1 MONTH OF
FREE
READING

at

www.ForgottenBooks.com

By purchasing this book you are
eligible for one month membership to
ForgottenBooks.com, giving you
unlimited access to our entire
collection of over 1,000,000 titles via
our web site and mobile apps.

To claim your free month visit:

www.forgottenbooks.com/free860075

ISBN 978-0-364-42563-3
PIBN 10860075

THE

ENCYCLOPÆDIA BRITANNICA

ELEVENTH EDITION

FIRST	edition, published in three		volumes,	1768—1771.
SECOND	„	„	ten	„	1777—1784.
THIRD	„	„	eighteen	„	1788—1797.
FOURTH	„	„	twenty	„	1801—1810.
FIFTH	„	„	twenty	„	1815—1817.
SIXTH	„	„	twenty	„	1823—1824.
SEVENTH	„	„	twenty-one	„	1830—1842.
EIGHTH	„	„	twenty-two	„	1853—1860.
NINTH	„	„,	twenty-five	„	1875—1889.
TENTH	„	ninth edition and eleven			
		supplementary volumes,		1902—1903.
ELEVENTH	„	published in twenty-nine volumes,			1910—1911.

THE

ENCYCLOPÆDIA BRITANNICA

A

DICTIONARY

OF

ARTS, SCIENCES, LITERATURE AND GENERAL INFORMATION

ELEVENTH EDITION

VOLUME XX

ODE to PAYMENT OF MEMBERS

NEW YORK

THE ENCYCLOPÆDIA BRITANNICA COMPANY

1911

INITIALS USED IN VOLUME XX. TO IDENTIFY INDIVIDUAL CONTRIBUTORS,[1] WITH THE HEADINGS OF THE ARTICLES IN THIS VOLUME SO SIGNED.

A. C. Se.	ALBERT CHARLES SEWARD, M.A., F.R.S. Professor of Botany in the University of Cambridge. Hon. Fellow of Emmanuel College, Cambridge. President of the Yorkshire Naturalists' Union, 1910.	**Palaeobotany:** *Mesozoic.*
A. F. P.	ALBERT FREDERICK POLLARD, M.A., F.R.Hist.S. Professor of English History in the University of London. Fellow of All Souls' College, Oxford. Assistant Editor of the *Dictionary of National Biography*, 1893–1901. Lothian Prizeman, Oxford, 1892; Arnold Prizeman, 1898. Author of *England under the Protector Somerset*; *Henry VIII.*; *Life of Thomas Cranmer*; &c.	**Parker, Matthew.**
A. G. D.	ARTHUR GEORGE DOUGHTY, M.A., LITT.D., C.M.G. Dominion Archivist of Canada. Member of the Geographical Board of Canada. Author of *The Cradle of New France*; &c. Joint-editor of *Documents relating to the Constitutional History of Canada*.	**Papineau.**
A. G. H.	ALBERT GEORGE HADCOCK. Late R.A. Manager, Gun Department, Elswick Works, Newcastle-on-Tyne. Lieut.-Col. commanding 1st Northumbrian Brigade, R.F.A. (Territorial Forces). Joint-author of *Artillery: its Progress and Present Position*; &c.	**Ordnance:** *History and Construction.*
A. Ha.	ADOLF HARNACK. See the biographical article: HARNACK, ADOLF.	**Origen.**
A. J. L.	ANDREW JACKSON LAMOUREUX. Librarian, College of Agriculture, Cornell University. Formerly Editor of the *Rio News*, Rio de Janeiro.	**Pará.**
A. Lu.	ACHILLE LUCHAIRE. See the biographical article: LUCHAIRE, DENIS J. ACHILLE.	**Papacy:** *1087–1305.*
A. Ma.	ALEXANDER MACALISTER, M.A., M.D., LL.D., D.Sc., F.R.S., F.S.A. Professor of Anatomy in the University of Cambridge, and Fellow of St John's College. Author of *Text-Book of Human Anatomy*; &c.	**Palmistry.**
A. M. Cl.	AGNES MURIEL CLAY (Mrs Wilde). Formerly Resident Tutor of Lady Margaret Hall, Oxford. Joint-author of *Sources of Roman History, 133–70 B.C.*	**Patron and Client** (*in part*).
A. N.	ALFRED NEWTON, F.R.S. See the biographical article: NEWTON, ALFRED.	**Oriole; Ornithology** (*in part*)**; Orthonyx; Ortolan; Osprey; Ostrich; Ousel; Owl; Oyster-catcher; Parrot; Partridge.**
A. P. H.	ALFRED PETER HILLIER, M.D., M.P. Author of *South African Studies*; *The Commonweal*; &c. Served in Kaffir War, 1878–1879. Partner with Dr L. S. Jameson in medical practice in South Africa till 1896. Member of Reform Committee, Johannesburg, and Political Prisoner at Pretoria, 1895–1896. M.P. for Hitchin division of Herts, 1910.	**Orange Free State:** *History* (*in part*).
A. S.-P.	ANTHYME ST PAUL. Author of *Histoire Monumentale de la France.*	**Paris:** *History* (*in part*).
A. S. Wo.	ARTHUR SMITH WOODWARD, LL.D., F.R.S. Keeper of Geology, Natural History Museum, South Kensington. Secretary of the Geological Society, London.	**Ostracoderms; Owen, Sir Richard; Palaeospondylus.**
A. Wa.	ARTHUR WAUGH, M.A. New College, Oxford. Newdigate Prize, 1888. Author of *Gordon in Africa*; *Alfred, Lord Tennyson.* Editor of Johnson's *Lives of the Poets*; and of editions of *Dickens, Tennyson, Arnold, Lamb*; &c.	**Pater, Walter; Patmore, Coventry.**
A. W. H.*	ARTHUR WILLIAM HOLLAND. Formerly Scholar of St John's College, Oxford. Bacon Scholar of Gray's Inn, 1900.	**Otto of Freising; Palatine; Paston Letters.**

[1] A complete list, showing all individual contributors, appears in the final volume.

E. H. M.	Ellis Hovell Minns, M.A. University Lecturer in Palaeography, Cambridge. Lecturer and Assistant Librarian at Pembroke College, Cambridge. Formerly Fellow of Pembroke College.	Olbia (*Euxine*).
Ed. M.	Eduard Meyer, Ph.D., D.Litt. (Oxon.), LL.D. Professor of Ancient History in the University of Berlin. Author of *Geschichte des Alterthums; Geschichte des alten Aegyptens; Die Israeliten und ihre Nachbarstämme.*	Orodes; Osroene; Osroes; Pacorus; Parthia; Parysatis; Pasargadae.
E. M. H.	Edward Morell Holmes. Curator of the Museum of the Pharmaceutical Society, London.	Opium.
E. M. T.	Sir Edward Maunde Thompson, G.C.B., I.S.O., D.C.L., Litt.D., LL.D. Director and Principal Librarian, British Museum, 1898–1909. Sandars Reader in Bibliography, Cambridge, 1895–1896. Hon. Fellow of University College, Oxford. Correspondent of the Institute of France and of the Royal Prussian Academy of Sciences. Author of *Handbook of Greek and Latin Palaeography.* Editor of *Chronicon Angliae.* Joint-editor of publications of the Palaeographical Society, the New Palaeographical Society, and of the Facsimile of the Laurentian Sophocles.	Palaeography; Palimpsest; Paper: *History*; Papyrus; Parchment.
E. M. W.	Rev. Edward Mewburn Walker, M.A. Fellow, Senior Tutor and Librarian of Queen's College, Oxford.	Olynthus.
E. O.*	Edmund Owen, M.B., F.R.C.S., LL.D., D.Sc. Consulting Surgeon to St Mary's Hospital, London, and to the Children's Hospital, Great Ormond Street, London. Chevalier of the Legion of Honour. Late Examiner in Surgery at the Universities of Cambridge, London and Durham. Author of *A Manual of Anatomy for Senior Students.*	Ovariotomy.
E. Pr.	Edgar Prestage. Special Lecturer in Portuguese Literature in the University of Manchester. Examiner in Portuguese in the Universities of London, Manchester, &c. Commendador, Portuguese Order of S. Thiago. Corresponding Member of Lisbon Royal Academy of Sciences, Lisbon Geographical Society; &c. Editor of *Letters of a Portuguese Nun;* Azurara's *Chronicle of Guinea;* &c.	Oliveira Martins; Osorio.
F. C. C.	Frederick Cornwallis Conybeare, M.A., D.Th. (Giessen). Fellow of the British Academy. Formerly Fellow of University College, Oxford. Editor of *The Ancient Armenian Texts of Aristotle.* Author of *Myth, Magic and Morals;* &c.	Paul of Samosata; Paulicians.
F. G. P.	Frederick Gymer Parsons, F.R.C.S., F.Z.S., F.R.Anthrop.Inst. Vice-President, Anatomical Society of Great Britain and Ireland. Lecturer on Anatomy at St Thomas's Hospital and the London School of Medicine for Women, London. Formerly Hunterian Professor at the Royal College of Surgeons.	Olfactory System; Pancreas.
F. K.*	Fernand Khnopff. See the biographical article: Khnopff, F. E. J. M.	Painting: *Modern Belgian*
F. R. C.	Frank R. Cana. Author of *South Africa from the Great Trek to the Union.*	Orange Free State (*in part*).
F. Wa.	Francis Watt, M.A. Barrister-at-Law, Middle Temple. Author of *Law's Lumber Room.*	Paterson, William.
F. W. Mo.	Frederick Walker Mott, F.R.S., M.D. Physician to Charing Cross Hospital. Pathologist to the London County Asylums. Fullerian Professor of Physiology at the Royal Institution.	Paralysis.
F. W. R.*	Frederick William Rudler, I.S.O., F.G.S. Curator and Librarian of the Museum of Practical Geology, London, 1879–1902. President of the Geologists' Association, 1887–1889.	Onyx; Opal.
F. X. K.	Franz Xaver Kraus (1840–1901). Professor of Church History, University of Freiburg-im-Breisgau, 1878–1901. Author of *Geschichte der christlichen Kunst;* &c.	Papacy: *1870–1900.*
G. A. Gr.	George Abraham Grierson, C.I.E., Ph.D., D.Litt. Member of the Indian Civil Service, 1873–1903. In charge of Linguistic Survey of India, 1898–1902. Gold Medallist, Royal Asiatic Society, 1909. Vice-President of the Royal Asiatic Society. Formerly Fellow of Calcutta University. Author of *The Languages of India;* &c.	Pahari.
G. A. C.*	Rev. George Albert Cooke, D.D. Oriel Professor of the Interpretation of Holy Scripture, and Fellow of Oriel College, Oxford. Canon of Rochester. Hon. Canon of St Mary's Cathedral, Edinburgh.	Palmyra.
G. B. B.	Gerard Baldwin Brown, M.A. Professor of Fine Art, University of Edinburgh. Formerly Fellow of Brasenose College, Oxford. Author of *The Fine Arts; The Arts in Early England;* &c.	Painting.
G. B. G.	George Brown Goode (1851–1896). Assistant Secretary of the Smithsonian Institution, Washington, 1887–1896. Author of *American Fishes.*	Oyster (*in part*).
G. Ch.	George Chrystal, M.A., LL.D. Professor of Mathematics and Dean of the Faculty of Arts, Edinburgh University. Hon. Fellow and formerly Fellow and Lecturer of Corpus Christi College, Cambridge.	Pascal (*in part*).
G. C. W.	George Charles Williamson, Litt.D. Chevalier of the Legion of Honour. Author of *Portrait Miniatures; Life of Richard Cosway, R.A.; George Engleheart; Portrait Drawings;* &c. Editor of the New Edition of Bryan's *Dictionary of Painters and Engravers.*	Oliver, Isaac; Oliver, Peter.

G. E.	Rev. George Edmundson, M.A., F.R.Hist.S. Formerly Fellow and Tutor of Brasenose College, Oxford. Ford's Lecturer, 1909. Hon. Member, Dutch Historical Society, and Foreign Member, Netherlands Association of Literature.	Oldenbarneveldt; Orange (House of); Ostend Company.
G. E. C.	George Earl Church. See the biographical article: Church, G. E.	{ Orinoco.
G. H. C.	George Herbert Carpenter, B.Sc. Professor of Zoology in the Royal College of Science, Dublin. Author of *Insects: their Structure and Life.*	Orthoptera.
G. Sa.	George Saintsbury, LL.D., D.C.L. See the biographical article: Saintsbury, George E. B.	{ Orleans, Charles, Duke of; { Pascal (*in part*).
G. S. W.	German Sims Woodhead, M.A., M.D., F.R.S. (Edin.). Professor of Pathology, Cambridge University. Fellow of Trinity Hall, Cambridge. Member of Royal Commission on Tuberculosis, 1902.	Parasitic Diseases.
H. A. B.	Henry Arthur Bethell. Lieut.-Col. Commanding 49th Brigade R.F.A. Associate Member of R.A. Committee. Awarded Lefroy Medal for Contributions to Artillery Science. Author of *Modern Guns and Gunnery; The Employment of Artillery*; &c.	Ordnance: Field Artillery Equipments.
H. Br.	Henry Bradley, M.A., Ph.D. Joint-editor of the *New English Dictionary* (Oxford). Fellow of the British Academy. Author of *The Story of the Goths; The Making of English;* &c.	Orm.
H. Ch.	Hugh Chisholm, M.A. Formerly Scholar of Corpus Christi College, Oxford. Editor of the 11th edition of the *Encyclopaedia Britannica.* Co-editor of the 10th edition.	Parliament (*in part*).
H. Cl.	Sir Hugh Charles Clifford, K.C.M.G. Colonial Secretary, Ceylon. Fellow of the Royal Colonial Institute. Formerly Resident, Pahang. Colonial Secretary, Trinidad and Tobago, 1903-1907. Author of *Studies in Brown Humanity; Further India,* &c. Joint-author of *A Dictionary of the Malay Language.*	Pantun.
H. E.	Karl Hermann Ethé, M.A., Ph.D. Professor of Oriental Languages, University College, Aberystwyth (University of Wales). Author of *Catalogue of Persian Manuscripts in the India Office Library,* London (Clarendon Press); &c.	Omar Khayyám (*in part*)
H. E. R.	Sir Henry Enfield Roscoe, LL.D. See the biographical article: Roscoe, Sir Henry Enfield.	Pasteur.
H. F. B.	Horatio Robert Forbes Brown, LL.D. Editor of the *Calendar of Venetian State Papers,* for the Public Record Office, London. Author of *Life on the Lagoons; Venetian Studies; John Addington Symonds, a Biography;* &c.	Padua.
H. F. G.	Hans Friedrich Gadow, F.R.S., Ph.D. Strickland Curator and Lecturer on Zoology in the University of Cambridge. Author of " Amphibia and Reptiles," in the *Cambridge Natural History.*	Odontornithes.
H. F. O.	Henry Fairfield Osborn, LL.D., D.Sc., F.R.S. (Edin.). Da Costa Professor of Zoology, Columbia University, New York. President, American Museum of Natural History, New York. Curator of Department of Vertebrate Palaeontology. Palaeontologist U.S. Geological Survey. Author of *From the Greeks to Darwin;* &c.	Palaeontology.
H. F. P.	Henry Francis Pelham, LL.D., D.C.L. See the biographical article: Pelham, Henry Francis.	{ Otho, Marcus S.
H. Ja.	Henry Jackson, Litt.D., LL.D., O.M. Regius Professor of Greek in the University of Cambridge. Fellow of Trinity College. Fellow of the British Academy. Author of *Texts to illustrate the History of Greek Philosophy from Thales to Aristotle.*	Parmenides of Elea.
H. L. H.	Harriet L. Hennessy, M.D. (Brux.), L.R.C.P.I., L.R.C.S.I.	{ Olfactory System: *Diseases.*
H. M. C.	Hector Munro Chadwick, M.A. Librarian and Fellow of Clare College, Cambridge. Reader in Scandinavian, Cambridge University. Author of *Studies on Anglo-Saxon Institutions.*	Odin.
H. N. D.	Henry Newton Dickson, M.A., D.Sc., F.R.S. (Edin.), F.R.G.S. Professor of Geography at University College, Reading. Formerly Vice-President, Royal Meteorological Society. Lecturer in Physical Geography, Oxford. Author of *Meteorology; Elements of Weather and Climate;* &c.	Pacific Ocean (*in part*).
H. R. T.	Henry Richard Tedder, F.S.A. Secretary and Librarian of the Athenaeum Club, London.	{ Pamphlets.
H. W. C. D.	Henry William Carless Davis, M.A. Fellow and Tutor of Balliol College, Oxford. Fellow of All Souls' College, Oxford, 1895-1902. Author of *England under the Normans and Angevins; Charlemagne.*	Odo of Bayeux; Orderic Vitalis.
H. Y.	Sir Henry Yule, K.C.S.I. See the biographical article, Yule, Sir Henry.	{ Odoric (*in part*).
J. A. C.	Sir Joseph Archer Crowe, K.C.M.G. See the biographical article: Crowe, Sir Joseph Archer.	{ Ostade (*in part*).

J. A. F.	JOHN AMBROSE FLEMING, M.A., D.SC., F.R.S. Pender Professor of Electrical Engineering in the University of London. Fellow of University College, London. Formerly Fellow of St John's College, Cambridge. Vice-President of the Institution of Electrical Engineers. Author of *The Principles of Electric Wave Telegraphy; Magnets and Electric Currents*; &c.	{ Ohmmeter; Oscillograph.
J. A. H.	JOHN ALLEN HOWE, B.SC. Curator and Librarian of the Museum of Practical Geology, London. Author of *Geology of Building Stones.*	{ Oligocene System; Oolite; Ordovician System; Oxfordian; Palaeozoic Era.
J. Bra.	JOSEPH BRAUN, S.J. Author of *Die Liturgische Gewandung* &c.	{ Pastoral Staff.
J. Bt.	JAMES BARTLETT. Lecturer on Construction, Architecture, Sanitation, Quantities, &c., at King's College, London. Member of Society of Architects. Member of Institute of Junior Engineers.	{ Painter-work.
J. B. A.	JOSEPH BEAVINGTON ATKINSON. Formerly art-critic of the *Saturday Review.* Author of *An Art Tour in the Northern Capitals of Europe; Schools of Modern Art in Germany.*	{ Overbeck.
J. C. van D.	JOHN CHARLES VAN DYKE. Professor of the History of Art, Rutgers College, New Brunswick, N.J. Formerly Editor of *The Studio* and the *Art Review.* Author of *Art for Art's Sake; History of Painting; Old English Masters*; &c.	{ Painting: *United States.*
J. E. S.	JOHN EDWIN SANDYS, M.A., LITT.D., LL.D. Public Orator in the University of Cambridge. Fellow of St John's College, Cambridge. Fellow of the British Academy. Author of *History of Classical Scholarship*; &c.	{ Pausanias: *Traveller.*
J. Fi.	JOHN FISKE, LL.D. See the biographical article: FISKE, JOHN.	{ Parkman, Francis.
J. F.-K.	JAMES FITZMAURICE-KELLY, LITT.D., F.R.HIST.S. Gilmour Professor of Spanish Language and Literature, Liverpool University. Norman McColl Lecturer, Cambridge University. Fellow of the British Academy. Member of the Royal Spanish Academy. Knight Commander of the Order of Alphonso XII. Author of *A History of Spanish Literature*; &c.	{ Palacio Valdés, Armando; Pardo Bazán.
J. H. A. H.	JOHN HENRY ARTHUR HART, M.A. Fellow, Theological Lecturer and Librarian, St John's College, Cambridge.	{ Palestine: *History (in part).*
J. H. F.	JOHN HENRY FREESE, M.A. Formerly Fellow of St John's College, Cambridge.	{ Orpheus *(in part).*
J. H. M.	JOHN HENRY MIDDLETON, M.A., LITT.D., F.S.A., D.C.L. (1846-1896). Slade Professor of Fine Arts in the University of Cambridge, 1886-1895. Director of the Fitzwilliam Museum, Cambridge, 1889-1892. Art Director of the South Kensington Museum, 1892-1896. Author of *The Engraved Gems of Classical Times; Illuminated Manuscripts in Classical and Medieval Times.*	{ Orcagna.
J. Hl. R.	JOHN HOLLAND ROSE, M.A., LITT.D. Christ's College, Cambridge. Lecturer on Modern History to the Cambridge University Local Lectures Syndicate. Author of *Life of Napoleon I.; Napoleonic Studies; The Development of the European Nations; The Life of Pitt*; &c.	{ Pasquier.
J. Ja.	JOSEPH JACOBS, LITT.D. Professor of English Literature in the Jewish Theological Seminary, New York. Formerly President of the Jewish Historical Society of England. Corresponding Member of the Royal Academy of History, Madrid. Author of *Jews of Angevin England; Studies in Biblical Archaeology*; &c.	{ Passover.
J. Lb.	JULIUS LEWKOWITSCH, M.A., PH.D. Examiner to the City and Guilds of London Institute. Vice-President of Chemical Society. Member of Council of Chemical Society; Institute of Chemistry; and Society of Public Analysts. Author of *Chemical Technology and Analysis of Oils, Fats, and Waxes*; &c.	{ Oils.
J. L. M.	JOHN LINTON MYRES, M.A., F.S.A., F.R.G.S. Wykeham Professor of Ancient History in the University of Oxford and Fellow of Magdalen College. Formerly Gladstone Professor of Greek and Lecturer in Ancient Geography, University of Liverpool. Lecturer of Classical Archaeology in the University of Oxford.	{ Paphos.
J. M.	JAMES MUIRHEAD, LL.D, (1831-1889). Scotch Advocate; Professor of Civil Law in the University of Edinburgh, 1862-1889. Author of *Historical Introduction to the Private Law of Rome*, and of an edition of the *Institutes of Gaius and Rules of Ulpian.*	{ Patron and Client (*in part*).
J. Ma.	JOHN MACPHERSON, M.A., M.D., M.R.C.S. (1817-1890). Formerly Inspector-General of Hospitals, Bengal. Author of *The Baths and Wells of Europe*; &c.	{ Paranoia.
J. M. M.	JOHN MALCOLM MITCHELL. Sometime Scholar of Queen's College, Oxford. Lecturer in Classics, East London College (University of London). Joint-editor of Grote's *History of Greece.*	{ Ostracism; Patricians.
J. P.-B.	JAMES GEORGE JOSEPH PENDEREL-BRODHURST. Editor of the *Guardian* (London).	{ Pawnbroking.
J. P. E.	JEAN PAUL HIPPOLYTE EMMANUEL ADHÉMAR ESMEIN. Professor of Law in the University of Paris. Officer of the Legion of Honour. Member of the Institute of France. Author of *Cours élémentaire d'histoire du droit français*; &c.	{ Parliament.

ROBERT SEYMOUR CONWAY, M.A., D.LITT. (Cantab.).
    Professor of Latin and Indo-European Philology in the University of Manchester. **Paelligni;**
    Formerly Professor of Latin in University College, Cardiff; and Fellow of Gonville **Osca Lingua.**
    and Caius College, Cambridge. Author of *The Italic Dialects.*

ROLAND TRUSLOVE, M.A.
    Formerly Scholar of Christ Church, Oxford. Fellow, Dean and Lecturer in Classics **Paris:** *Geography and*
    at Worcester College, Oxford. *Statistics.*

STANLEY ARTHUR COOK, M.A.
    Lecturer in Hebrew and Syriac, and formerly Fellow, Gonville and Caius College,
    Cambridge. Editor for the Palestine Exploration Fund. Examiner in Hebrew
    and Aramaic, London University, 1904–1908. Author of *Glossary of Aramaic*
    Inscriptions; The Law of Moses and the Code of Hammurabi; Critical Notes on
    Old Testament History; Religion of Ancient Palestine; &c.

SYDNEY R. FREMANTLE. **Ordnance:** *Naval Guns and*
    Captain, R.N. Naval Mobilization Department, Admiralty, London. *Gunnery.*

SIDNEY GEORGE OWEN, M.A.
    Student and Tutor of Christ Church, Oxford.

SIMON NEWCOMB, D.SC., LL.D. **Orbit;**
    See the biographical article: NEWCOMB, SIMON. **Parallax.**

STEPHEN PAGET, F.R.C.S.
    Surgeon to Throat and Ear Department, Middlesex Hospital. Hon. Secretary, **Paget, Sir James.**
    Research Defence Society. Author of *Memoirs and Letters of Sir James Paget;* &c.

    Olbia: *Sardinia;*

THOMAS ASHBY, M.A., D.LITT.
    Director of British School of Archaeology at Rome. Formerly Scholar of Christ
    Church, Oxford. Craven Fellow, 1897. Conington Prizeman, 1906. Member of
    the Imperial German Archaeological Institute. Author of *The Classical Topography*
    of the Roman Campagna.

T. Ba.

RT. HON. LORD FARNBOROUGH.
    See the biographical article: FARNBOROUGH, THOMAS ERSKINE MAY, BARON.

THEODORE FREYLINGHUYSEN COLLIER, PH.D. **Paul III., IV., V.** *(Popes).*
    Assistant Professor of History, Williams College, Williamstown, Mass.

THOMAS HODGKIN, LITT. D., LL.D., D.C.L. **Odoacar.**
    See the biographical article: HODGKIN, T.

SIR THOMAS HUNGERFORD HOLDICH, K.C.M.G., K.C.I.E., D.SC. **Oman; Oxus;**
    Superintendent, Frontier Surveys, India, 1892–1898. Gold Medallist, R.G.S., **Pamirs.**
    London, 1887. Author of *The Indian Borderland; The Countries of the King's*
    Award; India; Tibet.

REV. THOMAS KELLY CHEYNE, M.A., D.D., LL.D.
    See the biographical article: CHEYNE, T. K.

    Pahlavi.

THOMAS OKEY.
    Examiner in Basket Work for the City and Guilds of London Institute.

T. W. R. D. THOMAS WILLIAM RHYS DAVIDS, LL.D., PH.D.
    Professor of Comparative Religion, Manchester University. President of the
    Pali Text Society. Fellow of the British Academy. Secretary and Librarian of
    Royal Asiatic Society, 1885–1902. Author of *Buddhism; Sacred Books of the*
    Buddhists; Early Buddhism; Buddhist India; Dialogues of the Buddha; &c.

V. M.
    Ophicleide *(in part).*

W. Ar. SIR WALTER ARMSTRONG. **Orchardson.**
    Director of National Gallery of Ireland. Author of *Art in the British Isles;* &c.
    Joint-editor of Bryan's *Dictionary of Painters;* &c.

W. A. B. C. REV. WILLIAM AUGUSTUS BREVOORT COOLIDGE, M.A., F.R.G.S., PH.D. **Olivier, J. D.;**
    Fellow of Magdalen College, Oxford. Professor of English History, St David's **Orta,**
    College, Lampeter, 1880–1881. Author of *Guide du Haut Dauphiné; The Range* **Ortler.**
    of the Tödi; Guide to Grindelwald; Guide to Switzerland; The Alps in Nature and
    in History; &c. Editor to *The Alpine Journal*, 1880–1881; &c.

W. A. H. **Oneida Community.**
    President of the Oneida Community, Ltd.; Author of *American Communities;* &c.

PRINCIPAL UNSIGNED ARTICLES

ENCYCLOPÆDIA BRITANNICA

ELEVENTH EDITION

VOLUME XX

ODE (Gr. ᾠδή, from ἀείδειν, to sing), a form of stately and elaborate lyrical verse. As its name shows, the original signification of an ode was a chant, a poem arranged to be sung to an instrumental accompaniment. There were two great divisions of the Greek *melos* or song; the one the personal utterance of the poet, the other, as Professor G. G. Murray says, " the choric song of his band of trained dancers." Each of these culminated in what have been called odes, but the former, in the hands of Alcaeus, Anacreon and Sappho, came closer to what modern criticism knows as lyric, pure and simple. On the other hand, the choir-song, in which the poet spoke for himself, but always supported, or interpreted, by a chorus, led up to what is now known as ode proper. It was Alcman, as is supposed, who first gave to his poems a strophic arrangement, and the strophe has come to be essential to an ode. Stesichorus, Ibycus and Simonides of Ceos led the way to the two great masters of ode among the ancients, Pindar and Bacchylides. The form and verse-arrangement of Pindar's great lyrics have regulated the type of the heroic ode. It is now perceived that they are consciously composed in very elaborate measures, and that each is the result of a separate act of creative ingenuity, but each preserving an absolute consistency of form. So far from being, as critics down to Cowley and Boileau, and indeed to the time of August Böckh, supposed, utterly licentious in their irregularity, they are more like the *canzos* and *sirventes* of the medieval troubadours than any modern verse. The Latins themselves seem to have lost the secret of these complicated harmonies, and they made no serious attempt to imitate the odes of Pindar and Bacchylides. It is probable that the Greek odes gradually lost their musical character; they were accompanied on the flute, and then declaimed without any music at all. The ode, as it was practised by the Romans, returned to the personally lyrical form of the Lesbian lyrists. This was exemplified, in the most exquisite way, by Horace and Catullus; the former imitated, and even translated, Alcaeus and Anacreon, the latter was directly inspired by Sappho.

The earliest modern writer to perceive the value of the antique ode was Ronsard, who attempted with as much energy as he could exercise to recover the fire and volume of Pindar; his principal experiments date from 1550 to 1552. The poets of the Pleiad recognized in the ode one of the forms of verse with which French prosody should be enriched, but they went too far, and in their use of Greek words crudely introduced, and in their quantitative experiments, they offended the genius of the French language. The ode, however, died in France almost as rapidly as it had come to life; it hardly survived the 16th century, and neither the examples of J. B. Rousseau nor of Saint-Amant nor of Malherbe possessed much poetic life. Early in the 19th century the form was resumed, and we have the *Odes* composed between 1817 and 1824 by Victor Hugo, the philosophical and religious odes of Lamartine, those of Victor de Laprade (collected in 1844), and the brilliant *Odes funambulesques* of Théodore de Banville (1857).

The earliest odes in the English language, using the word in its strict form, were the magnificent *Epithalamium* and *Prothalamium* of Spenser. Ben Jonson introduced a kind of elaborate lyric, in stanzas of rhymed irregular verse, to which he gave the name of ode; and some of his disciples, in particular Randolph, Cartwright and Herrick, followed him. The great "Hymn on the Morning of Christ's Nativity," begun by Milton in 1629, may be considered an ode, and his lyrics "On Time" and " At a Solemn Music" may claim to belong to the same category. But it was Cowley who introduced into English poetry the ode consciously built up, on a solemn theme and as definitely as possible on the ancient Greek pattern. Being in exile in France about 1645, and at a place where the only book was the text of Pindar, Cowley set himself to study and to imitate the *Epinikia*. He conceived, he says, that this was " the noblest and the highest kind of writing in verse," but he was no more perspicacious than others in observing what the rules were which Pindar had followed. He supposed the Greek poet to be carried away on a storm of heroic emotion, in which all the discipline of prosody was disregarded: In 1656 Cowley published his Pindaric odes, in which he had not even regarded the elements of the Greek structure, with strophe, antistrophe and epode. His idea of an ode, which he impressed with such success upon the British nation that it has never been entirely removed, was of a lofty and tempestuous piece of indefinite poetry, conducted " without sail or oar " in whatever direction the enthusiasm of the poet chose to take it. These shapeless pieces became very popular after the Restoration, and enjoyed the sanction of Dryden in three or four irregular odes which are the best of their kind in the English language. Prior, in a humorous ode on the taking of Namur (1695), imitated the French type of this poem, as cultivated by Boileau. In 1705 Congreve published a *Discourse on the Pindarique Ode*, in which many of the critical errors of Cowley were corrected; and Congreve wrote odes, in strophe, antistrophe and epode which were the earliest of their kind in English; unhappily they were not very poetical. He was imitated by Ambrose Philips, but then the tide of Cowley-Pindarism rose again and swept the reform away. The attempts of Gilbert West (1703–1756) to explain the prosody of Pindar (1749) inspired Gray to write his "Progress of Poesy" (1754) and "The Bard" (1756). Collins, meanwhile, had in 1747 published a collection of odes devised in the Aeolian or Lesbian manner. The odes of Mason and Akenside were more correctly Pindaric, but frigid and formal. The odes of Wordsworth, Coleridge and Tennyson are entirely irregular. Shelley desired to revive the pure manner of the Greeks, but he understood the principle of the form so little that he began his noble "Ode to Naples" with two epodes, passed on to two strophes, and then indulged in four successive antistrophes. Coventry Patmore, in 1868, printed a volume of Odes, which he afterwards enlarged; these were irregularly built up on a musical system, the exact consistency of which is not always apparent. Finally Swinburne, although some of his odes, like those of Keats, are really elaborate lyrics, written in a succession of stanzas identical in form, has cultivated the Greek form also, and some of his political odes follow very closely the type of Bacchylides and Pindar.

See Philipp August Böckh, De metris Pindari (1811); Wilhelm Christ, Metrik der Griechen und Römer (1874); Edmund Gosse, English Odes, (1881). (E.G.)

ODENKIRCHEN, a town of Germany, in the Prussian Rhine province, 21 m. by rail S.W. of Düsseldorf, and at the junction of lines to Munich, Gladbach and Stolberg. Pop. (1905) 16,808. It has a Roman Catholic church, an Evangelical one, a synagogue and several schools. Its principal industries are spinning, weaving, tanning and dyeing. Odenkirchen became a town in 1856.

See Wiedemann, Geschichte der ehemaligen Herrschaft und, des Hauses Odenkirchen (Odenkirchen, 1879).

ODENSE, a city of Denmark, the chief town of the amt (county) of its name, which forms the northern part of the island of Fünen (Fyen). Pop. (1901) 40,138. The city lies 4 m. from Odense Fjord on the Odense Aa, the main portion on the north side of the stream, and the industrial Albani quarter on the south side. It has a station on the railway route between Copenhagen and Jutland and Schleswig-Holstein via Korsör. A canal, 15½ to 21 ft. deep, gives access to the town from the fjord. St Canute's cathedral, formerly connected with the great Benedictine monastery of the same name, is one of the largest and finest buildings of its kind in Denmark. It is constructed of brick in a pure Gothic style. Originally dating from 1081–1093, it was rebuilt in the 13th century. Under the altar lies Canute (Knud), the patron saint of Denmark, who intended to dispute with William of Normandy the possession of England, but was slain in an insurrection at Odense in 1086; Kings John and Christian II. are also buried within the walls. Our Lady's church, built in the 13th century and restored in 1851–1852 and again in 1864, contains a carved altarpiece (16th century) by Claus Berg of Lübeck. Odense Castle was erected by Frederick IV., who died there in 1730. In Albani are tanneries, iron-foundries and machine-shops. Exports, mostly agricultural produce (butter, bacon, eggs); imports, iron, petroleum, coal, yarn and timber.

Odense, or Odinsey, originally Odinsoe, i.e. Odin's island, is one of the oldest cities of Denmark. St Canute's shrine was a great resort of pilgrims throughout the middle ages. In the 16th century the town was the meeting-place of several parliaments, and down to 1805 it was the seat of the provincial assembly of Fünen.

ODENWALD, a wooded mountainous region of Germany, almost entirely in the grand duchy of Hesse, with small portions in Bavaria and Baden. It stretches between the Neckar and the Main, and is some 50 m. long by 20 to 30 broad. Its highest points are the Katzenbuckel (2057 ft.), the Neunkircher Höhe (1985 ft.) and the Krähberg (1965 ft.). The wooded heights overlooking the Bergstrasse are studded with castles and medieval ruins, some of which are associated with some of the most memorable adventures of German tradition. Among them are

Rodenstein, the reputed home of the wild huntsman, and near Grasellenbach, the spot where Siegfried of the Nibelungenlied is said to have been slain.

See F. Montanus, Der Odenwald (Mainz, 1894); T. Lorentzen, Der Odenwald in Wort und Bild (Stuttgart, 1904); G. Volk, Der Odenwald und seine Nachbargebiete (Stuttgart, 1900), and Windhaus, Führer durch den Odenwald (Darmstadt, 1903).

ODER (Lat. Viadua; Slavonic, Vjodr), a river of Germany, rises in Austria on the Odergebirge in the Moravian tableland at a height of 1950 ft. above the sea, and 14 m. to the east of Olmütz. From its source to its mouth in the Baltic it has a total length of 560 m., of which 480 m. are navigable for barges, and it drains an area of 43,300 sq. m. The first 45 m. of its course lie within Moravia; for the next 15 m., it forms the frontier between Prussian and Austrian Silesia, while the remaining 500 m. belong to Prussia, where it traverses the provinces of Silesia, Brandenburg and Pomerania. It flows at first towards the south-east, but on quitting Austria turns towards the north-west, maintaining this direction as far as Frankfort-on-Oder, beyond which its general course is nearly due north. As far as the frontier the Oder flows through a well-defined valley, but, after passing through the gap between the Moravian mountains, and the Carpathians and entering the Silesian plain, its valley is wide and shallow and its banks generally low. In its lower course it is divided into numerous branches, forming many islands. The main channel follows the left side of the valley and finally expands into the Pommersches, or Stettiner Haff, which is connected with the sea by three arms, the Peene, the Swine and the Dievenow, forming the islands of Usedom and Wollin. The Swine, in the middle, is the main channel for navigation. The chief tributaries of the Oder on the left bank are the Oppa, Glatzer Neisse, Katzbach, Bober and Lausitzer Neisse; on the right bank the Malapane, Bartsch and Warthe. Of these the only one of importance for navigation is the Warthe, which through the Netze is brought into communication with the Vistula. The Oder is also connected by canals with the Havel and the Spree. The most important towns on its banks are Ratibor, Oppeln, Brieg, Breslau, Glogau, Frankfort, Cüstrin and Stettin, with the seaport of Swinemünde at its mouth. Glogau, Cüstrin and Swinemünde are strongly fortified.

The earliest important undertaking with a view of improving the waterway was due to the initiative of Frederick the Great, who recommended the diversion of the river into a new and straight channel in the swampy tract of land known as the Oderbruch, near Cüstrin. The work was carried out in the years 1746–1753, a large tract of marshland being brought under cultivation, a considerable detour cut off, and the main stream successfully confined to the canal, 12 m. in length, which is known as the New Oder. The river at present begins to be navigable for barges at Ratibor, where it is about 100 ft. wide, and for larger vessels at Breslau, and great exertions are made by the government to deepen and keep open the channel, which still shows a strong tendency to choke itself with sand in certain places. The alterations made of late years consist of three systems of works:—(1) The canalization of the main stream (4 m.) at Breslau, and from the confluence of the Glatzer Neisse to the mouth of the Klodnitz canal, a distance of over 50 m. These engineering works were completed in 1896. (2) In 1887–1891 the Oder-Spree canal was made to connect the two rivers named. The canal leaves the Oder at Fürstenberg (132 m. above its mouth) at an altitude of 93 ft., and after 15 m. enters the Friedrich-Wilhelm canal (134 ft.). After coinciding with this for 7 m., it makes another cut of 5 m. to the Spree at Fürstenwalde (126 ft.). Then it follows the Spree for 15 m., and at Gross Tränke (121 ft.) passes out and goes to Lake Seddin (106 ft.), 15 m. (3) The deepening and regulation of the mouth and lower course of the stream, consisting of the Kaiserfahrt, 3 m. long, affording a waterway between the Stettiner Haff and the river Swine for the largest ocean-going vessels; a new cut, 4½ m. long, from Vietzig on the Stettiner Haff to Wollin Island; the Parnitz-Dunzig and Dunzig-Oder canals, together 1 m. long constituting the immediate approach to Stettin. Vessels drawing 24 ft. are now able to go right up to Stettin. In 1905 a project was sanctioned for improving the communication between Berlin and Stettin by widening and deepening the lower course of the river and then connecting this by a canal with Berlin. Another project, born at the same time, is one for the canalization of the upper course of the Oder. About 4,000,000 tons of merchandise pass through Breslau (up and down) on the Oder in the year.

See *Der Oderstrom, sein Stromgebiet und seine wichtigsten Nebenflüsse; hydrographische, wasserwirtschaftliche und wasserrechtliche Darstellung* (Berlin, 1896).

ODERBERG, a town of Germany, in the Prussian province of Brandenburg, on the Alte Oder, 2 m. from Bralitz, a station 44 m. N.W. from Frankfort-on-Oder, by the railway to Angermünde. Pop. (1905) 4,015. It has a fine Gothic church, dedicated to St Nicholas, and the ruins of an ancient castle, called Bärenkasten. Oderberg is an important emporium for the Russian timber trade.

ODESCALCHI-ERBA, the name of a Roman princely family of great antiquity. They are supposed to be descended from Enrico Erba, imperial vicar in Milan in 1165. Alessandro Erba married Lucrezia Odescalchi, sister of Pope Innocent IX., in 1709, who is believed to have been descended from Giorgio Odescalchi (*floruit* at Como in 1290). The title of prince of the Holy Roman Empire was conferred on Alessandro in 1714, and that of duke of Syrmium in Hungary in 1714, with the qualification of "serene highness." The head of the family now bears the titles of Fürst Odescalchi, duke of Syrmium, prince of Bassano, &c., and he is an hereditary magnate of Hungary and a grandee of Spain; the family, which is one of the most important in Italy, owns the Palazzo Odescalchi in Rome, the magnificent castle of Bracciano, besides large estates in Italy and Hungary.

See A. von Reumont, *Geschichte der Stadt Rom* (Berlin, 1868), and the *Almanach de Gotha*.

ODESSA, one of the most important seaports of Russia, ranking by its population and foreign trade after St Petersburg, Moscow and Warsaw. It is situated in 46° 28′ N. and 30° 44′ E., on the southern shore of a semi-circular bay, at the north-west angle of the Black Sea, and is by rail 1017 m. S.S.W. from Moscow and 610 S. from Kiev. Odessa is the seaport for the basins of two great rivers of Russia, the Dnieper, with its tributary the Bug, and the Dniester (20 m. to S.). The entrances to the mouths of both these offering many difficulties for navigation, trade has from the remotest antiquity selected this spot, which is situated half-way between the two estuaries, while the level surface of the neighbouring steppe allows easy communication with the lower parts of both rivers. The bay of Odessa, which has an area of 14 sq. m. and a depth of 30 ft. with a soft bottom, is a dangerous anchorage on account of its exposure to easterly winds. But inside it are six harbours—the quarantine harbour, new harbour, coal harbour and "practical" harbour, the first and last, on the S. and N. respectively, protected by moles, and the two middle harbours by a breakwater. Besides these, there are the harbour of the principal shipping company—the Russian Company for Navigation and Commerce, and the petroleum harbour. The harbours freeze for a few days in winter, as also does the bay occasionally, navigation being interrupted every year for an average of sixteen days; though this is materially shortened by the use of an ice-breaker. Odessa experiences the influence of the continental climate of the neighbouring steppes; its winters are cold (the average temperature for January being 23·2° F., and the isotherm for the entire season that of Königsberg), its summers are hot (72·8° in July), and the yearly average temperature is 48·5°. The rainfall is scanty (14 in. per annum). The city is built on a terrace 100 to 155 ft. in height, which descends by steep crags to the sea, and on the other side is continuous with the level of the "black earth" steppe. Catacombs, whence sandstone for building has been taken, extend underneath the town and suburbs, not without some danger to the buildings.

The general aspect of Odessa is that of a wealthy west-European city. Its chief embankment, the Nikolai boulevard, bordered with tall and handsome houses, forms a fine promenade. The central square is adorned with a statue of Armand, duc de Richelieu (1826), who was governor of Odessa in 1803–1814. A little back from the sea stands a fine bronze statue of Catherine II. (1900). A magnificent flight of nearly 200 granite steps leads from the Richelieu monument down to the harbours. The central parts of the city have broad streets and squares, bordered with fine buildings and mansions in the Italian style, and with good shops. The cathedral, founded in 1794 and finished in 1809, and thoroughly restored in 1903, can accommodate 5000 persons; it contains the tomb of Count Michael Voronstov, governor-general from 1823 to 1854, who contributed much towards the development and embellishment of the city. The "Palais Royal," with its parterre and fountains, and the spacious public park are fine pleasure-grounds, whilst in the ravines that lead down to the sea cluster the houses of the poorer classes. The shore is occupied by immense granaries, some of which look like palaces, and large storehouses take up a broad space in the west of the city. Odessa consists (i.) of the city proper, containing the old fort (now a quarantine establishment) and surrounded by a boulevard, where was formerly a wall marking the limits of the free port; (ii.) of the suburbs Novaya and Peresyp, extending northward along the lower shore of the bay; and (iii.) of Moldavanka to the south-west. The city, being in a treeless region, is proud of the avenues of trees that line several of its streets and of its parks, especially of the Alexander Park, with a statue of Alexander II. (1891), and of the summer resorts of Fontaine, Arcadia and Langeron along the bay. Odessa is rising in repute as a summer sea-bathing resort, and its mud-baths (from the mud of the *limans* or lagoons) are considered to be efficacious in cases of rheumatism, gout, nervous affections and skin diseases. The German colonies Liebenthal and Lustdorf are bathing-places.

Odessa is the real capital, intellectual and commercial, of so-called Novorossia, or New Russia, which includes the governments of Bessarabia and Kherson. It is the see of an archbishop of the Orthodox Greek Church, and the headquarters of the VIII. army corps, and constitutes an independent "municipal district" or captaincy, which covers 195 sq. m. and includes a dozen villages, some of which have 2000 to 3000 inhabitants each. It is also the chief town of the Novorossian (New Russian) educational district, and has a university, which replaced the Richelieu Lyceum in 1865, and now has over 1700 students.

In 1795 the town had only 2250 inhabitants; in 1814, twenty years after its foundation, it had 25,000. The population has steadily increased from 100,000 in 1850, 185,000 in 1873, 225,000 in 1884, to 449,673 in 1900. The great majority of inhabitants are Great Russians and Little Russians; but there are also large numbers of Jews (133,000, exclusive of Karaites), as well as of Italians, Greeks, Germans and French (to which nationalities the chief merchants belong), as also of Rumanians, Servians, Bulgarians, Tatars, Armenians, Lazes, Georgians. A numerous floating population of labourers, attracted at certain periods by pressing work in the port, and afterwards left unemployed owing to the enormous fluctuations in the corn trade, is one of the features of Odessa. It is estimated that there are no less than 35,000 people living from hand to mouth in the utmost misery, partly in the extensive catacombs beneath the city.

The leading occupations are connected with exporting, shipping and manufactures. The industrial development has been rather slow: sugar-refineries, tea-packing, oil-mills, tanneries, steam flour-mills, iron and mechanical works, factories of jute sacks, chemical works, tin-plate works, paper-factories are the chief. Commercially the city is the chief seaport of Russia for exports, which in favourable years are twice as high as those of St Petersburg, while as regards the value of the imports Odessa is second only to the northern capital. The total returns amount to 16 to 20 millions sterling a year, representing about one-ninth of the entire Russian foreign trade, and 14% if the coast trade be included as well. The total exports are valued at 10 to 11 millions sterling annually, and the imports at 6 to 9 millions sterling, about 8½ % of all the imports into Russia. Grain, and especially wheat, is the chief article of export. The chief imports are raw cotton, iron, agricultural machinery, coal, chemicals, jute, copra and lead. A new and spacious harbour, especially for the petroleum trade, was constructed in 1894–1900.

History.—The bay of Odessa was colonized by Greeks at a very early period, and their ports—*Istrianorum Portus* and *Isiacorum Portus* on the shores of the bay, and *Odessus* at the mouth of the Tiligul *liman*—carried on a lively trade with the neighbouring steppes. These towns disappeared in the 3rd and 4th centuries, and for ten centuries no settlements in these tracts are mentioned. In the 14th century this region belonged to the Lithuanians, and in 1396 Oigerd, prince of Lithuania, defeated in battle three Tatar chiefs, one of whom, Khaji Beg or Bey, had recently founded, at the place now occupied by Odessa, a fort which received his name. The Lithuanians, and subsequently the Poles, kept the country under their dominion until the 16th century, when it was seized by the Tatars, who still permitted, however, the Lithuanians to gather salt in the neighbouring lakes. Later on the Turks left a garrison here, and founded in 1764 the fortress Yani-dunya. In 1789 the Russians, under the French captain de Ribas, took the fortress by assault. In 1791 Khaji-bey and the Ochakov region were ceded to Russia. De Ribas and the French engineer Voland were entrusted in 1794 with the erection of a town and the construction of a port at Khaji-bey. In 1803 Odessa became the chief town of a separate municipal district or captaincy, the first captain being Armand, duc de Richelieu, who did very much for the development of the young city and its improvement as a seaport. In 1824 Odessa became the seat of the governors-general of Novorossia and Bessarabia. In 1866 it was brought into railway connexion with Kiev and Kharkov via Balta, and with Jassy in Rumania. In 1854 it was unsuccessfully attacked by the Anglo-Russian fleet, and in 1876–1877 by the Turkish, also unsuccessfully. In 1905–1906 the city was the scene of violent revolutionary disorders, marked by a naval insurrection. (P. A. K.; J. T. Be.)

ODEUM (Gr. *Odeion*), the name given to a concert hall in ancient Greece. In a general way its construction was similar to that of a theatre, but it was only a quarter of the size and was provided with a roof for acoustic purposes, a characteristic difference. The oldest known Odeum in Greece was the Skias at Sparta, so called from its resemblance to the top of a parasol, said to have been erected by Theodorus of Samos (600 B.C.); in Athens an Odeum near the spring Enneacrunus on the Ilissus was referred to the age of Peisistratus, and appears to have been rebuilt or restored by Lycurgus (c. 330 B.C.). This is probably the building which, according to Aristophanes (*Wasps*, 1109), was used for judicial purposes, for the distribution of corn, and even for the billeting of soldiers. The building which served as a model for later similar constructions was the Odeum of Pericles (completed c. 445) on the south-eastern slope of the rock of the Acropolis, whose conical roof, a supposed imitation of the tent of Xerxes, was made of the masts of captured Persian ships. It was destroyed by Aristion, the so-called tyrant of Athens, at the time of the rising against Sulla (87), and rebuilt by Ariobarzanes II., king of Cappadocia (Appian, *Mithrid.* 38). The most magnificent example of its kind, however, was the Odeum built on the south-west cliff of the Acropolis at Athens about A.D. 160 by the wealthy sophist and rhetorician Herodes Atticus in memory of his wife, considerable remains of which are still to be seen. It had accommodation for 8000 persons, and the ceiling was constructed of beautifully carved beams of cedar wood, probably with an open space in the centre to admit the light. It was also profusely decorated with pictures and other works of art. Similar buildings also existed in other parts of Greece; at Corinth, also the gift of Herodes Atticus; at Patrae, where there was a famous statue of Apollo; at Smyrna, Tralles, and other towns in Asia Minor. The first Odeum in Rome was built by Domitian, a second by Trajan.

ODILIENBERG, or **OTTILIENBERG** (called *Altitona* in the 8th century), a peak of the Vosges Mountains in Germany, in the imperial province of Alsace-Lorraine, immediately W. of the town of Barr. Its crest (2500 ft.) is surmounted by the ruins of the ancient Roman wall, the Heidenmauer, and by the convent and church of St Odilia, or Ottilia, the patron saint of Alsace, whose remains rest within. It is thus the object of frequent pilgrimages. The convent is said to have been founded by Duke Eticho I., in honour of his daughter St Odilia, about the end of the 7th century, and it is certain that it existed at the time of Charlemagne. Destroyed during the wars of the middle ages, it was rebuilt by the Premonstrants at the beginning of the 17th century, and was acquired later by the bishop of Strassburg, who restored the building and the adjoining church, in 1853. Since 1899 the convent has contained a museum of antiquities.

See Reinhard, *Le Mont Ste Odile* (Strassburg, 1888); Pfister, *Le Duché mérovingien d'Alsace et la légende de Sainte Odile* (Nancy, 1892); and R. Forrer, *Der Odilienberg* (Strassburg, 1899).

ODIN, or **OTHIN** (O. Norse *Óðinn*), the chief god of the Northern pantheon. He is represented as an old man with one eye. Frigg is his wife, and several of the gods, including Thor and Balder, are his sons. He is also said to have been the father of several legendary kings, and more than one princely family claimed descent from him. His exploits and adventures form the theme of a number of the Eddaic poems, and also of several stories in the prose Edda. In all these stories his character is distinguished rather by wisdom and cunning than by martial prowess, and reference is very frequently made to his skill in poetry and magic. In *Ynglinga Saga* he is represented as reigning in Sweden, where he established laws for his people. In notices relating to religious observances Odin appears chiefly as the giver of victory or as the god of the dead. He is frequently introduced in legendary sagas, generally in disguise, imparting secret instructions to his favourites or presenting them with weapons by which victory is assured. In return he receives the souls of the slain who in his palace, Valhalla (q.v.), live a life of fighting and feasting, similar to that which has been their desire on earth. Human sacrifices were very frequently offered to Odin, especially prisoners taken in battle. The commonest method of sacrifice was by hanging the victim on a tree; and in the poem *Hávamál* the god himself is represented as sacrificed in this way. The worship of Odin seems to have prevailed chiefly, if not solely, in military circles, i.e. among princely families and the retinues of warriors attached to them. It is probable, however, that the worship of Odin was once common to most of the Teutonic peoples. To the Anglo-Saxons he was known as Woden (q.v.) and to the Germans as Wodan (Wuotan), which are the regular forms of the same name in those languages. It is largely owing to the peculiar character of this god and the prominent position which he occupies that the mythology of the north presents so striking a contrast to that of Greece.

See TEUTONIC PEOPLES, *ad fin.*; and WODEN. (H. M. C.)

ODO, or **EUDES** (d. c. 736), king, or duke, of Aquitaine, obtained this dignity about 715, and his territory included the south-western part of Gaul from the Loire to the Pyrenees. In 718 he appears as the ally of Chilperic II., king of Neustria, who was fighting against the Austrasian mayor of the palace, Charles Martel; but after the defeat of Chilperic at Soissons in 719 he probably made peace with Charles by surrendering to him the Neustrian king and his treasures. Odo was also obliged to fight the Saracens who invaded the southern part of his kingdom, and inflicted a severe defeat upon them at Toulouse in 721. When, however, he was again attacked by Charles Martel, the Saracens renewed their ravages, and Odo was defeated near Bordeaux; he was compelled to crave protection from Charles, who took up this struggle and gained his momentous victory at Poitiers in 732. In 735 the king abdicated, and was succeeded by his son Hunold.

ODO, or **EUDES** (d. 898), king of the Franks, was a son of Robert the Strong, count of Anjou (d. 866), and is sometimes referred to as duke of France and also as count of Paris. For his skill and bravery in resisting the attacks of the Normans

Odo was chosen king by the western Franks when the emperor Charles the Fat was deposed in 887, and was crowned at Compiègne in February 888. He continued to battle against the Normans, whom he defeated at Montfaucon and elsewhere, but was soon involved in a struggle with some powerful nobles, who supported the claim of Charles, afterwards King Charles III., to the Frankish kingdom. To gain prestige and support Odo owned himself a vassal of the German king, Arnulf, but in 894 Arnulf declared for Charles. Eventually, after a struggle which lasted for three years, Odo was compelled to come to terms with his rival, and to surrender to him a district north of the Seine. He died at La Fère on the 1st of January 898.

See E. Lavisse, *Histoire de France,* tome H. (Paris, 1903); and E. Favre, *Eudes, comte de Paris et roi de France* (Paris, 1893).

ODO[1] OF BAYEUX (c. 1036–1097), Norman bishop and English earl, was a uterine brother of William the Conqueror, from whom he received, while still a youth, the see of Bayeux (1049). But his active career was that of a warrior and statesman. He found ships for the invasion of England and fought in person at Senlac; in 1067 he became earl of Kent, and for some years he was a trusted royal minister. At times he acted as viceroy in William's absence; at times he led the royal forces to chastise rebellions. But in 1083 he was suddenly disgraced and imprisoned for having planned a military expedition to Italy. He was accused of desiring to make himself pope; more probably he thought of serving as a papal condottiere against the emperor Henry IV. The Conqueror, when on his death-bed, reluctantly permitted Odo's release (1087). The bishop returned to his earldom and soon organized a rebellion with the object of handing over England to his eldest nephew, Duke Robert. William Rufus, to the disgust of his supporters, permitted Odo to leave the kingdom after the collapse of this design (1088), and thenceforward Odo was the right-hand man of Robert in Normandy. He took part in the agitation for the First Crusade, and started in the duke's company for Palestine, but died on the way, at Palermo (February 1097). Little good is recorded of Odo. His vast wealth was gained by extortion and robbery. His ambitions were boundless and his morals lax. But he was a patron of learning and, like most prelates of his age, a great architect. He rebuilt the cathedral of his see, and may perhaps have commissioned the unknown artist of the celebrated Bayeux tapestry.

See the authorities cited for WILLIAM I. and WILLIAM II., the biographical sketch in *Gallia Christiana,* xi. 353-360; H. Wharton *Anglia Sacra,* i. 334-339 (1691); and F. R. Fowke, *The Bayeux Tapestry* (London, 1898). (H. W. C. D.)

ODOACER, or **ODOVACAR** (c. 434–493), the first barbarian ruler of Italy on the downfall of the Western empire, was born in the district bordering on the middle Danube about the year 434. In this district the once rich and fertile provinces of Noricum and Pannonia were being torn piecemeal from the Roman empire by a crowd of German tribes, among whom we discern four, who seem to have hovered over the Danube from Passau to Pest, namely, the Rugii, Scyrri, Turcilingi and Heruli. With all of these Odoacer was connected by his subsequent career, and all seem, more or less, to have claimed him as belonging to them by birth; the evidence slightly preponderates in favour of his descent from the Scyrri.

His father was Aedico or Idico, a name which suggests Edeco the Hun, who was suborned by the Byzantine court to plot the assassination of his master Attila. There are, however,

[1] Odo must be distinguished from two English prelates of the same name and also from an English earl. Odo or Oda (d. 959), archbishop of Canterbury, was bishop of Ramsbury from 927 to 942, and went with King Æthelstan to the battle of Brunanburh in 937. In 942 he succeeded Wulfhelm as archbishop of Canterbury, and he appears to have been an able and conscientious ruler of the see. He had great influence with King Edwy, whom he had crowned in 956. Odo (d. 1200), abbot of Battle, was a monk of Christ Church, Canterbury, and was prior of this house at the time when Thomas Becket was murdered. In 1175 he was chosen abbot of Battle, and on two occasions the efforts of Henry II. alone prevented him from being elected archbishop of Canterbury. Odo or Odda (d. 1056), a relative of Edward the Confessor, during whose reign he was an earl in the west of England, built the minster at Deerhurst in Gloucestershire.

some strong arguments against this identification. A certain Edica, chief of the Scyrri, of whom Jordanes speaks as defeated by the Ostrogoths, may more probably have been the father of Odoacer, though even in this theory there are some difficulties, chiefly connected with the low estate in which he appears before us in the next scene of his life, when as a tall young recruit for the Roman armies, dressed in a sordid vesture of skins, on his way to Italy, he enters the cell of Severinus, a noted hermit-saint of Noricum, to ask his blessing. The saint had an inward premonition of his future greatness, and in blessing him said, "Fare onward into Italy. Thou who art now clothed in vile raiment wilt soon give precious gifts unto many."

Odoacer was probably about thirty years of age when he thus left his country and entered the imperial service. By the year 472 he had risen to some eminence, since it is expressly recorded that he sided with the patrician Ricimer in his quarrel with the emperor Anthemius. In the year 475, by one of the endless revolutions which marked the close of the Western empire, the emperor Nepos was driven into exile, and the successful rebel Orestes was enabled to array in the purple his son, a handsome boy of fourteen or fifteen, who was named Romulus after his grandfather, and nicknamed Augustulus, from his inability to play the part of the great Augustus. Before this puppet emperor had been a year on the throne the barbarian mercenaries, who were chiefly drawn from the Danubian tribes before mentioned, rose in mutiny, demanding to be made proprietors of one-third of the soil of Italy. To this request Orestes returned a peremptory negative. Odoacer now offered his fellow-soldiers to obtain for them all that they desired if they would seat him on the throne. On the 23rd of August 476 he was proclaimed king; five days later Orestes was made prisoner at Placentia and beheaded; and on the 4th of September his brother Paulus was defeated and slain near Ravenna. Rome at once accepted the new ruler. Augustulus was compelled to descend from the throne, but his life was spared.

Odoacer was forty-two years of age when he thus became chief ruler of Italy, and he reigned thirteen years with undisputed sway. Our information as to this period is very slender, but we can perceive that the administration was conducted as much as possible on the lines of the old imperial government. The settlement of the barbarian soldiers on the lands of Italy probably affected the great landowners rather than the labouring class. To the herd of *coloni* and *servi,* by whom in their various degrees the land was actually cultivated, it probably made little difference, except as a matter of sentiment, whether the master whom they served called himself Roman or Rugian. We have one most interesting example, though in a small way, of such a transfer of land with its appurtenant slaves and cattle, in the donation made by Odoacer himself to his faithful follower Pierius.[2] Few things bring more vividly before the reader the continuity of legal and social life in the midst of the tremendous ethnical changes of the 5th century than the perusal of such a record.

The same fact, from a slightly different point of view, is illustrated by the curious history (recorded by Malchus) of the embassies to Constantinople. The dethroned emperor Nepos sent ambassadors (in 477 or 478) to Zeno, emperor of the East, begging his aid in the reconquest of Italy. These ambassadors met a deputation from the Roman senate, sent nominally by the command of Augustulus, really no doubt by that of Odoacer, the purport of whose commission was that they did not need a separate emperor. One was sufficient to defend the borders of either realm. The senate had chosen Odoacer, whose knowledge of military affairs and whose statesmanship admirably fitted him for preserving order in that part of the world, and they therefore prayed Zeno to confer upon him the dignity of patrician, and entrust the "diocese" of Italy to his care. Zeno returned a harsh answer to the senate, requiring them to return to their allegiance to Nepos. In fact, however, he did nothing for the fallen emperor, but accepted the new order of things, and even addressed Odoacer as patrician. On the other hand, the latter

[2] Published in Marini's *Papiri diplomatici* (Rome, 1815. Nos. 82 and 83) and in Spangenberg's *Juris Romani Tabulae* (Leipzig, 1822. pp. 164-173). and well worthy of careful study.

sent the ornaments of empire, the diadem and purple robe, to Constantinople as an acknowledgment of the fact that he did not claim supreme power. Our information as to the actual title assumed by the new ruler is somewhat confused. He does not appear to have called himself king of Italy. His kingship seems to have marked only his relation to his Teutonic followers, among whom he was " king of the Turcilingi," " king of the Heruli," and so forth, according to the nationality with which he was dealing. By the Roman inhabitants of Italy he was addressed as " dominus noster," but his right to exercise power would in their eyes rest, in theory, on his recognition as patricius by the Byzantine Augustus. At the same time he marked his own high pretensions by assuming the prefix Flavius, a reminiscence of the early emperors, to which the barbarian rulers of realms formed out of the Roman state seem to have been peculiarly partial. His internal administration was probably, upon the whole, wise and moderate, though we hear some complaints of financial oppression, and he may be looked upon as a not altogether unworthy predecessor of Theodoric.

In the history of the papacy Odoacer figures as the author of a decree promulgated at the election of Felix II. in 483, forbidding the pope to alienate any of the lands or ornaments of the Roman Church, and threatening any pope who should infringe this edict with anathema. This decree was loudly condemned in a synod held by Pope Symmachus (502) as an unwarrantable interference of the civil power with the concerns of the church.

The chief events in the foreign policy of Odoacer were his Dalmatian and Rugian wars. In the year 480 the ex-emperor Nepos, who ruled Dalmatia, was traitorously assassinated in Diocletian's palace at Spalato by the counts Viator and Ovida. In the following year Odoacer invaded Dalmatia, slew the murderer Ovida, and reannexed Dalmatia to the Western state. In 487 he appeared as an invader in his own native Danubian lands. War broke out between him and Feletheus, king of the Rugians. Odoacer entered the Rugian territory, defeated Feletheus, and carried him and " his noxious wife " Gisa prisoners to Ravenna. In the following year Frederick, son of the captive king, endeavoured to raise again the fallen fortunes of his house, but was defeated by Onulf, brother of Odoacer, and, being forced to flee, took refuge at the court of Theodoric the Ostrogoth, at Sistova on the lower Danube.

This Rugian war was probably an indirect cause of the fall of Odoacer. His increasing power rendered him too formidable to the Byzantine court, with whom his relations had for some time been growing less friendly. At the same time, Zeno was embarrassed by the formidable neighbourhood of Theodoric and his Ostrogothic warriors, who were almost equally burdensome as enemies or as allies. In these circumstances arose the plan of Theodoric's invasion of Italy, a plan by whom originated it would be difficult to say. Whether the land when conquered was to be held by the Ostrogoth in full sovereignty, or administered by him as lieutenant of Zeno, is a point upon which our information is ambiguous, and which was perhaps intentionally left vague by the two contracting parties, whose chief anxiety was not to see one another's faces again. The details of the Ostrogothic invasion of Italy belong properly to the life of Theodoric. It is sufficient to state here that he entered Italy in August 489, defeated Odoacer at the Isontius (Isonzo) on the 28th of August, and at Verona on the 30th of September. Odoacer then shut himself up in Ravenna, and there maintained himself for four years, with one brief gleam of success, during which he emerged from his hiding-place and fought the battle of the Addua (11th August 490), in which he was again defeated. A sally from Ravenna (10th July 491) was again the occasion of a murderous defeat. At length, the famine in Ravenna having become almost intolerable, and the Goths despairing of ever taking the city by assault, negotiations were opened for a compromise (25th February 493). John, archbishop of Ravenna, acted as mediator. It was stipulated that Ravenna should be surrendered, that Odoacer's life should be spared, and that he and Theodoric should be recognized as joint rulers of the Roman state. The arrangement was evidently a precarious one, and

was soon terminated by the treachery of Theodoric. He invited his rival to a banquet in the palace of the Lauretum on the 15th of March, and there slew him with his own hand. " Where is God? " cried Odoacer when he perceived the ambush into which he had fallen. " Thus didst thou deal with my kinsmen," shouted Theodoric, and clove his rival with the broadsword from shoulder to flank. Onulf, the brother of the murdered king, was . shot down while attempting to escape through the palace garden, and Thelan, his son, was not long after put to death by order of the conqueror. Thus perished the whole race of Odoacer.

LITERATURE.—The chief authorities for the life of Odoacer are the so-called " Anonymus Valesii," generally printed at the end of Ammianus Marcellinus; the *Life of Severinus*, by Eugippius; the chroniclers, Cassiodorus and " Cuspiniani Anonymus " (both in Roncalli's collection); and the Byzantine historians, Malchus and John of Antioch. A fragment of the latter historian, unknown when Gibbon wrote, is to be found in the fifth volume of Müller's *Fragmenta Historicorum Graecorum*. There is a thorough investigation of the history of Odoacer in R. Pallmann's *Geschichte der Völkerwanderung*, vol. ii. (Weimar, 1864). See also T. Hodgkin, *Italy and her Invaders*, vol. iii. (Oxford, 1885).   (T. H.)

ODOFREDUS, an Italian jurist of the 13th century. He was born at Bologna and studied law under Balduinus and Accursius. After having practised as an advocate both in Italy and France, he became professor at Bologna in 1228. The commentaries on Roman law attributed to him are valuable as showing the growth of the study of law in Italy, and for their biographical details of the jurists of the 11th and 13th centuries. Odofredus died at Bologna on the 3rd of December 1265.

Over his name appeared *Lecturae in codicem* (Lyons, 1480) *Lecturae in digestum vetus* (Paris, 1504), *Summa de libellis formandis* (Strassburg, 1510), *Lecturae in tres libros* (Venice, 1514), and *Lecturae in digestum novum* (Lyons, 1552).

O'DONNELL, the name of an ancient and powerful Irish family, lords of Tyrconnel in early times, and the chief rivals of the O'Neills in Ulster. Like the family of O'Neill (*q.v.*), that of O'Donnell was descended from Niall of the Nine Hostages, king of Ireland at the beginning of the 5th century; the O'Neills, or Cinél Owen, tracing their pedigree to Owen (Eoghan), and the O'Donnells, or Cinél Connell, to Conall Gulban, both sons of Niall. Tyrconnel, the district named after the Cinél Connell, where the O'Donnells held sway, comprised the greater part of the modern county of Donegal except the peninsula of Inishowen; and since it lay conterminous with the territory ruled by the O'Neills of Tyrone, who were continually attempting to assert their supremacy over it, the history of the O'Donnells is for the most part a record of tribal warfare with their powerful neighbours, and of their own efforts to make good their claims to the overlordship of northern Connaught.

The first chieftain of mark in the family was Goffraidh (Godfrey), son of Donnell Mor O'Donnell (d. 1241). Goffraidh, who was " inaugurated " as " The O'Donnell," *i.e.* chief of the clan, in 1248, made a successful inroad into Tyrone against Brian O'Neill in 1252. In 1257 he drove the English out of northern Connaught, after a single combat with Maurice Fitzgerald in which both warriors were wounded. O'Donnell while still incapacitated by his wound was summoned by Brian O'Neill to give hostages in token of submission. Carried on a litter at the head of his clan he gave battle to O'Neill, whom he defeated with heavy loss in prisoners and cattle; but he died of his wound immediately afterwards near Letterkenny, and was succeeded in the chieftainship by his brother Donnell Oge, who returned from Scotland in time to withstand successfully the demands of O'Neill.

In the 16th century, when the English began to make determined efforts to bring the whole of Ireland under subjection to the crown, the O'Donnells of Tyrconnel played a leading part; co-operating at times with the English, especially when such co-operation appeared to promise triumph over their ancient enemies the O'Neills, at other times joining with the latter against the English authorities.

<hr />

[1] The Cinel, or Kinel, was a group of related clans occupying an extensive district. See P. W. Joyce, *A Social History of Ireland* (London, 1903), i. 166.

MANUS O'DONNELL (d. 1564), son of Hugh Dubh O'Donnell, was left by his father to rule Tyrconnel, though still a mere youth, when Hugh Dubb went on a pilgrimage to Rome about 1511. Hugh Dubh had been chief of the O'Donnells during one of the bitterest and most protracted of the feuds between his clan and the O'Neills, which in 1491 led to a war lasting more than ten years. On his return from Rome in broken health after two years' absence, his son Manus, who had proved himself a capable leader in defending his country against the O'Neills, retained the chief authority. A family quarrel ensued, and when Hugh Dubb appealed for aid against his son to the Maguires, Manus made an alliance with the O'Neills, by whose assistance he established his hold over Tyrconnel. But in 1522 the two great northern clans were again at war. Conn Bacach O'Neill, 1st earl of Tyrone, determined to bring the O'Donnells under thorough subjection. Supported by several septs of Munster and Connaught, and assisted also by English contingents and by the MacDonnells of Antrim, O'Neill took the castle of Ballyshannon, and after devastating a large part of Tyrconnel he encamped at Knockavoe, near Strabane. Here he was surprised at night by Hugh Dubh and Manus O'Donnell, and routed with the loss of 900 men and an immense quantity of booty. Although this was one of the bloodiest fights that ever took place between the O'Neills and the O'Donnells, it did not bring the war to an end; and in 1531 O'Donnell applied to the English government for protection, giving assurances of allegiance to Henry VIII. In 1537 Lord Thomas Fitzgerald and his five uncles were executed for rebellion in Munster, and the English government made every effort to lay hands also on Gerald, the youthful heir to the earldom of Kildare, a boy of twelve years of age who was in the secret custody of his aunt Lady Eleanor McCarthy. This lady, in order to secure a powerful protector for the boy, accepted an offer of marriage by Manus O'Donnell, who on the death of Hugh Dubh in July 1537 was inaugurated The O'Donnell. Conn O'Neill was a relative of Gerald Fitzgerald, and this event accordingly led to the formation of the Geraldine League, a federation which combined the O'Neills, the O'Donnells, the O'Briens of Thomond, and other powerful clans; the primary object of which was to restore Gerald to the earldom of Kildare, but which afterwards aimed at the complete overthrow of English rule in Ireland. In August 1539 Manus O'Donnell and Conn O'Neill were defeated with heavy loss by the lord deputy at Lake Bellahoe, in Monaghan, which crippled their power for many years. In the west Manus made unceasing efforts to assert the supremacy of the O'Donnells in north Connaught, where he compelled O'Conor Sligo to acknowledge his over-lordship in 1539. In 1542 he went to England and presented himself, together with Conn O'Neill and other Irish chiefs, before Henry VIII., who promised to make him earl of Tyrconnel, though he refused O'Donnell's request to be made earl of Sligo. In his later years Manus was troubled by quarrels between his sons Calvagh and Hugh MacManus; in 1555 he was made prisoner by Calvagh, who deposed him from all authority in Tyrconnel, and he died in 1564. Manus O'Donnell, though a fierce warrior, was hospitable and generous to the poor and the Church. He is described by the Four Masters as "a learned man, skilled in many arts, gifted with a profound intellect, and the knowledge of every science." At his castle of Portnattynod near Strabane he supervised if he did not actually dictate the writing of the *Life of Saint Columbkille* in Irish, which is preserved in the Bodleian Library at Oxford. Manus was several times married. His first wife, Joan O'Reilly, was the mother of Calvagh, and two daughters, both of whom married O'Neills; the younger, Margaret, was wife of the famous rebel Shane O'Neill. His second wife, Hugh's mother, by whom he was ancestor of the earls of Tyrconnel (see below), was Judith, sister of Conn Bacach O'Neill, 1st earl of Tyrone, and aunt of Shane O'Neill.

CALVAGH O'DONNELL (d. 1566), eldest son of Manus O'Donnell, in the course of his above-mentioned quarrel with his father and his half-brother Hugh, sought aid in Scotland from the MacDonnells, who assisted him in deposing Manus and securing the lordship of Tyrconnel for himself. Hugh then appealed to Shane O'Neill, who invaded Tyrconnel at the head of a large army in 1557, desiring to make himself supreme throughout Ulster, and encamped on the shore of Lough Swilly. Calvagh, acting apparently on the advice of his father, who was his prisoner and who remembered the successful night attack on Conn O'Neill at Knockavoe in 1522, surprised the O'Neills in their camp at night and routed them with the loss of all their spoils. Calvagh was then recognized by the English government as lord of Tyrconnel; but in 1561 he and his wife were captured by Shane O'Neill in the monastery of Kildonnell. His wife, Catherine Maclean, who had previously been the wife of the earl of Argyll, was kept by Shane O'Neill as his mistress and bore him several children, though grossly ill-treated by her savage captor; Calvagh himself was subjected to atrocious torture during the three years that he remained O'Neill's prisoner. He was released in 1564 on conditions which he had no intention of fulfilling; and crossing to England he threw himself on the mercy of Queen Elizabeth. In 1566 Sir Henry Sidney by the queen's orders marched to Tyrconnel and restored Calvagh to his rights. Calvagh, however, died in the same year, and as his son Conn was a prisoner in the hands of Shane O'Neill, his half-brother Hugh MacManus was inaugurated The O'Donnell in his place. Hugh, who in the family feud with Calvagh had allied himself with O'Neill, now turned round and combined with the English to crush the hereditary enemy of his family; and in 1567 he utterly routed Shane at Letterkenny with the loss of 1300 men, compelling him to seek refuge with the Mac-Donnells of Antrim, by whom he was treacherously put to death. In 1592 Hugh abdicated in favour of his son Hugh Roe O'Donnell (see below); but there was a member of the elder branch of the family who resented the passing of the chieftainship to the descendants of Manus O'Donnell's second marriage. This was Niall Garve, second son of Calvagh's son Conn. His elder brother was Hugh of Ramelton, whose son John, an officer in the Spanish army, was father of Hugh Baldearg O'Donnell (d. 1704), known in Spain as Count O'Donnell, who commanded an Irish regiment as brigadier in the Spanish service. This officer came to Ireland in 1690 and raised an army in Ulster for the service of James II., afterwards deserting to the side of William III., from whom he accepted a pension.

NIALL GARVE O'DONNELL (1569–1626), who was incensed at the elevation of his cousin Hugh Roe to the chieftainship in 1592, was further alienated when the latter deprived him of his castle of Lifford, and a bitter feud between the two O'Donnells was the result. Niall Garve made terms with the English government, to whom he rendered valuable service both against the O'Neills and against his cousin. But in 1601 he quarrelled with the lord deputy, who, though willing to establish Niall Garve in the lordship of Tyrconnel, would not permit him to enforce his supremacy over Cahir O'Dogherty in Inishowen. After the departure of Hugh Roe from Ireland in 1602, Niall Garve and Hugh Roe's brother Rory went to London, where the privy council endeavoured to arrange the family quarrel, but failed to satisfy Niall. Charged with complicity in Cahir O'Dogherty's rebellion in 1608, Niall Garve was sent to the Tower of London, where he remained till his death in 1626. He married his cousin Nuala, sister of Hugh Roe and Rory O'Donnell. When Rory fled with the earl of Tyrone to Rome in 1607, Nuala, who had deserted her husband when he joined the English against her brother, accompanied him, taking with her her daughter Grania. She was the subject of an Irish poem, of which an English version was written by James Mangan from a prose translation by Eugene O'Curry.

HUGH ROE O'DONNELL (1572–1602), eldest son of Hugh MacManus O'Donnell, and grandson of Manus O'Donnell by his second marriage with Judith O'Neill, was the most celebrated member of his clan. His mother was Ineen Dubh, daughter of James MacDonnell of Kintyre; his sister was the second wife of Hugh O'Neill, 2nd earl of Tyrone. These family connexions with the Hebridean Scots and with the O'Neills made the lord deputy, Sir John Perrot, afraid of a powerful combination against the English government, and induced him to establish garrisons in Tyrconnel and to demand hostages from Hugh MacManus O'Donnell, which the latter refused to hand over. In 1587 Perrot conceived a plan for kidnapping Hugh Roe (Hugh the Red), now a youth of fifteen, who had already given proof of exceptional manliness and sagacity. A merchant vessel laden with Spanish wines was sent to Lough Swilly, and anchoring off Rathmullan, where the boy was residing in the castle of MacSweeny his foster parent, Hugh Roe with some youthful companions was enticed on board, when the ship immediately set sail and conveyed the party to Dublin. The boys were kept in prison for more than three years In 1591 young O'Donnell made two attempts to escape, the second of which proved successful; and after enduring terrible privations from exposure in the mountains he made his way to Tyrconnel, where in the following year his father handed the chieftainship over to him. Red Hugh lost no time in leading an expedition against Turlough Luineach O'Neill, then at war with his kinsman Hugh, earl of Tyrone, with whom O'Donnell was in alliance. At the same time he sent assurances of loyalty to the lord deputy, whom he met in person at Dundalk in the summer of 1592. But being determined to vindicate the traditional claims of his family in north Connaught, he aided Hugh Maguire against the English, though on the advice of Tyrone he abstained for a time from committing himself too far. When, however, in 1594 Enniskillen castle was taken and the women and children flung into the river from its walls by order of Sir Richard Bingham, the English governor of Connaught, O'Donnell sent urgent messages to Tyrone for help, and while he himself hurried to Derry to withstand an invasion of Scots from the isles, Maguire defeated the English with heavy loss at Bellana-briska (The Ford of the Biscuits). In 1595 Red Hugh again invaded Connaught, putting to the sword every soul above fifteen years of age unable to speak Irish; he captured Longford and soon afterwards gained possession of Sligo, which placed north Connaught at his mercy. In 1596 he agreed in conjunction with Tyrone to a cessation of hostilities with the English, and consented to meet commissioners from the government near Dundalk. The terms he demanded were, however, refused; and his determination to continue the struggle was strengthened by the prospect of help from Philip II. of Spain; with whom he and Tyrone had been in correspondence. In the beginning of 1597 he made another inroad into Connaught, where O'Conor Sligo had been set up by the English as a counterpoise to O'Donnell. He devastated the country and returned to Tyrconnel with rich spoils; in the following year he shared in Tyrone's victory over the English at the Yellow Ford on the Blackwater; and in 1599 he defeated an attempt by the English under Sir Conyers Clifford, governor of Connaught, to succour O'Conor Sligo in Collooney castle, which O'Donnell captured, forcing Sligo to submission. The government now sent Sir Henry Docwra to Derry, and O'Donnell entrusted to his cousin Niall Garve the task of opposing him. Niall Garve, however, went over to the English, making himself master of O'Donnell's fortresses of Lifford and Donegal. While Hugh Roe was attempting to retake the latter place in 1601, he heard that a Spanish force had landed in Munster. He marched rapidly to the south, and was joined by Tyrone at Bandon; but a night-attack on the English besieging the Spaniards in Kinsale having utterly failed, O'Donnell, who attributed the disaster to the incapacity of the Spanish commander, took ship to Spain on the 6th of January 1602 to lay his complaint before Philip III. He was favourably received by the Spanish king, but he died at Simancas on the 10th of September in the same year.

RORY O'DONNELL, 1st earl of Tyrconnel (1575-1608), second son of Hugh MacManus O'Donnell, and younger brother of Hugh Roe, accompanied the latter in the above-mentioned expedition to Kinsale; and when his brother sailed for Spain he transferred his authority as chief to Rory, who led the O'Donnell contingent back to the north. In 1602 Rory gave in his allegiance to Lord Mountjoy, the lord deputy; and in the following summer he went to London with the earl of Tyrone,

where he was received with favour by James I., who created him earl of Tyrconnel. In 1605 he was invested with authority as lieutenant of the king in Donegal. But the arrangement between Rory and Niall Garve insisted upon by the government was displeasing to both O'Donnells, and Rory, like Hugh Roe before him, entered into negotiations with Spain. His country had been reduced to a desert by famine and war, and his own reckless extravagance had plunged him deeply in debt. These circumstances as much as the fear that his designs were known to the government may have persuaded him to leave Ireland. In September 1607 "the flight of the earls" (see O'NEILL) took place, Tyrconnel and Tyrone reaching Rome in April 1608, where Tyrconnel died on the 28th of July. His wife, the beautiful daughter of the earl of Kildare, was left behind in the haste of Tyrconnel's flight, and lived to marry Nicholas Barnewell, Lord Kingsland. By Tyrconnel she had a son Hugh; and among other children a daughter Mary Stuart O'Donnell, who, born after her father's flight from Ireland, was so named by James I. after his mother. This lady, after many romantic adventures disguised in male attire, married a man called O'Gallagher and died in poverty on the continent.

Rory O'Donnell was attainted by the Irish parliament in 1614, but his son Hugh, who lived at the Spanish Court, assumed the title of earl; and the last titular earl of Tyrconnel was this Hugh's son Hugh Albert, who died without heirs in 1642, and who by his will appointed Hugh Balldearg O'Donnell (see above) his heir, thus restoring the chieftainship to the elder branch of the family. To a still elder branch belonged Daniel O'Donnell (1666-1735), a general of the famous Irish brigade in the French service, whose father, Turlough, was a son of Hugh Dubh O'Donnell, elder brother of Manus, son of an earlier Hugh Dubh mentioned above. Daniel served in the French army in the wars of the period, fighting against Marlborough at Oudenarde and Malplaquet at the head of an O'Donnell regiment. He died in 1735.

The famous Cathach, or Battle-Book of the O'Donnells, was in the possession of General Daniel O'Donnell, from whom it passed to more modern representatives of the family, who presented it to the Royal Irish Academy, where it is preserved. This relic, of which a curious legend is told (see P. W. Joyce, *A Social History of Ancient Ireland*, vol. i. p. 501), is a Psalter said to have belonged to Saint Columba, a kinsman of the O'Donnells, which was carried by them in battle as a charm or talisman to secure victory. Two other circumstances connecting the O'Donnells with ancient Irish literature may be mentioned. The family of O'Clery, to which three of the celebrated "Four Masters" belonged, were hereditary Ollaves (doctors of history, music, law, &c.) attached to the family of O'Donnell; while the "Book of the Dun Cow" (*Lebor-na-h Uidhre*), one of the most ancient Irish MSS., was in the possession of the O'Donnells in the 14th century; and the estimation in which it was held at that time is proved by the fact that it was given to the O'Conors of Connaught as ransom for an important prisoner, and was forcibly recovered some years later.

See O'NEILL, and the authorities there cited.   (R. J. M.)

O'DONNELL, HENRY JOSEPH (1769-1834), count of La Bisbal, Spanish soldier, was descended from the O'Donnells who left Ireland after the battle of the Boyne.[1] Born in Spain, he early entered the Spanish army, and in 1810 became general; receiving a command in Catalonia, where in that year he earned his title and the rank of field-marshal. He afterwards held posts of great responsibility under Ferdinand VII., whom he served on the whole with constancy; the events of 1823 compelled his flight into France, where he was interned at Limoges, and where he died in 1834. His second son LEOPOLD O'DONNELL (1809-1867), duke of Tetuan, Spanish general and statesman, was born at Santa Cruz, Teneriffe, on the 12th of January 1809. He fought in the army of Queen Christina, where he attained the rank of general of division; and in 1840 he accompanied the queen into exile. He failed in an attempt to effect a rising in her favour at Pamplona in 1841, but took a more successful part in the movement which led to the overthrow and exile of

_____
[1] A branch of the family settled in Austria, and General Karl O'Donnell, count of Tyrconnel (1715-1771), held important commands during the Seven Years' War. The name of a descendant figures in the history of the Italian and Hungarian campaigns of 1848 and 1849.

Espartero in 1843. From 1844 to 1848 he served the new government in Cuba; after his return he entered the senate. In 1854 he became war minister under Espartero, and in 1856 he plotted successfully against his chief, becoming head of the cabinet from the July revolution until October. This rank he again reached in July 1858; and in December 1859 he took command of the expedition to Morocco, and received the title of duke after the surrender of Tetuan. Quitting office in 1863, he again resumed it in June 1865, but was compelled to resign in favour of Narvaez in 1866. He died at Bayonne on the 5th of November 1867.

There is a _Life_ of Leopold O'Donnell in _La Corona de laurel_, by Manuel Ibo Alfaro (Madrid, 1860).

O'DONOVAN, EDMUND (1844–1883), British war-correspondent, was born at Dublin on the 13th of September 1844, the son of John O'Donovan (1809–1861), a well-known Irish archaeologist and topographer. In 1866 he began to contribute to the _Irish Times_ and other Dublin papers. After the battle of Sedan he joined the Foreign Legion of the French army, and was wounded and taken prisoner by the Germans. In 1873 the Carlist rising attracted him to Spain, and he wrote many newspaper letters on the campaign. In 1876 he represented the London _Daily News_ during the rising of Bosnia and Herzegovina against the Turks, and in 1879, for the same paper, made his adventurous and famous journey to Merv. On his arrival at Merv, the Turcomans, suspecting him to be a Russian spy, detained him. It was only after several months' captivity that O'Donovan managed to get a message to his principals through to Persia, whence it was telegraphed to England. These adventures he described in _The Merv Oasis_ (1882). In 1883 O'Donovan accompanied the ill-fated expedition of Hicks Pasha to the Egyptian Sudan, and perished with it.

O'DONOVAN, WILLIAM RUDOLF (1844–   ), American sculptor, was born in Preston county, Virginia, on the 28th of March 1844. He had no technical art training, but after the Civil War, in which he served in the Confederate army, he opened a studio in New York City and became a well-known sculptor, especially of memorial pieces. Among these are statues of George Washington (in Caracas), Lincoln and Grant (Prospect Park, Brooklyn), the captors of Major André (Tarrytown, N.Y.), and Archbishop Hughes (Fordham University, Fordham, N.Y.), and a memorial tablet to Bayard Taylor (Cornell University). In 1878 he become an associate of the National Academy of Design.

ODONTORNITHES, the term proposed by O. C. Marsh (_Am. Journ. Sci._ ser 3, v. (1873) pp. 161–162) for birds possessed of teeth (Gr. ὀδούς, tooth, ὄρνις, ὄρνιθος, bird), notably the genera _Hesperornis_ and _Ichthyornis_ from the Cretaceous deposits of Kansas. In 1875 (_op. cit._ x. pp. 403–408) he divided the "subclass" into _Odontolcae_, with the teeth standing in grooves, and _Odontotormae_, with the teeth in separate alveoles or sockets. In his magnificent work, _Odontornithes: A monograph on the extinct toothed birds of North America_, New Haven, Connecticut, 1880, be logically added the Saururae, represented by _Archaeopteryx_, as a third order. As it usually happens with the selection of a single anatomical character, the resulting classification was unnatural. In the present case the Odontornithes are a heterogeneous assembly, and the fact of their possessing teeth proves nothing but that birds, possibly all of them, still had these organs during the Cretaceous epoch. This, by itself, is a very interesting point, showing that birds, as a class, are the descendants of well-toothed reptiles, to the complete exclusion of the Chelonia with which various authors persistently try to connect them. No fossil birds of later than Cretaceous age are known to have teeth, and concerning recent birds they possess not even embryonic vestiges.

E. Geoffroy St Hilaire stated in 1821 (_Ann. Gén. Sci. Phys._ viii. pp. 373–380) that he had found a considerable number of tooth-germs in the upper and lower jaws of the parrot _Palaeornis torquatus_. E. Blanchard ("Observations sur le système dentaire chez les oiseaux," _Comptes rendus_ 50, 1860, pp. 540–542) felt justified in recognizing flakes of dentine. However,

M. Braun (_Arbeit Zool. Inst._, Würzburg, v. 1879) and especially P. Fraisse (_Phys. Med. Ges._, Würzburg, 1880) have shown that the structures in question are of the same kind as the well-known serrated "teeth" of the bill of anserine birds. In fact the papillae observed in the embryonic birds are the soft cutaneous extensions into the surrounding horny sheath of the bill, comparable to the well-known nutritive papillae in a horse's hoof. They are easily exposed in the well-macerated under jaw of a parrot, after removal of the horny sheath. Occasionally calcification occurs in or around these papillae, as it does regularly in the "egg-tooth" of the embryos of all birds.

The best-known of the Odontornithes are _Hesperornis regalis_, standing about 3 ft. high, and the somewhat taller _H. crassipes_. Both show the general configuration of a diver, but it is only by analogy that _Hesperornis_ can be looked upon as ancestral to the Colymbiformes. There are about fourteen teeth in a groove of the maxilla and about twenty-one in the mandible; the vertebrae are typically heterocoelous; of the wing-bones only the very slender and long humerus is known; clavicles slightly reduced; coracoids short and broad, movably connected with the scapula; sternum very long, broad and quite flat, without the trace of a keel. Hind limbs very strong and of the Colymbine type, but the outer or fourth capitulum of the metatarsus is the strongest and longest, an unique arrangement in an otherwise typically steganopodous foot. The pelvis shows much resemblance to that of the divers, but there is still an incisura ischiadica instead of a foramen. The tail is composed of about twelve vertebrae, without a pygostyle. _Enaliornis_ of the Cambridge Greensand of England, and _Baptornis_ of the mid-Cretaceous of North America, are probably allied, but imperfectly known. The vertebrae are biconcave, with heterocoelous indications in the cervicals; the metatarsal bones appear still somewhat imperfectly anchylosed. The absence of a keel misled Marsh who suspected relationship of _Hesperornis_ with the Ratitae, and L. Dollo went so far as to call it a carnivorous, aquatic ostrich (_Bull. Sci. Départ. du Nord_, ser. 2, iv. 1881, p. 300), and this mistaken notion of the "swimming ostrich" was popularized by various authors. B. Vetter (_Festschr. Ges. Isis._, Dresden, 1885) rightly pointed out that _Hesperornis_ was a descendant of Carinatae, but adapted to aquatic life, implying reduction of the keel. Lastly, M. Fürbringer (_Untersuchungen_, Amsterdam, 1888, pp. 1543, 1505, 1580) relegated it, together with _Enaliornis_ and the Colymbo-Podicipedes, to his suborder Podicipitiformes. The present writer does not feel justified in going so far. On account of their various, decidedly primitive characters, he prefers to look upon the Odontolcae as a separate group, one of the three divisions of the Neornithes, as birds which form an early offshoot from the later Colymbo-Pelargomorphous stock; in adaptation to a marine, swimming life they have lost the power of flight, as is shown by the absence of the keel and by the great reduction of the wing-skeleton, just as in another direction, away from the later _Alectoromorphous_ stock the Ratitae have specialized as runners. It is only in so far as the loss of flight is correlated with the absence of the keel that the Odontolcae and the Ratitae bear analogy to each other.

There remain the Odontotormae, notably _Ichthyornis victor_, _I. dispar_, _Apatornis_ and _Graculavus_ of the middle and upper Cretaceous of Kansas. The teeth stand in separate alveoles; the two halves of the mandible are, as in _Hesperornis_, without a symphysis. The vertebrae are amphicoelous, but at least the third cervical has somewhat saddle-shaped articular facets. Tail composed of five free vertebrae, followed by a rather small pygostyle. Shoulder girdle and sternum well developed and of the typical carinate type. Pelvis still with incisura ischiadica. Marsh based the restoration of _Ichthyornis_, which was obviously a well-flying aquatic bird, upon the skeleton of a tern, a relationship which cannot be supported. The teeth, vertebrae, pelvis and the small brain are all so many low characters that the Odontotormae may well form a separate, and very low, order of the typical Carinatae, of course near the Colymbomorphous Legion.　　　　　　　　　　　　　　　(H. F. G.)

ODORIC (*c.* 1286–1331), styled "of Pordenone," one of the chief travellers of the later middle ages, and a *Beatus* of the Roman Church, was born at Villa Nuova, a hamlet near the town of Pordenone in Friuli, in or about 1286. According to the ecclesiastical biographers, in early years he took the vows of the Franciscan order and joined their convent at Udine, the capital of Friuli.

Friar Odoric was despatched to the East, where a remarkable extension of missionary action was then taking place, about 1316–1318, and did not return till the end of 1329 or beginning of 1330; but, as regards intermediate dates, all that we can deduce from his narrative or other evidence is that he was in western India soon after 1321 (pretty certainly in 1322) and that he spent three years in China between the opening of 1323 and the close of 1328. His route to the East lay by Trebizond and Erzerum to Tabriz and Sultanieh, in all of which places the order had houses. From Sultanieh he proceeded by Kashan and Yazd, and turning thence followed a somewhat devious route by Persepolis and the Shiraz and Bagdad regions, to the Persian Gulf. At Hormuz he embarked for India, landing at Thana, near Bombay. At this city four brethren of his order, three of them Italians and the fourth a Georgian, had shortly before met death at the hands of the Mahommedan governor. The bones of the martyred friars had been collected by Friar Jordanus of Séverac, a Dominican, who carried them to Supera—the *Suppara* of the ancient geographers, near the modern Bassein, about 26 m. north of Bombay—and buried them there Odoric tells that he disinterred these relics and carried them with him on his further travels. In the course of these he visited Malabar, touching at Pandarani (20 m. north of Calicut), at Cranganore, and at Kulam or Quilon, proceeding thence, apparently, to Ceylon and to the shrine of St Thomas at Maylapur near Madras. From India he sailed in a junk to Sumatra, visiting various ports on the northern coast of that island, and thence to Java, to the coast (it would seem) of Borneo, to Champa (South Cochin-China), and to Canton, at that time known to western Asiatics as *Chin-Kalan* or Great China (Mahachin). From Canton he travelled overland to the great ports of Fukien, at one of which, Zayton or Amoy harbour, he found two houses of his order; in one of these he deposited the bones of the brethren who had suffered in India. From Fuchow he struck across the mountains into Cheh-kiang and visited Hangchow, then renowned, under the name of Cansay, *Khansa*, or *Quinsai* (i.e. *Kingsze* or royal residence), as the greatest city in the world, of whose splendours Odoric, like Marco Polo, Marignolli, or Ibn Batuta, gives notable details. Passing northward by Nanking and crossing the Yangtsze-kiang, Odoric embarked on the Great Canal and travelled to *Cambalec* (otherwise *Cambaleth, Cambaluc,* &c.) or Peking, where he remained for three years, attached, no doubt, to one of the churches founded by Archbishop John of Monte Corvino, at this time in extreme old age. Returning overland across Asia, through the Land of Prester John and through Casan, the adventurous traveller seems to have entered Tibet, and even perhaps to have visited Lhasa. After this we trace the friar in northern Persia, in Millestorte, once famous as the Land of the Assassins in the Elburz highlands. No further indications of his homeward route (to Venice) are given, though it is almost certain that he passed through Tabriz. The vague and fragmentary character of the narrative, in this section, forcibly contrasts with the clear and careful tracing of the outward way. During a part at least of these long journeys the companion of Odoric was Friar James, an Irishman, as appears from a record in the public books of Udine, showing that shortly after Odoric's death a present of two marks was made to this Irish friar, *Socio beati Fratris Odorici, amore Dei et Odorici.* Shortly after his return Odoric betook himself to the Minorite house attached to St Anthony's at Padua, and it was there that in May 1330 he related the story of his travels, which was taken down in homely Latin by Friar William of Solagna. Travelling towards the papal court at Avignon, Odoric fell ill at Pisa, and turning back to Udine, the capital of his native province, died in the convent there on the 14th of January 1331. The fame of

his vast journeys appears to have made a much greater impression on the laity of his native territory than on his Franciscan brethren. The latter were about to bury him without delay or ceremony, but the *gastald* or chief magistrate of the city interfered and appointed a public funeral; rumours of his wondrous travels and of posthumous miracles were diffused, and excitement spread like wildfire over Friuli and Carniola; the ceremony had to be deferred more than once, and at last took place in presence of the patriarch of Aquileia and all the local dignitaries. Popular acclamation made him an object of devotion, the municipality erected a noble shrine for his body, and his fame as saint and traveller had spread far and wide before the middle of the century, but it was not till four centuries later (1755) that the papal authority formally sanctioned his beatification. A bust of Odoric was set up at Pordenone in 1881.

The numerous copies of Odoric's narrative (both of the original text and of the versions in French, Italian, &c.) that have come down to our time, chiefly from the 14th century, show how speedily and widely it acquired popularity. It does not deserve the charge of mendacity brought against it by some, though the adulation of others is nearly as injudicious. Odoric's credit was not benefited by the liberties which Sir John Mandeville took with it. The substance of that knight's alleged travels in India and Cathay is stolen from Odoric, though amplified with fables from other sources and from his own invention, and garnished with his own unusually clear astronomical notions. We may indicate a few passages which stamp Odoric as a genuine and original traveller. He is the first European, after Marco Polo, who distinctly mentions the name of Sumatra. The cannibalism and community of wives which he attributes to certain races of that island do certainly belong to it, or to islands closely adjoining. His description of sago in the archipelago is not free from errors, but they are the errors of an eye-witness. In China his mention of Canton by the name of *Censcolam* or *Censcalam* (Chin-Kalan), and his descriptions of the custom of fishing with tame cormorants, of the habit of letting the finger-nails grow extravagantly, and of the compression of women's feet, are peculiar to him among the travellers of that age; Marco Polo omits them all.

Seventy-three MSS. of Odoric's narrative are known to exist in Latin, French and Italian: of these the chief is in Paris, National Library, MSS. Lat. 2584, fols. 118 r.–127 v., of about 1350. The narrative was first printed at Pesaro in 1513, in what Apostolo Zeno calls *lingua inculta e rozza.* Ramusio's collection first contains it in the 2nd vol. of the 2nd edition (1574) (Italian version), in which are given two versions, differing curiously from one another, but without any prefatory matter or explanation. (See also edition of 1583, vol. ii. fols. 245 r.–256 r.) Another (Latin) version is given in the *Acta Sanctorum* (Bollandist) under the 14th of January. The curious discussion before the papal court respecting the beatification of Odoric forms a kind of blue-book issued *ex typographia rev. cameras apostolicas* (Rome, 1755). Professor Friedrich Kunstmann of Munich devoted one of his valuable papers to Odoric's narrative (*Histor.-polit. Blätter von Phillips und Görres,* vol. xxxviii. pp. 507–537). The best editions of Odoric are by G. Venni, *Elogio storico alle gesta del Beato Odorico* (Venice, 1761); H. Yule in *Cathay and the Way Thither,* vol. i. pp. 1–162, vol. ii. appendix, pp. 1–42 (London, 1866), Hakluyt Society; and H. Cordier, *Les Voyages ... du ... frère Odoric ...* (Paris, 1891) (edition of Old French version of *c.* 1350). The edition by T. Domenichelli (Prato, 1881) may also be mentioned; likewise those texts of Odoric embedded in the *Storia universale delle Missioni Francescane,* iii. 730–781, and in Hakluyt's *Principal Navigations* (1599), ii. 39–67. See also John of Viktring (Joannes Victoriensis) in *Fontes rerum Germanicarum,* ed. J. F. Boehmer; vol. i. ed. by J. G. Cotta (Stuttgart, 1843), p. 391; Wadding, *Annales Minorum,* A.D. 1331, vol. vii. pp. 123–126; Bartholomew Albizzi, *Opus conformitatum ... B. Francisci ...* bk. i. par. ii. conf. 8 (fol. 124 of Milan, edition of 1513); John of Winterthur in Eccard, *Corpus historicum medii aevi,* vol. i. cols. 1894–1897, especially 1894; C. R. Beazley, *Dawn of Modern Geography,* iii. 250–287, 548–549, 554, 565–566, 612–613, &c.

(H. Y.; C. R. B.)

ODYLIC FORCE, a term once in vogue to explain the phenomenon of hypnotism (*q.v.*). In 1845 considerable attention was drawn to the announcement by Baron von Reichenbach of a so-called new " imponderable " or " influence " developed by certain crystals, magnets, the human body, associated with heat, chemical action, or electricity, and existing throughout the universe, to which he gave the name of *odyl*. Persons sensitive to odyl saw luminous phenomena near the poles of magnets, or even around the hands or heads of certain persons in whose bodies the force was supposed to be concentrated. In Britain an impetus was given to this view of the subject by the translation in 1850 of Reichenbach's *Researches on Magnetism, &c., in relation to Vital Force*, by Dr Gregory, professor of chemistry in the university of Edinburgh. These *Researches* show many of the phenomena to be of the same nature as those described previously by F. A. Mesmer, and even long before Mesmer's time by Swedenborg.

ODYSSEUS (in Latin *Ulixes*, incorrectly written Ulysses), in Greek legend, son of Laërtes and Anticleia, king of Ithaca, a famous hero and typical representative of the Greek race. In Homer he is one of the best and bravest of the heroes, and the favourite of Athena, whereas in later legend he is cowardly and deceitful. Soon after his marriage to Penelope he was summoned to the Trojan war. Unwilling to go, he feigned madness, ploughing a field sown with salt with an ox and an ass yoked together; but Palamedes discovered his deceit by placing his infant child Telemachus in front of the plough; Odysseus afterwards revenged himself by compassing the death of Palamedes. During the war, he distinguished himself as the wisest adviser of the Greeks, and finally, the capture of Troy, which the bravery of Achilles could not accomplish, was attained by Odysseus' stratagem of the wooden horse. After the death of Achilles the Greeks adjudged his armour to Odysseus as the man who had done most to end the war successfully. When Troy was captured he set sail for Ithaca, but was carried by unfavourable winds to the coast of Africa. After encountering many adventures in all parts of the unknown seas, among the lotus-eaters and the Cyclopes, in the isles of Aeolus and Circe and the perils of Scylla and Charybdis, among the Laestrygones, and even in the world of the dead, having lost all his ships and companions, he barely escaped with his life to the island of Calypso, where he was detained eight years, an unwilling lover of the beautiful nymph. Then at the command of Zeus he was sent homewards, but was again wrecked on the island of Phaeacia, whence he was conveyed to Ithaca in one of the wondrous Phaeacian ships. Here he found that a host of suitors, taking advantage of the youth of his son Telemachus, were wasting his property and trying to force Penelope to marry one of them. The stratagems and disguises by which with the help of a few faithful friends he slew the suitors are described at length in the *Odyssey*. The only allusion to his death is contained in the prophecy of Teiresias, who promised him a happy old age and a peaceful death from the sea. According to a later legend, Telegonus, the son of Odysseus by Circe, was sent by her in search of his father. Cast ashore on Ithaca by a storm, he plundered the island to get provisions, and was attacked by Odysseus, whom he slew. The prophecy was thus fulfilled. Telegonus, accompanied by Penelope and Telemachus, returned to his home with the body of his father, whose identity he had discovered.

According to E. Meyer (*Hermes*, xxx. p. 267), Odysseus is an old Arcadian nature god identical with Poseidon, who dies at the approach of winter (retires to the western sea or is carried away to the underworld) to revive in spring (but see E. Rohde, *Rhein. Mus.* I. p. 631) A more suitable identification would be Hermes. Mannhardt and others regard Odysseus as a solar or summer divinity, who withdraws to the underworld during the winter, and returns in spring to free his wife from the suitors (the powers of winter) A. Gercke (*Neue Jahrbücher für das klassische Altertum*, xv. p. 331) takes him to be an agricultural divinity akin to the sun god, whose wife is the moon-goddess Penelope, from whom he is separated and reunited to her on the day of the new moon. His cult early disappeared; in Arcadia his place was taken by Poseidon. But although the personality of Odysseus may have had its origin in some primitive religious myth, chief interest attaches to him as the typical representative of the old sailor-race whose adventurous voyages educated and moulded the Hellenic race. The period when the character of Odysseus took shape among the Ionian bards

was when the Ionian ships were beginning to penetrate to the farthest shores of the Black Sea and to the western side of Italy, but when Egypt had not yet been freely opened to foreign intercourse. The adventures of Odysseus were a favourite subject in ancient art, in which he may usually be recognised by his conical sailor's cap.

See article by J. Schmidt in Roscher's *Lexikon der Mythologie* (where the different forms of the name and its etymology are fully discussed); O. Gruppe, *Griechische Mythologie*, ii. pp. 624, 705-718; J. E. Harrison, *Myths of the Odyssey in Art and Literature* (1881), with appendix on authorities. W. Mannhardt, *Wald- und Feldkulte* (1905), ii. p. 106; O. Seeck, *Gesch. des Untergangs der antiken Welt*, ii. p. 576; G. Fougères, *Mantinée et l'Arcadie orientale* (1898), according to whom Odysseus is an Arcadian chthonian divinity and Penelope a goddess of flocks and herds, akin to the Arcadian Artemis; S. Eitrem, *Die göttlichen Zwillinge bei den Griechen* (1902), who identifies Odysseus with one of the Dioscuri ('Οδυσσευς = Πολυδευκης); V. Bérard, *Les Phéniciens et l'Odyssée* (1902-1903), who regards the *Odyssey* as "the integration in a Greek νοστος (home-coming) of a Semitic periplus," in the form of a poem written 900-850 B.C. by an Ionic poet at the court of one of the Neleid kings of Miletus. For an estimate of this work, the interest of which is mainly geographical, see *Classical Review* (April 1904) and *Quarterly Review* (April 1905). It consists of two large volumes, with 240 illustrations and maps.

OEBEN, JEAN FRANÇOIS, French 18th-century cabinet-maker, is believed to have been of German or Flemish origin; the date of his birth is unknown, but he was dead before 1767. In 1752, twenty years after Boulle's death, we find him occupying an apartment in the Louvre sublet to him by Charles Joseph Boulle, whose pupil he may have been. He has sometimes been confused with Simon Oehen, presumably a relative, who signed a fine bureau in the Jones collection at the Victoria and Albert Museum. J. F. Oeben is also represented in that collection by a pair of inlaid corner-cupboards. These with a bureau and a chiffonier in the Garde Meuble in which bouquets of flowers are delicately inlaid in choice woods are his best-known and most admirable achievement. He appears to have worked extensively for the marquise de Pompadour by whose influence he was granted lodgings at the Gobelins and the title of " Ébéniste du Roi " in 1754. There he remained until 1760, when he obtained an apartment and workshops at the Arsenal. His work in marquetry is of very great distinction, but he would probably never have enjoyed so great a reputation had it not been for his connexion with the famous Bureau du Roi, made for Louis XV., which appears to have owed its inception to him, notwithstanding that it was not completed until some considerable time after his death and is signed by J. H. Riesener (*q.v.*) only. Documentary evidence under the hand of the king shows that it was ordered from Oeben in 1760, the year in which he moved to the Arsenal. The known work of Oehen possesses genuine grace and beauty; as craftsmanship it is of the first rank, and it is remarkable that, despite his Teutonic or Flemish origin, it is typically French in character.

OECOLAMPADIUS, JOHN (1482-1531), German Reformer, whose real name was Hussgen or Heussgen,[1] was born at Weinsberg, a small town in the north of the modern kingdom of Württemberg, but then belonging to the Palatinate. He went to school at Weinsberg and Heilbronn, and then, intending to study law, he went to Bologna, but soon returned to Heidelberg and betook himself to theology. He became a zealous student of the new learning and passed from the study of Greek to that of Hebrew, taking his bachelor's degree in 1503. He became cathedral preacher at Basel in 1515, serving under Christopher von Uttenheim, the evangelical bishop of Basel. From the beginning the sermons of Oecolampadius centred in the Atonement, and his first reformatory zeal showed itself in a protest (*De risu paschali*, 1518) against the introduction of humorous stories into Easter sermons. In 1520 he published his *Greek Grammar*. The same year he was asked to become preacher in the high church in Augsburg. Germany was then ablaze with the questions raised by Luther's theses, and his introduction into this new world, when at first he championed Luther's position especially in his anonymous *Canonici indocti* (1519), seems to have compelled Oecolampadius to severe self-examina-

[1] Changed to Hausschein and then into the Greek equivalent.

tion, which ended in his entering a convent and becoming a monk. A short experience convinced him that this was not for him the ideal Christian life (" amisi monachum, inveni Christianum "), and in February 1522 he made his way to Ebernburg, near Creuznach, where he acted as chaplain to the little group of men holding the new opinions who had settled there under the leadership of Franz von Sickingen.

The second period of Oecolampadius's life opens with his return to Basel in November 1522, as vicar of St Martin's and (in 1523) reader of the Holy Scripture at the university. Lecturing on Isaiah he condemned current ecclesiastical abuses, and in a public disputation (20th of August 1523) was so successful that Erasmus writing to Zürich said "Oecolampadius has the upper hand amongst us." He became Zwingli's best helper, and after more than a year of earnest preaching and four public disputations in which the popular verdict had been given in favour of Oecolampadius and his friends, the authorities of Basel began to see the necessity of some reformation. They began with the convents, and Oecolampadius was able to refrain in public worship on certain festival days from some practices he believed to be superstitious. Basel was slow to accept the Reformation; the news of the Peasants' War and the inroads of Anabaptists prevented progress; but at last, in 1525, it seemed as if the authorities were resolved to listen to schemes for restoring the purity of worship and teaching. In the midst of these hopes and difficulties Oecolampadius married, in the beginning of 1528, Wilibrandis Rosenblatt, the widow of Ludwig Keller, who proved to be *non rixosa vel garrula vel vaga*, he says, and made him a good wife. After his death she married Capito, and, when Capito died, Bucer. She died in 1564. In January 1528 Oecolampadius and Zwingli took part in the disputation at Berne which led to the adoption of the new faith in that canton, and in the following year to the discontinuance of the mass at Basel. The Anabaptists claimed Oecolampadius for their views, but in a disputation with them he dissociated himself from most of their positions. He died on the 24th of November 1531.

Oecolampadius was not a great theologian, like Luther, Zwingli or Calvin, and yet he was a trusted theological leader. With Zwingli he represented the Swiss views at the unfortunate conference at Marburg. His views on the Eucharist upheld the metaphorical against the literal interpretation of the new word " body," but he asserted that believers partook of the sacrament more for the sake of others than for their own, though later he emphasized it as a means of grace for the Christian life. To Luther's doctrine of the ubiquity of Christ's body he opposed that of the presence and activity of the Holy Spirit in the church. He did not minutely analyse the doctrine of predestination as Luther, Calvin and Zwingli did, contenting himself with the summary " Our Salvation is of God, our perdition of ourselves."

See J. J. Herzog, *Leben Joh. Oecolampads u. die Reformation der Kirche zu Basel* (1843); K. R. Hagenbach, *Johann Oecolampad u. Oswald Myconius, die Reformatoren Basels* (1859). For other literature see W. Hadorn's art. in Herzog-Hauck's *Realencyklopädie für prot. Rel. u. Kirche*.

OECOLOGY. or **ECOLOGY** (from Gr. οἶκος, house, and λόγος, department of science), that part of the science of biology which treats of the adaptation of plants or animals to their environment (see PLANTS: *Ecology*).

OECUMENICAL (through the Lat. from Gr. οἰκουμενικός, universal, belonging to the whole inhabited world, ἡ οἰκουμένη *sc.* γῆ, οἰκεῖν, to dwell), a word chiefly used in the sense of belonging to the universal Christian Church. It is thus specifically applied to the general councils of the early church (see COUNCIL). In the Roman Church a council is regarded as oecumenical when it has been summoned from the whole church under the presidency of the pope or his legates; the decrees confirmed by the pope are binding. The word has also been applied to assemblies of other religious bodies, such as the Occumenical Methodist Conferences, which met for the first time in 1881. "Oecumenical" has also been the title of the patriarch of Constantinople since the 6th century (see ORTHODOX EASTERN CHURCH).

OECUS, the Latinised form of Gr. οἶκος, house, used by Vitruvius for the principal hall or saloon in a Roman house, which was used occasionally as a triclinium for banquets. When of great size it became necessary to support its ceiling with columns; thus, according to Vitruvius, the tetrastyle oecus had four columns; in the Corinthian oecus there was a row of columns on each side, virtually therefore dividing the room into nave and aisles, the former being covered over with a semicircular ceiling. The Egyptian oecus had a similar plan, but the aisles were of less height, so that clerestory windows were introduced to light the room, which, as Vitruvius states, presents more the appearance of a basilica than of a triclinium.

OEDIPUS (Οἰδίπους, Οἰδιπόδης, Οἰδίπος, from Gr. οἰδεῖν swell, and πούς foot, *i.e.* " the swollen-footed ") [1] In Greek legend, son of Laïus, king of Thebes, and Jocasta (Iocastê). Laïus, having been warned by an oracle that he would be killed by his son, ordered him to be exposed, with his feet pierced, immediately after his birth. Thus Oedipus grew up ignorant of his parentage, and, meeting Laïus in a narrow way, quarrelled with him and slew him. The country was ravaged by a monster, the Sphinx; Oedipus solved the riddle which it proposed to its victims, freed the country, and married his own mother. In the *Odyssey* it is said that the gods disclosed the impiety. Epicastê (as Jocasta is called in Homer) hanged herself, and Oedipus lived as king in Thebes tormented by the Erinyes of his mother. In the tragic poets the tale takes a different form. Oedipus fulfils an ancient prophecy in killing his father; he is the blind instrument in the hands of fate. The further treatment of the tale by Aeschylus is unknown. Sophocles describes in his *Oedipus Tyrannus* how Oedipus was resolved to pursue to the end the mystery of the death of Laïus, and thus unravelled the dark tale, and in horror put out his own eyes. The sequel of the tale is told in the *Oedipus Coloneus*. Banished by his sons, he is tended by the loving care of his daughters. He comes to Attica and dies in the grove of the Eumenides at Colonus, in his death welcomed and pardoned by the fate which had pursued him throughout his life. In addition to the two tragedies of Sophocles, the legend formed the subject of a trilogy by Aeschylus, of which only the *Seven against Thebes* is extant; of the *Phoenissae* of Euripides; and of the *Oedipus* and *Phoenissae* of Seneca.

See A. Höfer's exhaustive article in Roscher's *Lexikon der Mythologie*; F. W. Schneidewin, *Die Sage von Oedipus* (1852); D. Comparetti, *Edipo e la mitologia comparata* (1867); M. Bréal, " Le Mythe d'Œdipe," in *Mélanges de mythologie* (1878), who explains Oedipus as a personification of light, and his blinding as the disappearance of the sun at the end of the day; J. Paulson in *Eranos, Acta philologica Suecana*, i. (Upsala, 1896) places the original home of the legend in Egyptian Thebes, and identifies Oedipus with the Egyptian god Seth, represented as the hippopotamus " with swollen foot," which was said to kill its father in order to take its place with the mother. O. Crusius (*Beiträge zur griechischen Mythologie*, 1886, p. 21) sees in the marriage of Oedipus with his mother an agrarian myth (with special reference to *Oed. Tyr.* 1497), while Höfer (in Roscher's *Lexikon*) suggests that the episodes of the murder of his father and of his marriage are reminiscences of the overthrow of Cronus by Zeus and of the union of Zeus with his own sister.

Medieval Legends.—In the *Golden Legend* of Jacobus de Voragine (13th century) and the *Mystère de la Passion* of Jean Michel (15th century) and Arnoul Gréban (15th century), the story of Oedipus is associated with the name of Judas. The main idea is the same as in the classical account. The Judas legend, however, never really became popular, whereas that of Oedipus was handed down both orally and in written national tales (Albanian, Finnish, Cypriote). One incident (the incest unwittingly committed) frequently recurs in connexion with the life of Gregory the Great. The Theban legend, which reached its fullest development in the *Thebais* of Statius and in Seneca, reappeared in the *Roman de Thèbes* (the work of an unknown imitator of Benoît de Sainte-More). Oedipus is also the subject of an anonymous medieval romance (15th century), *Le Roman d'Œdipus, fils de Layus*, in which the sphinx is depicted as a cunning and ferocious giant. The Oedipus legend was handed down to the period of the Renaissance by the Romans and its imitations, which then fell into oblivion. Even to the present day the legend has

[1] It is probable that the story of the piercing of his feet is a subsequent invention to explain the name, or is due to a false etymology (from οἶδα), οἶδιπους in reality meaning the " wise " (from οἶδα), chiefly in reference to his having solved the riddle, the syllable -πους having no significance.

survived amongst the modern Greeks, without any traces of the influence of Christianity (B. Schmidt, *Griechische Märchen,* 1877). The works of the ancient tragedians (especially Seneca, in preference to the Greek) came into vogue, and were slavishly followed by French and Italian imitators down to the 17th century.

See L. Constans, *La Légende d'Œdipe dans l'antiquité, au moyen âge, et dans les temps modernes* (1881); D. Comparetti's *Edipo* and Jebb's introduction for the *Oedipus* of Dryden, Corneille and Voltaire; A. Heintze, *Gregorius auf dem Steine, der mittelalterliche Oedipus* (progr., Stolp, 1877); V. Diederichs, "Russische Verwandte der Legende von Gregor auf dem Stein und der Sage von Judas Ischariot," in *Russische Revue* (1880); S. Novakovitch, "Die Oedipussage in der südslavischen Volksdichtung," in *Archiv für slavische Philologie* xi. (1888).

OEHLER, GUSTAV FRIEDRICH (1812–1872), German theologian, was born on the 10th of June 1812 at Ebingen, Württemberg, and was educated privately and at Tübingen where he was much influenced by J. C. F. Steudel, professor of Old Testament Theology. In 1837, after a term of Oriental study at Berlin, he went to Tübingen as *Repetent*, becoming in 1840 professor at the seminary and pastor in Schönthal. In 1845 he published his *Prolegomena zur Theologie des Alten Testaments,* accepted an invitation to Breslau and received the degree of doctor from Bonn. In 1852 he returned to Tübingen as director of the seminary and professor of Old Testament Theology at the university. He declined a call to Erlangen as successor to Franz Delitzsch (1867), and died at Tübingen on the 19th of February 1872. Oehler admitted the composite authorship of the Pentateuch and the Book of Isaiah, and did much to counteract the antipathy against the Old Testament that had been fostered by Schleiermacher. In church polity he was Lutheran rather than Reformed. Besides his *Old Testament Theology* (Eng. trans., 2 vols., Edinburgh, 1874–1875), his works were *Gesammelte Seminarreden* (1872) and *Lehrbuch Symbolik* (1876), both published posthumously, and about forty articles for the first edition of Herzog's *Realencyklopädie* which were largely retained by Delitzsch and von Orelli in the second.

OEHRINGEN, a town of Germany, in the kingdom of Württemberg, agreeably situated in a fertile country, on the Ohrn, 12 m. E. from Heilbronn by the railways to Hall and Crailsheim. Pop. (1905) 3,450. It is a quaint medieval place, and, among its ancient buildings, boasts a fine Evangelical church, containing carvings in cedar-wood of the 15th century and numerous interesting tombs and monuments; a Renaissance town hall; the building, now used as a library, which formerly belonged to a monastery, erected in 1034; and a palace, the residence of the princes of Hohenlohe-Oehringen.

Oehringen is the *Vicus Aurelii* of the Romans. Eastwards of it ran the old Roman frontier wall, and numerous remains and inscriptions dating from the days of the Roman settlement have been recently discovered, including traces of three camps.

See Keller, *Vicus Aurelii, oder Öhringen zur Zeit der Römer* (Bonn, 1872).

OELS, a town of Germany, in the Prussian province of Silesia, formerly the capital of a mediatized principality of its own name. It lies in a sandy plain on the Oelsbach, 20 m. N.E. of Breslau by rail. Pop. (1905) 10,940. The princely château, now the property of the crown prince of Prussia, dating from 1558 and beautifully restored in 1891–1894, contains a good library and a collection of pictures. Of its three Evangelical churches, the Schlosskirche dates from the 13th century and the Propstkirche from the 14th. The inhabitants are chiefly engaged in making shoes and growing vegetables for the Breslau market.

Oels was founded about 940, and became a town in 1255. It appears as the capital of an independent principality at the beginning of the 14th century. The principality, with an area of 700 sq. m. and about 130,000 inhabitants, passed through various hands and was inherited by the ducal family of Brunswick in 1792. Then on the extinction of this family in 1884 it lapsed to the crown of Prussia.

See W. Häusler, *Geschichte des Fürstentums Oels bis zum Aussterben der piastischen Herzogshinie* (Breslau; 1883); and Schulze, *Die Succession im Fürstentum Oels* (Breslau, 1884).

OELSCHLÄGER [OLEARIUS], **ADAM** (1600–1671), German traveller and Orientalist, was born at Aschersleben, near Magdeburg, in 1599 or 1600. After studying at Leipzig he became librarian and court mathematician to Duke Frederick III. of Holstein-Gottorp, and in 1633 he was appointed secretary to the ambassadors Philip Crusius, juriconsult, and Otto Brüggemann or Brugman, merchant, sent by the duke to Muscovy and Persia in the hope of making arrangements by which his newly-founded city of Friedrichstadt should become the terminus of an overland silk-trade. This embassy started from Gottorp on the 22nd of October 1633, and travelled by Hamburg, Lübeck, Riga, Dorpat (five months' stay), Revel, Narva, Ladoga and Novgorod to Moscow (August 14, 1634). Here they concluded an advantageous treaty with Michael Romanov, and returned forthwith to Gottorp (December 14, 1634–April 7, 1635) to procure the ratification of this arrangement from the duke, before proceeding to Persia. This accomplished, they started afresh from Hamburg on the 22nd of October 1635, arrived at Moscow on the 29th of March 1636; and left Moscow on the 30th of June for Nizhniy Novgorod, whither they had already sent agents (in 1634–1635) to prepare a vessel for their descent of the Volga. Their voyage down the great river and over the Caspian was slow and hindered by accidents, especially by grounding, as near Derbent on the 14th of November 1636; but at last, by way of Shemakha (three months' delay here), Ardebil, Sultanieh and Kasvin, they reached the Persian court at Isfahan (August 3, 1637), and were received by the shah (August 16). Negotiations here were not as successful as at Moscow, and the embassy left Isfahan on the 21st of December 1637, and returned home by Resht, Lenkoran, Astrakhan, Kazan, Moscow, &c. At Revel Oelschläger parted from his colleagues (April 15, 1639) and embarked direct for Lübeck. On his way he had made a chart of the Volga, and partly for this reason the tsar Michael wished to persuade, or compel, him to enter his service. Once back at Gottorp, Oelschläger became librarian to the duke, who also made him keeper of his Cabinet of Curiosities, and induced the tsar to excuse his (promised) return to Moscow. Under his care the Gottorp library and cabinet were greatly enriched in MSS., books, and oriental and other works of art: in 1651 he purchased, for this purpose, the collection of the Dutch scholar and physician, Bernard ten Broecke ("Paludanus"). He died at Gottorp on the 22nd of February 1671.

It is by his admirable narrative of the Russian and the Persian legation (*Beschreibung der muscovitischen und persischen Reise,* Schleswig, 1647, and afterwards in several enlarged editions, 1656, &c.) that Oelschläger is best known, though he also published a history of Holstein (*Kurtzer Begriff einer holsteinischen Chronic,* Schleswig, 1663), a famous catalogue of the Holstein-Gottorp cabinet (1666), and a translation of the Gulistan (*Persianisches Rosenthal,* Schleswig, 1654), to which was appended a translation of the fables of Lokman. A French version of the *Beschreibung* was published by Abraham de Wicquefort (*Voyages en Moscovie, Tartarie et Perse, par Adam Olearius,* Paris, 1656), an English version was made by John Davies of Kidwelly (*Travels of the Ambassadors sent by Frederic, Duke of Holstein, to the Great Duke of Muscovy and the King of Persia,* London, 1662); and ed., 1669), and a Dutch translation by Dieterius van Wageningen (*Beschrijvingh van de nieuwe Parciaensche ofte Orientaelsche Reyse,* Utrecht, 1651); an Italian translation of the Russian sections also appeared (*Viaggi di Moscovia,* Viterbo and Rome, 1658). Paul Flemming the poet and J. A. de Mandelslo, whose travels to the East Indies are usually published with those of Oelschläger, accompanied the embassy. Under Oelschläger's direction the celebrated globe of Gottorp (11 ft. in diameter) and armillary sphere were executed in 1654–1664; the globe was given to Peter the Great of Russia in 1713 by Duke Frederick's grandson, Christian Augustus. Oelschläger's unpublished works include a *Lexicon Persicum* and several other Persian studies. (C. R. B.)

OELSNITZ, a town of Germany, in the kingdom of Saxony, on the Weisse Elster, 26 m. by rail S.W. of Zwickau. Pop. (1905) 13,966. It has two Evangelical churches, one of them being the old Gothic Jakobskirche, and several schools. There are various manufactories. Oelsnitz belonged in the 14th and 15th centuries to the margraves of Meissen, and later to the electors of Saxony. Near it is the village of Voigtsberg, with the remains of a castle, once a residence of the governor (Vogt) of the Vogtland.

See Jahn, *Chronik der Stadt Ölsnitz* (1875).

OELWEIN, a city of Fayette county, Iowa, U.S.A., in the N.E. part of the state, about 132 m. N.E. of Des Moines. Pop. (1890) 830; (1900) 5142, of whom 789 were foreign-born; (1910 U.S. census) 6028. It is served by the Chicago, Rock Island & Pacific and the Chicago Great Western railways, the latter having large repair shops here, where four lines of its road converge. Oelwein was named in honour of its founder, August Oelwein, who settled here in 1873; it was incorporated in 1888, and chartered as a city in 1897.

OENOMAÜS, in Greek legend, son of Ares and Harpinna, king of Pisa in Elis and father of Hippodameia. It was predicted that he should be slain by his daughter's husband. His father, the god Ares-Hippius, gave him winged horses swift as the wind, and Oenomaüs promised his daughter to the man who could outstrip him in the chariot race, hoping thus to prevent her marriage altogether. Pelops, by the treachery of Myrtilus, the charioteer of Oenomaüs, won the race and married Hippodameia. The defeat of Oenomaüs by Pelops, a stranger from Asia Minor, points to the conquest of native Ares-worshippers by immigrants who introduced the new religion of Zeus.

See Diod. Sic. iv. 73; Pausanias vi. 21, and elsewhere; Sophocles, *Electra*, 504; Hyginus, *Fab.* 84. 253. Fig. 33 in article GREEK ART represents the preparations for the chariot race.

OENONE, in Greek legend, daughter of the river-god Kebren and wife of Paris. Possessing the gift of divination, she warned her husband of the evils that would result from his journey to Greece. The sequel was the rape of Helen and the Trojan War. Just before the capture of the city, Paris, wounded by Philoctetes with one of the arrows of Heracles, sought the aid of the deserted Oenone, who had told him that she alone could heal him if wounded. Indignant at his faithlessness, she refused to help him, and Paris returned to Troy and died of his wound. Oenone soon repented and hastened after him, but finding that she was too late to save him slew herself from grief at the sight of his dead body. Ovid (*Heroïdes*, 5) gives a pathetic description of Oenone's grief when she found herself deserted.

OERLAMS, the name (said to be a corruption of the Dutch *Oberlanders*) for a Hottentot tribal group living in Great Namaqualand. They came originally from Little Namaqualand in Cape Colony. They are of very mixed Hottentot-Bantu blood.

OESEL (in Esthonian *Kure-saare* or *Saare-ma*), a Russian island in the Baltic, forming with Worms, Mohn and Runö, a district of the government of Livonia, and lying across the mouth of the Gulf of Riga, 106 m. N.N.W. of the city of Riga. It has a length of 45 m., and an area of 1010 sq. m. The coasts are bold and steep, and, especially towards the north and west, form precipitous limestone cliffs. Like those of Shetland, the Oesel ponies are small, but prized for their spirit and endurance. The population, numbering 50,566 in 1870 and 60,000 in 1900, is mainly Protestant in creed, and, with the exception of the German nobility, clergy and some of the townsfolk, Esthonian by race. The chief town, Arensburg, on the south coast, is a place of 4600 inhabitants, with summer sea-bathing, mud baths and a trade in grain, potatoes, whisky and fish. In 1227 Oesel was conquered by the Knights of the Sword, and was governed by its own bishops till 1561, when it passed into the hands of the Danes. By them it was surrendered to the Swedes by the peace of Brömsebro (1645), and, along with Livonia, it was united to Russia in 1721.

OESOPHAGUS (Gr. οἴσω=I will carry, and φαγεῖν, to eat), in anatomy, the gullet; see ALIMENTARY CANAL for comparative anatomy. The human oesophagus is peculiarly liable to certain accidents and diseases, due both to its function as a tube to carry food to the stomach and to its anatomical situation (see generally DIGESTIVE ORGANS). One of the commonest accidents is the lodgment of foreign bodies in some part of the tube. The situations in which they are arrested vary with the nature of the body, whether it be a coin, fishbone, toothplate or a portion of food. An impacted substance may be removed by the oesophageal forceps, or by a coin-catcher; if it should be impossible to draw it up it may be pushed down into the stomach. When it is in the stomach a purgative should never be given, but soft food such as porridge. Should gastric symptoms develop it may have to be removed by the operation of gastrotomy. Charring and ulceration of the oesophagus may occur from the swallowing of corrosive liquids, strong acids or alkalis, or even of boiling water. Stricture of the oesophagus is a closing of the tube so that neither solids nor liquids are able to pass down into the stomach. There are three varieties of stricture; spasmodic, fibrous and malignant. *Spasmodic stricture* usually occurs in young hysterical women; difficulty in swallowing is complained of, and a bougie may not be able to be passed, but under an anaesthetic will slip down quite easily. *Fibrous stricture* is usually situated near the commencement of the oesophagus, generally just behind the cricoid cartilage, and usually results from swallowing corrosive fluids, but may also result from the healing of a syphilitic ulcer. Occasionally it is congenital. The ordinary treatment is repeated dilatation by bougies. Occasionally division of a fibrous stricture has been practised, or a Symond's tube inserted. Mikulicz recommends dilatation of the stricture by the fingers from inside after an incision into the stomach or a permanent gastric fistula may have to be made. *Malignant strictures* are usually epitheliomatous in structure, and may be situated in any part of the oesophagus. They nearly always occur in males between the ages of 40 and 70 years. An X-ray photograph taken after the patient has swallowed a preparation of bismuth will show the situation of the growth, and Killian and Brünig have introduced an instrument called the oesophagoscope, which makes direct examination possible. The remedy of constant dilatation by bougies must not be attempted here, the walls of the oesophagus being so softened by disease and ulceration that severe haemorrhage or perforation of the walls of the tube might take place. The patient should be fed with purely liquid and concentrated nourishment in order to give the oesophagus as much rest as possible, or if the stricture be too tight rectal feeding may be necessary. Symond's method of tubage is well borne by some patients, the tube having attached to it a long string which is secured to the cheek or ear. The most satisfactory treatment, however, is the operation of gastrotomy, a permanent artificial opening being made into the stomach through which the patient can be fed.

OETA (mod. *Kóiavotlera*), a mountain to the south of Thessaly, in Greece, forming a boundary between the valleys of the Spercheius and the Boeotian Cephissus. It is an offshoot of the Pindus range, 7080 ft. high. In its eastern portion, called Callidromus, it comes close to the sea, leaving only a narrow passage known as the famous pass of Thermopylae (*q.v.*). There was also a high pass to the west of Callidromus leading over into the upper Cephissus valley. In mythology Oeta is chiefly celebrated as the scene of the funeral pyre on which Heracles burnt himself before his admission to Olympus.

OETINGER, FRIEDRICH CHRISTOPH (1702–1782), German divine and theosophist, was born at Göppingen on the 6th of May 1702. He studied theology at Tübingen (1722–1728), and was much impressed by the works of Jakob Böhme. On the completion of his university course, Oetinger spent some years in travel. In 1730 he visited Count Zinzendorf at Herrnhut, remaining there some months as teacher of Hebrew and Greek. During his travels, in his eager search for knowledge, he made the acquaintance of mystics and separatists, Christians and learned Jews, theologians and physicians alike. At Halle he studied medicine. After some delay he was ordained to the ministry, and held several pastorates. While pastor (from 1746) at Waldorf near Berlin, he studied alchemy and made many experiments, his idea being to use his knowledge for symbolic purposes. These practices exposed him to the attacks of persons who misunderstood him. "My religion," he once said, "is the parallelism of Nature and Grace." Oetinger translated Swedenborg's philosophy of heaven and earth, and added notes of his own. Eventually (1766) he became prelate at Murrhardt, where he died on the 10th of February 1782.

Oetinger's autobiography was published by J. Hamberger in 1845. He published about seventy works, in which he expounded his theosophic views. A collected edition, *Sämtliche Schriften* (1st section, *Homiletische Schriften*, 5 vols., 1858–1866; 2nd section, *Theosophische Werke*, 6 vols., 1858–1863), was prepared by K. F. C. Ehmann, who also wrote Oetinger's *Leben und Briefe* (1859). See also C. A. Auberlen, *Die Theosophie Friedr. Chr. Oetinger's* (1847; 2nd ed., 1859), and Herzog, *Friedrich Christoph Oetinger* (1902).

OEYNHAUSEN, a town and watering-place of Germany, in the Prussian province of Westphalia, on the Werre, situated just above its confluence with the Weser, 9 m. W. from Minden by the main line of railway from Hanover to Cologne, with a station on the Löhne-Hameln line. Pop. (1905) 3894. The place, which was formerly called Rehme, owes its development to the discovery in 1830 of its five famous salt springs, which are heavily charged with carbonic acid gas. The waters are used both for bathing and drinking, and are particularly efficacious for nervous disorders, rheumatism, gout and feminine complaints.

OFFA, the most famous hero of the early Angli. He is said by the Anglo-Saxon poem *Widsith* to have ruled over Angel, and the poem refers briefly to his victorious single combat, a story which is related at length by the Danish historians Saxo and Svend Aagesen. Offa (Uffo) is said to have been dumb or silent during his early years, and to have only recovered his speech when his aged father Wermund was threatened by the Saxons, who insolently demanded the cession of his kingdom. Offa undertook to fight against both the Saxon king 's son and a chosen champion at once. The combat took place at Rendsburg on an island in the Eider, and Offa succeeded in killing both his opponents. According to *Widsith* Offa's opponents belonged to a tribe or dynasty called Myrgingas, but both accounts state that he won a great kingdom as the result of his victory. A somewhat corrupt version of the same story is preserved in the *Vitae duorum Offarum*, where, however, the scene is transferred to England. It is very probable that the Offa whose marriage with a lady of murderous disposition is mentioned in Beowulf is the same person; and this story also appears in the *Vitae duorum Offarum*, though it is erroneously told of a later Offa, the famous king of Mercia. Offa of Mercia, however, was a descendant in the 12th generation of Offa, king of Angel. It is probable from this and other considerations that the early Offa lived in the latter part of the 4th century.

See H. M. Chadwick, *Origin of the English Nation* (Cambridge, 1907), where references to the original authorities will be found.

OFFA (d. 796), king of Mercia, obtained that kingdom in A.D. 757, after driving out Beornred, who had succeeded a few months earlier on the murder of Æthelbald. He traced his descent from Pybba, the father of Penda, through Eowa, brother of that king, his own father's name being Thingferth. In 770 he was at war with Cynewulf of Wessex from whom he wrested Bensington. It is not unlikely that the Thames became the boundary of the two kingdoms about this time. In 787 the power of Offa was displayed in a synod held at a place called Cealchyth. He deprived Jænberht, archbishop of Canterbury, of several of his suffragan sees, and assigned them to Lichfield, which, with the leave of the pope, he constituted as a separate archbishopric under Hygeberht. He also took advantage of this meeting to have his son Ecgferth consecrated as his colleague, and that prince subsequently signed charters as *Rex Merciorum*. In 789 Offa secured the alliance of Berhtric of Wessex by giving him his daughter Eadburg in marriage. In 794 he appears to have caused the death of Æthelberht of East Anglia, though some accounts ascribe the murder to Cynethryth, the wife of Offa. In 796 Offa died after a reign of thirty-nine years and was succeeded by his son Ecgferth. It is customary to ascribe to Offa a policy of limited scope, namely the establishment of Mercia in a position equal to that of Wessex and of Northumbria. This is supposed to be illustrated by his measures with regard to the see of Lichfield. It cannot be doubted, however, that at this time Mercia was a much more formidable power than Wessex. Offa, like most of his predecessors,

probably held a kind of supremacy over all kingdoms south of the Humber. He seems, however, not to have been contented with this position, and to have entertained the design of putting an end to the dependent kingdoms. At all events we hear of no kings of the Hwicce after about 780, and the kings of Sussex seem to have given up the royal title about the same time. Further, there is no evidence for any kings in Kent from 784 until after Offa's death. To Offa is ascribed by Asser, in his life of Alfred, the great fortification against the Welsh which is still known as " Offa's dike." It stretched from sea to sea and consisted of a wall and a rampart. An account of his Welsh campaigns is given in the *Vitae duorum Offarum*, but it is difficult to determine how far the stories there given have an historical basis.

See *Anglo-Saxon Chronicle*, ed. J. Earle and C. Plummer (Oxford, 1899), *s.a.* 755, 777, 785, 787, 792, 794, 796, 836; W. de G. Birch, *Cartularium Saxonicum* (London, 1885–1893), vol. i.; Asser, *Life of Alfred*, ed. W. H. Stevenson (Oxford, 1904); *Vitae duorum Offarum* (in works of Matthew Paris, ed. W. Wats, London, 1640).

OFFAL, refuse or waste stuff, the " off fall," that which falls off (cf. Dutch *afval*, Ger. *Abfall*). The term is applied especially to the waste parts of an animal that has been slaughtered for food, to putrid flesh or carrion, and to waste fish, especially to the little ones that get caught in the nets with the larger and better fish, and are thrown away or used as manure. As applied to grain "offal" is used of grains too small or light for use for flour, and also in flour milling of the husk or bran of wheat with a certain amount of flour attaching, sold for feeding beasts (see FLOUR).

OFFENBACH, JACQUES (1819–1880), French composer of *opéra bouffe*, was born at Cologne, of German Jewish parents, on the 21st of June 1819. His talent for music was developed at a very early age; and in 1833 he was sent to Paris to study the violoncello at the conservatoire, where, under the care of Professor Yaslin, he became a fairly good performer. In 1834 he became a member of the orchestra of the Opéra Comique; but he turned his opportunities to good account, so that eventually he was made conductor at the Théâtre Français. There, in 1848, he made his first success as a composer in the *Chanson de Fortunio* in Alfred de Musset's play *Le Chandelier*. From this time forward his life became a ceaseless struggle for the attainment of popularity. His power of production was apparently inexhaustible. His first complete work, *Pepito*, was produced at the Opéra Comique in 1853. This was followed by a crowd of dramatic pieces of a light character, which daily gained in favour with Parisian audiences, and eventually effected a complete revolution in the popular taste of the period. Encouraged by these early successes, Offenbach boldly undertook the delicate task of entirely remodelling both the form and the style of the light musical pieces which had so long been welcomed with acclamation by the frequenters of the smaller theatres in Paris. With this purpose in view he obtained a lease of the Théâtre Comte in the Passage Choiseul, reopened it in 1855 under the title of the Bouffes Parisiens, and night after night attracted crowded audiences by a succession of brilliant, humorous trifles. Ludovic Halévy, the librettist, was associated with him from the first, but still more after 1860, when Halévy obtained Henri Meilhac's collaboration (see HALÉVY). Beginning with *Les Deux Aveugles* and *Le Violoneux*, the series of Offenbach's operettas was rapidly continued, until in 1867 its triumph culminated in *La Grande Duchesse de Gérolstein*, perhaps the most popular *opéra bouffe* that ever was written, not excepting even his *Orphée aux enfers*, produced in 1858. From this time forward the success of Offenbach's pieces became an absolute certainty, and the new form of *opéra bouffe*, which he had gradually endowed with as much consistency as it was capable of assuming, was accepted as the only one worth cultivating. It found imitators in Lecocq and other aspirants of a younger generation, and Offenbach's works found their way to every town in Europe in which a theatre existed. Tuneful, gay and exhilarating, their want of refinement formed no obstacle to their popularity, and perhaps even contributed to it. In 1866 his own connexion with the Bouffes Parisiens ceased, and he wrote for various theatres. In twenty-five years Offenbach produced no less than sixty-nine complete dramatic works, some of which were in three or even in four acts. Among the latest of these were *Le Docteur Ox*, founded on a story by Jules Verne, and *La Botte au lait*, both produced in 1877, and *Madame Favart* (1879). Offenbach died at Paris on the 5th of October 1880.

OFFENBACH, a town of Germany, in the grand-duchy of Hesse, on the left bank of the Main, 5 m. S.E. of Frankfort-on-Main, with which it is connected by the railway to Bebra and by a local electric line. Pop. (1905) 58,806, of whom about 20,000 were Roman Catholics and 1400 Jews. The most interest-ing building in the town is the Renaissance château of the counts of Isenburg. Offenbach is the principal industrial town of the duchy, and its manufactures are of the most varied description. Its characteristic industry, however, is the manufacture of portfolios, pocket-books, albums and other fancy goods in leather. The earliest mention of Offenbach is in a document of 970. In 1486 it came into the possession of the counts of Isenburg, who made it their residence in 1685, and in 1816, when their lands were mediatized, it was assigned to Hesse. It owes its prosperity in the first place to the industry of the French Protestant refugees who settled here at the end of the 17th, and the beginning of the 18th century, and in the second place to the accession of Hesse to the German Zollverein in 1828.

See Jöst, *Offenbach am Main in Vergangenheit und Gegenwart* (Offenbach, 1901); Hager, *Die Lederwarenindustrie in Offenbach* (Karlsruhe, 1905).

OFFENBURG, a town of Germany, in the grand-duchy of Baden, 27 m. by rail S.W. of Baden, on the river Kinzig. Pop. (1905) 15,434. It contains a statue of Sir Francis Drake, a mark of honour due to the fact that Drake is sometimes regarded as having introduced the potato into Europe. The chief industries of the town are the making of cotton, linen, hats, malt, machinery, tobacco and cigars and glass. Offenburg is first mentioned about 1100. In 1223 it became a town; in 1248 it passed to the bishop of Strassburg; and in 1289 it became an imperial free city. Soon, however, this position was lost, but it was regained about the middle of the 16th century, and Offenburg remained a free city until 1802, when it became part of Baden. In 1632 it was taken by the Swedes, and in 1689 it was destroyed by the French.

See Walter, *Kurzer Abriss der Geschichte der Reichsstadt Offenburg* (Offenburg, 1896).

OFFERTORY (from the ecclesiastical Lat. *offertorium*, Fr. *offertoire*, a place to which offerings were brought), the alms of a congregation collected in church, or at any religious service. Offertory has also a special sense in the services of both the English and Roman churches. It forms in both that part of the Communion service appointed to be said or sung, during the collection of alms, before the elements are consecrated. In music, an offertory is the vocal or instrumental setting of the offertory sentences, or a short instrumental piece played by the organist while the collection is being made.

OFFICE (from Lat. *officium*, "duty," "service," a shortened form of *opifacium*, from *facere*, "to do," and either the stem of *opes*, "wealth," "aid," or *opus*, "work"), a duty or service, particularly the special duty cast upon a person by his position; also a ceremonial duty, as in the rites paid to the dead, the "last offices." The term is thus especially used of a religious service, the "daily office" of the English Church or the "divine office" of the Roman Church (see BREVIARY). It is also used in this sense of a service for a particular occasion, as the Office for the Visitation of the Sick, &c. From the sense of duty or function, the word is transferred to the position or place which lays on the holder or occupier the performance of such duties. This leads naturally to the use of the word for the buildings or the separate rooms in which the duties are performed, and for the staff carrying on the work or business in such offices. In the Roman curia the department of the Inquisition is known as the Holy Office, in full, the Congregation of the Holy Office of the Inquisition (see INQUISITION and CURIA ROMANA).

Offices of Profit.—The phrase "office of profit under the crown" is used with a particular application in British parliamentary practice. The holders of such offices of profit have been subject in regard to the occupation of seats in the House of Commons to certain disabilities which were in their origin due to the fear of the undue influence exercised by the crown during the constitu-tional struggles of the 17th century. Attempts to deal with the danger of the presence of "place-men" in the House of Commons were made by the Place Bills introduced in 1672–1673, 1694 and 1743. The Act of Settlement 1700 (§ 3) laid it down that no person who has an office or place of profit under the king or receives a pension from the crown shall be capable of serving as a member of the House of Commons. This drastic clause, which would have had the disastrous effect of entirely separating the executive from the legislature, was repealed and the basis of the present law was laid down in 1706 by 6 Anne (c. 41). This first disqualifies (§ 24) from membership all holders of "new offices,"[1] *i.e.* those created after October 1705; secondly (§ 25) it renders void the election of a member who shall accept any office of profit other than "new offices" but allows the member to stand for re-election. The disqualification attaching to many "new offices" has been removed by various statutes, and by § 52 of the Reform Act 1867 the necessity of re-election is avoided when a member, having been elected subsequent to the accept-ance of any office named in a schedule of that act, is transferred to any other office in that schedule. The rules as to what offices disqualify from membership or render re-election necessary are exceedingly complicated, depending as they do on a large number of statutes (see Erskine May, *Parliamentary Practice*, 11th ed., pp. 632–645, and Rogers, *On Elections*, vol. ii., 1906). The old established rule that a member, once duly elected, cannot resign his seat is evaded by the acceptance of certain minor offices (see CHILTERN HUNDREDS).

OFFICERS. Historically the employment of the word "officer" to denote a person holding a military or naval com-mand as representative of the state, and not as deriving his authority from his own powers or privileges, marks an entire change in the character of the armed forces of civilized nations. Originally signifying an official, one who performs an assigned duty (Lat. *officium*), an agent, and in the 15th century actually meaning the subordinate of such an official (even to-day a constable is so called), the word seems to have acquired a military signific-ance late in the 16th century.[2] It was at this time that armies, though not yet "standing," came to be constituted almost exclusively of professional soldiers in the king's pay. Mercen-aries, and great numbers of mercenaries, had always existed, and their captains were not feudal magnates. But the bond between mercenaries and their captains was entirely personal, and the bond between the captain and the sovereign was of the nature of a contract. The non-mercenary portion of the older armies was feudal in character. It was the lord and not a king's officer who commanded it, and he commanded in virtue of his rights, not of a warrant or commission.

European history in the late 15th century is the story of the victory of the crown over the feudatories. The instrument of the crown was its army, raised and commanded by its deputies. But these deputies were still largely soldiers of fortune and, in the higher ranks, feudal personages, who created the armies them-selves by their personal influence with the would-be soldier or the unemployed professional fighting man. Thus the first system to replace the obsolete combination of feudalism and "free companies" was what may be called the proprietary system. Under this the colonel was the proprietor of his regiment, the captain the proprietor of his company. The king accepted them as his officers, and armed them with authority to raise men, but they themselves raised the men as a rule from experienced soldiers who were in search of employment, although, like

[1] This section also disqualifies colonial governors and deputy governors and holders of certain other offices.
[2] At sea the relatively clear partition of actual duties amongst the authorities of a ship brought about the adoption of the term "officer" somewhat earlier.

Falstaff, some captains and colonels ".misused the King's press damnably." All alike were most rigorously watched lest by showing imaginary men on their pay-sheets they should make undue profits. A " muster " was the production of a number of living men on parade corresponding to the number shown on the pay-roll. An inspection was an inspection not so much of the efficiency as of the numbers and the accounts of units. A full account of these practices, which were neither more nor less prevalent in England than elsewhere, will be found in J. W. Fortescue's *History of the British Army*, vol. I. So faithfully was the custom observed of requiring the showing of a man for a man's pay, that the grant of a special allowance to officers administering companies was often made in the form of allowing them to show imaginary John Does and Richard Roes on the pay-sheets.

The next step was taken when armies, instead of being raised for each campaign and from the qualified men who at each recruiting time offered themselves, became " standing " armies fed by untrained recruits. During the late 17th and the 18th centuries the crown supplied the recruits, and also the money for maintaining the forces, but the colonels and captains retained in a more or less restricted degree their proprietorship.

Thus, the profits of military office without its earlier burdens were in time of peace considerable, and an officer's commission had therefore a " surrender value." The practice of buying and selling commissions was a natural consequence, and this continued long after the system of proprietary regiments and companies had disappeared. In England " purchase " endured until 1873, nearly a hundred years after it had ceased on the continent of Europe and more than fifty after the clothing, feeding and payment of the soldiers had been taken out of the colonels' hands. The purchase system, it should be mentioned, did not affect artillery and engineer officers, either in England or in the rest of Europe. These officers, who were rather semi-civil than military officials until about 1715, executed an office rather than a command—superintended gun-making, built fortresses and so on. As late as 1780 the right of a general officer promoted from the Royal Artillery to command troops of other arms was challenged. In its original form, therefore, the proprietary system was a most serious bar to efficiency. So long as war was chronic, and self-trained recruits were forthcoming, it had been a good working method of devolving responsibility. But when drill and the handling of arms became more complicated, and, above all, when the supply of trained men died away, the state took recruiting out of the colonels' and captains' hands, and, as the individual officer had now nothing to offer the crown but his own potential military capacity (part of which resided in his social status, but by no means all), the crown was able to make him, in the full sense of the word, an officer of itself. This was most fully seen in the reorganization of the French army by Louis XIV. and Louvois. The colonelcies and captaincies of horse and foot remained proprietary offices in the hands of the nobles but these offices were sinecures or almost sinecures. The colonels, in peace at any rate, were not expected to do regimental duty. They were at liberty to make such profits as they could make under a stringent inspection system. But they were expected to be the influential figure-heads of their regiments and to pay large sums for the privilege of being proprietors. This classification of officers into two bodies, the poorer which did the whole of the work, and the richer upon which the holding of a commission conferred an honour that birth or wealth did not confer, marks two very notable advances in the history of army organization, the professionalization of the officer and the creation of the prestige attaching to the holder of a commission *because* he holds it and not for any extraneous reason.

The distinction between working and quasi-honorary officers was much older, of course, than Louvois's reorganization. Moreover it extended to the highest ranks. About 1600 the " general " of a European army[1] was always a king, prince or nobleman. The lieutenant-general, by custom the commander of the cavalry, was also, as a rule, a noble, in

[1] Except in the Italian republics.

virtue of his command of the aristocratic arm. But the commander of the foot, the " sergeant-major-general " or " major-general," was invariably a professional soldier. It was his duty to draw up the army (not merely the foot) for battle, and in other respects to act as chief of staff to the general. In the infantry regiment, the " sergeant-major " or " major" was second-in-command and adjutant combined. Often, if not always, he was promoted from amongst the lieutenants and not the (proprietary) captains. The lieutenants were the backbone of the army.

Seventy years later, on the organization of the first great standing army by Louvois, the " proprietors," as mentioned above, were reduced to a minimum both in numbers and in military importance. The word " major " in its various meanings had come, in the French service, to imply staff functions. Thus the sergeant-major of infantry became the " adjutant-major." The sergeant-major-general, as commander of the foot, had disappeared and given place to numerous lieutenant-generals and " brigadiers," but as chief of the staff he survived for two hundred years. As late as 1870 the chief of staff of a French army bore the title of " the major-general."

Moreover a new title had come into prominence, that of " marshal " or " field marshal." This marks one of the most important points in the evolution of the military officer, his classification by rank and not by the actual command he holds. In the 16th century an officer was a lieutenant *of*, not *in*, a particular regiment, and the higher officers were general, lieutenant-general and major-general *of* a particular army. When their army was disbanded they had no command and possessed therefore no rank—except of course when, as was usually the case, they were colonels of permanent regiments or governors of fortresses. Thus in the British army it was not until late in the 18th century that general officers received any pay as such. The introduction of a distinctively military *rank*[2] of " marshal " or " field marshal," which took place in France and the empire in the first years of the 17th century, meant the establishment of a list of general officers, and the list spread downwards through the various regimental ranks, in proportion as the close proprietary system broke up, until it became the general army list of an army of to-day. At first field marshals were merely officers of high rank and experience, eligible for appointment to the offices of general, lieutenant-general, &c., in a particular army. On an army being formed, the list of field marshals was drawn upon, and the necessary number appointed. Thus an army of Gustavus Adolphus's time often included 6 or 8 field marshals as subordinate general officers. But soon armies grew larger, more mobile and more flexible and more general officers were needed. Thus fresh grades of general arose. The next rank below that of marshal, in France, was that of lieutenant-general, which had formerly implied the second-in-command of an army, and a little further back in history the king's lieutenant-general or military viceroy.[2] Below the lieutenant-general was the *maréchal de camp*, the heir of the sergeant-major-general. In the imperial service the ranks were field marshal and lieutenant field marshal (both of which survive to the present day) and major-general. A further grade of general officer was created by Louis XIV., that of brigadier, and this completes the process of evolution, for the regimental system had already provided the lower titles.

The ranks of a modern army, with slight variations in title, are therefore as follows:

(a) *Field marshal*: in Germany, *Generalfeldmarschall*; in Spain " captain-general "; in France (though the rank is in abeyance) " marshal." The marshals of France, however, were neither so few in number nor so restricted to the highest commands as are marshals elsewhere. In Germany a new rank, " colonel-general "

[2] The title was, of course, far older.
[3] In England, until after Marlborough's death, rank followed command and not vice versa. The first field marshals were the duke of Argyll and the earl of Cadogan. Marlborough's title, or rather office, was that of captain-general.

(*Generaloberst*), has come into existence—or rather has been revived [1] —of late years. Most of the holders of this rank have the honorary style of general-field-marshal.[2]

(*b*) *General*: in Germany and Russia, "general of infantry," "general of cavalry," "general of artillery." In Austria generals of artillery and infantry were known by the historic title of *Feldzeugmeister* (ordnance-master) up to 1909, but the grade of general of infantry was created in that year, the old title being now restricted to generals of artillery. In France the highest grade of general officer is the "general of division." In the United States army the grade of full "general" has only been held by Washington, Grant, Sherman and Sheridan.

(*c*) *Lieutenant-general* (except in France): in Austria the old title of lieutenant field marshal is retained. In the United States army the title "lieutenant-general," except within recent years, has been almost as rare as "general." Winfield Scott was a brevet lieutenant-general. The substantive rank was revived for Grant whenever was placed in command of the Union Army in 1864. It was abolished as an American rank in 1907.

(*d*) *Major-general* (in France, general of brigade): this is the highest grade normally found in the United States Army, generals and lieutenant-generals being promoted for special service only.[3]

(*e*) *Brigadier-general*, in the United States and (as a temporary rank only) in the British services.

The above are the five grades of higher officers. To all intents and purposes, no nation has more than four of these five ranks, while France and the United States, the great republics, have only two. The correspondence between rank and functions cannot be exactly laid down, but in general an officer of the rank of lieutenant-general commands an army corps and a major-general a division. Brigades are commanded by major-generals, brigadier-generals or colonels. Armies are as a rule commanded by field marshals or full generals. In France generals of division command divisions, corps, armies and groups of armies.

The above are classed as general officers. The "field officers" (French *efficiers supérieurs*, German *Stabsofficiere*) are as follows:—

(*a*) *Colonel.*—This rank exists in its primitive significance in every army. It denotes a regimental commander, or an officer of corresponding status on the staff. In Great Britain, with the "linked battalion" system, regiments of infantry do not work as units, and the executive command of battalions, regiments of cavalry and brigades of field artillery is in the hands of lieutenant-colonels. Colonels of British regiments who are quasi-honorary (though no longer proprietary) chiefs are royal personages or general officers. Colonels in active employment as such are either on the staff, commanders of brigades or corresponding units, or otherwise extra-regimentally employed.

(*b*) *Lieutenant colonel*: in Great Britain "the commanding officer" of a unit. Elsewhere, where the regiment and not the battalion is the executive unit, the lieutenant-colonel sometimes acts as second in command, sometimes commands one of the battalions. In Russia all the battalion leaders are lieutenant-colonels.

(*c*) *Major.*—This rank does not exist in Russia, and in France is replaced by *chef de bataillon* or *chef d'escadron*, colloquially *commandant*. In the British infantry he preserves some of the characteristics of the ancient "sergeant-major," as a second in command with certain administrative duties. The junior majors command companies. In the cavalry the majors, other than the second-in-command, command squadrons; in the artillery they command batteries. In armies which have the regiment as the executive unit, majors command battalions (" wings " of cavalry, " groups " of artillery).

Lastly the "company officers" (called in France and Germany subaltern officers) are as follows:—

(*a*) *Captain* (Germany and Austria, *Hauptmann*, cavalry *Rittmeister*): in the infantry of all countries, the company commander. In Russia there is a lower grade of captain called "staff-captain," and in Belgium there is the rank of "second-captain." In all countries except Great Britain captains command squadrons and batteries. Under the captain, with such commands and powers as are delegated to them, are the subalterns, usually graded as—

[1] The 16th-century "colonel-general " was the commander of a whole section of the armed forces. In France there were several colonels-general, each of whom controlled several regiments, or indeed the whole of an " arm." Their functions were rather those of a war office than those of a troop-leader. If they held high commands in a field army, it was by special appointment *ad hoc.* Colonels-general were also proprietors in France of one company in each regiment, whose services they accepted.

[2] In Russia the rank of marshal has been long in abeyance.

[3] In the Confederate service the grades were general for army commanders, lieutenant-general for corps commanders, major-general for divisional commanders and brigadier-general for brigade commanders.

(*b*) *Lieutenant* (first lieutenant in U.S.A., *Oberleutnant* in Germany and Austria).

(*c*) *Sub-lieutenant* (second-lieutenant in Great Britain and U.S.A., *Leutnant* in Germany and Austria).

(*d*) Aspirants, or probationary young officers, not of full commissioned status.

The continental officer is on an average considerably older, rank for rank, than the British; but he is neither younger nor older in respect of command. In the huge "universal service " armies of to-day, the regimental officer of France or Germany commands, *in war*, on an average twice the number of men that are placed under the British officer of equal rank. Thus a German or French major of infantry has about 900 rifles to direct, while a British major may have either half a battalion, 450, or a double company, 220; a German captain commands a company of 250 rifles as against an English captain's 110 and so on. At the same time it must be remembered that at peace strength the continental battalion and company are maintained at little more than half their war strength, and the under-officering of European armies only makes itself seriously felt on mobilization.

It is different with the questions of pay and promotion, which chiefly affect the life of an army in peace. As to the former (see also PENSIONS) the Continental officer is paid at a lower rate than the British, as shown by the table of *ordinary pay* per annum (without special pay or allowances) below:—

	Great Britain.	France.	Germany.
Lieutenant-colonel [1]	328	263	292
Major [1]	248	224	292
Captain [1]	210	139 to 200	150 to 195
Oberleutnant (Lieutenant) [1]	118	101 to 120	78
Second Lieutenant (*Leutnant*, *Sous-lieutenant*) [1]	94	93	45 to 60

[1] Infantry, lowest scale, other arms and branches higher, often considerably higher.

It must be noted that in France and Germany the major is a battalion commander, corresponding to the British lieutenant-colonel. But the significance of this table can only be realized when it is remembered that promotion is rapid in the British army and very slow in the others. The senior *Oberleutnants* of the German army are men of 37 to 38 years of age; the senior captains 47 to 48. In 1908 the youngest captains were 36, the youngest majors 45 years of age. As another illustration, the captain's maximum pay in the French army, £10 per annum less than a British captain's, is only given after 12 years' service in that rank, *i.e.* to a man of at least twenty years' service. The corresponding times for British regular officers in 1905 (when the effects of rapid promotions during the South African War were still felt) were 6 to 7½ years from first commission to promotion to captain, and 14 to 19 years from first commission to promotion to major. In 1908, under more normal conditions, the times were 7 to 8½ years to captain, 15 to 20 to major. In the Royal Engineers and the Indian army a subaltern is automatically promoted captain on completing 9 years' commissioned service, and a captain similarly promoted major after 18.

The process of development in the case of naval officers (seeNAVY) presents many points of similarity, but also considerable differences. For from the first the naval officer could only offer to serve on the king's ship: he did not build a ship as a colonel raised a regiment, and thus there was no proprietary system. On the other hand the naval officer was even more of a simple office-holder than his comrade ashore. He had no rank apart from that which he held in the economy of the ship, and when the ship went out of commission the officers as well as the crew were disbanded. One feature of the proprietary system, however, appears in the navy organization; there was a marked distinction between the captain and the lieutenant who led the combatants and the master and the master's mate who sailed the ship. But here there were fewer "vested interests," and instead of remaining in the condition, so to speak, of distinguished passengers, until finally eliminated by the "levelling up " of the working class of officers, the lieutenants and captains were (in England) required to educate themselves thoroughly in the subjects of the sea officer's profession. When this process had gone on for two generations, that is, about 1670, the formation of a permanent staff of naval officers was begun by the institution of half-pay for the captains, and very soon afterwards the methods of admission and early training of naval officers were systematized.

The ranks in the British Royal Navy are shown with the relative ranks of the army in the following table (taken from *King's Regulations*), which also gives some idea of the complexity of the non-combatant branches of naval officers.

Training of British Army Officers.—This may be conveniently

by the Civil Service Commissioners as to their educational qualifications. This examination is competitive in so far that vacancies at the Royal Military College at Sandhurst (for Cavalry, Infantry and Army Service Corps), or the Royal Military Academy at Woolwich (for Engineers and Artillery), go to those who pass highest, if physically fit. Before presenting himself for this examination, the candidate must produce a " leaving certificate " from the school at which he was educated, showing that he already possesses a fair knowledge

Corresponding Ranks.

Army.		Navy.
1. Field Marshals . . .	Admirals of the Fleet	
2. Generals . . .	Admirals	
3. Lieutenant-Generals .	Vice-Admirals .	Engineer-in-Chief, if Engineer Vice-Admiral.
4. Major-Generals . .	Rear-Admirals .	Inspectors-General of Hospitals and Fleets. Engineer-in-Chief, if Engineer Rear-Admiral. Engineer Rear-Admiral.
5. Brigadier-Generals . .	Commodores	
6. Colonels . . .	Captains of 3 years' seniority .	Deputy Inspectors-General of Hospitals and Fleets. Secretaries to Admirals of the Fleet. Paymasters-in-Chief. Engineer Captains of 8 years' seniority in that rank.
7. Lieutenant-Colonels . .	Captains under 3 years' seniority .	Staff Captains of 4 years' seniority. Staff Captains under 4 years' seniority (navigating branch). Secretaries to Commanders-in-Chief, of 5 years' service as such. Engineer Captains under 8 years' seniority in that rank.
	Commanders, but junior of that rank .	Fleet-Surgeons.[1] Secretaries to Commanders-in-Chief under 5 years' service.[1] Fleet Paymasters.[1] Engineer Commanders.[1]
8. Majors . . .	Lieutenants of 8 years' seniority .	Naval Instructors of 15 years' seniority.[1] Engineer Lieutenants of 8 years' seniority, qualified and selected. Staff-Surgeons. Secretaries to Junior Flag Officers, Commodores, 1st Class.
9. Captains . . .	Lieutenants under 8 years' seniority .	Staff Paymasters and Paymaster. Naval Instructors of 8 years' seniority. Carpenter Lieutenant of 8 years' seniority. Surgeons. Secretaries to Commodores, 2nd Class. Naval Instructors under 8 years' seniority. Engineer Lieutenant under 8 years' seniority, or over if not duly qualified and selected. Assistant Paymasters of 4 years' seniority. Carpenter Lieutenant under 8 years' seniority.
10. Lieutenants . . .	Sub-Lieutenants . . .	Assistant Paymasters under 4 years' seniority. Engineer Sub-Lieutenants.
11. Second Lieutenants . .		Chief Gunner.[1] Chief Boatswain.[1] Chief Carpenter.[1] Chief Artificer Engineer.[2] Chief Schoolmaster.[1]
12. Higher ranks of Warrant Officers .		Midshipmen.[2] Clerks.[2] Gunners.[1] Boatswains.[1] Carpenters.[1] Artificer Engineer.[2] Head Schoolmaster.[1] Head Wardmaster.[1]

[1] But junior of the army rank. [2] But senior of the army rank.

divided into two parts: (I.) that which precedes the appointment to a commission; (II.) that which succeeds it.

I. Omitting those officers who obtain their commissions from the ranks, the training which precedes the appointment to a commission is subdivided into: (a) General Education; (b) Technical Instruction.

(a) *General Education.*—A fairly high standard of education is considered essential. Candidates from universities approved by the Army Council must have resided for three academic years at their university, and have taken a degree in any subject or group of subjects other than Theology, Medicine, Music and Commerce. A university candidate for a commission in the Royal Artillery must further be qualified in Mathematics. The obtaining of first-class honours is considered equivalent to one year's extra service in the army, and an officer can count that year for calculating his service towards his pension. University candidates are eligible for commissions in the Cavalry, Royal Artillery, Infantry, Indian Army and Army Service Corps. For other branches of the service special regulations are in force.

Those candidates who have not been at a university are examined

of the subjects of examination. Candidates who fail to secure admission to these institutions, but satisfy the examiners that they are sufficiently well educated, can obtain commissions in the Special Reserve.

Candidates for commissions in the Royal Army Medical Corps and the Army Veterinary Corps are not required to pass an educational examination, the ordinary course of medical or veterinary education being deemed sufficient, but the Army Council may reject a candidate who shows any deficiency in his general education.

Officers of the Colonial military forces wishing to obtain commissions in the British Army must either produce a school or college " leaving certificate " or pass an examination held by the Army Qualifying Board, or must show that they have passed one of certain recognized examinations.

(b) *Technical Instruction.*—In addition to general educational attainments, a fair knowledge of technical matters is expected from candidates.

For Cavalry, Infantry, Royal Engineers, Royal Artillery and Army Service Corps, an examination must be passed in administration and organisation; military history, strategy and tactics; military topography, engineering and law. In addition, the following conditions must be complied with: (1) *University candidates* are required to be members of the Senior Division of the Officers' Training Corps (see UNITED KINGDOM: *Army*) should there be a unit of that corps at the university to which they belong. They are further required to be attached for six weeks to a Regular unit during their residence at the university. If there is no Officers' Training Corps at his university, the candidate is attached to a Regular unit for twelve weeks (consecutively or in two stages). The final examination in military subjects is competitive. (2) *Cadets of the Royal Military College* are instructed in the following additional subjects: sanitation, French or German (or both), riding and horse management, musketry, physical training, drill and signalling. Hindustani may be taken instead of French or German. (3) *Cadets of the Royal Military Academy* are instructed in the same subjects as the cadets at the Royal Military College, with the addition of artillery, advanced mathematics, chemistry, light, heat, electricity and workshop practice. Cadets who pass highest in the final examination for commissions are as a rule appointed to the Royal Engineers, the remainder to the Royal Artillery. (4) *Officers of the Special Reserve, Territorial Force* and certain other forces must have completed a continuous period of attachment of twelve months to a Regular unit of Cavalry, Artillery, Engineers or Infantry, and have served and been trained for at least one year in the force to which they belong, before presenting themselves at the competitive examination in military subjects. The period of attachment to Regular units may be reduced if certain certificates are obtained. Candidates for commissions in the artillery must belong to the artillery branches of the above forces and have a certificate in riding and mathematics. They are not eligible for the Royal Engineers. (5) The conditions for *Officers of the Colonial Military Forces* are similar to those for the Special Reserve, &c., except that only two months' attachment to a Regular unit, or unit of the Permanent Colonial Forces, is required. (6) Commissions are also given to *Cadets of the Royal Military College, Kingston, Canada;* the training of that establishment being similar to that at the Royal Military College and the Royal Military Academy.

Candidates for commissions in the Royal Army Medical Corps and Army Veterinary Corps are not examined in military subjects, but must pass in the appropriate technical subjects; those for the Royal Army Medical Corps passing two written and two oral examinations, one each in medicine and surgery; those for the Army Veterinary Corps passing a written and an oral examination in veterinary medicine, surgery and hygiene. Candidates for the Royal Army Medical Corps have further to proceed to the Royal Army Medical College for instruction in recruiting duties, hygiene, pathology, tropical medicine, military surgery and military medical administration.

Royal Engineers attend the School of Military Engineering at Chatham, where long and elaborate courses of instruction are given in all subjects appertaining to the work of the corps, including practical work in the field and in fortresses.

II. The training which succeeds the appointment to a commission consists partly of more detailed instruction in the subjects already learned, partly of the practical application of those subjects, and partly of more advanced instruction with its practical application.

On first joining his unit the young officer is put through a course of preliminary drills, lasting, as a rule, for from three months (infantry) to six months (cavalry), though the time depends upon the individual officer's rate of progress. During this period, and for some considerable time afterwards, officers are instructed in " regimental duties," consisting of the interior economy of a regiment, such as financial accounts, stores, correspondence, the minor points of military law in their actual working, customs of the service, the management of regimental institutes, &c., with, in the case of the mounted branches, equitation and the care and management of horses. They are required to attend a number of courts-martial, as supernumerary members, before being permitted to attend one in the effective and official capacities of member or prosecutor, although from a legal point of view their qualification depends simply upon their rank and length of service. A course of musketry, theoretical and practical, is then gone through. Field training begins with lectures on the various evolutions of the squadron, battery or company, followed by actual practice in the field, arranged by the commanders of squadrons, batteries or companies.

Before promotion from the rank of second-lieutenant to lieutenant, an examination must be passed in " Regimental Duties " (practical, oral and written) and " Drill and Field Training " (practical only). The officer is then taken in hand by the commanding officer of his regiment, battalion or brigade. He is frequently examined in the subjects in which he has already been instructed, and is practically taught the more advanced stages of topography, engineering, tactics, law and organization. The next stage consists of regimental drills, which include every kind of practical work in the field which can be done by a unit under the command of a lieutenant-colonel. After this come brigade, division and army manœuvres. Officers have to pass examinations in-military subjects for promotion until they attain the rank of major. The chief of these subjects are tactics, military topography, military engineering, military law, administration and military history. For majors, before promotion to lieutenant-colonel, an examination in " Tactical Fitness for Command " has to be passed. This examination is a test of ability in commanding the " three arms " in the field; a course of attachment to the two arms to which the officer does not belong being a necessary preliminary.

Army Service Corps.—The officers of this corps have usually served for at least one year in the cavalry, infantry or Royal Marines, though commissions are also given to cadets of the Royal Military College. On joining, the officer first spends nine months on probation, during which he attends lectures and practical demonstrations in the following subjects: military administration and organization generally; and as regards Army Service Corps work, in detail; organization of the Field Army and Lines of Communication; war organization and duties of the A.S.C.; registry and care of correspondence; contracts; special purchases; precautions in receiving supplies, and care and issue of same; accounts, forms, vouchers and office work in general and in detail; barrack duties (including all points relating to coal, wood, turf, candles, lamps, gas, water, &c). A thorough and detailed description of all kinds of forage, breadstuffs, meat, groceries and other field supplies is given. The lectures and demonstrations in transport include, beside mounted and dismounted drill, wagon drill; carriages; embarkation and disembarkation of men and animals; entraining and detraining; harness and saddlery; transport, by rail and sea, with the office work involved. This course of instruction is given at the Army Service Corps Training Establishment at Aldershot.

A satisfactory examination having been passed, the officer is permanently taken into the corps. Before promotion to captain he is examined in accounts, correspondence and contracts; judging cattle and supplies; duties of an A.S.C. officer in charge of a sub-district; interior economy of a company; military vehicles and pack animals; embarkation, disembarkation and duties on board ship; convoys; duties of brigade supply and transport officer in war. Captains, before promotion to major, are examined in lines of communication of an army in war; method of obtaining supplies and transport in war, and formation and working of depots; organization of transport in war; schemes of supply and transport for troops operating from a fixed base; duties of a staff-officer administering supply, transport and barrack duties at home. These are in addition to general military subjects.

Royal Army Medical Corps.—On completion of the course of instruction at the Royal Army Medical College, lieutenants on probation proceed to the R.A.M.C. School of Instruction at Aldershot for a two months' course in the technical duties of the corps, and at the end of the course are examined in the subjects taught. This passed, their commissions are confirmed. After eighteen months' service, officers are examined in squad, company and corps drills and exercises; the Geneva Convention; the administration, organization and equipment of the army in its relation to the medical services; duties of wardmasters and stewards in military hospitals and returns, accounts and requisitions connected therewith; duties of executive medical officers; military law. These successful candidates are then eligible for promotion to captain. Before promotion to major the following examination must be passed, after a course of study under such arrangements as the director-general of the Army Medical Service may determine: (1) medicine, (2) surgery, (3) hygiene, (4) bacteriology, (5) one out of seven special subjects named, and (6) military law. The examination for promotion from major to lieutenant-colonel embraces army medical organization in peace and war; sanitation of towns, camps, transports, &c.; epidemiology and the management of epidemics; medical history of important campaigns; the Army Medical Service of the more important powers; the laws and customs of war, so far as they relate to the sick and wounded; and a tactical problem in field medical administration. Officers who pass these examinations with distinction are eligible for accelerated promotion.

Army Ordnance Department.—An officer of this department must have had at least four years' service in other branches of the army and must have passed for the rank of captain. They are then eligible to present themselves at an elementary examination in mathematics, after passing which they attend a one year's course at the Ordnance College, Woolwich. The course comprises the following: (a) *Gunnery* (including principles of gun construction and practical optics); (b) *Matériel*, guns, carriages, machine guns, small arms and ammunition of all descriptions; (c) *Army Ordnance Duties* (functions of the corps; supply, receipt and issue of stores, &c.); (d) *Machinery*; (e) *Chemistry and Metallurgy*; (f) *Electricity*. An advanced course follows in which officers take up any two of the subjects of applied mechanics, chemistry and electricity, combined with either small arms, optics or mechanical design. They are then appointed to the department and hold their appointments for four years, with a possible extension of an additional three years.

Army Veterinary Corps.—A candidate on appointment as veterinary officer, on joining at Aldershot, undergoes a course of special training at the Army Veterinary School. The course lasts one year, and consists of (a) hygiene; conformation of the foot and shoeing, conformation, points, colours, markings; stable construction and management; management of horses in the open and of large bodies of sick; saddles and sore backs; collars and sore shoulders; bits and bitting; transport by sea and rail; mules, donkeys, camels and oxen; remount depots; training of army horses; marching. (b) Diseases met with specially on active service. (c) Military etiquette and ethics; accounts and returns; administration and organization; veterinary hospitals, mobilization, map-reading and law. At the end of the course he is examined, and if found satisfactory, is retained in the service. Before promotion to captain he is examined in the duties of executive veterinary officers and in law; before promotion to major, in medicine, surgery, hygiene, bacteriology and tropical diseases, and in one special subject selected by the candidate; and before promotion to lieutenant-colonel, in law, duties of administrative veterinary officers at home and abroad, management of epizootics, sanitation of stables, horse-lines and transports.

Army Pay Department.—Officers are appointed to the department, on probation for a period not exceeding one year, after serving for five years in one of the other arms or branches of the service. At the end of this period the candidates are examined in the following subjects: examination of company pay lists and pay and mess book; method of keeping accounts and preparing balance-sheets and monthly estimates; knowledge of pay-warrant, allowance regulations and financial instructions, book-keeping, by double entry and the duties attending the payment of soldiers; aptitude for accounts, and quickness and neatness in work. On completion of five years' service, officers return to their regiments, unless they elect to remain with the department or are required by the Army Council to be permanently attached to it.

Schools and Colleges.—The training of the officer in his regiment is necessarily incomplete, owing to a far wider knowledge of his profession in general, and of his own branch of the service in particular, being essential, than can be acquired within the comparatively confined limits of his own unit. Accordingly, schools and colleges have been established, in which special courses of instruction are given, dealing more fully with the generalities and details of the various branches of the service.

There is a cavalry school at Netheravon.

Mounted Infantry schools have been established at Longmoor, Bulford and Kilworth, which train both officers and men in mounted infantry duties. The officers selected to be trained at these schools must have at least two years' service, have completed a trained soldier's course of musketry and should have some knowledge of horsemanship and be able to ride. The instruction consists for the most part of riding school and field training.

The *School of Gunnery* at Shoeburyness gives five courses of instruction per annum; one "Staff" course for Ordnance officers, lasting one month; two courses for senior officers of the Royal Artillery, lasting a fortnight each, and two courses for junior officers of the same regiment, lasting one month each. For Royal Garrison Artillery officers there is one "Staff" course lasting for seven months (this being a continuation of the previous "Staff" course), and two courses, lasting four months each, for junior officers. There is also a school of gunnery at Lydd, where two courses, lasting for three weeks each, in siege artillery, are given each year.

The *Ordnance College* at Woolwich provides various courses of instruction in addition to those intended for officers of the Ordnance Department. There is a "Gunnery Staff Course" for senior officers, in gunnery, guns, carriages, ammunition, electricity and machinery; two courses for junior officers of the Royal Artillery in the same subjects; a course for officers of the Army Service Corps in mechanical transport, which includes instruction in allied subjects, such as electricity and chemistry. It also gives courses of instruction to officers of the Royal Navy.

The *School of Military Engineering* at Chatham trains officers of the Royal Engineers, compiles official text-books on field defences, attack and defence of fortresses, military bridging, mining, encampments, railways.

The *School of Musketry* at Hythe (besides assisting and directing the musketry training of the army at large by revising regulations, experiments, &c.) trains officers of all branches of the service in theoretical and practical musketry, the courses lasting about a month each and embracing fire control, the training of the eye in quick perception, fire effect and so on. Courses in the Maxim gun usually follow.

The *Staff College* (see also STAFF) at Camberley is the most important of the military colleges. Only specially selected officers are eligible to attempt the entrance examination. The course lasts two years, and is divided into: (a) military history, strategy, tactics, imperial strategy, strategic distribution, coast defence, fortification, war organization, reconnaissance; (b) staff duties, administration, peace distribution, mobilization, movements of troops by land and sea, supply, transport, remounts, organization, law and topographical reconnaissance. Visits are paid to workshops, fortresses, continental battlefields, &c., and staff tours are carried out. Officers of the non-mounted branches attend riding school, and students can be examined in any foreign languages they may have previously studied. They are also attached for short periods to arms of the service other than those to which they belong, and attend at staff offices to ensure their being conversant with the work done there.

The *Army Service Corps Training Establishment* at Aldershot gives courses of instruction to senior officers of the corps at which

a limited number of officers of other corps may attend, provided they have passed through or been recommended for the Staff College. Other courses, in addition to the nine months' course for officers on probation for the corps are, one of twelve days for senior officers of the corps in mechanical transport; two (one long and one short) in the same subject for other officers; one for officers in other branches of the service in judging provisions; and one for lieutenants of the Royal Army Medical Corps in supply and transport.

Other colleges and schools are: the *Balloon School* at Farnborough, for officers of the Royal Engineers; *Schools of Electric Lighting* at Plymouth and Portsmouth; the *School of Signalling* at Aldershot, for officers of all branches of the service; the *School of Gymnastics*, also at Aldershot; and the *Army Veterinary School*, where a one month's course is given to officers of the mounted branches in the main principles of horsemastership, stable management and veterinary first aid, in addition to the one year's course for officers on probation for the Army Veterinary Corps.

To encourage the study of foreign languages, officers who pass a preliminary examination in any language they may select are allowed to reside in the foreign country for a period of at least two months. After such residence they may present themselves for examination, and if successful, receive a grant in aid of the expenses incurred. The grant is £80 for Russian, £50 for German, £24 for French and £30 for other languages. The final or "Interpretership" examination for which the grant is given is of a very high standard. In the case of Russian, £80 is paid to the officer during his residence in Russia, in addition to the grant. Special arrangements are made with regard to the Chinese and Japanese languages; three officers for the former and four officers for the latter being selected annually for a two years' residence in those countries. During such residence officers receive £150 per annum, in addition to their pay, and a reward of £175 on passing the "Interpretership" examination.

There has been a tendency of late years to give officers facilities for going through civilian courses of instruction; for example, at the London School of Economics and in the workshops of the principal railway companies. These courses enable the officer not only to profit by civilian experience and progress, but also to form an opinion as to his own knowledge, as compared with the knowledge of those outside his immediate surroundings.

Promotion from the Ranks.—In several armies aspirant officers may join as privates and pass through all grades. This is hardly promotion from the ranks, however, because it is understood from the first that the young *enseigneur*, as he is called in Germany, is a candidate for officer's rank, and he is treated accordingly, generally living in the officers' mess and spending only a brief period in each of the non-commissioned ranks. True promotion from the ranks, by mere merit and without any preferential treatment, is practically unknown in Germany. In France, on the other hand, one-third of the officers are promoted non-commissioned officers. In Italy also a large proportion of the officers comes from the ranks. In Great Britain, largely owing to the chances of distinction afforded by frequent colonial expeditions, a fair number of non-commissioned officers receive promotion to combatants' commissions. The number is, however, diminishing, as shown by the following extracts from a return of 1909 (combatants only):—

1885–1888	annual average	34	(Sudan Wars, &c.)
1889–1892	" "	25	
1893–1902	" "	19	
1899–1902	" "	35	(S. African War)
1903–1908	" "	14	

Quartermasters and riding masters are invariably promoted from the lower ranks.

Officers of reserve and second line forces are recruited in Great Britain both by direct appointment and by transfer from the regular forces. In universal service armies reserve officers are drawn from retired regular officers, selected non-commissioned officers, and most of all from young men of good social standing who are gazetted after serving their compulsory period as privates in the ranks.

FOREIGN ARMIES

The training of the officer of a foreign army differs very slightly from that of the British officer. Each country specializes according to its individual requirements, but in the main the training is much the same.

Germany.—The Germans attend more closely to detail—being even microscopical—and it has been said that a little grit in the German military machine would cause a cessation of its working. Unfortunately for this argument, the German army has not yet given any signs of cessation of work, so few deviations from the smooth working of the military machine being permitted that the introduction of grit into this air-tight casing is practically impossible. At the same time, the German officer is trained to have initiative and to use that initiative, but he is expected to be discreet in the use of it and consequently undue insistence on literal obedience to instructions (as distinct from formal orders), and undue reticence on the part of senior, especially staff, officers is held to be dangerous, in that the regimental officer, if ignorant of the military situation, may, by acts of initiative out of harmony with the general plan, seriously prejudice the issue. The Germans attach special importance to instruction in the tactical handling of artillery.

Italy.—The Italians make a speciality of horsemanship, their cavalry officers studying for two years at the cavalry school at Modena; later at the school at Pinerolo, and later still at the school at Tor di Quinto. They also attach much importance to mountain warfare.

France.—The formal training of the French officer does not appear to differ seriously from that of the British officer, with this exception, that as one-third or so of French officers are promoted from the non-commissioned ranks, a great feature of the educational system is the group of schools comprising the Saumur (cavalry), St Maixent (infantry) and Versailles (artillery and engineers), which are intended for under-officer candidates for commissions. The generality of the officers comes from the "special school" of St Cyr (infantry and cavalry) and the *École Polytechnique* (artillery and engineers).

(R. J. C.)

United States.—The principal source from which officers are supplied to the army is the famous Military Academy at West Point, N.Y. The President may appoint forty cadets and generally chooses sons of army and navy officers. Each senator and each representative and delegate in Congress may appoint one. These appointments are not made annually, but as vacancies occur through graduation of cadets, or their discharge before graduation. The maximum number of cadets under the Twelfth Census is 533. The commanding officer of the academy has the title of superintendent and commandant. He is detailed from the army, and has the temporary rank of colonel. The corps of cadets is organized as a battalion, and is commanded by an officer detailed from the army, having the title of commandant of cadets. He has the temporary rank of lieutenant-colonel. An officer of engineers and of ordnance are detailed as instructors of practical military engineering and of ordnance and gunnery respectively. The heads of the departments of instruction have the title of professors. They are selected generally from officers of the army, and their positions are permanent. The officers above mentioned and the professors constitute the academic board. The military staff and assistant instructors are officers of the army. The course of instruction covers four years and is very thorough. Theoretical instruction comprises mathematics, French, Spanish, English, drawing, physics, astronomy, chemistry, ordnance and gunnery, art of war, civil and military engineering, law (international, constitutional and military), history and drill regulations of all arms. Practical instruction comprises the service drills in infantry, cavalry and artillery, surveying, reconnaissances, field engineering, construction of temporary bridges, simple astronomical observations, fencing, gymnastics and swimming. Cadets are a part of the army, and rank between second lieutenants and the highest grade of non-commissioned officers. They receive from the government a rate of pay sufficient to cover all necessary expenses at the academy. About 50% of those entering are able to complete the course. The graduating class each year numbers, on an average, about 60. A class, on graduating, is arranged in order according to merit, and its members are assigned as second lieutenants to corps and arm, according to the recommendation of the academic board. A few at the head of the class go into the corps of engineers; the next in order generally go into the artillery, and the rest of the class into the cavalry and infantry. The choice of graduates as to arm of service and regiments is consulted as far as practicable. Any enlisted man who has served honestly and faithfully not less than two years, who is between twenty-one and thirty years of age, unmarried, a citizen of the United States and of good moral character, may aspire to a commission. To obtain it he must pass an educational and physical examination before a board of five officers. This board must also inquire as to the character, standing and record of the candidate. Many well-educated young men, unable to obtain appointments to West Point, enlist in the army for the express purpose of obtaining a commission. Vacancies in the grade of second lieutenant remaining, after the graduates of the Military Academy and qualified enlisted men have been appointed, are filled from civil life. To be eligible for appointment a candidate must be a citizen of the United States, unmarried, between the ages of twenty-one and twenty-seven years, and must be approved by an examining board of five officers as to habits, moral character, physical ability, education and general fitness for the service. In time of peace very few appointments from civil life are made, but in time of war there is a large number.

There are, in addition to the Engineer School at Washington, D.C. four service schools for officers. These are: the Coast Artillery School at Fort Monroe, Virginia; the General Service and Staff College at Fort Leavenworth, Kansas; the Mounted Service School at Fort Riley, Kansas; the Army Medical School at Washington. The commandants, staffs and instructors at these schools are officers specially selected. The garrison at Fort Monroe is composed of several companies of coast artillery. The lieutenants of these companies, who constitute the class, are relieved and replaced by others on 1st September of each year. The course of instruction comprises the following subjects: artillery, ballistics, engineering, steam and mechanics, electricity and mines, chemistry and explosives, military science, practical military exercises, photography, telegraphy and cordage (the use of ropes, the making of various kinds of knots

and lashings, rigging shears, &c., for the handling of heavy guns). July and August of each year are ordinarily devoted to artillery target practice. The course at the General Service and Staff College is for one year in each School. The class of student officers is made up of one lieutenant from each regiment of infantry and cavalry, and such others as may be detailed. They are assigned to the organizations comprising the garrison, normally a regiment of infantry, a squadron (four troops) of cavalry and a battery of field artillery. The departments of instruction are: military art, engineering, law, infantry, cavalry, military hygiene. Much attention is paid to practical work in the minor operations of war, the troops of the garrison being utilized in connexion therewith. At the close of the final examinations of each class at Fort Monroe and Fort Leavenworth, those officers most distinguished for proficiency are reported to the adjutant-general of the army. Two from each class of the Artillery School, and not more than five from each class at the General Service and Staff College, are thereafter, so long as they remain in the service, noted in the annual army register as "honour graduates." The work of the Mounted Service School at Fort Riley is mainly practical, and is carried on by the regular garrison, which usually, in time of peace, consists of two squadrons of cavalry and three field batteries. The government reservation at Fort Riley comprises about 40 sq. m. of varied terrain, so that opportunities are afforded, and taken advantage of, for all kinds of field operations. The Army Medical School is established at Washington. The faculty consists of four or more instructors selected from the senior officers of the medical department. The course of instruction covers a period of five months, beginning annually in November. The student officers are recently appointed medical officers, and such other medical officers, available for detail, as may desire to take the course. Instruction is by lecture and practical work, special attention being given to the following subjects: duties of medical officers in peace and war; hospital administration; military medicine, surgery and hygiene; microscopy and bacteriology; hospital corps drill and first aid to the wounded.

(W. A. S.)

OFFICIAL (Late Lat. *officialis*, for class. Lat. *apparitor*, from *officium*, office, duty), in general any holder of office under the state or a public body. In ecclesiastical law the word "official" has a special technical sense as applied to the official exercising a diocesan bishop's jurisdiction as his representative and in his name (see ECCLESIASTICAL JURISDICTION). The title of "official principal," together with that of "vicar-general," is in England now merged in that of "chancellor" of a diocese (see CHANCELLOR).

OFFICINAL, a term applied in medicine to drugs, plants and herbs, which are sold in chemists' and druggists' shops, and to medical preparations of such drugs, &c., as are made in accordance with the prescriptions authorized by the pharmacopoeia. In the latter sense, modern usage tends to supersede "officinal" by "official." The classical Lat. *officina* meant a workshop, manufactory, laboratory, and in medieval monastic Latin was applied to a general store-room (see Du Cange, *Gloss.*, *s.v.*); it thus became applied to a shop where goods were sold rather than a place where things were made.

OGDEN, a city and the county-seat of Weber county, Utah, U.S.A., at the confluence of the Ogden and Weber rivers, and about 35 m. N. of Salt Lake City. Pop. (1890) 14,889; (1900) 16,313, of whom 3302 were foreign-born; (1910 census) 25,580. It is served by the Union Pacific, the Southern Pacific, the Oregon Short Line, and the Denver & Rio Grande railways. It is situated at an elevation of about 4300 ft. in the picturesque region of the Wasatch Range, Ogden Cañon and the Great Salt Lake. Ogden is in an agricultural and fruit-growing region, and gold and silver are mined in the vicinity. It has various manufactures, and the value of the factory product increased from $1,242,214 in 1900 to $2,997,057 in 1905, or 141·3%. Ogden, which is said to have been named in honour of John Ogden, a trapper, was laid out under the direction of Brigham Young in 1850, and was incorporated in the next year; in 1861 it received a new charter, but since 1898 it has been governed under a general law of the state.

OGDENSBURG, a city and port of entry of St Lawrence county, New York, U.S.A., on the St Lawrence river, at the mouth of the Oswegatchie, 140 m. N. by E. of Syracuse, New York. Pop. (1890) 11,662; (1900) 12,633, of whom 3222 were foreign-born; (1910 census) 15,933. It is served by the New York Central & Hudson River and the Rutland railways, and by several lake and river steamboat lines connecting with ports on the Great Lakes, the city being at the head of lake navigation on the St Lawrence. Steam ferries connect Ogdensburg with Prescott, Ontario. The city is the seat of the St Lawrence State Hospital for the Insane (1890), and has a United States Customs House and a state armoury. The city became the see of a Roman Catholic bishop in 1872, and here Edgar Philip Wadhams (1817–1891) laboured as bishop in 1872–1891. It is the port of entry of the Oswegatchie customs district, and has an extensive commerce, particularly in lumber and grain. The city has various manufactures, including lumber, flour, wooden-ware, brass-ware, silks, woollens and clothing. The value of the factory products increased from $2,260,889 in 1900 to $3,057,371 in 1905, or 35·2%. The site of Ogdensburg was occupied in 1749 by the Indian settlement of La Presentation, founded by the Abbé François Piquet (1708–1781) for the Christian converts of the Iroquois. At the outbreak of the War of Independence the British built here Fort Presentation, which they held until 1796, when, in accordance with the terms of the Jay Treaty, the garrison was withdrawn. Abraham Ogden (1743–1798), a prominent New Jersey lawyer, bought land here, and the settlement which grew up around the fort was named Ogdensburg. During the early part of the War of 1812 it was an important point on the American line of defence. On the 4th of October 1812 Colonel Lethbridge, with about 750 men, prepared to attack Ogdensburg but was driven off by American troops under General Jacob Brown. On the 22nd of February 1813 both fort and village were captured and partially destroyed by the British. During the Canadian rising of 1837–1838 Ogdensburg became a rendezvous of the insurgents. Ogdensburg was incorporated as a village in 1818, and was chartered as a city in 1868.

OGEE (probably an English corruption of Fr. *ogive*, a diagonal groin rib, being a moulding commonly employed; equivalents in other languages are Lat. *cyma-reversa*, Ital. *gola*, Fr. *cymaise*, Ger. *Kehlleisten*), a term given in architecture to a moulding of a double curvature, convex and concave, in which the former is the uppermost (see MOULDING). The name "ogee-arch" is often applied to an arch formed by the meeting of two contrasted ogees (see ARCH).

OGIER THE DANE, a hero of romance, who is identified with the Frankish warrior Autchar (Autgarius, Auctarius, Otgarius, Oggerius) of the old chroniclers. In 771 or 772 Autchar accompanied Gerberga, widow of Carloman, Charlemagne's brother, and her children to the court of Desiderius, king of the Lombards, with whom he marched against Rome. In 773 he submitted to Charles at Verona. He finally entered the cloister of St Faro at Meaux, and Mabillon (*Acta SS. ord. St Benedicti*, Paris, 1677) has left a description of his monument there, which had figures of Ogier and his friend Benedict or Benoît, with smaller images of Roland and la belle Aude and other Carolingian personages. In the chronicle of the Pseudo Turpin it is stated that innumerable *cantilenae* were current on the subject of Ogier, and his deeds were probably sung in German as well as in French. The Ogier of romance may be definitely associated with the flight of Gerberga and her children to Lombardy, but it is not safe to assume that the other scattered references all relate to the same individual. Colour is lent to the theory of his Bavarian origin by the fact that he, with Duke Naimes of Bavaria, led the Bavarian contingent to battle at Roncesvaux.

In the romances of the Carolingian cycle he is, on account of his revolt against Charlemagne, placed in the family of Doon de Mayence, being the son of Gaufrey de "Dannemarche." The *Enfances Ogier* of Adenès le Rois, and the *Chevalerie Ogier de Dannemarche* of Raimbert de Paris, are doubtless based on earlier *chansons*. The *Chevalerie* is divided into twelve songs or branches. Ogier, who was the hostage for his father at Charlemagne's court, fell into disgrace, but regained the emperor's favour by his exploits in Italy. One Easter at the court of Laon, however, his son Balduinet was slain by Charlemagne's son, Charlot, with a chess-board (cf. the incident of Renaud and Bertholais in the *Quatre Fils Aymon*). Ogier in his rage slays the queen's nephew Loher, and would have slain Charlemagne himself but for the intervention of the knights, who connived

at his flight to Lombardy. In his stronghold of Castelfort he resisted the imperial forces for seven years, but was at last taken prisoner by Turpin, who incarcerated him at Reims, while his horse Broiefort, the sharer of his exploits, was made to draw stones at Meaux. He was eventually released to fight the Saracen chief Bréhus or Braihier, whose armies had ravaged France, and who had defied Charlemagne to single combat. Ogier only consented to fight after the surrender of Charlot, but the prince was saved from his barbarous vengeance by the intervention of St Michael. The giant Bréhus, despite his 17 ft. of stature, was overthrown, and Ogier, after marrying an English princess, the daughter of Angart (or Edgard), king of England, received from Charlemagne the fiefs of Hainaut and Brabant.

A later romance in Alexandrines (Brit. Mus. MS. Royal 15 E vi.) contains marvels added from Celtic romance. Six fairies visit his cradle, the sixth, Morgan la Fay, promising that he shall be her lover. He has a conqueror's career in the East, and after two hundred years in the "castle" of Avalon returns to France in the days of King Philip, bearing a firebrand on which his life depends. This he destroys when Philip's widowed queen wishes to marry him, and he is again carried off by Morgan la Fay. The prose romance printed at Paris in 1498 is a version of this later poem. The fairy element is prominent in the Italian legend of *Uggieri il Danese*, the most famous redaction being the prose *Libro dele bataglie del Danese* (Milan, 1498), and in the English *Famous and renowned history of Morvine, son to Oger the Dane*, translated by J. M. (London, 1612). The Spanish Urgel was the hero of Lope de Vega's play, the *Marques de Mantua*. Ogier occupies the third branch of the Scandinavian Karlamagnus saga; his fight with Brunamont (*Enfances Ogier*) was the subject of a Danish folk-song; and as *Holger Danske* he became a Danish national hero, who fought against the German Dietrich of Bern (Theodoric "of Verona"), and was invested with the common tradition of the king who sleeps in a mountain ready to awaken at need. Whether he had originally anything to do with Denmark seems doubtful. The surname le Danois has been explained as a corruption of l'Ardennois and Dannemarche as the marches of the Ardennes.

BIBLIOGRAPHY.—*La Chevalerie Ogier de Dannemarche*, ed. J. B. Barrois (2 vols., Paris, 1842); *Les Enfances Ogier*, ed. A. Scheler (Brussels, 1874); *Hist. litt. de la France*, vols. xx. and xxii.; G. Paris, *Hist. poët. de Charlemagne* (Paris, 1856); L. Gautier, *Les Epopées françaises* (2nd ed., 1878–1896); L. Pio, *Saguet om Holger Danske* (Copenhagen, 1870); H. L. Ward, *Catalogue of Romances*, vol. i. pp. 604–610; C. Voretzsch, *Über die Sage von Ogier dem Dänen* (Halle, 1891); F. Paris, "Recherches sur Ogier le Danois," *Bibl. de l'École des Chartes*, vol. iii.; P. Rajna, *Le Origini dell' epopea francese* (1884); Riezler, "Naimes v. Bayern und Ogier der Däne," in *Sitsungsberichte der phil. hist. Classe der kl. Akad. d. Wiss.*, vol. iv. (Munich, 1892).

OGILBY, JOHN (1600–1676), British writer, was born in or near Edinburgh in November 1600. His father was a prisoner within the rules of King's Bench, but by speculation the son found money to apprentice himself to a dancing-master and to obtain his father's release. He accompanied Thomas Wentworth, earl of Strafford, when he went to Ireland as lord deputy, and became tutor to his children. Strafford made him deputy-master of the revels, and he built a little theatre in St Werburgh Street, Dublin, which was very successful. The outbreak of the Civil War ruined his fortunes, and in 1646 he returned to England. Finding his way to Cambridge, he learned Latin from kindly scholars who had been impressed by his industry. He then ventured to translate Virgil into English verse (1649–1650), which brought him a considerable sum of money. The success of this attempt encouraged Ogilby to learn Greek from David Whitford, who was usher in the school kept by James Shirley the dramatist. *Homer his Iliads translated* . . . appeared in 1660, and in 1665 *Homer his Odysses translated* . . . Anthony à Wood asserts that in these undertakings he had the assistance of Shirley. At the Restoration Ogilby received a commission for the "poetical part" of the coronation. His property was destroyed in the Great Fire of 1666, but he rebuilt his house in Whitefriars, and set up a printing press, from which he issued many magnificent books, the most important of which were a series of atlases, with engravings and maps by Hollar and others. He styled himself "His Majesty's Cosmographer and Geographic Printer." He died in London on the 4th of September 1676.

Ogilby also translated the fables of Aesop, and wrote three epic poems. His bulky output was ridiculed by John Dryden in *Mac-Flecknoe* and by Alexander Pope in the *Dunciad*.

OGILVIE (or **OGILBY**), **JOHN** (c. 1580–1615), English Jesuit, was born in Scotland and educated mainly in Germany, where he entered the Society of Jesus, being ordained priest at Paris in 1613. As an emissary of the society he returned to Scotland in this year disguised as a soldier, and in October 1614 he was arrested in Glasgow. He defended himself stoutly when he was tried in Edinburgh, but he was condemned to death and was hanged on the 28th of February 1615.

A *True Relation of the Proceedings against John Ogilvie, a Jesuit* (Edinburgh, 1615), is usually attributed to Archbishop Spottiswoode. See also James Forbes, *L'Eglise catholique en Ecosse: martyre de Jean Ogilvie* (Paris, 1885); and W. Forbes-Leith, *Narratives of Scottish Catholics* (1885).

OGILVY, the name of a celebrated Scottish family of which the earl of Airlie is the head. The family was probably descended from a certain Gillebride, earl of Angus, who received lands from William the Lion. Sir Walter Ogilvy (d. 1440) of Lintrathen, lord high treasurer of Scotland from 1425 to 1431, was the son of Sir Walter Ogilvy of Wester Powrie and Auchterhouse, a man, says Andrew of Wyntoun, "stout and manfull, bauld and wycht," who was killed in 1392. He built a castle at Airlie in Forfarshire, and left two sons. The elder of these, Sir John Ogilvy (d. c. 1484), was the father of Sir James Ogilvy (c. 1430–c. 1504), who was made a lord of parliament in 1491; and the younger, Sir Walter Ogilvy, was the ancestor of the earls of Findlater. The earldom of Findlater, bestowed on James Ogilvy, Lord Ogilvy of Deskford, in 1638, was united in 1711 with the earldom of Seafield and became dormant after the death of James Ogilvy, the 7th earl, in October 1811 (see SEA-FIELD, EARLS OF).

Sir James Ogilvy's descendant, James Ogilvy, 5th Lord Ogilvy of Airlie (c. 1541–1606), a son of James Ogilvy, master of Ogilvy, who was killed at the battle of Pinkie in 1547, took a leading part in Scottish politics during the reigns of Mary and of James VI. His grandson, James Ogilvy (c. 1593–1666), was created earl of Airlie by Charles I. at York in 1639. A loyal partisan of the king, he joined Montrose in Scotland in 1644 and was one of the royalist leaders at the battle of Kilsyth. The destruction of the earl's castles of Airlie and of Forther in 1640 by the earl of Argyll, who "left him not in all his lands a cock to crow day," gave rise to the song " The bonny house o'Airlie." His eldest son, James, the 2nd earl (c. 1615–c. 1704) also fought among the royalists in Scotland; in 1644 he was taken prisoner, but he was released in the following year as a consequence of Montrose's victory at Kilsyth. He was again a prisoner after the battle of Philiphaugh and was sentenced to death in 1646, but he escaped from his captivity at St Andrews and was afterwards pardoned. Serving with the Scots against Cromwell he became a prisoner for the third time in 1651, and was in the Tower of London during most of the years of the Commonwealth. He was a fairly prominent man under Charles II. and James II., and in 1689 he ranged himself on the side of William of Orange. This earl's grandson, James Ogilvy (d. 1731), took part in the Jacobite rising of 1715 and was attainted; consequently on his father's death in 1717 he was not allowed to succeed to the earldom, although he was pardoned in 1725. When he died his brother John (d. 1761) became earl *de jure*, and John's son David (1725–1803) joined the standard of Prince Charles Edward in 1745. He was attainted, and after the defeat of the prince at Culloden escaped to Norway and Sweden, afterwards serving in the French army, where he commanded " *le regiment Ogilvy* " and was known as " *le bel Ecossais*." In 1778 he was pardoned and was allowed to return to Scotland, and his family became extinct when his son David died unmarried in April 1812. After this event David's cousin, another David Ogilvy

(1785–1849), claimed the earldom. He asserted that he was unaffected by the two attainders, but the House of Lords decided that these barred his succession; however, in 1826 the attainders were reversed by act of parliament and David became 6th earl of Airlie. He died on the 20th of August 1849 and was succeeded by his son, David Graham Drummond Ogilvy (1826–1881), who was a Scottish representative peer for over thirty years. The latter's son, David Stanley William Drummond Ogilvy, the 8th earl (1856–1900), served in Egypt in 1882 and 1885, and was killed on the 11th of June 1900 during the Boer War while at the head of his regiment, the 12th Lancers. His titles then passed to his son, David Lyulph Gore Wolseley Ogilvy, the 9th earl (b. 1893).

A word may be said about other noteworthy members of the Ogilvy family. John Ogilvy, called Powrie Ogilvy, was a political adventurer who professed to serve King James VI. as a spy and who certainly served William Cecil in this capacity. Mariota Ogilvy (d. 1575) was the mistress of Cardinal Beaton. Sir George Ogilvy (d. 1663), a supporter of Charles I. during the struggle with the Covenanters, was created a peer as lord of Banff in 1642; this dignity became dormant, or extinct, on the death of his descendant, William Ogilvy, the 8th lord, in June 1803. Sir George Ogilvy of Barras (d. c. 1679) defended Dunnottar Castle against Cromwell in 1651 and 1652, and was instrumental in preventing the regalia of Scotland from falling into his hands; in 1660 he was created a baronet, the title becoming extinct in 1837.

See Sir R. Douglas, *Peerage of Scotland*, new ed. by Sir J. B. Paul (1904 fol.).

OGIVE (a French term, of which the origin is obscure; *auge*, trough, from Lat. *augere*, to increase, and an Arabic astrological word for the " highest point." have been suggested as derivations), a term applied in architecture to the diagonal ribs of a vault. In France the name is generally given to the pointed arch, which has resulted in its acceptance as a title for Gothic architecture, there often called " *le style ogival*."

OGLETHORPE, JAMES EDWARD (1696–1785), English general and philanthropist, the founder of the state of Georgia, was born in London on the 21st of December 1696, the son of Sir Theophilus Oglethorpe (1650–1702) of Westbrook Place, Godalming, Surrey. He entered Corpus Christi College, Oxford, in 1714, but in the same year joined the army of Prince Eugène. Through the recommendation of the duke of Marlborough he became aide-de-camp to the prince, and he served with distinction in the campaign against the Turks, 1716–17, more especially at the siege and capture of Belgrade. After his return to England he was in 1722 chosen member of parliament for Haslemere. He devoted much attention to the improvement of the circumstances of poor debtors in London prisons; and for the purpose of providing an asylum for persons who had become insolvent, and for oppressed Protestants on the continent, he projected the settlement of a colony in America between Carolina and Florida (see GEORGIA). In 1745 Oglethorpe was promoted to the rank of major-general. His conduct in connexion with the Scottish rebellion of that year was the subject of inquiry by court-martial, but he was acquitted. In 1765 he was raised to the rank of general. He died at Cranham Hall, Essex, on the 1st of July 1785.

Sir Theophilus Oglethorpe, the father, had four sons and four daughters, James Edward being the youngest son, and another James (b. 1688) having died in infancy. Of the daughters, Anne Henrietta (b. 1680–1683), Eleanor (b. 1684) and Frances Charlotte (Bolingbroke's " Fanny Oglethorpe ") may be specified as having played rather curious parts in the Jacobitism of the time; their careers are described in the essay on " Queen Oglethorpe " by Miss A. Shield and A. Lang, in the latter's *Historical Mysteries* (1904).

OGOWÉ, one of the largest of the African rivers of the second class, rising in 3° S. in the highlands known as the Crystal range, and flowing N.W. and W. to the Atlantic, a little south of the equator, and some 400 m. following the coast, north of the mouth of the Congo. Its course, estimated at 750 m., lies wholly within the colony of Gabun, French Congo. In spite of its considerable size, the river is of comparatively little use for navigation, as rapids constantly occur as it descends the successive steps of the interior tablelands. The principal obstructions are the falls of Dume, in 13° E.; Bunji, in 12° 35'; Chengwe, in 12° 16'; Boué, in 11° 53'; and the rapids formed in the passes by which it breaks through the outer chains of the mountainous zone, between 10½° and 11½° E. In its lower course the river passes through a lacustrine region in which it sends off secondary channels. These channels, before reuniting with the main stream, traverse a series of lakes, one north, the other south, of the river. These lakes are natural regulators of the river when in flood. The Ogowé has a large number of tributaries, especially in its upper course, but of these few are navigable. The most important are the Lolo, which joins on the south bank in 12° 20' E., and the Ivindo, which enters the Ogowé a few miles lower down. Below the Ivindo the largest tributaries are the Ofowé, 400 yds. wide at its mouth (11° 47' E.), but unnavigable except in the rains, and the Ngunye, the largest southern tributary, navigable for 60 m. to the Samba or Eugénie Falls. Apart from the narrow coast plain the whole region of the lower Ogowé is densely forested. It is fairly thickly populated by Bantu tribes who have migrated from the interior. The fauna includes the gorilla and chimpanzee.

The Ogowé rises in March and April, and again in October and November; it is navigable for steamers in its low-water condition as far as the junction of the Ngunye. At flood time the river can be ascended by steamers for a distance of 235 m. to a place called N'Jole. The first person to explore the valley of the Ogowé was Paul du Chaillu, who travelled in the country during 1857-1859. The extent of the delta and the immense volume of water carried by the river gave rise to the belief that it must either be a bifurcation of the Congo or one of the leading rivers of Africa. However, in 1882 Savorgnan de Brazza (the founder of French Congo) reached the sources of the river in a rugged, sandy and almost treeless plateau, which forms the watershed between its basin and that of the Congo, whose main stream is only 140 m. distant. Since that time the basin of the Ogowé has been fully explored by French travellers.

OGRE, the name in fairy tales and folk-lore of a malignant monstrous giant who lives on human flesh. The word is French, and occurs first in Charles Perrault's *Histoires ou contes du temps passé* (1697). The first English use is in the translation of a French version of the *Arabian Nights* in 1713, where it is spelled *hogre.* Attempts have been made to connect the word with *Ugri,* the racial name of the Magyars or Hungarians, but it is generally accepted that it was adapted into French from the O. Span. *huerco, huergo, uergo,* cognate with Ital. *orco, i.e. Orcus,* the Latin god of the dead and the infernal regions (see PLUTO), who in Romance folk-lore became a man-eating demon of the woods.

OGYGES, or OGYGUS, in Greek mythology, the first king of Thebes. During his reign a great flood, called the Ogygian deluge, was said to have overwhelmed the land. Similar legends were current in Attica and Phrygia. Ogyges is variously described as a Boeotian autochthon, as the son of Cadmus, or of Poseidon.

O'HAGAN, THOMAS O'HAGAN, 1ST BARON (1812-1885), lord chancellor of Ireland, was born at Belfast, on the 29th of May 1812. He was educated at Belfast Academical Institution, and was called to the Irish bar in 1836. In 1840 he removed to Dublin, where he appeared for the repeal party in many political trials. His advocacy of a continuance of the union with England, and his appointment as solicitor-general for Ireland in 1861 and attorney-general in the following year, lost him the support of the Nationalist party, but he was returned to parliament as member for Tralee in 1863. In 1865 he was appointed a judge of common pleas, and in 1868 became lord chancellor of Ireland in Gladstone's first ministry. He was the first Roman Catholic to hold the chancellorship since the reign of James II., an act throwing open the office to Roman Catholics having been passed in 1867. In 1870 he was raised to the peerage, and held office until the resignation of the ministry in 1874. In 1880 he again became lord chancellor on Gladstone's return to office, but resigned in

1881. He died in London on the 1st of February 1885, and was succeeded by his eldest son, Thomas Towneley (1878-1900), and then by another son, Maurice Herbert Towneley (b. 1882).

O'HIGGINS, BERNARDO (1778-1842), one of the foremost leaders in the Chilean struggle for independence and head of the first permanent national government, was a natural son of the Irishman Ambrosio O'Higgins, governor of Chile (1788-1796), and was born at Chillan on the 20th of August 1778. He was educated in England, and after a visit to Spain he lived quietly on his estate in Chile till the revolution broke out. Joining the nationalist party led by Martinez de Rozas, he distinguished himself in the early fighting against the royalist troops despatched from Peru, and was appointed in November 1813 to supersede J. M. Carrera in command of the patriot forces. The rivalry that ensued, in spite of O'Higgins's generous offer to serve under Carrera, eventually resulted in O'Higgins being isolated and overwhelmed with the bulk of the Chilean forces at Rancagua in 1814. O'Higgins with most of the patriots fled across the Andes to Mendoza, where José de San Martin (q.v.) was preparing a force for the liberation of Chile. San Martin espoused O'Higgins's part against Carrera, and O'Higgins, recognizing the superior ability and experience of San Martin, readily consented to serve as his subordinate. The loyalty and energy with which he acted under San Martin contributed not a little to the organization of the liberating army, to its transportation over the Andes, and to the defeat of the royalists at Chacabuco (1817) and Maipo (1818). After the battle of Chacabuco O'Higgins was entrusted with the administration of Chile, and he ruled the country firmly and well, maintaining the close connexion with the Argentine, co-operating loyally with San Martin in the preparation of the force for the invasion of Peru, and seeking, as far as the confusion and embarrassments of the time allowed, to improve the welfare of the people. After the overthrow of the Spanish supremacy in Peru had freed the Chileans from fear of attack, an agitation set in for constitutional government. O'Higgins at first tried to maintain his position by calling a congress and obtaining a constitution which invested him with dictatorial powers. But popular discontent grew in force; risings took place in Concepcion and Coquimbo, and on the 28th of January 1823 O'Higgins was finally patriotic enough to resign his post of director-general, without attempting to retain it by force. He retired to Peru, where he was granted an estate and lived quietly till his death on the 24th of October 1842.

See B. Vicuña Machenna, *Vida de O'Higgins* (Santiago, 1882), and M. L. Armunátegni, *La Dictadura de O'Higgins* (Santiago, 1853); both containing good accounts of O'Higgins's career. Also P. B. Figueroa, *Diccionario biográfico de Chile,* 1550-1887 (Santiago, 1888), and J. B. Suarez, *Rasgos biográficos de hombres notables de Chile* (Valparaiso, 1886).

OHIO, a north central state of the United States of America, lying between latitudes 38° 27' and 41° 57' N. and between longitudes 80° 34' and 84° 49' W. It is bounded N. by Michigan and Lake Erie, E. by Pennsylvania and by the Ohio river which separates it from West Virginia, S. by the Ohio river which separates it from West Virginia and Kentucky, and W. by Indiana. The total area is 41,040 sq. m., 300 sq. m. being water surface.

Physiography.—The state lies on the borderland between the Prairie Plains and the Alleghany Plateau. The disturbances among the underlying rocks of Ohio have been slight, and originally the surface was a plain only slightly undulating; stream dissection changed the region to one of numberless hills and valleys; glacial drift then filled up the valleys over large broken areas, forming the remarkably level till plains of north-western Ohio; but at the same time other areas were broken by the uneven distribution of the drift, and south-eastern Ohio, which was unglaciated, retains its rugged hilly character, gradually merging with the typical plateau country farther S.E. The average elevation of the state above the sea is about 850 ft., but extremes vary from 425 ft. at the confluence of the Great Miami and Ohio rivers in the S.W. corner to 1540 ft. on the summit of Hogues Hill about 1½ m. E. of Bellefontaine in the west central part.

The main water-parting is formed by a range of hills which are composed chiefly of drift and extend W.S.W. across the state from Trumbull county in the N.E. to Darke county, or about the middle of the W. border. North of this water-parting the rivers flow into Lake Erie; S. of it into the Ohio river. Nearly all of the streams in the N.E. part of the state have a rapid current. Those that flow directly into the lake are short, but some of the rivers of this region, such as the Cuyahoga and the Grand, are turned by drift ridges into circuitous courses and flow through narrow valleys with numerous falls and rapids. Passing the village of Cuyahoga Falls the Cuyahoga river descends more than 200 ft. in 3 m.; a part of its course is between walls of sandstone 100 ft. or more in height, and near its mouth, at Cleveland, its bed has been cut down through 60 ft. of drift. In the middle N. part of the state the Black, Vermilion and Huron rivers have their sources in swamps on the water-parting and flow directly to the lake through narrow valleys. The till plains of north-western Ohio are drained chiefly by the Maumee and Sandusky rivers, with their tributaries, and the average fall of the Maumee is only 1·1 ft. per mile, while that of the Sandusky decreases from about 7 ft. per mile at Upper Sandusky to 2·5 ft. per mile below Fremont. South of the water-parting the average length of the rivers is greater than that of those N. of it, and their average fall per mile is much less. In the S.W. the Great Miami and Little Miami rivers have uniform falls through basins that are decidedly rolling and that contain the extremes of elevation for the entire state. The central and S. middle part is drained by the Scioto river and its tributaries. The basin of this river is formed mostly in Devonian shale, and is bounded on the W. by a limestone rim and on the E. by preglacial valleys filled with glacial drift. In its middle portion the basin is about 40 m. wide and only moderately rolling, but toward the mouth of the river the basin becomes narrow and is shut in by high hills. In the E. part of Ohio the Muskingum river and its tributaries drain an area of about 7750 sq. m. or nearly one-fifth of the entire state. Much of the unglacial or driftless portion of the state is embraced within its limits, and although the streams now have a gentle or even sluggish flow, they have greatly broken the surface of the country. The upper portion of the basin is about 100 m. in width, but it becomes quite narrow below Zanesville. The Ohio river flows for 436 m. through a narrow valley on the S. border of the state, and Lake Erie forms the N. boundary for a distance of 230 m. At the W. end of the lake are Sandusky and Maumee bays, each with a good natural harbour. In this vicinity also are various small islands of limestone formation which are attractive summer resorts. On Put-in-Bay Island are some interesting "hydration" caves, i.e. caves formed by the uplifting and folding of the rocks while gypsum was forming beneath, followed by the partial collapse of those rocks when the gypsum passed into solution. Ohio has no large lakes within its limits, but there are several small ones on the water-parting, especially in the vicinity of Akron and Canton, and a few large reservoirs in the W. central section.

Fauna.—Bears, wolves, bison, deer, wild turkeys and wild pigeons were common in the primeval forests of Ohio, but they long ago disappeared. Foxes are still found in considerable numbers in suitable habitats; opossums, skunks and raccoons are plentiful in some parts of the state; and rabbits and squirrels are still numerous. All the song-birds and birds of prey of the temperate zone are plentiful. Whitefish, bass, trout and pickerel are an important food supply obtained from the waters of the lake, and some perch, catfish and sunfish are caught in the rivers and brooks.

Flora.—Ohio is known as the "Buckeye State" on account of the prevalence of the buckeye (*Aesculus glabra*). The state was originally covered with a dense forest mostly of hardwood timber, and although the merchantable portion of this has been practically all cut away, there are still undergrowths of young timber and a great variety of trees. The white oak is the most common, but there are thirteen other varieties of oak, six of hickory, five of ash, five of poplar, three of pine, three of elm, three of birch, two of locust and two of cherry. Beech, black walnut, butternut, chestnut, catalpa, hemlock and tamarack trees are also common. Among native fruits are the blackberry, raspberry, elderberry, cranberry, wild plum and pawpaw (*Asimina triloba*). Buttercups, violets, anemones, spring beauties, trilliums, arbutus, orchids, columbine, laurel, honeysuckle, golden rod and asters are common wild flowers, and of ferns there are many varieties.

Climate.—The mean annual temperature of Ohio is about 51° F.; in the N., 49·5°, and in the S., 53·5°. But except where influenced by Lake Erie the temperature is subject to great extremes; at Coalton, Jackson county, in the S.E. part of the state, the highest recorded range of extremes is from 104° to −38° or 142°; at Wauseon, Fulton county, near the N.W. corner, it is from 104° to −32° or 136°; while at Toledo on the lake shore the range is only from 99° to −16° or 115° F. July is the warmest month, and in most parts of the state January is the coldest; in a few valleys, however, February has a colder record than January. The normal annual precipitation for the entire state is 38·4 in. It is greater in the S.E. and least in the N.W. At Marietta, for example, it is 42·1 in., but at Toledo it is only 30·8 in. Nearly 60 % of it comes in the spring and summer. The average annual fall of snow is about 37 in. in the N. and 22 in. in the S. The prevailing winds in most parts are westerly, but sudden changes, as well as the extremes of temperature, are caused mainly by the frequent shifting of the wind from N.W. to S.W. and from S.W. to N.W. At Cleveland and Cincinnati the winds blow mostly from the S.E.

Soil.—In the driftless area, the S.E. part of the state, the soil is largely a decomposition of the underlying rocks, and its fertility varies according to their composition; there is considerable limestone in the E. central portion, and this renders the soil very productive. In the valleys also are strips covered with a fertile alluvial deposit. In the other parts of the state the soil is composed mainly of glacial drift, and is generally deep and fertile. It is deeper and more fertile, however, in the basins of the Great Miami and Little Miami rivers, where there is a liberal mixture of decomposed limestone and where extensive areas with a clay subsoil are covered with alluvial deposits. North of the lower course of the Maumee river is a belt of sand, but Ohio drift generally contains a large mixture of clay.

Agriculture.—Ohio ranks high as an agricultural state. Of its total land surface 24,501,820 acres or nearly 94 %, was, in 1900, included in farms and 78·5 % of all the farm land was improved. There were altogether 276,719 farms; of these 93,028 contained less than 50 acres, 182,802 contained less than 100 acres, 150,060 contained less than 175 acres, 26,659 contained 175 acres or more, and 164 contained 1000 acres or more. The average size of the farms decreased from 125·2 acres in 1850 to 99·2 acres in 1880 and 88·5 acres in 1900. Nearly seven-tenths of the farms were worked in 1900 by owners or part owners, 24,051 were worked by cash tenants, 51,880 were worked by share tenants, and 1969 were worked by negroes as owners, tenants or managers. There is a great variety of produce, but the principal crops are Indian corn, wheat, oats, hay, potatoes, apples and tobacco. In 1900 the acreage of cereals constituted 68·4 % of the acreage of all crops, and the acreage of Indian corn, wheat and oats constituted 99·3 % of the total acreage of cereals. The Indian corn crop was 67,501,144 bushels in 1870; 152,055,330 bushels in 1899 and 153,062,000 in 1909, when it was grown on 3,875,000 acres and the state ranked seventh among the states of the Union in the production of this cereal. The wheat crop was 27,882,159 bushels in 1870; 50,376,800 bushels (grown on 3,209,014 acres) in 1899; and 23,532,000 bushels (grown on 1,480,000 acres) in 1909. The oat crop was 25,347,549 bushels in 1870; 42,050,910 bushels (grown on 1,115,149 acres) in 1899; and 56,225,000 bushels (grown on 1,730,000 acres) in 1909. The barley crop decreased from 1,715,221 bushels in 1870 to 1,053,240 bushels in 1899 and 829,000 bushels in 1909. The number of swine was 1,964,770 in 1850; 3,285,789 in 1900; and 2,047,000 in 1910. The number of cattle was 1,358,947 in 1850; 2,117,923 in 1900; and 1,625,000 in 1910. In 1900 there were 868,832 and in 1910 947,000 milch cows in the state. The number of sheep decreased slightly between 1870 and 1900, when there were 4,030,021; in 1910 there were 3,203,000 sheep in the state. The number of horses was 463,397 in 1850; 1,068,170 in 1900; and 977,000 in 1910. The cultivation of tobacco was of little importance in the state until about 1840; but the product increased from 10,454,449 ℔ in 1850 to 34,735,235 ℔ in 1880, and to 65,957,100 ℔ in 1899, when the crop was grown on 71,422 acres; in 1909 the crop was 83,250,000 ℔, grown on 90,000 acres. The value of all farm products in 1899 was $257,065,826. Indian corn, wheat and oats are grown in all parts, but the W. half of the state produces about three-fourths of the Indian corn and two-thirds of the wheat, and in the N. half, especially in the N.W. corner, are the best oat-producing counties. The N.E. quarter ranks highest in the production of hay. Domestic animals are evenly distributed throughout the state; in no county was their total value, in June 1900, less than $500,000, and in only three counties (Licking, Trumbull and Wood) did their value exceed $2,000,000; in 73 counties their value exceeded $1,000,000, but was less than $2,000,000. Dairying and the production of eggs are also important industries in all sections. Most of the tobacco is grown in the counties on or near the S.W. border.

Fisheries.—Commercial fishing is important only in Lake Erie. In 1903 the total catch there amounted to 10,748,986 ℔, valued at $317,027. Propagation facilities are being greatly improved, and there are stringent laws for the protection of immature fish. Inland streams and lakes are well supplied with game fish; state laws prohibit the sale of game fish and their being taken, except with hook and line.

Mineral Products.—The mineral wealth of Ohio consists largely of bituminous coal and petroleum, but the state also ranks high in the production of natural gas, sandstone, limestone, grindstone, lime and gypsum. The coal fields, comprising a total area of 10,000 sq. m. or more, are in the E. half of the state. Coal was discovered here as early as 1770, and the mining of it was begun not later than 1828, but no accurate account of the output was kept until 1872, in which year it was 5,315,294 short tons; this was increased to 18,988,150 short tons in 1900, and to 26,270,639 short tons in 1908—in 1907 it was 32,142,419 short tons. There are 29 counties in which coal is produced, but 81·4 % of it in 1908 came from Belmont, Athens, Jefferson, Guernsey, Perry, Hocking, Tuscarawas and Jackson counties. Two of the most productive petroleum fields of the United States are in part in Ohio; the Appalachian field in the E. and S. parts of the state, and the Lima-Indiana field in the N.W. part. Some petroleum was obtained in the S.E. as early as 1859, but the state's output was comparatively small until after petroleum

la ld

Environs of
COLUMBUS
Scale, 1:300,000
English Miles

Railways ...... +-+-+-+ Roads ....
Canals ....
Boundary of Columbus City ....

was discovered in the N.W. in 1884; in 1883 the output was only 47,632 barrels, four years later it was 5,022,632 barrels, and in 1896 it was 23,941,169 barrels, or 39% of the total output in the United States. For the next ten years, however, there was a decrease, and in 1908 the output had fallen to 10,858,797 barrels, of which 6,748,676 barrels (valued at $6,861,885) was obtained in the Lima district, 4,109,935 barrels (valued at $7,315,667) from the south-east district, and 186 barrels (valued at $950), suitable for lubricating purposes, from the Mecca-Belden district in Trumbull and Lorain counties. Natural gas abounds in the eastern, central and north-western parts of the state. That in the E. was first used in 1866, the N.W. field was opened in 1884, and the central field was opened in 1887. The value of the state's yearly flow increased steadily from $100,000 in 1885 to $5,215,669 in 1889, decreased from the latter year to $1,171,777 in 1897, and then increased to $8,244,835 in 1908. Some of the best sandstone in the United States is obtained from Cuyahoga and Lorain counties; it is exceptionally pure in texture (about 97% being pure silica), durable and evenly coloured light buff, grey or blue grey. From the Ohio sandstone known as Berea grit a very large portion of the country's grindstones and pulpstones has been obtained; in 1908 the value of Ohio's output of these stones was $482,128. Some of the Berea grit is also suitable for making oilstones and scythestones. Although the state has a great amount of limestone, especially in Erie and Ottawa counties, its dull colour renders it unsuitable for most building purposes. It is, however, much used as a flux for melting iron and for making quick lime. The quantity of Portland cement made in Ohio increased from 57,000 barrels in 1890 to 563,115 barrels in 1902 and to 1,531,764 barrels in 1908. Beds of rock gypsum extend over an area of 150 acres or more in Ottawa county. There is some iron ore in the eastern and south-eastern parts of the state, and the mining of it was begun early in the 19th century; but the output decreased from 254,294 long tons in 1889 to only 26,585 long tons (all carbonate) in 1908. Ohio, in 1908, produced 3,427,478 barrels of salt valued at $864,710. Other valuable minerals are clay suitable for making pottery, brick and tile (in 1908 the value of the clay working products was $26,622,490) and sand suitable for making glass. The total value of the state's mineral products in 1908 amounted to $134,499,335.

Manufactures.—The total value of the manufactures increased from $348,298,390 in 1880 to $641,688,064 in 1890, and to $832,438,113 in 1900. The value of the factory product was $748,670,855 in 1900 and $960,811,857 in 1905.[1] The most important manufacturing industry is that of iron and steel. This industry was established near Youngstown in 1804. The value of the product increased from $65,206,828 in 1890 to $138,935,256 in 1900 and to $152,859,124 in 1905. Foundry and machine-shop products, consisting largely of engines, boilers, metal-working machinery, wood-working machinery, pumping machinery, mining machinery and stoves, rank second among the state's manufactures; their value increased from $43,617,072 in 1890 to $72,399,632 in 1900, and to $94,507,691 in 1905. Flour and grist mill products rank third in the state; the value of the products decreased from $39,468,490 in 1890 to $37,390,367 in 1900, and then increased to $40,855,566 in 1905. Meat (slaughtering and packing) was next in the value of the product, and increased from $20,660,780 in 1900 to $28,729,044 in 1905. Clay products rank fifth in the state; they increased in value from $16,460,812 in 1900 to $25,686,870 in 1905. Boots and shoes rank sixth; their value increased from $8,489,728 in 1890 to $17,920,854 in 1900 and to $25,140,220 in 1905. Other leading manufactures are malt liquors ($21,620,794 in 1905), railway rolling-stock consisting largely of cars ($21,428,227), men's clothing ($18,496,173), planing mill products ($17,725,711), carriages and wagons ($16,096,125), distilled liquors ($15,976,523), rubber and elastic goods ($15,963,603), furniture ($13,322,608), cigars and cigarettes ($13,241,230), agricultural implements ($12,891,197), women's clothing ($12,803,582), lumber and timber products ($12,567,992), soap and candles ($11,791,223), electrical machinery, apparatus and supplies ($11,019,235), paper and wood pulp ($10,961,527) and refined petroleum ($10,948,864).

The great manufacturing centres are Cleveland, Cincinnati, Youngstown, Toledo, Columbus, Dayton and Akron, and in 1905 the value of the products of these cities amounted to 56.7% of that for the entire state. A large portion of the iron and steel is manufactured in Cleveland, Youngstown, Steubenville, Bellaire, Lorain and Ironton. Most of the automobiles are manufactured in Cleveland; most of the cash registers and calculating machines in Dayton; most of the rubber and elastic goods in Akron; nearly one-half of the liquors and about three-fourths of the men's clothing in Cincinnati. East Liverpool leads in the manufacture of pottery; Toledo in flour and grist mill products; Springfield in agricultural implements; Cincinnati and Columbus in boots and shoes; Cleveland in women's clothing.

Transportation and Commerce.—The most important natural means of transportation are the Ohio river on the S. border and Lake

---

Erie on the N. border. One of the first great public improvements made within the state was the connexion of these waterways by two canals—the Ohio & Erie Canal from Cleveland to Portsmouth, and the Miami & Erie Canal from Toledo to Cincinnati. The Ohio & Erie was opened throughout its entire length (309 m.) in 1832. The Miami & Erie was completed from Middletown to Cincinnati in 1827; in 1845 it was opened to the lake (250 m. from Cincinnati). The national government began in 1825 to extend the National Road across Ohio from Bridgeport, opposite Wheeling, West Virginia, through Zanesville and Columbus, and completed it to Springfield in 1837. Before the completion of the Miami & Erie Canal to Toledo, the building of railways was begun in this region, and in 1836 a railway was completed from that city to Adrian, Michigan. By the close of 1850 the railway mileage had increased to 575 m., and for the next forty years, with the exception of the Civil War period, more than 2000 m. of railways were built during each decade. At the close of 1908 there was a total mileage of 9,300·45 m. Among the railways are the Cleveland, Cincinnati, Chicago & St Louis, the Baltimore & Ohio, the Lake Shore & Michigan Southern, the New York, Chicago & St Louis, the Pittsburgh, Cincinnati, Chicago & St Louis (Pennsylvania), the Pittsburgh, Ft. Wayne & Chicago (Pennsylvania), the Nypano (Erie), the Wheeling & Lake Erie, the Cincinnati, Hamilton & Dayton, the Detroit, Toledo & Ironton, and the Norfolk & Western. As the building of steam railways lessened, the building of suburban and interurban electric railways was begun, and systems of these railways have been rapidly extended, until all the more populous districts are connected by them. Ohio has six ports of entry. They are Cleveland, Toledo, Sandusky, Cincinnati, Columbus and Dayton, and the value of the foreign commerce passing through these in 1909 amounted to $9,483,974 in imports (more than one-half to Cleveland) and $10,920,083 in exports (nearly eight-ninths from Cleveland). Of far greater volume than the foreign commerce is the domestic trade in coal, iron, lumber, &c., largely by way of the Great Lakes.

Population.—The population of Ohio in the various census years was: (1800) 45,365; (1810) 230,760; (1820) 581,434; (1830) 937,903; (1840) 1,519,467; (1850) 1,980,329; (1860) 2,339,511; (1870) 2,665,260; (1880) 3,198,062; (1890) 3,672,316; (1900) 4,157,545; (1910) 4,767,121. In 1900 and 1910 it ranked fourth in population among the states. Of the total population in 1900, 4,060,204 or 97·6% were white and 97,341 were coloured (96,901 negroes, 371 Chinese, 27 Japanese and 42 Indians). Of the same total 3,698,811 or 88·9% were native-born and 458,734 were foreign-born; 93·8% of the foreign-born consisted of the following: 204,160 natives of Germany, 65,553 of Great Britain, 55,018 of Ireland, 22,767 of Canada (19,864 English Canadian), 16,822 of Poland, 15,131 of Bohemia, 11,575 of Austria and 11,321 of Italy. In 1906 there were 1,742,873 communicants of different religious denominations, over one-third being Roman Catholics and about one-fifth Methodists. From 1890 to 1900 the urban population (i.e. population of incorporated places having 4000 inhabitants or more) increased from 1,387,884 to 1,864,519, and the semi-urban (i.e. population of incorporated places having less than 4000 inhabitants) increased from 458,033 to 549,741, but the rural (i.e. population outside of incorporated places) decreased from 1,836,412 to 1,743,285. The largest cities are Cleveland, Cincinnati, Columbus (the capital), Toledo, Dayton, Youngstown, Akron, Canton, Springfield, Hamilton, Lima and Zanesville.

Administration.—Ohio is governed under the constitution of 1851 as amended in 1875, 1883, 1885, 1902, 1903, and 1905. An amendment may be proposed at any time by either branch of the General Assembly, and if after being approved by three-fifths of the members of both branches it is also approved at a general election by a majority of those voting on the question it is declared adopted; a constitutional convention may be called after a favourable two-thirds vote of the members of each branch of the Assembly and a favourable popular vote—a majority of those voting on the question; and the question of calling such a convention must be submitted to a popular vote at least once every twenty years. Under the constitution of 1802 and 1851 the suffrage was limited to "white male" citizens of the United States, but since the adoption of the Fifteenth Amendment to the Federal Constitution (1870), negroes vote, though the constitution is unchanged. Since 1894 women who possess the usual qualifications required of men may vote for and be voted for as members of boards of education. The constitution requires that all elections be by ballot, and the Australian ballot system was adopted in 1891; registration is required in cities having a population of 11,800 or more. The executive department consists of a governor, lieutenant-governor, secretary of state, auditor, treasurer and attorney-general. As a result of the dispute between Governor Arthur St Clair and the Territorial legislature, the constitution of 1802 conferred nearly all of the ordinary executive functions on the legislature. The governor's control over appointments was strengthened by the constitution of 1851 and by the subsequent creation of statutory offices, boards and commissions, but the right of veto was not given to him until the adoption of the constitutional amendments of 1903. The power as conferred at that time, however, is broader than usual, for it extends not only to items in appropriation bills, but to separate sections in other measures, and, in addition to the customary provision for passing a bill over the governor's veto by a two-thirds vote of each house it is required that the votes for repassage in each house must not be less than those given on the original passage. The governor is elected in November of even-numbered years for a term of two years. He is commander-in-chief of the state's military and naval forces, except when they are called into the service of the United States. He grants pardons and reprieves on the recommendation of the state board of pardons. If he die in office, resign or be impeached, the officers standing next in succession are the lieutenant-governor, the president of the Senate, and the speaker of the House of Representatives in the order named.

Members of the Senate and House of Representatives are elected for terms of two years; they must be residents of their respective counties or districts for one year preceding election, unless absent on public business of the state or of the United States. The ratio of representation in the Senate is obtained by dividing the total population of the state by thirty-five, the ratio in the House by dividing the population by one hundred. The membership in each house, however, is slightly above these figures, owing to a system of fractional representation and to the constitutional amendment of 1903 which allows each county at least one representative in the House of Representatives. The constitution provides for a reapportionment every ten years beginning in 1861. Biennial sessions are held beginning on the first Monday in January of the even-numbered years. The powers of the two houses are equal in every respect except that the Senate passes upon the governor's appointments and tries impeachment cases brought before it by the House of Representatives. The constitution prohibits special, local and retroactive legislation, legislation impairing the obligation of contracts, and legislation levying a poll tax for county or state purposes or a tax on state, municipal and public school bonds (amendment of 1905), and it limits the amount and specifies the character of public debts which the legislature may contract.

The judicial department in 1910 was composed of a supreme court of six judges, eight circuit courts[1] of three judges each, ten districts (some with sub-divisions) of the common pleas court, the superior court of Cincinnati, probate courts, courts of insolvency in Cuyahoga and Hamilton counties, juvenile courts (established in 1904), justice of the peace courts and municipal courts. Under the constitution of 1802 judges were chosen by the legislature, but since 1851 they have been elected by direct popular vote—the judges of the supreme court being chosen at large. They are removable on complaint by a two-thirds majority in each house of the legislature. The constitution provides that the terms of supreme and circuit judges shall be such even number of years not less than six as may be prescribed by the legislature—the statutory provision is six years—that of the judges of the common pleas six years, that of the probate judges four years, that of other judges such even number of years not exceeding six as may be prescribed by the legislature—the statutory provision is six years—and that of justices of the peace such even number of years not exceeding four as may be thus prescribed—the statutory provision is four years.

Local Government.—The county and the township are the units of the rural, the city and the village the units of the urban local

[1] The provision for circuit courts was first made in the constitution by an amendment of 1883.

government. The chief county authority is the board of commissioners of three members elected for terms of two years. The other officials are the sheriff, treasurer and coroner, elected for two years; the auditor, recorder, clerk of courts, prosecuting attorney, surveyor and infirmary directors, elected for two years; and the board of school examiners (three) and the board of county visitors (six, of whom three are women), appointed usually by the probate judge for three years. The chief township authority is the board of trustees of three members, elected by popular vote for two years. In the parts of the state settled by people from New England township meetings were held in the early days, but their functions were gradually transferred to the trustees, and by 1820 the meetings had been given up almost entirely. The other township officials are the clerk, treasurer, assessor, supervisor of roads, justices of the peace, constables, board of education and board of health. Under the constitution of 1802, municipal corporations were established by special legislation. The constitution of 1851, however, provided for a general law, and the legislature in 1852 enacted a "general municipal corporations act," the first of its kind in the United States. The system of classification adopted in time became so elaborate that many municipalities became isolated, each in a separate class, and the evils of special legislation were revived. Of the two chief cities, Cleveland (under a special act providing for the government of Columbus and Toledo, also) in 1892-1902 was governed under the federal plan, which centralized power in the hands of the mayor; in Cincinnati there was an almost hopeless diffusion of responsibility among the council and various executive boards. The supreme court in June 1902 decided that practically all the existing municipal legislation was special in character and was therefore unconstitutional. (State *ex. rel.* Kniseley *vs.* Jones, 66 Ohio State Reports, 453. See also 66 Ohio State Reports, 491.) A special session of the legislature was called, and a new municipal code was adopted on the 22nd of October which went into effect in April 1903; it was a compromise between the Cleveland and the Cincinnati plans, with some additional features necessary to meet the conditions existing in the smaller cities. In order to comply with the court's interpretation of the constitution, municipalities were divided into only two classes, cities and villages, the former having a population of five thousand or more; the chief officials in both cities and villages were the mayor, council, treasurer and numerous boards of commissions. This was an attempt to devise a system of government that would apply to Cleveland, a city of 400,000 inhabitants, and to Painesville with its 5000 inhabitants. The code was replaced by the Paine Law of 1909, which provided for a board of control (something like that under the "federal plan" in Cleveland, Columbus and Toledo) of three members: the mayor and the directors (appointed and removable by the mayor) of two municipal departments—public service and public safety, the former including public works and parks, and the latter police, fire, charities, correction and buildings. The mayor's appointments are many, and are seldom dependent on the consent of the council. A municipal civil service commission of three members (holding office for three years) is chosen by the president of the board of education, the president of the city council, and the president of the board of sinking fund commissioners; the pay (if any) of these commissioners is set by each city. The city auditor, treasurer and solicitor are elected, as under the code.

In 1908 a direct primary law was passed providing for party primaries, those of all parties in each district to be held at the same time (annually) and, before the same election board, and at public expense, to nominate candidates for township and municipal offices and members of the school board; nominations to be by petition signed by at least 2% of the party voters of the political division, except that for United States senators ⅓ of 1% is the minimum. The law does not make the nomination of candidates for the United States Senate by this method mandatory nor such choice binding upon the General Assembly.

Laws.—The property rights of husband and wife are nearly equal; a wife may hold her property the same as if single, and a widower or a widow is entitled to the use for life of one-third of the real estate of which his or her deceased consort was seized at the time of his or her death. Among the grounds on which a divorce may be obtained are adultery, extreme cruelty, fraud, abandonment for three years, gross neglect of duty, habitual drunkenness, a former existing marriage, procurement of divorce without the state by one party, which continues marriage binding on the other, and imprisonment in a penitentiary. For every family in which there is a wife, a minor son, or an unmarried daughter, a homestead not exceeding $1000 in value, or personal property not exceeding $500 in value, is exempt from sale for the satisfaction of debts.

In 1908 an act was passed providing for local option in regard to the sale of intoxicating liquors, by an election to be called an initiative petition, signed by at least 35% of the electors of a county.

Charitable and Penal Institutions.—The state charitable and penal institutions are supervised by the board of charities of six members ("not more than three . . . from the same political party") appointed by the governor, and local institutions by boards of county visitors of six members appointed by the probate judge. Each state institution in addition has its own board of trustees appointed by the governor, and each county infirmary is under the charge of three infirmary directors chosen by popular vote. There are hospitals for the insane at Athens, Columbus, Dayton, Cleveland, Carthage (10 m. from Cincinnati; Longview Hospital), Massillon, Toledo and Lima; a hospital for epileptics at Gallipolis, opened in 1893; institutions for feeble-minded, for the blind (opened 1839) and for the deaf (opened 1829) at Columbus; a state sanatorium for tuberculous patients at Mt. Vernon (opened 1909); an institution for crippled and deformed children (authorized in 1907); a soldiers' and sailors' orphans' home at Xenia (organized in 1869 by the Grand Army of the Republic); a home for soldiers, sailors, marines, their wives, mothers and widows, and army nurses at Madison (established by the National Women's Relief Corps; taken over by the state, 1904); and soldiers' and sailors' homes at Sandusky (opened 1888), supported by the state, and at Dayton, supported by the United States. The state penal institutions are the boys' industrial school near Lancaster (established in 1834 as a Reform Farm), the girls' industrial home (1869) at Rathbone near Delaware, the reformatory at Mansfield (authorized 1884, opened 1896) and the penitentiary at Columbus (1816).

Education.—Congress in 1785 set apart 1 sq. m. in each township of 36 sq. m. for the support of education. The public school system, however, was not established until 1825, and then it developed very slowly. The office of state commissioner of common schools was created in 1837, abolished in 1840 and revived in 1843. School districts fall into four classes—cities, villages, townships and special districts—each of which has its own board of education elected by popular vote. Laws passed in 1877, 1890, 1893 and 1900 have made education compulsory for children between the ages of eight and fourteen. The school revenues are derived from the sale and rental of public lands granted by Congress, and of the salt and swamp lands devoted by the state to such purposes, from a uniform levy of one mill on each dollar of taxable property in the state, from local levies (averaging 7·2 mills in township districts and 10·07 mills in separate districts in 1908), from certain fines and licences, and from tuition fees paid by non-resident pupils. The total receipts from all sources in 1908 amounted to $25,987,021; the balance from the preceding year was $11,714,135, and the total expenditures were $24,695,157. Three institutions for higher education are supported in large measure by the state: Ohio University at Athens, founded in 1804 on the proceeds derived from two townships granted by Congress to the Ohio Company; Miami University (chartered in 1809) at Oxford, which received the proceeds from a township granted by Congress in the Symmes purchase; and Ohio State University (1873) at Columbus, which received the proceeds from the lands granted by Congress under the act of 1862 for the establishment of agricultural and mechanical colleges, and reorganized as a university in 1878. Wilberforce University (1856), for negroes, near Xenia, is under the control of the African Methodist Episcopal Church; but the state established a normal and industrial department in 1888, and has since contributed to its maintenance. Under an act of 1902 normal colleges, supported by the state, have also been created in connexion with Ohio and Miami universities. Among the numerous other colleges and universities in the state are Western Reserve University (1826) at Cleveland, the university of Cincinnati (opened 1873) at Cincinnati, and Oberlin College (1833) at Oberlin.

Finance.—The revenues of the state are classified into four funds: the general revenue fund, the sinking fund, the state common school fund and the university fund. The chief sources of the general revenue fund are taxes on real and personal property, og liquors and cigarettes, on corporations and on inheritances; in 1909 the net receipts for this fund were $8,043,257, the disbursements $9,103,301, and the cash balance at the end of the fiscal year $3,428,705. There is a tendency to reduce the rate on real property, leaving it as a basis for local taxation. The rate on collateral inheritances is 5% on direct inheritances 2% on the excess above $3000. There are state, county and municipal boards of equalization. A special tax is levied for the benefit of the sinking fund—one-tenth of a mill in 1909. The commissioners of the fund are the auditor, the secretary of state and the attorney-general. The public debt, which began to accumulate in 1825, was increased by the canal expenditures to $16,880,000 in 1845. The constitution of 1851 practically deprived the legislature of the power to create new obligations. The funded debt was then gradually reduced until the last installment was paid in 1903. There still remains, however, an irredeemable debt due to the common schools, Ohio University and Ohio State University, in return for their public lands. About one-half of the annual common school fund is derived from local taxes; the state levy for this fund in 1909 was one mill, and the total receipts were $2,382,353. The university fund is derived from special taxes levied for the four institutions which receive aid from the state; in 1909 the levy was 0·245 mills and the total receipts were $582,843. Several banks and trading houses with banking privileges were incorporated by special statutes between 1803 and 1817. Resentment was aroused by the establishment of branches of the Bank of the United States at Chillicothe and Cincinnati in 1817, and an attempt was made to tax them out of existence. State officials broke into the vaults of the Chillicothe branch in 1819 and took out $100,000 due for taxes. The Federal courts compelled a restoration of the money and pronounced the taxing law unconstitutional. In 1845 the legislature chartered for twenty years the State Bank of Ohio, based on the model of the

State Bank of Indiana of 1834. It became a guarantee of conservative banking, and was ighly successful. There were at one time thirty-six branches. Most of the state institutions secured Federal charters after the establishment of the national banking system (1863-1864), but the high price of government bonds and the large amount of capital required led to a reaction, which was only partially checked by the reduction of the minimum capital to $25,000 under the currency act of the 14th of March 1900.

History.—Ohio was the pioneer state of the old North-West Territory, which embraced also what are now the states of Indiana, Illinois, Michigan and Wisconsin, and the N.E. corner of Minnesota. When discovered by Europeans, late in the first half of the 17th century, the territory included within what is now Ohio was mainly a battle-ground of numerous Indian tribes and the fixed abode of none except the Eries who occupied a strip along the border of Lake Erie. From the middle to the close of the 17th century the French were establishing a claim to the territory between the Great Lakes and the Ohio river by discovery and occupation, and although they had provoked the hostility of the Iroquois Indians they had helped the Wyandots, Miamis and Shawnees to banish them from all territory W. of the Muskingum river. Up to this time the English had based their claim to the same territory on the discovery of the Atlantic Coast by the Cabots and upon the Virginia, Massachusetts and Connecticut charters under which these colonies extended westward to the Pacific Ocean. In 1701, New York, seeking another claim, obtained from the Iroquois a grant to the king of England of this territory which they claimed to have conquered but from which they had subsequently been expelled, and this grant was confirmed in 1726 and again in 1744. About 1730 English traders from Pennsylvania and Virginia began to visit the eastern and southern parts of the territory and the crisis approached as a French Canadian expedition under Céleron de Bienville took formal possession of the upper Ohio Valley by planting leaden plates at the mouths of the principal streams. This was in 1749 and in the same year George II. chartered the first Ohio Company, formed by Virginians and London merchants trading with Virginia for the purpose of colonizing the West. This company in 1750 sent Christopher Gist down the Ohio river to explore the country as far as the mouth of the Scioto river; and four years later the erection of a fort was begun in its interest at the forks of the Ohio. The French drove the English away and completed the fort (Fort Duquesne) for themselves. The Seven Years' War was the immediate consequence and this ended in the cession of the entire North-West to Great Britain. The former Indian allies of the French, however, immediately rose up in opposition to British rule in what is known as the Conspiracy of Pontiac (see PONTIAC), and the supression of this was not completed until Colonel Henry Bouquet made an expedition (1764) into the valley of the Muskingum and there brought the Shawnees, Wyandots and Delawares to terms. With the North-West won from the French Great Britain no longer recognized those claims of her colonies to this territory which she had asserted against that nation, but in a royal proclamation of the 7th of October 1763 the granting of land W. of the Alleghanies was forbidden and on the 22nd of June 1774 parliament passed the Quebec Act which annexed the region to the province of Quebec. This was one of the grievances which brought on the War of Independence and during that war the North-West was won for the Americans by George Rogers Clark (q.v.). During that war also, those states which had no claims in the West contended that title to these western lands should pass to the Union and when the Articles of Confederation were submitted for ratification in 1777, Maryland refused to ratify them except on that condition. The result was that New York ceded its claim to the United States in 1780; Virginia in 1784, Massachusetts in 1785 and Connecticut in 1786. Connecticut, however, excepted a strip bordering on Lake Erie for 120 m. and containing 3,250,000 acres. This district, known as the Western Reserve, was ceded in 1800 on condition that Congress would guarantee the titles to land already granted by the state. Virginia reserved a tract between the Little Miami and Scioto rivers, known as the Virginia Military District, for her soldiers in the War of Independence.

When the war was over and these cessions had been made a great number of war veterans wished an opportunity to repair their broken fortunes in the West, and Congress, hopeful of receiving a large revenue from the sale of lands here, passed an ordinance on the 20th of May 1785 by which the present national system of land-surveys into townships 6 m. sq. was inaugurated in what is now S.W. Ohio in the summer of 1786. In March 1786 the second Ohio Company (q.s.), composed chiefly of New England officers and soldiers, was organized in Boston, Massachusetts, with a view to founding a new state between Lake Erie and the Ohio river. The famous North-West Ordinance was passed by Congress on the 13th of July 1787. This instrument provided a temporary government for the Territory with the understanding that, as soon as the population was sufficient, the representative system should be adopted, and later that states should be formed and admitted into the Union. There were to be not less than three nor more than five states. Of these the easternmost (Ohio) was to be bounded on the N., E. and S. by the Lakes, Pennsylvania and the Ohio river, and on the W. by a line drawn due N. from the mouth of the Great Miami river to the Canadian boundary, if there were to be three states, or to its intersection with an E. and W. line drawn through the extreme S. bend of Lake Michigan, if there were to be five. Slavery was forbidden by the sixth article of the ordinance; and the third article read: " Religion, morality and knowledge being necessary to good government and the happiness of mankind, schools and the means of education shall for ever be encouraged." After the adoption of the North-West Ordinance the work of settlement made rapid progress. There were four main centres. The Ohio Company founded Marietta at the mouth of the Muskingum in 1788, and this is regarded as the oldest permanent settlement in the state. An association of New Jerseymen, organized by John Cleves Symmes, secured a grant from Congress in 1788–1792 to a strip of 248,540 acres on the Ohio between the Great Miami and the Little Miami, which came to be known as the Symmes Purchase. Their chief settlements were Columbia (1788) and Cincinnati (1789). The Virginia Military District, between the Scioto and the Little Miami, reserved in 1784 for bounties to Virginia continental troops, was colonized in large measure by people from that state. Their chief towns were Massieville or Manchester (1790) and Chillicothe (1796). A small company of Connecticut people under Moses Cleaveland founded Cleveland in 1796 and Youngstown was begun a few years later, but that portion of the state made very slow progress until after the opening of the Ohio & Erie Canal in 1832.

During the Territorial period (1787–1803) Ohio was first a part of the unorganized North-West Territory (1787–1799), then a part of the organized North-West Territory (1799–1800), and then the organized North-West Territory (1800–1803), Indiana Territory having been detached from it on the W. in 1800. The first Territorial government was established at Marietta in July 1788, and General Arthur St Clair (1734–1818), the governor, had arrived in that month. His administration was characterized by the final struggle with the Indians and by a bitter conflict between the executive and the legislature, which greatly influenced the constitutional history of the state. The War of Independence was succeeded by a series of Indian uprisings. Two campaigns, the first under General Josiah Harmar (1753–1813) in 1790, and the second under General St Clair in 1791, failed on account of bad management and ignorance of Indian methods of warfare, and in 1793 General Anthony Wayne (q.s.) was sent out in command of a large force of regulars and volunteers. The decisive conflict, fought on the 20th of August 1794, near the rapids of the Maumee, is called the battle of Fallen Timbers, because the Indians concealed themselves behind the trunks of trees which had been felled by a storm. Wayne's dragoons broke through the brushwood, attacked the left flank of the Indians and soon put them to flight. In the treaty of Greenville (3rd August 1795) the Indians ceded their claims to the territory E. and S. of the Cuyahoga, the Tuscarawas, and an irregular line from Fort

Laurens (Bolivar) in Tuscarawas county to Fort Recovery in Mercer county, practically the whole E. and S. Ohio. The Jay Treaty was ratified in the same year, and in 1796 the British finally evacuated Detroit and the Maumee and Sandusky forts. By cessions and purchases in 1804, 1808 and 1817–1818 the state secured all of the lands of the Indians except their immediate homes, and these were finally exchanged for territory W. of the Mississippi. The last remnant migrated in 1841. General Wayne's victory was followed by an extensive immigration of New Englanders, of Germans, Scotch-Irish and Quakers from Pennsylvania, and of settlers from Virginia and Kentucky, many of whom came to escape the evils of slavery. This rapid increase of population led to the establishment of the organized Territorial government in 1799, to the restriction of that government in Ohio in 1800, and to the admission of the state into the Union in 1803.

The Congressional Enabling Act of the 30th of April 1802 followed that alternative of the North-West Ordinance which provided for five states in determining the boundaries, and in consequence the Indiana and Michigan districts were detached. A rigid adherence to the boundary authorized in 1787, however, would have resulted in the loss to Ohio of 470 sq. m. of territory in the N.W. part of the state, including the lake port of Toledo. After a long and bitter dispute—the Toledo War (see TOLEDO)—the present line, which is several miles N. of the S. bend of Lake Michigan, was definitely fixed in 1837, when Michigan came into the Union. (For the settlement of the eastern boundary, see PENNSYLVANIA.)

After having been temporarily at Marietta, Cincinnati, Chillicothe and Zanesville the capital was established at Columbus in 1816.

Since Congress did not pass any formal act of admission there has been some controversy as to when Ohio became a state. The Enabling Act was passed on the 30th of April 1802, the first state legislature met on the 1st of March 1803, the Territorial judges gave up their offices on the 15th of April 1803, and the Federal senators and representatives took their seats in Congress on the 17th of October 1803. Congress decided in 1806 in connexion with the payment of salaries to Territorial officials that the 1st of March 1803 was the date when state government began. During the War of 1812 the Indians under the lead of Tecumseh were again on the side of the British. Battles were fought at Fort Meigs (1813) and Fort Stephenson (Fremont, 1813) and Commodore Oliver Hazard Perry's naval victory on Lake Erie in 1813 was on the Ohio side of the boundary line. Owing to the prohibition of slavery the vast majority of the early immigrants to Ohio came from the North, but, until the Mexican War forced the slavery question into the foreground, the Democrats usually controlled the state, because the principles of that party were more in harmony with frontier ideas of equality. The Whigs were successful in the presidential elections of 1836 and 1840, partly because of the financial panic and partly because their candidate, William Henry Harrison, was a " favourite son," and in the election of 1844, because of the unpopularity of the Texas issue. Victory was with the Democrats in 1848 and 1852, but since the organization of the Republican party in 1854 the state has uniformly given to the Republican presidential candidates its electoral votes. In the Civil War Ohio loyally supported the Union, furnishing 319,659 men for the army. Dissatisfaction with the President's emancipation programme resulted in the election of a Democratic Congressional delegation in 1862, but the tide turned again after Gettysburg and Vicksburg; Clement L. Vallandigham, the Democratic leader, was deported from the state by military order, and the Republicans were successful in the elections of 1863 and 1864. A detachment of the Confederate cavalry under General John Morgan invaded the state in 1863, but was badly defeated in the battle of Buffington's Island (July 18th). Democratic governors were elected in 1873, 1877, 1883, 1889, 1905, 1908 and 1910. Five presidents have come from Ohio, William Henry Harrison, Rutherford B. Hayes, James A. Garfield, William McKinley, Jr., and William Howard Taft.

GOVERNORS OF OHIO

Territorial Period (1787–1803).

Arthur St Clair . .	. 1787–1802	Federalist
Charles W. Byrd (Acting) .	. 1802–1803	Dem.-Repub.

Period of Statehood.

Edward Tiffin . . .	. 1803–1807	Dem.-Repub.
Thomas Kirker (Acting) .	. 1807–1809	,,
Samuel Huntington . .	. 1809–1811	,,
Return Jonathan Meigs .	. 1811–1814	,,
Othniel Looker (Acting) .	. 1814–1815	,,
Thomas Worthington . .	. 1815–1819	,,
Ethan Allen Brown . .	. 1819–1822	,,
Allen Trimble (Acting) .	. 1822–1823	,,
Jeremiah Morrow . .	. 1823–1827	Democrat.
Allen Trimble . . .	. 1827–1831	,,
Duncan McArthur . .	. 1831–1833	Nat.-Repub.
Robert Lucas . . .	. 1833–1837	Democrat
Joseph Vance . . .	. 1837–1839	Whig
Wilson Shannon . .	. 1839–1841	Democrat
Thomas Corwin . .	. 1841–1843	Whig
Wilson Shannon . .	. 1843–1844	Democrat
Thomas W. Bartley (Acting)	. 1844–1845	,,
Mordecai Bartley . .	. 1845–1847	Whig ,,
William Bebb . . .	. 1847–1849	,,
Seabury Ford . . .	. 1849–1851	,,
Reuben Wood . . .	. 1851–1853	Democrat
William Medill (Acting, 1853)	. 1853–1856	,,
Salmon P. Chase . .	. 1856–1860	Republican
William Dennison, Jr. .	. 1860–1862	,,
David Tod . . .	. 1862–1864	,,
John Brough . . .	. 1864–1865	,,
Charles Anderson (Acting) .	. 1865–1866	,,
Jacob D. Cox . .	. 1866–1868	,,
Rutherford B. Hayes .	. 1868–1872[1]	,,
Edward F. Noyes . .	. 1872–1874	,,
William Allen . .	. 1874–1876	Democrat
Rutherford B. Hayes .	. 1876–1877	Republican
Thomas L. Young (Acting) .	. 1877–1878	,,
Richard M. Bishop . .	. 1878–1880	Democrat
Charles Foster . .	. 1880–1884	Republican
George Hoadley . .	. 1884–1886	Democrat
Joseph B. Foraker . .	. 1886–1890	Republican
James E. Campbell . .	. 1890–1892	Democrat
William McKinley, Jr. .	. 1892–1896	Republican
Asa S. Bushnell . .	. 1896–1900	,,
George K. Nash . .	. 1900–1904	,,
Myron T. Herrick. .	. 1904–1906	,,
John M. Pattison[1] .	. 1906	Democrat
Andrew Lintner Harris .	. 1906–1909	Republican
Judson Harmon . .	. 1909–	Democrat

BIBLIOGRAPHY.—For a brief but admirable treatment of the physiography see Stella S. Wilson, *Ohio* (New York, 1902), and a great mass of material on this subject is contained in the publications of the Geological Survey of Ohio (1837 et seq.). For the administration see the *Constitution of the State of Ohio, adopted June 1851* (Norwalk, Ohio, 1897), and amendments of 1903 and 1905 published separately; the annual reports of the state treasurer, auditor, board of state charities and commissioner of common schools, the Ellis municipal code (1902) and the Harrison school code (1904). The Civil Code, issued 1852, the Criminal Code in 1869 and the Revised Statutes in 1879, have several times been amended and published in new editions. There are two excellent secondary accounts: Samuel P. Orth, *The Centralization of Administration in Ohio*, in the Columbia University Studies in History, Economics and Public Law, xvi. No. 3 (New York, 1903); and Wilbur H. Siebert, *The Government of Ohio, its History and Administration* (New York, 1904). B. A. Hinsdale's *History and Civil Government of Ohio* (Chicago, 1896) is more elementary. For local government see J. A. Wilgus, "Evolution of Township Government in Ohio," in the *Annual Report* of the American Historical Association for 1894, pp. 403–412 (Washington, 1895); D. F. Wilcox, *Municipal Government in Michigan and Ohio*, in the Columbia University Studies in History, Economics and Public Law, v. No. 3 (New York, 1895); J. A. Fairlie, "The Municipal Crisis in Ohio," in the *Michigan Law Review* for February 1903; and Thomas L. Sidlo, "Centralization in Ohio Municipal Government," in the *American Political Science Review* for November 1909. On education see George B. Germann, *National Legislation concerning Education, its Influence and Effect in the Public Lands east of the Mississippi River, admitted prior to 1820* (New York, 1899); J. J. Burns, *Educational History of Ohio* (Columbus, 1905).

Archaeology and History: P. G. Thomson's *Bibliography of Ohio* (Cincinnati, 1880) is an excellent guide to the study of Ohio's history. For archaeology see Cyrus Thomas's *Catalogue of Prehistoric Works*

[1] Died in office.

East of the Rocky Mountains (Washington, 1891), and his *Report on the Mound Explorations of the Bureau of Ethnology* in the 12th Report (1894) of that Bureau, supplementing his earlier bulletins, *Problem of the Ohio Mounds* and the *Circular, Square and Octagonal Earthworks of Ohio* (1889); and W. K. Moorehead, *Primitive Man in Ohio* (New York, 1892). The best history is Rufus King, *Ohio; First Fruits of the Ordinance of 1787* (Boston and New York, 1888), in the "American Commonwealths" series. Alexander Black's *Story of Ohio* (Boston, 1888) is a short popular account. B. A. Hinsdale, *The Old North-west* (2nd ed., New York, 1899), is good for the period before 1803. Of the older histories Caleb Atwater, *History of the State of Ohio, Natural and Civil* (Cincinnati, 1838), and James W. Taylor, *History of the State of Ohio: First Period 1650–1787* (Cincinnati, 1854), are useful. For the Territorial period, and especially for the Indian wars of 1790–1794, see W. H. Smith (ed.), *The St Clair Papers; Life and Services of Arthur St Clair* (2 vols., Cincinnati, 1882); Jacob Burnet, *Notes on the Early Settlement of the North-Western Territory* (Cincinnati, 1847), written from the Federalist point of view, and hence rather favourable to St Clair; C. E. Slocum, *Ohio Country between 1783 and 1815* (New York, 1910); and John Armstrong's *Life of Anthony Wayne* in Sparks' "Library of American Biography" (Boston, 1834–1838), series i. vol. iv. See also F. P. Goodwin, *The Growth of Ohio* (Cincinnati, 1907) and R. E. Chaddock, *Ohio before 1850* (New York, 1908). There is considerable material of value, especially for local history, in the *Ohio Archaeological and Historical Society Publications* (Columbus, 1887), and in Henry Howe, *Historical Collections of Ohio* (1st ed., Cincinnati, 1847; Centennial edition [enlarged], 2 vols., Columbus, 1889–1891). T. B. Galloway, "The Ohio-Michigan Boundary Line Dispute," in the *Ohio Archaeological and Historical Society Publications*, vol. iv. pp. 199–230, is a good treatment of that complicated question. W. F. Gephart's *Transportation and Industrial Development in the Middle West* (New York, 1909), in the Columbia University Studies in History, Economics and Public Law, is a commercial history of Ohio.

OHIO COMPANY, a name of two 18th century companies organized for the colonization of the Ohio Valley. The first Ohio Company was organized in 1749, partly to aid in securing for the English control of the valley, then in dispute between England and France, and partly as a commercial project for trade with the Indians. The company was composed of Virginians, including Thomas Lee (d. 1750) and the two brothers of George Washington, Lawrence (who succeeded to the management upon the death of Lee) and Augustine; and of Englishmen, including John Hanbury, a wealthy London merchant. George II. sanctioned a grant to the company of 500,000 acres generally N.W. of the Ohio, and to the eastward, between the Monongahela and the Kanawha rivers, but the grant was never actually issued. In 1750–1751 Christopher Gist, a skilful woodsman and surveyor, explored for the company the Ohio Valley as far as the mouth of the Scioto river. In 1752 the company had a pathway blazed between the small fortified posts at Will's Creek (Cumberland), Maryland, and at Redstone Creek (Brownsville), Pennsylvania, which it had established in 1750; but it was finally merged in the Walpole Company (an organization in which Benjamin Franklin was interested), which in 1772 had received from the British government a grant of a large tract lying along the southern bank of the Ohio as far west as the mouth of the Scioto river. The War of Independence interrupted colonization and nothing was accomplished.

The second company, the Ohio Company of Associates, was formed at Boston on the 3rd of March 1786. The leaders in the movement were General Rufus Putnam, Benjamin Tupper (1738–1792), Samuel Holden Parsons (1737–1789) and Manasseh Cutler. Dr Cutler was selected to negotiate with Congress, and seems to have helped to secure the incorporation in the Ordinance for the government of the North-West Territory of the paragraphs which prohibited slavery and provided for public education and for the support of the ministry. Cutler's original intention was to buy for the Ohio Company only about 1,500,000 acres, but on the 27th of July Congress authorized a grant of about 5,000,000 acres of land for $3,500,000; a reduction of one-third was allowed for bad tracts, and it was also provided that the lands could be paid for in United States securities. On the 27th of October 1787 Cutler and Major Winthrop Sargent (1753–1820), who had joined him in the negotiations, signed two contracts; one was for the absolute purchase for the Ohio Company, at 66⅔ cents an acre, of 1,500,000 acres of land lying along the north bank of the Ohio river, from a point near the site of the present Marietta, to a point nearly opposite the site of the present Huntington, Kentucky; the other was for an option to buy all the land between the Ohio and the Scioto rivers and the western boundary line of the Ohio Company's tract, extending north of the tenth township from the Ohio, this tract being pre-empted by " Manasseh Cutler and Winthrop Sargent for themselves and others "—actually for the Scioto Company (see GALLIPOLIS). On the same day 'Cutler and Sargent " for themselves and associates " transferred to William Duer,, then Secretary of the Treasury Board, and his associates " one equal moiety of the Scioto tract of land mentioned in the second contract," it being provided that both parties were to be equally interested in the sale of the land, and were to share equally any profit or loss. Colonists were sent out by the Ohio Company from New England, and Marietta, the first permanent settlement in the present state of Ohio, was founded in April 1788.

OHIO RIVER, the principal eastern tributary of the Mississippi river, U.S.A. It is formed by the confluence of the Allegheny and Monongahela rivers at Pittsburg, Pennsylvania, and flows N.W. nearly to the W. border of Pennsylvania, S.S.W. between Ohio and West Virginia, W. by N. between Ohio and Kentucky, and W.S.W. between Indiana and Illinois on the N. and Kentucky on the S. It is the largest of all the tributaries of the Mississippi in respect to the amount of water discharged (an average of about 158,000 cub. ft. per sec.), is first in importance as a highway of commerce, and in length (967 m.) as well as in the area of its drainage basin (approximately 210,000 sq. m.) It is exceeded only by the Missouri. The slope of the river at low water ranges from 1 ft. or more per mile in the upper section to about 0·75 ft. per mile in the middle section, and 0·29 ft. per mile in the lower section, and the total fall is approximately 500 ft. Nearly two-thirds of the bed is occupied by 187 pools, in which the fall is very gentle; and the greater part of the descent is made over intervening bars, which are usually composed of sand or gravel but occasionally of hard pan or rock. The greatest falls are at Louisville, where the river within a distance of 2·25 m. descends 23·9 ft. over an irregular mass of limestone. The rock floor of the valley is usually 30 to 50 ft. below low water level, and when it comes to the surface, as it occasionally does, it extends at this height only part way across the valley. In the upper part of the river the bed contains much coarse gravel and numerous boulders, but lower down a sand bed prevails. The ordinary width of the upper half of the river is quite uniform, from 1200 to 1500 ft., but it widens in the pool above Louisville, contracts immediately below the Falls, and then gradually widens again until it reaches a maximum width of more than a mile about 20 m. from its mouth. Islands are numerous and vary in size from an acre or less to 5000 acres; above Louisville there are fifty or more, and below it about thirty. Many of them are cultivated.

Besides its parent streams, the Allegheny and the Monongahela, the Ohio has numerous large branches. On the N. it receives the waters of the Muskingum, Scioto, Miami and Wabash rivers, and on the S. those of the Kanawha, Big Sandy, Licking, Kentucky, Green, Cumberland and Tennessee rivers.

The drainage basin of the Ohio, in which the annual rainfall averages about 43 in., is, especially in the S. part of the river, of the " quick-spilling " kind, and as the swift mountain streams in that section are filled in February or March by the storms from the Gulf of Mexico, while the northern streams are swollen by melting snow and rain, the Ohio rises very suddenly and not infrequently attains a height of 30 to 50 ft. or more above low water level, spreads out ten to fifteen times its usual width, submerges the bottom lands, and often causes great damage to property in the lower part of the cities along its banks.

Robert Cavelier, Sieur de La Salle, asserted that he discovered the Ohio and descended it until his course was obstructed by a fall (thought to be the Falls at Louisville); this was probably in 1670, but until the middle of the next century, when its strategic importance in the struggle of the French and the English for the possession of the interior of the continent became fully recognized, little was generally known of it. By the treaty of 1763 ending the Seven Years' War the English finally gained

undisputed control of the territory along its banks. After Virginia had bought, in 1768, the claims of the Six Nations to the territory south of the Ohio, immigrants, mostly Virginians, began to descend the river in considerable numbers, but the Shawnee Indians, whose title to the land was more plausible than that of the Six Nations ever was, resisted their encroachments until the Shawnees were defeated in October 1774 at the battle of Point Pleasant. By the treaty of 1783 the entire Ohio country became a part of the United States and by the famous Ordinance of 1787 the north side was opened to settlement. Most of the settlers entered the region by the headwaters of the Ohio and carried much of their market produce, lumber, &c., down the Ohio and Mississippi to New Orleans or beyond. Until the successful navigation of the river by steamboats a considerable portion of the imports was carried overland from Philadelphia or Baltimore to Pittsburg. The first steamboat on the Ohio was the " New Orleans," which was built in 1811 by Nicholas J. Roosevelt and sailed from Pittsburg to New Orleans in the same year, but it remained for Captain Henry M. Shreve (1785-1854) to demonstrate with the " Washington," which he built in 1816, the success of this kind of navigation on the river. From 1820 to the Civil War the steamboat on the system of inland waterways of which the Ohio was a part was a dominant factor in the industrial life of the Middle West. Cincinnati, Louisville and Pittsburg on its banks were extensively engaged in building these vessels. The river was dotted with floating shops—dry-goods boats fitted with counters, boats containing a tinner's establishment, a blacksmith's shop, a factory, or a lottery office. Until the Erie Canal was opened in 1825 the Ohio river was the chief commercial highway between the East and the West. It was connected with Lake Erie in 1832 by the Ohio & Erie Canal from Portsmouth to Cleveland, and in 1845 by the Miami & Erie Canal from Cincinnati to Toledo.

In the natural state of the river navigation was usually almost wholly suspended during low water from July to November, and it was dangerous at all times on account of the numerous snags. The Federal government in 1827 undertook to remove the snags and to increase the depth of water on the bars by the construction of contraction works, such as dikes and wing dams, and appropriations for these purposes as well as for dredging were continued until 1844 and resumed in 1866; but as the channel obtained was less than 3 ft. in 1870, locks with movable dams—that is, dams that can be thrown down on the approach of a flood—were then advocated, and five years later Congress made an appropriation for constructing such a dam, the Davis Island Dam immediately below Pittsburg, as an experiment. This was opened in 1885 and was a recognized success; and in 1895 the Ohio Valley Improvement Association was organized in an effort to have the system extended. At first the association asked only for a channel 6 ft. in depth; and between 1896 and 1905 Congress authorized the necessary surveys and made appropriations for thirty-six locks and dams from the Davis Island Dam to the mouth of the Great Miami river. As the association then urged that the channel be made 9 ft. in depth Congress authorized the secretary of war to appoint a board of engineers which should make a thorough examination and report on the comparative merits of a channel 9 ft. in depth, and one 6 ft. in depth. The board reported in 1908 in favour of a 9-ft. channel and stated that fifty-four locks and dams would be necessary for such a channel throughout the course of the river, and Congress adopted this project. At the Falls is the Louisville & Portland Canal, originally built by a private corporation, with the United States as one of the stockholders, and opened in 1830, with a width of 50 ft., a length of 500 ft., and three locks, each with a lift of about 8½ ft. The width was increased to 90 ft. and the three old locks were replaced by two new ones. The United States gradually increased its holdings of stock until in 1855 it became owner of all but five shares; it assumed the management of the canal in 1874, abolished tolls in 1880, and thereafter improved it in many respects. Sixty-eight locks and dams have been constructed on the principal tributaries, and the Allegheny, Monongahela, Cumberland, Tennessee,

Muskingum, Kanawha, Little Kanawha, Big Sandy, Wabash, and Green now afford a total of about 960 m. of slack-water navigation.

See the Board of Engineers' *Report of Examination of Ohio River with a view to obtaining Channel Depths of 6 and 9 ft. respectively* (Washington, 1908); A. B. Hulbert, *Waterways of Westward Expansion* (Cleveland, 1903) and *The Ohio River, a Course of Empire* (New York, 1906); also R. G. Thwaites, *Afloat on the Ohio* (New York, 1900).

OHLAU, a town of Germany, in the Prussian province of Silesia, 16 m. by rail S.E. of Breslau, on the left bank of the Oder. Pop. (1905) 9233. It has two Roman Catholic and two Evangelical churches, and a castle. Ohlau is the centre of a tobacco-growing district and has manufactures of tobacco and cigars, machinery, beer, shoes and bricks. It became a town in 1291 and passed to Prussia in 1742. In the 17th and 18th centuries it was often the residence of the dukes of Brieg and of the Sobieski family.

See Schulz, *Aus Ohlaus Vergangenheit* (Ohlau, 1902).

ÖHLENSCHLÄGER, ADAM GOTTLOB (1779–1850), Danish poet, was born in Vesterbro, a suburb of Copenhagen, on the 14th of November 1779. His father, a Schleswiger by birth, was at that time organist, and later became keeper, of the royal palace of Frederiksberg; he was a very brisk and cheerful man. The poet's mother, on the other hand, who was partly German by extraction, suffered from depressed spirits, which afterwards deepened into melancholy madness. Adam and his sister Sofia were allowed their own way throughout their childhood, and were taught nothing, except to read and write, until their twelfth year. At the age of nine Adam began to make fluent verses. Three years later, while walking in Frederiksberg Gardens, he attracted the notice of the poet Edvard Storm, and the result of the conversation was that he received a nomination to the college called "Posterity's High School," an important institution of which Storm was the principal. Storm himself taught the class of Scandinavian mythology, and thus Öhlenschläger received his earliest bias towards the poetical religion of his ancestors. He was confirmed in 1795, and was to have been apprenticed to a tradesman in Copenhagen. To his great delight there was a hitch in the preliminaries, and he returned to his father's house. He now, in his eighteenth year, suddenly took up study with great zeal, but soon again abandoned his books for the stage, where a small position was offered him. In 1797 he actually made his appearance on the boards in several successive parts, but soon discovered that he possessed no real histrionic talent. The brothers Örsted, with whom he had formed an intimacy fruitful of profit to him, persuaded him to quit the stage, and in 1800 he entered the university of Copenhagen as a student. He was doomed, however, to disturbance in his studies, first from the death of his mother, next from his inveterate tendency towards poetry, and finally from the attack of the English upon Copenhagen in April 1801, which, however, inspired a dramatic sketch (*April the Second 1801*) which is the first thing of the kind by Öhlenschläger that we possess. In the summer of 1802, when Öhlenschläger read an old Scandinavian romance, as well as a volume of lyrics, in the press, the young Norse philosopher, Henrik Steffens, came back to Copenhagen after a long visit to Schelling in Germany, full of new romantic ideas. His lectures at the university, in which Goethe and Schiller were for the first time revealed to the Danish public, created a great sensation. Steffens and Öhlenschläger met one day at Dreier's Club, and after a conversation of sixteen hours the latter went home, suppressed his two coming volumes, and wrote at a sitting his splendid poem *Guldhornene*, in a manner totally new to Danish literature. The result of his new enthusiasm speedily showed itself in a somewhat hasty volume of poems, published in 1803, now chiefly remembered as containing the lovely piece called *Sanct-Hansaften-Spil*. The next two years saw the production of several exquisite works, in particular the epic of *Thors Reise til Jotunheim*, the charming poem in hexameters called *Langelandsreisen*, and the bewitching piece of fantasy *Aladdin's Lampe* (1805). At the age of twenty-six Öhlenschläger was universally recognized, even by the opponents of the romantic revival, as the leading poet of Denmark. He

now collected his *Poetical Writings* in two volumes. He found no difficulty in obtaining a grant for foreign travel from the government, and he left his native country for the first time, joining Steffens at Halle in August 1805. Here he wrote the first of his great historical tragedies, *Hakon Jarl*, which he sent off to Copenhagen, and then proceeded for the winter months to Berlin, where he associated with Humboldt, Fichte, and the leading men of the day, and met Goethe for the first time. In the spring of 1806 he went on to Weimar, where he spent several months in daily intercourse with Goethe. The autumn of the same year he spent with Tieck in Dresden, and proceeded in December to Paris. Here he resided eighteen months and wrote his three famous masterpieces, *Baldur hin Gode* (1808), *Palnatoke* (1809), and *Axel og Valborg* (1810). In July 1808 he left Paris and spent the autumn and winter in Switzerland as the guest of Madame de Staël-Holstein at Coppet, in the midst of her circle of wits. In the spring of 1809 Öhlenschläger went to Rome to visit Thorwaldsen, and in his house wrote his tragedy of *Correggio*. He hurriedly returned to Denmark in the spring of 1810, partly to take the chair of aesthetics at the university of Copenhagen, partly to marry the sister-in-law of Rabbek, to whom he had been long betrothed. His first course of lectures dealt with his Danish predecessor Ewald, the second with Schiller. From this time forward his literary activity became very great; in 1811 he published the Oriental tale of *Ali og Gulhyndi*, and in 1812 the last of his great tragedies, *Staerkodder*. From 1814 to 1819 he, or rather his admirers, were engaged in a long and angry controversy with Baggesen, who represented the old didactic school. This contest seems to have disturbed the peace of Öhlenschläger's mind, and to have undermined his genius. His talent may be said to have culminated in the glorious cycle of verse-romances called *Helge*, published in 1814. The tragedy of *Hagbarth og Signe*, 1815, showed a distinct falling-off in style. In 1817 he went back to Paris, and published *Hroars Saga* and the tragedy of *Fostbrödrene*. In 1818 he was again in Copenhagen, and wrote the idyll of *Den lille Hyrdedreng* and the Eddaic cycle called *Nordens Guder*. His next productions were the tragedies of *Erik og Abel* (1820) and *Vaeringerne i Miklagaard* (1826), and the epic of *Hrolf Krake* (1829). It was in the last-mentioned year that, being in Sweden, Öhlenschläger was publicly crowned with laurel in front of the high altar in Lund cathedral by Bishop Esaias Tegnér, as the "Scandinavian King of Song." His last volumes were *Tordenskjold* (1833), *Dronning Margrethe* (1833), *Sokrates* (1835), *Olaf den Hellige* (1836), *Knud den Store* (1838), *Dina* (1842), *Erik Glipping* (1843), and *Kiartan og Gudrun* (1847). On his seventieth birthday, 14th November 1849, a public festival was arranged in his honour, and he was decorated by the king of Denmark under circumstances of great pomp. He died on the 20th of January 1850, and was buried in the cemetery of Frederiksberg. Immediately after his death his *Recollections* were published in two volumes.

With the exception of Holberg, there has been no Danish writer who has exercised so wide an influence as Öhlenschläger. His great work was to awaken in the breasts of his countrymen an enthusiasm for the poetry and religion of their ancestors, and this he performed to so complete an extent that his name remains to this day synonymous with Scandinavian romance. He supplied his countrymen with romantic tragedies at the very moment when all eyes were turned to the stage, and when the old-fashioned pieces were felt to be inadequate. His plays, partly, no doubt, in consequence of his own early familiarity with acting, fulfilled the stage requirements of the day, and were popular beyond all expectation. The earliest are the best—Öhlenschläger's dramatic masterpiece being, without doubt his first tragedy, *Hakon Jarl*. In his poems and plays alike his style is limpid, elevated, profuse; his flight is sustained at a high pitch without visible excitement. His fluent tenderness and romantic zest have been the secrets of his extreme popularity. Although his inspiration came from Germany, he is not much like a German poet, except when he is consciously following Goethe; his analogy is much rather to be found among the English poets, his contemporaries. His mission towards antiquity reminds us of Scott, but he is, as a poet, a better artist than Scott; he has sometimes touches of exquisite diction and of over-wrought sensibility which recall Coleridge to us. In his wide ambition and profuseness he possessed some characteristics of Southey, although his style has far more vitality. With all his faults he was a very great writer, and one of the principal pioneers of the romantic movement in Europe.   (E. G.)

OHLIGS, a town of Germany, in the Prussian Rhine Province, 17 m. by rail N. of Cologne, on the railway to Elberfeld. Pop. (1905) 24,264. Its chief manufactures are cutlery and hardware, and there are iron-foundries and flour-mills. Other industries are brewing, dyeing, weaving and brick-making. Before 1891 it was known as Merscheid.

OHM, GEORG SIMON (1787–1854), German physicist, was born at Erlangen on the 16th of March 1787, and was educated at the university there. He became professor of mathematics in the Jesuits' college at Cologne in 1817 and in the polytechnic school of Nuremberg in 1833, and in 1852 professor of experimental physics in the university of Munich, where he died on the 7th of July 1854. His writings were numerous, but, with one important exception, not of the first order. The exception is his pamphlet published in Berlin in 1827, with the title *Die galvanische Kette mathematisch bearbeitet*. This work, the germs of which had appeared during the two preceding years in the journals of Schweigger and Poggendorff, has exerted most important influence on the whole development of the theory and applications of current electricity, and Ohm's name has been incorporated in the terminology of electrical science. Nowadays "Ohm's Law," as it is called, in which all that is most valuable in the pamphlet is summarized, is as universally known as anything in physics. The equation for the propagation of electricity formed on Ohm's principles is identical with that of J. B. J. Fourier for the propagation of heat; and if, in Fourier's solution of any problem of heat-conduction, we change the word "temperature" to "potential" and write "electric current" instead of "flux of heat," we have the solution of a corresponding problem of electric conduction. The basis of Fourier's work was his clear conception and definition of conductivity. But this involves an assumption, undoubtedly true for small temperature-gradients, but still an assumption, viz. that, all else being the same, the flux of heat is strictly proportional to the gradient of temperature. An exactly similar assumption is made in the statement of Ohm's law, i.e. that, other things being alike, the strength of the current is at each point proportional to the gradient of potential. It happens, however, that with our modern methods it is much more easy to test the accuracy of the assumption in the case of electricity than in that of heat; and it has accordingly been shown by J. Clerk Maxwell and George Chrystal that Ohm's law is true, within the limits of experimental error, even when the currents are so powerful as almost to fuse the conducting wire.

OHMMETER, an electrical instrument employed for measuring insulation-resistance or other high electrical resistances. For the purpose of measuring resistances up to a few thousand ohms, the most convenient appliance is a Wheatstone's Bridge (q.v.), but when the resistance of the conductor to be measured is several hundred thousand ohms, or if it is the resistance of a so-called insulator, such as the insulating covering of the copper wires employed for distributing electric current in houses and buildings for electric lighting, then the ohmmeter is more convenient. An ohmmeter in one form consists of two pairs of coils, one pair called the series coil and the other called the shunt coil. These coils are placed with their axes at right angles to one another, and at the point where the axes intersect a small pivoted needle of soft iron is placed, carrying a longer index needle moving over a scale.

Suppose it is desired to measure the insulation-resistance of a system of electric house wiring; the ohmmeter circuits are then joined up as shown in fig. 1, where W represents a portion of the wiring of the building and I a portion of the insulating materials surrounding it. The object of the test is to discover the resistance of the insulator I, that is, to determine how much current flows through this insulator by leakage under a certain electromotive force or voltage which must not be less than that which will be employed in practice when the electric lights supplied through these wires are in operation. For this purpose the ohmmeter is provided with a small dynamo D, contained in a box, which produces a continuous electromotive force of from 200 to 500 volts when the handle of the instrument is steadily turned. In making the test, the whole of the copper wires belonging to any section of the wiring and the test must be connected together at some point and then connected through the series coil of the ohmmeter with one terminal of the dynamo. The shunt coil Sh and the series coil Se are connected together at one point, and the remaining terminals of

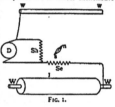

FIG. 1.

the dynamo and shunt coil must be connected to a "good earth," which is generally the gas or water pipes w of the building. On setting the dynamo in operation, a current passes through the shunt coil of the ohmmeter proportional to the voltage of the dynamo, and, if there is any sensible leakage through the insulator to earth, at the same time another current passes through the series coil proportional to the conductivity of the insulation of the wiring under the electromotive force used. The two coils, the shunt and the series coil, then produce two magnetic fields, with their lines of force at right angles to one another. The small pivoted iron needle is placed in their common field therefore takes up a certain position, dependent on the relative value of these fields. The tangent of the angle of deflection θ of this needle measured from its position, when the shunt coil is disconnected, is equal to the ratio of the voltage of the dynamo to the current through the insulator. If we call this last resistance R, the voltage of the working dynamo V, and the current through the insulator C, then tan θ = C/V = R. Hence the deflection of the needle is proportional to the insulation resistance, and the scale can be graduated to show directly this resistance in megohms.

The Evershed and Vignoles form of the instrument is much used in testing the insulation resistance of electric wiring in houses. In this case the dynamo and ohmmeter are combined in one instrument. The field magnet of the dynamo has two gaps in it. In one the exciting armature is rotated, producing the working voltage of 250, 500 or 1000 volts. In the other gap are pivoted two coils wound on an iron core and connected at nearly a right angle to each other. One of these coils is in series with the armature circuit and with the insulation or high resistance to be measured. The other is a shunt across the terminals of the armature. When the armature is rotated, these two coils endeavour to place themselves in certain directions in the field so as to be perforated by the greatest magnetic flux. The exact position of the core, and, therefore, of an index needle connected with it, is dependent on the ratio of the voltage applied to the terminals of the high resistance or insulator and the current passing through it. This, however, is a measure of the insulation-resistance. Hence the instrument can be graduated to show this directly.

In the Nalder ohmmeter the electrostatic principle is employed. The instrument consists of a high-voltage continuous-current dynamo which creates a potential difference between the needle and the two quadrants of a quadrant electrometer (see ELECTROMETER). These two quadrants are interconnected by the high resistance to be measured, and, therefore, themselves differ in potential. The exact position taken up by the needle is therefore determined by the potential difference, (P.D.) of the quadrants and the P.D. of the needle and each quadrant, and, therefore, by the ratios of the P.D. of the ends of the insulator and the current flowing through it, that is, by its insulation resistance.

The ohmmeter recommends itself by its portability, but in default of the possession of an ohmmeter the insulation-resistance can be measured by means of an ordinary mirror galvanometer (see GALVANOMETER) and insulated battery of suitable voltage. In this case one terminal of the battery is connected to the earth, and the other terminal is connected through the galvanometer with the copper wire, the insulation of which it is desired to test. If any sensible current flows through this insulator the galvanometer will show a deflection.

The meaning of this deflection can be interpreted as follows: If a galvanometer has a resistance R and is shunted by a shunt of resistance S, and the shunted galvanometer is placed in series with a large resistance R' of the order of a megohm, and if the same battery is applied to the shunted galvanometer, then the current C passing through the galvanometer will be given by the expression

$$C = \frac{SV}{R'(R+S)+RS}$$

where V is the electromotive force of the battery. It is possible so to arrange the value of the shunt and of the high resistance R' that the same or nearly the same deflection of the galvanometer is obtained as when it is used in series with the battery and the insulation-resistance. In these circumstances the current passing through the galvanometer is known, provided that the voltage of the battery is determined by means of a potentiometer (q.v.). Hence the resistance of the insulator can be ascertained, since it is expressed in ohms by the ratio of the voltage of the battery in volts to the current through the galvanometer in amperes. In applying this method to test the insulation of indiarubber-covered or of insulated copper wire, before employing it for electrical purposes, it is usual to place the coil of wire W (fig. 2) in an insulated tank of water T, which is connected

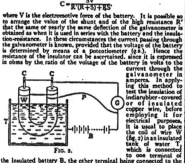

FIG. 2.

to one terminal of the insulated battery B, the other terminal being connected to the metallic conductor CC of the wire under test, through a galvanometer G. To prevent leakage over the surface of the insulating covering of the wire which projects above the surface of the water, it is necessary to employ a "guard wire" P, which consists of a piece of fine copper wire, twisted round the extremity of the insulated wire and connected to the battery. This guard wire prevents any current which leaks over the surface of the insulator from passing through the galvanometer G, and the galvanometer indication is therefore only determined by the amount of current which passes through the insulator, or by its insulation-resistance.

For further information on the measurement of high resistance, see J. A. Fleming, *A Handbook for the Electrical Laboratory and Testing Room* (2 vols., London, 1904); H. R. Kempe, *A Handbook of Electrical Testing* (London, 1900); H. L. Webb, *A Practical Guide to the Testing of Insulated Wires and Cables* (New York, 1902).

(J. A. F.)

OHNET, GEORGES (1848-   ), French novelist and man of letters, was born in Paris on the 3rd of April 1848. After the war of 1870 he became editor of the *Pays* and the *Constitutionnel* in succession. In collaboration with the engineer and dramatist Louis Denayrouze (b. 1848) he produced the play *Regina Sarpi*, and in 1877 *Marthe*. He was an admirer of Georges Sand and bitterly opposed to the realistic modern novel. He began a series of novels, *Les Batailles de la vie*, of a simple and idealistic character, which, although attacked by the critics as unreal and commonplace, were very popular. The series included *Serge Panine* (1881) which was crowned by the Academy; *Le Maître de forges* (1882), *La Grande Marnière* (1885), *Volonté* (1888), *Dernier amour* (1891). Many of his novels have been dramatized with great success, *Le Maître de forges*, produced at the Gymnase in 1883, holding the stage for a whole year. His later publications include *Le Crépuscule* (1902), *Le Marchand de poisons* (1903), *La Conquérante* (1905), *La Dixième Muse* (1906).

OHRDRUF, a town of Germany in the duchy of Saxe-Coburg-Gotha, 11 m. by rail S.E. of Gotha. Pop. (1905) 6114. It has a castle, two Evangelical churches, a technical and other schools, and manufactures of porcelain, paper, copper goods, shoes and small wares. Close by is the summer resort of Luisenthal. As early as 725 there was a monastery at Ohrdruf, which received municipal rights in 1399. With six neighbouring villages it forms the county of Obergleichen.

OIHENART, ARNAULD DE (1592-1668), Basque historian and poet, was born at Mauléon, and studied law at Bordeaux, where he took his degree in 1612. He practised first in his native town, and after his marriage with Jeanne d'Erdoy, the heiress of a noble family of Saint-Palais, at the bar of the parlement of Navarre. He spent his leisure and his fortune in the search for documents bearing on the old Basque and Bearnese provinces; and the fruits of his studies in the archives of Bayonne, Toulouse,

Pau, Perigord and other cities were embodied in forty-five MS. volumes, which were sent by his son Gabriel to Colbert. Twenty-three of these are in the Bibliothèque Nationale of Paris (Coll. Duchesne).

Oihenart published in 1625 a *Déclaration historique de l'injuste usurpation et retention de la Navarre par les Espagnols* and a fragment of a Latin work on the same subject is included in Galland's *Mémoires pour l'histoire de Navarre* (1648). His most important work is *Notitia utriusque Vasconiae, tum Ibericae, tum Aquitanicae, qua praeter situm regionis et alia scitu digna, Navarrae regum coeterarumque in iis insignum vetustate et dignitate familiarum* ... (Paris, 1638 and 1656), a description of Gascony and Navarre. His collection of over five hundred Basque proverbs, *Atsotiaec edo Refrauac*, included in a volume of his poems *O^en Gastaroa Neurthiizatan*, printed in Paris in 1657, was supplemented by a second collection, *Atsotizen Vrrhenquina*. The proverbs were edited by Francisque Michel (Paris, 1847), and the supplement by P. Hariston (Bayonne, 1892) and by V. Stempf (Bordeaux, 1894). See Julien Vinson, *Essai d'une bibliographie de la langue basque* (Paris, 1891); J. B. E. de Jaurgain, *Arnaud d'Oihenart et sa famille* (Paris, 1885).

OIL CITY, a city of Venango county, Pennsylvania, U.S.A., on the Allegheny river, at the mouth of Oil Creek, about 55 m. S.S.E. of Erie and about 135 m. N. of Pittsburg. Pop. (1890) 10,932; (1900) 13,264, of whom 2001 were foreign-born and 184 were negroes; (1910 census) 15,657. It is served by the Pennsylvania (two lines), the Erie, and the Lake Shore & Michigan Southern railways. The city lies about 1000 ft. above the sea, and is divided by the river and the creek into three sections connected by bridges. The business part of the city is on the low ground north of the river; the residential districts are the South Side, a portion of the flats, the West Side, and Cottage Hill and Palace Hill on the North Side. Oil City is the centre and the principal market of the Pennsylvania oil region. It has extensive oil refineries and foundries and machine shops, and manufactures oil-well supplies and a few other commodities. The city's factory products were valued at $5,164,059 in 1900 and at $3,217,208 in 1905, and in the latter year foundry and machine-shop products were valued at $2,317,505, or 72% of the total. Natural gas is used for power, heat and light. Oil City was founded in 1860, incorporated as a borough in 1863 and chartered as a city in 1874. The city was partially destroyed by flood in 1865, and by flood and fire in 1866 and again in 1892; on this last occasion Oil Creek was swollen by a cloud-burst on the 5th of June, and several tanks farther up the valley, which seem to have been struck by lightning, gave way and a mass of burning oil was carried by the creek to Oil City, where some sixty lives were lost and property valued at more than $1,000,000 was destroyed.

OIL ENGINE. Oil engines, like gas engines (q.v.), are internal combustion motors in which motive power is produced by the explosion or expansion of a mixture of inflammable material and air. The inflammable fluid used, however, consists of vapour produced from oil instead of permanent gas. The thermodynamic operations are the same as in gas engines, and the structural and mechanical differences are due to the devices required to vaporise the oil and supply the measured proportion of vapour which is to mix with the air in the cylinders

Light and heavy oils are used; light oils may be defined as those which are readily volatile at ordinary atmospheric temperatures, while heavy oils are those which require special heating or spraying processes in order to produce an inflammable vapour capable of forming explosive mixture to be supplied to the cylinders. Of the light oils the most important is known as petrol. It is not a definite chemical compound. It is a mixture of various hydrocarbons of the paraffin and olefine series produced from the distillation of petroleum and paraffin oils. It consists, in fact, of the lighter fractions which distil over first in the process of purifying petroleums or paraffins.

The specific gravity of the standard petrols of commerce generally ranges between 0·700 to about 0·740; and the heat value on complete combustion per 1/10 gallon burned varies from 14,240 to 14,850 British thermal units. The thermal value per gallon thus increases with the density, but the volatility diminishes. Thus, samples of petrol examined by Mr Blount of from ·700 to ·730 specific gravity showed that 98% of the lighter sample distilled over below 120° C. while only 88% of the heavier came over within the same temperature range. The heavier petrol is not so easily converted into vapour. The great modern development of the motor car gives the light oil engine a most important place as one of the leading sources of motive power in the world. The total petrol power now applied to cars on land and to vessels on sea amounts to at least two million H.P. The petrol engine has also enabled aeroplanes to be used in practice.

The earliest proposal to use oil as a means to produce motive power was made by an English inventor—Street—in 1794, but the first practical petroleum engine was that of Julius Hock of Vienna, produced in 1870. This engine, like Lenoir's gas engine, operated without compression. The piston took in a charge of air and light petroleum spray which was ignited by a flame jet and produced a low-pressure explosion. Like all non-compression engines, Hock's machine was very cumbrous and gave little power. In 1873, Brayton, an English engineer, who had settled in America, produced a light oil engine working on the constant pressure system without explosion. This appears to have been the earliest compression engine to use oil fuel instead of gas.

Shortly after the introduction of the "Otto" gas engine in 1876, a motor of this type was operated by an inflammable vapour produced by passing air on its way to the cylinder through the light oil then known as gasolene. A further air supply was drawn into the cylinder to form the required explosive mixture, which was subsequently compressed and ignited in the usual way. The Spiel petroleum engine was the first Otto cycle motor introduced into practice which dispensed with an independent vaporizing apparatus. Light hydrocarbon of a specific gravity of not greater than 0.725 was injected directly into the cylinder on the suction stroke by means of a pump. In entering it formed spray mixed with the air, was vaporized, and on compression an explosion was obtained just as in the gas engine.

Until the year 1883 the different gas and oil engines constructed were of a heavy type rotating at about 150 to 250 revolutions per minute. In that year Daimler conceived the idea of constructing very small engines with light moving parts, in order to enable them to be rotated at such high speeds as 800 and 1000 revolutions per minute. At that time engineers did not consider it practicable to run engines at such speeds; it was supposed that low speed was necessary to durability and smooth running. Daimler showed this idea to be wrong by producing his first small engine in 1883. In 1886 he made his first experiment with a motor bicycle, and on the 4th of March 1887 he ran for the first time a motor car propelled by a petrol engine. Daimler deserves great credit for realizing the possibility of producing durable and effective engines rotating at such unusually high speeds; and, further, for proving that his ideas were right in actual practice. His engines contained nothing new in their cycles of operation, but they provided the first step in the startlingly rapid development of petrol motive power, which we have seen in the last twenty years. The high-speed of rotation enabled motors to be constructed giving a very large power for a very small weight.

Fig. 1 is a diagrammatic section of an early Daimler motor. A is the cylinder, B the piston, C the connecting rod, and D the crank, which is entirely enclosed in a casing. A small fly-wheel is carried by the crank-shaft, and it serves the double purpose of a fly-wheel and a clutch. a is the combustion space, E the single port, which serves both for inlet of the charge and for discharge of exhaust. W is the exhaust valve, F the charge inlet valve, which is automatic in its action, and is held closed by a spring f, G the carburettor. H the igniter tube, I the igniter tube lamp, K the charge inlet passage, L the air filter chamber, and M an adjustable air inlet cap for regulating the air inlet area. The light oil—or petrol, as it is commonly called—is supplied to the float chamber N of the vaporiser by means of the valve O. So long as the level of the petrol is high, the float n, acting by levers about it, holds the valve O closed against oil forced by air pressure along the pipe, P When the level falls, however, the valve opens and more petrol is admitted. When the piston B makes its suction stroke, air passes from the atmosphere by the passage K through the valve F, which it opens automatically. The pressure falls within the passage K, and a spurt of petrol passes by the jet G¹, separate air at the same time passing by the passage K¹ round the jet. The petrol breaks up into spray by impact against the walls of the passage K, and then it vaporizes and passes into the cylinder A as an inflammable mixture. When the piston B returns it compresses the charge into a, and upon compression the incandescent igniter tube H fires the charge. H is a short platinum tube, which is always open to the compression space It is rendered incandescent by the burner I, fed with petrol from the pipe supplying the vaporizer. The open incandescent tube is found to act well for small engines, and it does not ignite the charge until the compression takes place, because the inflammable mixture cannot come into contact with the hot part till it is forced up the tube by the

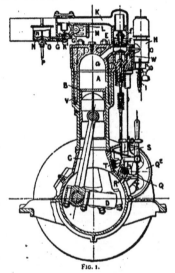

FIG. 1.

compression. The engine is started by giving the crank-shaft a smart turn round by means of a detachable handle. The exhaust is alone actuated from the valve shaft. The shaft Q is operated by pinion and a spur-wheel Q¹ at half the rate of the crank-shaft. The governing is accomplished by cutting out explosions as with the gas engine, but the governor operates by preventing the exhaust valve from opening, so that no charge is discharged from the cylinder, and therefore no charge is drawn in. The cam R operates the exhaust valve, the levers shown are so controlled by the governor (not shown) that the knife edge S is pressed out when speed is too high, and cannot engage the recess T until it falls. The engine has a water jacket V, through which water is circulated. Cooling devices are used to economize water.

Benz of Mannheim followed close on the work of Daimler, and in France Panhard and Levassor, Peugeot, De Dion, Delahaye and Renault all contributed to the development of the petrol engine, while Napier, Lanchester, Royce and Austin were the most prominent among the many English designers.

The modern petrol engine differs in many respects from the Daimler engine just described both as to general design, method of carburetting, igniting and controlling the power and speed. The carburettor now used is usually of the float and jet type shown in fig. 1, but alterations have been made to allow of the production of uniform mixture in the cylinder under widely varying conditions of speed and load. The original form of carburettor was not well adapted to allow of great change of volume per suction stroke. Tube ignition has been abandoned, and the electric system is now supreme. The favourite type at present is that of the high-tension magneto. Valves are now all mechanically operated; the automatic inlet valve has practically disappeared. Engines are no longer controlled by cutting out impulses; the governing is effected by throttling the charge, that is by diminishing the volume of charge admitted to the cylinder at one stroke. Broadly, throttling by reducing charge weight reduces pressure of compression and so allows the power of the explosion to be graduated within wide limits while maintaining continuity of impulses. The object of the throttle control is to keep up continuous impulses for each cycle of operation, while graduating the power produced by each impulse so as to meet the conditions of the load.

wick carburettor; and third, the jet carburettor. The surface carburettor has entirely disappeared. In it air was passed over a surface of light oil or bubbled through it; the air carried off a vapour to form explosive mixture. It was found, however, that the oil remaining in the carburettor gradually became heavier and heavier, so that ultimately no proper vaporization took place. This was due to the fractional evaporation of the oil which tended to carry away the light vapours, leaving in the vessel the oil, which produced heavy vapours. To avoid this fractionation the wick carburettor was introduced and here a complete portion of oil was evaporated at each operation so that no concentration of heavy oil was possible. The wick carburettor is still used in some cars, but the jet carburettor is practically universal. It has the advantage of discharging separate portions of oil into the air entering the engine, each portion being carried away and evaporated with all its fractions to produce the charge in the cylinder.

The modern jet carburettor appears to have originated with Butler, an English engineer, but it was first extensively used in the modification produced by Maybach as shown in fig. 1.

A diagrammatic section of a carburettor of the Maybach type is shown in a larger scale in fig. 2.

Petrol is admitted to the chamber A by the valve B which is controlled by the float C acting through the levers D, so that the valve

G

F

FIG. 2.

when
at an

portioned to give the desired volume of petrol to form the proper mixture with air. The device in this form works quite well when the range of speed required from the engine is not great; that is, within limits, the volume of petrol thrown by the jet is fairly proportional to the air passing the jet. When, however the speed range is great, such as in modern motors, which may vary from 300 to 1500 revolutions per minute under light and heavy loads, then it becomes impossible to secure proportionality sufficiently accurate for regular ignition. This implies not only a change of engine speed but a change of volume entering the cylinder at each stroke as determined by the position of the throttle. This introduces further complications. Throttle control implies a change of total charge volume per stroke, which change may occur either at a low or at a high speed. To meet this change the petrol jet should respond in such manner as to give a constant proportionality of petrol weight to air weight throughout all the variations—otherwise sometimes petrol will be present in excess with no oxygen to burn it, and at other times the mixture may be so dilute as to miss firing altogether. To meet these varying conditions many carburettors have been produced which seek by various devices to maintain uniformity of quality of mixture by the automatic change of throttle around the jet.

Fig. 3 shows in diagrammatic section one of the simplest of these contrivances, known as the Krebs carburettor. The petrol enters from the float chamber to the jet E; and, while the engine is running slowly, the whole supply of air enters by way of the passage F, mixes with the petrol and reaches the cylinders by way of the pipe G. The volume of charge entering the cylinder per stroke is controlled by the piston throttle valve H, operated by the rod I; and so long as the charge volume required remains small, air from the atmosphere enters only by F. When speed rises, however, and the throttle is sufficiently opened, the pressure within the apparatus falls and affects a spring-pressed diaphragm K, which actuates a piston valve controlling the air passages L, so that this valve opens to the atmosphere more and more with increasing pressure reduction, and additional air thus flows into the carburettor and mixes with the air and petrol entering through F. By this device the required proportion of air to petrol is maintained through a comparatively large volume range. This change of air admission is rendered necessary because of the difference between the laws of air and petrol flow. In order to give a sufficient weight of petrol at low speeds when the pressure drop is small, it is necessary to provide a somewhat large area of petrol jet. When suction increases owing to high speed, this large area discharges too much petrol, and so necessitates a device, such as that described, which admits more air.

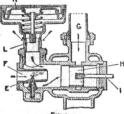

FIG. 3.

A still simpler device is adopted in many carburettors—that of an additional air inlet valve, kept closed until wanted by a spring. Fig. 4 shows a diagrammatic section as used in the Vauxhall carburettor. Here the petrol jet and primary and secondary air passages are lettered as before.

The same effect is produced by devices which alter the area of the petrol jet or increase or diminish the number of petrol jets exposed as required. Although engine designers have succeeded in proportioning mixture through a considerable range of speed and charge demand, so as to obtain effective power explosions under all these conditions, yet much remains to be done to secure constancy of mixture at all speeds. Notwithstanding much which has been said as to varying mixture, there is only one mixture of air and petrol which gives the best results—that in which there is some excess of oxygen, more than sufficient to burn all the hydrogen and carbon present. It is necessary to secure this mixture under all conditions, not only to obtain economy in running but also to maintain purity of exhaust gases. Most engines at certain speeds discharge considerable quantities of carbonic oxide into the atmosphere with their exhaust gases, and some discharge so much as to give rise to danger in a closed garage. Carbonic oxide is an extremely poisonous gas which should be reduced to the minimum in the interests of the health of our large cities. The enormous increase of motor traffic makes it important to render the exhaust gases as pure and innocuous as possible. Tests were made by the Royal Automobile Club some years ago which clearly showed that carbonic oxide should be kept down to 2% and under when carburettors were properly adjusted. Subsequent experiments have been made by Hopkinson, Clerk and

Watson, which clearly prove that in some cases as much as 30 % of the whole heat of the petrol is lost in the exhaust gases by im-

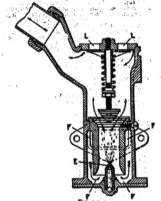

FIG. 4.

perfect combustion. This opens a wide field for improvement, and makes it probable that with better carburettors motor cars would

not only discharge purer exhaust gases but would work on very much less petrol than they do at present.

Practically all modern petrol engines are controlled by throttling the whole charge. In the earlier days several methods of control were attempted: (1) missing impulses as in fig. 1 of the Daimler engines; (2) altering the timing of spark; (3) throttling petrol supply, and (4) throttling the mixture of petrol and air. The last method has proved to be the best. By maintaining the proportion of explosive mixture, but diminishing the total volume admitted to the cylinder per stroke, graduated impulses are obtained without any, or but few, missed ignitions. The effect of the throttling is to reduce compression by diminishing total charge weight. To a certain extent the proportion of petrol to total charge also varies, because the residual exhaust gases remain constant through a wide range. The thermal efficiency diminishes as the throttling increases; but, down to a third of the brake power, the diminution is not great, because although compression is reduced the expansion remains the same. At low compressions, however, the engine works practically as a non-compression engine, and the point of maximum pressure becomes greatly delayed. The efficiency, therefore, falls markedly, but this is not of much importance at light loads. Experiments by Callendar, Hopkinson, Watson and others have proved that the thermal efficiency obtained from these small engines with the throttle full open is very high indeed; 28 % of the whole heat in the petrol is often given as indicated work when the carburettor is properly adjusted. As a large gas engine for the same compression cannot do better than 35 %, it appears that the loss of heat due to small dimensions is compensated by the small time of exposure of the gases of explosion due to the high speed of rotation. Throttle control is very effective, and it has the great advantage of diminishing maximum

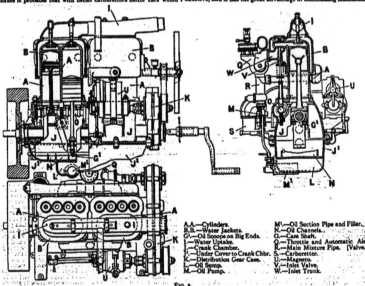

| A.A.—Cylinders. | M¹.—Oil Suction Pipe and Filler. |

A.A.—Cylinders.
B.B.—Water Jackets.
G¹.—Oil Scoops on Big Ends.
I.—Water Uptake.
J.—Crank Chamber.
J¹.—Under Cover to Crank Chbr.
K.—Distribution Gear Case.
L.—Oil Sump.
M.—Oil Pump.

M¹.—Oil Suction Pipe and Filler.
N.—Oil Channels.
O.—Cam Shaft.
Q.—Throttle and Automatic Air
R.—Main Mixture Pipe   [Valve.
S.—Carburetter.
U.—Magneto.
V.—Inlet Valve.
W.—Inlet Trunk.

FIG. 5.

pressures to which the piston and cylinders are exposed while the engine is running at the lower loads. This is important both for smooth running and good wearing qualities. Theoretically, better results could be obtained from the point of view of economy by retaining a constant compression pressure, constant charge of air, and producing ignition, somewhat in the manner of the Diesel engine. Such a method, however, would have the disadvantage of producing practically the same maximum pressure for all loads, and this would tend to give an engine which would not run smoothly at slow speeds.

As has been said, tube ignition was speedily abandoned for electric ignition by accumulator, induction coil distributor and sparking plug. This in its turn was largely displaced by the low-tension magneto system, in which the spark was formed between contacts which were mechanically separated within the cylinders. The separable contacts gave rise to complications, and at present the most popular system of ignition is undoubtedly that of the high-tension magneto. In this system the ordinary high-tension sparking plugs are used, and the high-tension current is generated in a secondary winding on the armature of the magneto, and reaches the sparking plugs by way of a rotary distributor. In many cases the high-tension magneto system is used for the ordinary running of the engine, combined with an accumulator or battery and induction coil for starting systems. Sometimes the same ignition plugs are adapted to spark from either source, and in other cases separate plugs are used. The magneto systems have the great advantage of generating current without battery, and by their use noise is reduced to a minimum. All electrical systems are now arranged to allow of advancing and retarding the spark from the steering wheel. In modern magneto methods, however, the spark is automatically retarded when the engine slows and advanced when the speed rises, so that less change is required from the wheel than is necessary with battery and coil.

Sir Oliver Lodge has invented a most interesting system of electric ignition, depending upon the production of an extra oscillatory current of enormous tension produced by the combined use of spark gap and condenser. This extra spark passes freely even under water, and it is impossible to stop it by any ordinary sooting or fouling of the ignition plug.

The most popular engines are now of the four and six cylinder types.

Fig. 5 shows a modern four-cylinder engine in longitudinal and transverse sections as made by the Wolseley Company. A, A are the cylinders; B, B, water jackets; G¹, oil scoops on the large ends of the connecting-rods. These scoops take up oil from the crank chamber. Forced lubrication is used. The oil pump M is of the toothed wheel type, and it is driven by skew gearing. An oil sump is arranged at L, and the oil is pumped from this sump by the pump described. The overflow from the main bearings supplies the channels in the crank case from which the oil scoops take their charge. It will be seen that the two inside pistons are attached to cranks of co-incident centres, and this is true of the two outside pistons also. This is the usual arrangement in four-cylinder engines. By this device the primary forces are balanced; but a small secondary unbalanced force remains, due to the difference in motion of the pistons at the up and down portions of their stroke. A six-cylinder engine has the advantage of getting rid of this secondary unbalanced force; but it requires a longer and more rigid crank chamber. In this engine the inlet and exhaust valves of each cylinder are placed in the same pocket and are driven from one cam-shaft. This is a very favourite arrangement; but many engines are constructed in which the inlet and exhaust valves operate on opposite sides of the cylinder in separate ports and are driven from separate cam-shafts. Dual ignition is applied to this engine; that is, an ignition composed of high-tension magneto and also battery and coil for starting. U is the high-tension magneto. Under the figure there is shown a list of parts which sufficiently indicate the nature of the engine.

An interesting and novel form of engine is shown at fig. 6. This is a well-known engine designed by Mr Knight, an American inventor, and now made by the Daimler and other companies. It will be observed in the figure that the ordinary lift valves are entirely dispensed with, and slide valves are used of the cylindrical shell type. The engine operates on the ordinary Otto cycle, and all the valve actions necessary to admit charge and discharge exhaust gases are accomplished by means of two sleeves sliding one within the other.

The outer sleeve slides in the main cylinder and the inner sleeve slides within the outer sleeve. The piston fits within the inner sleeve. The sleeves receive separate motions from short connecting links C and E, driven by eccentrics carried on a shaft W. This shaft is driven from the main crank-shaft by a strong chain so as to make half the revolutions of the crank-shaft in the usual manner of the Otto cycle. The inlet port is formed on one side of the cylinder and is marked I. The exhaust port is arranged on the other side and marked J. These ports are segmental. A water-jacketed cylinder head carries stationary rings L, K, which press outwards. These are clearly shown in the drawing. The inner sleeve ports run past the lower broad ring L, when compression is to be accomplished, and the contents of the cylinder are retained within the cylinder and compression space by the piston rings and the fixed rings referred to.

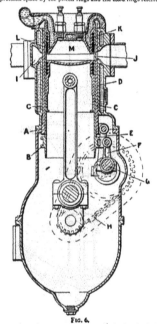

FIG. 6.

The outer sleeve does not require rings at all. Its function is simply to distribute the gases so that the exhaust port is closed by the outer sleeve when the inlet port is open. The outer sleeve acts really as a distributor; the inner sleeve supplies the pressure tightness required to resist compression and explosion. The idea of working exhaust and inlet by two sleeves within which the main piston operates is very daring and ingenious; and for these small engines the sleeve valve system works admirably. There are many advantages; the shape of the compression space is a most favourable one for reducing loss by cooling. All the valve ports required in ordinary lift valve engines are entirely dispensed with; that is, the surface exposed to the explosion causing loss of heat is reduced to a minimum. The engines are found in use to be very flexible and economical.

The petrol engines hitherto described, although light compared to the old stationary gas engines, are heavy when compared with recent motors developed for the purpose of aeroplanes. Many of these motors have been produced, but two only will be noticed here—the Anzani, because Bleriot's great flight across the Channel was accomplished by means of an Anzani engine, and the Gnome engine, because it was used in the aeroplane with which Paulhan flew from London to Manchester.

Fig. 7 shows transverse and longitudinal sections through the Anzani motor. Looking at the longitudinal section it will be observed that the cylinders are of the air-cooled type; the exhaust valves alone are positively operated, and the inlet valves are of the automatic lift kind. The transverse section shows that three radially arranged cylinders are used and three pistons act upon one crank-pin. The Otto cycle is followed so that three impulses are obtained for

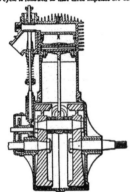

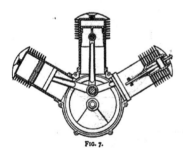

FIG. 7.

every two revolutions. The cylinders are spaced apart 60° and project from the upper side of the crank chamber. Although not shown in the drawing, the pistons overrun a row of holes at the out end of the stroke and the exhaust first discharges through these holes. This is a very common device in aeroplane engines, and it greatly increases the rapidity of the exhaust discharged and reduces the work falling upon the exhaust valve. The pistons and cylinders are of cast iron; the rings are of cast iron; the ignition is electric; and the petrol is fed by gravity. The engine used by Blériot in his Cross-Channel flight was 25 H.P., cylinders 105 mm. bore × 130 mm. stroke; revolutions, 1600 per minute; total weight, 145 ℔. The engine, it will be seen, is exceedingly simple, although air-cooling seems somewhat primitive for anything except short flights. The larger Anzani motors are water-cooled.

A diagrammatic transverse section of the Gnome motor is shown at fig. 8. In this interesting engine there are seven cylinders disposed radially round a fixed crank-shaft. The seven pistons are all connected to the same crank-shaft, one piston being rigidly connected to a big end of peculiar construction by a connecting-rod, while the other connecting-rods are linked on to the same big end by pins; that is, a hollow fixed crank-shaft has a single throw to which only one connecting-rod is attached; all the other connecting-rods work on pins let into the big end of that connecting-rod. The cylinders revolve round the fixed crank in the manner of the well-known engines first introduced to practice by Mr John Rigg. The explosive mixture is led from the carburettor through the hollow crank-shaft into the crank-case, and it is admitted into the cylinders by means of automatic inlet valves placed in the heads of the pistons. The exhaust valves are arranged on the cylinder heads. Dual ignition is provided by high tension magneto and storage battery and coil. The cylinders are ribbed outside like the Anzani, and are very effectively air-cooled by their rotation through the air as well as by the passage of the aeroplane through the atmosphere. The cylinders in the 35 H.P. motor are 110 mm. bore × 120 mm. stroke. The speed of rotation is usually 1200 revolutions per minute. The total weight of the engine complete is 180 ℔, or just over 5 ℔ per brake horse-power. The subject of aeroplane petrol engines is a most interesting one, and rapid progress is being made.

So far, only 4-cycle engines have been described, and they are almost universal for use in motor-cars and aeroplanes. Some motor cars, however, use 2-cycle engines. Several types follow the "Clerk" cycle (see GAS ENGINE) and others the "Day" cycle. In America the Day cycle is very popular for motor

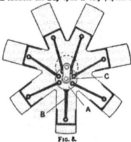

FIG. 8.

launches, as the engine is of a very simple, easily managed kind. At present, however, the two-cycle engine has made but little way in motor car or aeroplane work. It is capable of great development and the attention given to it is increasing.

So far, petrol has been alluded to as the main liquid fuel for these motors. Other hydrocarbons have also been used; benzol, for example, obtained from gas tar is used to some extent, and alcohol has been applied to a considerable extent both for stationary and locomotive engines. Alcohol, however, has not been entirely successful. The amount of heat obtained for a given monetary expenditure is only about half that obtained by means of petrol. On the continent of Europe, however, alcohol motors have been considerably used for public vehicles.

The majority of petrol motors are provided with water jackets around their cylinders and combustion spaces. As only a small quantity of water can be carried, it is necessary to cool the water as fast as it becomes hot. For this purpose radiators of various constructions are applied. Generally a pump is used to produce a forced circulation, discharging the hot water from the engine jackets through the radiator and returning the cooled water to the jackets at another place. The radiators consist in some cases of fine tubes covered with projecting fins or gills; the motion of the car forces air over the exterior of those surfaces and is assisted by the operation of a powerful fan driven from the engine. A favourite form of radiator consists of numerous small tubes set into a casing and arranged somewhat like a steam-engine condenser. Water is forced by the pump round these tubes, and air passes from the atmosphere through them. This type of radiator is sometimes known as the "honeycomb" radiator. A very large cooling surface is provided, so that the same water is used over and over again. In a day's run with a modern petrol engine very little water is lost from the system. Some engines dispense with a pump and depend on what is called the thermo-syphon. This is the old gas-engine system of circulation, depending on the different density of water when hot and cool. The engine shown at fig. 5 is provided with a water-circulation system of this kind. For the smaller engines the thermo-syphon works extremely well.

Heavy oil engines are those which consume oil having a flashing-point above 73° F.—the minimum at present allowed by act of parliament in Great Britain for oils to be consumed in ordinary illuminating lamps. Such oils are American and Russian petroleums and Scottish paraffins. They vary in specific gravity from ·78 to ·825, and in flashing-point from 75° to 152° F. Engines burning such oils may be divided into three distinct classes: (1) Engines in which the oil is subjected to a spraying operation before vaporization; (2) Engines in which the oil is injected into the cylinder and vaporized within the cylinder; (3) Engines in which the oil is vaporized in a device external to the cylinder and introduced into the cylinder in the state of vapour.

The method of ignition might also be used to divide the engines into those igniting by the electric spark, by an incandescent tube, by compression, or by the heat of the internal surfaces of the combustion space. Spiel's engine was ignited by a flame igniting device similar to that used in Clerk's gas engine, and it was the only one introduced into Great Britain in which this method was adopted, though on the continent flame igniters were not uncommon. Electrically-operated igniters have come into extensive use throughout the world.

The engines first used in Great Britain which fell under the first head were the Priestman and Samuelson, the oil being sprayed before being vaporized in both. The principle of the spray producer used is that so well and so widely known in connexion with the atomizers or spray producers used by perfumers. Fig. 9 shows such a spray producer in section. An air blast passing from the small jet A crosses the top of the tube B and creates within it a partial vacuum. The liquid contained in C

FIG. 9.—Perfume Spray Producer.

flows up the tube B and issuing at the top of the tube through a small orifice is at once blown into very fine spray by the action of the air jet. If such a scent distributor be filled with petroleum oil, such as Royal Daylight or Russoline, the oil will be blown into fine spray, which can be ignited by a flame and will burn, if the jets be properly proportioned, with an intense blue non-luminous flame. The earlier inventors often expressed the idea that an explosive mixture could be prepared without any vaporization whatever, by simply producing an atmosphere containing inflammable liquid in extremely small particles distributed throughout the air in such proportion as to allow of complete combustion. The familiar explosive combustion of lycopodium, and the disastrous explosions caused in the exhaustion rooms of flour-mills by the presence of finely divided flour in the air, have also suggested to inventors the idea of producing explosions for power purposes from combustible solids. Although, doubtless, explosions could be produced in that way, yet in oil engines the production of spray is only a preliminary to the vaporization of the oil. If a sample of oil is sprayed in the manner just described, and injected in a hot chamber also filled with hot air, it at once passes into a state of vapour within that chamber, even though the air be at a temperature far below the boiling-point of the oil; the spray producer, in fact, furnishes a ready means of saturating any volume of air with

heavy petroleum oil to the full extent possible from the vapour tension of the oil at that particular temperature. The oil engines described below are in reality explosion gas engines of the ordinary Otto type, with special arrangements to enable them to vaporize the oil to be used. Only such parts of them as are necessary for the treatment and ignition will therefore be described.

Fig. 10 is a vertical section through the cylinder and vaporizer of a Priestman engine, and fig. 11 is a section on a larger scale, showing the vaporizing jet and the air admission and regulation valve

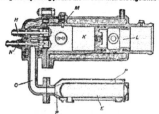

FIG. 10.—Priestman Oil Engine (vertical section through cylinder and vaporizer).

leading to the vaporizer. Oil is forced by means of air pressure from a reservoir through a pipe to the spraying nozzle a, and air passes from an air-pump by way of the annular channel b into the sprayer c, and there meets the oil jet issuing from a. The oil is thus broken up into spray, and the air charged with spray flows into the vaporizer E, which is heated up in the first place on starting the engine by means of a lamp. In the vaporizer the oil spray becomes oil vapour, saturating the air within the hot walls. On the out-charging stroke of the piston the mixture passes by way of the inlet valve H into the cylinder, air flowing into the vaporizer to replace it through the valve l (fig. 11). The cylinder K is thus charged with a mixture of air and hydrocarbon vapour, some of which may exist in the form of very fine spray. The piston L then returns and compresses the mixture, and when the compression is quite complete an electric spark is passed between the points M, and a compression explosion is obtained precisely similar to that obtained in the gas engine. The piston moves out, and on its return stroke the exhaust valve N is opened and the exhaust gases discharged by way of the pipe O, round the jacket P, enclosing the vaporizing chamber. The latter is thus kept hot by the exhaust gases when the engine is at work, and it remains sufficiently hot without the use of the lamp provided for starting. To obtain the electric spark a bichromate battery with an induction coil is used. The spark is timed by contact pieces operated by an eccentric rod, used to actuate the exhaust valve and the air-pump for supplying the oil chamber and the spraying jet. To start the engine a hand pump is worked until the pressure is sufficient to force the oil through the spraying nozzle, and oil spray

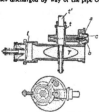

FIG. 11.—Priestman Oil Engine (section on a larger scale).

is formed in the starting lamp; the spray and air mixed produce a blue flame which heats the vaporizer. The fly-wheel is then rotated by hand and the engine moves away. The eccentric shaft is driven from the crank-shaft by means of toothed wheels, which reduce the speed to one-half the revolutions of the crank-shaft. The charging inlet valve is automatic. Governing is effected by throttling the oil and air supply. The governor operates on the butterfly valve T (fig. 11), and on the plug-cock t connected to it, by means of the spindle t'. The air and oil are thus simultaneously reduced, and the attempt is made to maintain the charge entering the cylinder at a constant proportion by weight of oil and air, while reducing the total weight, and therefore volume, of the charge entering. The Priestman engine thus gives an explosion on every second revolution in all circumstances, whether the engine be running light or loaded.

The compression pressure of the mixture before admission is, however, steadily reduced as the load is reduced, and at very light loads the engine is running practically as a non-compression engine.

A test by Professor Unwin of a 4½ nominal horse-power Priestman engine, cylinder 8·5 in. diameter, 12 in. stroke, normal speed 180 revolutions per minute, showed the consumption of oil per indicated horse-power hour to be 1·066 lb and per brake horse-power hour 1·243 lb. The oil used was that known as Broxburn Lighthouse, a Scottish paraffin oil produced by the destructive distillation of shale, having a density of ·81 and a flashing-point about 152° F. With a 5 H.P. engine of the same dimensions, the volume swept by the piston per stroke being ·395 cub. ft. and the clearance space in the cylinder at the end of the stroke ·210 cub. ft., the principal results were:—

	Daylight Oil	Russoline Oil
Indicated horse-power . . .	9·369	7·408
Brake horse-power . . .	7·722	6·765
Mean speed (revolutions per minute) .	204·33	207·73
Mean available pressure (revolutions per minute)	53·2	41·38
Oil consumed per indicated horse-power per hour	·694 lb	·864 lb
Oil consumed per brake horse-power per hour	·842 lb	·946 lb

With daylight oil the explosion pressure was 151·4 lb per square inch above atmosphere, and with Russoline 134·3 lb. The terminal pressure at the moment of opening the exhaust valve with daylight oil was 35·4 lb and with Russoline 33·7 per square inch. The compression pressure with daylight oil was 35 lb, and with Russoline 27·6 lb pressure above atmosphere. Professor Unwin calculated the amount of heat accounted for by the indicator as 18·8 % in the case of daylight oil and 15·2 in the case of Russoline oil.

The Hornsby-Ackroyd engine is an example of the class in which the oil is injected into the cylinder and there vaporized. Fig. 12

Fig. 12.—Hornsby-Ackroyd Engine (section through vaporizer and cylinder).

Fig. 13.—Hornsby-Ackroyd Engine (section through valves, vaporizer and cylinder).

is a section through the vaporizer and cylinder of this engine, and fig. 13 shows the inlet and exhaust valves also in section placed in front of the vaporizer and cylinder section. Vaporizing is conducted in the interior of the combustion chamber, which is so arranged that the heat of each explosion maintains it at a temperature sufficiently high to enable the oil to be vaporized by mere injection upon the hot surfaces. The vaporizer A is heated up by a separate lamp, the oil is injected at the oil inlet B, and the engine is rotated by hand. The piston then takes in a charge of air by the air-inlet valve into the cylinder, the air passing by the port directly into the cylinder without passing through the vaporizer chamber. While the piston is moving forward, taking in the charge of air, the oil thrown into the vaporizer is vaporizing and diffusing itself through the vaporizer chamber, mixing, however, only with the hot products of combustion left by the preceding explosion. During the charging stroke the air enters through the cylinder, and the vapour formed from the oil is almost entirely confined to the combustion chamber. On the return stroke of the piston air is forced through the somewhat narrow neck à into the combustion chamber, and is there mixed with the vapour contained in it. At first, however, the mixture is too rich in inflammable vapour to be capable of ignition. As the compression proceeds, however, more and more air is forced into the vaporizer chamber, and just as compression is completed the mixture attains proper explosive proportions. The sides of the chamber are sufficiently hot to cause explosion, under the pressure of which the piston moves forward. As the vaporizer A is not water-jacketed, and is connected to the metal of the back cover only by the small section or area of cast-iron forming the metal neck a, the heat given to the

surface by each explosion is sufficient to keep its temperature at about 700-800° C. Oil vapour mixed with air will explode by contact with a metal surface at a comparatively low temperature; this accounts for the explosion of the compressed mixture in the combustion chamber A, which is never really raised to a red heat. It has long been known that under certain conditions of internal surface a gas engine may be made to run with very great regularity, without incandescent tube or any other form of igniter, if some portion of the interior surfaces of the cylinder or combustion space be so arranged that the temperature can rise moderately; then, although the temperature may be too low to ignite the mixture at atmospheric temperature, yet when compression is completed the mixture will often ignite in a perfectly regular manner. It is a curious fact that with heavy oils ignition is more easily accomplished at a low temperature than with light oils. The explanation seems to be that, while in the case of light oils the hydrocarbon vapours formed are tolerably stable from a chemical point of view, the heavy oils very easily decompose by heat, and separate out their carbons, liberating the combined hydrogen, and at the moment of liberation the hydrogen, being in what chemists know as the *nascent* state, very readily enters into combination with the oxygen beside it. To start the engine the vaporizer is heated by a separate heating lamp, which is supplied with an air blast by means of a hand-operated fan. This operation should take about nine minutes. The engine is then moved round by hand, and starts in the usual manner. The oil tank is placed in the bed plate of the engine. The air and exhaust valves are driven by cams on a valve shaft. The governing is effected by a centrifugal governor which operates a by-pass valve, opening it when the speed is too high, and causes the oil pump to return the oil to the oil tank. At a test of one of these engines, which weighed 40 cwt. and was given as of 8 brake horse-power, with cylinder 10 in. in diameter and 15 in. stroke, according to Professor Capper's report, the revolutions were very constant, and the power developed did not vary one quarter of a brake horse-power from day to day. The oil consumed, reckoned on the average of the three days over which the trial extended, was ·919 lb per brake horse-power per hour, the mean power exerted being 8·35 brake horse. At another full-power trial of the same engine a brake horse-power of 8·57 was obtained, the mean speed being 239·66 revolutions per minute and the test lasting for two hours; the indicated power was 10·3 horse, the explosions per minute 119·83, the mean effective pressure 38·9 per sq. in., the oil used per indicated horse-power per hour was ·81 lb, and per brake horse-power per hour ·977 lb. In a test at half power, the brake horse-power developed was 4·57 at 235·9 revolutions per minute, and the oil used per blast horse-power was 1·48 lb. On a four hours' test, without a load, at 240 revolutions per minute, the consumption of oil was 4·23 lb per hour. Engines of this class are those manufactured by Messrs Crossley Bros., Ltd., and the National Gas Engine Co., Ltd.

Figs. 14 and 15 show a longitudinal section and detail views of the operative parts of the Crossley oil engine. On the suction stroke, air is drawn into the cylinder by the piston A through the automatic inlet valve D, and oil is then pumped into the heated vaporizer C through the oil sprayer G, as seen in section at fig. 15. The vaporizer C is bolted to the water-jacketed part B; and, like the Hornsby, this vaporizer is first heated by lamp and then the heat of the explosions keeps up its temperature to a sufficiently high point to vaporize the oil when sprayed against it. On the compression stroke

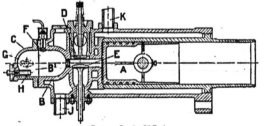

Fig. 14.—Crossley Oil Engine.

of the piston A the charge of air is forced into the combustion chamber B and the vaporizer chamber C, where it mixes with the oil vapour, and the mixture is ignited at the termination of the stroke by the ignition tube H. This tube is isolated to some extent from the vaporizer chamber C, and so it becomes hotter than the chamber C and is relied upon to ignite the mixture when formed at times when C would be too cold for the purpose. E is the exhaust valve, which operates in the usual way · The water circulation passes through the jacket by way of the pipes J and K. When the engine is running at heavy loads with full charges of oil delivered by the oil pump through the sprayer G, a second pump is caused to come into action, which discharges a very small quantity of water through the water sprayer valve F. This water passes into the vaporiser and combustion chamber, together with a little air, which enters by the automatic inlet valve, which serves as sprayer. This contrivance is found useful to prevent the vaporizer from overheating at heavy

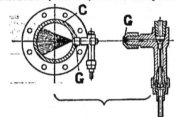

FIG. 15.—Crossley Oil Engine.

loads. The principal difference between this engine and the Hornsby engine already described lies in the use of the separate ignition tube H and in the water sprayer F, which acts as a snifting valve, taking in a little air and water when the engine becomes hot. Messrs Crossley inform the writer that the consumption of either crude or refined oil is about ·63 of a pint per horse-power on full load. They also give a test of a small engine developing 7 B.H.P., which consumed ·601 pint per B.H.P. per hour of Rock Light refined lamp oil and only ·603 pint per B.H.P. per hour of crude Borneo petroleum oil.

Engines in which the oil is vaporized in a device external to the cylinder have almost disappeared, because of the great success of the Hornsby-Ackroyd type, where oil is injected into, and vaporized within, the cylinder. It has been found, however, that many petrol engines having jet carburettors will operate with the heavier oils if the jet carburettor is suitably heated by means of the exhaust gases. In some engines it is customary to start with petrol, and then when the parts have become sufficiently heated to substitute paraffin or heavy petroleum oil, putting the heavy oil through the same spraying process as the petrol and evaporating the spray by hot walls before entering the cylinder.

Mr Diesel has produced a very interesting engine which departs considerably from other types. In it air alone is drawn into the cylinder on the charging stroke; the air is compressed on the return stroke to a very high pressure generally to over 400 ℔ per sq. in. This compression raises the air to incandescence, and then heavy oil is injected into the incandescent air by a small portion of air compressed to a still higher point. The oil ignites at once as it enters the combustion space, and so a power impulse is obtained, but without explosion. The pressure does not rise above the pressure of air and oil injection. The Diesel engine thus embodies two very original features; it operates at compression pressures very much higher than those used in any other internal combustion engines, and it dispenses with the usual igniting devices by rendering the air charge incandescent by compression. The engine operates generally on the Otto cycle, but it is also built giving an impulse at every revolution. Mr Diesel has shown great determination and perseverance, and the engine has now attained a position of considerable commercial importance. It is made on the continent, in England and in America in sizes up to 1000 H.P., and it has been applied to many purposes on land and also to the propulsion of small vessels. The engine gives a very high thermal efficiency. The present writer has calculated the following values from a test of a 500 B.H.P. Diesel oil engine made by Mr Michael Longridge, M.Inst.C.E. The engine had three cylinders, each of 22·05 in. diameter and stroke 29·52 in., each cylinder operating on the "Otto" cycle. The main results were as follows:—

Indicated power	.	.	.	.	595 horse
Brake power	.	.	.	.	459 "
Mechanical efficiency	.	.	.	.	77 %
Indicated thermal efficiency	.	.	.	.	41 %
Brake thermal efficiency	.	.	.	.	31·7 %

(D. C.)

OILLETS (from an O. Fr. diminutive of œil, eye, in Mod. Fr. œillet; other English variants are oylets, eyelets, or eyelet-holes), the architectural term given to the arrow slits in the walls of medieval fortifications, but more strictly applied to the round

hole or circle with which the openings terminate. The same term is applied to the small circles inserted in the tracery-head of the windows of the Decorated and Perpendicular periods, sometimes varied with trefoils and quatrefoils.

OILS (adopted from the Fr. oile, mod. huile, Lat. oleum, olive oil), the generic expression for substances belonging to extensive series of bodies of diverse chemical character, all of which have the common physical property of being fluid either at the ordinary temperature or at temperatures below the boiling-point of water. Formerly, when substances were principally classified by obvious characteristics, the word included such a body as " oil of vitriol " (sulphuric acid), which has of course nothing in common with what is now understood under the term oils. In its most comprehensive ordinary acceptation the word embraces at present the fluid fixed oils or fatty oils (e.g. olive oil), the soft fats which may be fluid in their country of origin (e.g. coco-nut oil, palm oil), the hard fats (e.g. tallow), the still harder vegetable and animal waxes (e.g. carnaúba wax, beeswax), the odoriferous ethereal (essential) oils, and the fluid and solid volatile hydrocarbons—mineral hydrocarbons—found in nature or obtained from natural products by destructive distillation.

The common characteristic of all these substances is that they consist principally, in some cases exclusively, of carbon and hydrogen. They are all readily inflammable and are practically insoluble in water. The mineral hydrocarbons found in nature or obtained by destructive distillation do not come within the range of this article (see NAPHTHA, PARAFFIN, PETROLEUM), which is restricted to the following two large groups of bodies, formed naturally within the vegetable and animal organisms, viz. (1) Fixed oils, fats and waxes, and (2) Essential, ethereal or volatile oils.

1. Fixed Oils, Fats and Waxes.

The substances to be considered under this head divide themselves naturally into two large classes, viz. fatty (fixed) oils and fats on the one hand, and waxes on the other, the distinction between the two classes being based on a most important chemical difference. The fixed oils and fats consist essentially of glycerides, i.e. esters formed by the union of three molecules of fatty acids with one molecule of the trihydric alcohol glycerin (q.v.), whereas the waxes consist of esters formed by the union of one molecule of fatty acid with one molecule of a monohydric alcohol, such as cetyl alcohol, cholesterol, &c. Only in the case of the wax coccerin two molecules of fatty acids are combined with one molecule of a dihydric (bivalent) alcohol. It must be pointed out that in common parlance this distinction does not find its ready expression. Thus Japan wax is a glyceride and should be more correctly termed Japan tallow, whereas sperm oil is, chemically speaking, a wax. Although these two classes of substances have a number of physical properties in common, they must be considered under separate heads. The true chemical constitution of oils and fats was first expounded by the classical researches of Chevreul, embodied in his work, Recherches sur les corps gras d'origine animale (1823, reprinted 1889).

(a) Fatty (fixed) Oils and Fats.—The fatty (fixed) oils and fats form a well-defined and homogeneous group of substances, passing through all gradations of consistency, from oils which are fluid even below the freezing-point of water, up to the hardest fats which melt at about 50° C. Therefore, no sharp distinction can be made between fatty oils and fats. Nevertheless, it is convenient to apply the term " oil " to those glycerides which are fluid below about 20° C., and the term " fat " to those which are solid above this temperature.

Chemical Composition.—No oil or fat is found in nature consisting of a single chemical individual, i.e. a fat consisting of the glyceride of one fatty acid only, such as stearin or tristearin, $C_3H_5(O \cdot C_{18}H_{35}O)_3$, the glycerin ester of stearic acid, $C_{17}H_{35} \cdot CO_2H$. The natural oils and fats are mixtures of at least two or three different triglycerides, the most important of which are tristearin, tripalmitin, $C_3H_5(O \cdot C_{16}H_{31}O)_3$ and triolein, C_3H_5 $(O \cdot C_{18}H_{33}O)_3$. These three glycerides have been usually considered the chief constituents of most oils and fats, but latterly there have been recognized as widely distributed trilinolin, the glyceride of linolic acid, and trillinolenin, the glyceride of linolenic acid. The two last-named glycerides are characteristic of the semi-drying and drying oils respectively. In addition to the fatty acids mentioned already there occur also, although in much smaller quantities, other fatty acids combined with glycerin, as natural glycerides, such as the glyceride of butyric acid in butter-fat, of caproic, caprylic and capric acids in butter-fat and in coco-nut oil, lauric acid in coco-nut and palm-nut oils, and myristic acid in mace butter. These glycerides are, therefore, characteristic of the oils and fats named.

In the classified list below the most important fatty acids occurring in oils and fats are enumerated (cf. *Waxes*, below).

Oils and fats must, therefore, not be looked upon as definite chemical individuals, but as representatives of natural species which vary, although within certain narrow limits, according to the climate and soil in which the plants which produce them are grown, or, in the case of animal fats, according to the climate, the race, the age of the animal, and especially the food, and also the idiosyncrasy of the individual animal. The oils and fats are distributed throughout the animal and vegetable kingdom from the lowest organism up to the most highly organized forms of animal and vegetable life, and are found in almost all tissues and organs. The vegetable oils and fats occur chiefly in the seeds, where they are stored to nourish the embryo, whereas in animals the oils and fats are enclosed mainly in the cellular tissues of the intestines and of the back.

		Boiling-point.		Melting-point. °C.	Characteristic of
		mm. Pressure.	°C.		
I. Acids of the Acetic series $C_nH_{2n}O_2$—					
Acetic acid	$C_2H_4O_2$	760	119	17	Spindle-tree oil, Macassar oil
Butyric acid	$C_4H_8O_2$	760	162·3	−6·5	Butter fat, Macassar oil
Isovaleric acid	$C_5H_{10}O_2$	760	173·7	−51	Porpoise and dolphin oils
Caproic acid	$C_6H_{12}O_2$	770	202–203	−8	
Caprylic acid	$C_8H_{16}O_2$	761	236–237	16·5	Butter fat, coco-nut oil,
Capric acid	$C_{10}H_{20}O_2$	760	268–270	31·3	palm nut oil
Lauric acid	$C_{12}H_{24}O_2$	100	225	43·6	Laurel oil, coco-nut oil
Myristic acid	$C_{14}H_{28}O_2$	100	250·5	53·8	Mace butter, nutmeg butter
Isocetic acid (?)	$C_{16}H_{32}O_2$	...	...	55	Purging nut
Palmitic acid	$C_{16}H_{32}O_2$	100	271·5	62–62	Palm oil, Japan wax, myrtle wax, lard, tallow, &c.
Stearic acid	$C_{18}H_{36}O_2$	100	291	69·32	Tallow, cacao butter, &c.
Arachidic acid	$C_{20}H_{40}O_2$	...	...	77·0	Arachis oil
Behenic acid	$C_{22}H_{44}O_2$	...	...	83–84	Ben oil
Lignoceric acid	$C_{24}H_{48}O_2$	...	...	80·5	Arachis oil
II. Acids of the Acrylic or Oleic series $C_nH_{2n-2}O_2$—					
Tiglic acid	$C_5H_8O_2$	760	198·5	64·5	Croton oil
Hypogaeic acid	$C_{16}H_{30}O_2$	15	236	33–34	Arachis oil
Physetoleic acid	$C_{16}H_{30}O_2$	...	...	30	Caspian seal oil
Oleic acid	$C_{18}H_{34}O_2$	100	285·5–286	14	Most oils and fats
Rapic acid	$C_{18}H_{34}O_2$	...	...	...	Rape oils
Erucic acid	$C_{22}H_{42}O_2$	30	281	33–34	Rape oils, fish oils
III. Acids of the Linolic series $C_nH_{2n-4}O_2$—					
Linolic acid	$C_{16}H_{28}O_2$	...	...	...	Maize oil, cotton-seed oil
Taririic acid	$C_{18}H_{32}O_2$	...	...	50·5	Oil of *Picramnia Camboita*
Telfairic acid	$C_{18}H_{32}O_2$	13	220–225	...	Koëme oil
Elaeomargaric acid	$C_{18}H_{32}O_2$	...	...	48	Tung oil
IV. Acids of the cyclic Chaulmoogric series $C_nH_{2n-4}O_2$—					
Hydnocarpic acid	$C_{16}H_{28}O_2$	...	...	59–60	Hydnocarpus, Lukrabo and
Chaulmoogric acid	$C_{18}H_{32}O_2$	20	247–248	68	Chaulmoogra oils
V. Acids of the Linolenic series $C_nH_{2n-6}O_2$—					
Linolenic acid	$C_{18}H_{30}O_2$	...	...	...	Linseed oil
Isolinolenic acid	$C_{18}H_{30}O_2$	...	...	...	
VI. Acids of the series $C_nH_{2n-8}O_2$—					
Clupanodonic acid	$C_{18}H_{28}O_2$	...	...	(liquid)	Fish, liver and blubber oils
VII. Acids of the Ricinoleic series $C_nH_{2n-2}O_3$—					
Ricinoleic acid	$C_{18}H_{34}O_3$	15	150	4–5	Castor oil
Quince oil acid	$C_{18}H_{34}O_3$	...	...	...	Quince oil
VIII. Dihydroxylated acids of the series $C_nH_{2n}O_4$—					
Dihydroxystearic acid	$C_{18}H_{36}O_4$	...	...	141–143	Castor oil
IX. Acids of the series $C_nH_{2n-2}O_4$—					
Japanic acid	$C_{21}H_{40}O_4$	...	...	117·7–117·9	Japan wax

Up to recently the oils and fats were looked upon as consisting in the main of a mixture of triglycerides, in which the three combined fatty acids are identical, as is the case in the above-named glycerides. Such glycerides are termed " simple glycerides." Recently, however, glycerides have been found in which the glycerin is combined with two and even three different acid radicals; examples of such glycerides are dis-tearo-olein, $C_3H_5(O·C_{18}H_{35}O)_2·(O·C_{18}H_{33}O)$, and stearo-palmito-olein, $C_3H_5(O·C_{18}H_{35}O)·(O·C_{16}H_{31}O)·(O·C_{18}H_{33}O)$. Such glycerides are termed " mixed glycerides." The glycerides occurring in natural oils and fats differ, therefore, in the first instance by the different fatty acids contained in them, and secondly, even if they do contain the same fatty acids, by different proportions of the several simple and mixed glycerides.

Since the methods of preparing the vegetable and animal fats are comparatively crude ones, they usually contain certain impurities of one kind or another, such as colouring and mucilaginous matter, remnants of vegetable and animal tissues, &c. For the most part these foreign substances can be removed by processes of refining, but even after this purification they still retain small quantities of foreign substances, such as traces of colouring matters, albuminoid and (or) resinous substances, and other foreign substances, which remain dissolved in the oils and fats, and can only be isolated after saponification of the fat. These foreign substances are comprised in the term " unsaponifiable matter." The most important constituents of the " unsaponifiable matter " are phytosterol $C_{26}H_{44}O$ or $C_{27}H_{46}O(?)$, and the isomeric cholesterol. The former occurs in all oils and fats of vegetable origin; the latter is characteristic of all oils and fats of animal origin. This important difference furnishes a method of distinguishing between vegetable oils and fats from animal oils and fats. This distinction will be made use of in the classification of the oils and fats. A second guiding principle is afforded by the different amounts of iodine (see *Oil Testing* below) the various oils and fats are capable of absorbing. Since this capacity runs parallel with one of the best-known properties of oils and fats, viz. the power of absorbing larger or smaller quantities of oxygen on exposure to the air, we arrive at the following classification:—

I. FATTY OILS OR LIQUID FATS

A. *Vegetable oils.*	B. *Animal oils.*
1. Drying oils.	1. Marine animal oils.
2. Semi-drying oils.	(a) Fish oils.
3. Non-drying oils.	(b) Liver oils
	(c) Blubber oils.
	2. Terrestrial animal oils.

II. SOLID FATS

A. *Vegetable fats.*	B. *Animal fats.*
	1. Drying fats.
	2. Semi-drying fats.
	3. Non-drying fats.

Physical Properties.—The specific gravities of oils and fats vary between the limits of 0·910 and 0·975. The lowest specific gravity is owned by the oils belonging to the rape oil group—from 0·913 to 0·916. The specific gravities of most non-drying oils lie between 0·916 and 0·920, and of most semi-drying oils between 0·920 and 0·925, whereas the drying oils have specific gravities of about 0·930. The animal and vegetable fats possess somewhat higher specific gravities, up to 0·930. The high specific gravity, 0·970, is owned by castor oil and cacao butter, and the highest specific gravity observed hitherto, 0·975, by Japan wax and myrtle wax.

In their liquid state oils and fats easily penetrate into the pores of dry substances; on paper they leave a translucent spot—'grease spot'—which cannot be removed by washing with water and subsequent drying. A curious fact, which may be used for the detection of the minutest quantity of oils and fats, is that camphor crushed between layers of paper without having been touched with the fingers rotates when thrown on clean water, the rotation ceasing immediately when a trace of oil or fat is added such as introduced by touching the water with a needle which has been passed previously through the hair.

The oils and fats are practically insoluble in water. With the exception of castor oil they are insoluble in cold alcohol; in boiling alcohol somewhat larger quantities dissolve. They are completely soluble in ether, carbon bisulphide, chloroform, carbon tetrachloride, petroleum ether, and benzene. Oils and fats have no distinct melting or solidifying point. This is not only due to the fact that they are mixtures of several glycerides, but also that even pure glycerides, such as tristearin, exhibit two melting-points, a so-called "double melting-point," the triglycerides melting at a certain temperature, then solidifying at a higher temperature to melt again on further heating. This curious behaviour was looked upon by Duffy as being due to the existence of two isomeric modifications, the actual occurrence of which has been proved (1907) in the case of several mixed glycerides.

The freezing-points of those oils which are fluid at the ordinary temperature range from a few degrees above zero down to –28° C (linseed oil). At low temperatures solid portions—usually termed "stearine"—separate out from many oils; in the case of cotton-seed oil the separation takes place at 12° C. These solid portions can be filtered off, and thus are obtained the commercial "demargarinated oils," or "winter oils."

Oils and fats can be heated to a temperature of 200° to 250° C. without undergoing any material change, provided prolonged contact with air is avoided. On being heated above 250° up to 300° some oils, like linseed oil, safflower oil, tung oil (Chinese or Japanese wood oil) and even castor oil, undergo a change which is most likely due to polymerization. In the case of castor oil solid products are formed. Above 300° C. all oils and fats are decomposed; this is evidenced by the evolution of acrolein, which possesses the well-known pungent odour of burning fat. At the same time hydrocarbons are formed (see PETROLEUM).

On exposure to the atmosphere, oils and fats gradually undergo certain changes. The *drying* oils absorb oxygen somewhat rapidly and dry to a film or skin, especially if exposed in a thin layer. Extensive use of this property is made in the paint and varnish trades. The *semi-drying* oils absorb oxygen more slowly than the drying oils, and are, therefore, useless as paint oils. Still, in course of time, they absorb oxygen distinctly enough to become thickened. The property of the semi-drying

oils to absorb oxygen is accelerated by spreading such oils over a large surface, notably over woollen or cotton fibres, when absorption proceeds so rapidly that frequently spontaneous combustion will ensue. Many fires in cotton and woollen mills have been caused thereby. The *non-drying* oils, the type of, which is olive oil, do not become oxidized readily on exposure to the air, although gradually a change takes place, the oils thickening slightly and acquiring that peculiar disagreeable smell and acrid taste, which are defined by the term "rancid." The changes conditioning rancidity, although not yet fully understood in all details, must be ascribed in the first instance to slow hydrolysis ("saponification") of the oils and fats by the moisture of the air, especially if favoured by insolation, when water is taken up by the oils and fats, and free fatty acids are formed. The fatty acids so set free are then more readily attacked by the oxygen of the air, and oxygenated products are formed, which impart to the oils and fats the rancid smell and taste. The products of oxidation are not yet fully known; most likely they consist of lower fatty acids, such as formic and acetic acids, and perhaps also of aldehydes and ketones. If the fats and oils are well protected from air and light, they can be kept indefinitely. In fact C. Friedel has found unchanged triglycerides in the fat which had been buried several thousand years ago in the tombs of Abydos. If the action of air and moisture is allowed free play, the hydrolysis of the oils and fats may become so complete that only the insoluble fatty acids remain behind, the glycerin being washed away. This is exemplified by adipocere, and also by Irish bog butter, which consist chiefly of free fatty acids.

The property of oils and fats of being readily hydrolysed is a most important one, and very extensive use of it is made in the arts (soap-making, candle-making and recovery of their by-products). If oils and ats are treated with water alone under high pressure (corresponding to a temperature of about 220° C.), or in the presence of water with caustic alkalis or alkaline earths or basic metallic oxides (which bodies act as "catalysers") at lower pressures, they are converted in the first instance into free fatty acids and glycerin. If an amount of the bases sufficient to combine subsequently with the fatty acids be present, then the corresponding salts of these fatty acids are formed, such as sodium salts of fatty acids (hard soap) or potassium salts of the fatty acids (soft soap), soaps of the alkaline earth (lime soap), or soaps of the metallic oxides (zinc soap, &c.). The conversion of the glycerides (triglycerides) into fatty acids and glycerin must be looked upon as a reaction which takes place in stages, one molecule of a triglyceride being converted first into diglyceride and one molecule of fatty acid, the diglyceride then being changed into monoglyceride, and a second molecule of fatty acid, and finally the monoglyceride being converted into one molecule of fatty acid and glycerin. All these reactions take place concurrently, so that one molecule of a diglyceride may still retain its ephemeral existence, whilst another molecule is already broken up completely into free fatty acids and glycerin.

The oils and fats used in the industries are not drawn from any very great number of sources. The tables on the following pages contain chiefly the most important oils and fats together with their sources, yields and principal uses, arranged according to the above classification, and according to the magnitude of the iodine value. It should be added that many other oils and fats are only waiting improved conditions of transport to enter into successful competition with some of those that are already on the market.

Extraction.—Since the oils and fats have always served the human race as one of the most important articles of food, the oil and fat industry may well be considered to be as old as the human race itself. The methods of preparing oils and fats range themselves under three heads: (1) Extraction of oil by "rendering," *i.e.* boiling out with water; (2) Extraction of oil by expression; (3) Extraction of oil by means of solvents.

Rendering.—The crudest method of rendering oils from seeds, still practised in Central Africa, in Indo-China and on some of the South Sea Islands, consists in heaping up oleaginous fruits and allowing them to melt by the heat of the sun, when the exuding oil runs off and is collected. In a somewhat improved form this process of rendering is practised in the preparation of palm oil, and the rendering the best (Cochin) coco-nut oil by boiling the fresh kernels with water. Since hardly any machinery, or only the simplest machinery, is required for these processes, this method has some fascination for inventors, and even at the present day processes are being patented, having for their object the boiling out of fruits with water or salt solutions, so as to facilitate the separation of the oil from the pulp by gravitation. Naturally these processes can only be applied to those seeds which contain large quantities of fatty matter, such as coco-nuts and olives. The rendering process is, however, applied on a very large scale to the production of animal oils and fats. Formerly the animal oils and fats were obtained by heating the tissues con-taining the oils or fats over a free fire, when the cell membranes burst and the liquid fat flowed out. The cave-dweller who first collected the fat dripping off the deer on the roasting spit may well be looked upon as the first manufacturer of tallow. This crude process is now classed amongst the noxious trades, owing to the offensive stench given off, and must be considered as almost extinct in this country. Even on whaling vessels, where up to recently whale oil, seal oil and sperm oil (see *Waxes*, below) were obtained exclusively by "trying," *i.e.* by melting the blubber over a free fire, the process of rendering is fast becoming obsolete, the modern prac-tice being to deliver the blubber in as fresh a state as possible to the "whaling establishments," where the oil is rendered by methods closely resembling those worked in the enormous rendering establish-ments (for tallow, lard, bone fat) in the United States and in South America. The method consists essentially in cutting up the fatty matter into small fragments, which are transferred into vessels containing water, wherein the comminuted mass is heated by steam, either under ordinary pressure in open vessels or under higher pressure in digestors. The fat gradually exudes and collects on the top of the water, whilst the membranous matter, "greaves," falls to the bottom. The fat is then drawn off the aqueous (gluey) layer, and strained through sieves or filters. The greaves are placed

VEGETABLE OILS

Name of Oil.	Source.	Yield per cent.	Iodine Value.	Principal Use.
	Drying Oils.			
Linseed	*Linum usitatissimum*	38–40	175–205	Paint, varnish, linoleum, soap
Tung (Chinese or Japanese wood)	*Aleurites cordata*	40–41	150–165	Paint and varnish
Candle nut	*Aleurites moluccana*	62–64	163	Burning oil, soap, paint
Hemp seed	*Cannabis sativa*	30–35	148	Paints and varnishes, soft soap
Walnut; Nut	*Juglans regia*	63–65	145	Oil painting
Safflower	*Carthamus tinctorius*	30–32	130–147	Burning, varnish (" roghan ")
Poppy seed	*Papaver somniferum*	41–50	123–143	Salad oil, painting, soft soap
Sunflower	*Helianthus annuus*	21–22	119–135	Edible oil, soap
Madia	*Madia sativa*	32–33	118·5	Soap, burning
	Semi-drying Oils.			
Cameline (German *Sesamé*)	*Camelina sativa*	31–34	135	Burning, soap
Soja bean	*Soja hispida*	..	122	Edible, burning
Maize; Corn	*Zea Mays*	6–10	113–125	Edible, soap
Beech nut	*Fagus sylvatica*	43–45	111–120	Food, burning
Kapok	*Bombax pentandrum (Eriodendron anfractuosum)*	30–32	116	Food, soap
Cotton-seed	*Gossypium herbaceum*	24–26	108–110	Food, soap
Sesamé	*Sesamum orientale, S. indicum*	50–57	103–108	Food, soap
Curcas, purging nut	*Jatropha curcas*	55–57	98–112	Medicine, soap
Brazil nut	*Bertholletia excelsa*	..	90–106	Edible, soap
Croton	*Croton Tiglium*	..	102–104	Medicine
Ravison	*Wild Brassica campestris*	53–56	105–117	Lubricant, burning
Rape (Colza)	*Brassica campestris*	33–40	94–102	Lubricant, burning
Jamba	*Brassica campestris var.?*	33–43	95	Burning, lubricant
		24		
	Non-drying Oils.			
Apricot kernel	*Prunus armeniaca*	40–45	96–108	Perfumery, medicine
Peach kernel	*Prunus persica*	32–35	93–100	Perfumery, medicine
Almond	*Prunus amygdalus*	45–55	93–100	Perfumery, medicine
Arachis (ground nut)	*Arachis hypogaea*	43–45	83–100	Edible, soap
Hazel nut	*Corylus avellana*	50–60	83–90	Edible, perfumery, lubricating
Olive	*Olea europaea*	40–60	79–88	Edible, lubricating, burning, soap
Olive kernel	*Olea europaea*	·12–15	87	Edible, lubricating, burning, soap
Ben	*Moringa oleifera*	35–36	82	Edible, perfumery, lubricating
Grape seed	*Vitis vinifera*	10–20	96	Food, burning
Castor	*Ricinus communis*	46–53	83–86	Medicine, soap, lubricating, Turkey red oil

ANIMAL OILS

Name of Oil.	Source.	Yield per cent.	Iodine Value.	Principal Use.
	Marine Animal Oils.			
Fish oils—				
Menhaden	*Alosa menhaden*	..	140–173	Currying leather
Sardine oil	*Clupea sardinus*	..	161–193	Currying leather
Salmon	*Salmo salar*	..	161	Currying leather
Herring	*Clupea harengus*	..	124–142	Currying leather
Liver oils—				
Cod liver	*Gadus morrhua*	..	167	Medicine, currying leather
Shark liver (Arctic)	*Scymnus borealis*	..	115	Currying leather
Blubber oils—				
Seal	*Phoca vitulina*	..	127–147	Burning, currying leather
Whale	*Balaena mysticetus, &c.*	..	121–136	Burning, soap-making, fibre dressing, currying leather
Dolphin, black fish, body oil	*Delphinus globiceps*	..	99–126	Lubricating oil for delicate machinery
Jaw oil		..	33	
Porpoise Body oil	*Delphinus phocaena*	..	119	
Porpoise Jaw oil		..	36	
	Terrestrial Animal Oils.			
Sheep's foot	*Ovis aries*.	..	74	Lubricating
Horses' foot	*Equus caballus*	..	74–90	Lubricating
Neat's foot	*Bos taurus*	..	67–73	Lubricating, leather dressing
Egg	*Gallus domesticus*	..	68–82	Leather dressing

VEGETABLE FATS

Name of Fat.	Source.	Yield per cent.	Iodine Value.	Principal Use.
Laurel oil	Laurus nobilis	24-26	68-80	Medicine
Mahua butter, Illipé butter	Bassia latifolia	50-55	53-67	Food, soap, candles
Mowrah butter	Bassia longifolia	50-55	50-62	Food, soap, candles
Shea butter (Galam butter)	Bassia Parkii	49-52	56	Food, soap, candles
Palm oil	Elaeis guineensis, E. melanococca	65-72	53	Candles, soap
Mace butter	Myristica officinalis	38-40	40-52	Medicine, perfumery
Ghee butter (Phulwara butter)	Bassia butyracea	50-52	42	Food
Cacao butter	Theobroma cacao	44-50	32-41	Chocolate
Chinese vegetable tallow	Stillingia sebifera (Croton sebiferum)	22	28-32	Soap, candles
Kokum butter (Goa butter)	Garcinia indica	49	33	Food
Borneo tallow	Shorea stenoptera, Hopea aspera	45-50	15-31	Food, candles
Mocaya oil	Cocos sclerocarpa	60-70	24	Food, soap
Maripa fat	Palma (?) Maripa	..	17	Food, soap
Palm kernel oil } Palm nut oil }	Elaeis guineensis, } E. melanococca	45-50	13-14	Food, soap
Coco-nut oil	Cocos nucifera, C. butyracea	20-25	8-9	Food, soap, candles
Japan wax	Rhus succedanea, R. vernicifera	25	4-10	Polishes
Dika oil (oba oil, wild mango oil)	Irvingia gabonensis	60-65	5-2	Food
Myrtle wax	Myrica cerifera, M. carolinensis	20-25	2-4	Soap, candles (?)

ANIMAL FATS

Name of Fat.	Source.	Yield per cent.	Iodine Value.	Principal Use.
	Drying Fats.			
Ice bear	Ursus maritimus	..	147	Pharmacy
Rattlesnake	Crotalus durissus	..	106	Pharmacy
	Semi-drying Fats.			
Horses' fat	Equus caballus	..	75-85	Food, soap
	Non-drying Fats.			
Goose fat	Anser cinereus	..	70	Food, pomades
Lard	Sus scrofa	..	50-70	Food, soap, candles
Beef marrow	Bos taurus	..	85	Pomades
Bone	Bos, Ovis	..	46-56	Soap, candles
Tallow, beef	Bos taurus	..	38-46	Food, soap, candles, lubricants
Tallow, mutton	Ovis aries	..	35-46	Food, soap, candles, lubricants
Butter	Bos taurus	..	26-38	Food

In hair or woollen bags and submitted to hydraulic pressure, by which a further portion of oil or fat is obtained (cf. *Pressing*, below). In the case of those animal fats which are intended for edible purposes, such as lard, suet for margarine, the greatest cleanliness must, of course, be observed, and the temperature must be kept as low as possible in order to obtain a perfectly sweet and pure material.

Pressing.—The boiling out process cannot be applied to small seeds, such as linseed and rape seed. Whilst the original method of obtaining seed oils may perhaps have been the same which is still used in India, viz. trituration of (rape) seeds in a mortar so that the oil can exude, it may be safely assumed that the process of expressing has been applied in the first instance to the preparation of olive oil. The first woman who expressed olives packed in a sack by heaping stones on them may be considered as the forerunner of the inventors of all the presses that subsequently came into use. Pliny describes in detail the apparatus and processes for obtaining olive oil in vogue among his Roman contemporaries, who used already a simple screw press, a knowledge of which they had derived from the Greeks. In the East, where vegetable oils form an important article of food and serve also for other domestic purposes, various ingenious applications of lever presses and wedge presses, and even of combined lever and wedge presses, have been used from the remotest time. At an early stage of history the Chinese employed the same series of operations which are followed in the most advanced oil mills of modern time, viz. bruising and reducing the seeds to meal under an edge-stone, heating the meal in an open pan, and pressing out the oil in a wedge press in which the wedges were driven home by hammers. This primitive process is still being carried out in Manchuria, in the production of soja bean cake and soja bean oil, one of the staple industries of that country. The olive press, which was also used in the vineyards for expressing the grape juice, found its way from the south of France to the north, and was employed there for expressing poppy seed and rape seed. The apparatus was then gradually improved, and thus were evolved the modern forms of the screw press, next the Dutch or stamper press, and finally the hydraulic press. With the screw press, even in its most improved form, the amount of pressure practically obtainable is limited from the failure of its parts under the severe inelastic strain. Hence this kind of press finds only limited application, as in the industry of olive oil for expressing the best and finest virgin oil, and in the production of animal fats for edible purposes, such as lard and oleomargarine. The Dutch or stamper press, invented in Holland in the 17th century, was up to the early years of the 19th century almost exclusively employed in Europe for pressing oil-seeds. It consists of two principal parts, an oblong rectangular box with an arrangement of plates, blocks and wedges, and over it a framework with heavy stampers which produce the pressure by their fall. The press box first consisted of strongly bound oaken planks, but later on cast-iron boxes were introduced. At each extremity of the box a bag of oil-meal was placed between two perforated iron plates, next to which were inserted filling-up pieces of wood, two of which were oblique, so that the wedges which exercised the pressure could be readily driven home. This press has had to yield place to the hydraulic press, although in some old-fashioned establishments in Holland the stamper press could still be seen at work in the 'eighties of the 19th century. The invention of the hydraulic press in 1795 by Joseph Bramah (Eng. pat., 30th April 1795) effected the greatest revolution in the oil industry, bringing a new, easily controlled and almost unlimited source of power into play; the limit of the power being solely reached by the limit of the strength of the material which the engineer is able to produce. Since then the hydraulic press has practically completely superseded all other appliances used for expression, and in consequence of this epoch-making invention, assisted as it was later on by the accumulator—invented by William George (later Lord) Armstrong in 1843—the seed-crushing industry reached a perfection of mechanical detail which soon secured its supremacy for England.

The sequence of operations in treating oil seeds, oil nuts, &c., for the separation of their contained oils is at the present time as follows: As a preliminary operation the oil seeds and nuts are freed from dust, sand and other impurities by sifting in an inclined revolving cylinder or sieving machine, covered with woven wire, having meshes varying according to the size and nature of the seed operated upon. This preliminary purification is of the greatest importance, especially for the preparation of edible oils and fats. In the case of those seeds amongst which are found pieces of iron (hammer beads amongst palm kernels, &c.), the seeds are passed over magnetic separators, which retain the pieces of iron. The seeds and nuts are then decorticated (where required), the shells removed, and the kernels ("meats") converted into a pulpy mass or meal (in older establishments by crushing and grinding between stones in edge-runners) on passing through a hopper over rollers consisting of five chilled iron or steel cylinders mounted vertically like the bowls of a calendar. These rollers are finely grooved so that the seed is cut up whilst passing in succession between the first and second rollers in the series, then between the second and the third, and so on to the last, when the grains are sufficiently bruised, crushed and ground. The distance between the rollers can be easily regulated so that the seed leaving the bottom roller has the desired fineness. The comminuted mass, forming a more or less coarse meal, is either expressed in this state or subjected to a preliminary heating, according to the quality of the product to be manufactured. For the preparation of *edible* oils and fats the meal is expressed in the cold, after having been packed into bags and placed in hydraulic presses under a pressure of three hundred atmospheres or even more. The cakes are allowed to remain under pressure for about seven minutes. The oil exuding in the cold dissolves the smallest amount of colouring matter, &c., and hence has suffered least in its quality. Oils so obtained are known in commerce as "cold drawn oils," " cold pressed oils," " salad oils," " virgin oils."

By pressing in the cold, obviously only part of the oil or fat is recovered. A further quantity is obtained by expressing the seed meal at a somewhat elevated temperature, reached by warming the comminuted seeds or fruits either immediately after they leave the five-roller mill, or after the "cold drawn oil" has been taken off. Of course the cold pressed cakes must be first disintegrated, which may be done under an edge-runner. The same operation may be repeated once more. Thus oils of the "second expression" and of the "third expression" are obtained.

In the case of oleaginous seeds of low value (cotton-seed, linseed) it is of importance to express in one operation the largest possible quantity of oil. Hence the bruised seed is, after leaving the five-roller mill, generally warmed at once in a steam-jacketed kettle fitted with a mixing gear, by passing steam into the jacket, and sending at the same time some steam through a rose, fixed inside the kettle, into the mass while it is being agitated. This practice is a survival of the older method of moistening the seed with a little water, while the seeds were bruised under edge-runners, so as to lower the temperature and facilitate the bursting of the cells. The warm meal is then delivered through measuring boxes into closed pressbags ("scourtins" of the "Marseilles" press), or through measuring boxes, combined with an automatic moulding machine, into cloths open at two sides (Anglo-American press), so that the preliminarily pressed cakes can be put at once into the hydraulic press. In the latest constructions of cage presses, the use of bags is entirely dispensed with, a measured-out quantity of seed falling direct into the circular press cage and being separated from the material forming the next cake by a circular plate of sheet iron. The essentials of proper oil pressing are a slowly accumulating pressure, so that the liberated oil may have time to flow out and escape, a pressure that increases in proportion as the resistance of the material increases, and that maintains itself as the volume of material decreases through the escape of oil.

Numerous forms of hydraulic presses have been devised. Horizontal presses have practically ceased to be used in this branch of industry. At present vertical presses are almost exclusively in vogue; the three chief types of these have been already mentioned. Continuously working presses (compression by a conical screw) have been patented, but hitherto they have not been found practicable. Of the vertical presses the Anglo-American type of press is most in use. It represents an open press fitted with a number (usually sixteen) of iron press plates, between which the cakes are inserted by hand. A hydraulic ram then forces the table carrying the cakes against a press-head, and the exuding oil flows down the sides into a tank below. The "Marseilles press" is largely used in the south of France. There the meal is packed by hand in "scourtins," bags made of plaited coco-nut leaves—replacing the woollen cloths used in England. The packing of the press requires more manual labour than in the case of the Anglo-American press; moreover, the Marseilles press offers inconvenience in keeping the bags straight, and the pressure cannot be raised to the same height as in the more modern hydraulic presses. Oil obtained from heated meal is usually more highly coloured and harsher to the taste than cold drawn oil, more of the extractive substances being dissolved and intermixed with the oil. Such oils are hardly suitable for edible purposes, and they are chiefly used for manufacturing processes. According to the care exercised by the manufacturer in the range of temperature to which the seed is heated, various grades of oils are obtained.

In the case of those seeds which contain more than 40% of oil, such as arachis nuts and sesame seed, the first expression in pressbags leads to difficulty, as the meal causes "spueing," i.e. the meal exudes and escapes from the press. Hence, in modern installations, the first expression of those seeds is carried out in so-called cage (clodding) presses, consisting of hydraulic presses provided with circular boxes or cages, into which the meal is filled. These cages or boxes are either constructed of metal staves held together by a number of steel rings, or consist of one cylinder having a large number of perforations. The presses having perforated cylinders, although presenting mechanically a more perfect arrangement, are not preferable to the press cages formed by staves, as the holes become easily clogged up by the meal, when the cylinder must be carefully cleaned out. Modern improvements, with a view to cheapening of cost, effect the transport of the cages from one press battery to another on rails. In order to dispense even with the charging of the presses by hand, in some systems the cages are first charged in a preliminary arrangement,

from which they are transferred mechanically by a swinging arrangement into the final press.

Whilst the meal is under pressure the oil works its way to the edge of the cake, whence it exudes. For this reason an oblong form is the most favourable one for the easy separation of the oil. The edges of the cakes invariably retain a considerable portion of oil; hence the soft edges are pared off, in the case of the oblong cake in a cake-paring machine, and the parings are returned to edge-runners, to be ground up and again pressed with fresh meal. Through the introduction of the cage (clodding) presses circular cakes have become fashionable, and as the material of these presses can be made much stronger and therefore higher pressure can be employed, more oil is expressed from the meal than in open presses. The oil flowing from the presses is caught in reservoirs placed under the level of the floor, from which it is pumped into storage tanks for settling and clarifying.

Extraction by Solvents.—The cakes obtained in the foregoing process still retain considerable proportions of oil, not less than 4 to 5%—usually, however, about 10%. If it be desired to obtain larger quantities than are yielded by the above-described methods, processes having for their object the extraction of the seeds by volatile solvents must be resorted to. Extraction by means of carbon bisulphide was first introduced in 1843 by Jesse Fisher of Birmingham. Thirteen years later E. Deiss of Brunswick again patented the extraction by means of carbon bisulphide (*Eng. Pat.* No. 390, 1856), and added "chloroform, ether, essences, or benzine or benzole" to the list of solvents. For several years afterwards the process made little advance, for the colour of the oils produced was higher and the taste much sharper. The oil retained traces of sulphur, which showed themselves disagreeably in the smell of soaps made from it, and in the blackening of substances with which it was used. Of course, the meal left by the process was so tainted with carbon bisulphide that it was absolutely out of the question to use the extracted meal as cattle food. With the improvement in the manufacture of carbon bisulphide, these drawbacks have been surmounted to a large extent, and the process of extracting with carbon bisulphide has especially gained much extension in the extraction of expressed olive marc in the south of France, in Italy and in Spain. Yet even now traces of carbon bisulphide are retained by the extracted meal, so that it is impossible to iced cattle with it. Carbon bisulphide is comparatively cheap, and it is heavier than water, hence there are certain advantages in storing so volatile and inflammable a liquid. But owing to the physiological effect carbon bisulphide has on the workmen, coupled with the chemical action of impure carbon bisulphide on iron which has frequently led to conflagrations, the employment of carbon bisulphide must remain restricted. In 1863 Richardson, Landy and Irvine secured a patent (*Eng. Pat.* No. 2315) for obtaining oil from crushed seeds, or from refuse cake, by the solvent action of volatile hydrocarbons from "petroleum, earth oils, asphaltum oil, coal oil or shale oil, such hydrocarbons being required to be volatile under 212° F." Since that time the development of the petroleum industry in all parts of the world and the large quantities of low boiling-point hydrocarbons—naphtha —obtained from the petroleum fields, and also the improvements in the apparatus employed, have raised this system of extraction to the rank of a competing practical method of oil production. Of the other proposed volatile solvents ordinary ether has found no practical application, as it is far too volatile and hence far too dangerous. Carbon tetrachloride, chloroform, acetone and benzene are far too expensive. Carbon tetrachloride would be an ideal solvent, as it is non-inflammable and shares with carbon bisulphide the advantage of being heavier than water. Efforts have been made during the last few years to introduce this solvent on a large scale, but its high price and its physiological effect on the workmen have hitherto militated against it. At the present time the choice lies practically only between the two solvents, carbon bisulphide and naphtha (petroleum ether). Naphtha is preferable for oil seeds, as it extracts neither resins nor gummy matters from the oil seeds, and takes up less colouring matter than carbon bisulphide. Yet even with naphtha traces of the solvents remain, so that the meal obtained cannot be used for cattle food, notwithstanding the many statements by interested parties to the contrary. It is true that on the continent extracted meal, especially rape meal from good Indian seed and palm kernel meal, are somewhat largely used as food for cattle in admixture with press cakes, but in England no extracted meal is used for feeding cattle, but finds its proper use in manuring the land.

The apparatus employed on a large scale depends on the temperature at which the extraction is carried out. In the main two types of extracting apparatus are differentiated, viz. for extraction in the cold and for extraction in the hot. The seed is prepared in a similar manner as for pressing, but it is not reduced to a fine meal, so as not to impede the percolation of the solvent through the mass. In the case of cold extraction the seed is placed in a series of closed vessels, through which the solvent percolates by displacement, on the "counter-current" system. A battery of vessels is so arranged that one vessel can always be made the last of the series to discharge finished meal and to be recharged with fresh meal, so that the process is practically a continuous one. The solution of the extracted oil or fat is then transferred to a steam-heated still, where the solvent is driven off and recovered by condensing the vapours in a cooling coil, to be used again. The last remnant of volatile solvent in the oil is driven off by a current of open steam blown through the oil in the warm state. The extracting process in the hot is carried out in apparatus, the principle of which is exemplified by the well-known Soxhlet extractor. The comminuted seed is placed inside a vessel connected with an upright refrigerator on trays or baskets, and is surrounded there by the volatile solvent. On heating the solvent with steam through a coil or jacket, the vapours rise through and around the meal. They pass into the refrigerator, where they are condensed and fall back as a condensed liquid through the meal, percolating it as they pass downwards, and reaching to the bottom of the vessel as a more or less saturated solution of oil in the solvent. The solvent is again evaporated, leaving the oil at the bottom of the vessel until the extraction is deemed finished. The solution of fat is then run off into a still, as described already, and the last traces of solvent are driven out. The solvent is recovered and used again.

With regard to the merits and demerits of the last two mentioned processes—expression and extraction—the adoption of either will largely depend on local conditions and the objects for which the products are intended. Wherever the cake is the main product, expression will commend itself as the most advantageous process. Where, however, the fatty material forms the main product, as in the case of palm kernel oil, or sesame and coco-nut oils from damaged seeds (which would no longer yield proper cattle food), the process of extraction will be preferred, especially when the price of oils is high. In some cases the combination of the two processes commends itself, as in the case of the production of olive oil. The fruits are expressed, and after the edible qualities and best class of oils for technical purposes have been taken off by expression, the remaining pulp is extracted by means of solvents. This process is known under the name of mixed process (*huilerie mixte*).

Refining and Bleaching.—The oils and fats prepared by any of the methods detailed above are in their fresh state, and, if got from perfectly fresh (" sweet ") material, practically neutral. If care is exercised in the process of rendering animal oils and fats or expressing oils in the cold, the products are, as a rule, sufficiently pure to be delivered to the consumer, after a preliminary settling has allowed any mucilaginous matter, such as animal or vegetable fibres or other impurities, and also traces of moisture, to separate out. This spontaneous clarification was at one time the only method in vogue. This process is now shortened by filtering oils through filter presses, or otherwise brightening them, *e.g.* by blowing with air. In many cases these methods still suffice for the production of commercial oils and fats.

In special cases; such as the preparation of edible oils and fats, a further improvement in colour and greater purity is obtained by filtering the oils over charcoal, or over natural absorbent earths, such as fuller's earth. Where this process does not suffice, as in the case of coco-nut oil or palm kernel oil, a preliminary purification in a current of steam must be resorted to before the final purification, described above, is carried out. Oils intended for use on the table which deposit " stearine " in winter must be freed from such solid fats. This is done by allowing the oil to cool down to a low temperature and pressing it through cloths in a press, when a limpid oil exudes, which remains proof against cold—" winter oil." Most olive oils are naturally non-congealing oils, whereas the Tunisian and Algerian olive oils deposit so much " stearine " that they must be " demarganarated." Similar methods are employed in the production of lard oil, edible cotton-seed oil, &c. For refining oils and fats intended for edible purposes only the foregoing methods, which may be summarized by the name of physical methods, can be used; the only chemicals permissible are alkalis or alkaline earths to remove free fatty acids present. Treatment with other chemicals renders the oils and fats unfit for consumption. Therefore all bleaching and refining processes involving other means than those enumerated can only be used for technical oils and fats, such as lubricating oils, burning oils, paint oils, soap-making oils, &c.

Bleaching by the aid of chemicals requires great circumspection. There is no universal method of oil-refining applicable to any and every oil or fat. Not only must each kind of oil or fat be considered as a special problem, but frequently even varieties of one and the same oil or fat are apt to cause the same difficulties as would a new individual. In many cases the purification by means of sulphuric acid, invented and patented

by Charles Gower in 1792 (frequently ascribed to Thénard), is still usefully applied. It consists in treating the oil with a small percentage of a more or less concentrated sulphuric acid, according to the nature of the oil or fat. The acid not only takes up water, but it acts on the suspended impurities, carbonizing them to some extent, and thus causing them to coagulate and fall down in the form of a flocculent mass, which carries with it mechanically other impurities which have not been acted upon. This method is chiefly used in the refining of linseed and rape oils. Purification by means of strong caustic soda was first recommended as a general process by Louis C. Arthur Barreswil, his suggestion being to beat the oil and add 2 % to 3 % of caustic soda. In most cases the purification consisted in removing the free fatty acids from rancid oils and fats, the caustic soda forming a soap with the fatty acids, which would either rise as a scum and lift up with it impurities, or fall to the bottom and carry down impurities. This process is a useful one in the case of cotton-seed oil. As a rule, however, it is a very precarious one, since emulsions are formed which prevent in many cases the separation of oil altogether. After the treatment with sulphuric acid or caustic soda, the oils must be washed to remove the last traces of chemicals. The water is then allowed to settle out, and the oils are finally filtered. The number of chemicals which have been proposed from time to time for the purification of oils and fats is almost legion, and so long as the nature of oils and fats was little understood, a secret trade in oil-purifying-chemicals flourished. With our present knowledge most of these chemicals may be removed into the limbo of useless things. The general methods of bleaching besides those mentioned already as physical methods, viz. filtration over charcoal or bleaching earth, are chiefly methods based on bleaching by means of oxygen or by chlorine. The methods of bleaching by oxygen include all those which aim at the bleaching by exposure to the air and to sunlight (as in the case of artists' linseed-oil), or where oxygen or ozone is introduced in the form of gas or is evolved by chemicals, as manganese dioxide, potassium bichromate or potassium permanganate and sulphuric acid. In the process of bleaching by means of chlorine either bleaching powder or bichromates and hydrochloric acid are used. It must again be emphasized that no general rule can be laid down as to which process should be employed in each given case. There is still a wide field open for the application of proper processes for the removal of impurities and colouring matters without running the risk of attacking the oil or fat itself.

Oil Testing.—Reliable scientific methods for testing oils and fats date back only to the end of the 'seventies of the 19th century. Before that time it was believed that not only could individual oils and fats be distinguished from each other by colour reactions, but it was also maintained that falsification could be detected thereby. With one or two exceptions (detection of sesame oil and perhaps also of cotton-seed oil) all colour reactions are entirely useless. The modern methods of oil testing rest chiefly on so-called " quantitative " reactions, a number of characteristic " values " being determined which, being based on the special nature of the fatty acids contained in each individual oil or fat, assist in identifying them and also in revealing adulteration. These " values," together with other useful methods, are enumerated in the order of their utility for the purposes of testing.

The *saponification value* (*saponification number*) denotes the number of milligrams which one gramme of an oil or fat requires for saponification, or, in other words, for the neutralization of the total fatty acids contained in an oil or fat. We thus measure the alkali absorption value of all fatty acids contained in an oil or fat. The saponification values of most oils and fats lie in the neighbourhood of 195. But the oils belonging to the rape oil group are characterized by considerably lower saponification values, viz. about 175 on account of their containing notable quantities of erucic acid, $C_{22}H_{42}O_2$. In the case of those oils which do not belong to the rape oils and yet show abnormally low saponification values, the suspicion is raised at once that a certain amount of mineral oils (which do not absorb

XX 2   3a alkali and are therefore termed " unsaponifiable ") has been admixed fraudulently. Their amount can be determined in a direct manner by exhausting the saponified mass, after dilution with water, with ether, evaporating the latter and weighing the amount of mineral oil left behind. A few of the blubber oils, like dolphin jaw and porpoise jaw oils (used for lubricating typewriting machines), have exceedingly high saponification values owing to their containing volatile fatty acids with a small number of carbon atoms. Notable also are coco-nut and palm-nut oils, the saponification numbers of which vary from 240 to 260, and especially butter-fat, which has a saponification value of about 227. These high saponification values are due to the presence of (glycerides of) volatile fatty acids, and are of extreme usefulness to the analyst, especially in testing butter-fat for added margarine and other fats. These volatile acids are specially measured by the *Reichert value (Reichert-Wollny value)*. To ascertain this value the volatile acids contained in 5 grammes of an oil or fat are distilled in a minutely prescribed manner, and the distilled-off acids are measured by titration with decinormal alkali. Whereas most of the oils and fats, viz. all those the saponification value of which lies at or below 195, contain practically no volatile acids,*i.e.* have extremely low Reichert-Wollny values, all those oils and fats having saponification values above 195 contain notable amounts of volatile fatty acids. Thus, the *Reichert-Meissl value* of butter-fat is 25-30, that of coco-nut oil 6-7, and of palm kernel oil about 5-6. This value is indispensable for judging the purity of a butter.

One of the most important values in oil testing is the *iodine value*. This indicates the percentage of iodine absorbed by an oil or fat when the latter is dissolved in chloroform or carbon tetrachloride, and treated with an accurately measured amount of free iodine supplied in the form of iodine chloride. By this means a measure is obtained of the unsaturated fatty acids contained in an oil or fat. On this value a scientific classification of all oils and fats can be based, as is shown by the above-given list of oils and fats. The unsaturated fatty acids which occur e, iefly in oils and fats are *oleic acid*, iodine value 90·07; *erucic acid*,iodine value 75·15; *linolic acid*, iodine value 181·42; *linolenic acid*, iodine value 274·1; and *clupanodonic acid*, iodine value 367·7. Oleic acid occurs in all non-drying oils and fats, and to some extent in the semi-drying oils and fats. Linolic acid is a characteristic constituent of all semi-drying, and to some extent of all drying oils. Linolenic acid characterises all vegetable drying oils; similarly clupanodonic acid characterises all marine animal oils.

If one individual oil or fat is given, the iodine value alone furnishes the readiest means of finding its place in the above system, and in many cases of identifying it. Even if a mixture of several oils and fats be present, the iodine value assists greatly in the identification of the components of the mixture, and furnishes the most important key for the attacking and resolving of this not very simple problem. Thus it points the way to the application of a further method to resolve the isolated fatty acids of an oil or fat into saturated fatty acids, which do not absorb iodine, and into unsaturated fatty acids, which absorb iodine in various proportions as shown above. This separation is effected by converting the alkali soaps of the fatty acids into lead soaps and treating the latter with ether, in which the lead salts of the saturated acids are insoluble, whereas the salts of the above-named unsaturated acids are soluble. The saturated fatty acids can then be further examined, and valuable information is gained by the determination of the melting-points and by treatment with solvents. Thus some individual fatty acids, such as stearic acid and arachidic acid (which is characteristic of ground nut oil) can be identified. In the mixture of unsaturated fatty acids, by means of some more refined methods, clupanodonic acid, linolenic acid, linolic acid and oleic acid can be recognized. By combining the various methods which have been outlined here, and by the help of some further additional special methods, and by reasoning in a strictly logical manner, it is possible to resolve a mixture of two oils and fats, and even of three and four, into their components and determine approximately their quantities. The methods sketched here do not yet exhaust the armoury of the analytical chemist, but it can only be pointed out in passing that the detection of hydroxylated acids enables the analyst to ascertain the presence of castor oil, just as the isolation and determination of oxidised fatty acids enables him to differentiate blown oils from other oils.

Tests such as the Maumené test, the elaïdin test and others, which formerly were the only resource of the chemist, have been practically superseded by the foregoing methods. The viscosity test, although of considerable importance in the examination of lubricating oils, has been shown to have very little discriminative value as a general test.

Commerce.—It may be safely said of the United Kingdom that it regards the foremost position in the world as regards the extent of the oil and fat industries. An estimate made by the writer (Cantor Lectures, " Oils and Fats, their Uses and Applications," *Society of Arts*, 1904, p. 795), and based on the most reliable information obtainable, led to the conclusion that the sums involved in the oil and fat trade exceeded £1,000,000 per week; in 1907 they approximated £1,250,000 per week. The great centres of the seed-oil trade (linseed, cotton-seed, rape-seed, castor-seed) are Hull, London, Liverpool, Bristol, Leith and Glasgow. Linseed is imported principally from the East Indies, Argentina, Canada, Russia and the United States; cotton-seed is chiefly supplied by Egypt and East India; rape-seed and castor-seed chiefly by East India. The importation of copra and palm kernels for the production of coco-nut oil and palm-nut oil is also considerable, but in these two cases Great Britain does not take the first place. Fish and blubber oils are principally produced in Dundee, London and Greenock. The manufacture of cod-liver oil for pharmaceutical purposes is naturally somewhat limited, as Norway, Newfoundland, and latterly also Japan, are more favourably situated as regards the supply of fresh cod, but the technical liver oils (cod oil, shark-liver oil) are produced in very large quantities in Grimsby, Hull, Aberdeen, and latterly also on the west coasts of the United Kingdom. The production of edible fats (margarine, lard compounds, and vegetable butters) has taken root in this country, and bids fair to extend rapidly. With regard to edible oils, edible cotton-seed oil is the only table oil produced in Great Britain. The United Kingdom is also one of the largest importers of fatty materials.

Practically the whole trade in palm oil, which comes exclusively from West Africa, is confined to Liverpool, and the bulk of the tallow imported into Europe from Australasia, South America and the United States, is sold in the marts of London and Liverpool. Lard reaches Great Britain chiefly from the United States. Amongst the edible oils and fats which are largely imported, butter takes the first rank (to an amount of almost £25,000,000 per annum). This food-stuff reaches Great Britain not only from all butter-exporting countries of the continent of Europe, but in increasing quantities also from Australia, Canada, Argentine, Siberia and the United States of America. Next in importance is margarine, the British production of which does not suffice for the consumption, so that large quantities must be imported from Holland, edible olive oil from Italy, the south of France, Spain and the Mediterranean ports generally. Coco-nut oil and copra, both for edible and technical purposes, are largely shipped to Great Britain from the East Indies and Ceylon, Java and the West Indies. Of lesser importance are greases, which form the by-product of the large slaughter-houses in the United States and Argentina, and American (Canadian) and Japanese fish oils.

On the continent of Europe the largest oil-trading centres are on the Mediterranean (Marseilles and Triest), which are geographically more favourably placed than England for the production of such edible oils (in addition to the home-grown olive oil) as arachis oil, sesame oil and coco-nut oil. Moreover, the native population itself constitutes a large consumer of these oils. In the north of Europe, Hamburg, Rotterdam, Antwerp and Copenhagen are the largest centres of the oil and fat trade. Hamburg and its neighbourhood produces, curiously enough, at present the largest amount of palm-nut oil. The United States takes the foremost place in the world for the production of cotton-seed and maize oils, lard, bone fat and fish oils. Canada is likely to outstrip the United States in the trade of fish and blubber oils, and in the near future Japan bids fair to become a very serious competitor in the supply of these oils. Vast stores of hard vegetable fats are still practically wasted in tropical countries, such as India, Indo-China and the Sunda Islands, tropical South America, Africa and China. With the improvement in transport these will no doubt reach European manufacturing centres in larger quantities than has been the case hitherto.

WAXES

The waxes consist chiefly of the fatty acid esters of the higher monohydric alcohols, with which are frequently associated free alcohols as also free fatty acids. In the following two tables the " acids " and " alcohols " hitherto identified in waxes are enumerated in a classified order:—

ACIDS

		Boiling Point.		Melting Point. °C.	Characteristic of
		mm. Pressure.	°C.		
I. Acids of the Acetic series CₙH₂ₙO₂—					
Ficocerylic acid	C₁₃H₂₆O₂	..	..	57	Gondang wax
Myristic acid	C₁₄H₂₈O₂	100	250·5	53·8	Wool wax
Palmitic acid	C₁₆H₃₂O₂	100	271·5	62·62	Beeswax, spermaceti
Carnaübic acid	C₂₄H₄₈O₂	..	..	·72·5	Carnaüba wax, wool wax
Pisangcerylic acid	C₂₆H₅₂O₂	..	..	71	Pisang wax
Cerotic acid	C₂₇H₅₄O₂	..	..	77·8	Beeswax, wool wax, insect wax
Melissic acid	C₃₀H₆₀O₂	..	..	91	Beeswax
Psyllostearylic acid	C₃₃H₆₆O₂	..	..	94-95	Psylla wax
II. Acids of the Acrylic or Oleic series CₙH₂ₙ₋₂O₂—					
Physetoleic acid	C₁₆H₃₀O₂	..	..	30	} Sperm oil
Doeglic acid (?)	C₁₉H₃₆O₂	..	..	..	
III. Hydroxylated acids of the series CₙH₂ₙO₃—					
Lanopalmic acid	C₁₆H₃₂O₃	..	..	87-88	Wool wax
Coceric acid	C₃₁H₆₂O₃	..	··	92-93	Cochineal wax
IV. Dihydroxylated acids of the series CₙH₂ₙO₄—					
Lanoceric acid	C₃₀H₆₀O₄	..		104-105	Wool wax

ALCOHOLS

		Boiling Point.		Melting Point. °C.	Characteristic of
		mm. Pressure.	°C.		
I. Alcohols of the Ethane series CₙH₂ₙ₊₂O—					
Pisangceryl alcohol	C₂₅H₅₂O	..	..	78	Pisang wax
Cetyl alcohol (Ethal)	C₁₆H₃₄O	760	344	·50	} Spermaceti
Octodecyl alcohol	C₁₈H₃₈O	15	210·5	59	
Carnaübyl alcohol	C₂₄H₅₀O	..	..	68-69	Wool wax
Ceryl alcohol	C₂₆H₅₄O	..	..	79	Chinese wax, opium wax, wool fat
Myricyl (Melissyl) alcohol	C₃₀H₆₂O	..	..	85-88	Beeswax, Carnaüba wax
Psyllostearyl alcohol	C₃₃H₆₈O	..	..	68-70	Psylla wax
II. Alcohols of the Allylic series CₙH₂ₙO—					
Lanolin alcohol	C₂₇H₅₄O	..	..	102-104	Wool wax
III. Alcohols of the series CₙH₂ₙ₋₄O—					
Ficoceryl alcohol	C₁₃H₂₄O	..	..	198	Gondang wax
IV. Alcohols of the Glycolic series CₙH₂ₙ₊₂O₂—					
Coceryl alcohol	C₃₀H₆₂O₂	..	··	101-104	Cochineal wax
V. Alcohols of the Cholesterol series—					
Cholesterol	C₂₆H₄₄O	..	..	148·4-150·8	} Wool wax
Isocholesterol	C₂₆H₄₄O	..	..	137-138	

Spermaceti consists practically of cetyl palmitate, Chinese wax of ceryl palmitate. The other waxes are of more complex composition, especially so wool wax.

The waxes can be classified similarly to the oils and fats as follows:—

    I. Liquid waxes.
    II. Solid waxes.
        A. Vegetable waxes.
        B. Animal waxes.

The table enumerates the most important waxes:—

WAXES

Name of Wax.	Source.	Iodine Value.	Principal Use.
	Liquid Waxes.		
Sperm oil	*Physeter macrocephalus*	81-90	Lubricant
Arctic sperm oil (Bottlenose oil)	*Hyperoödon rostratus*	67-82	Lubricant
	Solid Waxes.		
Vegetable Waxes—			
Carnaüba wax	*Corypha cerifera*	13	Polishes. Phonograph mass
Animal Waxes—			
Wool wax	*Ovis aries*	102	Ointment
Beeswax	*Apis mellifica*	8-11	Candles, polishes
Spermaceti (Cetin)	*Physeter macrocephalus*	0-4	Candles, surgery
Insect wax, Chinese wax	*Coccus ceriferus*	0-1·4	Candles, polishes, sizes

There are only two liquid waxes known, sperm oil and arctic sperm oil (bottlenose-whale oil), formerly always classed together with the animal oils. In their physical properties the natural waxes simulate the fatty oils and fats. They behave similarly to solvents; and in their liquid condition leave a grease spot on paper. An important property of waxes is that of easily forming emulsions with water, so that large quantities of water can be incorporated with them (lanolin).

The liquid waxes occur in the blubber of the sperm whale, and in the head cavities of those whales which yield spermaceti; this latter is obtained by cooling the crude oil obtained from the head cavities. Vegetable waxes appear to be very widely distributed throughout the vegetable kingdom, and occur mostly as a very thin film covering leaves and also fruits. A few only are found in sufficiently large quantities to be of commercial importance. So far carnaüba wax is practically the only vegetable wax which is of importance in the world's markets. The animal waxes are widely distributed amongst the insects, the most important being beeswax, which is collected in almost all parts of the world. An exceptional position is occupied by wool wax, the main constituent of the natural wool fat which covers the hair of sheep, and is obtained as a by-product in scouring the raw wool. Wool fat is now being purified on a large scale and brought into commerce, under the name of lanolin, as an ointment the beneficent properties of which were known to Dioscorides in the beginning of the present era. Its chemical composition is exceedingly complex, and specially remarkable on account of the considerable proportions of cholesterol and isocholesterol it contains.

Commerce.—The sperm oils are generally sold in the same markets as the fish and blubber oils (see above). For beeswax London is one of the chief marts of the world. In Yorkshire, the centre of the woollen industry, the largest amounts of wool-fat are produced, all attempts to recover the hitherto wasted material in Argentine and Australia having so far not been attended with any marked success. Spermaceti is a comparatively unimportant article of commerce; and of Chinese wax small quantities only are imported, as the home consumption takes up the bulk of the wax for the manufacture of candles, polishes and sizes.

2. Essential or Ethereal Oils.

The essential, ethereal, or "volatile" oils constitute a very extensive class of bodies, which possess, in a concentrated form, the odour characteristic of the plants or vegetable substances from which they are obtained. The oils are usually contained in special cells, glands, cavities, or canals within the plants either as such or intermixed with resinous substances; in the latter case the mixtures form oleo-resins, balsams or resins according as the product is viscid, or solid and hard. A few do not exist ready formed in the plants, but result from chemical change of inodorous substances; as for instance, bitter almonds and essential oil of mustard.

The essential oils are for the most part insoluble or only very sparingly soluble in water, but in alcohol, ether, fatty oils and mineral oils they dissolve freely. They ignite with great ease, emitting a smoke freely, owing to the large proportion of carbon they contain. Their chief physical distinction from the fatty oils is that they are as a rule not oleaginous to the touch and leave no permanent grease spot. They have an aromatic smell and a hot burning taste, and can be distilled unchanged. The crude oils are at the ordinary temperature mostly liquid, some are solid substances, others, again, deposit on standing a crystalline portion ("stearoptene" in contradistinction to the liquid portion ("elaeoptene"). The essential oils possess a high refractive power, and most of them rotate the plane of the polarized light. Even so nearly related oils as the oils of turpentine, if obtained from different sources, rotate the plane of the polarized light in opposite directions. In specific gravity the essential oils range from 0·850 to 1·143; the majority are, however, specifically lighter than water. In their chemical constitution the essential oils present no relationship to the fats and oils. They represent a large number of classes of substances of which the most important are: (1) *Hydrocarbons*, such as pinene in oil of turpentine, camphene in citronella oil, limonene in lemon and orange-peel oils, caryophyllene in clove oil and cumene in oil of thyme; (2) *ketones*, such as camphor from the camphor tree, and irone which occurs in orris root; (3) *phenols*, such as eugenol in clove oil, thymol in thyme oil, safrol in sassafras oil, anethol in anise oil; (4) *aldehydes*, such as citral and citronellal, the most important constituents of lemon oil and lemon-grass oil, benzaldehyde in the oil of bitter almonds, cinnamic aldehyde in cassia oil, vanillin in gum benzoin and heliotropin in the spiraea oil, &c.; (5) *alcohols* and their esters, such as geraniol (rhodinol) in rose oil and geranium oil, linalool, occurring in bergamot and lavender oils, and as the acetic ester in rose oil, terpineol in cardamom oil, menthol in peppermint oil, eucalyptol in eucalyptus oil and borneol in rosemary oil and Borneo camphor; (6) *acids and their anhydrides*, such as cinnamic acid in Peru balsam and coumarin in woodruff; and (7) *nitrogenous compounds*, such as mustard oil, indol in jasmine oil and anthranilic methyl-ester in neroli and jasmine oils.

Preparation from Plants.—Before essential oils could be prepared synthetically they were obtained from plants by one of the following methods: (1) distillation, (2) expression, (3) extraction, (4) enfleurage, (5) maceration.

The most important of these processes is the first, as it is applicable to a large number of substances of the widest range, such as oil of peppermint and camphor. The process is based on the principle that whilst the odoriferous substances are insoluble in water, their vapour tension is reduced on being treated with steam so that they are carried over by a current of steam. The distillation is generally performed in a still with an inlet for steam and an outlet to carry the vapours laden with essential oils into a condenser, where the water and oil vapours are condensed. On standing, the distillate separates into two layers, an aqueous and an oily layer, the oil floating on or sinking through the water according to its specific gravity. The process of *expression* is applicable to the obtaining of essential oils which are contained in the rind or skin of the fruits belonging to the citron family, such as orange and lemon oils. The oranges, lemons, &c. are peeled, and the peel is pressed against a large number of fine needles, the exuding oil being absorbed by sponges. It is intended to introduce machinery to replace manual labour. The process of *extraction* with volatile solvents is similar to that used in the extraction of oils and fats, but as only the most highly purified solvents can be used, this process has not yet gained commercial importance. The process of *enfleurage* is used in those cases where the odoriferous substance is present to a very small extent, and is so tender and liable to deterioration that it cannot be separated by way of distillation. Thus in the case of neroli oil the petals of orange blossom are loosely spread on trays covered with purified lard or with fine olive oil. The fatty materials then take up and fix the essential oil. This process is principally employed for preparing pomades and perfumed oils. Less tender plants can be treated by the analogous method of *maceration*, which consists in extracting the odoriferous substances by macerating the flowers in hot oil or molten fat. The essential oil is then dissolved by the fatty substances. The essential oil itself can be recovered from the perfumed oils, prepared either by enfleurage or maceration, by agitating the perfumed fat in a shaking machine with pure concentrated alcohol. The essential oil passes into the alcoholic solution, which is used as such in perfumery.

Synthetic Preparation.—Since the chemistry of the essential oils has been investigated in a systematic fashion a large number of the chemical individuals mentioned above have been isolated from the oils and identified.

This first step has led to the synthetical production of the most characteristic substances of essential oils in the laboratory, and the synthetical manufacture of essential oils bade fair to rival in importance the production of tar colours from the hydrocarbons obtained on distilling coal. One of the earliest triumphs of synthetical chemistry in this direction was the production of terpineol, the artificial lilac scent, from oil of turpentine. At present it is almost a by-product in the manufacture of artificial camphor. This was followed by the production of heliotropin, coumarin and vanillin, and later on by the artificial preparation of ionone, the most characteristic constituent of the violet scent. At present the manufacture of artificial camphor may be considered a solved problem, although it is doubtful whether such camphor will be able to compete in price with the natural product in the future. The aim of the chemist to produce essential oils on a manufacturing scale is naturally confined at present to the more expensive oils. For so long as the great bulk of oils is so cheaply produced in nature's laboratory, the natural products will hold their field for a long time to come.

Applications.—Essential oils have an extensive range of uses, of which the principal are their various applications in perfumery (q.v.). Next to that they play an important part in connexion with food. The value of flavouring herbs, condiments and spices is due in a large measure to the essential oils contained in them. The commercial value of tea, coffee, wine and other beverages may be said to depend largely on the delicate aroma which they owe to the presence of minute quantities of ethereal oils. Hence, essential oils are extensively used for the flavouring of liqueurs, aerated beverages and other drinks. Nor is their employment less considerable in the manufacture of confectionery and in the preparation of many dietetic articles. Most fruit essences now employed in confectionery are artificially prepared oils, especially is this the case with cheap confectionery (jams, marmalades, &c.) in which the artificial fruit esters to a large extent replace the natural fruity flavour. Thus amyl acetate is used as an imitation of the jargonelle-pear flavour; amyl valerate replaces apple flavour, and a mixture of ethyl and propyl butyrates yields the so-called pine-apple flavour. Formic ether gives a peach-like odour, and is used for flavouring fictitious rum. Many of the essential oils find extensive use in medicine. In the arts, oil of turpentine is used on the largest scale in the manufacture of varnishes, and in smaller quantities for the production of terpineol and of artificial camphor. Oil of cloves is used in the silvering of mirror glasses. Oils of lavender and of spike are used as vehicles for painting, more especially for the painting of pottery and glass.

The examination of essential oils is by no means an easy task. Each oil requires almost a special method, but with the progress of chemistry the extensive adulteration that used to be practised with fatty oils has almost disappeared, as the presence of fatty oils is readily detected. Adulteration of expensive oils with cheaper oils is now more extensively practised, and such tests as the determination of the saponification value (see above) and of the optical rotation, and in special cases the isolation and quantitative determination of characteristic substances, leads in very many cases to reliable results. The colour, the boiling-point, the specific gravity and solubility in alcohol serve as most valuable adjuncts in the examination with a view to form an estimate of the genuineness and value of a sample. Quite apart from the genuineness of a sample, its special aroma constitutes the value of an oil, and in this respect the judging of the value of a given oil may, apart from the purity, be more readily solved by an experienced perfumer than by the chemist. Thus roses of different origin or even of different years will yield rose oils of widely different value. The cultivation of plants for essential oils has become a large industry, and is especially practised as an industry in the south of France (Grasse, Nice, Cannes). The rose oil industry, which had been for centuries located in the valleys of Bulgaria, has now been taken up in Germany (near Leipzig), where roses are specially cultivated for the production of rose oil. India and China are also very large producers of essential oils. Owing to the climate other countries are less favoured, although lavender and peppermint are largely cultivated at Mitcham in Surrey, in Hertfordshire and Bedfordshire. Lavender and peppermint oils of English origin rank as the best qualities. As an illustration of the extent to which this part of the industry suffers from the climate, it may be stated that oil from lavender plants grown in England never produces more than 7 to 10% linalool acetate, which gives the characteristic scent to lavender oil, whilst oil from lavender grown in the south of France frequently yields as much as 35% of the ester. The proof that this is due mainly to climatic influences is furnished by the fact that Mitcham lavender transplanted to France produces an oil which year by year approximates more closely in respect of its contents of linalool acetate to the product of the French plant.

BIBLIOGRAPHY.—For the fixed oils, fats and waxes, see C. R. A. Wright, *Fixed Oils, Fats, Butters and Waxes* (London, 2nd ed. by C. A. Mitchell, 1903); W. Brannt, *Animal and Vegetable Fats and Oils* (London, 1896); J. Lewkowitsch, *Chemical Technology and Analysis of Oils, Fats and Waxes* (London, 4th ed., 3 vols., 1909; also German ed., Brunswick, 1905; French ed., Paris, vol. i. 1906, vol. ii. 1908, vol. iii. 1905); *Laboratory Companion to Fats and Oil Industries* (London, 1902); Cantor Lectures of the Society of Arts, *Oils and Fats, their Uses and Applications*; Groves and Thorp, *Chemical Technology*, vol. ii.; A. H. Gill, *Oil Analyses* (1909); G. Hefter, *Technologie der Fette und Öle* (Berlin, vol. i. 1906; vol. ii. 1908); L. Ubbelohde, *Handbuch der Chemie und Technologie der Öle und Fette* (Leipzig, vol. i. 1908); R. Benedikt and F. Ulzer, *Analyse der Fette und Wachsarten* (Berlin, 1908); J. Fritsch, *Les Huiles et graisses d'origine animale* (Paris, 1907).

For the essential oils, see F. B. Power, *Descriptive Catalogue of Essential Oils*; J. C. Sawer, *Odorographia* (London, 1892 and 1894); E. Gildemeister and F. Hoffmann, *Die aetherischen Öle* (Berlin, 1899), trans. (1900) by E. Kremers under the title *Volatile Oils* (Milwaukee, Wisconsin); F. W. Semmler, *Die aetherischen Öle nach ihren chemischen Bestandteilen unter Berücksichtigung der geschichtlichen Entwickelung* (Leipzig); M. Otto, *L'Industrie des parfums* (Paris, 1909); O. Aschan, *Chemie der alicyklischen Verbindungen* (Brunswick, 1905); F. R. Heussler (translated by Pond), *The Chemistry of the Terpenes* (London, 1904).
(J. Lh.)

OIRON, a village of western France, in the department of Deux-Sèvres, 7½ m. E. by S. of Thouars by road. Oiron is celebrated for its château, standing in a park and originally built in the first half of the 16th century by the Gouffier family, rebuilt in the latter half of the 17th century by Francis of Auhusson, duke of La Feuillade, and purchased by Madame de Montespan, who there passed the latter part of her life. Marshal Villeroy afterwards lived there. The château consists of a main building with two long projecting wings, one of which is a graceful structure of the Renaissance period built over a cloister. The adjoining church, begun in 1518, combines the Gothic and Renaissance styles and contains the tombs of four members of the Gouffier family. These together with other parts of the château and church were mutilated by the Protestants in 1568. The park contains a group of four dolmens.

For the Oiron pottery see CERAMICS.

OISE, a river of northern France, tributary to the Seine, flowing south-west from the Belgian frontier and traversing the departments of Aisne, Oise and Seine-et-Oise. Length, 187 m.; area of basin 6437 sq. m. Rising in Belgium, 5 m. S.E. of Chimay (province of Namur) at a height of 980 ft., the river enters France after a course of little more than 9 m. Flowing through the district of Thiérache, it divides below Guise into several arms and proceeds to the confluence of the Serre, near La Fère (Aisne). Thence as far as the confluence of the Ailette its course lies through well-wooded country to Compiègne,

a short distance above which it receives the Aisne. Skirting the forests of Compiègne, Halatte and Chantilly, all on its left bank, and receiving near Creil the Thérain and the Brèche, the river flows past Pontoise and debouches into the Seine 39 m. below Paris. Its channel is canalized (depth 6 ft. 6 in.) from Janville above Compiègne, to its mouth over a section 60 m. in length. Above Janville a lateral canal continued by the Sambre-Oise canal accompanies the river to Landrecies. It communicates with the canal system of Flanders and with the Somme canal by way of the St Quentin canal (Crozat branch) which unites with it at Chauny. The same town is its point of junction with the Aisne-Oise canal, by which it is linked with the Eastern canal system.

OISE, a department of northern France, three-fourths of which belonged to Île-de-France and the rest to Picardy, bounded N. by Somme, E. by Aisne, S. by Seine-et-Marne and Seine-et-Oise, and W. by Eure and Seine-Inférieure. Pop. (1906) 410,049; area 2272 sq. m. The department is a moderately elevated plateau with pleasant valleys and fine forests, such as those of Compiègne, Ermenonville, Chantilly and Halatte, all in the south-east. It belongs almost entirely to the basin of the Seine—the Somme and the Bresle, which flow into the English Channel, draining but a small area. The most important river is the Oise, which flows through a broad and fertile valley from north-east to south-west, past the towns of Noyon, Compiègne, Pont St Maxence and Creil. On its right it receives the Brèche and the Thérain, and on its left the Aisne, which brings down a larger volume of water than the Oise itself, the Authonne, and the Nonette, which irrigates the valley of Senlis and Chantilly. The Ourcq, a tributary of the Marne, in the south-east, and the Epte, a tributary of the Seine, in the west, also in part belong to the department. These streams are separated by ranges of slight elevation or by isolated hills, the highest point (770 ft.) being in the ridge of Bray, which stretches from Dieppe to Précy-sur-Oise. The lowest point is at the mouth of the Oise, only 66 ft. above sea-level. The climate is very variable, but the range of temperature is moderate.

Clay for bricks and earthenware, sand and building-stone are among the mineral products of Oise, and peat is also worked. Pierrefonds, Gouvieux, Chantilly and Fontaine Bonneleau have mineral springs. Wheat, oats and other cereals, potatoes and sugar beet are the chief agricultural crops. Cattle are reared more especially in the western districts, where dairying is actively carried on. Bee-keeping is general. Racing stables are numerous in the neighbourhood of Chantilly and Compiègne. Among the industries of the department of manufacture of sugar and alcohol from beetroot occupies a foremost place. The manufacture of furniture, brushes (Beauvais) and other wooden goods and of toys, fancy-ware, buttons, fans and other articles in wood, ivory, bone or mother-of-pearl are widespread industries. There are also woollen and cotton mills, and the making of woollen fabrics, blankets, carpets (Beauvais), hosiery and lace (Chantilly and its vicinity) is actively carried on. Creil and the neighbouring Montataire form an important metallurgical centre. Oise is served by the Northern railway, on which Creil is an important junction, and its commerce is facilitated by the Oise and its lateral canal and the Aisne, which afford about 70 m. of navigable waterway.

There are four arrondissements—Beauvais, Clermont, Compiègne and Senlis—with 35 cantons and 701 communes. The department forms the diocese of Beauvais (province of Reims) and part of the region of the II. army corps and of the académie (educational division) of Paris. Its court of appeal is at Amiens. The principal places are Beauvais, the capital, Chantilly, Clermont-en-Beauvoisis, Compiègne, Noyon, Pierrefonds, Creil and Senlis, which are treated separately. Among the more populous places not mentioned is Méru (5317), a centre for fancy-ware manufacture. The department abounds in old churches, among which, besides those of Beauvais, Noyon and Senlis, may be mentioned those at Morienval (11th and 12th centuries), Maignelay (15th and 16th centuries), Crépy-en-Valois (St Thomas, 12th, 13th and 15th centuries), St Leu d'Esserent (mainly 12th century), Tracy-le-Val (mainly 11th century), Villers St Paul (11th and 13th centuries), St Germer-de-Fly (a fine example of the transition from Romanesque to Gothic architecture), and St Martin-aux-Bois (13th, 14th and 15th centuries). Pontpoint preserves the buildings of an abbey founded towards the end of the 14th century and St Jean-aux-Bois the remains of a priory including a church of the 13th century. There are Gallo-Roman remains of Champlieu close to the forest of Compiègne. At Ermenonville there is a chateau of the 17th century where Rousseau died in 1778.

OJIBWAY (OJIBWA), or CHIPPEWAY (CHIPPEWA), the name given by the English to a large tribe of North American Indians of Algonquian stock. They must not be confused with the Chipewyan tribe of Athabascan stock settled around Lake Athabasca, Canada. They formerly occupied a vast tract of country around Lakes Huron and Superior, and now are settled on reservations in the neighbourhood. The name is from a word meaning " to roast till puckered " or " drawn up," in reference, it is suggested, to a peculiar seam in their mocassins, though other explanations have been proposed. They call themselves *Anishinabeg* (" spontaneous men "), and the French called them *Saulteurs* (" People of the Falls "), from the first group of them being met at Sault Ste Marie. Tribal traditions declare they migrated from the St Lawrence region together with the Ottawa and Potawatomi, with which tribes they formed a confederacy known as " The Three Fires." When first encountered about 1640 the Ojibway were inhabiting the coast of Lake Superior, surrounded by the Sioux and Foxes on the west and south. During the 18th century they conquered these latter and occupied much of their territory. Throughout the Colonial wars they were loyal to the French, but fought for the English in the War of Independence and the War of 1812, and thereafter permanently maintained peace with the Whites. The tribe was divided into ten divisions. They lived chiefly by hunting and fishing. They had many tribal myths, which were collected by Henry R. Schoolcraft in his *Algic Researches* (1839), upon which Longfellow founded his " Hiawatha."

See INDIANS, NORTH AMERICAN; also W. J. Hoffmann, "Midewiwin of the Ojibwa," in *7th Report of Bureau of American Ethnology* (1891); W. W. Warren, " History of the Ojibways," vol. v., *Minnesota Historical Society's Collections*; G. Copway, *History of the Ojibway Indians* (Boston, 1850); P. Jones, *History of the Ojebway Indians* (1861); A. E. Jenks, " Wild Rice Gatherers," *19th Report of Bureau of American Ethnology* (1900).

OKAPI, the native name of an African ruminant mammal (*Ocapia johnstoni*), belonging to the *Giraffidae*, or giraffe-family, but distinguished from giraffes by its shorter limbs and neck, the absence of horns in the females, and its very remarkable type of colouring. Its affinity with the giraffes is, however, clearly revealed by the structure of the skull and teeth, more especially the bilobed crown to the incisor-like lower canine teeth. At the shoulder the okapi stands about 5 ft. In colour the sides of the face are puce, and the neck and most of the body purplish, but the buttocks and upper part of both fore and hind limbs are transversely barred with black and white, while their lower portion is mainly white with black fetlock-rings, and the front pair a vertical black stripe on the anterior surface. Males have a pair of dagger-shaped horns on the forehead, the tips of which, in some cases at any rate, perforate the hairy skin with which the rest of the horns are covered. As in all forest-dwelling animals, the ears are large and capacious. The tail is shorter than in giraffes, and not tufted as at the tip. The okapi, of which the first entire skin sent to Europe was received in England from Sir H. H. Johnston in the spring of 1901, is a native of the Semliki forest, in the district between Lakes Albert and Albert Edward. From certain differences in the striping of the legs, as well as from variation in skull-characters, the existence of more than a single species has been suggested; but further evidence is required before such a view can be definitely accepted.

Specimens in the museum at Tervueren near Brussels show that in fully adult males the horns are subtriangular and inclined somewhat backwards; each being capped with a small polished epiphysis, which projects through the skin investing the rest of the horn. As regards its general characters, the skull of the okapi appears to be intermediate between that of the giraffe on the one hand and that of the extinct *Palaeotragus* (or *Samotherium*) of the Lower Pliocene deposits of southern Europe on the other. It has, for instance, a greater development of air-cells in the *diplöe* than in the latter, but much less than in the former. Again, in *Palaeotragus* the horns (present only in the male) are situated immediately over the eye-sockets, in *Ocapia* they are placed just behind the latter, while in *Giraffa* they are partly on the parietals. In general form, so far as can be judged from the disarticulated skeleton, the okapi was more like an antelope than a giraffe, the fore and hind cannon-bones, and consequently the entire limbs, being of approximately equal length. From this it seems probable that *Palaeotragus* and *Ocapia* indicate the ancestral type of the giraffe-line; while it has been further suggested that the apparently hornless *Helladotherium* of the

Female Okapi.

Grecian Pliocene may occupy a somewhat similar position in regard to the horned Sivatherium of the Indian Siwaliks.

For these and other allied extinct genera see PECORA; for a full description of the okapi itself the reader should refer to an illustrated memoir by Sir E. Ray Lankester in the *Transactions* of the Zoological Society of London (xvi. 6, 1902), entitled " On *Okapia*, a New Genus of *Giraffidae* from Central Africa."

Little is known with regard to the habits of the okapi. It appears, however, from the observations of Dr J. David, who spent some time in the Albert Edward district, that the creature dwells in the most dense parts of the primeval forest, where there is an undergrowth of solid-leaved, swamp-loving plants, such as arum, *Donax* and *Phrynium*, which, with orchids and climbing plants, form a thick and confused mass of vegetation. The leaves of these plants are blackish-green, and in the gloom of the forest, grow more or less horizontally, and are glistening with moisture. The effect of the light falling upon them is to produce along the midrib of each a number of short white streaks of light, which contrast most strongly with the shadows cast by the leaves themselves, and with the general twilight gloom of the forest. On the other hand, the thick layer of fallen leaves on the ground, and the bulk of the stems of the forest trees are bluish-brown and russet, thus closely resembling the decaying leaves in an European forest after heavy rain; while the whole effect is precisely similar to that produced by the russet head and body and the striped thighs and limbs of the okapi. The long and mobile muzzle of the okapi appears to be adapted for feeding on the low forest underwood and the swamp-vegetation. The small size of the horns of the males is probably also an adaptation to life in thick underwood. In Dr David's opinion an okapi in its native forest could not be seen at a distance of more than twenty or twenty-five paces. At distances greater than this it is impossible to see anything clearly in these equatorial forests, and it is very difficult to do so even at this short distance. This suggests that the colouring of the okapi is of purely protective type.

By the Arabianised emancipated slaves of the Albert Edward district the okapi is known as the kenge, ô-â-pi being the Pigmies' name for the creature. Dr David adds that Junker may undoubtedly claim to be the discoverer of the okapi, for, as stated on p. 299 of the third volume of the original German edition of his *Travels*, he saw in 1878 or 1879 in the Nepo district a portion of the skin with the characteristic black and white stripes. Junker, by whom it was mistaken for a large water-chevrotain or zebra-antelope, states that to the natives of the Nepo district the okapi is known as the makapé. (R. L.*)

OKEHAMPTON, a market town and municipal borough in the Tavistock parliamentary division of Devonshire, England, on the east and west Okement rivers, 22 m. W. by N. of Exeter by the London & South-Western railway. Pop. (1901) 2569. The church of All Saints has a fine Perpendicular tower, left uninjured when the nave and chancel were burned down in 1842. Glass is made from granulite found in the Meldon Valley, 3 m. distant. Both branches of the river abound in small trout. Okehampton Castle, one of the most picturesque ruins in Devon, probably dates from the 15th century, though its keep may be late Norman. It was dismantled under Henry VIII., but considerable portions remain of the chapel, banqueting hall and herald's tower. Immediately opposite are the traces of a supposed British camp, and of the Roman road from Exeter to Cornwall. The custom of tolling the curfew still prevails in Okehampton. The town is governed by a mayor, 4 aldermen and 12 councillors. Area, 503 acres.

Okehampton (Oakmanton) was bestowed by William the Conqueror on Baldwin de Brioniis, and became the caput of the barony of Okehampton. At the time of the Domesday Survey of 1086 it already ranked as a borough, with a castle, a market paying 4 shillings, and four burgesses. In the 18th century the manor passed by marriage to the Courtenays, afterwards earls of Devon, and Robert de Courtenay in 1220 gave the king a palfrey to hold an annual fair at his manor of Okehampton, on the vigil and feast day of St Thomas the Apostle. In the reign of Henry III. the inhabitants received a charter (undated) from the earl of Devon, confirming their rights "in woods and in uplands, in ways and in paths, in common of pastures, in waters and in mills. They were to be free from all toil and to elect yearly a portreeve and a beadle." A further grant of privileges was bestowed in 1292 by the earl of Devon, but no charter of incorporation was granted until that from James I. in 1623, and the confirmation of this by Charles II. in 1684 continued to be the governing charter, the corporation consisting of a mayor, seven principal burgesses and eight assistant burgesses, until the Municipal Corporations Act of 1882. On a petition from the inhabitants the town was reincorporated by a new charter in 1885. Okehampton returned two members to parliament in 1300, and again in 1312 and 1313, after which there was an intermission till 1640, from which date two members were returned regularly until by the Reform Act of 1832 the borough was disfranchised.

See *Victoria County History, Devonshire*; W. B. Bridges, *History of Okehampton* (1889).

OKEN, LORENZ (1779–1851), German naturalist, was born at Bohlsbach, Swabia, on the 1st of August 1779. His real name was Lorenz Ockenfuss, and under that name he was entered at the natural history and medical classes in the university of Würzburg, whence he proceeded to that of Göttingen, where he became a privat-docent, and abridged his name to Oken. As Lorenz Oken he published in 1802 his small work entitled *Grundriss der Naturphilosophie, der Theorie der Sinne, und der darauf*

gegründeten Classification der Thiere, the first of the series of works which placed him at the head of the "natur-philosophie" or physio-philosophical school of Germany. In it he extended to physical science the philosophical principles which Kant had applied to mental and moral science. Oken had, however, in this application been preceded by J. G. Fichte, who, acknowledging that the materials for a universal science had been discovered by Kant, declared that nothing more was needed than a systematic co-ordination of these materials; and this task Fichte undertook in his famous *Doctrine of Science* (Wissenschaftslehre), the aim of which was to construct a priori all knowledge. In this attempt, however, Fichte did little more than indicate the path; it was reserved for F. W. J. von Schelling fairly to enter upon it, and for Oken, following him, to explore its mazes yet further, and to produce a systematic plan of the country so surveyed.

In the *Grundriss der Naturphilosophie* of 1802 Oken sketched the outlines of the scheme he afterwards devoted himself to perfect. The position which he advanced in that remarkable work, and to which he ever after professed adherence, is that "the animal classes are virtually nothing else than a representation of the sense-organs, and that they must be arranged in accordance with them." Agreeably with this idea, Oken contended that there are only five animal classes: (1) the *Dermatozoa*, or invertebrates; (2) the *Glossozoa*, or Fishes, as being those animals in which a true tongue makes, for the first time, its appearance; (3) the *Rhinozoa*, or Reptiles, wherein the nose opens for the first time into the mouth and inhales air; (4) the *Otozoa*, or Birds, in which the ear for the first time opens externally; and (5) *Ophthalmozoa*, or Mammals, in which all the organs of sense are present and complete, the eyes being movable and covered with two lids.

In 1805 Oken made another characteristic advance in the application of the a priori principle, by a book on generation (*Die Zeugung*), wherein he maintained the proposition that "all organic beings originate from and consist of vesicles or cells. These vesicles, when singly detached and regarded in their original process of production, are the infusorial mass or protoplasma (*urschleim*) whence all larger organisms fashion themselves or are evolved. Their production is therefore nothing else than a regular agglomeration of *Infusoria*—not, of course, of species already elaborated or perfect, but of mucous vesicles or points in general, which first form themselves by their union or combination into particular species."

One year after the production of this remarkable treatise, Oken advanced another step in the development of his system, and in a volume published in 1806, in which D. G. Kieser (1779–1862) assisted him, entitled *Beiträge zur vergleichenden Zoologie, Anatomie, und Physiologie*, he demonstrated that the intestines originate from the umbilical vesicle, and that this corresponds to the vitellus or yolk-bag. Caspar Friedrich Wolff had previously proved this fact in the chick (*Theoria Generationis*, 1774), but he did not see its application as evidence of a general law. Oken showed the importance of the discovery as an illustration of his system. In the same work Oken described and recalled attention to the *corpora Wolffiana*, or "primordial kidneys."

The reputation of the young privat-docent of Göttingen had meanwhile reached the ear of Goethe, and in 1807 Oken was invited to fill the office of professor extraordinarius of the medical sciences in the university of Jena. He accepted the call, and selected for the subject of his inaugural discourse his ideas on the "Signification of the Bones of the Skull," based upon a discovery he had made in the previous year. This famous lecture was delivered in the presence of Goethe, as privy-councillor and rector of the university, and was published in the same year, with the title, *Ueber die Bedeutung der Schädelknochen*.

With regard to the origin of the idea, Oken narrates in his *Isis* that, walking one autumn day in 1806 in the Harz forest, he stumbled upon the blanched skull of a deer, picked up the partially dislocated bones, and contemplated them for a while, when the truth flashed across his mind, and he exclaimed, "It is a vertebral column!" At a meeting of the German naturalists held at Jena some years afterwards Professor Kieser gave an account of Oken's discovery in the presence of the grand-duke, which account is printed in the *Tageblatt*, or "proceedings," of that meeting. The professor stated that Oken communicated to him his discovery when journeying in 1806 to the island of Wangeroog. On their return to Göttingen Oken explained his ideas by reference to the skull of a turtle in Kieser's collection, which he disarticulated for that purpose with his own hands. "It is with the greatest pleasure," wrote Kieser, "that I am able to show here the same skull, after having it thirty years in my collection. The single bones of the skull are marked by Oken's own handwriting, which may be so easily known."

The range of Oken's lectures at Jena was a wide one, and they were highly esteemed. They embraced the subjects of natural philosophy, general natural history, zoology, comparative anatomy, the physiology of man, of animals and of plants. The spirit with which he grappled with the vast scope of science is characteristically illustrated in his essay *Ueber das Universum als Fortsetzung des Sinnensystems*, 1808. In this work he lays it down that "organism is none other than a combination of all the universe's activities within a single individual body." This doctrine led him to the conviction that "world and organism are one in kind, and do not stand merely in harmony with each other." In the same year he published his *Erste Ideen zur Theorie des Lichts*, &c., in which he advanced the proposition that "light could be nothing but a polar tension of the ether, evoked by a central body in antagonism with the planets, and heat was none other than a motion of this ether"—a sort of vague anticipation of the doctrine of the "correlation of physical forces." In 1809 Oken extended his system to the mineral world, arranging the ores, not according to the metals, but agreeably to their combinations with oxygen, acids and sulphur. In 1810 he summed up his views on organic and inorganic nature into one compendious system. In the first edition of the *Lehrbuch der Naturphilosophie*, which appeared in that and the following years, he sought to bring his different doctrines into mutual connexion, and to "show that the mineral, vegetable and animal kingdoms are not to be arranged arbitrarily in accordance with single and isolated characters, but to be based upon the cardinal organs or anatomical systems, from which a firmly established number of classes would necessarily be evolved; that each class, moreover, takes its starting-point from below, and consequently that all of them pass parallel to each other"; and that, "as in chemistry, where the combinations follow a definite numerical law, so also in anatomy the organs, in physiology the functions, and in natural history the classes, families, and even genera of minerals, plants, and animals present a similar arithmetical ratio." The *Lehrbuch* procured for Oken the title of *Hofrath*, or court-councillor, and in 1812 he was appointed ordinary professor of the natural sciences.

In 1816 he commenced the publication of his well-known periodical, entitled *Isis, eine encyclopädische Zeitschrift, vorzüglich für Naturgeschichte, vergleichende Anatomie und Physiologie*. In this journal appeared essays and notices not only on the natural sciences but on other subjects of interest; poetry, and even comments on the politics of other German states, were occasionally admitted. This led to representations and remonstrances from the governments criticized or impugned, and the court of Weimar called upon Oken either to suppress the *Isis* or resign his professorship. He chose the latter alternative. The publication of the *Isis* at Weimar was prohibited. Oken made arrangements for its issue at Rudolstadt, and this continued uninterruptedly until the year 1848.

In 1821 Oken promulgated in his *Isis* the first idea of the annual general meetings of the German naturalists and medical practitioners, which happy idea was realized in the following year, when the first meeting was held at Leipzig. The British Association for the Advancement of Science was at the outset avowedly organized after the German or Okenian model.

In 1828 Oken resumed his original humble duties as privat-docent in the newly-established university of Munich, and soon

afterwards he was appointed ordinary professor in the same university. In 1832, on the proposal by the Bavarian government to transfer him to a professorship in a provincial university of the state, he resigned his appointments and left the kingdom. He was appointed in 1833 to the professorship of natural history in the then recently-established university of Zurich. There he continued to reside, fulfilling his professional duties and promoting the progress of his favourite sciences, until his death on the 11th of August 1851.

All Oken's writings are eminently deductive illustrations of a foregone and assumed principle, which, with other philosophers of the transcendental school, he deemed equal to the explanation of all the mysteries of nature. According to him, the head was a repetition of the trunk—a kind of second trunk, with its limbs and other appendages; this sum of his observations and comparisons —few of which he ever gave in detail—ought always to be borne in mind in comparing the share taken by Oken in homological anatomy with the progress made by other cultivators of that philosophical branch of the science.

The idea of the analogy between the skull, or parts of the skull, and the vertebral column had been previously propounded and ventilated in their lectures by J. H. F. Autenreith and K. F. Kielmeyer, and in the writings of J. P. Frank. By Oken it was applied chiefly in illustration of the mystical system of Schelling—the "all-in-all" and "all-in-every-part." From the earliest to the latest of Oken's writings on the subject, "the head is a repetition of the whole trunk with all its systems: the brain is the spinal cord; the cranium is the vertebral column; the mouth is intestine and abdomen; the nose is the lungs and thorax; the jaws are the limbs; and the teeth the claws or nails." J. B. von Spix, in his folio *Cephalogenesis* (1818), richly illustrated comparative craniology, but presented the facts under the same transcendental guise; and Cuvier ably availed himself of the extravagances of these disciples of Schelling to cast ridicule on the whole inquiry into those higher relations of parts to the archetype which Sir Richard Owen called "general homologies."

The vertebral theory of the skull had practically disappeared from anatomical science when the labours of Cuvier drew to their close. In Owen's *Archetype and Homologies of the Vertebrate Skeleton* the idea was not only revived but worked out for the first time inductively, and the theory rightly stated, as follows: "The head is not a virtual equivalent of the trunk, but is only a portion, i.e. certain modified segments, of the whole body. The jaws are the 'haemal arches' of the first two segments; they are not limbs of the head" (p. 176).

Vaguely and strangely, however, as Oken had blended the idea with his a priori conception of the nature of the head, the chance of appropriating it seems to have overcome the moral sense of Goethe—unless indeed the poet deceived himself. Comparative osteology had attracted Goethe's attention. In 1786 he published at Jena his essay *Ueber den Zwischenkieferknochen des Menschen und der Thiere*, showing that the intermaxillary bone existed in man as well as in brutes. But not a word in this essay gives the remotest hint of his having then possessed the idea of the vertebral analogies of the skull. In 1820, in his *Morphologie*, he first publicly stated that thirty years before the date of that publication he had discovered the secret relationship between the vertebrae and the bones of the head, and that he had always continued to meditate on this subject. The circumstances under which the poet, in 1820, narrates having become inspired with the original idea are suspiciously analogous to those described by Oken in 1807, as producing the same effect on his mind. A bleached skull is accidentally discovered in both instances: in Oken's it was that of a deer in the Harz forest; in Goethe's it was that of a sheep picked up on the shores of the Lido, at Venice.

It may be assumed that Oken when a privat-docent at Göttingen in 1806 knew nothing of this unpublished idea or discovery of Goethe, and that Goethe first became aware that Oken had the idea of the vertebral relations of the skull when he listened to the introductory discourse in which the young professor, invited by the poet to Jena, selected this very idea for its subject. It is incredible that Oken, had he adopted the idea from Goethe, or been aware of an anticipation by him, should have omitted to acknowledge the source—should not rather have eagerly embraced so appropriate an opportunity of doing graceful homage to the originality and genius of his patron.

The anatomist having lectured for an hour plainly unconscious of any such anticipation, it seems hardly less incredible that the poet should not have mentioned to the young lecturer his previous conception of the vertebro-cranial theory, and the singular coincidence of the accidental circumstance which he subsequently alleged to have produced that discovery. On the contrary, Goethe permits Oken to publish his famous lecture, with the same unconsciousness of any anticipation as when he delivered it; and Oken, in the same state of belief, transmits a copy to Goethe (*Isis*, No. 7) who thereupon honours the professor with special marks of attention and an invitation to his house. No hint of any claim of the host is given to the guest; no word of reclamation in any shape appears for some years. In Goethe's *Tages- und Jahres-Hefte*, he refers to two friends, Reimer and Voigt, as being cognizant in 1807 of his theory. Why did not one or other of these make known to Oken that he had been so anticipated? "I told my friends to keep quiet," writes Goethe in 1825! Spix, in the meanwhile, in 1815, contributes his share to the development of Oken's idea in his *Cephalogenesis*. Ulrich follows in 1816 with his *Schildkrötenschädel*; next appears the contribution, in 1818, by L. H. Bojanus, to the vertebral theory of the skull, amplified in the *Paragon* to that anatomist's admirable *Anatome Testudinis Europaeae* (1821). And now for the first time, in 1818, Bojanus, visiting some friends at Weimar, there hears the rumour that his friend Oken had been anticipated by the great poet. He communicates it to Oken, who, like an honest man, at once published the statement made by Goethe's friends in the *Isis* of that year, offering no reflection on the poet, but restricting himself to a detailed and interesting account of the circumstances under which he himself had been led independently to make his discovery when wandering in 1806 through the Harz. It was enough for him thus to vindicate his own claims; he abstains from any comment reflecting on Goethe, and maintained the same blameless silence when Goethe ventured for the first time to claim for himself, in 1820, the merit of having entertained the same idea, or made the discovery, thirty years previously.

The German naturalists held their annual meeting at Jena in 1836, and there Kieser publicly bore testimony, from personal knowledge, to the circumstances and dates of Oken's discovery. However, in the edition of Hegel's works by Michelet (Berlin, 1842), there appeared the following paragraph: "The type-bone is the dorsal vertebra, provided inwards with a hole and outwards with processes, every bone being only a modification of it. This idea originated with Goethe, who worked it out in a treatise written in 1785, and published it in his *Morphologie* (1820), p. 162. Oken, *to whom the treatise was communicated, has pretended that the idea was his own property, and has reaped the honour of it.*" This accusation again called out Oken, who thoroughly refuted it in an able, circumstantial and temperate statement in part vii. of the *Isis* (1847). Goethe's osteological essay of 1785, the only one he printed in that century, is on a different subject. In the *Morphologie* of 1820-1824 Goethe distinctly declares that he had never published his ideas on the vertebral theory of the skull. He could not, therefore, have sent any such essay to Oken before the year 1807. Oken, in reference to his previous endurance of Goethe's pretensions, states that, "being well aware that his fellow-labourers in natural science thoroughly appreciated the true state of the case, he confided in quiet silence in their judgment. Meckel, Spix, Ulrich, Bojanus, Carus, Cuvier, Geoffroy St Hilaire, Albers, Straus-Durckheim, Owen, Kieser and Lichtenstein had recorded their judgment in his favour and against Goethe. But upon the appearance of the new assault in Michelet's edition of Hegel he could no longer remain silent."

Oken's bold axiom that heat is but a mode of motion of light, and the idea broached in his essay on generation (1805) that "all the parts of higher animals are made up of an aggregate of *Infusoria* or animated globular monads," are both of the same order as his proposition of the head being a repetition of the trunk, with its vertebrae and limbs. Science would have profited no more from the one idea without the subsequent experimental discoveries of H. C. Oersted and M. Faraday, or from the other without the microscopical observations of Robert Brown, J. M. Schleiden and T. Schwann, than from the third notion without the inductive demonstration of the segmental constitution of the skull by Owen. It is questionable, indeed, whether in either case the discoverers of the true theories were excited to their labours, or in any way influenced, by the *a priori* guesses of Oken; more probable is it that the requisite researches and genuine deductions therefrom were the results of the correlated fitness of the stage of the science and the gifts of its true cultivators at such particular stage.

The following is a list of Oken's principal works: *Grundriss der Naturphilosophie, der Theorie der Sinne, und der darauf gegründeten Classification der Thiere* (1802); *Die Zeugung* (1805); *Abriss der Biologie* (1805); *Beiträge zur vergleichenden Zoologie, Anatomie und Physiologie* (along with Kieser, 1806-1807); *Ueber die Bedeutung der Schädelknochen* (1807); *Ueber das Universum als Fortsetzung des Sinnensystems* (1808); *Erste Ideen zur Theorie des Lichts, der Finsterniss, der Farben und der Wärme* (1808); *Grundzeichnung des natürlichen Systems der Erze* (1809); *Ueber den Werth der Naturgeschichte* (1809); *Lehrbuch der Naturphilosophie* (1809-1811; 2nd ed., 1831; 3rd ed., 1843; Eng. trans., *Elements of Physiophilosophy*, 1847); *Lehrbuch der Naturgeschichte* (1813, 1815, 1825); *Handbuch der Naturgeschichte zum Gebrauch bei Vorlesungen* (1816-1820); *Naturgeschichte für Schulen* (1821); *Esquisse d'un Système d'Anatomie, de Physiologie, et d'Histoire Naturelle* (1821); *Allgemeine Naturgeschichte* (1833-1842, 14 vols.). He also contributed a large number of papers to the *Isis* and other journals. (R. O.)

OKHOTSK, SEA OF, a part of the western Pacific Ocean, lying between the peninsula of Kamchatka, the Kurile Islands, the Japanese island of Yezo, the island of Sakhalin, and the Amur province of East Siberia. The Sakhalin Gulf and Gulf of Tartary connect it with the Japanese Sea on the west of

the island of Sakhalin, and on the south of this island is the La Pérouse Strait.

OKI, a group of islands belonging to Japan, lying due north of the province of Izumo, at the intersection of 36° N. and 133° E. The group consists of one large island called Dogo, and three smaller isles—Chiburi-shima, Nishi-no-shima, and Naka-no-shima—which are collectively known as Dozen. These four islands have a coast-line of 182 m., an area of 130 sq. m., and a population of 63,000. The island of Dogo has two high peaks, Daimanji-mine (2185 ft.) and Omine-yama (2128 ft.). The chief town is Saigo in Dogo, distant about 40 m. from the port of Sakai in Izumo. The name Oki-no-shima signifies "islands in the offing," and the place is celebrated in Japanese history not only because the possession of the islands was much disputed in feudal days, but also because an ex-emperor and an emperor were banished thither by the Hojo regents in the 13th century.

OKLAHOMA (a Choctaw Indian word meaning "red people"), a south central state of the United States of America lying between 33° 35′ and 37° N. lat. and 94° 29′ and 103° W. long. It is bounded N. by Colorado and Kansas; E. by Missouri and Arkansas; S. by Texas, from which it is separated in part by the Red river; and W. by Texas and New Mexico. It has a total area of 70,057 sq. m., of which 643 sq. m. are water-surface. Although the extreme western limit of the state is the 103rd meridian, the only portion W. of the 100th meridian is a strip of land about 35 m. wide in the present Beaver, Texas and Cimarron counties, and formerly designated as "No Man's Land."

Physiography.—The topographical features of the state exhibit considerable diversity, ranging from wide treeless plains in the W. to rugged and heavily wooded mountains in the E. In general terms, however, the surface may be described as a vast rolling plain having a gentle southern and eastern slope. The elevations above the sea range from 4700 ft. in the extreme N.W. to about 350 ft. in the S.E. The southern and eastern slopes are remarkably uniform; between the northern and southern boundaries E. of the 100th meridian there is a general difference in elevation of from 200 to 300 ft., while from W. to E. there is an average decline of about 3 ft. to the mile. The state has a mean elevation of 1300 ft. with 34,930 sq. m. below 1000 ft; 25,400 sq. m. between 1000 and 2000 ft.; 6500 sq. m. between 2000 and 3000 ft.; and 3600 sq. m. between 3000 and 5000 ft.

The western portion of the Ozark Mountains enters Oklahoma near the centre of the eastern boundary, and extends W.S.W. half way across the state in a chain of hills gradually decreasing in height. In the south central part of the state is an elevated tableland known as the Arbuckle Mountains. In its western portion this tableland attains an elevation of about 1350 ft. above the sea and lies about 400 ft. above the bordering plains. At its eastern termination, where it merges with the plains, it has an elevation of about 750 ft. Sixty miles N.W. of this plateau lie the Wichita Mountains, a straggling range of rugged peaks rising abruptly from a level plain. This range extends from Fort Sill north-westward beyond Granite, a distance of 65 m., with some breaks in the second half of this area. The highest peaks are not more than 1500 ft. above the plain, but on account of their steep and rugged slopes they are difficult to ascend. A third group of hills, the Chautauqua Mountains, lie in the W. in Blaine and Canadian counties, their main axis being almost parallel with the North Fork of the Canadian river. With the exception of these isolated clusters of hills the western portion of the state consists almost entirely of rolling prairie. The extreme north-western part of Oklahoma is a lofty tableland forming part of the Great Plains region E. of the Rocky Mountains.

The prairies N. of the Arkansas and W. of the Neosho rivers are deeply carved by small streams, and in the western portion of this area, where the formation consists of alternating shales and sandstones, the easily eroded rocks have been carved into canyons, buttes and mesas. South of the Arkansas river these ledges of sandstone continue as far as Okmulgee, but the evidences of erosion are less noticeable. East of the Neosho river the prairies merge into a hilly woodland. In the N.W. four large salt plains form a striking physical feature. Of these the most noted is the Big Salt Plain of the Cimarron river, in Woodward county, which varies in width from ½ m. to 2 m. and extends along the river for 8 m. The plain is almost perfectly level, covered with snowy-white saline crystals, and contains many salt springs. The other saline areas are the Little Salt Plain, which lies on the Cimarron river, near the Kansas boundary; the Salt Creek Plain, 3 m. long and 100 yds. wide, in Blaine county; and the Salt Fork Plain, 6 m. wide and 8 m. long, so called from its position on the Salt Fork of the Arkansas river.

Following the slope of the land, the important streams flow from N.W. to S.E. The Arkansas river enters the state from the N. near the 97th meridian, and after following a general south-easterly course, leaves it near the centre of the eastern boundary. Its tributaries from the N. and E.—the Verdigris, Grand or Neosho and Illinois—are small and unimportant; but from the S. and W. it receives the waters of much larger streams—the Salt Fork, the Cimarron and the Canadian, with its numerous tributaries. The extreme southern portion of the state is drained by the Red River, which forms the greater part of the southern boundary, and by its tributaries, the North Fork, the Washita and the Kiamichi.

Fauna and Flora.—Of wild animals the most characteristic are the black bear, puma, prairie wolf, timber wolf, fox, deer, antelope, squirrel, rabbit and prairie dog. Hawks and turkey buzzards are common types of the larger birds, and the wild turkey, prairie chicken and quail are the principal game birds. The total woodland area of the state was estimated in 1900 at 24,400 sq. m., or 34·8 % of the land area. The most densely wooded section is the extreme E.; among the prairies of the W. timber is seldom found beyond the banks of streams. The most common trees are the various species of the oak and cedar. The pine is confined to the more mountainous sections of the E., and the black walnut is found among the river bottom lands. These four varieties are of commercial value. Other varieties, most of which are widely distributed, are the ash, pecan, cottonwood, sycamore, elm, maple, hickory, elder, gum, locust and river birch. The prairies are covered with valuable bunch, grama and dropseed grasses; in the extreme N.W. the cactus, sagebrush and yucca, types characteristic of more arid regions, are found.

Climate.—The climate of the state is of a continental type, with great annual variations of temperature and a rainfall which, though generally sufficient for the needs of vegetation, is considerably less than that of the Atlantic Coast or the Mississippi Valley. The western and central portions of the state are in general cooler and dryer than the E., on account of their greater elevation and greater distance from the Gulf Coast. Thus at Beaver, in the extreme N.W. the mean annual temperature is 57° F. and the mean annual rainfall 18·9 in.; while at Lehigh, in the S.E., these figures are respectively 62° and 35·1 in. At Oklahoma City, in the centre of the state, the mean annual temperature is 59°; the mean for the summer (June, July and August) is 78°, with an extreme recorded of 104°; the mean for the winter (December, January and February) is 38°, with an extreme recorded of −17°. At Mangum, in the S.W., the mean annual temperature is 61°; the mean for the summer is 81° and for the winter 41°, while the highest and lowest temperatures ever recorded are respectively 114° and −17°. The mean annual precipitation for the state is 31·7 in.; the variation between the E. and the W. being about 12 in.

Soils.—The prevailing type of soil is a deep dark-red loam, sometimes (especially in the east central part of the state) made up of a decomposed sandstone, and again (in the north central part) made up of shales and decomposed limestone. Not infrequently there are a belt of red sandy loam on uplands N. of a river, a rich deposit of black alluvium on valley bottom lands, a belt of red clay loam on uplands S. of a river, and a deposit of wind-blown loess on the water parting. Loess, often thin and always containing little humus, also covers large areas on the high, semi-arid plains in the western part of the state.

Agriculture and Stock-raising.—For some time before the first opening to settlement by white men in 1899, the territory now embraced in Oklahoma was largely occupied by great herds of cattle driven in from Texas, and since then, although the opening was piecemeal, the agricultural development has been remarkably rapid. By 1900, 22,988,339 acres, or 52·1 %, of the total land surface was included in farms, and 8,574,187 acres, or 37·7 %, of the farm land was improved.[1] The farm land was divided among 108,000 farms containing an average of 212·85 acres; 26,121 of them contained less than 50 acres, but the most usual size was 160 acres; and 48,083, or 45·35 %, contained from 100 to 174 acres. A considerable portion of the larger farms (there were 2390 containing 500 acres or more) were owned by Indians but leased to white men. Much land as late as 1900 was held in common by Indian tribes, but has since been allotted to the members of those tribes and most of it is leased to whites. In 1900, 59,367 (or a little more than one-half of all) farms were worked by owners or part owners, 33,347 were worked by share tenants, and 13,903 were worked by cash tenants. Indian corn, wheat, cotton, oats and hay are the principal crops, but the variety of farm and garden produce is great, and includes Kafir corn, broom corn, barley, rye, buckwheat, flax, tobacco, beans, castor beans, peanuts, pecans, sorghum cane, sugar cane, and nearly all the fruits and vegetables common to the temperate zone; stock-raising, too, is a very important industry. Of the total acreage of all crops in 1900, 4,431,819 acres, or 68·64 %, were of cereals; and of the cereal acreage 56·45 % was of Indian corn, 34·45 % was of wheat and 7·15 % was of oats. The acreage of Indian corn increased from

2,501,945 acres in 1900 to 5,950,000 acres in 1909;[2] between 1899 and 1909 the yield increased from 68,949,300 bushels to 101,250,000 bushels. The acreage of wheat decreased during this period from 1,704,969 acres to 1,225,000 acres, and the yield from 20,328,300 bushels to 15,680,000 bushels. The acreage of oats increased from 317,076 acres to 550,000 acres, and the yield increased from 9,511,340 bushels to 15,950,000 bushels. The hay crop of 1899 was grown on 1,095,706 acres and amounted to 1,617,905 tons, but nearly one-half of this was made from wild grasses; since then the amounts of fodder obtained from alfalfa, Kafir corn, sorghum cane and timothy have much increased, and that obtained from wild grasses has decreased; in 1909 the acreage was 900,000 and the crop 810,000 tons. Except in the W. section, where there is good grazing but generally an insufficient rainfall for growing crops, cattle-raising on the range has in considerable measure given way to stock-raising on the farm, and nearly everywhere the quality of the cattle has been greatly improved. The total number of cattle decreased from 3,236,008 in 1900 to 1,992,000 in 1910, but at the same time the number of dairy cows increased from 276,539 to 355,000. The number of horses increased from 557,153 in 1900 to 804,000 in 1910; of mules from 117,562 to 191,000; of swine from 1,265,189 to 1,302,000; and of sheep from 88,741 to 108,000. Winter wheat is used extensively for pasturage during the winter months with little or no damage to the crop. No other branch of agriculture in Oklahoma has advanced so rapidly as the production of cotton; the culture of this fibre was introduced in 1890, and the acreage increased from 682,743 acres in 1899 to 2,037,000 acres in 1909, and the yield increased from 277,741 bales to 617,000 bales (in 1907 it was 862,383 bales). There was only a very small crop of broom corn in 1889, but in 1899 the crop was 3,565,510 ℔. The state has risen to high rank in the production of sorghum cane and castor beans also; in 1899 16,477 acres of the cane yielded 40,259 tons, and 14,070 acres of castor beans yielded 774,09 bushels. Two crops of potatoes may be grown on the same ground in one year, and the acreage of potatoes increased from 15,360 acres in 1899 to 27,000 acres in 1909, and the yield from 1,191,997 bushels to 1,890,000 bushels. Oklahoma is already producing large crops of apples, peaches, grapes, water-melons and musk-melons, and many large apple and peach orchards and vineyards have been planted. Pears, plums, apricots, cherries, strawberries, blackberries, raspberries, currants, gooseberries, cabbages, onions, sweet potatoes, tomatoes and cucumbers are grown in considerable quantities. The cereals and most of the fruits and vegetables are grown throughout the greater portion of the middle and E. parts of the state, although the soil of the N. middle section yields the best crops of wheat. Kafir corn and sorghum cane are the most common in the W. sections, where the climate is too dry for other crops. Some cotton is grown N. of the middle of the state, but the S.E. quarter takes in most of the cotton belt. Broom corn grows best in Woods county on the N. border, and castor beans in the central and N. central sections. About 3000 acres (nearly one-half in the narrow extension in the N.W.) were already irrigated in 1909, and surveys had been made by the Federal Reclamation Service with a view to irrigating about 100,000 acres more—10,000 to 14,000 acres in Beaver and Woodward counties, under the Cimarron project, and 80,000 to 100,000 acres in Kiowa and Comanche counties, under the Red River project.

Lumber and Timber Products.—The merchantable timber is mostly in that part of the state which formerly constituted Indian Territory, and consists largely of black walnut and other valuable hard woods in the bottom lands, of black jack and post oak on the uplands and of pine on the higher elevations S. of the Arkansas river. The manufactured forest products of Indian Territory increased in value from $180,373 in 1900 to $588,078 in 1905, or 205·78 %.

Minerals.—The coal-fields extend from Kansas on the N. to Arkansas on the E., and have an area of about 20,000 sq. m. The principal mining centres are McAlester, Wilburton, Hartshorn, Coalgate and Phillips. In quality the coal varies from a low grade to a high grade bituminous, and some of the latter is good for coking. The output increased from 446,429 short tons in 1885 to 1,922,298 short tons in 1900, and to 2,948,116 short tons in 1908, the output for the last-named year being much less than for 1906 or 1907, when it was over 3,500,000 tons. The range of hills extending from the centre of the state N.W. to and beyond the Kansas border are composed chiefly of great deposits of rock gypsum. A similar but minor range extends parallel with it 40 to 50 m. S.W. There are also deposits in Greer county in the S.W. corner, and some gypsite in Kay county on the N. middle border. For working these extensive deposits there are, however, few mills; these are in Kay, Canadian and Blaine counties. Some petroleum was discovered in the N. part of Indian Territory near the Oklahoma border as early as 1890, but there was little development until 1901, when several wells were drilled in the vicinity of Bartlesville. Then wells were drilled to the W. on the Osage Reservation, and to the S., until in 1906 about 110 wells were drilled into the famous Glen Pool near Sapulpa. One of these wells has a flow of about 1000 barrels a day, and the total product from the Oklahoma oil-field (which includes wells in

---

[1] The statistics in this article were obtained by adding to those for Oklahoma those for Indian Territory, which was combined with it in 1907.

[2] The agricultural statistics for 1909 are taken from the *Year-Book* of the United States Department of Agriculture.

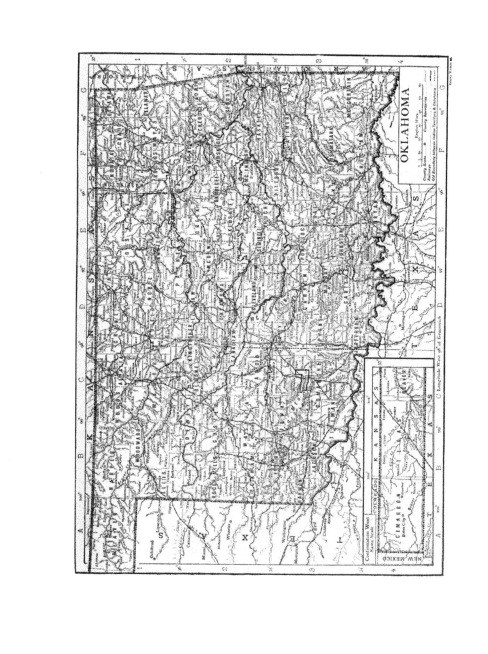

OKLAHOMA

what was Indian Territory) increased from 10,000 barrels in 1901 to 138,911 in 1903, 1,366,748 in 1904 and 45,798,765 in 1908, when it was valued at $17,694,843. Natural gas abounds in the same region, and several strong wells were developed in 1906, and immediately afterwards gas began to be used largely for industrial purposes for which in 1908 the price was from 1½ to 15 cents per 1000 ft. Pipe lines have been constructed. The value of the output increased from $360 in 1902 to $130,137 in 1905 and to $860,159 in 1908. In the central part of the state S. of the Canadian river are extensive deposits of asphaltum, but their development has been undertaken only on a small scale: in 1908, 2402 short tons were put on the market, the value being $23,820. Lead and zinc are found in the Miami district, the Peoria district and the Quapaw district; and in 1908 the lead (1409 tons) was valued at $118,336 and the zinc (2235 tons) at $210,090. The total value of the mineral products in 1908 was $26,586,751.

Manufactures.—The manufactures in 1905 were still largely such as are closely related to agriculture. Measured by the value of the products, 61·8% were represented by flour and grist mill products and cottonseed oil and cake. Among the manufacturing centres are Oklahoma City and Guthrie, and the combined value of their factory products increased from $1,493,098 in 1900 to $4,871,392 in 1905.

Transportation and Commerce.—The navigable waters in Oklahoma are of little importance, and the state is almost wholly dependent on railways as a means of transportation. The first railway was that of the Missouri, Kansas & Texas, which completed a line across the territory to Denison, Texas, in 1872. The railway mileage was slowly increased to 1260 m. in 1890, and on the 1st of January 1909 was 5829 m. The Missouri, Kansas & Texas railway crosses the E. part of the state, and somewhat parallel with this to the westward are the St Louis & San Francisco, the Atchison, Topeka & Santa Fé, two lines of the Chicago, Rock Island & Pacific, and the Kansas City, Mexico & Orient railways. The Chicago, Rock Island & Pacific also crosses the middle of the state from E. to W. The Atchison, Topeka & Santa Fé and the Chicago, Rock Island & Gulf cross the N.W. part. The St Louis & San Francisco crosses the S.E. quarter. A line of the Frisco system extends along the S. border from the Arkansas line to the middle of the state, and with these main lines numerous branches form an extensive network.

Population.—The population of the territory now embraced within the state increased from 258,657 in 1890, when the first census was taken, to 790,391 in 1900, or 205·6%, to 1,414,177 in 1907, and to 1,657,155 in 1910. Of the total population in 1900 769,853, or 97·4%, were native-born. The white population increased from 172,554 in 1890 to 1,054,376 in 1907, or 611%, the negro population during the same period from 21,609 to 112,160, or 419%, and the Indian population from 64,456 to 75,012, or 16·3%. In 1890 the Indians and negroes constituted 33·3% of the total population, but in 1907 they (with the Mongolians, who numbered 75) constituted only 13·2% of the total. The only Indians who are natives of this region are a few members of the Kiowa, Comanche and Apache tribes. The others are the remnants of a number of tribes collected here from various parts of the country: Choctaws, Chickasaws, Cherokees, Creeks, Seminoles, Osages, Kaws, Poncas, Otoes, Cheyennes, Iowas, Kickapoos, Sauk and Foxes, Sioux, Miamis, Shawnees, Pawnees, Ottawas and several others. Until 1906 the Osages lived on a reservation touching Kansas on the N. and the Arkansas river on the W. (since then almost all allotted); but to the greater portion of the Indians the government has made individual allotments. Only about one-fourth of the so-called Indians are full bloods. A large portion are one-half or more white blood and the Creeks and some others have more or less negro blood. In 1906 there were 257,100 communicants of various churches in Oklahoma and Indian Territory, the Methodist Episcopalians being the most numerous, and next to them the Baptists. The population in places having 4000 inhabitants or more increased from 29,978 in 1900 to 140,579 in 1907, or 368·9%, while the population outside of such places increased from 760,413 to 1,273,598, or only 67·5%. The principal cities in 1907 were Oklahoma City, Muskogee, Guthrie (the capital), Shawnee, Enid, Ardmore, McAlester and Chickasha.

Administration.—The constitution now in operation was adopted in September 1907, and is that with which the state was admitted into the Union in November of the same year. Amendments may be submitted through a majority of the members elected to both houses of the legislature or through a petition signed by 15% of the electorate, and a proposed amendment becomes a part of the constitution if the majority of the votes cast at a popular election are in favour of it. The legislature may also at any time propose a convention for amending or revising the constitution, but no such convention can be called without first obtaining the approval of the electorate. An elector must be able to read or write (unless he or an ancestor was a voter in 1866 or then lived in some foreign nation) and must be 21 years old, and a resident of the state for one year, in the county six months, and in the election precinct 30 days; and women have the privilege of voting at school meetings. General elections are held on the first Tuesday after the first Monday in November in odd-numbered years and party candidates for state, district, county and municipal offices and for the United States Senate are chosen at primary elections held on the first Tuesday in August. The Massachusetts ballot which had been in use in 1897–1899 was again adopted in 1909. Oklahoma has put into its constitution many things which in the older states were left to legislative enactment. The governor is elected for a term of four years but is ineligible for the next succeeding term. The number of officers whom he appoints is rather limited and for most of his appointments the confirmation of the Senate is required. He is not permitted to pardon a criminal until he has obtained the advice of the board of pardons which is composed of the state superintendent of public instruction, the president of the board of agriculture and the state auditor. He is a member of some important administrative boards, his veto power extends to items in appropriation bills, and to pass a bill over his veto a vote of two-thirds of the members elected to each house is required. A lieutenant-governor, secretary of state, treasurer, auditor, examiner, and inspector, commissioner of labour, commissioner of insurance, chief mine inspector, commissioner of charities and corrections, and president of the board of agriculture are elected each for a term of four years, and the secretary of state, auditor and treasurer are, like the governor, ineligible for the next succeeding term.

The law-making bodies are a Senate and a House of Representatives. One-half the senators and all the representatives are elected every two years, senators by districts and representatives by counties. Sessions are held biennially in even-numbered years and begin the first Tuesday after the first Monday in January. The constitution reserves to the people the privilege of rejecting any act or any item of any act whenever 5% of the legal voters ask that the matter be voted upon at a general election; and the people may initiate legislation by a petition signed by 8% of the electorate.

For the administration of justice there have been established a supreme court composed of six justices elected for a term of six years; a criminal court of appeals composed of three justices appointed by the governor with the advice and consent of the Senate; twenty-one district courts each with one or more justices elected for a term of four years; a county court in each county with one justice elected for a term of two years; a court of a justice of the peace, elected for a term of two years, in each of six districts of each county, and police courts in the cities. The supreme court has appellate jurisdiction in all civil cases, but its original jurisdiction is restricted to a general control of the lower courts. The criminal court of appeals has jurisdiction in all criminal cases appealed from the district and county courts. The district courts have exclusive jurisdiction in civil actions for sums exceeding $1000, concurrent jurisdiction with the county courts in civil actions for sums greater than $500 and not exceeding $1000, and original or appellate in criminal cases. The county courts have, besides the concurrent jurisdiction above stated, original jurisdiction in all probate matters, original jurisdiction in civil actions for sums greater than $200 and not exceeding $500, concurrent jurisdiction with the justices of the peace in misdemeanour cases, and appellate jurisdiction in all cases brought from a justice of the peace or a police court.

Local Government.—The general management of county affairs is intrusted to three commissioners elected by districts, but these commissioners are not permitted to incur extraordinary expenses or levy a tax exceeding five mills on a dollar without first obtaining the consent of the people at a general or special election. The other county officers are a treasurer, clerk, register of deeds, attorney, surveyor, sheriff, assessor and superintendent of public instruction. The counties have been divided into municipal townships, each of which elects a trustee, a clerk and a treasurer, who together constitute a board of directors for the management of township affairs. The trustee is also the assessor. Cities or towns having a population of 2000 or more may become cities of the first class whenever a favourable majority vote is obtained at a general or special election held in that city or town, and this question must be submitted at such an election whenever 35% of the legal voters petition for it.

Miscellaneous Laws.—The property rights of husband and wife are practically equal, and either may buy, sell or mortgage real estate, other than the homestead, without the consent of the other. Among the grounds for a divorce are adultery, extreme cruelty, habitual drunkenness, gross neglect of duty and imprisonment for felony. Article XII. of the constitution exempts from forced sale the homestead of any family in the state to the extent of 160 acres of land in the country, or 1 acre in a city, town or village, provided the value of the same does not exceed $5000 and that the claims against it are not for purchase money, improvements or taxes. A corporation commission of three members, elected for a term of six years, is intrusted with the necessary powers for a rigid control of public service corporations. A state board of arbitration, composed of two farmers, two employers and two employés is authorized to investigate the causes of any strike affecting the public interests, and publish what it finds to be the facts in the case, together with recommendations for settlement. Labour laws, passed by the first legislature (1908), were amended and made more radical by the legislature of 1909: a child labour law forbids the employment of children under 14 in factories, workshops, theatres, bowling-alleys, pool-halls, steam-laundries or other dangerous places (to be defined by the commissioner of labour), and no child under 16 is to be employed in such places unless able to read and write simple English sentences or without having attended school during the previous year; no child under 16 is to be employed in any of several (enumerated) dangerous occupations; no child under 16 is to be employed more than 8 hours in any one day, or more than 48 hours in any one week in any gainful occupation other than agriculture or domestic service; age and schooling certificates are required of children between 14 and 16 in certain occupations. A state dispensary system for the sale of intoxicating liquors was authorized by the constitution, but the popular vote in 1908 was unfavourable to the continuance of the system, the sentiment seeming to be for rigid prohibition of the sale of intoxicating liquors. A law passed in May 1908 against nepotism (closely following the Texas law of 1907) forbids public officers to appoint (or vote for) any person related to them by affinity or consanguinity within the third degree to any position in the government of which they are a part; makes persons thus related to public officers ineligible to positions in the branch in which their relative is an official; and renders any official making such an appointment liable to fine and removal from office.

Education.—The common school system is administered by a state superintendent of public instruction, a state board of education, county superintendents and district boards. The state board is composed of the state superintendent, who is president of the board; the secretary of state, who is secretary of the board; the attorney-general and the governor. Each district board is composed of three members elected for a term of three years, one each year. Each district school must be open at least three months each year, and children between the ages of eight and sixteen are required to attend either a public or a private school, unless excused because of physical or mental infirmity. There are separate schools for whites and negroes. In addition to instruction in the ordinary branches, the teaching in the district schools of the elementary principles of agriculture, horticulture, animal husbandry, stock-feeding, forestry, building country roads and domestic science is required. A law of 1908 requires that an agricultural school of secondary grade be established in each of the five supreme court judicial districts, and that an experimental farm be operated in connexion with each; and in 1909 the number of these districts was increased to six. There is a state industrial school for girls, teaching domestic science and the fine arts. The higher institutions of learning established by the state are the Oklahoma Agricultural and Mechanical College, a land grant college with an agricultural experiment station at Stillwater; the Oklahoma School of Mines at Wilburton; the Colored Agricultural and Normal University at Langston; the Central Normal School at Edmond; the North-western Normal School at Alva; the South-western Normal School at Weatherford, Custer county; the South-eastern Normal School at Durant, Bryan county; the East Central Normal School at Ada; the North-eastern Normal School at Tahlequah, Cherokee county; and the University of Oklahoma at Norman. The State University (established in 1892, opened in 1893) embraces a college of arts and sciences, and schools of fine arts, applied science, medicine, mines and pharmacy. In 1907–1908 it had 40 instructors and 790 students. There is a University Preparatory School (1901) at Tonkawa in Kay county, and there are state schools of agriculture at Tishomingo and

at Warner. The common schools are in large part maintained out of the proceeds of the school lands (about 1,200,000 acres), which are sections 16 and 36 in each township of that portion of the state which formerly constituted Oklahoma Territory, and a Congressional appropriation of $5,000,000 in lieu of these sections in what was formerly Indian Territory. The university, agricultural and mechanical college and normal schools also are maintained to a considerable extent out of the proceeds of section 13 in several townships. The university owns land valued at $3,670,000. Among the institutions of learning, neither maintained nor controlled by the state, are Epworth University (Methodist Episcopal, 1901) at Oklahoma City, and Kingfisher College at Kingfisher.

Charities and Correctional Institutions.—The state has a hospital for the insane at Fort Supply, the Whitaker Orphans' Home at Pryor Creek, the Oklahoma School for the Blind at Fort Gibson and the Oklahoma School for the Deaf at Sulphur; and the legislature of 1908 appropriated money for the East Oklahoma Hospital for the Insane at Vinita, a School for the Feeble-Minded at Enid, a State Training School for Boys at Wynnewood and a State Reformatory (at Granite, Greer county) for first-time convicts between the ages of sixteen and twenty-five. Under the constitution the supervision and inspection of charities and institutions of correction is in the hands of a State Commissioner of Charities and Corrections, elected by the people. The commissioner must inspect once each year all penal, correctional and eleemosynary institutions, including public hospitals, jails, poorhouses and corporations and organizations doing charitable work; and the commissioner appears as next friend in cases affecting the property of orphan minors, and has power to investigate complaints against public and private institutions whose charters may be revoked for cause by the commissioner. By act of legislature a State Board of Public Affairs was created; it is made of five members appointed by the governor, with charge of the fiscal affairs of all state institutions. Convicts were sent to the state penitentiary of Kansas until January 1909, when it was charged that they were treated cruelly there; in 1909 work was begun on a penitentiary at McAlester.

Banking and Finance.—The unique feature of the banking system (with amendments adopted by the second legislature becoming effective on the 11th of June 1909) is a fund for the guaranty of deposits. The state banking board, which is composed of the governor, lieutenant-governor, president of the board of agriculture, state treasurer and state auditor, levies against the capital stock of each state bank and trust company, organized or existing, under the laws of the state to create a fund equal to 5% of average daily deposits other than the deposits of state funds properly secured. One-fifth of this fund is payable the first year and one-twentieth each year thereafter; 1% of the increase in average deposits is collected each year. Emergency assessments, not to exceed 2%, may be made whenever necessary to pay in full the depositors in an insolvent bank; if the guaranty fund is impaired to such a degree that it is not made up by the 2% emergency assessment, the state banking board issues certificates of indebtedness which draw 6% interest and which are paid out of the assessment. Any national bank may secure its depositors in this manner if it so desires. The bank guarantee law was held to be valid by the United States Supreme Court in 1908 after the attorney-general of the United States had decided that it was illegal.

The revenue for state and local purposes is derived chiefly from taxes. The constitutional limit on the state tax levy is 3½ mills on a dollar, and legislation has fixed the limit of the county levy at 5 mills, of the levy in cities at 7, in incorporated towns at 5, in townships at 3, and in school districts at 5. There is a tax on the gross receipts of corporations, a graduated land tax on all holdings exceeding 640 acres, a tax on income exceeding $3500, and a tax on gifts and inheritances. The aggregate amount of indebtedness which the state may have at any time is limited by the constitution to $400,000, save when borrowing is necessary to repel an invasion, suppress an insurrection or defend the state in war.

History.—With the exception of the narrow strip N. of the most N. section of Texas the territory comprising the present state of Oklahoma was set apart by Congress in 1834, under the name of Indian Territory, for the possession of the five southern tribes (Cherokees, Creeks, Seminoles, Choctaws and Chickasaws) and the Quapaw Agency. Early in 1809 some Cherokees in the south-eastern states made known to President Jefferson their desire to remove to hunting grounds W. of the Mississippi, and at first they were allowed to occupy lands in what is now Arkansas, but by a new arrangement first entered into in 1828 they received instead, in 1838, a patent for a wide strip extending along the entire N. border of Indian Territory with the exception of the small section in the N.E. corner which was reserved to the Quapaw Agency. By treaties negotiated in 1820, 1825, 1830 and 1842 the Choctaws received for themselves and the Chickasaws a patent for all that portion of the territory which lies S. of the Canadian and Arkansas rivers, and by treaties negotiated in 1844, 1833 and 1851 the Creeks received for themselves and the Seminoles a part for the remaining or middle portion. Many of the Indians of these tribes brought slaves with them from the Southern states and during the Civil War they supported the Confederacy, but when that war was over the Federal government demanded not only the liberation of the slaves but new treaties, partly on the ground that the tribal lands must be divided with the freedmen. By these treaties, negotiated in 1866, the Cherokees gave the United States permission to settle other Indians on what was approximately the western half of their domain; the Seminoles, to whom the Creeks in 1855 had granted as their portion the strip between the Canadian river and its North Fork, ceded all of theirs, and the Creeks, Choctaws and Chickasaws ceded the western half of theirs back to the United States for occupancy by freedmen or other Indians. In the E. portion of the lands thus placed at its disposal by the Cherokees and the Creeks the Federal government within the next seventeen years made a number of small grants as follows: to the Seminoles in 1866, to the Sauk and Foxes in 1867, to the Osages, Kansas, Pottawatomies, Absentee Shawnees and Wichitas in 1871–1872, to the Pawnees in 1876, to the Poncas and Nes Percés in 1878, to the Otoes and Missouris in 1881, and to the Iowas and Kickapoos in 1883; in the S.W. quarter of the Territory, also, the Kiowas, Comanches and Apaches were located in 1867 and the Cheyennes and Arapahoes in 1869. There still remained unassigned the greater part of the Cherokee Strip besides a tract embracing 1,887,800 acres of choice land in the centre of the Territory, and the agitation for the opening of this to settlement by white people increased until in 1889 a complete title to the central tract was purchased from the Creeks and Seminoles. Soon after the purchase President Benjamin Harrison issued a proclamation announcing that this land would be opened to homestead settlement at twelve o'clock noon, on the 22nd of April 1889. At that hour no less than 20,000 people were on the border, and when the signal was given there ensued a remarkably spectacular race for homes. In the next year that portion of Indian Territory which lay S. of the Cherokee Strip and W. of the lands occupied by the five tribes, together with the narrow strip N. of Texas which had been denied to that state in 1850, was organized as the Territory of Oklahoma. In the meantime negotiations were begun for acquiring a clear title to the unoccupied portion of the Cherokee Strip, for individual allotments to the members of the several small tribes who had received tribal allotments since 1866, and for the purchase of what remained after such individual allotments had been made. As these negotiations were successful most of the land between the tract first opened and that of the Creeks was opened to settlement in 1891, a large tract to the W. of the centre was opened in 1892, a tract S. of the Canadian river and W. of the Chickasaws was opened in 1902, and by 1904 the entire Territory had been opened to settlement with the exception of a tract in the N.E. which was occupied by the Osages, Kaws, Poncas and Otoes. By the treaties with the five southern tribes they were to be permitted to make their own laws so long as they preserved their tribal relations, but since the Civil War many whites had mingled with these Indians, gained control for their own selfish ends of such government as there was, and made the country a refuge for fugitives from justice. Consequently, in 1893, Congress appointed the Dawes Commission to induce the tribes to consent to individual allotments as well as to a government administered from Washington, and in 1898 the Curtis Act was passed for making such allotments and for the establishment of a territorial government. When the allotments were nearly all made Congress in 1906 authorized Oklahoma and Indian Territories to qualify for admission to the Union as one state. As both Territories approved, a constitutional convention (composed of 100 Democrats and 12 Republicans) met at Guthrie on the 20th of November 1906. The constitution framed by this body was approved by the electorate on the 17th of September 1907, and the state was admitted to the Union on the 16th of November.

Governors of Oklahoma—Territorial.

George W. Steele	1890–1891
Robert Martin (acting)	1891–1892
Abraham J. Seay	1892–1893
William Cary Renfrow	1893–1897
Cassius McDonald Barnes . . .	1897–1901
William M. Jenkins	1901
Thompson B. Ferguson	1901–1906
Frank Frantz	1906–1907

State.

Charles Nathaniel Haskell, Democrat.	.	1907–1911
Lee Cruce, Democrat		1911–

BIBLIOGRAPHY.—See the *Biennial Reports* (Guthrie, 1904 sqq.) of the Oklahoma Department of Geology and Natural History; the Oklahoma Geological Survey, *Bulletin No. 1: Preliminary Report on the Mineral Resources of Oklahoma* (Norman, 1908); C. N. Gould, *Geology and Water Resources of Oklahoma* (Washington, 1905), being Water Supply and Irrigation Paper, No. 148 of the United States Geological Survey; A. J. Henry, *Climatology of the United States*, pp. 442-453 (Washington, 1906), being Bulletin Q of the Weather Bureau of the United States Department of Agriculture; *Mineral Resources of the United States*, annual reports published by the United States Geological Survey (Washington, 1883 sqq.); Charles Evans and C. O. Bunn, *Oklahoma Civil Government* (Ardmore, 1908); C. A. Beard, "Constitution of Oklahoma," in the *Political Science Quarterly*, vol. 24 (Boston, 1909); R. L. Owen, "Comments on the Constitution of Oklahoma," in the *Proceedings of the American Political Science Association*, vol. 5 (Baltimore, 1909); S. J. Buck, *The Settlement of Oklahoma* (Madison, 1907), reprinted from the *Transactions of the Wisconsin Academy of Sciences, Arts and Letters*; and D. C. Gideon, *Indian Territory, Descriptive, Biographical and Genealogical . . . with a General History of the Territory* (New York, 1901).

OKLAHOMA CITY, a city and the county-seat of Oklahoma County, Oklahoma, U.S.A., on the North Fork of the Canadian river, near the geographical centre of the state. Pop. (1890) 4151; (1900) 10,037; (1907) 32,452; (1910) 64,205. It is served by the Atchison, Topeka & Santa Fe, the Chicago, Rock Island & Pacific, the Missouri, Kansas & Texas, and the St Louis & San Francisco railways, and by inter-urban electric lines. It lies partly in a valley, partly on an upland, in a rich agricultural region. The city is the seat of Epworth University (founded in 1901 by the joint action of the Methodist Episcopal Church and the Methodist Episcopal Church, South). Oklahoma City's prosperity is due chiefly to its jobbing trade, with an extensive farming and stock-raising region, but it has also cotton compresses and cotton gins, and various manufactures. The total value of the factory products in 1905 was $3,670,730. Natural gas is largely used as a fuel. A large settlement was established here on the 22nd of April 1889, the day on which the country was by proclamation declared open for settlement. The city was chartered in 1890.

OKUBO TOSHIMITSU (1830–1878), Japanese statesman, a samurai of Satsuma, was one of the five great nobles who led the revolution in 1868 against the shogunate. He became one of the mikado's principal ministers, and in the Satsuma troubles which followed he was the chief opponent of Saigo Takamori. But the suppression of the Satsuma rebellion brought upon him the personal revenge of Saigo's sympathizers, and in the spring of 1878 he was assassinated by six clansmen. Okubo was one of the leading men of his day, and in 1872 was one of the Japanese mission which was sent round the world to get ideas for organizing the new régime.

OKUMA (SHIGENOBU), COUNT (1838–   ), Japanese statesman, was born in the province of Hizen in 1838. His father was an officer in the artillery, and during his early years his education consisted mainly of the study of Chinese literature. Happily for him, however, he was able to acquire in his youth a knowledge of English and Dutch, and by the help of some missionaries he succeeded in obtaining books in those languages on both scientific and political subjects. These works effected a complete revolution in his mind. He had been designed by his parents for the military profession, but the new light which now broke in upon him determined him to devote his entire energies to the abolition of the existing feudal system and to the establishment of a constitutional government. With impetuous zeal he urged his views on his countrymen, and though he took no active part in the revolution of 1868, the effect of his opinions exercised no slight weight in the struggle. Already he was a marked man, and no sooner was the government reorganized, with the mikado as the sole wielder of power, than he was appointed chief assistant in the department of foreign affairs. In 1869 he succeeded to the post of secretary of the joint departments of the interior and of finance, and for the next fourteen years he devoted himself wholly to politics. In 1870 he was made a councillor of state, and a few months later he accepted the office of president of the commission which represented the Japanese government at the Vienna Exhibition. In 1872 he was again appointed minister of finance, and when the expedition under General Saigō was sent to Formosa (1874) to chastise the natives of that island for the murder of some shipwrecked fishermen, he was nominated president of the commission appointed to supervise the campaign. By one of those waves of popular feeling to which the Japanese people are peculiarly liable, the nation which had supported him up to a certain point suddenly veered round and opposed him with heated violence. So strong was the feeling against him that on one occasion a would-be assassin threw at him a dynamite shell, which blew off one of his legs. During the whole of his public life he recognized the necessity of promoting education. When he resigned office in the early 'eighties he established the Semmon Gako, or school for special studies, at the cost of the 30,000 yen which had been voted him when he received the title of count, and subsequently he was instrumental in founding other schools and colleges. In 1896 he joined the Matsukata cabinet, and resigned in the following year in consequence of intrigues which produced an estrangement between him and the prime minister. On the retirement of Marquis Ito in 1898 he again took office, combining the duties of premier with those of minister of foreign affairs. But dissensions having arisen in the cabinet, he resigned a few months later, and retired into private life, cultivating his beautiful garden at Waseda near Tōkyō.

OLAF, the name of five kings of Norway.

OLAF I. TRYGGVESSÖN (969–1000) was born in 969, and began his meteoric career in exile. It is even said that he was bought as a slave in Esthonia. After a boyhood spent in Novgorod under the protection of King Valdemar, Olaf fought for the emperor Otto III. under the Wendish king Burislav, whose daughter he had married. On her death he followed the example of his countrymen, and harried in France and the British Isles, till, in a good day for the peace of those countries, he was converted to Christianity by a hermit in the Scilly Islands, and his marauding expeditions ceased since he would not harry those of his new faith. In England he married Gyda, sister of Olaf Kvaran, king of Dublin, and it was only after some years spent in administering her property in England and Ireland that he set sail for Norway, fired by reports of the unpopularity of its ruler Earl Haakon. Arriving in Norway in the autumn of 995, he was unanimously accepted as king, and at once set about the conversion of the country to Christianity, undeterred by the obstinate resistance of the people. It has been suggested that Olaf's ambition was to rule a united, as well as a Christian, Scandinavia, and we know that he made overtures of marriage to Sigrid, queen of Sweden, and set about adding new ships to his fleet, when negotiations fell through owing to her obstinate heathenism. He made an enemy of her, and did not hesitate to involve himself in a quarrel with King Sveyn of Denmark by marrying his sister Thyre, who had fled from her heathen husband Burislav in defiance of her brother's authority. Both his Wendish and his Irish wife had brought Olaf wealth and good fortune, but Thyre was his undoing, for it was on an expedition undertaken in the year 1000 to wrest her lands from Burislav that he was waylaid off the island Svöld, near Rügen, by the combined Swedish and Danish fleets, together with the ships of Earl Haakon's sons. The battle ended in the annihilation of the Norwegians. Olaf fought to the last on his great vessel, the "Long Snake," the mightiest ship in the North, and finally leapt overboard and was no more seen. Full of energy and daring, skilled in the use of every kind of weapon, genial and open-handed to his friends, implacable to his enemies, Olaf's personality was the ideal of the heathendom he had trodden down with such reckless disregard of his people's prejudices, and it was no doubt as much owing to the popularity his character won for him as to the strength of his position that he was able to force his will on the country with impunity. After his death he remained the hero of his people, who whispered that he was yet alive and looked for his return. "But however that may be," says the story, "Olaf Tryggvessön never came back to his kingdom in Norway."

OLAF (II.) HARALDSSÖN (995–1030), king from 1016–1029, called during his lifetime "the Fat," and afterwards known as St Olaf, was born in 995, the year in which Olaf Tryggvessön came to Norway. After some years' absence in England, fighting the Danes, he returned to Norway in 1015 and declared himself king, obtaining the support of the five petty kings of the Uplands. In 1016 he defeated Earl Sveyn, hitherto the virtual ruler of Norway, at the battle of Nesje, and within a few years had won more power than had been enjoyed by any of his predecessors on the throne. He had annihilated the petty kings of the South, had crushed the aristocracy, enforced the acceptance of Christianity throughout the kingdom, asserted his suzerainty in the Orkney Islands, had humbled the king of Sweden and married his daughter in his despite, and had conducted a successful raid on Denmark. But his success was short-lived, for in 1029 the Norwegian nobles, seething with discontent, rallied round the invading Knut the Great, and Olaf had to flee to Russia. On his return a year later he fell at the battle of Stiklestad, where his own subjects were arrayed against him. The succeeding years of disunion and misrule under the Danes explain the belated affection with which his countrymen came to regard him. The cunning and cruelty which marred his character were forgotten, and his services to his church and country remembered. Miracles were worked at his tomb, and in 1164 he was canonized and was declared the patron saint of Norway, whence his fame spread throughout Scandinavia and even to England, where churches are dedicated to him. The Norwegian order of knighthood of St Olaf was founded in 1847 by Oscar I., king of Sweden and Norway, in memory of this king.

The three remaining Norwegian kings of this name are persons of minor importance (see NORWAY: *History*).

OLAF, or **ANLAF** (d. 981), king of the Danish kingdoms of Northumbria and of Dublin, was a son of Sitric, king of Deira, and was related to the English king Æthelstan. As his name indicates he was of Norse descent, and he married a daughter of Constantine II., king of the Scots. When Sitric died about 927 Æthelstan annexed Deira, and Olaf took refuge in Scotland and in Ireland until 937, when he was one of the leaders of the formidable league of princes which was destroyed by Æthelstan at the famous battle of Brunanburh. Again he sought a home among his kinsfolk in Ireland, but just after Æthelstan's death in 940 he or Olaf Godfreyson was recalled to England by the Northumbrians. Both crossed over, and in 941 the new English king, Edmund, gave up Deira to the former. The peace between the English and the Danes did not, however, last long. Wulfstan, archbishop of York, sided with Olaf; but in 944 this king was driven from Northumbria by Edmund, and crossing to Ireland he ruled over the Danish kingdom of Dublin. From 949 to 952 he was again king of Northumbria, until he was expelled once more, and he passed the remainder of his active life in warfare in Ireland. But in 980 his dominion was shattered by the defeat of the Danes at the battle of Tara. He went to Iona, where he died probably in 981, although one account says he was in Dublin in 994. This, however, is unlikely. In the sagas he is known as Olaf the Red.

This Olaf must not be confused with his kinsman and ally, Olaf (d. 941), also king of Northumbria and of Dublin, who was a son of Godfrey, king of Dublin. The latter Olaf became king of Dublin in 934; but he was in England in 937, as he took part in the fight at Brunanburh. After this event he returned to Ireland, but he appears to have acted for a very short time as joint king of Northumbria with Olaf Sitricson. It is possible that he was the "Olaf of Ireland" who was called by the Northumbrians after Æthelstan's death, but both the Olafs appear to have accepted the invitation. He was killed in 941 at Tyningham near Dunbar.

See W. F. Skene, *Celtic Scotland*, vol. i. (1876), and J. R. Green, *The Conquest of England*, vol. i. (1899).

ÖLAND, an island in the Baltic Sea, next to Gotland the largest belonging to Sweden, stretching for 85 m. along the east coast of the southern extremity of that country, from which it is separated by Kalmar Sound which is from 5 to 15 m. broad. The greatest breadth of the island is 10 m., and its area 519 sq. m. Pop. (1900) 30,408. Consisting for the most part of Silurian limestone, and thus forming a striking contrast to the mainland with its granite and gneiss, Öland is further remarkable on account of the peculiarities of its structure. Down the west side for a considerable distance runs a limestone ridge, rising usually in terraces, but at times in steep cliffs, to an extreme height of 200 ft.; and along the east side there is a parallel ridge of sand, resting on limestone, never exceeding 90 ft. These ridges, known as the Western and Eastern Landborgar, are connected towards the north and the south by belts of sand and heath; and the hollow between them is occupied by a desolate and almost barren tract: the southern portion, or Alfvar (forming fully half of the southern part of the island), presents a surface of bare red limestone scored by superficial cracks and unfathomed fissures, and calcined by the heat refracted from the surrounding heights. The northern portion is covered at best with a copse of hazel bushes. Outside the ridges, however, Öland has quite a different aspect, the hillsides being not infrequently clothed with clumps of trees, while the narrow strip of alluvial coast-land, with its cornfields, windmills, villages and church towers, appears fruitful and prosperous. There are a few small streams in the island; and one lake, Hornsjö, about 3 m. long, deserves mention. Of the fir woods which once clothed a considerable area in the north the Böda crown-park is the only remnant. Grain, especially barley, and sandstone, are exported from the island, and there are cement works. A number of monuments of unknown age exist, including stones (*stensättningar*) arranged in groups to represent ships. The only town is Borgholm, a watering-place on the west coast, with one of the finest castle ruins in Sweden. The town was founded in 1817, but the castle, dating at least from the 13th century, was one of the strongest fortresses, and afterwards, as erected by the architect Nicodemus Tessin the elder (1615–1681), one of the most stately palaces in the country. The island was joined in 1824 to the administrative district (*län*) of Kalmar. Its inhabitants were formerly styled Öningar, and show considerable diversity of origin in the matter of speech, local customs and physical appearance.

From the raid of Ragnar Lodbrok's sons in 775 Öland is frequently mentioned in Scandinavian history, and especially as a battleground in the wars between Denmark and the northern kingdoms. In the middle ages it formed a separate legislative and administrative unity.

OLAUS MAGNUS, or MAGNI (Magnus, *i.e. Stora*, great, being the family name, and not a personal epithet), Swedish ecclesiastic and author, was born at Linköping in 1490 and died at Rome in 1558. Like his elder brother, Johannes Magnus, he obtained several ecclesiastical preferments (a canonry at Upsala and at Linköping, and the archdeaconry of Strengnes), and was employed on various diplomatic services (such as a mission to Rome, from Gustavus I., to procure the appointment of Johannes Magnus as archbishop of Upsala); but on the success of the reformation in Sweden his attachment to the old church led him to accompany his brother into exile. Settling at Rome, from 1527, he acted as his brother's secretary, and ultimately became his successor in the (now titular) archbishopric of Upsala. Pope Paul III., in 1546, sent him to the council of Trent; later, he became canon of St Lambert in Liége; King Sigismund I. of Poland also offered him a canonry at Posen; but most of his life, after his brother's death, seems to have been spent in the monastery of St Brigitta in Rome, where he

subsisted on a pension assigned him by the pope. He is best remembered as the author of the famous *Historia de Gentibus Septentrionalibus* (Rome, 1555), a work which long remained for the rest of Europe the chief authority on Swedish matters and is still a valuable repertory of much curious information in regard to Scandinavian customs and folk-lore.

The *Historia* was translated into Italian (Venice, 1565), German (Strassburg, 1567), English (London, 1658) and Dutch (Amsterdam, 1665); abridgments of the work appeared also at Antwerp (1558 and 1562), Paris (a French abridged version, 1561), Amsterdam (1586), Frankfort (1618) and Leiden (1652). Olaus also wrote a *Tabula terrarum septentrionalium . . .* (Venice, 1539).

OLBERS, HEINRICH WILHELM MATTHIAS (1758–1840), German astronomer, was born on the 11th of October 1758 at Arbergen, a village near Bremen, where his father was minister. He studied medicine at Göttingen, 1777–1780, attending at the same time Kaestner's mathematical course; and in 1779, while watching by the sick-bed of a fellow-student, he devised a method of calculating cometary orbits which made an epoch in the treatment of the subject, and is still extensively used. The treatise containing this important invention was made public by Baron von Zach under the title *Ueber die leichteste und bequemste Methode die Bahn eines Cometen zu berechnen* (Weimar, 1797). A table of eighty-seven calculated orbits was appended, enlarged by Encke in the second edition (1847) to 178, and by Galle in the third (1864) to 242. Olbers settled as a physician in Bremen towards the end of 1781, and practised actively for above forty years, finally retiring on the 1st of January 1823. The greater part of each night (he never slept more than four hours) was meantime devoted to astronomy, the upper portion of his house being fitted up as an observatory. He paid special attention to comets, and that of 1815 (period seventy-four years) bears his name in commemoration of its detection by him. He also took a leading part in the discovery of the minor planets, re-identified Ceres on the 1st of January 1802, and detected Pallas on the 28th of March following. His bold hypothesis of their origin by the disruption of a primitive large planet (*Monatliche Correspondenz*, vi. 88), although now discarded, received countenance from the finding of Juno by Harding, and of Vesta by himself, in the precise regions of Cetus and Virgo where the nodes of such supposed planetary fragments should be situated. Olbers was deputed by his fellow-citizens to assist at the baptism of the king of Rome on the 9th of June 1811, and was a member of the *corps législatif* in Paris 1812–1813. He died on the 2nd of March 1840, at the age of eighty-one. He was twice married, and one son survived him.

See *Biographische Skizzen verstorbener Bremischer Aerzte*, by Dr G. Barkhausen (Bremen, 1844); *Allgemeine geographische Ephemeriden*, iv. 283 (1799); *Abstracts Phil. Trans*. iv. 268 (1843); *Astronomische Nachrichten*, xxii. 265 (Bessel), also appended to A. Erman's *Briefwechsel zwischen Olbers und Bessel* (2 vols. Leipzig, 1852); *Allgemeine Deutsche Biographie* (S. Günther); R. Grant, *Hist. of Phys. Astr*. p. 239; R. Wolf, *Geschichte der Astronomie*, p. 517. The first two volumes of Dr C. Schilling's exhaustive work, *Wilhelm Olbers, sein Leben und seine Werke*, appeared at Berlin in 1894 and 1900, a third and later volume including his personal correspondence and biography. A list of Olbers's contributions to scientific periodicals is given at p. xxxv of the 3rd ed. of his *Leichteste Methode*, and his unique collection of works relating to comets now forms part of the Pulkowa library.

OLBIA, the chief Greek settlement in the north-west of the Euxine. It was generally known to the Greeks of Hellas as Borysthenes, though its actual site was on the right bank of the Hypanis (Bug) 4 m. above its junction with the estuary of the Borysthenes river (Dnieper). Eusebius says that it was founded from Miletus *c.* 650 B.C., a statement which is borne out by the discovery of Milesian pottery of the 7th century. It first appears as enjoying friendly relations with its neighbours the Scythians and standing at the head of trade routes leading far to the north-east (Herodotus iv.). Its wares also penetrated northward. It exchanged the manufactures of Ionia and, from the 5th century, of Attica for the slaves, hides and corn of Scythia. Changes of the native population (see SCYTHIA) interrupted this commerce, and the city was hard put to it to defend itself against the surrounding barbarians. We know of these difficulties and of the democratic constitution of the city from a decree in honour of Protogenes in the 3rd century B.C. (*C.I.G.* ii. 2058, *Inscr. Or. Septent. Pont. Euxin.* i. 16). In the following century it fell under the suzerainty of Scilurus, whose name appears on its coins, and when his power was broken by Mithradates VI. the Great, of Pontus, it submitted to the latter. About 50 B.C. it was entirely destroyed by the Getae and lay waste for many years. Ultimately at the wish of, and, to judge by the coins, under the protection of the natives themselves, it was restored, but Dio Chrysostom (*Or.* xxxvi.), who visited it about A.D. 83, gives a curious picture of its poor state. During the 2nd century A.D. it prospered better with Roman support and was quite flourishing from the time of Septimius Severus, when it was incorporated in Lower Moesia, to 248, when its coins came to an end, probably owing to its sack by the Goths. It was once more restored in some sort and lingered on to an unknown date. Excavations have shown the position of the old Greek walls and of those which enclosed the narrower site of the Roman city, an interesting Hellenistic house, and cemeteries of various dates. The principal cult was that of Achilles Pontarches, to whom the archons made dedications. It has another centre at Leuce (Phidonisi) and at various points in the north Euxine. Secondary was that of Apollo Prostates, the patron of the strategi; but the worship of most of the Hellenic deities is testified to in the inscriptions. The coinage begins with large round copper pieces comparable only to the Roman *aes grave* and smaller pieces in the shape of dolphins; these both go back into the 6th century B.C. Later the city adopted silver and gold coins of the Aeginetic standard.

See E. H. Minns, *Scythians and Greeks* (Cambridge, 1909); V. V. Latyshev, *Olbia* (St Petersburg, 1887, in Russian). For inscriptions, Boeckh, *C.I.G.* vol. ii.; V. V. Latyshev, *Inscr. Orae Septent. Ponti Euxini*, vols. i. and iv. For excavations, Reports of B. V. Pharmakovsky in *Compte rendu de la Comm. imp. archéolog.* (St Petersburg, 1901 sqq.), and *Bulletin* of the same, Nos. 8, 13, &c., summarized in *Archäologischer Anzeiger* (1903 sqq.). (E. H. M.)

OLBIA (Gr. ὀλβία, *i.e.* happy; mod. Terranova Pausania, *q.v.*), an ancient seaport city of Sardinia, on the east coast. The name indicates that it was of Greek origin, and tradition attributes its foundation to the Boeotians and Thespians under Iolaus (see SARDINIA). Pais considers that it was founded by the Phocaeans of Massilia before the 4th century B.C. (in Tamponi, *op. cit.* p. 83). It is situated on low ground, at the extremity of a deep recess, now called the Golfo di Terranova. It was besieged unsuccessfully by L. Cornelius Scipio in 259 B.C. Its territory was ravaged in 210 B.C. by a Carthaginian fleet. In Roman times it was the regular landing-place for travellers from Italy. Cicero notes the receipt of a letter from his brother from Olbia in 56 B.C., and obviously shared the prevailing belief as to the unhealthiness of Sardinia. Traces of the pre-Roman city have not been found. The line of the Roman city walls has been determined on the N. and E,. the N.E. angle being at the ancient harbour, which lay to the N. of the modern (*Notizie degli Scavi*, 1890, p. 224). Among the inscriptions are two tombstones, one of an imperial freedwoman,[1] the other of a freedman of Acte, the concubine of Nero; a similar tombstone was also found at Carales, and tiles bearing her name have been found in several parts of the island, but especially at Olbia, where in building a modern house in 1881 about one thousand were discovered. Pais (*op. cit.* 89 sqq.) attributes to Olbia an inscription now in the Campo Santo at Pisa, an epistyle bearing the words " Cereri sacrum Claudia Aug. lib. Acte," and made of Sardinian (?) granite. In any case it is clear that Acte must have had considerable property in the island (*Corp. Inscr. Lat.* x. 7980). Discoveries of buildings and tombs have frequently occurred within the area of the town and in its neighbourhood. Some scanty remains of an aqueduct exist outside the town, but hardly anything else of

[1] The freedwoman had been a slave of Acte before passing into the property of the emperor, and took the cognomen *Acteniana*—a practice which otherwise only occurs in the case of slaves of citizens of the highest rank or of foreign kings.

antiquity is to be seen *in situ*. A large number of milestones, fifty-one in all, with inscriptions, and several more with illegible ones, belonging to the first twelve miles of the Roman road between Olbia and Carales, have been discovered, and are now kept in the church of S. Simplicio (*Notizie degli Scavi*, 1888, p. 535; 1889, p. 258, 1892, pp. 217, 366; *Classical Review*, 1889, p. 228; 1890, p. 65, P. Tamponi, *Silloge Epigrafica, Olbiense*, Sassari, 1895). This large number may be accounted for by the fact that a new stone was often erected for a new emperor. They range in date from A.D. 245 to 375 (one is possibly of Domitian). The itineraries state that the main road from Carales to Olbia ran through the centre of the island to the east of Gennargentu (see SARDINIA); but a branch certainly diverged from the main road from Carales to Turris Libisonis (which kept farther west, more or less along the line followed by the modern railway) and came to Olbia. The distance by both lines is much the same; and all these milestones belong to the last portion which was common to both roads. (T. As.)

OLD-AGE PENSIONS. The provision of annuities for aged poor by the state was proposed in England in the 18th century—*e.g.* by Francis Maseres, cursitor baron of the Exchequer, in 1772, and by Mr Mark Rolle, M.P., in 1787. Suggestions for subsidizing friendly societies have also been frequent—*e.g.* by T. Paine in 1795, tentatively in Sturges Bourne's Report on the Poor Laws, 1817, and by Lord Lansdowne in 1837. The subject again became prominent in the latter part of the 19th century. Canon Blackley, who started this movement, proposed to compel every one to insure with a state department against sickness and old age, and essentially his scheme was one for the relief of the ratepayers and a more equitable readjustment of the poor-rate. The terms provisionally put forward by him required that every one in youth should pay £10, in return for which the state was to grant 8s. a week sick allowance and 4s. pension after seventy. These proposals were submitted to the Select Committee on National Provident Insurance, 1885–1887. This body reported unfavourably, more especially on the sick insurance part of the scheme, but the idea of old-age pension survived, and was taken up by the National Provident League, of which Mr (afterwards Sir) J. Rankin, M.P., was chairman. The subject was discussed in the constituencies and expectation was aroused. An unofficial parliamentary committee was formed, with Mr J. Chamberlain as chairman. This committee published proposals in March 1892, which show a very interesting change of attitude on the part of the promoters. Compulsion, which at the earlier period had found favour with Canon Blackley, Sir J. Rankin and even Mr Chamberlain, was no longer urged. The annuitant was no longer required to pay a premium adequate to the benefits promised, as in Canon Blackley's proposal. The benefit was no longer a pure annuity, but premiums were, in certain cases, returnable, and allowances were provided for widows, children (if any) and for the next of kin. Canon Blackley's professed object was to supersede the friendly societies, which, he alleged, were more or less insolvent; a proposal was now introduced to double every half-crown of pension derived by members from their friendly societies. This suggestion was criticized, even by supporters of the principle of state aid, on the ground that unless a pension was gratuitous, the class from which pauperism is really drawn could not profit by it. Mr Charles Booth in particular took this line. He accordingly proposed that there should be a general endowment of old age, 5s. a week to every one at the age of sixty-five. This proposal was calculated to involve an expenditure of £18,000,000 for England and Wales and £24,000,000 for the United Kingdom, exclusive of the cost of administration. While Mr Booth severely criticized the weak points of the contributory and voluntary schemes, their most influential advocate, Mr Chamberlain, did not spare Mr Booth's proposals. Speaking at Highbury, for instance, on the 24th of May 1899, he described Mr Booth's universal scheme as " a gigantic system of out-door relief for every one, good and bad, thrifty and unthrifty, the waster, drunkard and idler, as well as the industrious," and very forcibly stated his inability to support it.

In 1893 Mr Gladstone referred the whole question to a royal commission (Lord Aberdare, chairman). A majority report, adverse to the principle of state pensions, was issued in 1895. A minority report, signed by Mr Chamberlain and others, dissented, mainly on the ground that public expectation would be disappointed if nothing was done. In 1896 Lord Salisbury appointed a committee " of experts " (Lord Rothschild, chairman) to report on schemes submitted, and, if necessary, to devise a scheme. The committee were unable to recommend any of the schemes submitted, and added that, " we ourselves are unable, after repeated attempts, to devise any proposal free from grave inherent disadvantages." This second condemnation was not considered conclusive, and a select committee of the House of Commons (Mr Chaplin, chairman) was appointed to consider the condition of " the aged deserving poor." After an ineffectual attempt by Mr Chaplin to induce the committee to drop the pension idea, and to consider the provision made for the aged by the poor law, the committee somewhat hastily promulgated a scheme of gratuitous pensions for persons possessing certain qualifications. Of these the following were the most important: age of sixty-five; no conviction for, crime; no poor-law relief, " unless under exceptional circumstances," within twenty years; non-possession of income of 10s. a week; proved industry, or proved exercise of reasonable providence by some definite mode of thrift. The committee refrained from explaining the machinery and from estimating the cost, and suggested that this last problem should be submitted to yet another committee.

Accordingly a departmental committee (chairman, Sir E. Hamilton) was appointed, which reported in January 1900. The estimated cost of the above plan was, by this committee, calculated at £10,300,000 in 1901, rising to £15,650,000 in 1931. Mr Chaplin had publicly suggested that £2,000,000, the proceeds of a 1s. duty on corn, would go a long way to meet the needs of the case—a conjecture which was obviously far too sanguine. These unfavourable reports discouraged the more responsible advocates of state pensions. Mr Chamberlain appealed to the friendly societies to formulate a plan, an invitation which they showed no disposition to accept. Efforts continued to be made to press forward Mr Booth's universal endowment scheme or some modification of it. To this Mr Chamberlain declared his hostility. And here the matter rested, till in his Budget speech in 1907 Mr Asquith pledged the Liberal government to start a scheme in 1908.

In 1908 accordingly there was passed the Old-Age Pensions Act, which carried into effect a scheme for state pensions, payable as from the 1st of January 1909 to persons of the age of 70 years and over. The act grants a pension according to a graduated scale of not exceeding 5s. a week to every person, male and female, who fulfils certain statutory conditions, and at the same time is not subject to certain disqualifications. The statutory conditions, as set out in § 2 of the act, are: (1) The person must have attained the age of seventy; (2) must satisfy the pension authorities that for at least twenty years up to the date of receipt of pension he has been a British subject and has had his residence in the United Kingdom; and (3) the person must satisfy the pension authorities that his yearly means do not exceed £31, 10s. In § 4 of the act there are elaborate provisions for the calculation of yearly means, but the following may be particularly noticed: (1) in calculating the means of a person being one of a married couple living together in the same house, the means shall not in any case be taken to be a less amount than half the total means of the couple, and (2) if any person directly or indirectly deprives himself of any income or property in order to qualify for an old-age pension, it shall nevertheless be taken to be part of his means. The disqualifications are (1) receipt of poor-law relief (this qualification was specially removed as from the 1st of January 1911); (2) habitual failure to work (except in the case of those who have continuously for ten years up to the age of sixty made provision for their future by payments to friendly, provident or other societies or trade unions; (3) detention in a pauper or criminal lunatic asylum; (4) imprisonment without the option of a fine, which

disqualifies for ten years; and (5) liability to disqualification for a period not exceeding ten years in the case of an habitual drunkard. The graduated scale of pensions is given in a schedule to the act, and provide that when the yearly means of a pensioner do not exceed £21 he shall have the full pension of 5s. a week, which diminishes by 1s. a week for every addition of £2, 12s. 6d. to his income, until the latter reaches £31, 10s., when no pension is payable. The pension is paid weekly, on Fridays (§ 5), and is inalienable (§ 6).

All claims for, and questions relating to, pensions are determined by the pension authorities. They are (1) pension officers appointed by the Treasury from among inland revenue officers; (2) a central pension authority, which is the Local Government Board or a committee appointed by it, and (3) local pension committees appointed for every borough and urban district with a population of over 20,000, and for every county.

During the first three months of the year 1909, in which the act came into operation, there were 837,831 claims made for pensions: 490,755 in England and Wales, 85,408 in Scotland, and 261,668 in Ireland. Of these claims a total of 647,494 were granted: 393,700 in England and Wales, 70,294 in Scotland, and 183,500 in Ireland. The pensions in force on the 31st of March 1909 were as follows: 582,565 of 5s., 23,616 of 4s., 23,275 of 3s., 11,429 of 2s., and 6609 of 1s. By the 30th of September the total amount of money paid to 682,768 pensioners was £6,063,658, and in the estimates of 1909–1910 a sum of £8,750,000 was provided for the payment of pensions.

Germany.—The movement in favour of state aid to provision for old age has been largely due to the example of Germany. The German system (which for old age dates from 1891) is a form of compulsory and contributory insurance. One half of the premium payable is paid by the labourer, the other half by the employer. The state adds a subvention to the allowances paid to the annuitant. (See GERMANY.)

France.—By a law of April 1910 a system of old-age pensions, designed to come into operation in 1911, was adopted. It is a contributory system, embracing all wage-earners, with the exception of railway servants, miners and sailors on the special reserve list of the navy. It applies also to small landowners, tenant farmers and farm labourers. All are eligible for a pension at the age of 65, if in receipt of less than £120 a year. The actual *rente* or pension is calculated on the basis of the total obligatory contribution, together with a fixed viagère or state annuity. Male wage-earners are required to contribute 9 francs a year, and females 6 francs, the employers contributing a like amount. The largest pension obtainable is for life contributions and amounts to 414 francs. A clause in the act permits wage-earners to claim the *rente* at the age of 55 on a proportionately reduced scale without the viagère. The total cost of providing pensions in 1911 is estimated at over £5,500,000.

Denmark.—The Danish system of old-age pensions was instituted by a law of 1891, and has been extended by further acts of 1902 and 1908. By the law of 1891 the burden of maintaining the aged was in part transferred from the local to the national taxes, and relief from this latter source was called a pension. Recipients of public assistance must be over 60 years of age, they must be of good character and for 5 years previous to receipt must have had their domicile in Denmark without receiving public charity. Such public assistance may be granted either in money, or kind, or by residence in an institution, such as an hospital. The assistance given, whatever it may be, must be sufficient for maintenance, and for attendance in case of illness. The actual amount is determined by the poor-law authorities, but all private assistance amounting to more than 100 kroner (£5, 13s.) a year is taken into account in measuring the poverty of the applicant. The cost of assistance is met in the first case by the commune in which the recipient is domiciled, but half the amount is afterwards refunded by the state. In 1907–1903, 71,185 persons were assisted—53,008 by money and 18,177 otherwise. The total expenditure was £489,200, £242,660 being refunded by the state.

New Zealand.—In 1898 a bill, introduced by the Rt. Hon. R. J. Seddon, premier, became law which provided for the payment of an old-age pension out of the consolidated fund (revenue of the general government) to persons duly qualified, without contribution by the beneficiaries. The claimants must be 65 years of age, resident in the colony, and have so resided for 25 years. They must be free from conviction for lesser legal offences for 12 years, and for more serious breaches of the law for 25 years, previous to the application. They must be of good moral character and have a record of sobriety and respectability for five years. Their yearly income must not exceed £52, and they must not be owners of property exceeding in value £270. Aliens, aborigines, Chinese and Asiatics are excluded. The pensions are for £18 per annum. but for each £1 of yearly income over and above £34, and also for each £15 of capital over and above £50, £1 is deducted from the amount of the pension. Applications have to be made to the deputy registrars of one of 72 districts into which the colony is for this purpose divided. The claim is then recorded and submitted to a stipendiary magistrate, before whom the claimant has to prove his qualifications and submit to cross-examination. If the claim is admitted, a certificate is issued to the deputy registrar and in due course handed to the claimant. Payment is made through the local post-office as desired by the pensioner. The act came into force on the 1st of November 1898. An amending act of 1905 increased the amount of the maximum pension to £26 a year. See further, NEW ZEALAND. The authors of the measure maintain that it is a great success, while others point to the invidious character of the cross-examination required in proving the necessary degree of poverty, and allege that the arrangement penalizes the thrifty members of the poorer class, and is a direct incentive to transfer of property, of a more or less fraudulent character, between members of a family.

Victoria.—By the Old-Age Pensions Act 1900, £75,000 was appropriated for the purpose of paying a pension of not more than 10s. per week to any person who fulfilled the necessary conditions, of which the following were the principal: The pensioner must be 65 years of age or permanently disabled, must fill up a declaration that he has lived twenty years in the state; has not been convicted of drunkenness, wife-desertion, &c.; that his weekly income and his property do not exceed a given sum (the regulation of this and other details is intrusted to the governor in council). Further sums were subsequently appropriated to the purposes of the act.

AUTHORITIES.—Report and Evidence of Select Committee on National Provident Insurance (1887); Report of Royal Commission on Aged Poor (1895); Report of Lord Rothschild's Committee (1898); Report of the Select Committee on Aged Deserving Poor (1899); Report of Departmental Committee, &c., about the Aged Deserving Poor (1900); J. A. Spender, *The State and Pensions in Old Age* (1892); George King, *Old Age Pensions* (1899); Reports of Poor Law Conferences; Annual Reports of the Chief Registrar of Friendly Societies; E. W. Brabrook, *Provident Societies and the Public Welfare* (1898), ch. viii. For: Charles Booth, *The Aged Poor in England and Wales* (1894); *Old Age Pensions* (1899); Right Hon. Joseph Chamberlain, "The Labour Question," *Nineteenth Century* (November 1892); Speeches (21st April 1891 and 24th May 1899); Rev. J. Frome Wilkinson, *Pensions and Pauperism* (1892); Publications of the National Providence League. Against: C. J. Radley, *Self-Help versus State-Pensions* (3rd edition); *Plea for Liberty* (1892); *Report of Royal Commission from a Friendly Society Point of View*, reprint from *Oddfellows' Magazine* (1895); *The Foresters' Miscellany* (February 1902); *Unity, a Monthly Journal of Foresters,* &c. (February 1902); C. S. Loch, *Old-Age Pensions and Pauperism* (1892); Reply of Bradfield Board of Guardians to circular of National Provident League (1891); Publications of the Charity Organization Society.

OLDBURY, an urban district in the Oldbury parliamentary division of Worcestershire, England, 5 m. W. of Birmingham, on the Great Western and London & North-Western railways and the Birmingham canal. Pop. (1901) 25,191. Coal, iron and limestone abound in the neighbourhood, and the town possesses alkali and chemical works, railway-carriage works, iron, edge-tool, nail and steel works, maltings, corn-mills, and brick and tile kilns. The urban district includes the townships of Langley and Warley.

OLDCASTLE, SIR JOHN (d. 1417), English Lollard leader, was son of Sir Richard Oldcastle of Almeley in Herefordshire. He is first mentioned as serving in the expedition to Scotland in 1400, when he was probably quite a young man. Next year he was in charge of Builth castle in Brecon, and serving all through the Welsh campaigns won the friendship and esteem of Henry, the prince of Wales. Oldcastle represented Herefordshire in the parliament of 1404. Four years later he married Joan, the heiress of Cobham, and was thereon summoned to parliament as Lord Cobham in her right. As a trusted supporter of the prince, Oldcastle held a high command in the expedition which the young Henry sent to France in 1411. Lollardy had many supporters in Herefordshire, and Oldcastle himself had adopted Lollard opinions before 1410, when the churches on his wife's estates in Kent were laid under interdict for unlicensed preaching. In the convocation which met in March 1413, shortly before the death of Henry IV., Oldcastle was at once accused of heresy. But his friendship with the new king prevented any decisive action till convincing evidence was found in a book belonging to Oldcastle, which was discovered in a shop in Paternoster Row. The matter was brought before the king, who desired that nothing should be done till he had tried his personal influence. Oldcastle declared his readiness to submit to the king "all his fortune in this world," but was firm in his religious beliefs. When he fled from Windsor to his own castle at Cowling, Henry at last consented to a prosecution. Oldcastle refused to obey the archbishop's repeated citations, and it was only under a royal writ that he at last appeared before the ecclesiastical court on the 23rd of September. In a confession of his faith he declared his belief in the sacraments and the necessity of penance and true confession; but to put hope, faith or trust in images was the great sin of idolatry. But he would not assent to the orthodox doctrine of the sacrament as stated by the bishops, nor admit the necessity of confession to a priest. So on the 25th of September he was convicted as a heretic. Henry was still anxious to find a way of escape for his old comrade, and granted a respite of forty days. Before that time had expired Oldcastle escaped from the Tower by the help of one William Fisher, a parchment-maker of Smithfield (Riley, *Memorials of London*, 641). Old-castle now put himself at the head of a wide-spread Lollard conspiracy, which assumed a definitely political character. The design was to seize the king and his brothers during a Twelfth-night mumming at Eltham, and perhaps, as was alleged, to establish some sort of commonwealth. Henry, forewarned of their intention, removed to London, and when the Lollards assembled in force in St Giles's Fields on the 10th of January they were easily dispersed. Oldcastle himself escaped into Herefordshire, and for nearly four years avoided capture. Apparently he was privy to the Scrope and Cambridge plot in July 1415, when he stirred some movement in the Welsh Marches. On the failure of the scheme he went again into hiding. Oldcastle was no doubt the instigator of the abortive Lollard plots of 1416, and appears to have intrigued with the Scots. But at last his hiding-place was discovered and in November 1417 he was captured by the Lord Charlton of Powis. Oldcastle who was "sore wounded ere he would be taken," was brought to London in a horse-litter. On the 14th of December he was formally condemned, on the record of his previous conviction, and that same day was hung in St Giles's Fields, and burnt "gallows and all." It is not clear that he was burnt alive.

Oldcastle died a martyr. He was no doubt a man of fine quality, but circumstances made him a traitor, and it is impossible altogether to condemn his execution. His unpopular opinions and early friendship with Henry V. created a traditional scandal which long continued. In the old play *The Famous Victories of Henry V.*, written before 1588, Oldcastle figures as the prince's boon companion. When Shakespeare adapted that play in *Henry IV.*, Oldcastle still appeared; but when the play was printed in 1598 Falstaff's name was substituted, in deference, as it is said, to the then Lord Cobham. Though the fat knight still remains "my old lad of the Castle," the stage character has nothing to do with the Lollard leader.

BIBLIOGRAPHY.—The record of Oldcastle's trial is printed in *Fasciculi Zizaniorum* (Rolls series), and in Wilkins's *Concilia*, iii. 351-357. The chief contemporary notices of his later career are given in *Gesta Henrici Quinti* (Eng. Hist. Soc.) and in Walsingham's *Historia Anglicana*. There have been many lives of Oldcastle, mainly based on *The Actes and Monuments* of John Foxe, who in his turn followed the *Briefe Chronycle* of John Bale, first published in 1544. For notes on Oldcastle's early career, consult J. H. Wylie, *History of England under Henry IV.* For literary history see the Introductions to Richard James's *Iter Lancastrense* (Chetham Soc., 1845) and to Grosart's edition of the *Poems of Richard James* (1880). See also W. Baeske, *Oldcastle-Falstaff in der englischen Literatur bis zu Shakespeare* (Palaestra, i. Berlin, 1905). For a recent Life, see W. T. Waugh in the *English Historical Review*, vol. xx. (C. L. K.)

OLD CATHOLICS (Ger. *Altkatholiken*), the designation assumed by those members of the Roman Catholic Church who refused to accept the decrees of the Vatican Council of 1870 defining the dogma of papal infallibility (see VATICAN COUNCIL and INFALLIBILITY) and ultimately set up a separate ecclesiastical organization on the episcopal model. The Old Catholic movement, at the outset at least, differed fundamentally from the Protestant Reformation of the 16th century in that it aimed not at any drastic changes in doctrine but at the restoration of the ancient Catholic system, founded on the diocesan episcopate, which under the influence of the ultramontane movement of the 19th century had been finally displaced by the rigidly centralized system of the papal monarchy. In this respect it represented a tendency of old standing within the Church and one which, in the 18th century, had all but gained the upper hand (see FEBRONIANISM and GALLICANISM). Protestantism takes for its standard the Bible and the supposed doctrines and institutions of the apostolic age. Old Catholicism sets up the authority of the undivided Church, and accepts the decrees of the first seven general councils—down to the second council of Nicaea (787), a principle which has necessarily involved a certain amount of doctrinal divergence both from the standards of Rome and those of the Protestant Churches.

The proceedings of the Vatican council and their outcome had at first threatened to lead to a serious schism in the Church. The minority against the decrees included many of the most distinguished prelates and theologians of the Roman communion, and the methods by which their opposition had been overcome seemed to make it difficult for them to submit. The pressure put upon them was, however, immense, and the reasons for submission may well have seemed overwhelming; in the end, after more or less delay, all the recalcitrant bishops gave in their adhesion to the decrees.

The "sacrificio dell' intelletto," as it was termed—the subordination of individual opinion to the general authority of the Church—was the maxim adopted by one and all. Seventeen of the German bishops almost immediately receded from the position they had taken up at Rome and assented to the dogma, publishing at the same time a pastoral letter in which they sought to justify their change of sentiment on the ground of expediency in relation to the interests of the Church (Michelis, *Der neue Fuldaer Hirtenbrief*, 1870). Their example was followed by all the other bishops of Germany. Darboy, archbishop of Paris, and Dupanloup, bishop of Orléans, in France adopted a like course, and took with them the entire body of the French clergy. Each bishop demanded in turn the same submission from the clergy of his diocese, the alternative being suspension from pastoral functions, to be followed by deprivation of office. It may be urged as some extenuation of this general abandonment of a great principle, that those who had refused to subscribe to the dogma received but languid support, and in some cases direct discouragement, from their respective governments. The submission of the illustrious Karl Joseph. von Hefele was generally attributed to the influence exerted by the court of Württemberg.

The universities, being less directly under the control of the Church, were prepared to show a bolder front. Dr J. F. von Schulte, professor at Prague, was one of the first to publish a formal protest. A meeting of Catholic professors and distinguished scholars convened at Nuremberg (August 1870) recorded a like dissent, and resolved on the adoption of measures for bringing about the assembling of a really free council north of the Alps. The *Appel aux Evêques Catholiques* of M. Hyacinthe Loyson (better known as "Père Hyacinthe"), after referring to the overthrow of "the two despotisms," "the empire of the Napoleons and the temporal power of the popes," appealed to the Catholic bishops throughout the world to put an end to the schism by declaring whether the recent decrees were or were not binding on the faith of the Church. This appeal, on its appearance in *La Liberté* early in 1871, was suppressed by the order of the king of Italy. On the 28th of March Döllinger, in a letter of some length, set forth the reasons which com-

pelled him also to withhold his submission alike as " a Christian, a theologian, an historical student and a citizen." The publication of this letter was shortly followed by a sentence of excommunication pronounced against Döllinger and Professor Johannes Friedrich (*q.v.*), and read to the different congregations from the pulpits of Munich. The professors of the university, on the other hand, had shortly before evinced their resolution of affording Döllinger all the moral support in their power by an address (April 3, 1871) in which they denounced the Vatican decrees with unsparing severity, declaring that, at the very time when the German people had " won for themselves the post of honour on the battlefield among the nations of the earth," the German bishops had stooped to the dishonouring task of "forcing consciences in the service of an unchristian tyranny, of reducing many pious and upright men to distress and want, and of persecuting those who had but stood steadfast in their allegiance to the ancient faith " (Friedberg, *Aktenstücke z. ersten Vaticanischen Concil*, p. 187). An address to the king, drawn up a few days later, received the signatures of 12,000 Catholics. The refusal of the rites of the Church to one of the signatories, Dr Zenger, when on his deathbed, elicited strong expressions of disapproval;[1] and when, shortly after, it became necessary to fill up by election six vacancies in the council of the university, the feeling of the electors was indicated by the return of candidates distinguished by their dissent from the new decrees. In the following September the demand for another and a free council was responded to by the assembling of a congress at Munich. It was composed of nearly 500 delegates, convened from almost all parts of the world; but the Teutonic element was now as manifestly predominant as the Latin element had been at Rome. The proceedings were presided over by Professor von Schulte, and lasted three days. Among those who took a prominent part in the deliberations were Landammann Keller, Windscheid, Döllinger, Reinkens, Maassen (professor of canon law at Vienna), Friedrich and Huber. The arrangements finally agreed upon were mainly provisional; but one of the resolutions plainly declared that it was desirable if possible to effect a reunion with the Oriental Greek and Russian Churches, and also to arrive at an " understanding " with the Protestant and Episcopal communions.

In the following year lectures were delivered at Munich by various supporters of the new movement, and the learning and eloquence of Reinkens were displayed with marked effect. In France the adhesion of the abbé Michaud to the cause attracted considerable interest, not only from his reputation as a preacher, but also from the notable step in advance made by his declaration that, inasmuch as the adoption of the standpoint of the Tridentine canons would render reunion with the Lutheran and the Reformed Churches impossible, the wisest course would be to insist on nothing more with respect to doctrinal belief than was embodied in the canons of the first seven oecumenical councils. In the same year the Old Catholics, as they now began to be termed, entered into relations with the historical little Jansenist Church of Utrecht. Döllinger, in delivering his inaugural address as rector of the university of Munich, expressed his conviction that theology had received a fresh impulse and that the religious history of Europe was entering upon a new phase.

Other circumstances contributed to invest Old Catholicism with additional importance. It was evident that the relations between the Roman Curia and the Prussian government were becoming extremely strained. In February 1872 appeared the first measures of the Falk ministry, having for their object the control of the influence of the clergy in the schools, and in May the pope refused to accept Cardinal Hohenlohe, who during the council had opposed the definition of the dogma, as Prussian minister at the Vatican. In the same year two humble parish priests, Renftle of Mering in Bavaria and Tangermann of Unkel in the Rhineland, set an example of independence by refusing

---

[1] The rites were administered and the burial service conducted by Friedrich, who had refused to acknowledge his excommunication.

to accept the decrees. The former, driven from his parish church, was followed by the majority of his congregation, who, in spite of every discouragement, continued faithful to him; and for years after, as successive members were removed by death, the crosses over their graves recorded that they had died "true to their ancient belief." Tangermann, the poet, expelled in like manner from his parish by the archbishop of Cologne, before long found himself the minister of a much larger congregation in the episcopal city itself. These examples exercised no little influence, and congregations of Old Catholics were shortly after formed at numerous towns and villages in Bavaria, Baden, Prussia, German Switzerland, and even in Austria. At Warnsdorf in Bohemia a congregation was collected which still represents one of the most important centres of the movement. In September the second congress was held at Cologne. It was attended by some 500 delegates or visitors from all parts of Europe, and the English Church was represented by the bishops of Ely and Lincoln and other distinguished members. At this congress Friedrich boldly declared that the movement was directed "against the whole papal system, a system of errors during a thousand years, which had only reached its climax in the doctrine of infallibility."

The movement thus entered a new phase, the congress occupying itself mainly with the formation of a more definite organization and with the question of reunion with other Churches. The immediate effect was a fateful divergence of opinion; for many who sympathized with the opposition to the extreme papal claims shrank from the creation of a fresh schism. Prince Chlodwig Höhenlohe, who as prime minister of Bavaria had attempted to unite the governments against the definition of the dogma, refused to have anything to do with proceedings which could only end in the creation of a fresh sect, and would make the prospect of the reform of the Church from within hopeless; more important still, Döllinger refused to take part in setting up a separate organization, and though he afterwards so far modified his opinion as to help the Old Catholic community with sympathy and advice, he never formally joined it.

Meanwhile, the progress of the quarrel between the Prussian government and the Curia had been highly favourable to the movement. In May 1873 the celebrated Falk laws were enacted, whereby the articles 15 and 18 of the Prussian constitution were modified, so as to legalize a systematic state supervision over the education of the clergy of all denominations, and also over the appointment and dismissal of all ministers of religion. The measure, which was a direct response to the Vatican decrees, inspired the Old Catholics with a not unreasonable expectation that the moral support of the government would henceforth be enlisted on their side. On the 11th of August Professor J. H. Reinkens of Breslau, having been duly elected bishop of the new community,[1] was consecrated at Rotterdam by Bishop Heykamp of Deventer, the archbishop of Utrecht, who was to have performed the ceremony, having died a few days before. In the meantime the extension of the movement in Switzerland had been proceeding rapidly, and it was resolved to hold the third congress at Constance. The proceedings occupied three days (12th to 14th September), the subjects discussed being chiefly the institution of a synod[2] as the legislative and executive organ of the Church, and schemes of reunion with the Greek, the African and the Protestant communions. On the 20th of September the election of Bishop Reinkens was formally recognized by the Prussian government; and on the 7th of October he took the oath of allegiance to the king.

The following year (1874) was marked by the assembling of the first synod and a conference at Bonn, and of a congress

[1] Reinkens was elected at Cologne in primitive Christian fashion by clergy and people, the latter being representatives of Old Catholic congregations.

[2] The diocesan synod, under the presidency of the bishop, consists of the clergy of the diocese and one lay delegate for every 200 church members. It now meets twice a year and transacts the business prepared for it by an executive committee of 4 clergy and 5 laymen. In Switzerland the organization is still more democratic; the bishop does not preside over the synod and may be deposed by it.

at Freiburg-im-Breisgau. At the congress Bishop Reinkens spoke in hopeful terms of the results of his observations during a recent missionary tour throughout Germany. The conference, held on the 14th, 15th and 16th of September, had for its special object the discussion of the early confessions as a basis of agreement, though not necessarily of fusion, between the different communions above-named. The meetings, which were presided over by Döllinger, successively took into consideration the *Filioque* clause in the Nicene creed, the sacraments, the canon of Scripture, the episcopal succession in the English Church, the confessional, indulgences, prayers for the dead, and the eucharist (see DÖLLINGER). The synod (May 27-29) was the first of a series, held yearly till 1879 and afterwards twice a year, in which the doctrine and discipline of the new Church were gradually formulated. The tendency was, naturally, to move further and further away from the Roman model; and though the synod expressly renounced any claim to formulate dogma, or any intention of destroying the unity of the faith, the "Catholic Catechism" adopted by it in 1874 contained several articles fundamentally at variance with the teaching of Rome.[3] At the first synod, too, it was decided to make confession and fasting optional, while later synods pronounced in favour of using the vernacular in public worship, allowing the marriage of priests, and permitting them to administer the communion in both kinds to members of the Anglican Church attending their services. Of these developments that abolishing the compulsory celibacy of the clergy led to the most opposition; some opposed it as inexpedient, others—notably the Jansenist clergy of Holland—as wrong in itself, and when it was ultimately passed in 1878 some of the clergy, notably Tangermann and Reusch, withdrew from the Old Catholic movement.

Meanwhile the movement had made some progress in other countries—in Austria, in Italy and in Mexico; but everywhere it was hampered by the inevitable controversies, which either broke up its organization or hindered its development. In Switzerland, where important conferences were successively convened (at Solothurn in 1871, at Olten in 1872, 1873 and 1874), the unanimity of the "Christian Catholics," as they preferred to call themselves, seemed at one time in danger of being shipwrecked on the question of episcopacy. It was not until September 18th, 1876, that the conflict of opinions was so far composed as to allow of the consecration of Bishop Herzog by Bishop Reinkens. The reforms introduced by M. Hyacinthe Loyson in his church at Geneva received only a partial assent from the general body. Among the more practical results of his example is to be reckoned, however, the fact that in French Switzerland nearly all the clergy, in German Switzerland about one half, are married men.

The end of the *Kulturkampf* in 1878, and the new alliance between Bismarck and Pope Leo XIII. against revolutionary Socialism, deprived the Old Catholics of the special favour which had been shown them by the Prussian government; they continued, however, to enjoy the legal status of Catholics, and their communities retained the rights and the property secured to them by the law of the 4th of July 1875. In Bavaria, on the other hand, they were in March 1890, after the death of Döllinger, definitely reduced to the status of a private religious sect, with very narrow rights. When Bishop Reinkens died in January 1896 his successor Theodor Weber, professor of theology at Breslau, elected bishop on the 4th of March, was recognized only by the governments of Prussia, Baden and Hesse. The present position of the Old Catholic Church has disappointed the expectation of its friends and of its enemies. It has neither advanced rapidly, as the former had hoped, nor retrograded, as the latter have frequently predicted it would do. In Germany there are 90 congregations, served by 60 priests, and the number of adherents is estimated at about 60,000. In Switzerland there are 40 parishes (of which only one, that at Lucerne, is in the

[3] E.g. especially Question 164: "this (the Christian) community is invisible," and Question 167, "one may belong to the invisible Church (i.e. of those sharing in Christ's redemption) without belonging to the visible Church."

Roman Catholic cantons), 60 clergy and about 50,000 adherents. In Austria, though some accessions have been received since the *Los von Rom* movement began in 1899, the Old Catholic Church has not made much headway; it has some 15 churches and about 15,000 adherents. In Holland the Old Catholic or Jansenist Church has 3 bishops, about 30 congregations and over 8000 adherents. In France the movement headed by Loyson did not go far. There is but one congregation, in Paris, where it has built for itself a beautiful new church on the Boulevard Blanqin. Its priest is George Volet, who was ordained by Herzog, and it has just over 300 members. It is under the supervision of the Old Catholic archbishops of Utrecht. In Italy a branch of the Old Catholic communion was established in 1881 by Count Enrico di Campello, a former canon of St Peter's at Rome. A church was opened in Rome by Monsignor Savarese and Count Campello, under the supervision of the bishop of Long Island in the United States, who undertook the superintendence of the congregation in accordance with the regulations laid down by the Lambeth conference. But dissensions arose between the two men. The church in Rome was closed; Savarese returned to the Roman Church; and Campello commenced a reform work in the rural districts of Umbria, under the episcopal guidance of the bishop of Salisbury. This was in 1885. In 1900 Campello returned to Rome, and once more opened a church there. In 1902 he retired from active participation in the work, on account of age and bodily infirmity; and his place at the head of it was taken by Professor Cicchitti of Milan. Campello ultimately returned to the Roman communion. There are half-a-dozen priests, who are either in Roman or Old Catholic orders, and about twice as many congregations. Old Catholicism has spread to America. The Polish Romanists there, in 1899, complained of the rule of Irish bishops; elected a bishop of their own, Herr Anton Koslowski; presented him to the Old Catholic bishops in Europe for consecration; and he presides over seven congregations in Chicago and the neighbourhood. The Austrian and Italian churches possess no bishops, and the Austrian government refuses to allow the Old Catholic bishops of other countries to perform their functions in Austria. Every Old Catholic congregation has its choral union, its poor relief, and its mutual improvement society. Theological faculties exist at Bonn and Bern, and at the former a residential college for theological students was established by Bishop Reinkens. Old Catholicism has eight newspapers—two in Italy, two in Switzerland, and one each in Holland, Germany, Austria and France. It has held reunion conferences at Lucerne in 1892, at Rotterdam in 1894, and at Vienna in 1897. At these, members of the various episcopal bodies have been welcomed. It has also established a quarterly publication, the *Revue internationale de théologie*, which has admitted articles in French, German and English, contributed not merely by Old Catholics, but by members of the Anglican, Russian, Greek and Slavonic churches. Old Catholic theologians have been very active, and the work of Döllinger and Reusch on the Jesuits, and the history of the Roman Church by Professor Langen, have attained a European reputation.

An outline of the whole movement up to the year 1875 will be found in *The New Reformation*, by "Theodorus" (J. Bass Mullinger); and an excellent résumé of the main facts in the history of the movement in each European country, as connected with other developments of liberal thought, and with political history, is given in the second volume of Dr F. Nippold's *Handbuch der neuesten Kirchengeschichte*, vol. ii. (1883). See also A. M. E. Scarth, *The Story of the Old Catholic and Kindred Movements* (London, 1883); Bühler, *Der Altkatholicismus* (Leiden, 1880); J. F. von Schulte, *Der Altkatholinismus* (Giessen, 1887); and article in Hauck-Herzog's *Realencyk. für prot. Theol. und Kirche*, i. 415. For details the following sources may be consulted: (a) For the proceedings of the successive congresses: the *Stenographische Berichte*, published at Munich, Cologne, Constance, &c.; those of the congress of Constance were summarized in an English form, with other elucidatory matter, by Professor John Mayor. (b) For the questions involved in the consecration of Bishop Reinkens: *Rechtsgutachten über die Frage der Anerkennung des altkatholischen Bischofs Dr Reinkens in Bayern* (Munich, 1874); Emil Friedberg, *Der Staat und d. Bischofswahlen in Deutschland* (Leipzig, 1874); F. von Sybel, *Das altkatholische Bisthum und das Vermögen d. römischkatholischen. Kirchengesellschaften in*

Preussen (Bonn, 1874). (c) Reinkens's own speeches and pastorals, some of which have been translated into English, give his personal views and experiences; the *Life* of Huber has been written and published by Eberhard Stirngiebl; and the persecutions to which the Old Catholic clergy were exposed have been set forth in a pamphlet by J. Mayor, *Facts and Documents* (London, 1875). (d) For Switzerland, C. Herzog, *Beiträge zur Vorgeschichte der Christkathol, Kirche der Schweiz* (Bern, 1896).

OLD DEER, a parish and village in the district of Buchan, Aberdeenshire, Scotland. Pop. (1901), 4313. The village lies on the Deer or South Ugie Water, 10½ m. W. of Peterhead, and 2 m. from Mintlaw station on the Great North of Scotland Railway Company's branch line from Aberdeen to Peterhead. The industries include distilling, brewing, and the manufacture of woollens, and there are quarries of granite and limestone. Columba and his nephew Drostan founded a monastery here in the 6th century, of which no trace remains. A most interesting relic of the monks was discovered in 1857 in the Cambridge University library by Henry Bradshaw. It consisted of a small MS. of the Gospels in the Vulgate, fragments of the liturgy of the Celtic church, and notes, in the Gaelic script of the 12th century, referring to the charters of the ancient monastery, including a summary of that granted by David I. These are among the oldest examples of Scottish Gaelic. The MS. was also adorned with Gaelic designs. It had belonged to the monks of Deer and been in the possession of the University Library since 1715. It was edited by John Stuart (1813-1877) for the Spalding Club, by whom it was published in 1869 under the title of *The Book of Deer*. In 1218 William Comyn, earl of Buchan, founded the Abbey of St Mary of Deer, now in ruins, ⅜ m. farther up the river than the monastery and on the opposite bank. Although it was erected for Cistercians from the priory of Kinloss, near Forres, the property of the Columban monastery was removed to it. The founder (d. 1233) and his countess were buried in the church. The parish is rich in antiquities, but the most noted of them—the Stone of Deer, a sculptured block of syenite, which stood near the Abbey—was destroyed in 1854. The thriving village of NEW DEER (formerly called Auchriddie) lies about 7 m. W. of the older village; it includes the ruined castle of Fedderat.

OLDENBARNEVELDT, JOHAN VAN (1547-1619), Dutch statesman, was born at Amersfoort on the 14th of September 1547. The family from which he claimed descent was of ancient lineage. After studying law at Louvain, Bourges and Heidelberg, and travelling in France and Italy, Oldenbarneveldt settled down to practise in the law courts at the Hague. In religion a moderate Calvinist, he threw himself with ardour into the revolt against Spanish tyranny and became a zealous adherent of William the Silent. He served as a volunteer for the relief of Haarlem (1573) and again at Leiden (1574). In 1576 he obtained the important post of pensionary of Rotterdam, an office which carried with it official membership of the States of Holland. In this capacity his industry, singular grasp of affairs, and persuasive powers of speech speedily gained for him a position of influence. He was active in promoting the Union of Utrecht (1579) and the acceptance of the countship of Holland and Zeeland by William (1584). On the assassination of Orange it was at the proposal of Oldenbarneveldt that the youthful Maurice of Nassau was at once elected stadholder, captain-general and admiral of Holland. During the governorship of Leicester he was the leader of the strenuous opposition offered by the States of Holland to the centralizing policy of the governor. In 1586 he was appointed, in succession to Paul Buys, to the post of Land's Advocate of Holland. This great office, which he held for 32 years, gave to a man of commanding ability and industry unbounded influence in a many-headed republic without any central executive authority. Though nominally the servant of the States of Holland he made himself politically the personification of the province which bore more than half the entire charge of the union, and as its mouthpiece in the states-general he practically dominated that assembly. In a brief period he became entrusted with such large and far-reaching authority in all the details of administration, as to be virtually "minister of all affairs."

During the two critical years which followed the withdrawal of Leicester, it was the statesmanship of the advocate which kept the United Provinces from falling asunder through their own inherent separatist tendencies, and prevented them from becoming an easy conquest to the formidable army of Alexander of Parma. Fortunately for the Netherlands the attention of Philip was at their time of greatest weakness riveted upon his contemplated invasion of England, and a respite was afforded which enabled Oldenbarneveldt to supply the lack of any central organized government by gathering into his own hands the control of administrative affairs. His task was made the easier by the whole-hearted support he received from Maurice of Nassau, who, after 1589, held the Stadholderate of five provinces, and was likewise captain-general and admiral of the union. The interests and ambitions of the two men did not clash, for Maurice's thoughts were centred on the training and leadership of armies and he had no special capacity as a statesman or inclination for politics. The first rift between them came in 1600, when Maurice was forced against his will by the states-general, under the advocate's influence, to undertake an expedition into Flanders, which was only saved from disaster by desperate efforts which ended in victory at Nieuwport. In 1598 Oldenbarneveldt took part in special embassies to Henry IV. and Elizabeth, and again in 1605 in a special mission sent to congratulate James I. on his accession.

The opening of negotiations by Albert and Isabel in 1606 for a peace or long truce led to a great division of opinion in the Netherlands. The archdukes having consented to treat with the United Provinces " as free provinces and states over which they had no pretensions," Oldenbarneveldt, who had with him the States of Holland and the majority of burgher regents throughout the county, was for peace, provided that liberty of trading was conceded. Maurice and his cousin William Louis, stadholder of Frisia, with the military and naval leaders and the Calvinist clergy, were opposed to it, on the ground that the Spanish king was merely seeking an interval of repose in which to recuperate his strength for a renewed attack on the independence of the Netherlands. For some three years the negotiations went on, but at last after endless parleying, on the 9th of April 1609, a truce for twelve years was concluded. All that the Dutch asked was directly or indirectly granted, and Maurice felt obliged to give a reluctant and somewhat sullen assent to the favourable conditions obtained by the firm and skilful diplomacy of the advocate.

The immediate effect of the truce was a strengthening of Oldenbarneveldt's influence in the government of the republic, now recognized as a "free and independent state"; external peace, however, was to bring with it internal strife. For some years there had been a war of words between the religious parties, known as the Gomarists (strict Calvinists) and the Arminians (moderate Calvinists). In 1610 the Arminians drew up a petition, known as the Remonstrance, in which they asked that their tenets (defined in five articles) should be submitted to a national synod, summoned by the civil government. It was no secret that this action of the Arminians was taken with the approval and connivance of the advocate, who was what was styled a *libertine*, *i.e.* an upholder of the principle of toleration in religious opinions. The Gomarists in reply drew up a Contra-Remonstrance in seven articles, and appealed to a purely church synod. The whole land was henceforth divided into Remonstrants and Contra-Remonstrants; the States of Holland under the influence of Oldenbarneveldt supported the former, and refused to sanction the summoning of a purely church synod (1613). They likewise (1614) forbade the preachers in the Province of Holland to treat of disputed subjects from their pulpits. Obedience was difficult to enforce without military help, riots broke out in certain towns, and when Maurice was appealed to, as captain-general, he declined to act. He did more, though in no sense a theologian; he declared himself on the side of the Contra-Remonstrants, and established a preacher of that persuasion in a church at the Hague (1617).

The advocate now took a bold step. He proposed that the States of Holland should, on their own authority, as a sovereign province, raise a local force of 4000 men (*waardgelders*) to keep the peace. The states-general meanwhile by a bare majority (4 provinces to 3) agreed to the summoning of a national church synod. The States of Holland, also by a narrow majority, refused their assent to this, and passed (August 4, 1617) a strong resolution (*Scherpe Resolutie*) by which all magistrates, officials and soldiers in the pay of the province were required to take an oath of obedience to the states on pain of dismissal, and were to be held accountable not to the ordinary tribunals, but to the States of Holland. It was a declaration of sovereign independence on the part of Holland, and the states-general took up the challenge and determined on decisive action. A commission was appointed with Maurice at its head to compel the disbanding of the *waardgelders*. On the 31st of July 1618 the stadholder appeared at Utrecht, which had thrown in its lot with Holland, at the head of a body of troops, and at his command the local levies at once laid down their arms. His progress through the towns of Holland met with no opposition. The states party was crushed without a blow being struck. On the 23rd of August, by order of the states-general, the advocate and his chief supporters, de Groot and Hoogerbeets, were arrested.

Oldenbarneveldt was with his friends kept in the strictest confinement until November, and then brought for examination before a commission appointed by the states-general. He appeared more than sixty times before the commissioners and was examined most severely upon the whole course of his official life, and was, most unjustly, allowed neither to consult papers nor to put his defence in writing. On the 20th of February 1619 he was arraigned before a special court of twenty-four members, only half of whom were Hollanders, and nearly all of them his personal enemies. It was in no sense a legal court, nor had it any jurisdiction over the prisoner, but the protest of the advocate, who claimed his right to be tried by the sovereign province of Holland, whose servant he was, was disregarded. He was allowed no advocates, nor the use of documents, pen or paper. It was in fact not a trial at all, and the packed bench of judges on Sunday, the 12th of May, pronounced sentence of death. On the following day the old statesman, at the age of seventy-one, was beheaded in the Binnenhof at the Hague. Such, to use his own words, was his reward for serving his country forty-three years.

The accusations brought against Oldenbarneveldt of having been a traitor to his country, whose interests he had betrayed for foreign gold, have no basis in fact. The whole life of the advocate disproves them, and not a shred of evidence has ever been produced to throw suspicion upon the patriot statesman's conduct. All his private papers fell into the hands of his foes, but not even the bitterest and ablest of his personal enemies, Francis Aarssens (see AARSSENS), could extract from them anything to show that Oldenbarneveldt at any time betrayed his country's interests. That he was an ambitious man, fond of power, and haughty in his attitude to those who differed from him in opinion, may be granted, but it must also be conceded that he sought for power in order to confer invaluable services upon his country, and that impatience of opposition was not unnatural in a man who had exercised an almost supreme control of administrative affairs for upwards of three decades. His high-handed course of action in defence of what he conceived to be the sovereign rights of his own province of Holland to decide upon religious questions within its borders may be challenged on the ground of inexpediency, but not of illegality. The harshness of the treatment meted out by Maurice to his father's old friend, the faithful counsellor and protector of his own early years, leaves a stain upon the stadholder's memory which can never be washed away. That the prince should have felt compelled in the last resort to take up arms for the Union against the attempt of the province of Holland to defy the authority of the Generality may be justified by the plea *reipublicae salus suprema lex*. To eject the advocate from power was one thing, to execute him as a traitor quite another. The condemnation of Oldenbarneveldt was carried out with Maurice's consent and approval, and he cannot be acquitted of a prominent share in what posterity has pronounced to be a judicial murder.

Oldenbarneveldt was married in 1575 to Maria van Utrecht. He left two sons, the lords of Groeneveld and Stoutenburg, and two daughters. A conspiracy against the life of Maurice, in which the sons of Oldenbarneveldt took part, was discovered in 1623. Stoutenburg, who was the chief accomplice, made his escape and entered the service of Spain; Groeneveld was executed.

BIBLIOGRAPHY.—L. v. Deventer, *Gedenkstukken van Johan v. Oldenbarneveldt en zijn tijd* (1577–1609; 3 vols., 1860–1865); J. van Oldenbarneveldt, *Historie Warachtige van de ghevanchennisse ... leste wonder ende droevige dool van J.4 v. O. ... uyt de verklaringe van Z. E. dienaar Johan Francken* (1620); *Historie van het leven en sterven van den Heer Johan van Olden Barneveldt* (1648); Groen van Prinsterer, *Maurice et Barneveldt* (1875); J. L. Motley, *Life and Death of John of Barneveldt* (2 vols., 1874). (G. E.)

OLDENBURG, a grand-duchy of Germany, with an area of 2479 sq. m. It consists of three widely separated portions of territory—(1) the duchy of Oldenburg, (2) the principality of Lübeck, and (3) the principality of Birkenfeld. It ranks tenth among the states of the German empire and has one vote in the Bundesrat (federal council) and three members in the Reichstag.

I. The duchy of Oldenburg, comprising fully four-fifths of the entire area and population, lies between 52° 29′ and 53° 44′ N. and between 7° 37′ and 8° 37′ E., and is bounded on the N. by the North Sea and on the other three sides by Hanover, with the exception of a small strip on the east, where it is conterminous with the territory of the free city of Bremen. It forms part of the north-western German plain lying between the Weser and the Ems, and, except on the south, where the Dammersbirge attain a height of 478 ft., it is almost entirely flat, with a slight inclination towards the sea. In respect of its soil it is divided broadly into two parts—the higher and inland-lying *Geest*, consisting of sandy plains intermixed with extensive heaths and moors, and the marsh lands along the coast, consisting of rich but somewhat swampy alluvial soil. The latter, which compose about one-fifth of the duchy, are protected against the inroads of the sea by dikes as in Holland; and beyond these are the so-called *Watten*, generally covered at high tide, but at many points being gradually reclaimed. The climate is temperate and humid; the mean temperature of the coldest month at the town of Oldenburg is 26° F. of the warmest 66°. Storms are numerous, and their violence is the more felt owing to the almost entire absence of trees; and fogs and ague are prevalent in the marsh lands. The chief rivers are the Hunte, flowing into the Weser, and the Hase and Leda flowing into the Ems. The Weser itself forms the eastern boundary for 42 m., and internal navigation is greatly facilitated by a canal, passing through the heart of the duchy and connecting the Hunte and the Leda. On the north there are several small coast streams conducted through the dikes by sluices, the only one of importance being the Jade, which empties itself into the Jade Busen, a deep gulf affording good accommodation for shipping. The duchy also contains numerous small lakes, the chief of which is the Dümmer See in the south-east corner, measuring 4 m. in length by 2½ in width. About 30% of the area of the duchy is under cultivation and 17% under pasture and meadows, while the rest consists mainly of marsh, moor and heath. Forests occupy a very small proportion of the whole, but there are some fine old oaks. In the Geest the principal crops are rye, oats, potatoes and buckwheat, for which the heath is sometimes prepared by burning. Large tracts of moorland, however, are useful only as producing peat for fuel, or as affording pasture to the flocks of small coarse-woolled Oldenburg sheep. The rich soil of the marsh lands produces good crops of wheat, oats, rye, hemp and rape, but is especially adapted for grazing. The cattle and horses raised on it are highly esteemed throughout Germany, and the former are exported in large numbers to England. Bee-keeping is much in vogue on the moors. The live stock of Oldenburg forms a great part of its wealth, and the ratio of cattle, sheep and horses to the population is one of the highest

among the German states. There are few large estates, and the ground is mostly in the hands of small farmers, who enjoy the right of fishing and shooting on their holdings. Game is scarce, but fishing is fairly productive. The mineral wealth of Oldenburg is very small. Woollen and cotton fabrics, stockings, jute and cigars are made at Varel, Delmenhorst and Lohne; cork-cutting is extensively practised in some districts, and there are a few iron-foundries. Trade is relatively of more importance, chiefly owing to the proximity of Bremen. The agricultural produce of the duchy is exported to Scandinavia, Russia, England and the United States, in return for colonial goods and manufactures. Varel, Brake and Elsfleth are the chief commercial harbours.

II. The principality of Lübeck has an area of 209 sq. m. and shares in the general physical characteristics of east Holstein, within which it lies. On the east it extends to Lübeck Bay of the Baltic Sea, and on the south-east it is bounded by the Trave. The chief rivers are the Schwartau, a tributary of the Trave, and the Schwentine, flowing northwards to the Gulf of Kiel. The scenery of Lübeck is often picturesque, especially in the vicinity of the Plön See and the Eutin See, the most important of the small lakes with which it is dotted. Agriculture is practised here even more extensively than in the duchy of Oldenburg, about 75% of the area being cultivated. The population in 1905 was 38,583.

III. The principality of Birkenfeld, 312 sq. m. in extent, lies in the midst of the Prussian province of the Rhine, about 30 m. W. of the Rhine at Worms and 150 m. S. of the duchy of Oldenburg. The population in 1905 was 46,484. (See BIRKENFELD.)

The total population of the grand-duchy of Oldenburg in 1880 was 337,478, and in 1905 438,856. The bulk of the inhabitants are of the Saxon stock, but to the north and west of the duchy there are numerous descendants of the ancient Frisians. The differences between the two races are still to some extent perceptible, but Low German (*Platt-deutsch*) is universally spoken, except in one limited district, where a Frisian dialect has maintained itself. In general characteristics the Oldenburg peasants resemble the Dutch, and the absence of large landowners has contributed to make them sturdy and independent. The population of Oldenburg is somewhat unequally distributed, some parts of the marsh lands containing over 300 persons to the square mile, while in the Geest the number occasionally sinks as low as 40. About 70% of the inhabitants belong to the "rural" population. The town of Oldenburg is the capital of the grand-duchy. The war-harbour of Wilhelmshaven, on the shore of the Jade Busen, was built by Prussia on land bought from Oldenburg. The chief towns of Birkenfeld and Lübeck respectively are Birkenfeld and Eutin.

Oldenburg is a Protestant country, and the grand-duke is required to be a member of the Lutheran Church. Roman Catholicism, however, preponderates in the south-western provinces, which formerly belonged to the bishopric of Münster. Oldenburg Roman Catholics are under the sway of the bishops of Münster, who is represented by an official at Vechta. The educational system of Oldenburg is on a similar footing to that of north Germany in general, though the scattered position of the farmhouses interferes to some extent with school attendance.

The constitution of Oldenburg, based upon a decree of 1849, revised in 1852, is one of the most liberal in Germany. It provides for a single representative chamber (*Landtag*), elected indirectly by universal suffrage and exercising concurrent rights of legislation and taxation with the grand-duke. The chamber which consists of forty members, one for every 10,000 inhabitants, is elected every three years. The executive consists of three ministers, who are aided by a committee of the Landtag, when that body is not in session. The local affairs of Birkenfeld and Lübeck are entrusted to provincial councils of fifteen members each. All citizens paying taxes and not having been convicted of felony are enfranchised. The municipal communities enjoy an unusual amount of independence. The finances of each constituent state of the grand-duchy are managed separately, and there is also a fourth budget concerned with the joint administration. The total revenue and expenditure are each about £650,000 annually. The grand-duchy had a debt in 1907 of £2,958,409.

History.—The earliest recorded inhabitants of the district now called Oldenburg were a Teutonic people, the Chauci, who were afterwards merged in the Frisians. The chroniclers delight in tracing the genealogy of the counts of Oldenburg to the Saxon hero, Widukind, the stubborn opponent of Charlemagne, but their first historical representative is one Elimar (d. 1108) who is described as *comes in confinio Saxoniae et Frisiae.* Elimar's descendants appear as vassals, although sometimes rebellious ones, of the dukes of Saxony; but they attained the dignity of princes of the empire when the emperor Frederick I. dismembered the Saxon duchy in 1180. At this time the county of Delmenhorst formed part of the dominions of the counts of Oldenburg, but afterwards it was on several occasions separated from them to form an apanage for younger branches of the family. This was the case between 1262 and 1447, between 1463 and 1547, and between 1577 and 1617. The northern and western parts of the present grand-duchy of Oldenburg were in the hands of independent, or semi-independent, Frisian princes, who were usually heathens, and during the early part of the 13th century the counts carried on a series of wars with these small potentates which resulted in a gradual expansion of their territory. The free city of Bremen and the bishop of Münster were also frequently at war with the counts of Oldenburg.

The successor of Count Dietrich (d. 1440), called *Fortunatus,* was his son Christian, who in 1448 was chosen king of Denmark as Christian I. In 1450 he became king of Norway and in 1457 king of Sweden; in 1460 he inherited the duchy of Schleswig and the county of Holstein, an event of high importance for the future history of Oldenburg. In 1454 he handed over Oldenburg to his brother Gerhard (c. 1430–1499) a turbulent prince, who was constantly at war with the bishop of Bremen and other neighbours. In 1483 Gerhard was compelled to abdicate in favour of his sons, and he died whilst on a pilgrimage in Spain. Early in the 16th century Oldenburg was again enlarged at the expense of the Frisians. Protestantism was introduced into the county by Count Anton I. (1505–1573), who also suppressed the monasteries; however, he remained loyal to Charles V. during the war of the league of Schmalkalden, and was able thus to increase his territories, obtaining Delmenhorst in 1547. One of Anton's brothers, Count Christopher (c. 1506–1566), won some reputation as a soldier. Anton's grandson, Anton Günther (1583–1667), who succeeded in 1603, proved himself the wisest prince who had yet ruled Oldenburg. Jever had been acquired before he became count, but in 1624 he added Knyphausen and Varel to his lands, with which in 1647 Delmenhorst was finally united. By his prudent neutrality during the Thirty Years' War Anton Günther secured for his dominions an immunity from the terrible devastations to which nearly all the other states of Germany were exposed. He also obtained from the emperor the right to levy tolls on vessels passing along the Weser, a lucrative grant which soon formed a material addition to his resources.

When Count Anton Günther died in June 1667 Oldenburg was inherited by virtue of a compact made in 1649 by Frederick III., king of Denmark, and Christian Albert, duke of Holstein-Gottorp. Some difficulties, however, arose from this joint ownership, but eventually these were satisfactorily settled, and from 1702 to 1773 the county was ruled by the kings of Denmark only, this period being on the whole one of peaceful development. Then in 1773 another change took place. Christian VII. of Denmark surrendered Oldenburg to Paul, duke of Holstein-Gottorp, afterwards the emperor Paul of Russia,[1] and in return Paul gave up to Christian his duchy of Holstein-Gottorp and his claims on the duchies of Schleswig and Holstein. At once Paul handed over Oldenburg to his kinsman, Frederick Augustus, bishop of Lübeck, the representative of a younger branch of

the family,[2] and in 1777 the county was raised to the rank of a duchy. The bishop's son William, who succeeded his father as duke in 1785, was a man of weak intellect, and his cousin Peter Frederick, bishop of Lübeck, acted as administrator and eventually, in 1823, inherited the duchy. This prince is the direct ancestor of the present grand duke.

To Peter fell the onerous task of governing the duchy during the time of the Napoleonic wars. In 1806 Oldenburg was occupied by the French and the Dutch, the duke and the regent being put to flight; but in 1807 William was restored, and in 1808 he joined the Confederation of the Rhine. However, in 1810 his lands were forcibly seized by Napoleon because he refused to exchange them for Erfurt. This drove him to join the Allies, and at the congress of Vienna his services were rewarded by the grant of the principality of Birkenfeld, an addition to his lands due to the good offices of the tsar Alexander I. At this time Oldenburg was made a grand duchy, but the title of grand-duke was not formally assumed until 1829, when Augustus succeeded his father Peter as ruler. Under Peter's rule the area of Oldenburg had been increased, not only by Birkenfeld, but by the bishopric of Lübeck (secularized in 1802) and some smaller pieces of territory.

Oldenburg did not entirely escape from the revolutionary movement which swept across Europe in 1848, but no serious disturbances took place therein. In 1849 the grand-duke granted a constitution of a very liberal character to his subjects. Hitherto his country had been ruled in the spirit of enlightened despotism, which was strengthened by the absence of a privileged class of nobles, by the comparative independence of the peasantry, and by the unimportance of the towns; and thus a certain amount of friction was inevitable in the working of the new order. In 1852 some modifications were introduced into the constitution, which, nevertheless, remained one of the most liberal in Germany. Important alterations were made in the administrative system in 1855, and again in 1868, and church affairs were ordered by a law of 1853. In 1853 the grand-duke Peter II. (1827–1900), who had ruled Oldenburg since the death of his father Augustus in 1853, seemed inclined to press a claim to the vacant duchies of Schleswig and Holstein, but ultimately in 1867 he abandoned this in favour of Prussia, and received some slight compensation. In 1866 he had sided with this power against Austria and had joined the North German Confederation; in 1871 Oldenburg became a state of the new German empire. In June 1900 Frederick Augustus (b. 1852) succeeded his father Peter as grand-duke. By a law passed in 1904 the succession to Oldenburg was vested in Frederick Ferdinand, duke of Schleswig-Holstein-Sonderburg-Glücksburg, and his family, after the extinction of the present ruling house. This arrangement was rendered advisable because the grand-duke Frederick Augustus had only one son Nicholas (b. 1897), and his only brother George Louis (1855) was unmarried.

For the history of Oldenburg see Runde, *Oldenburgische Chronik* (Oldenburg, 1863); E. Pleitner, *Oldenburg im 19 Jahrhundert* (Oldenburg, 1899–1900); and *Oldenburgisches Quellenbuch* (Oldenburg, 1903). See also the *Jahrbuch für die Geschichte des Herzogtums Oldenburg* (1892 seq.).

OLDENBURG, a town of Germany, and capital of the grand-duchy of Oldenburg. It is a quiet and pleasant-looking town, situated 27 m. by rail W. of Bremen, on the navigable Hunte and the Hunte-Ems canal. Pop. (1905), including the suburbs, 28,555. The inner or old town, with its somewhat narrow streets, is surrounded by avenues laid out on the site of the former ramparts, beyond which are the villas, promenades and gardens of the modern quarters. Oldenburg has almost nothing to show in the shape of interesting old buildings. The

[1] His father, Charles Frederick of Holstein-Gottorp (1700–1739), a descendant of Christian I. of Denmark, married Anne, daughter of Peter the Great, and became tsar as Peter III. in 1762.

[2] To this branch belonged Adolphus Frederick, son of Christian Augustus bishop of Lübeck (d. 1726), who in 1751 became king of Sweden.

Another branch of the Oldenburg family, descended from John, son of Christian III. of Denmark, is that of Holstein-Sonderburg. This was subdivided into the lines of Sonderburg-Augustenburg and Sonderburg-Glücksburg. Prince Christian, who married Princess Helena of Great Britain, belongs to the former of them. To the latter belong the kings of Denmark, Greece and Norway.

Evangelical Lambertikirche, though dating from the 13th century, has been so transformed in the last century (1874–1886) as to show no trace of its antiquity. The palaces of the grand-duke and the old town-hall are Renaissance buildings of the 17th and 18th centuries. Among the other prominent buildings—all modern—are the palace of the heir apparent, the new town-hall, the theatre, the law-courts, the gymnasium, the commercial school, the three hospitals and the new Roman Catholic church. The grand-ducal picture gallery in the Augusteum includes works by Veronese, Velasquez, Murillo and Rubens, and there are collections of modern paintings and sculptures in the two palaces. The public library contains 110,000 volumes and the duke's private library 55,000. There is also a large natural history museum and a museum with a collection of antiquities. The industries of Oldenburg, which are of no great importance, include iron-founding, spinning and the making of glass, tobacco, gloves, soap and leather. A considerable trade is carried on in grain, and the horse fairs are largely frequented. According to popular tradition Oldenburg was founded by Walbert, grandson of the Saxon hero, Widukind, and was named after his wife Altburga, but the first historical mention of it occurs in a document of 1108. It was fortified in 1155, and received a municipal charter in 1345. The subsequent history of the town is merged in that of the grand-duchy.

See Sello, *Historische Wanderung durch die Stadt Oldenburg* (Oldenburg, 1896); and *Alt-Oldenburg* (Oldenburg, 1903); and Kohl, *Die Allmende der Stadt Oldenburg* (Oldenburg, 1903).

OLDFIELD, ANNE (1683–1730), English actress, was born in London, the daughter of a soldier. She worked for a time as apprentice to a semptress, until she attracted George Farquhar's attention by reciting some lines from a play in his hearing. She thereupon obtained an engagement at Drury Lane, where her beauty rather than her ability slowly brought her into favour, and it was not until ten years later that she was generally acknowledged as the best actress of her time. In polite comedy, especially, she was the unrivalled, and even the usually grudging Cibber acknowledged that she had as much as he to do with the success of the *Careless Husband* (1704), in which she created the part of Lady Modish, reluctantly given her because Mrs Verbruggen was ill. In tragedy, too, she won laurels, and the list of her parts, many of them original, is a long and varied one. She was the theatrical idol of her day. Her exquisite acting and lady-like carriage were the delight of her contemporaries, and her beauty and generosity found innumerable eulogists, as well as sneering detractors. Alexander Pope, in his *Sober Advice from Horace*, wrote of her—

"Engaging Oldfield, who, with grace and ease,
Could join the arts to ruin and to please."

It was to her that the satirist alluded as the lady who detested being buried in woollen, who said to her maid—

"No, let a charming chintz and Brussels lace
Wrap my cold limbs and shade my lifeless face;
One would not, sure, be frightful when one's dead,
And—Betty—give this cheek a little red."

She was but forty-seven when she died on the 23rd of October 1730, leaving all the court and half the town in tears.

She divided her property, for that time a large one, between her natural sons, the first by Arthur Mainwaring (1668–1712)—who had left her and his son half his fortune on his death—and the second by Lieut.-General Charles Churchill (d. 1745). Mrs Oldfield was buried in Westminster Abbey, beneath the monument to Congreve, but when Churchill applied for permission to erect a monument there to her memory the dean of Westminster refused it.

OLD FORGE, a borough of Lackawanna county, Pennsylvania, U.S.A., on the Lackawanna river, about 6 m. S.W. of Scranton. Pop. (1900) 5630 (2404 foreign-born, principally Italians); (1910) 11,324. It is served by the Delaware, Lackawanna & Western and the Lehigh Valley railways. The principal public buildings are the town-hall and the high school. The borough is situated in the anthracite coal region, and the mining of coal is the principal industry, though there are also various manufactures.

Old Forge was settled in 1830 and incorporated as a borough in 1899.

OLDHAM, JOHN (1653–1683), English satirist, son of a Presbyterian minister, was born at Shipton Moyne, near Tetbury, Gloucestershire, on the 9th of August 1653. He graduated from St Edmund Hall, Oxford, in 1674, and was for three years an usher in a school at Croydon. Some of his verses attracted the attention of the town, and the earl of Rochester, with Sir Charles Sedley and other wits, came down to see him. The visit did not affect his career apparently, for he stayed at Croydon until 1681, when he became tutor to the grandsons of Sir Edward Thurland, near Reigate. Meanwhile he had tried, he says, to conquer his inclination for the unprofitable trade of poetry, but in the panic caused by the revelations of Titus Oates, he found an opportunity for the exercise of his gift for rough satire. *Garnet's Ghost* was published as a broadside in 1679, but the other *Satires on the Jesuits*, although written at the same time, were not printed until 1681. The success of these dramatic and unsparing invectives apparently gave Oldham hope that he might become independent of teaching. But his undoubted services to the Country Party brought no reward from its leaders. He became tutor to the son of Sir William Hickes, and was eventually glad to accept the patronage of William Pierrepont, earl of Kingston, whose kindly offer of a chaplaincy he had refused earlier. He died at Holme-Pierrepoint, near Nottingham, on the 9th of December 1683, of smallpox.

Oldham took Juvenal for his model, and in breadth of treatment and power of invective surpassed his English predecessors. He was original in the dramatic setting provided for his satires. Thomas Garnet, who suffered for supposed implication in the Gunpowder Plot, rose from the dead to encourage the Jesuits in the first satire, and in the third Ignatius Loyola is represented as dictating his wishes to his disciples from his death-bed. Oldham wrote other satires, notably one "addressed to a friend about to leave the university," which contains a well-known description of the state of slavery of the private chaplain, and another "dissuading from poetry," describing the ingratitude shown to Edmund Spenser, whose ghost is the speaker, to Samuel Butler and to Abraham Cowley. Oldham's verse is rugged, and his rhymes often defective, but he met with a generous appreciation from Dryden, whose own satiric bent was perhaps influenced by his efforts. He says ("To the Memory of Mr Oldham," *Works*, ed. Scott, vol. xi. p. 99):—

"For sure our souls were near allied, and thine
Cast in the same poetic mould with mine."

The real wit and rigour of Oldham's satirical poetry are undeniable, while its faults—its frenzied extravagance and lack of metrical polish—might, as Dryden suggests, have been cured with time, for Oldham was only thirty when he died.

The best edition of his works is *The Compositions in Prose and Verse of Mr John Oldham . . .* (1770), with memoir and explanatory notes by Edward Thompson.

OLDHAM, THOMAS (1816–1878) British geologist, was born in Dublin on the 4th of May 1816. He was educated there at Trinity College, graduating B.A. in 1836, and afterwards studied engineering in Edinburgh, where he gained a good knowledge of geology and mineralogy under Jameson. On his return to Ireland in 1839 he became chief assistant to Captain (afterwards Major General) Portlock, who conducted the geological department of the Ordnance Survey, and he rendered much help in the field and office in the preparation of the *Report on the Geology of Londonderry, &c.* (1843). Subsequently he served under Captain (afterwards Sir Henry) James, the first local director of the Geological Survey of Ireland, whom he succeeded in 1846. Meanwhile in 1845 he was appointed professor of Geology in the university of Dublin. In 1848 he was elected F.R.S. In 1849 he discovered in the Cambrian rocks of Bray Head the problematical fossil named *Oldhamia*. In 1850 he was selected to take charge of the Geological Survey of India, which he organized, and in due course he established the *Memoirs*, the *Palaeontologia Indica* and the *Records*, to which he contributed many important articles. In 1864 he published an elaborate report *On the Coal Resources of India*. He retired in 1876, and died at Rugby on the 17th of July 1878.

OLDHAM, a municipal county and parliamentary borough of Lancashire, England, 7 m. N.E. of Manchester, on the London & North-Western, Great Central and Lancashire & Yorkshire railways and the Oldham canal. Pop. (1891) 131,463; (1901) 137,246. The principal railway station is called Mumps, but there are several others. The town lies high, near the source of the small river Medlock. Its growth as a manufacturing centre gives it a wholly modern appearance. Among several handsome churches the oldest dates only from the later 18th century. The principal buildings and institutions include the town-hall, with tetrastyle portico copied from the Ionic temple of Ceres near Athens, the reference library, art gallery and museum, the Union Street baths, commemorating Sir Robert Peel the statesman, and the county court. Of educational establishments the chief are the Lyceum, a building in Italian style, containing schools of art and science, and including an observatory; the largely-endowed blue-coat school founded in 1808 by Thomas Henshaw, a wealthy manufacturer of hats; the Hulme grammar school (1895), and municipal technical schools. The Alexandra Park, opened in 1865, was laid out by operatives who were thrown out of employment owing to the cotton famine in the years previous to that date. The site is picturesquely undulating and terraced. Oldham is one of the most important centres of the cotton manufactures, the consumption of cotton being about one-fifth of the total importation into the United Kingdom, the factories numbering some 230, and the spindles over 13 millions, while some 35,000 operatives are employed. The principal manufactures are fustians, velvets, cords, shirtings, sheetings and nankeens. There are also large foundries and mill and cotton machinery works; and works for the construction of gas-meters and sewing-machines; while all these industries are assisted by the immediate presence of collieries. There are extensive markets and numerous fairs are held. Oldham was incorporated in 1849, and became a county borough in 1888. The corporation consists of 4 mayor, 12 aldermen and 36 councillors. The parliamentary borough has returned two members since 1832. Area of municipal borough, 4736 acres.

A Roman road, of which some traces are still left, passes through the site of the township, but it does not appear to have been a Roman station. It is not mentioned in Domesday; but in the reign of Henry III. Alwardus de Aldholme is referred to as holding land in Vernet (Werneth). A daughter and co-heiress of this Alwardus conveyed Werneth Hall and its manor to the Cudworths, a branch of the Yorkshire family, with whom it remained till the early part of the 18th century. From the Oldhams was descended Hugh Oldham, who died bishop of Exeter in 1519. From entries in the church registers it would appear that linens were manufactured in Oldham as early as 1630. Watermills were introduced in 1770, and with the adoption of Arkwright's inventions the cotton industry grew with great rapidity.

OLD MAID, a game of cards. Any number may play, and the full pack is used, the Queen of Hearts being removed. The cards are dealt out one by one until exhausted, and each player then sorts his hand and discards the pairs. The dealer then offers his hand, spread out face downwards to the next player, who draws a card, which, if it completes a pair, is discarded, but otherwise remains in the hand. The process continues from player to player, until all the cards have been paired and discarded excepting the odd queen, the holder of which is the "Old Maid."

OLDMIXON, JOHN (1673–1742), English historian, was a son of John Oldmixon of Oldmixon, near Bridgwater. His first writings were poems and dramas, among them being *Amores Britannici; Epistles historical and gallant* (1703); and a tragedy, *The Governor of Cyprus.* His earliest historical work was *The British Empire in America* (1708 and again 1741), which was followed by *The Secret History of Europe* (1712–1715); by *Arcana Gallica, or the Secret History of France for the last Century*

(1714); and by other smaller writings. More important, however, although of a very partisan character, are Oldmixon's works on English history. His *Critical history of England* (1724–1726) contains attacks on Clarendon and a defence of Bishop Burnet, and its publication led to a controversy between Dr Zachary Grey (1688–1766) and the author, who replied to Grey in his *Clarendon and Whitlock compared* (1727). On the same lines he wrote his *History of England during the Reigns of the Royal House of Stuart* (1730). Herein he charged Bishop Atterbury and other of Clarendon's editors with tampering with the text of the *History.* From his exile Atterbury replied to this charge in a *Vindication,* and although Oldmixon continued the controversy it is practically certain that he was in the wrong. He completed a continuous history of England by writing the *History of England during the Reigns of William and Mary, Anne and George I.* (1735); and the *History of England during the Reign of Henry VIII., Edward VI., Mary and Elisabeth* (1739). Among his other writings are, *Memoirs of North Britain* (1715), *Essay on Criticism* (1728) and *Memoirs of the Press 1710–1740* (1742), which was only published after his death. Oldmixon had much to do with editing two periodicals, *The Muses Mercury* and *The Medley,* and he often complained that his services were overlooked by the government. He died on the 9th of July 1742.

OLD POINT COMFORT, a summer and winter resort, in Elizabeth City county, Virginia, U.S.A., at the southern end of a narrow, sandy peninsula projecting into Hampton Roads (at the mouth of the James river), about 12 m. N. by W. of Norfolk. It is served directly by the Chesapeake & Ohio railway, and indirectly by the New York, Philadelphia & Norfolk (Pennsylvania System), passengers and freight being carried by steamer from the terminus at Cape Charles; by steamboat lines connecting with the principal cities along the Atlantic coast, and with cities along the James river; by ferry, connecting with Norfolk and Portsmouth; and by electric railway (3 m.) to Hampton and (12 m.) to Newport News. There is a U.S. garrison at Fort Monroe, one of the most important fortifications on the Atlantic coast of the United States. Old Point Comfort is included in the reservation of Fort Monroe. The fort lies within the tract of 252 acres ceded, for coast defence purposes, to the Federal government by the state of Virginia in 1821, the survey for the original fortifications having been made in 1818, and the building begun in 1819. It was named in honour of President Monroe and was first regularly garrisoned in 1823; in 1824 the Artillery School of Practice (now called the United States Coast Artillery School) was established to provide commissioned officers of the Coast Artillery with instruction in professional work and to give technical instruction to the non-commissioned staff. During the Civil War the fort was the rendezvous for several military expeditions, notably those of General Benjamin F. Butler to Hatteras Inlet, in 1861; of General A. E. Burnside, to North Carolina, in 1862; and of General A. H. Terry, against Fort Fisher, in 1865; within sight of its parapets was fought the famous duel between the "Monitor" and the "Merrimac" (March 9, 1862). Jefferson Davis was a prisoner here for two years, from the 22nd of May 1865, and Clement Claiborne Clay (1819–1882), a prominent Confederate, from the same date until April 1866. Between Fort Monroe and Sewell's Point is Fort Wool, almost covering a small island called Rip Raps. The expedition which settled Jamestown rounded this peninsula (April 26, 1607), opened its sealed instructions here, and named the peninsula Poynt Comfort, in recognition of the sheltered harbour. (The "Old" was added subsequently to distinguish it from a Point Comfort settlement at the mouth of the York river on Chesapeake Bay). On the site of the present fortification a fort was occupied by the whites as early as 1630.

OLD TOWN, a city of Penobscot county, Maine, U.S.A., on the Penobscot river, about 12 m. N.E. of Bangor. Pop. (1890) 5312; (1900) 5763 (1247 foreign-born); (1910) 6317. It is served by the Maine Central and the Bangor & Aroostook railways, and by an electric line connecting with Bangor. The city proper is on an island (Marsh, or Old Town Island), but considerable territory on the W. bank of the river is included within the municipal limits. The manufacture of lumber is the principal industry of the city On Indian Island (opposite the city) is the principal settlement of the Penobscot Indians, an Abnaki tribe, now wards of the state. The abbé Louis Pierre Thury was sent here from Quebec about 1687 and built a church in 1688–1689; in 1705 the mission passed under the control of the Jesuits. The first white settler in the vicinity seems to have been John Marsh, who came about 1774, and who bought the island now known as Marsh Island. From 1806 to 1840, when it was incorporated as a separate township, Old Town was a part of Orono. In 1891 it was chartered as a city. One of the oldest railways in the United States, and the first in Maine, was completed to Old Town from Bangor in 1836.

OLDYS, WILLIAM (1696–1761), English antiquary and bibliographer, natural son of Dr William Oldys, chancellor of Lincoln, was born on the 14th of July 1696, probably in London. His father had also held the office of advocate of the admiralty, but lost it in 1693 because he would not prosecute as traitors and pirates the sailors who had served against England under James II. William Oldys, the younger, lost part of his small patrimony in the South Sea Bubble, and in 1724 went to Yorkshire, spending the greater part of the next six years as the guest of the earl of Malton. On his return to London he found that his landlord had disposed of the books and papers left in his charge. Among these was an annotated copy of Gerard Langbaine's *Dramatick Poets*. The book came into the hands of Thomas Coxeter (1689–1747), and subsequently into Theophilus Cibber's possession, and furnished the basis of the *Lives of the Poets* (1753) published with Cibber's name on the title page, though most of it was written by Robert Shiels. In 1731 Oldys sold his collections to Edward Harley, second earl of Oxford, who appointed him his literary secretary in 1738. Three years later his patron died, and from that time he worked for the booksellers. His habits were irregular, and in 1751 his debts drove him to the Fleet prison. After two years' imprisonment he was released through the kindness of friends who paid his debts, and in April 1755 he was appointed Norroy king-at-arms by the duke of Norfolk. He died on the 15th of April 1761.

Oldys's chief works are: *The British Librarian*, a review of scarce and valuable books in print and in manuscript (1737–1738); the *Harleian Miscellany* (1744–1746), a collection of tracts and pamphlets in the earl of Oxford's library, undertaken in conjunction with Dr Johnson; twenty-two articles contributed to the *Biographia Britannica* (1747–1760); an edition of Raleigh's *History of the World*, with a *Life* of the author (1736); *Life of Charles Cotton* prefixed to Sir John Hawkins's edition (1760) of the *Compleat Angler*. In 1727 Oldys began to annotate another Langbaine to replace the one he had lost. This valuable book, with a MS. collection of notes by Oldys on various bibliographical subjects, is preserved in the British Museum.

OLEAN, a city of Cattaraugus county, in south-western New York, U.S.A., on Olean Creek and the N. side of the Allegheny river, 70 m. S.E. of Buffalo. Pop. (1880), 3036; (1890), 7358; (1900), 9462, of whom 1514 were foreign-born and 122 were negroes; (1910 census), 14,743. The city is served by the Erie, the Pittsburg, Shawmut & Northern, and the Pennsylvania railways (the last has large car shops here); and is connected with Bradford, Pa., Allegany, Pa., Salamanca, N.Y., Little Valley, N.Y., and Bolivar, N.Y., by electric lines. Olean is situated in a level valley 1440 ft. above sea-level. The surrounding country is rich in oil and natural gas. Six miles from Olean and 2000 ft. above the sea-level is Rock City, a group of immense, strangely regular, conglomerate rocks (some of them pure white) covering about 40 acres. They are remnants of a bed of Upper Devonian Conglomerate, which broke along the joint planes, leaving a group of huge blocks. In the city are a public library, a general hospital and a state armoury; and at Allegany (pop. 1910, 1286), about 3 m. W of Olean, is St Bonaventure's College (1859; Roman Catholic). Olean's factory product was valued at $4,677,477 in 1905; the city is the terminus of an Ohio pipe line, and of a sea-board pipe line for petroleum; and among its industries are oil-refining and the refining of wood alcohol, tanning, currying, and finishing leather; and the manufacture of flour, glass (mostly bottles),

lumber, &c. The vicinity was settled in 1804, and this was the first township organized (1808), being then coextensive with the county. Olean Creek was called Ischue (or Ischua); the vicinity. Olean was suggested, possibly in reference to the oil-springs in the vicinity. The village was officially called Hamilton for a time, but Olean was the name given to the post-office in 1817, and Olean Point was the popular local name. In 1909 several suburbs, including the village of North Olean (pop. in 1905, 1761), were annexed to Olean, considerably increasing its area and population.

See *History of Cattaraugus County, New York* (Philadelphia, 1879).

OLEANDER, the common name for the shrub known to botanists as *Nerium Oleander*. It is a native of the Mediterranean and Levant, and is characterized by its tall shrubby habit and its thick lance-shaped opposite leaves, which exude a milky juice when punctured. The flowers are borne in terminal clusters, and are like those of the common periwinkle (*Vinca*), but are of a rose colour, rarely white, and the throat or upper edge of the tube of the corolla is occupied by outgrowths in the form of lobed and fringed petal-like scales. The hairy anthers adhere to the thickened stigma. The fruit or seed-vessel consists of two long pods, which, bursting along one edge, liberate a number of seeds, each of which has a tuft of silky hairs like thistle down at the upper end. The genus belongs to the natural order Apocynaceae, a family that, as is usual where the juice has a milky appearance, is marked by its poisonous properties. Cases are recorded by Lindley of children poisoned by the flowers. The same author also narrates how in the course of the Peninsular War some French soldiers died in consequence of employing skewers made from

Nerium Oleander.

freshly-cut twigs of oleander for roasting their meat. The oleander was known to the Greeks under three names, viz. *rhododendron*, *nerion* and *rhododaphne*, and is well described by Pliny (xvi. 20), who mentions its rose-like flowers and poisonous qualities, at the same time stating that it was considered serviceable as a remedy against snake-bite. The name is supposed to be a corruption of *lorandrum*, *lauridendrum* (Du Cange), influenced by *olea*, the olive-tree, *lorandrum* being itself a corruption of *rhododendron*. The modern Greeks still know the plant as ῥοδοδάφνη, although in a figure in the Rinuccini MSS. of Dioscorides a plant is represented under this name, which, however, had rather the appearance of a willow herb (*Epilobium*). The oleander has long been cultivated in greenhouses in England, being, as Gerard says, "a small shrub of a gallant shewe"; numerous varieties, differing in the colour of their flowers, which are often double, have been introduced.

OLEASTER, known botanically as *Elaeagnus hortensis*, a handsome deciduous tree, 15 to 20 ft. high, growing in the Mediterranean region and temperate Asia, where it is commonly cultivated for its edible fruit. The brown smooth branches are more or less spiny; the narrow leaves have a hoary look from the presence of a dense covering of star-shaped hairs; the small fragrant yellow flowers, which are borne in the axils of the leaves, are scaly on the outside. The genus contains other species of ornamental deciduous or evergreen shrubs or small trees. *E. argentea*, a native of North America, has leaves and fruit covered with shining silvery scales. In *E. glabra*, from Japan, the evergreen leaves are clothed beneath with rust-coloured scales; variegated forms of this are cultivated, as also of *E. pungens*, another Japanese species, a spiny shrub with leaves silvery beneath.

OLEFINE, in organic chemistry, the generic name given to open chain hydrocarbons having only singly and doubly linked pairs of carbon atoms. The word is derived from the French *oléfiant* (from *oléfier*, to make oil), which was the name given to ethylene, the first member of the series, by the Dutch chemists, J. R. Deiman, Paets van Troostwyk, N. Bondt and A. Lauwerenburgh in 1795. The simple olefines containing one doubly-linked pair of carbon atoms have the general formula (C_nH_{2n}; the di-olefines, containing two doubly-linked pairs, have the general formula C_nH_{2n-2} and are consequently isomeric with the simple acetylenes. Tri-, tetra- and more complicated members are also known. The name of any particular member of the series is derived from that of the corresponding member of the paraffin series by removing the final syllable "-ane," and replacing it by the syllable "ylene." Isomerism in the olefine series does not appear until the third member of the series is reached.

The higher olefines are found in the tar which is obtained by distilling bituminous shales, in illuminating gas, and among the products formed by distilling paraffin under pressure (T. E. Thorpe and J. Young, *Ann.*, 1873, 165, p. 1). The olefines may be synthetically prepared by eliminating water from the alcohols of the general formula C_nH_{2n+1}·OH, using sulphuric acid or zinc chloride generally as the dehydrating agent, although phosphorus pentoxide, syrupy phosphoric acid and anhydrous oxalic acid may frequently be substituted. In this method of preparation it is found that the secondary alcohols decompose more readily than the primary alcohols of the series, and when sulphuric acid is used, two phases are present in the reaction, the first being the building up of an intermediate sulphuric acid ester, which then decomposes into sulphuric acid and hydrocarbon: $C_2H_5OH \rightarrow C_2H_5·HSO_4 \rightarrow C_2H_4 + H_2SO_4$. As an alternative to the above method, V. Ipatiew (*Ber.*, 1901, 34, p. 596 et seq.) has shown that the alcohols break up into ethylenes and water when their vapour is passed through a heated tube containing some "contact" substance, such as graphite, kieselguhr, &c. (see also J. B. Senderens, *Comptes rendus*, 1907, 144, pp. 382, 1109).

They may also be prepared by eliminating the halogen hydride from the alkyl halides by heating with alcoholic potash, or with litharge at 320° C. (A. Eltekow, *Ber.*, 1878, 11, p. 414); by the action of metals on the halogen compounds $C_nH_{2n}Br_2$; by boiling the aqueous solution of nitrites of the primary amines (V. Meyer, *Ber.*, 1876, 9, p. 543). $C_2H_5NH_2 + HNO_2 = N_2 + 2H_2O + C_2H_4$; by the electrolysis of the alkali salts of saturated dicarboxylic acids; by the decomposition of β-haloid fatty acids with sodium carbonate, $CH_2CHBr·CH(CH_3)·CO_2H \rightarrow HBr + CH_3·CH:CH·CH_3$; by distilling the barium salts of acids $C_nH_{2n-1}O_2$ with sodium methylate *in vacuo* (I. Mai, *Ber.*, 1889, 22, p. 2135); from the higher halogens by converting them into esters which are then distilled (F. Krafft, *Ber.*, 1883, 16, p. 3018):

$C_{10}H_{21}·CH_2·CH_2·OH \rightarrow C_{10}H_{21}CH_2·CH_2·CH_2·CO·R \rightarrow$
$\qquad\qquad\qquad\qquad\qquad C_{10}H_{21}CH:CH_2 + R·COOH;$

from tertiary alcohols by the action of acetic anhydride in the presence of a small quantity of sulphuric acid (L. Henry, *Comptes rendus*, 1907, 144, p. 552):

$(CH_3)_2C(OH)·CH(CH_3)_2 \rightarrow (CH_3)_2C:C(CH_3)_2 + CH_3:C(CH_3)·CH$
$\qquad\qquad\qquad\qquad\qquad\qquad\qquad\qquad\qquad (CH_3)_2;$

from unsaturated alcohols by the action of metal-ammonium compounds (E. Chablay, *Comptes rendus*, 1906, 143, p. 123):
$2CH_2:CH·CH_2OH + 2NH_3·Na = CH_2:CH·CH_2·CH:CH·CH_2ONa$
$\qquad\qquad\qquad\qquad\qquad\qquad\qquad\qquad\qquad + NaOH + 2NH_3;$

from the lower members of the series by heating them with alkyl halides in the presence of lead oxide or lime; $C_2H_4 + 2CH_3I = 2HI + C_3H_8$; and by the action of the zinc alkyls upon the halogen substituted olefines.

A. Mailhe (*Chem. Zeit.*, 1906, 30, p. 37) has shown that on passing the monohalogen derivatives of the paraffins through a glass tube containing reduced nickel, copper or cobalt at 250° C., olefines are produced, together with the halogen acids, and recombination is prevented by passing the gases through a solution of potash. The reaction probably proceeds thus: $MCl_2 + C_nH_{2n+1}Cl \rightarrow HCl + Cl·M·C_nH_{2n}Cl \rightarrow MCl_2 + C_nH_{2n}$, since the haloid derivatives of the monovalent metals do not act similarly. The anhydrous chlorides of nickel, cobalt, cadmium, barium, iron and lead act in the same way as catalysts at about 300° C., and the bromides of lead, cadmium, nickel and barium at about 320° C.

In their physical properties, the olefines resemble the normal paraffins, the lower members of the series being inflammable gases, the members from C_5 to C_{16} liquids insoluble in water,

and from C_{16} upwards of solids. The chief normal members of the series are shown in the table.

Name.	Formula.	Melting-point. C.	Boiling-point. C.
Ethylene	$CH_2:CH_2$	−169°	−102·7° (757 mm.)
Propylene	$CH_2CH:CH_2$	..	−50·2° (749 mm.)
Butylene	$C_2H_5·CH:CH_2$	..	−5°
Amylene	$C_3H_7·CH:CH_2$	..	39°—40°
Hexylene	$C_4H_9·CH:CH_2$	..	68°—70°
Heptylene	$C_5H_{11}·CH:CH_2$	..	95°
Octylene	$C_6H_{13}·CH:CH_2$	..	122°—123°
Decylene	$C_8H_{17}·CH:CH_2$	..	172°
Undecylene	$C_9H_{19}·CH:CH_2$	..	84° (18 mm.)
Duodecylene	$C_{10}H_{21}CH:CH_2$	−31°	96° (15 mm.)

In chemical properties, however, they differ very markedly from the paraffins. As unsaturated compounds they can combine with two monovalent atoms. Hydrogen is absorbed readily at ordinary temperature in the presence of platinum black, and paraffins are formed; the halogens (chlorine and bromine) combine directly with them, giving dihalogen substituted compounds; the halogen halides to form monohalogen derivatives (hydriodic acid reacts most readily, hydrochloric acid, least); and it is to be noted that the haloid acids attach themselves in such a manner that the halogen atom unites itself to the carbon atom which is in combination with the fewest hydrogen atoms (W. Markownikow, *Ann.*, 1870, 153, p. 256).

They combine with hypochlorous acid to form chlorhydrins; and are easily soluble in concentrated sulphuric acid, giving rise to sulphuric acid esters; consequently if the solution be boiled with water, the alcohol from which the olefine was in the first place derived is regenerated. The oxides of nitrogen convert them into nitrosites and nitrosates (O. Wallach, *Ann.*, 1887, 241, p. 288, &c.) ; J. Schmidt, *Ber.*, 1902, 35, pp. 2323 et seq.). They also combine with nitrosyl bromide and chloride, and with many metallic haloid salts (platinum bichloride, iridium chloride), with mercury salts (see K. A. Hofmann and J. Sand, *Ber.*, 1900, 33, pp. 1340 et seq.), and those with a tertiary carbon atom yield double salts with zinc chloride. Dilute potassium permanganate oxidizes the olefines to glycols (G. Wagner, *Ber.*, 1888, 21, p. 3359). With ozone they form ozonides (C. Harries, *Ber.*, 1904, 37, p. 839). The higher members of the series readily polymerize in the presence of dilute sulphuric acid, zinc chloride, &c.

For the first member of the series see ETHYLENE.

Propylene, C_3H_6, may be obtained by passing the vapour of trimethylene through a heated tube (S. M. Tanatar, *Ber.*, 1899, 32, pp. 702, 1905). It is a colourless gas which may be liquefied by a pressure of 7 to 8 atmospheres. *Butylene*, C_4H_8, exists in three isomeric forms: normal butylene, $C_2H_5·CH:CH_2$; pseudo-butylene, $CH_3·CH:CH·CH_3$; and isobutylene, $(CH_3)_2C:CH_2$. Normal butylene is a readily condensible gas. Two spatial modifications of *pseudo-butylene*, $CH_3·CH:CH·CH_3$, are known, the *cis* and the *trans*; they are prepared by heating the sodium salts of hydro-iodo-tiglic and hydro-iodo-angelic acids respectively (J. Wislicenus, *Ann.*, 1900, 313, p. 228). *Isobutylene*, $(CH_3)_2C:CH_2$, is formed in the dry distillation of fats, and also occurs among the products obtained when the vapour of fusel oil is led through a heated tube. It is a gas at ordinary temperature, and may be liquefied, the liquid boiling at −5° C. It combines with acetyl chloride in the presence of zinc chloride to form a ketone, which on warming breaks down into hydrochloric acid and mesityl oxide (I. L. Kondakow, *Jour. Russ. phys. chem. Soc.* 26, p. 12). It polymerizes, giving isodibutylene, C_8H_{16}, and isotributylene, $C_{12}H_{24}$, liquids which boil at 110−113° and 178−181° C. *Amylene*, C_5H_{10}, exists in five isomeric forms, viz. (n) propylethylene, $C_3H_7·CH_2·CH_2·CH:CH_2$; isopropylethylene, $(CH_3)_2CH·CH:CH_2$; symmetrical methyl-ethyl-ethylene, $CH_3·CH:CH·C_2H_5$; unsymmetrical methyl-ethyl-ethylene, $(CH_3)(C_2H_5)C:CH_2$; and trimethyl ethylene, $(CH_3)_2C:CH·CH_3$. The highest members of the series as yet known are *cerotene*, $C_{26}H_{52}$ which is obtained by the distillation of Chinese wax and is a paraffin-like solid which melts at 57° C., and *melene*, $C_{30}H_{60}(?)$, which is obtained by the distillation of bees'-wax. It melts at 62° C. (B. J. Brodie, *Ann.*, 1848, 67, p. 210; 1849, 71, p. 156).

OLEG (?−912), prince of Kiev, succeeded Rurik, as being the eldest member of the ducal family, in the principality of Great Novgorod, the first Russian metropolis. Three years later he moved southwards and, after taking Smolensk and other places, fixed his residence at Kiev, which he made his capital. He then proceeded to build a fortress there and gradually compelled the surrounding tribes to pay him tribute, extending his conquests in all directions (883−903) at the expense of the Khazars, who hitherto had held all southern Russia to tribute. In 907, with a host made up of all the subject tribes, Slavonic and Finnic, he sailed against the Greeks in a fleet consisting, according to the *lyetopis*, of 2000 vessels, each of which held 40 men; but this estimate is plainly an exaggeration. On reaching Constantinople, Oleg disembarked his forces, mercilessly ravaged the suburbs of the imperial city, and compelled the emperor to pay tribute, provide the Russians with provisions for the return journey, and take fifty of them over the city. A formal treaty was then concluded, which the Slavonians swore to observe in the names of their gods Perun and Volos. Oleg returned to Kiev laden with golden ornaments, costly cloths, wines, and all manner of precious things. In 911 he sent an embassy of fourteen persons to Constantinople to get the former treaty confirmed and enlarged. The names of these ambassadors are preserved and they point to the Scandinavian origin of Oleg's host; there is not a Slavonic name among them. A new and elaborate treaty, the terms of which have come down to us, was now concluded between the Russians and Greeks, a treaty which evidently sought to bind the two nations closely together and obviate all possible differences which might arise between them in the future. There was also to be free trade between the two nations, and the Russians might enter the service of the Greek emperor if they desired it. The envoys returned to Kiev in 912 after being shown the splendours of the Greek capital and being instructed in the rudiments of the Greek faith. In the autumn of the same year Oleg died and was buried at Kiev.

See S. M. Solovev, *History of Russia* (Rus.), vol. i. (St Petersburg, 1895, &c.); M. F. Vladimirsky-Budanov, *Chrestomathy of the History of Russian Law* (Rus.), pt. i. (Kiev, 1889). (R. N. B.)

OLEIC ACID, $C_{18}H_{34}O_2$ or $C_8H_{17}CH:CH\cdot[CH_2]_7\cdot CO_2H$, an organic acid occurring as a glyceride, triolein, in nearly all fats, and in many oils—olive, almond, cod-liver, &c. (see OILS). It appears as a by-product in the manufacture of candles. To prepare it olive oil is saponified with potash, and lead acetate added; the lead salts are separated, dried, and extracted with ether, which dissolves the lead oleate; the solution is then treated with hydrochloric acid, the lead chloride filtered off, the liquid concentrated, and finally distilled under diminished pressure. Oleic acid is a colourless, odourless solid, melting at 14° and boiling at 223° (10 mm.). On exposure it turns yellow, becoming rancid. Nitric acid oxidizes it to all the fatty acids from acetic to capric. Nitrous acid gives the isomeric elaidic acid, $C_8H_{17}CH:CH\cdot(CH_2)_7\cdot CO_2H$, which is crystalline and melts at 51° Hydriodic acid reduces both oleic and elaidic acids to stearic acid.

Erucic acid, $C_8H_{17}CH:CH\cdot[CH_2]_{11}\cdot CO_2H$, and the isomeric brassidic acid, belong to the oleic acid series. They occur as glycerides in rape-seed oil, in the fatty oil of mustard, and in the oil of grape seeds. Linoleic acid, $C_{16}H_{29}O_2$, found as glyceride in drying oils, and ricinoleic acid, $C_{18}H_{33}(OH)O_2$, found as glyceride in castor oil, closely resemble oleic acid.

OLEN, a semi-legendary Greek bard and seer, and writer of hymns. He is said to have been the first priest of Apollo, his connexion with whom is indicated by his traditional birthplace—Lycia or the land of the Hyperboreans, favourite haunts of the god The Delphian poetess Boeo attributed to him the introduction of the cult of Apollo and the invention of the epic metre Many hymns, nomes (simple songs to accompany the circular dance of the chorus), and oracles, attributed to Olen, were preserved in Delos. In his hymns he celebrated Opis and Argé, two Hyperborean maidens who founded the cult of Apollo in Delos, and in the hymn to Eilythyia the birth of Apollo and Artemis and the foundation of the Delian sanctuary His reputed Lycian origin corroborates the view that the cult of Apollo was an importation from Asia to Greece. His poetry generally was of the kind called hieratic.

See Callimachus, *Hymn to Delos*, 305; Pausanias i. 18, ii. 13; v. 7; ix. 27; x. 5; Herodotus iv 35.

OLÉRON, an island lying off the west coast of France, opposite the mouths of the Charente and Seudre, and included in the department of Charente-Inférieure. In 1906 the population numbered 16,747. In area (66 sq. m.) it ranks next to Corsica among French islands. It is about 18 m. in length from N.W.

to S.E., and 7 in extreme breadth; the width of the strait (*Pertuis de Maumusson*) separating it from the mainland is at one point less than a mile. The island is flat and low-lying and fringed by dunes on the coast. The greater part is very fertile, but there are also some extensive salt marshes, and oyster culture and fishing are carried on. The chief products are corn, wine, fruit and vegetables. The inhabitants are mostly Protestants and make excellent sailors. The chief places are St Pierre (pop. 1582 in 1906), Le Château d'Oléron (1546), and the watering-place of St Trojan-les-Bains.

Oléron, the *Uliarus Insula* of Pliny, formed part of the duchy of Aquitaine, and finally came into the possession of the French crown in 1370. It gave its name to a medieval code of maritime laws promulgated by Eleanor of Guienne.

OLFACTORY SYSTEM, in anatomy. The olfactory system consists of the outer nose, which projects from the face, and the nasal cavities, contained in the skull, which support the olfactory mucous membrane for the perception of smell in their upper parts, and act as respiratory passages below.

The bony framework of the nose is part of the skull (*q.v.*), but the outer nose is only supported by bone above; lower down its shape is kept by an " upper " and " lower lateral cartilage " and two or three smaller plates known as " cartilagines minores."

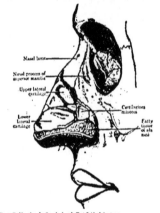

From R. Howden, in Cunningham's *Test-Book of Anatomy*.

FIG. 1.—Profile View of the Bony and Cartilaginous Skeleton of the Nose.

The expanded lower part of the side of the outer nose is known as the " ala " and is only formed of skin, both externally and internally, with fibro-fatty tissue between the layers. The inner nose or nasal cavities are separated by a septum, which is seldom quite median and is lower two-thirds by thick, highly vascular mucous membrane composed of columnar ciliated epithelium with masses of acinous glands (see EPITHELIAL TISSUES) embedded in it, while in its upper part it is covered by the less vascular but more specialized olfactory membrane. Near the front of the lower part of the septum a slight opening into a short blind tube, which runs upward and backward, may sometimes be found; this is the vestigial remnant of " Jacobson's organ," which will be noticed later. The supporting framework of the septum is made up of ethmoid above, vomer below, and the " septal cartilage " in front. The outer wall of each nasal cavity is divided into three meatūs by the overhanging turbinated bones (see fig.' 2) Above the superior turbinated is a space between it and the roof known as the "recessus spheno-ethmoidalis," into the back of which the "sphenoidal air sinus" opens. Between the superior and middle turbinated bones is the "superior meatus," containing the openings of the "posterior ethmoidal air cells," while between the middle and inferior turbinateds is the "middle meatus," which is the largest of the three and contains a rounded elevation known as the "bulla ethmoidalis:" Above and behind this is often an opening for the "middle ethmoidal cells," while below and in front a deep sickle-shaped gutter runs, the "hiatus semilunaris," which communicates above with the "frontal air sinus" and below with the opening into the "antrum of Highmore" or "maxillary antrum." So deep is this hiatus semilunaris that if, in the dead subject, water is poured into the frontal sinus it all passes into the

the sphenoidal turbinated bone separates the nasal cavity from the sphenoidal sinus above, and below there is an opening into the naso-pharynx known as the "posterior nasal aperture" or "choana." The mucous membrane of the outer wall is characteristic of the respiratory tract as high as the superior turbinated bone; it is ciliated all over and very vascular where it covers the inferior turbinated ; superficial to and above the superior turbinated the olfactory tract is reached and the specialised olfactory epithelium begins.

Embryology.

In the third week of intra-uterine life two pits make their appearance on the under side of the front of the head, and are known as the olfactory or nasal pits; they are the first appearance of the true olfactory region of the nose, and some of their epithelial lining cells send off axons (see NERVOUS SYSTEM) which arborise with the dendrites of the cells of the olfactory lobe of the brain and so form the olfactory nerves (see J. Disse, *Anal. Hefte*, 1897; also *P. Anal. Soc., J. Anat. and Phys.*, 1897, p. 12). Between the olfactory pits the broad median fronto-nasal process grows down from the forehead region to form the dorsum of the nose (see fig. 3), and the anterior part of the nasal septum, while outside them the lateral nasal processes grow down, and later on meet the maxillary processes from the first visceral arch. In this way the nasal cavities are formed, but for some time they are separated from the mouth by a thin bucconasal membrane which eventually is broken through; after this the mouth and nose are one cavity until the formation of the palate in the third month (see MOUTH AND SALIVARY GLANDS). In the third month Jacobson's organ may be seen as a well-marked tube lined with respiratory mucous membrane and running upward and backward, close to the septum, from its orifice, which is just above the foramen of Stensen in the anterior palatine canal. In man it never has any connexion with the olfactory membrane or olfactory nerves. Internally and below it is surrounded by a delicate sheet of cartilage, which is distinct from that of the nasal septum. No explanation of the function of Jacobson's organ in man is known, and it is probably entirely atavistic. At birth the nasal cavities are very shallow from above downward, but they rapidly deepen till the age of puberty. The external nose at birth projects very little from the plane of the face except at the tip, the button-like shape of which in babies is well known. In the second and third year the bridge becomes more prominent; but after puberty the nasal bones tend to tilt upward at their lower ends to form the eminence which is seen at its best in the Roman nose. (For further details see Quain's *Anatomy*, vol. i., London, 1908.)

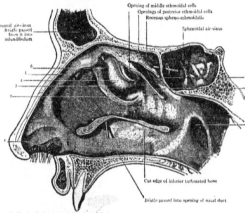

Opening of middle ethmoidal cells
Openings of posterior ethmoidal cells
Recessus spheno-ethmoidalis

Sphenoidal air-sinus

Frontal air-sinus
Bristle passed
from it into
infundibulum

Cut edge of inferior turbinated bone

Bristle passed into opening of nasal duct

From R. Howden, in Cunningham's *Test-Book of Anatomy.*

FIG. 2.—View of the Outer Wall of the Nose—the Turbinated Bones having been removed.

1. Vestibule.
2. Opening of antrum of Highmore.
3. Hiatus semilunaris.
4. Bulla ethmoidalis.
5. Agger nasi.
6. Opening of anterior ethmoidal cells
7. Cut edge of superior turbinated bone
8. Cut edge of middle turbinated bone
9. Pharyngeal orifice of Eustachian tube.

antrum and none escapes through the nostrils until that cavity is full. The passage from the frontal sinus to the hiatus semilunaris is known as the "infundibulum," and into this open the "anterior ethmoidal cells," so that the antrum acts as a sink for the secretion of these cells and of the frontal sinus. Running downward and forward from the front of the middle turbinated bone is a curved ridge known as the "agger nasi," which forms the anterior boundary of a slightly depressed area called the "atrium."

The "inferior meatus" is below the inferior turbinated bone, and, when that is lifted up, the valvular opening of the nasal duct (see EYE) is seen. In front of the inferior meatus there is a depression just above the nostril which is lined with skin instead of mucous membrane and from which short hairs grow; this is called the "vestibule." The roof of the nose is very narrow, and here the olfactory nerves pass in through the cribriform plate. The floor is a good deal wider so that a coronal section through each nasal cavity has roughly the appearance of a right-angled triangle. The anterior wall is formed by the nasal bones and the upper and lower lateral cartilages, while posteriorly

Comparative Anatomy.

In Amphioxus among the Acrania there is a ciliated pit above the anterior end of the central nervous system, which is probably a rudiment of an unpaired olfactory organ. In the Cyclostomata (lampreys and hags) the pit is at first ventral, but later becomes dorsal and shares a common opening with the pituitary invagination. It furthermore becomes divided internally into two lateral halves. In fishes there are also two lateral pits, the nostrils of which open sometimes, as in the elasmobranchs (sharks and rays), on to the ventral surface of the snout, and sometimes, as in the higher fishes, on to the dorsal surface. Up to this stage the olfactory organs are mere pits, but in the Dipnoi (mud-fish) an opening is established from them into the front of the roof of the mouth, and so they serve as respiratory passages as well as organs for the sense of smell. In the higher Amphibia the nasal organ becomes included in the skull and respiratory and olfactory parts are distinguished. In this class, too, turbinal ingrowths are found, and the naso-lachrymal duct appears. In the lizards, among the Reptilia, the olfactory and respiratory parts are very distinct, the latter being lined only by stratified epithelium unconnected with the olfactory nerves. There is one true turbinal bone growing from the outer wall, and close to this is a large nasal gland. In crocodiles the hard palate is formed, and there is henceforward a considerable distance between the openings of the external and internal nares. In this order, too (Crocodilia) air sinuses are first found extending from the olfactory cavities into the skull-bones. The birds' arrangement is very like that of the reptiles; olfactory and respiratory chambers are present, and into the latter projects the true turbinal, though there is a pseudo-turbinal in the upper or olfactory chamber. In mammals the olfactory chamber of the nose is variously developed; most of them are "macrosmatic," and have a large area of olfactory mucous membrane; some, like the seals, whalebone whales, monkeys and man are "microsmatic," while the toothed whales have the olfactory region practically suppressed in the adult, and are said to be "anosmatic." There are generally five turbinal bones in macrosmatic mammals, so that man has a reduced number. The lowest of the series or "maxillo-turbinal" is the equivalent of the single true turbinal bone of birds and reptiles, and in most mammals is a double scroll, one

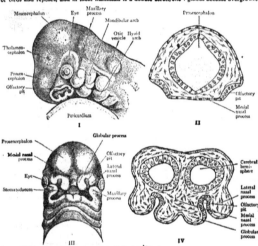

Misencephalon — Eye — Maxillary process — Mandibular arch — Otic vesicle — Hyoid arch — Prosencephalon — Tholamen-cephalon — Procen-cephalon — Olfactory pit — Perikardium — Olfactory pit — Mesial-nasal process

I — II

Prosencephalon — Globular process — Mesial nasal process — Olfactory pit — Lateral nasal process — Eye — Stomatodaeum — Maxillary process — Cerebral hemi-sphere — Lateral nasal process — Olfactory pit — Mesial nasal process — Globular process

III — IV

From A. H. Young and A. Robinson, in Cunningham's *Test-Book of Anatomy*

FIG. 3.

I. Side view of the head of human embryo about 27 days old, showing the olfactory pit and the visceral arches and clefts (from His).

II. Transverse section through the head of an embryo, showing the relation of the olfactory pits to the forebrain and to the roof of the stomatodaeal space.

III. Head of human embryo about 29 days old, showing the division of the lower part of the mesial frontal process into

the two globular processes, the intervention of the olfactory pits between the mesial and lateral nasal processes, and the approximation of the maxillary and lateral nasal processes, which, however, are separated by the oculo-nasal sulcus (from His).

IV. Transverse section of head of embryo, showing the deepening of the olfactory pits and their relation to the hemi-sphere vesicles of the fore-brain.

leaf turning upward and the other down. Jacobson's organ first appears in amphibians, where it is found as an anteroposterior gutter in the floor of the nasal cavity, sometimes being close to the septum, at other times far away, though the former position is the more primitive. In reptiles the roof of the gutter closes in on each side, and a tube is formed lying below and internal to the nasal cavity, opening anteriorly into the mouth and ending by a blind extremity, posteriorly to which branches of the olfactory and tri-geminal nerves are distributed. In the higher reptiles (crocodiles and chelonians) the organ is suppressed in the adult, and the same applies to birds; but in the lower mammals, especially the mono-tremes, it is very well developed, and is enclosed in a cartilaginous sheath, from which a turbinal process projects into its interior. In other mammals, with the exception of the Primates and perhaps the Chiroptera, the organ is quite distinct, though even in man, as has been shown, its presence can be demonstrated in the embryo. The special opening through which it communicates with the mouth is the foramen of Stenson in the anterior palatine canal.

See J. Symington on the organ of Jacobson in the Ornithorynchus,

P. Zool. Soc. (1891), and in the kangaroo, J. Anat. and Phys., vol. 26 (1891); also G. Eliot Smith on Jacobson's organ, Anatom. Anzeiger, xi. Band No. 6 (1895). For general literature on the comparative anatomy of the olfactory system up to 1906, see R. Wiedersheim's *Comparative Anatomy of Vertebrates*, translated and adapted by W. N. Parker (London, 1907).   (F. G. P.)

DISEASES OF OLFACTORY SYSTEM

External Affections and Injuries of the Nose.—Acne rosacea is one of the most frequent nasal skin affections. In an early stage it consists of dilatation or congestion of the capillaries, and later of a hypertrophy of the sebaceous follicles. This may be accompanied by the formation of pustules. In an exaggerated stage the sebaceous glands become overgrown, forming large protuberant nodular masses over which the dilated capillaries are plainly visible. This condition is termed lipoma nasi (rhinophyinia or hammer nose), though there is no increase in fatty tissue. Nasal acne occurs mainly in dyspeptics and tea drinkers, and the more advanced condition, lipoma nasi, chiefly in elderly men addicted to al-coholism. The treatment of acne is the removal of the dyspepsia with the local application of sulphur ointment or of a lotion of perchloride of mercury. Un-sightly capillaries may be destroyed by an application of the galvano-cautery or by electrolysis. Free dissection of the re-dundant tissue from around the nasal cartilages is necessary in lipoma nasi, skin being grafted on to the raw surface. The nasal bones are frequently frac-tured as the result of direct violence, as by a blow from a cricket ball or stick. The fracture is usually transverse, and may be communicated, leading to much deformity if left untreated. The treat-ment is the immediate reposition of the bony fragments. The old-standing cases where there is considerable depression wiring the fragments may be resorted to. In numerous cases the subcutaneous injection of paraffin may improve the shape of the organ. Deflection of the septum may also result from similar injuries, and lateral displacement may cause subsequent nasal obstruction and require the straightening of the septum. Lesions involving considerable loss of substance due to injury or to syphilitic or tuberculous disease have led to many methods being devised to supply the missing part. In the Indian method of rhinoplasty a flap is cut from the fore-head, to which it is left attached by a pedicle; the flap is then turned down-wards to cover the missing portion of the nose; when the parts have united, the pedicle is cut through. In the Italian operation devised by Tagliacotius (Taglia-cozzi), a flap was taken from the patient's arm, the arm being kept fixed to the head until the flap has united.

Diseases of the Interior of the Nose.—Epistaxis or bleeding of the nose may arise from many conditions. It is par-ticularly common in young girls at the time of puberty, being a form of vicarious menstruation. It also occurs in cerebral congestion, heart disease, scurvy, haemo-phylia, or as a sign of local disease. The treatment will depend upon the cause. In patients with high arterial tension epistaxis may be of direct benefit. In other cases rest on the back may be tried, with the local application of tanno-gallic acid or hazelin or adrenalin, either in a spray or on absorbent cotton. If these should not stop the haemorrhage the nose must be plugged. In cases which arise from specific forms of ulceration, such as tuberculosis and syphilis, the area should be rendered anaesthetic by cocaine, the bleeding points found, and the vessels obliterated by the electro-cautery. Polypi in the nasal passages are also a frequent cause of epistaxis.

Rhinitis, or inflammation of the mucous membrane of the nose, occurs both in acute and chronic forms. Of the acute the simple catarrhal form termed "coryza" forms the widely known "cold in the head." The tendency of acute coryza to affect entire families, and to be communicable from one person to another, points to its infectious nature, though probably some predisposing condition of health is necessary for its development. It is considered proved that the symptoms are due to the presence and development of several distinct micro-organisms. Of these the most important is the micrococcus catarrhalis described by Martin Kirchner in 1890, but Friedländer's pneumo-bacillus has also been found. In ordinary cases of coryza, sneezing, congestion of the nasal mucous membrane and a profuse watery discharge usher in the attack, and the inflammation may extend to the pharynx, larynx and trachea, blocking of the Eustachian tube producing a temporary deafness. Later the discharge may become muco-purulent. One attack of coryza conveys no immunity from subsequent attacks and some persons seem particularly susceptible. The treatment is directed towards increasing the action of the kidneys, skin and bowels. A brisk mercurial purgative is indicated, and salicin and aspirin are useful in many cases. Considerable relief may be obtained by washing out the nasal cavities several times a day with a warm lotion containing boric acid. Those who are unusually prone to catch cold should habituate themselves to an open air life by day and an open window by night, adenoids or enlarged tonsils should be removed, and the diet should be modified so as not to contain an excess of starchy foods. An acute croupous inflammation occasionally attacks the nasal mucous membrane when the Klebs-Löffler bacillus is not present, but the nasal membrane often shares in true diphtheria, or it may be the only organ to be infected thereby. The diagnosis is of course bacteriological.

As a result of frequent catarrhal attacks the nasal mucous membrane may become the seat of a chronic rhinitis in which the turbinals become swollen with oedema, and congested and finally thickened by increase in the fibrous tissue. There is an excessive muco-purulent discharge, and the patient is unable to breathe through the nose; deafness and adenoid vegetations may be the result. In the early stages the nasal cavity should be washed out night and morning with an alkaline lotion, such as bicarbonate of soda, or a caustic, such as chromic acid, should be used in swabbing over the affected part. The application of the galvano-cautery here is useful, but when the areas are much hypertrophied the hypertrophied portion of the inferior turbinals may have to be removed under cocaine. A special form of recurrent hypertrophic rhinitis is *hay fever* (q.v.).

Rhinitis Sicca is a form of chronic rhinitis in which there is but little discharge, crusts or scabs which may be difficult to remove forming in the nasal cavities; the pharynx may be also affected.

Atrophic rhinitis or ozaena usually attacks children and young adults, following on measles or scarlet fever. Crusts form, and favour the retention of the purulent discharge. The disease may extend to the nasal sinuses and septic absorption take place. The treatment is to keep the nasal cavity clean by irrigation with solution of permanganate of potash or carbolic acid lotion, the nose then being wiped and smeared with lanolin or partially plugged with a tampon of cotton-wool, the process being repeated at frequent intervals, the general treatment being that for anaemia. Disease of the middle turbinated bone is also a cause of an offensive nasal discharge, and rhinitis occurring in infants gives rise to the obstructed respiration known as "the snuffles."

Three forms of nasal polypi are described, the mucous, the fibrous and the malignant. The general symptoms of nasal polypus are a feeling of stuffiness in one or both nostrils, inability to breathe down the nose and a thin watery discharge. A nasal tone of voice, together with cough and asthma, may be present, or there may be partial or complete loss of the sense of smell (anosmia). The treatment of mucous polypi is their removal by the forceps or the snare, the base of the growth being afterwards carefully examined and cauterized with the galvano-cautery.

Fibrous polypi are usually very vascular, and may be a cause of severe epistaxis as well as of obstruction of breathing, "dead voice," sleepiness and deafness. The increasing growth may lead to expansion of the bridge of the nose and deformity of the facial bones, known as "frog-face." The tendency of fibrous polypi to take on malignant sarcomatous characters is specially noticeable. Extirpation of the growth as soon as its nature is recognized is therefore urgently demanded.

The chief diseases of the nasal septum are abscesses, due to the breaking down of haematomata, syphilitic gummata (leading to deep excavation and bony destruction), tuberculous disease in which a small yellowish grey ulcer forms and what is known as perforating ulcer of the septum, which is met with just within the nostril. The latter tends to run a chronic course, and the detachment of one of its crusts may cause epistaxis. Rhinoscleroma was first described by F. Hebra in 1870, and is endemic in Russian Poland, Galicia and Hungary, but is unknown in England, except amongst alien immigrants. The infecting organism is a specific bacillus, and the disease starts as a chronic smooth painless obstruction with the formation of dense plate-like masses of tissue of stony hardness. Treatment other than that of excision of the masses has proved useless, though the recent plan of introduction of the injection of a vaccine of the bacillus may in future modify the progress of the disease.

The accessory sinuses of the nose are also prone to disease. The maxillary antrum may become filled with muco-pus, forming an empyema, pus escaping intermittently by way of the nose. The condition causes pain and swelling, and may require the irrigation and drainage of the antrum. The frontal sinuses may become filled with mucous, owing to the swelling of the nasal mucous membrane

over the middle turbinated bone, or an acute inflammation may spread to the frontal sinuses, giving rise to an empyema in that locality. This is severe frontal pain, and in some cases a fulness on the forehead over the affected side, the pus often pointing in this site, or there may be a discharge of pus through the nose. The treatment is that of incision and irrigation of the sinus (in some cases scraping out of the sinus) and the re-establishment of communication with the nose, with free drainage. The ethmoidal and sphenoidal sinuses are also frequently the site of empyemata, giving rise to pain in the orbit and the back of the nose, and a discharge into the naso-pharynx. In the case of the ethmoidal sinus it may give rise to exophthalmus and to strabismus (squint), with the formation of a tumour at the inner wall of the orbit and fever and delirium at night. In the young the condition may become rapidly fatal. Suppuration in the sphenoidal sinus may lead to blindness from involvement of the sheath of the optic nerve, and dangerous complications such as septic basal meningitis and thrombosis of the cavernous sinus may occur. Acute ethmoiditis and sphenoiditis are serious conditions demanding immediate surgical intervention.   (H. L. H.)

OLGA, wife of Igor, prince of Kiev, and afterwards (from 945) regent for Sviatoslav her son, was baptized at Constantinople about 955 and died about 969. She was afterwards canonized in the Russian church, and is now commemorated on the 11th of July.

OLGIERD (d. 1377), grand-duke of Lithuania, was one of the seven sons of Gedymin, grand-duke of Lithuania, among whom on his death in 1341 he divided his domains, leaving the youngest, Yavnuty, in possession of the capital, Wilna, with a nominal priority. With the aid of his brother Kiejstut, Olgierd in 1345 drove out the incapable Yavnuty and declared himself grand-duke. The two and thirty years of his reign (1345–1377) were devoted to the development and extension of Lithuania, and he lived to make it one of the greatest states in Europe. Two factors contributed to produce this result, the extraordinary political sagacity of Olgierd and the life-long devotion of his brother Kiejstut. The Teutonic knights in the north and the Tatar hordes in the south were equally bent on the subjection of Lithuania, while Olgierd's eastern and western neighbours, Muscovy and Poland, were far more frequently hostile competitors than serviceable allies. Nevertheless, Olgierd not only succeeded in holding his own, but acquired influence and territory at the expense of both Muscovy and the Tatars, and extended the borders of Lithuania to the shores of the Black Sea. The principal efforts of this eminent empire-maker were directed to securing those of the Russian lands which had formed part of the ancient grand-duchy of Kiev. He procured the election of his son Andrew as prince of Pskov, and a powerful minority of the citizens of the republic of Novgorod held the balance in his favour against the Muscovite influence, but his ascendancy in both these commercial centres was at the best precarious. On the other hand he acquired permanently the important principalities of Smolensk and Bryansk in central Russia. His relations with the grand-dukes of Muscovy were friendly on the whole, and twice he married orthodox Russian princesses; but this did not prevent him from besieging Moscow in 1368 and again in 1372, both times unsuccessfully. Olgierd's most memorable feat was his great victory over the Tatars at Siniya Vodui on the Bug in 1362, which practically broke up the great Kipchak horde and compelled the khan to migrate still farther south and establish his headquarters for the future in the Crimea. Indeed, but for the unceasing simultaneous struggle with the Teutonic knights, the burden of which was heroically borne by Kiejstut, Russian historians frankly admit that Lithuania, not Muscovy, must have become the dominant power of eastern Europe. Olgierd died in 1377, accepting both Christianity and the tonsure shortly before his death. His son Jagiello ultimately ascended the Polish throne, and was the founder of the dynasty which ruled Poland for nearly 200 years.

See Kazimierz Stadnicki, *The Sons of Gedymin* (Pol.) (Lemberg, 1849–1853), Vladimir Bonifatevich Antonovich, *Monograph on the History of Western Russia* (Rus.), vol. i. (Kiev, 1885).   (R. N. B.)

OLHÃO, a seaport of southern Portugal, in the district of Faro; 5 m. E. of Faro, on the Atlantic coast. Pop. (1900) 10,609. Olhão has a good harbour at the head of the Barra Nova, a deep channel among the sandy islands which fringe the coast. Wine, fruit, cork, baskets and sumach are exported in small coasting vessels; there are important sardine and tunny fisheries; and boats, sails and cordage are manufactured

OLIGARCHY (Gr. ὀλίγος, few, ἀρχή, rule), in political philosophy, the term applied to a government exercised by a relatively small number of the members of a community. It is thus the appropriate term for what is now generally known as "aristocracy" (*q.v.*). The meaning of the terms has substantially altered since Plato's day, for in the *Republic* "oligarchy" meant the rule of the wealthy, and "aristocracy" that of the really best people.

OLIGOCENE SYSTEM (from the Gr ὀλίγος, few, and καινός, recent), in geology, the name given to the second division of the older Tertiary rocks, viz. those which occur above the Eocene and below the Miocene strata. These rocks were originally classed by Sir C. Lyell as "older Miocene," the term Oligocene being proposed by H. E Beyrich in 1854 and again in 1858. Following A. de Lapparent, the Oligocene is here regarded as divisible into two stages, an upper one, the Etampian (from Étampes), equivalent to the Rupélian of A Dumont (1849), and a lower one, the Sannoisian (from Sannois near Paris), equivalent to the Tongrian (from Tongris in Limburg) of Dumont (1859). This lower division is the Ligurian of some authors, and corresponds with the Lattorfian (Latdorf) of E. Mayer in north Germany; it is in part the equivalent of the older term Ludian of de Lapparent. It should be pointed out that several authors retain the Aquitanian stage (see MIOCENE) at the top of the Oligocene, but there are sufficiently good reasons for removing it to the younger system.

The Oligocene deposits are of fresh-water, brackish, marine and terrestrial origin; they include soft sands, sandstones, grits, marls, shales, limestones, conglomerates and lignites. The geographical aspect of Europe during this period is indicated on the accompanying map. Here and there, as in N. Germany,

Map of Europe in the early part of the Oligocene Period

Land or undifferentiated area
sea area

After A de Lapparent   Emery Walker sc

the sea gained ground that had been unoccupied by Eocene waters, but important changes, associated with the continuation of elevatory processes in the Pyrenees and Alps which had begun in the preceding period, were in progress, and a general relative uplifting took place which caused much of the Eocene sea floor to be occupied at this time by lake basins and lagoons. The movements, however, were not all of a negative character as regards the water areas, for oscillations were evidently frequent, and subsidence must have been considerable in some regions to admit of the accumulation of the great thickness of material found deposited there. Perhaps the most striking change from Eocene topography in Europe is to be seen in the extension of the Oligocene sea over North Germany, whence it extended eastward through Poland and Russia to the Aral-Caspian region, communicating thence with Arctic waters by way of a Ural depression. The Asian extension of the central mediterranean sea appears to have begun to be limited. It was later in the period when the wide-spread emersion set in.

天天 2*

In Britain Oligocene formations are found only in the Hampshire Basin and the Isle of Wight; from the admixture of fresh-water, marine and estuarine deposits, E. Forbes named these the "Fluviomarine series." The following are the more important subdivisions, in descending order: The Hamstead (Hampstead) beds, marine at the top, with *Ostrea callifera, Natica*, &c., estuarine and fresh-water below, with *Unio, Viviparus* and the remains of crocodiles, turtles and mammalia. The Bembridge marls, fresh-water, estuarine and marine, resting upon the Bembridge limestone, with many fresh-water fossils such as *Limnaea, Planorbis, Chara*, large land snails, *Amphidromus, Helix, Glandina*, and many insects and plant leaves. The Osborne beds, marls, clays and limestones, with *Unio, Limnaea*, &c. The Headon beds (upper), fresh-water clays, marls and limestones (middle), brackish and marine, more sandy (lower), brackish and fresh-water clays, marls, tufaceous limestones and sandstones. The clays and sands of the Bovey Basin in Devonshire were formerly classed as Miocene, but they are now regarded by C. Reid as Eocene on the evidence of the plant remains, though there is still a possibility that they may be found to be of Oligocene age.

In France the best-known tract of Oligocene rocks rests in the Paris basin in close relationship with the underlying Eocene. These rocks include the first and second gypsum beds, the source of "plaster of Paris"; at Montmartre the first or upper bed is 20 metres in thickness, and some of the beds contain siliceous nodules (fusils) and numerous mammalian remains. Above the gypsum beds is the travertine of Champigny-sur-Marne, a series of blue and white marls (supra-gypseous marls), followed by the "glaises verta" or greenish marls. At the top of the lower Oligocene of this district is the lacustrine "calcaire de Brie" or middle travertine, which at Ferté-sous-Jouane is exploited for millstones; this is associated with the Fontainebleau limestone, which at Chateau-Landon and Souppes is sufficiently compact to form an important building stone, used in the Arc de Triomphe and other structures in Paris. The upper Oligocene of Paris begins with the *marnes à huitres*, followed by the brackish and fresh-water molasse of Etrechy, and a series of sandy beds, of which the best known are those of Fontainebleau, Étampes and Ormoy; in these occur the groups of calcite crystals, charged with sand, familiar in all mineral collections. Elsewhere in France similar mixed marine, fresh-water and brackish beds are found: in Aquitaine there are marine and lacustrine marls, limestones and molasse; marine beds occur at Biarritz; lacustrine and fresh-water marls and limestones with lignite appear in the sub-Pyrenees; in Provence there are brackish red clays, conglomerates and lignites, with limestones in the upper parts; and in Limagne there are mottled sands, arkoses, clays and fresh-water limestones. In the Jura region and on the borders of the central *massif* a peculiar group of deposits, the *terrain sidérolithique*, is found in beds and in pockets in Jurassic limestones. Sometimes this deposit consists of red clay (bolus) with nests of pisolitic iron, as in Jura and Franche-comté, Alsace, &c.; occasionally, as in Bourgogne, Berry, the valley of the Aubois, Châtillon, it is made up of a breccia or conglomerate of Jurassic pebbles cemented with limonite and carbonate of lime or silica (an intimate mixture of marl and iron ore in these districts is called "castillard"). At Quercy the cementing material is phosphate of lime derived from the bones of mammals (*Adapis, Necrolemur, Palaeotherium, Xiphodon*, &c.), which are so numerous that it has been suggested that these animals must have been suffocated by gaseous emanations. Similar ferruginous deposits occur in South Germany.

In the Alpine region the Oligocene rocks assume the character of the Flysch, a complex assemblage of marly and sandy shales and soft sandstones with calcareous cement ("macigno"). The Flysch phase of deposition had begun before the close of the preceding period, but the bulk of it belongs to the Oligocene, and is especially characteristic of the lower part. The Flysch may attain a very great thickness; in Dauphiné it is said to be 2000 metres. Obscure plant-like impressions are common on certain horizons of this formation, and have received such names as *Chondrites, Fucoids, Helminthoidea*. The "grès de Taveyannaz" and "Wildflysch" of Lake Thun contain fragments of eruptive rocks. Marine beds occur at Barrême, Désert, Chambéry, &c., and parallel with the normal Flysch in the higher Alps of Vaudois is a nummulitic limestone; both here and near Interlaken, in the marble of Ralligstöcke, calcareous algae are abundant. Part of the "schistes des Grisons" (" Bündner Schiefer") have been regarded as of Oligocene age. In the Léman region the "Flysch rouge" at the foot of the Dent du Midi belongs to the upper part of the Flysch formation.

In North Germany the lower Oligocene consists largely of sandy marls, often glauconitic; typical localities are Egeln near Magdeburg and Latdorf near Bernburg; at Samland the glauconitic sand contains nodules of amber, with insects, derived from Eocene strata. The upper Oligocene beds, which cover a wide area, comprise the Stettin sands and Septarian Clay or Rupelton, marine beds tending to merge laterally one into another. In the Mainz basin is a petroleum-bearing sandy marl is found at Pechelbronn and Lobsann in Alsace underlying a fresh-water limestone which is followed by the marine "Meeressand" of Alzey. Lignites (*Braunkohl*) are widely spread in this region and appear at Latdorf, Leipzig, in Westphalia and Mecklenburg; at Halle is a variety called pyropissite, which is exploited at Weissenfels for the manufacture of paraffin.

In Belgium a sandy series (Wemmelian, Asschian, Henisian), mainly of brackish-water origin, is succeeded by the marine sands of Bergh (with the clay of Boom), which pass up through the inferior sands of Bolderberg into the Miocene. In Switzerland, beyond the limits of the Flysch, nearer the Alpine *massif*, is a belt of grits, limestones and clays in an uncompacted condition, to which the name "molasse" is usually given; mixed with the molasse is an inconstant conglomeratic littoral formation, called *Nagelfluh.* The molasse occurs also in Bavaria, where it is several thousand feet thick and contains lignites. Oligocene deposits occur in the Carpathian region and Tirol; as Flysch and brackish and lacustrine beds with lignite in Klausenburg, lignites at Häring in Tirol. In the Spanish Pyrenees they are well developed; in the Apennines the scaly clays ("argille scagliose") are of this age; while in Calabria they are represented by thick conglomerates and Flysch. Flysch appears also in Dalmatia and Istria (where it is called "tassello") and in North Bosnia, where it contains marine limestones. Lignites are found at Sotzka and Styria, marine beds in the Balkan peninsula, glauconitic sands prevail in South Russia, Flysch with sands and grits in the Caucasus, while marine deposits also occupy the Aral-Caspian region and Armenia, and are to be traced into Persia. Oligocene rocks are known in North Africa, Algeria, Tunis and Egypt, with the silicified trees and basalt sheets north of the Fayum. In North America the rocks of this period have not been very clearly differentiated, but they may possibly be represented by the White river beds of S. Dakota, the white and blue marls of Jackson on the Mississippi, the "Jacksonian" white limestone of Alabama, the limestone of Ocala in Florida, certain lacustrine clays in the Uinta basin, and by the ribband shales with asphalt and petroleum in the coastal range of California. In South America and the Antilles upper Oligocene is found, and the lignite beds of Coronel and Lota in Chile and in the Straits of Magellan may be of this age; in Patagonia are the lower Oligocene marine beds ("Patagonian") and beds with mammalian remains. In New Zealand the Oamaru series of J. Hutton is regarded as Oligocene; at its base are interstratified basic volcanic rocks.

A correlation of Oligocene strata is summarized in the following table:—

in the Eocene seas (*Coelopleurus, Echinolampas, Clypeaster, Scutella*). Corals were abundant, and nummulites still continued till near the close of the period, but they were diminished in size.

REFERENCES.—"Geology of the Isle of Wight," *Mem. Geol. Survey* (2nd ed. 1889); A. von Koenen, *Abhand. geol. Specialkart Preuss.* x. (1889–1894); M. Voliest, *Der Braunkohlenbergbaum* (Halle, 1880); E. van den Brocek, "Matériaux pour l'étude de l'Oligocène beige," *Bull. Soc. Belg. Géol.* (1894); also the works of O. Heer, H. Filhol, G. Vasseur, H. F. Osborn, A. Gaudry, H. Douvillé, R. B. Newton, H. Dall, M. Cossmann, G. Lambert, &c., and the article FLYSCH (J. A. H.)

OLIGOCLASE, a rock-forming mineral belonging to the plagioclase (*q.v.*) division of the felspars. In chemical composition and in its crystallographical and physical characters it is intermediate between albite ($NaAlSi_3O_8$) and anorthite ($CaAl_2Si_2O_8$), being an isomorphous mixture of three to six molecules of the former with one of the latter. It is thus a soda-lime felspar crystallizing in the anorthic system. Varieties intermediate between oligoclase and albite are known as oligoclase-albite. The name oligoclase was given by A. Breithaupt in 1826 from the Gr. ὀλίγος, little, and κλάν, to break, because the mineral was thought to have a less perfect cleavage than albite. It had previously been recognized as a distinct species by J. J. Berzelius in 1824, and was named by him soda-spodumene (*Natron-spodumen*), because of its resemblance in appearance to spodumene. The hardness is 6½ and the sp. gr. 2·65-2·67. In colour it is usually whitish, with shades of grey, green or red. Perfectly colourless and transparent glassy material found at Bakersville in North Carolina has occasionally been faceted as a gem-stone. Another variety more frequently used as a gem-stone is the aventurine-felspar or "sun-stone" (*q.v.*) found as reddish cleavage masses in gneiss at Tvedestrand in southern

OLIGOCENE SYSTEM 8.

	England.	Paris Basin.	Belgium.	North German Region.	Other Localities.	Alps and S. Europe.
Upper Oligocene. Tongrian. (Stampian.)	Hamstead Beds.	Sands and sandstones of Ormoy, Fontainebleau and Pierrefitte. Sands of Morigny, Falun of Jeurre, Oyster marls. Molasse of Etrechy.	Lower sands of Bolderberg. Sands of Bergh with Clay of Boom.	Septarian Clay, or Repelton. Stettin sands.	Cyrena marls of Mainz. Lignites of Häring, Gypsiferous limestone of Aix, and Lower marine Molasse of Basel.	Nummulitic formations. Flysch formations.
Lower Oligocene. Sannoisian. (Tongrian.)	Bembridge Beds. Osborne Beds. Headon Beds.	Limestone of Brie, marine beds of Sannois, "Glaise verte," and Cyrena marls. Supragypseous marls, limestones of Champigny, "First" and "Second" masses of gypsum.	Sands of Vieux-Jones. Clays of Henis. Sands of Grimmertingen. Sands of Wemmel.	Clays of Egeln and Latdorf. Amber-bearing Glauconitic sands of Samland.	Lignites of Celas (Languedoc). Lignites of Brunstatt. Marls of Priabona, limestones of Crosara.	

The land flora of this period was a rich one consisting largely of evergreens with characters akin to those of tropical India and Australia and subtropical America. Sequoias, sabal palms, ferns, cinnamon-trees, gum-trees, oaks, figs, laurels and willows were common. *Chara* is a common fossil in the fresh-water beds. The most interesting feature of the land fauna was undoubtedly the astonishing variety of mammalians, especially the long series from the White river beds and others in the interior of North America. Pachyderms were very numerous. Many of the mammals were of mixed types, *Hyaenodon* (between marsupials and placentals), *Adapis* (between pachyderms and lemurs), and many were clearly the forerunners of living genera. Rhinocerids were represented in the upper Oligocene by the hornless *Aceratherium; Palaeomastodon* and *Arsinoitherium,* from Egypt are early proboscidian forms which may have lived in this period; *Anchitherium, Anchippus,* &c., were forerunners of the horse. *Palaeotherium, Anthracotherium, Palaeogale, Steneofiber, Cynodictis, Dinictis, Ictops, Palaeolagus, Sciurus, Colodon, Hyopotamus, Oreodon, Poebrotherium, Protoceras, Hypertragulus* and the gigantic Titanotherids (*Titanotherium, Brontotherium,* &c.) are some of the important genera, representatives of most of the modern groups, including carnivores (*Canidae* and *Felidae*), insectivores, rodents, ruminants, camels. Tortoises were abundant, and the genus *Rana* made its appearance. Rays and dog-fish were the dominant marine fish; logconal brackish-water fish are represented by *Protebias, Smerdis,* &c. Insects abounded and arachnids were rapidly developing. Gasteropods were increasing in importance, most of the genera still existing (*Cerithium, Potamides, Melania,* large *Naticas, Pleurotomaria, Voluta, Turritella, Rostellaria, Pyrula*). Cephalopods, on the other hand, show a falling off. Pelecypods include the genera *Cardita, Pectunculus, Lucina, Ostrea, Cyrena, Cytherea.* Bryozoa were very abundant (*Membranipora, Lepralia, Hornera, Idmonea*). Echinoids were less numerous than

Norway; this presents a brilliant red metallic glitter, due to the presence of numerous small scales of haematite or göthite enclosed in the felspar.

Oligoclase occurs, often accompanying orthoclase, as a constituent of igneous rocks of various kinds; for instance, amongst plutonic rocks in granite, syenite, diorite; amongst dike-rocks in porphyry and diabase; and amongst volcanic rocks in andesite and trachyte. It also occurs in gneiss. The best developed and largest crystals are those found with orthoclase, quartz, epidote and calcite in veins in granite at Arendal in Norway. (L. J. S.)

OLIPHANT, LAURENCE (1829–1888), British author, son of Anthony Oliphant (1793–1859),[1] was born at Cape Town.

[1] The family to which Oliphant belonged is old and famous in Scottish history. Sir Laurence Oliphant of Aberdalgie, Perthshire, who was created a lord of the Scottish parliament before 1458, was descended from Sir William Oliphant of Aberdalgie and on the female side from King Robert the Bruce. Sir William (d. 1329) is renowned for his brave defence of Stirling castle against Edward I. in 1304. Sir Laurence was sent to conclude a treaty with England in 1484; he helped to establish the young king James IV. on his throne, and he died about 1500. His son John, the 2nd lord (d. 1516), having lost his son and heir, Colin, at Flodden, was succeeded by his grandson Laurence (d. 1566), who was taken prisoner by the English at the rout of Solway Moss in 1542. Laurence's son, Laurence, the 4th lord (1529–1593), was a partisan of Mary queen of Scots, and was succeeded by his grandson Laurence (1583–1631), who left no sons when he died. The 6th lord was Patrick Oliphant, a descendant of the 4th lord, and the title was held by his descendants

His father was then attorney-general in Cape Colony, but was soon transferred as chief justice to Ceylon. The boy's education was of the most desultory kind. Far the least useless portion of it belonged to the years 1848 and 1849, when he accompanied his parents on a tour on the continent of Europe. In 1851 he accompanied Jung Bahadur from Colombo to Nepaul. He passed an agreeable time there, and saw enough that was new to enable him to write his first book, *A Journey to Katmandu* (1852). From Nepaul he returned to Ceylon and thence to England, dallied a little with the English bar, so far at least as to eat dinners at Lincoln's Inn, and then with the Scottish bar, so far at least as to pass an examination in Roman law. He was more happily inspired when he threw over his legal studies and went to travel in Russia. The outcome of that tour was his book on *The Russian Shores of the Black Sea* (1853). Between 1853 and 1861 he was successively secretary to Lord Elgin during the negotiation of the Canada Reciprocity treaty at Washington, the companion of the duke of Newcastle on a visit to the Circassian coast during the Crimean War, and Lord Elgin's private secretary on his expedition to China. Each of these experiences produced a pleasant book of travel. In 1861 he was appointed first secretary in Japan, and might have made a successful diplomatic career if it had not been interrupted, almost at the outset, by a night attack on the legation, in which he nearly lost his life. It seems probable that he never properly recovered from this affair. He returned to England and resigned the service, and was elected to parliament in 1865 for the Stirling Burghs.

Oliphant did not show any conspicuous parliamentary ability, but made a great success by his vivacious and witty novel, *Piccadilly* (1870). He fell, however, under the influence of the spiritualist prophet Thomas Lake Harris (*q.v.*), who about 1861 had organized a small community, the Brotherhood of the New Life,[1] which at this time was settled at Brocton on Lake Erie and subsequently moved to Santa Rosa in California. Harris obtained so strange an ascendancy over Oliphant that the latter left parliament in 1868, followed him to Brocton, and lived there the life of a farm labourer, in obedience to the imperious will of his spiritual guide. The cause of this painful and grotesque aberration has never been made quite clear. It was part of the Brocton régime that members of the community should be allowed to return into the world from time to time, to make money for its advantage. After three years this was permitted to Oliphant, who, once more in Europe, acted as correspondent of *The Times* during the Franco-German War, and spent afterwards several years at Paris in the service of that journal. There he met Miss Alice le Strange, whom he married. In 1873 he went back to Brocton, taking with him his wife and mother. During the years which followed he continued to be employed in the service of the community and its head, but on work very different from that with which he had been occupied on his first sojourn. His new work was chiefly financial, and took him much to New York and a good deal to England. As late as December 1878 he continued to believe that Harris was an incarnation of the Deity. By that time, however, his mind was occupied with a large project of colonization in Palestine, and he made in 1879 an extensive journey in that country, going also to Constantinople,

in the vain hope of obtaining a lease of the northern half of the Holy Land with a view to settling large numbers of Jews there. This he conceived would be an easy task from a financial point of view, as there were so many persons in England and America " anxious to fulfil the prophecies, and bring about the end of the world." He landed once more in England without having accomplished anything definite; but his wife, who had been banished from him for years and had been living in California, was allowed to rejoin him, and they went to Egypt together. In 1881 he crossed again to America. It was on this visit that he became utterly disgusted with Harris, and finally split from him. He was at first a little afraid that his wife would not follow him in his renunciation of " the prophet," but this was not the case, and they settled themselves very agreeably, with one house in the midst of the German community at Haifa, and another about twelve miles off at Dalieh on Mount Carmel.

It was at Haifa in 1884 that they wrote together the strange book called *Sympneumata: Evolutionary Forces now active in Man*, and in the next year Oliphant produced there his novel *Masollam*; which may be taken to contain its author's latest views with regard to the personage whom he long considered as " a new Avatar." One of his cleverest works, *Altiora Peto*, had been published in 1883. In 1886 an attack of fever, caught on the shores of the Lake of Tiberias, resulted in the death of his wife, whose constitution had been undermined by the hardships of her American life. He was persuaded that after death he was in much closer relation with her than when she was still alive, and conceived that it was under her influence that he wrote the book to which he gave the name of *Scientific Religion*. In November 1887 he went to England to publish that book. By the Whitsuntide of 1888 he had completed it and started for America. There he determined to marry again, his second wife being a granddaughter of Robert Owen the Socialist. They were married at Malvern, and meant to have gone to Haifa, but Oliphant was taken very ill at Twickenham, and died on the 23rd of December 1888. Although a very clever man and a delightful companion, full of high aspiration and noble feeling, Oliphant was only partially sane. In any case, his education was ludicrously inappropriate for a man who aspired to be an authority on religion and philosophy. He had gone through no philosophical discipline in his early life, and knew next to nothing of the subjects with regard to which he imagined it was in his power to pour a flood of new light upon the world. His shortcomings and eccentricities, however, did not prevent his being a brilliant writer and talker, and a notable figure in any society.

See Mrs (Margaret) Oliphant, *Memoir of the Life of Laurence Oliphant and of Alice Oliphant his Wife* (1892). (M. G. D.)

OLIPHANT, MARGARET OLIPHANT (1828-1897), British novelist and historical writer, daughter of Francis Wilson, was born at Wallyford, near Musselburgh, Midlothian, in 1828. Her childhood was spent at Lasswade (near Dalkeith), Glasgow and Liverpool. As a girl she constantly occupied herself with literary experiments, and in 1849 published her first novel, *Passages in the Life of Mrs Margaret Maitland*. It dealt with the Scottish Free Church movement, with which Mr and Mrs Wilson both sympathized, and had some success. This she followed up in 1851 with *Caleb Field*, and in the same year met Major Blackwood in Edinburgh, and was invited by him to contribute to the famous *Blackwood's Magazine*. The connexion thus early commenced lasted during her whole lifetime, and she contributed considerably more than 100 articles to its pages. In May 1852 she married her cousin, Frank Wilson Oliphant, at Birkenhead, and settled at Harrington Square, in London. Her husband was an artist, principally in stained glass. He had very delicate health, and two of their children died in infancy, while the father himself developed alarming symptoms of consumption. For the sake of his health they moved in January 1859 to Florence, and thence to Rome, where Frank Oliphant died. His wife, left almost entirely without resources, returned to England and took up the burden of supporting her three

until the death of Francis, the 10th lord, in April 1748. It has since been claimed by several persons, but without success.

Another member of the family was Laurence Oliphant (1691-1767) the Jacobite, who belonged to a branch settled at Gask in Perthshire. He took part in the rising of 1715, and both he and his son Laurence (d. 1792) were actively concerned in that of 1745, being present at the battles of Falkirk and Culloden. After the ruin of the Stuart cause they escaped to France, but were afterwards allowed to return to Scotland. One of this Oliphant's descendants was Carolina, Baroness Nairne (*q.v.*).

[1] It should be mentioned that the unfavourable view of Harris taken by Oliphant's own biographer, and certainly not shaken by subsequent evidence, has been strongly repudiated by some who knew him. Mr J. Cuming Walters, for instance, in the *Westminster Gazette* (London, July 28, 1906) defends the purity of his character. It is difficult to arrive at the exact truth as to Oliphant's relations with him, or the financial scandal which ended them; and it must be admitted that Oliphant himself was at least decidedly cranky.

children by her own literary activity. She had now become a popular writer, and worked with amazing industry to sustain her position. Unfortunately, her home life was full of sorrow and disappointment. In January 1864 her only daughter died in Rome, and was buried in her father's grave. Her brother, who had emigrated to Canada, was shortly afterwards involved in financial ruin, and Mrs Oliphant offered a home to him and his children, and added their support to her already heavy responsibilities. In 1866 she settled at Windsor to be near her sons who were being educated at Eton. This was her home for the rest of her life, and for more than thirty years she pursued a varied literary career with courage scarcely broken by a series of the gravest troubles. The ambitions she cherished for her sons were unfulfilled. Cyril Francis, the elder, died in 1890, leaving a *Life of Alfred de Musset*, incorporated in his mother's *Foreign Classics for English Readers*. The younger, Frank, collaborated with her in the *Victorian Age of English Literature* and won a position at the British Museum, but was rejected by the doctors. He died in 1894. With the last of her children lost to her, she had but little further interest in life. Her health steadily declined, and she died at Wimbledon, on the 25th of June 1897.

In the course of her long struggle with circumstances, Mrs Oliphant produced more than 120 separate works, including novels, books of travel and description, histories and volumes of literary criticism. Among the best known of her works of fiction are *Adam Graeme* (1852), *Magdalen Hepburn* (1854), *Lilliesleaf* (1855), *The Laird of Norlaw* (1858) and a series of stories with the collective title of *The Chronicles of Carlingford*, which, originally appearing in *Blackwood's Magazine* (1862-1865), did much to widen her reputation. This series included *Salem Chapel* (1863), *The Rector; and the Doctor's Family* (1863), *The Perpetual Curate* (1864) and *Miss Marjoribanks* (1866). Other successful novels were *Madonna Mary* (1867), *Squire Arden* (1871), *He that will not when he may* (1880), *Hester* (1883), *Kirsteen* (1890), *The Marriage of Elinor* (1892) and *The Ways of Life* (1897). Her tendency to mysticism found expression in *The Beleaguered City* (1880) and *A Little Pilgrim in the Unseen* (1882). Her biographies of *Edward Irving* (1862) and *Laurence Oliphant* (1892), together with her life of Sheridan in the "English Men of Letters" (1883), have vivacity and a sympathetic touch. She also wrote historical and critical works of considerable variety, including *Historical Sketches of the Reign of George II.* (1869), *The Makers of Florence* (1876), *A Literary History of England from 1790 to 1825* (1882), *The Makers of Venice* (1887), *Royal Edinburgh* (1890), *Jerusalem* (1891) and *The Makers of Modern Rome* (1895), while at the time of her death she was still occupied upon *Annals of a Publishing House*, a record of the progress and achievement of the firm of Blackwood, with which she had been so long and honourably connected.

Her *Autobiography and Letters*, which present a touching picture of her domestic anxieties, appeared in 1899.

OLIPHANT, OLIFANT (Ger. *Helfant*), the large signal horn of the middle ages, made, as its name indicates, from the tusk of an elephant. The oliphant was the instrument of knights and men of high degree, and was usually ornamented with scenes of hunting or war carved either lengthways or round the horn in sections divided by bands of gold and studded with gems. The knights used their oliphants in the hunting field and in battle, and the loss of this precious horn was considered as shameful as the loss of sword or banner.

OLIVA, FERNAN PEREZ DE (1492?-1530), Spanish man of letters, was born at Cordoya about 1492. After studying at Salamanca, Alcalá, Paris and Rome, he was appointed rector at Salamanca, where he died in 1530. His *Diálogo de la dignidad del hombre* (1543), an unfinished work completed by Francisco Cervantes de Salazar, was written chiefly to prove the suitability of Spanish as a vehicle for philosophic discussion. He also published translations of the *Amphitruo* (1525), the *Electra* (1528) and the *Hecuba* (1528).

OLIVARES, GASPAR DE GUZMAN, count of Olivares and duke of San Lucar (1587-1645), Spanish royal favourite and minister, was born in Rome, where his father was Spanish ambassador, on the 6th of January 1587. His compound title is explained by the fact that he inherited the title of count of Olivares, but was created duke of San Lucar by the favour of Philip IV. He begged the king to allow him to preserve his inherited title in combination with the new honour—according to a practice of which there are a few other examples in Spanish history. Therefore he was commonly spoken of as *el conde-duque*. During the life of Philip III. he was appointed to a post in the household of the heir apparent, Philip, by the interest of his maternal uncle Don Baltasar de Zúñiga, who was the head of the prince's establishment. Olivares made it his business to acquire the most complete influence over the young prince. When Philip IV. ascended the throne in 1621, at the age of sixteen, he showed his confidence in Olivares by ordering that all papers requiring the royal signature should first be sent to the count-duke. Olivares could now boast to his uncle Don Baltasar de Zúñiga that he was "all." He became what is known in Spain as a *valido*—something more than a prime minister, the favourite and *alter ego* of the king. For twenty-two years he directed the policy of Spain. It was a period of constant war, and finally of disaster abroad and of rebellion at home. The Spaniards, who were too thoroughly monarchical to blame the king, held his favourite responsible for the misfortunes of the country. The count-duke became, and for long remained, in the opinion of which countrymen, the accepted model of a grasping and incapable favourite. Of late, largely under the inspiration of Don Antonio Canovas, there has been a certain reaction in his favour. It would certainly be most unjust to blame Olivares alone for the decadence of Spain, which was due to internal causes of long standing. The gross errors of his policy—the renewal of the war with Holland in 1621, the persistence of Spain in taking part in the Thirty Years' War, the lesser wars undertaken in northern Italy, and the entire neglect of all effort to promote the unification of the different states forming the peninsular kingdom—were shared by him with the king, the Church and the commercial classes. When he had fallen from power he wrote an apology, in which he maintained that he had always wished to see more attention paid to internal government, and above all to the complete unification of Portugal with Spain. But if this was not an afterthought, he must, on his own showing, stand accused of having carried out during long years a policy which he knew to be disastrous to his country, rather than risk the loss of the king's favour and his place. Olivares did not share the king's taste for art and literature, but he formed a vast collection of state papers, ancient and contemporary, which he endeavoured to protect from destruction by entailing them as an heirloom. He also formed a splendid aviary which, under the name of "hencoop," was a favourite subject of ridicule with his enemies. Towards the end of his period of favour he caused great offence by legitimizing a supposed bastard son of very doubtful paternity and worthless personal character, and by arranging a rich marriage for him. The fall of Olivares was immediately due to the revolts of Portugal and Catalonia in 1640. The king parted with him reluctantly, and only under the pressure of a strong court intrigue headed by Queen Isabella. It was noted with anxiety by his enemies that he was succeeded in the king's confidence by his nephew the count of Haro. There remains, however, a letter from the king, in which Philip tells his old favourite, with frivolous ferocity, that it might be necessary to sacrifice his life in order to avert unpopularity from the royal house. Olivares was driven from office in 1643. He retired by the king's order to Toro. Here he endeavoured to satisfy his passion for activity, partly by sharing in the municipal government of the town and the regulation of its commons, woods and pastures, and partly by the composition of the apology he published under the title of *El Nicandro*, which was perhaps written by an agent, but was undeniably inspired by the fallen minister. The *Nicandro* was denounced to the Inquisition, and it is not impossible that Olivares might have ended in the prisons of the Holy Office, or on the scaffold, if he had not died on the 22nd of July 1645.

See the *Estudios del reinado de Felipe IV.* of Don Antonio Canovas (Madrid, 1889); and Don F. Silvela's introduction, much less favourable to Olivares, to his edition of the *Cartas de Sor Maria de Agreda y del rey Felipe IV.* (Madrid, 1885-1886).

OLIVE (*Olea europaea*), the plant that yields the olive oil of commerce, belonging to a section of the natural order Oleaceae, of which it has been taken as the type. The genus *Olea* includes about thirty species, very widely scattered, chiefly over the Old World, from the basin of the Mediterranean to South Africa and New Zealand. The wild olive is a small tree or bush of rather straggling growth, with thorny branches and opposite oblong pointed leaves, dark greyish-green above and, in the young state, hoary beneath with whitish scales, the small white flowers, with four-cleft calyx and corolla, two stamens and bifid stigma, are borne on the last year's wood, in racemes springing from the axils of the leaves; the drupaceous fruit is small in the wild plant, and the fleshy pericarp, which gives the cultivated olive its economic value, is hard and comparatively thin. In the cultivated forms the tree acquires a more compact habit, the branches lose their spinous character, while the young shoots become more or less angular; the leaves are always

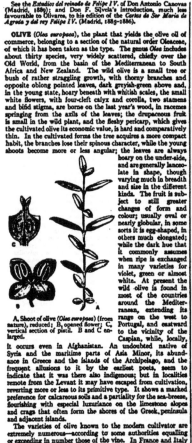

A, Shoot of olive (*Olea europaea*) (from nature), reduced; B, opened flower; C, vertical section of pistil. B and C enlarged.

hoary on the under-side, and are generally lanceolate in shape, though varying much in breadth and size in the different kinds. The fruit is subject to still greater changes of form and colour; usually oval or nearly globular, in some sorts it is egg-shaped, in others much elongated; while the dark hue that it commonly assumes when ripe is exchanged in many varieties for violet, green or almost white. At present the wild olive is found in most of the countries around the Mediterranean, extending its range on the west to Portugal, and eastward to the vicinity of the Caspian, while, locally, it occurs even in Afghanistan. An undoubted native of Syria and the maritime parts of Asia Minor, its abundance in Greece and the islands of the Archipelago, and the frequent allusions to it by the earliest poets, seem to indicate that it was there also indigenous; but in localities remote from the Levant it may have escaped from cultivation, reverting more or less to its primitive type. It shows a marked preference for calcareous soils and a partiality for the sea-breeze, flourishing with especial luxuriance on the limestone slopes and crags that often form the shores of the Greek peninsula and adjacent islands.

The varieties of the olive known to the modern cultivator are extremely numerous—according to some authorities equalling or exceeding in number those of the vine. In France and Italy at least thirty kinds have been enumerated, but comparatively few are grown to any large extent. None of these can be safely identified with ancient descriptions, though it is not unlikely that some of the narrow-leaved sorts that are most esteemed may be descendants of the famed "Licinian" (see below). Italy retains its old pre-eminence in olive cultivation; and, though its ancient Gallic province now excels it in the production of the finer oils, its fast-improving culture may restore the old prestige. The broad-leaved olive trees of Spain bear a larger fruit, but the pericarp is of more bitter flavour and the oil of ranker quality. The olive tree, even when free increase is

unchecked by pruning, is of very slow growth; but, where allowed for ages its natural development, the trunk sometimes attains a considerable diameter. De Candolle records one exceeding 23 ft. in girth, the age being supposed to amount to seven centuries. Some old Italian olives have been credited with an antiquity reaching back to the first years of the empire, or even to the days of republican Rome; but the age of such ancient trees is always doubtful during growth, and their identity with old descriptions still more difficult to establish. The tree in cultivation rarely exceeds 30 ft. in height, and in France and Italy is generally confined to much more limited dimensions by frequent pruning. The wood, of a yellow or light greenish-brown hue, is often finely veined with a darker tint, and, being very hard and close grained, is valued by the cabinetmaker and ornamental turner.

The olive is propagated in various ways, but cuttings or layers are generally preferred; the tree roots in favourable soil almost as easily as the willow, and throws up suckers from the stump when cut down. Branches of various thickness are cut into lengths of several feet each, and, planted rather deeply in manured ground, soon vegetate; shorter pieces are sometimes laid horizontally in shallow trenches, when, covered with a few inches of soil, they rapidly throw up sucker-like shoots. In Greece and the islands grafting the cultivated tree on the wild form is a common practice. In Italy embryonic buds, which form small swellings on the stems, are carefully excised and planted beneath the surface, where they grow readily, these "uovoli" soon forming a vigorous shoot. Occasionally the larger boughs are inarched, and young trees thus soon obtained. The olive is also sometimes raised from seed, the oily pericarp being first softened by slight rotting, or soaking in hot water or in an alkaline solution, to facilitate germination. The olives in the East receive little attention from the husbandman, the branches being allowed to grow freely and without curtailment by the pruning-knife; water, however, must be supplied in long droughts to ensure a crop; with this neglectful culture the trees bear abundantly only at intervals of three or four years; thus, although wild growth is favourable to the picturesque aspect of the plantation, it is not to be recommended on economic grounds. Where the olive is carefully cultivated, as in Languedoc and Provence, it is planted in rows at regular intervals, the distance between the trees varying in different "olivettes," according to the variety grown. Careful pruning is practised, the object being to preserve the flower-bearing shoots of the preceding year, while keeping the head of the tree low, so as to allow the easy gathering of the fruit; a dome or rounded form is generally the aim of the pruner. The spaces between the trees are occasionally manured with rotten dung or other nitrogenous matter; in France woollen rags are in high esteem for this purpose. Various annual crops are sometimes raised between the rows, and in Calabria wheat even is grown in this way; but the trees are better without any intermediate cropping. Latterly a dwarf variety, very prolific and with green fruit, has come into favour in certain localities, especially in America, where it is said to have produced a crop two or three seasons after planting. The ordinary kinds do not become profitable to the grower until from five to seven years after the cuttings are placed in the olive-ground. Apart from occasional damage by weather or organic foes, the olive crop is somewhat precarious even with the most careful cultivation, and the large untended trees so often seen in Spain and Italy do not yield that certain income to the peasant proprietor that some authors have attributed to them; the crop from these old trees is often enormous, but they seldom bear well two years in succession, and in many instances a luxuriant harvest can only be reckoned upon every sixth or seventh season. The fruit when ripe is, by the careful grower, picked by hand and deposited in cloths or baskets for conveyance to the mill; but in many parts of Spain and Greece, and generally in Asia, the olives are beaten down by poles or by shaking the boughs, or even allowed to drop naturally, often lying on the ground until the convenience of the owner admits of their removal; much of the inferior oil owes its bad quality to the carelessness of the proprietor of the trees. In southern Europe the olive harvest is in the winter months, continuing for several weeks; but the time varies in each country, and also with the season and the kinds cultivated. The amount of oil contained in the fruit differs much in the various sorts; the pericarp usually yields from 60 to 70%. The ancient agriculturists believed that the olive would not succeed if planted more than a few leagues from the sea (Theophrastus gives 300 stadia as the limit), but modern experience does not confirm the idea, and, though showing a preference for the coast, it has long been grown far inland. A calcareous soil, however dry or poor, seems best adapted to its healthy development, though the tree will grow in any light soil, and even on clay if well drained; but, as remarked by Pliny, the plant is more liable to disease on rich soils, and the oil is inferior to the produce of the poorer and more rocky ground the species naturally affects. The olive suffers greatly in some years from the attacks of various enemies. A fungoid growth has at times infested the trees for several successive seasons, to the great damage of the plantations. A species of coccus, *C. oleae*, attaches itself to the shoots, and certain lepidopterous caterpillars feed on the leaves, while the "olive-fly" attacks the fruit. In France the olivettes suffer occasionally from frost; in the early part of the 18th century many trees were cut to the ground by a winter of exceptional severity. Gales and long-continued rains during the gathering season also cause mischief.

The unripe fruit of the olive is largely used in modern as in ancient times as an article of dessert, to enhance the flavour of wine, and to renew the sensitiveness of the palate for other viands. For this purpose the fruit is picked while green, soaked for a few hours in an alkaline ley, washed well in clean water and then placed in bottles or jars filled with brine; the Romans added *amurca* to the salt to increase the bitter flavour of the olives, and at the present day spices are sometimes used.

The leaves and bark of the tree are employed in the south, as a tonic medicine, in intermittent fever. A resinous matter called "olive gum," or Lucca gum, formed by the exuding juice in hot seasons, was anciently in medical esteem, and in modern Italy is used as a perfume.

In England the olive is not hardy, though in the southern counties it will stand ordinary winters with only the protection of a wall, and will bear fruit in such situations; but the leaves are generally shed in the autumn, and the olive rarely ripen.

The genus *Olea* includes several other species of some economic importance. *O. paniculata* is a larger tree, attaining a height of 50 or 60 ft. in the forests of Queensland, and yielding a hard and tough timber. The yet harder wood of *O. laurifolia*, an inhabitant of Natal, is the black ironwood of the South African colonist.

At what remote period of human progress the wild olive passed under the care of the husbandman and became the fruitful garden olive it is impossible to conjecture. The frequent reference in the Bible to the plant and its produce, its implied abundance in the land of Canaan, the important place it has always held in the economy of the inhabitants of Syria, lead us to consider that country the birthplace of the cultivated olive. An improved variety, possessed at first by some small Semitic sept, it was probably slowly distributed to adjacent tribes; and, yielding profusely, with little labour, that oily matter so essential to healthy life in the dry hot climates of the East, the gift of the fruitful tree became in that primitive age a symbol of peace and goodwill among the warlike barbarians. At a later period, with the development of maritime enterprise, the oil was conveyed, as an article of trade, to the neighbouring Pelasgic and Ionian nations, and the plant, doubtless, soon followed.

In the Homeric world, as depicted in the *Iliad*, olive oil is known only as a luxury of the wealthy—an exotic product, prized chiefly for its value in the heroic toilet; the warriors anoint themselves with it after the bath, and the body of Patroclus is similarly sprinkled; but no mention of the culture of the plant is made, nor does it find any place on the Achillean shield, on which a vineyard is represented. But, although no reference to the cultivation of the olive occurs in the *Iliad*, the presence of the tree in the garden of Alcinous and other familiar allusions show it to have been known when the *Odyssey* was written. Whenever the introduction may have taken place, all tradition points to the limestone hills of Attica as the seat of its first cultivation on the Hellenic peninsula. When Poseidon and Athena contended for the future city, an olive sprang from the barren rock at the bidding of the goddess, the patron of those arts that were to bring undying influence to the rising state. That this myth has some relation to the first planting of the olive in Greece seems certain from the remarkable story told by Herodotus of the Epidaurians, who, on their crops failing, applied for counsel to the Delphic oracle, and were enjoined to erect statues to Damia and Auxesia (symbols of fertility) carved from the wood of the true garden olive, then possessed only by the Athenians, who granted their request for a tree on condition of their making an annual sacrifice to Athena, its patron; they thus obeyed the command of the Pythian, and their lands became again fertile. The sacred tree of the goddess long stood on the Acropolis, and, though destroyed in the Persian invasion, sprouted again from the root—some suckers of which were said to have produced those olive trees of the Academy in an after age no less revered. By the time of Solon the olive had

so spread that he found it necessary to enact laws to regulate the cultivation of the tree in Attica, from which country it was probably distributed gradually to all the Athenian allies and tributary states. To the Ionian coast, where it abounded in the time of Thales, it may have been in an earlier age brought by Phoenician vessels; some of the Sporades may have received it from the same source; the olives of Rhodes and Crete had perhaps a similar origin. Samos, if we may judge from the epithet of Aeschylus (Ἐλαιόφυτος), must have had the fruitful plant long before the Persian wars.

It is not unlikely that the valued tree was taken to Magna Graecia by the first Achaean colonists, and the assertion of Pliny (quoted from Fenestella), that no olives existed in Italy in the reign of Tarquinius Priscus, must be received with the caution due to many statements of that industrious compiler. In Latin Italy the cultivation seems to have spread slowly, for it was not until the consulship of Pompey that the production of oil became sufficient to permit of its exportation. In Pliny's time it was already grown abundantly in the two Gallic provinces and in Spain; indeed, in the earlier days of Strabo the Ligurians supplied the Alpine barbarians with oil, in exchange for the wild produce of their mountains; the plant may have been introduced into those districts by Greek settlers in a previous age. Africa was indebted for the olive mainly to Semitic agencies. In Egypt the culture never seems to have made much progress; the oil found in Theban tombs was probably imported from Syria. Along the southern shore of the great inland sea the tree was carried by the Phoenicians, at a remote period, to their numerous colonies in Africa—though the abundant olives of Cyrene, to which allusion is made by Theophrastus, and the glaucous foliage of whose descendants still clothes the rocks of the deserted Cyrenaica, may have been the offspring of Greek plants brought by the first settlers. The tree was most likely introduced into southern Spain, and perhaps into Sardinia and the Balearic Islands, by Phoenician merchants; and, if it be true that old olive trees were found in the Canaries on their rediscovery by medieval navigators, the venerable trees probably owed their origin to the same enterprising pioneers of the ancient world. De Candolle says that the means by which the olive was distributed to the two opposite shores of the Mediterranean are indicated by the names given to the plant by their respective inhabitants— the Greek ἐλαία passing into the Latin *olea* and *oliva*, that in its turn becoming the *ulivo* of the modern Italian, the *olivo* of the Spaniard, and the *olive*, *olivier*, of the French, while in Africa and southern Spain the olive retains appellatives derived from the Semitic *saii* or *seit*; but the complete subjugation of Barbary by the Saracens sufficiently accounts for the prevalence of Semitic forms in that region; and *aceytuno* (Arab. *seitūn*), the Andalusian name of the fruit, locally given to the tree itself, is but a vestige of the Moorish conquest.

Yielding a grateful substitute for the butter and animal fats consumed by the races of the north, the olive, among the southern nations of antiquity, became an emblem not only of peace but of national wealth and domestic plenty; the branches borne in the Panathenaea, the wild olive spray of the Olympic victor, the olive crown of the Roman conqueror at ovation, and those of the equites at their imperial review alike typified gifts of peace that, in a barbarous age, could be secured by victory alone. Among the Greeks the oil was valued as an important article of diet, as well as for its external use. The Roman people employed it largely in food and cookery—the wealthy as an indispensable adjunct to the toilet; and in the luxurious days of the later empire it became a favourite axiom that long and pleasant life depended on two fluids, "wine within and oil without." Pliny vaguely describes fifteen varieties of olive cultivated in his day, that called the "Licinian" being held in most esteem, and the oil obtained from it at Venafrum in Campania the finest known to Roman connoisseurs; the produce of Istria and Baetica was regarded as second only to that of the Italian peninsula. The *gourmet* of the empire valued the unripe fruit, steeped in brine, as a provocative to the palate, no less than his modern representative;

and ·pickled olives, retaining· their characteristic flavour, have been found among the buried stores of Pompeii. The bitter juice or refuse deposited during expression of the oil (called *amurca*), and the astringent leaves of the tree have many virtues attributed to them by ancient authors. The oil of the bitter wild olive was employed by the Roman physicians in medicine, but does not appear ever to have been used as food or in the culinary art.

In modern times the olive has been spread widely over the world; and, though the Mediterranean lands that were its ancient home still yield the chief supply of the oil, the tree is now cultivated successfully in many regions unknown to its early distributors. Soon after the discovery of the American continent it was conveyed into Chile by the Spanish settlers. In Chile it flourishes as luxuriantly as in its native land, the trunk sometimes becoming of large girth, while oil of fair quality is yielded by the fruit. To Peru it was carried at a later date, but has not there been equally successful. ·Introduced into Mexico by the Jesuit missionaries of the 17th century; it was planted by similar agency in Upper California, where it has prospered latterly under the more careful management of the Anglo-Saxon conqueror. Its cultivation has also been attempted in the south-eastern states, especially in S. Carolina, Florida and Mississippi. In the eastern hemisphere the olive has been established in many inland districts which would have been anciently considered ill-adapted for its culture. To Armenia and Persia it was known at a comparatively early period of history, and many olive-yards now exist in Upper Egypt. The tree has been introduced into Chinese agriculture, and has become an important addition to the resources of the Australian planter. In Queensland the olive has found a climate specially suited to its wants; in South Australia, near Adelaide, it also grows vigorously; and there are probably few coast districts of the vast island-continent where the tree would not flourish. It has·likewise been successfully introduced into some parts of Cape Colony.

OLIVEIRA MARTINS, JOAQUIM PEDRO DE (1845–1894), Portuguese writer, was born in Lisbon and received his early education at the Lycéo Nacional and the Academia das Bellas Artes. At the age of fourteen his father's death compelled him to seek a living as clerk in a commercial house, but he gradually improved his position until in 1870 he was appointed manager of the mine of St Eufemia near Cordova. In Spain he wrote *O. Socialismo*, and developed that sympathy for the industrial classes of which he gave proof throughout his life. Returning to Portugal in 1874, he became administrator of the railway from Oporto to Povoa, residing in Oporto. He had married when only nineteen, and for many years devoted his leisure hours to the study of economics, geography and history. In 1878 his memoir *A Circulação fiduciaria* brought him the gold medal and membership of the Royal Academy of Sciences of Lisbon. Two years later he was elected president of the Society of Commercial Geography of Oporto, and in 1884 he became director of the Industrial and Commercial Museum in that city. In 1885 he entered public life, and in the following year represented Vianna do Castello in parliament, and in 1887 Oporto. Removing to Lisbon in 1888, he continued the journalistic work which he had commenced when living in the north, by editing the *Reporter*, and· in 1889 he was named administrator of the Tobacco Régie. He represented Portugal at international conferences in Berlin and Madrid in 1890, and was chosen to speak at the celebration of the fourth centenary of Columbus held in Madrid in 1891, which gained him membership of the Spanish Royal Academy of History. He became minister of finance on the 17th of January 1892, and later vice-president of the Junta do Credito Publico. His health, however, began to break down as a result of a life spent in unremitting toil, and he died on the 24th of August 1894.

His youthful struggles and privations had taught him a serious view of life, which, with his acute sensibility, gave him a reserved manner, but Oliveira Martins was one of the most generous and noble of men. Like Anthero de Quental, he was impregnated with modern German philosophy, and his perception of the low moral standard prevailing in public life made him a pessimist who despaired of his country's future, but his sense of proportion, and the necessity which impelled him to work, saved him from the fate which befell his friend, and he died a believing Catholic. At once a gifted psychologist, a profound sociologist, a stern moralist, and an ardent patriot, Oliveira Martins deserved his European reputation. His *Bibliotheca das sciencias sociaes*, a veritable encyclopaedia, comprises literary criticism, socialism, economics, anthropology, histories of Iberian civilization, of the Roman Republic, Portugal and Brazil. Towards the end of his life he specialized in the 15th century and produced two notable volumes, *Os filhos de D. João I.* and *A vida de Nun'Alvares*, leaving unfinished *O''principe perfeito*, a study on King John II., which was edited by his friend Henrique de Barros Gomes.

As the literary leader of a national revival, Oliveira Martins occupied an almost unique position in Portugal during the last third of the 19th century. If he judged and condemned the parliamentary régime and destroyed many illusions in his sensational *Contemporary Portugal*, and if in his philosophic *History of Portugal* he showed, in a series of impressionist pictures, the slow decline of his country commencing in the golden age of the discoveries and conquests, he at the same time directed the gaze of his countrymen to the days of their real greatness under the House of Aviz, and incited them to work for a better future by describing the faith and patriotism which had animated the foremost men of the race in the middle ages. He had neither time nor opportunity for original research, but his powerful imagination and picturesque style enabled him to evoke the past and make it present to his readers.

The chief characteristics of the man—psychological imagination combined with realism and a gentle irony—make his strength as a historian and his charm as a writer. When some·critics objected that his *Historia de Portugal* ought rather to be named "Ideas on Portuguese History," he replied that a synthetic and dramatic picture of one of those collective beings called nations gives the mind a clearer, truer and more lasting impression than a summary narrative of successive events. But· just because he possessed the talents and temperament of a poet, Oliveira Martins was fated to make frequent mistakes as well as to discover important truths. ·He must be read with care because he is emotional, and cannot let facts speak for themselves, but interrupts the narrative with expressions of praise or blame. Some of his books resemble a series of visions, while, despite his immense erudition, he does not always supply notes or refer to authorities. He can draw admirable portraits, rich with colour and life; in his *Historia de Portugal* and *Contemporaneo Portugal* those of King Pedro I. and Herculano are among the best known. He describes to perfection such striking events as the Lisbon earthquake, and excels in ·the appreciation of an epoch. In these respects Castelar considered him superior to Macaulay, and declared that few men in Europe possessed the universal aptitude ·and the fullness of knowledge displayed by Oliveira Martins.

The works of Oliveira Martins include *Elementos de anthropologia, As Raças humanas e a civilisação primitiva, Systema das mythos religiosos, Quadro das instituições primitivas, O Regime das riquezas, Politica e economia nacional, Taboas de chronologia e geographia historica, O Hellenismo e a civilisação christã, Historia da Republica Romana, Historia da civilisação iberica, Historia de Portugal, Brazil e as colonias portuguesas, Portugal nos Mares, Portugal em Africa, Portugal contemporaneo, Camões os Lusiadas e a renascença em Portugal*—a brilliant commentary on the physiognomy of the poet and his poem, *Os Filhos de D. João I.*, the preface to which gives his views on the writing of history—*A Vida de Nun' Alvares*; and *A. Inglaterra de Hoje*—the result of a visit to England.

See Moniz Barreto, *Oliveira Martins, estudo de psychologia* (Paris, 1887), a remarkable study; F. Diniz D'Ayalla, *Os Ideaes de Oliveira Martins* (Lisbon, 1897), which contains an admirable statement of his ideas, philosophical and otherwise; Anthero de Quental, *Oliveira Martins* (Lisbon, 1894) and *Diccionario bibliographico portuguez*, xii. 125. (E. Pr.)

OLIVENITE, a mineral consisting of basic copper arsenate with the formula $Cu_2(OH)AsO_4$. It crystallizes in the orthorhombic system, and is sometimes found in small brilliant crystals of simple prismatic habit terminated by domal faces. More usually, however, it occurs as globular aggregates of acicular crystals, these fibrous forms often having a velvety lustre: sometimes it is lamellar in structure, or soft and earthy. A characteristic feature, and one to which the name alludes (German, *Olivenerz*, of A. G. Werner, 1789), is the olive-green colour, which varies in shade from blackish-green in the crystals to almost white in the finely fibrous variety known as "wood-copper." The hardness is 3, and the sp. gr. 4·3. The mineral was formerly found in some abundance, associated with limonite and quartz, in the upper workings in the copper mines of the St Day district in Cornwall; also near Redruth, and in the Tintic district in Utah. It is a mineral of secondary origin, having been formed by the alteration of copper ores and mispickel.

The arsenic of olivenite is sometimes partly replaced by a small amount of phosphorus, and in the species libethenite we have the corresponding basic copper phosphate $Cu_2(OH)PO_4$. This is found as small dark green crystals resembling olivenite at Libethen in Hungary, and in small amount also in Cornwall. Other members of this isomorphous group of minerals are adamite, $Zn_2(OH)AsO_4$, and descloizite (*q.v.*).   (L. J. S.)

OLIVER, ISAAC (*d.* 1566–1617), English miniature painter, was probably born in London, as in 1571 a certain Peter Olivier of Rouen was residing in London with his wife and had been there for three years with one "chylde" named "Isake." It would seem likely, therefore, that he was not at that time more than six years old. It has been suggested by Mr Lionel Cust, from the Huguenot records, that he is identical with one Isaac Oliver of Rouen, married at the Dutch church in Austin Friars in 1602. His death occurred in 1617, and he was buried in the church of St Anne, Blackfriars. He was probably a pupil of Nicholas Hilliard, and connected through his wife, whose name is unknown, with the artists Gheeraerts and De Critz. He was an exceedingly expert miniature painter, and splendid examples of his work can be seen at Montagu House, Windsor Castle, Sherborne Castle and in the collections of Mr J. Pierpont Morgan and the late Baroness Burdett-Coutts. Some of his pen drawings are in the British Museum.   (G. C. W.)

OLIVER, PETER (1594–1648), English miniature painter, was the eldest son of Isaac Oliver, probably by his first wife; and to him Isaac Oliver left his finished and unfinished drawings, with the hope that he would live to exercise the art of his father. The younger sons of the artist appear to have been under age at the time of his death, and were probably therefore sons by a later wife than the mother of Peter Oliver. He resided at Isleworth, and was buried beside his father at St Anne's, Blackfriars. He was even more eminent in miniature painting than his father, and is specially remarkable for a series of copies in water-colour he made after celebrated pictures by old masters. Most of these were done by the desire of the king, and seven of them still remain at Windsor Castle. A great many of Oliver's works were purchased by Charles II. from his widow; several of his drawings are in existence, and a leaf from his pocket-book in the collection of the earl of Derby. His most important work is the group of the three grandsons of the 1st Viscount Montacute with their servant, now belonging to the marquess of Exeter; and there are fine miniatures by him at Welbeck Abbey, Montagu House, Sherborne Castle, Minley Manor, Belvoir Castle and in the private collection of the queen of Holland.   (G. C. W.)

OLIVES, MOUNT OF, or **MOUNT OLIVET** (Ὄρος Ἐλαιῶν or τῶν Ἐλαιῶν; mod. Jebel-et-Tur), the ridge facing the Temple Mount at Jerusalem on the east, and separated from it by the Kidron. A basis of hard cretaceous limestone is topped with softer deposits of the same, quaternary deposits forming the summit. There are four distinct elevations in the ridge: traditionally the southernmost, which is separated by a cleft from the others, is called the "Hill of Offence," and said to be the scene of Solomon's idolatry. The summit to the north of this is often (wrongly) spoken of as Olivet proper. Still worse is the error of

calling the next hill but one to the north "Scopus." The top of the ridge affords a comprehensive view. There are four Old Testament references: 2 Sam. xv. 30 sqq., Neh. viii. 15, Ezek. xi. 23, Zech. xiv. 4. In the New Testament the place is mentioned in connexion with the last days of the life of Jesus. He crossed it on his kingly entry into Jerusalem, and upon it he delivered his great eschatological address (Mark xiii. 3). That the Ascension took place *from the summit* of the Mount of Olives is not necessarily implied in Acts i. 12; the words "over against Bethany" (Luke xxiv. 50) perhaps mean one of the secluded ravines on the eastern slope, beside one of which that village stands. But since Constantine erected the "Basilica of the Ascension" on the spot marked by a certain sacred cave (Euseb. *Vita Const.* iii. 41), the site of this event has been placed here and marked by a succession of churches. The present building is quite modern, and is in the hands of the Moslems. Close to the Chapel of the Ascension is the vault of St Pelagia, and a little way down the hill is the labyrinth of early Christian rock-hewn sepulchral chambers now called the "Tombs of the Prophets." During the middle ages Olivet was also shown as the mount of the Transfiguration. A chapel, bearing the name of the Caliph Omar, and said to occupy the place where he encamped when Jerusalem surrendered to the Moslems, formerly stood beside the Church of the Ascension. There are a considerable number of monasteries and churches of various religious orders and sects on the hill, from whose beauty their uniform and unredeemed ugliness detracts sadly. On Easter day 1907 was laid the foundation of a hospice for pilgrims, under the patronage of the German empress.

OLIVETANS, one of the lesser monastic orders following the Benedictine Rule, founded by St Bernard Tolomei, a Sienese nobleman. At the age of forty, when the leading man in Siena, he retired along with two companions to live a hermit's life at Accona, a desert place fifteen miles to the south of Siena, 1313. Soon others joined them, and in 1324 John XXII. approved of the formation of an order. The Benedictine Rule was taken as the basis of the life; but austerities were introduced beyond what St Benedict prescribed, and the government was framed on the mendicant, not the monastic, model, the superiors being appointed only for a short term of years. The habit is white. Partly from the olive trees that abound there, and partly out of devotion to the Passion, Accona was christened Monte Oliveto, whence the order received its name. By the end of the 14th century there were upwards of a hundred monasteries, chiefly in Italy; and in the 18th there still were eighty, one of the most famous being San Miniato at Florence. The monastery of Monte Oliveto Maggiore is an extensive building of considerable artistic interest, enhanced by frescoes of Signorelli and Sodoma; it is now a national monument occupied by two or three monks as custodians, though it could accommodate three hundred. The Olivetans have a house in Rome and a few others, including one founded in Austria in 1899. There are about 125 monks in all, 54 being priests. In America are some convents of Olivetan nuns.

See Helyot, *Hist. des ordres religieux* (1718), vi. c. 24; Max Heimbucher, *Orden u. Kongregationen* (1907), i. § 30; Wetzer u. Welte, *Kirchenlexicon* (ed. 2); J. A. Symonds, *Sketches and Studies in Italy* (1898), "Monte Oliveto"; B. M. Maréchaux, *Vie de bienheureux Bernard Tolomei* (1888).   (E. C. B.)

OLIVIER, JUSTE DANIEL (1807–1876), Swiss poet, was born near Nyon in the canton of Vaud; he was brought up as a peasant, but studied at the college of Nyon, and later at the academy of Lausanne. Though originally intended for the ministry, his poetic genius (foreshadowed by the prizes he obtained in 1825 and 1828 for poems on *Marcos Botzaris* and *Julia Alpinula* respectively) inclined him towards literary studies. He was named professor of literature at Neuchâtel (1830), but before taking up the duties of his post made a visit to Paris, where he completed his education and became associated with Ste Beuve, especially from 1837 onwards. He professed history at Lausanne from 1833 to 1846, when he lost his chair in consequence of the religious troubles. He then went to Paris, where he remained till 1870, earning his bread by various means, but being nearly forgotten in his native land, to which he remained tenderly attached. From 1845 till 1860 (when the magazine was merged in the *Bibliothèque universelle*) Olivier and his wife wrote in the *Revue suisse* the Paris letter, which had been started by Ste Beuve in 1843, when Olivier became the owner of the periodical. After the war of 1870 he settled down in Switzerland, spending his summers at his beloved Gryon, and died at Geneva on the 7th of January 1876. Besides some novels, a semi-poetical work on the Canton of Vaud (2 vols., 1837–1841), and a volume of historical essays entitled *Études d'histoire nationale* (1842), he published several volumes of poems, *Deux Voix* (1835), *Chansons lointaines* (1847) and its continuation *Chansons du soir* (1867), and *Sentiers de montagne* (Gryon, 1875). His younger brother, Urbain (1810–1888), was well known from 1856 onwards as the author of numerous popular tales of rural life in the Canton of Vaud, especially of the region near Nyon.

Life by Rambert (1877), republished in his *Écrivains de la Suisse romande* (1889), and also prefixed to his edition of Olivier's *Œuvres choisies* (Lausanne, 1879). (W. A. B. C.)

OLIVINE, a rock-forming mineral composed of magnesium and ferrous orthosilicate, the formula being $(Mg, Fe)_2SiO_4$. The name olivine, proposed by A. G. Werner in 1790, alludes to the olive-green colour commonly shown by the mineral. The transparent varieties, or "precious olivine" used in jewelry, are known as chrysolite (*q.v.*) and peridot (*q.v.*). The term olivine is often applied incorrectly by jewellers to various green stones.

Olivine crystallizes in the orthorhombic system, but distinctly developed crystals are comparatively rare, the mineral more often occurring as compact or granular masses or as grains and blebs embedded in the igneous rocks of which it forms a constituent part. There are indistinct cleavages parallel to the macropinacoid (M in the fig.) and the brachypinacoid. The

hardness is $6\frac{1}{2}$; and the sp. gr. 3.27–3.37, but reaching 3.57 in the highly ferruginous variety known as hyalosiderite. The amount of ferrous oxide varies from 5 (about 9 % in the gem varieties) to 30 % in hyalosiderite. The depth of the green, or yellowish-brown colour, also varies with the amount of iron. The lustre is vitreous. The indices of refraction (1.66 and 1.70) and the double refraction are higher than in many other rock-forming minerals; and these characters, together with the indistinct cleavage, enable the mineral to be readily distinguished in thin rock-sections under the microscope. The mineral is decomposed by hot hydrochloric acid with separation of gelatinous silica. Olivine often contains small amounts of nickel and titanium dioxide; the latter replaces silica, and in the variety known as titanolivine reaches 5 %.

Olivine is a common constituent of many basic and ultrabasic rocks, such as basalt, diabase, gabbro and peridotite: the dunite, of Dun Mountain near Nelson in New Zealand, is an almost pure olivine-rock. In basalts it is often present as small porphyritic crystals or as large granular aggregates. It also occurs as an accessory constituent of some granular dolomitic limestones and crystalline schists. With enstatite it forms the bulk of the material of meteoric stones; and in another type of meteorites large blebs of glassy olivine fill spaces in a cellular mass of metallic iron.

Olivine is especially liable to alteration into serpentine (hydrated magnesium silicate); the alteration proceeds from the outside of the crystals and grains or along irregular cracks in their interior, and gives rise to the separation of iron oxides and an irregular net-work of fibrous serpentine, which in rock-sections presents a very characteristic appearance. Large greenish-yellow crystals from Snarum in Buskerud, Norway, at one time thought to be crystals of serpentine, really consist of serpentine pseudomorphous after olivine. Many of the large rock-masses of

serpentine have been derived by the serpentinization of olivine-rocks. Olivine also sometimes alters, especially in crystalline schists, to a fibrous, colourless amphibole, to which the name pilite has been given. By ordinary weathering processes it alters to limonite and silica.

Closely related to olivine are several other species, which are included together in the olivine group : they have the orthosilicate formula R'_2SiO_4, where R' represents calcium, magnesium, iron, manganese and rarely zinc; they all crystallize in the orthorhombic system, and are isomorphous with olivine. The following may be mentioned:—

Monticellite, $CaMgSiO_4$, a rare mineral occurring as yellowish-grey crystals and grains in granular limestone at Monte Somma, Vesuvius.

Forsterite, Mg_2SiO_4, as colourless or yellowish grains embedded in many crystalline limestones.

Fayalite, Fe_2SiO_4, or iron olivine is dark brown or black in colour. It occurs as nodules in a volcanic rock at Fayal in the Azores, and in granite at the Mourne Mountains in Ireland; and as small crystals in cavities in rhyolite at the Yellowstone Park, U.S.A. It is a common constituent of crystalline iron slags.

Tephroite, Mn_2SiO_4, a grey (*τεφρός*, ash-coloured), cleavable mineral occurring with other manganiferous minerals in Sweden and New Jersey. (L. J. S.)

OLLIVIER, OLIVIER ÉMILE (1825–   ), French statesman; was born at Marseilles on the 2nd of July 1825. His father, Demosthènes Ollivier (1799–1884), was a vehement opponent of the July monarchy, and was returned by Marseilles to the Constituent Assembly in 1848. His opposition to Louis Napoleon led to his banishment after the *coup d'état* of December 1851, and he only returned to France in 1860. On the establishment of the short-lived Second Republic his father's influence with Ledru-Rollin secured for Émile Ollivier the position of commissary-general of the department of Bouches-du-Rhône. Ollivier was then twenty-three and had just been called to the Parisian bar. Less radical in his political opinions than his father, his repression of a socialist outbreak at Marseilles commended him to General Cavaignac, who continued him in his functions by making him prefect of the department. He was shortly afterwards removed to the comparatively unimportant prefecture of Chaumont (Haute-Marne), a semi-disgrace which he ascribed to his father's enemies. He therefore resigned from the civil service to take up practice at the bar, where his brilliant abilities assured his success.

He re-entered political life in 1857 as deputy for the 3rd circumscription of the Seine. His candidature had been supported by the *Siècle*, and he joined the constitutional opposition. With Alfred Darimon, Jules Favre, J. L. Hénon and Ernest Picard he formed the group known as *Les Cinq*, which wrung from Napoleon III. some concessions in the direction of constitutional government. The imperial decree of the 24th of November, permitting the insertion of parliamentary reports in the *Moniteur*, and an address from the Corps Législatif in reply to the speech from the throne, were welcomed by him as a first instalment of reform. This acquiescence marked a considerable change of attitude, for only a year previously a violent attack on the imperial government, in the course of a defence of Étienne Vacherot, brought to trial for the publication of *La Démocratie*, had resulted in his suspension from the bar for three months. He gradually separated from his old associates, who grouped themselves around Jules Favre, and during the session of 1866–1867 Ollivier formed a third party, which definitely supported the principle of a Liberal Empire. On the last day of December 1866, Count A. F. J. Walewski, acting in continuance of negotiations already begun by the duc de Morny, offered Ollivier the ministry of education with the function of representing the general policy of the government in the Chamber. The imperial decree of the 19th of January 1867, together with the promise inserted in the *Moniteur* of a relaxation of the stringency of the press laws and of concessions in respect of the right of public meeting, failed to satisfy Ollivier's demands, and he refused office. On the eve of the general election of 1869 he published a manifesto, *Le 19 janvier*, in justification of his policy. The *sénatus-consulte* of the 8th of September 1869 gave the two chambers the ordinary parliamentary rights, and was followed by the dismissal of Rouher and the formation in the last week of 1869 of a responsible ministry of which M. Ollivier was really premier, although that office was not nominally recognized by the constitution. The new cabinet, known as the ministry of the 2nd of January, had a hard task before it, complicated a week after its formation by the shooting of Victor Noir by Prince Pierre Bonaparte. Ollivier immediately summoned the high court of justice for the judgment of Prince Bonaparte and Prince Joachim Murat. The riots following on the murder were suppressed without bloodshed; circulars were sent round to the prefects forbidding them in future to put pressure on the electors in favour of official candidates; Baron Haussmann was dismissed from the prefecture of the Seine; the violence of the press campaign against the emperor, to whom he had promised a happy old age, was broken by the prosecution of Henri Rochefort; and on the 20th of April a *sénatus-consulte* was issued which accomplished the transformation of the Empire into a constitutional monarchy. Neither concessions nor firmness sufficed to appease the "Irreconcilables" of the opposition, who since the relaxation of the press laws were able to influence the electorate. On the 8th of May, however, the amended constitution was submitted, on Rouher's advice, to a plebiscite, which resulted in a vote of nearly seven to one in favour of the government. The most distinguished members of the Left in his cabinet—L. J. Buffet, Napoléon Daru and Talhouët Roy—resigned in April on the question of the plebiscite. Ollivier himself held the ministry of foreign affairs for a few weeks, until Daru was replaced by the duc de Gramont, destined to be Ollivier's evil genius. The other vacancies were filled by J. P. Mège and C. L. Plichon, both of them of Conservative tendencies.

The revival of the candidature of Prince Leopold of Hohenzollern-Sigmaringen for the throne of Spain early in 1870 disconcerted Ollivier's plans. The French government, following Gramont's advice, instructed Benedetti to demand from the king of Prussia a formal disavowal of the Hohenzollern candidature. Ollivier allowed himself to be gained by the war party. The story of Benedetti's reception at Ems and of Bismarck's manipulation of the Ems telegram is told elsewhere (see BISMARCK). It is unlikely that Ollivier could have prevented the eventual outbreak of war, but he might perhaps have postponed it at that time, if he had taken time to hear Benedetti's account of the incident. He was outmanœuvred by Bismarck, and on the 15th of July he made a hasty declaration in the Chamber that the Prussian government had issued to the powers a note announcing the rebuff received by Benedetti. He obtained a war vote of 500,000,000 francs, and used the fatal words that he accepted the responsibility of the war " with a light heart," saying that the war had been forced on France. On the 9th of August, with the news of the first disaster, the Ollivier cabinet was driven from office, and its chief sought refuge from the general rage in Italy. He returned to France in 1873, but although he carried on an active campaign in the Bonapartist *Estafette* his political power was gone, and even in his own party he came into collision in 1880 with M. Paul de Cassagnac. During his retirement he employed himself in writing a history of *L'Empire libéral*, the first volume of which appeared in 1895. The work really dealt with the remote and immediate causes of the war, and was the author's apology for his blunder. The 13th volume showed that the immediate blame could not justly be placed entirely on his shoulders. His other works include *Démocratie et liberté* (1867), *Le Ministère du 2 janvier, mes discours* (1875), *Principes et conduite* (1875), *L'Église et l'État au concile du Vatican* (2 vols. 1879), *Solutions politiques et sociales* (1893), *Nouveau Manuel du droit ecclésiastique français* (1885). He had many connexions with the literary and artistic world, being one of the early Parisian champions of Wagner. Elected to the Academy in 1870, he did not take his seat, his reception being indefinitely postponed. His first wife, Blandine Liszt, was the daughter of the Abbé Liszt by Mme d'Agoult (Daniel Stern). She died in 1862, and Ollivier married in 1869 Mlle Gravier.

Ollivier's own view of his political life is given in his *L'Empire libéral*, which must always be an important "document" for the history of his time; but the book must be treated with no less caution than respect.

OLMSTED, DENISON (1791–1859), American man of science, was born at East Hartford, Connecticut, U.S.A., on the 18th of June 1791, and in 1813 graduated at Yale, where he acted as college tutor from 1815 to 1817. In the latter year he was appointed to the chair of chemistry, mineralogy and geology in the university of North Carolina. This chair he exchanged for that of mathematics and physics at Yale in 1825; in 1836, when this professorship was divided, he retained that of astronomy and natural philosophy. He died at New Haven, Connecticut, on the 13th of May 1859.

His first publication (1824–1825) was the *Report* of his geological survey of the state of North Carolina. It was followed by various text-books on natural philosophy and astronomy, but he is chiefly known to the scientific world for his observations on hail (1830), on meteors and on the aurora borealis (see *Smithsonian Contributions*, vol. viii.).

OLMSTED, FREDERICK LAW (1822–1903), American landscape architect, was born in Hartford, Connecticut, on the 27th of April 1822. From his earliest years he was a wanderer. While still a lad he shipped before the mast as a sailor; then he took a course in the Yale Scientific School; worked for several farmers; and, finally, began farming for himself on Staten Island, where he met Calvert Vaux, with whom later he formed a business partnership. All this time he wrote for the agricultural papers. In 1850 he made a walking tour through England, his observations being published in *Walks and Talks of an American Farmer in England* (1852). A horseback trip through the Southern States was recorded in *A Journey in the Seaboard Slave States* (1856), *A Journey through Texas* (1857) and *A Journey in the Back Country* (1860). These three volumes, reprinted in England in two as *Journeys and Explorations in the Cotton Kingdom* (1861), gave a picture of the conditions surrounding American slavery that had great influence on British opinion, and they were much quoted in the controversies at the time of the Civil War. During the war he was the untiring secretary of the U.S. Sanitary Commission. He happened to be in New York City when Central Park was projected, and, in conjunction with Vaux, proposed the plan which, in competition with more than thirty others, won first prize. Olmsted was made superintendent to carry out the plan. This was practically the first attempt in the United States to apply art to the improvement or embellishment of nature in a public park; it attracted great attention, and the work was so satisfactorily done that he was engaged thereafter in most of the important works of a similar nature in America—Prospect Park, Brooklyn; Fairmount Park, Philadelphia; South Park, Chicago; Riverside and Morningside Parks, New York; Mount Royal Park, Montreal; the grounds surrounding the Capitol at Washington, and at Leland Stanford University at Palo Alto (California); and many others. He took the bare stretch of lake front at Chicago and developed it into the beautiful World's Fair grounds, placing all the buildings and contributing much to the architectural beauty and the success of the exposition. He was greatly interested in the Niagara reservation, made the plans for the park there, and also did much to influence the state of New York to provide the Niagara Park. He was the first commissioner of the National Park of the Yosemite and the Mariposa Grove, directing the survey and taking charge of the property for the state of California. He had also held directing appointments under the cities of New York, Boston, Philadelphia, Baltimore, Wilmington and San Francisco, the Joint Committee on Buildings and Grounds of Congress, the Niagara Falls Reservation Commission, the trustees of Harvard, Yale, Amherst and other colleges and public institutions. Subsequently to 1886 he was largely occupied in laying out an extensive system of parks and parkways for the city of Boston and the town of Brookline, and on a scheme of landscape improvement of Boston harbour. Olmsted received honorary degrees from Harvard, Amherst and Yale in 1864, 1867 and 1893. He died on the 28th of August 1903.

OLMÜTZ (Czech, *Olomouc* or *Holomouc*), a town of Austria, in Moravia, 67 m. N.E. of Brünn by rail. Pop. (1900) 21,033, of which two-thirds are Germans. It is situated on the March, and is the ecclesiastical metropolis of Moravia. Until 1886 Olmütz was one of the strongest fortresses of Austria, but the fortifications have been removed, and their place is occupied by a town park, gardens and promenades. Like most Slavonic towns, it contains several large squares, the chief of which is adorned with a trinity column, 115 ft. high, erected in 1740. The most prominent church is the cathedral, a Gothic building of the 14th century, restored in 1883-1886, with a tower 328 ft. high and the biggest church-bell in Moravia. It contains the tomb of King Wenceslaus III., who was murdered here in 1306. The Mauritius church, a fine Gothic building of the 15th century, and the St Michael church are also worth mentioning. The principal secular building is the town-hall, completed in the 15th century, flanked on one side by a Gothic chapel, transformed now into a museum. It possesses a tower 250 ft. high, adorned with an astronomical clock, an artistic and famous work, executed by Anton Pohl in 1422. The old university, founded in 1570 and suppressed in 1858, is now represented by a theological seminary, which contains a very valuable library and an important collection of manuscripts and early prints. Olmütz is an important railway junction, and is the emporium of a busy mining and industrial district. Its industries include brewing and distilling and the manufacture of malt, sugar and starch.

Olmütz is said to occupy the site of a Roman fort founded in the imperial period, the original name of which, *Mons Julii*, has been gradually corrupted to the present form. At a later period Olmütz was long the capital of the Slavonic kingdom of Moravia, but it ceded that position to Brünn in 1640. The Mongols were defeated here in 1241 by Yaroslav von Sternberg. During the Thirty Years' War it was occupied by the Swedes for eight years. The town was originally fortified by Maria Theresa during the wars with Frederick the Great, who besieged the town unsuccessfully for seven weeks in 1758. In 1848 Olmütz was the scene of the emperor Ferdinand's abdication, and in 1850 an important conference took place here between Austrian and German statesmen. The bishopric of Olmütz was founded in 1073, and raised to the rank of an archbishopric in 1777. The bishops were created princes of the empire in 1588. The archbishop is the only one in the Austrian empire who is elected by the cathedral chapter.

See W. Müller, *Geschichte der königlichen Hauptstadt Olmütz* (2nd ed., Olmütz, 1895).

OLNEY, RICHARD (1835-   ); American statesman, was born at Oxford, Massachusetts, on the 15th of September 1835. He graduated from Brown University in 1856, and from the Law School of Harvard University in 1858. In 1859 he began the practice of law at Boston, Massachusetts, and attained a high position at the bar. He served in the state house of representatives in 1874, and in March 1893 became attorney-general of the United States in the cabinet of President Cleveland. In this position, during the strike of the railway employés of Chicago in 1894, he instructed the district attorneys to secure from the Federal Courts writs of injunction restraining the strikers from acts of violence, and thus set a precedent for "government by injunction." He also advised the use of Federal troops to quell the disturbances in the city, on the ground that the government must prevent interference with its mails and with the general railway transportation between the states. Upon the death of Secretary W. Q. Gresham (1832-1895), Olney succeeded him as secretary of state on the 10th of June 1895. He became specially prominent in the controversy with Great Britain concerning the boundary dispute between the British and Venezuelan governments (see VENEZUELA), and in his correspondence with Lord Salisbury gave an extended interpretation to the Monroe Doctrine which went considerably beyond previous statements on the subject. In 1897, at the expiration of President Cleveland's term, he returned to the practice of the law.

OLNEY, a market town in the Buckingham parliamentary division of Buckinghamshire, England, 50 m. N.W. by N. of London, on a branch of the Midland railway. Pop. of urban district (1901) 2634. It lies in the open valley of the Ouse on the north (left) bank of the river. The church of St Peter and St Paul is Decorated. It has a fine tower and spire; and the chancel has a northerly inclination from the alignment of the nave. The town is chiefly noted for its connexion with William Cowper, who came to live here in 1767 and remained until 1786, when he removed to the neighbouring village of Weston Underwood. His house and garden at Olney retain relics of the poet, and the house at Weston also remains. In the garden at Olney are his favourite seat and the house in which he kept his tame hares. John Newton, curate of Olney, had the assistance of Cowper in the production of the collection of Olney Hymns. The trade of Olney is principally agricultural; the town also shares in the manufacture of boots and shoes common to many places in the neighbouring county of Northampton.

OLNEY, a city and the county-seat of Richland county, Illinois, U.S.A., about 30 m. W. of Vincennes, Indiana. Pop. (1890) 3831; (1900) 4260 (235 foreign-born); (1910) 5011. Olney is served by the Baltimore & Ohio South-western, the Illinois Central, and the Cincinnati, Hamilton & Dayton railways, and is a terminus of the Ohio River Division of the last. It has a Carnegie library and a city park of 55 acres. Olney is an important shipping point for the agricultural products of this district; oil is found in the vicinity; and the city has various manufactures. The municipality owns its water-works. Olney was settled about 1842 and was first chartered as a city in 1867.

OLONETS, a government of north-western Russia, extending from Lake Ladoga almost to the White Sea, bounded W. by Finland, N. and E. by Archangel and Vologda, and S. by Novgorod and St Petersburg. The area is 57,422 sq. m., of which 6794 sq. m. are lakes. Its north-western portion belongs orographically and geologically to the Finland region; it is thickly dotted with hills reaching 1000 ft. in altitude, and diversified by numberless smaller ridges and hollows running from north-west to south-east. The rest of the government is a flat plateau sloping towards the marshy lowlands of the south. The geological structure is very varied. Granites, syenites and diorites, covered with Laurentian metamorphic slates, occur extensively in the north-west. Near Lake Onega they are overlain with Devonian sandstones and limestones, yielding marble and sandstone for building; to the south of that lake Carboniferous limestones and clays make their appearance. The whole is sheeted with boulder-clay, the bottom moraine of the great ice-sheet of the Glacial period. The entire region bears traces of glaciation, either in the shape of scratchings and elongated grooves on the rocks, or of eskers (*äsar, selga*s) running parallel to the glacial striations. Numberless lakes occupy the depressions, while a great many more have left evidences of their existence in the extensive marshes. Lake Onega covers 3764 sq. m., and reaches a depth of 400 ft; Lakes Zeg, Vyg, Lacha, Loksha, Tulos and Vodl cover from 140 to 480 sq. m. each, and their crustacean fauna indicates a former connexion with the Arctic Ocean. The south-eastern part of Lake Ladoga falls also within the government of Olonets. The rivers drain to the Baltic and White Sea basins. To the former system belong Lakes Ladoga and Onega, which are connected by the Svir and receive numerous streams; of these the Vytegra, which communicates with the Mariinsk canal-system, and the Oyat; an affluent of Lake Ladoga, are important for navigation. Large quantities of timber, fire-wood, stone, metal and flour are annually shipped on waters belonging to this government. The Onega river, which has its source in the south-east of the government and flows into the White Sea, is of minor importance. Sixty-three per cent of the area of Olonets is occupied by forests; those of the crown, maintained for shipbuilding purposes, extend to more than 800,000 acres. The climate is harsh and moist, the average yearly temperature at Petrosavodsk (61° 8' N.) being 33·6° F. (17·0° in January, 57·4° in July); but the thermometer rarely falls below −30° F.

The population, which numbered 321,250 in 1881, reached 367,902 in 1897, and 401,100 (estimate) in 1906. They are principally Great Russians and Finns. The people belong mostly to the Orthodox Greek Church, or are Nonconformists. Rye and oats are the principal crops, and some flax, barley and turnips are grown, but the total cultivated area does not exceed 2¼% of the whole government. The chief source of wealth is timber, next to which come fishing and hunting. Mushrooms and berries are exported to St Petersburg. There are quarries and iron-mines, saw-mills, tanneries, iron-works, distilleries and flour-mills. More than one-fifth of the entire male population leave their homes every year in search of temporary employment. Olonets is divided into seven districts, of which the chief towns are Petrozavodsk, Kargopol, Lodeinoye Pole, Olonets, Povyenets, Pudozh and Vytegra. It includes the Olonets mining district, a territory belonging to the crown, which covers 432 sq. m. and extends into the Serdobol district of Finland; the ironworks were begun by Peter the Great in 1701–1714. Olonets was colonized by Novgorod in the 11th century, and though it suffered much from Swedish invasion its towns soon became wealthy trading centres. Ivan·III. annexed it to the principality of Moscow in the second half of the 16th century.

OLOPAN, OLOPUEN or OLOPEN (probably a Chinese form of the Syriac *Rabban, i.e.* monk: fl. A.D. 635), the first Christian missionary·in China (setting aside vague stories of St Thomas, St Bartholomew, &c.), and founder of the Nestorian Church in the Far¹East. According to the Si-ngan-fu inscription, our sole authority, Olopan came to China from Ta T'sin (the Roman empire) in the ninth year of the emperor T'ai-Tsung (A.D. 635), bringing sacred books and images. He was received with favour; his teaching was examined and approved; his Scriptures were translated for the imperial library; and in 638 an imperial edict declared Christianity a tolerated religion. T'ai-Tsung's successor, Kao-Tsung (650–683), was still more friendly, and Olopan now became a "guardian of the empire" and "lord of the great law." After this followed (c. 683–744) a time of disfavour and oppression for Chinese Christians, followed by a revival dating from the arrival of a fresh missionary, Kiho, from the Roman empire.

The Si-ngan-fu inscription, which alone records these facts, was erected in 781, and rediscovered in 1625 by workmen digging in the Chang-ngan suburb of Si-ngan-fu city. It consists of 1789 Chinese characters, giving a history of the Christian mission down to 781, together with a sketch of Nestorian doctrine, the decree of T'ai-Tsung in favour of Christianity, the date of erection, and names of various persons connected with the church in China when the monument was put up. Additional notes in Syriac (Estrangelo characters) repeat the date and record the names of the reigning Nestorian patriarch, the Nestorian bishop in China, and a number of the Nestorian clergy.

See Kircher, *China Illustrata*; G. Pauthier, *De l'authenticité de l'inscription nestorienne de Si-ngan-fou* (Paris, 1857) and *L'inscription syro-chinoise de Si-ngan-fou* (Paris, 1858); Henry Yule, *Cathay, Preliminary Essay,* xcii.–xciv. clxxxi.–clxxxiii. (London, Hakluyt Soc., 1866); F. Hirth, *China and the Roman Orient,* 323, &c.; Father Henri Havret, *La stèle chrétienne de Si-ngan-fou,* two parts (text and history) published out of three (Shanghai, 1895 and 1897); Dr James Legge's edition and translation of the text, *The Nestorian Monument of Hsi-an-Fu* (London, 1888); Yule and Cordier, *Marco Polo,* ii. 27–29 (London, 1903); C. R. Beazley, *Dawn of Modern Geography,* i. 215–218.

OLORON-SAINTE-MARIE, a town of south-western France, capital of an arrondissement in the department of Basses-Pyrénées, 21 m. S.W. of Pau on a branch of the Southern railway. It lies at the confluence of the mountain torrents (locally known as *gaves*) Aspe and Ossau, which, after dividing it into three parts, unite·to form the Oloron, a tributary of the Pau. The united population of the old feudal town of Sainte-Croix and Oloron proper, which is situated on an eminence between the two rivers, of Sainte-Marie on the left bank of the Aspe, and of the new quarters on the right bank of the Ossau, is 7715. Oloron has remains of old ramparts and pleasant promenades with beautiful views, and there are several old houses of the 15th,

16th and 17th centuries, one of which is occupied by the hôtel de ville. The church of Sainte-Croix, the building of most interest, belongs mainly to the 11th century; the chief feature of the exterior is the central Byzantine cupola; in the interior there is a large altar of gilded wood, constructed in the Spanish style of the 17th century. The church of Sainte-Marie, which formerly served as the cathedral of Oloroa, is in the old ecclesiastical quarter of Sainte-Marie. It is a medley of various styles from the 11th to the 14th century. A square tower at the west end shelters a fine Romanesque portal. In the new quarter there is the modern church of Notre-Dame. Remains of a castle of the 14th century are also still to be seen. Oloron is the seat of a sub-prefect, and its public institutions include tribunals of first instance and of commerce, and a chamber of arts and manufactures. It is the most important commercial centre of its department after Bayonne, and carries on a thriving trade with Spain by way of the passes of Somport and Anso.

A Celtiberian and then a Gallo-Roman town, known as *Iluro,* occupied the hill on which Sainte-Croix now stands. Devastated by the Vascones in the 6th and by the Saracens in the 8th century, it was abandoned, and it was not until the 11th century that the quarter of Sainte-Marie was re-established by the bishops. In 1080 the viscount of Béarn took possession of the old town. The two quarters remained distinct till the union of Béarn with the crown at the accession of Henry IV. At the Reformation the place became a centre of Catholic reaction. In the 17th century it carried on a considerable trade with Aragon, until the Spaniards, jealous of its prosperity, pillaged the establishments of the Oloron merchants at Saragossa in 1694—a disaster from which it only slowly recovered. The bishopric was suppressed in 1790.

OLSHAUSEN, HERMANN (1796–1839), German theologian, was born at Oldeslohe in Holstein on the 21st of August 1796, and was educated at the universities of Kiel (1814) and Berlin (1816), where he was influenced by Schleiermacher and Neander. In 1820 he became *Privatdocent* and in 1821 professor extraordinarius at Berlin; in 1827 professor at Königsberg, in 1834 at Erlangen. He died on the 4th of September 1839. Olshausen's department was New Testament exegesis; his Commentary (completed and revised by Ebrard and Wiesinger) began to appear at Königsberg in 1830, and was translated into English in 4 vols. (Edinburgh, 1847–1849). He had prepared for it by his other works, *Die Achtheit d. vier Kanon. Evangelien* (1823), *Ein Wort über tieferen Schriftsinn* (1824) and *Die biblische Schriftauslegung* (1825).

OLTENITZA (*Oltenita*), a town of Rumania, on the left bank of the river Argesh, 33 m. from its outflow into the Danube, and at a terminus of a branch railway from Bucharest. Pop. (1900) 5801. The principal trade is in grain, timber (floated down the Argesh) and fish. Lake Greca, famous for its carp, lies 10 m. E. and has an area of about 45 sq. m. Its waters reach the Danube through a network of streams, marshes and meres. Oltenitza is the ancient Constantiola, which was the seat of the first bishopric established in Dacia. In the Crimean War the Turks forced the river at this point and inflicted heavy losses on the Russians.

OLUSTEE, a village of Baker county, Florida, U.S.A., in the precinct of Olustee, about 46 m. W. by S. of Jacksonville. Pop. of the precinct (1910) 466. The village is served by the Seaboard Air Line. The battle of Olustee, or Ocean Pond (the name of a small body of water in the vicinity), one of the most sanguinary engagements of the Civil War in proportion to the numbers engaged, was fought on the 20th of February 1864, about 2 m. east of Olustee, between about 5500 Federal troops, under General·Truman Seymour (1824–1891), and about·5400 Confederates, under General Joseph Finegan, the Federal forces being decisively defeated, with a loss, in killed and wounded, of about one-third of their number, including several officers. The Confederate losses, in killed and wounded, were about 940.

OLYBRIUS, Roman emperor of the West from the 11th of July to the 23rd of October 472, was a member of a noble family and a native of Rome. After the sack of the city by Genseric

(Geiseric) in 455, he fled to Constantinople, where in 464 he was made consul, and about the same time married Placidia, daughter of Valentinian III. and Eudoxia. This afforded Genseric, whose son Hunneric had married Eudocia, the elder sister of Placidia, the opportunity of claiming the empire of the West for Olybrius. In 472 Olybrius was sent to Italy by the emperor Leo to assist the emperor Anthemius against his son-in-law Ricimer, but, having entered into negotiations with the latter, was himself proclaimed emperor against his will, and on the murder of his rival ascended the throne unopposed. His reign was as uneventful as it was brief.

See Gibbon, *Decline and Fall*, ch. xxxvi.; J. B. Bury, *Later Roman Empire.*

OLYMPIA, the scene of the famous Olympic games, is on the right or north bank of the Alpheus (mod. Ruphia), about 11 m. E. of the modern Pyrgos. The course of the river is here from E. to W., and the average breadth of the valley is about ⅔ m. At this point a small stream, the ancient Cladeus, flows from the north into the Alpheus. The area known as Olympia is bounded on the west by the Cladeus, on the south by the Alpheus, on the north by the low heights which shut in the Alpheus valley, and on the east by the ancient racecourses. One group of the northern heights terminates in a conical hill, about 400 ft. high, which is cut off from the rest by a deep cleft, and descends abruptly on Olympia. This hill is the famous *Cronion*, sacred to Cronus, the father of Zeus.

The natural situation of Olympia is, in one sense, of great beauty. When Lysias, in his *Olympiacus* (spoken here), calls it " the fairest spot of Greece," he was doubtless thinking also— or perhaps chiefly—of the masterpieces which art, in all its forms, had contributed to the embellishment of this national sanctuary. But even now the praise seems hardly excessive to a visitor who, looking eastward up the fertile and well-wooded valley of Olympia, sees the snow-crowned chains of Erymanthus and Cyllene rising in the distance. The valley, at once spacious and definite, is a natural precinct, and it is probable that no artificial boundaries of the Altis, or sacred grove, existed until comparatively late times.

History.—The importance of Olympia in the history of Greece is religious and political. The religious associations of the place date from the prehistoric age, when, before the states of Elis and Pisa had been founded, there was a centre of worship in this valley which is attested by early votive offerings found beneath the Heraeum and an altar near it. The earliest extant building on the site is the temple of Hera, which probably dates in its original form from about 1000 B.C. There were various traditions as to the origin of the games. According to one of them, the first race was that between Pelops and Oenomaus, who used to challenge the suitors of his daughter Hippodameia and then slay them. According to another, the festival was founded by Heracles, either the well-known hero or the Idaean Dactyl of that name. The control of the festival belonged in early times to Pisa, but Elis seems to have claimed association with it. Sixteen women, representing eight towns of Elis and eight of Pisatis, wove the festal robe for the Olympian Hera. Olympia thus became the centre of an amphictyony (q.v.), or federal league under religious sanction, for the west coast of the Peloponnesus, as Delphi was for its neighbours in northern Greece. It suited the interests of Sparta to join this amphictyony; and, before the regular catalogue of Olympic victors begins in 776 B.C., Sparta had formed an alliance with Elis. Aristotle saw in the temple of Hera at Olympia a bronze disk, recording the installation laws of the festival, on which the name of Lycurgus stood next to that of Iphitus, king of Elis. Whatever may have been the age of the disk itself, the relation which it indicates is well attested. Elis and Sparta, making common cause, had no difficulty in excluding the Pisatans from their proper share in the management of the Olympian sanctuary. Pisa had, indeed, a brief moment of better fortune, when Pheidon of Argos celebrated the 28th Olympiad under the presidency of the Pisatans. This festival, from which the Eleans and Spartans were excluded, was afterwards struck out of the official register,

as having no proper existence. The destruction of Pisa (before 572 B.C.) by the combined forces of Sparta and Elis put an end to the long rivalry. Not only Pisatis, but also the district of Triphylia to the south of it, became dependent on Elis. So far as the religious side of the festival was concerned, the Eleans had an unquestioned supremacy. It was at Elis, in the gymnasium, that candidates from all parts of Greece were tested, before they were admitted to the athletic competitions at Olympia. To have passed through the training (usually of ten months) at Elis was regarded as the most valuable preparation. Elean officials, who not only adjudged the prizes at Olympia, but decided who should be admitted to compete, marked the national aspect of their functions by assuming the title of *Hellanodicae.*

Long before the overthrow of Pisa the list of contests had been so enlarged as to invest the celebration with a Panhellenic character. Exercises of a Spartan type—testing endurance and strength with an especial view to war—had almost exclusively formed the earlier programme. But as early as the 25th Olympiad—*i.e.* several years before the interference of Pheidon on behalf of Pisa—the four-horse chariot-race was added. This was an invitation to wealthy competitors from every part of the Hellenic world, and was also the recognition of a popular or spectacular element, as distinct from the skill which had a merely athletic or military interest. Horse-races were added later. For such contests the *hippodrome* was set apart. Meanwhile the list of contests on the old racecourse, the *stadium,* had been enlarged. Besides the foot-race in which the course was traversed once only, there were now the *diaulos* or double course, and the "long" foot-race (*dolichos*): Wrestling and boxing were combined in the *pancration.* Leaping, quoit-throwing, javelin-throwing, running and wrestling were combined in the *pentathlon.* The festival was to acquire a new importance under the protection of the Spartans, who, having failed in their plans of actual conquest in the Peloponnese, sought to gain at least the hegemony (acknowledged predominance) of the peninsula. As the Eleans, therefore, were the religious supervisors of Olympia, so the Spartans aimed at constituting themselves its political protectors. Their military strength— greatly superior at the time to that of any other state—enabled them to do this. Spartan arms could enforce the sanction which the Olympian Zeus gave to the oaths of the amphictyones, whose federal bond was symbolized by common worship at his shrine. Spartan arms could punish any violation of that " sacred truce " which was indispensable if Hellenes from all cities were to have peaceable access to the Olympian festival. And in the eyes of all Dorians the assured dignity thus added to Olympia would be enhanced by the fact that the protectors were the Spartan Heraclidae.

Olympia entered on a new phase of brilliant and secure existence as a recognized Panhellenic institution. This phase may be considered as beginning after the establishment of Elean supremacy in 572 B.C. And so to the last Olympia always remained a central expression of the Greek ideas that the body of man has a glory as well as his intellect and spirit, that body and mind should alike be disciplined, and that it is by the harmonious discipline of both that men best honour Zeus. The significance of Olympia was larger and higher than the political fortunes of the Greeks who met there, and it survived the overthrow of Greek independence. In the Macedonian and Roman ages the temples and contests of Olympia still interpreted the ideal at which free Greece had aimed. Philip of Macedon and Nero are, as we shall see, among those whose names have a record in the Altis. Such names are typical of long series of visitors who paid homage to Olympia. According to Cedrenus, a Greek writer of the 11th century (Σύνοψις Ἱστορικῶν, i. 326), the Olympian festival ceased to be held after A.D. 393, the first year of the 293rd Olympiad. The list of Olympian victors, which begins in 776 B.C. with Coroebus of Elis, closes with the name of an Armenian, Varastad, who is said to have belonged to the race of the Arsacidae. In the 5th century the desolation of Olympia had set in. The chryselephantine statue of the Olympian Zeus, by Pheidias, was carried to Constantinople, and perished in a great fire, A.D. 476,

The Olympian temple of Zeus is said to have been dismantled, either by the Goths or by Christian zeal, in the reign of Theodosius II. (A.D. 402–450). After this the inhabitants converted the temple of Zeus and the region to the south of it into a fortress, by constructing a wall from materials found among the ancient buildings. The temple was probably thrown down by earthquakes in the 6th century A.D.

Excavations.—The German excavations were begun in 1875. After six campaigns, of which the first five lasted from September to June, they were completed on the 20th of March 1881. The result of these six years' labours was, first, to strip off a thick covering of earth from the *Altis*, the consecrated precinct of the Olympian Zeus. This covering had been formed, during some twelve centuries, partly by clay swept down from the Cronion, partly by deposit from the overflowings of the Cladeus. The coating of earth over the Altis had an average depth of no less than 16 ft.

The work could not, however, be restricted to the Altis. It was necessary to dig beyond it, especially on the west, the south and the east, where several ancient buildings existed, not included within the sacred precinct itself. The complexity of the task was further increased by the fact that in many places early Greek work had later Greek on top of it, or late Greek work had been overlaid with Roman. In a concise survey of the results obtained, it will be best to begin with the remains external to the precinct of Zeus.

1. REMAINS OUTSIDE THE ALTIS

A. *West Side.*—The wall bounding the Altis on the west belongs probably to the time of Nero. In the west wall were two gates, one at its northern and the other at its southern extremity. The latter must have served as the processional entrance. Each gate was πρόστυλος, having before it on the west a colonnade consisting of a row of four columns. There is a third and smaller gate at about the middle point of the west wall, and nearly opposite the Pelopion in the Altis.

West of the west Altis wall, on the strip of ground between the Altis and the river Cladeus (of which the course is roughly parallel to the west Altis wall), the following buildings were traced. The order in which they are placed here is that in which they succeed each other from north to south.

1. Just outside the Altis at its north-west corner was a *Gymnasium*. A large open space, not regularly rectangular, was enclosed on two sides—possibly on three—by Doric colonnades. On the south it was bordered by a portico with a single row of columns in front; on the east by a double portico, more than a stadium in length (220 yds.), and serving as a racecourse for practice in bad weather. At the south-east corner of the gymnasium, in the angle between the south and the east portico, was a Corinthian doorway, which a double row of columns divided into three passages. Immediately to the east of this doorway was the gate giving access to the Altis at its north-west corner. The gymnasium was used as an exercise ground for competitors during the last month of their training.

2. Immediately adjoining the gymnasium on the south was a Palaestra, the place of exercise for wrestlers and boxers. It was in the form of a square, of which each side was about 70 yds. long, enclosing an inner building surrounded by a Doric colonnade. Facing this inner building on north, east and west were rooms of different sizes, to which doors or colonnades gave access. The chief entrances to the palaestra were at south-west and south-east, separated by a double colonnade which extended along the south side.

3. Near the palaestra on the south a Byzantine church forms the central point in a complex group of remains. (a) The church itself occupies the site of an older brick building, which is perhaps a remnant of the "workshop of Pheidias" seen by Pausanias. (b) North of the church is a square enclosure with a well in the middle, of the Hellenic age. (c) West of this is a small circular structure, enclosed by square walls. An altar found (*in situ*) on the south side of the circular enclosure shows by an inscription that this was the *Heroum*, where worship of the heroes was practised down to a late period. (d) East of the court stood a large building, of Roman age at latest, arranged round an inner hall with colonnades. These buildings probably formed the Theocoleon, house of the priests. (e) There is also a long and narrow building on the south of the Byzantine church. This may have been occupied by the φαιδρύνται, those alleged "descendants of Pheidias" (Pausanias v. 14) whose hereditary privilege it was to keep the statue of Zeus clean. The so-called "workshop of Pheidias" (see a) evidently owed its preservation to the fact that it continued to be used for actual work,

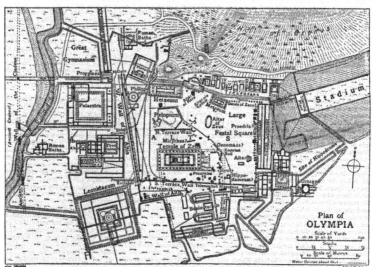

Plan of
OLYMPIA

an the adjacent building would have been a convenient lodging for the artists.

4. South of the group described above occur the remains of a large building shown by its inscription to be the Leonidaeum, dedicated by an Elean named Leonidas in the 4th century B.C., and probably intended for the reception of distinguished visitors during the games, such as the heads of the special missions from the various Greek cities. It is an oblong, of which the north and south sides measure about 250 ft., the east and west about 230. Its orientation differs from that of all the other buildings above mentioned, being not from N. to S., but from W.S.W. to E.N.E. Externally it is an Ionic peripteros, enclosing suites of rooms, large and small, grouped round a small interior Doric peristyle. In Roman times it was altered in such a way as to distribute the rooms into (apparently) four quarters, each having an atrium with six or four columns. Traces existing within the exterior porticos on north, west and east indicate much carriage traffic.

B. *South Side.*—Although the limits of the Altis on the south (*i.e.* on the side towards the Alpheus) can be traced with approximate accuracy, the precise line of the south wall becomes doubtful after we have advanced a little more than one-third of the distance from the west to the east end of the south side. The middle and eastern portions of the south side were places at which architectural changes, large or small, were numerous down to the latest times, and where the older buildings met with scant mercy.

1. The *Council Hall* (*Bouleuterium*), Paus. v. 23) was just outside the Altis, nearly at the middle of its south wall. It comprised two separate Doric buildings of different date but identical form, viz. oblong, having a single row of columns dividing the length into two naves and terminating to the west in a semicircular apse. The orientation of each was from west-south-west to east-north-east, one being south-south-east of the other. In the space between stood a small square building. In front, on the east, was a portico extending along the front of all three buildings; and east of this again a large trapeze-shaped vestibule or fore-hall, enclosed by a colonnade. This bouleuterium would have been available on all occasions when Olympia became the scene of conference or debate between the representatives of different states—whether the subject was properly political, as concerning the amphictyonic treaties, or related more directly to the administration of the sanctuary and festival. Two smaller Hellenic buildings stood immediately west of the bouleuterium. The more northerly of the two opened on the Altis. Their purpose is uncertain.

2. Close to the bouleuterium on the south, and running parallel with it from south-west by west to north-east by east, was the *South Colonnade*, a late but handsome structure, closed on the north side, open on the south and at the east and west ends. The external colonnade (on south, east and west) was Doric; the interior row of columns Corinthian. It was used as a promenade, and as a place from which to view the festal processions as they passed towards the Altis.

3. East of the bouleuterium was a triumphal gateway of Roman age, with triple entrance, the central being the widest, opening on the Altis from the south. North of this gateway, but at a somewhat greater depth, traces of a pavement were found in the Altis.

C. *East Side.*—The line of the east wall, running due north and south, can be traced from the north-east corner of the Altis down about three-fifths of the east side, when it breaks off at the remains known as " Nero's house." These are the first which claim attention on the east side.

1. To the south-east of the Altis is a building of 4th-century date and of uncertain purpose. This was afterwards absorbed into a Roman house which projected beyond the Altis on the east, the south part of the east Altis wall being destroyed to admit of this. A piece of leaden water-pipe found in the house bears NER. AVG. Only a Roman master could have dealt thus with the Altis, and with a building which stood within its sacred precinct. It cannot be doubted that the Roman house—from which three doors gave access to the Altis—was that occupied by Nero when he visited Olympia. Later Roman hands again enlarged and altered the building, which may perhaps have been used for the reception of Roman governors.

2' Following northwards the line of the east wall, we reach at the north-east corner of the Altis the entrance to the *Stadium*, which extends east of the Altis in a direction from west-south-west to east-north-east. The apparently strange and inconvenient position of the Stadium relatively to the Altis was due simply to the necessity of obeying the conditions of the ground, here determined by the curve of the lower slopes which bound the valley on the north. The German explorers excavated the Stadium so far as was necessary for the ascertainment of all essential points. Low embankment had originally been built on west, east and south, the north boundary being formed by the natural slope of the hill. These were afterwards thickened and raised. The space thus defined was a large oblong, about 234 yds. in length by 35 in breadth; There were no artificial seats. It is computed that from 40,000 to 45,000 spectators could have found sitting-room, though it is hardly probable that such a number was ever reached. The exact length of the Stadium itself—which was primarily the course for the foot-race—was about 210 yds. or 192·27 metres—an important result, as it determines

the Olympian foot to be 0·3204 metre or a little more than an English foot (1·05). In the Heraeum at Olympia, it may be remarked, the unit adopted was not this Olympian foot, but an older one of 0·297 metre, and in the temple of Zeus an Attic foot of 1·08 English foot was used. The starting-point and the goal in the Stadium were marked by limestone thresholds. Provision for drainage was made by a channel running round the enclosure. The Stadium was used not only for foot-races, but for boxing, wrestling, leaping, quoit-throwing and javelin-throwing.

The entrance to the Stadium from the north-east corner of the Altis was a privileged one, reserved for the judges of the games, the competitors and the heralds. Its form was that of a vaulted tunnel, 100 Olympian feet in length. It was probably constructed in Roman times. To the west was a vestibule, from which the Altis was entered by a handsome gateway.

3. The *Hippodrome*, in which the chariot-races and horse-races were held, can no longer be accurately traced. The overflowings of the Alpheus have washed away all certain indications of its limits. But it is clear that it extended south and south-east of the Stadium, and roughly parallel with it, though stretching far beyond it to the east. From the state of the ground the German explorers inferred that the length of the hippodrome was 770 metres or 4 Olympic stadia.

D. *North Side.*—If the northern limit of the Altis, like the west, south and east, had been traced by a boundary wall, this would have had the effect of excluding from the precinct a spot so sacred as the Cronion, " Hill of Cronus," inseparably associated with the oldest worship of Zeus at Olympia. It seems therefore unlikely that any such northern boundary wall ever existed. But the line which such a boundary would have followed is partly represented by the remains of a wall running from east to west immediately north of the treasure-houses (see below), which it was designed to protect against the descent of earth from the Cronion just above. This was the wall along which, about A.D. 157, the main water-channel constructed by Herodes Atticus was carried.

Having now surveyed the chief remains external to the sacred precinct on west, south, east and north, we proceed to notice those which have been traced within it.

II.—REMAINS WITHIN THE ALTIS

The form of the Altis, as indicated by the existing traces, is not regularly rectangular. The length of the west side, where the line of direction is from south-south-east to north-north-west, is about 215 yds. The south side, running nearly due east ·and ·west, is about equally long, if measured from the end of the west wall to the point which the east wall would touch when produced due south in a straight line from the place at which it was demolished to make way for " Nero's house." The east side, measured to a point just behind the treasure-houses, is the shortest, about 200 yds. The north side is the longest. A line drawn eastward behind the treasure-houses, from the Prytaneum at the north-west angle, would give about 275 yds.

The remains or sites within the Altis may conveniently be classed in three main groups, viz.—(A) the chief centres of religious worship; (B) votive buildings; (C) buildings, &c., connected with the administration of Olympia or the reception of visitors.

A. *Chief Centres of Religious Worship.*—1. There are traces of an altar near the Heraeum which was probably older than the great altar of Zeus; this was probably the original centre of worship. The great altar of Zeus was of elliptic form, the length of the lozenge being directed from south-south-west to north-north-east, in such a manner that the axis would pass through the Cronion. The upper structure imposed on this basis was in two tiers, and also, probably, lozenge-shaped. This was the famous " ash-altar " at which the iamidae, the hereditary gens of seers, practised those rights of divination by fire in virtue of which more especially Olympia is saluted by Pindar as " mistress of truth." The steps by which the priests mounted the altar seem to have been at north and south.

2. The *Pelopium*, to the west of the Altar of Zeus, was a small precinct in which sacrifices were offered to the hero Pelops. The traces agree with the account of Pausanias. Walls, inclined to each other at obtuse angles, enclosed a plot of ground having in the middle a low tumulus of elliptic form, about 33 metres from east to west by 20 from north to south. A Doric propylon with three doors gave access on the south-west side.

The three temples of the Altis were those of Zeus, Hera and the Mother of the gods. All were Doric. All, too, were completely surrounded by a colonnade, *i.e.* were " peripteral."

3. The *Temple of Zeus*, south of the Pelopium, stood on a high substructure with three steps. It was probably built about 470 B.C. The colonnades at the east and west side were of six columns each; those at the north and south sides (counting the corner columns again) of thirteen each. The cella had a pronaos on the east and an opisthodomos on the west. The cella itself was divided longitudinally (*i.e.* from east to west) into three partitions by a double row of columns. The central partition, which was the widest, consisted of three sections. The west section contained the throne and image of the Olympian Zeus. The middle section, next to the east, which was shut off by low screens, contained a table and stelae. Here, probably, the wreaths were presented to the victors.

The third or easternmost section was open to the public. This temple was most richly adorned with statues and reliefs. On the east front were represented in twenty-one colossal figures the moment before the contest between Oenomaus and Pelope. The west front exhibited the fight of the Lapithae and Centaurs. The statement of Pausanias that the two pediments were made by Paeonius and Alcamenes is now generally supposed to be an error. The Twelve Labours of Heracles were depicted on the metopes of the prodromos and opisthodomos; and of these reliefs much the greater part was found—enough to determine with certainty all the essential features of the composition. It was near this temple, at a point about 38 yds. E.S.E. from the south-east angle, that the explorers found the statue of a flying goddess of victory—the Nike of Paeonius.

4. The *Temple of Hera* (Heraeum), north of the Pelopium, was raised on two steps. It is probably the oldest of extant Greek temples, and may date from about 1000 B.C. It has colonnades of six columns each at east and west, and of sixteen each (counting the corner columns again) at north and south. It was smaller than the temple of Zeus, and, while resembling it in general plan, differed from it by its singular length relatively to its breadth. When Pausanias saw it, one of the two columns of the opisthodomos (at the west end of the cella) was of wood; and for a long period all the columns of this temple had probably been of the same material. A good deal of patch-work in the restoration of particular parts seems to have been done at various periods. Only the lower part of the cella wall was of stone, the rest being of unbaked brick; the entablature above the columns was of wood covered with terra-cotta. The cella—divided, like that of Zeus, into three partitions by a double row of columns—had four "tongue-walls," or small screens, projecting at right angles from its north wall, and as many from the south wall. Five niches were thus formed on the north side and five on the south. In the third niche from the east, on the north side of the cella, was found one of the greatest of all the treasures which rewarded the German explorers—the Hermes of Praxiteles (1878).

5. The *Temple of the Great Mother of the Gods* (Metroum) was again considerably smaller than the Heraeum. It stood to the east of the latter, and had a different orientation, viz. not west to east, but west-north-west to east-south-east. It was raised on three steps, and had a peripteros of six columns (east and west) by eleven (north and south), having thus a slightly smaller length relatively to its breadth than either of the other two temples. Here also the cella had prodomos and opisthodomos. The adornment and painting of this temple had once been very rich and varied. It was probably built in the 4th century, and there are indications that in Roman times it underwent a restoration.

B. *Votive Edifices.*—Under this head are placed buildings erected, either by states or by individuals, as offerings to the Olympian god.

1. The twelve *Treasure-houses* on the north side of the Altis, immediately under the Cronion, belong to this class.

The same general character—that of a Doric temple *in antis*, facing south—is traceable in all the treasure-houses. In the cases of several of these the fragments are sufficient to aid a reconstruction. Two—viz. the 2nd and 3rd counting from the west—had been dismantled at an early date, and their site was traversed by a roadway winding upward towards the Cronion. This roadway seems to have been older at least than A.D. 157, since it caused a deflexion in the watercourse along the base of the Cronion constructed by Herodes Atticus. Pausanias, therefore, would not have seen treasure-houses Nos. 2 and 3. This explains the fact that, though we can trace twelve, he names only ten.

As the temples of ancient Greece partly served the purposes of banks in which precious objects could be securely deposited, so the form of a small Doric chapel was a natural one for the "treasure-house" to assume. Each of these treasure-houses was erected by a Greek state, either as a thank-offering for Olympian victories gained by its citizens, or as a general mark of homage to the Olympian Zeus. The treasure-houses were designed to contain the various *draphara* or dedicated gifts (such as gold and silver plate, &c.), in which the wealth of the sanctuary partly consisted. The temple inventories recently discovered at Delos illustrate the great quantity of such possessions which were apt to accumulate at a shrine of Panhellenic celebrity. Taken in order from the west, the treasure-houses were founded by the following states: 1, Sicyon; 2, 3, unknown; 4, Syracuse (referred by Pausanias to Carthage); 5, Epidamnus; 6, Byzantium; 7, Sybaris; 8, Cyrene; 9, Selinus; 10, Metapontum; 11, Megara; 12, Gela. It is interesting to remark how this list represents the Greek colonies, from Libya to Sicily, from the Euxine to the Adriatic. Greece proper, on the other hand, is represented only by Megara and Sicyon. The dates of the foundations cannot be fixed. The architectural members of some of the treasure-houses have been found built into the Byzantine wall, or elsewhere on the site, as well as the terra-cotta plates that overlaid the stone-work in some cases, and the pedimental figures, representing the battle of the gods and giants, from the treasure-house of the Megarians.

2. The *Philippeum* stood near the north-west corner of the Altis, a short space west-south-west of the Heraeum. It was dedicated by Philip of Macedon, after his victory at Chaeronea (338 B.C.). As a thank-offering for the overthrow of Greek freedom, it might seem strangely placed in the Olympian Altis. But it is, in fact, only another illustration of the manner in which Philip's position and power enabled him to place a decent disguise on the real nature of the change. Without risking any revolt of Hellenic feeling, the new "captain-general" of Greece could erect a monument of his triumph in the very heart of the Panhellenic sanctuary. The building consisted of a circular Ionic colonnade (of eighteen columns), about 13 metres in diameter, raised on three steps and enclosing a small circular cella, probably adorned with fourteen Corinthian half-columns. It contained portraits by Leochares of Philip, Alexander, and other members of their family, in gold and ivory.

3. The *Exedra of Herodes Atticus* stood at the north limit of the Altis, close to the north-east angle of the Heraeum, and immediately west of the westernmost treasure-house (that of Sicyon). It consisted of a half-dome of brick, 54 ft. in diameter, with south-south-west aspect. Under the half-dome were placed twenty-one marble statues, representing the family of Antoninus Pius, of Marcus Aurelius, and of the founder, Herodes Atticus. In front of the half-dome on the south, and extending slightly beyond it, was a basin of water for drinking, 71½ ft. long. The ends of the basin at north-north-west and south-south-east were adorned by very small open temples, each with a circular colonnade of eight pillars. A marble bull, in front of the basin, bore an inscription saying that Herodes dedicates the whole to Zeus, in the name of his wife, Annia Regilla. The exedra must have been seen by Pausanias, but he does not mention it.

C. It remains to notice those features of the Altis which were connected with the management of the sanctuary or with the accommodation of its guests.

1. Olympia, besides its religious character, originally possessed also a political character, as the centre of an amphictyony. It was, in fact, a sacred πόλις. We have seen that it had a bouleuterion for purposes of public debate or conference. So also it was needful that, like a Greek city, it should have a public hearth or prytaneum, where fire should always burn on the altar of the Olympian Hestia, and where the controllers of Olympia should exercise public hospitality. The *Prytaneum* was at the north-west corner of the Altis, in such a position that its south-east angle was close to the north-west angle of the Heraeum. It was apparently a square building, of which each side measured 100 Olympian feet, with a south-west aspect. It contained a chapel of Hestia at the front or south-west side, before which a portico was afterwards built. The dining-hall was at the back (north-east), the kitchen on the north-west side. On the same side with the kitchen, and also on the opposite side (south-east), there were some smaller rooms.

2. The *Porch of Echo*, also called the "Painted Porch," extended to a length of 100 yds. along the east Altis wall. Raised on three steps, and formed by a single Doric colonnade, open towards the Altis, it afforded a place from which spectators could conveniently view the passage of processions and the sacrifices at the great altar of Zeus. It was built in the Macedonian period to replace an earlier portico which stood farther back. In front of it was a series of pedestals for votive offerings, including two colossal Ionic columns. These columns, as the inscriptions show, once supported statues of Ptolemy and Berenice.

3. The *Agora* was the name given to that part of the Altis which had the Porch of Echo on the east, the Altar of Zeus on the west, the Metroum on the north, and the precinct of the Temple of Zeus on the south-west. In this part stood the altars of Zeus Agoraios and Artemis Agoraia.

4. The *Zanes* were bronze images of Zeus, the cost of making which was defrayed by the fines exacted from competitors who had infringed the rules of the contest at Olympia. These images stood at the northern side of the Agora, in a row, which extended from the north-east angle of the Metroum to the gate of the private entrance from the Altis into the Stadium. Sixteen pedestals were here discovered *in situ*. A lesson of loyalty was thus impressed on aspirants to renown by the last objects which met their eyes as they passed from the sacred enclosure to the scene of their trial.

5. *Arrangements for Water-supply.*—A copious supply of water was required for the service of the altars and temples, for the private dwellings of priests and officials, for the use of the gymnasium, palaestra, &c., and for the thermae which arose in Roman times. In the Hellenic age the water was derived wholly from the Cladeus and from the small lateral tributaries of its valley. A basin, to serve as a chief reservoir, was built at the north-west corner of the Altis; and a supplementary reservoir was afterwards constructed a little to the north-east of this, on the slope of the Cronion. A new source of supply was for the first time made available by Herodes Atticus, c. A.D. 157. At a short distance east of Olympia, near the village of Miraka, small streams flow from comparatively high ground through the side-valleys which descend towards the right or northern bank of the Alpheus. From these side-valleys water was now conducted to Olympia, entering the Altis at its north-east corner by an arched canal which passed behind the treasure-houses to the reservoir at the back of the exedra. The large basin of drinking-water in front of the exedra was fed thence, and served to associate the name of Herodes with a benefit of the highest practical value. Olympia further possessed several fountains, enclosed by round or square walls,

chiefly, in connexion with the buildings outside the Altis. The
drainage of the Altis followed two main lines. One, for the west
part, passed from the south-west angle of the Heraeum to the south
portico outside the south Altis wall. The other, which served for the
treasure-houses, passed in front of the Porch of Echo parallel with
the line of the east Altis wall.

See the official *Die Ausgrabungen su Olympia* (5 vols., 1875–1881);
Laloux and Monceaux, *Restauration de l'Olympie* (1889); Curtius
and Adler, *Olympia die Ergebnisse der Ausgrabungen* (1890–1897),
I. "Topographie und Geschichte." II. "Baudenkmäler." III.
"Bildwerke in Stein und Thon" (Treu), IV. "Bronzen" (Furt-
wängler), V. "Inschriften" (Dittenberger and Purgold).
(R. C. J.; E. Gr.)

OLYMPIA, the capital of the state of Washington, U.S.A.,
and the county-seat of Thurston county, on the Des Chutes
river and Budd's Inlet, at the head of Puget Sound, about 50 m.
S.S.W. of Seattle. Pop. (1890) 4698, (1900) 3863, of whom
591 were foreign-born; (1910; U S. census) 6996. It is
served by the Northern Pacific and the Port Townsend Southern
railways, and by steamboat lines to other ports on the Sound
and along the Pacific coast. Budd's Inlet is spanned here by a
wagon bridge and a railway bridge. Among the prominent
buildings are the Capitol, which is constructed of native sandstone and stands in a park of considerable beauty, the county
court-house, St Peter's hospital, the governor's mansion and
the city hall. The state library is housed in the Capitol. At
Tumwater, the oldest settlement (1845) on Puget Sound, about
2 m. S. of Olympia, are the Tumwater Falls of the Des Chutes,
which provide good water power. The city's chief industry is
the cutting, sawing and dressing of lumber obtained from the
neighbouring forests. Olympia oysters are widely known in
the Pacific coast region; they are obtained chiefly from
Oyster Bay, Skookum Bay, North Bay and South Bay, all
near Olympia. Olympia was laid out in 1851, became the
capital of Washington in 1853, and was chartered as a city
in 1859.

OLYMPIAD, in Greek chronology, a period of four years, used
as a method of dating for literary purposes, but never adopted
in every-day life. The four years were reckoned from one
celebration of the Olympian games to another, the first Olympiad
beginning with 776 B.C., the year of Coroebus, the first victor in
the games after their suspension for 86 years, the last with
A.D. 394, when they were finally abolished during the reign of
Theodosius the Great. The system was first regularly used by
the Sicilian historian Timaeus (352–256 B.C.).

OLYMPIAS, daughter of Neoptolemus, king of Epirus, wife
of Philip II. of Macedon, and mother of Alexander the Great. It
is said that Philip fell in love with her in Samothrace, where
they were both being initiated into the mysteries (Plutarch,
Alexander, 2). The marriage took place in 359 B.C., shortly
after Philip's accession, and Alexander was born in 356. The
fickleness of Philip and the jealous temper of Olympias led to
a growing estrangement, which became complete when Philip
married a new wife, Cleopatra, in 337. Alexander, who sided
with his mother, withdrew, along with her, into Epirus, whence
they both returned in the following year, after the assassination
of Philip, which Olympias is said to have countenanced. During
the absence of Alexander, with whom she regularly corresponded
on public as well as domestic affairs, she had great influence, and
by her arrogance and ambition caused such trouble to the regent
Antipater that on Alexander's death (323) she found it prudent
to withdraw into Epirus. Here she remained until 317, when,
allying herself with Polyperchon, by whom her old enemy had
been succeeded in 319, she took the field with an Epirote army;
the opposing troops at once declared in her favour, and for a
short period Olympias was mistress of Macedonia. Cassander,
Antipater's son, hastened from Peloponnesus, and, after an
obstinate siege, compelled the surrender of Pydna, where she
had taken refuge. One of the terms of the capitulation had been
that her life should be spared; but in spite of this she was brought
to trial for the numerous and cruel executions of which she had
been guilty during her short lease of power. Condemned
without a hearing, she was put to death (316) by the friends
of those whom she had slain, and Cassander is said to have
denied her remains the rites of burial.

See Plutarch, *Alexander*, 9, 39, 68; Justin, vii. 6, ix. 7, xiv 5, 6,
Arrian, *Anab.* vii. 12; Diod, Sic. xviii. 49–65, xix. 11–51; also the
articles ALEXANDER III. THE GREAT and MACEDONIAN EMPIRE.

OLYMPIODORUS, the name of several Greek authors, of
whom the following are the most important. (1) An historical
writer (5th century A.D.), born at Thebes in Egypt, who was
sent on a mission to Attila by the emperor Honorius in 412,
and later lived at the court of Theodosius. He was the author
of a history ('Ιστορικοὶ λόγοι) in 22 books of the Western Empire
from 407 to 425. The original is lost, but an abstract is given
by Photius, according to whom he was an alchemist (ποιητής).
A MS. treatise on alchemy, reputed to be by him, is preserved
in the National Library in Paris, and was printed with a translation by P. E. M. Berthelot in his *Collection des alchimistes grecs*
(1887–1888). (2) A Peripatetic philosopher (5th century A.D.),
an elder contemporary of Proclus. He lived at Alexandria and
lectured on Aristotle with considerable success. His best-known
pupil was Proclus, to whom he wished to betroth his daughter.
(3) A Neoplatonist philosopher, also of Alexandria, who flourished
in the 6th century of our era, during the reign of Justinian. He
was, therefore, a younger contemporary of Damascius, and
seems to have carried on the Platonic tradition after the closing
of the Athenian School in 529, at a time when the old pagan
philosophy was at its last ebb. His philosophy is in close
conformity with that of Damascius, and, apart from great
lucidity of expression, shows no striking features. He is,
however, important as a critic and a commentator, and preserved
much that was valuable in the writings of Iamblichus, Damascius
and Syrianus. He made a close and intelligent study of the
dialogues of Plato, and his notes, formulated and collected by
his pupils (ἀπὸ φωνῆς Ὀλυμπιοδώρου τοῦ μεγάλου φιλοσόφου), are
extremely valuable. In one of his commentaries he makes the
interesting statement that the Platonic succession had not been
interrupted by the numerous confiscations it had suffered.
Zeller points out that this refers to the Alexandrian, not to the
Athenian, succession; but internal evidence makes it clear
that he does not draw a hard line of demarcation between
the two schools. The works which have been preserved are a
life of Plato, an attack on Strato and Scholia on the *Phaedo*,
Alcibiades I., *Philebus* and *Gorgias*. (4) An Aristotelian who
wrote a commentary on the *Meteorologica* of Aristotle. He also
lived at Alexandria in the 6th century, and from a reference
in his work to a comet must have lived after A.D. 564. But
Zeller (iii. 2, p. 582, n. 1) maintains that he is identical with the
commentator on Plato (2, above) in spite of the late date of his
death. His work, like that of Simplicius, endeavours to reconcile
Plato and Aristotle, and refers to Proclus with reverence. The
commentary was printed by the Aldine Press at Venice about
1550.

OLYMPUS, the name of many mountains in Greece and Asia
Minor, and of the fabled home of the gods, and also a city name
and a personal name.

I. Of mountains bearing the name the most famous
is the lofty ridge on the borders of Thessaly and Macedonia.
The river Peneus, which drains Thessaly, finds its way to the
sea through the great gorge of Tempe, which is close below the
south-eastern end of Olympus and separates it from Mount Ossa.
The highest peak of Olympus is nearly 10,000 ft. high; it is
covered with snow for great part of the year. Olympus is a
mountain of massive appearance, in many places rising in
tremendous precipices broken by vast ravines, above which
is the broad summit. The lower parts are densely wooded;
the summit is naked rock. Homer calls the mountain
ἀγάννιφος, μακρός, πολυδειράς: the epithets νιφόεις, πολυδένδρος,
φενδόσσος and *opacus* are used by other poets. The modern
name is Έλυμπο, a dialectic form of the ancient word.

The peak of Mount Lycaeus in the south-west of Arcadia
was called Olympus. East of Olympia, on the north bank of
the Alpheus, was a hill bearing this name; beside Sellasia in
Laconia another. The name was even commoner in Asia

Minor: a lofty chain in Mysia (Keshish Dagh), a ridge east of Smyrna (Nif Dagh), other mountains in Lycia, in Galatia, in Cilicia, in Cyprus, &c., were all called Olympus.

II. A lofty peak, rising high above the clouds of the lower atmosphere into the clear ether, seemed to be the chosen seat of the deity. In the *Iliad* the gods are described as dwelling on the top of the mountain, in the *Odyssey* Olympus is regarded as a more remote and less definite locality; and in later poets we find similar divergence of ideas, from a definite mountain to a vague conception of heaven. In the elaborate mythology of Greek literature Olympus was the common home of the multitude of gods. Each deity had his special haunts, but all had a residence at the court of Zeus on Olympus; here were held the assemblies and the common feasts of the gods.

III. There was a city in Lycia named Olympus; it was a bishopric in the Byzantine time.

OLYNTHUS, an ancient city of Chalcidice, situated in a fertile plain at the head of the Gulf of Torone, near the neck of the peninsula of Pallene, at some little distance from the sea, and about 60 stadia (7 or 8 m.) from Potidaea. The district had belonged to a Thracian tribe, the Bottiaeans, in whose possession the town of Olynthus remained till 479 B.C.[1] In that year the Persian general Artabazus, on his return from escorting Xerxes to the Hellespont, suspecting that a revolt from the Great King was meditated, slew the inhabitants and handed the town over to a fresh population, consisting of Greeks from the neighbouring region of Chalcidice (Herod. viii. 127). Olynthus thus became a Greek *polis*, but it remained insignificant (in the quota-lists of the Delian League it appears as paying on the average 2 talents, as compared with 9 paid by Scione, 8 by Mende, 6 by Torone) until the synoecism (συνοικισμός), effected in 432 through the influence of King Perdiccas of Macedon, as the result of which the inhabitants of a number of petty Chalcidian towns in the neighbourhood were added to its population(Thucyd. i. 58). Henceforward it ranks as the chief Hellenic city west of the Strymon. It had been enrolled as a member of the Delian League (*q.v.*) in the early days of the league, but it revolted from Athens at the time of its synoecism, and was never again reduced. It formed a base for Brasidas during his expedition (424). In the 4th century it attained to great importance in the politics of the age as the head of the Chalcidic League (τὸ κοινὸν τῶν Χαλκιδέων). The league may probably be traced back to the period of the peace of Nicias (421), when we find the Chalcidians (οἱ ἐπὶ Θρᾴκης Χαλκιδῆι) taking diplomatic action in common, and enrolled as members of the Argive alliance. There are coins of the league which can be dated with certainty as early as 405; one specimen may perhaps go back to 415-420. Unquestionably, then, the league originated before the end of the 5th century, and the motive for its formation is almost certainly to be found in the fear of Athenian attack. After the end of the Peloponnesian War the development of the league was rapid. About 390 we find it concluding an important treaty with Amyntas, king of Macedon (the father of Philip),[2] and by 382 it had absorbed most of the Greek cities west of the Strymon, and had even got possession of Pella, the chief city in Macedonia (Xenophon, *Hell.* v. 2, 12). In this year Sparta was induced by an embassy from Acanthus and Apollonia, which anticipated conquest by the league, to send an expedition against Olynthus. After three years of indecisive warfare Olynthus consented to dissolve the confederacy (379). It is clear, however, that the dissolution was little more than formal, as the Chalcidians (Χαλκιδῆι ἀπὸ Θρᾴκης) appear, only a year or two later, among the members of the Athenian naval confederacy of 378-377.[3] Twenty years later, in the reign of Philip, the power of Olynthus is asserted by Demosthenes to have been much greater than before the Spartan expedition.[4] The town itself at this period

is spoken of as a city of the first rank (πόλις μυριανδρος), and the league included thirty-two cities. When war broke out between Philip and Athens (357), Olynthus was at first in alliance with Philip. Subsequently, in alarm at the growth of his power, it concluded an alliance with Athens; but in spite of all the efforts of the latter state, and of its great orator Demosthenes, it fell before Philip, who razed it to the ground (348).

The history of the confederacy of Olynthus illustrates at once the strength and the weakness of that movement towards federation which is one of the most marked features of the later stages of Greek history. The strength of the movement is shown both by the duration and by the extent of the Chalcidic League. It lasted for something like seventy years; it survived defeat and temporary dissolution, and it embraced upwards of thirty cities. Yet, in the end, the centrifugal forces proved stronger than the centripetal; the sentiment of autonomy stronger than the sentiment of union. It is clear that Philip's victory was mainly due to the spirit of dissidence within the league itself, just as the victory of Sparta had been (cf. Diod. xvi. 53, 2 with Xen. *Hell.* v. 2, 24). The mere fact that Philip captured all the thirty-two towns without serious resistance is sufficient evidence of this. It is probable that the strength of the league was more seriously undermined by the policy of Athens than by the action of Sparta. The successes of Athens at the expense of Olynthus, shortly before Philip's accession, must have fatally divided the Greek interest north of the Aegean in the struggle with Macedon.

AUTHORITIES.—The chief passages in ancient literature are the Olynthiac Orations of Demosthenes, and Xenophon, *Hell.* v. 2. See E. A. Freeman, *History of Federal Government*, ch. iv.; A. H. J. Greenidge, *Handbook of Greek Constitutional History* (1896), p. 228; B. V. Head, *Historia Numorum*, pp. 184-186; G. Gilbert, *Griechische Staatsalterthümer*, vol. ii. pp. 197-198. The view taken by all these authorities as to the date of the formation of the Confederacy of Olynthus differs widely from that put forward above. Freeman and Greenidge suppose the league to have originated in 382, Head in 392, Hicks (*Manual of Greek Inscriptions*, No. 74) before 390. The decisive test is the numismatic one. There are coins of the league in the British Museum which are earlier than 400, and one in the possession of Professor Oman, of Oxford, which he and Mr Head are disposed to think may be as early as 415-420. (E. M. W.)

OMAGH, a market town and the county town of county Tyrone, Ireland, on the river Strule, 129½ m. N.W. by N. from Dublin by the Londonderry line of the Great Northern railway, here joined by a branch from Enniskillen. Pop. (1901) 4789. The greater part of the town is picturesquely situated on a steep slope above the river. The milling and linen industries are carried on, and monthly fairs are held. The Protestant church has a lofty and handsome spire, and the Roman Catholic church stands well on the summit of a hill. A castle, of which there are scanty remains, was of sufficient importance to stand sieges in 1509 and 1641, being rebuilt after its total destruction in the first case. The town is governed by an urban district council.

OMAGUAS, UMANAS or CAMBEVAS (flat-heads), a tribe of South American Indians of the Amazon valley. Fabulous stories about the wealth of the Omaguas led to several early expeditions into their country, the most famous of which were those of George of Spires in 1536, of Philip von Hutten in 1541 and of Pedro de Ursua in 1560. In 1645 Jesuits began work. In 1687 Father Fritz, "apostle of the Omaguas," established some forty mission villages. The Omaguas are still numerous and powerful around the head waters of the Japura and Uaupés.

OMAHA, the county-seat of Douglas county and the largest city in Nebraska, U.S.A., situated on the W. bank of the Missouri river, about 20 m. above the mouth of the Platte. Pop. (1880) 30,518, (1890) 66,536,[5] (1900) 102,555, of whom 23,552 (comprising 5522 Germans, 3068 Swedes, 2430 Danes, 2170 Bohemians, 2164 Irish, 1526 English, 1141 English Canadians,

---

[1] If Olynthus was one of the early colonies of Chalcis (and there is numismatic evidence for this view; see Head, *Hist. Numorum*, p. 185) it must have subsequently passed into the hands of the Bottiaeans.
[2] For the inscription see Hicks, *Manual of Greek Inscriptions*, No. 74.
[3] Hicks, No. 81; *C.I.A.* ii. 17.
[4] Demosthenes, *De falso legatione*, §§ 263-266.
[5] These are the figures given in Census Bulletin 71, *Estimates of Population, 1904, 1905, 1906* (1907), and are the arithmetical mean between the figures for 1880 and those for 1900, those of the census of 1890 being 140,452; these are substituted by the Bureau of the Census, as the 1890 census was in error. In 1910, according to the U.S. census, the population was 124,096.

997 Russians, &c.) were foreign-born and 3443 were negroes, (1906 estimate) 124,167. Originally, with Council Bluffs, Iowa, the eastern terminus of the first Pacific railway, Omaha now has outlets over nine great railway systems: the Chicago, Burlington & Quincy, the Union Pacific, the Chicago, Rock Island & Pacific, the Chicago Great-Western, the Chicago & North-Western, the Chicago, Milwaukee & St Paul, the Illinois Central, the Missouri Pacific and the Wabash. Bridges over the Missouri river connect Omaha with Council Bluffs. The original town site occupied an elongated and elevated river terrace, now given over wholly to business; behind this are hills and bluffs, over which the residential districts have extended.

Among the more important buildings are the Federal Building, Court House, a city-hall, two high schools, one of which is one of the finest in the country, a convention hall, the Auditorium and the Public Library. Omaha is the see of Roman Catholic and Protestant Episcopal bishoprics. Among the educational institutions are a state school for the deaf (1867); the medical department and orthopaedic branch of the University of Nebraska (whose other departments are at Lincoln); a Presbyterian Theological Seminary (1891); and Creighton University (Roman Catholic, under Jesuit control). This university, which was founded in honour of Edward Creighton (d. 1874) (whose brother, Count John A. Creighton, d. 1907, gave large sums in his lifetime and about $1,250,000 by his will), by his wife Mary Lucretia Creighton (d. 1876), was incorporated in 1879; it includes the Creighton Academy, Creighton College (1875), to which a Scientific Department was added in 1883, the John A. Creighton Medical College (1892), the Creighton University College of Law (1904), the Creighton University Dental College (1905) and the Creighton College of Pharmacy (1905). In 1909–1910 it had 120 instructors and 800 students. St Joseph's Hospital (Roman Catholic) was built as a memorial to John A. Creighton. The principal newspapers are the *Omaha Bee*, the *World-Herald* and the *News*. The *Omaha Bee* was established in 1871 by Edward Rosewater (1841–1906), who made it one of the most influential Republican journals in the West. The *World-Herald* (Democratic), founded in 1865 by George L. Miller, was edited by William Jennings Bryan from 1894 to 1896.

Omaha is the headquarters of the United States military department of the Missouri, and there are military posts at Fort Omaha (signal corps and station for experiments with war balloons), immediately north, and Fort Crook (infantry), 10 m. S. of the city. A carnival, the "Festival of Ak-Sar-Ben," is held in Omaha every autumn. Among the manufacturing establishments of Omaha are breweries (product value in 1905, $1,141,424) and distilleries, silver and lead smelting and refining works, railway shops, flour and grist-mills and dairies. The product-value of its manufactures in 1900 ($43,168,876) constituted 30% of the total output of the state, not including the greater product (48·7% of the total) of South Omaha (q.v.), where the industrial interests of Omaha are largely concentrated. The "factory" product of Omaha in 1905 was valued at $54,003,704, an increase of 41·8 % over that ($38,074,244) for 1900. The net debt of the city on the 1st of May 1909 was $5,770,000; its assessed value in 1909 (about ⅓ of cash value) was $26,749,148, and its total tax-rate was $5·73 per $1000.

In 1804 Meriwether Lewis and William Clark camped on the Omaha plateau. In 1825 a licensed Indian post was established here. In 1846 the Mormons settled at "Winter Quarters"—after 1854 called Florence (pop. in 1900, 668), in the immediate environs (6 m. N.) of the present Omaha—and by 1847 had built up camps of some 12,000 inhabitants on the Nebraska and Iowa sides of the Missouri. Compelled to remove from the Indian reservation within which Winter Quarters lay, they founded "Kanesville" on the Iowa side (which also was called Winter Quarters by the Mormons, and after 1853 was known as Council Bluffs), gradually emigrating to Utah in the years following. Winter Quarters (Florence) was deserted in 1848, but many Mormons were still in Nebraska and Iowa, and their local influence was strong for nearly a decade afterwards. Not all had

left Nebraska in 1853. Speculative land "squatters" intruded upon the Indian lands in that year, and a rush of settlers followed the opening of Nebraska Territory under the Kansas-Nebraska Bill of 1854. Omaha (named from the Omaha Indians) was platted in 1854, and was first chartered as a city in 1857. It was the provisional territorial capital in 1854–1855, and the regular capital in 1855–1867. Its charter status has often been modified. Since 1887 it has been the only city of the state governed under the general charter for metropolitan cities. Prairie freighting and Missouri river navigation were of importance before the construction of the Union Pacific railway, and the activity of the city in securing the freighting interest gave her an initial start over the other cities of the state. Council Bluffs was the legal, but Omaha the practical, eastern terminus of that great undertaking, work on which began at Omaha in December 1863. The city was already connected as early as 1863 by telegraph with Chicago, St Louis, and since 1861 with San Francisco. Lines of the present great Rock Island, Burlington and North-Western railway systems all entered the city in the years 1867–1868. Meat-packing began as early as 1871, but its first great advance followed the removal of the Union stock yards south of the city in 1884. South Omaha (q.v.) was rapidly built up around them. A Trans-Mississippi Exposition illustrating the progress and resources of the states west of the Mississippi was held at Omaha in 1898. It represented an investment of $2,000,000, and in spite of financial depression and wartime, 90 % of their subscriptions were returned in dividends to the stockholders.

OMAHAS, a tribe of North American Indians of Siouan stock. They were found on St Peter's river, Minnesota, where they lived an agricultural life. Owing to a severe epidemic of small-pox they abandoned their village, and wandered westward to the Niobrara river in Nebraska. After a succession of treaties and removals they are now located on a reservation in eastern Nebraska, and number some 1200.

OMALIUS D'HALLOY, JEAN BAPTISTE JULIEN D' (1783–1875), Belgian geologist, was born on the 16th of February 1783 at Liége, and educated firstly in that city and afterwards in Paris. While a youth he became interested in geology, and being of independent means he was able to devote his energies to geological researches. As early as 1808 he communicated to the *Journal des mines* a paper entitled *Essai sur la géologie du Nord de la France*. He became *maire* of Skeuvre in 1807, governor of the province of Namur in 1815, and from 1848 occupied a place in the Belgian senate. He was an active member of the Belgian Academy of Sciences from 1816, and served three times as president. He was likewise president of the Geological Society of France in 1852. In Belgium and the Rhine provinces he was one of the geological pioneers in determining the stratigraphy of the Carboniferous and other rocks. He studied also in detail the Tertiary deposits of the Paris Basin, and ascertained the extent of the Cretaceous and some of the older strata, which he for the first time clearly depicted on a map (1817). He was distinguished as an ethnologist, and when nearly ninety years of age he was chosen president of the Congress of Pre-historic Archaeology (Brussels, 1872). He died on the 15th of January 1875. His chief works were: *Mémoires pour servir à la description géologique des Pays-Bas, de la France et de quelques contrées voisines* (1828); *Éléments de géologie* (1831, 3rd ed. 1839); *Abrégé de géologie* (1853, 7th ed. 1862); *Des races humaines, ou éléments d'ethnographie* (5th ed., 1869).

Obituar by J. Gosselet, *Bull. soc. géol. de France*, ser. 3, vol. vi. (1878). y

OMAN, a kingdom occupying the south-eastern coast districts of Arabia, its southern limits being a little to the west of the meridian of 55° E. long., and the boundary on the north, the southern borders of El Hasa. Oman and Hasa between them occupy the eastern coast districts of Arabia to the head of the Persian Gulf. The Oman-Hasa boundary has been usually drawn north of the promontory of El Katr. This is, however, incorrect. In 1870 Katr was under Wahhabi rule, but in the year 1871 Turkish assistance was requested to aid the settlement of a family quarrel between certain Wahhabi chiefs, and the Turks thus obtained a footing in Katr, which they have retained ever since. Turkish occupation (now firmly established throughout El Hasa) includes Katif (the ancient Gerrha), and El Bidia on the coast of Katr. But the pearl fisheries of Katr are still under the protection of the chiefs of Bahrein, who are themselves under British suzerainty. In 1895 the chief of Katr (Sheikh Jasim ben Thaniy, instigated by the Turks, attacked Sheikh Isa of Bahrein, but his fleet of dhows was destroyed by a British gunboat, and Bahrein (like Zanzibar) has since been detached from Oman and placed directly under British protection.

Oman is a mountainous district dominated by a range called Jebel Akhdar (or the Green Mountain), which is 10,000 ft. in altitude, and is flanked by minor ranges running approximately parallel to the coast, and shutting off the harbours from the interior. They enclose long lateral valleys, some of which are fertile and highly cultivated, and traversed by narrow precipitous gorges at intervals, which form the only means of access to the interior from the sea. Beyond the mountains which flank the cultivated valleys of Semail and Tyin, to the west, there stretches the great Ruba el Khali, or Dahna, the central desert of southern Arabia, which reaches across the continent to the borders of Yemen, isolating the province on the landward side just as the rugged mountain barriers shut it off from the sea. The wadis (or valleys) of Oman (like the wadis of Arabia generally) are merely torrential channels, dry for the greater part of the year. Water is obtained from wells and springs in sufficient quantity to supply an extensive system of irrigation.

The only good harbour on the coast is that of Muscat, the capital of the kingdom, which, however, is not directly connected with the interior by any mountain route. The little port of Matrah, immediately contiguous to Muscat, offers the only opportunity for penetrating into the interior by the wadi Kahza, a rough pass which is held for the sultan or imam of Muscat by the Rehbayin chief. In 1883, owing to the treachery of this chief, Muscat was besieged by a rebel army, and disaster was only averted by the guns of H.M.S. "Philomel." About 50 m. south of Muscat the port of Kuryat is again connected with the inland valleys by the wadi Hail, leading to the gorges of the wadi Tbaika or "Devil's Gap." Both routes give access to the wadi Tyin, which, enclosed between the mountain of El Beideh and Hallowi (from 2000 to 3000 ft. high), is the garden of Oman. Fifty miles to the north-west of Muscat this interior region may again be reached by the transverse valley of Semail, leading into the wadi Munsab, and from thence to Tyin. This is generally reckoned the easiest line for travellers. But all routes are difficult, winding between granite and limestone rocks, and abounding in narrow defiles and rugged torrent beds. Vegetation is, however, tolerably abundant—tamarisks, oleanders, kafas, euphorbias, the milk bush, rhamnus and acacias being the most common and most characteristic forms of vegetable life, and pools of water are frequent. The rich oasis of Tyin contains many villages embosomed in palm groves and surrounded with orchards and fields.

In addition to cereals and vegetables, the cultivation of fruit is abundant throughout the valley. After the date, vines, peaches, apricots, oranges, mangoes, melons and mulberries find special favour with the Rehbayin, who exhibit all the skill and perseverance of the Arab agriculturist of Yemen, and cultivate everything that the soil is capable of producing.

The sultan, a descendant of those Yemenite imams who consolidated Arab power in Zanzibar and on the East African coast, and raised Oman to its position as the most powerful state in Arabia during the first half of the 19th century, resides at Muscat, where his palace directly faces the harbour, not far from the British residency. The little port of Gwadar, on the Makran coast of the Arabian Sea, a station of the Persian Gulf telegraph system, is still a dependency of Oman.

See Colonel Miles, *Geographical Journal*, vol. vii. (1896); Commander Stiffe, *Geographical Journal* (1899).   (T. H. H.")

OMAR (c. 581–644), in full 'OMAR IBN AL-KHATTAB, the second of the Mahommedan caliphs (see CALIPHATE, A, §§ 1 and 2).

Originally opposed to Mahomet, he became later one of the ablest advisers both of him and of the first caliph, Abu Bekr. His own reign (634–644) saw Islam's transformation from a religious sect to an imperial power. The chief events were the defeat of the Persians at Kadisiya (637) and the conquest of Syria and Palestine. The conquest of Egypt followed (see EGYPT and AMR IBN EL-ASS) and the final rout of the Persians at Nehāwend (641) brought Iran under Arab rule. Omar was assassinated by a Persian slave in 644, and though he lingered several days after the attack, he appointed no successor, but only a body of six Muhajirun who should select a new caliph. Omar was a wise and far-sighted ruler and rendered great service to Islam. He is said to have built the so-called "Mosque of Omar" ("the Dome of the Rock") in Jerusalem, which contains the rock regarded by Mahommedans as the scene of Mahomet's ascent to heaven, and by the Jews as that of the proposed sacrifice of Isaac.

'OMAR KHAYYĀM [in full, GHIYĀTHUDDĪN ABULFATH 'OMAR BIN IBRĀHĪM AL-KHAYYĀMĪ], the great Persian mathematician, astronomer, freethinker and epigrammatist, who derived the epithet Khayyām (the tentmaker) most likely from his father's trade, was born in or near Nishāpūr, where he is said to have died in A.H. 517 (A.D. 1123). At an early age he entered into a close friendship both with Nizām-ul-mulk and his school-fellow Hassan ibn Sabbāh, who founded afterwards the terrible sect of the Assassins. When Nizām-ul-mulk was raised to the rank of vizier by the Seljūk sultan Alp-Arslan (A.D. 1063–1073) he bestowed upon Hassan ibn Sabbāh the dignity of a chamberlain, whilst offering a similar court office to 'Omar Khayyām. But the latter contented himself with an annual stipend which would enable him to devote all his time to his favourite studies of mathematics and astronomy. His standard work on algebra, written in Arabic, and other treatises of a similar character raised him at once to the foremost rank among the mathematicians of that age, and induced Sultān Malik-Shāh to summon him in A.H. 467 (A.D. 1074) to institute astronomical observations on a larger scale, and to aid him in his great enterprise of a thorough reform of the calendar. The results of 'Omar's research were—a revised edition of the Zij or astronomical tables, and the introduction of the Ta'rīkh-i-Malikshāhī or Jalālī, that is, the so-called Jalālian or Seljūk era, which commences in A.H. 471 (A.D. 1079, 15th March).

'Omar's great scientific fame, however, is nearly eclipsed by his still greater poetical renown, which he owes to his *rubā'is* or quatrains, a collection of about 500 epigrams. The peculiar form of the *rubā'i*—viz. four lines, the first, second and fourth of which have the same rhyme, while the third usually (but not always) remains rhymeless—was first successfully introduced into Persian literature as the exclusive vehicle for subtle thoughts on the various topics of Sūfic mysticism by the sheikh Abū Sa'īd bin Abulkhair,[1] but 'Omar differs in its treatment considerably from Abū Sa'īd. Although some of his quatrains are purely mystic and pantheistic, most of them bear quite another stamp; they are the breviary of a radical freethinker, who protests in the most forcible manner both against the narrowness, bigotry and uncompromising austerity of the orthodox ulemā and the eccentricity, hypocrisy and wild ravings of advanced Sūfis, whom he successfully combats with their own weapons, using the whole mystic terminology simply to ridicule mysticism itself. There is in this respect a great resemblance between him and Hāfiz, but 'Omar is decidedly superior. He has often been called the Voltaire of the East, and cried down as materialist and atheist. As far as purity of diction, fine wit, crushing satire against a debased and ignorant clergy, and a general sympathy with suffering humanity are concerned, 'Omar certainly reminds us of the great Frenchman; but there the comparison ceases. Voltaire never wrote anything equal to 'Omar's fascinating rhapsodies in praise of wine, love and all earthly joys, and his passionate denunciations of a malevolent and inexorable

[1] Died Jan. 1049. Comp. Ethé's edition of his rubā'īs in *Sitzungsberichte der bayr. Akademie* (1875), pp. 145 seq., and (1878) pp. 38 seq.; and E. G. Browne's *Literary Hist. of Persia*, ii. 261.

fate which dooms to slow decay or sudden death and to eternal oblivion all that is great, good and beautiful in this world. There is a touch of Byron, Swinburne and even of Schopenhauer in many of his *rubā'īs*, which clearly proves that the modern pessimist is by no means a novel creature in the realm of philosophic thought and poetical imagination.

The Leiden copy of 'Omar Khayyām's work on algebra was noticed as far back as 1742 by Gerald Meerman in the preface to his *Specimen calculi fluxionalis*; further notices of the same work by Sédillot appeared in the *Nouv. Jour. As.* (1834) and in vol. xiii. of the *Notices et extraits des MSS. de la Bibl. roy.* The complete text, together with a French translation (on the basis of the Leiden and Paris copies, the latter first discovered by M. Libri, see his *Histoire des sciences mathématiques en Italie*, i. 300), was edited by F. Woepcke, *L'Algèbre d'Omar Alkhayyāmi* (Paris, 1851). Articles on 'Omar's life and works are found in Reinaud's *Géographie d'Aboulféda*, pref., p. 101; *Notices et extraits*, ix. 143 seq.; Garcin de Tassy, *Note sur les Rubā'iyāt de 'Omar Khaiyām* (Paris, 1857); Rieu, *Cal. Pers. MSS. in the Br. Mus.*, ii. 546; A. Christensen, *Recherches sur les Rubā'iyāt de 'Omar Hayyām* (Heidelberg, 1905); V. Zhukovski's *'Umar Khayyām and the "Wandering" Quatrains*, translated from the Russian by E. D. Ross in the *Journal of the Royal Asiatic Society*, xxx. (1898); E. G. Browne; *Literary History of Persia*, ii. 246. The quatrains have been edited at Calcutta (1836) and Teheran (1857 and 1862); text and French translation by J. B. Nicolas (Paris, 1867) (very incorrect and misleading); a portion of the same, rendered in English verse, by E. FitzGerald (London, 1859, 1872 and 1879). FitzGerald's translation has been edited with commentary by H. M. Batson (1900), and the 2nd ed. of the same (1868) by E. Heron Allen (1908). A new English version was published in Trübner's "Oriental" series (1882) by E. H. Whinfield, and the first critical edition of the text, with translation, by the same (1883). Important later works are N. H. Dole's *variorum* edition (1896), J. Payne's translation (1898), E. Heron Allen's edition (1898) and the Life by J. K. M. Shirazi (1905); but the literature in new translations and imitations has recently multiplied exceedingly. (H. E.; X.)

OMBRE, a card game, very fashionable at the end of the 18th century, but now practically obsolete. The following recommendation of the game is taken from the *Court Gamester*, a book published in 1720 for the use of the daughters of the prince of Wales, afterwards George II:—

"The game of Ombre owes its invention to the Spaniards, and it has in it a great deal of the gravity peculiar to that nation. It is called *Ombre*, or *The Man*. It was so named as requiring thought and reflection, which are qualities peculiar to many or rather alluding to him who undertakes to play the game against the rest of the gamesters, and is called *the man*. To play it well requires a great deal of application, and let a man be ever so expert, he will be apt to fall into mistakes if he think of anything else or is disturbed by the conversation of them that look on. . . . It will be found the most delightful and entertaining of all games to those who have anything in them of what we call the spirit of play."

Ombre is played by three players with a pack of 40 cards, the 8, 9 and 10 being dispensed with. The order of value of the hands is irregular, being different for trumps and suits not trumps. In a suit not trumps the order is, for red suits: K, Q, Kn, ace, 2, 3, 4, 5, 6, 7; for black suits: K, Q, Kn, 7, 6, 5, 4, 3, 2. In trump suits the ace of spades, called *spadille*, is always a trump, and the highest one, whichever of the four suits may be trumps. The order for red suit trumps is: ace of spades 7 (called *manille*), ace of clubs (called *basto*), ace (called *ponto*), K, Q, Kn, 2, 3, 4, 5, 6. For black suit trumps: ace of spades (*spadille*), 2 (*manille*), ace (*basto*), K, Q, Kn, 7, 6, 5, 4, 3. There is no ponto in black trumps. The three highest trumps are called *matadores* (or *mats*). The holder of them has the privilege of not following suit, except when a higher mat is played, which forces a lower one if the hand contains no other trump.

Cards are dealt round, and the receiver of the first black ace is the dealer. He deals (towards his right) nine cards, by threes, to each player. The remaining 13 cards form the stock or *talon*, as at piquet. Each deal constitutes a game. One hand plays against the other two, the solo player being called the *Ombre*. The player at the dealer's right has the first option of being Ombre, which entails two privileges: that of naming the trump suit, and that of throwing away as many of his cards as he chooses, receiving new ones in their place, as at poker. If, with clear advantages in mind, he thinks he can win against the other two hands, he says, " I ask leave," or " I play." But in this case his right-hand neighbour has the privilege of claiming

Ombre for himself, providing he is willing to play his hand without drawing new cards, or, as the phrase goes, *sans prendre*. If, however, the other player reconsiders and decides that he will himself play without drawing cards, he can still remain 'Ombre. If the second player passes, the dealer in his turn may ask to play *sans prendre*, as above. If all three pass a new deal ensues. After the Ombre discards (if he does not play *sans prendre*) the two others in turn do likewise, and, if any cards are left in the stock, the last discarder may look at them (as at piquet)-and the others after him. But if he does not look at them the others lose the privilege of doing so.

The manner of play is like whist, except that it is towards the right. The second and third players combine to defeat Ombre. If in the sequel Ombre makes more tricks than either of his opponents he wins. If one of his opponents makes more than Ombre the latter loses (called *codille*). If Ombre and one or both of his opponents make the same number of tricks the game is drawn. When Ombre makes all nine tricks he wins a *vole*. The game is played with counters having certain values, the pool being emptied by the winner. If all pass, a counter of low value is paid into the pool by each player. If Ombre wins he takes the entire pool. If he draws he forfeits to the pool a sum equal to that already in it, *i.e.* the pool is doubled. If either opponents majority of the tricks (*codille*), Ombre pays him a sum equal to that in the pool, which itself remains untouched until the next game. When the pool is emptied each player pays in three counters.

OMDURMAN, a town of the Anglo-Egyptian Sudan, on the west bank of the Nile, immediately north of the junction of the White and Blue Niles in $15°\ 38'$ N., $32°\ 29'$ E., 2 m. N. by W. of Khartum. Pop. (1909 census) 42,779, of whom 541 were Europeans. The town covers a large area, being over 5 m. long and 2 broad. It consists for the most part of mud huts, but there are some houses built of sun-dried bricks. Save for two or three wide streets which traverse it from end to end the town is a network of narrow lanes. In the centre facing an open space are the ruins of the tomb of the Mahdi and behind is the house in which he lived. The Khalifa's house (a two-storeyed building), the mosque, the Beit el Amana (arsenal) and other houses famed in the history of the town also face the central square. A high wall runs behind these buildings parallel with the Nile. Omdurman is the headquarters of the native traders in the Anglo-Egyptian Sudan, the chief articles of commerce being ivory, ostrich feathers and gum arabic from Darfur and Kordofan. There is also an important camel and cattle market. Nearly every tribe in the Sudan is represented in the population of the city. Among the native artificers the metal workers and leather dressers are noted. The government maintains elementary and technical schools. Mission work is undertaken by various Protestant and Roman Catholic societies.

Omdurman, then an insignificant village, was chosen in 1884 by the Mahdi Mahommed Ahmed as his capital and so continued after the fall of Khartum in January 1885. Its growth was rapid, the Khalifa (who succeeded the Mahdi) compelling large numbers of disaffected tribesmen to live in the town under the eye of his soldiery. Here also were imprisoned the European captives of the Mahdists—notably Slatin Pasha and Father Ohrwalder. On the 2nd of September 1898 the Anglo-Egyptian army under Lord Kitchener totally defeated the forces of the Khalifa at Kerreri, 7 m. N. of the town. A marble obelisk marks the spot where the 21st Lancers made a charge. Within the enclosure of the Khalifa's house is the tomb of Hubert Howard, son of the 9th earl of Carlisle, who was killed in the house at the capture of the city by a splinter of a shell fired at the Mahdi's tomb. (See SUDAN: *Anglo-Egyptian*.)

OMELETTE, sometimes Anglicized as "omelet," a French word of which the history is an example of the curious changes a word may undergo. The ultimate origin is Lat. *lamella*, diminutive of *lamina*, plate; this became in French *lamelle*, and a wrong division of *la lamelle* gave *alamelle*, *alemelle*, or *alumelle*; thence *alemette*, metathesized to *amelette* and *aumelete*, the form in which the word appears in the 15th and 16th centuries. The original meaning seems to be a pancake of a thin flat shape. Omelettes are made with eggs, beaten up lightly, with the addition of milk, flour, herbs, cheese, mushrooms, &c., according to the requirement, and cooked quickly in a buttered pan.

OMEN (a Latin word, either connected with *os*, mouth, or more probably with *auris* (Gr. *οὖς*, ear; apparently, meaning "a thing heard" or "spoken"), a sign in divination, favourable or unfavourable as the case may be (see DIVINATION, AUGURS and ORACLE). The taking of omens may be said to be a part of all systems of divination, in which the future is predicted by means of indications of one sort or another; and tradition has thus gathered round many subjects—events, actions, colours, numbers, &c.—which are considered "ominous," an adjective which generally connotes ill-fortune.

One of the oldest and most widespread methods of divining the future, both among primitive people and among several of the civilizations of antiquity, was the reading of omens in the signs noted on the liver of the animal offered as a sacrifice to some deity. The custom is vouched for by travellers as still observed in Borneo, Burma, Uganda and elsewhere, the animal chosen being a pig or a fowl. It constituted the most common form of divination in ancient Babylonia, where it can be traced back to the 3rd millennium B.C. Among the Etruscans the prominence of the rite led to the liver being looked upon as the trade-mark of the priest. From the Etruscans it made its way to the Romans, though as we shall see it was also modified by them. The evidence for the rite among the Greeks is sufficient to warrant the conclusion of its introduction at a very early period and its persistence to a late day.

The theory upon which the rite everywhere rests is clearly the belief, for which there is an abundance of concurrent testimony, that the liver was at one time regarded as the seat of vitality. This belief appears to be of a more primitive character than the view which places the seat of life in the heart, though we are accustomed to think that the latter was the prevailing view in antiquity. The fact, however, appears to be that the prominence given to the heart in popular beliefs dates from the time when in the course of the development of anatomical knowledge the important function of the heart in animal life came to be recognized, whereas the supposition that the liver is the seat of vitality rests upon other factors than anatomical knowledge, and, being independent of such knowledge, also antedates it. Among the reasons which led people to identify the liver with the very source of life, and hence as the seat of *all* affections and emotions, including what to us are intellectual functions, we may name the bloody appearance of that organ. Filled with blood, it was natural to regard it as the seat of the blood, and as a matter of fact one-sixth of the entire blood of man is in the liver, while in the case of some animals the proportion is even larger. Now blood was everywhere in antiquity associated with life, and the biblical passage, Genesis ix. 3, which identifies the blood with the soul of the animal and therefore prohibits its use fairly represents the current conception both among primitive peoples as well as among those who had advanced along the road of culture and civilization. The liver being regarded as the seat of the blood, it was a natural and short step to identify the liver with the soul as well as with the seat of life, and therefore as the centre of all manifestations of vitality and activity. In this stage of belief, therefore, the liver is the seat of all emotions and affections, as well as of intellectual functions, and it is only when with advancing anatomical knowledge the functions of the heart and then of the brain come to be recognized that a differentiation of functions takes place which had its outcome in the assignment of intellectual activity to the brain or head, of the higher emotions and affections (as love and courage) to the heart, while the liver was degraded to the rank of being regarded as the seat of the lower emotions and affections, such as jealousy, moroseness and the like.

Hepatoscopy, or divination through the liver, belongs therefore to the primitive period when that organ summed up *all* vitality and was regarded as the seat of *all* the emotions and affections—the higher as well as the lower—and also as the seat of intellectual functions. The question, however, still remains to be answered how people came to the belief or to the assumption that through the soul, or the seat of life of the sacrificial animal, the intention of the gods could be divined. There are two theories that may be put forward. The one is that the animal sacrificed was looked upon as a deity, and that, therefore, the liver represented the soul of the god; the other theory is that the deity in accepting the sacrifice identified himself with the animal, and that, therefore, the liver as the soul of the animal was the counterpart of the soul of the god. It is true that the killing of the god plays a prominent part in primitive cults, as has been shown more particularly through the valuable researches of J. G. Frazer (*The Golden Bough*). On the other hand, serious difficulties arise if we assume that every animal sacrificed represents a deity; and even assuming that such a belief underlies the rite of animal sacrifice, a modification of the belief must have been introduced when such sacrifices became a common rite resorted to on every occasion when a deity was to be approached. It is manifestly impossible to assume, *e.g.* that the daily sacrifices which form a feature of advanced cults involved the belief of the daily slaughter of some deity, and even before this stage was reached the primitive belief of the actual identification of the god with the animal must have yielded to some such belief as that the deity in accepting the sacrifice assimilates the animal to his own being, precisely as man assimilates the food that enters into his body. The animal is in a certain sense, indeed, the food of the god.

The theory underlying hepatoscopy therefore consists of these two factors: the belief (1) that the liver is the seat of life, or, to put it more succinctly, what was currently regarded as the soul of the animal; and (2) that the liver of the sacrificial animal, by virtue of its acceptance on the part of the god, took on the same character as the soul of the god to whom it was offered. The two souls acted in accord, the soul of the animal becoming a reflection, as it were, of the soul of the god. If, therefore, one understood the signs noted on a particular liver, one entered, as it were, into the mind—as one of the manifestations of soul-life—of the deity who had assimilated the being of the animal to his own being. To know the mind of the god was equivalent to knowing what the god in question proposed to do. Hence, when one approached a deity with an inquiry as to the outcome of some undertaking, the reading of the signs on the liver afforded a direct means of determining the course of future events, which was, according to current beliefs, in the control of the gods. That there are defects in the logical process as here outlined to account for the curious rite constitutes no valid objection to the theory advanced, for, in the first place, primitive logic in matters of belief is inherently defective and even contradictory, and, secondly, the strong desire to pierce the mysterious future, forming an impelling factor in all religions—even in the most advanced of our own day—would tend to obscure the weakness of any theory developed to explain a rite which represents merely one endeavour among many to divine the intention and plans of the gods, upon the knowledge of which so much of man's happiness and welfare depended.

Passing now to typical examples, the beginning must be made with Babylonia, which is also the richest source of our knowledge of the details of the rite. Hepatoscopy in the Euphrates valley can be traced back to the 3rd millennium before our era, which may be taken as sufficient evidence for its survival from the period of primitive culture, while the supreme importance attached to signs read on the livers of sacrificial animals—usually a sheep—follows from the care with which omens derived from such inspection on occasions of historical significance were preserved as guides to later generations of priests. Thus we have a collection of the signs noted during the career of Sargon I. of Agade (*c.* 2800 B.C.), which in some way were handed down till the days of the Assyrian king Assur-bani-pal (668-626 B.C.). One of the chief names for the priest was *bârû*—literally the "inspector"—which was given to him because of the prominence of his function as an inspector of livers for the purpose of divining the intention of the gods. It is to the collections formed by these *bârû*-priests as a guidance for themselves and as a basis of instruction for those in training for the priesthood that we owe our knowledge of the parts of the liver to which particular attention was directed, of the signs noted, and of the principles guiding the interpretation of the signs.

The inspection of the liver for purposes of divination led to the study of the anatomy of the liver, and there are indeed good reasons for believing that hepatoscopy represents the starting-point for the study of animal anatomy in general. We find in the Babylonian-Assyrian omen-texts special designations for the three main lobes of the sheep's liver—the *lobus dexter*, the *lobus sinister* and the *lobus caudatus*; the first-named being called "the right wing of the liver," the second "the left wing of the liver," and the third "the middle of the liver." Whether the division of the *lobus dexter* into two divisions—(1) *lobus dexter* proper and (2) *lobus quadratus*, as in modern anatomical nomenclature—was also assumed in Babylonian hepatoscopy, is not certain, but the groove separating the right lobe into two sections—the *fossa venae umbilicalis*—was recognized and distinguished by the designation of "river of the liver." The two appendixes attached to the upper lobe or *lobus pyramidalis*, and known in modern nomenclature as *processus pyramidalis* and *processus papillaris*, were described respectively as the "finger" of the liver and as the "offshoot." The former of these two appendixes plays an especially important part in hepatoscopy, and, according to its shape and peculiarities, furnishes a good or bad omen. The gall-bladder, appropriately designated as "the bitter," was regarded as a part of the liver, and the cystic duct (compared, apparently, to a "penis") to which it is joined, as well as the hepatic duct (pictured as an "outlet") and the *ductus choleductus* (described as a "yoke"), all had their special designations. The depression separating the two lower lobes from the *lobus caudatus*, and known as the *porta hepatis*, was appropriately designated as the "crucible" of the liver. Lastly, to pass over unnecessary details, the markings of various kinds to be observed on the lobes of the livers of freshly-slaughtered animals, which are due mainly to the traces left by the subsidiary hepatic ducts and hepatic veins on the liver surface, were described as "holes," "paths," "clubs" and the like. The constantly varying character of these markings, no two livers being alike in this respect, furnished a particularly large field for the fancy of the *bârû*-priest.

In the interpretation of these signs the two chief factors were association of ideas and association of words. If, for example, the *processus pyramidalis* was abnormally small and the *processus papillaris* abnormally large, it pointed to a reversion of the natural order, to wit, that the servant should control the master or that the son would be above the father. A long cystic duct would point to a long reign of the king. If the gall-bladder was swollen, it pointed to an extension or enlargement of some kind. If the *porta hepatis* was torn it prognosticated a plundering of the enemy's land. As among most people, a sign on the right side was favourable, but the sign on the left side unfavourable. If, for example, the *porta hepatis* was long on the right side and short on the left side, it was a good sign for the king's army, but if short on the right side and long on the left, it was unfavourable; and similarly for a whole series of phenomena connected with any one of the various subdivisions of the liver. Past experience constituted another important factor in establishing the interpretation of signs noted. If, for example, on a certain occasion when the liver of a sacrificial animal was examined, certain events of a favourable character followed, the conclusion was drawn that the signs observed were favourable, and hence the recurrence of these signs on another occasion suggested a favourable answer to the question put to the priests. With this in view, omens given in the reigns of prominent rulers were preserved with special care as guides to the priests.

In the course of time the collections of signs and their interpretation made by the *bârû*-priests grew in number until elaborate series were produced in which the endeavour was made to exhaust so far as possible all the varieties and modifications of the many signs, so as to furnish a complete handbook both for purposes of instruction and as a basis for the practical work of divination. Divination through the liver remained in force among the Assyrians and Babylonians down to the end of the Babylonian Empire.

Among the Greeks and Romans likewise it was the liver that continued throughout all periods to play the chief rôle in divination through the sacrificial animal. Blecher (*De Extispicio Capite Tria*, Giessen, 1905, pp. 3-22) has recently collected most of the references in Greek and Latin authors to animal divination, and an examination of these shows conclusively that, although the general term used for the inspection of the sacrificial animal was *iera* or *iereia* (i.e. "victims" or "sacred parts") in Greek, and *exta* in Latin, when *specific* illustrations are introduced, the reference is almost invariably to some sign or signs on the liver; and we have an interesting statement in Pliny (*Hist. Nat.* xi. § 186), furnishing the date (274 B.C.) when the examination of the heart was for the first time introduced by the side of the liver as a means of divining the future, while the lungs are not mentioned till we reach the days of Cicero (*de Divinatione*, i. 85). We are justified in concluding, therefore, that among the Greeks and Romans likewise the examination of the liver was the basis of divination in the case of the sacrificial animal. It is well known that the Romans borrowed their methods of hepatoscopy from the Etruscans, and, apart from the direct evidence for this in Latin writings, we have, in the case of the bronze model of a liver found near Piacenza in 1877, and of Etruscan origin, the unmistakable proof that among the Etruscans the examination of the liver was the basis of animal divination. Besides this object dating from about the 3rd century B.C., according to the latest investigator, G. Körte ("Die Bronzeleber von Piacenza," in *Mitt. d. K. D. Archaeol. Instituts*, 1905, xx. pp. 348-379), there are other Etruscan monuments, e.g. the figure of an Etruscan augur holding a liver in his hand as his trade-mark (Körte, *ib.* pl. xiv.), which point in the same direction, and indicate that the model of the liver was used as an object lesson to illustrate the method of divination through the liver. For further details the reader is referred to Thulin's monograph, *Die Etruskische Disciplin, II Die Haruspicin* (Gothenburg, 1906).

As for the Greeks, it is still an open question whether they perfected their method of hepatoscopy under Etruscan influence or through the Babylonians. In any case, since the Eastern origin of the Etruscans is now generally admitted, we may temporarily, at least, accept the conclusion that hepatoscopy as a method of divination owes its survival in advanced forms of culture to the elaborate system devised in the course of centuries by the Babylonian priests, and to the influence, direct and indirect, exerted by this system in the ancient world. But for this system hepatoscopy, the theoretic basis of which as above set forth falls within the sphere of ideas that belong to primitive culture, would have passed away as higher stages of civilization were reached; and as a matter of fact it plays no part in the Egyptian culture or in the civilization of India, while the liver as the seat of the soul are to be met with in the Old Testament, among which an allusion in the indirect form of a protest against the use of the sacrificial animal for purposes of divination in the ordinance (Exodus xxix. 13, 22; Leviticus iii. 4, 10, 15, &c.) to burn the *processus pyramidalis* of the liver, which played a particularly significant rôle in hepatoscopy, calls for special mention.

In modern times hepatoscopy still survives among primitive peoples in Borneo, Burma, Uganda, &c.

It but remains to call attention to the fact that the earlier view of the liver as the seat of the soul gave way among many ancient nations to the theory which, reflecting the growth of anatomical knowledge, assigned that function to the heart, while, with the further change which led to placing the seat of soul-life in the brain, an attempt was made to partition the various functions of manifestations of personality among the three organs, brain, heart and liver, the intellectual activity being assigned to the first-named, the higher emotions, as love and courage, to the second; while the liver, once the master of the entire domain of soul-life as understood in antiquity, was degraded to serve as the seat of the lower emotions, such as jealousy, anger and the like. This is substantially the view set forth in the *Timaeus* of Plato (§ 71 c). The addition of the heart to the liver as an organ of the revelation of the divine will, reflects the stage which assigned to the heart the position once occupied by the liver. By the time the third stage, which placed the seat of soul-life in the brain, was reached through the further advance of anatomical knowledge, the religious rites of Greece and Rome were too deeply incrusted to admit of further radical changes, and faith in the gods had already declined too far to bring new elements into the religion. In phrenology, however, as popularly carried on as an *unofficial* cult, we may recognize a modified form of divination, co-ordinate with the third stage in the development of beliefs regarding the seat of soul and based on the assumption that this organ is—as were its predecessors—a medium of revelation of otherwise hidden knowledge.

(M. JA.)

OMICHUND (d. 1767), an Indian whose name is indelibly associated with the treaty negotiated by Clive before the battle of Plassey in 1757. His real name was Amir Chand; and he was not a Bengali, as stated by Macaulay, but a Sikh from the Punjab. It is impossible now to unravel the intrigues in which he may have engaged, but some facts about his career can be stated. He had long been resident at Calcutta, where he had acquired a large fortune by providing the "Investment" for the Company, and also by acting as intermediary between the English and the native court at Murshidabad. In a letter of Mr Watts of later date he is represented as saying to the nawab (Suraj-ud-daula): "He had lived under the English protection these forty years; that he never knew them once to break their agreement, to the truth of which he took his oath by touching a Brahman's foot; and that if a lie could be proved in England upon any one, they were spit upon and never trusted." Several houses owned by him in Calcutta are mentioned in connexion with the fighting that preceded the tragedy of the Black Hole in 1756, and it is on record that he suffered heavy losses at that time. He had been arrested by the English on suspicion of treachery, but afterwards he was forward in giving help to the fugitives and also valuable advice. On the recapture of Calcutta he was sent by Clive to accompany Mr Watts as agent at Murshidabad. It seems to have been through his influence that the nawab gave reluctant consent to Clive's attack on Chandernagore. Later, when the treaty with Mir Jafar was being negotiated, he put in a claim for 5% on all the treasure to be recovered, under threat of disclosing the plot. To defeat him, two copies of the treaty were drawn up: the one, the true treaty, omitting his claim; the other containing it, to be shown to him, which Admiral Watson refused to sign, but Clive directed the admiral's signature to be appended. When the truth was revealed to Omichund after Plassey, Macaulay states (following Orme) that he sank gradually into idiocy, languished a few months, and then died. As a matter of fact, he survived for ten years, till 1767; and by his will he bequeathed £2000 to the Foundling Hospital (where his name may be seen in the list of benefactors as "a black merchant of Calcutta ") and also to the Magdalen Hospital in London. (J. S. Co.)

OMNIBUS (Lat. " for all "), a large closed public conveyance with seats for passengers inside and out (see CARRIAGE). The name, colloquially shortened to " bus," was, in the form *voiture omnibus*, first used for such conveyances in Paris in 1828, and was taken by Shillibeer for the vehicle he ran on the Paddington road in 1829. The word is also applied to a box at the opera which is shared by several subscribers, to a bill or act of parliament dealing with a variety of subjects, and in electrical engineering to the bar to which the terminals of the generators are attached and from which the current is taken off by the wires supplying the various consumers.

OMRI, in the Bible, the first great king of Israel after the separation of the two kingdoms of Israel and Judah, who flourished in the early part of the 9th century B.C. The dynasty of Jeroboam had been exterminated by Baasha (see ASA) at a revolt when the army was besieging the Philistines at Gibbethon, an unidentified Danite site. A quarter of a century later, Baasha's son Elah, after a reign of two years, was slain by Zimri, captain of the chariots, in a drinking bout, and again the royal family were put to the sword. Meanwhile, the general Omri, who was at Gibbethon, was promptly elected king by the army, and Zimri himself in a short while[1] met his death in the royal city of Tirzah. However, fresh disturbance was caused by Tibni ben Ginath (perhaps of Naphtali), and Israel was divided into rival factions. Ultimately Tibni and his brother Joram (1 Kings xvi. 22, LXX.) were overcome, and Omri remained in sole possession of the throne. The compiler of the biblical narratives takes little interest in Omri's work (1 Kings xvi. 15-28), and records briefly his purchase of Samaria, which became the capital of his dynasty (see SAMARIA). The inscription of Mesha throws welcome light upon his conquest of Moab (q.v.); the position of Israel during the reign of Omri's son Ahab (q.v.) bears testimony to the success of the father; and the fact that the land continued to be known to the Assyrians down to the time of Sargon as " house of Omri " indicates the reputation which this little-known king enjoyed. (S. A. C.)

OMSK, a town of Russia, capital of the province of Akmolinsk, capital of western Siberia from 1839 to 1882, and now capital of the general-governorship of the Steppes. Pop. (1881) 31,000, (1900) 53,050. It is the seat of administration of the Siberian Cossacks, and the see of the bishop of Omsk. Situated on the right bank of the Irtysh, at its confluence with the Om, at an altitude of 285 ft., and on the Siberian railway, 1862 m. via Chelyabinsk from Moscow, and 586 m. W.S.W. of Tomsk, it is the meeting-place of the highways to middle Russia, Orenburg and Turkestan. Steamers ply down the Irtysh and the Ob, and up the former to the Altai towns and Lake Zaisan. The climate is dry and relatively temperate, but marked by violent snow-storms and sand-storms. The average temperatures are, for the year, 31° F.; for January, 5°; for July, 68°; the annual rainfall is 12·4 in. The town is poorly built. Apart from the railway workshops, its industries are unimportant (steam saw-mill, tanneries); but the trade, especially since the construction of the railway, is growing. There are two yearly fairs. Omsk has a society for education, which organizes schools, kindergartens, libraries and lectures for the people. There are a corps of cadets, medical, dramatic and musical societies, and the west Siberian section of the Russian Geographical Society, with a museum.

The " fort " of Omsk was erected in 1716 to protect the block-houses on the Russian frontier, along the Ishim and the Irtysh. In consequence of the frequent incursions of the Kirghiz about the end of the 18th century, stronger earthworks were erected on the right bank of the Om; but these have now almost entirely disappeared.

ONAGRACEAE, in botany, an order of dicotyledons belonging to the series Myrtiflorae, to which belongs also the myrtle order, Myrtaceae. It contains about 36 genera and 300 species, and occurs chiefly in the temperate zone of the New World, especially on the Pacific side. It is represented in Britain by several species of *Epilobium* (willow-herb), *Circaea* (enchanter's nightshade), and *Ludwigia*, a small perennial herb very rare in boggy pools in Sussex and Hampshire. The plants are generally herbaceous, sometimes annual, as species of *Epilobium*, *Clarkia*, *Godetia*, or biennial, as *Oenothera biennis*—evening primrose—or sometimes become shrubby or arborescent, as Fuchsia (q.v.). The simple leaves are generally entire or inconspicuously toothed, and are alternate, opposite or whorled in arrangement; they are generally exstipulate, but small caducous stipules occur in Fuchsia, *Circaea* and other genera. The flowers are often solitary in the leaf-axils, as in many fuchsias, *Clarkia*, &c., or associated, as in *Epilobium* and *Oenothera*, in large showy terminal spikes or racemes; in *Circaea* the small white or red

[1] He is said to have reigned seven days, but the LXX. (B) in 1 Kings xvi. 15 read seven *years*. Further confusion is caused by the fact that the LXX. reads Zimri throughout for Omri.

flowers are borne in terminal and lateral racemes. The regular flowers have the parts in fours, the typical arrangement as illustrated by *Epilobium, Oenothera* and Fuchsia being as follows: 4 sepals, 4 petals, two alternating whorls of 4 stamens, and 4 inferior carpels. The floral receptacle is produced above the ovary into the so-called calyx-tube, which is often petaloid, as in Fuchsia, and is sharply distinguished from the ovary, from which it separates after flowering.

In *Clarkia* the inner whorl of stamens is often barren, and in an allied genus, *Eucharidium*, it is absent. In *Circaea* the flower has its parts

FIG. 1.—*Fuchsia coccinea* 1, Flower cut open after removal of sepals; 2, fruit; 3, floral diagram.

FIG. 2.—Floral diagram of *Circaea.*

in twos. Both sepals and petals are free; the former have a broad insertion, are valvate in bud, and reflexed in the flower; in Fuchsia they are petaloid. The petals have a narrow attachment, and are generally convolute in bud; they are entire (Fuchsia) or bilobed (*Epilobium*); in some species of Fuchsia they are small and scale-like, or absent (*F. apetala*). The stamens are free, and those of the inner whorl are generally shorter than those of the outer whorl. The flowers of *Lopezia* (Central America) have only one fertile stamen. The large spherical pollen grains are connected by viscid threads. The typically quadrilocular ovary contains numerous ovules on axile placentas; the 1-to-2-celled ovary of *Circaea* has a single ovule in each loculus. The long slender style has a capitate (Fuchsia), 4-rayed (*Oenothera, Epilobium*) or 4-notched (*Circaea*) stigma. The flowers, which have generally an attractive corolla and honey secreted by a swollen disk at the base of the style or on the lower part of the "calyx-tube," are adapted for pollination by insects, chiefly bees and lepidoptera; sometimes by night-flying insects when the flowers are pale and open towards evening, as in evening primrose. The fruit is generally a capsule splitting into 4 valves and leaving a central column on which the seeds are borne as in *Epilobium* and *Oenothera*—in the former the seeds are scattered by aid of a long tuft of silky hairs on the broader end. In Fuchsia the fruit is a berry, which is sometimes edible, and in *Circaea* a nut bearing recurved bristles. The seeds are exalbuminous. Several of

FIG. 3.
A. Young flower of *Epilobium hirsutum.* c, petals; f, inferior ovary; k, sepals; s, pedicel.
B, Fruit of *Epilobium* after dehiscence. w, outer wall; m, columella formed by the septa; se, seed with tufts of hairs.

From Vines' *Students' Text-Book of Botany*, by permission of Swan Sonnenschein & Co.

the genera are well known as garden plants, *e.g.* Fuchsia, *Oenothera, Clarkia* and *Godetia.* Evening primrose (*Oenothera biennis*), a native of North America, occurs apparently wild as a garden escape in Britain. *Jussieua* is a tropical genus of water- and marsh-herbs with well-developed aerating tissue.

ONATAS, a Greek sculptor of the time of the Persian wars, a member of the flourishing school of Aegina. Many of his works are mentioned by Pausanias; they included a Hermes carrying the ram, and a strange image of the Black Demeter made for the people of Phigalia; also some elaborate groups in bronze set up at Olympia and Delphi. For Hiero I., king of Syracuse, Onatas executed a votive chariot in bronze dedicated at Olympia. If we compare the descriptions of the works of Onatas given us by Pausanias with the well-known pediments of Aegina at Munich we shall find so close an agreement that we may safely take the pedimental figures as an index of the style of Onatas. They are manly, vigorous, athletic, showing great knowledge of the human form, but somewhat stiff and automaton-like.

ONEGA, the largest lake in Europe next to Ladoga, having an area of 3764 sq. m. It is situated in the government of Olonets in European Russia, and, discharging its waters by the Svir into Lake Ladoga, belongs to the system of the Neva. The lake basin extends north-west and south-east, the direction characteristic of the lakes of Finland and the line of glacier-scoring observed in that region. Between the northern and southern divisions of the lake there is a considerable difference: while the latter has a comparatively regular outline, and contains hardly any islands, the former splits up into a number of inlets, the largest being Povyenets Bay, and is crowded with islands (*e.g.* Klimetsk) and submerged rocks. It is thus the northern division which brings the coast-line up to 870 m. and causes the navigation of the lake to be so dangerous. The north-western shore between Petro-zavodsk and the mouth of the river Lumbosha consists of dark clay slates, generally arranged in horizontal strata and broken by protruding, parallel ridges of diorite, which extend far into the lake. The eastern shore, as far as the mouth of the Andoma, is for the most part alluvial, with outcroppings of granite and in one place (the mouth of the Pyalma) diorite and dolomite. To the south-east are sedimentary Devonian rocks, and the general level of the coast is broken by Mount Andoma and Cape Petro-pavlovskiy (160 ft. above the lake); to the south-west a quartz sandstone (used as a building and monumental stone in St Petersburg) forms a fairly bold rim. Lake Onega lies 115 ft. above the sea. The greatest depths, 318 to 408 ft., occur at the entrance to the double bay of Lishemsk and Unitsk. On the continuation of this line the depth exceeds 240 ft. in several places. In the middle of the lake the depth is 120 to 282 ft., and less than 120 ft. in the south. The lake is 145 m. long, with an average breadth of 50 m. The most important affluents, the Vodka, the Andoma and the Vytegra, come from the east. The Kumsa, a northern tributary, is sometimes represented as if it connected the lake with Lake Seg, but at the present time the latter drains to the White Sea. The Onega canal (45 m. long) was constructed in 1818-1851 along the southern shore in order to connect the Svir (and hence Lake Ladoga and the Baltic) with the Vytegra, which connects with the Volga. Lake Onega remains free from ice for 209 days in the year (middle of May to second week of December). The water is at its lowest level in the beginning of March; by June it has risen 2 ft. A considerable population is scattered along the shores of the lake, mainly occupied in the timber trade, fisheries and mining industries. Salmon, *palya* (a kind of trout), burbot, pike, perchpike and perch are among the fish caught in the lake. Steamboats were introduced in 1832.

The river Onega, which, after a course of 250 m., reaches the Gulf of Onega, an inlet of the White Sea, has no connexion with Lake Onega. At the mouth of this river (on the right bank) stands the town and port of Onega (pop. 2694 in 1897), which dates from settlements made by the people of Novgorod in the 15th century, and known in history as Ustenskaya or Ustyans-kaya. It has a cathedral, erected in 1796. (P. A. K.; J. T. Be.)

ONEIDA, a city of Madison county, New York, U.S.A., on Oneida Creek, about 6 m. S.E. of Oneida Lake, about 26 m. W. of Utica, and about 26 m. E.N.E. of Syracuse. Pop. (1890) 6083; (1900) 6364, of whom 784 were foreign-born; (1910, U.S. census) 8317. It is served by the New York Central & Hudson River, the New York, Ontario & Western, the West Shore and the Oneida (electric) railways .(the last connecting with Utica and Syracuse), and by the Erie Canal. The city lies about 440 ft. above the sea on a level site. Across Oneida Creek, to the south-east, in Oneida county, is the village of Oneida Castle (pop. in 1910, 303), situated in the township of Vernon (pop. in 1910, 3197), and the former gathering place of the Oneida Indians, some of whom still live in the township of Vernon and in the city of Oneida. In the south-eastern part of the city is the headquarters of the Oneida Community (*q v*), which controls important industries here, at Niagara Falls, and elsewhere. Immediately west of Oneida is the village of Wampsville (incorporated in 1908), the county-seat of Madison county. Among the manufactures of Oneida are wagons, cigars, furniture, caskets, silver-plated ware, engines and machinery, steel and wooden pulleys and chucks, steel grave vaults, hosiery; and milk bottle caps. In the vicinity the Oneida Community manufactures chains and animal traps. The site of Oneida was purchased in 1829-1830 by Sands Higinbotham, in honour of whom one of the municipal parks (the other is Allen Park) is named. Oneida was incorporated as a village in 1848 and chartered as a city in 1901.

ONEIDA (a corruption of their proper name *Oneyotka-ono*, " people of the stone," in allusion to the Oneida stone, a granite boulder near their former village, which was held sacred by them), a tribe of North American Indians of Iroquoian stock, forming one of the Six Nations. They lived around Oneida Lake in New York state, in the region southward to the Susquehanna. They were not loyal to the League's policy of friendliness to the English, but inclined towards the French, and were practically the only Iroquois who fought for the Americans in the War of Independence. As a consequence they were attacked by others of the Iroquois under Joseph Brant and took refuge within the American settlements till the war ended, when the majority returned to their former home, while some migrated to the Thames river district, Ontario. Early in the 19th century they sold their lands, and most of them settled on a reservation at Green Bay, Wisconsin, some few remaining in New York state. The tribe now numbers more than 3000, of whom about two-thirds are in Wisconsin, a few hundreds in New York state, and about 800 in Ontario. They are civilized and prosperous.

ONEIDA COMMUNITY (or Bible Communists), an American communistic society at Oneida, Madison county, New York, which has attracted wide interest on account of its pecuniary success and its peculiar religious and social principles (see COMMUNISM).

Its founder, John Humphrey Noyes (1811–1886), was born in Brattleboro, Vermont, on the 3rd of September 1811. He was of good parentage; his father, John Noyes (1763–1841), was a graduate of and for a time a tutor in Dartmouth College, and was a representative in Congress in 1815–1817; and his mother, Polly Hayes, was an aunt of Rutherford B. Hayes, president of the United States. The son graduated at Dartmouth in 1830, and studied law for a year, but having been converted in a protracted revival in 1831 he turned to the ministry, studied theology for one year at Andover. (where he was a member of " The Brethren," a secret society of students preparing for foreign missionary work, and in 1833 was licensed to preach by the New Haven Association; but his open preaching of his new religious doctrines, and especially that of present salvation from sin, resulted in the revocation of his license in 1834, and his thereafter being called a Perfectionist. He continued to promulgate his ideas of a higher Christian life, and soon had disciples in many places, one of whom, Harriet A. Holton, a woman of means, he married in 1838. In 1836 he returned to his father's home in Putney, Vt., and founded a Bible School; in 1843 he entered into

a " contract of Partnership " with his Putney followers; and in March 1845 the Putney Corporation or Association of Perfectionists was formed.

Although the Putney Corporation or Association was never a community in the sense of common-property ownership, yet it was practically a communal organization, and embodied the radical religious and social principles that subsequently gave such fame to the Oneida Community, of which it may justly be regarded as the beginning and precursor. These principles naturally excited the opposition of the churches in the small Vermont village where the Perfectionists resided, and indignation meetings against them were held; and although they resulted in no personal violence Mr Noyes and his followers considered it prudent to remove to a place where they were sure of more liberal treatment. They accordingly withdrew from Putney in 1847, and accepting the invitation of Jonathan Burt and others, settled near Oneida, Madison county, New York.

Here the community at first devoted itself to agriculture and fruit raising, but had little financial success until it began the manufacture of a steel trap, invented by one of its members, Sewall Newhouse; the manufacture of steel chains for use with the traps followed; the canning of vegetables and fruits was begun about 1854, and the manufacture of sewing and embroidery silk in 1866. Having started with a very small capital (the inventoried valuation of its property in 1857 was only $67,000), the community gradually grew in numbers and prospered as a business concern. Its relations with the surrounding population, after the first few years, became very friendly. The members won the reputation of being good, industrious citizens, whose word was always " as good as their bond "; against whom no charge of intemperance, profanity or crime was ever brought. But the communists claimed that among true Christians " mine and thine " in property matters should cease to exist, as among the early pentecostal believers; and, moreover, that the same unselfish spirit should pervade and control all human relations. And notwithstanding these very radical principles, which were freely propounded and discussed in their weekly paper, the communists were not seriously disturbed for a quarter of a century. But from 1873 to 1879 active measures favouring legislative action against the community, specially instigated by Prof. John W. Mears (1825–1881), were taken by several ecclesiastical bodies of Central New York. These measures culminated in a conference held at Syracuse University on the 14th of February 1879, when denunciatory resolutions against the community were passed and legal measures advised.

Mr Noyes, the founder and leader of the community, had repeatedly said to his followers that the time might come when it would be necessary, in deference to public opinion, to recede from the practical assertion of their social principles; and on the 20th of August of this year (1879) he said definitely to them that in his judgment that time had come, and he thereupon proposed that the community " give up the practice of Complex Marriage, not as renouncing belief in the principles and prospective finality of that institution, but in deference to public sentiment." This proposition was considered and accepted in full assembly of the community on the 26th of the same month. This great change was followed by other changes of vital importance, finally resulting in the transformation of the Oneida Community into the Incorporated Oneida Community, Limited, a co-operative joint-stock company, in which each person's interest was represented by the shares of stock standing in his name on the books of the company.

In the reorganization the adult members fared alike in the matter of remuneration for past services—those who by reason of ill-health had been unable to contribute to the common fund receiving the same as those who by reason of strength and ability had contributed most thereto; besides, the old and infirm had the option of accepting a life-guaranty in lieu of work; and hence there were no cases of suffering and want at the time, the transformation from a common-property interest to an individual stock interest was made; and in the new company all were guaranteed remunerative labour.

This occurred on the 1st of January 1881, at which time the business and property of the community were transferred to the incorporated stock company, and stock issued therefor to the amount of $600,000. In the subsequent twenty-eight years this capital stock was doubled, and dividends averaging more than 6% per annum were paid. Aside from the home buildings and the large acreage devoted to agriculture and fruit raising, the present capital of the company is invested, first, in its hardware department at Kenwood, N.Y., manufacturing steel game-traps, and weirless chains of every description; second, the silk department at Kenwood, N.Y., manufacturing sewing silk, machine twist and embroidery silks; third, the fruit department at Kenwood, N.Y., whose reputation for putting up pure, wholesome fruits and vegetables is probably the highest in the country; fourth, the tableware department, at Niagara Falls, N.Y., which manufactures the now celebrated Community Silver; fifth, the Canadian department, with factory at Niagara Falls, Ontario, Canada, where the hardware lines are manufactured for Canadian trade. The annual sales of all departments aggregate over $3,000,000. The officers of the company consist of a president, secretary, treasurer and assistant treasurer, and there were in 1909 eleven directors. Each of the five leading departments is managed by a superintendent, and all are under the supervision of the general manager. Nearly all the superintendents and the general manager were in 1909 young men who were born in the community, and have devoted their life-work to the interests of the company. Selling offices are maintained in New York City, Chicago, St Louis, Cleveland, O., Richmond, Va., Atlanta, Ga., and San Francisco.

In addition to the members of the society the company employs between 1500 and 2000 workmen. The policy has been to avoid trade-unions, but to pay higher wages and give better conditions than other employers in similar lines, and by so doing to obtain a better selection of workmen. The conditions of work as well as of living have been studied and developed with the idea of making both healthful and attractive. With this in view the company has laid out small villages, in many ways making them attractive and sanitary, and has encouraged the building of houses by its employés. Much has been accomplished in this direction by providing desirable building-sites at moderate expense, and paying a bonus of from $100 to $200 in cash to every employé who builds his own home. The company has also taken an interest in the schools in the vicinity of its factories, with the idea of offering to the children of its employés facilities for a good education.

The communism of John H. Noyes was based on his interpretation of the New Testament. In his pamphlet, Bible Communism (1848), he affirmed that the second coming of Christ occurred at the close of the apostolic age, immediately after the destruction of Jerusalem, and he argued from many New Testament passages, especially 1 John 1, 7, that after the second coming and the beginning of Christ's reign upon the earth, the true standard of Christian character was sinlessness, which was possible through vital union with Christ, that all selfishness was to be done away with, both in property in things and in persons, or, in other words, that communism was to be finally established in all the relations of life. But, while affirming that the same spirit which on the day of Pentecost abolished exclusiveness in regard to money tends to obliterate all other property distinctions, he had no affiliation with those commonly termed Free Lovers, because their principles and practices seemed to him to tend toward anarchy. "Our Communities," he said, "are families as distinctly bounded and separated from promiscuous society as ordinary households. The tie that binds us together is as permanent and sacred, to say the least, as that of common marriage, for it is our religion. We receive no new members (except by deception and mistake) who do not give heart and hand to the family interest for life and for ever. Community of property extends just as far as freedom of love. Every man's care and every dollar of the common property are pledged for the maintenance and protection of the women and the education of the children of the Community."

The community was much interested in the question of race improvement by scientific means, and maintained with much force of argument that at least as much scientific attention should be given to the physical improvement of human beings as is given to the improvement of domestic animals; and they referred to the results of their own incomplete stirpicultural experiments as indicative of what may be expected in the far future, when the conditions of human reproduction are no longer controlled by chance, social position, wealth, impulse or lust.

The community claimed to have solved among themselves the labour question, all kinds of service being regarded as equally honourable, and every person being respected according to his real character.

The members had some peculiarities of dress, mostly confined, however, to the women, whose costumes included a short dress and pantalets, which were appreciated for their convenience, if not for their beauty. The women also adopted the practice of wearing short hair, which it was claimed saved time and vanity. Tobacco, intoxicants, profanity, obscenity found no place in the community. The community diet consisted largely of vegetables and fruits; meat, tea and coffee being served only occasionally.

For securing good order and the improvement of the members, the community placed much reliance upon a very peculiar system of plain speaking they termed mutual criticism, which originated in a secret society of missionary brethren with which Mr Noyes was connected while pursuing his theological studies at Andover Seminary, and whose members submitted themselves in turn to the sincerest comment of one another as a means of personal improvement. Under Mr Noyes's supervision it became in the Oneida Community a principal means of discipline and government. There was a standing committee of criticism, selected by the community, and changed from time to time, thus giving all an opportunity to serve both as critics and subjects, and justifying the term "mutual" which they gave to the system. The subject was free to have others besides the committee present, or to have critics only of his own choice, or to invite an expression from the whole community.

Noyes edited The Perfectionist (New Haven, Connecticut, 1834, and Putney, Vermont, 1843-1846); The Witness (Ithaca, New York, and Putney, 1838-1843); The Spiritual Magazine (Putney, 1846-1847; Oneida, 1848-1850); The Free Church Circular (Oneida, 1850-1851); and virtually, though not always nominally, The Circular and The Oneida Circular (Brooklyn, 1851-1854; Oneida, N.Y., and Wallingford, Conn., 1854-1876); and The American Socialist (Oneida, 1876-1880). He was the author of The Way of Holiness (Putney, 1838); The Berean (Putney, 1847), containing an exposition of his doctrines of Salvation from Sin; the Second Coming of Christ; the Origin of Evil; the Atonement; the Second Birth; the Millennium; Our Relations to the Primitive Church, &c. &c.; History of American Socialism (Philadelphia, 1870); Home Talks (Oneida, 1876); and numerous pamphlets.

See a series of articles in the Manufacturer and Builder (New York, 1891-1894), by "C. R. Edson" (i.e. C. E. Robinson); The Oneida Community, by Allan Estlake (a member of the community) (1900); Morris Hillquit's History of Socialism in the United States (New York, 1903), and especially William A. Hinds' American Communities and Co-operative Colonies (3rd ed., Chicago, 1908). (W. A. H.)

O'NEILL, the name of an Irish family tracing descent from Niall, king of Ireland early in the 5th century, and known in Irish history and legend as Niall of the Nine Hostages. He is said to have made war not only against lesser rulers in Ireland, but also in Britain and Gaul, stories of his exploits being related in the Book of Leinster and the Book of Ballymote, both of which, however, are many centuries later than the time of Niall. This king had fourteen sons, one of whom was Eoghan (Owen), from whom the O'Neills of the later history were descended. The descendants of Niall spread over Ireland and became divided into two main branches, the northern and the southern Hy Neill, to one or other of which nearly all the high-kings (ard-ri) of Ireland from the 5th to the 12th century belonged; the descendants of Eoghan being the chief of the northern Hy Neill.[1] Eoghan was grandfather of Murkertagh (Muircheartach) (d. 533).

[1] A list of these kings will be found in P. W. Joyce's A Social History of Ancient Ireland (London, 1903), vol. i. pp. 70, 71.

said to have been the first Christian king of Ireland, whose mother, Eirc or Erca, became by a subsequent marriage the grandmother of St Columba. Of this monarch, known as Murkertagh MacNeill (Niall), and sometimes by reference to his mother as Murkertagh Mac Erca, the story is told, illustrating an ancient Celtic custom, that in making a league with a tribe in Meath he emphasized the inviolability of the treaty by having it written with the blood of both clans mixed in one vessel. Murkertagh was chief of the great north Irish clan, the Cinel Eoghain,[1] and after becoming king of Ireland about the year 517, he wrested from a neighbouring clan a tract of country in the modern County Derry, which remained till the 17th century in the possession of the Cinel Eoghain. The inauguration stone of the Irish kings, the Lia Fail, or Stone of Destiny, fabled to have been the pillow of the patriarch Jacob on the occasion of his dream of the heavenly ladder, was said to have been presented by Murkertagh to the king of Dalriada, by whom it was conveyed to Dunstaffnage Castle in Scotland (see Scone). A lineal descendant of Murkertagh was Niall Frassach (i.e. of the showers), who became king of Ireland in 763; his surname, of which several fanciful explanations have been suggested, probably commemorating merely weather of exceptional severity at his birth. His grandson, Niall (791–845), drove back the Vikings who in his time began to infest the coast of Donegal. Niall's son, Aedh (Hugh) Finnlaith, was father of Niall Glundubh (i.e. Niall of the black knee), one of the most famous of the early Irish kings, from whom the family surname of the O'Neills was derived. His brother Domhnall (Donnell) was king of Ailech, a district in Donegal and Derry; the royal palace, the ruined masonry of which is still to be seen, being on the summit of a hill 800 ft. high overlooking loughs Foyle and Swilly. On the death of Domhnall in 911 Niall Glundubh became king of Ailech, and he then attacked and defeated the king of Dalriada at Glarryford, in County Antrim, and the king of Ulidia near Ballymena. Having thus extended his dominion he became king of Ireland in 915. To him is attributed the revival of the ancient meeting of Irish clans known as the Fair of Telltown (see Ireland; Early History). He fought many battles against the Norsemen, in one of which he was killed in 919 at Kilmashoge, where his place of burial is still to be seen.

His son Murkertagh, who gained a great victory over the Norse in 926, is celebrated for his triumphant march round Ireland, the Moirthimchell Eireann, in which, starting from Portglenone on the Bann, he completed a circuit of the island at the head of his armed clan, returning with many captive kings and chieftains. From the dress of his followers in this expedition he was called "Murkertagh of the Leather Cloaks." The exploit was celebrated by Cormacan, the king's bard, in a poem that has been printed by the Irish Archaeological Society; and a number of Murkertagh's other deeds are related in the Book of Leinster. He was killed in battle against the Norse in 943, and was succeeded as king of Ailech by his son, Donnell Ua Niall (i.e. O'Neill, grandson of Neill, or Niall, the name O'Neill becoming about this time an hereditary family surname[2]), whose grandson, Flaherty, became renowned for piety by going on a pilgrimage to Rome in 1030.

Aedh (Hugh) O'Neill, chief of the Cinel Eoghain, or lord of Tir-Eoghain (Tir-Owen, Tyrone) at the end of the 11th century, was the first of the family to be brought prominently into conflict with the Anglo-Norman monarchy, whose pretensions he took the lead in disputing in Ulster. It was probably his son or nephew (for the relationship is uncertain, the genealogies of the O'Neills being rendered obscure by the contemporaneous occurrence of the same name in different branches of the family) Hugh O'Neill, lord of Tyrone, who was styled "Head of the liberality and valour of the Irish." Hugh's son, Brian, by gaining

the support of the earl of Ulster, was inaugurated[3] prince, or lord, of Tyrone in 1291; and his son Henry became lord of the Clann Aodha Buidhe (Clanaboy or Clandeboye) early in the 14th century. Henry's son Murkertagh the Strongminded, and his great-grandson Hugh, described as "the most renowned, hospitable and valorous of the princes of Ireland in his time," greatly consolidated the power of the O'Neills. Niall Og O'Neill, one of the four kings of Ireland, accepted knighthood from Richard II. of England; and his son Eoghan formally acknowledged the supremacy of the English crown, though he afterwards ravaged the Pale, and was inaugurated "the O'Neill" (i.e. chief of the clan) on the death of his kinsman Domhnall Boy O'Neill; a dignity from which he was deposed in 1455 by his son Henry, who in 1463 was acknowledged as chief of the Irish kings by Henry VII. of England. Contemporary with him was Neill Mor O'Neill (see below), lord of Clanaboy, from whose son Brian was descended the branch of the O'Neills who, settling in Portugal in the 18th century, became prominent among the Portuguese nobility, and who at the present day are the representatives in the male line of the ancient Irish kings of the house of O'Neill.

Conn O'Neill (c. 1480–1559), 1st earl of Tyrone, surnamed Bacach (the Lame), grandson of Henry O'Neill mentioned above, was the first of the O'Neills whom the attempts of the English in the 16th century to subjugate Ireland brought to the front as leaders of the native Irish. Conn, who was related through his mother with the earl of Kildare (Fitzgerald), became chief of the Tyrone branch of the O'Neills (Cinel Eoghain) about 1520. When Kildare became viceroy in 1524, O'Neill consented to act as his swordbearer in ceremonies of state; but his allegiance was not to be reckoned upon, and while ready enough to give verbal assurances of loyalty, he could not be persuaded to give hostages as security for his conduct; but Tyrone having been invaded in 1541 by Sir Anthony St Leger, the lord deputy, Conn delivered up his son as a hostage, attended a parliament held at Trim, and, crossing to England, made his submission at Greenwich to Henry VIII., who created him earl of Tyrone for life, and made him a present of money and a valuable gold chain. He was also made a privy councillor in Ireland, and received a grant of lands within the Pale. This event created a deep impression in Ireland, where O'Neill's submission to the English king, and his acceptance of an English title, were resented by his clansmen and dependents. The rest of the earl's life was mainly occupied by endeavours to maintain his influence, and by an undying feud with his son Shane (John), arising out of his transaction with Henry VIII. For not only did the nomination of O'Neill's reputed son Matthew as his heir with the title of baron of Dungannon by the English king conflict with the Irish custom of tanistry (q.v.) which regulated the chieftainship of the Irish clans, but Matthew, if indeed he was O'Neill's son at all, was illegitimate; while Shane, Conn's eldest legitimate son, was not the man to submit tamely to any invasion of his rights. The fierce family feud only terminated when Matthew was murdered by agents of Shane in 1558; Conn dying about a year later. Conn was twice married, Shane being the son of his first wife, a daughter of Hugh Boy O'Neill of Clanaboy. An illegitimate daughter of Conn married the celebrated Sorley Boy MacDonnell (q.s.).

Shane O'Neill (c. 1530–1567) was a chieftain whose support was worth gaining by the English even during his father's lifetime; but rejecting overtures from the earl of Sussex, the lord deputy, Shane refused to help the English against the Scottish settlers on the coast of Antrim, allying himself instead with the MacDonnells, the most powerful of these immigrants. Nevertheless Queen Elizabeth, on succeeding to the English throne, was disposed to come to terms with Shane, who after his father's death was de facto chief of the formidable O'Neill clan. She accordingly agreed to recognize his claims to the chieftainship, thus throwing over Brian O'Neill, son of the murdered Matthew,

---

[1] The Cinel, or Kinel, was a group of related clans occupying an extensive district. See Joyce, op. cit. i. 166.

[2] The adoption of hereditary names became general in Ireland, in obedience, it is said, to an ordinance of Brian Boru, about the end of the 10th century. For the method of their formation see Joyce, op. cit. ii. 19.

[3] The ceremony of "inauguration" among the ancient Irish clans was an elaborate and important one. A stone inauguration chair of the O'Neills is preserved in the Belfast Museum. See Joyce, op. cit. i. 46.

baron of Dungannon, if Shane would submit to her authority and that of her deputy. O'Neill, however, refused to put himself in the power of Sussex without a guarantee for his safety; and his claims in other respects were so exacting that Elizabeth consented to measures being taken to subdue him and to restore Brian. An attempt to foment the enmity of the O'Donnells against him was frustrated by Shane's capture of Calvagh O'Donnell, whom he kept a close prisoner for nearly three years. Elizabeth, whose prudence and parsimony were averse to so formidable an undertaking as the complete subjugation of the powerful Irish chieftain, desired peace with him at almost any price; especially when the devastation of his territory by Sussex brought him no nearer to submission. Sussex, indignant at Shane's request for his sister's hand in marriage, and his demand for the withdrawal of the English garrison from Armagh, was not supported by the queen, who sent the earl of Kildare to arrange terms with O'Neill. The latter, making some trifling concessions, consented to present himself before Elizabeth. Accompanied by Ormonde and Kildare he reached London on the 4th of January 1562. Camden describes the wonder with which O'Neill's wild gallowglasses were seen in the English capital, with their heads bare, their long hair falling over their shoulders and clipped short in front above the eyes, and clothed in rough yellow shirts. Elizabeth was less concerned with the respective claims of Brian and Shane, the one resting on an English patent and the other on the Celtic custom, than with the question of policy involved in supporting or rejecting the demands of her proud suppliant. Characteristically, she temporized; but finding that O'Neill was in danger of becoming a tool in the hands of Spanish intriguers, she permitted him to return to Ireland, recognizing him as " the O'Neill," and chieftain of Tyrone; though a reservation was made of the rights of Hugh O'Neill, who had meantime succeeded his brother Brian as baron of Dungannon, Brian having been murdered in April 1562 by his kinsman Turlough Luineach O'Neill.

There were at this time three powerful contemporary members of the O'Neill family in Ireland—Shane, Turlough and Hugh, 2nd earl of Tyrone. Turlough had been elected tanist (see TANISTRY) when his cousin Shane was inaugurated the O'Neill, and he schemed to supplant him in the higher dignity during Shane's absence in London. The feud did not long survive Shane's return to Ireland, where he quickly re-established his authority, and in spite of Sussex renewed his turbulent tribal warfare against the O'Donnells and others. Elizabeth at last authorized Sussex to take the field against Shane, but two several expeditions failed to accomplish anything except some depredation in O'Neill's country. Sussex had tried in 1561 to procure Shane's assassination, and Shane now laid the whole blame for his lawless conduct on the lord deputy's repeated alleged attempts on his life. Force having ignominiously failed, Elizabeth consented to treat, and hostilities were stopped on terms that gave O'Neill practically the whole of his demands. O'Neill now turned his hand against the MacDonnells, claiming that he was serving the queen of England in harrying the Scots. He fought an indecisive battle with Sorley Boy MacDonnell near Coleraine in 1564, and the following year marched from Antrim through the mountains by Clogh to the neighbourhood of Ballycastle, where he routed the MacDonnells and took Sorley Boy prisoner. This victory greatly strengthened Shane O'Neill's position, and Sir Henry Sidney, who became lord deputy in 1566, declared to the earl of Leicester that Lucifer himself was not more puffed up with pride and ambition than O'Neill. Preparations were made in earnest for his subjugation. O'Neill ravaged the Pale, failed in an attempt on Dundalk, made a truce with the MacDonnells, and sought help from the earl of Desmond. The English, on the other hand, invaded Donegal and restored O'Donnell. Failing in an attempt to arrange terms, and also in obtaining the help which he solicited from France, O'Neill was utterly routed by the O'Donnells at Letterkenny; and seeking safety in flight, he threw himself on the mercy of his enemies, the MacDonnells. Attended by a small body of gallowglasses, and taking his prisoner Sorley Boy with

him, he presented himself among the MacDonnells near Cushendun, on the Antrim coast. Here, on the 2nd of June 1567, whether by premeditated treachery or in a sudden brawl is uncertain, he was slain by the MacDonnells, and was buried at Glenarm. In his private character Shane O'Neill was a brutal, uneducated savage. He divorced his first wife, a daughter of James MacDonnell, and treated his second, a sister of Calvagh O'Donnell, with gross cruelty in revenge for her brother's hostility; Calvagh himself, when Shane's prisoner, he subjected to continual torture; and Calvagh's wife, whom he made his mistress, and by whom he had several children, endured ill-usage at the hands of her drunken captor, who is said to have married her in 1565.

TURLOUGH LUINEACH O'NEILL (c. 1530-1595), earl of Clanconnell, was inaugurated chief of Tyrone on Shane's death. Making professions of loyalty to the queen of England, be sought to strengthen his position by alliance with the O'Donnells, MacDonnells and MacQuillans. But his conduct giving rise to suspicions, an expedition under the earl of Essex was sent against him, which met with such doubtful success that in 1575 a treaty was arranged by which O'Neill received extensive grants of lands and permission to employ three hundred Scottish mercenaries. In 1578 he was created baron of Clogher and earl of Clanconnell for life; but on the outbreak of rebellion in Munster his attitude again became menacing, and for the next few years he continued to intrigue against the English authorities. The latter, as a counterpoise to Turlough, supported his cousin Hugh, brother of Brian, whom Turlough had murdered. After several years of rivalry and much fighting between the two relatives, Turlough resigned the headship of the clan in favour of Hugh, who was inaugurated O'Neill in 1593. Turlough died in 1595.

HUGH O'NEILL (c. 1540-1616), 2nd earl (known as the great earl) of Tyrone, was the second son of Matthew, reputed illegitimate son of Conn, 1st earl of Tyrone.[1] He succeeded his brother, Brian, when the latter was murdered by Turlough in 1562, as baron of Dungannon. He was brought up in London, but returned to Ireland in 1567 after the death of Shane, under the protection of Sir Henry Sidney. He served with the English against Desmond in Munster in 1580, and assisted Sir John Perrot against the Scots of Ulster in 1584. In the following year he was allowed to attend parliament as earl of Tyrone, though Conn's title had been for life only, and had not been assumed by Brian. Hugh's constant disputes with Turlough were fomented by the English with a view to weakening the power of the O'Neills, but after Hugh's inauguration as the O'Neill on Turlough's resignation in 1593, he was left without a rival in the north. His career was marked by unceasing duplicity, at one time giving evidence of submission to the English authorities, at another intriguing against them in conjunction with lesser Irish chieftains. Having roused the ire of Sir Henry Bagnal (or Bagenal) by eloping with his sister in 1591, he afterwards assisted him in defeating Hugh Maguire at Belleek in 1593; and then again went into opposition and sought aid from Spain and Scotland. Sir John Norris was accordingly ordered to Ireland with a considerable force to subdue him in 1595, but Tyrone succeeded in taking the Blackwater Fort and Sligo Castle before Norris was prepared; and he was thereupon proclaimed a traitor at Dundalk. In spite of the traditional enmity between the O'Neills and the O'Donnells, Tyrone allied himself with Hugh Roe O'Donnell, nephew of Shane's former enemy Calvagh O'Donnell, and the two chieftains opened communications with Philip II. of Spain, their letters to whom were intercepted by the viceroy, Sir William Russell. They put themselves forward as the champions of the Catholic religion, claiming liberty of conscience as well as political liberty for the native inhabitants of Ireland. In April 1596 Tyrone received promises of help from Spain. This increased his anxiety to temporize, which he did with signal success for more than two years, making

[1] The grave doubt as to the paternity of Matthew involved a doubt whether the great earl of Tyrone and his equally famous nephew Owen Roe had in fact any O'Neill blood in their veins.

from time to time as circumstances required, professions of loyalty which deceived Sir John Norris and the earl of Ormonde. In 1598 a cessation of hostilities was arranged, and a formal pardon granted to Tyrone by Elizabeth. Within two months he was again in the field, and on the 14th of August he destroyed an English force under Bagnal at the Yellow Ford on the Blackwater. If the earl had known how to profit by this victory, he might now have successfully withstood the English power in Ireland; for in every part of Ireland—and especially in the south, where James Fitzthomas Fitzgerald with O'Neill's support was asserting his claim to the earldom of Desmond at the head of a formidable army of Geraldine clansmen—discontent broke into flame. But Tyrone, who possessed but little generalship, procrastinated until the golden opportunity was lost. Eight months after the battle of the Yellow Ford, the earl of Essex landed in Ireland to find that Tyrone had done nothing in the interval to improve his position. Acting on the queen's explicit instructions, Essex, after some ill-managed operations, had a meeting with Tyrone at a ford on the Lagan on th 7th of September 1599, when a truce was arranged; but Elizabeth was displeased by the favourable conditions allowed to the O'Neill and by Essex's treatment of him as an equal. Tyrone continued to concert measures with the Irish leaders in Munster, and issued a manifesto to the Catholics of Ireland summoning them to join his standard; protesting that the interests of religion were his first care. After an inconclusive campaign in Munster in January 1600, he returned in haste to Donegal, where he received supplies from Spain and a token of encouragement from Pope Clement VIII. In May of the same year Sir Henry Docwra, at the head of a considerable army, took up a position at Derry, while Mountjoy marched from Westmeath to Newry to support him, compelling O'Neill to retire to Armagh, a large reward having been offered for his capture alive or dead.

The appearance of a Spanish fleet at Kinsale drew Mountjoy to Munster in 1601; Tyrone followed him, and at Bandon joined forces with O'Donnell and with the Spaniards under Don John D'Aquila. The attack of these allies on the English completely failed. O'Donnell went to Spain, where he died soon afterwards, and Tyrone with a shattered force made his way once more to the north, where he renewed his policy of ostensibly seeking pardon while warily evading his enemies. Early in 1603 Elizabeth instructed Mountjoy to open negotiations with the rebellious chieftains; and in April, Tyrone, in ignorance of Elizabeth's death, made his submission to Mountjoy. In Dublin, whither he proceeded with Mountjoy, he heard of the accession of King James, at whose court he presented himself in June accompanied by Rory O'Donnell, who had become chief of the O'Donnells after the departure of his brother Hugh Roe. The English courtiers were greatly incensed at the gracious reception accorded to these notable rebels by King James; but although Tyrone was confirmed in his title and estates, he had no sooner returned to Ireland than he again engaged in dispute with the government concerning his rights over certain of his feudatories, of whom Donnal O'Cahan was the most important. This dispute dragged on till 1607, when Tyrone arranged to go to London to submit the matter to the king. Warned, however, that his arrest was imminent, and possibly persuaded by Rory O'Donnell (created earl of Tyrconnel in 1603), whose relations with Spain had endangered his own safety, Tyrone resolved to fly from the country.

"The flight of the earls," one of the most celebrated episodes in Irish history, occurred on the 14th of September 1607, when Tyrone and Tyrconnel embarked at midnight at Rathmullen on Lough Swilly, with their wives, families and retainers, numbering ninety-nine persons, and sailed for Spain. Driven by contrary winds to take shelter in the Seine, the refugees passed the winter in the Netherlands, and in April 1608 proceeded to Rome, where they were welcomed and hospitably entertained by Pope Paul V., and where Tyrconnel died the same year. In 1613 Tyrone was outlawed and attainted by the Irish parliament, and he died in Rome on the 20th of July 1616. He was four times married, and had a large number both of legitimate and illegitimate children.

SIR PHELIM O'NEILL (c. 1603–1653), a kinsman and younger contemporary of the earl of Tyrone, took a prominent part in the rebellion of 1641. In that year he was elected member of the Irish parliament for Dungannon, and joined the earl of Antrim and other lords in concerting measures for supporting Charles I. in his struggle with the parliament. On the 22nd of October 1641 he surprised and captured Charlemont Castle; and having been chosen commander-in-chief of the Irish forces in the north, he forged and issued a pretended commission from Charles I. sanctioning his proceedings. Phelim and his followers committed much depredation in Ulster on the pretext of reducing the Scots; and he attempted without success to take Drogheda, being compelled by Ormonde to raise the siege in April 1642. He was responsible for many of the barbarities committed by the Catholics during the rebellion.[1] During the summer his fortunes ebbed, and he was soon superseded by his kinsman Owen Roe O'Neill, who returned from military service abroad at the end of July.

OWEN ROE O'NEILL (c. 1590–1649), one of the most celebrated of the O'Neills, the subject of the well-known ballad "The Lament for Owen Roe," was the son of Art O'Neill, a younger brother of Hugh, 2nd earl of Tyrone. Having served with distinction for many years in the Spanish army, he was immediately recognized on his return to Ireland as the leading representative of the O'Neills. Phelim resigned the northern command in his favour, and escorted him from Lough Swilly to Charlemont. But jealousy between the kinsmen was complicated by differences between Owen Roe and the Catholic council which met at Kilkenny in October 1642. Owen Roe professed to be acting in the interest of Charles I.; but his real aim was the complete independence of Ireland, while the Anglo-Norman Catholics represented by the council desired to secure religious liberty and an Irish constitution under the crown of England. Although Owen Roe O'Neill possessed the qualities of a general, the struggle dragged on inconclusively for three or four years. In March 1646 a cessation of hostilities was arranged between Ormonde and the Catholics; and O'Neill, furnished with supplies by the papal nuncio, Rinuccini, turned against the Scottish parliamentary army under General Monro, who had been operating with fluctuating success in Ireland since April 1642. On the 5th of June 1646 O'Neill utterly routed Monro at Benburb, on the Blackwater; but, being summoned to the south by Rinuccini, he failed to take advantage of the victory, and suffered Monro to remain unmolested at Carrickfergus. For the next two years confusion reigned supreme among the numerous factions in Ireland, O'Neill supporting the party led by Rinuccini, though continuing to profess loyalty to Ormonde as the king of England's representative. Isolated by the departure of the papal nuncio from Ireland in February 1649, he made overtures for alliance to Ormonde, and afterwards with success to Monck, who had superseded Monro in command of the parliamentarians in the north. O'Neill's chief need was supplies for his forces, and failing to obtain them from Monck he turned once more to Ormonde, and the Catholic confederates, with whom he prepared to co-operate more earnestly when Cromwell's arrival in Ireland in August 1649 brought the Catholic party face to face with serious danger. Before, however, anything was accomplished by this combination, Owen Roe died on the 6th of November 1649.

The alliance between Owen Roe and Ormonde had been opposed by Phelim O'Neill, who after his kinsman's death expected to be restored to his former position of command. In this he was disappointed; but he continued to fight against the parliamentarians till August 1652, when a reward was offered for his apprehension. Betrayed by a kinsman while hiding in Tyrone, he was tried for high treason in Dublin, and executed on the 10th of March 1653. Phelim married a daughter of the marquis of Huntly, by whom he had a son Gordon O'Neill, who was member of parliament for Tyrone in 1689; fought for the king at the siege of Derry and at the battles of Aughrim and the

[1] See W. E. H. Lecky, Hist. of Ireland in the Eighteenth Century, i. 66-68 (Cabinet edition, 5 vols., London, 1892).

Boyne; and afterwards commanded an Irish regiment in the French service, and died in 1704.

DANIEL O'NEILL (c. 1612–1664), son of Conn MacNeill MacFagartach O'Neill, a member of the Clanaboy branch of the family, whose wife was a sister of Owen Roe, was prominent in the Civil Wars. He spent much of his early life at the court of Charles I., and became a Protestant. He commanded a troop of horse in Scotland in 1639; was involved in army plots in 1641, for which he was committed to the Tower, but escaped abroad; and on the outbreak of the Civil War returned to England and served with Prince Rupert, being present at Marston Moor, the second battle of Newbury and Naseby. He then went to Ireland to negotiate between Ormonde and his uncle, Owen Roe O'Neill. He was made a major-general in 1649, and but for his Protestantism would have succeeded Owen Roe as chief of the O'Neills. He joined Charles II. at the Hague, and took part in the expedition to Scotland and the Scotch invasion of England in 1652. At the Restoration he received many marks of favour from the king, including grants of land and lucrative monopolies. He died in 1664.

HUGH O'NEILL (d. c. 1660), son of Owen Roe's brother Art Oge, and therefore known as Hugh Mac Art, had served with some distinction in Spain before he accompanied his uncle, Owen Roe, to Ireland in 1642. In 1646 he was made a major-general of the forces commanded by Owen Roe; and after the death of the latter he successfully defended Clonmel in 1650 against Cromwell, on whom he inflicted the latter's most severe defeat in Ireland. In the following year he so stubbornly resisted Ireton's attack on Limerick that he was excepted from the benefit of the capitulation, and, after being condemned to death and reprieved, was sent as a prisoner to the Tower of London. Released in 1652 on the representation of the Spanish ambassador that O'Neill was a Spanish subject, he repaired to Spain, whence he wrote to Charles II. in 1660 claiming the earldom of Tyrone. He probably died in Spain, but the date of his death is unknown.

The Clanaboy (or Clandeboye) branch of the O'Neills descended from the ancient kings through Neill Mor O'Neill, lord of Clanaboy in the time of Henry VIII., ancestor (as mentioned above) of the Portuguese O'Neills. Neill Mor's great-great-grandson, Henry O'Neill, was created baronet of Killeleagh in 1666. His son, Sir Neill O'Neill fought for James II. in Ireland, and died of wounds received at the battle of the Boyne. Through an elder line from Neill Mor was descended Brian Mac Phelim O'Neill, who was treacherously seized in 1573 by the earl of Essex, whom he was hospitably entertaining, and executed together with his wife and brother, some two hundred of his clan being at the same time massacred by the orders of Essex. (See ESSEX, WALTER DEVEREUX, 1st earl of.) Sir Brian Mac Phelim's son, Shane Mac Brian O'Neill, was the last lord of Clanaboy, and from him the family castle of Edenduffcarrick, on the shore of Lough Neagh in Co. Antrim, was named Shane's Castle. He joined the rebellion of his kinsman Hugh, earl of Tyrone, but submitted in 1586.

In the 18th century the commanding importance of the O'Neills in Irish history had come to an end. But John O'Neill (1740–1798), who represented Randalstown in the Irish parliament 1761–1783, and the county of Antrim from the latter year till his death, took an active part in debate on the popular side, being a strong supporter of Catholic emancipation. He was one of the delegates in 1789 from the Irish parliament to George, prince of Wales, requesting him to assume the regency as a matter of right. In 1793 he was raised to the peerage of Ireland as Baron O'Neill of Shane's Castle, and in 1795 was created a viscount. In defending the town of Antrim against the rebels in 1798 O'Neill received wounds from which he died on the 18th of June, being succeeded as Viscount O'Neill by his son Charles Henry St John (1779–1841), who in 1800 was created Earl O'Neill. Dying unmarried, when the earldom therefore became extinct, Charles was succeeded as Viscount O'Neill by his brother John Bruce Richard (1780–1855), a general in the British army; on whose death without issue in 1855 the male line in the United Kingdom became extinct. The estates then devolved on William Chichester, great-grandson of Arthur Chichester and his wife Mary, only child and heiress of Henry (d. 1721), eldest son of John O'Neill of Shane's Castle.

WILLIAM CHICHESTER (1813–1883), 1st Baron O'Neill, a clergyman, on succeeding to the estates as heir-general, assumed by royal licence the surname and arms of O'Neill; and in 1868 was created Baron O'Neill of Shane's Castle. On his death in 1883 he was succeeded by his son Edward, 2nd Baron O'Neill (b. 1839), who was member of parliament for Co. Antrim 1863–1880, and who married in 1873 Louisa, daughter of the 11th earl of Dundonald.

For the history of the ancient Irish kings of the Hy Neill see: The Book of Leinster, edited with introduction by R. Atkinson (Royal Irish Academy, Dublin, 1880); The Annals of Ulster, edited by W. M. Hennessy and B. MacCarthy (4 vols., Dublin, 1887–1901); The Annals of Loch Cé, edited by W. M. Hennessy (Rolls Series, London, 1871). For the later period see: P. W. Joyce, A Short History of Ireland (London, 1893), and A Social History of Ancient Ireland (2 vols., London, 1903); The Annals of Ireland by the Four Masters, edited by J. O'Donovan (7 vols., Dublin, 1851); Sir J. T. Gilbert, History of the Viceroys of Ireland (Dublin, 1865), and, especially for Owen Roe O'Neill, Contemporary History of Affairs in Ireland, 1641–1652 (Irish Archaeol. Soc., 3 vols., Dublin, 1879); also History of the Irish Confederation and the War in Ireland (Dublin, 1882); John O'Hart, Irish Pedigrees (Dublin, 1881); The Montgomery MSS. "The Flight of the Earls, 1607" (p. 767), edited by George Hill (Belfast, 1878); Thomas Carte, History of the Life of James, Duke of Ormonde (3 vols., London, 1735); C. P. Meehan, Fate and Fortunes of Hugh O'Neill, Earl of Tyrone, and Rory O'Donel, Earl of Tyrconnel (Dublin, 1886); Richard Bagwell, Ireland under the Tudors, with an Account of the Earlier History (3 vols., London, 1885–1890); J. F. Taylor, Owen Roe O'Neill (London, 1896); John Mitchell, Life and Times of Hugh, Earl of Tyrone, with an Account of his Predecessors, Con, Shane, Turlough (Dublin, 1846); L. O'Clery, Life of Hugh Roe O'Donnell (Dublin, 1893). For the O'Neills of the 18th century, and especially the 1st Viscount O'Neill, see The Charlemont Papers, and F. Hardy, Memoirs of J. Caulfield, Earl of Charlemont (2 vols., London, 1812). The O'Neills of Ulster: Their History and Genealogy, by Thomas Mathews (3 vols., Dublin, 1907), an ill-arranged and uncritical work, has little historical value, but contains a mass of traditional and legendary lore, and a number of translations of ancient poems, and genealogical tables of doubtful authority.   (R. J. M.)

O'NEILL, ELIZA (1791–1872), Irish actress, was the daughter of an actor and stage manager. Her first appearance on the stage was made at the Crow Street theatre in 1811 as the Widow Cheerly in The Soldier's Daughter, and after several years in Ireland she came to London and made an immediate success as Juliet at Covent Garden in 1814. For five years she was the favourite of the town in comedy as well as tragedy, but in the latter she particularly excelled, being frequently compared, not to her disadvantage, with Mrs Siddons. In 1819 she married William Wrixon Becher, an Irish M.P. who was created a baronet in 1831. She never returned to the stage, and died on the 29th of October 1872.

ONEONTA, a city in the township of the same name, in the south-central part of Otsego county, New York, U.S.A., on the N. side of the Susquehanna river, about 82 m. S.W. of Albany. Pop. (1880) 3002, (1890) 6272, (1900) 7147, of whom 456 were foreign-born, (1910, U.S. census) 9491. The city lies about 1100 ft. above sea-level. It is served by the Ulster & Delaware, by the Susquehanna division of the Delaware & Hudson, and by the Oneonta & Mohawk Valley (electric) railways. In Oneonta are a state normal school (1889), a state armoury, and the Aurelia Fox Memorial Hospital. The city is situated in a good agricultural region. The principal manufactures are machine-shop products (the Delaware & Hudson has repair and machine shops at Oneonta), knit goods, silk goods, lumber and planing mill products, &c. The first settlement was made about 1780. The township was erected in 1830 from parts of Milford and Otego. Oneonta was known as Milfordville until 1830, when it received its present name. It was first incorporated as a village in 1848, and was chartered as a city in 1908, the charter coming into effect on the 1st of January 1909. The name "Oneonta" is derived from Onahrenton or Onarenta, the Indian name of a creek flowing through the city.

See Edwin F. Bacon, Otsego County, N.Y. (Oneonta, 1902); and Dudley M. Campbell, A History of Oneonta (Oneonta, 1906).

ONESICRITUS, or **ONESICRATES**, of Aegina or Astypalaea (probably simply the "old city" of Aegina), one of the writers on Alexander the Great. At an advanced age he became a pupil of Diogenes the Cynic, and gained such repute as a student of philosophy that he was selected by Alexander to hold a conference with the Indian Gymnosophists. When the fleet was constructed on the Hydaspes, Onesicritus was appointed chief pilot (in his vanity he calls himself commander), and in this capacity accompanied Nearchus on the voyage from the mouth of the Indus to the Persian gulf. He wrote a diffuse biography of Alexander, which in addition to historical details contained descriptions of the countries visited, especially India. After the king's death, Onesicritus appears to have completed his work at the court of Lysimachus, king of Thrace. Its historical value was considered small, it being avowedly a panegyric, and contemporaries (including even Alexander himself) regarded it as untrustworthy. Strabo especially takes Onesicritus to task for his exaggeration and love of the marvellous. His *Paraplus* (or description of the coasts of India) probably formed part of the work, and, incorporated by Juba II. of Mauretania with the accounts of coasting voyages by Nearchus and other geographers, and circulated by him under the name of Onesicritus, was largely used by Pliny.

See Arrian, *Anabasis*, vi. 2; *Indica*, 32; Diogenes Laërtius vi. 75; Plutarch, *Alexander*, 46, 65; Strabo xv. 698; Pliny, *Nat. Hist.* vi. 26; Aulus Gellius ix. 4; fragments and life in C. W. Müller, appendix to F. Dübner's *Arrian* (1846); monograph by F. Lilie (Bonn, 1864); E. H. Bunbury, *Hist. of Ancient Geography*, i. (1879); Meier in Ersch and Gruber's *Allgemeine Encyclopädie.*

ONION (Fr. *oignon*, Lat. *unio*, literally unity, oneness, applied to a large pearl and to a species of onion), *Allium Cepa* (nat. ord. Liliaceae), a hardy bulbous biennial, which has been cultivated in Britain from time immemorial, and is one of the earliest of cultivated species; it is represented on Egyptian monuments, and one variety cultivated in Egypt was accorded divine honours. It is commonly cultivated in India, China and Japan. A. de Candolle, arguing from its ancient cultivation and the antiquity of the Sanskrit and Hebrew names, regards it as a native of western Asia.

The onion should be grown in an open situation, and on a light, rich, well-worked soil, which has not been recently manured. In England the principal crop may be sown at any time from the middle of February to the middle of March, if the weather is fine and the ground sufficiently dry. The seed should be sown in shallow drills, 10 in. apart, the ground being made as level and firm as possible, and the plants should be regularly thinned, hoed and kept free from weeds. At the final thinning they should be set from 3 to 6 in. apart, the latter distance in very rich soil. About the beginning of September the crop is ripe, which is known by the withering of the leaves; the bulbs are then to be pulled, and exposed on the ground till well dried, and they are then to be put away in a store-room, or loft, where they may be perfectly secured from frost and damp.

About the end of August a crop is sown to afford a supply of young onions in the spring months. Those which are not required for the kitchen, if allowed to stand, and if the flower-bud is picked out on its first appearance, and the earth stirred about them, frequently produce bulbs equal in size and quality to the large ones that are imported from the Continent. A crop of very large bulbs may also be secured by sowing about the beginning of September, and transplanting early in spring to very rich soil. Another plan is to sow in May on dry poor soil, when a crop of small bulbs will be produced; these are to be stored in the usual way, and planted in rich soil about February, on ground made firm by treading, in rows about 1 ft. apart, the bulbs being set near the surface, and about 6 in. asunder. The White Spanish and Tripoli are good sorts for this purpose.

To obtain a crop of bulbs for pickling, seed should be sown thickly in March, in rather poor soil, the seeds being very thinly covered, and the surface well rolled; these are not to be thinned, but should be pulled and harvested when ripe. The best sorts for this crop are the Silver-skinned, Early Silver-skinned, Nocera and Queen.

Onions may be forced like mustard and cress if required for winter salads, the seeds being sown thickly in boxes which are to be placed in a warm house or frame. The young onions are of course pulled while quite small.

The *Potato Onion, Allium Cepa* var. *aggregatum*, is propagated by the lateral bulbs, which it throws out, under ground, in considerable numbers. This variety is very prolific, and is useful when other sorts do not keep well. It is sometimes planted about midwinter, and then ripens in summer, but for use during the spring and early summer it is best planted in spring. It is also known as the underground onion, from its habit of producing its bulbs beneath the surface.

The *Tree Onion* or *Egyptian Onion, Allium Cepa* var. *proliferum*, produces small bulbs instead of flowers, and a few offsets also underground. These small stem bulbs are excellent for pickling.

The *Welsh Onion* or *Ciboule, Allium fistulosum*, is a hardy perennial, native of Siberia. It was unknown to the ancients, and must have come into Europe through Russia in the middle ages or later. It forms no bulbs, but, on account of its extreme hardiness, is sown in July or early in August, to furnish a reliable supply of young onions for use in salads during the early spring. These bulbless onions are sometimes called Scallions, a name which is also applied to old onions which have stem and leaves but no bulbs.

The following are among the best varieties of onions for various purposes:—

For Summer and Autumn.—Queen; Early White Naples: these two sorts also excellent for sowing in autumn for spring salading. Silver-skinned; Tripoli, including Giant Rocca.

For Winter.—Brown Globe, including Magnum Bonum; White Globe; Yellow Danvers; White Spanish, in its several forms; Trébons, the finest variety for autumn sowing, attaining a large size early, ripening well, and keeping good till after Christmas; Ailsa Craig; Roneham Park Hero; James's Keeping; Cranston's Excelsior; Blood Red, strong-flavoured.

For Pickling.—Queen, Early Silver-skinned, White Nocera, Egyptian.

ONOMACRITUS (c. 530–480 B.C.), seer, priest and poet of Attica. His importance lies in his connexion with the religious movements in Attica during the 6th century B.C. He had great influence on the development of the Orphic religion and mysteries, and was said to have composed a poem on initiatory rites. The works of Musaeus, the legendary founder of Orphism in Attica, are said to have been reduced to order (if not actually written) by him (Clem. Alex. *Stromata*, i. p. 143 [397]; Pausanias i. 22, 7). He was in high favour at the court of the Peisistratidae till he was banished by Hipparchus for making additions of his own in an oracle of Musaeus. When the Peisistratidae were themselves expelled and were living in Persia, he furnished them with oracles encouraging Xerxes to invade Greece and restore the tyrants in Athens (Herodotus vii. 6). He is also said to have been employed by Peisistratus in editing the Homeric poems, and to have introduced interpolations of his own (e.g. a passage in the episode of the visit of Odysseus to the world below). According to Pausanias (viii. 31, 37, 5; ix. 35, 5) he was also the author of poems on mythological subjects.

See F. W. Ritschl, "Onomakritos von Athen," in his *Opuscula*, i. (1866), and p. 35 of the same volume; U. von Wilamowitz-Möllendorff, "Homerische Untersuchungen" (pp. 190-226 on the Orphic interpolation in *Odyssey*, λ 566-631), in Kiessling-Möllendorff, *Philologische Untersuchungen*, Heft 7 (1884).

ONOMATOPOEIA, literally the making or formation of words (Gr. ὀνοματοποιία, from ὄνομα, name, word, ποιεῖν, to make), hence a term used in philology for the formation of words by imitation of natural sounds, e.g. "hiss," "hush," "click." Modern philologists prefer the term "echoism," "echoic" for this process, as suggesting the imitative repetition of the sounds heard. At one time there was an exaggerated tendency to find in echoism a principal source in the origin and growth of language, ridiculed as the "bow-wow" theory of language; it is now recognized that it has played only a limited part.

ONONDAGA, a tribe of North American Indians of Iroquoian stock, forming one of the Six Nations. The tribal headquarters was about the lake and creek of the same name in New York state. Their territory extended northward to Lake Ontario and southward to the Susquehanna river. They were the official guardians of the council-fire of the Iroquois. Their chief town, near the site of the present Onondaga, consisted of some 140 houses in the middle of the 17th century, when the tribe was estimated as numbering between 1500 and 1700. During the 18th century the tribe divided, part loyally supporting the Iroquois league, while part, having come under the influence of French missionaries, migrated to the Catholic Iroquois settlements in Canada. Of those who supported the league, the majority, after the War of Independence, settled on a reservation on Grand river, Ontario, where their descendants still are. About 500 are upon the Onondaga reservation in New York state. For Onondaga cosmology see *21st Ann. Report Bureau Amer. Ethnol.* (1899–1900).

ONOSANDER, or **ONASANDER**, Greek philosopher, lived during the 1st century A.D. He was the author of a commentary on the *Republic* of Plato, which is lost, but we still possess by him a short but comprehensive work (Στρατηγικός) on the duties of a general. It is dedicated to Quintus Veranius Nepos, consul 49, and legate of Britain. It was the chief authority for the military writings of the emperors Maurice and Leo, and Maurice of Saxony, who consulted it in a French translation, expressed a high opinion of it.

Edition by H. Köchly (1860); see also G. Rathgeber in Ersch and Gruber's *Allgemeine Encyclopädie*.

ONSLOW, EARL OF, a title borne by an English family claiming descent from Roger, lord of Ondeslowe in the liberty of Shrewsbury in the 13th century. Richard Onslow (1528–1571), solicitor-general and then Speaker of the House of Commons in the reign of Elizabeth, was grandfather of Sir Richard Onslow (1601–1664), who inherited the family estate on the death of his brother, Sir Thomas Onslow, in 1616. Sir Richard was a member of the Long Parliament, and during the great Rebellion was a colonel in the parliamentary army. He was a member of Cromwell's parliament in 1654 and again in 1656, and was also a member of his House of Lords. His son, Sir Arthur Onslow (1621–1688), succeeded in 1687 by special remainder to the baronetcy of his father-in-law, Sir Thomas Foot, lord mayor of London. Sir Arthur's son, Sir Richard (1654–1717), was Speaker of the House of Commons from 1708 to 1710, and chancellor of the exchequer in 1715. In 1716 he was created Baron Onslow of Onslow and of Clandon. He was uncle of Arthur Onslow, the famous Speaker (see below), whose only son George became 4th Baron Onslow on the death of his kinsman Richard in October 1776. The 4th baron (1731–1814) had entered parliament in 1754, and was very active in the House of Commons; and in May 1776, just before he succeeded to the family barony, he was created Baron Cranley of Imbercourt. He was comptroller and then treasurer of the royal household, and was present at the marriage of the prince of Wales, afterwards George IV., with Mrs Fitzherbert in 1785. In 1801 he was created Viscount Cranley and earl of Onslow, and he died at his Surrey residence, Clandon Park, on the 17th of May 1814. The second earl was his eldest son Thomas (1754–1827), whose son Arthur George (1777–1870), the 3rd earl, died without surviving male issue in October 1870. He was succeeded by his grand-nephew, William Hillier, 4th earl of Onslow (b. 1853), who was governor of New Zealand from 1888 to 1892; under-secretary for India from 1895 to 1900; and under-secretary for the Colonies from 1900 to 1903. From 1903 to 1905 he was a member of the Conservative cabinet as president of the board of agriculture.

ONSLOW, ARTHUR (1691–1768), English politician, elder son of Foot Onslow (d. 1710), was born at Chelsea on the 1st of October 1691. Educated at Winchester and at Wadham College, Oxford, he became a barrister and in 1720 entered parliament as a member for the borough of Guildford. Seven years later he became one of the members for Surrey, and he retained this seat until 1761. In 1728 he was elected Speaker of the House of Commons, being the third member of his family to hold this office; he was also chancellor to George II.'s queen, Caroline, and from 1734 to 1742 he was treasurer of the navy. He retired from the position of Speaker and from parliament in 1761, and enjoyed an annuity of £3000 until his death on the 17th of February 1768. As Speaker, Onslow was a conspicuous success, displaying knowledge, tact and firmness in his office; in his leisure hours he was a collector of books.

Speaker Onslow's nephew, GEORGE ONSLOW (1731–1792), a son of his brother Richard, was a lieutenant-colonel and member of parliament for Guildford from 1760 to 1784. He had a younger brother Richard (1741–1817), who entered the navy and was made an admiral in 1799.

ONTARIO, a province of Canada, having the province of Quebec to the E., the states of New York, Ohio, Michigan, Wisconsin, and Minnesota to the S., Manitoba to the W., and the district of Keewatin with James Bay to the N. In most cases the actual boundary consists of rivers or lakes, the Ottawa to the north-east, the St Lawrence and its chain of lakes and rivers to the south as far as Pigeon river, which separates Ontario from Minnesota. From this a canoe route over small rivers and lakes leads to the Lake-of-the-Woods, which lies between Ontario, Minnesota and Manitoba; and English and Albany rivers with various lakes carry the boundary to James Bay. From Lake Temiscaming northwards the boundary is the meridian of 79° 30′.

Physical Geography.—Ontario extends 1000 m. from E. to W. and more than 700 m. from N. to S., between latitudes 55° and 42°, including the most southerly point in Canada. Its area is 260,862 sq. m. (40,354 water), and it is the most populous of the provinces, nine-tenths of its inhabitants living, however, in one-tenth of its area, between the Great Lakes, the Ottawa and the St Lawrence. This forms part of the plain of the St Lawrence, underlain by Palaeozoic limestones and shales, with some sandstone, all furnishing useful building material and working up into a good soil. The lowest part of the plain, including an area of 4500 sq. m. lying between elevations of 100 and 400 ft., was covered by the sea at the close of the Ice Age, which left behind broad deposits of clay and sand with marine shells.

The south-western part is naturally divided into two tracts by the Niagara escarpment, a line of cliffs capped by hard Silurian limestones, running from Queenston Heights near the falls of Niagara west to the head of Lake Ontario near Hamilton, and then northwest to the Bruce Peninsula on Georgian Bay. The tract north-east of the escarpment has an area of 9000 sq. m. and an altitude of 400 to 1000 ft., and the south-western tract includes 15,000 sq. m. with an elevation of 600 to 1700 ft. In the last petroleum, natural gas, salt and gypsum are obtained, but elsewhere in southern Ontario no economic minerals except building materials are obtained. Covering the higher parts of the south-western Palaeozoic area in most places are rolling hills of boulder clay or stony moraines; while the lower levels are plains gently sloping toward the nearest of the Great Lakes and sheeted with silt deposited in more ancient lakes when the St Lawrence outlet was blocked with ice at the end of the glacial period. The old shore cliffs and gravel bars of these glacial lakes are still well-marked topographical features, and provide favourite sites for towns and cities. London, for example, is built on the old shore of Lake Warren, the highest of the extinct lakes; and St Catharines, Hamilton and Toronto are on the old shore of Lake Iroquois, the lowest. The Niagara escarpment mentioned above, generally called " the mountain " in Ontario, is the cause of waterfalls on all the rivers which plunge over it, Niagara Falls being, of course, the most important; and in most cases these falls have eaten their way back into the tableland, forming deep gorges or canyons like that below Niagara itself, through which the water pours as violent rapids. Between the Palaeozoic area near Ottawa, and Georgian Bay to the north of the region just referred to, there is a southward projection of the Archaean protaxis consisting of granite and gneiss of the Laurentian, enclosing bands of crystalline limestone and schists, which are of interest as furnishing the only mines of " Old Ontario." From these rocks in the Ottawa valley are quarried or mined granite, marble, magnificent blue sodalite, felspar, talc, actinolite, mica, apatite, graphite and corundum; the latter mineral, which occurs on a larger scale here than elsewhere, is rapidly replacing emery as an abrasive. Several metals have been mined also, including gold, copper, lead, iron and arsenic; but the amounts produced have not been great, and many of the mines are no longer working.

While all the larger cities and most of the manufacturing and farming districts of the province belong to old Ontario, there is now in process of development a " New Ontario," stretching for hundreds of miles to the north and north-west of the region just described and covering a far larger area, chiefly made up of Laurentian and Huronian rocks of the Archaean protaxis. The rocky hills of the tableland to the north long repelled settlement, the region being looked on by the thrifty farmers of the south as a wilderness useless except for its forests and its furs; and unfortunate settlers who ventured into it usually failed and went west or south in search of better land. Gradually, however, areas of good soil were opened up, in the Rainy river valley, near Lake Temiscaming and elsewhere, and mines of various kinds were discovered, as the Canadian Pacific railway and its branches extended through the region, and at length the finding of very rich silver mines attracted world-wide attention to northern Ontario. In the better explored parts along the great lakes and the railways, ores of gold, silver, nickel, cobalt, antimony, arsenic, bismuth and molybdenum have been obtained, and several important mines have been opened up. Gold has been found at many points across the whole province, from the mines of the Lake-of-the-Woods on the west to the discoveries at Larder Lake on the east; but, in most cases the returns have been unsatisfactory, and only a few of the gold mines are working. Silver mines have proved of far greater importance, in early days near Thunder Bay on Lake Superior, more recently in the cobalt region near Lake Temiscaming on the east side of the province. Silver Islet mine in Lake Superior produced in all $3,250,000 worth of silver, but this record will no doubt be surpassed by some of the mines in the extraordinarily rich cobalt district. The veins are small, but contain native silver and other rich silver ores running sometimes several thousand ounces per ton, the output being 5,500,000 oz. in 1906. Associated with the silver minerals are rich ores of cobalt and nickel, combined with arsenic, antimony and sulphur, which would be considered valuable if occurring alone, but are not paid for under present conditions, since they are difficult to separate and refine. The cobalt silver ores are found mainly in Huronian conglomerate, but also in older Keewatin rocks and younger diabase, and the silver-bearing region, which at first included only a few square miles, is found to extend 25 m. to the west and as much to the north. Up to the present the most important mineral product of Ontario is nickel, which is mined only in the neighbourhood of Sudbury, where the ores occur in very large deposits, which in 1905 produced 9503 tons, more than half of the world's supply of the metal. With the nickel copper is always found, and copper ores are worked on their own account in a few localities, such as Bruce mines. Iron ores have been discovered in many places in connexion with the "iron formation" of the Keewatin, but nowhere in amounts comparable with those of the same formation in Michigan and Minnesota. The total mineral output of Ontario, including building materials and cement, is larger than that of any other province of the dominion, and as more careful exploration is carried on in the northern parts, no doubt many more deposits of value will be discovered. It has been found that northern Ontario beyond the divide between the Great Lakes and Hudson Bay possesses many millions of acres of arable land, clay deposits in a post-glacial lake, like those in the southern part of the province, running from east to west from Lake Abitibbi to a point north of Lake Nipigon. Railways are opening up this tract. The clay belt is in latitudes south of Winnipeg, with a good summer climate but cold winters. The spruce timber covering much of the area is of great value, compensating for the labour of clearing the land.

Lakes and Rivers.—All parts of Ontario are well provided with lakes and rivers, the most important chain being that of the St Lawrence and the Great Lakes with their tributaries, which drain the more populous southern districts, and, with the aid of canals, furnish communication by fairly large vessels between the lower St Lawrence and the Lake Superior. Lake Nipigon, a beautiful body of water 852 ft. above the sea, 70 m. long and 50 m. wide, may be looked upon as the headwaters of the St Lawrence, since Nipigon river is the largest tributary of Lake Superior, though several other important rivers, such as the Kaministiquia, the Pic and the Michi-picoten, enter it from the north. All these rivers have high falls not far from Lake Superior, and Kakebeka Falls on the Kaministiquia supplies power to the twin cities of Fort William and Port Arthur, while the deep water of its mouth makes the great shipping port for western wheat during the summer. The north shore of Lake Superior is bold and rugged with many islands, such as Ignace and Michipicoten, but with very few settlements, except fishing stations, owing to its rocky character. At the south-eastern end St Mary's river carries its waters to Lake Huron, with a fall of 602 to 581 ft., most of which takes place at Sault Sainte Marie, where the largest locks in the world permit vessels of 10,000 tons to pass from one lake to the other, and where water-power has been greatly developed for use in the rolling mills and wood pulp industry. The north-east shores of Lake Huron and its large expansion Georgian Bay are fringed with thousands of islands, mostly small, but one of them, Manitoulin Island, is 80 m. long and 30 m. broad. French river, the outlet of Lake Nipissing, and Severn river, draining Lake Simcoe, come into Georgian Bay from the east, and canals have been projected to connect Lake Huron with the St Lawrence by each of these routes, the northern one to make use of the Ottawa and the southern one of Trent river. The Trent Valley canal is partly in operation. Georgian Bay is cut off from the main lake by Manitoulin Island and the long promontory of Bruce Peninsula. Lakes Superior and Huron both reach depths hundreds of feet below sea-level, but the next lake in the series, St Clair, towards which Lake Huron drains southward through St Clair river, is very shallow and marshy. Detroit river connects Lake St Clair with Lake Erie at an elevation of 570 ft.; and this comparatively shallow lake, running for 240 m. east and west, empties northwards by Niagara river into Lake Ontario, which is only 247 ft. above the sea.

Niagara Falls, with rapids above and below, carry the waters of the upper lakes over the Niagara escarpment. Power from the falls is put to use in New York state and Ontario, a large amount being sent to Toronto 80 m. away. Welland canal, between Port Colborne on Lake Erie and Dalhousie on Lake Ontario, carries vessels of 14 ft. draught from one lake to the other. From Lake Ontario the St Lawrence emerges through the meshes of the Thousand Islands, where it crosses Archaean rocks, after which follow several rapids separated by quieter stretches before Montreal is reached at the head of ocean navigation. Steamers not of too great draught can run the rapids going down, but vessels must come up through the canals. All the other rivers in southern Ontario are tributaries of the lakes or of the St Lawrence, the Ottawa, navigable in many parts, being the largest, and the Trent next in importance. In northern Ontario lakes are innumerable and often very picturesque, forming favourite summer resorts, such as Lake Temagami, the Muskoka Lakes and Lake-of-the-Woods. The latter lake with Rainy Lake and other connected bodies of water belong to the Hudson Bay system of waters, their outlet being by Winnipeg river to Lake Winnipeg, from which flows Nelson river. In Ontario the Albany, Moose, Missanabi and Abitibbi flow into Hudson Bay, but none of these rivers is navigable except for canoes.

Climate.—The climate of Ontario varies greatly, as might be expected from its wide range in latitude and the relationships of the Great Lakes to the southern peninsula of the province. The northern parts as far south as the north shore of Lake Superior have long and cold but bright winters, sometimes with temperatures reaching 90° F. below zero; while their summers are delightful, with much sunshine and some hot days but pleasantly cool nights. Between Georgian Bay and Ottawa the winters are less cold, but usually with a plentiful snowfall; while the summers are warm and sometimes even hot. The south-west peninsula of Ontario has its climate greatly modified by the lakes which almost enclose it. As the lakes never freeze, the prevalent cold north-west winds of North America are warmed in their passage over them, and often much of the winter precipitation is in the form of rain, so that the weather has much less certainty than in the north. The summers are often sultry, though the presence of the lakes prevents the intense heat experienced in the states to the west and south. Owing to the mildness of its winters, the south-west peninsula is a famous fruit country with many vineyards and orchards of apples, plums and peaches. Indian corn (maize) is an important field crop, and tobacco is cultivated on a large scale. Small fruits and tomatoes are widely grown for the city markets and for canning, giving rise to an important industry. The normal temperatures (Fahr.) for three points in the south-western, eastern and north-western portions are given below:—

	Toronto.	Ottawa.	Port Arthur.
December, January and February .	23·7	13·3	7·3
March, April and May . . .	40·6	38·5	31·1
June, July and August . . .	65·4	67·4	58·9
September, October and November	47·0	44·8	38·5
	in.	in.	in.
Average annual precipitation .	33·944	32·650	23·580

(A. P. C.)

Population.—The following table shows the population of the province:—

	1881.	1891.	1901.
[1] Townships . . .	1,346,623	1,283,281	1,247,190
[2] Towns and villages .	323,188	432,912	935,757
Cities	257,111	398,128	
	1,926,922	2,114,321	2,182,947

[1] The name given to the rural municipalities.
[2] Any town in Canada can become incorporated as a city on attaining a population of 10,000.

Ontario is thus pre-eminently an agricultural province, though the growth of manufactures has increased the importance of the towns and cities, and many of the farmers are seeking new homes in the provinces of Manitoba, Alberta and Saskatchewan. This emigration accounts in large measure for the slow increase of the population, though there has also been a slight decrease in the birth-rate. The population was long entirely confined to the southern and eastern sections of the province, which comprise an area of about 33,000 sq. m.; but in these districts it is now stationary or decreasing, whereas the northern and western portions are filling up rapidly. Toronto, the provincial capital, has grown from 59,000 in 1871 to about 300,000, partly through the absorption of neighbouring towns and villages. Other

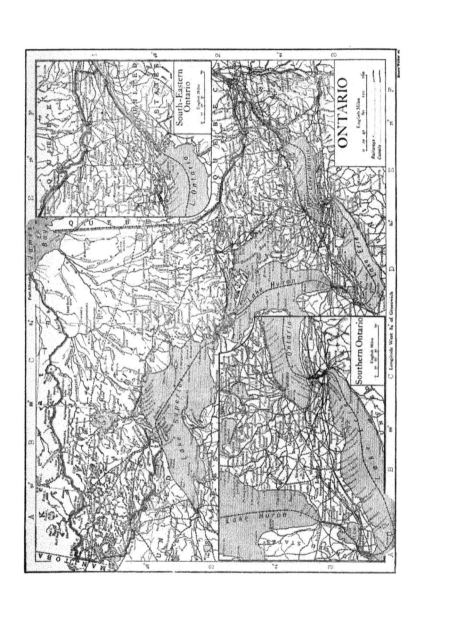

ONTARIO

English Miles
Railways
Canals

South-Eastern Ontario

Southern Ontario

English Miles

C Longitude West 84 of Greenwich D

important cities are Ottawa (the capital of the Dominion) (59,928 in 1901), Hamilton (52,634), London (37,981), Kingston (17,961). The number of males slightly exceeds that of females. The population is chiefly of British descent, though in the eastern counties numerous French Canadians are flocking in from Quebec and in some instances by purchase of farms replacing the British. There are also about 20,000 Indians, many of whom are civilised, enjoy the franchise and are enrolled in the Dominion militia. There is no state Church, though buildings devoted to religious purposes are almost wholly exempt from municipal taxation. The Methodists are, numerically, the strongest religious body, then come Presbyterians, Roman Catholics and Anglicans, in the order named.

Administration.—The executive power is vested in a lieutenant-governor appointed for five years by the federal government, and assisted by an executive council, who have seats in and are responsible to the local legislature. This consists of one house only, of 106 members, elected by what is practically manhood suffrage.

The municipal system still embodies the spirit and purpose of the Baldwin Municipal Act which originated it in 1849. Though based rather on the simple English model than on the more complicated municipal governments of the United States, it has certain features of its own, and is revised from year to year. On it have been modelled the municipal systems of the other provinces. Municipal ownership does not prevail to any extent, and in the larger cities the powers of certain great corporations have tended to cause friction, but such matters as the provision of electric power and light are gradually being taken in hand both by the municipalities and by the province, and a railway and municipal board appointed by the local legislature has certain powers over the railways and electric tramlines.

Finance.—By the British North America Act, which formed in 1867 the Dominion of Canada, the provinces have the right of direct taxation only. Against this, however, a strong prejudice exists, and in Ontario the only direct taxation takes the form of taxes on corporations (insurance, loan and railway companies), succession duties, liquor licences, &c. These, together with returns from various investments, earnings of provincial buildings, &c., yield about one-third of the revenue. Another third comes from the Dominion subsidy, granted in lieu of the power of indirect taxation, and the remainder from the sale or lease of crown lands, timber and minerals. Owing to the excellence of the municipal system there has been a tendency to devolve thereon, in whole or in part, certain financial burdens on the plea of decentralization. The finances of the province have been well administered, and only in recent years has a debt been incurred, chiefly owing to the construction of a provincial railway to aid in the development of the northern districts.

Education.—As early as 1797 500,000 acres of crown lands were set apart for educational purposes, and a well-organized system of education now exists, which, since 1876, has constituted a department of the provincial government. A laudable attempt has been made to keep the education department free from the vagaries and the strife of party politics, and the advantages of political control have been as much felt as its drawbacks. Since 1906 a superintendent has been appointed with large powers, independent of political control and with the assistance of an advisory council; attention is also paid to the advice of the provincial Educational Association, which meets yearly at Toronto.

School attendance is compulsory between the ages of eight and fourteen, and is enforced by truant officers. The primary or public schools are free and undenominational. They cannot, however, be called secular, as they are opened and closed with the Lord's Prayer and closed with the reading of the Bible. From these religious exercises any children may absent themselves whose parents profess conscientious objections. After a long and bitter struggle the Roman Catholics won in 1863 the right to separate schools. These may be set up in any district upon the request of not less than five heads of families. The rates levied on their supporters are devoted exclusively to the separate schools, which also share *pro rata* in the government grant. Although many Roman Catholic children attend the public schools, the number of separate schools is, under the influence of the priesthood, steadily increasing. Under certain conditions, Protestants and coloured persons may also claim separate schools, but of these only four or five exist. Numerous kindergartens have been established in the cities.

Secondary education is imparted in high schools and collegiate[1] institutes. These may exact fees or give free education at the

[1] A high school is raised to the rank of collegiate institute on complying with certain provisions, chief among which are the employment of at least four teachers with Degrees in Honours from a recognized Canadian university. Such an institution receives a slightly larger government grant.

option of the local trustees. There are also numerous private schools. Of these such as are incorporated are aided by exemption from municipal taxation. In and around Toronto are numerous boarding schools and colleges, of which those for boys are on the model of the great public schools of England. Of these the most celebrated is Upper Canada College, founded in 1829, and long part of the educational system of the province, but now under private control.

The provincial university is situated in Toronto, and since 1906 has been governed by an independent board, over which a power of veto is retained by the lieutenant-governor in council. With the affiliated colleges, it had in 1908 a staff of 356, and 3545 students. There are also numerous universities throughout the province, founded in early days by the various religious bodies. Of these Victoria (Methodist) and Trinity (Anglican) are in Toronto, and have become federated with the provincial university, in which they have merged their degree-conferring powers. MacMaster (Baptist) is also in Toronto, and retains its independence. The others are Queen's University, Kingston (Presbyterian); the Western University, London (Anglican); and the university of Ottawa (Roman Catholic). Women students are admitted to all the universities save Ottawa on the same terms as men, and form nearly one-third of the whole number of students. Theological colleges are supported by the various religious bodies, and are in affiliation with one or other of the universities.

The public and high schools tend rather to follow American than British methods, though less freedom is allowed to the local authorities than in most of the American states. Only those text books authorized by the central department may be used. Free text books may be issued at the discretion of the local authorities, but in most cases are provided by parents. Every school, public, separate or high, shares in the provincial grant, but the chief financial burden falls on the local authorities.

Owing to the low rate of salaries, the percentage of women teachers, especially in the public schools, is steadily increasing, and now amounts in these to almost 83%. The same cause has also reduced their age, and the teachers are in many cases exceedingly immature. The institution of a minimum salary for the provincial department led to such resistance that it was withdrawn, but a distinct advance in salaries has taken place since 1906. In the rural districts an attempt is being made to increase efficiency by the consolidation of several small schools and the conveyance of the children to one central building.

The curriculum, originally modelled on that of England, is being gradually modified by the necessities of a new country. In addition to the ordinary literary and scientific subjects, manual training, domestic science, agriculture and kindred subjects are taught in the public and high schools, and in the larger towns technical institutes are being founded. Many of the rural schools have gardens, in which the elements of agriculture, botany and kindred subjects are taught in a practical manner. Travelling libraries are sent through the country districts, and an attempt is being made to extend similar aid to the lumber-camps.

The training of teachers is carefully supervised. Numerous model and normal schools exist, and a well-equipped normal college at Toronto. The smaller county model schools have, since 1906–1907, been consolidated and centralized in the larger towns.

At Guelph is the Ontario Agricultural College, founded and endowed by the provincial government, and greatly enlarged and improved by the generosity of Sir William Macdonald (b. 1832). Its services in placing provincial agriculture on a scientific basis cannot be over-estimated. The government also maintains an institute for the deaf and dumb at Belleville and for the blind at Brantford. At Kingston it supports a dairy school and a large school of mining.

Agriculture.—About three-fifths of the inhabitants are engaged in agricultural pursuits, and in 1910 the amount invested in land, buildings, implements and stock was double that invested in the manufactures of the whole Dominion. Nearly all the farms are worked by their owners, and a simple and efficient system of land-transfer is in use. The farming population in the older parts of the province tends to decline in numbers, owing to emigration, partly to the towns, but especially to the newer lands of Manitoba and the west. Yet, owing to the increasing use of scientific implements and methods promoted by the federal and provincial governments, the total value of agricultural products increased by over 50% between 1881 and 1910. In general, the soil is fertile and the climate favourable. The district north of the Height of Land, long supposed to be a barren wilderness, has proved in part suitable for agriculture, and is steadily increasing in population. Mixed farming and the raising of live stock is becoming more and more the rule, so that the failure of any one crop becomes of less vital importance. The average farm varies in size from 100 to 200 acres. Wheat, barley, oats, peas, potatoes and other roots are staple crops, the average yield of wheat being about 20 bushels an acre; cattle are increasing in number and improving in quality, and all branches of dairy farming prosper. Owing to tariff restrictions, the United States market is being more and more abandoned, and improvements in cold storage are making it possible to export to Great Britain increasing quantities of butter and cheese. The collection of milk by the creameries and cheese-factories is carried on with great efficiency. The number of horses and sheep is stationary or declining, but the raising of hogs, formerly abandoned in great part to the western states, is becoming an increasing industry. Large quantities of peas, corn, tomatoes and other vegetables are canned, chiefly for home consumption. Three-quarters of the orchard lands of Canada are in Ontario, the chief crops being apples and peaches. The cultivation of the latter centres in the Niagara peninsula, but apples flourish along the great lakes and the St Lawrence from Goderich to Cornwall. In Essex and Kent, and along the shore of Lake Erie, tobacco and grapes form a staple crop, and wine of fair quality is produced.

Lumber.—Slightly less than half remains of the forest which once covered the whole province. The lumber industry exceeds that of any other part of the Dominion, though Quebec possesses greater timber areas untouched. The numerous lakes and rivers greatly facilitate the bringing of the timber to market. All trees were long little thought of in comparison with the pine, but of late years poplar and spruce have proved of great value in the making of paper pulp, and hard-wood (oak, beech, ash, elm, certain varieties of maple) is becoming increasingly valuable for use in flooring and the making of furniture. In the spring the making of syrup and sugar from the sap of the sugar-maple is a typical industry.

Much splendid timber has been needlessly destroyed, chiefly by forest-fires, but also by improvident farmers in their haste to clear the land. Increased attention is now being paid by both provincial and federal governments to preservation and to reforestation. Special areas have been set apart on which no timber may be cut, and on which the problems of scientific forestry may be studied. Of these, the earliest was the Algonquin National Park, which also forms a haven of refuge for the wild creatures.

Northern Ontario is still a valuable fur-bearing and hunting country, moose, caribou, fox, bear, otter, mink and skunk being found in large quantities. Wolves, once numerous, have now been almost extirpated, though a bounty on each head is still paid.

Minerals.—The geographical distribution of the great mineral wealth of Ontario has already been indicated (see *Physical Geography*, above). Save for beds of lignite, said to exist in the extreme north, coal is not found and has to be imported, chiefly from the states of Ohio and Pennsylvania, though Nova Scotia furnishes an increasing quantity. The production of iron is stimulated by federal and provincial bounties. The province supplies over two-thirds of the iron ore mined in the Dominion, but much is still imported. The output of gold is decreasing. The nickel mines in the neighbourhood of Sudbury are the largest in the world, outrivalling those of New Caledonia. In the same district, and chiefly in connexion with the nickel mines, large quantities of copper are produced. When in 1905 the rich silver area was found in northern Ontario, a rush was made to it, comparable to those to the Australian and Californian goldfields. Cobalt, the centre of this area, is 103 m. from North Bay by the provincial railway (Temiscaming & North Ontario railway). In the same neighbourhood are found cobalt, arsenic and bismuth. In the older districts of the province are found petroleum and salt. The district around Petrolea produces about 30,000,000 gallons of petroleum yearly, practically the whole output of the dominion. Salt is worked in the vicinity of Lake Huron, but the production is less than half that imported. Natural gas is produced in the counties of Welland and Essex, and exported in pipes to Buffalo and Detroit. Among the less important metals and minerals which are also mined, is corundum of especial purity.

Manufactures and Commerce.—Manufactures are becoming of increasing importance. The obstacle due to lack of coal is offset by the splendid water powers afforded by the rapid streams in all parts of the province. Save for the flour and grist mills, few do more than supply the markets of the Dominion, of which they control an increasing portion. Woollen mills, distilleries and breweries and manufactures of leather, locomotives and iron-work, implements, agricultural implements, cloth and paper are the chief. The great agricultural development of the western provinces, in which manufactures are little advanced, has given a great impetus to the industries of the older provinces, especially Ontario.

Communications.—Numerous lakes and rivers afford means of communication, and obstacles thereon have been largely overcome by canals (see CANADA). Railways gridiron the province, which contains over one-third the total mileage of the dominion; their construction is aided by provincial and municipal subsidies, in addition to that paid by the federal government. The provincial government owns a line running north from North Bay, operated by a board of commissioners. The other railways are owned by private companies, but are subject to the decisions of a federal railway commission. The provincial railway and municipal board also exercises control, especially over the city and suburban electric lines.

History.—The first white man known to have set foot in what is now Ontario was Champlain. In 1613 he explored the Ottawa river as far as Allumette Island; in 1615, starting from Montreal, he reached the Georgian Bay by way of the Ottawa river, Lake Nipissing and French river, and then by way of Lakes Couchiching and Simcoe and the Trent river system of lakes and streams made his way to Lake Ontario, called by him Entouhoronon. The

winter of 1615-1616 he spent among the Huron Indians, near the Georgian Bay. In 1615 a mission among these Indians was founded by the Recollet friars, and carried on with great success and devotion by the Jesuits, but in 1648-1650 the Huron nation was almost utterly destroyed by an invasion of their hereditary foes, the Iroquois. From its centre at Quebec French civilization extended along the Mississippi and the Great Lakes, and also northwards to Hudson's Bay. In the western country numerous posts were founded, wherein fur-trader and missionary were often at variance, the trader finding brandy his best medium of exchange, while the missionary tried in vain to stay its ravages among his flock. On the frontiers of what is now Ontario the chief points were at the strategic centres of Fort Frontenac (now Kingston), Niagara, Michilimackinac and Sault-Ste-Marie. Farther north, in what is now New Ontario, their English rivals, the Hudson's Bay Company, had more or less permanent posts, especially at Fort Albany and Moose Factory.

With the cession of French North America to Great Britain in 1763, the Indian lords of the soil rose under Pontiac in a last attempt to shake off the white man, and in 1763-1765 there was hard fighting along the western frontier from Sault-Ste-Marie to Detroit. Thereafter for almost twenty years, Ontario was traversed only by wandering bands of trappers, chiefly belonging to the Hudson's Bay Company; but in 1782 bands of American loyalists began to occupy the fertile country along the Bay of Quinté, and in the Niagara peninsula, the first settlement being made in 1782 at Kingston. Between 1782-1784 about 5000 loyalists entered Ontario, and were given liberal grants of land by the British government.

The oligarchic constitution established in Canada in 1774 by the Quebec Act did not suit men trained in the school of local self-government which Britain had unwittingly established in the American colonies, and the gift of representative institutions was soon necessary. In the debates in the British parliament Fox urged that the whole territory should remain one province, and of this the governor-general, the 1st baron Dorchester (q.v.), was on the whole in favour, but in 1791 Pitt introduced and carried the Constitutional Act, by which Upper and Lower Canada were separated. The Ottawa river was chosen as the main boundary between them, but the retention by Lower Canada of the seigneuries of New Longueuil and Vaudreuil, on the western side of the river, is a curious instance of the triumph of social and historical conditions over geographical. To the new province were given English civil and criminal law, a legislative assembly and council and a lieutenant-governor; in the words of its first governor, Colonel John Graves Simcoe, it had, "the British Constitution, and all the forms which secure and maintain it." Simcoe set to work with great energy to develop the province, but he quarrelled with the governor-general over his pet scheme of founding military colonies of retired soldiers in different parts of the province, and retired in 1796. Even before his retirement political feuds had broken out, which increased in bitterness year by year. In so far as these had other causes than the Anglo-Saxon love of faction, they were due to the formation by the loyalists, their descendants and hangers-on of a clique who more and more engrossed political and social power. The English church also formed a quasi-official clerical oligarchy, and the land reserved by the Constitutional Act for the support of " a protestant clergy " formed a fruitful source of bitterness.

For a time the War of 1812-1814 with the United States put an end to the strife. The war gave some heroic traditions to the province, and in special cemented that loyalty to Great Britain for which Ontario has been conspicuous. On the other hand, the natural dislike of the United States felt by the loyalists and their descendants was deepened and broadened, and has not yet wholly died away, especially among the women of the province. The jobbing of land by the official clique, whose frequent intermarriages won for them the name of "The Family Compact," the undoubted grievance of the " Clergy Reserves " and the well-meaning high-handedness and social exclusiveness of military governors, who tried hard but unavailingly to stay the democratic wave, soon revived political discord, which found a voice in that born agitator, William Lyon Mackenzie. A wiser but less vigorous reformer was Robert Baldwin, who saw that in responsible government lay the cure for the political green-sickness from which Upper Canada was suffering. But though Baldwin and Mackenzie were in the right, it is very doubtful whether their party could at the time have given the country as cheap and efficient a civil service as was given by the Family Compact, who had at least education and an honourable tradition.

In 1837 discontent flared up into a pitiful little rebellion, led by Mackenzie. This tragical farce was soon at an end and its author a fugitive in the United States, whence he instigated bands of hooligans to make piratical attacks upon the Canadian frontier. Thus forcibly reminded of the existence of Canada, the British government sent out Lord Durham to investigate, and as a result of his report the two Canadas were in 1841 united in a legislative union.

Meanwhile the southern part of the province had been filling up. In 1791 the population was probably under 10,000; in 1824 it was 150,066, and in 1841, 455,688. The eastern counties of Stormont and Glengarry, and parts of the western peninsula, had been settled by Highlanders; the Canada Company, organized in 1825 by the Scottish novelist, John Galt, had founded the town of Guelph, had cleared large tracts of land in the western peninsula, and settled thereon hundreds of the best class of English and Scotch settlers.

Once granted responsible government, and the liberty to make her own mistakes, Upper Canada went ahead. The population rose to 952,004 in 1851 and to 1,396,091 in 1861. Politically she found Lower Canada an uneasy yoke-fellow. The equality of representation, granted at the union, at first unfair to Lower Canada, became still more unfair to Upper Canada, as her population first equalled and then surpassed that of her sister province. The Roman Catholic claim to separate state-aided schools, at length conceded in 1863, long set the religious bodies by the ears. Materially the province prospered. The "Clergy Reserves" were secularized in 1854, and in 1851 began a railway development, the excitement and extravagance caused by which led in 1857 to a financial crisis and the bankruptcy of various municipalities, but which on the whole produced great and lasting benefit. The Reciprocity Treaty with the United States, in operation from 1854 to 1866, and the high prices for farm produce due to the American Civil War, brought about an almost hectic prosperity. In the discussions from which sprang the federation of 1867, Ontario was the one province strongly in favour of the union, which was only rendered possible by the coalition of her rival leaders, J. A. Macdonald and George Brown.

Since Federation Upper Canada has been known as the province of Ontario. The first provincial government, formed on coalition lines by John Sandfield Macdonald, was thrifty and not unprogressive, but in 1871 was defeated by a reorganized liberal party, which held power from 1871 to 1905, and on the whole worthily. Under Oliver Mowat, premier from 1873 to 1896, the government, though strongly partisan, was thrifty and honest. An excellent system of primary and secondary schools was organized by Egerton Ryerson (1803–1882) and G. W. Ross (q.v.), higher education was aided and a school of practical science established in Toronto and of mining in Kingston; agriculture was fostered, and an excellent agricultural college founded at Guelph in 1874.

The great struggle of the time was with the federal government on the question of provincial rights. Several questions in which Ontario and the Dominion came into conflict were carried to the Judicial Committee of the Privy Council, and in all of them Mowat was successful. Connected with this was the boundary struggle with Manitoba, the latter province being aided by the federal government, partly out of dislike for Mowat, partly because the crown lands in the disputed territory would, had it been adjudged to Manitoba, have been under federal control. Had Manitoba won, the boundary line would have been drawn about 6 m. east of Port Arthur, but in 1884 the Judicial Committee of the Privy Council unanimously decided in favour of Ontario; and in 1888 another decision gave her absolute control of the crown lands of New Ontario. Under Mowat's successors

the barnacles which always attach to a party long in power became unpleasantly conspicuous, and in January 1905 the conscience of Ontario sent the conservatives into power, more from disgust at their opponents than from any enthusiasm for themselves. The new government displayed unexpected energy, ability and strength. The primary and model schools were consolidated and improved; the provincial university was given increased aid from the succession duties; various public utilities, previously operated by private companies, were taken over by the province, and worked with vigour and success. At the election of the 8th of June 1908 the conservative government was returned by an increased majority.

BIBLIOGRAPHY.—Statistical: The various departments of the provincial government publish annual reports, and frequent special reports. Among these may be noted those of the Bureau of Mines and the archaeological reports by David Boyle (1886–1906). Since 1889 the university of Toronto has published numerous valuable studies on historical, economic and social questions, e.g. Adam Shortt, Municipal Government in Ontario.

Historical: The early history of the province is best given in the general histories of Canada by MacMullen and Kingsford (see CANADA). Ernest Cruikshanks has published numerous excellent studies on the Ontario section of the War of 1812. Lord Durham's celebrated Report (1839, reprinted 1902) is less trustworthy on Ontario than on Quebec. R. and K. M. Lizar's In the Days of the Canada Company depicts the life of the early settlers. Biographies exist of most of the chief men: C. R. W. Biggar, Sir Oliver Mowat (2 vols. 1905), is practically a history of Ontario from 1867 to 1896. The provincial government has issued an excellent Documentary History of Education in Ontario, by J. G. Hodgins (28 vols.). See also W. Kingsford, Early Bibliography of Ontario. (W. L. G.)

ONTARIO, LAKE, the smallest and most easterly of the Great Lakes of North America. It lies between 43° 11′ and 44° 12′ N. and 76° 12′ and 79° 40′ W., and is bounded on the N. by the province of Ontario and on the S. by the state of New York. It is roughly elliptical, its major axis, 180 m. long, lying nearly east and west, and its greatest breadth is 53 m. The area of its water surface is 7260 sq. m. and the total area of its basin 32,080 sq. m. Its greatest depth is 738 ft., its average depth much in excess of that of Lake Erie, and it is as a general rule free from outlying shoals or dangers.

On the north side of the lake the land rises gradually from the shore, and spreads out into broad plains, which are thickly settled by farmers. A marked feature of the topography of the south shore is what is known as the Lake ridge, or, as it approaches the Niagara river, the Mountain ridge. This ridge extends, with breaks, from Sodus to the Niagara river, and is distant from the lake 3 to 8 m. The low ground between it and the shore, and between the Niagara escarpment and the water on the Canadian shore, is a celebrated fruit growing district, covered with vineyards, peach, apple and pear orchards and fruit farms. The Niagara river is the main feeder of the lake; the other largest rivers emptying into the lake are the Genesee, Oswego and Black from the south side, and the Trent, which discharges into the upper end of the bay of Quinte, a picturesque inlet 70 m. long, on the north shore, between the peninsula of Prince Edward, near the eastern extremity of the lake, and the mainland. The east end of the lake, where it is 30 m. wide, is crossed by a chain of five islands; and the lake has its outlet near Kingston, where it discharges into the head of the St Lawrence river between a group of islands. Elsewhere the lake is practically free from islands. There is a general surface current down the lake towards the eastward of about 8 m. a day, strongest along the south shore, but no noticeable return current. As a result of its relatively great depth there are seldom any great fluctuations of level in this lake due to wind disturbance, but the lake follows the general rule of the Great Lakes (q.v.) of seasonal and annual variation. Standard high water (of 1870) is 2·77 ft. below the mean level, of 246·18 ft. above mean sea-level, and standard low water 3·24 ft. below the same plane. The lake never freezes over, and is less obstructed by ice than the other lakes, but the harbours are closed by ice from about the middle of December to the middle of April.

The commerce of Lake Ontario is limited in comparison with that of the lakes above Niagara Falls, and is restricted to vessels that can pass through the Welland canal locks, which are 270 ft. long, 45 ft. wide and 14 ft. deep. Freight consists principally of coal shipped from Charlotte, Great and Little Sodus bays and Oswego to Canadian ports in the lakes, and to ports on the St Lawrence river; of grain shipped through the Welland canal to the St Lawrence; and of lumber from Canadian ports. There is a large passenger traffic, including pleasure trips, principally radiating from Toronto. Ports on the lake are limited in capacity to vessels drawing not more than 14 ft. of water. The principal Canadian ports are Kingston, at the head of the St Lawrence river; Toronto, where the harbour is formed by an island with improved entrance channels constructed both east and west of it; and Hamilton, at the head of the lake, situated on a landlocked lagoon, connected with the main lake by Burlington channel, an artificial cut. The principal United States port is Oswego, where a breakwater has been built, making an outer harbour. The construction of a breakwater was undertaken in 1907 by the United States government at Cape Vincent to form a harbour where westbound vessels can shelter from storm before crossing the lake.

The difference of 327 ft. in level between Lake Ontario and Lake Erie is overcome by the Welland canal, which leads southward from Port Dalhousie. It accommodates vessels 255 ft. in length, with a draught of 14 ft. The Murray canal, opened for traffic on the 14th of April 1890, extends from Presqu'ile bay, on the north of the lake, to the head of the bay of Quinte, and enables vessels to avoid 70 m. of open navigation. It is 11 ft. deep below the lowest lake level, and has no locks. It is proposed to have the eastern terminus of the Trent canal system (see GREAT LAKES) at the head of the bay of Quinte, entering through the Trent river. At Kingston the Rideau canal, extending 128 m. to Ottawa, enters the St Lawrence river at the foot of the lake.

BIBLIOGRAPHY.—*Bulletin No. 17, Survey of Northern and North-western Lakes*, U.S. Lake Survey Office (Detroit, Mich., 1907): Publication No. 108 D., *Sailing Directions for Lake Ontario*, Hydrographic Office, U.S. Navy (Washington, D.C., 1902); *St Lawrence Pilot* (7th ed.), Hydrographic Office, Admiralty (London, 1906). (W. P. A.)

ONTENIENTE, a town of eastern Spain, in the province of Valencia; on the right bank of the Clariano or Onteniente, a sub-tributary of the Júcar, and on the Játiva-Villena railway. Pop. (1900) 11,430. Onteniente has a parish church remarkable for its lofty square tower, and a palace of the dukes of Almodóvar. There is a large modern suburb outside the old town, which was formerly a walled city; some vestiges of the ramparts still remain. Linen and woollen cloth, paper, brandy, furniture and earthenware are manufactured; and there is some trade in cereals, wine and oil.

ONTOLOGY (adapted from a modern Latin form *ontologia* used by Jean le Clerc 1692; Gr. ὤν, ὄντος, pres. part. of εἶναι, to be, and λόγος, science), the name given to that branch of philosophy which deals specially with the nature of being (οὐσία) *i.e.* reality in the abstract. The idea, denoted in modern philosophy by the term "ontology" in contrast to the broader "metaphysics" and the correlative "epistemology," goes back to such phrases as ὄντως ὄντα, which Plato uses to describe the absolute reality of ideas; Plato, however, uses the term "dialectic" for this particular branch of metaphysics. Aristotle, likewise, holding that the separate sciences have each their own subject matter, postulates a prior science of existence in general which he describes as "first philosophy." So far, therefore, the science of being is distinguished not from that of knowing but from that of the special forms of being: as to the possibility of objective reality there is no question. A new distinction arises in the philosophy of Wolff who first made "ontology" a technical term. Theoretical philosophy (metaphysics) is by him divided into that which deals with being in general whether objective or subjective, as contrasted with the particular entities, the soul, the world and God. The former is ontology. This intermediate stage in the evolution of the science of being gave place to the modern view that the first duty of the philosopher is to consider knowledge itself (see EPISTEMOLOGY), and that only in the light of conclusion as to this primary problem is it possible to consider the nature of being. The evolution of metaphysics has thus relegated ontology to a secondary place. On the other hand it remains true that the science of knowing is inseparable from, and in a sense identical with that of being. Epistemological conclusions cannot be expressed ultimately without the aid of ontological terms.

For the wider relations of ontology, see further PHILOSOPHY.

ONYX, a banded chalcedony or striped agate, composed of white layers alternating with others of black, brown or red colour. A typical onyx consists of two or more black and white strata, whilst the term sardonyx is applied to the stone if it contains red or brown bands (see SARDONYX). Probably those varieties which show red and white zones originally suggested the name "onyx," from Gr. ὄνυξ (a finger nail), since the colours of such stones may be not unlike those of the nail. The onyx when worked by the lapidary was often designated by the diminutive ὀνύχιον; and at the present day the term *nicolo*, a corruption of the Italian diminutive *onicolo*, is applied to an onyx which presents a thin layer of chalcedony deriving a bluish tint from the subjacent black ground. The Hebrew *soham* is translated in the authorized version of the Old Testament "onyx," but the revised version gives in some of the passages an alternative marginal reading of "beryl." The position of the land of Havilah, which yielded the onyx-stone, is uncertain.

India has for ages supplied the finest onyxes, and hence jewellers apply the expression "Oriental onyx" to any stone remarkable for beauty of colour and regularity of stratification, quite regardless of its locality. As far back as the 1st century the author of the *Periplus Maris Erythraei* mentions the onyx among the products of Plythanae, a locality probably identified with Paithan on the Godavari; and he further states that the stones were taken down to Barygaza, the modern Broach, where the agate trade still flourishes. It is probable that the early Greeks and Romans derived their prized agate-cups from this locality. The Indian onyx is found, with agate and jasper-pebbles, in river gravels derived from the disintegration of the amygdaloidal volcanic rocks of the Deccan. A great deal of onyx now sold is obtained from South American agates, cut in Germany. It often happens that the lower deposits in an agate-nodule are in horizontal layers, forming onyx, while the other deposits have adapted themselves to the curved contours of the cavity. The onyxes cut from agate-nodules are usually stained artificially, as explained under AGATE.

The onyx is largely used for heads, brooches, pins, ring-stones and other small ornamental objects, while the larger pieces are occasionally wrought in the form of cups, bowls, vases, &c. Onyx is the favourite stone for cameo work, advantage being taken of the differently-coloured layers to produce a subject in relief on a background of another colour. For fine examples of ancient cameo-work in onyx and sardonyx see CEM.

It should be noted that the term onyx, or onychite, was formerly, and is still sometimes, applied to certain kinds of banded marble, like the "oriental alabaster" (see ALABASTER). Such substances are quite distinct from the hard siliceous onyx, being much softer and less precious: they are, in fact, usually deposits of calcium carbonate like stalagmite and travertine. The ornamental stones known as Mexican onyx, or Tecali marble, and Algerian onyx are of this character; and in order to avoid any confusion with the true onyx it is well to distinguish all the calcareous "onyxes" as onyx-marble. The well-known "Gibraltar stone" is an onyx-marble, with brown bands, from caverns in the limestone of Gibraltar. The Tecali onyx, sometimes with delicate green shades, takes its name from the district of Tecali; one of its localities being La Pedrara, about 21 m. from the city of Puebla.

For onyx-marbles see Dr G. P. Merrill, *Rep. U.S. Nat. Mus.* for 1893 (1895), p. 539. (F. W. R.*)

OOLITE (Gr. ᾠόν, egg, λίθος, stone), in geology, a term having two distinct meanings. In petrology (*q.v.*) it denotes a type of rock structure characterized by the presence of minute spherical grains resembling the roe of a fish; if the grains become larger, the structure is said to be pisolitic (Gr. πίσος, pea). In stratigraphical geology, the oolite is a division of the Jurassic system (q.v.). The term appears to have been first applied in this latter sense by A. J. M. Brochant de Villiers in 1803, and through the labours of W. Smith, W. D. Conybeare, W. Buckland and others, it was gradually introduced for the calcareous rocks of the British Jurassic until it came to comprehend the whole system above the Lias. Custom still sanctions its use in England, but it has been objected that the Oolitic (Jurassic) system contains many strata that are not oolitic; and since oolitic structure occurs in limestones of all ages, it is misleading to employ the word in this way.

The oolites are usually divided into: the *Upper* or *Portland Oolite*, comprising the Purbeck, Portland and Kimeridge stages; the *Middle* or *Oxford Oolite*, including the Corallian, Oxfordian and Kellaways beds; and the *Lower Oolites*, with the Cornbrash, Great or Bath Oolite (Bathonian), Fullonian and the Inferior Oolite (Bajocian). The Great Oolite and Inferior Oolite are treated here.

The *Inferior Oolite*, called by William Smith the "Under Oolite" from its occurrence beneath the Great or "Upper Oolite" in the neighbourhood of Bath, received its present name from J. Townsend in 1813. It is an extremely variable assemblage of strata. In the Cotteswold Hills it is a series of marine deposits, 264 ft. thick near Cheltenham, but within 25 m. the strata thin out to 30 ft. at Fawler in Oxfordshire. A typical section N.E. of Dursley contains the following subdivisions:—

	Zone Fossils.
White Freestone . . .5 ft. Clypeus Grit . . . 6-15 ft.	Cosmoceras Parkinsoni.
Upper Trigonia Grit 2-12 ft. Gryphite Grit . . . 2-12 ft. LowerTrigonia Grit .2-12 ft.	Stephanoceras Humphriesianum.
Upper Freestone . 6-20 ft. Oolite Marl . . . 5-10 ft. Lower Freestone 45-130 ft.	Harpoceras Murchisonae.
Pea Grit . . . . 3-20 ft. Lower Limestone 10-25 ft.	
Cephalopod Limestone 2-7 ft. Cotteswold Sands 10-120 ft.	Lioceras opalinum. Lytoceras jurense.

The basal sandy series, which is closely related with the underlying Lias, is usually described as the Midford Sands (from Midford, near Bath), but it is also known locally as the Bradford, Yeovil or Cotteswold Sands. The Pea Grit series contains pisolitic limestone and coarse, iron-stained oolite and sandy limestone. The freestones are compact oolite limestones. The ragstones are fossiliferous, earthy and iron-stained oolitic limestones. The "grits" are really coarse-grained limestones or calciferous sandstones. Between Andoversford and Bourton-in-the-Water the Inferior Oolite is represented by ragstones (Ferruginous beds, Clypeus Grit, Trigonia bed, Notgrove Freestone, Gryphite Grit) and freestones (Upper Freestones and Harford Sands, Oolite Marl, Lower Freestone). Near Chipping Norton in Oxfordshire the "Chipping Norton Limestone" lies at the top of a very variable series of rocks. In Rutlandshire, Northamptonshire and Lincolnshire the following beds, in descending order, belong to the Inferior Oolite: Lincolnshire limestone (shelly, coral-bearing and oolitic), Collyweston slate, Lower Estuarine series and Northampton Sands (hard calcareous sandstones, blue and greenish ironstones and sandy limestones. The Collyweston slates are arenaceous limestones which have been used for roofing slates since the time of Henry VII.; Easton, Dene and Kirkby are important localities. The fissility of the rock is developed by exposure to frost. Similar beds are the Whittering Pendle and White Pendle or Duston slate.

The Inferior Oolite of Yorkshire differs from that of the Cotteswold district; in place of the marine limestones of the latter area there is a thick series of sands and sandstones with shales and beds of coal; these deposits are mainly estuarine with occasional marine beds. The principal subdivisions, in descending order, are: the Scarborough or Grey Limestone series, the Middle Estuarine series with their coal seams; the Millepore series and Whitwell or Cave Oolite; the Lower Estuarine series with the Eller Beck bed and Hydraulic Limestone; the Dogger and Blea Wyke beds. The last-named beds, like the Midford Sands, exhibit a passage between the Inferior Oolite and the Lias. In Skye and Raasay the Inferior Oolite is represented by sandstones.

The fossils of the Inferior Oolite are abundant. Over 200 species of Ammonite are known; gasteropods are numerous: *Trigonia, Lima, Ostrea, Gervillia, Pecten*, are common pelecypods; *Terebratula, Waldheimia* and *Rhynchonella* are the prevailing brachiopods. Corals are very numerous in some limestones (*Isastrea, Montivaultia*). Urchins are represented by *Cidaris, Acrosalenia, Nucleolites, Pygaster, Pseudodiadema, Hemicidaris*; starfish by *Solaster, Astropecten*, and Crinoids by *Pentacrinus, Apiocrinus*. Plant remains, cycads, ferns, Ginkgo and coniferous trees are found most abundantly in the Yorkshire area.

The economic products of the Inferior Oolite include many well-known building stones, notably those of Ham Hill, Doulting, Dundry, Painswick, Cheltenham, Duston, Weldon, Ketton, Barnack, Stamford, Casterton, Clipsham, Great Ponton, Ancaster, Aislaby (Lower Estuarine series). Several of the stones are used for road metal. Iron ores have been worked in the Grey Limestone, the Eller Beck bed, the Dogger and the Northampton beds, the latter being the most important.

The *Great or Bath Oolite* is typically developed in the neighbourhood of Bath, and except in a modified form it does not extend beyond the counties of Wiltshire, Somersetshire, Gloucestershire and Oxfordshire. It does not reach so far as Yorkshire, unless the Upper Estuarine series of that district is its representative. The principal subdivisions of the series are:—

	Wiltshire, Somersetshire, Gloucestershire, Oxfordshire.	Northamptonshire, Buckinghamshire, Bedfordshire, Lincolnshire.
Upper	False - bedded Oolites = Kemble beds, "White Limestone," pale, earthy Limestones, occasionally oolitic, and Marls. Upper Ragstones of Bath.	Great Oolite Clay = Blisworth Clay.
Lower	False - bedded Oolites = the principal building stones, Bath Freestone. Fissile calcareous Sandstones; oolitic Limestones and Clays; Lower Ragstones of Bath and Stonesfield Slate. Thickness, 100-130 ft.	Great Oolite Limestone (generally non-oolitic). Upper Estuarine series. Thickness, 20-100 ft.

An exact correlation of the Great Oolite strata in the N.E. area with those of the S.W. is not possible on account of the great variability and impersistence of the beds. Current bedding is very prevalent, and minor stratigraphical breaks are common. The absence of the typical Great Oolite from the N.E. district is probably due in part to contemporaneous erosion with overstep of the succeeding formation, and in part to local changes in the sediment in the shallow waters of this epoch. This may also explain the rapid thinning-out of the Great Oolite south of Bath, where its place may be taken, to some extent, by the Bradford Clay, Forest Marble and Fullonian.

The Great Oolite is not readily divisible into palaeontological zones, but the ammonite *Perisphinctes arbustigerus* may be taken as the characteristic form along with *Belemnites bessinus* and *Terebratula maxillata*. Corals (*Isastraea, Thamnastria*) and Polyzoa (*Stomatopora, Diastopora*) are abundant. *Hemicidaris, Cidaris, Acrosalenia, Clypeus* and other urchins are common: *Pentacrinus* and *Apiocrinus* represent the Crinoids. *Terebratula, Rhynchonella, Waldheimia, Crania* are the prevailing brachiopods: the common pelecypods, *Pecten, Ostrea, Lima, Trigonia, Modiola; Natica, Nerinea* and other gasteropods are found. *Perisphinctes grandis, Macrocephalites subcontractus, Oppelia discus* and *Nautilus dispansus* are among the more common cephalopods. The remains of fish (*Mesodon, Hybodus*), crocodiles (*Teliosaurus*), dinosaurs (*Cetiosaurus,*

Megalosaurus), pterosaurs (*Rhamphocephalus*), and in the Stonesfield slate the jaws of marsupial mammals (*Amphitherium, Amphilestes, Phascolotherium*) occur.

. The building stones of the Great Oolite are mainly oolitic freestones, viz. the varieties of "Bath stone " quarried and mined in the neighbourhood of that city (Corsham Down, Monks Park, Coombe Down, Odd Down, Box Ground, &c.) and more shelly limestones like the Taynton and Milton stone. The Stonesfield slate·has been largely worked near Woodstock in Oxfordshire and in Gloucestershire for roofing, &c. The "slates " are brown calcareous sandstone, grey and slightly oolitic calcareous sand-stone, and blue and grey oolitic limestone. A curious modification of the Great Oolite—White Limestone division—is characterized by irregular ramifying tubular cavities, usually filled with ochreous material; this rock occurs in blocks and layers, and is used for rockeries under the name of " Dagham stone " from Dagham Down north of Cirencester. (See also JURASSIC.)

(J.A.H.)

OOSTERZEE, JAN JACOB VAN (1817–1882), Dutch divine, was born at Rotterdam on the 1st of April 1817. After acting as pastor at Alkmaar and Rotterdam, in 1863 he was made professor of biblical and practical theology at the university of Utrecht. Oosterzee earned a reputation as a preacher, was editor of the *Theolog. Jahrbücher* from 1845, wrote a number of noteworthy books on religious history, and published poems in Dutch (1882). He died on the 29th of July 1882. A collected edition of Oosterzee's works was published in French, *Œuvres complètes*, in three volumes (1877–1880). His autobiography appeared in 1882.

OOTACAMUND, or UTAKAMAND, a town of British India, headquarters of the Nilgiris district in Madras, approached by a rack railway from the Mettapolliem station on the Madras railway. Pop. (1901) 18,596. It is the principal sanatorium of southern India, and summer headquarters of the Madras government. It is placed on a plateau about 7230 ft. above the sea, with a fine artificial lake, and mountains rising above 8000 ft. The mean annual temperature is 58° F., with a minimum of 38° in January and a maximum of 76° in May; average annual rainfall, 49 in. The houses are scattered on the hillsides amid luxuriant gardens, and there are extensive carriage drives. In the neighbourhood are plantations of coffee, tea and cinchona. There are a brewery and two dairy farms. The Lawrence asylum for the children of European soldiers was founded in 1858, and there are also the Breeks memorial and Basel Mission high schools.

See Sir F. Price, *Ootacamund: A History* (Madras, 1908).

OOZE (O. Eng. *wáse*, cognate with an obsolete *waise*, mud; cf. O. Nor. *veisa*, muddy pool), the slime or mud at the bottom of a river, stream, especially of a tidal river or estuary, and so particularly used in deep-sea soundings of the deposit of fine calcareous mud, in which remains of foraminifera are largely present. . The word " ooze " is also used as a technical term in tanning, of the liquor in a tan vat in which the hides are steeped, made of a solution of oak bark or other substances which yield tannin. This word is in origin different from " ooze " in its first sense. It appears in O. Eng. as *wós*, and meant the juice of plants, fruits, &c.

OPAH (*Lampris luna*), a pelagic fish, the affinities of which are still a puzzle to ichthyologists. The body is compressed and deep (more so than in the bream) and the scales are minute. A long dorsal fin, high and pointed anteriorly, runs along nearly the whole length of the back; the caudal is strong and deeply cleft. The ventral fin is also elongated, and all the fins are destitute of spines. The pelvic fins are abdominal in position, long and pointed in shape, and the pelvic bones are connected with the caracoids. These fins contain numerous (15–17) rays, a feature in which the fish differs from the Acanthopterygians. · In its gorgeous colours the opah surpasses even the dolphins, all the fins being of a bright scarlet. The sides are bluish green above, violet in the middle, red beneath, variegated with oval spots of brilliant silver. It is only occasionally found near the shore; its real home is the Atlantic, especially near Madeira and the Azores, but many captures are recorded from Great

Britain, Ireland and Scandinavia; it strays as far north as Iceland and Newfoundland, and probably southwards to the latitudes of the coast of Guinea. It is rare in the Mediterranean. The name opah, which is now generally used, is derived from the statement of a native of the coast of Guinea who happened to be in England when the first specimen was exhibited (1750), and who thought he recognized in it a fish well known by that name in his native country. From its habit of coming to the surface in calm weather, showing its high dorsal fin above the water, it has also received the name of " sun-fish," which it shares with *Orthagoriscus* and the basking shark. It grows to a length of 4 to 5 ft. and a weight exceeding 100 lb, and is highly esteemed on account of the excellent flavour of its flesh.

OPAL, an amorphous or non-crystalline mineral consisting of hydrated silica, occasionally displaying a beautiful play of colour, whence its value as a gem-stone. It is named from Lat. *opalus*, Gr. ὀπάλλιον, with which may be compared Sansk. *upala*, a precious stone. Opal commonly occurs in nodular or stalactitic masses, in the cavities of volcanic rocks, having been deposited in a gelatinous or colloidal condition. It is inferior to quartz in hardness (H. 5·5 to 6·5) and in density (S. G. 1·9 to 2·3), whilst it differs also by its solubility in caustic alkalis. The proportion of water in opal varies usually from 3 to 12%, and it is said that occasionally no water can be detected, the mineral having apparently suffered dehydration. Though normally isotropic, opal is frequently doubly refracting, the anomaly being due to tension set up during consolidation. The mineral when pure is transparent and colourless; as well seen in the variety which, from its vitreous appearance, was called by A. G. Werner *hyalite* (Gr. ὕαλος, glass), or popularly " Müller's glass," a name said to have been taken from its discoverer. This pellucid opaline silica occurs as an incrustation in small globules, and is by no means a common mineral, being chiefly found at certain localities in Bohemia, Mexico and Colorado, U.S.A. (Cripple Creek).

The beautiful variety known as " noble " or " precious opal " owes its value to the brilliant flashes of colour which it displays by reflected light. The colours are not due to the presence of any material pigment, but result from certain structural peculiarities in the stone, perhaps from microscopic fissures or pores or from delicate strain, but more probably from very thin lamellae of foreign matter, or of opaline silica, having a different index of refraction from that of the matrix. The origin of the colours in opal has been studied by Sir D. Brewster, Sir W. Crookes, Lord Rayleigh and H. Behrens. In the variety known, to jewellers as " harlequin opal," the rainbow-like tints are flashed forth from small angular masses, forming a kind of polychromatic mosaic, whilst in other varieties the colours are disposed in broad bands or irregular patches of comparatively large area. By moving the stone, a brilliant succession of fiery flashes may sometimes be obtained. The opal is usually cut with a convex surface, and, being a soft stone, should be protected from friction likely to produce abrasion; nor should it be exposed to sudden alternations of temperature. The loss of water, sometimes effected by heat, greatly impairs the colour, though moderate warmth may improve it. According to Pliny the opal ranked next in value to the emerald, and he relates that the rich Roman senator Nonius was exiled by Mark Antony for sake of his magnificent opal, as large as a hazel nut. The opal, on account of its unique characters, has been the subject of remarkable superstition, and even in modern times has often been regarded as an unlucky stone, but in recent years it has regained popular favour and is now when fine, among the most highly valued gem-stones.

Precious opal is a mineral of very limited distribution. Though ancient writers state that it was brought from India, and fine stones are still called in trade " Oriental opal," its occurrence is not known in the East. The finest opals seem to have been always obtained from Hungary, where the mineral occurs, associated with much common opal, in nests in an altered andesitic rock. The fine opals occur only at the Dubnyik mine, near the village of Vörösvágás (Czerwenitza). The workings have been carried on for centuries in the mountains near Eperjes, and some remarkable stones from this locality are preserved in the Imperial Natural History Museum in Vienna, including an uncut specimen weighing about 3000 carats. Precious opal is found also in Honduras, especially in trachyte near Gracias á Dios; and in Mexico, where it occurs in a porphyritic rock at Esperanza in the state of Queretaro. A remarkable kind of opal, of yellow or hyacinth-red colour, occurs in trachytic porphyry at Zimapan in Hidalgo, Mexico, and is known as "fire-opal." This variety is not only cut *en cabochon* but is also faceted. Fire-opal is sometimes called "girasol." Much precious opal is worked in Australia. In Queensland it is found lining cracks in nodules of brown ironstone in the Desert Sandstone, a rock of Upper Cretaceous age, and is distributed over a wide area near the Barcoo river. Bulla Creek is a well-known locality. The layer of opal, when too thin to be cut with a convex surface, is used for inlaid work or is carved into cameos which show to much advantage against the dark-brown matrix. The matrix penetrated by veins and spots of opal, and perhaps heightened in colour artificially, has been called "black opal"; but true black opal occurs in New South Wales. The "root of opal" consists of the mineral disseminated through the matrix. In New South Wales precious opal was accidentally discovered in 1889, and is now largely worked at White Cliffs, Yungnulgra county, where it is found in nodules and seams in a siliceous rock of the Upper Cretaceous series. It is notable that the opal sometimes replaces shells and even reptilian bones, whilst curious pseudomorphs, known as "pineapple opal," show the opal in the form of aggregated crystals, perhaps of gypsum, gaylussite or glauberite.

"Common opal" is the name generally applied to the varieties which exhibit no beauty of colour, and may be nearly opaque. It is frequently found in the vesicular lavas of the N.E. of Ireland, the west of Scotland, the Faroe Isles and Iceland. When of milky-white colour it is known as "milk opal"; when of resinous and waxy appearance as "resin opal"; if handed it is called "agate opal"; a green variety is termed "prase opal"; a dark red, ferruginous variety "jaspar opal"; whilst "rose opal" is a beautiful pink mineral, coloured with organic matter, found at Quincy, near Méhun-sur-Yèvre, in France. A brown or grey concretionary opal from Tertiary shales at Menilmontant, near Paris, is known as menilite or "liver opal." A dull opaque form of opal, with a fracture imperfectly conchoidal, is called "semi-opal"; whilst the opal which not infrequently forms the mineralizing substance of fossil wood passes as "wood opal." The name hydrophane is applied to a porous opal, perhaps partially dehydrated, which is almost opaque when dry but becomes more or less transparent when immersed in water. It has been sometimes sold in America as "magic stone." Cacholong is another kind of porous opal with a lustre rather like that of mother-of-pearl, said to have been named from the Cach river in Bokhara, but the word is probably of Tatar origin.

Opaline silica is frequently deposited from hot siliceous springs, often in cauliflower-like masses, and is known as geyserite. This occurs in Iceland, New Zealand and the Yellowstone National Park. The fiorite from the hot springs of Santa Fiora, in Tuscany, is opaline silica, with a rather pearly lustre. A variety containing an exceptionally small proportion of water, obtained from the Yellowstone Park, was named pealite, after the c. emist A. C. Peale. The siliceous deposits from springs, often due to organic agencies, are known generally as "siliceous sinter" or, if very loose in texture, as "siliceous tuff." Opaline silica forms the material of many organic structures, like the frustules of diatoms and the tests of radiolarians, which may accumulate as deposits of tripoli, and be used for polishing purposes. (F. W. R.*)

OPALINA (so named by J. E. Purkinjě and G. Valentin), a genus of Protozoa, without mouth or contractile vacuole, covered with nearly equal flagelliform cilia, and possessing numerous nuclei, all similar. It has been referred to Aspirotricha by Bütschli, but by M. Hartog (*Cambridge Natural History*, vol. ii., 1906) has been transferred to the Flagellates (*q.v.*). All the species are parasitic in cold-blooded Vertebrates.

See Bezzenberger in *Archiv. f. Protistenkunde* (1903), iii. 138.

OPATA ("enemies," so called by their neighbours the Pimas), a tribe of Mexican Indians of Piman stock. Their country is the mountainous district of north-eastern Sonora and northwestern Chihuahua, Mexico. Though usually loyal to the Mexican government, they rebelled in 1820, but after a gallant effort were defeated. They number now about 5000, and still largely retain their ancient autonomy.

OPERA (Italian for "work"), a drama set to music, as distinguished from plays in which music is merely incidental. Music has been a resource of the drama from the earliest times, and doubtless the results of researches in the early history of this connexion have been made very interesting, but they are hardly relevant to a history of opera as an art-form. If language has meaning, an art-form can hardly be said to exist under conditions where the only real connexions between its alleged origin and its modern maturity are such universal means of expression as can equally well connect it with almost everything else. We will therefore pass over the orthodox history of opera as traceable from the music of Greek tragedy to that of miracle-plays, and will begin with its real beginning, the first dramas that were set to music in order to be produced as musical works of art, at the beginning of the 17th century.

There seems no reason to doubt the story, given by Doni, of the meetings held by a group of amateurs at the house of the Bardi in Florence in the last years of the 16th century, with the object of trying experiments in emotional musical expression by the use of instruments and solo voices. Before this time there was no real opportunity for music-drama. The only high musical art of the 16th century was unaccompanied choral music: its expression was perfect within its limits, and its limits so absolutely excluded all but what may be called static or contemplative emotion that "dramatic music" was as inconceivable as "dramatic architecture." But the literary and musical *dilettanti* who met at the house of the Bardi were not mature musical artists; they therefore had no scruples, and their imaginations were fired by the dream of restoring the glories of Greek tragedy, especially on the side of its musical declamation. The first pioneer in the new "monodic" movement seems to have been Vincenzo Galilei, the father of Galileo. This enthusiastic amateur warbled the story of Ugolino to the accompaniment of the lute, much to the amusement of expert musicians; but he gained the respect and sympathy of those whose culture was literary rather than musical. His efforts must have been not unlike a wild caricature of Mr. W. B. Yeats's method of reciting poetry to the psaltery. The first public production in the new style was Jacopo Peri's *Euridice* (1600), which was followed by a less successful effort of Caccini's on the same subject. To us it is astonishing that an art so great as the polyphony of the 16th century could ever have become forgotten in a new venture so feeble in its first steps. Sir Hubert Parry has happily characterized the general effect of the new movement on contemporary imagination as something like that of laying a foundation-stone—the suggestion of a vista of possibilities so inspiriting as to exclude all sense of the triviality of the present achievement. Meanwhile those composers who retained the mastery of polyphonic music tried to find a purely vocal and polyphonic solution of the problem of music-drama; and the *Amfiparnasso* of Orazio Vecchi (written in 1594, the year of Palestrina's death, and produced three years later) is not alone, though it is by far the most remarkable, among attempts to make a music-drama out of a series of madrigals. From the woodcuts which adorn the first edition of the *Amfiparnasso* it has been conjectured that the actors sang one voice each, while the rest of the harmony was supplied by singers behind the stage[1]; and this may have been the case with other works of this kind. But the words of Vecchi's introductory chorus contradict this idea, for they tell the audience that "the theatre of this drama is the world" and that the spectators must "hear instead of seeing."

[1] The first story in Berlioz's *Soirées d'orchestre* is about a young 16th-century genius who revolts from this practice and becomes a pioneer of monody. The picture is brilliant, though the young genius evidently learnt all his music in Paris somewhere about 1830.

With the decadence of the madrigal, Monteverde brought a real musical power to bear on the new style. His results are now intelligible only to historians, and they seem to us artistically nugatory; but in their day they were so impressive as to render the further continuance of 16th-century choral art impossible. At the beginning of the 17th century no young musician of lively artistic receptivity could fail to be profoundly stirred by Monteverde's *Orfeo* (1602), *Arianna* (1608) and *Il Combattimento di Tancredi e Clorinda* (1624), works in which the resources of instruments were developed with the same archaic boldness, the same grasp of immediate emotional effect and the same lack of artistic organization as the harmonic resources. The spark of Monteverde's genius produced·in musical history a result more like an explosion than an enlightenment; and the emotional rhetoric of his art was so uncontrollable, and at the same time so much more impressive in suggestion than in realization, that we cannot be surprised that the next definite step in the history of opera took the direction of mere musical form, and was not only undramatic but anti-dramatic.

The system of free musical declamation known as *recitative* is said to have been used by Emilio del Cavalieri as early as 1588, and it was in the nature of things almost the only means of vocal expression conceivable by the pioneers of opera. Formal melody, such as that·of popular songs, was as much beneath their dignity as it had been beneath that of the high art from which they revolted; but, in the absence of any harmonic system but that of the church modes, which was manifestly incapable of assimilating the new "unprepared discords," and in the utter chaos of early experiments in instrumentation, formal melody proved a godsend as the novelty of recitative faded. Tunes were soon legalized at moments of dramatic repose when it was possible for the actors to indulge in either a dance or a display of vocalization; it was in the tunes that the strong harmonic system of modern tonality took shape; and by the early days of Alessandro Scarlatti, before the end of the 17th century, the art of tune-making had perennially blossomed into the musically safe and effective form of the *aria* (*q.v.*). From this time until the death of Handel the history of opera is simply the history of the aria; except in so far as in France, under Lully, it is also the history of ballet-music, the other main theatrical occasion for the art of tune-making. With opera before Gluck there is little interest in tracing schools and developments, for the musical art had as mechanical a connexion with drama as it had with the art of scene-painting, and neither it nor the drama which was attached to it showed any real development at all, though the librettist Metastasio presented as imposing a figure in 18th-century Italian literature as Handel presented in Italian opera. Before this period of stagnation we find an almost solitary and provincial outburst of life in the wonderful patch-work of Purcell's art (1658–1695). Whether he is producing genuine operas (as in the unique case of *Dido and Aeneas*) or merely incidental music to plays (as in the so-called opera *King Arthur*), his deeply inspired essays in dramatic music are no less interesting in their historic isolation from everything except the influence of Lully than they are admirable as evidences of a genius which, with the opportunities of 50 years later or 150 years earlier, might assuredly have proved one of the greatest in all music. Another sign of life has been appreciated by recent research in the interesting farcical operas (mostly Neapolitan) of certain early 18th-century Italian composers (see LEO, PERGOLESE, LOGROSCINO), which have some bearing on the antecedents of Mozart.

The real reason for the stagnation of high opera before Gluck is (as explained in the articles MUSIC and SONATA FORMS) that the forms of music known before 1750 could not express dramatic change without losing artistic organization. The "spirit of the age" can have had little to do with the difficulty, or why should Shakespeare not have had a contemporary operatic brother-artist during the "Golden Age" of music? The opportunity for reform came with the rise of the sonata style. It was fortunate for Gluck that the music of his time was too vigorously organised to be upset by new discoveries. Gluck was a much greater artist than Monteverde, but he too was not overloaded with academic mastery; indeed, though historians have denied it, Monteverde was by far the better contrapuntist, and seems rather to have renounced his musical powers than to have struggled for need of them. But instead of memories of a Golden Age, Gluck had behind him 150 years of harmonic and orchestral knowledge of good and evil. He also had almost as clear a sense of symphonic form as could find scope in opera at all; and his melodic power was generally of the highest order. It is often said that his work was too far in advance of his time to establish his intended reform; and, if this means that undramatic Italian operas continued to outnumber those dramatic masterpieces which no smaller man could achieve, the statement is as true as it is of every great artist. If, however, it is taken to mean that because Mozart's triumphs do not lie in serious opera he owes nothing to Gluck, then the statement. is misleading (see GLUCK). The influence of Gluck on Mozart was profound, not on˷ where it is relevant to the particular type of libretto, as in *Idomeneo*, but also on the broad dramatic basis which includes Greek tragedy and the 18th-century comedy of manners. Mozart, whose first impulse was always to make his music coherent in itself, far some time continued to cultivate side by side with his growing polyphony and freedom of movement certain Italian formalities which, though musically effective and flattering˜to singers, were dramatically vicious. But these features, though they spoil *Idomeneo*, correspond to much that in Gluck's operas shows mere helplessness; and in comic opera they may even become dramatically appropriate. Thus in *Così fan tutte* the florid arias in which the two heroines protest their fidelity are the arias of ladies who do protest too much; and in *Die Zauberflöte* the extravagant vocal fireworks of the Queen of Night are the displays of one who, in the words of the high priest Sarastro, "hopes to cajole the people with illusions and superstition." In the article MOZART we have discussed other evidences of his stagecraft and insight into character, talents for which his comic subjects gave him far more scope than those of classical tragedy had given to Gluck. Mozart always extracts the utmost musical effect from every situation in his absurd and often tiresome libretti (especially in vocal *ensemble*), while his musical effects are always such as give dramatic life to what in other hands are conventional musical forms. These merits would never have been gainsaid but for the violence of Wagner's earlier partisans in their revolt from the uncritical classicism of his denser and noisier opponents. Wagner himself stands as far aloof from Wagnerian Philistinism as from uncritical classicism. He was a fierce critic of social conditions and by no means incapable of hasty iconoclastic judgments; but he would have treated with scant respect the criticism that censures Mozart for superficiality in rejecting the radically unmusical element of mordant social satire which distinguishes the *Figaro* of Beaumarchais from the most perfect opera in all classical music.

It cannot be said that in any high artistic sense Italian comic opera has developed continuously since Mozart. The vocal athleticism of singers; the acceptance and great development by Mozart.of what we may call symphonic (as distinguished from Handelian) forms of aria and *ensemble*; and the enlargement of the orchestra; these processes gave the Italian composers of Mozart's and later times prosaically golden opportunities for lilting spectators and singers to the seventh heaven of flattered vanity, while the music, in itself no less than in its relation to the drama, was steadily degraded. The decline begins with Mozart's contemporary and survivor, D. Cimarosa, whose ideas are genuine and, in the main, refined, but who lacks power and resource. His style was by no means debased, but it was just so slight that contemporaries found it fairly easy. His most famous work, *Il Matrimonio Segreto*, is an *opera buffa* which is still occasionally revived, and it is very like the sort of thing that people who despise Mozart imagine *Figaro* to be. Unless it is approached with sympathy, its effect after *Figaro* is hardly more exhilarating than that of the once pilloried spurious " Second Part " to the *Pickwick Papers*. But this is harsh judgment; for it proves.to be a good semi-classic as soon as we take it on its own merits.

It is far more musical, if less vivacious, than Rossini's *Barbiere*; and the decline of Italian opera is more significantly foreshadowed in Cimarosa's other *chef-d'œuvre*, the remarkable *opera seria*, *Gli Orazi ed i Curiazi*. Here the arias and *ensembles* are serious art, showing a pale reflection of Mozart, and not wholly without Mozart's spirit; the choruses, notably the first of all, have fine moments; and the treatment of conflicting emotions at one crisis, where military music is heard behind the scenes, is masterly. Lastly, the abrupt conclusion at the moment of the catastrophe is good and was novel at the time, though it foreshadows that sacrifice of true dramatic and musical breadth to the desire for an "effective curtain," and that mortal fear of anti-climax which in classical French opera rendered a great musical finale almost impossible. But the interesting and dramatic features in *Gli Orazi* are unfortunately less significant historically than the vulgarity of its overture, and the impossibility, after the beautiful opening chorus, of tracing any unmistakably tragic style in the whole work except by the negative sign of dullness.

Before Cimarosa's overwhelming successor Rossini had retired from his indolent career, these tendencies had already reduced both composers and spectators to a supreme indifference to the mood of the libretto, an indifference far more fatal than mere inattention to the plot. Nobody cares to follow the plot of Mozart's *Figaro*; but then no spectator of Beaumarchais's *Mariage de Figaro* is prevented by the intricacy of its plot from enjoying it as a play. In both cases we are interested in the character-drawing and in each situation as it arises; and we do no justice to Mozart's music when we forget this interest, even in cases where the libretto has none of the literary merit that survives in the transformation of Beaumarchais's comedy into an Italian libretto. But with the Rossinian decline all charitable scruples of criticism are misplaced, for Italian opera once more became as purely a pantomimic concert as in the Handelian period; and we must not ignore the difference that it was now a concert of very vulgar music, the vileness of which was only aggravated by the growing range and interest of dramatic subjects. The best that can be said in defence of it was that the vulgarity was not pretentious and unhealthy, like Meyerbeer's; indeed, if the famous "Mad Scene" in Donizetti's *Lucia di Lammermoor* had only been meant to be funny it would not have been vulgar at all. Occasionally the drama pierced through the empty breeziness of the music; and so the spirit of Shakespeare, even when smothered in an Italian libretto unsuccessfully set to music by Rossini, proved so powerful that one spectator of Rossini's *Otello* is recorded to have started out of his seat at the catastrophe, exclaiming "Good Heavens! the tenor is murdering the soprano!" And in times of political unrest more than one opera became as dangerous as an over-censored theatre could make it. An historical case in point is brilliantly described in George Meredith's *Vittoria*. But what has this to do with the progress of music? The history of Italian opera from after its culmination in Mozart to its subsidence on the big drum and cymbals of the Rossinians is the history of a protected industry. Verdi's art, both in its burly youth and in its shrewd old age, is far more the crown of his native genius than of his native traditions; and, though opinions differ as to the spontaneity and depth of the change, the paradox is true that the Wagnerization of Verdi was the musical emancipation of Italy.

After Mozart the next step in the development of true operatic art was neither Italian nor German, but French. The French sense of dramatic fitness had a wonderfully stimulating effect upon every foreign composer who came to France. Rossini himself, in *Guillaume Tell*, was electrified into a dramatic and orchestral life of an incomparably higher order than the rollicking rattle of serious and comic Italian opera in its decline. He was in the prime of life when he wrote it, but it exhausted him and was practically his last important work, though he lived to a cheerful old age. The defects of its libretto were grave, but he made unprecedented efforts to remedy them, and finally succeeded, at the cost of an entire act. The experience was very significant; for, from the time of Gluck onwards, while it

cannot be denied that native and naturalized French operatic art has suffered from many forms of musical and dramatic debasement, we may safely say that no opera has met with success in France that is without theatrical merit. And the French contribution to musical history between Gluck and Rossini is of great nobility. If Cherubini and Méhul had had Gluck's melodic power, the classics of French opera would have been the greatest achievements in semi-tragic music-drama before Wagner. As it is, their austerity is not that of the highest classics. It is negative, and tends to exclude outward attractiveness rather because it cannot achieve it than because it contains all things in due proportion. Be this as it may, Cherubini had a real influence on Beethoven; not to mention that the libretti of *Fidelio* and *Les Deux Journées* were originally by the same author, though *Fidelio* underwent great changes in translation and revision. It is impossible to say what French opera might have done for music through Beethoven if *Fidelio* had not remained his solitary (because very nearly unsuccessful) operatic monument; but there is no doubt as to its effect on Weber, whose two greatest works, *Der Freischütz* and *Euryanthe*, are two giant strides from Cherubini to Wagner. *Euryanthe* is in respect of *Leit-motif* (see below) almost more Wagnerian than *Lohengrin*, Wagner's fourth published opera. It failed to make an epoch in history because of its dreary libretto, to which, however, the highly dramatic libretto of *Lohengrin* owes a surprising number of points.

The libretti of classical opera set too low a literary standard to induce critics to give sufficient attention to their aesthetic bearings; and perhaps the great scholar Otto Jahn is the only writer who has applied a first-rate literary analysis to the subject (see his *Life of Mozart*); a subject which, though of great importance to music, has, like the music itself, been generally thrust into the background by the countless externals that give theatrical works and institutions a national or political importance independent of artistic merit and historical development. Much that finds prominent place in the orthodox history of opera is really outside the scope of musical and dramatic discussion; and it may therefore be safely left to be discovered under non-musical headings elsewhere in this Encyclopaedia. Even when what passes for operatic history has a more real connexion with the art than the history of locomotion has with physical science, the importance of the connexion is often overrated. For example, much has been said as to the progress in German opera from the choice of remote subjects like Mozart's *Die Entführung aus dem Serail* to the choice of a subject so thoroughly German as *Der Freischütz*: but this is only part of the general progress made, chiefly in France, towards the choice of romantic instead of classical subjects. Whatever the intrinsic interest of musical ethnology, and whatever light it may throw upon the reasons why an art will develop and decline sooner in one country than in another, racial character will not suffice to produce an art for which no technique as yet exists. Nor will it suffice in any country to check the development or destroy the value of an art of which the principles were developed elsewhere. No music of Mozart's time could have handled Weber's romantic subjects, and all the Teutonism in history could not have prevented Mozart from adopting and developing those Italian methods that gave him scope. Again, in the time of Lully, who was the contemporary of Molière, the French genius of stagecraft was devoted to reducing opera to an effective series of ballets; yet so little did this hamper composers of real dramatic power that Quinault's libretto to Lully's very successful *Armide* served Gluck unaltered for one of his greatest works 90 years later. If Lully owes so little to Cambert as to be rightly entitled the founder of French opera, if Gluck is a greater reformer than his predecessor Rameau, if Cherubini is a more powerful artist than Méhul, and if, lastly, Meyerbeer developed the vices of the French histrionic machinery with a plausibility which has never been surpassed, then we must reconcile our racial theories with the historic process by which the French *Grand Opéra*, one of the most pronounced national types in all music, was founded by an Italian Jew, reformed by an Austrian, classicized by another Italian, and debased by a German Jew. This only enhances the significance of that French dramatic sense which stimulated foreign composers and widened their choice of subjects, as it also preserved all except the Italian forms of opera from falling into that elsewhere prevalent early 19th-century operatic style in which there was no means of guessing by the music whether any situation was tragic or comic. From the time of Meyerbeer onwards, trivial and vulgar opera has been as common in France as elsewhere; but there is a world of difference between, for example, a garish tune naively intended for a funeral march, and a similar tune used in a serious situation with a dramatic sense of its association with other incidents in the opera, and of its contrast with the sympathies of spectators and actors. The first case is as typical of 19th-century musical Italy as the second case is of musical France, and all that has come under French influence.

As Wagner slowly and painfully attained his maturity he learned to abhor the influence of Meyerbeer, and indeed it accounts for much of the inequality of his earlier work. But it can hardly have failed to stimulate his sense of effect; and without the help of Meyerbeer's outwardly successful novelties it is doubtful whether even Wagner's determination could have faced the task of his early work, a task so negative and destructive in its first stages. We have elsewhere (see MUSIC, SONATA FORMS *ad finem*, and SYMPHONIC POEM) described how if music of any kind, instrumental or dramatic, was to advance beyond the range of the classical symphony, there was need to devise a kind of musical motion and proportion as different from that of the sonata or symphony as the sonata style is different from that of the suite. All the vexed questions of the function of vocal ensemble, of the structure of the libretto, and of instrumentation, are but aspects and results of this change in what is as much a primary category of music as extension is a primary category of matter. Wagnerian opera, a generation after Wagner's death, was still an unique phenomenon, the rational influence of which was not yet sifted from the concomitant confusions of thought prevalent among many composers of symphony, oratorio, and other forms of which Wagner's principles can be relevant only with incalculable modifications. With Wagner the history of classical opera ends and a new history begins, for in Wagner's hands opera first became a single art-form, a true and indivisible music-drama, instead of a kind of dramatic casket for a collection of *objets d'art* more or less aptly arranged in theatrical tableaux.

Forms and Terminology of Opera.

The history of pre-Wagnerian opera is not, like that of the sonata forms, a history in which the technical terminology has a clear relationship to the aesthetic development. In order to understand the progress of classical opera we must understand the whole progress of classical music; and this not merely for the general reason that the development of an art-form is inseparable from the development of the whole art, but because in the case of opera only the most external terminology and the most natural and incoherent history of fashions and factions remain for consideration after the general development of musical art has been discussed. For completeness, however, the terminology must be included; and a commentary on it will complete our sketch in better historical perspective than any attempt to amplify details on the lines of a continuous history.

1. *Secco-recitative* is the delivery of ordinary operatic dialogue in prosaic recitative-formulas, accompanied by nothing but a harpsichord or pianoforte. In comic operas it was not so bad a method as some critics imagine; for the conductor (who sat at the harpsichord or pianoforte) would, if he had the wits expected of him by the composer, extemporize his accompaniments in an unobtrusively amusing manner, while the actors delivered their recitative rapidly in a conversational style known as *parlante*. In serious operas, however, the conductor dare not be frivolous; and accordingly secco-recitative outside comic opera is the dreariest of makeshifts, and is not tolerated by Gluck in his mature works. He accompanies his recitatives

with the string band, introducing other instruments freely as the situation suggests.

2. *Accompanied recitative* was used in all kinds of opera, as introductory to important arias and other movements, and also in the course of finales. Magnificent examples abound in *Idomeneo*, *Figaro* and *Don Giovanni*; and one of the longest recitatives before Wagner is that near the beginning of the finale of the first act of *Die Zauberflöte*. Beethoven's two examples in *Fidelio* are short but of overwhelming pathos.

3. *Melodrama* is the use of an orchestral accompaniment to spoken dialogue (see BENDA). It is wonderfully promising in theory, but generally disappointing in effect, unless the actors are successfully trained to speak without being dragged by the music into an out-of-tune sing-song. Classical examples are generally short and cautious, but very impressive; there is one in *Fidelio* in which the orchestra quotes two points from earlier movements in a thoroughly Wagnerian way (see *Leitmotif* below). But the device is more prominent in incidental music to plays, as in Beethoven's music for Goethe's *Egmont*. Mendelssohn's music for *A Midsummer Night's Dream* contains the most brilliant and resourceful examples yet achieved in this art; but they are beyond the musical capacity of the English stage, which, however, has practised the worst forms of the method until it has become a disease, many modern performances of Shakespeare attaining an almost operatic continuity of bad music.

4. *Opera buffa* is classical Italian comic opera with secco-recitative. Its central classics are, of course, *Figaro* and *Don Giovanni*, while Cimarosa's *Matrimonio Segreto* and Rossini's *Barbiere* are the most important steps from the culmination to the fall.

5. *Opera seria* is classical Italian opera with secco-recitative; almost always (like the Handelian opera from which it is derived) on a Greek or Roman subject, and, at whatever cost to dramatic or historic propriety, with a happy ending. Gluck purposely avoids the term in his mature works. The only great classic in *opera seria* is Mozart's *Idomeneo*, and even that is dramatically too unequal to be more than occasionally revived, though it contains much of Mozart's finest music.

6. The *Singspiel* is German opera with spoken dialogue. In early stages it advanced from the farcical to the comic. With Beethoven it came under French influence and adopted "thrilling" stories with happy endings; and from this stage it passed to specifically "Romantic" subjects. Its greatest classics are Mozart's *Entführung* and *Zauberflöte*, Beethoven's *Fidelio*, and Weber's *Freischütz*.

7. *Opéra comique*, being French opera with spoken dialogue. It did not originate in farce but in the refusal of the *Académie de Musique* to allow rival companies to infringe its monopoly of *Grand Opéra*; and it is so far from being essentially comic that one of its most famous classics, Méhul's *Joseph*, is on a Biblical subject; while its highest achievement, Cherubini's *Les Deux Journées*, is on a story almost as serious as that of *Fidelio*. All Cherubini's mature operas (except the ballet *Anacréon*, which is uninterrupted music from beginning to end) are *opéras comiques* in the sense of having spoken dialogue; though *Médée*, being, perhaps, the first genuine tragedy in the history of music-drama,[1] is simply called "*opéra*" on the title-page. In the smaller French works, especially those in one act, there is so much spoken dialogue that they are almost like plays with incidental music. But they never sink to the condition of the so-called operas of the English composers since Handel. When Weber accepted the commission to write *Oberon* for the English stage in 1815, he found that he was compelled to set the musical numbers one by one as they were sent to him, without the slightest information as to the plot, the situation, or even the order of the pieces! And, to crown his disgust, he found that this really did not matter.

[1] Even Gluck never contemplated any alternative to the absurd happy ending of *Orfeo*; and all his other operatic subjects include a *deus ex machina*.

8. *Grand opéra* is French opera in which every word is sung, and generally all recitative accompanied by the orchestra. It originated in the *Académie de Musique*, which, from its foundation in 1669 to the proclamation of the *liberté des théâtres* in 1791, claimed the monopoly of operas on the lines laid down by Lully, Rameau and Gluck. Rossini's *Guillaume Tell*, Spontini's *Vestale* and the works of Meyerbeer crown this theoretically promising art-form with what Sir Hubert Parry has justly if severely called a crown of no very precious metal. Weber's *Euryanthe*, Spohr's *Jessonda*, and others of his operas, are German parallel developments; and Wagner's first published work, *Rienzi*, is like an attempt to beat Meyerbeer on his own ground.

9. *Opéra bouffe* is not an equivalent of *opera buffa*, but is French light opera with a prominent strain of persiflage. Its chief representative is Offenbach. It seems to be as native to France as the austere *opéra comique* which it eclipsed. Sulliyan assimilated its adroit orchestration as Gilbert purified its literary wit, and the result became a peculiarly English possession.

10. The *finale* is that part of a classical opera where, some way before the end of an act, the music gathers itself together and flows in an unbroken chain of concerted movements. The "invention" has been ascribed to this or that composer before Mozart, and it certainly must have taken some time in the growing; but Mozart is the first classic whose finales are famous. The finales to the second act of *Figaro*, the first act of *Don Giovanni* and the second of the *Zauberflöte* remained unequalled in scale and in dramatic and symphonic continuity, until Wagner, as it were, extended the finale backwards until it met the *introduction* (see below) so that the whole act became musically continuous. This step was foreshadowed by Weber, in whose *Euryanthe* the numbering of the later movements of each act is quite arbitrary. Great finales are less frequent in *Singspiel* than in *opera buffa*. They can hardly be said to exist in *opera seria*, climax at the end of an act being there (even in Gluck) attained only by a collection of ballet movements, whereas the essence of Mozart's finale is its capacity to deal with real turning-points of the action. A few finales of the first and second acts of *opéras comiques* (which are almost always in three acts) are on the great classical lines, *e.g.* that to the first act of *Les Deux journées*; but a French finale to a last act is, except in Cherubini's works, hardly ever more than a short chorus, often so perfunctory that, for instance, when Méhul's *Joseph* was first produced by Weber at Dresden in 1817, a three-movement finale by Fränzl of Munich was added; and Weber publicly explained the difference between French and German notions of finality, in excuse for a course so repugnant to his principles in the performance of other works.

11. The *introduction* is sometimes merely an instrumental entr'acte in classical opera; but it is more especially an extension of continuous dramatic music at the beginning of an act, like the extension of the finale backwards towards the middle of the act, but much smaller. Beethoven, in his last version of *Fidelio*, used the term for the perfectly normal duet that begins the first act, and for the instrumental entr'acte which leads to the rise of the curtain on Florestan's great scene in the second act. The classical instances of the special meaning of "introduction" are the first number in *Don Giovanni* and, more typically, that in the *Zauberflöte*.

12. *Leit-motif*, or the association of musical themes with dramatic ideas and persons, is not only a natural means of progress in music drama, but is an absolute musical necessity as soon as the lines dividing an opera into separate formal pieces are broken down, unless the music is to become exclusively "atmospheric" and inarticulate. Without recurrence of themes a large piece of music could no more show coherent development than a drama in which the characters were never twice addressed by the same name nor twice allowed to appear in the same guise. Now the classical operatic forms, being mainly limited by the sonata style, were not such as could, when once worked out in appropriate designs of aria and ensemble, be worked out again in recognizable transformations without poverty and monotony of effect. And hence a system of *Leit-motif* was not appropriate

to that ingenious compromise which classical opera made between music that completed from 12 to 30 independent designs and the drama that meanwhile completed one. But when the music became as continuous as the drama the case was different. There are plenty of classical instances of a theme superficially marking some cardinal incident or personal characteristic, without affecting the independence of the musical forms; the commonest case being, of course, the allusion somewhere in the overture to salient points in the body of the opera; as, for instance, the allusion to the words "*così fan tutti*" in the overture to Mozart's opera of that name, and the Masonic three-fold chord in that to the *Zauberflöte*. Weber's overtures are sonata-form fantasias on themes to come: and in later and lighter operas such allusiveness, being childishly easy, is a meaningless matter of course. Within the opera itself, songs, such as would be sung in an ordinary non-musical play, will probably recur, as in *Les Deux journées*; and so will all phrases that have the character of a call or a signal, a remarkable and pathetic instance of which may be found in Méhul's *Médidore et Phrosine*, where the orchestra makes a true *Leit-motif* of the music of the heroine's name. But it is a long way from this to the system already clearly marked by Weber in *Der Freischütz* and developed in *Euryanthe* to an extent which Wagner did not surpass in any earlier work than *Tristan*, though in respect of the obliteration of sections his earliest works are in advance of Weber. Yet not only are there some thirteen recurrent musical incidents in the *Freischütz* and over twenty in *Euryanthe*, but in the latter the serpentine theme associated with the treacherous Eglantine actually stands the Wagnerian test of being recognizable when its character is transformed. This can hardly be claimed even for the organization of themes in *Lohengrin*.

Mature Wagnerian *Leit-motif* is a very different thing from the crude system of musical labels to which some of Wagner's disciples have reduced it, and Wagner himself had no patience with the catalogue methods of modern operatic analysis. The *Leit-motif* system of *Tristan*, the *Meistersinger*, the *Ring* and *Parsifal* is a profoundly natural and subtle cross-current of musical thought, often sharply contrasted with the externals of a dramatic situation, since it is free to reflect not only these externals, not only the things which the audience know and the persons of the drama do not know, not only those workings of the dramatic character's mind which he is trying to conceal from the other characters, but even those which he conceals from himself. There was nothing new in any one of these possibilities taken singly (see, for example, Gluck's ironic treatment of "*le calme rentre dans mon cœur*"), but polyphonic *Leit-motif* made them all possible simultaneously. Wagner's mind was not concentrated on the merely literary and theatrical aspects of music-drama; he fought his way to the topmost heights of the peculiar musical mastery necessary to his ideals; and so he realized that principle in which none but the very greatest musicians find freedom; the principle that, however constantly necessary and powerful homophonic music may be in passages of artificial simplicity, all harmonic music is by nature and origin polyphonic; and that in polyphony lies the normal and natural means of expressing a dramatic blending of emotions.

Wagnerian *Leit-motif* has proved rather a giant's robe for later composers; and the most successful of recent operas have, while aiming less at the sublime, cultivated Wagner's musical and dramatic continuity more than his principles of musical texture. Certainly Wagnerian continuity is a permanent postulate in modern opera; but it shows itself to be a thing attainable quite independently of any purely musical style or merit, so long as the dramatic movement of the play is good. This condition was always necessary, even where opera was most symphonic. Mozart was incessantly disputing with his librettists; and all his criticisms and changes, though apparently of purely musical purport, had a brilliant effect on the movement of the play. In one desperate case, where the librettist was obstinate, Mozart abandoned a work (*L'Oca del Cairo*) to the first act of which he had already sketched a great finale embodying a grandiose farcical figure that promised to be unique in classical opera.

Mozart's lesson of dramatic movement has been better learnt than anything peculiar to either music or literature; for, while his libretti show how little that quality has to do with poetic merit, the whole history of Italian opera from Rossini to Mascagni shows how little it has to do with good music. On the other hand, the musical coherence of the individual classical forms used in opera has caused many critics to miss the real dramatic ground of some of the most important operatic conventions. The chief instance of this is the repetition of words in arias and at climaxes, a convention which we are over-ready to explain as a device which prolongs situations and delays action for the sake of musical design. But in the best classical examples the case is almost the reverse, for the aria does not, as we are apt to suppose, *represent* a few words repeated so as to serve for a long piece of music. Without the music the drama would have required a long speech in its place; but the classical composer cannot fit intelligible music to a long string of different sentences, and so the librettist reduces the speech to mere headlines and the composer supplies the eloquence. Herein lies the meaning of Mozart's rapid progress from vocal concertos like "*Fuor del mar*" in *Idomeneo* and "*Martern aller Arten*" in *Die Entführung* to genuine musical speeches like "*Non più andrai*" in *Figaro*, in which the obvious capacity to deal with a greater number of words is far less important than the naturalness and freedom with which the pace of the declamation is varied—a freedom unsurpassed even in the *Elektra* of Richard Strauss.

With Wagnerian polyphony and continuity music became capable of treating words as they occur in ordinary speech, and repetitions have accordingly become out of place except where they would be natural without music. But it is not here that the real gain in freedom of movement lies. That gain has been won, not by Wagner's negative reforms alone, but by his combination of negative reform with new depths of musical thought; and modern opera is not more exempt than classical opera from the dangers of artistic methods that have become facile and secure. If the libretto has the right dramatic movement, the modern composer need have no care beyond what is wanted to avoid interference with that movement. So long as the music arouses no obviously incompatible emotion and has no breach of continuity, it may find perfect safety in being meaningless. The necessary stagecraft is indeed not common, but neither is it musical. Critics and public will cheerfully agree in ascribing to the composer all the qualities of the dramatist; and three allusions in the music of one scene to that of another will suffice to pass for a marvellous development of Wagnerian *Leit-motif*.

Modern opera of genuine artistic significance ranges from the light song-play type admirably represented by Bizet's *Carmen* to the exclusively "atmospheric" Impressionism of Debussy's *Pélleas et Mélisande*. Both these extremes are equally natural in effect, though diametrically opposite in method; for both types eliminate everything that would be inadmissible in ordinary drama. If we examine the libretto of *Carmen* as an ordinary play we shall find it to consist mainly of actual songs and dances, so that more than half of the music would be necessary even if it were not an opera at all. Debussy's opera differs from Maeterlinck's play only in a few omissions such as would probably be made in ordinary non-musical performances. His musical method combines perfect Wagnerian continuity with so entire an absence of *Leit-motif* that there are hardly three musical phrases in the whole opera that could be recognized if they recurred in fresh contexts. The highest conceivable development of Wagnerian continuity has been attained by Strauss in *Salome* and *Elektra*; these operas being actually more perfect in dramatic movement than the original plays of Wilde and Hofmannsthal. But their use of *Leit-motif*, though obvious and impressive, is far less developed than in Wagner; and the polyphony, as distinguished from the brilliant instrumental technique, is, like that technique, devoted mainly to realistic and physically exciting effects that crown the impression in much the same way as skilful lighting of the stage. Certainly Strauss does not in his whole time-limit of an hour and three-quarters use as many definite themes (even in the shortest of figures) as Wagner uses in ten minutes.

It remains to be seen whether a further development of Wagnerian opera, in the sense of addition to Wagner's resources in musical architecture, is possible. The uncompromising realism of Strauss does not at first sight seem encouraging in this direction; yet his treatment of Elektra's first invocation of Agamemnon produces a powerful effect of musical form, dimly perceived, but on a larger scale than even the huge sequences of Wagner. In any case, the best thing that can happen in a period of musical transition is that the leading revolutionaries should make a mark in opera. Musical revolutions are too easy to mean too much by themselves; there is no purely musical means of testing the sanity of the revolutionaries or of the critics. But the stage, while boundlessly tolerant of bad music, will stand no nonsense in dramatic movement. (The case of Handelian opera is no exception, for in it the stage was a mere topographical term.) In every period of musical fermentation the art of opera has instantly sifted the men of real ideas from the aesthetes and doctrinaires; Monteverde from the prince of Venosa, Gluck from Gossec, and Wagner from Liszt. As the ferment subsides, opera tends to a complacent decadence; but it will always revive to put to the first and most crucial test every revolutionary principle that enters into music to destroy and expand.

See also ARIA; OVERTURE; CHERUBINI; GLUCK; MOZART; VERDI; WAGNER; WEBER.   (D. F. T.)

OPHICLEIDE (Fr. *ophicléide, basse d'harmonie*; Ger. *Ophikleid*; Ital. *oficleide*), a brass wind instrument having a cup-shaped mouthpiece and keys, in fact a bass keyed-bugle. The name (from Gr. ὄφις, serpent, and κλείδες, keys), applied to it by Halary, the patentee of the instrument, is hardly a happy one, for there is nothing of the serpent about the ophicleide, which has the bore of the bugle and also owes the chromatic arrangement of the keys to a principle evolved by Halliday for the bugle, to be explained later on.

The ophicleide is almost perfect theoretically, for it combines the natural harmonic scale of the brass wind instruments having cup-shaped mouthpieces, such as the trumpet, with a system of keys, twelve in number, one for each chromatic semitone of the scale; it is capable of absolutely accurate intonation. It consists of a wooden, or oftener brass, tube with a conical bore having the same proportions as that of the bugle but not wide enough in proportion to its length to make the fundamental or first note of the harmonic series of much practical use. The tube, theoretically[1] 8 ft. long, is doubled upon itself once, terminating at the narrow end in a tight coil, from which protrudes the straight piece known as the crook, which bears the cup-shaped mouthpiece; the wide end of the tube terminates in a funnel-shaped bell pointing upwards.

The production of sound is effected in the ophicleide as in other instruments with cup- or funnel-shaped mouthpieces (see HORN). The lips stretched across the mouthpiece act as vibrating reeds or as the vocal chords in the larynx. The breath of the performer, compressed by being forced through the narrow opening between the lips, sets the latter in vibration. The stream of air, instead of proceeding into the cup in an even flow—in which case there would be no sound—is converted into a series of pulsations by the trembling of the lips. On being thrown into communication with the main stationary column of air at the bottom of the cup, the pulsating stream generates "sound waves," each consisting of a half wave of expansion and of a half wave of compression. On the frequency per second of the sound waves as they strike the drum of the ear depends the pitch of the note, the acuteness of the sound varying in direct proportion to the frequency. To ensure a higher frequency in the sound waves, their length must be decreased. Two things are necessary to bring this about without shortening the length of the tube: (1) the opening between the lips, fixed at each end by contact with the edges of

[1] For an explanation of the difference between theory and practice in the length of the tubes of wind instruments, see Victor Mahillon, "Le cor" (*Les instruments de musique au musée du conservatoire royal de musique de Bruxelles*, pt. ii. Brussels and London, 1907), pp. 27-29.

the mouthpiece, must be made narrower by greater tension; (2) the breath must be sent through the reduced aperture in a more compressed form and with greater force, so that the exciting current of air becomes more incisive. An exact proportion, not yet scientifically determined, evidently exists between the amount of pressure and the degree of tension, which is unconsciously regulated by the performer, excess of pressure in proportion to the tension of the lips producing a crescendo by causing amplitude of vibration instead of increased speed.

When the fundamental note of a pipe is produced, the tension of the lips and pressure of breath proportionally combined are at their minimum for that instrument. If both be doubled, a node is formed half way up the pipe, and the column of air no longer vibrates as a whole, but as two separate parts, each half the length of the tube, and the frequency of the sound waves is doubled in consequence. The practical result is the production of the second harmonic of the series an octave above the fundamental. The formation of three nodes and therefore of three separate sound waves produces a note a twelfth above the fundamental, known as the third harmonic, and so on in mathematical ratio. This harmonic series forms the natural scale of the instrument, and is for the ophicleide the following:

In some cases the fundamental is difficult to obtain, and the harmonics above the eighth are not used.

The ophicleide has in addition to its natural scale eleven or twelve lateral holes covered by keys, each of which, when successively opened, raises the pitch of the harmonic series a semitone, with the exception of the first, an open key, which on being closed lowers the pitch a semitone. There were ophicleides in C and in Bb, the former being the more common; contrabass ophicleides were also occasionally made in F and Eb. The keys of the ophicleide, being placed in the lowest register, are intended to bind together by chromatic degrees the first and second harmonics. The compass is a little over three octaves, from [music notation] with chromatic semitones throughout.

The unsatisfactory timbre of the ophicleide led to its being superseded by the bass tuba; but it seems a pity that an instrument so powerful, so easy to learn and understand, and capable of such accurate intonation, should have to be discarded. The lower register is rough, but so powerful that it can easily sustain above it masses of brass harmonics; the medium is coarse in tone, and the upper wild and unmusical.

Although a bass keyed-bugle, the ophicleide owes something of its origin to the application of keys to the serpent (q.v.), a wind instrument, the invention of which is generally attributed to Edme Guillaume, canon of Auxerre, about 1590. The serpent remained in its primitive form for nearly two centuries, and then only it was attempted to improve it by adding keys. It was a musician named Régibo[1] belonging to the orchestra of the church of St Pierre at Lille, who, about 1780, first thought of giving it the shape of a bassoon. The merit of this innovation was rapidly recognized in England and Germany. Still, to follow Gerber[2] one Frichot, who was established in London, published in 1800 a description of an instrument, entirely of brass, manufactured by J. Astor, which he claimed as his invention, calling it the basshorn, but which was no other in principle than the new serpent of Régibo. It only made its way to France and Belgium after the passage of the allied armies in 1815. The English bass basshorn was designated on the Continent the English or the Russian basshorn, the "serpent anglais" or the "basson russe." Under this last name all instruments of the form, whether of wood or brass, were later on confounded in France and Belgium. The "basson russe" remained in great vogue until the appearance of the ophicleide, to disappear with it in the complete revolution brought about by the invention of pistons.

The invention of the ophicleide is generally but falsely attributed to Alexandre Frichot, a professor of music at Lisieux, department of Calvados, France. The instrument, which the inventor called "basse-trompette," was approved of as early as 13th November 1806 by a commission composed of professors of the Paris Con-

servatoire, but the patent bears the date 31st December 1810. The "basse-trompette," which Frichot in his specification had at first, in imitation of the English basshorn, called "basse cor," was, like the English instrument, entirely of brass, and bad, like it, six holes; it only differed in a more favourable disposition brought about by the curvings of the tube, and by the application of four crooks which permitted the instrument to be tuned "in C low pitch and C high pitch for military bands, in C♯ for churches, and in D for concert use." The close relationship between the two instruments suggests the question whether this was the Frichot who worked with Astor in London in 1800.

The first idea of adding keys to instruments with cupped mouthpieces, unprovided with lateral holes, with the aim of filling up some of the gaps between the notes of the harmonic scale, goes back, according to Gerber (Lexicon of 1790), to Kölbel, a hornplayer in the Russian imperial band, about 1760. Anton Weidinger,[a] trumpeter in the Austrian imperial band, improved upon this first attempt, and applied it in 1800 to the trumpet. But the honour belongs to Joseph Halliday, bandmaster of the Cavan militia, of being the first to conceive, in 1810, the disposition of a certain number of keys along the tube, setting out from its lower extremity, with the idea of producing by their successive or simultaneous opening a chromatic scale throughout the extent of the instrument. The bugle-horn was the object of his reform; the scale of which, he says, in the preamble of his patent, "until my invention contained but five tones, viz. [music notation]. My improvements on that instrument are five keys, to be used by the performer according to the annexed scale, which, with its five original notes, render it capable of producing twenty-five separate tones in regular progression. Fig. 1 represents the keyed bugle of Joseph Halliday.

It was not until 1815 that the use of the new instrument spread upon the Continent. We find in the account-books of a Belgian maker, Tuerlinckx of Mechlin, that his first supply of a bugle-horn bears the date of 25th March 1815, and it was made "aen den Heer Muldener, lieutenant in het regiment due d'York."

The acoustic principle inaugurated by Halliday consisted in binding together by chromatic degrees the second and third harmonics, [music notation] to [music notation]. He attained it as we have just seen,

FIG. 1.—Keyed Bugle.

by the help of five keys. The principle once discovered, it became easy to extend it to instruments of the largest size, of which the compass, as in the "basson russe," began with the fundamental sound. It was simply necessary to bind this fundamental sound [music notation] to the next harmonic sound [music notation] by a larger number of keys. This was done in 1817 by Jean Hilaire Asté, known as Halary, a professor of music and instrument-maker at Paris. We find the description of the instruments for which he sought a patent in the Rapport de l'Académie Royale des Beaux-Arts de l'Institut de France, meeting of the 19th of July 1817. These instruments were three in number: (1) the clavi-tube, a keyed trumpet; (2) the quinti-tube, or quinti-clave; (3) the ophicleide, a keyed serpent. The clavi-tube was no other than the bugle-horn slightly modified in some details of construction, and reproduced in the different tonalities Ab, F, Eb, D, C, Bb, A and Ab. The quinti-tube had nearly the form of a bassoon, and was, in the first instance, armed with eight keys and constructed in two tonalities, F and Eb. This was the instrument afterwards named "alto ophicleide." The ophicleide (fig. 2) had the same form as the quinti-tube. It was at first adjusted with nine or ten keys, and the number was carried on to twelve—each key to give a semitone (additional patent of 16th August 1822). The ophicleide or bass of the harmony was made in C and in Bb, the contra-bass in F and in Eb.[4]

FIG. 2.—Ophicleide of Halary.

[a] The announcement of Weidinger's invention of a Klappentrompete, or trumpet with keys, appears in the Allg. musik. Ztg. (Leipzig, November 1802), p. 158; and further accounts are given in January 1803, p. 245, and 1815, p. 844.

[4] The report of the Académie des Beaux-Arts on the subject of this invention shows a strange misconception of it, which it is interesting to recall. "As to the two instruments which M. Halary designa

[1] Gerber, Lexicon der Tonkünstler (Leipzig, 1790).

[2] Lexikon, edition of 1812.

It is certain that from the point of view of invention Halary's labours had only secondary importance; but, if the principle of keyed chromatic instruments with cupped mouthpieces[1] goes back to Halliday, it was Halary's merit to know how to take advantage of the principle in extending it to instruments of diverse tonalities, in grouping them in one single family, that of the bugles, in so complete a manner that the improvements of modern manufacture have not widened its limits either in the grave or the acute direction. Keyed chromatic wind instruments made their way rapidly; to their introduction into military full or brass bands we can date the regeneration of military music. After pistons had been invented some forty years, instruments with keys could still reckon their partisans. Now these have utterly disappeared, and pistons or rotary cylinders remain absolute masters of the situation.

(V. M.; K. S.)

OPHIR, a region celebrated in antiquity for its gold, which was proverbially fine (Job xxii. 24, xxviii. 16; Psalms xlv. 9; Isa. xiii. 12). Thence Solomon's Phoenician sailors brought gold for their master (1 Kings ix. 28, x. 11; 2 Chron. viii. 18, ix. 10); Ophir gold was stored up among the materials for the Temple (1 Chron. xxix. 4). Jehoshaphat, attempting to follow his ancestors' example, was foiled by the shipwreck of his navy (1 Kings xxii. 48). The situation of the place has been the subject of much controversy.

The only indications whereby it can be identified are its connexion, in the geographical table (Gen. x. 29), with Sheba and Havilah, the latter also an auriferous country (Gen. ii. 11), and the fact that ships sailing thither started from Ezion-Geber at the head of the Red Sea. It must, therefore, have been somewhere south or east of Suez; and must be known to be a gold-bearing region. The suggested identification with the Egyptian Punt is in itself disputable, and it would be more helpful if we knew exactly where Punt was (see EGYPT).

(1) *East Africa.*—This has, perhaps, been the favourite theory in recent years, and it has been widely popularized by the sensational works of Theodore Bent and others, to say nothing of one of Rider Haggard's novels. The centre of speculation is a group of extensive ruins at Zimbabwe, in Mashonaland, about 200 m. inland from Sofala. Many and wild words have been written on these imposing remains. But the results of the saner researches of Randall MacIver, announced first at the South Africa meeting of the British Association (1905) and later communicated to the Royal Geographical Society, have robbed these structures of much of their glamour; from being the centres of Phoenician and Hebrew industry they have sunk to be mere magnified kraals, not more than three or four hundred years old.

(2) *The Far East.*—Various writers, following Josephus and the Greek version, have placed Ophir in different parts of the Far East. A chief argument in favour of this view is the length of the voyages of Solomon's vessels (three years were occupied in the double voyage, going and returning, 1 Kings x. 22) and the nature of the other imports that they brought—"almug-trees" (*i.e.* probably sandal-wood), ivory, apes and peacocks. This, however, proves nothing. It is nowhere said that these various imports all came from one place; and the voyages must have been somewhat analogous to those of modern "coasting tramps," which would necessarily consume a considerable time over comparatively short journeys. It has been sought at

under the names of ' quinti-clave ' and ' ophicleide, ' they bear a great resemblance to those submitted to the Academy in the sitting of the 11th of March 1811 by M. Dumas, which he designed under the names of ' basse et contrebasse guerrières.' . . . The opinion of our commission on the quinti-clave and ophicleide is that M. Halary can only claim the merit of an improvement and not that of an entire invention; still, for an equitable judgment on this point, we should compare the one with the other, and this our commission cannot do, not having the instruments of M. Dumas at our disposal." This is what the commission ought to have had, but it would have sufficed had they referred to the report of the sittings of 6th and 8th April, in which it is clearly explained that the instruments presented by M. Dumas were bass clarinets (*Moniteur Universel* of 19th April 1811).

[1] We designedly omit the use of the word "brass" to qualify these instruments. The substance which determines the form of a column of air is demonstrably indifferent for the *timbre* or quality of tone so long as the sides of the tubes are equally elastic and rigid.

Abhira, at the mouth of the Indus (where, however, there is no gold); at Supara, in Goa; and at a certain Mount Ophir in Johore.

(3) *Arabia.*—On the whole the most satisfactory theory is that Ophir was in some part of Arabia—whether south or east is disputed, and (with the indications at our disposal) probably cannot be settled. Arabia was known as a gold-producing country to the Phoenicians (Ezek. xxvii. 22); Sheba certainly, and Havilah probably, are regions of Arabia, and these are coupled with Ophir in Genesis x.; and the account of the arrival of the navy in 1 Kings x. 11, is strangely interpolated into the story of the visit of the queen of Sheba, perhaps because there is a closer connexion between the two events than appears at first sight.

Historians have been at a loss to know what Solomon could give in exchange for the gold of Ophir and the costly gifts of the queen of Sheba. Mr K. T. Frost (*Expos. Times,* Jan. 1905) shows that by his command of the trade routes Solomon was able to balance Phoenicians and Sabaeans against each other, and that his Ophir gold would be paid for by trade facilities and protection of caravans.

(R. A. S. M.)

OPHITES, or OPHIANS (Gr. ὄφις, Heb. אֹחַ, "snake"), known also as NAASENES, an early sect of Gnostics described by Hippolytus (*Philosoph.* v.), Irenaeus (*adv. Haer.* I. 11), Origen (*Contra Celsum,* vi. 25 seq. and Epiphanius (*Haer.* xxvi.). The account given by Irenaeus may be taken as representative of these descriptions which vary partly as referring to different groups, partly to different dates. The honour paid by them to the serpent is connected with the old mythologies of Babylon and Egypt as well as with the popular cults of Greece and the Orient. It was particularly offensive to Christians as tending to dishonour the Creator who is set over against the serpent as bad against good. The Ophite system had its Trinity: (1) the Universal God, the First Man, (2) his conception (ἔννοια), the Second Man, (3) a female Holy Spirit. From her the Third Man (Christ) was begotten by the First and Second. Christ flew upward with his mother, and in their ascent a spark of light fell on the waters as Sophia. From this contact came Ialdabaoth the Demiurgos, who in turn produced six powers and with them created the seven heavens and from the dregs of matter the Nous of serpent form, from whom are spirit and soul, evil and death. Ialdabaoth then announced himself as the Supreme, and when man (created by the six powers) gave thanks for life not to Ialdabaoth but to the First Man, Ialdabaoth created a woman (Eve) to destroy him. Then Sophia or Prunikos sent the serpent (as a benefactor) to persuade Adam and Eve to eat the tree of knowledge and so break the commandment of Ialdabaoth, who banished them from paradise to earth. After a long war between mankind aided by Prunikos against Ialdabaoth (this is the inner story of the Old Testament), the Holy Spirit sends Christ to the earth to enter (united with his sister Prunikos) the pure vessel, the virgin-born Jesus. Jesus Christ worked miracles and declared himself the Son of the First Man. Ialdabaoth instigated the Jews to kill him, but only Jesus died on the cross, for Christ and Prunikos had departed from him. Christ then raised the spiritual body of Jesus which remained on earth for eighteen months, initiating a small circle of elect disciples. Christ, received into heaven, sits at the right hand of Ialdabaoth, whom he deprives of glory and receives the souls that are his own. In some circles the serpent was identified with Prunikos. There are some resemblances to the Valentinian system, but whereas the great Archon sins in ignorance, Ialdabaoth sins against knowledge; there is also less of Greek philosophy in the Ophite system.

See King, *The Gnostics and their Remains* (London, 1887); G. Salmon, art. "Ophites " in *Dict. Chr. Biog.*

OPHTHALMOLOGY (Gr. ὀφθαλμός, eye), the science of the anatomy, physiology and pathology of the eye (see EYE and VISION). From the same Greek word come numerous other derivatives: *e.g.* ophthalmia, the general name for conjunctival inflammations (see *Eye diseases,* under EYE); and the instruments ophthalmometer and ophthalmoscope (see VISION).

OPIE, AMELIA (1769–1853), English author, daughter of James Alderson, a physician in Norwich, and was born there on the 12th of November 1769. Miss Alderson had inherited radical principles and was an ardent admirer of Horne Tooke. She was intimate with the Kembles and with Mrs Siddons, with Godwin and Mary Wollstonecraft. In 1798 she married John Opie, the painter. The nine years of her married life were very happy, although her husband did not share her love of society. He encouraged her to write, and in 1801 she produced a novel entitled *Father and Daughter*, which showed genuine fancy and pathos. She published a volume of graceful verse in 1802; *Adeline Mowbray* followed in 1804, *Simple Tales* in 1806, *Temper* in 1812, *Tales of Real Life* in 1813, *Valentine's Eve* in 1816, *Tales of the Heart* in 1818, and *Madeline* in 1822. At length, in 1825, through the influence of Joseph John Gurney, she joined the Society of Friends, and beyond a volume entitled *Detraction Displayed*, and contributions to periodicals, she wrote nothing more. The rest of her life was spent in travelling and in the exercise of charity. Mrs Opie retained her vivacity to the last, dying at Norwich on the 2nd of December 1853.

A *Life*, by Miss C. L. Brightwell, was published in 1854.

OPIE, JOHN (1761–1807), English historical and portrait painter, was born at St Agnes near Truro in May 1761. He early showed a taste for drawing, besides having at the age of twelve mastered Euclid and opened an evening school for arithmetic and writing. Before long he won some local reputation by portrait-painting; and in 1780 he started for London, under the patronage of Dr Wolcot (Peter Pindar). Opie was introduced to the town as " The Cornish Wonder," a self-taught genius. The world of fashion, ever eager for a new sensation, was attracted; the carriages of the wealthy blocked the street in which the painter resided, and for a time he reaped a rich harvest by his portraits. But soon the fickle tide of popularity flowed past him, and the painter was left neglected. He now applied himself with redoubled diligence to correcting the defects which marred his art, meriting the praise of his rival Northcote—" Other artists paint to live; Opie lives to paint." At the same time he sought to supplement his early education by the study of Latin and French and of the best English classics, and to polish the rudeness of his provincial manners by mixing in cultivated and learned circles. In 1786 he exhibited his first important historical subject, the " Assassination of James I.," and in the following year the " Murder of Rizzio," a work whose merit was recognized by the artist's immediate election as associate of the Academy, of which he became a full member in 1788. He was employed on five subjects for Boydell's " Shakespeare Gallery "; and until his death, on the 9th of April 1807, his practice alternated between portraiture and historical work. His productions are distinguished by breadth of handling and a certain rude vigour, individuality and freshness. They are wanting in grace, elegance and poetic feeling. Opie is also favourably known as a writer on art by his *Life of Reynolds* in Wolcot's edition of Pilkington, his *Letter on the Cultivation of the Fine Arts in England*, in which he advocated the formation of a national gallery, and his *Lectures* as professor of painting to the Royal Academy, which were published in 1809, with a memoir of the artist by his widow (see above).

OPINION (Lat. *opinio*, from *opinari*, to think), a term used loosely in ordinary speech for an idea or an explanation of facts which is regarded as being based on evidence which is good but not conclusive. In logic it is used as a translation of Gr. δόξα, which plays a prominent part in Greek philosophy as the opposite of knowledge (ἐπιστήμη or ἀλήθεια). The distinction is drawn by Parmenides, who contrasts the sphere of truth or knowledge with that of opinion, which deals with mere appearance, error, not-being. So Plato places δόξα between αἴσθησις and διάνοια, as dealing with phenomena contrasted with non-being and being respectively. Thus Plato confines opinion to that which is subject to change. Aristotle, retaining the same idea, assigns to opinion (especially in the *Ethics*) the sphere of things contingent, *i.e.* the future: hence opinion deals with that which is probable. More generally he uses

popular opinion—that which is generally held to be true (δοκεῖ) —as the starting-point of an inquiry. In modern philosophy the term has been used for various conceptions all having much the same connotation. The absence of any universally acknowledged definition, especially such as would contrast " opinion " with " belief," " faith " and the like, deprives it of any status as a philosophic term.

OPITZ VON BOBERFELD, MARTIN (1597–1639), German poet, was born at Bunzlau in Silesia on the 23rd of December 1597, the son of a prosperous citizen. He received his early education at the Gymnasium of his native town, of which his uncle was rector, and in 1617 attended the high school—" Schönaichianum "—at Beuthen, where he made a special study of French, Dutch and Italian poetry. In 1618 he entered the university of Frankfort-on-Oder as a student of *literae humaniores*, and in the same year published his first essay, *Aristarchus, sive De contemptu linguae Teutonicae*, a plea for the purification of the German language from foreign adulteration. In 1619 he went to Heidelberg, where he became the leader of the school of young poets which at that time made that university town remarkable. Visiting Leiden in the following year he sat at the feet of the famous Dutch lyric poet Daniel Heinsius (1580–1655), whose *Lobgesang Jesu Christi* and *Lobgesang Bacchi* he had already translated into alexandrines. After being for a short year (1622) professor of philosophy at the Gymnasium of Weissenburg (now Karlsburg) in Transylvania, he led a wandering life in the service of various territorial nobles. In 1624 he was appointed councillor to Duke George Rudolf of Liégnitz and Brieg in Silesia, and in 1625, as reward for a requiem poem composed on the death of Archduke Charles of Austria, was crowned laureate by the emperor Ferdinand II. who a few years later ennobled him under the title " von Boberfeld." He was elected a member of the *Fruchtbringende Gesellschaft* in 1629, and in 1630 went to Paris, where he made the acquaintance of Hugo Grotius. He settled in 1635 at Danzig, where Ladislaus IV. of Poland made him his historiographer and secretary. Here he died of the plague on the 20th of August 1639.

Opitz was the head of the so-called First Silesian School of poets (see GERMANY:*Literature*), and was during his life regarded as the greatest German poet. Although he would not to-day be considered a poetical genius, he may justly claim to have been the " father of German poetry " in respect at least of its form; his *Buch von der deutschen Poeterey* (1624) put an end to the hybridism that had until then prevailed, and established rules for the " purity " of language, style, verse and rhyme. Opitz's own poems are in accordance with the rigorous rules which he laid down. They are mostly a formal and sober elaboration of carefully considered themes, and contain little beauty and less feeling. To this didactic and descriptive category belong his best poems, *Trost-Gedichte in Widerwärtigkeit des Krieges* (written 1621, but not published till 1633); *Zlatna, oder von Ruhe des Gemüts* (1622); *Lob des Feldlebens* (1623); *Vielgut, oder vom wahren Glück* (1629), and *Vesuvius* (1633). These contain some vivid poetical descriptions, but are in the main treatises in poetical form. In 1624 Opitz published a German version of his poetry under the title *Acht Bücher deutscher Poematum* (though, owing to a mistake on the part of the printer, there are only five books); his *Dafne* (1627), to which Heinrich Schütz composed the music, is the earliest German opera. Besides numerous translations, Opitz edited (1639) *Das Annolied*, a Middle High German poem of the end of the 11th century, and thus preserved it from oblivion.

Collected editions of Opitz's works appeared in 1625, 1629, 1637, 1641, 1690 and 1746. His *Ausgewählte Dichtungen* have been edited by J. Tittmann (1869) and by H. Oesterley (Kürschner's *Deutsche Nationalliteratur*, vol. xxvii. 1889). There are modern reprints of the *Buch von der deutschen Poeterey* by W. Braune (2nd ed., 1882) and, together with *Aristarchus*, by G. Witkowski (1888), and also of the *Teutsche Poemata*, of 1624, by G. Witkowski (1902). See H. Palm, *Beiträge zur Geschichte der deutschen Literatur des 16ten und 17ten Jahrhunderts* (1877); K. Borinski, *Die Poetik der Renaissance* (1886); R. Beckherrn, *Opitz, Ronsard und Heinsius* (1888). Bibliography by H. Oesterley in the *Zentralblatt für Bibliothekswesen* for 1885.

OPIUM

OPIUM (Gr. ὄπιον, dim. from ὀπός, juice), a narcotic drug prepared from the juice of the opium poppy, *Papaver somniferum*, a plant probably indigenous in the south of Europe and western Asia, but now so widely cultivated that its original habitat is uncertain. The medicinal properties of the juice have been recognized from a very early period. It was known to Theophrastus by the name of μηκόνιον, and appears in his time to have consisted of an extract of the whole plant, since Dioscorides, about A.D. 77, draws a distinction between μηκόνειον, which he describes as an extract of the entire herb, and the more active ὀπός, derived from the capsules alone. From the 1st to the 12th century the opium of Asia Minor appears to have been the only kind known in commerce. In the 13th century *opium thebaicum* is mentioned by Simon Januensis, physician to Pope Nicholas IV., while *meconium* was still in use. In the 16th century opium is mentioned by Pyres (1516) as a production of the kingdom of Cous (Kuch Behar, south-west of Bhutan) in Bengal, and of Malwa.[1] Its introduction into India appears to have been connected with the spread of Islam. The opium monopoly was the property of the Great Mogul and was regularly sold. In the 17th century Kaempfer describes the various kinds of opium prepared in Persia, and states that the best sorts were flavoured with spices and called "theriaka." These preparations were held in great estimation during the middle ages, and probably supplied to a large extent the place of the pure drug. Opium is said to have been introduced into China by the Arabs probably in the 13th century, and it was originally used there as a medicine, the introduction of opium-smoking being assigned to the 17th century. In a

FIG. 1.—Opium Poppy (*Papaver somniferum*).

Chinese Herbal compiled before 1700 both the plant and its inspissated juice are described, together with the mode of collecting it, and in the *General History of the Southern Provinces of Yunnan*, revised and republished in 1736, opium is noticed as a common product. The first edict prohibiting opium-smoking was issued by the emperor Yung Cheng in 1729. Up to that date the amount imported did not exceed 200 chests, and was usually brought from India by junks as a return cargo. In the year 1757 the monopoly of opium cultivation in India passed into the hands of the East India Company through the victory of Clive at Plassey. Up to 1773 the trade with China had been in the hands of the Portuguese, but in that year the East India Company took the trade under their own charge, and in 1776 the annual export reached 1000 chests, and 5054 chests in 1790. Although the importation was forbidden by the Chinese imperial authorities in 1796, and opium-smoking punished with severe penalties (ultimately increased to transportation and death), the trade continued and had increased during 1820–1830 to 16,877 chests per annum. The trade was contraband, and the opium was bought by the Chinese from depôt ships at the ports. Up to 1839 no effort was made to stop the trade, but in that year the emperor Tao-Kwang sent a commissioner, Lin Tsze-sü, to Canton to put down the traffic. Lin issued a proclamation threatening hostile measures if the British opium ships serving as depôts were not sent away. The demand for removal not being complied with, 20,291 chests of opium (of 149½ ℔ each), valued at £2,000,000, were destroyed by the Chinese commissioner Lin; but still the British sought to

[1] *Aromatum Historia* (ed. Clusius, Ant., 1574).

smuggle cargoes on shore, and some outrages committed on both sides led to an open war, which was ended by the treaty of Nanking in 1842. The importation of opium continued and was legalized in 1858. From that time, in spite of the remonstrances of the Chinese government, the exportation of opium from India to China continued, increasing from 52,025 piculs (of 133½ ℔) in 1850 to 96,839 piculs in 1880. While, however, the court of Peking was honestly endeavouring to suppress the foreign trade in opium from 1839 to 1858 several of the provincial viceroys encouraged the trade, nor could the central government put a stop to the home cultivation of the drug. The cultivation increased so rapidly that at the beginning of the 20th century opium was produced in every province of China. The western provinces of Sze-ch'uen, Yun-nan and Kwei-chow yielded respectively 200,000, 30,000 and 15,000 piculs (of 133½ ℔); Manchuria 15,000; Shen-si, Chih-li and Shan-tung 10,000 each; and the other provinces from 5000 to 500 piculs each, the whole amount produced in China in 1906 being estimated at 330,000 piculs, of which the province of Sze-ch'uen produced nearly two-thirds. Of this amount China required for home consumption 325,270 piculs, the remainder being chiefly exported to Indo-China, whilst 54,225 piculs of foreign opium were imported into China. Of the whole amount of opium used in China, equal to 22,588 tons, only about one-seventh came from India.

The Chinese government regarding the use of opium as one of the most acute moral and economic questions which as a nation they have to face, representing an annual loss to the country of 856,250,000 taels, decided in 1906 to put an end to the use of the drug within ten years, and issued an edict on the 20th of September 1906, forbidding the consumption of opium and the cultivation of the poppy. As an indication of their earnestness of purpose the government allowed officials a period of six months in which to break off the use of opium, under heavy penalties if they failed to do so. In October of the same year the American government in the Philippines, having to deal with the opium trade, raised the question of the taking of joint measures for its suppression by the powers interested, and as a result a conference met at Shanghai on the 1st of February 1909 to which China, the United States of America, Great Britain, Austria-Hungary, France, Germany, Italy, Japan, the Netherlands, Persia, Portugal and Russia sent delegates. At this meeting it was resolved that it was the duty of the respective governments to prevent the export of opium to any countries prohibiting its importation; that drastic measures should be taken against the use of morphine; that anti-opium remedies should be investigated; and that all countries having concessions in China should close the opium divans in their possessions. The British government made an offer in 1907 to reduce the export of Indian opium to countries beyond the seas by 5100 chests, i.e. $\frac{1}{10}$th of the amount annually taken by China, each year until the year 1910, and that if during these three years the Chinese government had carried out its arrangements for proportionally diminishing the production and consumption of opium in China, the British government were prepared to continue the same rate of reduction, so that the export of Indian opium to China would cease in ten years; the restrictions of the imports of Turkish, Persian and other opiums being separately arranged for by the Chinese government, and carried out simultaneously. The above proposal was gratefully received by the Chinese government. A non-official report by Mr E. S. Little, after travelling through western China, which appeared in the newspapers in May 1910, stated that all over the province of Sze-ch'uen opium had almost ceased to be produced, except only in a few remote districts on the frontier (see further CHINA: § *History*).

The average annual import of Persian and Turkish opium into China is estimated at 1125 piculs, and if this quantity were to be reduced every year by one-ninth, beginning in 1909, in nine years the import into China would entirely cease, and the Indian, Persian and Turkish opiums no longer be articles of commerce in that country. One result of these regulations was that the price of foreign opium in China rose, a circumstance which was calculated to reduce the loss to the Indian revenue.

Thus in 1909–1910, with only 350,000 acres under cultivation and 40,000 chests of opium in stock, the revenue was £4,420,600 as against £3,572,944 in 1905–1906 with 613,996 acres under cultivation and a stock of 76,063 chests. No opium dens have been allowed since 1907 in their possessions or leased territories in China by Great Britain, France, Germany, Russia or Japan.

The difficulties of the task undertaken by the Chinese government to eradicate a national and popular vice, in a country whose population is generally estimated at 400,000,000, are increased by the fact that the opium habit has been indulged in by all classes of society, that opium has been practically the principal if not the only national stimulant; that it must involve a considerable loss of revenue, which will have to be made up by other taxes, and by the fact that its cultivation is more profitable than that of cereals, for an English acre will on the average produce raw dry opium of the value of £5, 16s. 8d. while it will yield grain valued only at £4, 5s. 6d.

Various remedies for the opium habit have been experimented with in China, but with doubtful success. Under the name of anti-opium cure various remedies containing morphine in the form of powder, or of little pills, have been introduced, as well as the subcutaneous injection of the alkaloid, so that the use of morphine is increasing in China to an alarming extent, and considerable difficulty is experienced in controlling the illicit traffic in it, especially that sent through the post. Its comparative cheapness, one dollar's worth being equal to three dollars' worth of opium in the effect produced, its portability and the facilities offered in obtaining it, are all in its favour. A good deal of morphine is exported to Japan from Europe, and generally passes into China by way of Manchuria, where Japanese products have a virtual monopoly. The effects of morphine are much more deleterious than those of opium-smoking. The smoke of opium, as shown by H. Moissan, contains only a trifling amount of morphia, and the effect produced by it is apparently due, not to that alkaloid, but to such decomposition products as pyrrol, acetone and pyridine and hydropyridine bases. F. Browne finds that after smoking "chandoo," containing 8·98 % of morphine, 7·63 % was left in the dross, so that only 1·35 % of morphia was carried over in the smoke or decomposed by the heat.

For many years two Scotch firms, Messrs J. D. Macfarlan and T. and H. Smith of Edinburgh, and T. Whiffen of London manufactured practically the world's supply of this alkaloid, but it is now made in the United States and Germany, although the largest amount is still probably made in Great Britain. A small amount of morphine and codeine is also manufactured in India for medicinal use. The prohibition of the general importation of morphia into China except on certain conditions was agreed to by the British government in Act XI. of the Mackay treaty, but only came into force on the 1st of January 1909. Unless the indirect importation of morphine into China from Europe and the United States is stopped, a worse habit and more difficult to cure than any other (except perhaps that of cocaine) may replace that of opium-smoking in China. It is worse even than opium-eating, in proportion as morphine is more active than opium. The sale and use of morphine in India and Burma is now restricted. The quantity of morphine that any one may legally possess, and then only for medicinal purposes, is in India 10 grams, and in Burma five. The possession of morphine by medical practitioners is also safeguarded by well-defined limitations.

Production and Commerce.—Although the collection of opium is possible in all places where there is not an excessive rainfall and the climate is temperate or subtropical, the yield is smaller in temperate than in tropical regions and the industry can only be profitably carried on where labour and land are sufficiently cheap and abundant; hence production on a large scale is limited to comparatively few countries. The varieties of poppy grown, the mode of cultivation adopted and the character of the opium produced differ so greatly that it will be convenient to consider the opiums of each country separately.

Turkey.—The poppy cultivated in Asia Minor is the variety *glabrum*, distinguished by the sub-globular shape of the capsule and by the stigmata or rays at the top of the fruit being ten or twelve in number. The flowers are usually of a purplish colour, but are sometimes white, and the seeds, like the petals, vary in tint from dark violet to white. The cultivation is carried on, both on the more elevated and lower lands, chiefly by peasant proprietors. A naturally light and rich soil, further improved by manure, is necessary, and moisture is indispensable, although injurious in excess, so that after a wet winter the best crops are obtained on hilly ground, and in a dry season on the plains. The land is ploughed twice, the second time crosswise, so that it may be thoroughly pulverized; and the seed, mixed with four times its quantity of sand, to prevent its being sown too thickly, is scattered broadcast, about ½ to 1 lb being used for every toloom (1600 sq. yds.). The crop is very uncertain owing to droughts, spring frosts and locusts, and, in order to avoid a total failure and to allow time for collecting the produce, there are three sowings at intervals from October to March—the crops thus coming to perfection in succession. But notwithstanding these precautions quantities of the drug are wasted when the crop is a full one, owing to the difficulty of gathering the whole in the short time during which collection is possible. The first sowing produces the hardiest plants, the yield of the other two depending almost entirely on favourable weather. In localities where there is hoar frost in autumn and spring the seed is sown in September or at latest in the beginning of October, and the yield of opium and seed is then greater than if sown later. After sowing, the land is harrowed, and the young plants are hoed and weeded, chiefly by women and children, from early spring until the time of flowering. In the plains the flowers expand at the end of May, on the uplands in July. At this period gentle showers are of great value, as they cause an increase in the subsequent yield of opium. The petals fall in a few hours, and the capsules grow so rapidly that in a short time—generally from nine to fifteen days—the opium is fit for collection. This period is known by the capsules yielding to pressure with the fingers, assuming a lighter green tint and exhibiting a kind of bloom called "cougak," easily rubbed off with the fingers; they are then about 1½ in. in diameter. The incisions are made by holding the capsule in the left hand and drawing a knife two-thirds round it, or spirally beyond the starting-point (see fig. 2, *a*), great care being taken not to let the incisions penetrate to the interior lest the juice should flow inside and be lost. (In this case also it is said that the seeds will not ripen, and that no oil can be obtained from them.) The operation is usually performed after the heat of the day, commencing early in the afternoon and continuing to nightfall, and the exuded juice is collected the next morning. This is done by scraping the capsule with a knife and transferring the concreted juice to a poppy-leaf held in the left hand, the edges of the leaf being turned in to avoid spilling the juice, and the knife-blade moistened with saliva by drawing it through the mouth after every alternate scraping to prevent the juice from adhering to it. When as much opium has been collected as the size of the leaf will allow, another leaf is wrapped over the top of the lump, which is then placed in the shade to dry for several days. The pieces vary in size from about 2 oz. to over 2 lb, being made larger in some districts than in others. The capsules are generally incised only once, but the fields are visited a second or third time to collect the opium from the poppy-heads subsequently developed by the branching of the stem. The yield of opium varies, even on the same piece of land, from ½ to 7½ chequis (of 1·62 lb) per toloom (1600 sq. yds.), the average being 1½ chequis of opium and 4 bushels (of 50 lb) of seed. The seed, which yields 35 to 42 % of oil, is worth about two-thirds of the value of the opium. The whole of the operation must, of course, be completed in the few days—five to ten—during which the capsules are capable of yielding the drug. A cold wind or a chilly atmosphere at the time of collection lessens the yield, and rain washes the opium off the capsules. Before the crop is all gathered in a meeting of buyers and sellers takes place in each district, at which the price to be asked is discussed and settled, and the opium handed to the buyers, who in many instances have advanced money on the standing crop. When sufficiently solid the pieces of opium are packed in cotton bags, a quantity of the fruits of a species of *Rumex* being thrown in to prevent the cakes from adhering together. The bags are then sealed up, packed in oblong or circular baskets and sent to Smyrna or other ports on mules. On the arrival of the opium at its destination, in the end of July or beginning of August, it is placed in cool warehouses to avoid loss of weight until sold. The opium is then of a mixed character and is known as talequale. When transferred to the buyer's warehouses the bags are opened and each piece is examined by a public inspector in the presence of both buyer and seller, the quality of the opium being judged by appearance, odour, colour and weight. It is then sorted into three qualities: (1) finest quality; (2) current or second; (3) chicanti or rejected pieces. A fourth sort consists of the very bad or wholly factitious pieces. The substances used to adulterate opium are grape-juice thickened with flour, fig-paste, liquorice, half-dried apricots, inferior gum tragacanth and sometimes clay or pieces of lead or other metals. The chicanti is returned to the seller, who disposes of it at 20 to 30 % discount to French and German merchants. After inspection the opium is hermetically sealed in tin-lined boxes containing about 150 lb. Turkey opium is principally used in medicine on account of its purity and the large percentage of morphia that it contains, a comparatively small quantity being exported for smoking purposes.

About three-quarters of the opium prepared in Turkey is produced in Anatolia, and is exported by way of Smyrna, and the remainder is produced in the hilly districts of the provinces near the southern coast of the Black Sea, and finds its way into Constantinople, the commercial varieties bearing the name of the district where they are produced. The Smyrna varieties include the produce of Afium Karahissar, Uschak, Akhissar, Taoushanli, Isbarta, Konia, Bulvadan, Hamid, Magnesia and Yerli, the last name being applied to opium collected in the immediate neighbourhood of Smyrna. The opium exported by way of Constantinople includes that of Hadjikeuy and Malatia; the Tokat kind, of good quality, including that produced in Yoegad, Sile and Niksar, and the current or second quality derived from Amasia and Oerek; the Karahissar kind including the produce of Mykalitch, Carabazar, Sivrahissar, Eskichehir and Nachlihan; the Balukesri sort, including that of Balukhissar and Bogaditch; also the produce of Beybazar and Angora. The average amount of Turkish opium exported is 7000 chests, but in rare seasons amounts to 12,000 chests, but the yield depends upon fine weather in harvest time, heavy rains washing the opium off the capsules, and lessening the yield to a considerable extent.

These commercial varieties differ in appearance and quality, and are roughly classified as Soft or Shipping opium, Druggists' and Manufacturers' opium. Shipping opium is distinguished by its soft character and clean paste, containing very little débris, or chaff, as it is technically called. The Hadjikeuy variety is at present the best in the market. The Malatia, including that of Kharput, second, and the Sile, third in quality. The chief markets for the soft or shipping varieties of opium are, China, Korea, the West Indian Islands, Cuba, British Guiana, Japan and Java; the United States also purchase for re-exportation as well as for home consumption. Druggists' opium includes the kinds purchased for use in medicine, which for Great Britain should, when dried and powdered, contain 9½-10½ % of morphine. That generally sold in this country for the purpose includes the Karahissar and Adet, Balukhissar, Amasia and Akhissar kinds, and for making the tincture and extract, that of Tokat. But the produce of Ghéve, Biledjik, Mondourlan, Konia, Tauschanli, Kutahlia and Karaman is often mixed with the kinds first mentioned. The softer varieties of opium are preferred in the American market, as being richer in morphine. In all Turkey opium the pieces vary much in size. On the continent of Europe, especially in Belgium, Germany and Italy, where pieces of small size are preferred, the Ghéve,[1] and the Yoghourma, *i.e.* opium remade into cakes, at the port of shipment, to contain 7, 8, 9, or 10 % of morphine, are chiefly sold. Manufacturers' opium includes any grade yielding not less than 10½ % of morphine, but the Yoghourma or "pudding" opium, on account of its paste being more difficult to work, is not used for the extraction of the active principles. For the extraction of codeine, the Persian opium is preferred when Turkey opium is dear, as it contains on the average 2½ % of that alkaloid, whilst Turkey opium yields only ½-¾ %. But codeine can also be made from morphine.

The ordinary varieties of Turkish opium are recognized in commerce by the following characteristics: Hadjikeuy opium occurs in pieces of about ¾ lb-1½ lb; it has an unusually pale-coloured paste of soft consistence, and is very rich in morphia. Malatia opium is in pieces of irregular size usually of a broadly conical shape, weighing from 1-2 lb. It has a soft paste with irregular layers of light and dark colour and is covered with unusually green poppy leaves. Tokat opium resembles that of Malatia, but the cakes are flatter, and the paste is similar in character, though the leaves covering it are of a yellower tint of green. Bogaditz opium occurs in smaller pieces, about 3 or 4 oz. in weight, but sometimes larger pieces of 1-1½ lb in weight are met with, approaching more nearly to the Kurgagatsch and Balukissar varieties. The surface is covered with a yellowish green leaf and many *Rumex* fruits. Karahissar opium, which usually includes the produce of Adet, Akhissar and Amasia, occurs in rather large shortly conical or more or less irregular lumps. Angora opium is met with in small smooth pieces, has generally a pale paste and is rich in morphia. Yerli opium is of good quality, variable in size and shape; the surface is usually rough with *Rumex* capsules. Ghéve opium formerly came over as a distinct kind, but is now mixed with other varieties; the pieces form small rounded cakes, smooth and shining like those of Angora, about 3-6 oz. in weight, with the midrib of the leaf they are wrapped in forming a median line on the surface. The interior often shows layers of light and dark colour.

In Macedonia opium culture was begun in 1865 at Istip with seed obtained from Karahissar in Asia Minor, and extended subsequently to the adjacent districts of Kotchava, Stroumnitza, Tikvish and Kinprulu-veles, most of the produce being exported under the name of Salonica opium. Macedonian opium, especially that produced at Istip, is very pure, and is considered equal to the Malatia opium, containing about 11 % of morphine. The pieces vary from ¾ lb to 1½ lb in weight. For some years past, however, it has been occasionally mixed with pieces of inferior opium, like that of Yoghourma, recognizable on cutting by their solidity and heavy character. The Turkish government encourage the development of the industry by remitting the tithes on opium and poppy-seed for one year on lands sown for the first time, and by distributing printed instructions for cultivating the poppy and preparing the opium. In these directions it is pointed out that the opium crop is ten times as profitable as that of wheat. Four varieties of poppy are distinguished—two with white flowers, large oval capsules without holes under their "combs" (stigmas) and bearing respectively yellow and white seed, and the other two having red or purple flowers and seeds of the same colour, one bearing small capsules perforated at the top, and the other larger oval capsules not perforated. The white varieties are recommended as yielding a more abundant opium of superior quality. The yellow seed is said to yield the best oil; that obtained by hot pressure is used for lamps and for paint, and the cold-pressed oil for culinary purposes.

Opium is also grown in Bulgaria, but almost entirely for home consumption; any surplus produce is, however, bought by Jews and Turks at low prices and sent to Constantinople, where it is sold as Turkish opium. It is produced in the districts of Kustendil, Lowtscha and Halitz, and is made into lumps weighing about 4 oz., of a light-brown colour internally and containing a few seeds; it is covered with leaves which have not been identified. Samples have yielded from 7 to 19 % of morphia, and only 2 to 3 % of ash, and are therefore of excellent quality.

India.—The poppy grown in India is usually the white-flowered variety, but in the Himalayas a red-flowered poppy with dark seeds is cultivated. The opium industry in Bengal is a government monopoly, under the control of officials residing respectively at Patna and Ghazipore. Any one may undertake the industry, but cultivators are obliged to sell the opium exclusively to the government agent at a price fixed beforehand by the latter, which, although small, is said to fully remunerate the grower. It is considered that with greater freedom the cultivator would produce too great a quantity, and loss to the government would soon result. Advances of money are often made by the government to enable the ryots to grow the poppy. The chief centres of production are Bihar in Bengal, and the district of the United Provinces of Agra and Oudh lying along the Gangetic valley, and north of it, of which the produce is known as Bengal opium. The opium manufactured at Patna is of two classes, viz. Provision opium manufactured for export, and Excise or Akbari opium intended for local consumption in India. These differ in consistence: Excise opium is prepared to contain 90 % of non-volatile solid matter and made up into cubes weighing one seer or 2 1/16 lb, and wrapped in oiled paper, whilst Provision opium is made up into balls, protected by a leafy covering, made of poppy petals, opium and "pussewah," or liquid drainings of the crude opium; that of Patna is made to contain 75 % of solid matter, and that of Ghazipore, which is known as Benares opium, 71 % only. Each ball consists of a little over 3½ lb of fine opium, in addition to other poppy products. The Benares ball opium has about 1½ oz. less of the external covering than the Patna sort. Forty of these balls are packed in each chest. The Excise opium not having a covering of poppy petals lacks the aroma of Provision opium. Malwa opium is produced in a large number of states in the Central India and Rajputana Agencies, chiefly Gwalior, Indore and Bhopal, in the former, and Mewar in the latter. It is also produced in the native state of Baroda, and in the small British territory of Ajmer Merwara. The cultivation of Malwa opium is free and extremely profitable, the crop realizing usually from three to seven times the value of wheat or other cereals, and in exceptionally advantageous situations, from twelve to twenty times as much. On its entering British territory a heavy duty is imposed on Malwa opium, so as to raise its price to an equality with the government article. It is shipped from Bombay to northern China, where nearly the whole of the exported Malwa opium is consumed. The poppy is grown for opium in the Punjab to a limited extent, but it has been decided to entirely abolish the cultivation there within a short time. In Nepal, Bashahr and Rampur, and at Doda Kashtwar in the Jammu territory, opium is produced and exported to Yarkand, Khotan and Aksu. The cultivation of the poppy is also carried on in Afghanistan, Kashmir, Nepal and the Shan states of Burma, but the areas and production are not known.

A small amount of opium alkaloids only is manufactured in India. The surplus above that issued to government medical institutions in India is sold in London. The amount manufactured in 1906-1907 was 346 lb of morphine hydrochlorate, 12 lb of the acetate and 61 lb of codeia.

The land intended for poppy culture is usually selected near villages, in order that it may be more easily manured and irrigated. On a rich soil a crop of maize or vegetables is grown during the rainy season, and after its removal in September the ground is prepared for the poppy-culture. Under less favourable circumstances the land is prepared from July till October by ploughing, weeding and manuring. The seed is sown between the 1st and

[1] Ghéve is the commercial name for opium from Geiveh on the river Sakaria, running into the Black Sea. It appears to find its way to Constantinople via the port of Ismid, and hence is known also by the latter name.

15th of November, and germinates in ten or fifteen days. The fields are divided for purposes of irrigation into beds about 10 ft. square, which usually are irrigated twice between November and February, but if the season be cold, with hardly any rain, the operation is repeated five or six times. When the seedlings are 2 or 3 in. high they are thinned out and weeded. The plants during growth are liable to injury by severe frost, excessive rain, insects, fungi and the growth of a root-parasite (*Orobanche indica*). The poppy blossoms about the middle of February, and the petals when about to fall are collected for the purpose of making "leaves" for the spherical coverings of the balls of opium. These are made by heating a circular-ridged earthen plate over a slow fire, and spreading the petals, a few at a time, over its surface. As the juice exudes, more petals are pressed on to them with a cloth until a layer of sufficient thickness is obtained. The leaves are forwarded to the opium-factories, where they are sorted into three classes, according to size and colour, the smaller and dark-coloured being reserved for the inside of the shells of the opium-balls, and the larger and least coloured for the outside. These are valued respectively at 10 to 7 and 5 rupees per maund of 82⅔ ℔. The collection of opium commences in Behar about 25th February, and continues to about 25th March. but in Malwa is performed in March and April. The capsules are scarified vertically (fig. 2, *b*) in most districts (although in some the incisions are made horizontally, as in Asia Minor), the "nushtur" or cutting instrument being drawn twice upwards for each incision, and repeated two to six times at intervals of two or three days. The nushtur (fig. 2, *c*) consists of three to five flattened

FIG. 2.—Opium Poppy Capsules, &c.; *a*, capsule showing mode of incision practised in Turkey; *b*, capsule as incised in India; *c*, nushtur, or instrument used in India for making the incisions. Drawn from specimens in the Museum of the Pharmaceutical Society of Great Britain.

blades forked at the larger end, and separated about one-sixteenth of an inch from each other by winding cotton thread between them, the whole being also bound together by thread, and the protrusion of the points being restricted to one-twelfth of an inch, by which the depth of the incision is limited. The operation is usually performed about three or four o'clock in the afternoon, and the opium collected the next morning. In Bengal a small sheet-iron scoop or "seetoah" is used for scraping off the dried juice, and, as it becomes filled, the opium is emptied into an earthen pot carried for the purpose. In Malwa a flat scraper is employed, a small piece of cotton soaked in linseed oil being attached to the upper part of the blade, and used for smearing the thumb and edge of the scraper to prevent adhesion of the juice; sometimes water is used instead of oil, but both practices injure the quality of the product. Sometimes the opium is in a fluid state by reason of dew, and in some places it is rendered still more so by the practice adopted by collectors of washing their scrapers, and adding the washings to the morning's collection. The juice, when brought home, is consequently a wet granular mass of pinkish colour, from which a dark fluid drains to the bottom of the vessel. In order to get rid of this fluid, called "pasewa" or "pussewah," the opium is placed in a shallow earthen vessel tilted on one side, and the pussewah drained off. The residual mass is then exposed to the air in the shade, and regularly turned over every few days, until it has reached the proper consistence, which takes place in about three or four weeks. The drug is then taken to the government factory to be sold. It is turned out of the pots into wide tin vessels or "tagars," in which it is weighed in quantities not exceeding 21 ℔. It is then examined by a native expert (purkhea) as to impurities, colour, fracture, aroma and consistence. To determine the amount of moisture, which should not exceed 30%, a weighed sample is evaporated and dried in a plate on a metallic surface heated by steam. Adulterations such as mud, sand, powdered charcoal, soot, cow-dung, powdered poppy petals and powdered seeds of various kinds are easily detected by breaking up the drug in cold water. Flour, potato-flour, ghee and ghoor (crude date-sugar) are revealed by their odour and the consistence they impart.

Various other adulterants are sometimes used, such as the inspissated juice of the prickly pear, extracts from tobacco, stramonium and hemp, pulp of the tamarind and bael fruit, mahwah flowers and gums of different kinds. The price paid to the cultivator is regulated chiefly by the amount of water contained in the drug. When received into the government stores the opium is kept in large wooden boxes holding about 50 maunds and occasionally stirred up, if only a little below the standard. If containing much water it is placed in shallow wooden drawers and constantly turned over. During the process it deepens in colour. From the store about 250 maunds are taken daily to be manufactured into cakes.

Various portions, each weighing 10 seers (of 2₁/₁₆ ℔), are selected by test assay so as to ensure the mass being of standard consistence (70% of the pure dry drug and 30% of water), and are thrown into shallow drawers and kneaded together. The mass is then packed into boxes all of one size, and a specimen of each again assayed, the mean of the whole being taken as the average. Before evening these boxes are emptied into wooden vats 20 ft. long, 3½ ft. wide and 1⅓ ft. deep, and the opium further kneaded and mixed by men wading through it from end to end until it appears to be of a uniform consistence. Next morning the manufacture of the opium into balls commences. The workman sits on a wooden stand, with a brass cup before him, which he lines with the leaves of poppy petals before-mentioned until the thickness of half an inch is reached, a few being allowed to hang over the cup; the leaves are agglutinated by means of "lewa," a pasty fluid which consists of a mixture of inferior opium, 8% of "pusaewah" and the "dhoe" or washings of the vessels that have contained opium, and the whole is made of such consistence that 100 grains evaporated to dryness over a water-bath leave 53 grains of solid residue. All the ingredients for the opium-ball are furnished to the workmen by measure. When the inside of the brass cup is ready a ball of opium previously weighed is placed on the leafy case in it, and the upper half of it covered with leaves in the same way that the casing for the lower half was made, the overhanging leaves of the lower half being pressed upwards and the sphere completed by one large leaf which is placed over the upper half. The ball, which resembles a Dutch cheese in size and shape, is now rolled in "poppy trash" made from the coarsely-powdered leaves, capsules and stalks of the poppy plant, and is placed in an earthen cup of the same size as the brass one; the cups are then placed in dishes and the opium exposed to the sun to dry for three days, being constantly turned and examined. If it becomes distended the ball is pierced to liberate the gas and again lightly closed. On the third evening the cups are placed in open frames which allow free circulation of the air. This operation is usually completed by the end of July. The balls thus made consist on the average of:—

Standard opium	.	.	.	1 seer 7·50 chittacks.
Lewa	.	.	.	0 „ 3·75 „
Leaves (poppy petals)	.	.	.	0 „ 5·43 „
Poppy trash	.	.	.	0 „ 0·50 „

2 seers 1·18 chittacks.

The average number of cakes that can be made daily by one man is about 70, although 90 to 100 are sometimes turned out by clever workmen. The cakes are liable to become mildewed, and require constant turning and occasional rubbing in dry "poppy trash" to remove the mildew, and strengthening in weak places with fresh poppy leaves. By October the cakes are dry and fairly solid, and are then packed in chests, which are divided into two tiers of twenty square compartments for the reception of as many cakes, which are steadied by a packing of loose poppy trash.[1] Each case contains about 120 catties (about 160 ℔). The chests need to be kept in a dry warehouse for a length of time, but ultimately the opium ceases to lose moisture to the shell, and the latter becomes extremely solid.

The care bestowed on the selection and preparation of the drug in the Bengal opium-factories is such that the merchants who purchase it rarely require to examine it, although permission is given to open at each sale any number of chests or cakes that they may desire. In Malwa the opium is manufactured by private enterprise, the government levying an export duty of 600 rupees (£60) per chest. It is not made into balls but into rectangular or rounded masses, and is not cased in poppy petals. It contains as much as 95% of dry opium, but is of much less uniform quality than the Bengal drug, and, having no guarantee as to purity, is not considered so valuable. The cultivation in Malwa does not differ in any important particular from that in Bengal. The opium is collected in March and April, and the crude drug or "chick" is thrown into an earthen vessel and covered with linseed oil to prevent evaporation. In this state it is sold to itinerant dealers. It is afterwards tied up in quantities of 25 ℔ and 50 ℔ in double bags of sheeting, which are suspended to a ceiling out of the light and draught to allow the excess of oil to drain off. This takes place in seven to ten days, but the bags are left for four to six weeks until the oil remaining on the opium has become oxidized and hardened. In June and July, when the rains begin, the bags are taken down and emptied

_____
[1] This is purchased from the ryots at 12 annas per maund.

into shallow vats 10 to 15 ft. across, and 6 to 8 in. deep, in which the opium is kneaded until uniform in colour and consistence and tough enough to be formed into cakes of 8 or 10 oz. in weight. These are thrown into a basket containing chaff made from the capsules. They are then rolled in broken leaves and stalks of the poppy and left, with occasional turning, for a week or so, when they become hard enough to bear packing. In October and November they are weighed and sent to market, packed in chests containing as nearly as possible 1 picul = 133½℔, the petals and leaves of the poppy being used as packing materials. The production is said to amount to about 20,000 chests annually.

The amount of opium revenue collected in India was £10,480,051 in 1881, but in 1907–1908 was only £5,244,986. It is a remarkable fact that the only Indian opium ever seen in England is an occasional sample of the Malwa sort, whilst the government monopoly opium is quite unknown; indeed, the whole of the opium used in medicine in Europe and the United States is obtained from Turkey. This is in some measure due to the fact that Indian opium contains less morphia. It has recently been shown, however, that opium grown in the hilly districts of the Himalayas yields 50 % more morphia than that of the plains, and that the deficiency of morphia in the Indian drug is due, in some measure, to the long exposure to the air in a semi-liquid state which it undergoes. In view, therefore, of the probable decline in the Chinese demand, the cultivation of the drug for the European market in the hilly districts of India, and its preparation after the mode adopted in Turkey, viz., by drying the concrete juice as quickly as possible, might be worthy of the consideration of the British government.

Persia.—The variety of poppy grown in Persia appears to be *P. somniferum*, var. *album*, having roundish ovate capsules. It is most largely produced in the districts of Ispahan, Shiraz, Yezd and Khonsar, and to a less extent in those of Khorasan, Kermanshah and Fars. The Yezd opium is considered better than that of Ispahan, but the strongest or *Theriak-e-Arabistani* is produced in the neighbourhood of Disful and Shuster, east of the river Tigris. Good opium is also produced about Sari and Balfarush in the province of Mazanderan. The capsules are incised vertically, or in some districts vertical cuts with diagonal branches are made. The crop is collected in May and June and reaches the ports for exportation between August and January. Although the cultivation of opium in Persia was probably carried on at an earlier date than in India, Persian opium was almost unknown in England until about the year 1870, except in the form of the inferior quality known as "Trebizond," which usually contains only 0·2 to 3 % of morphia. This opium is in the form of cylindrical sticks about 6 in. long and half an inch in diameter, wrapped in white waxed or red paper. Since 1870 Persian opium has been largely exported from Bushire and Bandar-Abbas in the Persian Gulf to London, the Straits Settlements and China. At that date the annual yield is said not to have exceeded 2600 cases; but, the profits on opium having about that time attracted attention, all available ground was utilized for this to the exclusion of cereals, cotton and other produce. The result was a severe famine in 1871–1872, which was further aggravated by drought and other circumstances. Notwithstanding the lesson thus taught, the cultivation is being extended every year, especially in Ispahan, which abounds in streams and rivers, an advantage in which Yezd is deficient. About Shiraz, Behbehan and Kermanshah it now occupies much of the land, and has consequently affected the price and growth of cereals. The trade—only 300 chests in 1859—gradually increased until 1877, when the Persian opium was much adulterated with glucose. The heavy losses on this inferior opium and, the higher prices obtained for the genuine article led to a great improvement in its preparation, and in 1907 the production had increased to 10,000 piculs. About half of the total produce finds its way to the Chinese market, chiefly by sea to Hongkong and the Federated Malay States, although some is carried overland through Bokhara, Khokand and Kashgar; a small quantity is exported by way of Trebizond and Samsun to Constantinople, and about 2000 piculs to Great Britain. The produce of Ispahan and Fars is carried for exportation to Bushire, and that of Khorasan and Kirman and Yezd partly to Bushire and partly to Bandar-Abbas. The Shuster opium is sent partly via Bushire to Muscat for transhipment to Zanzibar, and part is believed to be smuggled into India by way of Baluchistan and Mekrkn. Smaller quantities grown in Teheran, Tabriz and Kermanshah find their way to Smyrna, where it is said to be mixed with the local drug for the European market, the same practice being carried on at Constantinople with the Persian opium that arrives there from Samsun and Trebizond. For the Chinese market the opium is usually packed in chests containing 10½ shahmans (of 13½ ℔), so that on arrival it may weigh 1 Chinese picul (= 133½ ℔). 5 to 10 % being allowed for loss by drying. At Ispahan, Shiraz and Yezd the drug, after being dried in the sun, is mixed with oil in the proportion of 6 or 7 ℔ to 141 ℔ of opium, with the object, it is said, of suiting the taste of the Chinese—that intended for the London market being now always free from oil.

Persian opium, as met with in the London market, occurs in several forms, the most common being that of brick-shaped pieces. These occur wrapped separately in paper, and weighing 1 ℔ each; of these 140-160 are packed in a case. Ispahan opium also occurs

in the form of parallelopipeds weighing about 16-20 oz.; sometimes flat circular pieces weighing about 20 oz. are met with. The opium is usually of much firmer and smoother consistence than that of Turkey, of a chocolate-brown colour and cheesy appearance, the pieces bearing evidence of having been beaten into a uniform mass previously to being made into lumps, probably with the addition of Sarcocoll, as it is always harder when dry than Turkey opium. The odour differs but slightly, except in oily specimens, from that of Turkey opium. Great care is now taken to prevent adulteration, and consequently Persian opium can be obtained nearly as rich in morphia as the Turkish drug—on the average from 9-12 %. The greater proportion of the Persian opium imported into London is again exported, a comparatively small quantity being used, chiefly for the manufacture of codeine when Turkey opium is dear, and a little in veterinary practice. According to Dr Revell, Persian opium usually contains 75 to 84 % of matter soluble in water, and some samples contain from 13 to 30 % of glucose, probably due to an extract or syrup of raisins added to the paste in the pots in which it is collected, and to which the shining fracture of hard Persian opium is attributed.

Europe.—Experiments made in England, France, Italy, Switzerland, Greece, Spain, Germany, and even in Sweden, prove that opium as rich in morphia as that of Eastern countries can be produced in Europe. In 1830 Young, a surgeon at Edinburgh, succeeded in obtaining 56 ℔ of opium from an acre of poppies, and sold it at 36s. per ℔. In France the cultivation has been carried on since 1844 at Clermont-Ferrand by Aubergier. The juice, of which a workman is able to collect about 9·64 troy oz. in a day, is evaporated by artificial heat immediately after collection. The juice yields about one-fourth its weight of opium, and the percentage of morphia varies according to the variety of poppy used, the purple one giving the best results. By mixing assayed samples he is able to produce an opium containing uniformly 10 % of morphia. It is made up in cakes of 50 grammes, but is not produced in sufficient quantity to become an article of wholesale commerce. Some specimens of French opium have been found by Guibourt to yield 22·8 % of morphia, being the highest percentage observed as yet in any opium. Experiments made in Germany by Karsten, Jobst and Vulpius have shown that it is possible to obtain in that country opium of excellent quality, containing from 8 to 13 % of morphia. It was found that the method yielding the best results was to make incisions in the poppy-heads soon after sunrise, to collect the juice with the finger immediately after incision and evaporate it as speedily as possible, the colour of the opium being lighter and the percentage of morphia greater than when the juice was allowed to dry on the plant. Cutting through the poppy-head caused the shrivelling up of the young fruit, but the heads which had been carefully incised yielded more seed than those which had not been cut at all. Newly-manured soil was found to act prejudicially on the poppy. The giant variety of poppy yielded most morphia.

The difficulty of obtaining the requisite amount of cheap labour at the exact time it is needed and the uncertainty of the weather render the cultivation of opium too much a matter of speculation for it ever to become a regular crop in most European countries.

North America.—In 1865 the cultivation of opium was attempted in Virginia by A. Robertson, and a product was obtained which yielded 4 % of morphia. In 1867 H. Black grew opium in Tennessee which contained 10 % of morphia. Opium produced in California by H. Flint in 1873 yielded 7⅓ % of morphia, equal to 10 % in perfectly-dried opium. The expense of cultivation exceeded the returns obtained by its sale. As in Europe, therefore, the high price of labour militates against its production on a large scale.

(E. M. H.)

Chemistry of the Opium Alkaloids.—The chemical investigation of opium dates from 1803 when C. Derosne isolated a crystalline compound which he named "opium salt." In 1805 F. W. Sertürner, a German apothecary, independently isolated this same substance, naming it "morphium," and recognized its basic nature; he also isolated an acid, *meconic acid*. A second paper, published in 1817, was followed in the same year by the identification of a new base, *narcotine*, by P. J. Robiquet. Thebaine, another alkaloid, was discovered by Thiboumery in 1835; whilst, in 1848, Merck isolated papaverine from commercial narcotine. Subsequent investigations have revealed some twenty or more alkaloids, the more important of which are given in the following table (from A. Pictet, *Vegetable Alkaloids*):—

Morphine	9·0 %	Laudanine	0·01 %
Narcotine	5·0 %	Lanthopine	0·006 %
Papaverine	0·8 %	Protopine	0·003 %
Thebaine	0·4 %	Codamine	0·002 %
Codeine	0·3 %	Iritopine	0·0015 %
Narceine	0·2 %	Laudanosine	0·0008 %
Cryptopine	0·08 %	Meconine	0·3 %
Pseudomorphine	0·02 %		

Opium also contains a gum, pectin, a wax, sugar and similar substances, in addition to meconic and lactic acids.

The alkaloids fall into two chemical groups: (1) derivatives of isoquinoline, including papaverine, narcotine, gnoscopine (racemic narcotine), narceine, laudanosine, laudanine, cotarnine, hydrocotarnine (the last two do not occur in opium), and (2) derivatives of phenanthrene, including morphine, codeine; thebaine. The constitutions of the first series have been determined; of the second they are still uncertain.

Papaverine, $C_{20}H_{21}NO_4$, was investigated by G. Goldschmiedt (*Monats.*, 1883-1889), who determined its constitution (formula I., below) by a study of its oxidation products, showing that papaveraldine, which it gives with potassium permanganate, is a tetramethoxybenzoylisoquinoline. Its synthesis, and also that of *laudanosine*, $C_{21}H_{27}NO_4$, which is N-methyltetrahydropapaverine, was effected in 1909 by F. L. Pyman (*Jour. Chem. Soc.*, 95, p. 1610) and by A. Pictet and Mlle M. Finkelstein (*Compt. rend.* 1909, 148, p. 925). *Laudanine*, $C_{20}H_{25}NO_4$, is very similar to laudanosine, differing in having three methoxy groups and one hydroxy instead of four methoxy.

Narceine, $C_{23}H_{27}NO_8$, has been principally investigated by A. Matthiessen and G. C. Foster, and by W. Roser (*Ann.*, 1888, 249, p. 156; 1889, 254, p. 334.) By hydrolysis it yields opianic acid, $C_{10}H_{10}O_5$, and hydrocotarnine, $C_{12}H_{15}NO_3$; reduction gives meconine, $C_{10}H_{10}O_4$, and hydrocotarnine; whilst oxidation gives opianic acid and cotarnine, $C_{12}H_{15}NO_4$. Narcotine was shown to be methoxyhydrastine (II.) (hydrastine, the alkaloid of Golden seal, *Hydrastis canadensis*, was solved by E. Schmidt, M. Freund, and P. Fritsch) and cotarnine to be III.; the latter has been synthesized by A. H. Salway (*Jour. Chem. Soc.*, 1910, 97, p. 1208). *Narceine*, $C_{23}H_{29}NO_8$, obtained by the action of potash on the methyl iodide of narcotine, is probably IV. (see Pyman, *loc. cit.* pp. 1266, 1738; M. Freund and P. Oppenheim, *Ber.*, 1909, 42, p. 1084).

The proprietary drug "stypticin" is cotarnine hydrochloride, and "styptol" cotarnine phthalate; "antispasmin" is a sodium narceine combined with sodium salicylate, and "narcyl" narceine ethyl hydrochloride.

I.Papaverine   II.Narcotine   III.Cotarnine   IV.Narceine

The chemistry of morphine, codeine and thebaine is exceedingly complicated, and the literature enormous. That these alkaloids are closely related may be suspected from their empirical formulae, viz. morphine = $C_{17}H_{19}NO_3$, codeine = $C_{18}H_{21}NO_3$, thebaine = $C_{19}H_{21}NO_3$. As a matter of fact, Grimaux, in 1881, showed codeine to be a methylmorphine, and in 1903 Ach and L. Knorr (*Ber.*, 36, p. 3067) obtained identical substances, viz. thebaine and morphothebaine, from both codeine and thebaine, thereby establishing their connexion. Our knowledge of the constitution of these alkaloids largely depends on the researches of M. Freund, E. Vongerichten, L. Knorr and R. Pschorr. The presence of the phenanthrene nucleus and the chain system $CH_2.N.C.C.$ follows from the fact that these alkaloids, by appropriate treatment, yield a substituted phenanthrene and also dimethylaminoethanol $(CH_3)_2N·CH_2·CH_2OH$. Formulae have been proposed by Pschorr and Knorr explaining this and other decompositions (in Pschorr's formula the morphine ring system is a fusion of a phenanthrene and pyridine nucleus); another formula, containing a fusion of a phenanthrene with a pyrrol ring, was proposed by Bucherer in 1907. The problem is discussed by Pschorr and Einbeck (*Ber.*, 1907, 40, p. 1980), and by Knorr and Hörlein (*ibid.* p. 2042); see also *Ann. Reps. Chem. Soc.*

Morphine, or morphia, crystallizes in prisms with one molecule of water; it is soluble in 1000 parts of cold water and in 160 of boiling water, and may be crystallized from alcohol; it is almost insoluble in ether and chloroform. It has an alkaline reaction and behaves as a tertiary, monacid base; its salts are soluble in water and alcohol. The official hydrochloride, $C_{17}H_{19}NO_3·HCl+3H_2O$, forms delicate needles. Distilled with zinc dust morphine yields phenanthrene, pyridine and quinoline; dehydration gives, under certain conditions, apomorphine, $C_{17}H_{17}NO_2$, a white amorphous substance, readily soluble in alcohol, ether and chloroform. The drug "heroin" is a diacetylmorphine hydrochloride. Codeine, or codeia, crystallizes in orthorhombic prisms with one molecule of water; it is readily soluble in alcohol, ether and chloroform. Thebaine forms silvery plates, melting at 193°.   (C. E.*)

Medicine.—Of the opium alkaloids only morphine and codeine are used to any extent in medicine. . Thebaine is not so used, but is an important and sometimes very dangerous constituent of the various opium preparations, which are still largely employed, despite the complexity and inconstant composition of the drug. Of the other alkaloids narceine is hypnotic, like morphine and codeine, whilst thebaine, papaverine and narcotine have an action which resembles that of strychnine, and is, generally speaking, undesirable or dangerous if at all well marked. A drug of so complex a composition as opium is necessarily incompatible with a large number of substances. Tannic acid, for instance, precipitates codeine as a tannate, salts of many of the heavy metals form precipitates of meconates and sulphates, whilst the various alkali, alkaline carbonates and ammonia precipitate the important alkaloids.

The pharmacology of opium differs from that of morphine (q.v.) in a few particulars. The chief difference between the action of opium and morphine is due to the presence in the former of thebaine, which readily affects the more irritable spinal cord of very young children. In infants especially opium acts markedly upon the spinal cord, and, just as strychnine is dangerous when given to young children, so opium, because of the strychnine-like alkaloid it contains, should never be administered, under any circumstances or in any dose, to children under one year of age.

When given by the mouth, opium has a somewhat different action from that of morphine. It often relieves hunger, by arresting the secretion of gastric juice and the movements of the stomach and bowel, and it frequently upsets digestion from the same cause. Often it relieves vomiting, though in a few persons it may cause vomiting, but in far less degree than apomorphine, which is a powerful emetic. Opium has a more marked diaphoretic action than morphine, and is much less certain as a hypnotic and analgesic.

There are a few therapeutic indications for the use of opium rather than morphine, but they are far less important than those which make the opposite demand. In some abdominal conditions, for instance, opium is still preferred by the majority of practitioners, though certainly not in gastric cases, where morphine gives the relief for which opium often increases the need, owing to the irritant action of some of its constituents. Opium is often preferred to morphine in cases of diabetes, where prolonged administration is required. In such cases the soporific action is not that which is sought, and so opium is preferable. A Dover's powder, also, is hardly to be surpassed in the early stages of a bad cold in the head or bronchitis. Ten grains taken at bedtime will often give sleep; cause free diaphoresis and quieten the entire nervous system in such cases. The tincture often known as "paregoric" is also largely used in bronchial conditions, and morphine shows no sign of displacing it in favour. Opium rather than morphine is also usually employed to relieve the pain of haemorrhoids or fissure of the rectum. This practice is, however, obsolescent.

The alkaloid thebaine may here be referred to, as it is not used separately in medicine. Crum Brown and Fraser of Edinburgh showed that, whilst thebaine acts like strychnine, methyl and ethyl thebaine act like curara, paralysing the terminals of motor nerves. At present we say of such a substance as thebaine, " it acts on the anterior cornua of grey matter in the spinal cord," but why on them and not elsewhere we do not know.

Toxicology.—Under this heading must be considered acute poisoning by opium, and the chronic poisoning seen in those who eat or smoke the drug. Chronic opium poisoning by the taking of laudanum—as in the familiar case of De Quincey—need not be considered here, as the hypodermic injection of morphine has almost entirely supplanted it.

The acute poisoning presents a series of symptoms which are only with difficulty to be distinguished from those produced by alcohol, by cerebral haemorrhage and by several other morbid conditions. The differential diagnosis is of the highest importance, but very frequently time alone will furnish a sufficient criterion. The patient who has swallowed a toxic or lethal dose of laudanum, for instance, usually passes at once into the narcotic state, without any prior excitement. Intense drowsiness yields to sleep and coma, which ends in death from failure of the respiration. This last is the cardinal fact in determining treatment. The comatose patient has a cold and clammy skin, livid lips and ear-tips—a grave sign—and "pin-point pupils." The heart's action is feeble, the pulse being small, irregular and often abnormally slow. The action on the circulation is largely secondary, however, to the all-important action of opium on the respiratory centre in the medulla oblongata. The centre is directly poisoned by the circulation through it of opium-containing blood, and the patient's breathing becomes progressively slower, shallower and more irregular until finally it ceases altogether.

In *treating* acute opium poisoning the first proceeding is to empty the stomach. For this purpose the best emetic is apomorphine, which may be injected subcutaneously in a dose of about one-tenth of a grain. But apomorphine is not always to be obtained, and even if it be administered it may fail, since the gastric wall is often paralysed in opium poisoning, so that no emetic can act. It is therefore better to wash out the stomach, and this should be done, if possible, with a solution containing about ten grains of salt to each ounce of water. This must be repeated at intervals of about half an hour, since some of the opium is excreted into the stomach after its absorption into the blood. If apomorphine is obtainable, both of these measures may be employed. Potassium permanganate decomposes morphine by oxidation, the action being facilitated by the addition of a small quantity of mineral acid to the solution. The physiological as well as the chemical antidotes must be employed. The chief of these are coffee or caffeine and atropine. A pint of hot strong coffee may be introduced into the rectum, and caffeine in large doses—ten or twenty grains of the carbonate—may be given by the mouth. A twentieth, even a tenth of a grain of atropine sulphate should be injected subcutaneously, the drug being a direct stimulant of the respiratory centre. Every means must be taken to keep the patient awake. He must be walked about, have smelling salts constantly applied to the nose, or be stimulated by the faradic battery. But the final resort in cases of opium poisoning is artificial respiration, which should be persevered with as long as the heart continues to beat. It has, indeed, been asserted that, if relays of trained assistants are at hand, no one need die of opium poisoning, even if artificial respiration has to be continued for hours or days.

Opium-eating.—Opium, like many other poisons, produces after a time a less effect if frequently administered as a medicine, so that the dose has to be constantly increased to produce the same result on those who take it habitually. When it is used to relieve pain or diarrhoea, if the dose be not taken at the usual time the symptoms of the disease recur with such violence that the remedy is speedily resorted to as the only means of relief, and thus the habit is exceedingly difficult to break off. Opium-eating is chiefly practised in Asia Minor, Persia and India. Opinions differ widely as to the injurious effect of the habit; the weight of evidence appears, however, to indicate that it is much more deleterious than opium-smoking.

The following statistics collected by Vincent Richards regarding Balasor in Orissa throw some light on the influence of this practice on the health. He estimates that 1 in every 12 or 14 of the population uses the drug, and that the habit is increasing. Of the 613 opium-eaters examined by him he found that the average age at which the habit was commenced was 20 to 26 years for men and 24 to 30 years for women. Of this number 143 had taken the drug for from 10 to 20 years, 62 for from 20 to 30 years and 38 for more than 30 years. The majority took their opium twice daily, morning and evening, the quantity taken varying from 2 to 46 grains daily, large doses being the exception, and the average 5 to 7 grains daily. The dose, when large, had been increased from the beginning; when small, there had usually been no increase at all. The causes which first led to the increase of the drug were disease, example and a belief in its aphrodisiac powers. The diseases for which it was chiefly taken were malarial fever, dysentery, diarrhoea, spitting of blood, rheumatism and elephantiasis. A number began to take it in the famine year, 1866, as it enabled them to exist on less food and mitigated their sufferings; others used it to enable them to undergo fatigue and to make long journeys. Richards concludes that the excessive use of opium by the agricultural classes, who are the chief consumers in Orissa, is very rare indeed. Its moderate use may be and is indulged in for years without producing any decided or appreciable ill effect except weakening the reproductive powers, the average number of the children of opium-eaters being 1·11 after 11 years of married life. It compares favourably as regards crime and insanity with intoxicating drinks, the inhabitants of Balasor being a particularly law-abiding race, and the insane forming only 0·0009 % of the population. Dr W. Dymock of Bombay, speaking of western India, concurs in Richards's opinion regarding the moderate use of the drug. He believes that excessive indulgence in it is confined to a comparatively small number of the wealthier classes of the community. Dr Moore's experience of Rajputana strongly supports the same views. It seems probable that violent physical exercise may counteract in great measure the deleterious effect of opium and prevent it from retarding the respiration, and that in such cases the beneficial effects are obtained without the noxious results which would accrue from its use to those engaged in sedentary pursuits. There is no doubt that the spread of the practice is connected with the ban imposed in Mohammedan countries on the use of alcoholic beverages, and to some extent with the long religious fasts of the Buddhists, Hindus and Moslems, in which opium is used to allay hunger.

To break off the habit of opium-eating is exceedingly difficult, and can be effected only by actual external restraint, or the strongest effort of a powerful will, especially if the dose has been gradually increased.

Opium-smoking.—This is chiefly practised by the inhabitants of China and parts of the Indian Archipelago, and in countries where Chinese are largely employed. Opium-smoking began in China in the 17th century. Foreign opium was first imported by the Portuguese (early 18th century). In 1906 it was

estimated that 13,455,699 of Chinese smoked opium, or 27 % of adult males; but during 1908–1910 the consumption of opium is believed to have diminished by about one-third.

For smoking the Chinese use an extract of opium known as prepared opium or chandoo, and a cheaper preparation is made from 60 % used opium known as " opium dross " and 40 % native opium. This latter is chiefly used by the poorer classes.

The process of preparation is thus described by Hugh M'Callum, government analyst at Hong-Kong:—

" The opium is removed from its covering of leaves, &c., moistened with a little water, and allowed to stand for about fourteen hours; it is then divided into pans, 2½ balls of opium and about 10 pints of water going to each pan; it is now boiled and stirred occasionally until a uniform mixture having the consistence of a thin paste is obtained. This operation takes from five to six hours. The paste is at once transferred to a larger pan and cold water added to about 3 gallons, covered and allowed to stand for from fourteen to fifteen hours. A bunch of ' tang sani ' (lamp-wick, the pith of *Eriocaulon* or *Scirpus*) is then inserted well into the mass, and the pan slightly canted, when a rich, clear, brown fluid is thus drawn off, and filtered through ' chi mui ' (paper made from bamboo fibre). The residue is removed to a calico filter and thoroughly washed with boiling water, the wash water being reboiled and used time after time. The last washing is done with pure water; these washings are used in the next day's boiling.

" The residues on the calico filters are transferred to a large one of the same material and well pressed. This insoluble residue, called ' nai chai ' (opium dirt), is the perquisite of the head boiling coolie, who finds a ready market for it in Canton, where it is used for adulterating, or rather in manufacturing, the most inferior kinds of prepared opium. The filtrate or opium solution is concentrated by evaporation at the boiling point, with occasional stirring until of a proper consistence, the time required being from three to four hours; it is then removed from the fire and stirred with great vigour till cold, the cooling being accelerated by coolies with large fans. When quite cold it is taken to the hong and kept there for some months before it is considered in prime condition for smoking. As thus prepared it has the consistence of a thin treacly extract, and is called boiled or prepared opium. In this state it is largely exported from China to America, Australia, &c., being carefully sealed up in small pots having the name of the maker (i.e. hong) on each.

" The Chinese recognize the following grades of opium: (1) ' raw opium,' as imported from India; (2) ' prepared opium,' opium made as above; (3) ' opium dross,' the scrapings from the opium pipe; this is reboiled and manufactured as a second-class prepared opium; a Chinese doctor stated lately at a coroner's inquest on a case of poisoning that it was more poisonous than the ordinary prepared opium; (4) ' nai chai ' (opium dirt), the insoluble residue left on exhausting the raw opium thoroughly with water. The opium is sent every day from the hong (i.e. shop or firm) to the boiling-house, the previous day's boiling being then returned to the hong. The average quantity boiled each day is from six to eight chests of Patna opium, this being the only kind used."

By this process of preparation a considerable portion of the narcotine, caoutchouc, resin, oil or fatty and insoluble matters are removed, and the prolonged boiling, evaporating and baking over a naked fire tend to lessen the amount of alkaloids present in the extract. The only alkaloids likely to remain in the prepared opium, and capable of producing well-marked physiological results, are morphine, codeine and narceine. Morphine, in the pure state, can be sublimed, but codeine and narceine are said not to give a sublimate. Even if sublimed in smoking opium, morphine would, in M'Callum's opinion, probably be deposited in the pipe before it reached the mouth of the smoker. The bitter taste of morphine is not noticeable when smoking opium, and it is therefore possible that the pleasure derived from smoking the drug is due to some product formed during combustion. This supposition is rendered probable by the fact that the opiums most prized by smokers are not those containing most morphine, and that the quality is judged by the amount of soluble matter in the opium, by its tenacity or " touch," and by peculiarities of aroma—the Indian opium, especially the Patna kind, bearing much the same relation to the Chinese and Persian drug that champagne does to *vin ordinaire*. Opium-smoking is thus described by Theo. Sampson of Canton:—

" The smoker, lying on his side, with his face towards the tray and his head resting on a high hard pillow (sometimes made of earthenware, but more frequently of bamboo covered with leather), takes the pipe in his hand; with the other hand he takes a dipper and puts the *sharp* end of it into the opium, which is of a treacly consistency. Twisting it round and round he gets a large drop of the fluid to adhere to the dipper; still twisting it round to prevent it falling he brings the drop over the flame of the lamp, and twirling it round and round he roasts it; all this is done with acquired dexterity. The opium must not be burnt or made too dry, but roasted gently till it looks like burnt worsted; every now and then he takes it away from the flame and rolls it (still on the end of the dipper) on the flat surface of the bowl. When it is roasted and rolled to his satisfaction he gently heats the centre of the bowl, where there is a small orifice; then he quickly thrusts the end of the dipper into the orifice, twirls it round smartly and withdraws it; if this is properly done, the opium (now about the size of a grain of hemp-seed or a little larger) is left adhering to the bowl immediately over the orifice. It is now ready for smoking.

" The smoker assumes a comfortable attitude (lying down of course) at a proper distance from the lamp. He now puts the stem to his lips, and holds the bowl over the lamp. The heat causes the opium to frizzle, and the smoker takes three or four long inhalations, all the time using the dipper to bring every particle of the opium to the orifice as it burns away, but not taking his lips from the end of the stem, or the opium pellet from the lamp till all is finished. Then he uses the flattened end of the dipper to scrape away any little residue there may be left around the orifice, and proceeds to prepare another pipe. The preparations occupy from five to ten minutes, and the actual smoking about thirty seconds. The smoke is swallowed, and is exhaled through both the mouth and the nose."

FIG. 3.—Opium-smoking Apparatus. *a*, pipe; *b*, dipper; *c*, lamp.

So far as can be gathered from the conflicting statements published on the subject, opium-smoking may be regarded much in the same light as the use of alcoholic stimulants. To the great majority of smokers who use it moderately it appears to act as a stimulant, and to enable them to undergo great fatigue and to go for a considerable time with little or no food. According to the reports on the subject, when the smoker has plenty of active work it appears to be no more injurious than smoking tobacco. When carried to excess it becomes an inveterate habit; but this happens chiefly in individuals of weak will-power, who would just as easily become the victims of intoxicating drinks, and who are practically moral imbeciles, often addicted also to other forms of depravity. The effect in bad cases is to cause loss of appetite, a leaden pallor of the skin, and a degree of leanness so excessive as to make its victims appear like living skeletons. All inclination for exertion becomes gradually lost, business is neglected, and certain ruin to the smoker follows. There can be no doubt that the use of the drug is opposed by all thinking Chinese who are not pecuniarily interested in the opium trade or cultivation, for several reasons, among which may be mentioned the drain of bullion from the country, the decrease of population, the liability to famine through the cultivation of opium where cereals should be grown, and the corruption of state officials.

See *Pharmaceutical Journ.* [i] xi. p. 269, xiv. p. 395; [2] x. p. 434; Impey, *Report on Malwa Opium* (Bombay, 1848); *Rep.xi on Trade of Hankow* (1869); *New Remedies* (1876), p. 229; *Pharmacographia* (1879), p. 421; *Journal of the Society of Arts* (1882); *The Friend of China* (1883), &c.; *Report* of the Straits Settlements, Federated Malay States Opium Commission (1908), App. xxiii. and xxiv.; Allen, *Commercial Organic Analysis*, vol. iii. pt. iv. p. 355; Frank Browne, *Report on Opium* (Hong-Kong, 1908); G. Watt, *Dictionary of the Economic Products of India* (1892); H. Moissan, *Comptes rendus*, of the 5th of December 1892, iv. p. 33; Lalande, *Archives de médicine navale*, t. l. (1890); International Opium Commission (1909), vol. ii. " Report of the Delegations "; Squire, *Companion to the British Pharmacopeia* (1908) (18th edition).   (E. M. H.)

OPLADEN, a town of Germany, in the Prussian Rhine Province, 10 m. N.E. from Cologne by the railway to Elberfeld and at the junction of lines to Speldorf and Bonn. Pop. (1905) 6338. It has an Evangelical and a Roman Catholic church. It has dyeing works, and manufactures of dynamite, indigo products and railway plant. Before passing to Prussia, Opladen belonged to the duchy of Berg.

OPON, a town of the province of Cebu, Philippine Islands, on the small island of Mactan (area about 45 sq. m.), which is separated from the island of Cebu by a channel only about 1 m. wide. Pop (1903), after the annexation of Cordova and Santa Rosa, 20,166. There are forty-four *barrios*, or villages, in the town, and three of these had in 1903 more than 1000 inhabitants each. The language is Visayan. Opon is a shipping and commercial suburb of Cebu city, the harbour of which is sheltered by Mactan Island. The town has large groves of coco-nut trees, and its principal industries are the cultivation of Indian corn and maguey and fishing: In the N.E. part of the

town is a monument to Magellan, who discovered the Philippines in March 1521, and was slain here by the natives late in the following month.

OPORTO (*i.e. o porto*, " the port "), the second city of the kingdom of Portugal, the capital of the district of Oporto and formerly of Entre-Douro-e-Minho; on both banks of the river Douro, about 3 m. from its mouth, in 41° 8' N. and 8° 37' W. Pop. (1900) 167,955. In Portuguese the definite article is uncompounded in the name of the city, which in strict accuracy should always be written. *Porto*; the form *Oporto* has, however, been stereotyped by long usage in English and in some other European languages. The part of the city south of the Douro is known as Villa Nova de Gaia. Oporto is the see of a bishop, in the archiepiscopal province of Braga. It is the true capital of northern Portugal, and the commercial and political rival of Lisbon, in much the same way as Barcelona (*q.v.*) is the rival of Madrid. Three main railway lines meet here—from Lisbon, from Valença do Minho on the northern frontier, and from Barca d'Alva on the north-western frontier. The Valença line has branches to Guimarães and Braga, and affords access to Corunna and other cities of north-western Spain; the Barca d'Alva line has a branch to Mirandella and communicates with Madrid via Salamanca. Oporto is built chiefly on the north or right bank of the Douro; its principal suburbs are Bomfim on the E., Monte Pedral and Paranhos on the N., Villar Bicalho, Lordello and São João da Foz on the W., Ramalde, Villarinha, Matozinhos, Leça da Palmeira and the port of Leixões on the N.W. The mouth of the river is obstructed by a sandy spit of land which has been enlarged by the deposits of silt constantly washed down by the swift current; on the north side of this bar is a narrow channel varying in depth from 16 ft. to 19 ft. A fort in São João da Foz protects the entrance, and there is a lighthouse on a rock outside the bar. As large vessels cannot enter the river, a harbour of refuge has been constructed at Leixões (*q.v.*).

The approach to Oporto up the winding and fjord-like estuary is one of singular beauty. On the north the streets rise in terraces up the steep bank, built in many cases of granite overlaid with plaster, so that white is the prevailing colour of the city; on the south are the hamlets of Gaia and Furada, and the red-tiled wine lodges of Villa Nova de Gaia, in which vast quantities of " port " are manufactured and stored. The architecture of the houses and public buildings is often rather Oriental than European in appearance. There are numerous parks and gardens, especially on the outskirts of the city, in which palms, oranges and aloes grow side by side with the flowers and fruits of northern Europe, for the climate is mild and very equable, the mean temperatures for January and July—the coldest and the hottest months—being respectively about 50° and 70°. The Douro is at all seasons crowded with shipping, chiefly small steamers and large sailing vessels. The design of some of the native craft is peculiar—among them may be mentioned the high-prowed canoe-like fishing boats, the *rascas* with their three lateen sails, and the *barcos rabello*, flat-bottomed barges with huge rudders, used for the conveyance of wine down stream. Two remarkable iron bridges, the Maria Pia and the Dom Luiz I., span the river. The first was built by Messrs Eiffel & Company of Paris in 1876-1877; it rests on a granite substructure and carries the Lisbon railway line across the Douro ravine at a height of 200 ft. The second, constructed in 1881-1885 by a Belgian firm, has two decks or roadways, one 33 ft., the other 200 ft. above the usual water-level; its arch, one of the largest in Europe, has a span of 560 ft. and is supported by two massive granite towers. The Douro is liable in winter to sudden and violent floods; in 1909-1910 the water rose 40 ft. at Oporto, where it is confined in a deep and narrow bed.

Though parts of the city are modern or have been modernized, the older quarters in the east are extremely picturesque, with their steep and narrow lanes overshadowed by lofty balconied houses. Overcrowding and dirt are common, for the density of population is nearly 13,000 per sq. m., or greater than in any other city of Portugal. Until the early years of the 20th century, when a proper system of sewerage was installed, the condition of Oporto was most insanitary. Electric lighting and tramways were introduced a little before this, but the completion of the tramway system was long delayed, and in the hilly districts cars drawn by ten mules were not an uncommon sight. Ox-carts are used for the conveyance of heavy goods, and until late in the 19th century sedan-chairs were still occasionally used. A painful feature of the street-life of Oporto is the great number of the diseased and mutilated beggars who frequent the busiest thoroughfares. As a rule, however, the natives of Oporto are strong and of fine physique; they also show fewer signs of negro descent than the people of Lisbon.. Their numbers tend to increase very rapidly; in 1864 the population of Oporto was 86,751, but in 1878 it rose to 105,838, in 1890 to 138,860, and in 1900 to 167,955. Many of the men emigrate to South America, where their industry usually enables them to prosper, and ultimately to return with considerable savings. The local dialect is broader than the Portuguese of the educated classes, from which it differs more in pronunciation than in idiom. The poverty of the people is very great. Out of the 597,035 inhabitants of the district of Oporto (803 sq. m.), 422,320 were returned at the census of 1900 as unable to read or write. Much had been done, however, to remedy this defect, and besides numerous primary schools there are in the city two schools for teachers, a medical academy, polytechnic, art, trade and naval schools, and industrial institute, a commercial athenaeum, a lyceum for secondary education, an ecclesiastical seminary, and a meteorological observatory.

The cathedral, which stands at the highest point of eastern Oporto, on the site of the Visigothic citadel, was originally a Romanesque building of the 12th century; its cloisters are Gothic of the 14th century, but the greater part of the fabric was modernized in the 17th and 18th centuries. The interior of the cloisters is adorned with blue and white tiles, painted to represent scenes from the Song of Solomon. The bishop's palace is a large and lofty building conspicuously placed on a high rock; the interior contains a fine marble staircase. The Romanesque and early Gothic church of São Martinho de Cedo Feita is the most interesting ecclesiastical building in Oporto, especially noteworthy being the curiously carved capitals of its pillars. Though the present structure is not older, except in details, than the 11th century, the church is said to have been " hastily built " (cedo feita, cito facta) by Theodomir, king of the Visigoths, in 559, to receive the relics of St Martin of Tours, which were then on their way hither from France. The Torre dos Clerigos is a granite tower 246 ft. high, built in the middle of the 18th century at the expense of the local clergy (clerigos); it stands on a hill and forms a conspicuous landmark for sailors. Nossa Senhora da Lapa is a fine 18th-century church, Corinthian in style; São Francisco is a Gothic basilica dating from 1410; Nossa Senhora da Serra do Pilar is a secularized Augustinian convent used as artillery barracks, and marks the spot at which Wellington forced the passage of the Douro in 1809. The exchange (lonja) is another secularized convent, decorated with coloured marbles. Parts of the interior are floored and panelled with polished native-coloured woods from Brazil, which are inlaid in elaborate patterns; there is a very handsome staircase, and the fittings of one large room are an excellent modern copy of Moorish ornamentation.

Other noteworthy public buildings are the museum, library, opera-house, bull-ring, hospital and quarantine station. The crystal palace is a large glass and iron structure built for the industrial exhibition of 1865; its garden commands a fine view of the city and river, and contains a small menagerie. The English factory, built in 1790, has been converted into a club for the British residents—a large and important community whose members are chiefly connected with the wine and shipping trades. Lawn tennis, cricket, boat-racing on the Douro, and other British sports have been successfully introduced, and there is keen competition between the Oporto clubs and those of Lisbon and Carcavellos. The English club gave its name to the Rua Nova dos Inglezes, one of the busiest streets, which contains many banks, warehouses and steamship offices. The

Rua da Alfândega, skirting the right bank of the Douro and passing the custom house (alfândega), is of similar character; here may be seen characteristic types of the fishermen and peasants of northern Portugal. The Rua das Flores contains, on its eastern side, the shops of the cloth-dealers; on the west are the jewellers' shops, with a remarkable display of gold and silver filigree-work and enamelled gold. Oporto is famous for these ornaments, which are often very artistic, and are largely worn on holidays by women of the poorer classes, whose savings or dowries are often kept in this readily marketable form.

Oporto is chiefly famous for the export of the wine which bears its name. An act passed on the 29th of January 1906 defined " port," as a wine grown in the Douro district, exported from Oporto, and containing more than 16·5% of alcoholic strength. The vines from which it is made grow in the Paiz do Vinho, a hilly region about 60 m. up the river, and having an area of 27 m. in length by 5 or 6 in breadth, cut off from the sea, and shut in from the north-east by mountains. The trade was established in 1678, but the shipments for some years did not exceed 600 pipes (of 115 gallons each). In 1703 the British government concluded the Methuen treaty with Portugal, under which Portuguese wines were admitted on easier terms than French or German, and henceforward " port " began to be drunk (see PORTUGAL: History). In 1747 the export reached 17,000 pipes. In 1754 the great wine monopoly company of Oporto originated, under which the shipments rose to 33,000 pipes. At the beginning of the 19th century the policy of the government more and more favoured port wine, besides which the vintages from 1802 to 1815 were splendid both in Portugal and in Madeira—that of 1815 has, in fact, never been excelled. For the next few years the grape was not at all good, but the 1820 vintage was the most remarkable of any. It was singularly sweet and black, besides being equal in quality to that of 1815. This was long regarded as the standard in taste and colour for true port, and to keep up the vintage of following years to this exceptional standard adulteration by elder berries, &c., was resorted to. This practice did not long continue, for it was cheaper to adulterate the best wines with inferior sorts of port wine itself. In 1852 the Oidium which spread over Europe destroyed many of the Portuguese vineyards. In 1865 Phylloxera did much damage, and in 1867 the second monopoly company was abolished. From this time the exports again increased. (See WINE.)

A third of the population is engaged in the manufacture of cottons, woollens, leather, silk, gloves, hats, pottery, corks, tobacco, spirits, beer, aerated waters, preserved foods, soap or jewelry. Oporto gloves and hats are highly esteemed in Portugal. Cotton piece goods are sent to the African colonies, and, in small quantities, to Brazil; their value in 1905 was £120,360, but a larger quantity was retained for the home market. The fisheries —chiefly of hake, bream and sardines—are extensive. Steam-trawling, though unsuccessful in the 19th century, was resumed in 1904, and in 1906 there were 136 British, 10 Dutch and 3 Portuguese steamers thus engaged. The innovation was much resented by the owners of more than 350 small sailing boats, and protective legislation was demanded. In 1905 the combined port of Oporto and Leixões was entered by 1734 vessels of 1,562,724 tons, but in this total some vessels were counted twice over—i.e. once at each port. Nearly three-fourths of the tonnage was entered at Leixões. About the close of the 19th century there was an important development of tourist traffic from Liverpool and Southampton via Havre. Reduced railway rates and improved hotel accommodation have facilitated the growth of this traffic. Many tourists land at Oporto and visit Braga (q.v.), Bussaco (q.v.) and other places of interest, on their way to Lisbon. There is also a large tourist traffic from Germany. The exports of Oporto include wine, cottons, wood, pitwood, stone, cork, salt, sumach, onions, oranges, olives and beans. American competition has destroyed the export trade in live cattle for which Great Britain was the principal market. Dried codfish (bacalháo) is imported in great quantities from Newfoundland and Norway; other noteworthy imports are coal, iron, steel, machinery and textiles. The total yearly value of the foreign trade exceeds £5,000,000.

The history of Oporto dates from an early period. Before the Roman invasion, under the name of Portus Cale, Gaia or Cago, it was a town on the south bank of the Douro with a good trade; the Alani subsequently founded a city on the north bank, calling it *Castrum Novum*. About A.D. 540 the Visigoths under Leovigild obtained possession, but yielded place in 716 to the Moors. The Christians, however, recaptured Oporto in 997, and it became the capital of the counts of *Portucalia* for part of the period during which the Moors ruled in the southern provinces of Portugal. (See PORTUGAL: *History*.) The Moors once more became its masters for a short period, till in 1095 it was brought finally under Christian domination. The citizens rebelled in 1628 against an unpopular tax, in 1661 for a similar reason, in 1757 against the wine monopoly, and in 1808 against the French. The town is renowned in British military annals from the duke of Wellington's passage of the Douro, by which he surprised and put to flight the French army under Marshal Soult, capturing the city on the 12th of May 1809. Oporto sustained a severe siege in 1832–1833, being bravely defended against the Miguelites by Dom Pedro with 7000 soldiers; 16,000 of its inhabitants perished. In the constitutional crises of 1820, 1826, 1836, 1841, 1846–1847, 1891 and 1907–1908 the action of Oporto, as the capital of northern Portugal, was always of the utmost importance.

OPOSSUM, an American Indian name properly belonging to the American marsupials (other than *Caenolestes*), but in Australia applied to the phalangers (see PHALANGER). True opossums are found throughout the greater part of America from the United States to Patagonia, the number of species being largest in the more tropical parts (see MARSUPIALIA). They form the family *Didelphyidae*, distinguished from other marsupial families by the equally developed hind-toes, the nailless but fully opposable first hind-toe, and by the dentition, of which the formula is $i. \frac{5}{4}, c. \frac{1}{1}, p. \frac{3}{3}, m. \frac{4}{4}$; total 50. The peculiarity in the mode of succession of these teeth is explained in the article referred to. Opossums are small animals, varying from the size of a mouse to that of a large cat, with long noses, ears and tails, the latter being as a rule naked and prehensile, and with the first toe in the hind-foot so fully opposable to the other digits as to constitute a functionally perfect posterior " hand." These opposable first toes are without nail or claw, but their tips are expanded into broad flat pads, which are of great use to these climbing animals. On the anterior limbs all the five digits are provided with long sharp claws, and the first toe is but little opposable. The numerous cheek-teeth are crowned with minute sharply-pointed cusps, with which to crush the insects on which these creatures feed, for the opossums seem to take in South America the place in the economy of nature filled in other countries by hedgehogs, moles, shrews, &c. The true opossums are typically represented by *Didelphys marsupialis*, a species, with several local races, ranging over the greater part of North America (except the extreme north). It is of large size, and extremely common, being even found living in towns, where it acts as a scavenger by night, retiring for shelter by day upon the roofs or into the sewers. It produces in the spring from six to sixteen young ones, which are placed by the mother in her pouch immediately after birth, and remain there until able to take care of themselves; the period of gestation being from fourteen to seventeen days. A local race found in Central and tropical South America is known as the crab-eating opossum (*D. marsupialis cancrivora*). The second sub-genus, or genus, *Metachirus* contains a considerable number of species found all over the tropical parts of the New World. They are of medium size, with short, close fur, very long, scaly and naked tails, and have less developed ridges on their skulls They have, as a rule, no pouch in which to carry their young, and the latter therefore commonly ride on their mother's back, holding on by winding their prehensile tails round hers, as in the figure of the woolly opossum. The latter belongs to the sub-genus *Philander*, which is nearly allied to the last; its full title being *Didelphy*

(*Philander*) *lanigera*. The philander (*D. [P.] philander*) is closely related.

The fourth sub-genus (or genus) is *Marmosa* (*Micoureus*, or *Grymaeomys*), differing from the two last by the smaller size of its members and by certain slight differences in the shape of their teeth. Its best-known species is the murine opossum (*D. murina*), no larger than a mouse, of a bright-red colour, found as far north as central Mexico, and extending thence to the south of Brazil. A second well-known species is *D. cinerea*, which ranges from Central America to western Brazil, Peru and Bolivia. Yet another group (*Peramys*) is represented by numerous shrew-like species, of very small size, with short, hairy and non-prehensile tails, not half the length of the trunk, and unridged skulls. The most striking member of the group

The Woolly Opossum (*Didelphys lanigera*) and young.

is the Three-striped Opossum (*D. americana*) from Brazil, which is of a reddish grey colour, with three clearly-defined deep-black bands down its back, as in some of the striped mice of Africa. *D. dimidiata*, *D. nudicaudata*, *D. domestica*, *D. unistriata* and several other South American species belong to this group. Lastly we have the Chiloe Island opossum (*D. gliroides*), alone representing the sub-genus *Dromiciops*, which is most nearly allied to *Marmosa*, but differs from all other opossums by the short furry ears, thick hairy tail, doubly swollen auditory bulla, short canines and peculiarly formed and situated incisors.

Whatever difference of opinion there may be as to the right of the above-mentioned groups to generic separation from the typical *Didelphys*, there can be none as to the distinctness of the water-opossum (*Chironectes minimus*), which differs from all the other members of the family by its fully webbed feet, and the dark-brown transverse bands across the body (see WATER-OPOSSUM).

See O. Thomas, *Catalogue of Marsupialia and Monotremata* (British Museum, 1888); " On Micoureus griseus, with the Description of a New Genus and Species of Didelphyidae," *Ann. Mag. Nat. Hist.* ser. 6, vol. xiv. p. 184, and later papers in the same and other serials. (R. L.*)

OPPEL, CARL ALBERT (1831–1865), German palaeontologist, was born at Hohenheim in Württemberg, on the 19th of December 1831. After studying mineralogy and geology at Stuttgart, he entered the university of Tübingen, where he graduated Ph.D. in 1853. Here he came under the influence of Quenstedt and devoted his special attention to the fossils of the Jurassic system. With this object he examined in detail during 1854 and the following year the succession of strata in England, France and Germany and determined the various palaeontological stages or zones characterized by special guide-fossils, in most cases ammonites The results of his researches were published in his great work *Die Juraformation Englands, Frankreichs und des südwestlichen Deutschlands* (1856–1858). In 1858 he became an assistant in the Palaeontological Museum at Munich. In 1860 he became professor of palaeontology in the university at Munich, and in 1861 director of the Palaeontological Collection. There he continued his labours on the Jurassic fauna, describing new species of crustacea, ammonites, &c. To him also we owe the establishment of the Tithonian stage,. for strata (mainly equivalent to the English Portland and Purbeck Beds) that occur on the borders of Jurassic and Cretaceous. Of his later works the most important was *Paläontologische Mittheilungen aus dem Museum des Königl. Bayer. Staats.* (1862–1865). He died at Munich on the 23rd of December 1865.

OPPELN (Polish, *Oppolie*), a town of Germany, in the Prussian province of Silesia, lies on the right bank of the Oder, 51 m. S.E. of Breslau, on the railway to Kattowitz, and at the junction of lines to Beuthen, Neisse and Tarnowitz. Pop. (1905) 30,769. It is the seat of the provincial administration of Upper Silesia, and contains the oldest Christian church in the district, that of St Adalbert, founded at the close of the 10th century. It has two other churches and a ducal 15th-century palace in the town hall in the Oder. The most prominent among the other buildings are the offices of the district authorities, the town hall, the normal seminary and the hospital of St Adalbert. The Roman Catholic gymnasium is established in an old Jesuit college. The industries of Oppeln include the manufacture of Portland cement, machinery, beer, soap, cigars and lime; trade is carried on by rail and river in cattle, grain and the vast mineral output of the district, of which Oppeln is the chief centre. The upper classes speak German, the lower Polish.

Oppeln was a flourishing place at the beginning of the 11th century, and became a town in 1228. It was the capital of the duchy of Oppeln and the residence of the duke from 1163 to 1532, when the ruling family became extinct. Then it passed to Austria, and with the rest of Silesia was ceded to Prussia in 1742.

See Idzikowski, *Geschichte der Stadt Oppeln* (Oppeln, 1863); and Vogt, *Oppeln beim Eintritt in das Jahr 1900* (Oppeln, 1900).

OPPENHEIM, a town of Germany, in the grand duchy of Hesse, picturesquely situated on the slope of vine-clad hills, on the left bank of the Rhine, 20 m. S. of Mainz, on the railway to Worms. Pop. (1905) 3696. The only relic of its former importance is the Evangelical church of St Catherine, one of the most beautiful Gothic edifices of the 13th and 14th centuries in Germany, and recently restored at the public expense. The town has a Roman Catholic church, several schools and a memorial of the War of 1870–71. Its industries and commerce are principally concerned with the manufacture and export of wine. Above the town are the ruins of the fortress of Landskron, built in the 11th century and destroyed in 1689.

Oppenheim, which occupies the site of the Roman Bauconica, was formerly much larger than at present. In 1226 it appears as a free town of the Empire and later as one of the most important members of the Rhenish League. It lost its independence in 1375, when it was given in pledge to the elector palatine of the Rhine. During the Thirty Years' War it was alternately occupied by the Swedes and the Imperialists, and in 1689 it was entirely destroyed by the French.

See W. Franck, *Geschichte der ehemaligen Reichsstadt Oppenheim* (Darmstadt, 1859).

OPPERT, JULIUS (1825–1905), German Assyriologist, was born at Hamburg, of Jewish parents, on the 9th of July 1825. After studying at Heidelberg, Bonn and Berlin, he graduated at Kiel in 1847, and in the following year went to France, where he was teacher of German at Laval and at Reims. His leisure was given to Oriental studies, in which he had made great progress in Germany, and in 1852 he joined Fresnel's archaeological expedition to Mesopotamia. On his return in 1854 he occupied himself in digesting the results of the expedition in so far as they concerned cuneiform inscriptions, and published an important work upon them (*Déchiffrement des inscriptions cunéiformes*, 1861). In 1857 he was appointed professor of Sanscrit in the school of languages connected with the National Library in Paris, and in this capacity he produced a Sanscrit grammar; but his attention was chiefly given to Assyrian and cognate subjects, and he was especially prominent in establishing the Turanian character of the language originally spoken in Assyria. In 1869 Oppert was appointed professor of Assyrian philology and archaeology at the *Collège de France*. In 1865 he published

a history of Assyria and Chaldaea in the light of the results of the different exploring expeditions. At a later period he devoted much attention to the language and antiquities of ancient Media, writing *Le Peuple et la langue des Mèdes* (1879). He died in Paris on the 21st of August 1905. Oppert was a voluminous writer upon Assyrian mythology and jurisprudence, and other subjects connected with the ancient civilizations of the East. Among his other works may be mentioned: *Éléments de la grammaire assyrienne* (1868); *L'Immortalité de l'âme chez les Chaldéens*, (1875); *Salomon et ses successeurs* (1877); and, with J. Ménant, *Doctrines juridiques de l'Assyrie et de la Chaldée* (1877).

,**OPPIAN** (Gr. Ὀππιανός), the name of the authors of two (or three) didactic poems in Greek hexameters, formerly identified, but now generally regarded as two different persons. (1) Oppian of Corycus (or Anabarzus) in Cilicia, who flourished in the reign of Marcus Aurelius (emperor A.D. 161–180). According to an anonymous biographer, his father, having incurred the displeasure of Lucius Verus, the colleague of Aurelius, by neglecting to pay his respects to him when he visited the town, was banished to Malta. Oppian, who had accompanied his father into exile, returned after the death of Verus (169) and went on a visit to Rome. Here he presented his poems to Aurelius, who was so pleased with them that he gave the author a piece of gold for each line, took him into favour and pardoned his father. Oppian subsequently returned to his native country, but died of the plague shortly afterwards, at the early age of thirty. His contemporaries erected a statue in his honour, with an inscription which is still extant, containing a lament for his premature death and a eulogy of his precocious genius. His poem on fishing (*Halieutica*), of about 3500 lines, dedicated to Aurelius and his son Commodus, is still extant. (2) Oppian of Apamea (or Pella) in Syria. His extant poem on hunting (*Cynegetica*) is dedicated to the emperor Caracalla, so that it must have been written after 211. It consists of about 2150 lines, and is divided into four books, the last of which seems incomplete. The author evidently knew the *Halieutica*, and perhaps intended his poem as a supplement. Like his namesake, he shows considerable knowledge of his subject and close observation of nature; but in style and poetical merit he is inferior to him. His versification also is less correct. The improbability of there having been two poets of the same name, writing on subjects so closely akin and such near contemporaries, may perhaps be explained by assuming that the real name of the author of the *Cynegetica* was not Oppian, but that he has been confounded with his predecessor. In any case, it seems clear that the two were not identical.

A third poem on bird-catching (*Ixeutica*, from ἰξός, bird-lime), also formerly attributed to an Oppian, is lost; a paraphrase in Greek prose by a certain Eutecnius is extant. The author is probably one Dionysius, who is mentioned by Suidas as the author of a treatise on stones (*Lithiaca*).

The chief modern editions are J. G. Schneider (1776); F. S. Lehrs (1846); U. C. Bussemaker (Scholia, 1849); (*Cynegetica*) P. Boudreaux (1908). The anonymous biography referred to above will be found in A. Westermann's *Biographi Graeci* (1845). On the subject generally see A. Martin, *Études sur la vie et les œuvres d'Oppien de Cilicie* (1863); A. Ausfeld, *De Oppiano et scriptis sub ejus nomine traditis* (1876). There are translations of the *Halieutica*, in English by Diaper and Jones (1722), and in French by E. J. Bourquin (1877).

OPPIUS, GAIUS, an intimate friend of Julius Caesar. He managed the dictator's private affairs during his absence from Rome, and, together with L. Cornelius Balbus, exercised considerable influence in the city. According to Suetonius (*Caesar*, 56), many authorities considered Oppius to have written the histories of the Spanish, African and Alexandrian wars which are printed among the works of Caesar. It is now generally held that he may possibly be the author of the last (although the claims of Hirtius are considered stronger), but certainly not of the two first, although Niebuhr confidently assigned the *Bellum Africanum* to him; the writer of these took an actual part in the wars they described, whereas Oppius was in Rome at the time. He also wrote a life of Caesar and the elder Scipio.

For a discussion of the whole question, see M. Schanz, *Geschichte der römischen Literatur*, pt. i. p. 210 (2nd ed., 1898); Teuffel-Schwabe, *Hist. of Roman Literature* (Eng. trans.), § 197; see also Cicero, *Letters*, ed. Tyrrell and Purser, iv. introd. p. 69.

OPTICS, the science of light, regarded as the medium of sight (Gr. ὄψις). Generally the noun is qualified by an adjective so as to delimitate the principal groups of optical phenomena, *e.g.* geometrical optics, physical optics, meteorological optics, &c. Greek terminology included two adjectival forms—τὰ ὀπτικά, for all optical phenomena, including vision and the nature of light, and ἡ ὀπτική (*sc.* θεωρία), for the objective study of light, *i.e.* the nature of light itself and the theory of vision. See LIGHT and VISION.

OPTION (Lat. *optio*, choice, choosing, *optare*, to choose), the action of choosing or thing chosen, choice or power or opportunity of making a choice. The word had a particular meaning in ecclesiastical law, where it was used of a right claimed by an archbishop to select one benefice from the diocese of a newly appointed bishop, the next presentation to which would fall to his, the archbishop's, patronage. This right was abolished by various statutes in the early part of the 19th century. As a term in stock-exchange operations, " option " is used to express the privilege given to conclude a bargain at some future time at an agreed-upon price (see CALL and STOCK EXCHANGE). The phrase " local option " has been specifically used in politics of the power given to the electorate of a particular district to choose whether licences for the sale of intoxicating liquor should be granted or not. This form of " local option " has been also and more rightly termed " local veto " (see LIQUOR LAWS).

OPUS ('Οποῦς), in ancient Greece, the chief city of the Opuntian Locrians; the walls of the town may still be seen on a hill about 6 m. S.E. of the modern Atalante, and about 2 m. from the channel which separates the mainland from Euboea. It is mentioned in the Homeric catalogue among the towns of the Locrians, who were led by Ajax Oïleus; and there were games called Aiantea and an altar at Opus in honour of Ajax. Opus was also the birthplace of Patroclus. Pindar's Ninth Olympian Ode is mainly devoted to the glory and traditions of Opus. Its founder was Opus the son of Zeus and Protogeneia, the daughter of an Elian Opus, or, according to another version, of Deucalion and Pyrrha, and the wife of Locrus. The Locrians deserted the Greek side in the Persian Wars; they were among the allies of Sparta in the Peloponnesian War. In the struggle between Philip V. of Macedon and the Romans the town went over to the latter in 197 B.C., but the Acropolis held out for Philip until his defeat at Cynoscephalae (Livy xxxii. 32). The town suffered from earthquakes, such as that which destroyed the neighbouring Atalante in 1894.

ORACH, or MOUNTAIN SPINACH, known botanically as *Atriplex hortensis*, a tall-growing hardy annual, whose leaves, though coarsely flavoured, are used as a substitute for spinach, and to correct the acidity of sorrel. The white and the green are the most desirable varieties. The plant should be grown quickly in rich soil. It may be sown in rows 2 ft. apart, and about the same distance in the row, about March, and for succession again in June. If needful, water must be freely given; so as to maintain a rapid growth. A variety, *A. hortensis* var. *rubra*, commonly called red mountain spinach, is a hardy annual 3 to 4 ft. high with fine ornamental foliage.

ORACLE (Lat. *oraculum*, from *orare*, to pray; the corresponding Greek word is μαντεῖον or χρηστήριον), a special place where a deity is supposed to give a response, by the mouth of an inspired priest, to the inquiries of his votaries; or the actual response. The whole question of oracles—whether in the sense of the response or the sacred place—is bound up with that of magic, divination and omens, to the articles on which the reader is referred. They are commonly found in the earlier stages of religious culture among different nations. But it is as an ancient Greek institution that they are most interesting historically.

A characteristic feature of Greek religion which distinguishes it from many other systems of advanced cult was the wide prevalence of a ritual of divination and the prominence of certain oracular centres which were supposed to give voice to the will of Providence. An account of the oracles of Greece is concerned with the historical question about their growth, influence and career. But it is convenient to consider first the anthropologic question, as to the methods of divination practised in ancient Greece, their significance and the original ideas that inspired them. Only the slightest theoretical construction is possible here; and the true psychologic explanation of the mantic facts is of very recent discovery. In the Greek world these were of great variety, but nearly all the methods of divination found there can be traced among other communities, primitive and advanced, ancient and modern. The most obvious and useful classification of them is that of which Plato[1] was the author, who distinguishes between (*a*) the " sane " form of divination and (*b*) the ecstatic, enthusiastic or "insane" form. The first method appears to be cool and scientific, the diviner (μάντις) interpreting certain signs according to fixed principles of interpretation. The second is worked by the prophet, shaman or Pythoness, who is possessed and overpowered by the deity, and in temporary frenzy utters mystic speech under divine suggestion. To these we may add a third form (*c*), divination by communion with the spiritual world in dreams or through intercourse with the departed spirit: this resembles class (*a*) in that it does not necessarily involve ecstasy, and class (*b*) in that it assumes immediate *rapport* with some spiritual power.

It will be convenient first to give typical examples of these various processes of discovering the divine will, and then to sketch the history of Delphi, the leading centre of divination. We may subdivide the methods that fall under class (*a*), those that conform to the " omen "-system, according as they deal with the phenomena of the animate or the inanimate world; although this distinction would not be relevant in the period of primitive animistic thought. The Homeric poems attest that auguries from the flight and actions of birds were commonly observed in the earliest Hellenic period as they occasionally were in the later, but we have little evidence that this method was ever organized as it was at Rome into a regular system of state-divination, still less of state-craft. We can only quote the passage in the *Antigone* where Sophocles describes the method of Teiresias, who keeps an aviary where he studies and interprets the flight and the cries of the birds; it is probable that the poet was aware of some such practice actually in vogue. But the usual examples of Greek augury do not suggest deliberate and systematic observation; for instance, the phenomenon in the *Iliad* of the eagle seizing the snake and dropping it, or, in the *Agamemnon* of Aeschylus, of the eagles swooping on the pregnant hare. Other animals besides birds could furnish omens; we have an interesting story of the omen derived from the contest between a wolf and a bull which decided the question of the sovereignty of Argos when Danaus arrived and claimed the kingdom;[2] and the private superstitious man might be encouraged or depressed by any ominous sign derived from any part of the animal world. But it is very rare to find such omens habitually consulted in any public system of divination sanctioned by the state. We hear of a shrine of Apollo at Sura in Lycia,[3] where omens were taken from the movements of the sacred fish that were kept there in a tank; and again of a grove consecrated to this god in Epirus, where tame serpents were kept and fed by a priestess, who could predict a good or bad harvest according as they ate heartily or came willingly to her or not.[4]

But the method of animal divination that was most in vogue was the inspection of the inward parts of the victim offered upon the altar, and the interpretation of certain marks found there according to a conventional code. Sophocles in the passage referred to above gives us a glimpse of the prophet's procedure. A conspicuous example of an oracle organized on this principle was that of Zeus at Olympia, where soothsayers of the family of the Iamidai prophesied partly by the inspection of entrails,

[1] *Phaedrus*, p. 244.
[2] Serv. Verg. *Aen.* iv. 377; Paus. ii. 19. 3.
[3] Steph. Byz. *s.v.* Σοῦρα. Plut. *De sollert. anim.* p. 976 c. Ael. *Nat. anim.* xii. 1.
[4] Ael. *Nat. anim.* xi. 2.

partly by the observation of certain signs in the skin when it was cut or burned.[1] Another less familiar procedure that belongs to this subdivision is that which was known as divination διά κληδόνων, which might sometimes have been the cries of birds, but in an oracle of Hermes at the Achaean city of Pharae were the casual utterances of men. Pausanias tells us[2] how this was worked. The consultant came in the evening to the statue of Hermes in the market-place that stood by the side of a hearth-altar to which bronze lamps were attached; having kindled the lamps and put a piece of money on the altar, he whispered into the ear of the statue what he wished to know; he then departed, closing his ears with his hands, and whatever human speech he first heard after withdrawing his hands he took for a sign. The same custom seems to have prevailed at Thebes in a shrine of Apollo, and in the Olympian oracle of Zeus.[3]

Of omens taken from what we call the inanimate world salient examples are those derived from trees and water, a divination to be explained by an animistic feeling that may be regarded as at one time universal. Both were in vogue at Dodona, where the ecstatic method of prophecy was never used; we hear of divination there from the bubbling stream, and still more often of the "talking oak"; under its branches may once have slept the Selloi, who interpreted the sounds of the boughs, and who may be regarded as the depositories of the Aryan tradition of Zeus, the oak god who spoke in the tree.[4] At Korope in Thessaly we hear vaguely of an Apolline divination by means of a branch of the tamarisk tree,[5] a method akin no doubt to that of the divining rod which was used in Greece as elsewhere; and there is a late record that at Daphne near Antioch oracles were obtained by dipping a laurel leaf or branch in a sacred stream.[6] Water divination must have been as familiar at one time to the Greeks as it was to the ancient Germans; for we hear of the fountain at Daphne revealing things to come by the varying murmur of its flow,[7] and marvellous reflections of a mantic import might be seen in a spring on Tacnaron in Laconia;[8] from another at Patrae omens were drawn concerning the chances of recovery from disease.[9] Thunder magic, which was practised in Arcadia, is usually associated with thunder divination; but of this, which was so much in vogue in Etruria and was adopted as a state-craft by Rome, the evidence in Greece is singularly slight. Once a year watchers took their stand on the wall at Athens and waited till they saw the lightning flash from Harma, which was accepted as an auspicious omen for the setting out of the sacred procession to Apollo Pythius at Delphi; and the altar of Zeus Σημαλέος, the sender of omens, on Mount Parnes, may have been a religious observatory of meteorological phenomena.[10] No doubt such a rare and portentous event as the fall of a meteor-stone would be regarded as ominous, and the state would be inclined to consult Delphi or Dodona as to its divine import.

We may conclude the examples of this main department of μαντική by mentioning a method that seems to have been much in vogue in the earlier times, that which was called ἡ διὰ ψήφων μαντική, or divination by the drawing or throwing of lots; these must have been objects, such as small pieces of wood or dice, with certain marks inscribed upon them, drawn casually or thrown down and interpreted according to a certain code. This simple process of immemorial antiquity, for other Aryan peoples such as the Teutonic possessed it, was practised at Delphi and Dodona by the side of the more solemn procedure; we hear of it also in the oracle of Heracles at Bura in Achaea.[11] It is this method of "scraping" or "notching" (χόαειν) signs on wood

that explains probably the origin of the words χρησμός, χρῆσθαι, ἀναιρεῖν for oracular consultation and deliverance.

The processes described above are part of a world-wide system of popular divination. And most of them were taken up by the oracular shrines in Greece, Apollo himself having no special and characteristic mantic method, but generally adopting that which was of local currency. But much that is adopted by the higher personal religions descends from a more primitive and lower stage of religious feeling. And all this divination was originally independent of any personal divinity. The primitive diviner appealed directly to that mysterious potency which was supposed to inhere in the tree and spring, in the bird or beast, or even in a notched piece of wood. At a later stage, it may be, this power is interpreted in accordance with the animistic, and finally with the theistic, belief; and now it is the god who sends the sign, and the bird or animal is merely his organ. Hence the omen-seeker comes to prefer the sacrificed animal, as likely to be filled with the divine spirit through contact with the altar. And, again, if we are to understand the most primitive thought, we probably ought to conceive of it as regarding the omen not as a mere sign, but in some confused sense as a cause of that which is to happen. By sympathetic magic the flight of the bird, or the appearance of the entrails, is mysteriously connected, as cause with effect, with the event which is desired or dreaded. Thus in the Aztec sacrifice of children to procure rain, the victims were encouraged to shed tears copiously; and this was not a mere sign of an abundant rainfall, but was sympathetically connected with it. And in the same way, when of the three beasts over which three kings swore an oath of alliance, one died prematurely and was supposed thereby to portend the death of one of the kings,[12] or when in the Lacedaemonian sacrifice the head of the victim mysteriously vanished, and this portended the death of their naval commander,[13] these omens would be merely signs of the future for the comparatively advanced Hellene; but we may discern at the back of this belief one more primitive still, that these things were somehow casually or sympathetically connected with the kindred events that followed. We can observe the logical nexus here, which in most instances escapes us. This form of divination, then, we may regard as a special branch of sympathetic magic, which nature herself performs for early man, and which it concerns him to watch.

The other branch of the mantic art, the ecstatic or inspired, has had the greater career among the peoples of the higher religions; and morphologically we may call it the more advanced, as Shamanism or demoniac or divine possession implies the belief in spirits or divinities. But actually it is no doubt of great antiquity, and it is found still existing at a rather low grade of savagery. Therefore it is unsafe to infer from Homer's silence about it that it only became prevalent in Greece in the post-Homeric period. It did not altogether supersede the simpler method of divination by omens; but being far more impressive and awe-inspiring, it was adopted by some of the chief Apolline oracles, though never by Dodona.

The most salient example of it is afforded by Delphi. In the historic period, and perhaps from the earliest times, a woman known as the Pythoness was the organ of inspiration, and it was generally believed that she delivered her oracles under the direct afflatus of the god. The divine possession worked like an epileptic seizure, and was exhausting and might be dangerous; nor is there any reason to suspect that it was simulated. This communion with the divinity needed careful preparation. Originally, as it seems, virginity was a condition of the tenure of the office; for the virgin has been often supposed to be the purer vehicle for divine communication; but later the rule was established that a married woman over fifty years of age should be chosen, with the proviso that she should be attired as a maiden. As a preliminary to the divine possession, she appears to have chewed leaves of the sacred laurel, and then to have drunk water from the prophetic stream called Kassotis which flowed underground. But the culminating point of the afflatus was reached when she seated herself upon the tripod; and here, according to the belief

---

[1] Schol. Pind. *Ol.* 6, 111.   [2] vii. 22. 2.
[3] Farnell, *Cults of the Greek States,* iv., p. 221.
[4] Hom. *Il.* xvi. 233. *Od.* xiv. 327; Hesiod, *ap.* Schol. Soph. *Trach.* 1169; Aesch. *Prom. Vinc.* 829.
[5] Nikander, *Theriaka,* 612; Schol. *ibid.*
[6] See Robertson-Smith, *Religion of the Semites,* p. 128, quoting Sozomen v. 19.
[7] Ammian. Marcell, xxii. 12; cf. Plut. *Vita Caes.* c. 19.
[8] Paus. iii. 25. 8.   [9] Paus. vii. 21. 11.   [10] Paus. i. 32. 2.
[11] Cic. *De div.* i. 76. Suid. *s.v.* πύθι. Paus. vii. 25. 10.
[12] Plut. *Vita Pyrrh.* c. 6.   [13] Diod. Sic. xiii. 97.

of at least the later ages of paganism, she was supposed to be inspired by a mystic vapour that arose from a fissure in the ground. Against the ordinary explanation of this as a real mephitic gas producing convulsions, there seem to be geological and chemical objections;[1] nor have the recent French excavations revealed any chasm or gap in the floor of the temple. But the strong testimony of the later writers, especially Plutarch,[2] cannot wholly be set aside; and we can sufficiently reconcile it with the facts if we suppose a small crack in the floor through which a draught of air was felt to ascend. This, combining with the other mantic stimulants used, would be enough to throw a believing medium into a condition of mental seizure; and the difficulty felt by the older generation of scholars, who had to resort to the hypothesis of charlatanism or diabolic agency, no longer exists in the light of modern anthropology and the modern science of psychic phenomena. The Pythoness was no ambitious pretender, but ordinarily a virtuous woman of the lower class. It is probable that what she uttered were only unintelligible murmurs, 'and that these were interpreted into relevance and set in metric or prose sentences by the "prophet" and the "Holy Ones" or "Οσιοι as they were called, members of leading Delphic families, who sat round the tripod, who received the questions of the consultant beforehand, probably in writing, and usually had considered the answers that should be given.

Examples of the same enthusiastic method can be found in other oracles of Apollo. At Argos, the prophetess of the Apollo Pythius attained to the divine afflatus by drinking the blood of the lamb that was sacrificed in the night to him;[3] this is obviously a mantic communion, for the sacrificial victim is full of the spirit of the divinity. And we find the same process at the prophetic shrine of Ge at Aegae in Achaea, where the prophetess drank a draught of bull's blood for the same purpose.[4] In the famous oracle shrines of Apollo across the sea, at Klaros and Branchidae[5] near Miletus, the divination was of the same ecstatic type, but produced by a simple draught of holy water. The Clarian prophet fasted several days and nights in retirement and stimulated his ecstasy by drinking from a subterranean spring which is said by Pliny to have shortened the lives of those who used it.[6] Then, "on certain fixed nights after many sacrifices had been offered, he delivered his oracles, shrouded from the eyes of the consultants."[7]

The divination by "incubation" was allied to this type, because though lacking the ecstatic character, the consultant received direct communion with the god or departed spirit. He attained it by laying himself down to sleep or to await a vision, usually by night, in some holy place, having prepared himself by a course of ritualistic purification. Such consultation was naturally confined to the underworld divinities or to the departed heroes. It appears to have prevailed at Delphi when Ge gave oracles there before the coming of Apollo, and among the heroes Amphiaraus, Calchas and Trophonius are recorded to have communicated with their worshippers in this fashion. And it was by incubation that the sick and diseased who repaired to the temple of Epidaurus received their prescriptions from Asclepius, originally a god of the lower world.

After this brief account of the prevalent forms of prophetic consultation, it remains to consider the part played by the Greek oracles in the history of Greek civilization. It will be sufficient to confine our attention to Delphi, about which our information is immeasurably fuller than it is about the other shrines. In the earliest period Dodona may have had the higher prestige, but after the Homeric age it was eclipsed by Delphi, being consulted chiefly by the western Greeks, and occasionally in the 4th century by Athens.

The gorge of Delphi was a seat of prophecy from the earliest

[1] See Oppé on "The Chasm at Delphi," *Journ. of Hellenic Studies* (1904).
[2] *De defect. Orac.* c. 43.
[3] Paus. ii, 24, 1.
[4] Farnell, *op. cit.* iii. 11.
[5] The prophetic fountain at Branchidae is attested by Strabo, p. 814, and in a confused mystic passage of Iamblichus, *De Myst.* 3, 11.
[6] *Nat. Hist.* ii. 232.
[7] Iambl. *loc. cit.*

days of Greek tradition. Ge, Themis and perhaps Poseidon had given oracles here before Apollo. But it is clear that he had won it in the days before Homer, who attests the prestige and wealth of his Pythian shrine; and it seems clear that before the Dorian conquest of the Peloponnese a Dryopian migration had already carried the cult of Apollo Pythius to Asine in Argolis. Also the constitution of the Amphictyones, "the dwellers around the temple," reflects the early age when the tribe rather than the city was the political unit, and the Dorians were a small tribe of north Greece. The original function of these Amphictyones was to preserve the sanctity and property of the temple; but this common interest early developed a certain rule of intertribal morality. By the formula of the Amphictyonic oath preserved by Aeschines, which may be of great antiquity, the members bound themselves "not to destroy any city of the league, not to cut any one of them off from spring-water, either in war or peace, and to war against any who violated these rules." We discern here that Greek religion offered the ideal of a federal national union that Greek politics refused to realise.

The next stage in the history of the oracle is presented by the legend of the Dorian migration. For we have no right to reject the strong tradition of the Delphic encouragement of this movement, which well accounts for the devotion shown by Sparta to the Pythian god from the earliest days; and accounts also for the higher position that Delphi occupied at the time when Greek history is supposed to begin.

We have next to consider a valuable record that belongs to the end of the 8th century or beginning of the 7th, the Homeric hymn to Apollo, which describes the coming of the Dolphin-God —Δελφίνιος—to Pytho, and the organization of the oracle by Cretan ministers. Of this Cretan settlement at Delphi there is no other literary evidence, and the "Οσιοι who administered the oracle in the historic period claimed to be of aboriginal descent. Yet recent excavation has proved a connexion between Crete and Delphi in the Minoan period; and there is reason to believe that in the 8th century some ritual of purification, momentous for the religious career of the oracle, was brought from Crete to Delphi, and that the adoption of this latter name for the place which had formerly been called Πυθώ synchronised with the coming of Apollo Delphinius.

The influence of Delphi was great in various ways, though no scholar would now maintain the exaggerated dogma of Curtius, who imputed to the oracle a lofty religious enthusiasm and the consciousness of a religious political mission.

We may first consider its political influence upon the other states. The practice of a community consulting an oracle on important occasions undoubtedly puts a powerful weapon into the hands of the priesthood, and might lead to something like a theocracy. And there are one or two ominous hints in the *Odyssey* that the ruler of the oracle might overthrow the ruler of the land. Yet owing to the healthy temperament of the early Greek, the civic character of the priesthood, the strength of the autonomous feeling, Greece might flock to Delphi without exposing itself to the perils of sacerdotal control. The Delphic priesthood, content with their rich revenues, were probably never tempted to enter upon schemes of far-reaching political ambition, nor were they in any way fitted to be the leaders of a national policy. Once only, when the Spartan state applied to Delphi to sanction their attack on Arcadia, did the oracle speak as if, like the older papacy, it claimed to dispose of territory[1]—"Thou askest of me Arcadia; I will not give it thee." But here the oracle is on the side of righteousness, and it is the Spartan that is the aggressor. In the various oracles that have come down to us, many of which must have been genuine and preserved in the archives of the state that received them, we cannot discover any marked political policy consistently pursued by the "Holy Ones" of Delphi. As conservative aristocrats they would probably dislike tyranny; their action against the Peisistratidae was interested, but one oracle contains a spirited rebuke to Cleisthenes, while one or two others, perhaps not genuine, express the spirit of temperate constitutionalism. As exponents of an

[1] Herod; i. 66.

Amphictyonic system they would be sufficiently sensitive of the moral conscience of Greece to utter nothing in flagrant violation of the " jus gentium." In one department of politics, the legislative sphere, it has been supposed that the influence of Delphi was direct and inspiring. Plato and later writers imagined that the Pythoness had dictated the Lycurgean system, and even modern scholars like Bergk have regarded the ῥήτραι of Sparta as of Delphic origin. But a severer criticism dispels these suppositions. The Delphic priesthood had neither the capacity nor probably the desire to undertake so delicate a task as the drafting of a code. They might make now and again a general suggestion when consulted, and, availing themselves of their unique opportunities of collecting foreign intelligence, they might often recommend a skilful legislator or arbitrator to a state that consulted them at a time of intestine trouble. Finally, a legislator with a code would be well advised, especially at Sparta, in endeavouring to obtain the sanction and the blessing of the Delphic god, that he might appear before his own people as one possessed of a religious mandate. In this sense we can understand the stories about Lycurgus.

There is only one department of the secular history of Greece where Delphi played a predominant and most effective part, the colonial department. The great colonial expansion of Greece, which has left so deep an imprint on the culture of Europe, was in part inspired and directed by the oracle. For the proof of this we have not only the evidence of the χρησμοί preserved by Herodotus and others, such as those concerning the foundation of Cyrene, but also the worship of Apollo Ἀρχηγέτης, "the Founder," prevalent in Sicily and Magna Graecia, and the early custom of the sending of tithes or thanksgiving offerings by the flourishing western states to the oracle that had encouraged their settlements.

Apollo was already a god of ways—Ἀγυιεύς—who led the migration of tribes before he came to Delphi. And those legends are of some value that explain the prehistoric origin of cities such as Magnesia on the Maeander, the Dryopian Asine in the Peloponnese, as due to the colonization of temple-slaves, acquired by the Pythian god as the tithe of conquests, and planted out by him in distant settlements. The success of the oracle in this activity led at last to the establishment of the rule that Herodotus declares to be almost universal in Greece, namely, that no leader of a colony would start without consulting Delphi. Doubtless in many cases the priesthood only gave encouragement to a pre-conceived project. But they were in a unique position for giving direct advice also, and they appear to have used their opportunities with great intelligence.

Their influence on the state cults can be briefly indicated, for it was not by any means far-reaching. They could have felt conscious of no mission to preach Apollo, for his cult was an ancient heritage of the Hellenic stocks. Only the narrower duty devolved upon them of impressing upon the consultants the religious obligation of sending tithes or other offerings. Nevertheless their opportunity of directing the religious ritual and organization of the public worships was great; for Plato's view[1] that all questions of detail in religion should be left to the decision of the god " who sits on the omphalos " was on the whole in accord with the usual practice of Greece. Such consultations would occur when the state was in some trouble, which would be likely to be imputed to some neglect of religion, and the question to the oracle would commonly be put in this way—" to what god or goddess or hero shall we sacrifice?" The oracle would then be inclined to suggest the name of some divine personage hitherto neglected, or of one whose rites had fallen into decay. Again, Apollo would know the wishes of the other divinities, who were not in the habit of directly communicating with their worshippers; therefore questions about the sacred land of the goddesses at Eleusis would be naturally referred to him. From both these points of view we can understand why Delphi appears to have encouraged the tendency towards hero-worship which was becoming rife in Greece from the 7th century onwards. But the only high cult for which we can

[1] *Republ.* 427 A.

discover a definite enthusiasm in the Delphic priesthood was that of Dionysus. And his position at Delphi, where he became the brother-deity of Apollo, sufficiently explains this.

As regards the development of religious morality in Greece, we must reckon seriously with the part played by the oracle. The larger number of deliverances that have come down to us bearing on this point are probably spurious, in the sense that the Pythia did not actually utter them, but they have a certain value as showing the ideas entertained by the cultivated Hellene concerning the oracular god. On the whole, we discern that the moral influence of Delphi was beneficent and on the side of righteousness. It did nothing, indeed, to abolish, it may even have encouraged at times, the barbarous practice of human sacrifice, which was becoming abhorrent to the Greek of the 6th and 5th centuries; but a conservative priesthood is always liable to lag behind the moral progress of an age in respect of certain rites, and in other respects it appears that the " Holy Ones" of Delphi kept well abreast of the Hellenic advance in ethical thought. An oracle attributed to the Pythoness by Theopompus (Porph. *De abstinentia*, 2, 16 and 17) expresses the idea contained in the story of " the widow's mite," that the deity prefers the humble offering of the righteous poor to the costly and pompous sacrifice of the rich. Another, of which the authenticity is vouched for by Herodotus (vi. 86), denounces the contemplated perjury and fraud of a certain Glaucus, and declares to the terrified sinner that to tempt God was no less a sin than to commit the actual crime. A later χρησμός, for which Plutarch (*de Pyth. Or.* p. 404 B) is the authority, embodies the charitable conception of forgiveness for venial faults committed under excessive stress of temptation: " God pardons what man's nature is too weak to resist." And in one most important branch of morality, with which progressive ancient law was intimately concerned, namely, the concept of the sin of homicide, we have reason for believing that the Apolline oracle played a leading part. Perhaps so early as the 8th century, it came to lay stress on the impurity of bloodshed and to organise and impose a ritual of purification; and thus to assist the development and the clearer definition of the concept of murder as a sin and the growth of a theory of equity which recognises extenuating or justifying circumstances.[1] Gradually, as Greek ethics escaped the bondage of ritual and evolved the idea of spiritual purity of conscience, this found eloquent expression in the utterances imputed to the Pythoness.[2] Many of these are no doubt literary fictions; but even these are of value as showing the popular view about the oracular god, whose temple and tripod were regarded as the shrine and organ of the best wisdom and morality of Greece. The downfall of Greek liberty before Macedon destroyed the political influence of the Delphic oracle; but for some centuries after it still retained a certain value for the individual as a counsellor and director of private conscience. But in the latter days of paganism it was eclipsed by the oracles of Claros and Branchidae.

AUTHORITIES.—A. Bouché-Leclercq, *Histoire de la divination dans l'antiquité*, in 4 vols., is still the chief work: cf. L. R. Farnell, *Cults of the Greek States*, vol. iv. pp. 179-233; Buresch, *Apollo Klarios*; Bernard Haussoullier, *Études sur l'histoire de Milet et du Didymeion*; Legrand, " Questions oraculaires " in *Revue des études grecques*, vol. xiv.; Pomtow's article on " Delphoi " in Pauly-Wissowa *Realencyclopädie*.
ANCIENT AUTHORITIES.—Plutarch, *De Pythio Oraculo* and *De defectu oraculorum*; Cicero, *De divinatione*; Euseb. *Praep. Ev.* 4, 2, 14.
(L. R. F.)

ORAKZAI, a Pathan tribe on the Kohat border of the North-West Frontier Province of India. The Orakzais inhabit the mountains to the north-west of Kohat district, bounded on the N. and E. by the Afridis, on the S. by the Miranzai valley and on the W. by the Zaimukht country and the Safed Koh mountains. Their name means " lost tribes," and their origin is buried in obscurity; though they resemble the Afghans in language, features and many of their customs, they are rejected by them as brethren. One branch, the Ali Khel, has been traced to Swat, whence they were expelled by the other inhabitants,

[1] Farnell, *Cults*, vol. iv. p. 300. *Hibbert Lectures*, pp. 139-152.
[2] Aetian, *Var. Hist.* iii. 44: *Anth. Pal.* xiv. 71 and 74.

and it is not improbable that the whole tribe consists of refugee clans of the surrounding races. They are very wiry-looking mountaineers, but they are not as fine men or as brave fighters as their neighbours the Afridis. They cultivate a good deal of the Khanki and Kurmana valleys in the winter, but in the hot months retire to the heights of Tirah, of which they occupy the southern half called the Mastura valley. They have been estimated at 28,000 fighting men, but this estimate must be largely exaggerated, as the country could not possibly support the consequent population of over 100,000. They have been the object of various British military expeditions, notably in 1855, 1868, 1869, 1891, and the Tirah campaign of 1897.

ORAN (Arabic *Wahran*, i.e. ravine), a city of Algeria, capital of the department and military division of the same name. It stands at the head of the Gulf of Oran, on the Mediterranean in 35° 44' N., 0° 41' W. The city is 261 m. by rail W.S.W. of Algiers, 220 m. E. of Gibraltar and 130 m. S. of Cartagena, Spain. It is built on the steep slopes of the Jebel Murjajo, which rises to a height of 1900 ft. The city was originally cut in two by the ravine of Wad Rekhi, now for the most part covered by boulevards and buildings. West of the ravine lies the old port, and above this rises what was the Spanish town with the ancient citadel looking down on it; but few traces of Spanish occupation remain. The modern quarter rises, like an amphitheatre, to the east of the ravine. The place d'Armes, built on the plateau above the ravine, is the centre of the modern quarter. It contains a fine column commemorative of the battle of Sidi Brahim (1845), between the French and Abd-el-Kader. The Château Neuf, built in 1563 by the Spaniards, overlooks the old port. Formerly the seat of the beys of Oran, it is occupied by the general in command of the military division and also serves as barracks. The kasbah (citadel) or Château Vieux, used for military purposes, lies S.W. of the Château Neuf. It was partly destroyed by the earthquake of the 8th and 9th of October 1790. On the hills behind the kasbah are Fort St Grégoire, a votive chapel commemorative of the cholera of 1849, and Fort Santa Cruz, crowning at a height of 1312 ft. the summit of the Aidur. Fort de la Moune (so called from the monkeys said to have haunted the neighbourhood) is at the western end of the harbour, and commands the road from Oran to Mers-el-Kebir (see below). Fort St Philippe, south of the kasbah, replaces the old Castle of the Saints of the Spaniards. There is subterranean communication between all the ancient forts. The cathedral, dedicated to St Louis, and built in 1839, occupies the site of a chapel belonging in the days of Spanish dominion to a convent of monks of St Bernard. The Grand Mosque (in rue Philippe) was erected at the end of the 18th century to commemorate the expulsion of the Spaniards, and with money paid as ransom for Christian slaves. Other mosques have been turned into churches or utilized for military purposes. The military hospital, a large building adjoining the kasbah, contains 1400 beds. A house in the place de l'hôpital, now used by the military, was once the home of the Inquisition; it was built at the expense of Spain in 1772. The museum formed by the Oran Society of Geography and Archaeology (founded in 1878) has a fine collection of antiquities.

Oran is the seat of a large trade. There is regular communication with Marseilles, Cette, Barcelona, Valencia, Cartagena, Malaga, Gibraltar, and the various ports on the Barbary coast. The railway to Algiers is joined at Perrégaux (47 m. E. of Oran) by the line from Arzeu to Saida and Ain Sefra which serves the high plateau whence esparto is obtained. There is also a railway to Sidi-Bel-Abbes and Tlemçen. The export trade is chiefly in esparto grass, cereals, wines, olive oil, marbles, cattle and hides. The imports include manufactured goods, coal and other commodities. The inner harbour, or old port, contains two basins, one of 10 acres and another of 60 acres, formed by the construction of a pier eastward from Fort de la Moune, with two cross piers. In consequence of the growing importance of the port and the decision of the French government to make Oran the chief naval station in Algeria, it was decided to build an eastern harbour. This outer harbour, on which work was

begun in 1905, lies east of the old port and is about double its size. The least depth of water in the old harbour is 18 ft., the average depth in the new harbour is 30 ft., the depth at the entrance being 40 ft.

The population of the city in 1906 was 100,499, of whom 25,906 were French, and 23,071 Spanish. There were also 27,570 naturalized Frenchmen, mostly of Spanish origin. There is a negro colony in the city, numbering about 3000, included in the census in the native population of 16,206. Including the garrison and naval forces the total population of the commune was 106,517.

Four miles west of Oran a small promontory forms the harbour of Mers-el-Kebir, formerly a stronghold of the Barbary pirates. The promontory is strongly fortified and crosses fire with a battery erected to the east of Oran. A road along the east coast, cut for the most part out of the solid rock, connects Oran and Mers-el-Kebir.

Attempts have been made to identify Oran with the Quiza, and Mers-el-Kebir with the Portus Magnus, of the Romans. There are, however, no Roman ruins at Oran or at Mers-el-Kebir. The foundation of Oran is more properly ascribed to Andalusian Arabs, who settled there in the beginning of the 10th century, and gave it its name. Rapidly rising into importance as a seaport, Oran was taken and retaken, pillaged and rebuilt, by the various conquerors of northern Africa. Almoravides, Almohades and Marinides succeeded each other, and in the space of half a century the city changed hands nine times. In the latter half of the 15th century it became subject to the sultans of Tlemçen, and reached the height of its prosperity. Active commerce was maintained with the Venetians, the Pisans, the Genoese, the Marseillais and the Catalans, who imported the produce of their looms, glass-wares, tin-wares, and iron, and received in return ivory, ostrich feathers, gold-dust, tanned hides, grain and negro slaves. Admirable woollen cloth and splendid arms were manufactured. The magnificence of its mosques and other public buildings, the number of its schools, and the extent of its warehouses shed lustre on the city; but wealth and luxury began to undermine its prosperity, and its ruin was hastened by the conduct of the Moslem refugees from Spain. Under the influence of these refugees the legitimate trade of the town gave place to piracy, Mers-el-Kebir becoming the stronghold of the pirates.

Animated by the patriotic enthusiasm of Cardinal Ximenes, the Spaniards determined to put a stop to these expeditions which were carrying off their countrymen, destroying their commerce, and even ravaging their country. Mers-el-Kebir fell into their hands on the 23rd of October 1505, and Oran in May 1509. The latter victory, obtained with but trifling loss, was stained by the massacre of a third of the Mahommedan population. From 6000 to 8000 prisoners, 60 cannon, engines of war and a considerable booty from the wealth accumulated by piracy fell into the hands of the conquerors. Cardinal Ximenes introduced the Inquisition, &c., and also restored and extended the fortifications. Oran became the penal settlement of Spain, but neither the convicts nor the noblemen in disgrace who were also banished thither seem to have been under rigorous surveillance; contemporary accounts speak of constant fêtes, games and bull-fights. Meanwhile the Turks had become masters of Algeria, and expelled the Spaniards from all their possessions except Oran. The bey of Mascara watched his opportunity, and at length, in 1708, the weakness of Spain and the treason of the count of Vera Cruz obliged the city to capitulate. The Spaniards recovered possession in 1732, but found the maintenance of the place a burden rather than a benefit, the neighbouring tribes having ceased to deal with the Christians. The earthquake of 1790 furnished an excuse for withdrawing their forces. Commencing by twenty-two separate shocks at brief intervals, the oscillations continued from the 8th of October to the 22nd of November. Houses and fortifications were overthrown and a third of the garrison and a great number of the inhabitants perished. Famine and sickness had begun to aggravate the situation when the bey of Mascara appeared before the town with 30,000 men. By prodigies of energy the Spanish commander held out till August 1791, when the Spanish government having made terms with the bey of Algiers, he was allowed to set sail for Spain with his guns and ammunition. The bey Mahommed took possession of Oran in March 1792, and made it his residence instead of Mascara. On the fall of Algiers the bey (Hassan) placed himself under the protection of the conquerors, and shortly afterwards removed to the Levant. The French army entered the city on the 4th of January 1831, and took formal possession on the 17th of August. In 1832 a census of the town showed that it had but 3800 inhabitants, of whom more than two-thirds were Jews. Under French rule Oran has regained its ancient commercial activity and has become the second city in Algeria.

ORANGE, HOUSE OF. The small principality of Orange, a district now included in the French department of Vaucluse, traces back its history as an independent sovereignty to the time of Charlemagne. William, surnamed *le Cornet*, who lived towards the end of the 8th century, is said to have been the first prince of Orange, the succession is only certainly known after the time of Gerald Adhemar (fl. 1086). In 1174 the principality passed by marriage to Bertrand de Baux, and there were nine princes of this line. By the marriage of John of Chalons with Marie de Baux, the house of Chalons succeeded to the sovereignty in 1393. The princes of Orange-Chalons were (1) John I., 1393-1418, (2) Louis I., 1418-1463, (3) William VIII., 1463-1475, (4) John II., (1475-1502, (5) Philibert, 1502-1530. Philibert was a great warrior and statesman, who was held in great esteem by the emperor Charles V. For his services in his campaigns the emperor gave him considerable possessions in the Netherlands in 1522, and Francis I. of France, who had occupied Orange, was compelled, when a prisoner in Madrid, to restore it to him. Philibert had no children, and he was succeeded by his nephew Réné of Nassau-Chalons, son of Philibert's sister Claudia and Henry, count of Nassau, the confidential friend and counsellor of Charles V. He too died without an heir in 1544 at the siege of St Dizier, having devised all his titles and possessions to his first cousin William, the eldest son of William, count of Nassau-Dillenburg, who was the younger brother of Réné's father, and had inherited the German possessions of the family.

William of Orange-Nassau was but eleven years old when he succeeded to the principality. He was brought up at the court of Charles V. and became famous in history as William the Silent, the founder of the Dutch Republic. On his assassination in 1584 he was succeeded by his eldest son Philip William, who had been kidnapped by Philip II. of Spain in his boyhood and brought up at Madrid. This prince never married, and on his death in 1618 his next brother, Maurice, stadtholder in the United Netherlands and one of the greatest generals of his time, became prince of Orange. Maurice died in 1625, also unmarried. Frederick Henry, the son of Louise de Coligny, William's fourth wife, born just before his murder, now succeeded to the princedom of Orange and to all his brothers' dignities, posts and property in the Netherlands. Frederick Henry was both a great general and statesman. His only son, William, was married in 1641 to Mary, princess royal of England, he being fifteen and the princess nine years old at that date, and he succeeded to the title of prince of Orange on his father's death in 1647. At the very outset of a promising career he suddenly succumbed to an attack of smallpox on the 6th of November 1650, his son William III. being born a week after his father's death.

A revolution now took place in the system of government in the United Provinces, and the offices of stadtholder and captain-and admiral-general, held by four successive princes of Orange, were abolished. However, the counter revolution of 1672 called William III. to the head of affairs. At this time Louis XIV. conquered the principality of Orange and the territory was incorporated in France, the title alone being recognized by the treaty of Ryswick. William married his cousin Mary, the eldest daughter of James, duke of York, in 1677. In 1688 he landed in England, expelled his father-in-law, James II., from his throne, and reigned as king of Great Britain and Ireland until his death in 1702. He left no children, and a dispute arose among various

claimants to the title of prince of Orange. The king of Prussia claimed it as the descendant of the eldest daughter of Frederick Henry; John William Friso of Nassau-Dietz claimed it as the descendant of John, the brother of William the Silent, and also of the second daughter of Frederick Henry. The result was that at the peace of Utrecht in 1713, the king of Prussia abandoned the principality to the king of France in exchange for compensation elsewhere, and John William Friso gained the barren title and became William IV. prince of Orange. His sons William V. and William VI. succeeded him. William VI. in 1815 became William I. king of the Netherlands.

See Bastet, *Histoire de la ville et de la principauté d'Orange* (Orange 1856).   (G. E.)

ORANGE, a town of Wellington and Bathurst counties, New South Wales, Australia, 192 m. by rail W.N.W. of Sydney. It lies in a fruit and wheat-growing district, in which gold, copper and silver also abound. It is the centre of trade with the western interior and has a number of flourishing industries. Orange also has a great reputation as a health resort. Its suburb, East Orange, in the county of Bathurst, is a separate municipality. Pop., including East Orange (1901), 6331.

ORANGE, a town of south-eastern France, capital of an arrondissement in the department of Vaucluse, 18 m. N. of Avignon on the railway from Lyons to Marseilles. Pop. (1906) of the town, 6412; of the commune, 10,303. Orange is situated at some distance from the left bank of the Rhone, in the midst of meadows, orchards and mulberry plantations, watered by a stream called the Meyne, and overlooked by the majestic summit of Mount Ventoux, which lies 22 m. to the east. The district is highly fertile, and the town deals largely in fruit, and millet-stalks for brooms, as well as in wool, silk, honey and truffles.

Orange is interesting mainly from its Roman remains. The triumphal arch is not only far finer than any other in France, but ranks third in size and importance among those still extant in Europe. Measuring 72 ft. in height, 69 ft. in width, and 26 ft. in depth, it is composed of three arches supported by Corinthian columns. On three sides it is well preserved, and displays remarkable variety and elegance in its sculptured decorations. To judge from the traces of an inscription, the arch seems to have been erected in honour of Tiberius, perhaps to commemorate his victory over the Gallic chieftain Sacrovir in A.D. 21. It suffered from being used as a donjon in the middle ages. Another most imposing structure is the theatre, dating from the time of the emperor Hadrian and built against a hill from the summit of which a colossal figure of the Virgin commands the town. The façade, which is 121 ft. high, 340 ft. long and 13 ft. thick, is pierced by three square gates surmounted by a range of blind arches and a double row of projecting corbels, with holes in which the poles of the awning were placed. Of the seats occupied by the spectators, only the lower tiers remain. It was used as an out-work to the fortress built on the hill by Maurice of Nassau in 1622, and destroyed fifty years later by order of Louis XIV., whose troops in 1660 captured the town. Up to the beginning of the 19th century it was filled with hovels and stables; these were subsequently cleared out, and at the end of the century the building was restored, and now serves as a national theatre. In the neighbourhood of the theatre traces have been found of a hippodrome; and statues, bas-reliefs and ruins of an amphitheatre also serve to show the importance of the Roman town. Notre Dame, the old cathedral, originally erected by the prefect of Gaul, was ruined by the Barbarians, rebuilt in the 11th and 12th centuries, and damaged by the Protestants.

The town has a sub-prefecture, a tribunal of first instance, and a communal college among its institutions; and it has tile and mosaic works and flour-mills, and manufactories of boots and shoes and brooms. There is trade in truffles, fruit, wine, &c.

Orange (*Arausio*), capital of the Cavari, was in 105 B.C. the scene of the defeat of a Roman army by the Cimbri and Teutones. It became after Caesar an important Roman colony. Its ramparts and fine buildings were partly destroyed by the

Alamanni and Visigoths, and partly ruined by the erections of the middle ages. Orange was included in the kingdom of Austrasia, fell into the hands of the Saracens and was recovered by Charlemagne It became the seat of an independent countship in the 11th century. From the 14th century till the Revolution the town had a university. At the latter period the town suffered severely from the excesses of a popular commission.

See R. Peyre, *Nîmes, Arles et Orange* (Paris, 1903); A. de Pontbriant, *Histoire de la principauté d'Orange* (Avignon and Paris, 1891).

Councils of Orange.—In 441 a synod of sixteen bishops was held at Orange under the presidency of St Hilary of Arles, which adopted thirty canons touching the reconciliation of penitents and heretics; the ecclesiastical right of asylum, diocesan prerogatives of bishops, spiritual privileges of the defective or demoniac, the deportment of catechumens at worship, and clerical celibacy (forbidding married men to be ordained as deacons, and digamists to be advanced beyond the sub-diaconate). In 529 a synod of fifteen bishops, under the presidency of Caesarius of Arles, assembled primarily to dedicate a church, the gift of Liberius, the lieutenant of Theodoric, in Gaul, but proved to be one of the most important councils of the 6th century. Caesarius had sought the aid of Rome against semi-Pelagianism, and in response Pope Felix IV. had sent certain *capitula* concerning grace and free-will, drawn chiefly from the writings of Augustine and Prosper. These to the number of twenty-five the synod subscribed, and adopted a supplementary statement, reaffirming the Augustinian doctrines of corruption, human inability, prevenient grace and baptismal regeneration. Its acts were confirmed by Boniface II. on the " 25th of January 530," a date which is open to question.

See F. H. Woods, *Canons of the Second Council of Orange* (Oxford, 1882). (T. F. C.) d

ORANGE, a city of Essex county, New Jersey, U.S.A., in the N.E. part of the state, about 14 m. W. of New York City. Pop. (1890) 18,844, (1900) 24,141, of whom 6598 were foreign-born and 1903 were negroes, (1910 census) 29,630. It is served by the Morris & Essex Division of the Delaware, Lackawanna & Western railroad and by the Orange branch (of which it is a terminus) of the Erie railroad, and is connected with Newark, South Orange and Bloomfield by electric lines. The city lies at the base of the eastern slope of the first Watchung, or Orange, Mountain, and is primarily a residential suburb of New York and Newark; with East Orange, West Orange and South Orange it constitutes virtually a single community, popularly known as " the Oranges." The city has a good public school system and various private schools, including the Dearborn-Morgan School (for girls) and the Carteret Academy (for boys). Of historical interest is the First Presbyterian Church, erected in 1813, the third structure used by this church organization, whose history dates back to 1718. The value of the factory products of Orange increased from $2,995,688 in 1900 to $6,150,635 in 1905, or 105·3%, and the capital invested in manufacturing from $1,359,523 in 1900 to $3,441,183 in 1905, or 153·1%. Of the total product-value in 1905, $2,311,614 was the value of felt hats manufactured. Among other manufactures are beer, pharmaceutical supplies and lawn mowers. The city owns and operates its water-works and electric lighting plant. Settlements were made in or near the limits of the present city soon after the founding of Newark, in 1666, and, on account of the mountainous ridge in this region, they were generally referred to collectively as " Newark Mountain." As a disagreement soon arose between the people of Newark and those of "the mountain", on questions of church administration, the latter in 1718 severed their connexion with the church at Newark and formed an independent congregation, the " Mountain Society." The church, which was known also as " The Church of the New Ark Mountains," was at first Congregational, but in 1748 became Presbyterian. In 1782 occurs the earliest reference to the neighbourhood as " Orange Dale," and two years later it is sometimes referred to as " Orange." In 1806 the legislature incorporated the township of Orange. Parts of its territory were included in South Orange and Fairmount (now West Orange)

in 1861 and 1862 respectively, and in 1863 East Orange was created out of part of Orange. Orange was incorporated as a town in 1860 and was chartered as a city in 1872.

See H. Whittemore, *The Founders and Builders of the Oranges* (Newark, 1896); J. H. Condit, *Early Records of the Township of Orange* (1807–1845) (Orange, 1897); and S. Wickes, *History of the Oranges* (1666–1806), (Newark, 1892).

ORANGE, the longest river of South Africa, almost traversing the continent from ocean to ocean. It rises in Basutoland, less than 200 m. from the Indian Ocean, and flows west, with wide sweeps south and north, to the Atlantic. It drains, with its tributaries, an area estimated at over 400,000 sq. m., passing through more than twelve degrees of longitude or 750 m. in a straight line from source to mouth. The valley of the river exceeds 1000 m., and the stream has a length of not less than 1300 m. Its headstreams are in the highest part of the Drakensberg range, the principal source, the Senku, rising, at an elevation of more than 10,000 ft., on the south face of the Mont aux Sources in 28° 48' E., 28° 50' S. The other headstreams are S.E. of the Senku source, in Champagne Castle, Giant's Castle and other heights of the Drakensberg. The Giant's Castle source is not more than 130 m. west of the Indian ocean in a direct line. Rising on the inner slopes of the hills these rivulets all join the Senku, which receives from the north several streams which rise in the Maluti Mountains. Of these the largest are the Semene and Senkunyana (little Senku) and the best known the Maletsunyane, by reason of its magnificent waterfall—an unbroken leap of 630 ft. Increased by the perennial waters of these numerous torrents the Senku makes its way S.W. across the upland valleys between the Maluti and Drakensberg ranges. After a course of some 200 m., passing the S.W. corner of the Maluti Mountains, the Senku, already known as the Orange, receives the Makhaleng or Kornet Spruit (90 m.), which rises in Machacha Mountain. The Orange here enters the great inner plateau of South Africa, which at Aliwal North, the first town of any size on the banks of the river, 80 m. below the Kornet Spruit confluence, has an elevation of 4300 ft. Forty miles lower down the Orange is joined by the first of its large tributaries, the Caledon (230 m.), which, rising on the western side of the Mont aux Sources, flows, first west and then south, through a broad and fertile valley north of the Maluti Mountains. At the confluence the united stream has a width of 350 yards. Thirty miles lower down the Orange reaches, in 25° 40' E., its southernmost point— 30° 40' S., approaching within 20 m. of the Zuurberg range. In this part of its course the river receives from the south the streams, often intermittent, which rise on the northern slopes of the Stormberg, Zuurberg and Sneeuwberg ranges—the mountain chain which forms the water-parting between the coast and inland drainage systems of South Africa. Of these southern rivers the chief are the Kraai, which joins the Orange near Aliwal North, the Stormberg and the Zeekoe (Sea Cow), the last named having a length of 120 m. From its most southern point the Orange turns sharply N.W. for 200 m., when having reached 29° 3' S., 23° 36' E, it is joined by its second great affluent, the Vaal (q.v.). Here it bends south again, and with many a zigzag continues its general westerly direction, crossing the arid plains of Bechuana, Bushman and Namaqualand. Flowing between steep banks, considerably below the general level of the country, here about 3000 ft., it receives, between the Vaal confluence and the Atlantic, a distance of more than 400 m. in a direct line, no perennial tributary but on the contrary loses a great deal of its water by evaporation. In this region, nevertheless, skeleton river systems cover the country north and south. These usually dry sandy beds, which on many maps appear rivers of imposing length, for a few hours or days following rare but violent thunderstorms, are deep and turbulent streams. The northern system consists of the Nosob and its tributaries, the Molopo and the Kuruman. These unite their waters in about 20° 40' E. and 27° S., whence a channel known as the Molopo or Hygap runs south to the Orange. The southern system, which at one time rendered fertile the great plains of western Cape Colony, is represented by the Brak and Ongers rivers, and, farther west, by the Zak and Olifants rivers, which, united as the Hartebeest, reach the Orange about 25 m. above the mouth of the Molopo. These rivers, in the wet season and in places, have plenty of water, generally dissipated in *vleis, pans* and *vloers* (marshy and lake land).

Between the mouths of the Hartebeest and Molopo, in 28° 35' S., 20° 20' E., are the great waterfalls of the Orange, where in a series of cataracts and cascades the river drops 400 ft. in 16 m. The Aughrabies or Hundred Falls, as they are called, are divided by ledges, reefs and islets, the last named often assuming fantastic shapes. Below the falls the river rushes through a rocky gorge, and openings in the cliffs to the water are rare. These openings are usually the sandy beds of dried-up or intermittent affluents, such as the Bak, Ham, Houm, Aub (or Great Fish) rivers of Great Namaqualand. As it approaches the Atlantic, the Orange, in its efforts to pierce the mountain barrier which guards the coast, is deflected north and then south, making a loop of fully 90 m., of which the two ends are but 38 m. apart. Crossing the narrow coast plain the river, with a south-westerly sweep, enters the ocean by a single mouth, studded with small islands, in 28° 37′ S., 16° 30′ E. A large sand bar obstructs the entrance to the river, which is not quite 1 m. wide. The river when in flood, at which time it has a depth of 40 ft., scours a channel through the bar, but the Orange is at all times inaccessible to sea-going vessels. Above the bar it is navigable by small vessels for 30 or 40 m. In the neighbourhood of the Vaal confluence, where the river passes through alluvial land, and at some other places, the waters of the Orange are used, and are capable of being much more largely used, for irrigation purposes.

The Hottentots call the Orange the Garib (great water), corrupted by the Dutch into Gariep. The early Dutch settlers called it simply Groote-Rivier. It was first visited by Europeans about the beginning of the 18th century. In 1685 Simon van der Stell, then governor of the Cape, led an expedition into Little Namaqualand and discovered the Koper Berg. In 1704 and 1705 other expeditions to Namaqualand were made. Attempts to mine the copper followed, and the prospectors and hunters who penetrated northward sent to the Cape reports of the existence of a great river whose waters always flowed. The first scientific expedition to reach the Orange was that under Captain Henry Hop sent by Governor Tulbagh in 1761, partly to investigate the reports concerning a semi-civilized yellow race living north of the great river. Hop crossed the Orange in September 1761, but shortly afterwards returned. Andrew Sparrman, the Swedish naturalist, when exploring in the Sneeuwberg in 1776, learned from the Hottentots that eight or ten days′ journey north there was a large perennial stream, which he rightly concluded was the *groote-rivier* of Hop. The next year Captain (afterwards Colonel) R. J. Gordon, a Dutch officer of Scottish extraction, who commanded the garrison at Cape Town, reached the river in its middle course at the spot indicated by Sparrman and named it the Orange in honour of the prince of Orange. In 1778 Lieut. W. Paterson, an English traveller, reached the river in its lower course, and in 1779 Paterson and Gordon journeyed along the west coast of the colony and explored the mouth of the river. F. Le Vaillant also visited the Orange near its mouth in 1784. Mission stations north of the Orange were established a few years later, and in 1813 the Rev. John Campbell, after visiting Griqualand West for the London Missionary Society, traced the Harts river, and from its junction with the Vaal followed the latter stream to its confluence with the Orange, journeying thence by the banks of the Orange as far as Pella, in Little Namaqualand, discovering the great falls. These falls were in 1885 visited and described by G. A. Farini, from whom they received the name of the Hundred Falls. The source of the Orange was first reached by the French Protestant missionaries T. Arbousset and F. Daumas in 1836.

The story of Hop's expedition is told in the *Nouvelle description du Cap de Bonne Espérance* (Amsterdam, 1778). Lieut. Paterson gave his experiences in *A Narrative of Four Journeys into the Country of the Hottentots and Caffraria in the Years 1777–1778–1779* (London, 1789). See also Campbell's *Travels in South Africa* (London, 1815), Arbousset and Daumas' *Relation d'un voyage d'exploration au nord-est de la colonie du Cap de Bonne Espérance en 1836* (Paris, 1842), and Farini's *Through the Kalahari Desert* (London, 1886).

ORANGE (*Citrus Aurantium*). The plant that produces the familiar fruit of commerce is closely allied to the citron, lemon and lime, all the cultivated forms of the genus *Citrus* being so nearly related that their specific demarcation must be regarded as somewhat doubtful and indefinite. The numerous kinds of orange chiefly differing in the external shape, size and flavour of the fruit may all probably be traced to two well-marked varieties or sub-species—the sweet or China orange, var. *sinensis*, and the bitter orange or bigarade, var. *amara*.

The BITTER SEVILLE or BIGARADE ORANGE, *C. Aurantium*, var. *amara* (*C. vulgaris* of Risso), is a rather small tree, rarely exceeding 30 ft. in height. The green shoots bear sharp axillary spines,. and alternate evergreen oblong leaves, pointed at the extremity, and with the margins entire or very slightly serrated; they are of a bright glossy green tint, the stalks distinctly winged and, as in the other species, articulated with the leaf. The fragrant

white or pale pinkish flowers appear in the summer months, and the fruit, usually round or spheroidal, does not perfectly ripen until the following spring, so that flowers and both green and mature fruit are often found on the plant at the same time. The bitter aromatic rind of the bigarade is rough, and dotted closely over with concave oil-cells; the pulp is acid and more or less bitter in flavour.

The SWEET or CHINA ORANGE, including the Malta or Portugal orange, has the petioles less distinctly winged, and the leaves more ovate in shape, but chiefly differs in the fruit, the pulp of which is agreeably acidulous and sweet, the rind comparatively smooth, and the oil-cells convex. The ordinary round shape of the sweet orange fruit is varied greatly in certain varieties, in some being greatly elongated, in others much flattened; while several kinds have a conical protuberance at the apex, others are deeply ribbed or furrowed, and a few are distinctly " horned " or lobed, by the partial separation of the carpels. The two sub-species of orange are said to reproduce themselves infallibly by seed; and, where hybridizing is prevented, the seedlings of the sweet and bitter orange appear to retain respectively the more distinctive features of the parent plant.·

Though now cultivated widely in most of the warmer parts of the world, and apparently in many completely naturalized, the

Orange (*Citrus Aurantium*, var. *amara*), from nature, about one-third natural size. *s*, diagram of flower.

diffusion of the orange has taken place in comparatively recent historical periods. To ancient Mediterranean agriculture it was unknown; and, though the later Greeks and Romans were familiar with the citron as an exotic fruit, their " median apple " appears to have been the only form of the citrine genus with which they were acquainted. The careful researches of Gallesio have proved that India was the country from which the orange spread to western Asia and eventually to Europe. Oranges are at present found wild in the jungles along the lower mountain slopes of Sylhet, Kumaon, Sikkim and other parts of northern India, and, according to Royle, even in the Nilgiri Hills; the plants are generally thorny, and present the other characters of the bitter variety, but occasionally wild oranges occur with sweet fruit; it is, however, doubtful whether either sub-species is really indigenous to Hindustan, and De Candolle is probably correct in regarding the Burmese peninsula and southern China as the original home of the orange. Cultivated from a remote period in Hindustan, it was carried to south-western Asia by the Arabs, probably before the 9th century, towards the close of which the bitter orange seems to have been well known to that people; though, according to Mas'ûdî, it was not cultivated in Arabia itself until the beginning of the 10th century, when it was first planted in 'Omân, and afterwards carried to Mesopotamia and Syria. It spread ultimately, through the agency of the same race, to Africa and Spain, and perhaps to Sicily, following everywhere the tide of Mohammedan conquest and civilization. In the 11th century the bigarade was abundantly cultivated in all the Levant countries, and the returning soldiers of the Cross brought it from Palestine to Italy and Provence. An orange tree of this variety is said to have been planted by St Dominic in the year 1200, though the identity of the one still standing in the garden of the monastery of St Sabina at Rome, and now attributed to the energetic friar, may be somewhat doubtful. No allusion to the sweet orange occurs in contemporary literature at this early date, and its introduction to Europe took place at a considerably later period, though the exact time is unknown. It was commonly cultivated in Italy early in the 16th century, and seems to have been known there previously to the expedition of Da Gama (1497), as a Florentine narrator of that voyage appears to have been familiar with the fruit. The importation of this tree into Europe, though often attributed to the Portuguese, is with more probability referred to the enterprise of the Genoese merchants of the 15th century, who must have found it growing abundantly in the Levant. The prevailing European name of the orange is sufficient evidence of its origin and of the line taken in its migration westward. The Sanskrit designation *nagrunge*, becoming *narungee* in Hindustani, and corrupted by the Arabs into *nâranj* (Spanish *naranja*), passed by easy transitions into the Italian *arancia* (Latinised *aurantium*), the Romance *arangi*, and the later Provençal *orange*. The true Chinese variety, however, was undoubtedly brought by the Portuguese navigators direct from the East both to their own country and to the Azores, where now luxuriant groves of the golden-fruited tree give a modern realization to the old myth of the gardens of the Hesperides.[1] Throughout China and in Japan the orange has been grown from very ancient times, and it was found diffused widely when the Indian Archipelago was first visited by Europeans. In more recent days its cultivation has extended over most of the warmer regions of the globe, the tree growing freely and producing fruit abundantly wherever heat is sufficient and enough moisture can be supplied to the roots; where night-frosts occur in winter or spring the culture becomes more difficult and the crop precarious.

The orange flourishes in any moderately fertile soil, if it is well drained and sufficiently moist; but a rather stiff loam or calcareous marl, intermingled with some vegetable humus, is most favourable to its growth. Grafting or budding on stocks raised from the seed of some vigorous variety is the plan usually adopted by the cultivator. The seeds, carefully selected, are sown in well-prepared ground, and the seedlings removed to a nursery-bed in the fourth or fifth year, and, sometimes after a second transplantation, grafted in the seventh or eighth year with the desired variety. When the grafts have acquired sufficient vigour, the trees are placed in rows in the permanent orangery. Propagation by layers is occasionally adopted; cuttings do not readily root, and multiplication directly by seed is always doubtful in result, though recommended by some authorities. The distance left between the trees in the permanent plantation or grove varies according to the size of the plants and subsequent culture adopted. In France, when the trunks are from 5 to 6½ ft. in height, a space of from 16 to 26 ft. is left between; but the dwarfer trees admit of much closer planting. In the West Indies and Azores an interval of 24 or even of 30 ft. is often allowed. The ground is kept well stirred between the trunks, and the roots manured with well-rotted dung, guano or other highly nitrogenous matter; shallow pits are sometimes formed above the roots for the reception of liquid or other manures; in dry climates water must be abundantly and frequently supplied. The trees require regular and careful pruning, the heads being trained as nearly as possible to a spherical form. Between the rows melons, pumpkins and other annual vegetables are frequently raised. In garden culture the orange is often trained as an espalier, and with careful attention yields fruit in great profusion when thus grown. In favourable seasons the oranges are produced in great abundance, from 400 to 1000 being

[1] The modern Arabic name, Bortukân (that is, Portuguese), shows that the China apple reached the Levant from the West.

commonly borne on a single plant in full bearing, while on large trees the latter number is often vastly exceeded. The trees will continue to bear abundantly from fifty to eighty years, or even more; and some old orange trees, whose age must be reckoned by centuries, still produce their golden crop; these very ancient trees are, however, generally of the bitter variety. Oranges intended for export to colder climates are gathered long before the deep tint that indicates maturity is attained, the fruit ripening rapidly after picking; but the delicious taste of the mature China orange is never thus acquired, and those who have not eaten the fruit in a perfectly ripe state have little idea of its flavour when in that condition. Carefully gathered, the oranges are packed in boxes, each orange being wrapped in paper, or with dry maize husks or leaves placed between them. The immense quantities of this valuable fruit imported into Britain are derived from various sources, the Azores ("St Michael's" oranges), Sicily, Portugal, Spain and other Mediterranean countries, Jamaica, the Bahamas and Florida, California, &c. In Florida the bitter orange has grown, from an unknown period, in a wild condition, and some of the earlier botanical explorers regarded it as an indigenous tree; but it was undoubtedly brought by the Spanish colonists to the West India Islands, and was probably soon afterwards transplanted to Florida by them or their buccaneering enemies; its chief use in America is for stocks on which to graft sweet orange and other species of *Citrus*.

Orange cultivation has been attempted with success in several parts of Australia, especially in New South Wales, where the orange groves near Paramatta yield an abundant colonial supply. The orangeries of Queensland and South Australia likewise produce well. In many of the Pacific Islands the plant has been long established. There are numerous varieties of the sweet orange, a few of which deserve mention on account of some striking peculiarity. Maltese or Blood oranges are characterized by the deep-red tint of the pulp, and comprise some of the best varieties. Gallesio refers to the blood orange as cultivated extensively in Malta and Provence; they are largely grown in the Mediterranean region in the present day, and have been introduced into America. So-called navel oranges have an umbilical mark on the apex of the fruit due to the production of an incipient second whorl of carpels. Baptiste Ferrari, a Jesuit monk, in his work *Hesperides, sive De malorum aureorum cultura et usu Libri Quatuor*, published at Rome in 1646, figures and describes (pp. 403, 405) such an orange. The mandarin orange of China, sometimes regarded as a distinct species, *C. nobilis*, is remarkable for its very flat spheroidal fruit, the rind of which readily separates with the slightest pressure; the pulp has a peculiarly luscious flavour when ripe. The small Tangerine oranges, valued for their fine fragrance, are derived from the mandarin.

Diseases.—Several are caused by fungi, others by insects. Of the fungus diseases that known as foot-rot in Florida and mal-di-gomma in Italy is very widely distributed. It occurs on the lower part of the trunk and the main roots of the tree, and is indicated by exudation of gum on the bark covering the diseased spot. The diseased patches spread into the wood, killing the tissues, which emit a foetid odour; the general appearance of the tree is unhealthy, the leaves become yellow and the twigs and young branches die. A fungus, *Fusarium limonis* is found associated with the disease, which is also fostered by faulty drainage, a shaded condition of the soil, the use of rank manures and other conditions. For treatment the soil should be removed from the base of the tree, the diseased patches cut away and the wound treated with a fungicide. Decay of oranges in transit often causes serious losses; this has been shown to be due to a species of *Penicillium*, of which the germinating spores penetrate the skin of damaged fruits. Careful picking, handling and packing have much reduced the amount of loss from this cause. Another fungus disease, scab, has been very injurious to the lemon and bitter orange in Florida. It is caused by a species of *Cladosporium*, which forms numerous small warts on the leaves and fruits; spraying with a weak solution of Bordeaux mixture or with ammoniacal solution of carbonate of copper is recommended. The sooty mould of orange, which forms a black incrustation on the leaves and also the fruit, probably occurs wherever the orange is cultivated. It is caused by species of *Meliola*; in Europe and the United States, by *M. Penzigii* and *M. Camelliae*. The fruit is often rendered unsaleable and the plant is also injured as the leaves are unable properly to perform their functions. The fungus is not a parasite, but lives apparently upon the honey-dew secreted by aphides, &c., and is therefore dependent on the presence of these insects. Spraying with resin-wash is an effective preventive, as it destroys the insects. Several insect enemies attack the plant, of which the scale insect *Aspidiotus* is the most injurious in Europe and the Azores. In Florida another species, *Mytilaspis citricola* (purple scale), sometimes disfigures the fruit to such an extent as to make it unfit for market. Several species of *Aleyrodes* are insect pests on leaves of the orange; *A. citri*, the white fly of Florida, is described as the most important of all the insect pests of the crop in Florida at the present time; and another species, *A. Howardi*, is a very serious pest in Cuba. Cold weather in winter has sometimes proved destructive in Provence, and many plantations were destroyed by the hard frosts of 1789 and 1820.

Besides the widespread use of the fruit as an agreeable and wholesome article of diet, that of the sweet orange, abounding in citric acid, possesses in a high degree the antiscorbutic properties that render the lemon and lime so valuable in medicine; and the free consumption of this fruit in the large towns of England during the winter months has doubtless a very beneficial effect on the health of the people. The juice is sometimes employed as a cooling drink in fevers, as well as for making a pleasant beverage in hot weather.

The bitter orange is chiefly cultivated for the aromatic and tonic qualities of the rind, which render it a valuable stomachic. Planted long ago in Andalusia by the Moorish conquerors, it is still extensively grown in southern Spain—deriving its common English name of "Seville" orange from the abundant groves that still exist around that city, though the plant is now largely cultivated elsewhere. The fruit is imported into Great Britain and the United States in considerable quantities for the manufacture of orange marmalade, which is prepared from the pulp and rind, usually more or less mingled with the pulp of the China orange. In medicine the fresh peel is largely employed as an aromatic tonic, and often, in tincture and syrup and "orange wine," as a mere vehicle to disguise the flavour of more nauseous remedies. The chief constituents are three glucosides, hesperidin, isohesperidin and aurantiamarin, the latter being the bitter principle; and an oil which mainly consists of a terpene known as limonene. The essential oil of the rind is collected for the use of the perfumer, being obtained either by the pressure of the fresh peel against a piece of sponge, or by the process known as *écuelle*, in which the skin of the ripe fruit is scraped against a series of points or ridges arranged upon the surface of a peculiarly-shaped dish or broad funnel, when the oil flows freely from the broken cells. Another fragrant oil, called in France *essence de petit grain*, is procured by the distillation of the leaves, from which also an aromatic water is prepared. The flowers of both sweet and bitter orange yield, when distilled with water, the "oil of Neroli" of the druggist and perfumer, and likewise the fragrant liquid known as "orange-flower water," which is a saturated solution of the volatile oil of the fresh flowers. The candied peel is much in request by cook and confectioner; the favourite liqueur sold as "curaçoa" derives its aromatic flavour from the rind of the bigarade. The minute immature oranges that drop from the trees are manufactured into "issue-peas"; from those of the sweet orange in a fresh state a sweetmeat is sometimes prepared in France. Orange trees occasionally acquire a considerable diameter; the trunk of one near Nice, still standing in 1789, was so large that two men could scarcely embrace it; the tree was killed by the intense cold of the winter of that year. The wood of the orange is of a fine yellow tint, and, being hard and close-grained,

is valued by the turner and cabinetmaker for the manufacture of small articles; it takes a good polish.

Although the bitter "Poma de Orenge" were brought in small quantities from Spain to England as early as the year 1290, no attempt appears to have been made to cultivate the tree in Britain until about 1595, when some plants were introduced by the Carews of Beddington in Surrey, and placed in their garden, where, trained against a wall, and sheltered in winter, they remained until destroyed by the great frost of 1739-1740. In the 18th century the tree became a favourite object of conservatory growth; in the open air, planted against a wall, and covered with mats in winter, it has often stood the cold of many seasons in the southern counties, in such situations the trees occasionally bearing abundant fruit. The trees are usually imported from Italy, where, especially near Nervi, such plants are raised in great numbers for exportation; they are generally budded on the stocks of some free-growing variety, often on the lemon or citron.

The orange has been usually cultivated in England for the beauty of the plant and the fragrance of its blossoms, rather than for the purpose of affording a supply of edible fruit. The latter can, however, be easily grown in a hot-house, some of the fruits thus grown, especially those of the pretty little Tangerine variety, being superior in quality to the imported fruit. The best form of orange house is the span-roofed, with glass on both sides, the height and other conditions being similar to those recommended for stove plants. The trees may be planted out, a row on each side a central path, in a house of moderate width. They will flourish in a compost of good, light, turfy loam and well-decayed leaf-mould in equal proportions, to which a little broken charcoal may be added. Each year the trees should be top-dressed with a similar compost, removing some of the old soil beforehand. The trees, if intended to be permanent, should be placed 10 to 12 ft. apart. It will often be found more convenient to grow the plants in pots or tubs, and then bottom heat can be secured by placing them on or over a series of hot-water pipes kept near to or above the ground level. The pots or tubs should be thoroughly well drained, and should not be too large for the plants; and repotting should take place about every third year, the soil being top-dressed in intervening years. The temperature may be kept at about 50° or 55° in winter, under which treatment the trees will come into bloom in February; the heat must then be increased to 60° or 65° in the day time, and later on to 80° or 85°. Throughout the growing season the trees should be liberally watered, and thoroughly syringed every day; this will materially assist in keeping down insects. When the trees are in bloom, however, they must not be syringed, but the house must be kept moist by throwing water on the pathways a few times during the day. When the flowers have fallen the syringe may be used again daily in the early morning and late afternoon. The fruit may be expected to ripen from about the middle of October to January, and if the sorts are good will be of excellent quality. When the trees are at rest the soil must not be kept too wet, since this will produce a sickly condition, through the loss of the small feeding roots. The trees require little pruning or training. The tips of the stronger shoots are just pinched out when they have made about 6 in. of growth, but when a branch appears to be robbing the rest, or growing ahead of them, it should be shortened back or tied down.

When grown for the production of flowers, which are always in great request, the plants must be treated in a similar manner to that already described, but may do without bottom heat.

For details of orange varieties, cultivation, &c., see Risso and Poiteau, *Histoire et culture des orangers* (edited by A. Du Breuil, Paris, 1872); for early history and diffusion, G. Gallesio, *Traité du citrus* (Paris, 1811). A useful modern handbook is *Citrus Fruits and their Culture*, by Harold Hume (New York, 1907).

There are many varieties of the sweet orange that may be grown under glass in the British Isles. Amongst the best for dessert is the *St-Michaels*, a heavy cropper with large juicy fruits; and closely related are *Bittencourt*, *Egg*, *Dom Louise*, *Sustain*, *Excelsior* and *Brown's Orange*. The White Orange, so called from its pale skin, is excellent. *Silver* or *Plata* is a sweet, pale-coloured variety with a curious weal-like orange stripe, the fruit being rather small but heavy. *Embiguo*, or the *Washington Navel Orange*, produces splendid fruit under glass. The *Jaffa*, with large oblong fruits and large wavy crinkled leaves, although a shy bearer, makes up for this in the size of its fruits. The Maltese *Blood Orange* is remarkable for the blood-like stains in the pulp, although these are not present in every fruit even on the same tree.

Other kinds of oranges are the Tangerine with small aromatic fruits and willow-like leaves. The Seville orange is a handsome free-flowering tree, but its fruits are bitter and used only for preserving and marmalade.

ORANGEBURG, a city and the county-seat of Orangeburg county, South Carolina, U.S.A., on the North Edisto river, 50 m. S. by E. of Columbia. Pop. (1890) 2964; (1900) 4455 (2518 negroes); (1910) 5906. Orangeburg is served by the Atlantic Coast Line and the Southern railways. It is the seat of Claflin University for negroes, and of the State Colored Normal, Industrial, Agricultural and Mechanical College. Claflin University, incorporated in 1869, was named in honour of Lee Claflin (1791-1871) of Massachusetts, and is under the control of the Freedmen's Aid and Education Society of the Methodist Episcopal Church. In 1908 it had 25 instructors and 538 students (241 men and 297 women). The State Colored Normal, Industrial, Agricultural and Mechanical College was established here by the state in 1872 as the College of Agriculture and Mechanics' Institute (for negroes), on property immediately adjoining the campus of Claflin University, and the two schools were under one management (although otherwise distinct and separate) until 1896, when the present name of the state college was adopted. Among the city's manufactures are cotton-seed oil, cotton (yarn and cloth), lumber, bricks, concrete and turpentine. The municipality owns the water-works and the electric-lighting plant. A trader and trapper settled on the site of what is now Orangeburg in 1704. In 1735 a company of Germans and Swiss established the first real settlement and named it Orangeburg, in honour of the prince of Orange. Orangeburg was incorporated as a town in 1851, and was first chartered as a city in 1883.

ORANGE FREE STATE, an inland province of British South Africa; formerly—from 1854 to 1900—an independent republic. From May 1900 to June 1910 it was known as the Orange River Colony, since when under the style of Orange Free State it has formed a province of the Union of South Africa. It lies north of the Orange and south of the Vaal rivers, between 26° 30' and 30° 40' S. and 24° 20' and 29° 40' E., and has an area of 50,392 sq. m., being nearly the size of England. It is surrounded by other British possessions, being bounded N. by the Transvaal, E. by Natal, S.E. by Basutoland, S. and W. by the Cape province. Its greatest length is 356 m., its greatest breadth 304 m.

Physical Features.—The country forms part of the inner tableland of South Africa and has an elevation of between 4000 and 5000 ft. On the N.E. or Natal border the crest of the Drakensberg forms the frontier. The northern slopes of Mont aux Sources (11,000 ft.), the highest land in South Africa, are within the province, as are also the Draken's Berg (5682 ft.), the mountain from which the range takes its name, Melanies Kop (7500 ft.) and Platberg (about 8000 ft.), near Harrismith. Though rugged in places, with outlying spurs and secondary chains, the westward slopes of the Drakensberg are much gentler than the eastern or Natal versant of the chain. Several passes exist through the mountains, that of Van Reenen, 5500 ft., being traversed by a railway. From the mountainous eastern district the country dips gradually westward. No natural boundary marks the western frontier, a line across the veld (separating it from the Griqualand West district of the Cape) from the Orange to the Vaal rivers.

The aspect of the greater part of the country is that of vast undulating treeless plains, diversified by low rands and isolated tafelbergs and spitzkops, indicating the former level of the country. These hills are either of sandstone or ironstone and in altitude vary from about 4800 ft. to 5300 ft. Ironstone hills are numerous in the south-west districts. The whole country forms part of the drainage basin of the Orange river, its streams, with insignificant exceptions, being tributaries of the Vaal or Caledon affluents of that river. The watershed between the Vaal and Caledon is formed by chains of hills, which, leaving the main range of the Drakensberg at Mont aux Sources, sweep in semicircles west and south. These hills are known as the Roodebergen, Wittebergen, Korannaberg, Viervoet, &c., and rise to nearly 7000 ft. The well-known Thaba Nchu (Black Mountain) is an isolated peak between this range and Bloemfontein. Three-fourths of the country lies north of these hills and is typical veld; the valley of the Caledon, sheltered eastward by the Maluti Mountains in Basutoland, is well watered and extremely fertile. The Caledon, from its source in Mont aux Sources to Jammerberg Drift near Wepener, forms the boundary of the province, the southern bank being in Basutoland; below Wepener the land on both sides of the Caledon is in the province. Here, between the Caledon and the Orange, is the fertile district of Rouxville. The north bank of the Orange, from the Kornet Spruit confluence to a point a little east of the spot where the railway from Cape Town to Kimberley crosses the river, forms the southern frontier of the province. The chief tributaries of the Vaal (q.v.) wholly or partly within the province are, going from east to west, the Klip (this stream from near its source to its confluence with the Vaal divides the Free State from the Transvaal), the Wilge, Rhenoster, Vet, Modder and Reit. The Sand river, on whose banks the convention recognizing the independence of the Transvaal Boers was signed in 1852, is a tributary of the Vet and passes through the centre of the country. All the affluents of the Vaal mentioned flow north or west. The Vaal itself for the greater part of its course forms the boundary between the province and the Transvaal. From the Klip river confluence it flows west and south-west, entering Griqualand West above Kimberley. The river beds are generally 40 to 80 ft. below the level of the surrounding land. Most of the rivers have a considerable slope and none is navigable. Except the Caledon, Vaal and Orange, they are dry or nearly dry for three or four months in the year, but in the rainy season they are often raging torrents. The valleys of the Modder, Reit and the lower Caledon contain rich alluvial deposits. Besides the rivers water is obtained from numerous springs. A remarkable feature of the western plains is the large number of salt pans and salt springs grouped together in extensive areas, especially in the Boshof district.

Geology.—Except a small area around Vredefort in the north, the whole of the province is occupied by rocks of Karroo age. At Vredefort there is a granitic boss, belonging to the Swaziland series, regarded as being an intrusive in the overlying Witwatersrand series by G. A. F. Molengraaff, but to be of older date by F. A. Hatch. This boss is bounded, except on the south, by the Witwatersrand series, the lower portion of which consists of quartzites and slates and the upper portion of quartzites and conglomerates. At Hoopstad and at Stinkboschoom the Witwatersrand series is unconformably overlain by 500 ft. of boulder beds and amygdaloidal lavas belonging to the Vaal River System. The Black Reef series of quartzites and conglomerates and dolomite form a narrow outcrop resting unconformably upon the last-mentioned system. Of the Karroo System all the groups from the basal Dwyka Conglomerate to the Cave Sandstone of the Stormberg series (see CAPE COLONY) are represented; but these rocks have not been so minutely subdivided as in the Cape. The Dwyka Conglomerate forms a narrow outcrop in the north-west, and is known from boreholes to extend over large areas beneath the Ecca Shales and to rest directly on rocks of older age. At Vereeniging a seam of coal is worked above it. The Ecca series extends over the major portion of the province. It consists mainly of sandstones, but these are often thin-bedded and pass into shales. Impressions of plants and silicified stems are frequently found. The Beaufort series occupies a portion of the area formerly regarded as being composed of the Stormberg beds. The prevailing rocks are sandstones, mudstones and shales. Reptilian remains abound; plants are also plentiful. The Stormberg series is confined to the north-east.[1]

Climate.—Cut off from the warm, rain-bearing winds of the Indian Ocean by the Drakensberg, the country is swept by the winds from the dry desert regions to the west. It is also occasionally subject to hot, dry winds from the north. The westerly wind is almost constant and, in conjunction with the elevation of the land, greatly modifies the climatic conditions. The heat usual in sub-tropical countries is tempered by the cool breezes, and the atmosphere is dry and bracing. The climate indeed is noted for its healthiness, the chief drawback being dust-storms. The average temperature for the four winter months—May-August—is 49° F.; hard frosts at night are then common. For the other eight months the average temperature is 66°, December-February being the hottest months. The average daily range of the thermometer is from 25° to 30°,

[1] See for geology, A. H. Green, "A Contribution to the Geology and Physical Geography of the Cape Colony," *Quart. Journ. Geol. Soc.* vol. xliv., 1888; E. J. Dunn, *Geological Sketch Map of S. Africa* (Melbourne, 1887); D. Draper, "Notes on the Geology of South-Eastern Africa," *Quart. Journ. Geol. Soc.* vol. l., 1894; F. H. Hatch and G. S. Corstorphine, *The Geology of South Africa* (2nd ed. London, 1909).

the highest recorded range in one day being 74° (from 20° to 94°). Rain falls on from sixty to seventy days during the year, chiefly in the summer (December-April). Rain is generally preceded by thunder and lightning and falls heavily for a short period. Most of the water runs off the surface into the spruits and in a little while the veld is again dry. The western part of the province is driest, as the rain clouds often pass over the lower levels but are caught by the eastern hills. The average annual rainfall varies from 18 in. or less in the west to 24 in. in the central regions and 30 in the eastern highlands.

Flora and Fauna.—The flora is typical of a region of scanty rainfall. Over the greater part of the plains little now grows save veld, the coarse long grass of South Africa. Formerly, much of the country was covered with mimosa bush, but the trees were to a large extent cut down by the early white immigrants. Thorny acacias, euphorbias and aloes are still, however, found in patches on the plains. Timber trees are almost confined to the river valleys, where willows, yellow wood, iron wood, red wood, mimosas and, in deep gorges, the wild fig are found. The tobacco plant also grows wild. In moist regions ferns and mosses, the arum and other broad flat-leaved plants are found. The characteristic plants are thorny and small leaved, or else bulbous. Among veld plants the elands-boontje provides tanning material equal to oak bark. European fruit trees and vines flourish in certain localities, while in the drier regions the Australian wattle, gum trees and pepper trees have been introduced with success.

The fauna has undergone a great alteration since the first white settlers entered the country. Big game was then abundant. The elephant, giraffe, lion, leopard, hyena, zebra, buffalo, gnu, quagga, kudu, eland and many other kinds of antelope roamed the plains; the rhinoceros, hippopotamus and crocodile lived in or frequented the rivers, and ostriches and baboons were numerous. The immigrant farmers ruthlessly shot down game of all kinds and most of the animals named were exterminated, so far as the province was concerned. Of animals still found may be mentioned baboons and monkeys, the leopard, red lynx (*Felis caracal*), spotted hyena, aard wolf, wild cat, long-eared fox, jackals of various kinds, the dassie or rock rabbit, the scaly anteater, the ant bear (aardvaark), the mongoose and the spring haas, a rodent of the jerboa family. Antelope of any kind are now scarce; a few white-tailed gnu are preserved. None of the dangerous wild beasts is common, but there are several varieties of poisonous snakes. Scorpions and tarantulas are numerous, and lizards, frogs, beetles, ants, butterflies, moths and flies are abundant. Locusts are an intermittent plague. There are few earthworms or snails. The birds include eagles—some are called lammervangers from their occasional attacks on young lambs—vultures, hawks, kites, owls, crows, ravens, the secretary bird, cranes, a small white heron, quails, partridges, korhaans, wild geese, duck and guineafowl, swallows, finches, starlings, the mossie or Cape sparrow, and the widow bird, noted for the length of its tail in summer. Barbel and yellow mudfish are found in the rivers.

Inhabitants.—The Bushmen (*q.v.*) are, presumably, the oldest inhabitants of this, as of many other parts of South Africa. Next came the Hottentots (*q.v.*), and in the 16th century Bantu negroes of the Bechuana tribes appear to have established themselves in the country. The Barolong, one of the oldest Bechuana tribes, are believed to have entered the country subsequently to the Bakuena, the particular tribe from which the general name of the race is derived (see BECHUANA; and TRANSVAAL: *Inhabitants*). Clans representing the southern Bakuena were welded together into one tribe in the 19th century, and are now known as Basuto (see BASUTOLAND). The Basuto were already a strong force when the first white settlers, Dutch farmers from the Cape, entered the country in 1824; the white element has since been reinforced by a considerable strain of British, particularly Scottish, blood. Since the advent of the whites there has also been a considerable immigration of Zulus. The majority of the inhabitants live in the eastern part of the country; the arid regions west of the main railway line containing a scanty pastoral population and no towns of any size. The first census, taken in 1880, showed a total population of 133,518; in 1890 there were 207,503 inhabitants—an increase in ten years of 55·41%—and at the census of 1904 there were 387,315 inhabitants, a further increase of 85·56%. The density in 1904 was under 8 persons per sq. m. The inhabitants are officially divided into "Europeans or white," "aboriginal natives" and "mixed and other coloured races." Between 1880 and 1904 the proportion of whites dropped from 45·70% to 36·84%. Of the 142,679 white inhabitants in 1904, 85,036 were born in the province; 29,727 in the Cape; 3116 in the Transvaal; 1835 in Natal, and 18,487 in the United Kingdom. Of the 2726 European

immigrants born in non-British states 1095 came from Russian Poland.

According to the 1904 census classification the "aboriginal inhabitants" numbered in that year 229,149. In this term are included, however, Zulu-Kaffir immigrants. The tribe most largely represented was the Basuto (130,213 persons), former owners of considerable tracts in the eastern part of the country, now known as "The Conquered Territory." In the eastern districts of Harrismith, Bethlehem, Ficksburg and Ladybrand the Basutos are largely concentrated. Barolong numbered 37,008 and other Bechuana 5115. Of the Zulu-Kaffir tribes Zulus proper numbered 35,275, Fingoes 6275, and Ama Xosa 5376 (see KAFFIRS; and ZULULAND: *Inhabitants*). The Bushmen numbered 4048 persons. Of these 1131 were in the Bloemfontein district. The Bushmen have left in drawings on caves and in rocks traces of their habitation in regions where they are no longer to be found. In Thaba'nchu a petty Barolong state enjoyed autonomy up to 1884, and the majority of the Barolong are found in that district and the adjoining district of Bloemfontein. The Zulus are mostly found in that part of the country nearest Zululand. In 1904 the number of persons belonging to "mixed and other coloured races" was 15,487. The proportion between the sexes was, for all races, 84·35 females to 100 males; for white inhabitants only 74·91 females to 100 males; for aboriginal inhabitants only 90·86 females to 100 males. Of the population above fifteen years old 55·87% of the men and 33·69% of the women were unmarried. Among whites for every 100 unmarried men there were 65·33 unmarried women; there were 93·04 married women for every 100 married men, and 173·81 widows for every 100 widowers.

Classified by occupations the census of 1904 gave the following results: dependants, mainly young children, 28·53%; agriculture, 30·51%; commercial and industrial pursuits, 7·62%; professional, 3·18%; domestic (including women living at home other than those helping in farm work), 15·75%. Divided by races 8·19% of the whites were engaged in professional work and only 0·16% of the coloured classes.

Chief Towns.—The capital, Bloemfontein (pop. in 1904, 33,883), is fairly centrally situated on the trunk railway to Johannesburg. Kroonstad (pop. 7191) lies 127 m. N.N.E. of Bloemfontein on the same railway line. Harrismith, 8300, is in the N.E. of the colony, 60 m. by rail from Ladysmith, Natal. Jagersfontein, 3657, is in the S.W. of the province and owes its importance to the existence there of a diamond mine. Ladybrand, 3862, Ficksburg, 1954, and Wepener, 1366, lie in the valley of the Caledon near the Basutoland frontier. Winburg, 2762, lies between Bloemfontein and Kroonstad. All these towns are separately noticed. Other towns on the trunk railway, going from south to north, are Springfontein, 1000, an important railway junction; Trompsburg, 1378; Edenburg, 1562, and Brandfort, 1977. In the S.E. Thaba'nchu, 1134, Zastron, 1157, Dewetsdorp, 971 (named after the father of Christian De Wet), Reddersburg, 750, Smithfield, 999, and Rouxville, 990. These are all centres of fine agricultural regions. Bethulie, 1686, on the Orange river, in the "Conquered Territory," has been the scene of the labours of French Protestant missionaries since 1832, and possesses a fine park. Through it passes the main line from East London, 514 m. In the N.E. are: Bethlehem, 1777, on the railway, 57 m. W. of Harrismith, an agricultural and coal-mining centre; Senekal, 1039; Heilbron, 1544; Vrede, 1543; Frankfort, 747; Lindley, 646; and Reitz, 526. In the north-west of the trunk railway are: Parijs, 1732, finely situated on the Vaal, and Vredefort, 759. Farther west and south are: Hoopstad, 452, on the Vet river; Boshof, 1308, a fruit and vegetable centre, 30 m. N.E. of Kimberley; and Jacobsdal, 764. In the S.W. are: Philippolis, 809, at one time capital of the Griqua chief Adam Kok and named after the Rev. John Philip (*q.v.*). Fauresmith, 1363, a mining centre, 6 m. W. of Jagersfontein, and Koffyfontein, 1657, where is a diamond mine. Many of the towns were, the scenes of encounters between the Boers and British, March 1900-May 1902. At Boshof fell the leader of the Boers' European Legion, Colonel de Villebois Mareuil, on the 5th of April 1900. At the census of 1904 Harrismith and Kroonstad were the only towns where the white inhabitants outnumbered the coloured population. Nine towns contained more than 1000 white inhabitants, the total white population of these towns being 31,505, of whom 15,501 lived in Bloemfontein.

Communications.—Largely owing to its situation—being on the direct route between the Cape ports and the Transvaal, and between Durban and Kimberley—the province possesses an extensive network of railways. The railways are state owned and of the standard South African gauge—3 ft. 6 in. They may be divided into two systems, (1) those connecting the province with the Cape and the Transvaal, and (2) those linking it with Natal.

The first system consists of a trunk line, formed by the junction of lines from Cape Town and Port Elizabeth, which crosses the Orange at Norvals Pont, traverses the province from south to north, passing through Bloemfontein and Kroonstad, and enters the Transvaal at Viljoens Drift (331 m. from Norvals Pont), being continued thence to Johannesburg. This line is joined at Springfontein by a railway from East London which crosses the Orange near Bethulie. From Bloemfontein a line (102 m. long) runs west to Kimberley, on the main line from Cape Town to Rhodesia, and from Springfontein a branch (56 m. long) goes past Jagersfontein to Fauresmith.

The second system is formed by a line leaving the Natal trunk railway at Ladysmith which crosses the Drakensberg at Van Reenen's Pass and is continued thence through Harrismith to Bethlehem. At Bethlehem it divides, one branch going N.W. to Kroonstad (178 m. from the Natal border and 393 m. from Durban), the other S.W. along the Caledon valley to Modderpoort near Ladybrand, and thence directly west to Bloemfontein. The distance from Van Reenen's Pass to Bloemfontein by this route is 278 m. The two systems, it will be seen, are doubly connected, namely at Bloemfontein and at Kroonstad, and the lines running east from those towns afford the quickest connexion between Cape Town and Durban. Besides the lines enumerated there are various local lines, one branching at Sannah's Post station from the Bloemfontein-Bethlehem line running south-east to Wepener. Another branch from the same line crosses the Caledon to Maseru, Basutoland. In 1910 there were in all 1060 m. of railway open in the province. There are well-kept high-roads connecting all the towns, and a government service of mail carts to places not on the railway. The light Cape cart is largely used, and the wagon, drawn by a team of oxen, is still employed by farmers to bring their produce to market. There is an extensive telegraphic system and a well-organized postal service.

Agriculture.—The chief industry is agriculture, including sheep farming and stock raising. The dry western plains are best adapted for sheep rearing, while the well-watered eastern regions are specially suitable for the growing of cereals and also for horse breeding. The land under cultivation in 1904 was 371,515 morgen (a morgen is 2·11 acres) or about 1230 sq. m. The chief crop is mealies, the staple food of the natives; wheat, oathay, Kaffir corn and oats coming next. Little barley is cultivated. The " Conquered Territory," that is the valley of the Caledon, is the most fertile region and is styled the granary of South Africa. Here, in the districts of Ladybrand, Ficksburg, Bethlehem and Rouxville, most wheat is grown. The same regions, together with the adjoining regions of Harrismith and Thaba'nchu, produce the most oats and oathay. Besides grain the chief crops are those of pumpkins, potatoes and other table vegetables, and tobacco. The cultivation of potatoes and tobacco largely increased between the census years 1890 and 1904. The principal tobacco-growing regions are Vredefort, which produced 258,643 lb in 1904, and Kroonstad (80,385 lb), the districts of Bethlehem, Ladybrand and Winburg also producing considerable quantities. Fruit farming engages attention, about 8000 morgen being devoted to orchards in 1904. The fruit trees commonly cultivated are the peach, apricot, apple, orange, lemon, pear, fig and plum.

The rearing of live stock, the chief pursuit of the first Dutch settlers, is an important industry. Rinderpest and other epidemic diseases swept over the country in 1895–1896, and during the war of 1899–1902 the province was practically denuded of live stock. There was a rapid increase of stock after the close of hostilities. Sheep numbered over 5,000,000 in 1910, cattle over 600,000, horses over 100,000, goats (chiefly owned by natives) over 1,000,000. Large numbers of pigs are reared. Ostrich farming is growing in favour. The eastern and south-eastern districts have the greatest amount of stock per square mile, Ficksburg leading in cattle, horses and mules. Sheep are most abundant in the Rouxville, Wepener and Smithfield districts, goats in Philippolis. The dairying industry is increasing. The Afrikander cattle, powerful draught animals, large horned, bony and giving little milk, are being crossed with other stock. A government Department of Agriculture, created in 1904, affords help to the farmers in various ways, notably in combating insect plagues, in experimental farms, and in improving the breed of horses, sheep and cattle.

Land Settlement.—Under the provisions of a Land Settlements Ordinance of 1902 over 1,500,000 acres of crown land had been by 1907 allotted, and in September 1909 there were 642 families, of whom over 570 were British, settled on the land. In 1907 a Land Settlement Board was created to deal with the affairs of these settlers. At the end of five years the Board was to hand over its duties to the government.

Diamond Mining and other Industries.—Next to agriculture the most important industry is that of diamond mining. The chief diamond mines are at Jagersfontein (q.v.) and Koffyfontein. There are also diamond mines in the Winburg and Kroonstad districts, and near Ficksburg, where old workings have been found 40 ft. deep. The alluvial deposits on the banks of the Vaal, N.E. of Kimberley, yield occasional diamonds of great purity. The value of the output

from the diamond mines rose from £224,000 in 1890 to £1,508,000 in 1898. The war hindered operations, but the output was valued at £648,000 in 1904 and at £1,048,000 in 1909.

Coal-mines are worked in various districts in the north near the Vaal, notably at Vierfontein, and at Clydesdale, which lies a few miles south of Vereeniging. Before 1905 the mines were little worked; in that year the output was 118,000 tons, while in 1907 over 500,000 tons were raised. It dropped to 470,000 in 1909 owing to loss of railway contracts.

Of other minerals gold has been found, but up to 1909 was not worked; iron ore exists near Kroonstad and Vredefort, but it also is not worked. Petroleum has been found in the Ficksburg, Ladybrand and Harrismith districts, and is pumped to a limited extent. Good building stone is obtained near Bloemfontein, Ladybrand and other places, and excellent pottery clay near Bloemfontein.

Besides the industries mentioned flour-milling, soap-making, and the manufacture of jam and salt are carried on. During 1905 over 12,300,000 lb of salt were obtained from the salt springs at Zoutpan, near Jacobsdal, and Haagenstad, to the west of Brandfort. In 1907 the output had increased to nearly 23,000,000 lb.

Trade.—The bulk of the direct trade of the country is with the Cape and the Transvaal, Natal, however, taking an increasing share. Basutoland comes fourth. Its chief exports are diamonds, live stock (cattle, horses and mules, sheep and goats), wool, mohair, coal, wheat and eggs. Except the diamonds, which go to London via Cape Town, all the exports are taken by the neighbouring territories. The principal imports, over 90 % being of British origin, are cotton goods, clothing and haberdashery, leather, boots, &c., hardware, sugar, coffee, tea and furniture.

The volume of trade in 1898, as represented by imports and exports, was £3,114,000 (imports £1,190,000; exports £1,923,000). For the four years beginning on June 30, 1902, that is immediately after the close of hostilities, the imports increased from £2,460,000 to £4,053,000, the exports from £285,000 to £3,045,000. For the fiscal year 1908–1909 the imports were valued at £2,945,000, the exports at £3,558,000. About a third of the imports are the produce or manufactures of other South African countries. Imported goods re-exported are of comparatively slight value—some £381,000 in 1908–1909.

Constitution.—From July 1907 to June 1910 the province was a self-governing colony. It is now represented in the Union parliament by sixteen senators and seventeen members of the house of assembly. For parliamentary purposes the province is divided into single-member constituencies. The franchise is given to all adult white male British subjects. There is no property qualification, but six months' residence in the province is essential. There is a biennial registration of voters, and every five years the electoral areas are to be redivided, with the object of giving to each constituency an approximately equal number of voters. The qualifications for membership of the assembly are the same as those for voters.

At the head of the provincial government is an administrator (who holds office for five years) appointed by the Union ministry. This official is assisted by an executive committee of four members elected by the provincial council. The provincial council consists of 25 members (each representing a separate constituency) elected by the parliamentary voters and has a statutory existence of three years. Its powers are strictly local and delegated. The control of elementary education was guaranteed to the council for a period of five years following the establishment of the Union.

Justice.—The law of the province is the Roman-Dutch law, in so far as it has been introduced into and is applicable to South Africa, and as amended by local acts. Bloemfontein is the seat of the Supreme Court of the Union of South Africa and also of a provincial division of the same court. For judicial purposes the province is divided into twenty-four divisions, in each of which is a resident magistrate, who has limited civil and criminal jurisdiction. There are also special justices of the peace, having criminal jurisdiction in minor cases. The provincial court has jurisdiction in all civil and criminal matters, and is a court of appeal from all inferior courts. From it appeals can be made to the Appellate Division of the Supreme Court. Criminal cases are tried before one judge and a jury of nine, who must give a unanimous opinion. Circuit courts are also held by judges of the provincial court.

Finance.—The bulk of the revenue, e.g. that derived from customs and railways, is now paid to the Union government, but the provincial council has power to levy taxes and (with the consent of the Union ministry) to raise loans for strictly provincial purposes. In 1870–1871, when the province was an independent state and possessed neither railways nor diamond mines, the revenue was £78,000 and the expenditure £71,000; in 1884–1885 the revenue had risen to £228,000 and the expenditure to £229,000; in 1898, the last full year of the republican administration, the figures were: revenue, including railway profits, £799,000; expenditure, including outlay on new railways, £956,000. Omitting the figures during the war period, the figures for the year ending June 1903 were: revenue, £956,000; expenditure, £839,000. The depression in trade which followed caused a reduction in revenue, the average for the years 1904-1909 being: revenue, £820,000; expenditure, £819,000. These figures are exclusive of railway receipts and expenditure (see TRANSVAAL: *Finance*).

Religion.—The vast majority (over 95 %) of the white inhabitants are Protestants, and over 70 % belong to the Dutch Reformed Church, while another 3 % are adherents of the very similar organization, the Gereformeerde Kerk. Anglicans are the next numerous body, forming 12·53 % of the white population. The Wesleyans number nearly 4 % of the inhabitants. The Roman Catholics number 2·30 % of the whites, the head of their church in the province being a vicar apostolic. At the head of the Anglican community, which is in full communion with the Church of England, is the bishop of Bloemfontein, whose diocese, founded in 1863, includes not only the Orange Free State, but Basutoland, Griqualand West and British Bechuanaland. All the churches named have missions to the natives, and in 1904, 104,389 aboriginals and 10,909 persons of mixed race were returned as Protestants, and 1093 aboriginals and 117 of mixed race as Roman Catholics. The total number of persons in the country professing Christianity was 251,904 or 65 %. The Dutch Reformed Church had the largest number (21,272) of converts among the natives, the Wesleyans coming next. The African Methodist Episcopal (Ethiopian) Church had 4110 members, of whom only two were whites. The Jewish community numbered 1616. Nearly 33 % of the population, 127,637 persons, were returned officially at the census of 1904 as of "no religion," under which head are classed the natives who retain their primitive forms of belief, for which see KAFFIRS, BECHUANAS, &c.

Education.—At the census of 1904, 32·57 % of the total population could read and write; of the whites over fifteen years old 82·63 % could read and write. Of the aboriginals, 8·15 % could read and write; of the mixed and other races, 12·28 %. In the urban areas the proportion of persons, of all races, able to read and write was 50·67 %; in the 'rural areas the proportion was 26·43 %. By sexes, 35 % of males and 29·63 % of females 'could read and write.

Elementary education is administered by the provincial council, assisted by a permanent director of education. From 1900 to 1905 the schools were managed, teachers selected and appointed and all expenses borne by the government. They were of an undenominational character and English was the medium of instruction. The teaching of Dutch was optional. In 1904 the Dutch Reformed Church started Christian National (*i.e.* Denominational) Schools, but in March 1905 an agreement was come to whereby these schools were amalgamated with the government schools, and in June 1905 a further agreement was arrived at between the government and the leading religious denominations. By this arrangement " religious instruction of a purely historical character " was given in all government schools for two hours every week, and might be given in Dutch. Further, ministers of the various denominations might give, on the special request of the parents, instruction to the children of their own congregations for one hour on one day in each week. The attendance at government schools reached in 1908 a total of nearly 20,000, as against 8000 in 1898, the highest attendance recorded under republican government. On the attainment of self-government the colonial legislature passed an act (1908) which in respect to primary and secondary education made attendance compulsory on all white children, the fee system being national. English and Dutch were, nominally, placed on an equal footing as media of instruction. Every school was under the supervision of a committee elected by the parents of the children. Schools were grouped in districts, and for each district there was a controlling board of nine members, of whom five were elected by the committees of the separate schools and four appointed by the government. Religious instruction could only be given by members of the school staff. Dogmatic teaching was prohibited during school hours, except in rural schools when parents required such teaching to be given. The application of the provision as to the media of instruction gave rise to much friction, the English-speaking community complaining that instruction in Dutch was forced upon their children (see further, § *History*). Primary education for natives is provided in private schools, many of which receive government grants. In 1908 over 10,000 natives were in attendance at schools.

Provision is made for secondary education in all the leading town schools, which prepare pupils for matriculation. At Bloemfontein is a high school for girls, the Grey College school for boys, and a normal school for the training of teachers. The Grey University College is a state institution providing university education for the whole province. It is affiliated to the university of the Cape of Good Hope.

History

The country north of the Orange river was first visited by Europeans towards the close of the 18th century. At that time it was somewhat thinly peopled. The majority of the inhabitants appear to have been members of the Bechuana division of the Bantus, but in the valleys of the Orange and Vaal were Korannas and other Hottentots, and in the Drakensberg and on the western border lived numbers of Bushmen. Early in the 19th century Griquas established themselves north of the Orange. Between 1817 and 1831 the country was devastated by the chief Mosilikatze and his Zulus, and large areas were depopulated. Up to this time the few white men who had crossed the Orange had been chiefly hunters or missionaries. In 1824 Dutch farmers from Cape Colony seeking pasture for their flocks settled in the country. They were followed in 1836 by the first parties of the Great Trek. These emigrants left Cape Colony from various motives, but all were animated by the desire to escape from British sovereignty. (See SOUTH AFRICA, *History*; and CAPE COLONY, *History*.) The leader of the first large party of emigrants was A. H. Potgieter, who concluded an agreement with Makwana, the chief of the Bataung tribe of Bechuanas, ceding to the farmers the country between the Vet and Vaal rivers. The emigrants soon came into collision with the Bantus, raiding parties of Zulus attacking Boer hunters who had crossed the Vaal without seeking permission from that chieftain. Reprisals followed, and in November 1837 Mosilikatze was decisively defeated by the Boers and thereupon fled northward. In the meantime another party of emigrants had settled at Thaba'nchu, where the Wesleyans had a mission station for the Barolong. The emigrants were treated with great kindness by Moroko, the chief of that tribe, and with the Barolong the Boers maintained uniformly friendly relations. In December 1836 the emigrants beyond the Orange drew up in general assembly an elementary republican form of government. After the defeat of Mosilikatze the town of Winburg (so named by the Boers in commemoration of their victory) was founded, a volksraad elected, and Piet Retief, one of the ablest of the *voortrekkers*, chosen " governor and commandant-general." The emigrants already numbered some 500 men, besides women and children and many coloured servants. Dissensions speedily arose among the emigrants, whose numbers were constantly added to, and Retief, Potgieter and other leaders crossed the Drakensberg and entered Natal. Those that remained were divided into several parties intensely jealous of one another.

Early relations with British, Basutos and Griquas. Meantime a new power had arisen along the upper Orange and in the valley of the Caledon. Moshesh, a Bechuana chief of high descent, had welded together a number of scattered and broken clans which had sought refuge in that mountainous region, and had formed of them the Basuto nation. In 1833 he had welcomed as workers among his people a band of French Protestant missionaries, and as the Boer immigrants began to settle in his neighbourhood he decided to seek support from the British at the Cape. At that time the British government was not prepared to exercise effective control over the emigrants. Acting upon the advice of Dr John Philip, the superintendent of the London Missionary Society's stations in South Africa, a treaty was concluded in 1843 with Moshesh, placing him under British protection. A similar treaty was made with the Griqua chief, Adam Kok III. (See BASUTOLAND and GRIQUALAND.) By these treaties, which recognized native sovereignty over large areas on which Boer farmers were settled, it was sought to keep a check on the emigrants and to protect both the natives and Cape Colony. Their effect was to precipitate collisions between all three parties. The year in which the treaty with Moshesh was made several large parties of Boers recrossed the Drakensberg into the country north of the Orange, refusing to remain in Natal when it became a British colony. During their stay there they had inflicted a severe defeat on the Zulus under Dingaan (December 1838), an event which, following on the flight of Mosilikatze, greatly strengthened the position of Moshesh, whose power became a menace to that of the emigrant farmers. Trouble first arose, however, between the Boers and the Griquas in the Philippolis district. Many of the white farmers in this district, unlike their fellows dwelling farther north, were willing to accept British rule, and this fact induced Mr Justice Menzies, one of the judges of Cape Colony then on circuit at Colesberg, to cross the Orange and proclaim (October 1842) the country British·territory, a proclamation disallowed by the governor, Sir George Napier, who, nevertheless, maintained that the emigrant farmers were still British subjects. It was after this episode that the treaties with Adam Kok and Moshesh were negotiated. The treaties gave great offence to the Boers, who refused to acknowledge the sovereignty of the native chiefs. The majority of the white farmers in Kok's territory sent a deputation to the British commissioner in Natal, Henry Cloete, asking for equal treatment with the Griquas, and expressing the desire to come, on such terms, under British protection. Shortly afterwards hostilities between the farmers and the Griquas broke out. British troops were moved up to support the Griquas, and after a skirmish at Zwartkopjes (May 2, 1845) a new arrangement was made between Kok and Sir Peregrine Maitland, then governor of Cape Colony, virtually placing the administration of his territory in the hands of a British resident, a post filled in 1846 by Captain H, D. Warden. The place chosen by Captain (afterwards Major) Warden as the seat of his court was known as Bloemfontein, and it subsequently became the capital of the whole country.

The volksraad at Winburg during this period continued to claim jurisdiction over the Boers living between the Orange and the Vaal and was in federation with the volksraad at Potchefstroom, which made a similar claim upon the Boers living north of the Vaal. In 1846 Major Warden occupied Winburg for a short time, and the relations between the Boers and the British were in a continual state of tension. Many of the farmers deserted Winburg for the Transvaal. Sir Harry Smith became governor of the Cape at the end of 1847. He recognized the failure of the attempt to govern on the lines of the treaties with the Griquas and Basutos, and on the 3rd of February 1848 he issued a proclamation declaring British sovereignty over the country· between the Orange and the Vaal eastward to the Drakensberg. The justness of Sir Harry Smith's measures and his popularity among the Boers gained for his policy considerable support, but the republican party, at whose head was Andries Pretorius (q.v.), did not submit without a struggle. They were, however, defeated by Sir Harry Smith in an engagement at Boomplaats (August 29, 1848). Thereupon Pretorius, with those most bitterly opposed to British rule, retreated across the Vaal. In March 1849 Major Warden was succeeded at Bloemfontein as civil commissioner by Mr C. U. Stuart, but he remained British resident until July 1852. A nominated legislative council was created, a high court established and other steps taken for the orderly government of the country, which was officially styled the Orange River Sovereignty. In October 1849 Moshesh was induced to sign a new arrangement considerably curtailing the boundaries of the Basuto reserve. The frontier towards the Sovereignty was thereafter known as the Warden line. A little later the reserves of other chieftains were precisely defined. The British Resident had, however, no force sufficient to maintain his authority, and Moshesh and all the neighbouring clans became involved in hostilities with one another and with the whites. In 1851 Moshesh joined the republican party in the Sovereignty in an invitation to Pretorius to recross the Vaal. The intervention of Pretorius resulted in the Sand River Convention of 1852, which acknowledged the independence of the Transvaal but left the status of the Sovereignty untouched. The British government (the first Russell administration), which had reluctantly agreed to the annexation of the country, had, however, already repented its decision and had resolved to abandon the Sovereignty. Lord Grey (the 3rd earl), secretary of state ̄for the colonies, in a despatch to Sir Harry Smith dated the 21st of October 1851, declared, "The ultimate abandonment of the Orange Sovereignty should be a settled point in our policy." A meeting of representatives of all European inhabitants of the Sovereignty, elected on manhood suffrage, held at Bloemfontein in June 1852, never-

theless declared in favour of the retention of British rule. At the close of that year a settlement was at length concluded with Moshesh, which left, perhaps, that chief in a stronger position than he had hitherto been. (See BASUTOLAND: History.) There had been ministerial changes in England and the ministry then in power—that of Lord Aberdeen—adhered to the determination to withdraw from the Sovereignty. Sir George Russell Clerk was sent out in 1853 as special commissioner "for the settling and adjusting of the affairs" of the Sovereignty, and in August of that year he summoned a meeting of delegates to determine upon a form of self-government. At that time there were some 15,000 whites in the country, many of them recent emigrants from Cape Colony. There were among them numbers of farmers and tradesmen of British blood. The majority of the whites still wished for the continuance of British rule provided that it was effective and the country guarded against its enemies. The representations of their delegates, who drew up a proposed constitution retaining British control, were unavailing. Sir George Clerk announced that, as the elected delegates were unwilling to take steps to form an independent government, he would enter into negotiations with other persons. "And then," writes Dr Theal, "was seen the strange spectacle of an English commissioner addressing men who wished to be free of British control as the friendly and well-disposed inhabitants, while for those who desired to remain British subjects and who claimed that protection to which they believed themselves entitled he had no sympathizing word." While the elected delegates sent two members to England to try and induce the government to alter their decision Sir George Clerk speedily came to terms with a committee formed by the republican party and presided over by Mr J. H. Hoffman. Even before this committee met a royal proclamation had been signed (January 30, 1854) "abandoning and renouncing all dominion" in the Sovereignty. A convention recognizing the independence of the country was signed at Bloemfontein on the 23rd of February by Sir George Clerk and the republican committee, and on the 11th of March the Boer government assumed office and the republican flag was hoisted. Five days later the representatives of the elected delegates had an interview in London with the colonial secretary, the duke of Newcastle, who informed them that it was now too late to discuss the question of the retention of British rule. The colonial secretary added that it was impossible for England to supply troops to constantly advancing outposts, "especially as Cape Town and the port of Table Bay were all she really required in South Africa." In withdrawing from the Sovereignty the British government declared that it had "no alliance with any native chief or tribes to the northward of the Orange River with the exception of the Griqua chief Captain Adam Kok." Kok was not formidable in a military sense, nor could he prevent individual Griquas from alienating their lands. Eventually, in 1861, he sold his sovereign rights to the Free State for £4000 and removed with his followers to the district now known as Griqualand East. (F. R. C.)

On the abandonment of British rule representatives of the people were elected and met at Bloemfontein on the 28th of March 1854, and between that date and the 18th of April were engaged in framing a constitution. The country was declared a republic and named the Orange Free State. All persons of European blood possessing a six months' residential qualification were to be granted full burgher rights. The sole legislative authority was vested in a single popularly elected chamber styled the volksraad. Executive authority was entrusted to a president elected by the burghers from a list submitted by the volksraad. The president was to be assisted by an executive council, was to hold office for five years and was eligible for re-election. The constitution was subsequently modified but remained of a liberal character. A residence of five years in the country was required before aliens could become naturalized. The first president was Mr Hoffman, but he was accused of being too complaisant towards Moshesh and resigned, being succeeded in 1855 by Mr J. N. Boshof, one of the voortrekkers, who had previously taken an active part in the affairs of Natal.

Distracted among themselves, with the formidable Basuto power on their southern and eastern flank, the troubles of the infant state were speedily added to by the action of *A Transvaal raid into the Free State.* the Transvaal Boers. Marthinus Pretorius, who had succeeded to his father's position as commandant-general of Potchefstroom, wished to bring about a confederation between the two Boer states. Peaceful overtures from Pretorius were declined, and some of his partisans in the Free State were accused of treason (February 1857). Thereupon Pretorius, aided by Paul Kruger, conducted a raid into the Free State territory. On learning of the invasion President Boshof proclaimed martial law throughout the country. The majority of the burghers rallied to his support, and on the 25th of May the two opposing forces faced one another on the banks of the Rhenoster. President Boshof not only got together some eight hundred men within the Free State, but he received offers of support from Commandant Schoeman, the Transvaal leader in the Zoutpansberg district and from Commandant Joubert of Lydenburg. Pretorius and Kruger, realizing that they would have to sustain attack from both north and south, abandoned their enterprise. Their force, too, only amounted to some three hundred. Kruger came to Boshof's camp with a flag of truce, the "army" of Pretorius returned north and on the 2nd of June a treaty of peace was signed, each state acknowledging the absolute independence of the other. The conduct of Pretorius was stigmatized as "blameworthy." Several of the malcontents in the Free State who had joined Pretorius permanently settled in the Transvaal, and other Free Staters who had been guilty of high treason were arrested and punished. This experience did not, however, heal the party strife within the Free State. In consequence of the dissensions among the burghers President Boshof tendered his resignation in February 1858, but was for a time induced to remain in office. The difficulties of the state were at that time (1858) so great that the volksraad in December of that year passed a resolution in favour of confederation with the Cape Colony. This proposition received the strong support of Sir George Grey, then governor of Cape Colony, but his view did not commend itself to the British government, and was not adopted (see SOUTH AFRICA: *History*). In the same year the disputes between the Basutos and the Boers culminated in open war. Both parties laid claims to land beyond the Warden line, and each party had taken possession of what it could, the Basutos being also expert cattle-lifters. In the war the advantage rested with the Basutos; thereupon the Free State appealed to Sir George Grey, who induced Moshesh to come to terms. On the 15th of October 1858 a treaty was signed defining anew the boundary. The peace was nominal only, while the burghers were also involved in disputes with other tribes. Mr. Boshof again tendered his resignation (February 1859) and retired to Natal. Many of the burghers would have at this time welcomed union with the Transvaal, but learning from Sir George Grey that such a union would nullify the conventions of 1852 and 1854 and necessitate the reconsideration of Great Britain's policy towards the native tribes north of the Orange and Vaal rivers, the project dropped. Commandant Pretorius was, however, elected president in place of Mr Boshof. Though unable to effect a durable peace with the Basutos, or to realize his ambition for the creation of one powerful Boer republic, Pretorius saw the Free State begin to grow in strength. The fertile district of Bethulie as well as Adam Kok's territory was acquired, and there was a considerable increase in the white population. The burghers generally, however, had not learned the need of discipline, of confidence in their elected rulers, or that to carry on a government taxes must be levied. Wearied like Mr Boshof of a thankless task, and more interested in affairs in the Transvaal than in those of the Free State, Pretorius resigned the presidency in 1863, and after an interval of seven months Mr (afterwards Sir) John Henry Brand (*q.v.*), an advocate at the Cape bar, was elected president. He assumed office in February 1864. His election proved a turning-point in the history of the country,

which, under his beneficent and tactful guidance, became peaceful and prosperous and, in some respects, a model state. But before peace could be established an end had to be made of the difficulties with the Basutos. Moshesh continued *Brand elected President.* to menace the Free State border. Attempts at accommodation made by the governor of Cape Colony (Sir Philip Wodehouse) failed, and war between the Free State and Moshesh was renewed in 1865. The Boers gained considerable successes, and this induced Moshesh to sue for peace. The terms exacted were, however, too harsh for a nation yet unbroken to accept permanently. A treaty was signed at Thaba Bosigo in April 1866, but war again broke out in 1867, and the Free State attracted to its side a large number of adventurers from all parts of South Africa. The burghers thus reinforced gained at length a decisive victory over their great antagonist, every stronghold in Basutoland save Thaba Bosigo being stormed. Moshesh now turned in earnest to Sir Philip Wodehouse for preservation. His prayer was heeded, and in 1868 he and his country were taken under British protection. Thus the thirty years' strife between the Basutos and the Boers came to an end. The *Settlement of the troubles.* intervention of the governor of Cape Colony led to the conclusion of the treaty of Aliwal North (Feb. 12, 1869), which defined the borders between the Orange Free State and Basutoland. The country lying to the north of the Orange river and west of the Caledon, formerly a part of Basutoland, was ceded to the Free State (see BASUTOLAND). This country, some hundred miles long and nearly thirty wide, is a fertile stretch of agricultural land on the lower slopes of the Maluti mountains. It lies at an altitude of nearly 6000 ft., and is well watered by the Caledon and its tributaries. It has ever since been known as the Conquered Territory, and it forms to-day one of the richest corn-growing districts in South Africa. A year after the addition of the Conquered Territory to the state another boundary dispute was settled by the arbitration of Mr Keate, lieutenant-governor of Natal. By the Sand River Convention independence had been granted to the Boers living "north of the Vaal," and the dispute turned on the question as to what stream constituted the true upper course of that river. Mr Keate decided (Feb. 19, 1870) against the Free State view and fixed the Klip river as the dividing line, the Transvaal thus securing the Wakkerstroom and adjacent districts.

The Basutoland difficulties were no sooner arranged than the Free Staters found themselves confronted with a serious difficulty on their western border. In the years 1870-1871 a *Discovery of the Kimberley Diamond Fields.* large number of diggers had settled on the diamond fields near the junction of the Vaal and Orange rivers, which were situated in part on land claimed by the Griqua chief Nicholas Waterboer and by the Free State. The Free State established a temporary government over the diamond fields, but the administration of this body was satisfactory neither to the Free State nor to the diggers. At this juncture Waterboer offered to place the territory under the administration of Queen Victoria. The offer was accepted, and on the 27th of October 1871 the district, together with some adjacent territory to which the Transvaal had laid claim, was proclaimed, under the name of Griqualand West, British territory. Waterboer's claims were based on the treaty concluded by his father with the British in 1834, and on various arrangements with the Kok chiefs; the Free State based its claim on its purchase of Adam Kok's sovereign rights and on long occupation. The difference between proprietorship and sovereignty was confused or ignored. That Waterboer exercised no authority in the disputed district was admitted. When the British annexation took place a party in the volksraad wished to go to war with Britain, but the wiser counsels of President Brand prevailed. The Free State, however, did not abandon its claims. The matter involved no little irritation between the parties concerned until July 1876. It was then disposed of by the 4th earl of Carnarvon, at that time secretary of state for the colonies, who granted to the Free State £90,000 "in full satisfaction of all claims which it considers it may possess to Griqualand West." Lord Carnarvon declined to entertain the proposal made by Mr Brand that the territory should be given up by Great Britain. One thing at least is certain with regard to the diamond fields—they were the means of restoring the credit and prosperity of the Free State. In the opinion, moreover, of Dr Theal, who has written the history of the Boer Republics and has been a consistent supporter of the Boers, the annexation of Griqualand West was probably in the best interests of the Free State. "There was," he states, "no alternative from British sovereignty other than an independent diamond field republic."

At this time, largely owing to the exhausting struggle with the Basutos, the Free State Boers, like their Transvaal neighbours, had drifted into financial straits. A paper currency had been instituted, and the notes—currently known as "bluebacks"—soon dropped to less than half their nominal value. Commerce was largely carried on by barter, and many cases of bankruptcy occurred in the state. But as British annexation in 1877 saved the Transvaal from bankruptcy, so did the influx of British and other immigrants to the diamond fields, in the early 'seventies, restore public credit and individual prosperity to the Boers of the Free State. The diamond fields offered a ready market for stock and other agricultural produce. Money flowed into the pockets of the farmers. Public credit was restored. "Bluebacks" recovered par value, and were called in and redeemed by the government. Valuable diamond mines were also discovered within the Free State, of which the one at Jagersfontein is the richest. Capital from Kimberley and London was soon provided with which to work them.

The relations between the British and the Free State, after the question of the boundary was once settled, remained perfectly *Cordial relations with Great Britain.* amicable down to the outbreak of the Boer War in 1899. From 1870 onward the history of the state was one of quiet, steady progress. At the time of the first annexation of the Transvaal the Free State declined Lord Carnarvon's invitation to federate with the other South African communities. In 1880, when a rising of the Boers in the Transvaal was threatening, President Brand showed every desire to avert the conflict. He suggested that Sir Henry de Villiers, Chief Justice of Cape Colony, should be sent into the Transvaal to endeavour to gauge the true state of affairs in that country. This suggestion was not acted upon, but when war broke out in the Transvaal Brand declined to take any part in the struggle. In spite of the neutral attitude taken by their government a number of the Free State Boers, living in the northern part of the country, went to the Transvaal and joined their brethren then in arms against the British. This fact was not allowed to influence the friendly relations between the Free State and Great Britain. In 1888 Sir John Brand died. In him the Boers, not only in the Free State but in the whole of South Africa, lost one of the most enlightened and most upright rulers and leaders they have ever had. He realized the disinterested aims pursued by the British government, without always approving its methods. Though he had thrown the weight of his influence against Lord Carnarvon's federation scheme Brand disapproved racial rivalries.

During the period of Brand's presidency a great change, both political and economic, had come over South Africa. The renewal of the policy of British expansion had been answered by the formation of the Afrikander Bond, which represented the racial aspirations of the Dutch-speaking people, and had active branches in the Free State. This alteration in the political outlook was accompanied, and in part occasioned, by economic changes of great significance. The development of the diamond mines and of the gold and coal industries—of which Brand saw the beginning—had far-reaching consequences, bringing the Boer republics into vital contact with the new industrial era. The Free Staters, under Brand's rule, had shown considerable ability to adapt their policy to meet the altered situation. The one agreement was come to between the Free State and the Cape Colony government, whereby the latter were empowered to extend, at their own cost, their railway system to Bloemfontein. The Free State retained the right to purchase this extension at cost price, a right they exercised after the Jameson Raid.

Having accepted the assistance of the Cape government in constructing its railway, the state also in 1889 entered into a Customs Union Convention with them. The convention was the outcome of a conference held at Cape Town in 1888, at which delegates from Natal, the Free State and the Colony attended. Natal at this time had not seen its way to entering the Customs Union, but did so at a later date.

In January 1889 Mr F. W. Reitz was elected president of the Free State. His accession to the presidency marked the beginning of a new and disastrous line of policy in the external affairs of the country. Mr Reitz had no *Alliance with the Transvaal.* sooner got into office than a meeting was arranged with Mr Kruger, president of the Transvaal, at which various terms of an agreement dealing with the railways, terms of a treaty of amity and commerce and what was called a political treaty, were discussed and decided upon. The political treaty referred in general terms to a federal union between the Transvaal and the Free State, and bound each of them to help the other, whenever the independence of either should be assailed or threatened from without, unless the state so called upon for assistance should be able to show the injustice of the cause of quarrel in which the other state had engaged. While thus committed to a dangerous alliance with its northern neighbour no change was made in internal administration. The Free State, in fact, from its geographical position reaped the benefits without incurring the anxieties consequent on the settlement of a large *uitlander* population on the Rand. The state, however, became increasingly identified with the reactionary party in the Transvaal. In 1895 the volksraad passed a resolution, in which they declared their readiness to entertain a proposition from the Transvaal in favour of some form of federal union. In the same year Mr Reitz retired from the presidency of the Free State, and was succeeded in February 1896 by M. T. Steyn (*q.v.*), a judge of the High Court. In 1896 President Steyn visited Pretoria, where he received an ovation as the probable future president of the two Republics. A further offensive and defensive alliance between the two Republics was then entered into, under which the Free State took up arms on the outbreak of hostilities with the Transvaal in 1899.

In 1897 President Kruger, bent on still further cementing the union with the Free State, visited Bloemfontein. It was on this occasion that President Kruger, referring to the London Convention, spoke of Queen Victoria as a *kwaaje Vrouw*, an expression which caused a good deal of offence in England at the time, but which, to any one familiar with the homely phraseology of the Boers, obviously was not meant by President Kruger as insulting.

In order to understand the attitude which the Free State took at this time in relation to the Transvaal, it is necessary to review the history of Mr Reitz from an earlier date. Previously to his becoming president of the Free State *The Afrikander ideal.* he had acted as its Chief Justice, and still earlier in life had practised as an advocate in Cape Colony. In 1881 Mr Reitz had, in conjunction with Mr Steyn, come under the influence of a clever German named Borckenhagen, the editor of the *Bloemfontein Express.* These three men were principally responsible for the formation of the Afrikander Bond (see CAPE COLONY: *History*). From 1881 onwards they cherished the idea of an independent South Africa. Brand had been far too sagacious to be led away by this pseudo-nationalist dream, and did his utmost to discountenance the Bond. At the same time his policy was guided by a sincere patriotism, which looked to the true prosperity of the Free State as well as to that of the whole of South Africa. From his death may be dated the disastrous line of policy which led to the extinction of the state as a republic. The one prominent member of the volksraad who inherited the traditions and enlightened views of President Brand was Mr (Afterwards Sir) John G. Fraser. Mr Fraser, who was an unsuccessful candidate for the presidency in 1896, was the son of a Presbyterian minister, who had acted as a minister in the Dutch Reformed Church since the middle of the century. He grew up in the country of his father's adoption, and he consistently warned the Free State of the inevitable result—the loss of independence—which must follow their mischievous policy in being led by the Transvaal. The mass of Boers in the Free State, deluded by a belief in Great Britain's weakness, paid no heed to his remonstrances. Mr Fraser lived to see the fulfilment of these prophecies. After the British occupation of Bloemfontein he cast in his lot with the Imperial Government, realizing that it had fought for those very principles which President Brand and he had laboured for in bygone years. On entering Bloemfontein in 1900 the British obtained possession of certain state papers which contained records of negotiations between the Transvaal and the Orange Free State. The evidence contained in these state records so clearly marks the difference between the policy of Mr Kruger and the pacific, commercial policy of President Brand and his followers, that the documents call for careful consideration. From these papers it was found that, in 1887, two secret conferences had taken place between representatives of the Republics, dealing with various political and economical questions. At the first of these conferences, held in Pretoria, the object of the Free State deputies were to arrange a general treaty of amity and commerce which would knit the states more closely together, and to come to some agreement with reference to the scheme for building a railway across the Free State from the Cape, to connect with a farther extension in the Transvaal to Pretoria. The deputation also urged the Transvaal to join the South African Customs Union. Both of these suggestions were strongly disapproved by Mr Kruger, inasmuch as they meant knitting together the Boer republics and the British possessions, instead of merely bringing the Free State into completer dependence on the Transvaal. From the minutes of this conference it is clear that the two deputations were practically at cross purposes. In the minds of President Kruger and his immediate followers one idea was dominant, that of ousting and keeping out at all costs British influence and interests. On the part of the Free State there was obviously a genuine desire to further the best interests of the state, together with the general prosperity of the whole of South Africa. In President Kruger's eyes British trade meant ruin; he desired to keep it out of the Republic at all costs, and he begged the Free State to delay the construction of their railway until the Delagoa Bay line was completed. He said, " Delagoa is a life or death question for us. Help us; if you hook on to the Colony you cut our throat. . . How can our state exist without the Delagoa railway? Keep free." With regard to the Customs Union, President Kruger was equally emphatic; he begged the Free State to steer clear of it. " Customs Unions," he said, " are made between equal states with equal access to harbours. We are striving to settle the question of our own harbour peacefully. The English will only use their position to swindle the Transvaal of its proper receipts." In response, Mr Fraser, one of the Free State delegates, remarked that a harbour requires forts, soldiers, ships and sailors to man them, or else it would be at the mercy of the first gunboat that happened to assail it. President Kruger replied that once the Transvaal had a harbour foreign powers would intervene. Mr Wolmarans was as emphatic as President Kruger. " Wait a few years. . . . You know our secret policy. We cannot treat the [Cape] Colony as we would treat you. The Colony would destroy us. It is not the Dutch there we are fighting against. Time shall show what we mean to do with them; for the present we must keep them off."

The result of this conference was a secret session of the Transvaal volksraad and the proposition of a secret treaty with the Free State, by which each state should bind itself not to build railways to its frontier without the consent of the other, the eastern and northern frontiers of the Transvaal being excepted. The railway from Pretoria to Bloemfontein was to be proceeded with; neither party was to enter the Customs Union without the consent of the other. The Transvaal was to pay £30,000 annually to the Free State for loss incurred for not having the railway to Cape Colony. Such a treaty as the one proposed would simply have enslaved the Free State to the Transvaal, and it was rejected by the Free State volksraad. President Kruger

Anti-British designs.

determined on a still more active measure, and proceeded with Dr Leyds to interview President Brand at Bloemfontein. A series of meetings took place in October of the same year (1887). President Brand opened the proceedings by proposing a treaty of friendship and free trade between the two Republics, in which a number of useful and thoroughly practical provisions were set forth. President Kruger, however, soon brushed these propositions aside, and responded by stating that, in consideration of the common enemy and the dangers which threatened the Republic, an offensive and defensive alliance must be preliminary to any closer union. To this Brand rejoined that, as far as the offensive was concerned, he did not desire to be a party to attacking any one, and as for the defensive, where was the pressing danger of the enemy which Kruger feared? The Free State was on terms of friendship with its neighbours, nor (added Brand) would the Transvaal have need for such an alliance as the one proposed if its policy would only remain peaceful and conciliatory. At a later date in the conference (see TRANSVAAL) President Brand apparently changed his policy, and himself drafted a constitution resembling that of the United States. This constitution appears to have been modelled on terms a great deal too liberal and enlightened to please Mr Kruger, whose one idea was to have at his command the armed forces of the Free State when he should require them, and who pressed for an offensive and defensive alliance. Brand refused to allow the Free State to be committed to a suicidal treaty, or dragged into any wild policy which the Transvaal might deem it expedient to adopt. The result of the whole conference was that Kruger returned to Pretoria completely baffled, and for a time the Free State was saved from being a party to the fatal policy into which others subsequently drew it. Independent power of action was retained by Brand for the Free State in both the railway and Customs Union questions.

After Sir John Brand's death, as already stated, a series of agreements and measures gradually subordinated Free State interests to the mistaken ambition and narrow views of the Transvaal. The influence which the Kruger party had obtained in the Free State was evidenced by the presidential election in 1896, when Mr Steyn received forty-one votes against nineteen cast for Mr Fraser. That this election should have taken place immediately after the Jameson Raid probably increased Mr Steyn's majority. Underlying the new policy adopted by the Free State was the belief held, if not by President Steyn himself, at least by his followers, that the two republics combined would be more than a match for the power of Great Britain should hostilities occur.

In December 1897 the Free State revised its constitution in reference to the franchise law, and the period of residence necessary to obtain naturalization was reduced from five to three years. The oath of allegiance to the state was alone required, and no renunciation of nationality was insisted upon. In 1898 the Free State also acquiesced in the new convention arranged with regard to the Customs Union between the Cape Colony, Natal, Basutoland and the Bechuanaland Protectorate. These measures suggest that a slight reaction against the extreme policy of President Kruger had set in. But events were moving rapidly in the Transvaal, and matters had proceeded too far for the Free State to turn back. In May 1899 President Steyn suggested the conference at Bloemfontein between President Kruger and Sir Alfred Milner, but this act, if it expressed a genuine desire for reconciliation, was too late. President Kruger had got the Free State ensnared in his meshes. The Free Staters were practically bound, under the offensive and defensive alliance, in case hostilities arose with Great Britain, either to denounce the policy to which they had so unwisely been secretly party, or to throw in their lot with the Transvaal. War occurred, and they accepted the inevitable consequence. For President Steyn and the Free State of 1899, in the light of the *Boer War* negotiations we have recorded, neutrality was impossible. A resolution was passed by the volksraad on the 27th of September declaring that the state would observe its obligations to the Transvaal whatever might happen. Before war had actually broken out the Free State began to expel British subjects, and the very first act of war was committed by Free State Boers, who, on the 11th of October, seized a train upon the border belonging to Natal. The events of the war are given elsewhere (see TRANSVAAL: *History*).

After the surrender of Cronje at Paardeberg on the 27th of February 1900 Bloemfontein was occupied by the British troops under Lord Roberts (March 13,) and on the 28th of May a proclamation was issued annexing the Free State to the British dominions under the title of Orange River Colony. For nearly two years longer the burghers kept the field under Christian de Wet (*q.v.*), and other leaders, but by the articles of peace signed on the 31st of May 1902 British sovereignty was acknowledged. A civil administration of the colony was established early in 1901 with Sir Alfred Milner as governor. Major (afterwards Sir) H. J. Goold-Adams was appointed lieutenant-governor, Milner being governor also of the Transvaal, which country claimed most of his attention. A nominated legislative council was established in June 1902 of which Sir John Fraser and a number of other prominent ex-burghers became unofficial members. The railways and constabulary of the two colonies were (1903) placed under an inter-colonial council; active measures were taken for the repatriation of the prisoners of war and the residents in the concentration camps, and in every direction vigorous and successful efforts were made to repair the ravages of the war. Over £4,000,000 was spent by the British government in Orange Colony alone on these objects. At the same time efforts were made, with a fair measure of success, to strengthen the British element in the country by means of land settlements. Special attention was also devoted to the development of the resources of the country by building new lines of railway traversing the fertile south-eastern districts and connecting Bloemfontein with Natal and with Kimberley. The educational system was reorganized and greatly improved.

To a certain extent the leading ex-burghers co-operated with the administration in the work of reconstruction. The loss of their independence was, however, felt bitterly by the Boers, and the attitude assumed by the majority was highly critical of the work of the government. Having recovered from the worst effects of the war the Boers, both in the Transvaal and Orange Colony, began in 1904 to make organized efforts to regain their political ascendancy, and to bring pressure on the government in respect to compensation, repatriation, the position of the Dutch language, education and other subjects on which they alleged unfair treatment. This agitation, as far as the Orange River Colony was concerned, coincided with the return to South Africa of ex-President Steyn. Mr Steyn had gone to Europe at the close of the war and did not take the oath of allegiance to the British Crown until the autumn of 1904. A congress of ex-burghers was held at Brandfort in December 1904, when among other resolutions passed was one demanding the grant of self-government to the colony. This was followed in July 1905 by a conference at Bloemfontein, when it was resolved to form a national union. This organization, known as the *Oranje Unie*, was formally constituted in May 1906, but had been in existence for some months previously. A similar organization, called *Het Volk*, had been formed by the Transvaal Boers in January 1905. Both unions had constitutions almost identical with that of the Afrikander Bond, and their aims were similar—to secure the triumph of Boer ideals in state and society. Of the Oranjie Unie Mr Abraham Fischer became chairman, other prominent members being Messrs Hertzog, C. de Wet and Steyn. Mr Fischer, the leader of the party, was one of the ablest statesmen on the Boer side in the pre-war period. He was originally an attorney in Cape Colony and had joined the Free State bar in 1875. He became vice-president of the volksraad in 1893 and a member of the executive council of the state in 1896. He was one of the most trusted counsellors of Presidents Steyn and Kruger, and the ultimatum sent to the British on the eve of hostilities was recast by him. While the war was in progress he went to Europe to seek support for

the Boer cause. He returned to South Africa early in 1903 and was admitted to the bar of the Orange Colony.

A counter-organization was formed by the ex-burghers who had whole-heartedly accepted the new order of things. They took the title of the Constitutional party, and Sir John Fraser was chosen as chairman. In Bloemfontein the Constitutionalists had a strong following; elsewhere their supporters were numerically weak. It was noteworthy that the programmes of the two parties were very similar, the real difference between them being the attitude with which they regarded the British connexion. While the ideal of the Unie was an Afrikander state, the Constitutionalists desired the perfect equality of both white races.

The advent of a Liberal administration under Sir Henry Campbell-Bannerman in Great Britain in December 1905 completely altered the political situation in the late Boer states. The previous (Conservative) government had in March 1905 made public a form of representative government, intended to lead up to self-government for the Transvaal, and had intimated that a similar constitution would be subsequently conferred on the Orange Colony. The Campbell-Bannerman administration decided to do without this intermediary step in both colonies. In April 1906 a committee, under the chairmanship of Sir J. West-Ridgeway, was sent to South Africa to inquire into and report upon various questions regarding the basis of the franchise, single-member constituencies and kindred matters. There was in the Orange Colony a considerable body of opinion that the party system of government should be avoided, and that the executive should consist of three members elected by the single representative chamber it was desired to obtain, and three members nominated by the governor—in short, what was desired was a restoration as far as possible of the old Free State constitution. These views were laid before the committee on their visit to Bloemfontein in June 1906. When, however, the outline of the new constitution was made public in December 1906 it was found that the British government had decided on a party government plan which would have the inevitable and fully foreseen effect of placing the country in the power of the Boer majority. It was not until the 1st of July 1907 that the letters-patent conferring self-government on the colony were promulgated, the election for the legislative assembly taking place in November following. They resulted in the return of 29 members of the Oranjie Unie, 5 Constitutionalists and 4 Independents. The Constitutionalists won four of the five seats allotted to Bloemfontein, Sir John Fraser being among those returned. Following the elections the governor, Sir Hamilton Goold-Adams, sent for Mr Fischer, who formed a ministry, his colleagues being ex-General J.B.M. Hertzog, attorney-general and director of education; Dr A. E. W. Ramsbottom, treasurer; Christian de Wet, minister of agriculture, and Mr C. H. Wessels, minister of public works, &c. Mr Fischer, besides the premiership, held the portfolio of colonial secretary. The new ministry took office on the 27th of November. Of the members of the first legislative council five were supporters of the Oranjie Unie and five were regarded as Constitutionalists, the eleventh member holding the balance.

The responsible government entered upon its task in favourable conditions. Despite the many obstacles it had to meet, including drought, commercial depression and the hostility of many of the ex-burghers, the crown colony administration had achieved remarkable results. During each of its seven years of existence there had been a surplus of revenue over expenditure, despite the fact that taxation had not materially increased, save in respect to mining, which did not affect the general population. Custom duties were about the same as in 1898, but railway rates were materially lower and many new lines had been opened. The educational system had been placed on a sound basis. Departments of agriculture, mining, health and native affairs had been organized, and the civil service rendered thoroughly efficient. A substantial cash balance was left in the treasury for the use of the new government. Over 700 families had been settled on the land and thus an additional source of strength provided for the state. The first parliament under the new constitution met on the 18th of December 1907, when it was announced that the Transvaal and Orange Colony had each given notice of the termination of the intercolonial council with the intention of each colony to gain individual control of its railways and constabulary.

After a two days' session the legislature was prorogued until May 1908, when the chief measure submitted by the government *The* was an education bill designed to foster the knowledge *institu-* of the Dutch language. This measure became law *tion* (see above § *Education*). Parliament also passed a *move-* measure granting ex-President Steyn a pension of *ment.* £1000 a year and ex-President Reitz a pension of £500. In view of the dissolution of the intercolonial council a convention was signed at Pretoria on the 29th of May which made provision for the division of the common property, rights and liabilities of the Orange Colony and the Transvaal in respect to the railways and constabulary, and established for four years a joint board to continue the administration of the railway systems of the two colonies. The Orange Colony assumed responsibility for £7,700,000 of the guaranteed loan of £35,000,000 of 1903 (see TRANSVAAL: *Finance*). The colony took part during this month in an inter-state conference which met at Pretoria and Cape Town, and determined to renew the existing customs convention and to make no alteration in railway rates. These decisions were the result of an agreement to bring before the parliaments of the various colonies a resolution advocating the closer union of the South African states and the appointment of delegates to a national convention to frame a draft constitution. In this convention Mr Steyn took a leading and conciliatory part, and subsequently the Orange River legislature agreed to the terms drawn up by the convention for the unification of the four self-governing colonies. Under the imperial act by which unification was established (May 31, 1910) the colony entered the union under the style of the Free State Province. (For the union movement see SOUTH AFRICA: *History*.) Mr Fischer and General Hertzog became members of the first union ministry while Dr A. E. W. Ramsbottom, formerly colonial treasurer, became the first administrator of the Free State as a province of the union.

The period during which the province had been a self-governing colony had been one of steady progress in most directions, *Education* but was greatly embittered by the educational policy *contro-* pursued by General Hertzog. From the date of the *versy.* passing of the education act in the middle of 1908 until the absorption of the colony into the union, General Hertzog so administered the provisions of the act regarding the media of instruction as to compel every European child to receive instruction in every subject partly in the medium of Dutch. This policy of compulsory bilingualism was persisted in despite the vehement protests of the English-speaking community, and of the desire of many Dutch burghers that the medium of instruction for their children should be English. Attempts to adjust the difficulty were made and a conference on the subject was held at Bloemfontein in November 1909. It was fruitless, and in March 1910 Mr Hugh Gunn (director of education since 1904) resigned.[1] The action of General Hertzog had the support of his colleagues and of Mr Steyn and kept alive the racial spirit. Failing to obtain redress the English-speaking section of the community proceeded to open separate schools, the terms of the act of union leaving the management of elementary education to the provincial council.

AUTHORITIES.—A. H. Keane, *The Boer States; Land and People* (1900); The *Report* on the 1904 census (Bloemfontein, 1906); *The Statistical Year Book* (Bloemfontein) and other official publications; W. S. Johnson, *Orangia* (1906), a good elementary geography; *Précis of Information. Orange Free State and Griqualand West* (War Office, 1878); D. Aitton, "De Oranje Vrijstaat," *Tijds. K. Ned. Aard. Genoots.* Amsterdam, vol. xvii. (1900); H. Kloessel, *Die Südafrikanischen Republiken* (Leipzig, 1888). For a good early account of the country see Sir W. Cornwallis Harris, *Narrative of an Expedition into Southern Africa during 1836-37* (Bombay, 1838). For history see, in addition to the British, Cape and Orange

[1] See Mr Gunn's pamphlet, *The Language Question in the Orange River Colony, 1902-1910.*

Free State parliamentary papers, H. Dehérain, *L'Expansion des Boers au xixe siècle* (Paris, 1905); G. McCall Theal, *History of South Africa since 1795* (up to 1872), vols. ii., iii. and iv. (1908 ed.), and A. Wilmot's *Life and Times of Sir R. Southey* (1904). G. B. Beak's *The Aftermath of War* (1906) is an account of the repatriation work in the Orange River Colony. A. C. Murray and R. Cannon, *Map of the Orange River Colony* (6 sheets: 4 m. to 1 in., 1908). The place of publication, unless otherwise stated, is London. Consult also the bibliographies under GRIQUALAND, TRANSVAAL and SOUTH AFRICA.	(A. P. H.; F. R. C.)

ORANGEMEN, members of the Orange Society, an association of Irish Protestants, originating and chiefly flourishing in Ulster, but with ramifications in other parts of the United Kingdom, and in the British colonies. Orangemen derive their name from King William III. (Prince of Orange). They are enrolled in lodges in the ordinary form of a secret society. Their toasts, about which there is no concealment, indicate the spirit of the Orangemen. The commonest form is " the glorious, pious and immortal memory of the great and good King William, who saved us from popery, slavery, knavery, brass money and wooden shoes," with grotesque or truculent additions according to the orator's taste. The brass money refers to James II.'s finance, and the wooden shoes to his French allies. The final words are often " a fig for the bishop of Cork," in allusion to Dr Peter Browne, who, in 1715, wrote cogently against the practice of toasting the dead. Orangemen are fond of beating drums and flaunting flags with the legend " no surrender," in allusion to Londonderry. Orangeism is essentially political. Its original object was the maintenance of Protestant ascendancy, and that spirit still survives. The first regular lodges were founded in 1795, but the system existed earlier. The Brunswick clubs, founded to oppose Catholic emancipation, were sprigs from the original Orange tree. The orange flowers of the *Lilium bulbiferum* are worn in Ulster on the 1st and 12th July, the anniversaries of the Boyne and Aughrim. Another great day is the 5th of November, when William III. landed in Torbay.

ORANG-UTAN (" man of the woods "), the Malay name of the giant red man-like ape of Borneo and Sumatra, known to the Dyaks as the *mias*, and to most naturalists as *Simia satyrus*. The red, or brownish-red, colour of the long and coarse hair at once distinguishes the orang-utan from the African apes; a further point of distinction being the excessive length of the arms, which are of such proportions that the animal when in the upright posture (which it seldom voluntarily assumes) can rest on its bent knuckles. Very characteristic of the old males, which may stand as much as 5½ ft. in height, is the lateral expansion of the cheeks, owing to a kind of warty growth, thus producing an extraordinarily broad and flattened type of face. Such an expansion is however by no means characteristic of all the males of the species, and is apparently a feature of racial value. Another peculiarity of the males is the presence of a huge throat-sac or pouch on the front of the throat and chest, which may extend even to the arm-pits; although present in females, it does not reach nearly the same dimensions in that sex. More than half-a-dozen separate races of orang-utan are recognized in Borneo, where, however, they do not appear to be restricted to separate localities. In Sumatra the Deli and Langkat district is inhabited by *S. satyrus deliensis* and Abong by *S. s. abongensis*.

In Borneo the red ape inhabits the swampy forest-tract at the foot of the mountains. In confinement these apes (of which adult specimens have been exhibited in Calcutta) appear very slow and deliberate in their movements; but in their native forests they swing themselves from bough to bough and from tree to tree as fast as a man can walk on the ground beneath. They construct platforms of boughs in the trees, which are used as sleeping-places, and apparently occupied for several nights in succession. Jack-fruit or durian, the tough spiny hide of which is torn open with their strong fingers, forms the chief food of orang-utans, which also consume the luscious mangustin and other fruits. (See PRIMATES.)

ORANIENBAUM, a town of European Russia, in the government of St Petersburg, lying 100 ft. above the sea on the south

coast of the Gulf of Finland, opposite Kronstadt. Pop. (1897) 5333. It is well known for its imperial palace and as a summer resort for the inhabitants of St Petersburg, from which it is 25 m. W. by rail. In 1714 Menshikov, to whom the site was presented by Peter the Great, erected for himself the country-seat of Oranienbaum; but confiscated, like the rest of his estates, in 1727, it became an imperial residence. In 1743 the empress Elizabeth assigned the place to Peter III., who built there a castle, Peterstadt (now destroyed), for his Holstein soldiers.

ORAONS, an aboriginal people of Bengal. They call themselves Kurukh, and are sometimes also known as Dhangars. Their home is in Ranchi district and there are communities in the Chota Nagpur states and Palamau, while elsewhere they have scattered settlements, e.g. in Jalpaiguri and the Darjeeling Terai, whither they have gone to work in the tea-gardens. They number upwards of three quarters of a million. According to their traditions the tribe migrated from the west coast of India. The Oraons are a small race (average 5 ft. 2 in.); the usual colour is dark brown, but some are as light as Hindus. They are heavy-jawed, with large mouths, thick lips and projecting teeth. They reverence the sun, and acknowledge a supreme god, Dharmi or Dharmest, the holy one, who is perfectly pure, but whose beneficent designs are thwarted by evil spirits. They burn their dead, and the urn with the ashes is suspended outside the deceased's hut to await the period of the year especially set apart for burials. The language is harsh and guttural, having much connexion with Tamil. In 1901 the total number of speakers of Kurukh or Oraon in all India was nearly 600,000.

See E. T. Dalton, *Descriptive Ethnology of Bengal* (Calcutta, 1872), and his article "The Kols of Chota-Nagpore," in *Supplement to Journ. of Asiatic Soc. of Bengal*, vol. xxxv. (1887), part ii. p. 153; Batsch, "Notes on the Oraon Language" in *Journ. Roy. Asiatic Soc. of Bengal* for 1866; F. B. Bradley Birt, *The Story of an Indian Upland* (1905).

ORATORIO, the name given to a form of religious music with chorus, solo voices and instruments, independent or at least separable from the liturgy, and on a larger scale than the cantata (q.v.). Its early history is involved in that of opera (see ARIA and OPERA), though there is a more definite interest in its antecedents. The term is supposed, with good reason, to be derived from the fact that St Filippo Neri's Oratory was the place for which Animuccia's setting of the *Laudi Spirituali* were written; and the custom of interspersing these hymns among liturgical or other forms of the recitation of a Biblical story is certainly one of several sources to which the idea of modern oratorio may be traced. Further claim to the "invention" of the oratorio cannot be given to Animuccia. A more ancient source is the use of incidental music in miracle-plays and in such medieval dramatic processions as the 12th-century *Prose de L'Âne*, which on the 1st of January celebrated at Beauvais the Flight into Egypt. But the most ancient origin of all has hardly been duly brought into line, although it is the only form that led to classically artistic results before the time of Bach. This is the Roman Catholic rite of reciting, during Holy Week, the story of the Passion according to the Four Gospels, in such a manner that the words of the Evangelist are sung in Gregorian tones by a tenor, all directly quoted utterances are sung by voices appropriate to the speakers, and the *responso turbae* or utterances of the whole body of disciples (e.g. "Lord, is it I ?"). and of crowds, are sung by a chorus. The only portion of this scheme that concerned composers was the *responsa turbae*, to which it was optional to add polyphonic settings of the Seven Last Words or other special utterances of the Saviour. The narrative and the parts of single speakers were sung in the Gregorian tones appointed in the liturgy. Thus the settings of the Passion by Victoria and Soriano represent, in a very simple form, a perfect solution of the art-problem of oratorio, as that problem presented itself to an age in which "dramatic music," or even "epic music," would have been a contradiction in terms. It has been aptly said that the object of the composer in setting such words as "Crucify Him" was not to express the feelings of an infuriated crowd, but rather to express the contrition of devout Christians telling the story; though this view must be admitted to be,

like the 16th-century music itself, decidedly more modern than the quaintly dramatic traditional methods of performance. As an art-form this early Passion-music owes its perfection primarily to the church. The liturgy gives body to all the art-forms of 16th-century church music, and it is for the composer to spiritualize or debase them by his style.

With the monodic revolution at the beginning of the 17th century the history of oratorio as an art-form controlled by composers has its real beginning. There is nothing but its religious subject to distinguish the first oratorio from the first opera; and so Emilio del Cavaliere's *Rappresentazione di anima e di corpo* (1600) is in no respect outside the line of early attempts at dramatic music. In the course of the 17th century the differentiation between opera and oratorio increased, but not systematically. The gradual revival of choral art found its best opportunity in the treatment of sacred subjects; not only because it was with such subjects that the greatest 16th-century choral art was associated, but also because these subjects tended to discourage such vestiges of dramatic realism as had not been already suppressed by the aria form. This form arose as a concession to dire musical necessity and to the growing vanity of singers, and it speedily became almost the only possibility of keeping music alive, or at least embalmed, until the advent of Bach and Handel. The efforts of Carissimi (d. 1674) in oratorio clearly show the limited rise from the musical standards of opera that was then possible where music was emancipated from the stage. Yet in his art the corruption of church music by secular ideas is far more evident than any tendency to elevate Biblical music-drama to the dignity of church music. Normal Italian oratorio remains indistinguishable from serious Italian opera until as late as the boyhood of Mozart. Handel's *La Resurrezione* and *Il Trionfo del Tempo* contain many pieces almost simultaneously used in his operas, and they show not the slightest tendency to indulge in choral writing. Nor did *Il Trionfo del Tempo* become radically different from the musical masques of *Acis and Galatea* and *Semele*, when Handel at the close of his life dictated an adaptation of it to an English translation with several choral and other numbers interpolated from other works. Yet between these two versions of the same work lies more than half the history of classical oratorio. The rest lies in that specialized German art of which the text centres round the Passion and the music culminates in Bach; after which there is no very dignified connected history of the form, until the two streams, sadly silted up, and never afterwards quite pure, united in Mendelssohn.

One feature of the Reformation in Germany was that Luther was very musical. This had the curious result that, though the German Reformation was far from conservative in its attitude towards ancient liturgy, it retained almost everything which makes for musical coherence in a church service; while the English church, with all its insistence on historic continuity, so rearranged the liturgy that no possible music for an English church service can ever form a coherent whole. We are accustomed to think of German Passion-music as typically Protestant; yet the four *Passions* and the *Historia der Auferstehung Christi* of H. Schütz (who was born in 1585, exactly a century before Bach) are as truly the descendants of Victoria's Passions as they are the ancestors of Bach's. The difference between them and the Roman Catholic Passions is, of course, eminently characteristic of the Reformation: the language is German (so that it may be "understanded of the people"), and the narrative and dialogue is set to free composition instead of to forms of Gregorian chant, though it is written in a sort of Gregorian notation. Schütz's preface to the *Historia der Auferstehung Christi* shows that he writes his recitative for solo voices, though he calls it *Chor des Evangelisten* and *Chor der Personen Colloquenten*. The *Marcus-Passion* is, on internal evidence, of doubtful authenticity, being later in style and quite stereotyped in its recitative. But in the other Passions, and most of all in the *Auferstehung*, the recitative is wonderfully expressive. It was probably accompanied by the organ, though the Passions contain no hint of accompaniment at all. In the

Auferstehung the Evangelist is accompanied by four viols da gamba in preference to the organ. In any case, Schütz tells us, the players are to "execute appropriate runs or passages" during the sustained chords. Apart from their remarkable dramatic force, Schütz's oratorios show another approximation to the Passion oratorio of Bach's time in ending with a non-scriptural hymn-chorus, more or less clearly based on a chorale-tune. But in the course of the work the Scriptural narrative is as uninterrupted as it is in the Roman Catholic Passions. And there is one respect in which the *Auferstehung*, although perhaps the richest and most advanced of all Schütz's works, is less realistic than either the Roman Passions or those of later times; namely, that single persons, other than the Evangelist, are frequently represented by more than one voice. In the case of the part of the Saviour, this might, to modern minds, seem natural as showing a reverent avoidance of impersonation; and it was not without an occasional analogy in Roman Catholic Passion-music (in the polyphonic settings of special words). But Schütz's Passions show no such convention; this feature is peculiar to the *Auferstehung*; and, while the three holy women and the two angels in the scene at the tomb are represented realistically by three and two imitative voices, it is curious to see Mary Magdalene elsewhere always represented by two sopranos, even though Schütz remarks in his preface that "one of the two voices may be sung and the other done *instrumentaliter*, or, *si placet*, simply left out."

Shortly before Bach, Passion oratorios, not always so entitled, were represented by several remarkable and mature works of art, most notably by R. Keiser (1673-1739). Chorale-tunes, mostly in plain harmony, were freely interspersed in order that the congregation might take part in what was, after all, a musical church service for Holy Week. The feelings of devout contemplative Christians on each incident of the story were expressed in accompanied recitatives (*arioso*) leading to arias; and the Scriptural narrative was sung to dramatic recitative and ejaculatory chorus on the ancient Roman plan, exactly followed, even in the detail that the Evangelist was a tenor.

The difference between Bach's Passions and those of his predecessors and contemporaries is simply the difference between his music and theirs. Where his chorus represents the whole body of Christendom it has as peculiar an epic power as it is dramatic where it represents with brevity and rapid climax the *responsa turbae* of the Scriptural narrative. Take, for example, the double chorus at the beginning of the *Passion according to St Matthew*, where one chorus calls to the other to "come and behold" what has come to pass, and the other chorus asks "whom?" "what?" "whither?" to each exhortation, until at last the two choruses join, while above all is heard, phrase by phrase, the hymn "O Lamm Gottes unschuldig." Still more powerful, indeed unapproached even in external effect by anything else in classical or modern oratorio, is the duet with chorus that follows the narrative of the betrayal. Its tremendous final outburst in the brief indignant appeal to heaven for the vengeance of damnation on the traitor is met by the calm conclusion of the Evangelist's interrupted narrative and the overpowering tenderness of the great figured chorale ("O Mensch bewein' dein' Sünde gross"), which ends the first part with a call to repentance. Such contrasts might seem to be but the natural use of fine opportunities furnished by the librettist; but the composer appears to owe less to the librettist when we find that this chorale originally belonged to the *Passion according to St John*, where it was to follow Peter's denial of Christ. To modern ears the most striking device in the Matthew Passion is that by which the part of Christ is separated from all the rest by being accompanied with the string band, generally at a high pitch, though deepening at the most solemn moments with an effect of sublime euphony and tenderness. And a peculiarly profound and startling thought, which has not always met with the attention it deserves, is the omission of this musical halo at the words "Eli, Eli, lama sabacthani." These points are aesthetically parallel with Wagnerian *Leit-motif*, though entirely different in method. (See OPERA.)

In his amazing power of declamation Bach was not altogether unanticipated by Keiser, but no one before or since approached him in sustained elevation and variety of oratorio style. Analogies to the forms of Passion music may be found in many of Bach's church-cantatas; a very favourite form being the *Dialogus*; as, for instance, a dispute between a fearing and a trusting soul, with, perhaps, the voice of the Saviour heard from a distance; or a dialogue between Christ and the Church, on the lines of the Song of Solomon. The *Christmas Oratorio*, a set of six closely connected church-cantatas for performance on separate days, is treated in exactly the same way as the Passions, with a larger proportion of non-dramatic choruses expressive of the triumphant gratitude of Christendom. Many of the single church-cantatas are called oratorios. If it were not that Bach's idea of oratorio seems to be definitely connected with that of dialogue,[1] there is really no reason in musical terminology why the *B minor Mass* should not be so called, for it can never have been liturgical either in a Roman Catholic or in a Protestant church. But in all respects it stands alone; and we must now return to Handel's far more heterogeneous work, which forms the staple of almost everything else that has been understood by oratorio until the most recent times.

Handel discovered and matured every possibility of oratorio as an art-form, except such as may now be brought to light by those composers with whom the influence of Wagner is not too overwhelming for them to consider how far his principles are applicable to an art unconnected with the stage. Handel shows us that a definite oratorio style may exist in many different degrees. He was evidently impressed by the German forms of Passion-music as combining the utmost dramatic interest with the most intense contemplative devotion; and it is significant that it was after he came to England, and before his first English oratorio, that he set to music the famous poetic version of the Passion by Brockes, a version which had been adopted by all the German composers of the time, and, which, with very necessary and interesting improvements of taste, was largely drawn upon by Bach for the text of his *Johannes-Passion*. Handel's *Brockes-Passion* does not appear ever to have been performed, though Bach found access to it and made a careful copy; and it is difficult to see what motive, except interest in the form, Handel had for composing it. At all events it furnishes an important connecting-link between Bach's solution of the problem of oratorio and the various other solutions which Handel afterwards produced so successfully. He soon discovered how many kinds of oratorio were possible. The freedom from stage restrictions admitted of subjects ranging from semi-dramatic histories, like those of *Saul, Esther* and *Belshazzar*, to cosmic schemes based exclusively on the words of the Bible, such as *Israel in Egypt* and the *Messiah*. Between these types there is every gradation of organization; and it may be added, every gradation between sacred and secular subjects and treatment. The very name of Handel's first English oratorio, *Esther*, with the facts of its production as a masque and the origin of its libretto in Racine, show the transition from the stage to the church; and a really scandalous example of the converse transition may be found by any one rash enough to look for the source of some of Haman's music in the *Brockes-Passion*. Roughly speaking we may reduce the types of Handelian oratorio to a convenient three; not divisible among works as wholes, but always evident here and there. Firstly, there is the semi-operatic method, in which the arias are the utterances of characters in the story, while the conception of the chorus rarely diverges from that of multitudes of actors (*e.g. Athalia, Belshazzar, Saul*, &c.). The second method is a more or less recognisable application of the forms of the Passion-music to other subjects, without, however, the conception of a special rôle of narrator, but (as, for instance, in "Envy, eldest born of Hell" in *Saul*) with the definite conception of the choruses as descriptive of the feelings of spectators rather than of actors. Handel's

[1] It is possible that a false etymology may by Bach's time have given this colour to the word oratorio. Schütz inscribes a monodic sacred piece "in stilo Oratorio," meaning "in the style of recitative."

audience demanded an inconvenient number of arias; most of which are clumsily accounted for by a conventional assignment to dramatic rôles with a futile attempt at love-interest; which makes many of the best solos in *Saul* and *Joshua* rather absurd. The third Handelian method is that which has since become embodied in the modern type of sacred or secular cantata; a series of choruses and numbers on a subject altogether beyond the scope of dramatic narrative (as, for instance, the greater part of *Solomon*), and, in the case of the *Messiah* and *Israel in Egypt*, treated entirely in the words of Scripture.

After Bach and Handel the history of oratorio becomes disjointed. The rise of the sonata style, which brought life to the opera, was almost wholly bad for the oratorio; since not only did it cause a serious decline in choral art by distracting attention from that organization of texture which is essential even to mere euphony in choral writing (see COUNTERPOINT and CONTRAPUNTAL FORMS), but its dramatic power became more and more disturbing to the essentially epic treatment demanded by the conditions of oratorio. Bach and Handel (especially Handel) were as dramatic in characterization as the greatest epic poets, and were just as far removed from the theatre. Any doubt on this point is removed by the history of Handelian opera and the reforms of Gluck. But the power of later composers to rise above the growing swarms of 18th-century and 19th-century oratorio-mongers depended largely on the balance between their theatrical and contemplative sensibilities. Academicism naturally mistrusted the theatre, but, in the absence of any contemplative depth beyond that of a tactful asceticism, it has then and ever since made spasmodic concessions to theatrical effect, with the intention of avoiding pedantry, and with the effect of encouraging vulgarity. Philipp Emanuel Bach's oratorios, though not permanently convincing works of art, achieved a remarkably true balance of style in the earlier days of the conflict; indeed, with judicious reduction to the size of a large cantata, *Die Israeliten in der Wüste* (1769) would perhaps bear revival almost better than Haydn's *Tobias* (1774), in spite of the superior musical value of that ambitious forerunner of *The Creation* and *The Seasons*. These two great products of Haydn's old age owe their vitality not only to Haydn's combination of contrapuntal and choral mastery with his unsurpassable freedom of movement in the sonata style, but also to his priceless rediscovery of the fact (well known to Bach, the composer of " Mein gläubiges Herze," but since forgotten) that, in Haydn's own words, " God will not be angry with me for worshipping him in a cheerful manner." This is the very spirit of St Francis of Assisi, and it brings the naively realistic birds and beasts of *The Creation* into line with even the Bacchanalian parts of the mainly secular *Seasons*, and so removes Haydn from the dangers of a definitely, bad taste, which began to beset Roman Catholic oratorio on the one hand, and those of no taste at all, which engulfed Protestant oratorio on the other.

From the moment when music became independent of the church, Roman Catholic religious music, liturgical or other, lost its high artistic position. Some of the technical hindrances to greatness in liturgical music after the Golden Age are mentioned in the article MASS; but the status of Roman Catholic non-liturgical religious music was from the outset lowered by the use of the vulgar tongue, since that implied a condescension to the laity, and composers could not but be affected by the assumption that oratorio belonged to a lower sphere than Latin church music. With this element of condescension came a reluctance to foster the fault of intellectual pride by criticizing pious verse on grounds of taste. Even in Protestant England this reluctance still causes educated people to strain tolerance of bad hymns to an extent which apostles of culture denounce as positively immoral: but the initial impossibility of basing a non-Latin Roman Catholic oratorio directly on the Bible would already have been detrimental to good taste in religious musical texts even if criticism were not disarmed. It must be confessed that Protestant taste (as shown in the texts of many of Bach's cantatas) was often unsurpassably bad; but in its most morbid phases its badness was mainly barbarian, and could either be

ignored by composers and listeners, or easily improved away, as Bach showed in his alterations of Brockes's vile verses in the *Passion according to St John*. But the bad taste of the text of Beethoven's *Christus am Oelberge* (*The Mount of Olives*, c. 1800) is ineradicable, for it represents the standpoint of writers who may be very devout and innocent, but whose purest source of sacred art has been the pictures of Guido Reni. It was one thing for Sir Joshua Reynolds to admire the wrong period of Italian art: he had his own access to great ideas; but for Beethoven's librettist, who had no such access, it was very different. The real sacred subject has no chance of penetrating through a tradition which is neither naïve nor ecclesiastical, but is simply that of a long-tolerated comfortable vulgarity. An operatic tenor represents the Saviour; an operatic soprano represents the ministering angel; and in the garden of Gethsemane the two sing an operatic duet. The music is brilliant and well worthy of Beethoven's early powers, but he afterwards greatly regretted it; and indeed its circumstances are intolerable, and the English attempt at a new libretto (*Engedi*, or *David in the Wilderness*) only substituted ineptitude for irreverence.

Schubert's wonderful fragment *Lazarus* (1820) suffers less from the sickliness of its text; for the music seizes on a certain genuine quality aimed at by all typical Roman Catholic religious verse-writers, and embodies it in a kind of romantic mysticism unexampled in Protestant oratorio. Modern literature shows this peculiar strain in Cardinal Newman's *Dream of Gerontius*, just as Sir Edward Elgar's setting of that poem to music of Wagnerian continuity and texture presents the only parallel discoverable later or earlier to the slightly oppressive aroma of Schubert's unique experiment.[1] *Lazarus* also surprises us by a rather invertebrate continuity of flow, anticipating early Wagnerian opera; indeed, in almost every respect it is two generations ahead of its time; and, if only Schubert had finished it and allowed it to see publicity, the history of 19th-century oratorio might have become a more interesting subject than it is.

The ascendancy of Mendelssohn, as things happened, is really its main redeeming feature. Mendelssohn applied an unprecedented care and a wide general culture to the structure and criticism of his libretto (see his correspondence with Schubring, his principal helper with the texts of *St Paul* and *Elijah*), and was able to bear witness of his new-found gospel according to Bach by introducing chorales into *St Paul* as well as by disinterring and performing Bach's works. But he had not the strength to rescue oratorio from the slough into which it had now fallen, no less in Protestant than in Roman Catholic forms.

As the interest in Biblical themes becomes more independent of church and dogma, oratorio once more tends to become confused with Biblical opera. The singular fragrance and tenderness of the best parts of Berlioz's little masterpiece *L'Enfance du Christ* (put together from sections composed between 1847 and 1854) give it high artistic value; but if " oratorio " means " sacred music " Berlioz was incapable of anything of the sort; for the Christianity of his *Grande Messe des morts* and his *Te Deum* is the Christianity of Napoleon; and, if oratorio means a consistent treatment of a legend or subject in terms of musical epic, Berlioz can never fix his attention long enough to remember how he began by the time he has got half way through. Though Berlioz's essay in oratorio is not quite so irresponsible a vocal-symphonic-dramatic medley as his *Roméo et Juliette* and *Damnation de Faust*, it unmistakably marks a transition towards the complete secularizing of the Bible for musical purposes. But the long-continued prejudice in England against the representation of religious subjects on the stage has wrought peculiar confusion in the theory of their romantic treatment in music. It may be noted as a curiosity that Saint-Saëns's Biblical opera, *Samson et Dalila* (written in 1877), after being known in England for many quiet years as an oratorio, suddenly, in 1910, was permitted by the censor of plays, under royal command, to be produced at Covent Garden for what it was intended. It may

[1] Schubert's well-known cantata, *Miriam's Siegesgesang*, has been discussed as a small oratorio; but it is of slight artistic and no historic importance.

even be suggested that this occurred just early enough to prevent Strauss's *Salome* from being regarded by the British public as an oratorio.

The earnest efforts of César Franck prevented French oratorio from drifting entirely towards the stage; and meanwhile year by year Brahms's *Deutsches Requiem* (completed, except for one movement, in 1868) towers ever higher above all choral music since Beethoven's *Mass in D*, and draws us away from the semi-dramatic oratorio towards the musically perfectible form of an enlarged cantata in which a group of choral movements is concentrated on a set of religious ideas differing from liturgical forms only in free choice of text. Within the essentially non-theatrical limitations of dramatic or epic oratorio, we may note the spirited new departures of Sir Charles Stanford in *Eden* (1891), and of Sir Hubert Parry in *Judith* (1888), *Job* (1892) and *King Saul* (1894), which showed that Wagnerian *Leitmotif* and continuity might well avail to produce an oratorio style standing to Mendelssohn as Wagner stands to Mozart, if musical interest be retained in the foreground. Freedom from the restrictions of the stage also means absence of the resources of the stage, so that Wagnerian *Leitmotif* is no sufficient substitute for formal musical coherence when the audience has no action before its eyes. Accordingly these leaders of the English musical renascence are by no means exclusively Wagnerian in their oratorios. A fine and typical example of their peculiar non-theatrical resources may be seen in the end of *King Saul*, where Parry (who, like Wagner, is his own librettist) makes the Witch of Endor foresee the battle of Gilboa, and allows her tale to become real in the telling: so that it is followed immediately by the final dirge. (D. F. T.)

ORATORY (Lat. *oratoria*, sc. *ars*; from *orare*, to speak or pray), the art of speaking eloquently or in accordance with the rules of rhetoric (q.v.). From Lat. *oratorium*, sc. *templum*, a place of prayer, comes the use of the word for a small chapel or place of prayer for the use of private individuals, generally attached to a mansion and sometimes to a church. The name is also given to small chapels built to commemorate some special deliverance.

ORATORY OF ST PHILIP NERI, CONGREGATION OF THE, or ORATORIANS, a religious order consisting of a number of independent houses. The first congregation was formally organized in 1575 by the Florentine priest, Philip Neri. (See NERI, PHILIP.)

ORB, a circle or ring (Lat. *orbis*), hence a globe or disk or other spherical object. It is thus used, chiefly poetically, of any of the heavenly bodies, including the earth itself (Lat. *orbis terrarum*), or of the eye-ball or eye. The "orb," also known as the "mound" (Lat. *mundus*, "world"), consisting of a globe surmounted by a cross, forms part of many regalia, being a symbol of sovereignty (see REGALIA). In architecture the meaning to be attached to the word "orb" is doubtful. It is usually now taken to mean properly a blank or blind window, and thence a blank panel. If so the word represents Lat. *orbus*, "bereft of," "orphaned," *fenestra orba luminis*. It is also identified with a circular boss concealing the intersection of arches in a vault.

ORBETELLO, a town of Tuscany, Italy, in the province of Grosseto, 24 m. S. by E. of Grosseto by rail, 13 ft. above sea-level. Pop. (1901) 4188 (town), 5335 (commune). It is situated on a tongue of land projecting westward into a lagoon which is enclosed on the W. and S. by two long narrow sandy spits, and on the seaward (S.W.) side by the peninsula of Monte Argentario. A causeway connecting the town with this peninsula was built across the lagoon in 1842. On every side except the landward (E.) side the town is enclosed by an ancient terrace wall of polygonal work, and tombs have been discovered in the vicinity and even within the town itself. On the N. side of the promontory are the remains of a Roman villa partly below sea-level. The town must thus occupy an ancient site, the name of which is unknown. The town still has the bastions which the Spaniards built during the period (1557–1713) when they were masters of this corner of Italy. There is a large convict prison with which is connected another at Porto Ercole, on the east side of the peninsula. The mother house of the Passionist order crowns an eminence of Monte Argentario, now strongly fortified. The salt-water lagoon (11 sq. m. in extent), in the middle of which the town stands, abounds in white fish, soles and eels. On the eastern edge of the Monte Argentario is an active manganese iron ore mine, yielding some 30,000 tons per annum.

After the fall of the Republic of Siena, when the territory of Siena passed to Tuscany, Philip II. of Spain retained Orbetello, Talamone, Monte Argentario and the island of Giannutri until 1713, under the name of the Reali Stati dei Presidii. There are still many Spanish names among the inhabitants of Orbetello. In 1713 this district passed by treaty to the emperor, in 1736 to the king of the two Sicilies, in 1801 to the kingdom of Etruria, and in 1814 to the grand-duchy of Tuscany.

See G. Dennis, *Cities and Cemeteries of Etruria* (London, 1883), ii. 240; M. Carmichael, *In Tuscany* (London, 1901), 283, sqq.

(T. As.)

ORBIGNY, ALCIDE DESSALINES D' (1802–1857), French palaeontologist, was born at Couëron, Loire Inférieure, on the 6th of September 1802. He was educated at La Rochelle, where he became interested in the study of natural history, and in particular of zoology and palaeontology. His first appointment was that of travelling naturalist for the Museum of Natural History at Paris. In the course of his duties he proceeded in 1826 to South America, and gathered much information on the natural history and ethnology, the results being embodied in his great work *Voyage dans l'Amérique Méridionale* (1839–1842). Meanwhile he had decided to devote his time and energies to palaeontology, and he dealt in course of time with various invertebrata from foraminifera to crinoids and mollusca. In 1840 he commenced the publication of *Paléontologie Française, ou description des fossiles de la France*, a monumental work, accompanied by figures of the species. Eight volumes were published by him dealing with Jurassic and Cretaceous invertebrata, and since his death many later volumes have been issued. (See notes by C. D. Sherborn, " On the Dates of the *Paléontologie Française* of D'Orbigny," *Geol. Mag.*, 1899, p. 223.) Among his other works were *Cours élémentaire de paléontologie et de géologie stratigraphiques* (3 vols., 1849–1852), and *Prodrome de paléontologie stratigraphique* (3 vols., 1850–1852). D'Orbigny introduced (1852) a methodical system of nomenclature for geological formations based partly on the English terms—thus Bathonian for the Great or Bath Oolite, Bajocian from Bajocea or Bayeux in Calvados for the Inferior Oolite. Many of these names have been widely adopted, but some are of too local application to be generally used. In 1853 he was appointed professor of palaeontology at the Museum of Natural History in Paris, but died four years later, on the 30th of June 1857, at Pierresitte, near St Denis.

ORBILIUS, PUPILLUS, a Latin grammarian of the 1st century A.D., who had a school at Rome, where the poet Horace was one of his pupils. Horace (*Epistles*, ii.) criticizes his old schoolmaster and describes him as *plagosus* (a flogger), and Orbilius has become proverbial as a disciplinarian pedagogue.

ORBIT (from Lat. *orbita*, a track, *orbis*, a wheel), in astronomy, the path of any body, and especially of a heavenly body, revolving round an attracting centre. If the law of attraction is that of gravitation, the orbit is a conic section—ellipse, parabola or hyperbola—having the centre of attraction in one of its foci; and the motion takes place in accordance with Kepler's laws (see ASTRONOMY). But unless the orbit is an ellipse the body will never complete a revolution, but will recede indefinitely from the centre of motion. Elliptic orbits, and a parabolic orbit considered as the special case when the eccentricity of the ellipse is 1, are almost the only ones the astronomer has to consider, and our attention will therefore be confined to them in the present article. If the attraction of a central body is not the only force acting on the moving body, the orbit will deviate from the form of a conic section in a degree depending on the amount of the extraneous force; and the curve described may not be a re-entering curve at all, but one winding around so as to form an indefinite succession of spires. In all the cases which have yet arisen in astronomy the extraneous forces are so small compared with the gravitation of the central body that the orbit is approximately an ellipse, and the preliminary computations, as well as all determinations in which a high degree of precision is not necessary, are made on the hypothesis of elliptic orbits. Below are set forth the methods of determining and dealing with such orbits.

We begin by considering the laws of motion in the orbit itself, regardless of the position of the latter.

Let the curve represent an elliptic orbit, AB being the major axis, DE the minor axis, and F the focus in which the centre of attraction is situated, which centre we shall call the sun. From the

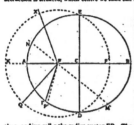

properties of the ellipse, A is the pericentre or nearest point of the orbit to the centre of attraction and B the apocentre or most distant point. The semi-major axis, CA or CB, is called the mean distance, and is represented by the symbol a. We put e for the eccentricity of the ellipse, represented by the ratio CF : CA. P is the position of the planet at any time, and we call r the radius vector FP. The angle AFP between the pericentre and the position P of the planet is the *anomaly* called v. By Kepler's second law the radius vector, FP, sweeps over equal areas in equal times. To do this the actual speed in the orbit, and in a yet higher degree the angular speed around F, must be greatest at pericentre, and continually diminish till the apocentre is reached. Let P, P' be two consecutive positions of the radius vector. Since the area of the triangle FPP' is one half the product of FP into the perpendicular p from P on FP', it follows that if these perpendiculars were equal all round the orbit, the areas described during the infinitesimal time would be smallest at the pericentre and continually increase during the passage of the body to B. It follows that p must be greatest at pericentre, where its distance from F is least. By geometrical consideration it can be shown that the angle subtended by p, as seen from F must be inversely as the square of its distance r. We therefore have the fundamental theorem that the angular velocity of the body around the centre of attraction varies inversely as the square of its distance, and is therefore at every point proportional to the gravitation of the sun. Another curious theorem proposed by Boulliand in 1625 as a substitute for Kepler's second law is that the angular motion of the body as measured around the empty focus F' is (approximately) uniform. That is to say an eye at F', the planet would seem to move around the sky with a nearly uniform speed.

The true anomaly, AFP, is commonly determined through the mean anomaly conceived thus: Describe a circle of radius a=CA around F, and let a fictitious planet start from K at the same moment that the actual planet passes A, and let it move with a uniform speed such that it shall complete its revolution in the same time T as the actual planet. From the law of angular motion of the latter its radius vector will run ahead of PQ near A, PQ will overtake and pass it at apocentre, and the two will again coincide at pericentre when the revolution is completed. The anomaly AFQ of Q at any moment is called the *mean anomaly*, and the angle QFP by which the true anomaly exceeds it at that moment is the *equation of the centre*.

Two elements define the position of the plane passing through the attracting centre in which the orbit lies. One of these is the position of the line MN through the sun at F in which the plane of the orbit cuts some fundamental plane of reference, commonly the ecliptic. This is called the *line of nodes*, and its position is specified by the angle which it makes with some fixed line FX in the fundamental plane. At one of the nodes, say N, the body passes from the south to the north side of the fundamental plane; this is called the ascending node. The other element is the inclination of the plane of the orbit to the fundamental plane, called the *inclination* simply. A fifth element is the position of the pericentre, which may be expressed by its angular distance XFN from the ascending node. A sixth is the position of the planet in the orbit at a given moment, for which may be substituted the moment at which it passed the pericentre. Another element is the time of revolution of the body in its orbit, called its *period*. Instead of the period it is common in astronomical practice to use the mean angular

speed, called the *mean motion* of the body. This is defined as the speed of revolution of the fictitious body already described, revolving with a uniform angular motion and the same periodic time as the planet. It follows that putting n for the mean motion and T for the period of revolution we shall have in degrees $nT = 360°$.

It is shown in the article ASTRONOMY (*Celestial Mechanics*) that the mean distance and mean motion or time of revolution of a planet are so related by Kepler's third law that, when one of these elements is given, the other can be found. Hence the number of independent elements assigned to a planet or other body moving around the sun is commonly six. But the same relation does not hold of a satellite the mass of whose primary is not regarded as an absolutely known quantity, or of a binary star. In these cases therefore the mean distance and mean motion are regarded as different elements, and the whole number of the latter is seven.

The process by which the position of a planet at any time is determined from its elements may now be conceived as follows:—The epoch of passage through pericentre being given, let t be the interval of time between this epoch and that for which the position of the body is required. Representing by P this position, it follows that the area of that portion of the ellipse contained between the radii vectores FB and FP will bear the same ratio to the whole area of the ellipse that t does to T, the time of revolution. The problem of finding a radius vector satisfying this condition is one which can be solved only by successive approximations, or tentatively. Its discussion may be found in any work on theoretical astronomy. The solution may be worked out directly or through the determination of the equation of the centre which, being added to the mean anomaly, gives the true anomaly. The angle from the pericentre to the actual radius vector, and the length of the latter being found, the angular distance of the planet from the node in the plane of the orbit is found by adding to the true anomaly the distance from the node to the pericentre. This, and the inclination of the orbit being given, we have all the geometrical data necessary to compute the coordinates of the planet itself. The coordinates thus found will in the case of a body moving around the sun be *heliocentric*. The reduction to the earth's centre is a problem of pure geometry.

When a new celestial body, say a planet or a comet is discovered, the astronomer who meets with the problem of determining the orbit from several observed positions of the body. To form a conception of this problem it is to be noted that since the position of the body in space can be computed from the six elements of the orbit at any time we may ideally conceive the coordinates of the body to be algebraically expressed as functions of the six elements and of the time. Since the distance of a body from the observer cannot be observed directly, but only the right ascension and declination, calling these a and δ we conceive ideal equations of the form

$$a = f(a, b, c, d, e, f, g, t) \text{ and } \delta = \phi(a, b, c, d, e, f, g, t),$$

the symbols $a, b, \ldots t$, representing the six elements and the time. If the values of a and δ, defining the position of the body on the celestial sphere, are observed at three different times, we may conceive six equations like the above, one for each of the three observed values of a and δ. Then by solving these equations, regarding the six elements as unknown quantities, the values of the latter may be computed. The actual process of solution is vastly more complex than is indicated by this description of it. Instead of the six ideal equations just described we have to combine a number of equations of various forms containing other quantities than the elements. But the logical framework of the process is that which we have set forth.

The problem of determining an orbit may be regarded as coeval with Hipparchus, who, it is supposed, found the moon's orbit. The problem of determining the apogee and perigee of the moon's orbit. The problem of determining a heliocentric orbit first presented itself to Kepler, who actually determined that of Mars. The modern method of determining orbits from three or four observations was first developed by C. F. Gauss in his celebrated work *Theoria Motus Corporum Coelestium*. This classical work is still a favourite among students, the improvements on its methods made since its publication being rather in details than in general principles.

AUTHORITIES.—Among recent works on the determination of orbits, J. C. Watson's *Theoretical Astronomy* is the most complete in the English language. The most complete existing work, an encyclopaedia of the subject in fact, is T. von Oppolzer's *Lehrbuch zur Bahnbestimmung der Kometen und Planeten* (2 vols.), which contains voluminous tables, formulae, and instructions for the computation of orbits in the many special cases that arise. More recent and better adapted to study is Bauschinger's *Bahnbestimmung der Himmelskörper* (1 vol., Leipzig, 1906), which, alone of the three, treats orbits of satellites and double stars.   (S. N.)

ORCAGNA (c. 1308-c. 1368 [1]), Italian painter, sculptor and architect, whose full name was ANDREA DI CIONE, called

[1] The dates of Orcagna's birth and death are not exactly known. According to Vasari, he died in 1389 at the age of sixty; but a document dated 1376 provides a guardian for Tessa and Romola, daughters of Orcagna's widow Francesca (see Bonaini, *Mem. Ined.* pp. 105-106). In that case 1376 was perhaps the year of his death; and if

ARCAGNUOLO,[1] was the son of a very able Florentine goldsmith, Maestro Cione, said to have been one of the principal artists who worked on the magnificent silver frontal of the high altar of San Giovanni, the Florentine Baptistery. The result of Orcagna's early training in the use of the precious metals may be traced in the extreme delicacy and refined detail of his principal works in sculpture. He had at least three brothers who all practised some branch of the fine arts: Lionardo or Nardo, the eldest, a painter; Matteo, a sculptor and mosaicist; and Jacopo, also a painter. They were frequently associated with Orcagna in his varied labours.

From the time of Giotto to the end of the 14th century Orcagna stands quite pre-eminent even among the many excellent artists of that time. In sculpture he was a pupil of Andrea Pisano; in painting, though indirectly, he was a disciple of Giotto. Few artists have practised with such success so many branches of the arts. Orcagna was not only a painter and sculptor, but also a worker in mosaic, an architect and a poet. His importance in the history of Italian art rests not merely on his numerous and beautiful productions, but also on his widespread influence, transmitted to his successors through a large and carefully-trained school of pupils. In style as a painter Orcagna comes midway between Giotto and Fra Angelico: he combined the dramatic force and realistic vigour of the earlier painter with the pure brilliant colour and refined unearthly beauty of Fra Angelico. His large fresco paintings are works of extreme decorative beauty and splendour—composed with careful reference to their architectural surroundings, arranged for the most part on one plane, without the strong foreshortening or effects of perspective with which the mural paintings of later masters are so often marred.

1. *Orcagna as a Painter.*—His chief works in fresco were at Florence, in the church of S Maria Novella. He first covered the walls of the retro-choir with scenes from the life of the Virgin. These, unfortunately, were much injured by damp very soon after their completion, and towards the end of the following century were replaced by other frescoes of the same subjects by Ghirlandaio, who, according to Vasari, made much use of Orcagna's motives and invention. Orcagna also painted three walls of the Strozzi chapel, at the north-east of the same church, with a grand series of frescoes, which still exist, though in a much injured and "restored" state. On the northern end wall is the Last Judgment, painted above and round the window, the light from which makes it difficult to see the picture. In the centre is Christ floating among clouds, surrounded by angels; below are kneeling figures of the Virgin and St John the Baptist, with the twelve apostles. Lower still are patriarchs, prophets and saints, with the resurrection of the blessed and the lost. The finest composition is that on the west wall, unbroken by any window. It represents paradise, with Christ and the Virgin enthroned in majesty among rows of brilliantly-coloured cherubim and seraphim tinged with rainbow-like rays of light. Below are long lines of the heavenly hierarchy mingled with angel musicians; and lower still a crowd of saints floating on clouds. Many of these figures are of exquisite beauty especially the few that have escaped restoration. Faces of the most divine tenderness and delicacy occur among the female saints; the two central angels below the Virgin are figures of wonderful grace in pose and movement; and the whole picture, lighted by a soft luminous atmosphere, seems to glow with an unearthly gladness and peace. Opposite to this is the fresco attributed by Vasari to Orcagna's brother Bernardo, or rather Nardo (*i.e.* Lionardo); it was completely repainted in 1530, so that nothing but the design remains, full of horror and weird imagination. To some extent the painter has followed Dante's scheme of successive circles.

These paintings were probably executed soon after 1350, and in 1357 Orcagna painted one of his finest panel pictures, as a retable for the altar of the same chapel, where it still remains.

Vasari is right about his age: his birth would have been in 1316. Milanesi, the editor of Vasari, is, however, inclined to think that Orcagna died in 1368, when he is known to have been seriously ill.
[1] Of this form, sometimes spelt Orcagnuolo, Orcagna is a corruption.

In the centre is Christ in majesty between kneeling figures of St Peter and St Thomas Aquinas, attended by angel musicians; on each side are standing figures of three other saints. It is a work of the greatest beauty both in colour and composition; it is painted with extreme miniature-like delicacy, and is on the whole very well preserved. This retable is signed, "Aō. dñi. mccclvii Andreas Cionis de Florentia me pinxit." Another fine altar-piece on panel by Orcagna, dated 1363, is preserved in the Cappella de' Medici; near the sacristy Sta Croce; it represents the four doctors of the Latin church. According to Vasari, Orcagna also painted some very fine frescoes in Sta Croce, similar in subjects to those attributed to him in the Campo Santo of Pisa, and full of fine portraits. These do not now exist. In the cathedral of Florence, on one of the northern piers, there hangs a nobly designed and highly finished picture on panel by Orcagna, representing S Zanobio enthroned, trampling under his feet Cruelty and Pride; at the sides are kneeling figures of SS Eugenius and Crescentius—the whole very rich in colour. The retable mentioned by Vasari as having been painted for the Florentine church of S Pietro Maggiore is now in the National Gallery of London. It is a richly decorative composition of the Coronation of the Virgin, between rows of saints, together with nine other subjects painted in miniature. Other paintings on panel by Orcagna were sent by the Pope to Avignon, but cannot now be traced. The frescoes also have been destroyed with which, according to Vasari, Orcagna decorated the façade of S Apollinare and the Cappella de' Cresci in the church of the Servi in Florence.[2]

2. *Orcagna as a Sculptor and Architect.*—In 1355 Orcagna was appointed architect to the chapel of Or San Michele in Florence. This curiously-planned building, with a large upper room over the vaulting of the lower part, has been begun by Taddeo Gaddi as a thank-offering for the cessation of the plague of 1348. It took the place of an earlier oratory designed by Arnolfo del Cambio, and was the gift of the united trade-gilds of Florence. As to the building itself, it is impossible to say how much is due to Taddeo Gaddi and how much to Orcagna, but the great marble tabernacle was wholly by Orcagna. This, in its combined splendour of architectural design, sculptured reliefs and statuettes, and mosaic enrichments, is one of the most important and beautiful works of art which even rich Italy possesses. It combines an altar, a shrine, a reredos and a baldacchino. In general form it is perhaps the purest and most gracefully designed of all specimens of Italian Gothic. It is a tall structure of white marble, with vaulted canopy and richly decorated gables and pinnacles, reaching almost to the vaulted roof of the chapel. The detail is extremely delicate, and brilliant gem-like colour is given by lavish enrichments of minute patterns in glass mosaic, inlaid in the white marble of the structure. It is put together with the greatest care and precision; Vasari especially notes the fact that the whole was put together without any cement, which might have stained the purity of the marble, all the parts being closely fitted together with bronze dowels. The spire-like summit of the tabernacle is surmounted by a figure of St Michael, and at a lower stage on the roof are statuettes of the apostles. The altar has a relief of Hope between panels with the Marriage of the Virgin and the Annunciation. On the right side, looking east, of the base of the tabernacle are reliefs of the Birth of the Virgin and her Presentation in the Temple; on the left, the Nativity and the Adoration of the Magi; and behind, the Presentation of Christ in the Temple, and the

[2] The magnificent but much injured frescoes of the Last Judgment, Hell, and the Triumph of Death in the Pisan Campo Santo, described with great minuteness and enthusiasm by Vasari, are attributed by him to Orcagna, but internal evidence seems to show that they are productions of the Sienese school. Crowe and Cavalcaselle attribute them to the two brothers Lorenzetti of Siena, but they have been so injured by wet, the settlement of the wall, and repeated retouchings that it is difficult to come to any clear decision as to their authorship. It appears, however, much more probable that they are the work of Bernardo Daddi.

[3] Orcagna was admitted as a member of the Sculptors' Gild in 1352. His name occurs in the roll as "Andreas Cionis vocatus Arcagnolus, pictor."

Angel warning the Virgin to escape into Egypt. Above the last two subjects are large reliefs of the Death of the Virgin, surrounded by the apostles, and higher still her Assumption; she stands in a vesica, and is borne by angels to heaven. On the base of the tabernacle is inscribed " Andreas Cionis pictor Florentinvs oratorii archimagister extitit hvjvs mcccliv." Orcagna's own portrait is given as one of the apostles. In addition to these richly-composed subject-reliefs the whole work is adorned with many other single figures and heads of prophets, angels, and the Virtues, all executed with wonderful finish and refinement. The shrine, which forms an aumbry in the reredos, contains a miraculous picture of the Madonna. A fine bronze screen, with open geometrical tracery, encloses the whole. No work of sculpture in Italy is more magnificent than this wonderful tabernacle, both in general effect and in the delicate beauty of the reliefs and statuettes with which it is so lavishly enriched. It cost the enormous sum of 96,000 gold florins. Unfortunately it is very badly placed and insufficiently lighted, so that a minute examination of its beauties is a work of difficulty.

No mention is made by Vasari of Orcagna's residence in Orvieto, where he was occupied for some time the post of " capo-maestro " to the duomo. He accepted this appointment on the 14th of June 1358 at the large salary (for that time) of 300 gold florins a year. His brother Matteo was engaged to work under him, receiving 8 florins a month. When Orcagna accepted this appointment at Orvieto he had not yet finished his work at Or San Michele, and so was obliged to make long visits to Florence, which naturally interfered with the satisfactory performance of his work for the Orvietans. The result was that on the 12th of September 1360 Orcagna, having been paid for his work up to that time, resigned the post of " capo-maestro " of the duomo, though he still remained a little longer in Orvieto to finish a large mosaic picture on the west front. When this mosaic (made of glass tesserae from Venice) was finished in 1362, it was found to be uneven in surface, and not fixed securely into its cement bed. An arbitration was therefore held as to the price Orcagna was to receive for it, and he was awarded 60 gold florins.

Vasari mentions as other architectural works by Orcagna the design for the piers in the nave of the Florentine duomo, a zecca or mint, which appears not to have been carried out, and the Loggia dei Lanzi in the Piazza della Signoria. It is, however, more than doubtful whether Orcagna had any hand in this last building, a very graceful vaulted structure, with three semicircular open arches on the side and one at each end, intended to form a sheltered meeting-place for the Priori during elections and other public transactions. This loggia was ordered by the General Council of Florence in 1356, but was not actually begun till the year 1376, after Orcagna's death. The architects were Benci di Cione (possibly a brother of Orcagna) and Simone di Francesco Talenti, both men of considerable reputation in Florence. The sculptured reliefs of the seven Virtues in the spandrels of the arches of the loggia, also attributed to Orcagna by Vasari, were later still. They were designed by Angelo Gaddi (1383-1386), and were carried out by three or four different sculptors.

Pupils of Orcagna named by Vasari are Bernardo Nello, a Pisan, Tommaso di Marco, a Florentine, and, chief of all, Francesco Traini, whose grand painting on panel of St Thomas Aquinas enthroned with the arch-heretics at his feet still hangs in the church for which it was painted—Sta Caterina at Pisa. Orcagna had, in addition to the two daughters mentioned above, a son named Cione, who was a painter of but little eminence. Some sonnets attributed to Orcagna exist in MS. in the Strozzi and Magliabecchian libraries in Florence. They have been published by Trucchi (*Poesie inedite*, ii. p. 25, Prato, 1846). They are graceful in language, but rather artificial and over-elaborated.

AUTHORITIES.—Vasari, ed. Milanesi, i. p. 593 (Florence, 1878); *Giornale degli Archivi Toscani*, iii. p. 282, &c.; Passerini, *Curiosità storico-artistiche*; Gaye, *Carteggio inedito*, i. pp. 500-513, ii. p. 5; Rosini, *Storia della pittura*, vol. ii.; Baldinucci, *Professori del disegno*, vol. i.; Rumohr, *Ricerche Italiane*, ii., and *Antologia di Firenze*, iii.; Crowe and Cavalcaselle, *Painting in Italy*, i. p. 425 (London, 1864); Perkins, *Tuscan Sculptors*, p. 77 (London, 1865). (J. H. M.)

ORCHARD (O. Eng. *ort-geard*, later *orceard*; a combination apparently of Lat. *hortus*, garden, and " yard " or " garth "), a piece of ground enclosed for the purposes of horticulture. The term was formerly used in a general way for a garden where herbs and fruit-trees were cultivated, but is now used exclusively for a piece of enclosed ground for fruit-trees only, and particularly for apples, pears, plums and cherries.

ORCHARDSON, SIR WILLIAM QUILLER (1835-1910), British painter, was born in Edinburgh, where his father was engaged in business, in 1835. " Orchardson " is a variation of " Urquhartson," the name of a Highland sept settled on Loch Ness, from which the painter is descended. At the age of fifteen he was sent to the Trustees' Academy, then under the mastership of Robert Scott Lauder, where he had as fellow-students most of those who afterwards shed lustre on the Scottish school of the second half of the 19th century. As a student he was not especially precocious or industrious, but his work was distinguished by a peculiar reserve, by an unusual determination that his hand should be subdued to his eye, with the result that his early things reach their own ideal as surely as those of his maturity. By the time he was twenty, Orchardson had mastered the essentials of his art, and had produced at least one picture which might be accepted as representative, a portrait of Mr John Hutchison, the sculptor. For seven years after this he worked in Edinburgh, some of his attention being given to " black and white," his practice in which had been partly acquired at a sketch club, which included among its members Mr Hugh Cameron, Mr Peter Graham, Mr George Hay, Mr M'Taggart, Mr John Hutchison and others. In 1862 he came to London, and established himself in 37 Fitzroy Square, where he was joined twelve months later by his friend John Pettie. The same house was afterwards inhabited by Ford Madox Brown.

The English public was not immediately attracted by Orchardson's work. It was too quiet to compel attention at the Royal Academy, and Pettie, Orchardson's junior by four years, stepped before him for a time, and became the most readily accepted member of the school. Orchardson confined himself to the simplest themes and designs, to the most reticent schemes of colour. Among his best pictures during the first eighteen years after his migration to London were " The Challenge," " Christopher Sly," " Queen of the Swords," " Conditional Neutrality," " Hard Hit "—perhaps the best of all—and portraits of Mr Charles Moxon, his father-in-law, and of his own wife. In all these good judgment and a refined imagination were united to a restrained but consummate technical dexterity. During these same years he made a few drawings on wood, turning to account his early facility in this mode. The period between 1862 and 1880 was one of quiet ambitions, of a characteristic *insouciance*, of life accepted as a thing of many-balanced interests rather than as a matter of *sturm und drang*. In 1865 Pettie married, and the Fitzroy Square *ménage* was broken up. In 1868 Orchardson was elected A.R.A. In 1870 he spent the summer in Venice, travelling home in the early autumn through a France overrun by the German armies. In 1873 he married Miss Helen Moxon, and in 1877 he was elected to the full membership of the Royal Academy. In this same year he finished building a house at Westgate-on-Sea, with an open tennis-court and a studio in the garden. He was knighted in June 1907, and died in London on the 13th of April 1910.

Orchardson's wider popularity dates from 1881. To that year's Academy he sent the large " On Board the *Bellerophon*," which now hangs in the Tate Gallery. Its success with the public was great and instantaneous, and for ten or twelve years Orchardson's work was more eagerly looked for at the Academy than that of any one else. He followed up the " Bellerophon " with the still finer " Voltaire," now in the Kunsthalle at Hamburg. Technically, the " Voltaire " is, perhaps, his high-water mark. Fine both in design and colour, it is carried out with a supple dexterity of hand which has scarcely been equalled in the British school since the death of Gainsborough. The subject is not entirely happy, for it does not explain itself, but requires a previous knowledge on the part of the spectator of how Voltaire was beaten by the servants of the Chevalier de Rohan-Cabot, and how the duc de Sully failed to avenge his guest. The painter was attracted by the opportunity it gave for effective opposition of character, line, colour and movement. The "Voltaire" was at the Academy of 1883; it was followed, in 1884, by the "Mariage de convenance," perhaps the most popular of all Orchardson's pictures; in 1885, by "The Salon of Madame Récamier"; in 1886, by "After," the sequel to the "Mariage de convenance," and "A Tender Chord," one of his most exquisite productions; in 1887, by "The First Cloud"; in 1888, by "Her Mother's Voice"; and in 1889, by "The Young Duke," a canvas on which he returned to much the same pictorial scheme as that of the "Voltaire." Subsequently he exhibited a series of pictures in which fine pictorial use was made of the furniture and costumes of the early years of the 19th century, the subjects, as a rule, being only just enough to suggest a title: "An Enigma," "A Social Eddy," "Reflections," "If music be the food of love, play on!" "Music, when sweet voices die, vibrates on the memory," "Her First Dance,"—in these, opportunities are made to introduce old harpsichords, spinets, early pianofortes, Empire chairs, sofas and tables, Aubusson carpets, short-waisted gowns, delicate in material and primitive in ornament. Between such things and Orchardson's methods as a painter the sympathy is close, so that the best among them, "A Tender Chord," for instance, or "Music, when sweet voices die," have a rare distinction.

As a portrait-painter Orchardson must be placed in the first class. His portraits are not numerous, but among them are a few which rise to the highest level reached by modern art. "Master Baby," a picture, connecting subject-painting with portraiture, is a masterpiece of design, colour and broad execution. "Mrs Joseph," "Mrs Ralli," "Sir Andrew Walker, Bart.," "Charles Moxon, Esq.," "Mrs Orchardson," "Conditional Neutrality" (a portrait of Orchardson's eldest son as a boy of six), "Lord Rookwood," "The Provost of Aberdeen," and, above all, "Sir Walter Gilbey, Bart.," would all deserve a place in any list of the best portraits of the 19th century. In this branch of art the "Sir Walter Gilbey" may fairly be called the painter's masterpiece, although the sumptuous full-length of the Scottish provost, in his robes, runs it closely. The scheme of colour is reticent; had the picture been exhibited at the time of the Boer War of 1900 the colour would have been called khaki; the design is simple, uniting nature to art with a rare felicity; and the likeness has been found satisfactory by the sitter's friends. The most important commission ever received by Orchardson as a portrait-painter was that for a group of Queen Victoria, with her son (afterwards King Edward VII.), grandson, and great-grandson, to be painted on one canvas for the Royal Agricultural Society. The painter hit upon a happy notion for the bringing of the four figures together, and as time goes on and the picture slowly turns into history, its merit is likely to be better appreciated. He continued painting to the end of his life, and had three portraits ready for the Royal Academy in 1910.

Orchardson's method was that of one who worked under a creative, decorative and subjective impulse, rather than under one derived from a wish to observe and record. His affiliation is with Watteau and Gainsborough, rather than with those who would base all pictorial art on a keen eye for actuality and "value." Among French painters his pictures have excited particular admiration.   (W. AR.)

ORCHESTRA (Fr. *Orchestre*; Ger. *Kapelle, Orchester*; Ital. *Orchestra*), in its modern acceptation (1) the place in a theatre or concert hall set apart for the musicians; (2) a carefully-balanced group of performers on stringed, wind and percussion instruments adapted for playing in concert and directed by a conductor. In ancient Greece the ὀρχήστρα was the space between the auditorium and the proscenium or stage, in which were stationed the chorus and the instrumentalists. The second sense is that which is dealt with here.

A modern orchestra is composed of (1) a basis of strings—first and second violins, violas, violoncellos and double basses;

(2) flutes, sometimes including a piccolo; (3) the reed contingent, consisting of two complete families, the oboes with their tenors and basses (the cor Anglais, the fagotto or bassoon and the contrafagotto or double bassoon), the clarinets with their tenor and basses (the basset horn and the bass and pedal clarinets) with the addition sometimes of saxophones; (4) the brass wind, consisting of the horns, a group sometimes completed by the tenor and tenor-bass Wagner tubas, the trumpet or cornet, the trombones (tenor, bass and contrabass), the tubas (tenor, bass and contrabass); (5) the percussion instruments, including the kettledrums, bells, Glockenspiel, cymbals, triangle, &c. Harps are added when required for special effects.

Although most of the instruments from the older civilizations of Egypt, Chaldea, Persia, Phoenicia and of the Semitic races were known to the ancient Greeks, their conception of music led them to discourage all imitation of their neighbours' love of orchestral effects, obtained by combining harps, lyres, guitars, tanburs, double pipes and long flutes, trumpets, bagpipes, cymbals, drums, &c., playing in unison or in octaves. The Greeks only cultivated to any extent the various kinds of citharas, lyres and auloi, seldom used in concert. To the predilection of the Romans for wind instruments of all kinds, we owe nearly all the wind instruments of the modern orchestra, each of which had its prototype among the instruments of the Roman Empire: the flute, oboe and clarinet, in the tibia; the trombone and trumpet in the buccina; the tubas in the tuba; and the French horn in cornu and buccina. The 4th century A.D. witnessed the downfall of the Roman drama and the debasement of instrumental music, which was placed under a ban by the Church. During the convulsions which the migrations of Goths, Vandals and Huns caused in Europe after the fall of Rome, instrumental music was preserved from absolute extinction by wandering actors and musicians turned adrift after the closing of the theatres by command of the Church. Later, as demand arose, reinforcements of instruments, instrumentalists and instrument makers filtered through the Byzantine Empire and the Christian East generally on the one side and from the Moors on the West. It is towards the dawn of the 11th century that we find the first definite indications of the status of instrumental music in Western and Central Europe. Everywhere are the evidences, so conspicuously absent from the catacombs and from Romano-Christian monuments, of the growing favour in which instrumental music was held, to instance only such sculptures as those of the Abbey of Boscherville in Normandy, of the portico of the Cathedral of Santiago da Compostella (12th century) with its orchestra of 24 musicians, and the full-page illuminations of Psalters representing David and his musicians and of the 24 elders in the Apocalypses.

The earliest instrumental compositions extant are certain 15th-century dances and pieces in contrapuntal style preserved in the libraries of Berlin and Munich. The late development of notation, which long remained exclusively in the hands of monks and troubadours, personally more concerned with vocal than with instrumental music, ensured the preservation of the former, while the latter was left unrecorded. Instrumental music was for centuries dependent on outcasts and outlaws, tolerated by Church and State but beyond the pale. Little was known of the construction and technique of the instruments, and their possibilities were undreamed. Nevertheless, the innate love and yearning of the people for tone-colour asserted itself with sufficient strength to overcome all obstacles. It is true that the development of the early forms of harmony, the *organum, diaphony*, the *discant* and the richer forms of polyphony grew up round the voice, but indications are not wanting of an independent energy and vitality which must surely have existed in unrecorded medieval instrumental music, since they can be so clearly traced in the instruments themselves. It is, for example, significant of the attitude of 10th-century instrumentalists towards musical progress that they at once assimilated Hucbald's innovation of the *organum*, a parallel succession of fourths and fifths, accompanied sometimes by the octave, for two or three voices respectively, and they produced in the same century the *organistrum*, named after Hucbald's *organum*, and specially constructed to reproduce it.

Shortly after the introduction of polyphony, instruments such as flûtes-à-bec, or flajols, cornets, cromornes, shawms, hunting horns, bagpipes, as well as lutes and bowed instruments began to be made in sizes approximately corresponding in pitch with the voice parts. It is probably to the same yearning of instrumentalists after a polyphonic ensemble, possible until the 14th century only on organs, hurdy-gurdies and bagpipes, that we owe the clavichord and clavicembalo, embodying the application of keys, respectively, to the dulcimer and the psaltery.

There are two reasons which account for the development of the brass wind proceeding more slowly. (1) These instruments, trumpets or busines, tubas and horns, were for many centuries mainly used in medieval Europe as military or hunting signal instruments, and as such the utmost required of them was a fanfare. Specimens of 14th-century tablature and 16th-century notation for the horn, for instance, show that for that instrument rhythm alone was taken into account. (2) Whereas in most of the instruments named above the notes of the diatonic scale were either fixed or easily obtained, the acoustic principles of tubes without lateral holes and blown by means of a cup mouthpiece do not allow of a diatonic scale, except for the fourth octave from the fundamental, and that only in trumpets and horns, the notes of the common chord with the addition of the flattened seventh being the utmost that can be produced without the help of valves, keys or slides. These instruments were, therefore, the last to be added to the orchestra, although they were extensively used for special military, civil and religious functions and were the most highly favoured of all.

The earliest improvement in the status of the roving instrumentalists came with the rise of minstrelsy. The courts of the counts of Toulouse, Provence and Barcelona were the first to foster the art of improvising or composing songs known as *trobar* (or *trouver* in the north of France), and Count Guillaume of Poitiers (1087–1127) is said to have been the first troubadour. The noble troubadour seldom sang the songs he composed himself, this duty devolving upon his professional minstrel skilled in singing and in playing upon divers instruments who interpreted and disseminated his master's verses. In this respect the troubadour differed from his German contemporary the Minnesinger, who frequently sang himself. The professional musicians were included under the general term of *jongleurs* or *jugleors*, *gleemen* or *minstrels*, whose function was to entertain and amuse, but there were among them many subtle distinctions and ranks, such as *chanteors* and *estrumanteors*. Love was the prevailing theme in the south, while in the north war and heroic deeds inspired the bards. To the former was due the rapid development of bowed instruments, which by reason of their singing quality were more suitable for accompanying passionate love songs, while instruments of which the strings were plucked accorded better with the declamatory and dramatic style of the north.

The first assertive move towards independence was made by the wandering musicians in the 13th century, when some of these, tired of a roving life, settled down in cities, forming gilds or brotherhoods for the protection of their mutual interests and privileges. In time they came to be recognized by the burgomasters and municipalities, by whom they were engaged to provide music at all civic and private festivities, wandering musicians being prohibited from playing within the precincts of the cities. The oldest of these gilds was the Brotherhood of Nicolai founded in Vienna in 1288. In the next century these pioneers chose as patron of their brotherhood Peter von Eberstorff, from 1354 to 1376 known as *Vogt der Musikanten*, who obtained for the members an imperial charter. This example was gradually followed in other parts of Germany and elsewhere in Europe. In England, John of Gaunt was in 1381 chosen King of the Minstrels. In France there was the Confrérie of St Julien des Menestriers, incorporated in 1321. Exalted patrons of instrumental music multiplied in the 15th century, to instance only the dukes of Burgundy, the emperors of the House of Austria, the dukes of Lorraine, of Este, Ferrara and Tuscany, the electors of Saxony and the kings of France with their renowned institutions *La Chapelle-Musique du Roi* (c. 1440), *la Musique de la Chambre, la Musique de la Grande Ecurie du Roi.*

At the time of the revival of the drama with music, afterwards modified and known as opera, at the end of the 16th century, there was as yet no orchestra in our sense of the word, but merely an abundance of instruments used in concert for special effects, without balance or grouping; small positive organs, regals, harpsichords, lutes, theorbos, archlutes and chittarone (bass and contrabass lutes), guitars, viols, lyras *da braccio* and *da gamba*, psalteries, citterns, harps, flutes, recorders, cornets, trumpets and trombones, drums and cymbals.

Monteverde was the first to see that a preponderance of strings is necessary to ensure a proper balance of tone. With the perfected models of the Cremona violins at his disposal, a quartett of strings was established, and all other stringed instruments not played with the bow were ejected from the orchestra with the exception of the harp. Under the influence of Monteverde and his successors, Cavalli and Cesti, the orchestra won for itself a separate existence with music and laws of its own. As instruments were improved, new ones introduced, and old ones abandoned, instrumentation became a new and favourite study in Italy and in Germany. Musicians began to find out the capabilities of various families of instruments and their individual value.

The proper understanding of the compass and capabilities of wind instruments, and more especially of the brass wind, was of later date (18th century). At first the scores contained but few indications for instruments other than strings; the others played as much as they could according to the compass of their instruments at the direction of the leader. The possibility of using instruments for solos, by encouraging virtuosi to acquire great skill, raised the standard of excellence of the whole orchestra.

At first the orchestra was an aristocratic luxury, performing privately at the courts of the princes and nobles of Italy; but in the 17th century performances were given in theatres, and Germany eagerly followed. Dresden, Munich and Hamburg successively built opera houses, while in England opera flourished under Purcell, and in France under Lully, who with the collaboration of Molière also greatly raised the status of the entertainments known as *ballets*, interspersed with instrumental and vocal music.

The revival of the drama seems to have exhausted the enthusiasm of Italy for instrumental music, and the field of action was shifted to Germany, where the perfecting of the orchestra was continued. Most German princes had at the beginning of the 18th century good private orchestras or *Kapelle*, and they always endeavoured to secure the services of the best available instrumentalists. Kaiser, Telemann, Graun, Mattheson and Handel contributed greatly to the development of German opera and of the orchestra in Hamburg during the first quarter of the century. Bach, Gluck and Mozart, the reformers of opera; Haydn, the father of the modern orchestra and the first to treat it independently as a power opposed to the solo and chorus, by scoring for the instruments in well-defined groups; Beethoven, who individualized the instruments, writing solo passages for them; Weber, who brought the horn and clarinet into prominence; Schubert, who inaugurated the conversations between members of the wood wind—all left their mark on the orchestra, leading the way up to Wagner and Strauss.

A sketch of the rise of the modern orchestra would not be complete without reference to the invention of the piston or valve by Stölzel and Blümel, both Silesians, in 1815. A satisfactory bass for the wind, and more especially for the brass, had long been a desideratum. The effect of this invention was felt at once: instrument-makers in all countries vied with each other in making use of the contrivance and in bringing it to perfection; and the orchestra was before long enriched by a new family of valved instruments, variously known as tubas, or euphoniums and bombardons, having a chromatic scale and a full sonorous tone of great beauty and immense volume, forming a magnificent bass.

(K. S.)

ORCHESTRION, a name applied to three different kinds of instruments. (1) A chamber organ, designed by Abt Vogler at the end of the 18th century, which in a space of 9 cub. ft. contained no less than 900 pipes, 3 manuals of 63 keys each and 39 pedals (see HARMONIUM). (2) A pianoforte with organ pipes attached, invented by Thomas Anton Kunz of Prague in 1791. This orchestrion comprised two manuals of 65 keys and 25 pedals, all of which could be used either independently or coupled. There were 21 stops, 230 strings and 360 pipes which produced 105 different combinations. The bellows were worked either by hand or by machinery. (3) A mechanical instrument, automatically played by means of revolving cylinders, invented in 1851 by F. T. Kaufmann of Dresden. It comprises a complete wind orchestra, with the addition of kettle-drums, side-drums, cymbals and triangle.   (K. S.)

ORCHHA, or URCHHA (also called *Tehri* or *Tikamgarh*), a native state of Central India, in the Bundelkhand agency. Orchha is the oldest and highest in rank of all the Bundela principalities, and was the only one not held in subjection by the peshwa. Area, 2080 sq. m.; pop. (1901) 321,634; estimated revenue, £47,000; no tribute. The maharaja, Sir Pratap Singh, G.S.C.I. (born in 1854, succeeded in 1874), took a great personal interest in the development of his state, and himself designed most of the engineering and irrigation works that have been executed here within recent years. He bears the hereditary title of "First of the Princes of Bundelkhand." The state exports grain, *ghi*, and cotton cloth, but trade suffers from imperfect communications. The town of Orchha, the former capital, is on the river Betwa, not far from Jhansi. It possesses an imposing fort, dating mainly from the early 17th century. This contains a number of palaces and other buildings connected one with another. The most noteworthy are the Rajmandir, a massive square erection of which the exterior is almost absolutely plain; and the Jahangirmahal, of the same form but far more ornate, a singularly beautiful specimen of Hindu domestic architecture. Elsewhere about the town are fine temples and tombs, among which may be noticed the Chaturbhuj temple on its vast platform of stone. The town of Tehri or Tikamgarh, where the chief now resides, is about 40 m. S. of Orchha; pop. (1901) 14,050. It contains the fort of Tikamgarh, by which name the town is generally called, to distinguish it from Tehri in the Himalayas.

ORCHIS. The word *Orchis* is used in a special sense to denote a particular genus of the Orchid family (*Orchidaceae*); very frequently, also, it is employed in a more general way to indicate any member of that large and very interesting group. It will be convenient here to use the word *Orchis* as applying to that particular genus which gives its name to the order or family, and to employ the term "orchid" in the less precise sense.

The flowers of all orchids, though extremely diverse within certain limits, and although superficially very different from those of other monocotyledons, are all formed upon one common plan, which is only a modification of that observable in such flowers as those of the narcissus or snowdrop (*Galanthus*). The conformation of those flowers consists essentially in the presence of a six-parted perianth, the three outer segments of which correspond to a calyx, the three inner ones to a corolla. These segments spring apparently from the top of the ovary—the real expansion, however, being that the end of the flower-stalk or "thalamus," as it grows, becomes dilated into a sort of cup or tube enclosing and indeed closely adhering to the ovary, so that the latter organ appears to be beneath the perianth instead of above it as in a lily, an appearance which has given origin to the term "inferior ovary." Within the perianth, and springing

FIG. 1.

A. Floral diagram of typical orchid flower; *l*, labellum; *a*, anther; *s*, rudiments of barren stamens (staminodes).
B. Diagram of the symmetrical trimerous flower of Fritillary (*Fritillaria*).

from its sides, or apparently from the top of the ovary, are six stamens whose anthers contain pulverulent pollen-grains. These stamens encircle a style which is the upward continuation of the ovary, and which shows at its free end traces of the three originally separate but now blended carpels of which the ovary consists. An orchid flower has an inferior ovary like that just

FIG. 2.—Diagram of the flower of *Orchis*.
s, sl, sl, The three divisions of the outer perianth.
pl, pl, The two lateral divisions of the inner perianth.
ps, The superior division or the labellum, which may become inferior by the twisting of the ovary.
e, The fertile stamen, with its two pollen-masses in the anther-lobes.
c, The one-celled ovary cut transversely, having three parietal placentas.

FIG. 3.—Flower of *Orchis*.
s, s, s, The three outer divisions of the perianth.
p, p, l, The three inner, *l* being the labellum, here inferior by the twisting of the ovary.
e, Spur of the labellum.
st, The twisted ovary.
si, The stigma.
a, The anther, containing pollen-masses.

described, but with the ovules on the walls of the cavity (not in its axis or centre), a six-parted perianth, a stamen or stamens and stigmas. The main distinguishing features consist in the fact that one of the inner pieces of the perianth becomes in course of its growth much larger than the rest, and usually different in colour, texture and form. So different is it that it receives a distinct name, that of the "lip" or "labellum." In place of the six stamens we commonly find but one (two in *Cypripedium*), and that one is raised together with the stigmatic surfaces on an elongation of the floral axis known as the "column." Moreover, the pollen, instead of consisting of separate cells or grains, consists of cells aggregated into "pollen-masses," the number varying in different genera, but very generally two, four, or eight, and in many of the genera provided at the base with a strap-shaped stalk or "caudicle" ending in a flattish gland or "viscid disk" like a boy's sucker. In *Cypripedium* all three stigmas are functional, but in the great majority of orchids only the lateral pair form receptive surfaces (*si*, fig. 3), the third being sterile and forming the rostellum which plays an important part in the process of pollination, often forming a peculiar pouch-like process (fig. 4, *r*) in which the viscid disk of the pollen-masses is concealed till released in the manner presently to be mentioned. It would appear, then, that the orchid flower differs from the more general monocotyledonous type in the irregularity of the perianth, in the suppression of five out of six stamens, and in the union of the one stamen and the stigmas. In addition to these modifications, which are common to nearly all orchids, there are others generally but not so universally met with; among them is the displacement of the flower arising from the twisting of the inferior ovary, in consequence of which the flower is so completely turned round that the "lip," which originates in that part of the flower, conventionally called the posterior or superior part, or that

FIG. 4.—Diagram illustrating arrangement of parts in flower of *Orchis*.
s, Sepals.
p, Petals.
a, Anther.
st, Two united stigmas.
r, Rostellum (barren stigma).

nearest to the supporting stem, becomes in course of growth turned to the anterior or lower part of the flower nearest to the bract, from whose axil it arises. Other common modifications arise from the union of certain parts of the perianth to each other, and from the varied and often very remarkable outgrowths from the lip. These modifications are associated with the structure and habits of insects and their visits to the flowers.

Cross fertilization, or the impregnation of any given flower by pollen from another flower of the same species on the same or on another plant, has been proved to be of great advantage to the plant by securing a more

FIG. 5.—Pollen-masses of an Orchid, with their caudicles *c* and common gland *g*.

numerous or a more robust offspring, or one better able to adapt itself to the varying conditions under which it has to live. This cross fertilization is often effected by the agency of insects. They are attracted to the flower by its colour or its perfume; they seek, collect or feed on its honey, and while so doing they remove the pollen from the anther and convey it to another flower, there to germinate on the stigma when its tubes travel down the style to the ovary where their contents ultimately fuse with the "oosphere" or immature egg, which becomes in consequence fertilized, and forms a seed which afterwards develops into a new plant (see article ANGIOSPERMS). To facilitate the operations of such insects, by compelling them to move in certain lines so as to secure the due removal of the pollen and its subsequent deposit on the right place, the form of the flower and the conformation of its several parts are modified in ways as varied as they are wonderful. Other insects visit the flower with more questionable result. For them the pollen is an attraction as food, or some other part of the flower offers an inducement to them for a like object. Such visitors are clearly prejudicial to the flower, and so we meet with arrangements which are calculated to repel the intruders, or at least to force them to enter the flower in such a way as not to effect mischief. See Darwin's *Fertilisation of Orchids* and similar works.

In the common orchids of British meadows, *Orchis Morio*, *mascula* (Shakespeare's long purples), &c., the general structure of the flower is as we have described it (figs. 2, 3). In addition there is in this particular genus, as indeed in many others, a long tubular spur or horn projecting downwards from the back of the lip, whose office it is to secrete and store a honeyed juice; the forepart of the lip forms an expanded plate, usually larger and more brightly coloured than the other parts of the flower, and with hairs or ridges and spots of various kinds according to the species. The remaining parts of the perianth are very much smaller, and commonly are so arranged as to form a hood over-arching the "column." This column stands up from the base of the flower, almost at right angles to the lip, and it bears at the top an anther, in the two hollow lobes of which are concealed the two pollen-masses, each with its caudicle terminating below in a roundish gland, concealed at first in the pouch-like rostellum at the front of the column. Below the anther the surface of the column in front is hollowed out into a greenish depression covered with viscid fluid—this is the two united stigmas. The other parts of the flower need not detain us. Such being in general terms the mechanism of the flower of a common orchid, let us now see how it acts. A bee, we will assume, attracted by the colour and perfume of the flower, alights on that part of it which is the first to attract its attention—the lip. There, guided by the hairs or ridges before-mentioned, it is led to the orifice of the spur with its store of honeyed juice. The position of this orifice, as we have seen, is at the base of the lip and of the column, so that the insect, if of sufficient size, while bending its head to insert the proboscis into the spur, almost of necessity displaces the pollen-masses. Liberated from the anthers, these adhere to the head or back of the insect by means of the sticky gland at the bottom of the caudicle (fig. 4). Having attained its object the insect withdraws, taking the pollen-masses, and visits another flower. And now occurs another device or adaptation no

less marvellous than those of which mention has been made. The two anther-cases in an orchis are erect and nearly parallel the one to the other; the pollen-masses within them are of course in like case, as may be thus represented ‖, but immediately the pollen-masses are removed movements take place at the base of the caudicle so as to effect the bending of this stalk and the placing the pollen-mass in a more or less horizontal position, thus ≕, or, as in the case of *O. pyramidalis*, the two pollen-masses originally placed parallel ‖ diverge from the base like the letter V. The movements of the pollen-masses may readily be seen with the naked eye by thrusting the point of a needle into the base of the anther, when the disks adhere to the needle as they would do to the antenna of an insect, and may be withdrawn. Sometimes the lip is mobile and even sensitive to impressions, as are also certain processes of the column. In such cases the contact of an insect or other body with those processes is sufficient to liberate the pollen often with elastic force, even when the anther itself is not touched. In other orchids movements take place in different ways and in other directions. The object of these movements will be appreciated when it is remembered that, if the pollen-masses retained the original direction they had in the anther in which they were formed, they would, when transported by the insect to another flower, merely come in contact with the anther of that flower, where of course they would be of no use; but, owing to the divergences and flexions above alluded to, the pollen-masses come to be so placed that, when transplanted to another flower of the same species, they come in contact with the stigma and so effect the fertilization of that flower. These illustrations are comparatively simple; it would have been easy to select others of a more complicated nature, but all evidently connected with the visits of insects and the cross fertilization of the flower. In some cases, as in *Catasetum*, male flowers are produced so different from the female that before the different flowers had been found on the same pike, and before the facts of the case were fully known, they were taken to be representatives of distinct genera.

The fruit is a capsule splitting generally by three longitudinal slits forming valves which remain united above and below. The seeds are minute and innumerable; they contain a small rudimentary embryo surrounded by a thin loose membraneous coat, of the valves which by their movements jerk out the seeds. The floral structure is so curious that perhaps less attention has been paid to the vegetative organs than the peculiarities of their organisation demand. We can only allude to some of these points. The orchids of British fields are all of terrestrial habit, and their roots are mostly tuberous (fig. 6), the tubers being partly radical partly budlike in their character. There is often a marked alternation in the production of vegetative and flowering shoots respectively; and, sometimes, from various circumstances, the flowering shoots are not produced for several years in succession. This fact will account for the profusion with which some orchids, like the common bee orchis for instance, are found in some seasons and their scarcity in others. Tropical orchids are mostly epiphytal—that is, they grow upon trees without deriving nourishment from them. They are frequently provided with "pseudo-bulbs," large solid swellings of the stem, in the tissues of which water and nutritive materials are stored. They

FIG. 6.—Tuberculars roots of *Orchis mascula*, a terrestrial Orchid.

derive this moisture from the air by means of aerial roots, developed from the stem and bearing an outer spongy structure, or *velamen*, consisting of empty cells kept open by spiral thickenings in the wall; this sponge-like tissue absorbs dew and rain and condenses the moisture of the air and passes it on to the internal tissues.

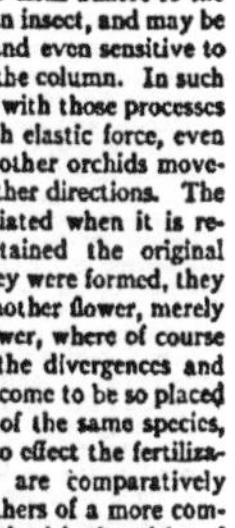

The number of species of orchids is greater than that of any other monocotyledonous order—not even excepting grasses—amounting to 6000, contained in 400 genera. This large number is partly accounted for by the diligent search in all countries that has been made for these plants for purposes of cultivation—being held at present in the greatest esteem by plant- and prices being paid for new or rare varieties which they the days of the tulipomania.

In this, economic uses of orchids are not remarkable. When we have mentioned vanilla (q.v.), which consists of the fleshy p°ds of an orchid, we have mentioned about the only economic product that now comes into market. Salep (q.v.), still used in the Levant, consists of the dried tubers of a terrestrial orchid, and contains a relatively large amount of nutritious matter. The cultivation of orchids is treated under HORTICULTURE.

The order is divided into two main groups based on the number of the stamens and stigmata. The first Diandreae, has two or rarely three fertile stamens and three functional stigmata. It contains two small genera of tropical Asia and Africa with almost regular flowers, and the large genus *Cypripedium* containing about 80 species in the north-temperate zone and tropical Asia and America. In *Cypripedium* two stamens are present, one on each side of the column instead of one only at the top, as in the group Monandreae, to which belong the remaining genera in which also only two stigmas are fertile. What may be considered the normal number of stamens is, as has been said, six, arranged in two rows. In most orchids the only stamen developed to maturity is the posterior one of the three opposite to the lip (anterior before the twisting of the ovary), the other two, as well as all three inner ones, being entirely absent, or present only in the form of rudiments. In *Cypripedium* two of the outer stamens are wanting; the third—the one, that is, which corresponds to the single fertile stamen in the Monandreae—forms a large sterile structure or staminode; the two lateral ones of the inner series are present, the third being undeveloped. This arrangement may be understood by reference to the following diagram, representing the relative position of the stamens in orchids generally and in *Cypripedium*. The letter L indicates the position of the labellum; the large figures indicate the developed stamens; the italic figures show the position of the suppressed stamens.

Arrangement of stamens in *Orchis*.   Arrangement of stamens in *Cypripedium*.

The Monandreae have been subdivided into twenty-eight tribes, the characters of which are based on the structure of the anther and pollinia, the nature of the inflorescence, whether terminal or lateral, the vernation of the leaf and the presence or absence of a joint between blade and sheath, and the nature of the stem. The most important are the following:

Ophrydineae, with about 45 genera, of terrestrial orchids, mainly north temperate, including the British genera *Orchis, Aceras, Ophrys, Herminium, Gymnadenia* and *Habenaria*. Also some genera mainly represented in South and tropical Africa, such as *Satyrium, Disa* and others.

Neottiineae, including 90 genera, also terrestrial, contains thirteen more or less widely distributed tropical or subtropical subtribes, some of which extend into temperate zones; one, *Cephalanthereae*, which includes our British genera *Cephalanthera* and *Epipactis* is chiefly north temperate. The British genera *Spiranthes, Listera* and *Neottia* are also included in this tribe, as is also *Vanilla*, the elongated stem of which climbs by means of tendril-like aerial roots—the long fleshy pod is the vanilla used for flavouring.

Coelogynineae, 7 genera, mostly epiphytes, and inhabitants of tropical Asia. A single internode of each shoot is swollen to form a pseudobulb.

Liparidineae, 9 genera, terrestrial, two, *Malaxis* and *Corallorhiza*, are British. *Liparis* is a large genus widely distributed in the tropics.

Pleurothallidineae, characterized by a thin stem bearing one leaf which separates at a distinct joint; the sepals are usually much larger than the petals and lip. Includes 30 genera, natives of tropical America, one of which, *Pleurothallis*, contains about 400 species. *Masdevallia* is common in cultivation and has often brilliant scarlet, crimson or orange flowers.

Laeliineae, with 22 genera, natives of the warmer parts of America, including three of those best known in cultivation, *Epidendrum, Cattleya* and *Laelia*. The jointed leaves are fleshy or leathery; the flowers are generally large with a well-developed lip.

Phajineae, includes 15 genera chiefly tropical Asiatic, some—*Phajus* and *Calanthe*—spreading northwards into China and Japan.

Cystopodiinae, includes 9 genera tropical, but extending into north temperate Asia and South Africa; *Eulophia* and *Lissochilus* are important African genera.

Catasetinae, with three tropical American genera, two of which, *Catasetum* and *Cycnoches*, have di- or tri-morphic flowers. They are cultivated for their strange-looking flowers.

Dendrobiinae, with six genera in the warmer parts of the Old World; the chief is *Dendrobium*, with 300 species, often with showy flowers.

Cymbidiinae, with 8 genera in the tropics of the Old World. The leaves are generally long and narrow. *Cymbidium* is well known in cultivation.

Oncidiinae, with 44 genera in the warmer parts of America. *Odontoglossum* and *Oncidium* include some of the best-known cultivated orchids.

Sarcanthinae, with 42 genera in the tropics. *Vanda* (Asia) and *Angraecum* (Africa and Madagascar) are known in cultivation. The flower of *Angraecum sesquipedale* has a spur 18 in. in length.

The order is well represented in Britain by 18 genera, which include several species of *Orchis*—*Gymnadenia* (fragrant orchis), *Habenaria* (butterfly and frog orchis), *Aceras* (man orchis), *Herminium* (musk orchis), *Ophrys* (bee, spider and fly orchis), *Epipactis* (Helleborine), *Cephalanthera, Neottia* (bird's-nest orchis), one of the few saprophytic genera, which have no green leaves, but derive their nourishment from decaying organic matter in the soil, *Listera* (Tway blade), *Spiranthes* (lady's tresses), *Malaxis* (bog-orchis), *Liparis* (fen-orchis), *Corallorhiza* (coral root), also a saprophyte, and *Cypripedium* (lady's slipper), represented by a single species now very rare in limestone districts in the north of England.

ORCHOMENUS (local form on coins and inscriptions, *Erchomenos*), the name borne by two cities of ancient Greece.

1. A Boeotian city, situated in an angle between the Cephissus and its tributary the Melas, on a long narrow hill which projects south from Mount Acontium. Its position is exceedingly strong, being defended on every side by precipice or marsh or river, and it was admirably situated to be the stronghold of an early kingdom. The acropolis is at the north end of the hill, on a peak which is overhung by Acontium, but at a distance sufficient to be safe from an enemy with the weapons of early warfare posted on the mountain. At the foot of the acropolis are the springs of the Melas.

In prehistoric times Orchomenus, as is proved alike by archaeological finds and by an extensive cycle of legends, was one of the most prosperous towns of Greece. It was at once a continental and a maritime power. On the mainland it controlled the greater part of Boeotia and drew its riches from the fertile lowlands of Lake Copaïs, upon the drainage of which the early kings of Orchomenus bestowed great care. Its maritime connexions have not been as yet determined, but it is clear that its original inhabitants, the Minyae, were a seafaring nation, and in historical times Orchomenus remained a member of the Calaurian League of naval states. At the end of the second millennium the Minyae were more or less supplanted by the incoming stock of Boeotians. Henceforth Orchomenus no longer figures as a great commercial state, and its political supremacy in Boeotia passed now, if not previously, to the people of Thebes. Nevertheless, owing perhaps to its strong military position, it long continued to exercise some sort of overlordship over other towns of northern Boeotia, and maintained an independent attitude within the Boeotian League. In 447 it served as the headquarters of the oligarchic exiles who freed Boeotia from Athenian control. In the 4th century Orchomenus was actuated throughout by an anti-Theban policy, which may have been nothing more than a recrudescence of old-time rivalry, but seems chiefly inspired by aversion to the newly established democracy at Thebes. In the Corinthian War the city supported Lysander and Agesilaus in their attacks upon Thebes, and when war was renewed between the Thebans and Spartans in 379 Orchomenus again sided with the latter. After the battle of Leuctra it was left at the mercy of the Thebans, who first, on Epaminondas's advice, readmitted it into the Boeotian League, but in 368 destroyed the town and exterminated or enslaved its people. By 353 Orchomenus had been rebuilt, probably by the Phocians, who used it as a bulwark against Thebes. After the subjection of the Phocians in 346 it was again razed by the Thebans, but was restored by Philip of Macedon as a check upon the latter (338). Orchomenus springs into prominence once again in 85 B.C., when it provided the battle-field on which the Roman general Sulla destroyed an army of Mithradates VI. of Pontus. Apart from this event·its later history is obscure, and its decadence is further attested by the neglectful drainage of the plain and the consequent encroachments of Lake Copaïs. Since medieval times the site has been occupied by a village named Skripou. Since 1867 drainage operations have been resumed, and the land thus reclaimed has been divided into small holdings. The most remarkable relic of the early power of Orchomenus is the so-called "treasury" (of "Minyas") which resembles the buildings of similar style at Mycenae (see MYCENAE), and is almost exactly the same size as the treasury of Atreus. The admiration which Pausanias expresses for it is justified by the beautiful ornamentation, especially of the roof, which has been brought to light by Schliemann's excavations in the inner chamber opening out of the circular vaulted tomb. The monument, undoubtedly the tomb of some ancient ruler, or of a dynasty, lies outside the city walls. Other remains of early date have been found upon this site.

The worship of the Charites (see GRACES) was the great cultus of Orchomenus, and the site of the temple is now occupied by a chapel, the Κοίμησις τῆς Παναγίας. The Charites were worshipped under the form of rude stones, which had fallen from heaven during the reign of Eteocles; and it was not till the time of Pausanias that statues of the goddesses were placed in the temple. Near this was another temple dedicated to Dionysus, in whose festival, the Ἀγριώνια, are apparent the traces of human sacrifice in early times (see AGRIONIA).

See Strabo viii. p. 374, ix. pp. 407, 414-416; Pausanias ix. 34-38; Thucydides i. 12, iv. 76; Xenophon, *Hellenica*, iii. 5, iv. 3, vi. 4; Diodorus xv., xvi.; Plutarch, *Sulla*, chs. 30-31; K. O. Müller, *Orchomenos und die Minyer* (Breslau, 1844); B. V. Head, *Historia numorum* (Oxford, 1877), pp. 293-294; *Journal of Hellenic Studies*, vol. ii. pls. xii., xiii.

2. An Arcadian city, situated in a district of the same name, north of Mantineia and west of Stymphalus. The district was mountainous, but embraced two valleys—the northern containing a lake which is drained, like all Arcadian lakes, by a *katavothron*; the southern lying under the city, separated from Mantineia by a mountain ridge called Anchisia. The old city occupied a strong and lofty situation; in the time of Strabo it was a ruin, but Pausanias mentions that a new town was built below the old. A primitive wooden image of Artemis Cedreatis stood in a large cedar tree outside the city. Orchomenus is mentioned in the Homeric catalogue with the epithet πολύμηλος.

In early history Orchomenus figures as a town of some importance, for its kings until the late 7th century B.C. held some sort of sovereignty over all Arcadia. In the 5th century it was overshadowed by its southern neighbour Mantineia, with whom it is henceforth generally found to be at variance. In 418 B.C. Orchomenus fell for a time into·the hands of the Mantineians; in 370 it held aloof from the new Arcadian League which the Mantineians were organizing. About this time it further declined in importance through the loss of some possessions on the east Arcadian watershed to the new Arcadian capital Megalopolis. In the 3rd century Orchomenus belonged in turn to the Aetolian League, to the Lacedaemonians, and, since 222, to the Achaean League. Though a fairly extensive settlement still existed on the site in the 2nd century A.D., its history under the Roman rule is quite obscure.

See Pausanias, viii. chs. 5, 11-13, 27; B. V. Head, *Historia numorum* (Oxford, 1887), pp. 377-378.

ORCIN, a dioxytoluene, $C_6H_2(CH_3)(OH)_2$ (1:3:5), found in many lichens, e.g. *Rocella tinctoria*, *Lecanora*, and formed by fusing extract of aloes with potash. It may be synthesized from toluene; more interesting is its production when acetone dicarboxylic ester is condensed with the aid of sodium. It crystallizes in colourless prisms with one molecule of water, which redden on exposure. Ferric chloride gives a bluish-violet coloration with the aqueous solution. Unlike resorcin it does not give a fluorescein with phthalic anhydride. Oxidation of the ammoniacal solution gives *orcein*, $C_7H_7N_2O_2$, the chief constituent of the natural dye archil (q.v.). Homo-pyrocatechin

is an isomer $(CH_3:OH:OH=1:3:4)$, found as its methyl ether (creosol) in beech-wood tar.

ORDEAL (O.Eng. *ordal*, *ordæl*, judgment), a term corresponding to modern Ger. *Urteil*, but bearing the special sense of the medieval Lat. *Dei judicium*, a miraculous decision as to the truth of an accusation or claim. The word is adopted in the late Lat. *ordalium*, Fr. *ordalie*. The ordeal had existed for many ages before it was thus named in Europe. In principle, and often in the very forms used, it belongs to ancient culture, thence flourishing up to the medieval European and modern Asiatic levels, but dying out before modern civilization. Some ordeals, which possibly represent early stages of the practice, are simply magical, being processes of divination turned to legal purpose. Thus in Burma suits are still determined by plaintiff and defendant being each furnished with a candle, equal in size and both lighted at once—he whose candle outlasts the other being adjudged, amid the acclamations of his friends, to have won his cause (Shway Yoe, *The Burman*, ii. 254). Even quainter is a Dyak ordeal in Borneo, where the two parties are represented by two shell-fish on a plate, which are irritated by pouring on some lime-juice, and the one first moving settles the guilt or innocence (as has been before arranged) of its owner (St John, *Forests of the Far East*, i. 89). The administration of ordeals has been much in the hands of priests, and they are more often than not worked on a theological basis, the intervention of a deity being invoked and assumed to take place even when the process is in its nature one of symbolic magic. For instance, an ancient divining instrument consisted of a sieve held suspended by a thread or by a pair of shears with the points stuck into its rim, and considered to move at the mention of the name to be discovered, &c. Thus girls consulted the "sieve-witch" (κοσκινόμαντις) about lovers (Theocr., *Idyll*. iii. 31). This *coscinomancy* served in the same way to discover a thief, when, with prayer to the gods for direction, the names of the suspected persons were called over to it (Potter, *Greek Antiquities*, i. 352). When a suspended hatchet was used in the same way to turn to the guilty, the process was called *axinomancy*. The sieve-ordeal remained popular in the middle ages (see the description and picture in Cornelius Agrippa, *De Occ. Phil.*); it is mentioned in Hudibras (ii. 3):

"... th' oracle of sieve and shears
That turns as certain as the spheres."

From this ancient ordeal is evidently derived the modern Christian form of the key and Bible, where a Psalter or Bible is suspended by a key tied in at Psalm l. 18: "When thou sawest a thief, then thou consentedst with him "; the bow of the key being balanced on the fingers, and the names of those suspected being called over, he or she at whose name the book turns or falls is the culprit (see Brand, *Popular Antiquities*, ed. Bohn, iii. 351).

One of the most remarkable groups of divinations passing into ordeals are those which appeal to the corpse itself for discovery of its murderer. The idea is rooted in that primitive state of mind which has not yet realized the full effect of death, but regards the body as still able to hear and act. Thus the natives of Australia will ask the dead man carried on his bier of boughs, who bewitched him; if he has died by witchcraft he will make the bier move round, and if the sorcerer who killed him be present a bough will touch him (Eyre, *Australia*, ii. 344). That this is no isolated fancy is shown by its recurrence among the negroes of Africa, where, for instance, the corpse causes its bearers to dash against some one's house, which accuses the owner of the murder (J. L. Wilson; *Western Africa*, p. 231; Waitz, ii. 193). This somewhat resembles the well-known ordeal of the bier in Europe in the middle ages, which, however, seems founded on a different principle, the imagination that a sympathetic action of the blood causes it to flow at the touch or neighbourhood of the murderer. Apparently the liquefaction of the blood which in certain cases takes place after death may have furnished the ground for this belief. On Teutonic ground, this ordeal appears in the *Nibelungenlied*, where the murdered Siegfried is laid on his bier, and Hagen is called on to prove his innocence by going to the corpse, but at his approach the dead chief's wounds bleed afresh. The typical instance in English history is the passage of Matthew Paris, that after Henry II.'s death at Chinon his son Richard came to view the body, " Quo superveniente, confestim erupit sanguis ex naribus regis mortui; ac si indignaretur spiritus in adventu ejus, qui ejusdem mortis causa esse credebatur, ut videretur sanguis clamare ad Deum." In Shakespeare (*Rich. III.*, act 1, sc. 2):

" O gentlemen, see, see! dead Henry's wounds
Open their congeal'd mouths, and bleed afresh!"

At Hertford assizes (1628) the deposition was taken as to certain suspected murderers being required to touch the corpse, when the murdered woman thrust out the ring finger three times and it dropped blood on the grass (Brand, iii. 231); and there was a case in the Scottish High Court of Justiciary as late as 1668 (T. F. Thiselton Dyer, *Folklore of Shakespeare*, p. 487). Durham peasants, apparently remembering the old belief, still expect those who come to look at a corpse to touch it, in token that they bear no ill-will to the departed (W. Henderson, *Folklore of Northern Counties*, p. 57). .

Certain ordeals are closely related to oaths, so that the two shade into one another. Let the curse which is to fall on the oath-breaker take effect at once, it then becomes a sign condemning the swearer— in fact, an ordeal. Thus the drinking of water on which a curse or magical penalty has been laid is a mere oath so long as the time of fulfilment is unfixed (see OATH). But it becomes an ordeal when, as in Brahmanic India, the accused drinks three handfuls of water in which a sacred image has been dipped; if he is innocent nothing happens, but if he is guilty sickness or misfortune will fall on him within one to three weeks (for accounts of these and other Hindu ordeals see Ali Ibrahim Khan in *Asiatic Researches*, i. 389, and Stenzler's summary in *Z. D. M. G.*, vol. ix.). The earliest account of such an ordeal is in Numbers v., which describes the mode of administering to a woman charged with unfaithfulness the bitter water mixed with the dust of the tabernacle floor, with the curse laid on it to cause her belly to swell and her thigh to fall if guilty. Ewald (*Antiquities of Israel*, 236) regards the draught as in itself harmless, and the operation of this curse on the guilty as due to the influence of the mind on the body. But the term " bitter " is applied to the water before it has been cursed, which suggests that it already contained some drug, as in the poison-water ordeal still in constant use over a great part of Africa. Thus the red water of Guinea is a decoction made by pounding in a wooden mortar and steeping in water the inner bark of one of the mimosas, producing a liquor like that of a tan-vat, astringent, narcotic, and when taken in sufficient quantity emetic. The accused, with solemn ceremony and invocation, drinks freely of it; if it nauseates him and he throws it up he is triumphantly acquitted, but if he becomes dizzy he is guilty, and the assembly fall on him, pelt him with stones and even drag him over the rocks till he is dead. Here the result of the ordeal depends partly on the patient's constitution, but more on the sorcerer who can prepare the proper dose to prove either guilt or innocence. Among the various drugs used in different parts of Africa are the *mbundu* root, the Calabar bean, the tangena nut (*Tanghinia venenifiua*, a strong poison and emetic) The sorcerers who administer this ordeal have in their hands a power of inflicting or remitting judicial murder, giving them boundless influence (details in J. L. Wilson, *Western Africa*, pp. 275, 398; Burton, *Lake Regions of Central Africa*, ii. 357; Bosman, " Guinea," in *Pinkerton's Voyages*, xvi. 398, &c.). The poison-ordeal is also known to Brahmanic law, decoction of aconite root being one of the poisons given, and the accused if not sickening being declared free (Stenzler, l.c.). Theoretically connected with the ordeal by cursed drink is that by cursed food, which is, however, distinguished among this black catalogue by being sometimes an effectual means of discovering the truth. The ordeal by bread and cheese, practised in Alexandria about the 2nd century, was practically the same as that known to English law five to ten centuries later as the *corsnaed* or " trial slice " of consecrated bread and cheese which was administered from the altar, with

the curse that if the accused were guilty God would send the angel Gabriel to stop his throat, that he might not be able to swallow that bread and cheese. In fact, if guilty and not a hardened offender he was apt to fail, dry-mouthed and choking through terror, to get it down. The remembrance of this ancient ordeal still lingers in the popular phrase, " May this bit choke me if I lie! " In India the corresponding trial by rice is prescribed in the old laws to be done by suspected persons chewing the consecrated grains of rice and spitting them out, moist and untinged with blood, on a banyan leaf; this or the mere chewing and swallowing of a mouthful of rice-grains is often used even by the English as a means of detecting a thief. A classical mention of the ordeals by carrying hot iron in the hands and by passing through the fire is made more interesting by the guards who offer to prove their innocence in this way offering further to take oath by the gods, which shows the intimate connexion between oaths and ordeals (Soph.. *Ant.* 264, see also Aeschyl., *fr.* 284).

ᾖμεν δ' ἕτοιμοι καὶ μύδρους αἴρειν χεροῖν
καὶ πῦρ διέρπειν, καὶ θεοὺς ὁρκωμοτεῖν
τὸ μήτε δρᾶσαι μήτε τῷ ξυνειδέναι
τὸ πρᾶγμα βουλεύσαντι μήτ' εἰργασμένῳ.

The passing through the fire is described in the Hindu codes of Yâjnavalkya and others, and is an incident in Hindu poetry, where in the *Râmâyana* the virtuous Sîtâ thus proves her innocence to her jealous husband Râma (Stenzler, p. 669; Pictet, *Origines Indo-Européennes*, part ii. p. 457). It was not less known to European law and chronicle, as where Richardis, wife of Charles the Fat, proves her innocence by going into a fire clothed in a waxed shift, and is unhurt by the fire (Grimm, *Deutsche Rechtsalterthümer*, p. 912). Yet more minutely prescribed in the Hindu ordeal-books is the rite of carrying the glowing hot iron seven steps, into the seven or nine circles traced on the ground, the examination of the hands to see if they show traces of burning, and the binding them up in leaves. The close historical connexion of the Hindu ordeal laws with the old European is shown by the correspondence of minute details, as where in a Scandinavian law it is prescribed that the red-hot iron shall be carried nine steps (*Grimm, op. cit.*, p. 918). In Anglo-Saxon laws the iron to be carried was at first only one pound weight, but Athelstan's law (in *Ancient Laws and Institutes of England*, iv. 6) enacts that it be increased to weigh three pounds. Another form well known in old Germany and England was the walking barefoot over glowing ploughshares, generally nine. The law-codes of the early middle ages show this as an ordinary criminal procedure (see the two works last referred to), but it is perhaps best remembered in two non-historical legends. The German queen Kunigunde, " haec dicens stupentibus et flentibus universis qui aderant, vomeres candentes nudo vestigio calcavit et sine adustionis molestia transiit " (*Vita Henrici*, ap. Canisium, vi. 387). Queen Emma, mother of Edward the Confessor, accused of familiarity with Alwyn bishop of Winchester, triumphantly purges herself and him by the help of St Swithin—each of the two thus acquitted giving nine manors to the church of Winchester, in memory of the nine ploughshares, and the king being corrected with stripes (John Bromton; see Freeman's *Norm. Conq.*, vol. ii. App.). To dip the hand in boiling water or oil or melted lead and take out a stone or ring is another ordeal of this class. The traveller may find some of these fiery trials still in use, or at least in recent memory, in barbaric regions of Africa or further Asia—the negro plunging his arm into the caldron of boiling oil, the Burman doing feats with melted lead, while the Bedouin will settle a conflict of evidence by the opposing witnesses licking a glowing hot-iron spoon (Burckhardt, *Arabien*, pp. 98, 233). This latter feat may be done with safety by any one, provided the iron be clean and thoroughly white hot, while if only red-hot it would touch and burn the tongue. Probably the administerers of the ordeal are aware of this, and of the possibility of dipping the hand in melted metal; and there are stories of arts of protecting the skin (see the recipe in Albertus Magnus, *De Mirabilibus*), though it is not known what can be really done beyond making it horny, like a smith's, which would serve as a defence in stepping on coals, but not in serious trials like that of carrying a heavy hot-hot iron. The fire-ordeals are still performed by mountebanks, who very likely keep up the same means of trickery which were in official use when the accused was to be acquitted. The actual practice of the fire-ordeal contrasts shamefully with its theory, that the fire rather than harm the innocent restrained its natural action. Thus it stands in the Hindu code of Manu (viii. 115): "He whom the flame does not burn, whom the water does not cast up, or whom no harm soon befals, is to be taken as truthful in his oath." The water-ordeal here referred to is that well known in Europe, where the accused is thrown bound into the water, which receives him if innocent, but rejects him if guilty. The manner of carrying out this test is well explained in the directions given by Archbishop Hincmar in the 9th century: he who is let down into the water for trial is to be fastened by a rope, that he may not be in danger if the water receives him as innocent, but may be pulled out. In the later middle ages this ordeal by "swimming" or "fleeting" became the most approved means of trying a suspected witch: she was stripped naked and cross bound, the right thumb to the left toe, and the left thumb to the right toe. In this state she was cast into a pond or river, in which it was thought impossible for her to sink (Brand iii. 21). The cases of "ducking" witches which have occurred in England within the last few years are remains of the ancient ordeal.

If there is one thing that may be predicated of man in a state of nature it is that two disputants tend to fight out their quarrel. When in the warfare of Greeks and Trojans, of Jews and Philistines, of Vandals and Alamans, heroes come out from the two sides and their combat is taken to mark the powers of the opposing war-gods and decide the victory, then the principle of the ordeal by battle has been practically called in. Among striking instances of the Teutonic custom which influenced the whole of medieval Europe may be cited the custom of the Franks that the princes, if they could not quell the strife, had to fight it out between themselves, and Wipo's account of the quarrel between the Christian Saxons and the Pagan Slavs as to which broke the peace, when both sides demanded of the emperor that it should be settled by duel, which was done by choosing a champion on each side, and the Christian fell. The Scandinavian term "holmgang" refers to the habit of fighting duels on an island. A passage from old German law shows the single combat accepted as a regular legal procedure: "If there be dispute concerning fields, vineyards, or money, that they avoid perjury let two be chosen to fight, and decide the cause by duel" (Grimm, Rechtsaltert., p. 928). In England, after the Conquest, trial by combat superseded other legal ordeals, which were abolished in the time of Henry III. Among famous instances is that of Henry de Essex, hereditary standard-bearer of England, who fled from a battle in Wales, in 1158, threw from him the royal standard, and cried out that the king was slain. Robert de Montfort afterwards, accusing him of having done this with treasonable intent, offered to prove his accusation by combat, and they fought in presence of Henry II. and his court, when Essex was defeated, but the king spared his life, and his estate being confiscated, he became a monk in Reading Abbey. A lord often sent his man in his stead to such combats, and priests and women were ordinarily represented by champions. The wager of battle died out so quietly in England without being legally abolished that in the court of king's bench in 1818 it was claimed by a person charged with murder, which led to its formal abolition (Ashford v. Thornton in Barnewall and Alderson 457; see details in H. C. Lea, Superstition and Force, ii.). A distinct connexion may, however, be traced between the legal duel and the illegal private duel, which has disappeared from England, but still flourishes in France and Germany (see Duel). (E. B. T.)

ORDER (through Fr. ordre, for earlier ordene, from Lat. ordo, ordinis, rank, service, arrangement; the ultimate source is generally taken to be the root seen in Lat. oriri, rise, arise, begin; cf. "origin"), a row or series, hence grade, class or rank, succession, sequence or orderly arrangement; from these, the original meanings of ordo, have developed the numerous applications attached to the word, many, if not most, of which appear in classical and medieval Latin. In the sense of a class or body of persons or things united by some common status, rank or distinguishing characteristics, or as organized and living under some common rules and regulations, we find the term applied, in such expressions as "lower" or "higher orders," to the class divisions of society; to the various grades of persons exercising spiritual functions in the Christian church (see Order, Holy, below); to the bodies of persons bound by vows to a religious life (see Monasticism, and separate articles on the chief religious orders); to the military and monastic fraternities of the middle ages, such as the Templars, Hospitallers, &c., and to those institutions, founded by sovereigns or states, in part imitation of these fraternities, which are conveniently divided into orders of knighthood, or orders of merit (see Knighthood). The term "order" is thus used, in an easily transferred sense, for the various insignia, badge, star, collar, worn by the members of the institution. As applied to a group of objects, an "order" in zoological, botanical and mineral classification ranks next below a "class," and above a "family." The use of the word in architecture is treated in a separate article below.

The word has several technical mathematical usages. In number-theory it denotes a relative rank between the elements of an aggregate so that the collection becomes an ordered aggregate (see Number). The order of a plane curve is the number of points (real or imaginary) in which the curve is intersected by a straight line; it is equal to the degree (or coefficient of the highest power) of the Cartesian equation expressing the curve. The order of a non-plane curve is the number of points (real or imaginary) in which the curve intersects a plane (see Curve). The order of a surface is the number of points in which the surface intersects a straight line. For the order of a congruence and complex see Surface. The order of a differential equation is the degree of its highest differential coefficient (see Differential Equation).

Another branch of the sense-development of the word starts from the meaning of orderly, systematic or proper arrangement, which appears in the simplest form in such adverbial expressions as "in order," "out of order" and the like. More particular instances are the use of the word for the customary procedure observed in the conduct of the business of a public meeting, or of parliamentary debates, and for the general maintenance and due observance of law and authority, "public order."

In liturgical use "order" is a special form of divine service prescribed by authority, e.g. the "Order of Confirmation," in the English Prayer Book.

The common use of "order" in the sense of a command, instruction or direction is a transference from that of arrangement, in accordance with intention to the means for attaining it. It is a comparatively late sense-development; it does not appear in Latin, and the earliest quotations in the New English Dictionary are from the 16th century. Particular applications of the term are, in commercial usage, to a direction in writing to a banker or holder of money or goods, by the person in whom the legal right to them lies, to pay or hand over the same to a third person named or to his order. A bill or negotiable instrument made "payable to order" is one which can be negotiated by the payee by endorsement. At common law a negotiable instrument must contain words expressly authorizing transfer. By the Bills of Exchange Act 1882, § 8, "a bill is payable to order which is expressed to be so payable, or which is expressed to be payable to a particular person, and does not contain words prohibiting transfer or indicating an intention that it should not be transferable." Other applications are to a direction for the supply of goods and to a pass for free admission to a place of amusement, a building, &c.

In law an "order of the court" is a judicial direction on matters outside the record; as laid down by Esher, M.R., in Onslow v. Inland Revenue, 50, L.J.Q.B. 556, a "judgment" is a decision obtained in an action and every other decision is an "order." For "Order in Council" see below.

ORDER, in classic architecture the term employed (Lat. *genus*, Ital. *ordine*, Sp. *orden*, Ger. *Ordnung*) to distinguish the varieties of column and entablature which were employed by the Greeks and Romans in their temples and public buildings. The first attempt to classify the architectural orders was made by Vitruvius, who, to those found in Greek buildings, viz. the Doric, Ionic and Corinthian, added a fourth, the Tuscan. On the revival of classic art in Italy, the revivalists translated Vitruvius's work *De Architectura*, and added a fifth example, the Composite, so that nominally there are five orders. The Tuscan, however, is only an undeveloped and crude modification of the Doric order, and the Composite is the same as the Corinthian with the exception of the capital, in which the volutes of the Ionic order were placed above the acanthus leaves of the Corinthian.

An order in architecture consists of several parts, constructive in their origin, but, as employed afterwards, partly constructive and partly decorative; its principal features are the column, consisting of base (except in the Greek Doric order), shaft and capital, and the entablature, subdivided into the architrave (the supporting member), the frieze (the decorative member) and the cornice (the crowning and protecting member). Two only of the orders were independently evolved, viz. the Doric in Greece and Magna Grecia, and the Ionic in Ionia. For the Corinthian order, the Greeks borrowed with slight variations the entablature for their Ionic order, and the Romans employed this modified entablature for their Composite order. Owing to a certain resemblance in form, it was at one time thought that the Greeks owed the origin of the Doric order to Egypt, but the Egyptian column has no echinus under its abacus, which in the earliest Doric examples is an extremely important element in its design, owing to its great size and projection; moreover, the Doric column ceased to be employed in Egypt after the XIXth Dynasty, some seven or eight centuries before the first Greek colony was established there. Dr Arthur Evans's discoveries in the palace of Cnossus in Crete have shown that the earliest type of the Doric column (c. 1500 B.C.) is that painted in a fresco which represents the façades of three temples or shrines, the truth of this representation being borne out by actual remains in the palace; the columns were in timber, tapered from the top downwards, and were crowned by a projecting abacus supported by a large torus moulding, probably moulded in stucco. The next examples of the order are those in stone, which flank the entrance doorway of the tomb of Agamemnon at Mycenae (c. 1200 B.C.), the greater portions of which are now set up in the British Museum, and here both capital and shaft are richly decorated with the chevron pattern, probably derived from the metal plates which in Homeric times sheathed the wood columns. The columns of the Mycenae tombs are semi-detached only, and of very slender proportions, averaging 10 to 11 diameters in height; as isolated columns, therefore, they would have been incapable of carrying any weight, so that in the next examples known, those of the temple at Corinth, where the columns had to carry an entablature in stone supporting a stone ceiling over the peristyle, the relation of diameter to height is nearly one to four, so diffident were the Greek architects as to the bearing power of the stone. In the temple of Apollo at Syracuse, also a very archaic example, the projection of the capital was so great that the abaci nearly touched one another, and the columns are less than one diameter apart. The subsequent development which took place was in the lightening of the column and the introduction of many refinements, so that in the most perfected example known, the Parthenon, the columns are 1½ diameters apart and nearly 5½ diameters high. In a somewhat later example, the temple of the Nemaean Zeus (Argos) the columns are 6½ diameters high. A similar lightening of the structure took place in the entablature, which in the earliest temple in Sicily is about half the height of the columns, in the Parthenon less than a third, and in the Temple of the Nemaean Zeus a little over a fourth.

The origin of the Ionic order is not so clear, and it cannot be traced beyond the remains of the archaic temple of Diana at Ephesus (c. 560 B.C.), now in the British Museum, in which the capitals and the lower drum of the shaft enriched with sculpture in their design and execution suggest many centuries of development. Here again attempts have been made to trace the source to Egypt, but the volute capital of the archaic temple of Diana at Ephesus and the decorative lotus bud of Egypt are entirely different in their form and object. The latter is purely decorative and vertical in its tendency, the former is a feature intended to carry a superincumbent weight, and is extended horizontally so as to perform the function of a bracket-capital, viz. to lessen the bearing of the architrave or beam which it carries. A similar constructive expedient is found in Persian work at Persepolis, which, however, dates about forty years later than the Ephesian work. The volutes of the capitals of the Lycian tombs are none of them older than the 4th century, being copies of Greek stone examples. As with the Doric order, the columns became more slender than at first, those of the archaic temple being probably between 6 and 7 diameters high, of the temple on the Ilissus (c. 450 B.C.) 8½, and of the temple of Athena Polias at Priene (c. 345 B.C.) over 10 diameters high.

The employment of the two orders in Athens simultaneously, and sometimes in the same building, led to a reciprocal influence one on the other. In the Doric order to an increased refinement in the contour of its mouldings, in the Ionic order to greater severity in treatment, more particularly in the bedmould, the members of which were reduced in number and simplified, the dentil course (which in Ionia was a very important feature) being dispensed with in the temple on the Ilissus and in that of Nike Apteros, and employed only in the caryatide portico of the Erechtheum. The capital of the Corinthian order, its only original feature, may have been derived from the Egyptian bell-capital, which was constantly employed there, even in Roman times, its decoration was, however, purely Greek, and would seem to have been based on the application to the bell of foliage and ornament derived from metallic forms. The inventor of the capital is said to have been Callimachus of Corinth, who was a craftsman in metal and designed the bronze lamp and its cover for the Erechtheum in Corinthian bronze, which may account for the origin and title of the capital. The earliest example of the Corinthian capital is that found at Bassae by Cockerell, dating from about 430 B.C., and the more perfected type is that of the Tholos of Epidaurus (400 B.C.).

Whilst the entablatures of the Doric and Ionic orders suggest their origin from timber construction, that of the Corinthian was simply borrowed from the Ionic order, and its subsequent development by the Romans affords the only instance of their improvement of a Greek order (so far as the independent treatment of it was concerned) by the further enrichment of the bedmould of the cornice, where the introduction of the modillion gave an increased support to the corona and was a finer crowning feature.

The Greek Doric order was not understood by the Romans, and was, with one or two exceptions, utilized by them only as a decorative feature in their theatres and amphitheatres, where in the form of semi-detached columns they formed divisions between the arches; the same course was taken with the Ionic order, which, however, would seem to have been employed largely in porticoes. On the other hand, the Corinthian order, in consequence of its rich decoration, appealed more to the Roman taste; moreover, all its lines were the same, and it could be employed in rectangular or in circular buildings without any difficulty. The earliest examples are found in the temple of Castor and Pollux at Cora, near Rome, which is Greek in the style of its carving, and in the portico of the Pantheon at Rome erected by Agrippa (27 B.C.), where the Roman order is fully developed. The next developments of the orders are those which followed the revival of classic architecture in the 16th century, and these were largely influenced by the discovery in 1456 of the manuscript of Vitruvius, an architect who flourished in the latter half of the 1st century B.C. In his work *De Architectura* he refers constantly to drawings which he had prepared to illustrate his descriptions; these, however, have never been found, so that the translators of his work put their own interpretation on his text and published woodcuts representing the Roman orders as defined by him. They did not, however, confine themselves to the actual remains, which in their day were in much better preservation than at present, but attempted to complete the orders by the addition of pedestals to the columns, which were not employed by the Greeks, and only under special conditions by the Romans; as, however, they are included in the two chief authorities on the subject, Palladio and Vignola, the text-book of the former being the standard in England, and that of the latter in France, the rules and proportions set forth in them for pedestals, as also for the employment of the superposing of the orders with arches between, will follow the analysis of the Greek and Roman orders.

The Greek Doric Order.—The Doric was the favourite order of the Greeks, and the one in which they introduced all their principal refinements; these were of so subtle a nature that until the site was cleared in 1837 their existence was not known, and the earlier explorers, though recognizing the extreme beauty of the proportions and some of the refinements, were unable to grasp the extent to which they were carried, and it was reserved for Penrose in 1846 to verify by micrometrical studies the theories put forward by Pennethorne and other authors. The whole structure of the Doric temple (which consisted of the columns, subdivided into shaft and capital, and the entablature, subdivided into architrave, frieze and cornice) rested on a platform of three steps, of which the upper step was the stylobate or column base (fig. 1). The tread and rise of the steps varied in accordance with the diameter of the column; in temples of great dimensions, therefore, supplementary steps were provided for access to the stylobate, or, as found in many temples, slight inclined planes. Resting on the stylobate was the shaft of the column, which was either monolithic or composed of frusta or drums. The shaft tapered as it rose, the diminution of the upper diameter being more pronounced in early examples, as in one of the temples at Selinus and in the great temple at Paestum. In the Parthenon at Athens the lower diameter is 6 ft. 3 in. and the upper 4 ft. 9 in., which gives a diminution slightly over one-quarter of the lower diameter. The shaft was always fluted, with two or three exceptions, where the temples were not completed, and there were usually twenty flutes. In two temples at Syracuse, the most ancient temple at Selinus, the temple at Assos, and the temple at Sunium there are only sixteen flutes; the flutes were elliptic in section and intersected with an arris. In order to correct an optical illusion, which arises in a diminishing shaft, a slight entasis or swelling in the centre was given, the greatest departure from the straight line being about one-third up the shaft. The shaft was crowned by the capital, the juncture of the two being marked by a groove (one in the Parthenon, but up to three in more ancient examples) known as the hypotrachelion. Above this the trachelion or necking curves over, constructing what is known as the apophyge up to the fillets, round the base of the echinus, which forms the transition to the square abacus. The varying curve of the echinus, from the earliest times down to the later examples, is shown in the article on mouldings. The relative proportions of the lower diameter and the height of the columns vary according to the date of the example, in the early examples the column

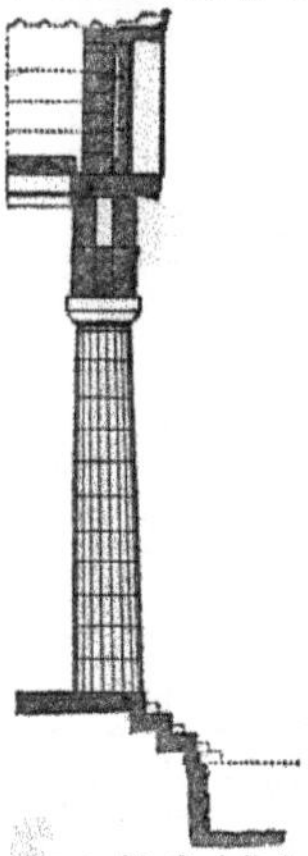

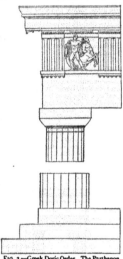

FIG. 1.—The Greek Doric Order. The Parthenon, Athens; section through front.

being just on 4 diameters high, in the Parthenon nearly 5½ diameters, and in the Temple of Jupiter Nemaeus 6½ diameters high. The distance between the columns or intercolumniation varied also according to the date, that of the earliest examples in Sicily being about 1 diameter (that between the angle columns being always less), in the Parthenon in the proportion of 1 to 1·24, and in the temple at Argos as 1 to 1·53.

Above the columns rested the entablature (fig. 2), of which the lower member, the architrave, was plain and crowned by a projecting fillet, known as the regula; under which, and below the triglyph, was a fillet (taenia), with six guttae underneath. The proportional height of the architrave, which was the chief supporting member, varied according to date, in one of the earliest examples at Syracuse being of greater depth than the diameter of the column, and in the Parthenon about two-thirds of the diameter. Above the architrave was the frieze, divided into triglyphs, so called because they are divided into three bands by two vertical grooves, and metopes or spaces between the triglyphs. It is supposed that the triglyphs represented the beams in the primitive cella before the peristyle was

FIG. 2.—Greek Doric Order. The Parthenon, Athens.

added, the spaces between being filled with shutters or boards to prevent the temple being entered by birds. The face of the metopes, which are nearly square, is set back behind that of the triglyphs, and is sometimes decorated with sculpture in high relief. There is generally one triglyph over each column and one between, but at each end of the temple there is a triglyph at the angle, so that the intercolumniation at the angle columns is less than that of the others, which gives a sense of increased strength. Above the frieze is the cornice, which projects forward about one-third of the diameter of the column and slopes downwards at an angle generally the same as the slope of the roof. On its under surface are mutules, one over each triglyph and one between, which are studded with guttae, probably representing the wood pins which secured the rafters in their position. Generally speaking, in the Doric temples there is no cymatium or gutter, and the rain fell directly off the roof; in order to prevent it trickling down there was an upper moulding, throated, with a bird's beak moulding behind and a second throating near the bottom, so that the corona had an upper fillet projecting, and a lower fillet receding, from its fascia plane. The roof itself was covered with tiles in terra-cotta or marble, which consisted of flat slabs with raised edges and covering tiles over the joints; the lower ends of the covering tiles were decorated with antefixae, and the top of the roof was protected by ridge tiles, on the top of which were sometimes additional antefixae placed parallel with the ridge tile. As the mouldings of the pediment were returned for a short distance along the side, there was a small cymatium or gutter with lions' heads, through the mouth of which the water ran. In the principal and rear front of the temple the lines of the cornice were repeated up the slope of the pediment, which coincided with that of the roof, and the tympanum, which they enclosed, was enriched with sculpture. On the centre of the pediment and at each end were pedestals (acroteria), on which figures, or conventional ornaments, were placed. Supplementary to the order at the back of the peristyle were antae, slightly projecting pilasters which terminated the walls of the pronaos; these had a small base, were of the same diameter from the top to the bottom, and had a simple moulded capital.

The Greek Ionic Order.—The Ionic order, like the Doric, owes its origin to timber prototypes, but varies in its features; the columns are more slender, being from 8 to 9 diameters high, with an intercolumniation of sometimes as much as 2 diameters; the architrave also is subdivided into three fascia, which suggests that in its origin it consisted of three beams superposed, in contradistinction to that of the Doric architrave, which consisted of a single beam. As in the Doric order, the Ionic temple rested on a stylobate of three steps (fig. 3). The columns consisted of base, shaft and capital. In the Ionic examples the base consisted of a torus moulding, fluted horizontally, beneath which were three double astragals divided by the scotia, sometimes, as in the temple at Priene, resting on a square plinth. In the Attic base employed in Athens, under the upper torus, which is either plain, fluted or carved with the guilloche, is a fillet and deep scotia, with a second torus underneath. The shaft tapers much less than in the Doric order; it has a slighter entasis, and is fluted, the flutes being elliptical in section but subdivided by fillets. The number of flutes is generally 24. The lower and upper parts of the shaft have an apophyge and a fillet, resting on the base in the former case and supporting the capital in the latter. The capital consists of an astragal, sometimes carved with the bead and reel, and an echinus moulding above enriched with the egg-and-dart, on which rests the capital with spiral volutes at each end, and from front to back with cushions which vary in design and enrichment. In the capitals of the angle columns the end volute is turned round on the diagonal, so as to present the same appearance on the front and the side; this results in an awkward arrangement at the back, where two half-volutes intersect one another at right angles. A small abacus, generally carved with ornament, crowns the capital. In early examples the channels between the fillets of the spiral are convex, in later examples concave. In the capitals of the Erechtheum (fig. 4), a greater richness is given by intermediary fillets. In all great examples the second fillet dips down in the centre of the front and a small anthemion ornament marks the receding of the echinus moulding, which is circular and sometimes nearly merged into the cushion. In the Erechtheum the enrichment of the capital is carried further in the

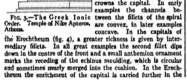

FIG. 3.—The Greek Ionic Order. Temple of Nike Apteros, Athens.

necking, which is decorated with the anthemion and divided off from the upper part of the shaft by a bead and reel. The entablature is divided, like that of the Doric order, into architrave, frieze and cornice. The architrave is subdivided into three fasciae, the upper one projecting slightly beyond the lower, and crowned by small mouldings, the lower one sometimes carved with the Lesbian leaf. Above this is the frieze, sometimes plain and at other times enriched with figure sculpture in low relief. In the Ionian examples there was no frieze, its place being taken by dentils of great size and projection. The cornice consists of bedmould, corona and cymatium; in the Ionian examples the bedmould is of great richness, consisting of a lower moulding of egg-and-dart with bead and reel, a dentil course above, and another egg-and-dart with bead and reel above, sinking into the soffit of the corona, which projects in the Ionian examples more than half a diameter. The corona consists of a plain fascia with moulding and cymatium above, and as the cymatium or gutter is carried through from end to end of the temple it is provided with lions' heads to throw off the water, and sometimes enriched with

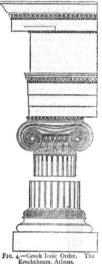

FIG. 4.—Greek Ionic Order. The Erechtheum, Athens.

the anthemion ornament. In the Attic examples much greater simplicity, ascribed to Dorian influence, is given to the bedmould, in which only the cyma-reversa with the Lesbian leaf carved on it and the bead and reel are retained. The mouldings of the cornice, including the cymatium, are carried up as a pediment, as in the Doric temple, and the roofs are similar. The base and capital of the antae are more elaborate than in those of the Doric order, and are sometimes, both in Ionic and Attic examples, richly carved with the Lesbian leaf and egg-and-dart, in both cases with the bead and reel underneath. The chief variation from the usual entablature is found in that of the caryatide portico of the Erechtheum, where the frieze is omitted, dentils are introduced in the bedmould, paterae are carved on the upper fascia of the architrave, and the covering was a flat marble roof. The caryatide figures, the drapery of which recalls the fluting of the columns, stood on a podium which enriched cornice and base.

The Greek Corinthian Order (fig. 5).—As the entablature of this order was adapted by the Greeks from that of the Ionic order, the capital only need be described, and its evolution from the earliest examples known, that in the temple at Bassae, to the fully developed type in the temple of Zeus Olympius at Athens, can be easily traced. It consisted of either a small range of leaves at the bottom, or of a bead-and-reel moulding, a bell decorated in various ways and a moulded abacus, the latter as a rule being concave in plan on each face and generally terminating in an arris or point. In the Bassae capital we find the first example of the spiral tendrils which rise up and support the abacus with other spirals crossing to the centre and the acanthus leaf and flower. In the more perfected example of the Choragic monument of Lysicrates (fig. 6), there is a lower range of small leaves of some river plant, between which and the tops of the flutes (which here are turned over as leaves) is a sinking which was probably filled with a metal band. From the lower range of leaves spring eight acanthus leaves, bending forward at the top, with small flowers between, representing the heads of nails which in the metal prototype fastened these leaves to the bell; from the caulicolae, on the right and left, spring spiral tendrils rising to the angles under the abacus, and from the same caulicolae double spirals which cross to the centre of the bell, the upper ones carrying the anthemion flower, which rises across the abacus. The abacus in this capital has a deep scotia with fillet, and an echinus above, and is one of the few great examples in which the angles are canted. The architrave, frieze and cornice are adaptations from the Ionic order. The corona has in the place of the cymatium a cresting of antefixae, which is purely decorative, as there are no covering tiles, the roof of the monument being

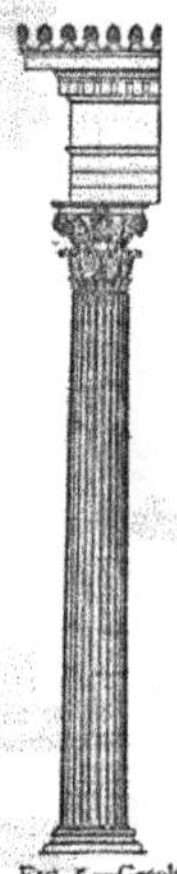

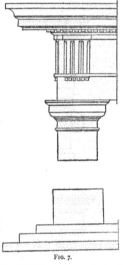

FIG. 5.—Greek Corinthian Order Choragic monument of Lysicrates.

FIG. 6.

in one block of marble carved with leaves. Set back and on the same plane as the architrave and frieze is a second cresting with the Greek wave scroll. There are other types of Greek Corinthian capital, of which the finest example is in the interior of the Tholos at Epidaurus (c. 400 B.C.), with two rows of leaves round the lower part, angle and central spirals, and a flower in the centre of the abacus. Of other examples the capitals of the interior of the temple of Apollo Branchidae in Asia Minor, and of the vestibule at Eleusis, and of the two porches of the temple of Winds at Athens, are the best known. Except for the pointed ends of the abacus, which are Greek, the capital of the temple of Zeus Olympius might almost be classed among the Roman examples, and it is thought to have been the model copied by the Romans from those which Sulla took to Rome for the temple of Jupiter Capitolinus.

The Roman Doric Order.—The earliest example of this order is probably that of the temple at Cora, about 20 m. from Rome,

attributed to Sulla (80 B.C.), in which the leading features of the Greek Doric order are employed, but extremely degraded in style. The temple was raised on a podium with a flight of steps in front; the shaft has 20 flutes and is carried on a small torus base, and the echinus of the capital is very poor. The architrave and triglyph-frieze are cut out of the same stone, the former being much too shallow to allow of its carrying the frieze and cornice. Two other early examples are those employed in the decoration of the arcades of the Tabularium and of the theatre of Marcellus (fig. 7); they are only semi-detached. The Doric order was not a favourite with the Romans, and did not appeal to their tastes for rich decoration; the only other examples known are those at Praeneste, at Albano, and in the thermae of Diocletian. At Albano the echinus of the capital is carved with the egg and anchor, and in the

FIG. 7.

thermae a cyma-recta carved with a leaf ornament takes the place of the echinus. There is no base to any of these examples, the Albano base consisting only of an apophyge and fillet, and only the Diocletian example is fluted.

The Roman Ionic Order.—The complete degradation of the Ionic order is clearly shown in the so-called temple of Fortuna Virilis (ascribed to about 100 B.C.), in the profuse decoration of architrave, frieze and cornice with coarse ornament, and, in the capital, the raising of the echinus to the same level as the top of the second fillet of the volute, so that it is no longer visible under the cushion. The shaft has twenty flutes, the fillet being much wider than in the Greek examples, and the flute is semi-circular. Much more refinement is shown in the order as employed on the upper storey of the theatre of Marcellus (fig. 8), where the only part enriched with ornament is in the egg and tongue of the bedmould. In the capital the fillet of the volute runs across above the echinus, and the canalis is stopped at each end over the volute, an original treatment. The most corrupt example of the Roman Ionic capital is that of the temple of Saturn on the Forum Romanum, which fortunately does not seem to have been copied later. The base of all the Roman Ionic columns is that known as the Attic base, viz. a lower and upper torus with scotia and fillets between, always raised on a square plinth.

The Roman Corinthian Order.—The great varieties of design in the Greek Corinthian capital (fig. 9), and the fact that its entablature was copied from Ionic examples, suggests that no definite type sufficient to constitute an order had been evolved by the Greeks; it remained therefore a problem to be worked out by the Romans, who, with the assistance of Greek artists, employed generally by the Romans, not only in Rome but throughout Greece, Asia Minor and Syria, developed an order which, though wanting in the refinement and subtlety found in Greek work, is one of the most monumental kind, and has in its adoption by the Italian revivalists had more influence than any other in the raising of palatial structures. Even in Rome itself the portico of the Pantheon, erected by Agrippa (27 B.C.), and the temple of Castor (rebuilt by Domitian A.D. 86) in the Forum, are remarkable instances of early work, which hold their own with some of the later examples even of Greek art.

The development of the Roman Corinthian order will be best understood by a description in detail similar to that given of the

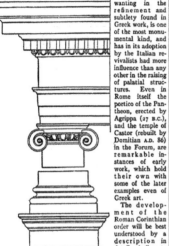

FIG. 8.

great Doric and Ionic orders. Taking the Pantheon portico as the earlier example, the base consists of an upper and lower torus separated by a double astragal with scotia and fillet above and below, and resting on a square plinth. The shaft, a monolith, is unfluted, tapering upwards, 9⅓ diameters in height, with apophyge and fillet at the bottom, and an apophyge, fillet and astragal at the top. The capital consisted of a square abacus with concave sides carried on a circular inverted bell, two rows of acanthus leaves, rising three-fifths of the bell, being carved round it (fig. 10), the stems of the upper range of eight leaves lying in the axis of each face and of the diagonals, and those of the lower range between them; the stems of the caulicolae from which spring the spirals, which rise to support the angles of the abacus, and to the centre of the capital, carrying the central flower, start from between the upper range of leaves. The abacus has concave sides, canted angles,

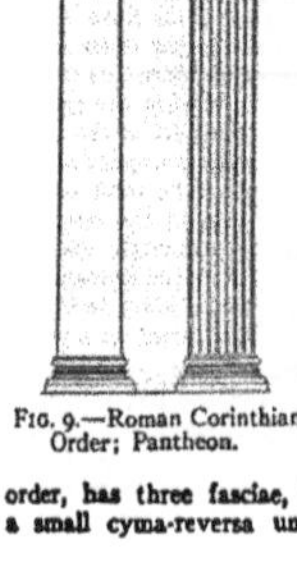

FIG. 9.—Roman Corinthian Order; Pantheon.

and is moulded, with a quarter round, fillet and cavetto. The architrave, like that of the Greek Ionic order, has three fasciae, but they are further elaborated by a small cyma-reversa under the upper fascia and a bead

under the second fascia. The architrave is crowned with a moulding, consisting of a fillet with cyma-reversa and bead underneath. The frieze is plain, its only decoration being the well-known inscription of Agrippa. The bedmould consists of a bead, cyma-reversa and fillet, under a plain dentil course, in which the dentils are not carved; bead-and-reel and egg-and-dart above these carried a plain face on which is found the new feature introduced by the Romans, viz. the modillion. This, though carved out of one solid block with the whole bedmould, suggested an appropriate support to the projecting cornice. The modillion was a bracket, a horizontal version of the ancones which supported the cornice of the Greek doorway cornice, and was here crowned by a small cyma-reversa carved with leaves which profiled round the modillion and along the upper part of the plain face. The cornice is simple, consisting of a corona, fillet and cymatium, the latter omitted across the front of the temple, but carried up over the cornice of the pediment. All the columns are equidistant with an intercolumniation of 2⅓ diameters. The order of the interior of the rotunda built by Hadrian (A.D. 121) is similar to that of the portico, the lower moulding of the bedmould being carved, and the tongue or anchor taking the place of the dart between the eggs.

The order of the temple of Castor (fig. 11) was enriched to a far greater extent, and parts were carved with ornament, which in Greek examples was probably only painted. The base was similar, but the columns (10 diameters high) had twenty-four flutes, with fillets between. The capital was further enriched with

FIG. 10.—The Roman Corinthian Order; Pantheon.

foliage, which rising from the caulicolae was carried along the cavetto of the abacus, whose upper moulding was carved with the egg-and-dart. The middle fascia of the architrave was carved with a version of the Greek anthemion, the cyma-reversa under the upper fascia being carved with leaves and bead-and-reel under. The lower moulding of the bedmould was carved with the egg-and-tongue; the dentil course was carved with finely proportioned dentils, the cyma-reversa and mouldings above being similar to those of the Pantheon portico. In the latter, on the soffit of the corona, square panels are sunk with a flower in the centre. In the temple of Castor the panel is square, but there is a border in front and back, which shows that the cornice had a greater projection. The corona was carved with fluting, departing from the simplicity of the Pantheon example, but evidently more to the taste of the Romans, as it is found in many subsequent examples. The intercolumniation is only two and one-third of the diameter. Though not quite equal to Greek foliage, that of the capitals of the temple of Castor is of great beauty, and there is one other feature in the capital which is unique, the spirals of the centre are larger than usual and interlace one another. A variety of the bedmould of the cornice is found in the so-called Temple of the Sun on the Quirinal Hill, although of late date, the entablature has the character of the Renaissance of the Augustan era, so fine and simple are

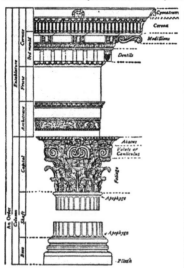

FIG. 11.—The Roman Corinthian Order; Temple of Castor.

its proportions and details; there are only two fasciae to the architrave, and the upper feature of the bedmould consisted of large projecting blocks with two fascia and an upper egg-and-tongue moulding, like the Ionic dentil, these blocks projecting half-way between the fascia and the edge of the corona.

The Roman Composite Order.—As already noted, the Composite order differs from the Corinthian only in the design of its capital, which is a compound of the foliage of the Corinthian and the volutes of the Ionic capital. Already, in the Ionic capital of the Erechtheum, a further enrichment with the anthemion was provided round the necking; this was copied in the capitals of the interior of Trajan's basilica; in Asia Minor at Aizani (1st century A.D.) a single row of leaves was employed round the capitals of the pronaos under the volutes of an Ionic capital; the architect of the Arch of Titus (A.D. 81) went one step farther and introduced the double row of leaves; both examples exist in the Arch of Septimius Severus (fig. 12), in the tepidarium of the thermae of Diocletian; and, to judge by the numerous examples still existing in the churches at Rome, it would seem to have been the favourite capital. The Byzantine architects also based most of their capitals on the Roman Composite examples. There are other hybrid Roman capitals, in which figures of a winged Victory, rams' heads or cornucopia, take the place of the angle spirals of the Corinthian capital.

The Arcade Order.—This, which was defined by Fergusson as the true Roman order, is a compound of two distinct types of construction, the arcuated and the trabeated, the former

derived from the Etruscans, the latter from the Greeks. . Whilst, however, the arcade was a constructive feature, the employ-ment of the semi- or, three-quarter detached column with its entablature complete, as a decorative screen, was a travesty of its original constructive function, without even the excuse of its adding in any way to the solidity of the structure, for the whole screen could be taken off from the Roman theatres and amphi-theatres without in any sense interfering with their stability The employment of the attached column only, as a vertical decorative feature subdividing the arches, might have been admissible, but to add the entablature was a mistake, on account of the intercolumniation, which was far in excess of that em-ployed in any order, so that not only was it necessary to cut the architrave into voussoirs, thus forming a flat arch, but the stones composing it had to be built into the wall to ensure their stability, the entablature thus became an element of weakness instead of strength (fig 13) The earliest example of the Arcade order is the Tabularium in Rome (80 B.C.) where it was employed to light a vaulted corridor running from one end to the other of the structure and raised some 50 ft from the ground. The column is semi-detached, 7½ diameters high with an intercolumniation of nearly 4 diameters, and an entablature with an architrave which is less than half a diameter, quite incapable, therefore, of carrying itself, much less than the rest of the entablature; the impost pier of the arch is half a diameter, and the height of the open arcade a little more than half its width. The shaft

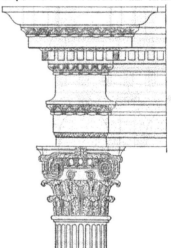

FIG. 12.—The Composite Order; Arch of Septimius Severus.

had twenty-four flutes with arrises, and rested on a square plinth, and in the capital the echinus was only about one-twelfth of the diameter, the shallowest known. The frieze was divided by triglyphs, there being four between those over the axis of each column; the correct number in the Greek Doric order being one. In the theatre of Marcellus there were three triglyphs; the impost pier was ⅝ diameter, thus giving greater solidity to the wall, but resulting in a narrower opening. The Tabularium had originally a second arcade above that now existing, with semi-detached columns of the Ionic order, and these are found in the upper storey of the theatre of Marcellus, the earliest example existing of the superposed orders. A certain proportion exists between the orders employed; thus the upper diameter of the Doric column (which is 7½ diameters high with a diminution of between one-fifth and one-sixth of the lower diameter) is the same as the lower diameter of the Ionic column, which is 8½ diameters high and a much slighter diminution In the Colosseum

FIG. 13.—The Arcade Order; Theatre of Marcellus.

there were three storeys pierced with arcades, with the Corinthian order on the third storey, and a superstructure (added at a later date) without an arcade, and decorated with Corinthian pilasters only. Apparently this scheme of decoration was considered to be the best for the purpose, and with some slight changes was employed for all the amphitheatres throughout the Empire. The intercolumniation, on which the design is made, varies in the examples of later date. With an intercolumniation of 6 diameters, the arcades are wider and a lighter effect is obtained, and this is the proportion in the Colosseum.

The Five Orders; Italian.—The two Italian architects whose text-books with illustrations of the five orders have been accepted generally as the chief authorities on the subject are Vignola

and Palladio, the former in France and the latter in England, the dates of the publication of their works being 1563 and 1570 respectively In 1759 Sir William Chambers published a treatise on civil architecture, in which he set forth his interpretation of the five orders, and his treatise is still consulted by students They all of them based their conjectural restorations on the descriptions given by Vitruvius, who, however, avoids using the same term throughout, the words *genus, ratio, species, mores* being employed, from which it may be concluded that the Greeks themselves had no such term as that which is now defined as "order," especially as in his book he invariably quotes the Greek name when describing various parts of the temple. In the preface to the fourth book he speaks only of the three orders (*genus*), so that the Tuscan described in Book IV chap. vii. would seem to have been an afterthought, and his description of the entablature shows that it was entirely in wood and therefore an incomplete development. The Italian revivalists, however, evolved one of their orders out of it and added a fifth, the Composite, of which there was no example in Rome before A.D. 82 In the description which follows it must be understood that it refers only to the Italian version of what the revivalists considered the Roman orders to consist of, and as a rule Vignola's interpretation will be given, because he seems to have kept closer to Vitruvius's descriptions and to have taken as his models the finest examples then existing in Rome.

The Tuscan Order—The base consists of a torus moulding, resting on square plinths; the shaft is terminated below by an apophyge and fillet and tapers upwards, the diminution being between one-quarter and one-fifth of the lower diameter, with an apophyge, fillet and astragal at the top, the capital consists of a square abacus with fillet and cavetto, an echinus, fillet and a necking; the whole column being 7 diameters high. The intercolumniation given by Vignola is 2½ diameters, instead of the 3½ diameters of Vitruvius's areostyle. The architrave, frieze and cornice, are simple versions of the Doric, except that there are no triglyphs in the frieze.

The Doric Order.—In his Doric order Vignola has followed the Roman Doric order of the theatre of Marcellus, but he gives it a base consisting of an astragal and torus resting on a square plinth; in his shaft he copies the fluting (24 flutes) with the arris of the columns of the thermae of Diocletian; his capital, except the flowers decorating the necking and his entablature, are entirely taken from the theatre of Marcellus; in a second study he introduces an Attic base, carves the echinus of the capital with the egg-and-tongue, introduces two fasciae in his architrave, and to support the cornice provides shallow plain modillions with guttae on the soffits. In both the examples given the columns taper upwards and are 8 diameters high.

The Ionic Order.—For the Ionic order Vignola discards the temple of Fortuna Virilis, but enriches the order of the theatre of Marcellus, adopting the base of the temple of Castor and the fluted columns of the same; in his frieze he introduces that of the Corinthian temple of Antoninus and Faustina, and in the bedmould and cornice copies that of the thermae of Diocletian. Palladio in his entablature introduces the convex friezes and adopts a single uncarved modillion under the cornice. In both cases the columns are fluted and 9 diameters high.

The Corinthian Order.—In this order Vignola, for his base, returns to the temple of Castor, makes his columns 10 diameters high, copies the capital of the portico of the Pantheon, introduces a rib frieze with winged female figures and a bull about to be sacrificed, and adopts the bedmould of the temple of Castor, reversing the carving of two of the mouldings and the cornice, and omitting the fluting of the corona of that temple. In Palladio's Corinthian order the frieze is too narrow and the bedmould, though copied from the temple of Castor, is of smaller scale.

The Composite Order.—As in the Roman Composite order the only original feature was the capital, there were no new versions to be given of the entablature, but unfortunately they were unable to copy the many examples in Rome. In the three best-known capitals, those of the arches of Titus and Septimus

Tuscan.　　　Doric.　　　Ionic.　　　Corinthian.　　　Composite.

FIG. 14.—The Italian Orders.

Severus and in the thermae of Diocletian, the upper fillet of the volute runs straight across the capital, being partially sunk in the cavetto of the abacus; in the canalis of the volutes of all these examples is a band of foliage which dips down to carry the centre flower, and, on account of its projection, it hides, from those looking only from below, the upper fillet of the volute. The architects of the Revival, therefore, in their studies of the capital, turned the volutes (which they would seem, like Ruskin, to have thought were borns) down on to the top of the echinus, producing a composition which is not in accordance with ancient examples and shows ignorance of the origin and development of the Ionic volute; unfortunately their interpretations of the Composite capital were followed by Inigo Jones, and are employed even in Regent Street, London, at the present day; there are, however, two or three Renaissance examples in Paris, in which the true Composite capital has been retained.

The Pedestal.—The architects of the Revival would seem to have conceived the idea that no order was complete without a pedestal. The only Roman examples of isolated columns with pedestals known are those of the columns of Trajan, Marcus Aurelius, Antoninus Pius and others of less importance, but they carried statues only and had no structural functions as supports to an entablature; the pedestals under the columns which decorated the arches of triumph were built into and formed part of the structure of the arch. The columns of the tepidarium of the Roman thermae had pedestals of moderate height (about 3 to 4 ft.) which bore no proportional relation to the diameter of the column. Vignola, however, gave definite proportions for the pedestal, which in the Doric order was to be 2 diameters in height, in the Ionic 2½ diameters, and in the Corinthian order 3 diameters, the result being that in the front of the church of St John Lateran, where the Corinthian pilasters are of great height, the pedestals are 12 to 13 ft. high. In conjunction with the arcade there was more reason for pedestals to the semi-detached columns on the upper storeys, but none was employed on the ground storey, either in the theatre of Marcellus or in the Colosseum. (R. P. S.)

ORDER, HOLY. "Holy Orders" (*ordines sacri*) may be defined as the rank or status of persons empowered by virtue of a certain form or ceremony to exercise spiritual functions in the Christian church. Thus Tertullian (*Idol.* 7, *Monog.* 11) mentions the "ecclesiastical order," including therein those who hold office in the church, and (*Exhort. Cast.* 7:) he distinguishes this *ordo* from the Christian *plebs* or laity. We may compare the common use of the word *ordo* in profane writers, who refer, *e.g.*, to the *ordo senatorius, ordo equester*, &c. It is true that the evidence of Tertullian does not carry us back farther than the close of the 2nd or opening of the 3rd century A.D. But a little before Tertullian, Irenaeus, though he does not use the word *ordo*, anticipates in some measure Tertullian's abstract term, for he recognizes a *magisterii locus*, "a place of magistracy" or "presidency" in the church. Indeed, phrases more or less equivalent occur in the sub-apostolic literature, and even in the New Testament itself, such as those who are "over you in the Lord" (1 Thess. v. 12), those "that bear the rule" (Heb. xiii. 7; cf. 1 Clem. i. 3; Herm. *Vis.* ii. 2, 6). Here we pause to remark that in Tertullian's view the church as a whole possesses the power of self-government and administration, though in the interest of discipline and convenience it delegates that power to special officers. It is, he says, the "authority of the church" which has constituted the difference between the governing body and the laity, and in an emergency a layman may baptize and celebrate (*Exhort. Cast.* 7), nor can this statement be lightly set aside on the plea that Tertullian, when he so wrote, had lapsed into Montanism. The fact is that the Montanists represented the conservatism of their day, and even now the Roman Church admits the right of laymen to baptize when a priest cannot be had. The *Apostolic Constitutions* (viii. 32) allow a layman to preach, if he be skilful and reverent, and the language of St Ignatius (*Ad Smyrn.* 8), " Let that be esteemed a valid Eucharist which is celebrated in the presence of the bishop or of some one commissioned by him," is really inconsistent with any firmly established principle that celebration by a layman was in itself absolutely null (see also EUCHARIST).

When we go on to inquire what special offices the church from the beginning, or almost from the beginning, adopted and recognized, two points claim preliminary attention. In the first place, much would be done in practical administration by persons who held no definite position formally assigned to them, although they wielded great influence on account of their age, talents and character. Next, it must be carefully remembered that the early church was, in a sense hard for us even to understand, ruled and edified by the direct action of the Holy Spirit. St Paul (1 Cor. xii. 28) furnishes us with a list of church offices very different from those which obtain in any church at the present day.[1] " God," he says, " hath set some in the church, first apostles, secondly prophets, thirdly teachers, then miracles, then gifts of healing, helps, governments, (divers) kinds of tongues." Ministry of this sort is not to be confounded with " order," of which this article treats. It died out very gradually, and the *Didache* or *Teaching of the Apostles*, compiled probably between A.D. 130 and 160, gives clear information on the nature of this prophetic or charismatic ministry. The title of " apostle " was not limited to the immediate disciples of our Lord, but was given to missionaries or evangelists who went about founding new churches; the prophets spoke by revelation; the teachers were enabled by supernatural illumination to instruct others. All of these men were called to their work by the internal voice of the Holy Spirit: none of them was appointed or elected by their fellows: none of them, and this is an important feature, was necessarily confined to a local church. Nevertheless, side by side with this prophetic ministry there was another, mediately at least of human appointment, and local in its character. Here we have the germ of orders in the technical sense. At first this local ministry was twofold, consisting of presbyters and bishops and deacons. Christian presbyters first appear (Acts xi. 30) in the church of Jerusalem, and most likely the name and office were adopted from the Jewish municipalities, perhaps from the Jewish synagogues (see PRIEST). Afterwards St Paul and St Barnabas in their first missionary journey " appointed[2] (Acts xiv. 23) presbyters in every church." Further, we find St Paul about A.D. 62 addressing the " saints " at Philippi " with the bishops and deacons." The word ἐπίσκοπος or overseer may be of Gentile origin, just as presbyter may have been borrowed from the Jews. There is strong proof that presbyter and *episcopus* are two names for the same office. It has indeed been maintained by eminent scholars, chiefly by Hatch and Harnack, that the word *episcopus* was given originally to the chief officer of a club or a confraternity, so that the *episcopus* was a financial officer, whereas the presbyters regulated the discipline. To this it may be objected that presbyters and bishops are never mentioned together, and that the names were interchangeable (Acts xx. 17 and 28; 1 Pet. v, 1, 2; 1 Tim. iii. 1-7 and v. 17-19; Tit. i. 5-7). The work of the presbyter or bishop was concerned at first with discipline rather than with teaching, which was largely in the hands of the charismatic ministry; nevertheless, the Pastoral Epistles (1 Tim. iii. 2) insist that an *episcopus* must be " apt to teach," and some presbyters (1 Tim. v, 17) not only ruled but also " laboured in the word and in teaching." They also " offered the gifts " (1 Clem. 44), i.e. to adopt Bishop Lightfoot's interpretation, " they led the prayers and thanksgivings of the congregation, presented the alms and contributions to God and asked His blessing on them in the name of the whole body." Under the bishops or presbyters stood the deacons or " helpers " (Philipp. i. 1,; 1 Tim. iii. 8-13). Whether they were the successors, as most of the Fathers believed, of the seven chosen by the church of Jerusalem

to relieve the apostles in the administration of alms (Acts vi.) is a question still disputed and uncertain. Be that as it may, the deacon was long considered to be the " servant of the widows and the poor " (Jerome, *Ep.* 146), and the archdeacon, who first appears towards the end of the 4th century, owes the greatness of his position to the fact that he was the chief administrator of church funds (see ARCHDEACON). This ancient idea of the diaconate, ignored in the Roman Pontifical, has been restored in the English ordinal. The growth of sacerdotal theories, which were fully developed in Cyprian's time, fixed attention on the bishop as a sacrificing priest, and on the deacon[3] as his assistant at the altar.

Out of the twofold grew the threefold ministry, so that each local church was governed by one *episcopus* surrounded by a council of presbyters. James, the Lord's brother, who, partly because of his relationship to Christ, stood supreme in the church at Jerusalem, as also Timothy and Titus, who acted as temporary delegates of St Paul at Ephesus and in Crete, are justly considered to have been forerunners of the monarchical episcopate. The episcopal rule in this new sense probably arose in the lifetime of St John, and may have had his sanction. At all events the rights of the monarchical bishop are strongly asserted in the Ignatian epistles (about A.D. 110), and were already recognized in the contemporary churches of Asia Minor. We may attribute the origin of the episcopate to the need felt of a single official to preside at the Eucharist, to represent the church before the heathen state and in the face of rising heresy, and to carry on correspondence with sister churches. The change of constitution occurred at different times in different places. Thus St Ignatius in writing to the Romans never refers to any presiding bishop, and somewhat earlier Clement of Rome in his epistles to the Corinthians uses the terms presbyter and *episcopus* interchangeably. Hermas (about A.D. 140) confirms the impression that the Roman Church of his day was under presbyteral rule. . Even when introduced, the monarchical episcopate was not thought necessary for the ordination of other bishops or presbyters. St Jerome (*Ep.* 146) tells us that as late as the middle of the 3rd century the presbyters of Alexandria, when the see was vacant, used to elect one of their own number and without any further ordination set him in the episcopal office. So the canons of Hippolytus (about A.D. 250) decree that a confessor who has suffered torment for his adherence to the Christian faith should merit and obtain the rank of presbyter forthwith—" Immo confessio est ordinatio ejus." Likewise in A.D. 314 the thirteenth canon of Ancyra (for the true reading see Bishop Wordsworth's *Ministry of Grace*, p. 140) assumes that city presbyters may with the bishop's leave ordain other presbyters. Even among the medieval schoolmen, some (Gore, *Church and Ministry*, p. 377) maintained that a priest might be empowered by the pope to ordain other priests.

The threefold[4] ministry was developed in the 2nd, a sevenfold ministry in the middle of the 3rd century. There must, says Cornelius (*apud* Euseb., *H.E.* vi. 43), be one bishop in the Catholic Church; and he then enumerates the church officers subject to himself as bishop of Rome. These are 46 presbyters, 7 deacons, 7 subdeacons, 42 acolytes, 52 exorcists and readers, together with doorkeepers. The subdeacons, no doubt, became a necessity when the deacons, whose number was limited to seven in memory of their original institution, were no longer equal to their duties in the " regions " of the imperial city, and left their lower work, such as preparation of the sacred vessels, to their subordinates. The office of acolyte may have been suggested by the attendant assigned to heathen priests. The office of doorkeeper explains itself, though it must be remembered that it was the special duty of the Christian *ostiarius* to exclude the unbaptized and persons undergoing penance from the more solemn part of the Eucharistic service. But readers and exorcists claim

---

[1] A partial exception may be made in favour of the ¥ Catholic Apostolic Church " founded by Edward Irving.

[2] Josephus, e.g. *Antiq.* vi. 4. 2, abundantly justifies this translation.

[3] " Fixed attention " on the deacon's ministration, the ministration itself being much more ancient. See Justin, *Apol.* i. 65.

[4] The Nestorians may be said to have a fourfold ministry, for they reconsecrated a bishop when he was made catholicos or patriarch. Chardon, v. p. 222

special notice. The reader is the only minor official mentioned by Tertullian (*Praescr.* 41). An ancient church order which belongs to the latter part of the 2nd century (see Harnack's *Sources of Apostolic Canons*, Engl. Transl. p. 54 seq.) mentions the reader before the deacon, and speaks of him as filling "the place of an evangelist." We are justified in believing that both exorcists and readers, whose functions differed essentially from the mechanical employments of the other minor clerics, belonged originally to the "charismatic" ministry, and sank afterwards to a low rank in the "orders" of the church (see EXORCIST and LECTOR). There were also other minor orders in the ancient church which have fallen into oblivion or lost their clerical character. Such were the *copiatae* or grave-diggers, the *psalmistae* or chaunters, and the *parabolani*, who at great personal risk—whence the name—visited the sick in pestilence. The modern Greek Church recognizes only two minor orders, viz. those of subdeacons and readers, and this holds good of the Oriental churches generally, with the single exception of the Armenians.[1] The Anglican Church is content with the threefold ministry of bishops, priests and deacons, but in recent times the bishops have appointed lay-readers, licensed to read prayers and preach in buildings which are not consecrated. The Latins, and Armenians who have borrowed from the Latins, have subdeacons, acolytes, exorcists, readers and doorkeepers. Since the pontificate of Innocent III., however, the Latin Church has placed the subdiaconate among the greater or sacred orders, the subdeacon being obliged to the law of celibacy and bound to the daily recitation of the breviary offices. The minor orders, and even the subdiaconate and diaconate, are now regarded as no more than steps to the priesthood. Roman theologians generally reckon only seven orders, although, if we count the episcopate an order distinct from the presbyterate, the sum is not seven, but eight. The explanation given by St Thomas (*Supp.* xl. 5.) is that, whereas all the orders have reference to the body of Christ present on the altar, the episcopate, so far forth, is not a separate order, since a simple priest no less than a bishop celebrates the Eucharist. The Council of Trent takes the same view; it enumerates (Sess. xxiii. cap. 2) only seven orders, and yet maintains (cap. 4) the ecclesiastical hierarchy of bishops, priests and ministers, the bishops as successors of the Apostles holding the highest place. The Roman Church forbids ordination to higher grades unless the candidate has received all the inferior orders. Further, a cleric is bound to exercise the minor orders for a year before he can be ordained subdeacon, he must be subdeacon for a year before he is ordained deacon, deacon for a year before he is made priest. However, instances of men elevated at once from the condition of laymen to the priesthood were known in the early church, and Chardon (*Hist. des sacrements*, vol. v. part 2, ch. v.) shows that in exceptional cases men were consecrated bishops without previous ordination to the priesthood.

Passing to the effect of ordination, we meet with two views, each of which still finds advocates. According to some, ordination simply entitles a man to hold an office and perform its functions. It corresponds to the form by which, *e.g.*, a Roman official was put in possession of his magistracy. This theory is clearly stated by Cranmer: "In the New Testament he that is appointed bishop or priest needed no consecration, by the Scripture, for election or appointment thereto is sufficient."[2] This view, widely held among modern scholars, has strong support in the fact that the words used for ordination in the first three centuries (χειροτονεῖν, καθιστάναι, κληροῦσθαι, constituunt, ordinare) also expressed appointment to civil office. Very different is the medieval theory, which arose from the gradual acceptance of the belief that the Jewish was the prototype of the Christian priest. According, then, to the Roman view,

holy order is a sacrament, and as such instituted by Christ; it confers grace and power, besides setting a mark or character upon the soul, in consequence of which ordination to the same office cannot be reiterated. Such is the teaching of the Roman Church, accepted by the Greeks and with certain modifications by Anglicans of the High Church school, who appeal to 1 Tim. iv. 14, 2 Tim. i. 6. We may conclude with brief reference to the most important aspects of the Roman doctrine.

The ordinary minister of orders is a bishop. The tonsure and minor orders are, however, still sometimes conferred by abbots, who, though simple priests, have special faculties for the ordination of their monks. Some account has been already given of scholastic opinion on presbyteral ordination to the diaconate and even to the priesthood. Can a heretical or schismatical bishop validly ordain? Is a simoniacal ordination valid? All modern theologians of the Roman Church answer these questions in the affirmative, but from the 8th to the beginning of the 13th century they were fiercely agitated with the utmost divergence of opinion and practice. Pope Stephen reconsecrated bishops consecrated in the usual way by his schismatical predecessor Constantine. Pope Nicholas declared orders given by Photius of Constantinople null. St Peter Damian was grievously perplexed about the validity of simoniacal ordinations. Similarly William of Paris held that degradation deprived a priest of power to consecrate.[3] St Thomas, on the contrary, contends that "heretics and persons cut off from the church" (*Summ. Suppl.* xxxviii. 2) may ordain validly, and that a priest who has been degraded can still celebrate the Eucharist (*Summ.* iii. 82. 8) validly, though of course not lawfully. This opinion, defended by Bonaventura, Alexander of Hales, Scotus and others, soon became and is now generally accepted.

The Schoolmen had no historical sense and little historical information; hence they fell into one error after another on the essentials in the rite of ordination. Some of them believed that the essential matter in the consecration of a bishop consisted in the placing the book of the gospels on his head and shoulders. True, this rite was used both in East and West as early as the 4th century; it was not, however, universal. According to common opinion, the matter and form of ordination to the episcopate were the imposition of the consecrating bishop's hands with the words, "Receive the Holy Ghost." The words in question, and indeed any imperative form of this kind, are still unknown to the East and were of very late introduction in the West. The final imposition of hands and the bestowal of power to forgive sins at the end of the ordination rite for priests in the Roman Pontifical is later even than the tradition of instruments. For like reasons the tradition of the instruments, *i.e.* the handing over of paten and chalice in ordination to the priesthood, are admittedly non-essential, unless we adopt the opinion of some Roman theologians that our Lord left the determination of matter and form to the church, which has insisted on different rites at different times.

The necessity of reference to sacerdotal power in the ordination of priests and bishops will be considered a little farther on in connexion with Anglican orders.

Deaconesses in the East received the imposition of the bishop's hands, but could not ascend to the priesthood. The Roman theologians regard them as incapable of true ordination, alleging 1 Tim. ii. 12. An unbaptized person is also incapable of valid ordination. On the other hand, St Thomas holds that orders may be validly conferred on children who have not come to the use of reason. For lawful ordination in the Roman Church, a man must be confirmed, tonsured, in possession of all orders lower than that which he proposes to receive, of legitimate birth, not a slave or notably mutilated, of good life and competent knowledge. By the present law (Concil. Trid. Sess. xxiii. de Ref. cap. 12) a subdeacon must have begun his twenty-second, a deacon his twenty-third, a priest his twenty-fifth year.[4] The

[1] The Syrian Jacobites and the Maronites also ordain "singers." Denzinger, *Rit. Oriental.* i. p. 116 seq.; Silbernagl, *Kirchen des Orients*, pp. 254. 315.

[2] Cranmer's works are to be found in Burnet, "Collection of Records" appended to his *History of the Reformation* (ed. Pocock), iv. 478. Cranmer also maintained that "bishops and priests are but both one office in the beginning of Christ's religion," *ib.* p. 471.

[3] In reality this is a survival of the primitive view that holy order is institution for an office which the local church confers and can therefore take away.

[4] The canon law fixes the thirtieth year as the lowest age for episcopal consecration.

Council of Trent also requires that any one who receives holy orders must have a "title," i.e. means of support. The chief titles are poverty, i.e. solemn profession in a religious order, patrimony and benefice. Holy orders are to be conferred on the Ember Saturdays, on the Saturday before Passion Sunday or on Holy Saturday .(Easter Eve).¹ The ancient and essential rule that a bishop must be "chosen by all the people " (Can. Hipp. ii. 7) has fallen into disuse, partly by the right of confirmation allowed to the bishops of the province, partly by the influence of Christian emperors, who controlled the elections in the capital where they resided, most of all by the authority exercised by kings after the invasion of the northern tribes and the dissolution of the empire (see CHURCH HISTORY).

Such in brief were the doctrine and use of the early churches, gradually systematized, developed and transformed in the churches of the Roman obedience. The Reformation brought in radical changes, which were on the whole a return to the primitive type. Calvin states his views clearly in the fourth book of his Institutes, cap. iii. Christ, as he holds, has established in His church certain offices which are always to be retained. First comes the order of presbyters or elders. These are sub-divided into pastors, who administer the word and sacraments, doctors, who teach and expound the Bible, elders pure and simple, who exercise rule and discipline. The special care of the poor is committed to deacons. Ordination is to be effected by imposition of hands. The monarchical episcopate is rejected. This view of order was accepted in the Calvinistic churches, but with various modifications. Knox, for example, did away with the imposition of hands (M'Crie's Knox, period vii.), though the rite was restored by the Scottish Presbyterian Church in the Second Book of Discipline. Knox also provided the Church of Scotland with superintendents or visitors, as well as readers and exhorters, offices which soon fell into disuse. Nor do Scottish presbyterians now recognize any special class of doctors, unless we suppose that these are represented by professors of theology. Independents acknowledge the two orders of presbyters and deacons, and differ from the Calvinistic presbyterians chiefly in this, that with them the church is complete in each single con-gregation, which is subject to no control of presbytery or synod. Luther was not, like Calvin, a man of rigid system. He refused to look upon any ecclesiastical constitution as binding for all time. The keys, as he believed, were entrusted to the church as a whole, and from the church as a whole the "ministers of the word and sacraments " are to derive their institution and authority. The form of government was not essential. Pro-vided that the preaching of the gospel was free and full, Luther was willing to tolerate episcopacy and even papacy. Hence the Lutheran churches exhibit great variety of constitution. In Scandinavia they are under episcopal rule. The Lutheran Bugenhagen, who was in priest's orders, ordained seven super-intendents, afterwards called bishops, for Denmark in 1527, and Norway, then under the same crown, derives its present episcopate from the same source. Sweden stands in a different position. There three bishops were consecrated in 1528 by Peter Magnusson, who had himself been consecrated by a cardinal with the pope's approval at Rome in 1524, for the see of Westirås, to which he had been elected by the chapter. J. A. Nicholson (Apostolical Succession in the Church of Sweden, 1880) seems to have proved so much from contemporary evidence. A reply to Mr Nicholson was made in Swedish by a Roman priest, Bern-hard, to whom Mr Nicholson replied in 1887. Unfortunately Mr Nicholson gives no detailed account of the form used in con-secration, and on this and other points fuller information is needed. We may say, however, that Mr Nicholson has presented a strong case for the preservation of episcopal succession in the Swedish Church.

If the Swedish Church has preserved the episcopal succession, it does not make much of that advantage, for it is in communion with the Danish and Norwegian bodies, which can advance no such claim. On the other hand, the Church of England adheres closely to the episcopal constitution. It is true that in articles xix. and xxxvi. she defines the church, without any express

reference to the episcopate, as a "congregation of faithful men in which the pure word of God is preached and the sacraments be duly administered according to Christ's ordinance," and simply adds that the ordinal of Edward VI. for the consecration of bishops, priests and deacons, contains all that is necessary for such ordination and nothing which is of itself superstitious. The preface to the ordinal (1550) goes farther. Therein we are told that the threefold ministry of bishops, priests and deacons may be traced back to apostolic times, and in the final revision of 1662 a clause was added to the effect that no one is to be accounted "a lawful bishop, priest or deacon in the Church of England," unless he has had episcopal consecration or ordination. The words " in the Church of England " deserve careful notice. Nothing is said to condemn the opinion of Hooker (Eccl. Pol. vii. 14. 11) that "there may be sometimes very just and sufficient reason to allow ordination made without a bishop," or of the High Church Thorndike (apud Gibson on the Articles, ii. 74), who " neither justifies nor condemns the orders of foreign Protestants." The church lays down a rule of domestic policy, and neither gives nor pretends to give any absolute criterion for the validity of ordination.

But while the Church of England has declined communion with non-episcopal churches, she has been involved in a long controversy with the Church of Rome on the validity of her own orders. It will be best to give first the leading facts, and then the inferences which may be drawn from them.

The English Church derives its orders through Matthew Parker, archbishop of Canterbury, who was consecrated in 1559 by William Barlow, bishop-elect of Chichester. We may assume that the rite employed was serious and reverent, and there is no longer any need to refute the fable of a ludicrous consecration at the "Nag's Head" tavern. We may further take for granted that Barlow was a bishop in the Catholic sense of the word. He had been nominated bishop of St Asaph in 1536, translated to St David's in the same year, and to Bath and Wells in 1547. He also sat in the upper house of Convocation and in the House of Peers. Now if Barlow all this time was not consecrated—and so far the only form of consecration known in England was according to the Roman rite—he would have incurred the penalties of praemunire, let alone the fact that Henry VIII. would not have tolerated such a defiance of Catholic order for a moment. The registers at St David's make no mention of his consecration, but this counts for nothing. No reference in the registers can be produced for many ordinations of undoubted validity. Parker thus was consecrated by a true bishop according to the Edwardine ordinal, i.e. he received imposition of hands with the words," Take the Holy Ghost and remember that thou stir up the grace of God which is in thee by imposition of hands." The corresponding form for the ordination of a priest was " Receive thou the Holy Ghost: whose sins thou dost forgive," &c. These were the sole forms in use from 1552 to 1562.

Roman authorities have from the beginning and throughout consistently repudiated orders given according to the Edwardine ordinal. The case first came under consideration when Cardinal Pole returned to England early in Mary's reign with legatine authority for reconciling the realm to the Holy See. In his instructions to the bishops (Burnet Collect., pt. iii., bk. v., 33; see also Dixon, Hist. Ch. of England, v. 238 seq.²) he clearly recognizes orders schismatical but valid, i.e. those conferred in Henry's reign, and so distinguishes them by implication from invalid orders, i.e. those given according to the Edwardine book. In the former alone were " the form and intention of the church preserved." He could not doubt for a moment the utter invalidity of Edwardine ordinations to the priesthood. He knew very well that the theologians of his church almost without exception held that the handing over of the paten and chalice with the words, " Receive power of offering sacrifice," &c., were the essential matter and form of ordination to the priesthood; indeed he published the decree of Eugenius IV. to that effect

¹ Compare also the article on Anglican orders in the Catholic Encyclopedia, vol. i., especially at p. 492.

(Wilkins, *Concil.* iv. 111). The Anglican priesthood being gone, the episcopate also lapses. For according to the Pontifical, the episcopate is the "*summum sacerdotium*"; the bishop in consecration receives "the sacerdotal grace"; it is "his office to consecrate, ordain, offer, baptize, confirm." Thus in the Pontifical the words "Receive the Holy Ghost" are determined and defined by the context. There is nothing in the Anglican ordinal to show that the Holy Ghost is given for the consecration of a bishop in the Roman sense. In 1704 John Gordon, formerly Anglican bishop of Galloway, gave to the Holy Office an account of the manner in which he had been consecrated. The Sacred Congregation, with the pope's approval, declared his orders to be null. The constant practice has been to reordain unconditionally Anglican priests and deacons. In 1896 Leo XIII. summoned eight divines of his own communion to examine the question anew. Four of those divines were, it is said, decidedly opposed to the admission of Anglican orders as valid; four were more or less favourably disposed to them. The report of this commission was then handed over to a committee of cardinals, who pronounced unanimously for the nullity of the orders in question. Thereupon the pope published his bull *Apostolicae curae*. In it he lays the chief stress on the indeterminate nature of the Anglican form "Receive the Holy Ghost" at least. from 1552 till the addition of the specific words, "for the office and work of a bishop (or priest) in the church of God,"; as also on the changes made in the Edwardine prayer "with the manifest intention. . . of rejecting what the church does." His conclusion is that Anglican orders are "absolutely null and utterly void." Moreover, in a letter to Cardinal Richard, archbishop of Paris, the pope affirms that his solemn decision is "firm, authoritative and irrevocable."

For Roman Catholics the decision necessarily carries great weight, and it may perhaps have its influence on Anglicans of the school which approximates most closely to Roman belief. It need not affect the opinion of dispassionate students. It is not the judgment of experts. The rejection of Anglican orders in the 16th and 17th centuries was based on a theory about the "tradition of instruments," which has long ceased to be tenable in the face of history, and is abandoned by Romanists themselves. The opinion of a liturgical scholar like Mgr. Louis Duchesne, who was a member of the papal commission, on the general question would be interesting in the highest degree. Unfortunately we know nothing of his vote or of the reasons he gave for it, and outside of the Roman pale the unanimous decision of a committee of cardinals counts for very little. We may grant the pope's contention that the Edwardine church had no belief in priests who offered in sacrifice the body and blood of Christ or in bishops capable of ordaining such priests. We may grant further that the medieval offices have been deliberately altered to exclude this view. But then the liturgy of Serapion, the friend of Athanasius, recently discovered, contains forms for the ordination of priests and bishops which do not say a word about power to sacrifice, much less about power to sacrifice Christ's literal body and blood. The canons of Hippolytus, which are about 150 years older, and indeed all the oldest forms for celebration, absolutely ignore any such power of sacrifice. If they speak of sacrifice at all, it is a sacrifice of the gifts brought by the faithful and distributed in the congregation and among the poor, or again they refer to those spiritual sacrifices which a bishop is to offer "day and night." The *Didache* and Justin Martyr are no less unsatisfactory from the Roman point of view. In short, the English reformers knew very well that the ordinal and communion office which they drew up could not satisfy the requirements of medieval theology. They appealed not to the school divines, but to Scripture and primitive antiquity. That is the standard by which we are to test their work.

AUTHORITIES.—For holy order in the apostolic and sub-apostolic age the reader may consult R. Rothe, *Anfänge der christlichen Kirche* (1837); A. Ritschl's *Entstehung der altkatholischen Kirche* (2nd ed., 1857); J. B. Lightfoot's dissertation on the "Christian Ministry" in his commentary on the Philippians (1868). A new era was opened by E. Hatch's *Organisation of the Early Christian Church*

(1880); to this Bishop C. Gore's *Church and Ministry* (1888) is a reply. The facts are judicially stated and weighed in Bishop J. Wordsworth's *Ministry of Grace* (1902). Dr T. M. Lindsay's *Church and Ministry in Early Centuries* (1902) on the whole agrees with Hatch, but is too eager to find modern Presbyterianism in the early church. A. Harnack's edition of the *Didache* (1884), his *Sources of the Apostolic Canons* (Eng. trans., 1895), the edition of the Canons of Hippolytus by H. Achelis, in *Texte und Untersuchungen*, vol. vi. (1891), the translation of Serapion's Prayer-book (translated by Bishop J. Wordsworth, 1899), are indispensable for serious study of the subject.

Joann Morinus, *De sacris ordinationibus* (1655) and A. C. Chardon, *Histoire des sacramenis*, vol. v. (1745), are rich in material chiefly relating to the patristic and medieval periods.

For the controversy on Anglican orders see P. F. Courayer, *Validité des ordinations anglaises* (1732), and two works in reply by M. Le Quien, *Nullité des ordinations anglicanes* (1725), *Nullité des ordinations anglicanes démonstrée de nouveau* (1730). In recent times Anglican orders have been defended by A. W. Haddan, *Apostolical Succession in the Church of England*; F. W. Puller, *The Bull Apostolicae Curae and the Edwardine Ordinal*. They have been attacked by E. E. Estcourt, *Question of Anglican Ordinations* (1873), and by A. W. Hutton, *The Anglican Ministry*, with a preface by Cardinal J. H. Newman (1879). (W. E. A.*)

ORDER IN COUNCIL, in Great Britain, an order issued by the sovereign on the advice of the privy council, or more usually on the advice of a few selected members thereof. It is the modern equivalent of the medieval ordinance and of the proclamation so frequently used by the Tudor and Stewart sovereigns. It is opposed to the statute because it does not require the sanction of parliament; it is issued by the sovereign by virtue of the royal prerogative. But although theoretically orders in council are thus independent of parliamentary authority, in practice they are only issued on the advice of ministers of the crown, who are, of course, responsible to parliament for their action in the matter. Orders in council were first issued during the 18th century, and their legality has sometimes been called in question, the fear being evidently prevalent that they would be used, like the earlier ordinances and proclamations, to alter the law. Consequently in several cases parliament has subsequently passed acts of indemnity to protect the persons responsible for issuing them, and incidentally to assert its own authority. At the present time the principle seems generally accepted that orders in council may be issued on the strength of the royal prerogative, but they must not seriously alter the law of the land.

The most celebrated instance of the use of orders in council was in 1807 when Great Britain was at war with France. In answer to Napoleon's Berlin decree, the object of which was to destroy the British shipping industry, George III. and his ministers issued orders in council forbidding all vessels under penalty of seizure to trade with ports under the influence of France. Supplementary orders were issued later in the same year, and also in 1808. Orders in council are used to regulate the matters which need immediate attention on the death of one sovereign and the accession of another.

In addition to these and other orders issued by the sovereign by virtue of his prerogative, there is another class of orders in council, viz. those issued by the authority of an act of parliament, many of which provide thus for carrying out their provisions. At the present day orders in council are extensively used by the various administrative departments of the government, who act on the strength of powers conferred upon them by some act of parliament. They are largely used for regulating the details of local government and matters concerning the navy and the army, while a new bishopric is sometimes founded by an order in council. They are also employed to regulate the affairs of the crown colonies, and the lord-lieutenant of Ireland, the viceroy of India, the governor-general of Canada, and other representatives of the sovereign may issue orders in council under certain conditions.

In times of emergency the use of orders in council is indispensable to the executive. In September 1766, a famine being feared, the export of wheat was forbidden by an order in council, and the Regulation of the Forces Act 1871 empowers the government in a time of emergency to take possession of the railway system of the country by the issue of such an order.

ORDERIC VITALIS (1075–c. 1142), the chronicler, was the son of a French priest, Odeler of Orleans, who had entered the service of Roger Montgomery, earl of Shrewsbury, and had received from his patron a chapel in that city. Orderic was the eldest son of his parents. They sent him at the age of five to learn his letters from an English priest, Siward by name, who kept a school in the church of SS Peter and Paul at Shrewsbury. When eleven years old he was entered as a novice in the Norman monastery of St Evroul en Ouche, which Earl Roger had formerly persecuted but, in his later years, was loading with gifts. The parents paid thirty marks for their son's admission; and he expresses the conviction that they imposed this exile upon him from an earnest desire for his welfare. Odeler's respect for the monastic profession is attested by his own retirement, a few years later, into a religious house which Earl Roger had founded at his persuasion. But the young Orderic felt for some time, as he tells us, like Joseph in a strange land. He did not know a word of French when he reached Normandy; his book though written many years later, shows that he never lost his English cast of mind or his attachment to the country of his birth. His superiors rechristened him Vitalis (after a member of the legendary Theban legion) because they found a difficulty in pronouncing his baptismal name. But, in the title of his Ecclesiastical History he prefixes the old to the new name and proudly adds the epithet Angligena. His cloistered life was uneventful. He became a deacon in 1093, a priest in 1107. He left his cloister on several occasions, and speaks of having visited Croyland, Worcester, Cambrai (1105) and Cluny (1132). But he turned his attention at an early date to literature, and for many years he appears to have spent his summers in the scriptorium. His superiors (at some time between 1099 and 1122) ordered him to write the history of St Evroul. The work grew under his hands until it became a general history of his own age. St Evroul was a house of wealth and distinction. War-worn knights chose it as a resting-place of their last years. It was constantly entertaining visitors from southern Italy, where it had planted colonies of monks, and from England, where it had extensive possessions. Thus Orderic, though he witnessed no great events, was often well informed about them. In spite of a cumbrous and affected style, he is a vivid narrator; and his character sketches are admirable as summaries of current estimates. His narrative is badly arranged and full of unexpected digressions. But he gives us much invaluable information for which we should search the more methodical chroniclers in vain. He throws a flood of light upon the manners and ideas of his own age; he sometimes comments with surprising shrewdness upon the broader aspects and tendencies of history. His narrative breaks off in the middle of 1141, though he added some finishing touches in 1142. He tells us that he was then old and infirm. Probably he did not long survive the completion of his great work.

The *Historia ecclesiastica* falls into three sections. (1) Bks. i., ii., which are historically valueless, give the history of Christianity from the birth of Christ. After 855 this becomes a bare catalogue of popes, ending with the name of Innocent I. These books were added, as an afterthought, to the original scheme; they were composed in the years 1136–1141. (2) Bks. iii.-vi. form a history of St Evroul, the original nucleus of the work. Planned before 1122, they were mainly composed in the years 1123–1131. The fourth and fifth books contain long digressions on the deeds of William the Conqueror in Normandy and England. Before 1067 these are of little value, being chiefly derived from two extant sources. William of Jumièges' *Historia Normannorum* and William of Poitiers' *Gesta Guilelmi*. For the years 1067–1071 Orderic follows the last portion of the *Gesta Guilelmi*, and is therefore of the first importance. From 1071 he begins to be an independent authority. But his notices of political events in this part of his work are far less copious than in (3) Bks. vii.-xiii., where ecclesiastical affairs are relegated to the background. In this section, after sketching the history of France under the Carolingians and early Capets, Orderic takes up the events of his own times, starting from about 1082. He has much to say concerning the empire, the papacy, the Normans in Italy and Apulia, the First Crusade (for which he follows Fulcher of Chartres and Baudri of Bourgueil). But his chief interest is in the histories of Duke Robert of Normandy, William Rufus and Henry I. He continues his work, in the form of annals, up to the defeat and capture of Stephen at Lincoln in 1141.

The *Historia ecclesiastica* was edited by Duchesne in his *Historiae*

Normannorum scriptores (Paris, 1619). This is the edition cited by Freeman and in many standard works. It is, however, inferior to that of A. le Prévost in five vols. (*Soc. de l'histoire de France*, Paris, 1838–1855). The fifth volume contains excellent critical studies by M. Leopold Delisle, and is admirably indexed. Migne's edition (*Patrologia latina*, clxxxviii.) is merely a reprint of Duchesne. There is a French translation (by L. Dubois) in Guizot's *Collection des mémoires relatifs à l'histoire de France* (Paris, 1825–1827); and one in English by T. Forester in Bohn's Antiquarian Library (4 vols., 1853–1856). In addition to the *Historia* there exists, in the library at Rouen, a manuscript edition of William of Jumièges' *Historia Normannorum* which Leopold Delisle assigns to Orderic (see this critic's *Lettre à M Jules Lair* (1873). (H. W. C. D.)

ORDINANCE, or ORDONNANCE, in architecture, a composition of some particular order or style. It need not be restricted to columnar composition, but applies to any kind of design which is subjected to conventional rules for its arrangement.

ORDINANCE, in medieval England, a form of legislation. The ordinance differed from the statute because it did not require the sanction of parliament, but was issued by the sovereign by virtue of the royal prerogative, although, especially during the reign of Edward I., the king frequently obtained the assent of his council to his ordinances. Dr Stubbs (*Const. Hist.* vol. ii.) defines the ordinance as " a regulation made by the king, by himself or in his council or with the advice of his council, promulgated in letters patent or in charter, and liable to be recalled by the same authority." But after remarking that " these generalizations do not cover all the instances of the use of ordinance," he adds: " The statute is primarily a legislative act, the ordinance is primarily an executive one." Legislation by ordinance was very common during the reigns of Henry III. and Edward I. when laws were issued by the king in council or enacted in parliament indifferently. Both were regarded as equally binding. Soon, however, legislation by ordinance aroused the jealousy of parliament, especially when it was found that acts of parliament were altered and their purpose defeated by this means. Consequently in 1389 the Commons presented a petition to King Richard II. asking that no ordinance should be made contrary to the common law, or the ancient customs of the land, or the statutes ordained by parliament. For this and other reasons this form of legislation fell gradually into disuse, becoming obsolete in the 15th century. The modern equivalent of the ordinance is the order in council.

In 1310, when Edward II. was on the throne and England was in a very disturbed condition, a committee of twenty-one bishops, earls and barons was chosen to make certain ordinances for the better government of the country. These men were called ordainers.

In the 17th century the use of the word ordinance was revived, and was applied to some of the measures passed by the Long Parliament, among them the famous self-denying ordinance of 1645. This form was used probably in conformity with the opinion of Sir Edward Coke, who says in his *Fourth Institute* " an ordinance in parliament wanteth the threefold consent, and is ordained by one or two of them " (*i.e.* king, lords and commons). The ordinances of the Long Parliament did not, of course, obtain the assent of the king. At the present time the word ordinance is used to describe a body of laws enacted by a body less than sovereign. For example, the ordinances of Southern Nigeria are issued by the governor of that colony with the assent of his council.

Before 1789 the kings of France frequently issued *ordonnances*. These were acts of legislation, and were similar to the ordinances of the English kings in medieval times.

ORDINARY (med. Lat. *ordinarius*, Fr. *ordinaire*), in canon law, the name commonly employed to designate a superior ecclesiastic exercising " ordinary " jurisdiction (*jurisdictionem ordinariam*), *i.e.* in accordance with the normal organization of the church. It is usually applied to the bishop of a diocese and to those who exercise jurisdiction in his name or by delegation of his functions. Thus, in Germany, the term *ordinariat* is applied to the whole body of officials, including the bishop, through whom a diocese is administered. In English law, however, the term ordinary is now confined to the bishop and the chancellor of his court. The pope is the *ordinarius* of the whole Roman Catholic Church, and is sometimes described as *ordinarius ordinariorum*. Similarly in the Church of England the king is legally the supreme ordinary, as the source of jurisdiction.

The use of the term ordinary is not confined to ecclesiastical jurisdiction. In the civil law the *judex ordinarius* is a judge who has regular jurisdiction as of course and of common right as opposed to persons extraordinarily appointed. The term survived throughout the middle ages wherever the Roman law gained a foothold. In the Byzantine empire it was applied to any one filling a regular office (*e.g.* ὕπατος ὀρδινάριος=consul ordinarius, ἄρχων ὀρδινάριος=praefectus ordinarius); but it also occasionally implied rank as distinct from office, all those who had the title of *clarissimus* being sometimes described as ὀρδινάριοι. In England the only case of the term being employed in its civil use was that of the office of judge ordinary created by the Divorce Act of 1857, a title which was, however, only in existence for the space of about eighteen years owing to the incorporation of the Divorce Court with the High Court of Justice by the Judicature Act 1875. But in Scotland the ordinary judges of the Inner and Outer Houses are called lords ordinary, the junior lord ordinary of the Outer House acts as lord ordinary of the bills, the second junior as lord ordinary on teinds, the third junior as lord ordinary on Exchequer causes. In the United States the ordinary possesses, in the states where such an officer exists, powers vested in him by the constitution and acts of the legislature identical with those usually vested in the courts of probate. In South Carolina he was a judicial officer, but the office no longer exists, as South Carolina has now a probate court.

In the German universities the *Professor ordinarius* is the occupant of one of the regular and permanent chairs in any faculty.

ORDINATE, in the Cartesian system of co-ordinates, the distance of a point from the horizontal axis (axis of x) measured parallel to the axis of y. Thus PR is the *ordinate* of P. The word appears to have been first used by René Descartes, and to be derived from *lineae ordinatae*, a term used by Roman surveyors for parallel lines. (See GEOMETRY: *Analytical.*)

ORDNANCE (a syncopated form of "ordinance" or "ordonnance," so spelt in this sense since the 17th century), a general term for great guns for military and naval purposes, as opposed to "small arms" and their equipment; hence the term also includes miscellaneous stores under the control of the ordnance department as organized. In England the Master-General of the Ordnance, from Henry VIII.'s time, was head of a board, partly military, partly civil, which managed all affairs concerning the artillery, engineers and *matériel* of the army; this was abolished in 1855, its duties being distributed. The making of surveys and maps (see MAP) was, for instance, handed over eventually (1889) to the Board of Agriculture, though the term "ordnance survey" still shows the origin.

I. HISTORY AND CONSTRUCTION

The efficiency of any weapon depends entirely on two factors: (1) its power to destroy men and material, (2) the moral effect upon the enemy. Even at the present day the moral effect of gun fire is of great importance, but when guns were first used the noise they made on discharge must have produced a bewildering fear in those without previous experience of them; more especially would this be the case with horses and other animals. Villani wrote of the battle of Cressy that the "English guns made a noise like thunder and caused much loss in men and horses" (Hime, *Proc. R. A. Institution*, vol. 26). Now, the moral effect may be considered more or less constant, for, as men are educated to the presence of artillery, the range of guns, their accuracy, mobility and on shore their invisibility, so increase that there is always the ever present fear that the stroke will fall without giving any evidence of whence it came.

On the other hand, the development of the gun has always had an upward tendency, which of late years has been very marked, the demand for the increase of energy has kept pace with—or rather in recent times may be said to have caused—improvements in metallurgical science.

The evolution of ordnance may be divided roughly into three epochs. The first includes that period during which stone shot were principally employed; the guns during this period (1313 to 1520) were mostly made of wrought iron, although the art of casting bronze was then well known. This was due to the fact that guns were made of large size to fire heavy stone shot, and, in consequence, bronze guns would be very expensive, besides which wrought iron was the stronger material. The second epoch was that extending from 1520 to 1854, during which cast iron round shot were generally employed. In this epoch, both bronze and cast iron ordnance were used, but the progress achieved was remarkably small. The increase of power actually obtained was due to the use of corn, instead of serpentine, powder, but guns were undoubtedly much better proportioned towards the middle and end of this period than they were at the beginning. The third or present epoch may be said to have commenced in 1854, when elongated projectiles and rifled guns were beginning to be adopted. The rapid progress made during this period is as remarkable as the unproductiveness of the second epoch. Even during recent years the call for greater power has produced results which were believed to be impossible in 1890.

The actual date of the introduction of cannon, and the country in which they first appeared, have been the subject of much antiquarian research; but no definite conclusion has been arrived at. Some writers suppose (see Brackenbury, "Ancient Cannon in Europe" in *Proc. Royal Artillery Inst.*, vol. iv.) that gunpowder was the result of a gradual development from incendiary compounds, such as Greek and sea fire of far earlier times, and that cannon followed in natural sequence. Other writers attribute the invention of cannon to the Chinese or Arabs. In any case, after their introduction into Europe a comparatively rapid progress was made. Early in the 14th century the first guns were small and vase shaped; towards the end they had become of huge dimensions firing heavy stone shot of from 200 to 450 lb weight.

The earliest known representation of a gun in England is contained in an illuminated manuscript "De Officiis Regum" at Christ Church, Oxford, of the time of Edward II. (1326). This clearly shows a knight in armour firing a short primitive weapon shaped something like a vase and loaded with an incendiary arrow. This type of gun was a muzzle loader with a vent channel at the breech end. There seems to be undoubted evidence that in 1338 there existed breech-loading guns of both iron and brass, provided with one or more movable chambers to facilitate loading (*Proc. R. A. I.*, vol. iv. p. 291). These fire-arms were evidently very small, as only 2 lb of gunpowder were provided for firing 48 arrows, or about seven-tenths of an ounce for each charge.

The great Bombarde of Ghent, called "Dulle Griete" (fig. 1) is believed to belong to the end of the century, probably about

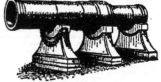

FIG. 1.—Dulle Griete, Ghent.

1382, and, according to the *Guide des voyageurs dans la ville d Gand* (Voisin) the people of Ghent used it in 1411. This gun, which weighs about 13 tons, is formed of an inner lining of wrought iron longitudinal bars arranged like the staves of a cask and welded together, surrounded by rings of wrought iron driven or shrunk on. The chamber portion is of smaller diameter, and some suppose it to be screwed to the muzzle portion. The length of the gun is 197 in., the diameter of the bore 25 in., and the chamber 10 in. at the front and tapering to 6 in. diameter at the breech end. It fired a granite ball weighing about 700 ℔. Two wrought iron guns left by the English in 1423 when they had to raise the siege of Mont St Michel in Normandy belong to about the same period; the larger of these guns has a bore of 19 in. diameter.

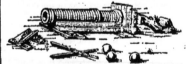

FIG. 2.—Mons Meg.

"Mons Meg" (fig. 2) in Edinburgh Castle is a wrought iron gun of a little later period; it is built up in the same manner of iron bars and external rings. It has a calibre of 20 in. and fired a granite shot weighing 330 ℔.

Bronze guns of almost identical dimensions to the "Dulle Griete" were cast a little later (1468) at Constantinople (see Lefroy, *Proc. R. A. I.*, vol. vi.). One of these is now in the Royal Military Repository, Woolwich. It is in two pieces screwed together: the front portion has a calibre of 25 in. and is for the reception of the stone shot, which weighed 672 ℔; and a rear portion, forming the powder chamber, of 10 in. diameter. The whole gun weighs nearly 18¾ tons.

To give some idea of the power of these guns, the damage done by them to Sir John Duckworth's squadron in 1807 when the Dardanelles were forced may be instanced. In this engagement six men-of-war were more or less damaged and some 126 men were killed or wounded. The guns were too unwieldy to lay for each round and were consequently placed in a permanent position; they were often kept loaded for months.

The 16th century was remarkable from the fact that the large bombard type was discarded and smaller wrought iron guns were made. This was due to the use of iron projectiles, which enabled a blow to be delivered from a comparatively small gun as destructive as that from the very weighty bombards throwing stone shot.

Bronze guns also now came into great favour. They were first cast in England in 1521 (Henry VIII.), and iron cannon about 1540, foreign founders being introduced for the purpose of teaching the English the art. The "Mary Rose," which sank off Spithead in 1545, had on board both breech-loading wrought-iron and muzzle-loading bronze guns.

The smaller guns cast at this period were of considerable length, probably on account of the large charges of meal powder which were fired. The long bronze gun in Dover Castle known as "Queen Elizabeth's pocket pistol" has a calibre of 4·75 in.; its bore is 23 ft. 1 in. long or 58 calibres, but its total length including the cascable is 24 ft. 6 in. It was cast at Utrecht in 1544 and presented by Charles V. to Henry VIII.

Little or no classification of the various types of guns was attempted during the 15th century. The following century saw some attempt made at uniformity and the division of the several calibres into classes, but it was not until about 1730, when Maritz of Geneva introduced the boring of guns from the solid, that actual uniformity of calibre was attained, as up to this date they were always cast hollow and discrepancies naturally occurred. In France organization was attempted in 1732 by Vallière, but to Gribeauval (*q.v.*) is due the credit of having simplified artillery and introduced great improvements in the equipment.

It is not possible to compare properly the power of the earlier guns; at first small and feeble, they became later large and unwieldy, but still feeble. The gunpowder called "serpentine" often compounded from separate ingredients on the spot at the time of loading, burnt slowly without strength and naturally varied from round to round. The more fiercely burning granulated or corned powder, introduced into Germany about 1429, and

into England shortly after, was too strong for the larger pieces of that date, and could be used only for small firearms for more than a century after. These small guns were often loaded with a lead or lead-coated ball driven down the bore by hammering.

The bronze and cast iron ordnance which followed in the 16th century were strengthened in the 17th century, and so were more adapted to use the corned powder. By this means some access of energy and greater effective ranges were obtained.

In the 18th century and in the first half of the 19th no change of importance was made. Greater purity of the ingredients and better methods of manufacture had improved gunpowder; the windage between the shot and the bore had also been reduced, and guns had been strengthened to meet this progress, but the principles of construction remained unaltered until the middle of the 19th century. Metallurgical science had made great progress, but cast iron was still the only metal considered suitable for large guns, whilst bronze was used for field guns. Many accidents, due to defects developing during practice, had, however, occurred, in order to prevent which experimental guns constructed of stronger material such as forged iron and steel had been made. Some of these weapons were merely massive solid blocks, with a hole bored in for the bore, and only withstood a few rounds before bursting. This result was attributed to the metal being of an indifferent quality—quite a possible reason as the treatment of large masses of steel was then in its infancy, and even with the best modern appliances difficulties have always existed in the efficient welding of large forgings of iron. Forged iron, however, always gave some evidence of its impending failure whereas the steel burst in pieces suddenly; steel was, therefore, considered too treacherous a material for use in ordnance. This view held for many years, and steel was only again employed after many trials had been made to demonstrate its reliability. It will be seen later that the ill success of these experiments was greatly due to a want of knowledge of the correct principles of gun construction.

The progress made since 1854 is dependent on and embraces improvements in gun construction, rifling and breech mechanisms.

Considerable obscurity exists as regards the means adopted for mounting the first cannon. From illuminations in contemporary manuscripts it appears that the earliest guns, which were trunnionless, were simply laid on the ground and supported by a timber framing at each side, whilst the flat breech end rested against a strong wood support let into the ground to prevent recoil. This arrangement was no doubt inconvenient, and in the later small guns were fastened in a wooden stock by iron bands; larger guns were supported in massive timber cradles (fig. 3) and

Redrawn from *Mallet's Construction of Artillery.*

FIG. 3.—Primitive Gun-mounting.

secured thereto by iron straps or ropes. The ponderous weight to be moved and the deficiency of mechanical means prevented these large cannon and their cradles from being readily moved when once placed in position. Laying was of the most primitive kind, and the bombard was packed up in its wood cradle to the required elevation once for all. When it was desired to breach a wall the bombard with its bed would be laid on the ground at about 100 yds. distance, the breech end of the gun or the rear end of the bed abutting against a solid baulk of wood fixed to the ground. "Mons Meg" was originally provided with a wood cradle.

It is by no means certain when wheeled carriages were

introduced. They must have gradually appeared as a means of surmounting the difficulties engendered by the recoil of the piece and of transport of the early guns and their cradles. Andrea Redusio mentions in *Chronicon Tarvisinum* the use of two wheeled bombard carriages at the siege of Quero by the Venetians in 1376. It does not follow that these weapons were of large dimensions, as the term " bombard " was applied to small guns as well as to the more ponderous types.

The ancient carriages used on land are remarkable from the fact that in general design they contain the main principles which have been included in field carriages up to the present day. Until 1870 the body of all field carriages was made of wood. In an early type the trail portion was made of a solid baulk of timber supported at the front by a hard wood axletree, on the arms of which the wheels were placed (iron axletrees were introduced by Gribeauval in 1765). The gun resting in its wooden cradle was carried in bearings on the trail immediately over the axletree (fig. 4), the cradle being provided with an

From Clephan, Early Ordnance.

FIG. 4.—Early Field Gun.

axle or trunnions for the purpose. For giving elevation a wood arc was fixed to the trail towards the rear end, and the breech end could be moved up and down along this arc and fixed at certain positions by a pin passing through both cradle and arc.

About the middle of the 15th century the trunnions were formed with the gun—the wood cradle therefore became unnecessary and was discarded. The carriage was then formed of two strong cheeks or sides of wood fastened together by four wood transoms. At the front end the cheeks were secured to the wooden axletree, which was strengthened by a bar of iron let into its under side. Trunnion bearings were cut in the upper surface of the cheeks over the axletree, and these were lined with iron, while the trunnions were secured in position by iron cap-squares. Elevation was given by a wedge or " quoin " being placed under the breech and supported by a transom or stool bed. For transport the trail end of the carriage was supported on a limber, a pintle on the limber body passing through a hole in the trail. One set of shafts were fixed to the limber, and a single horse was harnessed to them; the remainder of the team were attached in pairs in front. A driver was provided for every two pairs of horses. In Italy oxen were often yoked to the larger guns instead of horses. Tartaglia mentions in his *Nova scientia* (1562) that 28 oxen were required for a gun 15 ft. in length and weighing 13,000 lb; horses were used for small guns only.

For service on board ship the difficulties of the cramped situation seem to have been surmounted in an ingenious manner In the " Mary Rose, " sunk in the reign of Henry VIII, the brass guns with trunnions were mounted on short wood carriages provided with four small wood wheels called " trucks " and fastened to the gun ports by rope breechings. The iron breech-loading guns were employed in restricted positions where loading

at the muzzle would be difficult. They had no trunnions and were mounted in a wood cradle, the under side of which was grooved to enable it to slide on a directing bar.

At the end of the 17th century not much progress had been made. The larger guns were mounted on short wood carriages having two or four " trucks. " The guns and carriages recoiled along the vessel's deck, and where this endangered the masts or other structures the recoil was hindered by soft substances being laid down in the path of the recoil.

The small guns were mounted in iron Y pieces—the upper arms being provided with bearings for the gun trunnions—and the stalk formed a pivot which rested in a socket in the vessel's side or on a wall, so that the gun could be turned to any quarter.

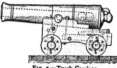

FIG. 5.—Truck Carriage.

Similar carriages (fig. 5) existed until the advent of rifled guns, but a few small improvements, such as screw elevating gear in place of the quoin, had been approved. Cast iron standing carriages were also, about 1825, used on land for hot climates and situations not much exposed.

The earliest guns were not provided with sights or other means for directing them. This was not important, as the range seldom exceeded 100 yds. As, however, ranges became longer, some means became necessary for *Sighting.* giving the correct line and elevation (see also SIGHTS). The direction for line was easily obtained by looking over the gun and moving the carriage trail to the right or left as was necessary. For elevation an instrument invented by Tartaglia called a Gunner's Quadrant (sometimes also called a Gunner's Square) was used; this was a graduated quadrant of a circle (fig. 6) connecting a long and short arm forming a right angle; a line with a plummet hung from the angle in such a manner that on the long arm being placed along the bore near the muzzle the plummet hung down against the quadrant and indicated the de-

FIG. 6.—Gunner's Quadrant.

grees of elevation given to the piece. The quadrant was divided into 90° and also into 12 parts; it was continued past the short arm for some degrees to enable depression to be given to the gun. The instrument was also used for surveying in obtaining the heights of buildings, and is still much employed for elevating guns in its clinometer form, in which a level takes the place of the plummet.

For short range firing a dispart sight was in use early in the 17th century. A notch was cut on the top of the breech or base ring, and on the muzzle ring a notched fore sight (called the dispart sight) was placed in the same vertical plane as the notch, and of such a height that a line stretched from the top of the breech ring notch to the notch of the foresight was parallel to the axis of the bore. These sights were well enough for close, horizontal fire and so long as the enemy were within what was called " point blank " range; that is the range to the first graze, on a horizontal plane, of the shot when fired from a gun the axis of which is horizontal. As this range depends entirely, other things being equal, on the height of the gun's axis above the horizontal plane, it is not very definite. When, however, the enemy were at a greater distance, elevation had to be given to the gun, and, as a quadrant was slow and not easy to use, there was introduced an instrument, called a Gunner's Rule (see *The Art of Gunnery*, by Nathanael Nye, 1670), which was really a primitive form of tangent sight. This was a flat brass scale 12 or 14 in. long divided on its flat surface into divisions proportional to the tangents of angles with a base equal to the distance from the notch on the base ring to the dispart notch. A slit was made along the rule, and a thread with a bead on it was mounted on a slider so that it could be moved in the slit to any required graduation. By sighting along the bead to the dispart the gun could be laid on any object. Later still, the requisite elevation was obtained by cutting a series of notches on the side of the base ring and one on the muzzle ring. These were called "Quarter Sights" and allowed of elevations up to 3°; the lowest notch with the one on the muzzle swell gave a line parallel to the axis of the bore but above it so as to clear the cap-squares of the trunnions. This system was also used in bronze field guns and in all cast iron guns up to the 32-pdr. Difficulties in laying occurred unless the direction was obtained by looking over the top or dispart sight and the elevation then given by the quarter sights. This was the system of sighting in use during the great naval actions of the end of the 18th century and the beginning of the 19th century. A pointed dispart sight was often used, and for naval purposes it was fixed on the reinforce near the trunnions, as the recoil of the gun through the port would destroy it if fixed on the muzzle swell.

The double sighting operation was rendered unnecessary by the use of "tangent scales" introduced by Gribeauval. Similar scales were soon adopted in the English land service artillery, but they were not fully adopted in the English navy until about 1854 (see *Naval Gunnery*, by Sir Howard Douglas, p. 390), although in the United States navy a system of sighting, which enabled the guns to be layed at any degree of elevation, had been applied as early as 1812. These tangent scales were of brass fitting into sockets on the breech end of the gun; they were used in conjunction with the dispart fore sight and gave elevation up to 4° or 5° over the top of the gun. For greater elevation a wooden tangent scale was provided which gave elevation up to 8° or 10°.

In the British navy, before tangent sights were used, the plan often adopted for rapidly laying the guns was by sighting, with the notch on the breech ring and the dispart sight, on some part of the masts of the enemy's vessel at a height corresponding to the range.

With sailing ships about the middle of the 19th century the angle of heel of the vessel when it was sailing on a wind was ascertained from the ship's pendulum, and the lee guns elevated or the weather guns depressed to compensate by means of a graduated wooden stave called a "heel scale" of which one end was placed on the deck or last step of the carriage whilst the upper end read in connection with a scale of degrees engraved on the flat end of the cascable.

Subsequently the term "tangent sight" was given to the "tangent scales," and they were fitted into holes made in the body of the gun—the foresight usually being fitted to a hole in the gun near the trunnions. Two pairs of sights—one at each side—were generally arranged for, and in rifled guns the holes for the tangent sight bars were inclined to compensate for the drift of the projectile. As the drift angle varies with the muzzle velocity, the tangent sights of howitzers were set vertically, so that for the various charges used the deflection to compensate for drift had to be given on the head of the sight bar. Modern forms of sights are described and illustrated in the article SIGHTS.

Breech-loading ordnance dates from about the end of the 14th century, or soon after the introduction of cannon into
Breech-
loading
Ordnance.
England (Brackenbury, *Proc. R.A.I.* v. 32). The gun body, in some cases, was fixed to a wood cradle by iron straps and the breech portion kept in position between the muzzle portion and a vertical block of wood fixed to the end of the cradle, by a wedge. Accidents must have been common, and improvements were made by dropping the breech or chamber of the weapon into a receptacle, solidly forged on or fastened by lugs to the rear end of the gun (fig. 7) This system was used for small guns only, such as wall pieces, &c., which could not be easily loaded at the

muzzle owing to the position in which they were placed, and in order to obtain rapidity each gun was furnished with several chambers.

Guns of this nature, called Petrieroes a Brazu, were used in particular positions even at the end of the 17th century. Moretti states that they carried a stone ball of from 2 lb to 14 lb, which

FIG. 7.—Early Breech-loader.

was placed in the bore of the gun and kept in position by wads. The chambers, resembling an ordinary tankard in shape, had a spigot formed on their front end which entered into a corresponding recess at the rear end of the bore and so formed a rude joint. Each chamber was nearly filled with powder and the mouth closed by a wood stopper driven in; it was then inserted into the breech of the gun and secured by a wedge. Even with feeble gunpowder this means of securing the chamber does not commend itself, but as powder improved there was a greater probability of the breech end of the gun giving way; besides which the escape of the powder gas from the imperfect joint between the chamber and gun must have caused great inconvenience. To these causes must be attributed the general disuse of the breech-loading system during the 18th and first half of the 19th centuries.

Robins mentions (*Tracts of Gunnery*, p. 337) that experimental breech-loading rifled pieces had been tried in 1745 in England to surmount the difficulty of loading from the muzzle. In these there was an opening made in the side of the breech which, after the loading had been completed, was closed by a screw. The breech arrangement (fig. 8) of the rifled gun in-

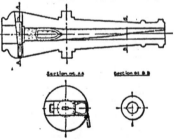

Section at A A　　　　Section at B B

FIG. 8.—Cavalli Gun, 1845.

vented by Major Cavalli, a Sardinian officer, in 1845, was far superior to anything tried previously. After the projectile and charge had been loaded into the gun through the breech, a cast iron cylindrical plug, cupped on the front face, was introduced into the chamber; a copper ring was placed against its rear face; finally a strong iron wedge was passed through the body of the gun horizontally just in rear of the plug, and prevented it being blown out of the gun. In England the breech of one of the experimental guns was blown off after only a few rounds had been fired. In Wahrendorff's gun, invented in 1846, the breech arrangement (fig. 9) was very similar in principle to the Cavalli gun. In addition to the breech plug and horizontal wedge there was an iron door, hinged to the breech face of the gun, which carried a rod attached to the rear of the breech plug. The horizontal wedge had a slot cut from its right side to the centre, so that it might freely pass this rod. After loading,

Fig. 15.—Forging Process.

PLATE II. UR

Fig. 18.—Shrinking-on Process.

Fig. 60.—British 18-pr. Quick-firing Gun.

Fig. 61.—British 18-pr. Quick-firing Gun and Limber.

Fig. 62.—French 75-mm. Quick-firing Gun and Wagon Body in Action.

Fig. 64.—Danish (Krupp) 7.5-cm. Quick-firing Field Gun and Wagon Body in Action.

Fig. 67.—Ehrhardt 4.7-in. Quick-firing Field Howitzer (Controlled Recoil).

Fig. 68.—Krupp 7.5-cm. Mountain Gun.

PLATE V.

From Lieut.-Col. Ormond M. Lissak's *Ordnance and Gunnery*.

Fig. 69.—4.7-In. Siege Gun, Travelling Position (U.S.A.).

PLATE VI.   ORDNANCE

From Lieut.-Col. Ormond M. Lissak's *Ordnance and Gunnery*.

Fig. 70.—4.7-in. Siege Gun, in Action (U.S.A.).

Fig. 83.—Krupp 11.2-in. Howitzer and Shield. From photograph by Friedrich Krupp, A. G., Essen/Ruhr.

PLATE VIII.

ORDNANCE

Fig. 77.—Krupp 8.26-in. Mortar, Firing Position.

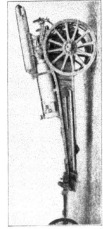

Fig. 76.—Krupp 8.26-in. Mortar, Travelling.

Fig. 88.—Krupp 3.4-in. Automatic Gun.   From photographs by Friedrich Krupp, A. G., Essen/Ruhr.

the hinged door, with the breech plug resting against its front face, was swung into the breech opening, and the plug was pushed forward to its position in the chamber of the gun; the

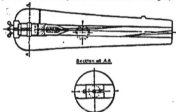

Section at AA

FIG. 9.—Wahrendorff Gun, 1846.

wedge was then pushed across to prevent the plug being blown back, and, finally, a nut screwed to the rear end of the plug rod was given a couple of turns so that all was made tight and secure. After firing, the breech was opened by reversing these operations.

The Armstrong system of breech-loading introduced in 1854 was the first to give satisfactory results; its simple design and few parts produced a favourable effect in the minds of artillerists, which was increased by the excellent accuracy obtained in shooting. The gun (fig. 10) had a removable breech block having

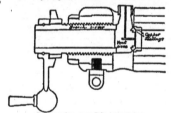

FIG. 10.—Armstrong B.L. Arrangement.

on its front face a coned copper ring which fitted into a coned seating at the breech end of the powder chamber. The breech block was secured by means of a powerful breech-screw; a hole was made through the screw so that, in loading, the shell and cartridge could be passed through it after the breech block had been removed. After loading, the block was dropped into its place and the breech screw turned rapidly so that it might jam the block against its seating, and so prevent the escape of powder gas when the gun was fired. This gun was most successful, and a great number of guns of this type were soon introduced into the British army and navy.

They were employed in the China campaign of 1860, and satisfactory reports were made as to their serviceableness; but while the breech-loading system had obtained a firm footing on the Continent of Europe, there was a strong prejudice against it in England, and about 1864 M.L.R. guns were adopted. Breech-loaders did not again find favour until about 1882, when a demand was made for more powerful guns than the M.L.R. In consequence, M.L. guns having enlarged chambers for burning large charges of prismatic powder were experimented with by the Elswick Ordnance Co. and subsequently by the War Office. The results were so promising that means were sought for further improvements, and breech-loading guns, having the Elswick cup obturation, were reintroduced.

Up to about 1850 the dimensions of canon had been proportioned by means of empirical rules, as the real principles underlying the construction of ordnance had been little understood. It was known of course that a gun was **Built-up guns.** subjected to two fundamental stresses—a circumferential tension tending to split the gun open longitudinally, and a longitudinal tension tending to pull the gun apart lengthwise; the longitudinal strength of a gun is usually greatly in excess of any requirements. It is easy to demonstrate that any so-called homogeneous gun, i.e. a gun made of solid material and not built up, soon reaches a limit of thickness beyond which additional thickness is practically useless in giving strength to resist circumferential stress. This is due to the fact that the stress on the metal near the bore is far higher than that on the outer portion and soon reaches its maximum resistance which additional thickness of metal does not materially increase. The gun can, however, be arranged to withstand a considerably higher working pressure by building it up on the principle of initial tensions. The inner layers of the metal are thereby compressed so that the gas pressure has first to reverse this compression and then to extend the metal. The gun barrel supported by the contraction of the outer hoops will then be able to endure a gas pressure which can be expressed as being proportional to the initial *compression* plus the *extension*, whereas in the old type solid gun it was proportional to the *extension* only. The first to employ successfully this important principle for all parts of a gun was Lord Armstrong (q.v.), who in 1855–1856 produced

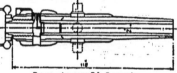

FIG. 11.—Armstrong B.L. Construction.

a breech-loading field gun with a steel barrel strengthened by wrought iron hoops. In this system (fig. 11) wrought iron coils were shrunk over one another so that the inner tube, or barrel, was placed in a state of compression and the outer portions in a state of tension—the parts so proportioned that each performs its maximum duty in resisting the pressure from within. Further, by forming the outer parts of wrought iron bar coiled round a mandril and then welding the coil into a solid hoop, the fibre of the iron was arranged circumferentially and was thus in the best position to resist this stress. These outer coils were shrunk over a hollow breech-piece of forged iron, having the fibre running lengthwise to resist the longitudinal stress. The several cylinders were shrunk over the steel inner tube or barrel. To obtain the necessary compression the exterior diameter of the inner portion is turned in a lathe slightly greater than the interior diameter of the outer coil. The outer coil is heated and expands; it is then slipped over the inner portion and contracts on cooling. If the strength of the two parts has been properly adjusted the outer will remain in a state of tension and the inner in a state of compression.

Every nation has adopted this fundamental principle which governs all systems of modern gun construction. The winding, at a high tension, of thin wire or ribbon on the barrel or on one of the outer coils may be considered as having an exactly similar effect to the shrinking of thin hoops over one another. The American, Dr Woodbridge, claims to have originated the system of strengthening guns by wire in 1850; Brunel, the great railway engineer, also had similar plans; to Longridge, however, belongs the credit of pointing out the proper mode of winding on the wire with initial tension so adjusted as to make the firing tension (i.e. the tension which exists when the gun is fired) of the wire uniform for the maximum proof powder pressure. Great success attended the early introduction of the coil system. Large numbers (about 3500) of breech-loading Armstrong guns from 2·5 in. to 7 in. calibre were manufactured for England alone; most of these had barrels of coiled iron, but solid forged iron barrels were also employed and a few were of steel. This manufacture continued until 1867, when M.L. guns built up on the coil system (fig. 12) with the French form of rifling were adopted; but as the knowledge of the proper treatment and the quality of the steel had improved, steel barrels bored from a solid steel forging were mostly used; the exterior layers were still iron hoops with the fibre of the metal disposed as in the original type. In order to cheapen manufacture the coils were thickened by Mr Fraser of Woolwich Arsenal, so that a few thick coils were used instead of a number of thin ones (fig. 13).

In the Fraser system an attempt was made to obtain rigidity of construction and additional longitudinal strength by interlocking the various coils from breech to muzzle; this feature still exists in all designs adopted by the English government, but foreign designers do not favour it altogether, and many of their guns of the latest type have a number of short independent hoops shrunk on, especially over the chase. Their view is that movements—such as stretching of the inner parts—are bound to take place under the huge forces acting upon the tubes, and that it is better to allow freedom for these to take place naturally rather than to make any attempt to retard them. On the other hand it cannot be denied that the rigid construction is

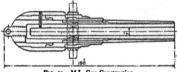

FIG. 12.—M.L. Gun Construction.

conducive to strength and durability, but it is essential that massive tubes of the highest quality of steel should be employed.

The actual building up of a gun entails operations which are exactly similar, whether it be of the M.L. or B.L. system; and the hardening treatment of the steel is also the same—the coiled iron hoops when welded, of course, received no such treatment.

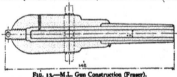

FIG. 13.—M.L. Gun Construction (Fraser).

Fig. 14 shows the various stages of building up a B.L. gun and illustrates at the same time the principle of the interlocking system.

The steel barrels of the M.L. guns were forged solid; the material was then tested so as to determine the most suitable temperature at which the oil hardening treatment should be carried out after the barrel had been bored. The bored barrel was simply heated to the required temperature and plunged vertically into a tank of oil. The subsequent annealing process was not introduced until some years after; it is therefore not to be wondered at that steel proved untrustworthy and so was used with reluctance.

Since 1880 the steel industry has made so much progress that this material is now regarded as the metal most to be relied on. The long high-power guns, however, require to be worked at a greater chamber pressure than the older B.L. guns, with which 15 tons or 16 tons per square inch was considered the maximum. With the designs now produced 18·5 tons to 20 tons per square inch working pressure in the chamber is the general rule.

A stronger material than ordinary carbon gun steel was consequently demanded from the steel-makers, in order to keep the weights of the heavier natures of guns within reasonable limits. The demand was met by the introduction of a gun steel having about 4 % of nickel in addition to about 0·4 % of carbon. This alloy gives great

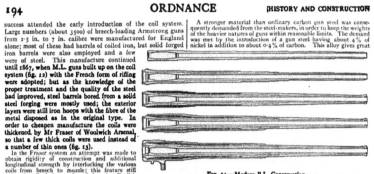

FIG. 14.—Modern B.L. Construction.

toughness and endurance under a suitable oil hardening and annealing process, the yielding stress being about 26 tons to 28 tons and the breaking stress from 45 tons to 55 tons per square inch, with an elongation of 16 %. The tests for ordinary carbon gun steel are: "yield not less than 21 tons, breaking stress between 34 tons and 44 tons per square inch, and elongation 17 %."

The toughness of nickel steel forgings renders them much more difficult to machine, but the advantages have been so great that practically all barrels and hoops (except jackets) of modern guns are now made of this material.

The gun steel, whether of the carbon or nickel quality, used in England and most foreign countries, is prepared by the open hearth method in a regenerative gas furnace of the Siemens-Martin type (see IRON AND STEEL). The steel is run from the furnace into a large ladle, previously heated by gas, and from this it is allowed to run into a cast iron ingot mould of from 10 to 12 ft. high and 2 ft. or more in diameter. With very large ingots two furnaces may have to be employed. The external shape of these ingots varies in different steel works, but they are so arranged that, as the ingot slowly cools, the contraction of the metal shall not set up dangerous internal stresses. The top of the ingot is generally porous, and consequently, after cooling, it is usual for about one-third of the length of the ingot to be cut from the top and remelted; a small part of the bottom is also often discarded. The centre of the larger ingots is also inclined to be unsound, and a hole is therefore bored through them to remove this part. In the Whitworth and Harmet methods of fluid compressed steel, this porosity at the top and centre of the ingot does not occur to the same extent, and a much greater portion can therefore be utilised.

The sound portion of the ingot is now heated in a reheating gas furnace, which is usually built in close proximity to a hydraulic forging press (fig. 15, Plate I.). This press is now almost exclusively used for forging the steel in place of the steam hammers which were formerly an important feature in all large works. The largest of these steam hammers could not deliver a blow of much more than some 500 ft. tons of energy; with the hydraulic press, however, the pressure amounts to, for ordinary purposes, from 1000 tons to 5000 tons, while for the manufacture of armour plates it may amount to as much as 10,000 or 12,000 tons.

For forgings of 8-in. internal diameter and upwards, the bored out ingot, just mentioned, is forged hollow on a tubular mandril, kept cool by water running through the centre; from two to four hours forging work can be performed before the metal has cooled down too much. Generally one end of the ingot is forged down to the proper size; it is then reheated and the other end similarly treated.

The forging of the steel and the subsequent operations have a very marked influence on the structure of the metal, as will be seen from the micro-photographs shown in the article ALLOYS, where (a) and (b) show the structure of the cast steel of the actual ingot; from this it will be noticed that the crystals are very large and prominent, but, as the metal passes through the various operations, these crystals become smaller and less pronounced. Thus (c) and (d) show the metal after forging; (e) shows the pearlite structure with a magnification of 1000 diameters, which disappears on the steel being oil hardened, and (f) shows the oil hardened and annealed crystals. At the Bofors Works in Sweden, gun barrels up to 24 cm. (9·5 in.) calibre have been formed of an unforged cast steel tube; but this practice, although allowing of the production of an inexpensive gun, is not followed by other nations.

After the forging is completed, it is annealed by reheating and cooling slowly, and test pieces are cut from each end tangentially to the circumference of the bore; these are tested to ascertain the quality of the steel in the soft state.

It is found that the quality of the steel is greatly improved by forging, so long as this is not carried so far as to set up a laminar structure in the metal, which is thereby rendered less suitable for gun construction—being weaker across the laminae than in the other directions. It is then termed over-forged.

If the tests are satisfactory the forging is rough-turned and bored, then reheated to a temperature of about 1600° F., and hardened by plunging it into a vertical tank of rape oil. This process is a somewhat critical one and great care is observed in uniformly heating, to the required temperature, the whole of the forging in a furnace in close proximity to the oil tank, into which it is plunged and completely submerged as rapidly as possible. In some cases the oil in the tank is circulated by pumping, so that uniformity of cooling is ensured; and, in addition, the oil tank is surrounded by a water jacket which also helps to keep it at a uniform heat. The forging is subsequently again heated to about 1200° F. and allowed to cool slowly by being placed in warm sand, &c. This last operation is termed annealing, and is intended to dissipate any internal stress which may have been induced in the forging by any of the previous processes, especially that of oil-hardening. After this annealing process a second set of test pieces, two for tensile and two for bending test, are cut from each end of the forging in the positions above mentioned; for guns of less than 5-in. calibre only half this number of test pieces is taken; and with hoops of less than 48 in. in length the test pieces are taken only from the end which formed the upper part of the cast ingot.

In all cases of annealed steel the test pieces of 2 in. length and 0·533 in. diameter must give the stipulated tests according to the character of the steel. For breech screws the steel is made of a harder quality, as it has to resist a crushing stress. These are the tests required in England, but they differ in different countries; for instance in France a harder class of carbon steel is employed for hoops, in which the tensile strength must not be less than 44·5 tons, nor the elastic limit less than 28·5 tons per square inch, neither must the elongation fall below 12%.

Assuming that the tests of the annealed forging are satisfactory, the forging, which we will suppose to be a barrel, is tested for straightness and if necessary rectified. It is then rough-turned in a lathe (fig. 16) " to break the skin " (as it is termed technically) and so

interior of the covering tube or hoop finished to suit. The covering hoop is allowed usually only a small shrinkage, or sometimes none, as it is simply intended as a protection to the wire and to give longitudinal strength; but in order to place it over the wire it must be heated and thus some little contraction always does take place on cooling. The heat to which these hoops are brought for shrinking never exceeds that used in annealing, otherwise the modifying effects of this process would be interfered with.

In the earliest modern type B.L. guns, the breech screw engaged directly with a screw thread cut in the barrel, which thus had to resist a large portion, if not all, of the longitudinal stress. This was also the system first adopted in France, but there are certain objections to it, the principal being that the barrel must be made of large diameter to meet the longitudinal stress, and this in consequence reduces the circumferential strength of the gun. Again, the diameter of the screw is always considerably larger than the breech opening, and so an abrupt change of section takes place, which it is always best to avoid in structures liable to sudden shocks. The thick barrel, however, gives stiffness against bending and, moreover, does not materially lengthen with firing; thin barrels on the other hand are gradually extended by the drawing out action of the shot as it is forced through the gun. In some large guns with excessively thin barrels this action was so pronounced as to entail considerable inconvenience. In the English system the breech screw is engaged either in the breech piece, i.e. the hoop which is shrunk on over the breech end of the barrel, or in a special bush screwed into the breech piece. This latter method suits the latest system of construction in which the breech piece is put on the barrel from the muzzle, while with the earlier type it was put on from the breech end.

With the earlier modern guns short hoops were used whenever possible, as, for instance, over the chase, principally because the steel in short lengths was less likely to contain flaws, but as the metallurgical processes of steel making developed the necessity for this disappeared, and the hoops became gradually longer. This has however, increased correspondingly the difficulties in boring and turning, and, to a much greater extent, those encountered in building up the gun. In this operation the greatest care has to be taken, or warping will occur during heating. The tubes are heated in a vertical cylindrical furnace, gas jets playing both on the exterior and interior of the tube. When sufficiently hot, known by the diameter of the tube expanding to equal previously prepared gauges, the tube is

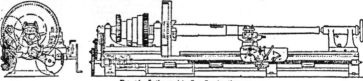

FIG. 16.—Lathe used in Gun Construction.

prevent warping during the subsequent operations. It is then bored out to nearly the finished dimension and afterwards fine turned on the exterior. In the meantime the other portions of the gun are in progress, and as it is far easier to turn down the outside of a tube than to bore out the interior of the superimposed one to the exact measurements required to allow for shrinkage, the interior of the jacket and other hoops are bored out and finished before the exterior of the internal tubes or of the barrel is fine turned. The process of boring is illustrated in fig. 17. The barrel or hoop A, to be bored, is passed through the revolving headstock B and firmly held by jaws C, the other end being supported on rollers D. A head E, mounted on the end of a boring bar F, is drawn gradually through the barrel, as it revolves, by the leading screw K actuated by the gear G. The boring head is provided with two or more

raised out of the furnace and dropped vertically over the barrel or other portion of the gun (fig. 18, Plate II.). In cooling it shrinks longitudinally as well as circumferentially, and in order to avoid gaps between adjoining tubes the tube is, after being placed in position, cooled at one end by a ring of water jets to make it grip, while the other portions are kept hot by rings of burning gas flames, which are successively extinguished to allow the hoop to shorten gradually and thus prevent internal longitudinal stress. A stream of water is also directed along the interior of the gun during the building up process, in order to ensure the hoop cooling from the interior. After the building up has been completed, the barrel is fine-bored, then chambered and rifled. The breech is then screwed either for the bush or breech screw and the breech mechanism fitted to the gun.

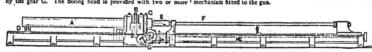

FIG. 17.—Boring.

cutting tools, and also with a number of brass pins or pieces of hard wood to act as guides, in order to keep the boring head central after it has entered the barrel. The revolving headstock B is driven by a belt and suitable gearing.

With wire guns the procedure is somewhat different. The wire is wound on to its tube, which has been previously fine turned, the exterior diameter of the wire is then carefully measured and the

In order to obtain additional longitudinal strength the outer tubes are so arranged that each hooks on to its neighbour from muzzle to breech. Thus, the chase hoop hooks on to the barrel by a step, and the succeeding hoops hook on to each other until the jacket is reached which is then secured to the breech piece by a strong screwed ring. In all the latest patterns of English guns there is a single chase hoop covering the forward portion of the gun and a jacket covering the breech portion, an arrangement which simplifies the design but increases the difficulties of manufacture.

Wire guns are now made of almost all calibres, ranging from 3 in. to 12 in. Many authorities objected to guns of less calibre than

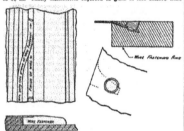

Elswick System   *Woolwich System*
FIG. 19.—Wire Fastening.

4·7 in. being wound with wire, as they considered that on diameters so small the interior surface of each layer of wire is over-compressed, while the exterior is too much extended; but by proportioning the thickness of the wire to the diameter of the tube on which it is wound there is no reason for this to be so.

The wire is wound on the barrel at a certain tension, ascertained by calculation, and varying from about 50 tons per square inch for the layers first wound on the gun, to about 35 or 40 for the outer layers. To fasten the wire at the beginning and several methods are adopted. In the Woolwich system a narrow annular ring (fig. 19), with slots cut into one of its faces, is shrunk on to the gun; into these slots one end of the wire is inserted and secured in position by a steel screwed plug. The wire is wound on for the distance desired and then back again to the ring, where the end is fastened off in the same way. At Elswick the wire is fastened by bending it into a shunt cut groove in a similar annular ring, but the wire is only fastened off in the same way after several layers have been wound.

With each succeeding layer of wire the interior layers are compressed, and these in turn **compress the** barrel. It is therefore

necessary, in order to prevent the fatigue of the material, to make the barrel comparatively thick, or, better still, to have an outer barrel superimposed on the inner one. This latter arrangement is now used in all guns of 4 in. calibre and upwards. It is not so important with smaller guns as the barrel is always relatively thick, and therefore meets the conditions.

With many modern guns the interior of the outer barrel, termed the " A " tube, is taper bored, the larger end being towards the breech; and the exterior of the inner barrel or liner, called the " inner A tube," is made tapered to correspond. The latter is, after careful fitting, inserted in the outer barrel while both are cold, and forced into position by hydraulic pressure or other mechanical means.

The details of the machines for winding on the wire (see fig. 20) differ somewhat in different works, but all are arranged so that any desired tension can be given to the wire as it is being wound on to the gun. The wire is manufactured in much the same way as ordinary wire. A red-hot bar of steel, gradually rolled down between rollers to a section about double that which it is finally intended to have, is annealed and carefully pickled in an acid bath to detach any scale. It is then wound on a drum, ready for the next process, which consists in drawing it through graduated holes made in a hardened steel draw-plate, the wire being often annealed and pickled during this process. The drawplate holes vary in size from slightly smaller than the rolled bar section to the finished size of the wire, and, as a rule, the sharp corners of the wire are only given by the last draw. It is found that considerable wear takes place in the holes of the draw-plate, and a new plate may be required for each hank of 500 or 600 yds. of wire. Great importance is attached to the absence of scale from the wire when it is being drawn, and, after pickling, the rolled bar and wire are treated with lime or some similar substance to facilitate the drawing. The tests for the finished wire are as follows: it has to stand a tensile stress of from **90 to 110 tons per square inch of section, and a test for ductility in which a short length of wire is twisted a considerable number of turns in one direction, then unwound and re-twisted in the opposite direction, without showing signs of fracture.** It will be seen that the wire is extremely strong and the moderate stress of from 35 to 50 tons per square inch, which at most it is called upon to withstand in a gun, is far less than what it could endure with perfect safety.

The wire after being manufactured is made up into hanks for storage purposes; but when required for gun construction it is thoroughly cleaned and wound on a drum R about 3 ft. 6 in. in diameter, which is placed in one portion of the machine in connexion with a powerful band friction brake M. The wire is then led to the gun A placed between centres or on rollers B.B, parallel to the axis of the wire drum. By rotating the gun the wire is drawn off from the drum against the resistance of the band brake, which is so designed that, by adjusting the weight S suspended from the brake strap, any desired resistance can be given in order to produce the necessary tension in the wire as it is being wound on the gun. The stress on

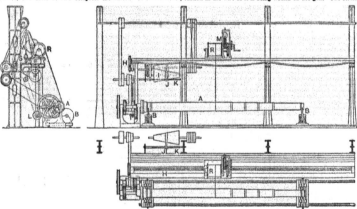

FIG. 20.—Wire-winding Machine.

the wire is indicated on a dial, and the headstock, containing the drum of wire, is capable of being moved along the bed G by a leading screw H, driven by a belt through variable speed cones I; the belt is moved along the cones by forks J, traversed by screws K, which in their turn are actuated by chain belts from the hand wheel L. The traversing speed is regulated to suit the speed of winding by moving the belt along the speed cones.

The wire is rectangular in section, 0·25 in. wide and 0·06 in. thick, and after it has been wound on to the gun it presents a very even surface which requires little further preparation. The diameter over the wire is gauged and the jacket or other covering hoop is carefully bored equal to this, if no shrinkage is to be allowed; or the dimension is diminished in accordance with the amount of shrinkage to be arranged for.

The gun is built up, after wiring, in the same manner as a gun without wire, the jacket or other hoop being heated in the vertical gas furnace and when hot enough dropped into place over the wire, cooled by the ring of water jets at the end first required to grip and kept hot at the other, exactly as before described.

The machine arranged for rifling modern guns is very similar to that employed for the old muzzle-loaders; it is a special tool *Rifling operations.* used in gun construction only (fig. 21), and is in reality a copying machine. A steel or cast-iron bar J which forms the copy of the developed rifling curve is first made. The copying bar—which is straight if the rifling is to be uniform but curved if it is to be increasing—is fixed, inclined at the

bullet, from the muzzle. In 1836 Russia made a large number of experiments with a rifled gun invented by Montigny, a Belgian; this was not a success, but in England the guns invented by Major Cavalli, in 1845, and by Baron Wahrendorff in 1846, obtained some measure of favour. Both these guns were breech-loaders. The Cavalli gun had a bore of 6·5 in. diameter; it was rifled in two grooves having a uniform twist of 1 in 25 calibres, and the elongated projectile had two ribs cast with it to fit the grooves, but no means were taken to prevent windage. The Wahrendorff gun had an enlarged chamber and the bore of 6·37 in. diameter was rifled in 2 grooves; the projectile had ribs similar to that for the Cavalli gun; but Wahrendorff had also tried lead-coated projectiles, the coating being attached by grooves undercut in the outside of the shell. In 1854 Lancaster submitted his plan of rifling; in this (fig. 22) the bore was made of an oval section which twisted round the axis of the gun from the breech to the muzzle; a projectile having an oval section was fired. Several old cast-iron guns bored on this system burst in the Crimean War from the projectile wedging in the gun. In 1855 Armstrong experimented with a breech-loading rifled gun, firing a lead-coated projectile. The rifling consisted

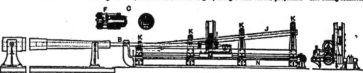

FIG. 21.—Rifling Machine.

proper angle, to standards K on the machine. The cutting tool is carried at one end C of a strong hollow cylindrical rifling bar B, the other end of which is fixed to a saddle M. This is moved along the bed of the machine by a long screw N, and the rifling bar is consequently either pushed into the gun or withdrawn by the motion of the saddle along the machine. During this motion it is made to rotate slowly by being connected to the copying bar by suitable gearing I. It will thus be seen that the cutting tool will cut a spiral groove along the bore of the gun in strict conformity with the copy. In most English machines the cutting tool cuts only as the rifling bar is drawn out of the gun; during the reverse motion the cutter F is withdrawn out of action by means of a wedge arrangement actuated by a rod passing through the centre of the rifling bar, which also pushes forward the cutter at the proper time for cutting. One, two or more grooves may be cut at one time, the full depth being attained by slowly feeding the tool after each stroke. After each set of grooves is cut the rifling bar or the gun is rotated so as to bring the cutters to a new position. In some foreign machines the cut is taken as the rifling bar is pushed into the gun.

Rifling is the term given to the numerous shallow grooves cut spirally along the bore of a gun; the rib between two *Rifling.* grooves is called the "land." Rifling has been known for many years; it was supposed to increase the range, and no doubt did so, owing to the fact that the bullet having to be forced into the gun during the loading operation became a mechanical fit and prevented to a great extent the loss of gas by windage which occurred with ordinary weapons. Kotter (1520) and Danner (1552), both of Nuremberg, are respectively credited as being the first to rifle gun barrels; and there is at the Rotunda, Woolwich, a muzzle-loading barrel dated 1547 rifled with six fine grooves. At this early period, rifling was applied only to small arms, usually for sporting purposes. The disadvantage of having, during loading, to force a soft lead (or lead-covered) ball down a bore of smaller diameter prevented its general employment for military use. In 1661 Prussia experimented with a gun rifled in thirteen shallow grooves, and in 1696 the elliptical bore—similar to the Lancaster—had been tried in Germany. In 1745 Robins was experimenting with rifled guns and elongated shot in England. During the Peninsular War about 1809, the only regiment (the "Rifle Brigade," formerly called the 95th) equipped with rifled arms, found considerable difficulty in loading them with the old spherical lead

of a large number of shallow grooves having a uniform twist of 1 in 38 calibres. When the gun was fired the lead-coated projectile, which was slightly larger in diameter than the bore of the gun, was forced into the rifling and so gave rotation to the elongated projectile. Whitworth in 1857 brought out his

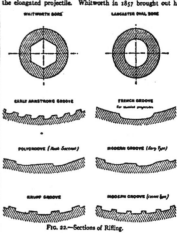

WHITWORTH BORE   LANCASTER OVAL BORE

EARLY ARMSTRONG GROOVE   FRENCH GROOVE for studded projectiles

POLYGROOVE (Flush Section)   MODERN GROOVE (Krupp Type)

KRUPP GROOVE   MODERN GROOVE (Sweet Type)

FIG. 22.—Sections of Rifling.

hexagonal bore method of rifling and a projectile which was a good mechanical fit to the bore. Good results were obtained, but although this system had certain advantages it did not fulfil all requirements.

In 1863, England re-opened the whole question, and after exhaustive trials of various inventions decided on the adoption of the muzzle-loading type for all guns, with the French system of rifling. This system was invented in 1842 by Colonel Treüille de Beaulieu and consisted of a few wide and deep grooves which gave rotation to a studded projectile. At the first trials two grooves only were tried, but the number was afterwards increased to three or more, as it was found that two grooves only would not correctly centre the projectile. The adoption of the muzzle-loading system with studded shot was a distinctly retrograde step, as a considerable amount of clearance was necessary between the bore and projectile for the purposes of loading, and this resulted in the barrel being seriously eroded by the rush of gas over the shot, and also led to a considerable loss of energy. In the Wahrendorff and Armstrong systems however the lead-coated projectiles entirely prevented windage, besides which the projectile was perfectly centred and a high degree of accuracy was obtained.

Shunt rifling was a brief attempt to make loading by the muzzle easy without forfeiting the centring principle: in this the rifling varied in width and in depth, at different portions of the bore in such a manner that, during loading, the studs on the projectile could move freely in the bore. When the gun was fired the studs of the projectile were forced to travel in the shallow part of the rifling, thus gripping and centring the projectile as it left the muzzle.

With uniform rifling on the French system, the few studs—generally two per groove—had to bear so high a pressure to produce rotation that they sometimes gave way. This subject was investigated by Captain (Sir Andrew) Noble, who showed that by making the rifling an increasing twist, commencing with no twist and gradually increasing until the necessary pitch was obtained, the maximum pressure due to rotation was much reduced. Increasing rifling was consequently adopted, with beneficial results.

In order to prevent the heavy erosion due to windage, a gas check was adopted which was attached to the base end of the studded projectiles. In some guns the number of grooves of the rifling was sufficiently great to admit of rotation being insured by means of the gas check alone; in these guns studded projectiles were not employed, but the gas check, called "automatic," to distinguish it from that fitted to studded projectiles was usually indented around its circumference to correspond with the rifling of the gun. It was found that the studless projectile had considerably greater range and accuracy than the studded projectile, with the additional advantage that the shell was not weakened by the stud holes.

The introduction of the plain copper driving band for rotating projectiles with breech-loading guns included a return to the polygroove system with shallow grooves; this still exists, but the continuous demand for greater power has had the effect of increasing the number of grooves from that at first considered necessary, in order to keep the rotating pressure on the driving band within practical limits.

Many ingenious devices for giving rotation and preventing the escape of gas past the projectile were tried in the early days of modern rifling. Experiments of this nature still continue to be made with a view to improving the shooting and to prevent the erosion of the bore of the gun. Briefly considered, without going into any detail of the numerous plans, all rotating devices fitted to projectiles can be divided into three classes—the "centring," the "compressing" and the "expansion" systems. The two last named almost invariably include the "centring" type. Studded (fig. 23) and Whitworth (fig. 24) hexagonal projectiles, which can freely slide in the bore, come under the first system.

In the compression class the coating or rings on the projectile are larger in diameter than the bore and when fired the coating (or rings) is squeezed or engraved by the rifling to fit the bore—the projectile is consequently also centred. The old-fashioned

lead-coated shell (fig. 25), and the modern system of plain copper driving bands (fig. 26), come under this class. Most variety exists in the expansion type, where the pressure of the powder gas acts on the base of the projectile or on the driving ring and compresses a lead, copper or asbestos ring into the rifling grooves. One of the earliest was the Hotchkiss (1865) shell (fig. 27), in which a separate base end B was driven forward by the gas pressure and squeezed out the lead ring L into the rifling. The automatic gas check (fig. 28), and the gas check driving band (fig. 29), belong to this system; in the last the lip L is expanded into the rifling groove. In fig. 30 a copper driving band is

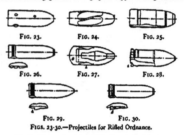

FIG. 23.　　　FIG. 24.　　　FIG. 25.

FIG. 26.　　　FIG. 27.　　　FIG. 28.

FIG. 29.　　　FIG. 30.

FIGS. 23-30.—Projectiles for Rifled Ordnance.

associated with an asbestos packing A, contained in a canvas bag or copper casing made in the form of a ring on the principle of the de Bange obturator; but the results of this have not been entirely satisfactory.

It will be seen that with breech-loading guns the projectile is better centred, and the copper driving band forms a definite stop for the projectile; and, in consequence, the capacity of the gun chamber is practically constant. In addition, the use of a copper driving band ensures a uniform resistance while this is being engraved and the projectile forced through the gun, and also prevents the escape of gas. These elements have a very great influence on the accuracy of the shooting, and fully account for the vastly superior results obtained from breech-loading ordnance when compared with the muzzle-loading type. Driving bands of other materials such as cupro-nickel and ferro-nickel have also been tried.

Many authorities believe that the best results are obtained when the projectile is fitted with two bands, one near the head and the other near the base, and no doubt it is better centred when so arranged, but such shot can only be fired from guns rifled with a uniform twist, and it must also not be forgotten that the groove formed for the front band in the head of the projectile necessarily weakens that part of the projectile which should be strongest.

Projectiles with a driving band at the base only can be fired from guns rifled either uniformly or with increasing twist.

The introduction of cordite (q.v.) about 1890 again brought into special prominence the question of rifling. The erosion caused by this explosive soon obliterated the rifling for some 4 or 5 calibres at the breech end. The driving band of the shell consequently started with indifferent engraving, and with the increasing twist, then in general use, it was feared that the wear would quickly render the gun useless. To remedy this the late Commander Younghusband, R.N., proposed straight rifling, which was adopted in 1895, for that portion of the rifling mostly affected by the erosion, with a gradual increase of the twist thence to the required pitch at the muzzle. Thus, any erosion of the straight part of the rifling would not affect that portion giving rotation, and it was argued that the gun would remain efficient for a longer period. The defect in this system is that when the projectile arrives at the end of the straight rifling it has a considerable forward velocity and no rotation. Rotation is then imparted by the increasing twist of rifling, and the resulting pressure on the engraved ribs of the driving band rises suddenly to a maximum which, in high velocity guns, the driving band is unable to resist. For this reason the straight portion at the commencement of the rifling has been discarded, and with high power guns firing a slow burning propellant uniform rifling has again found favour.

It is evident that in order that a projectile may have a definite amount of spin as it leaves the gun a determinate amount of work must be imparted to rotate it during its passage along the rifled portion of the bore. Put briefly, this work is the sum of the products of the pressure between the engraved ribs on the driving band and the lands of the rifling in the gun multiplied by the length of the rifling over which this pressure acts. Sir Andrew Noble has proved theoretically and experimentally (see *Phil. Mag.*, 1863 and 1873; also *Proc. Roy. Soc.* vol. 50) that the rotating pressure depends on the propelling pressure of the powder gas on the base of the projectile and on the curve of the rifling. If this curve was so proportioned as to make the rotating pressure approximately constant along the bore, the result was an increasing or progressive curve partaking of the nature of a parabola, in which case it was usual to make the last two or three calibres of rifling at the muzzle of uniform twist for the purpose of steadying the projectile and aiding accuracy.

In uniform rifling the curve is a straight line and the rotating pressure is consequently mainly proportional to the propelling gas pressure. The pressure for rotation with uniform rifling therefore rises to a maximum with the propelling pressure and falls as it becomes less towards the muzzle.

With increasing rifling, owing to the angle of twist continually changing as the projectile travels along the bore, the ribs originally engraved by the rifling on the driving band are forced to change their direction correspondingly, and this occurs by the front surface of the ribs wearing away. They are therefore weakened considerably, and it is found that with high velocities the engraved part of the band often entirely disappears through this progressive action.

It will thus be seen that although an increasing twist of rifling may be so arranged as to give uniform pressure, it is evident that if wear takes place, the engraved rib becomes weaker to resist shearing as the shot advances, and the rate of wear also increases owing to the increase of heat by friction. With the very narrow driving bands used for low velocity guns this action was not so detrimental.

With the long modern guns and the high muzzle velocities required, the propelling gas pressures along the bore rise comparatively slowly to a maximum and gradually fall until the muzzle is reached. The pressure of the gas at all points of the bore is now considerably higher than with the older patterns of B.L. guns.

For modern conditions, in order to obtain an increasing curve giving an approximately constant driving pressure between the rifling and driving band, this pressure becomes comparatively high. The maximum rotating pressure, with uniform rifling, is certainly somewhat higher, but not to a very great extent, and as it occurs when the projectile is still moving slowly, the wear due to friction will be correspondingly low; the pressure gradually falls until the muzzle is reached, where it is much lower than with increasing rifling. The projectile thus leaves the gun without any great disturbance from the rifling pressure. Further, as the band is engraved once for all with the angle it will have all along the bore the pressure is distributed equally over the driving face of the ribs instead of being concentrated at the front of the ribs as in progressive or increasing rifling.

The following formulae showing the driving pressures for increasing and uniform rifling are calculated from Sir Andrew Noble's formula, which Sir G. Greenhill has established independently by another method.

Let R = total pressure, in tons, between rifling and driving band.
G = gaseous pressure, in tons, on the base of the projectile.
r = radius, in feet, of the bore.
μ = coefficient of friction.
ρ = radius of gyration of projectile.
δ = angle between the normal to the driving surface of groove and radius.
k = the pitch of the rifling, in feet.
h = cotangent of angle of rifling at an point of rifling.
M = weight of the projectile in pounds.
s = the length, in feet, travelled by the projectile.

Then for parabolic rifling

$$R = \frac{2p^2(Gz + M z^2)}{\frac{(r^2 h^2 + \frac{1}{4}p^2 h^2) \sin \delta}{(\frac{1}{4}z^2 \sin^2 \delta + k^2)^{\frac{1}{2}}} + \frac{2\mu_1 k z (p^2 - r^2)}{(4z^2 + k^2)^{\frac{1}{2}}}}$$

For uniform rifling

$$R = \frac{2\pi p^2 G}{\frac{\mu_1 (2\pi p^2 k - rh)}{(1 + h^2)^{\frac{1}{2}}} + \frac{(2\pi p^2 + rhk) \sin \delta}{(k^2 + \sin^2 \delta)^{\frac{1}{2}}}}$$

For modern rifling δ = 90°; therefore sin δ = 1; by which the above expressions may be considerably simplified.

For parabolic rifling

$$R = \frac{2p^3(4z^2 + k^2)^{\frac{1}{2}}(Gz + M z^2)}{k^2 (k - 2\mu_1 z) + 2p^2 z(2z + \mu_1 k)},$$

For uniform rifling we can write $hk = 2\pi r$ and the expression reduces to

$$R = \frac{p^2(1 + k^2)^{\frac{1}{2}}}{\mu_1 \left(p^2 k - \frac{r^2}{k}\right) + p^2 + r^2} . G.$$

Fig. 31 shows graphically the calculated results obtained for a 4·7-in. 50-calibre gun which has a shot travel of 17·3 ft.; the pressure

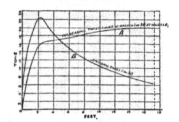

4·7 INCH 50 CALIBRE GUN
FIG. 31.—Pressure Curves (uniform and increasing twist).

curve A is for a rifling twist increasing from 1 in 60 calibres at the breech to 1 in 30 calibres at the muzzle; curve B is for rifling having a uniform twist of 1 in 30 calibres.

It must be remembered that this comparison is typical for modern conditions; with old-fashioned guns firing black or brown powder the maximum rotating pressure for uniform rifling could attain a value 50 % above that for increasing rifling.

In this example, with the increasing twist there is a loss of energy of about 11 % of the total muzzle energy, and for the uniform rifling a loss of about 8 %. This explains the reason for uniformly rifled guns giving a higher muzzle velocity than those with increasing rifling, supposing the guns to be otherwise similar.

The pitch of the rifling or the amount of twist to be given to it depends altogether on the length of the projectile; if this is short a small amount of twist only is necessary, if long a greater amount of twist must be arranged for, in order to spin the shell more rapidly. Sir G. Greenhill has shown that the pitch of the rifling necessary to keep a projectile in steady motion is independent of the velocity, of the calibre, or of the length of the gun, but depends principally on the length of the shell and on its description, so that for similar projectiles one pitch would do for all guns.

Table I., on following page, has been calculated from Greenhill's formula.

In most modern guns the projectile varies in length from 3·5 to 4 calibres, so that the rifling is made to terminate at the muzzle with a twist of 1 turn in 30 calibres, which is found ample to give a steady flight to the projectile. In the United States a terminal twist of 1 in 25 calibres is often adopted; Krupp also uses this in some guns. With howitzers the projectile may be 4·5 calibres long, and the rifling has to be made of a quicker twist to suit.

If the gun has, as is usually the case, a right-hand twist of rifling , the projectile drifts to the right; if it has a left-hand twist the **Drift.** drift takes place to the left. The drift increases with the range but in a greater ratio; further, the greater the twist (*i.e.* the smaller the pitch of rifling) the greater the drift. On the other hand the smooth B.L. projectiles drift less than studded M.L. projectiles.

To find the angle, usually called the *permanent angle of deflection*, at which the sights must be inclined to compensate for the drift, a number of shots are fired at various ranges. The results obtained are plotted on paper, and a straight line is then drawn from the point representing the muzzle through the mean value of the plotted curve.

The early guns were fired by inserting a red-hot wire into the vent, or by filling the vent with powder and firing it by a red-hot iron. Slow match held in a cleft stick afterwards **Firing** took the place of the hot iron, and this again was **arrange-** replaced by a port-fire. Filling the vent with loose **ments.** powder was inconvenient and slow, and to improve matters the powder was placed in a paper, tin or quill tube which was simply pushed into the vent and fired by the slow match or port-fire.

The first attempt to fire guns by mechanical means was made in 1781 by Sir Charles Douglas, who fitted flint locks, similar to musket locks, but with the trigger actuated by a lanyard, to the guns on board his ship H.M.S. "Duke." A double flint lock introduced in 1818 by Sir Howard Douglas, R.A., continued to

TABLE I.

Length of projectile in calibres.	Minimum twist at muzzle of gun requisite to give stability of rotation — one turn in n calibres or a pitch of n calibres.			
	Cast-iron common shell, cavity ~7⁄16 vol. of shell (s.g. of iron = 7·2).	Palliser shell, cavity ~¼ vol. (s.g. = 8·0).	Solid steel bullet (s.g. = 8·0).	Solid lead and tin bullets of similar composition to M.-H. bullets (s g = 10·9).
	n.	n.	n.	n.
2·0	63·87	71·08	72·21	84·29
·1	59·84	66·59	67·66	78·98
·2	56·31	62·67	63·67	74·32
·3	53·19	59·19	60·14	70·20
·4	50·41	56·10	57·00	66·53
·5	47·91	53·32	54·17	63·24
·6	45·65	50·81	51·62	60·26
·7	43·61	48·53	49·30	57·55
·8	41·74	46·45	47·19	55·09
·9	40·02	44·54	45·25	52·72
3·0	38·45	42·79	43·47	50·74
·1	36·99	41·16	41·82	48·82
·2	35·64	39·66	40·30	47·04
·3	34·39	38·27	38·84	45·38
·4	33·22	36·97	37·56	43·84
·5	32·13	35·75	36·33	42·40
·6	31·11	34·62	35·17	41·05
·7	30·15	33·55	34·09	39·79
·8	29·25	32·55	33·07	38·61
·9	28·40	31·61	32·11	37·48
4·0	27·60	30·72	31·21	36·43
·1	26·85	29·88	30·36	35·43
·2	26·13	29·08	29·55	34·49
·3	25·45	28·33	28·78	33·59
·4	24·81	27·61	28·05	32·74
·5	24·20	26·93	27·36	31·94
·6	23·65	26·32	26·74	31·21
·7	23·06	25·66	26·08	30·44
·8	22·53	25·08	25·48	29·74
·9	22·03	24·51	24·91	29·07
5·0	21·56	23·98	24·36	28·44
·1	21·08	23·46	23·84	27·83
·2	20·64	22·97	23·34	27·24
·3	20·22	22·50	22·86	26·68
·4	19·81	22·05	22·40	26·14
·5	19·42	21·61	21·96	25·63
·6	19·04	21·19	21·53	25·18
·7	18·68	20·79	21·12	24·66
·8	18·33	20·40	20·73	24·20
·9	18·00	20·03	20·35	23·75
6·0	17·67	19·67	19·98	23·33
7·0	14·99	16·68	16·95	19·78
8·0	13·02	14·48	14·72	17·18
9·0	11·50	12·80	13·00	15·18
10·0	10·31	11·47	11·65	13·60

be used until about 1842, when it was replaced by a percussion lock invented by an American named Hiddens. In this lock one pull on the lanyard caused the hammer to fall and strike a percussion patch or cap hung on a small hook over the vent, and afterwards caused the hammer to be drawn backwards out of the way of the blast from the vent. These somewhat clumsy contrivances were swept away on the adoption in 1853 of friction tubes (see AMMUNITION), which had simply to be placed in the vent and the friction bar withdrawn by means of a lanyard.

Friction tubes continued to be used with all muzzle-loading ordnance except in one or two natures with which the charge was ignited axially at the breech of the gun. In these a vent sealing friction tube retained in the vent by a tube holder was employed. With breech-loading field guns ordinary friction tubes were also used until the introduction of cordite, which eroded the vents so quickly by the escape of the gases that vent sealing tubes became a necessity.

In all other breech-loading ordnance and with the latest pattern field guns the firing gear forms part of the breech mechanism.

All modern breech mechanisms form two groups (a) the sliding type as with the Krupp wedge system, (b) the swinging type as in the interrupted screw system. Either type may be used with B.L. guns (i.e. those with which the charge is not contained in a metallic cartridge case) and Q.F. guns (i.e. those with which a metallic cartridge case is used). **_Breech mechanism._**

Sliding mechanisms may be divided into two forms: (1) those having the block or wedge sliding horizontally, and (2) those in which the block works in a vertical direction. (1) is that used principally by Krupp; (2) is best illustrated by the Hotchkiss system for small Q.F.; guns; the Nordenfelt, Skoda and the Driggs-Schroeder mechanisms for small Q.F. guns are an adaptation of the same principle.

The Krupp gear is in reality an improved Cavalli mechanism; it is capable of being worked rapidly, is simple, with strong parts not liable to derangement, except perhaps the obturator. The breech end of the gun, however, occupies valuable space especially when these guns are mounted in the restricted turrets or gun houses on board ship.

Later it will be seen that owing to the difficulty of arranging a convenient and efficient obturating device for the smokeless nitro-powders, which have a peculiarly severe, searching effect, a metal cartridge case has to be used with even the heaviest guns; naturally this assumes large dimensions for the 305 m/m. gun.

The wedge (fig. 32) is housed in the breech piece, which covers the breech part of the barrel, made very massive and extended to the rear of the barrel. A slot, cut transversely through the extended portion, forms a seat for the sliding block. The slot is formed so that its front is a plane surface perpendicular to the axis of the gun, while the rear is rounded and slightly inclined to the axis. One or more ribs similarly inclined on the upper and lower surfaces of the slot guide the breech block in its movements. For traversing the block a quick pitched screw is fitted to its upper surface and works in a nut attached to the upper part of the slot (in small guns this traversing screw is dispensed with, as the block can be easily moved by hand). As the rear seat of the sliding block is inclined, there is a tendency for the block to be moved sideways, when the gun is fired by the pressure in the chamber acting on the front face of the wedge; this is prevented by a locking gear, consisting of a cylinder, having a series of interrupted collars, which is mounted on a screw. When the breech has been traversed into position, the collars are rotated, by a cross handle at the side of the block, into grooves cut in the rear surface of the slot; a further movement makes the screw jam the collars hard in contact with the gun and secures the breech. With small guns having no traversing gear a short strong screw takes the place of the collars, and on the handle being turned enters a threaded portion at the rear surface of the slot, actuates the breech for the last (or first in opening) portion of its movement in closing and secures it. To open the gun the movements are reversed.

The gun is fired by a friction tube, screwed into an axial vent bored through the sliding block, or, in field guns, by a copper friction tube through an oblique vent drilled through the top of the breech end of the gun and through the block.

There is also fitted in some guns a percussion arrangement for firing a percussion tube.

The obturation is effected by a Broadwell ring or some modification of it; this is placed in a groove cut in the gun and rests against a hard steel plate fitted in the breech block.

For modern Krupp mechanisms, for use with cartridge cases, the arrangement (fig. 33) is very similar to that described above, but some improvements have added to its simplicity. The transporting screw is fitted with a strong projection which, at the end of the movement for closing the breech, locks with a recess cut in the upper surface of the slot and secures the breech. The extra locking device is consequently dispensed with. The firing gear consists of a striker fitted in the sliding block in line with the axis of the gun; the striker is pushed back by a lever contained in the block and, on release, is driven forward against the primer of the cartridge case by a spiral spring.

In the Hotchkiss gun the mechanism has a vertical breech block of a rectangular section. The actuating lever F (fig. 34) is on the right side of the gun, and connected to a powerful crank arm C working in a groove E cut on the right side of the breech block. By pulling the lever towards the rear, the crank arm forces down the block A and extracts the fired case by an extractor X, which is actuated by a cam groove Y cut on one side or on both sides of the block. As the mechanism is opened the hammer H is cocked ready for the next round. To close the mechanism the lever is pushed over to the front, and by releasing the trigger scar by pulling the lanyard the hammer falls and fires the cap of the cartridge case.

Automatic gear is now generally fitted which opens the breech as the gun runs up after recoil and extracts the fired case by means of a supplementary mechanism and strong spring actuated by the recoil of the gun, and on pushing a new cartridge into the gun the breech which was retained by the extractor is released and closes automatically.

The Nordenfelt mechanism consists of a breech block (fig. 35) and a wedge to secure it. A hand lever on the shaft is pulled to the rear, and this works the action cam, which pulls down the wedge; the breech block is then caused to rotate and falls back to the rear. This motion of the breech block actuates the extractor

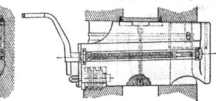

FIG. 32—Krupp Breech Action.

and extracts the case. While the **wedge is being withdrawn the** firing pin is pulled back and cocked for the next round. The mechanism is closed by reversing the hand lever; this rotates the breech block upwards and pushes home the cartridge case, and the wedge is then forced up and secures the breech block.

These small type Q.F. guns, which were introduced to cope with torpedo boats, are now, however, of little account, since experiment has proved that nothing smaller than a 12-pounder is sufficient so to injure a modern torpedo boat as to stop it. Most of these small guns are therefore in the English and in some other Services being converted into "sub-calibre" guns for exercise purposes. These sub-calibre guns retain their ordinary breech mechanism, but the bodies are fitted with a strong steel plug screwed on the outside in a similar manner to the breech screw of the parent gun. The sub-calibre gun is placed in the parent gun and the screwed plug engages in the threads of the breech opening.

There has been a gradual development of ideas regarding the repelling power required by a vessel against torpedo boat attack. The 12-pounder Q.F. 40-calibre guns were replaced by the more powerful 12-pounder Q.F. 50-calibre gun; this again by the 4-in. high power gun of 50 calibres, and now 6-in. guns are being used.

One other form of sliding mechanism is of importance owing to its adoption for the 75 m/m. French long recoil field gun (see below: *Field equipments*). This mechanism is on the Nordenfelt eccentric screw system and is very similar to that proposed by Clay about 1860; it has a breech screw (fig. 36) of large diameter mounted in the breech opening, which is eccentric to the bore. For loading, the breech block has a longitudinal opening cut through it, so that when the mechanism is in the open position this opening coincides with the chamber, while a half turn of the breech screw brings its solid part opposite the chamber and closes the gun. The mechanism is very simple and strong, but it is only suitable for small Q.F. guns using cartridge cases; the firing gear is similar to that applied to other types of mechanism, and the fired case is extracted by an extractor actuated by the face of the breech screw as it is opened.

With the swinging type of breech mechanism we are confronted with numberless patterns, many of undoubted merit and claiming certain advantages over others, and all showing the vast amount of ingenuity expended in so designing them that they may be as simple, and, at the same time, as effective and quick acting as possible. It is impossible to deal with all these, and therefore only the more important systems will be described. The special feature of this type is that the breech is closed by an interrupted breech screw; the screw is either supported in a carrier ring or tray hinged near the breech opening, or on a carrier arm which is hinged near the outer circumference of the gun.

The screw may be of the cylindric interrupted, Welin and coned types; these, or their modifications, practically embrace the various forms used. The cylindric form (fig. 37) is the simplest; it consists of a strong screwed plug engaging with a corresponding screw

thread cut on the interior of the breech opening of the gun. The screw surface of the breech plug is cut away in sections equally divided and alternating with the threaded portions. The screw surface of the breech opening is similarly cut away, so that the plug can be pushed nearly home into the breech opening without trouble; by then revolving the breech screw through a small angle the screwed portions of the plug and breech opening engage. Thus if there are three screwed sections alternate with three plain sections the angle of revolution necessary to ensure a full engagement of the screw surfaces will be 60°. The Welin screw (fig. 38) is an ingenious adaptation of the cylindric type; in this the surface is divided into sections each formed of two or three cylindrical steps with a single plain portion; thus if there are three sections, each section of which has one plain division and two screwed divisions, there will be in all six screwed portions and three plain. The breech opening is correspondingly formed so that the screwed threads would fully engage with 40° of movement. There is consequently a greater amount of screwed circumferential surface with the Welin screw than with the ordinary cylindric interrupted type; the latter form has 50 % screw surface while the Welin has 60 %. For equal screw surface the Welin can therefore be made shorter.

For medium guns the Elswick type of coned screw (fig. 39) has found much favour, and this mechanism has been fitted to guns of all calibres from 3-inch to 6-inch, both for the British and numerous other governments. The coned breech screw is formed with the front part conical and the rear cylindrical, to facilitate its entrance into the gun, and also its exit; this form, moreover, is taken advantage of by cutting the interruptions in the screwed surface alternately on the coned part and on the cylindrical part, so that there is a screwed surface all round the circumference of the breech screw. By this means the stress is taken all round the circumference, both of the breech screw and in the gun, instead of in portions alternately, as with other forms.

The Bolors breech screw is a modification. The surface is formed of a truncated ogive instead of a cylinder and cone, and the threaded portions are not alternate.

In the older types of mechanism for heavy B.L. guns the breech was opened in from three to four different operations which involved considerable loss of time. Fig. 40 shows the general type for 9·2-in., 10-in. and 12-in. B.L. guns. To open the breech the cam lever C was folded up so that it engaged the **pin B in connexion with the**

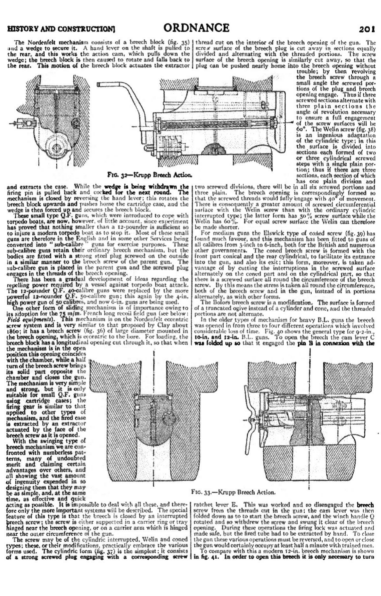

FIG. 33.—Krupp Breech Action.

ratchet lever E. This was worked and so disengaged the **breech** screw from the threads cut in the gun; the cam lever was then folded down, as to to start the breech screw, and the winch handle O rotated and so withdrew the screw and swung it clear of the breech opening. During these operations the firing lock was actuated and made safe, but the fired tube had to be extracted by hand. To close the gun these various operations must be reversed, and to open or close the gun would certainly occupy at least half a minute with trained men.

To compare with this a modern 12-in. breech mechanism is shown in fig. 41. In order to open this breech it is only necessary to turn the handwheel continuously in one direction, and to close it again the motion of the handwheel is simply reversed; either closing or opening the breech by hand occupies about 6 seconds. Supposing the breech closed, the handwheel when rotated gives motion to the link G through the worm wheel S and crank F. By this means the

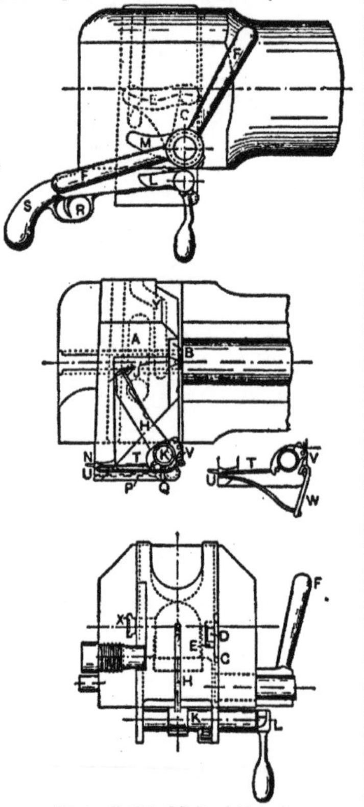

required for opening the breech. Thus, with the 6-in. B.L. gun Mark IV., introduced about 1885 (fig. 42) the breech is opened in three separate operations—(a) the cam lever, which also locks the breech, is raised into the vertical position and pulled over to the left; this disengages the screw threads; (b) the cam lever is folded down so

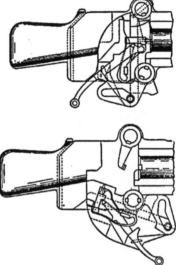

FIG. 35.—Nordenfeldt Q.F. Breech Mechanism.

that the cam acting on the rear face of the gun releases the de Bange obturator, and the screw is then pulled by hand through the carrier ring out of the breech; (c) the carrier ring and breech screw are revolved together to the right, clear of the breech opening.

In a modern 6-in. gun fitted with de Bange obturator all these operations are combined and the mechanism (fig. 43) worked by a horizontal hand lever which is moved from left to right through an angle of about 200°. The hand lever A moves a link B connected to a pin C on the breech screw D and disengages the screw from the gun; a small lateral movement is then given to the axis pin of the carrier so as to allow the obturator pad E to swing out of its seating; when

FIG. 36.—Eccentric Screw, Breech Mechanism.

this is quite free, the whole mechanism revolves on the axis pin and thus clears the breech opening. The firing lock F is actuated at the same time and ejects the fired tube G. A new tube is inserted while the gun is being loaded, so that immediately the breech is closed the charge can be fired without loss of time. In the old mechanisms the breech had to be closed first, and the firing tube inserted after.

FIG. 34.—Hotchkiss Q.F. Breech Mechanism.

tooth B is moved from its extreme left position to the right, and so disengages the breech screw A from the threads in the gun; the rack A² on the breech screw then comes into gear with the pinion E and draws the breech screw out of the gun into the carrier ring C, which finally swings on the axis pin and clears the breech opening. While the opening is being performed the firing lock L is operated by the cam groove A²; this puts the firing mechanism, either electric or percussion, to safety by withdrawing the firing needle, extracts the fired tube and leaves the primer chamber open for a fresh primer. All these operations are performed in the reverse order on closing.

With both these types of mechanism the de Bange system of obturation, with the pad only slightly coned, is used.

With smaller guns the mechanism is simpler, as less power is

The breech mechanism for Q.F. guns firing metallic cartridge cases is worked on similar principles, but is somewhat simpler than that for the de Bange obturation, due principally to the fact of the firing primer being already contained in the cartridge case when this is introduced into the gun.

In the English service the later patterns of breech mechanism for medium and heavy B.L. guns have a Welin screw, with a " steep

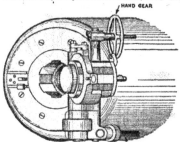

FIG. 37.—Interrupted Breech Screw—Cylindrical.

cone " de Bange obturator, supported on a carrier arm. This arrangement allows the mechanism (fig. 44) to swing clear of the breech opening immediately the threads of the breech screw are disengaged from those in the breech in a similar manner to the Q.F. guns fitted with a cone screw. The mechanism is actuated by the handwheel L which rotates the hinge pin; this in turn, through gearing, moves a crank arm D connected, by a link B, to the pin on the breech screw. By continuously moving the handwheel the link B is drawn towards the hinge pin until the breech screw threads are disengaged; the catch C then drops into a pocket on the breech screw and fixes it to the carrier arm. The whole of the mechanism then rotates around the hinge pin and leaves the breech open ready for loading. As the breech screw threads are being disengaged the electric or percussion lock W is operated by a cam groove in a similar manner to that already described. In the latest modification of this mechanism a roller at the end of the crank arm D works a long lever connected to the breech screw by two pins. This forms what is termed a " pure-couple " mechanism and it is claimed that greater ease of working is ensured by its use. While the loading is going on a new firing tube is placed in the vent, so that on closing the gun, by turning the handwheel in the opposite direction, the gun is ready for firing. For 9·2-in. guns and those of smaller calibre the handwheel is replaced by a hand lever pivoted on the carrier (fig. 45). By giving this lever a single motion from left to right the mechanism is opened.

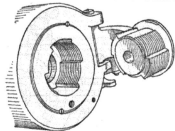

For 6-in. and 4-in. guns a shot support is attached to the breech face which is operated by the breech mechanism so that when the breech is open the shot support is in position for loading, and it falls out of the way when the breech is being closed.

In the larger types of all breech mechanisms ball bearings are employed in various parts, such as the hinge pin bearings, &c., to reduce friction and in most of the modern heavy guns on board ship the breech mechanism is arranged to be worked by a hydraulic cylinder placed on the breech face, or by a small hydraulic engine or electric motor placed in some convenient position on the mounting. The hand gear, however, is always retained for emergency and a clutch is provided so that it can be put into action at a moment's notice.

The Welin screw is largely used in the United States, but in heavy guns the ordinary cone (not " steep cone ") de Bange obturator is employed. The screw is mounted either in a carrier ring or on a carrier tray. In France the ordinary type of interrupted screw is adopted and this rests in a carrier tray. The operations of opening and closing are very similar to those already described.

All the recent patterns of mechanism have an extractor fitted to extract the empty cartridge case with Q.F. guns or the fired tube with B.L. guns. In Q.F. field guns it generally takes the form of a lever working on an axis pin. The longer arm of the lever is formed into a jaw which rests on the inner face of the breech opening beneath the rim of the cartridge case, and the short arm is so arranged that when the breech is opened the carrier, in swinging mechanisms, or the breech block itself, in sliding systems, suddenly comes in contact with it; the long arm is thus jerked backwards and extracts the case. In B.L. mechanisms the tube extractor is

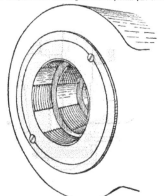

FIG. 38.—Welin Breech Screw.

arranged on the same principle but in this case usually forms part of the box slide, i.e. that portion of the mechanism attached by interrupted collars to the rear end of the vent axial, in which the firing lock slides as it is actuated by the opening or closing of the breech mechanism. When the breech is being opened the firing pin of the lock is drawn back to safety and the lock is moved aside from over the tube; a tripper then actuates the extractor and ejects the fired tube. The extractor and tripper are so contrived that when a new tube is pushed home the extractor is also pushed back into the closed position, or, if the tube is somewhat stiff to insert, the action of closing the mechanism moves the lock over the primer and forces it home.

The firing lock used in B.L. guns is an important part of the

FIG. 39.—Elswick Coned Screw.

mechanism. They are all designed on the same principle, with a view to safety and rapidity, and may be regarded as a miniature sliding breech mechanism. In the older types the lock or its substitute was manipulated by hand, and with electric firing the wires from the tubes were joined up to the loose ends of the firing circuit;

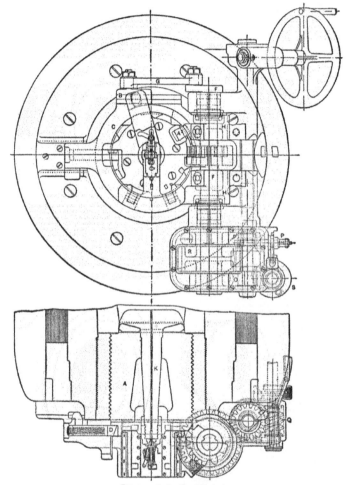

FIG. 41.—12-in. Gun, Breech Mechanism.

safety depended therefore on everything being in order and all operations correctly performed. The gun could, however, be fired before the breech was properly secured and a serious accident caused; to prevent this all the movements of modern locks are arranged to be automatic, and wireless electric tubes are used so that immediately the breech mechanism commences to open, the lock itself is moved in the box slide so as to uncover the vent opening. During the first part of this movement a foot on the striker rides up an incline I (fig. 45) on the box slide and thus pushes back the striker from contact with the tube. The extractor described above is actuated at the same time. Most locks

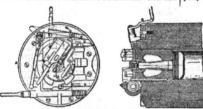

FIG. 40.—Breech Mechanisms, Heavy Guns.

consist of a steel frame with a socket for containing the striker and main spring. They are contrived so as to be capable of firing both electric and percussion tubes, but others are arranged for firing only electric, separate locks being employed for use with percussion tubes. The construction of both is very similar, but with the percussion lock, or the combined lock, a trigger is provided

FIG. 42.—Breech Mechanism, 6-in. B.L. Mark IV.

which drops into a notch in the striker when this is pulled back by the lugs E E (fig. 43) on the outer attachment of the striker. On the trigger being pulled by a lanyard the striker is released and fires the tube.

For Q.F. guns with interrupted or coned breech screws the striker is contained in the breech screw, but, in order to provide for safety, a small lever cam or other contrivance is fitted which, when the mechanism commences to open, is operated by the hand lever and withdraws the striker from contact with the primer inserted in the cartridge case.

The striker consists of a steel needle, with the stem insulated by ebonite or some similar material, contained in an outer steel sheath. The sheath is formed with a foot or lug which is acted upon by the safety gear; a collar is also provided for taking the thrust of the main spring.

Another form of lock now much in favour, especially for field-gun mechanisms, is that known as a trip lock. It is mainly used for percussion firing but can also be combined for use with electric tubes. In this pattern the striker is withdrawn, cocked and released by the continuous pull of a hand lever attached to the mounting or by a lanyard attached to the lock. Should a miss-fire occur the striker may be actuated as often as necessary by releasing the hand lever or lanyard and again giving a continuous pull (fig. 46).

In all modern heavy guns, especially when firing to windward, there is a tendency, when the breech is opened
Back flash. rapidly after firing, for a sheet of flame to issue from the open breech. It was practically unknown with the old black powders, but is of frequent occurrence with all smokeless propellants. If the gun is loaded immediately after the breech is opened the fresh charge may be ignited and an accident caused. Several serious accidents have already been traced to this cause, notably one on the United States battleship " Missouri " on 13th April 1904, when 33 lives were lost. The flame is due to the large amount of highly heated carbonic oxide remaining in the gun from the explosion of the charge; this mixing with the oxygen of the air when the breech is opened burns readily as a sheet of flame in rear of the gun, and should wind be blowing down the gun the action is more intense. By looking into the gun from the muzzle, before the breech is opened, the gas can often be seen burning with a pale-blue flame as it slowly mixes with air and a

curious singing noise is heard at the same time. It is now usual to fit a special apparatus on the gun, so that directly the breech is partly opened a blast of compressed air is allowed to enter the rear end of the chamber and thus sweep the whole of the residual gas out at the muzzle.

The purpose of the obturator is to render the breech end of the gun gas-tight, and to prevent any escape of gas past the breech mechanism. In the first **Obturators.** Armstrong B.L. gun this object was attained by fitting to the breech block a copper ring coned on the exterior; the coned surface was forcibly pressed by screwing up the breech screw against a corresponding copper ring fitted at the breech opening of the gun chamber. It is only possible to use this method when the copper surfaces can be jammed together by a powerful screw.

Except the above, all obturators in use are arranged to act automatically, i.e. the pressure set up in the gun when it is fired expands the arrangement and seals the opening; immediately the projectile leaves the bore the pressure is relieved and the obturator, by its elasticity, regains its original shape, so that the breech mechanism can be opened or closed with ease. In the French naval service B.L. guns have been in use since 1864, and the system of obturation was arranged on the same expansion principle as the leather packing ring of the hydraulic press. A steel ring A (fig. 47) of cupped form was fastened by a screwed plug to a thick steel plate, carried on the face of the breech screw, so that it could rotate when the breech screw was rotated in opening or closing the gun. The outer lip of the cup fitted against a slightly coned seating formed in the breech end of the gun chamber. When the gun was fired, the gas pressure expanded the cup ring and forced it into close bearing against the seating in the gun and the thick steel plate on the breech screw, thus preventing any escape of gas. Very similar to this was the Elswick cup obturator (fig. 48) introduced by the Elswick Ordnance Company in 1881; its rear surface was flat and it was held by a central bolt against the front of the breech screw which was slightly rounded. The cup yielded to the gas pressure until it was supported by the breech screw; this action expanded the lip against a copper seating, let into the gun, which could be renewed when necessary. Many of both types are still in use and act perfectly efficiently if carefully treated. The use of modern smokeless powder renders them and similar devices, such as the Broadwell ring (fig. 49), &c., peculiarly liable to damage, as a slight abrasion of the lip of the cup or ring, or of its seating, allows gas to escape, and so accentuates the defect with each round fired. Unless, therefore, the fault be immediately remedied considerable damage may be caused to the gun. The Broadwell gas ring is still in use in the French naval service, where

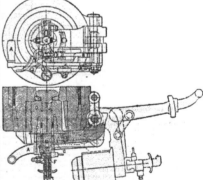

FIG. 43.—Breech Mechanism, Modern 6-in. Gun.

it is made of copper (fig. 50), and also of steel in a modified form (Piorkowski) in the German service (fig. 51); in the last-named service, owing to the defect already named, all the latest guns, both light and heavy, use metal cartridge cases. In the French navy, as in most 'other services, cartridge cases are used for the smaller and medium guns only.

One of the most efficient obturators not liable to damage is the plastic device introduced by Colonel de Bange of the French service and adopted by the French army and also by the British and other governments. It consists of a pad (fig. 52) made up of a strong annular-shaped canvas bag A, containing a mixture of asbestos fibre and mutton suet; the bag with its contents is placed in a properly formed die and subjected to hydraulic pressure by which it becomes hard and firm. The pad so made is then placed on the front of the breech screw B, and it is protected on its faces by disks C, C, of metallic tin or copper having steel wedge rings on the outer edges; the circumference of the complete pad and disks is

steel wedge ring into which the axial head fits. On firing the gun the head is forced into the wedge ring and expands it against the seating in the gun.

One other means of obturation has to be considered, viz. metallic cartridge cases. These are made of a kind of brass; aluminium cases have been experimented with, but have not proved satisfactory. The case (fig. 54) acts on the same principle as the cup obturation and is extremely efficient for the purpose; moreover, they have certain advantages conducive to rapid firing when used for small guns. The idea has developed from the use of such cartridges in small arms, and larger cartridges of the same type were introduced for 3-pounder and 6-pounder guns by Hotchkiss and Nordenfelt about the year 1880 for the purpose of rapid firing against torpedo boats. Then in 1886 the Elswick Company produced a 36-pounder (soon converted to a 45-pounder) of 4·7-in. calibre with the powder charge contained in metallic cases, and about 1888 a 6-in. 100-pounder gun using similar cartridges. A special advantage of the cartridge case is that it contains the firing primer by which the charge is ignited and consequently renders the firing gear of the gun more simple; on the other hand, should a miss-fire occur the gun must be opened to replace the primer. This is a proceeding liable to produce an accident, unless a long enough time is allowed to elapse before attempting to open the breech; guns having de Bange obturators and firing tubes inserted after the breech is closed are therefore safer in this respect.

Some means of extracting the case after firing must be fitted to the gun; this is simple enough with small guns, but with those of heavy natures the extractor becomes a somewhat ponderous piece of gear.

Metallic cases of a short pattern have been tried for large calibre guns; although their action is quite efficient, they are difficult to handle, and if a case must be used it is preferable to employ a fairly long one. It was for this reason that in England up to 1898 it was considered that for guns above 6-in. calibre the de Bange obturation was the most advantageous. Since then the de Bange obturator has been employed in guns of 4-in. calibre and above, the cartridge case being retained only for 3-in. and smaller guns. Krupp, however, uses cartridge cases with all guns even up to 12-in. calibre, but this is undoubtedly due to the difficulties, which have already been noticed, attending the use of smokeless powder with the ordinary forms of obturation applicable to the wedge breech system. In the most modern Krupp 12-in. guns the charge is formed in two pieces; the piece forming the front portion of the charge is contained in a consumable envelope, while the rear portion is contained in a brass cartridge case, which forms the obturator, about 48 in. long.

It will be seen that such large and heavy cases add to the difficulties which occur in handling or stowing the ammunition of large calibre guns, and although the use of cartridge cases with small guns adds to their rapidity of firing this is not the case with heavy guns. It seems, therefore, that the balance of advantages is certainly in favour of the de Bange system, for all guns except those of small calibre. With ordinary field guns cartridge cases are now considered obligatory owing to their convenience in loading.

While the ordinary types of plastic obturators last for an indefinite time a cartridge case can be used for a limited number of rounds only, depending on the calibre of the gun; with field guns from ten to twenty rounds or even more may be fired from one case if care is taken to reform it after each round; with large guns they will not, of course, fire so many. Cartridge cases are an expensive addition to the ammunition, so that there should be no doubt about the advantages they offer before they are definitely adopted for heavy guns.

The rapidity with which modern guns can be fired and the enormous energy they develop is especially striking when one

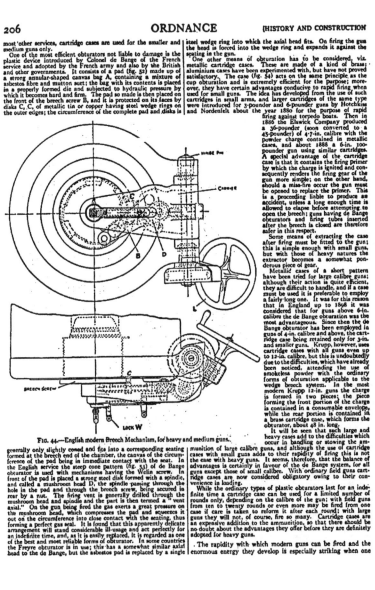

FIG. 44.—English modern Breech Mechanism, for heavy and medium guns.

generally only slightly coned and fits into a corresponding seating formed at the breech end of the chamber, the canvas of the circumference of the pad being in immediate contact with the seat. In the English service the steep cone pattern (fig. 53) of de Bange obturator is used with mechanisms having the Welin screw. In front of the pad is placed a strong steel disk formed with a spindle, and called a mushroom head D, the spindle passing through the hole in the pad and through the breech screw, being secured in rear by a nut. The firing vent is generally drilled through the mushroom head and spindle and the part is then termed a "vent axial." On the gun being fired the gas exerts a great pressure on the mushroom head, which compresses the pad and squeezes it out on the circumference into close contact with the seating, thus forming a perfect gas seal. It is found that this apparently delicate arrangement will stand considerable ill-usage and act perfectly for an indefinite time, and, as it is easily replaced, it is regarded as one of the best and most reliable forms of obturator. In some countries the Freyre obturator is in use; this has a somewhat similar axial head to the de Bange, but the asbestos pad is replaced by a single

considers the same facts in connexion with the early guns. Favé states in his *Histoire et tactique des trois armes* (p. 23) that during the invasion of Italy in 1494 by Charles VIII. the guns were so unwieldy and the firing so slow that the damage caused by one shot could be repaired before the next could be fired. The range, too, about 100 yds. for battering purposes, now seems absurdly short; even at Waterloo 1200 yds. was all that separated the antagonists at the commencement of the battle, but they approached to within 200 or 300 yds. without suffering serious loss from either musketry or gun fire. Nelson fought his ships side by side with the enemy's; and fifty years after Nelson's day a range of 1000 yds. at sea was looked upon as an extreme distance at which to engage an enemy. Contrast this with the range of 12,000 yds. at which the opposing Russian and Japanese fleets more than once commenced a naval battle in 1904, while the critical part of the action took place at a distance of 7000 yds.

Range and power.

These long ranges naturally intensified the requirements of the British and other navies, and, so that they shall not be outclassed and beaten by an enemy's long-range fire, guns of continually increasing power were demanded. In 1900 a 12-in. gun of 40 calibres was considered all that was necessary. After the Russo-Japanese War the demand rose first for a 45-calibre gun and then for a 50-calibre gun, and muzzle velocities from about 2400 f.s. to about 3000 f.s. In 1910 greater shell power was demanded, to meet which new type guns of 13·5-in. and 14-in. calibre were being made.

In the days of M.L. heavy guns one of the most difficult problems was that of loading. The weight of the shell and powder was such that some mechanical power had to be employed for moving and ramming them home, and as hydraulic gear had by that date been introduced it was generally used for all loading operations. To load, the guns had to be run back until their muzzles were within the turret, or, in the case of the 16-in. 80-ton guns of H.M.S. "Inflexible," until they were just outside the turret. The guns were then depressed to a fixed angle so as to bring the loading gear, which was protected below the gun deck, in line with the bore; the charge was first rammed home and then the projectile. With this arrangement, and in order to keep the turret of manageable dimensions, the guns had to be made short. Thus the 12·5-in. 38-ton M.L. gun had a length of bore of but 16 calibres, and the largest English service gun of 16-in. diameter had a bore of 18 calibres in length; while the largest of the type weighing 100 tons, built by Sir W. G. Armstrong & Co., for the Italian navy, had a bore of 17·72 in. and a length of 20 calibres. The rate of fire was fairly rapid— two rounds could be fired from one turret with the 12·5-in. guns in about three minutes, while it took about four minutes to fire the same number from the 80-ton and 100-ton gun turrets.

The possibility of double loading M.L. guns was responsible for the bursting on the 2nd January 1879 of a 38-ton gun in a turret on H.M.S. "Thunderer"; and it was partly due to this

accident that B.L. guns were subsequently more favourably regarded in England, as it was argued that the double loading of a B.L. gun was an impossibility.

With the B.L. system guns gradually grew to be about 30 calibres in length of bore, and they were not made longer because this was considered a disadvantage, not to be compensated for by the small additional velocity which the old black and brown prismatic powders were capable of imparting with guns of greater length. Increase in the striking energy of the projectile was consequently sought by increasing the weight of the projectile, and, to carry this out with advantage, a gun of larger calibre had to be adopted. Thus the 12-in. B.L. gun of about 25 calibres in length gave place to the 13·5-in. gun of 30 calibres and weighing 67 tons, and to the 16 25-in. also of 30 calibres and weighing 111 tons. The 10,000- or 12,000-ton battleships

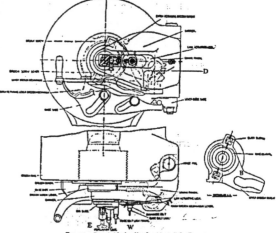

FIG. 45.—Breech Mechanism for 6-inch B.L. Gun

carrying these enormous pieces were, judged by our present-day standard, far too small to carry such a heavy armament with their ponderous armoured machinery, which restricted the coal supply and rendered other advantages impossible; even the 24,000-ton battleships are none too large to carry the number of heavy guns now required to form the main armament.

The weight and size of the old brown prismatic charges had also reached huge dimensions; thus, while with heavy M.L. guns the weight of the full charge was about one-fourth that of the projectile, it had with heavy B.L. guns become one-half of the weight of the shell or even a greater proportion. The introduction of smokeless powder about 1890, having more than three times the amount of energy for the same weight of the older powders, allowed longer guns to be used, which fired a much smaller weight of charge but gave higher velocities; the muzzle or striking energy demanded for piercing hard-faced armour could consequently be obtained from guns of more moderate calibre. The 13·5-in. and 16·25-in. guns were therefore gradually discarded and new ships were armed with 12-in. guns of greater power. As the ballistic requirements are increased the weight of the charge becomes proportionately greater; thus for the present high velocity guns it has reached a ratio of about 0·4 of the weight of the projectile.

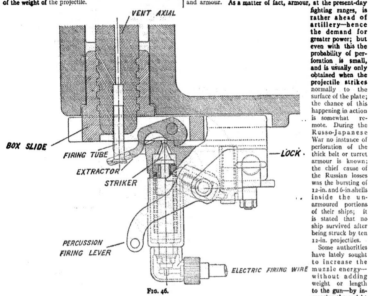

VENT AXIAL

BOX SLIDE

FIRING TUBE

EXTRACTOR

STRIKER

LOCK

PERCUSSION FIRING LEVER

ELECTRIC FIRING WIRE

FIG. 46.

the case at the present time as regards both projectiles and armour. As a matter of fact, armour, at the present-day fighting ranges, is rather ahead of artillery—hence the demand for greater power; but even with this the probability of perforation is small, and is usually only obtained when the projectile strikes normally to the surface of the plate; the chance of this happening in action is somewhat remote. During the Russo-Japanese War no instance of perforation of the thick belt or turret armour is known; the chief cause of the Russian losses was the bursting of 12-in. and 6-in. shells inside the unarmoured portions of their ships; it is stated that no ship survived after being struck by ten 12-in. projectiles.

Some authorities have lately sought to increase the muzzle energy—without adding weight or length to the gun—by increasing the weight of the projectile. This can be done to a limited extent with beneficial results, but it is impossible to carry the idea very far, as the projectile becomes very long and difficulties may be encountered with the rifling; or, if these are avoided, the thickness of the walls of the shell is increased so much that

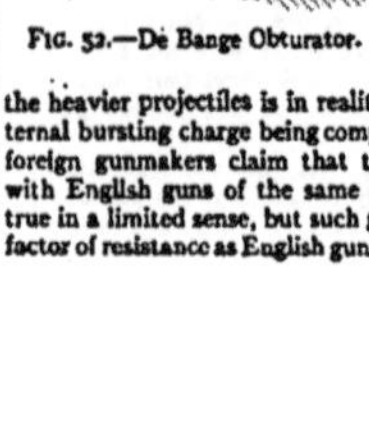

The progress of artillery and the improvements made in armour have been reciprocal; as the protective value of iron and

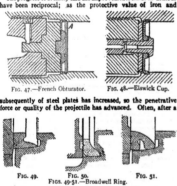

FIG. 47.—French Obturator.   FIG. 48.—Elswick Cup.

subsequently of steel plates has increased, so the penetrative force or quality of the projectile has advanced. Often, after a

FIG. 49.   FIG. 50.   FIG. 51.
FIGS. 49-51.—Broadwell Ring.

period of apparent inactivity, fresh ideas or new metallurgical processes have enabled further progress to be made; this is

FIG. 52.—De Bange Obturator. 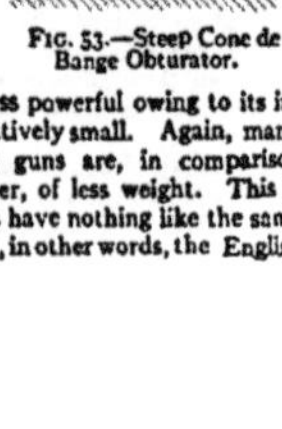   FIG. 53.—Steep Cone de Bange Obturator.

the heavier projectiles is in reality less powerful owing to its internal bursting charge being comparatively small. Again, many foreign gunmakers claim that their guns are, in comparison with English guns of the same power, of less weight. This is true in a limited sense, but such guns have nothing like the same factor of resistance as English guns, or, in other words, the English guns are much stronger. This is an obvious advantage, but an equally solid one is the fact that owing to the greater weight of the home-made weapon the recoil energy is less and consequently

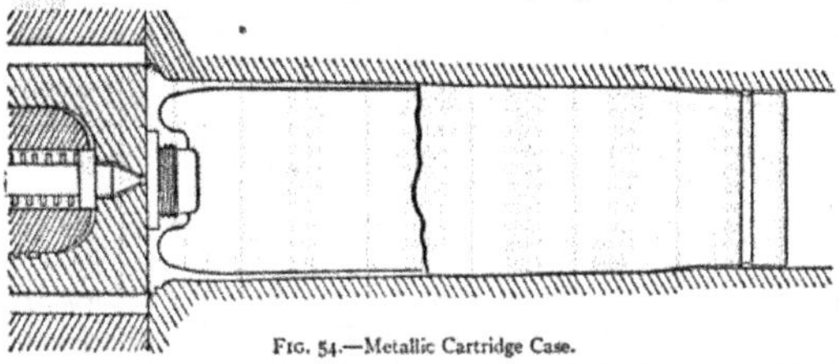

Fig. 54.—Metallic Cartridge Case.

the mounting can be made of a lighter pattern. Besides, the weight of the gun is so disposed as to bring its centre of gravity as near the breech end as possible; by this means the radius of the gun house is reduced to the smallest dimension and, in consequence, there is a great saving of weight of armour. The extra weight of the gun is therefore more than compensated for.

Until late into the 16th century the calibres of the guns were not regulated with a view to the interchangeability of shot. In the following century ordnance was divided into classes, but even then, owing no doubt to manufacturing difficulties, there was no fixed size for the bore. The Tables II.-VII. give some idea of the size and weight of these pieces.

Table II. is taken from Cleveland's Notes, but corrected from "An Old Table of Ordnance" (Proc. R.A.I., vol. xxviii. p. 365); the last column gives the range in scores of paces at point-blank, a term used in those days to denote the first part of the trajectory which was supposed to be a straight line. Later the point-blank range was that distance from the gun on its carriage to the first graze of the shot on the horizontal plane when the axis of the gun was placed horizontal; this depended on the height of the gun above the ground plane, but it was the only method of determining the relative power of these early guns.

In power, smooth-bore guns in Europe did not differ very much from each other, and it may be taken for granted that the progress made since has been much the same in all.

D'Antoni, in his Treatise of Fire Arms (translated by Captain Thomson, R.A.), gives particulars of Italian guns of about 1746, which are shown in Table III..

It will be seen that the velocities given in Table III. are not inferior to those obtained from guns actually in use in 1860 (see Table IV.). They were considerably higher than those for elongated rifled projectiles (Table V.) for many years after their introduction; the last-named, however, during flight only lost their velocity slowly, while the spherical shot lost their velocity so rapidly that at 2000 yds. range only about one-third of the initial velocity was retained.

TABLE II.—Names and Weights of English Cannon, 1574.

Names.	Weight.	Diameter of Bore.	Diameter of Shot.	Weight of Shot.	Weight of Charge, Serpentine.	Scores of Paces at point-blank.
	lb	in.	in.	lb	lb	
Robinet	200	1¼	1	1	1	...
Falconet	800	2	1½	2	1½	14
Falcon	800	2¾	2½	2½	2¾	16
Minion	1100	3¼	3	4½	4½	17
Sacre	1500	3½	3½	5	5	18
Demi-Culverin	2500	4¼	4	9	9	20
Culverin	4000	5	5	18	18	25
Demi-Cannon	6000	6½	6½	30	28	28
Cannon	7000	7¼	7¼	60	40	20
Eliza-Cannon	8000	8	7¾	63	42	20
Basiliske	9000	8¾	8¾	60	60	21

TABLE III.

Gun.	Weight of Charge.	Weight of Shot.	Muzzle Velocity.
	lb.	lb.	f.s.
27-pr. 66 cwt.	13·125	27	1517
13½-pr. 37·5 cwt.	6·562	13·5	1618
6¼ pr. 20 cwt.	4·922	6·75	1696
3¼ pr. 11 cwt.	2·469	3·375	1720

TABLE IV.—British Smooth Bore Guns, 1860.

Official Designation of Gun.	Calibre.	Weight of Gun.	Weight of Charge.	Weight of Projectile.	Muzzle Velocity.	Muzzle Energy.
	In.	Tons.	lb.	lb.	Ft. Secs.	Ft. Tons.
10 in. 87 cwt.	10	4·35	12	88·31	1292	1022
68 pr. 95 "	8·12	4·75	16	66·25	1579	1145
8 in. 65 "	8·05	3·22	10	49·875	1464	742
32 pr. 58 "	6·375	2·9	10	31·375	1690	621
24 " 50 "	5·823	2·5	8	23·5	1720	482
18 " 38 "	5·292	1·9	6	17·69	1690	350
12 " 18 "	4·623	0·9	4	12·66	1769	275
9 " 13 "	4·20	0·65	2·5	9·36	1614	169
6 " 6 "	3·668	0·3	1·5	6·23	1484	95

TABLE V.—British B.L. Ordnance, 1860. Armstrong System.

Official Designation of Gun.	Calibre.	Weight of Gun.	Weight of Charge.	Weight of Projectile.	Muzzle Velocity.	Muzzle Energy.
	In.	Tons.	lb.	lb.	Ft. Secs.	Ft. Tons.
100 pr.	7	{4·1 / 3·6} *	12	103·75	1166	978
40 "	4·75	{1·75 / 1·6} *	5	41·5	{1164 / 1134}	{399 / 370}
20 "	3·75	{0·8 / 0·65} *	2·5	21·22	{1114 / 997}	{162 / 146}
12 "	3·0	0·425	1·5	11·56	1184	112
9 "	3·0	0·3	1·125	9·0	1141	81
6 "	2·5	0·175	0·75	6·0	946	37

At a later date the velocities of these guns were altered.   * Two patterns were in existence.

TABLE VI.—*British Rifled Ordnance, 1890.*

Official Designation of Gun.	Calibre.	Weight of Gun.	Weight of Charge.	Weight of Projectile.	Muzzle Velocity.	Muzzle Energy.	Perforation of Wrought Iron.	Rate of Firing Rounds.	Propellant.
	In.	Tons.	lb.	lb.	Ft. Secs.	Ft. Tons.	In.	Per Minute.	
M.L. Guns—									
17.72 in.	17.72	100	450	2000	1548	33,233	24.5		Prism Black
16 „	16	80	450	1700	1540	29,806	25.0		Prism Brown
12.5 „	12.5	38	210	818	1575	14,140	19.2		Prism Black
12 „	12	35	140	714	1390	9,563	15.2		Pr.
11 „	11	25	85	548	1360	6,510	13.5		Pebble
10 „	10	18	70	410	1379	5,406	12.5		„
9 „	9	12	50	256	1440	3,695	11.0		„
8 „	8	9	35	179	1390	2,391	9.2		„
7 „	7	7	30	114.6	1525	1,854	9.2	1	„
64-pr.¹	6.3	3.2	10	66.9	1390	897	6.4	1	R.L.G.⁴
B.L. Guns—									
16.25 in.	16.25	110.5	960	1800	2087	54,390	38		S.B.C.
13.5 „	13.5	67	630	1250	2016	35,230	33		„
12 „	12	45	295	714	1914	18,137	24.5	1	Prism Brown
10 „	10	29	252	500	2100	15,290	25.8	1	„
9.2 „	9.2	22	166	380	2036	10,915	22.3	1½	„
8 „	8	14	118	210	2200	7,046	20.0	2	„
6 „	6	5	48	100	1960	2,435	13.5	3	E.X.E.
5 „	5	2	16	50	1800	1,113	9.2	3	S.P.
4 „	4	1.3	12	25	1900	626	7.8	3	„
Q.F. Guns—									
4.7 in.	4.72	2.1	12	45	1786	995	8.8	8	Q.F.
6-pr.	2.24	0.4		6	1837	141.2	5.3	20	„
3 „	1.85	0.25	1.5	3.3	1873	80.2	4.0	20	„

¹ And many smaller guns.

TABLE VII.—*British B.L. Ordnance, 1900.*

Official Designation of Gun.	Calibre.	Weight of Gun.	Weight of Charge.	Weight of Projectile.	Muzzle Velocity.	Muzzle Energy.	Perforation of Wrought Iron.	Rate of Firing Rounds.	Propellant.
	In.	Tons.	lb.	lb.	Ft. Secs.	Ft. Tons.	In.	Per Minute.	
16.25 in.	16.25	110.5	960	1800	2087	54,390	38		S.B.C. Cordite
13.5 in.	13.5	67	187	1250	2016	35,230	33		„
12 in. Mark VIII.	12	46	167.5	850	2367	33,000	36.9	1	„
10 in.	10	29	76	500	2040	14,391	24.8	1½	„
9.2 in. Mark X.	9.2	28	103	380	2601	17,826	32.3	2½	„
8 in.	8	14	32.625	210	2200	7,046	20.0	.	„
6 in. Mark VII.	6	7	20	100	2493	4,335	19.25	7	„
5 in.	5	2	4.45	50	1750	1,062	8.8	3	„
4 in.	4	1.3	3.06	25	1900	626	7.8	3	„
Q.F. Guns—									
6 in.	6	7	13.25	100	2200	3,356	16.0	6	„
4.7 „	4.72	2.1	5.43	45	2188	1,494	12.0	8	„
4 „	4	1.3	3.75	25	2456	1,046	11.6	9	„
12-pr.	3	0.6	1.94	12.5	2210	433	8.0	15	„
6 „	2.24	0.4	0.483	6	1818	137	4.8	20	„
3 „	1.81	0.25	0.396	3.3	1873	80.2	4.0	20	„

As regards rapidity of aimed fire—and no shooting is worth consideration which is not aimed—much depends on the quickness with which the gun can be opened, loaded and closed again ready for firing, but quite as much depends on the ease and convenience of moving to any required direction the gun with its mounting; also on the system of recoil adopted and the method of sighting. Two identically similar guns may consequently give entirely different rates of firing, unless mounted and sighted on the same system—without taking into consideration the personal element or the gun detachment or crew. The rates of firing shown in many tables are therefore not always a trustworthy criterion of the guns' capabilities. The advantage of the Q.F. system (i.e. a gun firing charges contained in metallic cases), when suitably mounted, over the old B.L. guns was exhibited in a very marked manner in 1887, when the first 4.7-in. Q.F. gun fired ten rounds in 47.5 seconds and subsequently fifteen rounds in one minute. The 5-in. B.L. gun when fired as rapidly as possible only fired ten rounds in 6 minutes 16 seconds; so that the Q.F. gun fired its tenth round before the 5-in. B.L. gun fired its second shot. Recent improvements made in the mechanism of the B.L. gun enable it to compete with the Q.F. system.

The tabulated armour-piercing value of a gun is based on the

TABLE VIII.—*British Ordnance, 1910.*

Official Designation of Gun.	Calibre.	Weight of Gun.	Weight of Charge.	Weight of Projectile.	Muzzle Velocity.	Muzzle Energy.	Perforation of Wrought Iron.	Rate of Firing Rounds.	Propellant.
	In.	Tons.	lb.	lb.	Ft. Secs.	Ft. Tons.	In.	Per Minute.	
12 in. Mark XI.	12	66	..	850	2959	51,580	51.5	2	M.D.Cordite
12 in. Mark X.	12	58	300	850	2900	47,697	51.0	2	„
10 in.	10	31	148	500	2800	27,205	39.5	2	„
9.2 Mark X.	9.2	28	103	380	2640	18,400	33.3	3	„
7.5 in.	7.5	16	69.5	200	2800	10,883	29.0	4	„
6 in. Mark VII.	6	7.4	20	100	2493	4,308	19.6	6	„
4 in.	4	1.3	3.75	25	2456	1,046	11.6	9	„

Q.F. guns as in 1900.

results given by various formulas. These often vary considerably, so in order that a direct comparison in the tables may be made, this value is obtained for wrought iron plate only, using Tresidder's formula, which is one of the most trustworthy. The equivalent thickness of Krupp cemented steel armour can be obtained immediately by dividing the tabulated value for wrought iron by a "factor of effect" of 2·3 to 2·4 for uncapped armour piercing

shot, and about 2·0 for capped armour piercing shell. These factors are dependent on the nature of the projectile and **must** therefore be taken as approximate.

Tables VIII.-XXII. are obtained from trustworthy sources, but as great secrecy is now observed in many countries there may be a few inaccuracies; in some cases the whole of the data are not available.

TABLE IX.—*French Naval Ordnance*, 1910.

Official Designation of Gun.	Calibre.	Weight of Gun.	Weight of Charge.	Weight of Projectile.	Muzzle Velocity.	Muzzle Energy.	Perforation of Wrought Iron.	Rate of firing Rounds.	Propellant.
	In.	Tons.	lb.	lb.	Ft.-Secs.	Ft.-Tons.	In.	Per Minute.	
305 mm.	12·01	..	..	750	2870	42,890	46·0	1·5	Smokeless
274 ,,	10·8	34·5	..	562	2650	27,186	38·8	1·5	B. Powder
240 ,,	9·45	23·6	..	375	2870	21,445	37·0	2	,,
194 ,,	7·64	12·5	..	190	2870	10,890	29·0	2	,,
164·7 ,,	6·46	8·5	..	115	3000	7,185	26·3	4	,,
Q.F. Guns—									
164·7 mm.	6·46	8·1	..	115	2870	6,568	24·5	5	,,
140 ,,	5·44	4·13	..	66	2625	3,153	20·0	6	,,
100 ,,	3·94	..	..	31	2395	1,232	12·4	6	,,
75 ,,	2·9	..	..	14	3116	943	14·5	12	,,
65 ,,	2·57	..	..	8·8	2871	503	10·8	12	,,
47 ,,	1·85	..	..	3·3	2871	188	7·9	15	,,

TABLE X.—*German Naval Ordnance.*

Official Designation of Gun.	Calibre.	Weight of Gun.	Weight of Charge.	Weight of Projectile.	Muzzle Velocity.	Muzzle Energy.	Perforation of Wrought Iron.	Rate of firing Rounds.	Propellant.
	In.	Tons.	lb.	lb.	Ft.-Secs.	Ft.-Tons.	In.	Per Minute.	Nitro-Glycerine powder
Q.F. Guns—									
28 cm.	11·02	33·3	..	529	2854	29,878	40·2	1	
24 ,,	9·45	25·4	88·2	309	2740	16,086	31·0	1½	,,
21 ,,	8·2	15·75	49·5	242	2526	10,707	26·1	3	,,
17 ,,	6·7	7·8	41·1	132	2887	7,629	26·1	5	,,
15 ,,	5·9	4·73	19·83	88	2461	3,696	18·0	7	,,
10·5 ,,	4·13	1·645	7·27	38·35	2297	1,403	12·75	8	,,
8·8 ,,	3·42	1·34	4·85	23·6	2789	1,273	14·7	10	,,
5 ,,	1·97	0·236	0·66	3·86	2165	125	5·4	11	,,

Note.—It is stated that the new German 28 cm. 50 calibre naval gun weighing 43·9 tons fires, with a charge of 291 lb, a projectile of 760 lb with a velocity of 2871 f.s.

TABLE XI.—*Italian Naval Ordnance*, 1910.

Official Designation of Gun.	Calibre.	Weight of Gun.	Weight of Charge.	Weight of Projectile.	Muzzle Velocity.	Muzzle Energy.	Perforation of Wrought Iron.	Rate of firing Rounds.	Propellant.
	In.	Tons.	lb.	lb.	Ft.-Secs.	Ft.-Tons.	In.	Per Minute.	Strip Ballistite
343 mm.	13·5	67·9	187·2	1215	2067	36,050	34·0	..	
305 ,,	12	51	231·5	850	2580	59,220	42·0	..	,,
254 ,,	10	30	85	450	2461	19,000	31·0	..	,,
203 ,,	8	19	57	250	2526	11,060	27·0	..	,,
152 ,,	6	5·7	17·6	100	2296	3,655	17·0	..	,,
120 ,,	4·72	2·1	5·5	45	2116	1,397	11·4	..	,,
76 ,,	3·0	0·6	2·17	12·5	2296	457	8·5	..	,,
57 ,,	2·24	0·4	1·05	6	2198	201	6·3	..	,,
47 ,,	1·81	0·25	0·67	3·3	2330	124	5·8	..	,,

TABLE XII.—*Russian Naval Ordnance*, 1910.

Official Designation of Gun.	Calibre.	Weight of Gun.	Weight of Charge.	Weight of Projectile.	Muzzle Velocity.	Muzzle Energy.	Perforation of Wrought Iron.	Rate of firing Rounds.	Propellant.
	In.	Tons.	lb.	lb.	Ft.-Secs.	Ft.-Tons.	In.	Per Minute.	Nitro-Cellulose
12 in.	12	59	..	720	2600	33,730	39·0	..	
10 ,,	10	32	..	488	2550	22,003	34·0	..	,,
8 ,,	8	14	87	188	2950	11,345	29·5	..	,,
6 ,,	6	6·28	50·6	91·5	2118	2,849	14·4	..	,,
9 pr.	4·2	0·87	4·88	27·75	1226	289	4·2	..	,,
4 ,,	3·43	0·45	3·1	15·0	1451	219	4·6	..	,,
Q.F. Guns—									
6 in.	6	5·75	28	91·5	2502	3,970	18·5	..	,,
4·7 ,,	4·72	2·95	15·4	45·0	2502	1,953	14·6	..	,,
2·9 ,,	..	0·87	3·53	10·8	2700	546	10·3	..	,,
1·81 ,,	1·81	0·323	..	3·3	2003	91·8	4·6	..	,,

TABLE XIII.—*Austrian Naval Ordnance, 1910.*

Official Designation of Gun.	Calibre.	Weight of Gun.	Weight of Charge.	Weight of Projectile.	Muzzle Velocity.	Muzzle Energy.	Perforation of Wrought Iron.	Rate of firing Rounds.	Propellant.
	In.	Tons.	lb.	lb.	Ft.-Secs.	Ft.-Tons.	In.	Per Minute.	
30·5 cm.	12·01	..	..	990	2625	47,300	46·0	..	
24 "	9·45	21·5	130·6	474	2595	22,121	34·5	..	
19 "	7·5	11·6	56	198	2700	10,025	27·3	3	
15 "	5·91	5·2	28·8	112·5	2608	5,308	22·0	10	
12 "	4·72	2·0	9·7	52·4	2264	3,554	13·7	10	
7 "	2·75	..	3·3	15·2	2378	..	10·4	..	
4·7 "	1·85	0·253	0·79	3·3	2329	..	5·8	..	
3·7 "	1·46	..	..	1·0	2346	..	..	..	

TABLE XIV.—*Austrian Coast Artillery, 1910.*

Official Designation of Gun.	Calibre.	Weight of Gun.	Weight of Charge.	Weight of Projectile.	Muzzle Velocity.	Muzzle Energy.	Perforation of Wrought Iron.	Rate of firing Rounds.	Propellant.
	In.	Tons.	lb.	lb.	Ft.-Secs.	Ft.-Tons.	In.	Per Minute.	
30·5 cm.	12·01	..	198·4	981	2297	35,860	37·8	..	Tubular
28 "	11·024	38	220	760	1722	15,615	22·5	..	Prism
15 "	5·906	4·28	18·28	100	2297	3,059	17·2	4	

TABLE XV.—*United States Naval Guns, 1910.*

Official Designation of Gun.	Calibre.	Weight of Gun.	Weight of Charge.	Weight of Projectile.	Muzzle Velocity.	Muzzle Energy.	Perforation of Wrought Iron.	Rate of firing Rounds.	Propellant.
	In.	Tons.	lb.	lb.	Ft.-Secs.	Ft.-Tons.	In.	Per Minute.	Nitro-Cellulose
13 · in.	13	61·4	180	1130	2000	31,333	31·8	..	
12 "	12	56·1	340	870	2950	52,483	52·	..	"
10 "	10	34·6	207·5	510	2700	25,772	38	..	"
8 "	8	18·7	98·5	260	2750	13,630	31·1	..	"
7 "	7	12·7	58	165	2700	8,340	25·9	..	"
6 "	6	8·6	37	105	2800	8,710	23·5	..	"
5 "	5	..	23·8	50	3150	3,439	21·1	..	"
4·7 "	4·72	..	..	45	2600	2,110	15·5	..	"
4 "	4	2·9	12·3	33	2800	1,794	16·1	..	"
3 "	3	1·0	3·85	13	2700	657	11·0	..	"
6 pr.	2·24	..	..	6	2240	209	6·6	..	"
3 "	1·81	..	..	3	2200	100	5·4	..	"

TABLE XVI.—*United States Coast Defence Guns.*

Official Designation of Gun.	Calibre.	Weight of Gun.	Weight of Charge.	Weight of Projectile.	Muzzle Velocity.	Muzzle Energy.	Perforation of Wrought Iron	Rate of firing Rounds.	Propellant.
	In.	Tons.	lb.	lb.	Ft.-Secs.	Ft.-Tons.	In.	Per Minute.	Nitro-Cellulose
16 in.	16	127	612	2400	2150	77,000	46·4	..	
14 "	14	59	280	1660	2150	53,220	41·0	..	"
12 "	12	59	310	1046	2250	36,730	37·6	..	"
10 "	10	34·3	205	604	2350	21,200	31·5	..	"
8 "	8	14·4	80	316	2200	10,600	24·5	..	"
6 "	6	9·45	35	106	2600	4,970	21·1	..	"
5 "	5	4·96	20	58	2600	2,718	17·2	..	"
4·72 "	4·72	2·75	10·5	45	2600	2,110	15·5	..	"
4 "	4	1·61	7·5	33	2300	1,210	12·0	..	"
3 "	3	1·2	6·0	15	2600	704	11·25	..	"
2·24 "	2·24	0·38	1·35	6	2400	240	7·3	..	"
12 " mortar	12	13	54 / 67	1046 / 824	1150 / 1325	9,390 / 10,025	..	..	"

TABLE XVII.—*Japanese Naval Ordnance, 1910.*

Official Designation of Gun.	Calibre.	Weight of Gun.	Weight of Charge.	Weight of Projectile.	Muzzle Velocity.	Muzzle Energy.	Perforation of Wrought Iron.	Rate of firing Rounds.	Propellant.
	In.	Tons.	lb.	lb.	Ft.-Secs.	Ft.-Tons.	In.	Per Minute.	M.D. Cordite
12·5	66	..	990	2308	36,500	37·3	0·2		
12	59	305	850	2800	46,200	47·2	2·0	"	
10	34	166·5	500	2850	28,170	40·9	3·0	"	
8	17·5	44	250	2750	13,015	30·3	2·0	"	
6	7	35	100	2800	5,436	29·3	7·0	"	
4·72	2·1	5·5	45	2188	1,494	12·0	8	"	
3	0·6	1·94	13·5	2210	423	8·0	12	"	
2·24	0·9	..	10·8	2716	551	10·2	..	"	
1·35	0·4	0·5	6·0	1818	138	4·8	20	"	
	0·25	3·3	1873	80	4·25	20	"		

Note.—The Japanese fleet has mainly been armed by Armstrong's Works, but the "Katori" was armed by Vickers', and those ships taken from the Russians during the late war are armed with guns from Krupp or Obuchoff. Guns of all sizes are now, however, being constructed in Japan, so that the country is no longer dependent on foreign factories.

TABLE XVIII.—*Sir W. G. Armstrong, Whitworth & Co.'s Guns. Abridged Table.*

Official Designation of Gun.	Calibre.	Weight of Gun.	Weight of Charge.	Weight of Projectile.	Muzzle Velocity.	Muzzle Energy.	Perforation of Wrought Iron.	Rate of firing Rounds.	Propellant.
	In.	Tons.	lb.	lb.	Ft.-Secs.	Ft.-Tons.	In.	Per Minute.	
12 in.	12	69	318	850	2960	51,640	51·5	2	
10 „	10	36	200	500	3000	35,318	44·0	3	
9·2 „	9·2	28	138	380	3030	24,190	40·8	4	
8 „	8	21	90	250	3000	15,660	34·9	5	
7·5 „	7·5	15·75	76	200	3000	12,481	32·1	6	
6 „	6	8·75	35·5	100	3050	6,492	26·0	9	
4·7 „	4·7	3·3	15	45	3000	2,808	19·1	12	
4 „	4	2·1	11	31	3000	1,934	17·3	12	
3 „	3	1·1	5·75	14·3	3050	922	13·9	30	Semi-automatic
6 pr.	2·24	·52	1.13	6	2400	240	7·3	25	
3 „	1·85	·25	·625	3·3	2300	121	5·7	25	

Note.—The most powerful gun of each calibre has been selected.

TABLE XIX.—*Vickers, Sons and Maxim's Guns. Abridged Table.*

Official Designation of Gun.	Calibre.	Weight of Gun.	Weight of Charge.	Weight of Projectile.	Muzzle Velocity.	Muzzle Energy.	Perforation of Wrought Iron.	Rate of firing Rounds.	Propellant.
	In.	Tons.	lb.	lb.	Ft.-Secs.	Ft.-Tons.	In.	Per Minute.	
12 in.	12	65·85	344	850	3010	53,400	53·0	2	
10 „	10	27·85	172	496·6	2863	28,275	41·0	3	
9·2 „	9·2	27·8	184	380	3070	24,835	41·3	4	
8 „	8	13·15	60	216·7	3090	14,350	33·9	6	
7·5 „	7·5	16·0	80·05	200	3007	12,540	32·3	8	
6 „	6	7·8	43	100	3190	7,056	27·9	10	
4·7 „	4·72	3·1	17	45·14	3050	2,910	18·5	12	
4 „	4	2·1	11·25	31	3030	1,975	17·6	15	
3 „	3	0·95	3·625	12·5	2760	632	10·8	25	Semi-automatic
6 pr.	2·24	0·46	1·55	6	2600	281	8·2	28	
3 „	1·85	0·28	1·066	3·3	2800	179·4	7·5	30	

Note.—The most powerful gun of each calibre has been selected.

TABLE XX.—*Krupp's Naval and Coast-Defence Ordnance. Abridged from Table of Ordnance, 1906.*

Official Designation of Gun.	Calibre.	Weight of Gun.	Weight of Charge.	Weight of Projectile.	Muzzle Velocity.	Muzzle Energy.	Perforation of Wrought Iron.	Rate of firing.	Propellant.
	In.	Tons.	lb.	lb.	Ft.-Secs.	Ft.-Tons.	In.	Per Minute.	
30·5 cm.	12·01	{47 / 52·2}	357	771·6 / 981·0	3251 / 2884	56,540	53·0	2–3	
28 „	11·02	{36·4 / 40·4}	276	595·2 / 760·6	3255 / 2881	43,754	52·0 / 49·0	2–3	The explosive for the charges of guns of 10·5 cm. and upwards contains 25% of nitroglycerin
24 „	9·45	{22·93 / 25·45}	173·6	374·8 / 474·0	3255 / 2894	27,540	44·5 / 42·0	3–4	
21 „	8·27	{15·20 / 16·90}	115·2	249·1 / 308·6	3251 / 2920	18,101	38·6 / 36·5	4–5	
19 „	7·48	{11·37 / 12·04}	86·2	187·4 / 235·9	3241 / 2890	13,572	35·0 / 33·1	5–6	
17 „	6·7	{8·55 / 9·48}	64·6	141·1 / 176·4	3238 / 2897	10,259	32·0 / 30·3	6–7	
15 „	5·91	{5·5 / 6·1}	41·7	99·4 / 112·4	3245 / 2910	6,603	27·4 / 26·1	6–8	
12 „	4·72	{2·86 / 3·18}	21·72	46·3 / 59·5	3274 / 2887	3,442	22·2 / 20·8	15–20	
10·5 „	4·13	{1·92 / 2·13}	14·55	30·9 / 39·7	3281 / 2897	2,306	19·5 / 18·3	20–25	
9 „	3·54	{1·28. / 1·45}	7·72 / 7·94	19·84 / 25·13 / 19·84 / 25·13	3163 / 2812 / 3248 / 2887	1,377 / 1,452	16·0 / 15·0 / 16·5 / 15·6	25–30	The explosive for charges of guns up to 9·5 cm. contains 40% nitroglycerin
7·5 „	2·95	{·74 / ·84}	4·48 / 4·61	11·46 / 14·55 / 11·46 / 14·55	3165 / 2812 / 3251 / 2887	297 / 840	13·3 / 13·6 / 13·9 / 13·0	30–40	
5·7 „	2·24	{·325 / ·367}	1·96 / 2·03	5·07 / 6·4 / 5·07 / 6·4	3156 / 2808 / 3242 / 2882	350 / 369	10·1 / 9·5 / 10·5 / 8·9	40–50	
5·0 „	1·97	{·220 / ·248}	1·32 / 1·37	3·42 / 4·3 / 3·42 / 4·3	3156 / 2814 / 3242 / 2890	236 / 249	8·7 / 8·4 / 9·0 / 8·75	40–50	

Note.—The above table includes a light and heavy type of gun, but for each the length of bore is 50 calibres; in the unabridged table guns of 40 and 45 calibres are included. The particulars of the shorter pieces can be easily obtained from Table XX., as the construction of Krupp's complete table is based on very simple rules. Thus, for the same relative length of gun, the weight of the projectile and of the charge are, with few exceptions, in proportion to the cube of the calibre. Again, the weight of the gun varies as the cube of the calibre multiplied by the length. The muzzle velocity is practically identical for guns of the same relative length, and varies as the square root of the length; consequently the muzzle energy varies directly as the length. Two weights of projectile are given for every gun, but the muzzle energy of each, for the same charge, is identical; this result is never the case in actual practice. Similar arithmetical processes are utilised for the Schneider-Canet, Bofors and Skoda tables, and only the first named is therefore given.

TABLE XXI.—*Schneider-Canet Guns. Abridged Table.*

Official Designation of Gun.	Calibre.	Weight of Gun.	Weight of Charge.	Weight of Projectile.	Muzzle Velocity.	Muzzle Energy	Perforation of Wrought Iron.	Rate of firing Rounds.	Propellant.
	In.	Tons.	lb.	lb.	Ft.-Secs.	Ft.-Tons.	In.	Per Minute.	
305 mm.	12·01	57·6	..	826	3116	55,717	54·8		
274·4 ,,	10·9	41·9	..	606	3116	40,859	49·1		
240 ,,	9·45	28·0	..	407	3116	27,487	43·2		
200 ,,	7·87	16·25	..	231	3116	15,601	35·9		
175 ,,	6·89	10·8	..	165	3116	11,143	32·1		
150 ,,	5·91	6·8	..	99	3116	6,686	27·0		
120 ,,	4·72	3·5	..	48	3116	3,268	21·0		
100 ,,	3·94	2·0	..	28·6	3116	1,931	17·8		
75 ,,	2·95	1·2	..	14·3	3116	917	14·6		
57 ,,	2·24	·55	..	6·0	3116	400	10·7		
47 ,,	1·85	·30	..	3·3	3116	223	8·9		

Note.—The unabridged table gives only 45 and 50 calibre guns; the above table gives the particulars for 50 calibre guns.

TABLE XXII.—*Bethlehem Steel Co.'s Guns. Abridged Table.*

Official Designation of Gun.	Calibre.	Weight of Gun.	Weight of Charge.	Weight of Projectile.	Muzzle Velocity.	Muzzle Energy.	Perforation of Wrought Iron.	Rate of firing Rounds.	Propellant.
	In.	Tons.	lb.	lb.	Ft.-Secs.	Ft.-Tons.	In.	Per Minute.	
18 in.	18	60	..	2000	2250	70,185	42·7		
12 ,,	12	53	..	850	2800	46,195	47·4		
10 ,,	10	35	..	500	2800	27,174	39·8		
8 ,,	8	18·6	..	250	2800	13,587	31·5		
7 ,,	7	14·5	..	165	2900	9,619	28·8		
6 ,,	6	8·4	..	105	2900	6,180	24·9		
5 ,,	5	4·75	..	60	2900	3,490	20·5		
4·724 ,,	4·724	4·2	..	45	2900	2,623	18·3		
4 ,,	4	2·6	..	33	2900	1,924	17·0		
3 ,,	3	·85	..	13	2800	707	11·7		
2·24 ,,	2·24	·43	..	6	2400	240	7·3		
1·85 ,,	1·85	·245	..	3	2600	142	6·4		

Note.—The most powerful gun of each calibre has been selected.

Modern naval artillery may be looked upon as the high water mark of gun construction, and keeps pace with the latest scientific improvements. For coast defence the latest patterns of ordnance is not of the same importance; in general very similar guns are employed, although perhaps of an older type. Formerly in the British Service the heaviest guns have been used for this purpose; but of late years, where fortifications could be erected in suitable situations, the largest gun favoured is the 9·2-in. of the latest model. Other governments have, however, selected still heavier pieces up to 12-in. calibre, mounted in heavily armoured cupolas or gunhouses.

As regards field material, mobility is still one of the primary conditions, and, as high power is seldom required, ordnance of medium calibre is all that is necessary. For siege purposes guns of 4-in. to 6-in. calibre are generally sufficient, but howitzers up to 28 cm. (11·02 in.) were used at the siege of Port Arthur, 1904. All authorities seem agreed that for ordinary field guns 75 mm. or 3-in. calibre is the smallest which can be efficiently employed for the purpose, and the muzzle velocity is in nearly all equipments about 500 m.s. (1640 f.s.).

For mountain equipments all foreign governments have selected a 75-millimetre gun with a velocity of about 350 m.s. (1148 f.s.); in England, however, a 2·75-in. has been supplied to mountain batteries; this fires a projectile of 10 lb with 1440 f.s.

Field Howitzer batteries abroad have pieces of from 10 to 12 centimetres calibre and a low velocity; in England a 5-in. howitzer is at present used, but it is intended to adopt a 4·5-in. howitzer of 17 calibres in length for future manufacture.

Heavy shell power and long range fighting render the work of the gun designer particularly difficult, especially when this is *Theory of gun-making.* combined with conditions restricting length and weight; and, in addition, other considerations, especially for naval guns, may have to be taken into account such as the allowable weight of the armament, and the size of the gun house or turret. These and other similar conditions are important factors in deciding on the type of design

which embodies most advantages for a heavy gun intended for the main armament. For land defence more latitude is allowed so long as this is combined with economy. With both heavy and medium naval guns the length is often limited to 45 calibres on account of peculiarities in the design of the vessel, but usually great rapidity of fire, high velocity and large shell power are insisted upon. Again for Q.F. field guns, where high velocity is not of importance, ease of manipulation, rapidity of working and reliability even after months of arduous service are essential. Supposing, however, that the initial conditions, imposed by the shipbuilder or by the exigency of the case, can be fulfilled, it still remains to so design the gun that, when it is fired, there is an ample margin of safety to meet the various stresses to which the several portions of the structure are subject. The two principal stresses requiring special attention are the circumferential stress, which tends to burst open the gun longitudinally, and the longitudinal stress. The calculation for the last named is based on the supposition that the gun is a hollow cylinder, closed at one end by the breech screw and at the other by the shot, both being firmly fixed to the cylinder. The gas pressure exerts its force on the face of the breech screw and on the base of the shot thus tending to pull the walls of the cylinder asunder. But besides these there is the special stress on the threads of the breech screw which must receive very careful consideration.

Regard must also be had to the fact that in building up the gun, the smaller the diameter of the hoop and the longer it is, the higher must be the temperature to which it is heated before shrinking. This is necessary in order that the dilatation may allow sufficient clearance to place the hoop correctly in position on the gun, without the possibility of its contracting and gripping before being so placed. Should it warp while being heated or while being placed in position the hoop may prematurely grip on the gun and may consequently have to be sacrificed by cutting it off and shrinking on another.

The dilatation must be so adjusted that the required temperature to obtain it is not higher than that used for annealing the forging, otherwise the effect of this annealing will be modified. There is, therefore, for this reason, considerable risk in shrinking up long hoops of small diameter.

Before heating hoops of large diameter two or three narrow reference bands are turned on the exterior and their diameter measured; special gauges are prepared to measure these plus the dilatation required. After heating the hoop but before shrinking it, the diameter of the reference bands when tested by these gauges should not be in excess of them. The temperature can then be easily ascertained by dividing the dilatation by the coefficient of expansion of steel per degree F. or C., taking of course the diameter into account.

For small hoops this method is not convenient, as the hoop cools too quickly; the dilatation must then be obtained by ascertaining the temperature, and this is best done by the use of some form of pyrometer, such as a Siemens water pyrometer, before the hoop is withdrawn from the furnace.

It may also be desired to obtain a given striking energy or velocity at some definite range—then, the weight of the projectile being decided upon, the muzzle velocity is found from the formulas (see BALLISTICS) given in Exterior Ballistics. From this and the length of the gun allowable the designer has, with the aid of former experience and the formulas given in Internal Ballistics, to decide on the weight and nature of the powder charge necessary and the internal dimensions of the powder chamber and bore. These data are used to plot what is termed a "gunmakers' curve," i.e. the curve of pressures along the bore which the powder charge decided upon will give. The factor of safety and the maximum allowable stress of the steel forgings or steel wire also being known, the necessary strength of each section of the gun can be easily found and it remains to so proportion each part as to conform to these conditions and to meet certain others, such as facilities for manufacture, which experience only can determine.

When the second course consists of a single long tube into which a tapered barrel is driven, as in the system adopted by the English government, the two tubes are treated as a single tube equal in thickness to the two together; but when the second course consists of several tubes shrunk on to the barrel the additional strength, obtained by the initial tension of the shrunk tubes, is sometimes taken account of in the calculation, or the two may be treated as one thick tube.

The gunmakers' formulas for the strength of the gun are obtained from considering the strength of a thick cylinder exposed to unequal internal and external pressures. Supposing a transverse section of the gun to cut through n tubes, the internal radius of the barrel is r_0 in., the external radius r_1 in.; the external radius of the second course is r_2 and so on; and the external radius of the jacket is r_n. Then if $T = a$ circumferential stress (tension) in tons per square inch, $T_n = a$ circumferential stress at radius r_n in., $P = a$ radial stress (pressure) in tons per square inch, and $P_n = a$ radial stress at radius r_n in. the formulas used in the calculation of the strength of built-up guns are as follows:—

$$T = \frac{P_{n-1}r_{n-1}^2 - P_n r_n^2}{r_n^2 - r_{n-1}^2} + \frac{r_{n-1}^2 r_n^2}{r^2} \frac{P_{n-1} - P_n}{r_n^2 - r_{n-1}^2}$$ (1)

$$P = \frac{r_{n-1}^2 r_n^2}{r^2} \frac{P_{n-1} - P_n}{r_n^2 - r_{n-1}^2} - \frac{P_{n-1}r_{n-1}^2 - P_n r_n^2}{r_n^2 - r_{n-1}^2}$$ (2),

where r is any intermediate radius in the thickness of a tube

$$T_n - P_n = T - P$$ (3)

in the same tube; also the pressure between the $(n-1)^{th}$ and n^{th} hoops is

$$P_{n-1} = \frac{r_n^2 - r_{n-1}^2}{r_n^2 + r_{n-1}^2}(T_{n-1} + P_n) + P_n$$ (4).

Equation (4) is usually known as the *Gunmakers' formula* and from it, when P_n and T_{n-1}, T_{n-1} . . . are known the other pressures can be found. The proof tension of the material is kept well below the yielding stress. For ordinary carbon gun steel it is usual to

consider that the proof tension of the barrel should not exceed 15 tons and of the outer hoops 18 tons per square inch; with nickel gun steel these become 20 tons and 24 tons respectively. If the nth hoop is the exterior tube then $P_n = 0$; neglecting the atmospheric pressure.

In all gun calculations for strength three cases must be considered:

(a) When the built-up gun is fired, the stress is called the *Firing Stress* and is obtained by the repeated use of equation (4);

(b) When the gun, supposed to be a solid homogeneous block of metal is fired, the stress is termed the *Powder Stress* and is obtained from the equations (1) and (2);

(c) When the built-up gun is in repose, the stress is then called the *Initial Stress* or *Stress of Repose*.

Between these three cases the following relations hold:—

Initial Stress + Powder Stress = Firing Stress   (5).

It is best to use different symbols to distinguish each kind of stress. We will use for the Firing Stress P, T; for Powder Stress p, t; and for the Initial Stress (p), (t).

The method of working will be illustrated by a practical example. Take, for instance, a section across the chamber of a 4·7-in. Q.F. gun, for which the diameter of the chamber is 5 in., that of the barrel 8·2 in., and the external diameter of the jacket 15 in.

Here
$$r_0 = 2·5; \ r_1 = 4·1; \ r_2 = 7·5$$
$$T_0 = 15; \ T_1 = 18; \ P_2 = 0.$$

From (4) for the *Firing Stress*

$$P_1 = \frac{(7·5)^2 - (4·1)^2}{(7·5)^2 + (4·1)^2} \times 18 = 9·72 \text{ tons per square inch.}$$

$$P_0 = \frac{(4·1)^2 - (2·5)^2}{(4·1)^2 + (2·5)^2} \times (15 + 9·72) + 9·72 = 21 \text{ tons per square inch.}$$

From (3) the tension T'_2 of the outer fibres of the hoops is obtained; thus

$$T'_2 = P_2 + T_1 - P_1 = 18 - 9·72 = 8·28 \text{ tons per square inch.}$$
$$T'_1 = P_1 + T_0 - P_0 = 9·72 + 15 - 21 = 3·72 \text{ tons per square inch.}$$

For any intermediate radius r the stress can be found by using equations (1) and (2) or (1) or (2) and (3).

For the *Powder Stress* equations (1) and (2) are used by putting $n = 1$, and then $p_1 = 0$ (also remembering that, as there are two hoops, the outer radius must be written r_2); the formulas become

$$t = \frac{r_2^2 + r^2}{r^2} \frac{r_2^2 + r^2}{r_2^2 - r_0^2} p_0$$ (6)

$$p = \frac{r_2^2}{r^2} \frac{r_2^2 - r^2}{r_2^2 - r_0^2} p_0$$ (7).

When $r = r_0 = 2·5$, $t = t_0$, $p_0 = P_0$ already found and:

$$t_0 = \frac{(7·5)^2 + (2·5)^2}{(7·5)^2 - (2·5)^2} \times 21 = 26·25 \text{ tons.}$$

For the tension of the fibres at the outer circumference

$$t'_2 = 26·25 - 21 = 5·25 \text{ tons,}$$

from (3) and for a radius $r_2 = 7·5$ inches.

The stress for any intermediate radius r can be obtained from (6) and (7) or, from (6) or (7) and (3).

Subtracting the *Powder Stress* from the *Firing Stress* the *Initial Stress* is obtained, and the various results can be tabulated as follows:—

At Radius.		Tensions.			Pressures.		
		Firing Stress.	Powder Stress.	Initial Stress.	Firing Stress.	Powder Stress.	Initial Stress.
Barrel	$r_0 = 2·5$	15·0	26·25	−11·25	21·0	21·0	0
	$r_1 = 4·1$	3·72	11·57	− 7·85	9·72	6·32	3·4
Jacket	$r_1 = 4·1$	18·0	11·57	6·43	9·72	6·32	3·4
	$r_2 = 7·5$	8·28	5·25	3·03	0	0	0

It is generally stipulated that the initial compression of the material at the interior surface of the barrel shall not exceed 26 tons per square inch, i.e. $(t_0) = 26$ tons; in the example above $(t_0) = -11·25$ tons only, but in wire-wound guns special attention to this condition is necessary.

It now remains for the designer so to dimension the several hoops that they shall, when shrunk together, give the stresses found by calculation. To do this the exterior diameter of the barrel must be a little larger than the interior diameter of the covering hoop; after this hoop is shrunk on to the barrel its exterior diameter is turned in a lathe so that it is slightly larger than the interior of the next course hoop and so on. It will be seen that the fibres of the barrel must be compressed while the fibres of the superimposed hoop are extended, and thus produce the *Initial Stress*. The shrinkage S may be defined as the excess of the external diameter of the tube over the internal diameter of the hoop, when separate and both are in the cold state. Then

If S_{n+1} denotes the shrinkage between the nth and $(n+1)^{th}$ hoops

$$S_{n+1} = \frac{2r_r}{M}[(l_n) - (l'_n)] \quad (8)$$

$$= \frac{2r_r}{M}\left[(l_n) - (l_{n-1}) + \frac{r_n^2 - r_s^2}{r_n^2 + r_s^2}\{(l_{n-1}) + (p_n)\}\right] \quad (9).$$

Here M can be taken as 12,500 tons per square inch for gun steel. In the example already calculated the shrinkage between the jacket and barrel is 0·009 in.

$$S = \frac{2 \times 4 \cdot 1}{12,500}\left[6 \cdot 43 + 11 \cdot 25 + \frac{(4 \cdot 1)^2 - (2 \cdot 5)^2}{(4 \cdot 1)^2 + (2 \cdot 5)^2}(-11 \cdot 25 + 3 \cdot 4)\right]$$
$$= 0 \cdot 009 \text{ in.}$$

In that portion of the gun in which wire is used in the construction, exactly the same principles are involved. It may be *Wire* assumed that the tube on which the wire is wound is so *guns.* large, in comparison to the thickness of the wire, that the compression of the concave surface of the wire and the extension of its convex surface may be neglected without sensible error.

The greatest advantage is obtained from the wire, coils when in the Firing Stress the tension T is uniform throughout the thickness of the wiring. The Firing Stress T in the wire may be as low as 25 tons per square inch and as high as 50 tons, but as the yielding strength of the wire is never less than 80 tons per square inch nor its breaking strength less than 90 tons, there is still an ample margin especially when it is remembered that the factor of safety is included in the calculation.

If the wire is wound direct on to the barrel and is covered by a jacket, r_0, r_1 being the radii in inches of the barrel, r_1, r_2 the radii of the internal and external layers of wire, and r_2, r_3 the radii of the jacket; then for the Firing Stress in the wire

$$T(r_2 - r) = P r - P_2 r_2 \quad (9),$$

or

$$T(r - r_1) = P_1 r_1 - P r \quad (10).$$

By combining these the gunmakers' formula for the wire is obtained

$$P_1 = \frac{r_2 - r}{r_1}(T + P_2) + P_2 \quad (10a).$$

As T is to be uniform, when the gun is fired, the Initial Tensions of the wire are arranged accordingly, and the tensions at which the wire must be wound on to the guns have now to be determined.

Let θ = the winding tension at radius r in.
(l) = the initial tension at radius r in.
(p) = the radial pressure between any two layers of wire at radius r in.

It is assumed that M is uniform for the gun steel and wire. Then

$$\theta = (l) + (p)\frac{r^2 + r_0^2}{r^2 - r_0^2} \quad (11),$$

where

$$(l) = T - P_2 \frac{r_2^2}{r^2}\frac{r^2 + r_0^2}{r_2^2 - r_0^2} \quad (12),$$

and

$$(p) = P - P_2 \frac{r_2^2}{r^2}\frac{r^2 - r_0^2}{r_2^2 - r_0^2} \quad (13).$$

By means of these two equations and (9) the expression (11) becomes

$$\theta = \frac{E}{r} + \frac{F}{r - r_0} + \frac{G}{r + r_0} \quad (14),$$

where

$$E = -(T + P_2)r_2$$
$$F = (T + P_2)r_0 - (T + P_2)r_2$$
$$G = (T + P_2)r_0 + (T + P_2)r_2$$

To compare with the previous example, the stress for a 4·7-in. Q.F. wire gun will be calculated. This consists of a barrel, intermediate layer of wire and jacket.

Here $r_0 = 2 \cdot 5$; $r_1 = 3 \cdot 75$; $r_2 = 5 \cdot 5$; $r_3 = 7 \cdot 5$ inches; the firing tension T_1 to T_2 of the wire = 25 tons per square inch, suppose.

Take $P_2 = 21$ tons per square inch and consider that the jacket fits tightly over the wire, but has no shrinkage. Then for the Firing Stress, from (2), $P_3 = 2 \cdot 25$ tons, and from (9) and (10), $T_1(r_2 - r_1) = P_1 r_1 - P_2 r_2$

$$P_1 = 14 \cdot 97, \text{ say 15 tons;}$$

from (4) we can obtain T_2 and T_1 since P_2, P_1 and P_3 are known; from (3) $T_2 = 0 \cdot 6$ tons. $T_1 = 7 \cdot 5$ tons.

$$T'_1 = -5 \cdot 4 \text{ tons (a compression),}$$

and

$$T_2 = 5 \cdot 25 \text{ tons.}$$

The *Powder Stress* is obtained in the same way as in the previous example, so also is the *Initial Stress*; therefore we may tabulate as follows:—

At Radius.		Tensions.			Pressures.		
		Firing Stress.	Powder Stress.	Initial Stress.	Firing Stress.	Powder Stress.	Initial Stress.
Barrel	$r_0 = 2 \cdot 5$	0·6	26·25	-25·65	21·0	21·0	0
	$r_1 = 3 \cdot 75$	-5·4	13·125	-18·525	15·0	7·875	7·125
Wire	$r_1 = 3 \cdot 75$	25·0	13·125	11·875	15·0	7·875	7·125
	$r_2 = 5 \cdot 5$	25·0	7·5	17·5	2·25	2·25	0
Jacket	$r_2 = 5 \cdot 5$	7·5	7·5	0	2·25	2·25	0
	$r_3 = 7 \cdot 5$	5·25	5·25	0	0	0	0

As the wire is wound on, the pressure of the external layers will compress those on the interior, thus producing an extension in the wire which is equivalent to a reduction in the winding tension θ of the particular layer at radius r considered. If τ represents this reduction then

$$\theta = (l) - \tau,$$

where

$$\tau = \frac{r^2 + r_0^2}{r^2 - r_0^2}(p).$$

At the interior layer of wire r is the initial stress on the exterior of the barrel and the winding tension must commence at

$$\theta = 11 \cdot 875 + 18 \cdot 525 = 30 \cdot 4 \text{ tons per square inch.}$$

As the jacket is supposed to have no shrinkage $T = 0$ and consequently

$$\theta = (l) = 17 \cdot 5 \text{ tons per square inch.}$$

These winding tensions can be found directly from formula (14) and then

$$E = -149 \cdot 875; \quad F = 34 \cdot 875; \quad G = 264 \cdot 875.$$

Sir G. Greenhill has put these formulas, both for the built-up and wire-wound guns, into an extremely neat and practical geometrical form, which can be used instead of the arithmetical processes; for these see *Text-Book of Gunnery*, *Treatise of Service Ordnance*, 1893, and *Journal of the United States Artillery*, vol. iv.

The longitudinal strength of the gun is very important especially at the breech end; along the forward portion of the gun the thickness of the barrel and the interlocking of the covering hoops *Longi-* provide ample strength, but at the breech special pro- *tudinal* vision must be made. It is usual to provide for this by *stress.* means of a strong breech piece or jacket in small guns or by both combined in large ones. Its amount is easily calculated on the hypothesis that the stress is uniformly distributed throughout the thickness of the breech piece, or jacket, or of both. If r_3 is the largest radius of the gun chamber, r_0 the radius of the obturator seating, r_1 the external radius of the barrel, and P_0 the maximum powder pressure, then, with the usual form of chamber adopted with guns fitted with obturation other than cartridge cases, there will be a longitudinal stress on the barrel at the breech end of the chamber due to the action of the pressure P_0 on the rear slope of the chamber, of

$$\frac{\pi}{4}(r_3^2 - r_0^2)P_0 \text{ tons}$$

this is resisted by the barrel of section $\frac{\pi}{4}(r_1^2 - r_0^2)$ so that the resistance

$$R = \frac{r_3^2 - r_0^2}{r_1^2 - r_0^2}P_0 \text{ tons.}$$

This portion of the longitudinal stress is not of great importance as the breech end of the barrel is supported in all modern designs by the breech bush. In Q.F. guns, *i.e.* those firing cartridge cases, the breech end of the chamber has the largest diameter, and $r_3 = r_0$ so that there is no longitudinal stress on the chamber part of the barrel.

For the breech piece or outer tube of radii r_1 and r_3, the resistance

$$R = \frac{r_0^2}{r_3^2 - r_1^2}P_0 \text{ tons for B.L. guns.}$$

$$R = \frac{r_3^2}{r_3^2 - r_1^2}P_0 \text{ tons in Q.F. guns.}$$

If the longitudinal stress is taken by a jacket only, the resistance is found in the same way.

Generally for ordinary gun steel, the longitudinal stress on the material is always kept below 10 tons per square inch or 13 tons for nickel steel; but even with these low figures there is also included a factor of safety of 1·5 to 2. In large guns it is best to consider the jacket as an auxiliary aid only to longitudinal resistance, as, owing to the necessary connexions between it and the breech bush and its distance from the centre of pressure, there is a possibility that it may not be taking its proportionate share of the stress.

The thread of the breech screw and of the breech bush (or opening) must be so proportioned as to sustain the full pressure on the maximum obturator area; V or buttress shaped threads are always used as they are stronger than other forms, but V threads have the great advantage of centring the breech screw when under pressure.

In most modern B.L. guns fitted with de Bange obturation the diameter of the seating is made just large enough to freely admit the projectile; this is usually considerably smaller than the maximum diameter of the chamber, consequently a less area is exposed to the gas pressure and less screw thread section is required.

The principal features of the various systems of construction of modern heavy guns may be briefly described.

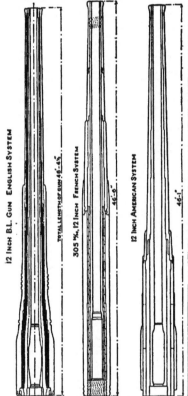

FIGS. 55-57.—British, French and American Construction.

Fig. 55 is that adopted in England. The barrel or "inner A tube" is surmounted by a second layer which is either shrunk on in two or three pieces, as at Elswick, or is formed of one long piece called the "A tube," as in the Woolwich system. This second layer is covered with wire, and over this is shrunk the chase hoop or B tube and the jacket. The breech bush is screwed into the rear end of the A tube so that the principal longitudinal stress is taken by this tube.

Fig. 56 is the system adopted in the French service. In this the barrel is surmounted over the breech end with two layers of short thin hoops, which consequently approximate to the wire system.

Systems of construction.

Over the muzzle end two or three long tubes are shrunk; the chase hoop is also screwed to the barrel near the muzzle. A jacket is shrunk over the breech portion of the gun, and the breech bush is screwed into it at the rear end. The gun is further strengthened by a long tube in front of the jacket to which it is attached by a screwed collar.

Fig. 57 shows the design adopted for the United States navy. Here the barrel is surmounted by a second course in two lengths, and over the breech a third and fourth layer are shrunk. The breech screw is screwed into the rear end of the second course.

Fig. 58 is the Krupp system, of which,however,it is an old example; it is believed, however, that Krupp still retains the essential peculiarities of this design, viz. that over the breech end of the barrel is shrunk a solid breech piece, made particularly massive in rear where the breech wedge is seated. The remainder of the layers consist of hoops which are comparatively short but may be covered with longer thin tubes.

FIG. 58.—Krupp Construction.

When guns are fired, the interior surface is gradually worn away by the action of the powder gases; the breech end of the rifled portion of the bore becomes enlarged, and the rifling itself partly obliterated. The ballistics suffer in consequence of the enlarged diameter of the bore, and the rifling may be worn so much as not to properly rotate the projectile.

Erosion.

In all modern gun designs provision has, therefore, to be made for repairing or replacing the barrel when it is worn out. There are two methods of providing for the repair in the original design—the first is by replacing the whole of the barrel by an entirely new one; the second is to make the original barrel thick so that when it is worn the interior can be bored out, either over a portion of its length to cover the eroded part, or the full length for "through lining." In large guns it is usual to make the original barrel, if it is intended to be removed as a whole, tapered from end to end, so that by warming the gun in a vertical position breech downwards to about 300° F. and then suddenly cooling the barrel by a jet of water it can be knocked out by heavy blows from a falling weight. A new tapered barrel can then be inserted by driving it in. When a gun which had originally a thick barrel is lined part of the barrel is bored out in a machine, and it is usual to make the hole tapered so that a new tapered liner can be inserted and driven home.

The wearing of the barrel owing to erosion is one of the most difficult problems the gun constructor has to face. Sir Andrew Noble (see "Some Modern Explosives," a paper read at the Royal Institution, 1900, also "Researches on Explosives," part iii., *Phil. Trans. Roy. Soc.*) has conclusively proved that the erosion is mainly dependent on the very high temperature to which the interior surface of the gun is raised and on the quantity of this heat. Both these factors are, for any particular explosive, determined by some function of the proportion of the weight of the charge to the extent of the exposed surface. The passage for the products of combustion gradually reduces from the maximum diameter of the chamber to the diameter of the bore. The highly heated gases therefore impinge more directly on that part of the bore which forms the seating for the shot and acts on it for the longest time, *i.e.* for the whole time the shot is in the gun. Consequently this part suffers most wear.

It may be assumed that the weights of the charges vary as the cube of the diameters of the bore, while the circumference of the bore varies directly as the calibre; now as the wear depends principally on the weight of the charge in relation to the exposed surface at the shot seating it varies as the square of the calibre. It is evident too that the allowable wear will vary as the calibre, so that the life of the gun or the number of rounds which can be fired is inversely proportionate to the calibre.

The heat of combustion and the time of burning of the explosive are factors in determining the amount of heat developed per unit of time, and thus influence the proportion of heat conducted away from the interior surface of the gun. The time of burning of the explosive depends on the size and form of the explosive and on the density of loading, while the heat of combustion depends on its composition and cannot be treated of here, but it may be stated generally that for equal weights Ballistite is more erosive than Cordite Mark I., and Cordite Mark I. than Cordite M.D. All of these explosives contain a fairly large proportion of nitro-glycerine, and it is found that as the proportion of this ingredient is reduced the erosion also decreases, so that for pure nitro-cellulose powders it is less still. Unfortunately pure nitro-cellulose powders are not ballistically equal to the same weight of nitroglycerin powder; the advantage of the less erosive action is lost owing to the greater weight of pure nitro-cellulose explosive required to obtain the same ballistics.

The effect of erosion on large high-power guns is serious, for in a

12-in. gun after some 150 or fewer rounds are fired with a full charge the barrel is worn so much as to need replacing. In the British service it is considered that the wear produced by firing sixteen half charges is equivalent to that of one full charge.

In small high-velocity guns the number of rounds with full charge which can be fired without replacing the barrel is considerably greater; while for low-velocity guns the number is higher still. In some guns this number appears abnormally high; in others of exactly similar type it may be low and for no apparent reason.

The first effect of the powder gases on the steel is a very characteristic hardening of the surface of the whole of the bore; so much is this the case that it is difficult to carry out any mechanical operation, except grinding, after a gun has been fired. When ignited the explosive contained in the chamber of the gun burns fiercely, and as the projectile travels along the bore the highly heated gases follow. The surface of the bore near the chamber is naturally the most highly heated and for the longest time; here too the rush of gas is greatest. There is in consequence a film of steel swept off from the surface, but this becomes less as the distance from the chamber becomes greater, owing to the abstraction of heat by the bore. It is a noticeable fact that only where a decided movement of gas takes place is there any erosion: thus, towards the breech end of the chamber where no rush of gas occurs there is no perceptible erosion, even after many rounds have been fired. Again, at the muzzle end there is very little erosion, as here the gases are in contact with the bore for a minute fraction of time.

As the firing proceeds, the interior surface of the bore, where the erosion is greatest, becomes covered with a network of very fine cracks running both longitudinally and circumferentially. The sides of these cracks in their turn become eroded and gradually fissures are formed. With the old black and brown powders these fissures were a feature of the erosion, while with the new type smokeless powders the eroded surface is usually smooth, and it is only after prolonged firing that fissures occur although fine cracks occur after a comparatively few rounds have been fired.

BIBLIOGRAPHY.—English: Nye, *The Art of Gunnery* (1670); Norton, *The Gunner, showing the whole Practice of Artillerie* (London, 1628); Sir Jonas Moore, *Treatise of Artillery* (London, 1683); Robins, *New Principles of Gunnery* (London, 1742); Hutton, *Tracts* (London, 1812); Sir Howard Douglas, R.A., *Naval Gunnery* (London, 1855); Mallet, *Construction of Artillery* (London, 1856); Boxer, *Treatise on Artillery* (London, 1856); Owen, *Modern Artillery* (London, 1871); *Text-Book Rifled Ordnance* (London, 1877); *Treatise on Construction of Ordnance* (London, 1879); Lloyd and Hadcock, *Artillery: its Progress and Present Position* (Portsmouth, 1893); *Treatise on Service Ordnance* (London, 1893–1904); *Catalogue of Museum of Artillery in the Rotunda* (Woolwich, 1906); Sir Andrew Noble, *Artillery and Explosives* (1906); Brassey, *Naval Annual*. United States: A. L. Holley, *Ordnance and Armour* (New York, 1865); E. Simpson, *Ordnance and Naval Gunnery* (New York, 1862); *Resistance of Guns to Tangential Rupture* (Washington, 1892); *Annual Reports of Chief of Ordnance*; Fullam and Hart, *Text-Book of Ordnance and Gunnery* (Annapolis, 1905); O. M. Lissak, *Ordnance and Gunnery* (New York, 1907). French: Jacob, *Resistance et construction des bouches à feu* (Paris, 1909); De Lagabbe, *Matériel d'artillerie* (Paris, 1903); *Manuel du canonnier* (1907); Alvin, *Leçons sur l'artillerie* (Paris, 1908). German and Austrian: Kaiser, *Konstruktion der gezogenen Geschützröhre* (Vienna, 1900); Indra, *Die wahre Gestalt der Spannungskurve* (Vienna, 1901). Italian: Tartaglia, *La Nuova Scienta* (Venice, 1562); Bianchi, *Materiale d'artiglieria* (Turin, 1905).   (A. G. H.)

II. FIELD ARTILLERY EQUIPMENTS

General Principles.—A field gun may be considered as a machine for delivering shrapnel bullets and high-explosive shell at a given distant point. The power of the machine is limited by its weight, and this is limited by the load which a team of six horses is able to pull at a trot on the road and across open country. For under these conditions it is found that six is the maximum number of horses which can work in one team without loss of efficiency. The most suitable load for a gun-team is variously estimated by different nations, according to the size of the horses available and to the nature of the country in the probable theatre of war. Thus in England the field artillery load is fixed at 43 cwt. behind the traces; France, 41·5 cwt., Germany 42 cwt., and Japan (1903) 30 cwt. This load consists of the gun with carriage and shield, the limber with ammunition and entrenching tools, and the gunners with their kits and accoutrements. The weights may be variously distributed, subject to the condition that for case of draught the weight on the gun wheels must not greatly exceed that on the limber wheels. It is still usual to carry two gunners on seats on the gun axletree, and two on the limber. But a Q.F. gun capable of firing 20 rounds a minute requires to be constantly accompanied by an ammunition wagon, and the modern tendency is to take advantage of this to carry some of the gunners on the wagon. Thus in the British field artillery two gunners are carried on the gun limber, two on the wagon limber, one on the wagon body and none on the gun. These five gunners, with the sergeant, called the No. 1, on his horse, make a full gun-detachment. Three wagons for each gun usually are provided, two of which, with the spare gunners and non-commissioned officers, are posted under cover at some distance behind the battery. The weight on the gun, the presence of the wagon allows the number of rounds in the limber to be reduced. The result of this redistribution of weights is that field artillery may now be equipped with a much heavier and more powerful gun than was formerly the case. A gun weighing 24 cwt. in action is about as heavy as a detachment of six can man-handle.

The power of a field gun is measured by its muzzle energy, which is proportional to the weight of the shell multiplied by the square of its velocity. The muzzle energy varies in different equipments from 230 to 380 foot-tons. Details of the power, weight and dimensions of the guns of the principal military nations are given in Table A.

A gun of given weight and power may fire a heavy shell with a low velocity, or a light shell with a high velocity. High velocity is the gunner's ideal, for it implies a flat trajectory and a small angle of descent. The bullets when blown forward out of the shrapnel fly at first almost parallel to the surface of the ground, covering at medium ranges a depth of some 350 yards, as against half that distance for a low-velocity gun. Under modern tactical conditions a deep zone of shrapnel effect is most desirable. On the other hand, for a given power of gun, flatness of trajectory means a corresponding reduction in the weight of the shell; that is, in the number of shrapnel bullets discharged per minute. We have accordingly to compromise between high velocity and great shell power. Thus the British field gun fires an 18½ lb shell with muzzle velocity of 1590 ft. per second, while the French gun, which is practically of the same power, fires a 16 lb shell with M.V. of 1740 f.s. Again, a shell of given weight may be fired either from a large-bore gun or from a small-bore gun; in the latter case the length of the shell will be proportionately increased. The small-bore gun is naturally the lighter of the two. But the longer the shell the thicker must its walls be, in order not to break up or collapse in the gun. The shorter the shell, the higher is the percentage of useful weight, consisting of powder and bullets, which it contains. We must, therefore, compromise between these antagonistic conditions, and select the calibre which gives the maximum useful weight of projectiles for a given weight of equipment. In practice it is found that a calibre of 3 in. is best suited to a shell weighing 15 lb; and that, starting with this ratio, the calibre should vary as the cube root of the weight of the shell.

As to rifling, the relative advantages of uniform and increasing twist are disputed. The British field guns are rifled with uniform twist, but the balance of European opinion is in favour of a twist increasing from 1 turn in 50 calibres at the breech to 1 in 25 at the muzzle. Mathematically, the development of the groove is a parabola.

For field guns the favourite breech actions are the interrupted screw and the wedge. The latter is simpler, but affords a less powerful extractor for throwing out the empty cartridge case. This point is of importance, since cartridge cases hastily manufactured in war time might not all be true to gauge. Modern guns have percussion locks, in which a striker impinges upon a cap in the base of the metallic cartridge. All Q.F. guns have repeating trip-locks. In these, when the firing-lever or lanyard is pulled, the striker is first drawn back and then released, allowing it to fly forward against the cap. The gun is usually fired by the gun-layer; it is found that he lays more steadily if he knows that the gun cannot go off till he is ready. A field gun has to be sighted (see SIGHTS) for laying (a) by direct vision (b) by clinometer and aiming-point (see ARTILLERY). The first purpose is served by the ordinary and telescopic sights; the second by the goniometric sight or the panorama sight. The

TABLE A—FIELD GUNS

(Corrected to May 1, 1910, in accordance with Bethell's "Modern Guns and Gunnery," 3rd edition.)

	Austria 1905	Belgium 1905	Brazil 1904	Denmark 1902	France 1898–1902	Germany 1906	Great Britain F.A. 1903	Great Britain H.A. 1903	Italy 1906	Japan 1905	Rumania 1904	Russia 1903	Spain 1906	Switzerland 1903	United States 1902
Calibre, inches	3·01	2·95	2·95	2·95	2·95	3·03	3·3	3·3	2·95	2·95	2·95	3	2·95	2·95	3
Weight of shrapnel, lb.	14·72	14·3	12·1	14·85	15·96	15	18·48	12·54	14·3	14·3	14·3	14·41*	14·3	14	15
Number of bullets	316–416	300	338	595	300	300	364	263	300	210	295	260	294	210	252
Number of bullets to the lb.	50 and 35	50	42	41½	38	45	42	42	50	56¼	42	42	45	52½	36½
Whether H.E. shell carried	Yes	Yes	Yes	No	Yes	Yes	No	No	Yes	Yes	Yes	Yes	Yes	Yes	Yes
Muzzle velocity, f.-s.	1640	1640	1600	1640	1739	1525	1590	1658	1675	1706	1640	1930	1640	1590	1700
Muzzle energy, ft.-tons	275	266	215	277	334	242	324	239	279	288	267	373	267	267	300
Weight of gun, cwt.	7	6·67	5·7	6·42	9	7·66	9	8	6·9	6·8*	7·37	7·85	6·67	6·48	6·9
Weight of gun and limber	20	20	16·3	20·5	22·4	18·6	24·75	19·5	19·75	19·7	21	20·75	20·4	19·75	21
Maximum elevation, degrees	37·5	34·5	26·7	36·6	37	34·4	40	33·5	33·45	33·25	34·8	38·5	34·2	35·5	37·3
Traverse each way, degrees	18	15	17	15	17	16	16	17	17	17*	16	16½	16	16	16
Length of recoil, inches	4	3½	3	3½	3	4	4	3	3½	3	3½	2½	3	2	4
Height of wheels	55·3	55·3	4·3	54·3	43	44	48	48	57	55	55	4·5	50	55	50
Line of sight, whether independent	4·3	4·31*		4·3*	4*	4·51*	4·6*	4·8*	4·31*	4·31*	4·31*	4*	4·31*	4·31*	4·8*
Sights, goniometric, telescopic, panoramic, or ordinary	No	Yes	No	No	Yes	Yes	Yes	Yes	Yes	No	No	No	Yes	No	No
Length of gun, calibres	P. 30	P. 30	T.G. 28	T.G. 30	G. 36	T.G. 27·3	T.P. 29·4	T.P. 24·4	T.P. 30	T.G. 30	T.G. 30	O.P. 30	T.G. 30	O. 30	O.P. 29·2
Breech action, wedge, swinging block, or eccentric screw	W. 0·18	W. 0·2	W. 0·177	W. 0·236	E.S. 0·2	W. 0·135	S.R. 0·155*	S.R. 0·155*	W. 0·1575	W. 0·118	W. 0·236	S.R. 0·2	S.R. 0·16	W. 0·17	S.R. 0·2
Thickness of shield, inches	P.	P.	P.	P.	A.	P.	P.	P.	P.	P.	P.	A.	A.	P.	P.
Traverse on pivot or along axle	33	40	32	44	24	36	24	24	32	36	24	36	38	40	36
Number of rounds in limber	30	40	40	48	24	36	28	28	32	36	24	40	38	48	36
Number of rounds in wagon limber	60	61	40	72	72	52	48	48	64	60	64	48	60	48	70
Number of rounds in wagon body	168	242	192	284	312	1261	176	176	224	228	288	212	278	280	358*
Weight of wagon, packed cwt.	38·5	35·3	24	39·4	38·5	35	36·75	30·5	36	34·5*	34	36	34	35·3	37
No. of guns in battery	6	4	4	4	4	6	6	6	12	12	12	8	4	4	4
No. of wagons in battery	9	8	8	8	12	61	12	12	12	12	12	16	10	10	12
Maker	State, Skoda & Ehrhardt	Krupp & Cockerill	Krupp	Krupp	State	State	State, Elswick Ordnance Co., Vickers, Maxim and Coventry Ordnance Works		Krupp	State and Krupp	Krupp	Putilow	Schneider	Krupp	State and Ehrhardt

These weights do not include the gunners and kits.   Doubtful figures are marked thus.*

† In addition to the wagons with light ammunition column, now raised to 6½ per battery.   * Including four rounds with gun

independent line of sight is an arrangement of sights and elevating gear found in many modern field guns, which divides between two gunners the work of aiming (called *laying*) the gun, and of giving it the elevation required to hit the target.

In fig. 59 the gun is shown mounted on an intermediate carriage elevated and depressed by the screw A. The telescopic

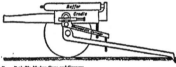

From Bethell's *Modern Guns and Gunnery*.

FIG. 59.—Diagram illustrating the independent line of sight.

or ordinary sight is fixed to this carriage. The gun, in its cradle, is elevated and depressed by the screw B. To lay the gun, the layer works the laying screw A till the telescope points at the target; the gun also, if no elevation has been given, is then pointing straight at the target. To give the gun the elevation necessary for the range, the elevating number on the right of the gun now works the elevating screw B till the gun is sufficiently elevated, the amount given being shown in yards of range on a drum. The motion given to the gun does not disturb the intermediate carriage with the telescope attached to it, and the telescope still remains layed on the target. Once the sights are layed on the target, the elevation of the gun may be changed in a moment by a turn of the elevating wheel, without disturbing the laying. The layer does not have to concern himself about the elevation; he has only to keep his sights on the target while the other numbers continue the service of the gun. This device is especially valuable when firing at moving targets, when the range and the laying have to be altered simultaneously.

The same result may also be obtained by other mechanical devices without the use of the intermediate carriage. Thus the British field guns have a long elevating screw with the sight connected to its centre, the lower end passing through a nut at the side of the upper carriage, the upper end through a nut at the side of the cradle. Then, if the lower nut be turned by the laying wheel, the screw, the sight and the gun will go up or down together; if the upper nut be turned by the elevating wheel, the gun will go up or down the screw without moving the sights. Colonel Scott's "automatic" line of sight is an improvement on the ordinary gear in that the sight can be cross-levelled to eliminate the error due to difference of level of wheels. Krupp has a similar device in which the sight-socket is on the cradle so that it can be cross-levelled. The sight itself is connected to the elevating gear, and is screwed out of its socket as the breech of the gun is depressed, so that the sight remains in the same place.

Construction of the Gun.—Field guns are made of steel, usually containing a small percentage of nickel or chromium, or both, and having a tensile breaking strain of about 50 tons per square inch. In Austria, for facility of local manufacture, hard-drawn bronze is still used, although this is considerably heavier than steel.

The Carriage (see ARTILLERY, Plate I.).—The first field guns used in war were supported by crossed stakes under the muzzle and anchored by a spike on the breech which penetrated into the ground. The next improvement was to mount the gun on a sleigh. This method is still used in Norway and in Canada. The next step was to mount the gun on a two-wheeled carriage, connected to a second two-wheeled carriage (the limber) by a flexible coupling. For centuries the gun-carriage was a rigid construction, recoiling on firing, and having to be run up by hand after each round. In 1895 spring-spade equipments were introduced. In these a spade attached to a helical spring was set under the carriage; on discharge the spade dug into the ground, compressing the spring as the carriage recoiled. The extension of the spring ran the gun up again without assistance from the gunners.

The British 15 pr. used in the South African War (1899–1902) had a spring spade carriage designed by Sir George Clark. Similar equipments were introduced by several continental powers. The Japanese gun used in Manchuria (1904) had dragshoes attached by wire ropes passing round drums on the wheels to a strong spring in the trail. On recoil the wheels revolved backwards, compressing the spring; after recoil the pull of the spring on the wire ropes revolved the wheels forward and returned the gun to its former position. The Italian 1902 semi-Q.F. carriage was constructed on a very similar principle. All these semi-Q.F. equipments were open to the objection that the gunners had to stand clear of the shield every time the gun was fired. They have since been superseded by Q.F. gun-recoil equipments.

The gun-carriage must be strong enough to carry the gun across country, and it must be so constructed as not to move when the gun is fired. If the gun-carriage were allowed to recoil to the rear on discharge, the gunners would have to stand clear on firing, abandoning the protection of the shield, and, moreover, the loss of time entailed by running and relaying the gun would render the fire slow. The requirement of steadiness of the carriage is met by allowing the gun itself to recoil on its carriage. Its motion is gradually checked by the hydraulic buffer (see below) and the gun is returned to the firing position by helical springs, or, in the French, Spanish and Portuguese equipments, by compressed air. The carriage is held from recoiling by a spade fixed to the point of the trail, which digs into the earth on discharge, and (usually) by brakes on the wheels. This is known as the gun-recoil system, and is now universally adopted. Field guns constructed on this principle are styled Q.F., or quick-firing, guns.

Steadiness of Carriage.—In the gun-recoil equipment the constructional difficulty lies not in preventing the carriage from recoiling but in preventing the wheels from rising off the ground on the shock of discharge. The force of recoil of the gun, acting in the line of motion of the centre of gravity of the recoiling parts, tends to turn the carriage over backwards about the point of the trail, or, more correctly, about the centre of the spade. This force is resisted by the weight of the gun and carriage, which tends to keep the wheels on the ground. The leverage with which the overturning force acts is that due to the distance of its line of motion above the centre of the spade; the leverage with which the steadying force acts is that due to the horizontal distance of the centre of gravity of the gun and carriage from the centre of the spade. If the force of recoil be 6 ft.-tons, and if it be absorbed during a recoil of 3 ft., the average overturning force is 2 tons; since the weight of the gun in action may not greatly exceed 1 ton, the trail must be so long as to give a leverage of at least two to one in favour of the steadying force. It follows from the above that the steadiness of the carriage, for a given muzzle energy, may be promoted by four factors. (a) Increasing the weight of the gun and recoiling parts. This reduces the recoil-energy. (b) Increasing the length of recoil allowed. This reduces the overturning pull. (c) Keeping the gun as low as possible, either by reducing the height of the wheels, or by cranking the axle-tree downwards. This reduces the leverage of the overturning force. (d) Increasing the length of the trail. This increases the leverage of the steadying force.

It will be seen from Table A that the condition of steadiness is satisfied in the various Q.F. equipments by not very dissimilar combinations of the above factors.

The *cradle* is the portion of the carriage upon which the gun slides when it recoils. It also contains the buffer and running-up springs, which are fixed either above or below the gun. The latter method gives the stronger and simpler construction, and is favoured by all nations except Great Britain. By putting the buffer on top the gun can be set lower on the carriage, which is an advantage as regards steadiness. A top-socket cradle is of ring section, surrounding the gun; the gun is formed with ribs or guides extending for its whole length, which, on recoil, slide in grooves in the cradle. The cradle is pivoted on horizontal trunnions to the intermediate carriage and carries the buffer and springs on top. This construction is shown in the illustration of the 18 pr. Q.F. gun (fig. 60, Plate III.).

In carriages having the buffer under the gun the cradle is a trough of steel plate, usually closed in at the top. It has guides formed on the upper edges fitted to take guide-blocks on the gun. The cradle contains the buffer-cylinder, which is fixed to a horn projecting downwards from the breech of the gun, and recoils with it; the piston-rod is fixed to the front of the cradle. The running-up springs are usually coiled round the buffer-cylinder, and, on recoil, are compressed between a shoulder on the front end of the cylinder and the rear plate of the cradle.

The cradle is mounted on a vertical pivot set in a saddle pivoted on horizontal trunnions between the sides of the trail (Krupp) or, as in the earlier Ehrhardt equipments, the vertical pivot is set in the axletree itself, which has then to turn when the gun is elevated or depressed. The Krupp cradle is shown in the drawing of the German gun.

The *buffer* consists of a steel cylinder nearly filled with oil or glycerine. In this cylinder works a piston with piston-rod attached to the carriage; the cylinder is attached to the gun. On recoil the piston is drawn fron one end of the cylinder to the other, so that the liquid is forced to flow past the piston. The friction thus caused gradually absorbs the energy of recoil of the gun and brings it gently to a standstill. As the gun recoils the centre of gravity of the gun and carriage shifts to the rear, reducing the stability. The buffer-resistance has to be gradually reduced proportionately to the reduced stability. To allow the liquid to flow past the piston, grooves (called *ports*) are formed in the sides of the cylinder, and by varying the depth of the grooves at different points the resistance can be adjusted as required.

Running-up Gear.—In compressed-air equipments a separate piston is attached to the gun, working in a cylinder on the carriage connected with a reservoir of air at a pressure of about 300 ℔ to the square inch. This gear is much lighter than the springs, but the difficulty of keeping the piston and gland tight is a serious objection to it, although this difficulty is partly overcome by filling the cylinder with glycerine so that the air has no direct access to the piston or the gland. In spring equipments the principal difficulty lies in providing a sufficient length of recoil without undue compression of the column of springs. Thus if the spring column be 6 ft. long and the gun recoils 4½ ft. the springs are compressed into a space of 1½ ft., or a quarter of their working length. This treatment is liable to crush the springs. German gun-makers get over this difficulty by the use of very high-class springs made of steel having a tenacity of about 140 tons to the square inch with an elastic limit of 90 tons. They also use a valve in the buffer piston which relieves the springs of resistance in running-up, and so allows slighter springs to be used. But in England the telescopic spring-case patented by the Elswick Ordnance Company is preferred. Suppose that the spring-columns before firing are each 4 ft. long; then if the telescopic gear be pulled out for a distance of 4 ft. on recoil, each spring column will be compressed to 2 ft., or only to half its length. Tensile running-up springs are used by some firms, as Cockerill of Seraing (Liége). They are open to the objection that if a spring breaks the gun is for the time being rendered useless, which is not the case with compression springs.

The intermediate carriage is used chiefly in equipments with buffer above the gun; it serves as a means of connecting the cradle to the lower carriage. When the spade is fixed in the ground it is impossible to shift the carriage laterally in order to correct the aim, the intermediate carriage is therefore pivoted so that it can traverse laterally about 3 degrees each way. Instead of using an intermediate carriage the direction may be given to the gun by shifting the whole carriage sideways along the axle in an arc about the point of the trail, which is fixed by the spade. This system is used in guns of French manufacture and in the 1902 Russian gun. It is simple in action, but requires the shield to be cut away on either side to clear the wheels at extreme traverse.

The trail is either a drawn steel tube, of circular section as in the 18 pr., or of closed U section as in the Ehrhardt carriages, or else a box trail built up of sheet steel. In the Krupp equipments the trail is bent downwards to give a greater range of elevation to the gun.

Elevating Gear, in order to save space, is usually of the telescopic screw pattern, in which one screw is inside the other so that the two pack into half the length of a single screw. The angle is of the shape shown in the illustration of the 18 pr. Q F. gun. For equipments which may have to be used on rock, such as the Swiss gun, the spade is made to fold upwards when desired. The axletree is usually a hollow steel forging with the ends tapered to receive the wheels. The wheels are of wood, with naves of stamped steel. Steel wheels have been tried but are less elastic than wood and have been found unsuitable. England and the United States use 4 ft. 8 in. wheels; most European nations use wheels 4 ft. 3½ in. in diameter.

The *shield* is made of hard steel, from 0·12 to 0·236 in. thick. The size and thickness of the shield are limited by considerations of weight. Thus if 150 ℔ of weight be available this will provide a shield about 5 ft. square and 3½ mm. or 0·138 in. thick, proof against rifle bullets at distances over 600 yds., and against shrapnel bullets at all distances. The present tendency, since the introduction of the French D bullet and German S bullet (see AMMUNITION: *Bullet*), is to make shields thicker than this, 5 mm. or 0·2 in. being the usual thickness.

Recent Developments of the Q.F. Gun-Carriage.—The principle of "differential" recoil gear is as follows: Suppose an ordinary Q.F. field gun held in the recoil position by a catch, loaded, released and allowed to fly forward under the action of the running-up springs. A valve in the buffer relieves the gun of any resistance to running-up. While in rapid motion forward the gun is fired by a tripper which catches the firing lever. The gun then returns to the recoil position and is again held by the catch. On firing, the recoil-velocity is reduced by the amount of the forward velocity previously imparted to the gun. Thus if the ordinary recoil-velocity of a Q.F. gun be 30 f.s., and if it be fired while running up at a velocity of 10 f.s., the recoil-velocity with respect to the carriage will be only 20 f.s. And since the recoil-energy is proportional to the weight of the gun multiplied by the square of the recoil-velocity, the recoil-energy is reduced in the proportion of 900 to 400, or roughly by one-half. This halves the overturning stress on the carriage, and renders it possible to make the gun and carriage lighter for the same power, or to obtain greater power for the same weight. This increase of efficiency is due to the fact that the whole of the recoil-energy is not, as in ordinary Q.F. guns, absorbed by the friction in the buffer, but that part of it is stored up and used to counteract the recoil of the next round. If the hydraulic buffer be dispensed with, and the whole of the recoil taken on the springs or compressed air gear,

the overturning stress is reduced to one-fourth of its normal amount. One practical difficulty in the way of applying the differential system to field guns lies in the vibration and slight lateral motion of the carriage during running-up. Since this motion takes place after laying and before firing, it is liable to cause inaccuracy. The only equipment on this principle as yet in use is the French 1907 mountain gun referred to below.

"Semi-automatic" Q.F. field and mountain guns are made by the leading firms, but have not been generally introduced. In these equipments the breech is thrown open by tripping gear during the run-up, and the cartridge case is ejected. When the gun is reloaded the action of introducing the cartridge releases the breech-block, which is closed by a spring. In the Krupp semi-automatic gun the breech-block is set vertically to facilitate loading. This equipment is capable of firing thirty rounds per minute. The principal advantage of the semi-automatic system lies not in the increased rate of fire but in the fact that three gunners are sufficient to carry out the service of the gun. This is of importance in mountain equipments, where the size of the shield is limited.

The introduction of airships into military operations has produced the anti-airship gun, which differs from the ordinary field gun in almost every respect. The attack of airships presents special problems. High elevation, higher even than the howitzer's, may have to be given, and, unlike the howitzer, the airship gun must be a high-velocity weapon, both ranging power and flatness of trajectory being essential. As regards the shell, to bring down a gas-bag, or even to kill a crew, with time shrapnel is difficult, owing to the speed of the airship and the difficulty of observing bursts. Direct hits with ordinary shell are equally hard to obtain, unless the balloon is stationary and the range known. Even if such a hit were got, the ordinary fuse would not act on encountering the slight resistance of the balloon envelope. As regards the equipment, the absorption of recoil at high elevations presents difficulties, the exaggeration of the angle of sight makes the sighting arrangements complicated, and rapidity in changing the line of fire is essential. The most powerful equipment that, in June 1910, had been constructed to meet these conditions was the Krupp 75 mm., which is mounted on a motor lorry, the weight of the equipment and carriage, without gunners, being about 4⅓ tons. The equipment is constructed on the differential principle, with rear trunnions on the cradle. The shell is a 12 ℔ H.E., fitted with a highly sensitive fuse and containing, beside the H.E. burster, a quantity of composition which gives off a trail of smoke to facilitate ranging.

The British 18-pr. Q.F. Field Gun (1905) (see Plate III., figs. 60 and 61) also ARTILLERY, Plate II.).—Taking fig. 60 from the top, we see the buffer, telescopic spring-case and springs on top of the cradle, the buffer being attached to the horn projecting upwards from the breech. The cradle, of bronze, surrounds the gun, and is pivoted on horizontal trunnions on the upper carriage. The gun recoils in the cradle on the guide ribs, which extend for its whole length. The upper carriage is pivoted vertically on the trail and is traversed by the handle seen below the breech. The long elevating screw is formed as a telescopic screw at its lower end to avoid any downward projection; the screw does not turn, but the nut at bottom raises the gun, screw and sights for laying, while the nut at top raises and lowers the gun alone for giving elevation. The tubular trail supports the brake-arms, which also carry the seats for the layer and elevating number. The spade and traversing hand-spike are seen at the end of the trail. The telescopic sight is on the left of the gun. The shield is curved well back to give as much protection as possible to the detachment. The lower portion of the shield is hinged and folds up for travelling.

The French Q.F. Field Gun (1898) (fig. 62, Plate III.; see also ARTILLERY, Plate II.).—This is a powerful gun, of unusual length, namely 36 calibres. The breech mechanism is of the eccentric screw type (see Part I. of this article). The gun has compressed-air running-up gear and traverses along the axletree. The carriage is anchored by a trail spade and two brake-blocks which are arranged so as to go under the wheels, forming dragshoes, on firing. This method of anchoring causes some delay on coming into action and considerable delay in changing on to a fresh target. The gun has a goniometric sight with independent line of sight. The body of the ammunition wagon is tilted alongside the gun, and, with its armoured bottom and steel doors, forms a good protection for the gunners supplying ammunition.

The German Q.F. Field Gun (1906) (fig. 63).—This is the 1896 gun remounted on a Q.F. carriage. It is not a powerful gun, the ballistics being the same as those of the British 15-pr. B.L. of 1893. It has a single-motion wedge breech action. The gun is mounted on a cradle with buffer and springs under the gun; the cradle traverses on a vertical pivot set in a traversing bed which turns about the axletree. The gun has an arc sight with prismatic telescope and a clinometer mounted on it, and a circular laying-plane for laying on an auxiliary mark. It has not the independent line of sight. The shield is in three pieces, the top flap folding down for travelling. The carriage stands perfectly steady on discharge.

The Russian Q.F. Field Gun (1903) is intended as an improvement on the French gun, being of even greater power. Springs are used for running-up instead of compressed air. To ensure steadiness the gun is kept very low on the carriage; this is effected by the use of a cranked axletree. The gun has not the independent line of sight, but has a panorama sight. It traverses on the axletree.

The Danish Q.F. Field Gun (fig. 64, Plate IV.) is a good example of the heavier or more powerful type of Krupp field gun. The gun may be seen supported on the cradle, which contains the hydraulic buffer and running-up springs. The wedge breech-block is open.

Horse Artillery Guns.—A horse artillery gun must be mobile enough to accompany cavalry. This is secured partly by the adoption of a light type of gun, partly by carrying the gunners on horseback instead of on the carriage. It is considered that the weight behind the team should not exceed 30 cwt. The Germans have declined to introduce a special type of light gun, as they

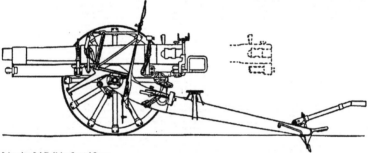

Redrawn from Bethell's *Modern Guns and Gunnery.*

Fig. 63.—The German Q.F. Gun. C. 96. n./A. (1906).

The arc sight with panorama telescope is seen behind the shield, which is curved backwards for better protection. The seats for the gunners who lay and attend to the breech are on either side of the trail. At the point of the trail are the spade, the traversing lever and the trail eye by which the gun is limbered up.

The American Q.F. Field Gun.—This is an example of the Ehrhardt type of gun. It is considerably more powerful than the field guns adopted by most European powers. Steadiness is ensured by making the trail 10½ ft. long, or 1½ ft. longer than the Krupp trail. The construction is otherwise very similar to that of the Krupp gun shown in fig. 64, Plate IV. Four rounds are carried in tubes on the carriage.

Other Q.F. Equipments.—These closely resemble the standard types of their makers, as given in the above table of field guns. The Swiss and Dutch guns are light Krupps; the Spanish and Portuguese guns, by Schneider of Creusôt, are improved and lighter models of the French gun.

The new Italian gun is a medium Krupp. The Austrian gun is similar to the American (Ehrhardt) but the gun itself is of bronze.

object to the complication entailed by the supply of two natures of ammunition on the battlefield. The H.A. guns of other nations are merely lighter and less powerful editions of their field guns.

The Q.F. Field Howitzer.—A field howitzer is a gun capable of throwing a shell weighing 35 to 45 lb at high angles of elevation, and light enough to manœuvre at a trot across open country. The permissible weight of the equipment is but slightly greater than that of a field gun. The object of the howitzer is to throw a heavy shell with an angle of descent of not less than 25°, so as to destroy overhead cover with high-explosive shell, and to search entrenchments and reach gunners behind their gun-shields with shrapnel. Effect is obtained, not by the striking velocity of the shell, but by the amount of its high-explosive burster, or, in the case of shrapnel fire, by the use of a large driving charge in the base of the shell which gives the necessary forward and downward velocity to the bullets.

Since the muzzle energy of a howitzer is limited by the weight of the equipment, the heavy shell can only be fired with a low velocity,

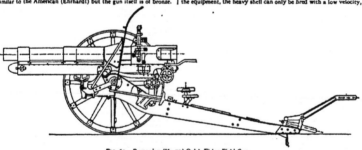

Fig. 65.—Rumanian (Krupp) Quick-Firing Field Gun.

The Rumanian Q.F. field gun (fig. 65) is a recent type of medium Krupp gun. The shield is set well back, and has a hood projecting forwards and fitting close to the gun. The brake is used for travelling only; the brake-wheel is seen in front of the shield. The panorama telescope is mounted on top of the arc sight; no foresight is used. There are no axletree seats, the gunners being carried on the gun limber and wagon limber. The wagon body (fig. 66) is tipped beside the gun in action.

usually not exceeding 1000 ft. per second. And in order to secure a steep angle of descent at short ranges this velocity is still further reduced by using half and quarter charges.

The construction of the howitzer is much the same as that of a gun. The calibre is usually between 4·3 and 4·7 in., and the length does not much exceed 12 calibres. Case ammunition is used, and the breech action is similar to that of a Q.F. gun. Howitzers are usually provided with shields in order to enable them to come into action in the open when necessary. At short ranges, with full charge, they make very powerful guns.

Construction of the Carriage.—The gun-recoil system is used as in a gun equipment. There is however one important difference. If the recoil allowed be sufficient to keep the carriage steady at low elevations, then when fired at an elevation of 45° the breech will strike the ground. This may be to some extent avoided by placing the trunnions of the cradle which supports the howitzer at the extreme rear end, so that when elevated the breech of the howitzer is not brought any nearer the ground (Krupp). One objection to this is that the forward preponderance of the howitzer has to be balanced by a spring to enable it to be elevated.

A second method is known as *controlled recoil*. The buffer-liquid, on recoil, has to pass through holes in the piston. The access of the buffer-liquid to these holes is controlled by a disk valve rotated by rifled grooves in the cylinder. By connecting the piston-rod to the carriage so as to rotate the piston when the gun is elevated, the area of the holes exposed by the disk valve can be decreased at high elevations so as to shorten the recoil. This is known as the Vavasseur-Ehrhardt control valve. Messrs Cockerill use a channel through which the liquid is forced on recoil, which is partly closed by a stopcock connected to the left trunnion when the howitzer is elevated. The running-up springs require to be strong in order to lift the weight of the howitzer at 45° elevation In most equipments twin columns of springs are used.

The Ehrhardt Q.F. Field Howitzer, fig. 67 (Plate IV.), may be taken as a type of the light field howitzer with controlled recoil, as opposed

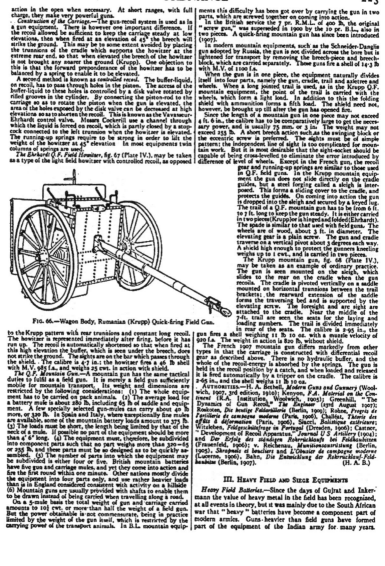

FIG. 66.—Wagon Body, Rumanian (Krupp) Quick-firing Field Gun.

to the Krupp pattern with rear trunnions and constant long recoil. The howitzer is represented immediately after firing, before it has run up. The recoil is automatically shortened so that when fired at this high elevation the buffer, which is seen under the breech, does not strike the ground. The sights are on the bar which passes through the shield. . The calibre is 4·7 in.: the howitzer fires a 46 lb shell with M.V. 985 f.s., and weighs 25 cwt. in action with shield.

The Q.F. Mountain Gun.—A mountain gun has the same tactical duties to fulfil as a field gun. It is merely a field gun sufficiently mobile for mountain transport. Its weight and dimensions are restricted by the following considerations: (1) The whole equipment has to be carried on pack animals. (2) The average load for a battery mule is about 280 lb, including 65 lb of saddle and equipment. A few specially selected gun-mules can carry about 40 lb more, or 320 lb. In Spain and Italy, where exceptionally fine mules are available, some of the mountain battery loads amount to 375 lb. (3) The loads must be short, the length being limited by that of the neck of a mule. If possible no part of the equipment should be more than 4′ 6″ long. (4) The equipment must, therefore, be subdivided into component parts such that no part weighs more than 320–65 or 255 lb, and these parts must be so designed as to be quickly assembled. (5) The number of parts into which the equipment may be subdivided is either four or five. British mountain batteries have five gun and carriage mules, and yet they come into action and fire the first round within one minute. Other nations mostly divide the equipment into four parts only, and use rather heavier loads than is in England considered consistent with activity on a hillside (6) Mountain guns are usually provided with shafts to enable them to be drawn instead of being carried when travelling along a road.

On a 5-mule basis the total weight of gun and carriage carried amounts to 10½ cwt. or more than half the weight of a field gun. But the power obtainable is not commensurate, being in practice limited by the weight of the gun itself, which is restricted by the carrying power of the transport animals. In B.L. mountain equip-

ments this difficulty has been got over by carrying the gun in two parts, which are screwed together on coming into action.

In the British service the 7 pr. R.M.L. of 400 lb, the original " screw gun," was superseded in 1900 by the 10 pr. B.L., also in two pieces. A quick-firing mountain gun has since been introduced (1907).

In modern mountain equipments, such as the Schneider-Danglis gun adopted by Russia, the gun is not divided across the bore but is lightened for transport by removing the breech-piece and breech-block, which are carried separately. These guns fire a shell of 14·3 lb with M.V. of 1100 f.s.

When the gun is in one piece, the equipment naturally divides itself into four parts, namely the gun, cradle, trail and axletree and wheels. When a long jointed trail is used, as in the Krupp Q.F. mountain equipment, the point of the trail is carried with the wheels, which form a light load. In addition to this the folding shield with ammunition forms a fifth load. The shield need not, however, be brought up till after the gun has opened fire.

Since the length of a mountain gun in one piece may not exceed 4 ft. 6 in., the calibre has to be comparatively large to get the necessary power, and is usually 75 mm. or 3 in. The weight may not exceed 255 lb. A short breech action such as the swinging block or the eccentric screw is preferred. The sights must be of simple pattern; the independent line of sight is too complicated for mountain work. But it is most desirable that the sight-socket should be capable of being cross-levelled to eliminate the error introduced by difference of level of wheels. Except in the French gun, the recoil gear and running-up springs are similar to those used in Q.F. field guns. In the Krupp mountain equipment the gun does not slide directly on the cradle guides, but a steel forging called a sleigh is interposed. This forms a sliding cover to the cradle, and protects the guides. On coming into action the gun is dropped into the sleigh and secured by a keyed lug. The trail of a Q.F. mountain gun has to be from 6 ft. to 7 ft. long to keep the gun steady. It is either carried in two pieces (Krupp) or is hinged and folded (Ehrhardt). The spade is similar to that used with field guns. The wheels are of wood, about 3 ft. in diameter. The elevating gear is a plain screw. The gun and cradle traverse on a vertical pivot about 3 degrees each way. A shield high enough to protect the gunners kneeling weighs up to 1 cwt. and is carried in two pieces.

The Krupp mountain gun, fig. 68 (Plate IV.), may be taken as an example of ordinary practice. The gun is seen mounted on the sleigh, which slides to the rear on the cradle when the gun recoils. The cradle is pivoted vertically on a saddle mounted on horizontal trunnions between the trail brackets; the rearward extension of the saddle forms the traversing bed and is supported by the elevating screw. The foresight and arc sight are attached to the cradle. Near the middle of the 7-ft. trail are seen the seats for the laying and loading numbers. The trail is divided immediately in rear of the seats. The calibre is 2·95 in., the gun fires a shell weighing 11 lb 10 oz. with a muzzle velocity of 920 f.s. The weight in action is 820 lb, without shield.

The French 1907 mountain gun differs markedly from other types in that the carriage is constructed with differential recoil gear as described above. There is no hydraulic buffer, and the whole of the recoil-energy is absorbed by the springs. The gun is held in the recoil position by a catch, and when loaded and released it is fired automatically by a tripper on the cradle. The calibre is 2·95 in., and the shell weighs 11 lb 10 oz.

AUTHORITIES.—H. A. Bethell, *Modern Guns and Gunnery* (Woolwich, 1907, 3rd edition, 1910); Kenyon, *F.A. Material on the Continent* (R.A. Institution, Woolwich, 1905); Greenhill, " The Dynamics of Gun Recoil," *The Engineer* (23rd August 1907); Rookoten, *Die heutige Feldartillerie* (Berlin, 1909); Rohne, *Progrès de l'artillerie de campagne moderne* (Paris, 1906), Challéat, *Théorie des affûts à déformation* (Paris, 1906), Sacci, *Balistique extérieure*; Witzleben, *Feldgeschützfrage im Portugal* (Dresden, 1906); Castner, " Development of Recoil Apparatus." *Journal U S Artillery* (1904); and *Der Erfolg des ständigen Rohrrücklaufs bei Feldhaubitzen* (Frauenfeld, 1906); v. Reichenau, *Munitionsausrüstung* (Berlin, 1905), *Shrapnels et boucliers* and *L'Obusier de campagne moderne* (Lucerne, 1906), Bahn, *Die Entwicklung der Rohrrücklauf-Feldhaubitze* (Berlin, 1907). (H. A. B.)

III. HEAVY FIELD AND SIEGE EQUIPMENTS

Heavy Field Batteries.—Since the days of Gujrat and Inkermann the value of heavy metal in the field has been recognized, at all events in theory, but it was mainly due to the South African war that " heavy " batteries have become a component part of modern armies. Guns heavier than field guns have formed part of the equipment of the Indian army for many years.

but they have existed for a specific purpose, and ordnance originally designed for quite other functions has, from the exigencies of war, been occasionally utilized in the field, as was the case in South Africa and Manchuria, but the heavy field battery as we know it to-day is a new military product. Its rôle is an extensive one, as it embraces many of the functions of ordinary field guns as well as some of those usually attributed to light siege pieces. In the heavy field armaments of the Powers as they stand at the present time will be found guns, howitzers and mortars, and projectiles that vary from 50 ℔ to more than five times that weight, and no boundary line can be assigned which will separate these field equipments from those of the light units of a siege train It will be convenient to consider in turn the three natures of ordnance (guns, howitzers and mortars) employed and to quote some typical instances of each kind

The United States 60 pr. Gun.—This gun and its equipment are of modern type (1904) Its general appearance is shown in figs. 69 and 70, Plate V. The calibre is 4·7″; the charge 5·94 ℔ of smokeless powder and the muzzle velocity developed is 1700 f.s. Fixed ammunition is employed, and with an elevation of 15° the range is 7600 yds The weight of the equipment limbered up is given as 71½ cwt.: it is known as a siege gun

In its general aspect the carriage resembles a field carriage, but of stronger type, with a special arrangement of cradle.

In fig. 71 two sections are given; the cradle, it will be seen, consists of three cylinders (seen in section in the upper figure) which

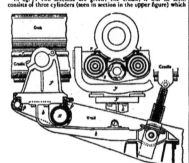

FIG. 71.—Diagram of 4·7-in. Siege Gun, U.S.A.

b, Traversing bracket.   *r,* Rails.   *z,* Axle.
p, Pintle bearing.   *s,* Spring cylinders.   *t,* Pintle yoke.

are bound together by broad steel bands; the two outer cylinders carry rails *r* upon which the gun slides in recoil. The centre cylinder contains the hydraulic gear for checking recoil, the two outer contain the running-up springs *s.* These springs are arranged in three concentric columns, the front end of each outer column being connected to the rear end of the next inner column by a steel tube, flanged outwardly at the front end and inwardly at the rear end. A rod carrying a head which acts on the inner coil only passes through the centre of the cylinder and is fixed to a yoke that is connected with a lug at the breech of the gun. The flanged tubes thus convey the pressure from the innermost coil to the next outer coil and finally to the outermost coil, so that in each cylinder the springs work in tandem and have a long stroke with short assembled length. It is thus seen that the recoil takes place partially on the carriage and only a portion of the energy remains to tend to cause movement in the mounting.

The cradle is supported by trunnions in the casting *y,* which is itself seated in the casting *p,* which forms a bearing for it. This bearing is mounted between the front ends of the trail brackets, its rear end embracing the hollow axle *z.* Attached to the lower surface of *y* is the traversing bracket *b,* which extends to the rear under the axle and forms a support for the traversing shaft *t* and for the elevating mechanism.

For travelling (Plate V., fig. 69) the gun is withdrawn to the rear and the breech is attached to a holding-down arrangement about the middle of the trail. A spade is hinged at the point of the trail.

The British 60 pr. Gun.—This is known as a heavy battery gun; its calibre is 5″, its length 32 calibres, its weight 39 cwt.; its charge is 9¾ ℔ of cordite, its muzzle velocity 2080 f.s. and its effective shrapnel range 10,000 yds. The weight behind the team is 106 cwts., 3 qrs.

The German 10 cm. Gun is called a heavy battery gun; its calibre is 4″, its effective shrapnel range is 5750 yds., but common shell can be used up to 11,000 yds. The organization is a six-gun battery, but a platform has always to be used.

A howitzer is a comparatively light piece that fires a comparatively heavy shell with a comparatively low muzzle velocity, and changes in range are effected sometimes by alteration of charge **Howitzers.** as well as of elevation. On the continent of Europe howitzers are more popular than guns for heavy field batteries and light siege units.

The French 15 cm. (Rimailho) Howitzer.—This piece is at the present time very popular in France, where, in 1907, some 170 batteries of the field army were said to be armed with it. It came into being from the conversion of an old pattern siege howitzer and its adaptation to a new form of carriage, according to the plans of Commandant Rimailho. The gun (*canon de 155 R*) is a short piece, made of steel, with a calibre of 6·1″; the shell weighs about 94 ℔ and has an effective range of 7000 yds. The breech opens automatically after each round and a rapidity of fire of from 4 to 5 rounds a minute is claimed. The howitzer is supported on two trunnions near its rear end so that the weight pivots about a point near the breech, with the result that the latter remains nearly 5 ft. above the ground level at all angles of elevation; space is thus left for recoil, which is checked by a buffer, the construction of which is a secret; running-out springs are provided to return the gun to the firing position. The piece recoils in a cradle to which is attached the elevation scale, but the elevating gear is independent of the carriage proper; the line of sight is also independent. The howitzer has a special transporting carriage, but it can be placed on its firing carriage, it is said, in two minutes. The weight behind the teams is in each case about 47 cwt. On a war looting three ammunition wagons per howitzer would be provided.

The German 15 cm. Howitzer.—The Germans also possess a 15 cm. howitzer of modern type; its rate of fire is 2 to 3 rounds a minute; its shell is 87½ ℔ in weight and the weight behind the team is about 53 cwt.

The British 6″ B.L. Howitzer.—This piece is made of steel, it weighs 36 cwt., its shell weighs 122 ℔ and has an effective range of 7000 yds. The weight behind the team is 84 cwt.

Fig. 72 shows the howitzer and cradle A mounted on the travelling carriage, from which it can be fired up to an angle of 35°: in fig. 73

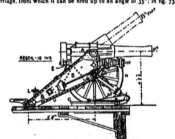

FIG. 72.—Diagram of British 6-in. B.L. Howitzer.

the wheels have been removed, the trail B has been lowered on to the pivot plate C and secured to a pivot plug screwed into the plate: to the trail is fitted the top carriage D, and when the howitzer and cradle are thus mounted 70° elevation can be given. The howitzer recoils through the cradle, in which are two hydraulic buffers side by side, fig. 74, whose piston rods E are attached to the howitzer so that the recoil of the latter draws the pistons J to the rear. Consider now, in fig. 74, the right buffer only; forged in one piece with the piston and piston rod is a tail rod F of larger diameter than the piston rod, and in the front of the cylinder is an annular bronze casting G, called a floating piston, which bears against the rear of the springs. On discharge, the howitzer slides along the cradle to the rear, the piston rod E is drawn out of the cylinder and the tail rod F is drawn in, and from its larger diameter causes a pressure of oil against the floating piston G, which slides forward and compresses the springs which are prevented moving by the rods H. The action is the same in each buffer. After recoil the springs expand and return the howitzer into the firing position.

The floating pistons are tapered slightly inside towards the front to prevent violence in the running out action. The elevating gear, which can be placed on the left side of either the trail or the top carriage, actuates the arc K, bolted to the left side of the cradle. When the gun is fired on wheels (fig. 72) an anchorage buffer M, attached to the platform, checks the recoil, whilst the springs with which it is provided cause the carriage to return to its position.

The United States 6"-Howitzer.—This is a more modern equipment, its date being 1905. The howitzer is a short piece, 13 calibres long; it fires a 120-lb shell with a muzzle velocity of 900 f.s. It has an

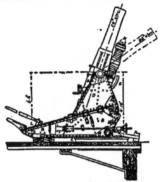

FIG. 73.—Diagram of British 6-in. B.L. Howitzer
(70° elevation).

extreme elevation of 45° and an effective range of 7000 yds. The weight behind the team is 70½ cwt. The carriage is of peculiar construction (fig. 75). The howitzer is supported under its cradle, which is carried on trunnions seated in the top carriage. The cradle consists of three cylinders generally similar in arrangement and in functions to those described for the 4·7" 60 pr. gun: the howitzer is made in a single forging and carries a lug on its breech end for the attachment of the recoil piston rod and the yoke for the rods of the spring cylinders; flanged rails are formed on its upper surface, which support it on its cradle. The top carriage rests on a framework called a " pintle bearing." Flanges in the former engage under clips in the latter; the pintle bearing is riveted to the front part of the trail brackets, and forms a turn-table upon which the top carriage and all supported by it have a movement of 3° traverse on either side.

This movement of traverse is effected by a shaft and worm: the former is supported in a fixture attached to the left trail bracket, and the latter works in a nut pivoted to the top carriage.

Elevation is effected by a forging called the rocker. The rear part of the latter is U-shaped and passes under the gun, being

FIG. 74.—Hydraulic buffers of British 6-in. B.L. Howitzer.
(N.B.—Spiral, instead of volute springs, are now used.)

attached to the cradle by a pivoted hook A. From either side of the U arms extend which embrace the cradle trunnions between the cradle and the cheeks of the top carriage so that the rocker can rotate about the cradle trunnions. The elevating gear is contained in lugs on the under side of the top carriage, while the upper end of the elevating screw is attached to the bottom of the rocker. The rocker thus moves in elevation in the top carriage and gives elevation to the cradle, and therefore to the gun, by means of the pivoted hook above referred to.

The brackets of the trail extend separately to the rear, sufficiently providing for free movements of recoil at any elevation; they are then joined by transoms and top and bottom plates and terminate

in a detachable spade which is secured to the top of the trail in travelling. The axle is of special shape to admit of the movements of the cradle; it is lower in the middle than at the sides and is made in three parts, held together by shrinkage in cylinders formed in the sides of the pintle bearing.

A peculiarity of this carriage is that recoil is automatically shortened as elevation increases. Thus the length of recoil is 50" at angles of firing from —5° to 0°, from 0° to 25° the 50" is gradually reduced to 28", which is not changed for higher angles. This is effected as follows: Four apertures are made in the piston of the recoil cylinder and there are two longitudinal throttling grooves in the walls of the cylinder. All apertures being open and deepest part of grooves in use would correspond to a 50" recoil; apertures closed and grooves alone at work would mean a 28" recoil. A rotating disk with apertures similar and similarly placed to those on the piston is carried by the piston rod and rests against the front of the piston, and is actuated during recoil by two lugs projecting into helical guide slots cut in the walls of the recoil cylinder. The latter is mounted so as to be capable of rotation in the cradle, and its outer surface carries teeth which engage with similar teeth in a ring surrounding the right spring cylinder. When the elevation is between 0° and 25° these latter teeth engage in special gearing which is seated in the hollow trunnion of the cradle and is attached to the right cheek of the top carriage. The buffer conditions are thus made to correspond with the elevation.

The mortar is a short piece of ordnance that is always fired from a bed. Changes in range are usually effected by varying the charge. *Mortars.*

United States 3·6" Mortar.—This equipment is not modern; the piece was intended for vertical fire against troops in entrenchments; the mortar weighs 245 lb, and its bed, which is made in a single casting of steel, 300 lb. The latter rests in action on a wooden platform and is held down by ropes and pickets.

The German 8·4" Mortar.—This equipment is perhaps the heaviest field equipment existing. The mortar in action weighs about 4·9 tons; it has to be transported in a special vehicle and can only be fired from a platform; four hours are required for bringing it into action. Two platform wagons are attached to each mortar, weighing respectively 2·9 and 4·9 tons. The equipment can be moved at a walk on good roads, but two companies of infantry are always attached for haulage in case of need. A battery consists of 4 mortars, and 160 rounds are carried. The shell weighs 250 lb and carries a heavy charge of high explosive, with or without delay action fuze.

A special equipment designed by Messrs Krupp is shown in Plate vi., figs. 76 and 77. It is a mobile mounting for an 8·26" mortar with constant long recoil, which is fired, like a howitzer, from its travelling carriage without a platform. This equipment weighs about 5 tons in action.

All the foregoing equipments may be considered *mobile*; that is to say, the batteries in which they are organized are self-contained, can move from place to place without external assistance, and may be employed on either field or siege duties. Their uses may be summed up as follows: The first object of the heavy artillery accompanying an army is to demolish the barrier forts or other frontier fortifications of a permanent nature in order to enable the army to penetrate into the enemy's country. After this has been done, a small portion of this artillery will be employed in connexion with the siege of fortresses, while another, by far the more considerable portion, will accompany the advance of the field army.

Heavy Siege Units.—When a serious siege has to be undertaken it is necessary to organize one or more siege trains in addition to the troops of the field army. Both heavy and light siege units enter into the composition of a siege train. As to the armament of the latter, we have said that it is not exactly distinguishable from that of heavy field units, and it has already been described. That of the former is less definite. Heavy siege units are seldom mobile in the sense that light siege units are: the ordnance comprising the former has usually to be transported by some special means; thus it might be conveyed by ordinary rail or ship to some place from which special siege railways would admit of its conveyance to its place in battery, and probably great variety of calibre and mounting would exist. For example, during the siege of Sevastopol a civil engineer, Robert Mallet (1810–1881), designed a 36" mortar; it did not, however, reach the seat of war; and in 1904 the Japanese made use of their 11·1" coast howitzers at Port Arthur. At the siege manœuvres in France in 1906 the heavy siege units were represented by their 6·1" gun and their 10·7" howitzer. The official British pieces are a 6" gun and a 9·4" howitzer. Generally speaking, whereas the most suitable armament of the light units can as a rule be foreseen, that of the heavy would depend very much on circumstances.

The French 10·7″ Howitzer.—As a typical piece the 10·7″ howitzer may be taken, which the French transported by special horse draught, as it was found too heavy for the type of siege railway made use of at the mock siege of Langres in 1907. Its total equipment weighs 22 tons and it is transported in four components, namely, the piece, the carriage, the slide and the platform. A battery of six pieces would thus require, exclusive of ammunition

hydraulic buffer is attached to the front of the slide and also to the bed.

The fighting units of siege artillery in the British service are companies and brigades; each company would be armed with from 4 to 6 light siege pieces or from 2 to 4 heavy pieces. A company is usually a major's command. Three such companies would form a siege brigade under a lieutenant-colonel. If a siege train of any magnitude were organized it might be necessary to combine two or more brigades into a division under a colonel or brigadier. In the French service each siege train consists of three divisions. A division is divided into groups and comprises some 50 pieces of ordnance, heavy and light. (J. R. J. J.)

IV. GARRISON MOUNTINGS

The armament of modern coast fronts consists of (*a*) heavy B.L. guns, 9″ and upwards; (*b*) medium guns, 4″ and upwards, and (*c*) light Q.F. guns; all these being for direct fire; and (*d*) guns, howitzers or mortars of various calibres for high angle fire. Typical guns of type (*a*) are the Krupp 12″ gun and the British 9·2 B.L. gun. The Krupp 12″ gun is built up of crucible cast nickel steel, not wire wound. It is 45 calibres long and has the Krupp wedge-shaped breech-closing apparatus. It is fitted with a repeating trip lock. The cartridge is a metallic case containing a charge of 290 lb of tubular powder. The projectiles are of two weights, 770 lb and 980 lb, and the respective muzzle velocities are 3025 f.s. and 2700 f.s. The British 9·2 B.L. gun is of wire-wound construction and is over 48 calibres long. It has the asbestos pad and Welin screw system of obturation, and its charge of 103 lb of cordite, contained in a cartridge of silk cloth, fires a 380 lb projectile with a muzzle velocity of 2643 f.s. A typical gun of class (*b*) is the British 6″ mark VII. It is similar in construction and breech mechanism to the last-named and fires a 100 lb projectile with a charge of 23 lb cordite, giving a muzzle velocity of 2493 f.s. A typical gun of class (*c*) is the British 12 pr. Q.F.; its weight is 12 cwt., it is made of steel, is 10·3 calibres long, and with a cordite charge of 1 lb 15 oz. it fires a projectile 12½ lb in weight with a muzzle velocity of 2197 f.s. and a possible rate of 15 aimed rounds a minute. A typical piece of class (*d*) is the 11″ Krupp howitzer. It is 12 calibres long, has a charge of 28¾ lb smokeless powder and fires steel shell weighing 470 lb or 760 lb. It is provided with a shrapnel shell of the former weight which contains 1880 bullets.

The methods of mounting of coast ordnance are many; space only permits of referring to certain typical arrangements.

1. *The Moncrieff Principle.*—The disappearing carriage originated, at all events in England, with Colonel Sir A. Moncrieff, who, about 1864, proposed to utilize the energy of recoil to bring a gun into a protected position and at the same time to store up sufficient energy to raise it to a firing position when loading was completed. To effect this a heavy counter-weight was so adjusted that its tendency was to raise the gun; when the latter was fired, it raised the counterweight and a ratchet and pawl followed the action up; when the pawl was released the counterweight brought the gun back to the firing position; this application of the principle had many drawbacks, and never had any success with guns over 7 tons in weight. It was not until Moncrieff invented the hydropneumatic appliances that any real progress was made. In 1888 was introduced into the British service the first of a large group of disappearing mountings for guns of types (*a*) and (*b*), where the energy of recoil was absorbed chiefly by forcing a large volume of liquid through a narrow opening or recoil valve, and also by further compressing a large volume of already highly compressed air; when recoil was completed the recoil valve closed and the air was retained at very high pressure: the energy thus stored up returned the gun to the firing position. The action will be understood from the following example.

The British 6″ B.L. Gun on H.P. Mounting, Mark IV.—Fig. 78 shows a general view of the mounting; fig. 79 is a vertical and

Disappearing mountings.

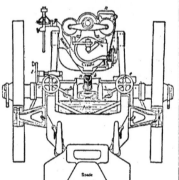

Fig. 75.—Diagram of 6-in. Siege Howitzer, U.S.A.

From Lieut.-Colonel Ormond M. Lissak's *Ordnance and Gunnery.*

b, Hand-wheel actuating wheel
c, Elevating hand-wheel.
h, Handle.
k, Hook, 1, 2, 3, 4 and 5, mechanism for loading position.
n, Elevating screw.
t, Traversing wheel.

transport, 24 vehicles that would weigh 130 tons. The howitzer was designed originally for coast defence; it weighs about 5¾ tons and its bed weighed 6½ tons: to this equipment was added a slide and a platform, consisting of a thick plate of iron upon which the slide moves. The platform is provided with a pivot upon which the front part of the slide fits. The latter consists of an iron framework, having lateral movement around the aforesaid pivot; its rear portion is provided with rollers to facilitate its movement on the platform. Its upper portion consists of two inclined rails along which the bed or carriage of the howitzer slides. To check recoil a

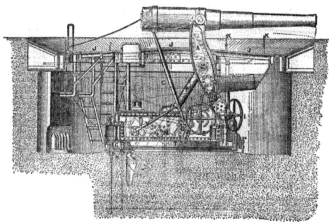

FIG. 78.—British 6″ B.L. Gun on H.P. Mounting, Mark IV.

fig. 80 a transverse section through the recoil cylinder. The gun trunnions (fig. 78) are supported by the two arms of the elevator A, which is pivoted to the front of the lower carriage at B. The breech is supported by the two elevating bars C whose lower ends are attached to the elevating arcs D. These arcs are worked by the elevating gear actuated by the hand-wheel E. The arcs are struck with the bars C as radii, their centres being points at the upper end of the bars when the gun is in the loading position. Elevation can thus be given to the gun whilst it is being loaded. The lower carriage rests on a ring of live rollers G, which are free to traverse round on a circular racer H, motion being given by traversing gear actuated by the hand-wheel I. Supported by vertical stanchions attached to the lower carriage is a horizontal circular shield J through which the gun rises to the firing position. The manganese bronze ram F which is attached to the elevators A by the cross-head L is forced on recoil into the central chamber of the recoil cylinder (see fig. 79), which is supported by trunnions M resting in the brackets of the lower carriage. There are ten chambers N (figs. 79 and 80), all of which are connected at the bottom with the recoil valve chamber O, and consequently with each other. Nine of these contain liquid in their lower portions and highly compressed air above, and are connected at the top by a channel P to equalize the pressure in each chamber. The tenth chamber N′, which is situated lowest in the cylinder, contains liquid alone and has at its upper end the raising valve Q. On recoil the liquid in the central chamber is forced by the ram through the recoil valve R into the outer chambers N, thus further compressing the air. As R is a non-return valve the air is maintained in this highly compressed state during loading. The gun is raised by pushing the lever S (fig. 78) to the front which actuates the rack T (fig. 79), thus opening Q, which allows the air in the nine chambers to force liquid from the tenth chamber N′ into the centre ram chamber, lifting the ram. U is a pump (fig. 79) by which the gun can be pumped down at drill. The liquid employed in the buffer is a mixture of methylated spirits, mineral oil, distilled water and carbonate of soda, and its aeration, due to the churning it receives on recoil, is a serious drawback to this class of mounting. From a 6″ B.L. gun mounted in this fashion somewhat more than one aimed round a minute can be obtained; from a 9·2″ B.L. about four such rounds in five minutes.

The foregoing description is now, however, principally interesting as showing an ingenious application of mechanical principles for military purposes. Mountings of this type are being gradually withdrawn from the British service.

The Buffington-Crozier Principle.—In the United States a type of disappearing carriage known as the Buffington-Crozier (fig. 81) is used. Here, as in the earlier types of Moncrieff carriage, a counterweight is employed, but the energy of recoil is partly absorbed by a buffer, and the counterweight, which is constrained by guides to move vertically up and down, is just able to raise the gun to the

firing position. A satisfactory rate of fire is claimed for this mounting, which has recently been improved.

Balanced Pillar.—Another type of disappearing mounting for guns of type (b) or (c), known as the balanced pillar, is found on the continent of Europe and in the United States, where it is used for 5″ guns and under. A long steel cylinder, which supports the gun and its carriage, has a vertical movement of about 3½ ft. in an outer cylinder. The inner cylinder and all that it carries is balanced by a counterweight. After the gun is fired it can be brought with its length parallel to the parapet. Then by the action of the mechanism the inner cylinder can be made to sink

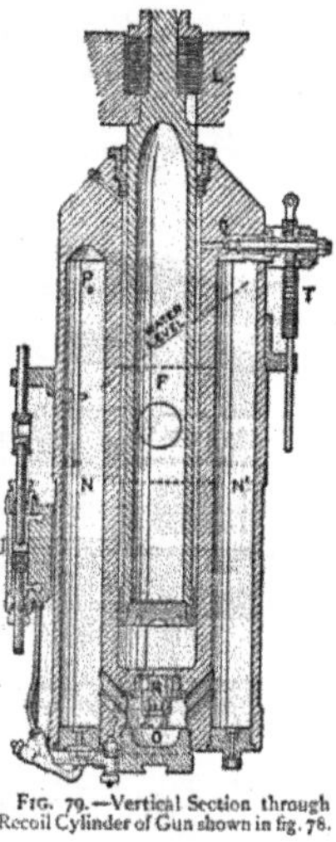

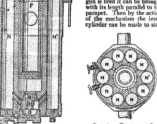

FIG. 79.—Vertical Section through Recoil Cylinder of Gun shown in fig. 78.

FIG. 80.—Transverse Section through Recoil Cylinder of Gun shown in fig. 78.

in the outer cylinder and the gun is brought down to the loading position; the release of the counterweight will cause it to rise again. The gun has the usual motion of traverse round the common axis of the two cylinders.

The heavy gun cupola is found on the continent of Europe in the armaments of various Powers for guns of type (a), the German

A heavy chilled cast-iron collar protects the under side of the armoured structure and the working mechanism of the guns. Fig. 83, Plate VI., represents a Krupp mounting for an 11·2″ howitzer, with a cupola-like shield. This is worked both electrically and by hand. Vertical fire from a weapon of this type is sufficiently powerful to penetrate the protective deck of a vessel. Light and medium guns, types (b) and (c), are sometimes mounted in cupolas, especially on land fronts (see below), and disappearing cupolas have also been proposed for them: in the latter the whole structure is made to sink by the action of mechanism till the top of the cupola is level with the ground. Types and further details will be found in the article FORTIFICATION AND SIEGE-CRAFT.

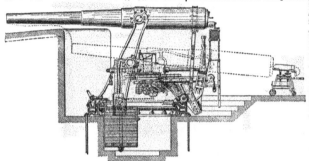

FIG. 81.—Buffington-Crozier Disappearing Carriage for 10″ B.L.-Gun, U.S.A.

practice being occasionally to mount two 11″ guns in the same cupola. The cast-iron cupola was introduced by Gruson of Magdeburg, but nickel steel is now generally employed by Krupp. In Gruson's design the gun and mounting are placed upon a turn-table upon which also rest the bases of a series of cast-iron plates; these are very massive, are curvilinear in section, and are built up into a shallow dome which completely covers the mountings as with a cap: the whole structure turns together, being traversed round a central pivot. The chase of the gun emerges through a port which admits of the necessary play of elevation. A notable example of a cupola was erected at Spezzia containing two 120-ton Krupp guns, the structure complete weighing 2050 tons. A Krupp cupola of chilled cast-iron for two 28-cm. (11″) is shown in fig. 82. These are designed principally for coast defence in low sites. The cupola, which is built up like a Gruson cupola of several heavy iron masses, is revolved and the guns laid by hydraulic power.

Cupolas.

Mountings of the barbette type are much favoured in the British service for guns of types (a) and (b); one of the most modern is shown in fig. 84, where a 9·2″ B.L. gun, Mark X., is placed upon a Mark V. mounting, a combination which admits of over five aimed rounds in two minutes.

Barbette mountings.

The British 9·2″ B.L. Gun.—Fig. 84 shows a general view of the mounting, fig. 85 a longitudinal section through the cradle on a larger scale. The gun, which is trunnionless, carries a cross-head A and recoils in the cradle C, being supported by its guides D, which slide in longitudinal grooves in the cradle. To this cross-head is attached the buffer cylinder B (see fig. 85) which recoils with the gun, while the piston rod L is attached to the front of the cradle: engaging with the buffer cylinder and in the same axial line is a bronze casting containing two air chambers F and G; the casting is attached to the rear of the cradle, which is supported by trunnions E in the lower carriage. Thus on firing, the gun carries the buffer

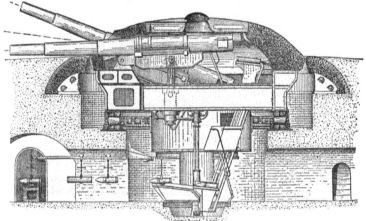

FIG. 82.—Krupp Cupola for two 28-cm. Guns.

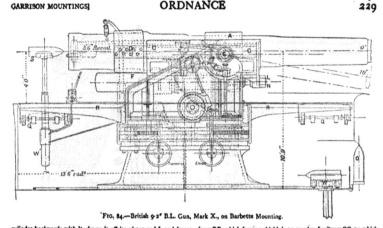

'FIG. 84.—British 9·2" B.L. Gun, Mark X., on Barbette Mounting.

cylinder backwards with it, draws it off its piston rod L and forces it into the air chamber F. The air in the chambers F and G is at a high initial tension and, on recoil, the air in F is further compressed and forced through the valve H into the chamber G. At the conclusion of recoil the air expands and forces the buffer cylinder to the front, which carries with it the gun into its loading position; but the valve H closes and the air has to make its way through a narrow hole before it can act on the end of the buffer, thus preventing violent action, which is further guarded against by the "control ram" M which is bolted into the rear end of the buffer. To prevent leakage of air between the air chamber and the buffer at the gland K the packing employed is a viscous liquid which is in communication by means of the pipe J with the intensifier I. The latter consists of a cylinder containing a piston and rod free to move; the front face of this piston is subject to the pressure of the air in the air chamber, the rear face is in communication with the liquid in the gland. Now, as the piston head is held in position by the pressures on either side of it, and as the effective area of the front face is greater than that of the rear—on account of the rod—the liquid pressure per square inch of the fluid in the gland, &c., must be greater than that of the air in the air chamber, hence the latter cannot escape through the former. The pressure in the chambers F and G is adjusted on preparing for action by an air pump worked by hand. The energy of recoil is further utilised as follows: hydraulic cylinders called compressors are held in the cradle, and in them work rams connected with the cross-head A (see fig. 85); they are

form RR, which forms a shield, is an overhead railway QQ, on which run trollies, each taking a projectile. The projectiles are stored in the recess shown in section at O. By means of a shell barrow any projectile can be placed on the lift W and raised to a trolley which can be run round over the lift W", which raises the projectile, as shown at S, to a point suitable for loading.

The British 6" B.L. Gun.—A typical mounting for guns of type (b) is afforded by the British C.P. (central pivot), Mark II. mounting for the 6" B.L. Mark VII. gun, a combination which admits of six rounds a minute aimed fire. Fig. 86 shows a side elevation of the mounting with half the shield removed; fig. 87 a longitudinal section of part of the cradle through the axis of the buffer. The gun, which is trunnionless, recoils in the cradle A; the latter contains a buffer B and two cylindrical boxes containing springs S. Attached to the breech of the gun is a piston rod C with piston D, the latter having an opening or "port" E, through which the oil passes on recoil, the pressure in the buffer, which would otherwise vary with the velocity of the recoil, being kept constant by the variation in the area of aperture afforded by E. This area is governed by the action of the valve key strip F of varying section, which is inserted in the buffer in such a way that as the gun recoils the port E is constrained to pass over it. On recoil the rods J, which are attached to the gun in rear and screwed into the flanged cylinder H in front, force back the front of the springs S, whose rear ends butt up against the rear of the spring boxes. After recoil the springs return the gun to the firing position. To check the violence of this action a control ram G is made use of; the piston rod has a cylindrical hole in front which, as the gun recoils, becomes filled with oil, and before the piston can come up against the front of the buffer this oil has to be displaced by the thrust of the ram G which checks the forward movement of the gun. The cradle A rests on its trunnions in seatings in the lower carriage and is elevated or depressed by the gear K'. The last-named drives the elevating arc L, which is attached to the cradle at M, the axis of the gun moving parallel to the axis of the cradle. In fig. 86 the lower carriage is almost entirely hidden by the gears carried on it, namely, the elevating gear K, the traversing gear N, which works a spur pinion, gearing into the rack O attached to the pedestal P; the elevation indicators Q and R for recording the angle of elevation of the gun

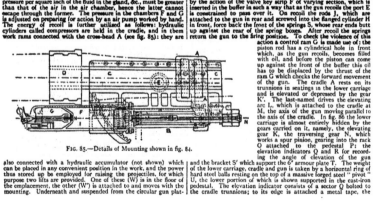

FIG. 85.—Details of Mounting shown in fig. 84.

also connected with a hydraulic accumulator (not shown) which can be placed in any convenient position in the work, and the power thus stored up be employed for raising the projectiles, for which purpose two lifts are provided. One of these (W) is in the floor of the emplacement, the other (W") is attached to and moves with the mounting. Underneath and suspended from the circular gun plat-

and the bracket S' which support the 6" armour plate T. The weight of the lower carriage, cradle and gun is taken by a horizontal ring of hard steel balls resting on the top of a massive forged steel "pivot" U, the lower portion of which is shown supported in the cast-iron pedestal. The elevation indicator consists of a sector Q bolted to the cradle trunnions; to its edge is attached a metal tape, the

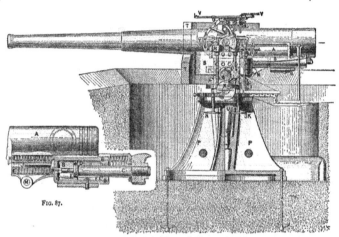

FIG. 87.

FIG. 86.

FIG. 86.—British Mark II. Barbette Mounting for 6″ B.L. Gun.
FIG. 87.—Longitudinal Section of Part of Cradle of Gun shown in fig. 13, through Axis of Buffer.

other end of which is fixed to the spindle supporting a pointer, reading angles of elevation on the drum R. As the gun elevates the tape is paid out, the slack being taken in and the pointer revolved by the action of a clock spring.[1] The mounting carries an automatic sight (see SIGHTS, *Gun Sights*).

The British 12-pr. Q.F. Gun.—A typical mounting for guns of class (*c*) is the British pedestal mounting for the 12-pr. Q.F. gun. This mounting consists of a cradle, a pivot, a pedestal and holdfast. The cradle is a gunmetal casting, provided with trunnions that rest in bearings on the pivot; the gun recoils in the upper portion of the cradle and the lower part of the latter is bored at the rear for an hydraulic buffer and at the front for a running-out spring. The pivot is of steel, is fork-shaped at the top end, where are the trunnion bearings for the cradle; its lower end is conical and fits into bushes in the pedestal, where it is free to revolve but is prevented from lifting by a holding-down screw.[2] The pedestal is bolted down to the platform. The gun has a shoulder-piece and it can be trained and elevated by the layer. It has also an automatic sight.

A typical Krupp mounting of this kind is shown in fig. 88, Plate VI., which represents an 8·8-cm. (3·4″) automatic gun firing, it is stated, 40 aimed rounds in the minute.

The United States 12″ Mortar.—A typical mounting for pieces of class (*d*) is afforded by the United States mounting, model of 1896, for the 12″ B.L. mortar. The piece is mounted in a top carriage or saddle consisting of two arms connected by a heavy web. This saddle is hinged on a heavy bolt and is connected to the front of the turntable (fig. 89). The saddle inclines to the rear and upwards at an angle of 45°, the upper ends forming trunnion bearings: it is supported at a point about one-third of its length from the bolt or fulcrum by five columns of double springs arranged in a row, side by side. The recoil is checked by two hydraulic cylinders, one on each side, the pistons of which are attached to the saddle near the trunnions of the piece. When the mortar is fired the saddle revolves about its fulcrum to the rear and downwards, carrying the mortar and compressing the spring columns until the action is stopped by the hydraulic buffers; the springs then assert themselves and return the piece to the firing position. The mortar must always be brought horizontal for loading.

[1] The elevation indicators are now read on a plate provided with a spiral groove, which guides a stud on the reader along the scale of graduations.
[2] In a later mark there is no holding-down screw for pivot.

The fighting units of coast artillery in the British service are the fire command, the battery command and the group. The limits of a fire command are governed by the possibility of efficient surveillance and control that can be exercised by an individual, and these limits vary much from time to time. Usually a number of forts or emplacements are included in a fire command. The fire command is broken up into battery commands, in every one of which it must be possible for its commander actually to take charge of the guns therein contained in all phases of action. The battery command is divided up into gun groups, each consisting of one or more pieces of like calibre, nature and shooting qualities. As a rule a fire commander is a field officer, a battery commander a major or a captain, a gun group commander a subaltern or senior N.C. officer. In connexion with coast artillery range-finders (*q.v.*) and electric lights (see COAST DEFENCE) are installed and electric communications established for the chain of command. (J. R. J. J.)

V. NAVAL GUNS AND GUNNERY

In dealing with naval guns and gunnery, we shall take the British navy as the basis. At the close of the 19th and at the beginning of the 20th century it appeared that a type of British battleship (see SHIP) had been evolved which was stable as regards disposition of armament, and that further advance would consist merely in greater efficiency of individual guns, in improvements of armour rendering possible the protection of greater areas, and in changes of engine and boiler design resulting in higher speeds. The "Majestic," "Glory," "Exmouth," "London" and "Bulwark" classes differed from each other only in such details, all of them subordinate to the main *raison d'être* of the battleship, *i.e.* the number and nature of the guns which she carries.

The strength and disposition of the armaments of the ships of these classes were identical except in small details (see fig. 90). In every case the main armament consisted of a pair of 12-in. guns forward and a pair aft, each pair enclosed in a hooded barbette, which was more commonly designated a turret. The turrets were on the midship line, and the guns in each commanded an arc of fire of 240°, *i.e.* from right ahead to 30° abaft the beam on either side in the case of the fore turret, and from astern to 30° before either beam in the case of the after turret. The secondary armament, consisting of twelve 6-in. guns, was also symmetrically disposed. Two guns on either side (four in the " Majestic " class) were mounted with arcs of fire of from 60°

capacity which were to kill and demoralize his personnel, pierce his funnels, destroy any navigational or sighting appliances which were exposed, set his woodwork on fire and render extinction of the fires impossible, and by piercing or bursting on

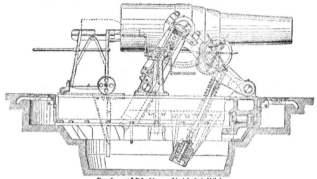

FIG. 89.—12″ B.L. Mortar, Model 1896, U.S.A.

before to 60° abaft the beam, while two guns each side forward and two aft (one forward and one aft in the " Majestic " class) fired through similar arcs to the turret guns, but on their own sides only. Four of these 6-in. guns were mounted on either side of the main deck and two on either side of the upper deck, all being enclosed in casemates.

In the armoured and large protected cruisers built contemporaneously with these classes of battleships, the 9·2-in. gun had been largely mounted, and it was the improvements brought about by practical experience in the rate and accuracy of fire of this gun that suggested its adoption in battleships to replace the whole or a part of the 6-in. armament. During the period in which the battleships referred to above were constructed, the idea of the

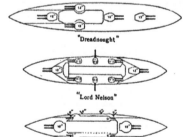

"Dreadnought"

"Lord Nelson"

"London"

FIG. 90.—Diagrams showing Disposition of Armament in Typical Ships.

functions of the respective divisions of the armament was that the 12-in. guns were to injure the enemy's vitals by piercing his armour with armour-piercing shot or shell, while the business of the 6-in. guns was to cover him with a bail of shells of large

unarmoured portions of his side diminish his reserve of buoyancy and so impair his sea-going qualities.

These ideas were gradually losing favour; it was realized that the damage done by an armour-piercing shot, whether or not it hit and pierced armour, was limited to its own path, while that done by an armour-piercing shell striking an unarmoured portion of the ship's side was inconsiderable as compared with that effected by a common shell of the same calibre. Further, the area of side, by piercing which an armour-piercing projectile would reach any portion of the propelling machinery or magazines of an enemy, was so small compared with the whole exposed area of his side and upper works that it was scarcely advantageous to fire at it projectiles, the effectiveness of which, if they struck another portion of the enemy, was small in comparison with that of other projectiles which might equally well be fired from the same gun. Again, the lessons of practical experience showed that ships might be and were defeated by shell fire alone, while their armour remained unpierced, and propelling machinery and magazines intact.

All these considerations led to the conclusion that it was to intensity of shell-fire, and especially to the fire of large capacity and high explosive shell, that attention should be directed. At the same time, while the rate of fire of the 6-in. guns, to which great attention had been paid, remained stationary or nearly so, the rate of fire of the 9·2-in. and 12-in. guns had considerably improved, and their ballistic powers rendered possible more accurate firing at long ranges than could be effected with the 6-in. guns. The explosive effect of a shell is said to vary as the square of the weight of its bursting charge. The bursting charge, with shell of the same type, bears a constant proportion to the weight of the shell. Now the weight of the 12-in. shell is 850 lb, that of the 9·2-in. 380 lb, that of the 6-in. 100 lb. Hence it would require fourteen 6-in. shells to produce the same effect as one 9·2-in., and seventy-two to produce the same effect as one 12-in. shell, consequently the 6-in. gun to produce the same shell effect as the 12-in. or 9·2-in. gun must fire 72 times, or 14 times, respectively, faster. The rate of fire of guns in action depends upon a variety of conditions, an important one being that of smoke interference, which tends to reduce the maximum rate of fire of the smaller guns nearer to that practicable with the heavier guns, but the rate of fire of the three guns in question, under battle conditions, is in the approximate proportions of 1: 1·5: 4, which would thus produce a shell effect (supposing the hits made by each type of gun to bear a fixed proportion to the rounds fired), in the proportions of 72: 22: 4, for the 12-in., 9·2-in. and 6-in. guns respectively. This argument of course takes no account of the probably greater effect produced by the dispersion of the larger number of hits of the smaller gun over the exposed area of the target, nor, on the other hand, does it take account of the greater armour-piercing power of the 12-in. shell which would have the result that a larger proportion of the hits from the smaller gun would be defeated by the enemy's armour, and so prove innocuous.

The shell effect forms a strong argument for the weight available for the heavy gun armament of a ship being disposed of in the form only of the heaviest gun available. Another strong argument is that deduced from the fact already stated, that, as the calibre of the gun increases, its ballistic powers enable accurate shooting to be made at a longer range.

The accuracy of a gun at any range depends mainly, for practical naval purposes, on what is known as the "dangerous space," or the limit within which the range must be known in order that a target of a given height may be struck. Again, the dangerous space at any range depends upon the remaining velocity of the projectile at that range, which, as between guns of different calibres but with the same initial muzzle velocity, is greater, the greater the calibre of the gun and weight of projectile, the advantage possessed by the larger gun in this respect being much increased at great ranges. As a practical example, for a target 30 ft. high at a range of 8000 yds., the dangerous spaces of modern 12-in., 9·2-in. and 6-in. guns, which do not differ greatly in muzzle velocity, are 75, 65 and 40 yds. respectively. At whatever range a naval action is to be fought, it is evident that there must be a period during which the enemy is within the practical 12-in. gun range, and outside the practical 6-in. gun range, and that during this period the weight allotted to 6-in. guns will be wasted, and this at the outset of an action, when it is more important than at any time during its progress to inflict damage on the enemy as a means of preventing him from inflicting damage on ourselves. But if all the weight available be allotted to 12-in. guns, the whole of the armament which will bear on the enemy will come into action at the same time, and that the earliest, and consequently most advantageous, time possible. This train of argument led to the substitution of 9·2-in. guns in the 8 "King Edward VII." class (the first of which was completed in 1905) for the upper deck 6-in. guns, and eventually in the "Lord Nelson" and "Agamemnon" (completed in 1908) to the abolition of the 6-in. armament, which was replaced by ten 9·2-in. guns.

At the beginning of the present century the subject of "fire control" began to receive considerable attention, and a short statement is necessary of the causes which render essential an accurate and reliable system of controlling the fire of a ship if hits are to be made at long ranges. In the first place, even with the 12-in. gun, the range must be known with considerable nicety for a ship to be hit. At a target 30 ft. high, at 8000 yds., for example, the range on the sights must be correct within 75 yds. or the shot will fall over or short of the target. No range-finder has yet proved itself reliable, under service conditions, to such a degree, and even if one were found, it could not be relied upon to do more than place the first shot in fair proximity to the target. The reason for this lies in the distinction which must be drawn between the distance of a target and its "gun range," or, in other words, the distance to which the sights must be adjusted in order that the target may be hit.

This gun range varies with many conditions, foremost among which are the wear of the gun, the temperature of the cordite, the force and direction of the wind and other atmospheric conditions. It can only be ascertained with certainty by a process of "trial and error," using the gun itself. The error, or distance which a shot falls short of or beyond the target, can be estimated with a greater approach to accuracy the greater the height of the observer. It is the process of forming this estimate which is termed "spotting," a duty the performance of which calls for the exercise of the most accurate judgment on the part of the "spotter," and which requires much practice in order that efficiency may be secured. In practice, the first shot is fired with the sights adjusted for the distance of the target given by the range-finder, corrected as far as is practicable for the various conditions affecting the gun range. The first shot is spotted, and the result of the spotting observations governs the adjustment of the sights for the next shot, which is spotted in its turn, and the sights are readjusted until the target is hit. From this time onwards it is (in theory) only necessary to apply the change in range, due to the movements of our own ship and of the enemy, for the interval between successive shots, in order to continue hitting. This change of range, which may be considerable (e.g. 1000 yds. per minute in the extreme case of ships approaching each other directly, and both steaming at the rate of 15 knots), is in practice extremely difficult to estimate correctly, and the spotting is consequently continued in order to rectify errors in estimating the rate of change in range. For various reasons the "gun range" which has been referred to is not the same for different natures of guns. This is mainly on account of the difference in the height attained by their projectiles in the course of their respective trajectories. While it is possible, by careful calibration (i.e. the firing from the several guns of carefully aimed rounds at a fixed target with known range and under favourable conditions for practice), to make the shots from all guns of the same nature fall in very close proximity to each other when the sights of all are similarly adjusted, it has not been found possible in practice to achieve this result with guns of different natures. Consequently guns of each nature must be spotted for independently, and it is obvious that this adds considerably to the elaboration and complication of the fire control system.

This constitutes one of the reasons for the adoption of the uniform armament in the "Dreadnought" and her successors; another important reason lies in the fact that with the weight available for the heavy gun armament disposed of in a small number of very large guns, a greater proportion of these guns can be mounted on the midship line, and consequently be available for fire on either side of the ship (see fig. 90). Thus in the "Dreadnought," eight of her ten 12-in. guns can bear through a considerable arc on either beam, while in the "Lord Nelson," although all her four 12-in. guns can bear on either beam, half at least of her 9·2-in. armament (i.e. that half on the opposite side to the enemy) will be at any moment out of bearing, and consequently be for the time a useless weight. The same principle of a uniform armament of 12-in. guns has been adopted in the "Invincible" type, the only large cruisers designed since the inception of the "Dreadnought." Thus the 12-in. gun forms the sole heavy gun armament of all battleships and large cruisers of the "Dreadnought" era. The gun so carried is known as the Mark X., it is 45 calibres in length, and fires a projectile weighing 850 lb with a charge of cordite of 260 lb, resulting in a muzzle velocity of 2700 ft. per second. The Mark XI. gun was designed to be mounted in the later "Dreadnoughts." Following the same line of development as resulted in the Mark X. gun, it is longer, heavier, fires an increased charge of cordite, and has a higher muzzle velocity, viz. of 2960 ft. per second. This gun appears to mark the climax of development along the present lines, since the price to be paid in greater weight, length and diminished durability of rifling is out of all proportion to the small increase in muzzle velocity. Further developments would therefore be looked for in some other direction, such as the adoption either of a new form of propellant or of a gun of larger calibre. A modern gun of 10-in. calibre is found in the battleships "Triumph" and "Swiftsure." The next gun in importance to the 12-in. is the 9·2-in., which forms part of the armament of the "Lord Nelson" and "King Edward VII." classes of battleships, and the principal armament of all armoured cruisers (excepting the "County" class) antecedent to the "Invincibles." The latest gun of this calibre has developed from earlier types in a similar manner to the 12-in.; that is to say, it has experienced a gradual increase in length, weight, and weight of charge, with a consequently increased muzzle velocity. The latest type, which is known as the Mark XI., and is mounted in the " Lord Nelson " and " Agamemnon," is 50 calibres in length, weighs 28 tons, and with a charge of cordite of 130 ℔ gives to a projectile of 380 ℔ a muzzle velocity of 2875 ft. per second. The 7·5-in. gun forms the secondary armament of the " Triumph " and " Swiftsure," and is mounted in the armoured cruisers of the " Minotaur," " Duke of Edinburgh " and " Devonshire " classes. The 6-in. gun, of which there are a very large number afloat in modern, though not the most recent, battleships, and in armoured and first and second class cruisers, is the largest gun which is worked by hand power alone. For this reason, and on account of its rapidity of fire, it was for many years popular as an efficient weapon. It was evolved from the 6-in. 80-pounder B.L. gun, constructed at Elswick, which was the first breech-loader adopted by the Royal Navy, and whose development has culminated in the 6-in. Mark XI. gun of the " King Edward VII." class and contemporary cruisers, which fires a 100-℔ projectile with a muzzle velocity of 2900 ft. per second. It has only now passed out of favour on account of its inferior hitting power at long range as compared with that of guns of larger calibre, and as a secondary armament of 6-in. guns is still being included in the latest battleship designs of more than one foreign navy—notably that of the Japanese, with their practical experience of modern war at sea—its abandonment in the British Navy can scarcely be considered final. The 4-in. Q.F. gun is mounted in the third-class cruisers of the " P " class as their main armament, and an improved gun of this calibre, with muzzle velocity of about 2800 ft. per second, is mounted in the later " Dreadnoughts," as their anti-torpedo-boat armament.

The increase in size of modern torpedo craft and the increased range of modern torpedoes has led to a reconsideration of the type of gun suitable for the protection of large ships against torpedo attack. The conditions under which the anti-torpedo-boat armament comes into play are the most unfavourable possible for accurate gun-fire. The target is a comparatively small one; it comes into view suddenly and unexpectedly; it is moving rapidly, and the interval during which the boat must be stopped, i.e. that between her being first sighted and her arrival at the distance at which she can expect to fire her torpedo with success, is in all probability a very short one. Moreover, in the great majority of cases the attack will be made at night, when the difficulties of rapid and correct adjustment of sight, and of range-finding and spotting, are intensified. Two requirements then are paramount to be satisfied by the ideal anti-torpedo-boat gun: (1) it must have a low trajectory, so that its shooting will not be seriously affected by a small error in the range on the sights; (2) one hit from it must suffice to stop a hostile destroyer.

For many years it was considered that these requirements would be met by the 12-pounder, which was the anti-torpedo-boat gun for battleships from the " Majestics " to the " Dreadnought," the 12-pounders mounted in the " King Edwards " and the " Dreadnought " being of a longer and heavier type, giving a higher muzzle velocity. The introduction of a larger gun has, however, been considered desirable, and a 4-in. gun of new type is mounted in the later " Dreadnoughts," while in the older battleships and large cruisers with secondary armaments it is considered by many officers that the 6-in. guns will prove to be the most effective weapon against torpedo craft. The gun armament of destroyers being required to answer much the same purpose as the anti-torpedo-boat armament of large ships, namely, to disable hostile torpedo craft, the type of gun used has followed a similar line of development.

Starting with 6-pounders in the first destroyers built, the majority of the new destroyers have a fixed armament consisting of one 12-pounder forward, and four 6-pounders. This armament has been changed in the larger destroyers to one of 12-pounders only, while the latest ocean-going destroyers have two 4-in. guns. Owing, however, to the strength of the decks of such craft being insufficient to withstand the stresses set up by the discharge of a gun giving very high muzzle velocity, the 4-in. gun for use in

light craft is one giving 2300 ft. per second muzzle velocity only and has a very long recoil. The 6-pounder and 3-pounder Q.F. guns are no longer being mounted as part of the armaments of modern ships. A very high rate of fire was attained in the " semi-automatic " mounting of the 3-pounder, which was last fitted in the " Duke of Edinburgh " class, but for reasons already given guns of this type are no longer required, and the 3-pounder is retained only as a boat gun for sub-calibre practice.

All double-banked pulling boats and all steam-boats are fitted with arrangements for mounting one or two guns, according to the size of the boat; the object of the boat armaments being for use in river operations, for covering a landing, or in guard-boats. Three descriptions of gun are used, the 12-pounder 8 cwt. and 3-pounder, light Q.F. guns, and the Maxim rifle-calibre machine gun.

Gun-Mountings.—Gun mountings in the British navy may be divided broadly into two classes, power-worked and hand-worked mountings. The former class includes the mountings of guns of all calibres mounted in turrets or barbettes, also of 9·2-in. guns mounted behind shields; the latter class includes mountings of guns of all sizes up to the 7·5-in. which are mounted in batteries, casemates or behind shields.

Hydraulic power has been adopted almost universally in the British navy for power-worked mountings, although electricity has been experimented with, and has been largely applied in some foreign navies. The principal advantages of hydraulic, as compared with electric, power are its comparative noiselessness and reliability, and the ease with which defects can be diagnosed and rectified. On the other hand, electric power is more easily transmitted, and is already installed in all ships for working electric light and other machinery, whereas hydraulic power, when used, is generally installed for the purpose of working the guns only. The 12-in. guns in the " Majestic " class, following the practice with the earliest heavy B.L. guns, were loaded normally at extreme elevation of 13½°, and the turret had to be trained to the fore and aft line and locked there for each occasion of loading. An alternative loading position was also provided, in which the guns could be loaded at 1° of elevation and with the turret trained in any direction. Loading in the alternative position could, however, only be continued until the limited supply of projectiles which could be stowed in the turret was exhausted. Experience showed that a greater rapidity of fire could be obtained by the use of this " all round " loading position, as it was termed, and in the latest ships of the " Majestic " class, and in subsequent battleships, the fixed loading position has been abandoned.

The details of recent 12-in. mountings vary considerably, a drawing of one of the most recent being shown in fig. 91, for which thanks are due to Messrs Vickers, Sons & Maxim, but in the majority of cases there is a " working chamber " revolving with the turret. A fixed ammunition hoist brings the shell and cartridges from shell-room and magazine respectively into the working chamber, where they are transferred to a cage which takes them up, by hydraulic power, to the rear of the gun. The gun is strapped by steel bands to a cradle (see fig. 91) which moves in and out along a slide on recoil, the gun always remaining parallel to the slide. Gun, slide and cradle are pivoted for elevation on trunnions carried in trunnion bearings fixed to the structure of the turret, and the whole moving weight is balanced with the gun in the " run out " position. The recoil of the gun on firing is taken up by a hydraulic press placed underneath the slide, and the gun is run out again into the firing position by hydraulic power. Loading is carried out by means of a hydraulic rammer, with the gun in the " run out " position, and at an angle of elevation which varies with different mountings. In the most recent mountings loading can be carried out with the gun at any elevation, thus affording considerably greater facility to the gun-layer for keeping his sights on the target during the process of loading, and so increasing the rate of fire by enabling the gun to be discharged immediately the loading operations are completed. Elevating is by hydraulic power, and is effected by cylinders placed underneath the slide, the pistons working on an arm projecting downwards. Turret turning engines are also hydraulic, and much attention has been given of late years to the perfection of elevating and turning gear such as will enable the turret or gun to respond instantly to the wish of the gun-layer, and to move either with considerable rapidity, or very slowly and steadily as would be the case when following a target at long range and with but little motion on the ship. The breech is opened and closed by hand or by hydraulic

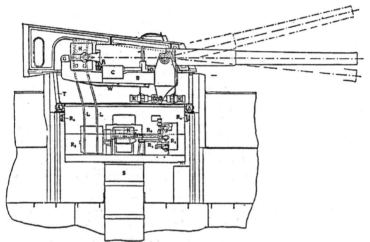

From a drawing supplied by Messrs. Vickers, Sons & Maxim.

FIG. 91.—Diagram of 12-in. Gun Mounting, " Dreadnought " type.

A,	Roller ring.	K,	Elevating presses.	R₁,	Transferring rammer projectiles from trunk cage to gun-loading cage.	Rₐ,	Transferring chamber.

A, Roller ring.
B, Gun slide.
C, Recoil buffer.
D, Gun cradle.
G, Rammer.
H, Loading cage.

K, Elevating presses.
L, Guide rail for loading cage.
N, Trunk cage.
P₁, Breech block in open position.
P₂, Breech operating hand wheel.

R₁, Transferring rammer projectiles from trunk cage to gun-loading cage.
Rₐ, Transferring rammer for powder charges from trunk cage to gun-loading cage.

Rₐ, Transferring chamber.
R₄, Training rack.
R₄, Training engine.
S, Rotating trunk.
T, Turntable.
W, Casing for chain rammer.

power, and a douche of water or blast of air, or a combination of both, removes any smouldering fragments of cordite or cartridge material before a fresh round is loaded.

Although there is little difference in principle between the arrangements of the mountings in the later " Majestics " and those in the " Dreadnought," improvements in detail have enabled the interval between successive rounds to be reduced from about 55 seconds in the former case to 25 or 30 seconds in the latter.

In the turrets containing 9·2-in. and 7·5-in. guns, which exist in most British armoured and first-class protected cruisers, the moving weights are, of course, not so large, and, as might be expected, the assistance of hydraulic machinery is not necessary in so many operations. A drawing of a typical 9·2-in. gun and mounting is shown in fig. 92.

Training the turret and elevating the guns are, however, in all cases performed by hydraulic power, as is the raising of the projectiles to their place on the loading tray in rear of the gun, but the breech is opened and closed, and the charge and projectile rammed home, by hand power only, while the gun, after recoil, is forced out again to its firing position by means of springs. A ready supply of thirty-two projectiles is stowed in a " shell carrier," which is a circular trough running on rollers round the turret, but independently of it. When a projectile is required to be loaded into the gun, the shell carrier is rotated until the required projectile is under a hatch in rear of the gun, when the projectile is raised by a hydraulic press on to a swinging loading tray. It is intended that the shell carrier shall be replenished direct from the shell-room during the pauses of an engagement. A new type of 9·2-in. mounting has been installed in the " Lord Nelson " and " Agamemnon," in which greater use is made of hydraulic power with a view to improving rapidity of fire. In this mounting, each projectile is brought up from the shell-room as it is required, and the loading operations are performed by hydraulic power instead of by hand.

The " King Edward VII." class of battleships and " Duke of Edinburgh " class of cruisers are the last ships in which any 6-in. guns have been mounted, and with the exception of the 7·5-in. guns in the " Triumph " and " Swiftsure," these are the largest guns which are worked entirely by hand. Other hand-worked guns are

the 4-in. and 12-pounder, which are mounted in small cruisers and destroyers.

The principles of the 6-in., 4-in. and 12-pounder mountings are similar. The rear part of the gun is partially enclosed in a metal cradle, which carries the recoil cylinder and running out spring box. The gun and cradle are balanced for elevation about trunnions on the cradle, which fit into trunnion bearings on the carriage. The latter carries the elevating and training gear, and the whole moving weight is borne by a pivot pin which rotates on a ball bearing. The gun recoils in the line of fire, and the energy of recoil is absorbed by means of the recoil piston, whose rod is secured to the gun, passing over a valve key secured to the cradle, in such a way as to produce a channel of varying sectional area through which the liquid in the recoil cylinder must pass from one side of the piston to the other. Springs run the gun out again after firing into its original position. The breech is opened by the single motion of a hand lever. A " bare !" charge is used in the 6-in. and 4-in. guns, with the de Bange type of obturation, while a brass cartridge case has been retained with the 12-pounder, as with the earlier Q.F. guns.

Firing is by electricity, percussion being available as an alternative if required, and the current is usually taken off the dynamo mains of the ship.

Sighting.—The great advances recently made in accuracy of fire have been rendered possible, to a very great extent, by the use of telescopic sighting apparatus. Arrangements are made in all modern sights for the bars or disks which carry the range graduations to be of considerable length or diameter respectively, in order that no difficulty may be found in adjusting the sights for every 25 or 50 yds. of range. In the larger hand-worked mountings, where the laying of the gun for elevation and for direction is effected by two men on opposite sides of the gun, the sights used by them are " cross-connected, " i.e. connected by rods and gearing to one another in such a way that, initial parallelism of the axes of the two telescopes having

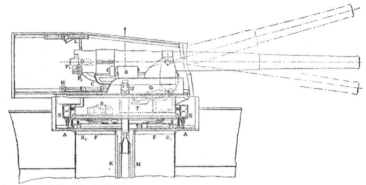

From a drawing supplied by Messrs Vickers, Sons & Maxim.

FIG. 92.—Diagram of a 9·2-in. Gun and Mounting. "Hogue" type.

A, Roller ring.
B, Recoil buffer.
C, Gun cradle slide frame.
D, Loading tray.
E, Shell carrier.
F, Pressure water pivot pipes.
G, Elevating press.
H, Shell-lifting press.
K, Fixed armoured trunk.
L, Radial shell-lifting crane.
M, Axial powder hoist.
P₁, Breech block.
P₂, Breech operating hand-wheel.
R₁, Training rack.
R₂, Training engine.
T, Turntable.
U, Powder door.

been secured, the adjustments to one sight made by the sight-setter are simultaneously effected at the sight on the opposite of the gun.

In practice with the 6-in. and 4-in. guns, one man is responsible for the laying of the gun for direction, and has consequently only to think about the coincidence of the vertical cross-wire with the target, while another man, who also fires, keeps the gun laid for elevation, and is responsible only for the coincidence of the target with the horizontal cross-wire. The 12-pounder has one sight only, one man being considered sufficient to keep the gun laid for elevation as well as for direction, and to fire. It is essential that the sights shall be unaffected by the recoil of the gun, so that they can be adjusted up to the moment of firing by the sight-setter, and that it shall not be necessary for the gun-layer to remove his eye from the telescope while the gun is being fired and reloaded. It is also essential that the sights shall move automatically in elevation and direction with the gun. These two requirements are easily met in the hand-worked mountings by the attachment of the sights to the cradle, which does not move on recoil, and remains constantly parallel to the gun; but in turret mountings the case is more complicated and involves greater complexity of gearing.

The older turret sighting arrangement consisted of two horizontal shafts, one for each gun, running across the turret, which were rotated by pinions gearing into racks underneath the gun-slides, the latter remaining of course always parallel to the guns. Pinions keyed to these shafts geared in their turn into racks formed on vertical sighting columns in the sighting positions, these columns, which carried the sighting telescopes, accordingly moving up and down with the guns. With this arrangement an appreciable amount of backlash was found to be inevitable, owing to the play between the teeth of the several racks and pinions, and to the torsion of the shafts, and the arrangement was also open to the objection that the telescopes were much exposed to possible injury from an enemy's fire. These defects have been very largely obviated by the "rocking motion sights," which have been fitted in the turrets of the latest British battleships and cruisers. In these sights a sight-bracket is secured to and rotates with the trunnion of the mounting; the sight-carrier and telescope move along the top of the sight-bracket, on a curved arc of which the trunnion is not the centre. When the sight is at zero, the telescope is parallel to the axis of the gun, while to adjust the sight, the sight-carrier with telescope is moved along the curved arc by means of a rack and pinion a distance corresponding

to the graduations shown on the range dial, which is concentric with the pinion.

Organisation.— The organization of a large ship for action is necessarily highly elaborate. Among the officers, next to the captain, the most important duties are probably those of the fire-control officer. He is in communication by telephone or voice tube with each of the several units composing the ship's armament. This office is usually filled by the gunnery lieutenant. In the conning tower with the captain is the navigating officer, who attends to the course and speed of the ship, assisted by petty officers to work the wheel and engine-room telegraphs. The torpedo lieutenant, or another officer at the torpedo director, is also in the conning tower, prepared to fire the torpedoes if opportunity offers. Other officers of the military branch, and marine officers, are in charge of various sections of the "quarters."

The rate of advance in naval gunnery has been much accelerated since 1902. The construction of the "Dreadnought," which embodied a new principle both in nature and disposition of armament, the rise of the United States and Japanese navies to the first rank, and the practical experience of the Russo-Japanese war, were all factors which contributed to the increase of the normal rate of advance due to progress in metallurgy and engineering science. In the British as well as in other navies, notably those of Germany, the United States and Japan, ever-increased attention is being devoted to the attainment of a rapid and accurate shell-fire, and large sums are being expended upon fire control instruments and elaborate aiming and sighting appliances. Size of armaments, power of guns, resistance of armour, efficiency of projectiles, and, above all, rapidity and accuracy of fire, all seem to be advancing with giant strides. But there are two important ingredients of naval gunnery which are not subject to change: the human factor, and the factor of the elements—wind, sea and weather. The latter ensures at any rate one datum point to the student of the science, that is, that the extreme range in action is limited by the maximum distance at which the enemy can be clearly seen, which may be considered to be a distance of 8000 to 10,000 yds. The permanence of the human factor assures that, however great the advance in material, and, provided that no great discrepancies exist in this respect between opposing navies, success at sea will be the lot of the nation whose officers are the coolest and most intelligent, whose men are the best disciplined and best trained, and whose navy is in all respects the most imbued with the habits and traditions of the sea.   (S. Fr.)

ORDOVICIAN SYSTEM, in geology, the group of strata which occur normally between the Cambrian below and the Silurian above; it is here regarded as including in ascending order the Arenig, Llandeilo, and Caradoc or Bala series (*qq.v.*). The name was introduced by C. Lapworth in 1879 to embrace those rocks—well developed in the region formerly inhabited by the Ordovices—which had been classed by Sir R. Murchison as Lower Silurian and by A. Sedgwick in his Cambrian system. The term is convenient and well established, but Lower Silurian is still used by some authors. The line of demarcation between the Ordovician and the Cambrian is not sharply defined, and beds on the Tremadoc horizon of the Cambrian are placed by many writers at the base of the Ordovician, with good palaeontological reasons.

The rocks of this system include all types of sedimentation; when they lie flat and undisturbed, as in the Baltic region and Russia, the sands and clays are as soft and incoherent as the similar rocks of Tertiary age in the south of England; where they have been subjected to powerful movements, as in Great Britain, they are represented by slates, greywackes, quartzites, chlorite-, actinolite- and garnet-schists, amphibolites and other products of metamorphism. In Europe the type of rock varies rapidly from point to point, limestones, shales, sandstones, current-bedded grits and conglomerates or their metamorphosed equivalents are all found within limited areas; but in northern Europe particularly the paucity of limestones is a noteworthy feature in contrast with the rocks of like age in the south, and still more with the Ordovician of North America, in which limestones are prevalent. In the Highlands of Scotland, north-west England, in Wales and Ireland, there are enormous developments of contemporaneous lavas and tuffs and their metamorphosed representatives; tuffs occur also in Brittany, and lavas on a large scale in Nova Scotia and New Brunswick.

Distribution.—The Ordovician system is widely distributed. The accompanying map indicates roughly the relative positions of the principal land-masses and seas, but it must be accepted with reserve.

A study of the fossils appears to point to the existence of definite faunal regions or marine basins. The Ordovician rocks

waters, embracing China, Siberia and the Himalayas; concerning the last-named marine area not much is known. In the opposite direction, the Baltic basin may have communicated, through Greenland, with the North American and Arctic seas. Over central and eastern North America another large body of water probably lay, with open communications with the north and west, and with a more constricted connexion with the

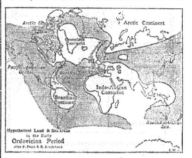

Hypothetical Land & Sea areas
in the Early
Ordovician Period
After F. Frech & R. Renevier.

Atlantic sea. The lagoonal character of some of the rocks of the Tunguska region of Siberia may perhaps be indicative of continental border conditions in that quarter.

Some of the principal subdivisions of the Ordovician rocks are enumerated in the table. Owing to the universal distribution of the graptolites, the correlation of widely separated areas has been rendered possible wherever the muds and shales, in which their remains are preserved, are found. Where they are absent the correlation of the minor local subdivisions of distant deposits is more difficult. In Great Britain, through

ORDOVICIAN SYSTEM.

Ordovician Rocks: Generalized Correlation Table.

England and Wales.	Graptolite Zones.	Scotland.	Scandinavia.	Bohemia.	N.-W. France.	W. Russia.	North American Continent.		
							New York.		Quebec.
Caradoc or Bala group.	Dicellograptus anceps. D. complanatus. Pleurograptus linearis. Dicranograptus clingani.	Hartfell Shales. Ardmillan Series. and Lowther Shales.	Brachiopod beds, Trinucleus beds, and Leptaena limestone. Trinucleus limestone.	D3. D4. D3.	Grès de May. Calcaire de Rosan.	Borkholm and Lyckholm beds. Wesenberg beds.	Richmond beds and Hudson river Shales. Lorraine beds. Utica Shale.	Cincinnatian	Lowest Antikosti limestone and Hudson river beds.
Llandeilo group.	Coenograptus gracilis. Didymograptus Murchisoni.	Glenkiln Shales. and Barr Series.	Middle Graptolite beds and Chasmops limestone. Cystidean limestone.	Dz. Dry.	Schistes des Gothlieux and Ironstone.	Jewe, Itfer, and Kuckers beds. Echinosphaerite limestone.	Trenton beds. Galena limestone. Black river beds. Lowville limestone.	Mohawkian	Trenton limestone. Coenograptus Shales.
(Lanvirn) and Arenig group.	Didymograptus bifidus. Tetragraptus beyondei.	Radiolarian Cherts and Ballantrae Series.	Lower Graptolite beds and Orthoceras limestone.	D4K	Grès Armoricain (part).	Vaginatus limestone and Glauconite limestone.	Chazy limestone (part). St Peter's sandstone.	Canadian	Levis Shales with Tetragraptus, and Phyllograptus.

Tremadoc beds, *Ceratopyge* beds, and beds with *Euloma-Niobe* fauna here regarded as Cambrian: not invariably present.

of the British Isles seem to have been deposited in a North Atlantic sea which embraced also the north of France and Belgium. Confluent with this sea on the east was a rather peculiar basin which included Bohemia, southern France, Spain, Portugal, the eastern Alps, Thuringia, Fichtelgebirge and the Keller Wald. Another European basin, probably separated from the Bohemian or Mediterranean area in early Ordovician times, lay over the Baltic region, Scandinavia, the Baltic provinces and north Germany, and communicated eastwards by way of Russian Poland and central Russia with far eastern

C. Lapworth and his school, and J. E. Marr and the Cambridge school, and in Scandinavia and the Baltic region, through W. C. Brögger, S. A. Tulberg, F. Schmidt and others, the most elaborate subdivision of the Ordovician rocks has been attained.

In the Baltic provinces of Russia, F. Schmidt describes the following stages, in descending order: (Stage F) the Lyckholm and Borkholm zones, a highly fossiliferous series, equivalent to the Middle Bala of Britain; many of the limestones are largely formed of *Rhabdoporella* and other calcareous algae. (E) Wesenberg zone = Bala. (D) Jewe and Kegel zone. (C) Itfer beds, Kuckers Shale (bituminous limestones and marls = Brandschiefer), Echinosphaerite limestone—Upper Orthoceratite limestone of Sweden. (B) Ortho-ceratite (Vaginaten) limestone—Orthoceratite limestone of Sweden, Glauconitic limestone, Glauconitic sand (Greensand). The last-mentioned reposes on Cambrian *Dictyonema* shales. While the Ordovician rocks in Scania, the Baltic provinces and north-central Russia are undisturbed and level-bedded, those on the western side of the Scandinavian axis and in the Urals have suffered movement and are metamorphosed into schists, phyllites, quartzite, marble, &c.; and, especially in Scandinavia, have been extensively thrust. The Bohemian Ordovician, " stage D " of Barrande, consists mainly of greywackes and shales with some ironstone beds and eruptive rocks in the lower parts. In Germany the only large areas are found in the Thuringer Wald, Fichtelgebirge, Frankenwald and Vogtland, where they consist principally of unfossiliferous greywackes and shales with some oolites and glauconitic ironstone (chamosite) in the lower part. They are divisible into the Hauptschiefer or Lederschiefer and the Ober-Thuringit beds above, and the Griffelschiefer and Unter-Thuringit beds below, which rest upon the Leitmitzschiefer of the Euloma-Niobe (Cambrian) horizon. Across northern Russia Ordovician rocks cover a great area; they consist of clays, bitumin-ous and calcareous shales, sands and marls, which in the Ural region have been metamorphosed; the Bukowka sandstone of Russian Poland is of this age. In north-west France this system is represented in Brittany and Normandy by the slates of Riadan, the *grès de Mey*, the *schistes à calymènes* (with an ironstone bed at the base) and the *grès armoricain*. In the Ardennes are the *schistes de Gembloux*, resting upon graptolitic shales of Arenig age. Sandstones and shales occur in Languedoc, and various rocks in the Pyrenees. In the Iberian peninsula Ordovician rocks are widely spread, represented by sandstones, slates and shales covering the whole of the period; they are well developed in Asturia and Galicia. In the eastern Alps about Graz are found calcareous shales with crinoids, the "Schock-elkalk" and "Semriacher" shales; the Marthener beds of the Carnic Alps are of this age. In China (Kiang-su, Kian-chang), in Burma (Mandalay) and in the Himalayas (Niti and Spiti) Ordo-vician fossil-bearing rocks are known.

On the North American continent Ordovician rocks cover a very large area in the central, eastern and northern parts (north of lat. 30°). As regards the classification and correlation of the strata, which change in character from point to point, as is natural over so large an area, much remains to be done. In the table the divisions of the system that obtain in the New York district are enumerated; but in each state there is a local nomenclature for the beds. Thus in Iowa, Wisconsin and Minnesota we find (1) Lower Magnesian lime-stone, St Peter's sandstone; (2) Trenton limestone, Galena lime-stone; (3) Hudson river shales; in Arkansas, the California or Magnesian limestone, Saccaroidal limestone, Izard limestone and Polk Bayou limestone; in Oklahoma, the Arbuckle limestone, Simpson series, Viola limestone and Sylvan shales; and in east Tennessee, the Chickamauga limestone, Athens shale, Tellia sand-stone, Sievier shale and Bays sandstone. In Massachusetts there are enormous series of schists which have been assigned to this period. In west Virginia are the Martinsburg shales (1000 ft or more). In Canada the Ordovician rocks (Quebec group) are thickly developed. In the upper division there are the lowest of the Anticosti limestones, the Hudson river beds, and Trenton limestone; to the middle division belong the *Coenograptus* shales; and the lower division consists of the Levis shales with Sillery beds at the base. In Nova Scotia and New Brunswick are the lower and upper divisions of the Cobequid group, a series of shales, quartzites and conglomer-ates with igneous rocks. In the polar regions Ordovician rocks are represented by the Trenton limestone in Boothia and King William's Land; by limestones with *Caryocystis granetum* in east Greenland; and in the Barrow Straits by beds with *Asaphus* and *Maclurea*.

In North Africa Ordovician rocks are probably present, and in New Zealand the Arorere series (Wanaka group), and in Australia (Victoria) the graptolitic, gold-bearing shales and slates belong to this period. During this period there appears to have been a general tendency for the sea to transgress on the land, a tendency which increased towards its close, especially in the northern hemisphere (Europe and the Appalachian regions). One of the results of this movement was the interchange and commingling of many previously separated faunal groups. About the beginning of the period the sea withdrew from the land in Texas and south of the Rocky Mountains. The folding of the Appalachians was in progress early in Ordovician times and later in the period the first synchronous of the Scandinavian and British folding set in.

Volcanic Activity.—This period was one of great volcanic activity in several widely separated regions. " In Ayrshire and the south-western districts (of the southern uplands), where the volcanic constituents attain a great development, they consist of basic lavas (diabase, &c.), with intercalated tuffs and agglomerates. A characteristic feature of these lavas is the development of ellipsoidal or pillow-structure in them. This volcanic platform appears to underlie the Silurian region over an area of at least 2000 sq. m., inasmuch as it comes to the surface wherever the crests of the anticlines bring up suffi-

ciently deep parts of the formations. It is thus one of the most extensive as well as one of the most ancient volcanic tracts of Europe " (Sir A. Geikie, *Text-book of Geology*, 4th ed. vol. ii. p. 951). In the west of England and in Wales there was also a very active volcanic centre. In the Snowdon district thousands of feet of contemporaneous felsitic lavas and tuffs occur in the Bala beds; while in Cader Idris, the Arenig Mountains and the Arans there are similar eruptions of felsitic and rhyolitic lavas, tuffs and agglomerates—probably many of them sub-marine—interstratified in the Arenig formation. In the Lake district a great series of lavas and ashes—the Borrowdale series—was erupted during the middle of the period; the earlier effusions were andesitic, the later ones felsitic and rhyolitic. In Ireland the Arenig lavas of Tyrone resemble some of those in Scotland. Volcanic rocks (porphyrites, syenites and lavas) occur in considerable force in the Ordovician rocks of Nova Scotia and New Brunswick and New Zealand. Tuffs of this age are found in Brittany, and diabase in Bohemia.

The *economic products* obtained from rocks of this period include gold in Australia, New Zealand and Wales; iron ore in France; lead and zinc from the Galena and Trenton horizons in Wisconsin, Iowa and Illinois; manganese in Arkansas; oil and gas from the Trenton stage in Ohio and east Indiana; roofing slates and slate pencils in Wales and the Lake district; limestone in Great Britain and Tennessee; phosphate beds in Wales and Tennessee; marble in the Appalachian district; graphite (plumbago) in the Lake district; and jasper in Wales and southern Scotland.

Ordovician Life.—Compared with the preceding Cambrian period, the Ordovician is remarkable for the great expansion in numbers and variety of organisms, apart from the fact that fossils are better preserved in the younger formations.

All the great classes of molluscs were represented, the most numer-ous being the brachiopods, which, in addition to the simple forms of the Cambrian, began at this time to develop spire-bearing genera (*Choneles, Orthis, Orthisina, Strophomena, Crania, Schizotreta, Porambonites, Rafinesquina, Leptaena, Zygospira*). The gasteropoda now developed all the leading types of shell (*Pleurotomaria, Ophtalo-trochus*); but both this class and the pelecypods (*Lyrodesma, Clenodonta, Modiolopsis*) were subordinate in importance to the cephalopods. These molluscs were probably the most powerful living creatures in the Ordovician seas; straight-shelled, slightly curved, and nautiloid forms predominated (*Orthoceras, Cyrtoceras, Gyroceras, Trocholites, Endoceras, Lituoceras, Listuiles, Actinoceras*). Some of the straight shells were of enormous size, 12 to 15 ft. long and as much as 1 ft. in diameter, in the widest part. Trilobites were present in great abundance, and in this period they reached the climax of their development. In the lower stage we find *Agnostus, Calymene, Asaphus, Illaenus, Placoparis*; on the Llandeilo horizon, *Calymene, Asaphus, Megalaspis, Dalmanites*; and, at the summit, *Trinucleus* and *Homalonotus*. In the transition zone between Ordovician and Cambrian, *Dalmania, Ceratopyge, Euloma, Niobe*, flourished. Other important genera are *Ogygia, Cheirurus, Harpes, Acidaspis, Ostracoda* (*Leperditia, Beyrichia*), cyprids (*Bairdia, Macrocypris*), phyllocarida (*Ceratiocaris, Peltocaris*), cirripeds (*Lepidocoleus*), and, later, eurypterids represented other crustacean groups. The bryozoans, *Stomatopora, Monticulipora, Phylloporina, Fenestella* and others, were abundant and frequently formed beds of limestone. Among the echinoderms the cystoids were the most prominent (*Pleurocystis, Aristocystis*) and at this period reached their climax; crinoids (*Archaeocrinus, Dendrocrinus*) became more important; while ophiuroids, echinoids (*Bothriocidaris*) and asteroids (*Taeniaster, Palaeaster*) made their appearance. Corals (*Streptelasma, Colum-naria*) were scarce, and sponges (*Aulocopium, Caryospongia, Archaeo-cyathus*) were not particularly important; *Receptaculites, Ischadites*, are well-known fossils doubtfully referred to this group. Radiolaria assisted in the formation of certain beds of chert, and foraminifera have been observed. The remarkable group, the graptolites, evi-dently inhabited the seas in countless numbers and have left their remains in the dark shales of this period all over the world. At this time the diprionidian forms alone were represented by such genera as *Tetragraptus, Phyllograptus, Didymograptus, Dicellograptus, Diplo-graptus* and others. Of great interest are the earliest known indica-tions of vertebrate life in the form of dermal plates and teeth of fish-like organisms from the Ordovician of Colorado. The terrestrial life of the period is very meagrely represented by the remains of land plants, mostly poorly preserved in certain sandstones, and by scorpions and several orders of insects, *Protocimex* (Sweden), *Palaeoblattina* (Colorado).

One of the most striking facts brought out by the study of the distribution of Ordovician fossils is the wide range of the northern or " periarctic " faunal assemblage. This periarctic fauna prevails over the whole world—so far as our present knowledge shows—with the exception of the peculiar Bohemian or Mediterranean region, which includes north-west and south-west France, Spain, Italy, the Alps, the Fichtelgebirge, east Thuringia, Harz and Rhenish Mountains.

AUTHORITIES.—Sir R. I. Murchison, *Silurian System* (1839) and *Siluria* (1854, 1867); A. Sedgwick, *Synopsis of the Classification of the British Palaeozoic Rocks* (1855); J. Barrande, *Système silurien du centre de la Bohême* (1852–1887); J. J. Bigsby, *Thesaurus Siluricus* (London, 1868); J. E. Marr, *The Classification of the Cambrian and Silurian Rocks* (Cambridge, 1883); Charles Lapworth, "On the Geological Distribution of the Rhabdophora," *Annals and Mag. Nat. Hist.* ser. 5, vols. iii., iv., v., vi. (1879–1880); B. N. Peach, J. Horne, J. J. H. Teall, "The Silurian Rocks of Great Britain," vol. i., Scotland, *Mem. Geol. Survey* (1899); F. Frech and others, "Lethaea geognostica," Theil I. Band 2 (*Lethaea palaeozoica*) (Stuttgart, 1897–1902); Sir A. Geikie, *Text-book of Geology* (4th ed., 1903); and for recent papers, *Geological Literature*, Geol. Soc. (London, annual). See also CAMBRIAN and SILURIAN SYSTEMS.   (J. A. H.)

ORDU (anc. *Cotyora*, where the "Ten Thousand" embarked for home), a town on the N. coast of Asia Minor, between Samsun and Kerasund, connected with Zara, and so with Sivas, by a carriage road, and with Constantinople and Trebizond by steamer. Pop. about 6000, more than half Christian. Ordu has exceptionally good Greek schools, and a growing trade in filberts.

ORDUIN - NASHCHOKIN, ATHANASY LAVRENTEVICH (?–1680), Russian statesman, was the son of a poor official at Pskov, who saw to it that his son was taught Latin, German and mathematics. Athanasy began his public career in 1642 as one of the delineators of the new Russo-Swedish frontier after the peace of Stolbova. Even then he had a great reputation at Moscow as one who thoroughly understood "German ways and things." He was one of the first Muscovites who diligently collected foreign books, and we hear of as many as sixty-nine Latin works being sent to him at one time from abroad. He attracted the attention of the young tsar Alexius by his resourcefulness during the Pskov rebellion of 1650, which he succeeded in localizing by personal influence. At the beginning of the Swedish War, Orduin was appointed to a high command, in which he displayed striking ability. In 1657 he was appointed minister-plenipotentiary to treat with the Swedes on the Narova river. He was the only Russian statesman of the day with sufficient foresight to grasp the fact that the Baltic seaboard, or even a part of it, was worth more to Muscovy than ten times the same amount of territory in Lithuania, and, despite ignorant jealousy of his colleagues, succeeded (Dec. 1658) in concluding a three-years' truce whereby the Muscovites were left in possession of all their conquests in Livonia. In 1660 he was sent as pleni-potentiary to a second congress, to convert the truce of 1658 into a permanent peace. He advised that the truce with Sweden should be prolonged and Charles II. of England invited to mediate a northern peace. Finally he laid stress upon the immense importance of Livonia for the development of Russian trade. On being overruled he retired from the negotiations. He was the chief plenipotentiary at the abortive congress of Durovicha, which met in 1664, to terminate the Russo-Polish War; and it was due in no small measure to his superior ability and great tenacity of purpose that Russia succeeded in concluding with Poland the advantageous truce of Andrussowo (Feb. 11, 1667). On his return to Russia he was created a boyar of the first class and entrusted with the direction of the foreign office, with the title of "Guardian of the great Tsarish Seal and Director of the great Imperial Offices." He was, in fact, the first Russian chancellor. It was Orduin who first abolished the onerous system of tolls on exports and imports, and established a combination of native merchants for promoting direct commercial relations between Sweden and Russia. He also set on foot a postal system between Muscovy, Courland and Poland, and introduced gazettes and bills of exchange into Russia. With his name, too, is associated the building of the first Russian merchant-vessels on the Dvina and Volga. But his whole official career was a constant struggle with narrow routine and personal jealousy on the part of the boyars and clerks of the council. He was last employed in the negotiations for confirming the truce of Andrussowo (September 1669; March 1670). In January 1671 we hear of him as in attendance upon the tsar on the occasion of his second marriage; but in February the same year he was dismissed, and withdrew to the Kruipetsky monastery near Kiev, where he took the tonsure under the name of Antony, and occupied himself with good works till his death in 1680. In many things he anticipated Peter the Great. He was absolutely incorruptible, thus standing, morally as well as intellectually, far above the level of his age.

See S. M. Solovev, *History of Russia* (Rus.), vol. xi. (St Petersburg, 1895, seq.); V. Ikonnikov, "Biography of Orduin-Nashchokin" (in *Russkaya Starina*, Nos. 11–12) (St Petersburg, 1883); R. Nisbet Bain, *The First Romanovs* (London, 1905, chaps. 4 and 6).   (R. N. B.)

ÖREBRO, a town of Sweden, capital of the district (*län*) of Örebro, lying on both banks of the Svartå a mile above its entrance into Lake Hjelmar, 135 m. W. of Stockholm by rail. Pop. (1900), 22,013. In great part rebuilt since a fire in 1854, it has a modern appearance. An ancient castle, however, with four round towers, remains on an island in the stream. It is used as a museum. There may be mentioned also the church of St Nicholas, of the 13th century; and the King's House (*Kungstuga*), an old and picturesque timber building. In front of the modern town hall stands a statue, by Karl Gustav Qvarnström (1810–1867), of the patriot Engelbrecht (d. 1436), who was born here. The Swedish reformers of the 16th century, Olaus and Laurentius Petri, are commemorated by an obelisk. Örebro is in close connexion with the iron-mining district of central Sweden; it has mechanical works and a technical college. A large trade is carried on, by way of the Örebro canal and lakes Hjelmar and Mälar, with Stockholm.

Örebro was in existence in the 11th century. Its castle, erected by Birger jarl in the 13th century, played an important part in the early annals of Sweden; and no fewer than twenty diets or important assemblies were held either in the castle or in the town. Such were the Örebro *concilium* of 1537, the diet of 1540 in which the crown was declared hereditary, and that of 1810 when Bernadotte was elected crown prince.

ORE-DRESSING, one of the principal processes in the work of mining (*q.v.*). When the miner hoists his ore[1] to the surface, the contained metal may be either in the native uncombined state, as, for example, native gold, native silver, native copper, or combined with other substances forming minerals of more or less complex composition, as, for example, telluride of gold, sulphide of silver, sulphide of copper. In both cases the valuable mineral is always associated with minerals of no value. The province of the ore-dresser is to separate the "values" from the waste—for example, quartz, felspar, calcite—by mechanical means, obtaining thereby "concentrates" and "tailings." The province of the metallurgist is to extract the pure metal from the concentrates by chemical means, with or without the aid of heat. There are also a number of non-metallic minerals which do not have any value, or at best do not reach their highest value until they have been subjected to some form of mechanical preparation; among them are diamonds, graphite, corundum, garnet, asbestos and coal. Ore-dressing, for the purposes of this article, may be divided into three parts: (1) properties of minerals which render aid in their separation; (2) simple operations; (3) operations combined to form processes or mills.

1. The *specific gravity* of minerals varies greatly, some being heavy, others light. The rate of settling in water is affected by the specific gravity in this way: of two particles of the same *Properties.* size but different specific gravity, the heavier settles more rapidly than the lighter, while of two particles of different specific gravity which settle at the same rate in water, that of higher specific gravity is of smaller diameter than the other. The same statements are true in regard to settling in air, and in regard to momentum in air when the particles are thrown out in a horizontal direction. *Colour*, *lustre* and *fracture* are of especial value in hand-picking, to aid the eye in selecting the mineral sought. Instances are, of colours, the white of quartz, the pale straw colour of felspar, the dull yellow of limonite, the brass yellow of chalcopyrite, the pale metallic yellow of pyrite; of lustres, the vitreous of quartz, the adamantine of diamond and cerussite, the resinous of blende, the earthy of limonite, and the metallic of pyrite; and of fractures, the cleavage planes of felspar and galena, the conchoidal fracture of quartz and pyrite, the granular of some forms of magnetite and blende. *Magnetism* is a most direct and simple method of separating minerals where it is available. The discovery that by the use of electro-magnets of great

[1] The O. Eng. word was *óra*, corresponding with Du. *oer*, the origin of which is unknown. The form "ore" represents the O Eng. *ár*, brass; cf. Lat. *aes*, Skt. *ayas*.

power minerals formerly regarded as non-magnetic are attracted, has made it possible to separate several classes of minerals present in an ore; for example, the strongly magnetic mineral may first be taken out, then the mildly magnetic, and last the weakly magnetic, the non-magnetic being left behind. *Adhesion* acts when brightly burnished particles of gold issuing with the sand from the stamp mill come in contact with an amalgamated copper plate, for they are instantly plated with mercury and adhere to the copper, while the sand is carried forward by the water. In this way a very perfect separation of the gold from the sand is effected. In the South African diamond fields it has been found that if the diamond-bearing sand is taken in a stream of water over a smooth surface covered with a suitable coating of grease, the diamonds will adhere to the grease while the sand does not.

2. The concentration of ores always proceeds by steps or stages. Thus the ore must be crushed before the minerals can be separated, and certain preliminary steps, such as sizing and classify- *Simple Operations.* ing, must precede the final operations which produce the finished concentrates. The more important of these simple operations will now be described.

The ore as mined contains the valuable minerals attached to and enclosed in lumps of waste rock. The province of *crushing* or *disintegrating* is to sever or unlock the values from the waste, so that the methods of separation are then able to part the one from the other. In crushing ores it is found wise to progress by stages, coarse crushing being best done by one class of machine, medium by another, and fine by a third. Coarse crushing is accomplished by *breakers* of the Blake type (fig. 1) or of the Gates Comet type (fig. 2). All of these machines break by direct pressure, caused by a movable jaw,

FIG. 1.—Blake Breaker
a, Movable jaw.
b, Fixed jaw.

a (figs. 1, 2), approaching towards and receding from a fixed jaw, b. The largest size ever fed to a breaker is 24 in. in diameter, and the smallest size to which the finest crushing commonly done by these machines brings the ore is about 3/4 in. diameter. The machine is generally supplied with ore in lumps not larger than 9 in. in diameter, and crushes them to about 1 1/4 in. in diameter. Medium-size crushing is done mostly by rolls or steam stamps. *Rolls* (fig. 3) crush by direct pressure caused by the ore being drawn between two revolving rolls held closely together. They make the least fine slimes or fines to be lost in the subsequent treatment, and are therefore preferred for all brittle minerals. The *steam stamp* works upon the same principle as a steam hammer, the pestle being forced down by steam pressure acting through piston and cylinder with great crushing force in the mortar. Steam stamps have been very successful with the native copper rock, because they break up the little leaves, flakes and filaments of copper, and render them susceptible of concentration, which rolls do not. Fine crushing is done by gravity stamps, pneumatic stamps, by centrifugal roller mills, by amalgamating pans, by ball mills, by Chile edgestone mills, by tube mills and by arrastras. The *gravity stamp* (fig. 4) is a pestle of 900-lb weight more or less, which is lifted by a revolving loose fit on the cam and falls by the force of gravity to strike a heavy blow on the ore resting on the die in the mortar and do the work

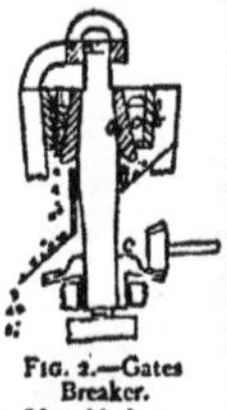

FIG. 2.—Gates Breaker.
a, Movable jaw.
b, Fixed jaw.
c, Gear with eccentric hub and with loose fit on the spindle.

of crushing; the frequent revolution of the cam gives a more or less rapid succession of blows. Gravity stamps are especially adapted to the fine crushing of gold ores, which they reduce to 1/16-in. and sometimes even to 1/30-in. grains. The blow of the stamp upon the fragments of quartz not only liberates the fine particles of gold, but brightens them so that they are quickly caught upon the amalgamated plates. The *centrifugal roller mills* are suited to fine crushing of middle products, namely by-products composed of grains containing both values and waste, since they avoid making much fine slimes. They crush by the action of a roller, rolling on the inside

FIG. 3.—Crushing Rolls.

of a steel ring, both having vertical axes. The *amalgamating pan* is suitable for grinding silver ore for amalgamation where the finest grinding is sought, together with the chemical action from the contact with iron. It crushes by a true grinding action of one surface sliding upon another. The *Chile edgestone mill* is employed for the finest grinding ever used preparatory to concentration. The *arrastra* or drag-stone mill grinds still finer for amalgamating. The *ball mill*

is a horizontal revolving cylinder with iron balls in it which do the grinding; the pulverized ore passes out through screens in the cylinder wall. It is a fine grinder, making a small amount of impalpable slimes. It is used for preparation for concentrating. The *tube mill* is of similar construction, but it is fed through the hollow shaft at one end and discharged through the hollow shaft at the other; the finely ground ore is floated out by water and contains a large proportion of impalpable slimes. It is used for preparation for cyaniding of gold.

A considerable class of workable minerals, among which are surface ores of iron and surface phosphates, contain worthless clay mixed with the valuable material, the removal of which is accomplished by the *log washer.* This is a disintegrator consisting of a long narrow cylinder revolving in a trough which is nearly horizontal. Upon the cylinder are knives or paddles set at an angle, which serve the double purpose of bruising and disintegrating the clay and of conveying the cleaned lump ore to be discharged at the upper end of the trough, while water meanwhile washing away the clay at the lower end.

Roasting for Friability.—When two minerals—for example, pyrite and cassiterite (tin ore)—one of which is decomposed and rendered porous and friable by heat and oxygen—are roasted in a furnace, the pyrite becomes porous oxide of iron, while the cassiterite is not changed. A gentle crushing and washing operation will then break and float away the lighter iron oxide, leaving the cleaned cassiterite behind.

FIG. 4.—Gravity Stamp.

Sizing.—This is the first of the preliminary operations of separation. It is found useful in concentration, for dividing an ore into a number of portions graded from coarser sizes down to finer sizes. Each portion is made suitable for treatment on its respective machine. If crushed ore be sifted upon a screen with holes of definite size, two products will result—the oversize, which is unable to pass through the screen, and the undersize, which does pass. If the latter size be sifted upon another screen with smaller holes, it will again make oversize and undersize. The operation can be repeated with more sieves until the desired number of portions is obtained. P. von Rittinger adopted for close sizing the following diameters in millimetres for the holes in a set of screens: 64, 45·2, 32, 22·6, 16, 11·3, 8, 5·6, 4, 2·8, 2, 1·4, 1. Each of these holes has an area double that of the one next below it; this may be called the screen ratio. A process which does not need such close sizing might use every other screen of the above set, and in extreme cases even every fourth screen. In mills the screen ratio for coarse sizes often differs from that for fine. Sizing is done by cylindrical screens revolving upon their inclined axes (fig. 5) by flat shaking screens, and by fixed screens with a comparatively steel slope. Either wire cloth or square holes or steel plate punched with round holes is used. To remove the largest lumps in the preliminary sizing, fixed-bar screens (grizzlies) are preferred, on account of their strength and durability.

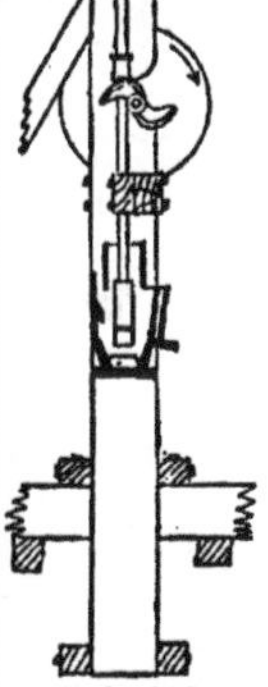

FIG. 5.—Trommel or Revolving Screen.

Sizes smaller than can be satisfactorily graded by screens are treated by means of *hydraulic classifiers* and *box classifiers.* The lower limit of screening and therefore the beginning of this work

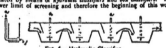

FIG. 6.—Hydraulic Classifier.

varies from grains of 5 millimetres to grains of 1 millimetre in diameter. A hydraulic classifier (fig. 6) is a trough-like washer through which the water and sand flow from one end to the other. In the bottom, at regular intervals, are pockets or pits with hydraulic devices which hinder the outflowing discharge of sand, b, by an inflowing stream of clear water, a. By regulating the speed of these water currents, the size of the grains in the several discharges can be regulated, the first being the coarsest and the overflow at the end the finest. Box classifiers (*spitzkasten*) are similar, except that the pockets are much larger and no inflowing clear water is used, they therefore do their work much less perfectly. Classifiers do not truly size the ore, but merely class together grains which have equal settling power. In any given product, except the first, the grain of high specific gravity will always be smaller than that of low. The box classifiers are suited to treating finer sizes than the hydraulic classifiers, and therefore follow them in the mill treatment.

Picking Floors, the first of the final operations of separation, are areas on which men, boys or girls pick out the valuable mineral which is rich enough to ship at once to the smelter. The picking is often accompanied and aided by breaking with a hammer. *Picking tables* are generally so constructed that the pickers can sit still and have the ore pass before them on a moving surface, such as a revolving circular table or travelling belt. Stationary picking tables require the ore to be wheeled to and dumped in front of the pickers. Picking out the values by hand has the double advantage that it saves the power and time of crushing, and prevents the formation of a good deal of fine slimes which are difficult to save.

Jigs treat ores ranging from 1½ in. in diameter down to $\frac{1}{25}$ in. If an intermittently pulsating current of water is passed up through a horizontal sieve on which is a bed of ore, the heavy mineral and the quartz quickly form layers, the former beneath the latter. The machine by which this work is done is called a jig, and the operation is called jigging. In the hand jig the sieve is moved up and down in a tank of water to get the desired separation. In the power jig (fig. 7) the sieve, *a*, is stationary and the pulsating current is obtained by placing a vertical longitudinal partition, *c*, extending part of the way down to the bottom of the jig box. The sieve, *a*, is firmly fastened on one side of the partition, and on the other a piston or plunger, *d*, is moved rapidly up and down by an eccentric, causing an up-and-down current of water through the sieve, *a*. The sieve is fed at one end, *e*, with a constant supply of water and ore, and the quartz overflows at the other. Clear water ("hydraulic water") is brought by the pipe, *i*, into the space, *g*, below called the hutch, to regulate the condition of the bed of ore on *a*. The constantly accumulating bed of concentrates is either discharged through the sieve into the hutch, *g*, or by some special device at the side. On jigs where the concentrates pass through the sieve, a bed of heavy mineral grains too large to pass holds back the lighter quartz. The quartz overflow from one sieve, *a*, generally carries too much value to be thrown away, and it is therefore jigged again upon a second sieve, *b*. In jigging difficult ores, three, four, five and even six sieves are used. A succession of sieves gives a set of products graded both in kind and in richness, the heavier mineral, as galena, coming first, the lighter, as pyrites and blende, coming later. The best jigging is done upon closely sized products using a large amount of clear water added beneath the sieve. Very good jigging may, however, be done upon the products of hydraulic classifiers, where the heavy mineral is in small grains and the quartz is large, by using a bed on the sieve and diminished hydraulic water, which increases the suction or downward pull by the returning plunger.

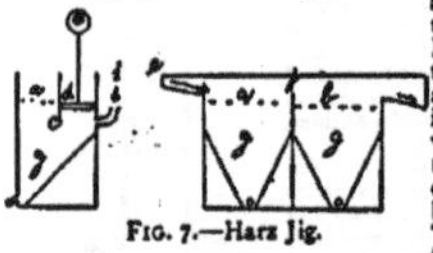

FIG. 7.—Harz Jig.

Bumping Tables.—Rittinger's table is a rectangular gently sloping plane surface which by a bumping motion throws the heavy particles to one side while the current of water washes down the quartz to another, a wedge-shaped divider separating and guiding the concentrates and tailings into their respective hoppers. The capacity on pulp of $\frac{1}{10}$ to $\frac{1}{25}$ in. size is some 4 tons in twenty-four hours. In the Wilfley table (fig. 8) and those derived from it a gentler vanning motion is substituted for the harsh bump; they have a greatly increased width and a set of riffle blocks, *b*, at right angles to the direction of flow, *c*, tapering in height towards the side where the concentrates are discharged, *d*. This combination has produced a table of great efficiency and capacity for treating grains from ¼ in. in diameter down to $\frac{1}{200}$ in. or even finer. The capacity on $\frac{1}{25}$ in. pulp is from 15 to 25 tons in twenty-four hours.

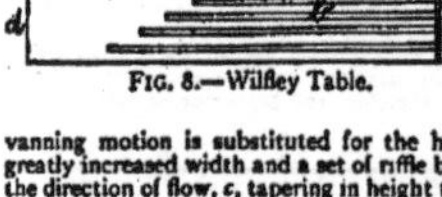

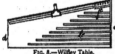

FIG. 8.—Wilfley Table.

Vanners are machines which treat ores on endless belts, generally of rubber with flanges on the two sides. The belt (fig. 9) travels up a gentle slope, *a*, on horizontal transverse rollers, and is shaken about 200 times a minute, either sidewise or endwise, to the extent of about 1 in. The lower 10 ft. is called the concentrating plane, *b*, and slopes 2·78% more or less from the horizontal; the upper 2 ft. of length is called the cleaning plane, *c*, and slopes 4·45% more or less. The fine ore is fed on with water (technically called pulp) at the intersection of the two planes, *d*. The vibration separates the ore into layers, the heavy minerals beneath and the light above. The downward flow of the water carries the light waste off and discharges it over the tail roller *e* into the waste launder, while the upward travel of the belt carries up the heavy mineral. On the cleaning plane the latter passes under a row of jets, *f*, of clean water, which remove the last of the waste rock; it clings to the belt while it passes over the head roller, and only leaves it when the belt is forced by the dipping roller to dip in the water of the concentrates tank, *g*. The cleaned belt then continues its return journey over the guide roller *h* to the tail roller *e*, which it passes round, and again does concentration duty. Experience proves that for exceedingly fine ores the end shake with steep slope and rapid travel does better work than the side-shake vanner. For ordinary gold stamp-mill pulp, where cleanness of tailings is the most important end, and where to gain it the engineer is willing to throw a little quartz into the concentrates, the end-shake vanner is again probably a little better than the side-shake, but where cleanness of concentrates is sought the side-shake vanner is the most satisfactory. The latter is much the most usual form.

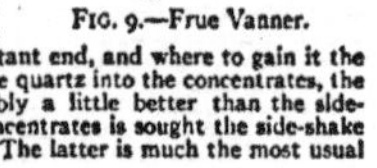

FIG. 9.—Frue Vanner.

Slime-Tables are circular revolving tables (fig. 10) with flattened conical surfaces, and a slope of 1½ in. more or less per foot from centre to circumference; a common size is 17 ft. in diameter, and a common speed one revolution per minute. These tables treat material of $\frac{1}{60}$ in. and less in diameter coming from box classifiers. The principle on which the table works is that the film of water upon the smooth surface rolls the larger grains (quartz) towards the margin of the table faster than the smaller grains (heavy mineral) which are in the slow-moving bottom current. The revolution of the table then discharges the quartz earlier at *a*, *a*, *a*, *a*, an intermediate middling product next at *b*, and the heavy mineral last at *c*. Suitable launders or troughs and catch-boxes are supplied for the three products. The capacity of such a table is 12 tons or more of pulp, dry weight, in twenty-four hours. *Frames*, used in concentrating tin ore in Cornwall, are rectangular slime-tables which separate the waste from the concentrates on the same principle as the circular tables, though they run intermittently. They treat very fine pulp, and after being fed for a short period (about fifteen minutes) the pulp is shut off, the concentrates are flushed off with a douche of water and caught in a box, and the feed pulp is again turned on. *Canvas tables* are rectangular tables with plane surfaces covered with cotton duck (canvas) free from seams, they slope about 1½ in. to the foot. They are fed with stamp-mill pulp, with the tailings of vanners, or, best of all, with very fine pulp overflowing from a fine classifier. The rough surface of the duck is such an efficient catching surface that they can run for an hour before the concentrates are removed—an operation which is effected by shutting off the feed pulp, rinsing the surface with a little clean water, and hosing or brooming off the concentrates into a catch-box. The feed-pulp is then again turned on and the work resumed. They have been more successful than any other machine in treating the finest pulp, especially when their concentrates are finally cleaned on a steep slope end-shake vanner (the G. G. Gates canvas table system of California).

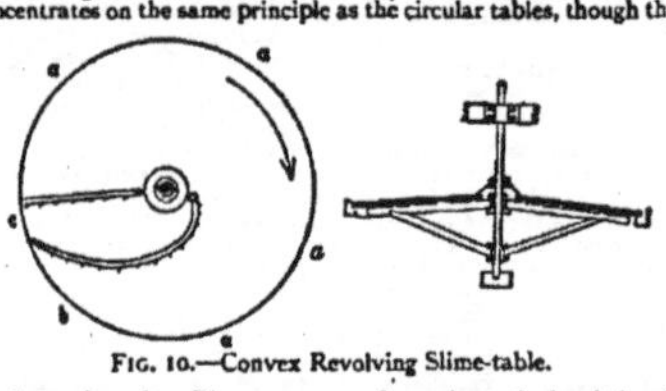

FIG. 10.—Convex Revolving Slime-table.

Buddles act in principle like slime-tables, but they are stationary, and they allow the sand to build itself up upon the conical surface, which is surrounded by a retaining wall. When charged, the tailings are shovelled from the outer part of the circle, the middlings from the intervening annular part, and the concentrates from the inner part. They treat somewhat coarser sizes than the slime-table. The term *buddle* is sometimes applied to the slime-tables, but the majority confine the phrase to the machine on which the sand builds up in a deep layer.

Riffles.—When wooden blocks or cobble-stones of uniform size are placed in the bottom of a sluice, the spaces between them are called *riffles*; and when gold-bearing gravel is carried through the sluice by a current of water, a great many eddies are produced, in which the gold and other heavy minerals settle.

Kieves.—The *kieve* or *dolly-tub* is a tub as large or larger than an ordinary oil-barrel, with sides flaring slightly upwards all the way from the bottom. In the centre is a little vertical shaft, with hand-crank at the top and stirring blades like those of a propeller at the bottom. Fine concentrates from buddles or slime-tables are still further enriched by treatment in the kieve. The kieve is filled perhaps half full of water, and the paddles set in motion; concentrates are now shovelled in until it is nearly full, the rotation is continued a little longer and then the shaft is quickly withdrawn and the side of the kieve steadily thumped by a bumping-bar as long as settling contiques. When this is completed, the water is siphoned off, the top sand skimmed off and sent back to the buddle, and the enriched bottom shovelled out and sent to the smelter.

Combined operations.

3. In designing concentration works, the millwright seeks so to combine the various methods of coarse and fine crushing and of preliminary and final concentration that he will obtain the maximum return from the ore with the minimum cost. Some of the more important of these mill schemes will now be described.

The hand-jig process used for the zinc and lead ores of Missouri is first to clean the ore from adhering clay by raking it back and forth in a sluice with a running stream of water, and then shovel it upon a sloping screen with holes of about 1 in., where it yields oversize and undersize. The former is hand-picked into lead ore, zinc ore and waste, while the latter is jigged upon a hand-jig and yields several layers of minerals removed by a hand-skimmer. The top skimmings are waste, the middle skimmings come back with the next charge to be jigged over, and the bottom skimmings go to a second jig with finer screen. The coarsest of the hutch product, *i.e.* the product which passed through the sieve and settled at the bottom of the tank, goes to the second jig, the finest is sold to a sludge mill to be finished on buddles. The second jig makes top skimmings which are sent back to the first jig, middle skimmings which are zinc concentrates, and bottom skimmings and hutch, which are lead concentrates.

In the Missouri zinc-concentrating mill the ore carrying blende and calamine with a little galena is in very large crystallizations and contains, when crushed, very little in the way of included grains. It is crushed by Blake breaker and rolls, to pass through a sieve with holes $\frac{3}{8}$ in. in diameter, and is then treated on a power jig with six consecutive sieves, yielding discharge and hutch products from each sieve, and tailings to waste. The earlier discharges are finished products, while the later are re-crushed and re-treated on the same jig. The hutch products are treated on a finishing-jig with five sieves, and yield galena from the first discharge and hutch, and zinc ore from the others. The capacity of such jigs is very large, even to 75 or 100 tons per day of ten hours.

In the diamond washing of Kimberley, South Africa, the material taken from the mine is weathered by exposure to the air and rain for several months, and the softening and disintegration thus well started are completed by stirring in vats with water. Breaker and rolls were tried in order to hasten the process, but the larger diamonds were broken and ruined thereby. The material from the vats is screened and jigged, and of the jig concentrates containing about 2% of diamonds the coarser are hand-picked and the finer are treated on a greased surface.

Lead and copper ores contain their values in brittle minerals, and are concentrated in mills which vary somewhat according to local conditions; the one here outlined is typical of the class. The ore is crushed by breaker and rolls, and separated into a series of products diminishing in size by a set of screens, hydraulic classifier and box classifier. All the products of screens and hydraulic classifiers are jigged on separate jigs yielding concentrates, middlings and tailings; those of the box classifier are treated on the slime-table, vanner or Wilfley table, yielding concentrates and tailings and perhaps middlings. The coarser middlings contain values attached to grains of quartz and are therefore sent back to be re-crushed and re-treated. The finer middlings contain values difficult to save from their shape only, and are sent back to the same machine or to another to be finished.

The native copper rock of Lake Superior is broken by powerful breakers, sometimes preceded by a heavy drop-hammer weighing a ton, more or less. The operation is accompanied by hand-picking, yielding rich nuggets with perhaps 75% of copper ready for the smelter; at some mines a second grade is also picked out which goes to a steam finishing-hammer and yields cleaned mass copper for the smelter and rich stamp stuff. The run of rock which passes by the hand-pickers is of a size that will pass through a bar screen with bars 3 in. apart, and goes to the steam stamps. The stamp crushes the rock and discharges coarse copper through a pipe 4 in. in diameter, in which it descends against a rising stream of water which lifts out the lighter rock. The copper is let out about once an hour by opening a gate at the bottom. The rest of the rock is crushed to pass through a screen with round holes $\frac{3}{16}$ in. in diameter, more or less. This sand is treated in hydraulic classifiers with four pockets, the products from the pockets being jigged by four roughing-jigs yielding finished mineral copper for the smelter, included grains for the grinder, partially concentrated products for the finishing-jigs, and tailings which go to waste. The overflow of the hydraulic classifier runs to a tank of which the overflow is sent to waste in order to diminish the quantity of water, while the discharge from beneath, treated upon slime-tables, yields concentrates, middlings and tailings. The middlings are re-treated. All the finished concentrates put together will assay from 60 to 80% of copper according to circumstances. The extraction from the rock is from 50 to 80% of the copper contained in it.

Cornwall Tin.—Tinstone in Cornwall occurs associated with sulphides, wolfram, quartz, felspar, slate, &c., and is broken by spalling-hammers to 3-in. lumps. Hammers make less slimes than the rock-breakers, and they also break the ore more advantageously for the hand-picking. The latter rejects waste, removes as far as possible the hurtful wolfram, and classes the values into groups according to richness. Gravity or pneumatic stamps then crush the ore to $\frac{1}{16}$ in., and stripes (a species of long rectangular buddle) yield heads, middlings, tailings and fine slimes: the first three are sent separately to circular buddles, and the last to frames. The buddles yield concentrates, middlings and tailings: the middlings are re-treated, the tailings are all waste; the concentrates are still further enriched by kieves, which yield tops to the buddle again and bottoms shipped to the smelter. The fine slimes are treated on frames, the concentrates of which go to buddles; of these the concentrates go to kieves.

The Missouri zinc-lead sludge mill takes the finest part of the hutch product of the hand-jigs. The treatment begins on revolving screens with two sizes of holes, 25 mm. and 1 mm.: these take out two coarser sizes, of which the coarser is waste and the other is jigged, yielding concentrates and waste. The main treatment begins with the finest size, which is much the largest product. It is fed to a convex circular buddle (first buddle), and yields a coarser product at the outer part of the circle and a finer product in the inner. The finer product is treated by a series of buddlings which vary somewhat, but in general are as follows: fed to a second buddle it yields zinc and lead ore in the centre, next zinc ore, next middlings which come back, and, outside of all, tailings. The zinc-lead ore is set on one side until enough has accumulated to make a buddle run, when it is run upon a third buddle yielding in the central part pure lead concentrates, next lead ore (which is returned to this treatment), next zinc ore, and outside of all a zinc product which is fed to the second buddle. The coarse outside product of the first buddle is treated in much the same way as the fine, but it yields practically no lead zinc product, which simplifies the series of buddlings necessary.

Gold Mill.—Gold ores usually contain their value in two conditions—the free gold, which can be taken out by mercury, and the combined gold, in which the metal is either coated with or combined with compounds of sulphur, tellurium, &c. The usual gold-milling scheme is to crush the ore by rock-breaker to about $1\frac{1}{2}$ in. diameter, and then to crush with water by gravity stamps, a little mercury being added to the mortar from time to time to begin the amalgamation at the first moment the gold is liberated. The pulp leaves the mortar through a screen with holes or slots $\frac{1}{40}$ to $\frac{1}{60}$ in. in width, and is then passed over amalgamated plates of copper or silver-plated copper. The free gold, amalgamated by the mercury, adheres to the mercurial surface on the plate; the rest of the pulp flows on through mercury traps to catch any of the mercury, which drains off the end of the plate. The plates and mortar are periodically cleaned up, the plates being scraped to recover the amalgam and leave them in good condition to do their work: if plates are used inside the mortar, they are cleaned in the same way. The residue of partly crushed ore in the mortar, with amalgam and free mercury scattered through it, is ground for a time in a ball mill, panned to recover the amalgam, and returned to the mortar. The pulp flowing away from the mercury traps flows to a Frue vanner or Wilfley table, on which it yields concentrates for the chlorination plant or smelter and tailings: these are waste when the heavy mineral is of low grade, but if the vanner concentrates are of high grade, they still contain values in very fine sizes which can and should be saved. Recent improvements in California for saving this material have been made. The vanner tailings are sent to a fine classifier, from which the light overflow only is saved; this is treated upon canvas tables yielding concentrates and tailings, and these concentrates, treated upon a little end-shake vanner with steep slope and rapid travel, give clean, very fine, high-grade concentrates for the chlorination works.

Iron Ores.—The brown ores of iron from surface deposits are contaminated with a considerable amount of clay and some quartz. The crude ore from surface pits or shallow underground workings is treated in a log-washer and yields the fine clay, which runs to waste, and the coarse material which is caught upon a screen and hand-picked, to free it from the little quartz, or jigged if it contains too much quartz. The magnetic oxide of iron occurs associated with felspar and quartz, and can often be separated from them by the magnet. The ore, after being broken by breaker and rolls to a size varying from $\frac{1}{4}$ to $\frac{1}{16}$ of an inch in diameter, goes to a magnetic machine which yields (1) the strongly magnetic, (2) the weakly magnetic, and (3) the non-magnetic portions. The second or middlings product contains grains of magnetite attached to quartz, and is therefore re-crushed and sent back to the magnets; the strongly magnetic portion is shipped to the furnace; and the waste to the dump heap. In concentrating by water certain zinc sulphides, siderite (carbonate of iron) follows the zinc, and would seriously injure the furnace work. By a carefully adjusted roasting of the product in a furnace the siderite is converted into magnetic oxide of iron, and can then be separated by magnet from the zinc ore. A special magnet of very high power, known from its inventor as the Wetherill magnet, has been designed for treating the franklinite of New Jersey, a mineral which is non-magnetic in the usual machines. The ore, crushed by breaker and rolls and hand-picked to remove garnet, is treated upon a belt with a roughing magnet to take out the most magnetic portion, and then very closely sized by screens with

16, 24, 30 and 50 meshes per linear inch. The several products are treated each on its own magnetic machine, yielding the franklinite for the zinc oxide grates, and followed by spiegel furnace; the residue, which is jigged, yields the zinc silicate and oxide for the spelter furnaces, and waste carrying the calcite, quartz and mica.

Asbestos, when of good quality, is in compact masses, which by suitable bruising and beating are resolved into fine flexible fibres. The Canadian asbestos is associated with serpentine, and is crushed by breakers to ⅛ in., screened on ₁/₁₆-in. screens to reject fines. The values are removed by hand-picking and are crushed by rolls carefully set so as not to break the fibre; this product is then sized by screens and the various sizes are sent to the Cyclone pulverizer, which by beating liberates the individual fibres. It then goes to a screen with eleven holes to the linear inch, and yields a granular undersize and oversize, and a fibrous oversize which is drawn off by a suction fan to a settling-chamber with air outlets covered by fine screen cloth. This fibrous product is the clean mineral for the market. A special treatment separates the fibres of different lengths.

The usual method of dressing *corundum* and *emery*, after the preliminary breaking, is to treat the material in an edge-stone mill fitted with light wooden rollers. The action is that of grinding one particle against another, whereby the talc, chlorite, mica, &c., are worn off from the harder mineral. A constant current of *water* carries off the light impurities. This is called the "muller" process. At Corundum Hill, North Carolina, the first step in removing the impurities from "sand" corundum is to subject it to the scouring action of a stream of water while it is being sluiced from the mine to the mill, the action being increased by several vertical drops of 5 to 10 ft. in the sluice. After reaching the mill all that will not pass through a 14-mesh screen is crushed by rolls, and the undersize of the screen is treated in a washing trough; this removes part of the light waste, and the "mullers" mentioned above complete the cleaning.

Graphite occurs in schist, but being of less specific gravity than the other minerals which enter into the composition of the schist, it settles later than they do. It also breaks into thin scales, which reduces its settling rate still further. The ore is broken by breakers, and by Chile edge-stone mills or by gravity stamps, to a size varying with the character of the minerals from perhaps ₁/₁₀ to ₁/₁ in. in diameter. The pulp is then conveyed through a series of settling tanks of which the later are larger than the earlier. The quartz and other waste minerals settle in the earlier tanks, while the graphite settles later; the latest tank gives the best graphite. In the Dixon Company's works in New York some forms of concentrators are believed to have replaced the slower settling tanks.

The *phosphates* of Florida are of four kinds: hard rock, soft rock, land pebble and river pebble. The hard rock is crushed by toothed rolls, and cleaned in log washers. The washed product is screened; the sizes finer than ¼ in. are thrown away because too poor; the other sizes are dried and sold, some waste having been picked out of the coarsest. The soft rock is simply dried, ground and sold. Land pebble is treated by log washers, any clay balls remaining being removed by a screen, and the phosphate dried and sold. In special cases land pebble is treated by hydraulicking, followed by a log washer, and this again by a powerful jet washer, to remove the last of the clay. River pebble is taken from the river by centrifugal pumps, and screened on two screens with 1-in. and ₃/₁₆-in. holes respectively; the oversize of the first sieve and the undersize of the second sieve are thrown away because of too low grade.　(R. H. R.)

OREGON, a North-Western state of the American Union, on the Pacific slope, lying between 42° and 46° 18′ N. lat. and 116° 35′ and 124° 32′ W. long. It is bounded N. by the state of Washington, from which it is separated in part by the Columbia river, the 46th parallel forming the rest of the boundary; E., by Idaho, from which it is separated in part by the Snake river; S., by Nevada and California, and W., by the Pacific Ocean. It has an extreme length, E. and W., of 375 m., an extreme width, N. and S., of 290 m., and a total area of 96,699 sq. m., of which 1092 sq. m. are water-surface.

Topography.—The coast of the state extends in a general N. and S. direction for about 300 m., and consists of long stretches of sandy beach broken occasionally by lateral spurs of the Coast Range, which project boldly into the sea and form high rocky headlands. With the exception of the mouth of the Columbia river, the bays and inlets by which the shore is indented are small and of very little importance. Parallel with the coast and with its main axis about 20 m. inland is an irregular chain of hills known as the Coast Range. It does not attain a great height, but has numerous lateral spurs, especially toward the W. Euchre Peak (Lincoln county), probably the highest point in the range in Oregon, rises 3962 ft. above the sea. In southern Oregon the general elevation of this range is greater than in the N., but the individual peaks are less prominent, and the range in some respects resembles a plateau. Its western slope is generally longer and more gentle than the eastern. A number of small streams, among them the Nehalem, Coquille and Umpqua rivers, cut their way through the Coast Range to reach the ocean. For the greater portion of its length in Oregon, in the northern half of the state, the Coast Range is bordered on the E. by the Willamette Valley, a region about 200 m. long and about 30 m. wide, and the most thickly populated portion of the state; here, therefore, the range is easily defined, but in the S., near the Rogue river, it merges apparently with the Cascade and the Sierra Nevada Mountains in a large complex group designated as the Klamath Mountains, lying partly in Oregon and partly in California, and extending from the northern extremity of the Sierra Nevada to the sea. The Klamath Mountains separate topographically southern Oregon from northern California. A number of ridges and peaks bearing special names, such as the Rogue river, Umpqua and Siskiyou Mountains, belong to this group. The Cascade Mountains, the most important range in Oregon, extend parallel with the coast and lie about 100 m. inland. The peaks of this system are much higher than those of the Coast Range, varying from 5000 to 11,000 ft., and the highest of them are cones of extinct volcanoes. Mount Hood (11,225 ft.), which is the highest point in the state, Mount Jefferson (10,200 ft.), the Three Sister Peaks, Mount Adams, Bachelor Mountain, and Diamond Peak (8807 ft.) all have one or more glaciers on their sides. The Calapooya Mountains, forming the water-parting between the Willamette and the Umpqua rivers, are a lateral spur of the Cascades, and extend westward as far as the Coast Range. The Cascade Mountains divide the state topographically into two sharply contrasted parts. West of this range the country exhibits a great variety of surface structure, and is humid and densely wooded; east of the range it consists of a broken tableland, arid or semiarid, with a general elevation of 5000 ft. This eastern tableland, though really very rugged and mountainous, seems to have few striking topographic features when compared with the more broken area to the W. In the north-eastern part of this eastern plateau lie the Blue Mountains, which have an average elevation of about 6000 ft. and decline gradually toward the N. A south-western spur, about 100 m. in length, and the principal ridge together enclose on several sides a wide valley drained by the tributaries of the John Day river. South of these mountains lies the northern limit of the Great Basin region. In Oregon this area extends from the Nevada boundary northward for about 160 m., to the head of the Silvies river, and embraces an area of about 16,000 sq. m. None of its streams reaches the sea, but all lose their waters by seepage or evaporation. On the E., N., and N.W. the Great Basin is bounded by the drainage systems of the tributaries of the Columbia river, and on the S.W. by the drainage system of the Klamath river. Its boundaries, however, cannot be definitely fixed, as they change with the periods of humidity and drought. Goose Lake, for example, lies in the Great Basin at some seasons; but at other times it overflows and becomes a part of the drainage system of the Sacramento river. Many of the mountains within the Basin region consist of great faulted crust blocks, with a general N. and S. trend. One face of these mountains is usually in the form of a steep palisade, while the other has a very gradual slope. Between these ridges lie almost level valleys, whose floors consist partly of lava flows, partly of volcanic fragmental material, and partly of detritus from the bordering mountains. During the wet season the valleys often contain ephemeral lakes, whose waters on evaporating leave a playa, or mud flat, often covered with an alkaline encrustation of snowy whiteness. Some large permanent lakes occupy the troughs between faulted blocks in southern Oregon. The greatest level, or approximately level, area in the Great Basin region of Oregon is the so-called Great Sandy Desert, a tract about 150 m. long and from 30 to 50 m. wide, lying in parts of Crook, Lake and Harney counties. Its surface consists of a thick sheet of pumiceous sand and dust, from which arise occasional buttes and mesas. On account of the small amount of precipitation, the fissured condition of the underlying lava sheets, and the porous soil, the Great Sandy Desert has practically no surface streams even in the wet season, and within its limits no potable waters have been found. The most prominent mountain range in the Oregon portion of the Great Basin is the Steens Mountains in the S.E., which attain an altitude of about 9000 ft. above the sea and of 5000 ft. above Alvord Valley, which lies along the eastern base. This range is a large monoclinal block, with a trend almost N.E. and S.W., presenting a steep escarpment toward the E., and sloping very gradually toward the W. It exhibits much evidence of powerful erosion, having deep canyons in its sides, and it bears evidence of previous glaciers. The region adjoining the Great Basin on the E. is usually known as the Snake River Plains, and embraces an area of about 1200 sq. m. in Malheur county. Here the hills are deeply sculptured and the valleys much carved by streams which often flow through deep canyons. Where the streams cut their way through sheets of basaltic lava their banks are steep, almost vertical cliffs, but where they cut through sedimentary rocks the sides have a more gentle slope. When several alternate layers of hard and soft rock are cut through by a stream its banks sometimes have the form of steps. The destruction of the grasses on the hillsides by overgrazing in recent years has increased the flooding by temporary streams, and consequently has tended to deepen and increase the gulleys and channels of the mountains and valleys.

The state as a whole has an average elevation of 3300 ft.; with 20,300 sq. m. below 1000 ft.; 19,200 sq. m. between 1000 and 3000 ft.; 33,500 sq. m. between 3000 and 5000 ft.; and 23,030 sq. m. between 5000 and 9000 ft.

The most important stream is the Columbia river, which forms the northern boundary for 300 m. and receives directly the waters of all the important rivers in the state except a few in the S.W. **Rivers.** and a few in the extreme E. About 160 m. from its mouth are the Cascades, where the river cuts through the lava beds of the Cascade Mountains and makes a descent of about 300 ft. through a canyon 6 m. long and nearly 1 m. deep. The passage of vessels through the river at this point is made possible by means of locks. Fifty-three m. farther up the stream is a second set of rapids known as the Dalles, where the stream for about 2 m. is confined within a narrow channel from 130 to 200 ft. wide. The largest tributary of the Columbia is the Snake river, which for nearly 200 m. of its course forms the boundary between Oregon and Idaho. It flows through a canyon from 2000 to 5000 ft. deep, with steep walls of basaltic and kindred rocks. The powerful erosion has often caused the columnar black basalt to assume weird and fantastic shapes. The chief tributaries of the Snake river in Oregon are the Grand Ronde, Powder, Burnt, Malheur and Owyhee rivers. The principal tributaries of the Columbia E. of the Cascade Mountains and lying wholly within the state are the John Day river, which rises in the Blue Mountains and enters the Columbia 29 m. above the Dalles after pursuing a winding course of about 250 m.; and the Deschutes river, which rises on the eastern slope of the Cascade Mountains, and after flowing northward for about 320 m. enters the Columbia 12 m. above the Dalles. The Deschutes river drains a region which is less arid than the plateau farther E., and which contains a number of small lakes. A peculiar feature of the stream is the uniformity of its volume throughout the year; the great crevasses in the lava bed through which it flows form natural spillways and check any tendency of the stream to rise within its banks. The Willamette river, W. of the Cascade Mountains, is the most important stream lying wholly within the state. It rises on the western slope of the Cascades and enters the Columbia river about 100 m. above its mouth, having with its branches a length of about 300 m. In the western part of the state a number of short streams flow directly into the Pacific Ocean, the most important of these being the Rogue and the Umpqua rivers, which have their sources in the Cascades.

In Southern Oregon, especially in the Great Basin region, there are numerous lakes. Malheur Lake, in Harney county, during the wet **Lakes.** season is about 25 m. long and has an average width of 5 or 6 m. It is not over 10 ft. deep in any part, and is only a few inches in depth a mile from the shore. In the summer most of its bed is a playa or mud flat. Almost continuous with this body of water on the S.W. is Harney Lake, roughly circular in form and about 7-8 m. in diameter. The waters of both lakes are alkaline, but Malheur Lake is often freshened by overflowing into Harney Lake, while the latter, having no outlet, is growing continually more alkaline. East of the Steens Mountains there is a chain of very small lakes, such as the Juniper, Manns and Alvord lakes, and also a playa known as the Alvord Desert, which in the spring is covered with a few inches, or perhaps 1 or 2 ft., of water, and becomes a lake with an area of 50 or 60 sq. m. In the summer the dry bed is smooth and very hard, and when the skies are clear the monotony of the landscape is sometimes broken by a mirage. In Lake county, occupying fault-made troughs, are several large bodies of water—Lake Abert (about 5 m. by 15 m.), Warner Lake (50 m. long, 4-8 m. wide), Summer Lake (a little smaller than Abert), and Goose Lake, the one last named lying partly in California and draining into the Sacramento system. The Upper and the Lower Klamath lakes of Klamath county are noted for their scenic beauty. Near the north-western boundary of Klamath county is the famous Crater Lake, whose surface is 6239 ft. above the sea. This lake lies in a great pit or caldera created by the wrecking in prehistoric times of the volcano Mount Mazama, which according to geologists once had an altitude of about 14,000 ft. above the sea and of 8000 ft. above the surrounding tableland; the upper portion of the mountain fell inward, possibly owing to the withdrawal of interior lava, and left a crater-like rim, or caldera, rising 2000 ft. above the surrounding country. The lake is 4 m. wide and 6 m. long, has a depth in some places of nearly 2000 ft., and is surrounded by walls of rock from 500 to 2000 ft. high. In spite of its great elevation the lake has never been known to freeze, and though it has no visible outlet its waters are fresh.

Fauna and Flora.—Large game has disappeared from the settled areas, but is still fairly abundant on the plains of the east and among the mountains of the west. In the mountain forests of south-western Oregon bears, deer, elk, pumas, wolves and foxes are plentiful. Among the south-eastern plateaus antelope are found at all seasons, and deer and big-horn (mountain sheep), and occasionally a few elk, in the winter. Bears, wolves, lynxes and foxes are also numerous in the east, and there the coyote is found in disagreeable numbers. The pocket-gopher and the jack-rabbit are so numerous as to be great pests. The principal varieties of game-birds are ducks, geese, grouse and California quail. Sage-hens are occasionally seen on the dry plateaus and valleys, especially in Harney county. The Oregon robin (*Merula naevia*) and the Oregon snowbird (*Junco Oregonus*) are common in Oregon and northward. On the rocky headlands and islands of the coast nest thousands of gulls, cormorants, puffins, guillemots, surf-ducks (*Oedemia*), dotterels, terns, petrels and numerous other birds. There, too, the Steller's sea-lion (*Eumetopias stelleri*) spends the mating season. The marine fauna is abundant

and of great economic importance. The river fauna of the coast is of two distinct types: the type of the Columbia fauna in rivers north of the Rogue; and another type in the Klamath and its tributaries. Typical of the Columbia river is *Catostomus macrocheilus* and of the Klamath, *C. rimiculus.* Lampreys, sticklebacks, cattoids, sturgeons —the white sturgeon (*Acipenser transmontanus*) is commonly known as the " Oregon sturgeon,"—trout and salmon are the principal anadromous fish, the salmon and trout being the most important economically. The best varieties of the salmon for canning are: the king, Chinook or quinnat (*Oncorhynchus tschawytscha*), far better than any other variety; and the steel-head, blue back or sukkegh (*O. nerka*).

The total woodland area of the state according to the United States census of 1900. was 54,300 sq. m. or 56·8 % of the land area. The Federal government established in 1907 and 1908 thirteen forest reserves in the state, ten of which had an area of more than 1,000,000 acres each; their total area on the 1st of January 1910 was 25,345 sq. m. From the coast to the eastern base of the Cascade Mountains the state is heavily timbered, except in small prairies and clearings in the Willamette and other valleys, and the most important tree is the great Douglas fir, pine or spruce (*Pseudotsuga Douglasii*), commonly called Oregon pine, which sometimes grows to a height of 300 ft., and which was formerly in great demand for masts and spars of sailing-vessels and for bridge timbers; the Douglas fir grows more commercial timber to the acre than any other American variety, and constitutes about five-sevenths of the total stand of the state. Timber is also found on the Blue Mountains in the north-east and on a number of mountains in the central and south-eastern parts of the state. East of the Cascades the valleys are usually treeless, save for a few willows and cottonwoods in the vicinity of streams. Over the greater part of this region the sage-brush is the most common plant, and by its ubiquity it imparts to the landscape the monotonous greyish tint so characteristic of the arid regions of the western United States. West of the Cascades most of the trees of commercial value consist of Douglas fir. Cedar and hemlock also are commercially valuable. There are small amounts of sugar pine, yellow pine, red fir and silver fir (*Abies grandis* and *A. nobilis*) and spruce; and among the broad-leaved varieties the oak, ash, maple, mahogany-birch or mountain mahogany (*Cercocarpus ledifolia*), aspen, cotton-wood and balsam are the most common. East of the Cascades the forests consist for the most part of yellow pine. In the south-east the hills and lower slopes of the mountains are almost bare of trees. At higher altitudes, however, the moisture increases and scattered junipers begin to appear. Blending with these at their upper limit and continuing above them are clumps of mountain mahogany, which sometimes attains a height of 20 or 30 ft. Above this belt of mahogany, pines and firs are commonly found. In this region the mountains have an upper, or cold, timber line, the height of which depends upon the severity of the climate; and a lower, or dry, timber line, which is determined by the amount of rainfall. These upper and lower limits of the timber belt are sometimes very sharply defined, so that tall mountains may be marked by a dark girdle of forest, above and below which appear walls of bare rock. In a very arid region the dry timber line may rise above the cold timber line, and in such a case the mountain will contain no forests. Of this phenomenon the Steens Mountains furnish a conspicuous example. It was estimated that the forests of Oregon contained in 1900 about 150,000,000,000 ft. of Douglas fir or spruce, 40,000,000,000 ft. of yellow pine and 35,000,000,000 ft. of other species—chiefly cedar, hemlock and spruce. In the most heavily wooded region along the Pacific coast and the lower course of the Columbia river are forests of the Douglas fir with stands of 100,000 ft. of timber per acre. The value of the lumber and timber products increased from $1,014,211 in 1870 to $6,530,757 in 1890, to $10,257,169 in 1900, and to $12,183,908 in 1905.

Climate.—Perhaps no state in the union has such great local variations in its climate as has Oregon. Along the coast the climate is humid, mild and uniform, and, as has often been remarked, very like the climate of the British Isles; in the eastern two-thirds of the state, from which the moisture-laden winds are excluded by the high coastwise mountains, the climate is dry and marked by great daily and annual ranges of temperature. The mean annual temperature varies with the elevation and the distance from the sea, being highest along the western slope of the Coast Range at altitudes below 2000 ft., and lowest in the elevated regions E. of the Cascade Mountains. The temperatures along the coast are never as high as 100° F. or as low as zero. In the valleys between the Coast Range and the Cascade Mountains the range of temperature is much greater than it is along the coast; the absolute maximum and minimum being respectively 102° and -2° at Portland, in the N.W., and 108° and -4° at Ashland, in the S.W. Owing to its greater elevation the southern portion of Oregon experiences greater extremes of temperature than the northern. In that part of the state E. of the Cascades the climate is of a continental type, with much greater ranges of temperature than in the W., although in a few low valleys, as at the Dalles, the extremes are somewhat modified. While flowers bloom throughout the year at Portland, frosts have occurred in every month of the year at Lakeview, in the Great Basin. At Astoria, near the mouth of the Columbia river, the mean annual temperature is 52° F., with extremes recorded of 97° and 10°; but at Silver Lake, in the Great

Basin region, while the mean annual temperature is 44°, the highest and lowest ever recorded are respectively 104° and −32°. These records afford a striking illustration of the moderating influence of the ocean upon climate.

As is the case in all the Pacific states, the amount of rainfall decreases from N. to S., and is greatest on the seaward slopes of the hills and mountains. As the winds from the ocean are deprived of their moisture on reaching the Coast and Cascade ranges, the amount of annual precipitation, which in the coast counties varies from 75 to 138 in., constantly diminishes toward the E. until in the extreme south-eastern part of the state it amounts to only about 8 in. No other state, except perhaps Washington, has such a great variation in the amount of its rainfall. Precipitation on the Coast Range at altitudes above 2000 ft. amounts to about 138 in. annually; in the valleys E. of this range it varies from 20-2 in. at Ashland to 78-2 in. at Portland. On the western slope of the Cascades it varies from 50 in. in the S. to 100 in. in the N.; in the Columbia Valley the amount is from 10 to 15 in.; in the valleys and foothills of the Blue Mountains, 12 to 25 in.; and in the plateau region of central and south-eastern Oregon, 8 to 22 in. In the region W. of the Cascade Mountains there is a so-called wet season, which lasts from October to March, and the summers are almost rainless. In the rest of the state there is a maximum rainfall in the winter and a secondary wet season in May and June, with the rest of the summer very dry. During the winter the prevailing winds are from the S. and bring moisture; during the summer they are from the N.W. and are accompanied by cloudless skies and moderate temperatures. Winds from the N.E. bring hot weather in the summer and intense cold in the winter.

Soils.—The state has almost as great a variety of soils as of climate. In the Willamette Valley the soils are mostly clay loams, of a basaltic nature on the foothills and greatly enriched in the river bottom lands by washings from the hills and by deposits of rich black humus. In south-western Oregon, in the Rogue and Umpqua valleys, the characteristic soil is a reddish clay, though other varieties are numerous. In eastern Oregon the soils are of an entirely different type, being usually of a greyish appearance, lacking in humus, and composed of volcanic dust and alluvium from the uplands. They are deep, of fine texture, easily worked and contain abundant plant food in the form of soluble compounds of calcium, sodium and potassium. At times, however, these salts are present in such excess as to render the soils too alkaline for plant growing. Where there is no excess of alkali and the water supply is sufficient, good crops can be grown in this soil without the use of fertilizers.

Agriculture and Stock-Raising.—Oregon has some of the most productive agricultural lands in the United States, but they are rather limited in extent, being confined for the most part to the valleys west of the Cascade Mountains and the counties bordering on the Columbia river east of those mountains. The other parts of the state are generally too dry or too mountainous for growing crops, but contain considerable areas suitable for grazing. In 1900 only about one-sixth of the total land surface was included in farms, and a trifle less than one-third of the farm land was improved. There were 35,837 farms, and their average size was 281 acres. Of the whole number 33·0 % (11,827) contained less than 100 acres each, 30·5 % (11,055) contained from 100 to 175 acres each, and 10·4 % (3777) devoted mainly to stock-raising, contained 500 acres or more each. Nearly four-fifths of the farms (28,636) were operated by owners or part owners, 3729 were operated by share tenants, 2637 by cash tenants and 835 by owners and tenants or managers. The principal crops are wheat, oats, hay, fruits, hops, potatoes and miscellaneous vegetables. Sheep and cattle are raised extensively on ranches in the semi-arid regions, large herds of cattle are kept on lands too wet for cultivation in the western counties, and stock-raising and dairying have become important factors in the operation of many of the best farms. The acreage of wheat was 810,000 in 1909 and the crop was 16,377,000 bushels. The oat crop was 10,886,000 bushels. The barley crop was 1,984,000 bushels. The nights are so cool that Indian corn is successfully grown only by careful cultivation, and the crop amounted to only 552,000 bushels in 1909. The hay crop, 865,000 tons in 1909, is made quite largely from wild grasses and grains cut green; on the irrigated lands alfalfa is grown extensively for the cattle and sheep, which are otherwise almost wholly dependent for sustenance upon the bunch grass of the semi-arid plains. Both cattle and sheep ranches in the region east of the Cascade Mountains have been considerably encroached upon by the appropriation of lands for agricultural purposes, and the cattle, also, have been forced to the south and east by the grazing of sheep on lands formerly reserved for them; but the numbers of both cattle and sheep on the farms have become much larger. The whole number of sheep in the state was 2,581,000 in 1910. The number of cattle other than dairy cows was 698,000 and that of dairy cows 174,000. The dairy business is a promising industry in the farming regions, especially in the Willamette Valley. The number of swine in 1910 was 308,000. The small number of swine (267,000 in 1910) is partly due to the small crop of Indian corn. Fruit-growing has been an increasingly important industry in the region between the Cascade and Coast Ranges and (to a less degree) east of the Cascade Range; and the cultivation of apples is especially important. The cultivation of hops was begun in Oregon about 1850; the soil and climate of the Willamette Valley

were found to be exceedingly favourable to their growth, and the product increased to 20,500,000 ℔ in 1905, when the state ranked first in the Union in this industry.

The agricultural resources of the state may be considerably increased by irrigation east of the Cascade Mountains. The irrigated areas, which are widely distributed, increased from a total of 177,944 acres in 1889 to 388,310 acres in 1902. In 1894 Congress passed the "Carey Act" which authorizes the Secretary of the Interior, with the approval of the President, to donate to each of the states in which there are Federal desert lands as much of such lands (less than 1,000,000 acres) as the state may apply for, on condition that the state reclaim by irrigation, cultivation and occupancy not less than 20 acres of each 160-acre tract within ten years, and under the operation of this Act the state chose 432,203 acres for reclamation, mostly in the basin of the Deschutes river. Furthermore there is a state association engaged in irrigation projects, and the United States Reclamation Service, established by an Act of Congress in 1902, has projects for utilizing the flood waters of the Umatilla, Malheur, Silvies and Grande Ronde rivers, the waters of the Owyhee and Wallowa rivers and Willow Creek, and the waters of some of the lakes in the central part of the state. Two of these projects had been begun by 1909: the Umatilla project in Umatilla county, to irrigate 20,440 acres with water diverted from the Umatilla river by a dam (98 ft. high, 3500 ft. long) 2 m. above Echo, with a reservoir of 1500 acres, was authorized in 1905 and was 85⅓ % finished in 1909; the Klamath project, to irrigate 181,000 acres in Klamath county, Oregon (about 145,000 acres) and Siskiyou and Modoc counties, California, by two canals from Upper Klamath Lake and by a storage dam (33 ft. high, 940 ft. long) in the Clear Lake reservoir of 25,000 acres, was authorized in 1905 and was 38 % completed in 1909. It has been estimated that the irrigated and irrigable area under private canals is about 80,000 acres, and that that still undisposed of in 1909, irrigated by the state under the Carey Act, amounted to 180,000 acres.

Fisheries.—The Columbia river has long been famous for its salmon, and as the supply seemed threatened with exhaustion for several years following the maximum catch in 1883, the state legislature in 1907 passed an act establishing a close season both early in the spring and late in the summer and prohibiting any fishing, except with hook and line, at any time, without a licence. In 1908 two laws proposed by initiative petition were passed, stopping all fishing by night and fishing in the navigable channels of the lower river, limiting the length of seines to be used in the lower river and abolishing the use of gear by fishermen of the upper river—the mouth of the Sandy river, in Multnomah county, being the dividing line between the upper and lower Columbia. Several hatcheries have been established by the state authorities of Oregon and Washington and by the Federal government for propagating the best varieties: the Chinooks (*O. tschawytscha*), the bluebacks (*O. nerka*) and, when the bluebacks became scarce, silversides (*O. kisutch*). The total catch of salmon on the Oregon side of the Columbia river in 1901 was 16,725,435 ℔; from this it rose to 24,575,228 ℔ in 1903, but fell to 18,151,743 ℔ in 1907 and 18,463,546 ℔ in 1908. Salmon are caught in smaller quantities in the coast streams: 4,371,618 ℔ in 1901 and 8,043,690 ℔ in 1906, but only 6,738,682 ℔ in 1907 and 6,422,511 ℔ in 1908. Some catfish, shad, smelt, halibut, herring, perch, sturgeon, flounders, oysters, clams, crabs and crawfish are also obtained from Oregon waters.

Minerals.—Gold was discovered in the Rogue and Klamath rivers in the S. part of Oregon in 1852, and placer-mining was prosecuted here without interruption until 1860, when the metal was found in larger quantities on the streams in Baker and Grant counties in the north-eastern part of the state. Quartz-mining has since very largely taken the place of placer-mining, but the two principal gold-producing districts are still that traversed by the Blue Mountains in the north-eastern quarter and that drained by the Rogue river in the south-western corner, a continuation of the California field. The value of the total output of the state was $2,113,356 in 1894, but only $865,076 in 1908. Silver is obtained almost wholly in the form of alloy with gold, and in 1908 the value of the output was only $23,109. Lignitic coal was discovered on or near the coast of Coos Bay as early as 1855, and this is still the only productive coalfield within the state, although there are outcroppings of the mineral all along the Coast Range N. of the Rogue river, along the W. foothills of the Cascade Range and in the Blue Mountains; this coal is suitable for steam and heating purposes but will not coke. The quantity of the output was 86,329 short tons in 1908. Copper ores are known to be quite widely distributed in the mountain districts, but there has been little work on any except some in Josephine and Grant counties. In 1908 the state's output amounted to 291,377 ℔ of copper. Iron ore, platinum, lead, quicksilver and cobalt have been obtained in the state in merchantable quantities, and there is some zinc ore in the Cascade Range. In Union county is a great amount of blue limestone, and there is limestone, also, in Baker, Grant, Wallowa, Jackson and Josephine counties. Sandstone is abundant, and there is some granite, in the Coast Range. A variegated marble is obtained in Douglas county, and other marbles are found in several counties. Clays suitable for making brick and tile are found in nearly every part of the state: in 1908 the clay products of the state were valued at $555,768. Soapstone is abundant in both the E. and W. counties. Ochre, or mineral paint, and mineral waters, too, are widely distributed. There is some roofing slate along the Rogue river, natural cement, nickel ore, bismuth and wolframite in Douglas county, gypsum in Baker county, fire-clay in Clatsop county, borate of soda on the marsh lands of Harney county, infusorial earth and tripoli in the valley of the Deschutes river, chromate of iron in Curry and Douglas counties, molybdenite in Union county, bauxite in Clackamas county, borate of lime in Curry county, manganese ore in Columbia county, and asbestos in several of the southern and eastern counties. The total value of all mineral products in 1908 was $2,743,434.

Manufactures.—Manufacturing is encouraged both by the variety and abundance of raw material furnished by the mines, the forests, the farms and the fisheries, and by the coal and water-power available for operating the machinery. The total value of manufactures increased from $10,931,232 in 1880 to $41,432,174 in 1890, or 279 % in ten years, and although progress was slow from 1890 to 1900 there was a rapid advance again from 1900 to 1905, when the value of factory products increased from $36,592,714 to $55,525,123. The manufactures of greatest value are lumber and timber products ($12,483,908 in 1905). Portland and Astoria are the chief manufacturing centres; in 1905 the value of the factory products of these two cities was 57·2 % of that of the factory products of the entire state.

Transportation and Commerce.—For 110 m. from the mouth of the Columbia river to Portland, 12 m. up the Willamette river, is a channel which in 1909 was navigable (20-22 ft. deep) by large ocean-going vessels, and which will have a minimum depth of 25 ft. at low water upon the completion of the Federal project of 1902. From the mouth of the Willamette river vessels of light draft ascend the Columbia (passing the Cascade Falls through a lock canal, which was opened in 1896 and has a depth of 8 ft., a width of 92 ft. and two locks, each 462 ft. long) to the mouth of the Snake river (in the state of Washington), up that river to the mouth of the Imnaha, in Wallowa county, on the eastern boundary of Oregon, and, when the water is high, up the Imnaha river to the town of Imnaha, 516 m. from the sea. The Willamette river is navigable to Harrisburg, 152 m. above Portland, but boats seldom go farther up the river than Corvallis, 119 m. above Portland, and the depth at low water to Corvallis is only 3 ft. On the coast, Coos Bay, a tidal estuary, is the principal harbour between the mouth of the Columbia and San Francisco; it admits vessels drawing 14 to 16 ft. of water, and both the north and south forks of the Coos river are navigable for vessels of light draft (the depth at low water is only 1·5 ft.) 14 m. from the mouth of that river, and 8·5 m. on each fork. Farther north, Yaquina Bay and Tillamook Bay also admit small steamboats. The Coquille river is navigable for about 37 m., the Yaquina river for 23 m. with a depth of 13 to 15 ft., the Siuslaw river for 6 m. (for vessels drawing less than 6 ft., 15 m. farther for very light draft vessels) and a few other coast streams for short distances. The beginning of railway building in Oregon was delayed a few years by a contest between parties desiring a line on the east side of the Willamette river and parties desiring one on the west side. Finally, on the 14th of May 1868, ground was broken for the proposed line on the west side, and two days later it was broken for one on the east side; that on the east side was completed for 20 m. south of Portland in 1869 and that on the west side was completed to the Yamhill river in 1872. In 1870 the mileage was 159 m. The principal period of railway building was from 1880 to 1890, during which 931·97 m. were built and the state's mileage increased from 508 m. to 1,439·97 m. In 1909 the total mileage was 2080·46 m. There is a state railway commission. The principal railways are: that of the Oregon Railroad & Navigation Company (controlled by the Union Pacific), which crosses the north-eastern corner of the state and then runs along the bank of the Columbia river to Portland; three lines of the Southern Pacific in the Willamette Valley, the main line connecting Portland with San Francisco; the Astoria & Columbia River, connecting Portland and Astoria; the Coos Bay, Roseburg & Eastern Railroad & Navigation Company (owned by the Southern Pacific), connecting Coos Bay with one of the Southern Pacific lines; and the Corvallis & Eastern (owned by the Southern Pacific), connecting Yaquina Bay with all three lines of the Southern Pacific. Throughout the Cascade Mountain Region and the great semi-arid region east of those mountains, which together embrace more than two-thirds of the state's area, there is not a railway.

The state carries on an extensive commerce with the Orient and with the Canadian provinces. Its exports are principally lumber, wheat, live-stock, fish and wool; its imports are largely a variety of products of the Oriental countries. There are four customs districts: southern Oregon, with Coos Bay as the port of entry; Willamette, with Portland as the port of entry; Oregon, with Astoria as the port of entry; and Yaquina, at the mouth of the Yaquina river.

Population.—The population of Oregon was 13,294 in 1850; 52,465 in 1860; 90,923 in 1870; 174,768 in 1880; 317,704 in 1890; 413,536 in 1900, an increase of 30·2 % in the decade; and 672,765 in 1910, a further increase of 62·7 %. Of the total population in 1900, 347,788, or 84·1 %, were native-born, 65,748 were foreign-born, 394,582, or 95·4 %, were of the white race, and 18,954

were coloured. Of those born within the United States only 164,431, or less than one-half, were natives of Oregon, and of those born in other states of the Union 128,654, or about seven-tenths, were natives of one or another of the following states: Missouri, Illinois, Iowa, Ohio, California, New York, Indiana, Kansas, Washington, Wisconsin and Pennsylvania. Nearly three-fourths of the foreign-born were composed of the following: 13,292 Germans, 9365 Chinese, 9007 Scandinavians, 7508 Canadians, 5663 English and 4210 Irish. The coloured population consisted of 10,397 Chinese, 4951 Indians, 2501 Japanese and 1105 negroes.

The Indians are remnants of a large number of tribes, most of which are aboriginal to this region, and they represent ten or more distinct linguistic stocks. Most of them have been collected under five government schools: the Clackamas, Cow Creek, Calapooya, Lakmiut, Mary's River, Molala, Nestucca, Rogue River, Santiam, Shasta, Tumwater, Umpqua, Wapato and Yamhill, numbering 145 in 1909, under the Grande Ronde school, on the Grande Ronde reservation in Polk and Yamhill counties; the Klamath (658), Modoc (216), Paiute (103), and Pit River or Achomawi (56), under the Klamath school on the Klamath reservation (1362·8 sq. m.) in Klamath and Lake counties; the Alsea, Coquille, Kusan, Kwatami, Rogue River, Skoton, Shasta, Saiustkea, Siuslaw, Tututni, Umpqua and several other small tribes, numbering 442 in 1909, under the Siletz school, on the Siletz reservation (5 sq. m.) in Lincoln county; the Cayuse, Umatilla and Wallawalla, numbering 1205 in 1908, under the Umatilla school, on the Umatilla reservation (124·73 sq. m.) in Umatilla county, and the Paiute, Tenino, Warm Springs and Wasco Indians, numbering 765 in 1909, under the Warm Springs school on the Warm Springs reservation (503·29 sq. m.) in Wasco and Crook counties. Most of the Indians are engaged in farming and stock-raising, but a few still derive their maintenance mainly from fishing and hunting.

Roman Catholics are the most numerous religious sect in the state (in 1906 out of a total of 170,229 communicants of all religious bodies, they numbered 35,317). The rural population (*i.e.* population outside of incorporated places) is very sparse, only about 2½, in 1900, to the square mile, and while it increased from 203,973 in 1890 to 229,894 in 1900, or only 11·3 %, the urban (*i.e.* population of places having 4000 inhabitants or more) together with the semi-urban (*i.e.* population of incorporated places having less than 4000 inhabitants) increased during the same decade from 113,731 to 183,642, or 61·5 %. The principal cities are Portland, Astoria, Baker City and Salem, which is the capital.

Administration.—The state is still governed under its original constitution of 1857, with the amendments adopted in 1902, 1906 and 1908. This constitution may be amended: by a majority of the popular vote at a regular general election, if the amendment has been passed by a majority vote of all the elected members of each house of the legislature; or by an initiative petition; or by a constitutional convention, which may not be called, however, unless the law providing for it is approved by popular vote. The right of suffrage is conferred by the constitution upon all white male citizens twenty-one years of age and over who have resided in the state during the six months immediately preceding the election, and upon every white male of the required age who has been a resident of the state for six months, and who, one year before the election, has declared his intention of becoming a citizen and who has resided in the United States for one year and in the state for six months prior to the election. Idiots, insane persons and persons convicted of serious crimes are disfranchised. The clause excluding negroes and Chinese from the suffrage has never been repealed, although it has been rendered nugatory by the Fifteenth Amendment to the Federal Constitution. Another provision which has been annulled by amendment to the Federal Constitution, but which still remains in the state constitution, is a clause forbidding free negroes or mulattoes, not residing in the state at the time of the adoption of the constitution, to enter the state or to own real estate or make contracts and maintain suits therein, and bidding the legislature provide for the removal of such negroes and mulattoes and for the punishment of persons bringing them into the state, or employing or harbouring them. The constitution provides that no Chinaman, not a resident of the state at the time of the adoption of the constitution, shall ever hold any real estate or mining claim, or work any mining claim in the state.

The chief executive functions are vested in a governor, who is elected for a term of four years, and who must be at least 30 years old and must have been a resident of the state for three years before his election. He is not eligible to the office for more than eight years in any period of twelve years. He has the right of pardon and a veto of legislative acts, which may be overridden by a two-thirds vote of the members present of each house of the legislature. The other important administrative officers are the secretary of state (who succeeds the governor if he dies or resigns—there is no lieutenant-governor), treasurer, attorney-general, superintendent of public instruction and labour commissioner. No public officer may be impeached, but for sufficient cause the governor may remove a justice of the supreme court or a prosecuting attorney from office, upon a joint resolution of the legislature adopted by a two-thirds vote in each house. A public official may be tried for incompetence, corruption or malfeasance according to the regular procedure in criminal cases, and if convicted he may be dismissed from office and receive such other penalties as the law provides.

The legislative department (officially called "the legislative assembly") consists of a Senate of thirty[1] members chosen for four years, with half the membership retiring every two years, and a House of Representatives with sixty[1] members elected biennially. A senatorial district, if it contains more than one county, must be composed of contiguous counties, and no county may be divided between different senatorial districts. The sessions of the legislature are biennial. Bills for raising revenue must originate in the House of Representatives, but the Senate may offer amendments. Until 1902 the legislature was the sole law-making body in the state, but on the 2nd of June of this year the voters adopted a constitutional amendment which declared that "the people reserve to themselves power to propose laws and amendments to the constitution, and to enact or reject the same at the polls, independent of the legislative assembly, and also reserve power at their own option to approve or reject at the polls any act of the legislative assembly." This provision for the initiative and the referendum was made effective by a legislative act of 1903. Eight per cent of the number of voters who at the last preceding election voted for a justice of the supreme court, by filing with the secretary of state a petition for the enactment of any law or constitutional amendment—the petition must contain the full text of the law and must be filed at least four months before the election at which it is to be voted upon—may secure a vote on the proposed measure at the next general election, and if it receives the approval of the voters it becomes a law without interposition of the legislature, and goes into effect from the day of the governor's proclamation announcing the result of the election. A referendum of legislative enactments may be ordered in two ways: the legislature itself may refer any of its acts to the people for approval or rejection at the next regular election, in which case the act may not be vetoed by the governor and does not go into effect until approved at the polls; or 5 % of the number of voters at the last election for a supreme court justice may by petition order any act, except such as are "necessary for the immediate preservation of the public peace, health or safety," to be referred to the voters for their approval or rejection. Such a petition must be filed within ninety days after the adjournment of the session in which the act was passed. The secretary of state is required to mail to every voter whose address he has a pamphlet containing the text of the laws to be voted upon at the ensuing election. Along with the text of the law, the state will print arguments in its favour if any are submitted by the persons initiating the measure and the cost of the extra printing is paid by the initiators. In like manner, any one who will defray the expense of the printing may submit arguments in opposition to any proposed measure, and these will be included in the pamphlet and distributed by the state at its own expense. This "text-book" for the voters contained 60 pages in 1906 and 126 pages in 1908.

The power of the initiative was first exercised by the people of Oregon in 1904, when they proposed and enacted a local option liquor law and a direct primary law. As a result of the first of these measures, in 1908 nineteen of the thirty-three counties of the state had prohibited the sale of intoxicants since 1905. The most important effect of the direct primary law has been the choice of United States senators by what is practically a popular vote. Candidates for the United States Senate are voted for in the primaries, and between 1904 and 1907 candidates for the state legislature were required to say whether or not they would support the people's choice for United States senator regardless of their own preferences.[2] In the state election in June 1908 a Democrat received the highest popular vote for the senatorship, and as a majority of the legislature of 1909 had committed itself to vote for the people's choice, he was elected by that body, although five-sixths of its members were Republicans.[3] This was an anomaly in American politics. In June 1906 five laws and five amendments to the constitution, proposed by initiative petitions, and one law on which the referendum was ordered by petition, were submitted to a popular vote. An amendment giving women the right to vote was defeated, and among those adopted was one providing for the initiative upon special and local laws and parts of laws, and another giving cities and towns the exclusive right to enact or amend their own charters, subject only to the constitution and the criminal laws. Oregon was thus the first American state to grant complete home rule to its municipalities. At the election in June 1908 the number of initiative and referendum measures amounted to nineteen, and the ballot required forty-one separate marks and was over 2½ ft. long.

The measures to be voted on consisted of eleven laws or constitutional amendments proposed by initiative petition, four constitutional amendments referred to the people by the legislature, and four laws upon which the voters had ordered a referendum. Among the measures defeated were the fourth woman's suffrage amendment voted down in Oregon, a single-tax bill and an "open town" bill designed to defeat the purpose of the local option liquor law. Among the measures adopted were: a law (of doubtful constitutionality) requiring legislators to vote for the people's choice for a United States senator—this was adopted by a vote of 69,668 to 21,162; a corrupt practices act, regulating the expenditure of moneys in political campaigns and limiting a candidate's expenses to one-fourth of one year's salary; an amendment permitting the establishment of state institutions elsewhere than at the capital; an amendment changing the time of state elections from June to November; an amendment permitting the legislature to pass a law providing for proportional representation, i.e. representation for each political party in proportion to its numerical strength, by providing for first and second choice in voting—the system of preferential voting adopted in Idaho in 1909; and the "recall," by which the voters may remove from office after six months' service by a special election any local official.[4]

Judiciary.—The judicial department of the state consists of a supreme court, circuit courts, county courts (held by a county judge in each county) and the courts of local justices of the peace. The supreme court consists of five (before 1909 the number was three) justices elected for a term of six years, and its jurisdiction extends only to appeals from the decisions of the circuit courts. The judges of the circuit courts were formerly supreme court justices on circuit; they also are chosen for six years, and they have cognizance over all cases, including appeals from inferior courts, not specifically reserved by law for some other tribunal. The judges of the county courts are elected for four years, and their courts have jurisdiction over probate matters, civil cases involving amounts not exceeding $500, and criminal cases in which the offence is not punishable by death or imprisonment in the penitentiary. Each county is divided into a number of districts or precincts, for each of which there is a justice of the peace, elected biennially and having jurisdiction in minor cases.

Local Government.—For the purposes of local government the state is divided into thirty-four counties. The constitution provides that no county may have an area of less than 400 sq. m., and that no new county may be created unless its population is at least 1200. County affairs are administered by the county judge acting with two commissioners. Any portion of a county containing as many as 150 inhabitants may be incorporated as a town or city, and as such it possesses complete self-government in all purely local matters, even

---

[1] The constitution set 30 as the maximum number of senators, 60 as the maximum number of representatives, and provided for 16 senators and 34 representatives in 1857-1860. It provided for an enumeration and a reapportionment each tenth year after 1865.

[2] Before 1904, under a law of 1901, the people voted for candidates for the United States Senate, but the legislative assembly was in no way bound to carry out the decision of the popular vote; and in 1904 the legislature chose as United States senator a candidate for whom no vote had been cast in the popular election.

[3] It is to be noted that the Republican party had not favoured requiring a pledge from members of the legislature that they would vote for the people's choice for senator; that the Democratic candidate for senator (Gov. G. E. Chamberlain) was a prominent advocate of the initiative, the referendum and the direct election of United States senators; and that a wing of the Republican party worked for the choice of the Democratic candidate by the people in the hope that the (Republican) legislature would not ratify the popular choice and so would nullify the direct primary law.

[4] At times the two law-making bodies—the legislature and the people—have come into conflict. In 1906, for example, the people by the initiative secured a law forbidding public officers from accepting free passes from railways. In 1907 the legislature repealed all laws on this subject and required railways to furnish free transportation to certain officials. Upon this measure, however, the people ordered a referendum and it was rejected at the polls. In 1908 the people voted against increasing the number of supreme court judges; in 1909 the legislature increased the number.

having the power to revise its own charter. A constitutional amendment of 1906 forbids the formation of corporations by special laws (formerly the constitution provided that corporations " shall not be created by special laws except for municipal purposes ") and says: " The legislative assembly shall not enact, amend or repeal any charter or act of incorporation for any municipality, city or town." The initiative and the referendum are employed in municipal ordinances as well as in state laws; towns and cities make their own provisions as to " the manner of exercising the initiative and referendum powers as to their own municipal legislation "; but " not more than 10 % of the legal voters may be required to order the referendum nor more than 15 % to propose any measure by the initiative, in any city or town."

Miscellaneous Laws.—The value of the homestead exempt from judicial sale for the satisfaction of liabilities is limited to $1500; the homestead must be owned and occupied by some member of the family claiming the exemption and may not exceed in area one block in a town or city or 160 acres outside of a municipality. The exemption is not valid against a mortgage, but the mortgage must be executed by both husband and wife, if the householder is married. The debtor claims the exemption where the levy is made, but if the sheriff deems the homestead greater in value than the law allows, he may choose three disinterested persons to appraise it and sell any portion that may be adjudged in excess of the legal limit. The constitution provides that the property and pecuniary rights of every married woman, at the time of her marriage, or afterwards, acquired by gift, devise or inheritance, shall not be subject to the debts or contracts of the husband; and that laws shall be passed providing for the registration of the wife's separate property. Marriages between whites and persons of negro descent, between whites and Indians, and between first cousins are forbidden or are void. One year's residence is necessary to secure a divorce, for which the causes recognized are a conviction of felony, habitual drunkenness for one year, physical incapacity, desertion for one year and cruelty or personal indignities.

Education.—The public school system (organized 1873) is administered by the state superintendent of public instruction, who exercises a general supervision over the schools, and by the state board of education, which prescribes the general rules and regulations for their management. For the support of the schools there is a school fund, amounting on the 1st of April 1909 to $5,861,475, and consisting of the moneys derived from the sale of lands donated by the Federal government and of small sums derived from miscellaneous sources. The fund is administered by a board consisting of the governor, the secretary of state and the state treasurer, and the income from it is apportioned among the counties according to the number of children of school age. The counties are also required to levy special school taxes, the aggregate annual amount of which shall be equivalent to at least seven dollars for every child between the ages of four and twenty years. If the total annual fund for a school district amounts to less than $300, the district must levy a special tax to bring the fund up to that sum. Each school district in the state is required to have a school term of six months or more. Special county taxes are levied for the maintenance of public school libraries also. For all children between the ages of nine and fourteen inclusive, school attendance is compulsory.

The total number of teachers in the public schools in 1908 was 4213; the total school enrollment, 107,493; the average daily attendance 94,333. In 1908 there was paid for the support of common schools $3,061,994; the average monthly salary of rural teachers was $49.60, and of school principals, $80-87. The proportion of illiterates is low: in 1900 of the total population 10 years of age or over only 3·3 % was illiterate; of the male population of the same age 3·9 %, of the female 2·3 % and of the native white population only 0·8 % were illiterate.

In addition to the public schools, the state maintains: the University of Oregon at Eugene (q.v.); the State Agricultural College (1870), at Corvallis (pop. 1900, 1819), the county-seat of Benton county, and the State Normal School (1882) at Monmouth (pop. in 1900, 606), in Polk county. Among the institutions not receiving state aid are Albany College (Presbyterian, 1867), at Albany; Columbia University (Roman Catholic, 1901), at Portland; Dallas College (United Evangelical, 1900), at Dallas; Pacific University (Congregational, 1853), at Forest Grove; McMinnville College (Baptist, 1858), at McMinnville; Pacific College (Friends, founded in 1885 as an academy, college opened in 1891), at Newberg; Philomath College (United Brethren, 1866), at Philomath; and Willamette University (Methodist Episcopal, 1844), at Salem.

Charitable and Correctional Institutions.—The state supports the following charitable and correctional institutions: a soldiers' home (1894) at Roseburg and a school for deaf mutes (1870), an institute for the blind (1873), a reform school, an insane asylum and a penitentiary at Salem, the capital of the state. These institutions (except the penitentiary, of which the governor of the state is an inspector) are governed each by a board of three trustees, the governor of the state and the secretary of state serving on all boards, and the third trustee being the state treasurer on the boards for the state insane asylum, the state reform school and the institute for the feeble-minded, and the superintendent of public instruction on the boards for the school for deaf mutes and the institute for the blind.

Finance.—The constitution forbids the establishment or incorporation by the legislative assembly of any bank or banking company; and it forbids any bank or banking company in the state from issuing bills, checks, certificates, promissory notes or other paper to circulate as money. Except in case of war the legislative assembly may not contract a state debt greater than $50,000. To pay bounties to soldiers in the Civil War a debt of $237,000 was contracted; but in 1870 only $90,000 of it was still outstanding. An issue of bonds (to be redeemed from the sale of public lands) for a privately built canal at Oregon City was authorized in 1870. About $175,000 more of debt was incurred by Indian wars in 1874 and 1878; in the latter year the public debt amounted to more than $650,000, but about $350,000 of this was in 10 % warrants for road-building, &c.; the bonds and warrants (with the exception of some never presented for redemption) were speedily redeemed by a special property tax. Revenues for the support of the government are derived from the following sources: the general property tax, the poll tax (the proceeds of which accrue to the county in which it is collected), the inheritance tax, corporation taxes, business taxes and licenses and fees. By far the most important source of revenue is the general property tax, which is assessed for state, county and municipal purposes. The amount of revenue to be raised for state purposes each year by this tax is computed by a board consisting of the governor, the secretary of state and the state treasurer, and it is apportioned among the counties on the basis of their average expenditures for the previous five years. At the close of the year 1907 the state was free from bonded indebtedness; receipts into the treasury during the year were $2,851,471, and the expenditure was $2,697,645.

History.—As to the European who first saw any portion of the present Oregon there is some controversy and doubt. It is known that within thirty years after the discovery of the Pacific Ocean the Spaniards had explored the western coasts of the American continent from the isthmus to the vicinity of the forty-second parallel of north latitude, and it is possible that the Spanish pilot Bartolomé Ferrelo (or Ferrer), who in 1543 made the farthest northward voyage in the Pacific recorded in the first half of the 16th century, may have reached a point on the Oregon coast. The profitable trade between the Spanish colonies and the Far East, however, soon occupied the whole attention of the Spaniards, and caused them to neglect the exploration of the coast of north-western América for many years. In 1579 the Englishman, Francis Drake, came to this region seeking a route home by way of the North-west Passage, and in his futile quest he seems to have gone as far north as 43°.[1] He took possession of the country in the name of Queen Elizabeth and called it Albion. Near the end of the century persistent stories of a North-west Passage caused the Spanish rulers to plan further explorations of the Pacific coast, so as to forestall other nations in the discovery of the alleged new route and thus retain their monopoly of the South Sea (Pacific Ocean). In 1603 Sebastian Viscaino, acting under orders of the viceroy of Mexico, reached the latitude of 42° N., and Martin Aguilar, with another vessel of the fleet, reached a point near latitude 43° which he called Cape Blanco and claimed to have discovered there a large river. For the next century and a half Spain again neglected this region, until the fear of English and Russian encroachment caused her to resume the work of exploration. In 1774 Juan Perez sailed up the coast as far as 54° N. lat., and on his return followed the shore line very closely, thus making the first real and undisputed exploration of the Oregon coast of which there is any record. In the following year Bruno Heceta landed off what is now called Point Grenville and took formal possession of the country, and later, in lat. 46°0', he discovered a bay whose swift currents led him to suspect that he was in the mouth of a large river or strait. In 1778 Jonathan Carver (q.v.) published in London *Travels throughout the Interior Parts of North America,* in which, following the example of the Spaniards, he asserted that there was a great river on the western coast, although, so far as is known, no white man had then ever seen such a stream. Whether his declaration was based on stories told by the Indians of the interior, or upon reports of Spanish sailors, or had no basis at all, is not known; its chief importance lies in the fact that Carver called this undiscovered stream the Oregon, and thus

[1] Some early writers assert that Drake even reached the lat. of 48° N. and anchored in the Straits of Juan de Fuca.

this name was eventually applied to the territory drained by this great western river. The name, like the whole story, may have been of Spanish or Indian origin, or it may have been purely fanciful.[1]

The Spaniards made no effort to colonize north-western America or to develop its trade with the Indians, but toward the end of the 18th century the traders of the great British fur companies of the North were gradually pushing overland to the Pacific. Upon the sea, too, the English were not idle. Captain James Cook in March 1778 sighted the coast of Oregon in the lat. of 44°, and examined it between 47° and 48° in the hope of finding the Straits of Juan de Fuca described in Spanish accounts. Soon after the close of the War of Independence American merchants began to buy furs along the north-west coast and to ship them to China to be exchanged for the products of the East. It was in the prosecution of this trade that Captain Robert Gray (1755-1806), an American in the service of Boston merchants, discovered in 1792 the long-sought river of the West, which he named the Columbia, after his ship. By the discovery of this stream Gray gave to the United States a claim to the whole territory drained by its waters. Other explorers had searched in vain for this river. Cook had sailed by without suspecting its presence; Captain John Meares (c. 1756-1809), another English navigator, who visited the region in 1788, declared that no such river existed, and actually called its estuary "Deception Bay"; and George Vancouver, who visited the coast in 1792, was sceptical until he learned of Gray's discovery.

Spanish claims to this part of North America did not long remain undisputed by England and the United States. By the Nootka Convention of 1790 Spain acknowledged the right of British subjects to fish, trade and settle in the parts of the northern Pacific coast not already occupied; and under the treaty of 1819 (proclaimed in 1821) she ceded to the United States all the territory claimed by her N. of 42°. But even before these agreements had been reached, Alexander Mackenzie, in the service of the North-west Company, in 1793 had explored through Canada to the Pacific coast in lat. about 52° 20′ N., and Meriwether Lewis and William Clark, American explorers acting under the orders of President Jefferson, in 1805-1806 had passed west of the Rocky Mountains and down the Columbia river to the Pacific Ocean. Both British and American adventurers were attracted to the region by the profitable fur trade. In 1808 the North-west Company had several posts on the Fraser river, and in the same year the American Fur Company was organized by John Jacob Astor, who was planning to build up a trade in the West. In 1811 the Pacific Fur Company, a kind of western division of the American Fur Company, founded a trading post at the mouth of the Columbia which they called Astoria, and set up a number of minor posts on the Willamette, Spokane and Okanogan rivers. On hearing of the war between England and the United States, Astor's associates, deeming Astoria untenable, sold the property in October 1813 to the North-west Company. In the following month a British ship arrived, and its captain took formal possession of the post and renamed it Fort George.

Soon after the restoration of peace between England and the United States by the treaty of Ghent (1814), there arose the so-called "Oregon question" or "North-western boundary dispute," which agitated both countries for more than a generation and almost led to another war. As that treaty had stipulated that all territory captured during the war should be restored to its former owner, the American government in 1817 took

steps to reoccupy the Columbia Valley. The British government at first protested, on the ground that Astoria was not captured territory, but finally surrendered the post to the United States in 1818. The United States was willing at the time to extend the north-western boundary along the forty-ninth parallel from the Lake of the Woods to the Pacific, but to this the British government would not consent; and on the 20th of October 1818 both nations agreed to a convention providing for the "joint occupation" for ten years of the country "on the north-west coast of America, westward of the Stony [Rocky] Mountains." In the following year, as already stated, Spain waived her claim to the territory north of 42° in favour of the United States. In 1821, however, Russia asserted her claim to all lands as far south as the fifty-first parallel. Against this claim both England and the United States protested, and in 1824 the United States and Russia concluded a treaty by which Russia agreed to make no settlements south of 54° 40′, and the United States agreed to make none north of that line. From this time until the final settlement of the controversy the Americans were disposed to believe that their title was clear to all the territory south of the Russian possessions; that is, to all the region west of the Rocky Mountains between 42° and 54° 40′ N. lat. In 1827 the agreement of 1818 between Great Britain and the United States as to joint occupation was renewed for an indefinite term, with the proviso that it might be terminated by either party on twelve months' notice.

For the next two decades the history of Oregon is concerned mainly with the British fur traders and the American immigrants. The Hudson's Bay Company absorbed its rival, the North-west Company, in 1821, and thus secured a practical monopoly of the fur trade of the North and West. Its policy was to discourage colonization so as to maintain the territory in which it operated as a vast game preserve. Fortunately for the Americans, however, the company in 1824 sent to the Columbia river as its chief factor and governor west of the Rocky Mountains Dr John McLoughlin (1784-1857), who ruled the region with an iron hand, but with a benevolent purpose, for twenty-two years. On the northern bank of the Columbia in 1824-1825 he built Fort Vancouver, which became a port for ocean vessels and a great entrepôt for the western fur trade; in 1829 he began the settlement of Oregon City; and, most important of all, he extended a hearty welcome to all settlers and aided them in many ways, though this was against the company's interests.

In 1832 four Indian chiefs from the Oregon country journeyed to St Louis to obtain a copy of the white man's Bible; and this incident aroused the missionary zeal of the religious denominations. In 1834 Jason Lee (d. 1845) and his nephew, Daniel Lee, went to Oregon as Methodist missionaries, and with McLoughlin's assistance they established missions in the Willamette valley. Samuel Parker went as a Presbyterian missionary in 1835, and was followed in the next year by Marcus Whitman and Henry H. Spalding (c. 1801-1874), who were accompanied by their wives, the first white women, it is said, to cross the American continent. Whitman settled at Wai-i-lat-pu, about 5 m. W. of the present Walla Walla and 25 m. from the Hudson's Bay Company's Fort Walla Walla, and Spalding at Lapwai, near the present Lewiston, Idaho. Roman Catholic missions were established near Fort Walla Walla in 1838. In this year Jason Lee returned to the Eastern states and carried back to Oregon with him by sea over fifty people, missionaries and their families. It is significant, if true, that part of the money for chartering his vessel was supplied from the secret-service fund of the United States government.

As early as 1841 the Americans in Oregon began to feel the need of some form of civil government, as the regulations of the Hudson's Bay Company were the only laws then known to the country. After several ineffectual attempts a provisional government was finally organized by two meetings at Champoeg (in what is now Marion county, north-east of Salem) on the 2nd of May and on the 5th of July 1843. The governing body was at first an executive committee of three citizens, but in 1845 this committee was abolished and a governor was chosen. In

[1] There have been many ingenious, but quite unsatisfactory, efforts to explain the derivation of the word *Oregon*. They are enumerated at length in Bancroft's *History of Oregon*, vol. i. pp. 17-25. It seems that after the publication of Carver's book the word Oregon did not appear again in print until William Cullen Bryant employed it in his poem *Thanatopsis*, in 1817. It was applied to the territory drained by the Columbia river for the first time perhaps, by Hall J. Kelley, a promoter of immigration into the North-west, who in memorials to Congress and numerous other writings referred to the country as Oregon

the "fundamental laws" of the provisional government were incorporated a number of Articles from the Ordinance of 1787, among them the one prohibiting slavery. The new government encountered the opposition of the missionaries and of the non-American population, but it was soon strengthened by the "Great Immigration" in 1843, when nearly nine hundred men, women and children, after assembling at Independence, Missouri, crossed the plains in a body and settled in the Columbia Valley. After this year the flow of immigrants steadily increased, about 1400 arriving in 1844, and 3000 in 1845.[1] Signs of hostility to the Hudson's Bay Company now began to appear among the American population, and in 1845 the provisional government sought to extend its jurisdiction north of the Columbia river, where the Americans had hitherto refrained from settling. A compromise was finally reached, whereby the company was to be exempt from taxes on all its property except the goods sold to settlers, and the officers and employees of the company and all the British residents were to become subject to the provisional government. Meanwhile the western states had inaugurated a movement in favour of the immediate and definite settlement of the Oregon question, with the result that the Democratic national convention of 1844 declared that the title of the United States to "the whole of the territory of Oregon" was "clear and unquestionable," and the party made "Fifty-four forty or fight" a campaign slogan. The Democrats were successful at the polls, and President Polk in his inaugural address asserted the claim of the United States to all of Oregon in terms suggesting the possibility of war. Negotiations, however, resulted in a treaty, drafted by James Buchanan, the American Secretary of State, and Richard Pakenham, the British envoy, which the president in June 1846 submitted to the Senate for its opinion and which he was advised to accept. By this instrument the northern boundary of Oregon was fixed at the forty-ninth parallel, extending westward from the crest of the Rocky Mountains to the middle of the channel separating Vancouver's Island from the mainland, "and thence southerly through the middle of the said channel, and of Fuca's Straits, to the Pacific Ocean."

Although President Polk immediately urged the formation of a territorial government for Oregon, the bill introduced for this purpose was held up in the Senate on account of the opposition of Southern leaders, who were seeking to maintain the abstract principle that slavery could not be constitutionally prohibited in any territory of the United States, although they had no hope of Oregon ever becoming slave territory. Indian outbreaks, however, which began in 1847, compelled Congress to take measures for the defence of the inhabitants, and on the 14th of August 1848 a bill was enacted providing a territorial government. As then constituted, the Territory embraced the whole area to which the title of the United States had been confirmed by the treaty of 1846, and included the present states of Oregon, Washington and Idaho, and parts of Wyoming and Montana. Its area was reduced in 1853 by the creation of the Territory of Washington. The discovery of gold in California drew many Oregon settlers to that country in 1848-1850, but this exodus was soon offset as a result of the enactment by Congress in 1850 of the "land donation law," by which settlers in Oregon between 1850 and 1853 were entitled to large tracts of land free of cost. The number of claims registered under this act was over eight thousand.

In 1856 the people voted for statehood; and in June 1857 they elected members of a constitutional convention which drafted a constitution at Salem in August and September 1857; the constitution was ratified by popular vote in November

1857; and on the 14th of February 1859 Oregon was admitted into the Union with its present boundaries. The new state was at first Democratic in politics, and the southern faction of the Democratic party in 1860 made a bid for its support by nominating as their candidate for vice-president, on the ticket with John C. Breckinridge, Joseph Lane (1801-1881), then a senator from Oregon and previously its territorial governor. The Douglas Democrats and the Republicans, however, worked together as a union party, and Lincoln carried the state by a small majority. The so-called union party broke up after the Civil War, and by 1870 the Democrats were strong enough to prevent the ratification by Oregon of the Fifteenth Amendment to the Federal Constitution. In 1876, after the presidential election, two sets of electoral returns were forwarded from Oregon, one showing the choice of three Republican electors, and the other (signed by the governor, who was a Democrat) showing the election of two Republicans and one Democrat. The popular vote was admittedly for the three Republican electors, but one of the Republican electors (Watts) was a deputy-postmaster and so seemed ineligible under the constitutional provision that "no . . . person holding an office of trust or profit under the United States shall be an elector." Watts resigned as deputy-postmaster, and the secretary of state of Oregon, who under the state law was the canvassing officer, certified the election of the three Republican electors. On the 6th of December the three met, Watts resigned, and was immediately reappointed by the other two. The Democratic claimant, with whom the two Republican electors whose election was conceded, refused to meet, met alone, appointed two other Democrats to fill the two "vacancies," and the "electoral college" of the state so constituted forthwith cast two votes for Hayes and one for Tilden. The Electoral Commission decided that the three votes should be counted for Hayes—if the one Democratic elector had been adjudged chosen, the Democratic candidate for the presidency, S. J. Tilden, would have been elected. The political complexion of the state has generally been Republican, although the contests between the two leading parties have often been very close. The Indian outbreaks which began in 1847 continued with occasional periods of quiet for nearly a generation, until most of the Indians were either killed or placed on reservations. The Indians were very active during the Civil War, when the regular troops were withdrawn for service in the eastern states, and Oregon's volunteers from 1861 to 1865 were needed for home defence. The most noted Indian conflicts within the state have been the Modoc War (1864-73) and the Shoshone War (1866-68). During the Spanish-American War Oregon furnished a regiment of volunteers which served in the Philippines.

GOVERNORS OF OREGON

Under the Provisional Government.

George Abernethy .	1845-1849

Under the Territorial Government.

Joseph Lane .	1849-1850
Kintzing Pritchett (acting) .	1850
John P. Gaines .	1850-1852
Joseph Lane .	1853[2]
George Law Curry (acting) .	1853
John W. Davis .	1853-1854
George Law Curry .	1854-1859

Under the State Government.

John Whiteaker, Dem.	1859-1862
Addison Crandall Gibbs, Rep.	1862-1866
George Lemuel Woods, Rep.	1866-1870
La Fayette Grover, Dem.	1870-1877
Stephen Fowler Chadwick (acting)	1877-1878
William Wallace Thayer, Dem.	1878-1882
Zenas Ferry Moody, Rep.	1882-1887
Sylvester Pennoyer, Dem.	1887-1895
William Paine Lord, Rep.	1895-1899
Theodore Thurston Geer, Rep.	1899-1903
George Earle Chamberlain, Dem.	1903-1909
Frank W. Benson, Rep.	1909-1911[3]
Oswald West, Dem.	1911-

[1] For many years it was generally believed that the administration at Washington was prevented from surrendering its claims to Oregon, in return for the grant by Great Britain of fishing stations in Newfoundland, by Marcus Whitman, who in 1842-1843 made a journey across the entire continent in the depth of winter to dissuade the government from this purpose. This story seems to have no foundation in fact; it was not Whitman, but the great influx of settlers in 1843-1844 that saved Oregon, if, indeed, there was then any danger of its being given up. (See WHITMAN, MARCUS.)

[2] Held office only three days, May 16-19.

[3] Secretary of State; succeeded G. E. Chamberlain, who resigned to become a member of the U.S. Senate.

BIBLIOGRAPHY.—See generally W. Nash, *The Settler's Handbook to Oregon* (Portland, 1904); and publications and reports of the various national and state departments. For administration: J. R. Robertson, " The Genesis of Political Authority and of a Commonwealth Government in Oregon " in the *Quarterly of the Oregon Historical Society*, vol. i. (Salem, 1901); *Journal of the Constitutional Convention of the State of Oregon held at Salem in 1857* (Salem, 1882); C. B. Bellinger and W. W. Cotton, *The Codes and Statutes of Oregon* (2 vols., San Francisco, 1902); and Frank Foxcroft, " Constitution Mending and the Initiative," in the *Atlantic Monthly* for June 1906. For history: H. H. Bancroft's *History of the North-west Coast* (2 vols., San Francisco, 1884) and *History of Oregon* (2 vols., San Francisco, 1886–1888); William Barrows's *Oregon: The Struggle for Possession* (Boston, 1883) in the "American Commonwealths" series; J. Dunn's *Oregon Territory and the British North American Fur Trade* (Philadelphia, 1845); W. H. Gray's *History of Oregon, 1792–1849* (Portland, Oregon, 1870); H. S. Lyman's *History of Oregon* (4 vols., New York, 1903), the best complete history of the state; Joseph Schafer's " Pacific Slope and Alaska," vol. x. of G. C. Lee's *History of North America* (Philadelphia, 1904), more succinct. On special features of the state's history see W. R. Manning's " The Nootka Sound Controversy," pp. 279-478 of the *Annual Report for 1904* (Washington, 1905) of the American Historical Association; F. V. Holman's *Dr John McLoughlin, the Father of Oregon* (Cleveland, 1907); J. H. Gilbert's *Trade and Currency in Early Oregon*, in the Columbia University Studies in Economics, vol. xxvi., No. 1 (New York, 1907); and P. J. de Smet's " Oregon Missions and Travels over the Rocky Mountains in 1845–1846," in vol. xxix. of R. G. Thwaites's *Early Western Travels* (Cleveland, 1906). For the Whitman controversy see WHITMAN, MARCUS. Much historical material may be found in the publications of the Oregon Historical Society, especially in the Society's *Quarterly* (1900 sqq.), and of the Oregon Pioneer Association.

OREGON CITY, a city and the county-seat of Clackamas county, Oregon, U.S.A., on the E. bank of the Willamette river, and S. of the mouth of the Clackamas river, about 15 m. S. by E. of Portland. Pop. (1890) 3062; (1900) 3494 (535 being foreign-born); (1910) 4287. It is served by the Southern Pacific railway, by an electric line to Portland, by other electric lines, and by small river steamboats. The principal business streets are Main Street, on level ground along the river, and Seventh Street, on a bluff which rises abruptly 100 ft. above the river and is reached by four stairways elevated above the tracks of the Southern Pacific. The residences are for the most part on this bluff, which commands views of the peaks of the Cascade Mountains. The river here makes a picturesque plunge of about 40 ft. over a basalt ridge extending across the valley, and then flows between nearly vertical walls of solid rock 20-50 ft. high; it is spanned by a suspension bridge nearly 100 ft. above the water. A lock canal enables vessels to pass the falls. The water-power works woollen-mills, flour-mills, paper-mills, and an electric power plant (of the Portland Railway, Light and Power Company), which lights the city of Portland and transmits power to that city for street railways and factories. The municipality owns the waterworks. Next to Astoria, Oregon City is the oldest settlement in the state. In 1829 Dr John McLoughlin (1784–1857), chief agent of the Hudson's Bay Company, established a claim to the water-power at the Falls of the Willamette and to land where Oregon City now stands, and began the erection of a mill and several houses. After 1840, in which year McLoughlin laid out a town here and named it Oregon City, a Methodist Mission disputed his claim. He aided many destitute American immigrants, left the service of the company, and removed to Oregon City. In 1850 Congress gave a great part of his claim at Oregon City for the endowment of a university, and in 1862 the legislature of Oregon reconveyed the land to McLoughlin's heirs on condition that they should give $1000 to the university fund; but the questionable title between 1840 and 1862 hindered the growth of the place, which was chartered as a city in 1850.

O'REILLY, JOHN BOYLE (1844–1890), Irish-American politician and journalist, was born near Drogheda on the 28th of June 1844, the son of a schoolmaster. After some years of newspaper experience, first as compositor, then as reporter, during which he became an ardent revolutionist and joined the Fenian organization known as the Irish Republican Brotherhood, he enlisted in a British cavalry regiment with the purpose of winning over the troops to the revolutionary cause (1863).

At this period wholesale corruption of the army, in which there was a very large percentage of Irishmen, was a strong feature in the Fenian programme, and O'Reilly, who soon became a great favourite, was successful in disseminating disaffection in his regiment. In 1866 the extent of the sedition in the regiments in Ireland was discovered by the authorities. O'Reilly was arrested at Dublin, where his regiment was then quartered, tried by court-martial for concealing his knowledge of an impending mutiny, and sentenced to be shot, but the sentence was subsequently commuted to twenty years' penal servitude. After confinement in various English prisons, he was transported in 1867 to Bunbury, Western Australia. In 1869 he escaped to the United States, and settled in Boston, where he became editor of *The Pilot*, a Roman Catholic newspaper. He subsequently organized the expedition which rescued all the Irish military political prisoners from the Western Australia convict establishments (1876), and he aided and abetted the American propaganda in favour of Irish nationalism. O'Reilly died in Hull, Mass., on the 10th of August 1890. His reputation in America naturally differed very much from what it was in England, towards whom he was uniformly mischievous. He was the author of several volumes of poetry of considerable merit, and of a novel of convict life, *Moondyne*, which achieved a great success. He was also selected to write occasional odes in commemoration of many American celebrations.

See J. J. Roche, *Life of John Boyle O'Reilly*, (Boston, 1891).

OREL, or ORLOV, a government of central Russia, bounded by the governments of Smolensk, Kaluga and Tula on the N., and by Voronezh and Kursk on the S., with an area of 18,036 sq. m. The surface is an undulating plateau sloping gently towards the west; the highest hills barely exceed 900 ft., and none of the valleys is less than 450 ft. above the sea. The principal rivers are the Don, which forms part of the eastern boundary, and its tributary the Sosna; the Oka, which rises in the district of Orel and receives the navigable Zusha; and the Desna, with the Bolva, draining the marshy lowlands in the west. Geologically Orel consists principally of Lower Devonian limestones, marls and sandstones, covered with Jurassic clays, the last appearing at the surface, however, only as isolated islands, or in the valleys, being concealed for the most part under thick beds of Cretaceous chalk, marls and sands. The Carboniferous limestones and clays (of the so-called Moscow basin) show in the north-west only at a great depth. The Jurassic clays and marls are overlain at several places with a stratum of clay containing good iron-ore, while the Devonian sandstones and limestones are worked for building purposes. The whole is buried under a bed, 30 to 40 ft. thick, of boulder-clay and loess, the last covering extensive areas as well as the valleys. The soil—a mixture of " black earth " with clay—is fertile, except in the Desna region in the west, where sands and tenacious 'clays predominate. On the Oka, Zusha, Desna and Bolva there is a brisk traffic in corn, oil, hemp, timber, metal, glass, china, paper and building-stone. Marshes occupy large areas in the basin of the Desna; as also in several parts of that of the Oka; they are mostly covered with forests, which run up to 50 to 65% of the area in the districts of Bryansk, Trubchevsk and Karachev, while towards the east, in the basin of the Don, wood is so scarce that straw is used for fuel The climate is moderate, the average yearly temperature at Orel being 41·2° (14·8° in January and 67·0° in July).

The estimated population in 1906 was 2,365,700. It consists almost exclusively of Great Russians, belonging to the Orthodox Greek Church; the Nonconformists are reckoned at about 12,000, the Roman Catholics at 3000 and the Jews at 1000. The chief occupation is agriculture, which is most productive in the east and towards the centre of the government. The principal crops are rye, oats, barley, wheat, hemp, potatoes, hops, vegetables, tobacco and fruit. Of the grain not used in the area the government. Hemp and hemp-seed oil are extensively exported from the west to Riga, Libau and St Petersburg. Tobacco is cultivated with profit. Cattle and horse-breeding flourishes better than in the neighbouring governments—the Orel breeds of both carriage and draught horses being held in estimation throughout Russia. Bee-keeping is widely diffused in the forest districts, as are also the timber-trade and the preparation of tar and pitch. Manufactures are rapidly increasing; they produce cast-iron rails, machinery, locomotive engines and railway wagons, glass, hemp-yarn and ropes, leather, timber, soap, tobacco and chemical produce. There are also distilleries and a great many smaller oil-works and flour-mills. Karachev and Syevsk are important centres for hemp-carding; Bolkhov and Elets are the chief centres of the tanning industry; while the districts of Elets, Dmitrov and partly Mtsensk supply flour and various foodpastes. At Bryansk there is a government cannon-foundry. The " Maltsov works " in the district of Bryansk are an industrial colony (20,000), comprising several iron, machinery, glass and rope works, where thousands of peasants find temporary or permanent employment; they have their own technical school, employ engineers of their own training, and have their own narrow-gauge railways and telegraphs, both managed by boys of the technical school. Numerous petty trades are carried on by the peasants, along with agriculture. The government is divided into twelve districts, of which the chief towns are Orel, the capital, Bolkhov, Bryansk, Dmitrovsk, Elets, Karachev, Kromy, Livny, Malo-arkhangelsk, Mtsensk, Syevsk and Trubchevsk.

In the 9th century the country was inhabited by the Slav tribes of the Syeveryanes on the Desna and the Vyatichis on the Oka, who both paid tribute to the Khazars. The Syeveryanes recognised the rule of the princes of the Rurik family from 884, and the Vyatichis from the middle of the 10th century; but the two peoples followed different historical lines, the former being absorbed into the Suzdal principality, while the latter fell under the rule of that of Chernigov. In the 11th century both had wealthy towns and villages; during the Mongol invasion of 1239-1242 these were all burned and pillaged, and the entire territory devastated. With the decay of the Great Horde of the Mongols the western part of the country fell under Lithuanian rule, and was the object of repeated struggles between Lithuania and Moscow. In the 16th century the Russians began to erect new forts and fortify the old towns, and the territory was rapidly colonised by immigrants from the north. In 1610 the towns of the present government of Orel (then known as the Ukrayna Ukraine, i.e. " border-region,") took an active share in the insurrection against Moscow under the false Demetrius, and suffered much from the civil war which ensued. They continued, however, to be united with the rest of Russia.

(P. A. K.; J. T. Bᴇ.)

OREL, a town of Russia, capital of the government of the same name, lies at the confluence of the Oka with the Orlik, on the line of railway to the Crimea, 238 m. S.S.W. from Moscow. Pop. (1875) 45,000, (1900) 70,075. It was founded in 1566, but developed slowly, and had only a very few houses at the beginning of the 18th century. The cathedral, begun in 1794, was finished only in 1861. The town possesses a military gymnasium (corps of cadets), a public library, and storehouses for grain and timber. The manufactures are rapidly increasing, and include hempcarding and spinning, rope-making, flour-mills and candle factories. Orel is one of the chief markets of central Russia for corn, hemp, hempseed oil, and tallow, exported; metal wares, tobacco, kaolin, and glass ware are also exported, while salt, groceries and manufactured goods are imported.

O'RELL, MAX, the *nom-de-plume* of PAUL BLOUET (1848-1903), French author and journalist, who was born in Brittany in 1848. He served as a cavalry officer in the Franco-German War, was captured at Sedan, but was released in time to join the Versailllist army which overcame the Commune, and was severely wounded during the second siege of Paris. In 1872 he went to England as correspondent of several French newspapers, and in 1876 became the very efficient French master at St Paul's school, London, retaining that post until 1884. What induced him to leave was the brilliant success of his first book, *John Bull et son Ile*, which in its French and English forms was so widely read as to make his pseudonym a household word in England and America.

Several other volumes of a similar type dealing in a like spirit with Scotland, America and France followed. He married an Englishwoman, who translated his books. But the main work of the years between 1890 and 1900 was lecturing. Max O'Rell was a ready and amusing speaker, and his easy manner and his humorous gift made him very successful on the platform. He lectured often in the United Kingdom and still more often in America. He died in Paris, where he was acting as correspondent of the *New York Journal*, on the 25th of May 1903.

ORELLI, HANS KONRAD VON (1846-   ), Swiss theologian, was born at Zürich on the 25th of January 1846 and was educated at Lausanne, Zürich and Erlangen. He also visited Tübingen for theology and Leipzig for oriental languages. In 1869 he was appointed preacher at the orphan house, Zürich, and in 1871 *Privatdocent* at the university. In 1873 he went to Basel as professor extraordinarius of theology, becoming ordinary professor in 1881. His chief work is on the Old Testament; in addition to commentaries on Isaiah, Jeremiah (1886), Ezekiel and the Twelve Prophets (1888), most of which have been translated, he wrote *Die alttestamentliche Weissagung von der Vollendung des Gottesreiches* (Vienna, 1882; Eng. trans. Edinburgh, 1885), *Die himmlischen Heerschaaren* (Basel, 1889), and a journal of Palestinian travel, *Durchs Heilige Land* (Basel, 1878).

ORELLI, JOHANN CASPAR VON (1787-1849), Swiss classical scholar, was born at Zürich on the 13th of February 1787. He belonged to a distinguished Italian family, which had taken refuge in Switzerland at the time of the Reformation. His cousin, JOHANN CONRAD ORELLI (1770-1826), was the author of several works in the department of later Greek literature. From 1807 to 1814 Orelli worked as preacher in the reformed community of Bergamo, where he acquired the taste for Italian literature which led to the publication of *Contributions to the History of Italian Poetry* (1810) and a biography (1812) of Vittorino da Feltre, his ideal of a teacher. In 1814 he became teacher of modern languages and history at the cantonal school at Chur (Coire); in 1819, professor of eloquence and hermeneutics at the Carolinum in Zürich, and in 1833 professor at the new university, the foundation of which was largely due to his efforts. His attention during this period was mainly devoted to classical literature and antiquities. He had already published (1814) an edition, with critical notes and commentary, of the *Antidosis* of Isocrates, the complete text of which, based upon the MSS. in the Ambrosian and Laurentian libraries, had recently been made known by Andreas Mystoxedes of Corfu. The three works upon which his reputation rests are the following. (1) A complete edition of Cicero in seven volumes (1826-1838). The first four volumes contained the text (new ed., 1845-1863), the fifth the old Scholiasts, the remaining three (called *Onomasticon Tullianum*) a life of Cicero, a bibliography of previous editions, indexes of geographical and historical names, of laws and legal formulae, of Greek words, and the consular annals. After his death, the revised edition of the text was completed by J. G. Baiter and C. Halm, and contained numerous emendations by Theodor Mommsen and J. N. Madvig. (2) The works of Horace (1837-1838; 4th ed., 1886-1892). The exegetical commentary, although confessedly only a compilation from the works of earlier commentators, shows great taste and extensive learning, although hardly up to the exacting standard of modern criticism. (3) *Inscriptionum Latinarum Selectarum Collectio* (1828; revised edition by W. Henzen, 1856), extremely helpful for the study of Roman public and private life and religion. His editions of Plato (1839-1841, including the old scholia, in collaboration with A. W. Winckelmann) and Tacitus (1846-1848, new ed. by various scholars, 1875-1894) also deserve mention. Orelli died at Zürich on the 6th of January 1849. He was a most liberal-minded man, both in politics and religion, an enthusiastic supporter of popular education and a most inspiring teacher. He took great interest in the struggle of the Greeks for independence, and strongly favoured the appointment of the notorious J. F. Strauss to the chair of dogmatic theology at Zürich, which led to the disturbance of the 6th of September 1839 and the fall of the liberal government.

See *Life* by his younger brother Conrad in *Neujakrsblatt der Stadtbibliothek Zürich* (1851); J. Adert, *Essai sur la Vie et les Travaux de J.C.O.* (Geneva, 1849); H. Schweizer-Sidler, *Gedächtnissrede auf J.C.O.* (Zürich, 1874); C. Bursian, *Geschichte der klassischen Philologie in Deutschland* (1883).

ORENBURG, a government of south-eastern Russia, bounded N. by the governments of Ufa and Perm, E. by Tobolsk, S.E. by Turgai, and W. by Uralsk and Samara, with an area of 73,794 sq. m. Situated at the southern extremity of the Urals and extending to the north-east on their eastern slope, Orenburg consists of a hilly tract bordered on both sides by steppes. The central ridge occasionally reaches an elevation of 5000 ft.; there are several parallel ridges, which, however, nowhere exceed 2600 ft., and gradually sink towards the south. A great variety of geological formations are represented within the government, which is rich in minerals. Diorites and granites enter it from the north and crop out at many places from underneath the Silurian and Devonian deposits. The Carboniferous limestones and sandstones, as well as softer Permian, Jurassic and Cretaceous deposits, have a wide extension in the south and east. Coal has been found on the Miyas (in N.) and near Iletsk (in S.). The extremely rich layers of rock salt at Iletsk yield about 24,000 tons every year. Very fertile "black earth" covers wide areas around the Urals. The government is traversed from north to south by the Ural river, which also forms its southern boundary; the chief tributaries are the Sakmara and the Ilek. The upper courses of the Byelaya and Samara, tributaries of the Kama and the Volga, also lie within the government, as well as affluents of the Tobol on the eastern slope of the Ural range. Numerous salt lakes occur in the district of Chelyabinsk; but several parts of the flat lands occasionally suffer from want of water. Sixteen per cent of the surface is under wood. The climate is continental and dry, the average temperature at Orenburg being 37·4° Fahr. (4·5° in January, 69·8° in July). Frosts of −33° and heats of 98° are not uncommon.

The estimated population in 1906 was 1,836,500, mainly Great Russians, with Bashkirs and Meshcheryaks (25%). Gold is extracted chiefly from alluvial deposits, about 116,500 oz. every year; also some silver. Nearly one-fifth of all the copper ore extracted in Russia comes from Orenburg (about 16,000 tons annually); and every year 16,000 to 20,000 tons of cast iron and 11,500 tons of iron are obtained. Agriculture is carried on on a large scale, the principal crops being wheat, rye, oats, barley and potatoes. Horses, cattle and sheep are kept in large numbers and camels are bred: Kitchen-gardening gives occupation to nearly 11,000 persons. Various kinds of animal produce are largely exported, and by knitting "Orenburg shawls" of goats' wool the women earn £10,000 every year. The growth of the industries is slow, but trade, especially with the Kirghiz, is prosperous. The chief towns of the five districts into which the government is divided are Orenburg, Orsk, Chelyabinsk, Troitsk and Verkhne-Uralsk.

The government of Orenburg was formerly inhabited by the Kirghiz in the south, and by the Bashkirs in the north. The latter were brought under the rule of Russia in 1557, and a few years later the fort of Ufa was erected in order to protect them against the raids of the Kirghiz. The frequent risings of the Bashkirs, and the continuous attacks of the Kirghiz, led the Russian government in the 18th century to erect a line of forts and blockhouses on the Ural and Sakmara rivers, and these were afterwards extended south-westwards towards the Caspian, and eastwards towards Omsk. The central point of these military lines was the fort of Orenburg, originally founded in 1735 at the confluence (now Orsk) of the Or with the Ural, and removed in 1740–1743 120 m. lower down the Ural river to its present site. In 1773 it was besieged by Pugachev, the leader of the revolt of the peasantry.   (P. A. K.; J. T. BE.)

ORENBURG, a town of Russia, capital of the government of the same name, on the Ural river; connected by rail with Samara (262 m.), and since 1905 with Tashkent (1150 m.). Pop. (1900) 65,906, of whom about 30% were Tatars, Jews, Bashkirs, &c. The town now includes the former suburbs of Golubinaya and Novaya. It is an episcopal see of the Orthodox Greek Church and the headquarters of the hetman of the Orenburg Cossacks. To a "barter house," 3 m. from the town, the camel caravans bring carpets, silks, cottons, lambskins, dried fruits, &c., from Bokhara, Khiva, Kokand and Tashkent, to be bartered against the textiles, metallic goods, sugar and manufactured wares of Russia. From 20,000 to 100,000 horses, 40,000 to 160,000 cattle, and 450,000 to 750,000 sheep are also sold every year at the barter house. Formerly most of these were sent alive to Russia; now some 200,000 head of cattle and sheep are killed every year, and exported in cold-storage wagons. Cattle are also bought by wandering merchants in the Steppe provinces and Turkestan. Every year many tons of tallow, hams, sausages, butter, cheese and game are exported by rail to Samara. Besides these, nearly a million hides and sheepskins, goat and astrakhan skins, as well as wool, horsehair, bristles, down, horns, bones, &c., are exported. There are two cadet corps, a theological seminary, seminaries for Russian and Kirghiz teachers, a museum, branches of the Russian Geographical Society and the Gardening Society, and a military arsenal.

ORENDEL, a Middle High German poem, of no great literary merit, dating from the close of the 12th century. The story is associated with the town of Treves (Trier), where the poem was probably written. The introduction narrates the story of the Holy Coat, which, after many adventures, is swallowed by a whale. It is recovered by Orendel, son of King Eigel of Treves, who had embarked with twenty-two ships in order to woo the lovely Brida, the mistress of the Holy Sepulchre, as his wife. Suffering shipwreck, he falls into the hands of the fisherman Eise, and in his service catches the whale that has swallowed the Holy Coat. The coat has the property of rendering the wearer proof against wounds, and Grendel successfully overcomes innumerable perils and eventually wins Brida for his wife. A message brought by an angel summons both back to Treves, where Orendel meets with many adventures and at last disposes of the Holy Coat by placing it in a stone sarcophagus. Another angel announces both his and Brida's approaching death, when they renounce the world and prepare for the end.

The poem exists in a single manuscript of the 15th century, and in one print, dated 1512. It has been edited by von der Hagen (1844); L. Etzmüller (1858) and A. E. Berger (1888); there is a modern German translation by K. Simrock (1845). See H. Harkensee, *Untersuchungen über das Spielmannsgedicht Orendel* (1879); F. Vogt, in the *Zeitschrift für deutsche Philologie*, vol. xxii. (1890); R. Heinzel, *Über das Gedicht vom König Orendel* (1892); and K. Müllenhoff, in *Deutsche Alterlumskunde*, vol. I. (2nd ed., 1890), pp. 32 seq.

ORENSE, an inland province of north-western Spain, formed in 1833 of districts previously included in Galicia, and bounded on the N. by Pontevedra and Lugo, E. by Leon and Zamora, S. by Portugal, and W. by Portugal and Pontevedra. Pop. (1900) 404,311; area 2694 sq. m. The surface of the province is almost everywhere mountainous. Its western half is traversed in a south-westerly direction by the river Miño (Portuguese *Minho*), which flows through Portugal to the Atlantic; the Sil, a left-hand tributary of the Miño, waters the north-eastern districts; and the Limia rises in the central mountains and flows west-south-west, reaching the sea at the Portuguese port of Vianna do Castello. The upper valley of the Limia is the only large tract of level country. The climate is very varied; mild in some valleys, cold and damp in the highlands, rainy near the northern border, and subject to rapid changes of temperature. The railway from Monforte to Vigo runs through the province. There are a few iron foundries of a primitive sort, but lack of transport and of cheap coal hinder the growth of mining and manufactures.

Though the soil is fertile and well watered, agricultural products are not so important as arboriculture. The oak, beech, pine, chestnut, walnut and plane grow in abundance on the hills and mountains; pears, apples, cherries, almonds, figs, roses and olives in the valleys, and even oranges and lemons in sheltered spots. The chief towns are the capital, Orense, Allariz, Carballino, Viana, Nogueira de Ramuin, Boborás, Cartella and La Vega. See also GALICIA.

ORENSE, an episcopal see and the capital of the Spanish province of Orense; on the left bank of the river Miño, and on the Tuy-Monforte railway. Pop. (1900) 15,194. The river is here crossed by a bridge—one of the most remarkable in Spain—of seven arches, 1319 ft. in length, and at its highest point 135 ft. above the bed of the river. This bridge was built by Bishop Lorenzo in 1230, but has frequently been repaired. The Gothic cathedral, also dating from Bishop Lorenzo's time, is a comparatively small building, but has an image, El Santo Cristo, which was brought from Cape Finisterre in 1330 and is celebrated throughout Galicia for its miraculous powers. The city contains many schools, a public library and a theatre. In the older streets there are some interesting medieval houses. Chocolate and leather are manufactured, and there are saw-mills, flour-mills and iron foundries. The three warm springs to the west, known as Las Burgas, attract many summer visitors; the waters were well known to the Romans, as their ancient name, Aquae Originis, Aquae Urentes, or perhaps Aquae Salientis, clearly indicates.

The Romans named Orense Aurium, probably from the alluvial gold found in the Miño valley. The bishopric, founded in the 5th century by the Visigoths, was named the Sedes Auriensis (see of Aurium), and from this the modern Orense is derived. The city became the capital of the Suevi in the 6th century; it was sacked by the Moors in 716, and rebuilt only in 884.

OREODON (i.e. "hillock-tooth"), the name of an Oligocene genus of North American primitive ruminants related to the camels, and typifying the family *Oreodontidae*. Typical oreo-donts were long-tailed, four-toed, partially plantigrade ruminants with sharp-crowned crescentic molars, of which the upper ones carry four cusps, and the first lower premolar canine-like both in shape and function. In the type genus there are forty-four teeth, forming an uninterrupted series. The vertebral artery pierces the neck-vertebrae in the normal manner. The name *Oreodon* is preoccupied by *Orodus*, the designation of a genus of Palaeozoic fishes, and is likewise antedated by *Merycoidodon*, which is now used by some writers. See TYLOPODA.

ORESME, NICOLAS (c. 1320–1382), French bishop, celebrated for his numerous works in both French and Latin on scholastic, scientific and political questions, was born in Normandy at the opening of the 14th century. In 1348 he was a student in the college of Navarre at Paris, of which he became head in 1356. In 1361 he was named dean of the cathedral of Rouen. Charles V. had him appointed bishop of Lisieux on the 16th of November 1377. He died in that city on the 11th of July 1382. One of his works, of great importance for the history of economic conceptions in the middle ages, was the *De origine, natura, jure et mutationibus monetarum,* of which there is also a French edition. Oresme was the author of several works on astrology, in which he showed its falseness as a science and denounced its practice. At the request of Charles V. he translated the *Ethics, Politics* and *Economics* of Aristotle. In December 1363 he preached before Urban V. a sermon on reform in the church, so severe in its arraignment that it was often brought forward in the 16th century by Protestant polemists.

See Francis Meunier, *Essai sur la vie et les ouvrages de Nicole Oresme* (Paris, 1857); Feret, *La Faculté de théologie de l'Université de Paris* (Paris, 1896, t. iii. p. 290 sqq.); Émile Bridrey, *Nicole Oresme. Étude des doctrines et des faits économiques* (Paris, 1906).

ORESTES, in Greek legend, son of Agamemnon and Clytaem-nestra. According to the Homeric story he was absent from Mycenae when his father returned from the Trojan War and was murdered by Aegisthus. Eight years later he returned from Athens and revenged his father's death by slaying his mother, and her paramour (*Odyssey,* iii. 306; xi. 542). According to Pindar (*Pythia,* xi. 25) he was saved by his nurse, who conveyed him out of the country when Clytaemnestra wished to kill him. The tale is told much more fully and with many variations in the tragedians. He was preserved by his sister Electra from his father's fate, and conveyed to Phanote on Mount Parnassus, where King Strophius took charge of him.

In his twentieth year he was ordered by the Delphic oracle to return home and revenge his father's death. According to Aeschylus, he met his sister Electra before the tomb of Agamem-non, whither both had gone to perform rites to the dead; a recognition takes place, and they arrange how Orestes shall accomplish his revenge. Orestes, after the deed, goes mad, and is pursued by the Erinyes, whose duty it is to punish any violation of the ties of family piety. He takes refuge in the temple at Delphi; but, though Apollo had ordered him to do the deed, he is powerless to protect his suppliant from the consequences. At last Athena receives him on the acropolis of Athens and arranges a formal trial of the case before twelve Attic judges. The Erinyes demand their victim; he pleads the orders of Apollo; the votes of the judges are equally divided, and Athena gives her casting vote for acquittal. The Erinyes are propitiated by a new ritual, in which they are worshipped as Eumenides (the Kindly), and Orestes dedicates an altar to Athena Areia. With Aeschylus the punishment ends here, but, according to Euripides, in order to escape the persecutions of the Erinyes, he was ordered by Apollo to go to Tauris, carry off the statue of Artemis which had fallen from heaven, and bring it to Athens. He repairs to Tauris with Pylades, the son of Strophius and the intimate friend of Orestes, and the pair are at once imprisoned by the people, among whom the custom is to sacrifice all strangers to Artemis. The priestess of Artemis, whose duty it is to perform the sacrifice, is his sister Iphigeneia (q.v.). She offers to release Orestes if he will carry home a letter from her to Greece; he refuses to go, but bids Pylades take the letter while he himself will stay and be slain. After a conflict of mutual affection, Pylades at last yields, but the letter brings about a recognition between brother and sister, and all three escape together, carrying with them the image of Artemis. After his return to Greece, Orestes took possession of his father's kingdom of Mycenae, to which were added Argos and Laconia. He is said to have died of the bite of a snake in Arcadia. His body was conveyed to Sparta for burial (where he was the object of a cult), or, according to an Italian legend, to Aricia, whence it was removed to Rome (Servius on *Aeneid,* ii. 116). The story of Orestes was the subject of the *Oresteia* of Aeschylus (*Agamem-non, Choephori, Eumenides*), of the *Electra* of Sophocles, of the *Electra, Iphigeneia in Tauris,* and *Orestes,* of Euripides. There is extant a Latin epic poem, consisting of about 1000 hexa-meters, called *Orestis Tragoedia,* which has been ascribed to Dracontius of Carthage.

Orestes appears also as a central figure in various legends connected with his madness and purification, both in Greece and Asia. In these Orestes is the guilt-laden mortal who is purified from his sin by the grace of the gods, whose merciful justice is shown to all persons whose crime is mitigated by extenuating circumstances. These legends belong to an age when higher ideas of law and of social duty were being established; the implacable blood-feud of primitive society gives place to a fair trial, and in Athens, when the votes of the judges are evenly divided, mercy prevails.

The legend of Orestes is the subject of a lengthy monograph by T. Zielinski, "Die Orestessage und die Rechtfertigungsidee" in *Neue Jahrbücher für das klassische Altertum,* ii. (1899). Orestes, according to Zielinski, is the son of the sky-god Zeus-Agamemnon, who over-comes his wife the earth-goddess Gaia-Clytaemnestra; with the assistance of the dragon Aegisthus, she slays her husband, whose murder is in turn avenged by his son. The religion of Zeus is then reformed under the influence of the cult of Apollo, who slays the dragon brought up by the earth-goddess on Parnassus, the seat of one of her oldest sanctuaries. Parnassus becomes the holy mountain of Apollo, and Orestes himself an hypostasis of Apollo "of the mountain," just as Pylades is Apollo "of the plain"; similarly Electra, Iphigeneia and Chrysothemis are hypostases of Artemis. Zeus being firmly seated on his throne as the result of the slaying of the dragon by Orestes, the theological significance of the myth is forgotten, and the identifications Zeus-Agamemnon and Gaia-Clytaemnestra are abandoned. In the Homeric Oresteia the soul of the murdered wife has no claim to vengeance, and Orestes rules unmolested in Argos. But the Apolline religion introduces the theory of the rights of the soul and revenge for bloodshed. Apollo, who has urged Orestes to parricide and has himself expiated the crime of slaying the dragon, is able to purify others in similar case. Hence

Orestes, freed from the guilt of blood, is enabled to take possession of the throne of his father. This is the Delphic Oresteia. But a new idea is introduced by the Attic Oresteia. The claim that Apollo can in every case purify from sin is met by Athena with a counterclaim on behalf of the state. It is the community of which murdered and murderer were members which has the right to exact revenge and retribution, an idea which found expression in the foundation of the Areopagus. If the accused is acquitted, the state undertakes to appease the soul of the murdered person or its judicial representative, the Erinys.

Others attach chief importance to the slaying of Neoptolemus (Pyrrhus) by Orestes at Delphi; according to Radermacher (*Das Jenseits im Mythos der Hellenen*, 1903), Orestes is an hypostasis of Apollo, Pyrrhus the principle of evil, which is overcome by the god; on the other hand, Usener (*Archiv für Religionswesen*, vii., 1899, 334) takes Orestes for a god of winter and the underworld, a double of the Phocian Dionysus the " mountain " god (among the Ionians a summer-god, but in this case corresponding to Dionysus μελαναιγίς), who subdues Pyrrhus " the light," the double of Apollo, the whole being a form of the well-known myths of the expulsion of summer by winter, S. Reinach (reviewing P. Mazan's *L'Orestie d'Eschyle*, 1902) defends the theory of Bachofen, who finds in the legend of Orestes an indication of the decay of matriarchal ideas.

See article by Höfer in Roscher's *Lexikon der Mythologie*; A. Olivieri, " Sul mito di Oreste nella letteratura classica " (with a section on modern literature) in *Rivista di Filologia*, xxvi. (1898), and Jebb's edition of the *Electra* of Sophocles.

ORFILA, MATHIEU JOSEPH BONAVENTURE (1787–1853), French toxicologist and chemist, was by birth a Spaniard, having been born at Mahon in Minorca on the 24th of April 1787. An island merchant's son, he looked naturally first to the sea for a profession; but a voyage at the age of fifteen to Sardinia, Sicily and Egypt did not prove satisfactory. He next took to medicine, which he studied at the universities of Valencia and Barcelona with such success that the local authorities of the latter city made him a grant to enable him to follow his studies at Madrid and Paris, preparatory to appointing him professor. He had scarcely settled for that purpose in Paris when the outbreak of the Spanish war, in 1807, threatened destruction to his prospects. But he had the good fortune to find a patron in the chemist L. N. Vauquelin, who claimed him as his pupil, guaranteed his conduct, and saved him from expulsion from Paris. Four years afterwards he graduated, and immediately became a private lecturer on chemistry in the French capital. In 1819 he was appointed professor of medical jurisprudence, and four years later he succeeded Vauquelin as professor of chemistry in the faculty of medicine at Paris. In 1830 he was nominated dean of that faculty, a high medical honour in France. Under the Orleans dynasty, honours were lavishly showered upon him; he became successively member of the council of education of France, member of the general council of the department of the Seine, and commander of the Legion of Honour. But by the republic of 1848 he was held in less favour, and chagrin at the treatment he experienced at the hands of the governments which succeeded that of Louis Philippe is supposed to have shortened his life. He died, after a short illness, in Paris on the 12th of March 1853.

Orfila's chief publications are *Traité des poisons, or Toxicologie générale* (1813); *Éléments de chimie médicale* (1817); *Leçons de médécine légale* (1823); *Traité des exhumations juridiques* (1830); and *Recherches sur l'empoisonnement par l'acide arsénieux* (1841). He also wrote many valuable papers, chiefly on subjects connected with medical jurisprudence. His fame rests mainly on the first-named work, published when he was only in his twenty-seventh year. It is a vast mine of experimental observation on the symptoms of poisoning of all kinds, on the appearances which poisons leave in the dead body, on their physiological action, and on the means of detecting them. Few branches of science, so important on their bearings on every-day life and so difficult of investigation, can be said to have been created and raised at once to a state of high advancement by the labours of a single man.

ORFORD, EDWARD RUSSELL, EARL OF (1653–1727), British admiral, was born in 1653, the son of Edward Russell, a younger brother of the 1st duke of Bedford. He was one of the first gentleman officers of the navy regularly bred to the sea. In 1671 he was named lieutenant of the " Advice " at the age of eighteen, captain in the following year. He continued in active service against the Dutch in the North Sea in 1672–73, and in the Mediterranean in the operations against the Barbary Pirates

with Sir John Narborough and Arthur Herbert, afterwards earl of Torrington, from 1676 to 1682. In 1683 he ceased to be employed, and the reason must no doubt be looked for in the fact that all members of the Russell family had fallen into disfavour with the king, after the discovery of William, Lord Russell's connexion with the Rye House Plot. The family had a private revenge to take which sharpened their sense of the danger run by British liberties from the tyranny of King James II. Throughout the negotiations preceding the revolution of 1688 Edward Russell appears acting on behalf and in the name of the head of this great Whig house, which did so much to bring it about, and profited by it so enormously in purse and power. He signed the invitation which William of Orange insisted on having in writing in order to commit the chiefs of the opposition to give him open help. Edward Russell's prominence at this crisis was of itself enough to account for his importance after the Revolution. When the war began with France in 1689, he served at first under the earl of Torrington. But during 1690, when that admiral avowed his intention of retiring to the Gunfleet, and of leaving the French in command of the Channel, Russell was one of those who condemned him most fiercely. In December 1690 he succeeded Torrington, and during 1691 he cruised without meeting the French under Tourville (*q.v.*), who made no attempt to meet him. At this time Russell, like some of the other extreme Whigs, was discontented with the moderation of William of Orange and had entered into negotiations with the exiled court, partly out of spite, and partly to make themselves safe in case of a restoration. But he was always ready to fight the French, and in 1692 he defeated Tourville in the battle called La Hogue, or Barfleur. Russell had Dutch allies with him, and they were greatly superior in number, but the chief difficulty encountered was in the pursuit, which Russell conducted with great resolution. His utter inability to work with the Tories, with whom William III. would not quarrel altogether, made his retirement imperative for a short time. But in 1694 he was appointed to the command of the fleet which, taking advantage of the inability of the king of France to maintain a great fleet in the Channel from want of money, followed the French into the Mediterranean, confined them to Toulon for the rest of the war, and co-operated with the Spanish armies in Catalonia. He returned in 1695, and in 1697 was created earl of Orford. For the rest of his life he filled posts of easy dignity and emolument, and died on the 26th of November 1727. He married his cousin, Mary Russell; but his title became extinct on his death without issue.

See Charnock, *Biog. Nav.* i. 354; Campbell's *Lives of the Admirals*, ii. 317.   (D. H.)

ORFORD, ROBERT WALPOLE, 1st EARL OF (1676–1745), generally known as SIR ROBERT WALPOLE, prime minister of England from 1721 to 1742, was the third but eldest surviving son of Robert Walpole, M.P., of Houghton in Norfolk, by Mary, only daughter and heiress of Sir Jeffery Burwell, of Rougham, in Suffolk. The father, a jolly old squire of Whig politics who revelled in outdoor sport and the pleasures of the table, transmitted to his son the chief traits in his own character. The future statesman was born at Houghton on the 26th of August 1676, was an Eton colleger from 1690 to 1695 and was admitted at King's College, Cambridge, as scholar on the 22nd of April 1696. At this time he was destined, as a younger son, for the church, but his two elder brothers died young and he became the heir to an estate producing about £2000 a year, whereupon on the 25th of May 1698 he resigned his scholarship, and was soon afterwards withdrawn by his father from the university. In classical attainments he was excelled by Pulteney, Carteret, and many others of his contemporaries in politics.

On his father's death in November 1700 the electors of the family borough of Castle Rising returned him (January 1701) to the House of Commons as their representative, but after two short-lived parliaments he sought the suffrages of the more important constituency of King's Lynn (July 23, 1702), and was elected as its member at every subsequent dissolution until he left the Lower House. From the first his shrewdness in counsel and his zeal for the interests of the Whigs were generally recognised. In June 1705 he was appointed one of the council to Prince George of Denmark, the inactive husband of Queen Anne, and then lord high admiral of England. Complaints against the administration of the navy were then loud and frequent (Burton's *Queen Anne*, ii. 22-31), and the responsibilities of his new position tested his capacity for public life. His abilities justified his advancement, in succession to his lifelong rival, Henry St John, to the more important position of secretary-at-war (February 25, 1708), which brought him into immediate contact with the duke of Marlborough and the queen. With this post he held for a short time (1710) the treasurership of the navy, and by the discharge of his official duties and by his skill in debate became admitted to the inmost councils of the ministry. He could not succeed, however, in diverting Harley from the great error of that statesman's career, the impeachment of Sacheverell, and when the committee was appointed in December 1709 for elaborating the articles of impeachment Walpole was nominated one of the managers for the House of Commons. On the wreck of the Whig party which ensued, Walpole shared in the general misfortune, and in spite of the flattery, followed by the threats, of Harley he took his place with his friends in opposition. His energies now shone forth with irresistible vigour; both in debate and in the pamphlet press he vindicated Godolphin from the charge that thirty-five millions of public money were not accounted for, and in revenge for his zeal his political opponents brought against him an accusation of personal corruption. On these charges, now universally acknowledged to have proceeded from party animosity, he was in January 1712 expelled from the House and committed to the Tower. His prison cell now became the rendezvous of the Whigs among the aristocracy, while the populace heard his praises commemorated in the ballads of the streets. The ignominy which the Tories had endeavoured to inflict upon him was turned into augmented reputation. In the last parliament of Queen Anne he took the leading part in defence of Sir Richard Steele against the attacks of the Tories.

After the accession of George, the Whigs for nearly half a century retained the control of English politics. Walpole obtained the lucrative if unimportant post of paymaster-general of the forces in the administration which was formed under the nominal rule of Lord Halifax, but of which Stanhope and Townshend were the guiding spirits. A committee of secrecy was appointed to inquire into the acts of the late ministry, and especially into the Peace of Utrecht, with a view to the impeachment of Harley and St John, and to Walpole was entrusted the place of chairman. Most of his colleagues in office were members of the House of Lords, and the lead in the Commons quickly became the reward of his talents and assiduity. Halifax died on the 19th of May 1715, and after a short interval Walpole was exalted into the conspicuous position of first lord of the treasury and chancellor of the exchequer (October 11, 1715). Jealousies, however, prevailed among the Whigs, and the German favourites of the new monarch quickly showed their discontent with the heads of the ministry. Townshend was forced into resigning his secretaryship of state for the dignified exile of viceroy of Ireland, but he never crossed the sea to Dublin, and the support which Sunderland and Stanhope, the new advisers of the king, received from him and from Walpole was so grudging that Townshend was dismissed from the lord-lieutenancy (April 9, 1717), and Walpole on the next morning withdrew from the ministry. They plunged into opposition with unflagging energy, and in resisting the measure by which it was proposed to limit the royal prerogative in the creation of peerages (March-December 1718) Walpole exerted all his powers. This display of ability brought about a partial reconciliation of the two sections of the Whigs. To Townshend was given the presidency of the council, and Walpole once again assumed the paymastership of the forces (June 1720).

On the financial crash which followed the failure of the South Sea scheme, the public voice insisted that he should assume a more prominent place in public life. At this crisis in England's fortunes Stanhope and James Craggs, the two secretaries of state, were seized by death, John Aislabie, the chancellor of

the exchequer, was committed to the Tower, and Sunderland, though acquitted of corruption, was compelled to resign the lead. Walpole, at first lord of the treasury and chancellor of the exchequer (April 1721), became with Townshend responsible for the country's government (though for some years they had to contend with the influence of Carteret), the danger arising from the panic in South Sea stock was averted by its amalgamation with Bank and East India-stock, and during the rest of the reign of George I. they remained at the head of the ministry. The hopes of the Jacobites, which revived with these financial troubles, soon drooped in disappointment. Atterbury, their boldest leader, was exiled in 1723; Bolingbroke, in dismay at their feebleness, sued for pardon, and was permitted to return to his own country. The troubles which broke out in Ireland over Wood's patent for a copper coinage were allayed through the tact of Carteret, who had been banished in April 1724 as its lord-lieutenant by his triumphant rivals. The continent was still troubled with wars and rumours of wars, but a treaty between England, Prussia and France was successfully effected at Hanover in 1725.

England was kept free from warfare, and in the general prosperity which ensued Walpole basked in the royal favour. His eldest son was raised to the peerage as Baron Walpole (June 10, 1723) and he himself became a Knight of the Bath on the 27th of May 1725, and was rewarded with the Garter in May 1726. Next year the first King George died, and Walpole's enemies fondly believed that he would be driven from office, but their expectations were doomed to disappointment. The confidence which the old king had reposed in him was renewed by his successor, and in the person of Queen Caroline, the discreet ruler of her royal spouse, the second George, the Whig minister found a faithful and lifelong friend. For three years he shared power with Townshend, but the jealous Walpole brooked no rival near the throne, and his brother-in-law withdrew from official life to Norfolk in May 1730. Before and after that event the administration was based on two principles; sound finance at home and freedom from the intrigues and wars which raged abroad. On the continent congresses and treaties were matters of annual arrangement, and if the work of the plenipotentiaries soon faded it was through their labours that England enjoyed many years of peace. Walpole's influence received a serious blow in 1733. The enormous frauds on the excise duties forced themselves on his attention, and he proposed to check smuggling and avoid fraud by levying the full tax on tobacco and wine when they were removed from the warehouses for sale. His opponents fastened on these proposals with irresistible force, and so serious an agitation stirred the country that the ministerial measure was dropped amid general rejoicing. Several of his most active antagonists were dismissed from office or deprived of their regiments, but their spirits remained unquenched, as the incessant attacks in the *Craftsman* showed, and when Walpole met a new House of Commons in 1734 his supporters were far less numerous. The Gin Act of 1736, by which the tax on that drink was raised to an excessive amount, led to disorders in the suburbs of London; and the imprisonment of two notorious smugglers in the Tolbooth at Edinburgh resulted in those Porteous riots which have been rendered famous in the *Heart of Midlothian*. These events weakened his influence with large classes in England and Scotland, but his parliamentary supremacy remained unimpaired, and was illustrated in 1737 by his defeat of Sir John Barnard's plan for the reduction of the interest on the national debt, and by his passing of the Playhouse Act, under which the London theatres are still regulated. That year, however, heralded his fall from power. His constant friend Queen Caroline died on the 20th of November 1737, and the prince of Wales, long discontented with his parents and their minister, flung himself into active opposition. Many of the boroughs within the limits of the duchy of Cornwall were obedient to the prince's will, and he quickly attracted to his cause a considerable number of adherents, of whom Pitt and the Grenvilles were the most influential. The leading orators of England thundered against Walpole in the senate, and. the press resounded with the taunts of the poet and pamphleteer, illustrious and obscure, who found abundant food for their invectives in the troubles with Spain over its exclusive pretensions to the continent of America and its claim to the right of searching English vessels. The minister long resisted the pressure of the opposition for war, but at the close of 1739 he abandoned his efforts to stem the current, and with a divided cabinet was forced, as the king would not allow him to resign, into hostility with Spain. The Tory minority known as " the patriots " had seceded from parliament in March 1739, but at the commencement of the new session, in November 1739, they returned to their places with redoubled energies. The campaign was prosecuted with vigour, but the successes of the troops brought little strength to Walpole's declining popularity, and when parliament was dissolved in April 1741 his influence with his fellow-countrymen had faded away. His enemies were active in opposition, while some of his colleagues were lukewarm in support. In the new House of Commons political parties were almost evenly balanced. Their strength was tried immediately on the opening of parliament. After the ministry had sustained some defeats on election petitions, the voting on the return from Chippenham was accepted as a decisive test of parties, and, as Walpole was beaten in the divisions, he resolved on resigning his places. On the 9th of February 1742 he was created earl of Orford, and two days later he ceased to be prime minister. A committee of inquiry into the conduct of his ministry for the previous ten years was ultimately granted, but its deliberations ended in nought. Although he withdrew to Houghton for a time, his influence over public affairs was unbroken and he was still consulted by the monarch. He died at Arlington Street, London, on the 18th of March 1745 and was buried at Houghton on the 25th of March. With the permanent places, valued at £15,000 per annum, which he had secured for his family, and with his accumulations in office, he had rebuilt the mansion at great expense, and formed a gallery of pictures within its walls at a cost of £40,000, but the collection was sold by his grandson for a much larger sum in 1779 to the empress of Russia, and the estate and house of Houghton passed to Lord Cholmondeley, the third earl having married the premier's younger daughter.

Walpole was twice married—in 1700 to Catherine, eldest daughter of John Shorter and grand-daughter of Sir John Shorter, lord mayor of London, who died in 1737, having had issue three sons and two daughters, and in March 1738 to Maria, daughter of Thomas Skerret, a lady often mentioned in the letters of Lady Mary Wortley Montagu. He was succeeded in his earldom and other titles by his eldest son Robert (1701-1751), who had been created Baron Walpole of Walpole in 1723; the 3rd earl was the latter's only son George (1730-1791), " the last of the English nobility who practised the ancient sport of hawking," and the 4th earl was the famous Horace Walpole (q.v.) the youngest son of the great Sir Robert. Horace Walpole died unmarried on the 2nd of March 1797, when the earldom became extinct, but the barony of Walpole of Walpole passed to his cousin, Horatio (1723-1809), who had already succeeded his father, Horatio Walpole, 1st Baron Walpole of Wolterton in that barony. In 1806 he was created earl of Orford, and this title still remains in the possession of his descendants, Robert Horace Walpole (b. 1854) becoming the 5th earl in 1894. When Horace Walpole died his splendid residence at Houghton and the Norfolk estates did not pass with the title, but were inherited by George James Cholmondeley, 4th earl and afterwards 1st marquess of Cholmondeley.

Sir R. Walpole's life has been written by Archdeacon William Coxe (1798 and 1800, 3 vols.), A. C. Ewald (1878) and John Viscount Morley (1889). See also *Walpole, a Study in Politics*, by Edward Jenks (1894); *English Hist. Rev.* xv. 251, 479, 665, xvi. 67, 308, 439 (his foreign policy, by Basil Williams); *Bolingbroke*, by Walter Sichel (1901-1902, 2 vols.); the histories, letters and reminiscences by his son, Horace Walpole; and the other lives of the chief political personages of the period. (W. P. C.)

ORFORD, a small town, once of greater importance, in the south-eastern parliamentary division of Suffolk, England,

21 m. E. by N. of Ipswich. Pop. (1901) 987. It lies by the right bank of the river Alde, where that river flows south-west-ward on the inner side of the great beach which has blocked its direct outflow to the sea, and swells out seaward in the blunt promontory of Orford Ness. The church of St Bartholomew is of much interest. It retains a ruined Norman chancel of rich and unusual design, while the body of the church is Decorated. Of Orford castle the keep remains, standing high on a mound; it is partly of Caen stone and partly of flint work, and is of Norman date.

ORGAN, in music, the name (from Gr. ὄργανον, Lat. *organum*, instrument) given to the well-known wind-instrument. The notes of the organ are produced by *pipes*, which are blown by air under pressure, technically called *wind*.

Pipes differ from one another in two principal ways—(1) in *pitch*, (2) in *quality* of tone. (1) Consider first a series of pipes producing notes of similar quality, but differing in pitch. Such a series is called a *stop*. Each stop of the organ is in effect a musical instrument in itself. (2) The pipes of different stops differ, musically speaking, in their quality of tone, as well as sometimes in their pitch. Physically, they differ in shape and general arrangement. The sounding of the pipes is determined by the use of *keys*, some of which are played by the hands, some by the feet. A complete stop possesses a pipe for every key of some one row of manuals or pedals. If one stop alone is caused to sound, the effect is that of performance on a single instrument. There are such things as incomplete stops, which do not extend over a whole row of keys; and also there are stops which have more than one pipe to each key. Every stop is provided with mechanism by means of which the wind can be cut off from its pipes, so that they cannot sound even when the keys are pressed. This mechanism is made to terminate in a *handle*, which is commonly spoken of as the *stop*. When the handle is pushed in, the stop does not sound; when the handle is pulled out, the stop sounds if the keys are pressed. An organ may contain from one to four *manuals* or *keyboards* and one set of pedals. There are exceptional instruments having five manuals, and also some having two sets of pedals. The usual compass of the manuals approximates to five octaves, from C to c''''' inclusive. The compass of the pedal is two and a half octaves, from C to f'. This represents the pitch in which the notes of the pedal are written; but the pedal generally possesses stops sounding one octave lower than the written note, and in some cases stops sounding two octaves below the written note. Each manual or pedal has as a rule one *soundboard*, on which all its pipes are placed. Underneath the soundboard is the *windchest*, by which the wind is conveyed from the bellows, through the soundboard to the pipes. The windchest contains the mechanism of valves by which the keys control the admission of wind to the soundboard. The soundboard contains the grooves which receive the wind from the valves, and the slides by which the handles of the stops control the transmission of the wind through the soundboard to the pipes of the different stops.

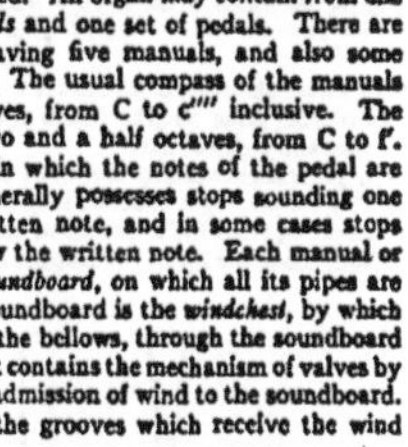

The *grooves* of the soundboard are spaces left between wooden bars glued on to the *table* of the soundboard. There is usually one groove for every key. The grooves of the bass notes, which have to supply wind for large pipes, are broader than those of the treble.

FIG. 1.—A portion of the Table with the open grooves seen from above.

The bass bars are also thicker than those of the treble, that they may the better support the great weight which rests on the bass portion of the soundboard. The table forms the top of the grooves. The grooves are generally closed below with key-valve or *pallet:*

The sliders are connected with the draw-stops or stop-handles, which are covered in with stout *upper boards,* on which the pipes

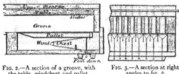

FIG. 2.—A section of a groove, with the table, windchest and pallet.

FIG. 3.—A section at right angles to fig. 2.

stand. The stop-handles are pulled out, and holes are then bored straight down through the upper boards, sliders and table to admit the wind from the grooves to the pipes. When the sliders are shifted by pushing in the handles, the holes no longer correspond, and the pipes are silenced.

Pipes are divided first into *flue-pipes* and *reed-pipes.* Flue-pipes are blown by a wind mouthpiece characteristic of the organ, while in reed-pipes the wind acts on a metal tongue vibrating on a reed, and the motion of the tongue determines the speech of the pipe.

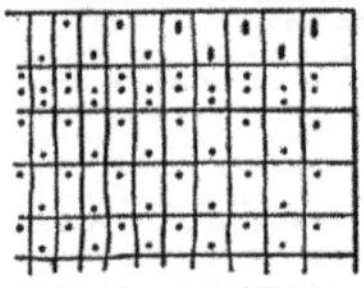

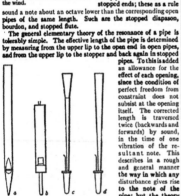

FIG. 4.—A portion of the table as it appears from above, with the places for the sliders of the stops; the small circles show the holes for the wind.

Pipes are made either of wood or of metal. Wood flue-pipes are generally of the form of a rectangular parallelepiped, metal flue-pipes of a cylindrical shape. Reed-pipes are conical or pyramidal, and widen towards the top. Some flue-pipes are made with stopped ends; these as a rule sound a note about an octave lower than the corresponding open pipes of the same length. Such are the stopped diapason, bourdon, and stopped flute.

The general elementary theory of the resonance of a pipe is tolerably simple. The effective length of the pipe is determined by measuring from the upper lip to the open end in open pipes, and from the upper lip to the stopper and back again in stopped pipes. To this is added an allowance for the effect of each opening, since the condition of perfect freedom from constraint does not subsist at the opening itself. The corrected length is traversed twice (backwards and forwards) by sound, in the time of one vibration of the resultant note. This describes in a rough and general manner the way in which any disturbance gives rise to the note of the pipe; but the theory of the mouth-pieces is a much more difficult matter, into which we cannot here enter.

FIG. 5.—*a,* An open diapason; *b,* a stopped diapason; *c,* an oboe; and *d,* a trumpet—*c* and *d* being forms of reed-pipes.

In reed-pipes which are simply conical the resonance of the body is nearly the same as that of an open pipe of the same length. Where the form is irregular no simple rule can be given.

But the resonance of the body of the pipe is generally the same as the note produced. The tongue of a reed-pipe alternately opens and closes the aperture of the reed. In this way it admits pulses of wind to the body of the pipe; these, if they recur at the proper intervals, maintain its vibration, which takes place when the note produced corresponds to the resonance of the pipe. The reed itself has its vibrating length determined by a wire which presses against it. The free end of this wire is touched with the tuning tool until a satisfactory note is produced.

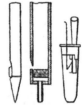

FIG. 6.—Mouthpieces in somewhat greater detail.

The pitch of the different stops is commonly denoted by the conventional approximate length of the pipe sounded by C, the lowest key of the manual. Even in incomplete stops which have no bass, the length of the pipe which C would have if the stop were extended down serves to indicate the pitch.

The conventional length of the C-pipe for stops having the normal pitch of the keys is 8 ft.; a pipe having twice this length sounds the octave below, a pipe having half that length the octave above, and so on. Thus stops which sound the octave below the normal pitch of the keys are spoken of as 16-foot stops. Even where the pipes are stopped so that the actual length is only 8 ft., they are spoken of as having "16-ft. tone." Similarly 32-ft. stops sound two octaves below the normal pitch of the keys. But if these notes are produced by stopped pipes, whose actual length is only 16 ft., they are spoken of as having "32-ft. tone." Sixteen-foot and 32-ft. stops are specially characteristic of the pedal, where the names also signify the length of the open pipe which would sound the note actually produced by the lowest C. Of stops higher than the normal pitch of the keys, the octave is denoted by 4 ft. if made with open pipes, 4-ft. tone if stopped; the twelfth is commonly spoken of as 2⅔, the fifteenth or double octave as 2 ft. Higher-sounding stops are occasionally used, but these generally form part of "mixtures," and the foot-lengths of the separate ranks are not usually given.

The true or accurate lengths of the pipes vary within considerable limits. The base of the scales (dimensions) varies according to the standard of pitch, and the voicing and the complicated natural laws of pipes produce other deviations from simple relations, so that the conventional dimensions can only be regarded as a simple means of classifying the stops according to their pitch-relations. For this purpose they are essential; they are continually appealed to in discussion and description; and they are almost invariably marked on the stop-handles in all countries, so that a moderate knowledge of foreign nomenclatures, combined with the habit of seizing the meaning of the figures such as 16, 8, 4, on the stop-handles, will frequently suffice as a key to the complexities of a foreign organ.

Each of the manuals, or rows of keys, of an organ constitutes a separate organ, which is more or less complete in itself. The names of the different manuals or organs are *great organ, swell organ, choir organ* and *solo organ.* The fifth manual, where it occurs, is the *echo organ.* The above is the usual order in point of development and frequency of occurrence, although the solo is sometimes preferred to the choir organ. The great organ is in a certain sense the principal department of the organ. It may be regarded as formed by a completely developed series of those fundamental stops which constitute the solid basis of the tone of the instrument. If an instrument be constructed with only a single manual this necessarily assumes, in general, the characteristics of a great organ. The great organ is called "grande orgue" in French, and first manual or "haupt-werk" in German.

It is proposed to describe the principal organ-stops under the heads of the manuals to which they belong. The enumeration will not be exhaustive, but will include all the usual types.

The great organ begins generally with stops of 16 ft. in large instruments. In some cases a 32-foot sounding stop is introduced, but this cannot be said to be a proper characteristic of the great organ. The foundation tone is of 8 ft.; the stops of higher pitch serve to add brilliancy; those of 16 ft., which sound the octave below the normal pitch, serve to add gravity and weight to the tone. Sixteen-foot stops are commonly spoken of as "doubles," their conventional length being twice that of stops of normal pitch.

The 16-ft. stops are the 16 double open diapason, and the 16 bourdon or double stopped diapason, to which, in very large instruments, there may be added a 16 double trumpet. The double open diapason on the great organ consists usually of metal pipes, having moderate "scale," or transverse dimensions. These are of the same general character as the pipes of the ordinary open diapason, though they are made somewhat less powerful. In the better instruments of the second class as to size this stop alone would probably be regarded as representing suitably and sufficiently the class of doubles on the great organ. It gives great body to the general tone, and appears decidedly preferable to the bourdon, which frequently takes its place.

The 16 bourdon, when used on the great organ, is made of rather small scale and light tone. It gives great body to a large great organ and affords interesting combinations with other stops, such as the 4-ft. flute. It is used either alone in smaller organs of the second class, or in addition to a double open in larger instruments.

The 16 double trumpet is a trumpet (large reed stop) sounding the octave below the normal pitch. It is used generally in instruments of the largest size, but is somewhat more common in Germany. It is useful in giving a massive character to the tone of the full great organ, which is apt to become disagreeable on account of the great development of stops of a piercing character. If, however, the double trumpet is rough in tone, it is apt to communicate to the whole a corresponding impression.

We now proceed to the 8-ft. stops (the reeds come at the end according to ordinary usage). An ordinary great organ may contain 8 stopped diapason, 8 open diapason (one or more), 8 gamba and 8 hohlflöte. The 8 stopped diapason on the great organ is usually of moderate scale, and some considerable fulness of tone. Few stops admit of more variety and individuality in their quality of tone than the stopped diapason; but too frequently the great organ stopped diapason fails to attract attention on its merits, being regarded simply as an inconsiderable portion of the foundation tone.

If there is any one stop which in itself represents the organ as a whole it is the open diapason. The pipes of this stop are the typical metal pipes which have always been characteristic of the appearance of the organ. A single open diapason stop is capable of being used as an organ of sufficient power for many purposes, though of course without variety. The pipes of this stop are called "principal" in German, this appellation apparently corresponding to the fact that "diapason" has been taken to mean that these are the normal pipes which run through the whole compass. This, however, does not appear to be the actual derivation of the term; originally it is technically applied to the organ-builder's rule, which gives the dimensions of pipes; and it appears that the application to the stop followed on this meaning.

The scales, character and voicing of the open diapason vary with fashion, and are different in different countries. We may distinguish three principal types. The old English diapasons of the days before the introduction of pedal organs into England were characterised by a rich sweet tone, and were not very powerful. They were generally voiced on a light wind, having a pressure equivalent to that of a column of water of from 2 to 2½ in. The scale was in some cases very large, as in Green's two open diapasons in the old organ at St George's, Windsor; in these the wind was light, and the tone very soft. In other cases the scale was smaller and the voicing bolder, as in Father Smith's original diapasons in St Paul's Cathedral. But on the whole the old English diapasons presented a lovely quality of tone. English travellers of those days, accustomed to these diapasons, usually found foreign organs harsh, noisy and uninteresting. And there are many still in England who, while recognizing the necessity of a firmer diapason tone in view of the introduction of the heavy pedal bass, and the corresponding strengthening of the upper departments of the organ tone, lament the disappearance of the old diapason tone. However, it is possible with care to obtain diapasons presenting the sweet characteristics of the old English tone, combined with sufficient fulness and power to form a sound general foundation. And there can be no doubt that this should be one of the chief points to be kept in view in organ design.

The German diapason was of an entirely different character from the English. The heavy bass of the pedals has been an essential characteristic of the German organ for at least two or three centuries, or, as it is said, for four. The development of the piercing stops of high pitch was equally general. Thus foundation work of comparatively great power was required to maintain the balance of tone; the ordinary German diapason was very loud, and we may

almost say coarse, in its tone when compared with the old English diapason. The German stop was voiced as a rule on from 3½ to 4 in. of wind, not quite twice the pressure used in England.

The French diapason is a modern variety. It may be described as presenting rather the characteristics of a loud gamba than of a diapason. In other words the tone tends towards a certain quality which may be described as "nasal" or metallic, or as approaching to that of a string instrument of rather coarse character. Some modern English builders appear to aim at the same model, and not without success.

The tone of a diapason must be strong enough to assert itself. It is the foundation of the whole organ tone. It is the voicer's business to satisfy this condition in conjunction with the requirement that the tone shall be full and of agreeable quality.

The spitzflöte may be regarded as a variety of open diapason. The pipes taper slightly towards the top, and the quality is slightly stringy. This stop was much used at one time in place of a second open diapason. But it appears better that, where two open diapasons are desirable, they should both be of full diapason quality, though possibly of different strengths and dimensions. The admixture of stringy qualities of tone with the diapasons is always to be deprecated.

The 8 gamba was originally an imitation of the viola da gamba, a sort of violoncello. When made of a light quality of tone it is a pleasing stop; but its use in the great organ instead of a second open diapason is greatly to be deprecated for the reasons just stated.

The 8 hohlflöte is an open flute, usually of wood, and of small scale. If made to a moderate scale and fully voiced it possesses a full pleasant tone, which is a useful support to the foundation tone of the great organ. The 8 clarabella differs from the hohlflöte in being usually of rather large scale, and having the open pipes only in the treble. In old organs. a separate bass was generally provided; now it is more usual to supply the stop with a stopped bass.

The 4-ft. stops of the great organ comprise the 4 principal and the 4 flute. The 4 principal is the octave of the open diapason, generally of somewhat reduced scale and light but bright quality of tone. The use of the word "principal" in connexion with this stop is purely English, and is said to be connected with the use made of it as the standard of tuning for the whole organ. The Germans and French both designate this stop as "octave."

Of the 4 flute there are several varieties—open, stopped, wood, metal and harmonic. The harmonic flute has open metal pipes of double the conventional length, which speak their octave. This is determined partly by the voicing, partly by making a small hole about the middle of the length, which determines the motion as that of the two separate lengths between which the hole lies. Harmonic flutes have a sweet but full and powerful tone. Other flutes are generally rather light, except the waldflöte, which is a powerful stop of a somewhat hooting quality.

The great organ flute is frequently used to give brilliancy to light combinations. Thus it may be used with the stopped diapason alone, or with the 16 bourdon alone, or with any of these and either or both of the open diapasons.

The ordinary use of the 4-ft. stops is to add a degree of loudness to the diapasons. This is accompanied with a certain measure of keenness, which may become disagreeable if the 4-ft. tone is disproportionately strong. The ordinary practice is to use the 4-ft. tone very freely.

The 2⅔ twelfth stop sounds fiddle g on the C key. It is composed of diapason pipes, rather small and gently voiced. Its use is said to be to thicken the tone, which it certainly does. But how far the particular effect produced is desirable is another question. It is generally necessary that this stop should be accompanied by the fifteenth or other octave sounding stop of higher pitch.

The 2 fifteenth, or superoctave, of the great organ consists of diapason pipes sounding notes two octaves above the normal pitch of the keys. The 2 piccolo is a fluty stop of less power, having the same pitch. The 2-ft. tone is commonly used as giving a degree of loudness to the great organ beyond that obtainable with the 4-ft. tone.

The modern great organ fifteenth is generally a very powerful stop, and requires great caution in its use in organs of moderate size, or in limited spaces. The old English high pitched stops had little power, and their brilliancy was capable of pleasing without offence. The modern great organ up to fifteenth can only be heard with comfort in very large spaces. Under such suitable circumstances the fifteenth is capable of giving to the whole tone a ringing or silvery character, which lends itself specially to contrast with the tone of reeds. This peculiar keen tone requires for its full development the mixtures.

Mixture, sesquialtera, furniture, cymbal, scharf, cornet, are various names applied to a description of stop which possesses several ranks or several pipes to each note. The pipes of each note sound a chord which is generally composed of concordant notes of the harmonic series whose fundamental is the proper note of the key. Modern mixtures generally consist of fifths and octaves. Their composition is not the same throughout the whole range of the keyboard. A three-rank mixture may consist of the following (the numbers signify intervals, reckoned along the scale)—

C—c̄ (tenor) 15—19—22
c♯ to top   8—12—15

For a somewhat larger full mixture this may be modified as follows—

C—c̄ (middle)   15—19—22
c♯ to top   1—8—12—15.

A sharp mixture suitable for a large instrument may be as follows—

Five Ranks.

C—f̄   15—19—22—26—29
c♯—f♯   8—12—15—19—22
f♯—c̄²   1—8—12—15—19
c̄² to top   1—5—8—12—15.

The last two compositions are given by Hopkins in his great treatise on the organ.

The early mixtures generally included the tierce (17th, or two octaves and a third). The German practice was to unite this with a twelfth, carrying the combination 12-17 throughout the keyboard under the name of sesquialtera. The combination is not now usually provided. The old English sesquialtera was ordinarily simply a form of mixture, as was the furniture. The mounted cornet consisted usually of five ranks—

1—8—12—15—17.

It extended from middle c upwards. The pipes were raised on a small soundboard of their own. The stop was used for giving out a melody. It is now obsolete.

The question of the employment and composition of mixtures is of the greatest importance with respect to the good effect of the full organ proper, i.e. without reeds. With reference to the whole question of keen-toned stops it may be laid down that their free employment in the great organ does not produce a good effect unless the organ is situated in a very large space. If this is the case, properly proportioned mixtures are capable of giving to the tone of the full diapason work a character which is brilliant without being overpowering. The contrast between this class of tone and that afforded by the reeds is one of the most charming and legitimate effects within the range of the instrument.

We now pass to the reeds. The 16-ft. trumpet has been already alluded to, and there remain 8 trumpet and 4 clarion or octave
Great organ reeds. trumpet. These are both stops of great power. The best trumpets possess also richness and smoothness of tone. Stops of this class can be used with the diapasons only, producing what may be described as a rich-toned blare of moderate strength. The more usual employment of the reeds is in connexion with the entire great organ, the whole forming the ordinary fortissimo of the instrument.

The second department of the English organ is the swell organ. The whole of the swell pipes are enclosed in a box, faced on one or
Swell organ. more sides with a set of balanced shutters. When these are closed the tone is almost completely muffled. When the shutters are opened, by means of a pedal usually, the sound bursts out. In order that the use of the swell may be effective, it is necessary that the shutters should close tightly, and that there should be a sufficient volume of tone to produce an effect when they are opened. The swell is of entirely English origin; it has been introduced in Germany to a very small extent, but more widely in France. It is usually called " recitatif " on the Continent. The chief characteristic of the swell is the rich and powerful volume of reed-tone of a peculiar character which it contains. But other stops are also of importance. We consider them in order. The 16 bourdon, small scale, is very commonly used in swells. It assists in giving body to the tone. It occupies, however, a large space within the swell box; and where the choice between it and a 16-ft. reed has to be made there can be no doubt that the reed should be preferred, as it contributes so much more to the development of the characteristic swell tone. The 16 contra fagotto is the usual name of this stop. It imparts great richness to the tone of the other swell reeds.

The 8-ft. diapason work is principally valuable for the soft effects obtained from it. The diapasons are voiced less loudly than for the great organ; and with the shutters closed they sound very soft. The dulciana is the softest stop generally available; and either this or some similar stop is introduced into the swell for the purpose of obtaining effects of the most extreme softness. Space within the swell box has generally to be economised. The complete bass of the open diapason or dulciana requires an 8-ft. swell box, whereas even a 16-ft. reed can be bent round so as to go within a smaller box if necessary. The open diapason and the dulciana are therefore often cut short at tenor c, and completed, if desired, with stopped pipes. The 4 principal and the 4 flute stops are similar to the corresponding stops in the great organ, but are somewhat lighter in tone.

The 2 fifteenth and mixtures are much more pleasing in the swell than in the great organ. The shutters tone them down, so that they cannot easily become offensive. Added to the reeds, they give a peculiar brilliancy to the full swell. But perhaps their most pleasing use is when all the diapason work of the swell is used alone, and as a contrast to the reeds.

The usual reeds are as follows, besides the doubles already mentioned: 8 oboe, 8 cornopean, 8 trumpet and 4 clarion (octave trumpet). The oboe (hautboy) is a conventional imitation of the orchestral instrument. It is a stop of delicate tone, and perhaps is at its best in solo passages, softly accompanied on another manual. The cornopean has a powerful horn-like tone. It is the stop which, more than any other, gives to the English swell its peculiar character. The trumpet is used in addition to the cornopean in large instruments. The clarion serves to add brightness and point to the whole. The vox humana is also frequently placed on the swell.

The third department is the choir organ. The 8-ft.
Choir organ. work may contain 8 stopped diapason, 8 open diapason, 8 gamba, 8 keraulophon and 8 hohlflöte.

As a rule no open diapason is provided for choir organs, unless they are larger than usual; but a small open is most useful as a means of obtaining a better balance than usual against the other manuals. The stopped diapason is generally made to contrast in some way with that on the great organ. The hohlflöte, or its representative, is generally a lighter stop than what would be put on the great organ. The gamba is better placed in the choir organ than in the great or the swell. Such stops as the gamba and the keraulophon are frequently placed in the swell with the idea of adding to the reediness of the tone. But this is fallacious. Their tone is not strong enough to assert itself through the shutters, and their peculiar character is therefore lost. On the choir organ, on the other hand, the sort of strength required is just about what they possess, and they show to advantage. The keraulophon is a stop invented by Gray and Davison, and has been widely adopted for many years. It has a hole made in each pipe near the top, and gives a peculiar tone very well described by its name (horn-flute). Though not very like the gamba, its tone is so far of the same type of quality that the two stops would hardly be used together. It is generally the case that similar stops of exceptional characters do not combine well, whereas stops of opposed qualities do combine well. Thus a gamba and a keraulophon would not combine well, whereas either of them forms an excellent combination with a stopped diapason or a hohlflöte.

The 4 principal is sometimes very useful. A light combination on the choir, with excess of 4-ft. tone, may often be advantageously contrasted with the more full and solid tone of the great diapasons, or with other attainable effects. The 2 flute is constantly used. The 2 piccolo is frequently found on the choir organ, but is not particularly useful.

In organs which have no solo manual there is usually a clarionet (cremona, cromorne or krumhorn, in old organs sometimes corno di bassetto) on the choir, and often an orchestral oboe (real imitation of the instrument). These are reed-stops. The dulciana and another soft stop, the salicional, salicet or salicet (of similar strength, but slightly more pungent quality), are often placed on the choir. They are, however, hardly strong enough to be of much use there, and in the swell they are useful for effects of extreme softness. In very large instruments a fifteenth and a mixture are sometimes placed on the choir, which in this case has a complete series of diapason work. If the fifteenth and the mixtures are light enough the result is a sort of imitation of the tone of the old English organ. It also forms a useful echo to the great organ, i.e. a passage played on the great may be repeated on the similar but fainter tone of the choir with the effect of an echo. In instruments of the largest size the choir is sometimes provided with a very small bourdon of 16-ft. tone, which helps to give to the tone the character of that of a small full organ without reeds.

The solo organ is comparatively modern, at all events in its present usual form. A fourth manual was not unknown in old German organs; but the contents of all four resembled
Solo organ. each other in a general sort of way, and there was nothing like the English swell or the modern solo. The solo appears to have arisen with Cavaillé-Coll in France, and Hill in England, as a vehicle for the powerful reed-stops on heavy wind introduced by these builders. Thus the French term for the solo is " clavier des bombardes "; and in the earlier English solos the " tuba mirabilis " was usually prominent. A solo organ may suitably contain any of the following stops: 8 tromba (a powerful reed on heavy wind), 8 harmonic flute (powerful tone and heavy wind), 8 clarionet and 8 orchestral oboe (real imitations of the instruments) and 8 vox humana (conventional imitation of the human voice). The last three stops are reeds. They may be with advantage enclosed in a swell box, having a separate pedal. In very large instruments a complete series of both diapason and reed stops is occasionally placed on the solo. But there does not seem to be much advantage in this arrangement.

We now come to the pedal. This forms the general bass to the whole organ. Thirty-two foot stops only occur in the largest
Pedal organ. instruments; they are as follows: 32 open diapason (wood or metal), 32-ft. tone bourdon and 32 contra trombone, posaune, bombardo, sackbut (reed). The 32-ft. open diapason, whether wood or metal, is usually made of large scale, and produces true musical notes throughout. Its musical effect in the lower part of its range is, however, questionable, so far as this depends on the possibility of recognizing the pitch of the notes. It adds great richness to the general effect, particularly in large spaces. The 32-ft. tone bourdon is not usually a successful stop.

It rarely produces its true note in the lower part of its range. The 32-ft. reed on the pedal has long been a characteristic of the largest instruments. With the old type of reed it was rarely pleasant to hear. The manufacture has been greatly improved, and these large reeds are now made to produce a fairly smooth effect. Deep reed notes, when rich and good, undoubtedly form one of the principal elements in giving the impression of power produced by large organs. From this point of view they are of great importance. Nevertheless the effect of large pedal reeds is generally more satisfactory to the performer than to the listener.

The 16-ft. pitch may be regarded as the normal pitch of the pedal; the principal stops are as follows: 16 open diapason (wood or metal), 16-ft. tone bourdon, 16 violone (imitation of double bass) and 16 trombone or posaune (reed). The 16-ft. open diapason on the pedal assumes different forms according to circumstances. As a rule the character is sufficiently indicated by the stop being of wood or metal. The wooden open is generally of very large scale, and produces a ponderous tone of great power and fulness, which is only suitable for the accompaniment of the full organ, or of very powerful manual combinations. Such a stop is, as a rule, unsuitable in organs of moderate size, unless supplemented by lighter 16s for ordinary purposes. The metal open is of considerably smaller scale (in fact all metal pipes are effectively of much smaller scale than wooden pipes of similar diameter). The metal gives a clear tone, lighter than that of large wooden pipes, and pleasanter for ordinary purposes. The metal open combines advantageously with a bourdon. In the largest organs both wood and metal open 16s may be suitably provided. Where metal pipes are made a feature in the organ-case, both the double open diapason in the great organ and the metal 16 of the pedal may be properly made of good metal (polished tin or spotted metal), and worked in to the design of the organ-case.¹ The same applies to the 32-ft. metal opens of the largest instruments. This saves space in the interior, and gives the large pipes room to speak, which is apt to be wanting when they are placed inside. The 16-ft. tone bourdon on the pedal may be made of any scale according to circumstances. If it is the chief bass of the organ it is made very large and with great volume of tone. Such stops are unsuitable for soft purposes, and a soft 16, usually a violone, is required in addition. If the loud department of the 16 tone is otherwise provided for the bourdon may be made of moderate strength. It may also be made very soft, like a manual bourdon. These three different strengths ought always to be provided for in an instrument of a complete character. The violone is also made of all three strengths. In a few cases it furnishes the moderate element; and it is often applied to obtain a very soft 16-ft. tone. The 16-ft. reed is very common. The observations made as to the effect of 32-ft. reeds are applicable also in this case.

The 8-ft. department of the pedal is only less important than the 16, because it is possible to replace it to a certain extent by coupling or attaching the manuals to the pedals. The usual 8-ft. pedal-stops are as follows: 8 principal bass (metal or wood), 8 bass flute (stopped), 8 violoncello (imitation of the instrument) and 8 trumpet. The remarks made above as to the scale of open 16s apply with little change to the pedal principal. Only, since the manuals are generally coupled, it is perhaps best to provide the large scale wood-stop, which presents the powerful class of tone in which the manual diapasons are deficient. The bass flute is almost a necessity in combination with the light 16-ft. tone. A composition ought to be provided by which the pedal can be reduced to these two elements by a single movement. The violoncello is sometimes used instead of the bass flute for the last-named purpose, for which, however, it is not so suitable. It is a favourite stop for some solo purposes, but is not of much general utility. The 8-ft. trumpet serves to give clearness and point to the tone of the 16-ft. reed.

In the short preface to Mendelssohn's *Organ Sonatas* it is stated that everywhere, even in pianissimo, it is intended that the 16-ft. tone of the pedal should be accompanied by 8-ft. tone. For the purpose of realizing this as a general direction the soft 16-ft. and 8-ft. stops are required; large instruments are, however, occasionally found which possess nothing of the kind.

The following stops of higher pitch are occasionally found on the pedal: 5⅓ twelfth bass, 4 fifteenth bass, mixture and 4 clarion. These serve to make the pedal tone practically independent of coupling to the manual, which is a matter of great importance, especially in the performance of certain compositions of Bach and other writers, who appear to have been independent of couplers.

In some instruments two sets of pedals are provided, which may **Second** be described as great and choir pedals. The great pedal is in the **pedal.** usual position; the choir pedal is in front of the other, and sloping. It is so placed that the feet rest on it naturally when stretched out in front of the performer. There is a choir pedal of this kind in the organ in the minster at Ulm, built by Walcker of Ludwigsburg. It is a very large instrument, having 100

¹ Anything down to one-third tin and two-thirds lead is called tin. But "pure tin" should have over 90% of tin. Absolutely pure tin could not be worked. Spotted metal is said to have from one-third to two-thirds tin. Under one-third tin no spots are said to rise, and the mixture has the general characters of lead.

sounding stops. It has no compositions, which indeed are but little known in Germany; and without some arrangement such as this a soft pedal would hardly be obtainable. There are a few other instruments which have choir pedals, but they have not been introduced into England.

In organs which have a single manual the characteristics of the great and choir organs are usually united. In organs which have two manuals the lower usually represents the united great and choir, the upper is the swell. In organs which have **Arrange-** three manuals the lower is usually the choir, but some- **ment of** times combines choir and solo, the middle is the great, **manuals.** and the top is the swell. In organs which have four manuals the order is solo, swell, great, choir, the solo being at the top and the choir at the bottom.

Compositions are mechanical contrivances for moving the stop-handles in groups at a time. The ordinary form consists of pedals, which project from the front just above the pedal keys. The arrangements are various. We may refer to the **Composi-** arrangement in the organ at Windsor, given later on. **tions.** A species of composition was introduced by Willis some years ago, and has been adopted in many large English instruments, which acts by means of a series of brass disks placed just under the front of the keys of each manual, within reach of the thumb. These act by means of pneumatic levers. A slight pressure on one of the disks sets the machine attached to it in action, and the required change in the stops is made without any exertion on the part of the performer.

The connexion between the keys and their pallets is made by various mechanisms, some of which are very ancient. In *square and trackerwork* (fig. 7) the old squares were **General** made of wood. They **mechan-** resemble in function the **ism.** squares used for taking bell-wires round a corner. The trackers are slight strips of wood, having screwed wires whipped on to their ends, which hold by leather buttons. The trackers play the part of the bell-wires. Where pressure has to be transmitted instead of a pull, thin but broad slips of wood are used, having pins stuck into their ends to keep them in their places: These are *stickers* (fig. 8). *Backfalls* (fig. 9) are narrow wooden levers turning on pins which pass through their centres.

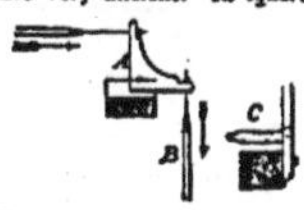

FIG. 7.—A, square, B, tracker; C, metal square.

The *fan frame* (fig. 10) is a set of backfalls having one set of ends close together, usually corresponding to the keys; the other ends are spread widely apart. The *roller board* (fig. 11) is a more general mode of shifting the movements sideways. The roller is a slip of wood, or a bit of metal tube, which turns on two pins inserted into its ends. It has two arms projecting at right angles to its length. One of these receives the pull at one point, the other gives it off at another. In case a pull has to be transmitted to more than one quarter, a roller will sometimes have more than two arms. The name of *couplers* (fig. 12) is given to the mechanical stop by which the keys of one manual are made to take down those of another, or those of the pedal to take down those of the manuals. Some old forms of the mechanism could not be put on while any of the keys were depressed; others had a tendency to throw the fingers off the keys. These forms have been entirely superseded. That now used consists of a series of backfalls centred on a movable support. The one set of ends is connected with the moving keys; the other set of ends is pierced by the wires of the trackers or stickers from the keys to be moved. In the one position of the support these ends play freely over the wires; in the other they are brought up against the buttons of the trackers or against the stickers to be moved. The usual couplers are —each of the manuals to the pedal, swell to great, swell to great sub-octave, swell to great, choir, choir to great sub-octave, and solo to great. The swell octave and sub-octave couplers are sometimes placed on the swell itself. The objection to this is, that if they are used when the swell is coupled to

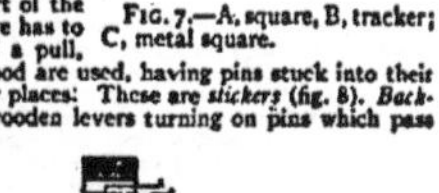

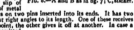

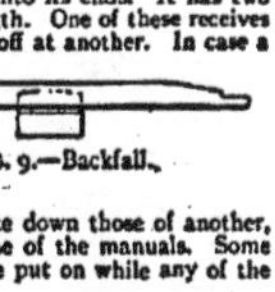

FIG. 8.—A and B as in fig. 7; C, sticker.

FIG. 9.—Backfall.

FIG. 10.—Fan Frame.

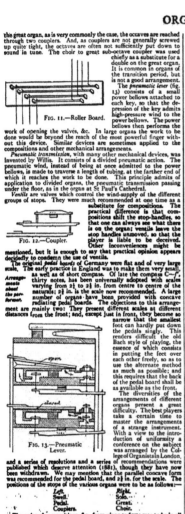

the great organ, as is very commonly the case, the octaves are reached through two couplers. And, as couplers are not generally screwed up quite tight, the octaves are often not sufficiently put down to sound in tune. The choir to great sub-octave coupler was used chiefly as a substitute for a double on the great organ. It is common in organs of the transition period, but is not a good arrangement.

The *pneumatic lever* (fig. 13) consists of a small power bellows attached to each key, so that the depression of the key admits high-pressure wind to the power bellows. The power bellows then performs the work of opening the valves, &c. In large organs the work to be done would be beyond the reach of the most powerful finger without this device. Similar devices are sometimes applied to the compositions and other mechanical arrangements.

FIG. 11.—Roller Board.

Pneumatic transmission, with many other mechanical devices, was invented by Willis. It consists of a divided pneumatic action. The pneumatic wind, instead of being at once admitted to the power bellows, is made to traverse a length of tubing, at the farther end of which it reaches the work to be done. This principle admits of application to divided organs, the pneumatic transmission passing under the floor, as in the organ at St Paul's Cathedral.

Ventils are valves which control the wind-supply of the different groups of stops. They were much recommended at one time as a substitute for compositions. The practical difference is that compositions shift the stop-handles, so that one can always see what there is on the organ; ventils leave the stop handles unmoved, so that the player is liable to be deceived. Other inconveniences might be mentioned, but it is enough to say that practical opinion appears decidedly to condemn the use of ventils.

FIG. 12.—Coupler.

The original *pedal boards* of Germany were flat and of very large scale. The early practice in England was to make them very small, as well as of short compass. Of late the compass C—f¹, thirty notes, has been universally adopted with scales varying from 2½ to 2½ in. from centre to centre of the naturals; 2½ in. is the scale now recommended. A large number of organs have been provided with concave radiating pedal boards. The objections to this arrangement are mainly two: They present different scales at different distances from the front; and, except just in front, they become so narrow that the smallest foot can hardly put down the pedals singly. This renders difficult the old Bach style of playing, the essence of which consists in putting the feet over each other freely, so as to use the alternate method as much as possible; and this requires that the back of the pedal board shall be as available as the front.

The diversities of the arrangements of different organs present a great difficulty. The best players take a certain time to master the arrangements of a strange instrument. With a view to the introduction of uniformity a conference on the subject was arranged by the College of Organists in London,

FIG. 13.—Pneumatic Lever.

and a series of resolutions and a series of recommendations were published which deserve attention (1881), though they have now been withdrawn. We may mention that the parallel concave form was recommended for the pedal board, and 2½ in. for the scale. The positions of the stops of the various organs were to be as follows:—

Left.	Right.
Swell.	Solo.
Pedal.	Great.
Couplers.	Choir.

The order of compositions, &c., from piano to forte was to be in all cases from left to right. The groups of compositions were to be in the order from left to right—pedal, swell, couplers, great.

Two other points of detail may be alluded to. One is the position of the pedal board with reference to the keys. The height from the

middle of the pedals to the great organ keys, it is agreed, should be 32 in. But as to the forward position there is a difference. The resolutions said that " a plumb-line dropped from the front of the great organ sharp keys falls 2 in. nearer the player than the front of the centre short key of the pedal board." The old arrangement gave usually 1½ in. for this distance. But it is thought that the change has not gone far enough, and 4 in. has been found preferable. There is scarcely any single arrangement which is so important for the comfort of the player as having sufficient space in this direction (fig. 14). The second matter is the provision of some other means of acting on the swell than by the swell pedal. The use of the swell pedal is inconsistent with the proper use of both feet on the pedal keys; and there is no doubt that incorrect habits in this respect are commonly the result of the English use of the swell pedal. In fact, players sometimes keep one foot on the swell pedal all the time, so that proper pedal playing is impossible. Arrangements have been devised by means of which a movable back to the seat can be made the means of acting on the swell. The first " recommendation " of the College of Organists illustrated the requirement; it was, that " the consideration of organ-builders be directed to the widely-expressed desire for some means of operating on the swell in addition to the ordinary swell pedal." G. Cooper had a movable back to the seat of the organ at St Sepulchre's, London. The swell was opened by leaning back, so that it could only be used when the swell was coupled to the great. The writer has had an organ for more than twenty years in which the movable back is provided with a strap passing over one shoulder and buckling in front. It opens the swell when the player leans forward. It is most valuable, particularly in such things as accompanying the service. The emphasis required is obtained when wanted without taking the feet from their other duties. Young people pick it up easily; older people have difficulty.

As an example of an organ of a complete but not enormously large character, we give the details of the organ at St George's Chapel, Windsor, which was rebuilt by Messrs Gray and Davidson, according to Sir Walter Parratt's designs, in the year 1883.

FIG. 14.—Relative Position of Manual and Pedal.

Great Organ

Old arrangement

1 Old arrangement

2 College of Organists

Magdalen College & S¹ Georges Windsor

Four manuals, C to a‴, 58 notes. Pedal, C to f¹, 30 notes.

Great Organ (3½-in. wind).	
Double open diapason	16
Large open diapason	8
Open diapason	8
Stopped diapason	8
Clarabella	8
Principal	4
Harmonic flute	4
Twelfth	2⅔
Fifteenth	2
Sesquialtera[1]	III ranks
Harmonic piccolo	2
Posaune	8
Clarion	4

Swell Organ (3-in. wind).	
Lieblich bourdon	16
Open diapason	8
Stopped diapason	8
Dulciana	8
Vox coelestis[1]	8
Principal	4
Octave dulciana	4
Fifteenth	2
Mixture[1]	III ranks
Contra fagotto	16
Oboe	8
Vox humana	8
Clarion	4

Choir Organ (2½-in. wind).	
Dulciana	8
Keraulophon	8
Stopped diapason	8
Viol d'orchestre	8
Flute	4
Piccolo	2
Corno di bassetto (reed)	8

Solo Organ (6-in. wind).	
Harmonic flute	8
Orchestral oboe	8
Tromba	8

Pedal Organ (4-in. wind).	
Open diapason (wood)	16
Violone (metal)	16
Bourdon (wood)	16
Wood flute	8
Trombone (wood tubes)	16

Couplers.

Solo to great.	Swell to pedal.
Swell to great.	Great to pedal.
Solo to pedal.	Choir to pedal.

Pneumatic action to great organ and its couplers. The arrangement of the stops and compositions is as follows:—

Left.	Over the keys.	Right.
Solo.	Couplers.	Swell.
Choir.	Tremulant.	Great.
Pedal.	(Knob below swell keys.)	

[1] These are the old mixtures.

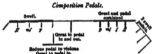

Composition Pedals.

One swell pedal controls two sides of the swell box. The other controls the box in which the orchestral oboe is placed. The vox humana is in a box which is always shut, inside the swell box.

History of the Modern Organ.

The history of the ancient organ is dealt with in a separate section below. The first keyboard is said to have been introduced into the organ in the cathedral at Magdeburg about the close of the 11th century. There were sixteen keys; and a drawing exists in a work of the 17th century[1] which purports to represent them. They are said to have been an ell long and 3 in. broad. The drawing represents a complete octave with naturals and short keys (semitones), arranged in the same relative positions as in the modern keyboard. In early organs with keyboards the keys are said to have required blows of the fist to put them down. In these cases probably sounding the notes of the plain song was all that could be accomplished.

As to the precise time and conditions under which the keyboard assumed its present form we know nothing. It is commonly said that the change to narrow keys took place in the course of the 14th century, and the semitones were introduced about the same time.

Many examples of organ keyboards still exist, both in England and on the Continent, which have black naturals and white short keys (semitones). The organ in the church at Heiligenblut in Tirol had in 1870 two manuals, one having black naturals and white semitones, the other white naturals and black semitones. In this organ the stops were acted on by iron levers which moved right and left. It had a beautiful tone; it possessed a reservoir bellows of great capacity, and was altogether a remarkable instrument. Harpsichords with black keyboards also exist.

The mode of blowing practised about the time of the introduction of the first keyboard appears to have been that which ultimately developed into the method still generally **Bellows.** used in Germany. There were a great many separate bellows, each like a magnified kitchen-bellows, but provided with a valve, so that the wind could not return into the bellows. One man had charge of two of these. Each foot was attached to one bellows, and the blower held on by a bar above. It was possible, by raising each of the two bellows in turn and then resting his weight upon it, to produce a constant supply of wind with the pressure due to his weight. A great many such bellows were provided, and it seems that each pair required one man; so that great numbers of blowers were employed. A slight modification is enough to change this method into the German one. Instead of fastening the feet to the bellows and pulling them up, the blower treads on a lever which raises the bellows. The bellows being loaded then supplies the wind of itself. The bellows thus used have diagonal hinges, and various expedients are employed to make them furnish steady wind. But the English system of horizontal reservoirs and feeders appears far superior.

The invention of the pedal may be set down to the 15th century. About that time the organ assumed on the Continent of Europe **Pedal.** the general form which it has retained till lately, more especially in Germany. This may be described generally as having a compass of about four octaves in the manuals and of two octaves in the pedal, with occasionally extra notes at the top in both, and frequently "short octaves" at the bottom. German short octaves are as follows. The manual and pedal appear to terminate on E instead of C. Then the E key sounds C, F = F, F♯ = D, G = G, G♯ = E, and the rest as usual. There were often three, sometimes four, manuals in large organs.

[1] Praetorius, *Theatrum Instrumentorum.*

The character of all these was in general much the same, but they were more softly voiced in succession, the softest manual being sometimes spoken of as an echo organ. There are one or two examples of the echo as a fourth or fifth manual in England at the present time, in organs which have been designed more or less under German inspiration. The old echo was long ago superseded by the swell in England.

A few ancient cases survive in a more or less altered condition. Of these the following are worthy of mention, as **Cases.** bearing on the question of date.

Sion (Switzerland). Gothic. A small instrument . .	1390
Amiens. Originally Gothic. Large, with 16-ft. pipes . .	1429
Perpignan. Gothic. Large, with 32-ft. pipes	1490
Lübeck. One of the finest Gothic organs in Europe. 32a.	1504
(or, according to Hopkins, 1518).	

In all these the cases are sufficiently preserved to make it almost certain that pipes of the same lengths were originally employed. The actual pipes are generally modern. Shortly after this date we find Renaissance cases. At La Ferté Bernard (dep. Sarthe) part of the substructure is Gothic, and is known to be of date 1501; the organ above is Renaissance, and is known to be of date 1536. At St Maurice, Angers, an organ was built in 1511, with Renaissance case, two towers of 32-ft. pipes, 48 stops and a separate pedal. An account of the instrument in a procès verbal of 1533 furnishes good evidence. In the 16th century, therefore, the organ had attained great completeness, and the independent pedal was general on the Continent.

We cannot follow the history of German organs through the intervening centuries; but we propose to give the items of one of the principal organs of the Silbermanns, the great **German** builders of the 18th century—namely, that standing **organ.** in the Royal Catholic Church, Dresden. Without being an enormously large instrument it is complete in its way, and gives a very good idea of the German organ. The account is taken from Hopkins. The date is 1754.[2]

Great.

Principal	.	.	16	Octave	.	.	.	2
Bourdon	.	.	16 tone	Tertia	.	.	.	1⅗
Principal	.	.	8	Mixtur	.	.	.	IV ranks
Viola da Gamba	.	8	Cymbel	.	.	.	III
Rohrflöte	.	.	8 tone	Cornet	.	.	.	V
Octave	.	.	4	Fagott	.	.	.	16
Spitzflöte	.	.	4	Trumpet	.	.	.	8
Quinta	.	.	2⅔	Clarin	.	.	.	4

Echo.

Quintaton	.	.	16 tone	Octave	.	.	.	2
Principal	.	.	8	Tertia	.	.	.	1⅗
Gedackt	.	.	8 tone	Flageolet	.	.	1
Unda Maris	.	8 tone	Mixtur	.	.	.	IV ranks
Octave	.	.	4	Echo	.	.	.	V
Rohrflöte	.	.	4 tone	Vox humana	.	8 tone
Nassat	.	.	2⅔					

Choir.

Gedackt	.	.	8 tone	Quinta	.	.	.	1⅓
Principal	.	.	4	Siffflöte	.	.	.	1
Rohrflöte	.	.	4 tone	Mixtur	.	.	.	III ranks
Nassat	.	.	2⅔	Sesquialtera	.	II
Octave	.	.	2	Chalumeaux	.	8 tone

Pedal.

Untersatz	.	.	32 tone	Mixtur	.	.	IV ranks
Principal	.	.	16	Pausan (trombune)	16
Octave-bass	.	8	Trompette	.	.	8
Octave	.	.	4	Clarin	.	.	4

Accessories.

Echo to great.	Tremulant echo.
Great to pedal.	Tremulant great.

Compass.

Manuals—C to d''' in alt.   Pedal—C₁ to tenor c.

The chief difference between English organs and those of the Continent was that until the 19th century the pedal was absolutely unknown in England. The heavy bass given by the **English** pedal being absent, a lighter style of voicing was **organs.** adopted, and the manuals were usually continued down below the 8-ft. C so as to obtain additional bass by

[2] The writer heard this instrument as a boy, and has a very pleasant recollection of the general effect.

playing octaves with the hands. Thus the old organ (date 1697) of Father Smith in St Paul's Cathedral had manuals descending to the 16-ft. C (C₁), with two open diapasons throughout. Green's old organ at St George's, Windsor, had manuals descending to the 12-ft. F, also two open diapasons throughout, no F♯. But the more usual practice was to make the manual descend to the 10⅔ G, leaving out the G♯. At the Revolution most of the organs in England had been destroyed. Shortly afterwards Bernard Smith, a German, commonly called Father Smith, and Thomas and René Harris, Frenchmen, were largely employed in building organs, which were wanted everywhere. Father Smith perhaps had the greatest reputation of any builder of the old time, and his work has lasted wonderfully. There is a list in Rimbault of forty-five organs built for churches by him. The list of René Harris is scarcely less extensive.

The most important step in the development of the old English organ was the invention of the swell. This was first introduced into an organ built by two Jordans, father and son, for St Magnus's church near London Bridge, in 1712.

Burney writes (1771):—

" It is very extraordinary that the swell, which has been introduced into the English organ more than fifty years, and which is so capable of expression and of pleasing effects that it may be well said to be the greatest and most important improvement that was ever made in any keyed instrument, should be utterly unknown in Italy; and, now I am on this subject, I must observe that most of the organs I have met with on the Continent seem to be inferior to ours by Father Smith, Byfield or Snetzler, in everything but size! As the churches there are very often immense, so are the organs; the tone is indeed somewhat softened and refined by space and distance; but, when heard near, it is intolerably coarse and noisy; and, though the number of stops in these large instruments is very great, they afford but little variety, being for the most part duplicates in unisons and octaves to each other, such as the great and small 12ths, flutes and 15ths; hence in our organs, not only the touch and tone, but the imitative stops, are greatly superior to those of any other organs I have met with."

(As to these opinions, compare what is said on great organ open diapasons above.)

In the course of the 18th century most of the old echoes were altered into swells, and the swell came into almost universal use in England. The development of the swell is inseparably associated with the peculiar quality of English swell reeds. These must have originated during the development of the swell. We hear of a " good reed voicer " named Hancock, who worked with Crang, changing echoes into swells. However it originated, the English reed is beautiful when properly made. The original swells were usually short in compass downwards, frequently extending only to fiddle g. It is only lately that the value of the bass of the swell has been properly appreciated. Short-compass swells may be said to have now disappeared.

Avery's old English organ. The organ in St Stephen's, Coleman Street, was probably nearly in its original condition at the date when it was described by Hopkins. It was built by Avery in 1775. At all events the following arrangements might very well have been the original ones. The pedal clavier without pipes is no doubt a subsequent addition, and is omitted.

Great.	
Open diapason.	Sesquialtera—III ranks.
Stopped diapason.	Mixture—II ranks.
Principal.	Trumpet.
Twelfth.	Clarion.
Fifteenth.	Cornet to middle c—V ranks.

Choir.	
Stopped diapason.	Fifteenth.
Principal.	Cremona to tenor c.
Flute.	

Swell.	
Open diapason.	Cornet—III ranks.
Stopped diapason.	Trumpet.
Principal.	Hautboy.

Compass.	
Great and choir—G₁ to e''' no G₁♯.	Swell—fiddle g to e'''.

This gives an excellent idea of the old English organ. There are several different accounts of the introduction of pedals into England. It took place certainly before the end of the 18th century, but only in a few instances; and for long after the usual arrangement was simply to provide a pedal clavier, usually from F₁ or G₁ to tenor c or d, which took down the notes of the great organ. Unison diapason pipes (12-ft.) were occasionally used. In one or two cases, as in the transition states of the old organ at St George's, Windsor, a 24-ft. open diapason was employed as well as the unison stop. But a more usual arrangement, of a most objectionable character, was to combine the G₁—c pedal-board with a single octave of so-called pedal-pipes, extending from the 16-ft. to the 8-ft. C; so that, instead of a uniform progression in ascending the scale, there was always a break or repetition in passing C.

Pedals in England.

About the middle of the 19th century it began to be generally admitted that the German arrangement of the pedal was the better, and the practice gradually became general of providing a complete pedal-board of 2½ octaves (C—f'), with at least one stop of 16-ft. tone throughout, even on the smallest organs that pretended to be of any real use. The study of the classical works of Bach and Mendelssohn went hand in hand with this change; for that study was impossible without the change, and yet the desire for the study was one of the principal motives for it. In the meantime Bishop, an English builder, had invented composition pedals, which so greatly facilitate dealing with groups of stops. About the same time (1850) the mechanics of the organ were advanced by the general introduction of the pneumatic lever into large instruments; the whole mechanism of the organ was revolutionized by Willis's improvements; and the organ-builders of England, having obtained from the Continent the fundamental ideas necessary for completeness, advanced to a point at which they appear to have been decidedly ahead.

In the early part of the last quarter of the 19th century, the future of the English organ appeared to be one of great promise. Much confidence was felt in the brilliant combinations of Willis's mechanism. The employment of electricity had reached a certain stage, and the necessary fundamental mechanism, under the name of the electro-pneumatic lever, was to be obtained in a practical form. Several new devices were in the air, by means of which the control of the various valves was accomplished by the action of wind, traversing channels, with complete abolition of trackers, and even of stop slides; and Willis's classical mechanisms, including those for acting on stop slides pneumatically without direct mechanical connexion between slide and handle, were almost universally adopted in large organs. The delicate device of pneumatic lever on pneumatic lever, by which alone the small electromagnetic impulses available could be made to do heavy work, had obtained recognition. If there was an occasional failure, it was thought to be no more than might be expected with work of a novel and delicate character. And it was confidently expected that these devices would, in time, with the improvements associated with practical use, come to be reliable. This expectation has not been realized. The objections to the modern pneumatic, and still more to the electropneumatic machinery, are of two kinds—noise and inefficiency.

Present day organs.

Noise in the Key Action.—We take as the standard of comparison the old tracker organ, without pneumatics. There was always a certain amount of noise. Now, even in the best instruments of Willis himself during his lifetime, and still more in the best instruments of the present day, the noise of the key action is judged to be as bad as in the old tracker organ. The pneumatics have to be driven by a powerful wind; the consequence is they get home with a knock.

Noise in the Stop Action.—If in a large instrument with pneumatic drawstop action one of the compositions which affects several stops is put in action, the movement of the stops is followed by a blow like a hammer, which is caused by the pneumatics getting home under the powerful force employed. This is much worse than anything there was in the old organ.

Inefficiency in the Key Action; Delay and Cyphering.—This chiefly shows itself in delay, both at the depressing and at the recovery of the key. Some of the causes are the size of the pneumatic bellows, which takes time to fill and time to empty; and, very often, defective regulation of the valves. The regulation of the valves is an art in itself, and it is often the case that the performance in this respect can be greatly improved by going over the regulation. The test is the possibility of executing shakes and repetitions. It is quite common to find mechanism by the first organ-builders of the day on which shakes or repetitions cannot be executed.

Pneumatic transmission is also specially liable to cause delay. In divided organs the swell is usually on the far side from the keys, and the pneumatic transmission tubes pass it under the floor. The swell touch is then considerably worse than the great. In all cases there must be some delay on account of the time the pulse takes to traverse the transmission tube with the velocity of sound. And if a pneumatic bellows has to be filled at the far end the delay will be more. Some of the delay experienced in large buildings may be due to the time taken in supplying the energy necessary for setting up and maintaining the vibrations of the air in the building. This should, however, have been the same with the old tracker action; and the opinion of old players is unanimous that they never experienced anything of the kind. The shake and repetition are the only real tests so far as the action is concerned.

Inefficiency in the key action also takes the form of "cyphering," i.e. a note sticks down. With the old tracker organ this could generally be cured without much difficulty by working on the action, and with the separate pneumatic lever something could be done. But the modern types of elaborated action are entirely enclosed in wind-chest and sound-board. It was always foreseen that these types would be dangerous, unless they could be made quite perfect, and they have not been made perfect. When a note sticks, there is no way of curing it except to get at the inside of the wind-chest, or to remove all the pipes belonging to the note. A case happened recently where, during a performance on an organ by a first-rate modern builder, two cypherings took place. To cure the first all the pipes belonging to a Bach fugue were played with a note cyphering all the time; and such cases are of frequent occurrence.

Inefficiency in the Stop Action.—In this case the power provided is insufficient to move the stop slide. As there is no direct connexion between slide and handle, nothing can be done but to get inside the organ and move the slide by hand. A case has recently occurred where an organ by a first-rate builder, in constant use, and perfectly cared for, got one of the slides stuck while in use. The organ was locked, so nothing could be done. The same happened to another slide a couple of days later. It is also an everyday experience that the pneumatic compositions are insufficient to move the stops; sometimes they move the stops about halfway, when a sort of wail is heard.

One practical result is—where an organ is not too large to be dealt with by the old mechanical methods, there is much to be said for adhering to them.

It seems worth while to mention two suggestions by which these imperfections in large organs might be reduced to a minimum.

For blowing, motors for stop action, &c., the writer would suggest the employment of the *Armstrong hydraulic accumulator system*, at a pressure of say 600 ℔ on the square inch. The pumping of the system would be done by external power (electricity, gas, oil or steam), quite away from the building containing the organ. The blowing would be done by the hydraulic system at a point near the organ. The small hydraulic motors attached to the stop slides, swell, &c., might have almost infinite power and be perfectly noiseless. The key-work should be pneumatic and should use *Willis's floating lever*. The swell pedal should be hydraulic, with the floating lever, as also the action of the back of the seat if employed for opening the swell. The effect of the floating lever is that the movement of the work corresponds exactly with the movement of the part connected with key or pedal. The connexion with the key would have a regulation so that the lever would begin to move a little later than the key, the regulation being adjusted by trial so as to give shakes and repetitions.

The principle of the floating lever is the same as that of the steam steering gear in ships. The control of the power is attached to the floating centre. It is always such that the movement of the work brings back the floating centre into its standard position, and it acts like a fixed centre with added power.

As to the general arrangement of the instrument, it is desired to make two protests. Firstly, the organ chamber is a monstrosity. Shutting up the organ in a confined space is simply throwing money away. An organ of a quarter the size would do the work better if not shut up in an organ chamber. Secondly, it has become customary to separate the different parts of an organ, putting the pipes of the pedal, great and swell perhaps in different places at a distance from one another, and the soft choir organ, which should be close to the singers, perhaps, as in one actual case, in a remote position where it cannot be heard at all and is useless for accompaniment. The parts of an organ so dispersed will not give a tone which blends into a whole. The practice is undesirable. The divided organ with pneumatic or electric transmission is to be avoided for all reasons.

GENERAL REMARKS ON ORGAN TREATMENT

The organ probably presents more difficulties than any other instrument in the way of a sound elementary mastery. A

person of ordinary capacity may work at it for years before being able to play passages of moderate difficulty with confidence and correctness. The special difficulty appears to be chiefly mental, and arises from the number of things that have to be thought of simultaneously. It does not lie in the execution least not chiefly; for to play a hymn-tune correctly, the $\frac{-\text{at}}{}$ being taken with the pedals, the tenor with the left hand, bass the two upper parts with the right, is a matter in which there is no execution required; but it is of great difficulty to an inexperienced player. Other distributions of parts—such as bass with pedals, treble with right hand on a solo stop (e.g. clarinet), two inner parts with a soft open diapason, or something of the kind—are of much greater difficulty in the first instance. Another distribution is bass with pedals, melody with reed or solo combination in the tenor with left hand (an octave below its true pitch), inner parts with right hand on a soft open diapason, or something that balances. This is of far greater difficulty, as it requires rearrangement of parts to avoid those faults of inversion the avoidance of which is known as double counterpoint. All this can be practised with common hymn-tunes; but the performer who can do these things with ease is in some respects an advanced player.

There is a natural gift, which may be called the polyphonic ear-brain. It is possessed by (roughly) about one in fifty of musical students, by students of the organ in much the largest proportion, and probably by a much smaller proportion of the unsifted population. For the polyphonic ear-brain these difficulties have no existence, or take little trouble to surmount. It consists of the power of hearing the notes of a combination simultaneously, each being heard as an ordinary person hears a single note. When a composition is played or sung in parts, each part is heard as a separate tune; and the effect is realized in a manner quite different from the single melody with accompaniment, which is all that an ordinary person usually hears. This is in many but not all cases associated with the rare power of remembering permanently the actual pitch of notes heard.

The observations made in the 9th edition of this *Encyclopædia* on "Balance of tone" do not now call for the stress there laid on them, as there is an improvement in this respect. But it is still desirable to insist on the importance of balance in the performance of organ trios such as the organ-sonatas of Bach. In these compositions there are generally three notes sounding, which may be regarded as belonging to three different voices, of nearly equal strength but different mean pitch, and, if possible, different quality; of these one is appropriated by each hand and one by the pedal. They are written in three lines, and are intended to be played on two manuals and the pedal.

The fugues of Bach are the classical organ music *par excellence*. As to those nothing has come down to us as to the composer's intentions, except that he generally played the fugues on the full organ with doubles. It does not seem clear that this was the case with the preludes; and, any way, the modern organ, with its facilities for managing the stops, appears to countenance a different treatment. The effect of doubles when a subject or tune is given out in solo on a manual is very bad. The doubles may be drawn with advantage when the parts are moving in massive chords. The usual practice is perhaps to employ various manual effects of a light character until the pedal enters, and then to produce full organ in its various modifications, but always to aim at variety of tone. If a prelude begins with heavy chords and pedal, then produce full organ at once. If it then passes to lighter matter, reduce to some extent. Some begin a fugue on the stopped diapason of the great organ, add more as the parts enter, and continue working up throughout. But perhaps it is the better practice to throw in loud organ during the pedal parts, and soften between times.

One of the greatest requisites in organ-playing is dignity of treatment. This is continually competing with clearness. The chief mode of keeping the different parts distinct, where that is necessary, is by using reeds of a pronounced character. These reeds sometimes verge on the comic, and anything more than the most sparing and careful employment of them is undesirable.[1] Expression is not possible unless the stops are enclosed in a swell box—a most desirable arrangement. In all cases hurry is to be avoided. A calm steadiness, a minute finish of all the phrasing, forms most of the difference between first- and second-rate players.

With reference to the general treatment of modern music we quote the preface to Mendelssohn's *Organ Sonatas*: " In these sonatas very much depends on the correct choice of the stops; but, since every organ with which I am acquainted requires in this respect special treatment, the stops of given names not producing the same effect in different instruments, I have only indicated certain limits, without specifying the names of the stops. By *fortissimo* I mean the full organ; by *pianissimo* usually one soft 8-foot stop alone; by *forte*, full organ without some of the most powerful stops; by *piano*, several soft 8-foot stops together; and so on. In the pedal I wish everywhere, even in pianissimo, 8-foot and 16-foot (tone) together, except where the contrary is expressly indicated, as in the sixth sonata [this refers to a passage where an 8-foot pedal is used without 16]. It is therefore left to the player to combine the stops suitably for the different pieces, but particularly to see that, in the simultaneous use of two manuals, the one keyboard is distinguished from the other by its quality, without forming a glaring contrast."

Importance is attached to the above directions as to single stops. The habit of mixing up two or more stops unnecessarily results in the loss of the characteristic qualities of tone which reach their highest value in single stops.

A habit is prevalent of using couplers in excess. One hears the swell coupled to the great during an entire service. The characteristics of the two manuals, which, separated, lend themselves to such charming contrasts, are lost in the mixture, just as the characteristics of single stops are lost when employed in groups. It is common to see an English organist keep the right foot on the swell pedal and hop about with the left on the pedals. This cannot be called pedal-playing. Both feet should be used, except where the swell pedal is actually required. It is a common habit to hold a note down when it should be repeated. It should be struck again when indicated. The repetition is a relief to the ear.

The older organists commonly filled up their chords, striking pretty nearly every concordant note within reach. The effect of this was in many cases to destroy effects of parts, or effects of restraint leading to contrasts intended by the composer. There is a well-known case of a climax about a line before the end of Bach's " Passacaglia." Here there is a pause on a chord of four notes; one low in the bass (podal); two forming a major third in the middle; and one high in the treble. Some players fill in every concordant note within the reach of both hands. Others consider the effect of Bach's four notes superior. The writer thinks that the average listener prefers the full chord, and the polyphonic hearer the thin arrangement of parts. Of course the parts are lost if thick chords are used. Restraint in the use of the pedal is also sometimes intended to lead up to a contrast which is lost if the pedal is introduced too soon.

Contrast and variety are essential elements in organ effects. A suitable phrase repeated on solo stops of different characters; a see-saw in a series of rhythmical chords between two manuals of different characters—contrasts generally—are charming when suitably employed. Phrasing we cannot describe here. It is just as important in the organ as in any solo instrument, or in song.

There has been a tendency to attempt too much in the imitation of orchestral instruments. While such stops as good flutes and good imitations of wind instruments have their value, the imitation of stringed instruments and of the orchestra in general

[1] As some difficulty has been felt as to what is here meant, an instance is given. The writer has heard a first-rate player emphasise the entrance of a chorale in the pedal (Mendelssohn's 3rd sonata in A) by coupling the choir clarinet to the pedal. The effect was coarse and disagreeable, and would have been ridiculous if it had not been so ugly. It was clear, but not dignified.

is undesirable. The organ's own proper tones are unequalled, and it is a pity to make it a mere caricature of the orchestra.

The writer has had the opportunity of inspecting two of the installations known by the name of R. Hope-Jones; both under the care of an able enthusiast in the matter, Mr Collinson, of Edinburgh. The Hope-Jones system consists of two parts: a mechanism, and a system of pipe-work. These must be considered separately. The mechanism is entirely electric. One example consisted of an application of this mechanism to a fine organ by Willis. The conditions were as favourable as possible, with temperature regulation and constant use. Yet even in this case the contacts failed occasionally. The difficulty about repetition appeared to have been entirely got over, the performance being satisfactory when the contact was in good order. These contacts appear to be the weak part of the system. All the mechanism, couplers and all, is worked by means of these contacts. With the care which is taken no difficulty is found in getting the arrangement to work in the case of the Willis instrument. The system is very complicated, with double touch couplers throughout, by means of which a solo can be effected on one manual by varying the pressure. The study of the double touch appears very difficult. Stop handles are done away with. They are replaced by rockers, the faces of which are about the size of small railway tickets. The appearance is as if the surface where the stop handles would be was plastered over with these rockers. They turn on a horizontal axis through the middle, and a touch of the finger at top or bottom opens or closes the stop. The other instrument was Hope-Jones thoughout, pipes and mechanism. The curator was the same as in the case of the Willis instrument. But, the hall being little used, there was no temperature regulation, and very little use. The state of the mechanism was inferior, the contacts failing freely. It could not be regarded as an admissible mechanism from the writer's point of view. As to the pipe-work, the effect was remarkable; but it could not be regarded as genuine organ work, as the player admitted. Our requirement in the matter of action is a perfectly unfailing connexion between key and pipe. And in this respect we adhere to a preference for the old tracker action, where possible. Anything that leaves a possibility of failure in the connexion we regard as inadmissible.

The writer desires to acknowledge his obligations to Sir Walter Parratt for much assistance in the preparation of this article.

(R. H. M. B.)

History of the Ancient Organ.

The earliest authentic records of the organ itself do not extend beyond the second century B.C., but the evolution of the instrument from the *Syrinx* or Pan-pipe goes back to a remote period. The hydraulic and pneumatic organs of the ancients were practically the same instrument, differing only in the method adopted for the compression of the wind supply; in the former this was effected by the weight of water, and in the latter by the more primitive expedient of working the bellows by hand or foot. What is known, therefore, of the evolution of the organ before hydraulic power was applied to it is common to both hydraulic and pneumatic organs. The organ of the ancients was a simple contrivance, consisting, in order of evolution, of three essential parts: (1) a sequence of pipes graduated in length and made of reed, wood or bronze; (2) a contrivance for compressing the wind and for supplying it to the pipes in order to make them speak, the ends of such pipes as were required to be silent being at first stopped by the fingers; and (3) a system for enabling the performer to store the wind and to control the distribution of the supply separately to the several pipes at will. The pipes of the syrinx were the prototypes of No. 1; the bellows and the bag-pipe—which was but the application of the former to the reed—foreshadowed No. 2. The third part of the organ was composed of contrivances and common objects used by carpenters, such as boxes having sliding lids running in grooves, levers, &c.

It seems probable that the syrinx was recognized by the ancients as the basis of the organ. Hero of Alexandria, in his description of the hydraulic organ, calls it a syrinx. Philo of Alexandria (c. 200 B.C.), mentioning the invention of the hydraulis(us) by Ctesibius, says, "the kind of syrinx played by hand which we call hydraulis." The fact that the syrinx was an assemblage of independent stopped pipes, which in their original condition could not be mechanically blown, since the movable lip of the player used to direct the air stream against the sharp edge of the open end of the pipe was a necessity, is no bar to the suggested derivation. Wind projected into a pipe can produce no musical sound unless the wind be first compressed and the even flow of the stream be interrupted and converted into a series of pulses. In order to produce these pulses in an organ-pipe, it is necessary to make use of some such contrivance as a reed, flute or whistle mouthpiece (q.v.).

In the earliest organs there is no doubt that the pipes consisted of lengths of the large reed known as *καλαμος* used for the syrinx, but converted into open flue-pipes. Instead of cutting off the reed immediately under the knot, as for syrinx pipes, a little extra length was left and shaped to a point to form a foot or mouthpiece, which was placed over the aperture in the wind-chest, so that it caused the stream of air to split in two as it was driven through the hole into the pipe by the action of the bellows. A narrow fissure was made through the knot near the bottom of the pipe, and above it a horizontal slit was cut in the reed, the two edges being bevelled inwards. When the wind was pumped into the chest it found an outlet through one of the holes in the lid, and the current, being divided by the foot of the pipe, became compressed and was forced through the fissure in the knot. It then ascended the pipe in an even stream, as yet silent, until thrown into commotion by another obstacle, the upper sharp edge or lip of the notch, which produced the regular flutterings or pulses requisite for the emission of a note. The very simplicity of this process disposes of any difficulty in accepting the syrinx as an important factor in the evolution of the organ. The conversion of a syrinx pipe is, in fact, a simpler and more natural expedient than the more elaborate construction of a wooden flue-pipe.

In order to convert the syrinx into a mechanically played instrument, the addition of the actuating principle of the bag-pipe was necessary. It is probable that in the earliest attempts the leather bag was actually retained and that the supply of wind was still furnished by the mouth through an insufflation pipe. Such an instrument is described and illustrated by Father Athanasius Kircher,[1] but his drawing should be accepted with reserve, as it was probably only an effort of the imagination to illustrate the text. In the instrument, which he calls the *Magrekelha* or *Mashrokitha* of the Chaldees, the bag is described as being inside the wind-chest, the insufflation pipe being carried through a hole in the side of the box. Little wooden sliders manipulated by the fingers formed a primitive means of controlling the escape of the wind through any given pipe.

We have two pottery figures of musicians playing on primitive organs in the next stage of development, namely with bellows, and a description in the Talmud. The quotation as given by Blasius Ugolinus states that the instrument known as the *Magrepha* d'Aruchis[2] consisted, as the Schlite Haggiborim teaches, of several rows of pipes and was blown by bellows. It had, besides, holes and small sliders answering to each pipe, which were set in motion by the pressure of the organist; the vent-holes being open, a wonderful variety of sounds were produced." The spurious letter of St Jerome to Dardanus might also be consulted in this connexion. At Tarsus in Asia Minor pottery and coins dating from c. 200 B.C. were excavated by W. Burckhardt Barker,[3] and amongst them is the fragment of a figure of a musician playing upon an instrument fastened to his breast, and having seven pipes set in a rectangular wind-chest, in the centre of which appear to be two bellows of unequal sizes. Unfortunately both drawing and description are somewhat vague; nevertheless, there is no room for doubt that this was an organ, perhaps without sliders or keys, the pipes being stopped at the open end, nearest the player's mouth, by the fingers, supposing that there was only one bellows. Another piece of pottery from Tarsus, discovered in 1852, during excavations carried out at Kusick-Kolah by M. M. Marvillier and V. Langlois,[4] and preserved in the Louvre, shows the back of an organ having fifteen pipes. Two models of organs of more recent date recall the instrument of that found by Mr Barker. One found in Chinese Turkestan on the site of ancient Khotan[5] (fig. 1) represents a musician holding the instrument to his breast; both hands seem to be pressing what might be bellows; and there are seven pipes below the bellows. The other instrument (fig. 2) is of Roman origin, and forms part of the decoration on a medallion on a yellow pottery vase, which was excavated at Orange (Dauphiné, France), and is now preserved in the collection of M. Emilien Dumas de Sommières. The subject represented in the

medallion is an amphitheatre, and in the centre a pneumatic organ with bellows is plainly visible (fig 2).

This brings us to a point in the history of the organ when the existence of the hydraulic organ can no longer be ignored. Some writers consider that the invention of the hydraulis in the 2nd century B.C. by Ctesibius[6] of Alexandria constitutes the invention of the organ, and that the pneumatic organ followed as an improvement or variety. Such an assertion would seem to be untenable in the face of what has been said above. It is most improbable that a man busy with the theory and practice of hydraulics would invent a highly complex musical instrument in which essential parts lying outside his realm, such as the flue-pipes, the balanced keyboard, the wind-chest for the distribution of the wind, are all in a highly developed state; it would be a case for which no parallel exists in the history of musical instruments, all of which have evolved slowly and surely through the ages. On the other hand, given a pneumatic organ in which the primitive unweighted bellows worked unsatisfactorily, an engineer would be prompt to see an opportunity for the advantageous application of his art.

From Marc Aurel Stein, *Ancient Khotan*, by permission of the Clarendon Press.

FIG. 1.

From Orange.

FIG. 2.—Roman Pneumatic Organ.

There are two detailed and duly accredited descriptions of the hydraulis extant, both of which presuppose the existence of a pneumatic organ. One is in Greek by Hero of Alexandria,[7] said to be a pupil of Ctesibius,[8] and the other in Latin by Vitruvius (*De Arch.* lib. x. cap. ii.). In both accounts reference is made to drawings now lost. Mr Woodcroft states that in each MS. the diagrams are said to have been copied faithfully, and that on consulting four MSS. and three early printed editions[9] he found that the mechanical parts in all agree essentially, and that it is only the case of the organ and the arrangement of the pipes which vary according to the fancy of the artist.

The principle of the hydraulis, which remained a complete mystery until recently, is now well understood. Representations of Roman hydraulic organs abound, but they were not always identified as such.[10] As the front of the organ (the performer sat or stood at the back) was invariably represented, there had been no indication of the manner in which the pipes were made to sound. A clue was furnished by a little baked clay model of an hydraulus, and parts of the performer, excavated in 1885 on the ruins of Carthage and now preserved in the Musée Lavigerie, attached to the cathedral of S. Louis of Carthage. This little clay model, measuring 7¼ in. by 2½ in. (figs. 3 and 4), modelled by Possessoria, a potter working at the beginning of the 2nd century A.D., whose name appears on the front, below the ends of the sliders, is so accurately designed that it tallies in every point with the description of the instrument by Hero and Vitruvius. The number and relative sizes of the three

---

[1] See *Musurgia*, bk. ii. ch. iv. § 3, p. 3.

[2] or Eruchin. Treatise XXXIII. of Babyl. Talmud. See *Thesaurus Antiquitatum Sacrarum* (Venice, 1744–1769), xxxiii. 11 and 21.

[3] See *Lares and Penates* (London, 1853), p. 260, fig. 60.

[4] See W. Froehner, *Monuments antiques du musée de France* (Paris, 1873), pl. 32; also *Archives des missions scientifiques*, iv. 64-67.

[5] See *Ancient Khotan, detailed report of archaeological explorations in Chinese Turkestan, carried out by H.M. Indian Government*, by Marc. Aurel Stein (Oxford, 1907), plate xliii.

[6] Tertullian (*De anima*, 14) names Archimedes, which is probably an error. See in this connexion Hermann Degering, who devotes considerable space to the question, *Die Orgel, ihre Erfindung und ihre Geschichte* (Muenster, 1905).

[7] See *The Pneumatics of Hero of Alexandria*, translated from the original Greek by Bennett Woodcroft (London, 1851), with diagrams.

[8] Edward Buhle in *Die musikalischen Instrumente in den Miniaturen des frühen Mittelalters*, pt. i. (Leipzig, 1903), p. 55. Note 1 corrects this as an error, assigning Hero's activity to the beginning of our era, in which case the description by Vitruvius would be the earlier in spite of the fact that the hydraulus, as he describes it, contains an improvement on that of Hero, i.e. registers, and two pumps instead of one, and that he omits to explain the purpose for which water is used. Buhle gives as his authority Diels, "Das phys. System des Strabon," p. 291, in *Berliner Monatsberichte* (Feb. 1893).

[9] For an exhaustive and careful compilation of these editions, and of the literature of the hydraulus generally, see Dr Charles Maclean's article, "The Principle of the Hydraulic Organ," *Intern. Mus. Ges.* Sbd. vi. 2, pp. 183–237; also John W. Warman, *Bibliography of the Organ*, who, however, takes the erroneous view that the medieval editions of Vitruvius and Hero may be taken as evidence that the instrument itself was in use until about the middle or end of the 17th century. See *Proc. Mus. Assoc.* (1903–1904), p. 40.

[10] The present writer was apparently the first in England to draw attention to this identity by introducing the drawing from the Utrecht Psalter and the model of the Carthage Organ, &c. See *Music* (London, Sept. 1898), p. 438.

rows of pipes, gauged by the remains of the organist, give the requisite compass for the production of the six Greek scales in use at that date.[1] A working reproduction based on the proportions of the remains of the organist, but at half scale for the sake of portability (the real organ must have measured 10 ft. in height by 4½ ft. in width), was successfully carried out by the Rev. F. W. Galpin in 1900–1901 by the help of photographs and of the text of Vitruvius.

The principle of the hydraulus is simple. An inverted funnel, or bell of metal, standing on short feet and immersed in water within the altar-like receptacle forming the base or pedestal, communicates by means of a pipe, with the wind-chest, placed above it. When the air is pumped into the funnel by

FIG. 3.—Pottery Model of the Hydraulus—Carthage. c. A.D. 150.

FIG. 4. Carthage. c. A.D. 150.

the alternate action of two pumps, one on each side of the organ, constructed bucket within bucket and fitted with valves, the water retreating before the compressed air, rises in the receptacle and by its weight holds the air in a state of compression in the funnel, whence it travels through the pipe into the wind-chest. The rest of the process is common also to the pneumatic organ. As there are two pumps worked alternately, these conditions remain unchanged, until by pressure on a key working a slider under the apertures leading to the pipes, the compressed air is afforded an exit through the latter, thus producing the desired note. It will be seen, therefore, that water acts on the air as a compressor exactly in the same manner as lead weights are used on the wind reservoir of modern pneumatic organs. The discovery of the Carthage model was of the greatest importance to the history of the keyboard (q.v.), for it proved beyond a doubt the use at the beginning of our era of balanced keys (seen in front of the organist) on the principle described by Vitruvius. What appears to be a second keyboard with smaller keys on the side of the hydraulus labelled Possessoris (fig. 4) is simply the ends of the sliders, which are pushed out or drawn in by the action of the keys.

The principle of the hydraulus made it possible to construct large organs of powerful tone more suitable for use in the arena than the small pneumatic instruments, but the hydraulic organ never entirely supplanted the pneumatic, which was probably not so imperfect at the beginning of our era as has been thought, since it outlived the former and seems to have differed from it only in the matter of pressure. The hydraulus, on the other hand, must have had many drawbacks, that of causing damp in the instrument being of a serious nature; it was also unwieldy and difficult to carry about.

From the Church of St Paul extra muros, Rome. 4th or 5th cent. A.D.

FIG. 5.

Of the pneumatic organ in portable and portative form, traces have been found during the palmy days of the Roman empire, and the art of organ-building, of which the organ in fig. 5 is an example, never seems to have quite died out during the decline of classic Rome and the dawn of Western civilization. This illustration is derived from a 4th- or 5th-century slab in the church of St Paul extra muros at Rome. It is evident that the hydraulic organ was widely known and used in the East during the early centuries of our era, but it never won a footing in the

West, although a few solitary specimens found their way into the palaces of kings and princes. On account of its association with the theatre, gladiatorial combats and pagan amusements of corrupt Rome, it was placed under a ban by the Church. The ignorance and misinformation displayed on the subject by writers and miniaturists of the early and late middle ages leave no room for doubt that the instrument itself was unknown to them except from hearsay.

Venice seems to have been famed for its organ-builders during the 9th century, for Louis le Débonnaire (778–840) sent there, it is recorded, for a certain monk, Georgius Benevento,[4] to construct an hydraulic organ for his palace at Aix-la-Chapelle.

No progress in the art of organ-building is recorded until the use of organs in the churches had long been established. The recognition of the value of the organ in Christian worship proved an incentive which led to the rapid development of the instrument.

In France and Germany the Romans must have used organs and have introduced them to the conquered tribes as they did in Spain, but the art of making them was soon lost after Roman influence and civilization were withdrawn. Pippin, when he wished to introduce the Roman ritual into the churches of France, felt the need of an organ and applied to the Byzantine emperor, Constantine Copronymus, to send him one, which arrived by special embassy in 757 and was placed in the church of St Corneille at Compiègne; the arrival of this organ was obviously considered a great event; it is mentioned by all the chroniclers of his reign. Charlemagne received a similar present from the emperor of the East in 812, of which a description has been preserved.[5] The bellows were of hide, the pipes of bronze; its tone was as loud as thunder and as sweet as that of lyre and psaltery. This organ must have had registers like those of the hydraulus of Vitruvius and the portative from Pompeii. In 826 we hear that his son Louis le Débonnaire obtained a pneumatic organ for the church at Aix-la-Chapelle, not to be confounded with the hydraulus installed in his palace.

The statement that the organ was introduced into the Roman Church by Pope Vitalian at the end of the 7th century, which has been generally accepted, is rejected by Buhle[6] on the ground of insufficient proof. There is abundant evidence to show that the organ had taken its place in the churches in the 10th century, not only in England but in Germany, where the construction by monks had become so general that we find no fewer than three treatises on organ-building[7] written by monks, followed by three more in the 11th century.[8]

Considerable activity was displayed in England in the 10th century in organ-building on a large scale for churches and monasteries, such as the monster organ for Bishop Alphege at Winchester, which had 400 bronze pipes, 26 bellows and 2 manuals of 10 keys, each governing 10 pipes.[9] There is also the elaborate organ presented by St Dunstan to his monastery at Malmesbury.[10]

[1] See Anonymi scriptio de musica, ed. Bellermann, p. 35.
[2] See "Notes on a Roman Hydraulus," Reisquary (1904); also the writer's "Researches into the Origin of the Organs of the Ancients" in Intern. Mus. Ges., Sbd. ii. 2, pp. 167–202 (Leipzig, 1901), and Proc. Mus. Assoc. (1903–1904), pp. 54–55.
[3] For a more complete explanation of the action of the hydraulus, with diagrams, see Victor Loret, Revue archéol. (Paris, 1890); W. Chappell, History of Music (London, 1874), pp. 325–361.

[4] "Vita Hludovici Imperatoris," Mon. Germ. ii. pp. 629–630; see also Buhle, op. cit. p. 58, note 4, where fuller references are given.
[5] Gesta Karoli Monachi Sangallensis, lib. ii. cap. x. p. 751.
[6] Op. cit. p. 61, note 2, where the evidence is carefully sifted.
[7] (1) by Notker of St Gallen (see Hattemer, Denkmäler, Bd. iii. pp. 568 seq.; Hugo Riemann, Studien z. Gesch. der Notenschrift, pp. 397 seq.; Martin Gerbert, i. pp. 100 seq. (2) By Bernelinius (see Gerbert, i. pp. 318 and 325). The third is an anonymous 9th-century tract, the earliest of all, De mensura fistularum, giving only the proportions of organ pipes. MS. Lat. 12949 fol. 43ᵛ. Paris Bibl. Nat. reproduced by Buhle, op. cit. p. 104 (Latin only).
[8] (1) De fistulis organicis, introduced in a MS. copy of Mart. Cap. by a Bernese monk; see A. Schubiger, Musikal. Spicilegien, pp. 82 seq. Reproduced also by Buhle, op. cit. Beilage iv. pp. 114–116, collated with a German translation. (2) Theophilus. De divers. artibus, edited and translated into English by Robert Hendrie (London, 1847); reproduced by Buhle, op. cit. Beilage iii. pp. 105 seq., Latin and German collated, who gives the title as Schedula artium. (3) Tractatus de mensura fistularum, by Bishop Eberhard of Freising. Martin Gerbert, op. cit. ii. pp. 279–281.
[9] See Wolstani, monachi Ventani, De Vita S. Swithuni; Coussemaker. "Essai sur les instruments de musique du moyen-âge," in Ann. Archéol., iii. pp. 281–282.
[10] William of Malmesbury, Gest. Pontif., lib. v.

Earl Elwin gave money "*triginta libras*" to the monastery at Ramsay for copper pipes for a great pneumatic organ to be played on high days and holidays.[1]

The great activity recorded in the 12th and 13th centuries in Germany is probably due to the influence and teaching of Byzantine masters during the 9th century. Pope John VIII. (872–880) applied to Bishop Anno of Freising to send him an organ and an organist.[2] Organs were installed in Cologne (10th century), in Halberstadt, in Erfurt, in Augsburg, Weltenburg (11th century); in Utrecht, Constance, Petershausen (12th century); Peters-

From the Bible of St. Etienne Harding at Dijon. 12th cent.
FIG. 6.

berg, Cologne Cathedral, 13th century.[3] The rest of the literary and archaeological material—treatises, monuments, miniatures—available during the later middle ages yields very scant authenticated information as to the progressive steps which lie between the 12th-century organ as described by Theophilus and the large church organs of the days of Praetorius[4] (1618).

Brit. Mus. Cotton MSS. Tiberius A vi. fol. 104b. 14th century.
FIG. 7.

The *keyboard* is the principal feature concerning which miniatures offer any evidence. Here and there a 13th-century miniature gives a hint of balanced keys on small portative organs which already abound during that and the next century. The Bernese monk in his treatise on the organ, to which reference was made in the note above, clearly describes balanced keys, *depressa lamina*, pressed down, not pulled out, as were those mentioned by Theophilus; his description conforms strictly with that of Hero, which suggests that he was borrowing from classical authorities rather than describing an actual instrument with which he was well acquainted, an expedient to which

Brit. Mus. Add. MS. 17695. 14th century.
FIG. 8.

many medieval writers had recourse. In the 14th-century miniatures, balanced keys are general for the larger portable organs. The adoption of narrower keys in the larger organs may no doubt be traced to the influence of the portatives, in which they in

---

most cases resemble the white keys of the modern pianoforte. There is no miniature on record in which the fast action on the keys is indicated, the performer during the 10th, 11th and 12th centuries being depicted in the act of drawing out the stop-like sliders—as for instance, in the 12th-century manuscript Bible of St Etienne Harding at Dijon[1] (fig. 6), where the organist is playing the notes D and F, the sliders being lettered from C to G. From the 13th century the keys are shown pressed down by means of one finger or of finger and thumb (fig. 7). In the beautiful Spanish MS. said to have been compiled for Alphonso XII. (*c.* 1237), known as the *Cantigas de Santa Maria*, a portative is shown having balanced keys, one of which is being lightly pressed by the thumb, the instrument resting on the palm—while the left hand manipulates the bellows.

The keys themselves varied in shape, being either like a T; a wide rectangle, with or without the corners rounded off, or a narrow rectangle. The earliest instance of chromatic keyboard is that of the organ at Halberstadt[2] built in 1361 and restored in 1495. An inscription on the keyboard states that it formed part of the original organ, which had the semitonal arrangement of keys.[3]

It must not, however, be inferred from these isolated cases that balanced keys were general from the 13th century, nor that the chromatic keys were common in the 14th. The St Cecilia in the altarpiece in Ghent by the brothers Hubert and Jan van Eyck (15th cent.) is represented as playing upon an organ with a modern-looking keyboard.

Brit. Mus. Add. MS. 29902, fol. 6. 14th century.
FIG. 9.

A picture by Fra Angelico (15th cent.) in the National Gallery shows a portative with accidentals. It will probably be found that the earliest development of the organ took place in Germany and in the Netherlands. (K. S.)

ORGANISTRUM, the medieval Latin name for the earliest known form of the hurdy-gurdy (*q.v.*). The organistrum was large enough to rest on the knees of two performers sitting side by side, one of whom turned the crank setting the wheel in motion, while the other, the artist, manipulated the keys. The word organistrum is derived from *organum* and *instrumentum*; the former term was applied to the primitive harmonies, consisting of octaves accompanied by fourths or fifths, first practised by Hucbald in the 10th century. This explanation enables us to fix with tolerable certainty the date of the invention of the organistrum, at the end of the 10th or beginning of the 11th century, and also to understand the construction of the instrument. A stringed instrument of the period—such as a guitar-fiddle, a rotta or oval vielle—being used as model, the proportions were increased for the convenience of holding the instrument and of dividing the performance between two persons. Inside the body was the wheel, having a tire of leather well rosined, and working easily through an aperture in the sound-board. The three strings resting on the wheel and supported besides on a bridge of the same height all sounded at once as the wheel revolved, and in the earliest examples the wooden tangents taking the place of fingers on the frets of the neck acted upon all three strings at once, thus producing the harmony known as organum.

The organistrum appears on a bas-relief from the abbey of St Georges de Boscherville (11th cent.), now preserved in the museum of Rouen, where it is played by a royal lady, her maid turning the crank. It has the place of honour in the centre of the band of musicians representing the twenty-four elders of the Apocalypse in the tympanum of the Gate of Glory of the cathedral of Santiago da Compostella (12th cent.). There is also a fine example in a miniature of a psalter of English workmanship (12th cent.), forming part of the Hunterian collection in Glasgow University; this was shown at the Exhibition of Illuminated MSS. at the Burlington Fine Arts Club in 1908. (K. S.)

---

[1] *Vita S. Oswaldi:* see Mabillon Acta S. scl. v. p. 756.
[2] See Baluze, *Miscell.* v. p. 490.
[3] Buhle (*op. cit.*) gives a list with quotations from authorities; see pp. 66 and 67.
[4] See Michael Praetorius *Syntagma Musicum* (Wolfenbüttel, 1618).

[1] See also for other organs with sliders being drawn out, A. Haseloff, *Eine Sachsischthüringische Malerschule um die Wende des XIII. Jahrh.*, pl. xxvi. No. 37, part of *Studien zu der Kunstgeschichte*; the same is reproduced in Gori's *Thesaurus diptychorum*, Bd. iii. Tab. 16, where it is falsely ascribed to the 9th century.
[2] Praetorius mentions the Halberstadt and Erfurt organs as having been built 600 years before his time (1618), and still bearing on them the date inscribed. See *op. cit.* p. 93.
[3] See A. J. Hipkins, *History of the Pianoforte* (London, 1896).

ORGANON (Gr. ὄργανον, instrument, from ἔργον, work), the name given to. Aristotle's logical treatises. They are so called because logic is itself neither a speculative science nor a practical art in the ordinary sense, but an aid or instrument to all scientific thought. Francis Bacon, regarding the Aristotelian logic as he understood it as of no avail, gave to his own treatise the name *Novum Organum* in the belief that he had discovered a new inductive logic which would lead necessarily to the acquisition of new scientific knowledge. Compare also Whewell's *Novum Organum Renovatum* and Lambert's *Neues Organon*. In medieval music the term was applied in a similar sense to early attempts at improvised counterpoint *i.e.* a part sung as an accompaniment above or below the melody or plainsong; it consisted of 8ths and 5ths (or 4ths) added to the plainsong.

ORGY (through French from Lat. *orgia*, Gr. ὄργια, in derivation connected probably with ἔργον, work; cf. Lat. *operari*, to sacrifice), a term originally denoting the secret rites or ceremonies connected with the worship of certain deities, especially those of Dionysus-Bacchus. The Dionysiac orgies, which were restricted to women, were celebrated in the winter among the Thracian hills or in spots remote from city life. The women met, clad in fawn-skins, with hair dishevelled, swinging the thyrsus and beating the cymbal; they danced and worked themselves up to a state of mad excitement. The holiest rites took place at night by the light of torches. A bull, the representative of the god, was torn in pieces by them as Dionysus-Zagreus had been torn; his bellowing reproduced the cries of the suffering god. The women tore the bull with their teeth, and the eating of the raw flesh was a necessary part of the ritual. Some further rites, which varied in different districts, represented the resurrection of the god in the spring. On Mount Parnassus the women carried back Dionysus-Licnites, the child cradled in the winnowing fan. The most famous festival of the kind was the τριετηρίς celebrated every second winter on Parnassus by the women of Attica and Phocis. The celebrants were called Maenads or Bacchae. The ecstatic enthusiasm of the Thracian women, Κλώδωνες or Μιμαλλόνες, was especially distinguished. The wild dances, songs, drinking and other "orgiastic" ceremonies which were characteristic of these rites have given rise to the use of the word "orgy" for any drunken, wild revel or festivity (see DIONYSUS and MYSTERY).

ORIA, a town of Apulia, Italy, in the province of Lecce, 25 m. E. of Taranto and 19 m. S.W. of Brindisi by rail, 540 ft. above sea-level. Pop. (1901), 8838. It occupies the site of the ancient Uria, the chief town of the Sallentini, which stood in a commanding position in the centre of the peninsula of the ancient Calabria (*q.v.*), almost midway between Brundusium and Tarentum on the Via Appia. Strabo mentions that he saw there the old palace of the Messapian kings (vi. 3. 6, p. 282). The town contains a small museum and a fine castle of Frederick II., erected in 1227. The Doria family of Genoa and Rome is said to derive its name from a certain Tommaso d'Oria, who led the rebellion against Frederick's son Manfred. Much damage was done by a cyclone in 1878.

ORIBI, or OUREBI, the local name of a small South African antelope (*Oribia scoparia*), standing about 24 in. at the shoulder, and characterized by the presence of a bare glandular spot below the ear, the upright horns of the bucks, which are ringed for a short distance above the face, and the tufted bushy tail, of which the terminal two-thirds are black. The name is extended to include the other members of the same genus, such as the Abyssinian, *O. montana*; the Gambian, *O. nigricaudata*; the British East African, *O. haggardi*; and the Mozambique, *O. peteri*.

ORIEL, JOHN FOSTER, BARON (1740–1828), Irish politician, was the son of Anthony Foster of Louth, an Irish judge. He was returned to the Irish parliament in 1761, and made his mark in financial and commercial questions, being appointed chancellor of the Irish exchequer in 1784. His law giving bounties on the exportation of corn and imposing heavy taxes on its importation is noted by Lecky as responsible for making Ireland an arable instead of a pasture country. In 1785 he became Speaker. He opposed the Union, and ultimately refused to surrender the Speaker's mace, which was kept by his family. He was returned to the united parliament, and in 1804 became chancellor of the Irish exchequer under Pitt. In 1821 he was created a peer of the United Kingdom as Baron Oriel of Ferrard in the county of Louth, and died on the 23rd of August 1828. His wife (d. 1824) had in 1790 been created an Irish peeress, as Baroness Oriel, and in 1797 Viscountess Ferrard; and their son, Thomas Henry (d. 1843), who married Viscountess Massereene (in her own right) and took the name of Skeffington, inherited all these titles; the later Viscounts Massereene being their descendants.

ORIEL, in architecture, a projecting bay window on an upper storey, which is carried by corbels or mouldings. It is usually polygonal or semicircular in plan, but at Oxford in some of the colleges there are examples which are rectangular and rise through two or three storeys. In Germany it forms a favourite feature, and is sometimes placed at the angle of a building, carried up through two or three floors and covered with a lofty roof. The oriel is also said to have been provided as a recess for an altar in an oratory or small chapel. In the 15th century oriels came into general use, and are frequently found over entrance gateways.

The origin of the word is unknown. The suggested derivation from Lat. *aureolum*, with the supposed meaning of a gilded chamber or room, is not, according to the *New English Dictionary*, borne out by any historical evidence, and early French forms —such as *eurieul*—do not point to an origin in a word beginning with *au*. Du Cange (*Glossarium, s.v. Oriolum*) quotes Matthew of Paris (1251, *Vitae Abbatum S. Albani*): *adjacet atrium nobilissimum in introitu, quod porticus vel Oriolum appellatur*; and also a French use of 1338, where a licence to build an *oriel* is granted to one Jehan Bourgos. The earliest meaning seems to be a gallery, portico or corridor, and the application of the term to a particular form of window apparently arose from such a window being in an "oriel." In Cornwall "orrel" is still used of a balcony or porch at the head of an outside staircase leading to an upper story in a fisherman's cottage. The name of Oriel College, at Oxford, comes from a tenement known as Seneschal Hall or La Oriole, and granted to the college in 1327. There is no trace of the reason why the tenement was so called, but it would seem that it referred to one of the earlier applications of the word, to a gallery or porch, rather than to a window.

ORIENTATION, the term in architecture given to the position of a building generally with reference to the points of the compass, and more especially (as the word implies) to that of the East. It would seem that some of the Egyptian temples were orientated in the direction of the sun or of some selected star, the exact position of which on some particular day would be an indication to the priest of the exact time of the year—a matter of great importance in an agricultural country, when the calendar was not known. The orientation of Greek temples has enabled astronomers to calculate the dates of the foundation of early temples, allowance being made for the gradual changes which in the course of centuries had taken place in the precession of the equinox. The principal front of the Greek temple always faced east; and the rays of the rising sun, passing through the great doorway of the naos, lighted up the statue at the further end, this being the only occasion on which the people who came to witness the event were able to gaze on the sculptured figure of the deity.

In early Christian architecture, in the five first basilicas built by Constantine, the apse of the church was at the west end, and the priest, standing behind the altar, faced the east; this orientation being probably derived from that of the church of the Holy Sepulchre at Jerusalem and the church at Bethlehem. Three-fourths of the early churches in Rome followed this orientation, but in many it was reversed at a later date. In Sta. Sophia, Constantinople, and all the Byzantine churches, the apse was always at the east end, and the same custom obtains in the early churches in Syria and the Coptic churches in Egypt.

In Spain, Germany and England generally the eastern

orientation is generally observed, but in France and Italy there are many variations. In Scotland it was the custom to fix a pole in the ground over night, and in the morning at sunrise to note the direction taken by the shadow of the pole, which was followed when setting out the axis of the choir; if such a custom had been followed in an early church, when setting out another of later date there should be some difference in the orientation of the two, on account of the variation of the obliquity of the ecliptic in the interval, and this in some cases accounts for the change of the axial line which is found in some churches, either when the east end has been rebuilt, as was constantly the case throughout Europe, or when a nave has been added to an earlier structure. In describing churches it is usual to use the terms east, west, north and south, on the assumption.that the altar is at the east end, although this may not be the real bearing of the edifice.

Indirectly also the term is sometimes used in the planning of houses and the relation of the windows of the various rooms to the sunshine and the weather—in other words, to the points of the compass; thus an eastward aspect should be provided for the morning- and dining-rooms, a south-western aspect for the drawing-room, a westward for the library, and north by west for the kitchen, larder, &c.   (R. P. S.)

ORIENTE, or LA REGION ORIENTALE, a large undefined territory of Ecuador, comprising all that part of the republic lying east of the Andes. Pop. (1887 estimate), 80,000. The territory was formed in 1884 from the older territories of Napo, Canelos and Zamora, but its boundaries with the neighbouring republics of Colombia and Peru are disputed. The territory is covered with great forests, inhabited by wild Indians, and its climate is hot and exceptionally humid. There are some mission settlements and trading stations in the Andean foothills and on some of the river courses, one of which is Archidona, on a small tributary of the Napo, which is the nominal capital.

ORIGEN (c. 185–c. 254), the most distinguished and most influential of all the theologians of the ancient church, with the possible exception of Augustine. He is the father of the church's science; he is the founder of a theology which was brought to perfection in the 4th and 5th centuries, and which still retained the stamp of his genius when in the 6th century it disowned its author. It was Origen who created the dogmatic of the church and laid the foundations of the scientific criticism of the Old and New Testaments. He could not have been what he was unless two generations before him had laboured at the problem of finding an intellectual expression and a philosophic basis for Christianity (Justin, Tatian, Athenagoras, Pantaenus, Clement). But their attempts, in comparison with his, are like a schoolboy's essays beside the finished work of a master. Like all great epoch-making personalities, he was favoured by the circumstances of his life, notwithstanding the relentless persecution to which he was exposed. He lived in a time when the Christian communities enjoyed almost uninterrupted peace and held an acknowledged position in the world. By proclaiming the reconciliation of science with the Christian faith, of the highest culture with the Gospel, Origen did more than any other man to win the Old World to the Christian religion. But he entered into no diplomatic compromises; it was his deepest and most solemn conviction that the sacred oracles of Christendom embraced all the ideals of antiquity. His character was as transparent as his life was blameless; there are few church fathers whose biography leaves so pure an impression on the reader. The atmosphere around him was a dangerous one for a philosopher and theologian to breathe, but he kept his spiritual health unimpaired, and even his sense of truth suffered less injury than was the case with most of his contemporaries. To us, indeed, his conception of the universe, like that of Philo, seems a strange medley, and one may be at a loss to conceive how he could bring together such heterogeneous elements; but there is no reason to doubt that the harmony of all the essential parts of his system was obvious enough to himself. It is true that in addressing the Christian people he used different language from that which he employed to the cultured; but there was no dissimulation in

that—on the contrary, it was a requirement of his system. Orthodox theology has never, in any of the confessions, ventured beyond the circle which the mind of Origen first measured out. It has suspected and amended its author, it has expunged his heresies; but whether it has put anything better or more tenable in their place may be gravely questioned.

Origen was born, perhaps at Alexandria, of Christian parents in the year 185 or 186. As a boy he showed evidence of remarkable talents, and his father Leonidas gave him an excellent education. At a very early age, about the year 200, he listened to the lectures of Pantaenus and Clement in the catechetical school. This school, of which the origin (though assigned to Athenagoras) is unknown, was the first and for a long time the only institution where Christians were instructed simultaneously in the Greek sciences and the doctrines of the holy Scriptures. Alexandria had been, since the days of the Ptolemies, a centre for the interchange of ideas between East and West—between Egypt, Syria, Greece and Italy; and, as it had furnished Judaism with an Hellenic philosophy, so it also brought about the alliance of Christianity with Greek philosophy. Asia Minor and the West developed the strict ecclesiastical forms by means of which the church closed her lines against heathenism, and especially against heresy; in Alexandria Christian ideas were handled in a free and speculative fashion and worked out with the help of Greek philosophy. Till near the end of the 2nd century the line between heresy and orthodoxy was less rigidly drawn there than at Ephesus, Lyons, Rome or Carthage. In the year 202 a persecution arose, in which the father of Origen became a martyr, and the family lost their livelihood. Origen, who had distinguished himself by his intrepid zeal, was supported for a time by a lady of rank, but began about the same time to earn his bread by teaching; and in 203 he was placed, with the sanction of the bishop Demetrius, at the head of the catechetical school. Even then his attainments in the whole circle of the sciences were extraordinary. But the spirit of investigation impelled him to devote himself to the highest studies, philosophy and the exegesis of the sacred Scriptures. With indomitable perseverance he applied himself to these subjects; although himself a teacher, he regularly attended the lectures of Ammonius Saccas, and made a thorough study of the books of Plato and Numenius, of the Stoics and the Pythagoreans. At the same time he endeavoured to acquire a knowledge of Hebrew, in order to be able to read the Old Testament in the original. His manner of life was ascetic; the sayings of the Sermon on the Mount and the practical maxims of the Stoics were his guiding stars. Four oboli a day, earned by copying manuscripts, sufficed for his bodily sustenance. A rash resolve led him to mutilate himself that he might escape from the lusts of the flesh, and work unhindered in the instruction of the female sex. This step he afterwards regretted. As the attendance at his classes continually increased—pagans thronging to him as well as Christians—he handed over the beginners to his friend Heracles, and took charge of the more advanced pupils himself. Meanwhile the literary activity of Origen was increasing year by year. He commenced his great work on the textual criticism of the Scriptures; and at the instigation of his friend Ambrosius, who provided him with the necessary amanuenses, he published his commentaries on the Old Testament and his dogmatic investigations. In this manner he laboured at Alexandria for twenty-eight years (till 231–232). This period, however, was broken by many journeys, undertaken partly for scientific and partly for ecclesiastical objects. We know that he was in Rome in the time of Zephyrinus, again in Arabia, when a Roman official wanted to hear his lectures, and in Antioch, in response to a most flattering invitation from Julia Mammaea (mother of Alexander Severus, afterwards emperor), who wished to become acquainted with his philosophy. In the year 216—the time when the imperial executioners were ravaging Alexandria—we find Origen in Palestine. There the bishops of Jerusalem and Caesarea received him in the most friendly manner, and got him to deliver public lectures in the churches. In the East, especially in Asia Minor, it was still no unusual thing for laymen, with permission of the bishop, to address the people in the church. In Alexandria, however, this custom had been given up, and Demetrius took occasion to express his disapproval and recall Origen to Alexandria. Probably the bishop was jealous of the high reputation of the teacher; and a coolness arose between them which led, fifteen years later, to an open rupture. On his way to Greece (apparently in the year 230) Origen was ordained a presbyter in Palestine by his friends the bishops. This was undoubtedly an infringement of the rights of the Alexandrian bishop; at the same time it was simply a piece of spite on the part of the latter that had kept Origen so long without any ecclesiastical consecration. Demetrius convened a synod, at which it was resolved to banish Origen from Alexandria. Even this did not satisfy his displeasure. A second synod, composed entirely of bishops, determined that Origen must be deposed from the presbyterial status. This decision was communicated to the foreign churches, and seems to have been justified by referring to the self-mutilation of Origen and adducing objectionable doctrines which he was said to have promulgated. The details of the incident are, however, unfortunately very obscure. No formal excommunication of Origen appears to have been decreed; it was considered sufficient to have him degraded to the position of a layman. The sentence was approved by most of the churches, in particular by that of Rome. At a later period Origen sought to vindicate his teaching in a letter to the Roman bishop Fabian, but, it would seem, without success. Even Heracles, his former friend and sharer of his views, took part against him; and by this means he procured his own election shortly afterwards as successor to Demetrius.

In these circumstances Origen thought it best voluntarily to retire from Alexandria (231-232). He betook himself to Palestine, where his condemnation had not been acknowledged by the churches any more than it had been in Phoenicia, Arabia and Achaea. He settled in Caesarea, and very shortly he had a flourishing school there, whose reputation rivalled that of Alexandria. His literary work, too, was prosecuted with unabated vigour. Enthusiastic pupils sat at his feet (see the Panegyric of Gregory Thaumaturgus), and the methodical instruction which he imparted in all branches of knowledge was famous all over the East. Here again his activity as a teacher was interrupted by frequent journeys. Thus he was for two years together at Caesarea in Cappadocia, where he was overtaken by the Maximinian persecution; here he worked at his recension of the Bible. We find him again in Nicomedia, in Athens, and twice in Arabia. He was called there to combat the unitarian christology of Beryllus, bishop of Bostra, and to clear up certain eschatological questions. As he had formerly had dealings with the house of Alexander Severus, so now he entered into a correspondence with the emperor Philip the Arabian and his wife Severa. But through all situations of his life he preserved his equanimity, his keen interest in science, and his indefatigable zeal for the instruction of others. In the year 250 the Decian persecution broke out, Origen was arrested, imprisoned and maltreated. But he survived these troubles—it is a malicious invention that he recanted during the persecution—and lived a few years longer in active intercourse with his friends. He died, probably in the year 254 (consequently under Valerian), at Tyre, where his grave was still shown in the middle ages.

Writings.—Origen is probably the most prolific author of the ancient church. "Which of us," asks Jerome, "can read all that he has written?" The number of his works was estimated at 6000, but that is certainly an exaggeration. Owing to the increasing unpopularity of Origen in the church, a comparatively small portion of these works have come down to us in the original. We have more in the Latin translation of Rufinus; but this translation in by no means trustworthy, since Rufinus, assuming that Origen's writings had been tampered with by the heretics, considered himself at liberty to omit or amend heterodox statements. Origen's real opinion, however, may frequently be gathered from the *Philocalia*—a sort of anthology from his works prepared by Basil the Great and Gregory Nazianzenus. The fragments in Photius and in the *Apology* of Pamphilus serve

for comparison. The writings of Origen consist of letters, and of works in textual criticism, exegesis, apologetics, dogmatic and practical theology.

1. Eusebius (to whom we owe our full knowledge of his life) collected more than a hundred of Origen's letters, arranged them in books, and deposited them in the library at Caesarea (*H. E.* vi. 36). In the church library at Jerusalem (founded by the bishop Alexander) there were also numerous letters of this father (Euseb. *H. E.* vi. 20). But unfortunately they have all been lost except two—one to Julius Africanus (about the history of Susanna) and one to Gregory Thaumaturgus. There are, besides, a couple of fragments.

2. Origen's textual studies on the Old Testament were undertaken partly in order to improve the manuscript tradition, and partly for apologetic reasons, to clear up the relation between the LXX and the original Hebrew text. The results of more than twenty years' labour were set forth in his *Hexapla* and *Tetrapla*, in which he placed the Hebrew text side by side with the various Greek versions, examined their mutual relations in detail, and tried to find the basis for a more reliable text of the LXX. The *Hexapla* was probably never fully written out, but excerpts were made from it by various scholars at Caesarea in the 4th century; and thus large sections of it have been saved.[1] Origen worked also at the text of the New Testament, although he produced no recension of his own.

3. The exegetical labours of Origen extend over the whole of the Old and New Testaments. They are divided into *Scholia* (σημειώσεις, short annotations, mostly grammatical), *Homilies* (edifying expositions grounded on exegesis), and *Commentaries* (τόμοι). In the Greek original only a very small portion has been preserved; in Latin translations, however, a good deal. The most important parts are the homilies on Jeremiah, the books of Moses, Joshua and Luke, and the commentaries on Matthew, John and Romans. With grammatical precision, antiquarian learning and critical discernment Origen combines the allegorical method of interpretation—the logical corollary of his conception of the inspiration of the Scriptures. He distinguishes a threefold sense of scripture, a grammatico-historical, a moral and a pneumatic—the last being the proper and highest sense. He thus set up a formal theory of allegorical exegesis, which is not quite extinct in the churches even yet, but in his own system was of fundamental importance. On this method the sacred writings are regarded as an inexhaustible mine of philosophical and dogmatic wisdom; in reality the exegete reads his own ideas into any passage he chooses. The commentaries are of course intolerably diffuse and tedious, a great deal of them is now quite unreadable; yet, on the other hand, one has not unfrequently occasion to admire the sound linguistic perception and the critical talent of the author.[2]

4. The principal apologetic work of Origen is his book κατὰ Κέλσου (eight books), written at Caesarea in the time of Philip the Arabian. It has been completely preserved in the original. This work is invaluable as a source for the history and situation of the church in the 2nd century; for it contains nearly the whole of the famous work of Celsus (Λόγος ἀληθής) against Christianity. What makes Origen's answer so instructive is that it shows how close an affinity existed between Celsus and himself in their fundamental philosophical and theological presuppositions. The real state of the case is certainly unsuspected by Origen himself; but many of his opponent's arguments he is unable to meet except by a speculative reconstruction of the church doctrine in question. Origen's apologetic is most effective when he appeals to the spirit and power of Christianity as an evidence of its truth. In details his argument is not free from sophistical subterfuges and superficial reasoning.[3]

---

[1] Field, *Origenis Hexaplorum quae supersunt* (2 vols., Oxon., 1867-1874).

[2] See Reuss, *Geschichte der heil. Schriften d. N.T.* (5th ed.), § 511.

[3] Keim, *Celsus* (1873); Aubé, *Hist. des persécut. de l'église*, vol. ii. (1875); Ornsby, "Origen against Celsus," *Dublin Review* (July 1879). p. 38; Pélagaud, *Étude sur Celse* (1878); Lebedeff, *Origen's Book against Celsus* (Moscow, 1878) (Russian); Overbeck in the *Theolog. Lit. Zeitung* (1878), No. 22 (1879), No. 9; *Orig. c. Cels.*, ed. Selwyn (1876).

5. Of the dogmatic writings we possess only one in its integrity, and that only in the translation of Rufinus,[1] Περὶ ἀρχῶν (On the Fundamental Doctrines). This work, which was composed before 228, is the first attempt at a dogmatic at once scientific and accommodated to the needs of the church. The material is drawn from Scripture, but in such a way that the propositions of the *regula fidei* are respected. This material is then formed into a system by all the resources of the intellect and of speculation. Origen thus solved, after his own fashion, a problem which his predecessor Clement had not even ventured to grapple with. The first three books treat of God, the world, the fall of spirits, anthropology and ethics. "Each of these three books really embraces, although not in a strictly comprehensive way, the whole scheme of the Christian view of the world, from different points of view, and with different contents." The fourth book explains the divinity of the Scriptures, and deduces rules for their interpretation. It ought properly to stand as first book at the beginning. The ten books of *Stromata* (in which Origen compared the teaching of the Christians with that of the philosophers, and corroborated all the Christian dogmas from Plato, Aristotle, Numenius and Cornutus) have all perished, with the exception of small fragments; so have the tractates on the resurrection and on freewill.[2]

6. Of practical theological works we have still the Προτρεπτικὸς εἰς μαρτύριον and the Σύνταγμα περὶ εὐχῆς. For a knowledge of Origen's Christian estimate of life and his relation to the faith of the church these two treatises are of great importance. The first was written during the persecution of Maximinus Thrax, and was dedicated to his friends Ambrosius and Protoctetus. The other also dates from the Caesarean period; it mentions many interesting details, and concludes with a fine exposition of the Lord's Prayer.

7. In his own lifetime Origen had to complain of falsifications of his works and forgeries under his name. Many pieces still in existence are wrongly ascribed to him; yet it is doubtful whether a single one of them was composed on purpose to deceive. The most noteworthy are the *Dialogues* of a certain Adamantius "de recta in Deum fide," which seem to have been erroneously attributed to Origen so early as the 4th century, one reason being the fact that Origen himself also bore that name. (Eusebius, *H.E.* vi. 14.)

Outline of Origen's View of the Universe and of Life.—The system of Origen was formulated in opposition to the Greek philosophers on the one hand, and the Christian Gnostics on the other.[3] But the science of faith, as expounded by him, bears unmistakably the stamp both of Neo-Platonism and of Gnosticism. As a theologian, in fact, Origen is not merely an orthodox traditionalist and believing exegete, but a speculative philosopher of Neo-Platonic tendencies. He is, moreover, a judicious critic. The union of these four elements gives character to his theology, and in a certain degree to all subsequent theology. It is this combination which has determined the peculiar and varying relations in which theology and the faith of the church have stood to each other since the time of Origen. That relation depends on the predominance of one or other of the four factors embraced in his theology.

As an orthodox traditionalist Origen holds that Christianity is a practical and religious saving principle, that it has unfolded itself in an historical series of revealing facts, that the church has accurately embodied the substance of her faith in the *regula fidei*, and that simple faith is sufficient for the renewal and salvation of man. As a philosophical idealist, however, he transmutes the whole contents of the faith of the church into ideas which bear the mark of Neo-Platonism, and were accordingly recognized by the later Neo-Platonists as Hellenic.[4] In Origen, however,

[1] There are, however, extensive fragments of the original in existence.

[2] See Redepenning, *Origenis de principiis*, first sep. ed. (Leipzig, 1836); Schnitzer, *Orig. über die Grundlehren des Glaubens*, an attempt at reconstruction (1835).

[3] The opposition to the unitarians within the church must also be kept in mind.

[4] Porphyry says of Origen, κατὰ τὰς περὶ πραγμάτων καὶ τοῦ θείου δόξας Ἑλληνίζων (Euseb. *H.E.* vi. 19).

the mystic and ecstatic element is held in abeyance. The ethico-religious ideal is the sorrowless condition, the state of superiority to all evils, the state of order and of rest. In this condition man enters into likeness to God and blessedness; and it is reached through contemplative isolation and self-knowledge, which is divine wisdom. "The soul is trained as it were to behold itself in a mirror, it shows the divine spirit, if it should be found worthy of such fellowship, as in a mirror, and thus discovers the traces of a secret path to participation in the divine nature." As a means to the realization of this ideal, Origen introduces the whole ethics of Stoicism. But the link that connects him with churchly realism, as well as with the Neo-Platonic mysticism, is the conviction that complete and certain knowledge rests wholly on divine revelation, *i.e.* on oracles. Consequently his theology is cosmological speculation and ethical reflection based on the sacred Scriptures. The Scriptures, however, are treated by Origen on the basis of a matured theory of inspiration in such a way that all their facts appear as the vehicles of ideas, and have their highest value only in this aspect. That is to say, his gnosis neutralizes all that is empirical and historical, if not always as to its actuality, at least absolutely in respect of its value. The most convincing proof of this is that Origen (1) takes the idea of the immutability of God as the regulating idea of his system, and (2) deprives the historical "Word made flesh" of all significance for the true Gnostic. To him Christ appears simply as the Logos who is with the Father from eternity, and works from all eternity, to whom alone the instructed Christian directs his thoughts, requiring nothing more than a perfect—*i.e.* divine—teacher. In such propositions historical Christianity is stripped off as a mere husk. The objects of religious knowledge are beyond the plane of history, or rather—in a thoroughly Gnostic and Neo-Platonic spirit—they are regarded as belonging to a supra-mundane history. On this view contact with the faith of the church could only be maintained by distinguishing an exoteric and an esoteric form of Christianity. This distinction was already current in the catechetical school of Alexandria, but Origen gave it its boldest expression, and justified it on the ground of the incapacity of the Christian masses to grasp the deeper sense of Scripture, or unravel the difficulties of exegesis. On the other hand, in dealing with the problem of bringing his heterodox system into conformity with the *regula fidei* he evinced a high degree of technical skill. An external conformity was possible, inasmuch as speculation, proceeding from the higher to the lower, could keep by the stages of the *regula fidei*, which had been developed into a history of salvation. The system itself aims in principle at being thoroughly monistic; but, since matter, although created by God out of nothing, was regarded merely as the sphere in which souls are punished and purified, the system is pervaded by a strongly dualistic element. The immutability of God requires the eternity of the Logos and of the world. At this point Origen succeeded in avoiding the heretical Gnostic idea of God by assigning to the Godhead the attributes of goodness and righteousness. The pre-existence of souls is another inference from the immutability of God, although Origen also deduced it from the nature of the soul, which as a spiritual potency must be eternal. Indeed this is the fundamental idea of Origen—"the original and indestructible unity of God and all spiritual essences." From this follows the necessity for the created spirit, after apostasy, error and sin, to return always to its origin in God. The actual sinfulness of all men Origen was able to explain by the theological hypothesis of pre-existence and the premundane fall of each individual soul. He holds that freedom is the inalienable prerogative of the finite spirit; and this is the second point that distinguishes his theology from the heretical Gnosticism. The system unfolds itself like a drama, of which the successive stages are as follows: the transcendental fall, the creation of the material world, inaugurating the history of punishment and redemption, the clothing of fallen souls in flesh, the dominion of sin, evil and the demons on earth, the appearing of the Logos, His union with a pure human soul, His esoteric preaching of salvation, and His death in the flesh, then the imparting of the

Spirit, and the ultimate restoration of all things. The doctrine of the restoration appeared necessary because the spirit, in spite of its inherent freedom, cannot lose its true nature, and because the final purposes of God cannot be foiled. The end, however, is only relative, for spirits are continually falling, and God remains through eternity the creator of the world. Moreover the end is not conceived as a transfiguration of the world, but as a liberation of the spirit from its unnatural union with the sensual. Here the Gnostic and philosophical character of the system is particularly manifest. The old Christian eschatology is set aside; no one has dealt such deadly blows to Chiliasm and Christian apocalypticism as Origen. It need hardly be said that he spiritualized the church doctrine of the resurrection of the flesh. But, while in all these doctrines he appears in the character of a Platonic philosopher, traces of rational criticism are not wanting. Where his fundamental conception admits of it, he tries to solve historical problems by historical methods. Even in the christology, where he is treating of the historical Christ, he entertains critical considerations; hence it is not altogether without reason that in after times he was suspected of " Ebionitic " views of the Person of Christ. Not unfrequently he represents the unity of the Father and the Son as a unity of agreement and harmony and "identity of will."

Although the theology of Origen exerted a considerable influence as a whole in the two following centuries, it certainly lost nothing by the circumstance that several important propositions were capable of being torn from their original setting and placed in new connexions. It is in fact one of the peculiarities of this theology, which professed to be at once churchly and philosophical, that most of its formulae could be interpreted and appreciated *in utramque partem*. By arbitrary divisions and rearrangements the doctrinal statements of this " science of faith " could be made to serve the most diverse dogmatic tendencies. This is seen especially in the doctrine of the Logos. On the basis of his idea of God Origen was obliged to insist in the strongest manner on the personality, the eternity (eternal generation) and the essential divinity of the Logos.[1] On the other hand, when he turned to consider the origin of the Logos he did not hesitate to speak of Him as a κτίσμα, and to include Him amongst the rest of God's spiritual creatures. A κτίσμα, which is at the same time ὁμοσύσιον τῷ Θεῷ, was no contradiction to him, simply because he held the immutability, the pure knowledge and the blessedness which constituted the divine nature to be communicable attributes. In later times both the orthodox and the Arians appealed to his teaching, both with a certain plausibility; but the inference of Arius, that an imparted divinity must be divinity in the second degree, Origen did not draw. With respect to other doctrines also, such as those of the Holy Spirit and the incarnation of Christ, &c., Origen prepared the way for the later dogmas. The technical terms round which such bitter controversies raged in the 4th and 5th centuries are often found in Origen lying peacefully side by side. But this is just where his epoch-making importance lies, that all the later parties in the church learned from him. And this is true not only of the dogmatic parties; solitary monks and ambitious priests, hard-headed critical exegetes,[2] allegorists, mystics, all found something congenial in his writings. The only man who tried to shake off the theological influence of Origen was Marcellus of Ancyra, who did not succeed in producing any lasting effect on theology.

The attacks on Origen, which had begun in his lifetime, did not cease for centuries, and only subsided during the time of the fierce Arian controversy. It was not so much the relation between pistis and gnosis—faith and knowledge—as defined by Origen that gave offence, but rather isolated propositions, such as his doctrines of the pre-existence of souls, of the soul and body of Christ, of the resurrection of the flesh, of the final restoration,

[1] " Communis substantiae est filio cum patre; ὁμοούσιος enim ὁμοούσιος videtur, *i.e.* unius substantiae cum illo corpore ex quo est ὁμοούσιος."

[2] *E.g.* Dionysius of Alexandria; compare his judicious verdict on the Apocalypse.

ΚΛ 9 Λ

and of the plurality of worlds. Even in the 3rd century Origen's view of the Trinity and of the Person of Christ was called in question, and that from various points of view. It was not till the 5th century, however, that objections of this kind became frequent. In the 4th century Pamphilus, Eusebius of Caesares, Athanasius, the Cappadocians, Didymus, and Rufinus were on the side of Origen against the attacks of Methodius and many others. But, when the zeal of Epiphanius was kindled against him, when Jerome, alarmed about his own reputation, and in defiance of his past attitude, turned against his once honoured teacher, and Theophilus, patriarch of Alexandria, found it prudent, for political reasons, and out of consideration for the uneducated monks, to condemn Origen—then his authority received a shock from which it never recovered. There were, doubtless, in the 5th century church historians and theologians who still spoke of him with reverence, but such men became fewer and fewer. In the West Vincent of Lerins held up Origen as a warning example (*Commonit.* 23), showing how even the most learned and most eminent of church teachers might become a misleading light. In the East the exegetical school of Antioch had an aversion to Origen; the Alexandrians had utterly repudiated him. Nevertheless his writings were much read, especially in Palestine. The monophysite monks appealed to his authority, but could not prevent Justinian and the fifth oecumenical council at Constantinople (553) from anathematising his teaching. It is true that many scholars (*e.g.* Hefele, *Concilien-gesch.* ii. p. 858 sq.) deny that Origen was condemned by this council; but Möller rightly holds that the condemnation is proved (*Realencyklop. f. protest. Theol. u. Kirche*, xl. 113).

SOURCES AND LITERATURE.—Next to the works of Origen (see Redepenning, " Des Hieronymus wiederaufgefundenes Verzeichnis der Schriften des Origens," in *Zeit. f. d. hist. Theol.* (1851), pp. 66 seq.) the most important sources are: Gregory Thaumat., *Panegyricus in Orig.*; Eusebius, *H.E.* vi.; Epiphanius, *Haer.* 64; the works of Methodius, the Cappadocians, Jerome (see *De vir. ill.* 54, 61) and Rufinus; Vincent. Lerin. *Commonit.* 23; Palladius, *Hist. Laus.* 147; Justinian, *Ep. ad Mennam* (Mansi, ix. p. 487 seq.); Photius, *Biblioth.* 118, &c. There is no complete critical edition of Origen's works. The best edition is that of Car. and C. Vinc. Delarue (4 vols. fol.) (Paris, 1733–1759), reprinted by Lommatzsch (25 vols. 8vo) (Berlin, 1831–1848) and by Migne, *Patrol. curs. compl.* ser. Gr., vols. xi.–xvii. Several new pieces have been edited by Gallandi and A. Mai. Amongst the older works on Origen those of Huetius (printed in Delarue, vol. iv.) are the best; but Tillemont, Fabricius, Walch (*Historie d. Ketzereien*, vii. pp. 362–760) and Schröckh also deserve to be mentioned. In recent times the doctrine of Origen has been expounded in the great works on church history by Baur, Dorner, Böhringer, Neander, Möller (*Geschichte der Kosmologie in der griechischen Kirche*) and Kahnis (*Die Lehre vom h. Geist*, vol. i.); compare with these the works on the history of philosophy by Ritter, Erdmann, Ueberweg and Zeller. Of monographs, the best and most complete is Redepenning, *Origenes, eine Darstellung seines Lebens und seiner Lehre* (2 vols., 1841, 1846). Compare Thomasius, *Orig.* (1837); Krüger, " Über das Verhältnis des Orig. zu Ammonius Sakkas," in the *Zischr. f. hist. Theol.* (1843), i. p. 46 seq.; Fischer, *Comment. de Orig. theologia et cosmologia* (1846); Ramers, *Orig. Lehre von der Auferstehung das Fleisches* (1851); Knittel, " Orig. Lehre von der Menschwerdung," in the *Theol. Quartalschr.* (1872); Schultz, " Christologie des Orig.," in the *Jahrb. f. protest. Theol.* (1875); Mehlhorn, " Die Lehre von der menschlichen Freiheit nach Orig.," in *Zeitschr. f. Kirchengesch.* vol. ii. (1878); Freppel, *Origène*, vol. i. 2nd ed. (Paris, 1875). A full list of the later bibliography will be found in Harnack's *Dogmengeschichte* and *Chronologie.* (A. HA.)

ORIGINAL PACKAGE, a legal term in America, meaning, in general usage, the package in which goods, intended for interstate commerce, are actually transported wholesale. The term is used chiefly in determining the boundary between Federal and state jurisdiction in the regulation of commerce, and derives special significance by reason of the conflict between the powers of Congress to regulate commerce and the police legislation of the several states with respect to commodities considered injurious to public health and morals, such as intoxicating liquors, cigarettes and oleomargarine. By the Federal constitution Congress is vested with the power " to regulate commerce with foreign nations and among the several states, and with the Indian tribes," and each state is forbidden, without the consent of Congress, to " lay any imposts or duties on imports or exports, except what may be absolutely necessary for executing its inspection laws," and the basis of the law on the subject of "original package" was laid when, in 1827, Chief Justice Marshall interpreted these clauses in his decision of the case of *Brown* v. *Maryland*,[1] which tested the constitutionality of an act of the legislature of Maryland requiring a licence from importers of foreign goods by bale or package and from persons selling the same by wholesale, bale, package, hogshead, barrel or tierce. After pronouncing such a licence to be in effect a tax, the chief justice observed that so long as the thing imported remained " the property of the importer, in his warehouse, in the original form or package in which it was imported," a tax upon it was too plainly a duty on imports to escape the prohibition of the Constitution, that imported commodities did not become subject to the taxing power of the state until they had " become incorporated and mixed with the mass of property in the country," that the right to sell a thing imported was incident to the right to import it, and consequently that a state tax upon the sale was repugnant to the power of Congress to regulate foreign commerce; and he added that the court supposed the same principles applied equally to interstate commerce. Later decisions agree that the right to import commodities or to ship them from one state to another carries with it the right to sell them and have established the boundary line between Federal and state control of both foreign imports and interstate shipments at a sale in the original package[2] or at the breaking of the original package before sale for other purposes than inspection.[3] A state or a municipality may, however, tax while in their original packages any commodities which have been shipped in from another state provided there be no discrimination against such commodities; this permission being granted on the theory that a general non-discriminating tax is not a regulation of commerce and therefore not repugnant to the power of Congress to regulate interstate commerce.[4] The first cases involving a serious conflict between the power of Congress to regulate interstate commerce and the police powers of the several states were the Licence Cases adjudicated by the Supreme Court of the United States in January 1847.[5] They were to test the constitutionality of a law of Massachusetts requiring a licence for the sale of wines or spirituous liquors in a less quantity than 28 gallons, of a law of Rhode Island requiring a licence for the sale of such liquors in a less quantity than 10 gallons, and a law of New Hampshire requiring a licence for the sale of wines or spirituous liquors in any quantity whatever, and in this case a barrel of gin had been bought in Boston Mass., carried to Dover, N.H., and there sold in the same barrel. Although the justices based their opinions on different principles, the court pronounced the laws constitutional. The justices did not even agree that the power of Congress to regulate an interstate shipment included the power to authorize a sale after shipment, which is the basis of the original package doctrine as applied to interstate commerce, and Chief Justice Taney with two other justices who were of this opinion held that a state might nevertheless in the exercise of its police powers regulate such sales so long as Congress did not pass an act for that purpose. In this confused and uncertain state the matter rested until the adjudication of *Leisy* v. *Hardin*[6] in 1889. In this case beer had been shipped from Illinois into Iowa and then sold in the original kegs and cases by an agent of the Illinois firm when Iowa had a law absolutely prohibiting the sale of intoxicating liquors within its limits except for pharmaceutical, medicinal, chemical or sacramental purposes. None of the justices now denied that the power of Congress to regulate an interstate shipment included the power to authorize a sale after shipment, and although there was disagreement with reference to the right of a state to regulate the sale in the absence of an act of Congress for that purpose, the

majority of the court were of the opinion that: " Whenever a particular power of the general government is one which must necessarily be exercised by it, and Congress remains silent, this is not only not a concession that the powers reserved by the states may be exerted as if the specific power had not been elsewhere reposed, but, on the contrary, the only legitimate conclusion is that the general government intended that power should not be affirmatively exercised, and that the action of the states cannot be permitted to effect that which would be incompatible with such intention. Hence, inasmuch as interstate commerce, consisting in the transportation, purchase, sale and exchange of commodities, is national in its character and must be governed by a uniform system, so long as Congress does not pass any law to regulate it, or allowing the states so to do, it thereby indicates its will that such commerce shall be free and untrammelled." The opinion of Chief Justice Taney in *Pierce* v. *New Hampshire* was therefore in part overruled and the Iowa law in so far as it applied to the sale in the original packages of liquors shipped in from another state was pronounced unconstitutional. As a consequence of this decision, Congress, in 1890, passed the Wilson Act providing that all fermented, distilled, or other intoxicating liquors or liquids transported into any state or Territory for use, consumption, sale or storage therein should, even though in the original packages, be subject to the police laws of the state or Territory to the same extent as those produced within the state or Territory. Even with this act, however, a state is not permitted to interfere with an interstate shipment of liquor direct to the consumer.[7]

What constitutes an original package was the principal question in *Austin* v. *Tennessee*[8] which was decided in November 1900. The general assembly of Tennessee had in this case made it a misdemeanour for any party to sell or to bring into the state for selling or giving away any cigarettes. The defendant had purchased at Durham, North Carolina, a quantity of cigarettes. They were packed in pasteboard boxes containing ten cigarettes each. The boxes were then placed in an open basket and in this manner the cigarettes were delivered at the defendant's place of business in Tennessee where he sold a package without breaking it. The court decided against the defendant because it held that the manner of transportation was evidently for the purpose of evading the state law and that the boxes were not original packages within the meaning of the Federal law, and in this connexion it observed that " The whole theory of the exemption of the original package from the operation of the state laws is based upon the idea that the property is imported in the ordinary form in which, from time to time immemorial, foreign goods have been brought into the country. These have gone at once into the hands of the wholesale dealers, who have been in the habit of breaking the package and distributing their contents among the several retail dealers throughout the state. It was with reference to this method of doing business that the doctrine of the exemption of the original package grew up." In the case of *Schollenberger* v. *Pennsylvania*,[9] however, the court decided that the state of Pennsylvania could not prohibit the sale of oleomargarine by retail when it had been shipped from Rhode Island in packages containing only 10 lb each, and the original package doctrine has been sharply criticized because of the difficulty in determining what constitutes an original package as well as because of the conflict between the doctrine and the police powers of the several states. It has been urged that the doctrine be abandoned and that commodities shipped into one state from another " be treated just like other goods already there are treated."

See J. D. Uhle, " The Law Governing an Original Package," in *The American Law Register*, vol. xxix. (Philadelphia, 1890); Shackelford Miller, " The Latest Phase of the Original Package Doctrine," and M. M. Townley, " What is the Original Package Doctrine?" both in *The American Law Review*, vol. xxxv. (St Louis, 1901); also F. H. Cooke, *The Commerce Clause of the Federal Constitution* (New York, 1908).

[1] 12 Wheaton 419.
[2] Waring v. Mobile, 8 Wall. 110.
[3] May v. New Orleans, 178 U.S. 498 and *in re* McAllister (C.C.Md.), 51 Fed. 282.
[4] Woodruff v. Parham, 8 Wallace 123, and Hinson v. Lott, 8 Wallace 148.
[5] 5 Howard 504.
[6] 135 U.S. 100.

[7] See Vance v. W. A. Vandercook Company, 170 U.S. 438.
[8] 179 U.S. 343.
[9] 171 U.S. 1.

ORIHUELA, a town and episcopal see of eastern Spain, in the province of Alicante; 13 m. N.E. of Murcia and about 15 m. from the Mediterranean Sea, on the Murcia-Elche railway. Pop. (1900) 28,530. Orihuela is situated in a beautiful and exceedingly fertile *huerta*, or tract of highly cultivated land, at the foot of a limestone bridge, and on both sides of the river Segura, which divides the city into two parts, Róig and San Augusto, and is spanned by two bridges. There are remains of a Moorish fort on the hill commanding the town; and the north gateway—the Puerta del Colegio—is a fine lofty arch, surmounted by an emblematic statue and the city arms. The most prominent buildings are the episcopal palace (1733), with a frontage of 600 ft.; the town house (1843), containing important archives; and the cathedral, a small Gothic structure built on the site of a former mosque in the 14th century, and enlarged and tastelessly restored in 1829. The university of Orihuela, founded in 1568 by the archbishop of Valencia, was closed in 1835, part of the revenue being applied to the support of a college affiliated to the university of Valencia. Besides numerous primary schools there are a theological seminary and a normal school. The trade in fruit, cereals, oil and wine is considerable. There are also tanneries, dye-works and manufactures of silk, linen and woollen fabrics, leather and starch.

Orihuela was captured by the Moors in 713, and retaken by James I. of Aragon, for his father-in-law Alphonso of Castile, in 1265. It was sacked during the disturbances at the beginning of the reign of Charles V. (1520), and again in the War of Succession (1706). Local annals specially mention the plague of 1648, the flood of 1651 and the earthquake of 1829.

ORILLIA, a town and port of entry of Simcoe county, Ontario, Canada, situated 84 m. N. of Toronto, on Lake Couchiching and on the Grand Trunk railway. Pop. (1901) 4907. It is a favourite summer resort, and has steamboat communication with other ports on Lakes Simcoe and Couchiching. It contains an asylum maintained by the provincial government; also saw and grist mills and iron foundries.

ORINOCO, a river in the north of South America, falling north-east into the Atlantic between 60° 30′ and 62° 30′ W. It is approximately 1500 m. long, but it is several hundred miles longer if measured by its Guaviare branch. Lying south and east of the main stream is a vast, densely forested region called Venezuelan Guiana, diversified by ranges of low mountains, irregular broken ridges and granitic masses, which define the courses of many unexplored tributaries of the Orinoco.

In 1498, Columbus, when exploring the Gulf of Pária, which receives a large part of the outflow of the Orinoco, noted the freshness of its waters, but made no examination of their origin. The caravels of Ojeda which, in 1499, followed almost the same track as that of Columbus, probably passed in sight of one or more of the mouths of the Orinoco. The first to explore any portion of the mighty river was the reckless and daring adventurer Ordaz. In his expedition (1531-1532) he entered its principal outlet, the Boca de Navios, and, at the cost of many lives, ascended to the junction of the Meta with the parent stream. From Ordaz up to recent times the Orinoco has been the scene of many voyages of discovery, including those in quest of El Dorado, and some scientific surveys have been made, especially among its upper waters, by José Solano and Diaz de la Fuente of the Spanish boundary line commission of Yturriaga and Solano (1757-1763), Humboldt (1800) and Michelena y Rojas (1855-1857). The last ascended to the Mawaca, a point about 170 m. above the northern entrance to the Casiquiare canal, and then a few miles up the Mawaca. A little knowledge about its sources above these points was given by the savages to de la Fuente in 1759 and to Mendoza in 1764, and we are also indebted to Humboldt for some vague data.

' At the date of the discovery, the Orinoco, like the Amazon, bore different names, according to those of the tribes occupying its margins. The *conquistador* Ordaz found that, at its mouth, it was called the Uriaparia, this being the name of the cacique of the tribe there. The Caribs, holding a certain section of the river, named it the Ibirinoco, corrupted by the Spaniards into Orinoco. It was known to other tribes as the Barraguán and to others as the Maraguaca. The Cabres called it the Paragua, because it flooded such a vast area of country.

The principal affluent of the Orinoco from the Guiana district is the Ventuari, the head-waters of which are also unknown. It is an important stream, which, running south-west, joins the Orinoco about 90 m. above its Guaviare branch. Two other large tributaries of the Orinoco flow north from the interior of this mysterious Guiana region, the Caura and the Caroni. The former has recently been explored by André, who found it greatly obstructed by falls and rapids; the latter is about 800 m. long, 400 of which are more or less navigable.

South of the Guaviare, as far as the *divortium aquarum*, between it and the Rio Negro branch of the Amazon, the country is dry and only partially swept by moisture-laden winds, so that few streams of moment are found in its southern drainage area; but north of it, as far as 6° 30′ N., the north-east trade winds, which have escaped condensation in the hot lower valley of the Orinoco, beat against the cold eastern slopes of the lofty Colombian Andes, and ceaselessly pour down such vast volumes of water that the almost countless streams which flow across the plains of Colombia and western Venezuela are taxed beyond their capacity to carry it to the Orinoco, and for several months of the year they flood tens of thousands of square miles of the districts they traverse. Among these the Apure, Arauca, Meta and Guaviare hold the first rank.

The Apure is formed by two great rivers, the Uribante and Sarare. The former, which rises in the Sierra de Merida, which overlooks the Lake of Maracaibo, has 16 large affluents; the latter has its sources near the Colombian city of Pamplona, and they are only separated from the basin of the river Magdalena by the " Oriental " Andean range. From the Uribante-Sarare junction to the Orinoco the length of the Apure is 645 m., of which Codazzi makes the doubtful claim that 564 are navigable, for there are some troublesome rapids 114 m. above its mouth, where the Apure is 3 m. wide. The numerous affluents which enter it from the north water the beautiful eastern and southern slopes of the Merida, Carabobo and Caracas mountain ranges. A few of them are navigable for a short distance; among them the most important is the many-armed Portuguesa, on the main route south from the Caribbean coast to the *llanos*. A few large streams enter the lower Apure from the south, but they are frequently entangled in lateral canals, due to the slight elevation of the plains above sea-level, the waters of the Apure, especially during flood time, having opened a great number of *caños* before reaching the Orinoco.

The " Oriental " Andes of Colombia give birth to another great affluent of the Orinoco, the Arauca, which soon reaches the plain and parallels the Apure on the south. Perez says that the Sarare branch of the Apure has formed a gigantic dam across its own course by prodigious quantities of trees, brush, vines and roots, and thus, impounding its own waters, has cut a new channel to the southward across the lowlands and joined the Arauca, from which the Sarare may be reached in small craft and ascended to the vicinity of Pamplona. The Arauca is navigable for large boats and barges up to the Andes, and by sail to its middle course. In floods, unable to carry the additional water contributed by the Sarare, it overflows its banks, and by several caños gives its surplus to the Capanaparo, which, about 18 m. farther south, joins the Orinoco.

The Meta is known as such from the union of two Andean streams, the Negro and Humadea, which rise near Bogotá. At their junction, 700 ft. above sea-level, it is 1000 ft. wide and 7 ft. deep in the dry season, but in flood the Meta rises 30 ft. It is navigable up to the old " Apostadero," about 150 m. above its mouth, but launches may ascend it, in the wet season, about 900 m., to the junction of the Negro with the Humadea. In the dry season, however, it is obstructed by reefs, sandbanks, shallows, snags, trees and floating timber from the " Apostadero " up, so that even canoes find its ascent difficult, while savage hordes along its banks add to the dangers to be encountered.

The Guaviare is the next great western tributary of the Orinoco. Eugenio Alvarado, a Spanish commissioner for the boundary delimitation of Colombia with Brazil in 1759, informed the viceroy at Bogotá that the rivers Arivari and Guayabero rise between Neiva and Popayan, and unite to take the composite name of Guaviare. In those times they called it Gualbari, or Guayuare. The Guaviare is about 500 m. long, of which 300 are called navigable, although not free from obstructions. Its upper portion has many rapids and falls. The banks are fringed throughout, and the river is infested by numerous alligators, so ferocious that they attack canoes. Two-thirds of the way up, it receives its Ariari tributary from the north-west, which is navigable for large boats. Near its mouth the Guaviare is joined by its great south-western affluent, the Ynirida. Above its rapid of Mariapiri, 180 m. up, this stream runs swiftly through a rough country, but for a long distance is a succession of lakes and shallow, overflowed areas. Its head-waters do not reach the Andes.

Between the Guaviare and the Meta the Orinoco is obstructed by the famous Maipures cataract, where, in several channels, it breaks through a granite spur of the Guiana highlands for a length of about

4 m., with a total fall of about 40 ft., and then, after passing two minor reefs, reaches the Atures rapids, where it plunges through a succession of gorges for a distance of about 6 m., winding among confused masses of granite boulders, and falling about 30 ft. At the mouth of the Meta it is about 1 m. wide, but as it flows northwards it increases its width until, at the point where it receives its Apure affluent, it is over 2 m. wide in the dry season and about 7 m. in floods. It rises 32 ft. at Cariben, but at the Angostura, or narrows, where the river is but 800 ft. wide, the difference between high and low river is 50 ft., and was even 60 in 1892.

The Orinoco finds its way to the ocean through a delta of about 700 sq. m. area, so little above sea level that much of it is periodically flooded. The river is navigable for large steamers up to the raudal or rapid of Cariben, 700 m. from the sea, and to within 6 m. of the mouth of the Meta. Maintaining its eastern course from the Apure, the main stream finds its way along the southern side of the delta, where it is called the Corosimi river, and enters the sea at the Boca Grande; but in front of the Tortola island, at the beginning of the Corosimi and 100 m. from the sea, it throws northwards to the Gulf of Paria another great arm which, about 100 m. long, and known as the Rio Vagre, bounds the western side of the delta. *En route* to the gulf the Vagre sends across the delta, east and north, two *caños* or canals of considerable volume, called the Macareo and Cucuino. The delta is also cut into many irregular divisions by other canals which derive their flow from its great boundary rivers, the Corosimi and Vagre, and its numerous islands and vast swamps are covered with a dense vegetation. The Boca Grande outlet is the deepest, and is the main navigable entrance to the Orinoco at all seasons, the muddy bar usually maintaining a depth of 16 ft.

The Spanish *conquistador* and his descendants have not been a blessing to the basin of the Orinoco: All they can boast of is the destruction of its population and products, so that the number of inhabitants of one of the richest valleys in the world is less to-day than it was four centuries ago. The entire river trade centres upon Ciudad Bolivar, on the right bank of the Orinoco, 373 m. above its mouth. The only other river port of any importance is San Fernando, on the Apure. It is a stopping-point for the incipient steamer traffic of the valley, which is principally confined to the Apure and lower Orinoco. It occupies, however, but a few small steam craft. There is steam connexion between Ciudad Bolivar and the island of Trinidad. Cattle are carried by vessels from the valley to the neighbouring foreign colonies, and a few local steamers do a coasting trade between the river and the Caribbean ports of Venezuela. A transit trade with Colombia, via the Meta river, has been carried on by two small steamers, but subject to interruptions from political causes. (G. E. C.)

ORIOLE (O. Fr. *Oriol*, Lat. *aureolus*), the name once applied to a bird, from its golden colouring—the *Oriolus galbula* of Linnaeus—but now commonly used in a much wider sense. The golden oriole, which is the type of the *Passerine* family *Oriolidae*, is a far from uncommon spring-visitor to the British Islands, but has very rarely bred there. On the continent of Europe it is a well-known if not an abundant bird, and its range in summer extends so far to the east as Irkutsk, while in winter it is found in Natal and Damaraland. In India it is replaced by a closely allied form, O. *kundoo*, the mango-bird, chiefly distinguishable by the male possessing a black streak behind as well as in front of the eye; and both in Asia and Africa are several other species more or less resembling O. *galbula*, but some depart considerably from that type, assuming a black head, or even a glowing crimson, instead of the ordinary yellow colouring, while others again remain constant to the dingy type of plumage which characterizes the female of the more normal form. Among these last are the aberrant species of the group *Mimetes* or *Mimeta*, belonging to the Australian Region, respecting which A. R. Wallace pointed out, first in the Zoological Society's *Proceedings* (1863, pp. 26–28), and afterwards in his *Malay Archipelago* (ii. pp. 150–153), the very curious signs of "mimicry" (see HONEY-EATER). It is a singular circumstance that this group *Mimeta* first received its name from P. P. King (*Survey, &c. of Australia*, ii. 417) under the belief that the birds composing it belonged to the family *Meliphagidae*, which had assumed the appearance of orioles, whereas Wallace's investigations tend to show that the imitation (unconscious, of course) is on the part of the latter. The external similarity of the *Mimeta* and the *Tropidorhynchus* of the island of Bouru, one

of the Moluccas, is perfectly wonderful, and has again and again deceived some of the best ornithologists, though the birds are structurally far apart. Another genus which has been referred to the *Oriolidae*, and may here be mentioned, is *Sphecotheres*, peculiar to the Australian Region, and distinguishable from the more normal orioles by a bare space round the eye. Orioles are shy and restless birds, frequenting gardens and woods, and living on insects and fruit. The nest is pocket-shaped, of bark, grass and fibres, and the eggs are white or salmon-coloured with dark spots. The "American orioles" (see ICTERUS) belong to a different Passerine family, the *Icteridae*. (A. N.)

ORION (or OARION), in Greek mythology, son of Hyrieus (Eponymus of Hyria in Boeotia), or of Poseidon, a mighty hunter of great beauty and gigantic strength, perhaps corresponding to the "wild huntsman" of Teutonic mythology. He is also sometimes represented as sprung from the earth. He was the favourite of Eos, the dawn-goddess, who loved him and carried him off to Delos; but the gods were angry, and would not be appeased till Artemis slew him with her arrows (*Odyssey*, v. 121). According to other accounts which attribute Orion's death to Artemis, the goddess herself loved him and was deceived by the angry Apollo into shooting him by mistake; or he paid the penalty of offering violence to her, or of challenging her to a contest of quoit-throwing (Apollodorus i. 4; Hyginus, *Poet. astron.* ii. 34; Horace, *Odes*, iii. 4, 71). In another legend he was blinded by Oenopion of Chios for having violated his daughter Merope; but having made his way to the place where the sun rose, he recovered his sight (Hyginus, *loc. cit.*; Parthenius, *Erotica*, 20). He afterwards retired to Crete, where he lived the life of a hunter with Artemis; but having threatened to exterminate all living creatures on the island, he was killed by the bite of a scorpion sent by the earth-goddess (Ovid, *Fasti*, v. 537). In the lower world his shade is seen by Odysseus driving the wild beasts before him as he had done on earth (*Odyssey*, xi. 572). After his death he was changed into the constellation which is called by his name. It took the form of a warrior, wearing a girdle of three stars and a lion's skin, and carrying a club and a sword. When it rose early it was a sign of summer; when late, of winter and stormy weather; when it rose about midnight it heralded the season of vintage.

See Küentzle, *Über die Sternsagen der Griechen* (1897), and his article in Roscher's *Lexikon*; he shows that in the oldest legend Orion the constellation and Orion the hero are quite distinct, without deciding which was the earlier conception. The attempt sometimes made to attribute an astronomical origin to the myths connected with his name is unsuccessful, except in the case of Orion's pursuit of Pleione and her daughters (see PLEIADES) and his death from the bite of the scorpion; see also C. O. Müller, *Kleine Deutsche Schriften*, ii. (1848); O. Gruppe, *Griechische Mythologie*, ii. pp. 945, 952; Preller-Robert, *Griechische Mythologie* (1894), pp. 448–454; Grimm, *Teutonic Mythology* (Eng. trans., 1883), ii. p. 726, iii. p. 948.

In Astronomy.—The constellation Orion is mentioned by Homer (*Il.* xviii. 486, xxii. 29; *Od.* v. 274), and also in the Old Testament (Amos v. 8, Job ix. 9). The Hebrew name for Orion also means " fool," in reference perhaps to a mythological story of a "foolhardy, heaven-daring rebel who was chained to the sky for his impiety" (Driver). For the Assyrian names see CONSTELLATION. Ptolemy catalogued 38 stars, Tycho Brahe 42 and Hevelius 62. Orion is one of the most conspicuous constellations. It consists of three stars of the 1st magnitude, four of the 2nd, and many of inferior magnitude. a *Orionis*, or Betelgeuse, is a bright, yellowish-red star of varying magnitude (0·5 to 1·4, generally 0·9). β *Orionis* or Regel is a 1st magnitude star. γ *Orionis* or Bellatrix, and κ *Orionis* are stars of the 2nd magnitude. These four stars, in the order a, β, γ, κ, form an approximate rectangle. Three collinear stars ζ, ε and δ *Orionis* constitute the "belt of Orion"; of these ε, the central star, is of the 1st magnitude, δ of the 2nd, while ζ *Orionis* is a fine double star, its components having magnitudes 2 and 6; there is also a faint companion of magnitude 10. σ *Orionis*, very close to ζ *Orionis*, is a very fine multiple star, described by Sir William Herschel as two sets of treble stars; more stars have been revealed by larger telescopes. θ *Orionis* is a multiple star, situated in the famous nebula of Orion, one of the most beautiful in the heavens. (See NEBULA.)

ORION and ORUS, the names of several Greek grammarians, frequently confused. The following are the most important. (1) Orion of Thebes in Egypt (5th century A.D.), the teacher of Proclus the neo-Platonist and of Eudocia, the wife of the younger Theodosius. He taught at Alexandria, Caesarea in Cappadocia and Byzantium. He was the author of a partly extant etymological Lexicon (ed. F. W. Sturz, 1820), largely used by the compilers of the *Etymologicum Magnum*, the *Etymologicum Gudianum* and other similar works; a collection of maxims in three books, addressed to Eudocia, also ascribed to him by Suidas, still exists in a Warsaw MS. (2) Orus of Miletus, who, according to Ritschl, flourished not later than the 2nd century A.D., and was a contemporary of Herodian and a little junior to Phrynichus (according to Reitzenstein he was a contemporary of Orion). His chief works were treatises on orthography; on Atticisms, written in opposition to Phrynichus; on the names of nations.

See F. Ritschl, *De Oro et Orione Commentatio* (1834); R. Reitzenstein, *Geschichte der griechischen Etymologika* (1897); and article " Orion " in Smith's *Dictionary of Greek and Roman Biography.*

ORISKANY, a village of Oneida county, New York, U.S.A., about 7 m. N W. of Utica. Pop. about 800. Oriskany is served by the New York Central & Hudson River railway. There are malleable iron works and a manufactory of paper makers' felts here. In a ravine, about 2 m. west of Oriskany, was fought on the 6th of August 1777 the battle of Oriskany, an important minor engagement of the American War of Independence. On the 4th of August Gen. Nicholas Herkimer, who had been colonel of the Tyrone county (New York) militia in 1775, and had been made a brigadier-general of the state militia in 1776, had gathered about 800 militiamen at Fort Dayton (on the site of the present Herkimer, New York) for the relief of Fort Schuyler (see ROME, N.Y.) then besieged by British and Indians under Colonel Barry St Leger and Joseph Brant. On the 6th General Herkimer's force, on its march to Fort Schuyler, was ambushed by a force of British under Sir John Johnson and Indians under Joseph Brant in the ravine above mentioned. The rear portion of Herkimer's troops escaped from the trap, but were pursued by the Indians, and many of them were overtaken and killed. Between the remainder and the British and Indians there was a desperate hand-to-hand conflict, interrupted by a violent thunderstorm, with no quarter shown by either side. On hearing the firing near Fort Schuyler (incident to a sortie by Lieut.-Colonel Marinus Willett) the British withdrew, after about 200 Americans had been killed and as many more taken prisoners, the loss of the British being about the same. General Herkimer (who had advised advancing slowly, awaiting signal shots announcing the sortie, and had been called " Tory " and " coward " in consequence), though his leg had been broken by a shot at the beginning of the action, continued to direct the fighting on the American side, but died on the 16th of August as a result of the clumsy amputation of his leg. The battle, though indecisive, had an important influence in preventing St Leger from effecting a junction with General Burgoyne. The battlefield is marked by a monument erected in 1884.

See *Orderly Book of Sir John Johnson during the Oriskany Campaign* (Albany, 1882), with notes by W. L. Stone and J. W. De Peyster; *Publications* of the Oneida Historical Society, vol. I. (Utica, N.Y., 1877); and Phoebe S. Cowen, *The Herkimers and Schuylers* (Albany, 1903).

ORISSA, a tract of India, in Bengal, consisting of a British division and twenty-four tributary states. The historical capital is Cuttack; and Puri, with its temple of Jagannath, is world-famous. Orissa differs from the rest of Bengal in being under temporary settlement of land revenue. A new settlement a term of thirty years was concluded in 1900, calculated to raise the total land revenue by more than one half; the greater part of this increase being levied gradually during the first eleven years of the term. To obviate destructive inundations and famines, the Orissa system of canals has been constructed, with a capital outlay of nearly two millions sterling.

(See MAHANADI). The province is traversed by the East Coast railway, which was opened throughout from Calcutta to Madras in 1901.

The DIVISION OF ORISSA consists of the five districts of Cuttack, Puri, Balasore, Sambalpur and the forfeited state of Angul. Total area 13,770 sq. m.; pop. (1901) 5,003,121, showing an increase of 7% in the decade. According to the census of 1901 the total number of persons in all India speaking Oriya was more than 9½ millions, showing that the linguistic area (extending into Madras and the Central Provinces) is much larger than the political province.

The whole of Orissa is holy ground. On the southern bank of the Baitarani shrine rises after shrine in honour of Siva, the All-Destroyer. On leaving the stream the pilgrim enters Jajpur, literally the city of sacrifice, the headquarters of the region of pilgrimage sacred to the wife of the All-Destroyer. There is not a fiscal division in Orissa without its community of cenobites, scarcely a village without consecrated lands, and not a single ancient family that has not devoted its best acres to the gods. Every town is filled with temples, and every hamlet has its shrine. The national reverence of the Hindus for holy places has been for ages concentrated on Puri, sacred to Vishnu under his title of Jagannath, the Lord of the World. Besides its copious water-supply in time of high flood, Orissa has an average rainfall of 62½ in. per annum. Nevertheless, the uncontrolled state of the water-supply has subjected the country from time immemorial to droughts no less than to inundation. Thus the terrible famine of 1865-1866, which swept away one-fourth of the entire population, was followed in 1866 by a flood which destroyed crops to the value of £3,000,000. Since then much has been done by government to husband the abundant water-supply.

The early history of the kingdom of Orissa (Odra-desa), as recorded in the archives of the temple of Jagannath, is largely mythical. A blank in the records from about 50 B.C. to A.D. 319 corresponds to a period of Yavana occupation and Buddhist influence, during which the numerous rock monasteries of Orissa were excavated. The founder of the Kesari or Lion dynasty, which ruled from A.D. 474 to 1132, is said to have restored the worship of Jagannath, and under this line the great Sivaite temple at Bhuvaneswar was constructed. In 1132 a new line (the Gajapati dynasty) succeeded, and Vishnu took the place of Siva in the royal worship. This dynasty was extinguished in 1532-1534, and in 1578, after half a century of war, Orissa became a province of the Mogul empire. It nominally passed to the British in 1765, by the Diwani grant of Bengal, Bhar and Orissa; but at that time it was occupied by the Mahratta raja of Nagpur, from whom it was finally conquered in 1803.

The TRIBUTARY STATES OF ORISSA, known also as the Tributary Mahals, or the Garhjats, occupy the hills between the British districts and the Central Provinces. The most important are Mayurbhanj, Keonjhar, Dhenkanal, Baud and Nayagarh. In 1905 five Oriya-speaking states (Bamra, Rairakhol, Sonpur, Patna and Kalahandi) were added from the Central Provinces and two (Gangpur and Bonai) from the Chota Nagpur states. This made the total area 28,046 sq. m. and the pop. (1901) 3,173,395.

Up to the year 1888 some doubt existed as to the actual position of the Tributary states of Orissa; but in that year the secretary of state accepted the view that they did not form part of British India, and modified powers were handed over to the Orissa chiefs under the control of a superintendent.

See Sir W. W. Hunter, *Orissa* (1872).

ORISTANO, a town and archiepiscopal see of Sardinia, situated 23 ft. above sea-level, about 3 m. from the eastern shore of a gulf on the W. coast, to which it gives its name, and 59 m. N. by W. of Cagliari by rail. Pop. (1901) 7107. The town preserves some scanty remains of the walls (dating from the end of the 13th century), by which it was surrounded, and two gates, the Porta Manna, surmounted by a lofty square tower, known also as the Torre S. Cristoforo, and the Porta Marina. The houses are largely constructed of sun-dried bricks, and are low, so that the area of the town is considerable in proportion to its population.

The cathedral was reconstructed in 1733 in the baroque style, and scanty traces of the original building of the 12th century exist (see D. Scano in *L' Arte*, 1901, p. 359, 1903, p. 15): and also in *Storia dell' arte in Sardegna dal XI. al XIV. secolo*, Cagliari-Sássari, 1907). Some statuettes and sculptured slabs partly belonging to its pulpit, perhaps the work of Andrea Pisano, have been found; upon the reverse side of two of the slabs are still older reliefs of the 8th or 9th century; so that the slabs perhaps originally came from Tharros. In the sacristy is some fine silverwork. The church of S. Francesco also dates from the end of the 13th century, but has been altered. A fine statue by Nino, son of Andrea, is preserved here. Two m. south of Oristano is the village of S. Giusta, with a beautiful Romanesque church of the Pisan period dedicated to this saint (D. Scano, *Bollettino dell' arte*, Feb. 1907, p. 8), containing several antique columns. It was once an independent episcopal see. The lagoons on the coast are full of fish, but are a cause of malaria. The environs are fertile, and a quantity of garden produce is grown, while good wine (*vernaccia*) is also made, and also ordinary pottery in considerable quantities, supplying most of the island. The bridge crossing the river Tirso, a little to the north of the town, over 300 ft. long, with five arches, took the place, in 1870, of an old one which is said to have been of Roman origin. A m. south of the mouth of this river is the landing-place for shipping. The large orange groves of Milis lie 13 m. N of Oristano at the base of Monte Ferru, where they are sheltered from the wind. The finest belong to the Marchese Boyl, whose plantation contains some 500,000 orange and lemon trees. The inhabitants of Milis manufacture reed baskets and mats, which they sell throughout Sardinia.

Oristano occupies the site of the Roman Othoca, the point at which the inland road and the coast road from Carales to Turris Libisonis bifurcated, but otherwise an unimportant place, overshadowed by Tharros. The medieval town is said to have been founded in 1070. It was the seat from the 11th century onwards of the *giudici* (judges) of Arborea, one of the four divisions of the island. Almost the last of these judges was Eleonora (1347–1403); after her death Oristano became the seat of a marquisate, which was suppressed in 1478. The frontier castles of Monreale and Sanluri, some 20 and 30 m. respectively to the S.S.E., were the scene of much fighting between the Aragonese government and the *giudici* and marquises of Arborea in the 14th and 15th centuries. (T A.)

ORIYA (properly *Oṛiyā*), the Aryan language of Odra or Orissa in India. It is the vernacular not only of that province but also of the adjoining districts and native states of Madras and of the Central Provinces. In 1901 it was spoken by 9,687,429 people. It is closely related to Bengali and Assamese, and with them and with Bihari it forms the Eastern Group of the Indo-Aryan vernaculars. See BENGALI.

ORIZABA (Aztec, *Citlaltepetl*, "star mountain"), an extinct or dormant volcano, on the boundary between the Mexican states of Puebla and Vera Cruz and very nearly on the 19th parallel. It rises from the south-eastern margin of the great Mexican plateau to an elevation of 18,314 ft., according to Scovell and Bunsen's measurements in 1891–1892, or 18,250 and 18,209 ft. according to other authorities, and 18,701 (5700 metres) by the Comisión Geográfica Exploradora. It is the highest peak in Mexico and the second highest in North America. Its upper timber line is about 13,500 ft. above sea-level, and Hans Gadow found patches of apparently permanent snow at an elevation of 14,400 ft. on its S.E. side in 1902. The first ascent of Orizaba was made by Reynolds and Maynard in 1848, since when other successful attempts have been made and many failures have been recorded. Its last eruptive period was 1545–1566, and the volcano is now considered to be extinct, although Humboldt records that smoke was seen issuing from its summit as late as the beginning of the 19th century.

ORIZABA (Indian name *Ahuaializ-apan*, pleasant waters), a city of Mexico in the state of Vera Cruz, 82 m. by rail W.S.W. of the port of Vera Cruz. Pop. (1900) 32,894, including a large percentage of Indians and half-breeds. The Mexican railway affords frequent communication with the City of Mexico and Vera Cruz, and a short line (4½ m.) connects with Ingenio, an industrial village. Orizaba stands in a fertile, well-watered, and richly wooded valley of the Sierra Madre Oriental, 4025 ft. above sea-level, and about 18 m. S. of the snow-crowned volcano that bears its name. It has a mild, humid and healthful climate. The public edifices include the parish church of San Miguel, a chamber of commerce, a handsome theatre, and some hospitals. The city is the centre of a rich agricultural region which produces sugar, rum, tobacco and Indian corn. In colonial times, when tobacco was one of the crown monopolies, Orizaba was one of the districts officially licensed to produce it. It is also a manufacturing centre of importance, having good water power from the *Rio Blanco* and producing cotton and woollen fabrics. Its cotton factories are among the largest in the republic. Paper is also made at Cocolapan in the canton of Orizaba. The forests in this vicinity are noted for orchids and ferns. An Indian town called *Ahuaializapan*, subject to Aztec rule, stood here when Cortes arrived on the coast. The Spanish town that succeeded it did not receive its charter until 1774, though it was one of the stopping-places between Vera Cruz and the capital. In 1862 it was the headquarters of the French.

ORKHON INSCRIPTIONS, ancient Turkish inscriptions of the 8th century A.D., discovered near the river Orkhon to the south of Lake Baikal in 1889. They are written in an alphabet derived from an Aramaic source and recount the history of the northern branch of the Turks or Tu-kiue of Chinese historians. See TURKS.

ORKNEY, EARL OF, a Scottish title held at different periods by various families, including its present possessors the Fitz-maurices. The Orkney Islands (q.v.) were ruled by jarls or earls under the supremacy of the kings of Norway from very early times to about 1360, many of these jarls being also earls of Caithness under the supremacy of the Scottish kings. Perhaps the most prominent of them were a certain Paul (d. 1099) who assisted the Norwegian king, Harald III. Haardraada, when he invaded England in 1066; and his grandson Paul the Silent, who built, at least in part, the cathedral of St Magnus at Kirkwall. They were related to the royal families of Scotland and Norway.

In its more modern sense the earldom dates from about 1380, and the first family to hold it was that of Sinclair, Sir Henry Sinclair (d. c. 1400) of Roslin, near Edinburgh, being recognized as earl by the king of Norway. Sir Henry was the son of Sir William Sinclair, who was killed by the Saracens whilst accompanying Sir James Douglas, the bearer of the Bruce's heart, to Palestine in 1330, and on the maternal side was the grandson of Malise, who called himself earl of Strathearn, Caithness and Orkney. He ruled the islands almost like a king, and employed in his service the Venetian travellers Nicolo and Antonio Zeno. His son Henry (d. 1418) was admiral of Scotland and was taken prisoner by the English in 1406, together with Prince James, afterwards King James I.; his grandson William, the 3rd earl (c. 1404–1480), was chancellor of Scotland and took some part in public affairs. In 1455 William was created earl of Caithness, and in 1470 he resigned his earldom of Orkney to James III. of Scotland, who had just acquired the sovereignty of these islands through his marriage with Margaret, daughter of Christian I., king of Denmark and Norway. In 1567 Queen Mary's lover, James Hepburn, earl of Bothwell, was created duke of Orkney, and in 1581 her half-brother Robert Stewart (d. 1592), an illegitimate son of James V., was made earl of Orkney. Robert, who was abbot of Holyrood, joined the party of the reformers and was afterwards one of the principal enemies of the regent Morton. His son Patrick acted in a very arbitrary manner in the Orkneys, where he set the royal authority at defiance; in 1609 he was seized and imprisoned, and, after his bastard son Robert had suffered death for heading a rebellion, he himself was executed in February 1614, when his honours and estates were forfeited.

In 1696 Lord George Hamilton was created earl of Orkney (see below). He married Elizabeth Villiers (see below), and he was succeeded by his daughter Anne (d. 1756), the wife of

William O'Brien, 4th earl of Inchiquin. Anne's daughter Mary (*c.* 1721–1791) and her granddaughter Mary (1755–1831) were both countesses of Orkney in their own right; the younger Mary married Thomas Fitzmaurice (1742–1793), son of John Petty, earl of Shelburne, and was succeeded in the title by her grandson, Thomas John Hamilton Fitzmaurice (1803–1877), whose descendants still hold the earldom.

ORKNEY, ELIZABETH HAMILTON, COUNTESS OF (*c.* 1657–1733), mistress of the English King William III., daughter of Colonel Sir Edward Villiers of Richmond, was born about 1657. Her mother, Frances Howard, daughter of the 2nd earl of Suffolk, was governess to the princesses Mary and Anne, and secured place and influence for her children in Mary's household. Edward Villiers, afterwards created 1st earl of Jersey (1656–1711), became master of the horse, while his sisters Anne and Elizabeth were among the maids of honour who accompanied Mary to the Hague on her marriage. Elizabeth Villiers became William's acknowledged mistress in 1680. After his accession to the English crown he settled on her a large share of the confiscated Irish estates of James II. This grant was revoked by parliament, however, in 1699. Mary's distrust of Marlborough was fomented by Edward Villiers, and the bitter hostility between Elizabeth Villiers and the duchess of Marlborough perhaps helped to secure the duke's disgrace with William. Shortly after Mary's death, William, actuated, it is said, by his wife's expressed wishes, broke with Elizabeth Villiers, who was married to her cousin, Lord George Hamilton, fifth son of the 3rd duke of Hamilton, in November 1695. The husband was gratified early in the next year with the titles of earl of Orkney, viscount of Kirkwall and Baron Dechmont. The countess of Orkney served her husband's interests with great skill, and the marriage proved a happy one. She died in London on the 19th of April 1733.

ORKNEY, GEORGE HAMILTON, EARL OF (1666–1737), British soldier, was the fifth son of William, duke of Hamilton, and was trained for the military career by his uncle, Lord Dumbarton, in the 1st Foot. In 1689 he became lieut.-colonel and a few months later brevet colonel. He served at the battles of the Boyne and of Aughrim, and, at the head of the Royal Fusiliers, at Steinkirk. As colonel of his old regiment, the 1st Foot, he took part in the battle of Landen or Neerwinden, and in the siege of Namur, serving also at Athlone and Limerick in the Irish war. At Namur Hamilton received a severe wound, and in recognition of his services was made a brigadier. In 1695 he married Elizabeth Villiers (see above), who was "the wisest woman" Swift "ever knew." The following year he was made earl of Orkney in the Scottish peerage. As a major-general he took the field with Marlborough in Flanders, and on January 1st, 1703–1704 he became lieutenant-general. At Blenheim it was Orkney's command which carried the village, and in June 1705 he led a flying column which marched from the Moselle to the rescue of Liége. At Ramillies he headed the pursuit of the defeated French, at Oudenarde he played a distinguished part and in 1708 he captured the forts of St Amand and St Martin at Tournay. At the desperately fought battle of Malplaquet Lord Orkney's battalions led the assault on the French entrenchments, and suffered very severe losses. He remained with the army in Flanders till the end of the war, as " general of the foot," and at the peace he was made colonel-commandant of the 1st Foot as a reward for his services. He occupied various civil and military posts of importance, culminating with the appointment of " field marshal of all His Majesty's forces " in 1736. This appointment is the first instance of field marshal's rank (as now understood) in the British Service. A year later he died in London.

ORKNEY ISLANDS, a group of islands, forming a county, off the north coast of Scotland. The islands are separated from the mainland by the Pentland Firth, which is 6½ m. wide between Brough Ness in the island of South Ronaldshay and Duncansbay Head in Caithness-shire. The group is commonly estimated to consist of 67 islands, of which 30 are inhabited (though in the case of four of them the population comprises only the light-house attendants), but the number may be increased to as many as 90 by including rocky islets more usually counted with the islands of which they probably once formed part. The Orkneys lie between 58° 41' and 59° 24' N., and 2° 22' and 3° 26' W., measure 50 m. from N.E. to S.W. and 29 m. from E. to W., and cover 240,476 acres or 375·5 sq. m. Excepting on the west coasts of the larger islands, which present rugged cliff scenery remarkable both for beauty and for colouring, the group lies somewhat low and is of bleak aspect, owing to the absence of trees. The highest hills are found in Hoy. The only other islands containing heights of any importance are Pomona, with Ward Hill (880 ft.), and Wideford (740 ft.) and Rousay. Nearly all of the islands possess lakes, and Loch Harray and Loch Stenness in Pomona attain noteworthy proportions. The rivers are merely streams draining the high land. Excepting on the west fronts of Pomona, Hoy and Rousay, the coast-line of the islands is deeply indented, and the islands themselves are divided from each other by straits generally called *sounds* or *firths*, though off the north-east of Hoy the designation *Bring Deeps* is used, south of Pomona is Scapa *Flow* and to the south-west of Eday is found the *Fall* of Warness. The very names of the islands indicate their nature, for the terminal *a* or *ay* is the Norse *ey*, meaning " island," which is scarcely disguised even in the words Pomona and Hoy. The islets are usually styled *holms* and the isolated rocks *skerries*. The tidal currents, or races, or *roost* (as some of them are called locally, from the Icelandic) off many of the isles run with enormous velocity, and whirlpools are of frequent occurrence, and strong enough at times to prove a source of danger to small craft. The charm of the Orkneys does not lie in their ordinary physical features, so much as in beautiful atmospheric effects, extraordinary examples of light and shade, and rich coloration of cliff and sea.

Geology.—All the islands of this group are built up entirely of Old Red Sandstone. As in the neighbouring mainland of Caithness, these rocks rest upon the metamorphic rocks of the eastern schists, as may be seen on Pomona, where a narrow strip is exposed between Stromness and Inganess, and again in the small island of Graemsay; they are represented by grey gneiss and granite. The upper division of the Old Red Sandstone is found only in Hoy, where it forms the Old Man and neighbouring cliffs on the N.W. coast., The Old Man presents a characteristic section, for it exhibits a thick pile of massive, current-bedded red sandstones, resting near the foot of the pinnacle, upon a thin bed of amygdaloidal porphyrite, which in its turn lies unconformably upon steeply inclined flagstones. This bed of volcanic rock may be followed northward in the cliffs, and it may be noticed that it thickens considerably in that direction. The Lower Old Red Sandstone is represented by well-bedded flagstones over most of the islands; in the south of Pomona these are faulted against an overlying series of massive red sandstones, but a gradual passage from the flagstones to the sandstones may be followed from Westray S.E. into Eday. A strong synclinal fold traverses Eday and Shapinsay, the axis being N. and S. Near Haco's Ness in Shapinsay there is a small exposure of amygdaloidal diabase which is of course older than that in Hoy. Many indications of ice action are found in these islands; striated surfaces are to be seen on the cliffs in Eday and Westray, in Kirkwall Bay and on Stennie Hill in Eday; boulder clay, with marine shells, and with many boulders of rocks foreign to the islands (flint, oolitic limestone, flint, &c.), which must have been brought up from the region of Moray Firth, rests upon the old strata in many places. Local moraines are found in some of the valleys in Pomona and Hoy.

Climate and Industries.—The climate is remarkably temperate and equable for so northerly a latitude. The average temperature for the year is 46° F., for winter 39° F. and for summer 54° 3' F. The winter months are January, February and March, the last being the coldest. Spring never begins till April, and it is the middle of June before the heat grows genial. September is frequently the finest month, and at the end of October or beginning of November occurs the peerie (or little) summer, the counterpart of the St Martin's summer of more southerly climes. The average annual rainfall varies from 33·4 in. to 37 in. Fogs occur during summer and early autumn, and furious gales may be expected four or five times in the year, when the crash of the Atlantic waves is audible for 20 m. To tourists one of the fascinations of the islands is their " nightless summers." On the longest day the sun rises at 3 o'clock A.M. and sets at 9.25 P.M., and darkness is unknown, it being possible to read at midnight. Winter, however, is long and depressing. On the shortest day the sun rises at 9.10 A.M. and sets at 3.17 P.M. The soil generally is a sandy loam or a strong but friable clay, and very fertile. Large quantities of seaweed as well as lime and marl are available for manure. Until the middle of the 19th century the methods of agriculture were of a primitive character, but since then they have been entirely transformed, and Orcadian farming is now not below the average standard of the Scottish lowlands. The crofters' houses have been rebuilt of stone and lime, and are superior to those in most parts of the Highlands. The holdings run fairly small, the average being between 30 and 40 acres. Practically the only grain crops that are cultivated are oats (which greatly predominate) and barley, while the favoured root crops are turnips (much the most extensively grown) and potatoes. Not half of the area has been brought under cultivation, and the acreage under wood is insignificant. The raising of live stock is rigorously pursued. Shorthorns and polled Angus are the commonest breeds of cattle; the sheep are mostly Cheviots and a Cheviot-Leicester cross, but the native sheep are still reared in considerable numbers in Hoy and South Ronaldshay, pigs are also kept on several of the islands, and the horses—as a rule hardy, active and small, though larger than the famous Shetland ponies—are very numerous, but mainly employed in connexion with agricultural work. The woollen trade once promised to reach considerable dimensions, but towards the end of the 18th century was superseded by the linen (for which flax came to be largely grown); and when this in turn collapsed before the products of the mills of Dundee, Dunfermline and Glasgow, straw-plaiting was taken up, though only to be killed in due time by the competition of the south. The kelp industry, formerly of at least minor importance, has ceased. Sandstone is quarried on several islands, and distilleries are found in Pomona (near Kirkwall and Stromness). But apart from agriculture the principal industry is fishing. For several centuries the Dutch practically monopolized the herring fishery, but when their supremacy was destroyed by the salt duty, the Orcadians failed to seize the opportunity thus presented, and George Barry (d. 1805) says that in his day the fisheries were almost totally neglected. The industry, however, has now been organized, and over 2000 persons are employed in the various branches of it. The great catches are herring, cod and ling, but lobsters and crabs are also exported in large quantities. There is a regular communication by steamer between Stromness and Kirkwall, and Thurso, Wick, Aberdeen and Leith, and also between Kirkwall and Lerwick and other points of the Shetlands.

Population and Administration.—In 1891 the population numbered 30,453, and in 1901 it was 28,699, or 67 persons to the sq. m. In 1901 there were 70 persons who spoke Gaelic and English, but none who spoke Gaelic only. Orkney unites with Shetland to send one member to parliament, and Kirkwall, the county town and the only royal burgh, is one of the Wick district groups of parliamentary burghs. There is a combination poorhouse at Kirkwall, where there are also two hospitals. Orkney forms a sheriffdom with Shetland and Caithness, and a resident sheriff-substitute sits at Kirkwall. The county is under the school-board jurisdiction, but at Kirkwall and Stromness there are public schools giving secondary education.

The Inhabited Islands.—Premising that they are more or less scattered, and that several lie on the same plane, the following list gives the majority of the inhabited islands from south to north, the number within brackets indicating the population. Sule Skerry (3) and the Pentland Skerries (8) lie at the eastern entrance of the Pentland Firth; Swona (23), 1½ m. from the mainland, belongs to Caithness and is situated in the parish of Canisbay; South Ronaldshay (1991) is the best cultivated and most fertile of the southern isles of the group. On Hoxa Head, to the west of the large village of St Margaret's Hope, is a *broch*, or round tower, and the island contains, besides, examples of Picts' houses and standing stones. Hoy (*q.v.*; 1216) is the southernmost of the larger islands. Flotta (372), east of Hoy, was the home for a long time of the Scandinavian compiler of the *Codex Flatticensis*, which furnished Thormodr Torfaeus (1636-1719), the Icelandic antiquary, with many of the facts for his *History of Norway*, more particularly with reference to the Norse occupation of Orkney. Pharay (59) also lies E. of Hoy Burray (677) is famous for the *broch* from which the island takes its name (Borgarey, Norse, " island of the broch "). The tower stands on the north-western shore, is 15 ft. high, has walls from 15 to 20 ft. thick, built of layers of flat stones without cement or mortar, and an interior diameter of 40 ft. It is entered from the east by a passage, on each side of which there is a small chamber constructed within the thickness of the wall. Similar chambers occur on the west, north and south sides, accessible only from the interior. Adjoining the southern chamber is the inside stair conducting to the top of the *broch*; of this stair some twenty steps remain. Between Hoy and Pomona are Hunda (8), Cava (17), and Graemsay (195), which has excellent soil and is mostly under cultivation. The isle is surrounded by shoals, and high-level and low-level lighthouses have been erected, the one at the north-west and the other at the north-east corner. The cliffs of Copinshay (10) are a favourite haunt of sea-birds, which are captured by the cragsmen for their feathers and eggs. Half a mile to the N.E. is the great rock which, from a fancied resemblance to a horse rearing its head from the sea, is called the Horse of Copinshay. Pomona (*q.v.*; 16,235) is the principal

island, and as such is known also as Mainland. Shapinshay (765) was the birthplace of William Irving, father of Washington Irving. It possesses several examples of Pictish and Scandinavian antiquities, such as the " Odin stone " and the *broch* of Burrowstone. Balfour Castle, a mansion in the Scottish Baronial style built in 1848, is situated near the south-western extremity of the island. The island takes its name from Hjalpand, a Norse viking. Gairsay (33) was the residence of Sweyn Asleifson, the rover, celebrated in the *Orkneyinga Saga* for his exploits as a trencherman and his feats in battle. Stronsay (1159) is a busy station of the herring fishery, and is also largely under cultivation. At Lamb Head, its south-easterly point, is a broch and Pictish pier, and about 2 m. farther north, on Odin Bay, is a round pit in the rocks called the Vat of Kirbuster. The well of Kildinguie was once resorted to as a specific for leprosy. Papa Stronsay (16) commemorates in its name, as others of both the Orkneys and Shetlands do, the labours of the Celtic *papae*, or missionaries, who preached the Christian gospel before the arrival of the Northmen. The adjacent Veira or Wire has a population of 60. Egilshay (142) is the island on which St Magnus was murdered by his cousin Hacco in 1115. It derives its name— Church (*ecclesia*) Island—from the little church of St Magnus, now in ruins, consisting of a chancel 15 ft. long, and nave 30 ft. long. The building has a round tower at the west end of the nave. The tower resembles similar constructions found beside Irish churches of the 7th and 8th centuries and has walls 3 ft. thick. It is doubtful whether it must be ascribed to the Celtic evangelists or to a much later period—not earlier than the 12th century. On Rousay (627) the cairn of Blotchnie Field (811 ft.), the highest point of the island, commands a beautiful survey of the northern isles of the archipelago. At the southern base of the hill stands the fine mansion of Trumbland House. Eday (596) contains several specimens of weems, mounds and standing stones. It affords good pasturage and has sandstone quarries. Carrick village, once a burgh of barony, with salt pans and other manufactures, was named after the earl of Carrick, brother of Patrick Stewart, 2nd earl of Orkney (d. 1614). It was off this island that John Gow, the pirate, was taken in 1725. Sanday (1727), with an area of 19 sq. m., is one of the largest of the northern isles, and yields excellent crops of potatoes and grain. It has safe harbours, in the north at Otterwick and in the south at Kettletoft. The antiquities include a *broch* in Elsness. Pharay (47) lies W. of Edey. Westray (1956), one of the seats of the cod fishery, has a good harbour at Pier-o'-wall. Noltland Castle, in the vicinity, is interesting as having been proposed as the refuge of Queen Mary after her flight from Loch Leven. It dates from the 15th century or even earlier, and was at one time the property of Sir Gilbert Balfour, the Master of Queen Mary's Household. The building, now in ruins, was never completed. On one side of the inner court, to which a finely ornamental doorway gives access, is a large hall with a vaulted ceiling of stone, 30 ft. high. The cliffs and overhanging crags at Noup Head (250 ft.), the most westerly point, are remarkably picturesque. An isolated portion, divided from the headland by a narrow chasm, is known as the Stack of Noup. Gentleman's Cave, 1 m. to the south, was so called from the circumstance that it afforded shelter to five of the leading followers of Prince Charles Edward, who lay here during the winter of 1745-1746. Papa Westray (295) and North Ronaldshay (442) are the most northerly islands of the group. The latter is only reached from Sanday, from which it is separated by a dangerous firth 2½ m. wide. The monumental stone with Ogham inscription, which was discovered in the *broch* of Burrian, must date from the days of the early Christian missionaries.

History.—The Orkneys were the *Orcades* of classical writers, and the word is probably derived from the Norse *Orka*, seal, and *ey*, island. The original inhabitants were Picts, evidence of whose occupation still exists in numerous weems or underground houses, chambered mounds, barrows or burial mounds, brochs or round towers, and stone circles and standing stones. Such implements as have survived are of the rudest description, and include querns or stone handmills for grinding corn, stone worls and bone combs employed in primitive forms of woollen manufacture, and specimens of simple pottery ware. If, as seems likely, the Dalriadic Scots towards the beginning of the 6th century established a footing in the islands, their success was short-lived, and the Picts regained power and kept it until dispossessed by the Norsemen in the 9th century In the wake of the Scots incursionists followed the Celtic missionaries about 565. They were companions of St Columba and their efforts to convert the folk to Christianity seem to have impressed the popular imagination, for several islands bear the epithet " Papa " in commemoration of the preachers. Norse pirates having made the islands the headquarters of their buccaneering expeditions indifferently against their own Norway and the coasts and isles of Scotland, Harold Haarfager (" Fair Hair ") subdued the rovers in 875 and both the Orkneys and Shetlands to Norway. They remained under the rule of Norse earls until 1231, when the line of the jarls became extinct. In that year the earldom of Caithness was granted to Magnus, second son of the earl of Angus, when the king of Norway apparently confirmed in the title. In 1468 the Orkneys and Shetlands were pledged by Christian I. of Denmark for the payment of the dowry of his daughter Margaret, betrothed to James III. of Scotland, and as the money was never paid, their connexion with the crown of Scotland has been perpetual. In 1471 James bestowed the castle and lands of Ravenscraig in Fife on William, earl of Orkney, in exchange for all his rights to the earldom of Orkney, which, by act of parliament passed on the 20th of February of the same year, was annexed to the Scottish crown. In 1564 Lord Robert Stewart, natural son of James V., who had visited Kirkwall twenty-four years before, was made sheriff of the Orkneys and Shetlands, and received possession of the estates of the *udallers*; in 1581 he was created earl of Orkney by James IV., the charter being ratified ten years later to his son Patrick, but in 1615 the earldom was again annexed to the crown. The islands were the *rendezvous* of Montrose's expedition in 1650 which culminated in his imprisonment and death. During the Protectorate they were visited by a detachment of Cromwell's troops, who initiated the inhabitants into various industrial arts and new methods of agriculture. In 1707 the islands were granted to the earl of Morton in mortgage, redeemable by the Crown on payment of £30,000, and subject to an annual feu-duty of £500; but in 1766 his estates were sold to Sir Lawrence Dundas, ancestor of the earls of Zetland. In early times both the archbishop of Hamburg and the archbishop of York disputed with the Norwegians ecclesiastical jurisdiction over the Orkneys and the right of consecrating bishops; but ultimately the Norwegian bishops, the first of whom was William the Old, consecrated in 1102, continued the canonical succession. The see remained vacant from 1580 to 1606, and from 1638 till the Restoration, and, after the accession of William III., the episcopacy was finally abolished (1697), although many of the clergy refused to conform. The topography of the Orkneys is wholly Norse, and the Norse tongue, at last extinguished by the constant influx of settlers from Scotland, lingered until the end of the 18th century. Readers of Scott's *Pirate* will remember the frank contempt which Magnus Troil expressed for the Scots, and his opinions probably accurately reflected the general Norse feeling on the subject. When the islands were given as security for the princess's dowry, there seems reason to believe that it was intended to redeem the pledge, because it was then stipulated that the Norse system of government and the law of St Olaf should continue to be observed in Orkney and Shetland. Thus the *udal* succession and mode of land tenure (or, that is, absolute freehold as distinguished from feudal tenure) still obtain to some extent, and the remaining *udallers* hold their lands and pass them on without written title. Among well-known Orcadians may be mentioned James Atkine (1613-1687), bishop first of Moray and afterwards of Galloway; Murdoch McKenzie (d. 1797), the hydrographer; Malcolm Laing (1762-1818), author of the *History of Scotland from the Union of the Crowns to the Union of the Kingdoms*; Mary Brunton (1778-1818), author of *Self-Control, Discipline* and other novels; Samuel Laing (1780-1868), author of *A Residence in Norway*, and translator of the *Heimskringla*, the Icelandic chronicle of the kings of Norway; Thomas Stewart Traill (1781-1862), professor of medical jurisprudence in Edinburgh University and editor of the 8th edition of the *Encyclopaedia Britannica*; Samuel Laing (1812-1897), chairman of the London, Brighton & South Coast railway, and introducer of the system of "parliamentary" trains with fares of one penny a mile; Dr John Rae (1813-1893), the Arctic explorer; and William Balfour Baikie (1825-1864), the African traveller.

BIBLIOGRAPHY.—*The Orkneyinga Saga*, ed. G. Vigfusson, translated by Sir George Dasent (1887-1894), and the edition of Dr Joseph Anderson (1873); James Wallace, *Account of the Islands of Orkney* (1700; new ed., 1884); George Low, *Tour through the Islands of Orkney and Shetland in 1774* (1879); G. B...ry, *History of Orkney* (1805, 1867); Daniel Gorrie, *Summers and Winters in the Orkneys*

(1868); D. Balfour, *Odal Rights and Feudal Wrongs* (1860); J. Fergusson, *The Brochs and Rude Stone Monuments of the Orkney Islands* (1877); J. B. Craven, *History of the Episcopal Church in Orkney* (1883); J. R. Tudor, *Orkney and Shetland* (1883).

ORLÉANAIS, one of the provinces into which France was divided before the Revolution. It was the country around Orleans, the *pagus Aurelianensis*; it lay on both banks of the Loire, and for ecclesiastical purposes formed the diocese of Orleans. It was in the possession of the Capet family before the advent of Hugh Capet to the throne of France in 987, and in 1344 Philip VI. gave it with the title of duke to Philip (d. 1375), one of his younger sons. In a geographical sense the region around Orleans is sometimes known as Orléanais, but this is somewhat smaller than the former province.

See A. Thomas, *Les États provinciaux de la France centrale* (1879).

ORLEANISTS, a French political party which arose out of the Revolution, and ceased to have a separate existence shortly after the establishment of the third republic in 1872. It took its name from the Orleans branch of the house of Bourbon, the descendants of the duke of Orleans, the younger brother of Louis XIV., who were its chiefs. The political aim of the Orleanists may be said to have been to find a common measure for the monarchical principle and the "rights of man" as set forth by the revolutionary leaders in 1789. The articles on Philippe, nicknamed Égalité (see ORLEANS, L.P.J., duke of), and his son LOUIS PHILIPPE, king of the French (1830-1848), will show the process of events by which it came to pass that the Orleans princes became the more or less successful advocates of this attempted compromise between old and new. It may be noted here, however, that a certain attitude of opposition, and of patronage of " freedom," was traditional in this branch of the house of Bourbon. Saint-Simon tells us that the regent Orleans who died in 1723 was in the habit of avowing his admiration for English liberty—at least in safe company and private conversation. Égalité, who had reasons to dislike King Louis XVI. and his queen, Marie Antoinette, stepped naturally into the position of spokesman of the liberal royalists of the early revolutionary time, and it was a short step from that position to the attitude of liberal candidates for the throne, as against the elder branch of the royal house which claimed to reign by divine right. The elder branch as represented by Louis XVIII. was prepared to grant (*octroyer*), and did grant, a charter of liberties. The count of Chambord, the last of the line (the Spanish Bourbons who descended directly from Louis XIV. were considered to be barred by the renunciation of Philip V. of Spain), was equally ready to grant a constitution. But these princes claimed to rule "in chief of God" and to confer constitutional rights on their subjects of their own free will, and mere motion. This feudal language and these mystic pretensions offended a people so devoted to principles as the French, and so acute in drawing deductions from premises, for they concluded, not unreasonably, that rights granted as a favour were always subject to revocation as a punishment. Therefore those of them who considered a monarchical government as more beneficial to France than a republic, but who were not disposed to hold their freedom subject to the pleasure of a king, were either Bonapartists who professed to rule by the choice of the nation, or supporters of the Orleans princes who were ready to reign by an " original compact " and by the will of the people. The difference therefore between the supporters of the elder line, or Legitimists, and the Orleanists was profound, for it went down to the very foundations of government.

The first generation of Orleanists, the immediate supporters of Philippe Égalité, were swamped in the turmoil of the great revolution. Yet it has been justly pointed out by Albert Sorel in his *L'Europe et la révolution française*, that they subsisted under the Empire, and that they came naturally to the front when the revival of liberalism overthrew the restored legitimate monarchy of Louis XVIII. and Charles X. During the Restoration, 1815-1830, everything tended to identify the liberals with the Orleanists. Legitimism was incompatible with constitutional freedom. Bonapartism was in eclipse, and was moreover essentially a Caesarism which in the hands of the great Napoleon had been a despotism, calling itself democratic for no better reason than because it reduced all men to an equality of submission to a master. Those rights of equality before the law, and in social life, which had been far dearer to Frenchmen of the revolutionary epoch than political freedom, were secured. The next step was to obtain political freedom, and it was made under the guidance of men who were Orleanists because the Orleans princes seemed to them to offer the best guarantee for such a government as they desired—a government which did not profess to stand above the people and to own it by virtue of a divine and legitimate hereditary right, nor one which, like the Bonapartists, implied a master relying on an army, and the general subjection of the nation. The liberals who were Orleanists had the advantage of being very ably led by men eminent in letters and in practical affairs—Guizot, Thiers, the Broglies, the banker Laffitte and many others. When the unsurpassed folly of the legitimate rulers brought about the revolution of 1830, the Orleanists stepped into its place, and they marked the profound change which had been made in the character of the government by calling the king. "King of the French" and not "King of France and Navarre." He was chief of the people by compact with the people, and not a territorial lord holding, in feudal phrase, "in chief of God."

The events of the eighteen years of Orleanist rule cannot be detailed here. They were on the whole profitable to France. That they ended in another "general overturn" in 1848 was due no doubt in part to errors of conduct in individual princes and politicians, but mainly to the fact that the Orleanist conception of what was meant by the word "people" led them to offend the long-standing and deeply-rooted love of the French for equality. It had been inevitable that the Orleanists, in their dislike of "divine right" on the one hand, and their fear of democratic Caesarism on the other, should turn for examples of a free government to England, and in England itself to the Whigs, both the old Whigs of the Revolution Settlement of 1689, and the new Whigs who extorted political franchises for the middle classes by the Reform Bill. They saw there a monarchy based on a parliamentary title, governing constitutionally and supported by the middle classes, and they endeavoured to establish the like in France under the name of a *juste-milieu*, a *via media* between absolutism by divine right, and a democracy which they were convinced would lead to Caesarism. The French equivalent for the English middle-class constituencies was to be a *pays légal* of about a quarter of a million of voters by whom all the rest of the country was to be "virtually represented." The doctrine was expounded and acted upon by Guizot with uncompromising rigour. The Orleanist monarchy became so thoroughly middle-class that the nation outside of the *pays légal* ended by thinking that it was being governed by a privileged class less offensive, and also a great deal less brilliant, than the aristocracy of the old monarchy.

The revolution of 1848 swept the Orleanist party from power for ever. The Orleanists indeed continued throughout the Second Republic and the Empire (1848–1870) to enjoy a marked social and literary prestige, on the strength of the wealth and capacity of some of their members, their influence in the French Academy and the ability of their organs in the press—particularly the *Revue des deux mondes*, the *Journal des débats*, and the papers directed by E. Hervé. During the Empire the discreet opposition of the Orleanists, exercised for the most part with infinite dexterity and tact, by reticences, omissions, and historical studies in which the Empire was attacked under foreign or ancient names, was a perpetual thorn in the side of Napoleon III. Yet they possessed little hold on the country and outside of a cultivated liberal circle in Paris. Their weakness was demonstrated when the second empire was swept away by the German War of 1870–71. The country in its disgust at the Bonapartists and its fear of the Republicans, chose a great many royalists to represent it in the Assembly which met in Bordeaux on the 12th of February 1871. In this body the Orleanists again exercised a kind of leadership by virtue of individual capacity, but they were counterbalanced by the Legitimists. The most effective

proof of power they gave was to render possible the expulsion from power of Thiers on the 24th of May 1873, as punishment for his dexterous imposition of the Republic on the unwilling majority of the Assembly. Their real occupation was to endeavour to bring about a fusion between themselves and the Legitimists which should unite the two royalist parties for the confusion of the Bonapartists and Republicans. The belief that a fusion would strengthen the royalists was natural and was not new. As far back as 1850 Guizot had proposed, or had thought of proposing, one, but it was on the condition that the comte de Chambord would resign his divine pretentions. When a fusion was arranged in 1873 it was on quite another footing. After much exchange of notes and many agitated conferences in committee rooms and drawing-rooms, the comte de Paris, the representative of the Orleanists, sought an interview with the comte de Chambord at Frohsdorff, and obtained it by giving a written engagement that he came not only to pay his respects to the head of his house, but also to "accept his principle." It has been somewhat artlessly pleaded by the Orleanists that this engagement was given with mental reservations. But there were no mental reservations on the part of the comte de Chambord, and the country showed its belief that the liberal royalists had been fused by absorption in the divine right royalists. It returned republicans at by-elections till it transformed the Assembly. The Orleanist princes had still a part to play, more particularly after the death of the comte de Chambord in 1883 left them heads of the house of France, but the Orleanist party ceased to exist as an independent political organization.

AUTHORITIES.—The Orleanists are necessarily more or less dealt with in all histories of France since 1789, and in most political memoirs, but their principles can be learnt and their fortunes followed from the following: A. Sorel, *L'Europe et la révolution française* (Paris, 1885–1904); F. Guizot, *Histoire parlementaire de la France* (Paris, 1819–1848) and *Mémoires pour servir à l'histoire de mon temps* (Paris, 1858–1867); P. de la Gorce, *Histoire du second empire* (Paris, 1894–1904); and G. Hanotaux, *Histoire de la France contemporaine* (Paris, 1903, &c.).   (D. H.)

ORLEANS, DUKES OF. The title of duke of Orleans was first created by King Philip VI. in favour of his son Philip, who died without legitimate issue in 1375. The second duke of Orleans, created in 1392, was Louis, a younger son of Charles V., whose heir was his son, the poet Charles of Orleans. Charles's son Louis, the succeeding duke, became king of France as Louis XII. in 1498, when the duchy of Orleans was united with the royal domain. In 1626 Louis XIII. created his brother, Jean Baptiste Gaston, duke of Orleans, and having become extinct on the death of this prince in 1660 the title was revived in the following year by Louis XIV. in favour of his brother Philip. Descendants of this duke have retained the title until the present day, one of them becoming king of France as Louis Philippe in 1830. Two distinguished families are descended from the first house of Orleans: the counts of Angoulême, who were descended from John, a son of Duke Louis I., and who furnished France with a king in the person of Francis I.; and the counts and dukes of Longueville, whose founder was John, count of Dunois, the bastard of Orleans, a natural son of the same duke. In addition to the dukes of Orleans the most important members of this family are: Anne Marie Louise, duchess of Montpensier; Francis, prince of Joinville; Louis Philippe Albert, count of Paris; and the traveller Prince Henry of Orleans. See the genealogical table to the article BOURBON.

See below for separate articles on the chief personages.

ORLÉANS, CHARLES, DUKE OF (1391–1465), commonly called Charles d'Orléans, French poet, was the eldest son of Louis, duke of Orleans (brother of Charles VI. of France), and of Valentina Visconti, daughter of Gian Galeazzo, duke of Milan. He was born on the 26th of May 1391. Although many minor details are preserved of his youth, nothing except his reception in 1403, from his uncle the king, of a pension of 12,000 livres d'or is worth noticing, until his marriage three years later (June 29, 1406) with Isabella, his cousin, widow of Richard II. of England. The bride was two years older than her husband, and is thought to have married him unwillingly.

but she brought him a great dowry—it is said, 500,000 francs. She died three years later, leaving Charles at the age of eighteen a widower and father of a daughter. He was already duke of Orleans, for Louis had been assassinated by the Burgundians two years before (1407). He soon saw himself the most important person in France, except the dukes of Burgundy and Brittany, the king being a cipher. This position his natural temperament by no means qualified him to fill. His mother desired vengeance for her husband, and Charles did his best to carry out her wishes by filling France with intestine war. Of this, however, he was only nominally one of the leaders, the real guidance of his party resting with Bernard VII., the great count of Armagnac, whose daughter, Bonne, he married, or at least formally espoused, in 1410. Five years of confused negotiations, plots and fightings passed before the English invasion and the battle of Agincourt, where Charles was joint commander-in-chief. According to one account he was dangerously wounded and narrowly escaped with his life. He was certainly taken prisoner and carried to England, which country was his residence thenceforward for a full quarter of a century. Windsor, Pontefract, Ampthill, Wingfield (Suffolk) and the Tower are named among other places as the scenes of his captivity, which, however, was anything but a rigorous one. He was maintained in the state due not merely to one of the greatest nobles of France but to one who ranked high in the order of succession to the crown. He hunted and hawked and enjoyed society amply, though the very dignities which secured him these privileges made his ransom great, and his release difficult to arrange. Above all, he had leisure to devote himself to literary work. But for this he would hardly be more than a name.

This work consists wholly of short poems in the peculiar artificial metres which had become fashionable in France about half a century or more before his birth, and which continued to be fashionable till nearly a century after his death. Besides these a number of English poems have been attributed to him, but without certainty. They have not much poetical merit, but they exhibit something of the smoothness of versification not uncommon in those who write, with care, a language not their own. The ingenuity of a single English critic has striven to attribute to him a curious book in prose, called *Le Débat des hérauts de France et d'Angleterre*, but Paul Meyer, in his edition of the book in question, has completely disposed of this theory. For all practical purposes, therefore, Charles's work consists of some hundreds of short French poems, a few in various metres, but the majority either ballades or rondels. The chronology of these poems is not always clear, still less the identity of the persons to whom they are addressed, and it is certain that some, perhaps the greater part of them, belong to the later years of the poet's life. But many are expressly stated in the manuscripts to have been "composed in prison," others are obviously so composed, and, on the whole, there is in them a remarkable unity of literary flavour. Charles d'Orléans is not distinguished by any extraordinary strength of passion or originality of character; but he is only the more valuable as the last and not the least accomplished representative of the poetry of the middle of the middle ages, in which the form was almost everything, and the personality of the poet, save in rare instances, nothing. Yet he is not entirely without *differentia*. He is a capital example of the cultivated and refined—it may almost be called the lettered—chivalry of the last chivalrous age, expert to the utmost degree in carrying out the traditional details of a graceful convention in love and literature. But he is more than this; in a certain easy grace and truth of expression, as well as in a peculiar mixture of melancholy, which is not incompatible with the enjoyment of the pleasures, even the trifling pleasures, of life, with listlessness that is fully able to occupy itself about those trifles, he stands quite alone. He has the urbanity of the 18th century without its vicious and prosaic frivolity, the poetry of the middle ages without their tendency to tediousness. His best-known rondels—those on Spring, on the Harbingers of Summer, and others—rank second to nothing of their kind.

Poetry, however, could hardly be an entire consolation, and Charles was perpetually scheming for liberty. But the English government had too many reasons for keeping him, and it was not till his hereditary foe Philip the Good of Burgundy interested himself in him that the government of Henry VI., which had by that time lost most of its hold on France, released him in return for an immediate payment of 80,000 *saluts d'or*, and an engagement on his part to pay 140,000 crowns at a future time. The agreement was concluded on the 2nd of July, 1440. He was actually released on the 3rd of November following, and almost immediately cemented his friendship with Duke Philip by marrying his niece, Mary of Cleves, who brought him a considerable dowry to assist the payment of his ransom. He had, however, some difficulty in making up the balance, as well as the large sum required for his brother, Jean d'Angoulême, who also was an English prisoner. The last twenty-five years of his life (for, curiously enough, it divides itself into three almost exactly equal periods, each of that length) were spent partly in negotiating, with a little fighting intermixed, for the purpose of gaining the Italian county of Asti, on which he had claims through his mother, partly in travelling about, but chiefly at his principal seat of Blois. Here he kept a miniature court which, from the literary point of view at least, was not devoid of brilliancy. At this most of the best-known French men-of-letters at the time—Villon, Olivier de la Marche, Chastelain, Jean Meschinot and others—were residents or visitors or correspondents. His son, afterwards Louis XII., was not born till 1462, three years before Charles's own death. He had become, notwithstanding his high position, something of a nullity in politics, and tradition ascribes his death to vexation at the harshness with which Louis XI. rejected his attempt to mediate on behalf of the duke of Brittany. At any rate he died, on the 4th of January, 1465, at Amboise. Many of his later poems are small occasional pieces addressed to his courtiers and companions, and in not a few cases answers to them by those to whom they were addressed exist.

The best edition of Charles d'Orléans's poems, with a brief but sufficient account of his life, is that of C. d'Héricault in the *Nouvelle collection Jannet* (Paris, 1874). For the English poems see the edition by Watson Taylor for the Roxburghe Club (1827). (G. Sa.)

ORLEANS, FERDINAND PHILIP LOUIS CHARLES HENRY, DUKE OF (1810–1842), born at Palermo on the 3rd of September 1810, was the son of Louis Philippe, duke of Orleans, afterwards king of France, and Marie Amélie, princess of the Two Sicilies. Under the Restoration he bore the title of duke of Chartres, and studied classics in Paris at the Collège Henri IV. At the outbreak of the Revolution, which in 1830 set his father on the throne, he was colonel of a regiment of Hussars. He then assumed the title of duke of Orleans, and was sent by the king to Lyons to put down the formidable riots which had broken out there (1831), and then to the siege of Antwerp (1832). He was appointed lieutenant-general, and made several campaigns in Algeria (1835, 1839, 1840). On his return to France he organized the battalions of light infantry known as the *chasseurs d'Orléans*. He died as the result of a carriage accident at Neuilly, near Paris, on the 13th of July 1842.

The duke of Orleans had married (May 30, 1837) Hélène Louise Elisabeth of Mecklenburg-Schwerin, and had by her two sons, the count of Paris and the duke of Chartres. On the 24th of February 1848, after the abdication of Louis Philippe, the duchess of Orleans went to the Chamber of Deputies assembled in the Palais Bourbon in the hope of having her eldest son proclaimed and of obtaining the regency; but the threatening attitude of the populace forced her to flee. She took refuge in England, and died at Richmond on the 18th of May 1858.
(M. P.°)

ORLEANS, HENRI, PRINCE OF (1867–1901), eldest son of Robert, duke of Chartres, was born at Ham, near Richmond, Surrey, on the 16th of October 1867. In 1889, at the instance of his father, who paid the expenses of the tour, he undertook, in company with MM. Bonvalot and Dedecken, a journey through Siberia to Siam. In the course of their travels they crossed the mountain range of Tibet, and the fruits of their observations, submitted to the Geographical Society of Paris (and later incorporated in *De Paris ou Tonkin à travers le Tibet inconnu*, published in 1892), brought them conjointly the gold medal of that society. In 1892 the prince made a short journey of exploration in East Africa, and shortly afterwards visited Madagascar, proceeding thence to Tongking. From this point he set out for Assam, and was successful in discovering the sources of the river Irrawaddy, a brilliant geographical achievement which secured the medal of the Geographical Society of Paris and the cross of the Legion of Honour. In 1897 he revisited Abyssinia, and political differences arising from this trip led to a duel with the comte de Turin, in which both combatants were wounded. While on a trip to Assam in 1901 he died at Saigon on the 9th of August. Prince Henri was a somewhat violent Anglophobe, and his diatribes against Great Britain contrasted rather curiously with the cordial reception which his position as a traveller obtained for him in London, where he was given the gold medal of the Royal Geographical Society.

ORLEANS, HENRIETTA, Duchess of (1644-1670), third daughter of the English king, Charles I., and his queen, Henrietta Maria, was born during the Civil War at Exeter on the 16th of June 1644. A few days after her birth her mother left England, and provision for her maintenance having been made by Charles she lived at Exeter under the care of Lady Dalkeith (afterwards countess of Morton) until the surrender of the city to the parliamentarians, when she was taken to Oatlands in Surrey. Then in July 1646 Lady Dalkeith carried the princess in disguise to France, and she rejoined her mother in Paris, where her girlhood was spent and where she was educated as a Roman Catholic. Henrietta was present at the coronation of Louis XIV., and was mentioned as a possible bride for the king, but she was betrothed, not to Louis, but to his only brother Philip. After the restoration of her brother Charles II., she returned to England with her mother, but a few months later she was again in Paris, where she was married to Philip, now duke of Orleans, on the 30th of March 1661. The duchess was very popular at the court of Louis XIV., and was on good terms with the grand monarch himself; she shared in the knowledge of state secrets, but was soon estranged from her husband, and at the best her conduct was very imprudent. In 1670, at the instigation of Louis, she visited England and obtained the signature of Charles II.'s ministers to the treaty of Dover; her success in this matter greatly delighted Louis, but it did not improve her relations with Philip, who had long refused his consent to his wife's visit to England. Shortly after returning to France, Henrietta died at St Cloud on the 30th of June 1670. She was buried at St Denis, her funeral oration being pronounced by her friend Bossuet, and it was asserted that she had been poisoned by order of her husband. She left two daughters, Marie Louise, wife of Charles II. of Spain, and Anne Marie, wife of Victor Amadeus II. of Savoy. According to legitimist principles, the descendants of Henrietta, through her daughter Marie of Savoy, are entitled to wear the British crown.

ORLEANS, JEAN BAPTISTE GASTON, Duke of (1608-1660), third son of the French king Henry IV., and his wife Marie de Medici, was born at Fontainebleau on the 25th of April 1608. Known at first as the duke of Anjou, he was created duke of Orleans in 1626, and was nominally in command of the army which besieged La Rochelle in 1628, having already entered upon that course of political intrigue which was destined to occupy the remainder of his life. On two occasions he was obliged to leave France for conspiring against the government of his mother and of Cardinal Richelieu; and after waging an unsuccessful war in Languedoc, he took refuge in Flanders. Reconciled with his brother Louis XIII., he plotted against Richelieu in 1635, fled from the country, and then submitted to the king and the cardinal. Soon afterwards the same process was repeated. Orleans stirred up Cinq-Mars to attempt Richelieu's murder, and then deserted his unfortunate accomplice. In 1643, on the death of Louis XIII., Gaston became lieutenant-general of the kingdom, and fought against Spain on the northern frontiers of France; but during the wars of the Fronde he passed with great facility from one party to the other. Then exiled by Mazarin to Blois in 1652 he remained there until his death on the 2nd of February 1660. Gaston's first wife was Marie (d. 1627), daughter and heiress of Henri de Bourbon, duc de Montpensier (d. 1608), and his second wife was Marguerite (d. 1672), sister of Charles III., duke of Lorraine. By Marie he left a daughter, Anne Marie, duchesse de Montpensier (*q.v.*); and by Marguerite he left three daughters, Marguerite Louise (1645-1721), wife of Cosimo III., grand duke of Tuscany; Elizabeth (1646-1696), wife of Louis Joseph, duke of Guise; and Françoise Madeleine (1648-1664), wife of Charles Emmanuel II., duke of Savoy.   (M. P.*)

ORLEANS, LOUIS, Duke of (1372-1407), younger son of the French king, Charles V., was born on the 13th of March 1372. Having been made count of Valois and of Beaumont-sur-Oise, and then duke of Touraine, he received the duchy of Orleans from his brother Charles VI. in 1392, three years after his marriage with Valentina (d. 1408), daughter of Gian Galeazzo Visconti, duke of Milan. This lady brought the county of Asti to her husband; but more important was her claim upon Milan, which she transmitted to her descendants, and which furnished Louis XII. and Francis I. with a pretext for interference in northern Italy. When Charles VI. became insane in 1392, Orleans placed himself in opposition to his uncle Philip II., duke of Burgundy, who was conducting the government; and this quarrel was not only the dominating factor in the affairs of France, but extended beyond the borders of that country. Continued after Philip's death in 1404 with his son and successor, John the Fearless, it culminated in the murder of Orleans by one of John's partisans on the 23rd of November 1407. The duke, who was an accomplished and generous prince, was suspected of immoral relations with several ladies of the royal house, among them Isabella of Bavaria, the queen of Charles VI. He had eight children by Valentina Visconti, including his successor, Charles of Orleans, the poet, and one of his natural sons was the famous bastard of Orleans, John, count of Dunois.

See E. Jarry, *La Vie politique de Louis d'Orléans* (Paris, 1889).

ORLEANS, LOUIS, Duke of (1703-1752), only son of Duke Philip II., the regent Orleans, was born at Versailles on the 4th of August 1703. A pious, charitable and cultured prince, he took very little part in the politics of the time, although he was conspicuous for his hostility to Cardinal Dubois in 1723. In 1730 Cardinal Fleury secured his dismissal from the position of colonel-general of the infantry, a post which he had held for nine years; and retiring into private life, he spent his time mainly in translating the Psalms and the epistles of St Paul. Having succeeded his father as duke of Orleans in 1723, he died in the abbey of St Geneviève at Paris on the 4th of February 1752. His wife Augusta (d. 1726), daughter of Louis William, margrave of Baden, bore him an only son, Louis Philippe, who succeeded his father as duke of Orleans.

ORLEANS, LOUIS PHILIPPE, Duke of (1725-1785), son of Louis, duke of Orleans, was born at Versailles on the 12th of May 1725, and was known as the duke of Chartres until his father's death in 1752. Serving with the French armies he distinguished himself in the campaigns of 1742, 1743 and 1744, and at the battle of Fontenoy in 1745, retiring to Bagnolet in 1757, and occupying his time with theatrical performances and the society of men of letters. He died at St Assise on the 18th of November 1785. The duke married Louise Henriette de Bourbon-Conti, who bore him a son Philip (Égalité), duke of Orleans, and a daughter, who married the last duke of Bourbon. His second wife, Madame de Montesson, whom he married secretly in 1773, was a clever woman and an authoress of some repute. He had two natural sons, known as the abbot of St Far and the abbot of St Albin.

See *L'Aumône d'un prince*, a collection of letters from the duke to his second wife, edited by J. Hermand (1910).

ORLEANS, LOUIS PHILIPPE JOSEPH, Duke of (1747-1793), called Philippe Égalité, son of Louis Philippe, duke of Orleans, and of Louise Henriette of Bourbon-Conti, was born at St Cloud on the 13th of April 1747. Having borne the title of duke of Montpensier until his grandfather's death in 1752, he became duke of Chartres, and in 1769 married Louise Marie Adelaide de Bourbon-Penthièvre, daughter and heiress of the duke of Penthièvre, grand admiral of France, and the richest heiress of the time. Her wealth made it certain that he would be the richest man in France, and he determined to play a part equal to that of his great-grandfather, the regent, whom he resembled in character and debauchery. As duke of Chartres he opposed the plans of Maupeou in 1771, and was promptly exiled to his country estate of Villers-Cotterets (Aisne). When Louis XVI. came to the throne in 1774 Chartres still found himself looked on coldly at court; Marie Antoinette hated him, and envied him for his wealth, wit and freedom from etiquette, and he was not slow to return her hatred with scorn. In 1778 he served in the squadron of D'Orvilliers, and was present in the naval battle of Ushant on the 27th of July 1778. He hoped to see further service, but the queen was opposed to this, and he was removed from the navy, and given the honorary post of colonel-general of hussars. He then abandoned himself to pleasure; he often visited London, and became an intimate friend of the prince of Wales (afterwards George IV.); he brought to Paris the "anglo-mania," as it was called, and made jockeys as fashionable as they were in England. He also made himself very popular in Paris by his large gifts to the poor in time of famine, and by throwing open the gardens of the Palais Royal to the people. Before the meeting of the notables in 1787 he had succeeded his father as duke of Orleans, and showed his liberal ideas, which were largely learnt in England, so boldly that he was believed to be aiming at becoming constitutional king of France. In November he again showed his liberalism in the *lit de justice*, which Brienne had made the king hold, and was again exiled to Villers-Cotterets. The approaching convocation of the states-general made his friends very active on his behalf; he circulated in every *bailliage* the pamphlets which F. J. Sieyès had drawn up at his request, and was elected in three—by the noblesse of Paris, Villers-Cotterets and Crépy-en-Valois. In the estate of the nobility he headed the liberal minority under the guidance of Adrien Duport, and led the minority of forty-seven noblemen who seceded from their own estate (June 1789) and joined the Tiers État. The part he played during the summer of 1789 is one of the most debated points in the history of the Revolution. The court accused him of being at the bottom of every popular movement, and saw the "gold of Orleans" as the cause of the Reveillon riot and the taking of the Bastille, as the republicans later saw the "gold of Pitt" in every germ of opposition to themselves. There can be no doubt that he hated the queen, and bitterly resented his long disgrace at court, and also that he sincerely wished for a thorough reform of the government and the establishment of some such constitution as that of England; and no doubt such friends as Adrien Duport and Choderlos de Laclos, for their own reasons, wished to see him king of France. The best testimony for the behaviour of Orleans during this summer is the testimony of an English lady, Mrs Grace Dalrymple Elliott, who shared his heart with the comtesse de Buffon, and from which it is absolutely certain that at the time of the riot of the 12th of July he was on a fishing excursion, and was rudely treated by the king on the next day when going to offer him his services. He indeed became so disgusted with the false position of a pretender to the crown, into which he was being forced, that he wished to go to America, but, as the comtesse de Buffon would not go with him, he decided to remain in Paris. He was again accused, unjustly, of having caused the march of the women to Versailles on the 5th of October. La Fayette, jealous of his popularity, persuaded the king to send the duke to England on a mission, and thus got him out of France, and he accordingly remained in England from October 1789 to July 1790. On the 7th of July he took his seat in the Assembly, and on the 2nd of October both he and Mirabeau were declared by the Assembly entirely free of any complicity in the events of October. He now tried to keep himself as much out of the political world as possible, but in vain, for the court would

suspect him, and his friends would talk about his being king. The best proof of his not being ambitious of such a doubtful piece of preferment is that he made no attempt to get himself made king, regent or lieutenant-general of the kingdom at the time of the flight to Varennes in June 1791. He, on the contrary, again tried to make his peace with the court in January 1792, but he was so insulted that he was not encouraged to sacrifice himself for the sake of the king and queen, who persisted in remembering all old enmities in their time of trouble. In the summer of 1792 he was present for a short time with the army of the north, with his two sons, the duke of Chartres and the duke of Montpensier, but had returned to Paris before the 10th of August. After that day he underwent great personal risk in saving fugitives; in particular, he saved the life of the count of Champcenetz, the governor of the Tuileries, who was his personal enemy, at the request of Mrs Elliott. It was impossible for him to recede, and, after accepting the title of Citoyen Égalité, conferred on him by the commune of Paris, he was elected twentieth and last deputy for Paris to the Convention. In that body he sat as quietly as he had done in the National Assembly, but on the occasion of the king's trial he had to speak, and then only to give his vote for the death of Louis. His compliance did not save him from suspicion, which was especially aroused by the friendship of his eldest son, the duke of Chartres, with Dumouriez, and when the news of the desertion of Chartres with Dumouriez became known at Paris all the Bourbons left in France, including Égalité, were ordered to be arrested on the 5th of April. He remained in prison till the month of October, when the Reign of Terror began. He was naturally the very sort of victim wanted, and he was decreed "of accusation" on the 3rd of October. He was tried on the 6th of November and was guillotined on the same day, with a smile upon his lips and without any appearance of fear. No man ever was more blamed than Orleans during the Revolution, but the faults of ambition and intrigue were his friends', not his own; it was his friends who wished him to be on the throne. Personally he possessed the charming manners of a polished grand seigneur: debauched and cynical, but never rude or cruel, full of gentle consideration for all about him but selfish in his pursuit of pleasure, he has had to bear a heavy load of blame, but it is ridiculous to describe the idle and courteous voluptuary as being a dark and designing scoundrel, capable of murder if it would serve his ambition. The execution of Philippe Égalité made the friend of Dumouriez, who was living in exile, duke of Orleans.

AUTHORITIES.—Baschet, *Histoire de Philippe Égalité*; *Journal of Mrs Grace Dalrymple Elliott* (1859); A. Nettement, *Philippe-Égalité* (Paris, 1842); Laurentie, *Histoire des ducs d'Orléans* (Paris, 1832); G. Peignot, *Précis historique de la maison d'Orléans* (Paris, 1830); L. C. R(ousselet), *Correspondance de Louis-Philippe Joseph d'Orléans avec Louis XVI* (Paris, 1800); Rivarol, *Portrait du duc d'Orléans et de Madame de Genlis*; Tournois, *Histoire du Louis Philippe Joseph duc d'Orléans* (Paris, 1842).

ORLEANS, LOUIS PHILIPPE ROBERT, DUKE OF (1869–), eldest son of the comte de Paris, was born at York House, Twickenham, on the 6th of February 1869. The law of exile against the French princes having been abrogated in 1871, he returned with his parents to France. He was first educated by a private tutor, and then followed the courses of the municipal college at Eu. In 1882 he entered the Collège Stanislas, Paris, and took a first prize in a competitive Latin translation. On the death of the comte de Chambord, the comte de Paris became head of the Bourbons; and in 1886 he and his son were exiled from France. Queen Victoria appointed the duke of Orleans a supernumerary cadet at the Royal Military College, Sandhurst. After passing his examinations he received a commission in the 4th battalion of the 60th Rifles, then quartered in India. In January 1888 the duke went out to India, accompanied by Colonel de Parseval as military governor and adviser. At Bombay he was received by the duke of Connaught and Lord Reay, and at Calcutta he became the guest of the viceroy, the marquess of Dufferin, who organized for the duke and his cousin, Prince Henry of Orleans, a grand tiger-shooting expedition in Nepaul. The duke now reported himself to the commander-in-chief,afterwards Earl Roberts,and joined his regiment at Chakrata. After seeing service, the duke ceased his connexion with the Indian army in February 1889, and returned to England. On attaining his majority, he entered Paris (February 7, 1890), and proceeding to the *mairie*, expressed his desire, as a Frenchman, to perform his military service. This act caused great excitement, and he was arrested in conformity with the law of 1886, which forbade the soil of France to the direct heirs of the families which had reigned there. He was tried, and sentenced to two years' imprisonment; but he was liberated by President Carnot after a few months' nominal incarceration (June 4), and conducted to the Swiss frontier. This escapade won for him the title of " Le Premier Conscrit de France." After the comte de Paris's funeral (September 12, 1894) the duke received his adherents in London, and then removed to Brussels, as being nearer France. On the 5th of November 1896 the duke married the archduchess Maria Dorothea Amalia of Austria, the ceremony taking place at Vienna. It was alleged that some of his followers were implicated in the conspiracies against the French Republic in 1899. A letter which the duke wrote in 1900, approving the artist whose caricatures were grossly insulting to Queen Victoria, excited great indignation both in England and in many French circles, and estranged him from many with whom he had formerly been upon friendly terms; but after Queen Victoria's death it was allowed to become known that this affair had been forgotten and forgiven by the British royal family. The duke of Orleans made several long exploring journeys, being particularly interested in polar discoveries. In 1905 he published *Une croisière au Spitsberg*, and, later, another account of his travels, under the title *A travers la Banquise*.

ORLEANS, PHILIP I., DUKE OF (1640–1701), son of the French king Louis XIII., was born at St Germain-en-Laye on the 21st of September 1640. In 1661 he was created duke of Orleans, and married Henrietta, sister of Charles II. of England; but the marriage was not a happy one, and the death of the duchess in 1670 was attributed to poison. Subsequently he married Charlotte Elizabeth, daughter of Charles Louis, elector palatine of the Rhine. Having fought with distinction in Flanders in 1667, Monsieur, as Orleans was generally called, returned to military life in 1672, and in 1677 gained a great victory at Cassel and took St Omer. Louis XIV., it was said, was jealous of his brother's success; at all events Orleans never commanded an army again. He died at St Cloud on the 8th of June 1701, leaving a son, Philip, the regent Orleans, and two daughters: Anne Marie (1669–1728), wife of Victor Amadeus II., duke of Savoy; and Elizabeth Charlotte (1676–1744), wife of Leopold, duke of Lorraine. His eldest daughter, Marie Louise (1662–1689), wife of Charles II. of Spain, died before her father.   (M. P.*)

ORLEANS, PHILIP II., DUKE OF (1674–1723), regent of France, son of Philip I., duke of Orleans, and his second wife, the princess palatine, was born on the 2nd of August 1674, and had his first experience of arms at the siege of Mons in 1691. His marriage with Mlle de Blois, the legitimized daughter of Louis XIV., won him the favour of the king. He fought with distinction at Steinkerk, Neerwinden and Namur (1692–1695). During the next few years, being without employment, he studied natural science. He was next given a command in Italy (1706) and in Spain (1707–1708) where he gained some important successes, but he cherished lofty ambitions and was suspected of wishing to take the place of Philip V. on the throne of Spain. Louis XIV. was angry at these pretensions, and for a long time held him in disfavour. In his will, however, he appointed him president of the council of regency of the young King Louis XV. (1715). After the death of the king, the duke of Orleans went to the parlement, had the will annulled, and himself invested with absolute power. At first he made a good use of this, counselling economy, decreasing taxation, disbanding 25,000 soldiers and restoring liberty to the persecuted Jansenists. But the inquisitorial measures which he had begun against the financiers led to disturbances. He was, moreover, weak enough to countenance

the risky operations of the banker John Law (1717), whose bankruptcy led to such a disastrous crisis in the public and private affairs of France.

There existed a party of malcontents who wished to transfer the regency from Orleans to Philip V., king of Spain. A conspiracy was formed, under the inspiration of Cardinal Alberoni, first minister of Spain, and directed by the prince of Cellamare, Spanish ambassador in France, with the complicity of the duke and duchess of Maine; but in 1718 it was discovered and defeated. Dubois, formerly tutor to the duke of Orleans, and now his all-powerful minister, caused war to be declared against Spain, with the support of the emperor, and of England and Holland (Quadruple Alliance). After some successes of the French marshal, the duke of Berwick, in Spain, and of the imperial troops in Sicily, Philip V. made peace with the regent (1720).

On the majority of the king, which was declared on the 15th of February 1723, the duke of Orleans resigned the supreme power; but he became first minister to the king, and remained in office till his death on the 23rd of December 1723. The regent had great qualities, both brilliant and solid, which were unfortunately spoilt by an excessive taste for pleasure. His dissolute manners found only too many imitators, and the regency was one of the most corrupt periods in French history.

See J. B. H. R. Capefigue, *Histoire de Philippe d'Orléans, régent de France* (2 vols., Paris, 1838); A. Baudrillart, *Philippe V. et la cour de France*, vol. ii. (Paris, 1890); and L. Wiesener, *Le régent, l'abbé Dubois et les Anglais* (3 vols., Paris, 1891–1899).   (M. P.*)

ORLEANS, a city of north central France, chief town of the department of Loiret, on the right bank of the Loire, 77 m. S.S.W. of Paris by rail. Pop. (1906), town, 57,544; commune, 68,614. At Les Aubrais, a mile to the north, is one of the chief railway junctions in the country. Besides the Paris and Orleans railway, which there divides into two main lines—a western to Nantes and Bordeaux via Tours, and a southern to Bourges and Toulouse via Vierzon—branches leave Les Aubrais eastwards for Pithiviers, Châlons-sur-Marne and Gien, north-west for Châteaudun and Rouen. The whole town of Orleans is clustered together on the right bank of the river and surrounded by fine boulevards, beyond which it sends out suburbs along the various roads. It is connected with the suburb of St Marceau on the left bank by a handsome stone bridge of nine arches, erected in the 18th century. Farther up is the railway bridge. The river is canalized on the right, and serves as a continuation of the Orleans Canal, which unites the Loire with the Seine by the canal of the Loing.

Owing to its position on the northernmost point of the Loire Orleans has long been the centre of communication between the Loire basin and Paris. The chief interest of the place lies in its public buildings and the historical events of which it has been the scene. Proceeding from the railway station to the bridge over the Loire, the visitor crosses Orleans from north to south and passes through the Place du Martroi, the heart of the city. In the middle of the square stands an equestrian statue of Joan of Arc, in bronze, resting on a granite pedestal surrounded by bas-reliefs representing the leading episodes in her life. In 1855 it took the place of an older statue executed in the beginning of the century, which was then transferred to the left bank of the Loire at the end of the bridge, a few paces from the spot where a simple cross marks the site of the *Fort des Tourelles* captured by Joan of Arc in 1429. From the Place du Martroi, the Rue Jeanne d'Arc leads to the cathedral of Ste Croix. This church, begun in 1287, was burned by the Huguenots in 1567 before its completion. Henry IV., in 1601, laid the first stone of the new structure, the building of which continued until 1829. It consists of a nave, a nave with double aisles, a corresponding choir, a transept and an apse. Its length is 472 ft., its width at the transept 220 ft. and the height of the central vaults 112 ft. The west front has two flat-topped towers, each of three storeys, of which the first is square, the second octagonal and the third cylindrical. The whole front is Gothic, but was designed and constructed in the 18th century and exhibits all the defects of the period, though its proportions are impressive. A central spire (19th century) 318 ft. high, on the other hand, recalls the pure Gothic style of the 13th century. In the interior the choir chapels and the apse, dating from the original erection of the building, and the fine modern tomb of Mgr. F. A. P. Dupanloup, bishop from 1849 to 1878, are worthy of note. In the episcopal palace and the higher seminary are several remarkable pictures and pieces of wood-carving; and the latter building has a crypt of the 9th century, belonging to the church of St Avit demolished in 1428. The church of St Aignan consists of a transept and choir of the second half of the 15th century; it contains in a gilded and carved wooden shrine the remains of its patron saint, who occupied the see of Orleans at the time of Attila's invasion. The crypt dates from the 9th to the beginning of the 11th century. The once beautiful sculpture of the exterior has been altogether ruined; the interior has been restored, but not in keeping with the original style. A third church, St Euverte, dedicated to one of the oldest bishops of Orleans (d. 391), is an early Gothic building dating from the 13th, completely restored in the 15th century. St Pierre-le-Puellier dates in its oldest portions from the 10th or even the 9th century. To the west of the Rue Royale stand the church of St Paul, whose façade and isolated tower both bear fine features of Renaissance work, and Notre-Dame de Recouvrance, rebuilt between 1517 and 1519 in the Renaissance style and dedicated to the memory of the deliverance of the city. The hôtel de ville, built under Francis I. and Henry II. and restored in the 19th century, was formerly the residence of the governors of Orleans, and was occupied by the kings and queens of France from Francis II. to Henry IV. The front of the building, with its different coloured bricks, its balconies supported by caryatides attributed to Jean Goujon, its gable-ends and its windows, recalls the Flemish style. There are several niches with statues. Beneath, between the double flight of steps leading up to the entrance, stands a bronze reproduction of the statue of Joan of Arc, a masterpiece of the princess Mary of Orleans, preserved in the Versailles museum. The richly-decorated apartments of the first storey contain paintings, interesting chimneys, and a bronze statuette (also by the princess Mary) representing Joan of Arc mounted on a caparisoned horse and clothed in the garb of the knights of the 15th century. The great hall in which it is placed also possesses a chimney decorated with three bas-reliefs of Domremy, Orleans and Reims, all associated with her life. The historical museum at Orleans is one of the most interesting of provincial collections, the numismatic, medieval and Renaissance departments, and the collection of ancient vases being of great value. The city also possesses a separate picture gallery, a sculpture gallery and a natural history museum, which are established in the former hôtel de ville, a Renaissance building of the latter half of the 15th century. The public library comprises among its manuscripts a number dating from the 7th century, and obtained in most cases from St Benoît on the Loire. The general hospital is incorporated with the Hôtel Dieu, and forms one of the finest institutions of the kind in France. The salle des fêtes, formerly the corn-market, stands within a vast cloister formed by 15th-century arcades, once belonging to the old cemetery. The salle des Thèses (1411) of the university is the meeting-place of the Archaeological Society of the city. Among the old private houses numerous at Orleans, that of Agnes Sorel (15th and 16th century), which contains a large collection of objects and works of art relating to Joan of Arc, that of Francis I., of the first half of the 16th century, that occupied by Joan of Arc during the siege of 1429, and that known as the house of Diane de Poitiers (16th century), which contains the historical museum, are of special interest. The hôtel de la Vieille-Intendance, built in the 15th and 16th centuries, served as residence of the intendants of Orleans in later times. The "White Tower" is the last representative of the towers rendered famous by the siege. A statue to the jurisconsult, R. J. Pothier (1699–1772), one of the most illustrious of the natives of Orleans, stands in front of the hôtel de ville. The anniversary of the raising of the siege in 1429 by Joan of Arc is celebrated every year with great pomp. After the English had

retired, the popular enthusiasm improvised a procession, which marched with singing of hymns from the cathedral to St Paul, and the ceremony is still repeated on the 8th of May by the clergy and the civil and military functionaries. Orleans is the seat of a bishopric, a prefect, a court of appeal, and a court of assizes and headquarters of the V. army corps. There are tribunals of first instance and of commerce, a board of trade-arbitration, a chamber of commerce and a branch of the Bank of France; and training colleges for both sexes, a lycée for boys, a technical school and an ecclesiastical seminary.

The more important industries of the town are the manufacture of tobacco (by the state), blankets, hairpins, vinegar, machinery, agricultural implements, hosiery, tools and ironware, and the preparation of preserved vegetables. Wine, wool, grain and live stock are the commercial staples of the city, round which there are important nurseries.

The site of Orleans must have been occupied very early in history by a trading post for commerce between northern and central and southern Gaul. At the time of the Roman conquest the town was known as Genabum, and was the starting-point of the great revolt against Julius Caesar in 52 B.C. In the 5th century it had taken the name Aurelianum from either Marcus Aurelius or Aurelian. It was vainly besieged in 451 by Attila, who was awed by the intercession of its bishop, St Aignan, and finally driven off by the patrician Aetius. Odoacer and his Saxons also failed to take it in 471, but in 498 it fell into the hands of Clovis, who in 511 held here the first ecclesiastical council assembled in France. The dignity which it then obtained, of being the capital of a separate kingdom, was lost by its union with that of Paris in 613. In the 10th century the town was given in fief to the counts of Paris, who in 987 ousted the Carolingian line from the throne of France. In 999 a great fire devastated the town. Orleans remained during all the medieval period one of the first cities of the French monarchy; several of the kings dwelt within its walls, or were consecrated in its cathedral; it had a royal mint, was the seat of councils, and obtained for its schools the name of university (1300), and for its soldiery an equal standing with those of Paris. Philip, fifth son of Philip VI., was the first of the dukes of Orleans. After the assassination of his successor Louis by Jean Sans-Peur, duke of Burgundy (1407), the people of Orleans sided resolutely with the Armagnacs, and in this way brought upon themselves the attacks of the Burgundians and the English. Joan of Arc, having entered the beleaguered city on the 29th of April 1429, effected the raising of the siege by means of an attack on the 7th of May on the Fort des Tourelles, in the course of which she was wounded. Early in the 16th century the town became a centre of Protestantism. After the Amboise conspiracy (1560) the states-general were convoked at Orleans, where Francis II. died. In 1562 it became the headquarters of Louis I. of Bourbon, prince of Condé, the Protestant commander-in-chief. In 1563 Francis, duke of Guise, laid siege to it, and had captured the tête-du-pont on the left bank of the Loire when he was assassinated. Orleans was surrendered to the king, who had its fortifications razed. It was held by the Huguenots from 1567 to 1568. The St Bartholomew massacre there in 1572 lasted a whole week. It was given as a lieu de sûreté to the League under Henry III., but surrendered to Henry IV. in person in 1594. During the Revolution the city suffered from the sanguinary excesses of Bertrand Barère and Collot d'Herbois. It was occupied by the Prussians in 1815 and in 1870, the latter campaign being discussed below.

See E. Bimbenet, Histoire de la ville d'Orléans (Orleans, 1884–1888).

THE ORLEANS CAMPAIGN OF 1870

Orleans was the central point of the second portion of the Franco-German War (q.v.), the city and the line of the Loire being at first the rendezvous of the new armies improvised by the government of National Defence and afterwards the starting-point of the most important attempt made to relieve Paris. The campaign has thus two well-marked phases, the first ending with the first capture of Orleans on the 10th of October, and the second with the second and final capture on the night of the 4th of December.

Shortly after the fall of the empire the government of National Defence, having decided that it must remain in Paris in spite of the impending siege, despatched a delegation to Tours to direct the government and the war in the provinces. This was originally composed (10-15 September) of two aged lawyers, Crémieux and Glais-Bizoin, and a naval officer, Vice-Admiral Fourichon, who had charge of both the war and the marine ministries. A retired general, de la Motte-Rouge, was placed in command of the "territorial division of Tours." He found, scattered over the south and west of France, a number of regular units, mostly provisional regiments, squadrons and batteries, assembled from the depôts, and all exceedingly ill supplied and equipped; but of such forces as he could muster he constituted the 15th corps. There were also ever-growing forces of mobiles, but these were wholly untrained and undisciplined, scarcely organized in battalions and for the most part armed with old-pattern weapons.

In these circumstances—the relative unimportance of the provincial war, the senility of the directors, the want of numbers, equipment and training in the troops available outside the walls of Paris—the rôle of the delegation was at first restricted to the establishment of a cordon of weak posts just out of reach of the German cavalry, with the object of protecting the formation of new corps and divisions in the interior. At the time of the investment of Paris part of the provincial forces were actually called in to reinforce the garrison. Only Reyau's weak cavalry division was sent out from Paris into the open country.

On their side the Germans had not enough forces left, after investing the capital with the III. and IV. Armies and Metz with the I. and II., to undertake a long forward stride to the Loire or the Cher. The only covering force provided on the south side of their Paris lines was the I. Bavarian corps, which had also to act as the reserve of the III. Army, and the cavalry divisions (6th, 4th, 2nd), whose chief work was the collection of supplies for the besiegers.

Shortly after this, near the end of September, francs-tireurs and small parties of National Guards became very active in Beauce, Perche and Gâtinais, and the German 4th cavalry division between Étampes and Toury was reinforced by some Bavarian battalions in consequence. But no important assemblies of French troops were noted, and indeed Orleans was twice evacuated on the mere rumour of the German advance. Moltke and every other German soldier gave no credence to rumours of the formation of a 15th corps behind the Loire—Trochu himself disbelieved in its existence—and the cavalry divisions, with their infantry supports, went about their ordinary business of gathering supplies.

In reality, however, the Delegation, unready as were its troops, was on the point of taking the offensive. In deference to popular clamour, a show of force in Beauce was decided upon. This was carried out by a force of all arms under Reyau on the 5th of October. It succeeded only too well. Prince Albert of Prussia, commander of the 4th cavalry division, which engaged Reyau at Toury, was so much impressed that he gave back 20 m. and sent alarming reports to army headquarters, which thereupon lost its incredulity and announced in army orders that the French "Army of the Loire" was advancing from Orleans. Von der Tann, the commander of the I. Bavarian corps, was ordered to take up a defensive position at Monthléry and to send out a detachment to cover Prince Albert's retreat. The 22nd infantry division was added to his command, and the 2nd and 6th cavalry divisions warned to protect his flanks. Thus the Germans were led to pay attention to the existence of the 15th corps when that corps was not only itself incomplete but also unsupported by the 16th, 17th and other still merely potential formations.

The preparations of the Germans were superfluous, for the demonstration ended in nothing. Reyau drew away leisurely towards Fontainebleau forest, and only a part of the 15th corps was sent up from Bourges to Orleans. Further, the fears of a sortie from Paris, which had occupied the German headquarters for some time, having for a moment ceased, Moltke on the 7th ordered von der Tann, with the I. Bavarian corps, 22nd division, and the three cavalry divisions, to advance. Next day these orders expanded. Orleans and, if possible, Tours itself were to be captured.

The punishment for the military promenade in Beauce was at hand. The main body of the 15th corps, which had not been *First* required to take part in it, was kept back at Bourges *capture of* and Vierzon, and only the miscellaneous troops *Orleans.* actually in Beauce were available to meet the blow they had provoked. On the 10th von der Tann attacked Reyau, who had returned from Fontainebleau towards Orleans, at Artenay. Had it not been that von der Tann believed that the 15th corps was in front of him, and therefore attacked deliberately and carefully, Reyau's resistance would have been even more brief than it was. The French were enormously outnumbered, and, after a brave resistance, were driven towards

Orleans in great disorder. Being still without any real offensive intentions, the Delegation and La Motte-Rouge decided, the same night, to evacuate Orleans. On the 11th, therefore, von der Tann's advance had to deal with no more than a strong rearguard on the outskirts of Orleans. But he was no longer on the plain of Beauce; villas, hedges and vineyards, as well as the outskirts of the great forest of Orleans, gave excellent cover to the. French infantry, all of which showed steadiness and some battalions true heroism, and the attack developed so slowly that the final positions of the defenders were not forced till close upon nightfall. The Germans lost at least 1000 men, and the harvest of prisoners proved to be no more than 1500. So far from pressing on to Tours, the Germans were well content with the occupation of Orleans.

The defeated enemy disappeared into Sologne, whither the assailants could not follow. Rumours of all sorts began to assail the German commander, who could not collect reliable news by means of the agencies under his own control because of the fluctuating but dense cordon of mobiles and francs-tireurs all around him. Moltke and Blumenthal wished him to strike out southward towards the arsenals of Bourges, the depôts of vehicles at Châteauroux and the improvised government offices at Tours. But he represented that he could not maintain himself nine or ten marches away from his nearest supports, and he was therefore allowed to stay at Orleans. The 22nd division and the 4th cavalry division, however, were withdrawn from him, and under these conditions von der Tann became uneasy as to his prospects of retaining even Orleans. His uneasiness was emphasized by reports of the appearance of heavy masses of French troops on the Loire above and below Orleans—reports that were true as regards the side of Blois, and more or less false as regards the Gien country. This news was obtained by the III. Army headquarters on the 19th of October, and next day von der Tann was ordered "not to abandon Orleans unless threatened by a greatly superior force." Such a threat soon became pronounced.

A new directing influence was at work at Tours in the person of Léon Gambetta, who arrived there by balloon from Paris and took control of the Delegation on the 11th. With de Freycinet (who was appointed deputy minister of war) as his most valued assistant, Gambetta at once became not merely the head of the government in the provinces, but the actual director of the war, in virtue of the fact that he was the very incarnation of the spirit of resistance to the invader. De la Motte-Rouge was replaced at the head of the 15th corps by General d'Aurelle de Paladines, under whom at the same time the embryo 16th corps was placed. The new commander with practically dictatorial powers occupied himself first of all with the organization and training of his motley troops. The Delegation indeed planned an advance from Gien on Fontainebleau, but this was given up on d'Aurelle's representations, and the 15th corps drew back to a strong position at Salbris in front of *The Camp* Bourges. There by dint of personal ascendancy, relent- *of Salbris.* less drilling and a few severe courts-martial, d'Aurelle produced an enormous improvement in the quality of his troops. Gambetta reinforced the troops at Salbris to the figure of 60,000, for the camp there was not merely a rendezvous but a school, the atmosphere of which profoundly affected even troops that only spent three or four days within its bounds. Meantime the 16th corps was formed at Blois and Vendôme, covered by a screen of francs-tireurs and National Guards. On October 23 a large force was sent over to the 16th corps from Salbris. This step was the first in a new plan of campaign.

A few days before it was taken, there had occurred an incident which led Moltke to a fresh misunderstanding of the situation towards the Loire. As mentioned above, the 22nd infan- *Château-* try and 4th cavalry divisions had been withdrawn from *dun.* von der Tann's command and ordered back to Paris, and on their way thither they were told to clear the country round Châteaudun and Chartres. General von Wittich, therefore, with the 22nd division and some cavalry, appeared before Châteaudun on the 18th of October. The little town was strongly held and repulsed the first attack. Wittich then prepared a second assault so carefully that sunset was at hand when it was made. It would seem indeed that at this period, when the Germans were hoping for a speedy return to their fatherland, the spirit of the offensive in all ranks had temporarily died away. The assailants carried the edge of the town, only to find themselves involved in a painful struggle in the streets. House-to-house fighting went on long after dark, but at last the inhabitants gave way, and the Germans punished the town for its unconventional resistance by subjecting it to what was practically a sack.[1] After this von Wittich passed on to Chartres, which, making his preparations more carefully, he was able to occupy after a few shells had been fired. These events, and the presence of a French force at Dreux, as a matter of fact signified nothing, for the 15th and 16th corps were still on the Loire and at Salbris, but they

---

[1] In 1879 the government added the cross of the Legion of Honour to the town arms of Châteaudun.

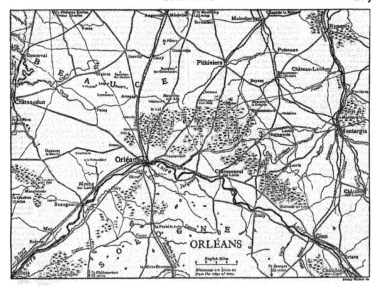

ORLÉANS

bewildered the German headquarters and conjured up a phantom "Army of the West," just as the promenade in Beauce had fashioned "the Army of the Loire" out of the small force under Reyau. Once more, indeed, as so often in the war, the Germans tried to solve the French problem by German data, and in their devotion to the net idea of "full steam ahead," could not conceive of military activity being spasmodic or unaimed. But this time the Versailles strategists were wrong only in their guess as to the direction of the blow. A blow was certainly impending.

By now the deliverance of Paris had become the defined objective of the "new formations" and of the provincial Delegation. Many plans were discussed, both at Paris and at Tours, for a combined effort, but each strategist had to convince the rest of the soundness of his own views, and the interchange of information and plans between Trochu and Gambetta was necessarily precarious. In the end, however, a few clear principles were accepted—Paris must be relieved, not merely revictualled, and the troops must be set in motion with that object at the earliest possible moment. For 200,000 French regulars were closely invested in Metz with the I. and II. Armies, if they passed into captivity, the veterans of Vionville and St Privat could be brought over to the Loire, and already there were strange rumours of intrigues between Bazaine, Bismarck and the empress Eugénie. But de Freycinet and d'Aurelle had different views as to the method of recapturing Orleans, which was agreed upon as the first thing to be done, and a compromise had to be made, by which 25,000 men were to advance by Gien and Châteauneuf and the main mass (75,000) from Blois by Beaugency, the hazards of this double movement being minimized by the weakness of the forces under von der Tann (the highest estimate of these that reached Tours was 60,000 and their real number only 26,000). The preliminary movements were to be completed by the 29th of October, when one strong division of the 15th corps was to be set at Gien and the remainder of the 15th and 16th corps between Blois and Vendôme.

This was duly carried out, and the Germans were confirmed in their suspicions of a concentration to the west of Paris by the despatch of dummy troop-trains to Le Mans. But bad weather, the news of the disastrous capitulation of Bazaine and the opening of a series of futile peace negotiations delayed the dénouement, the Gien column

was hastily recalled, and the French armies stood fast all along the line in their original grouping, 75,000 men (15th and 16th corps) at Blois-Vendôme, 10,000 men in Sologne and 25,000 at Gien. The Germans round Orleans were some 25,000 strong. Between Monthéry and Chartres were 21,000 more; but these were paralysed by the fictitious "Western Army" of the French, and von Wittich even thought of obtaining assistance from von der Tann. The activity of the irregulars, and the defiant attitude of the civil population everywhere, presaged a blow to be delivered by the once despised "new formations," but the direction of this blow was misconceived by the German headquarters, by the staff of the III. Army and by von der Tann alike, till the eve of its delivery. The halt of the French army allowed this uneasiness to grow, and, in default of a target, Moltke was unable to assign a definite task to the II. Army, now on its way from Metz. One of its corps, therefore, was sent to the lines before Paris to release the 17th and 22nd infantry divisions from siege duties, and these, with the I. Bavarian corps and the 2nd, 4th and 6th cavalry divisions, were constituted into a special detachment of the III. Army, under Friedrich Franz, grand duke of Mecklenburg-Schwerin. The duke was ordered to cover the siege of Paris and to break up the "new formations," but he was directed, not towards Orleans or even Tours, but towards Le Mans, concentrating with that object between Châteaudun and Chartres.

D'Aurelle, if cautious and slow, at least employed spare time well. The 16th corps was disciplined to the standard attained by the 15th and Chanzy was placed at the head of it, General Fiéreck, commanding at Le Mans, was ordered to attract the enemy's notice to the west by demonstrations, the defence of localities by irregulars was thoroughly organized, and in the first days of November, on de Freycinet's demand, the general advance was resumed. There was a difference of opinion between d'Aurelle and Chanzy as to the objective, the latter wishing to make the main effort by the left, so as to cut off the Bavarians from Paris, the former, to make it by the right with a view to recapturing Orleans, and, as on the German side at Gravelotte, a compromise was made whereby the army was deployed in equal force all along the line.

The début was singularly encouraging. Part of the German 2nd cavalry division, with its infantry supports, was severely handled by the French advanced guard near the hamlet of St Laurent des Bois (November 8). The half-heartedness of the Germans, evidenced by the number of prisoners taken unwounded, greatly encouraged the "new formations," who cheerfully submitted to a cold bivouac in anticipation of victory. Next morning the advance was resumed, d'Aurelle with the 15th corps on the right wing, Chanzy with the 16th on the left and Reyau's cavalry to the front. The march was made straight across country, in battle order, each brigade in line of battalion columns covered by a dense skirmish line. The French generals were determined that no accident should occur to shake the *moral* of the young troops they commanded.

At Orleans, meanwhile, von der Tann, in ever-growing suspense, had, rightly or wrongly, decided to stand his ground. He had been instructed by the headquarters staff not to fall back except under heavy pressure. He had his own reputation, dimmed by the failure of 1866, to retrieve, and national honour and loyalty seemed to him to require, in the words of his own staff officer, that "ere actual conflict had taken place with the 'greatly superior' enemy, no hostile force should enter the city placed under the protection of the Bavarians." But he could not allow himself to be enveloped in Orleans itself, and therefore, calling upon the far-distant III. Army reserves for support, he took up his position with 23,500 men around Coulmiers, leaving 2500 men to hold Orleans. The line of defence was from St Péravy on the Châteaudun road through Coulmiers to La Renardière, and thence along the Mauve stream, and here he was attacked in force on the 9th of November. The French approached from the south-west, and when their right had taken contact, the remainder gradually swung round and attacked the Bavarian centre and right. The result was foregone, given the

Battle of disparity of force, but the erratic movements of Reyau's
Coulmiers cavalry on the extreme left of d'Aurelle's line exposed Chanzy to a partial repulse and saved the Bavarian right. When at last the French stormed Coulmiers, and von der Tann had begun to retire, it was already nightfall, and the exhausted remnant of the I. Bavarian corps was able to draw off unpursued. The Orleans garrison followed suit, and the French army, gathering in its two outlying columns from Sologne and Gien, reoccupied the city. So ended the first blow of the Republic's armies. Coulmiers would indeed have been a crushing victory had Reyau's cavalry performed its part in the scheme and above all had d'Aurelle, adopting unreservedly either his own plan or Chanzy's, massed his troops here, economized them there, in accordance with the plan, instead of arraying them in equal strength at all points. But d'Aurelle wished above all to avoid what is now called a "regrettable incident" —hence his advance across country *en bataille*—and to thin out his line at any point might have been disastrous. And incomplete as it was, the victory had a moral significance which can scarcely be overrated. The "new formations" had won the first battle, and it was confidently hoped by all patriots that the spell of defeat was broken.

But d'Aurelle and the government viewed their success from the standpoint of their own side, and while von der Tann, glad to escape from the trap, fell back quickly to Angerville, d'Aurelle's only fear was an offensive return. Not even when von der Tann's defensive intentions were established did d'Aurelle resume the advance. The columns from Gien and the Sologne peacefully reoccupied Orleans, while the victors of Coulmiers went into cold and muddy bivouacs north of the city, for d'Aurelle feared that their dispersion in comfortable quarters would weaken the newly forged links of discipline. The French general knew that he had only put his hand to the plough, and he thought that before ploughing in earnest he must examine and overhaul his implement. In this opinion he was supported not only by soldiers who, like Chanzy, distrusted the staying power of the men, but even by the government, which knew that the limit of the capital's resistance was still distant, and felt the present vital necessity of protecting Bourges, Châteauroux and Tours from Prince Frederick Charles, who with the II. Army was now approaching from the east. The plan of General Borel, the chief of staff, for a lateral displacement of the whole army towards Chartres and Dreux, which would have left the prince without an animate target and concentrated the largest possible force on the weakest point of Moltke's position, but would have exposed the arsenals of the south, was rejected, and d'Aurelle organized a large fortified camp of instruction to the north of the captured city, to which came, beside the 15th and 16th corps, the new 17th and 18th.

To return to the Germans. An army at the halt, screened by active irregulars, is invisible, and the German commanders were

German again at a loss. It has been mentioned that a day or two
plans before the battle of Coulmiers Moltke had created an
after Army Detachment under the grand duke of Mecklenburg
Coulmiers for operations south of Paris. His objects in so doing
must now be briefly summarized. On November the 1st he had written to the II. Army to the effect that "the south of France would hardly make great efforts for Paris," and that the three disposable corps of the *army* were to range over the country as far as Chalon-sur-Saône, Nevers and Bourges. By the 7th his views had so far changed that he sanctioned t e formation of the "Detachment" with a view to breaking up the Army of the Loire by a march into the west towards Le Mans, the right wing of the II. Army at the same time harrying on to Fontainebleau to cover the

south side of the Paris investment. The king, however, less convinced than Moltke of the position of the Army of the Loire, suspended the westward deployment of the Detachment, with the result that on the 10th the retreating Bavarians were reinforced by two fresh divisions. But the same day all touch with the French was lost—perhaps deliberately, in accordance with the maxim that defeated troops should avoid contact with the victor. The curtain descended, and next day a few vague movements of small bodies misled the grand duke into seeking his target towards Chartres and Dreux, directly away from d'Aurelle's real position. Once more the king intervened and brought him back to the Orleans-Paris road (Nov. 13-14), but Moltke hurried forward the IX. corps (II. Army) from Fontainebleau to Étampes so as to release the grand duke from covering duties while satisfying the king's wishes for direct protection towards Orleans.

Moltke's views of the problem had not fundamentally changed since the day when he ordered the II. Army to spread out over southern France. He now told the grand duke to beat the Army of the Loire or Army of the West near Dreux or Chartres, and, that done, to sweep through a broad belt of country on the line Alençon-Verneuil towards Rouen, the outer wing of the II. Army meanwhile, after recapturing Orleans and destroying Bourges, to descend the Loire and Cher valleys towards Tours (14 Nov.).- On the 15th a fresh batch of information and surmises caused the leader of the Detachment, who had not yet received orders to do so, to leave the Paris-Orleans road to take care of itself and to swing out northwestward at once. The Detachment reached Chartres, Rambouillet and Auneau that night, and headquarters, having meanwhile been mystified by the news of a quite meaningless fight between German cavalry and some mobiles at Dreux, did not venture to reimpose the veto. The adventures of the Detachment need not be traced in detail. It moved first north towards the line Mantes-Dreux, and delivered a blow in the air. Then, hoping to find a target

Move- towards Nogent le Rotrou, it swung round so as to face
ments of south-west. Everywhere it met with the sharpest resist-
the De- ance from small parties, nowhere it found a large body
tachment. of all arms to attack. Matters were made worse by staff blunders in the duke's headquarters, and on the 19th, after a day of indescribable confusion, he had to halt to sort out his divisions. Moltke gave him the rest day he asked for the more readily as he was beginning to suspect that the king was right, that there were considerable forces still at Orleans, and that the Detachment might be wanted there after all.

This alteration in his views had been brought about by the reports from the II. Army during its advance from Champagne to the Gâtinais. At the time of the first order indicating Chalon,

Advance Nevers and Bourges as its objectives this army had just
of the II. opened out into line from its circular position round
Army. Metz, and it therefore naturally faced south. Moving forward, it reached the line Troyes-Neufchâteau about the time Coulmiers was fought, and was ordered to send in its right (IX. corps) to Fontainebleau. The II. corps had already been taken to strengthen the besiegers, thereby releasing the two Prussian divisions (17th and 22nd) that joined von der Tann on the 10th. The II. Army next changed front, in accordance with Moltke's directions, so as to face S.E. towards Orleans and Gien, and on the 16th the IX. corps and 1st cavalry division were at Méréville and on the Orleans-Paris road, the III. at Sens and the X. at Toonerre. The III. and X. from this time onward marched, camped and slept in the midst of a population so hostile that von Voigts-Rhetz kept his baggage in the midst of the fighting troops, and Prince Frederick Charles himself, with an escort, visited the villages lying off the main roads to gauge for himself the temper of the inhabitants.

From prisoners it was gleaned that the French 18th corps, supposed by the Germans to be forming in the Dijon-Lyons region, had arrived on the Loire, and a deserter said that there were 40,000 men encamped at Chevilly, just north of Orleans. Moltke's faith in his own reading of the situation was at last shaken; whether the Army of the Loire had joined the Army of the West or was still on the Loire, he did not yet know, but it was almost certain that from wherever they came, considerable French forces were around Orleans. He warned the prince to check the southward swing of the X. corps "because it cannot yet be foreseen whether the whole army will not have to be employed towards Châteaudun and Orleans," and turned to the Detachment for further information, cautioning the grand duke at the same time to keep touch with the II. Army. But, ignoring the hint, the grand duke, thinking that he had at last brought the elusive "Army of the West" to bay in the broken ground round Nogent-le-Rotrou, opened out, in accordance with German strategic principles, for a double envelopment of the enemy. He struck another blow in the air. The "Army of the West" had never really existed as an army, and its best-organised units had been sent back to join the new 21st corps at Le Mans ere the Detachment came into action at all, while the older mobiles continued the "small war" in front of the Germans, and sniped their sentries and trapped their atrols as before. Almost simultaneously with the news of this disappointment, the prince, who had meanwhile used his cavalry vigorously, sent word to Versailles on the 20th that the French 15th, 16th, 17th and 18th corps (in all over 150,000 men) were round Orleans. At this moment the III. corps was close to the

Forest of Orleans, the IX. corps away to the right rear at Angerville, and the X. equally distant to the south-east, as well as separated in three self-contained columns a day's march apart.. It seemed as if another Vionville was at hand, but this time Alvensleben and Voigts-Rhetz did not attack an obscure objective *codis que codis.* They stood fast, by the prince's order, to close up for battle and to wait on events in front of the Detachment.

The Germans had now discovered their target, and their strategical system, uncomplicated by past nightmares, should have worked smoothly to a decisive result. But there was nearly as much confusion between the various high officers as before. Prince Frederick Charles, in possession of the facts and almost in contact with the enemy, wrote to the grand duke to say that the II. Army was about to attack the enemy, and to suggest that the Detachment, which he knew to be heading for Le Mans, should make a " diversion " in his favour towards Tours, reserving to himself and his own army, as on the 2nd of July 1866 before Königgrätz, the perils and the honours of the battle. The grand duke meanwhile, whose temper was now roused, was making a last attempt to bring the phantom " Army of the West " to action. Rejecting Blumenthal's somewhat timidly worded advice to go slowly, the grand duke spread out his forces for the last time for an enveloping advance on Le Mans.

He had not gone far when, on the 23rd, he received a peremptory order from the king, through the III. Army headquarters, to bring *The De-* back his forces to Beauce and to be on the middle Loire *tachment* at latest by the 26th. In vain he pleaded for a day to *ordered* close up; the king replied that the march must go on, *towards* for much depended on it. Moltke, in fact, had seized *Orleans.* the reins more firmly at the critical moment, and given directions to the army commanders that the II. Army and the Detachment were to make a combined and concerted attack as soon as possible after the 26th. By that date the last brigades of the II. Army would have come up, and the Detachment was to time its own march accordingly. Yet even at this step Blumenthal, the original author of the Western expedition, in transmitting the king's order to the grand duke, assigned not Orleans but Beaugency, some miles down the river, as the objective of the Detachment.

D'Aurelle meanwhile had resolutely maintained his policy of inaction, confirmed in that course by the miserable and ill-equipped *French* condition of the troops that came from the east and the *plans.* west to double the numbers of the relatively well-disciplined army of Coulmiers. In the grand duke's move to the west, d'Aurelle saw only a trap to lure him into the plains and to offer him up as a victim to the approaching II. Army, the force of which he at first greatly exaggerated. All this time Gambetta and de Freycinet were receiving messages from Paris that spoke of desperate sorties being planned, and assigned December 15th as the last day of resistance. On the 19th of November de Freycinet wrote to d'Aurelle urging him to form a plan of active operations without delay, and even suggesting one (which was, in fact, vicious), but in reply the general merely promised to study the civilian's scheme. A severe letter from Gambetta, which followed this, had no better effect. D'Aurelle had, in fact, become a pessimist, and the Delegation, instead of removing him, merely suggested fresh plans.

On the 24th, however, the French at last took the offensive, in the direction of Fontainebleau Forest, to co-operate with the great sortie from Paris which was now definitely arranged. But owing to d'Aurelle's objections, the first orders were modified so far that on attaining the points ordered, Chilleurs (15th corps) Boiscommun-Bellegarde (20th), the troops were to await the order to advance. Shortly afterwards the 18th corps from Gien was ordered to advance on the line Montargis-Ladon. The rest of d'Aurelle's huge army was scarcely affected by these movements. Meanwhile Prince Frederick Charles, to clear up the situation, had pushed out strong reconnaissances of all arms from the front of the II. Army, and these naturally developed strong forces of the defenders. The advanced troops of the X. corps had severe engagements with fractions of the 20th corps at Ladon and Maizières, and those of the III. corps were sharply repulsed at Neuville and drew the fire of several battalions and batteries at Artenay. The French offensive slowly developed on the 25th and 26th, for the Germans were not ready to advance, and in addition greatly puzzled. The erratic movements of the grand duke towards Le Mans before he was recalled to the Loire had seriously disquieted both the Delegation and d'Aurelle, and the 17th corps, under a young and energetic leader, de Sonis, was moved restlessly hither and thither in the country south and west of Châteaudun. A fight at Brou (10 m. W. of Bonneval) provoked the grand duke into another false move. This time the Detachment, then near Droué (12 m. W. of Châteaudun) and Authon (22 m. W. of Bonneval), swung round north-east in defiance of the order to go to Beaugency, and had to be brought back by the drastic method of placing it under the orders of Prince Frederick Charles. General von Stosch of the headquarters staff was at the same time sent to act as Moltke's representative with the duke's headquarters, and Lieut.-Colonel von Waldersee to Prince Frederick Charles's to report thence direct to the king, who was dissatisfied with the diluted information with which the various staff officers furnished him. Still, the upshot was that Prince Frederick Charles was entrusted with affairs on the Loire, and all

superior control was voluntarily surrendered. The prince had very clear ideas, at the outset, of the task before him. If the French advanced towards Fontainebleau or elsewhere, he expected *Prince* to be able to repeat Napoleon's strategy of 1814, fighting *Frederick* containing actions with the IX. and X. corps and deliver- *Charles in* ing blow after blow at different points on d'Aurelle's line *general* of march with the III. If the French, as seemed more *command.* likely, stood fast, he thought his task more formidable, and therefore, abandoning the idea of a strategic envelopment, he ordered the Detachment inwards with the intention of directly attacking the Orleans position from the north-west.

As regards the method of the offensive, there is herein no material advance on the prince's first scheme; the detachment is simply added to the forces making the attack, and the diversion on Tours is abandoned. But the prince was at any rate a leader who enjoyed the responsibilities of director of operations—he even said that he would find the shuttle-play of the III. corps alluded to above " an interesting novelty in his experience of Army command "—while at the same time the unfortunate d'Aurelle was asking the Delegation to give orders direct to his generals.

It was now November 27th. The Versailles headquarters were in a state of intense nervous exaltation waiting for the sortie of 70,000 men that was daily expected to be launched at the investing line, and the king's parting words to von Waldersee indicate sufficiently the gravity of the decision that was now entrusted to the most resolute troop-leader in the service: " We are on the eve of a decisive moment. I know well that my troops are better than the French, but that does not relieve me into supposing that we have not a crisis before us. . . . If Prince Frederick Charles is beaten, we must give up the investment of Paris. . . . " The II. Army was waiting events on a dangerously extended front from Toury on the Paris-Orleans road (which the prince still thought it his duty to cover) to Beaune-la-Rolande. The Detachment, which never yet had concentrated save to deliver blows in the air, was approaching Châteaudun and Bonneval when von Stosch arrived and gave it the encouragement, the reforms in the staff work and the rest-day it needed. The French, who themselves had suffered from over-extension, had by now condensed on the extreme right. In these general conditions the battle of Beaune-la-Rolande took place—an engagement almost as honourable to Voigts-Rhetz and the X. corps as Vionville to Alvensleben and the III. The French attack began early on the morning of the 28th, under command of General Crouzat. It was directed on Beaune-la-Rolande from three sides, and only the want of combination between the various units of the French *Beaune-* and the arrival in the afternoon of part of the III. corps *la-* saved the X. from annihilation. As it was, the Germans *Rolande.* engaged were utterly exhausted, and the X. corps had but three rounds of ammunition per man left. But the magnificent resistance of the men of Vionville prolonged the fight until night had fallen and Crouzat, thinking the battle lost, ordered his troops to evacuate the battlefield. As at Coulmiers, and with even more deplorable results, and feared to hazard the issue of the campaign on the mere supposition that the enemy was even more exhausted. There was another resemblance, too, between Coulmiers and Beaune-la-Rolande, in that the French forces on the outer flank towards Artenay stood idle without attempting to influence the decision.

Prince Frederick Charles himself took only a cursory survey of the battlefield, and failed to realize that the whole of the enemy's right wing had been engaged, in spite of what Waldersee, who had been in Beaune, told him of events there. So far, therefore, from considering the battle as a great victory to be followed up by an energetic pursuit, he still feared a more round his left flank from Gien and Montargis towards Fontainebleau. The II. Army orders issued on the night of the battle actually had in view a farther extension *eastward.* Beaune-la-Rolande was a French defeat without being a German victory, and for the fact that it was a defeat, not a mere check, there was no cause but Crouzat's impressions of the state of the 20th corps, which, composed as it was of the newest levies in his army, was the most susceptible of unreasoning bravery and unreasoning depression.

In view of this, d'Aurelle and de Freycinet decided that the offensive was to be continued not towards Beaune-Nemours, but from the front of the steadier 15th and 16th corps towards Pithiviers, and with that object, on the 29th—a day of inaction for the Germans —the 18th and 20th corps began to close on the centre. There was sharp fighting on the 30th at various points along the north-eastern and eastern fringes of the Forest of Orleans, in which for the most part the French were successful. On the 29th the II. Army was inactive in spite of almost frantic appeals from Versailles to go forward (the great sortie from Paris had begun), and the Detachment, in accordance with the prince's orders and not with the views held by von Stosch, headed eastward to prolong the right of the II. Army, halting on the 29th in the area Orgères-Toury. The prince's message to the grand duke contained the significant phrase, " my plans to drive the enemy out of Orleans "—he no longer thought of a strategical envelopment of the Army of the Loire in Orleans. Disillusioned during the 30th as to the supposed danger on the side of Montargis, he closed from both wings towards the centre, but still defensively and well clear of the edge of the dangerous forest.

On this day d'Aurelle and the French generals assembled to receive de Freycinet's orders for the next advance. The 18th and 20th corps were to attack Beaune-la-Rolande, the 15th and 16th Pithiviers, while the 17th, aided by the 21st from Le Mans, was to look after the security of Orleans against a possible southward advance of the Detachment. A wise modification was arranged between d'Aurelle and Chanzy, whereby the first day's operations should be directed to driving away the Detachment with the 17th and 16th corps, preparatory to the move on Pithiviers. On the 1st of December, then, no events of importance took place on the front of the II. Army, the centre of gravity having shifted to Orgères-Toury and the direction of events to the grand duke and Stosch. Fortunately for the Germans the cavalry general von Schmidt, who had been called upon to return to the II. Army with his division, managed to impress Stosch, in a farewell interview, with the imminence of the danger, and a still more urgent argument was the action of Villepion-Terminiers, in which Chanzy with one infantry and one cavalry division attacked part of the I. Bavarian corps and drove it to Orgères with a loss of 1000 men. Von Stosch, therefore, so far from literally obeying the waiting policy indicated in the orders from Prince Frederick Charles, cautiously led the grand duke to prepare for a battle, and the grand duke, seeing the chance of which he had been cheated so often, and secure in his royal rank and in the support of Moltke, Stosch and Blumenthal, took control again. Lastly, von Stosch called back the 22nd division, which had been taken from the Detachment to form the reserve of the II. Army.

The result of the decision thus made at the Detachment headquarters was of the highest importance. The French main body moving north-westward in the general direction of Toury encountered first the I. Bavarian corps, then the 17th division, and finally the 22nd division, and the leadership of the German generals, who took every advantage of the disconnected and spasmodic movements of the enemy, secured a complete success (battle of Loigny-Poupry, 2nd Dec.). Meanwhile, and long before victory had declared itself, Prince Frederick Charles, still keeping the III. and X. corps on the side of Boiscommun and Bellegarde, had sent the IX. corps westward to support the Detachment, and halted von Schmidt's returning cavalry division on the Paris road. But from this point there began an interchange of telegrams which almost nullified the strategical effect of the battle. The grand duke and von Stosch, desirous above all of enveloping—that is, driving into Orleans—the target that after so many disappointments they had found and struck, wished to expand westwards so as to prevent the escape of the French towards Châteaudun, and with that object asked the II. Army "to attack Artenay and to take over the protection of the great road." Both von Stosch and von Waldersee had reported to the II. Army the importance of the French troops west of the main road, and Prince Frederick Charles, as above mentioned, had already moved the IX. corps and 6th cavalry division towards the Detachment. But when after the battle the grand duke's request to the II. Army arrived at the prince's headquarters, the reply was a curt general order for a direct concentric attack on Orleans by all forces under his command.

This was Moltke's doing. Before Waldersee's telegrams from the front arrived at Versailles, he had sent to the prince a peremptory order "to attack Orleans and thus to bring about the decision." This order was based on Moltke's view that the main body of the French had, after Beaune-la-Rolande, gathered on the west side of the great road, and although the king, in spite of the repulse of the great sortie from Paris, was still uneasy as to the possibility of a French offensive on Fontainebleau, he allowed the chief of his staff to have his way. The order, consequently, went forth. Long before it could be translated into action, the battle of Loigny-Poupry had completely changed the situation. Yet it was obeyed, and no attempt was made by the prince either to obtain its cancellation or to override it by the exercise of the beloved "initiative." At the prince's headquarters it was construed as a reflection upon the lethargy of that army after Beaune-la-Rolande, and—although it was the incompleteness of his own reports of that action that had misled Moltke as to the magnitude of the effort that had been expended to win it—the prince, bitterly resentful, fell into that dangerous condition of mind which induces a punctilious execution of orders to the letter, at whatever cost and without regard to circumstances. Hence the order to the Detachment, which allowed the French field army to escape, and substituted for a decisive victory the barren "second capture of Orleans."

The plan for this second capture was simple: III. corps to fight its way from Pithiviers to Chilleurs-aux-Bois and thence down the Pithiviers-Orleans road through the forest, IX. corps to advance on Artenay and thence down the main road, Detachment to fight its way southward over the plains, X. corps in rear of the centre as reserve. Only a small force was left on the side of Montargis, and the III. and X. corps, which were many miles away to the south and south-east, had to get into position at once (evening of the 2nd) by night marches if necessary. In short, a single grand line of battle, 40 m. long, supported only by one corps in rear of the centre, was to sweep over all obstacles, woods, fields, orchards and enemy, at a uniform rate

Advance of the French left wing.

Battle of Loigny-Poupry.

The III. corps in Orleans Forest.

of progress, and on the evening of the second day to converge on Orleans.[1] The advance opened on the morning of the 3rd of December. The French left or main group included the 15th, 16th and 17th corps, the right of the 15th corps being in advance of the forest edge near Santeau. The right group, now under Bourbaki, consisted of the 18th and 20th corps, and faced north-east towards Beaune-la-Rolande and Montargis, the left flank being at Chambon. Fortunately for the III. corps, which numbered barely 13,000 rifles in all, the thinnest part of the opposing cordon was its centre, and the adventurous march of this corps carried it far into the forest to Loury. Only at Chilleurs was any serious resistance met with; elsewhere the French sheered off to their left, leaving the Pithiviers-Orleans road clear. In the night of the 3rd–4th isolated fractions of the enemy came accidentally in contact with von Alvensleben's outposts, but a sudden night encounter in woods was too much for the half-trained French, and a panic ensued, in which five guns were abandoned. But, as Alvensleben himself said, when he marched into the forest from Chilleurs he " went with open eyes into a den " from which it was more than probable he would never emerge—Chilleurs was, in fact, reoccupied behind him by part of the 15th corps. By the fortune of war the III. corps actually did emerge safely, but only thanks to the inactivity of the French right group under Bourbaki,[2] and to the almost entire absence of direct opposition, not to Prince Frederick Charles's dispositions.

On the main road, meantime, the IX. corps had captured a series of villages, and at nightfall of the short December day reached the N.W. corner of the Forest. The Detachment, slowly pushing before it part of the army it had defeated at Loigny, and protecting itself on the outer flank by a flank guard (I. Bavarians) against the rest, had closed in towards Chevilly. Prince Frederick Charles, angered by the slow, painful and indecisive day's work, ordered the advance to be continued and the French positions about Chevilly stormed in the dark, but fortunately was dissuaded by von Stosch, who rode over to his headquarters. But the prince never (except perhaps for a brief moment during the battle of Loigny-Poupry) believed that there was any serious obstacle in the way of the Detachment except its own fears, and repeatedly impressed upon Stosch the fact that Orleans was the watchword and the objective for every one.

In pursuance of the *idée fixe*, the prince issued orders for the 4th to the following effect: III. corps to advance on Orleans and to " bring artillery into action against the city," at the same time carefully guarding his left flank; IX. and 6th cavalry division to go forward along the general line of the main road; Detachment to make an enveloping attack on Gidy in concert with the attack of the IX. corps. In the forest Alvensleben, knowing that he could not capture Orleans single-handed, guarded his left with a whole division and with the other advanced on the city, stormed the village of Vaumainbert, which was stubbornly defended by a small French force, and close upon nightfall perfunctorily threw a few shells into Orleans. The flank-guard division had meanwhile been gravely imperilled by the advance of Crouzat's 20th corps, but once again the III. corps was miraculously saved, for Bourbaki, receiving word from d'Aurelle that the left group could not hold its position in advance of the Loire, and that the line of retreat of the right group was by Gien, ordered the fight to be broken off.

In the centre the IX. corps, after fighting hard all day, progressed no farther than Cercottes. The prince and the grand duke had a short interview, but, being personal enemies, their intercourse was confined to the prince's issuing his orders without inquiring closely into the positions of the Detachment and its opponents. Thus while the main body of the French left group, under the determined Chanzy, slipped away to the left, to continue the struggle for three months longer, the Detachment was compelled to conform to the movements of the IX. corps. But it was handled resolutely, and in the afternoon its right swung in to Ormes. The 2nd cavalry division, finding a target and open ground, charged the demoralized defenders with great effect, a panic began and spread, and by nightfall, when the prince, who was with the IX. corps, had actually given up hope of capturing Orleans that day and had issued orders to suspend the fight, his rival and subordinate was marching into Orleans with bands playing and colours flying. There was no pursuit, and the severed wings of the French army thenceforward carried on the campaign as two separate armies under Chanzy and Bourbaki respectively.

See F. Hoenig, *Volkskrieg an der Loire*, and L. A. Hale, *The People's War*, besides general and special histories and memoirs referred to in FRANCO-GERMAN WAR. (C. F. A.)

Second Battle of Orleans.

ORLEY, BERNARD VAN (1491?–1542), Flemish painter, the son and pupil of the painter Valentyn van Orley, was born at

---

[1] The same night Moltke received copies of the prince's orders and also news of the victory of Loigny-Poupry, but for some reason that is still unknown he let events take their course.

[2] With all his faults, Bourbaki was hardly responsible for this failure. Gambetta had for some days been giving orders to the 18th and 20th corps direct, but precisely at the moment he handed back the control of the group to d'Aurelle, this being arranged over the wires while the III. corps was advancing.

Brussels and completed his art education in Rome in the school of Raphael. He returned to Brussels, where he held an appointment as court painter to Margaret of Austria until 1527, in which year he lost this position and left the city. He only returned to it upon being reinstated by Mary of Hungary in 1532, and died there in 1542. Whilst in his earlier work he continued the tradition of the Van Eycks and their followers, he inaugurated a new era in Flemish art by introducing into his native country the Italian manner of the later Renaissance, the style of which he had acquired during his sojourn in Rome. His art marks the passing from the Gothic to the Renaissance period; he is the chief figure in the period of decline which preceded the advent of Rubens. Meticulously careful execution, brilliant colouring, and an almost Umbrian sense of design are the chief characteristics of his work.

Van Orley, together with Michael Coxcie, superintended the execution of van Aelst's tapestries for the Vatican, after Raphael's designs, and is himself responsible for some remarkable tapestry designs, such as the panels at Hampton Court. His also are the designs for some of the stained glass windows in the cathedral of Ste Gudule, in Brussels, at the museum of which city are a number of his principal works, notably the triptych representing "The Patience of Job" (1521). Among his finest paintings are a "Trinity" at Lübeck cathedral, a "Pietà" at Brussels, a Madonna at Munich and another at Liverpool.

The National Gallery owns a "Magdalen, reading," another version of the same subject being at the Dublin National Gallery. Lord Northbrook possesses a portrait of Charles V. by the master.

ORLOV, the name of a noble Russian family that produced several distinguished statesmen, diplomatists and soldiers.

GREGORY (*Grigorii*) GRIGORIEVICH ORLOV, COUNT (1734–1783), Russian statesman, was the son of Gregory Orlov, governor of Great Novgorod. He was educated in the corps of cadets at St Petersburg, began his military career in the Seven Years' War, and was wounded at Zorndorf. While serving in the capital as an artillery officer he caught the fancy of Catherine II., and was the leader of the conspiracy which resulted in the dethronement and death of Peter III. (1762). After the event, Catherine raised him to the rank of count and made him adjutant-general, director-general of engineers and general-in-chief. At one time the empress thought of marrying her favourite, but the plan was frustrated by Nikita Panin. Orlov's influence became paramount after the discovery of the Khitrovo plot to murder the whole Orlov family. Gregory Orlov was no statesman, but he had a quick wit, a fairly accurate appreciation of current events, and was a useful and sympathetic counsellor during the earlier portion of Catherine's reign. He entered with enthusiasm, both from patriotic and from economical motives, into the question of the improvement of the condition of the serfs and their partial emancipation. He was also their most prominent advocate in the great commission of 1767; though he aimed primarily at pleasing the empress, who affected great liberality in her earlier years. He was one of the earliest propagandists of the Slavophil idea of the emancipation of the Christians from the Turkish yoke. In 1771 he was sent as first Russian plenipotentiary to the peace-congress of Focshani; but he failed in his mission, owing partly to the obstinacy of the Turks, and partly (according to Panin) to his own outrageous insolence. On returning without permission to St Petersburg, he found himself superseded in the empress's favour by Vasil'chikov. When Potemkin, in 1771, superseded Vasil'chikov, Orlov became of no account at court and went abroad for some years. He returned to Russia a few months previously to his death, which took place at Moscow in 1780. For some time before his death he was out of his mind. Late in life he married his niece, Madame Zinoveva, but left no children.

See A. P. Barsukov, *Narratives from Russian History in the 18th Century* (Rus.) (St Petersburg, 1885).

ALEXIS GRIGORIEVICH ORLOV, COUNT (1737–1808), brother of the above, was by far the ablest member of the Orlov county family, and was also remarkable for his athletic strength and dexterity. In the revolution of 1762 he played an even more important part than his brother Gregory. It was he who conveyed Peter III. to the château of Ropsha and murdered him there with his own hands. In 1770 he was appointed commander-in-chief of the fleet sent against the Turks, whose far superior navy he annihilated at Cheshme (July 5th 1770), a victory which led to the conquest of the Greek archipelago. For this exploit he received, in 1774, the honorific epithet *Chesmensky*, and the privilege of quartering the imperial arms in his shield. The same year he went into retirement and settled at Moscow. He devoted himself to horse-breeding, and produced the finest race of horses then known by crossing Arab and Frisian, and Arab and English studs. In the war with Napoleon during 1806–07 Orlov commanded the militia of the fifth district, which was placed on a war footing almost entirely at his own expense. He left an estate worth five millions of roubles and 30,000 serfs.

See article, "The Associates of Catherine II.," No. 2, in *Russkaya Starina* (Rus.) (St Petersburg, 1873).

THEODORE (*Fedor*) GRIGORIEVICH ORLOV, COUNT (1741–1796), Russian general, first distinguished himself in the Seven Years' War. He participated with his elder brothers, Gregory and Alexis, in the *coup d'état* of 1762, after which he was appointed chief procurator of the senate. During the first Turkish War of Catherine II. he served under Admiral Spiridov, and was one of the first to break through the Turkish line of battle at Cheshme. Subsequently, at Hydra, he put to flight eighteen Turkish vessels. These exploits were, by the order of Catherine, commemorated by a triumphal column, crowned with naval trophies, erected at Tsarskoe Selo. In 1775 he retired from the public service. Orlov was never married, but had five natural children, whom Catherine ennobled and legitimatized.

ALEXIS FEDOROVICH ORLOV, PRINCE (1787–1862), Russian statesman, the son of a natural son of Count Theodore Grigorievich Orlov, took part in all the Napoleonic wars from 1805 to the capture of Paris. For his services as commander of the cavalry regiment of the Life Guards on the occasion of the rebellion of 1825 he was created a count, and in the Turkish War of 1828–29 rose to the rank of lieutenant-general. It is from this time that the brilliant diplomatic career of Orlov begins. He was the Russian plenipotentiary at the peace of Adrianople, and in 1833 was appointed Russian ambassador at Constantinople, holding at the same time the post of commander-in-chief of the Black Sea fleet. He was, indeed, one of the most trusty agents of Nicholas I, whom in 1837 he accompanied on his foreign tour. In 1854 he was sent to Vienna to bring Austria over to the side of Russia, but without success. In 1856 he was one of the plenipotentiaries who concluded the peace of Paris. The same year he was raised to the dignity of prince, and was appointed president of the imperial council of state and of the council of ministers. In 1857, during the absence of the emperor, he presided over the commission formed to consider the question of the emancipation of the serfs, to which he was altogether hostile.

His only son, PRINCE NIKOLAI ALEKSYEEVICH ORLOV (1827–1885), was a distinguished Russian diplomatist and author. He first adopted a military career, and was seriously wounded in the Crimean War. Subsequently he entered the diplomatic service, and represented Russia successively at Brussels (1860–1870), Paris (1870–1882) and Berlin (1882–1885). As a publicist he stood in the forefront of reform. His articles on corporal punishment, which appeared in *Russkaya Starina* in 1881, brought about its abolition. He also advocated tolerance towards the dissenters. His historical work, *Sketch of Three Weeks' Campaign in 1806* (St Petersburg, 1856) is still of value. (R. N. B.)

ORM, or ORMIN, the author of an English book, called by himself *Ormulum* ("because Orm made it"), consisting of metrical homilies on the gospels read at mass. The unique MS., now in the Bodleian Library, is certainly Orm's autograph, and contains abundant corrections by his own hand. On palaeographical grounds it is referred to about A.D. 1200, and this date is supported by the linguistic evidence. The dialect is midland, with some northern features. It is marked in an unparalleled degree by the abundance of Scandinavian words, while the French element in its vocabulary is extraordinarily small. The precise determination of the locality is not free from difficulty, as it is now recognized that the criteria formerly relied on for distinguishing between the eastern and the western varieties of the midland dialect are not valid, at least for this early period. The *Ormulum* certainly contains a surprisingly large number of words that are otherwise nearly peculiar to western texts; but the inference that might be drawn from this fact appears to be untenable in face of the remarkable lexical affinities between this work and *Havelok*, which is certainly of north-east midland origin. On the whole, the language of the *Ormulum* seems to point to north Lincolnshire as the author's native district.

The work is dedicated to a certain Walter, at whose request it was composed, and whom Orm addresses as his brother in a threefold sense—"according to the flesh," as his fellow-Christian, and as being a member of the same religious fraternity, that of the Augustinian Canons. The present writer has suggested (*Athenaeum*, 19th May 1906) that Orm and Walter may have been inmates of the Augustinian priory of Elsham, near the Humber, which was established about the middle of the 12th century by Walter de Amundeville. In his foundation charter (Dugdale's *Monasticon*, ed. Caley and Bandinel, vi. 560) Walter endows the priory with lands, and also grants to it the services of certain villeins, among whom are his steward (*praepositus*) William, son of Leofwine, and his wife and family. As this William is said to have had an uncle named Orm, and probably owed his Norman name to a godfather belonging to the Amundeville family, it seems not unlikely that the author of the *Ormulum* and his brother Walter were his sons, named respectively after their father's uncle and his lord, and that they entered the religious house of which they had been made subjects. The name Orm is Scandinavian (Old Norse *Ormr*, literally "serpent," corresponding to the Old Eng. *wyrm*, "worm"), and was not uncommon in the Danish parts of England. It occurs once in the book. The Gallicized form Ormin is found only in one passage, where the author gives it as the name by which he was christened. If this statement be meant literally (*i.e.* if the writer was not merely treating the two names as equivalent), it shows that he must, like his brother, have had a Norman godfather. The ending -*in* was frequently appended to names in Old French, *e.g.* in *Johannin* for *Johan*, John. The title *Ormulum* for the book which Orm made was probably an imitation of *Speculum*, a common medieval name for books of devotion or religious edification.

The Ormulum is written in lines alternately of eight and seven syllables, without either rhyme or alliteration. The rhythm may be seen from the opening couplet:

Nu, broþerr Wallterr, broþerr min
Affterr þe flæshess kinde.

The extant portion of the work, not including the dedication and introduction, consists of about 20,000 lines. But the table of contents refers to 242 homilies, of which only 31 are preserved; and as the dedication implies that the book had been completed, and that it included homilies on the gospels for nearly all the year, it would seem that the huge fragment which we possess is not much more than one-eighth of this extraordinary monument of pious industry.

The *Ormulum* is entirely destitute of poetic merit, though the author's visible enjoyment of his task renders it not uninteresting reading. To the history of biblical interpretation and of theological ideas it probably contributes little or nothing that is not well-known from other sources. For the philologist, however, the work is of immense value, partly as a unique specimen of the north-midland dialect of the period, and partly because the author had invented an original system of phonetic spelling, which throws great light on the contemporary pronunciation of English. In closed syllables the shortness of a vowel is indicated by the doubling of the following consonant. In open syllables this method would have been misleading, as it would have suggested a phonetic doubling of the consonant. In such

cases Orm had recourse to the device of placing the mark ˇ over the vowel. Frequently, but apparently not according to any discoverable rule, he distinguishes long vowels by one, two or three accents over the letter. Like some earlier writers, he retained the Old English form of the letter g (ʒ) where it expressed a spirant sound (not, however, distinguishing between the guttural and the palatal spirant), and used the continental g for the guttural stop and the sound *dzh*. He was, however, original in distinguishing the two latter sounds by using slightly different forms of the letter. This fact was unfortunately not perceived by the editors, so that the printed text confounds the two symbols throughout. The discovery was made by Professor A. S. Napier in 1890. It must be confessed that Orm often forgets his own rules of spelling, and although hundreds of oversights are corrected by interlineation, many inconsistencies still remain. Nevertheless, the orthography of the *Ormulum* is the most valuable existing source of information on the development of sounds in Middle English.

The *Ormulum* was edited for the first time by R. M. White in 1854. A revised edition, by R. Holt, was published in 1878. Many important corrections of the text were given by E. Kölbing in the first volume of *Englische Studien*. With reference to the three forms of the letter g, see A. S. Napier, *Notes on the Orthography of the Ormulum*, printed with *A History of the Holy Rood Tree* (Early English Text Society, 1894). (H. Br.)

ORMAZD, or ORMUZD (O. Persian *Auramazda* or *Ahuramazda*), the supreme deity of Zoroastrianism. He is represented as the god and creator of good, light, intelligence, in perpetual opposition to Ahriman the lord of evil, darkness and ignorance. The dualism of the earlier Zoroastrians, which may be compared with the Christian doctrine of God and Satan, gradually tended in later times towards monotheism. At all times it was believed that Ormazd would ultimately vanquish Ahriman. See further ZOROASTER.

ORME, ROBERT (1728–1801), English historian of India, was born at Anjengo on the Malabar coast on the 25th of December 1728, the son of a surgeon in the Company's service. Educated at Harrow, he was appointed to a writership in Bengal in 1743. He returned to England in 1753 in the same ship with Clive, with whom he formed a close friendship. From 1754 to 1758 he was a member of council at Madras, in which capacity he largely influenced the sending of Clive to Calcutta to avenge the catastrophe of the Black Hole. His great work—*A History of the Military Transactions of the British Nation in Indostan from 1745*—was published in three volumes in 1763 and 1778 (Madras reprint, 1861–1862). This was followed by a volume of *Historical Fragments* (1781), dealing with an earlier period. In 1769 he was appointed historiographer to the East India Company. He died at Ealing on the 13th of January 1801. His valuable collections of MSS. are in the India Office library. The characteristics of his work, of which the influence is admirably shown in Thackeray's *The Newcomes*, are thus described by Macaulay: "Orme, inferior to no English historian in style and power of painting, is minute even to tediousness. In one volume he allots, on an average, a closely printed quarto page to the events of every forty-eight hours. The consequence is that his narrative, though one of the most authentic and one of the most finely written in our language, has never been very popular, and is now scarcely ever read." Not a few of the most picturesque passages in Macaulay's own Essay on Clive are borrowed from Orme. (J. S. Co.)

ORMEROD, ELEANOR A. (1828–1901), English entomologist, was the daughter of George Ormerod, F.R.S., author of *The History of Cheshire*, and was born at Sedbury Park, Gloucestershire, on the 11th of May 1828. From her earliest childhood insects were her delight, and the opportunity afforded for entomological study by the large estate upon which she grew up and the interest she took in agriculture generally soon made her a local authority upon this subject. When, in 1868, the Royal Horticultural Society began forming a collection of insect pests of the farm for practical purposes, Miss Ormerod largely contributed to it, and was awarded the Flora medal of the society. In 1877 she issued a pamphlet, *Notes for Observations* *on Injurious Insects,* which was distributed among persons interested in this line of inquiry, who readily sent in the results of their researches, and was thus the beginning of the well-known *Annual Series of Reports on Injurious Insects and Farm Pests.* In 1881 Miss Ormerod published a special report upon the " turnip-fly," and in 1882 was appointed consulting entomologist to the Royal Agricultural Society, a post she held until 1892. For several years she was lecturer on scientific entomology at the Royal Agricultural College, Cirencester. Her fame was not confined to England: she received silver and gold medals from the university of Moscow for her models of insects injurious to plants, and her treatise on *The Injurious Insects of South Africa* showed how wide was her range. In 1899 she received the large silver medal from the Société Nationale d' Acclimatation de France. Among others of her works are the *Cobden Journals, Manual of Injurious Insects,* and *Handbook of Insects injurious to Orchard and Bush Fruits.* Almost the last honour which fell to her was the honorary degree of LL.D. of Edinburgh University—a unique distinction, for she was the first woman upon whom the university had conferred this degree. The dean of the legal faculty in making the presentation aptly summoned up Miss Ormerod's services as follows: " The pre-eminent position which Miss Ormerod holds in the world of science is the reward of patient study and unwearying observation. Her investigations have been chiefly directed towards the discovery of methods for the prevention of the ravages of those insects which are injurious to orchard, field and forest. Her labours have been crowned with such success that she is entitled to be hailed the protectress of agriculture and the fruits of the earth—a beneficent Demeter of the 19th century." She died at St Albans on the 19th of July 1901.

ORMOC, a town of the province of Leyte, island of Leyte, Philippine Islands, on the W. coast about 35 m. S.W. of Tacloban. Pop. (1903), after the annexation of Albuera, 20,761. There are thirty-three barrios or villages in the town, and the largest of them had a population in 1903 of 5410. The language is Visayan. Ormoc is in a great hemp-producing region and is open to coast trade.

ORMOLU (Fr. *or moulu,* gold ground or pounded), an alloy of copper and zinc, sometimes with an addition of tin. The name is also used to describe gilded brass or copper. The tint of ormolu approximates closely to that of gold; it is heightened by a wash of gold lacquer, by immersion in dilute sulphuric acid, or by burnishing. The principal use of ormolu is for the mountings of furniture. With it the great French *ébénistes* of the 18th century obtained results which, in the most finished examples, are almost as fine as jewelers' work. The mounts were usually cast and then chiselled with extraordinary skill and delicacy.

ORMOND, a village and winter resort of Volusia county, Florida, U.S.A., about 68 m. by rail S. of St Augustine. It is situated on the Halifax river, an arm of the Atlantic Ocean extending for 25 m. along the E. coast of Florida. Pop. (1900) 505; (1905) 680; (1910) 780. It is served by the Florida East Coast Railway. The Halifax river region is famous for its excellent oranges and grape-fruit. The hard and compact Ormond-Daytona beach, about 200 ft. wide at low tide and about 20 m. long, offers exceptional facilities for driving, motoring and bicycling; on it are held the annual tournaments of the Florida East Coast Automobile Association. The old King's Road, built by the English between 1763 and 1783, from St Mary's, Georgia, some 400 m. to the south, has been improved for automobiles between Ormond and Jacksonville. About 2 m. west of Ormond are the ruins of an old sugar mill, probably dating from the last quarter of the 18th century and not, as is frequently said, from the Spanish occupation in the 16th century. About 5 m. south of Ormond and also on the Halifax river is another popular winter resort, Daytona (pop. 1900, 1690; 1905, 2199; 1910, 3181), founded in 1870 as Tomoka by Mathias Day of Mansfield, Ohio, in whose honour it was renamed Daytona in 1871. Its streets and drives are shaded by live oaks, palmettos, hickories and magnolias.

ORMONDE, EARL AND MARQUESS OF, titles still held by the famous Irish family of Butler (*q.v.*), the name being taken from a district now part of Co. Tipperary. In 1328 James Butler (*c.* 1305–1337), a son of Edmund Butler, was created earl of Ormonde, one reason for his elevation being the fact that his wife Eleanor, a daughter of Humfrey Bohun, earl of Hereford, was a granddaughter of King Edward I. His son James, the 2nd earl (1331–1382), was four times governor of Ireland; the latter's grandson James, the 4th earl (d. 1452), held the same position several times, and won repute not only as a soldier, but as a scholar. His son James, the 5th earl (1420–*c.* 1461), was created an English peer as earl of Wiltshire in 1440. A truculent partisan of the house of Lancaster, he was lord high treasurer of England in 1455 and again in 1459, and was taken prisoner after the battle of Towton in 1461. He and his two brothers were than attainted, and he died without issue, the exact date of his death being unknown. The attainder was repealed in the Irish parliament in 1476, when his brother Sir John Butler (*c.* 1422–1478), who had been pardoned by Edward IV. a few years previously, became 6th earl of Ormonde. John, who was a fine linguist, served Edward IV. as ambassador to many European princes, and this king is said to have described him as "the goodliest knight he ever beheld and the finest gentleman in Christendom." His brother Thomas, the 7th earl (*c.* 1424–1515), a courtier and an English baron under Richard III. and Henry VII., was ambassador to France and to Burgundy; he left no sons, and on his death in August 1515 his earldom reverted to the crown.

Margaret, a daughter of this earl, married Sir William Boleyn of Blickling, and their son Sir Thomas Boleyn (1477–1539) was created earl of Ormonde and of Wiltshire in 1529. He went on several important errands for Henry VIII., during one of which he arranged the preliminaries for the Field of the Cloth of Gold; he was lord privy seal from 1530 to 1536, and served the king in many other ways. He was the father of Henry's queen, Anne Boleyn, but both this lady, and her only brother, George Boleyn, had been put to death before their father died in March 1539.

Meanwhile in 1515 the title of earl of Ormonde had been assumed by Sir Piers Butler (*c.* 1467–1539), a cousin of the 7th earl, and a man of great influence in Ireland. He was lord deputy, and later lord treasurer of Ireland, and in 1528 he surrendered his claim to the earldom of Ormonde and was created earl of Ossory. Then in 1538 he was made earl of Ormonde, this being a new creation; however, he counts as the 8th earl of the Butler family. In 1550 his second son Richard (d. 1571) was created Viscount Mountgarret, a title still held by the Butlers. The 8th earl's son, James, the 9th earl (*c.* 1490–1546), lord high treasurer of Ireland, was created Viscount Thurles in 1536. In 1544 an act of parliament confirmed him in the possession of his earldom, which, for practical purposes, was declared to be the creation of 1328, and not the new creation of 1538.

Thomas, the 10th earl (1532–1614), a son of the 9th earl, was lord high treasurer of Ireland and a very prominent personage during the latter part of the 16th century. He was a Protestant and threw his great influence on the side of the English queen and her ministers in their efforts to crush the Irish rebels, but he was perhaps more anxious to prosecute a fierce feud with his hereditary foe, the earl of Desmond, this struggle between the two factions desolating Munster for many years. His successor was his nephew Walter (1569–1633), who was imprisoned from 1617 to 1625 for refusing to surrender the Ormonde estates to his cousin Elizabeth, the wife of Sir R. Preston and the only daughter of the 10th earl. He was deprived of the palatine rights in the county of Tipperary, which had belonged to his ancestors for 400 years, but he recovered many of the family estates after his release from prison in 1625.

Walter's grandson, James, the 12th earl, was created marquess of Ormonde in 1642 and duke of Ormonde in 1661 (see below); his son was Thomas Butler, earl of Ossory (*q.v.*), and his grandson was James Butler, 2nd duke of Ormonde (see below).

When Charles Butler, earl of Arran (1671–1758), the brother and successor of the 2nd duke, died in December 1758, the dukedom and marquessate became extinct, but the earldom was claimed by a kinsman, John Butler (d. 1766). John's cousin, Walter (1703–1783), inherited this claim, and Walter's son John (1740–1795) obtained a confirmation of it from the Irish House of Lords in 1791. He is reckoned as the 17th earl. His son Walter, the 18th earl (1770–1820), was created marquess of Ormonde in 1816, a title which became extinct on his death, but was revived in favour of his brother James (1774–1838) in 1825. James was the grandfather of James Edward William Theobald Butler (b. 1844), who became the 3rd marquess in 1854. The marquess sits in the House of Lords as Baron Ormonde of Llanthony, a creation of 1821.

See J. H. Round on "The Earldoms of Ormonde" in Joseph Foster's *Collectanea Genealogica* (1881–1883).

ORMONDE, JAMES BUTLER, 1st Duke of (1610–1688), Irish statesman and soldier, eldest son of Thomas Butler, Viscount Thurles, and of Elizabeth, daughter of Sir John Poyntz, and grandson of Walter, 11th earl of Ormonde (see above), was born in London on the 19th of October 1610. On the death of his father by drowning in 1619, the boy was made a royal ward by James I., removed from his Roman Catholic tutor, and placed in the household of Abbot, archbishop of Canterbury, with whom he stayed until 1625, residing afterwards in Ireland with his grandfather. In 1629, by his marriage with his cousin, the Lady Elizabeth Preston, daughter and heiress of Richard, earl of Desmond, he put an end to the long-standing quarrel between the families and united their estates. In 1632 on the death of his grandfather he succeeded him to the earldom.

He was already noted in Ireland, as had been many of his race, for his fine presence and great bodily vigour. His active career began in 1633 with the arrival of Strafford, by whom he was treated, in spite of his independence of character, with great favour. Writing to the king, Strafford described him as "young, but take it from me, a very staid head," and Ormonde was throughout his Irish government his chief friend and support. In 1640 during Strafford's absence he was made commander-in-chief of the forces, and in August he was appointed lieutenant-general. On the outbreak of the rebellion in 1641 he rendered admirable service in the expedition to Naas, and in the march into the Pale in 1642, though much hampered by the lords justices, who were jealous of his power and recalled him after he had succeeded in relieving Drogheda. He was publicly thanked by the English parliament and presented with a jewel of the value of £620. On the 15th of April 1642 he gained the battle of Kilrush against Lord Mountgarret. On the 30th of August he was created a marquess, and on the 16th of September was appointed lieutenant-general with a commission direct from the king. On the 18th of March 1643 he won the battle of New Ross against Thomas Preston, afterwards Viscount Tara. In September, the civil war in England having meanwhile broken out, Ormonde, in view of the successes of the rebels and the uncertain loyalty of the Scots in Ulster, concluded with the latter, in opposition to the lords justices, on the 15th of September, the "cessation" by which the greater part of Ireland was given up into the hands of the Catholic Confederation, leaving only small districts on the east coast and round Cork, together with certain fortresses in the north and west then actually in their possession, to the English commanders. He subsequently, by the king's orders, despatched a body of troops into England (shortly afterwards routed by Fairfax at Nantwich) and was appointed in January 1644 lord lieutenant, with special instructions to do all in his power to keep the Scotch army occupied. In the midst of all the plots and struggles of Scots, Old Irish, Catholic Irish of English race, and Protestants, and in spite of the intrigues of the pope's nuncio as well as of attempts by the parliament's commissioners to ruin his power, Ormonde showed the greatest firmness and ability. He assisted Antrim in his unsuccessful expedition into Scotland. On the 28th of March 1646 he concluded a treaty with the Irish which granted religious concessions and removed various grievances. Mean-

while the difficulties of his position had been greatly increased by Glamorgan's treaty with the Roman Catholics on the 25th of August 1645, and it became clear that he could not long hope to hold Dublin against the Irish rebels. He thereupon applied to the English parliament, signed a treaty on the 19th of June 1647, gave Dublin into their hands upon terms which protected the interests of both Protestants and Roman Catholics so far as they had not actually entered into rebellion, and sailed for England at the beginning of August. He attended Charles during August and October at Hampton Court, but subsequently, in March 1648, in order to avoid arrest by the parliament, he joined the queen and prince of Wales at Paris. In September of the same year, the pope's nuncio having been expelled, and affairs otherwise looking favourable, he returned to Ireland to endeavour to unite all parties for the king. On the 17th of January 1649 he concluded a peace with the rebels on the basis of the free exercise of their religion, on the execution of the king proclaimed Charles II. and was created a knight of the Garter in September. He upheld the royal cause with great vigour though with slight success, and on the conquest of the island by Cromwell he returned to France in December 1650.

Ormonde now, though in great straits for want of money, resided in constant attendance upon Charles and the queen-mother in Paris, and accompanied the former to Aix and Cologne when expelled from France by Mazarin's treaty with Cromwell in 1655. In 1658 he went disguised, and at great risk, upon a secret mission into England to gain trustworthy intelligence as to the chances of a rising. He attended the king at Fuenterrabia in 1659 and had an interview with Mazarin; and was actively engaged in the secret transactions immediately preceding the Restoration. On the return of the king he was at once appointed a commissioner for the treasury and the navy, made lord steward of the household, a privy councillor, lord lieutenant of Somerset (an office which he resigned in 1672), high steward of Westminster, Kingston and Bristol, chancellor of Dublin University, Baron Butler of Llanthony and earl of Brecknock in the peerage of England; and on the 30th of March 1661 he was created duke of Ormonde in the Irish peerage and lord high steward of England. At the same time he recovered his enormous estates in Ireland, and large grants in recompense of the fortune he had spent in the royal service were made to him by the king, while in the following year the Irish parliament presented him with £30,000. His losses, however, according to Carte, exceeded his gains by £868,000. On the 4th of November 1661 he once more received the lord lieutenancy of Ireland, and was busily engaged in the work of settling that country. The most important and most difficult problem was the land question, and the Act of Explanation was passed through the Irish parliament by Ormonde on the 23rd of December 1665. His heart was in his government, and he vehemently opposed the bill prohibiting the importation of Irish cattle which struck so fatal a blow at Irish trade; and retaliated by prohibiting the import into Ireland of Scottish commodities, and obtained leave to trade with foreign countries. He encouraged Irish manufactures and learning to the utmost, and it was to his efforts that the Irish College of Physicians owes its incorporation.

Ormonde's personality had always been a striking one, and in the new reign his virtues and patriotism became still more conspicuous. He represented almost alone the older and nobler generation. He stood aloof while the counsels of the king were guided by dishonour; and proud of the loyalty of his race which had remained unspotted through five centuries, he bore with silent self-respect calumny, envy and the loss of royal favour, declaring, "However ill I may stand at court I am resolved to lye well in the chronicle."

He soon became the mark for attack from all that was worst in the court. Buckingham especially did his utmost to undermine his influence. Ormonde's almost irresponsible government of Ireland during troublous times was no doubt open to criticism. He had billeted soldiers on civilians, and had executed martial law. The impeachment, however, threatened by Buckingham in 1667 and 1668 fell through. Nevertheless by

1669 constant importunity had had its usual effect upon Charles, and on the 14th of March Ormonde was removed from the government of Ireland and from the committee for Irish affairs. He made no complaint, insisted that his sons and others over whom he had influence should retain their posts, and continued to fulfil with dignified persistence the duties of his other offices, while the greatness of his character and services was recognized by his election as chancellor of Oxford University on the 4th of August.

In 1670 an extraordinary attempt was made to assassinate the duke by a ruffian and adventurer named Thomas Blood, already notorious for an unsuccessful plot to surprise Dublin Castle in 1663, and later for stealing the royal crown from the Tower. Ormonde was attacked by this person and his accomplices while driving up St James's Street on the night of the 6th of December, dragged out of his coach, and taken on horseback along Piccadilly with the intention of hanging him at Tyburn. Ormonde, however, succeeded in overcoming the horseman to whom he was bound, and his servants coming up, he escaped. The outrage, it was suspected, had been instigated by the duke of Buckingham, who was openly accused of the crime by Lord Ossory, Ormonde's son, in the king's presence, and threatened by him with instant death if any violence should happen to his father; and some colour was given to these suspicions by the improper action of the king in pardoning Blood, and in admitting him to his presence and treating him with favour after his apprehension while endeavouring to steal the crown jewels.

In 1671 Ormonde successfully opposed Richard Talbot's attempt to upset the Act of Settlement. In 1673 he again visited Ireland, returned to London in 1675 to give advice to Charles on affairs in parliament, and in 1677 was again restored to favour and reappointed to the lord lieutenancy. On his arrival in Ireland he occupied himself in placing the revenue and the army upon a proper footing. Upon the outbreak of the popish terror in England, he at once took the most vigorous and comprehensive steps, though with as little harshness as possible, towards rendering the Roman Catholics, who were in the proportion of 15 to 1, powerless; and the mildness and moderation of his measures served as the ground of an attack upon him in England led by Shaftesbury, from which he was defended with great spirit by his son Lord Ossory. In 1682 Charles summoned Ormonde to court. The same year he wrote "A Letter ... in answer to the earl of Anglesey, his Observations upon the earl of Castlehaven's Memoires concerning the Rebellion of Ireland," and gave to Charles a general support. On the 9th of November 1682 an English dukedom was conferred upon him, and in June 1684 he returned to Ireland; but he was recalled in October in consequence of fresh intrigues. Before, however, he could give up his government to Rochester, Charles II. died; and Ormonde's last act as lord lieutenant was to proclaim James II. in Dublin. Subsequently he lived in retirement at Cornbury in Oxfordshire, lent to him by Lord Clarendon, but emerged from it in 1687 to offer a firm and successful opposition at the board of the Charterhouse to James's attempt to assume the dispensing power, and force upon the institution a Roman Catholic candidate without taking the oaths according to the statutes and the act of parliament. He also refused the king his support in the question of the Indulgence; notwithstanding which James, to his credit, refused to take away his offices, and continued to hold him in respect and favour to the last.

Ormonde died on the 21st of July 1688, not having, as he rejoiced to know, "outlived his intellectuals"; and with him disappeared the greatest and grandest figure of the times. His splendid qualities were expressed with genuine felicity in verses written on welcoming his return to Ireland and printed in 1682:

"A Man of Plato's grand nobility,
An inbred greatness, innate honesty;
A Man not form'd of accidents, and whom
Misfortune might oppress, not overcome ...
Who weighs himself not by opinion
But conscience of a noble action."

He was buried in Westminster Abbey on the 1st of August.

He had, besides two daughters, three sons who grew to maturity. The eldest of these, Thomas, earl of Ossory (1634-1680) predeceased him, his eldest son succeeding as and duke of Ormonde. The other two, Richard, created earl of Arran, and John, created earl of Gowran, both dying without male issue, and the male descent of the 1st duke becoming extinct in the person of Charles, 3rd duke of Ormonde, the earldom subsequently reverted to the descendants of Walter, 11th earl of Ormonde.

AUTHORITIES.—*Life of the Duke of Ormonde*, by Thomas Carte; the same author's *Collection of Original Letters, found among the Duke of Ormonde's Papers* (1739), and the Carte MSS. in the Bodleian Library at Oxford: *Life of Ormonde*, by Sir Robert Southwell, printed in the *History of the Irish Parliament*, by Lord Mountmorres (1792), vol. i.; *Correspondence between Archbishop Williams and the Marquess of Ormonde*, ed. by B. H. Beedham (reprinted from *Archaeologia Cambrensis*, 1869); *Observations on the Articles of Peace between James, Earl of Ormonde, and the Irish Rebels*, by John Milton; *Hist. MSS. Comm.* Reps. ii.-iv. and vi.-x., esp. Rep. viii., appendix, p. 499, and Rep. xiv. App.: pt. vii., *MSS. of Marquis of Ormonde*, together with new series; *Notes and Queries*, vi. ser. v., pp. 343, 431; Gardiner's *Hist. of the Civil War*; *Calendar of State Papers (Domestic)* and *Irish,1633-1662*,with introductions; *Biographia Britannica* (Kippis); *Scottish Hist. Soc. Publications: Letters and Papers* of 1650, ed. by S. R. Gardiner, vol. xvii. (1894).

ORMONDE, JAMES BUTLER, 2ND DUKE OF (1665-1745), Irish statesman and soldier, son of Thomas, earl of Ossory, and grandson of the 1st duke, was born in Dublin on the 29th of April 1665, and was educated in France and afterwards at Christ Church, Oxford. On the death of his father in 1680 he became earl of Ossory by courtesy. He obtained command of a cavalry regiment in Ireland in 1684, and having received an appointment at court on the accession of James II., he served against the duke of Monmouth. Having succeeded his grandfather as duke of Ormonde in 1688, he joined William of Orange, by whom he was made colonel of a regiment of horse-guards, which he commanded at the battle of the Boyne. In 1691 he served on the continent under William, and after the accession of Anne he was placed in command of the land forces co-operating with Sir George Rooke in Spain. Having been made a privy councillor, Ormonde succeeded Rochester as viceroy of Ireland in 1703, a post which he held till 1707. On the dismissal of the duke of Marlborough in 1711, Ormonde was appointed captain-general in his place, and allowed himself to be made the tool of the Tory ministry, whose policy was to carry on the war in the Netherlands while giving secret orders to Ormonde to take no active part in supporting their allies under Prince Eugene. Ormonde's position as captain-general made him a personage of much importance in the crisis brought about by the death of Queen Anne. Though he had supported the revolution of 1688, he was traditionally a Tory, and Lord Bolingbroke was his political leader. During the last years of Queen Anne he almost certainly had Jacobite leanings, and corresponded with the duke of Berwick. He joined Bolingbroke and Oxford, however, in signing the proclamation of King George I., by whom he was nevertheless deprived of the captain-generalship. In June 1715 he was impeached, and fled to France, where he for some time resided with Bolingbroke, and in 1716 his immense estates were confiscated to the crown by act of parliament, though by a subsequent act his brother, Charles Butler, earl of Arran, was enabled to repurchase them. After taking part in the Jacobite invasion in 1715, Ormonde settled in Spain, where he was in favour at court and enjoyed a pension from the crown. Towards the end of his life he resided much at Avignon, where he was seen in 1733 by Lady Mary Wortley Montagu. Ormonde died on the 16th of November 1745, and was buried in Westminster Abbey.

With little of his grandfather's ability, and inferior to him in elevation of character, Ormonde was nevertheless one of the great figures of his time. Handsome, dignified, magnanimous and open-handed, and free from the meanness, treachery and venality of many of his leading contemporaries, he enjoyed a popularity which, with greater stability of purpose, might have enabled him to exercise commanding influence over events.

See Thomas Carte, *Hist. of the Life of James, Duke of Ormonde* (6 vols., Oxford, 1851), which contains much information respecting the life of the second duke; Earl Stanhope, *Hist of England, comprising the Reign of Queen Anne until the Peace of Utrecht* (London, 1870); F. W. Wyon, *Hist. of Great Britain during the Reign of Queen Anne* (2 vols., London, 1876); William Coxe, *Memoirs of Marlborough* (3 vols., new edition, London; 1847).

ORMSKIRK, a market town and urban district in the Ormskirk parliamentary division of Lancashire, England, 11 m. N.E. of Liverpool by the Lancashire and Yorkshire railway   Pop. (1901), 6857.   The church of St Peter and St Paul is a spacious building in various styles of architecture, but principally Perpendicular. It possesses the rare feature of two western towers, the one square and embattled, the other octagonal and bearing a short spire.   There are various Norman fragments, including a fine early window in the chancel. To the south-east of the church, and divided from it by a screen, is the Derby chapel, the exclusive property of the earls of Derby, whose vault is contained within. A free grammar school was founded about 1614. Rope and twine making, iron-founding and brewing are carried on, and the town has long been famous for its gingerbread.

The name and church existed in the time of Richard I., when the priory of Burscough was founded. A few fragments of this remain about 2 m. N. of Ormskirk. The prior and convent obtained from Edward I. a royal charter for a market at the manor of Ormskirk. On the dissolution of the monasteries the manor was granted to the earl of Derby.

ORNAMENT (Lat. *ornare*, to adorn), in decorative art, that element which adds an embellishment of beauty in detail. Ornament is in its nature accessory, and implies a thing to be ornamented, which is its active cause and by rights suggests its design (*q.v.*). It does not exist apart from its application. Nor is it properly *added* to a thing already in existence (that is but a makeshift for design), but is rather such modification of the thing *in the making* as may be determined by the consideration of beauty. For example, the construction and proportions of a chair are determined by use (by the necessity of combining the maximum of strength with the minimum of weight, and of fitting it to the proportions of the human body, &c.); and any modification of the plan, such as the turning of legs, the shaping of arms and back, carving, inlay, mouldings, &c.—any reconsideration even of the merely utilitarian plan from the point of view of art—has strictly to do with Ornament, which thus, far from being an afterthought, belongs to the very inception of the thing. Ornament is good only in so far as it is an indispensable part of something, helping its effect without hurt to its use. It is begotten of use by the consideration of beauty. The test of ornament is its *fitness*. It must occupy a space, fulfil a purpose, be adapted to the material in which and the process by which it is executed. This implies *treatment*. The treatment befitting a wall space does not equally befit a floor space of the same dimensions. What is suitable to hand-painting is not equally suitable to stencilling; nor what is proper to mosaic proper to carpet-weaving. Neither the purposes of decoration nor the conditions of production allow great scope for naturalism in ornament. Its forms are derived from nature, more or less; but repose is best secured by some removedness from nature—necessitated also by the due treatment of material after its kind and according to its fashioning. In the case of recurring ornament it is inept to multiply natural flowers, &c., which at every repetition lose something of their natural attraction. The artist in ornament does not imitate natural forms. Such as he may employ he transfigures. He does not necessarily set out with any idea of natural form (this comes to him by the way); his first thought is to solve a given problem in design, and he solves it perhaps most surely by means of abstract ornament—witness the work of the Greeks and of the Arabs. The extremity of tasteless naturalism, reached towards the beginning of the Victorian era, was the opportunity of English reformers, prominent amongst whom was Owen Jones, whose fault was in insisting upon a form of ornament too abstract to suit English ideas. William Morris and others led the way

back to nature, but to nature trained in the way of ornament. The Styles of ornament, so-called, mark the evolution of design, being the direct outcome of Greek, Roman, Byzantine, Gothic or other conditions, in days when fashion moved slowly. Post-Renaissance ornament goes by the name of the reigning king; but the character of the historic periods was not sought by artists; it came of their working in the way natural to them and doing their best. "Style," as distinguished from "the Styles," comes of an artist's intelligent and sympathetic treatment of his material, and of his personal sincerity and strength. International traffic has gone far to do away with national characteristics in ornament, which becomes yearly more and more alike all the world over. The subsidiary nature of ornament and its subjection to conditions lead to its frequent repetition, which results in *pattern*, repeated forms falling inevitably into lines, always self-asserting, and liable to annoy in proportion as they were not foreseen by the designer. He cannot, therefore, safely disregard them. Indeed, his first business is to build pattern upon lines, if not intrinsically beautiful, at least helpful to the scheme of decoration. He may disguise them, but capable designers are generally quite frank, about the construction of their pattern, and not afraid of pronounced lines. Of course, adaptation being all-essential to pattern, an artist must be versed in the technique of any manufacture for which he designs. His art is in being equal to the occasion.   (L. F D.)

ORNE, a department of the north-west of France, about half of which formerly belonged to the province of Normandy and the rest to the duchy of Alençon and to Perche. Pop. (1906) 315,993. Area, 2371 sq. m. It is bounded N. by Calvados, N.E. by Eure, E. and S.E. by Eure-et-Loir, S by Sarthe and Mayenne and W. by Manche. Geologically there are two distinct regions: to the west of the Orne and the railway from Argentan to Alençon lie primitive rocks connected with those of Brittany, to the east begin the Jurassic and Cretaceous formations of Normandy. The latter district is agriculturally the richest part of the department; in the former the poverty of the soil has led the inhabitants to seek their subsistence from industrial pursuits. Between the northern portions, draining to the Channel, and the southern portion, belonging to the basin of the Loire, stretch the hills of Perche and Normandy, which generally have a height of from 800 to 1000 ft. The highest point in the department, situated in the forest of Écouves north of Alençon, reaches 1368 ft. The department gives birth to three Seine tributaries—the Eure, its affluent the Iton, and the Risle, which passes by Laigle. The Touques, passing by Vimoutiers, the Dives and the Orne fall into the English Channel, the last passing Sées and Argentan, and receiving the Noireau with its tributary the Vère, which runs past Flers. Towards the Loire flows the Huisne, a feeder of the Sarthe passing by Mortagne, the Sarthe, which passes by Alençon, and the Mayenne, some of whose affluents make their way to the north of the dividing range and make their way through it by the most picturesque defiles. The department, indeed, with its beautiful forests containing oaks several centuries old, its meadows, streams, deep gorges and stupendous rocks, is one of the most picturesque of all France. In the matter of climate Orne belongs to the Seine region. The mean temperature is 50° F.; the summer heat is never extreme; the west winds are the most frequent; the rainfall, distributed over about a hundred days in the year, amounts to 36 in. or about 5 in. more than the average for France.

Horse-breeding is the most flourishing business in the rural districts; there are three breeds—those of Perche, Le Merlerault and Brittany. The great government stud of Le Pin-au-Haras (established in 1714), with its school of horse-breeding, is situated between Le Merlerault and Argentan. Several horse-training establishments exist in the department. A large number of lean cattle are bought in the neighbouring departments to be fattened; the farms in the vicinity of Vimoutiers, on the borders of Calvados, produce the famous Camembert cheese, and others excellent butter. The bee industry is very flourishing. Oats, wheat, barley and buckwheat are the chief cereals, besides which fodder in great quantity and variety, potatoes and some hemp are grown. The variety of production is due to the great natural diversity of the soils. Small farms are the rule, and the fields in those cases are surrounded by hedges relieved by pollard trees. Along the roads or in the enclosures are planted numerous pear and apple trees, the latter yielding cider, part of which is manufactured into brandy. Beech, oak, birch and pine are the chief timber trees in the extensive forests of the department. Orne has iron mines and freestone quarries; a kind of smoky quartz known as Alençon diamond is found. Its most celebrated mineral waters are those of the hot springs of Bagnoles, which contain salt, sulphur and arsenic, and are employed for tonic and restorative purposes in cases of general debility. In the forest of Bellême is the chalybeate spring of La Hesse, which was used by the Romans.

Cotton and linen weaving, principally carried on at Flers (q.v.) and La Ferté-Macé (pop. 4355), forms the staple industry of Orne. Alençon and Vimoutiers are engaged in the production of linen and canvas. Vimoutiers has bleacheries, which, together with dye-works, are found in the textile centres. Only a few workmen are now employed at Alençon in the making of the lace which takes its name from the town. Foundries and wire-works also exist in the department, and articles in copper, zinc and lead are manufactured. Pins, needles, wire and hardware are produced at Laigle (pop. 4416), and Tinchebray is also a centre for hardware manufacture. There are also glass-works, paper-mills, tanneries (the waters of the Orne being reputed to give a special quality to the leather) and glove-works. Coal, raw cotton, metals and machinery are imported into the department, which exports its woven and metal manufacture, live stock and farm produce.

The department is served by the Western railway. There are four arrondissements, with Alençon, the capital, Argentan, Domfront and Mortagne as their chief towns, 36 cantons and 512 communes. The department forms the diocese of Sées (province of Rouen) and part of the académie (educational division) of Caen, and the region of the IV. army corps; its court of appeal is at Caen: The chief places are Alençon, Argentan, Mortagne, Flers and Sées. Carrouges has remains of a château of the 15th and 17th centuries; Chambois has a donjon of the 12th century; and there is a fine Renaissance château at O. A church in Laigle has a fine tower of the 15th century. There are a great number of megalithic monuments in the department.

ORNITHOLOGY,[1] properly the methodical study and consequent knowledge of birds with all that relates to them; but the difficulty of assigning a limit to the commencement of such study and knowledge gives the word a very vague meaning, and practically procures its application to much that does not enter the domain of science. This elastic application renders it impossible in the following sketch of the history of ornithology to draw any sharp distinction between works that are emphatically ornithological and those to which that title can only be attached by courtesy; for, since birds have always attracted far greater attention than any other group of animals with which in number or in importance they can be compared, there has grown up concerning them a literature of corresponding magnitude and of the widest range, extending from the recondite and laborious investigations of the morphologist and anatomist to the casual observations of the sportsman or the schoolboy.

Though birds make a not unimportant appearance in the earliest written records of the human race, the painter's brush has preserved their counterfeit presentment for a still longer period. A fragmentary fresco taken from a tomb at Medum was deposited some years ago, though in a decaying condition, in the Museum of Egyptian Antiquities, Cairo. This Egyptian picture was said to date from the time of the third or fourth dynasty, some three thousand years before the Christian era. In it were depicted with a marvellous fidelity, and thorough appreciation of form and colouring (despite a certain conventional

[1] *Ornithologia*, from the Greek ὄρνις, crude form of ὄρνις, a bird, and -λογία, allied to λέγειν, commonly Englished a discourse. The earliest known use of the word Ornithology seems to be in the third edition of Blount's *Glossographia* (1670), where it is noted as being "the title of a late Book."

treatment), the figures of six geese. Four of these figures can be unhesitatingly referred to two species (*Anser albifrons* and *A. ruficollis*) well known at the present day. In later ages the representations of birds of one sort or another in Egyptian paintings and sculptures become countless, and the *bassi-rilievi* of Assyrian monuments, though mostly belonging of course to a subsequent period, are not without them. No figures of birds, however, seem yet to have been found on the incised stones, bones or ivories of the prehistoric races of Europe.

History of Ornithology to End of 18th Century.

Aristotle was the first serious author on ornithology with whose writings we are acquainted, but even he had, as he tells us, predecessors; and, looking to that portion of his **Early works.** works on animals which has come down to us, one finds that, though more than 170 sorts of birds are mentioned,[2] yet what is said of them amounts on the whole to very little, and this consists more of desultory observations in illustration of his general remarks (which are to a considerable extent physiological or bearing on the subject of reproduction) than of an attempt at a connected account of birds. One of his commentators, C. J. Sundevall—equally proficient in classical as in ornithological knowledge—was, in 1863, compelled to leave more than a score of the birds of which Aristotle wrote unidentified. Next in order of date, though at a long interval, comes Pliny the Elder, in whose *Historia Naturalis* Book X. is devoted to birds. Neither Aristotle nor Pliny attempted to classify the birds known to them beyond a very rough and for the most part obvious grouping. Aristotle seems to recognize eight principal groups: (1) *Gampsonyches*, approximately equivalent to the *Accipitres* of Linnaeus; (2) *Scolecophaga*, containing most of what would now be called *Oscines*, excepting indeed the (3) *Acanthophaga*, composed of the goldfinch, siskin and a few others; (4) *Scnipophaga*, the woodpeckers; (5) *Peristeroïde*, or pigeons; (6) *Schizopoda*, (7) *Steganopoda*, and (8) *Barea*, nearly the same respectively as the Linnaean *Grallae*, *Anseres* and *Gallinae*. Pliny, relying wholly on characters taken from the feet, limits himself to three groups—without assigning names to them—those which have "hooked tallons, as Hawkes; or round long clawes, as Hennes; or else they be broad, flat, and whole-footed, as Geese and all the sort in manner of water-foule"—to use the words of Philemon Holland, who, in 1601, published a quaint and, though condensed, yet fairly faithful English translation of Pliny's work.

About a century later came Aelian, who died about A.D. 140, and compiled in Greek (though he was an Italian by birth) a number of miscellaneous observations on the peculiarities of animals. His work is a kind of commonplace book kept without scientific discrimination. A considerable number of birds are mentioned, and something said of almost each of them; but that something is too often nonsense according to modern ideas. The twenty-six books *De Animalibus* of Albertus Magnus (Groot), printed in 1478, are founded mainly on Aristotle. The twenty-third of these books is *De Avibus*, and therein a great number of birds' names make their earliest appearance, few of which are without interest from a philologist's if not an ornithologist's point of view, but there is much difficulty in recognising the species to which many of them belong. In 1485 was printed the first dated copy of the volume known as the *Ortus sanitatis*, to the popularity of which many editions testify.[3] Though said by its author, Johann Wonnecke von Caub (Latinised as Johannes de Cuba), to have been composed from a study of the

[2] This is Sundevall's estimate; Drs Aubert and Wimmer in their excellent edition of the Ἰστορίαι περὶ ζῴων (Leipzig, 1868) limit the number to 126.

[3] Absurd as much that we find both in Albertus Magnus and the *Ortus* seems to modern eyes, if we go a step lower in the scale and consult the "Bestiaries" or treatises on animals which were common from the 12th to the 14th century we shall meet with many more absurdities. See for instance that by Philippe de Thaun (Philippus Taonensis), dedicated to Adelaide or Alice, queen of Henry I. of England, and probably written soon after 1121, as printed by the late Mr Thomas Wright, in his *Popular Treatises on Science written during the Middle Ages* (London, 1841).

collections formed by a certain nobleman who had travelled in Eastern Europe, Western Asia and Egypt—possible Breidenbach, an account of whose travels in the Levant was printed at Ments in 1486—it is really a medical treatise, and its zoological portion is mainly an abbreviation of the writings of Albertus Magnus, with a few interpolations from Isidorus of Seville (who flourished in the beginning of the 7th century, and was the author of many works highly esteemed in the middle ages) and a work known as *Physiologus* (q.v.). The third *tractatus* of this volume deals with· birds—including among them bats, bees and other flying creatures; but as it is the first printed book in which figures of birds are introduced it merits notice, though most of the illustrations, which are rude woodcuts, fail, even in the coloured copies, to give any ·precise indication of the species intended to be represented.

The revival of learning was at hand, and William Turner, a Northumbrian, while residing abroad to avoid persecution at home, printed at Cologne in 1544 the· first commentary on the birds mentioned by Aristotle and Pliny conceived in anything like the spirit that moves modern naturalists.[1] In the same year and from the same press was issued a *Dialogus de Auibus* by Gybertus Longolius, and in 1570 Caius brought out in London his treatise *De rariorum animalium atque stirpium historia*. In this last work, small though it be, ornithology has a good share; and all three may still be consulted with interest and advantage by its votaries.[2] Meanwhile the study received a great impulse from the appearance, at Zurich in 1555, of the third book of Conrad Gesner's *Historia Animalium* " qvi est de Auium natura," and at Paris in the same year of Pierre Belon's (Bellonius) *Histoire de la nature des Oyseaux*. Gesner brought an amount of erudition, hitherto unequalled, to bear upon his subject; and, making due allowance for the times in which he wrote, his judgment must in most respects be deemed excellent. In his work, however, there is little that can be called systematic treatment. Like nearly all his predecessors since Aelian, he adopted an alphabetical arrangement, though this was not too pedantically preserved, and did not hinder him from placing together the kinds of birds which he supposed (and generally supposed rightly) to have the most resemblance to that one whose name, being best known, was chosen for the headpiece (as it were) of his particular theme, thus recognizing to some extent the principle of classification.[3] Belon, with perhaps less book-learning than his contemporary, was evidently no mean scholar, and undoubtedly had more practical knowledge of birds—their internal as well as external structure. Hence his work, written in French, contains a far greater amount of original matter; and his personal observations made in many countries, from England to Egypt, enabled him to avoid most of the puerilities which disfigure other works of his own or of a preceding age. Besides this, Belon disposed the birds known to him according to a definite system, which (rude as we now know it to be) formed a foundation on which several of his successors were content to build, and even to this day traces of its influence may still be discerned in the arrangement followed by writers who have faintly appreciated the principles on which modern taxonomers rest the outline of their schemes. Both his work and that of Gesner were ·illustrated with woodcuts, many of which display much spirit and regard to accuracy.

Belon, as has just been said, had a knowledge of the anatomy

of birds, and he seems to have been the first to institute a direct comparison of their skeleton with that of man; but in this respect he only anticipated by a few years the more precise researches of Volcher Coiter, a Frisian, who in 1573 and 1575 published at Nuremberg two treatises, in one of which the internal structure of birds in general is very creditably described, while in the other the osteology and myology of certain forms is given in considerable detail, and illustrated by carefully drawn figures. The first is entitled *Externarum et internarum principalium humani corporis Tabulae*, &c. while the second, which is the most valuable, is merely appended to the *Lectiones Gabrielis. Fallopii de partibus similaribus humani corporis*, &c., and thus, the scope of each work being regarded as medical, the author's labours were wholly overlooked by the mere naturalhistorians who followed, though Coiter introduced a table, " De differentiis Auium," furnishing a key to a rough classification of such birds as were known to him, and this as nearly the first attempt of the kind deserves notice here.

Contemporary with these three men was Ulysses Aldrovandus, a Bolognese, who wrote an *Historia Naturalium* in sixteen folio volumes, most of which were not printed till after his death in 1605; but those on birds appeared between 1599 and 1603. The work is almost wholly a compilation, and that not of the most discriminative kind, while a peculiar jealousy of Gesner is continuously displayed, though his statements are ·very constantly quoted—nearly always as those of " Ornithologus," his name appearing but few times in the text, and not at all in the list of authors cited. With certain modifications in principle not very important, but characterized by much more elaborate detail, Aldrovandus adopted Belon's method of arrangement, but in a few respects there is a manifest retrogression. The work of Aldrovandus was illustrated by copperplates, but none of his figures approach those of his immediate predecessors in character or accuracy. Nevertheless the book was eagerly sought, and several editions of it appeared.[4]

Mention must be made of a medical treatise by Caspar Schwenckfeld, published at Liegnitz in 1603, under the title of *Theriotrophæum Silesiæ*, the fourth book of which consists of an " Aviarium Silesiae," and is the earliest of the works we now know by the name of fauna. The author was well acquainted with the labours of his predecessors, as his list of over one hundred of them testifies. Most of the birds he describes are characterized with accuracy sufficient to enable them to be identified, and his observations upon them have still some interest; but he was innocent of any methodical system, and was not exempt from most of the professional fallacies of his time.[5]

Hitherto, with the exception of the case, the works aforesaid treated of scarcely any but the birds belonging to the *orbis veteribus notus*; but the geographical discoveries of the 16th century began to bear fruit, and many animals of kinds unsuspected were, about one hundred years later, made known. Here there is only space to name Bontius, Clusius, Hernandez (or Fernandez), Marcgrave, Nieremberg and Piso,[6] whose several works describing the natural products of both the Indies—whether the result of their own observation or compilation—together with those of Olina and Worm, produced a marked effect, since they led up to what may be deemed the foundation of scientific ornithology.[7]

[1] This was reprinted at Cambridge in 1823 by Dr George Thackeray.

[2] The Seventh of Wotton's *De differentiis animalium Libri Decem*, published at Paris in 1552, treats of birds; but his work is merely a compilation from Aristotle and Pliny, with references to other classical writers who have more or less incidentally mentioned birds and other animals. The author in his preface states—" Veterum scriptorum sententias in unum quasi cumulum coaceruaui, de meo nihil addidi:" Nevertheless he makes some attempt at a systematic arrangement of birds, which, according to his lights, is far from despicable.

[3] For instance, under the title of " Accipiter " we have to look, not only for the sparrow-hawk and gos-hawk, but for many other birds of the family (as we now call it) removed comparatively far from those species by modern ornithologists.

[4] The *Historia Naturalis* of Johannes Johnstonus, said to be of Scottish descent but by birth a Pole, ran through several editions during the 17th century, but is little more than an epitome of the work of Aldrovandus.

[5] The *Hierozoicon* of Bochart—a treatise on the animals named in Holy Writ—was published in 1619.

[6] For Lichtenstein's determination of the birds described by Marcgrave and Piso see the *Abhandlungen* of the Berlin Academy for 1817 (pp. 155 seq.).

[7] The earliest list of British birds seems to be that in the *Pinax Rerum Naturalium* of Christopher Merrett, published in 1667. In the following year appeared the *Onomasticon Zooicon* of Walter Charleton, which contains some information on ornithology An enlarged edition of the latter, under the title of *Exercitationes*, &c., was published in 1677, but neither of these writers is of much authority. In 1684 Sibbald in his *Scotia illustrata* published the earliest Fauna of Scotland.

This foundation was laid by the joint labours of Francis Willughby (1635-1672) and John Ray (1628-1705), for it is impossible to separate their share of work in natural **Willughby** history more than to say that, while the former more **and Ray.** especially devoted himself to zoology, botany was the favourite pursuit of the latter. Together they studied, together they travelled and together they collected. Willughby, the younger of the two, and at first the other's pupil, seems to have gradually become the master; but, he dying before the promise of his life was fulfilled, his writings were given to the world by his friend Ray, who, adding to them from his own stores, published the *Ornithologia* in Latin in 1676, and in English with many emendations in 1678. In this work birds generally were grouped in two great divisions—"land-fowl" and "water-fowl"—the former being subdivided into those which have a crooked beak and talons, and those which have a straighter bill and claws, while the latter was separated into those which frequent waters and watery places, and those that swim in the water—each subdivision being further broken up into many sections, to the whole of which a key was given. Thus it became possible for almost any diligent reader without much chance of error to refer to its proper place nearly every bird he was likely to meet with. Ray's interest in ornithology continued, and in 1694 he completed a *Synopsis Methodica Avium*, which, through the fault of the booksellers to whom it was entrusted, was not published till 1713, when Derham gave it to the world.[1]

Two years after Ray's death, Linnaeus, the great reformer of natural history, was born, and in 1735 appeared the first **Linnæus.** edition of the celebrated *Systema Naturae*. Successive editions of this work were produced under its author's supervision in 1740, 1748, 1758 and 1766. Impressed by the belief that verbosity was the bane of science, he carried terseness to an extreme which frequently created obscurity, and this in no branch of zoology more than in that which relates to birds. Still the practice introduced by him of assigning to each species a diagnosis by which it ought in theory to be distinguishable from any other known species, and of naming it by two words—the first being the generic and the second the specific term, was so manifest an improvement upon anything which had previously obtained that the Linnaean method of differentiation and nomenclature established itself before long in spite of all opposition, and in principle became almost universally adopted. In his classification of birds Linnaeus for the most part followed Ray, and where he departed from his model he seldom improved upon it.

In 1745 P. Barrère brought out a little book called *Ornithologiae Specimen novum*, and in 1752 Möhring published at Aurich one still smaller, his *Avium Genera*. Both these works (now rare) are manifestly framed on the Linnaean method, so far as it had then reached; but in their arrangement of the various forms of birds they differed greatly from that which they designed to supplant, and they deservedly obtained little success. Yet as systematists their authors were no worse than Klein, whose *Historiae Avium Prodromus*, appearing at Lübeck in 1750, and *Stemmata Avium* at Leipzig in 1759, met with considerable favour in some quarters. The chief merit of the latter work lies in its forty plates, whereon the heads and feet of many birds are indifferently figured.[2]

But, while the successive editions of Linnaeus's great work were revolutionizing natural history, and his example of precision in language producing excellent effect on scientific writers, several other authors were advancing the study of ornithology in a very different way—a way that pleased the eye even more than his labours were pleasing the mind. Between 1731 and

1743 Mark Catesby brought out in London his *Natural History of Carolina*—two large folios containing highly coloured plates of the birds of that colony, Florida and the Bahamas.[3] Eleazar Albin between 1738 and 1740 produced a *Natural History of Birds* in three volumes of more modest dimensions; but he seems to have been ignorant of ornithology, and his coloured plates are greatly inferior to Catesby's. Far better both as draughtsman and as authority was George Edwards, who in 1743 began, under the same title as Albin, a series of plates with letterpress, which was continued by the name of *Gleanings in Natural History*, and finished in 1760, when it had reached seven parts, forming four quarto volumes, the figures of which are nearly always quoted with approval.[4]

The year which saw the works of Edwards completed was still further distinguished by the appearance in France, where little had been done since Belon's days,[?] in six quarto volumes, **Brisson.** of the *Ornithologie* of Mathurin Jacques Brisson—a work of very great merit so far as it goes, for as a descriptive ornithologist the author stands even now unsurpassed; but it must be said that his knowledge, according to internal evidence, was confined to books and to the external parts of birds' skins. It was enough for him to give a scrupulously exact description of such specimens as came under his eye, distinguishing these by prefixing two asterisks to their name, using a single asterisk where he had only seen a part of the bird, and leaving unmarked those that he described from other authors. His attempt at classification was certainly better than that of Linnaeus; and it is rather curious that the researches of the latest ornithologists point to results in some degree comparable with Brisson's systematic arrangement, for they refuse to keep the birds-of-prey at the head of the Class *Aves*, and they require the establishment of a much larger number of "Orders" than for a long while was thought advisable. Of such "Orders" Brisson had twenty-six and he gave pigeons and poultry precedence of the birds which are plunderers and scavengers. But greater value lies in his generic or sub-generic divisions, which, taken as a whole, are far more natural than those of Linnaeus, and consequently capable of better diagnosis. More than this, he seems to be the earliest ornithologist, perhaps the earliest zoologist, to conceive the idea of each genus possessing what is now called a "type" —though such a term does not occur in his work; and, in like manner, without declaring it in so many words, he indicated unmistakably the existence of subgenera—all this being effected by the skilful use of names. Unfortunately he was too soon in the field to avail himself, even had he been so minded, of the convenient mode of nomenclature brought into use by Linnaeus. Immediately on the completion of his *Règne Animale* in 1756, Brisson set about his *Ornithologie*, and it is only in the last two volumes of the latter that any reference is made to the tenth edition of the *Systema Naturae*, in which the binomial method was introduced. It is certain that the first four volumes were written if not printed before that method was promulgated, and when the fame of Linnaeus as a zoologist rested on little more than the very meagre sixth edition of the *Systema Naturae* and the first edition of his *Fauna Suecica*. Brisson has been charged with jealousy of, if not hostility to, the great Swede, and it is true that in the preface to his *Ornithologie* he complains of the insufficiency of the Linnaean characters, but, when one considers how much better acquainted with birds the Frenchman was, such criticism must be allowed to be pardonable if not wholly just. Brisson's work was in French, with a parallel translation (edited, it is said, by Pallas) in Latin, which last was reprinted separately at Leiden three years afterwards.

---

[1] To this was added a supplement by Petiver on the Birds of Madras, taken from pictures and information sent him by one Edward Buckley of Fort St George, being the first attempt to catalogue the birds of any part of the British possessions in India.

[2] After Klein's death his *Prodromus*, written in Latin, had the unwonted fortune of two distinct translations into German, published in the same year 1760, the one at Leipzig and Lübeck by Behn, the other at Danzig by Reyger—each of whom added more or less to the original.

[?] Several birds from Jamaica were figured in Sloane's *Voyage*, &c. (1705-1725), and a good many exotic species in the *Thesaurus*, &c., of Seba (1734-1765), but from their faulty execution these plates had little effect upon Ornithology.

[4] The works of Catesby and Edwards were afterwards reproduced at Nuremberg and Amsterdam by Seligmann, with the letterpress in German, French and Dutch.

[?] Birds were treated of in a worthless fashion by one D. B. in a *Dictionnaire raisonné et universel des animaux*, published at Paris in 1759.

In 1767 there was issued at Paris a book entitled *L'Histoire naturelle éclaircie dans une de ses parties principales, l'ornithologie*. This was the work of Salerne, published after his death, and is often spoken of as being a mere translation of Ray's *Synopsis*, but a vast amount of fresh matter, and mostly of good quality, is added.

The success of Edwards's very respectable work seems to have provoked competition, and in 1765, at the instigation of Buffon, the younger d'Aubenton began the publication known as the *Planches enluminées d'histoire naturelle*, which appearing in forty-two parts was not completed till 1780, when the plates[1] it contained reached the number of 1008—all coloured, as its title intimates, and nearly all representing birds. This enormous work was subsidized by the French government; and, though the figures are utterly devoid of artistic merit, they display the species they are intended to depict with sufficient approach to fidelity to ensure recognition in most cases without fear of error, which in the absence of any text is no small praise.[2]

But Buffon was not content with merely causing to be published this unparalleled set of plates. He seems to have regarded the work just named as a necessary precursor to his own labours in ornithology. His *Histoire naturelle, générale et particulière*, was begun in 1749, and in 1770 he brought out, with the assistance of Guénau de Montbeillard,[3] the first volume of his great *Histoire naturelle des oiseaux*. Buffon was the first man who formed any theory that may be called reasonable of the geographical distribution of animals. He proclaimed the variability of species in opposition to the views of Linnaeus as to their fixity, and moreover supposed that this variability arose in part by degradation.[4] Taking his labours as a whole, there cannot be a doubt that he enormously enlarged the purview of naturalists, and, even if limited to birds, that, on the completion of his work upon them in 1783, ornithology stood in a very different position from that which it had before occupied.

Great as were the services of Buffon to ornithology in one direction, those of a wholly different kind rendered by John Latham must not be overlooked. In 1781 he began a work the practical utility of which was immediately recognized. This was his *General Synopsis of Birds*, and, though formed generally on the model of Linnaeus, greatly diverged in some respects therefrom. The classification was modified, chiefly on the old lines of Willughby and Ray, and certainly for the better; but no scientific nomenclature was adopted, which, as the author subsequently found, was a change for the worse. His scope was co-extensive with that of Brisson, but Latham did not possess the inborn faculty of picking out the character wherein one species differs from another. His opportunities of becoming acquainted with birds were hardly inferior to Brisson's, for during Latham's long lifetime there poured in upon him countless new discoveries from all parts of the world, but especially from the newly-explored shores of Australia and the islands of the Pacific Ocean. The British Museum had been formed, and he had access to everything it contained in addition to the abundant materials afforded him by the private museum of Sir Ashton Lever.[5] Latham entered, so far as the limits of his work would allow, into the

[1] They were drawn and engraved by Martinet, who himself began in 1787 a *Histoire des oiseaux* with small coloured plates which have some merit, but the text is worthless.

[2] Between 1767 and 1776 there appeared at Florence a *Storia Naturale degli Uccelli*, in five folio volumes, containing a number of ill-drawn and ill-coloured figures from the collection of Giovanni Gerini, an ardent collector who died in 1751, and therefore must be acquitted of any share in the work, which, though sometimes attributed to him, is that of certain learned men who did not happen to be ornithologists (cf. Savi, *Ornitologia Toscana*, i. Introduzione, p. v.).

[3] He retired on the completion of the sixth volume, and thereupon Buffon associated Bexon with himself.

[4] See St George Mivart's address to the Section of Biology, *Rep. Brit Association* (Sheffield Meeting, 1879), p. 356.

[5] In 1792 Shaw began the *Museum Leverianum* in illustration of this collection, which was finally dispersed by sale, and what is known to remain of it found its way to Vienna. Of the specimens in the British Museum described by Latham it is to be feared that scarcely any exist. They were probably very imperfectly prepared.

history of the birds he described, and this with evident zest whereby he differed from his French predecessor; but the number of cases in which he erred as to the determination of his species must be very great, and not unfrequently the same species is described more than once. His *Synopsis* was finished in 1785; two supplements were added in 1787 and 1802,[6] and in 1790 he produced an abstract of the work under the title of *Index Ornithologicus*, wherein he assigned names on the Linnaean method to all the species described. Not to recur again to his labours, it may be said here that between 1821 and 1828 he published at Winchester, in eleven volumes, an enlarged edition of his original work, entitling it *A General His ory of Birds*; but his defects as a compiler, which had been manifest before, rather increased with age, and the consequences were not happy.[7]

About the time that Buffon was bringing to an end his studies of birds, Mauduyt undertook to write the *Ornithologie* of the *Encyclopédie méthodique*—a comparatively easy task, considering the recent works of his fellow-countrymen on that subject, and finished in 1784. Here it requires no further comment, especially as a new edition was called for in 1790, the ornithological portion of which was begun by Bonnaterre, who, however, had only finished three hundred and twenty pages of it when he lost his life in the French Revolution; and the work thus arrested was continued by Vieillot under the slightly changed title of *Tableau encyclopédique et méthodique des trois règnes de la Nature*—the *Ornithologie* forming volumes four to seven, and not completed till 1823. In the former edition Mauduyt had taken the subjects alphabetically; but here they are disposed according to an arrangement, with some few modifications, furnished by d'Aubenton, which is extremely shallow and unworthy of consideration.

Several other works bearing upon ornithology in general, but of less importance than most of those just named, belong to this period. Among others may be mentioned the *Genera of Birds* by Thomas Pennant, first printed at Edinburgh in 1773, but best known by the edition which appeared in London in 1781; the *Elementa Ornithologica* and *Museum Ornithologicum* of Schäffer, published at Ratisbon in 1774 and 1784 respectively; Peter Brown's *New Illustrations of Zoology* in London in 1776; Hermann's *Tabulae Affinitatum Animalium* at Strasburg in 1783, followed posthumously in 1804 by his *Observationes Zoologicae*; Jacquin's *Beytraege sur Geschichta der Voegel* at Vienna in 1784, and in 1790 at the same place the larger work of Spalowsky with nearly the same title; Sparrman's *Museum Carlsonianum* at Stockholm from 1786 to 1789; and in 1794 Hayes's *Portraits of rare and curious Birds* from the menagery of Child the banker at Osterley near London. The same draughtsman (who had in 1775 produced a *History of British Birds*) in 1822 began another series of *Figures of rare and curious Birds*.[8]

The practice of Brisson, Buffon, Latham and others of neglecting to name after the Linnaean fashion the species they described gave great encouragement to compilation, and led to what has proved to be of some inconvenience to modern ornithologists. In 1773 P. L. S. Müller brought out at Nuremberg a German translation of the *Systema Naturae*, completing it in 1776 by a *Supplement* containing a list of animals thus described, which had hitherto been technically anonymous, with diagnoses and names on the Linnaean model. In 1783 Boddaert printed at Utrecht a *Table des planches enluminées*,[9] in which he attempted to refer every species of bird figured in that extensive series to its proper Linnaean genus, and to assign it a scientific name if it did not already possess one. In like manner in 1786, Scopoli—already the author of a little book published at Leipzig in 1769 under the title of *Annus I. Historico-naturalis*, in which are described many birds, mostly from his

[6] A German translation by Bechstein subsequently appeared.

[7] He also prepared for publication a second edition of his *Index Ornithologicus*, but this was never printed, and the manuscript came into A. Newton's possession.

[8] *The Naturalist's Miscellany* or *Vivarium Naturale*, in English and Latin, of Shaw and Nodder, the former being the author, the latter the draughtsman and engraver, was begun in 1789 and carried on till Shaw's death, forming twenty-four volumes. It contains figures of more than 280 birds, but very poorly executed. In 1814 a sequel, *The Zoological Miscellany*, was begun by Leach, Nodder continuing to do the plates. This was completed in 1817, and forms three volumes with 149 plates, 27 of which represent birds.

[9] Of this work only fifty copies were printed, and it is one of the rarest known to the ornithologist. Only two copies are believed to exist in England, one in the British Museum, the other in private hands. It was reprinted in 1874 by Mr Tegetmeier.

own collection or the Imperial vivarium at Vienna—was at the pains to print at Pavia in his miscellaneous *Deliciae Florae et Faunae Insubricae* a *Specimen Zoologicum*[1] containing diagnoses, duly named, of the birds discovered and described by Sonnerat in his *Voyage aux Indes orientales* and *Voyage à la Nouvelle Guinée*, severally published at Paris in 1772 and 1776. But the most striking example of compilation was that exhibited by J. F. Gmelin, who in 1788 commenced what he called the Thirteenth Edition of the celebrated *Systema Naturae*, which obtained so wide a circulation that, in the comparative rarity of the original, the additions of this editor have been very frequently quoted, even by expert naturalists, as though they were the work of the author himself. Gmelin availed himself of every publication he could, but he perhaps found his richest booty in the labours of Latham, neatly condensing his English descriptions into Latin diagnoses, and bestowing on them binomial names. Hence it is that Gmelin appears as the authority for so much of the nomenclature now in use. He took many liberties with the details of Linnaeus's work, but left the classification, at least of the birds, as it was—a few new genera excepted.[2]

During all this time little had been done in studying the internal structure of birds;[3] but the foundations of the science of embryology had been laid by the investigations into the development of the chick by the great Harvey. Between 1666 and 1669 Perrault edited at Paris eight accounts of the dissection by du Verney of as many species of birds, which, translated into English, were published by the Royal Society in 1702, under the title of *The Natural History of Animals*. After the death of the two anatomists just named, another series of similar descriptions of eight other species was found among their papers, and the whole were published in the *Mémoires* of the French Academy of Sciences in 1733 and 1734. But in 1681 Gerard Blasius had brought out at Amsterdam an *Anatome Animalium*, containing the results of all the dissections of animals that he could find; and the second part of this book, treating of *Volatilia*, makes a respectable show of more than one hundred and twenty closely-printed quarto pages, though nearly two-thirds is devoted to a treatise *De Ovo et Pullo*, containing among other things a reprint of Harvey's researches. and the scientific rank of the whole book may be inferred from bats being still classed with birds. In 1720 Valentini published, at Frankfort-on-the-Main, his *Amphitheatrum Zootomicum*, in which again most of the existing accounts of the anatomy of birds were reprinted. But these and many other contributions,[4] made until nearly the close of the 18th century, though highly meritorious, were unconnected as a whole, and it is plain that no conception of what it was in the power of Comparative Anatomy to set forth had occurred to the most diligent dissectors.

It was reserved for Georges Cuvier, who in 1798 published at Paris his *Tableau élémentaire de l'histoire naturelle des animaux*, to lay the foundation of a thoroughly and correct hitherto unknown mode of appreciating the value of the various groups of the animal kingdom. Yet his first attempt was a mere sketch.[5] Though he made a perceptible advance on the classification of Linnaeus, at that time predominant, it is now easy to see in how many ways—want of sufficient material being no doubt one of the chief—Cuvier failed to produce a really natural arrangement. His principles, however, are those which must still guide taxonomers, notwithstanding that they have in so great a degree overthrown the entire scheme which he propounded. Confining our attention here to ornithology, Cuvier's arrangement of the class *Aves* is now seen to be not very much better than any which it superseded. But this view is gained by following the methods which Cuvier taught. In the work just mentioned few details are given; but even the more elaborate classification of birds contained in his *Leçons d'anatomie comparée* of 1805 is based wholly on external characters, such as had been used by nearly all his predecessors; and the *Règne Animal* of 1817, when he

[1] This was reprinted in 1882 by the Willughby Society.
[2] Daudin's unfinished *Traité élémentaire et complet d'ornithologie* appeared at Paris in 1800. and therefore is the last of these general works published in the 18th century
[3] A succinct notice of the older works on ornithotomy is given by Professor Selenka in the introduction to that portion of Dr Bronn's *Klassen und Ordnungen des Thierreichs* relating to birds (pp. 1-9) published in 1869: and Professor Carus's *Geschichte der Zoologie*, published in 1872, may also be usefully consulted for further information on this and other heads.
[4] The treatises of the two Bartholinis and Borrichius published at Copenhagen deserve mention if only to record the activity of Danish anatomists in those days.
[5] It had no effect on Lacépède, who in the following year added a *Tableau méthodique* containing a classification of birds to his *Discours d'ouverture* (*Mém. de l'Institut*, iii. pp. 454-468, 503-519).

was in his fullest vigour, afforded not the least evidence that he had ever dissected a couple even of birds[6] with the object of determining their relative position in his system, which then, as before, depended wholly on the configuration of bills, wings and feet. But, though apparently without such a knowledge of the anatomy of birds as would enable him to apply it to the formation of that natural system which he was fully aware had yet to be sought, he seems to have been an excellent judge of the characters afforded by the bill and limbs, and the use he made of them, coupled with the extraordinary reputation he acquired on other grounds, procured for his system the adhesion for many years of the majority of ornithologists.[7]

Hitherto mention has chiefly been made of works on general ornithology, but it will be understood that these were largely aided by the enterprise of travellers, and as there were many of them who published their narratives in separate forms their contributions have to be considered. Of those travellers then the first to be here especially named is Marsigli, the fifth volume of whose *Danubius Pannonico-Mysicus* is devoted to the birds he met with in the valley of the Danube, and appeared at the Hague in 1725, followed by a French translation in 1744.[8] Most of the many pupils whom Linnaeus sent to foreign countries submitted their discoveries to him, but Kalm, Hasselqvist and Osbeck published separately their respective travels in North America, the Levant and China.[9] The incessant journeys of Pallas and his colleagues—Falk, Georgi, S. G. Gmelin, Güldenstädt, Lepechin and others—in the exploration of the recently extended Russian empire supplied not only much material to the *Commentarii* and *Acta* of the Academy of St Petersburg, but more that is to be found in their narratives—all of it being of the highest interest to students of Palaearctic or Nearctic ornithology. Nearly the whole of their results, it may here be said, were summed up in the important *Zoographia Rosso-Asiatica* of the first-named naturalist, which saw the light in 1811—the year of its author's death—but, owing to circumstances over which he had no control, was not generally accessible till twenty years later. Of still wider interest are the accounts of Cook's three famous voyages, though unhappily much of the information gained by the naturalists who accompanied him on one or more of them seems to be irretrievably lost: the original observations of the elder Forster were not printed till 1844, and the valuable collection of zoological drawings made by the younger Forster still remains unpublished in the British Museum. The several accounts by John White, Collins, Phillips, Hunter and others of the colonization of New South Wales at the end of the last century ought not to be overlooked by any Australian ornithologist. The only information at this period on the ornithology of South America is contained in the two works on Chile by Molina, published at Bologna in 1776 and 1782. The travels of Le Vaillant in South Africa having been completed li. 1785, his great *Oiseaux d'Afrique* began to appear in Paris in 1797: but it is hard to speak properly of this work, for several of the species described in it are certainly not, and never were in his time, inhabitants of that country, though he sometimes gives a long account of the circumstances under which he observed them.[10]

From travellers who employ themselves in collecting the animals of any distant country the zoologists who stay at home and study those of their own district, be it great or small, are really not so much divided as at first might appear. Both may well be named "Faunists," and of the latter there were not a few who having turned their attention more or less to ornithology should here be

[6] So little regard did he pay to the osteology of birds that, according to de Blainville (*Jour. de Physique*, xcii. p. 187, note), the skeleton of a fowl to which was attached the head of a hornbill was for a long time exhibited in the Museum of Comparative Anatomy at Paris! Yet, in order to determine the difference of structure in their organs of voice, Cuvier, as he says in his *Leçons* (iv. 464), dissected more than one hundred and fifty species of birds. Unfortunately for him, as will appear in the sequel, it seems not to have occurred to him to use any of the results he obtained as the basis of a classification.
[7] It is unnecessary to enumerate the various editions of the *Règne Animal*. Of the English translations, that edited by Griffiths and Pidgeon is the most complete. The ornithological portion of it contained in these volumes received many additions from John Edward Gray, and appeared in 1829.
[8] Though much later in date, the *Iter per Poseganam Sclavoniae* of Piller and Mitterpacher, published at Buda in 1783, may perhaps be here most conveniently mentioned.
[9] The results of Forskål's travels in the Levant, published after his death by Niebuhr, require mention, but the ornithology they contain is but scant.
[10] It has been charitably suggested that, his collection and notes having suffered shipwreck, he was induced to supply the latter from his memory and the former by the nearest approach to his lost specimens that he could obtain. This explanation, poor as it is, fails, however, in regard to some species.

mentioned, and first among them Rzaczynski, who in 1721 brought out at Sandomirsk the *Historia naturalis curiosa regni Poloniae*, to which an *Auctuarium* was posthumously published at Danzig in 1742. This also may be perhaps the most proper place to notice the *Historiae avium Hungaricae* of Grossinger, published at Posen in 1793. In 1734 J. L. Frisch began the long series of works on the birds of Germany with which the literature of ornithology is enriched, by his *Vorstellung der Vögel Teutschlands*, which was only completed in 1763, and, its coloured plates proving very attractive, was again issued at Berlin in 1817. The little fly-sheet of *Zorn*—for it is scarcely more—on the birds of the Hercynian Forest made its appearance at Pappenheim in 1745. In 1756 Kramer published at Vienna a modest *Elenchus* of the plants and animals of Lower Austria, and J. D. Petersen produced at Altona in 1766 a *Verzeichniss holsteiescher Vögel*; while in 1791 J. B. Fischer's *Versuch einer Naturgeschichte von Livland* appeared at Königsberg, next year BESEKE brought out at Mitau his *Beytrag zur Naturgeschichte der Vögel Kurlands*, and in 1794 Siemssen's *Handbuch* of the birds of Mecklenburg was published at Rostock. But these works, locally useful as they may have been, did not occupy the whole attention of German ornithologists, for in 1791 Bechstein reached the second volume of his *Gemeinnützige Naturgeschichte Deutschlands*, treating of the birds of that country, which exiled with the fourth in 1795. Of this an abridged edition by the name of *Ornithologisches Taschenbuch* appeared in 1802 and 1803, with a supplement in 1812; while between 1805 and 1809 a fuller edition of the original was issued. Moreover in 1795 J. A. Naumann humbly began at Cöthen a treatise on the birds of the principality of Anhalt, which on its completion in 1804 was found to have swollen into an ornithology of northern Germany and the neighbouring countries. Eight supplements were successively published between 1805 and 1817, and in 1822 a new edition was required. This *Naturgeschichte der Vögel Deutschlands*, being almost wholly rewritten by his son J F Naumann, is by far the best thing of the kind as yet produced in any country. The fulness and accuracy of the text, combined with the neat beauty of its coloured plates, have gone far to promote the study of ornithology in Germany, and while essentially a popular work, since it is suited to the comprehension of all readers, it is throughout written with a simple dignity that commends it to the serious and scientific. Its twelfth and last volume was published in 1844—by no means too long a period for so arduous and honest a performance, and a supplement was begun in 1847; but, the editor—or author as he may be fairly called—dying in 1857, this continuation was finished in 1860 by the joint efforts of J H. Blasius and Dr Baldamus. In 1800 Borkhausen with others commenced at Darmstadt a *Teutsche Ornithologie* in folio which appeared at intervals till 1812, and remains unfinished, though a reissue of the portion published took place between 1837 and 1841

Other European countries, though not quite so prolific as Germany, bore some ornithological fruit at this period; but in all southern Europe only four faunistic products can be named: the *Saggio di storia naturale Bresciana* of Pilati, published at Brescia in 1769; the *Ornitologia dell' Europa meridionate* of Bernini, published at Parma between 1772 and 1776; the *Uccelli di Sardegna* of Cetti, published at Sassari in 1776; and the *Romana ornithologia* of Gilius, published at Rome in 1781—the last being in great part devoted to pigeons and poultry. More appeared in the North, for in 1770 Amsterdam sent forth the beginning of Nozeman's *Nederlandsche Vogelen*, a fairly illustrated work in folio, but only completed by Houttuyn in 1829, and in Scandinavia most of all was done. In 1746 the great Linnaeus had pro uce a *Fauna Suecica*, of which a second edition appeared in 1761, and althird, revised by Retzius, in 1800. In 1764 Brünnich published at Copenhagen his *Ornithologia borealis*, a compendious sketch of the birds of all the countries then subject to the Danish crown. At the same place occurred in 1767 Leem's work, *De Lapponibus Finmarchiae*, to which Gunnerus contributed some good notes on the ornithology of northern Norway, and at Copenhagen and Leipzig was published in 1780 the *Fauna Groenlandica* of Otho Fabricius.

Of strictly American origin can here be cited only W. Bartram's *Travels through North and South Carolina*, and B. S. Barton's *Fragments of the Natural History of Pennsylvania*,[1] both printed at Philadelphia, one in 1791, the other in 1799; but J. R. Forster published a *Catalogue of the Animals of North America* in London in 1771, and the following year described in the *Philosophical Transactions* a few birds from Hudson Bay.[2] A greater undertaking was Pennant's *Arctic Zoology*, published in 1785, with a supplement in 1787. The scope of this work was originally intended to be limited to North America, but circumstances induced him to include all the species of Northern Europe and Northern Asia, and though not free from errors it is a praiseworthy performance. A second edition appeared in 1792.

The ornithology of Britain naturally demands greater attention.

---

[1] His earlier work under the title of *Petinotheologie* can hardly be deemed scientific.

[2] This extremely rare book has been reprinted by the Willughby Society.

[3] Both of these treatises have been also reprinted by the Willughby Society.

The earliest list of British birds we possess is that given by Merrett in his *Pinax rerum naturalium Britannicarum*, printed in London in 1667.[4] In 1677 Plot published his *Natural History of Oxfordshire*, which reached a second edition in 1705, and in 1686 that of *Staffordshire*. A similar work on *Lancashire, Cheshire and the Peak* was sent out in 1700 by Leigh, and one on *Cornwall* by Borlae in 1758—all these four being printed at Oxford. In 1766 appeared Pennant's *British Zoology*, a well-illustrated folio, of which a second edition in octavo was published in 1768, and considerable additions (forming the nominally third edition) in 1770, while in 1777 there were two issues, one in octavo, the other in quarto, each called the fourth edition. In 1812, long after the author's death, another edition was printed, of which his son-in-law Hanmer was the reputed editor, but he received much assistance from Latham, and through carelessness many of the additions herein made have often been ascribed to Pennant. In 1769 Berkenhout gave to the world his *Outlines of the Natural History of Great Britain and Ireland*, which reappeared under the title of *Synopsis* of the same in 1795. Tunstall's *Ornithologia Britannica*, which appeared in 1771, is little more than a list of names.[5] Hayes's *Natural History of British Birds*, a folio with forty plates, appeared between 1771 and 1775, but was of no scientific value. In 1781 Nash's *Worcestershire* included a few ornithological notices; and Walcott in 1789 published an illustrated *Synopsis of British Birds*, coloured copies of which are rare. Simultaneously William Lewin began his seven quarto volumes on the *Birds of Great Britain*, a reissue in eight volumes following between 1795 and 1801. In 1791 J. Heysham added to Hutchins's *Cumberland* a list of birds of that county, whilst in the same year began Thomas Lord's valueless *Entire New System of Ornithology*, the text of which was written or corrected by Dr Dupree, and in 1794 Donovan began a *History of British Birds* which was only finished in *Donovan*. 1819—the earlier portion being reissued about the same time. Bolton's *Harmonia ruralis*, an account of British song-birds, first appeared between 1794 and 1796, but subsequent editions appeared up to 1846.

All the foregoing publications yield in importance to two that remain to be mentioned, a notice of which will fitly conclude this part of our subject. In 1767 Pennant, several of whose works have already been named, entered into correspondence with Gilbert White, receiving from him much information, almost wholly drawn from his own observation, for the succeeding editions of the *British Zoology*. In 1769 White began exchanging letters of a similar character with Barrington. The epistolary intercourse with the former continued until 1780 and with the latter until 1787. In 1789 White's share of the correspondence, together with some miscellaneous matter, was published as *The Natural History of Selborne*—from the name of the village in which he lived. Observations on birds form the principal though by no means the whole theme of this book, which may be safely said to have done more to promote a love of ornithology in England than any other work that has been written, nay more than all the other works (except one next to be mentioned) put together. It has passed through a far greater number of editions than any other work on natural history in the English, and has become emphatically an English classic—the graceful simplicity of its style, the elevating tone of its spirit, and the sympathetic chords it strikes recommending it to every lover of Nature, while the severely scientific reader can scarcely find an error in any statement it contains, whether of matter of fact or opinion. It is almost certain that more than half the zoologists of the British Islands for many years past have been infected with their love of the study of Gilbert White; and it can hardly be supposed that his influence will cease.

The other work to the importance of which on ornithology in England allusion has been made is Bewick's *History of British Birds*. The first volume of this, containing the land-birds, appeared in 1797—the text being, it is understood, by Beilby—the second, containing the water-birds, in 1804. The woodcuts illustrating this work are generally of surpassing excellence, and it takes rank in the category of artistic publications. Fully admitting the extraordinary execution of the engravings, every ornithologist may perceive that as a portraits of the birds they are of very unequal merit. Some of the figures were drawn from stuffed specimens, and accordingly perpetuate all the imperfections of the original; others represent species with the appearance of which the artist was not

---

[4] In this year there were two issues of this book; one, nominally a second edition, only differs from the first in having a new title-page. No real second edition ever appeared, but in anticipation of it Sir Thomas Browne prepared in or about 1671 (?) his " Account of Birds found in Norfolk," of which the draft, now in the British Museum, was printed in his collected works by Wilkin in 1835. If a fair copy was ever made its resting-place is unknown.

[5] It has been republished by the Willughby Society.

[6] There were two issues—virtually two editions—of this with the same date on the title-page, though one of them is said not to have been published till the following year. Among several other *indicia* this may be recognized by the woodcut of the " sea eagle " at page 11, bearing at its base the inscription " Wycliffe, 1791," and by the additional misprint on page 145 of *Sahaeniclus* for *Schaeniclus*.

familiar, and these are either wanting in expression or are caricatures;[1] but those that were drawn from live birds, or represent species which he knew in life, are worthy of all praise. It is well known that the earlier editions of this work, especially if they be upon large paper, command extravagant prices; but in reality the copies on smaller paper are now the rarer, for the stock of them has been consumed in nurseries and schoolrooms, where they have been torn up or worn out with incessant use. Moreover, whatever the lovers of the fine arts may say, it is nearly certain that the " Bewick Collector " is mistaken in attaching so high a value to these old editions, for owing to the want of skill in printing—in different ink being especially assigned as one cause—many of the earlier issues fail to show the most delicate touches of the engraver, which the increased care bestowed upon the edition of 1847 (published under the supervision of John Hancock) has revealed—though it must be admitted that certain blocks have suffered from wear of the press so as to be incapable of any more producing the effect intended. Of the text it may be said that it is respectable, but no more.

The existence of these two works explains the widely-spread taste for ornithology in England, which is to foreigners so puzzling, and the zeal—not always according to knowledge, but occasionally reaching to serious study—with which that taste is pursued.

Ornithology in the 19th Century.

On reviewing the progress of ornithology since the end of the 18th century, the first thing that will strike us is the fact that general works, though still undertaken, have become proportionally fewer, while special works, whether relating to the ornithic portion of the fauna of any particular country, or limited to certain groups of birds—works to which the name of " Monograph " has become wholly restricted—have become far more numerous. Another change has come over the condition of ornithology, as of kindred sciences, induced by the multiplication of learned societies which issue publications as well as of periodicals of greater or less scientific pretension. A number of these must necessarily be left unnoticed here. Still it seems advisable to furnish some connected account of the progress made in the ornithological knowledge of the British Islands and those parts of the European continent which lie nearest to them or are most commonly sought by travellers, the Dominion of Canada and the United States of America, South Africa, India, together with Australia and New Zealand. The more important monographs will usually be found cited in the separate articles on birds contained in this work, though some, by reason of changed views of classification, have for practical purposes to be regarded now as general works.

It will perhaps be most convenient to begin by mentioning some of these last, and in particular a number of them which appeared at Paris very early in the 19th century. First in order of them is the *Histoire naturelle d'une partie d'oiseaux nouveaux et rares de l'Amérique et des Indes*, a folio volume[2] published in 1801 by Le Vaillant. This is devoted to the very distinct and not nearly-allied groups of hornbills and of birds which for want of a better name we must call " Chatterers," and is illustrated, like those works of which a notice immediately follows, by coloured plates, done in what was then considered to be the highest style of art and by the best draughtsmen procurable. The first volume of a *Histoire naturelle des perroquets*, a companion work by the same author, appeared in the same year, and is truly a monograph, since the parrots constitute a family of birds so naturally severed from all others that there has rarely been anything else confounded with them. The second volume came out in 1805, and a third was issued in 1837–1838 long after the death of its predecessor's author, by Bourjot St-Hilaire. Between 1803 and 1806 Le Vaillant also published in just the same style two volumes with the title of *Histoire naturelle des oiseaux de Paradis et des rolliers, suivie de celle des toucans et des barbus*, an assemblage of forms, which, miscellaneous as it is, was surpassed in incongruity by a fourth work on the same scale, the *Histoire naturelle des promerops et des guêpiers, des couroucous et des touracos*, for herein are found jays, waxwings, the rock-of-the-rock (*Rupicola*), and what not beside. The plates in this last are by Barraband, for many years regarded as the perfection of ornithological artists, and indeed the figures, when they happen to have been drawn from the life, are not bad; but his skill was quite unable to vivify the preserved specimens contained in museums, and when he had only these as subjects he simply copied the distortions of the " bird-stuffer." The following year, 1806, being aided by Temminck of Amsterdam, of whose son we shall presently hear more, Le Vaillant brought out the sixth volume of

[1] This is especially observable in the figures of the birds of prey.
[2] There is also an issue of this, as of the same author's other works, on large quarto paper.

x x 6

his *Oiseaux d'Afrique*, already mentioned. Four more volumes of this work were promised; but the means of executing them were denied to him, and, though he lived until 1824, his publications ceased.

A similar series of works was projected and begun about the same time as that of Le Vaillant by Audebert and Vieillot, though the former, who was by profession a painter and illustrated *Audebert* the work, was already dead more than a year before the *and* appearance of the two volumes, bearing date 1802, and *Vieillot.* entitled *Oiseaux dorés ou à reflets métalliques*, the effect of the plates in which he sought to heighten by the lavish use of gilding. The first volume contains the " Colibris, Oiseaux-mouches, Jacamars et Promerops," the second the " Grimpereaux " and " Oiseaux de Paradis "—associations which set all the laws of systematic method at defiance. His colleague, Vieillot, brought out in 1805 a *Histoire naturelle des plus beaux chanteurs de la Zone Torride* with figures by Langlois of tropical finches, grosbeaks, buntings and other hard-billed birds; and in 1807 two volumes of a *Histoire naturelle des oiseaux de l'Amérique septentrionale*, without, however, paying much attention to the limits commonly assigned by geographers to that part of the world. In 1805 Anselme Desmarest published a *Histoire naturelle des tangaras, des manakins* *Desmarest* *et des todiers*, which, though belonging to the same category as all the former, differs from them in its more scientific treatment of the subjects to which it refers; and, in 1808, K. J. Temminck, whose father's aid to Le Vaillant has already *Temminck.* been noticed, brought out at Paris a *Histoire naturelle des pigeons* illustrated by Madame Knip, who had drawn the plates for Desmarest's volume.[3]

Since we have begun by considering these large illustrated works in which the text is made subservient to the coloured plates, it may be convenient to continue our notice of such others of similar character as it may be expedient to mention here, though thereby we shall be led somewhat far afield. Most of them are but luxuries, and there is some degree of truth in the remark of Andreas Wagner in his *Report on the Progress of Zoology for 1843*, drawn up for the Ray Society (p. 60), that they " are not adapted for the extension and promotion of science, but must inevitably, on account of their unnecessary costliness, constantly tend to reduce the number of naturalists who are able to avail themselves of them, and they thus enrich ornithology only to its ultimate injury." Earliest in date as it is greatest in bulk stands Audubon's *Birds of* *Audubon.* *America* four volumes, containing four hundred and thirty-five plates, of which the first part appeared in London in 1827 and the last in 1838. It does not seem to have been the author's original intention to publish any letterpress to this enormous work, but to let the plates tell their own story, though finally, with the assistance, as is now known, of William Macgillivray, a text, on the whole more than respectable, was produced in five large *Macgil-* octavo volumes under the title of *Ornithological Biography*, of *livray.* which more will be said in the sequel. Audubon has been greatly extolled as an ornithological artist; but he was far too much addicted to representing his subjects in violent action and in postures that outrage nature, while his drawing is very frequently defective.[4] In 1866 D. G. Elliot began, and in 1869 finished, a sequel *Elliot.* to Audubon's great work in two volumes, on the same scale—*The New and Hitherto unfigured Species of the Birds of North America*, containing life-size figures of all those which had been added to its fauna since the completion of the former.

In 1830 John Edward Gray commenced the *Illustrations of* *Indian Zoology*, a series of plates of vertebrated animals, *Gray and* but mostly of birds, from drawings, it is believed by *Hardwicke.* native artists in the collection of General Hardwicke, whose name is therefore associated with the work. Scientific names are assigned to the species figured; but no text *Lear.* was ever supplied. In 1832 Edward Lear, afterwards well known as a humorist, brought out his *Illustrations of the Family of Psittacidae*, a volume which deserves especial notice from the extreme fidelity to nature and the great artistic skill with which the figures were executed.

This same year (1832) saw the beginning of the marvellous series of illustrated ornithological works by which the name of John *Gould* is likely to be always remembered. *A Century of* *Gould.* *Birds from the Himalaya Mountains* was followed by The

[3] Temminck subsequently reproduced, with many additions, the text of this volume in his *Histoire naturelle des pigeons et des gallinacées*, published at Amsterdam in 1813–1815, in 3 vols. 8vo. Between 1838 and 1848 M. Florent-Prevost brought out at Paris a further set of illustrations of pigeons by Mme Knip.

[4] On the completion of these two works, for they must be regarded as distinct, an octavo edition in seven volumes under the title of *The Birds of America* was published in 1840–1844. In this the large plates were reduced by means of the *camera lucida*, the text was revised, and the whole systematically arranged. Other reprints have since been issued, but they are vastly inferior both in execution and value. A sequel to the octavo *Birds of America*, corresponding with it in form, was brought out in 1853–1855 by Cassin as *Illustrations of the Birds of California, Texas, Oregon, British and Russian America.*

20

Birds of Europe in five volumes, published between 1832 and 1837, while in the interim (1834) appeared *A Monograph of the Ramphastidae*, of which a second edition was some years later called for, then the *Icones avium*, of which only two parts were published (1837–1838), and *A Monograph of the Trogonidae* (1838), which also reached a second edition. Sailing in 1838 for New South Wales, on his return in 1840 he at once commenced the greatest of all his works, *The Birds of Australia*, which was finished in 1848 in seven volumes, to which several supplementary parts, forming another volume, were subsequently added. In 1849 he began *A Monograph of the Trochilidae or Humming-birds* extending to five volumes, the last of which appeared in 1861, and was followed by a supplement by Mr Salvin. *A Monograph of the Odontophorinae or Partridges of America* (1850); *The Birds of Asia*, in seven volumes, the last completed by Mr Sharpe (1850–1883); *The Birds of Great Britain*, in five volumes (1863–1873); and *The Birds of New Guinea*, begun in 1875, and, after the author's death in 1881, undertaken by Mr Sharpe, make up the wonderful tale consisting of more than forty folio volumes, and containing more than three thousand coloured plates. The earlier of these works were illustrated by Mrs Gould, and the figures in them are fairly good; but those in the later, except when (as he occasionally did) he secured the services of Mr Wolf, are not so much to be commended. There is, it is true, a smoothness and finish about them not often seen elsewhere; but, as though to avoid the exaggerations of Audubon, Gould usually adopted the tamest of attitudes in which to represent his subjects, whereby expression as well as vivacity is wanting. Moreover, both in drawing and in colouring there is frequently much that is untrue to nature, so that it has not uncommonly happened for them to fail in the chief object of all zoological plates, that of affording sure means of recognizing specimens on comparison. In estimating the letterpress, which was severely held to be of secondary importance to the plates, we must bear in mind that, to ensure the success of his works, it had to be written to suit a very peculiarly composed body of subscribers. Nevertheless a scientific character was so adroitly assumed that scientific men—some of them even ornithologists—have thence been led to believe the text had a scientific value, and that of a high class. However, it must also be remembered that, throughout the whole of his career, Gould consulted the convenience of working ornithologists by almost invariably refraining from including in his folio works the technical description of any new species without first publishing it in some journal of comparatively easy access.

An ambitious attempt to produce in England a general series of coloured plates on a large scale was Louis Fraser's *Zoologia Typica*, the first part of which bears date 1841–1842. Others **Fraser.** appeared at irregular intervals until 1849, when the work, which seems never to have received the support it deserved, was discontinued. The seventy plates (forty-six of which represent birds) composing, with some explanatory letterpress, the volume, are by C. Cousens and H. N. Turner—the latter (as his publications prove) a zoologist of much promise, who in 1851 died, a victim to his own zeal for investigation, of a wound received in dissecting. The chief object of the author, who had been naturalist to the Niger-Expedition, and curator to the Museum of the Zoological Society of London, was to figure the animals contained in its gardens or described in its *Proceedings*, until the year 1848 were not illustrated.

The publication of the *Zoological Sketches* of Joseph Wolf, from animals in the gardens of the Zoological Society of London, was **Wolf.** begun about 1855, with a brief text by D. W. Mitchell, at that time the Society's secretary, in illustration of them: After his death in 1859, the explanatory letterpress was rewritten by P. L. Sclater, his successor in that office, and a volume was completed in 1861. Upon this a second series was commenced, and brought to an end in 1868. Though a comparatively small number of species of birds are figured in this magnificent work (seventeen only in the first series, and twenty-two in the second), it must be mentioned here, for their likenesses are so admirably executed as to place it in regard to ornithological portraiture at the head of all others. There is not a single plate that is unworthy of the greatest of all animal painters.

Proceeding to illustrated works generally of less pretentious size, but of greater ornithological utility than the books last mentioned, which are fitter for the drawing-room than the study, we next have to consider some in which the text is not wholly subordinated to the plates, though the latter still form a conspicuous feature of the publication. First of these in point of time as well as in importance is the *Nouveau recueil des planches coloriées d'oiseaux* of Temminck **Temminck** and Langier, intended as a sequel to the *Planches en-* **and** *luminées* of D'Aubenton before noticed, and like that **Langier.** work issued both in folio and quarto size. The first portion of this was published at Paris in 1820, and of its one hundred and two *livraisons*, which appeared with great irregularity (*Ibis*, 1868, p. 500), the last was issued in 1839, containing the titles of the five volumes that the whole forms, together with a "Tableau méthodique" which but indifferently serves the purpose of an index. There are six hundred plates, but the exact number of species figured (which has been computed at six hundred and sixty-one) is not so easily ascertained. Generally the subject of

each plate has letterpress to correspond, but in some cases this is wanting, while on the other hand descriptions of species not figured are occasionally introduced, and usually observations on the distribution and construction of each genus or group are added. The plates, which show no improvement in execution on those of Martinet, are after drawings by Huet and Prêtre, the former being perhaps the less bad draughtsman of the two, for he seems to have had an idea of what a bird when alive looks like, though he was not able to give his figures any vitality, while the latter simply delineated the stiff and dishevelled specimens from museum shelves. Still the colouring is pretty well done, and experience has proved that generally speaking there is not much difficulty in recognizing the species represented. The letterpress is commonly limited to technical details, and is not always accurate; but it is of its kind useful, for in general knowledge of the outside of birds Temminck probably surpassed any of his contemporaries. The "Tableau méthodique" offers a convenient concordance of the old *Planches enluminées* and **Oudart.** its successor, and is arranged after the system set forth by Temminck in the first volume of the second edition of his *Manuel d'ornithologie*, of which something must presently be said.

The *Galerie des oiseaux*, a rival work, with plates by Oudart, seems to have been begun immediately after the former. The original project was apparently to give a figure and **Oudart.** description of every species of bird; but that was soon found to be impossible; and, when six parts had been issued, with text by some unnamed author, the scheme was brought within practicable limits, and the writing of the letterpress was **Vieillot.** entrusted to Vieillot, who, proceeding on a systematic plan, performed his task very creditably, completing the work, which forms two quarto volumes, in 1825, the original text and fifty-seven plates being relegated to the end of the second volume as a supplement. His portion is illustrated by two hundred and ninety-nine coloured plates that, wretched as they are, have been continually reproduced in various text-books—a fact possibly due to their subjects having been judiciously selected. It is a tradition that, this work not being favourably regarded by the authorities of the Paris Museum, its draughtsman and author were refused closer access to the specimens required, and had to draw and describe them through the glass as they stood on the shelves of the cases.

In 1825 Jardine and Selby began a series of *Illustrations of Ornithology*, the several parts of which appeared at long and irregular **Jardine** intervals, so that it was not until 1839 that three volumes **and Selby.** containing one hundred and fifty plates were completed. Then they set about a Second Series, which, forming a single volume with fifty-three plates, was finished in 1843. These authors, being zealous amateur artists, were their own draughtsmen to the extent even of lithographing the figures. In 1828 James Wilson (author of the article Ornithology in the 7th and **Wilson.** 8th editions of the present work) began, under the title of *Illustrations of Zoology*, the publication of a series of his own drawings (which he did not, however, himself engrave) with corresponding letterpress. Of the thirty-six plates illustrating this volume, a small folio, twenty are devoted to Ornithology, and contain figures, which, it must be allowed, are not very successful, of several species rare at the time.

Though the three works last mentioned fairly come under the same category as the *Planches enluminées* and the *Planches coloriées*, no one of them can be properly deemed their rightful **Des Murs.** heirs. The claim to that succession was made in 1845 by Des Murs for his *Iconographie ornithologique*, which, containing seventy-two plates by Prévot and Oudart[1] (the latter of whom had marvellously improved in his drawings since he worked with Vieillot), was completed in 1849. Simultaneously with this Du Bus began a work on a plan precisely similar, the *Esquisses ornitho-* **Du Bus.** *logiques*, illustrated by Severeyns, which, however, stopped short in 1849 with its thirty-seventh plate, while the letterpress unfortunately does not go beyond that belonging to the twentieth. In 1866 the succession was again taken up by the *Exotic Ornithology* of Messrs Sclater and Salvin, containing one **Sclater** hundred plates, representing one hundred and four **and** species, all from Central or South America, which are **Salvin.** neatly executed by J. Smit. The accompanying letterpress is in some places copious, and useful lists of the species of various genera are occasionally subjoined, adding to the definite value of the work, which, forming one volume, was completed in 1869. Rowley's *Ornithological Miscellany* in three quarto volumes, profusely illustrated, appeared between 1875 and 1878. The **Rowley.** contents are as varied as the authorship, and, most of the leading English ornithologists having contributed to the work, some of the papers are extremely good, while in the plates, which are in Keulemans's best manner, many rare species of birds are figured, some of them for the first time.

More recent monographs have been more exact, and some of them equally sumptuous. Amongst these may be mentioned F. E. Blaauw's *Monograph of the Cranes* (1897, folio); St G. Mivart's *Monograph of the Lories* (1898, folio); the Hon. W. Rothschild's *Monograph of the Genus Casuarius* (1899, quarto); R. B Sharpe's

[1] On the title-page credit is given to the latter alone, but only two-thirds of the plates (from pl. 25 to the end) bear his name.

Monographs of the Paradiseidae (1898, folio); H. Seebohm's *Monograph of the Thrushes* (1900, imp. quarto); J. G. Millais' *British Surface-feeding Ducks* (1902, folio); and the Hon. W. Rothschild's *Extinct Birds* (1907, quarto).

Most of the works lately named, being very costly, are not easily accessible. The few next to be mentioned, being of smaller size (octavo), may be within reach of more persons, and, therefore, can be passed over in a briefer fashion without detriment. In many ways, however, they are nearly as important. Swainson's *Zoological Illustrations* in three volumes, containing one hundred *Swainson.* and eighty-two plates, whereof seventy represent birds, appeared between 1820 and 1821, and in 1829 a second series of the same was begun by him, which, extending to another three volumes, contained forty-eight more plates of birds out of one hundred and thirty-six, and was completed in 1833. All the figures were drawn by the author, who as an ornithological artist had no rival in his time. Every plate is not beyond criticism, but his worst drawings show more knowledge of bird-life than do the best of his English or French contemporaries. A work of somewhat similar character, but one in which the letterpress is of greater value, is the *Lesson.* *Centurie zoologique* of Lesson, a single volume that, though bearing the date 1830 on its title-page, is believed to have been begun in 1829,[1] and was certainly not finished until 1831. It received the benefit of Isidore Geoffroy St-Hilaire's assistance. Notwithstanding its name it only contains eighty plates, but of them forty-two, all by Prêtre and in his usual stiff style, represent birds. Concurrently with this volume appeared Lesson's *Traité d'ornithologie*, which is dated 1831, and may perhaps be here most conveniently mentioned. Its professedly systematic form strictly relegates it to another group of works, but the presence of an "Atlas" (also in octavo) of one hundred and nineteen plates to some extent justifies its notice in this place. Between 1831 and 1834 the same author brought out, in continuation of his *Centurie*, his *Illustrations de zoologie* with sixty plates, twenty of which represent birds. In 1832 Kittlitz began to publish some *Kupferlafeln zur Naturgeschichte der Vögel*, in which many new *Kittlitz.* species are figured; but the work came to an end with its thirty-sixth plate in the following year. In 1845 Reichenbach commenced with his *Praktische Naturgeschichte der Vögel* *Reichen-* the extraordinary series of illustrated publications which, *bach.* under titles far too numerous here to repeat, ended in or about 1855, and are commonly known collectively as his *Vollständigste Naturgeschichte der Vögel*.[2] Herein are contained more than nine hundred coloured and more than one hundred uncoloured plates, which are crowded with the figures of birds, a large proportion of them reduced copies from other works, and especially those of Gould.

It now behoves us to turn to general and particularly systematic works in which plates, if they exist at all, form but an accessory to the text. These need not detain us for long, since, however well some of them may have been executed, regard being had to their epoch, and whatever repute some of them may have achieved, they are, so far as general information and especially classification is concerned, wholly obsolete, and most of them almost useless except as matters of antiquarian interest. It will be enough merely to name Duméril's *Zoologie analytique* (1806) and Gravenhorst's *Vergleichende Übersicht des linneischen und einiger neuern zoologischen Systeme* (1807); nor need we linger over Shaw's *General* *Shaw and* *Zoology*, a pretentious compilation continued by Stephens. *Stephens.* The last seven of its fourteen volumes include the Class *Aves*, and the first part of them appeared in 1809, but, the original author dying in 1815, when only two volumes of birds were published, the remainder was brought to an end in 1826 by his successor, who afterwards became well known as an entomologist. The engravings which these volumes contain are mostly bad copies, often of bad figures, though many are piracies from Bewick, and the whole is a most unsatisfactory performance. Of a very different kind is the next we have to notice, the *Prodromus systematis mammalium et* *Illiger.* *avium* of Illiger, published at Berlin in 1811, which must in its day have been a valuable little manual, and on many points it may now be consulted to advantage—the characters of the genera being admirably given, and good explanatory lists of the technical terms of ornithology furnished. The classification was quite new, and made a step distinctly in advance of anything that had before appeared.[3] In 1816 Vieillot published *Vieillot.* at Paris an *Analyse d'une nouvelle ornithologie élémentaire*, containing a method of classification which he had tried in vain to get printed before, both in Turin and in London.[4] Some of the

ideas in this are said to have been taken from Illiger; but the two systems seem to be wholly distinct. Vieillot's was afterwards more fully expounded in the series of articles which he contributed between 1816 and 1819 to the second edition of the *Nouveau dictionnaire d'histoire naturelle* containing much valuable information. The views of neither of these systematizers pleased Temminck, who in 1817 replied rather sharply to Vieillot in some *Observations* *Tem-* *sur la classification méthodique des oiseaux*, a pamphlet *minck.* published at Amsterdam, and prefixed to the second edition of his *Manuel d'ornithologie*, which appeared in 1820, an *Analyse du système général d'ornithologie*. This proved a great success, and his arrangement, though by no means simple,[5] was not only adopted by many ornithologists of almost every country, but still has some adherents. The following year Ranzani of Bologna, in his *Elementi* *di zoologia*—a very respectable compilation—came to *Ranzani.* treat of birds, and then followed to some extent the plan of De Blainville and Merrem (concerning which much more has to be said by and by), placing the Struthious birds in an Order by themselves. In 1827 Wagler brought out the first part *Wagler.* of a *Systema avium*, in this form never completed, consisting of forty-nine detached monographs of as many genera, the species of which are most elaborately described. The arrangement he subsequently adopted for them and for other groups is to be found in his *Natürliches System der Amphibien* (pp. 77-128), published in 1830, and is too fanciful to require any further attention. The several attempts at system-making by Kaup, from his *Allgemeine Zoologie* in 1829 to his *Über Classification* *Kaup.* *der Vögel* in 1849, were equally arbitrary and abortive; but his *Skizzirte Entwickelungs-Geschichte* in 1829 must be here named, as it is so often quoted on account of the number of new genera which the peculiar views he had embraced compelled him to invent. These views he shared more or less with Vigors and Swainson, and to them attention will be immediately especially invited, while consideration of the scheme gradually developed from 1831 onward by Charles Lucien Bonaparte, and still not without its *Bona-* influence, is deferred until we come to treat of the rise *parte.* and progress of what we may term the reformed school of ornithology. Yet injustice would be done to one of the ablest of those now to be called the old masters of the science if mention were not here made of the *Conspectus generum avium*, begun in 1850 by the naturalist last named, with the help of Schlegel, and unfortunately interrupted by its author's death at years later.[6] The systematic publications of George Robert Gray, so long in charge of the ornithological collection of the *G. R.* British Museum, began with *A List of the Genera of Birds* *Gray.* published in 1840. This, having been closely, though by no means in a hostile spirit, criticized by Strickland (*Ann. Nat. History*, vi. p. 410; vii. pp. 26 and 159), was followed by a second edition in 1841, in which nearly all the corrections of the reviewer were adopted, and in 1844 began the publication of *The Genera of Birds*, beautifully illustrated—first by Mitchell and afterwards by Mr Wolf—which will always keep Gray's name in remembrance. The enormous labour required for this work seems scarcely to have been appreciated, though it remains to this day one of the most useful books in an ornithologist's library. Yet it must be confessed that its author was hardly an ornithologist, but for the accident of his calling. He was a thoroughly conscientious clerk, devoted to his duty and unsparing of trouble. However, to have conceived the idea of executing a work on so grand a scale as this—it forms three folio volumes, and contains one hundred and eighty-five coloured and one hundred and forty-eight uncoloured plates, with references to upwards of two thousand four hundred generic names—was in itself a mark of genius, and in having it executed to a successful conclusion in 1849. Costly as it necessarily was, it has been of great service to working ornithologists. In 1855 Gray brought out, as one of the Museum publications, *A Catalogue of the Genera and Subgenera of Birds*, a handy little volume, naturally founded on the larger works. Its chief drawback is that it does not give any more reference to the authority for a generic term than the name of its inventor and the year of its application, though of course more precise information would have at least doubled the size of the book. The same deficiency became still more apparent when, between 1869 and 1871, he published his *Hand-List of Genera and Species of Birds* in three

---

[1] In 1828 he had brought out, under the title of *Manuel d'ornithologie*, two handy duodecimos which are very good of their kind.

[2] Technically speaking they are in quarto, but their size is so small that they may be well spoken of here. In 1879 Dr A. B. Meyer brought out an *Index* to them

[3] Illiger may be considered the founder of the school of nomenclatural purists. He would not tolerate any of the "barbarous" generic terms adopted by other writers, though some had been in use for many years.

[4] The method was communicated to the Turin Academy, on 10th January 1814, and was ordered to be printed (*Mém. Ac. Sc. Turin*,

1813-1814, p. xxviii.); but, through the derangements of that stormy period, the order was never carried out (*Mem. Accad. Sc. Torino*, xxiii. p. xcvii.). The minute-book of the Linnean Society of London shows that his *Prelusio* was read at meetings of that Society between the 15th of November 1814 and the 21st of February 1815. Why it was not at once accepted is not told, but the entry respecting it, which must be of much later date, in the "Register of Papers" is "Published already." It is due to Vieillot to mention these facts, as he has been accused of publishing his method in haste to anticipate some of Cuvier's views, but he might well complain of the delay in London. Some reparation has been made to his memory by the reprinting of his *Analyse* by the Willughby Society.

[5] He recognized sixteen Orders of Birds, while Vieillot had been content with five, and Illiger with seven.

[6] To this very indispensable work a good index was supplied in 1863 by Dr Finsch.

octavo volumes (or parts, as they are called). Giebel's *Thesaurus ornithologiae*, also in three volumes, published between 1872 and 1877, is a slight advance, but both works have been completely superseded by the *British Museum Catalogue of Birds*, the twenty-seventh and final volume of which was published in 1895, and by the compact and invaluable British Museum *Hand-List*, the four volumes of which were completed by Dr R. B. Sharpe in 1903.

It may be convenient here to deal with the theory of the Quinary System, which was promulgated with great zeal by its upholders during the end of the first and early part of the second quarter of the 19th century, and for some years seemed likely to carry all before it. The success it gained was doubtless due in some degree to the difficulty which most men had in comprehending it, for it was enwrapped in alluring mystery, but more to the confidence with which it was announced as being the long-looked-for key to the wonders of creation, since its promoters did not hesitate to term it the discovery of " *the* Natural System," though they condescended, by way of explanation to less exalted intellects than their own, to allow it the more moderate appellation of the Circular or Quinary System.

A comparison of the relation of created beings to a number of intersecting circles is as old as the days of Nieremberg, who in 1635 wrote (*Historia naturae*, lib. iii. cap. 3)—" Nullus hiatus est, nulla fractio, nulla dispersio formarum, laviceum connexa sunt velut annulus annulo "; but it is almost clear that he was thinking only of a chain. In 1806 Fischer de Waldheim, in his *Tableaux synoptiques de zoognosie* (p. 161), quoting Nieremberg, extended his figure of speech, and, while justly deprecating the notion that the series of forms belonging to any particular group of creatures—the *Mammalia* was that whence he took his instance—could be placed in a straight line, imagined the various genera to be arrayed in a series of contiguous circles around Man as a centre. Though there is nothing to show that Fischer intended, by what is here said, to do anything else than illustrate more fully the marvellous interconnexion of different animals, or that he attached any realistic meaning to his metaphor, his words were eagerly caught up by the prophet of the new faith. This was William Sharpe Macleay, a man of education and real genius, who in 1819 and 1821 brought out a work under the title of *Horae Entomologicae*, which was soon after hailed by Vigors as containing a new revelation, and applied by him to ornithology in some " Observations on the Natural Affinities that connect the Orders and Families of Birds," read before the Linnean Society of London in 1823, and afterwards published in its *Transactions* (xiv. pp. 395-517). In the following year Vigors returned to the subject in some papers published in the recently established *Zoological Journal*, and found an energetic condisciple and coadjutor in Swainson, who, for more than a dozen years—to the end, in fact, of his career as an ornithological writer—was instant in season and out of season in pressing on all his readers the views he had, through Vigors, adopted from Macleay, though not without some modification of detail if not of principle. What these views were it would be manifestly improper for a sceptic to state except in the terms of a believer. Their enunciation must therefore be given in Swainson's own words, though it must be admitted that space cannot be found here for the diagrams, which it was alleged were necessary for the right understanding of the theory. This theory, as originally propounded by Macleay, was said by Swainson in 1835 (*Geog. and Classif. of Animals*, p. 202) to have consisted of the following propositions:—

" 1. That the series of natural animals is continuous, forming, as it were, a circle; so that, upon commencing at any one given point, and thence tracing all the modifications of structure, we shall be imperceptibly led, after passing through numerous forms, again to the point from which we started.

" 2. That no groups are natural which do not exhibit, or show an evident tendency to exhibit, such a circular series.

" 3. That the primary divisions of every large group are ten, five of which are composed of comparatively large circles, and five of smaller: these latter being termed osculant, and being intermediate between the former, which they serve to connect.

" 4. That there is a tendency in such groups as are placed at the opposite points of a circle of affinity ' to meet each other.'

" 5. That *one* of the five larger groups into which every natural circle is divided ' bears a resemblance to all the rest, or, more strictly speaking, consists of types which represent those of each of the four other groups, together with a type peculiar to itself.' "

---

¹ We prefer giving them here in Swainson's version, because he seems to have set them forth more clearly and concisely than Macleay ever did, .and., moreover, Swainson's application of them to ornithology—a branch of science that lay outside of Macleay's proper studies—appears to be more suitable to the present occasion.

As subsequently modified by Swainson (*tom. cit.* pp. 224, 225), the foregoing propositions take the following form:—

" 1. That every natural series of beings in its progress from a given point, either actually returns, or evinces a tendency to return, again to that point, thereby forming a circle.

" II. The primary circular divisions of every group are three actually, or five apparently.

" III. The contents of such a circular group are symbolically (or analogically) represented by the contents of all other circles in the animal kingdom.

" IV. That these primary divisions of every group are characterized by definite peculiarities of form, structure and economy, which, under diversified modifications, are uniform throughout the animal kingdom, and are therefore to be regarded as the primary types of nature.

" V. That the different ranks or degrees of circular groups exhibited in the animal kingdom are NINE in number, each being involved within the other."

Though, as above stated, the theory here promulgated owed its temporary success chiefly to the extraordinary assurance and pertinacity with which it was urged upon a public generally incapable of understanding what it meant, that it received some support from men of science must be admitted. A " circular system " was advocated by the eminent botanist Fries, and the views of Macleay, met with the partial approbation of the celebrated entomologist Kirby, while at least as much may be said of the imaginative Oken, whose mysticism far surpassed that of the Quinarians. But it is obvious to every one who nowadays indulges in the profitless pastime of studying their writings that, as a whole, they failed in grasping the essential difference between *homology* (or " affinity," as they generally termed it) and *analogy*—though this difference had been fully understood and set forth by Aristotle himself—and, moreover, that in seeking for analogies on which to base their foregone conclusions they were often put to hard shifts. Another singular fact is that they often seemed to be totally unaware of the tendency if not the meaning of some of their own expressions: thus Macleay could write, and doubtless in perfect good faith (*Trans. Linn. Society*, xvi. p. 9, note), " Naturalists have nothing to do with mysticism, and but little with a priori reasoning." Yet his followers, if not he himself, were ever making use of language in the highest degree metaphorical, and were always explaining facts in accordance with preconceived opinions. Fleming, already the author of a harmless and extremely orthodox *Philosophy of Zoology*, pointed out in 1829 in the *Quarterly Review* (xli. pp. 302-327) some of the fallacies of Macleay's method, and in return provoked from him a reply, in the form of a letter addressed to Vigors *On the Dying Struggle of the Dichotomous System*, couched in language the force of which no one even at the present day can deny, though to the modern naturalist its invective power contrasts ludicrously with the strength of its ratiocination. But, confining ourselves to what is here our special business, it is to be remarked that perhaps the heaviest blow dealt at these strange doctrines was that delivered by Rennie, who, in an edition of Montagu's *Ornithological Dictionary* (pp. xxxiii.-lv.), published in 1831 and again issued in 1833, attacked the Quinary System, and especially its application to ornithology by Vigors and Swainson, in a way that might perhaps have demolished it, had not the author mingled with his undoubtedly sound reason much that is foreign to any question with which a naturalist, as such, ought to deal—though that herein he was only following the example of one of his opponents, who had constantly treated the subject in like manner, is to be allowed. This did not hinder Swainson, who had succeeded in getting the ornithological portion of the first zoological work ever published at the expense of the British government (namely, the *Fauna Borealli-Americana*) executed in accordance with his own opinions, from maintaining them more strongly than ever in several of the volumes treating of Natural History which he contributed to the *Cabinet Cyclopaedia*—among others that from which we have just given some extracts—and in what may be deemed the culmination in England of the Quinary System, the volume of the " Naturalist's Library " on *The Natural Arrangement and History of Flycatchers*, published in 1838, of which unhappy performance mention has already been made in this present work (vol. x. p. 584, note). This seems to have been his last attempt; for, two years later, his *Bibliography of Zoology* shows little trace of his favourite theory, though nothing he had uttered in its support was retracted. Appearing almost simultaneously with this work, an article by Strickland (*Mag. Nat. History*, ser. 2, iv. pp. 219-226) entitled *Observations upon the Affinities and Analogies of Organized Beings* administered to the theory a shock from which it never recovered, and from which it never recovered, and then made by its adherents to revive it; and, even ten years or more later, Kaup, one of the few foreign ornithologists who had embraced Quinary principles, was by mistaken kindness allowed to publish Monographs of the Birds-of-Prey (Jardine's *Contributions to Ornithology*, 1849, pp. 68-75, 96-121; 1850, pp. 51-80; 1851, pp. 119-130; 1852, pp. 103-122; and *Trans. Zool. Society*, iv. pp. 201-260), in which its absurdity reached the climax.

The mischief caused by this theory of a Quinary System was very great, but was chiefly confined to Britain, for (as has been already stated) the extraordinary views of its adherents found little favour on the continent of Europe. The purely artificial character of the System of Linnaeus and his successors had been perceived, and men were at a loss to find a substitute for it. The new doctrine, loudly proclaiming the discovery of a "Natural" System, led away many from the steady practice which should have followed the teaching of Cuvier (though he in ornithology had not been able to act up to the principles he had laid down) and from the extended study of Comparative Anatomy. Moreover, it veiled the honest attempts that were making both in France and Germany to find real grounds for establishing an improved state of things, and consequently the labours of De Blainville, Etienne, Geoffroy St-Hilaire and L'Herminier, of Merrem, Johannes Müller and Nitzsch—to say nothing of others—were almost wholly unknown on this side of the Channel, and even the value of the investigations of British ornithotomists of high merit, such as Macartney and Macgillivray, was almost completely overlooked. True it is that there were not wanting other men in these islands whose common sense refused to accept the metaphorical doctrine and the mystical jargon of the Quinarians, but so strenuously and persistently had the latter asserted their infallibility, and so vigorously had they assailed any who ventured to doubt it, that most peaceable ornithologists found it best to bend to the furious blast, and in some sort to acquiesce at least in the phraseology of the self-styled interpreters of Creative Will. But, while thus lamenting this unfortunate perversion into a mistaken channel of ornithological energy, we must not overblame those who caused it. Macleay indeed never pretended to a high position in this branch of science, his tastes lying in the direction of Entomology; but few of their countrymen knew more of birds than did Swainson and Vigors; and, while the latter, as editor for many years of the *Zoological Journal*, and the first secretary of the Zoological Society, has especial claims to the regard of all zoologists, so the former's indefatigable pursuit of Natural History, and conscientious labour in its behalf—among other ways by means of his graceful pencil—deserve to be remembered at a set-off against the injury he unwittingly caused.

It is now incumbent upon us to take a rapid survey of the ornithological works which come more or less under the designation of "Faunae "; but these are so numerous that it *Faunae.* will be necessary to limit this survey, as before indicated, to those countries alone which form the homes of English people, or are commonly visited by them in ordinary travel.

Beginning with New Zealand, it is hardly needful to go further back than Sir W. L. Buller's beautiful *Birds of New Zealand* (4to, 1872–*New* 1873), with coloured plates by Keulemans, since the publi-*Zealand.* cation of which the same author has issued a *Manual of the Birds of New Zealand* (8vo, 1882), founded on the former; but justice requires that mention be made of the labours of G. R. Gray, first in the Appendix to Dieffenbach's *Travels in New Zealand* (1843) and then in the ornithological portion of the *Zoology of the Voyage of H.M.S.* "*Erebus*" and "*Terror*," begun in 1844, but left unfinished from the following year until completed by Mr Sharpe in 1876. A considerable number of valuable papers on the ornithology of the country by Sir W. L. Buller, Drs Hector and Von Haast, F. W. Hutton, Mr Potts and others are to be found in the *Transactions and Proceedings of the New Zealand Institute.* Sir W. L. Buller's *Supplement to the Birds of New Zealand* (1905–1906) completes the great work of this author.

Passing to Australia, we have the first good description of some of its birds in the several old voyages and in Latham's works before *Australia.* mentioned. Shaw's *Zoology of New Holland* (4to, 1794) added those of a few more, as did J. W. Lewin's *Natural History of the Birds of New South Wales* (4to, 1822), which reached a third edition in 1838. Gould's great *Birds of Australia* has been already named, and he subsequently reproduced with some additions the text of that work under the title of *Handbook to the Birds of Australia* (2 vols. 8vo, 1865). In 1866 Mr Diggles commenced a similar publication, *The Ornithology of Australia*, but the coloured plates, though fairly drawn, are not comparable to those of his predecessor. This is still incomplete, though the parts that have appeared have been collected to form two volumes and issued with title-pages. Some notices of Australian birds by Mr Ramsay and others are to be found in the *Proceedings of the Linnaean Society of New South Wales* and of the *Royal Society of Tasmania.*

Coming to British Indian possessions, and beginning with Ceylon, we have Kelaart's *Prodromus faunae Zeylanicae* (8vo, 1852), and *Ceylon.* the admirable *Birds of Ceylon* by Captain Legge (4to, 1878–1880), with coloured plates by Mr Keulemans of all the peculiar species. It is hardly possible to name any book that has been more conscientiously executed than this. Blyth's *Mammals and Birds of Burma* (8vo, 1875)[2] contains much valuable information. Jerdon's *Birds of India* (8vo, 1862–1864;

[1] A very useful list of more general scope is given as the Appendix to an address by Mr Sclater to the British Association in 1875 (*Report*, pt. ii. pp. 114–133).

[2] This is a posthumous publication, nominally forming an extra number of the *Journal of the Asiatic Society*; but, since it was separately issued, it is entitled to notice here.

repriated 1877) is a comprehensive work on the ornithology of the peninsula. A very fairly executed compilation on the subject by an anonymous writer is to be found in a late edition of *India.* the *Cyclopaedia of India*, published at Madras, and W. T. Blanford's *Birds of British India* (1898) remains the standard work. *Stray Feathers*, an ornithological journal for India and its dependencies, contains many interesting and some valuable papers.

In regard to South Africa, besides the well-known work of Le Vaillant already mentioned, there is the second volume of Sir Andrew Smith's *Illustrations of the Zoology of South South* *Africa* (4to, 1838–1842), which is devoted to birds. This *Africa.* is an important but cannot be called a satisfactory work. Its one hundred and fourteen plates by Ford truthfully represent one hundred and twenty-two of the mounted specimens obtained by the author in his explorations into the interior. Layard's handy *Birds of South Africa* (8vo, 1867), though by no means free from faults, has much to recommend it. A so-called new edition of it by R. B. Sharpe appeared in 1875–1884, but was executed on a plan so wholly different that it must be regarded as a distinct work. C. J. Andersson's *Notes on the Birds of Damara Land* (8vo, 1872), edited by J. H. Gurney, was useful in its day, but has been superseded by the more comprehensive and extremely accurate volumes, the *Birds of Africa*, by G. E. Shelley (1900–1907), and the German work on the same subject by Anton Reichenow (1900–1905).

Of special works relating to the British West Indies, C. Waterton's well-known *Wanderings* has passed through several editions since its first appearance in 1825, and must be mentioned here, *West* though, strictly speaking, much of the country he traversed *Indies.* was not British territory. To Dr Cabanis we are indebted for the ornithological results of Richard Schomburgk's researches given in the third volume (pp. 662–765) of the latter's *Reisen in Britisch-Guiana* (8vo, 1848), and then in Léotaud's *Oiseaux de l'île de la Trinidad* (8vo, 1866). Of the Antilles there is only to be named P. H. Gosse's excellent *Birds of Jamaica* (12mo, 1847), together with its *Illustrations* (sm. fol., 1849) beautifully executed by him. A nominal list, with references, of the birds of the island is contained in the *Handbook of Jamaica.*

An admirable "List of Faunal Publications relating to North American Ornithology" up to 1878 has been given by Elliott Coues as an appendix to his *Birds of the Colorado Valley* *North* (pp. 567–784). Special mention should be made of the *America.* following works most of which have appeared since that time: S. F. Baird, T. M. Brewer and Robert Ridgway, *History of North American Birds: The Land Birds* (3 vols. Boston, 1875), *The Water Birds* (2 vols. Boston, 1884); Elliott Coues, *Check List of North American Birds* (Boston, 1882); *Key to North American Birds* (Boston, 1887); *Birds of the Northwest*, U.S. Geological Survey, Misc. pubs., No. 3 (1874) and *Birds of the Colorado Valley*, ibid. No. 11 (1878); Robert Ridgway, *Manual of North American Birds* (Philadelphia, 1887); Frank M. Chapman, *Color Key to North American Birds* (New York, 1903); *Handbook of Birds of Eastern North America* (ibid, 1895) and *The Warblers of North America* (ibid, 1907), with notable coloured illustrations by L. A. Fuertes and Bruce Horsfall; Dr. A. K. Fisher, *Hawks and Owls of the United States in their Relation to Agriculture*, U.S. Department of Agriculture, Bull. No. 3 (Washington, 1893), a very important work; D. G. Elliot, *Gallinaceous Game Birds of North America* (New York, 1897) and *Wild Fowl of the United States and British Possessions* (1898), and Robert Ridgway's learned and invaluable *Birds of North and Middle America*, published by the Smithsonian Institution, Bull. No. 50 (Washington, 1901 sqq.). Among contemporary writers in a more popular style are John Burroughs (q.v.); Herbert K. Job and A. R. Dugmore who have done much remarkable work in bird photography; Dallas Lore Sharp, Bradford Torrey, E. H. Parkhurst, Mrs Florence Merriam Bailey, Olive Thorne Miller (Mrs Harriet Mann Miller) and Mrs Mabel Osgood Wright. Alexander Wilson's *American Ornithology*, originally published between 1808 and 1814, has gone through many editions including those issued in Great Britain, by Jameson (4 vols. 16 mo, 1831), and Jardine (3 vols. 8vo, 1832). The former of these has the entire text, but no plates; the latter reproduces the plates, but the text is in places much condensed, and excellent notes are added. A continuation of Wilson's work was issued by Bonaparte between 1825 and 1833, and most of the later editions include the work of both authors. The works of Audubon, and the *Fauna Boreali-Americana* of Richardson and Swainson have already been noticed, but they need naming here, as also do Nuttall's *Manual of the Ornithology of the United States and of Canada* (2 vols., Boston, 1832–1834; 2nd ed., 1840); and the *Birds of Long Island* (8 vo, New York, 1844) by J. P. Giraud, remarkable for its excellent account of the habits of shore-birds. The *Bulletin of the Nuttall Ornithological Club* was published from 1876 to 1884, when it was superseded by *The Auk*, a bi-monthly, *Bird-Lore*, established in 1899, is edited by Frank M. Chapman. A recent valuable work is that of Mary B. Beebe and C. W. Beebe, *Our Search for a Wilderness* (New York, 1910) which deals with the birds of Venezuela and British Guiana, while Central America is fully treated in the comprehensive and beautiful *Biologia Centrali-Americana* of F. du Cane Godman and O. Salvin (1898–1905). X.]

Returning to the Old World, we have first Iceland, the fullest—indeed the only full—account of the birds of which is

Faber's *Prodromus der isländischen Ornithologie* (8vo, 1822), though the island has since been visited by several good ornithologists—Proctor, Krüper and Wolley among them. A list of its birds, with some notes, bibliographical and biological, has been given as an Appendix to Baring-Gould's *Iceland, its Scenes and Sagas* (8vo, 1862); and Shepherd's *North-west Peninsula of Iceland* (8vo, 1867) recounts a somewhat profitless expedition made thither expressly for ornithological objects. For the birds of the Faeroes there is H. C. Müller's *Faerôernes Fuglefauna* (8vo, 1862), of which a German translation has appeared. The ornithology of Norway has been treated in a great many papers by Herr Collett, some of which may be said to have been separately published as *Norges Fugle* (8vo, 1868; with a supplement, 1871), and *The Ornithology of Northern Norway* (8vo, 1872)—this last in English. For Scandinavia generally Herr Collin's *Skandinaviens Fugle* (8vo, 1873) is a greatly bettered edition of the very moderate *Danmarks Fugle* of Kjaerbölling; but the ornithological portion of Nilsson's *Skandinavisk Fauna, Foglarna* (3rd ed., 2 vols. 8vo, 1858), is of great merit; while the text of Sundevall's *Svenska Foglarna* (obl. fol., 1856-1873), unfortunately unfinished at his death, and Herr Holmgren's *Skandinaviens Foglar* (2 vols. 8vo, 1866-1875) deserve naming.

Works on the birds of Germany are far too numerous to be recounted. That of the two Naumanns stands at the head of all, and perhaps at the head of the "Faunal" works of all countries. It has been added to by C. R. Hennicke—Naumann's *Birds of Middle Europe* (1907). For want of space it must here suffice simply to name some of the ornithologists who have elaborated, to an extent elsewhere unknown, the science as regards their own country: Altum, Baldamus, Bechstein, Blasius (father and two sons), Bolle, Borggreve, whose *Vogel-Fauna von Norddeutschland* (8vo, 1869) contains what is practically a bibliographical index to the subject, Brehm (father and sons), Von Droste, Gätke, Gloger, Hintz, Alexander and Eugen von Homeyer, Jäckel, Koch, König-Warthausen, Krüper, Kutter, Landbeck, Landois, Leisler, Von Maltzan, Bernard Meyer, Von der Mühle, Neumann, Tobias, Johann Wolf and Zander. Were we to extend the list beyond the boundaries of the German empire, and include the ornithologists of Austria, Bohemia and the other states subject to the same monarch, the number would be nearly doubled; but that would overpass our proposed limits, though Herr von Pelzeln must be named. Passing onward to Switzerland, we must content ourselves by referring to the list already known, forming a *Bibliographia ornithologica Helvetica*, drawn up by Dr Stölker for Dr Fatio's *Bulletin de la Société Ornithologique Suisse* (ii. pp. 90-119).

As to Italy, we can but name here the *Fauna d'Italia*, of which the second part, *Uccelli* (8vo, 1872), by Count Salvadori, contains an excellent bibliography of Italian works on the subject, and the posthumously published *Ornitologia italiana* of Savi (3 vols. 8vo, 1873-1877). Coming to the Iberian peninsula we must, in default of separate works depart from our rule of not mentioning contributions to journals, for of the former there are only Colonel Irby's *Ornithology of the Straits of Gibraltar* (8vo, 1875) and Mr A. C. Smith's *Spring Tour in Portugal* to be named, and these only partially cover the ground. However, Dr A. E. Brehm has published a list of Spanish birds (*Allgem. deutsche naturhist. Zeitung*, iii. p. 431), and *The Ibis* contains several excellent papers by Lord Lilford and by H. Saunders, the latter of whom there records (1871, p. 55) the few works on ornithology by Spanish authors, and in the *Bulletin de la Société Zoologique de France* (i. p. 315; ii. pp. 11, 89, 185) has given a list of the Spanish birds known to him. Returning northwards, we have of the birds of the whole of France nothing of real importance more recent than the various *Oiseaux* in Vieillot's *Faune française* (8vo, 1822-1829); but there is a great number of local publications of which Mr Saunders has furnished (*Zoologist*, 1878, pp. 95-99) a catalogue.

[1] *Journal für Ornithologie* (1869), pp. 107, 341, 381. One may almost say an English translation also, for Major. Feilden's contribution to the *Zoologist* for 1872 on the same subject gives the most essential part of Herr Müller's information.

[2] This is, of course, no complete list of German ornithologists. Some of the most eminent of them have written scarcely a line on the birds of their own country, as Cabanis (editor since 1853 of the *Journal für Ornithologie*), Finsch, Hartlaub, Prince Max of Wied, A. B. Meyer, Nathusius, Nehrkorn, Reichenbach, Reichenow and Schalow among others.

[3] A useful ornithological bibliography of the Austrian-Hungarian dominions was printed in the *Verhandlungen* of the Zoological and Botanical Society of Vienna for 1878, by Victor Ritter von Tschusi zu Schmidhofen. A similar bibliography of Russian ornithology by Alexander Brandt was printed at St Petersburg in 1877 or 1878.

[4] A useful compendium of Greek and Turkish ornithology by Drs Krüper and Hartlaub is contained in Mommsen's *Griechische Jahreszeiten* for 1875 (Heft III.). For other countries in the Levant there are Canon Tristram's *Fauna and Flora of Palestine* (4to, 1884) and Captain Shelley's *Handbook to the Birds of Egypt* (8vo, 1872).

[5] In the final chapter of this work the author gives a list of Portuguese birds, including besides those observed by him those recorded by Professor Barboza du Bocage in the *Gazeta medica de Lisboa* (1861), pp. 17-21.

Some of these seem only to have appeared in journals, but many have certainly been issued separately. Those of most interest to English ornithologists naturally refer to Britanny, Normandy and Picardy, and are by Baillon, Benoist, Blandin, Bureau, Canivet, Chesnon, Degland, Demarle, De Norguet, Gentil, Hardy, Lemetteil, Lemonnicier, Lesauvage, Maignon, Marcotte, Nourry and Tasié, while perhaps the *Ornithologie parisienne* of M. René Paquet, under the pseudonym of Nérée Quépat, should also be named. Of the rest the most important are the *Ornithologie provençale* of Roux (2 vols. 4to, 1825-1830): Risso's *Histoire naturelle ... des environs de Nice* (5 vols. 8vo, 1826-1827); the *Ornithologie du Dauphiné* of Bouteille and Labatie (2 vols. 8vo, 1843-1844); the *Faune méridionale* of Crespon (2 vols. 8vo, 1844); the *Ornithologie de la Savoie* of Bailly (4 vols. 8vo, 1853-1854), and *Les Richesses ornithologiques du midi de la France* (4to, 1859-1861) of MM. Jaubert and Barthélemy-Lapommeraye. For Belgium the *Faune belge* of Baron De Selys-Longchamps (8vo, 1842), old as it is, remains the classical work, though the *Planches coloriées des oiseaux de la Belgique* of M. Dubois (8vo, 1851-1860) is so much later in date. In regard to Holland we have Schlegel's *De Vogels van Nederland* (3 vols. 8vo, 1854-1858; 2nd ed., 2 vols., 1878), besides his *De Dieren van Nederland: Vogels* (8vo, 1861).

Before considering the ornithological works relating solely to the British Islands, it may be well to cast a glance on a few of those that refer to Europe in general, the more so since most of them are of Continental origin. First we have the already-mentioned *Manuel d'ornithologie* of Temminck, which originally appeared as a single volume in 1815; but that was speedily superseded by the second edition of 1820, in two volumes. Two supplementary parts were issued in 1835 and 1840 respectively, and the work for many years deservedly maintained the highest position as the authority on European ornithology—indeed in England-it may almost without exaggeration be said to have been nearly the only foreign ornithological work known; but, as could only be expected, grave defects are now to be discovered in it. Some of them were already manifest when one of its author's colleagues, Schlegel (who had been employed to write the text for Susemihl's plates, originally intended to illustrate Temminck's work), brought out his bilingual *Revue critique des oiseaux d'Europe* (8vo, 1844), a very remarkable volume, since it correlated and consolidated the labours of French and German, to say nothing of Russian, ornithologists. Of Gould's *Birds of Europe* (5 vols. fol., 1832-1837) nothing need be added to what has been already said. The year 1849 saw the publication of Degland's *Ornithologie européenne* (2 vols. 8vo), a work fully intended to take the place of Temminck's; but of which Bonaparte, in a caustic but by no means ill-deserved *Revue critique* (12 mo, 1850), said that the author had performed a miracle since he had worked without a collection of specimens and without a library. A second edition, revised by M. Gerbe (2 vols. 8vo, 1867), strove to remedy, and to some extent did remedy, the grosser errors of the first, but enough still remain to make few statements in the work trustworthy unless corroborated by other evidence. Meanwhile in England Dr Bree had in 1858 begun the publication of *The Birds of Europe not observed in the British Isles* (4 vols. 8vo), which was completed in 1863, and in 1875 reached a second and improved edition (5 vols.). In 1862 M. Dubois brought out a similar work on the "Espèces non observées en Belgique," being supplementary to that of his above named. In 1870 Anton Fritsch completed his *Naturgeschichte der Vögel Europas* (8vo, with atlas in folio); and in 1871 Messrs Sharpe and Dresser began the publication of their *Birds of Europe*, which was completed by the latter in 1879 (8 vols. 4to), and is unquestionably the most complete work of its kind; both for fulness of information and beauty of illustration—the coloured plates being nearly all by Keulemans. This work has since been completed by H. E. Dresser's *Supplement to the Birds of Europe* (1896). H. Noble's *List of European Birds* (1898) is a useful compilation, and Dresser's magnificent *Eggs of the Birds of Europe* is another great contribution by that author to European ornithology.

Coming now to works on British birds only, the first of the present century that requires remark is Montagu's *Ornithological Dictionary* (2 vols. 8vo, 1802; supplement 1813), the merits of which have been so long and so fully acknowledged both abroad and at home that no further comment is here wanted. In 1831 Rennie brought out a modified edition of 'it (reissued in 1833), and Jenyns another in 1866 (reissued in 1882); but those who wish to know the author's views had better consult the original. Next in order come the very inferior *British Ornithology* of Graves (3 vols. 8vo, 1811-1821), and a work with the same title by Hunt (3 vols. 8vo, 1815-1822), published at Norwich, but never finished. Then we have Selby's *Illustrations of British Ornithology*, two folio volumes of coloured plates engraved by himself, between 1821 and 1833, with letterpress also in two volumes (8vo, 1825-1833), a second edition of the first volume being also issued (1833), for the author, having yielded to the pressure of the "Quinarian" doctrines then in vogue, thought it necessary to adjust his classification accordingly, and it must be admitted that for information the

[6] Copies are said to exist bearing the date 1814.

second edition is best. In 1828 Fleming brought out his *History of British Animals* (8vo), in which the birds are treated at considerable length (pp. 41-146), though not with great success. In 1835 Mr Jenyns (afterwards Blomefield) produced an excellent *Manual of British Vertebrate Animals*, a volume (8vo) executed with great scientific skill, the birds again receiving due attention (pp. 49-286), and the descriptions of the various species being as accurate as they are terse. In the same year began the *Coloured Illustrations of British Birds and their Eggs* of H. L. Meyer (4to), which was completed in 1843, whereof a second edition (7 vols. 8vo, 1842-1850) was brought out, and subsequently (1852-1857) a reissue of the latter. In 1836 appeared Eyton's *History of the rarer British Birds*, intended as a sequel to Bewick's well-known volumes, to which no important additions had been made since the issue of 1821. The year 1837 saw the beginning of two remarkable works by Macgillivray and Yarrell respectively, and each entitled *A History of British Birds*. Of Yarrell's work in three volumes, a second edition, was published in 1845, a third in 1856, and a fourth, begun in 1871, and almost wholly rewritten. Of the compilations based upon this work, without which they could not have been composed, there is no need to speak. One of the few appearing since, with the same scope, that are not borrowed is Jardine's *Birds of Great Britain and Ireland* (4 vols. 8vo, 1838-1843), forming part of his *Naturalist's Library*; and Gould's *Birds of Great Britain* has been already mentioned. The local works on English birds are too numerous to be mentioned; almost every county has had its ornithology recorded. Of more recent general works there should be mentioned A. G. Butler's *British Birds with their Nests and Eggs* (6 vols., 1896), the various editions of Howard Saunders's *Manual of British Birds*, and Lord Lilford's beautifully illustrated *Coloured Figures of the Birds of the British Islands* (1885-1897).

Taxonomy.

The good effects of "Faunal" works such as those named in the foregoing rapid survey none can doubt, but important as they are, they do not of themselves constitute ornithology as a science; and an inquiry, no less wide and far more recondite, still remains. By whatever term we choose to call it—Classification, Arrangement, Systematizing or Taxonomy—that inquiry which has for its object the discovery of the natural groups into which birds fall, and the mutual relations of those groups, has always been one of the deepest interest. It is now for us to trace the rise of the present more advanced school of ornithologists, whose labours yet give signs of far greater promise.

It would probably be unsafe to place its origin further back than a few scattered hints contained in the "Pterographische Fragmente" of Christian Ludwig Nitzsch, published

Nitzsch. in the *Magazin für den neuesten Zustand der Naturkunde* (edited by Voigt) for May 1806 (xi. pp. 393-417), and even these might be left to pass unnoticed, were it not that we recognize in them the germ of the great work which the same admirable zoologist subsequently accomplished. In these "Fragments," apparently his earliest productions, we find him engaged on the subject with which his name will always be especially identified, the structure and arrangement of feathers. In the following year another set of hints—of a kind so different that probably no one then living would have thought it possible that they should ever be brought in correlation with those of Nitzsch—are contained in a memoir on Fishes contributed to the tenth volume of the *Annales*

É. G. St- *du Muséum d'histoire naturelle* de Paris by, Étienne
Hilaire. Geoffroy St-Hilaire in 1807.[1] Here we have it stated as a general truth (p. 100) that young birds have the sternum formed of five separate pieces—one in the middle, being its keel, and two "annexes" on each side to which the ribs are articulated—all, however, finally uniting to form the single "breast-bone." Further on (pp. 101, 102) we find observations as to the number of ribs which are attached to each of the "annexes"—there being sometimes more of them articulated to the anterior than to the posterior, and in certain forms no ribs belonging to one, all being applied to the other. Moreover, the author goes on to remark that in adult birds trace of the origin of the sternum from five centres of ossification is always more or less indicated by sutures, and that, though these sutures had been generally regarded as ridges for the attachment of the sternal muscles, they indeed mark the extreme points of the five primary bony pieces of the sternum.

[1] In the *Philosophie anatomique* (i. pp. 69-101, and especially pp. 135, 136), which appeared in 1818, Geoffroy St-Hilaire explained the views he had adopted at greater length.

In 1810 appeared at Heidelberg the first volume of F. Tiedemann's carefully-wrought *Anatomie und Naturgeschichte der Vögel*—which shows a remarkable advance upon

Tiede- the work which Cuvier did in 1805, and in some respects
mann. is superior to his later production of 1817. It is, however, only noticed here on account of the numerous references made to it by succeeding writers, for neither in this nor in the author's second volume (not published until 1814) did he propound any systematic arrangement of the Class. More germane to our present subject are the *Osteographische Beiträge zur Naturgeschichte der Vögel* of C. L. Nitzsch, printed at Leipzig in

Nitzsch. 1811—a miscellaneous set of detached essays on some peculiarities of the skeleton or portions of the skeleton of certain birds—one of the most remarkable of which is that on the component parts of the foot (pp. 101-105) pointing out the aberration from the ordinary structure exhibited by the Goatsucker (*Caprimulgus*) and the Swift (*Cypselus*)—an aberration which, if rightly understood, would have conveyed a warning to those ornithological systematists who put their trust in birds' toes for characters on which to erect a classification, that there was in them more of importance, hidden in the integument, than had hitherto been suspected; but the warning was of little avail, if any, till many years had elapsed. However, Nitzsch had not as yet seen his way to proposing any methodical arrangement of the various groups of birds, and it was not until some eighteen months later that a scheme of classification in the main anatomical was attempted.

This scheme was the work of Blasius Merrem, who, in a communication to the Academy of Sciences of Berlin on the

10th December 1812, which was published in its
Merrem. *Abhandlungen* for the following year (pp. 237-259), set forth a *Tentamen systematis naturalis avium*, no less modestly entitled than modestly executed. The attempt of Merrem must be regarded as the virtual starting-point of the latest efforts in Systematic Ornithology, and in that view its proposals deserve to be stated at length. Without pledging ourselves to the acceptance of all its details—some of which, as is only natural, cannot be sustained with our present knowledge—it is certainly not too much to say that Merrem's merits are almost incomparably superior to those of any of his predecessors. Premising then that the chief characters assigned by this systematist to his several groups are drawn from almost all parts of the structure of birds, and are supplemented by some others of their more prominent peculiarities, we present the following abstract of his scheme:[2]

I. AVES CARINATAE:
　　1. Aves aereae.
　　　　A. Rapaces.—a. Accipitres—*Vultur, Falco, Sagittarius.* b. Strix.
　　　　B. Hymenopodes—a. Chelidones: α. C. nocturnae—*Caprimulgus*; β. C. diurnae—*Hirundo.*
　　　　　　b. Oscines: α. O. conirostres—*Loxia, Fringilla, Emberiza, Tanagra*; β. O. tenuirostres—*Alauda, Motacilla, Muscicapa, Todus, Lanius, Ampelis, Turdus, Paradisea, Buphaga, Sturnus, Oriolus, Gracula, Coracias, Corvus, Pipra?, Parus, Sitta, Certhiae* quaedam.
　　　　C. Melliisugae.—*Trochilus, Certhiae* et *Upupae* plurimae.
　　　　D. Dendrocolaptae.—*Picus, Yunx.*
　　　　E. Brevilingues.—a. *Upupa*; b. *Ispidae.*
　　　　F. Levirostres.—a. *Ramphastus, Scythrops?*; b. *Psittacus.*
　　　　G. Coccyges.—*Cuculus, Trogon, Bucco, Crotophaga.*
　　2. Aves terrestres.
　　　　A. *Columba.*
　　　　B. *Gallinae.*
　　3. Aves aquaticae.
　　　　A. Odontorhynchi: a. *Boscades*—*Anas*; b. *Mergus*; c. *Phoenicopterus.*

[2] The names of the genera are, he tells us, for the most part those of Linnaeus, as being the best-known, though not the best. To some of the Linnaean genera he dare not, however, assign a place, for instance, *Buceros, Haematopus, Merops, Glareola* (Brisson's genus, by the by) and *Palamedea.*

B. Platyrhynchl.—*Pelicanus, Phaeton, Plotus.*
C. *Aptenodytes.*
D. Urinatrices: *a.* Cepphi—*Alca, Colymbi* pedibus palmatis; *b. Podiceps, Colymbi* pedibus lobatis.
E. Stenorhynchl.—*Procellaria, Diomedea, Larus, Sterna, Rhynchops.*
4. Aves palustres.
A. Rusticolae: *a.* Phalarides—*Rallus, Fulica, Parra; b.* Limosugae—*Numenius, Scolopax, Tringa, Charadrius, Recurvirostra.*
B. Grallae: *a.* Erodii—*Ardeae* ungue intermedio serrato, *Cancroma; b.* Pelargi—*Ciconia, Mycteria, Tantali* quidam, *Scopus, Platalea; c.* Gerani—*Ardeae* cristatae, *Grues, Psophia.*
C. Otis.
II. Aves ratitae.—*Struthio.*

The most novel feature, and one the importance of which most ornithologists of the present day are fully prepared to admit, is the separation of the class *Aves* into two great divisions, which from one of the most obvious distinctions they present were called by its author *Carinatae*[1] and *Ratitae*,[2] according as the sternum possesses a keel (*crista* in the phraseology of many anatomists) or not. But Merrem, who subsequently communicated to the Academy of Berlin a more detailed memoir on the "flat-breasted" birds,[3] was careful not here to rest his divisions on the presence or absence of their sternal character alone. He concisely cites (p. 238) no fewer than *eight* other characters of more or less value as peculiar to the Carinate Division, the first of which is that the feathers have their barbs furnished with hooks, in consequence of which the barbs, including those of the wing-quills, cling closely together; while among the rest may be mentioned the position of the furcula and coracoids,[4] which keep the wing-bones apart; the limitation of the number of the lumbar vertebra to *fifteen*, and of the carpals to *two*; as well as the divergent direction of the iliac bones—the corresponding characters peculiar to the Ratite Division being the disconnected condition of the barbs of the feathers, through the absence of any hooks whereby they might cohere; the non-existence of the furcula, and the coalescence of the coracoids with the scapulae (or, as he expressed it, the extension of the scapulae to supply the place of the coracoids, which he thought were wanting); the lumbar vertebrae being *twenty* and the carpals *three* in number; and the parallelism of the iliac bones.

As for Merrem's partitioning of the inferior groups there is less to be said in its praise as a whole, though credit must be given to his anatomical knowledge for leading him to the perception of several affinities, as well as differences, that had never before been suggested by superficial systematists. But it must be confessed that (chiefly, no doubt, from paucity of accessible material) he overlooked many points, both of alliance and the opposite, which since his time have gradually come to be admitted.

Notice has next to be taken of a Memoir on the Employment of Sternal Characters in establishing Natural Families among Birds, which was read by De Blainville before the De Blainville. Academy of Sciences of Paris in 1815,[5] but not published in full for more than five years later (*Journal de physique . . . et des arts*, xcii. 185-215), though an abstract forming part of a *Prodrome d'une nouvelle distribution du règne animal* appeared earlier (*op. cit.* lxxxiii. 252, 253, 258, 259; and *Bull. soc. philomath. de Paris*, 1816, p. 110). This is a very disappointing performance, since the author observes that, notwithstanding his new classification of birds is based on a study of the form of the sternal apparatus, yet, because that lies wholly within the body, he is compelled to have recourse to such outward characters as are afforded by the

[1] From *carina*, a keel.
[2] From *rates*, a raft or flat-bottomed barge.
[3] "Beschreibung des Gerippes eines Casuars nebst einigen beiläufigen Bemerkungen über die flachbrüstigen Vögel," *Abhandl. der Berlin. Akademie, Phys. Klasse* (1817), pp. 179-198, tabb. i.-iii.
[4] Merrem, as did many others in his time, calls the coracoids "*claviculas*"; but it is now well understood that in birds the real *claviculae* form the furcula or "merry-thought."
[5] Not 1812, as has sometimes been stated.

proportion of the limbs and the disposition of the toes—even as had been the practice of most ornithologists before him! It is evident that the features of the sternum of which De Blainville chiefly relied were those drawn from its posterior margin, which no very extensive experience of specimens is needed to show are of comparatively slight value; for the number of "*échancrures*"—notches as they have sometimes been called in English—when they exist, goes but a very short way as a guide, and is so variable in some very natural groups as to be even in that short way occasionally misleading.[6] There is no appearance of his having at all taken into consideration the far more trustworthy characters furnished by the anterior part of the sternum, as well as by the coracoids and the furcula. Still De Blainville made some advance in a right direction, as for instance by elevating the parrots[7] and the pigeons as "*Ordres*," equal in rank to that of the birds of prey and some others. According to the testimony of L'Herminier (for whom see later) he divided the "*Passereaux*" into two sections, the "*faux*" and the "*vrais*"; but, while the latter were very correctly defined, the former were most arbitrarily separated from the "*Grimpeurs*." He also split his *Grallatores* and *Natatores* (practically identical with the *Grallae* and *Anseres* of Linnaeus) each into four sections; but he failed to see—as on his own principles he ought to have seen—that each of these sections was at least equivalent to almost any one of his other "*Ordres*." He had, however, the courage to act up to his own professions in collocating the rollers (*Coracias*) with the bee-eaters (*Merops*), and had the sagacity to surmise that *Menura* was not a Gallinaceous bird. The greatest benefit conferred by this memoir is probably that it stimulated the efforts, presently to be mentioned, of one of his pupils, and that it brought more distinctly into what that other factor, originally discovered by Merrem, of which it now clearly became the duty of systematizers to take cognizance.

Following the chronological order we are here adopting, we next have to recur to the labours of Nitzsch, who, in 1820, in a treatise on the nasal glands of birds—a subject that Nitzsch had already attracted the attention of Jacobson (*Nouv. Bull. soc. philomath. de. Paris*, iii. 267-269)—first put forth in Meckel's *Deutsches Archiv für die Physiologie* (vi. 251-269) a statement of his general views on ornithological classification which were based on a comparative examination of those bodies in various forms. It seems unnecessary here to occupy space by giving an abstract of his plan,[8] which hardly includes any but European species, because it was subsequently elaborated with no inconsiderable modifications in a way that must presently be mentioned at greater length. But the scheme, crude as it was, possesses some interest. It is not only a key to much of his later work—to nearly all indeed that was published in his lifetime—but in it are founded several definite groups (for example, *Passerinae* and *Picariae*) that subsequent experience has shown to be more or less natural; and it further serves as additional evidence of the breadth of his views, and his trust in the teachings of anatomy.

That Nitzsch took this extended view is abundantly proved by the valuable series of ornithotomical observations which he must have been for some time accumulating, and almost immediately afterwards began to contribute to the younger Naumann's excellent *Naturgeschichte der Vögel Deutschlands*, already noticed above. Besides a concise general treatise on the organization of birds to be found in the Introduction to this work (i. 23-52), a brief description from Nitzsch's pen of the peculiarities of the internal structure of nearly every genus is incorporated with the author's prefatory remarks, as each passed under consideration,

[6] Cf. *Philos. Transactions* (1869), p. 337, note.
[7] This view of them had been long before taken by Willughby, but abandoned by all later authors.
[8] This plan, having been repeated by Schöpss in 1829 (*op. cit.* xii. p. 73), became known to Sir R. Owen in 1835, who then drew to it the attention of Kirby (*Seventh Bridgewater Treatise*, ii. pp. 444, 445), and in the next year referred to it in his own article "Aves" in Todd's *Cyclopaedia of Anatomy* (i. p. 266), so that Englishmen need no excuse for not being aware of one of Nitzsch's labours, though his more advanced work of 1829, presently to be mentioned, was not referred to by Sir R. Owen.

and these descriptions being almost without exception so drawn up as to be comparative are accordingly of great utility to the student of classification, though they have been so greatly neglected. Upon these descriptions he was still engaged till death, in 1837, put an end to his labours, when his place as Naumann's assistant for the remainder of the work was taken by Rudolph Wagner; but, from time to time, a few more, which he had already completed, made their posthumous appearance in it, and, in subsequent years, some selections from his unpublished papers were through the care of Giebel presented to the public. Throughout the whole of this series the same marvellous industry and scrupulous accuracy are manifested, and attentive study of it will show how many times Nitzsch anticipated the conclusions of modern taxonomers. Yet over and over again his determination of the affinities of several groups even of European birds was disregarded; and his labours, being contained in a bulky and costly work, were hardly known at all outside of his own country, and within it by no means appreciated so much as they deserved [1]—for even Naumann himself, who gave them publication, and was doubtless in some degree influenced by them, utterly failed to perceive the importance of the characters offered by the song-muscles of certain groups, though their peculiarities were all duly described and recorded by his coadjutor, as some indeed had been long before by Cuvier in his famous dissertation [2] on the organs of voice in birds (Leçons d'anatomie comparée, iv. 450-491). Nitzsch's name was subsequently dismissed by Cuvier without a word of praise, and in terms which would have been applicable to many another and inferior author, while Temminck, terming Naumann's work an "ouvrage de luxe"—it being in truth one of the cheapest for its contents ever published—effectually shut it out from the realms of science. In Britain it seems to have been positively unknown until quoted some years after its completion by a catalogue-compiler on account of some peculiarities of nomenclature which it presented.

Now we must return to France, where, in 1827, L'Herminier, a creole of Guadaloupe and a pupil of De Blainville's, contributed L'Herminier. to the Actes of the Linnaean Society of Paris for that year (vi. 3-93) the "Recherches sur l'appareil sternal des Oiseaux," which the precept and example of his master had prompted him to undertake, and Cuvier had found for him the means of executing. A second and considerably enlarged edition of this very remarkable treatise was published as a separate work in the following year. We have already seen that De Blainville, though fully persuaded of the great value of sternal features as a method of classification, had been compelled to fall back upon the old pedal characters so often employed before; but now the scholar had learnt to excel his teacher, and not only to form an at least provisional arrangement of the various members of the Class, based on sternal characters, but to describe these characters at some length, and to give a reason for the faith that was in him. There is no evidence, so far as we can see, of his having been aware of Merrem's views; but like that anatomist he without hesitation divided the class into two great "coupes," to which he gave, however; no other names than " Oiseaux normaux " and " Oiseaux anomaux "—exactly corresponding with his predecessor's Carinatae and Ratitae—and, moreover, he had a great advantage in founding these groups, since he had discovered, apparently from his own investigations, that the mode of ossification in each was distinct; for hitherto the statement of there being five centres of ossification in every bird's sternum seems to have been accepted as a general truth, without contradiction, whereas in the ostrich and the rhea, at any rate, L'Herminier found that there were but two such primitive points,[3] and from analogy

---

[1] Their value was, however, understood by Gloger, who in 1834, as will presently be seen, expressed his regret at not being able to use them.
[2] Cuvier's first observations on the subject seem to have appeared in the Magasin encyclopédique for 1795 (ii. pp. 330, 358).
[3] This fact in the ostrich appears to have been known already to Geoffroy St-Hilaire from his own observation in Egypt, but does not seem to have been published by him.

he judged that the same would be the case with the cassowary and the emeu, which, with the two forms mentioned above, made up the whole of the " Oiseaux anomaux ", whose existence was then generally acknowledged.[4] These are the forms which composed the family previously termed Cursores by De Blainville; but L'Herminier was able to distinguish no fewer than thirty-four families of " Oiseaux normaux," and the judgment with which their separation and definition were effected must be deemed on the whole to be most creditable to him. It is to be remarked, however, that the wealth of the Paris Museum, which he enjoyed to the full, placed him in a situation incomparably more favourable for arriving at results than that which was occupied by Métrem, to whom many of the most remarkable forms were wholly unknown, while L'Herminier had at his disposal examples of nearly every type then known to exist. But the latter used this privilege wisely and well—not, after the manner of De Blainville and others subsequent to him, relying solely or even chiefly on the character afforded by the posterior portion of the sternum, but taking also into consideration those of the anterior, as well as of the in some cases still more important characters presented by the pre-sternal bones, such as the furcula, coracoids and scapulae. L'Herminier thus separated the families of " Normal Birds ":—

1.	"Accipitres" — Accipitres, Linn.		18.	"Passereaux" — Passeres, Linn.
2.	"Serpentaires" — Gypogeranus, Illiger.		19.	"Pigeons"—Columba, Linn.
3.	"Chouettes"—Strix, Linn.		20.	"Gallinacés"—Gallinacea.
4.	"Touracos"—Opaetus, Vieillot.		21.	"Tinamous" — Tinamus, Latham.
5.	"Perroquets" — Psittacus, Linn.		22.	"Foulques ou Poules d'eau" —Fulica, Linn.
6.	"Colibris "—Trochilus, Linn.		23.	"Grues"—Grus, Pallas.
7.	"Martinets "—Cypselus, Illiger.		24.	"Hérodions"—Herodii, Illiger.
8.	"Engoulevents " — Caprimulgus, Linn.		25.	No name given, but said to include " les ibis et les spatules."
9.	"Coucous "—Cuculus, Linn.		26.	"Cralles ou Échassiers " Grallae.
10.	"Couroucous"—Trogon,Linn.		27.	"Mouettes "—Larus, Linn.
11.	"Rolliers"—Galgulus, Brisson.		28.	"Pétrels"—Procellaria,Linn.
12.	"Guêpiers "—Merops, Linn.		29.	"Pélicans"—Pelecanus,Linn.
13.	"Martins-Pêcheurs"—Alcedo, Linn.		30.	"Canards "—Anas, Linn.
14.	"Calao "—Buceros, Linn.		31.	"Grèbes" — Podiceps, Latham.
15.	"Toucans "— Ramphastos, Linn.		32.	"Plongeons " — Colymbus, Latham.
16.	"Pics "—Picus, Linn.		33.	"Pingouins "—Alca,Latham.
17.	"Épopsides " — Epopsides, Vieillot.		34.	"Manchots " — Aptenodytes, Forster.

The preceding list is given to show the very marked agreement of L'Herminier's results compared with those obtained fifty years later by another investigator, who approached the subject from an entirely different, though still osteological, basis. Many of the excellencies of L'Herminier's method could not be pointed out without too great a sacrifice of space, because of the details into which it would be necessary to enter; but the trenchant way in which he showed that the " Passereaux "—a group of which Cuvier had said, " Son caractère semble d'abord purement négatif," and had then failed to define the limits—differed so completely from every other assemblage, while maintaining among its own innumerable members an almost perfect essential homogeneity, is very striking, and shows how admirably he could grasp his subject. Not less conspicuous are his merits in disposing of the groups of what are ordinarily known as water-birds, his indicating the affinity of the rails (No. 22) to the cranes (No. 23), and the severing of the latter from the hérons (No. 24). His union of the snipes, sandpipers and plovers into one group (No. 26) and the alliance, especially dwelt upon, of that group with the gulls (No. 27) are steps which, though indicated by Merrem, are here for the first time clearly laid down; and the separation of the gulls from the petrels (No. 28)—step in advance already taken; it is true, by Illiger—is here placed on indefeasible ground. With all this, perhaps on account of all this, L'Herminier's efforts did not

---

[4] Considerable doubts were at that time entertained in Paris as to the existence of the Apteryx.

find favour with his scientific superiors, and for the time things remained as though his investigations had never been carried on.

Nitzsch's grouping. Two years later Nitzsch, who was indefatigable in his endeavour to discover the natural families of birds and had been pursuing a series of researches into their vascular system, published the result, at Halle in Saxony, in his *Observationes de avium arteria carotide communi*, in which is included a classification drawn up in accordance with the variation of structure which that important vessel presented in the several groups that he had opportunities of examining. By this time he had visited several of the principal museums on the Continent, among others Leyden (where Temminck resided) and Paris (where he had frequent intercourse with Cuvier), thus becoming acquainted with a considerable number of exotic forms that had hitherto been inaccessible to him. Consequently his labours had attained to a certain degree of completeness in this direction, and it may therefore be expedient here to name the different groups which he thus thought himself entitled to consider established. They are as follows:—

I. AVES CARINATAE [L'H. "Oiseaux normaux"].

A. Aves Carinatae aereae.

1. *Accipitrinae* [L'H. 1, 2 partim, 3]; 2. *Passerinae* [L'H. 18]; 3. *Macrochires* [L'H. 6, 7]; 4. *Cuculinae* [L'H. 8, 9, 10 (qu. 11, 12?)]; 5. *Picinae* [L'H. 15, 16]; 6. *Psittacinae* [L'H. 5]; 7. *Lipoglossae* [L'H. 13, 14, 17]; 8. *Amphibolae* [L'H. 4].

B. Aves Carinatae terrestres.

1. *Columbinae* [L'H. 19]; 2. *Gallinaceae* [L'H. 20].

C. Aves Carinatae aquaticae.

Grallae.

1. *Alectorides* (= *Dicholophus* + *Otis*) [L'H. 2 partim, 26 partim]; 2. *Gruinae* [L'H. 23]; 3. *Fulicariae* [L'H. 22]; 4. *Herodiae* [L'H. 24 partim]; 5. *Pelargi* [L'H. 24 partim, 25]; 6. *Odontoglossi* (= *Phoenicopterus*) [L'H. 26 partim]; 7. *Limicolae* [L'H. 26 paene omnes].

Palmatae.

8. *Longipennes* [L'H. 27]; 9. *Nasutae* [L'H. 28]; 10. *Unguirostres* [L'H. 30]; 11. *Steganopodes* [L'H. 29]; 12. *Pygopodes* [L'H. 31, 32, 33, 34].

II. AVES RATITAE [L'H. "Oiseaux anomaux"].

To enable the reader to compare the several groups of Nitzsch with the families of L'Herminier, the numbers applied by the latter to his families are suffixed in square brackets to the names of the former; and, disregarding the order of sequence, which is here immaterial, the essential correspondence of the two systems is worthy of all attention, for it obviously means that these two investigators, starting from different points, must have been on the right track, when they so often coincided as to the limits of what they considered to be, and what we are now almost justified in calling, natural groups.[1] But it must be observed that the classification of Nitzsch, just given, rests much more on characters furnished by the general structure than on those furnished by the carotid artery only. Among all the species (188, he tells us, in number) of which he examined specimens, he found only *four* variations in the structure of that vessel, namely:—

1. That in which both a right carotid artery and a left are present. This is the most usual fashion among the various groups of birds, including all the "aerial" forms excepting *Passerinae*, *Macrochires* and *Picinae*.

2. That in which there is but a single carotid artery, springing from both right and left trunk, but the branches soon coalescing, to take a midway course, and again dividing near the head. This form Nitzsch was only able to find in the bittern (*Ardea stellaris*).

3. That in which the right carotid artery alone is present, of which, according to our author's experience, the flamingo (*Phoenicopterus*) was the sole example.

4. That in which the left carotid artery alone exists, as found in all other birds examined by Nitzsch, and therefore as regards species and individuals much the most common—since into this category come the countless thousands of the passerine birds—a group which outnumbers all the rest put together.

Berthold. Considering the enormous stride in advance made by L'Herminier, it is very disappointing for the historian to have to record that the next inquirer into the osteology of birds achieved a disastrous failure in his attempt to throw light on their arrangement by means of a comparison of their sternum. This was Berthold, who devoted a long chapter of his *Beiträge zur Anatomie*, published at Göttingen in 1831, to a consideration of the subject. So far as his introductory chapter went—the development of the sternum—he was, for his time, right enough and somewhat instructive. It was only when, after a close examination of the sternal apparatus of one hundred and thirty species, which he carefully described, that he arrived (pp. 177-183) at the conclusion—astonishing to us who know of L'Herminier's previous results—that the sternum of birds cannot be used as a help to their classification on account of the egregious anomalies that would follow the proceeding—such anomalies, for instance, as the separation of *Cypselus* from *Hirundo* and its alliance with *Trochilus*, and the grouping of *Hirundo* and *Fringilla* together.

Cuvier and Geoffroy. At the very beginning of the year 1832 Cuvier laid before the Academy of Sciences of Paris a memoir on the progress of ossification in the sternum of birds, of which memoir an abstract will be found in the *Annales des sciences naturelles* (xxv. pp. 260-272). Herein he traced in detail, illustrating his statements by the preparations he exhibited, the progress of ossification in the sternum of the fowl and of the duck, pointing out how it differed in each, and giving his interpretation of the differences. It had hitherto been generally believed that the mode of ossification in the fowl was that which obtained in all birds—the ostrich and its allies (as L'Herminier, we have seen, had already shown) excepted. But it was now made to appear that the struthious birds in this respect resembled, not only the duck, but a great many other groups—waders, birds-of-prey, pigeons, passerines and perhaps all birds not gallinaceous—so that, according to Cuvier's view, the five points of ossification observed in the *Gallinae*, instead of exhibiting the normal process, exhibited one quite exceptional, and that in all other birds, so far as he had been enabled to investigate the matter, ossification of the sternum began at two points only, situated near the anterior upper margin of the side of the sternum, and gradually crept towards the keel, into which it presently extended; and, though he allowed the appearance of detached portions of calcareous matter at the base of the still cartilaginous keel in ducks at a certain age, he seemed to consider this an individual peculiarity. This fact was fastened upon by Geoffroy in his reply, which was a week later presented to the Academy, but was not published in full until the following year, when it appeared in the *Annales du Muséum* (ser. 3, ii. pp. 1-22). Geoffroy here maintained that the five centres of ossification existed in the duck just as in the fowl, and that the real difference of the process lay in the period at which they made their appearance, a circumstance which, though virtually proved by the preparations Cuvier had used, had been by him overlooked or misinterpreted. The fowl possesses all five ossifications at birth, and for a long while the middle piece forming the keel is by far the largest. They all grow slowly, and it is not until the animal is about six months old that they are united into one firm bone. The duck, on the other hand, when newly hatched, and for nearly a month after, has the sternum wholly cartilaginous. Then, it is true, two lateral points of ossification appear at the margin, but subsequently the remaining three are developed, and when once formed they grow with much greater rapidity than in the fowl, so that by the time the young duck is quite independent of its parents, and can shift for itself, the whole sternum is completely bony. Nor, argued Geoffroy, was it true to say, as Cuvier had said, that the like occurred in the pigeons and true passerines. In their case the sternum begins to ossify from three very distinct points—one of which is the centre of ossification of

[1] Whether Nitzsch was cognizant of L'Herminier's views is in no way apparent. The latter's name seems not to be even mentioned by him, but Nitzsch was in Paris in the summer of 1827, and it is almost impossible that he should not have heard of L'Herminier's labours, unless the relations between the followers of Cuvier to whom Nitzsch attached himself, and those of De Blainville, whose pupil L'Herminier was, were such as to forbid any communication between the rival schools. Yet we have L'Herminier's evidence that Cuvier gave him every assistance. Nitzsch's silence, both on this occasion and afterwards, is very curious; but he cannot be accused of plagiarism, for the scheme given above is only an amplification of that foreshadowed by him (as already mentioned) in 1820—a scheme which seems to have been equally unknown to L'Herminier, perhaps through linguistic difficulty.

the keel. As regards the struthious birds, they could not be likened to the duck, for in them at no age was there any indication of a single median centre of ossification, as Geoffroy had satisfied himself by his own observations made in Egypt many years before. Cuvier seems to have acquiesced in the corrections of his views made by Geoffroy, and attempted no rejoinder; but the attentive and impartial student of the discussion will see that a good deal was really wanting to make the latter's reply effective, though, as events have shown, the former was hasty in the conclusions at which he arrived, having trusted too much to the first appearance of centres of ossification, for, had his observations in regard to other birds been carried on with the same attention to detail as in regard to the fowl, he would certainly have reached some very different results.

In 1834 C. W. L. Gloger brought out at Breslau the first (and unfortunately the only) part of a *Vollständiges Handbuch der Naturgeschichte der Vögel Europa's*, treating of the land-birds. In the Introduction to this book (p. xxxvii., note) he expressed his regret at not being able to use as fully as he could wish the excellent researches of Nitzsch which were then appearing (as has been above said) in the successive parts of Naumann's great work. Notwithstanding this, to Gloger seems to belong the credit of being the first author to avail himself in a book intended for practical ornithologists of the new light that had already been shed on Systematic Ornithology; and accordingly we have the second order of his arrangement, the *Aves Passerinae*, divided into two suborders: singing passerines (*melodusae*), and passerines without an apparatus of song-muscles (*anomalae*)—the latter including what some later writers called *Picariae*. For the rest his classification demands no particular remark; but that in a work of this kind he had the courage to recognize, for instance, such a fact as the essential difference between swallows and swifts lifts him considerably above the crowd of other ornithological writers of his time.

An improvement on the old method of classification by purely external characters was introduced to the Academy of Sciences of Stockholm by C. J. Sundevall in 1835, and was published the following year in its *Handlingar* (pp. 43-130). This was the foundation of a more extensive work of which, from the influence it still exerts, it will be necessary to treat later at some length, and there will be no need now to enter much into details respecting the earlier performance. It is sufficient here to remark that the author, even than a man of great erudition, must have been aware of the turn which taxonomy was taking; but, not being able to divest himself of the older notion that external characters were superior to those furnished by the study of internal structure, and that Comparative Anatomy, instead of being a part of zoology, was something distinct from it, he seems to have endeavoured to form a scheme which, while not running wholly counter to the teachings of Comparative Anatomists, should yet rest ostensibly on external characters. With this view he studied the latter most laboriously, and in some measure certainly not without success, for he brought into prominence several points that had hitherto escaped the notice of his predecessors. He also admitted among his characteristics a physiological consideration (apparently derived from Oken [1]) dividing the class *Aves* into two sections *Altrices* and *Praecoces*, according as the young were fed by their parents or, from the first, fed themselves. But at this time he was encumbered with the hazy doctrine of analogies, which, if it did not act to his detriment, was assuredly of no service to him. He prefixed an "Idea Systematis" to his "Expositio"; and the former, which appears to represent his real opinion, differs in arrangement very considerably from the latter. Like Gloger, Sundevall in his ideal system separated the true passerines from all other birds, calling them *Volucres*; but he took a step further, for he assigned to them the highest rank, wherein nearly every recent authority agrees with him; out of them, however, he chose the thrushes and warblers to stand first as his ideal "Centrum"—a selection which, though in the opinion of the present writer erroneous, is still largely followed.

The points at issue between Cuvier and Étienne Geoffroy St-Hilaire before mentioned naturally attracted the attention of L'Herminier, who in 1836 presented to the French Academy the results of his researches into the mode of growth of that bone which in the adult bird he had already studied to such good purpose. Unfortunately the full account of his diligent investigations was never published. We can best judge of his labours from an abstract reprinted in the *Comptes rendus* (iii. pp. 12-20) and reprinted in the *Annales des sciences naturelles* (ser. 2, vol. vi. pp. 107-115), and from the report upon them by Isidore Geoffroy

[1] He says from Oken's *Naturgeschichte für Schulen*, published in 1821, but the division is to be found in that author's earlier *Lehrbuch der Zoologie* (ii. p. 371), which appeared in 1816.

St-Hilaire, to whom with others they were referred. This report is contained in the *Comptes rendus* for the following year (iv. pp. 565-574), and is very critical in its character.

L'Herminier arrived at the conclusion that, so far from there being only two or three different modes by which the process of ossification in the sternum is carried out, the number of different modes is very considerable—almost each natural group of birds having its own. The principal theory which he hence conceived himself justified in propounding was that instead of *five* being (as had been stated) the maximum number of centres of ossification in the sternum, there are no fewer than *nine* entering into the composition of the perfect sternum of birds in general, though in every species some of these nine are wanting, whatever be the condition of development at the time of examination. These nine theoretical centres or "pieces" L'Herminier deemed to be disposed in *three* transverse series (*rangées*), namely the anterior or "prosternal," the middle or "mesosternal" and the posterior or "metasternal," —each series consisting of *three* portions, one median piece and two side-pieces. At the same time he seems, according to the abstract of his memoir, to have made the somewhat contradictory assertion that sometimes there are more than three pieces in each series, and in certain groups of birds as many as six. It would occupy more space than can here be allowed to give even the briefest abstract of the numerous observations which follow the statement of his theory and on which it professedly rests. They extend to more than a score of natural groups of birds, and nearly each of them presents some peculiar characters. Thus of the first series of pieces he says that when all exist they may be developed simultaneously, or that the two side-pieces may precede the median, or again that the median may precede the side-pieces—according to the group of birds, but that the second mode is much the commonest. The same variations are observable in the second or middle series, but its side-pieces are said to exist in all groups of birds without exception. As to the third or posterior series, when it is complete the three constituent pieces are developed almost simultaneously; but its median piece is said often to originate in two, which soon unite, especially when the side-pieces are wanting. By way of examples of L'Herminier's observations, what he says of the two groups that had been the subject of Cuvier's and the elder Geoffroy's contest may be mentioned. In the *Gallinae* the five well-known pieces or centres of ossification are said to consist of the two side-pieces of the second or middle series, and the three of the posterior. On two occasions, however, there was found in addition, what may be taken for a representation of the first series, a little "*noyau*" situated between the coracoids—forming the only instance of all three series being present in the same bird. As regards the ducks, L'Herminier agreed with Cuvier that there are commonly only two centres of ossification—the side-pieces of the middle series; but as these grow to meet one another a distinct median "*noyau*," also of the same series, sometimes appears, which soon forms a connexion with each of them. In the ostrich and its allies no trace of this median centre of ossification ever occurs; but with these exceptions its existence is invariable in all other birds. Here the matter must be left; but it is undoubtedly a subject which demands further investigation, and naturally any future investigator of it should consult the abstract of L'Herminier's memoir and the criticisms upon it of the younger Geoffroy.

Hitherto our attention has been given wholly to Germany and France, for the chief ornithologists of this time were occupying themselves at this time in a very useless way—not but that there were several distinguished men who were paying due heed at this time to the internal structure of birds, and some excellent descriptive memoirs on special forms had appeared from their pens, to say nothing of more than one general treatise on ornithic anatomy.[a] Yet no one in Britain

[a] We shall perhaps be justified in assuming that this apparent inconsistency, and others which present themselves, would be explicable if the whole memoir with the necessary illustrations had been published.

[b] Sir Richard Owen's celebrated article "Aves," in Todd's *Cyclopaedia of Anatomy and Physiology* (i. pp. 265-358), appeared in 1836, and, as giving a general view of the structure of birds, needs no praise here; but its object was not to establish a classification, or throw light especially on systematic arrangement. So far from that being the case, its distinguished author was content to adopt, as he tells us, the arrangement proposed by Kirby in the *Seventh Bridgewater Treatise* (ii. pp. 443-474), being that, it is true, of an estimable zoologist, but of one who had no special knowledge of ornithology. Indeed it is, as the latter says, that of Linnaeus, improved by Cuvier, with an additional modification of Illiger's—all these three authors having totally ignored any but external characters. Yet it was regarded "as being the one which facilitates the expression of the leading anatomical differences which obtain in the class of birds, and which therefore may be considered as the most natural."

seems to have attempted to found any scientific arrangement of birds on other than external characters until, in 1837, William Macgillivray issued the first volume of his *History of British Birds*, wherein, though professing (p. 19) "not to add a new system to the many already in partial use, or that have passed away like their authors," he propounded (pp. 16–18) a scheme for classifying the birds of Europe at least founded on a "consideration of the digestive organs, which merit special attention, on account, not so much of their great importance in the economy of birds, as the nervous, vascular and other systems are not behind them in this respect; but because, exhibiting great diversity of form and structure, in accordance with the nature of the food, they are more obviously qualified to afford a basis for the classification of the numerous species of birds " (p. 52). Fuller knowledge has shown that Macgillivray was ill-advised in laying stress on the systematic value of adaptive characters, but his contributions to anatomy were valuable, and later investigators, in particular H. Gadow and P. Chalmers Mitchell, have shown that useful systematic information can be obtained from the study of the alimentary canal. Macgillivray himself it was, apparently, who first detected the essential difference of the organs of voice presented by some of the New-World Passerines (subsequently known as *Clamatores*), and the earliest intimation of this seems to be given in his anatomical description of the Arkansas Flycatcher, *Tyrannus verticalis*, which was published in 1838 (*Ornithol. Biography*, iv. p. 425), though it must be admitted that he did not—because he then could not—perceive the bearing of their difference, which was reserved to be shown by the investigation of a still greater anatomist, and of one who had fuller facilities for research, and thereby almost revolutionized, as will presently be mentioned, the views of systematists as to this order of birds. There is only space here to say that the second volume of Macgillivray's work was published in 1839, and the third in 1840; but it was not until 1852 that the author, in broken health, found an opportunity of issuing the fourth and fifth. His scheme of classification, being as before stated partial, need not be given in detail. Its great merit is that it proved the necessity of combining another and hitherto much-neglected factor in any natural arrangement, though vitiated as so many other schemes have been by being based wholly on one class of characters.

But a bolder attempt at classification was that made in 1838 by Blyth in the New Series (Charlesworth's) of the *Magazine of Natural History* (ii. pp. 256-268, 314-319, 351-361, 420-426, 589-601; iii. pp. 76-84). It was limited, however, to what he called *Insessores*, being the group upon which that name had been conferred by Vigors (*Trans. Linn. Society*, xiv. p. 405) in 1823, with the addition, however, of his *Raptores*, and it will be unnecessary to enter into particulars concerning it, though it is as equally remarkable for the insight shown by the author into the structure of birds as for the philosophical breadth of his view, which comprehends almost every kind of character that had been at that time brought forward. It is plain that Blyth saw, and perhaps he was the first to see it, that geographical distribution was not unimportant in suggesting the affinities and differences of natural groups (pp. 258, 259); and, undeterred by the precepts and practice of the hitherto dominant English school of Ornithologists, he declared that "anatomy, when aided by every character which the manner of propagation, the progressive changes, and other physiological data supply, is the only sure basis of classification." He was quite aware of the taxonomic value of the vocal organs of some groups of birds, presently to be especially mentioned, and he had himself ascertained the presence and absence of caeca in a not inconsiderable number of groups, drawing thence very justifiable inferences. He knew at least the earlier investigations of L'Herminier, and, though the work of Nitzsch, even if he had ever heard of it, must (through ignorance of the language in which it was written) have been to him a sealed book, he had followed out and extended the hints already given by Temminck as to the differences which various groups of birds display in their moult. With all this it is not surprising to find, though the fact has

been generally overlooked, that Blyth's proposed arrangement in many points anticipated conclusions that were subsequently reached, and were then regarded as fresh discoveries. It is proper to add that at this time the greater part of his work was carried on in conjunction with A. Bartlett, the superintendent of the London Zoological Society's Gardens, and that, without his assistance, Blyth's opportunities, slender as they were compared with those which others have enjoyed, must have been still smaller. Considering the extent of their materials, which was limited to the bodies of such animals as they could obtain from dealers and the several menageries that then existed in or near London, the progress made in what has since proved to be the right direction is very wonderful. It is obvious that both these investigators had the genius for recognizing and interpreting the value of characters; but their labours do not seem to have met with much encouragement; and a general arrangement of the class laid by Blyth before the Zoological Society at this time [1] does not appear in its publications. The scheme could hardly fail to be a crude performance—a fact which nobody would know better than its author; but it must have presented much that was objectionable to the opinions then generally prevalent. Its line to some extent may be partly made out—very clearly, for the matter of that, so far as its details have been published in the series of papers to which reference has been given—and some traces of its features are probably preserved in his *Catalogue* of the specimens of birds in the museum of the Asiatic Society of Bengal, which, after several years of severe labour, made its appearance at Calcutta in 1849; but, from the time of his arrival in India, the onerous duties imposed upon Blyth, together with the want of sufficient books of reference, seem to have hindered him from seriously continuing his former researches, which, interrupted as they were, and born out of due time, had no appreciable effect on the views of systematisers generally.

Next must be noticed a series of short treatises communicated by Johann Friedrich Brandt, between the years 1836 and 1839, to the Academy of Sciences of St Petersburg, and published in its *Mémoires*. In the year last mentioned the greater part of these was separately issued under the title of *Beiträge zur Kenntniss der Naturgeschichte der Vögel*. Herein the author first assigned anatomical reasons for rearranging the order *Anseres* of Linnaeus and *Natatores* of Illiger, who, so long before as 1811, had proposed a new distribution of it into six families, the definitions of which, as was his wont, he had drawn from external characters only. Brandt now retained very nearly the same arrangement as his predecessor; but, notwithstanding that he could trust to the firmer foundation of internal framework, he took at least two retrograde steps. First he failed to see the great structural difference between the penguins (which Illiger had placed as a group, *Impennes*, of equal rank to his other families) and the auks, divers and grebes, *Pygopodes*—combining all of them to form a "Typus" (to use his term) *Urinatores*: and secondly he admitted among the *Natatores*, though as a distinct "Typus" *Podoidae*, the genera *Podoa* and *Fulica*, which are now known to belong to the *Rallidae*—the latter indeed (see COOT) being but very slightly removed from the moorhen (q.v.). At the same time he corrected the error made by Illiger in associating the Phalaropes with these forms, rightly declaring their relationship to *Tringa* (see SANDPIPER), a point of order which other systematists were long in admitting. On the whole Brandt's labours were of no small service in asserting the principle that consideration must be paid to osteology for his position was such as to gain more attention to his views than some of his less favourably placed brethren had succeeded in doing.

In the same year (1839) another slight advance was made in the classification of the true Passerines. Keyserling and Blasius briefly pointed out in the *Archiv für Naturgeschichte* (v. pp. 332-334) that, while all the other birds provided with perfect song-muscles had the "planta" or hind part of the "tarsus" covered with two long and undivided horny plates, the larks (q.v.) had this part divided by many transverse sutures, so as to be scutellated behind as well as in front; just as is the case in many of the passerines which have not the singing-apparatus, and also in the hoopoe (q.v.). The importance of this singular but superficial departure from the normal structure has been so needlessly exaggerated as a character that at the present time its value is apt to be unduly depreciated. So large and so homogeneous a group as that of the true Passerines, a constant

<hr>

[1] An abstract is contained in the Minute-book of the Scientific Meetings of the Zoological Society, 26th June and 10th July 1838. The class was to contain fifteen orders, but only three were dealt with in any detail.

Marginal notes: *Bartlett.* / *Blyth.* / *Brandt.* / *Keyserling and Blasius.*

character of this kind is not to be despised as a practical mode of separating the birds which possess it; and, more than this, it would appear that the discovery thus announced was the immediate means of leading to a series of investigations of a much more important and lasting nature—those of Johannes Müller to be presently mentioned.

Again we must recur to that indefatigable and most original investigator Nitzsch, who, having never intermitted his study of the particular subject of his first contribution to science, long ago noticed, in 1833 brought out at Halle, where he was professor of Zoology, an essay with the title *Pterylographiae Avium Pars prior*. It seems that this was issued as much with the object of inviting assistance from others in view of future labours, since the materials at his disposal were comparatively scanty, as with that of making known the results to which his researches had already led him. Indeed, he only communicated copies of this essay to a few friends, and examples of it are comparatively scarce. Moreover, he stated subsequently that he thereby hoped to excite other naturalists to share with him the investigations he was making on a subject which had hitherto escaped notice or had been wholly neglected, since he considered that he had proved the disposition of the feathered tracts in the plumage of birds to be the means of furnishing characters for the discrimination of the various natural groups as significant and important as they were new and unexpected. There was no need for us here to quote this essay in its chronological place, since it dealt only with the generalities of the subject, and did not enter upon any systematic details. These the author reserved for a second treatise which he was destined never to complete. He kept on diligently collecting materials, and as he did so was constrained to modify some of the statements he had published. He consequently fell into a state of doubt, and before he could make up his mind on some questions which he deemed important he was overtaken by death.[1] Then his papers were handed over to his friend and successor Professor Burmeister, now *Burmeister*. and for many years past of Buenos Aires, who, with much skill, elaborated from them the excellent work known as Nitzsch's *Pterylographie*, which was published at Halle in 1840, and translated into English for the Ray Society in 1867. There can be no doubt that Professor Burmeister discharged his editorial duty with the most conscientious scrupulosity; but, from what has been just said, it is certain that there were important points on which Nitzsch was as yet undecided—some of them perhaps of which no trace appeared in his manuscripts, and therefore as in every case of works posthumously published, unless (as rarely happens) they have received their author's "*imprimatur*," they cannot be implicitly trusted as the expression of his final views. It would consequently be unsafe to ascribe positively all that appears in this volume to the result of Nitzsch's mature consideration. Moreover, as Professor Burmeister states in his preface, Nitzsch by no means regarded the natural sequence of groups as the highest problem of the systematist, but rather their correct limitation. Again, the arrangement followed in the *Pterylographie* was of course based on pterylographical considerations, and we have its author's own word for it that he was persuaded that the limitation of natural groups could only be attained by the most assiduous research into the species of which they are composed from every point of view. The combination of these three facts will of itself explain some defects, or even retrogressions, observable in Nitzsch's later systematic work when compared with that which he had formerly done. On the other hand, some manifest improvements are introduced, and the abundance of details into which he enters in his *Pterylographie* render it far more instructive and valuable than the older performance. As an abstract of that has already been given, it may be sufficient here to point out the chief changes made in his newer arrangement. To begin with,

[1] Though not relating exactly to our present theme, it would be improper to dismiss Nitzsch's name without reference to his extraordinary labours in investigating the insect and other external parasites of birds, a subject which as regards British species was subsequently elaborated by Denny in his *Monographia Anoplurorum Britanniae* (1842) and in his list of the specimens of British *Anoplura* in the collection of the British Museum.

the three great sections of aerial, terrestrial, and aquatic birds are abolished. The "*Accipitres*" are divided into two groups, Diurnal and Nocturnal; but the first of these divisions is separated into three sections: (1) the Vultures of the New World, (2) those of the Old World, and (3) the genus *Falco* of Linnaeus. The "*Passerinae*," that is to say, the true *Passeres*, are split into eight families, not wholly with judgment,[2] but of their taxonomy more is to be said presently. Then a new order "*Picariae*" is instituted for the reception of the *Macrochires*, *Cuculinae*, *Picinae Psittacinae* and *Amphiboloe* of his old arrangement, to which are added three[3] others—*Caprimulginae*, *Todidae* and *Lipoglossae*—the last consisting of the genera *Buceros*, *Upupa* and *Alcedo*. The association of *Alcedo* with the other two is no doubt a misplacement, but the alliance of *Buceros* to *Upupa*, already suggested by Gould and Blyth in 1838[4] (*Mag. Nat. History*, ser. 2, ii. pp. 422 and 589), though apparently unnatural, has been corroborated by many later systematisers, and taken as a whole the establishment of the *Picariae* was certainly a commendable proceeding. For the rest there is only one considerable change, and that forms the greatest blot on the whole scheme. Instead of recognizing, as before, a subclass in the *Ratitae* of Merrem, Nitzsch now reduced them to the rank of an order under the name "*Platysternae*," placing them between the "*Gallinaceae*" and "*Grallae*," though admitting that in their pterylosis they differ from all other birds, in ways that he is at great pains to describe, in each of the four genera examined by him—*Struthio, Rhea, Dromaeus* and *Casuarius*.[5] It is significant that notwithstanding this he did not figure the pterylosis of any one of them, and the thought suggests itself that, though his editor assures us he had convinced himself that the group must be here shoved in (*eingeschoben* is the word used), the intrusion is rather due to the necessity which Nitzsch, in common with most men of his time (the Quinarians excepted), felt for deploying the whole series of birds into line, in which case the proceeding may be defensible on the score of convenience. The extraordinary merits of this book, and the admirable fidelity to his principles which Professor Burmeister showed in the difficult task of editing it, were unfortunately overlooked for many years, and perhaps are not sufficiently recognised now. Even in Germany, the author's own country, there were few to notice seriously what is certainly one of the most remarkable works ever published on the science, much less to pursue the investigations that had been so laboriously begun.[6] Andreas Wagner, in his report on the progress of

[2] A short essay by Nitzsch on the general structure of the Passerines, written, it is said, in 1836, was published in 1862 (*Zeitschr. Ges. Naturwissenschaft*, xix. pp. 389-408). It is probably to this essay that Professor Burmeister refers in the *Pterylographie* (p. 102, note; Eng. trans., p. 72, note) as forming the basis of the article "Passerinae" which he contributed to Ersch and Gruber's *Encyklopädie* (sect. iii. bd. xiii. pp. 139-144), and published before the *Pterylographie*.

[3] By the numbers prefixed it would look as if there should be four new members of this order; but that seems to be due rather to a slip of the pen or to a printer's error.

[4] This association is one of the most remarkable in the whole series of Blyth's remarkable papers on classification in the volume cited above. He states that Gould suspected the alliance of these two forms "from external structure and habits alone"; otherwise one might suppose that he had obtained an intimation to that effect on one of his Continental journeys. Blyth "arrived at the same conclusion, however, by a different train of investigation," and this is beyond doubt.

[5] He does not mention *Apteryx*, at that time so little known on the Continent.

[6] Some excuse is to be made for this neglect. Nitzsch had of course exhausted all the forms of birds commonly to be obtained, and specimens of the less common forms were too valuable from the curator's or collector's point of view to be subjected to a treatment that might end in their destruction. Yet it is said, on good authority, that Nitzsch had the patience so to manipulate the skins of many rare species that he was able to ascertain the characters of their pterylosis by the inspection of their inside only, without in any way damaging them for the ordinary purpose of a museum. Nor is this surprising when we consider the marvellous skill of Continental and especially German taxidermists, many of whom have elevated their profession to a height of art inconceivable to most Englishmen, who are only acquainted with the miserable mockery of Nature which is the most sublime result of all but a few "bird-stuffers."

ornithology, as might be expected from such a man as he was, placed the *Pterylographie* at the summit of those publications the appearance of which he had to record for the years 1839 and 1840, stating that for "Systematik" it was of the greatest importance.[1] On the other hand Oken (*Isis*, 1842, pp. 391–394), though giving a summary of Nitzsch's results and classification, was more sparing of his praise, and prefaced his remarks by asserting that he could not refrain from laughter when he looked at the plates in Nitzsch's work, since they reminded him of the plucked fowls hanging in a poulterer's shop, and goes on to say that, as the author always had the luck to engage in researches of which nobody thought, so had he the luck to print them where nobody sought them. In Sweden Sundevall, without accepting Nitzsch's views, accorded them a far more appreciative greeting in his annual reports for 1840–1842 (i. pp. 152–160); but, of course, in England and France[2] nothing was known of them beyond the scantiest notice, generally taken at second hand, in two or three publications. Thanks to Mr Sclater, the Ray Society was induced to publish, in 1867, an excellent translation by Mr Dallas of Nitzsch's *Pterylography*, and thereby, however tardily, justice was at length rendered by British ornithologists to one of their greatest foreign brethren.[3] Nitzsch's work on feathers has been carried farther by many later observers, and its value is now generally accepted (see FEATHER).

The treatise of Kessler on the osteology of birds' feet, published in the *Bulletin* of the Moscow Society of Naturalists for 1841, next
Kessler.   claims a few words, though its scope is rather to show differences than affinities; but treatment of that kind is undoubtedly useful at times in indicating that alliances generally admitted are unnatural; and this is the case here, for, following Cuvier's method, the author's researches prove the artificial character of some of its associations. While furnishing—almost unconsciously, however—additional evidence for overthrowing that classification, there is, nevertheless, no attempt made to construct a better one; and the elaborate tables of dimensions, both absolute and proportional, suggestive as is the whole tendency of the author's observations, seem not to lead to any very practical result, though the systematist's need to look beneath the integument, even in parts that are so comparatively little hidden as birds' feet, is once more made beyond all question apparent.

It has already been mentioned that Macgillivray contributed to Audubon's *Ornithological Biography* a series of descriptions of
Mac-   some parts of the anatomy of American birds, from
gillivray   subjects supplied to him by that enthusiastic naturalist,
and   whose zeal and prescience, it may be called, in this
Audubon.   respect merits all praise. Thus he (prompted very likely by Macgillivray) wrote: " I believe the time to be approaching when much of the results obtained from the inspection of the exterior alone will be laid aside; when museums filled with stuffed skins will be considered insufficient to afford a knowledge of birds; and when the student will go forth, not only to observe the habits and haunts of animals, but to preserve specimens of them to be carefully dissected" (*Ornith. Biography*, iv., Introduction, p. xxiv). As has been stated, the first of this series of anatomical descriptions appeared in the fourth volume of his work, published in 1838, but they were continued until its completion with the fifth volume in the following year, and the whole was incorporated into what may be termed its second edition, *The Birds of America*, which appeared between 1840 and 1844. Among the many species whose anatomy Macgillivray thus partly described from autopsy were at least half a dozen[4] of those now referred to the family *Tyrannidae* (see KING-

[1] *Archiv für Naturgeschichte*, vii. 2, pp. 60, 61.
[2] In 1836 Jacquemin communicated to the French Academy (*Comptes rendus*, ii. pp. 374, 375 and 472) some observations on the order in which feathers are disposed on the body of birds; but, however general may have been the scope of his investigations, the portion of them published refers only to the crow, and there is no mention made of Nitzsch's former work.
[3] The Ray Society had the good fortune to obtain the ten original copper-plates, all but one drawn by the author himself, wherewith the work was illustrated. It is only to be regretted that the Society did not also adopt the quarto size in which it appeared, for by issuing their English version in folio they needlessly put an impediment in the way of its common and convenient use.
[4] These are, according to modern nomenclature, *Tyrannus caroli- nensis* and (as before mentioned) *T. verticalis, Myiarchus crinitus, Sayornis fuscus, Contopus virens* and *Empidonax acadicus*.

BIRD), but then included, with many others, according to the irrational, vague and rudimentary notions of classification of the time, in what was termed the family "*Muscicapinae*." In all these species he found the vocal organs to differ essentially in structure from those of other birds of the Old World, which we now call Passerine, or, to be still more precise, OSCININE. But by him these last were most arbitrarily severed, dissociated from their allies, and wrongly combined with other forms by no means nearly related to them (*Brit. Birds*, i. pp. 17, 18) which he also examined, and he practically, though not literally,[5] asserted the truth, when he said that the general structure, but especially the muscular appendages, of the lower larynx was "similarly formed in all other birds of this family" described in Audubon's work. Macgillivray did not, however, assign to this essential difference any systematic value. Indeed he was so much prepossessed in favour of a classification based on the structure of the digestive organs that he could not bring himself to consider vocal muscles to be of much taxonomic use, and it was reserved to Johannes Müller to point out that the contrary was
   the fact. Thus the great German comparative anato-   *Johannes*
mist did in two communications to the Academy of   *Müller.*
Sciences of Berlin, one on the 26th June 1845 and the other on the 14th May 1846, which, having been first briefly published in the Academy's *Monatsbericht*, were afterwards printed in full, and illustrated by numerous figures, in its *Abhandlungen*, though in this latter and complete form they did not appear in public until 1847. This very remarkable treatise forms the groundwork of almost all later or recent researches in the comparative anatomy and consequent arrangement of the *Passeres*, and, though it is certainly not free from imperfections, many of them, it must be said, arise from want of material, notwithstanding that its author had command of a much more abundant supply than was at the disposal of Nitzsch. Carrying on the work from the anatomical point at which he had left it, correcting his errors, and utilizing to the fullest extent the observations of Keyserling and Blasius, to which reference has already been made, Müller,[6] though hampered by mistaken notions of which he seems to have been unable to rid himself, propounded a scheme for the classification of this group, the general truth of which has been admitted by all his successors, based, as the title of his treatise expressed, on the hitherto unknown different types of the vocal organs in the Passerines. He freely recognized the prior discoveries of, as he thought, Audubon, though really, as has since been ascertained, of Macgillivray; but Müller was able to perceive their systematic value, which Macgillivray did not, and taught others to know it. At the same time Müller showed himself, his power of discrimination notwithstanding, to fall behind Nitzsch in one very crucial point, for he refused to the latter's *Picariae* the rank that had been claimed for them, and imagined that the groups associated under that name formed but a third " tribe"—*Picarii*—of a great order *Insessores*, the others being (1) the *Oscines* or *Poly- myodi*—the singing birds by emphasis, whose inferior larynx was endowed with the full number of five pairs of song-muscles, and (2) the *Tracheophones*, composed of some South-American families. Looking on Müller's labours as we now can, we see that such errors as he committed are chiefly due to his want of special knowledge of ornithology, combined with the absence in several instances of sufficient materials for investigation. Nothing whatever is to be said against the composition of his first and second " tribes" ; but the third is an assemblage still more heterogeneous than that which Nitzsch brought together under a name so like that of Müller—for the fact must never be allowed to go out of sight that the extent of the *Picarii* of the latter is not at all that of the *Picariae* of the former[7] For
[6] Not literally, because a few other forms such as the genera *Polio- ptila* and *Ptilogonys*, now known to have no relation to the *Tyranni- dae*, were included, though these forms, it would seem, had never been dissected by him. On the other hand, he declares that the American redstart, *Muscicapa*, or, as it now stands, *Setophaga ruticilla*, when young, has its vocal organs like the rest—an extraordinary statement which is worthy the attention of the many able American ornithologists.
[7] It is not needless to point out this fine distinction, for more than one modern author would seem to have overlooked it.

instance, Müller places in his third "tribe" the group which he called *Ampelidae*, meaning thereby the peculiar forms of South America that are now considered to be more properly named *Cotingidae*, and herein he was clearly right, while Nitzsch, who (misled by their supposed affinity to the genus *Ampelis*—peculiar to the Northern Hemisphere, and a purely Passerine form) had kept them among his *Passerinae*, was as clearly wrong. But again Müller made his third "tribe" *Picariæ* also to contain the *Tyrannidae*, of which mention has just been made, though it is so obvious as now to be generally admitted that they have no very intimate relationship to the other families with which they are there associated. There is no need here to criticise more minutely this projected arrangement, and it must be said that, notwithstanding his researches, he seems to have had some misgivings that, after all, the separation of the *Insessores* into those "tribes" might not be justifiable. At any rate he wavered in his estimate of their taxonomic value, for he gave six alternative proposals, arranging all the genera in a single series, a proceeding in those days thought not only defensible and possible, but desirable or even requisite, though now utterly abandoned. Just as Nitzsch had laboured under the disadvantage of never having any example of the abnormal *Passeres* of the New World to dissect, and, therefore, was wholly ignorant of their abnormality, so Müller never succeeded in getting hold of an example of the genus *Pitta* for the same purpose, and yet, acting on the clue furnished by Keyserling and Blasius, he did not hesitate to predict that it would be found to fill one of the gaps he had to leave, and this to some extent it has been since proved to do.

It must not be supposed that the vocal muscles were first discovered by Müller; on the contrary, they had been described long before, and by many writers on the anatomy of birds. To say nothing of foreigners, or the authors of general works on the subject, an excellent account of them had been given to the Linnean Society by W. Yarrell in 1829, and published with elaborate figures in its *Transactions* (xvi. 305-321, pls. 17, 18), an abstract of which was subsequently given in the article "Raven" in his *History of British Birds*, and Macgillivray also described and figured them with the greatest accuracy ten years later in his work with the same title (ii. 21-37, pls. x.-xii.), while Blyth and Nitzsch had (as already mentioned) seen some of their value in classification. But Müller has the merit of clearly outstriding his predecessors, and with his accustomed perspicuity made the way even plainer for his successors to see than he himself was able to see it. What remains to add is that the extraordinary celebrity of its author actually procured for the first portion of his researches notice in England (*Ann. Nat. History*, xvii. 499), though it must be confessed not then to any practical purpose; but more than thirty years after there appeared an English translation of his treatise by F. Jeffrey Bell, with an appendix by Garrod containing a summary of the latter's own continuation of the same line of research.[1]

It is now necessary to revert to the year 1842, in which Dr Cornay of Rochefort communicated to the French Academy of Sciences a memoir on a new classification of birds, of which, however, nothing but a notice has been preserved (*Comptes rendus*, xiv. p. 164). Two years later this was followed by a second contribution from him on the same subject, and of this only an extract appeared in the official organ of the Academy (*ut supra*, xvi. pp. 94, 95), though an abstract was inserted in one scientific journal (*L'Institut*, xii. p. 21), and its first portion in another (*Journal des Découvertes*, i. p. 250). The *Revue Zoologique* for 1847 (pp. 360-369) contained the whole, and enabled naturalists to consider the merits of the author's project, which was to found a new classification of birds on the form of the anterior palatal bones, which he declared to be subjected more evidently than any other to certain fixed laws. These laws, as formulated by him, are that (1) there is a coincidence of form of the anterior palatal and of the cranium in birds of the same order; (2) there is a likeness between the anterior palatal bones in birds of the same order, (3) there are relations of likeness

between the anterior palatal bones in groups of birds which are near to one another. These laws, he added, exist in regard to all parts that offer characters fit for the methodical arrangement of birds, but it is in regard to the anterior palatal bone that they unquestionably offer the most evidence. In the evolution of these laws Dr Cornay had most laudably studied, as his observations prove, a vast number of different types, and the upshot of his whole labours, though not very clearly stated, was such as to wholly subvert the classification at that time generally adopted by French ornithologists. He of course knew the investigations of L'Herminier and De Blainville on sternal formation, and he also seems to have been aware of some pterylological differences exhibited by birds—whether those of Nitzsch or those of Jacquemin is not stated. True it is the latter were never published in full, but it is quite conceivable that Dr Cornay may have known their drift. Be that as it may, he declares that characters drawn from the sternum or the pelvis—hitherto deemed to be, next to the bones of the head, the most important portions of the bird's framework—are scarcely worth more, from a classificatory point of view, than characters drawn from the bill or the legs; while pterylological considerations, together with many others to which some systematists had attached more or less importance, can only assist, and apparently must never be taken to control, the force of evidence furnished by this bone of all bones—the anterior palatal.

That Dr Cornay was on the brink of making a discovery of considerable merit will by and by appear, but, with every disposition to regard his investigations favourably, it cannot be said that he accomplished it. Whatever proofs Dr Cornay may have had to satisfy himself of his being on the right track, these proofs were not adduced in sufficient number nor arranged with sufficient skill to persuade a somewhat stiff-necked generation of the truth of his views—(or it was a generation whose leaders, in France at any rate, looked with suspicion upon any one who professed to go beyond the bounds which the genius of Cuvier had been unable to overpass, and regarded the notion of upsetting any of the positions maintained by him as verging almost upon profanity. Moreover, Dr Cornay's scheme was not given to the world with any of those adjuncts that not merely please the eye but are in many cases necessary, for, though on a subject which required for its proper comprehension a series of plates, it made even its final appearance unadorned by a single explanatory figure, and in a journal, respectable and well-known indeed, but one not of the highest scientific rank.

The same year which saw the promulgation of the crude scheme just described, as well as the publication of the final researches of Müller, witnessed also another attempt at the classification of birds, much more limited indeed in scope, but, so far as it went, regarded by most ornithologists of the time as almost final in its operation. Under the vague title of "Ornithologische Notizen" Professor Cabanis of Berlin contributed to the *Archiv für Naturgeschichte* (xiii. 1, pp. 186-256, 308-352) an essay in two parts, wherein, following the researches of Müller's on the syrinx, in the course of which correlation had been shown to exist between the whole or divided condition of the *planta* or hind part of the "tarsus," first noticed, as has been said, by Keyserling and Blasius, and the presence or absence of the perfect song-apparatus, the younger author found an agreement which seemed almost invariable in this respect, and he also pointed out that the *planta* of the different groups of birds in which it is divided is divided in different modes, the mode of division being generally characteristic of the group. Such a coincidence of the internal and external features of birds was naturally deemed a discovery of the greatest value by those ornithologists who thought most highly of the latter, and it was unquestionably of no little practical utility. Further examination also revealed the fact[2] that in certain groups the number of "primaries," or quill-feathers growing from the *manus* or distal segment of the wing, formed another characteristic easy of observation. In the *Oscines* or *Polymyodi* of Müller the number was either nine or ten—and if the latter the outermost of them was generally very small. In two of the other groups of which Professor Cabanis especially treated—groups which had been hitherto more or less confounded with the *Oscines*—the number of primaries was invariably ten, and the outermost of them was comparatively large. This observation was also hailed as the discovery of a fact of extraordinary importance; and, from the results of these investigations, taken altogether, ornithology was declared by Sundevall, undoubtedly a man who had a right to speak with authority, to have made greater progress than had been achieved since the days of Cuvier. The final disposition of the "Sub-class *Insessores*"—all the

---

[1] The title of the English translation is *Johannes Müller on Certain Variations in the Vocal Organs of the Passeres that have hitherto escaped notice*. It was published at Oxford in 1878. By some unaccountable accident, the date of the original communication to the Academy of Berlin is wrongly printed. It has been rightly given above.

[2] On the other hand, Müller makes several references to the labours of Professor Cabanis. The investigations of both authors must have been proceeding simultaneously, and it matters little which actually appeared first.

[3] This seems to have been made known by Professor Cabanis the preceding year to the *Gesellschaft der Naturforschender Freunde* (cf. Müller, *Stimmorganen der Passerinen*, p. 65). Of course the variation to which the number of primaries was subject had not escaped the observation of Nitzsch, but he had scarcely used it as a classificatory character.

perching birds, that is to say, which are neither birds of prey nor pigeons—proposed by Professor Cabanis, was into four "Orders," as follows:—

1. *Oscines*, equal to Müller's group of the same name;

2. *Clamatores*, being a majority of that division of the *Picariae* of Nitzsch, so called by Andreas Wagner, in 1841,[1] which have their feet normally constructed;

3. *Strisores*, a group now separated from the *Clamatores* of Wagner, and containing those forms which have their feet abnormally constructed; and

4. *Scansores*, being the *Grimpeurs* of Cuvier, the *Zygodactyli* of several other systematists.

The first of these four "Orders" had been already indefeasibly established as one perfectly natural, but respecting its details more must presently be said. The remaining three are now seen to be obviously artificial associations, and the second of them, *Clamatores*, in particular, containing a very heterogeneous assemblage of forms; but it must be borne in mind that the internal structure of some of them was at that time still more imperfectly known than now.

This will perhaps be the most convenient place to mention another kind of classification of birds, which, based on a principle wholly **Bona-** different from those that have just been explained, **parte.** requires a few words, though it has not been productive, nor is likely, from all that appears, to be productive of any great effect. So long ago as 1831, Prince C. L. Bonaparte, in his *Saggio di una distribuzione metodica degli Animali Vertebrati*, published at Rome, and in 1837 communicated to the Linnean Society of London, "A new Systematic Arrangement of Vertebrated Animals," which was subsequently printed in that Society's *Transactions* (xviii. pp. 247-304), though before it appeared there was issued at Bologna, under the title of *Synopsis Vertebratorum Systematis*, a Latin translation of it. Herein he divided the class *Aves* into two subclasses, to which he applied the names of *Insessores* and *Grallatores* (hitherto used by their inventors Vigors and Illiger in a different sense), in the latter work relying chiefly for this division on characters which had not before been used by any systematist, namely that in the former group monogamy generally prevailed and the helpless nestlings were fed by their parents, while the latter group were mostly polygamous, and the chicks at birth were active and capable of feeding themselves. This method, which in process of time was dignified by the title of a Physiological Arrangement, was insisted upon with more or less pertinacity by the author throughout a long series of publications, some of them separate books, some of them contributed to the memoirs issued by many scientific bodies of various European countries, ceasing only at his death, which in July 1857 found him occupied upon a *Conspectus Generum Avium*, that in consequence remains unfinished. In the course of this series, however, he saw fit to alter the name of his two subclasses, since those which he at first adopted were open to a variety of meanings, and in a communication to the French Academy of Sciences in 1853 (*Comptes rendus*, xxxvii. pp. 641-647) the denomination *Insessores* was changed to *Altrices*, and *Grallatores* to *Praecoces*—the terms now preferred by him being taken from Sundevall's treatise of 1835 already mentioned. The views of Bonaparte were, it appears, also shared by an ornithological amateur **Hogg.** of some distinction, John Hogg, who propounded a scheme which, as he subsequently stated (*Zoologist*, 1850, p. 2797), was founded strictly in accordance with them; but it would seem that, allowing his convictions to be warped by other considerations, he abandoned the original " physiological " basis of his system, so that this, when published in 1846 (*Edinb. N. Philosoph. Journal*, xli. pp. 50-71), was found to be established on a single character of the feet only; though he was careful to point out, immediately after formulating the definition of his subclasses *Constrictipedes* and *Inconstrictipedes*, that the former " make, in general, compact and well-built nests, wherein they bring up their very weak, blind, and mostly naked young, which they feed with care, by bringing food to them for many days, while they are fledged and sufficiently strong to leave their nest," observing also that they " are principally monogamous " (pp. 55, 56); while of the latter he says that they " make either a poor and rude nest, in which they lay their eggs, or else none, depositing them on the bare ground. The young are generally born with their full sight, covered with down, strong, and capable of running or swimming immediately after they leave the egg-shell." He adds that the parents, which " are mostly polygamous," attend their young and direct them where to find their food (p. 63). The numerous errors in these assertions hardly need pointing out. The herons, for instance, are much more " *Constrictipedes* " than are the larks or the kingfishers, and, so far from the majority of " *Inconstrictipedes* " being polygamous, there is scarcely any evidence of polygamy obtaining as a habit among birds in a state of nature except in certain of the *Gallinae* and a very few others. Furthermore, the young of the goatsuckers are

at hatching far more developed than are those of the herons or the cormorants; and, in a general way, nearly every one of the asserted peculiarities of the two subclasses breaks down under careful examination. Yet the idea of a " physiological " arrangement on the same kind of principle found another follower, or, as he thought, **Newman.** inventor, in Edward Newman, who in 1850 communicated to the Zoological Society of London a plan published in its *Proceedings* for that year (pp. 46-48), and reprinted also in his own journal *The Zoologist* (pp. 2780-2782), based on exactly the same considerations, dividing birds into two groups, " Heathogenous "—a word so vicious in formation as to be incapable of amendment, but intended to signify those that were hatched with a clothing of down—and " Gymnogenous," or those that were hatched naked. These three systems are essentially identical; but, plausible as they may be at the first aspect, they have been found to be practically useless, though such of their characters as their upholders have advanced with truth deserve attention. Physiology may one day very likely assist the systematist; but it must be real physiology and not a sham.

In 1856 Paul Gervais, who had already contributed to the *Zoologie* of M. de Castelnau's *Expédition dans les parties centrales de l'Amérique* **Gervais.** *du Sud* some important memoirs describing the anatomy of the hoactzin and certain other birds of doubtful or anomalous position, published some remarks on the characters which could be drawn from the sternum of birds (*Ann. Sc. Nat. Zoologie*, ser. 4, vi. pp. 5-13). The considerations are not very striking from a general point of view; but the author adds to the weight of evidence which some of his predecessors had brought to bear on certain matters, particularly in aiding to abolish the artificial groups " Déodactyls," " Syndactyls," and " Zygodactyls," on which so much reliance had been placed by many of his countrymen; and it is with him a great merit that he was the first apparently to recognize publicly that characters drawn from the posterior part of the sternum, and particularly from the " *échancrures*," commonly called in English " notches " or " emarginations," are of comparatively little importance, since their number is apt to vary in forms that are most closely allied, and even in species that are usually associated in the same genus or unquestionably belong to the same family, while these " notches " sometimes become simple *foramina*, as in certain pigeons, or on the other hand *foramina* may exceptionally change to " notches," and not unfrequently disappear wholly. Among his chief systematic determinations we may mention that he refers the tinamous to the rails, because apparently of their deep " notches," but otherwise takes a view of that group more correct according to modern notions than did most of his contemporaries. The bustards he would place with the " Limicolæ," as also *Dromas* and *Chionis*, the sheath-bill (*q.v.*), *Phæthon*, the tropic-bird (*q.v.*), he would place with the " Larides " and not with the " Pelecanides," which it only resembles in its feet having all the toes connected by a web. Finally divers, auks and penguins, according to him, form the last term in the series, and it seems fit to him that they should be regarded as forming a separate order. It is a curious fact that even at a date so late as this, and by an investigator so well informed, doubt should still have existed whether *Apteryx* (see KIWI) should be referred to the group containing the cassowary and the ostrich. On the whole the remarks of this esteemed author do not go much beyond such as might occur to any one who had made a study of a good series of specimens; but many of them are published for the first time, and the author is careful to insist on the necessity of not resting solely on sternal characters, but associating with these those drawn from other parts of the body.

Three years later in the same journal (xi. 11-145, pls. 2-4) M. Blanchard published some *Recherches sur les caractères ostéologiques des oiseaux appliqués à la classification naturelle* **Blan-** *de ces animaux*, strongly urging the superiority of such **chard.** characters over those drawn from the bill or feet, which, he remarks, though they may have sometimes given correct notions, have mostly led to mistakes, and, if observations of habits and food have sometimes afforded happy results, they have often been inceptive, so that, should more be wanted than to draw up a mere inventory of creation or trace the distinctive outline of each species, zoology without anatomy would remain a barren study. At the same time he states that authors who have occupied themselves with the sternum alone have often produced uncertain results, especially when they have neglected its anterior for its posterior part, for in truth every bone of the skeleton ought to be studied in all its details. Yet this distinguished zoologist selects the sternum as furnishing the key to his primary groups or " Orders " of the class, adopting, as Merrem had done long before, the same two divisions *Carinatae* and *Ratitae*, naming, however, the former *Tropidosternis* and the latter *Homalosternis*.[2] Some unkind fate has hitherto hindered

---

[1] *Archiv für Naturgeschichte*, vi. 2, pp. 93, 94. The division seems to have been instituted by this author a couple of years earlier in the second edition of his *Handbuch der Naturgeschichte* (a work not seen by the present writer), but not then to have received a scientific name. It included all *Picariae* which had not " zygodactylous " feet, that is to say, toes placed in pairs, two before and two behind.

[1] He cites the cases of *Machetes pugnax* and *Scolopax rusticola* among the " Limicolæ," and *Larus cataractes* among the " Laridæ," as differing from their nearest allies by the possession of only one " notch " on either side of the keel. Several additional instances are cited in *Philos. Transactions* (1869), p. 337, note.

[2] These terms were explained in his great work *L'Organisation du règne animal*, *oiseaux*, begun in 1855, to mean exactly the same as those applied by Merrem to his two primary divisions.

him from making known to the world the rest of his researches in regard to the other bones of the skeleton till he reached the head, and in the memoir cited he treats of the sternum of only a portion of his first " Order." This is the more to be regretted by all ornithologists, since he intended to conclude with what to them would have been a very great boon—the showing in what way external characters coincided with those presented by osteology. It was also within the scope of his plan to have continued on a more extended scale the researches on ossification begun by L'Herminier, and thus M. Blanchard's investigations, if completed, would obviously have taken extraordinarily high rank among the highest contributions to ornithology. As it is, so much of them as we have are of considerable importance; for, in this unfortunately unfinished memoir, he describes in some detail the several differences which the sternum in a great many different groups of his *Tropidosternii* presents, and to some extent makes a methodical disposition of them accordingly. Thus he separates the birds of prey into three great groups—(1) the ordinary Diurnal forms, including the *Falconidae* and *Vulturidae* of the systematist of his time, but distinguishing the American Vultures from those of the Old World; (2) *Gypogeranus*, the secretary-bird (*q.v.*); and (3) the owls (*q.v.*). Next he places the parrots (*q.v.*), and then the vast assemblage of " Passereaux "—which he declares to be all of one type, even genera like *Pipra* (manakin, *q.v.*) and *Pitta*—and concludes with the somewhat heterogeneous conglomeration of forms, beginning with *Cypselus* (swift, *q.v.*), that so many systematists have been accustomed to call *Picariae*, though to them as a group he assigns no name. A continuation of the treatise was promised in a succeeding part of the *Annales*, but a quarter of a century has passed without its appearance.[1]

Important as are the characters afforded by the sternum, that bone even with the whole sternal apparatus should obviously not be considered alone. To aid ornithologists in their studies

Eytos. in this respect, T. C. Eyton, who for many years had been forming a collection of birds' skeletons, began the publication of a series of plates representing them. The first part of this work, *Osteologia Avium*, appeared early in 1859, and a volume was completed in 1867. A Supplement was issued in 1869, and a Second Supplement, in three parts, between 1873 and 1875. The whole work contains a great number of figures of birds' skeletons and detached bones; but they are not so drawn as to be of much practical use, and the accompanying letterpress is too brief to be satisfactory.

That the eggs laid by birds should offer to some extent characters of utility to systematists is only to be expected, when it is considered that those from the same nest generally bear an extraordinary family likeness to one another, and also that in certain groups the essential peculiarities of the egg-shell are constantly and distinctively characteristic. Thus no one who has ever examined the egg of a duck or of a tinamou would ever be in danger of not referring another tinamou's egg or another duck's, that he might see, to its proper family, and so on with many others. But at the same time many of the shortcomings of oology in this respect must be set down to the defective information and observation of its votaries, among whom some have been very lax, not to say incautious, in not ascertaining on due evidence the parentage of their specimens, and the author next to be named is open to this charge. After several minor notices that appeared in journals at various times, Des Murs

Des Murs. in 1860 brought out at Paris his ambitious *Traité général d'oologie ornithologique au point de vue de la classification*, which contains (pp. 529-538) a " Systema Oologicum " as the final result of his labours. In this scheme birds are arranged according to what the author considered to be their natural method and sequence; but the result exhibits some unions as ill-assorted as can well be met with in the whole range of tentative arrangements of the class, together with some very unjustifiable divorces. Its basis is the classification of Cuvier, the modifications of which by Des Murs will seldom commend themselves to systematists whose opinion is generally deemed worth having. Few, if any, of the faults of that classification are removed, and the improvements suggested, if not established by his successors, those especially of other countries than France, are ignored, or, as is the case with some of those of L'Herminier, are only cited to be set aside. Oologists have no reason to be thankful to Des Murs, notwithstanding his zeal in behalf of their study. It is perfectly true that in several or even in many instances he acknowledges and deplores the poverty of his information, but this does not excuse him for making assertions (and such assertions are not unfrequent) based on evidence that is either wholly untrustworthy or needs further inquiry before it can be accepted (*Ibis*, 1860, pp. 331-335). This being the case, it would seem useless to take up further space by analysing the several proposed modifications of Cuvier's arrangement. The great merit of the work is that the author shows the necessity of treating oology into account when investigating the classification of birds; but it also proves that in so doing the paramount consideration lies in the thorough sifting of evidence as to the parentage of the eggs which

are to serve as the building stones of the fabric to be erected. The attempt of Des Murs was praiseworthy, but in effect it has utterly failed, notwithstanding the encomiums passed upon it by friendly critics (*Rev. de Zoologie*, 1860, pp. 176-183, 313-325, 370-373).[2]

Until about this time systematists, almost without exception, may be said to have been wandering with no definite purpose. At least their purpose was indefinite compared with *Results of* that which they now have before them. No doubt *Doctrine of* they all agreed in saying that they were prosecuting *Evolution.* a search for what they called the true system of nature; but that was nearly the end of their agreement, for in what that true system consisted the opinions of scarcely any two would coincide, unless to own that it was some shadowy idea beyond the present power of mortals to reach or even comprehend. The Quinarians, who boldly asserted that they had fathomed the mystery of creation, had been shown to be no wiser than other men, if indeed they had not utterly befooled themselves; for their theory at best could give no other explanation of things than that they were because they were. The conception of such a process as has now come to be called by the name of evolution was certainly not novel; but except to two men the way in which that process was or could be possible had not been revealed.[3] Here there is no need to enter into details of the history of evolution; but there was possibly no branch of zoology in which so many of the best informed and consequently the most advanced of its workers sooner accepted the principles of evolution than ornithology, and of course the effect upon its study was very marked. New spirit was given to it. Ornithologists now felt they had something before them that was really worth investigating. Questions of affinity, and the details of geographical distribution, were endowed with a real interest, in comparison with which any interest that had hitherto been taken was a trifling pastime. Classification assumed a wholly different aspect. It had up to this time been little more than the shuffling of cards, the ingenious arrangement of counters in a pretty pattern. Henceforward it was to be the serious study of the workings of nature in producing the beings we see around us from beings more or less unlike them, that had existed in bygone ages and had been the parents of a varied and varying offspring—our fellow-creatures of to-day. Classification for the first time was something more than the expression of a fancy, not that it had not also its imaginative side. Men's minds began to figure to themselves the original type of some well-marked genus or family of birds. They could even discern dimly some generalized stock whence had descended whole groups that now differed strangely in habits and appearance—their discernment aided, may be, by some isolated form which yet retained undeniable traces of a primitive structure. More dimly still visions of what the first bird may have been like could be reasonably entertained; and, passing even to a higher antiquity, the reptilian parent whence all birds have sprung was brought within reach of man's consciousness. But, relieved as it may be by reflections of this kind—dreams some may perhaps still call them—the study of ornithology has unquestionably become harder and more serious; and a corresponding change in the style of investigation, followed in the works that remain to be considered, will be immediately perceptible.

That this was the case is undeniably shown by some remarks of Canon Tristram, who, in treating of the *Alaudidae* and *Saxicolinae* of Algeria (whence he had recently brought *Tristram.* a large collection of specimens of his own making), stated (*Ibis*, 1859, pp. 429-433) that he could " not help feeling convinced of the truth of the views set forth by Messrs Darwin and Wallace," adding that it was " hardly possible, I should think, to illustrate this theory better than by the larks and chats of North Africa." It is unnecessary to continue the

[1] M. Blanchard's animadversions on the employment of external characters, and on trusting to observations on the habits of birds, called forth a rejoinder from A. R. Wallace (*Ibis*, 1864, pp. 36-41), who successfully showed that they are not altogether to be despised.

[2] In this historical sketch of the progress of ornithology it has not been thought necessary to mention other oological works, since they have not a taxonomic bearing, and some of them have been already named (see BIRDS).

[3] Neither Lamarck nor Robert Chambers (the now acknowledged author of *Vestiges of Creation*), though thorough evolutionists, rationally indicated any means whereby, to use the old phrase, " the transmutation of species " could be effected.

quotation; the few words just cited are enough to assure to their author the credit of being (so far as is known) the first ornithological specialist who had the courage publicly to recognize and receive the new and at that time unpopular philosophy.

Parker. But greater work was at hand. In June 1860 W. K. Parker broke, as most will allow, entirely fresh ground by communicating to the Zoological Society a memoir "On the Osteology of *Balæniceps*," subsequently published in that Society's *Transactions* (iv. 269-351). Of this contribution to science, as of all the rest which have since proceeded from him, may be said in the words he himself has applied (*ut supra*, p. 271) to the work of another labourer in a not distant field: "This is a model paper for unbiassed observation, and freedom from that pleasant mode of *supposing* instead of *ascertaining* what is the true nature of an anatomical element."[1] Indeed, the study of this memoir, limited though it be in scope, could not fail to convince any one that it proceeded from the mind of one who taught with the authority derived directly from original knowledge, and not from association with the scribes—a conviction that has become strengthened as, in a series of successive memoirs, the stores of more than twenty years' silent observation and unremitting research were unfolded, and, more than that, the hidden forces of the science of morphology were gradually brought to bear upon almost each subject that came under discussion. These different memoirs, being technically monographs, have strictly no right to be mentioned in this place; but there is scarcely one of them, if one indeed there be, that does not deal with the generalities of the study; and the influence they have had upon contemporary investigation is so strong that it is impossible to refrain from noticing them here, though want of space forbids us from enlarging on their contents.

For some time past rumours of a discovery of the highest interest had been agitating the minds of zoologists, for in 1861 *Wagner.* Andreas Wagner had sent to the Academy of Sciences of Munich (*Sitzungsberichte*, pp. 146-154; *Ann. Nat. History*, series 3, ix. 261-267) an account of what he conceived to be a feathered reptile (assigning to it the name *Griphosaurus*), the remains of which had been found in the lithographic beds of Solenhofen; but he himself, through failing health, had been unable to see the fossil. In 1862 the slabs containing the remains were acquired by the British Museum, *Owen.* and towards the end of that year Sir R. Owen communicated a detailed description of them to the *Philosophical Transactions* (1863, pp. 33-47), proving their bird-like nature, and referring them to the genus *Archæopteryx* of Hermann von Meyer, hitherto known only by the impression of a single feather from the same geological beds. Wagner foresaw the use that would be made of this discovery by the adherents of the new philosophy, and, in the usual language of its opponents at the time, strove to ward off the "misinterpretations" that they would put upon it. His protest, it is needless to say, was unavailing, and all who respect his memory must regret that the sunset of life failed to give him that insight into the future which is poetically ascribed to it. To Darwin and those who believed with him scarcely any discovery could have been more welcome; but that is beside our present business. It was quickly seen—even by those who held *Archæopteryx* to be a reptile—that it was a form intermediate between existing birds and existing reptiles; while those who were convinced by Sir R. Owen's researches of its ornithic affinity saw that it must belong to a type of birds wholly unknown before, and one that in any future for the arrangement of the class must have a special rank reserved for it.[2]

to the Zoological Society in 1866, and published in its *Proceedings* for that year (pp. 5-20), since it was immediately after reprinted by the Smithsonian Institution, and with that authoriza- *Lilje-* tion has exercised a great influence on the opinions of *berg.* American ornithologists. Otherwise the scheme would hardly need notice here. This paper is indeed little more than an English translation of one published by the author in the annual volume (*Ärsskrift*) of the Scientific Society of Upsala for 1860, and belonging to the pre-Darwinian epoch should perhaps have been more properly treated before, but that at the time of its original appearance it failed to attract attention. The chief merit of the scheme perhaps is that, contrary to nearly every precedent, it begins with the lower and rises to the higher groups of birds, which is of course the natural mode of proceeding, and one therefore to be commended. Otherwise the " principles " on which it is founded are not clear to the ordinary zoologist. One of them is said to be " irritability," and, though this is explained to mean, not " muscular strength alone, but vivacity and activity generally,"[3] it does not seem to form a character that can be easily appreciated either as to quantity or quality; in fact, most persons would deem it quite immeasurable, and, as such, removed from practical consideration. Moreover, Professor Lilljeborg's scheme, being actually an adaptation of that of Sundevall, of which we shall have to speak at some length almost immediately, may possibly be left for the present with these remarks.

In the spring of the year 1867 Professor T. H. Huxley, to the delight of an appreciative audience, delivered at the Royal College of Surgeons of England a course of lectures *Huxley.* on birds, and a few weeks after presented an abstract of his researches to the Zoological Society, in whose *Proceedings* for the same year it will be found printed (pp. 415-472) as a paper " On the Classification of Birds, and on the taxonomic value of the modifications of certain of the cranial bones observable in that Class." Starting from the basis " that the phrase 'birds are greatly modified reptiles' would hardly be an exaggerated expression of the closeness " of the resemblance between the two classes, which he had previously brigaded under the name of *Sauropsida* (as he had brigaded the *Pisces* and *Amphibia* as *Ichthyopsida*), he drew in bold outline both their likenesses and their differences, and then proceeded to inquire how the *Aves* could be most approximately subdivided into orders, suborders and families. In this course of lectures he had already dwelt at some length on the insufficiency of the characters on which such groups as had hitherto been thought to be established were founded; but for the consideration of this part of his subject there was no room in the present paper, and the reasons why he arrived at the conclusion that new means of philosophically and successfully separating the class must be sought are herein left to be inferred. The upshot, however, admits of no uncertainty: the class *Aves* is held to be composed of *three* " Orders "—

I. SAURURAE, Häckel;
II. RATITAE, Merrem; and
III. CARINATAE, Merrem.

The *Saururae* have the metacarpals well developed and not anchylosed, and the caudal vertebrae are numerous and large, so that the caudal region of the spine is longer than the body. The furcula is complete and strong, the feet very passerine in appearance. The skull and sternum were at the time unknown, and indeed the whole order, without doubt entirely extinct, rested exclusively on the celebrated fossil, then unique, *Archæopteryx*.

The *Ratitae* comprehend the struthious birds, which differ from all others now extant in the combination of several peculiarities, some of which have been mentioned in the preceding pages. The sternum has no keel, and ossifies from lateral and paired centres only; the axes of the scapula and coracoid have the same general direction; certain of the cranial bones have characters very unlike those possessed by the next order—the vomer, for example, being broad posteriorly and generally intervening between the basisphenoidal rostrum and the palatals and pterygoids; the barbs of the feathers are disconnected; there is no syrinx or inferior larynx; and the diaphragm is better developed than in other birds.[4]

---

[1] It behoves us next to mention the " Outlines of a Systematic Review of the Class of Birds," communicated by W. Lilljeborg

[2] It is fair to state that some of Professor Parker's conclusions respecting *Balæniceps* were contested by the late Professor J. T. Reinhardt (*Overs. K. D. Vid. Selsk. Forhandlinger*, 1861, pp. 135-154; *Ibis*, 1862, pp. 158-175), and as it seems to the present writer not ineffectually. Professor Parker replied to his critic (*Ibis*, 1862, pp. 297-299).

[3] This was done shortly afterwards by Professor Haeckel, who proposed the name *Saururæ* for the group containing it.

[4] On this ground it is stated that the *Passeres* should be placed highest in the class. But those who know the habits and demeanour of many of the *Limicolæ* would no doubt rightly claim for them much more " vivacity and activity " than is possessed by most *Passeres*.

[5] This peculiarity had led some zoologists to consider the struthious birds more nearly allied to the *Mammalia* than any others.

The *Carinatae* are divided, according to the formation of the palate, into four "Suborders," and named (i.) *Dromaeognathae*, (ii.) *Schizognathae*, (iii.) *Desmognathae*, and (iv.) *Aegithognathae*.[1] The *Dromaeognathae* resemble the *Ratitae*, and especially the genus *Dromaeus*, in their palatal structure, and are composed of the forms belonging to the Linnaean Orders *Gallinae*, *Grallae* and *Anseres*. In them the vomer, however variable, always tapers to a point anteriorly, while behind it includes the basisphenoidal rostrum between the palatals; but neither these nor the pterygoids are borne by its posterior divergent ends. The maxillo-palatals are usually elongated and lamellar, uniting with the palatals, and, bending backward along their inner edge, leave a cleft (whence the name given to the "Suborder") between the vomer and themselves. In the *Desmognathae*, the vomer is either abortive or so small as to disappear from the skeleton. When it exists it is always slender, and tapers to a point anteriorly. The maxillo-palatals are bound together (whence the name of the "Suborder") across the middle line, either directly or by the ossification of the nasal septum. The posterior ends of the palatals and anterior of the pterygoids articulate directly with the rostrum. The *Aegithognathae*, the fourth and last of the "Suborders," is characterized by a form of palate in some respects intermediate between the two preceding. The vomer is broad, abruptly truncated in front, and deeply cleft behind, so as to embrace the rostrum of the sphenoid; the palatals have produced postero-external angles; the maxillo-palatals are slender at their origin, and extend obliquely inwards and forwards over the palatals, ending beneath the vomer in expanded extremities, not united either with one another or with the vomer, nor does the latter unite with the nasal septum, though that is frequently ossified.

The above abstract shows the general drift of this very remarkable contribution to ornithology, and it has to be added that for by far the greater number of his minor groups Huxley relied solely on the form of the palatal structure, the importance of which Dr Cornay had before urged, though to so little purpose. That the palatal structure must be taken into consideration by taxonomers as affording hints of some utility there can no longer be a doubt; but perhaps the characters drawn thence owed more of their worth to the extraordinary perspicuity with which they were presented by Huxley than to their own intrinsic value, and if the same power had been employed to elucidate in the same way other parts of the skeleton—say the bones of the sternal apparatus or even of the pelvic girdle—either set might have been made to appear quite as instructive and perhaps more so. Adventitious value would therefore seem to have been acquired by the bones of the palate through the fact that so great a master of the art of exposition selected them as fitting examples upon which to exercise his skill.[2] At the same time it must be stated this selection was not premeditated by Huxley, but forced itself upon him as his investigations proceeded.[3] In reply to some critical remarks (*Ibis*, 1868, pp. 85-96), chiefly aimed at showing the inexpediency of relying solely on one set of characters, especially when those afforded by the palatal bones were not, even within the limits of families, wholly diagnostic, the author (*Ibis*, 1868, pp. 357-362) announced a slight modification of his original scheme, by introducing three more groups into it, and concluded by indicating how its bearings upon the great question of "genetic classification" might be represented so far as the different groups of *Carinatae* are concerned:—

[1] These names are compounded respectively of *Dromaeus*, the generic name applied to the emu, σχίζω, a split or cleft, δέσμα, a bond or tying, αἴγυθος, a finch, and, in each case, γνάθος, a jaw.
[2] The notion of the superiority of the palatal bones to all others for purposes of classification has pleased many persons, from the fact that these bones are not unfrequently retained in the dried skins of birds sent home by collectors in foreign countries, and are therefore available for study, while such bones as the sternum and pelvis are rarely preserved. The common practice of ordinary collectors, until at least very recently, has been tersely described as being to "shoot a bird, take off its skin, and throw away its characters."
[3] Perhaps this may be partially explained by the fact that the Museum of the College of Surgeons, in which these investigations were chiefly carried on, like most other museums of the time, contained a much larger series of the heads of birds than of their entire skeletons, or of any other portion of the skeleton. Consequently the materials available for the comparison of different forms consisted in great part of heads only.

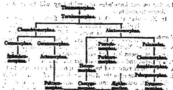

Huxley regarded the above scheme as nearly representing the affinities of the various Carinate groups—the great difficulty being to determine the relations to the rest of the *Coccygomorphae*, *Psittacomorphae* and *Aegithognathae*, which he indicated "only in the most doubtful and hypothetical fashion." Almost simultaneously with this he expounded more particularly before the Zoological Society, in whose *Proceedings* (1868, pp. 294-319) his results were soon after published, the groups of which he believed the *Alectoromorphae* to be composed and the relations to them of some outlying forms usually regarded as Gallinaceous, the *Turnicidae* and *Pteroclidae*, as well as the singular hoactzin, for all three of which he had to institute new groups—the last forming the sole representative of his *Heteromorphae*. More than this, he entered upon their geographical distribution, the facts of which important subject are here, almost for the first time, since the attempt of Blyth already mentioned,[4] brought to bear practically on classification.

Here we must mention the intimate connexion between classification and geographical distribution as revealed by the palaeontological researches of Alphonse Milne-Edwards, whose magnificent *Oiseaux Fossiles de la France* began to appear in 1867, and was completed in 1871— the more so, since the exigencies of his undertaking compelled him to use materials that had been almost wholly neglected by other investigators. A large proportion of the fossil remains, the determination and description of which was his object, were what are very commonly called the "long bones," that is to say, those of the limbs. The recognition of these, minute and fragmentary as many were, and the referring them to their proper place, rendered necessary an attentive study of the comparative osteology and myology of birds in general, that of the "long bones," whose sole characters were often a few muscular ridges or depressions, being especially obligatory. Hence it became manifest that a very respectable classification can be found in which characters drawn from these bones play a rather important part. Limited by circumstances as is that followed by Milne-Edwards, the details of his arrangement do not require setting forth here. It is enough to point out that we have in his work another proof of the multiplicity of the factors which must be taken into consideration by the systematist, and another proof of the fallacy of trusting to one set of characters alone. But this is not the only way in which the author has rendered service to the advanced student of ornithology. The unlooked-for discovery in France of remains which he has referred to, forms now existing it is true, but existing only in countries far removed from Europe, forms such as *Collocalia*, *Leptosomis*, *Psittacus*, *Serpentarius* and *Trogon*, is perhaps even more suggestive than the finding that France was once inhabited by forms that are wholly extinct, of which in the older formations there is abundance. Unfortunately none of these, however, can be compared for singularity with *Archaeopteryx* or with some American fossil forms next to be noticed, for their particular

[4] It is true that from the time of Buffon, though he scorned any regular classification, geographical distribution had been occasionally held to have something to do with systematic arrangement; but the way in which the two were related was never clearly put forth, though people who could read between the lines might have guessed the secret from Darwin's *Journal of Researches*, as well as from his introduction to the *Zoology of the "Beagle" Voyage*.

bearing on our knowledge of ornithology will be most conveniently treated here.

In November 1870 O. C. Marsh, by finding the imperfect fossilized tibia of a bird in the middle cretaceous shale of Kansas, **Marsh.** — began a series of wonderful discoveries of great importance to ornithology. Subsequent visits to the same part of North America, often performed under circumstances of discomfort and occasionally of danger, brought to this intrepid and energetic explorer the reward he had so fully earned. Brief notices of his spoils appeared from time to time in various volumes of the *American Journal of Science and Arts* (Silliman's), but it is unnecessary here to refer to more than a few of them. In that *Journal* for May 1872 (ser. 3, iii. p. 360) the remains of a large swimming bird (nearly 6 ft. in length, as afterwards appeared) having some affinity, it was thought, to the *Colymbidae* were described under the name of *Hesperornis regalis*, and a few months later (iv. p. 344) a second fossil bird from the same locality was indicated as *Ichthyornis dispar*—from the fish-like, biconcave form of its vertebrae. Further examination of the enormous collections gathered by the author, and preserved in the Museum of Yale University at New Haven, Connecticut, showed him that this last bird, and another to which he gave the name of *Apatornis*, had possessed well-developed teeth implanted in sockets in both jaws, and induced him to establish (v. pp. 161, 162) for their reception a "subclass" *Odontornithes* and an order *Ichthyornithes*. Two years more and the originally found *Hesperornis* was discovered also to have teeth, but these were inserted in a groove. It was accordingly regarded as the type of a distinct order *Odontolcae* (x. pp. 403-408), to which were assigned as other characters vertebrae of a saddle-shape and not biconcave, a keelless sternum, and wings consisting only of the humerus. In 1880 Marsh brought out *Odontornithes*, a monograph of the extinct toothed birds of North America. Herein remains, attributed to no fewer than a score of species, which were referred to eight different genera, are fully described and sufficiently illustrated, and, instead of the ordinal name *Ichthyornithes* previously used, that of *Odontormae* was proposed. In the author's concluding summary he remarks on the fact that, while the *Odontolcae*, as exhibited in *Hesperornis*, had teeth inserted in a continuous groove—a low and generalized character as shown by reptiles, they had, however, the strongly differentiated saddle-shaped vertebrae such as all modern birds possess. On the other hand the *Odontormae*, as exemplified in *Ichthyornis*, having the primitive biconcave vertebrae, yet possessed the highly specialized feature of teeth in distinct sockets. "*Hesperornis* too, with its keelless sternum, had aborted wings but strong legs and feet adapted for swimming, while *Ichthyornis* had a keeled sternum and powerful wings, but diminutive legs and feet. These and other characters separate the two forms so widely as quite to justify the establishment of as many orders for their reception. Marsh states that he had fully satisfied himself that *Archaeopteryx* belonged to the *Odontornithes*, which he thought it advisable for the present to regard as a subclass, separated into three orders—*Odontolcae, Odontormae* and *Saururae*—all well marked, but evidently not of equal rank, the last being clearly much more widely distinguished from the first two than they are from one another. But that these three oldest-known forms of birds should differ so greatly from each other unmistakably points to a great antiquity for the class.

The former efforts at classification made by Sundevall have already several times been mentioned, and a return to their consideration was promised. In 1872 and 1873 he brought **Sundevall.** out at Stockholm a *Methodi naturalis avium dispionendarum tentamen*, two portions of which (those relating to the diurnal birds-of-prey and the *Cichlomorphae*, or forms related to the thrushes) he found himself under the necessity of revising and modifying in the course of 1874, in as many communications to the Swedish Academy of Sciences (*K. V.-Ak. Förhandlingar*, 1874 No. 2, pp. 21-30; No. 3, pp. 27-30). This *Tentamen*, containing his complete method of classifying birds in general, naturally received much attention, the more so perhaps, since,

with its appendices, it was nearly the last labour of its respected author, whose industrious life came to an end in the course of the following year. From what has before been said of his works it may be gathered that, while professedly basing his systematic arrangement of the groups of birds on their external features, he had hitherto striven to make his schemes harmonize if possible with the dictates of internal structure as evinced by the science of anatomy, though he uniformly and persistently protested against the inside being better than the outside. In thus acting he proved himself a true follower of his great countryman Linnaeus; but, without disparagement of his efforts in this respect, it must be said that when internal and external characters appeared to be in conflict he gave, perhaps with unconscious bias, a preference to the latter, for he belonged to a school of zoologists whose natural instinct was to believe that such a conflict always existed. Hence his efforts, praiseworthy as they were from several points of view, and particularly so in regard to some details, failed to satisfy the philosophic taxonomer when generalizations and deeper principles were concerned, and in his practice in respect of certain technicalities of classification he was, in the eyes of the orthodox, a transgressor. Thus instead of contenting himself with terms that had met with pretty general approval, such as class, subclass, order, suborder, family, subfamily, and so on, he introduced into his final scheme other designations, "agmen," "cohorts," "phalanx," and the like, which to the ordinary student of ornithology convey an indefinite meaning, if any meaning at all. He also carried to a very extreme limit his views of nomenclature, which were certainly not in accordance with those held by most zoologists, though this is a matter so trifling as to need no details in illustration. His *Tentamen* was translated into English by F. Nicholson in 1889, and had a considerable influence on later writers, especially in the arrangement of the smaller groups. In the main it was an artificial system. Birds were divided into *Gymnopaedes* and *Dasypaedes*, according as the young were hatched naked or clothed. The *Gymnopaedes* are divided into two "orders"—*Oscines* and *Volucres*—the former intended to be identical with the group of the same name established by older authors, and, in accordance with the observations of Keyserling and Blasius already mentioned, divided into two "series"—*Laminiplantares*, having the hinder part of the "tarsus" covered with two horny plates, and *Scutelliplantares*, in which the same part is scutellated. These *Laminiplantares* are composed of six cohorts as follows:—

Cohors 1. *Cichlomorphae*.
Cohors 2. *Conirostres*.
Cohors 3. *Coliomorphae*.
Cohors 4. *Certhiomorphae.*—3 families: tree-creepers, nut-hatches.
Cohors 5. *Cinnyrimorphae.*—5 families: sun-birds, honey-suckers.
Cohors 6. *Chelidonomorphae.*—1 family: swallows.

The *Scutelliplantares* include a much smaller number of forms, and, with the exception of the first "cohort" and a few groups of the fourth and fifth, all are peculiar to America.

Cohors 1. *Holaspideae*.
Cohors 2. *Endaspideae*.
Cohors 3. *Exaspideae*.
Cohors 4. *Pycnaspideae*.
Cohors 5. *Taxaspideae*.

We then arrive at the second order *Volucres*, which is divided into two "series." Of these the first is made to contain, under the name *Zygodactyli*,

Cohors 1. *Psittaci*.
Cohors 2. *Pici*.
Cohors 3. *Coccyges*.
Cohors 4. *Coenomorphae*.
Cohors 5. *Ampliligulares*.
Cohors 6. *Longilingues* or *Mellisugae*.
Cohors 7. *Syndactylae*.
Cohors 8. *Peristeroideae*.

The *Dasypaedes* of Sundevall are separated into six "orders"; but these will occupy us but a short while. The first of them, *Accipitres*, comprehending all the birds-of-prey, were separated into 4 "cohorts" in his original work, but these were reduced in his appendix to two—*Nyctharpages* or owls with 4 families divided into 2 series, and *Hemeroharpages* containing all the rest, and comprising 10 families (the last of which is the seriema, *Dicholophus*) divided into 2 groups as *Rapaces* and *Saprophagi*—the latter including the vultures. Next stands the order *Gallinae* with 4 "cohorts";

(1) *Tetraonomorphae*, comprising 2 families, the sand-grouse (*Pterocles*) and the grouse proper, among which the Central American *Oreophasis* finds itself; (2) *Phasianomorphae*, with 4 families, pheasants pea-cocks, turkeys, guinea fowls, partridges, quails, and hemipodes (*Turnix*); (3) *Macronyches*, the megapodes, with 2 families; (4) the *Duodecimpennatae*, the curassows and guans, also with 2 families; (5) the *Struthioniformes*, composed of the tinamous; and (6) the *Subgrallatores* with 2 families, one consisting of the curious South American genera *Thinocorus* and *Attagis* and the other of the sheath-bill (*Chionis*). The fifth order (the third of the *Dasypaedes*) is formed by the *Grallatores*, divided into 2 " series "—(1) *Alinares*, consisting of 2 "cohorts," *Herodii* with 1 family, the herons, and *Pelargi* with 4 families, spoonbills, ibises, storks, and the umbre (*Scopus*), with *Balaniceps*; (2) *Humilinares*, also consisting of 2 " cohorts, *Limicolae* with 2 families, sandpipers and snipes, stilts and avocets, and *Cursores* with 8 families, including plovers, bustards, cranes, rails, and all the other " waders." The sixth order, *Natatores*, consists of all the birds that habitually swim and a few that do not, containing 6 " cohorts "; *Longipennes* and *Pygopodes* with 3 families each; *Totipalmatae* with 1 family; *Tubinares* with 3 families; *Impennes* with 1 family, penguins; and *Lamellirostres* with 2 families, flamingoes and ducks. The seventh order, *Proceres*, is divided into 2 " cohorts "—*Veri* with 2 families, ostriches and emeus; and *Subnobiles*, consisting of the genus *Apteryx*. The eighth order is formed by the *Saururae*.

Later systems of classification owe much to anatomy, and the pioneers in the modern advances in this respect were A. H. Garrod and W. A. Forbes, two brilliant and short-lived young men who occupied successively the post of prosector to the Zoological Society of London, and who made a rich use of the material provided by the collection of that society. Garrod was the more skilled and ingenious anatomist, Forbes had a greater acquaintance with the ornith-ology of museums and collectors. Garrod founded his system (1874) on muscular anatomy, making the two major divisions of Aves (his *Homalogonatae* and *Anomalogonatae*, depend in the first instance on the presence or absence of a peculiar muscular slip in the leg, known as the *ambiens*, although indeed he expressly stated that this was not on account of the intrinsic importance of the muscle in question, but because of its invariable association with other peculiarities. The system of Forbes was reconstructed after his death from notebook jottings, and neither Garrod nor Forbes have left any permanent mark on the classification of birds, although the material they furnished and the lines they indicated have proved valuable in later hands. In 1880 Dr P. L. Sclater published in the *Ibis* a classification which was mainly a revision of the system of Huxley, modified by the investigations of Garrod and Forbes and by his own large acquaintance with museum specimens.

Later Systems.

In the article " Ornithology" in the ninth edition of this encyclopaedia, A. Newton accepted the three subclasses of Huxley, *Saururae*, *Ratitae* and *Carinatae*, and made a series of cautious but critical observations on the minor divisions of the Carinates. In 1882 A. Reichenow in *Die Vögel der zoolo-gischen Gärten* published a classification of birds with a phylo-genetic tree. In this he departed considerably from the lines that had been made familiar by English workers, and made great use of natural characteristics. The next attempt of import-ance appeared in the American *Standard Natural History*, pub-lished in Boston in 1885. The volume on birds was written by Dr L. Stejneger and was founded on Elliot Coues's *Key to North American Birds*. Apart from its intrinsic merits as a learned and valuable addition to classification, this work is interesting in the history of ornithology because of the wholesale changes of nomenclature it introduced as the result of much diligence and zeal in the application of the strict rule of priority to the names of birds.

In 1888 there was published the huge monograph by Max Fürbringer entitled *Untersuchungen zur Morphologie und Systematik der Vögel*. In addition to an enormous body of new information chiefly on the shoulder girdle, the alar muscles and the nerve plexuses of birds, this work contained a critical and descriptive summary of practically the whole pre-existing literature on the structure of birds, and it is hardly necessary for the student of ornithology to refer to earlier literature at first hand. Fürbringer supposes that birds must have begun with toothed forms of small or moderate size, with long tails and four lizard-like feet and bodies clothed with a primitive kind of down. To these succeeded forms where the down had developed into body feathers for warmth, not flight, whilst the fore-limbs had become organs of prehension, the hind-limbs of progression. In such bipedal creatures the legs and pelvis became transformed to a condition similar to that of Dinosaurian reptiles. Many of them were climbing animals, and from these true birds with the power of flight were developed. In the course of this evolution there were many cases of arrest or degradation, and one of the most novel of the ideas of Fürbringer, and one now accepted by not a few anatomists, was that the ratites or ostrich-like birds were not a natural group but a set of stages of arrested development or of partial degradation. It is impossible to reproduce here Fürbringer's elaborate details and phylogenetic trees with their various horizontal sections, but the following tables give the main outlines:—

Classis AVES
I. Subclassis SAURURAE

Order.	Suborder.	Gens.	Family.
ARCHORNITHES . . .	Archaeopterygiformes	Archaeopteryges	Archaeopterygidae.

II. Subclassis ORNITHURAE

Order.	Suborder.	Gens.	Family.
STRUTHIORNITHES . .	Struthioniformes	Struthiones	Struthionidae.
RHEORNITHES . . .	Rheiformes	Rheae	Rheidae.
HIPPALECTRYORNITHES .	Casuariiformes	Casuarii	(Dromaeidae + Casuariidae + Dro-mornithidae).
	Intermediate suborder:— Aepyornithiformes. . . .	Aepyornithes	Aepyornithidae.
	Intermediate suborder:— Palamedeiformes . . .	Palamedae	Palamedeidae.
	Anseriformes	Gastornithes	Gastornithidae.
		Anseres or Lamellirostres .	Anatidae.
		Enaliornithes	Enaliornithidae.
	Podicipitiformes	Hesperornithes . . .	Hesperornithidae.
		Colymbo-Podicipites . .	Colymbidae. Podicipidae.
		Phoenicopteri	Palaeolodidae. Phoenicopteridae.
PELARGORNITHES.		Pelargo-Herodii . . .	Plataleidae or Hemiglottides. Ciconiidae or Pelargi. Scopidae. Ardeidae or Herodii. Balaenicipitidae.
	Ciconiiformes	Accipitres (*Hemeroharpages*, *Pelargoharpages*) . . .	Gypogeranidae. Cathartidae. Gypo-Falconidae.
		Steganopodes	Phaetontidae. Phalacrocoracidae. Pelecanidae. Fregatidae.

Order.	Suborder.	Gens.	Family.
	Intermediate suborder:— Procellariiformes	Procellariae or Tubinares.	Procellariidae.
	Intermediate suborder:— Aptenodytiformes	Aptenodytes or Impennes	Aptenodytidae.
	Intermediate suborder:— Ichthyornithiformes	Ichthyornithes	Ichthyornithidae. Apatornithidae.
	Charadriiformes	Charadrii	Charadriidae. Glareolidae. Dromadidae.
		Laro-Limicolae	Chionididae. Laridae. Alcidae. Thinocoridae.
CHARADRIORNITHES (Aegialornithes)		Parrae	Paridae.
		Otides	Oedicnemidae. Otididae.
	Intermediate suborder:— Gruiformes	Eurypygae	Eurypygidae. Rhinochetidae. Aptornithidae. Gruidae.
		Grues	Psophiidae. Cariamidae.
	Intermediate suborder:— Ralliformes	Fulicariae	Heliornithidae. Rallidae. Mesitidae.
		Hemipodii	Hemipodiidae.
ALECTORORNITHES (Chamaeornithes)	Apterygiformes	Apteryges	Apterygidae. Dinornithidae.
	Crypturiformes	Crypturi	Crypturidae.
	Galliformes	Callidae Opisthocomidae	Megapodiidae. Cracidae. Gallidae or Alectoropodes.
	Intermediate suborder:— Columbiformes	Pterocletes Columbae	Pteroclidae. Dididae. Columbidae.
	Intermediate suborder:— Psittaciformes	Psittaci	Psittacidae.
	Coccygiformes	Coccyges	Musophagidae. Cuculidae.
		Intermediate gens:— Galbulae	Bucconidae. Galbulidae. Capitonidae. Rhamphastidae. Indicatoridae.
	Pico-Passeriformes	Pici Pico-Passeres	Picidae. Pseudoscines.
CORACORNITHES (Dendrornithes)		Passeres	Passeridae or Passeres.
		Makrochires	Cypselidae. Trochilidae.
		Colii Intermediate gens:— Trogones	Coliidae. Trogonidae.
	Halcyoniformes	Halcyones	Halcyonidae. Alcedinidae.
		Bucerotes	Upupidae. Bucerotidae.
		Meropes Intermediate gens:— Todi	Meropidae. Momotidae. Todidae.
	Coraciiformes	Coraciae	Coraciidae. Leptosomidae.
		Caprimulgi	Caprimulgidae. Steatornithidae. Podargidae.
		Striges	Strigidae.

Whilst Fürbringer was engaged on his gigantic task, Dr Hans Gadow was preparing the ornithological volume of Bronn's *Thier-Reich.* The two authors were in constant communication, and the classifications they adopted had much in common. It is unnecessary here to discuss the views of Gadow, as that author himself has contributed the article BIRD to this edition of the *Encyclopaedia Britannica,* and has there set forth his revised scheme. (A. N.; P. C. M.)

ORODES (also called HYRŌDES, Pers. *Hurauda*), the name of two Parthian kings.

1. ORODES I., son of Phraates III., whom he murdered in 57 B.C., assisted by his brother Mithradates III. This Mithradates was made king of Media, but soon afterwards was expelled by Orodes and fled into Syria. Thence he invaded the Parthian kingdom, but having reigned for a short time (55) was besieged by Surenas, general of Orodes, in Seleucia, and after a prolonged resistance was captured and slain. Meanwhile Crassus had begun his attempt to conquer the east, but he was defeated and killed in 53 at Carrhae by Surenas, while Orodes himself invaded Armenia and forced King Artavasdes, the son of Tigranes, to abandon the Romans. By the victory of Carrhae the countries east of the Euphrates were secured to the Parthians. In the next year they invaded Syria, but with little success, for Surenas, whose achievements had made him too dangerous, was killed by Orodes (Plut. *Crass.* 33), and Pacorus, the young son of the king, was defeated by C. Cassius in 51. During the civil war the Parthians sided first with Pompey and then with Brutus and Cassius, but took no action until 40 B.C., when Pacorus, assisted by the Roman deserter Labienus, conquered a great part of Syria and Asia Minor, but was defeated and killed by Ventidius in 38 (see PACORUS). The old king, Orodes, who was deeply afflicted by the death of his gallant son, appointed

his son Phraates IV. successor, but was soon afterwards killed by him (37 B.C.; Dio. Cass. 49. 23; Justin 42. 4; Plut. *Crassus*, 33). Plutarch relates that Orodes understood Greek very well; after the death of Crassus the *Bacchae* of Euripides were represented at his court (Plut. *Crass.* 33).

2, ORODES II., raised to the throne by the magnates after the death of Phraates V. about A.D. 5, was killed after a short reign "on account of his extreme cruelty" (Joseph. *Ant.* xviii. 2, 4). (ED. M.)

OROGRAPHY (Gr. ὄρος, mountain, γράφειν, to write), that part of physical geography which deals with the geological formation, the surface features and description of mountains. The terms "oreography," "orology" and "oreology" are also sometimes used.

ORONTES, the ancient name of the chief Syrian river, also called DRACO, TYPHON and AXIUS, the last a native form, from whose revival, or continuous employment in native speech, has proceeded the modern name ' Āsī ("rebel"), which is variously interpreted by Arabs as referring to the stream's impetuosity, to its unproductive channel, or to the fact that it flows away from Mecca. The Orontes rises in the great springs of Labweh on the east side of the Buka'a, or inter-Lebanon district, very near the fountains of the southward-flowing Litani, and it runs due north, parallel with the coast, falling 2000 ft. through a rocky gorge. Leaving this it expands into the Lake of Homs, having been dammed back in antiquity. The valley now widens out into the rich district of Hamah (*Hamath-Epiphaneia*), below which lie the broad meadow-lands of Ghāb, containing the sites of ancient Apamea and Larissa. This central Orontes valley ends at the rocky barrier of Jisr al-Hadid, where the river is diverted to the west, and the plain of Antioch opens. Two large tributaries from the N., the Afrin and Kara Su, formerly reach it through the former Lake of Antioch, which is now drained through an artificial channel (Nahr al-Kowsit). Passing N. of the modern Antakia (Antioch) the Orontes plunges S.W. into a gorge (compared by the ancients to Tempe), and falls 150 ft. in 10 m. to the sea just south of the little port of Suedia (anc. *Seleucia Pieriae*), after a total course of 170 m. Mainly unnavigable and of little use for irrigation, the Orontes derives its historical importance solely from the convenience of its valley for traffic from N. to S. Roads from N. and N.E., converging at Antioch, follow the course of the stream up to Homs, where they fork to Damascus and to Coelo-Syria and the S.; and along its valley have passed the armies and traffic bound to and from Egypt in all ages. (See ANTIOCH and HOMS.) (D. G. H.)

OROPUS, a Greek seaport, on the Euripus, in the district Παραλία, opposite Eretria. It was a border city between Boeotia and Attica, and its possession was a continual cause of dispute between the two countries; but at last it came into the final possession of Athens, and is always alluded to under the Roman-empire as an Attic town. The actual harbour, which was called Delphinium, was at the mouth of the Asopus, about a mile north of the city. A village still called Oropo occupies the site of the ancient town. The famous oracle of Amphiaraus was situated in the territory of Oropus, 12 stadia from the city. The site has been excavated by the Greek Archaeological Society; it contained a temple, a sacred spring, into which coins were thrown by worshippers, altars and porticoes, and a small theatre, of which the proscenium is well preserved. Worshippers used to consult the oracle of Amphiaraus by sleeping on the skin of a slaughtered ram within the sacred building.

OROSIUS, PAULUS (fl. 415), historian and theologian, was born in Spain (possibly at Braga in Galicia) towards the close of the 4th century. Having entered the Christian priesthood, he naturally took an interest in the Priscillianist controversy then going on in his native country, and it may have been in connexion with this that he went to consult Augustine at Hippo in 413 or 414. After staying for some time in Africa as the disciple of Augustine, he was sent by him in 415 to Palestine with a letter of introduction to Jerome, then at Bethlehem. The

ostensible purpose of his mission (apart, of course, from those of pilgrimage and perhaps relic-hunting) was that he might gain further instruction from Jerome on the points raised by the Priscillianists and Origenists; but in reality, it would seem, his business was to stir up and assist Jerome and others against Pelagius, who, since the synod of Carthage in 411, had been living in Palestine, and finding some acceptance there. The result of his arrival was that John, bishop of Jerusalem, was induced to summon at his capital in June 415 a synod at which Orosius communicated the decisions of Carthage and read such of Augustine's writings against Pelagius as had at that time appeared. Success, however, was scarcely to be hoped for amongst Orientals who did not understand Latin, and whose sense of reverence was unshocked by the question of Pelagius, *si quis est mihi Augustinus?* All that Orosius succeeded in obtaining was John's consent to send letters and deputies to Innocent of Rome; and, after having waited long enough to learn the unfavourable decision of the synod of Diospolis or Lydda in December of the same year, he returned to north Africa, where he is believed to have died. According to Gennadius he carried with him recently discovered relics of the protomartyr Stephen from Palestine to Minorca, where they were efficacious in converting the Jews.

The earliest work of Orosius, *Consultatio sive commonitorium ad Augustinum de errore Priscillianistarum et Origenistarum*, explains its object by its title; it was written soon after his arrival in Africa, and is usually printed in the works of Augustine along with the reply of the latter, *Contra Priscillianistas et Origenistas liber ad Orosium*. His next treatise, *Liber apologeticus de arbitrii libertate*, was written during his stay in Palestine, and in connexion with the controversy which engaged him there. It is a keen but not always fair criticism of the Pelagian position from that of Augustine. The *Historiae adversum Paganos* was undertaken at the suggestion of Augustine, to whom it is dedicated. When Augustine proposed this task he had already planned and made some progress with his own *De civitate Dei*; it is the same argument that is elaborated by his disciple, namely, the evidence from history that the circumstances of the world had not really become worse since the introduction of Christianity. The work, which is thus a pragmatical chronicle of the calamities that have happened to mankind from the fall down to the Gothic period, has little accuracy or learning, and even less of literary charm to commend it; but it was the first attempt to write the history of the world as a history of God guiding humanity. Its purpose gave it value in the eyes of the orthodox, and the *Hormesta*, *Ormesta*, or *Ormista* as it was called, no one knows why (from Or[osii] M[undi] Hist[oria] or from *oi miseria mundi?* see Mörner, p. 180, for list of guesses), speedily attained a wide popularity. Nearly two hundred MSS. of it have survived. A free abridged translation by King Alfred is still extant (Old English text, with original in Latin, edited by H. Sweet, 1883). The *editio princeps* of the original appeared at Augsburg (1471); that of Haverkamp (Leiden, 1738 and 1767) has now been superseded by C. Zangemeister, who has edited the *Hist.* and also the *Lib. apol.* in vol. v. of the *Corp. scr. eccl. Lat.* (Vienna, 1882), as well as an edit. min. (Leipzig, Teubner, 1889). The "sources" made use of by Orosius have been investigated by T. de Mörner (*De Orosii vita ejusque hist. libr. vii. adversus Paganos*, 1844); besides the Old and New Testaments, he appears to have consulted Caesar, Livy, Justin, Tacitus, Suetonius, Florus and a cosmography, attaching also great value to Jerome's translation of the *Chronicles* of Eusebius.

ORPHAN, the term used of one who has lost both parents by death, sometimes of one who has lost father or mother only. In Law, an orphan is such a person who is under age. The Late Lat. *orphanus*, from which the word, chiefly owing to its use in the Vulgate, was adopted into English, is a transliteration of ὀρφανός, in the same sense, the original meaning being "bereft of," "destitute," classical Lat. *orbus*. The Old English word for an orphan was *stēopcild*, stepchild. By the custom of the city of London, the lord mayor and aldermen, in the Court of Orphans, have the guardianship of the children still under age of deceased freemen. Orphans' courts exist for the guardianship of orphans and administration of their estates in Delaware, Maryland, New Jersey and Pennsylvania in the United States. In other states these are performed by officers of the Probate Court, known as "surrogates," or by other titles.

ORPHEUS, in Greek legend, the chief representative of the art of song and playing on the lyre, and of great importance in the religious history of Greece. The derivation of the name is uncertain, the most probable being that which connects it with ὀρφ-("dark," ὀρφναῖος, ὀρφνη). In accordance with this, Orpheus may have been originally a god of darkness; or the liberator from the power of darkness by his gift of song; or he may have been so called because his rites were celebrated by night (cf. Dionysus Nyctelius). It is possible, but very improbable, that Orpheus was an historical personage; even in ancient times his existence was denied. According to Maass, he was a chthonian deity, the counterpart of Dionysus, with whom he is closely connected; J. E. Harrison, however, regards him as a religious reformer from Crete, who introduced the doctrine of *ecstasis* without intoxication amongst the Thracians and was slain by the votaries of the frenzied ritual. S. Reinach sees in him the fox roaming "in the darkness," to the Thracians a personification of the wine-god, torn in pieces by the Bassarae (fox-maidens). Although by some he was held to be a Greek, the tradition of his Thracian origin was most generally accepted. His name does not occur in Homer or Hesiod, but he was known in the time of Ibycus (c. 530 B.C.), and Pindar (522–442 B.C.) speaks of him as "the father of songs." From the 6th century onwards he was looked upon as one of the chief poets and musicians of antiquity, the inventor or perfecter of the lyre, who by his music and singing was able not only to charm the wild beasts, but even to draw the trees and rocks from their places, and to arrest the rivers in their course. As one of the pioneers of civilization, he was supposed to have taught mankind the arts of medicine, writing and agriculture. As closely connected with religious life, he was an augur and seer; practised magical arts, especially astrology; founded or rendered accessible many important cults, such as those of Apollo and Dionysus; instituted mystic rites, both public and private; prescribed initiatory and purificatory ritual. He was said to have visited Egypt, and to have become acquainted there with the writings of Moses and with the doctrine of a future life.

According to the best-known tradition, Orpheus was the son of Oeagrus, king of Thrace, and the muse Calliope. During his residence in Thrace he joined the expedition of the Argonauts, whose leader Jason had been informed by Chiron that only by the aid of Orpheus would they be able to pass by the Sirens unscathed. His numerous services during the journey are described in the *Argonautica* that goes under his name. But the most famous story in which he figures is that of his wife Eurydice. While fleeing from Aristaeus, she was bitten by a serpent and died. Orpheus went down to the lower world and by his music softened the heart of Pluto and Persephone, who allowed Eurydice to return with him to earth. But the condition was attached that he should walk in front of her and not look back until he had reached the upper world. In his anxiety he broke his promise, and Eurydice vanished again from his sight. The story in this form belongs to the time of Virgil, who first introduces the name of Aristaeus. Other ancient writers, however, speak of his visit to the underworld; according to Plato, the infernal gods only "presented an apparition" of Eurydice to him.

After the death of Eurydice, Orpheus rejected the advances of the Thracian women, who, jealous of his faithfulness to the memory of his lost wife, tore him to pieces during the frenzy of the Bacchic orgies. His head and lyre floated "down the swift Hebrus to the Lesbian shore," where the inhabitants buried his head and a shrine was built in his honour near Antissa. The lyre was carried to heaven by the Muses, and was placed amongst the stars. The Muses also gathered up the fragments of his body and buried them at Leibethra below Olympus, where the nightingales sang over his grave, while yet another legend places his tomb at Dium, near Pydna in Macedonia. Other accounts of his death are: that he killed himself from grief at the failure of his journey to Hades; that he was struck with lightning by Zeus for having revealed the mysteries of the gods to men; or he was torn to pieces by the Maenads for having abandoned the cult of Dionysus for that of Apollo.

According to Gruppe, the legend of the death of Orpheus is a late imitation of the Adonis-Osiris myth. Osiris, like Orpheus, is torn in pieces, and his head floats down every year from Egypt to Byblus; the body of Attis, the Phrygian counterpart of Adonis, like that of Orpheus, does not suffer decay. The story is repeated of Dionysus; he is torn in pieces, and his head is carried down to Lesbos. Without going so far as to assert that Orpheus is a hypostasis of Dionysus, there is no doubt that a close connexion existed between them from very early times. According to Fraser, these traditions may be "distorted reminiscences" of the practice of human sacrifice, especially of divine kings, the object of which was to ensure fertility in the animal and vegetable worlds. Orpheus, in the manner of his death, was considered to personate the god Dionysus, and was thus the representative of the god torn to pieces every year, a ceremony enacted by the Bacchae in the earliest times with a human victim, afterwards with a bull to represent the bull-formed god. A distinct feature of this ritual was ὠμοφαγία (eating the flesh of the victim raw), whereby the communicants imagined that they consumed and assimilated the god represented by the victim, and thus became filled with the divine ecstasy. A. W. Bather (*Journ. Hell. Studies*, xiv. p. 254) sees in the myth an allusion to a ritual, the object of which is the expulsion of death or winter. It is possible that the floating of the head of Orpheus to Lesbos has reference to the fact that the island was the first home of lyric poetry, and may be symbolical of the route taken by the Aeolian emigrants from Thessaly on their way to their new home in Asia Minor.

The name of Orpheus is equally important in the religious history of Greece. He was the mythic founder of a religious school or sect, with a code of rules of life, a mystic eclectic theology, a system of purificatory and expiatory rites, and peculiar mysteries. This school is first observable under the rule of Peisistratus at Athens in the 6th century B.C. Its doctrines are founded on two elements: the Thraco-Phrygian religion of Dionysus with its enthusiastic orgies, its mysteries and its purifications, and the tendency to philosophic speculation on the nature and mutual relations of the numerous gods, developed at this time by intercourse with Egypt and the East, and by the quickened intercourse between different tribes and different religions in Greece itself. These causes produced similar results in different parts of Greece. The close analogy between Pythagoreanism and Orphism has been recognized from Herodotus (ii. 81) to the latest modern writers. Both inculcated a peculiar kind of ascetic life; both had a mystical speculative theory of religion, with purificatory rites, abstinence from beans, &c.; but Orphism was more especially religious, while Pythagoreanism, at least originally, inclined more to be a political and philosophical creed.

The rules of the Orphic life prescribed abstinence from beans, flesh, certain kinds of fish, &c., the wearing of a special kind of clothes, and numerous other practices and abstinences. The ritual of worship was peculiar, not admitting bloody sacrifices. The belief was taught in the homogeneity of all living things, in the doctrine of original sin, in the transmigration of souls, in the view that the soul is entombed in the body (σῶμα σῆμα), and that it may gradually attain perfection during connexion with a series of bodies. When completely purified, it will be freed from this "circle of generation" (κύκλος γενέσεως), and will again become divine, as it was before its entrance into a mortal body.

The chief ceremonies of the nightly ritual were sacrifice and libation; prayer and purification; the representation of sacred legends (e.g. the myth of Zagreus, the chief object of worship, who was identified with most of the numerous gods of the Orphic pantheon); the rape of Persephone; and the descent into Hades. These were introduced as a "sacred explanation" (ἱερὸς λόγος) of the rules and prescriptions. To these also belong the rite of ὠμοφαγία, and the communication of liturgical formulae for the guidance of the soul of the dead man on his way to the underworld, which also served as credentials to the gods below. Some of the so-called "Orphic tablets," metrical inscriptions engraved on small plates of gold, chiefly dating from the 4th and 3rd centuries B.C., have been discovered in tombs in southern Italy, Crete and Rome.

It does not appear, however, that a regularly organized or numerous Orphic sect ever existed, nor that Orphism ever became popular; it was too abstract, too full of symbolism. On the other hand, the genuine Orphica, a fraternity of religious ascetics, found unscrupulous imitators and impostors, who preyed upon the credulous and ignorant. Such were the Orpheotelestae or Metragyrtae, wandering priests who went round the country with an ass carrying the sacred properties (Aristophanes, *Frogs*, 159) and a bundle of sacred books. They promised an easy expiation for crimes to both living and dead on payment of a fee, undertook to punish the enemies of their clients, and held out to them the prospect of perpetual banqueting and drinking-bouts in Paradise.

A large number of writings in the tone of the Orphic religion were ascribed to Orpheus. They dealt with such subjects as the origin of the gods, the creation of the world, the ritual of purification and initiation, and oracular responses. These poems were recited at rhapsodic contests together with those of Homer and Hesiod, and Orphic hymns were used in the Eleusinian mysteries.[1] The best-known name in connexion with them is that of Onomacritus (q.v.), who, in the time of the Peisistratidae, made a collection (including forgeries of his own) of Orphic songs and legends. In later times Orphic theology engaged the attention of Greek philosophers—Eudemus the Peripatetic, Chrysippus the Stoic, and Proclus the Neoplatonist, but it was an especially favourite study of the grammarians of Alexandria, where it became so intermixed with Egyptian elements that Orpheus came to be looked upon as the founder of mysticism. The "rhapsodic theogony" in particular exercised great influence on Neoplatonism. The Orphic literature (of which only fragments remain) was united in a corpus, called τὰ Ὀρφικά, the chief poem in which was ὁ τοῦ Ὀρφέως θεολογία. It also included a collection of Orphic hymns, liturgic songs, practical treatises, and poems on various subjects. The so-called Orphic Poems, still extant, are of much later date, probably belonging to the 4th century A.D.; they consist of: (1) an Argonautica, glorifying the deeds of Orpheus on the "Argo," (2) a didactic poem on the magic powers of stones, called Lithica, (3) eighty-seven hymns on various divinities and personified forces of nature. Some of these hymns are probably earlier (1st and 2nd centuries). The Orphic poems also played an important part in the controversies between Christian and pagan writers in the 3rd and 4th centuries after Christ; pagan writers quoted them to show the real meaning of the multitude of gods, while Christians retorted by reference to the obscene and disgraceful fictions by which the former degraded their gods.

BIBLIOGRAPHY.—C. A. Lobeck's Aglaophamus (1829) is still indispensable. Of more modern writings on Orpheus and Orphism the following may be consulted. The articles by O. Gruppe in Roscher's Lexikon der Mythologie and by P. Monceaux in Daremberg and Saglio's Dictionnaire des antiquités; "Orphica" in Smith's Dictionary of Greek and Roman Antiquities (3rd ed.; 1891), by L. C. Purser; J. E. Harrison, Prolegomena to the Study of Greek Religion (2nd ed., 1908, with a critical appendix by Gilbert Murray on the Orphic tablets); E. Rohde, Psyche, ii. (1907), and article in Heidelberger Jahrbücher (1896); E. W. Maass, Orpheus (1895); S. Reinach, "La mort d'Orphée" in Cultes, mythes, et religions, ii. (1906); O. Gruppe; Griechische Mythologie, ii. (1906), pp. 1028-1041, I. Gomperz, Greek Thinkers, i. (Eng. trans., 1901), pp. 84-90, 123-147; E. Gerhard, Über Orpheus und die Orphiker (1861); A. Dieterich, Nekyia (1893), pp. 72-108, 136-162, 225-232; O. Kern, De Orphei, Epimenidis, Pherecydis theogoniis (1888); O. Gruppe, Die rhapsodische Theogonie (1890); A. Dieterich, De hymnis Orphicis (1891); C. F. Schömann, Griechische Alterthümer, ii. (ed. J. H. Lipsius, 1902), p. 378; P. Stengel, Die griechischen Kultusalterthümer (1898), p. 159.

There is an edition of the Orphic Fragments and of the poems by E. Abel (1885). The Argonautica has been edited separately by J. W. Schneider (1803), the Lithica by T. Tyrwhitt (1791), and there is an English translation of the Hymns by T. Taylor (reprinted, 1896).

On the representations of Orpheus in heathen and Christian art (in which he is finally transformed into the Good Shepherd with his sheep), see A. Baumeister, Denkmäler des classischen Alterthums, ii. p. 1120; P. Knapp, Über Orpheusdarstellungen (Tübingen, 1895); F. X. Kraus, Realencyklopädie der christlichen Alterthums, ii. (1886); J. A. Martigny, Dictionnaire des antiquités chrétiennes (1880); A. Heussner, Die altchristlichen Orpheusdarstellungen (Leipzig, 1893); and the articles in Roscher's and Daremberg and Saglio's Lexicons.

The story of Orpheus, as was to be expected of a legend told both by Ovid and Boethius, retained its popularity throughout the middle ages and was transformed into the likeness of a northern fairy tale. In English medieval literature it appears in three somewhat different versions: Sir Orpheo, a "lay of Brittany" printed from the Harleian MS. in J. Ritson's Ancient English Metrical Romances, vol. ii. (1802); Orpheo and Heurodis from the Auchinleck MS. in David Laing's Select Remains of the Ancient Popular Poetry of Scotland (new ed., 1885); and Kyng Orfew from the Ashmolean MS. in J.O. Halliwell's Illustrations of Fairy Mythology (Shakespeare Soc., 1842). The poems show traces of French influence.

(J. H. F.: X.)

ORPHREY, gold or other richly ornamented embroidery, particularly an embroidered border on an ecclesiastical vestment (see VESTMENTS). The word is from O. Fr. orfreis, mod. orfroi, from med. Lat. aurifrisium, aurifrigium, &c., for auriphrygium,

[1] For Orphism in relation to the Eleusinian and other mysteries see MYSTERY.

aurum, gold, and phrygium, Phrygian; a name given to gold-embroidered tissues, also known as vestes Phrygiae, the Phrygians being famous for their skill in embroidering in gold.

ORPIMENT (auripigmentum), arsenic trisulphide, As_2S_3, or yellow realgar (q.v.), occurring in small quantities as a mineral crystallizing in the rhombic system and of a brilliant golden-yellow colour in Bohemia, Peru, &c. For industrial purposes an artificial orpiment is manufactured by subliming one part of sulphur with two of arsenic trioxide. The sublimate varies in colour from yellow to red, according to the intimacy of the combination of the ingredients; and by varying the relative quantities used many intermediate tones may be obtained. These artificial preparations are highly poisonous. Formerly, under the name of "king's yellow," a preparation of orpiment was in considerable use as a pigment, but now it has been largely superseded by chrome-yellow. It was also at one time used in dyeing and calico-printing, and for the unhairing of skins, &c.; but safer and equally efficient substitutes have been found.

ORPINGTON, a town in the Dartford parliamentary division of Kent, England, 13¾ m. S.E. of London, and 2½ m. S. by E. of Chislehurst, on the South-Eastern & Chatham railway. Pop. (1901), 4250. The church (Early English) contains some carved woodwork and ancient brasses. An old mansion called the Priory dates in part from 1393. The oak-panelled hall and the principal rooms are of the 15th century. In 1873 John Ruskin set up at Orpington a private publishing house for his works, in the hands of his friend George Allen. Fruit and hops are extensively grown in the neighbourhood. From its pleasant situation in a hilly, wooded district near the headwaters of the Cray stream, Orpington has become in modern times a favourite residential locality for those whose business lies in London. A line of populous villages extends down the valley between Orpington and Bexley—St Mary Cray (pop. 1894), St Paul's Cray (1207), Foots Cray (an urban district, 5817), and North Cray.

ORRERY,[1] **CHARLES BOYLE, 4TH EARL OF** (1676-1731), the second son of Roger, 2nd earl, was born at Chelsea in 1676. He was educated at Christ Church, Oxford, and soon distinguished himself by his learning and abilities. Like the first earl, he was an author, soldier and statesman. He translated Plutarch's life of Lysander, and published an edition of the epistles of Phalaris, which engaged him in the famous controversy with Bentley. He was three times member for the town of Huntingdon; and on the death of his brother, Lionel, 3rd earl, in 1703, he succeeded to the title. He entered the army, and in 1709 was raised to the rank of major-general, and sworn one of her Majesty's privy council. At the battle of the Wood he acted with distinguished bravery. He was appointed queen's envoy to the states of Brabant and Flanders; and having discharged this trust with ability, he was created an English peer, as Baron Boyle of Marston, in Somersetshire. He received several additional honours in the reign of George I.; but having had the misfortune to fall under the suspicion of the government he was committed to the Tower, where he remained six months, and was then admitted to bail. On a subsequent inquiry it was found impossible to criminate him, and he was discharged. He died on the 28th of August 1731. Among the works of Roger, earl of Orrery, will be found a comedy, entitled As you find it, written by Charles Boyle. His son John (see CORK, EARLS OF), the 5th earl of Orrery, succeeded to the earldom of Cork on the failure of the elder branch of the Boyle family, as earl of Cork and Orrery.

ORRERY, ROGER BOYLE, 1ST EARL OF (1621-1679), British soldier, statesman and dramatist, 3rd surviving son of Richard Boyle, 1st earl of Cork, was born on the 25th of April 1621, created baron of Broghill on the 28th of February 1627, and educated at Trinity College, Dublin, and, according to Wood,

[1] The orrery, an astronomical instrument—consisting of an apparatus which illustrates the motions of the solar system by means of the revolution of balls moved by wheelwork—invented, or at least constructed, by Graham, was named after the earl.

also at Oxford. He travelled in France and Italy, and coming home took part in the expedition against the Scots. He returned to Ireland on the outbreak of the rebellion in 1641 and fought with his brothers at the battle of Liscarrol in September 1642. On the resignation of the marquis of Ormonde, Lord Broghill consented to serve under the parliamentary commissioners till the execution of the king, when he retired altogether from public affairs and took up his residence at Marston in Somersetshire. Subsequently he originated a scheme to bring about the Restoration, but when on his way abroad to concert measures with Charles he was unexpectedly visited by Cromwell in London, who, after informing him that his plans were well known to the council, and warning him of the consequence of persisting in them, offered him a command in Ireland against the rebels, which, as it entailed no obligations except faithful service, was accepted. His assistance in Ireland proved invaluable. Appointed master of the ordnance, he soon assembled a body of infantry and horse, and drove the rebels into Kilkenny, where they surrendered. On the 10th of May 1650 he completely defeated at Macroom a force of Irish advancing to the relief of Clonmell, and joining Cromwell assisted in taking the latter place. On Cromwell's departure for Scotland he co-operated with Ireton, whom he joined at the siege of Limerick, and defeated the force marching to its relief under Lord Muskerry, thus effecting the capture of the town. By this time Broghill had become the fast friend and follower of Cromwell, whose stern measures in Ireland and support of the English and Protestants were welcomed after the policy of concession to the Irish initiated by Charles I. He was returned to Cromwell's parliaments of 1654 and 1656 as member for the county of Cork, and also in the latter assembly for Edinburgh, for which he elected to sit. He served this year as lord president of the council in Scotland, where he won much popularity; and when he returned to England he was included in the inner cabinet of Cromwell's council, and was nominated in 1657 a member of the new house of Lords. He was one of those most in favour of Cromwell's assumption of the royal title, and proposed a union between the Protector's daughter Frances and Charles II. On Cromwell's death he gave his support to Richard; but as he saw no possibility of maintaining the government he left for Ireland, where by resuming his command in Munster he secured the island for Charles and anticipated Monk's overtures by inviting him to land at Cork. He sat for Arundel in the Convention and in the parliament of 1661, and at the Restoration was taken into great favour. On the 5th of September 1660 he was created earl of Orrery. The same year he was appointed a lord justice of Ireland and drew up the Act of Settlement. He continued to exercise his office as lord-president of Munster till 1668, when he resigned it on account of disputes with the duke of Ormonde, the lord-lieutenant. On the 25th of November he was impeached by the House of Commons for "raising of money by his own authority upon his majesty's subjects," but the prorogation of parliament by the king interrupted the proceedings, which were not afterwards renewed. He died on the 26th of October 1679. He married Lady Margaret Howard, 3rd daughter of Theophilus, 2nd earl of Suffolk, whose charms were celebrated by Suckling in his poem "The Bride." By her he had besides five daughters, two sons, of whom the eldest, Roger (1646-1681 or 1682), succeeded as 2nd earl of Orrery.

In addition to Lord Orrery's achievements as a statesman and administrator, he gained some reputation as a writer and a dramatist. He was the author of An Answer to a Scandalous Letter . . . A Full Discovery of the Treachery of the Irish Rebels (1662), printed with the letter itself in his State Letters (1742), another answer to the same letter entitled Irish Colours Displayed . . . being also ascribed to him; Parthenissa, a novel (1654); English Adventures by a Person of Honour (1676), whence Otway drew his tragedy of the Orphan; Treatise of the Art of War (1677), a work of considerable historical value; poems, of little interest, including verses On His Majesty's Happy Restoration (unprinted), On the Death of Abraham Cowley (1677), The Dream (unprinted), Poems on most of the Festivals of the Church (1681); plays in verse, of some literary but no dramatic merit, of which Henry V. (1664), Mustapha (1665), Tryphon (acted 1668), The Black Prince (1669), Herod the Great (published 1694), and Altemira (1702) were tragedies, and Guzman (1669) and Mr Anthony

comedies. A collected edition was published in 1737, to which was added the comedy As you find it. The General is also attributed to him.

AUTHORITIES.—State Letters of Roger Boyle, 1st Earl of Orrery, ed. with his life by Th. Morrice (1742); Add. MSS. (Brit. Mus.) 25,287 (letter-book when governor of Munster), and 32,095 seq. 109-188 (letters); article in the Dict. of Nat. Biog. and authorities there collected; Wood's Athenae Oxonienses, iii. 1200; Biographia Britannica (Kippis); Orrery Papers, ed. by Lady Cork and Orrery (1903) (Preface); Contemporary Hist. of Affairs in Ireland, ed. by John T. Gilbert (1879-1880); Cal. of State Pap., Irish and Domestic.

ORRIS-ROOT (apparently a corruption of "iris root"), the rhizomes or underground stems of three species of Iris, I. germanica, I. florentina and I. pallida, closely allied plants growing in subtropical and temperate latitudes, but principally identified with North Italy. The three plants are indiscriminately cultivated in the neighbourhood of Florence as an agricultural product under the name of "ghiaggiuolo." The rhizomes are in August dug up and freed of the rootlets and brown outer bark; they are then dried and packed in casks for sale. In drying they acquire a delicate but distinct odour of violets. As it comes into the market, orris-root is in the form of contorted sticks and irregular knobby pieces up to 4 in. in length, of a compact chalky appearance. It is principally powdered for use in dentifrices and other scented dry preparations.

ORSEOLO, the name of a Venetian family, three members of which filled the office of doge.

PIETRO ORSEOLO I. (c. 928-997) acted as ambassador to the emperor Otto I. before he was elected doge in August 976. Just previous to this event part of Venice had been burned down and Pietro began the rebuilding of St Mark's church and the ducal palace. He is chiefly celebrated, however, for his piety and his generosity, and after holding office for two years he left Venice secretly and retired to a monastery in Aquitaine, where he passed his remaining days. He was canonized in 1731.

PIETRO ORSEOLO II. (d. 1009), a son of the previous doge, was himself elected to this office in 991. He was a great builder, but his chief work was to crush the pirates of the Adriatic Sea and to bring a long stretch of the Dalmatian coast under the rule of Venice, thus relieving the commerce of the republic from a great and pressing danger. The fleet which achieved this result was led by the doge in person; it sailed on Ascension Day, the 9th of May 1000, and its progress was attended with uninterrupted success. In honour of this victory the Venetians instituted the ceremony which afterwards grew into the sposalizio del mar, or marriage of the sea, and which was celebrated each year on Ascension Day, while the doge added to his title that of duke of Dalmatia. In many other ways Pietro's services to the state were considerable, and he may be said to be one of the chief founders of the commercial greatness of Venice. The doge was on very friendly terms with the emperor Otto III. and also with the emperors at Constantinople; and in 1003 he sailed against the Saracens and compelled them to raise the siege of Bari. In 1005 his son Giovanni was associated with him in the dogeship, and on Giovanni's death in 1007 another son, Ottone, succeeded to this position.

OTTONE ORSEOLO (d. 1032), whose godfather was the emperor Otto III., became sole doge on his father's death in 1009. He married a sister of St Stephen, king of Hungary, and under his rule Venice was powerful and prosperous. One of his brothers, Orso, was patriarch of Grado, another, Vitalis, was bishop of Torcello, but the growing wealth and influence of the Orseolo family soon filled the Venetians with alarm. About 1024 Ottone and Orso were driven from Venice, but when Orso's rival, Poppo, patriarch of Aquileia, seized Grado, the exiled doge and his brother was recalled and Grado was recovered. In 1026 Ottone was banished; he found a refuge in Constantinople, where he remained until his death, although in 1030 an embassy invited him to return to Venice, where his brother Orso acted as agent for fourteen months. Orso remained patriarch of Grado until his death in 1045, and another member of the Orseolo family, Domenico, was doge for a single day in 1031. After the fall of the Orseoli the Venetians decreed that no doge should name his successor, or associate any one with him in the dogeship.. Ottone's son, Pietro, was king of Hungary for some time after the death of his uncle, St Stephen, in 1038.

See Kohlschütter, *Venedig unter dem Herzog Peter II. Orseolo* (Göttingen, 1868); H. F, Brown, *Venice* (1893); F. C. Hodgson, *The Early History of Venice* (1901); and W. C. Hazlitt, *The Venetian Republic* (1900).

ORSHA (Polish-Orsza), a town of Russia, in the government of Mogilev, 74 m. by rail W.S.W. of Smolensk on the Moscow-Warsaw railway, and on the Dnieper. Pop. (1897), 13,161. It is an important entrepôt for grain, seeds and timber. It is a very old town, mentioned in the annals under the name of Rsha in 1067. In the 13th century it was taken by the Lithuanians, who fortified it. In 1604 the Poles founded there a Jesuit college. The Russians besieged Orsha more than once in the 16th and 17th centuries, and finally annexed it in 1772.

ORSINI, the name of a Roman princely family of great antiquity, whose perpetual feuds with the Colonna are one of the dominant features of the history of medieval Rome. According to tradition the popes Paul I. (757) and Eugenius II. (824) were of the Orsini family, but the probable founder of the house was a certain Ursus (the Bear), about whom very little is known, and the first authentic Orsini pope was Giacinto Orsini, son of Petrus Bobo, who assumed the name of Celestin III. (1191).

The [text cut] latter endowed his nephews with church lands and founded [text] of the family, which alone of the Guelf houses [text] confront the Ghibelline Colonna. "Orsini for the fortunes their war-cry" in opposition to "Colonna for the able to the 13th century the "Sons of the Bear" were [text]-powerful and rich, and under Innocent III. they waged incessant war against other families, including that of the pope himself (Conti) In 1241 Matteo Orsini was elected senator of Rome, and sided with Pope Gregory IX. against the Colonna and the Emperor Frederick II., saving Rome for the Guelfic cause. · In 1266 the family acquired Marino, and in 1277 Giovanni Orsini was elected pope as Nicholas III. When Boniface VIII. proclaimed a crusade against the Colonna in 1297, the Orsini played a conspicuous part in the expedition and captured Nepi, which the pope granted them as a fief. · On the death of Benedict XI. (1304) fierce civil warfare broke out in Rome and the Campagna for the election of his successor, and Cardinal Napoleone Orsini appears as the leader of the French faction at the conclave. The Campagna was laid waste by the feuds of the Orsinis, the Colonnas and the Caetanis. At this time the Orsini held the castle of S. Angelo, and a number of palaces on the Monte Giordano, which formed a fortified and walled quarter. In 1332, during the absence of the popes at Avignon, the feuds between Orsini and Colonna, in which even Giovanni Orsini, although cardinal legate, took part, reduced Rome to a state of complete anarchy. We find the Orsini again at war with the Colonna at the time of Rienzi. In 1435 Francesco Orsini was appointed prefect of Rome, and created duke of Gravina by Pope Eugenius IV. In 1484 war between the Orsini and the Colonna broke out once more, the former supporting the pope (Sixtus IV.). Virginio Orsini led his faction against the rival house's strongholds, which were stormed, the Colonna being thereby completely defeated. The Orsini fortunes waxed and waned many times, and their property was often confiscated, but they always remained a powerful family and gave many soldiers, statesmen and prelates to the church. The title of prince of Solofra was conferred on them in 1620, and that of prince of the Holy Roman Empire in 1629. In 1724 Vincenzo Maria Orsini was elected pope (Benedict XIII.) and gave his family the title of Roman princes.

AUTHORITIES.—F. Sansovino, *Storia di casa Orsina* (Venice, 1565); F. Gregorovius, *Geschichte der Stadt Rom* (Stuttgart, 1872); A. von Reumont, *Geschichte der Stadt Rom* (Berlin, 1868); *Almanach de Gotha.*

ORSINI, FELICE (1819-1858), Italian revolutionist, was born at Meldola in Romagna. He was destined for an ecclesiastical career, but he soon abandoned that prospect, and became an ardent liberal, joining the Giovane Italia, a society founded by Giuseppe Mazzini. Implicated together with his father in revolutionary plots, he was arrested in 1844 and condemned to

imprisonment for life. The new pope, Pius IX., however, set him free, and he led a company of young Romagnols in the first war of Italian independence (1848), distinguishing himself in the engagements at Treviso and Vicenza. He was elected member of the Roman Constituent Assembly in 1849, and after the fall of the republic he conspired against the papal autocracy once more in the interest of the Mazzinian party. Mazzini sent him on a secret mission to Hungary, but he was arrested in 1854 and imprisoned at Mantua, escaping a few months later. In 1857 he published an account of his prison experiences in English under the title of *Austrian Dungeons in Italy*, which led to a rupture between him and Mazzini. He then entered into negotiations with Ausonio Franchi, editor of the *Ragione* of Turin, which he proposed to make the organ of the pure republicans. But having become convinced that Napoleon III. was the chief obstacle to Italian independence and the principal cause of the anti-liberal reaction throughout Europe, he went to Paris in 1857 to conspire against him. On the evening of the 14th of January 1858, while the emperor and empress were on their way to the theatre, Orsini and his accomplices threw three bombs at the imperial carriage. The intended victims were unhurt, but several other persons were killed or wounded. Orsini himself was wounded, and at once arrested; on the 11th of February he wrote his famous letter to Napoleon, in which he exhorted him to take up the cause of Italian freedom. He addressed another letter to the youth of Italy, stigmatizing political assassination. He was condemned to death and executed on the 13th of March 1858, meeting his fate with great calmness and bravery. Of his accomplices Pieri also was executed, Rudio was condemned to death but obtained a commutation of sentence, and Gomez was condemned to hard labour for life. The importance of Orsini's attempt lies in the fact that it terrified Napoleon, who came to believe that unless he took up the Italian cause other attempts would follow and that sooner or later he would be assassinated. This fear contributed not a little to the emperor's subsequent Italian policy.

BIBLIOGRAPHY.—*Memoirs and Adventures of Felice Orsini written by himself* (Edinburgh, 1857, 2nd ed., edited by Ausonio Franchi, Turin, 1858); *Lettere edite e inedite di F. O.* (Milan, 1861); Enrico Montazio, *I contemporanei Italiani-Felice Orsini* (Turin, 1862); *La vérité sur Orsini, par un ancien proscrit* (1879); Angelo Arboit, *Tesin e la fuga di Felice Orsini* (Cagliari, 1893).

ORTA, LAKE OF, in N. Italy, W. of Lago Maggiore. It has been so named since the 16th century, but was previously called the *Lago di San Giulio,* the patron of the region—*Cusio* is a merely poetical name. Its southern end is about 22 m. by rail N.W. of Novara on the main Turin-Milan line, while its north end is about 4 m. by rail S. of the Gravellona-Toce railway station, half-way between Omavasso and Omegna. It has an area of about 6½ sq. m., it is about 8 m. in length, its greatest depth is 482 ft., and the surface is 951 ft. above sea-level, while its width varies from ½ to 1½ m. Its scenery is characteristically Italian, while the large island of San Giulio (just W. of the village of Orta) has some very picturesque buildings, and takes its name from the local saint, who lived in the 4th century. The chief place is Orta, built on a peninsula projecting from the east shore of the lake, while Omegna is at its northern extremity. It is supposed that the lake is the remnant of a much larger sheet of water by which originally the waters of the Toce or Tosa flowed south towards Novara. As the glaciers retreated the waters flowing from them sank, and were gradually diverted into Lago Maggiore. This explains why no considerable stream feeds the Lake of Orta, while at its north end the Nigoglia torrent flows out of it, but in about ½ m. it falls into the Strona, which in turn soon joins the Toce or Tosa, a short distance before this river flows into Lago Maggiore. (W. A. B. C.)

ORTELIUS (ORTELS, WORTELS), **ABRAHAM,** next to Mercator the greatest geographer of his age, was born at Antwerp on the 14th of April 1527, and died in the same city on the 4th of July 1598. He was of German origin, his family coming from Augsburg. He travelled extensively in western Europe, especially in the Netherlands; south and west Germany (e.g. 1560, 1575, 1578); France (1559-1560, &c.); England and Ireland

(1577), and Italy (1578, and perhaps twice or thrice between 1550 and 1558). Beginning as a map-engraver (in 1547 he enters the Antwerp gild of St Luke as *afsetter van Karten*), his early career is that of a business man, and most of his journeys before 1560 are for commercial purposes (such as his yearly visits to the Frankfort fair). In 1560, however, when travelling with Gerhard Kremer (Mercator) to Trier, Lorraine and Poitiers, he seems to have been attracted, largely by Mercator's influence, towards the career of a scientific geographer; in particular he now devoted himself, at his friend's suggestion, to the compilation of that atlas or *Theatre of the World* by which he became famous. In 1564 he completed a *mappemonde*, which afterwards appeared in the *Theatrum*. He also published a map of Egypt in 1565 a plan of Britenburg Castle on the coast of Holland, and perhaps a map of Asia, before the appearance of his great work. In 1570 (May 20) was issued, by Gilles Coppens de Diest at Antwerp, Ortelius' *Theatrum Orbis Terrarum*, the "first modern atlas" (of 53 maps). Three Latin editions of this (besides a Flemish, a French and a German) appeared before the end of 1572; twenty-five editions came out before Ortelius' death in 1598; and several others were published subsequently, for the vogue continued till about 1612. Most of the maps were admittedly reproductions (a list of 87 authors is given by Ortelius himself), and many discrepancies of delineation or nomenclature occur. Errors, of course, abound, both in general conceptions and in detail; thus South America is very faulty in outline, and in Scotland the Grampians lie between the Forth and the Clyde; but, taken as a whole, this atlas with its accompanying text was a monument of rare erudition and industry. Its immediate precursor and prototype was a collection of thirty-eight maps of European lands, and of Asia, Africa, Tartary and Egypt, gathered together by the wealth and enterprise, and through the agents, of Ortelius' friend and patron, Gilles Hooftman, lord of Cleydael and Aertselaér: most of these were printed in Rome, eight or nine only in Belgium. In 1573 Ortelius published seventeen supplementary maps under the title of *Additamentum Theatri Orbis Terrarum*. By this time he had formed a fine collection of coins, medals and antiques, and this produced (also in 1573, published by Philippe Galle of Antwerp) his *Deorum dearumque capita . . . ex Museo Ortelii* (reprinted in Gronovius, *Thes. Gr. Ant.* vol. vii.). In 1575 he was appointed geographer to the king of Spain, Philip II., on the recommendation of Arius Montanus, who vouched for his orthodoxy (his family, as early as 1535, had fallen under suspicion of Protestantism). In 1578 he laid the basis of a critical treatment of ancient geography by his *Synonymia geographica* (issued by the Plantin press at Antwerp and republished as *Thesaurus geographicus* in 1596). In 1584 he brought out his *Nomenclator Ptolemaicus*, his *Parergon* (a series of maps illustrating ancient history, sacred and secular), his *Itinerarium per nonnullas Galliae Belgicae partes* (published at the Plantin press, and reprinted in Hegenitius, *Itin. Frisio-Holl.*), a record of a journey in Belgium and the Rhineland made in 1575. Among his last works were an edition of Caesar (*C. I. Caesaris omnia quae extant*, Leiden, Raphelingen, 1593), and the *Aurei saeculi imago, sive Germanorum veterum vita* (Philippe Galle, Antwerp, 1596). He also aided Welser in his edition of the Peutinger Table in 1598. In 1596 he received a presentation from Antwerp city, similar to that afterwards bestowed on Rubens; his death and burial (in St Michael's Abbey church) in 1598 were marked by public mourning.

See Emmanuel van Meteren, *Historia Belgica* (Amsterdam, 1670); General Wauwermans, *Histoire de l'école cartographique belge et anversoise* (Antwerp, 1895), and article "Ortelius" in *Biographie nationale* (Belgian), vol. xvi. (Brussels, 1901); J. H. Hessels, *Abrahami Ortelii epistulae* (Cambridge, England, 1887); Max Rooses, *Ortelius et Plantin* (1880); Génard, "Généalogie d'Ortelius," in the *Bulletin de la Soc. roy. de Géog. d'Anvers* (1880 and 1881).   (C. R. B.)

ORTHEZ, a town of south-western France, capital of an arrondissement in the department of Basses-Pyrénées, 25 m. N.W. of Pau on the Southern railway to Bayonne. Pop. (1906) town 4159; commune 6254. It is finely situated on the right bank of the Gave de Pau which is crossed at this point by a bridge of the 14th century, having four arches and surmounted at its centre by a tower. Several old houses, and a church of the 12th, 14th and 15th centuries are of some interest, but the most remarkable building is the Tour de Moncade, a pentagonal tower of the 13th century, once the keep of a castle of the viscounts of Béarn, and now used as a meteorological observatory. A building of the 16th century is all that remains of the old Calvinist university (see below). The hôtel de ville is a modern building containing the library.

Orthez has a tribunal of first instance and is the seat of a subprefect. The spinning and weaving of cotton, especially of the fabric called *toile de Béarn*, flour-milling, the manufacture of paper and of leather, and the preparation of hams known as *jambons de Bayonne* and of other delicacies are among its industries. There are quarries of stone and marble in the neighbourhood, and the town has a thriving trade in leather, hams and lime.

At the end of the 11th century Orthez passed from the possession of the viscounts of Dax to that of the viscounts of Béarn, whose chief place of residence it became in the 13th century. Froissart records the splendour of the court of Orthez under Gaston Phoebus in the latter half of the 14th century. Jeanne d'Albret founded a Calvinist university in the town and Theodore Beza taught there for some time. An envoy sent in 1569 by Charles IX. to revive the Catholic faith had to stand a siege in Orthez which was eventually taken by assault by the Protestant captain, Gabriel, count of Montgomery. In 1684 Nicholas Foucault, intendant under Louis XIV., was more successful, as the inhabitants, ostensibly at least, renounced Protestantism, which is nevertheless still strong in the town. In 1814 the duke of Wellington defeated Marshal Soult on the hills to the north of Orthez.

ORTHOCLASE, an important rock-forming mineral belonging to the felspar group (see FELSPAR). It is a potash-felspar, $KAlSi_3O_8$, and crystallizes in the monoclinic system. Large and distinctly developed crystals are frequently found in the drusy cavities of granites and pegmatites. Crystals differ somewhat in habit; for example, they may be prismatic with an orthorhombic aspect (fig. 1), as in the variety adularia (from the Adular Mountains in the St Gotthard region); or tabular (fig. 2); being flattened parallel to the clino-pinacoid or plane of symmetry b (010), as in the variety sanidine (σάνίς, σανίδος, a board); or again the crystals may be elongated in the direction of the edge between b and the basal plane c (001), which is a characteristic habit of orthoclase from the granite quarries at Baveno in Italy. Twinning is frequent, and there are three well-defined twin-laws: (1) *Carlsbad twins* (fig. 4). Here the two individuals of the twin interpenetrate or are united parallel to the clino-

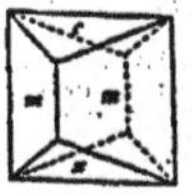

FIG. 1. 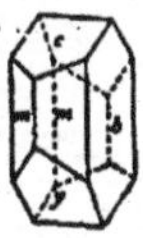   FIG. 2. 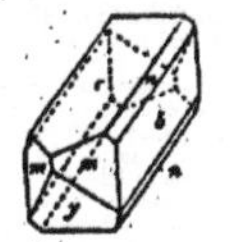   FIG. 3.

pinacoid: one individual may be brought into the position of the other by a rotation of 180° about the vertical crystallographic axis or prism-edge. Such twinned crystals are found at Carlsbad in Bohemia and many other places. (2) *Baveno twins* (fig. 5). These twins, in which n (021) is the twin-plane, are common at Baveno. (3) *Manebach twins* (fig. 6). The twin-plane here is c (001); examples of this rarer twin were first found at Manebach in Thuringia.

An important character of orthoclase is the cleavage. There is a direction of perfect cleavage parallel to the basal plane c, on which plane the lustre is consequently often pearly; and one less highly developed parallel to the plane of symmetry b.

The angle between these two cleavages is 90°, hence the name orthoclase (from the Gr. ὀρθός, right, and κλάω, to break), given by A. Breithaupt in 1823, who was the first to distinguish orthoclase from the other felspars. There are also imperfect cleavages parallel to the faces of the prism *m* (110).

The hardness is 6, and the sp. gr. 2·56. Crystals are sometimes colourless and transparent with a glassy aspect, as in the varieties adularia, sanidine and the rhyacolite of Monte Somma, Vesuvius.

The optical characters are somewhat variable, the plane of the optic axes being perpendicular to the plane of symmetry in

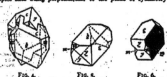

FIG. 4.   FIG. 5.   FIG. 6.
Twinned Crystals of Orthoclase.

some crystals and parallel to it in others; further, when some crystals are heated, the optic axes gradually change from one position to the other. In all cases, however, the acute negative bisectrix of the optic axes lies in the plane of symmetry and is inclined to the edge *b/c* at 5-7°, or, in varieties rich in soda, at 10-12°. The mean refractive index is 1·524, and the double refraction is weak (0·006).

Analyses of orthoclase usually prove the presence of small amounts of soda and lime in addition to potash. These constituents are, however, probably present as plagioclase (albite and oligoclase) intergrown with the orthoclase. The two minerals are interlaminated parallel to the ortho-pinacoid (100) or the pinacoid (801), and they may readily be distinguished in the flesh-red aventurine-felspar, known as perthite, from Perth in Lanark county, Ontario. Frequently, however, as in microperthite and cryptoperthite, this is on a microscopic scale or so minute as to be no longer recognizable. These directions (100) and (801) are planes of parting in orthoclase, and along them alteration frequently takes place, giving rise to *schiller* effects. Moon-stone (*q.v.*) shows a pearly opalescent reflection on these planes; and brilliant coloured reflections in the same directions are exhibited by the labradorescent orthoclase from the augite-syenite of Fredriksvärn and Laurvik in southern Norway, which is much used as an ornamental stone. The same effect is shown to a lesser degree by murchisonite, named in honour of Sir R.I. Murchison, from the Triassic conglomerate of Heavitree near Exeter.

Orthoclase forms an essential constituent of many acidic igneous rocks (granite, syenite, porphyry, trachyte, phonolite, &c.) and of crystalline schists and gneisses. In porphyries and in some granites (*e.g.* those of Shap in Westmorland, Cornwall, &c.) it occurs as embedded crystals with well-defined outlines, but usually it presents no crystalline form. In the trachyte of the Drachenfels and the Laacher See in Rhenish Prussia there are large porphyritic crystals of glassy sanidine. The best crystals are those found in the crystallined cavities and veins of granites, pegmatites and gneisses, for example, at Baveno and Elba in Italy, Alabashka near Mursinka in the Urals, Hirschberg in Silesia, Tanokami-yama in the province Omi, Japan, and the Mourne Mountains in Ireland. As a mineral of secondary origin orthoclase is sometimes found in cavities in basaltic rocks, and its occurrence in metalliferous mineral-veins has been observed. It has been formed artificially in the laboratory and is sometimes met with in furnace products.

The commonest alteration product of orthoclase is kaolin (*q.v.*); the frequent cloudiness or opacity of crystals is often due to partial alteration to kaolin. Mica and epidote also result by the alteration of orthoclase.   (L. J. S.)

ORTHODOX EASTERN CHURCH (frequently spoken of as " the Greek Church," and described officially as " The Holy Orthodox[1]

[1] The Orthodox Eastern Church has always laid especial stress upon the unchanging tradition of the faith, and has claimed orthodoxy as its especial characteristic. The " Feast of Orthodoxy " (ἡ κυριακὴ τῆς ὀρθοδοξίας), celebrated annually on the first Sunday of the Greek Lent, was founded in honour of the restoration of the

Catholic Apostolic Eastern Church "), the historical representative of the churches of the ancient East. It consists of (*a*) those churches which have accepted all the decrees of the first seven general councils, and have remained in full communion with one another, (*b*) such churches as have derived their origin from these by missionary activity, or by abscission without loss of communion. The Eastern Church is both the source and background of the Western. Christianity arose in the East, and Greek was the language of the Scriptures and early services of the church, but when Latin Christianity established itself in Europe and Africa, and when the old Roman empire fell in two, and the eastern half became separate in government, interests and ideas from the western, the term Greek or Eastern Church acquired gradually a fixed meaning. It denoted the church which included the patriarchates of Antioch, Alexandria, Jerusalem and Constantinople, and their dependencies. The ecclesiastical division of the early church, at least within the empire, was based upon the civil. Constantine introduced a new partition of the empire into dioceses, and the church adopted a similar division. The bishop of the chief city in each diocese naturally rose to a pre-eminence, and was commonly called *exarch*—a title borrowed from the civil jurisdiction. In process of time the common title *patriarch* was restricted to the most eminent of these exarchs, and councils decided who were worthy of the dignity. The council of Nicaea recognized three patriarchs—the bishops of Rome, Alexandria and Antioch To these were afterwards added the bishops of Constantinople and Jerusalem. When the empire was divided, there was one patriarch in the West; the bishop of Rome, while in the East there were at first two, then four and latterly five. This geographical fact has had a great deal to do in determining the character of the Eastern Church. It is not a despotic monarchy governed from one centre and by a monarch in whom plenitude of power resides. It is an oligarchy of patriarchs. It is based, of course, on the great body of bishops; but episcopal rule, through the various grades of metropolitan, primate, exarch, attains to sovereignty only in the five patriarchal thrones. Each patriarch is, within his diocese, what the Gallican theory makes the pope in the universal church. He is supreme, and not amenable to any of his brother patriarchs, but is within the jurisdiction of an oecumenical synod. This makes the Eastern Church quite distinct in government and traditions of polity from the Western. It has ever been the policy of Rome to efface national distinctions; but under the shadow of the Eastern Church national churches have grown and flourished. Revolts against Rome have always implied a repudiation of the ruling principles of the papal system; but the schismatic churches of the East have always reproduced the ecclesiastical polity of the church from which they seceded.

The Greek Church, like the Roman, soon spread far beyond the imperial dioceses which at first fixed its boundaries, but it was far less successful than the Roman in preserving its conquests for Christianity. This was due in the main to the differing quality of the forces by which the area covered by the two churches was respectively invaded. The northern barbarians by whom the Western empire was overrun had long stood in awe of the power and the civilization of Rome, which they recognized as superior; the conquerors were thus predisposed to enter into the heritage of the law and the religion of the conquered empire and, whether they were pagans or Arian heretics, became in the end Catholic Christians. In the East it was otherwise. The empire maintained itself long, and died hard; but its decline and fall meant not only the overthrow of the emperors of the East, but largely that of the civilization and Christianity which they represented. The Arabs, and after them the Turks, attacked the empire as the armed missionaries of what they regarded as a superior religion; Christianity survived in the vast territories they

Holy Images to the churches after the downfall of Iconoclasm (February 19, 842); but it has gradually assumed a wider significance as the celebration of victory over all heresies, and is now one of the most characteristic festivals of the Eastern Church.

conquered only as a despised and tolerated superstition, its ecclesiastical organization only as a convenient mechanism for governing a subject and tributary population. It is true that the Eastern Church made up in some sort for her losses by missionary conquests elsewhere. Greek Christianity became the religion of the Slavs as Latin Christianity became that of the Germans; but the Orthodox Church never conquered her conquerors, and the historian is too apt to enlarge on her past glories and forget her present strength.

Early History.—The early history of the Eastern Church is outlined in the article CHURCH HISTORY. Here it is proposed only to give in somewhat more detail the causes of division which led (1) to the formation of the schismatic churches of the East, and (2) to the open rupture with Latin Christianity.

The great dogmatic work of the Eastern Church was the definition of that portion of the creed of Christendom which concerns *theology proper*—the doctrines of the essential nature of the Godhead, and the doctrine of the Godhead in relation with manhood in the incarnation, while it fell to the Western Church to define *anthropology*, or the doctrine of man's nature and needs. The controversies which concern us are all related to the person of Christ, the Theanthropos, for they alone are represented in the schismatic churches of the East. These controversies will be best described by reference to the oecumenical councils of the ancient and undivided church.

Controversies and schisms.

All the churches of the East, schismatic as well as orthodox, accept unreservedly the decrees of the first two councils. The schismatic churches protest against the additions made to the creeds of Nicaea and Constantinople by succeeding councils. The Nicaeo-Constantinopolitan creed declared that Christ was *consubstantial* (ὁμοούσιος) with the Father, and that He *had become man* (ἐνανθρωπήσας). Disputes arose when theologians tried to explain the latter phrase. These differences took two separate and extreme types, the one of which forcibly separated the two natures so as to deny anything like a real union, while the other insisted upon a mixture of the two, or an absorption of the human in the divine. The former was the creed of Chaldaea and the latter the creed of Egypt; Chaldaea was the home of Nestorianism, Egypt the land of Monophysitism. The Nestorians accept the decisions of the first two councils, and reject the decrees of all the rest as unwarranted alterations of the creed of Nicaea. The Monophysites accept the first three councils, but reject the decree of Chalcedon and all that come after it.

The council of Ephesus (A.D. 431), the third oecumenical, had insisted upon applying the term Theotokos to the Virgin Mary, and this was repeated in the symbol of Chalcedon, which says that Christ was born of the Virgin Mary, the Theotokos, " according to the manhood." The same symbol also declares that Christ is " to be acknowledged in two natures . . . indivisibly and inseparably." Hence the Nestorians, who insisted upon the duality of the natures to such a degree as to lose sight of the unity of the person, and who rejected the term Theotokos, repudiated the decrees both of Ephesus and of Chalcedon, and upon the promulgation of the decrees of Chalcedon formally separated from the church. Nestorianism had sprung from an exaggeration of the theology of the school of Antioch, and the schism weakened that patriarchate and its dependencies. It took root in Chaldaea, and became very powerful. No small part of the literature and science of the Mahommedan Arabs came from Nestorian teachers, and Nestorian Christianity spread far and wide through Asia (see NESTORIUS and NESTORIANS).

The council of Chalcedon (451), the fourth oecumenical, declared that Christ is to be acknowledged " in two natures—unconfusedly, unchangeably," and therefore decided against the opinions of all who either believed that the divinity is the sole nature of Christ, or who, rejecting this, taught only one composite nature of Christ (one nature and one person, instead of two natures and one person). The advocates of the one nature theory were called Monophysites (q.v.), and they gave rise to numerous sects, and to at least three separate national

churches—the Jacobites of Syria, the Copts of Egypt and the Abyssinian Church, which are treated under separate headings.

The decisions of Chalcedon, which were the occasion of the formation of all these sects outside, did not put an end to Christological controversy inside the Orthodox Greek Church. The most prominent question which emerged in attempting to define further the person of Christ was whether the will belonged to the nature or the person, or, as it came to be stated, whether Christ had two wills or only one. The church in the sixth oecumenical council at Constantinople (680) declared that Christ had two wills. The Monothelites (q.v.) refused to submit, and the result was the formation of another schismatic church—the Maronite Church of the Lebanon range. The Maronites, however, were reconciled to Rome in the 12th century, and are reckoned as Roman Catholics of the Oriental Rite.

Later History.—The relation of the Byzantine Church to the Roman may be described as one of growing estrangement from the 5th to the 11th century, and a series of abortive attempts at reconciliation since the latter date. The estrangement and final rupture may be traced to the increasing claims of the Roman bishops and to Western innovations in practice and in the doctrine of the Holy Spirit, accompanied by an alteration of creed. In the early church three bishops stood forth prominently, principally from the political eminence of the cities in which they ruled—the bishops of Rome, Alexandria and Antioch. The transfer of the seat of empire from Rome to Constantinople gave the bishops of Rome a possible rival in the patriarch of Constantinople, but the absence of an overawing court and of meddling statesmen did more than recoup the loss to the head of the Roman Church. The theological calmness of the West, amid the violent theological disputes which troubled the Eastern patriarchates, and the statesmanlike wisdom of Rome's greater bishops, combined to give a unique position to the pope, which councils in vain strove to shake, and which in time of difficulty the Eastern patriarchs were fain to acknowledge and make use of, however they might protest against it and the conclusions deduced from it. But this pre-eminence, or rather the Roman idea of what was involved in it, was never acknowledged in the East; to press it upon the Eastern patriarchs was to prepare the way for separation, to insist upon it in times of irritation was to cause a schism. The theological genius of the East was different from that of the West. The Eastern theology had its roots in Greek philosophy, while a great deal of Western theology was based on Roman law. The Greek fathers succeeded the Sophists, the Latin theologians succeeded the Roman advocates (Stanley's *Eastern Church*, ch. i.). This gave rise to misunderstandings, and at last led to two widely separate ways of regarding and defining one important doctrine—the procession of the Holy Spirit from the Father or from the Father and the Son. Political jealousies and interests intensified the disputes, and at last, after many premonitory symptoms, the final break came in 1054, when Pope Leo IX. smote Michael Cerularius and the whole of the Eastern Church with an excommunication. There had been mutual excommunications before, but they had not resulted in permanent schism. Now, however, the separation was final, and the ostensible cause of its finality was the introduction by the Latins of two words *Filioque* into the creed.[1] It is this addition which was and which still remains the permanent cause of separation. Ffoulkes has pointed out in his second volume (ch. 1-3) that there was a resumption of intercourse more than once between Rome and Constantinople after 1054, and that the overbearing character of the Norman crusaders, and finally the horrors of the sack of Constantinople in the fourth crusade

Conflict with Rome.

[1] After the words " and in the Holy Ghost " of the Apostles' Creed the Constantinopolitan creed added " who proceedeth from the Father." The Roman Church, without the sanction of an oecumenical council and without consulting the Easterns, added " and the Son." The addition was first made at Toledo (589) in opposition to Arianism. The Easterns also resented the Roman enforcement of clerical celibacy, the limitation of the right of confirmation to the bishop and the use of unleavened bread in the Eucharist.

(1204), were the real causes of the permanent estrangement. It is undeniable, however, that the *Filioque* question has always come up to bar the way in any subsequent attempts at inter-communion. The theological question involved is a very small one, but it brings out clearly the opposing characteristics of Eastern and Western theology, and so has acquired an importance far beyond its own worth. The question is really one about the relations subsisting between the persons of the Trinity and their hypostatical properties. The Western Church affirms that the Holy Spirit "proceeds from" the Father and from the Son. It believes that the Spirit of the Father must be the Spirit of the Son also. Such a theory seems alone able to satisfy the practical instincts of the West, which did not concern itself with the metaphysical aspect of the Trinity, but with Godhead in its relation to redeemed humanity. The Eastern Church affirms that the Holy Spirit proceeds from the Father only, and takes its stand on John xv. 26. The Eastern theologian thinks that the Western double procession degrades the Deity and destroys the perfection of the Trinity. The double procession, in his eyes, means two active principles (ἀρχαί) in the Deity, and it means also that there is a confusion between the hypostatical properties; a property possessed by the Father and distinctive of the First Person is attributed also to the Second. This is the theological, and there is conjoined with it an historical and moral dispute. The Easterns allege that the addition of the words *Filioque* was made, not only without authority, and therefore unwarrantably, but also for the purpose of forcing a rupture between East and West in the interests of the barbarian empire of the West.

Attempts at reconciliation were made from time to time afterwards, but were always wrecked on the two points of papal supremacy, when it meant the right to impose Western usages upon the East, and of the addition to the creed. First there was the negotiation between Pope Gregory IX. (1227–1241) and Germanus, patriarch of Constantinople. The Roman conditions were practically recognition of papal jurisdiction, the use of unleavened bread and permission to omit *Filioque* if all books written against the Western doctrine were burnt. The patriarch refused the terms. Then, later in the 13th century, came negotiations under Innocent IV. and Clement IV., in which the popes proposed the same conditions as Gregory IX., with additions. These proposals were rejected by the Easterns, who regarded them as attempts to enforce new creeds on their church.

The negotiations at the council of Lyons (1274) were, strictly speaking, between the pope and the Byzantine emperor, and were more political than ecclesiastical. Michael Palaeologus ruled in Constantinople while Baldwin II., the last of the Latin emperors, was an exile in Europe. Palaeologus wished the pope to acknowledge his title to be emperor of the East, and in return promised submission to the papal supremacy and the union of the two churches on the pope's own terms. This enforced union lasted only during the lifetime of the emperor. The only other attempt at union which requires to be mentioned is that made at the council of Florence. It was really suggested by the political weakness of the Byzantine empire and the dread of the approach of the Turks. John Palaeologus the emperor, Joseph the patriarch of Constantinople, and several Eastern bishops came to Italy and appeared at the council of Florence—the papal council, the rival of that of the council of Basel. As on former occasions the representatives of the East were at first deceived by false representations; they were betrayed into recognition of papal supremacy, and tricked into signing what could afterwards be represented as a submission to Western doctrine. The natural consequences followed—a repudiation of what had been done; and the Eastern bishops on their way home took care to make emphatic their ritualistic differences from Rome. Soon after came the fall of Constantinople, and with this event an end to the political reasons for the submission of the Orthodox clergy. Rome's schemes for a union which meant an unconditional submission on the part of the Orthodox Church did not cease, however, but they were no

longer attempted on a grand scale. Jesuit missionaries after the Reformation stirred up schisms in some parts of the Eastern Church, and in Austria, Poland and elsewhere large numbers of Orthodox Christians submitted, either willingly or under compulsion to the see of Rome (see ROMAN CATHOLIC CHURCH, section *Uniat Oriental Churches*).

Doctrines and Creeds.—The Eastern Church has no creeds in the modern Western use of the word, no *normative* summaries of what must be believed. It has preserved the older idea that a creed is an adoring confession of the church engaged in worship; and, when occasion called for more, the belief of the church was expressed more by way of public testimony than in symbolical books. Still the doctrines of the church can be gathered from these confessions of faith. The Eastern creeds may thus be roughly placed in two classes—the oecumenical creeds of the early undivided church, and later testimonies defining the position of the Orthodox Church of the East with regard to the belief of the Roman Catholic and of Protestant Churches. These testimonies were called forth mainly by the protest of Greek theologians against Jesuitism on the one hand, and against the reforming tendencies of the patriarch Cyril Lucaris on the other. The Orthodox Greek Church adopts the doctrinal decisions of the seven oecumenical councils, together with the canons of the Concilium Quinisextum or second Trullan council (692); and they further hold that all these definitions and canons are simply explanations and enforcements of the Nicaeo-Constantinopolitan creed and the decrees of the first council of Nicaea. The first four councils settled the orthodox faith on the doctrines of the Trinity and of the Incarnation; the fifth supplemented the decisions of the first four. The sixth declared against Monothelitism; the seventh sanctioned the worship (δουλεία, not ἀληθινὴ λατρεία) of images; the council held in the Trullus (a saloon in the palace at Constantinople) supplemented by canons of discipline the doctrinal decrees of the fifth and sixth councils.

The Reformation of the 16th century was not without effect on the Eastern Church. Some of the Reformers, notably Melanchthon, expected to effect a reunion of Christendom by means of the Easterns, cherishing the same hopes as the modern Old Catholic divines and their English sympathisers. Melanchthon himself sent a Greek translation of the Augsburg Confession to Joasaph, patriarch of Constantinople, and some years afterwards Jacob Andreae and Martin Crusius began a correspondence with Jeremiah, patriarch of Constantinople, in which they asked an official expression of his opinions about Lutheran doctrine. The result was that Jeremiah answered in his *Censura Orientalis Ecclesiae* condemning the distinctive principles of Lutheranism.

The reformatory movement of Cyrillos Lucaris (φ.ν.), patriarch of Constantinople (1621), brought the Greek Church face to face with Reformation theology. Cyril conceived the plan of reforming the Eastern Church by bringing its doctrines into harmony with those of Calvinism, and by sending able young Greek theologians to Switzerland, Holland and England to study Protestant theology. His scheme of reform was opposed chiefly by the intrigues of the Jesuits, who in the end brought about his death. The church anathematized his doctrines; and in its later testimonies repudiated his confession on the one hand and Jesuit ideas on the other. The most important of these testimonies are (1) the Orthodox confession or catechism of Peter Mogilas, confirmed by the Eastern patriarchs and by the synod of Jerusalem (1643); and (2) the decree of the synod of Jerusalem or the confession of Dositheus (1672). Besides these, the catechisms of the Russian Church should be consulted, especially the catechism of Philaret, which since 1839 has been used in all the churches and schools in Russia. Founding on these doctrinal sources the teaching of the Orthodox Eastern Church is [1]:—

---

[1] This summary has been taken, with corrections, from G. B. Winer, *Comparative Darstellung des Lehrbegriffs der verschiedenen Kirchenparteien* (Leipzig, 1824, Eng. tr., Edin., 1873). Small capitals denote differences from Roman Catholic, italics differences from Protestant doctrine.

Christianity is a Divine revelation communicated to mankind through Christ; its saving truths are to be learned from the Bible *and tradition*, the former having been written, *and the latter maintained uncorrupted through the influence of the Holy Spirit; the interpretation of the Bible belongs to the Church, which is taught by the Holy Spirit,* but every believer may read the Scriptures.

According to the Christian revelation, God is a Trinity, that is, the Divine Essence exists in Three Persons, perfectly equal in nature and dignity, the Father, the Son and the Holy Ghost; THE HOLY GHOST PROCEEDS FROM THE FATHER ONLY. Besides the Triune God there is no other object of divine worship, *but homage (ὑπερδουλία) may be paid to the Virgin Mary, and reverence (δουλία) to the saints and to their pictures and relics.*

Man is born with a corrupt bias which was not his at creation; the first man, when created, possessed IMMORTALITY, PERFECT WISDOM, AND A WILL REGULATED BY REASON. Through the first sin Adam and his posterity lost IMMORTALITY, AND HIS WILL RECEIVED A BIAS TOWARDS EVIL. In this natural state man, who even before he actually sins is a sinner before God by original or inherited sin, commits manifold actual transgressions; *but he is not absolutely without power of will towards good, and is not always doing evil.*

Christ, the Son of God, became man in two natures, which internally and inseparably united make One Person, and, according to the eternal purpose of God, has obtained for man reconciliation with God, and eternal life, inasmuch as He by His vicarious death has made satisfaction to God for the world's sins, and this satisfaction was PERFECTLY COMMENSURATE WITH THE SINS OF THE WORLD. Man is made partaker of reconciliation in spiritual regeneration, which he attains to, being led and kept by the Holy Ghost. This divine help is offered *to all men without distinction, and may be rejected.* In order to attain to salvation, man is justified, and when so justified CAN DO NO MORE THAN THE COMMANDS OF GOD. He may fall from a state of grace through mortal sin.

Regeneration is offered by the word of God and in the sacraments, *which under visible signs communicate God's invisible grace to Christians when administered cum intentione.* There are *seven* mysteries or sacraments. Baptism *entirely destroys* original sin. In the Eucharist *the true body and blood of Christ are substantially present, and the elements are changed into the substance of Christ, whose body and blood are corporeally partaken of by communicants.* ALL Christians should receive the bread and the WINE. *The Eucharist is also an expiatory sacrifice.* The new birth when lost may be restored through repentance, which is not merely (1) sincere sorrow, but also (2) *confession of each individual sin to the priest,* and (3) *the discharge of penances imposed by the priest for the removal of the temporal punishment which may have been imposed by God and the Church.* Penance accompanied by the judicial absolution of the priest makes a *true sacrament.*

The Church of Christ is the fellowship of ALL THOSE WHO ACCEPT AND PROFESS ALL THE ARTICLES OF FAITH TRANSMITTED BY THE APOSTLES AND APPROVED BY GENERAL SYNODS. *Without this visible Church there is no salvation.* It is under the abiding influence of the Holy Ghost, and *therefore cannot err in matters of faith.* Specially appointed persons are necessary in the service of the Church, *and they form a threefold order, distinct jure divino from other Christians, of Bishops, Priests and Deacons.* THE FOUR PATRIARCHS, OF EQUAL DIGNITY, HAVE THE HIGHEST RANK AMONG THE BISHOPS, AND THE BISHOPS *united in a General Council represent the Church and infallibly decide,* under the guidance of the Holy Ghost, all matters of faith and ecclesiastical life. All ministers of Christ must be regularly called and appointed to their office, and are consecrated *by the sacrament of orders. Bishops must be unmarried,* and PRIESTS AND DEACONS MUST NOT CONTRACT A SECOND MARRIAGE. To all priests in common belongs, besides the preaching of the word, the administration of the SIX SACRAMENTS—BAPTISM, CONFIRMATION, PENANCE, EUCHARIST, MATRIMONY, UNCTION OF THE SICK. The bishops alone can administer the sacrament of orders. *Ecclesiastical ceremonies are part of the divine service; most of them have apostolic origin; and those connected with the sacrament must not be omitted by priests under pain of mortal sin.*

Liturgy and Worship.—The ancient liturgies of the Eastern Church were very numerous, and have been frequently classified. J. M. Neale makes three divisions—the liturgy of Jerusalem or of St James, that of Alexandria or of St Mark, and that of Edessa or of St Thaddaeus; and Daniel substantially agrees with him. The same passion for uniformity which suppressed the Gallican and Mozarabic liturgies in the West led to the almost exclusive use of the liturgy of St James in the East. It is used in two forms, a shorter revised by Chrysostom, and a longer called the liturgy of St Basil. This liturgy and the service generally are either in Old Greek or in Old Slavonic, and frequent disputes have arisen in particular districts about the language to be employed. Both sacred languages differ from the language of the people, but it cannot be said that in

the Eastern Church worship is conducted in an unknown tongue —"the actual difference," says Neale, "may be about that between Chaucer's English and our own." There are eleven chief service books, and no such compendium as the Roman breviary. Fasting is frequent and severe. Besides Wednesdays and Fridays, there are four fasting seasons, Lent, Pentecost to SS. Peter and Paul, August 1-15 preceding the Feast of the Sleep of the Theotokos, and the six weeks before Christmas. Indulgences are not recognized; an intermediate and purificatory state of the dead is held but not systematized into a doctrine of purgatory. The Virgin receives homage, but the dogma of her Immaculate Conception is not admitted. While ikons of the saints are found in the churches there is no "graven image" apart from the crucifix. There is plenty of singing but no instrumental music. Prayer is offered standing towards the East; at Pentecost, kneeling. The celebration of the Eucharist is an elaborate symbolical representation of the Passion. The consecrated bread is broken into the wine, and both elements are given together in a spoon.

The ritual generally is as magnificent as in the West, but of a more archaic type. (For the liturgical dress see VESTMENTS and subsidiary articles.)

Monastic Life.—Monasticism is, as it has always been, an important feature in the Eastern Church. An Orthodox monastery is perhaps the most perfect extant relic of the 4th century. The simple idea that possesses the monks is that of fleeing the world; they have no distinctions of orders, and though they follow the rule of St Basil object to being called Basilians. A few monasteries (Mt Sinai and some on Lebanon) follow the rule of St Anthony. K. Lake in *Early Days of Monasticism on Mount Athos* (1909) traces the development through three well-defined stages in the 9th and 10th centuries— (a) the hermit period, (b) the loose organization of hermits in lauras, (c) the stricter rule of the monastery, with definite buildings and fixed rules under an ἡγούμενος or abbot. The monasteries now have taken over the name lauras. They are under the jurisdiction of the metropolitan; a few of the most important deal direct with the patriarch and are called *Stauropegia*. The convent on Mt Sinai is absolutely independent. Apart from hermits there are (1) κοινοβιακοί, monks who possess nothing, live and eat together, and have definite tasks given them by their superiors; (2) ἰδιορυθμοί, monks who live apart from each other, each receiving from the monastery fuel, vegetables, cheese, wine and a little money. They only meet for the Divine Office and on great feasts, and are the real successors of the laura system. The most famous monasteries are those on Mount Athos; in 1902 there were twenty lauras with many dependent houses and 7522 monks there, mainly Russian and Greek. The monks are, for the most part, ignorant and unlettered, though in the dark days of Mahommedan persecution it was in the monasteries that Greek learning and the Greek nationality were largely preserved. Since priests *must* be married and bishops must *not,* only monks are eligible for appointment to bishoprics in the Eastern Church. See further, MONASTICISM.

The Branches of the Church.—In addition to the ancient churches which have separated themselves from the Orthodox faith, many have ceased to have an independent existence, owing either to the conquests of Islam or to their absorption by other churches. For example, the church of Mount Sinai may be regarded as all that survives of the ancient church of northern Arabia; the autocephalous Slavonic churches of Ipek and Okhrida, which derived their ultimate origin from the missions of Cyril and Methodius, were absorbed in the patriarchate of Constantinople in 1766 and 1767 respectively; and the Church of Georgia has been part of the Russian Church since 1801-1802. At the present day, then, the Orthodox Eastern Church consists of twelve mutually independent churches (or thirteen if we reckon the Bulgarian Church), using their own language in divine service (or some ancient form of it, as in Russia) and varying not a little in points of detail, but standing in full communion with one another, and united as equals in what has been described as one great ecclesiastical federation. However, in using such language it must be remembered that we are not dealing with bodies which were originally separated from one another and have now entered into fellowship, but with bodies which have grown naturally from a single origin and have not become estranged.

A. THE FOUR ANCIENT PATRIARCHATES

1. The Patriarchate of Constantinople or New Rome.—The ancient patriarchate of Constantinople included the imperial dioceses of Pontus, Asia, Thrace and Eastern Illyricum—i.e. speaking roughly, the greater part of Asia Minor, European Turkey, and Greece, with a small portion of Austria. The imperial diocese of Pontus was governed by the exarch of Caesarea, who ruled over thirteen metropolitans with more than 100 suffragans. Asia was governed by the exarch of Ephesus, who ruled over twelve metropolitans with more than 350 suffragan bishops. In Asia Minor the church maintains but a small remnant of her former greatness; in Europe it is otherwise. The old outlines, however, are effaced wherever the Christian races have emancipated themselves from the Turkish rule, and the national churches of Greece, Servia and Rumania have re-organized themselves on a new basis. Where the Turkish rule still prevails the church retains her old organization, but greatly impaired. Still, the Oecumenical Patriarch, as he has been called since early in the 6th century, is the most exalted ecclesiastic of the Eastern churches, and his influence reaches far outside the lands of the patriarchate. His jurisdiction extends over the dominions of the Sultan in Turkey, together with Asia Minor and the Turkish islands of the Aegean; there are eighty-two metropolitans under him, and the " monastic republic " of Mount Athos. He has great privileges and responsibilities as the recognized head of the Greek community in Turkey, and enjoys also many personal honours which have survived from the days of the Eastern emperors.

The patriarch under the old Ottoman system had his own court at Phanar, and his own prison, with a large civil jurisdiction over, and responsibility for, the Greek community. In ecclesiastical affairs he acts with two governing bodies—(a) a permanent Holy Synod ('Ιερά Σύνοδος, ἡ 'Ενδημοῦσα Κωνσταντινουπόλεως), consisting of twelve metropolitans, six of whom are re-elected every year from the whole number of metropolitans, arranged in three classes according to a fixed cycle; (b) the Permanent National Mixed Council (Διαρκὲς Ἐθνικὸν Μικτὸν Συμβούλιον), a remarkable assembly, which is at once the source of great power by introducing a strong lay element into the administration, and of a certain amount of weakness by its liability to sudden changes of popular feeling. It consists of four metropolitans, members of the Holy Synod, and eight laymen. All of these are chosen by an electoral body, consisting of all the members of the Holy Synod and the National Mixed Council, and twenty-five representatives of the parishes of Constantinople. The election of the patriarch is also, to a considerable extent, popular. An electoral assembly is formed for the purpose consisting of the twelve members of the Holy Synod, the eight lay members of the National Mixed Council, twenty-eight representatives of as many dioceses (the remaining dioceses having only the right to nominate a candidate by letter), ten representatives of the parishes of Constantinople, ten representatives of all persons who possess political rank, ten representatives of the Christian trades of Constantinople, the two representatives of the secretariat of the patriarchate, and such metropolitans, to the number of ten but not more, as happen to be in Constantinople at the time for some canonical reason (ἐνδημοῦντες). On the death or deposition of the patriarch, the Holy Synod and the National Mixed Council at once meet and elect a temporary substitute for the patriarch (Τοποτηρητής). Forty days afterwards the electoral assembly meets, under his presidency, and proceeds to make a list of twenty candidates (at the present day they must be metropolitans); who may be proposed either by the members of the electoral assembly or by any of the metropolitans of the patriarchate by letter. This list is sent to the sultan, who has by prescription the right to strike out five names. From the fifteen which remain the electoral assembly chooses three. These names are then submitted to the clerical members of the assembly, i.e. to the members of the Holy Synod and the ἐνδημοῦντες, who meet in church and, after the usual service, make the final selection. The patriarch-elect is presented to the Porte, which thereupon grants the berat or diploma of investiture and several customary presents; after which the new ruler is enthroned. The patriarch has the assistance and support of a large household, a survival from Byzantine times. Amongst them, actually or potentially, are the grand steward (μέγας οἰκονόμος), who serves him as deacon in the liturgy and presents candidates for orders; the grand visitor (μέγας σακελλάριος), who superintends the monasteries; the sacristan (σακελλίον); the chancellor (χαρτοφύλαξ), who superintends ecclesiastical causes; the deputy-visitor (ὁ τοῦ σακελλίου), who visits the nunneries; the protonotary (πρωτονοτάριος); the logothete (λογοθέτης), a most important lay officer, who represents the patriarch at the Porte and elsewhere outside; the censer-bearer, who seems to be also a kind of captain of the guard (ἀμνητίκων or ἀμνητίκαρος); the referendary (ῥεφερενδάριος); the secretary (ὑπομνηματογράφος); the chief syndic (πρωτέκδικος),

¹ The numbers have varied from time to time.

xx 6*

who is a judge of lesser causes; the recorder (ἱερομνήμων); and so on, down to the cleaners of the lamps (λαμπαδάριοι), the attendant of the lights (κηροστρογκάριος), and the bearer of the images (βαστάγιος) and of the holy ointment (μύρελαιος).

2. The Patriarchate of Alexandria, consisting of Egypt and its dependencies, was at one time the most powerful, as it was the most centralized, of all, and the patriarch still preserves his ancient titles of " pope " and " father of fathers, pastor of pastors, archpriest of archpriests, thirteenth apostle, and oecumenical judge." But the secession of the greater part of his church to Monophysitism [COPTIC CHURCH], and the Mahommedan conquest of Egypt, have left him but the shadow of his former greatness; and at the present time he has only the bishop of Libya under him, and rules over some 20,000 people at the outside, most of whom are settlers from elsewhere.

3. The Patriarchate of Antioch has undergone most changes in extent of jurisdiction, arising from the transfer of sees to Jerusalem, from the progress of the schismatic churches of the East and from the conquests of the Mahommedans. At the height of his power the patriarch of Antioch ruled over 12 metropolitans and 250 suffragan bishops. In the time of the first crusade 153 still survived; now there are scarcely 20, 14 of which are metropolitan sees. The patriarch, though he is " father of fathers and pastor of pastors," thus retains little of his old importance. His jurisdiction includes Cilicia, Syria (except Palestine) and Mesopotamia. Cyprus has been independent of Antioch since the council of Ephesus.

4. The Patriarchate of Jerusalem.—In the earlier period of the church, ecclesiastical followed civil divisions so closely that Jerusalem, in spite of the sacred associations connected with it, was merely an ordinary bishopric dependent on the metropolitan of Caesarea. Ambitious prelates had from time to time endeavoured to advance the pretensions of their see, but it was not until the council of Chalcedon, in 451, that Jerusalem was made a patriarchate with jurisdiction over Palestine. From this time on to the inroad of the Saracens the patriarchate of Jerusalem was highly prosperous. It ruled over three metropolitans with eighty suffragans. The modern patriarch has under his jurisdiction 5 archbishops and 5 bishops. The chief importance of the patriarchate is derived from the position of Jerusalem as a place of pilgrimage.

B. THE NINE NATIONAL CHURCHES

G. Finlay, in his History of Greece, has shown that there has been always a very close relation between the church and national life. Christianity from the first connected itself with the social organisation of the people, and therefore in every province assumed the language and the usages of the locality. In this way it was able to command at once individual attachment and universal power. This feeling died down to some extent when Constantine made use of the church to consolidate his empire. But it revived under the persecution of the Arian emperors. The struggle against Arianism was not merely a struggle for orthodoxy. Athanasius was really at the head of a national Greek party resisting the domination of a Latin-speaking court. From this time onwards Greek patriotism and Greek orthodoxy have been almost convertible terms, and this led naturally to revolts against Greek supremacy in the days of Justinian and other emperors. Dean Stanley was probably correct when he described the heretical churches of the East as the ancient national churches of Egypt, Syria, and Armenia in revolt against supposed innovations in the earlier faith imposed on them by Greek supremacy. In the East, as in Scotland, the history of the church is the key to the history of the nation, and in the freedom of the church the Greek saw the freedom and supremacy of his race. For this very reason Orthodox Eastern Christians of alien race felt compelled to resist Greek domination by means of independent ecclesiastical organisation, and the structure of the church rather favoured than interfered with the coexistence of separate national churches professing the same faith. Another circumstance favoured the creation of separate national churches. While the Greek empire lasted the emperors had a right of investiture on the election of a new patriarch, and this right was retained by the Turkish sultans after the conquest of Constantinople. The Russian people, for example, could not contemplate with calmness as the head of their church a bishop appointed by the hereditary enemy of their country. In this way the jealousies of race and the necessities of nations have produced various national churches which are independent or autocephalous and yet are one in doctrine.

1. The ancient Church of Cyprus (see CYPRUS, CHURCH OF).

2. The Church of Mount Sinai, consisting of little more than the famous monastery of St Catherine, under an archbishop who frequently resides in Egypt. It has, however, a few branch houses (μετόχια) in Turkey and Greece. The archbishop is chosen, from a list of candidates submitted by the monks of St Catherine, by the patriarch of Jerusalem and his Synod; and the patriarch consecrates him.

3. The Hellenic Church.—The constitution of the Church of Modern Greece is the result of the peculiar position of the patriarch of Constantinople. The war of liberation was sympathized in, not merely by the inhabitants of Greece, but by all the Greek-speaking Christians in the East. But the patriarch was in the hands of the Turks; he had been appointed by the sultan, and he was compelled by the Turkish authorities to ban the movement for freedom. When the Greeks achieved independence they refused to be subject ecclesiastically to a patriarch who was nominated by the sultan (June 9, 1828); and, to add to their difficulties, there were in the country twenty-two bishops who had been consecrated by the patriarch, twelve bishops who had been consecrated irregularly during the war, and about twenty bishops who had been deprived of their sees during the troubles—*i.e.* fifty-three bishops claimed to be provided for. In these circumstances the government and people resolved that there should be ten diocesan bishops and forty additional provisional sees. They also resolved that the church should be governed after the fashion of the Russian Church by a synod; and they decreed that the king of Greece was to be head of the church. All these ideas were carried out with some modifications, and gradually. The patriarch of Constantinople in 1850 acknowledged the independence of the church, which gradually grew to be more independent of the state. By the Greek constitution of 16th/28th November 1864 " the Orthodox Church of Greece remains indissolubly united, as regards dogmas, to the great Church of Constantinople, and to every other church professing the same doctrines, and, like these churches, it preserves in their integrity the apostolical constitutions and those of the councils of the Church, together with the holy traditions; it is αὐτοκέφαλος, it exercises its sovereign rights independently of every other church, and it is governed by a synod of bishops."

4. *The Servian Church.*—After the suppression of the Church of Ipek in 1766 Servia became ecclesiastically subject to Constantinople; but in 1830 the sultan permitted the Serbs to elect a patriarch (as a matter of fact he is merely styled metropolitan), subject to the confirmation of the patriarch of Constantinople. Eight years later the seat of ecclesiastical government was fixed at Belgrade; and when Servia gained its independence its church became autocephalous.

5. *The Rumanian Church.*—The fall of the church of Okhrida in 1767 had made Moldavia and Wallachia ecclesiastically subject to Constantinople. On the union of the two principalities under Alexander Couza (December 1861) the Church was declared autocephalous under a metropolitan at Bucharest; and the fact was recognized by the patriarchs, as it was in the case of Servia, after the treaty of Berlin had guaranteed their independence.

6. *The Church of Montenegro* has from early times been independent under its bishops, who from 1516 to 1851 were also the temporal rulers, under the title of Vladikas, or prince-bishops.

7. *The Orthodox Church in Austria-Hungary,* which, however, really consists of four independent sections: the Servians of Hungary and Croatia, under the patriarch of Karlowitz; the Rumanians of Transylvania, under the archbishop of Hermannstadt; the Ruthenians of Bukovina, under the metropolitan of Czernowitz; and the Serbs of Bosnia-Herzogovina, where there are four sees, that of Sarajevo holding the primacy.

8. *The Russian Church* dates from 992, when Prince Vladimir and his people accepted Christianity. The metropolitan, who was subject to the patriarch of Constantinople, resided at Kiev on the Dnieper. During the Tatar invasion the metropolis was destroyed, and Vladimir became the ecclesiastical capital. In 1320 the metropolitans fixed their seat at Moscow. In 1582 Jeremiah, patriarch of Constantinople, raised Job, 46th metropolitan, to the patriarchal dignity; and the act was afterwards confirmed by a general council of the East. In this way the Russian Church became autocephalous, and its patriarch had immense power. In 1700 Peter the Great forbade the election of a new patriarch, and in 1721 he established the Holy Governing Synod to supply the place of the patriarch. This body now governs the Russian Church, and consists of a procurator representing the emperor, the metropolitans of Kiev, Moscow and St Petersburg, the exarch of Georgia and five or six other bishops appointed by the emperor. There are moreover some 90 bishops and about 40 auxiliary bishops called vicars. There are 481 monasteries for men and 249 convents of nuns. The Church of Georgia, which has existed from a very early period, and was dependent first on the patriarch of Antioch and then on the patriarch of Constantinople, has since 1802 been incorporated in the Russian Church. Its head, the archbishop of Tiflis, bears the title of exarch of Georgia, and has under him four suffragans. A petition was presented to the emperor by the Georgians in 1904 asking for the restoration of their church and their language, but nothing came of it.

9. *The Bulgarian Church,* unless indeed it be classed with the separated churches. It differs from the national churches already mentioned in that it had its origin in a revolt of Turkish subjects against the patriarchal authority. From the earliest times the Bulgarians had occupied an anomalous position on the borders of Eastern and Western Christendom, but they had ultimately become subject to Constantinople. The revival of Bulgarian national feeling near the middle of the 19th century led to a movement for religious independence, the leaders of which were the archimandrite Neophit Bosveli and the bishop Ilarion Mikhailovsky. The Porte espoused the cause of the Bulgarians, partly to pacify them, but still more to strengthen its hold on all the Christians of Turkey by fostering their differences. Ultimately, on 28th February 1870, the sultan issued a firman constituting a new church, including all Bulgarians

who desired to join it within the vilayet of the Danube (*i.e.* the subsequently-formed principality of Bulgaria), and those of Adrianople, Salonica, Kossovo and Monastir (*i.e.* part of Macedonia, Eastern Rumelia and a tract farther south). The members of this Church were to constitute a *millet* or community, enjoying equal rights with the Greeks and Armenians; and its head, the Bulgarian exarch, was to reside at Constantinople. Naturally, this was resented by the patriarch Anthimus, who stigmatized the racial basis of the Bulgarian Church as the heresy of Phyletism. A local synod at Constantinople, in August 1872, pronounced it schismatical; Antioch, Alexandria and Greece followed suit; Jerusalem pronounced a modified condemnation; and the Servian and Rumanian churches avoided any definite expression of opinion. Russia was more favourable. It never actually acknowledged the Bulgarian Church, and Bulgarian prelates may not officiate publicly in Russian churches; on the other hand, the Holy Synod of Moscow refused to recognize the patriarch's condemnation, and Russian ecclesiastics have secretly supplied the Bulgarians with the holy oil. Above all, when Prince Boris, the heir-apparent of the principality, was received into the Bulgarian Church on 14th February 1896, the emperor of Russia was his godfather. The position is further complicated by the fact that many Bulgarians, both within and without the kingdom of Bulgaria, still remain subject to the patriarch. Nevertheless, the Bulgarian Church has made great headway both in Bulgaria itself and in Macedonia. The curious thing is that the Russian Church is in communion with both sides. The patriarch of Constantinople dares not excommunicate Russia, but the chief of its many grievances against that country is its patronage of the Bulgarian exarchate. The Bulgarians of course say they are not schismatics, but a national branch of the Greek Catholic, using their sacred right to manage their own affairs in their own way. They have never excommunicated the Patriarchists. On the whole it seems likely that the patriarch will ultimately have to yield, in spite of the strong Greek feeling against the Bulgars.[1]

Present Position of the Orthodox Church.—Although the signs of weakness which have characterized the past are still present, there are some indications of improvement. The encyclical on unity of Pope Leo XIII. (1895) called forth a reply from the patriarch Anthimus V. of Constantinople and his Synod, which was eminently learned, dignified and charitable.[2] The theological school of the patriarchate, at Halkí, is not undistinguished, and the university of Athens has a good record. Whilst the parochial clergy are still as unlearned as ever, there are not a few amongst the higher clergy who are distinguished for their learning beyond the limits of their own communion: for example, the metropolitan Ph. Bryennios, who discovered and edited the *Didachè*; the archbishop N. Kalogeras, who discovered and edited the second part of the commentary of Euthymius Zigabenus (d. *c.* 1118) on the New Testament; the archimandrite D. Latas, author of a valuable work on Christian archaeology (Athens, 1883); and the logothete S. Aristarchi, who edited a valuable collection of 83 newly discovered homilies of the patriarch Photius. This was published in 1900 at the Phanar press, erected as a memorial to Theodore of Tarsus, archbishop of Canterbury, by Greek and English churchmen, which was set up by the patriarch Constantine V. in 1899. An authorized version of the Scriptures in ancient Greek is also one of the works undertaken by this institution. On the other hand, the attempt made in 1901 by the Holy Synod at Athens, with the co-operation of Queen Olga of Greece (a Russian princess), to circulate a modern Greek version of the Gospels was resented as a symptom of a Pan-Slavist conspiracy, and led to an ebullition of popular feeling which could only be pacified by the withdrawal of the obnoxious version and the abdication of the metropolitan of Athens. The patriarch Constantine V. was deposed on the 12th of April 1901, and was succeeded on the 28th of May by Joachim III. (and V.), who had previously occupied the patriarchal throne from 1878 to 1884, when he was deposed through the ill-will of the Porte and banished to Mount Athos. His re-election had therefore no little importance. His progressive sympathies, illustrated by his proposals to reform the monasteries and the calendar, to modify the four long fasts and treat for union (especially with the Old Catholics), were not very well received, and in 1905 an attempt was made to depose him. The sultan Abd-ul-Hamid, to whom the different parties appealed,

[1] H. Brailsford in *Macedonia* (London, 1906) brings a crushing indictment against the Patriarchist party.
[2] For a different opinion see A. Fortescue, *The Orthodox Eastern Church*, 435 sqq.

lectured them on charity and concord! The patriarch's great rival was Joachim of Ephesus. Undoubtedly the question of the most pressing importance with regard to the future of Eastern Christendom is the relation between Russia and Constantinople. The Oecumenical Patriarch is, of course, officially the superior; but the Russian Church is numerically by far the greatest, and the tendency to regard Russia as the head, not only of the Slav races, but of all orthodox nations, inevitably reacts upon the church in the form of what has been called pan-Orthodoxy. The Russian Church is the only one which is in a position to display any missionary activity. It has been a powerful factor in the development of several of the churches already spoken of, especially those of Servia and Montenegro, which are usually very much subject to Russian influences ('Ρωσόφρονες or 'Ρωσόφιλοι). It has taken great interest in non-orthodox churches, such as those of Assyria, Abyssinia and Egypt. Above all, it has shown an increasing tendency to intervene in the affairs of the three lesser patriarchates.

In America the Russian archbishop, who resides in New York, has (on behalf of the Holy Synod) the oversight of some 152 churches and chapels in the United States, Alaska *Orthodox Church in America.* and Canada. He is assisted by two bishops, one for Alaska residing at Sitka, one for Orthodox Syrians residing in Brooklyn. There are 75 priests and 46,000 registered parishioners. The English language is increasingly used in the services. The increase of Orthodox communities has been very marked since 1888 owing to the immigration of Austrian Slavonians. Those of Greek nationality have churches in New Orleans, Chicago, New York, Boston, Lowell (Massachusetts) and other places. If, as seemed likely in 1910, in addition to the Russian and Syrian bishops, Greek and Servian ones were appointed, an independent synod could be formed, and the bishops could elect their own metropolitan. The total number of "Orthodox" Christians in North America is estimated at 300,000. Many of them were Austrian and Hungarian Uniats, who, after emigrating, have shown a tendency to separate from Rome and return to the Eastern Confession. One reason for this tendency is the attempt of the Roman Church to deprive the Uniats in America of their married priests.

The Catholic reaction represented by the Oxford movement in the Church of England early raised the question of a possible *The question of Anglican reunion.* union between the Anglican and Eastern Orthodox Churches. Into the history of the efforts to promote this end, which have never had any official sanction on the one side or the other, it is impossible to enter here. The obstacles would seem, indeed, to be insurmountable. From the point of view of Orthodoxy the English Church is schismatical, since it has seceded from the Roman patriarchate of the West, and doubly heretical, since it retains the obnoxious *Filioque* clause in the creed while rejecting many of the doctrines and practices held in common by Rome and the East; moreover, the Orthodox Church has never admitted the validity of Anglican orders, while not denying it. Union would clearly only be possible in the improbable event of the English Church surrendering most of the characteristic gains of the Reformation in order to ally herself with a body, the traditions of which are almost wholly alien to her own. At the same time, especially as against the universal claims of the papacy, the two churches have many interests and principles in common, and efforts to find a *modus vivendi* have not been wanting on either side. The question of union was, for instance, more than once discussed at the unofficial conferences connected with the Old Catholic movement (see OLD CATHOLICS). These and other discussions could have no definite result, but they led to an increase of good feeling and of personal intercourse. Thus, on the coronation of the emperor Nicholas II. of Russia in 1895, Dr Creighton, bishop of Peterborough, as representative of the English Church, was treated with peculiar distinction, and the compliment of his visit was returned by the presence of a high dignitary of the Russian Church at the service at St Paul's in London on the occasion of Queen Victoria's "diamond" jubilee in 1897. In 1890 there was further an interchange of courtesies between the archbishop of Canterbury and Constantine V., patriarch of Constantinople. To promote the "brotherly feeling between the members of the two churches," for which the patriarch expressed a desire, a committee was formed under the presidency of the Anglican bishop of Gibraltar.

On this question of reunion see A. Fortescue, *The Orthodox Eastern Church,* 257 sqq., 429 sqq.

AUTHORITIES.—For the origins of the Eastern Church and the early controversies see the authorities cited in the article CHURCH HISTORY. For the *Filioque* controversy, J. G. Walch, *Historia controversiae de Processu Spiritus Sancti* (Jena, 1751); E. S. Foulkes, *Historical Account of the Addition of Filioque to the Creed* (London, 1867); C. Adams, *Filioque* (Edinburgh, 1884); W. Norden, *Das Papsttum und Byzanz* (Berlin, 1903); also P. Schaff's *History of the Creeds of Christendom.* The following are devoted specially to the history and condition of the Eastern Church: M. le Quien, *Oriens Christianus* (Paris, 1740); J. S. Assemani, *Bibliotheca Orientalis* (Rome, 1719–1728); A. P. Stanley's *Eastern Church* (1861); J. M. Neale, *The Holy Eastern Church* (*General Introduction*, 2 vols.; *Patriarchate of Alexandria,* 2 vols.; and, published posthumously in 1873, *Patriarchate of Antioch*). For liturgy, see H. A. Daniel, *Codex Liturgicus Eccl. Univ. in epitomen redactus* (4 vols., 1847–1855); Leo Allatius, *De libris et rebus Eccles. Graecarum dissertationes*; F. E. Brightman, *Eastern Liturgies* (Oxford, 1896). For hymnology see Daniel, *Thesaurus Hymnologicus* (4 vols.); Neale's translations of *Eastern Hymns*; B. Pick, *Hymns and Poetry of the Eastern Church* (New York, 1908).

See also J. Pargoire, *L'Église Byzantine de 527 à 847* (Paris, 1905); I. Silbernagl, *Verfassung u. gegenwärtiger Bestand sämtlicher Kirchen des Orients* (1865; 2nd ed., Regensburg, 1904); W. F. Adeney, *The Greek and Eastern Churches* (Edinburgh, 1908); Adrian Fortescue, *The Orthodox Eastern Church* (London, 1907), with a full bibliography; F. G. Cole, *Mother of All Churches* (London, 1908); and M. Tamarati, *L'Église Géorgienne, des origines jusqu'à nos jours.* An interesting estimate of the Orthodox Church is given by A. Harnack in *What is Christianity?* For the festivals of the Greek Church see Mary Hamilton, *Greek Saints and their Festivals* (1910).

ORTHOGRAPHY (from Gr. ὀρθός, correct, right or straight, and γράφειν, to write), spelling which is correct according to accepted use. The word is also applied, in architecture, to the geometrical elevation of a building or of any part of one in which all the details are shown in correct relative proportion and drawn to scale. When the representation is taken through a building it is known as a section, and when portions of the structure only are drawn to a large scale they are called details.

ORTHONYX, the scientific name given in 1820, by C. J. Temminck, to a little bird, which, from the straightness of its claws—a character somewhat exaggerated by him—its large feet and spiny tail, he judged to be generically distinct from any other form. The typical species, *O. spinicauda,* is from south-eastern Australia, where it is very local in its distribution, and strictly terrestrial in its habits. It is rather larger than a skylark, coloured above not unlike a hedge-sparrow. The wings are, however, barred with white, and the chin, throat and breast are in the male pure white, but of a bright reddish-orange in the female. The remiges are very short, rounded and much incurved, showing a bird of weak flight. The rectrices are very broad, the shafts stiff, and towards the tip divested of barbs. *O. spaldingi* from Queensland is of much greater size than the type, and with a jet-black plumage, the throat being white in the male and orange-rufous in the female.

Orthonyx is a semi-terrestrial bird of weak flight, building a domed nest on or near the ground. Insects and larvae are its chief food, and the males are described as performing dancing antics like those of the lyre-bird (*q.v.*). Orthonyx belongs to the Oscines division of the *Passeres* and is placed in the family *Timeliidae.*   (A. N.)

ORTHOPTERA (Gr. ὀρθός, straight, and πτερόν, a wing), a term used in zoological classification for a large and important order of the class *Hexapoda.* The cockroaches, grasshoppers, crickets and other insects that are included in this order were first placed by C. Linné (1735) among the Coleoptera (beetles), and were later removed by him to the Hemiptera (bugs, &c.). J. C. Fabricius (1775) was the first to recognize the unnaturalness of these arrangements, and founded for the reception of the group an order Ulonata. In 1806 C. de Geer applied to these insects the name Dermaptera (δέρμα, a skin, and πτερόν); and A. G.

Olivier subsequently used for the assemblage the same Orthoptera, which is now much better known than the earlier terms. W. Kirby (1815) founded an order Dermaptera for the earwigs, which had formed part of de Geer's Dermaptera, accepting Olivier's term Orthoptera for the rest of the assemblage, and as modern research has shown that the earwigs undoubtedly deserve original separation from the cockroaches, grasshoppers, crickets, &c., this terminology will probably become established. W. E. Erichson and other writers added to the Orthoptera a number of families which Linné had included in his order, Neuroptera. These families are described and their affinities discussed in the articles NEUROPTERA and HEXAPODA. (q.v.). In the present article a short account of the characters of the Dermaptera and Orthoptera is given, while for details the reader is referred to special articles on the more interesting families or groups.

The Dermaptera and the Orthoptera agree in having well-developed mandibles, so that the jaws are adapted for biting; in the incomplete fusion of the second maxillae (which form the labium) so that the parts of a typical maxilla can be easily made out (see the description and figures of the cockroach's jaws under HEXAPODA); in the presence of a large number of excretory (Malpighian) tubes; in the firm texture of the forewings; in the presence of appendages (cerci) on the tenth abdominal segment; and in the absence of a metamorphosis, the young insect after hatching closely resembling the parent.

Order Dermaptera.

In addition to the characters just enumerated, the Dermaptera are distinguished by the presence of small but distinct maxillulae (fig. 2, see HEXAPODA, APTERA) in association with the tongue (hypopharynx); by the forewings when present being modified into short quadrangular elytra without nervuration, the complex hind-wings (fig. 1) being folded beneath these both longitudinally and transversely so that nearly the whole abdomen is left uncovered; and by the entirely mesodermal nature of the genital ducts, which,

From Carpenter's *Insects.* Dent & Co.

FIG. 1.—Common Earwig (*Forficula auricularia*). Male. Magnified.

FIG. 2.—Hypopharynx and Maxillulae (*m*) of common earwig (*Forficula auricularia*). Magnified about twenty-seven times.

according to the observations of F. Meinert, open to the exterior by a median aperture, the terminal part of the duct being single, either by the fusion of the primitive paired ducts or by the suppression of one of them. In the vast majority of winged insects the terminal part of the genital system (vagina and ductus ejaculatorius) is unpaired and ectodermal. Thus the condition in the Dermaptera is more primitive than in any other Pterygote order except the Ephemeroptera (Mayflies) which are still more generalized, the primitive mesodermal ducts (oviducts and vasa deferentia) opening by paired apertures as in the Crustacea. In the vast majority of the Dermaptera the cerci are—in the adult insect at least—stout, unjointed appendages forming a strong forceps (fig. 1) which the insect uses in arranging the hindwings beneath the elytra. In at least one genus the unjointed pincers of the forceps are preceded, in the youngest instar by jointed cerci. Very many members of the order are entirely wingless.

There are two families of Dermaptera. The *Hemimeridae* include the single genus *Hemimerus* (q.v.), which contains only two species of curious wingless insects with long, jointed cerci, found among the hair of certain West African rodents. The other family is that of the *Forficulidae* or earwigs (q.v.), all of which have the cerci modified as a forceps, while wings of the characteristic form described above are present in many of the species.

Order Orthoptera.

The bulk of de Geer's "Dermaptera" form the order Orthoptera of modern systematists, which includes some 10,000 described species. The insects comprised in it are distinguished from the earwigs by their elongate, rather narrow forewings, which usually cover, or nearly cover, the abdomen when at rest, and which are firmer in texture than the hindwings. The hindwings have a firm costal area, and a more delicate anal area which folds fanwise,

so that they are completely covered by the forewings when the insect rests. Rarely (in certain cockroaches) the hindwing undergoes transverse folding also. Wingless forms are fairly frequent in the order, but their relationship to the allied winged species is evident. The female of the common cockroach (fig. 3a) shows an interesting vestigial condition of the wings, which are but poorly developed in the male (fig. 3b). More important characters of the Orthoptera than the nature of the wings—characters in which they differ from

After Marlatt, *Ent. Bull.* 4, n. s. U.S. Dept. Agr.

FIG. 3.—Common Cockroach (*Blatta orientalis*); *a*, female, *b*, male; *c*, female (side view); *d*, young. Natural size.

the Dermaptera and agree with the vast majority of winged insects—are the absence of distinct maxillulae and the presence of an unpaired ectodermal tube as the terminal region of the genital system in both sexes. The cerci are nearly always jointed, and a typical insectan ovipositor with its three pairs of processes is present in connexion with the vagina of the female. In many Orthoptera this ovipositor is very long and conspicuous (fig. 5). Information as to the internal structure of a typical orthopteron—the cockroach—will be found under HEXAPODA.

Classification.—Six families of Orthoptera are here recognized, but most special students of the order consider that these should be rather regarded as super-families, and the number of families greatly multiplied. Those who wish to follow out the classification in detail should refer to some of the recent monographs mentioned below in the bibliography. There is general agreement as to the division of the Orthoptera into three sub-orders or tribes.

¶ I. *Phasmodea.*—This division includes the single family of the *Phasmidae* whose members, generally known as "stick-insects" (q.v.) and "leaf-insects" (q.v.), are among the best-known examples of "protective resemblance" to be found in the whole animal kingdom. The prothorax is short and the mesothorax very long, the three pairs of legs closely similar, the wings often highly modified or absent, and the cerci short and unjointed. Each egg is contained in a separate, curiously formed, seed-like capsule, provided with a lid which is raised to allow the escape of the newly-hatched insect.

II. *Oothecaria.*—In this tribe are included Orthoptera with a large prothorax, whose eggs are enclosed in a common purse or capsule formed by the hardening of a maternal secretion. The *Mantidae* or "praying insects" have the prothorax elongate and the fore-legs powerful and raptorial, while the large, broad head is prominent. The eggs are enclosed in a case attached to a twig or stone and containing many chambers. From this curious habitation the young mantids hang by threads till after their first moult (see MANTIS). The *Blattidae* (fig. 3) or cockroaches (q.v.) form the second family of this division.

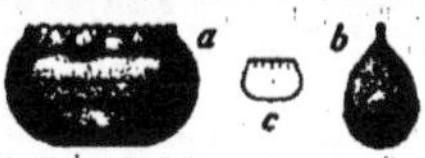

After Howard, *Ent. Bull.* 4, n. s. U.S. Dept. Agr.

FIG. 4.—Egg-purse of American Cockroach (*Periplaneta americana*). Magnified. *a*, Side view; *b*, end view; the outline *c* shows natural size.

They are readily distinguished by the somewhat rounded prothorax beneath which the head is usually concealed, while the forelegs are unmodified. Sixteen eggs are enclosed together in a compact capsule or "purse" (fig. 4).

III. *Saltatoria.*—The three families included in this tribe are distinguished by their elongate and powerful hindlegs (fig. 5) which enable them to leap far and high. They are remarkable for the possession of complex ears (described in the article HEXAPODA) and stridulating organs which produce chirping notes (see CRICKET). The families are the *Acrididae* and *Locustidae*—including the insects familiarly known as locusts and grasshoppers (q.v.) and the *Gryllidae* or crickets (q.v.). The Acrididae have the feelers and the ovipositor relatively short, and possess only three tarsal segments; their ears are situated on the first abdominal segment and the males stridulate by scraping rows of pegs on the inner aspect of the hind thigh, over the sharp edges of the forewing nervures. The Locustidae

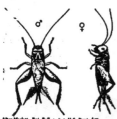

FIG. 5.—House Cricket (*Gryllus domesticus*); ♂ male; ♀, female. Natural size.

(see GRASSHOPPER, KATYDID) have the feelers and often also the ovipositor very elongate; the foot is four-segmented; the ears are placed at the base of the foreshin and the stridulation is due to the friction of a transverse "file" beneath the base of the left forewing over a sharp ridge on the upper aspect of the right. In some of these insects the wings are so small as to be useless for flight, being modified altogether for stridulation. The Gryllidae (fig. 5) are nearly related to the Locustidae, having long feelers and ovipositors,

Altus Marlatt, *Ent. Bull.* 4, n. s. U.S. Dept. Agr.

and agreeing with the latter family in the position of the ears. The forewings are curiously arranged when at rest, the anal region of the wing lying dorsal to the insect and the rest of the wing being turned downwards at the sides (see CRICKET).

Fossil History.—The Orthoptera are an exceedingly interesting order of insects as regards their past history. In Palaeozoic rocks of Carboniferous age the researches of S. H. Scudder have revealed insects with the general aspect of cockroaches and phasmids, but with the two pairs of wings similar to each other in texture and form. In the Mesozoic rocks (Trias and Lias) there have been discovered remains of insects intermediate between those ancient forms and our modern cockroaches, the differentiation between forewings and hindwings having begun. The Orthopteroid type of wings appears therefore to have arisen from a primitive Isopteroid condition.

BIBLIOGRAPHY.—A description and enumeration of all known Dermaptera has been lately published by A. de' Bormans and H. Kraus, *Das Tierreich*, xi. (Berlin, 1900). See also W. F. Kirby, *Synonymic Catalogue of Orthoptera*, pt. i. (London, Brit. Mus., 1904). See also, for earwigs, Kirby, *Journ. Linn. Soc. Zool.*, xxiii. (1890); E. E. Green, *Trans. Entom. Soc.* (1898); K. W. Verhoeff, *Abhandl. K. Leopold-Carol. Akad.*, lxxxiv. (1905); and M. Burr, *Science Gossip*, iv. (N.S., 1897); for Hemimerus, see H. J. Hansen, *Entom. Tidsk.*, xv. (1894). For Orthoptera generally, see C. Brunner von Wattenwyl, *Prodromus der europäischen Orthopteren* (Leipzig, 1882), and *Ann. Mus. Genov.* xiii. (1892), &c. R. Tümpel, *Die Geradflügler Mitteleuropas* (Eisenbach, 1901). The Orthoptera have been largely used for anatomical and embryological researches, the more important of which are mentioned under Hexapoda (q.v.). Of memoirs on special groups of Orthoptera may be mentioned here—J. O. Westwood, *Catalogue of Phasmidae* (London, Brit. Mus., 1859), and *Revisio Familias Mantidarum* (London, 1889); L. C. Miall and A. Denny, *The Cockroach* (London, 1886); E. B. Poulton, *Trans. Ent. Soc.* (1896); A. S. Packard, "Report on the Rocky Mountain Locust " in *9th Rep. U.S. Survey of Territories* (1875). For our native species see M. Burr, *British Orthoptera* (Huddersfield, 1897); D. Sharp's chapters (viii.-xiv.) *Cambridge Nat. History*, vol. v. (1895), give an excellent summary of our knowledge. (G. H. C.)

ORTHOSTATAE (Gr. ὀρθοστάτης, standing upright), the term in Greek architecture given to the lowest course of masonry of the external walls of the naos or cella, consisting of vertical slabs of stone or marble equal in height to two or three of the horizontal courses which constitute the inner part of the wall.

ORTHOSTYLE (Gr. ὀρθός, straight, and στῦλος, a column), in architecture, a range of columns placed in a straight row, as for instance those of the portico or flanks of a classic temple.

b **ORTIGUEIRA**; a seaport of north-western Spain, in the province of Corunna; on the northern slope of the Sierra de la Faladoira, on the river Nera and on the eastern shore of the Ría de Santa Marta—a winding, rock-hound and much indented inlet of the Bay of Biscay, between Capes Ortegal and Vares, the northernmost headlands of the Peninsula. The official total of the in-

habitants of Ortigueira (18,426 in 1900) includes many families which dwell at some distance; the actual urban population does not exceed 2000. The industries are fishing and farming. Owing to the shallowness of the harbour large vessels cannot enter, but there is an important coasting trade, despite the dangerous character of the coast-line and the prevalence of fogs and gales. The sea-bathing and magnificent scenery attract visitors in summer even to this remote district, which has no railway and few good roads.

ORTLER, the highest point (12,802 ft.) in Tirol, and so in the whole of the Eastern Alps. It is a great snow-clad mass, which rises E. of the Stelvio Pass, and a little S. of the upper valley of the Adige (whence it is very conspicuous) between the valleys of Trafoi (N.W.) and of Sulden (N.E.). It was long considered to be wholly inaccessible, but was first conquered in 1804 by three Tirolese peasants, of whom the chief was Josef Pichler. The first traveller to make the climb was Herr Gebhard in 1805 (sixth ascent). In 1826 Herr Schebelka, and in 1834 P. K. T. Thurwieser attained the summit, but it was only after the discovery of easier routes in 1864 by F. F. Tuckett, E. N. and H. E. Buxton, and in 1865 by Herr E. von Mojsisovics that the expedition became popular. Many routes to the summit are now known, but that usually taken (from the Payer Club hut, easily accessible from either Sulden or Trafoi) from the north is daily traversed in summer and offers no difficulties to moderately experienced walkers. (W. A. B. C.)

ORTNIT, or OTNIT, German hero of romance, was originally Hertnit or Hartnit, the elder of two brothers known as the Hartungs, who correspond in German mythology to the Dioscuri. His seat was at Holmgard (Novgorod), according to the *Thidreks-saga* (chapter 45), and he was related to the Russian saga heroes. Later on his city of Holmgard became Garda, and in ordinary German legend he ruled in Lombardy. Hartnit won his bride, a Valkyrie, by hard fighting against the giant Isungs, but was killed in a later fight by a dragon. His younger brother, Hardherf (replaced in later German legend by Wolfdietrich), avenged Ortnit by killing the dragon, and then married his brother's widow. Ortnit's wooing was corrupted by the popular interest in the crusades to an Oriental *Brautfahrtsaga*, hearing a very close resemblance to the French romance of Huon of Bordeaux. Both heroes receive similar assistance from Alberich (Oberon), who supplanted the Russian Ilya as Ortnit's epic father in middle high German romance. Neumann maintained that the Russian Ortnit and the Lombard king were originally two different persons, and that the incoherence of the tale is due to the welding of the two legends into one.

See editions of the *Heldenbuch* and one of *Ortnit* and *Wolfdietrich* by Dr. J. L. Edlen von Lindhausen (Tübingen, 1906); articles in the *Zeitschrift für deutsches Altertum* by K. Müllenhoff (xii. pp. 344-354, 1865; xiii. pp. 185-192, 1867), by J. Seemüller (xxvi. 201-211, 1882), and by E. H. Meyer (xxxviii. pp. 85-87, 1894), and in *Germania* by F. Neumann (vol. xxvii. pp. 191-219, Vienna, 1882). See also the literature dealing with Huon of Bordeaux.

ORTOLAN, JOSEPH LOUIS ELZÉAR (1802–1873), French jurist, was born at Toulon, on the 21st of August 1802. He studied law at Aix and Paris, and early made his name by two volumes, *Explication historique des instituts de Justinien* (1827), and *Histoire de la législation romaine* (1828), the first of which has been frequently republished. He was made assistant librarian to the court of cassation, and was promoted after the Revolution of 1830 to be secretary-general. He was also commissioned to give a course of lectures at the Sorbonne on constitutional law, and in 1836 was appointed to the chair of comparative criminal law at the university of Paris. He published many works on constitutional and comparative law, of which the following may be mentioned: *Histoire du droit constitutionnel en Europe pendant le moyen âge* (1831); *Introduction historique au cours de législation pénale comparée* (1841); he was the author of a volume of poetry *Les enfantines* (1845). He died in Paris, on the 27th of March 1873.

ORTOLAN (Fr. *ortolan*, Lat. *hortulanus*, the gardener bird, from *hortus*, a garden), the *Emberiza hortulana* of Linnaeus, a bird celebrated for the delicate flavour of its flesh, and a member of the *Emberizidae*, a Passerine family not separated by most modern authors from the *Fringillidae*. A native of most European countries—the British Islands (in which it occurs but rarely) excepted—as well as of western Asia, it emigrates in autumn presumably to the southward of the Mediterranean, though its winter quarters cannot be said to be accurately known, and returns about the end of April or beginning of May. Its distribution throughout its breeding-range seems to be very local, and for this no reason can be assigned. It was long ago said in France, and apparently with truth, to prefer wine-growing districts; but it certainly does not feed upon grapes, and is found equally in countries where vineyards are unknown—reaching in Scandinavia even beyond the arctic circle—and then generally frequents corn-fields and their neighbourhood. In appearance and habits it much resembles its congener the yellow-hammer, but wants the bright colouring of that species, its head for instance being of a greenish-grey, instead of a lively yellow. The somewhat monotonous song of the cock is also much of the same kind; and, where the bird is a familiar object to the country people, who usually associate its arrival with the return of fair weather, they commonly apply various syllabic interpretations to its notes, just as our boys do to those of the yellow-hammer. The nest is placed on or near the ground, but the eggs seldom show the hair-like markings so characteristic of those of most buntings. Its natural food consists of beetles, other insects and seeds. Ortolans are netted in great numbers, kept alive in an artificially lighted or darkened room, and fed with oats and millet. In a very short time they become enormously fat and are then killed for the table. If, as is supposed, the ortolan be the *Miliaria* of Varro, the practice of artificially fattening birds of this species is very ancient. In French the word *Ortolan* is used so as to be almost synonymous with the English " bunting "—thus the *Ortolan-de-neige* is the snowbunting (*Plectrophanes nivalis*), the *Ortolan-de-ris* is the rice-bird or " bobolink " of North America (*Dolichonyx oryzivorus*), so justly celebrated for its delicious flavour; but the name is also applied to other birds much more distantly related, for the *Ortolan* of some of the Antilles, where French is spoken, is a little ground-dove of the genus *Chamaepelia*.

In Europe the *Beccafico* (fig-eater) shares with the ortolan the highest honours of the dish, and this may be a convenient place to point out that the former is a name of equally elastic signification. The true *Beccafico* is said to be what is known in England as the garden-warbler (the *Motacilla salicaria* of Linnaeus, the *Sylvia hortensis* of modern writers); but in Italy any soft-billed small bird that can be snared or netted in its autumnal emigration passes under the name in the markets and cook-shops. The " beccafico," however, is not as a rule artificially fattened, and on this account is preferred by some sensitive tastes to the Ortolan. (A. N.)

ORTON, JOB (1717–1783), English dissenting minister, was born at Shrewsbury on the 4th of September 1717. He entered the academy of Dr Philip Doddridge at Northampton (*q.v.*), became minister of a congregation formed by a fusion of Presbyterians and Independents at High Street Chapel, Shrewsbury (1741), received Presbyterian ordination there (1745), resigned in 1766 owing to ill-health, and lived in retirement at Kidderminster until his death. He exerted great influence both among dissenting ministers and among clergy of the established church. He was deeply read in Puritan divinity, and adopted Sabellian doctrines on the Trinity. Old-fashioned in most of his views, he disliked the tendencies alike of the Methodists and other revivalists and of the rationalizing dissenters, yet he had a good word for Priestley and Theophilus Lindsey.

Among his numerous works are *Letters to Dissenting Ministers* (ed. by S. Palmer, 2 vols., 1806), and *Practical Works* (2 vols., with letters and memoir, 1842).

ORTONA A MARE, a small seaport and episcopal see of the Abruzzi, Italy, in the province of Chieti, 12 m. direct E. of that town and 105 m. by rail S.S.E. of Ancona. Pop. (1901) 8667 (town); 15,523 (commune). It is situated on a promontory 230 ft. above sea-level, and connected with the port below by a wire-rope railway. From the ruined castle magnificent views to the south as far as the Punta di Penna can be obtained,

The cathedral has been restored at various times, but preserves a fine portal of 1312 by a local artist, Nicolò Mancini. At one side of it is the Palazzo de Pirris with five pointed windows.

The town occupies the site of the ancient Ortona, a seaport of the Frentani; it lay on the Roman coast-road, which here turned inland to Anxanum (Lanciano), 10 m. to the S. The town suffered much from the ravages of the Turks, who laid it in ruins in 1566, and also from frequent earthquakes.

For discoveries in the neighbourhood see A. de Nino in *Notizie degli Scavi* (1888), 646. (T. As.)

ÖRTZEN, GEORG, BARON VON (1820–), German poet and prose-writer, was born at Brunn in Mecklenburg-Schwerin. He served as an officer of Prussian hussars (1850–1855), entered the consular service and after employment at New York (1879) and Constantinople (1880) was appointed to Marseilles (1881), and then to Christiania (1889), retiring in 1891. He published about thirty volumes, mostly of lyrics and aphorisms, including *Gedichte* (3rd ed. 1861), *Aus den Kämpfen des Lebens* (1868), *Deutsche Träume, deutsche Siege* (1876), *Epigramme und Epiloge in Prosa* (1880), *Es war ein Traum* (1902). His *Erlebnisse und Studien in der Gegenwart* (Leipzig, 1875) appeared under the pseudonym Ludwig Robert, and *Nacht* (Stuttgart, 1899), a collection of sonnets, under that of Stephen Ervésy.

ORURO, a department and town of Bolivia. The department is bounded N. by La Paz, E. by Cochabamba and Potosí, S. by Potosí, and W. by Chile; it forms a part of the ancient Titicaca lacustrine basin, and has an area of 19,127 sq. m., the greater part of which is semi-arid and covered with extensive saline deposits. It is bordered by Cordilleras on the E. and W., and by transverse ridges and detached groups of elevations on the N. and S. The slope and drainage is toward the S., but many of the streams are waterless in the dry season. The outlet of Lake Titicaca, the Desaguadero river, flows southward into Lake Pampa-Aullaguas, or Poópo, on the eastern side of the department near the Cordillera de los Frailes. Lake Poópo is 12,139 ft. above sea-level, or 506 ft. lower than Titicaca, and its waters discharge through a comparatively small outlet, called the Lacahahutra, into the lagoon and saline morasses of Coipasa (12,057 ft. elevation) in the S.W. corner of the department. Oruro is almost exclusively a mining department, the country being too arid for agriculture, with the exception of a narrow strip in the foothills of the Cordillera de los Frailes, where a few cattle, mules and llamas, and a considerable number of sheep are reared. The mineral wealth has not been fully developed except in the vicinity of the capital, in the north-east part of the department, where there are large deposits of tin, silver and copper, Oruro being the second largest producer of tin in the republic. There are borax deposits in the western part of the department, but the output is small.

The capital of the department is ORURO, 115 m. S.S.E. (direct) of La Paz; it is an old mining town dating from the 17th century; when it is said to have had a population of 70,000. The census of 1900 gave it a population of 13,575, the greater part of whom are Indians. A considerable number of foreigners are interested in the neighbouring mines. The elevation of Oruro is 12,250 ft. above sea-level, and its climate is characterized by a short cool summer and a cold rainy winter, with severe frosts and occasional snow-storms. The mean annual temperature is about 43° F. Oruro is the Bolivian terminus of the Antofagasta railway (0·75 metre gauge), 574 m. long, the first constructed in Bolivia. A law of the 27th of November 1906 provided for the construction of other lines, of metre gauge, from La Paz (Viacha) to Oruro, from Oruro to Cochabamba, and from Oruro to Tupiza, making Oruro the most important railway centre in Bolivia. Oruro enjoys the nominal distinction of being one of the four capitals of the republic, an anomaly which was practically ended by the revolution of 1898, since which time the government has remained at La Paz.

ORVIETO (anc. *Volsinii* (*q.v.*), later *Urbs Vetus*, whence the modern name), a town and episcopal see of the province of Perugia, Italy, on the Paglia, 78 m. by rail N. by W of Rome. Pop. (1901) 8830 (town); 18,108 (commune). It crowns an isolated rock, 1033 ft. above sea-level, 640 ft. above the plain.

commanding splendid views, and is approached on the east by a funicular railway from the station. The town is very picturesque, both from its magnificent position and also from the unusually large number of fine 13th-century houses and palaces which still exist in its streets. The chief glory of the place is its splendid cathedral, dedicated to the Virgin; it was begun before 1285, perhaps by Arnolfo di Cambio, on the site of an older church; and from the 13th till the 16th century was enriched by the labours of a whole succession of great Italian painters and sculptors. The exterior is covered with black and white marble; the interior is of grey limestone with bands of a dark basaltic stone. The plan consists of a large rectangular nave, with semicircular recesses for altars, opening out of the aisles, north and south. There are two transeptal chapels and a short choir. The most magnificent part of the exterior and indeed the finest polychrome monument in existence is the west façade, built of richly-sculptured marble from the designs of Lorenzo Maitani of Siena, and divided into three gables with intervening pinnacles, closely resembling the front of Siena cathedral, of which it is a reproduction, with some improvements. With the splendour of the whole, the beauty of the composition is marvellous, and it may rank as the highest achievement of Italian Gothic. It was begun in 1310, but the upper part was not completed till the 16th century. The mosaics are modern, and the whole church has suffered greatly from recent restoration. The four wall-surfaces that flank the three western doorways are decorated with very beautiful sculpture in relief, once ornamented with colour, the designs for which, according to Burckhardt, must be ascribed to the architect of the whole, though executed by other (but still Sienese, not Pisan) hands. The Madonna above the principal portal falls into the same category. The subjects are scenes from the Old and New Testaments, and the Last Judgment, with Heaven and Hell. In the interior on the north, the Cappella del Corporale possesses a large silver shrine, resembling in form the cathedral façade, enriched with countless figures in relief and subjects in translucent coloured enamels—one of the most important specimens of early silversmith's work that yet exists in Italy. It was begun by Ugolino Vieri of Siena in 1337; and was made to contain the Holy Corporal from Bolsena, which, according to the legend, became miraculously stained with blood during the celebration of mass to convince a sceptical priest of the truth of the doctrine of transubstantiation. This is supposed to have happened in 1263, while Urban IV. was residing at Orvieto; and it was to commemorate this miracle that the existing cathedral was built. On the south side is the chapel of S. Brizio, separated from the nave by a late 14th-century wrought-iron screen. The walls and vault of this chapel are covered with some of the best-preserved and finest frescoes in Italy—among the noblest works of Fra Angelico and Luca Signorelli, mainly painted between 1450 and 1501—the latter being of especial importance in the history of art owing to their great influence on Michelangelo in his early days. The choir stalls are fine and elaborate specimens of *tarsia* and rich wood-carving—the work of Antonio and Pietro della Minella (1431–1441). In 16th-century sculpture the cathedral is especially rich, containing many statues, groups and altar-reliefs by Simone Mosca and Ippolito Scalza. Close by are two Gothic buildings, the bishop's palace (1264) and the Palazzo dei Papi (begun in 1296), the latter with a huge hall now containing the Museo Civico, with various medieval works of art, and also objects from the Etruscan necropolis of the ancient Volsinii (q.v.). The Palazzo Faina has another interesting Etruscan collection. The Palazzo del Comune is Romanesque (13th century), but has been restored. S. Andrea and S. Giovenale are also Romanesque churches of the 11th century, both contain later frescoes. To the 12th century belongs the ruined abbey of S. Severo, 1 m. south of the town. The church of S. Domenico contains one of the finest works in sculpture by Arnolfo del Cambio. This is the tomb with recumbent effigy of the Cardinal Brago or De Braye (1282), with much beautiful sculpture and mosaic. It is signed HOC OPVS FECIT ARNVLFVS. It was imitated by Giovanni Pisano in his monument to Pope Benedict XI. at Perugia. Among the later

buildings, a few may be noted by Sanmicheli of Verona, who was employed as chief architect of the cathedral from 1509 to 1528. The fortress built in 1364 by Cardinal Albornos has been converted into a public garden. The well, now disused, called Il pozzo di S. Patrizio, is one of the chief curiosities of Orvieto. It is 200 ft. deep to the water-level and 42 ft. in diameter, cut in the rock, with a double winding inclined plane, so that asses could ascend and descend to carry the water from the bottom. It was begun by the architect Antonio da San Gallo the younger in 1527 for Clement VII., who fled to Orvieto after the sack of Rome, and was finished by Simone Mosca under Paul III.

The town appears under the name Οὐρβιβεντὸς in Procopius (Bell. Goth. ii. 11, &c.); who gives a somewhat exaggerated description of the site, and as *Urbs Vetus* elsewhere after his time. Belisarius starved out Vitiges in 539, and became master of it. In 606 it fell to the Lombards, and was recovered by Charlemagne. It formed part of the donation of the Countess Matilda to the papacy. Communal independence had probably been acquired as early as the end of the 10th century, but the first of the popes to reside in Orvieto and to recognize its communal administration was Hadrian IV. in 1157. It was then governed by consuls, but various changes of constitution supervened in the direction of enlarging the governing body. Its sympathies were always Guelphic, and it was closely allied with Florence, which it assisted in the battle of Monteaperto (1260), and its constitution owed much to her model. In 1199 the first *podestà* was elected, and in 1251 the first *capitano del popolo*. There were considerable Guelph and Ghibelline struggles even at Orvieto, the latter party being finally destroyed in 1313, and the representatives of the former, the Monaldeschi, obtaining the supreme power. The territory of Orvieto extended from Chiusi to the coast at Orbetello, to the Lake of Bolsena and the Tiber. The various branches of the Monaldeschi continually fought among themselves, however, and the quarrels of two of them divided the city into two factions under the names of Muffati and Mercorini, whose struggles lasted until 1460, when peace was finally made between them. After this period Orvieto was peaceably ruled by papal governors, and had practically no history. Owing to the strong Guelphic sympathies of the inhabitants, and the inaccessible nature of the site, Orvieto was constantly used as a place of refuge by the popes. In 1814 it became the chief town of a district, in 1831 of a province, and in 1860 with Umbria became part of the kingdom of Italy, and became a subprefecture.

See L. Fumi, *Il Duomo d' Orvieto e i suoi restauri* (Rome, 1891); *Orvieto, note storiche e biografiche* (Città di Castello, 1891), and other works. (T. As.)

ORYX (Gr. ὄρυξ, a pickaxe, hence applied to the animal), the scientific name of a group of African antelopes or relatively large size with long straight or scimitar-shaped horns, which are present in both sexes, and long tufted tails. They are all desert animals. The true oryx of classical writers was probably the East and North-east African beisa-oryx (*Oryx beisa*), which is replaced in South Africa by the gemsbuck (*oryx gazella*). In Northern Africa the group is represented by the scimitar-horned *O. leucoryx* or *O. algazal*, and in Arabia by the small white oryx (*O. beatrix*). See ANTELOPE.

ORZESZKO or **ORZESZKO, ELIZA** (1842–   ), Polish novelist, was born near Grodno, of the noble family of Pawlowski. In her sixteenth year she married Piotr Orzesako, a Polish nobleman, who was exiled to Siberia after the insurrection of 1863. She wrote a series of powerful novels and sketches, dealing with the social conditions of her country. *Eli Makower* (1875) describes the relations between the Jews and the Polish nobility, and *Meir Ezofowics* (1878) the conflict between Jewish orthodoxy and modern liberalism. *On the Niemen* (1888), perhaps her best work, deals with the Polish aristocracy, and *Lost Souls* (1886) and *Cham* (1888) with rural life in White Russia. Her study on *Patriotism and Cosmopolitanism* appeared in 1880. A uniform edition of her works appeared in Warsaw, 1884–1888.

OSAKA, or **OZAKA,** a city of Japan in the province of Settsu. Pop. (1908) 1,226,590. It lies in a plain bounded, except westward, where it opens on Osaka Bay, by hills of considerable height, on both sides of the Yodogawa, or rather its headwater the Aji (the outlet of Lake Biwa), and is so intersected by river-branches and canals as to suggest a comparison with a Dutch town. Steamers ply between Osaka and Kobe-Hiogo or Kobe, and Osaka is an important railway centre. The opening of the railway (1873) drew foreign trade to Kobe, but a harbour for ocean-steamers has been constructed at Osaka. The houses are mainly built of wood, and on the 31st of July 1900 some 12,000 houses and other buildings were destroyed by fire. Shin-sai Bashi Suji, the principal thoroughfare, leads from Kitahama, the district lying on the south side of the Tosabori, to the iron suspension bridge (Shin-sai Bashi) over the Dotom-bori. The foreign settlement is at Kawaguchi at the junction of the Shirinashi and the Aji. It is the seat of a number of European mission stations. Buddhist and Shinto temples are numerous. The principal secular buildings are the castle, the mint and the arsenal. The castle was founded in 1583 by Hideyoshi; the enclosed palace, probably the finest building in Japan, survived the capture of the castle by Iyeyasu (1615), and in 1867 and 1868 witnessed the reception of the foreign legations by the Tokugawa shoguns; but in the latter year it was fired by the Tokugawa party. It now provides military headquarters, containing a garrison and an arsenal. The whole castle is protected by high and massive walls and broad moats. Huge blocks of granite measuring 40 ft. by 10 ft. or more occur in the masonry. The mint, erected and organized by Europeans, was opened in 1871. Osaka possesses iron-works, sugar refineries, cotton spinning mills, ship-yards and a great variety of other manufactures. The trade shows an increase commensurate with that of the population, which in 1877 was only 284,105.

Osaka owes its origin to Rennio Sbonin, the eighth head of the Shin-Shu sect, who in 1495-1496 built on the site now occupied by the castle, a temple which afterwards became the principal residence of his successors. In 1580, after ten years' successful defence of his position, Kenryo, the eleventh " abbot," was obliged to surrender; and in 1583 the victorious Hideyoshi made Osaka his capital. The town was opened to foreign trade in 1868.

OSAWATOMIE, a city of Miami county, Kansas, U.S.A., about 45 m. S. by W. of Kansas City, on the Missouri Pacific railway. Pop. (1900) 4191 (227 negroes); (1905, state census) 4857; (1910) 4046. A state hospital for the insane (1866) is about 1 m. N.E. of the city. The region is a good one for general farming, and natural gas and petroleum are found in abundance in the vicinity. Osawatomie was settled about 1854 by colonists sent by the Emigrant Aid Company, and was platted in 1855; its name was coined from parts of the words " Osage " and " Pottawatomie." It was the scene of two of the " battles " of the " Border War," and of much of the political violence resulting from the clashes between the "pro-slavery " and the " free-state " factions of Missouri and Kansas. On the 7th of June 1856 it was plundered by about 170 pro-slavery men from Missouri. On the 30th of August 1856 General John W. Reid, commanding about 400 Missourians, attacked the town. The attack was resisted by Captain John Brown (who had come to Osawatomie in the autumn of 1855) at the head of about 40 men, who were soon overpowered. Of Captain Brown's men, four were killed and two were executed. The town was looted and practically destroyed. A park commemorating the battle was dedicated here on the 31st of August 1910.

OSBORN, SHERARD (1822-1875), English admiral and Arctic explorer, the son of an Indian army officer, was born on the 25th of April 1822. Entering the navy as a first-class volunteer in 1837, he was entrusted in 1838 with the command of a gunboat at the attack on Kedah in the Malay Peninsula, and was present at the reduction of Canton in 1841, and at the capture of the batteries of Woosung in 1842. From 1844 till 1848 he was gunnery mate and lieutenant in the flag-ship of Sir George Seymour in the Pacific. He took a prominent part in 1849 in advocating a new search expedition for Sir John Franklin, and in 1850 was appointed to the command of the steam-tender " Pioneer " in the Arctic expedition under Captain Austin, in the course of which he performed (1851) a remarkable sledge-journey to the western extremity of Prince of Wales Island. He published an account of this voyage, entitled *Stray Leaves from an Arctic Journal* (1852), and was promoted to the rank of commander shortly afterwards. In the new expedition (1852-1854) under Sir Edward Belcher he again took part as commander of the " Pioneer." In 1856 he published the journals of Captain Robert M'Clure, giving a narrative of the discovery of the North-West Passage. Early in 1855 he was called to active service in connexion with the Crimean War, and being promoted to post-rank in August of that year was appointed to the " Medusa," in which he commanded the Sea of Azoff squadron until the conclusion of the war. For these services he received the C.B., the Cross of the Legion of Honour, and the Medjidie of the fourth class. As commander of the " Furious " he took a prominent part in the operations of the second Chinese War, and performed a piece of difficult and intricate navigation in taking his ship 600 m. up the Yangtse-kiang to Hankow (1858). He returned to England in broken health in 1859, and at this time contributed a number of articles on naval and Chinese topics to *Blackwood's Magazine*, and wrote *The Career, Last Voyage and Fate of Sir John Franklin* (1860). In 1861 he commanded the " Donegal " in the Gulf of Mexico during the trouble there, and in 1862 undertook the command of a squadron fitted out by the Chinese government for the suppression of piracy on the coast of China; but owing to the non-fulfilment of the conditions that he should receive orders from the imperial government only, he threw up the appointment. In 1864 he was appointed to the command of the " Royal Sovereign " in order to test the turret system of ship-building, to which this vessel had been adapted. In 1865 he became agent to the Great Indian Peninsula Railway Company, and two years later managing director of the Telegraph Construction and Maintenance Company. In 1873 he attained flag-rank. His interest in Arctic exploration had never ceased, and in 1873 he induced Commander Albert Markham to undertake a summer voyage for the purpose of testing the conditions of ice-navigation with the aid of steam, with the result that a new Arctic expedition, under Sir George Nares, was determined upon. He was a member of the committee which made the preparations for this expedition, and died a few days after it had sailed.

OSBORNE, a mansion and estate in the Isle of Wight, England, S.E. of the town of East Cowes. The name of the manor in early times is quoted as Austerborne or Oysterborne, and the estate comprised about 2000 acres when, in 1845, it was purchased from Lady Isabella Blackford by Queen Victoria. The queen subsequently extended the estate to nearly 3000 acres, and a mansion, in simple Palladian style, was built from designs of Mr T. Cubitt. Here the queen died in 1901, and by a letter dated Coronation Day 1902, King Edward VII. presented the property to the nation. By his desire part of the house was transformed into a convalescent home for officers of the navy and army, opened in 1904.

In 1903 there was opened on the Osborne estate a Royal Naval College. The principal buildings lie near the Prince of Wales's Gate, the former royal stables being adapted to use as class-rooms, a mess-room, and other apartments, while certain adjacent buildings were also adapted, and a gymnasium and a series of bungalows to serve as dormitories, each accommodating thirty boys, were erected, together with quarters for officers, and for an attached body of marines. By the river Medina, on the Kingsdown portion of the estate, a machine shop and facilities for boating are provided.

At the church of St Mildred, Whippingham, 1¼ m. S.S.E. of East Cowes, there are memorials to various members of the royal family.

OSCA LINGUA, or **OSCAN,** the name given by the Romans to the language of (1) the Samnite tribes, and (2) the inhabitants of Campania (excluding the Greek colonies) from the 4th century

B.C. onwards. We know from inscriptions that it extended southwards over the whole of the Peninsula, except its two extreme projections (see BRUTTII and MESSAPII) covering the districts known as Lucania and Frentanum, and the greater part of Apulia (see LUCANIA, FRENTANI, APULIA). Northward, a very similar dialect was spoken in the Central Apennine region by the PAELIGNI, VESTINI (q.v.) and others. But there is some probability that both in the North and in the South the dialect spoken varied slightly from what we may call the standard or central Oscan of Samnium. There can also be no reasonable doubt, though doubt has strangely been raised, that the popular farces at Rome called Atellanae were acted in Oscan; Strabo (v. p. 233) records this most explicitly as a curious survival.

This name, for what ought probably to be called the Samnite or Safine speech, is due to historical causes, but is, in fact, incorrect. The Osci proper were not Samnites, but the Italic, Pre-Tuscan and Pre-Greek inhabitants of Campania. This is the sense in which Strabo regularly uses the name Ὀσκοι (cf. v. 247), so that it is quite possible that we should connect them with the other tribes whose Ethnica were formed with the -co- suffix and with the plebs of Rome (see VOLSCI and ROME).

For further evidence as to the history of the names Osci, Opsci, Opici, see R. S. Conway, The Italic Dialects, p. 149.

The chief monuments of the language, as spoken in Campania, come from Pompeii, Nola, Capua and Cumae (q.v.). From the two towns last mentioned we have the interesting group of heraldic inscriptions known as Iovilae (q.v.), and two interesting curses inscribed on lead plates and, so to speak, posted in graves, for conveyance to the deities of the Underworld. One of these may be quoted as a typical specimen of the Oscan of Campania:

From the memnim-Curse:—

> luvikis úhlavis
> statiis gaviis nep faṣtum nep delkum puṣtans;
> luvkis uhlavis uvellum velliam
> nep delkum nep faṣtum paṣtad,
> nep memnim nep úlam sífeí keriiad.

("(Lucius Octauius,) Statius Gauius neue memorare neue indicare possit, Lucius Octauius Nouellum Velliam neue memorare neue indicare possit, neue monumentum neue sepulcrum (?) sibi adipiecatur.")

The language as spoken in Samnium may be illustrated by a few sentences from the Tabula Agnonensis, now in the British Museum:—

> statús pús set húrím kerríín;
> diíuel verehasiúl statíf, diíuel regatureí statíf,
> herchiú kerríiúí statíf, patanaí piístíaí statíf,
> debeaí genetaí statíf. aasaí purasiaí saahúm
> tefúrúm alttreí púkereípíd akneí suakhker.
> fiuusasiaís az húrúm sakaraíer;
> pernaí kerríaí statíf, ammaí kerríaí statíf,
> fiuusaí kerríaí statíf, euklúí paúreí statíf.

("Qui erecti sunt in horto Cereali. Ioui vigiliarum patrono (?) statua, Ioui Rectori statua, Herculi Cereali statua, Pandae Ibero (?) statua, Diuae Genetae statua. In ara crematio sancta altero quoque festo (an 'anno'?) sancitur (an 'sanciatur'?). Deabus Floralibus iuxta hortum sacratur (an 'sacrantur'?). Anteuortae (?) Cereali statua, Nutrici Cereali statua, Florae Cereali statua, Mercurio patri statua.")

It remains to notice briefly (1) the chief characteristics which mark off the Osco-Umbrian, or, as they might more conveniently be termed, the Safine group of dialects, from the Latinian, and (2) the features which distinguish Oscan and the dialects most closely allied to it, e.g. North-Oscan (see PAELIGNI), from the Umbrian or (more strictly) Iguvine dialect (see IOUVIUM).

(A.) Phonology.—1. The conversion of the Indo-European velars into labials, e.g. Oscan and Umbrian pis = Lat. quis, Osc. Umb. pod = Lat. quod.

Umb. petur-pursus = Lat. quadrupedibus; Osc. kombened = Lat. conuēnit, from the Indo-European root *g*em-, Eng. come, Sanskrit gam-; Umb. accusative bum = Sanskrit gām, Eng. cow, the Lat. bōs, bouis having been borrowed from some Safine dialect, since the pure Latin form would have been *uōs.

2. The extrusion or syncope (a) of short vowels in the second syllable of a word, e.g. Oscan opsd, Umbrian osd-, from an Italic stem *opesd-, "to work, build," cf. Lat. opero, "work," and operāri (although this verb appears in Latin to have been invented only at a late period); Osc. actud, Umb. aitu = Lat. agito; Umb. marsio-, from Italic *medesio-, "iustus," beside Lat. modestus. (b) Of short vowels before final i, Osc. húrs (pronounced horis) = Lat. hortus; Umb. ikuvins = Lat. Iguvinus; Osc. nom. pl. humuns, O. Lat. homōnes; Umb. abl. pl. avis for *ovifos = Lat. auibus.

3. The preservation of s before n, m and l (whereas in Latin it is lost with compensatory lengthening " of the previous vowel when the change is medial): Umb. ahesnes, abl. pl. = Lat. ahenis; Paelignian prismu (nom. sing. fem.) = Lat. prima; Osc. Slabiis = Lat. Labius.

4. Instead of Lat. -nd- we have in Osco-Umbrian nn—which the Umbrian poet Plautus reproduces as a vulgarism in the well-known line (Miles Glor., v. 14, l. 1399), dispennite hominem, et dispennite; hence the gerundives, Osc. opsannam = Lat. operandam, So Umbrian pihaner, from pihanneis (gen. sing. masc.), equivalent to Lat. piandi. It is not certain what the original group of sounds was which appears in the shape of -nn- in Osco-Umbrian and -nd- in Latin, nor whether this group of sounds, whatever it was (possibly -nj-), became -nd- before it became -nn-.

5. Final ā became o in both Oscan (ú) and Umbrian (often written u), e.g. Oscan víú = Lat. uia; Umb. adro (nom. pl. neut.) = Lat. atra.

6. Italic ō became closer in Osco-Umbrian; in the Oscan alphabet it is denoted by a special sign ≻, which is best reproduced by ŭ (although the misleading symbol í with an accent upon it is frequently used). In the Umbrian alphabet (see IOUVIUM) it is variously written e and í, and in the Latin alphabet, when used to write Oscan and Umbrian, we have e, i, and occasionally even ei, e.g. Osc. ligatúis = Lat. legatis, but ligis (in Latin alphabet) = Lat. legibus; Umb. tref and trif = Lat. tres; N. Osc. sefei = Lat. sibi.

7. An original short i in Osco-Umbrian became identical in quality, though not in quantity, with the vowel just described, and is written with just the same symbols in all the alphabets, e.g. Osc. píd, Umb. pod = Lat. quid.

8. Precisely analogous changes happened with Italic ō and ŏ; the resulting vowel being denoted in Oscan alphabet both by u and by ú (≻), in Umbrian alphabet by u, in Latin alphabet by o.

It is well to add here one or two other characteristics in which Oscan alone is more primitive, not merely than Latin, but even than Umbrian.

(a) Oscan retains s between vowels, whereas in both Latin and Umbrian it became r. In Oscan it seems to have become voiced, as it is represented by z in Latin alphabet, e.g. gen. pl. fem. egmazum, "rerum"; esum, in Oscan alphabet eisom, pres. infin. " esse."

(b) Oscan retains the diphthongs ai, ei, oi, ou (representing both original eu and ou) and au even in unaccented syllables, e.g. abl. pl. feíhúis, " muris "; dat. pl. diumpais, " lymphis "; infin. deicum, " dicere."

(c) Oscan retains final, d, e.g. abl. masc. sing. dolud = Lat. dolo.

(B.) Morphology.—I. In nouns. (a) Considerable levelling has taken place between the consonantal and the -o- stems; thus the gen. sing. masc. of Osc. teerum (neut. = Lat. " terra ") is teereis, just like that of the consonantal stem tangin-, gen. tangineis. Conversely we have the abl. tangino on the pattern of o- stem ablatives, like dolud. (b) In the ō-stems and the ā-stems we have several primitive forms which are obscured in Latin, e.g. Osc. sing. fem. eítuas, " pecuniae"; gen. pl. masc. Núvlanúm, " Nolanorum "; and the locative is still a living case in both declensions, e.g. Osc. tereí " in terra," víaí " in via."

II. In verbs. (a) The formation of the infinitive in -um-, e.g. Osc. ezum, Umb. erom, " esse "; opsaum, " operari, facere " (cf. art LATIN LANGUAGE, § 32). (b) The formation of the future, and future perfect indicative respectively, with stems in -es- and -us-: Oscan didest, "dabit "; deiuast " iurabit "; censaz (n)t, " censebunt "; Umb. ferest, " feret "; fut. perf. Osc. sçfacust, " fecerit "; Osc. and Umb. fust, " fuerit "; Umb. fakust, " fecerit, fakurent, " fecerint "; furent, " fuerint." (c) Several new methods of forming the perfect from vowel stems, e.g. the Oscan and Umbrian -f- perfects. Osc. 1st sing. perf. manafum, " mandaui "; 3rd sing. aamanaffed, " mandauit, imperauit "; 3rd pl. Osc. fufens, " fuerunt " (cf. Umb. perf. subj. passive impersonal pihafei, " piatum sit "). One other formation occurs frequently in Oscan (from ā- verbs), whose origin is obscure. In this the perfect characteristic is -tt-, e.g. prúfatted, " probauit." (d) The peculiar and interesting impersonal or semi-personal forms which ultimately developed into a full passive, e.g. Osc. sakrafír, " sacrauerit aliquis " governing an accusative; Umb. ferar, " ferat aliquis " (see the section on the passive under Latin Language).

(C.) Syntax.—It may be said generally that there are very few if any peculiarities in the syntax of the Oscan and Umbrian inscriptions as compared with Latin usage, though a large number of familiar Latin idioms appear, such as the abl. absolute; the abl.

of circumstance, the genitive in judicial phrases, the use of the neut. adj. as an abstract substantive, *e.g.* Oscan *salaemom louicom*, "optimum publicum," i.e. "optima rei publicae ratio." In verbal forms the same use of the gerundive combined with the noun to represent the total verbal action, e.g. Umb. *ocrer pehaner paca*, "arcus pandae causa"; the usual sequence of tenses, *e.g.* the imperfect subj in Oratio Obliqua representing the fut. indic. in Oratio Recta (see *Cippus Abellanus* § 23, 25), and finally the use of the perf. subj in Oscan in prohibitions (*nep fefacid*, "neue fecerit "), but also in positive commands (Osc. *aakrafir*, see above).

Fuller accounts of the dialects in all these aspects will be found most exhaustively in Von Planta, *Grammatik der Oskisch-umbrischen Dialekte* (Strassburg, 1892–1897). Less fully, but very clearly and acutely in C. D. Buck's *Osca* and *Umbrian Grammar* (Boston, U.S.A., 1904). R. S. Conway, *The Italic Dialects*, vol. ii. (Cambridge, 1897), gives a fuller account of the alphabets and their history, a Conspectus of the Accidence and an account of the Syntax at some length.   (R. S. C.)

OSCAR I. (1799–1859), king of Sweden and Norway, was the son of General Bernadotte, afterwards King Charles XIV. of Sweden, and his wife, Eugénie Désirée Clary, afterwards Queen Desideria. When, in August 1810, Bernadotte was elected crown prince of Sweden, Oscar and his mother removed from Paris to Stockholm (June 1811). From Charles XIII. the lad received the title of duke of Södermanland (Sudermania). He quickly acquired the Swedish language, and, by the time he reached manhood, had become a general favourite. His very considerable native talents were developed by an excellent education, and he soon came to be regarded as an authority on all social-political questions. In 1839 he wrote a series of articles on popular education, and (in 1841) an anonymous work, *Om Straff och straffanstalter*, advocating prison reforms. Twice during his father's lifetime he was viceroy of Norway. On the 19th of June 1823 he married the princess Josephine, daughter of Eugène de Beauharnais, duke of Leuchtenberg, and granddaughter of the empress Josephine. In 1838 the king began to suspect his heir of plotting with the Liberal party to bring about a change of ministry, or even his own abdication. If Oscar did not actively assist the Opposition on this occasion, his disapprobation of his father's despotic behaviour was notorious, though he avoided an actual rupture. Yet his liberalism was of the most cautious and moderate character, as the Opposition, shortly after his accession (March 8th, 1844), discovered to their great chagrin. He would not hear of any radical reform of the cumbrous and obsolete constitution. But one of his earliest measures was to establish freedom of the press. Most of the legislation during Oscar I.'s reign aimed at improving the economic position of Sweden, and the *riksdag*, in its address to him in 1857, rightly declared that he had promoted the material prosperity of the kingdom more than any of his predecessors. In foreign affairs Oscar I. was a friend of the principle of nationality. In 1848 he supported Denmark against Germany; placed Swedish and Norwegian troops in cantonments in Fünen and North Schleswig (1849–1850); and mediated the truce of Malmö (August 26th, 1848). He was also one of the guarantors of the integrity of Denmark (London protocol, May 8th, 1852). As early as 1850 Oscar I. had conceived the plan of a dynastic union of the three northern kingdoms, but such difficulties presented themselves that the scheme had to be abandoned. He succeeded, however, in reversing his father's obsequious policy towards Russia. His fear lest Russia should demand a stretch of coast along the Varanger Fjord induced him to remain neutral during the Crimean War, and, subsequently, to conclude an alliance with Great Britain and France (November 25th, 1855) for preserving the territorial integrity of Scandinavia. Oscar I. left four sons, of whom two, Carl (Charles XV.) and Oskar Fredrik (Oscar II.), succeeded to his throne.

See T. Almén, *Åtten Bernadotte* (Stockholm, 1896); and C. E. Akrell, *Minnen från Carls XIV's, Oscars I. och Carls XV. Lagar* (Stockholm, 1884, 1885). Also NORWAY (*history*) and SWEDEN (*history*).

OSCAR II. (1829–1907), king of Sweden and Norway, son of Oscar I., was born at Stockholm on the 21st of January 1829. He entered the navy at the age of eleven, and was appointed junior lieutenant in July 1845. Later he studied at the univer-

sity of Upsala, where he distinguished himself in mathematics. In 1857 he married Princess Sophia Wilhelmina, youngest daughter of Duke William of Nassau. He succeeded his brother, Charles XV. on the 18th of September 1872, and was crowned in the Norwegian cathedral of Drontheim on the 18th of July 1873. At his accession he adopted as his motto *Brödrafolkens Val*, "the welfare of the brother folk," and from the first he realized the essential difficulties in the maintenance of the union between Sweden and Norway. The political events which led up to the final crisis in 1905, by which the thrones were separated, are dealt with in the historical articles under NORWAY and SWEDEN. But it may be said that the peaceful solution eventually adopted could hardly have been attained but for the tact, and patience of the king himself. He declined, indeed, to permit any prince of his house to become king of Norway, but better relations between the two countries were restored before his death, which took place at Stockholm on the 8th of December 1907. His acute intelligence and his aloofness from the dynastic considerations affecting most European sovereigns gave the king considerable weight as an arbitrator in international questions. At the request of Great Britain, Germany and the United States in 1889 he appointed the chief justice of Samoa, and he was again called in to arbitrate in Samoan affairs in 1899. In 1897 he was empowered to appoint a fifth arbitrator if necessary in the Venezuelan dispute, and he was called in to act as umpire in the Anglo-American arbitration treaty that was quashed by the senate. He won many friends in England by his outspoken and generous support of Great Britain at the time of the Boer War (1899–1902), expressed in a declaration printed in *The Times* of the 2nd of May 1900, when continental opinion was almost universally hostile.

Himself a distinguished writer and musical amateur, King Oscar proved a generous friend of learning, and did much to encourage the development of education throughout his dominions. In 1858 a collection of his lyrical and narrative poems, *Memorials of the Swedish Fleet*, published anonymously, obtained the second prize of the Swedish Academy. His "Contributions to the Military History of Sweden in the Years 1711, 1712, 1713," originally appeared in the *Annals* of the Academy, and were printed separately in 1865. His works, which included his speeches, translations of Herder's *Cid* and Goethe's *Torquato Tasso*, and a play, *Castle Cronberg*, were collected in two volumes in 1875–1876, and a larger edition, in three volumes, appeared in 1885–1888. His Easter hymn and some other of his poems are familiar throughout the Scandinavian countries. His *Memoirs of Charles XII.* were translated into English in 1879. In 1885 he published his *Address to the Academy of Music*, and a translation of one of his essays on music appeared in *Literature* on the 19th of May 1900. He had a valuable collection of printed and MS. music, which was readily accessible to the historical student of music.

His eldest son, Oscar Gustavus Adolphus, duke of Wärmland (b. 1858), succeeded him as Gustavus V. His second son, Oscar (b. 1859), resigned his royal rights on his marriage in 1888 with a lady-in-waiting, Fröken Ebba Munck, when he assumed the title of Prince Bernadotte. From 1892 he was known as Count Wisborg. The king's other sons were Charles, duke of Westergötland (b. 1861), who married Princess Ingeborg of Denmark; and Eugène, duke of Nerike (b. 1865), well known as an artist.

OSCEOLA (a corruption of the Seminole *As-se-he-ho-lar*, meaning black drink) (c. 1804–1838), a Seminole American Indian, leader in the second Seminole War, was born in Georgia, near the Chattahoochee river. His father was an Englishman named William Powell; his mother a Creek of the Red Stick or Mikasuki division. In 1808 he removed with his mother into northern Florida. When the United States commissioners negotiated with the Seminole chiefs the treaties of Payne's Landing (9th of May 1832) and Fort Gibson (28th of March 1833) for the removal of the Seminoles to Arkansas, Osceola seized the opportunity to lead the opposition of the young warriors, and declared to the U.S. agent, General Wiley Thompson, that any chief who prepared to remove would be killed. At the Agency (Fort King, in Marion county) he became more violent, and in the summer of 1835 Thompson put him in irons. From this confinement he obtained his release by a profession of penitence and of willingness to emigrate. Late in November 1835 he murdered Charley Emathla (or Emartla), a chief who was preparing to emigrate with his people, and on the 28th of December he and a few companions shot and killed General Thompson. On the same day two companies of infantry under Major Francis L. Dade were massacred at the Wahoo Swamp near the Withlacoochee river, while marching from Fort Brooke on Tampa Bay to the relief of Fort King. In a battle fought three days later at a ford of the Withlacoochee, Osceola was at the head of a negro detachment, and although the Indians and negroes were repulsed by troops under General Duncan L. Clinch (1787–1849), they continued, with Osceola as their most crafty and determined leader, to murder and devastate, and occasionally to engage the troops. In February 1836 General Edmund P. Gaines (1777–1849), with about 1100 men from New Orleans, marched from Fort Brooke to Fort King. When he attempted to return to Fort Brooke, because there were not the necessary provisions at Fort King, the Indians disputed his passage across the Withlacoochee. In the same year Generals Winfield Scott and Richard K. Call (1791–1862) conducted campaigns against them with little effect, and the year closed with General Thomas Sidney Jesup (1788–1860) in command with 8000 troops at his disposal. With mounted troops General Jesup drove the enemy from the Withlacoochee country and was pursuing them southward toward the Everglades when several chiefs expressed a readiness to treat for peace. In a conference at Fort Dade on the Withlacoochee on the 6th of March 1837 they agreed to cease hostilities, to withdraw south of the Hillsborough river, and to prepare for emigration to Arkansas, and gave hostages to bind them to their agreement. But on the 2nd of June Osceola came to the camp at the head of about 200 Mikasuki (Miccosukees) and effected the flight of all the Indians there, about 700 including the hostages, to the Everglades. Hostilities were then resumed, but in September Brigadier General Joseph M. Hernandez captured several chiefs, and a few days later there came from Osceola a request for an interview. This was granted, and by command of General Jesup he was taken captive at a given signal and carried to Fort Moultrie, at Charleston, South Carolina, where he died in January 1838. The war continued until 1842, but after Osceola's death the Indians sought to avoid battle with the regular troops and did little but attack the unarmed inhabitants.

See J. T. Sprague, *The Origin, Progress and Conclusion of the Florida War* (New York, 1848).

OSCHATZ, a town in the kingdom of Saxony, in the valley of the Döllnitz, 36 m. N.W. of Dresden, on the trunk railway to Leipzig. Pop. (1905) 10,854. One of its three Evangelical churches is the handsome Gothic church of St Aegidius, with twin spires. Sugar, felt, woollens, cloth and leather are manufactured, and there is considerable trade in agricultural produce. Four miles west lies the Kolmberg, the highest eminence in the north of Saxony.

See C. Hoffmann, *Historische Beschreibung der Stadt Oschatz* (Oschatz, 1873–1874); and Gurlitt, *Bau- und Kunstdenkmäler der Amtsmannschaft Oschatz* (Dresden, 1905).

OSCHERSLEBEN, a town of Germany, in the Prussian province of Saxony, on the Bode, 24 m. by rail S.W. of Magdeburg, and at the junction of lines to Halberstadt and Jerxheim. Pop. (1905) 13,271. Among its industrial establishments are sugar-refineries, iron-foundries, breweries, machine-shops and brick works. Oschersleben is first mentioned in 803, and belonged in the later middle ages to the bishops of Halberstadt.

OSCILLA, a word applied in Latin usage to small figures, most commonly masks or faces, which were hung up as offerings to various deities, either for propitiation or expiation, and in connexion with festivals and other ceremonies. It is usually taken as the plural of *oscillum* (dimin. of *os*), a little face. As the *oscilla* swung in the wind, *oscillare* came to mean to swing, hence

in English "oscillation," the act of swinging backwards and forwards, periodic motion to and fro, hence any variation or fluctuation, actual or figurative. For the scientific problems connected with oscillation see MECHANICS and OSCILLOGRAPH.

Many *oscilla* or masks, representing the head of Bacchus or of different rustic deities, are still preserved. There is a marble *oscillum* of Bacchus in the British Museum. Others still in existence are made of earthenware, but it seems probable that wax and wood were the ordinary materials. Small rudely shaped figures of wool, known as *pilae*, were also hung up in the same way as the *oscilla*.

The festivals at which the hanging of *oscilla* took place were: (1) The *Sementivae Feriae*, or sowing festivals, and the *Paganalia*, the country festivals of the tutelary deities of the pagi; both took place in January. Here the oscilla were hung on trees, such as the vine and the olive, oak and the pine, and represented the faces of Liber, Bacchus or other deity connected with the cultivation of the soil (Virg. *Georg.* ii. 382-396). (2) The *Feriae Latinae*: in this case games were played, among them swinging (*oscillatio*); cf. the Greek festival of *Aeora* (see ERIGONE). Festus (*s.v. Oscillum*, ed. Müller, p. 194) says that this swinging was called *oscillatio* because the swingers masked their faces (*os celare*) out of shame. (3) At the *Compitalia*, Festus says (*Paul. ex Fest.* ed. Müller, p. 239) that *pilae* and *effigies viriles et muliebres* made of wool were hung at the cross-roads to the Lares, the number of *pilae* equalling that of the slaves of the family, the *effigies* that of the children; the purpose being to induce the Lares to spare the living, and to be content with the *pilae* and images. This has led to the generally accepted conclusion that the custom of hanging these *oscilla* represents an older practice of expiating human sacrifice. There is also no doubt a connexion with lustration by the purifying with air.

OSCILLOGRAPH. In connexion with the study of alternating or varying electric current, appliances are required for determining the mode in which the current varies. An instrument for exhibiting optically or graphically these variations is called an oscillograph, or sometimes an ondograph. Several methods have been employed for making observations of the form of alternating current curves—(1) the point-by-point method, ascribed generally to Jules Joubert; (2) the stroboscopic methods, of which the wave transmitter of H. L. Callendar, E. B. Rosa, and E. Hospitalier are examples; (3) methods employing a high-frequency galvanometer or oscillograph, which originated with A. E. Blondel, and are exemplified by his oscillograph and that of W. Duddell; and (4) purely optical methods, such as those of I. Fröhlich and K. F. Braun.

In the point-by-point method the shaft of an alternator, or an alternating current motor driven in step with it, is furnished with an insulating disk having a metallic slip inserted in its edge. Against this disk press two springs which are connected together at each revolution by the contact of the slip at an assigned instant during the phase of the alternating current. This contact may be made to close the circuit of a suitable voltmeter, or to charge a condenser in connexion with it, and the reading of the voltmeter will therefore not be the average or effective voltage of the alternator, but the instantaneous value of the electromotive force corresponding to that instant during the phase, determined by the position of the rotating contact slip with reference to the poles of the alternator. If the contact springs can be moved round the disk so as to vary the instant of contact, we can plot out the value of the observed instantaneous voltage of the machine or circuit in a wavy curve, showing the wave form of the electromotive force of the alternator. This process is a tedious one, and necessarily only gives the average form of thousands of different alternations.

In the Hospitalier ondograph,[1] a synchronous electric motor driven in step with the periodic current in the circuit being tested drives a cylinder of insulating material having a metallic slip let into its edge. This cylinder is driven at a slightly lower speed than that of synchronism. Three springs press against the cylinder and make contact for a short time during each revolution, so that a condenser is charged by the circuit at an assigned instant during the alternating current phase, and then subsequently connected to a voltmeter. This process, so to speak, samples or tests the varying electromotive force of the alternating current at one particular instant during the phase and measures it on a voltmeter. Owing to the fact that the cylinder is losing or gaining slightly in speed on the circuit periodicity, the voltmeter goes slowly, say in one minute, through all the phases

[1] E. Hospitalier, "The Slow Registration of Rapid Phenomena by Stroboscopic Methods," *Journ. Inst. Elec. Eng.* (London, 1904), 33, 175. In this paper the author describes the "Ondographe" and "Puissancegraphe." See also a description of the ondograph in the *Electrical Review*, (1902), 50, 969.

of voltage which are performed rapidly during each period by the alternating current. The voltmeter needle may then be made to record its variations graphically on a drum covered with paper and so to delineate the wave form of the current. The process is analogous to the optical experiment of looking at a quickly rotating wheel or engine through slits in a disk, rotating slightly faster or slower than the object observed. We then see the engine going through all its motions but much more slowly, and can follow them easily. In another form devised by Callendar,[1] a revolving contact disk is placed on the shaft of an alternator, or of a synchronous motor driven by the alternating current under test. A pair of contact springs are slowly shifted over so as to close the circuit at successive assigned instants during a complete phase. The electromotive force so selected is balanced against the steady potential difference produced between a fixed and a sliding contact on a wire traversed by another steady current, and if there is any difference between this last, the potential difference, and the instantaneous potential difference balanced against it, a relay is operated and sets in action a motor which shifts the contact point along the potentiometer wire and so restores the balance. This contact point also carries a pen which moves over a rotating drum covered with paper. As the brushes are slowly shifted over on the revolving contact so as to select different phases of the alternating electromotive force, the pen follows and draws a curve delineating the wave form of that electromotive force or current. An instrument devised by E. B. Rosa is not very different in construction.[2] A commutator method has also been devised by T. R. Lyle (*Phil. Mag.*, November 1903, 6. 517) in which at an assigned instant during the phase a selection is made from the periodic current and measured on a galvanometer.

The oscillographs of A. E. Blondel[3] and W. Duddell operate on a different principle. They consist essentially of a galvanometer of which the needle or coil has such a short natural periodic time that it can follow all the variations of a current which runs through its cycle in say 1/100th second. This needle or coil must be so damped that when the current is cut off it returns to zero at once without overshooting the mark. By means of an attached mirror and reflected ray of light the motion of the movable system can be indicated on a screen. This ray is also given a periodic motion of the same frequency by reflection from a separate oscillating mirror so as to make the two motions at right angles to one another, and thus we have depicted on the screen a bright line having the same form as the periodic current being tested. In W. Duddell's oscillograph[4] (fig. 1) the galvanometer part consists of an electromagnet in the field of which is stretched a loop of very fine wire. To this is attached a mirror; hence, if a current goes up one side of a loop and down another, the wires are oppositely displaced in the field. The loop and mirror move in a cavity full of oil to render the system dead-beat. A ray of light is reflected from this mirror and from another mirror which is rocked by a small motor driven off the same circuit, so that the ray has two vibratory motions imparted to it at right angles, one a simple harmonic motion and the other a motion imitating the variation of the current or electromotive force under test. This ray can be received on a screen or photographic plate, and thus the wave form of the current is recorded. In the Duddell oscillograph it is usual to place a pair of loops in the magnetic field, each with its own mirror, so that a pair of curves can be delineated at the same time, and if there is any difference in phase between them, it will be detected. Thus we can take two curves, one showing the potential difference at the end of an inductive circuit, and the other the current flowing through the circuit. In one form of Blondel's oscillograph, the vibrating system is a small magnetic needle carrying a mirror, but the principle on which it operates is the same as that of the instrument above described. The oscillograph can be made to exhibit optically the form of the current curve in non-cyclical phenomena, such as the discharge of a condenser. In this case the large vibrating mirror must be oscillated by a current from an alternator, on the shaft of which is a disk of non-conducting material with brass slips let into it and so arranged with contact brushes that in each period of the alternator a contact is made, charging up a condenser and discharging it through the oscillograph. In this way an optical representation is obtained of the oscillatory discharge of the condenser. A form of thermal oscillograph has been devised by J. T. Irwin (*Jour. Inst. Elec. Eng. Lond.* 1907, 39. 617). In this instrument the periodic current, the time variation of which is being studied, passes through a pair of fine wires or strips, going up one wire and down the other. These wires are also traversed in the same direction by a constant current from a battery. The two currents are therefore added in one wire and subtracted in the other, and produce a differential heating effect which causes unequal expansion, and this in turn is made to tilt a

mirror which reflects a ray of light on to a screen or photographic plate as in the Duddell oscillograph.

Finally, purely optical methods have been employed. Braun[5] devised a form of cathode ray tube, consisting of a vacuum tube having a narrow tubular portion and a bulbous end. The cathode terminal is connected to the negative pole of an electrostatic machine, such as a Wimshurst or Voss machine, giving a steady pressure. A cathode discharge is projected through two small holes in plates in the narrow part of the tube on a fluorescent screen at the end of the enlarged end, and the cathode ray or pencil depicts on it a small bright greenish patch of light. If a pair of coils of wire through which an alternating current is passing are placed on either side of the tube, just beyond one of the plates with a hole in it, the field

FIG. 1.

causes a periodic displacement of the cathode ray and elongates the patch of light into a bright line. If this patch is also given a displacement in the direction of right angles by examining it in a steadily vibrating mirror, we see a wavy or oscillatory line of light which is an optical representation of the wave form of a current in the coils embracing the Braun tube.

References.—See J. A. Fleming, *A Handbook for the Electrical Laboratory and Testing Room*, vol. i. (London, 1901), which contains a list of original papers on the oscillograph; Id., *The Principles of Electric Wave Telegraphy* (London, 1906), which gives illustrations of the use of the oscillograph and the Braun cathode ray tube in depicting condenser discharges; also, for the development of the oscillograph, A. E. Blondel, "Oscillographs : New Apparatus for registering Electrical Oscillations" (a short description of the bifilar and soft iron oscillographs), *Comptes rendus* (1893), 116. 502; Id., "On the Determination and Photographic Registration of Periodic Curves," *La Lumière électrique* (August 29th, 1901); Id.,

[1] H. L. Callendar, "An Alternating Cycle Curve Recorder," *Electrician*, 41. 582.
[2] E. B. Rosa, "An Electric Curve Tracer," *Electrician*, 40. 126.
[3] See *Assoc. Franç. pour l'Avanc. des Sciences* (1898), for a paper on oscillographs describing Blondel's original invention of the oscillograph in 1891.
[4] *Electrician* (1897). 39. 636.

[5] See K. F. Braun, *Wied. Ann.* (1897), 60. 552; H. M. Varley, *Phil. Mag.* (1902), 3500; and J. M. Varley and W. H. F. Murdock, "On some Applications of the Braun Cathode Ray Tube," *Electrician* (1905), 55. 335.

"New Oscillographs," *L'Éclairage électrique* (May, 1902); Id., "Theory of Oscillographs," *L'Éclairage électrique* (October 28th, 1902). "Hot Wire Wattmeters and Oscillographs," J. T. Irwin, *Jour. Inst. Elec. Eng.* (1907), 39. 617. (J. A. F.)

OSH, a town of Russian Turkestan, in the government of Ferghana, 31 m. S.E. of Andijan railway terminus, at an altitude of 4030 ft. Pop. (1900) 37,397. It consists of two parts, native and Russian. Here begins a good road up to the Pamirs, practicable for artillery The trade with China is considerable.

O'SHANASSY, SIR JOHN (1818–1883), British colonial statesman, was born in 1818 at Holycross Abbey, near Thurles, Tipperary, his father being a land surveyor. He married in 1839, and the same year emigrated to the Port Phillip district of New South Wales, where he was for some time engaged in farming, and subsequently commenced business in Melbourne. Dr Geoghegan, afterwards Roman Catholic bishop of Adelaide, induced him to take part in public affairs. He was one of the founders, and later the president, of the St Patrick's Society of Melbourne, and represented the Roman Catholic body on the denominational board of education. When Port Phillip was separated from New South Wales in 1851 and became the colony of Victoria, O'Shanassy was returned to the Legislative Council as one of the members for Melbourne. A few weeks after the new colony began its independent existence gold was discovered, and the local government had to solve a number of difficult problems. The legislature was composed partly of elected representatives, and partly of nominees appointed by the governor in council. The great natural ability of O'Shanassy forced him to the front, and for some time the policy of the country was virtually shaped by him and by Mr (afterwards Sir) W. F. Stawell, the attorney-general. It was very much owing to the strong position taken by O'Shanassy that the Legislative Council was allowed to control not only the ordinary revenue raised by taxation, but also the territorial revenue derived from the sale and occupation of crown lands. From that date the Legislative Council, led by O'Shanassy, became virtually supreme. After the Ballarat riots in 1854, O'Shanassy was one of the members of a commission appointed to inquire into the condition of the gold-fields. The commission's report was the foundation of the mining legislation which, initiated in Victoria, was gradually followed by all the Australasian colonies. O'Shanassy, together with Sir Andrew Clarke, was one of the framers of the responsible government constitution. Under this constitution O'Shanassy was returned in 1856 to the Legislative Assembly for Melbourne and Kilmore, but took his seat for the latter constituency. Early in 1857 the Haines ministry, the first formed after the concession of responsible government, was defeated, and O'Shanassy formed a ministry of which he became the premier. But he was defeated after holding office for little more than six weeks. He returned to power in 1858 as chief secretary and premier. One of the first duties of the new ministry was to inaugurate the system of railways, and to raise the necessary funds for their construction. O'Shanassy decided to float a loan of eight millions sterling through the instrumentality of six of the Melbourne banks, and he began the series of borrowings by the Australian governments which subsequently attained such large proportions. In 1859 the ministry resigned, but in August 1861 O'Shanassy formed his third administration. During the two years that it held office the government passed an Education, a Local government, a Civil Service and a Land Act. The object of this last act was to abolish the system of selling the crown lands by auction, and to substitute another which insisted rather upon residence and cultivation than upon obtaining the highest possible price. The act did not carry out all the intentions of its framers, but it was a step in the right direction. The O'Shanassy government was defeated in June 1863, and its chief never again succeeded in regaining office. He did not stand at the general election of 1866, and paid a visit to Europe. In 1867 he returned to Victoria, and was elected to the Legislative Council. In 1870 he was created C.M.G., and in 1874 K.C.M.G. In the latter year he resigned his seat in the council, and did not re-enter public life until 1877, when he was returned to the

Assembly for Belfast. His strongly expressed Conservative opinions and his devotion to the interests of the Roman Catholic church impaired his influence in the legislature, which had become extremely democratic during the eleven years that he had been absent from it; and although Sir John was a fearless critic of the policy of the government, he never succeeded in defeating it. He had a singularly comprehensive grasp of all constitutional questions, was an eloquent speaker and an ardent free-trader. He retired from parliament in 1880, and died in 1883.

O'SHAUGHNESSY, ARTHUR WILLIAM EDGAR (1844–1881), English poet, was born in London on the 14th of March 1844, and at the age of seventeen obtained through the first Lord Lytton, who took a peculiar interest in him, the post of transcriber in the library of the British Museum. Two years later he was appointed to be an assistant in the natural history department, where he specialised in ichthyology. But his natural bent was towards literature. He published his *Epic of Women* in 1870, *Lays of France*, a free version of the *Lais* of Marie de France, in 1872, and *Music and Moonlight* in 1874. In his thirtieth year he married a daughter of John Westland Marston, and during the last seven years of his life printed no volume of poetry. *Songs of a Worker* was published posthumously in 1881, O'Shaughnessy dying on the 30th of January in that year from the effects of a chill upon a delicate constitution. O'Shaughnessy was a true singer; but his poems lack importance in theme and dignity in thought. His melodies are often magnificent; and, as in *The Fountain of Tears*, the richness of his imagery conceals a certain vagueness and indecision of the creative faculty. He was very felicitous in bold uses of repetition and echo, by which he secured effects which for haunting melody are almost inimitable. His spirit is that of a mild melancholy, drifting helplessly through the realities of life and spending itself in song. By some critics he has been disparaged, but reparation was done to his memory by Francis Turner Palgrave, who, in the second series of the *Golden Treasury*, said with some exaggeration that his metrical gift was the finest, after Tennyson, of any of the later poets, and that he had "a haunting music all his own."

OSHAWA, a manufacturing town and port of entry of Ontario county, Ontario, Canada, on Lake Ontario and the Grand Trunk railway, 30 m. E.N.E. of Toronto. Pop. (1901) 4394. It contains flour, woollen and grist-mills, piano, farm implement and carriage factories, foundries, tanneries, canning factories, &c. There are a ladies' college and good schools.

OSHIMA, a group of three small islands belonging to Japan, lying southwards of Kiushiu, in 30° 50′ N. and 130° E. Their names, from west to east, are Kuroshima, Iwo-shima and Takashima. Kuro-shima rises to a height of 2475 ft., and Iwo-shima has an active volcano 2480 ft. high. These islands are not to be confounded with Oshima, the most northerly island of the Izu-noshichito, or with the northern group of the Luchu Islands. There are several other islands of the same name in Japan, Oshima signifying "big island." One of the best known lies off the Kii promontory, and has been the scene of many maritime disasters.

OSHKOSH, a city and the county-seat of Winnebago county, Wisconsin, U.S.A., about 75 m. N.N.W. of Milwaukee, on the W. shore of Lake Winnebago at the mouth of the Upper Fox river. Pop. (1900) 28,284, of whom 7356 were foreign-born (including 4500 from Germany), and 16,042 of foreign parentage (including 10,655 of German and 1015 of Bohemian parentage); (1910 census) 33,062. Oshkosh is served by the Chicago, Milwaukee & St Paul, the Chicago & Northwestern and the Minneapolis, St Paul & Sault Ste. Marie railways, by river steamboat lines connecting with other Fox River Valley cities, with the Wisconsin river at Portage, and with the Great Lakes at Green Bay, and by interurban electric lines connecting with Fond du Lac on the S., Green Bay on the N. and Omro on the W. The city lies on both sides of the Fox river, here spanned by six steel bridges, and stretches back to Lake Butte des Morts, an expansion of the Fox. North Park (60 acres), on the lake front, is the most noteworthy of its parks; and there are Chautauqua grounds on the lake front. Yacht races take place annually on Lake Winnebago. Among the public buildings are the City Hall, Post Office, Winnebago County Court House, Public Library (22,000 volumes). Oshkosh is the seat of a State Normal School (1871), the largest in the state. The principal industries are the manufacture of lumber and of lumber products, although the former, which was once of paramount importance, has declined with the cutting of neighbouring forests. In 1905 the value of the city's factory product was $8,706,705, the lumber, timber and planing mill products being valued at $4,671,003, the furniture at $751,511 and the waggons and carriages at $475,935. Oshkosh is an important wholesale distributing centre for a large part of central Wisconsin. Farming and dairying are important industries in the vicinity.

Under the French régime the site of Oshkosh was on the natural route of travel for those who crossed the Fox-Wisconsin portage, and was visited by Marquette, Joliet and La Salle on their way to the Mississippi. There were temporary trading posts here in the 18th century. About 1827 the first permanent settlers came, and in 1830 there were a tavern, a store and a ferry across the river to Algoma, as the S. side of the river was at first called. The settlement was first known as Saukeer, but in 1840 its name was changed to Oshkosh in honour of a Menominee chief who had befriended the early settlers and who lived in the vicinity until his death in 1856. The real prosperity of the place began about 1845 with the erection of two saw mills; in 1850 Oshkosh had 1400 inhabitants, and between 1860 and 1870 the population increased from 6086 to 12,663. In July 1874 and April 1875 the city was greatly damaged by fire.

OSIANDER, ANDREAS (1498–1552), German reformer, was born at Gunzenhausen, near Nuremberg, on the 19th of December 1498. His German name was Heiligmann, or, according to others, Hosemann. After studying at Leipzig, Altenburg and Ingolstadt, he was ordained priest in 1520 and appointed Hebrew tutor in the Augustinian convent at Nuremberg. Two years afterwards he was appointed preacher in the St Lorenz Kirche, and about the same time he publicly joined the Lutheran party, taking a prominent part in the discussion which ultimately led to the adoption of the Reformation by the city. He married in 1525. He was present at the Marburg conference in 1529, at the Augsburg diet in 1530 and at the signing of the Schmalkald articles in 1537, and took part in other public transactions of importance in the history of the Reformation; that he had an exceptionally large number of personal enemies was due to his vehemence, coarseness, and arrogance in controversy. The introduction of the Augsburg Interim in 1548 necessitated his departure from Nuremberg; he went first to Breslau, and afterwards settled at Königsberg as professor in its new university at the call of Duke Albert of Prussia. Here in 1550 he published two disputations, the one *De lege et evangelio* and the other *De justificatione*, which aroused a controversy still unclosed at his death on the 17th of October 1552. While he was fundamentally at one with Luther in opposing both Romanism and Calvinism, his mysticism led him to interpret justification by faith as not an imputation but an infusion of the essential righteousness or divine nature of Christ. His party was afterwards led by his son-in-law Johann Funck, but disappeared after the latter's execution for high treason in 1566. Osiander's son Lukas (1534–1604), and grandsons Andreas (1562–1617) and Lukas (1571–1638), were well-known theologians.

Osiander, besides a number of controversial writings, published a corrected edition of the Vulgate, with notes, in 1522, and a *Harmony* of the Gospels—the first work of its kind—in 1537. The best-known work of his son Lukas was an *Epitome of the Magdeburg Centuries*. See the *Life* by W. Möller (Elberfeld, 1870).

OSIER (through Fr. from Late Lat. *osaria, ausaria*, a bundle of osier or willow twigs; the common term under which are included the various species, varieties and hybrids of the genus Salix, used in the manufacture of baskets. The chief species in cultivation are: *Salix viminalis* (the common osier) and *S. triandra, S. amygdalina, S. purpurea* and *S. fragilis*, which

botanically are willows and not osiers. The first named with some forty of its varieties, formed until recent times the staple basket-making material in England. It is an abundant cropper, sometimes attaining on low-lying soils 13 ft. in height. Full-topped and smooth, it is by reason of its pithy nature mainly cultivated for coarse work and is generally used as brown stuff. Some harder varieties, known as stone osiers and raised on drier upland soils, are peeled and used for fine work. *S. fragilis*, with some half-score varieties, is almost exclusively used by market gardeners for bunching greens, turnips and other produce. Owing to the increased demand for finer work much attention has been given (see BASKET) in recent years to the cultivation of the more ligneous and tougher species, *S. triandra, S. purpurea* and *S. amygdalina* with their many varieties and hybrids.

It is commonly supposed that osiers or willows will prove remunerative and flourish with little attention on any poor, wet, marshy soil. This is, however, not the case. No crop responds more readily to careful husbandry and skilful cultivation. For the successful raising of the finer sorts of willows good, well-drained, loamy upland soil is desirable, which before planting should be deeply trenched and cleared of weeds. J. A. Krabe of Prummern near Aachen, the most scientific and practical of German cultivators, the results of whose experiments have been published in his admirable *Lehrbuch der rationellen Weidenkultur* (Aix-la-Chapelle, 1886, et seq.) went so far as to assert that willows prefer a dry to a wet soil. T. Selby of Oxford, Kent, in a report dated the 18th of November 1800 (see *Jour. Soc. Arts*, 1801, xix., 75) stated that all kinds of willows invariably throve best on the driest spots of some yet land planted by him. Krabe found that in addition to loam, willows did well on dry ferrugineous, sandy ground with a good top soil of about 6 in. in depth; on poor loamy clay, and even on peaty moors.

At any time, from late winter to early spring, the ground may be planted with "sets," i.e. cuttings of about 9 to 16 in. in length, taken from clean, well-ripened rods. These are firmly set to within 3 to 6 in. of the top in rows, 16 to 20 in. apart and spaced at intervals of 8 to 12 in. Yearling sets are largely planted, but the experiments of Krabe tend to prove, and the practice of the best Midland and West of England growers confirms, the superior productiveness of sets cut from two yearling rods. W. P. Ellmore of Leicester, the most experienced and enterprising of Midland cultivators, preferred to plant his sets in squares, 18 to 20 in. apart, in order to admit of the use of the horse hoe in both directions and a freer play of sun and air. Great care should be exercised in planting lest the bark be fractured, loosened or removed from the wood. The ground should be kept free of weeds by frequent hoeing and, if not subject to periodical alluvial floods, manured yearly. The coarser *S. viminalis* may be raised on lowland soil if not water-logged or marshy, but the same attention to trenching and weeding is imperative. Approved varieties of willows cost from 5s. to 17s. 6d. per 1000 sets. The more valuable kinds are known as: New kind, Black mauls, Spaniards, Glibskins, Long-bud, Long-skin, Lancashire red-bud, French, Italians, Pomeranians and Councillors and scores of other local names. A hybrid of *S. viminalis* and *S. triandra*, known as Black-top and introduced by Ellmore has been found to produce the heaviest crops on the best Leicestershire grounds.

Cutting and binding take place in early winter after the fall of the leaf, the crop being known as green whole stuff. The coarser kinds are sorted, cured (dried in the sun and wind) and stacked ready for market. These are known as brown rods. The finer kinds, after the more shrubby or ill-grown rods, termed Ragged, have been rejected, are peeled or buffed. Two methods of stripping are chiefly practised: from the heads (sets) and from the pit. By the former method the rods are left on the ground until spring advances, when a rapid growth of the cork cambium begins. They are then cut direct from the head and the bark is easily removed by drawing the rods through a bifurcated hand-brake of smooth, well-rounded steel, framed in wood. Improved brakes worked by a treadle strip two rods at a time. For the smaller sizes, rubber brakes are sometimes used and, for the very smallest, the fingers either bare or protected by linen bands. This method ensures a clean-butted untractured rod, but unless great judgment is exercised in selecting the proper time for cutting, the rods will remain double-skinned and the head may bleed. By the "pit" process the green rods are stood upright in shallow pits of water at a depth of about 6 to 9 in. until the sap rises and growth begins, when they are ready for the brake. The defects of this method are that the tops are liable to split in the brake and the butts to remain foul. A third, known as the "pit" system enables the grower to bridge over the interval, and so keep his hands employed, between the end of the "head" and the beginning of the "pit" stripping. The willows are cut at the first indication of the sap rising and "couched" in rotten peelings and soil at a slight angle, the butts being on the ground, which should be strewn with damp straw from a manure heap. The tops are covered lightly with rotted peelings and by periodical application of water, fermentation is induced at the bottom, heat is engendered, the leaves force their way through the covering and peeling may begin. Peeling is chiefly done by women and lasts from early May to the middle of July. After stripping, the rods are bleached in the sun and stored for sale as White. If the rods are to be buffed they are immersed in large tanks of boiling water from 4 to 6 hours. They are then allowed to cool and mellow, are stripped and carefully dried in sun and air and remain dyed a rich tawny brown or buff colour. Brown rods may also be buffed by sinking them in cold water which is heated to boiling point, and maintained at that temperature for the requisite period. Sticks (two or three yearling osiers) are also grown for whitening and buffing; the less ligneous varieties of *S. viminalis* are best adapted for this purpose. Osiers or willows when tied for market vary locally in girth. In the west of England, the Thames valley, Cambridgeshire and Norfolk a "bolt" of green stuff measures 42 to 45 in. in circumference at 10 in. from the butt; a bolt of white or brown, 40 in. In the northern and midland counties the stuff is invariably sold by weight. On the continent of Europe osiers or willows are bunched in sizes of one metre in girth at the butts and (except in Belgium) are also sold by weight.

The cost of planting an acre of fine willows varies greatly; it was estimated by R. L. and R. Cotterell of Ruscombe, Berks, as follows: trenching and cleaning ground, £12; sets, 20,000 at 5s. per 1000, £5; planting and levelling £1. Hoeing, first year, £2; succeeding years about £3, 15s. per annum. After 12 to 15 years the heads become "tired," and should be grubbed up. The first year's crop, known as the "maiden" crop, is of small value but should be cut and the ensuing years of maturity will yield crops of about 130 bolts, green, per acre, worth £9, 15s. If whitened, the loss in bulk and in rejection being two-thirds, this would produce about 44 bolts, which at £30 per load of 80 bolts, the appreciated market value of 1907, would be worth £16, 10s. The cost of whitening is 1s. 6d. per bolt, but against this the value of the rejected Ragged, and as Brown, should be set off. In years of abundant crops and short demand, prices have fallen to £24 per load.

The cost of planting and the outlay for manuring and weeding during the years of maturity of the crop, are higher in the Midlands and the yield was estimated by Ellmore at 6 to 10 tons per acre, green, worth from £3, 10s. to £6, per ton. White rods, costing from £3, to £3, 7s. 6d. per ton for extra labour, will realize from £22 to £24 per ton. Buff rods costing (with coal at 10s. per ton) £5 per ton extra, will realize from £22 to £32 per ton. From 2½ to 3 tons of green are required to produce one ton white or buff. Wm. Scaling of Notts estimated the entire cost of an osier plantation at £33, 12s. per acre for the first year and the outlay for the next two years at £7, 5s. and £6, 15s. respectively. The maiden crop he valued at £8, 12s. and the second and third years' crop at £17 and £22.

A table given by Krabe, based on results obtained for 12 plantations amounting to 20 hectares (50 English acres) during 20 years showed the value of produce per Prussian acre (2553 of an hectare) to be in the 1st year, £3, 6s. In the 2nd year the value of the produce was £8, 19s; in the 3rd year, £9, 15s.; in the 4th year, £8, 10s.; in the 5th year, £8, 1s.; in the 6th year, £7, 6s.; in the 7th year, £5, 19s.; in the 8th year, £8, 9s.; in the 9th year, £5, 5s.; in the 10th year, £6, 10s.; in the 11th year, £5, 11s.; in the 12th year, £4; in the 13th year, £6, 1s.; in the 14th year, £2, 9s.; in the 15th year, £2, 8s.; in the 16th year, £1, 18s.; in the 17th year, £2, 7s.; in the 18th year, £2, 2s.; in the 19th year, £3, 13s.1s.; and in the 20th year, £1, 11s.

The cultivation of osiers is attended with many disturbing causes— winter floods, spring frosts, ground vermin and insect pests of various kinds, sometimes working great havoc to the crop.

The best comprehensive work on the subject is that by Krabe, which has passed through several editions. A pamphlet on the cultivation of osiers in the Fen districts is issued in England by the Board of Agriculture. (T. O.)

OSIMO (anc. *Auximum*, q.s.); a town and episcopal see of the Marches, Italy, in the province of Ancona, 10 m. S. of that town by rail. Pop. (1901) 6404 (town); 18,475 (commune). It is situated on the top of a hill 870 ft. above sea-level, whence there is a beautiful view, and it retains a portion of its ancient town wall (2nd century B.C.). The restored cathedral has a portal with sculptures of the 13th century, an old crypt, a fine bronze font of the 16th century and a series of portraits of all the bishops of the see; the town hall contains a number of statues found on the site of the ancient forum and also a few good pictures. The castle (1489) was built by Baccio Pontelli. Silk-spinning and the raising of cocoons are carried on.

OSIRIS, one of the principal gods of the ancient Egyptians. See EGYPT, section *Egyptian Religion*.

OSKALOOSA, a city and the county-seat of Mahaska county, Iowa, U.S.A., about 62 m. S.E. of Des Moines. Pop. (1900) 9212, of whom 649 were foreign-born and 344 were negroes; ((1910 U.S. census) 9466. It is served by the Chicago, Burlington & Quincy, the Chicago, Rock Island & Pacific, and the Iowa Central railways, and by interurban electric lines. The city is built on a fertile prairie in one of the principal coal-producing regions of the state. At Oskaloosa is held the Iowa yearly meeting of the Society of Friends; and the city is the seat of Penn College (opened 1873), a Friends' institution, and of the Iowa Christian College (incorporated as Oskaloosa College in 1856 and reincorporated under its present name in 1902). At the village of University Park (incorporated in 1909), a suburb adjoining the city on the E., is the Central Holiness University (1906; coeducational), where the annual camp meeting of the National and Iowa Holiness Associations is held. Coal-mining is the most important industry in the surrounding region. There are deposits of clay and limestone in the vicinity, and among the city's manufactures are drain and sewer tile, paving and building bricks, cement blocks, and warm-air furnaces; in 1905 the factory products were valued at $770,894. Oskaloosa was first settled in 1843; it was selected in 1844 by the county commissioners as a site for the county-seat, and was chartered as a city in 1853. It is said to have been named in honour of the wife of the Indian chief Mahaska (of the Iowa tribe), in whose honour the county was named; a bronze statue of Mahaska (by Sherry E. Fry, an Iowa sculptor) was erected here in 1909.

See W. A. Hunter, "History of Mahaska County," in *Annals of Iowa*, vols. vi.-vii. (Davenport, Iowa, 1868-1869), published by the Iowa State Historical Society.

OSMAN ('UṢMĀN), the usual form of the Arabic name 'OTHMĀN, as representing the Turkish and Persian pronunciation of the name. It is used, therefore, for (1) the founder of the Osmanli or Ottoman dynasty, Osman I., who took the title of sultan, ruled in Asia Minor, and died in 1326, and (2) the sixteenth sultan Osman II., who reigned 1616-1621 (see TURKEY: *History*). For the third Mahommedan caliph see OTHMAN and CALIPHATE.

OSMAN (1837-1900), Turkish pasha and mushir (field marshal), was born at Tokat, in Asia Minor, in 1832. Educated at the military academy at Constantinople, he entered the cavalry in 1853, and served under Omar Pasha in the Russian War of 1853-56, in Wallachia and the Crimea. Appointed a captain, in the Imperial Guard, he went through the campaigns of the Lebanon in 1860 and of Crete in 1867 to 1869, under Mustapha Pasha, when he distinguished himself at the capture of the convent of Hagia Georgia, and was promoted lieut.-colonel. He served under Redif Pasha in suppressing an insurrection in Yemen in 1871, was promoted major-general in 1874, and general of division in 1875. Appointed to command the army corps at Widin in 1876 on the declaration of war by Servia, he defeated Tchnernaieff at Saitschar and again at Yavor in July, invaded Servia and captured Alexinats and Deligrad in October, when the war ended. Osman was promoted to be mushir, and continued in the command of the army corps at Widin. When the Russians crossed the Danube in July 1877, Osman moved his force to Plevna, and, with the assistance of his engineer, Tewfik Pasha, entrenched himself there on the right flank of the Russian line of communication, and gradually made the position a most formidable one. He repulsed the three general assaults of the Russians on the 20th and 30th July and the 11th September, inflicting on them great loss— some 30,000 men in the three battles. He held the position, after being closely invested, until the 9th December, when, compelled by want to cut his way out, he was severely wounded and forced to capitulate. This famous improvised defence of a position delayed the Russians for five months, and entailed their crossing the Balkan range in the depth of winter after the third battle of Plevna. The sultan conferred on Osman the Grand Cross of the Osmanie in brilliants and the title of "Ghazi" (victorious), and, when he returned from imprisonment in Russia, made him commandant of the Imperial Guard, grand-master of the artillery and marshal of the palace. In December 1878 he became war minister, and held the post, with a small break, until 1885. He died at Constantinople, in the palace built for him by the sultan near Yildiz Kiosk, on the 14th of April 1900, and his body was buried with great pomp in the Sultan Muhammad Mosque.

OSMIUM [symbol Os, atomic weight 190·9 (O = 16)], in chemistry, a metallic element, found in platinum ore in small particles, consisting essentially of an alloy of osmium and iridium and known as osmiridium. It was first obtained in 1803 by Smithson Tennant (*Phil. Trans.*, 1804, 94, p. 411). It may be prepared from osmiridium by fusing the alloy with zinc, the zinc being afterwards removed by distillation. The residue so obtained is then powdered and ignited with barium nitrate, which converts the iridium into its oxide and the osmium into barium osmiate. The barium salt is extracted by water and boiled with nitric acid, when the osmium volatilizes in the form of its tetroxide. As an alternative the osmiridium is fused with zinc, the regulus treated with hydrochloric acid, and then heated with barium nitrate and barium peroxide. After fusion, the mass is finely powdered and treated with cold dilute hydrochloric acid; and when action has finished, nitric and sulphuric acids are added, the precipitated barium sulphate removed, the liquid distilled and the osmium precipitated as sulphide. The sulphide is converted into sodium osmichloride by fusion with salt, in a current of chlorine, the sodium salt transformed into ammonium salt by precipitation with ammonium chloride, and the ammonium salt finally heated strongly (H. Sainte-Claire-Deville and H. J. Debray, *An. min.*, 1859 [5], 16, 74; see also C. E. Claus, *Jour. prakt. Chem.*, 1862, 85, p. 142; F. Wöhler, *Pogg.* 31, p. 161; E. Leidie and L. Quenessen, *Bull. soc. chim.*, 1903 (8), 29, p. 801). The tetroxide, OsO₄, can be easily reduced to the metal by dissolving it in hydrochloric acid and adding zinc, mercury, or an alkaline formate to the liquid, or by passing its vapour, mixed with carbon dioxide and monoxide, through a red-hot porcelain tube. The metal has a blue-grey colour, and may be obtained in the crystalline state by solution in tin. Its specific gravity is 21·3-22·48 (Deville and Debray) and its specific heat is 0·03113 (Regnault). It can be distilled in the electric furnace. In the massive state it is insoluble in all acids, but when freshly precipitated from solutions it dissolves in fuming nitric acid. On fusion with caustic potash it yields potassium osmiate. It combines with fluorine at 100° C., and when heated with chlorine it forms a mixture of chlorides. A colloidal variety was obtained by A. Gutbier and G. Hofmeier (*Jour. prakt. Chem.*, 1905, (2), 71, p. 452) by reducing osmium compounds with hydrazine hydrate in the presence of gum arabic.

Several oxides of osmium are known. The protoxide, OsO, is obtained as a dark grey insoluble powder when osmium sulphite is heated with sodium carbonate in a current of carbon dioxide. The sesquioxide, Os₂O₃, results on heating osmium with an excess of the tetroxide. The dioxide, OsO₂, is formed when potassium osmichloride is heated with sodium carbonate in a current of carbon dioxide, or by electrolysis of a solution of the tetroxide in the presence of alkali. It is insoluble in acids and exists in several hydrated forms. The osmiates, corresponding to the unknown trioxide OsO₃, are red or green coloured salts; the solutions are only stable in the presence of excess of caustic alkali; on boiling an aqueous solution of the potassium salt it decomposes readily, forming a black precipitate of osmic acid: H₂OsO₄. *Potassium osmiate*, K₂OsO₄2H₂O, formed when an alkaline solution of the tetroxide is decomposed by alcohol, or by potassium nitrite, crystallizes in red octahedra. It is stable in dry air, but in moist air rapidly decomposes. The tetroxide, OsO₄, is formed when osmium compounds are heated in air, or with aqua regia, or fused with caustic alkali and nitre. It is obtained as a yellowish coloured mass and can be sublimed in the form of needles which melt at 40° C. It possesses an unpleasant smell and its vapour is extremely poisonous. It dissolves slowly in water, and the aqueous solution is reduced by most metals with precipitation of osmium. It acts as an oxidising agent, liberating iodine from potassium iodide, converting alcohol into acetaldehyde, &c.

Osmium dichloride, OsCl₂, is obtained as a dark coloured powder when the metal is heated in a current of chlorine. Its solution in water is deep blue in colour, but the colour changes rapidly to green and yellow. The *trichloride*, OsCl₃, is only known in solution and is formed by the reducing action of mercury on ammoniacal solutions of the tetroxide. A hydrated form of composition OsCl₃.3H₂O has been described. The *tetrachloride*, OsCl₄, is obtained as a dark red sublimate (mixed with the dichloride) when osmium is heated in dry chlorine. It is soluble in water, but the dilute solution readily decomposes on standing. It combines with the chlorides of the alkali metals to form characteristic double salts of the type OsCl₄.2MCl (osmichlorides). *Potassium osmichloride*, K₂OsCl₆, is formed when a mixture of osmium and potassium chloride is heated in a current of chlorine, or on adding potassium chloride and alcohol to a solution of the tetroxide in hydrochloric acid. It crystallizes in dark red octahedra which are almost insoluble in cold water. The aqueous solution decomposes rapidly on boiling. Iodine has no action on osmium, but on warming the tetroxide with a mixture of potassium iodide and hydrochloric acid a deep emerald green colour is produced, due to the formation of a compound OsI₄.2HI; this reaction is a delicate test for osmium (E. Pinerua Alvarez, *Comptes rendus*, 1905, 140, p. 1254). *Osmium disulphide*, OsS₂, is obtained as a dark brown precipitate, insoluble in water, by passing sulphuretted hydrogen into a solution of an osmichloride. The *tetrasulphide*, OsS₄, is similarly prepared when sulphuretted hydrogen is passed into acid solutions of the tetroxide. It is a brownish black solid, insoluble in solutions of the alkaline sulphides. The atomic weight of the metal has been determined by K. Seubert (*Ber.*, 1888, 21, p. 1839) from the analysis of potassium and ammonium osmichlorides, the values obtained being approximately 191.

OSNABRÜCK, a town and episcopal see of Germany, in the Prussian province of Hanover, situated on the Hase, 30 m. W. of the city of Hanover, 31 m. by rail N.E. of Münster, and at the junction of the lines Hamburg-Cologne and Berlin-Amsterdam. Pop. (1905) 59,580. The older streets contain many interesting examples of Gothic and Renaissance domestic architecture, while the substantial houses of the modern quarters testify to the present prosperity of the town. The old fortifications have been converted into promenades. The Roman Catholic cathedral, with its three towers, is a spacious building of the 13th century, partly in the Romanesque and partly in the Transitional style; but it is inferior in architectural interest to the Marienkirche, a fine Gothic structure of the 14th and 15th centuries. The town hall, a 13th-century Gothic building, contains portraits of some of the plenipotentiaries engaged in concluding the peace of Westphalia, the negotiations for which were partly carried on here from 1644 to 1648. Other important buildings are the museum, erected in 1888–1889 and containing scientific and historical collections; the episcopal palace and the law courts. The lunatic asylum on the Gertrudenberg occupies the site of an ancient nunnery. The town has an equestrian statue of the emperor William I., a statue of Justus Möser (1720–1794) and a memorial of the war of 1870–1871. Linen was formerly the staple product, but it no longer retains that position. The manufactures include machinery, paper, chemicals, tobacco and cigars, pianos and beer. Other industries are spinning and weaving. The town has large iron and steel works and there are coal mines in the neighbourhood. A brisk trade is carried on in grain and wood, textiles, iron goods and Westphalian hams, while important cattle and horse fairs are held here.

Osnabrück is an ancient place and in 888 received the right to establish a mint, a market and a toll-house. Surrounded with walls towards the close of the 11th century, it maintained an independent attitude towards its nominal ruler, the bishop, and joined the Hanseatic League, reaching the height of its prosperity in the 13th century. The decay inaugurated by the dissensions of the Reformation was accelerated by the ravages of the Thirty Years' War; but a new period of prosperity began about the middle of the 18th century. The bishopric of Osnabrück was founded by Charlemagne about 800, after he had subdued the Saxons. It embraced the district between the Ems and the Hunte, and was included in the archbishopric of Cologne. By the peace of Westphalia it was decreed that it should be held by a Roman Catholic and a Protestant bishop alternately, and this state of affairs lasted until the secularization of the see in 1803. In 1815 the bishopric was given to Hanover. The last bishop was Frederick, duke of York, a son of the English king George III. Since 1857 Osnabrück has been the seat of a Roman Catholic bishop.

See Friederici and Stieve, *Geschichte der Stadt Osnabrück* (Osnabrück, 1816–1826); Wurm, *Osnabrück, seine Geschichte, seine Bau- und Kunstdenkmäler* (Osnabrück, 1906), and Hoffmeyer, *Geschichte der Stadt und des Regierungsbezirks Osnabrück* (Osnabrück, 1904). See also the *Osnabrücker Geschichtsquellen* (Osnabrück, 1891 fol.); the *Osnabrücker Urkundenbuch*, edited by F. Philippi and M. Bär (Osnabrück, 1892–1902); and the publications of the *Verein für Geschichte und Landeskunde von Osnabrück* (Osnabrück, 1882 fol.). For the history of the bishopric see J. C. Möller, *Geschichte der Weihbischöfe von Osnabrück* (Lingen, 1887); and C. Stüve, *Geschichte des Hochstifts Osnabrück* (Jena, 1872–1882).

OSNABURG, the name given to a coarish type of plain fabric, originally made from flax yarns. It is now made from either flax, tow or jute yarns—sometimes flax or tow warp with mixed or jute weft, and often entirely of jute. The finer and better qualities form a kind of common sheeting, and the various kinds may contain from 20 to 36 threads per inch and 10 to 15 picks per inch.

OSORIO, JERONYMO (1506–1580), Portuguese historian, was a native of Lisbon and son of the Ouvidor Geral of India. In 1519 his mother sent him to Salamanca to study civil law, and in 1525 he went on to Paris to study philosophy, and there became intimate with Peter Fabre, one of the founders of the Society of Jesus. Returning to Portugal, Osorio next proceeded for theology to Bologna, where he made such a name that King John III. invited him in 1536–1537 to lecture on scripture in the reorganized university of Coimbra. He returned to Lisbon in 1540, and acted as secretary to Prince Luis, and as tutor to his son, the prior of Crato, obtaining also two benefices in the diocese of Vizeu. In 1542 he printed in Lisbon his treatise *De nobilitate*. After the death of Prince Luis in 1553, he withdrew from court to his churches. He was named archdeacon of Evora in 1560, and much against his will became bishop of Silves in 1564. The Cardinal Prince Henry, who had bestowed these honours, desired to employ him at Lisbon in state business when King Sebastian took up the reins of power in 1568, but Osorio excused himself on the ground of his pastoral duties, though he showed his zeal for the commonwealth by writing two letters, one in which he dissuaded the king from going to Africa, the other sent during the latter's first expedition there (1574), in which he called on him to return to his kingdom. Sebastian looked with disfavour on opponents of his African adventure, and Osorio found it prudent to leave Portugal for Parma and Rome on the pretext of a visit *ad limina*. His scruples regarding residence, and the appeals of the king and the Cardinal Prince, prevented him enjoying for long the hospitality of Pope Gregory XIII., and he returned to his diocese and died at Tavira on the 20th of August 1580. An exemplary prelate, a learned scholar and an able critic, Osorio gained a European reputation by writing in Latin, then the *lingua franca* of the studious throughout Christendom, and the perfection of his prose style caused him to be named by contemporaries "the Portuguese Cicero." His well-stocked library was carried off from Faro when the earl of Essex captured the town in 1596, and many of the books were bestowed on the Bodleian at Oxford.

His principal works written in Latin include: (1) *De gloria et nobilitate civile et christiana*, an English version of which by W. Blandie appeared in London in 1576. (2) *De justitia*. (3) *De regis institutione et disciplina*. (4) *De vera sapientia*. (5) *De rebus Emmanuelis* (1586), a history of the reign of King Emanuel which is little more than a translation of the chronicle on the same subject by Damião de Goes. Osorio's book was turned into Portuguese by F. M. do Nascimento (q.v.), into French by J. Crispin (2 vols. Geneva, 1610), and an English paraphrase in 2 vols. by J. Gibbs came out in London in 1752. His *Opera omnia* were published by his nephew (4 vols., Rome, 1592). Two of his polemical treatises have been translated into English, his *Epistle to Elizabeth Queene of England* by R. Shacklock (Antwerp, 1565), and his *Confutation of M. W. Haddon* by J. Fen (Louvain, 1568). His Portuguese epistles, including the two before mentioned, were printed in Lisbon in two editions in 1818 and 1819, and in Paris in 1859. For his biography see *Obras de D. F. A. Lobo*, bishop of Vizeu, i. 293–301 (Lisbon, 1848).   (F P.)

OSPREY, or OSPRAY, a word said to be corrupted from "Ossifrage," Lat. *ossifraga*, bone-breaker. The *Ossifraga* of Pliny (*H.N.* x. 3) and some other classical writers seems to have

been the Lämmergeyer (q.v.); but the name, not inapplicable in that case, has been transferred to another bird which is no breaker of bones, save incidentally those of the fishes it devours.[1] The osprey is a rapacious bird, of middling size and of conspicuously marked plumage, the white of its lower parts, and often of its head, contrasting sharply with the dark brown of the back and most of its upper parts when the bird is seen on the wing It is the *Falco haliaetus* of Linnaeus, but was, in 1810, established by J. C. Savigny (*Ois. de l'Égypte*, p. 35) as the type of a new genus *Pandion*. It is closely related to the family *Falconidae*, but is the representative of a separate family, *Pandionidae* Pandion differs from the *Falconidae* not only pterylologically, as observed by C. L. Nitzsch, but also osteologically, as pointed out by A. Milne-Edwards (*Ois. foss. France*, ii. pp. 413, 419). In some of the characters in which it differs structurally from the *Falconidae*, it agrees with certain of the owls, but the most important parts of its internal structure, as well as of its pterylosis, forbid a belief that there is any near alliance of the two groups. The special characters of the family are the presence of a reversible outer toe, the absence of an aftershaft and the feathering of the tibiae.

The osprey is one of the most cosmopolitan birds-of-prey. From Alaska to Brazil, from Lapland to Natal, from Japan to Tasmania, and in some of the islands of the Pacific, it occurs as a winter-visitant or as a resident. Though migratory in Europe at least, it is generally independent of climate. It breeds equally on the half-thawed shores of Hudson's Bay and on the cays of Honduras, in the dense forests of Finland and on the barren rocks of the Red Sea, in Kamchatka and in West Australia. Among the countries it does not frequent are Iceland and New Zealand. Where, through abundance of food, it is numerous—as in former days was the case in the eastern part of the United States—the nests of the fish-hawk (to use its American name) may be placed on trees to the number of three hundred close together. Where food is scarcer and the species accordingly less plentiful, a single pair will occupy an isolated rock, and jealously expel all intruders of their kind, as happens in Scotland.[2] Few birds lay eggs so beautiful or so rich in colouring: their white or pale ground is spotted, blotched or marbled with almost every shade of purple, orange and red—passing from the most delicate lilac, buff and peach-blossom, through violet, chestnut and crimson, to a nearly absolute black. The fierceness with which ospreys defend their eggs and young, in addition to the dangerous situation not infrequently chosen for the eyry, make the task of robbing the nests difficult.

The term "osprey," applied to the nuptial plumes of the egrets in the feather trade, is derived from the French *esprit*; it has nothing to do with the osprey bird, and its use has been supposed to be due to a confusion with "spray."   (A. N.)

OSROENE, or OSRHOENE, a district of north-western Mesopotamia, in the hill country on the upper Bilechas (Belichus; mod. *Nahr Belik*, Bilikh), the tributary of the Euphrates, with its capital at Edessa (q.v.), founded by Seleucus I. About 130 B.C. Edessa was occupied by a nomadic Arabic tribe, the Orrhoei (Plin. v. 85; vi. 25, 117; 129), who founded a small state ruled by their chieftains with the title of kings. After them the district was called Orrhoene (thus in the inscriptions, in Pliny and Dio Cassius), which occasionally has been changed into Osroene, in assimilation to the Parthian name Osroes or Chosroes (Khosrau). The founder of the dynasty is therefore called Osroes by Procop. *Bell Pers.* i. 17; but Orhâi or Urhâi, son of Hewyâ (*i.e.* "the

[1] Another supposed old form of the name is "Orfraie"; but that is said by M. Rolland (*Faune popul. France*, ii. p. 9, note), quoting M. Suchier (*Zeitschr. röm. Philol.* i. p. 432), to arise from a mingling of two wholly different sources: (1) *Oripelargus, Oripelargus, Orpraie* and (2) *Ossifraga*. "Orfraie" again is occasionally interchanged with *Effraie* (which, through such dialectical forms as *Fresoie, Pressoia*, is said to come from the Latin *praesaga*), the ordinary French name for the barn-owl, *Aluco flammeus* (see Owl). According to Skeat's *Dictionary* (i. p. 408), "Asprey" is the oldest English form; but "Osprey" is given by Cotgrave, and is found as early as the 15th century.

[2] Two good examples of the different localities chosen by this bird for its nest are illustrated in *Ootheca Wolleyana*, pls. B. & H.

snake "), in the chronicle of Dionysius of Tellmahre; he is no historical personality, but the eponym of the tribe. In the Syrian *Doctrine of Addas* (ed. Philipps 1876, p. 46) he is called Arjaw, i.e. "the lion." The kings soon became dependants of the Parthians; their names are mostly Arabic (Bekr, Abgar, Ma'nu), but among them occur some Iranian (Parthian) names, as Pacorus and Phratamaspates. Under Tigranes of Armenia they became his vassals, and after the victories of Lucullus and Pompey, vassals of the Romans. Their names occur in all wars between Romans and Parthians, when they generally inclined to the Parthian side, e.g. in the wars of Crassus and Trajan. Trajan deposed the dynasty, but Hadrian restored it. The kings generally used Greek inscriptions on their coins, but when they sided with the Parthians, as in the war of Marcus Aurelius and Verus (A.D. 161-165), an Aramaic legend appears instead. Hellenism soon disappeared and the Arabs adopted the language and civilization of the Aramaeans. This development was hastened by the introduction of Christianity, which is said to have been brought here by the apostle Judas, the brother of James, whose tomb was shown in Edessa. In 190 and 201 we hear of Christian churches in Edessa. King Abgar IX. (or VIII.) (179-214) himself became a Christian and abolished the pagan cults, especially the rite of castration in the service of Atargatis, which was now punished by the loss of the hands (see Bardesanes, "Book of the Laws of Countries," in Cureton, *Spicilegium Syriacum*, p. 31). His conversion has by the legend been transferred to his ancestor Abgar V. in the time of Christ himself, with whom he is said to have exchanged letters and who sent him his miraculous image, which afterwards was fixed over the principal gate of the city (see ABGAR; Lipsius, *Die edessenische Abgarsage* (1880); Dobschütz, *Christusbilder* (1896)) Edessa now became the principal seat of Aramaic-Christian (Syriac) language and literature; the literary dialect of Syriac is the dialect of Edessa.

Caracalla in 216 abolished the kingdom of Osroene (Dio Cass. 77, 12. 14) and Edessa became a Roman colony. The list of the kings of Osroene is preserved in the Syrian chronicle of Dionysius of Tellmahre, which is checked by the coins and the data of the Greek and Roman authors; it has been reconstructed by A. v. Gutschmid, "Untersuchungen über die Geschichte des Königreichs Osroene," in *Mémoires de l'Acad. de St Pétersbourg*, t. xxxv. (1887). Edessa remained Roman till it was taken by Chosroes II. in 608; but in 625 Heraclius conquered it again. In 638 it was taken by the Arabs.   (ED. M.)

OSROES (also OSDROES or CHOSROES), the Greek form of the Persian name Khosrau (see CHOSROES). The form Osroes is generally used for a Parthian king who from his coins appears to have reigned from about A.D. 106-129, as successor of his brother Pacorus. But during all this time another king, Vologaeses II. (77-147) maintained himself in a part of the kingdom. Osroes occupied Armenia, and placed Exedares, a son of Pacorus, and afterwards his brother Parthamasiris on the throne. This encroachment on the Roman sphere led to the Parthian war of Trajan. In 114 Parthamasiris surrendered to Trajan and was killed. In Mesopotamia a brother of Osroes, Meherdates (Mithradates IV.), and his son Sanatruces II. took the diadem and tried to withstand the Romans. Against them Trajan united with Parthamaspates, whom he placed on the throne, when he had advanced to Ctesiphon (116). But after the death of Trajan (117) Hadrian acknowledged Osroes and made Parthamaspates king of Edessa (Osroene); he also gave back to Osroes his daughter who had been taken prisoner by Trajan (Dio Cass. 68, 17, 22. 33; Malalas, p. 270 ff.; Spartian, *Vita Hadr.* 5. 13; Pausan. v. 12, 6). But meanwhile Vologaeses II. had regained a dominant position; his coins begin again in 122 and go on to 146, whereas after 121 we have no coins of Osroes except in 128.

By Procopius, *Pers.* i. 17, 24, the name of the territory of Osroene is derived from a dynast Osroes, but this is a false etymology (see OSROENE).   (ED. M.)

OSSA (mod. *Kissovo* or *Kissavo*), a mountain in the district of Magnesia in Thessaly, between Pelion and Olympus, from which it is separated by the valley of Tempe. Height about 6400 ft. The Giants are said to have piled Pelion upon it in their attempt to scale Olympus.

OSSETT, a municipal borough in the Morley parliamentary division of the West Riding of Yorkshire, England, 3 m. W. of Wakefield, on the Great Northern and (Horbury and Ossett station) the Lancashire and Yorkshire railways. Pop. (1901) 12,903. It includes the contiguous townships of Ossett, South Ossett and Gawthorpe. The church of the Holy Trinity, a fine cruciform structure in the Early Decorated style, was erected in 1865. Woollen cloth mills, and extensive collieries in the neighbourhood, employ the large industrial population. There are medicinal springs similar in their properties to those of Cheltenham. The municipal borough, incorporated in 1890, is under a mayor, 4 aldermen and 12 councillors. Area 3238 acres.

OSSIAN, OSSIN or OISIN, the legendary Irish 3rd-century hero of Celtic literature, son of Finn. According to the legend embodied in the Ossianic or Oisinic poems and prose romances which early spread over Ireland and Scotland, Ossian and his Fenian followers were defeated in 283 at the battle of Gabhra by the Irish king Carbery, and Ossian spent many years in fairyland, eventually being baptized by St Patrick. As Oisin he was long celebrated in Irish song and legend, and in recent years the Irish literary revival has repopularized the Fenian hero. In Scotland the Ossianic revival is associated with the name of James Macpherson (q.v.).

See CELT *Literature*; also Nutt's *Ossian and the Ossianic Literature* (1899).

OSSINGTON, JOHN EVELYN DENISON, VISCOUNT (1800-1873), English statesman, was the eldest son of John Denison (d. 1820) of Ossington, Nottinghamshire, where he was born on the 27th of January 1800. Educated at Eton and Christ Church, Oxford, he became member of parliament for Newcastle-under-Lyme in 1823, being returned for Hastings three years later, and holding for a short time a subordinate position in Canning's ministry. Defeated in 1830 both at Newcastle-under-Lyme and then at Liverpool, Denison secured a seat as one of the members for Nottinghamshire in 1831; and after the great Reform Act he represented the southern division of that county from 1832 until the general election of 1837. He represented Malton from 1841 to 1857, and North Nottinghamshire from 1857 to 1872. In April 1857 Denison was chosen Speaker of the House of Commons. Re-elected at the beginning of three successive parliaments he retained this position until February 1872, when he resigned and was created Viscount Ossington. He refused, however, to accept the pension usually given to retiring Speakers. In 1827 he had married Charlotte (d. 1889), daughter of William, 4th duke of Portland, but he left no children. He died on the 7th of March 1873, and his title became extinct.

OSSINING, a village of Westchester county, New York, U.S.A., 30 m. N. of New York city, on the E. bank of the Hudson river. Pop. (1900) 7930, of whom 1642 were foreign-born; (1910, U.S. census) 11,480. It is served by the New York Central & Hudson River railway, and by river steamboats. It is finely situated overlooking the Tappan Zee, an expansion of the Hudson river, and has excellent facilities for boating, sailing and yachting. The village is the seat of Mount Pleasant Academy (1814), Holbrook School (1866) and St John's School (1843), all for boys, and has a fine public library. The Croton Aqueduct is here carried over a stone arch with an eighty-foot span. At Ossining, near the river front, is the Sing Sing Prison, the best-known penitentiary in the United States. In 1906 a law was enacted providing for a new prison in the eastern part of the state in place of Sing Sing. The site of Ossining, originally a part of the Phillipse Manor, was first settled about 1700, taking the name of Sing Sing from the Sin Sinck Indians. The village was incorporated in 1813, and was reincorporated, with enlarged boundaries and a considerably increased population, in 1906, the name being changed from Sing Sing to Ossining in 1901.

OSSORY, THOMAS BUTLER, EARL OF (1634-1680), eldest son of James Butler, 1st duke of Ormonde, was born at Kilkenny on the 8th or 9th of July 1634. His early years were spent in

Ireland and France, and he became an accomplished athlete and by no means an indifferent scholar. Having come to London in 1652 he was rightly suspected of sympathizing with the exiled royalists, and in 1655 was put into prison by Cromwell; after his release about a year later he went to Holland and married a Dutch lady of good family, accompanying Charles II. to England in 1660. In 1661 Butler became a member of both the English and the Irish Houses of Commons, representing Bristol in the former and Dublin University in the latter House; and in 1662 was made an Irish peer as earl of Ossory. He held several military appointments, in 1665 was made lieutenant-general of the army in Ireland, and in 1666 was created an English peer as Lord Butler; but almost as soon as he appeared in the House of Lords he was imprisoned for two days for challenging the duke of Buckingham. In 1665 a fortunate accident had allowed Ossory to take part in a big naval fight with the Dutch, and in May 1672, being now in command of a ship, he fought against the same enemies in Southwold Bay, serving with great distinction on both occasions. The earl was partly responsible for this latter struggle, as in March 1672 before war was declared he had attacked the Dutch Smyrna fleet, an action which he is said to have greatly regretted later in life. Whilst visiting France in 1672 he rejected the liberal offers made by Louis XIV to induce him to enter the service of France, and returning to England he added to his high reputation by his conduct during a sea-fight in August 1673. The earl was intimate with William, prince of Orange, and in 1677 he joined the allied army in the Netherlands, commanding the British section and winning great fame at the siege of Mons in 1678. He acted as deputy for his father, who was lord-lieutenant of Ireland, and in parliament he defended Ormonde's Irish administration with great vigour. In 1680 he was appointed governor of Tangier, but his death on the 30th of July 1680 prevented him from taking up his new duties. One of his most intimate friends was John Evelyn, who eulogizes him in his *Diary*. Ossory had eleven children, and his eldest son James became duke of Ormonde in 1688.

See T. Carte, *Life of James, duke of Ormonde* (1851); and J. Evelyn, *Diary*, edited by W. Bray (1890).

OSSORY (*Osraighe*), an ancient kingdom of Ireland, in the south-west of Leinster. The name is preserved by dioceses of the Church of Ireland and the Roman Catholic Church. The kingdom of Ossory was founded in the 2nd century A.D., and its kings maintained their position until 1110.

OSTADE, the name of two Dutch painters whose ancestors were settled at Eyndhoven, near the village of Ostaden. Early in the 17th century Jan Hendricx, a weaver, moved from Eyndhoven to Haarlem, where he married and founded a large family. The eldest and youngest of his sons became celebrated artists.

1. ADRIAN OSTADE (1610–1685), the eldest of Jan Hendricx's sons, was born and died at Haarlem. According to Houbraken he was taught by Frans Hals, at that time master of Adrian Brouwer. At twenty-six he joined a company of the civic guard at Haarlem, and at twenty-eight he married. His wife died in 1640 and he speedily re-married, but again became a widower in 1666. He took the highest honours of his profession, the presidency of the painters' gild at Haarlem, in 1662. Among the treasures of the Louvre collection, a striking picture represents the father of a large family sitting in state with his wife at his side in a handsomely furnished room, surrounded by his son and five daughters, and a young married couple. It is an old tradition that Ostade here painted himself and his children in holiday attire; yet the style is much too refined for the painter of boors, and Ostade had but one daughter. The number of Ostade's pictures is given by Smith at three hundred and eighty-five, but by Hofstede de Groot (1910) at over 900. At his death the stock of unsold pieces was over two hundred. His engraved plates were put up to auction, with the pictures, and fifty etched plates—most of them dated 1647–1648—were disposed of in 1686. Two hundred and twenty of his pictures are in public and private collections, of which one hundred

and four are signed and dated, while seventeen are signed with the name but not with the date.

Adrian Ostade was the contemporary of David Teniers and Adrian Brouwer. Like them he spent his life in the delineation of the homeliest subjects—tavern scenes, village fairs and country quarters. Between Teniers and Ostade the contrast lies in the different condition of the agricultural classes of Brabant and Holland, and the atmosphere and dwellings that were peculiar to each region. Brabant has more sun, more comfort and a higher type of humanity; Teniers, in consequence, is silvery and sparkling; the people he paints are fair specimens of a well-built race. Holland, in the vicinity of Haarlem seems to have suffered much from war; the air is moist and hazy, and the people, as depicted by Ostade, are short, ill-favoured and marked with the stamp of adversity on their features and dress. Brouwer, who painted the Dutch boor in his frolics and passion, imported more of the spirit of Frans Hals into his delineations than his colleague; but the type is the same as Ostade's. During the first years of his career Ostade displayed the same tendency to exaggeration and frolic as his comrade, but he is to be distinguished from his rival by a more general use of the principles of light and shade, and especially by a greater concentration of light on a small surface in contrast with a broad expanse of gloom. The key of his harmonies remains for a time in the scale of greys. But his treatment is dry and careful, and in this style he shuns no difficulties of detail, representing cottages inside and out, with the vine leaves covering the poorness of the outer walls, and nothing inside to deck the patchwork of rafters and thatch, or tumble-down chimneys and ladder staircases, that make up the sordid interior of the Dutch rustic of those days. The greatness of Ostade lies in the fact that he often caught the poetic side of the life of the peasant class, in spite of its ugliness, and stunted form and misshapen features. He did so by giving their vulgar sports, their quarrels, even their quieter moods of enjoyment, the magic light of the sungleam, and by clothing the wreck of cottages with gay vegetation.

It was natural that, with the tendency to effect which marked Ostade from the first, he should have been fired by emulation to rival the masterpieces of Rembrandt. His early pictures are not so rare but that we can trace how he glided out of one period into the other. Before the dispersion of the Gsell collection at Vienna in 1872, it was easy to study the steel-grey harmonies and exaggerated caricature of his early works in the period intervening between 1632 and 1638. There is a picture of a "Countryman having his Tooth Drawn," in the Vienna Gallery, unsigned, and painted about 1632; a "Bagpiper" of 1635 in the Liechtenstein Gallery at Vienna; cottage scenes of 1635 and 1636, in the museums of Karlsruhe, Darmstadt and Dresden; and "Card Players" of 1637 in the Liechtenstein palace at Vienna, which make up for the loss of the Gsell collection. The same style marks most of those pieces. About 1638 or 1640 the influence of Rembrandt suddenly changed his style, and he painted the "Annunciation" of the Brunswick museum, where the angels appearing in the sky to Dutch boors half asleep amidst their cattle, sheep and dogs, in front of a cottage, at once recall the similar subject by Rembrandt and his effective mode of lighting the principal groups by rays propelled to the earth out of a murky sky. But Ostade was not successful in this effort to vulgarize Scripture. He might have been pardoned had he given dramatic force and expression to his picture; but his shepherds were only boors without much emotion, passion or surprise. His picture was an effect of light, as such masterly, in its sketchy rubbings, of dark brown tone relieved by strongly impasted lights, but without the very qualities which made his usual subjects attractive. When, in 1642, he painted the beautiful interior at the Louvre, in which a mother tends her child in a cradle at the side of a great chimney near which her husband is sitting, the darkness of a country loft is dimly illumined by a beam from the sun that shines on the casement; and one might think the painter intended to depict the Nativity, but that there is nothing holy in all the surroundings, nothing attractive indeed except the wonderful Rembrandtesque transparency, the brown tone, and the admirable keeping of the minutest parts. Ostade was more at home in a similar effect applied to the commonplace incident of the "Slaughtering of a Pig," one of the masterpieces of 1643, once in the Gsell collection. In this and similar subjects of previous and succeeding years, he returned to the homely subjects in which his power and wonderful observation made him a master. He does not seem to have gone back to gospel illustrations till 1667, when he produced an admirable "Nativity," which is only surpassed as regards arrangement and colour by Rembrandt's "Carpenter's Family" at the Louvre, or the

" Woodcutter and Children ' in the gallery of Cassel. Innumerable almost are the more familiar themes to which he devoted his brush during this interval, from small single figures, representing smokers or drinkers, to vulgarized allegories of the five senses (Hermitage and Brunswick galleries), half-lengths of fishmongers and bakers and cottage brawls, or scenes of gambling, or itinerant players and quacks, and nine-pin players in the open air. The humour in some of these pieces is contagious, as in the " Tavern Scene " of the Lacaze collection (Louvre, 1653). His art may be studied in the large series of dated pieces which adorn every European capital, from St Petersburg to London. Buckingham Palace has a large number, and many a good specimen lies hidden in the private collections of England. But if we should select a few as peculiarly worthy of attention, we might point to the " Rustics in a Tavern " of 1662 at the Hague, the " Village School " of the same year at the Louvre, the " Tavern Court-yard " of 1670 at Cassel, the " Sportsmen's Rest " of 1671 at Amsterdam and the " Fiddler and his Audience " of 1673 at the Hague. At Amsterdam we have the likeness of a painter, sitting with his back to the spectator, at his easel. The colour-grinder is at work in a corner, a pupil prepares a palette and a black dog sleeps on the ground. A replica of this picture, with the date of 1666, is in the Dresden gallery. Both specimens are supposed to represent Ostade himself. But unfortunately we see the artist's back and not his face. In his etching (Bartsch, 32) the painter shows himself in profile, at work on a canvas. Two of his latest dated works, the " Village Street " and " Skittle Players," which were noteworthy items in the Ashburton and Ellesmere collections, were executed in 1676 without any sign of declining powers. The prices which Ostade received are not known, but pictures which were worth £40 in 1750 were worth £1000 a century later, and Earl Dudley gave £4120 for a cottage interior in 1876. The signatures of Ostade vary at different periods. But the first two letters are generally interlaced. Up to 1635 Ostade writes himself Ostaden, e.g. in the " Bagpiper " of 1635 in the Liechtenstein collection at Vienna. Later on he uses the long s (f), and occasionally he signs in capital letters. His pupils are his own brother Isaac, Cornelis Bega, Cornelis Dusart and Richard Brakenburg.

2. ISAAC OSTADE (1621–1649) was born in Haarlem, and began his studies under Adrian, with whom he remained till 1641, when he started on his own account. At an early period he felt the influence of Rembrandt, and this·is apparent in a " Slaughtered Pig " of 1639, in the gallery of Augsburg. But he soon reverted to a style more suited to his brush. He produced pictures in 1641–1642 on the lines of his brother—amongst these, the " Five Senses," which Adrian afterwards represented by a " Man reading a Paper," a " Peasant tasting Beer," a " Rustic smearing his Sores with Ointment " and a " Countryman sniffing at a Snuff-box." A specimen of Isaac's work at this period may be seen in the " Laughing Boor with a Pot of Beer," in the museum of Amsterdam; the cottage interior, with two peasants and three children near a fire, in the Berlin museum; a " Concert;" with people listening to singers accompanied by a piper and flute player, and a " Boor stealing a Kiss from a Woman," in the Lacaze collection at the Louvre. The interior at Berlin is lighted from a casement in the same Rembrandtesque style as Adrian's interior of 1643 at the Louvre. The low price he received for his pictures of this character—in which he could only hope to remain a satellite of Adrian—induced him gradually to abandon the cottage subjects of his brother for landscapes in the fashion of Esaias Van de Velde and Salomon Ruisdael. Once only, in 1645, he seems to have fallen into the old groove, when he produced the " Slaughtered Pig," with the boy puffing out a bladder, in the museum of Lille. But this was an exception. Isaac's progress in his new path was greatly facilitated by his previous experience as a figure painter; and, although he now selected his subjects either from village high streets or·frozen canals, he gave fresh life to the scenes he depicted by groups of people full of movement and animation, which he relieved in their coarse humours and sordid appearance by a refined and searching study of picturesque contrasts. He did not live long enough to bring his art to the highest perfection. He died on the 16th October 1649 having painted about 400 pictures (see H. de Groot, 1910). .

. The first manifestation of Isaac's surrender of Adrian's style is apparent in 1644 when the skating and sledging scenes were executed which we see in the Lacaze collection and the galleries of the Hermitage, Antwerp and Lille. Three of these examples bear the artist's name, spelt Isack van Ostade, and the dates of 1644 and 1645. The roadside inns, with halts of travellers, form a compact

series from 1646 to 1649. · In this, the last form of his art, Isaac has very distinct peculiarities. The air which pervades his composition is warm and sunny, yet mellow and hazy, as if the sky were veiled with a vapour coloured by moor smoke. The trees are rubbings of umber, in which the prominent foliage is tipped with touches hardened in a liquid state by amber varnish mediums. · The same principle applied to details such as glazed bricks or rents in the mud lining of cottages gives an unreal and conventional stamp to those, particular parts. But these blemishes are forgotten when one looks at the broad contrasts of light and shade and the masterly figures ; of horses and riders, and travellers and rustics, or quarrelling children and dogs, poultry. and cattle, amongst which a favourite place is always given to the white horse, which seems as invariable an accompaniment as the grey in the skirmishes and fairs of Wouverman. But it is in winter scenes that Isaac displays the best qualities. The absence of foliage, the crisp atmosphere, the calm air of cold January days, unsullied by smoke or vapour, preclude the use of the brown tinge, and leave the painter no choice but to ring the changes on opal tints of great variety, upon which the figures emerge with masterly effect on the light background upon which they are thrown. Amongst the roadside inns which will best repay attention we should notice those of Buckingham Palace, the National Gallery; the Wallace and Holford collections in England, and those of the; Louvre, Berlin, Hermitage and Rotterdam museums and the Rothschild collection at Vienna on the Continent. The finest of the ice scenes is the famous one at the Louvre.

For paintings and etchings see Les Frères Ostade, by Marguerite van de Wiele (Paris, 1893). For his etchings see L'Œuvre d'Ostade, ou description des eaux-fortes de ce maître, &c., by Auguste·d'Orange (1860), and Catalogue raisonné de toutes les estampes qui forment· l'œuvre· gravé d'Adrian von Ostade, by L. E. Faucheux (Paris,: 1862). ·   (J. A. C.; P. G. K.)

OSTASHKOV, a town of Russia, in· the government of Tver, on Lake Seliger, 108 m. W.N.W. of the city·of Tver; pop. 10,457. The climate is damp and unhealthy. The town has tanneries, and is a centre for the making of boots and shoes, for agricultural implements, fishing-nets and the building of boats. The advantageous site, the proximity of the Smolenskiy Zhitnyi monastery, a pilgrim resort on an island of the lake and the early development of certain petty trades combined· to bring prosperity to Ostashkov. Its cathedral (1672–1685)· contains valuable offerings, as also do two other churches of the same century.

OSTEND (Flemish and French Ostende), a town of Belgium in the province of West Flanders. Pop. (1904) 41,181. It is the most fashionable seaside resort and the second port of the kingdom. . Situated on the North Sea it forms almost the central point on the 42 m. of sea-coast that belong to Belgium. In the middle ages it was strongly fortified and underwent several sieges, the most notable was that of 1601–1604, when it only surrendered by order of the states to Spinola. In 1865 the last vestiges of its ramparts were removed, and since that date, but more especially since 1898, a new town has been created. The digue or parade, constructed of solid granite, extends for over 2 m. along the shore in a southerly direction from the long, jetty which protects the entrance to the port. A fine casino and the royal châlet are prominent objects along the sea front, and the sea-bathing is unsurpassed. In the rear of the town is a fine park to which a race-course has.been added. Extensive works were begun in 1900 for the purpose of carrying the harbour back 2 m., and a series of large docks were excavated and extensive quays constructed. The docks accommodate ships of large tonnage. Apart from these docks Ostend has a very considerable passenger and provision traffic with England, and is the head-quarters of the Belgian fishing fleet, estimated to employ 400 boats and 1600 men and boys. Ostend is in direct railway communication with Brussels, Cologne and Berlin. It is also the starting point of several light railways along the coast·and to the southern towns of Flanders.

OSTEND COMPANY. The success of the Dutch, English and French East India Companies led the merchants and shipowners, of Ostend to desire to establish direct commercial relations with, the Indies. A private company was accordingly formed in, 1717 and some ships sent to the East. The emperor Charles VI. encouraged his subjects to raise subscriptions for the new, enterprise, but did not grant a charter or letters patent. Some success attended these early efforts, but the jealousy of the, neighbouring nations was shown by the seizure of an Ostend merchantman with its rich cargo by the Dutch in 1719 off the coast of Africa, and of another by the English near Madagascar. The Ostenders, however, despite these losses, persevered in their project. The opposition of the Dutch made Charles VI. hesitate for some time to grant their requests, but on the 19th of December 1722 letters-patent were granted by which the company of Ostend received for the period of thirty years the privilege of trading in the East and West Indies and along the coasts of Africa on this side and on that of the Cape of Good Hope. Six directors were nominated by the emperor, and subscriptions to the company flowed in so rapidly that the shares were at the end of August 1723 at 12% to 15% premium. Two factories were established, one at Coblom on the coast of Coromandel near Madras, the other at Bankibazar on the Ganges. At the outset the prospects of the company appeared to be most encouraging, but its promoters had not reckoned with the jealousy and hostility of the Dutch and English. The Dutch appealed to the treaty of Westphalia (1648) by which the king of Spain had prohibited the inhabitants of the southern Netherlands from trading with the Spanish colonies. The transference of the southern Netherlands to Austria by the peace of Utrecht (1713) did not, said the Dutch, remove this disability. The Spanish government, however, after some hesitation concluded a treaty of commerce with Austria and recognized the company of Ostend. The reply to this was a defensive league concluded at Herrenhausen in 1725 by England, the United Provinces and Prussia. Confronted with such formidable opposition the court of Vienna judged it best to yield. By the terms of a treaty signed at Paris on the 31st of May 1727 the emperor suspended the charter of the company for seven years, and the powers in return guaranteed the Pragmatic Sanction. The company, after nominally existing for a short time in this state of suspended animation, became extinct. The Austrian Netherlands were condemned to remain excluded from maritime commerce with the Indies until their union with Holland in 1815.   (G. E.)

OSTEOLOGY (Gr. ὀστέον, bone), that part or branch of the science of anatomy which has for its subject the bony framework of the body (see BONE, SKELETON, ANATOMY, &c.).

OSTERMAN, ANDREI IVANOVICH, COUNT (1686–1747), Russian statesman, was born at Bochum in Westphalia, of middle-class parents, his name being originally Heinrich Johann Friedrich Ostermann. He became secretary to Vice-Admiral Cornelis Kruse, who had a standing commission from Peter the Great to pick up promising young men, and in 1767 entered the tsar's service. His knowledge of the principal European languages made him the right hand of Vice-Chancellor Shafirov, whom he materially assisted during the troublesome negotiations which terminated in the peace of the Pruth (1711). Osterman, together with General Bruce, represented Russia at the Åland peace congress of 1718. Shrewdly guessing that Sweden was at exhaustion point, and that Görtz, the Swedish plenipotentiary, was acting *ultra vires*, he advised Peter to put additional pressure on Sweden to force a peace. In 1721 Osterman concluded the peace of Nystad with Sweden, and was created a baron for his services. In 1723 he was made vice-president of the ministry of foreign affairs for bringing about a very advantageous commercial treaty with Persia. Peter also constantly consulted him in domestic affairs, and he introduced many administrative novelties, e.g. "the table of degrees," and the reconstruction of the College of Foreign Affairs on more modern lines. During the reign of Catherine I. (1725–1727) Osterman's authority still further increased. The conduct of foreign affairs was left entirely in his hands, and he held also the posts of minister of commerce and postmaster-general. On the accession of Peter II. Osterman was appointed governor to the young emperor, and on his death (1730) he refused to participate in the attempt of Demetrius Golitsuin and the Dolgorukis to convert Russia into a limited constitutional monarchy. He held aloof till the empress Anne was firmly established on the throne as autocrat. Then he got his reward. His unique knowledge of foreign affairs made him indispensable to the empress and her counsellors, and even as to home affairs his advice was almost invariably

followed. It was at his suggestion that the cabinet system was introduced into Russia. All the useful reforms introduced between 1730 and 1740 are to be attributed to his initiative. He improved the state of trade, lowered taxation, encouraged industry and promoted education, ameliorated the judicature and materially raised the credit of Russia. As foreign minister he was cautious and circumspect, but when war was necessary he prosecuted it vigorously and left nothing to chance. The successful conclusions of the War of the Polish Succession (1733–1735) and of the war with Turkey (1736–39) were entirely due to his diplomacy. During the brief regency of Anna Leopoldovna (October 1740–December 1741) Osterman stood at the height of his power, and the French ambassador, La Chetardie, reported to his court that " it is not too much to say that he is tsar of all Russia." Osterman's foreign policy was based upon the Austrian alliance. He had, therefore, guaranteed the Pragmatic Sanction with the deliberate intention of defending it. Hence the determination of France to remove him at any cost. Russia, as the natural ally of Austria, was very obnoxious to France; indeed it was only the accident of the Russian alliance which, in 1741, seemed to stand between Maria Theresa and absolute ruin. The most obvious method of rendering the Russian alliance unserviceable to the queen of Hungary was by implicating Russia in hostilities with her ancient rival, Sweden, and this was brought about, by French influence and French money, when in August 1741 the Swedish government, on the most frivolous pretexts, declared war against Russia. The dispositions previously made by Osterman enabled him, however, to counter the blow, and all danger from Sweden was over when, early in September, Field-Marshal Lacy routed the Swedish general Wrangel under the walls of the frontier-fortress of Villmanstrand, which was carried by assault. It now became evident to La Chetardie that only a revolution would overthrow Osterman, and this he proposed to promote by elevating to the throne the tsesarevna Elizabeth, who hated the vice-chancellor because, though he owed everything to her father, he had systematically neglected her. Osterman was therefore the first and the most illustrious victim of the *coup d'état* of the 6th of December 1741. Accused, among other things, of contributing to the elevation of the empress Anne by his cabals and of suppressing a supposed will of Catherine I. made in favour of her daughter Elizabeth, he threw himself on the clemency of the new empress. He was condemned first to be broken on the wheel and then beheaded; but, reprieved on the scaffold, his sentence was commuted to lifelong banishment, with his whole family, to Berezov in Siberia, where he died six years later.

See S. Shubinsky, "Count A. I. Osterman" (Rus.) in *Syevernoyé Siyanïe*, vol. ii. (St Petersburg, 1863); D. Korsakov, *From the Lives of Russian Statesmen of the XVIIIth Century* (Rus.) (Kazan, 1891); A. N. Filippov, " Documents relating to the Cabinet Ministers of the Empress Anne " (Rus.) (St Petersburg, 1898) in the collections of the Russ. Hist. Soc. vol. 104; A. A. Kochubinsky, *Count A. I. Osterman and the proposed Partition of Turkey* (Rus.) (Odessa, 1889); Hon. C. Finch, *Diplomatic Despatches from Russia, 1740–1742* (St Petersburg, 1893–1894) in the collections of the Russ. Hist. Soc. vols. 85 and 91; R. Nisbet Bain, *The Pupils of Peter the Great* (London, 1897); and *The Daughter of Peter the Great* (London, 1899), chapters 1-3.   (R. N. B.)

OSTERODE, a town in the Prussian province of East Prussia, 75 m. by rail N.E. of Thorn, on Lake Drewenz, and at the junction of lines to Memel, Elbing and Schönsee. Pop. (1905) 13,957. It has a castle built by the Teutonic knights in 1270, to whom the town owes its birth. Its principal manufactures are railway plant, machinery, beer, spirits and bricks, while it has several saw-mills. Osterode has a lively trade in cattle, grain and timber.

See J. Müller, *Osterode und Ostpreussen* (Osterode, 1905).

OSTERODE, a town in the Prussian province of Hanover, at the south foot of the Harz Mountains, 34 m. N.W. of Nordhausen by rail. Pop. (1905) 7467. The church of St Aegidius (Evangelical), founded in 724 and rebuilt after a fire in 1578, contains some fine tombs of the dukes of Brunswick-Grubenhagen, who made Osterode their residence from 1361 to 1452. Other buildings are the fine town-hall and the hospital. There are manufactures of cotton and woollen goods, cigars and leather, and tanneries, dyeworks and gypsum quarries. In recent years Osterode has become celebrated as a health resort.

ÖSTERSUND, a town of Sweden, capital of the district (*län*) of Jemtland, on the east shore of Storsjö (Great Lake), 364 m. N. by W. of Stockholm by rail. Pop. (1900) 6866. It lies at an elevation of about 1000 ft. and is the metropolis of a mountainous and beautiful district. Immediately facing the town is the lofty island of Frös, with which it is connected by a bridge 1148 ft. long. A runic stone commemorates the building of a bridge here by a Christian missionary, Austmader, son of Gudfast. Östersund was founded in 1786. It has a considerable trade in timber, and a local trade by steamers on Storsjö. Electricity is obtained for lighting and other purposes by utilizing the abundant water-power in the district.

OSTERVALD, JEAN FRÉDÉRIC (1663-1747), Swiss Protestant divine, was born at Neuchâtel on the 25th of November 1663. He was educated at Zürich and at Saumur (where he graduated), studied theology at Orleans under Claude Pajon, at Paris under Jean Claude and at Geneva under Louis Tronchin, and was ordained to the ministry in his native place in 1683. As preacher, pastor, lecturer and author, he attained a position of great influence in his day, he and his friends, J. A. Turretin of Geneva and S. Werenfels (1657-1740) of Basel, forming what was once called the "Swiss triumvirate." He was thought to show a leaning towards Socinianism and Arminianism. He died on the 14th of April 1747.

His principal works are *Traité des sources de la corruption qui règne aujourd'hui parmi les Chrétiens* (1700), translated into English, Dutch and German, practically a plea for a more ethical and less doctrinal type of Christianity; *Catéchisme ou instruction dans la religion chrétienne* (1702), also translated into English, Dutch and German; *Traité contre l'impureté* (1707); *Sermons sur divers textes* (1722-1724); *Theologica compendium* (1739); and *Traduction de la Bible* (1724). All his writings attained great popularity among French Protestants; many were translated into various languages; and "Ostervald's Bible," a revision of the French translation, in particular, was long well known and much valued in Britain.

OSTIA, an ancient town and harbour of Latium, Italy, at the mouth of the river Tiber on its left bank. It lies 14 m. S.W. from Rome by the Via Ostiensis, a road of very ancient origin still followed by a modern road which preserves some traces of the old pavement and remains of several ancient bridges. It was the first colony ever founded by Rome—according to the Romans themselves, by Ancus Martius—and took its name from its position at the mouth (*ostium*) of the river. Its origin is connected with the establishment of the salt-marshes (*salinae*— see SALARIA, VIA) which only ceased to exist in 1875, though it acquired importance as a harbour in very early times. When it began to have magistrates of its own is not known: nor indeed have we any inscriptions from Ostia that can be certainly attributed to the Republican period. Under the empire, on the other hand, it had the ordinary magistrates of a colony, the chief being *duoviri*, charged with the administration of justice, whose place was taken every fifth year by *duoviri censoria potestate quinquennales*, then *quaestores* (or financial officials); and then *aediles* (building officials). There were also the usual *decuriones* (town councillors) and *Augustales*. We learn much as to these magistrates from the large number of inscriptions that have been found (over 2000 in Ostia and Portus taken together) and also as to the cults. Vulcan was the most important—perhaps in early times the only—deity worshipped at Ostia, and the priesthood of Vulcan was held sometimes by Roman senators. The Dioscuri too, as patrons of mariners, were held in honour. Later we find the worship of Isis and of Cybele, the latter being especially flourishing, with large corporations of *dendrophori* (priests who carried branches of trees in procession) and *canephori* (basket-carriers); the worship of Mithras, too, had a large number of followers. There was a temple of Serapis at Portus. No traces of Jewish worship have been found at Ostia, but at Portus a considerable number of Jewish inscriptions in Greek have come to light.

Of the church in Ostia there is no authentic record before the 4th century A.D., though there are several Christian inscriptions of an earlier date; but the first bishop of Ostia of whom we have any certain knowledge dates from A.D. 313. The see still continues, and is indeed held by the dean of the sacred college of cardinals. A large number of the inscriptions are also connected with the various guilds—firemen (*centonarii*), carpenters and metal workers (*fabri*), boatmen, lightermen and others (see J. P. Waltzing, *Les Corporations professionelles*, Brussels and Liége).

Until Trajan formed the port of Centumcellae (Civitavecchia) Ostia was the best harbour along the low sandy coast of central Italy between Monte Argentario and Monte Circeo. It is mentioned in 354 B.C. as a trading port, and became important as a naval harbour during the Punic Wars. Its commerce increased with the growth of Rome, and this, and the decay of agriculture in Italy, which obliged the capital to rely almost entirely on imported corn (the importation of which was, from 267 B.C. onwards, under the charge of a special quaestor stationed at Ostia), rendered the possession of Ostia the key to the situation on more than one occasion (87 B.C., A.D. 409 and 537). The inhabitants of the colony were thus regarded as a permanent garrison, and at first freed from the obligations of ordinary military service, until they were later on obliged to serve in the fleet. Ostia, however, was by no means an ideal harbour; the mouth of the Tiber is exposed to the south-west wind, which often did damage in the harbour itself; in A.D. 62 no less than 200 ships with their cargoes were sunk, and there was an important guild of divers (*urinatores*) at Ostia. The difficulties of the harbour were increased by the continued silting up, produced by the enormous amount of solid material brought down by the river. Even in Strabo's time (v. 3. 5, p. 231) the harbour of Ostia had become dangerous: he speaks of it as a "city without a harbour owing to the silting up brought about by the Tiber . . . : the ships anchor at considerable risk in the roads, but the love of gain prevails: for the large number of lighters which receive the cargoes and reload them renders the time short before they can enter the river, and having lightened a part of their cargoes they sail in and ascend to Rome."

Caesar had projected remedial measures, but (as in so many cases) had never been able to carry them out, and it was not until the time of Claudius that the problem was approached. That emperor constructed a large new harbour on the right bank, 2½ m. N. of Ostia, with an area of 170 acres enclosed by two curving moles, with an artificial island, supporting a lofty lighthouse, in the centre of the space between them. This was connected with the Tiber by an artificial channel, and by this work Claudius, according to the inscriptions which he erected in A.D. 46, freed the city of Rome from the danger of inundation. The harbour was named by Nero, Portus Augusti. Trajan found himself obliged in A.D. 103, owing to the silting up of the Claudian harbour, and the increase of trade, to construct another port further inland—a hexagonal basin enclosing an area of 97 acres with enormous warehouses—communicating with the harbour of Claudius and with the Tiber by means of the channel already constructed by Claudius; this channel being prolonged so as to give also direct access to the sea. This became blocked in the middle ages, but was reopened by Paul V. in 1612, and is still in use. Indeed it forms the right arm of the Tiber, by which navigation is carried on at the present day, and is known as the Fossa Trajana. The island between the two arms acquired the name of *Insula Sacra* (still called Isola Sacra) by which Procopius mentions it.

Ostia thus lost a considerable amount of its trade, but its importance still continued to be great. The 2nd and 3rd centuries, indeed, are the high-water mark of its prosperity; and it still possessed a mint in the 4th century A.D. During the Gothic wars, however, trade was confined to Portus, and the ravages of pirates led to its gradual abandonment. Gregory IV. constructed in 830 a fortified enceinte, called Gregoriopolis, in the eastern portion of the ancient city, and the Saracens were signally defeated here under Leo IV. (847-856). The battle is represented in Giulio Romano's fresco from Raphael's design in the Stanza dell' Incendio in the Vatican.

In the middle ages Ostia regained something of its importance, owing to the silting up of the right arm of the Tiber. In 1483–1486 Giuliano della Rovere (nephew of Pope Sixtus IV., and afterwards himself Pope Julius II.) caused the castle to be erected by Baccio Pontelli, a little to the east of the ancient city. It is built of brick and is one of the finest specimens of Renaissance fortification, and exemplifies especially the transition from the old girdle walls to the system of bastions; it still has round corner towers, not polygonal bastions (Burckhardt). Under the shelter of the castle lies the modern village. The small cathedral of St Aurea, also an early Renaissance structure, with Gothic windows, is by some ascribed to Meo del Caprina (1430–1501). Hitherto Ostia does not seem to have been very unhealthy. In 1557, however, a great flood caused the Tiber to change its course, so that it no longer flowed under the walls of the castle, but some half a mile farther west; and its old bed (Fiume Morto) has ever since then served as a breeding ground for the malarial mosquito (*Anopheles claviger*). An agricultural colony, founded at Ostia after 1875, and consisting mainly of cultivators from the neighbourhood of Ravenna, has produced a great change for the better in the condition of the place. The modern village is a part of the commune of Rome. The marshes have been drained, and a pumping station erected near Castel Fusano. An electric tramway has been constructed from Rome to Ostia and thence to the seashore, now some 2 m. distant, where sea-bathing is carried on.

Excavations on the site of Ostia were only begun towards the close of the 18th century, and no systematic work was done until 1854, when under Pius IX. a considerable amount was done (the objects are now in the Lateran museum). The Italian government, to whom the greater part of it now belongs, laid bare many of the more important buildings in 1880–1889; but much was left undone. Owing to the fact that the site is largely covered with sand and to the absence of any later alterations, the preservation of the buildings excavated is very good, and Ostia is, with the exception of Pompeii, the best example in Italy of a town of the Roman period. On the east the site is approached by an ancient road, flanked by tombs. On the right (N.) are some small well-preserved thermae, and the barracks of the firemen (*vigiles*), a special cohort of whom was stationed here. On one side of the central courtyard of the latter building is a chapel with inscribed pedestals for imperial statues (2nd and 3rd century A.D.) and a well-preserved black and white mosaic representing a sacrifice (see J. Carcopino in *Mélanges de l'École Française*, 1907).

To the south-west is the Forum, an area 265 ft. square surrounded by colonnades, in which were placed the offices of the various *collegia* or guilds of boatmen, raftmen and others, which had a special importance at Ostia; the names of the guilds may still be read in inscriptions in the mosaic pavements of the chambers. In the centre of the area are the substructions of a temple, and on the south-east side are the remains of the theatre, built in the early imperial period, restored by Septimius Severus in 196–197 and again in the 4th or 5th century. To the south-west of the Forum are the remains of three small temples, one dedicated to Venus, and a well-preserved Mithraeum, with mosaics representing the seven planets, &c. To the south-west again is the conspicuous brick cella of a lofty temple, on arched substructures, generally supposed to be that of Vulcan, with a threshold block of *africano* (Euboean) marble over 15 ft. long: from it a street over 20 ft. wide leads north-west to the river. It is flanked on each side by well-preserved warehouses, another group of which, surrounding a large court, lies to the south-west. The brick and *opus reticulatum* facing of the walls is especially fine. Hence an ancient road, leading between warehouses (into which the Tiber is encroaching), in one room of which a number of well-preserved large jars may be seen embedded in the floor, runs close to the river to a large private house with *thermae*, in which five mosaics were found: it (groundlessly) bears the name of "imperial palace." Farther to the south-west are remains of other warehouses, and (possibly) of the docks—long narrow chambers, which may have served

to contain ships. Here are remains of (earlier) structures in *opus quadratum* whereas the great bulk of the ruins are in brick work and belong to the imperial period. The medieval Torre Boacciana marks approximately the mouth of the river in Roman times. The south-eastern portion of the city has been excavated only very partially. To the south-west of the conspicuous temple alluded to are the remains of a temple of Cybele, with a portico. This lay close to the commencement of the Via Severiana (see SEVERIANA, VIA), and the line of tombs which flanked it soon begins. Farther south-east, a line of sand dunes, covering the ruins of ancient villas, marks the coastline of the Roman period. Some 2 m. to the south-east is the pine forest of Castel Fusano, taking its name from a castle erected by the marchese Sacchetti in the 16th century. It is now the property of the Chigi and is leased to the king (see LAURENTINA, VIA). Here Drs Lowe and Sambon made the decisive experiments which proved that the propagation of malaria was due to the mosquito *Anopheles claviger*.

See *Notizie degli scavi, passim*: H. Dessau in *Corp. inscript. Latin.* xiv. (Berlin, 1887), pp. 1 sqq., and the works of M. Jerome Carcopino. (T. As.)

OSTIAKS, or OSTYAKS, a tribe who inhabit the basin of the Ob in western Siberia belonging to the Finno-Ugric group and related to the Voguls. The so-called Ostyaks of the Yenisei speak an entirely different language. The best investigators (Gastrén, Lerberg, A. Schrenck) consider the trans-Uralian Ostiaks and Samoyedes as identical with the Yugra of the Russian annals. During the Russian conquest their abodes extended much farther south than now, forty-one of their fortified places having been destroyed by the Cossacks in 1501, in the region of Obdorsk alone. Remains of these "towns" are still to be seen at the Kunovat river, on the Ob 20 m. below Obdorsk and elsewhere. The total number of the Ostiaks may be estimated at 27,000. Those on the Irtysh are mostly settled, and have adopted the manner of life of Russians and Tatars. Those on the Ob are mostly nomads; along with 8000 Samoyedes in the districts of Berezov and Surgut, they own large herds of reindeer. The Ob Ostiaks are russified to a great extent. They live almost exclusively by fishing, buying from Russian merchants corn for bread, the use of which has become widely diffused.

The Ostiaks call themselves As-yakh (people of the Ob), and it is supposed that their present designation is a corruption of this name. By language they belong (Castrén, *Reiseberichte, Reisebriefe*; Ahlqvist, *Ofvers. af Finska Vet.-Soc. Förh.* xxi.) to the Ugrian branch of the eastern Finnish stem. All the Ostiaks speak the same language, mixed to some extent with foreign elements; but three or four leading dialects can be distinguished.

The Ostiaks are middle-sized, or of low stature, mostly meagre, and not ill made, however clumsy their appearance in winter in their thick fur-clothes. The extremities are fine, and the feet are usually small. The skull is brachycephalic, mostly of moderate size and height. The hair is dark and soft for the most part, fair and reddish individuals being rare; the eyes are dark, generally narrow; the nose is flat and broad; the mouth is large and with thick lips; the beard is scanty. The Mongolian type is more strongly pronounced in the women than in the men. On the whole, the Ostiaks are not a pure race; the purest type is found among the fishers on the Ob, the reindeer-breeders of the tundra being largely intermixed with Samoyedes. Investigators describe them as kind, gentle and honest; rioting is almost unknown among them, as also theft, this last occurring only in the vicinity of Russian settlements, and the only penalty enforced being the restitution twofold of the property stolen.

They are very skilful in the arts they practice, especially in carving wood and bone, tanning (with egg-yolk and brains), preparation of implements from birch-bark, &c. Some of their carved or decorated bark implements (like those figured in Middendorff's *Sibirische Reise*, iv. 2) show considerable artistic skill.

Their folk-lore, like that of other Finnish stems, is imbued with a feeling of natural poetry, and reflects also the sadness, or even the despair, which has been noticed among them. Christianity has made some progress among them and St Nicholas is a popular saint, but their ancient pagan observances are still retained.

For the language see Ahlqvist, *Über die Sprache der Nord-Ostyaken* (1880) and for customs, religion, &c., the *Journal de la Société Finno-Ougrienne*, particularly papers by Sirelius and Karjalainen, and the papers by Munkácsi, Gennep, Fuchs and others in the *Revue orientale pour les études Ouralo-Altaïques*; Patkanov, *Die Irtysch-Ostiaken und ihre Volkspoesie* (Petersburg, 1900); Patkanov, *Irtisch-Ostjaken und ihre Volkspoesie* (1897–1900); Papay, *Sammlung ostjakischer Volksdichtungen* (1906).

OSTRA, an ancient town of Umbria, Italy, near the modern Montenovo, S.E. of Sena Gallica (Sinigaglia). It is hardly mentioned by ancient authors, but excavations have brought to light remains of various buildings and some inscriptions exist. Pliny mentions with it another ancient town, Suasa, 5 m. W., which also did not survive the classical period.

OSTRACISM, a political device instituted, probably by Cleisthenes in 508 B.C., as a constitutional safeguard for the Athenian democracy. Its effect was to remove from Athens for a period of ten years any person who threatened the harmony and tranquillity of the body politic. A similar device existed at various times in Argos, Miletus, Syracuse and Megara, but in these cities it appears to have been introduced under Athenian influence. In Athens in the sixth prytany of each year the representatives of the Boulé asked the Ecclesia whether it was for the welfare of the state that ostracism should take place. If the answer was in the affirmative, a day was fixed for the voting in the eighth prytany. No names were mentioned, but it is clear that two or three names at the most could have been under consideration. The people met, not as usual in the Pnyx, but in the Agora, in the presence of the Archons, and recorded their votes by placing in urns small fragments of pottery (which in the ancient world served the purpose of waste-paper) (*ostraca*) on which they wrote the name of the person whom they wished to banish. As in the case of other *privilegia*, ostracism did not take effect unless six thousand votes in all were recorded. Grote and others hold that six thousand had to be given against one person before he was ostracized, but it seems unlikely that the attendance at the Ecclesia ever admitted of so large a vote against one man, and the view is contradicted by Plut. *Arist.* c. 7. The ostracized person was compelled to leave Athens for ten years, but he was not regarded as a traitor or criminal. When he returned, he resumed possession of his property and his civic status was unimpaired. The adverse vote simply implied that his power was so great as to be injurious to the state. Ostracism must therefore be carefully distinguished from *exile* in the Roman sense, which involved loss of property and status, and was for an indefinite period (*i.e.* generally for life). Certain writers have even spoken of the "honour" of ostracism. At the same time it was strictly unjust to the victim, and a heavy punishment to a cultured citizen for whom Athens contained all that made life worth living. Its political importance really was that it transferred the protection of the constitution from the Areopagus to the Ecclesia: its place was afterwards taken by the *Graphè Paranomôn*.

There is no doubt that Cleisthenes' object was primarily to get rid of the Peisistratid faction without perpetual recourse to armed resistance (so Androtion, *Ath. Pol.* 22, Ephorus, Theopompus, Aristotle, *Pol.* iii. 13, 1284 a 17 and 36; viii. (v.), 3, 1302 b 15). Aristotle's *Constitution of Athens* (c. 22) gives a list of ostracized persons, the first of whom was a certain Hipparchus of the Peisistratid family (488 B.C.). It is an extraordinary fact that, if ostracism was introduced in 508 B.C. for the purpose of expelling Hipparchus it was not till twenty years later that he was condemned. This has led some critics (see Lugebil in *Das Wesen . . . der Ostrakismos*, who arrives at the conclusion that ostracism could not have been introduced till after 496 B.C.) to suspect the unanimous evidence of antiquity that Cleisthenes was the inventor of ostracism. The problem is difficult, and no satisfactory answer has been given. Aelian's story that Cleisthenes himself was the first to be ostracized is attractive in view of his overtures to Persia (see CLEISTHENES), but it has little historical value and conflicts with the chapter in Aristotle's *Constitution*—which, however, may conceivably be simply the list of those recalled from ostracism at the time of Xerxes' Invasion, all of whom must have been ostracized less than ten years before 481 (*i.e.* since Marathon). With the end of the Persian Wars, the original object of ostracism was removed, but it continued in use for forty years and was revived in 417 B.C. It now became a mere party weapon and the farcical result of its use in 417 in the case of Hyperbolus led to its abolition either at once, or, as Lugebil seeks to prove, in the archonship of Euclides

(403 B.C.). Such a device inevitably lent itself to abuse (see Aristotle, *Pol.* 38, 1284 b 22 στασιαστικῶς ἐχρῶντο).

Grote maintains that ostracism was a useful device, on the grounds that it removed the danger of tyranny, and was better than the perpetual civil strife of the previous century. The second reason is strictly beside the point, and the first has no force after the Persian Wars. As a factor in party politics it was both unnecessary and injurious to the state. Thus in the Persian Wars, it deprived Athens of the wisdom of Xanthippus and Aristides, while at the battle of Tanagra and perhaps at the time of the Egyptian expedition the assistance of Cimon was lacking. Further, it was a blow to the fair-play of party politics; the defeated party, having no leader, was reduced to desperate measures, such as the assassination of Ephialtes. To defend it on the ground that it created and stimulated the national consciousness is hardly reconcilable with the historic remark of the voter who voted against Aristides because he wished to hear no more of his incorruptible integrity; moreover in democratic Athens the "national consciousness" was, if anything, too frequently stimulated in the ordinary course of government. Aristotle, admitting its usefulness, rightly describes ostracism as in theory tyrannical; Montesquieu (*Esprit des lois*, xii. cc. 19, 20, &c.) defends it as a mild and reasonable institution. On the whole, the history of its effect in Athens, Argos, Miletus, Megara and Syracuse (where it was called *Petalismus*), furnishes no sufficient defence against its admitted disadvantages. The following is a list of persons who suffered ostracism:—Hipparchus (488); Megacles (487); Xanthippus (485), Aristides (483), Themistocles (471?); Cimon (461?) Thucydides, son of Melesias (444), Damon, Hyperbolus (417) and possibly Cleisthenes himself (*q.v.*).

AUTHORITIES.—For the procedure in O. see Appendix Photii (Porson, p. 675); see also, besides authorities quoted above, Busolt, i. 620; Müller's *Handbuch*, iv. 1, 121; Gilbert, *Gr. St.* i. 446–466 and *Greek Constitutional Antiquities* (Eng. trans., 1895); A. H. J. Greenidge, *Handbook of Greek Constitutional Antiquities* (1896); histories of Greece in general. The view maintained in the text as to the number of votes necessary is supported by Duruy (*H. of G.* ii. 1, 360), Boeckh, Wachsmuth, &c.; opposed by Grote, Oman and (on the whole) by Evelyn Abbott. On the danger of privilegia in general see Cicero, *de Legibus*, iii. 4, and note that in Athens, ostracism gratuitously anticipated a crime which, if committed, would have been punishable in the popular Heliaea. Cf. also article EXILE. (J. M. M.)

OSTRACODERMS or OSTRACOPHORES, the earliest and most primitive group of fish-like animals, found as fossils in Upper

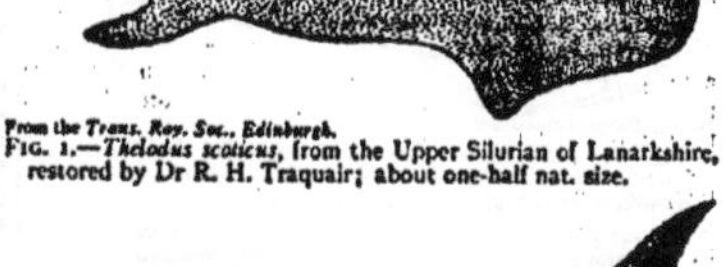

From the Trans. Roy. Soc., Edinburgh.
FIG. 1.—*Thelodus scoticus*, from the Upper Silurian of Lanarkshire, restored by Dr R. H. Traquair; about one-half nat. size.

From the Proc. Geol. Assoc.
FIG. 2.—*Cephalaspis murchisoni*, from the Lower Old Red Sandstone of Herefordshire, restored by Dr A. S. Woodward; about one-half nat. size.

Silurian and Devonian formations both in Europe and in North

America. They are so named (Gr. shell-skins or shell-bearers) in allusion to the nacreous shell-like appearance of the inner face of the plates of armour which cover the more common

FIG. 3.—*Pteraspis rostrata*, from the Lower Old Red Sandstone of Herefordshire; restored by Dr A. S. Woodward; about one-third nat. size.

members of the group. The Ostracoderms are, indeed, known only by the hard armature of the skin, but this sometimes bears impressions of certain internal soft parts which have perished

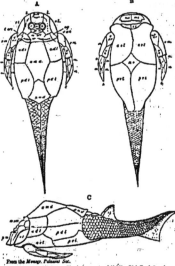

FIG. 4.—*Pterichthys milleri*, from the Middle Old Red Sandstone of Scotland, restored by Dr R. H. Traquair: upper (A), lower (B), and left-side view (C), about one-half nat. size.

ag.,	Angular.	*m.occ.*, Median occipital.
a.d.l.,	Anterior dorso-lateral.	*m.v.*, Median ventral.
a.m.d.,	Anterior median dorsal.	*mx.*, Maxilla.
a.v.l.,	Anterior ventro-lateral.	*o.*, Ocular.
c.,	Central.	*p.d.l.*, Posterior dorso-lateral.
d.a.,	Dorsal anconeal.	*p.m.*, Pre-median.
d.ar.,	Dorsal articular.	*p.m.d.*, Posterior median
e.l.,	Extra lateral.	dorsal.
e.m.,	External marginal.	*p.v.l.*, Posterior ventro-lateral.
i.m.,	Internal marginal.	*pt.m.*, Post-median.
l.,	Lateral.	*s.l.*, Semilunar.
l.occ.,	Lateral occipital.	*t.*, Terminal.
m.,	Median.	*v.a.*, Ventral anconeal.
m.m.,	Marginals of lower limb.	*v.ar.*, Ventral articular.

during fossilization. They agree with fishes in the possession of median fins, and resemble the large majority of early fishes in their unequal-lobed (heterocercal) tail, but they have no ordinary paired fins. They must also have been provided with the usual gill-apparatus, but there is reason to believe that their lower jaw was not on the fish plan. They are, therefore, at least as low in the zoological scale as the existing lampreys, with which Cope, Smith, Woodward and others have associated them. They are all small animals, many of them only a few centimetres in length.

The oldest and lowest family of Ostracoderms, that of Coelolepidae, is known by nearly complete skeletons of *Thelodus* (fig. 1) and *Lanarkia* from the Upper Silurian mudstones of Lanarkshire, Scotland. The body is completely and uniformly covered with minute granules which resemble the shagreen of sharks, and were erroneously ascribed to sharks when they were first discovered in the Upper Silurian bone-bed at Ludlow, Shropshire. The head and anterior part of the trunk are depressed and shown from above or below in the fossils, and this region sharply contracts behind into the slender tail, which is generally seen in side view, with one small dorsal fin and a forked heterocercal tail. The eyes are far forwards and wide apart. In another family, that of the Cephalaspidae (fig. 2), the animals resemble the Coelolepids in shape, but their skin-granules are fused into small plates, which are polygonal where there must have been much flexibility, and in rings round the tail where the underlying successive plates of muscle necessitated this arrangement. The eyes are close together. At the opening of the gill-cavity on each side at the back of the head, there is a flexible flap, which is sometimes interpreted as a paired limb. Part of the armour of the Cephalaspidians contains bone-cells, but the dermal plates of two other families, the Pteraspidae (fig. 3) and Drepanaspidae, consist merely of fused shagreen granules without any advance towards bone. The Pteraspidae are interesting as showing on the inner side of the dorsal shield impressions which suggest that the gill-cavities extended unusually far forwards to the front of the head. Another family, known only by nearly complete skeletons from the Upper Silurian mudstones of Lanarkshire, is that of the Birkeniidae, comprising small fusiform species which are covered with granules disposed in curiously-arranged rows. The highest Ostracoderms are the Asterolepidae, which occur only in Devonian rocks and include the familiar *Pterichthys* (fig. 4) from the Middle Old Red Sandstone of Scotland. In this family the primitive skin-tubercles seem to have fused, not into polygonal plates, but along the lines of the slime-canals. The Asterolepid armour consists of symmetrically arranged, overlapping plates on the top of the head and round the body, with a pair of flippers similarly armoured and appended to the latter. The tail resembles that of other Ostracoderms and is sometimes covered with scales.

See E. Ray Lankester, *The Cephalaspidae* (Monogr. Palaeont. Soc. 1868, 1870); R. H. Traquair, *The Asterolepidae* (Monogr. Palaeont. Soc. 1894, 1904, 1906) and papers in *Trans. Roy. Soc. Edinb.* vol. xxxix. No. 32 (1899), vol. xl. Nos. 30, 33 (1903, 1905); A. S. Woodward, *Catal. Foss. Fishes, B.M.* pt. ii. (1891); W. H. Gadell, *Origin of Vertebrates* (London, 1908). (A. S. Wo.)

OSTRAU, the name of two Austrian towns in the Ostrau-Karwin coal-mining district. (1) Mährisch-Ostrau (Moravian Ostrau), a town in Moravia, 95 m. N.E. of Brünn by rail. Pop. (1900) 30,125. It is situated on the right bank of the Ostrawitza, near its confluence with the Oder, and it derives its importance from the neighbouring coal mines, and the blast furnaces and iron-works which they have called into existence. The manufactures comprise sheet-iron, boilers, zinc, brick and tiles, paraffin, petroleum, soap and candles. The Rothschild iron-works at Witkowitz are in the vicinity. (2) Polnisch-Ostrau (Polish Ostrau), a mining town in Austrian Silesia, opposite Mährisch-Ostrau. Pop. (1900) 18,761, mostly Czech. It has large coal mines, which form the south-western portion of the extensive Upper Silesian coal fields, the largest Austrian deposit.

OSTRICH (O. Eng. *estridge*; Fr. *autruche*; Span. *avestruz*; Lat. *avis struthio*; Gr. στρουθίων or ὁ μέγας στρουθός); the *Struthio camelus* of Linnaeus, and the largest of living birds, an adult male standing nearly 8 ft. high and weighing 300 lb.

The genus *Struthio* forms the type of the group of Ratite birds, characterized chiefly by large size, breast-bone without a keel, strong running legs, rudimentary wings and simple feathers (see BIRD). The most obvious distinctive character presented by the ostrich is the presence of two toes only, the third and fourth, on each foot—a character absolutely peculiar to the genus *Struthio*. In South America another large Ratite bird, the rhea, is called ostrich; it can be distinguished at once from the true ostrich by its possession of three toes.

The wild ostrich[1] is disappearing before the persecution of man, and there are many districts, some of wide extent, frequented by the ostrich in the 19th century—especially towards the extremities of its African range—in which it no longer occurs, while in Asia there is evidence, more or less trustworthy, of its former existence in most parts of the south-western desert-tracts, in few of which it is now to be found. Xenophon's notice of its abundance in Assyria (*Anabasis*, I. 5) is well known. It is probable that it still lingers in the wastes of Kirwan in eastern Persia, whence examples may occasionally stray northward to those of Turkestan,[2] even near the Lower Oxus, but the assertion, often repeated, as to its former occurrence in Baluchistan or Sind seems to rest on testimony too slender

Ostrich.

for acceptance. Apparently the most northerly limit of the ostrich's ordinary range at the present day is that portion of the Syrian Desert lying directly eastward of Damascus; and, within the limits of what may be called Palestine, H. B. Tristram (*Fauna and Flora of Palestine*, p. 139) regards it as but a straggler from central Arabia, though we have little information as to its distribution in that country.

Africa is still, as in ancient days, the continent in which the ostrich chiefly flourishes. There it appears to inhabit every waste sufficiently extensive to afford it the solitude it loves. Yet even there it has to contend with the many species of carnivora which prey upon its eggs and young—the latter especially; and H. Lichtenstein long ago remarked[3] that if it

[1] A good summary of the present distribution is contained in the *Ostriches and Ostrich Farming* of De Mosenthal and Harting, from which the accompanying figure is, with permission, taken. Von Heuglin, in his *Ornithologie Nordost-Afrikas* (pp. 925-935), and A. Reichenow in *Die Vögel Afrikas*, have given more particular details of the ostrich's distribution in Africa.

[2] Drs Finsch and Hartlaub quote a passage from Remusat's *Remarques sur l'extension de l'empire chinoise*, stating that in about the 7th century of our era a live "camel-bird" was sent as a present with an embassy from Turkestan to China.

[3] H. Lichtenstein, *Reise im südlichen Africa*, ii. 42-45 (Berlin, 1812).

were not for its numerous enemies "the multiplication of ostriches would be quite unexampled."

Though sometimes assembling in troops of from thirty to fifty, and then generally associating with zebras or with some of the larger antelopes, ostriches commonly, and especially in the breeding season, live in companies of not more than four or five, one of which is a cock and the rest are hens. The latter lay their eggs in one and the same nest, a shallow pit scraped out by their feet, with the earth heaped around to form a kind of wall against which the outermost circle of eggs rest. As soon as ten or a dozen eggs are laid, the cock begins to brood, always taking his place on them at nightfall surrounded by the hens, while by day they relieve one another, more it would seem to guard their common treasure from jackals and small beasts of prey than directly to forward the process of hatching, for that is often left wholly to the sun.[4] Some thirty eggs are laid in the nest, and round it are scattered perhaps as many more. These last are said to be broken by the old birds to serve as nourishment for the newly-hatched chicks, whose stomachs cannot bear the hard food on which their parents thrive. The greatest care is taken to place the nest where it may not be discovered, and the birds avoid being seen when going to or from it, while they display great solicitude for their young. C. J. Andersson in his *Lake N'gami* (pp. 253-269) has given a lively account of the pursuit by himself and Francis Galton of a brood of ostriches, in the course of which the male bird feigned being wounded to distract their attention from his offspring. Though the ostrich ordinarily inhabits the most arid districts, it requires water to drink; more than that, it will frequently bathe, and sometimes even, according to Von Heuglin, in the sun.

The question whether to recognize more than one species of ostrich has been continually discussed without leading to a satisfactory solution. While eggs from North Africa present a perfectly smooth surface, those from South Africa are pitted. Moreover northern birds have the skin of the parts not covered with feathers flesh-coloured, while this skin is bluish in southern birds, and hence the latter have been thought to need specific designation as *S. australis*. Examples from the Somali country have been described as forming a distinct species under the name of *S. molybdophanes* from the leaden colour of their naked parts.

The great mercantile value of ostrich-feathers, and the increasing difficulty, due to the causes already mentioned, of procuring them from wild birds, has led to the formation in Cape Colony, Egypt, the French Riviera and elsewhere of numerous "ostrich-farms," on which these birds are kept in confinement, and at regular intervals deprived of their plumes. In favourable localities and with judicious management these establishments yield very considerable profit (see FEATHER).

See, besides the works mentioned, E. D'Alton, *Die Skelete der Straussartigen Vögel abgebildet und beschrieben* (Bonn, 1827); P. L. Sclater, "On the Struthious Birds living in the Zoological Society's Menagerie," *Transactions*, iv. p. 353, containing a fine representation (pl. 67), by J. Wolf, of the male *Struthio camelus*; J. Forest, *L'Autruche* (Paris, 1894); A. Douglass, *Ostrich Farming in South Africa* (London, 1881); modern anatomical work on the group is referred to in the article BIRDS.　　　　(A. N.)

OSTROG, a town of Russia, in the government of Volhynia, 95 m. W. of Zhitomir, at the confluence of the Vilya with the Goryn. Pop. (1897) 14,530. It is an episcopal see of the Orthodox Greek Church, and in the 16th century had a classical academy, converted later into a Jesuit college. Here was made and printed in 1581 the first translation of the Bible into old Slav. In the town is a brotherhood of Cyril and Methodius, which maintains schools of its own. The tanning of light leather is an active domestic trade; other industries are potteries, oil-works, soap, candle and tobacco factories. After being plundered by the Cossack chieftain Khmelnitski in 1648, and conquered by the Russians seven years later, the town fell into decay.

OSTROGOTHS, or EAST GOTHS, one of the two main branches into which the Goths were divided, the other being the Visigoths, or West Goths. See GOTHS.

OSTROVSKIY, ALEXANDER NIKOLAIVICH (1823-1886), Russian dramatic author, was born on the 12th of April 1823 in Moscow, where his father was an official of the senate. He studied

[4] By those whose experience is derived from the observation of captive ostriches this fact has been often disputed. But, the difference of circumstances under which they find themselves, and in particular their removal from the heat-retaining sands of the desert and its burning sunshine, is quite enough to account for the change of habit. Von Heuglin also (p. 933) is explicit on this point.

law in the university of that city, which he quitted without having submitted to the final examination. He was then employed as a clerk in the office of the "Court of Conscience," and subsequently in that of the Commercial Court at Moscow. Both tribunals were called upon to settle disputes chiefly among the Russian merchant class, from which Ostrovskiy was thus enabled to draw the chief characters for his earliest comedies. Among these are *Byednaya Nivesta* ("The Poor Bride "), *Byednost ne Porok* ("Poverty not a Vice "), and *Ne v'svoi sani ne sadis* (literally "Don't put yourself in another's sledge," meaning." Don't put yourself in a position for which you are not suited "). Of this last Nicholas I. said, " it was not a play, but a lesson." The uncultured, self-satisfied Moscow merchants are strikingly portrayed in *Groza* ("The Tempest ") and *Swoyi lyudi sochtyomrya* ("Between near relatives, no accounts are needed "), which was originally called "The Bankrupt." The last-mentioned comedy was prohibited for ten years, until the accession of Alexander II., and Ostrovskiy was dismissed the government service and placed under the supervision of the police. The Liberal tendencies of the new reign, however, soon brought relief, Ostrovskiy was one of several well-known literary men who were sent into the provinces to report on the condition of the people. Ostrovskiy's field of inquiry lay along the upper Volga, a part of the country memorable for some of the most important events in Russian history. This mission induced him to write several historical dramas of great merit, such as *Kusma Zakharich Minin Soukhorouk* (the full name of the famous butcher who saved Moscow from the Poles); "The False Demetrius" and " Vassily Shuisky "; *Vassilisa Melentiena* (the name of a favourite court lady of Ivan the Terrible), and the comedy, *Voivoda celi Son na Volge* ("The Military Commander," or "A dream on the Volga "). Many of his later works treat of the Russian nobility, and include *Byeshani Dengi* (literally "Mad Money "), *Vospontivitsa* ("A Girl brought up in a Stranger's Family "), and *Volki e Outsi* ("Wolves and Sheep "); others relate to the world of actors, such as *Less* ("Forest "), *Bei vini vinovatya* (" Guiltlessly guilty "), and *Talenti e Pokloniki* ("Talents and their Admirers "). Ostrovskiy enjoyed the patronage of Alexander III., and received a pension of 3000 roubles a year. With the help of Moscow capitalists he established in that city a model theatre and school of dramatic art, of which he became the first director. He also founded the Society of Russian Dramatic Art and Opera Composers. His death took place on the 24th of June 1886, while travelling to his estate in Kostroma.

OSTUNI, a picturesque walled city of Apulia, Italy, in the province of Lecce, 23 m. by rail N.W. of Brindisi. Pop. (1901) 7734 (town); 22,811 (commune). It has a cathedral of the 15th century with a fine Romanesque façade, and a municipal library with a collection of antiquities. The see has been amalgamated with that of Brindisi.

OSUNA, PEDRO TELLEZ GIRON, 3rd duke of (1575–1624), Spanish viceroy of Sicily and Naples, was born at Osuna, and baptized on the 18th of January 1575. He was the son of Juan Tellez Giron, the 2nd duke, and of his wife Ana Maria de Velasco, a daughter of the constable of Castile. When a boy he accompanied his grandfather, the 1st duke, to Naples, where he was viceroy. He saw service at the age of fourteen with the troops sent by Philip II. to put down a revolt in Aragon, and was married while still young to Doña Catarina Enriquez de Ribera, a grand-daughter on her mother's side of Hernan Cortes, the conqueror of Mexico. In 1598 he inherited the dukedom. Before and after his marriage he was known for the reckless dissipation of his life. The scandals to which his excesses gave rise led to his imprisonment at Arévalo in 1600. This sharp lesson had a wholesome effect on the duke, and in the same year he left for Flanders, with a body of soldiers raised at his own expense. His appearance in Flanders as a grandee with a following of his own caused some embarrassment to the king's officers. But Osuna displayed unexpected docility and good sense in the field. He was content to serve as a subordinate, and took a full share of work and fighting both by land and sea.

When peace was made with England in 1604 he is said to have visited London. He is said also to have paid a visit to Holland during the armistice arranged to allow of the negotiations for the twelve years' truce of 1609; but, as he was back in Spain by that year, he cannot have seen much of the country. His services had purged his early offences, and he had been decorated with the Golden Fleece. On the 18th of September 1610 he was named viceroy of Sicily, and he took possession of his post at Melazzo on the 9th of March 1611. In 1616 he was promoted to the viceroyalty of Naples, and held the office till he was recalled on the 28th of March 1620. The internal government of Osuna in both provinces was vigorous and just. During his Sicilian viceroyalty he organized a good squadron of galleys with which he freed the coast for a time from the raids of the Mahommedan pirates of the Barbary States and the Levant. After his transfer to Naples Osuna continued his energetic wars with the pirates, but he became concerned in some of the most obscure political intrigues of the time. He entered into a policy of unmeasured hostility to Venice, which he openly attacked in the Adriatic. The princes of the Spanish branch of the Habsburgs were at all times anxious to secure safe communication with the German possessions of their family. Hence their anxiety to dominate all northern Italy and secure possession of the Alpine passes. It would have suited them very well if they could have reduced Venice to the same state of servitude as Genoa. Osuna threw himself into this policy with a whole heart. There can be no reasonable doubt that he was engaged with the Spanish ambassador, and the viceroy of Milan, in the mysterious conspiracy against Venice in 1618. As usual, the Spanish government had miscalculated its resources, and was compelled to draw back. It then found extreme difficulty in controlling its fiery viceroy. Osuna continued to act against Venice in an almost piratical fashion, and treated orders from home with scant respect. Serious fears began to be entertained that he meant to declare himself independent in Naples, and had he tried he could have brought about a revolt which the enfeebled Spanish government could hardly have suppressed. It is, however, unlikely that he had treasonable intentions. He allowed his naval forces to be gradually reduced by drafts, and when superseded returned obediently to Madrid. After his return he was imprisoned on a long string of charges, and largely at the instigation of the Venetians. No judgment was issued against him, as he died in prison on the 24th of September 1624. The "great duke of Osuna," as he is always called by the Spaniards, impressed the imagination of his countrymen profoundly as a vigorous, domineering and patriotic leader of the stamp of the 16th century, and he was no less admired by the Italians. His ability was infinitely superior to that of the ordinary politicians and courtiers of the time, but he was more energetic than really wise, and he was an intolerable subordinate to the bureaucratic despotism of Madrid.

The *Vita di Don Pietro Giron, duca d' Ossuna, vicere di Napoli e di Sicilia* of Gregorio Leti (Amsterdam, 1699) is full of irrelevances, and contains much gossip, as well as speeches which are manifestly the invention of the author. But it is founded on good documents, and Leti, an Italian who detested the Spanish rule, knew the state of his own country well. See also Don C. Fernandez Duro, *El Gran Duque de Osuna y su Marina* (Madrid, 1885), and *Documentos inéditos para la historia de España* (Madrid, 1842, &c.), vols. xliv.–xlvii.

OSUNA, a town of southern Spain, in the province of Seville; 57 m. by rail E.S.E. of Seville. Pop. (1900) 18,072. Osuna is built on a hill, overlooking the fertile plain watered by the Salado, a sub-tributary of the Guadalquivir. On the top of the hill stands the collegiate church, dating from 1534 and containing interesting Spanish and early German paintings. These, however, as well as the sculptures over the portal, suffered considerably during the occupation of the place by the French under Soult. The vaults, which are supported by Moorish arches, contain the tombs of the Giron family, by one of whom, Don Juan Tellez, the church was founded in 1534. The university of Osuna, founded also by him in 1549, was suppressed in 1820; but its large building is still used as a secondary school.

The industries are agriculture and the making of esparto mats, pottery, bricks, oil, soap, cloth, linen and hats.

Osuna, the Urso of Hirtius, famous in the 1st century B.C. for its long resistance to the troops of Caesar, and its fidelity to the Pompeians, was subsequently called by the Romans Orsona and Gemina Urbanorum, the last name being due, it is said, to the presence of two urban legions here. Osuna was taken from the Moors in 1239, and given by Alphonso X. to the knights of Calatrava in 1264. Don Pedro Giron appropriated it to himself in 1445. One of his descendants, Don Pedro Tellez, was the first holder of the title duke of Osuna, conferred on him by Philip II. in 1562.

Estepa (pop. 8591), a town 6 m. E.N.E. is the Iberian and Carthaginian Astepa or Ostipo, famous for its siege in 207 B.C. by the Romans under Publius Cornelius Scipio. When further resistance became impossible, the people of Astepa set fire to their town, and all perished in the flames.

OSWALD (c. 605–642), king of Northumbria, was one of the sons of Æthelfrith and was expelled from Northumbria on the accession of Edwin, though he himself was a son of Edwin's sister Acha. He appears to have spent some of his exile in Iona, where he was instructed in the principles of Christianity. In 634 he defeated and slew the British king Ceadwalla at a place called by Bede Denisesburn, near Hefenfelth, which has been identified with St Oswald's Cocklaw, near Chollerford, Northumberland. By this he avenged his brother, Eanfrith, who had succeeded Edwin in Bernicia, and became king of Northumbria. Oswald reunited Deira and Bernicia, and soon raised his kingdom to a position equal to that which it had occupied in the time of Edwin, with whom he is classed by Bede as one of the seven great Anglo-Saxon kings. His close alliance with the Celtic church is the characteristic feature of his reign. In 635 he sent to the elders of the Scots for a bishop. On the arrival of Aidan in answer to this request he assigned to him the island of Lindisfarne as his see, near the royal city of Bamborough. He also completed the minster of St Peter at York which had been begun by Paulinus under Edwin. Bede declares that Oswald ruled over " all the peoples and provinces of Britain, which includes four languages, those of the Britons, Picts, Scots and Angles." His relationship to Edwin may have helped him to consolidate Deira and Bernicia. Early in his reign, he was sponsor to the West Saxon king Cynegils, whose daughter he married. In 642 he was defeated and slain at a place called Maserfeld, probably Oswestry in Shropshire, by Penda of Mercia.

See Bede, *Historia Ecclesiastica*, ed. C. Plummer (Oxford, 1896), ii. 5, 14, 20; iii. 2, 3, 5, 6, 7, 9–14; *Anglo-Saxon Chronicle*, ed. J. Earle and C. Plummer (Oxford, 1899), s.a., 617, 634, 635, 642, 654.

OSWALD (d. 992), archbishop of York, was a nephew of Oda, archbishop of Canterbury, and at an early age became, by purchase, head of the Old Minster at Winchester. Desiring to become a monk, he went with Oda's approval to the monastery of Fleury on the Loire—at that time the great centre of reviving Benedictinism. Here he soon distinguished himself by the monastic austerity of his life. In 959 he returned to England at the request of Oda, who, however, died before his arrival. He now went to York to his kinsman the Archbishop Oskytel, who took him with him on a pilgrimage to Rome. Soon after his return he was appointed bishop of Worcester at the recommendation of Dunstan, his predecessor in the see (961). As bishop he took a prominent part in that revival of monastic discipline on Benedictine lines of which Aethelwold, bishop of Winchester, was the most ardent leader. His methods, however, were less violent than those of Aethelwold. Among other religious houses he founded that of Ramsey in conjunction with Aethelwine, Ealdorman of East Anglia. In 972 he was translated (again at Dunstan's recommendation) to the archbishopric of York, with which he continued to hold the see of Worcester. He died on the 29th of February 992 and was buried at Worcester.

See *Memorials of St Dunstan*, edited by W. Stubbs, Rolls series (London, 1874).

OSWALDTWISTLE, an urban district in the Accrington parliamentary division of Lancashire, England, on the Leeds and Liverpool Canal, 3½ m. E.S.E. of Blackburn. Pop. (1901) 14,192. It possesses cotton-mills, printworks, bleachworks and chemical works, and in the neighbourhood are collieries, stone quarries and potteries. At Peelfold, in the township, was born (1750) Sir Robert Peel, first baronet, who, as a factory-owner, effected wide developments in the cotton industry.

OSWEGO, a city, port of entry, and the county-seat of Oswego county, New York, U.S.A., on the S.E. shore of Lake Ontario, at the mouth of the Oswego river, about 35 m. N.W. of Syracuse. Pop. (1900) 22,199, of whom 3989 were foreign born; (1910 census) 23,368. It is served by the New York Central & Hudson River, the Delaware, Lackawanna & Western, and the New York, Ontario & Western railways, by several lines of lake steamboats, and by the Oswego Canal, which connects Lake Ontario with the Erie Canal at Syracuse. There is an inner harbour of 9·35 acres and an outer harbour of 140 acres, which are defended by Fort Ontario. The city lies at an altitude of 300 ft., and is divided into two parts by the Oswego river. Oswego is the seat of a state Normal and Training School (founded as the City Training School in 1861, and a state school since 1867), a state armoury, and a United States life-saving station; among the public buildings are the City Library (about 14,000 volumes in 1909), founded by Gerrit Smith in 1855, the Federal Building and Custom House, the City Hall, the City Hospital, the County Court House, an Orphan Asylum, and a business college. The Oswego river has here a fall of 34 ft. and furnishes excellent water power. Among the principal manufactures are starch (the city has one of the largest starch factories in the world), knit goods, railway car springs, shade-cloth, boilers and engines, wooden-ware, matches, paper-cutting machines, and eau de cologne. The factory products were valued in 1905 at $7,594,145. Oswego has a considerable trade with Canada; in 1908 its exports were valued at $2,880,553 and its imports at $999,164. Lake commerce with other American Great Lake ports is also of some importance, the principal articles of trade being lumber, grain and coal.

The site of Oswego was visited by Samuel de Champlain in 1616. Subsequently it was a station for the Jesuit missionaries and the *coureurs des bois*. In 1722 a regular trading post was established here by English traders, and in 1727 Governor William Burnet of New York erected the first Fort Oswego (sometimes called Fort Burnet, Chouaguen or Pepperrell). It was an important base of operations during King George's War and the French and Indian War. In the years 1755–1756 the British erected two new forts at the mouth of the river, Fort Oswego (an enlargement of the earlier fort) on the east and Fort Ontario on the west. In August 1756 Montcalm, marching rapidly from Ticonderoga with a force of 3000 French and Indians, appeared before the forts, then garrisoned by 1000 British and colonial troops, and on the 14th of August forced the abandonment of Fort Ontario. On the following day he stormed and captured Fort Oswego, and, dismantling both, returned to Ticonderoga. The British restored Fort Ontario in 1759, and maintained a garrison here until 1796, when, with other posts on the lakes, they were, in accordance with the terms of Jay's Treaty, made over to the United States. It was here in 1766 that Pontiac formally made to Sir William Johnson his acknowledgment of Great Britain's authority. On the 6th of May 1814 Sir James Yeo, with a superior force of British and Canadians, captured the fort, but soon afterwards withdrew. In 1839 the fort was rebuilt and occupied by United States troops; it was abandoned in 1899, but, after having been reconstructed, was again garrisoned in 1905. The modern city may be said to date from 1796. Oswego became the county-seat in 1816, was incorporated as a village in 1828 (when the Oswego Canal was completed), and was first chartered as a city in 1848.

See Churchill, Smith and Child, *Landmarks of Oswego County* (Syracuse, 1895).

OSWESTRY, a market town and municipal borough in the Oswestry parliamentary division of Shropshire, England, on the borders of Wales, 18 m. N.W. from Shrewsbury. Pop. (1901) 9579. It is on a branch from the Chester line of the Great Western railway, and on the Cambrian main line. The situation is pleasant and the neighbouring district well wooded and hilly. The church of St Oswald, originally conventual, is Early English and Decorated, but has been greatly altered by restoration. There is a Roman Catholic chapel with presbytery, convent and school. The grammar school, founded in the reign of Henry IV., occupies modern buildings. The municipal buildings (1893) include a library, and a school of science and art. On a hill W. of the town are the castle grounds, laid out in 1890, but of the castle itself only slight remains are seen. The Cambrian railway engine and carriage works are here; and there are tanneries, malting works, machinery works and iron foundries. Frequent agricultural fairs are held. The town is governed by a mayor, 6 aldermen and 18 councillors. Area, 1887 acres.

Old Oswestry, also called Old Fort (Welsh Hên Dinas), is a British earthwork about a mile from the modern town. There are various unsatisfactory accounts of the early history of Oswestry (Blaneminster, or Album Monasterium), as that it was called Trer Cadeirau by the Britons and Osweiling after Cunelda Wledig, prince of North Wales, had granted it to his son Osweil. It derives its present name from Oswald, king of Northumbria, who is said to have been killed here in 642, although it was not definitely known as Oswestry until the 13th century. In the Domesday Survey it is included in the manor of Maesbury, which Rainald, sheriff of Shropshire, held of Roger, earl of Shrewsbury; but Rainald or his predecessor Warin had already raised a fortification at Oswestry called Louvre. This manor passed in the reign of Henry I. to Alan Fitz-Flaad, in whose family it continued until the death of Henry Fitzalan, earl of Arundel, without male issue in 1580. The first charter, of which a copy only is preserved among the corporation records, is one given in 1263 by John Fitzalan granting the burgesses self-government. Richard II. by a charter dated 1398 granted all the privileges which belonged to Shrewsbury, and a similar charter was obtained from Thomas, earl of Arundel in 1407. The town was incorporated by Elizabeth in 1582 under the government of two bailiffs and a common council of 24 burgesses, and her charter was confirmed by James I. in 1616. A charter granted by Charles II. in 1672 appointed a mayor, 12 aldermen and 15 common councilmen, and remained the governing charter until the Municipal Corporations Act of 1835 changed the corporation. In 1228 John Fitzalan obtained the right of holding a market every week on Monday instead of Thursday. The market rights were held by the lord of the manor until 1819, when Earl Powis sold them to the corporation. In the 15th and 16th centuries a weekly market was held at Oswestry for the sale of woollen goods manufactured in North Wales, but in the 17th century the drapers of Shrewsbury determined to get the trade into their own town, and although an Order in the Privy Council was passed to restrain it to Oswestry they agreed in 1621 to buy no more cloth there. The town was walled by the time of Edward I., but was several times burnt during Welsh invasions. In 1642 it was garrisoned for Charles I., but two years later surrendered to the parliamentary forces.

See William Cathrall, *The History of Oswestry* (1855); William Price, *The History of Oswestry from the Earliest Period* (1815); *Victoria County History, Shropshire.*

OSWIO (c. 612–670), king of Northumbria, son of Æthelfrith and brother of Oswald, whom he succeeded in Bernicia in 642 after the battle of Maserfield, was the seventh of the great English kings enumerated by Bede. He succeeded in making the majority of the Britons, Picts and Scots tributary to him. At Gilling in 651 he caused the murder of Oswine, a relative of Deira, who had become king of Deira, and a few years later took possession of that kingdom. He appears to have consolidated his power by the aid of the Church and by a series of judicious matrimonial alliances. It was probably in 642 that he married Eanfled, daughter of Edwin, thus uniting the two rival dynasties of Northumbria. His daughter Alhfled he married to Peada, son of Penda, king of Mercia, while another

daughter, Osthryth, became the wife of Æthelred, third son of the same king. Oswio was chiefly responsible for the reconversion of the East Saxons. He is said to have convinced their king Sigeberht of the truth of Christianity by his arguments, and at his request sent Cedd, a brother of Ceadda, on a mission to Essex. In 655 he was attacked by Penda, and, after an unsuccessful attempt to buy him off, defeated and slew the Mercian king at the battle of the Winwaed. He then took possession of part of Mercia, giving the rest to Peada. As a thank-offering he dedicated his daughter Ælfled to the Church, and founded the monastery of Whitby. About this time he is thought by many to have obtained some footing in the kingdom of the Picts in succession to their king Talorcan, the son of his brother Eanfrid. In 660 he married his son Ecgfrith to Æthelthryth, daughter of the East Anglian king Anna. In 664 at the synod of Whitby, Oswio accepted the usages of the Roman Church, which led to the departure of Colman and the appointment of Wilfrid as bishop of York. Oswio died in 670 and was succeeded by his son Ecgfrith.

See Bede, *Historia Ecclesiastica*, ii., iii., iv., v., edited by C. Plummer (Oxford, 1896); *Anglo-Saxon Chronicle*, edited by Earle and Plummer (Oxford, 1899).

OTHMAN (c. 574–656), in full Othmän ibn 'Affän, the third of the Mahommedan caliphs, a kinsman and son-in-law of Mahomet and cousin of Abu Sofian, whose son Moawiya became the first of the Omayyad dynasty. He was elected caliph in succession to Omar in 644, but owing to his alternate weakness and cruelty and his preference of the Koreish for all responsible positions irrespective of their capacity, he produced strife throughout the empire which culminated in his assassination by Mahommed, son of Abu Bekr. He was succeeded by Ali (q.v.). See CALIPHATE, A. § 3.

OTHNIEL, in the Bible, a clan settled at Debir or Kirjath-sepher in S. Palestine (Judg. i. 12 sqq.; Josh. xv. 16 sqq., contrast Josh. x. 38 seq.), described as the "brother" of Caleb. The name appears in Judg. iii. 7–11 (see JUDGES), as that of a hero who delivered Israel from a North Syrian king. That a king from the Euphrates who had subjugated Canaan should have been defeated by a clan of the south of Palestine has been doubted. There is no evidence of such a situation, and it has been conjectured that Cushan-Rishathaim (the name suggests "C. of double wickedness"!) of Aram (ארם) has arisen from some king (cp. Husham, Gen. xxxvi. 34) or clan (cp. Cush, Num. xii. 1; Cushan, Hab. iii. 7) of Edom (אדם) to the south or south-east of Palestine. Othniel recurs in 1 Chron. iv. 13.

See A. Klostermann, *Gesch. d. Volkes Israel* (1896), p. 122; Cheyne, *Ency. Bib.* col. 969 seq. and references; also the literature to JUDGES.

OTHO, MARCUS SALVIUS (32–69), Roman emperor from the 15th of January to the 15th of April A.D. 69, was born on the 28th of April A.D. 32. He belonged to an ancient and noble Etruscan family settled at Ferentinum in Etruria. He appears first as one of the most reckless and extravagant of the young nobles who surrounded Nero, whose friendship with Nero was brought to an abrupt close in 58, when Otho refused to divorce his beautiful wife Poppaea Sabina at the bidding of Nero, who at once appointed him governor of the remote province of Lusitania. Here Otho remained ten years, and his administration was marked by a moderation unusual at the time. When in 68 his neighbour Galba, the governor of Hispania Tarraconensis, rose in revolt against Nero, Otho accompanied him to Rome. Resentment at the treatment he had received from Nero may have impelled him to this course, but to this motive was added before long that of personal ambition. Galba was far advanced in years, and Otho, encouraged by the predictions of astrologers, aspired to succeed him. But in January 69 his hopes were dissipated by Galba's formal adoption of L. Calpurnius Piso as the fittest man to succeed him. Nothing remained for Otho but to strike a bold blow. Desperate as was the state of his finances, thanks to his previous extravagance, he found money to purchase the services of some three-and-twenty soldiers of the praetorian guard. On the morning of January 15, five days only after the adoption of Piso, Otho attended as usual to pay his respects to the emperor, and then hastily excusing himself on the score of private business hurried from the Palatine to meet his accomplices. By them he was escorted to the praetorian camp, where, after a few moments of surprise and indecision, he was saluted imperator. With an imposing force he returned to the Forum, and at the foot of the Capitol encountered Galba, who, alarmed by vague rumours of treachery, was making his way through a dense crowd of wondering citizens towards the barracks of the guard. The cohort on duty at the Palatine, which had accompanied the emperor, instantly deserted him, Galba, Piso and others were brutally murdered by the praetorians. The brief struggle over, Otho returned in triumph to the camp, and on the same day was duly invested by the senators with the name of Augustus, the tribunician power and the other dignities belonging to the principate. Otho had owed his success, not only to the resentment felt by the praetorian guards at Galba's well-meant attempts to curtail their privileges in the interests of discipline, but also largely to the attachment felt in Rome for the memory of Nero; and his first acts as emperor showed that he was not unmindful of the fact. He accepted, or appeared to accept, the cognomen of Nero conferred upon him by the shouts of the populace, whom his comparative youth and the effeminacy of his appearance reminded of their lost favourite. Nero's statues were again set up, his freedmen and household officers reinstalled, and the intended completion of the Golden House announced. At the same time the fears of the more sober and respectable citizens were allayed by Otho's liberal professions of his intention to govern equitably, and by his judicious clemency towards Marius Celsus, consul-designate, a devoted adherent of Galba.

But any further development of Otho's policy was checked by the news which reached Rome shortly after his accession, that the army in Germany had declared for Vitellius, the commander of the legions on the lower Rhine, and was already advancing upon Italy. After in vain attempting to conciliate Vitellius by the offer of a share in the empire, Otho, with unexpected vigour, prepared for war. From the remoter provinces, which had acquiesced in his accession, little help was to be expected; but the legions of Dalmatia, Pannonia and Moesia were eager in his cause, the praetorian cohorts were in themselves a formidable force and an efficient fleet gave him the mastery of the Italian seas. The fleet was at once despatched to secure Liguria, and on the 14th of March Otho, undismayed by omens and prodigies, started northwards at the head of his troops in the hopes of preventing the entry of the Vitellian troops into Italy. But for this he was too late, and all that could be done was to throw troops into Placentia and hold the line of the Po. Otho's advanced guard successfully defended Placentia against Alienus Caecina, and compelled that general to fall back on Cremona. But the arrival of Fabius Valens altered the aspect of affairs. The Vitellian commanders now resolved to bring on a decisive battle, and their designs were assisted by the divided and irresolute counsels which prevailed in Otho's camp. The more experienced officers urged the importance of avoiding a battle, until at least the legions from Dalmatia had arrived. But the rashness of the emperor's brother Titianus and of Proculus, prefect of the praetorian guards, added to Otho's feverish impatience, overruled all opposition, and an immediate advance was decided upon, Otho himself remaining behind with a considerable reserve force at Brixellum, on the southern bank of the Po. When this decision was taken the Othonian forces had already crossed the Po and were encamped at Bedriacum (or Betriacum), a small village on the Via Postumia, and on the route by which the legions from Dalmatia would naturally arrive. Leaving a strong detachment to hold the camp at Bedriacum, the Othonian forces advanced along the Via Postumia in the direction of Cremona. At a short distance from that city they unexpectedly encountered the Vitellian troops. The Othonians, though taken at a disadvantage, fought desperately, but were finally forced to fall back in disorder upon their camp at Bedriacum. Thither on the next day the victorious Vitellians followed them, but only to come to terms at once with their disheartened enemy, and to be welcomed into the camp as friends. More unexpected still was the effect produced at

Brixellum by the news of the battle. Otho was still in command of a formidable force—the Dalmatian legions had already reached Aquileia; and the spirit of his soldiers and their officers was unbroken. But he was resolved to accept the verdict of the battle which his own impatience had hastened. In a dignified speech he bade farewell to those about him, and then retiring to rest slept soundly for some hours. Early in the morning he stabbed himself to the heart with a dagger which he had concealed under his pillow, and died as his attendants entered the tent. His funeral was celebrated at once, as he had wished, and not a few of his soldiers followed their master's example by killing themselves at his pyre. A plain tomb was erected in his honour at Brixellum, with the simple inscription "Diis Manibus Marci Othonis." At the time of his death (the 15th of April 69) he was in his thirty-eighth year, and had reigned just three months. In all his life nothing became him so well as his manner of leaving it, but the fortitude he then showed, even if it was not merely the courage of despair, cannot blind us to the fact that he was little better than a reckless and vicious spendthrift, who was not the less dangerous because his fiercer passions were concealed beneath an affectation of effeminate dandyism. (H. F. P.)

See Tacitus, *Historiae*, i. 12-50, 71-90, ii. 11-51; *Lives* by Suetonius and Plutarch; Dio Cassius lxiv.; Merivale, *History of the Romans under the Empire*, ch. 56; H. Schiller, *Geschichte der römischen Kaiserzeit* (1883); L. Paul, "Kaiser M. Salvius Otho" in *Rhein. Mus.* lvii. (1902); W. A. Spooner, *On the Characters of Galba, Otho, and Vitellius*, in Introd. to his edition (1891) of the *Historiae* of Tacitus; B. W. Henderson, *Civil War and Rebellion in the Roman Empire*, A.D. 69-70 (1908).

OTIS, HARRISON GRAY (1765-1848), American politician, was born in Boston, Massachusetts, on the 8th of October 1765. He was a nephew of James Otis, and the son of Samuel Allyne Otis (1740-1814), who was a member of the Confederation Congress in 1787-1788 and secretary of the United States Senate from its first session in 1789 until his death. Young Otis graduated from Harvard College in 1783, was admitted to the bar in 1786, and soon became prominent as a Federalist in politics. He served in the Massachusetts House of Representatives in 1796-1797, in the National House of Representatives in 1797-1801, as district-attorney for Massachusetts in 1801, as speaker of the state House of Representatives in 1803-1805, as a member of the state Senate from 1805 to 1811, and as president of that body in 1805-1806 and 1808-1811, as a member of the United States Senate from 1817 to 1822, and as mayor of Boston in 1829-1832. He was strongly opposed to the War of 1812, and was a leader in the movement culminating in the Hartford Convention, which he defended in a series of open letters published in 1824, and in his inaugural address as mayor of Boston. A man of refinement and education, a member of an influential family, a popular social leader and an eloquent speaker—at the age of twenty-three he was chosen by the town authorities of Boston to deliver the Independence Day oration—Otis yet lacked conspicuous ability as a statesman. He died in Boston on the 28th of October 1848.

OTIS, JAMES (1725-1783), American patriot, was born at West Barnstable, Massachusetts, on the 5th of February 1725. He was the eldest son of James Otis (1702-1778), fourth in descent from John Otis (1581-1657), a native of Barnstable, Devon, and one of the first settlers (in 1635) of Hingham, Mass. The elder James Otis was elected to the provincial General Court in 1758, was its speaker in 1760-1762, and was chief justice of the Court of Common Pleas from 1764 until 1776; he was a prominent patriot in the colony of Massachusetts. The son graduated at Harvard in 1743; and after studying law in the office of Jeremiah Gridley (1702-1767), a well-known lawyer with Whig sympathies, rose to great distinction at the bar, practising first at Plymouth and after 1750 at Boston. In 1760 he published *Rudiments of Latin Prosody*, a book of authority in its time. He wrote a similar treatise upon Greek prosody; but this was never published, because, as he said, there was not a font of Greek letters in the country, nor, if there were, a printer who could have set them up. Soon after the accession of George III. to the throne of England in 1760, the British government decided upon a rigid enforcement of the navigation acts, which had long been disregarded by the colonists and had been almost wholly evaded during the French and Indian War. The Writs of Assistance issued in 1755 were about to expire, and it was decided to issue new ones, which would empower custom house officers to search any house for smuggled goods, though neither the house nor the goods had to be specifically mentioned in the writs. Much opposition was aroused in Massachusetts, the legality of the writs was questioned, and the Superior Court consented to hear argument. Otis held the office of advocate-general at the time, and it was his duty to appear on behalf of the government. He refused, resigned his office, and appeared for the people against the issue of the writs, Gridley appearing on the opposite side. The case was argued in the Old Town House of Boston in February 1761, and the chief speech was made by Otis. His plea was fervid in its eloquence and fearless in its assertion of the rights of the colonists. Going beyond the question at issue, he dealt with the more fundamental question of the relation between the English in America and the home government, and argued that even if authorized by act of parliament such writs were null and void. The young orator was elected in May of the same year a representative from Boston to the Massachusetts General Court. To that position he was re-elected nearly every year of the remaining active years of his life, serving there with his father. In 1766 he was chosen Speaker of the House of Representatives, but the choice was negatived. In September 1762 the younger Otis published *A Vindication of the Conduct of the House of Representatives of the Province of Massachusetts Bay*, in defence of the action of that body in sending to the governor a message (drafted by Otis) rebuking him for asking the assembly to pay for ships he had (with authorization of the Council and not of the representatives) sent to protect New England fisheries against French privateers; according to this message "it would be of little consequence to the people whether they were subject to George or Louis, the king of Great Britain or the French king, if both were as arbitrary as both would be if both could levy taxes without parliament." He also wrote various state papers addressed to the colonies to enlist them in the common cause, or sent to the government in England to uphold the rights or set forth the grievances of the colonists. His influence at home in controlling and directing the movement of events which led to the War of Independence was universally felt and acknowledged; and abroad no American was so frequently quoted, denounced, or applauded in parliament and the English press before 1769 as the recognized head and chief of the rebellious spirit of the New England colonists. In 1765 Massachusetts sent him as one of her representatives to the Stamp Act Congress at New York, which had been called by a Committee of the Massachusetts General Court, of which he was a member; and here he was a conspicuous figure, serving on the committee which prepared the address sent by that body to the British House of Commons. In 1769 he denounced in the Boston *Gazette* certain customs commissioners who had charged him with treason. Thereupon he became involved in an altercation in a public-house with Robinson, one of the commissioners; the altercation grew into an affray, and Otis received a sword cut on the head, which is considered to have caused his subsequent insanity. Robinson was mulcted in £2000 damages, but in view of his having made a written apology, Otis declined to take this sum from him. From 1769 almost continuously until his death Otis was harmlessly insane, though he had occasional lucid intervals, serving as a volunteer in the battle of Bunker Hill in 1775 and arguing a case in 1778. He was killed by lightning (it is said that he had often expressed a wish that he might die in this way) at Andover, Mass., on the 23rd of May 1783.

Otis's political writings were chiefly controversial and exercised an enormous influence, his pamphlets being among the most effective presentations of the arguments of the colonists against the arbitrary measures of the British ministry. His more important pamphlets were *A Vindication of the Conduct of the House of Representatives of the Province of Massachusetts Bay* (1762); *The Rights of the British Colonies Asserted and Proved* (1764); *A Vindication of the British Colonies against the Aspersions of the Halifax Gentleman in*

his *Letter to a Rhode Island Friend*—a letter known at the time as the "Halifax Libel" (1765); and *Considerations on Behalf of the Colonists in a Letter to a Noble Lord* (1765).

The best biography is that by William Tudor (Boston, 1823); there is a shorter one by Francis Bowen (Boston, 1847). The best account of Otis's characteristics and influence as a writer may be found in M. C. Tyler's *Literary History of the American Revolution* (New York, 1897). See also the notes on the Writs of Assistance by Horace Gray, Jr., in Quincy's *Massachusetts Reports, 1761-1772* (Boston, 1865). Otis's speech on the writs, reprinted from rough notes taken by John Adams, appears in *Appendix A* of vol. ii. of C. F. Adams's edition of the *Works of John Adams* (Boston, 1850).

OTLEY, a market town in the Otley parliamentary division of the West Riding of Yorkshire, England, 13 m. N.W. of Leeds on the Midland and the North-Eastern railways. Pop. of urban district (1901) 9230. It is picturesquely situated on the south bank of the Wharfe, at the foot of the precipitous Chevin Hill, 925 ft. in height. In this neighbourhood excellent building-stone is quarried, which was used for the foundations of the Houses of Parliament in London, and is despatched to all parts of England. The church of All Saints has Norman portions, and a cross and other remains of pre-Norman date were discovered in restoring the building. There are interesting monuments of members of the Fairfax family and others. Worsted spinning and weaving, tanning and leather-dressing, paper-making and the making of printing-machines are the principal industries. The scenery of Wharfedale is very pleasant. In the dale, 7 m. below Otley, are the fine ruins of Harewood Castle, of the 14th century. The neighbouring church contains a noteworthy series of monuments of the 15th century in alabaster.

OTRANTO, a seaport and archiepiscopal see of Apulia, Italy, in the province of Lecce, from which it is 29½ m. S.E. by rail, 49 ft. above sea-level. Pop. (1901) 2295. It is beautifully situated on the east coast of the peninsula of the ancient Calabria (*q.v.*). The castle was erected by Alphonso of Aragon; the cathedral, consecrated in 1088, has a rose window and side portal of 1481. The interior, a basilica with nave and two aisles, contains columns said to come from a temple of Minerva and a fine mosaic pavement of 1166, with interesting representations of the months, Old Testament subjects, &c. It has a crypt supported by forty-two marble columns. The church of S. Pietro has Byzantine frescoes. Two submarine cables start from Otranto, one for Valona, the other for Corfu. The harbour is small and has little trade.

Otranto occupies the site of the ancient Hydrus or Hydruntum, a town of Greek origin. In Roman times it was less important than Brundusium as a point of embarkation for the East, though the distance to Apollonia was less than from Brundusium. It remained in the hands of the Byzantine emperors until it was taken by Robert Guiscard in 1068. In 1480 it was utterly destroyed by the Turkish fleet, and has never since recovered its importance. About 30 m. S.E. lies the promontory of S. Maria di Leuca (so called since ancient times from its white cliffs), the S.E. extremity of Italy, the ancient Promontorium Iapygium or Sallentinum. The district between this promontory and Otranto is thickly populated, and very fertile. (T. As.)

OTTAKAR I. (d. 1230), king of Bohemia, was a younger son of King Vladislav II. (d. 1174) and a member of the Premyslide family, hence he is often referred to as Premysl Ottakar I. His early years were passed amid the anarchy which prevailed everywhere in his native land; after several struggles, in which he took part, he was recognized as ruler of Bohemia by the emperor Henry VI. in 1192. He was, however, soon overthrown, but renewing the fight in 1196 he forced his brother, King Vladislav III., to abandon Bohemia to him and to content himself with Moravia. Although confirmed in the possession of his kingdom by the German king, Philip, duke of Swabia, Ottakar soon deserted Philip, who thereupon declared him deposed. He then joined the rival German king, Otto of Brunswick, afterwards the emperor Otto IV., being recognized as king of Bohemia both by Otto and by his ally, Pope Innocent III. Philip's consequent invasion of Bohemia was a great success. Ottakar, having been compelled to pay a fine, again ranged himself among Philip's partisans and still later was among the supporters of the young king, Frederick II. He united Moravia with Bohemia in 1222, and when he died in December 1230 he left to his son, Wenceslaus I., a kingdom united and comparatively peaceable.

OTTAKAR II., or PREMYSL OTTAKAR II. (c. 1230-1278), king of Bohemia, was a son of King Wenceslaus I., and through his mother, Kunigunde, was related to the Hohenstaufen family, being a grandson of the German king, Philip, duke of Swabia. During his father's lifetime he ruled Moravia, but when in 1248 some discontented Bohemian nobles acknowledged him as their sovereign, trouble arose between him and his father, and for a short time Ottakar was imprisoned. However, in 1251 the young prince secured his election as duke of Austria, where he strengthened his position by marrying Margaret (d. 1267), sister of Duke Frederick II., the last of the Babenberg rulers of the duchy and widow of the German king, Henry VII. Some years later he repudiated this lady and married a Hungarian princess. Both before and after he became king of Bohemia in succession to his father in September 1253 Ottakar was involved in a dispute with Bela IV., king of Hungary, over the possession of Styria, which duchy had formerly been united with Austria. By an arrangement made in 1254 he surrendered part of it to Bela, but when the dispute was renewed he defeated the Hungarians in July 1260 and secured the whole of Styria for himself, owing his formal investiture with Austria and Styria to the German king, Richard, earl of Cornwall. The Bohemian king also led two expeditions against the Prussians. In 1269 he inherited Carinthia and part of Carniola; and having made good his claim, contested by the Hungarians, on the field of battle, he was the most powerful prince in Germany when an election for the German throne took place in 1273. But Ottakar was not the successful candidate. He refused to acknowledge his victorious rival, Rudolph of Habsburg, and urged the pope to adopt a similar attitude, while the new king claimed the Austrian duchies. Matters reached a climax in 1276. Placing Ottakar under the ban of the empire, Rudolph besieged Vienna and compelled Ottakar in November 1276 to sign a treaty by which he gave up Austria and the neighbouring duchies, retaining for himself only Bohemia and Moravia. Two years later the Bohemian king tried to recover his lost lands; he found allies and collected a large army, but he was defeated by Rudolph and killed at Dürnkrut on the March on the 26th of August 1278. Ottakar was a founder of towns and a friend of law and order, while he assisted trade and welcomed German immigrants. Clever, strong and handsome, he is a famous figure both in history and in legend, and is the subject of a tragedy by F. Grillparzer, *König Ottokars Glück und Ende*. His son and successor was Wenceslaus II.

See O. Lorenz, *Geschichte König Ottokars*, ii. (Vienna, 1866); A. Huber, *Geschichte Oesterreichs*, Band i. (Gotha, 1885); and F. Palacky, *Geschichte von Böhmen*, Band i. (Prague, 1844).

OTTAVA RIMA, a stanza of eight iambic lines, containing three rhymes, invariably arranged as follows:—*a b a b a b c c*. It is an Italian invention, and we find the earliest specimens of its use in the poetry of the fourteenth century. Boccaccio employed it for the *Teseide*, which he wrote in Florence in 1340, and for the *Filostrato*, which he wrote at Naples some seven years later. These remarkable epics gave to *ottava rima* its classic character. In the succeeding century it was employed by Politian, and by Boiardo for his famous *Orlando Innamorato* (1486). It was Pulci, however, in the *Morgante Maggiore* (1487), who invented the peculiar mock-heroic, or rather half-serious, half-burlesque, style with which *ottava rima* has been most commonly identified ever since and in connexion with which it was introduced into England by Frere and Byron. The measure, which was now recognized as the normal one for all Italian epic poetry, was presently wielded with extraordinary charm and variety by Berni, Ariosto and Tasso. The merits of it were not perceived by the English poets of the 16th and 17th centuries, although the versions of Tasso by Carew (1594) and Fairfax (1600) and of Ariosto by Harington (1591) preserve its external construction. The stanzaic forms invented by Spenser and by the Fletchers have less real relation to *ottava rima* than is commonly asserted, and it is quite incorrect to say that the author of the *Fairy Queen* adopted *ottava rima* and added a ninth line to prevent the sound from being monotonously iterative. A portion of Browne's *Britannia's Pastorals* is composed in pure *ottava rima*, but this is the only important specimen in original Elizabethan literature. Two centuries later a very successful attempt was made to introduce in English poetry the flexibility and gaiety of *ottava rima* by John Hookham Frere, who had studied Pulci and Casti, and had caught the very movement of their diverting measure. His *Whistlecraft* appeared in 1817. This is a specimen of the *ottava rima* of Frere:—

But chiefly, when the shadowy moon had shed
O'er woods and waters her mysterious hue,
Their passive hearts and vacant fancies fed
With thoughts and aspirations strange and new,
Till their brute souls with inward working bred
Dark hints that in the depths of instinct grew
Subjection—not from Locke's associations,
Nor David Hartley's doctrine of vibrations.

Byron was greatly impressed by the opportunities for satire involved in Frere's experiment, and in October 1817, in imitation of *Whistlecraft*, but keeping still closer to Pulci, he wrote *Beppo*. By far the greatest monument in *ottava rima* which exists in English literature is *Don Juan* (1819-1824). Byron also employed this measure, which was peculiarly adaptable to the purposes of his genius, in *The Vision of Judgment* (1822). Meanwhile Shelley also became attracted by it, and in 1820 translated the *Hymns* of Homer into *ottava rima*. The curious burlesque epic of William Tennant (1784-1848), *Anster Fair* (1812), which preceded all these, is written in what would be *ottava rima* if the eighth line were not an alexandrine. The form has been little used in other languages than Italian and English. It was employed by Boscán (1490-1542), who imitated Bembo vigorously in Spanish, and the very fine *Araucana* of Ercilla y Zúñiga (1533-1595) is in the same measure. Lope de Vega Carpio wrote plentifully in *ottava rima*. In Portuguese poetry of the 16th and 17th centuries this measure obtained the sanction of Camoens, who wrote in it his immortal *Lusiads* (1572). *Ottava rima* has been attempted in German poetry by Uhland and others, but not for pieces of any considerable length. (E. G.)

OTTAWA, a tribe of North American Indians of Algonquian stock, originally settled on the Ottawa river, Canada, and later on the north shore of the upper peninsula of Michigan. They were driven in 1650 by the Iroquois beyond the Mississippi, only to be forced back by the Dakotas. Then they settled on Manitoulin Island, Lake Huron, and joined the French against the English. During the War of Independence, however, they fought for the latter. Some were moved to Indian Territory (Oklahoma), but the majority live to-day in scattered communities throughout lower Michigan and Ontario.

OTTAWA, the largest tributary of the river St Lawrence; ranking ninth in length among the rivers of Canada, being 685 m. long. It flows first westward to Lake Temiscaming; thence south-east and east. The principal tributaries on the left bank are the Rouge (115 m.), North Nation (60), Lievre (205), Gatineau (240), Coulonge (135), Dumoine (80); and on the right bank, the South Nation (90), Mississippi (105), Madawaska (130) and Petawawa (95). Canals at Ste Anne, Carillon and Grenville permit the passage of vessels drawing 9 ft., from Montreal up to the city of Ottawa. At Ottawa the river is connected with Lake Ontario by the Rideau Canal. The Chaudière Falls, and the Chats and other rapids, prevent continuous navigation above the capital, but small steamers ply on the larger navigable stretches. The Montreal, Ottawa and Georgian Bay Canal is designed to surmount these obstructions and provide a navigable channel from Georgian Bay up French river, through Lake Nipissing and over the height of land to the Ottawa, thence down to Montreal, of sufficient depth to enable vessels drawing 20 on 21 ft. to carry cargo from Chicago, Duluth, Fort William, &c. to Montreal, or, if necessary, to Europe, without breaking bulk. Except the suggested Hudson Bay route, this canal would form the shortest route to the Atlantic seaboard from the great grain-producing areas of western America.

The Ottawa was first explored by Samuel de Champlain in 1613. Champlain describes many of its tributaries, the Chaudière and Rideau Falls, the Long Sault, Chats and other rapids, as well as the character of the river and its banks, with minuteness and reasonable accuracy. He places the Chaudière Falls in 45° 38', the true position being 45° 27'. The Long Sault Rapids on the Ottawa, about midway between Montreal and the capital, were the scene of one of the noblest exploits in Canadian history, when in 1661 the young Sieur des Ormeaux with sixteen comrades and a handful of Indian allies deliberately gave their lives to save New France from an invasion of the Iroquois. They intercepted the war party at the Long Sault, and for nearly a week held them at bay. When finally the last Frenchman fell under a shower of arrows, the Iroquois were thoroughly disheartened and returned crestfallen to their own country. For a hundred and fifty years thereafter the Ottawa was the great highway from Montreal to the west for explorers and fur-traders. The portage paths around its cataracts and rapids were worn smooth by the moccasined feet of countless *voyageurs*; and its wooded banks rang with the inimitable *chansons* of Old Canada, as the canoe brigades swept swiftly up and down its broad stream. Throughout the 19th century the Ottawa was the thoroughfare of the lumbermen, whose immense rafts were carried down from its upper waters to Montreal and Quebec.

OTTAWA, a city of Carleton county, province of Ontario, and the capital of the Dominion of Canada, on the right bank of the Ottawa river, 101 m. W. of Montreal and 217 m. N.E. of Toronto. The main tower of the parliament building is in 45° 25' 28" N., and 75° 42' 03" W.

The city stands for the most part on a cluster of hills, 60 to 155 ft. above the river. It is on the main line of the Canadian Pacific railway, which affords direct communication with Montreal by two routes, the North Shore and the Short Line, one on either side of the Ottawa river. Branches of the same railway lead to Brockville, on the St. Lawrence river, passing through the town of Smith's Falls where connexion is made with the direct line from Montreal to Toronto; to Prescott, also on the St Lawrence; northward through the Gatineau valley to Maniwaki, in the heart of a famous sporting country, and westward to Waltham, on the north side of the Ottawa. The Grand Trunk offers a third route to Montreal, and another line of the same railway leads to Parry Sound, on Georgian Bay. The Ottawa and New York (New York Central) runs to Cornwall, on the St Lawrence, thence to New York. Electric railways afford communication with all parts of the city and extend eastward to Rockliffe Park and the rifle ranges, westward to Britannia on Lake Deschenes, and through the neighbouring town of Hull to Aylmer and Victoria Park. During the summer months steamers ply down the Ottawa to Montreal, and by way of the Rideau canal and lakes to Kingston on the St Lawrence. A road bridge, partially destroyed in the great fire of 1900, connects Ottawa with Hull; a railway bridge spans the river above the Chaudière Falls; and the Royal Alexandra Bridge, below the falls, carries both steam and electric railway tracks, as well as roadways for vehicular and pedestrian traffic. The site of the city is exceedingly picturesque. For 3 m. it follows the high southern bank of the Ottawa, from the Chaudière Falls, whose mist-crowned cauldron is clearly visible from the summit of Parliament Hill, to and beyond the Rideau Falls, so named by early French explorers because of their curtain-like appearance. The Rideau, a southern tributary of the Ottawa, once formed the eastern boundary of the city, which, however, is now absorbing a string of suburbs, that lie along its eastern banks. The Rideau Canal cuts the city in two; the western portion being known as Upper Town and the eastern as Lower Town. Roughly speaking the canal divides the two sections of the population, the English occupying Upper Town and the French Lower Town, though Sandy Hill, a fashionable residential district, east of the canal, is mainly occupied by the English. Opposite and a little below the mouth of the Rideau, the Gatineau flows into the

Ottawa from the north. Above the Chaudière Falls the river is broken by the Deschenes Rapids, and beyond these again it expands into Lake Deschenes, a favourite summer resort for the people of the city. To the north lie the Laurentian Hills, broken by the picturesque Gatineau Valley.

The crowning architectural feature of the city is the splendid group of Gothic buildings on the summit of Parliament Hill, whose limestone bluffs rise 150 ft. sheer from the river. The three blocks of these buildings form sides of a great quadrangle, the fourth side remaining open. The main front of the central or Parliament building is 470 ft. long and 40 ft. high, the Victoria Tower (180 ft. high) rising over the principal entrance. Behind and connected with the Parliament building is an admirably proportioned polygonal hall, 90 ft. in diameter, in which the library of parliament is housed. The corner stone of the main building was laid by the then prince of Wales in 1860. The buildings forming the eastern and western sides of the quadrangle are devoted to departments of the Dominion government. To the south, but outside the grounds of Parliament Hill, stands the Langevin Block, a massive structure in brown sandstone, also used for departmental purposes. The increasing needs of the government have made necessary the erection of several other buildings and an effort has been made to bring as many of these as possible into a harmonious group. The Archives building and the Royal Mint stand on the commanding eminence of Nepean Point, to the eastward of Parliament Hill; the Rideau Canal lying between. Two large departmental buildings occupy ground south of the Archives building and facing Parliament Hill, one containing the Supreme Court as well as the Federal Department of Justice. At the foot of Metcalfe Street, south of Parliament Hill, stands the Victoria Museum, with the department of mines, with the splendid collections of the Geological and Natural History Museum the departmental library, and the National Art Gallery. The Dominion Observatory stands outside the city, in the grounds of the Central Experimental Farm. Plans were approved in 1909 by the government for a union railway station east of the canal, and immediately south of Rideau Street, and a large hotel (Grand Trunk Railway), the Chateau Laurier, at the southern end of Major's Hill Park. Other prominent buildings are the city hall, post office, Carnegie library, normal and model schools, government printing bureau, county court house, the Basilica or Roman Catholic cathedral, and Christ Church cathedral (Church of England), the Roman Catholic university of Ottawa and the collegiate institute.

The city charities include four large general hospitals, two of which are under Protestant auspices; one is controlled by Roman Catholics; the fourth is devoted to contagious diseases. Ottawa is the seat of the Church of England bishop of Ottawa, and of the Roman Catholic archbishop of Ottawa. Several of the philanthropic and educational orders of the latter church are established here, in nunneries, convents or monasteries. As elsewhere in Ontario, the educational system is divided into public schools (undenominational), and separate schools (Roman Catholic), the latter supported by Roman Catholic taxpayers, the former by all other members of the community. The collegiate institute is common to both, and is used as a preparatory school for the universities.

Ottawa has been a great seat of the lumber trade, and the manufacture of lumber still forms an important part of the industrial life of the city, but the magnificent waterpowers of the Chaudière and Rideau Falls are now utilized for matchworks, flour-mills, foundries, carbide factories and many other flourishing industries, as well as for the development of electric light and power, for the lighting of the city and the running of the electric railways.

The people of Ottawa possess a number of public parks, both within and outside the city, partly the result of their own foresight, and partly due to the labours of the Government Improvement Commission. Parliament Hill itself constitutes a park of no mean proportions, one of the noted features of which is the beautiful Lover's Walk, cut out of the side of the cliff half way between the river and the summit. The grounds above contain

2a

statues of Queen Victoria, as well as of Sir John Macdonald, Alexander Mackenzie, Sir George Cartier and other Canadian political leaders. On the eastern side of the canal is Major's Hill Park, maintained by the government. Below Sandy Hill, on the banks of the Rideau, lies Strathcona Park, an admirable piece of landscape gardening constructed out of what was once an unsightly swamp. Crossing the bridges above the Rideau Falls, and passing the heavily wooded grounds of Rideau Hall, the official residence of the governor-general, we come to Rock-liffe Park, beyond which lies the government rifle ranges. Rock-liffe Park is the easternmost point of an ambitious scheme of landscape gardening planned by the Improvement Commission. From here a driveway extends to Rideau Hall; thence it crosses the Rideau river to a noble thoroughfare cut through the heart of Lower Town, and known as King Edward Avenue. Crossing the canal by the Laurier bridge, the driveway turns south and follows the west bank of the canal for 4 m. to the Central Experimental Farm, an extensive tract of land upon which experiments in model farming are carried out by government specialists, for the benefit of Canadian farmers. From the Experimental Farm the driveway will be carried around the western side of the city to the banks of the Ottawa, connecting by light bridges with a group of islands above the Chaudière Falls which are to be converted into a park reserve.

Ottawa is governed by a mayor, elected by the city at large; a board of control consisting of four members, similarly elected and a board of 16 aldermen, 2 elected by each of the 8 wards. The city returns 2 members to the Dominion House of Commons and two to the provincial legislature.

The population, of which one-third is French-speaking, the remainder English (with the exception of a small German element), has increased rapidly since the incorporation of the city in 1854. It was 59,028 in 1901; 67,572 in 1906; and in 1907, including the suburbs and the neighbouring town of Hull, over 100,000.

The earliest description of the site of Ottawa is that of Samuel de Champlain, in his *Voyages*. In June 1613, on his way up the river, he came to a tributary on the south side, " at the mouth of which is a marvellous fall. For it descends a height of twenty or twenty-five fathoms with such impetuosity that it makes an arch nearly four hundred paces broad. The savages take pleasure in passing under it, not wetting themselves, except from the spray that is thrown off." This was the Rideau Falls, but a good deal of allowance must be made for exaggeration in Champlain's account. Continuing up the river, " we passed," he says, " a fall, a league from there, which is half a league broad and has a descent of six or seven fathoms. There are many little islands. The water falls in one place with such force upon a rock that it has hollowed out in course of time a large and deep basin, in which the water has a circular motion and forms large eddies in the middle, so that the savages call it *Asticou*, which signifies boiler. This cataract produces such a noise in this basin that it is heard for more than two leagues." The present name, Chaudière, is the French equivalent of the old Indian name. For two hundred years and more after Champlain's first visit the Chaudière portage was the main thoroughfare from Montreal to the great western fur country; but it was not until 1800 that any permanent settlement was made in the vicinity. In that year Philemon Wright, of Woburn, Massachusetts, built a home for himself at the foot of the portage, on the Quebec side of the river, where the city of Hull now stands; but for some time the precipitous cliffs on the south side seem to have discouraged settlement there. Finally about 1820 one Nicholas Sparks moved over the river and cleared a farm in what is now the heart of Ottawa. Seven years later Colonel John By, R.E., was sent out to build a canal from a point below the Chaudière Falls to Kingston on Lake Ontario. The canal, completed at a cost of $2,500,000, has never been of any great commercial importance; it has never been called upon to fulfil its primary object, as a military work to enable gun-boats and military supplies to reach the lakes from Montreal without being exposed to attack along the St Lawrence frontier. The building of the canal created a fair-sized settlement at its Ottawa end, which came to be known as Bytown. As the lumber trade developed Bytown rapidly increased in wealth and importance. In 1854 it was incorporated as a city, the name being changed to Ottawa; and four years later Queen Victoria selected Ottawa as the capital of Canada. Ottawa was admirably situated for a capital from a political and military point of view; but there is reason to believe that the deciding factor was the pressure exerted by the four other rival claimants, Montreal, Quebec, Toronto and Kingston, any three of which would have fiercely resented the selection of the fourth. The first session of parliament in the new capital was opened in 1865.

BIBLIOGRAPHY.—J. D. Edgar, *Canada and its Capital* (Toronto, 1898); A. S. Bradley, *Canada in the Twentieth Century* (London, 1903), pp. 130-140; F. Gertrude Kenny, " Some account of Bytown," *Transactions*, vol. i., *Women's Canadian Historical Society of Ottawa*; Mrs H. J. Friel, " The Rideau Canal and the Founder of Bytown," *ibid.*; M. Jamieson, " A glimpse of our city fifty years ago," *ibid.*; J. M. Oxley, " The Capital of Canada," *New England Magazine*, N.S., 22, 315-323; Godfrey T. Vigne, *Six Months in America* (London, 1832), pp. 191-198; Andrew Wilson, *History of Old Bytown* (Ottawa, 1876); Chas. Pope, *Incidents connected with Ottawa* (Ottawa, 1868); Wm. P. Lett, *Recollections of Bytown* (Ottawa, 1874); Wm. S. Hunter, *Ottawa Scenery* (Ottawa, 1855); Joseph Tassé, *Vallée de l'Oulaouais* (Montreal, 1873). (L. J. B.)

OTTAWA, a city and the county-seat of La Salle county, Illinois, U.S.A., on the Illinois river, at the mouth of the Fox, about 84 m. S.W. of Chicago. Pop. (1900) 10,588, of whom 1804 were foreign-born; (1910 census) 9535. It is served by the Chicago, Burlington & Quincy, and the Chicago, Rock Island & Pacific railways, by interurban electric railways, and by the Illinois & Michigan Canal. There is a monument at Ottawa to the 1400 soldiers from La Salle county who died in the Civil War, and among the public buildings are the County Court House, the Court House for the second district of the Illinois Appellate Court, and Reddick's Library, founded by William Reddick. Ottawa is the seat of the Pleasant View Luther College (co-educational), founded in 1896 by the Norwegian Lutherans of Northern Illinois. There is a medicinal spring, the water of which is called " Sanicula " water. The water supply of the city is derived from eight deep wells. There are about 150 privately owned artesian wells. In the vicinity are large deposits of coal, of glass-sand, and of clay suitable for brick and tile. The city's manufactures include glass, brick, tile, carriages and wagons, agricultural implements, pianos and organs and cigars. The value of the factory products increased from $1,737,884 in 1900 to $2,078,139 in 1905, or 19.6%.

The mouth of the Fox was early visited by French explorers, and Father Hennepin is said to have discovered here in 1680 the first deposit of coal found in America. On Starved Rock, a bold hillock about 125 ft. high, on the southern bank of the Illinois, about midway between Ottawa and La Salle, the French explorer La Salle, assisted by his lieutenant Henri de Tonty and a few Canadian voyageurs and Illinois Indians, established (in December 1682) Fort St Louis, about which he gathered nearly 20,000 Indians, who were seeking protection from the Iroquois. The plateau-like summit, which originally could be reached only from the south by a steep and narrow path, was rendered almost impregnable to Indian attack by a sheer cliff on the river side of the hill, a deep ravine along its eastern base and steep declivities on the other sides. On the summit La Salle built store-houses and log huts, which he surrounded by intrenchments and a log palisade. The post was used by fur traders as late as 1718. The hill has borne its present name since about 1770, when it became the last refuge of a small band of Illinois flying before a large force of Pottawattomies, who believed that an Illinois had assassinated Pontiac, in whose conspiracy the Pottawattomies had taken part. Unable to dislodge the Illinois, the Pottawattomies cut off their escape and let them die of starvation. Ottawa was laid out in 1830, incorporated as a village in 1838 and chartered as a city in 1853. On the 21st of August 1858 the first of the series of political debates between Abraham Lincoln and Stephen A. Douglas, in their contest for the United States senatorship, was held at

Ottawa. The semi-centennial of this debate was celebrated in 1908, when the Illini Chapter, Daughters of the American Revolution, caused a suitably inscribed boulder weighing 23 tons to be set up in Washington Park as a memorial.

OTTAWA, a city and the county-seat of Franklin county, eastern Kansas, U.S.A., situated on the Osage (Marais des Cygnes) river, about 58 m. (by rail) S.W. of Kansas City. Pop. (1900) 6934, of whom 333 were foreign born; (1905) 7727; (1910) 7670. It is served by the Atchison, Topeka & Santa Fé (which has large repair shops here) and the Missouri Pacific railways. There is a Carnegie library, and Forest Park, within the city limits, is a popular meeting place of conventions and summer gatherings, including the annual Ottawa Chautauqua Assembly. Ottawa University (Baptist) was established here in 1865, as the outgrowth of Roger Williams University, which had been chartered in 1860 for the education of Indians on the Ottawa Reservation, and had received a grant of 20,000 acres from the Federal government in 1862. The university comprises an academy, a college, a school of fine arts and a commercial college, and in 1909 had 406 students. Ottawa has an important trade in grain and live-stock; soft coal and natural gas are found in the vicinity; the manufactures include flour, wind-mills, wire-fences, furniture, bricks, brooms and foundry products. Ottawa was settled in 1854, and was first chartered as a city in 1866.

OTTER (O. Eng. *ote, otor,* a common Teutonic word, cf. Dutch and Ger. *Otter,* Dan. *odder,* Swed. *utter;* it is to be referred to the root seen in Gr. *ὕδωρ,* water), a name properly given to the well-known European carnivorous aquatic mammal (*Lutra vulgaris,* or *L. lutra*), but also applicable to all the members of the lutrine section of the family *Mustelidae* (see CARNIVORA). The otter has an elongated, low body, short broad feet, with five toes on each, connected together by webs, and all with short, moderately strong, compressed, curved, pointed claws. Head rather small, broad and flat; muzzle very broad; whiskers thick and strong; eyes small and black; ears short and rounded. Tail a little more than half the length of the body and head together, broad and strong at the base, and gradually tapering to the end, somewhat flattened horizontally. The fur is of fine quality, consisting of a short soft whitish grey under-fur, brown at the tips, interspersed with longer, stiffer and thicker hairs, shining, greyish at the base, bright rich brown at the points, especially on the upper-parts and outer surface of the legs; the throat, cheeks, under-parts and inner surface of the legs brownish grey throughout. Individual otters vary in size. The total length from the nose to the end of the tail averages about 3½ ft., of which the tail occupies 1 ft. 3 or 4 in. The weight of a full-sized male is from 18 to 24 ℔, that of a female about 4 ℔ less.

As the otter lives almost exclusively on fish, it is rarely met with far from water, and usually frequents the shores of brooks, rivers, lakes and, in some localities, the sea itself. It is a most expert swimmer and diver, easily overtaking and seizing fish in the water; but when it has captured its prey it brings it to shore to devour. When lying upon the bank, it holds the fish between its fore-paws, commences at the head and then eats gradually towards the tail, which it is said to leave. The female produces three to five young ones in March or April, and brings them up in a nest formed of grass or other herbage, usually placed in a hollow place in the bank of a river, or under the shelter of the roots of some overhanging tree. The otter is found in localities suitable to its habits throughout Great Britain and Ireland, though less abundantly than formerly, for, being destructive to fish, it is rarely allowed to live in peace when its haunts are discovered. Otter-hunting with packs of hounds of a special breed, and trained for the purpose, is a pastime in many parts of the country. It was formerly the practice to kill the otter with long spears, which the huntsmen carried; now the quarry is picked up and "tailed," or run into by the pack.

The otter ranges throughout the greater part of Europe and Asia; and a closely allied but larger species, *L. canadensis,* is extensively distributed throughout North America, where it is pursued for its fur. An Indian species, *L. nair,* is trained by the natives of some parts of Bengal to assist in fishing, by driving the fish into the nets. In China otters are taught to catch fish, being let into the water for the purpose attached to a long cord.

Otters are widely distributed, and, as they are much alike in size and coloration, their specific distinctions are by no means well defined. Besides those mentioned above, the following have been described, *L. californica,* North America; *L. felina,* Central America. Peru, and Chili; *L. brasiliensis,* Brazil; *L. maculicollis,* South Africa; *L. whiteleyi,* Japan; *L. chinensis,* China and Formosa, and other species. Some, with the feet only slightly webbed, and the claws exceedingly small or altogether wanting on some of the toes, and also with some difference in dental characters, have been separated as a distinct genus, *Aonyx.* These are *L. inunguis* from South Africa and *L. cinerea* from India, Java, and Sumatra.

More distinct still is the sea-otter (*Latax,* or *Enhydra, lutris*). The entire length of the animal from nose to end of tail is about 4 ft., so that the body is considerably larger and more massive than that of the English otter. The skin is peculiarly loose, and stretches when removed from the animal. The fur is remarkable for the preponderance of the beautifully soft woolly under-fur, the longer stiffer hairs being scanty. The general colour is deep liver-brown, silvered or frosted with the hoary tips of the longer stiff hairs. These are, however, removed when the skin is dressed for commercial purposes.

Sea-otters are only found upon the rocky shores of certain parts of the North Pacific Ocean, especially the Aleutian Islands and Alaska, extending as far south on the American coast as

The Sea-Otter (*Latax,* or *Enhydra, lutris*). From Wolf.

Oregon; but, owing to the persecution to which they are subjected for the sake of their valuable skins, their numbers are greatly diminishing. The otters are captured by spearing, clubbing, nets and bullets. They do not feed on fish, like true otters, but on clams, mussels, sea-urchins and crabs; and the female brings forth but a single young one at a time, apparently at any season of the year. They are excessively shy and wary; young cubs are often captured by the hunters who have killed the dam, but all attempts to rear them have hitherto failed.

See Elliott Coues, *Monograph on North American Fur-bearing Animals* (1877).　(W. H. F.; R. L.*)

OTTERY ST MARY, a market town in the Honiton parliamentary division of Devonshire, England, 15 m. E. by N. of Exeter, on a branch of the London & South-Western railway. Pop. of urban district (1901) 3405. It is pleasantly situated in the rich valley of the small river Otter. The parish church, the finest in the county, is cruciform, and has the unique feature of transeptal towers, imitated from Exeter Cathedral. The northern has a low spire. The church, which is Early English, with Decorated and Perpendicular additions, contains several ancient tombs. The manor of Ottery belonged to the abbey of Rouen in the time of Edward the Confessor. The church was dedicated in 1260 by Walter Bronescombe, bishop of Exeter; and c. 1335 Bishop John Grandisson, on founding a secular college here, greatly enlarged the church; it has been thought that, by copying the Early English style, he is responsible for more of the building than is apparent. The town has a large agricultural trade. It is the birthplace of Samuel Taylor Coleridge (1772); and W. M. Thackeray stayed in the vicinity in youth, his knowledge of the locality appearing in *Pendennis*.

OTTIGNIES, a town of Belgium, in the province of Brabant. It is an important station on the main line from Brussels to Namur, and forms the point of junction with several cross lines. It has extensive modern flower and vegetable gardens. Pop. (1904) 2405.

OTTO, king of Greece (1815–1867), was the second son of Louis I., king of Bavaria, and his wife Teresa of Saxe-Altenburg. He was born at Salzburg on the 1st of June 1815, and was educated at Munich. In 1832 he was chosen by the conference of London to occupy the newly-erected throne of Greece, and on the 6th of February 1833 he landed at Nauplia, then the capital of independent Greece. Otto, who was not yet eighteen, was accompanied by a council of regency composed of Bavarians under the presidency of Count Josef Ludwig von Armansperg (1787–1853), who as minister of finance in Bavaria had succeeded in restoring the credit of the state at the cost of his popularity. The task of governing a semi-barbarous people, but recently emancipated, divided into bitter factions, and filled with an exaggerated sense of their national destiny, would in no case have been easy; it was not facilitated by the bureaucratic methods introduced by the regents. Though Armansperg and his colleagues did a good deal to introduce system and order into the infant state, they contrived to make themselves hated by the Greeks, and with sufficient reason. That the regency refused to respond to the demand for a constitution was perhaps natural, for the experience of constitutional experiments in emancipated Greece had not been encouraging. The result, however, was perpetual unrest; the regency, too, was divided into a French and a Russian party, and distracted by personal quarrels, which led in 1834 to the recall by King Louis of G. L. von Maurer and Karl von Abel, who had been in bitter opposition to Armansperg. Soon afterwards the Mainotes were in open revolt, and the money obtained from foreign loans had to be spent in organizing a force to preserve order. On the 1st of June 1835 Otto came of age, but, on the advice of his father and under pressure of Great Britain and of the house of Rothschild, who all believed that a capable finance minister was the supreme need of Greece, he retained Armansperg as chancellor of state. The wisdom of this course was more than doubtful; for the expenses of government, of which the conversion of Athens into a dignified capital was not the least, exceeded the resources of the exchequer, and the state was only saved from bankruptcy by the continual intervention of the powers. Though King Louis, as the most exalted of Philhellenes, received an enthusiastic welcome when he visited Greece in the winter of 1835, his son's government grew increasingly unpopular. The Greeks were more heavily taxed than under Turkish rule, they had exchanged government by the sword, which they understood, for government by official regulations, which they hated; they had escaped from the sovereignty of the Mussulman to fall under that of a devout Catholic, to them a heretic. Otto was well intentioned, honest and inspired with a genuine affection for his adopted country; but it needed more than mere amiable qualities to reconcile the Greeks to his rule.

In 1837 Otto visited Germany and married the beautiful and talented Princess Amalie of Oldenburg. The union was unfruitful, and the new queen made herself unpopular by interfering in the government. Meanwhile, at the instance of the Swiss Philhellene Eynard, Armansperg had been dismissed by the king immediately on his return, but a Greek minister was not put in his place, and the granting of a constitution was still postponed. The attempts of Otto to conciliate Greek sentiment by efforts to enla. e the frontiers of his kingdom, *e.g.* by the suggested acquisition of Crete in 1841, failed of their object and only succeeded in embroiling him with the powers.

His power rested wholly on Bavarian bayonets; and when, in 1843, the last of the German troops were withdrawn, he was forced by the outbreak of a revolutionary movement in Athens to grant a constitution and to appoint a ministry of native Greeks.

With the grant of the constitution Otto's troubles increased. The Greek parliament, like its predecessors during the War of Liberation, was the battleground of factions divided, not by national issues, but by their adherence to one or other of the great powers who made Greece the arena of their rivalry for the control of the Mediterranean. Otto thought to counteract the effects of political corruption and incompetence by overriding the constitution to which he had sworn. The attempt would have been perilous even for a strong man, a native ruler and an Orthodox believer; and Otto was none of these. His prestige, moreover, suffered from the "Pacifico incident" in 1850, when Palmerston caused the British fleet to blockade the Peiraeus, to exact reparation for injustice done to a Levantine Jew who happened also to be a British subject. For the ill-advised intervention in the Crimean War, which led to a second occupation of the Peiraeus, Otto was not responsible; his consent had been given under protest as a concession to popular clamour. His position in Greece was, however, becoming untenable. In 1861 a student named Drusios attempted to murder the queen, and was hailed by the populace as a modern Harmodios. In October 1862 the troops in Acarnania under General Theodore Srivas declared for the king's deposition; those in Athens followed suit; a provisional government was set up and summoned a national convention. The king and queen, who were at sea, took refuge on a British war-ship, and returned to Bavaria, where they were lodged by King Louis in the palace of the former bishops of Bamberg. Here, on the 26th of July 1867, Otto died. He had become strangely persuaded that he held the throne of Greece by divine right; and, though he made no effort to regain it, he refused to acknowledge the validity of the election of Prince George of Denmark.

See E. A. Thouvenel, *La Grèce du roi Othon* (Paris, 1890); G. L. von Maurer, *Das griechische Volk*, &c. (1836); C. W. P. Mendelssohn-Bartholdy, "Die Verwaltung König Ottos von Griechenland und sein Sturz" (in *Preuss. Jahrbücher*, iv. 365); K. T. v. Heigel, *Ludwig I., König von Baiern*, pp. 149 et seq. (Leipzig, 1872); H. H. Parish, *The Diplomatic History of the Monarchy of Greece from the Year 1830* (London, 1838), the author of which was attached to the British Legation at Athens.

OTTO I. (912–973), surnamed the Great, Roman emperor, eldest son of King Henry I. the Fowler by his second wife Matilda, said to be a descendant of the Saxon hero Widukind, was born on the 23rd of November 912. Little is known of his early years, but he probably shared in some of his father's campaigns. In 929 he married Edith, daughter of Edward the Elder, king of the English, and sister of the reigning sovereign Æthelstan. It is said that Matilda wished her second son Henry to succeed his father, as this prince, unlike his elder brother, was born the son of a king. However this may be, Henry named Otto his successor, and after his death in July 936 Otto was chosen German king and crowned by Hildebert, archbishop of Mainz. This ceremony, according to the historian Widukind, was followed by a banquet at which the new king was waited upon by the dukes of Lorraine, Bavaria, Franconia and Swabia. Otto soon showed his intention of breaking with the policy of his father, who had been content with a nominal superiority over the duchies, in 937 he punished Eberhard, duke of Franconia, for an alleged infringement of the royal authority; and in 938 deposed Eberhard, who had recently become duke of Bavaria. During these years the Bohemians and other Slavonic tribes ravaged the eastern frontier of Germany, but although one expedition against them was led by the king in person, the defence of this district was left principally to agents. Trouble soon arose in Saxony, probably owing to Otto's refusal to give certain lands to his half-brother, Thankmar, who, although the king's senior, had been passed over in the succession as illegitimate. Thankmar, aided by an influential Saxon noble named Wichmann, and by Eberhard of Franconia, seized the fortress of Eresburg and took Otto's brother Henry prisoner; but soon afterwards he was defeated by the king and killed whilst taking sanctuary. The other conspirators were pardoned, but in 939 a fresh revolt broke out under the leadership of Henry, and Giselbert, duke of Lorraine. Otto gained a victory near Xanten, which was followed by the surrender of the fortresses held by his brother's adherents in Saxony, but the rebels, joined by Eberhard of Franconia and Archbishop Frederick of Mainz continued the struggle, and Giselbert of Lorraine transferred his allegiance to Louis IV., king of France. Otto's precarious position was saved by a victory near Andernach when Eberhard was killed, and Giselbert drowned in the subsequent flight. Henry took refuge with Louis of France, but was soon restored to favour and entrusted with the duchy of Lorraine, where, however, he was unable to restore order. Otto therefore crossed the Rhine and deprived his brother of authority. Henry then became involved in a plot to murder the king, which was discovered in time, and the good offices of his mother secured for him a pardon at Christmas 941. The deaths of Giselbert of Lorraine and of Eberhard of Franconia, quickly followed by those of two other dukes, enabled Otto to unite the stem-duchies more closely with the royal house. In 944 Lorraine was given to Conrad, surnamed the Red, who in 947 married the king's daughter Liutgard; Franconia was retained by Otto in his own hands; Henry married a daughter of Arnulf, duke of Bavaria, and received that duchy in 947; and Swabia came in 949 to the king's son Ludolf, who had married Ida, a daughter of the late duke, Hermann. During these years the tribes living between the Elbe and the Oder were made tributary, bishoprics were founded in this district, and in 950 the king himself marched against the Bohemians and reduced them to dependence. Strife between Otto and Louis IV. of France had arisen when the French king sought to obtain authority over Lorraine and aided the German rebels in 939; but after the German king had undertaken an expedition into France, peace was made in 942. Afterwards, when Louis became a prisoner in the hands of his powerful vassal Hugh the Great, duke of France, Otto attacked the duke, who, like the king, was his brother-in-law, captured Reims, and negotiated a peace between the two princes; and in subsequent struggles between them his authority was several times invoked.

In 945 Berengar I., margrave of Ivrea, left the court of Otto and returned to Italy, where he soon obtained a mastery over the country. After the death in 950 of Lothair, king of Italy, Berengar sought the hand of his widow Adelaide for his son Adalbert; and Henry of Bavaria and Ludolf of Swabia had already been meddling independently of each other in the affairs of northern Italy. In response to an appeal from Adelaide, Otto crossed the Alps in 951. He assumed the title of king of the Lombards, and having been a widower since 946, married Adelaide and negotiated with pope Agapetus II. about his reception in Rome. The influence of Alberic, prince and senator of the Romans, prevented the pope returning a favourable answer to the king's request. But when Otto returned to Germany in 952 he was followed by Berengar, who did homage for Italy at Augsburg. The chief advisers of Otto at this time were his wife and his brother Henry. Henry's influence seems to have been resented by Ludolf, who in 946 had been formally designated as his father's successor. When Adelaide bore a son, and a report gained currency that Otto intended to make this child his heir, Ludolf rose in revolt and was joined by Conrad of Lorraine and Frederick of Mainz. Otto fell into the power of the rebels at Mainz and was compelled to agree to demands made by them, which, however, he promptly revoked on his return to Saxony. Ludolf and Conrad were declared deposed, and in 953 war broke out in Lorraine and Swabia, and afterwards in Saxony and Bavaria. Otto failed to take Mainz and Augsburg; but an attempt on the part of Conrad and Ludolf to gain support from the Magyars, who had seized the opportunity to invade Bavaria, alienated many of their supporters. Otto's brother Bruno, archbishop of Cologne, was successful in restoring the royal authority in Lorraine, so that when Conrad and Frederick soon afterwards submitted to Otto, the struggle was confined to Bavaria. Ludolf was not long in

following the example of Conrad; and with the capture of Regensburg in 955 the rising ended. Conrad and Ludolf retained their estates, but their duchies were not restored to them. Meanwhile the Magyars had renewed their ravages and were attacking Augsburg. Otto marched against them, and in a battle fought on the Lechfeld on the 10th of August 955 the king's troops gained a brilliant victory which completely freed Germany from these invaders; while in the same year Otto also defeated the Slavs who had been ravaging the Saxon frontier.

About this time the king seems to have perceived the necessity of living and ruling in closer union with the church, a change of policy due perhaps to the influence of his brother Bruno, or forced upon him when his plans for uniting the duchies with the royal house brought rebellion in their train. Lands and privileges were granted to prelates, additional bishoprics were founded, and some years later Magdeburg was made the seat of an archbishop. In 960 Otto was invited to come to Italy by Pope John XII., who was hard pressed by Berengar, and he began to make preparations for the journey. As Ludolf had died in 957 and Otto, his only son by Adelaide, had been chosen king at Worms, the government was entrusted to Bruno of Cologne, and Archbishop William of Mainz, a natural son of the king. Reaching Pavia at Christmas 961, the king promised to defend and respect the church. He then proceeded to Rome, where he was crowned emperor on the 2nd of February 962. After the ceremony he confirmed the rights and privileges which had been conferred on the papacy, while the Romans promised obedience, and Pope John took an oath of fidelity to the emperor. But as he did not long observe his oath he was deposed at a synod held in St Peter's, after Otto had compelled the Romans to swear they would elect no pope without the imperial consent; and a nominee of the emperor, who took the name of Leo VIII., was chosen in his stead. A pestilence drove Otto to Germany in 965, and finding the Romans again in arms on his return in 966, he allowed his soldiers to sack the city, and severely punished the leaders of the rebellion. His next move was against the Greeks and Saracens of southern Italy, but seeking to attain his objects by negotiation, sent Liudprand, bishop of Cremona, to the eastern emperor Nicephorus II. to arrange for a marriage treaty between the two empires. Nicephorus refused to admit the validity of Otto's title, and the bishop was roughly repulsed; but the succeeding emperor, John Zimisces, was more reasonable, and Theophano, daughter of the emperor Romanus II., was married to the younger Otto in 972. The same year witnessed the restoration of peace in Italy and the return of the emperor to Germany, where he received the homage of the rulers of Poland, Bohemia and Denmark; but he died suddenly at Memleben on the 7th of May 973, and was buried at Magdeburg.

Otto was a man of untiring perseverance and relentless energy, with a high idea of his position. His policy was to crush all tendencies to independence in Germany, and this led him to grant the stem-duchies to his relatives, and afterwards to ally himself with the church. Indeed the necessity for obtaining complete control over the church was one reason which induced him to obtain the imperial crown. By this step the pope became his vassal, and a divided allegiance was rendered impossible for the German clergy. The Roman empire of the German nation was indeed less universal and less theocratic under Otto, its restorer, than under Charlemagne, but what it lacked in splendour it gained in stability. His object was not to make the state religious but the church political, and the clergy must first be officials of the king, and secondly members of an ecclesiastical order. He shared the piety and superstition of the age, and did much for the spread of Christianity. Although himself a stranger to letters he welcomed scholars to his court and eagerly seconded the efforts of his brother Bruno to encourage learning; and while he neither feared nor shirked battle, he was always ready to secure his ends by peaceable means. Otto was of tall and commanding presence, and although subject to violent bursts of passion, was liberal to his friends and just to his enemies.

BIBLIOGRAPHY.—See Widukind, *Res gestae Saxonicae*; Liudprand of Cremona, *Historia Ottonis*; Flodoard of Rheims, *Annales*;

Hrotsuit of Gandersheim, *Carmen de gestis Oddonis*—all in the *Monumenta Germaniae historica. Scriptores*, Bände iii. and iv. (Hanover and Berlin, 1826 fol.); *Die Urkunden des Kaisers Otto I.*, edited by Th. von Sickel in the *Monumenta Germaniae historica. Diplomata* (Hanover, 1879); W. von Giesebrecht, *Geschichte der deutschen Kaiserzeit* (Leipzig, 1881); R. Köpke and E. Dümmler, *Jahrbücher des deutschen Reichs unter Otto I.* (Leipzig, 1876); Th. von Sickel, *Das Privilegium Otto I. für die römische Kirche* (Innsbruck, 1883); H. von Sybel, *Die deutsche Nation und das Kaiserreich* (Düsseldorf, 1862); O. von Wydenbrugk, *Die deutsche Nation und das Kaiserreich* (Munich, 1862); J. Ficker, *Das deutsche Kaiserreich in seinen universalen und nationalen Beziehungen* (Innsbruck, 1861); and *Deutsches Königthum und Kaiserthum* (Innsbruck, 1862); G. Maurenbrecher, "Die Kaiserpolitik Otto I." in the *Historische Zeitschrift* (Munich, 1859); G. Waitz, *Deutsche Verfassungsgeschichte* (Kiel, 1844); J. Ficker, *Forschungen zur Reichs- und Rechtsgeschichte Italiens* (Innsbruck, 1868–1874); F. Fischer, *Über Otto I. Zug in die Lombardei vom Jahre 951* (Eisenberg, 1891); and K. Kötler, *Die Ungarnschlacht auf dem Lechfelde* (Augsburg, 1884).

OTTO II. (955–983), Roman emperor, was the son of the emperor Otto the Great, by his second wife Adelaide. He received a good education under the care of his uncle, Bruno, archbishop of Cologne, and his illegitimate half-brother, William, archbishop of Mainz. He was chosen German king at Worms in 961, crowned at Aix-la-Chapelle on the 26th of May 961, and on the 25th of December 967 was crowned joint emperor at Rome by Pope John XIII. On the 14th of April 972 he married Theophano, daughter of the eastern emperor Romanus II., and after sharing in various campaigns in Italy, returned to Germany and became sole emperor on the death of his father in May 973. After suppressing a rising in Lorraine, difficulties arose in southern Germany, probably owing to Otto's refusal to grant the duchy of Swabia to Henry II., the Quarrelsome, duke of Bavaria. The first conspiracy was easily suppressed, and in 974 an attempt on the part of Harold III., king of the Danes, to throw off the German yoke was also successfully resisted; but an expedition against the Bohemians led by the king in person in 975 was a partial failure owing to the outbreak of further trouble in Bavaria. In 976 Otto deposed Duke Henry, restored order for the second time in Lorraine, and made another expedition into Bohemia in 977, when King Boleslaus II. promised to return to his earlier allegiance. Having crushed an attempt made by Henry to regain Bavaria, Otto was suddenly attacked by Lothair, king of France, who held Aix in his possession for a few days; but when the emperor retaliated by invading France he met with little resistance. He was, however, compelled by sickness among his troops to raise the siege of Paris, and on the return journey the rearguard of his army was destroyed and the baggage seized by the French. An expedition against the Poles was followed by peace with France, when Lothair renounced his claim on Lorraine. The emperor then prepared for a journey to Italy. In Rome, where he restored Pope Benedict VII., he held a splendid court, attended by princes and nobles from all parts of western Europe. He was next required to punish inroads of the Saracens on the Italian mainland, and in September 981 he marched into Apulia, where he met at first with considerable success; but an alliance between the Arabs and the Eastern Empire, whose hostility had been provoked by the invasion of Apulia, resulted in a severe defeat on Otto's troops near Stilo in July 982. Without revealing his identity, the emperor escaped on a Greek vessel to Rossano. At a diet held at Verona, largely attended by German and Italian princes, a fresh campaign was arranged against the Saracens. Proceeding to Rome, Otto secured the election of Peter of Pavia as Pope John XIV. Just as the news reached him of a general rising of the tribes on the eastern frontier of Germany, he died in his palace in Rome on the 7th of December 983. He left a son, afterwards the emperor Otto III., and three daughters. He was buried in the atrium of St Peter's, and when the church was rebuilt his remains were removed to the crypt, where his tomb may still be seen. Otto, who is sometimes called the "Red," was a man of small stature, by nature brave and impulsive, and by training an accomplished knight. He was generous to the church and aided the spread of Christianity in many ways.

See *Die Urkunden des Kaisers Otto II.*, edited by Th. von Sickel, in the *Monumenta Germaniae historica. Diplomata* (Hanover, 1879);

L. von Ranke, *Weltgeschichte*, Part vii. (Leipzig, 1886); W. von Giesebrecht, *Geschichte der deutschen Kaiserzeit* (Leipzig, 1881–1890); and *Jahrbücher des deutschen Reichs unter Kaiser Otto II.* (Berlin, 1837–1840); H. Detmer, *Otto II. bis zum Tode seines Vaters* (Leipzig, 1878); J. Moltmann, *Theophano die Gemahlin Otto II. in ihrer Bedeutung für die Politik. Otto I. and Otto II.* (Göttingen, 1878); and A. Matthaei, *Die Händel Ottos II. mit Lothar von Frankreich* (Halle, 1888).

OTTO III. (980–1002), Roman emperor, son of the emperor Otto II. and Theophano, daughter of the eastern emperor Romanus II., was born in July 980, chosen as his father's successor at Verona in June 983 and crowned German king at Aix-la-Chapelle on the 25th of the following December. Otto II. had died a few days before this ceremony, but the news did not reach Germany until after the coronation. Early in 984 the king was seized by Henry II., the Quarrelsome, the deposed duke of Bavaria, who claimed the regency as a member of the reigning house, and probably entertained the idea of obtaining the kingly dignity himself. A strong opposition was quickly aroused, and when Theophano and Adelaide, widow of the emperor Otto the Great, appeared in Germany, Henry was compelled to hand over the young king to his mother. Otto's mental gifts were considerable, and were so carefully cultivated by Bernward, afterwards bishop of Hildesheim, and by Gerbert of Aurillac, archbishop of Reims, that he was called "the wonder of the world." The government of Germany during his minority was in the hands of Theophano, and after her death in June 991 passed to a council in which the chief influence was exercised by Adelaide and Willigis, archbishop of Mainz. Having accompanied his troops in expeditions against the Bohemians and the Wends, Otto was declared of age in 995. In 996 he crossed the Alps and was recognized as king of the Lombards at Pavia. Before he reached Rome, Pope John XV., who had invited him to Italy, had died, whereupon he raised his own cousin Bruno, son of Otto duke of Carinthia, to the papal chair as Pope Gregory V., and by this pontiff Otto was crowned emperor on the 21st of May 996. On his return to Germany, the emperor learned that Gregory had been driven from Rome, which was again in the power of John Crescentius, patrician of the Romans, and that a new pope, John XVI., had been elected. Leaving his aunt, Matilda, abbess of Quedlinburg, as regent of Germany, Otto, in February 998, led Gregory back to Rome, took the castle of St Angelo by storm and put Crescentius to death. A visit to southern Italy, where many of the princes did homage to the emperor, was cut short by the death of the pope, to whose chair Otto then appointed his former tutor Gerbert, who took the name of Sylvester II. In the palace which he built on the Aventine, Otto sought to surround himself with the splendour and ceremonial of the older emperors of Rome, and dreamed of making Rome once more the centre of a universal empire. Many names and customs were introduced into his court from that of Constantinople; he proposed to restore the Roman senate and consulate, revived the office of patrician, called himself "consul of the Roman senate and people" and issued a seal with the inscription, "restoration of the Roman empire." Passing from pride to humility he added "servant of the apostle," and "servant of Jesus Christ" to the imperial title, spent a fortnight in prayer in the grotto of St Clement and did penance in various Italian monasteries. Leaving Italy in the summer preceding the year 1000, when it was popularly believed that the end of the world was to come, Otto made a pilgrimage to the tomb of his old friend Adalbert, bishop of Prague, at Gnesen, and raised the city to the dignity of an archbishopric. He then went to Aix, and opened the tomb of Charlemagne, where, according to a legendary tale, he found the body of the great emperor sitting upright upon a throne, wearing the crown and holding the sceptre. Returning to Rome, trouble soon arose between Otto and the citizens, and for three days the emperor was besieged in his palace. After a temporary peace, he fled to the monastery of Classe near Ravenna. Troops were collected, but whilst conducting a campaign against the Romans, Otto died at Paterno near Viterbo on the 23rd of January 1002, and was buried in the cathedral at Aix-la-Chapelle. Tradition says he was ensnared and poisoned by Stephania, the widow of Crescentius. The mystic erratic temperament of Otto, alternating between the most magnificent schemes of empire and the lowest depths of self-debasement, was not conducive to the welfare of his dominions, and during his reign the conditions of Germany deteriorated. He was liberal to the papacy; and was greatly influenced by the eminent clerics with whom he eagerly associated.

See Thangmar, *Vita Bernwardi episcopi Hildesheimensis* in the *Monumenta Germaniae historica. Scriptores*, Band iv. (Hanover and Berlin, 1826 fol.); *Lettres de Gerbert*, edited by J. Havet (Paris, 1889); *Die Urkunden Kaisers Ottos III.*, edited by Th. von Sickel in the *Monumenta Germaniae historica. Diplomata* (Hanover, 1879); R. Wilmans, *Jahrbücher des deutschen Reichs unter Kaiser Otto III.* (Berlin, 1837–1840); P. Kehr, *Die Urkunden Otto III.* (Innsbruck, 1890).

OTTO IV. (*c.* 1182–1218), Roman emperor, second son of Henry the Lion, duke of Saxony, and Matilda, daughter of Henry II., king of England, was most probably born at Argenton in central France. His father died when he was still young, and he was educated at the court of his uncle Richard I., king of England, under whose leadership he gained valuable experience in war, being appointed duke of Aquitaine, count of Poitou and earl of Yorkshire. When the emperor Henry VI. died in September 1197, some of the princes under the leadership of Adolph, archbishop of Cologne, were anxious to find a rival to Philip, duke of Swabia, who had been elected German king. After some delay their choice fell upon Otto, who was chosen king at Cologne on the 9th of June 1198. Hostilities broke out at once, and Otto, who drew his main support from his hereditary possessions in the Rhineland and Saxony, seized Aix-la-Chapelle, and was crowned there on the 12th of July 1198. The earlier course of the war was unfavourable to Otto, whose position was weakened by the death of Richard of England in April 1199; but his cause began to improve when Pope Innocent III. declared for him and placed his rival under the ban in April 1201. This support was purchased by a capitulation signed by Otto at Neuss, which ratified the independence and decided the boundaries of the States of the Church, and was the first authentic basis for the practical authority of the pope in central Italy. In 1200 an attack made by Philip on Brunswick was beaten off, the city of Worms was taken, and subsequently the aid of Ottakar I., king of Bohemia, was won for Otto. The papal legate Guido worked energetically on his behalf, several princes were persuaded to desert Philip and by the end of 1203 his success seemed assured. But after a period of reverses, Otto was wounded during a fight in July 1206 and compelled to take refuge in Cologne. Retiring to Denmark, he obtained military assistance from King Waldemar II., and a visit to England procured monetary aid from King John, after which he managed to maintain his position in Brunswick. Preparations were made to drive him from his last refuge, when he was saved by the murder of Philip in June 1208. Many of the supporters of Philip now made overtures to Otto, and an attempt to set up Henry I. duke of Brabant having failed, Otto submitted to a fresh election and was chosen German king at Frankfort on the 11th of November 1208 in the presence of a large gathering of princes. A general reconciliation followed, which was assisted by the betrothal of Otto to Philip's eldest daughter Beatrix, but as she was only ten years old, the marriage was deferred until the 22nd of July 1212. The pope who had previously recognized the victorious Philip, hastened to return to the side of Otto; the capitulation of Neuss was renewed and large concessions were made to the church.

In August 1209 the king set out for Italy. Meeting with no opposition, he was received at Viterbo by Innocent, but refused the papal demand that he should concede to the church all the territories which, previous to 1197, had been in dispute between the Empire and the Papacy, consenting, however, not to claim supremacy over Sicily. He was crowned emperor at Rome on the 4th of October 1209, a ceremony which was followed by fighting between the Romans and the German soldiers. The pope then requested the emperor to leave Roman territory;

but he remained near Rome for some days, demanding satisfaction for the losses suffered by his troops. The breach with Innocent soon widened, and in violation of the treaty made with the pope Otto attempted to recover for the Empire all the property which Innocent had annexed to the Church, and rewarded his supporters with large estates in the disputed territories. Having occupied Tuscany he marched into Apulia, part of the kingdom of Frederick of Hohenstaufen, afterwards the emperor Frederick II., and on the 18th of November 1210 was excommunicated by the pope. Regardless of this sentence Otto completed the conquest of southern Italy, but the efforts of Innocent had succeeded in arousing considerable opposition in Germany, where the rebels were also supported by Philip Augustus, king of France. A number of princes assembled at Nuremberg declared Otto deposed, and invited Frederick to fill the vacant throne. Returning to Germany in March 1212, Otto made some headway against his enemies until the arrival of Frederick towards the close of the year. The death of his wife in August 1212 had weakened his hold on the southern duchies, and he was soon confined to the district of the lower Rhine, although supported by money from his uncle King John of England. The final blow to his fortunes came when he was decisively defeated by the French at Bouvines in July 1214. He escaped with difficulty from the fight and took refuge in Cologne. His former supporters hastened to recognize Frederick; and in 1216 he left Cologne for Brunswick, which he had received in 1202 by arrangement with his elder brother Henry. The conquest of Hamburg by the Danes, and the death of John of England, were further blows to his cause. On the 19th of May 1218 he died at the Harzburg after being loosed from the ban by a Cistercian monk, and was buried in the church of St Blasius at Brunswick. He married for his second wife in May 1214 Marie, daughter of Henry I., duke of Brabant, but left no children.

See *Regesta imperii V.*, edited by J. Ficker (Innsbruck, 1881); L. von Ranke, *Weltgeschichte*, Part viii. (Leipzig, 1887–1888); W. von Giesebrecht, *Geschichte der deutschen Kaiserzeit*, Band v. (Leipzig, 1888); O. Abel, *Kaiser Otto IV. und König Friedrich II.* (Berlin, 1856); E. Winkelmann, *Philipp von Schwaben und Otto IV. von Braunschweig* (Leipzig, 1873–1878); G. Langefeldt, *Kaiser Otto der Vierte* (Hanover, 1872); R. Schwemer, *Innocenz III. und die deutsche Kirche während des Thronstreites* (Strassburg, 1882); and A. Luchaire, *Innocent III., la papauté et l'empire* (Paris, 1906); and *Innocent III., la question d'Orient* (Paris, 1906).

OTTO OF FREISING (*c.* 1114–1158), German bishop and chronicler, was the fifth son of Leopold III., margrave of Austria, by his wife Agnes, daughter of the emperor Henry IV. By her first husband, Frederick I. of Hohenstaufen, duke of Swabia, Agnes was the mother of the German king Conrad III., and grandmother of the emperor Frederick I.; and Otto was thus related to the most powerful families in Germany. The notices of his life are scanty and the dates somewhat uncertain. He studied in Paris, where he took an especial interest in philosophy, is said to have been one of the first to introduce the philosophy of Aristotle into Germany, and he served as provost of a new foundation in Austria. Having entered the Cistercian order, Otto became abbot of the Cistercian monastery of Morimond in Burgundy about 1136, and soon afterwards was elected bishop of Freising. This diocese, and indeed the whole of Bavaria, was then disturbed by the feud between the Welfs and the Hohenstaufen, and the church was in a deplorable condition; but a great improvement was brought about by the new bishop in both ecclesiastical and secular matters. In 1147 he took part in the disastrous crusade of Conrad III. The section of the crusading army led by the bishop was decimated, but Otto reached Jerusalem, and returned to Bavaria in 1148 or 1149. He enjoyed the favour of Conrad's successor, Frederick I.; was probably instrumental in settling the dispute over the duchy of Bavaria. In 1156 he was present at the famous diet at Besançon in 1157, and, still retaining the dress of a Cistercian monk, died at Morimond on the 22nd of September 1158. In 1857 a statue of the bishop was erected at Freising.

Otto wrote a *Chronicon*, sometimes called *De duabus civitatibus*, an historical and philosophical work in eight books, which follows to some extent the lines laid down by Augustine and Orosius.

Written during the time of the civil war in Germany, it contrasts Jerusalem and Babel, the heavenly and the earthly kingdoms, but also contains much valuable information about the history of the time. The chronicle, which was held in very high regard by contemporaries, goes down to 1146, and from this date until 1209 has been continued by Otto, abbot of St Blasius (d. 1223). Better known is Otto's *Gesta Friderici imperatoris*, written at the request of Frederick I., and prefaced by a letter from the emperor to the author. The *Gesta* is in four books, the first two of which were written by Otto, and the remaining two, or part of them, by his pupil Ragewin, or Rahewin; it has been argued that the third book and the early part of the fourth were also the work of Otto. Beginning with the quarrel between Pope Gregory VII. and the emperor Henry IV., the first book takes the history down to the death of Conrad III. in 1152. It is not confined to German affairs, as the author digresses to tell of the preaching of Bernard of Clairvaux, of his zeal against the heretics, and of the condemnation of Abelard; and discourses on philosophy and theology. The second book opens with the election of Frederick I. in 1152, and deals with the history of the first five years of his reign, especially in Italy, in some detail. From this point (1156) the work is continued by Ragewin. Otto's Latin is excellent, and in spite of a slight partiality for the Hohenstaufen, and some minor inaccuracies, the *Gesta* has been rightly described as a "model of historical composition." First printed by John Cuspinian at Strassburg in 1515, Otto's writings are now found in the *Monumenta Germaniae historica*, Band xx. (Hanover, 1868), and have been translated into German by H. Kohl (Leipzig, 1881–1886). The *Gesta Friderici* has been published separately with introduction by G. Waitz. Otto is also said to have written a history of Austria (*Historia Austriaca*).

See J. Hashagen, *Otto von Freising als Geschichtsphilosoph und Kirchenpolitiker* (Leipzig, 1900); J. Schmidlin, *Die geschichtsphilosophische und kirchenpolitische Weltanschauung Otto von Freising* (Freiburg, 1906); W. Wattenbach, *Deutschlands Geschichtsquellen*, Band ii. (Berlin, 1894); and for full bibliography, A. Potthast, *Bibliotheca historica* (Berlin, 1896). (A. W. H.[2])

OTTO OF NORDHEIM (d. 1083), duke of Bavaria, belonged to the rich and influential Saxon family of the counts of Nordheim, and having distinguished himself in war and peace alike, received the duchy of Bavaria from Agnes, widow of the emperor Henry III., in 1061. In 1062 he assisted Anno, archbishop of Cologne, to seize the person of the German king, Henry IV.; led a successful expedition into Hungary in 1063; and took a prominent part in the government during the king's minority. In 1064 he went to Italy to settle a papal schism, was largely instrumental in securing the banishment from court of Adalbert, archbishop of Bremen, and crossed the Alps in the royal interests on two other occasions. He neglected his duchy, but added to his personal possessions, and in 1069 shared in two expeditions in the east of Germany. In 1070 Otto was accused by a certain Egino of being privy to a plot to murder the king, and it was decided he should submit to the ordeal of battle with his accuser. The duke asked for a safe-conduct to and from the place of meeting, and when this was refused he declined to appear, and was consequently deprived of Bavaria, while his Saxon estates were plundered. He obtained no support in Bavaria, but raised an army among the Saxons and carried on a campaign of plunder against Henry until 1071, when he submitted; in the following year he received back his private estates. When the Saxon revolt broke out in 1073 Otto is represented by Bruno, the author of *De bello Saxonico*, as delivering an inspiring speech to the assembled Saxons at Wormsleben, after which he took command of the insurgents. By the peace of Gerstungen in 1074 Bavaria was restored to him; he shared in the Saxon rising of 1075, after which he was again pardoned and made administrator of Saxony. After the excommunication of Henry IV. in 1076 Otto attempted to mediate between Henry and the Saxons, but when these efforts failed he again placed himself at their head. He assented to the election of Rudolph, count of Rheinfelden, as German king, when his restoration to Bavaria was assured, and by his skill and bravery inflicted defeats on Henry's forces at Mellrichstadt, Flarchheim and Hohenmölsen. He remained in arms against the king until his death on the 11th of January 1083. Otto is described as a noble, prudent and warlike man, and he possessed great abilities. His repeated pardon showed that Henry could not afford to neglect such a powerful personality, and his military talents were repeatedly displayed. By his wife Richenza, widow of Hermann, count of Werla, he left three sons and three daughters.

See W. von Giesebrecht, *Geschichte der deutschen Kaiserzeit*, Band iii. (Leipzig, 1881–1890); H. Mehmel, *Otto von Nordheim, Herzog von Bayern* (Göttingen, 1870); E. Neumann, *De Ottone de Nordheim* (Breslau, 1871); S. Riezler, *Geschichte Bayerns* (Gotha, 1878); and A. Vogeler, *Otto von Nordheim* (Göttingen, 1880).

OTTOMAN, a form of couch which usually has a head but no back, though sometimes it has neither. It may have square or semicircular ends, and as a rule it is what upholsterers call "stuffed over"—that is to say no wood is visible. It belongs to the same order of ideas as the divan (q.v.); its name indeed betokens its Oriental origin. It was one of the luxurious appointments which Europe imported from the East in the 18th century; the first mention that has been found of it is in France in 1729. In the course of a generation it made its way into every boudoir, but it appears originally to have been much larger than at present. The word is also applied to a small foot-stool covered with carpet, embroidery or beadwork.

OTTUMWA, a city and the county-seat of Wapello county, Iowa, U.S.A., on both sides of the Des Moines river, in the S.E. part of the state, about 85 m. S.E. of Des Moines. Pop. (1900) 18,197, of whom 1759 were foreign-born; (1910 census) 22,012. It is served by the Chicago, Burlington & Quincy, the Chicago, Milwaukee & Saint Paul, the Chicago, Rock Island & Pacific, and the Wabash railways. The site on which it is built forms a succession of terraces receding farther and farther from the river. In the city are a Carnegie library, a city hospital and St Joseph's Academy. Ottumwa is the headquarters of the Ottumwa Division of the Southern Federal Judicial District of Iowa, and terms of United States District and Circuit courts are held there. The city is in one of the richest coal regions of the state, and ranks high as a manufacturing centre, pork-packing, and the manufacture of iron and steel, machinery and agricultural and mining implements being the leading industries. The value of the factory product in 1905 was $10,374,183, an increase of 19·5% since 1900. Ottumwa was first settled in 1843, was incorporated as a town in 1851, and first chartered as a city in 1857.

OTWAY, THOMAS (1652–1685), English dramatist, was born at Trotton, near Midhurst, Sussex, on the 3rd of March 1652. His father, Humphrey Otway, was at that time curate of Trotton, but Otway's childhood was spent at Woolbeding, a parish 3 m. distant, of which his father had become rector. He was educated at Winchester College, and in 1669 entered Christ Church, Oxford, as a commoner, but left the university without a degree in the autumn of 1672. At Oxford he made the acquaintance of Anthony Cary, 5th viscount Falkland, through whom, he says in the dedication to *Caius Marius*, he first learned to love books. In London he made acquaintance with Mrs Aphra Behn, who in 1672 cast him for the part of the old king in her *Forc'd Marriage*, or *The Jealous Bridegroom*, at the Dorset Garden Theatre, but he had a bad attack of stage fright, and never made a second appearance. In 1675 Thomas Betterton produced at the same theatre Otway's first dramatic attempt, *Alcibiades*, which was printed in the same year. It is a poor tragedy, written in heroic verse, but was saved from absolute failure by the actors. Mrs Barry took the part of Draxilla, and her lover, the earl of Rochester, recommended the author of the piece to the notice of the duke of York. He made a great advance on this first work in *Don Carlos, Prince of Spain* (licensed June 15, 1676; an undated edition probably belongs to the same year). The material for this rhymed tragedy Otway took from the novel of the same name, written in 1672 by the Abbé de Saint-Réal, the source from which Schiller also drew his tragedy of *Don Carlos*. In it the two characters familiar throughout his plays make their appearance. Don Carlos is the impetuous, unstable youth, who seems to be drawn from Otway himself, while the queen's part is the gentle pathetic character repeated in his more celebrated heroines, Monimia and Belvidera. "It got more money," says John Downes (*Roscius Anglicanus*, 1708) of this play, "than any preceding modern tragedy." In 1677 Betterton produced two adaptations from the French by Otway, *Titus and Berenice* (from Racine's *Bérénice*), and the *Cheats of Scapin* (from Molière's *Fourberies de Scapin*). These were printed together, with a dedication to Lord Rochester. In 1678 he produced an original comedy, *Friendship in Fashion*, popular at the moment, though it was hissed off the stage for its gross indecency when it was revived at Drury Lane in 1749. Meanwhile he had conceived an overwhelming passion for Mrs Barry, who filled many of the leading parts in his plays. Six of his letters to her survive, the last of them referring to a broken appointment in the Mall. Mrs Barry seems to have coquetted with Otway, but she had no intention of permanently offending Rochester. In 1678, driven to desperation by Mrs Barry, Otway obtained a commission through Charles, earl of Plymouth, a natural son of Charles II., in a regiment serving in the Netherlands. The English troops were disbanded in 1679, but were left to find their way home as best they could. They were also paid with depreciated paper, and Otway arrived in London late in the year, ragged and dirty, a circumstance utilized by Rochester in his "Sessions of the Poets," which contains a scurrilous attack on his former protégé. Early in the next year (February 1680) was produced at Dorset Garden the first of Otway's two tragic masterpieces, *The Orphan, or The Unhappy Marriage*, Mrs Barry playing the part of Monimia. Written in blank verse, which shows a study of Shakespeare, its success was due to the tragic pathos, of which Otway was a master, in the characters of Castalio and Monimia. *The History and Fall of Caius Marius*, produced in the same year, and printed in 1692, is a curious grafting of Shakespeare's *Romeo and Juliet* on the story of Marius as related in Plutarch's *Lives*. In 1680 Otway also published *The Poet's Complaint of his Muse, or A Satyr against Libels*, in which he retaliated on his literary enemies. An indifferent comedy, *The Soldier's Fortune* (1681), was followed in February 1682 by *Venice Preserved, or A Plot Discover'd*. The story is founded on the *Histoire de la conjuration des Espagnols contre la Venise en 1618*, by the Abbé de Saint-Réal, but Otway modified the story considerably. The character of Belvidera is his own, and the leading part in the conspiracy, taken by Bedamor, the Spanish ambassador, is given in the play to the historically insignificant Pierre and Jaffier. The piece has a political meaning, enforced in the prologue. The Popish Plot was in Otway's mind, and Anthony, 1st earl of Shaftesbury, is caricatured in Antonio. The play won instant success. It was translated into almost every modern European language, and even Dryden said of it: "Nature is there, which is the greatest beauty." *The Orphan* and *Venice Preserved* remained stock pieces on the stage until the 19th century, and the leading actresses of the period played Monimia and Belvidera. One or two prefaces, another weak comedy, *The Atheist* (1684), and two posthumous pieces, a poem, *Windsor Castle* (1685), a panegyric of Charles II., and a *History of the Triumvirates* (1686), translated from the French, complete the list of Otway's works. He apparently ceased to struggle against his poverty and misfortunes. The generally accepted story regarding the manner of his death was first given in Theophilus Cibber's *Lives of the Poets*. He is said to have emerged from his retreat at the Bull on Tower Hill to beg for bread. A passer-by, learning who he was, gave him a guinea, with which Otway hastened to a baker's shop. He began too hastily to satisfy his ravenous hunger, and choked with the first mouthful. Whether this account of his death be true or not, it is certain that he died in the utmost poverty, and was buried on the 16th of April 1685 in the churchyard of St Clement Danes. A tragedy entitled *Heroick Friendship* was printed in 1686 as Otway's work, but the ascription is unlikely.

The Works of Mr Thomas Otway with some account of his life and writings, published in 1712, was followed by other editions (1757, 1768, 1812). The standard edition is that by T. Thornton (1813). A selection of his plays was edited for the Mermaid series (1891 and 1903) by Roden Noel. See also E. Gosse, *Seventeenth Century Studies* (1883); and Genest, *History of the Stage*.

OUBLIETTE, a French architectural term (from *oublier*, to forget), used in two senses of a dungeon or cell in a prison or castle which could only be reached by a trap-door from another dungeon, and of a concealed opening or passage leading from a dungeon to the moat or river, into which bodies of prisoners who were to be secretly disposed of might be dropped. Viollet le

Duc (*Dict. de l'architecture*) gives a diagram of such an oubliette at the castle of Pierrefonds, France. Many so-called "oubliettes" in medieval castles were probably outlets for the disposal of drainage, refuse, &c., which at times may have served for the getting rid of prisoners.

OUCH, a brooch, clasp or buckle, especially one ornamented with jewels, enamels, &c., and used to clasp a cope or other ecclesiastical vestment. It is also used, as in Exod. xxxix. 6, of the gold or silver setting of jewels. The word is an example of the misdivision of a substantive and the indefinite article, being properly "nouche," "a nouche" being divided into "an ouche," as a napron into an apron, a nadder into an adder, and, reversely, an ewt, *i.e.* eft, into a newt. "Nouche" was adapted into O. Fr.; whence English took the word, from the Late Lat. *nusca*; brooch; probably the original is Celtic, cf. O. Irish *nasc*, ring, *nasgaim*, fasten.

OUDENARDE (Flemish *Oudenaerde*), a town of Belgium in the province of East Flanders, 18 m. S. of Ghent. Pop. (1904) 6571. While it is best known for the great victory gained by Marlborough and Eugene over the French under Vendôme in 1708, Oudenarde has many features of interest. The town hall, which took ten years to build (1525-1535), has after that of Louvain the most elaborately decorated façade in Belgium. It was designed by H. van Peede and G. de Ronde, and is in tertiary Gothic style. The belfry tower of five storeys with three terraces, surmounted by a golden figure, is a striking feature. The council chamber contains a fine oak door and Gothic chimney-piece, both *c.* 1530. There are also two interesting old churches, St Walburga, partly of the 12th and partly of the 14th century, and Notre Dame, dating from the 13th century. The former contains several fine pictures by Craeyer and other old Flemish masters.

The *Battle of Oudenarde* (June 30th-July 11th 1708) was fought on the ground north-west and north of the town, which was then regularly fortified and was garrisoned by a force of the Allies. The French army under the duke of Burgundy and Marshal Vendôme, after an abortive attempt to invest Oudenarde, took up a defensive position north of the town when Marlborough and Eugene, after a forced march, arrived with the main Allied army. The advanced guard of the Allies under General (Lord) Cadogan promptly crossed the Scheldt and annihilated an outlying body of French troops, and Cadogan established himself on the ground he had won in front of the French centre. But the Allied main army took a long time to defile over the Scheldt and could form up (on the left of Cadogan's detachment) only slowly and by degrees. Observing this, Burgundy resolved to throw forward his right towards Oudenarde to engage and hold the main body of the Allies before their line of battle could be formed. This effected, it was hoped that the remainder of the French army could isolate and destroy Cadogan's detachment, which was already closely engaged with the French centre. But he miscalculated both the endurance of Cadogan's men (amongst whom the Prussians were conspicuous for their tenacity) and the rapidity with which in Marlborough's and Eugene's hands the wearied troops of the Allies could be made to move. Marlborough, who personally directed the operations on his left wing, not only formed his line of battle successfully, but also began seriously to press the forces that had been sent to check his deployment. Before long, while the hostile left wing still remained inactive, the unfortunate troops of the French centre and right were gradually hemmed in by the whole force of the Allies. The decisive blow was delivered by the Dutch marshal, Overkirk, who was sent by Marlborough with a large force (the last reserve of the Allies) to make a wide turning movement round the extreme right of the French, and at the proper time attacked them in rear. A belated attempt of the French left to intervene was checked by the British cavalry, and the pressure on the centre and right, which were now practically surrounded, continued even after nightfall. A few scattered units managed to escape, and the left wing retreated unmolested, but at the cost of about 3000 casualties the Allies inflicted a loss of 6000 killed and wounded and 9000 prisoners on the enemy, who were, moreover, so shaken that they never recovered their confidence to the end of the campaign. The battle of Oudenarde was not the greatest of Marlborough's victories, but it affords almost the best illustration of his military character. Contrary to all the rules of war then in vogue, he fought a piecemeal and unpremeditated battle, with his back to a river, and with wearied troops, and the event justified him. An ordinary commander would have avoided fighting altogether, but Marlborough saw beyond the material conditions and risked all on his estimate of the moral superiority of his army and of the weakness of the French leading. His conduct of the battle, once it had opened, was a model of the "partial" victory—the destruction of a part of the enemy's forces under the eyes of the rest—which was in the 17th and 18th centuries the tactician's ideal, and was sufficient to ensure him the reputation of being the best general of his age. But it is in virtue of having fought at all that he passes beyond the criteria of the time and becomes one of the great captains of history.

OUDINÉ, EUGÈNE ANDRÉ (1810–1887), French sculptor and medallist, was born in Paris in 1810, and devoted himself from the beginning to the medallist's branch of sculpture, although he also excelled in monumental sculpture and portrait busts. Having carried off the grand prize for medal engraving in 1831, he had a sensational success with his "Wounded Gladiator," which he exhibited in the same year. He subsequently occupied official posts as designer, first to the Inland Revenue Office, and then to the Mint. Among his most famous medals are that struck in commemoration of the annexation of Savoy by France, and that on the occasion of the peace of Villafranca. Other remarkable pieces are "The Apotheosis of Napoleon I.," "The Amnesty," "Le Duc d'Orléans," "Bertholet," "The Universal Exposition," "The Second of December, 1851," "The Establishment of the Republic," "The Battle of Inkermann," and "Napoleon's Tomb at the Invalides." For the Hotel de Ville in Paris he executed fourteen bas-reliefs, which were destroyed in 1871. Of his monumental works, many are to be seen in public places in and near Paris. In the Tuileries gardens is his group of "Daphnis and Hebe"; in the Luxembourg gardens the "Queen Bertha"; at the Louvre the "Buffon"; and in the courtyard of the same palace the "Bathsheba." A monument to General Espagne is at the Invalides, and a King Louis VIII. at Versailles. Oudiné, who may be considered the father of the modern medal, died in Paris in 1887.

OUDINOT, CHARLES NICOLAS (1767–1847), duke of Reggio, marshal of France, came of a bourgeois family in Lorraine, and was born at Bar-le-duc on the 25th of April 1767. He had a passion for a military career, and served in the regiment of Médoc from 1784 to 1787, when, having no hope of promotion on account of his non-noble birth, he retired with the rank of sergeant. The Revolution changed his fortunes, and in 1792, on the outbreak of war, he was elected lieutenant-colonel of the 3rd battalion of the volunteers of the Meuse. His gallant defence of the little fort of Bitsch in the Vosges in 1792 drew attention to him; he was transferred to the regular army in November 1793, and after serving in numerous actions on the Belgian frontier he was promoted general of brigade in June 1794 for his conduct at the battle of Kaiserslautern. He continued to serve with the greatest distinction on the German frontier under Hoche, Pichegru and Moreau, and was repeatedly wounded and once (in 1795) made prisoner. He was Masséna's right hand all through the great Swiss campaign of 1799—first as a general of division, to which grade he was promoted in April, and then as chief of the staff—and won extraordinary distinction at the battle of Zürich. He was present under Masséna at the defence of Genoa, and so distinguished himself at the combat of Monzambano that Napoleon presented him with a sword of honour. He was made inspector-general of infantry, and, on the establishment of the empire, given the Grand Cross of the Legion of Honour, but was not included in the first creation of marshals. He was at this time elected a member of the chamber of deputies, but he had little time to devote to politics. He took a conspicuous part in the war of 1805 in command of the famous division

of the "grenadiers Oudinot," formed of picked troops and organized by him, with which he seized the Vienna bridges, received a wound at Hollabrünn, and delivered the decisive blow at Austerlitz. In 1806 he won the battle of Ostrolenka, and fought with resolution and success at Friedland. In 1808 he was made governor of Erfurt and count of the Empire, and in 1809, after displaying brilliant courage at Wagram, he was promoted to the rank of marshal. He was made duke of Reggio, and received a large money grant in April 1810. Oudinot administered the government of Holland from 1810 to 1812, and commanded the II. corps of the *Grande Armée* in the Russian campaign. He was present at Lützen and Bautzen, and when holding the independent command of the corps directed to take Berlin was defeated at Gross Beeren (see NAPOLEONIC CAMPAIGNS). He was then superseded by Ney, but the mischief was too great to be repaired, and Ney was defeated at Dennewitz. Oudinot was not disgraced, however, holding important commands at Leipzig and in the campaign of 1814. On the abdication of Napoleon he rallied to the new government, and was made a peer by Louis XVIII., and, unlike many of his old comrades, he did not desert to his old master in 1815. His last active service was in the French invasion of Spain in 1823, in which he commanded a corps and was for a time governor of Madrid. He died as governor of the Invalides on the 13th of September 1847. Oudinot was not, and made no pretence of being, a great commander, but he was a great general of division. He was the beau-ideal of an infantry general, energetic, thoroughly conversant with detail, and in battle as resolute and skilful as any of the marshals of Napoleon.

Oudinot's eldest son, CHARLES NICOLAS VICTOR, 2nd duke of Reggio (1791–1863), lieutenant-general, served through the later campaigns of Napoleon from 1809 to 1814, being in the latter year promoted major for gallant conduct. Unlike his father he was a cavalryman, and as such held command of the cavalry school at Saumur (1822–1830), and the inspector-generalcy of cavalry (1836–1848). He is chiefly known as the commander of the French expedition which besieged and took Rome in 1849 and re-established the temporal power of the pope. After the *coup d'état* of the 2nd of December 1851, in resistance to which he took a prominent part, he retired from military and political life, dying at Paris on the 7th of June 1863. The 2nd duke wrote *Aperçu historique sur la dignité de maréchal de France* (1833): *Considérations sur les ordres militaires de Saint Louis, &c.* (1833); *L'Emploi des troupes aux grands travaux d'utilité publique* (1839); *De la Cavalerie et du casernement des troupes à cheval* (1840); *Des Remontes de l'armée* (1840); and a brief account of his Italian operations of 1849.

OUGHTRED, WILLIAM (fl. 1575–1660), English mathematician, was born at Eton, and educated there and at King's College, Cambridge, of which he became fellow. Being admitted to holy orders, he left the university about 1603, and was presented to the rectory of Aldbury, near Guildford in Surrey; and about 1628 he was appointed by the earl of Arundel to instruct his son in mathematics. He corresponded with some of the most eminent scholars of his time on mathematical subjects; and his house was frequently full of pupils from all quarters. It is said that he expired in a sudden transport of joy upon hearing the news of the vote at Westminster for the restoration of Charles II.

He published, among other mathematical works, *Clavis Mathematica*, in 1631, in which he introduced new signs for certain mathematical operations (see ALGEBRA); a treatise on navigation entitled *Circles of Proportion*, in 1632; works on trigonometry and dialling, and his *Opuscula Mathematica*, published posthumously in 1676.

OUIDA, the pen name—derived from a childish attempt to pronounce "Louisa"—of Maria Louise [de la] Ramée (1839–1908), English novelist, born at Bury St Edmunds, where her birth was registered on the 7th of January 1839. Her father, Louis Ramée, was French, and her mother, Susan Sutton, English. At an early age she went to live in London, and there began to contribute to the *New Monthly* and *Bentley's Magazine*. In 1860 her first story, afterwards republished as *Held in Bondage* (1863), appeared in the *New Monthly* under the title of *Granville de Vigne*, and this was followed in quick succession by *Strathmore*

(1865), *Chandos* (1866) and *Under Two Flags* (1867). The list of Ouida's subsequent works is a very long one; but it is sufficient to say that, together with *Moths* (1880), those already named are not only the most characteristic, but also the best. In a less dramatic genre, her *Bimbi: Stories for Children* (1882) may also be mentioned; but it was by her more flamboyant stories, such as *Under Two Flags* and *Moths*, that her popular success was achieved. By purely literary critics and on grounds of morality or taste Ouida's novels may be condemned. They are generally flashy, and frequently unwholesome. It is impossible, however, to dismiss books like *Chandos* and *Under Two Flags* merely on such grounds. The emphasis given by Ouida to motives of sensual passion was combined in her with an original gift for situation and plot, and also with genuine descriptive powers which, though disfigured by inaccurate observation, literary solecisms and tawdry extravagance, enabled her at her best to construct a picturesque and powerful story. The character of " Cigarette " in *Under Two Flags* is full of fine touches, and this is not an isolated instance. In 1874 Ouida made her home in Florence, and many of her later novels have an Italian setting. She contributed from time to time to the magazines, and wrote vigorously on behalf of anti-vivisection and on Italian politics; but her views on these subjects were marked by characteristic violence and lack of judgment. She had made a great deal of money by her earlier books, but had spent it without thought for the morrow; and though in 1907 she was awarded a Civil List pension, she died at Viareggio in poverty on the 25th of January 1908.

OUNCE. (1) (Through O. Fr. *unce*, modern *once*, from Lat. *uncia*, twelfth part, of weight, of a pound, of measure, of a foot, in which sense it gives the O.Eng. *ynce*, inch), a unit of weight, being the twelfth part of a pound troy, = 480 grains; in avoirdupois = 437·5 grains, $\frac{1}{16}$ of a pound. The *fluid ounce* is a measure of capacity; in the United Kingdom it is equivalent to an avoirdupois ounce of distilled water at 62° F.; in the United States of America it is the 128th part of the gallon, = ½ gill, = 456·033 grains of distilled water at its maximum density (see WEIGHTS AND MEASURES). (2) A name properly applied to the *Felis uncia* or snow leopard (*q.v.*). It appears to have been originally used of various species of lynx, and is still sometimes the name of the Canada lynx. The word appears in O. Fr. and Ital. as *once* and *lonce*, *onsa* and *lonsa* respectively, and it is usually explained as being due to the confusion of the *l* with the article, *lonce* and *lonsa* being changed to *l'once* or *l'onsa*, and the *l'* subsequently dropped. If this be so the word is the same as " lynx," from the popular Lat. *luncia* = *lyncia*, Gr. λύγξ. On the other hand *once* and *onsa* may be nasalised forms of *yds*, the Persian name of the panther.

OUNDLE, a market-town in the Northern parliamentary division of Northamptonshire, England, 30¾ m. N.E. of Northampton by a branch of the London & North-Western railway. Pop. of urban district (1901) 2404. It is picturesquely situated on an eminence, two sides of which are touched by the river Nene, which here makes a deep bend. The church of St Peter is a fine building with Early English, Decorated and Perpendicular porticos, with a western tower and lofty spire. Oundle School, one of the English public schools, was founded under the will of Sir William Laxton, Lord Mayor of London (d. 1556). There are about 200 boys. The school is divided into classical and modern sides, and has exhibitions to Oxford and Cambridge universities. A second-grade school was instituted out of the foundation in 1878. Oundle has a considerable agricultural trade.

Wilfrid, archbishop of York, is said to have been buried in 711 at a monastery in Oundle (*Undale*) which appears to have been destroyed shortly afterwards, and was certainly not in existence at the time of the Conquest. The manor, with a market and tolls, was among the possessions confirmed in 972 by King Edgar to the abbot of Peterborough, to whom it still belonged in 1086. The market was then worth 20s. yearly and is shown by the *quo warranto* rolls to have been held on Saturday, the day being changed to Thursday in 1835. After the Dissolu-

tion the market was granted with the manor to John, earl of Bedford, and still belongs to the lord of the manor. The abbot of Peterborough about the 13th century confirmed to his men of Oundle freedom from tallage, " saving to himself pleas of portmannoot and all customs pertaining to the market," and they agreed to pay 8 marks, 12s. 11d., yearly for their privileges. The town was evidently governed by bailiffs in 1401, when the " bailiffs and good men " received a grant of pontage for the repair of the bridge called " Asheconbrigge," but the town was never incorporated and never sent members to parliament.

OURO PRETO (" Black Gold "), a city of the state of Minas Geraes, Brazil, 336 m. by rail N. by W. of Rio de Janeiro, and about 300 m. W. of Victoria, Espirito Santo, on the eastern slope of the Serra de Espinhaço and within the drainage basin of the Rio Doce. Pop. (1890) 17,860; (1900) 11,116. Ouro Preto is connected with Miguel Burnier, on the Central of Brazil railway, by a metre-gauge line 31 m. in length. The city is built upon the lower slope of the Serra do Ouro Preto, a spur of the Espinhaço, deeply cut by ravines and divided into a number of irregular hills, up which the narrow, crooked streets are built and upon which groups of low, old-fashioned houses form each a separate nucleus. From a mining settlement the city grew as the inequalities of the site permitted. R. F. Burton (*Highlands of Brazil*, London, 1869) says that its shape " is that of a huge serpent, whose biggest end is about the Praça. . . . The extremities stretch two good miles, with raised convolutions. . . . The ' streeting ' of both upper and lower town is very tangled, and the old thoroughfares, mere ' wynds ' . . . show how valuable once was building ground." The rough streets are too steep and narrow for vehicles, and even riding on horseback is often difficult. Several rivulets follow the ravines and drain into the Ribeirão do Carmo, a sub-tributary of the Rio Doce. The climate is sub-tropical and humid, though the elevation (3700-3800 ft.) gives a temperate climate in winter. The days are usually hot and the nights cold, the variations in temperature being a fruitful cause of bronchial and pulmonary diseases. Ouro Preto has several historic buildings; they are of antiquated appearance and built of the simplest materials—broken stone and mortar, with an exterior covering of plaster. The more noteworthy are the old government house (now occupied by the school of mines), the legislative chambers, municipal hall and jail—all fronting on the Praça da Independencia—and elsewhere the old Casa dos Contos (afterwards the public treasury), a theatre (the oldest in Brazil, restored in 1861-1862) and a hospital. There are 15 churches in the city, some occupying the most conspicuous sites on the hills, all dating from the more prosperous days of the city's history, but all devoid of architectural taste. Ouro Preto is the seat of the best mining school in Brazil.

The city dates from 1701, when a gold-mining settlement was established in its ravines by Antonio Dias of Taubaté. The circumstance that the gold turned black on exposure to the humid air (owing to the presence of silver) gave the name of Ouro Preto to the mountain spur and the settlement. In 1711 it became a city with the name of Villa Rica, a title justified by its size and wealth. At one period of its prosperity its population was estimated at 25,000 to 30,000. In 1720 Villa Rica became the capital of the newly created captaincy of Minas Geraes, and in 1823 the capital of the province of the same name under the empire of Dom Pedro I. When the empire was overthrown in 1889 and Minas Geraes was reorganized as a republican state, it was decided to remove the capital to a more favourable site and Bello Horizonte was chosen, but Ouro Preto remained the capital until 1898, when the new town (also called Cidade de Minas) became the seat of government. With the decay of her mining industries, Ouro Preto had become merely the political centre of the state. The removal of the capital was a serious blow, as the city has no industries to support its population and no trade of importance. The event most prominent in the history of the city was the conspiracy of 1789, in which several leading citizens were concerned, and for which one of its less influential members, an *alferes* (ensign) of cavalry named Joaquim José da Silva Xavier, nicknamed "Tira-dentes" (teeth-puller), was executed in Rio de Janeiro in 1792. The conspiracy originated in a belief that the Portuguese crown was about to enforce payment of certain arrears in the mining tax known as the "royal fifths," and its object was to set up a republic in Brazil. Although a minor figure in the conspiracy, Tira-dentes was made the scapegoat of the thirty-two men arrested and sent to Rio de Janeiro for trial, and posterity has made him the proto-martyr of republicanism in Brazil.

OUSE, the name of several English rivers.

(1) The Great Ouse rises in Northamptonshire, in the slight hills between Banbury and Brackley, and falls only about 500 ft. in a course of 160 m. (excluding lesser windings) to its mouth in the Wash (North Sea). With an easterly direction it flows past Brackley and Buckingham and then turns N.E. to Stony Stratford, where the Roman Watling Street forded it. It receives the Tove from the N.W., and the Ouzel from the S. at Newport Pagnell. It then follows an extremely sinuous course past Olney to Sharnbrook, where it turns abruptly S. to Bedford. A north-easterly direction is then resumed past St Neot's to Godmanchester and Huntingdon, when the river trends easterly to St Ives. Hitherto the Ouse has watered an open fertile valley, and there are many beautiful wooded reaches between Bedford and St Ives, while the river abounds in coarse fish. Below St Ives the river debouches suddenly upon the Fens; its fall from this point to the mouth, a distance of 55 m. by the old course, is little more than 20 ft. (the extensive system of artificial drainage cuts connected with the river is considered under FENS). From Earith to Denver the waters of the Ouse flow almost wholly in two straight artificial channels called the Bedford Rivers, only a small head passing, under ordinary conditions, along the old course, called the Old West River. This is joined by the Cam from the S. 4 m. above Ely. In its northward course from this point the river receives from the E. the Lark, the Little Ouse, or Brandon river, and the Wissey. Below Denver sluice, 16 m. from the mouth, the Ouse is tidal. It flows past King's Lynn, and enters the Wash near the S.E. corner. The river is locked up to Bedford, a distance of 74½ m. by the direct course. In the lower part it bears a considerable traffic, but above St Ives it is little used, and above St Neot's navigation has ceased. The drainage area of the Great Ouse is 2607 sq. m.

(2) A river of Yorkshire. The river Ure, rising near the N.W. boundary of the county in the heart of the Pennines, and traversing the lovely valley famous under the name Wensleydale, unites with the river Swale to form the Ouse near the small town of Boroughbridge, which lies in the rich central plain of Yorkshire. The course of the Swale, which rises in the north of the county on the eastern flank of the Pennines, is mostly through this plain, and that of the Ouse is wholly so. It flows S.E. to York, thence for a short distance S. by W., then mainly S.E. again past Selby and Goole to the junction with the Trent; the great estuary so formed being known as the Humber. The course of the Ouse proper, thus defined, is 61 m. The Swale and Ure are each about 60 m. long. Goole is a large and growing port, and the river bears a considerable traffic up to York. There is also some traffic up to Boroughbridge, from which the Ure Navigation (partly a canal) continues up to Ripon. The Swale is not navigable. The chief tributaries are the Nidd, the Wharfe, the Don and the Aire from the W., and the Derwent from the N.E., but the detailed consideration of these involves that of the hydrography of the greater part of Yorkshire (q.v.). All, especially the western tributaries, traverse beautiful valleys, and the Aire and Don, with canals, are of importance as affording communications between the manufacturing district of south Yorkshire and the Humber ports. The Derwent is also navigable. The drainage area of the Ouse is 4133 sq. m. It is tidal up to Naburn lock, a distance of 37 m. from the junction with the Trent, and the total fall from Boroughbridge is about 40 ft.

(3) A river of Sussex, rising in the Forest Ridges between

Horsham and Cuckfield, and draining an area of about 200 sq. m., mostly in the Weald. Like other streams of this locality, it breaches the South Downs, and reaches the English Channel at Newhaven after a course of 30 m. The eastward drift of beach-building material formerly diverted the mouth of this river from its present place to a point to the east near Seaford. The Ouse is navigable for small vessels to Lewes, and Newhaven is an important harbour.

OUSEL, or OUZEL, Anglo-Saxon *ósle*, equivalent of the German *Amsel* (a form of the word found in several old English books), apparently the ancient name for what is now more commonly known as the blackbird (q.v.), *Turdus merula*, but at the present day not often applied to that species, though used in a compound form for birds belonging to another genus and family.

The water-ousel, or water-crow, is now commonly named the "dipper"—a term apparently invented and bestowed in the first edition of T. Bewick's *British Birds* (ii. 16, 17)—not, as is commonly supposed, from the bird's habit of entering the water in pursuit of its prey, but because "it may be seen perched on the top of a stone in the midst of the torrent, in a continual dipping motion, or short courtesy often repeated." The English dipper, *Cinclus aquaticus*, is the type of a small family, the *Cinclidae*, probably more nearly

Cinclus mexicanus.

akin to the wrens (q.v.) than to the thrushes, and with examples throughout the more temperate portions of Europe and Asia, as well as North and South America. The dipper haunts rocky streams, into which it boldly enters, generally by deliberately wading, and then by the strenuous combined action of its wings and feet makes its way along the bottom in quest of its living prey—fresh-water molluscs and aquatic insects in their larval or mature condition. Complaints of its attacks on the spawn of fish have not been justified by examination of the stomachs of captured specimens. Short and squat of stature, active and restless in its movements, dusky above, with a pure white throat and upper part of the breast, to which succeeds a broad band of dark bay, it is a familiar figure to most fishermen on the streams it frequents. The water-ousel's nest is a very curious structure—outwardly resembling a wren's, but built on a wholly different principle—an ordinary cup-shaped nest of grass lined with dead leaves, placed in some convenient niche, but encased with moss so as to form a large mass that covers it completely except a small hole for the bird's passage. The eggs laid within are from four to seven in number, and are of a pure white. The young are able to swim before they are fully fledged. (A. N.)

OUSELEY, SIR FREDERICK ARTHUR GORE (1825–1889), English composer, was the son of Sir Gore Ouseley, ambassador to Persia, and nephew to Sir William Ouseley, the Oriental scholar. He was born on the 12th of August 1825 in London, and manifested an extraordinary precocity in music, composing an opera at the age of eight years. In 1844, having succeeded to the baronetcy, he entered at Christ Church, and graduated B.A. in 1846 and M.A. in 1849. He was ordained in the latter year, and, as curate of St Paul's, Knightsbridge, served the parish of St Barnabas, Pimlico, until 1851. In 1850 he took the degree of Mus.B. at Oxford, and four years afterwards that of Mus.D., his exercise being the oratorio *St Polycarp*. In 1855 he succeeded Sir Henry Bishop as professor of music in the University of Oxford, was ordained priest and appointed precentor of Hereford. In 1856 he became vicar of St Michael's, Tenbury, and warden of St. Michael's College, which under him became an important educational institution both in music and general subjects. His works include a second oratorio, *Hagar* (Hereford, 1873), a great number of services and anthems, chamber music, songs, &c., and theoretical works of great importance, such as *Harmony* (1868) and *Counterpoint* (1869) and *Musical Form* (1875). One of his most useful works is a series of chapters on English music added to the translation of Emil Naumann's *History of Music*, the subject having been practically ignored in the German treatise. A profoundly learned musician, and a man of great general culture, Ouseley's influence on younger men was wholly for good, and he helped forward the cause of musical progress in England perhaps more effectually than if he himself had been among the more enthusiastic supporters of " advanced " music. The work by which he is best known, *St Polycarp*, shows, like most compositions of its date, the strong influence of Mendelssohn, at least in its plan and scope; but if Ouseley had little individuality of expression, his models in other works were the English church writers of the noblest school. He died at Hereford on the 6th of April 1889.

OUSELEY, SIR WILLIAM (1769–1842), British Orientalist, eldest son of Captain Ralph Ouseley, of an old Irish family, was born in Monmouthshire. After a private education he went to Paris, in 1787, to learn French, and there laid the foundation of his interest in Persian literature. In 1788 he became a cornet in the 8th regiment of dragoons. At the end of 1794 he sold his commission and went to Leiden to study Persian. In 1795 he published *Persian Miscellanies*; in 1797–1799, *Oriental Collections*; in 1799, *Epitome of the Ancient History of Persia*; in 1800, *The Oriental Geography of Ebn Haukal*; and in 1801, a translation of the *Bakhtiyār Nama* and *Observations on Some Medals and Gems*. He received the degree of LL.D. from the university of Dublin in 1797, and in 1800 he was knighted. When his brother, Sir Gore Ouseley, was sent, in 1810, as ambassador to Persia, Sir William accompanied him as secretary. He returned to England in 1813, and in 1819–1823 published, in three volumes, *Travels in Various Countries of the East, especially Persia, in 1810, 1811 and 1812*. He also published editions of the *Travels* and *Arabian Proverbs* of Burckhardt. He contributed a number of important papers to the *Transactions* of the Royal Society of Literature.' He died at Boulogne in September 1842.

OUSTER (from Anglo-Fr. *ouster*, to remove, take away, O. Fr. *oster*, mod. Fr. *ôter*, Eng. " oust," to eject, exclude; the derivation is not known; Lat. *obstare*, to stand in the way of, resist, would give the form but does not suit the sense; a more probable suggestion connects with a supposed *haustare*, from *haurire*, to draw water; cf. " exhaust "), a legal term signifying dispossession, especially the wrong or injury suffered by a person dispossessed of freeholds or chattels real. The wrong-doer by getting into occupation forces the real owner to take legal steps to regain his rights. Ouster of the freehold may be effected by *abatement*; i.e. by entry on the death of the person seized before the entry of the heir, or devisee, by *intrusion*, entry after the death of the tenant for life before the entry of the reversioner or remainderman, by *disseisin*, the forcible or fraudulent expulsion of the occupier or person seized of the property. Ouster of chattels real is effected by *disseisin*, the turning out by force or fraud of the legal proprietor before his estate is determined. In feudal law, the term *ouster-le-main* (Lat. *amovere manum*, to take away the hand) was applied to a writ or judgment granting the livery of land out of the sovereign's hand on the plea that he has no title to it, and also to the delivery by a guardian of land to a ward on his coming of age.

OUTLAWRY, the process of putting a person out of the protection of the law; a punishment for contemptuously refusing to appear when called in court, or evading justice by disappearing. It was an offence of very early existence in England, and was the punishment of those who could not pay the *wers* or blood-money to the relatives of the deceased. By the Saxon law, an outlaw, or *laughlesman*, lost his *libera lex* and had no protection from the frank-pledge in the decennary in which he was sworn. He was, too, a *frendlesman*, because he forfeited

his friends;' for if any of them rendered him any assistance, they became liable to the same punishment. He was, at one time, said to be *caput lupinum*, or to have a wolf's head, from the fact that he might be knocked on the head like a wolf by any one that should meet him; but so early as the time of Bracton an outlaw might be killed if he defended himself or ran away; once taken, his life was in the king's hands, and any one killing him had to answer for it as for any other homicide. The party guilty of outlawry suffered forfeiture of chattels in all cases, and in cases of treason or murder forfeiture of real property: for other offences the profits of land during his lifetime. In cases of treason or felony, outlawry was followed also by corruption of blood. An outlaw was *civiliter mortuus*. He could not sue in any court, nor had he any legal rights which could be enforced, but he was personally liable upon all causes of action. An outlawry might be reversed by proceedings in error, or by application to a court. It was finally abolished in civil proceedings in 1879, while in criminal proceedings it has practically become obsolete, being unnecessary through the general adoption of extradition treaties. A woman was said to be *waived* rather than outlawed.

In Scotland outlawry or fugitation may be pronounced by the supreme criminal court in the absence of the panel on the day of trial. In the United States outlawry never existed in civil cases, and in the few cases where it existed in criminal proceedings it has become obsolete.

OUTRAGE (through O. Fr. *ultrage*, *oltrage*, *oultrage*, from Lat. *ultra*, beyond, exceeding, cf. Ital. *oltraggio*; the meaning has been influenced by connexion with " rage," anger), originally extravagance, violence of behaviour, language, action, &c., hence especially a violent injury done to another.

OUTRAM, SIR JAMES (1803–1863), English general, and one of the heroes of the Indian Mutiny, was the son of Benjamin Outram of Butterley Hall, Derbyshire, civil engineer, and was born on the 29th of January 1803. His father died in 1805; and his mother, a daughter of Dr James Anderson, the Scottish writer on agriculture, removed in 1810 to Aberdeenshire. From Udny school the boy went in 1818 to the Marischal College, Aberdeen; and in 1819 an Indian cadetship was given him. Soon after his arrival at Bombay his remarkable energy attracted notice, and in July 1820 he became acting adjutant to the first battalion of the 12th regiment on its embodiment at Poona, an experience which he found to be of immense advantage to him in his after career. In 1825 he was sent to Khandesh, where he trained a light infantry corps, formed of the wild robber Bhils, gaining over them a marvellous personal influence, and employing them with great success in checking outrages and plunder. Their loyalty to him had its principal source in their boundless admiration of his hunting achievements, which in cool daring and hairbreadth escapes have perhaps never been equalled. Originally a " puny lad," and for many years after his arrival in India subject to constant attacks of sickness, Outram seemed to win strength by every new illness, acquiring a constitution of iron, " nerves of steel, shoulders and muscles worthy of a six-foot Highlander." In 1835 he was sent to Gujarat to make a report on the Mahi Kantha district, and for some time he remained there as political agent. On the outbreak of the first Afghan War in 1838 he was appointed extra aide-de-camp on the staff of Sir John Keane, and, besides many other brilliant deeds performed an extraordinary exploit in capturing a banner of the enemy before Ghazni. After conducting various raids against Afghan tribes, he was in 1839 promoted major, and appointed political agent in Lower Sind, and later in Upper Sind. Here he strongly opposed the policy of his superior, Sir Charles Napier, which led to the annexation of Sind. But when war broke out he heroically defended the residency at Hyderabad against 8000 Baluchis; and it was Sir C. Napier who then described him as " the Bayard of India." On his return from a short visit to England in 1843, he was, with the rank of brevet lieutenant-colonel, appointed to a command in the Mahratta country, and in 1847 he was transferred from Satara to Baroda, where he incurred the resentment of the Bombay government by his fearless exposure of corruption.

In 1854 he was appointed resident at Lucknow, in which capacity two years later he carried out the annexation of Oudh and became the first chief commissioner of that province. Appointed in 1857, with the rank of lieutenant-general, to command an expedition against Persia, he defeated the enemy with great slaughter at Khushab, and conducted the campaign with such rapid decision that peace was shortly afterwards concluded, his services being rewarded by the grand cross of the Bath.

From Persia he was summoned in June to India, with the brief explanation— "We want all our best men here." It was said of him at this time that "a fox is a fool and a lion a coward by the side of Sir J. Outram." Immediately on his arrival in Calcutta he was appointed to command the two divisions of the Bengal army occupying the country from Calcutta to Cawnpore; and to the military control was also joined the commissionership of Oudh. Already the mutiny had assumed such proportions as to compel Havelock to fall back on Cawnpore, which he only held with difficulty, although a speedy advance was necessary to save the garrison at Lucknow. On arriving at Cawnpore with reinforcements, Outram, "in admiration of the brilliant deeds of General Havelock," conceded to him the glory of relieving Lucknow, and, waiving his rank, tendered his services to him as a volunteer. During the advance he commanded a troop of volunteer cavalry, and performed exploits of great brilliancy at Mangalwar, and in the attack at the Alambagh; and in the final conflict he led the way, charging through a very tempest of fire. The volunteer cavalry unanimously voted him the Victoria Cross, but he refused the choice on the ground that he was ineligible as the general under whom they served. Resuming supreme command, he then held the town till the arrival of Sir Colin Campbell, after which he conducted the evacuation of the residency so as completely to deceive the enemy. In the second capture of Lucknow, on the commander-in-chief's return, Outram was entrusted with the attack on the side of the Gumti, and afterwards, having recrossed the river, he advanced "through the Chattar Manzil to take the residency," thus, in the words of Sir Colin Campbell, "putting the finishing stroke on the enemy." After the capture of Lucknow he was gazetted lieutenant-general. In February 1858 he received the special thanks of both houses of parliament, and in the same year the dignity of baronet with an annuity of £1000. When, on account of shattered health, he returned finally to England in 1860, a movement was set on foot to mark the sense entertained, not only of his military achievements, but of his constant exertions on behalf of the natives of India, whose "weal," in his own words, "he made his first object." The movement resulted in the presentation of a public testimonial and the erection of statues in London and Calcutta. He died on the 11th of March 1863, and was buried in Westminster Abbey, where the marble slab on his grave bears the pregnant epitaph "The Bayard of India."

See Sir F. J. Goldsmid, *James Outram, a Biography* (2 vols., 1880), and L. J. Trotter, *The Bayard of India* (1903).

OVAL (Lat. *ovum*, egg), in geometry, a closed curve, generally more or less egg-like in form. The simplest oval is the ellipse; more complicated forms are represented in the notation of analytical geometry by equations of the 4th, 6th, 8th . . . degrees. Those of the 4th degree, known as bicircular quartics, are the most important, and of these the special forms named after Descartes and Cassini are of most interest. The Cartesian ovals presented themselves in an investigation of the section of a surface which would refract rays proceeding from a point in a medium of one refractive index into a point in a medium of a different refractive index. The most convenient equation is $lr = mr' = n$, where r, r' are the distances of a point on the curve from two fixed and given points, termed the foci, and l, m, n are constants. The curve is obviously symmetrical about the line joining the foci, and has the important property that the normal at any point divides the angle between the radii into segments whose sines are in the ratio $l : m$. The Cassinian oval has the equation $rr' = a^2$, where r, r' are the radii of a point on the curve from two given foci, and a is a constant. This curve is symmetrical about two perpendicular axes. It may consist of a single closed curve or of two curves, according to the value of a; the transition between the two types being a figure of 8, better known as Bernoulli's lemniscate (*q.v.*).

See CURVE; also Salmon, *Higher Plane Curves.*

OVAR, a town of Portugal, in the district of Aveiro and at the northern extremity of the Lagoon of Aveiro (*q.v.*); 21 m. S. of Oporto by the Lisbon-Oporto railway, Pop. (1900) 10,462. Ovar is the centre of important fisheries and has some trade in wine and timber. It is visited by small coasting vessels which ply to and from north-west Africa. Millet, wheat and vegetables —especially onions—are the chief products of the low-lying and unhealthy region, in which Ovar is situated.

OVARIOTOMY, the operation for removal of one or of both of the female ovaries (for anatomy see REPRODUCTIVE SYSTEM). The progress of modern surgery has been conspicuously successful in this department. From 1701, the date when Houston of Carluke, Lanarkshire, carried out his successful partial extirpation, progress was arrested for some time, although the Hunters (1780) indicated the practicability of the operation. In 1809 Ephraim M'Dowell of Kentucky, inspired by the lectures of John Bell, his teacher in Edinburgh, performed ovariotomy, and, continuing to operate with success, established the possibility of surgical interference. He was followed by others in the United States. The cases brought forward by Lizars of Edinburgh were not sufficiently encouraging; the operation met with great opposition; and it was not until Charles Clay, Spencer Wells, Baker Brown and Thomas Keith began work that the procedure was placed on a firm basis and was regarded as justifiable. Improved methods were introduced, and surgeons vied with one another in trying to obtain good results. Eventually, by the introduction of the antiseptic system of treating wounds, this operation, formerly regarded as one of the most grave and anxious in the domain of surgery, came to be attended with a lower mortality than any other of a major character.

To give an idea of the terrible record associated with the operation in the third quarter of the 19th century, a passage may be quoted from the English translation of the *Life of Pasteur*: "As it was supposed that the infected air of the hospitals might be the cause of the invariably fatal results of the operation, the Assistance Publique hired an isolated house in the Avenue de Meudon, near Paris, a salubrious spot. In 1863, ten women in succession were sent to that house; the neighbouring inhabitants watched those ten patients entering the house, and a short time afterwards their ten coffins being taken away." But as time went on, the published statistics showed an increasing success in the practice of almost every operator. Spencer Wells states that in his first five years one patient in three died; in his second and third five years one in four; in his fourth five years one in five; in 1876-1877, one in ten. After the introduction of antiseptics (1878-1884) he lost only 10.9% of his operation cases, but this series showing a marked absence of septic complications. These figures have been greatly improved upon in later years, and at the present time the mortality may be taken at somewhere about 5, 7 or 9%.

Removal of the ovaries is performed when the ovaries are the seat of cystic and other morbid changes; for fibroid tumours of the womb, in which case, by operating, one hastens the menopause and causes the tumours to grow smaller; and in cases where dysmenorrhoea is wearing out and rendering useless the life of the patient—less severe treatment having proved ineffectual. *Oophorectomy,* by which is meant removal of the ovaries with the view of producing a curative effect upon some other part, was introduced in 1872 by Robert Battey of Georgia (1828-1895). The operation is sometimes followed by loss of sexual feeling, and has been said to unsex the patient, hence strong objections have been urged against it. The patient and her friends should clearly understand the object of the operation and the results likely to be gained by it. Lastly, the ovaries are sometimes removed with the hope of checking the progress of inoperable cancer of the breast.

From the time that the operation of ovariotomy was first established as a recognized and lawful surgical procedure, there has been much disputation as to how the pedicle of the ovary, which consists of a fold of peritoneum (the broad ligament) with included blood-vessels, should be treated. Some operators were in favour of tying it with strong silk, and bringing the ends of the ligatures outside the abdomen. Others were in favour of having a strong metal clamp upon those structures, or of searing them with the actual cautery, whilst others claimed that the best results were to be obtained by firmly tying the pedicle, cutting the ligatures short, dropping the pedicle into the abdomen and closing the wound. This last method is now almost universally adopted.   (E. O.")

OVATION (Lat. *ovatio*), a minor form of Roman "triumph." It was awarded either when the campaign, though victorious, had not been important enough for the higher honour; when the war was not entirely put an end to; when it had been waged with unworthy foes; or when the general was not of rank sufficient to give him the right to a triumph. The ceremonial was on the whole similar in the two cases, but in an ovation the general walked or more commonly rode on horseback, wore a simple magisterial robe, carried no sceptre and wore a wreath of myrtle instead of laurel. Instead of a bull, a sheep was sacrificed at the conclusion of the ceremony. The word is not, however, derived from *ovis*, sheep, but probably means "shouting" (cp. αὔω) as a sign of rejoicing.

OVEN (O. Eng. *ofn*, Ger. *Ofen*, cf. Gr. ἰπνός, oven), a close chamber or compartment which may be raised to a considerable temperature by heat generated either within or without it. In English the term generally refers to a chamber for baking bread and other food substances, but it is also used of certain appliances employed in manufacturing operations, as in coking coal or making pottery. See HEATING.

OVERBECK, JOHANN FRIEDRICH (1789–1869), German painter, the reviver of "Christian art" in the 19th century, was born in Lübeck on the 4th of July 1789. His ancestors for three generations had been Protestant pastors; his father was doctor of laws, poet, mystic pietist and burgomaster of Lübeck. Within a stone's throw of the family mansion in the Königstrasse stood the gymnasium, where the uncle, doctor of theology and a voluminous writer, was the master; there the nephew became a classic scholar and received instruction in art.

The young artist left Lübeck in March 1806, and entered as student the academy of Vienna, then under the direction of F. H. Füger, a painter of some renown, of the pseudo-classic school of the French David. Here was gained thorough knowledge, but the teachings and associations proved unendurable to the sensitive, spiritual-minded youth. Overbeck wrote to a friend that he had fallen among a vulgar set, that every noble thought was suppressed within the academy and that losing all faith in humanity he turned inwardly on himself. These words are a key to his future position and art. It seemed to him that in Vienna, and indeed throughout Europe, the pure springs of Christian art had been for centuries diverted and corrupted, and so he sought out afresh the living source, and, casting on one side his contemporaries, took for his guides the early and pre-Raphaelite painters of Italy. At the end of four years, differences had grown so irreconcilable that Overbeck and his band of followers were expelled from the academy. True art, he writes, he had sought in Vienna in vain—" Oh! I was full of it; my whole fancy was possessed by Madonnas and Christs, but nowhere could I find response." Accordingly he left for Rome, carrying his half-finished canvas " Christ's Entry into Jerusalem," as the charter of his creed—" I will abide by the Bible; I elect it as my standing-point."

Overbeck in 1810 entered Rome, which became for fifty-nine years the centre of his unremitting labour. He was joined by a goodly company, including Cornelius, Wilhelm Schadow and Philip Veit, who took up their abode in the old Franciscan convent of San Isidoro on the Pincian Hill, and were known among friends and enemies by the descriptive epithets—" the Nazarites," " the pre-Raphaelites," " the new-old school," " the German-Roman artists," " the church-romantic painters," " the German patriotic and religious painters." Their precept was hard and honest work and holy living; they eschewed the antique as pagan, the Renaissance as false, and built up a severe revival on simple nature and on the serious art of Perugino, Pinturicchio, Francia and the young Raphael. The characteristics of the style thus educed were nobility of idea, precision

and even hardness of outline, scholastic composition, with the addition of light, shade and colour, not for allurement, but chiefly for perspicuity and completion of motive. Overbeck was mentor in the movement; a fellow-labourer writes: " No one who saw him or heard him speak could question his purity of motive, his deep insight and abounding knowledge; he is a treasury of art and poetry, and a saintly man." But the struggle was hard and poverty its reward. Helpful friends, however, came in Niebuhr, Bunsen and Frederick Schlegel. Overbeck in 1813 joined the Roman Catholic Church, and thereby he believed that his art received Christian baptism.

Faith in a mission begat enthusiasm among kindred minds, and timely commissions followed. The Prussian consul, Bartholdi, had a house on the brow of the Pincian, and he engaged Overbeck, Cornelius, Veit and Schadow to decorate a room 24 ft. square with frescoes (now in the Berlin gallery) from the story of Joseph and his Brethren. The subjects which fell to the lot of Overbeck were the " Seven Years of Famine " and " Joseph sold by his Brethren." These tentative wall-pictures, finished in 1818, produced so favourable an impression among the Italians that in the same year Prince Massimo commissioned Overbeck, Cornelius, Veit and Schnorr to cover the walls and ceilings of his garden pavilion, near St John Lateran, with frescoes illustrative of Tasso, Dante and Ariosto. To Overbeck was assigned, in a room 15 ft. square, the illustration of Tasso's *Jerusalem Delivered*; and of eleven compositions the largest and most noteworthy, occupying one entire wall, is the " Meeting of Godfrey de Bouillon and Peter the Hermit." The completion of the frescoes—very unequal in merit—after ten years' delay, the overtaxed and enfeebled painter delegated to his friend Joseph Führich. The leisure thus gained was devoted to a thoroughly congenial theme, the " Vision of St Francis," a wall-painting 20 ft. long, figures life size, finished in 1830, for the church of Sta Maria degli Angeli near Assisi. Overbeck and the brethren set themselves the task of recovering the neglected art of fresco and of monumental painting; they adopted the old methods, and their success led to memorable revivals throughout Europe.

Fifty years of the artist's laborious life were given to oil and easel paintings, of which the chief, for size and import, are the following: " Christ's Entry into Jerusalem " (1824), in the Marien Kirche, Lübeck; " Christ's Agony in the Garden " (1835), in the great hospital, Hamburg; " Lo Sposalizio " (1836), Raczynski gallery, Berlin; the " Triumph of Religion in the Arts " (1840), in the Städel Institut, Frankfort; " Pietà " (1846), in the Marien Kirche, Lübeck; the " Incredulity of St Thomas " (1851), in the possession of Mr Beresford Hope, London; the " Assumption of the Madonna " (1855), in Cologne Cathedral; " Christ delivered from the Jews " (1858), tempera, on a ceiling in the Quirinal Palace—a commission from Pius IX., and a direct attack on the Italian temporal government, therefore now covered by a canvas adorned with Cupids. All the artist's works are marked by religious fervour, careful and protracted study, with a dry, severe handling, and an abstemious colour.

Overbeck belongs to eclectic schools, and yet was creative; he ranks among thinkers, and his pen was hardly less busy than his pencil. He was a minor poet, an essayist and a voluminous letter-writer. His style is wordy and tedious; like his art it is borne down with emotion and possessed by a somewhat morbid " subjectivity." His pictures were didactic, and used as means of propaganda for his artistic and religious faith, and the teachings of such compositions as the " Triumph of Religion and the Sacraments " he enforced by rapturous literary effusions. His art was the issue of his life: his constant thoughts, cherished in solitude and chastened by prayer, he transposed into pictorial forms, and thus were evolved countless and much-prized drawings and cartoons, of which the most considerable are the Gospels, forty cartoons (1852); Via Crucis, fourteen water-colour drawings (1857); the Seven Sacraments, seven cartoons (1861). Overbeck's compositions, with few exceptions, are engraved. His life-work he sums up in the words—" Art to me is as the harp of David, whereupon I would desire that psalms should at all times be sounded to the praise of the Lord." He died in Rome in

1869, aged eighty, and lies buried in San Bernardo, the church wherein he worshipped.

There are biographies by J. Beavington Atkinson (1882) and Howitt (1886).   (J. B. A.)

OVERBURY, SIR THOMAS (1581–1613), English poet and essayist, and the victim of one of the most sensational crimes in English history, was the son of Nicholas Overbury, of Bourton-on-the-Hill, and was born in 1581 at Compton Scorpion, near Ilmington, in Warwickshire. In the autumn of 1595 he became a gentleman commoner of Queen's College, Oxford, took his degree of B.A. in 1598 and came to London to study law in the Middle Temple. He found favour with Sir Robert Cecil, travelled on the Continent and began to enjoy a reputation for an accomplished mind and free manners. About the year 1601, being in Edinburgh on a holiday, he met Robert Carr, then an obscure page to the earl of Dunbar; and so great a friendship was struck up between the two youths that they came up to London together. The early history of Carr remains obscure, and it is probable that Overbury secured an introduction to Court before his young associate contrived to do so. At all events, when Carr attracted the attention of James I., in 1606, by breaking his leg in the tilt-yard, Overbury had for some time been servitor-in-ordinary to the king. He was knighted in June 1608, and in 1609 he travelled in France and the Low Countries. He seems to have followed the fortunes of Carr very closely, and "such was the warmth of the friendship, that they were inseparable, . . . nor could Overbury enjoy any felicity but in the company of him he loved [Carr]." When the latter was made Lord Rochester in 1610, the intimacy seems to have been sustained. But it was now destroyed by a new element. Early in 1611 the Court became aware of the mutual attraction between Rochester and the infamous and youthful countess of Essex, who seemed to have bewitched the handsome Scots adventurer. To this intrigue Overbury was from the first violently opposed, pointing out to Rochester that an indulgence in it would be hurtful to his preferment, and that the woman, even at this early stage in her career, was already "noted for her injury and immodesty." He went so far as to use, in describing her, a word which was not more just than scandalous. But Rochester was now infatuated, and he repeated to the countess what Overbury had said. It was at this time, too, that Overbury wrote, and circulated widely in MS., the poem called "His Wife," which was a picture of the virtues which a young man should demand in a woman before he has the rashness to marry her. It was represented to Lady Essex that Overbury's object in writing this poem was to open the eyes of Rochester to her defects. The situation now resolved itself into a deadly duel for the person of Rochester between the mistress and the friend. The countess contrived to lead Overbury into such a trap as to make him seem disrespectful to the king, and she succeeded so completely that he was thrown into the Tower on the 22nd of April 1613. It was not known at the time, and it is not certain now, how far Rochester participated in this first crime, or whether he was ignorant of it. But the queen, by a foolish phrase, had sown discord between the friends; she had called Overbury Rochester's "governor." It is, indeed, apparent that Overbury had become arrogant with success, and was no longer a favourite at Court. Lady Essex, however, was not satisfied with having had him shut up; she was determined that "he should return no more to this stage." She had Sir William Wade, the honest Governor of the Tower, removed to make way for a creature of her own, Sir Gervaise Elvis (or Helwys); and a gaoler, of whom it was ominously said that he was "a man well acquainted with the power of drugs," was set to attend on Overbury. This fellow, afterwards aided by Mrs Turner, the widow of a physician, and by an apothecary called Franklin, plied the miserable poet with sulphuric acid in the form of copper vitriol. But his constitution long withstood the timid doses they gave him, and he lingered in exquisite sufferings until the 15th of September 1613, when more violent measures put an end to his existence. Two months later Rochester, now earl of Somerset, married the chief murderess, Lady Essex. More than a year passed before

suspicion was roused, and when it was, the king showed a hateful disinclination to bring the offenders to justice. In the celebrated trial which followed, however, the wicked plot was all discovered. The four accomplices were hanged; the countess of Somerset pleaded guilty but was spared, and Somerset himself was disgraced. Meanwhile, Overbury's poem, The Wife, was published in 1614, and ran through six editions within a year, the scandal connected with the murder of the author greatly aiding its success. It was abundantly reprinted within the next sixty years, and it continued to be one of the most widely popular books of the 17th century. Combined with later editions of The Wife, and gradually adding to its bulk, were "Characters" (first printed in the second of the 1614 editions), "The Remedy of Love" (1620), and "Observations in Foreign Travels" (1626). Later, much that must be spurious was added to the gathering snowball of Overbury's Works. Posterity has found the praise of his contemporaries for the sententious and graceful moral verse of Overbury extravagantly expressed. The Wife is smooth and elegant, but uninspired. There is no question that the horrible death of the writer, and the extraordinary way in which his murderers were brought to justice, gave an extraneous charm to his writings. Nor can we be quite sure that Overbury was in fact such a "glorious constellation" of all the religious virtues as the 17th century believed. He certainly kept very bad company, and positive evidence of his goodness is wanting. But no one was ever more transcendently canonized by becoming the victim of conspirators whose crimes were equally détestable and unpopular.   (E. G.)

OVERDOOR, the name given to any ornamental moulding placed over a door. The overdoor is usually architectural in form, but is sometimes little more than a moulded shelf for the reception of china or curiosities.

OVERMANTEL, the name given to decorative cabinet work, or joinery, applied to the upper part of a fireplace. The overmantel is derived from the carved panelling formerly applied to chimney-pieces of importance, but the word is now generally restricted to a movable fitment, often consisting of a series of shelves and niches for the reception of ornaments.

OVERSOUL (Ger. Überseele), the name adopted by Emerson to describe his conception of that transcendent unity which embraces subject and object, mind and matter, and in which all the differences in virtue of which particular things exist are absorbed. The idea is analogous to the various doctrines of the absolute, and to the idia of Plato.

OVERSTONE, SAMUEL JONES LOYD, 1st BARON (1796–1883), English banker, the only son of the Rev. Lewis Loyd, a Welsh dissenting minister, was born on the 25th of September 1796. He was educated at Eton and Trinity College, Cambridge. His father, who had married a daughter of John Jones, a banker of Manchester, had given up the ministry to take a partnership in his father-in-law's bank, and had afterwards founded the London branch of Jones, Loyd & Co., afterwards incorporated in the London and Westminster Bank. Loyd, who had joined his father in the banking business, succeeded to it on the latter's retirement in 1844. He conducted the business so successfully that on his death he left personal property of over £2,000,000. He sat in parliament as liberal member for Hythe from 1819 to 1826, and unsuccessfully contested Manchester in 1832. As early as 1832 he was recognized as one of the foremost authorities on banking, and he enjoyed much influence with successive ministries and chancellors of the exchequer. He was created Baron Overstone in 1850. He died in London on the 17th of November 1883, leaving one daughter, who married Robert James Loyd-Lindsay, afterwards Lord Wantage.

OVERT ACT (O. Fr. overt, from ouvrir, to open), in law, an open act, one that can be clearly proved by evidence, and from which criminal intent can be inferred, as opposed to a mere intention in the mind to commit a crime (see INTENT). The term is more particularly employed in cases of treason (q.v.), which must be demonstrated by some overt or open act.

OVERTURE (Fr. ouverture, opening), in music, the instrumental introduction to a dramatic or choral composition. The notion of an overture thus has no existence until the 17th century. The *toccata* at the beginning of Monteverde's *Orfeo* is a barbaric flourish of every procurable instrument, alternating with a melodious section entitled *ritornello*; and, in so far as this constitutes the first instrumental movement prefixed to an opera, it may be called an overture. As an art-form the overture began to exist in the works of J. B. Lully. He devised a scheme which, although he himself did not always adhere to it, constitutes the typical French overture up to the time of Bach and Handel (whose works have made it classical). This French overture consists of a slow introduction in a marked " dotted rhythm" (*i.e.* exaggerated iambic, if the first chord is disregarded), followed by a lively movement in fugato style. The slow introduction was always repeated, and sometimes the quick movement concluded by returning to the slow tempo and material, and was also repeated (see Bach's French Overture in the *Klavierübung*).

The operatic French overture was frequently followed by a series of dance tunes before the curtain rose. It thus naturally became used as the prelude to a suite; and the *Klavierübung* French Overture of Bach is a case in point, the overture proper being the introduction to a suite of seven dances. For the same reason Bach's four orchestral suites are called overtures; and, again, the prelude to the fourth partita in the *Klavierübung* is an overture.

Bach was able to use the French overture form for choruses, and even for the treatment of chorales. Thus the overture, properly so called, of his fourth orchestral suite became the first chorus of the church cantata *Unser Mund sei voll Lachens*; the choruses of the cantatas *Preise Jerusalem den Herrn* and *Höchst erwünschtes Freudenfest* are in overture form; and, in the first of the two cantatas entitled *Nun komm der Heiden Heiland*, Bach has ingeniously adapted the overture form to the treatment of a chorale.

With the rise of dramatic music and the sonata style, the French overture became unsuitable for opera; and Gluck (whose remarks on the function of overtures in the preface to *Alceste* are historic) based himself on Italian models, of loose texture, which admit of a sweeping and massively contrasted technique (see SYMPHONY). By the time of Mozart's later works the overture in the sonata style had clearly differentiated itself from strictly symphonic music. It consists of a quick movement (with or without a slow introduction), in sonata form, loose in texture, without repeats, frequently without a development section, but sometimes substituting for it a melodious episode in slow time. Instances of this substitution are Mozart's " symphony " in G (Köchel's catalogue 318), which is an overture to an unknown opera, and his overtures to *Die Entführung* and to *Lo Sposo deluso*, in both of which cases the curtain rises at a point which throws a remarkable dramatic light upon the peculiar form. The overture to *Figaro* was at first intended to have a similar slow middle section, which, however, Mozart struck out as soon as he had begun it. In Beethoven's hands the overture style and form increased its distinction from that of the symphony, but it no longer remained inferior to it; and the final version of the overture to *Leonora* (that known as No. 3) is the most gigantic single orchestral movement ever based on the sonata style.

Overtures to plays, such as Beethoven's to Collin's *Coriolan*, naturally tend to become detached from their surroundings; and hence arises the concert overture, second only to the symphony in importance as a purely orchestral art-form. Its derivation associates it almost inevitably with external poetic ideas. These, if sufficiently broad, need in no way militate against musical integrity of form; and Mendelssohn's *Hebrides* overture is as perfect a masterpiece as can be found in any art. The same applies to Brahms's *Tragic Overture*, one of his grandest orchestral works, for which a more explanatory title would be misleading as well as unnecessary. His *Academic Festival Overture* is a highly organized working out of German student songs.

In modern opera the overture, *Vorspiel*, *Einleitung*, *Introduction*, or whatever else it may be called, is generally nothing more definite than that portion of the music which takes place before the curtain rises. *Tannhäuser* is the last case of high importance in which the overture (as originally written) is a really complete instrumental piece prefixed to an opera in tragic and continuous dramatic style. In lighter opera, where sectional forms are still possible, a separable overture is not out of place, though even *Carmen* is remarkable in the dramatic way in which its overture foreshadows the tragic end and leads directly to the rise of the curtain. Wagner's Vorspiel to *Lohengrin* is a short self-contained movement founded on the music of the Grail. With all its wonderful instrumentation, romantic beauty and identity with subsequent music in the first and third acts, it does not represent a further departure from the formal classical overture than that shown fifty years earlier by Méhul's interesting overtures to *Ariodant* and *Uthal*, in the latter of which a voice is several times heard on the stage before the rise of the curtain. The Vorspiel to *Die Meistersinger*, though very enjoyable by itself and needing only an additional tonic chord to bring it to an end, really loses incalculably in refinement by so ending in a concert room. In its proper position its otherwise disproportionate climax leads to the rise of the curtain and the engaging of the listener's mind in a crowd of dramatic and spectacular sensations amply adequate to account for that long introductory instrumental *crescendo*. The Vorspiel to *Tristan* has been very beautifully finished for concert use by Wagner himself, and the considerable length and subtlety of the added page shows how little calculated for independent existence the original Vorspiel was. Lastly, the *Parsifal* Vorspiel is a composition which, though finished for concert use by Wagner in a few extra bars, asserts itself with the utmost lucidity and force as a prelude to some vast design. The orchestral preludes to the four dramas of the *Ring* owe their whole meaning to their being mere preparations for the rise of the curtain; and these works can no more be said to have overtures than Verdi's *Falstaff* and Strauss's *Salome*, in which the curtain rises at the first note of the music.
(D. F. T.)

OVERYSEL, or **OVERIJSEL**, a province of Holland, bounded S. and S.W. by Gelderland, N.W. by the Zuider Zee, N. by Friesland and Drente, and E. by the Prussian provinces of Hanover and Westphalia respectively; area 1291 sq. m.; pop. (1904) 359,443. It includes the island of Schokland in the Zuider Zee. Like Drente on the north and Gelderland on the south, Overysel consists of a sandy flat relieved by hillocks, and is covered with waste stretches of heath and patches of wood and high fen. Along the shores of the Zuider Zee, however, west of the Zwolle-Leeuwarden railway, the country is low-lying and covered for the most part with fertile pasture lands. Cattle-rearing and butter and cheese making are consequently the chief occupations, while on the coast many of the people are engaged in making mats and besoms. The river system of the province is determined by two main ridges of hills. The first of these extends from the southern border at Markelo to the Lemeler bill (262 ft.) near the confluence of the Vecht and Regge, and forms the watershed between the Regge and the Salland streams (Sala, whence Salis, Isala, Ysel), which unite at Zwolle to form the Zwarte Water. The other ridge of hills extends through the south-eastern division of the province called Twente, from Enschede to Ootmarsum, and divides the basin of the Almelosche Aa from the Dinkel and its streams. The river Vecht crosses the province from E. to W. and joins the Zwarte Water, which communicates with the Zuider Zee by the Zwolsche Diep and with the Ysel by the Willemsvaart. Everywhere along the streams is a strip of fertile grass-land, from which agriculture and cattle-rearing have gradually spread over the sand-grounds. A large proportion of the sand-grounds, however, is waste. Forest culture is practised on parts of them, especially in the east, and pigs are largely bred. The deposits of the Salland and the Dinkel streams are found to contain iron ore, which is extracted and forms an article of export to Germany. Peat-digging and fen reclamation have been carried on from an early period, and the area of high fen which formerly covered the portion of the province to the north of the Vecht in the neighbourhood of Dedemsvaart has been mostly reclaimed. This industry is now most active on the eastern borders between Almelo and Hardenberg, Vriezenveen being the chief fen colony. Cotton-spinning, together with bleaching-works, has come into prominence in the 19th century in the district of Twente. The reason of its isolated settlement here is to be found in the former general practice of weaving as a home craft and its organization as an industry by capitalist Baptist refugees who arrived in the 17th and 18th centuries. The chief town of the province is Zwolle, and other thriving industrial centres are Deventer, famous for its carpets and cake, and Almelo, Enschede, Hengelo and Oldenzaal in Twente. Kampen, Genemuiden, Vollenhove and Blokzyl, on the Zuider Zee, carry on some fishing trade. Near Vollenhove was the castle of Toutenburg, built in 1502–1533 by the famous stadtholder of the emperor Charles V., George Schenk. The castle was demolished in the beginning of the 19th century and the remains are slight. The railway system of the province is supplemented by steam tram-lines between Zwolle, Dedemsvaart and Hardenberg.

OVID [PUBLIUS OVIDIUS NASO] (43 B.C.–A.D. 17), Roman poet, the last of the Augustan age, was born in 43 B.C., the last year of the republic, the year of the death of Cicero. Thus the only form of political life known to Ovid was that of the absolute rule of Augustus and his successor. His character was neither strengthened nor sobered, like that of his older contemporaries, by personal recollection of the crisis through which the republic passed into the empire. There is no sense of political freedom in his writings. The spirit inherited from his ancestors was that of the Italian country districts, not that of Rome. He was born on the 20th of March (his self-consciousness has preserved the exact day of the month)[1] at Sulmo, now Sulmona, a town of the Paeligni, picturesquely situated among the mountains of the Abruzzi: its wealth of waters and natural beauties seem to have strongly affected the young poet's imagination (for he often speaks of them with affectionate admiration) and to have quickened in him that appreciative eye for the beauties of nature which is one of the chief characteristics of his poems. The Paeligni were one of the four small mountain peoples whose proudest memories were of the part they had played in the Social War. But in spite of this they had no old race-hostility with Rome, and their opposition to the senatorial aristocracy in the Social War would predispose them to accept the empire. Ovid, whose father was of equestrian family, belonged by birth to the same social class as Tibullus and Propertius, that of old hereditary landowners; but he was more fortunate than they in the immunity which his native district enjoyed from the confiscations made by the triumvirs. His vigorous vitality was apparently a gift transmitted to him by heredity; for he tells us that his father lived till the age of ninety, and that he performed the funeral rites to his mother after his father's death. While he mentions both with the piety characteristic of the old Italian, he tells us little more about them than that " their thrift curtailed his youthful expenses,"[2] and that his father did what he could to dissuade him from poetry, and force him into the more profitable career of the law. He and his brother had been brought early to Rome for their education, where they attended the lectures of two most eminent teachers of rhetoric, Arellius Fuscus and Porcius Latro, to which influence is due the strong rhetorical element in Ovid's style. He is said to have attended these lectures eagerly, and to have shown in his exercises that his gift was poetical rather than oratorical, and that he had a distaste for the severer processes of thought.

Like Pope, " he lisped in numbers,"[3] and he wrote and destroyed many verses before he published anything. The earliest edition of the *Amores*, which first appeared in five books, and the *Heroides* were given by him to the world at an early age. " Virgil," he informs us, " he had only seen "; but Virgil's friend and contemporary Aemilius Macer used to read his didactic poems to him; and even the fastidious Horace some-

[1] *Trist.* iv. 10. 13.   [3] *Am.* i. 3. 10.
[2] *Trist.* iv. 10. 26 " et quod temptabam scribere, versus erat."

times delighted his ears with the music of his verse. He had a close bond of intimacy with the younger poets of the older generation—Tibullus, whose death he laments in one of the few pathetic pieces among his earlier writings, and Propertius, to whom he describes himself as united in the close ties of comradeship. The name of Maecenas he nowhere mentions. The time of his influence was past when Ovid entered upon his poetical career. But the veteran politician Messalla, the friend of Tibullus, together with his powerful son Cotta Messallinus and Fabius Maximus, who are mentioned together by Juvenal[4] along with Maecenas as types of munificent patrons of letters, and other influential persons whose names are preserved in the *Epistles from Pontus*, encouraged his literary efforts and extended to him their support. He enjoyed also the intimacy of poets and literary men, chiefly of the younger generation, whose names he enumerates in *Ex Ponto*, iv. 16, though, with the exception of Domitius Marsus and Grattius, they are scarcely more than names to us. With the older poet, Macer, he travelled for more than a year. Whether this was immediately after the completion of his education, or in the interval between the publication of his earlier poems and that of the *Medea* and *Ars amatoria* is unknown, but it is in his later works, the *Fasti* and *Metamorphoses*, that we chiefly recognize the impressions of the scenes he visited. In one of the *Epistles from Pontus* (ii. 10) to his fellow-traveller there is a vivid record of the pleasant time they had passed together. Athens was to a Roman then what Rome is to an educated Englishman of the present day. Ovid speaks of having gone there under the influence of literary enthusiasm, and a similar impulse induced him to visit the supposed site of Troy. The two friends saw together the illustrious cities of Asia, which had inspired the enthusiasm of travel in Catullus, and had become familiar to Cicero and Horace during the years they passed abroad. They spent nearly a year in Sicily, which attracted him, as it had attracted Lucretius[5] and Virgil,[6] by its manifold charm of climate, of sea-shore and inland scenery, and of legendary and poetical association. He recalls with a fresh sense of pleasure the incidents of their tour, and the endless delight which they had in each other's conversation. We would gladly exchange the record of his life of pleasure in Rome for more of these recollections. The highest type of classic Roman culture shows its affinity to that of modern times by nothing more clearly than the enthusiasm for travel among lands famous for their natural beauty, their monuments of art and their historical associations.

When settled at Rome, although a public career leading to senatorial position was open to him, and although he filled various minor judicial posts and claims to have filled them well, he had no ambition for such distinction, and looked upon pleasure and poetry as the occupations of his life. He was three times married; when little more than a boy to his first wife, whom he naïvely describes as unworthy of himself;[7] but he was soon separated from her and took a second wife, with whom his union, although through no fault of hers, did not last long. She was probably the mother of his one daughter. Later he was joined to a third wife, of whom he always speaks with affection and respect. She was a lady of the great Fabian house, and thus connected with his powerful patron Fabius Maximus, and was a friend of the empress Livia. It therefore seems likely that he may have been admitted into the intimacy of the younger society of the Palatine, although in the midst of his most fulsome flattery he does not claim ever to have enjoyed the favour of Augustus. His liaison with his mistress Corinna, whom he celebrates in the *Amores*, took place probably in the period between his first and second, or between his second and third marriages. It is doubtful whether Corinna was, like Catullus' Lesbia, a lady of recognized position, or whether she belonged to

[4] Juv. vii. 95.
[5] Lucret. i. 726—
     " quae cum magna modis multis miranda videtur
         gentibus humanis regio visendaque fertur."
[6] Sueton. (Donatus), *Vita Virg.* 13 " quamquam secessu Campaniae Siciliaeque plurimum uteretur."
[7] *Trist.* iv. 10. 69-70.

the same class as the Chloes and Lalages of Horace's artistic fancy. If we can trust the poet's later apologies for his life, in which he states that he had never given occasion for any serious scandal, it is probable that she belonged to the class of *libertinae*. However that may be, Ovid is not only a less constant but he is a less serious lover than his great predecessors Catullus, Tibullus and Propertius. His tone is that either of mere sensuous feeling or of irony. In his complete emancipation from all restraint he goes beyond them, and thus reflects the tastes and spirit of fashionable Rome between the years 20 B.C. and the beginning of our era. Society was then bent simply on amusement; and, as a result partly of the loss of political interests, women came to play a more important and brilliant part in its life than they had done before. Julia, the daughter of the emperor, was by her position, her wit and beauty, and her reckless dissipation, the natural leader of such a society. But the discovery of her intrigue (2 B.C.) with Iulus Antonius, the son of Mark Antony, was deeply resented by Augustus as being at once a shock to his affections and a blow to his policy of moral reform. Julia was banished and disinherited; Antonius and her many lovers were punished; and the Roman world awoke from its fool's paradise of pleasure. Nearly coincidently with this scandal appeared Ovid's *Ars amatoria*, perhaps the most immoral work ever written by a man of genius, though not the most demoralizing, since it is entirely free from morbid sentiment. By its brilliancy and heartlessness it appealed to the prevailing taste of the fashionable world; but its appearance excited deep resentment in the mind of the emperor, as is shown by his edict, issued ten years later, against the book and its author. Augustus had the art of dissembling his anger; and Ovid appears to have had no idea of the storm that was gathering over him. He still continued to enjoy the society of the court and the fashionable world; he passed before the emperor in the annual procession among the ranks of the *equites*; and he developed a richer vein of genius than he had shown in his youthful prime. But he was aware that public opinion had been shocked, or professed to be shocked, by his last work; and after writing a kind of apology for it, called the *Remedia amoris*, he turned to other subjects, and wrote during the next ten years the *Metamorphoses* and the *Fasti*. He had already written the *Heroides*, in which he had imparted a modern and romantic interest to the heroines of the old mythology,[1] and a tragedy, the *Medea*, which must have afforded greater scope for the dramatic and psychological treatment of the passion with which he was most familiar. In the *Fasti* Ovid assumes the position of a national poet[2] by imparting poetical life and interest to the ceremonial observances of the Roman religion; but it is as the brilliant narrator of the romantic tales that were so strangely blended with the realistic annals of Rome that he succeeds in the part assumed by him. The *Metamorphoses* is a narrative poem which recounts legends in which the miraculous involved transformations of shape. Beginning with the change from Chaos to Cosmos, legends first Greek and then Roman are passed in review, concluding with the metamorphosis of Julius Caesar into a star and a promise of immortality to Augustus. The long series of stories, which consist to a large extent of tales of the love adventures of the gods with nymphs and the daughters of men, is strongly tinged with Alexandrine influence, being in fact a succession of *epyllia* in the Alexandrine manner. This work, which Ovid regards as his most serious claim to immortality, had not been finally revised at the time of his disgrace, and in his despair he burnt it; but other copies were in existence, and when he was at Tomi it was published at Rome by one of his friends. He often regrets that it had not received his final revision. The *Fasti* also was broken off by his exile, after the publication of the first six books, treating of the first six months of the year.

Ovid assigns two causes for his banishment, his *Ars amatoria*, and an actual offence.[3] What this was is not known, but his

frequent references to it enable us to conjecture its character. He tells us that there was no breach of law on his part; he distinctly disclaims having been concerned in any treasonable plot: his fault was a mistake of judgment (*error*), an unpremeditated act of folly. He had been an unintentional witness of some culpable act committed by another or others—of some act which nearly affected the emperor, and the mention of which was likely to prove offensive to him. Ovid himself had reaped no personal gain from his conduct. Though his original act was a pardonable error, he had been prevented by timidity from atoning for it subsequently by taking the straightforward course. In a letter to an intimate friend, to whom he had been in the habit of confiding all his secrets, he says that had he confided this one he would have escaped condemnation.[4] In writing to another friend he warns him against the danger of courting too high society. This offence, which excited the anger of Augustus, was connected in some way with the publication of the *Ars amatoria*, since that fact was recited by the emperor in his sentence. All this points to his having been mixed up in a scandal affecting the imperial family, and seems to connect him with one event, coincident with the time of his disgrace (A.D. 9), the intrigue of the younger Julia, granddaughter of Augustus, with D. Silanus, mentioned by Tacitus.[5] Augustus deeply felt these family scandals, looking upon them as acts of treason and sacrilege. Julia was banished to the island of Trimerus, off the coast of Apulia. Silanus withdrew into voluntary exile. The chief punishment fell on Ovid, who was banished. The poet at the worst could only have been a confidant of the intrigue; but Augustus must have regarded him and his works as, if not the corrupter of the age, at least the most typical representative of that corruption which had tainted so direly even the imperial family. Ovid's form of banishment was the mildest possible (*relegatio*); it involved no deprivation of civic rights, and left him the possession of his property. He was ordered to remove to the half-Greek, half-barbaric town of Tomi, near the mouth of the Danube. He recounts vividly the agony of his last night in Rome, and the hardships of his November voyage down the Adriatic and up the Gulf of Corinth to Lechacum, where he crossed the isthmus and took ship again from Cenchreae to Samothrace, whence in the following spring he proceeded overland through Thrace to his destination. For eight years he bore up in his dreary solitude, suffering from the unhealthiness of the climate and the constant alarm of inroads of barbarians. In the hope of procuring a remission of his punishment he wrote poetical complaints, first in the series of the five books of the *Tristia*, sent successively to Rome, addressed to friends whose names he suppresses; afterwards in a number of poetical epistles, the *Epistulae ex Ponto*, addressed by name to friends who were likely to have influence at court. He believed that Augustus had softened towards him before his death, but his successor Tiberius was inexorable to his appeals. His chief consolation was the exercise of his art, though as time goes on he is painfully conscious of failure in power. But although the works written by him in exile lack the finished art of his earlier writings, their personal interest is greater. They have, like the letters of Cicero to Atticus, the fascination exercised by those works which have been given to the world under the title of Confessions; they are a sincere literary expression of the state of mind produced by a unique experience—that of a man, when well advanced in years but still retaining extraordinary sensibility to pleasure and pain, withdrawn from a brilliant social and intellectual position, and cast upon his own resources in a place and among people affording the dreariest contrast to the brightness of his previous life. How far these confidences are to be regarded as equally sincere expressions of his affection or admiration for his correspondents is another question. Even in those addressed to his wife, though he speaks of her with affection and respect, there may perhaps be detected a certain ring of insincerity in his conventional comparisons of her to the Penelopes and Laodamias of ancient legend. Had she been a Penelope or Laodamia she would have accompanied him in

---

[1] The essentially modern character of the work appears in his making a heroine of the time of the Trojan war speak of visiting "learned " Athens (*Heroid.* ii. 83).

[2] " Animos ad publica carmina flexi " (*Trist.* v. i. 23).

[3] *Trist.* ii. 209.

[4] *Trist.* iii. 6. 11.   [5] *Ann.* iii. 24.

his exile, as we learn from Tacitus was done by other wives[1] in the more evil days of which he wrote the record. The letters, which compose the *Tristia* and *Epistulae ex Ponto*, are addressed either to his wife, the emperor, or the general reader, or to his patrons and friends. To his patrons he writes in a vein of supplication, beseeching them to use their influence on his behalf. To his rather large circle of intimate acquaintances he writes in the language of familiarity, and often of affectionate regard; he seeks the sympathy of some, and speaks with bitterness of the coldness of others, and in three poems[2] he complains of the relentless hostility of the enemy who had contributed to procure his exile, and whom he attacked in the *Ibis*. There is a note of true affection in the letter to the young lyric poetess Perilla, of whose genius and beauty he speaks with pride, and whose poetic talents he had fostered by friendly criticism.[3] He was evidently a man of gentle and genial manners; and, as his active mind induced him to learn the language of the new people among whom he was thrown, his active interest in life enabled him to gain their regard and various marks of honour. One of his last acts was to revise the *Fasti*, and re-edit it with a dedication to Germanicus. The closing lines of the *Epistulae ex Ponto* sound like the despairing sigh of a drowning man who had long struggled alone with the waves:—

"Omnia perdidimus: tantummodo vita relicta est,
Praebeat ut sensum materiamque mali."

Shortly after these words were written he died in his sixty-first year in A.D. 17, the fourth year of the reign of Tiberius.

The temperament of Ovid, as indicated in his writings, has more in common with the suppleness of the later Italian than with the strength and force of the ancient Roman. That stamp of her own character and understanding which Rome impressed on the genius of those other races which she incorporated with herself is fainter in Ovid than in any other great writer. He ostentatiously disclaims the manliness which in the republican times was regarded as the birthright not of Romans only but of the Sabellian races from which he sprang. He is as devoid of dignity in his abandonment to pleasure as in the weakness with which he meets calamity. He has no depth of serious conviction, no vein of sober reflection, and is sustained by no great or elevating purpose. Although the beings of a supernatural world fill a large place in his writings, they appear stripped of all sanctity and mystery. It is difficult to say whether the tone of his references to the gods and goddesses of mythology implies a kind of half-believing return to the most childish elements of paganism, or is simply one of mocking unbelief. He has absolutely no reverence, and consequently inspires no reverence in his reader. With all a poet's feeling for the life, variety and subtlety of nature, he has no sense of her mystery and majesty. The love which he celebrates is sensual and superficial, a matter of vanity as much as of passion. He prefers the piquant attraction of falsehood and fickleness to the charm of truth and constancy. Even where he follows the Roman tendencies in his art he perverts them. The *Fasti* is a work conceived in the prosaic spirit of Roman antiquarianism. It is redeemed from being prosaic by the picturesqueness and vivacity with which the legends are told. But its conception might have been more poetical if it had been penetrated by the religious and patriotic spirit with which Virgil invests ancient ceremonies, and the mysticism with which he accepts the revelations of science. In this respect the contrast is great between the reverential treatment which the trivialities of legend and science receive in the *Georgics* and *Aeneid*, and the literal definiteness of the *Fasti*. These defects in strength and gravity show a corresponding result in Ovid's writings. Though possessing diligence, perseverance and literary ambition, he seems incapable of conceiv-

ing a great and serious whole. Though a keen observer of the superficial aspects of life, he has added few great thoughts to the intellectual heritage of the world.[4] But with all the levity of his character he must have had qualities which made him, if not much esteemed, yet much liked in his own day, and which are apparent in the genial amiability of his writings. He claims for himself two virtues highly prized by the Romans, *fides* and *candor*—the qualities of social honour and kindly sincerity. There is no indication of anything base, ungenerous or morose in his relations to others. Literary *candor*, the generous appreciation of all sorts of excellence, he possesses in a remarkable degree. He heartily admires everything in literature, Greek or Roman, that had any merit. In him more than any of the Augustan poets we find words of admiration applied to the rude genius of Ennius and the majestic style of Accius. It is by him, not by Virgil or Horace, that Lucretius is first named and his sublimity is first acknowledged.[5] The image of Catullus that most haunts the imagination is that of the poet who died so early—

"hedera iuvenalia cinctus
Tempora,"

as he is represented by Ovid coming to meet the shade of the young Tibullus in Elysium.[6] To his own contemporaries, known and unknown to fame, he is as liberal in his words of recognition.[7] He enjoyed society too in a thoroughly amiable and unenvious spirit. He lived on a friendly footing with a large circle of men of letters, poets, critics, grammarians, &c., but he showed none of that sense of superiority which is manifest in Horace's estimate of the "tribes of grammarians" and the poetasters of his day. Like Horace too he courted the society of the great, though probably not with equal independence; but unlike Horace he expresses no contempt for the humbler world outside. With his irony and knowledge of the world it might have been expected that he would become the social satirist of his age. But he lacked the censorious and critical temper, and the admixture of gall necessary for a successful satirist. In his exile he did retaliate on one enemy and persistent detractor in the *Ibis*, a poem written in imitation of a similar work by Callimachus; but the *Ibis* is not a satire, but an invective remarkable rather for recondite learning than for epigrammatic sting.

But Ovid's chief personal endowment was his vivacity, and his keen interest in and enjoyment of life. He had no grain of discontent in his composition; no regrets for an ideal past, or longings for an imaginary future. The age in which he lived was, as he tells us, that in which more than any other he would have wished to live.[8] He is its most gifted representative, but he does not rise above it. The great object of his art was to amuse and delight it by the vivid picture he presented of its fashions and pleasures, and by creating a literature of romance which reflected them, and which could stimulate the curiosity and fascinate the fancy of a society too idle and luxurious for serious intellectual effort. The sympathy which he felt for the love adventures of his contemporaries, to which he probably owed his fall, quickened his creative power in the composition of the *Heroides* and the romantic tales of the *Metamorphoses*. None of the Roman poets can people a purely imaginary world with such spontaneous fertility of fancy as Ovid. In heart and mind he is inferior to Lucretius and Catullus, to Virgil and Horace, perhaps to Tibullus and Propertius; but in the power and range of imaginative vision he is surpassed by no ancient and by few modern poets. This power of vision is the counterpart of his lively sensuous nature. He has a keener eye for the apprehension of outward beauty, for the life and colour and forms of nature, than any Roman or perhaps than any Greek poet. This power, acting upon the wealth of his varied reading, gathered with eager curiosity and received into a singularly retentive mind, has enabled him to depict with consummate skill and sympathy legendary scenes of the most varied and picturesque beauty. If his tragedy, the

[1] Tac. *Hist.* L 3 "comitatae profugos liberos matres, secutae maritos in exilia coniuges."
[2] *Trist.* iii. 11, iv. 9, v. 8.
[3] *Trist.* iii. 7. Perilla has by many been erroneously supposed to have been the poet's own daughter; but this is impossible, since she is described as young and still living under her mother's roof, whereas at the time of Ovid's exile his daughter was already married to her second husband.

[4] There are found in him some exceptionally fine expressions, such as *Her.* iii. 106 "qui bene pro patria cum patriaque iacent"; and *Met.* vii. 20 "video meliora proboque, deteriora sequor."
[5] *Am.* i. 15. 19 ff.   [6] *Am.* iii. 9. 61.
[7] *Ex Ponto*, iv. 16.   [8] *Ars amatoria*, iii. 121 ff.

Medea, highly praised by ancient critics, had been preserved, we should have been able to judge whether Roman art was capable of producing a great drama. In many of the *Heroides*, and in several speeches scattered through his works, he gives evidence of true dramatic creativeness. Unlike his great predecessor Catullus, he has little of the idyllic in his art, or whatever of idyllic there is in it is lost in the rapid movement of his narrative. But he is one, among the poets of all times, who can imagine a story with the most vivid inventiveness and tell it with the most unflagging animation. The faults of his verse and diction are those which arise from the vitality of his temperament—too facile a flow, too great exuberance of illustration. He has as little sense of the need of severe restraint in his art as in his life. He is not without mannerism, but he is quite unaffected, and, however far short he might fall of the highest excellence of verse or style, it was not possible for him to be rough or harsh, dull or obscure.

As regards the school of art to which he belongs, he may be described as the most brilliant representative of Roman Alexandrinism. The latter half of the Augustan age was, in its social and intellectual aspects, more like the Alexandrine age than any other era of antiquity. The Alexandrine age was like the Augustan, one of refinement and luxury, of outward magnificence and literary dilettantism flourishing under the fostering influence of an absolute monarchy. Poetry was the most important branch of literature cultivated, and the chief subjects of poetry were mythological tales, various phases of the passion of love, the popular aspects of science and some aspects of the beauty of nature. These two were the chief subjects of the later Augustan poetry. The higher feelings and ideas which found expression in the poetry of Virgil, Horace and the writers of an older generation no longer acted on the Roman world. It was to the private tastes and pleasures of individuals and society that Roman Alexandrinism had appealed both in the poetry of Catullus, Cinna, Calvus and their school, and in that of Gallus, Tibullus and Propertius. Ovid was the last of this class of writers.

His extant works fall naturally into three divisions, those of his youth, of middle life and of his later years. To the first of these divisions belong the amatory poems: (1) the three books of *Amores* (originally five, but reduced in a later recension to three) relating to his amours with his mistress Corinna; (2) the *Medicamina formae*, or, as it is sometimes called *Medicamina faciei*, a fragment of a hundred lines on the use of cosmetics; (3) the three books of the *Ars amatoria*, rules for men and women by which they may gain the affections of the other sex; (4) the *Remedia amoris* (one book), a kind of recantation of the *Ars amatoria*. To the second division belong (5) the fifteen books of the *Metamorphoses*, and (6) the six books of the *Fasti*, which was originally intended to be in twelve books, but which breaks off the account of the Roman calendar with the month of June. To the third division belong (7) the five books of the *Tristia*, (8) the *Ibis*, an invective against an enemy who had assisted to procure his fall, written in elegiac couplets probably soon after his exile; (9) the four books of *Epistulae ex Ponto*. Of these the first three were published soon after the *Tristia*, while the fourth book is a collection of scattered poems published by some friend soon after the author's death. The *Halieutica* is a didactic fragment in hexameters on the natural history of fishes, of doubtful genuineness, though it is certain that Ovid did begin such a work at the close of his life.[1]

In his extant works Ovid confined himself to two metres—the elegiac couplet and the hexameter. The great mass of his poetry is written in the first; while the *Metamorphoses* and the *Halieutica* are composed in the second. Of the elegiac couplet he is the acknowledged master. By fixing it into a uniform mould he brought it to its highest perfection; and the fact that the great mass of elegiac verse written subsequently has endeavoured merely to reproduce the echo of his rhythm is evidence of his pre-eminence. In the direct expression and illustration of feeling his elegiac metre has more ease, vivacity and sparkle than that of any of his predecessors, while he alone has communicated to it, without altering its essential characteristic of recurrent and regular pauses, a fluidity and rapidity of movement which make it an admirable vehicle for pathetic and picturesque narrative. It was impossible for him to give to the hexameter greater perfection, but he imparted to it also a new character, wanting indeed the weight and majesty and intricate harmonies of Virgil, but rapid, varied, animated in complete accord with the swift, versatile and fervid movement of his imagination. One other proof he gave of his irrepressible energy by composing during his exile a poem in the Getic (Gothic) language in praise of Augustus, Tiberius and the imperial family, the loss of which, whatever it may have been to literature, is much to be regretted in the interests of philology.

It was in Ovid's writings that the world of romance and wonder created by Greek imagination was first revealed to modern times. The vivid fancy, the transparent lucidity, the liveliness, ease and directness through which he reproduced his models made his works the most accessible and among the most attractive of the recovered treasures of antiquity. His influence was first felt in the literature of the Italian Renaissance. But in the most creative periods of English literature he seems to have been read more than any other ancient poet, not even excepting Virgil, and it was on minds such as those of Marlowe, Spenser, Shakespeare,[2] Milton and Dryden that he acted most powerfully. His influence is equally unmistakable during the classical era of Addison and Pope. The most successful Latin verse of modern times has been written in imitation of him; the faculty of literary composition and feeling for ancient Roman culture has been largely developed in the great schools of England and France by the writing of Ovidian elegiacs. His works afforded also abundant stimulus and materials to the great painters who flourished during and immediately after the Renaissance. Thus his first claim on the attention of modern readers is the influence which he has exercised on the development of literature and art; for this, if for no other reason, his works must always retain an importance second only to those of Virgil and Horace.

He is interesting further as the sole contemporary exponent of the last half of the Augustan age, the external aspects and inner spirit of which is known from the works, not of contemporary historians or prose-writers, but from its poets. The successive phases of Roman feeling and experience during this critical period are revealed in the poetry of Virgil, Horace and Ovid. Virgil throws an idealizing and religious halo around the hopes and aspirations of the nascent empire. Horace presents the most complete image of its manifold aspects, realistic and ideal. Ovid reflects the life of the world of wealth and fashion under the influence of the new court, its material prosperity, its refinement, its frivolity and its adulation. For the continuous study of the Roman world in its social and moral relations his place is important as marking the transition between the representation of Horace, in which the life of pleasure and amusement has its place, but is subordinate to the life of reflection and serious purpose, and that life which reveals itself in the cynicism of Martial and the scornful indignation of Juvenal. He is the last true poet of the great age of Roman literature, which begins with such vivacity and fertility of fancy; in respect of these two qualities we recognize in him the countryman of Cicero and Livy. But the type of genius of which he affords the best example is more familiar in modern Italian than in ancient Roman literature. While the serious spirit of Lucretius and Virgil reappeared in Dante, it is Ariosto who may be said to reproduce the light-hearted gaiety and brilliant fancy of Ovid.

BIBLIOGRAPHY.—The life of Ovid was first treated systematically by J. Masson, *Ovidii vita ordine chronologico digesta* (1780) (often reprinted, *e.g.* in Burmann's edition). Modern literature on this subject will be found in Teuffel's *History of Roman Literature* (Eng. trans., ed. 2), § 247, and S. G. Owen's edition of *Tristia*, bk. i. The very numerous manuscripts of Ovid are chiefly of late date, 13th to 15th century. The earliest and best are: for the *Heroides* a Paris MS. of the 9th, a Wolfenbüttel MS. of the 12th and an Eton

[1] Plin. *Hist. Nat.* xxxii. 152.

[2] The influence of Ovid on Shakespeare is shown conclusively by T. S. Baynes, *Shakespeare Studies* (1894), p. 195 ff.

fragmentary MS. of the 11th century (the *Epistula Sapphus*, found in no early MS., is best preserved in a 13th-century Frankfort, and a 15th-century Harleian MS.); for the *Amores, Ars amatoria, Remedia amoris*, two Paris MSS. of the 9th and 10th century respectively; for the *Medicamina formae* a Florence MS. (Marcianus) of the 11th; for the *Metamorphoses* two Florence MSS. (Marcianus and Laurentianus) and a Naples MS., all of the 11th century; for the *Fasti* two Vatican MSS. of the 10th and 11th century; for the *Tristia* a Florence MS. of the 11th; for the *Epistulae ex Ponto* a fragmentary Wolfenbüttel MS. of the 6th and a Hamburg and two Munich MSS. of the 12th; for the *Ibis* a Trinity College, Cambridge, MS. of the 12th; for the *Halieutica* a Paris MS. of the 9th or 10th, and a Vienna MS. of the 9th century. Important for the text of the *Heroides* and *Metamorphoses* is the interesting paraphrase written in Greek by the monk Maximus Planudes in the latter half of the 13th century at Constantinople; that of the *Heroides* is printed in Palmer's edition of the *Heroides* (1898), that of the *Metamorphoses* in Lemaire's edition of *Ovid*, vol. v., edited by Boissonade. See also Gudeman, *De Heroidum Ovidii codice Planudeo* (Berlin, 1888).

Two independent *editiones principes* of Ovid were published contemporaneously in 1471, one at Rome, printed by Sweynheym and Pannartz, and one at Bologna by Balthasar Azoguidius: these present entirely different texts. See Owen's *Tristium libri*, v. p. lv. ff. The following are the most important editions; those marked with an asterisk have explanatory notes. Of the whole works: *Heinsius-Burmann (1727); *Amar-Lemaire (1820–1824); Merkel-Ehwald (1874–1888); Riese (1871–1889); Postgate's *Corpus poetarum Latinorum*, by various editors (1894), reprinted separately (1898). Of separate works: *Amores*, *Némethy (1907); *Heroides*, Sedlmayer (critical) (1886); *Palmer (1898); *Epistula Sapphus (separately), *De Vries (1888); *Ars amatoria*, *P. Brandt (1902); *Medicamina formae* (critical), Kunz (1881); *Metamorphoses*, *J. C. Jahn (1821); *Loers (1843); Korn (critical) (1880); *Magnus (1885); *Haupt-Ehwald (1898–1903); *Fasti*, *Gierig (1812); Merkel (1841) (critical, with learned prolegomena on the sources, the Roman calendar, &c.); *Keightley (1848); *Paley (1854); *Peter (1889); *Tristia*, *Loers (1839); S. G. Owen (1889) (critical) *Bk. i. (1885), *Bk. iii. (1889); *Cocchia (1900); *Epistulae ex Ponto*, Korn (1868) (critical), Bk. I. Keene (1887); *Ellis (1881); *Halieutica*, *Birt, *De Halieuticis Ovidio poetae falso adscriptis* (1878). The following verse translations in English deserve mention: *Amores*, C. Marlowe (1600) (?); *Heroides*, Turberville (1579); Saltonstall (1639); Sherburne (1639), various hands, preface by Dryden (3rd edition, 1683); *Art of Love and Remedy of Love*, Creed (1600); Dryden and others (1709); *Metamorphoses*, Golding (1567); Sandys (1626); Dryden and others (1717); King (1871); *Fasti*, Gower (1640); Rose (1866); *Tristia*, Saltonstall (1633); Catlin (1639); Churchyarde (1816); *Epistles from Pontus*, Saltonstall (1639); Jones (1658).

The special treatises on matters connected with Ovid are very numerous; a fairly complete list up to the time of publication is given in Owen's *Tristia* (critical edition), p. cviii. ff.; in Teuffel's *History of Roman Literature* (trans. by Warr) and in Schanz's *Geschichte der römischen Litteratur*; and in the excellent critical digests of recent literature by Ehwald in the *Jahresbericht über die Fortschritte der classischen Altertumswissenschaft*, xxxi. (1884) pp. 157 ff., lxxx. (1894) pp. 2 ff., cix. (1902) pp. 157 ff. The following deserve special mention. On the history of the text: Ehwald, *Ad historiam carminum Ovidianorum symbolae* (1889); *Kritische Beiträge zu Ovids Epistulae ex Ponto* (1896); Sedlmayer, *Prolegomena ad Heroidas* (1878); Gruppe, *Minos*, pp. 441 ff. (on interpolations). On style: Ovid's diction in connexion with other writers,—A. Zingerle, *Ovidius und sein Verhältnis zu den Vorgängern* (1869–1871); *Martial's Ovid-Studien* (1877); W. Zingerle, *Untersuchungen zur Echtheitsfrage der Heroiden Ovids* (1878); W. Vollgraff, *Nikander und Ovid* (Groningen, 1909 foll.). Peculiarities of Ovid's style: van Idekeinge, *De Ovidii Romani turis peritia* (1811); Washieit, *De similitudinibus imaginibusque Ovidianis* (1885); M'Crea, *On Ovid's Use of Colour and Colour Terms* (Classical studies in honour of H. Drisler) (1894). Metre: the structure of the Ovidian pentameter examined in relation to the textual criticism,—Hilberg, *Gesetze der Wortstellung im Pentameter des Ovid* (1894) (fully reviewed by Ellis, *Classical Review*, ix. 157). Literary appreciation: Sellar, *Roman Poets of the Augustan Age*; Lafaye, *Les Métamorphoses d'Ovid et leurs modèles grecs*. Ovid's relation to works of art: Wunderer, *Ovids Werke in ihrem Verhältnis zur antiken Kunst* (1890–1891); Engelmann, *Bilder-Atlas zu Ovid's Metamorphosen* (1890). Cause of exile: the most interesting discussion is by Boissier in his *L'Opposition sous les Césars*. See also Nageotte, *Ovide, sa vie, ses œuvres* (1872); Huber, *Die Ursachen der Verbannung des Ovid* (1888). Influence of Ovid upon Shakespeare: T. S. Baynes, *Shakespeare Studies* (1894), pp. 195 ff.; Constable, Shakespeare's "Venus and Adonis" in *Verhältnis zu Ovid's Metamorphosen* (1890). (S. G. O.)

OVIEDO, a maritime province of northern Spain, bounded on the N. by the Bay of Biscay, E. by Santander, S. by Leon and W. by Lugo. Pop. (1900) 627,069; area, 4205 sq. m. In popular speech Oviedo is often called by its ancient name of

Asturias, which only ceased to be the official title of the province in 1833, when the Spanish system of local government was reorganized. An account of the physical features, history and inhabitants of this region is given under Asturias (q.v.). Oviedo is rich in forests, coal, streams and waterfalls, which have largely contributed to its modern industrial development. The climate is generally mild, but overcharged with humidity, and in the higher regions the winters are protracted and severe. The broken character of the surface prevents anything like extensive agricultural industry, but abundant pasturage is found in the valleys. The wheat crop frequently fails. Rye succeeds better, and is often mixed with the maize which forms the principal food of all but the higher classes. Chestnuts— here, as elsewhere in Spain, an important article of diet— are very abundant on the hills, and the trees supply valuable timber. Apples are abundant, and cider forms the common drink of the people; but little attention is paid to vines. The horses of Oviedo rank among the best in Spain. Wild deer, boars and bears were formerly common among the mountains; and the sea-coasts, as well as the streams, abound with fish, including salmon and lampreys, which are sent to the markets of Madrid. Large quantities of sardines and tunny are also cured and exported. Although no trace exists of the gold for which Asturias was celebrated under its Roman rulers, Oviedo possesses valuable coal measures, which are worked at Langreo, Mieres, Santo Firme, Siero and elsewhere. More than 1,400,000 tons of coal were produced in 1903, besides a considerable amount of iron, mercury and cinnabar. The copper mines near Avilés and Cangas de Onis, and the copper works which long supplied the fairs of Leon and Castile with kettles, pots and similar utensils, have lost their importance; but lead, magnesia, arsenic, cobalt, lapis lazuli, alum, antimony, jet, marble and rock-crystal are found in various parts of the province, while amber and coral are gathered along the coast. There are manufactures of fine textiles, coarse cloth and ribbons in Salas, Piloña, Casas and Avilés; of paper in Pianton; of porcelain and glass in Gijón, Avilés and Pola de Surro; of arms in Oviedo and Trubia; while foundries and works for the manufacture of agricultural implements, rails and pig-iron are numerous. An important highway is the 16th-century *Camino real*, or royal road, leading from Gijón to Leon and Madrid, which cost so much that the emperor Charles V. inquired if it were paved with silver. A railway from Madrid to Oviedo, Gijón and Avilés runs through some of the most difficult parts of the Cantabrian chain. There are also several branch railways, including numerous narrow-gauge lines.

OVIEDO, an episcopal city and capital of the Spanish province of Oviedo; 16 m. S. of the Bay of Biscay, on the river Nalon, and on the Leon-Gijón Oviedo-Trubia and Oviedo-Infiesto railways. Pop. (1900) 48,103. Oviedo is built on a hill rising from a broad and picturesque valley, which is bounded on the north-west by the Sierra de Naranco. The four main streets of Oviedo, which meet in a central square called the Plaza Mayor or Plaza de la Constitucion, are the roads connecting Gijón and Leon (north and south) and Santander and Grado (east and west). The streets are clean and well lighted; the projecting roofs of the houses give a characteristic effect, and some portions of the old Calle de la Plateria are highly picturesque. In the Plaza Mayor is the handsome Casa Consistorial or town hall dating from 1662; the Jesuit church of San Isidro (1578), and some ancient palaces of the Asturian nobility are architecturally interesting. The university was founded by Philip III. in 1604; connected with it are a fine library and physical and chemical museums. The Gothic cathedral, founded in 1388, occupies the site of a chapel founded in the 8th century, of which only the Camara Santa remains. The west front has a fine portico of ornamented arches between the two towers. The interior contains some fine stained glass, but has been much disfigured with modern rococo additions. The Camara Santa (dating from 802) contains the famous *arca* of Oviedo, an 11th-century Byzantine chest of cedar, overlaid with silver reliefs of scenes in the lives of Christ, the Virgin and the apostles. In it are preserved some highly sacred relics, two crosses dating from the 8th and 9th centuries and other valuable pieces of gold and silver plate. The cathedral library has some curious old MSS., including a deed of gift made by Alphonso II. of Asturias in 817, and a collection of illuminated documents of the 12th century, called the *Libro gótico*. On the Sierra de Naranco is the ancient Santa Maria de Naranco, originally built by Ramiro I. of Asturias in 850 as a palace, and afterwards turned into a church. Higher up the hill is San Miguel de Lino, also of the 9th century; and on the road to Gijón, about a mile outside the town, is the Santullano or church of St Julian, also of very early date. Few towns in Spain have better schools for primary and higher education, and there are a literary and scientific institute, a meteorological observatory, a school for teachers, a school of art, adult classes for artisans, an archaeological museum and several public libraries. Oviedo is the centre of a thriving trade in agricultural products; its other industries are marble-quarrying, and the manufacture of arms, cotton and woollen fabrics, iron goods, leather and matches.

Oviedo, founded in the reign of Fruela (762), became the fixed residence of the kings of the Asturias in the time of Alphonso II., and continued to be so until about 924, when the advancing reconquest of Spain from the Moors led them to remove their capital to Leon. From that date the history of the city was comparatively uneventful, until the Peninsular War, when it was twice plundered by the French—under Ney in 1809 and under Bonnet in 1810.

OVIEDO Y VALDÉS, GONZALO FERNÁNDEZ DE (1478–1557), Spanish historian, was born at Madrid in August 1478. Educated at the court of Ferdinand and Isabella, in his thirteenth year he became page to their son, the Infante Don John, was present at the siege of Granada, and there saw Columbus previous to his voyage to America. On the death of Prince John (4th of October 1497), Oviedo went to Italy, and there acted as secretary to Gonzalo Fernandez de Cordoba. In 1514 he was appointed supervisor of gold-smeltings at San Domingo, and on his return to Spain in 1523 was appointed historiographer of the Indies. He paid five more visits to America before his death, which took place at Valladolid in 1557.

Besides a romance of chivalry entitled *Claribalte* (1519) Oviedo wrote two extensive works of permanent value: *La General y natural historia de las Indias* and *Las Quinquagenas de la nobleza de España*. The former work was first issued at Toledo (1526) in the form of a summary entitled *La Natural hystoria de las Indias*; the first part of *La Historia general de las Indias* appeared at Seville in 1535; but the complete work was not published till 1851–1855, when it was edited by J. A. de los Rios for the Spanish Academy of History. Though written in a diffuse style, it embodies a mass of curious information collected at first hand, and the incomplete Seville edition was widely read in the English and French versions published by Eden and Poleur respectively in 1555 and 1556. Las Casas describes it as "containing almost as many lies as pages," and Oviedo undoubtedly puts the most favourable interpretation on the proceedings of his countrymen; but, apart from a patriotic bias which is too obvious to be misleading, his narrative is both trustworthy and interesting. In his *Quinquagenas* he indulges in much lively gossip concerning eminent contemporaries: this collection of quaint, moralizing anecdotes was first published at Madrid in 1880, under the editorship of Vicente de la Fuente.

OVOLO (adapted from Ital. *uovolo*, diminutive of *uovo*, an egg; other foreign equivalents are Fr. *ove*, *échine*, *quart de rond*; Lat. *echinus*), in architecture, a convex moulding known also as the echinus, which in Classic architecture was invariably carved with the egg and tongue. In Roman and Italian work the moulding is called by workmen a quarter round. It must not be confounded with the echinus of the Greek Doric capital, as this was of a more varied form and of much larger dimensions than the ovolo, which was only a subordinate moulding.

OWATONNA, a city and the county-seat of Steele county, Minnesota, U.S.A., on the Straight river, in the S.E. part of the state, about 67 m. S. of Minneapolis and St Paul. Pop. (1900) 5561, of whom 1160 were foreign-born; (1905) 5651; (1910) 5658. It is served by the Chicago, Milwaukee & St Paul, the Chicago & North-Western, the Chicago, Rock Island & Pacific and the Minneapolis, Rochester & Dubuque (electric) railways. Four fine steel bridges span the river at or near the city. Among the public buildings are a handsome county court-house, a city

hall, an armoury, a city hospital and a public library. Owatonna is the seat of the Pillsbury Academy (Baptist), the Sacred Heart Academy (Roman Catholic) and the Canfield Commercial School, and immediately west of the city is the State Public School for Dependent and Neglected Children (1886). The city's commercial importance is largely due to its situation in a rich dairying and farming district, for which it is the shipping centre. It has also various manufactures. There are valuable mineral springs in the vicinity. The municipality owns and operates the water-works. Owatonna was settled about 1855, was incorporated as a village in 1865, was chartered as a city in 1875 and received a new charter in 1909. Its name is a Sioux word meaning "straight," the river having been previously named Straight river.

OWEGO, a village and the county-seat of Tioga county, New York, U.S.A., on the Owego Creek and on the N. side of the Susquehanna river, 21 m. W. of Binghamton. Pop. (1910, U.S. census) 4633. It is served by the Erie, the Lehigh Valley and the Delaware, Lackawanna & Western railways; a branch of the last connects with Ithaca, N.Y. Owego occupies the site of an Indian (probably Tuscarora) village named "Ah-wa-ga," which was destroyed by General James Clinton in 1779. The name, of which "Owego" is a corruption, is said to mean "where the valley widens." A white settlement and trading post were set up here in 1785, and the village of Owego was incorporated in 1827.

OWEN, SIR HUGH (1804–1881), Welsh educationist, was born near Talyfoel Ferry, Anglesey, on the 14th of January 1804. Educated at a private school at Carnarvon, he became clerk in 1825 to a barrister in London. In 1836 he entered the office of the Poor Law Commission, eventually becoming chief clerk of the Poor Law Board, and retiring in 1872 to devote himself exclusively to educational work. As early as 1839 he had become secretary for an association to start a National school in Islington, and in 1843 he had published *A Letter to the Welsh People* on the need of educational activity, which was widely read. Successful in arousing the interest of the British and Foreign School Society, he became in 1846 honorary secretary of its newly-formed branch, the Cambrian School Society. He was one of the founders of the Bangor Normal College, for the training of teachers, and of the University College of Wales at Aberystwith, of which for many years he was honorary secretary and treasurer. He was for three years a member of the London School Board. His scheme for secondary education, formulated in 1881, was almost wholly adopted after his death in the Welsh Intermediate Education Act of 1889. The revival of the Honourable Cymrodorion Society, the National Eisteddfod Association and the Social Science Section of the National Eisteddfod was due to Owen. He was knighted in recognition of his service to Welsh education in August 1881; but died at Mentone on the 20th of November. A bronze statue was erected at Carnarvon in 1888 by public subscription.

OWEN, JOHN (OUENUS or AUDOENUS) (c. 1560–1622), Welsh epigrammatist, was born at Plas Dhu, Carnarvonshire, about 1560. He was educated under Dr Bilson at Winchester School, and at New College, Oxford. He was a fellow of his college from 1584 to 1591, when he became a schoolmaster, first at Trelleck, near Monmouth, and then at Warwick, where he was master of the school endowed by Henry VIII. He became distinguished for his perfect mastery of the Latin language, and for the humour, felicity and point of his epigrams. The Continental scholars and wits of the day used to call him "the British Martial." He was a staunch Protestant besides, and could not resist the temptation of turning his wit against the Roman Catholic Church. This practice caused his book to be placed on the *Index prohibitorius* in 1654, and led a rich old uncle of the Roman Catholic communion to cut him out of his will. When the poet died in 1622, his countryman and relative, Bishop Williams of Lincoln, who is said to have supported him in his later years, erected a monument to his memory in St Paul's cathedral with a Latin epitaph.

Owen's *Epigrammata* are divided into twelve books, of which the first four were published in 1606, and the rest at four different times. Owen frequently adapts and alters to his own purpose the lines of his predecessors in Latin verse, and one such borrowing has become celebrated as a quotation, though few know where it is to be found. It is the first line of this epigram:—

> " Tempora mutantur, nos et mutamur in illis:
> Quo modo? fit semper tempore pejor homo."
>   (Lib. i. ad Edoardum Noel, epig. 58.)

This first line is altered from an epigram by Matthew Borbonius, one of a series of mottoes for various emperors, this one being for Lothaire I.

> " Omnia mutantur, nos et mutamur in illis:
> Illa vices quasdam res habet, illa vices."

There are editions of the *Epigrammata* by Elzevir and by Didot; the best is that edited by Renouard (2 vols., Paris, 1795). Translations into English, either in whole or in part, were made by Vicars (1619); by Pecke, in his *Parnassi Puerperium* (1659); and by Harvey in 1677, which is the most complete. La Torre, the Spanish epigrammatist, owed much to Owen, and translated his works into Spanish in 1674. French translations of the best of Owen's epigrams were published by A. L. Lebrun (1709) and by Kérivalant (1819).

OWEN, JOHN (1616–1683), English Nonconformist divine, was born at Stadham in Oxfordshire in 1616, and was educated at Queen's College, Oxford (B.A. 1632, M.A. 1635), noted, as Fuller tells us, for its metaphysicians. A Puritan by training and conviction, in 1637 Owen was driven from Oxford by Laud's new statutes, and became chaplain and tutor in the family of Sir Robert Dormer and then in that of Lord Lovelace. At the outbreak of the civil troubles he sided with the parliament, and thus lost both his place and the prospects of succeeding to his Welsh royalist uncle's fortune. For a while he lived in Charterhouse Yard, in great unsettlement of mind on religious questions, which was removed at length by a sermon preached by a stranger in Aldermanbury Chapel whither he had gone to hear Edmund Calamy. His first publication, *The Display of Arminianism* (1642), was a spirited defence of rigid Calvinism. It was dedicated to the committee of religion, and gained him the living of Fordham in Essex, from which a " scandalous minister " had been ejected. At Fordham he remained engrossed in the work of his parish and writing only *The Duty of Pastors and People Distinguished* until 1646, when, the old incumbent dying, the presentation lapsed to the patron, who gave it to some one else. He was now, however, coming into notice, for on the 29th of April he preached before the Long parliament. In this sermon, and still more in his *Country Essay for the Practice of Church Government*, which he appended to it, his tendency to break away from Presbyterianism to the more tolerant Independent or Congregational system is plainly seen. Like Milton he saw little to choose between " new presbyter " and " old priest," and disliked a rigid and arbitrary polity by whatever name it was called. He became pastor at Coggeshall in Essex, where a large influx of Flemish tradesmen provided a congenial Independent atmosphere. His adoption of Congregational principles did not effect his theological position, and in 1647 he again attacked the Arminians in *The Death of Death in the Death of Christ*, which drew him into long debate with Richard Baxter. He made the friendship of Fairfax while the latter was besieging Colchester, and urgently addressed the army there against religious persecution. He was chosen to preach to parliament on the day after the execution of Charles, and succeeded in fulfilling his delicate task without directly mentioning that event. Another sermon preached on the 19th of April, a vigorous plea for sincerity of religion in high places, won not only the thanks of parliament but the friendship of Cromwell, who carried him off to Ireland as his chaplain, that he might regulate the affairs of Trinity College. He pleaded with the House of Commons for the religious needs of Ireland as some years earlier he had pleaded for those of Wales. In 1650 he accompanied Cromwell on his Scottish campaign. In March 1651 Cromwell, as chancellor of Oxford, gave him the deanery of Christ Church, and made him vice-chancellor in September 1652; in both offices he succeeded the Presbyterian Edward Reynolds.

During his eight years of official Oxford life Owen showed himself a firm disciplinarian, and infused a new spirit of thoroughness into dons and undergraduates alike, though, as John Locke testifies, the Aristotelian traditions in education suffered

no change. With Philip Nye he unmasked the popular astrologer, William Lilly, and in spite of his share in condemning two Quakeresses to be whipped for disturbing the peace, his rule was not intolerant.[1] Anglican services were conducted here and there, and at Christ Church itself the Anglican chaplain remained in the college. While little encouragement was given to a spirit of free inquiry,[2] it is unhistorical to say that Puritanism at Oxford was simply " an attempt to force education and culture into the leaden moulds of Calvinistic theology." It must be remembered, too, that Owen, unlike many of his contemporaries, found his chief interest in the New Testament rather than the Old. During his Oxford years he wrote *Justitia Divina* (1653), an exposition of the dogma that God cannot forgive sin without an atonement; *Communion with God* (1657), which has been called a " piece of wire-drawn mysticism"; *Doctrine of the Saints' Perseverance* (1654), his final attack on Arminianism; *Vindiciae Evangelicae*, a treatise written by order of the Council of State against Socinianism as expounded by John Bidle; *On the Mortification of Sin in Believers* (1656), an introspective and analytic work; *Schism* (1657), one of the most readable of all his writings; *Of Temptation* (1658), an attempt to recall Puritanism to its cardinal spiritual attitude from the jarring anarchy of sectarianism and the pharisaism which had followed on popularity and threatened to destroy the early simplicity.

Besides all his academic and literary concerns Owen was continually in the midst of affairs of state. In 1651, on October 24 (after Worcester), he preached the thanksgiving sermon before parliament. In 1652 he sat on a council to consider the condition of Protestantism in Ireland. In October 1653 he was one of several ministers whom Cromwell summoned to a consultation as to church union.[3] In December the degree of D.D. was conferred upon him by his university. In the parliament of 1654 he sat, but only for a short time, as member for Oxford university, and, with Baxter, was placed on the committee for settling the " fundamentals " necessary for the toleration promised in the Instrument of Government. In the same year he was chairman of a committee on Scottish Church affairs. He was, too, one of the Triers, and appears to have behaved with kindness and moderation in that capacity. As vice-chancellor he acted with readiness and spirit when a Royalist rising in Wiltshire broke out in 1655; his adherence to Cromwell, however, was by no means slavish, for he drew up, at the request of Desborough and Pride, a petition against his receiving the kingship. Thus, when Richard Cromwell succeeded his father as chancellor, Owen lost his vice-chancellorship. In 1658 he took a leading part in the conference of Independents which drew up the Savoy Declaration.

On the death of Cromwell Owen joined the Wallingford House party, and though he denied any share in the deposition of Richard Cromwell, he threw all his weight on the side of a simple republic as against a protectorate. He assisted in the restoration of the Rump parliament, and, when Monk began his march into England, Owen, in the name of the Independent churches, to whom Monk was supposed to belong, and who were keenly anxious as to his intentions, wrote to dissuade him from the enterprise.

In March 1660, the Presbyterian party being uppermost, Owen was further deprived of his deanery, which was given back to Reynolds. He retired to Stadham, where he wrote various controversial and theological works, in especial the laborious *Theologoumena Pantodapa*, a history of the rise and progress of theology. The respect in which many of the authorities held his intellectual eminence won him an immunity denied to other Nonconformists. In 1661 was published the celebrated *Fiat Lux*, a work by the Franciscan monk John

[1] H. L. Thompson, *Christ Church* (" Oxford College Histories ") pp. 70 seq.
[2] Owen made a very unhappy attack on Brian Walton's Polyglot Bible.
[3] Owen probably drew up the scheme for a national church surrounded by bodies of tolerated dissent which was presented to parliament. See D. Masson, *Milton*, iv. 390, 566.

Vincent Cane, in which the oneness and beauty of Roman Catholicism are contrasted with the confusion and multiplicity of Protestant sects. At Clarendon's request Owen answered this in 1662 in his *Animadversions*; and so great was its success that he was offered preferment if he would conform. Owen's condition for making terms was liberty to all who agree in doctrine with the Church of England; nothing therefore came of the negotiation.

In 1663 he was invited by the Congregational churches in Boston, New England, to become their minister, but declined. The Conventicle and Five Mile Acts drove him to London; and in 1666, after the. Fire, he, like other leading Nonconformist ministers, fitted up a room for public service and gathered a congregation, composed chiefly of the old Commonwealth officers. Meanwhile he was incessantly writing; and in 1667 he published his *Catechism*, which led to a proposal, " more acute than diplomatic," from Baxter for union. Various papers passed, and after a year the attempt was closed by the following laconical note from Owen: " I am still a well-wisher to these mathematics." It was now, too, that he published the first part of his vast work upon the Epistle to the Hebrews, together with his exposition of Psalm 130 and his searching book on *Indwelling Sin*.

In 1669 Owen wrote a spirited remonstrance to the Congregationalists in New England, who, under the influence of Presbyterianism, had shown themselves persecutors. At home, too, he was busy in the same cause. In 1670 Samuel Parker's *Ecclesiastical Polity* attacked the Nonconformists in a style of clumsy intolerance. Owen answered him (*Truth and Innocence Vindicated*); Parker replied with personalities as to Owen's connexion with Wallingford House. Then Andrew Marvell with banter and satire finally disposed of Parker in *The Rehearsal Transposed*. Owen himself produced a tract *On the Trinity* (1669), and *Christian Love and Peace* (1672).

At the revival of the Conventicle Acts in 1670, Owen was appointed to draw up a paper of reasons which was submitted to the House of Lords in protest. In this or the following year Harvard College invited him to become its president; he received similar invitations from some of the Dutch universities.

When Charles issued his Declaration of Indulgence in 1672, Owen drew up an address of thanks. This indulgence gave the dissenters an opportunity for increasing their churches and services, and Owen was one of the first preachers at the weekly lectures which the Independents and Presbyterians jointly held at Princes' Hall in Broad Street. He was held in high respect by a large number of the nobility (one of the many things which point to the fact that Congregationalism was by no means the creed of the poor and insignificant), and during 1674 both Charles and James held prolonged conversations with him in which they assured him of their good wishes to the dissenters. Charles gave him 1000 guineas to relieve those upon whom the severe laws had chiefly pressed, and he was even able to procure the release of John Bunyan, whose preaching he ardently admired. In 1674 Owen was attacked by William Sherlock, dean of St Paul's, whom he easily vanquished, and from this time until 1680 he was engaged upon his ministry and the writing of religious works. The chief of these were *On Apostasy* (1676), a sad account of religion under the Restoration; *On the Holy Spirit* (1677-1678) and *The Doctrine of Justification* (1677). In 1680, however, Stillingfleet having on May 11 preached his sermon on " The Mischief of Separation," Owen defended the Nonconformists from the charge of schism in his *Brief Vindication*. Baxter and Howe also answered Stillingfleet, who replied in *The Unreasonableness of Separation*. Owen again answered this, and then left the controversy to a swarm of eager combatants. From this time to his death he was occupied with continual writing, disturbed only by suffering from stone and asthma, and by an absurd charge of being concerned in the Rye House Plot. His most important work was his *Treatise on Evangelical Churches*, in which were contained his latest views regarding church government. He died at Ealing on the 24th

of August 1683, just twenty-one years after he had gone out with so many others on St Bartholomew's day in 1662, and was buried on the 4th of September in Bunhill Fields.

For engraved portraits of Owen see first edition of S. Palmer's *Nonconformists' Memorial* and Vertue's *Sermons and Tracts* (1721). The chief authorities for the life are Owen's *Works*; W. Orme's *Memoirs of Owen*; A. Wood's *Athenae Oxonienses*; R. Baxter's *Life*; D. Neal's *History of the Puritans*; T. Edwards's *Gangraena*; and the various histories of the Independents. See also *The Golden Book of John Owen*, a collection of extracts prefaced by a study of his life and age, by James Moffatt (London, 1904).

OWEN, SIR RICHARD (1804-1892), English biologist, was born at Lancaster on the 20th of July 1804, and received his early education at the grammar school of that town. In 1820 he was apprenticed to a local surgeon and apothecary, and in 1824 he proceeded as a medical student to the university of Edinburgh. He left the university in the following year, and completed his medical course in St Bartholomew's Hospital, London, where he came under the influence of the eminent surgeon, John Abernethy. He then contemplated the usual professional career; but his bent was evidently in the direction of anatomical research, and he was induced by Abernethy to accept the position of assistant to William Clift, conservator of the museum of the Royal College of Surgeons. This congenial occupation soon led him to abandon his intention of medical practice, and his life henceforth was devoted to purely scientific labours. He prepared an important series of catalogues of the Hunterian collection in the Royal College of Surgeons; and in the course of this work he acquired the unrivalled knowledge of comparative anatomy which enabled him to enrich all departments of the science, and specially facilitated his researches on the remains of extinct animals. In 1836 he was appointed Hunterian professor in the Royal College of Surgeons, and in 1849 he succeeded Clift as conservator. He held the latter office until 1856, when he became superintendent of the natural history department of the British Museum. He then devoted much of his energies to a great scheme for a National Museum of Natural History, which eventually resulted in the removal of the natural history collections of the British Museum to a new building at South Kensington, the British Museum (Natural History). He retained office until the completion of this work in 1884, when he received the distinction of K.C.B., and thenceforward lived quietly in retirement at Sheen Lodge, Richmond Park, until his death on the 18th of December 1892.

While occupied with the cataloguing of the Hunterian collection, Owen did not confine his attention to the preparations before him, but also seized every opportunity of dissecting fresh subjects. He was especially favoured with the privilege of investigating the animals which died in the Zoological Society's gardens; and when that society began to publish scientific proceedings in 1831, he was the most voluminous contributor of anatomical papers. His first notable publication, however, was his *Memoir on the Pearly Nautilus* (London, 1832), which was soon recognized as a classic. Henceforth he continued to make important contributions to every department of comparative anatomy and zoology for a period of over fifty years. In the sponges Owen was the first to describe the now well-known " Venus's flower basket " or *Euplectella* (1841, 1857). Among Entozoa his most noteworthy discovery was that of *Trichina spiralis* (1835), the parasite infesting the muscles of man in the disease now termed trichinosis (see also, however, the article on PAGET, SIR JAMES). Of Brachiopoda he made very special studies, which much advanced knowledge and settled the classification which has long been adopted. Among Mollusca, he not only described the pearly nautilus, but also *Spirula* (1850) and other Cephalopoda, both living and extinct; and it was he who proposed the universally-accepted subdivision of this class into the two orders of Dibranchiata and Tetrabranchiata (1832). The problematical Arthropod *Limulus* was also the subject of a special memoir by him in 1873.

Owen's technical descriptions of the Vertebrata were still more numerous and extensive than those of the invertebrate animals. His *Comparative Anatomy and Physiology of Verte-brates* (3 vols., London, 1866–1868) was indeed the result of more personal research than any similar work since Cuvier's *Leçons d'anatomie comparée*. He not only studied existing forms, but also devoted great attention to the remains of extinct groups, and immediately followed Cuvier as a pioneer in verte-brate palaeontology. Early in his career he made exhaustive studies of teeth, both of existing and extinct animals, and pub-lished his profusely illustrated work on *Odontography* (1840–1845). He discovered and described the remarkably complex structure of the teeth of the extinct animals which he named Labyrintho-donts. Among his writings on fishes, his memoir on the African mud-fish, which he named *Protopterus*, laid the foundations for the recognition of the Dipnoi by Johannes Müller. He also pointed out later the serial connexion between the teleostean and ganoid fishes, grouping them in one sub-class, the Teleostomi. Most of his work on reptiles related to the skeletons of extinct forms, and his chief memoirs on British specimens were reprinted in a connected series in his *History of British Fossil Reptiles* (4 vols., London, 1849–1884). He published the first important general account of the great group of Mesozoic land-reptiles, to which he gave the now familiar name of Dinosauria. He also first recognized the curious early Mesozoic land-reptiles, with affinities both to amphibians and mammals, which he termed Anomodontia. Most of these were obtained from South Africa, beginning in 1845 (*Dicynodon*), and eventually furnished materials for his *Catalogue of the Fossil Reptilia of South Africa*, issued by the British Museum in 1876. Among his writings on birds, his classical memoir on the *Apteryx* (1840–1846), a long series of papers on the extinct Dinornithidae of New Zealand, other memoirs on *Aptornis*, *Notornis*, the dodo, and the great auk, may be specially mentioned. His monograph on *Archaeopteryx* (1863), the long-tailed, toothed bird from the Bavarian lithographic stone, is also an epoch-making work. With regard to living mammals, the more striking of Owen's contributions relate to the monotremes, marsupials, and the anthropoid apes. He was also the first to recognize and name the two natural groups of typical Ungulata, the odd-toed (Perissodactyla) and the even-toed (Artiodactyla), while describ-ing some fossil remains in 1848. Most of his writings on mammals, however, deal with extinct forms, to which his attention seems to have been first directed by the remarkable fossils collected by Darwin in South America. *Toxodon*, from the pampas, was then described, and gave the earliest clear evidence of an extinct generalized hoof animal, a "pachyderm with affinities to the Rodentia, Edentata, and Herbivorous Cetacea." Owen's interest in South American extinct mammals then led to the recognition of the giant armadillo, which he named *Glyptodon* (1839), and to classic memoirs on the giant ground-sloths, *Mylodon* (1842) and *Megatherium* (1860), besides other important contributions. At the same time Sir Thomas Mitchell's dis-covery of fossil bones in New South Wales provided material for the first of Owen's long series of papers on the extinct mammals of Australia, which were eventually reprinted in book-form in 1877. He discovered *Diprotodon* and *Thylacoleo*, besides extinct kangaroos and wombats of gigantic size. While occupied with so much material from abroad, Owen was also busily collecting facts for an exhaustive work on similar fossils from the British Isles, and in 1844–1846 he published his *History of British Fossil Mammals and Birds*, which was followed by many later memoirs, notably his *Monograph of the Fossil Mammalia of the Mesozoic Formations* (Palaeont. Soc., 1871). One of his latest publications was a little work entitled *Antiquity of Man as deduced from the Discovery of a Human Skeleton during Excavations of the Docks at Tilbury* (London, 1884).

Owen's detailed memoirs and descriptions require laborious attention in reading, on account of their nomenclature and ambiguous modes of expression; and the circumstance that very little of his terminology has found universal favour causes them to be more generally neglected than they otherwise would be. At the same time it must be remembered that he was a pioneer in concise anatomical nomenclature; and, so far

at least as the vertebrate skeleton is concerned, his terms were based on a carefully reasoned philosophical scheme, which first clearly distinguished between the now familiar phenomena of "analogy" and "homology." Owen's theory of the *Arche-type and Homologies of the Vertebrate Skeleton* (1848), subsequently illustrated also by his little work *On the Nature of Limbs* (1849), regarded the vertebrate frame as consisting of a series of funda-mentally identical segments, each modified according to its position and functions. Much of it was fanciful, and failed when tested by the facts of embryology, which Owen systematically ignored throughout his work. However, though an imperfect and distorted view of certain great truths, it possessed a distinct value at the time of its conception. To the discussion of the deeper problems of biological philosophy he made scarcely any direct and definite contributions. His generalities rarely extended beyond strict comparative anatomy, the phenomena of adaptation to function, and the facts of geographical or geological distribution. His lecture on "virgin reproduction" or parthenogenesis, however, published in 1849, contained the essence of the theory of the germ-plasm elaborated later by August Weismann; and he made several vague statements concerning the geological succession of genera and species of animals and their possible derivation one from another. He referred especially to the changes exhibited by the successive forerunners of the crocodiles (1884) and horses (1868); but it has never become clear how much of the modern doctrines of organic evolution he admitted. He contented himself with the bare remark that "the inductive demonstration of the nature and mode of operation" of the laws governing life would "henceforth be the great aim of the philosophical naturalist."

See *The Life of Richard Owen*, by his grandson, Rev. Richard Owen (2 vols., London, 1894).   (A. S. Wo.)

OWEN, ROBERT (1771–1858), English social reformer, was born at Newtown, Montgomeryshire, in North Wales, on the 14th of May 1771. His father had a small business in Newtown as saddler and ironmonger, and there young Owen received all his school education, which terminated at the age of nine. After serving in a draper's shop for some years he settled in Manchester. His success was very rapid. When only nineteen years of age he became manager of a cotton mill in which five hundred people were employed, and by his administrative intelligence and energy soon made it one of the best establishments of the kind in Great Britain. In this factory Owen used the first bags of American sea-island cotton ever imported into the country; it was the first sea-island cotton from the Southern States. Owen also made remarkable improvement in the quality of the cotton spun; and indeed there is no reason to doubt that at this early age he was the first cotton-spinner in England, a position entirely due to his own capacity and knowledge of the trade. In 1794 or 1795 he became manager and one of the partners of the Chorlton Twist Company at Manchester. During a visit to Glasgow he had fallen in love with the daughter of the proprietor of the New Lanark mills, David Dale. Owen induced his partners to purchase New Lanark; and after his marriage with Miss Dale he settled there, as manager and part owner of the mills (1800). Encouraged by his great success in the management of cotton factories in Manchester, he had already formed the intention of conducting New Lanark on higher principles than the current commercial ones.

The factory of New Lanark had been started in 1784 by Dale and Arkwright, the water-power afforded by the falls of the Clyde being the great attraction. Connected with the mills were about two thousand people, five hundred of whom were children, brought, most of them, at the age of five or six from the poor-houses and charities of Edinburgh and Glasgow. The children especially had been well treated by Dale, but the general condition of the people was very unsatisfactory. Many of them were the lowest of the population, the respectable country people refusing to submit to the long hours and demoralizing drudgery of the factories; theft, drunkenness, and other vices were common; education and sanitation were alike neglected; most families lived only in one room. It was this population, thus committed to his care, which Owen now set himself to elevate and ameliorate. He greatly improved their houses, and by the unsparing and benevolent exertion of his personal influence trained them to habits of order, cleanliness and thrift. He opened a store, where the people could buy goods of the soundest quality at little more than cost price; and the sale of drink was placed under the strictest supervision. His greatest success, however, was in the education of the young, to which he devoted special attention. He was the founder of infant schools in Great Britain; and, though he was anticipated by reformers on the continent of Europe, he seems to have been led to institute them by his own views of what education ought to be, and without hint from abroad. In all these plans Owen obtained the most gratifying success. Though at first regarded with suspicion as a stranger, he soon won the confidence of his people. The mills continued to be a great commercial success, but it is needless to say that some of Owen's schemes involved considerable expense, which was displeasing to his partners. Tired at last of the restrictions imposed on him by men who wished to conduct the business on the ordinary principles, Owen formed a new firm, who, content with 5% of return for their capital, were ready to give freer scope to his philanthropy (1813). In this firm Jeremy Bentham and the well-known Quaker, William Allen, were partners. In the same year Owen first appeared as an author of essays, in which he expounded the principles on which his system of educational philanthropy was based. From an early age he had lost all belief in the prevailing forms of religion, and had thought out a creed for himself, which he considered an entirely new and original discovery. The chief points in this philosophy were that man's character is made not by him but for him; that it has been formed by circumstances over which he had no control ; that he is not a proper subject either of praise or blame,—these principles leading up to the practical conclusion that the great secret in the right formation of man's character is to place him under the proper influences—physical, moral and social—from his earliest years. These principles—of the irresponsibility of man and of the effect of early influences—are the keynote of Owen's whole system of education and social amelioration. As we have said, they are embodied in his first work, *A New View of Society, or Essays on the Principle of the Formation of the Human Character,* the first of these essays (there are four in all) being published in 1813. It is needless to say that Owen's new views theoretically belong to a very old system of philosophy, and that his originality is to be found only in his benevolent application of them. For the next few years Owen's work at New Lanark continued to have a national and even a European significance. His schemes for the education of his workpeople attained to something like completion on the opening of the institution at New Lanark in 1816. He was a zealous supporter of the factory legislation resulting in the act of 1819, which, however, greatly disappointed him. He had interviews and communications with the leading members of government, including the premier, Lord Liverpool, and with many of the rulers and leading statesmen of Europe. New Lanark itself became a much-frequented place of pilgrimage for social reformers, statesmen, and royal personages, including Nicholas, afterwards emperor of Russia. According to the unanimous testimony of all who visited it, the results achieved by Owen were singularly good. The manners of the children, brought up under his system, were beautifully graceful, genial and unconstrained; health, plenty, and contentment prevailed; drunkenness was almost unknown, and illegitimacy was extremely rare. The most perfect good feeling subsisted between Owen and his workpeople, and all the operations of the mill proceeded with the utmost smoothness and regularity; and the business was a great commercial success.

Hitherto Owen's work had been that of a philanthropist, whose great distinction was the originality and unwearying unselfishness of his methods. His first departure in socialism took place in 1817, and was embodied in a report communicated to the committee of the House of Commons on the poor law.

The general misery and stagnation of trade consequent on the termination of the great war was engrossing the attention of the country. After clearly tracing the special causes connected with the war which had led to such a deplorable state of things, Owen pointed out that the permanent cause of distress was to be found in the competition of human labour with machinery, and that the only effective remedy was the united action of men, and the subordination of machinery. His proposals for the treatment of pauperism were based on these principles. He recommended that communities of about twelve hundred persons each should be settled on quantities of land from 1000 to 1500 acres, all living in one large building in the form of a square, with public kitchen and mess-rooms. Each family should have its own private apartments, and the entire care of the children till the age of three, after which they should be brought up by the community, their parents having access to them at meals and all other proper times. These communities might be established by individuals, by parishes, by counties, or by the state; in every case there should be effective supervision by duly qualified persons. Work, and the enjoyment of its results, should be in common. The size of his community was no doubt partly suggested by his village of New Lanark; and he soon proceeded to advocate such a scheme as the best form for the reorganization of society in general. In its fully developed form—and it cannot be said to have changed much during Owen's lifetime—it was as follows. He considered an association of from 500 to 3000 as the fit number for a good working community. While mainly agricultural, it should possess all the best machinery, should offer every variety of employment, and should, as far as possible, be self-contained. "As these townships," as he also called them, "should increase in number, unions of them federatively united shall be formed in circles of tens, hundreds and thousands," till they should embrace the whole world in a common interest.

His plans for the cure of pauperism were received with great favour. *The Times* and the *Morning Post* and many of the leading men of the country countenanced them; one of his most steadfast friends was the duke of Kent, father of Queen Victoria. He had indeed gained the ear of the country, and had the prospect before him of a great career as a social reformer, when he went out of his way at a large meeting in London to declare his hostility to all the received forms of religion. After this defiance to the religious sentiment of the country, Owen's theories were in the popular mind associated with infidelity, and were henceforward suspected and discredited. Owen's own confidence, however, remained unshaken; and he was anxious that his scheme for establishing a community should be tested. At last, in 1825, such an experiment was attempted under the direction of his disciple, Abram Combe, at Orbiston near Glasgow; and in the next year Owen himself commenced another at New Harmony (*q.v.*), Indiana, U.S.A. After a trial of about two years both failed completely. Neither of them was a pauper experiment; but it must be said that the members were of the most motley description, many worthy people of the highest aims being mixed with vagrants, adventurers, and crotchety, wrong-headed enthusiasts. After a long period of friction with William Allen and some of his other partners, Owen resigned all connexion with New Lanark in 1828. On his return from America he made London the centre of his activity. Most of his means having been sunk in the New Harmony experiment, he was no longer a flourishing capitalist, but the head of a vigorous propaganda, in which socialism and secularism were combined. One of the most interesting features of the movement at this period was the establishment in 1832 of an equitable labour exchange system, in which exchange was effected by means of labour notes, the usual means of exchange and the usual middlemen being alike superseded. The word "socialism" first became current in the discussions of the Association of all Classes of all Nations, formed by Owen in 1835. During these years also his secularistic teaching gained such influence among the working classes as to give occasion for the statement in the *Westminster Review* (1839) that his principles were the actual creed of a great portion of them. His views on marriage, which were certainly lax, gave just ground for offence. At this period some more communistic experiments were made, of which the most important were that at Ralahine, in the county of Clare, Ireland, and that at Tytherly in Hampshire. It is admitted that the former (1831) was a remarkable success for three and a half years, till the proprietor, having ruined himself by gambling, was obliged to sell out. Tytherly, begun in 1839, was an absolute failure. By 1846 the only permanent result of Owen's agitation, so zealously carried on by public meetings, pamphlets, periodicals, and occasional treatises, was the co-operative movement, and for the time even that seemed to have utterly collapsed. In his later years Owen became a firm believer in spiritualism. He died at his native town on the 17th of November 1858.

Owen left four sons, Robert Dale, William, David Dale and Richard, all of whom became citizens of the United States. ROBERT DALE OWEN, the eldest (1801–1877), was for long an able exponent in his adopted country of his father's doctrines. In 1836–39 and 1851–52 he was a member of the Indiana House of Representatives and in 1844–47 was a Representative in Congress, where he drafted the bill for the founding of the Smithsonian Institution. He was elected a member of the Indiana Constitutional Convention in 1850, and was instrumental in securing widows and married women control of their property, and the adoption of a common free school system. He later succeeded in passing a state law giving greater freedom in divorce. From 1853 to 1858 he was United States minister at Naples. He was a strong believer in spiritualism and was the author of two well-known books on the subject: *Footfalls on the Boundary of Another World* (1859) and *The Debateable Land Between this World and the Next* (1872). Owen's third son, DAVID DALE OWEN (1807–1860), was in 1839 appointed United States geologist, and made extensive surveys of the north-west, which were published by order of Congress. The youngest son, RICHARD OWEN (1810–1890), was a professor of natural science in Nashville University.

Of R. Owen's numerous works in exposition of his system, the most important are the *New View of Society*; the *Report* communicated to the Committee on the Poor Law; the *Book of the New Moral World*; and *Revolution in the Mind and Practice of the Human Race*. See *Life of Robert Owen written by himself* (London, 1857), and *Threading my Way, Twenty-seven Years of Autobiography*, by Robert Dale Owen (London, 1874). There are also *Lives of Owen* by A. J. Booth (London, 1869), W. L. Sargant (London, 1860), Lloyd Jones (London, 1889), F. A. Packard (Philadelphia, 1866) and F. Podmore (London, 1906). See also H. Simon, *Robert Owen: sein Leben und seine Bedeutung für die Gegenwart* (Jena, 1905); E. Dolléans, *Robert Owen* (Paris, 1905); G. J. Holyoake, *History of Co-operation in England* (London, 1906); and the article COMMUNISM.

OWENS, JOHN (1790–1846), English merchant, was born at Manchester in 1796, the son of a prosperous merchant. Early in life he became a partner in his father's business and was soon noted for his ability as a cotton buyer. His business prospered, and the firm traded with China, India, South America and the United States, dealing in many other commodities. His large fortune he suggested leaving to his friend and partner George Faulkner (1790–1860), already a rich man. But by the latter's advice he bequeathed it to trustees for the foundation of a college (Owens College, Manchester, opened 1851, now part of Victoria University), based upon his own ideas of education. He died in Manchester on the 29th of July 1846. His bequests to friends and charities amounted to some £52,000, while for the college he left £96,654. Among the conditions for its foundation the most important was that which discountenanced any sort of religious test for students or teachers.

OWENSBORO, a city and the county-seat of Daviess county, Kentucky, U.S.A., on the Ohio river, 112 m. by rail W.S.W. of Louisville. Pop. (1890) 9837; (1900) 13,189, of whom 3061 were negroes; (1910 census) 16,011. The city is served by the Illinois Central, the Louisville & Nashville, and the Louisville, Henderson & St Louis railways, and by steamboat lines to river ports. At Owensboro are the Owensboro College for women (non-sect.), opened in 1890, Saint Francis Academy, and a Roman Catholic school for boys. Two miles S. of the city is Hickman Park (70 acres), a pleasure resort, and E. of the city is a summer

Chautauqua park. Owensboro is situated in a good agricultural region; coal, iron, building stone, clay, oil, lead and zinc abound in the vicinity; and the city has a notably large trade in tobacco (especially strip tobacco) and has various manufactures. The value of the city's factory products increased from $1,740,128 in 1900 to $4,187,700 in 1905, or 140·6%. The municipality owns and operates its electric-lighting plant and water-works. Owensboro was settled about 1798, and for several years was commonly known as Yellow Banks; in 1816 it was laid out as a town and named Rossborough, and two years later the present name was adopted in honour of Colonel Abraham Owen (1769–1811), a Virginian who removed to Kentucky in 1785, served in several Indian campaigns, and was killed in the battle of Tippecanoe. Owensboro was incorporated as a city in 1866.

OWEN SOUND, a town and port of entry in Ontario, Canada, and capital of Grey county, situated 99 m. N.W. of Toronto, on Georgian Bay. Pop. (1901) 8776. It is the terminus of branches of the Canadian Pacific and Grand Trunk railways, and of the Canadian Pacific and other steamship lines plying to ports on Lakes Huron and Superior. Its harbour is one of the best on Lake Huron, and navigable by lake vessels of the largest size. It is a flourishing town, containing shipbuilding yards, and manufactories of mill machinery, agricultural implements, furniture and sewing-machines, flour-mills, saw-mills and large grain elevators.

OWL (O. Eng. *Ûle*, Swed. *Ûggla*, Ger. *Eule*—all allied to Lat. *Ulula*, and evidently of imitative origin), the general English name for every nocturnal bird of prey, of which group nearly two hundred species have been recognized. The owls form a very natural assemblage, and one about the limits of which no doubt has for a long while existed. They were formerly placed with the Accipitres or diurnal birds of prey, but are now known to belong to a different group of birds, and are placed as a suborder *Striges* of Coraciiform birds, their nearest allies being the goatsuckers. The subdivision of the group has always been a fruitful matter of discussion, owing to the great resemblance obtaining among all its members, and the existence of safe characters for its division has only lately been at all generally recognized. By the older naturalists, it is true, owls were divided, as was first done by F. Willughby, into two sections—one in which all the species exhibit tufts of feathers on the head, the so-called "ears" or "horns," and the second in which the head is not tufted. The artificial and therefore untrustworthy nature of this distinction was shown by Isidore Geoffroy St-Hilaire (*Ann. Sc. Naturelles*, xxi. 194-203) in 1830. The later work of C. L. Nitzch on pterylography and of A. Milne-Edwards on osteology has led to a division of the family *Strigidae* into the sub-families *Striginae*, in which the unnotched sternum has its broad keel joined to the furcula, and *Buboninae*, in which the sternum is notched posteriorly, the clavicles do not always meet to form a furcula, nor meet the sternum. The *Striginae* contain the screech- or barn-owls (*Strix*) and the partly intermediate *Heliodilus* of Madagascar, whilst all the other genera are now placed with the *Buboninae*.

Among owls are found birds which vary in length from 5 in. —as *Glaucidium cobanense*, which is therefore much smaller than a skylark—to more than 2 ft., a size that is attained by many species. Their plumage, none of the feathers of which possesses an aftershaft, is of the softest kind, rendering their flight almost noiseless. But one of the most characteristic features of this whole group is the ruff, consisting of several rows of small and much curved feathers with stiff shafts—originating from a fold of the skin, which begins on each side of the base of the beak, runs above the eyes, and passing downwards round and behind the ears turns forward, and ends at the chin—and serving to support the longer feathers of the "disk" or space immediately around the eyes, which extend over it. A considerable number of species of owls, belonging to various genera, and natives of countries most widely separated, are remarkable for exhibiting two phases of coloration—one in which the prevalent browns have a more or less rusty-red tinge, and the other in which they incline to grey. Another characteristic of owls is the reversible property of their outer toes, which are when perching quite backwards. Many forms have the legs and toes thickly clothed to the very claws; others have the toes, and even the tarsi, bare, or only sparsely beset by bristles. Among the bare-legged owls those of the Indian *Ketupa* are conspicuous, and this feature is usually correlated with their fish-catching habits; but certainly other owls that are not known to catch fish present much the same character.

Among the multitude of owls there is only room here to make further mention of a few of the more interesting. First must be noticed the tawny owl—the *Strix stridula* of Linnaeus, the type, as has been above said, of the whole group, and especially of the Strigine section as here understood. This is the *Syrnium aluco* of some authors, the *chat-huant* of the French, the species whose tremulous hooting "tu-whit, to-who," has been celebrated by Shakespeare, and, as well as the plaintive call, "keewick," of the young after leaving the nest, will be familiar sounds to many readers, for the bird is very generally distributed throughout most parts of Europe, extending its range through Asia Minor to Palestine, and also to Barbary—but not belonging to the Ethiopian Region or to the eastern half of the Palaearctic. It

Fig. 1.—*Strix occidentalis.*

is the largest of the species indigenous to Britain, and is strictly a woodland bird, only occasionally choosing any other place for its nest than a hollow tree. Its food consists almost entirely of small mammals, chiefly rodents; but, though on this account most deserving of protection from all classes, it is subject to the stupid persecution of the ignorant; and is rapidly declining in numbers.[1] Its nearest allies in North America are the *S. nebulosa*, with some kindred forms, one of which, the *S. occidentalis* of California and Arizona, is figured above; but none of them seem to have the "merry note" that is uttered by the European species. Common to the most northerly forest-tracts of both continents (for, though a slight difference of coloration is observable between American examples and those from the Old World, it is impossible to consider it specific) is the much larger *S. cinerea* or *S. lapponica*, whose iron-grey plumage, delicately mottled with dark brown, and the concentric circles of its facial disks make it one of the most remarkable of the group. Then may be noticed the genus *Bubo*—containing several species

which from their size are usually known as eagle-owls. Here the Nearctic and Palaearctic forms are sufficiently distinct—the latter, *B. ignavus*,[2] the *duc* or *grand duc* of the French, ranging over the whole of Europe and Asia north of the Himalayas, while the former, *B. virginianus*, extends over the whole of North America. A contrast to the generally sombre colour of these birds is shown by the snowy owl, *Nyctea scandiaca*, a circumpolar species, and the only one of its genus, which disdains the shelter of forests and braves the most rigorous arctic climate, though compelled to migrate southward in winter when no sustenance is left for it. Its large size and white plumage, more or less mottled with black, distinguish this from every other owl. Then may be mentioned the birds commonly known in English as "horned" owls—the *hibous* of the French, belonging to the genus *Asio*. One, *A. otus* (the *Otus vulgaris* of some authors), inhabits woods, and, distinguished by its long tufts, usually borne erected, would seem to be common to both America and Europe—though experts profess their ability to distinguish between examples from each country. Another species, *A. accipitrinus* (the *Otus brachyotus* of many authors), has much shorter tufts on its head, and they are frequently carried depressed so as to escape observation. This is the "woodcock-owl" of English sportsmen, for, though a good many are bred in Great Britain, the majority arrive in autumn from Scandinavia, just about the time that the immigration of woodcocks occurs. This species frequents heaths, moors and the open country generally, to the exclusion of woods, and has an enormous geographical range, including not only all Europe, North Africa and northern Asia, but the whole of America—reaching also to the Falklands, the Galapagos and the Sandwich Islands—for the attempt to separate specifically examples from those localities only shows that they possess more or less well-defined local races. Commonly placed near *Asio*, but whether really akin to it cannot be stated, is the genus *Scops*, of which nearly forty species, coming from different parts of the world, have been described; but this number should probably be reduced by one half. The type of the genus *S. giu*, the *petit duc* of the French, is a well-known bird in the south of Europe, about as big as a thrush, with very delicately pencilled plumage, occasionally visiting Britain, emigrating in autumn across the Mediterranean, and ranging very far to the eastward. Farther southward, both in Asia and Africa, it is represented by other species of very similar size, and in the eastern part of North America by *S. asio*, of which there is a tolerably distinct western form, *S. kennicotti*, besides several local races. *S. asio* is one of the owls that especially exhibits the dimorphism of coloration above mentioned, and it was long before the true state of the case was understood. At first the two forms were thought to be distinct, and then for some time the belief obtained that the ruddy birds were the young of the greyer form which was called *S. naevia*; but now the "red owl" and the "mottled owl" of the older American ornithologists are known to be one species.[3] One of the most remarkable of American owls is *Speotyto cunicularia*, the bird that in the northern part of the continent inhabits the burrows of the prairie dog, and in the southern those of the biscacha, where the latter occurs—making holes for itself, says Darwin, where that is not the case—rattlesnakes being often also joint tenants of the same abodes. The odd association of these animals, interesting as it is, cannot here be more than noticed, for a few words must be said, ere we leave the owls of this section, on the species which has associations of a very different kind—the bird of Pallas Athene, the emblem of the city to which science and art were so welcome. There can be no doubt, from the many representations on coins and sculptures, as to their subject being the *Carine noctua* of modern ornithologists, but those who know the grotesque actions and ludicrous expression of this veritable buffoon of birds can never

[1] All owls have the habit of casting up the indigestible parts of the food swallowed in the form of pellets, which may often be found in abundance under the owl-roost, and reveal without any manner of doubt what the prey of the birds has been. The result in nearly every case shows the enormous service they render to man in destroying rats and mice. Details of many observations to this effect are recorded in the *Bericht über die XIV. Versammlung der Deutschen Ornithologen-Gesellschaft* (pp. 30-34).

[2] This species bears confinement very well, and propagates freely therein. To it belong the historic owls of Arundel Castle.

[3] See the remarks of Mr Ridgway in the work before quoted (*B. N. America*, iii. 9, 10), where also response is made to the observations of Mr Allen in the Harvard *Bulletin* (ii. 338, 339).

cease to wonder at its having been seriously selected as the symbol of learning, and can hardly divest themselves of a suspicion that the choice must have been made in the spirit of sarcasm. This little owl (for that is its only name—though it is not even the smallest that appears in England), the *chevêche* of the French, is spread throughout the greater part of Europe, but it is not a native of Britain. It has a congener in *C. brama*, a bird well known to all residents in India.

Finally, we have owls of the second section, those allied to the screech-owl, *Strix flammea*, the *Effraie*[1] of the French. This, with its discordant scream, its snoring, and its hissing, is far too well known to need description, for it is one of the most widely-spread of birds, and is the owl that has the greatest geographical range, inhabiting almost every country in the world—Sweden and Norway, America north of lat. 45°, and New Zealand being the principal exceptions. It varies, however, not inconsiderably, both in size and intensity of colour, and several ornithologists have tried to found on these variations more than half-a-dozen distinct species. Some, if not most of them, seem, however, hardly worthy to be considered geographical races, for their differences do not always depend on locality. R. Bowdler Sharpe, with much labour and in great detail, has given his reasons (*Cat. B. Brit. Museum*, ii. 291-309; and *Ornith. Miscellany*, i. 269-298; ii. 1-21) for acknowledging four "subspecies" of *S. flammea*, as well as five other species. Of these last, *S. tenebricosa* is peculiar to Australia, while *S. novae-hollandiae* inhabits also New Guinea, and has a "subspecies," *S. castanops*, found only in Tasmania; a third, *S. candida*, has a wide range from Fiji and northern Australia through the Philippines and Formosa to China, Burmah and India; a fourth, *S. capensis*, is peculiar to South Africa; while *S. thomensis* is said to be confined to the African island of St Thomas. To these may perhaps have to be added a species from New Britain, described by Count Salvadori as *Strix aurantia*, but it may possibly prove on further investigation not to be a strigine owl at all.　(A. N.)

FIG. 2.—*Strix flammea.*

OWLING, in English law, the offence of transporting wool or sheep out of the kingdom, to the detriment of the staple manufacture of wool. The name is said to owe its origin to the fact that the offence was usually carried on at night-time, when the owls were abroad. The offence was stringently regulated by a statute of Edward III. (1336–7), while many subsequent statutes also dealt with it. In 1566 the offence was made punishable by the cutting off of the left hand and nailing it in a public place. By a statute of 1660 the ship and cargo were to be forfeited. In the reign of George I. (1717–1718) the penalty was altered to transportation for seven years. The offence was abolished in 1824.

OWOSSO, a city of Shiawassee county, Michigan, U.S.A., on Shiawassee river, about 79 m. N.W. of Detroit and 28 m. N.E. of Lansing. Pop. (1900) 8696, of whom 1396 were foreign-born; (1910 census) 9639. It is served by the Michigan Central, the Grand Trunk, and the Ann Arbor railways, and is a division

[1] Through the dialectic forms *Fresaie* and *Presaie*, the origin of the word is easily traced to the Latin *praesaga*—a bird of bad omen; but it has also been confounded with *Orfraie*, a name of the Osprey (*q.v.*).

point of the last. It is situated in the coal area of Michigan, and has various manufactures, including beet-sugar, for which Owosso is an important centre. The value of the city's factory products increased from $2,055,052 in 1900 to $3,109,232 in 1905, or 51.3%. The municipality owns and operates its water-works. Owosso was settled about 1834 and chartered as a city in 1859.

OX, strictly speaking, the Saxon name for the males of domesticated cattle (*Bos taurus*), but in a zoological sense employed so as to include not only the extinct wild ox of Europe but likewise bovine animals of every description, that is to say true oxen, bison and buffaloes. The characteristics of the sub-family *Bovinae*, or typical section of the family *Bovidae*, are given in the article BOVIDAE (q.v.); for the systematic position of that family see PECORA.

In the typical oxen, as represented by the existing domesticated breeds (see CATTLE) and the extinct aurochs (q.v.), the horns are cylindrical and placed on an elevated crest at the very vertex of the skull, which has the frontal region of great length. The aurochs was a black animal, with a lighter dorsal streak, and horns directed upwards in the shape of a pitchfork, black at their tips, but otherwise whitish. The fighting bulls of Spain, the black Pembroke cattle of Wales, with their derivatives the white park-cattle of Chillingham in Northumberland, are undoubtedly the direct descendants of the aurochs. The black Kerry breed and the black or brown Scotch cattle are also more or less nearly related; and a similar kinship is claimed for the Siemental cattle of Switzerland, although their colour is white and fawn. Short-horns are a modern derivative from cattle of the same general type. Among other British breeds may be mentioned the Devons and Herefords, both characterized by their red colour; the long-horned and Sussex breeds, both with very large horns, showing a tendency to grow downwards; and the Ayrshire. Polled, or hornless, breeds, such as the polled Angus and polled Suffolk, are of interest, as showing how easily the horns can be eliminated, and thus indicating a hornless ancestry. The white cattle formerly kept at Chartley Park, Staffordshire, exhibit signs of affinity with the long-horn breed. The Channel Island cattle, which are either black or fawn, would seem to be nearly allied to the Spanish fighting breed, and thus to the aurochs. The great white or cream coloured cattle of Italy, Austria, Hungary and Poland, which have very long black-tipped horns, are also probably not far removed from the aurochs stock.

On the other hand, the great tawny draught cattle of Spain seem to indicate mixture with a different stock, the horns having a double curvature, quite different from the simple one of the aurochs type. There are reports as to these cattle having been formerly crossed with the humped eastern species; and their characteristics are all in favour of such an origin. Humped cattle are widely spread over Africa, Madagascar and India, and form a distinct species, *Bos indicus*, characterized by the presence of a fleshy hump on the shoulders, the convexity (instead of concavity) of the first part of the curve of the horns, the very large size of the dewlap; and the general presence of white rings round the fetlocks, and light circles surrounding the eyes. The voice and habits of these cattle are also markedly different from those of European cattle. Whether humped cattle are of Indian or African origin cannot be determined, and the species is known only in the domesticated condition. The largest horns are found in the Galla cattle, in which they attain enormous dimensions. In Europe the name zebu is generally applied to the Indian breed, although no such designation is known in India itself.

A third type is apparently indicated by the ancient Egyptian cattle, which were not humped, and for which the name *Bos aegyptiacus* has been suggested. The cattle of Ankole, on the Uganda frontier, which have immense horns, conform to this type.

A second group of the genus *Bos* is represented by the Indo-Malay cattle included in the sub-genus *Bibos* (see BANTIN, GAUR and GAYAL); they are characterized by the more or less marked flattening of the horns, the presence of a well-marked ridge on the anterior half of the back, and the white legs,

More distinct are the bisons, forming the sub-genus *Bison*, represented by the European and the American species (see BISON), the forehead of the skull being much shorter and wider, and the horns not arising from a crest on the extreme vertex, while the number of ribs is different (14 pairs in bisons, only 13 in oxen), and the hair on the head and neck is long and shaggy. Very close to this group, if indeed really separable, is the Tibetan yak (q.v.), forming by itself the sub-genus *Poephagus*.

The most widely different from the true oxen are, however, the buffaloes (see BUFFALO), which have consequently the most claim to generic distinction. From all other *Bovinae* they differ by the triangular section of their horns. They are divisible into two groups, an African and an Asiatic, both of which are generally included in the sub-genus, or genus, *Bubalus*, although the latter are sometimes separated as *Buffelus*. The smallest member of the group is the anoa (q.v.) of Celebes.

As regards the origin of the ox-tribe we are still in the dark. The structure of their molar teeth affiliates them to the antelopes of the *Oryx* and *Hippotragus* groups; but the early bovines lack horns in the female, whereas both sexes of these antelopes are horned.

Remains of the wild ox or aurochs are abundant in the superficial deposits of Europe, Western Asia, and Northern Africa; those from the brick-earths of the Thames valley indicating animals of immense proportions. Side by side with these are found remains of a huge bison, generally regarded as specifically distinct from the living European animal and termed *Bos (Bison) priscus*. In the Pleistocene of India occurs a large ox (*Bos namadicus*), possibly showing some affinity with the *Bibos* group, and in the same formation are found remains of a buffalo, allied to, but distinct from the living Indian species. Large oxen also occur in the Lower Pliocene of India, although not closely allied to the living kinds; while in the same formation are found remains of bison (or [?] yak) and buffaloes, some of the latter being nearly akin to the anoa, although much larger. Perhaps, however, the most interesting are the remains of certain oxen from the Lower Pliocene of Europe and India, which have been described under the sub-generic (or generic) title of *Leptobos*, and are characterized by the absence of horns in the females. In other respects they appear to come nearest to the bantin. Remains of extinct bisons, some of gigantic size, occur in the superficial formations of North America as far south as Texas. See R. Lydekker, *Wild Oxen, Sheep and Goats* (London, 1898).

(R. L.*)

OXALIC ACID, $H_2C_2O_4 \cdot 2H_2O$, one of the oldest known organic acids. Scheele prepared it by oxidizing sugar with nitric acid, and showed it to be identical with the acetosellic acid obtained from wood-sorrel. It is found in the form of its acid potassium salt in many plants, especially in wood-sorrel (*Oxalis acetosella*) and in varieties of *Rumex*; as ammonium salt in guano; as calcium salt in rhubarb root, in various lichens and in plant cells; as sodium salt in species of *Salicornia* and as free acid in varieties of *Boletus*. It is also present in urine and in urinary calculi. It is formed in the oxidation of many organic compounds (e.g. sugar, starch and cellulose) by nitric acid, and also by the fusion of many oxygen-holding compounds with caustic alkalis, this latter method being employed for the manufacture of oxalic acid. In this process cellulose (in the form of sawdust) is made into a stiff paste with a mixture of strong caustic potash and soda solution and heated in flat iron pans to 200-250° C. The somewhat dark-coloured mass is lixiviated with a small amount of warm water in order to remove excess of alkali, the residual alkaline oxalates converted into insoluble calcium oxalate by boiling with milk of lime, the lime salt separated, and decomposed by means of sulphuric acid. It is found that the sawdust obtained from soft woods is the best material for use in this process. It may be obtained synthetically by heating sodium in a current of carbon dioxide to 360° C.; by the oxidation of ethylene glycol; by heating sodium formate to 400° C. (V. Merz and W. Weith, *Ber.*, 1882, 15, p. 1513), and by the spontaneous hydrolysis of an aqueous solution of cyanogen gas.

The hydrated acid crystallizes in prisms which effloresce in air, and are readily soluble in water. It loses its water of crystallization at 100° C., and begins to sublime at about 150-160° C., whilst on heating to a still higher temperature it partially decomposes into carbon dioxide and formic acid, or into carbon dioxide, carbon monoxide and water; the latter decomposition being also brought about by heating oxalic acid with concentrated sulphuric acid. The anhydrous acid melts at 189·5° C. (E. Bamberger, *Ber.*, 1888, 21, p. 1901) and is frequently used as a condensing agent. Phosphorus pentachloride decomposes it into carbon monoxide and dioxide, the reaction being the one generally applied for the purpose of preparing phosphorus oxychloride. When heated with glycerin to 100° C. it yields formic acid and carbon dioxide; above this temperature, allyl alcohol is formed. Nascent hydrogen reduces it to glycollic acid. Potassium permanganate in acid solution oxidizes it to carbon dioxide and water; the manganese sulphate formed has a catalytic accelerating effect on the decomposition.

Oxalic acid is very poisonous, and by reason of its great similarity in appearance to Epsom salts, it has been very frequently mistaken for this substance with, in many cases, fatal results. The antidotes for oxalic acid poisoning are milk of lime, chalk, whiting, or even wall-plaster, followed by evacuation brought about by an enema or castor oil. Only the salts of the alkali metals are soluble in water. Beside the ordinary acid and neutral salts, a series of salts called quadroxalates is known, these being salts containing one molecule of acid salt, in combination with one molecule of acid, one of the most common being "salt of sorrel," $KHC_2O_4 \cdot H_2C_2O_4 \cdot 2H_2O$. The oxalates are readily decomposed on heating, leaving a residue of carbonate, or oxide of the metal. The silver salt decomposes with explosive violence, leaving a residue of the metal.

Potassium ferrous oxalate, $FeK_2(C_2O_4)_2 \cdot H_2O$, is a strong reducing agent and is used as a photographic developer. *Potassium ferric oxalate*, $FeK_3(C_2O_4)_3$, is used in the preparation of platinotypes, owing to the fact that its solution is rapidly decomposed by sunlight, $2FeK_3(C_2O_4)_3 = 2FeK_2(C_2O_4)_2 + K_2C_2O_4 + 2CO_2$. *Ethyl oxalate*, $(CO \cdot OC_2H_5)_2$, prepared by boiling anhydrous oxalic acid with absolute alcohol, is a colourless liquid which boils at 186° C. *Methyl oxalate* $(CO \cdot OCH_3)_2$, which is prepared in a similar manner, is a solid melting at 54° C. It is used in the preparation of pure methyl alcohol. On treatment with zinc and alkyl iodides or with zinc alkyls they are converted into esters of hydroxy-dialkyl acetic acids. An impure *oxalyl chloride*, a liquid boiling at 70° C., has been obtained by the action of phosphorus pentachloride on ethyl oxalate. *Oxamic acid*, $HO_2C \cdot CONH_2$, is obtained on heating acid ammonium oxalate; by boiling oxamide with ammonia; and among the products produced when amino-acids are oxidized with potassium permanganate (J. T. Halsey, *Zeit. f. physiol. Chem.*, 1898, 25, p. 325). It is a crystalline powder difficultly soluble in water and melting at 210° C. (with decomposition). Its ethyl ester, known as oxamaethane, crystallizes in rhombic plates which melt at 114-115° C. Phosphorus pentachloride converts it into cyan-carbonic ester, the ethyl oxamine chloride first formed being unstable; $ROOC \cdot CONH_2 \rightarrow ROOC \cdot C(Cl_2) \cdot NH_2 \rightarrow CN \cdot COOR$. *Oximide*, $(CO)_2NH$, produced by the action of a mixture of phosphorus pentachloride and oxychloride on oxamic acid (H. Ost and A. Mente, *Ber.*, 1886, 19, p. 3229), crystallizes in prisms, and when boiled with water is rapidly hydrolysed to oxamide and oxalic acid. *Oxamide*, $(CONH_2)_2$, is best prepared by the action of ammonia on the esters of oxalic acid. It is also obtained by the action of hydrogen peroxide on hydrocyanic acid, or of manganese dioxide and sulphuric acid on potassium cyanide. It is a white crystalline powder which is almost insoluble in cold water. It melts at 417-419° C. (with decomposition) when heated in a sealed tube (A. Michael, *Ber.*, 1895, 28, p. 1632). When heated with phosphorus pentoxide it yields cyanogen. It is readily hydrolysed by hot solutions of the caustic alkalis. Substituted oxamides are produced by the action of primary amines on ethyl oxalate. *Semioxamazide*, $H_2N \cdot CO \cdot CO \cdot NH \cdot NH_2$, is prepared by the action of hydrazine hydrate on oxamaethane (W. Kerp and K. Unger, *Ber.*, 1897, 30, p. 586). It crystallizes in plates which melt at 220-221° C. (with decomposition). It is only slightly soluble in water, but is readily soluble in acids and alkalis. It reduces silver salts rapidly. It condenses with aldehydes and ketones to produce semioxamazones.

OXALIS, in botany, a large genus of small herbaceous plants, comprising, with a few small allied genera, the natural order Oxalidaceae. The name is derived from Gr. $\delta\xi\dot{\upsilon}\varsigma$, acid, the plants being acid from presence of acid calcium oxalate. It contains about 220 species, chiefly South African and tropical and South American. It is represented in Britain by the wood-sorrel, a small stemless plant with radical trefoil-like leaves growing from a creeping scaly rootstock, and the flowers borne singly on an axillary stalk; the flowers are regular with five sepals, five obovate, white, purple-veined, free petals, ten stamens and a central five-lobed, five-celled ovary with five free styles. The fruit is a capsule, splitting by valves; the seeds have a fleshy coat, which curls back elastically, ejecting the true seed. The leaves, as in the other species of the genus, show a "sleep-movement," becoming pendulous at night.

Oxalis crenata, Oca of the South Americans, is a tuberous-rooted half-hardy perennial, native of Peru. Its tubers are comparatively small, and somewhat acid; but if they be exposed in the sun from six to ten days they become sweet and floury. In the climate of England they can only be grown by starting them in heat in March, and planting out in June in a light soil and warm situation. They grow freely enough, but few tubers are formed, and these of small size. The fleshy stalks, which have the acid flavour of the family, may, however, be used in the same way as rhubarb for tarts. The leaves may be eaten in salads. It is easily propagated by cuttings of the stems or by means of sets like the potato.

Oxalis Deppei or *O. tetraphylla*, a bulbous perennial, native of Mexico, has scaly bulbs, from which are produced fleshy, tapering, white, semi-transparent roots, about 4 in. in length and 3 to 4 in. in diameter. They strike down into the soil, which should therefore be made light and rich with abundance of decayed vegetable matter. The bulbs should be planted about the end of April, 6 in. apart, in rows 1 ft. asunder, being only just covered with soil and having a situation with a southern aspect. The roots should be dug up before

Wood-sorrel (*Oxalis Acetosella*). 1, Fruit which has a split open; the seeds are shot out by the elastic contractions of their outer coat, 2.

they become affected by frost, but if protected they will continue to increase in size till November. When taken up the bulbs should be stored in a cool dry place for replanting and the roots for use. The roots are gently boiled with salt and water, peeled and eaten like asparagus with melted butter and the yolks of eggs, or served up like salsafy and scorzonera with white sauce.

Many other species are known in cultivation for edgings, rockwork or as pot-plants for the greenhouse, the best hardy and half-hardy kinds being *O. arenaria*, purple; *O. Bowiei*, crimson; *O. enneaphylla*, white or pale rose; *O. floribunda*, rose; *O. lasiandra*, pink; *O. luteola*, creamy yellow; *O. variabilis*, purple, white, red; and *O. violacea*, violet.

OXAZOLES, a group of organic compounds containing a ring complex (shown below) composed of three carbon atoms, and one oxygen and one nitrogen atom; they are isomeric with the isoxazoles (*q.v.*). They are obtained by condensing a halogen derivatives of ketones with acid-amides (M. Lewy, *Ber.* 1887, 20, p. 2576; 1888, 21, p. 2195)

$$R \cdot C \underset{OH}{\overset{NH}{<}} + \overset{HO \cdot C \cdot R'}{\underset{Br \cdot CH}{}} = R \cdot C \underset{O \cdot CH}{\overset{N \cdot CR'}{<}};$$

by the action of concentrated sulphuric acid on nitriles and benzoin (F. Japp, *Jour. Chem. Soc.* 1893, 63, p. 469); and by passing hydrochloric acid gas into a mixture of aromatic aldehydes and their cyanhydrins (E. Fischer, *Ber.* 1896, 29, p. 205).

$$R \cdot CH \underset{OH}{\overset{CN}{<}} + OHC \cdot R = R \cdot C \underset{O \cdot C \cdot R}{\overset{CH \cdot N}{<}}$$

They are weak bases, and the ring system is readily split by evaporation with hydrochloric acid, or by the action of reducing and oxidizing agents.

The dihydro-oxazoles or oxazolines are similarly formed when β-halogen alkyl amides are condensed with alkali (S. Gabriel, *Ber.* 1889, 22, p. 2220), or by the action of alkali on the compounds formed by the interaction of ethylene chlorhydrin on nitriles. They

are strong bases characterized by a quinoline-like smell. The amino-oxazolines are known as alkylene-ψ-ureas and are formed by the action of potassium cyanate on the hydrobromides of the bromalkylamines (S. Gabriel, *Ber.* 1895, 28, p. 1899). They are strong bases. *Tetrahydro-oxazoles* or oxazolidines result from the action of aldehydes on amino-alcohols (L. Knorr, *Ber.* 1901, 34, p. 3484). The above types of compounds may be represented by the following formulae:—

$$\underset{\text{oxazole}}{\overset{N = CH}{\underset{CH = CH}{<}}O} \quad \underset{\text{oxazoline}}{\overset{N = CH}{\underset{CH_2 \cdot CH_2}{<}}O} \quad \underset{\text{amino-oxazoline}}{\overset{N = C(NH_2)}{\underset{CH_2 - CH_2}{<}}O} \quad \underset{\text{oxazolidine}}{\overset{NH - CH_2}{\underset{CH_2 - CH_2}{<}}O}$$

The *benzoxazoles* are formed when ortho-aminophenols are condensed with organic acids (A. Ladenburg, *Ber.* 1876, 9, p. 1524; 1877, 10, p. 1113), or by heating aldehydes and ortho-aminophenols to high temperature (C. Mazzara and A. Leonardi, *Gazz.* 1871, 21, p. 251). They are mostly crystalline solids which distil unchanged. When warmed with acids they split into their components. They behave as weak bases. By the condensation of ortho-aminophenols with phosgene or thiophosgene, oxy and thio-derivatives are obtained, the (OH) and (SH) groups being situated in the μ position, and these compounds on treatment with amines yield amino derivatives.

OXE, PEDER (1520–1575), Danish Finance Minister, was born in 1520. At the age of twelve he was sent abroad to complete his education, and resided at the principal universities of Germany, Holland, France, Italy and Switzerland for seventeen years. On his return he found both his parents dead, and was appointed the guardian of his eleven young brothers and sisters, in which capacity, profiting by the spoliation of the church, he accumulated immense riches. His extraordinary financial abilities and pronounced political capacity soon found ample scope in public life. In 1552 he was raised to the dignity of *Rigsraad* (councillor of state); in 1554 he successfully accomplished his first diplomatic mission, by adjusting the differences between the elector of Saxony and the margrave of Brandenburg. The same year he held the post of governor of Copenhagen and shared with Byrge Trolle the control of the treasury. A few years later he incurred the royal disfavour for gross malversation in the administration of public property, and failing to compromise matters with the king, fled to Germany and engaged in political intrigues with the adventurer Wilhelm von Grumbach (1503–1567) for the purpose of dethroning Frederick II. in favour of Christina of Lorraine, the daughter of Christian II. But the financial difficulties of Frederick II. during the stress of the Scandinavian Seven Years' War compelled him, in 1566, to recall the great financier, when his confiscated estates were restored to him and he was reinstated in all his offices and dignities. A change for the better immediately ensued. The finances were speedily put on an excellent footing, means were provided for carrying on the war to a successful issue (one of the chief expedients being the raising of the Sound tolls) and on the conclusion of peace Oxe, as lord treasurer, not only reduced the national debt considerably, but redeemed a large portion of the alienated crown-lands. He reformed the coinage, developed trade and commerce and introduced numerous agricultural reforms, especially on his own estates, which he was never weary of enlarging, so that on his death he was the wealthiest landowner in Denmark. Oxe died on the 24th of October 1575, after contributing, more than any other statesman of his day, to raise Denmark for a brief period to the rank of a great power.

See P. Oxe's *Live og Levnet* (Copenhagen, 1675); *Danmarks riges historie*, vol. 3 (Copenhagen, 1897–1905).

OXENBRIDGE, JOHN (1608–1674), English Nonconformist divine, was born at Daventry, Northamptonshire, on the 30th of January 1608, and was educated at Emmanuel College, Cambridge, and Magdalen Hall, Oxford (B.A. 1628, M.A. 1631). As tutor of Magdalen Hall he drew up a new code of articles referring to the government of the college. He was deprived of his office in May 1634, and began to preach, with a similar disregard for constituted authority. After his voyages to the Bermudas he returned to England (1641), and after exercising an itinerant and unattached ministry settled for some months in Great Yarmouth and then at Beverley. He was minister at Berwick-on-Tweed when in October 1652 he was appointed a fellow of Eton College. There in 1658 he preached the funeral sermon of Francis Rous, the provost, and thence in 1660 he was ejected. He returned to his preaching at Berwick-on-Tweed, but was expelled by the Act of Uniformity in 1662, and after spending some time in the West Indies settled (1670) at Boston, Massachusetts, where he was ordained minister of the First Church. He died on the 28th of December 1674. A few sermons are all that he published. His first wife (d. 1658) was " a scholar beyond what was usual in her sex," and Andrew Marvell, who was their friend, wrote an epitaph for her tomb at Eton which was defaced at the Restoration; his second wife (d. 1659) was Frances Woodward, daughter of the famous vicar of Bray; his third wife a widow whom he met at Barbados.

OXENFORD, JOHN (1812-1877), English dramatist, was born at Camberwell on the 12th of August 1812. He began his literary career by writing on finance. He was an excellent linguist, and the author of many translations from the German, notably of Goethe's *Dichtung und Wahrheit* (1846) and Eckermann's *Conversations of Goethe* (1850). He did much by his writing to spread the fame of Schopenhauer in England. His first play was *My Fellow Clerk*, produced at the Lyceum in 1835. This was followed by a long series of pieces, the most famous of which was perhaps the *Porter's Knot* (1858) and *Twice Killed* (1835). About 1850 he became dramatic critic of *The Times.* He died in Southwark on the 21st of February 1877.

Many references to his pieces will be found in *The Life and Reminiscences of E. L. Blanchard* (ed. C. Scott and C. Howard, 1891).

OXENHAM, HENRY NUTCOMBE (1829-1888), English ecclesiologist, son of a master at Harrow, was born there on the 15th of November 1829. From Harrow he went to Balliol College, Oxford. He took Anglican orders in 1854, but became a Roman Catholic in 1857. At first his thoughts turned towards the priesthood, and he spent some time at the London Oratory and at St Edmund's College, Ware; but being unable to surrender his belief in the validity of Anglican orders, he proceeded no further than minor orders in the Roman Church. In 1863 he made a prolonged visit to Germany, where he studied the language and literature, and formed a close friendship with Döllinger, whose *First Age of the Christian Church* he translated in 1866. Oxenham was a regular contributor to the *Saturday Review.* A selection of his essays was published in *Short Studies in Ecclesiastical History and Biography* (1884), and *Short Studies, Ethical and Religious* (1885). He also translated in 1876 the 2nd vol. of Bishop Hefele's *History of the Councils of the Church,* and published several pamphlets on the reunion of Christendom. His *Catholic Doctrine of the Atonement* (1865) and *Catholic Eschatology and Universalism* (1876) are standard works. Oxenham died at Kensington on the 23rd of March 1888.

See J. Gillow's *Bibliographical Dictionary of English Catholics,* vol. v. An interesting obituary notice on Oxenham was written by *Vicesimus, i.e.* Dean John Oakley of Manchester, for the *Manchester Guardian,* and published in pamphlet form (Manchester, 1888).

OXENSTJERNA, an ancient Swedish senatorial family, the origin of which can be traced up to the middle of the 14th century, which had vast estates in Södermanland and Uppland, and began to adopt its armorial designation of *Oxenstjerna* (" Ox-forehead ") as a personal name towards the end of the 16th century. Its most notable members were the following.

1. COUNT AXEL GUSTAFSSON (1583-1654), chancellor of Sweden, was born at Fönö in Uppland, and was educated with his brothers at the universities of Rostock, Jena and Wittenberg. On returning home in 1603 he was appointed *kammerjunker* to King Charles IX. In 1606 he was entrusted with his first diplomatic mission, to Mecklenburg, was appointed a senator during his absence, and henceforth became one of the king's most trusted servants. In 1610 he was sent to Copenhagen to prevent a war with Denmark, but was unsuccessful. This embassy is important as being the beginning of Oxenstjerna's long diplomatic struggle with Sweden's traditional rival in the north, whose most formidable enemy he continued to be throughout life. Oxenstjerna was appointed a member of Gustavus Adolphus's council of regency. High aristocrat as he was, he would at first willingly have limited the royal power.

An oligarchy guiding a limited monarchy was ever his ideal government, but the genius of the young king was not to be fettered, so Oxenstjerna was content to be the colleague instead of the master of his sovereign. On the 6th of January 1612 he was appointed chancellor. His controlling, organizing hand was speedily felt in every branch of the administration. For his services as first Swedish plenipotentiary at the peace of Knäred, 1613, he was richly rewarded. During the frequent absences of Gustavus in Livonia and Finland (1614-1616) Oxenstjerna acted as his vice-regent, when he displayed manifold abilities and an all-embracing activity. In 1620 he headed the brilliant embassage despatched to Berlin to arrange the nuptial contract between Gustavus and Mary Eleanora of Brandenburg. It was his principal duty during the king's Russian and Polish wars to supply the armies and the fleets with everything necessary, including men and money. By this time he had become so indispensable that Gustavus, in 1622, bade him accompany him to Livonia, where Oxenstjerna was appointed governor-general and commandant of Riga. His services in Livonia were rewarded with four castles and the whole bishopric of Wenden. He was entrusted with the peace negotiations which led to the truce with Poland in 1623, and succeeded, by skilful diplomacy, in averting a threatened rupture with Denmark in 1624. On the 7th of October 1626 he was appointed governor-general of the newly-acquired province of Prussia. In 1629 he concluded the very advantageous truce of Altmark with Poland. Previously to this (September 1628) he arranged with Denmark a joint occupation of Stralsund, to prevent that important fortress from falling into the hands of the Imperialists. After the battle of Breitenfeld (September 7th, 1631) he was summoned to assist the king with his counsels and co-operation in Germany. During the king's absence in Franconia and Bavaria in 1632 he was appointed *legatus* in the Rhine lands, with plenipotentiary authority over all the German generals and princes in the Swedish service. Although he never fought a battle, he was a born strategist, and frustrated all the efforts of the Spanish troops by his wise regulations. His military capacity was strikingly demonstrated by the skill with which he conducted large reinforcements to Gustavus through the heart of Germany in the summer of 1632. But it was only after the death of the king at Lützen that Oxenstjerna's true greatness came to light. He inspired the despairing Protestants both in Germany and Sweden with fresh hopes. He reorganized the government both at home and abroad. He united the estates of the four upper circles into a fresh league against the common foe (1634), in spite of the envious and foolish opposition of Saxony. By the patent of the 12th of January 1633 he had already been appointed legate plenipotentiary of Sweden in Germany with absolute control over all the territory already won by the Swedish arms. No Swedish subject, either before or after, ever held such an unrestricted and far-reaching authority. Yet he was more than equal to the extraordinary difficulties of the situation. To him both warriors and statesmen appealed invariably as their natural and infallible arbiter. Richelieu himself declared that the Swedish chancellor was " an inexhaustible source of well-matured counsels." Less original but more sagacious than the king, he had a firmer grasp of the realities of the situation. Gustavus would not only have aggrandized Sweden, he would have transformed the German empire. Oxenstjerna wisely abandoned these vaulting ambitions. His country's welfare was his sole object. All his efforts were directed towards procuring for the Swedish crown adequate compensation for its sacrifices. Simple to austerity in his own tastes, he nevertheless recognized the political necessity of impressing his allies and confederates by an almost regal show of dignity; and at the abortive congress of Frankfort-on-Main (March 1634), held for the purpose of uniting all the German Protestants, Oxenstjerna appeared in a carriage drawn by six horses, with German princes attending him on foot. But from first to last his policy suffered from the slenderness of Sweden's material resources, a cardinal defect which all his craft and tact could not altogether conceal from the vigilance of her enemies. The success of his system

·postulated an uninterrupted series of triumphs, whereas a single reverse was likely to be fatal to it. Thus the frightful disaster of Nördlingen (September 6th, 1634; see SWEDEN: *History*) brought him, for an instant, to the verge of ruin, and compelled him, for the first time, so far to depart from his policy of independence as to solicit direct assistance from France. But, well aware that Richelieu needed the Swedish armies as much as he himself needed money, he refused at the conference of Compiègne (1635) to bind his hands in the future for the sake of some slight present relief. In 1636, however, he concluded a fresh subsidy-treaty with France at Wismar. The same year he returned to Sweden and took his seat in the Regency. His presence at home overawed all opposition, and such was the general confidence inspired by his superior wisdom that for the next nine years his voice, especially as regarded foreign affairs, was omnipotent in the council of state. He drew up beforehand the plan of the Danish War of 1643–1645, so brilliantly executed by Lennart Torstensson, and had the satisfaction of severely crippling Denmark by the peace of Brömsebro (1645). His later years were embittered by the jealousy of the young Queen Christina, who thwarted the old statesman in every direction. He always attributed the exiguity of Sweden's gains by the peace of Osnabrück to Christina's undue interference. Oxenstjerna was opposed at first to the abdication of Christina, because he feared mischief to Sweden from the unruly and adventurous disposition of her appointed successor, Charles Gustavus. The extraordinary consideration shown to him by the new king ultimately, however, reconciled him to the change. He died at Stockholm on the 28th of August 1654.

See *Axel Oxenstjernas skriften och brefvexling* (Stockholm, 1888 et seq.); A. de Marny, *Oxenstjerna et Richelieu à Compiègne* (Paris, 1878).

2. COUNT JOHAN AXELSSON (1611–1657), son of the foregoing, completed his studies at Upsala in 1631, and was sent by his father on a grand tour through France, the Netherlands and Great Britain. He served under Count Gustavus Horn in the Thirty Years' War from 1632, and was subsequently employed by his father in various diplomatic missions, though his instructions were always so precise and minute that he was little more than the executor of the chancellor's wishes. He was one of the commissioners who signed the truce of 1635 with Poland, and in 1639, much against his father's will, was made a senator. Along with Salvius he represented Sweden at the great peace congress of Osnabrück, but as he received his instructions direct from his father, whereas Salvius was in the queen's confidence, the two "legates" were constantly at variance. From 1650 to 1652 he was governor-general of Pomerania. Charles X. made him earl marshal.

3. GABRIEL GUSTAFSSON (1587–1640), brother of (1), was from 1612 to 1618 the chief adviser of Duke John, son of King John III., and Gustavus Adolphus's competitor for the Swedish throne. After the duke's death he became, virtually, the *locum-tenens* of the chancellor (with whom he was always on the most intimate terms) during Axel's frequent absences from Sweden. He was also employed successfully on numerous diplomatic missions. He was most usually the intermediary between his brother and the *riksdag* and senate. In 1634 he was created lord high steward. His special department, "Svea Hofret," the supreme court of justice, was ever a model of efficiency, and he frequently acted as chancellor and lord high treasurer as well.

See *Gabriel Gustafssons bref till Riks Kansler Axel Oxenstjerna, 1611–1640* (Stockholm, 1890).

4. COUNT BENGT or BENEDICT GABRIELSSON (1623–1702), was the son of Axel Oxenstjerna's half-brother, Gabriel Bengtsson (1586–1656). After a careful education and a long residence abroad, he began his diplomatic career at the great peace congress of Osnabrück. During his stay in Germany he made the acquaintance of the count palatine, Charles Gustavus, afterwards Charles X., whose confidence he completely won. Two years after the king's accession (1654), Oxenstjerna was sent to represent Sweden at the *Kreistag* of Lower Saxony. In 1655 he accompanied Charles to Poland and was made governor

of the conquered provinces of Kulm, Kujavia, Masovia and Great Poland. The firmness and humanity which he displayed in this new capacity won the affectionate gratitude of the inhabitants, and induced the German portion of them, notably the city of Thorn, to side with the Swedes against the Poles. During Charles's absence in Denmark (1657), Oxenstjerna, in the most desperate circumstances, tenaciously defended Thorn for ten months, and the terms of capitulation ultimately obtained by him were so advantageous that they were made the basis of the subsequent peace negotiations at Oliva, between Poland and Sweden, when Oxenstjerna was one of the chief plenipotentiaries of the Swedish regency. During the domination of Magnus de la Gardie he played but a subordinate part in affairs. From 1662 to 1666 he was governor-general of Livonia. In 1674 he was sent to Vienna to try and prevent the threatened outbreak of war between France and the empire. The connexions which he formed and the sympathies which he won here had a considerable influence on his future career, and resulted in his appointment as one of the Swedish envoys to the congress of Nijmwegen (1676). His appointment was generally regarded as an approximation on the part of Sweden to Austria and Holland. During the congress he laboured assiduously in an anti-French direction; a well-justified distrust of France was, indeed, henceforth the keynote of his policy, a policy diametrically opposed to Sweden's former system. In 1680 Charles XI. entrusted him absolutely with the conduct of foreign affairs, on the sole condition that peace was to be preserved, an office which he held for the next seventeen years to the very great advantage of Sweden. His leading political principles were friendship with the maritime powers (Great Britain and Holland) and the emperor, and a close anti-Danish alliance with the house of Holstein. Charles XI. appointed Oxenstjerna one of the regents during the minority of Charles XII. The martial proclivities of the new king filled the prudent old chancellor with alarm and anxiety. His protests were frequent and energetic, and he advised Charles in vain to accept the terms of peace offered by the first anti-Swedish coalition. Oxenstjerna has been described as "a shrewd and subtle little man, of gentle disposition, but remarkable for his firmness and tenacity of character."

See F. F. Carlson, *Sveriges historia under Konungarne af Pfalziska huset* (Stockholm, 1883, 1885); O. Sjögren, *Karl den elfte och Svenska folket* (Stockholm, 1897); and *Négociations du comte d'Avaux pendant les années 1693, 1697–1698* (Utrecht, 1882, &c.). (R. N. B.)

. OXFORD, EARLS OF, an English title held successively by the families of Vere and Harley. The three most important earls of the Vere line (see VERE) are noticed separately below. The Veres held the earldom from 1142 until March 1703, when it became extinct on the death of Aubrey de Vere, the 20th earl. In 1711 the English statesman Robert Harley (see below) was created earl of Oxford; but the title became extinct in this family on the death of the 6th earl in 1853.

OXFORD, EDWARD DE VERE, 17TH EARL [1] OF (1550–1604), son of John de Vere, the 16th earl, was born on the 12th of April 1550. He matriculated at Queen's College, Cambridge, but he removed later to St John's College, and was known as Lord Bolebec or Bulbeck until he succeeded in 1562 to the earldom and to the hereditary dignity of great chamberlain of England. As one of the royal wards the boy came under the care of Lord Burghley, at whose house in London he lived under the tutorship of his maternal uncle, Arthur Golding, the translator of Ovid. His violent temper and erratic doings were a constant source of anxiety to Burghley, who nevertheless in 1571 gave him his eldest daughter, Anne, in marriage. Oxford more than once asked for a military or a naval command, but Burghley hoped that his good looks together with his skill in dancing and in feats of arms would win for him a high position at court. His accomplishments did indeed secure Elizabeth's favour, but he offended her by going to Flanders without her consent in 1574, and more seriously in 1582 by a duel with one of her gentlemen, Thomas Knyvet. Among his other escapades was a futile

[1] *I.e.* in the Vere line.

plot to rescue from the Tower Thomas Howard, 4th duke of Norfolk, with whom he was distantly connected. In 1579 he insulted Sir Philip Sidney by calling him a "puppy" on the tennis-court at Whitehall. Sidney accordingly challenged Oxford, but the queen forbade him to fight, and required him to apologise on the ground of the difference of rank between the disputants. On Sidney's refusal and consequent disgrace Oxford is said to have schemed to murder him. The earl sat on the special commission (1586) appointed for the trial of Mary queen of Scots; in 1589 he was one of the peers who tried Philip Howard, earl of Arundel, for high treason; and in 1601 he took part in the trial of Essex and Southampton. It has been suggested that Oxford was the Italianated Englishman ridiculed by Gabriel Harvey in his *Speculum Tuscanismi*. On his return from a journey to Italy in 1575 he brought back various inventions for the toilet, and his estate was rapidly dissipated in satisfying his extravagant whims. His first wife died in 1588, and from that time Burghley withdrew his support, Oxford being reduced to the necessity of seeking help among the poor men of letters whom he had at one time or another befriended. He was himself a lyric poet of no small merit. His fortunes were partially retrieved on his second marriage with Elizabeth Trentham, by whom he had a son, Henry de Vere, 18th earl of Oxford (1593–1625). He died at Newington, near London, on the 24th of June 1604.

His poems, scattered in various anthologies—the *Paradise of Dainty Devices, England's Parnassus, Phoenix Nest, England's Helicon*—and elsewhere, were collected by Dr A. B. Grosart in vol. iv. of the Fuller Worthies Library (1876).

OXFORD, JOHN DE VERE, 13TH EARL OF (1443–1513), was second son of John, the 12th earl, a prominent Lancastrian, who, together with his eldest son Aubrey de Vere, was executed in February 1462. John de Vere the younger was himself attainted, but two years later was restored as 13th earl. But his loyalty was suspected, and for a short time at the end of 1468 he was in the Tower. He sided with Warwick, the king-maker, in the political movements of 1469, accompanied him in his exile next year, and assisted in the Lancastrian restoration of 1470–1471. As constable he tried John Tiptoft, earl of Worcester, who had condemned his father nine years before. At the battle of Barnet, Oxford was victorious in command of the Lancastrian right, but his men got out of hand, and before they could be rallied Warwick was defeated. Oxford escaped to France. In 1473 he organized a Lancastrian expedition, which, after an attempted landing in Essex, sailed west and seized St Michael's Mount in Cornwall. It was only after a four months' siege that Oxford was forced to surrender in February 1474. He was sent to Hammes near Calais, whence, ten years later, in August 1484, he escaped and joined Henry Tudor in Brittany. He fought for Henry in high command at Bosworth, and was rewarded by restoration to his title, estates and hereditary office of Lord Chamberlain. At Stoke on the 16th of June 1486 he led the van of the royal army. In 1492 he was in command in the expedition to Flanders, and in 1497 was foremost in the defeat of the Cornish rebels on Blackheath. Bacon (*Hist. of Henry VII.* p. 192, ed. Lumby) has preserved a story that when in the summer of 1498 Oxford entertained the king at Castle Hedingham, he assembled a great number of his retainers in livery; Henry thanked the earl for his reception, but fined him 15,000 marks for the breach of the laws. Oxford was high steward at the trial of the earl of Warwick, and one of the commissioners for the trial of Sir James Tyrell and others in May 1502. Partly through ill-health he took little part afterwards in public affairs, and died on the 10th of March 1513. He was twice married, but left no children.

Oxford is frequently mentioned in the *Paston Letters*, which include twenty written by him, mostly to Sir John Paston the younger. See *The Paston Letters*, ed. J. Gairdner; *Chronicles of London*, ed. C. L. Kingsford (1905); Sir James Ramsay, *Lancaster and York*; and *The Political History of England*, vols. iv. and v. (1906). (C. L. K.)

OXFORD, ROBERT DE VERE, 9TH EARL OF (1362–1392), English courtier, was the only son of Thomas de Vere, 8th earl of

Oxford, and Maud (d. 1413), daughter of Sir Ralph de Ufford (d. 1346), and a descendant of King Henry III. He became 9th earl of Oxford on his father's death in 1371, and married Philippa (d. 1412), daughter of his guardian Ingelram de Couci, earl of Bedford, a son-in-law of Edward III., quickly becoming very intimate with Richard II. Already hereditary great chamberlain of England, Oxford was made a member of the privy council and a Knight of the Garter; while castles and lands were bestowed upon him, and he was constantly in the company of the young king. In 1385 Richard decided to send his friend to govern Ireland, and Oxford was given extensive rights in that country and was created marquess of Dublin for life; but although preparations were made for his journey he did not leave England. Meanwhile the discontent felt at Richard's incompetence and extravagance was increasing, one of the contributory causes thereto being the king's partiality for Oxford, who was regarded with jealousy by the nobles and who made powerful enemies about this time by divorcing his wife, Philippa, and by marrying a Bohemian lady. The king, however, indifferent to the gathering storm, created Vere duke of Ireland in October 1386, and gave him still more extensive powers in that country, and at once matters reached a climax. Richard was deprived of his authority for a short time, and Vere was ordered in vain to proceed to Ireland. The latter was then among those who were accused by the king's uncle Thomas of Woodstock, duke of Gloucester, and his supporters in November 1387; and rushing into the north of England he gathered an army to defend his royal master and himself. At Radcot Bridge in Oxfordshire, however, his men fled before the troops of Gloucester, and Oxford himself escaped in disguise to the Netherlands. In the parliament of 1388 he was found guilty of treason and was condemned to death, but as he remained abroad the sentence was never carried out. With another exile, Michael de la Pole, duke of Suffolk, he appears to have lived in Paris until after the treaty between England and France in June 1389, when he took refuge at Louvain. He was killed by a boar whilst hunting, and left no children. In 1395 his body was brought from Louvain to England, and was buried in the priory at Earl's Colne, Essex.

See T. Walsingham, *Historia Anglicana*, edited by H. T. Riley (London, 1863–1864); J. Froissart, *Chroniques*, edited by S. Luce and G. Raynaud (Paris, 1869–1897); H. Wallon, *Richard II.* (Paris, 1864); and W. Stubbs, *Constitutional History*, vol. ii. (Oxford, 1896).

OXFORD, ROBERT HARLEY, 1ST EARL[1] OF (1661–1724), English statesman, commonly known by his surname of HARLEY, eldest son of Sir Edward Harley (1624–1700), a prominent land-owner in Herefordshire, and grandson of the celebrated letter-writer Lady Brilliana Harley (*c.* 1600–1643), was born in Bow Street, Covent Garden, London, on the 5th of December 1661. His school days were passed at Shilton, near Burford, in Oxford-shire, in a small school which produced at the same time a lord high treasurer (Harley), a lord high chancellor (Simon Harcourt) and a lord chief justice of the common pleas (Thomas Trevor). The principles of Whiggism and Nonconformity were instilled into his mind at an early age, and if he changed the politics of his ancestors he never formally abandoned their religious opinions. At the Revolution of 1688 Sir Edward and his son raised a troop of horse in support of the cause of William III., and took possession of the city of Worcester in his interest. This recommended Robert Harley to the notice of the Boscawen family, and led to his election, in April 1689, as the parliamentary representative of Tregony, a borough under their control. He remained its member for one parliament, when he was elected by the constituency of New Radnor, and he continued to represent it until his elevation to the peerage in 1711.

From the first Harley gave great attention to the conduct of public business, bestowing especial care upon the study of the forms and ceremonies of the House. His reputation marked him out as a fitting person to preside over the debates of the House, and from the general election of February 1701 until the dissolution of 1705 he held with general approbation the office

[1] *I.e.* in the Harley line.

of speaker. For a part of this period, from the 18th of May 1704, he combined with the speakership the duties of a principal secretary of state for the northern department, displacing in that office the Tory earl of Nottingham. In 1703 Harley first made use of Defoe's talents as a political writer, and this alliance with the press proved so successful that he afterwards called the genius of Swift to his aid in many pamphlets against his opponents in politics. While he was secretary of state the union with Scotland was effected. At the time of his appointment as secretary of state Harley had given no outward sign of dissatisfaction with the Whigs, and it was mainly through Marlborough's good opinion of his abilities that he was admitted to the ministry. For some time, so long indeed as the victories of the great English general cast a glamour over the policy of his friends, Harley continued to act loyally with his colleagues. But in the summer of 1707 it became evident to Godolphin that some secret influence behind the throne was shaking the confidence of the queen in her ministers. The sovereign had resented the intrusion into the administration of the impetuous earl of Sunderland, and had persuaded herself that the safety of the church depended on the fortunes of the Tories. These convictions were strengthened in her mind by the new favourite Abigail Hill (a cousin of the duchess of Marlborough through her mother, and of Harley on her father's side), whose soft and silky ways contrasted only too favourably in the eyes of the queen with the haughty manners of her old friend, the duchess of Marlborough. Both the duchess and Godolphin were convinced that this change in the disposition of the queen was due to the sinister conduct of Harley and his relatives; but he was for the present permitted to remain in his office. Subsequent experience showed the necessity for his dismissal and an occurrence supplied an opportunity for carrying out their wishes. An ill-paid and poverty-stricken clerk, William Gregg, in Harley's office, was detected in furnishing the enemy with copies of many documents which should have been kept from the knowledge of all but the most trusted advisers of the court, and it was found that through the carelessness of the head of the department the contents of such papers became the common property of all in his service. The queen was thereupon informed that Godolphin and Marlborough could no longer serve in concert with him. They did not attend her next council, on the 8th of February 1708, and when Harley proposed to proceed with the business of the day the duke of Somerset drew attention to their absence, when the queen found herself forced (February 11,) to accept the resignations of both Harley and St John.

Harley went out of office, but his cousin, who had now become Mrs Masham, remained by the side of the queen, and contrived to convey to her mistress the views of the ejected minister. Every device which the defeated ambition of a man whose strength lay in his aptitude for intrigue could suggest for hastening the downfall of his adversaries was employed without scruple, and not employed in vain. The cost of the protracted war with France, and the danger to the national church, the chief proof of which lay in the prosecution of Sacheverell, were the weapons which he used to influence the masses of the people. Marlborough himself could not be dispensed with, but his relations were dismissed from their posts in turn. When the greatest of these, Lord Godolphin, was ejected from office, five commissioners to the treasury were appointed (August 10, 1710), and among them figured Harley as chancellor of the exchequer. It was the aim of the new chancellor to frame an administration from the moderate members of both parties, and to adopt with but slight changes the policy of his predecessors; but his efforts were doomed to disappointment. The Whigs refused to join in an alliance with the man whose rule began with the retirement from the treasury of the finance minister idolized by the city merchants, and the Tories, who were successful beyond their wildest hopes at the polling booths, could not understand why their leaders did not adopt a policy more favourable to the interests of their party. The clamours of the wilder spirits, the country members who met at the "October Club," began to be re-echoed even by those who were attached to the person of Harley, when, through an

unexpected event, his popularity was restored at a bound. A French refugee, the ex-abbé de la Bourlie (better known by the name of the marquis de Guiscard), was being examined before the privy council on a charge of treachery to the nation which had befriended him, when he stabbed Harley in the breast with a penknife (March 8, 1711). To a man in good health the wounds would not have been serious, but the minister had been for some time indisposed—a few days before the occurrence Swift had penned the prayer "Pray God preserve his health, everything depends upon it"—and the joy of the nation on his recovery knew no bounds. Both Houses presented an address to the crown, suitable response came from the queen, and on Harley's reappearance in the Lower House the speaker made an oration which was spread broadcast through the country. On the 23rd of May 1711 the minister became Baron Harley of Wigmore and earl of Oxford and Mortimer; on the 29th of May he was created lord treasurer, and on the 25th of October 1712 became a Knight of the Garter. Well might his friends exclaim that he had "grown by persecutions, turnings out, and stabbings."

With the sympathy which this attempted assassination had evoked, and with the skill which the lord treasurer possessed for conciliating the calmer members of either political party, he passed through several months of office without any loss of reputation. He rearranged the nation's finances, and continued to support her generals in the field with ample resources for carrying on the campaign, though his emissaries were in communication with the French king, and were settling the terms of a peace independently of England's allies. After many weeks of vacillation and intrigue, when the negotiations were frequently on the point of being interrupted, the preliminary peace was signed, and in spite of the opposition of the Whig majority in the Upper House, which was met by the creation of twelve new peers, the much-vexed treaty of Utrecht was brought to a conclusion the 31st of March 1713. While these negotiations were under discussion the friendship between Oxford and St John, who had become secretary of state in September 1710, was fast changing into hatred. The latter had resented the rise in fortune which the stabs of Guiscard had secured for his colleague, and when he was raised to the peerage with the title of Baron St John and Viscount Bolingbroke, instead of with an earldom, his resentment knew no bounds. The royal favourite, whose husband had been called to the Upper House as Baron Masham, deserted her old friend and relation for his more vivacious rival. The Jacobites found that, although the lord treasurer was profuse in his expressions of good will for their cause, no steps were taken to ensure its triumph, and they no longer placed reliance on promises which were repeatedly made and repeatedly broken. Even Oxford's friends began to complain of his habitual dilatoriness, and to find some excuse for his apathy in ill-health, aggravated by excess in the pleasures of the table and by the loss of his favourite child. By slow degrees the confidence of Queen Anne was transferred from Oxford to Bolingbroke; on the 27th of July 1714 the former surrendered his staff as lord treasurer, and on the 1st August the queen died.

On the accession of George I. the defeated minister retired to Herefordshire, but a few months later his impeachment was decided upon and he was committed to the Tower on the 16th of July 1715. After an imprisonment of nearly two years the prison doors were opened in July 1717 and he was allowed to resume his place among the peers, but he took little part in public affairs, and died almost unnoticed in London on the 21st of May 1724. He married, in May 1685, Edith, daughter of Thomas Foley, of Witley Court, Worcester. She died in November 1691. His second wife was Sarah, daughter of Simon Middleton, of Edmonton. His son Edward (1689–1741), who succeeded to the title, married Henrietta (d. 1755), daughter and heiress of John Holles, duke of Newcastle; and his only child, a daughter Margaret (1715–1785), married William Bentinck, 2nd duke of Portland, to whom she brought Welbeck Abbey and the London property which she inherited from her mother. The earldom then passed to a cousin, Edward, 3rd earl (c. 1699-1755), and eventually became extinct with Alfred, the 6th earl (1809-1853).

Harley's statesmanship may seem but intrigue and finesse, but his character is set forth in the brightest colours in the poems of Pope and the prose of Swift. The Irish dean was his discriminating friend in the hours of prosperity, his unswerving advocate in adversity. The books and manuscripts which the 1st earl of Oxford and his son collected were among the glories of their age. The manuscripts became the property of the nation in 1753 and are now in the British Museum; the books were sold to a bookseller called Thomas Osborne in 1742 and described in a printed catalogue of five volumes (1743-1745), Dr Johnson writing an account of the library. A selection of the rarer pamphlets and tracts, which was made by William Oldys, was printed in eight volumes (1744-1746), with a preface by Johnson. The best edition is that of Thomas Park, ten volumes (1808-1813). In the recollection of the Harleian manuscripts, the Harleian library and the *Harleian Miscellany*, the family name will never die.

BIBLIOGRAPHY.—The best life of Harley is by E. S. Roscoe (1902). Articles relating to him are in *Engl. Hist. Rev.* xv. 238-250 (Defoe and Harley by Thomas Bateson); *Trans. of the Royal Hist. Soc.* xiv. N.S. 69-121 (development of political parties *temp.* Q. Anne by W. Frewen Lord); *Edinburgh Review*, clxxxvii. 151-178, cxciii. 457-488 (Harley papers). For his relations with St John see Walter Sichel's *Bolingbroke* (1901-1902, 2 vols.); for those with Swift, consult the *Journal to Stella* and Sir Henry Craik's *Life of Swift* (2nd ed., 1894, 2 vols.). (W. P. C.)

OXFORD, a city, municipal and parliamentary borough, the county town of Oxfordshire, England, and the seat of a famous university.[1] Pop. (1901) 49,336. It is situated on the river Thames, 51 m. by road and 63¼ m. by rail W.N.W. of London. It is served by the main northern line of the Great Western railway, and by a branch from the London & North-Western system at Bletchley; while the Thames, and the Oxford canal, running north from it, afford water communications. The ancient nucleus of the city stands on a low gravel ridge between the Thames and its tributary the Cherwell, which here flow with meandering courses and many branches and backwaters through flat meadows. Modern extensions of Oxford cross both rivers, the suburbs of Osney and Botley lying to the west, Grandpont to the south, and St Clement's to the east beyond the Cherwell. To the north is a large modern residential district. The low meadow land is bounded east and west by well-wooded hills, rising rather abruptly, though only to a slight elevation, seldom exceeding 500 ft. Several points on these hills command celebrated views, such as that from Bagley Hill to the S.W., or from Elsfield to the N.E., from which only the inner Oxford is visible, with its collegiate buildings, towers and spires—a peerless city.

Main roads from east to west and from north to south intersect near the centre of ancient Oxford at a point called Carfax,[2] and form four principal streets, High Street (east), Queen Street (west), Cornmarket Street (north) and St Aldate's (south).[3] Cornmarket Street is continued northward by Magdalen Street, and near their point of junction Magdalen Street is intersected by a thoroughfare formed, from west to east, by George Street, Broad Street, Holywell Street and Long Wall Street, the last of which sweeps south to join High Street not far from Magdalen Bridge over the Cherwell. This thoroughfare is thus detailed, because it approximately indicates the northern and northeastern confines of the ancient city. The old walls indeed (of which there are many fragments, notably a very fine range in New College garden) indicate a somewhat smaller area than that defined by these streets. Their line, which slightly varied, as excavations have shown, in different ages, bent south-westward from Cornmarket Street, where stood the north gate, till it reached the enceinte of the castle, which lies at the west of the old city,

[1] See also UNIVERSITIES.
[2] This word, which occurs elsewhere in England, means a place where four roads meet. Its ultimate origin is the Latin *quadrifurcus*, four-forked. Earlier English forms are *carfuks, carrefore*. The modern French is *carrefour*.
[3] In the common speech of the university some streets are never spoken of as such, but, e.g., as "the High," "the Corn" (i.e. Cornmarket), "the Broad." St Aldate's is pronounced St Olds, and the Cherwell (pronounced Charwell) is called "the Char."

flanked on one side by a branch of the Thames. From the castle the southern wall ran east, along the modern Brewers' Street; the south gate of the city was in St Aldate's Street, where it is joined by this lane, and the walls then continued along the north side of Christ Church meadow, and north-eastward to the east gate, which stood in High Street near the junction of Long Wall Street. Oxford had thus a strong position: the castle and the Thames protected it on the east; the two rivers, the walls and the water-meadows between them on the south and east; and on the north the wall and a deep ditch, of which vestiges may be traced, as between Broad and Ship Streets.

An early rivalry between the universities of Oxford and Cambridge led to the circulation of many groundless legends respecting their foundation. For example, those which connected Oxford with "Brute the Trojan," King Mempric (1009 B.C.), and the Druids, are not found before the 14th century. The town is as a fact much older than the university. The historian, John Richard Green, epitomizes the relation between the two corporations when he shows[4] that "Oxford had already seen five centuries of borough life before a student appeared within its streets. . . . The university found Oxford a busy, prosperous borough, and reduced it to a cluster of lodging-houses. It found it among the first of English municipalities, and it so utterly crushed its freedom that the recovery of some of the commonest rights of self-government has only been brought about by recent legislation." A poor Romano-British village may have existed on the peninsula between Thames and Cherwell, but no Roman road of importance passed within 3 m. of it. In the 8th century an indication of the existence of Oxford is found in the legend of St Frideswide, a holy woman who is said to have died in 735, and to have founded a nunnery on the site of the present cathedral. Coins of King Alfred have been discovered (though not at Oxford) bearing the name Oksnaforda or Orsnaforda, which seems to prove the existence of a mint at Oxford. It is clear, at any rate, that Oxford was already important as a frontier town between Mercia and Wessex when the first unquestionable mention of it occurs, namely in the English Chronicle under the year 912, when Edward the Elder "took to himself" London and Oxford. The name points to a ford for oxen across the Thames, though some have connected the syllable "ox-" with a Celtic word meaning "water," comparing it with Ouse, Osney and Exford. The first mention of the townsmen of Oxford is in the English Chronicle of 1013, and that of its trade in the Abingdon Chronicle, which mentions the toll paid from the 11th century to the abbot of Abingdon by boats passing that town. Notices during that century prove the growing importance of Oxford. As the chief stronghold in the upper Thames valley it sustained various attacks by the Danes, being burned in 979, 1002 and 1010, while in 1013 Sweyn took hostages from it. It had also a considerable political importance, and several gemots were held here, as in 1015, when the two Danish thanes Sigfrith and Morkere were treacherously killed by the Mercian Edric; in 1020, when Canute chose Oxford as the scene of the confirmation of "Edgar's law" by Danes and English; in 1036, when Harold I. was chosen king, and in 1065. But Oxford must have suffered heavily about the time of the Conquest, for according to the Domesday Survey (which for Oxford is unusually complete) a great proportion of the "mansions" (106 out of 297) and houses (478 out of 721) were ruined or unoccupied. The city, however, had already a market, and under the strong hand of the Norman sheriff Robert d'Oilli (c. 1070-1119) it prospered steadily. He made heavy exactions on the townsfolk, though it may be noted that they withheld from him Port Meadow, the great meadow of 440 acres which is still a feature of the low riverside tract north of Oxford. But d'Oilli did much for Oxford, and the strong tower of the castle and possibly that of St Michael's church are extant relics of his building activity. His nephew, another Robert, who held the castle after him, founded in 1129 the most notable building that

[4] In his essay on "The Early History of Oxford," reprinted from *Stray Studies*, in *Studies in Oxford History*, by the Oxford Historical Society (1901).

Oxford has lost. This was the priory (shortly afterwards the abbey) of Osney, which was erected to the branch of the Thames next west of that by which the castle stands. In its finished state it had a splendid church, with two high towers and a great range of buildings, but only slight fragments may now be traced. About 1130 Henry I. built for himself Beaumont Palace, the site of which is indicated by Beaumont Street, and the same king gave Oxford its first known charter (not still extant), in which mention is made of a gild merchant. This charter is alluded to in another of Henry II., in which the citizens of Oxford and London are associated in the possession of similar customs and liberties. The most notable historical incident connected with the city in this period is the escape of the empress Matilda from the castle over the frozen river and through the snow to Abingdon, when besieged by Stephen in 1142.

It is about this time that an indication is first given of organized teaching in Oxford, for in 1133 one Robert Pullen is said to have instituted theological lectures here. No earlier facts are known concerning the origin of the university, though it may. with probability be associated with schools connected with the ecclesiastical foundations of Osney and St Frideswide; and the tendency for Oxford to become a centre of learning may have been fostered by the frequent presence of the court at Beaumont. A chancellor, appointed by the bishop of Lincoln, is mentioned in 1214, and an early instance of the subordination of the town to the university is seen in the fact that the townsfolk were required to take oaths of peace before this official and the archdeacon. It may be mentioned here that the present practice of appointing a non-resident chancellor, with a resident vice-chancellor, did not come into vogue till the end of the 15th century. In the 13th century a number of religious orders, which here as elsewhere exercised a profound influence on education, became established in Oxford. In 1221 came the Dominicans, whose later settlement (c. 1260) is attested by Blackfriars Street, Preacher's Bridge and Friars' Wharf. In 1224 the Franciscans settled near the present Paradise Square. In the middle of the century the Carmelites occupied part of the present site of Worcester College, but their place here was taken by the Benedictines when, about 1315, they were given Beaumont by Edward II., and removed there. The Austin Friars settled near the site of Wadham College; for the Cistercians Rewley Abbey, scanty remains of which may be traced near the present railway stations, was founded c. 1280. During the same century the political importance of Oxford was maintained. Several parliaments were held here, notably the Mad Parliament of 1258, which enforced the enactment of the Provisions of Oxford. Again, the later decades of the 13th century saw the initiation of the collegiate system. Merton, University and Balliol were the earliest foundations under this system. The paragraphs below, dealing with each college successively, give the dates and circumstances of foundation for all. As to the relations between the university and the city, in 1248 a charter of Henry III. afforded students considerable privileges at the expense of townsfolk, in the way of personal and financial protection. Moreover, the chancellor already possessed juridical powers; even over the townsfolk he shared jurisdiction with the mayor. Not unnaturally these peculiar conditions engendered rivalry between "town and gown ; rivalry led to violence, and after many lesser encounters a climax was reached in the riot on St Scholastica's and the following day, February 10th and 11th, 1354/5. Its immediate cause was trivial, but the townsmen gave rein to their long-standing animosity, severely handled the scholars, killing many, and paying the penalty, for Edward III. gave the university a new charter enhancing its privileges. Others followed from Richard II. and Henry IV. A charter given by Henry VIII. in 1523 at the instigation of Wolsey conferred such power on the university that traders of any sort might be given its privileges, so that the city had no jurisdiction over them. In 1571 was passed the act of Elizabeth which incorporated and reorganized the universities of Oxford and Cambridge. In 1635 a charter of Charles I. confirmed its privileges to the university of Oxford, of which William Laud had

become chancellor in 1630. Vestiges of these exaggerated powers (as distinct from the more equable division of rights between the two corporations which now obtains) long survived. For example, it was only in 1825 that the ceremony of reparation enforced on the municipality after the St Scholastica riots was discontinued.

During the reign of Mary, in 1555, there took place, on a s ot in Broad Street, the famous martyrdom of Ridley and Latimer. Cranmer followed them to the stake in 1556, and the three are commemorated by the ornate modern cross, an early work of Sir G. G. Scott (1841), in St Giles Street beside the church of St Mary Magdalen. A period such as this must have been in many ways harmful to the university, but it recovered prosperity under the care of Elizabeth and Wolsey. During the civil war, however, Oxford, as a city, suddenly acquired a new prominence as the headquarters of the Royalist party and the meeting-place of Charles I.'s parliament. This importance is not incomparable with that which Oxford possessed in the Mercian period. However the frontier shifted, between the districts held by the king and by the parliament, Oxford was always close to it. It was hither that the king retired after Edgehill, the two battles of Newbury and Naseby; from here Prince Rupert made his dashing raids in 1643. In May 1644 the earl of Essex and Sir William Waller first approached the city from the east and south, but failed to enclose the king, who escaped to Worcester, returning after the engagement at Copredy Bridge. The final investment of the city, when Charles had lost every other stronghold of importance, and had himself escaped in disguise, was in May 1646, and on the 24th of June it surrendered to Fairfax. Throughout the war the secret sympathies of the citizens were Parliamentarian, but there was no conflict within the walls. The disturbances of the war and the divisions of parties, however, had bad effects on the university, being subversive of discipline and inimical to study; nor were these effects wholly removed during the Commonwealth, in spite of the care of Cromwell, who was himself chancellor in 1651-1657. The Restoration led to conflicts between students and citizens. Charles II. held the last Oxford parliament in 1681. James II.'s action in forcing his nominees into certain high offices at last brought the university into temporary opposition to the crown. Later, however, Oxford became strongly Jacobite. In the first year of George I.'s reign there were serious Jacobite riots, but from that time the city becomes Hanoverian in opposition to the university, the feeling coming to a head in 1755 during a county election, which was ultimately the subject of a parliamentary inquiry. But George III., visiting Oxford in 1785, was well received by both parties, and this visit may be taken as the termination of the purely political history of Oxford. Details of the history of the university may be gathered from the following description of the colleges, the names of which are arranged alphabetically.

All Souls College was founded in 1437 by Henry Chicheley (q.v.), archbishop of Canterbury, for a warden, 40 fellows, 2 chaplains, and clerks. The charter was issued in the name of Henry VI., and it has been held that Chicheley wished, by founding the college, to expiate his own support of the disastrous wars in France during the reign of Henry V. and the ensuing regency. Fifty fellowships in all were provided for by the modern statutes, besides the honorary fellowships to which men of eminence are sometimes elected. Some of the fellowships are held in connexion with university offices; but the majority are awarded on examination, and are among the highest honours in the university offered by this method. The only undergraduate members of the college are four bible-clerks,[1] so that the college occupies a peculiar position as a society of graduates. The college has its beautiful original front upon High Street; the first quadrangle, practically unaltered since the foundation, is one of the most characteristic in Oxford. The chapel has a splendid reredos occupying the whole eastern wall, with tiers of figures in niches. After the original figures had been destroyed during the Reformation the reredos was plastered over, but

[1] Here and in some other colleges this title is connected with the duties of reading the Bible in chapel and saying grace in hall.

when the plaster was removed, Sir Gilbert Scott found enough remains to render it possible to restore the whole. The second quadrangle is divided from Radcliffe Square by a stone screen and cloister. From the eastern range of buildings twin towers rise in graduated stages. On the north side is the library. The whole is in a style partly Gothic, partly classical, fantastic, but not without dignity. The architect was Sir Christopher Wren's pupil, Nicholas Hawksmoor; the building was spread over the first half of the 18th century. The fine library originated in a bequest of Sir Christopher Codrington (d. 1710), and bears his name. One of the traditional customs surviving in Oxford is found at All Souls. Legend states that a mallard was discovered in a drain while the foundations were being dug. A song (probably Elizabethan) on this story is still sung at college gaudies, and later it is pretended to hunt the bird. With such a foundation as All Souls, a great number of eminent names are naturally associated (see Montagu Burrows, *Worthies of All Souls*, 1874).

Balliol College is one of the earliest foundations. About 1263 John de Baliol (see BALIOL, family) began, as part of a penance, to maintain certain scholars in Oxford. Dervorguila, his wife, developed his work after his death in 1269 by founding the college, whose statutes date from 1282, though not brought into final form (apart from modern revision) until 1504. There are now twelve fellowships and fifteen scholarships on the old foundation. Two fellowships, to be held by members already holding fellowships of the college, were founded by James Hozier, second Lord Newlands, in 1906, in commemoration of Benjamin Jowett, master of the college. The buildings, which front upon Broad Street, Magdalen Street and St Giles Street, are for the most part modern, and mainly by Alfred Waterhouse, Anthony Salvin and William Butterfield. The college has a high reputation for scholarship. Its master and fellows possess the unique right of electing the visitor of the college. In 1887 Balliol College absorbed New Inn Hall, one of the few old halls which had survived till modern times. In the time of the civil wars a royal mint was established in it.

Brasenose College (commonly written and called B.N.C.) was founded by William Smith, bishop of Lincoln, and Sir Richard Sutton of Prestbury, Cheshire, in 1509. Its name, however, perpetuates the fact that it took the place of a much earlier community in the university. There were several small halls on its site, all dependent on other colleges or religious houses except one—Brasenose Hall. The origin of this hall is not known, but it existed in the middle of the 12th century. In 1334 certain students, wishing for peace from the faction-fights which were then characteristic of their life in Oxford, migrated to Stamford, where a doorway remains of the house then occupied by them as Brasenose Hall. From this an ancient knocker in the form of a nose, which may have belonged to the hall at Oxford, was brought to the college in 1890. It presumably gave name to the hall, though a derivation from *brasinium* (Latin for a brew-house) was formerly upheld. The original foundation of the college was for a principal and twelve fellows. This number is maintained, but supernumerary fellowships are added. Of a number of scholarships founded by various benefactors several are confined to certain schools, notably Manchester Grammar School. William Hulme (1691) established a foundation which provides for twelve scholars and a varying number of exhibitioners on entrance, and also for eight senior scholarships open under certain conditions to members of the college already in residence. The main front of the college faces Radcliffe Square; the whole of this and the first quadrangle, excepting the upper storey, is of the time of the foundation; and the gateway tower is a specially fine example. The hall and the chapel, with its fine fan-tracery roof, date from 1663 and 1666, and are attributed to Sir Christopher Wren. In both is seen a curious attempt to combine Gothic and Grecian styles. Modern buildings (by T. G. Jackson) have a frontage upon High Street. Robert Burton, author of *The Anatomy of Melancholy*, became an undergraduate of the college in 1593; Reginald Heber in 1800; Walter Pater became a fellow in 1864.

Christ Church, in point of the number of its members the largest collegiate foundation in Oxford, is also eminent owing to its unique constitution, the history of which involves that of the see of Oxford. Mention has been made of the priory of St Frideswide and its very early foundation, also of the later but more magnificent foundation of Osney Abbey. Both of these were involved in the sweeping changes initiated by Wolsey and carried on by Henry VIII. Wolsey projected the foundation of a college on an even grander scale than that of the present house. In 1524-1525 he obtained authority from Pope Clement VII. to suppress certain religious houses for the purpose of this new foundation. These included St Frideswide's, which occupied part of the site which Wolsey intended to use. The new college, under the name of Cardinal College, was licensed by the king in 1525. Its erection began immediately. The monastic buildings were in great part removed. Statutes were issued and appointments were made to the new offices. But in 1529 Wolsey fell from power. Cardinal College was suppressed, and in 1532 Henry VIII. established in its place another college, on a reduced foundation, called King Henry VIII.'s College. Oxford had been, and was at this time, in the huge diocese of Lincoln. But in 1542, on the suppression of Osney Abbey, a new see was created, and the abbey church was made its cathedral. This arrangement obtained only until 1545, when both the new cathedral church and the new college which took the place of Wolsey's foundation were surrendered to the king. In 1546 Henry established the composite foundation which now (subject to certain modern alterations) exists. He provided for a dean and eight canons and 100 students, to which number one was added in 1664. The church of St Frideswide's foundation became both the cathedral of the diocese and the college chapel. The establishment was thus at once diocesan and collegiate,[1] and it remains so, though now the foundation consists of a dean, six canons, and the usual cathedral staff, a reduced number of students (corresponding to the fellows of other colleges) and scholars. Five of the canons are university professors. The disciplinary administration of the collegiate part of the foundation is under the immediate supervision of two students who hold the office of censors. Queen Elizabeth established the connexion with Westminster School by which not more than three scholars are elected thence each year to Christ Church. There is also a large number of valuable exhibitions. The great number of eminent men associated with Christ Church can only be indicated here by the statement that its books have borne the names of several members of the British and other royal families, including that of King Edward VII. as prince of Wales and of Frederick VIII. of Denmark as crown prince; also of ten prime ministers during the 19th century. The stately front of Christ Church is upon St Aldate's Street. The great gateway is surmounted by a tower begun by Wolsey, but only completed in 1682 from designs of Sir Christopher Wren. Though somewhat incongruous in detail, it is of singular and beautiful form, being octagonal and surmounted by a cupola. It contains the great bell "Tom" (dedicated to St Thomas of Canterbury), which, though recast in 1680, formerly belonged to Osney Abbey. A clock strikes the hours on it, and at five minutes past nine o'clock in the evening it is rung 101 times by band, to indicate the hour of closing college gates, the number being that of the former body of students. The gate, the tower, and the first quadrangle are all commonly named after this bell. Tom Quadrangle is the largest in Oxford, and after various restorations approximates to Wolsey's original design, though the cloisters which he intended were never built. On the south side lies the hall, entered by a staircase under a magnificent fan-tracery roof dating from 1640. The hall itself is one of the finest refectories in England; its roof is of ornate timberwork (1529) and a splendid series of portraits of eminent *alumni* of the house adorn the walls, together with Holbein's portraits

[1] As a whole it is therefore proper to be spoken of as Christ Church, not Christ Church College. In the common speech of the university it has become known as The House, though all the colleges are technically " houses."

of Henry VIII. and Wolsey. With the hall is connected the great kitchen, the first building undertaken by Wolsey. An entry through the eastern range of Tom Quadrangle forms the west portal of the Cathedral Church of Christ.

The cathedral, of which the nave and choir serve also as the college chapel, is the smallest English cathedral, but is of high architectural interest. The plan is cruciform, with a northward extension from the north choir aisle, comprising the Lady chapel and the Latin chapel. It has been seen that probably in the 8th century St Frideswide founded a religious house. In the east end of the north choir aisle and Lady chapel may be seen two blocked arches, rude, narrow and low. Excavations outside the wall in 1887 revealed the foundations of three apses corresponding with these two arches and another which has been traced between them, and in this wall, therefore, there is clearly a remnant of the small Saxon church, with its eastward triple-apsidal termination. In 1002 there took place the massacre of the Danes on St Brice's day at the order of Æthelred II. Some Danes took refuge in the tower of St Frideswide's church, which was fired to ensure their destruction. In 1004 the king undertook the rebuilding of the church. There is full reason to believe that he had assistance from his brother-in-law, Richard II., duke of Normandy, and that much of his work remains, notably in some of the remarkable capitals in the choir. About 1160, however, there was an extensive Norman restoration. The arcades of the choir and of the nave, which was shortened by Wolsey for the purpose of his collegiate building, have massive pillars and round arches. Within these arches, not, as usual, above them, a blind arcade forms the triforium, and below this a lower set of arches springs from the outer side of the main pillars. The Norman stone-vaulted aisles conform in height with these lower arches. Over all is a clerestory with passage. The east end is a striking Norman restoration by Sir Gilbert Scott, consisting of two windows and a rose window above them, with an intervening arcade. The choir has a Perpendicular fan-tracery roof in stone, one of the finest extant, and the early clerestory is here altered to conform with this style. The nave roof is woodwork of the 16th century, and there is a fine Jacobean pulpit. The lower part of the tower, with internal arcades in the lantern, is Norman; the upper stage is Early English, as is the low spire, possibly the earliest built in England. St Lucy's chapel in the south transept aisle contains a rich flamboyant Decorated window. In the north choir aisle are the fragments which have been discovered and roughly reconstructed of St Frideswide's shrine, of marble, with foliage beautifully carved, representing plants symbolical of the life of the saint. The Latin chapel is of various dates, but mainly of the 14th century. The north windows contain contemporary glass; the east window is a rich early work of Sir E. Burne-Jones, set in stonework of an inharmonious Venetian design. There are other beautiful windows by Burne-Jones at the east ends of the aisles and Lady chapel, and at the west end of the south nave aisle. The corresponding window of the north aisle is a curious work by the Dutch artist Abraham van Ling (1630). There are many fine ancient monuments, notably those of Bishop Robert King (d. 1557), and of Lady Elizabeth Montacute (d. 1355). The so-called watching-chamber for St Frideswide's shrine is a rich structure in stone and wood dating from c. 1500. The peculiar arrangement of the collegiate seats in the cathedral, the nave and choir being occupied by modern carved pews or stalls running east and west, and the position of the organ on a screen at the west end, add to the distinctive interior appearance of the building. Small cloisters adjoin the cathedral on the south, and an ornate Norman doorway gives access from them to the chapter-house, a beautiful Early English room. Above the cloisters on the south rises the "old library," originally the monastic refectory, which has suffered conversion into dwelling and lecture-rooms.

To the north-east of Tom Quadrangle is Peckwater Quadrangle, named from an inn upon the site, and built from the design of the versatile Dean Henry Aldrich (1705) with the exception of the library (1716–1761), which forms one side of it. The whole is classical in style. The library contains some fine pictures by Cimabue, Holbein, Van Dyck and others, and sculpture by Rysbrack, Roubillac, Chantrey and others. The small Canterbury Quadrangle, to the east, was built in 1773–1783, and marks the site of Canterbury College or Hall, founded by Archbishop Islip in 1363, and absorbed in Henry VIII.'s foundation. To the south of the hall and old library are the modern Meadow Buildings (1862–1865), overlooking the beautiful Christ Church Meadows, whose avenues lead to the Thames and Cherwell.

Corpus Christi College (commonly called Corpus) was founded in 1516 by Richard Fox, bishop of Winchester (1500–1528). He at first intended his foundation to be a seminary connected with St Swithin's priory at Winchester, but Hugh Oldham,

bishop of Exeter, foresaw the dissolution of the monasteries and advised against this. Fox had especially in view the object of classical education, and his foundation, besides a president, 20 fellows and 20 scholars, included 3 professors—in Greek, Latin and theology—whose lectures should be open to the whole university. This arrangement fell into desuetude, but was revived in 1854, when fellowships of the college were annexed to the professorial chairs of Latin and jurisprudence. The foundation now consists of a president, 16 fellows, 26 scholars and 3 exhibitioners. The college has its front upon Merton Street. The first quadrangle, with its gateway tower, is of the period of the foundation, and the gateway has a vaulted roof with beautiful tracery. In the centre of the quadrangle is a curious cylindrical dial in the form of a column surmounted by a pelican (the college symbol), constructed in 1581 by Charles Turnbull, a mathematician who entered the college in 1573. The hall has a rich late Perpendicular roof of timber; the chapel, dating from 1517, contains an altar-piece ascribed to Rubens, and the small library includes a valuable collection of rare printed books and MSS. The college retains its founder's crozier, and a very fine collection of old plate, for the preservation of which it is probable that Corpus had to pay a considerable sum in aid of the royalist cause. Behind the main quadrangle are the classical Turner buildings, erected during the presidency of Thomas Turner (1706), from a design attributed to Dean Aldrich. The picturesque college garden is bounded by the line of the old city wall. There are modern buildings (1885) by T. G. Jackson on the opposite side of Merton Street from the main buildings. Among the famous names associated with the college may be mentioned those of four eminent theologians—Reginald Pole, afterwards cardinal (nominated fellow in 1523); John Jewel, bishop of Salisbury (fellow 1542–1553), Richard Hooker (scholar, 1573) and John Keble (scholar, 1806). Thomas Arnold, the famous headmaster of Rugby school, was a scholar of the college (1811).

Exeter College was founded, as Stapeldon Hall, by Walter Stapeldon, bishop of Exeter, in 1314, but by the middle of the century it had become known as Exeter Hall. The foundation was extended by Sir William Petre in 1565. Stapeldon's original foundation for 12 scholars provided that 8 of them should be from Devonshire and 4 from Cornwall. There are still 8 "Stapeldon" scholarships confined to persons born or educated within the diocese of Exeter. The foundation consists of a rector, 12 fellowships and 21 scholarships or more. There are also a number of scholarships and exhibitions on private foundations, several of which are limited in various ways, including 3 confined to persons born in the Channel Islands or educated in Victoria College, Jersey, or Elizabeth College, Guernsey. The college has its front, which is of great length, upon Turl[1] Street. It has been extensively restored, and its gateway tower was rebuilt in 1703, while the earliest part of the quadrangle is Jacobean, the hall being an excellent example dating from 1618. The chapel (1857–1858) is an ornate structure by Sir Gilbert Scott; it is in Decorated style, of great height, with an eastern apse, and has some resemblance to the Sainte Chapelle in Paris. The interior contains mosaics by Antonio Salviati and tapestry by Sir E. Burne-Jones and William Morris. Scott's work is also seen in the frontage towards Broad Street, and in the library (1856). The college has a beautiful secluded garden between its own buildings and those of the divinity school or Bodleian library.

Hertford College, in its present form, is a modern foundation. There were formerly several halls on the site, and some-time between 1283 and 1300 Elias of Hertford acquired one of them, which became known as Hert or Hart Hall. In 1312 it was sold to Bishop Stapeldon, the founder of Exeter, and was occupied by his scholars for a short time. Again, some of William of Wykeham's scholars were lodged here while New College was building. The dependence of the hall on Exeter College was maintained until the second half of the 16th century. In 1710

1 "The Turl" takes its name from a postern (Turl or Thorold Gate) in the city wall, to which the street led.

Richard Newton, formerly a Westminster student of Christ Church, became principal, and in 1740, in spite of opposition from Exeter, he obtained a charter establishing Hertford as a college. The foundation, however, did not prosper, and by an inquisition of 1816 it was declared to have lapsed in 1805. With part of its property the university was able to endow the Hertford scholarship in 1834. Magdalen Hall, which had become independent of the college of that name in 1602, acquired the site and buildings of the dissolved Hertford College and occupied them, but was itself dissolved in 1874, when its principal and scholars were incorporated as forming the new Hertford College. An endowment was provided by Thomas Charles Baring, then M.P. for South Essex, for 15 fellows and 30 scholars, 7 lecturers and dean and bursar. The foundation now consists of a principal, 17 fellows and 40 scholars. Of the college buildings, which face those of the Bodleian library and border each side of New College Lane, no part is earlier than Newton's time. Modern buildings by T. G. Jackson (1903) incorporate remains of the little early Perpendicular chapel of Our Lady at Smith Gate (incorrectly called St Catherine's), which probably stood on the outer side of the town ditch. There is a striking modern chapel.

Jesus College has always had an intimate association with Wales. Queen Elizabeth figures as its foundress in its charter of 1571, but she was inspired by Hugh ap Rice (Price), a native of Brecon, who endowed the college. The original foundation was for a principal, 8 fellows and 8 scholars. It now consists of a principal and not less than 8 or more than 14 fellows, and there are 24 foundation scholarships, besides other scholarships and exhibitions, mainly on the foundation of Edmund Meyricke, a native of Merionethshire, who entered the college in 1656 and was a fellow in 1662. Not only his scholarships but others also are restricted (unless in default of suitable candidates) to persons born or educated in Wales, or of Welsh parentage. At Jesus, as at Exeter, there are also some "King Charles I." scholarships for persons born or educated in the Channel Islands. The college buildings face Turl Street; the front is an excellent reconstruction of 1856. The chapel dates from 1621, the hall from about the same time, and the library from 1677, being erected at the expense of the eminent principal (1661-1673) Sir Leoline Jenkins. He and his predecessor, Sir Eubule Thelwall (1621-1630), were prominent in raising the college from an early period of depression.

Keble College is modern; it received its charter in 1870. It was erected by subscription as a memorial to John Keble (q.v.). Its stated object was to provide an academical education combined with economical cost in living and a "training based upon the principles of the Church of England." The college is governed by a warden (who has full charge of the internal administration) and a council. There is a staff of tutors, and a number of scholarships and exhibitions on private foundations. The buildings lie somewhat apart from other collegiate buildings towards the north of the city, facing the university parks, which extend from here down to the river Cherwell. They are from the designs of William Butterfield, and are principally in variegated brick. The chapel has an elaborate scheme of decoration in mosaic; and the library contains a great number of books collected by Keble; and Holman Hunt's picture, "The Light of the World."

Lincoln College was founded in 1427 by Richard Flemyng, bishop of Lincoln. It was an outcome of the reaction against the doctrines of Wycliffe, of which the founder of the college, once their earnest supporter, was now an equally earnest opponent. He died (1431) before his schemes were fully carried out, and the college was struggling for existence when Thomas Rotherham, while bishop of Lincoln and visitor of the college, reconstituted and re-endowed it in 1478. The foundation consists of a rector, 12 fellows and 14 scholars. The buildings face Turl Street. The hall dates from 1436, but its wainscoting within was added in 1701. The chapel, in the back quadrangle, is an interesting example of Perpendicular work of very late date (1630). The interior is wainscoted in cedar, and the windows are filled with Flemish glass introduced at the time of the building. There is a modern library building in a classic Jacobean style, completed in 1906; the collection of books was originated by Dean

John Forest, who also built the hall. Among the eminent associates of this college was John Wesley, fellow 1726-1751.

Magdalen College (pronounced *Maudlen*; in full, St Mary Magdalen) was founded in 1458 by William of Waynflete, bishop of Winchester and lord chancellor of England. In 1448 he had obtained the patent authorizing the foundation of Magdalen Hall. In the college he provided for a president, 40 fellows, 30 demies,[1] and, for the chapel, chaplains, clerks and choristers. To the college he attached a grammar-school with a master and usher. The foundation now consists of a president, from 30 to 40 fellowships, of which 5 are attached to the Waynflete professorships in the university,[2] senior demies up to 8 and junior demies up to 35 in number. The choir, &c., are maintained, and the choral singing is celebrated. In order to found his college, Waynflete acquired the site and buildings of the hospital of St John the Baptist, a foundation or refoundation of Henry III. for a master and brethren, with sisters also, for "the relief of poor scholars and other miserable persons." The Magdalen buildings, which are among the most beautiful in Oxford, have a long frontage on High Street, while one side rises close to or directly above a branch of the river Cherwell. The chief feature of the front is the bell-tower, a structure which for grace and beauty of proportion is hardly surpassed by any other of the Perpendicular period. It was begun in 1492, and completed in about thirteen years. From its summit a Latin hymn is sung at five o'clock on May-day morning annually. Various suggestions have been made as to the origin of this custom; it may have been connected with the inauguration of the tower, but nothing is certainly known. The college is entered by a modern gateway, giving access to a small quadrangle, at one corner of which is an open pulpit of stone. This was connected with the chapel of St John's Hospital, which was incorporated in the front range of buildings. Adjoining this is the west front of the college chapel.[3] This chapel was begun in 1474, but has been much altered, and the internal fittings are in the main excellent modern work (1833 seq.). At the north-west corner of the entrance quadrangle is a picturesque remnant of the later buildings of Magdalen Hall. To the west is the modern St Swithun's quadrangle, the buildings of which were designed by G. F. Bodley and T. Garner, and begun in 1880, and to the west again a Perpendicular building erected for Magdalen College school in 1849. To the east lies the main quadrangle, called the cloister quadrangle, from the cloisters which surround it. These have been in great part reconstructed, but in accordance with the plan of the time of the foundation. Above the west walk rises the beautiful "founder's" tower, low and broad. On this side also is the valuable library. The south walk is bounded by the chapel and the hall, which lie in line, adjoining each other. The hall is a beautiful room, improved in 1906 by the substitution of an open timber roof for one of plaster erected in the 18th century. The panelling dates mainly from 1541; there is a tradition that the part at the west end came from the dissolved Reading Abbey. A curious series of figures which surmount the buttresses on three sides of the cloisters date from 1508-1509. Some are apparently symbolical, others scriptural, others again heraldic. To the north of the cloister quadrangle (a garden with broad lawns intervening) stand the so-called New Buildings, a massive classical range (1733). To the north and west of these extends the Grove or deer park, where the first deer were established probably c. 1700; to the east, across a branch of the Cherwell, is the meadow surrounded by Magdalen Walks, part of which is called Addison's Walk after Joseph Addison (demy and fellow). Perhaps the most notable period in the history of the college is that of 1687-1688, when the fellows resisted James II.'s attempt to force a president upon them, in place of their own choice, John Hough (1651-1743), successively bishop of Oxford,

---

[1] Singular *demy*, the last syllable accented. They correspond to the scholars of other colleges. The name is derived from the fact that their allowance was originally half (demi-) that of fellows.

[2] Waynflete himself had founded three readerships, in natural and moral philosophy and in theology.

[3] It actually faces about N.W.; the same deviation applies to other buildings described.

Lichfield, and Worcester. Cardinal Wolsey was a fellow of the college about the time when the bell-tower was building, but the attribution of the design to him, or even of any active part in the erection, is not borne out by evidence. Among *alumni* of the college were William Camden, Sir Thomas Bodley, John Hampden, at the time of whose matriculation (1610) Magdalen was strongly Puritan, Joseph Addison, Dr Sacheverell, and for a short period Gibbon the historian. Mention should be made of the eminent president, Martin Joseph Routh, who was elected to the office in 1791, and held it till his death in his 100th year in 1854. Magdalen College school had new buildings opened for it in 1894.

Merton College is of peculiar interest as regards its foundation, which is generally cited as the first on the present collegiate model. At some time before 1264 Walter de Merton,[1] a native of Merton, Surrey, devoted estates in that county to the maintenance of scholars in Oxford. Thus far he followed an established practice. In 1264 he founded at Malden a "house of scholars of Merton" for those who controlled the estates in the interest of the scholars, who should study preferably at Oxford, though any centre of learning was open to them. By 1268 the Oxford community had acquired the present site of the college; in 1270 new statutes laid down rules of living and study, and in 1274 the whole foundation was established under a final set of statutes at Oxford—*i.e.* the society ceased to be administered from the house in Surrey. The society was under a warden, and certain other officers were established, but no limit was set on the number of scholars. The foundation now consists of a warden, from 19 to 26 fellows, and 20 or more postmasterships. The postmasters of Merton correspond to the scholars of other colleges; they had their origin in the *portionistae* (*i.e.* foundationers who had a smaller portion or emolument than fellows), instituted in 1380 on the foundation of John Wyllyot (fellow 1334, chancellor 1349). The college is adjacent to Corpus, with its front upon Merton Street, and some of its buildings are of the highest interest, notably the chapel and library. The chapel consists of a choir and transepts with a tower at the crossing; but a nave, though intended, was never built. The choir is of the purest Decorated workmanship (dating probably from the last decade of the 13th century), with beautiful windows exhibiting most delicate tracery. The transepts show the appearance of Perpendicular work, but there is also work of the earlier style in them; the massive tower is wholly of the later period (*c.* 1450). The library, which lies on two sides of the so-called "mob" quadrangle, dates from 1377–1378, and was mainly the gift of William Rede, bishop of Chichester (1369–1386). It occupies two beautiful rooms and is of great interest from its early foundation and the preservation of its ancient character. The treasury is a small room coeval with the foundation, with a curious high-pitched ashlar roof. The other buildings, which are of various dates, are mainly disposed about four quadrangles, including that of St Alban's Hall, which, possibly dating from the early part of the 15th century, was incorporated with Merton College in 1882. The college hall retains an original door with fine ironwork, but the building is in great part modernized. A beautiful garden lies east of the buildings, being separated from the meadows to the south by part of the old city wall. Modern buildings (1907) have a frontage upon Merton Street; others (1864) overlook the meadows. Traditionally the names of Roger Bacon, Duns Scotus and Wycliffe have been associated with this college. Anthony Wood (1632–1695), the antiquary and historian of the university, was a postmaster of the college.

New College was founded by William of Wykeham in 1379. The founder's name for it, which it still bears in its corporate title, is the College of St Mary of Winchester. This house thus soon became known as the New College, and the substantive is still retained in the ordinary speech of the university, whereas in mentioning the titles of other colleges it is generally omitted:

[1] He was chancellor of the kingdom in 1261–1263, and again in 1272–1274, justiciar in 1271 and bishop of Rochester in 1274. He died in 1277.

Wykeham designed an exclusive connexion between his Oxford college and his school at Winchester. This connexion is maintained in a modified form. Wykeham's foundation was for a warden, and 70 fellows and scholars, with chaplains and a choir. The present foundation consists of a warden, and not more than 36 fellows, while 10 to 16 scholarships 6 elections· are made annually from Winchester and 4 from elsewhere. The choir is maintained, as at Magdalen. Five of the fellowships were attached to university professorships, of which three (logic, ancient history and physics) are called Wykeham professorships. The buildings of New College remain in great measure as designed by the founder, and illustrate the magnificence of his scheme. The main gateway tower fronts New College Lane. The chapel and hall stand in line (as at Magdalen), on the north side of the front quadrangle. The period of building was that of the development of the Perpendicular style. In shape the chapel was the prototype of a form common in Oxford, consisting of a choir, with transepts forming an antechapel, but with no nave. The remarkable west window in monochrome was erected, *c.* 1783, from a design by Sir Joshua Reynolds. The reredos, with its tiers of figures in niches, had a history similar to that at All Souls, being plastered over in 1567. In the same way, too, it was restored *c.* 1890; but previously James Wyatt had discovered traces of the original, and had unsuccessfully attempted the restoration of the niches in plaster, carrying out also, as elsewhere in Oxford, other extensive alterations of which the obliteration was demanded by later taste. Portions of the old woodwork were incorporated in the excellent new work of 1879 (Sir Gilbert Scott). In the chapel is preserved the beautiful pastoral staff of the founder, and there is a fine series of memorial brasses, mainly of the 15th century, in the antechapel. To the west of the chapel are the cloisters, consecrated in 1400, and the detached tower, a tall massive building on the line of the city wall. As already mentioned, a fine remnant of this wall adds to the picturesqueness of the college garden. The hall was completed in 1568, and has a Tudor screen and wainscoting. The garden quadrangle, the east side of which is open to the gardens, dates from 1682–1708. On the north side of the college precincts, facing Holywell Street, are extensive modern buildings by Sir G. G. Scott and B. Champneys. In 1642, when Oxford was playing its prominent part in the Civil War, the tower and cloisters of New College became a royalist magazine.

Oriel College was founded by Edward II. in 1326. The originator of the scheme and the prime mover in it was Adam de Brome, the king's almoner, who in 1324 had obtained royal licence to found a college; but in 1326 he surrendered his rights to the king, who issued charter and statutes, and created Brome the first provost. This foundation was for a provost and 10 fellows, but a number of bequests extending over nearly a century from 1445 enabled additional fellowships to be established. The foundation, however, now consists of the provost, 12 fellows and 2 professorial fellows, with at least 12 scholars and a number of exhibitioners. St Mary Hall, which had been the manse of St Mary's church, was given with the church to the college by the founder, and was opened as a hall with a principal of its own. It was, however, incorporated with the college in 1902. Oriel College was dedicated to St Mary the Virgin, and the name by which it is now known appears first in 1349. It was derived from a tenement called La Oriole (but the origin of this name is unknown), which had occupied part of the college site, had belonged to Eleanor of Provence, wife of Edward I., and had been given by her to her chaplain, James of Spain (Jacobus de Ispania). The buildings of Oriel, which face Oriel Street, are not coeval with the foundation. The first quadrangle, with its elaborate battlements, dates from 1620–1637. The inner quadrangle has buildings of 1719, 1729 and later dates. The modern extension on Cecil Rhodes's foundation faces High Street. Early in the 19th century a number of eminent men associated with Oriel gave the college its well-known connexion with the "Oxford Movement." Edward Copleston, elected fellow in 1795, became provost in 1814. In 1811 John Keble and Richard Whately were elected fellows, the one from Corpus; the other had been at Oriel. · Again in 1815 Thomas Arnold, afterwards headmaster of Rugby, was elected from Corpus, with Renn Dickson Hampden of Oriel. Later fellows were John Henry Newman (1822) and Edward Pusey (1823). James Anthony Froude entered the college in 1835; Matthew Arnold became a fellow in 1845. Cecil John Rhodes matriculated in 1873, and, besides his foundation of Rhodes scholarships, made a large bequest to the college.

Pembroke College was founded in 1624. Thomas Tesdale (1547–1609) of Glympton, Oxfordshire, left money for the support of scholars in Oxford, indicating Balliol College as his preference, but not insisting on this. Richard Wightwick (d. 2650), rector of East Ilsley, Berkshire, added to Tesdale's bequest, and though Balliol College desired to benefit by it, James I. preferred to figure as the founder of a new college with these moneys. Pembroke, which was named after William Herbert, earl of Pembroke, then chancellor of the university, was thus developed out of Broadgates Hall, which had long been eminent as the residence of students in law. ·The original college foundation was for a master, 10 fellows and 10 scholars, but a number of scholarships and exhibitions has been added by benefactors. Of the scholarships some are awarded by preference to candidates possessing certain qualifications, notably that of education at Abingdon school, which Tesdale intended to benefit by his bequest. The buildings of Pembroke lie south and west of St Aldate's Church, opposite Christ Church; they surround two picturesque quadrangles, but are in great part modern. The college preserves some relics of Samuel Johnson, who entered it in 1728.

Queen's College was founded in 1340–1341 by Robert de Eglesfield, chaplain of Philippa, queen-consort of Edward III., and was named in her honour. Her son, Edward the Black Prince, was entered on the books of the college, and Henry V. received education here. Several queens were among the benefactors of the college—Henrietta Maria, Caroline, Charlotte. The queen-consort is always the patroness of the college. The foundation consists of a provost, from 14 to 16 fellows, and about .25 scholars. There was formerly an intimate connexion between this college and the north of England. Five scholarships, called Eglesfield scholarships, are now given by preference to natives of Cumberland or Westmoriand, and the Hastings exhibitions founded by Lady Elisabeth Hastings (1682–1739) are open only to candidates from various schools in these counties and in Yorkshire. This connexion dates from the foundation. Eglesfield (d. 1349) was probably a native of Eaglesfield in Cumberland, and provided that the 12 fellows or scholars ·of his foundation were preferably to be natives of this county or Westmorland. During the time of Wycliffe, who while rector of Lutterworth resided for two years in the college, the foundation was by a ruling of the visitor (the archbishop of York) actually confined to the two counties mentioned, and so remained until 1854. The buildings date mainly from the close of the 17th century and the beginning of the 18th. They front High Street with a massive classical screen, flanked by the ends of the east and west ranges of buildings of the front quadrangle, and surmounted in the centre by a statue of Queen Caroline under a cupola. The buildings are the work of Sir Christopher Wren and Nicholas Hawksmoor. The library contains a valuable collection, especially of historical works, and is fitted with wood-carving by Grinling Gibbons. There is also here an interesting contemporary statue in wood of Queen Philippa. · The chapel retains several medieval windows from the former Gothic chapel, and some stained glass painted by Abraham van Ling (1635). The college preserves two early customs—on Christmas day a dinner is held at which a boar's head is carried in state into the hall, and an appropriate ancient carol is sung; and on New Year's day a threaded needle, with the motto " Take this and be thrifty," is presented to members in the college hall. The origin of this custom is traced to a rebus on the founder's name—*aiguille et fil* (needle and thread).

St John's College was founded in 1555 by Sir Thomas White, Kt., alderman of London (1492–1567). It occupied the site

of a house for Cistercian students in the university, founded by Archbishop Chicheley in 1437 and dedicated to St Bernard of Clairvaux. White's foundation was originally for a president, 50 fellows and scholars, and a chaplain, choir, &c., for the chapel. White established the intimate connexion which still exists between his college and the Merchant Taylors' school in London, in the foundation of which, as a prominent officer in the Merchant Taylors' Company, he had a share. The college foundation now consists of a president, from 14 to 18 fellowships, not less than 28 scholarships, of which 15 are appropriated to Merchant Taylors' school, and 4 senior scholarships, similarly appropriated. The buildings incorporate some of Chicheley's work, as in the front upon St Giles's Street, with its fine gateway. Similarly, in the front quadrangle, the hall and chapel belonged to the house of St Bernard, though subsequently much altered. A passage with a rich fan-traceried roof gives access from the front to the back quadrangle, on the south and east sides of which is the library. The south wing dates from 1596, the east from 1631. The latter is of the greater interest; it was built at the charge of William Laud, and the designs have been commonly attributed to Inigo Jones. The north and west sides of the quadrangle, of the same period, have cloisters. The union of the classical style, which predominates here, with the characteristic late Perpendicular of the period, makes this quadrangle architecturally one of the most interesting in Oxford, as the college gardens, which its east front overlooks, are among the most picturesque. The most notable period of the history of the college is associated with Laud, who entered the college in 1589, was elected a fellow in 1593, became president in 1611 and chancellor of the university in 1629. · Relics of him are preserved in the library, and he is buried in the chapel, together with White, the founder, and William Juxon, president 1621–1633, and afterwards archbishop of Canterbury.

Trinity College was founded in 1555 by Sir Thomas Pope, Kt. (d. 1559), of Tittenhanger, Hertfordshire. · He acquired and used for his college the ground and buildings of Durham College, the Oxford house of Durham Abbey, originally founded in the 13th century (see DURHAM, city). Trinity is therefore one of the instances of collegiate foundation forming a sequel to the dissolution of the monasteries, for Durham had been surrendered in 1540. Pope's foundation provided for a president, 12 fellows and 12 scholars. There are now 16 scholarships and a number of exhibitions. · There are also some scholarships in natural science, on the foundation (1873) of Thomas Millard, whose bequest also provides for a lecturer and laboratory. The front quadrangle of Trinity lies open to Broad Street; on its east side are modern buildings (by T. G. Jackson, 1887), on the north, the president's house and the chapel in a classic style, dating from 1694. It contains a rich alabaster tomb of Pope, the founder, and his third wife, and has a fine carved screen and altar-piece by Grinling Gibbons. The remainder of the buildings, forming two small quadrangles north of the chapel, includes parts of the old Durham college, but these have been much altered. Gardens extend to the east. John Henry Newman was a commoner of this college; Edward Augustus Freeman, the historian, and William Stubbs, bishop of Oxford, were among its fellows.

University College (commonly abbreviated Univ.) has claimed to find its origin in a period far earlier than that to which the earliest historical notice of the university itself can be assigned. In a petition to Richard II., respecting a dispute as to property the members of the " mickel universitie hall in Oxford " quote King Alfred as the founder of the house, for 26 divines. The date of 872 was claimed, and in 1872 a millenary celebration was held by the college. Moreover, in 1727 a dispute as to the mastership of the college led to an appeal to the Court of King's Bench to determine the right of visitation, and it was found that this right rested with the crown (as it now does) on the ground of the foundation by Alfred. Leaving tradition, however, it is found that William of Durham, archdeacon of Durham, dying in 1249, bequeathed money to the university to support masters at Oxford. In 1253 the university acquired its first tenement on this bequest; further acquisitions followed; and in 1180 an inquiry was held as to the disposition of the bequest, and statutes were issued to the society on Durham's foundation, the university finding it necessary to make provision for its individual governance. This intimate connexion between the university and the early development of a college has no parallel, and to it the college owes its name. The college, as it may now be called, developed slowly, further statutes being found necessary in 1292 and 1311; unlike other foundations which were established, with a definite code of statutes from the outset, by individual founders. It is possible, however, to maintain that the founders of Merton and Balliol were influenced in their work by that of William of Durham. The foundation consists of a master, 13 fellows and 16 scholars, and there are a large number of exhibitions. The buildings have a long frontage upon High Street. The oldest part of the buildings was begun in 1634. The chapel, built not long after, was altered in Decorated style by Sir Gilbert Scott, but contains fine woodwork of 1694, and windows by Abraham van Ling (1641). The old library dates from 1668-1670, but a new library was built by Scott, in Decorated style, and contains great statues of Lord Eldon and Lord Stowell, members of the college, the design of which was by Sir Francis Chantrey. The hall dates from 1657, but has been greatly altered. The extension of the college has necessitated that of its buildings in modern times. A chamber built for the purpose contains a statue, by Onslow Ford, of Percy Bysshe Shelley, presenting him lying drowned. The poet entered the college in 1810.

Wadham College was founded in 1612[1] by Nicholas Wadham (d. 1609) of Merifield, near Ilminster, Somersetshire, and Dorothy his wife, who as his executrix carried out his plans. The original foundation consisted of a warden, 15 fellows, 15 scholars, with 2 chaplains and 2 clerks. It now consists of a warden, 8 to 10 fellows and 18 scholars. The college, which has its frontage upon Parks Road, occupies the site of the house of the Austin Friars. No part of their buildings is retained. The erection of the college occupied the years 1610-1613, and while the buildings are in the main an excellent example of their period, the chapel (as distinct from the antechapel) is of peculiar interest. This appears and was long held to be pure Perpendicular work of the 15th century, but the record of its building in 1611 is preserved, and as the majority of the builders seem to have been natives of Somersetshire it is supposed that in the chapel they closely imitated the style which is so finely developed in that county. The buildings of Wadham have remained practically unchanged since the foundation, either by alteration of the existing fabric or by addition. Beautiful gardens lie to the east and north of them; the warden's garden is especially fine. In the quadrangle is a clock designed by Christopher Wren, who entered the college in 1649. It was in this year that John Wilkins, warden (1648-1659), initiated a weekly philosophical club, out of the meetings of which grew the Royal Society, which received its charter in 1662.

Worcester College was founded in its present form in 1714, out of a bequest by Sir Thomas Cookes, Bart. (d. 1701) of Bentley Pauncefoot, Worcestershire. On part of the site, in 1283, Gloucester Hall had been founded for Benedictine novices from Gloucester. After the dissolution of the monasteries, the buildings were used by Robert King, first bishop of Oxford, as a palace (1542); later it was acquired by Sir Thomas White, founder of St John's College, and again became a hall. This fell into difficulties, and was in great poverty when the present foundation superseded it. Cookes's foundation provided for a provost, 6 fellows and 6 scholars; there are now from 6 to 10 fellows, and from 10 to 18 scholars. Four of the scholarships are appropriated to Bromsgrove school, of which Cookes was a benefactor. The frontage of the buildings, in Worcester Street, is in a classical style, but the quadrangle retains some of the old buildings of Gloucester Hall. The gardens, with their lake, are fine.

[1] The year in which the statutes were issued; Dorothy Wadham had received the royal charter in 1610.

The academical halls, which were of very early origin, were originally in the nature of lodging-houses, in which students lived under a principal chosen by themselves. But they were gradually absorbed by the colleges as these became firmly established. The only remaining academical hall is that of St Edmund, which is said to have been founded in 1226, and to derive its name from Edmund Rich, archbishop of Canterbury, who is known to have taught at Oxford, and was canonized in 1248. The hall came into the possession of Queen's College in 1557, and the principal is nominated by that society. The buildings, which form a small quadrangle east of Queen's College, date mainly from the middle of the 18th century. There are three private halls in Oxford, established under a university statute of 1882, which provides for such establishment by any member of convocation under certain conditions and under licence from the vice-chancellor. Non-collegiate students,[2] i.e. members of the university, possessing all its privileges without being members of any college, were first admitted in 1868. As a body they are under the care of a delegacy and the supervision of a censor. Women are admitted to lectures and university examinations but not to its degrees; they have four colleges or halls—Somerville College (1879), Lady Margaret Hall (1879), St Hugh's Hall (1886) and St Hilda's Hall (1893). Among foundations independent of university jurisdiction and intended primarily for the teaching of theology are the Pusey House (1884, founded in memory of Edward Bouverie Pusey), St Stephen's House (1876) and Wycliffe Hall (1878), both theological colleges; Mansfield College (Congregational, founded to take the place of Spring Hill College, Birmingham, in 1889) and Manchester College (1893), also a nonconformist institution. The buildings of Mansfield, especially the chapel, should be noticed as of very good design in Decorated and Perpendicular styles. None of these houses is a residence for undergraduates. There is a theological college at Cuddesdon, near Oxford, where also is the bishop of Oxford's palace.

A notable group of buildings connected with the university stands between Broad Street and High Street, and between Exeter and Brasenose and All Souls colleges. Among these the principal are the old schools buildings, which form a fine quadrangle, and are now mainly occupied by the Bodleian Library, more extensive accommodation for the schools (examinations, &c.) being provided in the modern range of buildings facing High Street and King Street, completed in 1882 from the designs of T. G. Jackson. The erection of the old schools quadrangle was begun in 1613, and the architecture combines late Gothic with classical details. On the inner face of the gateway towers are seen the five Roman orders, in tiers, one above another. The windows, parapet and rich pinnacles, however, are Gothic. The quadrangle was founded by Sir Thomas Bodley, who conceived the addition of schools to the celebrated library which bears his name. The main chamber of the Bodleian Library is entered from the quadrangle. The library (see LIBRARIES) was opened in 1602. The central part of the room dates from 1480, when it was completed to contain the library given to the university by Humphrey, duke of Gloucester (d. 1447). This library was destroyed in the time of Edward VI. Bodley added the east wing, the west wing followed in 1634-1640, being built to house the collection of John Selden, one of the principal of many benefactors of the library. The whole forms a most beautiful room, enhanced by the finely painted ceiling and the excellent design of the fittings. In the storey above the library is the picture-gallery, containing portraits of chancellors, founders and benefactors of the university. The basement of the central part of the library is formed by the Divinity School, a splendid chamber (1480), in which the most notable feature is the groined roof, divided into compartments by widely splayed arches, and adorned with rich tracery and carved pendants. The Convocation House, below the west wing of the library, and entered from the west end of the school, has a roof with fan tracery. To the north of these buildings, flanking Broad Street, are the Sheldonian Theatre, the old building of the Clarendon Press and the Old Ashmolean building. "The Sheldonian" was built in 1664-1669 at the charge of Gilbert Sheldon (1598-1677), chancellor of the university and archbishop of Canterbury, from the design of Sir Christopher Wren. The principal public ceremonies of the university, including the "Encaenia," the annual commemoration of benefactors, accompanied by the conferring of honorary degrees and the recitation of prize compositions, are generally held in this building, which is particularly well adapted for its purpose. The university printing press was

[2] This title was given by a statute of 1884.

early established in its upper part. This institution bears the name of the Clarendon Press from the fact that it was founded partly from the proceeds of the sale of the earl of Clarendon's *History of the Rebellion*, the copyright of which was given to the university by his son Henry, the second earl. In 1713 it occupied the building erected for it close to the theatre; in 1830 it was moved to the larger buildings it now occupies in Walton Street. Printing in Oxford dates from the seventh or eighth decade of the 15th century, but was only carried on spasmodically until 1585, when the first university printer was Joseph Barnes. All the subsidiary processes of type-founding, stereotyping, &c., are carried on in the buildings of the press, and paper is supplied from the university mill at Wolvercote. The press is to a large extent a commercial firm, in which the university has a preponderating influence, governing it through a delegacy. The Broad Street building is used for other purposes of the university, as is the adjacent Old Ashmolean building, which originally (1683) contained the Ashmolean Museum, described hereafter; and now affords rooms for the School of Geography (1899). To the south of the old schools, between Brasenose and All Souls' colleges, is the fine classical rotunda known as the Radcliffe Library or camera, founded in 1737 by the eminent physician John Radcliffe (1650–1714). The architect was James Gibbs. In 1861 the building was devoted to the purpose it now serves, that of a reading room to the Bodleian Library, the collection of medieval and scientific works it contained being removed to the University Museum. The exterior gallery round the dome is celebrated as a view-point.

To the south of the Radcliffe Library, bordering High Street, is the church of St Mary the Virgin, commonly called the University church, on a site which is traditionally said to have been occupied by a church even from King Alfred's time. Its principal feature is a fine Decorated tower and spire, dating from the early part of the 13th century. The body of the church, however, is mainly an excellent example of Perpendicular work. The main entrance from High Street is beneath a classical porch erected in 1637 by Morgan Owen, a chaplain of Archbishop Laud; the statue of the Virgin and Child above it was alluded to in the impeachment of the archbishop. On the north side of the chancel is a building of earlier date than the present church; it is Decorated, of two storeys, and has served various purposes connected with the university, including that of housing a library before the foundation by Humphrey, duke of Gloucester. The university sermons are preached in St Mary's church.

A massive pile of classical buildings (1845) at the corner of Beaumont and St Giles's Streets is devoted to the Taylor Institution, the University Galleries and the Ashmolean Museum. Sir Robert Taylor, architect (1714–1788), left a bequest to establish the teaching of modern European languages in Oxford, and to provide a building for the purpose, and the eastern wing is devoted to this purpose, containing a library. In the University Galleries the most notable features are the celebrated Arundel marbles, a large series of drawings for pictures by Raphael and Michelangelo, and models for busts and statues by Sir Francis Chantrey. The new building for the Ashmolean Museum was added in 1895; and in connexion both with the building and with subsequent additions to the collections the benefactions of Charles Drury Edward Fortnum (1820–1899) should be remembered. The nucleus of this collection was formed by John Tradescant, a traveller and botanist (1608–1662), who left it to Elias Ashmole (q.v.), who added books, paintings and other objects, and presented the whole to the university in 1679. When the museum was moved from the Old Ashmolean building, the collection was in great part distributed; thus, books were sent to the Bodleian Library, and natural history objects to the University Museum. The Ashmolean Museum now contains excellent collections of Egyptian, Greek, Roman and British antiquities, and many other objects, among which perhaps the most widely famous is the Alfred Jewel, an ornament of crystal, enamel and gold, bearing King Alfred's name, and found at Athelney. The University Museum is an extensive building close to the parks, opposite Keble College. Its foundation was the outcome of the necessity of keeping pace in the university with the extended range of modern scientific study. It was built in 1856 seq., and contains the following departments—medicine and public health, comparative anatomy, physiology, human anatomy, zoology, experimental philosophy, physics, chemistry, geology, mineralogy and pathology. There is also here the Pitt-Rivers ethnographical museum, which had its origin in the collection of Augustus Henry Lane Fox Pitt-Rivers, presented to the university in 1883. Additional buildings contain the Radcliffe Library and various laboratories. The university observatory is in the parks, not far from the museum, but an older observatory is that called the Radcliffe (1772–1795), built by the trustees of the Radcliffe bequest, as was the Radcliffe Infirmary (1770) standing near the observatory, in Woodstock Road. Opposite Magdalen College, by the banks of the Cherwell, is the beautiful botanic garden founded by Henry Danvers, earl of Danby, in 1622, with which are connected a library, herbarium and museum. The Indian Institute (1882), in Broad Street, was founded as a centre for the study of Indian subjects, and for the use of native students in the university and prospective university civil servants. The Oxford Union Society, the principal university club, founded in 1825, has its rooms, with library and debating hall, near Cornmarket Street.

Ancient buildings in Oxford, apart from collegiate and university buildings, are mainly ecclesiastical, but there are a few notable exceptions. The castle, which, as already indicated, was erected by Robert d'Oili at the west of the ancient city, retains its massive tower, standing picturesquely by the river, and a mound within which is a curious chamber containing a well. There is also a Norman crypt-chapel, but the county court and gaol buildings adjacent are modern. Among old houses, of which not a few survive in Holywell Street and elsewhere, Bishop King's palace in St Aldate's Street may be mentioned; it has been in great part defaced by modern alterations, while the remaining front is a beautiful half-timbered and gabled example dated 1628; but ornate ceilings preserved in some of the rooms date from the erection in the time of Edward VI. Kettell Hall in Broad Street is another fine house, now used as a private residence, but formerly put to collegiate use, having been built by Ralph Kettell, president of Trinity (1599–1643). Among ancient churches in Oxford, after the cathedral and St Mary's, the chief in interest is St Peter's-in-the-East, which has a fine Norman chancel, crypt and south doorway, with additions of Early English and later date. St Michael's church, the body of which as now existing is of little interest, has a very early tower (11th century) of massive construction, which probably served as a defence for the north gate of the city. St Giles's church has Norman remains, but is chiefly notable for the excellent character of its Early English portions and for a beautiful font of that period. Holywell church retains a fine Norman chancel arch; and the churches of St Mary Magdalen, St Aldate's, St Ebbe's and St Thomas the Martyr are all of some antiquarian interest in spite of extensive modern alteration. Only the 14th century tower remains of St Martin's church at Carfax, the body of the church, which was a complete reconstruction of 1820, being removed at the close of the century, in the course of street-widening. Some of the modern churches are on sites of early dedication. The church of All Saints in High Street was rebuilt in 1706–1708 from the design of Dean Aldrich, and is a good classical example. Beneath several buildings in this part of the city the crypts of earlier halls or other buildings remain. In the suburb of Cowley are remains, including the chapel, of the hospital of St Bartholomew, originally a foundation for lepers (1126). The village church at Iffley, not far beyond the eastern outskirts of the city, with its ornate west end, tower and chancel, is one of the most notable small Norman churches in England. Of modern city buildings, the only one of special note is the town hall (1893–1897), which has a striking frontage upon St Aldate's Street.

"The Chancellor, Masters and Scholars of the University of Oxford" form a corporate body, within which the colleges are so many individual corporations. The university was *University constitution and administration.* governed by statutes of its own making, which were codified and brought out of the confusion into which they had fallen in the course of centuries in 1636, during Laud's chancellorship. A commission was appointed to inquire fully into the condition of the university in 1850; it reported in 1852, and in 1854 the constitution was amended by the Oxford University Act. In 1876 another commission was appointed, and in 1877 the Universities of Oxford and Cambridge Act was passed. This act provided for the appointment of commissioners who (1882) made statutes for each college, excepting Hertford, Keble and Lincoln, the first and second of which are modern foundations, while the third is governed under statutes of 1855. The highest officer of the university is the chancellor, who is elected by the members of convocation, holds office for life, and is generally a distinguished member of the university. He does not take an active part in the details of administration, delegating this to the vice-chancellor, who is, therefore, practically the head. He is nominated annually by the chancellor, and must be the head of a college. He appoints four pro-vice-chancellors, also heads of colleges, to exercise his authority in case of necessity. The high steward is appointed for life, with the duty of trying grave criminal cases when the accused is a resident member of the university. Two proctors are appointed annually by two of the colleges in rotation; their special duty is a disciplinary surveillance over members of the university in *statu pupillari* when there are not within the jurisdiction of their colleges. They are assisted by four pro-proctors. The principal duty of the public orator is that of presenting those who are to receive an honorary master's degree, and of making speeches in the name of the university on ceremonial occasions. The registrar acts as the recorder of the various administrative bodies of the university, and the secretary to the Board of Faculties has similar duties with regard to these boards, his work being closely associated with that of the registrar. The chancellor's court exercises civil jurisdiction in cases in which one of the parties is a resident member of the university. The university returns two members (burgesses) to parliament, the privilege dating from 1604.

The Hebdomadal [1] Council consists of the vice-chancellor, immediate ex-vice-chancellor and proctors as official members, and of eighteen other members (heads of houses, professors, &c.) elected for terms of six years by the congregation of the university. The council takes the initiative in promulgating,

_____
[1] From Greek ἑβδομάς, the number seven; the Hebdomadal Board instituted in 1631 was appointed to hold a weekly meeting.

discussing and submitting to Convocation all the legislation of the university. The Ancient House of Congregation consists of "regents," i.e. doctors and masters of arts for two years after the term in which they take their degrees, professors, heads of colleges and other resident officers, &c. The house thus includes all those who are concerned with education and discipline in the university, but it now has practically no functions beyond the granting of degrees. It lost its wider powers under the act of 1854, when the Congregation of the university was created. This body, which includes besides certain officials all members of Convocation who have resided for a fixed period within one mile and a half of Carfax, approves or amends legislation submitted by the Hebdomadal Council previously to its submission to Convocation; it also has considerable powers in the election of the various administrative boards. The House of Convocation consists of all masters of arts and doctors of the higher faculties who have their names on the university books, and has the final control over all acts and business of the university. There are boards of curators for the Bodleian Library, the university chest and other institutions, delegates of the common university fund, the museum and the press, for extension teaching, local examinations and other similar purposes, visitors for the Ashmolean Museum and university galleries, and many other administrative bodies. There are boards for the following faculties: theology, law, medicine, natural science and arts (including literæ humaniores, oriental languages and modern history). Among the numerous professorships and readerships in the various subjects of study, the oldest foundation is the Margaret professorship of divinity, founded in 1502 by Margaret, countess of Richmond and mother of Henry VII. This was followed by the five Regius professorships of divinity, civil law, medicine, Hebrew and Greek, founded by Henry VIII. in 1546.

The colleges, as already seen, consist of a head, whose title varies in different colleges, fellows (who form the governing body) and scholars. To these are to be added the commoners, who are not "on the foundation," i.e. those who either receive no emoluments, or hold exhibitions which do not (generally) entitle them to rank with the scholars. The college officer who is immediately concerned with the disciplinary surveillance of members of the college in statu pupillari is the dean (except at Christ Church). Each undergraduate (this term covering all who have not yet proceeded to a degree) is, as regards his studies, under the immediate supervision of one of the fellows as tutor. The university terms are four—Michaelmas (which begins the academic year, and is therefore the term in which the majority of undergraduates begin residence), Hilary or Lent, Easter and Trinity. The last two run consecutively without interval, and for certain purposes count as one; they are kept by three weeks' residence in each, while the two first are kept by six weeks' residence in each, though the terms properly speaking are longer. The examinations required to be passed in order to obtain the first or bachelor's degree may be summarized thus:—(a) Responsions, usually taken very early in the course of study. Exemption is in many cases granted when a candidate has passed a certificate examination held by university examiners at the school where he has been educated. (b) First public examination or School of Moderations, usually taken after four or six terms. (c) Second public examination or final school (this in the case of literæ humaniores is commonly called "Greats") usually takes place at the end of the fourth year of residence. "Pass" schools and "honour" schools are distinguished; in the latter candidates are grouped in classes according to merit. No further examination or other exercise is required for the degree of master of arts. Among the numerous scholarships and prizes offered by the university (as distinct from the colleges) a few of the most noted may be mentioned—the Craven and the Ireland classical scholarships (founded respectively by John, Lord Craven (d. 1648), who also founded the travelling fellowships which bear his name for the study of antiquities, and of John Ireland, dean of Westminster (1825); the scholarship commemorating Edward, earl of Derby (chancellor 1852-1869); the law scholarship commemorating John, first earl of Eldon; the chancellor's prizes in Latin verse and English prose (initiated by the earl of Lichfield, chancellor 1762-1772) and in Latin prose (by Lord Grenville, 1809); the Newdigate prize for English verse, founded by Sir Roger Newdigate (1806); the Gaisford prizes in Greek verse and prose (1856), commemorating Thomas Gaisford, dean of Christ Church; the Arnold historical essay (1850), commemorating Thomas Arnold, headmaster of Rugby school; and the theological foundations of Edward Bouverie Pusey and Edward Ellerton, fellow of Magdalen. University scholarships, such as those mentioned, are awarded to persons who are already members of the university (who must in some cases already have taken a degree); they thus differ from college scholarships, which are generally open to persons who have not yet matriculated. The Rhodes scholarships (see RHODES, CECIL) stand alone. They are an adaptation of the college scholarship to a special purpose, but are not in the award of any one college. Arrangements exist whereby members of the universities of Cambridge or Dublin may be "incorporated" as members of Oxford University; and whereby the period of necessary academical residence at Oxford University is reduced in the case of students from "affiliated" colleges within the United Kingdom. Special provisions are also made in the case of

students from any foreign university and from certain colonial and Indian universities. The number of persons who matriculate at Oxford University is about 850 annually.

The principal social functions in the university take place in "Eights' Week," when, during the summer term (Easter and Trinity), the college eight-oared bumping races are held, and also, more especially, in "Commemoration Week," at the close of the same term, when the university ceremonies connected with the commemoration of benefactors, the conferring of degrees honoris causa, &c., are held, and balls are given in some of the colleges.

The city of Oxford (as distinct from the university) returns one member to parliament, having lost its second member under the Redistribution Act of 1885, before which date it had been entirely disfranchised for a year owing to bribery at the election of 1881. The municipal government is in the hands of a mayor, 15 aldermen (including 3 from the university) and 45 councillors (9 from the university). Area, 4676 acres.

AUTHORITIES.—See the Oxford University Calendar (annually) and the Oxford Historical Register, Oxford. The Oxford Historical Society has issued various works dealing with the history. In the "College History" series, London, the story of each college forms a volume by a member of the foundation. The principal earlier authority is Anthony à Wood (q.v.). See also James Ingram (president of Trinity, 1824-1850), Memorials of Oxford (Oxford, 1837); A. Lang, Oxford (London, 1885); H. C. Maxwell Lyte, History of the University of Oxford to 1530 (London, 1886); Hon. G. C. Brodrick, History of the University of Oxford in "Epochs of Church History" series (London, 1886); C. W. Boase, Oxford, in "Historic Towns" series (London, 1887); Oxford and Oxford Life, ed. J. Wells (London, 1892).   (O. J. R. H.)

OXFORD, a village in Butler county, Ohio, U.S.A., about 40 m. N.W. of Cincinnati. Pop. (1900) 2009; (1910) 2017. Oxford is served by the Cincinnati, Hamilton & Dayton railway. It is the seat of Miami University (co-educational; chartered in 1809, opened as a grammar school in 1818, and organized as a college in 1824), which had 40 instructors and 1076 students in 1909. At Oxford also are the Oxford College for Women, chartered in 1906, an outgrowth, after various changes of name, of the Oxford Female Academy (1839); and the Western College for Women (chartered in 1904), an outgrowth of the Western Female Seminary (opened in 1855). The first settlement on the site was made about 1800.

OXFORD, PROVISIONS OF, the articles constituting a preliminary scheme of reform enacted by a parliament which met at Oxford (England) on the 11th of June 1258. King Henry III. had promised on the 2nd of May that the state of his realm should be rectified and reformed by twenty-four counsellors who were to meet at Oxford for this purpose five weeks later. Twelve of these counsellors were chosen by the king, and twelve by the earls and barons. When the parliament met each twelve of these twenty-four chose two from the other twelve, and this committee of four was empowered, subject to the approval of the whole body, to elect a king's council of fifteen members. The twenty-four then provided that the new council should meet three times a year in parliaments in which twelve commissioners were to be summoned to discuss the affairs of the realm on behalf of the whole community. Another body of twenty-four was appointed to treat of an aid, which was probably the aid which had been demanded earlier in the year. On the 22nd of June the king appointed new wardens of some of the castles which were then in the custody of his Poitevin half-brothers and their friends, and on the same day he gave directions that the twenty-four should proceed with the work of reform, and the committee of four with the election of the council of fifteen. Meanwhile it was provided that the sheriffs and the three great officers of state were to hold office for a year only, and to render accounts at the expiration of their terms of office. On the 24th of August in pursuance of a provision by the parliament the king directed four knights in each county to inquire into the trespasses and wrongs which had been committed by sheriffs, bailiffs and other officials. For many of the grievances of the barons the Oxford parliament provided no remedy; and they were only partly redressed by the Provisions of Westminster in the autumn of 1259. The king declared his adhesion to the Provisions of Oxford on the 18th of October by proclamations in English, French and Latin, but in 1261, having obtained a papal dispensation from his oath of observance, he entirely repudiated them. The barons, however, insisted on his obligation to observe the provisions, and the dispute was eventually referred to the arbitration of Louis IX. of France, who formally annulled them on the 23rd of January 1264, but expressly declared that his decision was not to invalidate the privileges, liberties and laudable customs of the realm of England, which had existed before the time of the provisions.

No official record of the Provisions of Oxford has been preserved, and our knowledge of them is chiefly derived from a series of notes and extracts entered in the Annals of Burton Abbey, which are probably neither exhaustive nor in correct order. See the *Annales monastici*, vol. i. (Burton), edited by H. R. Luard for the Rolls series; *Patent Rolls, Henry III.* (printed text); *Foedera* (Record Commission edition); W. Stubbs, *Constitutional History* and *Select Charters*, and Charles Bémont, *Simon de Montfort* (1884).

OXFORDIAN, in geology, the name given to a series of strata in the middle Oolites which occur between the Corallian beds and the Cornbrash; the division is now taken to include the Oxford Clay with the underlying Callovian stage (*q.v.*). The argillaceous beds were called "Clunch Clay and Shale" by William Smith (1815-1816); in 1818 W. Buckland described them under the unwieldy title "Oxford, Forest or Fen Clay." The term Oxfordian was introduced by d'Orbigny in 1844. The name is derived from the English county of Oxford, where the beds are well developed, but they crop out almost continuously from Dorsetshire to the coast of Yorkshire, generally forming low, broad valleys. They are well exposed at Weymouth, Oxford, Bedford, Peterborough, and in the cliffs at Scarborough, Red Cliff and Gristhorpe Bay. Rocks of this age are found also in Uig and Skye.

The Oxford Clay is usually bluish or greenish-grey in colour, weathering brown or yellow; in the lower portions it is somewhat more shaly. The beds frequently tend to be calcareous and bituminous, while in places there is a considerable amount of lignite. Septaria of large size are common, they have been cut and polished at Radipole and Melbury Osmund in Dorsetshire, where they are known as Melbury marble or "turtle-stones"; they were used to form table-tops, &c. In Yorkshire the Oxford Clay is usually a grey sandy shale. In the central and southern English counties the Oxford Clay is divisible as follows:—

Upper zone of *Cardioceras cordatum*	Clays with septaria and limestone nodules. Clays with pyritized fossils (subzone of *Quenstedticeras Lamberti*).
Lower zone of *Cosmoceras ornatum*	Shales with pyritized fossils (subzone of *Cosmoceras Jason*).

The upper zone contains also *Gryphaea dilatata* (large forms), *Serpula vertebralis*, *Belemnites hastatus*, *Aspidoceras perarmatum*, *Cardioceras vertebrale*. The lower zone yields *Reineckia anceps*, *Peltoceras athleta*, *Quenstedtoceras Mariae*, *Cosmoceras Jason*, *Cardioceras mariccatum*, and a small form of *Gryphaea dilatata*. The remains of fishes and saurian reptiles have been found. The Oxford Clay is dug for brick-making at Weymouth, Trowbridge, Chippenham, Oxford, Bedford, Peterborough and Fletton.

The "Oxfordian" of the continent of Europe is divided according to A. de Lapparent into an upper (Argovian) and a lower (Neuvizyen) substage. In the former he includes part of the English Coralline Oolite and in the latter the lower Calcareous Grit, while a portion of the lower Oxford Clay is placed in the Divesian or upper substage of the Callovian. In north-west Germany the Oxford Clay is represented by the Hersumer beds. Most of the European formations on this horizon are clays and marls with occasional limestone and ironstone beds.

See JURASSIC, CALLOVIAN, CORALLIAN.   J. A. H.)

OXFORDSHIRE (or OXON), an inland county of England, bounded N.E. by Northamptonshire, N.W. by Warwickshire, W. by Gloucestershire, S.S.W. and S.E. by Berkshire, and E. by Buckinghamshire; area 755·7 sq. m. The county lies almost wholly in the basin of the upper Thames. This river forms its southern boundary for 71 m., from Kelmscot near Lechlade (Gloucestershire) to Remenham below Henley-on-Thames, excepting for very short distances at two points near Oxford. The main stream is the boundary line, but from Oxford upward the river often sends out branches through the flat watermeadows. The principal tributaries joining the Thames on the Oxfordshire side do not in any case rise within the county, but have the greater part of their courses through it.

These tributaries are as follows, pursuing the main river downwards. (1) The Windrush, rising in Gloucestershire, follows a narrow and pleasant valley as far as Witney, after which it meanders in several branches through rich flat country, to join the Thames at Newbridge. (2) The Evenlode, also rising in Gloucestershire, forms the western county boundary for a short distance, and follows

a similar but more beautiful valley to the Thames below Eynsham. From the north it receives the Glyme, which joins it on the confines of Blenheim Park, where the woodland scenery is of peculiar richness. (3) The Cherwell, rising in Northamptonshire, forms some 10 m. of the eastern boundary, and with a straight southerly course joins the Thames at Oxford. From the east it receives the Ray, which drains the flat tract of Ot Moor. (4) The Thame, rising in Buckinghamshire, runs south-west and west, forming 6 m. of the eastern boundary, after which it turns south to join the Thames near Dorchester. Above the point of junction the Thames is often called the Isis. Lastly, a small part of the north-eastern boundary is formed by the Great Ouse (which discharges into the North Sea), here a very slight stream, some of whose head-feeders rise within Oxfordshire.

The low hills which lie south of the Windrush, and those between it and the Evenlode (which attain a greater height) are foothills of the Cotteswold range, the greater part of which lies in Gloucestershire. Between the Windrush and Evenlode they are clothed with the remaining woods of Wychwood Forest, one of the ancient forests of England, which was a royal preserve from the time of John, and was disafforested in 1862. Its extent was 3735 acres of forest proper. The hills continued north of the Evenlode (but not under the name of Cotteswold) at an average elevation over 500 ft. The range terminates at Edge Hill, just outside the county in Warwickshire. The hills bordering the Cherwell basin on the east are of slight elevation, until, running east from Oxford into Buckinghamshire, a considerable line of heights is found north of the Thame valley, reaching 560 ft. in Shotover hill, overlooking Oxford. Across the south-east of the county stretches the bold line of the Chiltern Hills, running N.E. and S.W. On the western brow, Nettlebed Common, an extensive plateau, reaches at some points nearly 700 ft. in altitude. The district was probably once covered with forest, and there are still many fine beeches, oaks and ash trees. William Camden in his survey of the British Isles (1586) mentions forests as a particular feature of Oxfordshire scenery, and there are traces still left of natural woodland in various parts of the county.

The Thames flows through a deep gap from about Goring downwards, between the Chilterns and the Berkshire Downs. Here, as above at Nuneham and other points, the sylvan scenery is fine, and Henley and Goring are favourite riverside resorts on the Oxfordshire shore. The western feeders of the Thames and Cherwell have much rich woodland in their narrow valleys, and the sequestered village of Great Tew, on a tributary of the Cherwell river, may be singled out as having a situation of exceptional beauty.

Geology.—The influence of the rocky substratum upon the character of the scenery and soil is clearly marked. It is sufficient to point, on the one hand, to the dry chalky upland of the Chiltern Hills and the oolitic limestone hills in the north-west, or the Cornbrash with its rich, fertile soil; and, on the other hand, to the dreary scenery of the Oxford Clay land with its cold, unproductive soil. Cretaceous rocks occupy the south-eastern corner of the county; Jurassic rocks prevail over the remainder. The general dip is towards the south-east, and the strike of the strata is S.W.–N.E.; therefore in passing from south to north, beds are traversed which are successively lower and older. The Chiltern Hills, with a strong scarp facing the north-west, are formed of Chalk, the Lower Chalk at the foot and the hard Chalk rock at the summit; from the top of the hills the Upper Chalk-with-Flints descends steadily towards the Thames. Here and there, as at Shiplake and Nettlebed, outliers of Tertiary clays rest upon it. The Upper Greensand forms a low feature at the foot of the Chalk hills; this is succeeded by the Gault, with an outcrop varying from 4 m. to 1½ m. wide between Dorchester and Sydenham; it is a pale blue clay, dug for bricks at Culham. The Lower Greensand appears from beneath the Gault at Culham and Nuneham Courtney and in outliers north of Cuddesdon. The Kimmeridge clay, in the grass-covered vales between Sandford and Waterperry, is separated from the Lower Greensand by the Portland limestone and Portland sands and by the thin Purbeck beds; it is dug for bricks at Headington. Both Portland and Purbeck beds may be observed in Shotover hill; the Portland limestone is quarried at Garsington. The Coral Rag, with calcareous grit at the base, is a shelly, coral-bearing limestone, traceable from Sandford to Wheatley; it has been extensively quarried at Headington hill. North-west of the last-named formation a broad outcrop of Oxford Clay crosses the county; while this is mostly under pasture, the next lower formation, the Cornbrash, a brownish rubbly limestone, gives rise to a loose brown soil very suitable for the cultivation of wheat. Exposures of Cornbrash occur at Norton

Bridge, Woodstock and Shipton; it forms a broad plateau between Middleton Stoney and Bicester. Inliers also lie in the Oxford Clay plain at Islip, Charlton, Merton and Black Horse Hill. Wychwood Forest has given its name to the "Forest Marble," an inconstant series of limestones which thin out eastward and become argillaceous. The Great Oolite limestones, with the "Stonesfield Slate" at the base and occasional marls, form the higher ground in the north-west. An excellent freestone is quarried at Tainton and Milton. The Inferior Oolite series of sands and limestones forms the Rollright Ridge and caps Shenlow and Epwell hills; it also reaches down to Chipping Norton and eastward to Steeple Aston. The three divisions of the Lias are represented in the N.W. of the county. The most important is the middle member with marlstone, which, being a hard calcareous bed at the top, forms an elevated ridge along the limit of the outcrop. The marlstone is quarried for building stone at Hornton, and for road metal in many places, and, as it contains a considerable amount of iron oxide, it has been extensively worked for iron at Adderbury, Fawler and elsewhere. The Upper Lias clays occur mostly as unimportant outliers. The Lower Lias clays have been exposed by the Evenlode near Charlbury and by the Cherwell in the upper part of its valley. A hard shelly limestone called Banbury marble occurs in this part of the Lias. Glacial drift is sparingly scattered over the south-western part of the county, but is more plentiful in the north-eastern portion. Valley gravels are associated with the main stream courses and gravel, clay-with-flints and brick earth rest upon much of the chalk slope. Coal Measures have been proved at a depth of about 1200 ft. near Burford.

Climate and Agriculture.—The climate is healthy and generally dry except in the low ground bordering the Thames, as at Oxford; but colder than the other southern districts of England, especially in the bleak and exposed regions of the Chilterns. Crops are later in the uplands than in more northerly situations at a lower elevation. In the northern districts there is a strong yet friable loam, well adapted for all kinds of crops. The centre of the county is occupied for the most part by a good friable but not so rich soil, formed of decomposed sandstone, chalk and limestone. A large district in the south-east is occupied by the chalk of the Chiltern Hills, partly wooded, partly arable, and partly used as sheep-walks. The remainder of the county is occupied by a variety of miscellaneous soils ranging from coarse sand to heavy tenacious clay, and occasionally very fertile. Nearly seven-eighths of the area of the county, a high proportion, is under cultivation. The acreage under grain crops is nearly equally divided between barley, oats and wheat. There is a considerable acreage under beans. More than half the total acreage under green crops is occupied by turnips, and vetches and tares are also largely grown. Along the smaller streams there are very rich meadows for grazing, but those on the Thames and Cherwell are subject to floods. The dairy system prevails in many places, but the milk is manufactured into butter, little cheese being made. The improved shorthorn is the most common breed, but Alderney and Devonshire cows are largely kept. Of sheep, Southdowns are kept on the lower grounds, and Leicesters and Cotteswolds on the hills. Pigs are extensively reared, the county being famous for its brawn.

Manufactures.—Blankets are manufactured at Witney, and tweed, girths and horsecloths at Chipping Norton. There are paper mills at Shiplake, Sandford-on-Thames, Wolvercot and Eynsham, using water power, as do the blanket works and many mills on the tributary streams of the Thames. Agricultural implements and portable engines are made at Banbury, and gloves at Woodstock, the last a very ancient industry. Banbury has been long celebrated for the manufacture of a peculiar cake. Some iron ore is raised (from the middle Lias), and the quarries and clays for brick-making are important, as already indicated. A large number of women and girls are employed in several of the towns and villages in the lace manufacture.

Communications.—The northern line of the Great Western railway, leaving the main line at Didcot Junction in Berkshire, runs north through Oxfordshire by the Cherwell valley. Oxford is the junction for the Worcester line, running north-west by the Evenlode valley, with branches from Chipping Norton Junction into Gloucestershire (Cheltenham), and across the north-west of the county to the northern line at King's Sutton. From Oxford also the East Gloucester line serves Witney and the upper Thames. Another Great Western line, from Maidenhead and London, enters the county on the east, has a branch to Watlington, serves the town of Thame, and runs to Oxford. The Great Central railway has a branch from its main line at Woodford in Northamptonshire to Banbury, the north and south expresses using the Great Western route southward. Branches of the London and North Western railway from Bletchley terminate at Oxford and Banbury. As regards water-communications, the Thames is navigable for large launches to Oxford, and for barges over the whole of its Oxfordshire course. None of its tributaries in this county is commercially navigable. The Oxford Canal, opened in 1790, follows the Cherwell north from Oxford and ultimately connects with the Grand Junction and Warwick canals.

Population and Administration.—The area of the ancient county is 483,626 acres, with a population in 1891 of 185,240

and in 1901 of 181,120. The area of the administrative county is 480,687 acres. The municipal boroughs are Banbury (pop. 12,968), Chipping Norton (3780), Henley-on-Thames (5984), Oxford, a city and the county town (49,336) and Woodstock (1684). The urban districts are Bicester (3023), Caversham (6580), Thame (2911), Wheatley (872), Witney (3574). Bampton (1167) and Burford (1146) in the west, and Watlington (1154) in the south-east, are the other principal country towns. The county is in the Oxford circuit, and assizes are held at Oxford. It has one court of quarter-sessions, and is divided into 11 petty sessional divisions. The borough of Banbury and the city of Oxford have separate courts of quarter-sessions and commissions of the peace, and the borough of Henley-on-Thames has a separate commission of the peace. The total number of civil parishes is 304. Oxfordshire is in the diocese of Oxford, and contains 244 ecclesiastical parishes or districts, wholly or in part. The ancient county is divided (since 1885) into three parliamentary divisions: Banbury or northern, Woodstock or mid, and Henley or southern, each returning one member. It also includes part of the parliamentary borough of Oxford, returning one member, in addition to which the university of Oxford returns two members.

Education.—On account of the famous university of Oxford and other educational institutions there, the county as regards education holds as high a position as any in England. In connexion with the university there is a day training college for schoolmasters, and there is also in Oxford a residential training college for schoolmistresses (diocesan), which takes day students. There is a training college for schoolmasters in the diocese of Oxford and Gloucester, at Culham. At Cuddesdon, where is the palace of the bishops of Oxford, there is a theological college, opened in 1854. At Bloxham is the large grammar school of All Saints, and there are several boys' schools in Oxford.

History.—The origin of the county of Oxford is somewhat uncertain; like other divisions of the Mercian kingdom, the older boundaries were entirely wiped out, and the district was renamed after the principal town. The boundaries, except for the southern one, which is formed by the Thames, are artificial. There are fourteen hundreds in Oxfordshire, among them being five of the Chiltern hundreds. The jurisdiction over these five belonged to the manor of Benson, and in 1199 to Robert de Hare-court, a name which is still to be found in the county in the Harcourts of Stanton-Harcourt and Nuneham. The county includes small portions of Berkshire and Buckinghamshire, which lie in the hundreds of Bampton and Ploughley respectively. There has been little change in the county boundary; but acts of William IV. and Victoria slightly increased its area.

The district was overrun in the 6th century by the victorious West Saxons, who took Benson and Eynsham, as may be seen in the *Saxon Chronicle* for 571. In the 7th century the Mercians held all the northern border of the Thames, and during the 8th century this district twice changed hands, falling to Wessex after the battle of Burford, and to Mercia after a battle at Benson. As part of the Mercian kingdom it was included in the diocese of Lincoln. A bishopric had been established at Dorchester as early as 634, when Birinus, the apostle of Wessex, was given an episcopal seat there, but when a bishop was established at Winchester this bishopric seems to have come to an end. Before the Mercian conquest in 777, Oxfordshire was in the diocese of Sherborne. In 873 the jurisdiction of Dorchester reached to the Humber, and when the Danes were converted it extended over Leicestershire and Lincolnshire, Oxfordshire forming about an eighth of the diocese. At the Conquest there was no alteration, but in 1092 the seat was transferred to Lincoln. In 1542 a bishopric of Osney and Thame was established, taking its title from Oxford, the last abbot of Osney being appointed to it. In 1546 the existing bishopric of Oxford was established. The ecclesiastical boundaries remain as they were when archdeacons were first appointed—the county and archdeaconry being conterminous—and the county being almost entirely in the diocese of Oxford. The Danes overran the county during the 11th century; Thurkell's army burnt Oxford in 1010, and the combined armies of Sweyn and Olaf crossed Watling Street and ravaged the district, Oxford and

Winchester submitting to them. In 1018 Danes and English-men chose Eadgar's law at an assembly in Oxford, and in 1036, on Canute's death, his son Harold was chosen king. Here also took place the stormy meeting following the assembly (gemot) at Northampton, in which Harold allowed Tostig to be outlawed and Morkere to be chosen earl in his place, thus preparing the way for his own downfall and for the Norman Conquest. The destruction of houses in Oxford recorded in the Domesday Survey may possibly be accounted for by the ravages of the rebel army of Eadwine and Morkere on this occasion, there being no undisputed mention of a siege by William. Large possessions in the county fell to the Conqueror, and also to his rapacious kinsman, Odo, bishop of Winchester. The bishop of Lincoln also had extensive lands therein, while the abbeys of Abingdon, Osney and Godstow, with other religious houses, held much land in the county. Among lay tenants in chief, Robert D'Oili, heir of Wigod of Wallingford, held many manors and houses in Oxford, of which town he was governor. The importance of Oxford was already well established; the shire-moot there is mentioned in Canute's Oxford laws, and it was undoubtedly the seat of the county court from the first, the castle being the county gaol. The principal historical events between this period and the Civil War belong less to the history of the county than to that of the city of Oxford (q.v.). The dissolution of the monasteries, though it affected the county greatly, caused no general disturbance.

When King Charles I. won the first battle of the Civil War at Edgehill (23rd of October 1642), Oxford at once became the material and moral stronghold of the royalist cause. Every manor house in the district became an advanced work, and from Banbury in the north to Marlborough in the west and Reading in the south the walled towns formed an outer line of defence. For the campaign of 1643 the rôle of this strong position was to be the detention of the main parliamentary army until the royalists from the north and the west could come into line on either hand, after which the united royal forces were to close upon London on all sides, and in the operations of that year Oxfordshire successfully performed its allotted functions. No serious breach was made in the line of defence, and more than once, notably at Chalgrove Field (18th of June 1643), Prince Rupert's cavalry struck hard and successfully. In the campaign of Newbury which followed, the parliamentary troops under Essex passed through north Oxfordshire on their way to the relief of Gloucester, and many confused skirmishes took place between them and Rupert's men; and when the campaign closed with the virtual defeat of the royalists, the fortresses of the county offered them a refuge which Essex was powerless to disturb. The following campaign witnessed a change in Charles' strategy. Realizing his numerical weakness he abandoned the idea of an envelopment, and decided to use Oxfordshire as the stronghold from which he could strike in all directions. The commanding situation of the city itself prevented any serious attempt at investment by dividing the enemy's forces, but material wants made it impossible for Charles to maintain permanently his central position. Plans were continually resolved upon and cancelled on both sides, and eventually Essex headed for the south-west, leaving Waller to face the king alone. The battle of Cropredy Bridge followed (29th of Jan.), and the victorious king turned south to pursue and capture Essex at Lostwithiel in Cornwall. In the remaining operations of 1644 Oxfordshire again served as a refuge and as a base (Newbury and Donnington). With the appearance on the scene of Cromwell and the New Model army a fresh interest arose. Having started from Windsor on the 30th of April 1645, the future Protector carried out a daring cavalry raid. He caught and scattered the royalists unawares at Islip; then he pursued the fugitives to Bletchington and terrified the governor into surrendering. He swept right round Oxford, fought again at Bampton, and finally rejoined his chief, Fairfax, in Berkshire. A few days later Charles again marched away northwards, while Fairfax was ordered to besiege Oxford. In spite of the difficulties of the besiegers Charles was compelled to turn back to relieve the city, and the consequent

delay led to the campaign and disaster of Naseby. Yet even after Naseby the actual position of Oxfordshire was practically un-shaken. It is true that Abingdon with its parliamentary garrison was a standing menace, but the districts east of the Cherwell and Thames, and the triangle bounded by Oxford, Faringdon and Banbury, still retained its importance, till early in 1646 the enemy closed from all sides on the last stronghold of royalism. Stow-on-the-Wold witnessed the final battle of the war. On the 9th of May Banbury surrendered, and two days later Oxford itself was closely invested. On the 24th of June the city capitulated, and three days later Wallingford, the last place to give in, followed its example.

The war left the county in an exceedingly impoverished condition. Its prosperity had steadily declined since the early 14th century, when it had been second in prosperity in the kingdom, owing its wealth largely to its well-watered pastures, which bred sheep whose wool was famous all over England, and to its good supply of water power. Salt is mentioned as a product of the county in Domesday Book. Various small industries grew up, such as plush-making at Banbury, leather works at Bampton and Burford, gloves at Woodstock, and malt at Henley. Glass was made at Benson and Stokenchurch in the reign of Henry VI., and the wool trade continued, though not in so flourishing a state, Witney retaining its fame in blanket-making. The pestilence of 1349, the conversion of arable into pasture land, and the enclosure of common land in the early 16th century had led to agricultural depression and discontent. In 1830 the enclosure of Otmoor led to serious riots, in which the people gathered in Oxford at St Giles' fair joined. The county was represented in parliament in 1289 by two members.

Antiquities.—The remains of castles are scanty. The majority of them were probably built for defence in the civil strife of Stephen's reign (1100–1135), and were not maintained after order was restored. Considerable portions of the Norman Oxford Castle survive, however, while there are slighter remains of the castle at Bampton, the seat of Aylmer de Valence in 1313. Among remains of former mansions there may be noted the 14th century Greys Court near Henley-on-Thames, Minster Lovell, on the Windrush above Witney, and Rycote, between Thame and Oxford. Minster Lovell, the extensive ruins of which make an exquisite picture by the river-side, was the seat of Francis, Lord Lovel, who, being the son of a Lancastrian father, incurred the hatred of that party by serving Richard III., and afterwards assisted the cause of Lambert Simnel, mysteri-ously disappearing after the battle of Stoke. The remains of Rycote (partly incorporated with a farmhouse) are of fine Elizabethan brick, and in the chapel attached to the manor there is remarkable Jacobean woodwork; the entire fittings of the church, including the canopied pews and altar-table, being of this period. Here Elizabeth was kept in 1554, before her accession, and afterwards resided as queen. Of ancient mansions still inhabited, the finest is Broughton Castle near Banbury, dating from 1301. Others are Shirburn Castle, begun in 1377, but mainly Perpendicular of the next century; Stanton Har-court, dating from 1450, with a gatehouse of 1540, a vast kitchen, and Pope's Tower, named from the poet, who stayed here more than once. Mapledurham, on the Thames above Reading, is a fine Tudor mansion of brick; and Water Eaton, on the Cher-well above Oxford, is a singularly perfect Jacobean house of stone, with a chapel of the same period resembling pure Per-pendicular. Of other mansions in the county Blenheim Palace, near Woodstock, must be mentioned. The former Holton House (now replaced by a Georgian building), near Wheatley, was the scene in 1646 of the wedding of Ireton, the soldier of Cromwell, with his leader's daughter Bridget.

The influence of such a centre of learning as the university was naturally very great upon the ecclesiastical history of the neighbourhood. A large number of monastic foundations arose, such as those of Augustinian canons at Bicester, Cavers-ham, Cold Norton, Dorchester, Osney (a magnificent foundation just outside the walls of Oxford) and Wroxton; of Cistercians, at Bruern and Thame; of Benedictines, at Cogges, Eynsham, Milton; of Mathurins, at Nuffield; of Gilbertines, at Clattercote; of Templars, at Sandford-on-Thames. There was at Gosford one of the only two preceptories of female Templars in England. Of all these, excepting the abbey church at Dorchester, remains are scanty. A few domestic buildings remain at Studley; the boundary walls still stand of Godstow Nunnery on the Thames, the retreat and burial-place of Rosamund Clifford or "Fair Rosamund," the object of Henry II.'s famous courtship; and there are traces of Rewley Abbey within Oxford.

In ecclesiastical architecture Oxfordshire, apart from Oxford itself, is remarkably rich, but there is no dominant style, nearly all the churches being of mixed dates. In fact, of the most important churches only Iffley, Adderbury and Minster Lovell need be taken as types of a single style. Iffley, picturesquely placed above the Thames 1 m. S. of Oxford, is one of the finest examples of pure Norman in England, with a highly ornate west front. Adderbury, 4 m. S. of Banbury, is a great cruciform Decorated church with a massive central tower and spire. Minster Lovell, also cruciform, is pure Perpendicular; its central tower is supported, with beautiful and unusual effect, on four detached piers. For the rest, one feature common to several is to be noticed. The short ungainly spire of Oxford cathedral was among the earliest, if not the first, constructed in England, and served as a model from which were probably developed the splendid central spires of the great churches at Witney, Bampton, Shipton-under-Wychwood and Bradwell. There are also three fine spires in the north: Bloxham, Adderbury and King's Sutton (across the border in Northamptonshire), which are locally proverbial as typifying length, strength and beauty. Bloxham church, mainly Decorated, with Norman portions and a remarkable Early English west front, is one of the largest and most beautiful in the county. In the west Burford (Norman and later) is noteworthy, and in the porch of the fine Norman church of Langford is seen the rare feature of a crucifix with the figure cloaked. At South Leigh are remarkable mural paintings of the 15th century. About 5 m. N. of Oxford there are Kidlington (Decorated) with a beautiful needle-like Perpendicular spire, and Islip, which, as the birthplace of Edward the Confessor, retains a connexion with his Abbey of Westminster, the Dean and Chapter of which are lords of the manor and patrons of the living. In the south-east, Dorchester Abbey, with its nave of transitional Norman, has a curious Decorated Jesse window, the tracery representing the genealogical tree of the patriarch. At Cuddesdon there is another large cruciform church, Norman and later. Ewelme church (Perpendicular) is remarkable for the tomb of Alice, Duchess of Suffolk (1475), gorgeous with tracery and gilded canopy, and that of Sir Thomas Chaucer (1434), ornamented with enamelled coats of arms. Here William de la Pole, Duke of Suffolk, founded in 1436 the picturesque hospital and free school still standing.

Authorities.—*The Natural History of Oxfordshire* (Oxford, 1677, 2nd ed. 1705); Shelton, *Engraved Illustrations of the principal Antiquities of Oxfordshire, from drawings by T. Mackenzie* (Oxford, 1823); Sir T. Phillips, *Oxfordshire Pedigrees* (Evesham, 1825); J. M. Davenport, *Lords Lieutenant and High Sheriffs of Oxford, 1086* (Oxford, 1868), and *Oxfordshire Annals* (Oxford, 1869).

OXIDE, in chemistry, a binary compound of oxygen and other elements. In general, oxides are the most important compounds with which the chemist has to deal, a study of their composition and properties permitting a valuable comparative investigation of the elements. It is possible to bring about the direct combination of oxygen with most of the elements (the presence of traces of water vapour is generally necessary according to the researches of H. B. Baker), and when this is not so, indirect methods are available, except with bromine and fluorine (and also with the so-called inert gases—argon, helium, &c.), which so far have yielded no oxides. Most of the elements combine with oxygen in several proportions, for example nitrogen has five oxides: N_2O, NO, N_2O_3, NO_2, N_2O_4; for classificatory purposes, however, it is advantageous to assign a typical oxide to each element; which, in general, is the highest-having a basic or acid character. Thus in Group I. the typical oxide is M_2O, of Group II. MO, of Group III. M_2O_3, of Group IV. MO_2, of Group V. M_2O_5, of Group VI. MO_3.

Five species of oxides may be distinguished: (1) basic oxides, (2) acidic oxides, (3) neutral oxides, (4) peroxides, (5) mixed anhydrides and salts. Basic oxides combine with acids or acidic oxides to form salts; similarly acidic oxides combine with basic oxides to form salts also. The former are more usually yielded by the metals (some metals, however, form oxides belonging to the other groups), whilst the latter are usually associated with the non-metals. An oxide may be both acidic and basic, i.e. combine with bases as well as acids; this is the case with elements occurring at the transi-

tion between basigenic and oxygenic elements in the periodic classification, e.g. aluminium and zinc. Neutral oxides combine neither with acids nor bases to give salts nor with water to give a base or acid. A typical member is nitric oxide; carbon monoxide and nitrous oxide may also be put in this class, but it must be remembered that these oxides may be regarded, in some measure at least, as the anhydrides of formic and hyponitrous acid, although, at the same time, it is impossible to obtain these acids by simple hydration of those oxides. Peroxides may in most cases be defined as oxides containing more oxygen than the typical oxide. The failure of this definition is seen in the case of lead dioxide, which is certainly a peroxide in properties, but it is also the typical oxide of Group IV. to which lead belongs. All peroxides have oxidizing properties. Peroxides may be basic or acidic. Some basic oxides yield hydrogen peroxide with acids, others yield oxygen (these also liberate chlorine from hydrochloric acid), and may combine with lower acidic oxides to form salts of the normal basic oxide with the higher acidic oxide. Examples are $BaO_2+H_2SO_4=BaSO_4+H_2O_2$; $2MnO_2+2H_2SO_4=2MnSO_4+2H_2O+O_2$, $MnO_2+4HCl=MnCl_4+2H_2O+Cl_2$; $PbO_2+SO_2=PbSO_4$, i.e. $PbO+SO_3$. Two species of basic peroxides may be distinguished: (1) the superoxides or peroxides, containing the oxygen atoms in a chain, e.g. $Na \cdot O \cdot O \cdot Na$, $O \cdot Ba \cdot O$, which yield hydrogen peroxide with acids; and (2) the polyoxides, having the oxygen atoms doubly linked to the metallic atom, e.g. $O:Mn:O$, $O,O:Pb:O$, and giving oxygen with sulphuric acid, and chlorine with hydrochloric. L. Marino (*Zeit. anorg. Chem.*, 1907, 56, p. 233) pointed out that manganese and lead dioxide behaved differently with sulphur dioxide, the former giving dithionate and the latter sulphate, and suggested the following formulae: $O:Mn:O$, $O \cdot Pb:O$, as explaining this difference. A simpler explanation is that the manganese dioxide first gives a *normal* sulphite which rearranges to dithionate, thus: $MnO_2+2SO_2=Mn(SO_3)_2 \rightarrow MnS_2O_6$, whilst the lead dioxide gives a *basic* sulphite which rearranges to sulphate, thus: $PbO+SO_3=PbOSO_3 \rightarrow PbSO_4$. Acidic peroxides combine with basic oxides to form "per" salts, and by loss of oxygen yield the acidic oxide typical of the element. Mixed anhydrides are oxides, which yield with water two oxides, or are salts composed of a basic and acidic oxide of the same metal. Examples of mixed anhydrides are ClO_2 and NO_2, which give chlorous and chloric acid, and nitrous and nitric acid: $2ClO_2+H_2O=HClO_2+HClO_3$, $2NO_2+H_2O=HNO_2+HNO_3$; and of mixed salts Pb_3O_4 and Pb_2O_3, which may be regarded as lead meta- and ortho-plumbate: $PbO \cdot 2PbO_2$, $2PbO \cdot PbO_2$.

Oxidation and Reduction.—In the narrow sense "oxidation" may be regarded as the combination of a substance with oxygen, and conversely, "reduction" as the abstraction of oxygen; in the wider sense oxidation includes not merely the addition of oxygen, but also of other electro-negative elements or groups, or the removal of hydrogen or an electro-positive element or group. In inorganic chemistry oxidation is associated in many cases with an increase in the active valency. Ignoring processes of oxidation or reduction simply brought about by heat or some other form of energy, we may regard an oxidizing agent as a substance having a strong affinity for electro-positive atoms or groups, and a reducing agent as having a strong affinity for electro-negative atoms or groups; in the actual processes the oxidizing agent suffers reduction and the reducing agent oxidation.

Many substances undergo simultaneous oxidation and reduction when treated in a particular manner; this is known as self- or auto-oxidation. For example, on boiling an aqueous solution of a hypochlorite, a chlorate and a chloride results, part of the original salt being oxidized and part reduced: $3NaOCl=NaClO_3+2NaCl$. Similarly phosphorous and hypophosphorous acids give phosphoric acid and phosphine, whilst nitrous acid gives nitric acid and nitric oxide: $4H_3PO_3=3H_3PO_4+PH_3$; $2H_3PO_2=H_3PO_4+PH_3$; $3HNO_2=HNO_3+2NO+H_2O$. In organic chemistry, a celebrated example is Cannizzaro's reaction wherein an aromatic aldehyde gives an acid and an alcohol: $2C_6H_5CHO+H_2O=C_6H_5CO_2H+C_6H_5CH_2OH$.

The important oxidizing agents include: oxygen, ozone, peroxides, the halogens chlorine and bromine, oxyacids such as nitric acid, those of chlorine, bromine and iodine, and also chromic and permanganic acid. The important reducing agents include hydrogen, hydrides such as those of iodine, sulphur, phosphorus, &c., carbon, many metals, potassium, sodium, aluminium, magnesium, &c., salts of lower oxyacids, lower salts of metals and lower oxides.

OXIMES, in organic chemistry, compounds containing the grouping $>C:N \cdot OH$, derived from aldehydes and ketones by condensing them with hydroxylamine. Those derived from aldehydes are known as aldoximes, those from ketones as ketoximes. They were first prepared by V. Meyer in 1882 (*Ber.*, 1882, 15, pp. 1324, 1525, 2778). They are either colourless liquids, which boil without decomposition, or crystalline solids; and are both basic and acidic in character. On reduction by sodium amalgam in glacial acetic acid solution they yield primary amines. They are hydrolysed by dilute mineral acids yielding hydroxylamine and the parent aldehyde or ketone. The aldoximes are converted by the action of dehydrating agents into nitriles: $RCH:NOH \rightarrow RC \vdots N + H_2O$. The ketoximes by the action of acetyl chloride undergo a peculiar intramolecular re-arrangement known as the Beckmann transformation (E. Beckmann, *Ber.*, 1886, 19, p. 989; 1887, 20, p. 2580), yielding as final products an acid-amide or anilide, thus:

$$RC(:N \cdot OH)R' \rightarrow RC(OH):NR' \rightarrow RCONHR'.$$

As regards the constitution of the oximes, two possibilities exist, namely $>C:NOH$, or $>C\overset{NH}{\underset{O}{<}}$, and the first of these is presumably correct, since on alkylation and subsequent hydrolysis an alkyl hydroxylamine of the type $NH_2 \cdot OR$ is obtained, and consequently it is to be presumed that in the alkylated oxime, the alkyl group is attached to oxygen, and the oxime itself therefore contains the hydroxyl group. It is to be noted that the oximes of aromatic aldehydes and of unsymmetrical aromatic ketones frequently exist in isomeric forms. This isomerism is explained by the Hantzsch-Werner hypothesis (*Ber.*, 1890, 23, p. 11) in which the assumption is made that the three valencies of the nitrogen atom do not lie in the same plane. Thus in the case of the simple aldoximes two configurations are possible, namely:

$$\underset{N \cdot OH}{\overset{R \cdot C \cdot H}{\vert \vert}} \quad \text{and} \quad \underset{HO \cdot N}{\overset{R \cdot C \cdot H}{\vert \vert}}, \text{ the former,}$$

where the H atom and OH group are contiguous, being known as *syn*-aldoximes and the latter as the *anti*-aldoximes. The syn-aldoximes on treatment with acetyl chloride readily lose water and yield nitriles; the anti-aldoximes as a rule are acetylated and do not yield nitriles. The isomerism of the oximes of unsymmetrical ketones is explained in the same manner, and their configuration is determined by an application of the Beckmann transformation (see *Ber.*, 1891, 24, p. 13); thus:

$$\underset{N \cdot OH}{\overset{R \cdot C \cdot R'}{\vert \vert}} \rightarrow R \cdot C(OH):NR' \rightarrow R \cdot CONHR'(R' \text{ and } OH, \text{ "}syn\text{ "}).$$

$$\underset{HO \cdot N}{\overset{R \cdot C \cdot R'}{\vert \vert}} \rightarrow RN \vdots C(OH)R' \rightarrow RNH \cdot COR'(R \text{ and } OH, \text{ "}syn\text{ "}).$$

Aldoximes are generally obtained by the action of hydroxylamine hydrochloride on the aldehyde in presence of sodium carbonate; the oxime being then usually extracted from the solution by ether. They may also be prepared by the reduction of primary nitro compounds with stannous chloride and concentrated hydrochloric acid; by the reduction of unsaturated nitro compounds with aluminium amalgam or zinc dust in the presence of dilute acetic acid (L. Bouveault, *Comptes rendus*, 1902, 134, p. 1145): $R_2C:CHNO_2 \rightarrow R_2C:CH \cdot NHOH \rightarrow R_2CH \cdot CH:NOH$, and by the action of alkyl iodides on the sodium salt of nitro-hydroxylamine (A. Angeli, *Rend. Accad. d. Lincei*, 1905, (5), 14, ii. p. 411), the cycle of reactions probably being as follows:

$$NO_2 \cdot NHOH \rightarrow HNO_2 + HNO; HNO + RI \rightarrow HI + RNO$$
$$(CH_2CH_2NO \rightarrow CH_2CH:N \cdot OH).$$

Formaldoxime, $CH_2:NOH$, was obtained by W. R. Dunstan (*Jour. Chem. Soc.*, 1898, 73, p. 352) as a colourless liquid by the addition of hydroxylamine hydrochloride to an aqueous solution of formaldehyde in the presence of sodium carbonate; the resulting solution was extracted with ether and the oxime hydrochloride precipitated by gaseous hydrochloric acid, the precipitate being then dissolved in water, the solution exactly neutralized and distilled. It boils at 83-85° C. and burns with a green coloured flame. It is readily transformed into a solid polymer, probably $(CH_2:NOH)_3$. In the absence of water, it forms salts of the type $(CH_2:NOH)_n \cdot HCl$ with acids. It behaves as a powerful reducing agent, and on hydrolysis with dilute mineral acids is decomposed into formaldehyde and hydroxylamine, together with some formic acid and ammonia, the amount of each product formed varying with temperature, time of reaction, amount of water present, &c. This latter reaction is probably due to some of the oxime existing in the form of the isomeric formamide $HCO \cdot NH_2$. Acetyl- and benzoyl-formaldoxime are derivatives of the threefold polymeric form. The acetyl compound on reduction yields two of its nitrogen atoms in the form of ammonia and the third in the form of methylamine.

Acetaldoxime, $CH_3CH:NOH$, crystallizes in needles which melt at 47° C. On continued fusion the melting point gradually sinks to about 13° C., probably owing to conversion into a polymeric form.

Chloraloxime, $CCl_3CH:NOH$, is obtained when one molecular proportion of chloral hydrate is warmed with four molecular proportions of hydroxylamine hydrochloride and a little water. It crystallizes in prisms which melt at 39° C. A chloral hydroxylamine, $CCl_3 \cdot CHOH \cdot NHOH$, melting at 98° C. is obtained by allowing a mixture of one molecular proportion of chloral hydrate with two molecular proportions of hydroxylamine hydrochloride and one of sodium carbonate to stand for some time in a desiccator.

Glyoxime, $HON:CH \cdot CH:NOH$, obtained from glyoxal and hydroxylamine, or by boiling amidothiazole with excess of hydroxylamine hydrochloride and water, melts at 178° C. and is readily soluble in hot water.

Succinic aldehyde dioxime, $HON:CH \cdot CH_2 \cdot CH_2 \cdot CH:NOH$, is obtained by boiling an alcoholic solution of pyrrol with hydroxylamine hydrochloride and anhydrous sodium carbonate (G. Ciamician, *Ber.*, 1884, 17, p. 534). It melts at 173° C.; and on reduction with sodium in alcoholic solution yields tetramethylene diamine. A boiling solution of caustic potash hydrolyses it to ammonia and succinic acid.

Benzaldoximes.—The α-oxime (benz-*anti*-aldoxime) is formed by the action of hydroxylamine on benzaldehyde. It melts at 35° C. and boils at 117° C. (14 mm.). Acids convert it into the β-oxime (benz-*syn*-aldoxime) which melts at 125° C. When distilled under diminished pressure the β-form reverts to the α-modification (see Beckmann, *Ber.*, 1887, 20, p. 2766; 1889, 22, pp. 429, 513, 1531, 1588).

Ketoximes are usually rather more difficult to prepare than aldoximes, and generally require the presence of a fairly concentrated alkaline solution. They may also be prepared by the reduction of pseudo-nitrols (R. Scholl, *Ber.*, 1896, 29, p. 87), the reaction probably being:

$$RR:C(NO_2)NO \rightarrow RR:C:(NHOH)_2 \rightarrow RR:C:NOH + NH_2OH.$$

Acetoxime, $(CH_3)_2C:NOH$, melts at- 58-59° C. and is readily soluble in water. Its sodium salt is obtained by the action of sodamide on the oxime, in presence of benzene (A. W. Titherley, *Jour. Chem. Soc.*, 1897, 71, p. 461).

Mesityl oxime, $(CH_3)_2C:CH \cdot C(:NOH)CH_3$, exists in two modifications. The β-form is obtained by the direct action of hydroxylamine hydrochloride on mesityl oxide, the hydrochloride so formed being decomposed by sodium carbonate. It crystallizes in plates which melt at 48-49° C. and boil at 92° C. (9 mm.). When boiled for some time with caustic soda, it is converted into the oily α-oxime, which boils at 83-84° C. (9 mm.). Both forms are volatile in steam. The α-oxime, on long continued boiling with a concentrated solution of a caustic alkali, is partially decomposed with formation of some acetone and acetoxime (C. Harries, *Ber.*, 1898, 31, pp. 1381, 1808; 1899, 32, p. 1331). By the direct action of hydroxylamine on a methyl alcohol solution of mesityl oxide in the presence of sodium methylate a hydroxylamino-ketone, *diacetone hydroxylamine*, $(CH_3)_2C(NHOH) \cdot CH_2COCH_3$, is formed. In a similar manner phorone gives rise to *triacetone hydroxylamine*, $CO:[CH_2 \cdot C(CH_3)_2]_2:NOH$.

Acetophenonoxime, $C_6H_5 \cdot C(:NOH)CH_3$, melts at 59° C. In glacial acetic acid solution, on the addition of concentrated sulphuric acid, it is converted into acetanilide. *Benzophenone oxime*, $C_6H_5C(:NOH)C_6H_5$, exists only in one modification which melts at 140° C.; whereas the unsymmetrical benzophenones each yield two oximes. O. Wallach (*Ann.*, 1900, 312, p. 171) has shown that the saturated cyclic ketones yield oximes which by an application of the Beckmann reaction are converted into isoximes, and these latter on hydrolysis with dilute mineral acids are transformed into acyclic amino-acids; thus from cyclohexanone, ε-amidocaproic acid (ε-leucine) may be obtained:—

$$CH_2\overset{CH_2 \cdot CH_2}{\underset{CH_2 \cdot CH_2}{<}}C:NOH \rightarrow CH_2\overset{CH_2 \cdot CH_2 \cdot CO}{\underset{CH_2 \cdot CH_2 \cdot NH}{<}}$$
$$\rightarrow \overset{CH_2 \cdot CH_2 \cdot CO_2H}{\underset{CH_2 \cdot CH_2 \cdot NH_2}{<}}$$

An ingenious application of the fact that oximes easily lose the elements of water and form nitriles was used by A. Wohl (*Ber.*, 1893, 26, p. 730) in the " breaking down " of the sugars. Glucose-oxime on warming with acetic anhydride is simultaneously acetylated and dehydrated, yielding an acetylated gluconitrile, which when warmed with ammoniacal silver nitrate loses hydrocyanic acid and is transformed into an acetyl pentose. The pentose is then obtained from the acetylated compound by successive treatment with ammonia and dilute acids:—

$$CH_2OH \cdot (CHOH)_4 \cdot CHOH \cdot CH:NOH \rightarrow CH_2OH \cdot (CHOH)_3 \cdot$$
$$CHOH \cdot CN \rightarrow CH_2OH(CHOH)_3CHO.$$

In order to arrive at the configuration of the stereoisomeric ketoximes, A. Hantzsch (*Ber.*, 1891, 24, p. 13) has made use of the Beckmann reaction, whereby they are converted into acid-amides. Thus, with the tolylphenylketoximes, one yields the anilide of toluic acid and the other the toluidide of benzoic acid, the former necessitating the presence of the phenyl and hydroxyl radicals in the *syn* position and the latter the tolyl and hydroxyl radicals in the *syn* position, thus:

$$\underset{N \cdot OH}{\overset{CH_3 \cdot C_6H_4 \cdot C \cdot C_6H_5}{\vert \vert}} \rightarrow CH_3C_6H_4 \cdot CONHC_6H_5;$$

Syn-phenyltolylketoxime

$$\underset{HO \cdot N}{\overset{CH_3 \cdot C_6H_4 \cdot C \cdot C_6H_5}{\vert \vert}} \rightarrow CH_3C_6H_4 \cdot NHCOC_6H_5.$$

Anti-tolylphenylketoxime

In the case of the aldoximes, that one which most readily loses the elements of water on dehydration is assumed to contain its hydroxyl radical adjacent to the movable hydrogen atom and is designated the *syn*-compound.

On the oxyamido-oximes see H. Ley, *Ber.*, 1898, 31, p. 2126; G. Schroeter, *Ber.*, 1900, 33, p. 1975.

OXUS, or AMU DARYA, one of the great rivers of Central Asia. Prior to the meeting of the commissions appointed for the determination of the Russo-Afghan boundary in 1885, no very accurate geographical knowledge of the upper Oxus regions existed, and the course of the river itself was but roughly mapped. Russian explorers and natives of India trained for geographical reconnaissance, and employed in connexion with the great trigonometrical· survey of India, had done so much towards clearing away the mists which enveloped the actual course of the river, that all the primary affluents were known, although their relative value was misunderstood, but the nature of the districts which bordered the river in Afghan Turkestan was so imperfectly mapped as to give rise to considerable political complication in framing the boundary agreement between Great Britain and Russia. From Lake Victoria (Sor-Kul) in the Pamirs, which was originally reckoned as the true source of the river, to Khamiab, on the edge of the Andkhui district of Afghan Turkestan, for a distance of about 680 m., the Oxus forms the boundary between Afghanistan and Russia. For another 550 m. below Khamiab it follows an open and sluggish course till it is lost in the Sea of Aral, being spanned at Charjui, 150 m. below Khamiab, by the wooden bridge which carries the Russian railway from Merv to Samarkand. The level of Lake Victoria is 13,400 ft. above sea. At Khamiab the river is probably rather less than 500 ft.

For many years a lively geographical controversy circled about the sources of the Oxus, and the discussion derived some political significance from the fact that the true source, wherever *Sources.* it might be found, was claimed as a point in the Russo-Afghan boundary. The final survey of the Pamir region (wherein the heads of all the chief tributaries of the river lay hidden), by the Pamir boundary commission of 1895 established the following topographical facts in connexion with this question. The elevated mountain chain which is now called the Nicolas range, which divides the Great from the Little Pamir, is a region of vast glaciers and snow-fields, from which the lakes lying immediately north and south derive the greater part of their water-supply. On the north the principal glacial tributary of Lake Victoria forms, within the folds of the gigantic spurs of the Nicolas mountains, a series of smaller lakes, or lakelets, before joining the great lake itself. On the south a similar stream starting farther east, called Burgutai (denoting the position of a difficult and dangerous pass across the range) sweeps downwards towards Lake Chakmaktin, the lake of the Little Pamir, which is some 400 ft. lower than Victoria. But at the foot of the mountain this stream bifurcates in the swamps which lie to the west of Chakmaktin, and part of its waters find their way eastwards into the lake, and part flow away westwards into the Ab-i-Panja, which joins the Pamir river from Lake Victoria at Kala Panja. This at any rate is the action of the Burgutai stream during certain seasons of the year, so that the glaciers and snowfields of the Nicolas range may be regarded as the chief fountain-head of at least two of the upper tributaries of the Oxus, namely, the Aksu (or Murghab) and the Pamir river, and as contributing largely to a third, the Ab-i-Panja. Neither Lake Victoria nor Lake Chakmaktin derives any very large contributions from glacial sources other than those of the Nicolas range. It is possible that there may be warm springs on the bed of Lake Victoria, as such springs are of frequent occurrence in the Pamirs; but there is no indication of them in the Chakmaktin basin, and the latter lake must be regarded rather as an incident in the course of the Aksu—a widening of the river channel in the midst of this high-level, glacier-formed valley—than as·the fountain-head of the infant stream. There are indications that the bed of Lake Victoria, as well as that of Chakmaktin, is rapidly silting, and that the shores of the latter are gradually receding farther from the foot of the hills. The glacial origin of the Pamir valleys is everywhere apparent in their terrace formations and the erratic blocks and boulders that lie scattered about their surface. It is probable that the lakes themselves are evidence of (geologically) a comparatively recent deliverance from the thraldom of the ice covering, which has worn and rounded the lower ridges into the smooth outlines of undulating·downs.

Another important source of the river (considered by Curzon to be the chief source) is to be found in the enormous glaciers which lie about the upper or main branch of the Ab-i-Panja (called the Ab-i-Wakhjir or Wakhan), which rises under the mountains enclosing the head of the Taghdumbash Pamirs. Although the superficial area of glacial ice from which the Ab-i-Wakhjir derives the greater part of its volume is not equal to that found on the Nicolas range, it is quite impossible to frame any estimate of comparative depth or bulk, or to separate the volume of its contributions at any time from those which, combined, derive their origin from·the Nicolas range. If the Aksu (or Murghab) and the Pamir river from Lake Victoria are to be considered in the light of independent tributaries, it is probable that the Ab-i-Panja contributes as large a volume of glacial flood to the Oxus as either of them.

From the point where the rivers of the Great and Little Pamirs join their forces at Kala Panja to Ishkashim, at the elbow of the great bend of the Oxus northwards, the river valley has *Surveys.* been surveyed by Woodthorpe; and the northern slopes of the Hindu Kush, which near Ishkashim extend in slopes of barely 10 m. in length from the main watershed to the river banks, have been carefully mapped. These slopes represent the extent of Afghan territory which exists north of the Hindu Kush between Kala Panja and Ishkashim. From Ishkashim northwards the river passes through the narrow rock-bound valleys of Shignan and Roshan ere it sweeps north and west through the mountains and defiles of Darwaz. By the terms of the boundary agreement with Russia this part of the river now parts Badakshan and Darwaz from the districts of Roshan, Shignan, and Bokhara, which formerly maintained an uncertain claim over a part of the territory on the left bank of the river. All this part of the Oxus, until the river once again emerges from the Bokhara hills into the open plains bordering Badakshan on the north, falls within the area of Russian surveys, with which a junction from India has been effected both on the Pamirs and in Turkestan.

At Langar Kisht, a little to the east of the Oxus bend, there is a small Russian post of observation. About 50 m. north of the bend, where the Suchan or Ghund joins the Oxus from the *Russian Posts on the Oxus.* Alichur Pamir, there is another and larger post called Charog. On the left bank of the river the Afghans maintain a frontier post at the fort of Kala Bar Panja. ·A road will connect Charog with the Alichur Pamir, following the general course of the Ghund stream, a road which will form a valuable link in the chain of communications between Bokhara and Sarikol. Eighty-five miles north of Ishkashim, at Kala Wamar, the river which rises in the Little Pamir, and which is called Aksu, Murghab, or Bartang, joins the Oxus from the east. It is on this river that the Russian outpost, Murghabi (or Pamirski), is situated, at an elevation of 12,150 ft. above the sea. Fort Murghabi is connected by a good military road with Osh. At this point the measurement of the comparative lengths of the chief Pamir tributaries of the Oxus is as follows:—

To the head of the Aksu at Lake Chakmaktin .	260 miles.
To the head of the most easterly tributary of Lake Victoria, in the Great Pamir, about .	230 "
To the glacial sources of the Ab-i-Wakhjir, about .	230 "

For 120 m. the two latter are united in the main stream of the Oxus, the volume of which has been further increased by the united forces of the Ghund and Shakhdara draining the Alichur Pamir and the heights of Shignan.

The narrow cramped valley of the river between Ishkashim and Kala Wamar is hedged in on the west by a long ridge flanking the highlands of Badakshan; on the east the buttresses and *Nature of the Oxus Valley.* spurs of the Shignan mountains (of which the strike is transverse to the direction of the river and more or less parallel to that of the main Hindu Kush watershed) overhang its channel like a wall, and afford but little room either for cultivation or for the maintenance of a practicable road. Yet the lower elevation (for this part of the Oxus stream is not more than about 7000 ft. above sea-level) and comparatively mild climate give opportunities to the industrious Tajik population for successful agriculture, of which they are not slow to avail themselves, and a track exists on the left bank of the river to Kala Bar Panja opposite the Ghund (or Suchan) debouchment, which is practicable for mules. There are no bridges, and the transit of the river from bank to bank can only be effected by the use of inflated skins. Beyond the Bartang (or Murghab) confluence the valley narrows, and the difficulties of the river route increase. Between Kala Wamar (6580 ft.) and Kala Khum (4400 ft.), where the Oxus again bends southwards, its course to the north-west is almost at right angles to the general strike of the Darwaz mountains, which is from north-east to south-west, following the usual conformation of all this part of high Asia. Thus its Ishkari affluents from the north-east, the Wanj and the Yaz Ghulam, drain valleys which are comparatively open, and which are said to be splendidly fertile. At

Kala Khum the river is 480 ft. wide, narrowing to 350 ft. in the narrowest gorge. Its level varies with the obstructions formed by ice, falling as much as 28 ft. when its upper channels are blocked.

The climate of eastern Bokhara and Darwaz is delightful in summer, and Dr Regel writes of its Alpine scenery and flora in terms of enthusiastic admiration. In the valleys of the Waksh **Climate and Productions.** and the Surkhab to the north of Darwaz, which form an important part of the province of Karategin, maple, ash, hawthorn, pistachio, and juniper grow freely in the mountain forests, and beetroot, kohl rabi, and other vegetables are widely cultivated. About the cliffs and precipices of the Panja valley near Kala Khum the wild vine, cerasus, and pomegranate are to be found, and the plane tree and mulberry flourish in groups near the villages. Here also, amongst other plants, the sunflower decorates village gardens. The houses are built of stone and mortar, and above the thatched straw-roof which surmounts the double-storeyed buildings the square water-tower rises gracefully. Every house possesses its staircase, its well, and cisterns for irrigation; and on the whole the Aryan Tajiks of this northern section of the Oxus valley seem to be well provided with most of the comforts, if not the luxuries, of life. Their language is the language of Bokhara and Samarkand. Bokharan supremacy was re-established in 1878, when Kala Khum was occupied by Bokharan troops. Since then the right bank of the river has been politically divided from the left, and the latter now belongs to Afghanistan.

From Kala Khum, which fort about marks the most northerly point of the great bend of the Oxus round Badakshan, the river follows a south-westerly course for another 50 m. through a close mountainous region ere it widens into the more open valley to the south of Kolab. It now becomes a river of the plains from which the mountains on either side stand back.

The topography of Darwaz south of the river is not accurately known, but at least one considerable stream of some 60 m. in length drains to the north-east, parallel to the general strike of **Darwaz Affluents.** the mountain system into the transverse course of the Oxus, which it joins nearly opposite to the lateral valleys of Yaz Ghulam and Wanj. This stream is called Pangi-Shiwa, or Shiwa, but not much is known about it. Another of about equal length, starting from the same central water-parting of this mountain block, and included within the Oxus bend, follows a transverse direction at almost right angles to the Shiwa, and joins the Oxus valley near its debouchment into the more open Kolab plains, where the course of the Oxus has again assumed a direction parallel to the mountain strike. All that we know about this river (which is called the Ragh or Sadda) is that towards its junction with the Oxus it cuts through successive mountain ridges, which renders its course impracticable as a roadway. It is necessary to avoid the river, and to pass by mountain tracks which surmount a series of local spurs or offshoots from the central plateau, in order to reach the Oxus. The existence of this route, which traverses the Darwaz mountains from east to west, cutting off the northern bend of the Oxus, and connecting those easterly routes which intersect the Pamirs by means of the Ghund and Shakhdara (and which concentrate about Lake Shiwa) with Kolab in eastern Bokhara, is important. (See BADAKSHAN.)

From about the point where the Oxus commences to separate the Bokharan province of Kolab from the comparatively open Afghan districts of Rustak and Kataghan, the channel of the **Karategin Affluents.** river is no longer confined within walls of mountains of volcanic and schistose formation. The Kolab and the Surkhab (or Waksh) flow into it in broad muddy streams from the highlands of Karateghin, and the river at once commences to adopt an uncertain channel wherever the out-stretched arms of the hills fall to confine it within definite limits. It divides its waters, splitting into many channels, leaving broad central islands; and as the width increases, and the depth during dry seasons diminishes, opportunities for fords become comparatively frequent. Between Kolab and Pata Kesar, immediately north of the Turkestan capital of Mazar-i-Sharif, there are at least three well-known " guzars " or fords, and there are probably more. Besides the great muddy affluents from Karateghin on the north, the Kabadian, the Surkhan, and the Darbant are all of them very considerable tributaries from Bokhara. The last of the three is the river on which the well-known trade centre of Shirabad is built, some 20 m. north of the river. Near the junction of the Surkhan with the Oxus are the ruins of the ancient city of Termez, on the northern or Bokharan bank, and the ferry at Pata Kesar (not far from the ruins of an old bridge) is the connecting link between Bokhara and Mazar hereabouts. A Russian branch railway is said to have been recently built from Samarkand to Termez.

From the south two very remarkable affluents of the Oxus join their streams to the main river between Kolab and the Mazar crossings. The Kokcha and the Khanabad (or Kunduz) **Badakshan Affluents.** are the two great rivers of Badakshan. The valley of the Kokcha leads directly from the Oxus to Faizabad, the capital of Badakshan, and its head is close above Ishkashim at the southern elbow of the great Oxus bend, a low pass of only 9500 ft. dividing its waters from those of the main river. This undoubtedly was a section of the great central trade route of Asia, which once connected Ferghana and Herat with Kashgar and China. (See BADAKSHAN.) Both these rivers tap the northern slopes of the Hindu Kush, and claim their sources in the unmapped mountain wilderness of Kafiristan. The Khanabad, or Kunduz, is also called locally the Aksarai. All the rivers of Central Asia are known by several names. To the west of the Kunduz no rivers find their way through the southern banks of the Oxus. Throughout the plains of Afghan Turkestan the drainage from the southern hills is arrested and lost in the desert sands.

The only island of any size in the bed of the river is the island of Paighambar, a little below the ruins of Termez. The inhabitants of this island, and of a smaller one in the neighbourhood called Zarshol, wash for gold in the bed of the river.

At Airatan, a little above the Pata Kesar ferry, there are ruins, as also at Khisht Tapa (where the road from Kabadian to Tashkurghan leaves the river) and at Kalukh Tapa. At Khisht Tapa there is a tradition of a bridge having once existed.

The Oxus river, as seen in flood at this part of its course, is an imposing stream. It is rarely less than 1000 yards wide, and in some places it is fully a mile across. Its winter channel **Channel of the Oxus.** may be estimated at from two-thirds to three-fourths of its flood channel, except where it is confined within narrow limits by a rocky bed, as at Kilif, where its unvarying width is only 540 yards. The average strength of the current in flood is about 4 m. per hour, varying from 2½ to 5 m. The left bank of the Oxus above Kilif is, as a rule, low and flat, with reed swamps bordering the stream and a strip of jungle between the reeds and the edge of the elevated sandy desert. The jungle is chiefly tamarisk and radak (willow). Swamp deer, pheasants and occasionally tigers are found in it. The right bank is generally higher, drier, more fertile and more populated than the left.

A wide belt of blown sand (or Chul), sprinkled with saxaul jungle, separates the swamps on the south side of the river from the cultivated plains of Afghan Turkestan; but in places, notably for **Cultivation.** about 12 m. above Khamiab, where the Russo-Afghan boundary touches the river, through the districts which are best known by the name of Khwaja Salar, and again in a less degree for 50 m. above the ferry at Kilif, a very successful war has been waged by the agricultural Turkman (of the Ersari tribes) against the encroaching sand-waves of the desert; and a strip of riverain soil averaging about a mile in width has been reclaimed and cultivated by irrigation. The cultivation, supported by canals drawn from the Oxus, the heads of which are constantly being destroyed by flood and again renewed, is of a very high order. Wheat and barley spread in broad crops over many square miles of rich soil; the fields are intersected by narrow little water-walled lanes, bright with wayside flowers, amongst which the poppy and the purple thistle of Badghis are predominant; the houses are neatly built of stone, and stand scattered about the landscape in single homesteads, substantial and comfortable; and the spreading willow and the mulberry offer a most grateful shade to the wayfarer in summer time, when the heat is often insupportable. The fiery blasts of summer, furnace-heated over the red-hot Kizil Kum, are hardly less to be feared than the ice-cold shamshir (or north-western blizzard) of winter, which freezes men when it finds them in the open desert, and frequently destroys whole caravans.

The principle on which the Oxus ferries are worked is peculiar to those regions. Large flat-bottomed boats are towed across the river by small horses attached to an outrigger projecting **Oxus Ferries.** beyond the gunwale by means of a surcingle or bellyband. They are thus partially supported in the water whilst they swim. The horses are guided from the boat, and a twenty- or thirty-foot barge with a heavy load of men and goods will be towed across the river at Kilif (where, as already stated, the width of the river is between 500 and 600 yards only) with ease by two of these animals. The Kilif ferry is on the direct high-road between Samarkand and Akcha. It is perhaps the best-used ferry on the Oxus.

Khwaja Salar derives some historical significance from the fact that it presented a substantial difficulty to the settlement of the Russo-Afghan boundary, in which it was assigned by agreement **Khwaja Salar.** as the point of junction between that boundary and the Oxus. It had been defined in the agreement as a " post " on the river banks, and had been so described by Burnes in his writings some fifty years previously. But no post such as that indicated could be discovered. There was a district of that name extending from Khamiab to the neighbourhood of Kilif, and at the Kilif end of the district was a ziarat sacred to the Khwaja who bore the name. It was only after long inquiry amongst local cultivators and landowners that, about 2 m. below the ziarat, and nearly opposite to the site of the present Karkin bazaar, the position of a lost ferry was identified, which had once been marked by a riverside hamlet called by the name of the saint. The ferry had long disappeared, and with it a considerable slice of the riverside alluvial soil, which had been washed into the stream by the action of floods. The post had, in fact, subsided to the bottom of the river, but the consequences of its disappearance had both far-reaching and expensive.

Below Khamiab, to its final disappearance in the Aral Sea, the great river rolls in silent majesty through a vast expanse of sand and desert. Under Russian auspices a considerable strip of alluvial soil on the left bank has been brought under cultivation, measuring 4 or 5 m. in width, and there is more cultivation on the banks of the Oxus now than there is in the Merv oasis itself, but it is confined to the immediate neighbourhood of the river, for no affluents of any considerable size exist. The river is navigable below Charjui, and takes its place as an important unit in the general scheme of Russian frontier communications. There is now a regular steamer service, twice a week in summer and once a week in winter, as far as Pata Kasar. The steamers are flat-bottomed paddle boats drawing 3 ft.

Lower Oxus.

An important feature in connexion with the course of the Oxus is the discussion that has arisen with regard to its former debouchment into the Caspian Sea. On this point much recent evidence has been collected, and it appears certain that there was a time in the post-Pliocene Age when a long gulf of the Caspian Sea protruded eastwards nearly as far as the longitude of Merv, covering the Kara Kum sands, but not the Kara Kum plateau to the north of the sands, which is separated from the sands by a distinct sea beach. At the same time another branch of the same gulf protruded northwards in the direction of the Aral, probably as far as the Sary Kamish depression, which lies to the west of the Khivan delta of the Oxus, separated from it by wide beds of loess, clays and gravel, covering rocks of an unknown age. The Murghab river and the Hari Rud, which terminate in the oases of Merv and Sarakhs, almost certainly penetrated to the gulf of the Kara Kum, but the question whether the Oxus was ever deflected so as to enter the gulf with the Murghab cannot be said to be answered decisively at present. The former connexion between the Caspian and Aral by means of the gulf now represented by the Sary Kamish depression seems to be admitted by Russian scientists, nor would there appear to be much doubt about the connexion between the Khivan oasis and the northern extremity of the Sary Kamish. In this discussion the names of Kaulbars, Lessar, Annenkov, Konshin and other Russian geographers are conspicuous. The general conclusions are ably summed up by P. Kropotkin in the September number of the *Journal* of the Royal Geographical Society for 1898.

Junction with the Aral Sea.

History.—In the most remote ages to which written history carries us, the regions on both sides of the Oxus were subject to the Persian monarchy. Of their populations Herodotus mentions the Bactrians, Chorasmians, Sogdians and Sacae as contributing their contingents to the armies of the great king Darius. The Oxus figures in Persian romantic history as the limit between Iran and Turan, but the substratum of settled population to the north as well as the south was probably of Iranian lineage. The valley is connected with many early Magian traditions, according to which Zoroaster dwelt at Balkh, where, in the 7th century B.C., his proselytizing efforts first came into operation. Buddhism eventually spread widely over the Oxus countries, and almost entirely displaced the religion of Zoroaster in its very cradle. The Chinese traveller Hsuen Tsang, who passed through the country in A.D. 630-644, found Termez, Khulm, Balkh, and above all Bamian, amply provided with monasteries, stupas and colossal images, which are the striking characteristics of prevalent Buddhism; even the Pamir highlands had their monasteries.

Christianity penetrated to Khorasan and Bactria at an early date; episcopal sees are said to have existed at Merv and Samarkand in the 4th and 5th centuries, and Cosmas (c. 545) testifies to the spread of Christianity among the Bactrians and Huns.

Bactria was long a province of the empire which Alexander the Great left to his successors, but the Greek historians give very little information of the Oxus basin and its inhabitants. About 250 B.C. Diodotus, the "governor of the thousand cities of Bactria," declared himself king, simultaneously with the revolt of Arsaces which laid the foundation of the Parthian monarchy. The Graeco-Bactrian dominion was overwhelmed entirely about 126 B.C. by the Yue-chi (q.v.), a numerous people who had been driven westwards from their settlements on the borders of China by the Hiungnu (q.v.). From the Yue-chi arose, about the Christian era, the great Indo-Scythian dominion which extended across the Hindu Kush southwards, over Afghanistan and Sind. The history of the next five centuries is a blank. In 571 the Haiathalah (Ephthalites, q.v.) of the Oxus, who are supposed to be descendants of the Yue-chi, were shattered by an invasion of the Turkish khakan; and in the following century the Chinese pilgrim Hsuen Tsang found the former empire of the Haiathalah

broken up into a great number of small states, all acknowledging the supremacy of the Turkish khakan, and several having names identical with those which still exist. The whole group of states he calls Tukhara, by which name in the form Tokharistan, or by that of Haiathalah, the country continued for centuries to be known to the Mahommedans. At the time of his pilgrimage Chinese influence had passed into Tokharistan and Transoxiana. Yazdeged, the last of the Sassanid kings of Persia, who died in 651, when defeated and hard pressed by the Moslems, invoked the aid of China; the Chinese emperor, Taitsung, issued an edict organizing the whole country from Ferghana to the borders of Persia into three Chinese administrative districts, with 126 military cantonments, an organization which, however, probably only existed on paper.

In 711-712 Mahommedan troops were conducted by Kotaiba, the governor of Khorasan, into the province of Khwarizm (Khiva), after subjugating which they advanced on Bokhara and Samarkand, the ancient Sogdians, and are said to have even reached Ferghana and Kashgar, but no occupation then ensued. In 1016-1025 the government of Khwarizm was bestowed by Sultan Mahmud of Ghazni upon Altuntash, one of his most distinguished generals.

Tokharistan in general formed a part successively of the empires of the Sassanid dynasty (terminated A.D. 999), of the Ghaznevid dynasty, of the Seljuk princes of Persia and of Khorasan, of the Ghori or Shansabanya kings, and of the sultans of Khwarizm. The last dynasty ended with Sultan Jalal-ud-din, during whose reign (1221-1231) a division of the Mogul army of Jenghiz Khan first invaded Khwarizm, while the khan himself was besieging Bamian; Jalal-ud-din, deserted by most of his troops, retired to Ghazni, where he was pursued by Jenghiz Khan, and again retreating towards Hindustan was overtaken and driven across the Indus.

The commencement of the 16th century was marked by the rise of the Uzbeg rule in Turkestan. The Uzbegs were no one race, but an aggregation of fragments from Turks, Mongols and all the great tribes constituting the hosts of Jenghiz and Batu. They held Kunduz, Balkh, Khwarizm and Khorasan, and for a time Badakshan also; but Badakshan was soon won by the emperor Baber, and in 1529 was bestowed on his cousin Suleiman, who by 1555 had established his rule over much of the region between the Oxus and the Hindu Kush. The Mogul emperors of India occasionally interfered in these provinces, notably Shah Jahan in 1646; but, finding the difficulty of maintaining so distant a frontier, they abandoned it to the Uzbeg princes. About 1765 the wazir of Ahmad Shah Abdali of Kabul invaded Badakshan, and from that time until now the domination of the countries on the south bank of the Oxus from Wakhan to Balkh has been a matter of frequent struggles between Afghans and Uzbegs.

The Uzbeg rule in Turkestan has during the last fifty years been rapidly dwindling before the growth of Russian power. In 1863 Russia invaded the Khokand territory, taking in rapid succession the cities of Turkestan, Chimkent and Tashkend. In 1866 Khojend was taken, the power of Khokand was completely crushed, a portion was incorporated in the new Russian province of Turkestan, while the remainder was left to be administered by a native chief almost as a Russian feudatory; the same year the Bokharians were defeated at Irdjar. In 1867 an army assembled by the amir of Bokhara was attacked and dispersed by the Russians, who in 1868 entered Samarkand, and became virtually rulers of Bokhara. In 1873 Khiva was invaded, and as much of the khanate as lay on the right bank of the Oxus was incorporated into the Russian empire, a portion being afterwards made over to Bokhara. Russia acquired the right of the free navigation of the Oxus throughout its entire course, on the borders of both Khiva and Bokhara. The administration of the whole of the states on the right bank of the Oxus, down to the Russian boundary line at Ichka Yar, is now in the hands of Bokhara, including Karateghin—which the Russians have transferred to it from Khokand—and Darwaz at the entrance to the Pamir highlands.

AUTHORITIES.—Although much has been written of late years about the sources of the Oxus within the region of the Pamirs, there is very little to be found in the writings of geographers of modern date descriptive of that part of its course which separates Darwaz and Afghan Turkestan from Bokhara, and that little is chiefly in the pages of reports and gazettes, &c., which are not available to the public. The following authorities may be consulted: The *Report* of the Pamir Boundary Commission of 1895, published at Calcutta (1897); Dr A. Regel, "Journey in Karateghin and Darwaz," *Iswestia*, Russian Geog. Soc., vol. xiii. (1882); translation, vol. iv. *Proc. R.G.S.*; Michell, "Regions of the Upper Oxus," vol. vi. *Proc. R.G.S.* (1884); Griesbach, "Geological Field Notes," No. 3, Afghan Boundary Commission (1885); C. Yate, *Northern Afghanistan* (London, 1888); Curzon, "The Pamirs," vol. viii. *Jour. R.G.S.* (1896); Kropotkin, "Old Beds of the Oxus," *Jour. R.G.S.* (September 1898); Cobbold, *Innermost Asia* (London, 1900). To the above may be added the Reports of the Russo-Afghan Boundary Commission of 1884-1885, and that of Lockhart's Mission in 1885, and the Indian Survey Reports. (T. H. H.*)

OXYGEN (symbol O, atomic weight 16), a non-metallic chemical element. It was apparently first obtained in 1727 by Stephen Hales by strongly heating minium, but he does not seem to have recognized that he had obtained a new element, and the first published description of its properties was due to J. Priestley in 1774, who obtained the gas by igniting mercuric oxide, and gave it the name "dephlogisticated air." K. W. Scheele, working independently, also announced in 1775 the discovery of this element which he called "empyreal air" (*Crells' Annalen*, 1785, 2, pp. 229, 291). A. L. Lavoisier repeated Priestley's experiments and named the gas "oxygen" (from Gr. ὀξύς, sour, γεννάω, I produce) to denote that in a large number of cases, the products formed by the combustion of substances in the gas were of an acid character. Oxygen occurs naturally as one of the chief constituents of the atmosphere, and in combination with other elements it is found in very large quantities; it constitutes approximately eight-ninths by weight of water and nearly one-half by weight of the rocks composing the earth's crust. It is also disengaged by growing vegetation, plants possessing the power of absorbing carbon dioxide, assimilating the carbon and rejecting the oxygen. Oxygen may be prepared by heating mercuric oxide; by strongly heating manganese dioxide and many other peroxides; by heating the oxides of precious metals; and by heating many oxy-acids and oxy-salts to high temperatures, for example, nitric acid, sulphuric acid, nitre, lead nitrate, zinc sulphate, potassium chlorate, &c. Potassium chlorate is generally used and the reaction is accelerated and carried out at a lower temperature by previously mixing the salt with about one-third of its weight of manganese dioxide, which acts as a catalytic agent. The actual decomposition of the chlorate is not settled definitely; the following equations give the results obtained by P. F. Frankland and Dingwall (*Chem. News*, 1887, 55, p. 67):—at a moderate heat: $8KClO_3 = 5KClO_4 + 3KCl + 2O_2$, succeeded by the following reactions as the temperature increases: $2KClO_3 = KClO_4 + KCl + O_2$ and $2KClO_3 = 2KCl + 3O_2$ (see also F. Teed, ibid., 1887, 55, p. 91; H. N. Warren, ibid., 1888, 58, p. 247; W. H. Sodeau, *Proc. Chem. Soc.*, 1901, 17, p. 149). It may also be obtained by heating manganese dioxide or potassium bichromate or potassium permanganate with sulphuric acid; by the action of cobalt salts or manganese dioxide on a solution of bleaching powder (Th. Fleitmann, *Ann.*, 1865, 134, p. 64); by the action of a ferrous or manganous salt with a salt of cobalt, nickel or copper on bleaching powder (G. F. Jaubert, Ger. pat. 157171); by passing chlorine into milk of lime (C. Winkler, *Jour. prakt. Chem.*, 1866, 98, p. 340); by the action of chlorine on steam at a bright red heat; by the decomposition of hydrogen peroxide by bleaching powder, manganese dioxide, potassium ferricyanide in alkaline solution, or potassium permanganate in acid solution; by beating barium peroxide with an aqueous solution of potassium ferricyanide (G. Kassner, *Zeit. angew. Chem.*, 1890, p. 448) $BaO_2 + 2K_3Fe(CN)_6 = Ba[FeK_3(CN)_6] + O_2$; by the decomposition of sodium and potassium peroxides with a solution of potassium permanganate in the presence of a trace of nickel salts (G. F. Jaubert, *Comptes rendus*, 1902, 134, p. 778).

Numerous methods have been devised for the manufacture of oxygen. The more important are as follows: by decomposing strongly heated sulphuric acid in the presence of a contact substance; by heating an intimate mixture of one part of sodium nitrate with two parts of zinc oxide (T. H. Pepper, *Dingler's Jour.*, 1863, 167, p. 39): $2ZnO + 4NaNO_3 = 2Zn(ONa)_2 + 2N_2 + 5O_2$; by the use of cuprous chloride which when mixed with clay and sand, moistened with water and heated in a current of air at 100-200° C. yields an oxychloride, which latter yields oxygen when heated to 400° C (A. Mallet, *Comptes rendus*, 1867, 64, p. 226; 1868, 66, p. 349); by the electrolysis of solutions of sodium hydroxide, using nickel electrodes; by heating calcium plumbate (obtained from litharge and calcium carbonate) in a current of carbon dioxide (G. Kassner, *Monit. Scient.*, 1890, pp. 503, 614); and from air by the process of Tessié du Motay (*Ding. Jour.*, 1870, 196, p. 230), in which air is drawn over a heated mixture of manganese dioxide and sodium hydroxide, the sodium manganate so formed being then heated to about 450° C. in a current of steam, the following reversible reaction takes place: $4NaOH + 2MnO_2 + O_2 \rightleftharpoons 2Na_2MnO_4 + 2H_2O$. Oxygen is largely prepared by Brin's process (*Mém. soc. des Ingén. civ.*, 1881, p. 450) in which barium monoxide is heated in a current of air, forming the dioxide, which when the retorts are exhausted yields up oxygen and leaves a residue of monoxide; but this method is now being superseded, its place being taken by the fractional distillation of liquid air (*The Times, Engin. Suppl.*, April 14, 1909, p. 13) as carried out by the Linde method (Eng. Pat. 14111; 1902).

Oxygen is a colourless, odourless and tasteless gas. It is somewhat heavier than air, its specific gravity being 1·10523 (A. Leduc, *Comptes rendus*, 1896, 123, p. 805). It is slightly soluble in water and more so in alcohol. It also dissolves quite readily in some molten metals, especially silver. Oxygen does not burn, but is the greatest supporter of combustion known, nearly all the other elements combining with it under suitable conditions (cf. OXIDE). These reactions, however, do not take place if the substances are *absolutely* dry. Thus H. B. Baker (*Proc. Chem. Soc.*, 1902, 18, p. 40) has shown that perfectly dry oxygen and hydrogen will not combine even at a temperature of 1000° C. It is the only gas capable of supporting respiration. For the properties of liquid oxygen see LIQUID GASES.

It is found, more especially in the case of organic compounds, that if a substance which oxidizes readily at ordinary temperature be mixed with another which is not capable of such oxidation, then both are oxidized simultaneously, the amount of oxygen used being shared equally between them; or in some cases when the substance is spontaneously oxidized an equivalent amount of oxygen is converted into ozone or hydrogen peroxide. This phenomenon was first noticed by C. F. Schonbein (*Jour. prakt. Chem.*, 1858-1868), who found that on oxidizing lead in the presence of sulphuric acid, the same quantity of oxygen is used to form lead oxide as is converted into hydrogen peroxide. In a similar manner M. Traube (*Ber.*, 1882-1893) found that when zinc is oxidized in presence of water equivalent quantities of zinc hydroxide and hydrogen peroxide are formed at first, thus: $Zn + H_2O + O_2 = ZnO + H_2O_2$, followed by $ZnO + H_2O = Zn(OH)_2$. $Zn + H_2O_2 = Zn(OH)_2$. The oxygen uniting with the substance undergoing oxidation is generally known as "bound oxygen," whilst that which is transformed into ozone or hydrogen peroxide is usually called "active oxygen." C. Engler (*Ber.*, 1897, 30, p. 1669) calls the substance which undergoes oxidation the "autoxidizer" and the substance which unites with the active oxygen the "acceptor": in the oxidation of metals he expresses results as: $M + O_2 = MO_2$, followed by $MO_2 = M-O + O$, and if water be present, $O + H_2O = H_2O_2$. Various theories have been developed in order to account for these phenomena. Schonbein (*loc. cit.*) assumed that the ordinary oxygen molecule is decomposed into two parts which carry electrical charges of opposite kinds, the one with the positive charge being called "antozone" and the other carrying the negative charge being called "ozone," one variety being preferentially used up by the oxidizing compound or element and the other for the secondary reaction. J. H. Van't Hoff (*Zeit. phys. Chem.*, 1895, 16, p. 411) is of the opinion that the oxygen molecule is to a certain extent ionized and that the ions of one kind are preferably used by the oxidizing compound. This *loc. cit.*), on the other hand, concludes that the oxygen molecule enters into action as a whole and that on the oxidation of metals, hydrogen peroxide and the oxide of the metal are the primary products of the reaction. A. Bach (*Comptes rendus*, 1897, 124, p. 2) considers that the first stage in the reaction consists in the production of a peroxide which then interacts with water to form hydrogen peroxide (see also W. Manchot, *Ann.*, 1901, 314, p. 177; 1902, 325, p. 95).

Oxygen is a member of the sixth group in the periodic classification, and consequently possesses a maximum valency of six. In most cases it behaves as a divalent element, but it may also be quadrivalent. A. v. Baeyer and V, Villiger (*Ber.*, 1901, 34, pp. 2679, 3612) showed that many organic compounds (ethers, alcohols, aldehydes, ketones, &c.) behave towards acids, particularly the more complex acids, very much like bases and yield crystallized salts in which quadrivalent oxygen must be assumed as the basic element. These salts are considered to be derived from the hypothetical base OH$_2$·OH, oxonium hydroxide (compare sulphonium salts). Further see J. Schmidt, " Über die basischen Eigenschaften des Sauerstoffs " (Berlin, 1904). Baeyer and Villiger assume for the configuration of the salts of carbonyl compounds the arrangement $>C:O<^H_X$, whilst J. W. Bruhl and P. W. Walden point out from the physico-chemical standpoint that in water and hydrogen peroxide the oxygen atom is probably quadrivalent.

The atomic weight of oxygen is now generally taken as 16, and as such is used as the standard by which the atomic weights of the other elements are determined, owing to the fact that most elements combine with oxygen more readily than with hydrogen (see ELEMENT).

Oxygen is widely used in medical practice as well as in surgery. Inhalations of the gas are of service in pneumonia, bronchitis, heart disease, asthma, angina and other conditions accompanied by cyanosis and dyspnoea. They often avert death from asphyxia, or render the end less distressing. Oxygen is also administered in chloroform poisoning, and in threatened death from the inhalation of coal gas or nitrous oxides. It is of value in cyanide and opium poisoning and in the resuscitation of the apparently drowned. The mode of administration is by an inhaler attached to an inhalation bag, which serves to break the force with which the oxygen issues from the cylinders in which it is sold in a compressed form. It can be administered pure or mixed with air as required. If given in too great quantity a temporary condition of apnoea (cessation of breathing) is produced, the blood being fully charged with the gas. Oxygen may be applied locally as a disinfectant to foul and diseased surfaces by the use of the peroxide of hydrogen, which readily parts with its oxygen; a solution of hydrogen peroxide therefore forms a valuable spray in diphtheria, tonsillitis, laryngeal tuberculosis and oxaena. It can also be used with advantage in inoperable uterine cancer, favus and lupus, and as an injection in gonorrhoea and suppurative conditions of the ear. It relieves the pain of wasp and bee stings. Internally hydrogen peroxide is used in various diseased conditions of the gastro-intestinal tract, such as dyspepsia, diarrhoea and enteric fever. The B.P. preparation *Liquor Hydrogenii Peroxidi* dose $\frac{1}{2}$ to 2 drs. is synonymous with the *Aqua Hydrogenii Dioxidi* of the U.S.P. and the ten-volume solution termed *eau oxygenée* in France. It is customary to use oxygen in combination with chloroform, or nitrous oxide in order to produce insensibility to pain (see ANAESTHETICS).

OXYHYDROGEN FLAME, the flame attending the combustion of hydrogen and oxygen, and characterized by a very high temperature. Hydrogen gas readily burns in oxygen or air with the formation of water. The quantity of heat evolved, according to Julius Thomsen, is 34,116 calories for each gram of hydrogen burned. This heat-disturbance is quite independent of the mode in which the process is conducted; but the temperature of the flame is dependent on the circumstances under which the process takes place. It obviously attains its maximum in the case of the firing of pure " oxyhydrogen " gas (a mixture of hydrogen with exactly half its volume of oxygen, the quantity it combines with in becoming water, German *Knall-gas*). It becomes less when the " oxyhydrogen " is mixed with excess of one or the other of the two reacting gases, or an inert gas such as nitrogen, because in any such case the same amount of heat spreads over a larger quantity of matter. Many forms of oxyhydrogen lamps have been invented, but the explosive nature of the gaseous mixture rendered them all more or less dangerous. It acquired considerable application in platinum works, this metal being only fusible in the oxyhydrogen flame and the electric current; and also for the production of limelight, as in optical (magic) lanterns. But these applications are being superseded by the electric furnace, and electric light.

OYAMA, IWAO, PRINCE (1842–   ), Japanese field-marshal, was born in Satsuma. He was a nephew of Saigo, with whom his elder brother sided in the Satsuma insurrection of 1877, but he nevertheless remained loyal to the imperial cause and commanded a brigade against the insurgents. When war broke out between China and Japan in 1894, he was appointed commander-in-chief of the second Japanese army corps, which, landing on the Liaotung Peninsula, carried Port Arthur by storm, and, subsequently crossing to Shantung, captured the fortress of Wei-hai-wei. For these services he received the title of marquess, and, three years later, he became field-marshal. When (1904) his country became embroiled in war with Russia, he was appointed commander-in-chief of the Japanese armies in Manchuria, and in the sequel of Japan's victory the mikado bestowed on him (1907) the rank of prince. He received the British Order of Merit in 1906.

OVER AND TERMINER, the Anglo-French name, meaning " to hear and determine," for one of the commissions by which a judge of assize sits (see ASSIZE). By the commission of oyer and terminer the commissioners (in practice the judges of assize, though other persons are named with them in the commission) are commanded to make diligent inquiry into all treasons, felonies and misdemeanours whatever committed in the counties specified in the commission, and to hear and determine the same according to law. The inquiry is by means of the grand jury; after the grand jury has found the bills submitted to it, the commissioners proceed " to hear and determine " by means of the petty jury. The words oyer and terminer are also used to denote the court which has jurisdiction to try offences within the limits to which the commission of oyer and terminer extends.

By the Treason Act 1708 the crown has power to issue commissions of oyer and terminer in Scotland for the trial of treason and misprision of treason. Three of the lords of justiciary must be in any such commission. An indictment for either of the offences mentioned may be removed by certiorari from the court of oyer and terminer into the court of justiciary.

In the United States oyer and terminer is the name given to courts of criminal jurisdiction in some states, *e.g.* New York, New Jersey, Pennsylvania, and Georgia.

OYSTER. The use of this name in the vernacular is equivalent to that of *Ostrea* (Lat. from Gr. ὄστρεον, oyster, so called from its shell, ὄστεον, bone, shell) in zoological nomenclature; there are no genera so similar to *Ostrea* as to be confounded with it in ordinary language. *Ostrea* is a genus of Lamellibranch Molluscs. The degeneration produced by sedentary habits in all lamellibranchs has in the oyster reached its most advanced stage. The valves of the shell are closed by a single large adductor muscle, the anterior adductor being absent. The muscular projection of the ventral surface called the foot, whose various modifications characterize the different classes of *Mollusca*, is almost entirely aborted. The two valves of the shell are unequal in size, and of different shape; the left valve is larger, thicker and more convex, and on it the animal rests in its natural state. This valve, in the young oyster, is attached to some object on the sea-bottom; in the adult it is sometimes attached, sometimes free. The right valve is flat, and smaller and thinner than the left. In a corresponding manner the right side of the animal's body is somewhat less developed than the left, and to this extent there is a departure from the bilateral symmetry characteristic of Lamellibranchs.

The organization of the oyster, as compared with that of a typical lamellibranch such as *Anodon* (see LAMELLIBRANCHIA), is brought about by the reduction of the anterior part of the body accompanying the loss of the anterior adductor, and the enlargement of the posterior region. The pedal ganglia and auditory organs have disappeared with the foot, at all events have never been detected; the cerebral ganglia are very minute, while the parieto-splanchnic are well developed, and constitute the principal part of the nervous system.

According to Spengel, the pair of ganglia near the mouth, variously called labial or cerebral, represent the cerebral pair and pleural pair of a gastropod combined, and the parieto-splanchnic pair correspond to the visceral ganglia, the commissure which connects them with the cerebro-pleural representing the visceral commissure. Each of the visceral ganglia is connected or combined with an olfactory ganglion underlying an area of specialized epithelium, which constitutes the olfactory organ, the osphradium. The heart and pericardial chamber in the oyster lie along the anterior face of the adductor muscle, almost perpendicular to the direction of the gills, with which in *Anodon* they are parallel. In *Anodon* and the majority of lamellibranchs the ventricle surrounds the intestine; in the oyster the two are quite independent, the intestine passing above the pericardium. The renal organs of the oyster were discovered by Hoek to agree in their morphological relations with those of other lamellibranchs.

The generative organs of the oyster consist of a system of branching cavities on each side of the body lying immediately beneath the surface. All the cavities of a side are ultimately in communication with an efferent duct opening on the surface of the body a little above the line of attachment of the gills. The genital opening on each side is situated in a depression of the surface into which the renal organ also opens. The genital products are derived from the cells which line the cavities of the genital organs. The researches of Hoek have shown that in the same oyster the genital organs at one time produce ova, at another spermatozoa, and that consequently the oyster does not fertilize itself. How many times the alternation of sex may take place in a season is not known. It must be borne in mind that in what follows the species of the European coasts, *Ostrea edulis*, is under consideration. The ova are fertilized in the genital duct, and before their escape have undergone the earliest stages of segmentation. After escaping from the genital aperture they find their way into the infra-branchial part of the mantle cavity of the parent, probably by passing through the supra-branchial chamber to the posterior extremity of the gills, and then being conducted by the inhalent current caused by the cilia of the gills into the infra-branchial chamber. In the latter they accumulate, being held together and fastened to the gills by a white viscid secretion. The mass of ova thus contained in the oyster is spoken of by oyster fishers as "white spat," and an oyster containing them is said to be "sick." While in this position the ova go through the earlier stages of development. At the end of a fortnight the white spat has become dark-coloured from the appearance of coloured patches in the developing embryos. The embryos having then reached the condition of "trochospheres" escape from the mantle cavity and swim about freely near the surface of the water among the multitude of other creatures, larval and adult, which swarm there. The larvae are extremely minute, about $\frac{1}{125}$ in. long and of glassy transparency, except in one or two spots which are dark brown. From the trochosphere stage the free larvae pass into that of "veligers." How long they remain free is not known; Huxley kept them in a glass vessel in this condition for a week. Ultimately they sink to the bottom and fix themselves to shells, stones or other objects, and rapidly take on the appearance of minute oysters, forming white disks $\frac{1}{50}$ in. in diameter. The appearance of these minute oysters constitutes what the fishermen call a "fall of spat." The experiment by which Hoek conclusively proved the change of sex in the oyster was as follows. In an oyster containing white spat microscopic examination of the genital organs shows nothing but a few unexpelled ova. An oyster in this condition was kept in an aquarium by itself for a fortnight, and after that period its genital organs were found to contain multitudes of spermatozoa in all stages of development.

The breeding season of the European oyster lasts from May to September. The rate of growth of the young oyster is, roughly speaking, an inch of diameter in a year, but after it has attained a breadth of 3 in. its growth is much slower. Professor Möbius is of opinion that oysters over twenty years of age are rare, and that most of the adult Schleswig oysters are seven to ten years old.

The development of the American oyster, *O. virginiana*, and of the Portuguese oyster, *O. angulata*, is very similar to that of *O. edulis*, except that there is no period of incubation within the mantle cavity of the parent in the case of these two species. Hence it is that so-called artificial fertilization is possible; that is to say, fertilization will take place when ripe eggs and milt are artificially pressed from the oysters and allowed to fall into a vessel of sea-water. But if it is possible to procure a supply of spat from the American oyster by keeping the swarms of larvae

in confinement, it ought to be possible in the case of the European oyster. All that would be necessary would be to take a number of mature oysters containing white spat and lay them down in tanks till the larvae escape. This would be merely carrying oyster culture a step farther back, and instead of collecting the newly fixed oysters, to obtain the free larvae in numbers and so insure a fall of spat independently of the uncertainty of natural conditions. This method has been tried several times in England, in Holland and in France, but always without permanent success.

Natural beds of oysters occur on stony and shelly bottoms at depths varying from 3, to 20 fathoms. In nature the beds are liable to variations, and, although Huxley was somewhat sceptical on this point, it seems that they are easily brought into an unproductive condition by over-dredging. Oysters do not flourish in water containing less than 3% salt; and hence they are absent from the Baltic. The chief enemies of oysters are the dog-whelk, *Purpura lapillus*, and the whelk-tingle, *Murex erinaceus*, which bore through the shells. Starfishes devour large numbers; they are able to pull the valves of the shell apart and then to digest the body of the oyster by their everted stomach. *Cliona*, the boring sponge, destroys the shells and so injures the oyster; the boring annelid *Leucodore* also excavates the shell.

The wandering life of the larvae makes it uncertain whether any of the progeny of a given oyster-bed will settle within its area and so keep up its numbers. It is known from the history of the Limfjord beds that the larvae may settle 5 m. from their place of birth.

The genus *Ostrea* has a world-wide distribution, in tropical and temperate seas; seventy species have been distinguished. Its nearest allies are *Pinna* among living forms, *Eligmus* among fossils. For the so-called pearl-oyster see PEARL.

Oyster Industry.—Oysters are more valuable than any other single product of the fisheries, and in at least twenty-five countries are an important factor in the food-supply. The approximate value of the world's oyster crop approaches £4,000,000 annually, representing over 30,000,000 bushels, or nearly 10 billion oysters. Not less than 150,000 persons are engaged in the industry, and the total number dependent thereon is fully half a million. The following table shows in general terms the yearly oyster product of the world:—

Country.	Bushels.	Value.
United States	26,853,760	£2,533,481
Canada	134,140	43,405
Great Britain and Ireland	113,700	154,722
France	3,260,190	716,778
Holland	200,000	84,400
Italy	68,750	44,000
Other European countries	29,930	40,250
Asia, Africa and Oceania	275,000	111,400
Total	30,835,470	£3,728,436

United States.—The oyster is the chief fishery product in the United States. The states which lead in the quantity of oysters taken are Maryland, Virginia, New York, New Jersey and Connecticut; the annual value of the output in each of these is over $1,000,000. Other states with important oyster interests are Rhode Island, North Carolina, Louisiana and California. The oyster fisheries give employment to over 56,000 fishermen, who man 4000 vessels, valued at $4,000,000, and 23,000 boats, valued at $1,470,000; the value of the 11,000 dredges and 37,000 tongs, rakes and other appliances used is $365,000. The quantity of oysters taken in 1898 was 26,853,760 bushels, with a value of $12,667,405. The output of cultivated oysters in 1899 was about 9,800,000 bushels, worth $8,700,000.

Canada.—Oyster banks of some importance exist in the Gulf of St Lawrence and on the coast of British Columbia. All of the grounds have suffered depletion, and cultural methods to maintain the supply have been instituted. The oyster output of the Dominion has never exceeded 200,000 bushels in a single year, and in 1898 was 134,140 bushels, valued at $217,024.

United Kingdom.—The natural oyster beds of Great Britain and Ireland have been among the most valuable of the fishery resources, and British oysters have been famous from time immemorial. The most important oyster region is the Thames estuary, the site of extensive planting operations. The present supply is largely from cultivated grounds. Important oyster-producing centres are

Whitstable, Colchester and Brightlingsea. The oysters landed on the coasts of England and Wales in 1898 numbered 35,809,000, valued at £122,320, and in 1899, 38,978,000, valued at £143,841. The Scottish fishery has its centre at Inveraray and Ballantrae, and in 1905 yielded 218,000 oysters, valued at £865. Public oyster grounds of Ireland in 1903 produced 2,532,800 oysters, valued at £5030. The fishery is most extensive at Wicklow, Queenstown, Ballyheige, Galway and Moville. Planting is carried on in seven counties; the oysters taken from cultivated beds in 1903 numbered 2,687,500 oysters, valued at £5420.

France.—The industry owes its importance to the attention given to oyster cultivation. In the fishery on public grounds in 1896 only 6370 fishermen were engaged, employing 1627 vessels and boats, valued at 1,473,449 francs, and apparatus worth 211,495 francs, while only 13,127,217 kilograms of oysters were taken, or about 320,000 bushels, valued at 414,830 francs. In the parks, claires and reservoirs the private culture of oysters has attained great perfection. Fully 40,000 men, women and children are employed, and the output in 1896 was 1,536,417,968 oysters, worth 17,537,778 francs. The principal centre is Arcachon.

Oyster Culture.—The oyster industry has passed from the hands of the fisherman into those of the oyster culturist. The oyster being sedentary, except for a few days in the earliest stages of its existence, is easily exterminated in any given locality; since, although it may not be possible for the fishermen to rake up from the bottom every individual, wholesale methods of capture soon result in covering up or otherwise destroying the oyster banks or reefs, as the communities of oysters are technically termed. The main difference between the oyster industry of America and that of Europe lies in the fact that in Europe the native beds have long since been practically destroyed, perhaps not more than 6 or 7% of the oysters of Europe passing from the native beds directly into the hands of the consumer. It is probable that 60 to 75% are reared from the spat in artificial parks, the remainder having been laid down for a time to increase in size and flavour in shoal waters along the coasts. In the United States, on the other hand, from 30 to 40% are carried from the native beds directly to market. The oyster fishery is everywhere, except in localities where the natural beds are nearly exhausted, carried on in the most reckless manner, and in all directions oyster grounds are becoming deteriorated, and in some cases have been entirely destroyed. At present the oyster is one of the cheapest articles of diet in the United States; and, though it can hardly be expected that the price of American oysters will always remain so low, still, taking into consideration the great wealth of the natural beds along the entire Atlantic coast, it seems certain that a moderate amount of protection would keep the price of seed oysters far below European rates, and that the immense stretches of submerged land especially suited for oyster planting may be utilized and made to produce an abundant harvest at much less cost than that which accompanies the complicated system of culture in vogue in France and Holland.

The simplest form of oyster culture is the preservation of the natural oyster-beds. Upon this, in fact, depends the whole future of the industry, since it is not probable that any system of artificial breeding can be devised which will render it possible to keep up a supply without at least occasional recourse to seed oysters produced under natural conditions. It is the opinion of almost all who have studied the subject that any natural bed may in time be destroyed by overfishing (perhaps not by removing all the oysters, but by breaking up the colonies, and delivering over the territory which they once occupied to other kinds of animals), by burying the breeding oysters, by covering up the projections suitable for the reception of spat, and by breaking down, through the action of heavy dredges, the ridges which are especially fitted to be seats of the colonies.[1] The

[1] Even Huxley, the most ardent of all opponents of fishery legislation, while denying that oyster-beds had been permanently annihilated by dredging, practically admitted that a bed may be reduced to such a condition that the oyster will only be able to recover its former state by a long struggle with its enemies and competition—in fact that it must re-establish itself much in the same way as they have acquired possession of new grounds in Jutland, a process which, according to his own statement, occupied thirty years (Lecture at the Royal Institution, May 11th, 1883, printed with additions in the *English Illustrated Magazine*, i. pp. 47-55; 112-121).

immense oyster-beds in Pocomoke Sound, Maryland, have practically been destroyed by over-dredging, and many of the other beds of the United States are seriously damaged. The same is doubtless true of all the beds of Europe. It has also been demonstrated that under proper restriction great quantities of mature oysters, and seed oysters as well, may be taken from any region of natural oyster-beds without injurious effects. Parallel cases in agriculture and forestry will occur to every one. Möbius, in his most admirable essay *Die Auster und Die Austernwirthschaft*, has pointed out the proper means of preserving natural beds, declaring that, if the average profit from a bed of oysters is to remain permanently the same, a sufficient number of mother oysters must be left in it, so as not to diminish the capacity of maturing. He further shows that the productive capacity of a bed can only be maintained in one of two ways: (1) by diminishing the causes which destroy the young oysters, in which case the number of breeding oysters may safely be decreased; this, however, is practicable only under such favourable conditions as occur at Arcachon, where the beds may be kept under the constant control of the oyster-culturist; (2) by regulating the fishing on the natural beds in such a manner as to make them produce permanently the highest possible average quantity of oysters. Since the annual increase of half-grown oysters is estimated by him to be four hundred and twenty-one to every thousand full-grown oysters, he claims that not more than 42% of these latter ought to be taken from a bed during a year.

The Schleswig-Holstein oyster-beds are the property of the state, and are leased to a company whose interest it is to preserve their productiveness. The French beds are also kept under government control. Not so the beds of Great Britain and America, which are as a general rule open to all comers,[1] except when some close-time regulation is in force. Huxley has illustrated the futility of "close-time" in his remark that the prohibition of taking oysters from an oyster-bed during four months of the year is not the slightest security against its being stripped clean during the other eight months. "Suppose," he continues, "that in a country infested by wolves, you have a flock of sheep, keeping the wolves off during the lambing season will not afford much protection if you withdraw shepherd and dogs during the rest of the year." The old close-time laws were abolished in England in 1866, and returned to in 1876, but no results can be traced to the action of parliament in either case. Huxley's conclusions as regards the future of the oyster industry in Great Britain are doubtless just as applicable to other countries—that the only hope for the oyster consumer lies in the encouragement of oyster-culture, and in the development of some means of breeding oysters under such conditions that the spat shall be safely deposited. Oyster culture can evidently be carried on only by private enterprise, and the problem for legislation to solve is how to give such rights of property upon those shores which are favourable to oyster culture as may encourage competent persons to invest their money in that undertaking. Such property right should undoubtedly be extended to natural beds, or else an area of natural spawning territory should be kept under constant control and surveillance by government, for the purpose of maintaining an adequate supply of seed oysters.

The extension of the area of the natural beds is the second step in oyster culture. As is well known to zoologists, and as has been very lucidly set forth by Möbius, the location of oyster banks is sharply defined by absolute physical conditions. Within certain definite limits of depth, temperature and salinity, the only requirement is a suitable place for attachment. Oysters cannot thrive where the ground is composed of moving sand or where mud is deposited; consequently, since the size and number of these places are very limited, only a very small percentage of the young oysters can find a resting-place, and the remainder perish. Möbius estimates that for every oyster brought to

[1] Connecticut has greatly benefited its oyster industry by giving to oyster-culturists a fee simple title to the lands under control by them.

market from the Holstein banks, 1,045,000 are destroyed or die. By putting down suitable "cultch" or "stools" immense quantities of the wandering fry may be induced to settle, and are thus saved. As a rule the natural beds occupy most of the suitable space in their own vicinity. Unoccupied territory may, however, be prepared for the reception of new beds, by spreading sand, gravel and shells over muddy bottoms, or, indeed, beds may be kept up in locations for permanent natural beds, by putting down mature oysters and cultch just before the time of breeding, thus giving the young a chance to fix themselves before the currents and enemies have had time to accomplish much in the way of destruction.

The collection of oyster spat upon artificial stools has been practised from time immemorial. As early as the 7th century, and probably before, the Romans practised a kind of oyster culture in Lake Avernus, which still survives to the present day in Lake Fusaro. Piles of rocks are made on the muddy bottoms of these salt-water lakes, and around these are arranged circles of stakes, to which are often attached bundles of twigs. Breeding oysters are piled upon the rookeries, and their young become attached to the stakes and twigs provided for their reception, where they are allowed to remain until ready for use, when they are plucked off and sent to the market. A similar though ruder device is used in the Poquonock river in Connecticut. Birch trees are thrown into the water near a natural bed of oysters, and the trunks and twigs become covered with spat; the trees are then dragged out upon the shore by oxen, and the young fry are broken off and laid down in the shallows to increase in size. In 1858 the methods of the Italian lakes were repeated at St Brieuc under the direction of Professor P. Coste, and from these experiments the art of artificial breeding as practised in France has been developed. There is, however, a marked distinction between oyster-culture and oyster-breeding.

In considering the oyster-culture in France it is necessary to distinguish the centres of production from the centres of rearing or fattening. The chief centres or regions of oyster production are two, (1) Arcachon, (2) Brittany. The basin of Arcachon has an area of about 38,000 acres at high water, and only about 15,000 acres are under water at low tide. The water is salter than the sea. At the beginning of the 19th century there were only natural oyster beds in the basin, and these produced 75 million oysters per annum. But in the middle of the century the natural beds had been almost exhausted and the system of government control, letting "parks" to private tenants, and artificial cultivation was instituted. Certain beds in the basin are reserved and kept under government control. Cultch is placed upon them every year, and gathering of oysters upon them is allowed only at intervals of two or more years, when the authority thinks they are sufficiently stocked to permit of it. These beds supply spat for the private cultivators. The latter collect the spat on tiles: these are made of earthenware and concave on one side. One of the most important points in the system is the coating of the tiles with lime. It is necessary to detach the young oysters from the tiles when they are nearly a year old (détroquage): this could not be done without destroying the young if they were attached directly to the surface of the tile. The coating of lime or mortar is soft and brittle, and consequently the young oysters can easily be detached with a stout knife. The method of liming the tiles (chaulage) consists in dipping them into a liquid mixture of lime and water. Sometimes lime only is used, sometimes equal quantities of lime and sand, or lime and mud. Often it is necessary to repeat the dipping, and for the second coat hydraulic lime may be employed.

The tiles coated with lime are set out on the shore near the low-water mark of spring tides, at the beginning of the spatting season. This is earlier in the south of France than in England: at Arcachon the collectors are put in position about the middle of June. Various methods are adopted for keeping the tiles in place and for arranging them in the position most favourable to the collection of spat. At Arcachon they are arranged in piles each layer being transverse to the one below, so that the space formed by the concavity of the tile is kept open. A wooden frame-work often surrounds the heap of tiles to prevent them being scattered by the waves.

In the following season, about April, the young oysters, then from ½ to 1 in. in diameter, are separated or détroqués. They may then be placed in oyster cases (caisses ostrophiles) or in shallow ponds (claires) made on the fore-shore. The cases are about 8 in. deep, made with a wooden frame-work, and galvanized wire netting top and bottom, the lid being hinged. These cases about 8 ft. by 4 ft. in dimensions are fixed on the fore-shore by means of short posts driven into the ground, so that they are raised about 9 in. or 1 ft. from the latter. The young oysters grow rapidly in these cases, and have to be thinned out as they grow larger. When they have been in the boxes a year they are large enough to be placed in the claires or simply scattered along the fore-shore.

In Brittany the chief seat of oyster production is the gulf of Morbihan, where the estuaries of numerous small rivers furnish fore-shores suitable to the industry. Here the prevalence of mud is one of the chief obstacles, and for this reason the tile-collectors are usually fastened together by wire and suspended to posts (tuiles en bouquets). The collectors are not set out before the middle of July. The natural beds from which the supply of spat is derived are reserved, but apparently are insufficiently protected, so that much poaching goes on.

These two regions of production, Arcachon and Morbihan supply young oysters for "relaying," i.e. rearing, not only to numerous places on the coast of France, but also to England, Ireland and elsewhere. Among rearing districts Marennes and La Tremblade are specially celebrated on account of the extensive system of claires or oyster ponds, in which the green oysters so much prized in Paris are produced. The irrigation of the claires is entirely under control, and the claires undergo a special preparation for the production of the green oysters, whose colour seems to be derived from a species of Diatom which abounds in the claires.

In Holland the French system of oyster-culture is followed in the estuary of the Scheldt, with some modifications in detail. The tiles used are flat and heavy, and are placed on the foreshores in an oblique position resting on their edges and against each other. The tiles with the young oysters on them are placed in enclosures during the winter, and détrouguage is carried out in the following summer.

In England the use of tiles has been tried on various occasions, in Cornwall on the river Fal, at Hayling Island and in Essex, but has nowhere become permanently established. The reasons for this are that the fall of spat is not usually very abundant, and the kind of labour required cannot be obtained at a sufficiently cheap rate. In many places oysters are simply imported from France and Holland and laid down to grow, or are obtained by dredging from open grounds. At Whitstable most of the stock is thus obtained, but cultch (i.e. dead shells) is here and elsewhere scattered over the ground to serve for the attachment of spat. The use of cultch as collector is a very ancient practice in England, and is still almost universally maintained. In the estuaries of Essex there are many private or semi-private oyster fisheries, where the method of culture is to dredge up the oysters in autumn and place them in pits, where they are sorted out, and the suitable ones are selected for the market. Just before the close season the young oysters and all the rest that remain are scattered over the beds again, with quantities of cultch, and in many cases the fishery is maintained by the local fall of spat, without importation. In some places where the ground is suitable cultch is spread over the foreshores also to collect spat. The genuine English "native" is produced in its greatest perfection in the Essex fisheries, and is probably the highest priced oyster in the world.

In addition to the literature quoted see also the following: *Rapport sur les recherches concernant l'huître et l'ostréiculture publié par la Commission de la Société Néerlandaise de Zoologie* (Leiden, 1883–1884); P. Brocchi, *Traité de l'ostréiculture* (Paris, 1883); Bashford Dean, *European Oyster Culture*, Bulletin U.S. Fish Commission, vol. x. for 1890, vol. xi. for 1891; J. T. Cunningham, Report of the Lecturer on Fishery Subjects, in *Report of Technical Instruction Committee of Cornwall* (1899, 1900). (G. B. G.; J. T. C.)

OYSTER BAY, a township of Nassau (formerly of Queens) county, New York, on Long Island, about 25 m. E.N.E. of Long Island City. Pop. (1890) 13,870, (1900) 16,334; (1910 census) 21,802. The township reaches from N. to S. across the island (here about 10 m. wide) in the shape of a rough wedge, the larger end being on Long Island Sound at the N.; on the northern shore is the tripartite Oyster Bay, whose western arm is Mill Neck creek, whose central branch is Oyster Bay harbor, and whose easternmost arm, called Cold Spring harbor, separates the township of Oyster Bay from the township of Huntington. On the south side of the township is South Oyster bay, immediately east of the main body of the Great South bay; and between South Oyster Bay and the ocean lie several island beaches, the smaller and northernmost ones being marshy, and the southern, Jones or Seaford beach, being sandy and having on the ocean side the Zach's inlet and Jones Beach life-saving stations. The township is served by four branches of the Long Island railway; the Oyster Bay branch of the north shore to the village of Sea Cliff (incorporated in 1883; pop. 1910, 1694), on the E. side of Hempstead harbor, to Glen Cove, a large unincorporated village, immediately N.E. of Sea Cliff, to Locust Valley and to Mill Neck farther E., and to the village of Oyster Bay, the terminus of the branch, on Oyster Bay harbor; the Wading

River branch to Hicksville and to Syosset; a third branch to Farmingdale, which also has direct communication by railway with Hicksville; and the Montauk division to Massapequa, in the south-western part of the township on Massapequa Lake and Massapequa Creek, which empties into South Oyster Bay. The villages served by the railway are the only important settlements; those on the hilly north shore are residential. To the north of the village of Oyster Bay, on a long peninsular beach called Centre Island, are the headquarters of the Seawanhaka Yacht Club; and to the east of the same village, especially on Cove Neck, between Oyster Bay Harbor and Cold Spring Harbor, are many summer residences with fine grounds. Massapequa, on the south shore, is a residential summer resort. The villages of Hicksville and Farmingdale are rural; the former has many German settlers. Jericho, N.E. of Hicksville, is a stronghold of the Hicksite Quakers, who are mostly wealthy landowners. In Locust Valley is Friends' Academy (1876), a secondary school for boys and girls. There are a few truck farms in the township, potatoes, cabbages and cucumbers for pickling being the principal crops; ' Oyster Bay asparagus " was once a famous crop. Oysters are cultivated on the Sound Shore and there are clam beds in Oyster Bay and South Oyster Bay. In the village of Glen Cove there is a large leather-belting factory.

David Pieterssen de Vries, in his *Voyages from Holland to America*, makes the first mention of Oyster Bay Harbor, which he explored in June 1639. In the same month Matthew Sinderland (or Sunderland) bought from James Forrett, deputy of William Alexander, earl of Stirling, " two little necks of land, the one upon the east side of Oyster Bay Harbor "; but Sinderland made no settlement. A settlement from Lynn, Mass., was attempted in 1640 but was prevented by Governor William Kieft. By the treaty signed at Hartford, Connecticut, on the 29th of September 1650 by the Commissioners of the United colonies of New England and those of New Netherland all land east of the west side of Oyster Bay was granted to the English, and all land west to the Dutch; but the Dutch placed Oyster Bay, according to a letter of Pieter Stuyvesant written in 1659, two and a half leagues farther east than the New Englanders did. In 1653 an Indian deed granted land at Oyster Bay to Peter Wright and others of Salem and Sandwich, Mass., who made a permanent settlement here; in 1663 another sale was made to Captain John Underhill (d. 1672), who first went to Long Island about 1653, when he led a force which fought the only important engagement ever fought with the Indians on Long Island, in which the colonists destroyed the fortification at Fort Neck near the present Massapequa, of Tackapousha, chief of the Massapequas, an Algonquian tribe, whose name meant " great pond." Oyster Bay was for a time closely connected politically with New Haven, but in 1664 with the remainder of Long Island it came under the New York government of Richard Nicolls, to whose success Underhill had largely contributed by undermining Dutch influence on Long Island. In 1680 a Friends' meeting-house was built at Jericho, the home of Elias Hicks, near the present Hicksville, the site of which was owned by his family and which was named in his honour; and the Dutch built their first church in Oyster Bay in 1732. The harbour of Oyster Bay was a famous smuggling place at the close of the 17th century, when there was a customs house here. The first settlement on the " south side " of the township was made about 1693, when the Massapequa Indians sold 6000 acres at Fort Neck to Thomas Townsend, and his son-in-law Thomas Jones (1665-1713), who had fought for James II. at Boyne and Aghrim, who became a high sheriff of Queen's county in 1704, and who was the founder of the family of Jones and Floyd-Jones, whose seat was Tryon Hall (built at South Oyster Bay, now Massapequa, in 1770); Thomas Jones (1731-1792), grandson of the first Thomas Jones, was a prominent Loyalist during the War of Independence and wrote a valuable *History of New York during the Revolutionary War*, first published in 1879.

OYSTER-CATCHER, a bird's name which does not seem to occur in books until 1731, when M. Catesby (*Nat. Hist. Carolina*, i. p. 85) used it for a species which he observed to be abundant

on the oyster-banks left bare at low water in the rivers of Carolina, and believed to feed principally upon those molluscs. In 1776 T. Pennant applied the name to the allied British species, which he and for nearly two hundred years many other English writers had called the " Sea-Pie." The change, in spite of the misnomer —for, whatever may be the case elsewhere, in England the bird does not feed upon oysters—met with general approval, and the new name has, at least in books, almost wholly replaced what seems to have been the older one.[1] The Oyster-catcher of Europe is the *Haematopus*[2] *ostralegus* or Linnaeus, belonging to the group now called *Limicolae*, and is generally included in the family *Charadriidae*; though some writers have placed it in one of its own, *Haematopodidae*, chiefly on account of its peculiar bill—a long thin wedge, ending in a vertical edge. Its feet also are much more fleshy than are generally seen in the Plover family. In its strongly-contrasted plumage of black and white, with a coral-coloured bill, the Oyster-catcher is one of the most conspicuous birds of the European coasts, and in many parts is still very common. It is nearly always seen paired, though the pairs collect in prodigious flocks; and, when these are broken up, its shrill but musical cry of " tu-lup," " tu-lup," somewhat pettishly repeated, helps to draw attention to it. Its wariness, however, is very marvellous, and even at the breeding-season, when most birds throw off their shyness, it is not easily approached within ordinary gunshot distance. The hen-bird commonly lays three clay-coloured eggs, blotched with black, in a very slight hollow on the ground not far from the sea. As incubation goes on the hollow is somewhat deepened, and perhaps some haulm is added to its edge, so that at last a very fair nest is the result. The young, as in all *Limicolae*, are at first clothed in down, so mottled in colour as closely to resemble the shingle to which, if they be not hatched upon it, they are almost immediately taken by their parents, and there, on the slightest alarm, they squat close to elude observation. This species occurs on the British coasts (very seldom straying inland) all the year round; but there is some reason to think that those we have in winter are natives of more northern latitudes, while our home-bred birds leave us. It ranges from Iceland to the shores of the Red Sea, and lives chiefly on marine worms, crustacea and such molluscs as it is able to obtain. It is commonly supposed to be capable of prizing limpets from their rock, and of opening the shells of mussels; but, though undoubtedly it feeds on both, further evidence as to the way in which it procures them is desirable. J. E. Harting informed the present writer that the bird seems to lay its head sideways on the ground, and then, grasping the limpet's shell close to the rock between the mandibles, use them as scissor-blades to cut off the mollusc from its sticking-place. The Oyster-catcher is not highly esteemed as a bird for the table.

Differing from this species in the possession of a longer bill, in having much less white on its back, in the paler colour of its mantle, and in a few other points, is the ordinary American species, with at least three races, *Haematopus palliatus*. Except that its call-note, judging from description, is unlike that of the European bird, the habits of the two seem to be perfectly similar; and the same may be said indeed of all the other species. The Falkland Islands are frequented by a third, *H. leucopus*, very similar to the first, but with a black wing-lining and paler legs, while the Australian Region possesses a fourth, *H. longirostris*, with a very long bill as its name intimates, and no white on its

[1] It seems, however, very possible, judging from its equivalents in other European languages, such as the Frisian *Oestervisscher*, the German *Augsterman*, *Austernfischer*, and the like, that the name " Oyster-catcher " may have been not a colonial invention but indigenous to the mother-country, though it had not found its way into print before. The French *Huîtrier*, however, appears to be a word coined by Brisson. " Sea-Pie " has its analogues in the French *Pie-de-Mer*, the German *Meerelster*, *Seeelster*, and so forth.
[2] Whether it be the *Haematopus*, whose name is found in some editions of Pliny (lib. x. cap. 47) is at best doubtful. Other editions have *Himantopus*; but Hardouin prefers the former reading. Both words have passed into modern ornithology, the latter as the generic name of the STILT (*q.v.*); and some writers have blended the two in the strange and impossible compound *Haemantopus.* . .

primaries. China, Japan and possibly eastern Asia in general have an Oyster-catcher which seems to be intermediate between the last and the first. This has received the name of *H. osculans*; but doubts have been expressed as to its deserving specific recognition. Then we have a group of species in which the plumage is wholly or almost wholly black, and among them only do we find birds that fulfil the implication of the scientific name of the genus by having feet that may be called blood-red. *H. niger*, which frequents both coasts of the northern Pacific, has, it is true, yellow legs, but towards the extremity of South America its place is taken by *H. ater*, in which they are bright red, and this bird is further remarkable by its laterally compressed and much upturned bill. The South African *H. capensis* has also scarlet legs; but in the otherwise very similar bird of Australia and New Zealand, *H. unicolor*, these members are of a pale brick-colour. (A. N.)

OYSTERMOUTH, or THE MUMBLES, an urban district and seaside resort in the Gower division of Glamorganshire, south Wales, situated on the western bend of Swansea Bay, 4½ m. S.W. of Swansea, with which it is connected by the steam-tramway of the Swansea and Mumbles Railway Company, constructed in 1804. The London and North-Western railway has also a station at Mumbles Road, 2¼ m. N. of Oystermouth. Pop. (1901) 4461. The castle, which belongs to the duke of Beaufort as lord of the seigniory of Gower, is an imposing ruin, nobly situated on a rocky knoll overlooking the bay. Its great hall and chapel with their traceried Gothic windows are fairly well preserved. The earliest structure (probably only a " peel " tower), built in the opening years of the 12th century, probably by Maurice de Londres, was destroyed by the Welsh in 1215. The early English features of the square keep indicate that it was soon rebuilt, by one of the De Breos lords (see GOWER). In 1284 Edward I. stayed here two days as the guest of William de Breos, and from that time on it became the chief residence in Gower of the lords seignior and subsequently of their stewards, and their chancery was located here till its abolition in 1535. The parish church, which has an embattled tower, was restored in 1860, when fragments of Roman tesselated pavement were found in various parts of the churchyard. Roman coins were also found in the village in 1822 and 1837—all indicating that there had been a small settlement here in Roman times. The name of the castle appears in the Welsh chronicles as Ystum Llwynarth, which, by the elision of the penultimate, was probably changed by false analogy into Oystermouth—the bay being noted for its oyster beds. Its church is mentioned in the cartulary of Gloucester (1141) as Ostrenuwe.

The village itself is straggling and uninteresting, but the high ground between it and the pretty bays of Langland and Caswell on the southern side of the headland fronting the open channel is dotted with well-built villas and commands magnificent views. The headland terminates in two rocky islands, which to sailors coming up the channel would appear like the breasts of " mammals," whence the comparatively modern name, The Mumbles, is supposed to be derived. On the outer of these rocks is a lighthouse erected in 1794 and maintained by the Swansea Harbour Trust. The district is rapidly increasing in popularity as a seaside resort. A pier was erected by the Mumbles Railway Company at a cost of £12,000 in 1898. The fishing industry, once prosperous, has much diminished in importance, but there are still oyster-beds in the bay.

OZANAM, ANTOINE FRÉDÉRIC (1813–1853), French scholar, was born at Milan on the 23rd of April 1813. His family, which was of Jewish extraction, had been settled in the Lyonnais for many centuries, and had reached distinction in the third generation before Frédéric through Jacques Ozanam (1640–1717), an eminent mathematician. Ozanam's father, Antoine, served in the armies of the republic, but betook himself, on the advent of the empire, to trade, teaching, and finally medicine. The boy was brought up at Lyons and was strongly influenced by one of his masters, the Abbé Noirot. His conservative and religious instincts showed themselves early, and he published a pamphlet against Saint-Simonianism in 1831, which attracted the attention of Lamartine. In the following year he was sent to study law at Paris, where he fell in with the Ampère family, and through them with Chateaubriand, Lacordaire, Montalembert, and other leaders of the neo-Catholic movement. Whilst still a student he took up journalism and contributed considerably to Bailly's *Tribune catholique*, which became (November 1, 1833) *L'univers*. In conjunction with other young men he founded in May 1833 the celebrated charitable society of St Vincent de Paul, which numbered before his death upwards of two thousand members. He received the degree of doctor of law in 1836, and in 1838 that of doctor of letters with a thesis on Dante, which was the beginning of one of his best-known books. A year later he was appointed to a professorship of commercial law at Lyons, and in 1840 assistant professor of foreign literature at the Sorbonne. He married in June 1841, and visited Italy on his wedding tour. At Fauriel's death in 1844 he succeeded to the full professorship of foreign literature. The short remainder of his life was extremely busy with his professorial duties, his extensive literary occupations, and the work, which he still continued, of district-visiting as a member of the society of St Vincent de Paul. During the revolution of 1848, of which he took an unduly sanguine view, he once more turned journalist for a short time in the *Ère nouvelle* and other papers. He travelled extensively, and was in England at the time of the Exhibition of 1851. His naturally weak constitution fell a prey to consumption, which he hoped to cure by visiting Italy; but he died on his return at Marseilles on the 8th of September 1853.

Ozanam was the leading historical and literary critic in the neo-Catholic movement in France during the first half of the 19th century. He was more learned, more sincere, and more logical than Chateaubriand; less of a political partisan and less of a literary sentimentalist than Montalembert. In contemporary movements he was an earnest and conscientious advocate of Catholic democracy and socialism and of the view that the church should adapt itself to the changed political conditions consequent to the Revolution. In his writings he dwelt upon important contributions of historical Christianity, and maintained especially that, in continuing the work of the Caesars, the Catholic church had been the most potent factor in civilizing the invading barbarians and in organizing the life of the middle ages. He confessed that his object was " to prove the contrary thesis to Gibbon's," and, although any historian who begins with the desire to prove a thesis is quite sure to go more or less wrong, Ozanam no doubt administered a healthful antidote to the prevalent notion, particularly amongst English-speaking peoples, that the Catholic church had done far more to enslave than to elevate the human mind. His knowledge of medieval literature and his appreciative sympathy with medieval life admirably qualified him for his work, and his scholarly attainments are still highly esteemed.

His works were published in eleven volumes (Paris, 1860–1865). They include *Deux chanceliers d'Angleterre*, *Bacon de Verulam et Saint Thomas de Cantorbéry* (Paris, 1836); *Dante et la philosophie catholique au XIIIᵐᵉ siècle* (Paris, 1839; 2nd ed., enlarged 1845); *Études germaniques* (2 vols., Paris, 1847–1849), translated by A. C. Glyn as *History of Civilization in the Fifth Century* (London, 1868); *Documents inédits pour servir à l'histoire de l'Italie depuis le VIIIᵐᵉ siècle jusqu'au XIIIᵐᵉ* (Paris, 1850); *Les poètes franciscains en Italie au XIIIᵐᵉ siècle* (Paris, 1852). His letters have been partially translated into English by A. Coates (London, 1886).

There are French lives of Ozanam by his brother, C. A. Ozanam (Paris, 1882); Mme. E. Humbert (Paris, 1880); C. Huit (Paris, 1882); M. de Lambel (Paris, 1887); L. Curnier (Paris, 1888); and B. Faulquier (Paris, 1903). German lives by F. X. Karker (Paderborn, 1867) and E. Hardy (Mainz, 1878); and an interesting English biography by Miss K. O'Meara (Edinburgh, 1867; 2nd ed., London, 1878). (C. H. HA.)

OZIERI, a town of Sardinia in the province of Sassari, from which it is 34 m. E.S.E. by rail. Pop. (1901) 9555. It is situated 1280 ft. above sea-level on a steep slope, but faces north, and so is not very healthy. In the centre of the town is a square with a fine fountain of 1594. The cathedral was restored in 1848; it is the seat of the diocese of Bisarcio. The former cathedral of this diocese lies some distance to the N.W.; it is a fine Romanesque building of the 12th and 13th centuries. The district of Ozieri

Is famous for its butter—the only butter made in Sardinia—cheese; and other pastoral products; cattle are also bred here.

See D. Scano, *Storia dell' arte in Sardegna dal xi. al xix. secolo* (Cagliari-Sassari, 1907). p. 200.

OZOKERITE, or OZOCERITE (Gr. ὄζειν, to emit odour, and κηρός, wax), mineral wax, a combustible mineral, which may be designated as crude native paraffin (q.v.), found in many localities in varying degrees of purity. Specimens have been obtained from Scotland, Northumberland and Wales, as well as from about thirty different countries. Of these occurrences the ozokerite of the island of Tcheleken, near Baku, and the deposits of Utah, U.S.A., deserve mention, though the last-named have been largely worked out. The sole sources of commercial supply are in Galicia, at Boryslaw, Dzwiniacs and Starunia, though the mineral is found at other points on both flanks of the Carpathians. Ozokerite-deposits are believed to have originated in much the same way as mineral veins, the slow evaporation and oxidation of petroleum having resulted in the deposition of its dissolved paraffin in the fissures and crevices previously occupied by the liquid. As found native, ozokerite varies from a very soft wax to a black mass as hard as gypsum. Its specific gravity ranges from ·85 to ·95, and its melting point from 58° to 100° C. It is soluble in ether, petroleum, benzene, turpentine, chloroform, carbon bisulphide, &c. Galician ozokerite varies in colour from light yellow to dark brown, and frequently appears green owing to dichroism. It usually melts at 62° C. Chemically, ozokerite consists of a mixture of various hydrocarbons, containing 85·7% by weight of carbon and 14·3% of hydrogen.

The mining of ozokerite was formerly carried on in Galicia by means of hand-labour, but in the modern ozokerite mines owned by the Boryslaw Actien Gesellschaft and the Galizische Kreditbank, the workings of which extend to a depth of 200 metres, and 225 metres respectively, electrical power is employed for hauling, pumping and ventilating. In these mines there are the usual main shafts and galleries, the ozokerite being reached by levels driven along the strike of the deposit. The wax, as it reaches the surface, varies in purity, and, in new workings especially, only hand-picking is needed to separate the pure material. In other cases much earthy matter is mixed with the material, and then the rock or shale having been eliminated by hand-picking, the "wax-stone" is boiled with water in large coppers, when the pure wax rises to the surface. This is again melted without water, and the impurities are skimmed off, the material being then run into slightly conical cylindrical moulds and thus made into blocks for the market. The crude ozokerite is refined by treatment first with Nordhausen oil of vitriol, and subsequently with charcoal, when the ceresine or cerasin of commerce is obtained. The refined ozokerite or ceresine, which usually has a melting-point of 61° to 78° C., is largely used as an adulterant of beeswax, and is frequently coloured artificially to resemble that product in appearance.

On distillation in a current of superheated steam, ozokerite yields a candle-making material resembling the paraffin obtained from petroleum and shale-oil but of higher melting-point, and therefore of greater value if the candles made from it are to be used in hot climates. There are also obtained in the distillation light oils and a product resembling vaseline (q.v.). The residue in the stills consists of a hard, black, waxy substance, which in admixture with india-rubber is employed under the name of *okonite* as an electrical insulator. From the residue a form of the material known as *heel-ball*, used to impart a polished surface to the heels and soles of boots, is also manufactured.

According to published statistics, the output of crude ozokerite in Galicia in 1906 and 1907 was as follows:

District.	1906. Metric Tons.	1907. Metric Tons.
Boryslaw .	2,205	2,740
Dzwiniacz .	260	270
Starunia . .	210	135

(H. R.)

OZONE, allotropic oxygen, O_3. The first recorded observations of the substance are due to Van Marum (1785), who found that oxygen gas through which a stream of electric sparks had been passed, tarnished mercury and emitted a peculiar smell. In 1840 C. F. Schonbein (*Pogg. Ann.* 50, p. 616) showed that this substance was also present in the oxygen liberated during the electrolysis of acidulated water; and gave it the name ozone (Gr. ὄζειν, to smell). Ozone mixed with an excess of oxygen is obtained by submitting dry oxygen to the silent electric discharge [at the temperature of liquid air, E. Briner and E. Durand (*Comptes rendus*, 1907, 145, p. 1277) obtained a 90% yield]; by the action of fluorine on water at 0° C. (H. Moissan, *Comptes rendus*, 1899, 129, p. 570); by the action of concentrated sulphuric acid or barium peroxide or on other peroxides and salts of peracids (A. v. Baeyer and V. Villiger, *Ber.* 1901, 34, p. 355); by passing oxygen over some heated metallic oxides, and by distilling potassium permanganate with concentrated sulphuric acid in vacuo. It is also formed during many processes of slow oxidation. For a description of the various forms of ozonizers used on the large scale see N. Otto, *Rev. gén. de chemie pure et appliquée*, 1900, ii. p. 405; W. Elworthy, *Elekt. Zeits.*, 1904, ii. p. 1), and H. Guilleminot (*Comptes rendus*, 1903, 136, p. 1653). Ozone is also produced by the action of cathode and ultra-violet rays on oxygen. These methods of preparation give an ozone diluted with a considerable amount of unaltered oxygen; A. Ladenburg (*Ber.* 1898, 31, pp. 2508, 2830) succeeded in liquefying ozonized oxygen with liquid air and then by fractional evaporation obtained a liquid containing between 80 and 90% of ozone.

Ozone is a colourless gas which possesses a characteristic smell. When strongly cooled it condenses to an indigo blue liquid which is extremely explosive (see LIQUID GASES). In ozonizing oxygen the volume of the gas diminishes, but if the gas be heated to about 300° C, it returns to its original volume, and is found to be nothing but oxygen. The same change of ozone into oxygen may be brought about by contact with platinum black and other substances. Ozone is only very slightly soluble in water. It is a most powerful oxidizing agent, which rapidly attacks organic matter (hence in preparing the gas, rubber connexions must not be used, since they are instantly destroyed), bleaches vegetable colouring matters and acts rapidly on most metals. It liberates iodine from solutions of potassium iodide, the reaction in neutral solution proceeding thus: $O_3 + 2KI + H_2O = O_2 + I_2 + 2KHO$ whilst in acid solution, the decomposition takes the following course: $4O_3 + 10HI = 5I_2 + H_2O + 4H_2O + 3O_2$ (A. Ladenburg, *Ber.* 1901, 34, p. 1184). Ozone is decomposed by some metallic oxides, with regeneration of oxygen. It combines with many unsaturated carbon compounds to form ozonides (C. Harries, *Ber.* 1904, 37, pp. 839 et seq.).

The constitution of ozone has been determined by J. L. Soret (*Ann. chim. phys.*, 1866 [4], 7, p. 113; 1868 [4], 13, p. 257), who showed that the diminution in volume when ozone is absorbed from ozonized oxygen by means of oil of turpentine is twice as great as the increase in volume observed when ozone is reconverted into oxygen on heating. This points to the gas possessing the molecular formula O_3. Confirmation was obtained by comparing the rate of diffusion of ozone with that of chlorine, which gave 24·8 as the value for the density of ozone, consequently the molecular formula must be O_3 (cf. B. C. Brodie, *Phil. Trans.*, 1872, pt. ii. p. 435). More recently A. Ladenburg (*Ber.* 1901, 34, p. 631) has obtained as a mean value for the molecular weight the number 47·78, which corresponds with the above molecular formula. Ozone is used largely for sterilizing water.

P The sixteenth letter of the English alphabet, the fifteenth in the Latin and the sixteenth in the Greek alphabet, the latter in its ordinary form having the symbol for *x* before *o*. In the Phoenician alphabet, from which the Western alphabets are directly or indirectly derived, its shape, written from right to left, is ¶. In the Greek alphabet, when written from left to right, it takes the form Γ or Π, the second form being much rarer in inscriptions than the first. Only very rarely and only in inscriptions of the 7th and 6th centuries B.C. are rounded forms Γ, Π found. In Italy the Etruscan and Umbrian form ¶ (written from right to left), though more angular than the Phoenician symbol, resembles it more closely than it does the Greek. The earliest Roman form—on the inscription found in the Forum in 1899—is Greek in shape ¶, though the second leg is barely visible. The Oscan Π is identical with the rarer Greek form. As time goes on the Roman form becomes more and more rounded P, but not till Imperial times is the semicircle completed so as to form the symbol in the shape which it still retains P. The Semitic name *Pé* became in Greek πεῖ, and has in the course of ages changed but little. The sound of *p* throughout has been that of the breathed labial stop, as in the English *pin*. At the end of English words like *lip* the breath is audible after the consonant, so that the sound is rather that of the ancient Greek φ, i.e. *p-h*, not *f*, as φ is ordinarily now pronounced. This sound is found initially also in some dialects of English, as in the Irish pronunciation of *pig* as *p-hig*. For a remarkable interchange between *p* and *qu* sounds which is found in many languages, see under Q. (P. Gi.)

PAARL, a town of the Cape Province, South Africa, 36 m. by rail E.N.E. of Cape Town. Pop. (1904), 11,293. The town is situated on the west bank of the Berg river, some 400 ft. above the sea. It stands on the coast plain near the foot of the Drakenstein mountains. West of the town the Paarl Berg rises from the plain. The berg is crowned by three great granite boulders, known as the Paarl, Britannia and Gordon Rock. The town is beautifully situated amid gardens, orange groves and vineyards. The chief public buildings are the two Dutch Reformed churches, the old church being a good specimen of colonial Dutch architecture, with gables, curves and thatched roof. Paarl is a thriving agricultural and viticultural centre, among its industries being the manufacture of wine and brandy, wagon and carriage building and harness making. South-east of the town are granite quarries. The wines produced in the district are among the best in South Africa, ranking second only to those of Constantia.

The Paarl is one of the oldest European towns in South Africa. It dates from 1687, the site for the new settlement being chosen by the governor, Simon van der Stell. It was named Paarl by the first settlers from the fancied resemblance of one of the boulders on the top of the hill, when glistening in the sun, to a gigantic pearl. Shortly afterwards several of the Huguenots who had sought refuge at the Cape after the revocation of the edict of Nantes were placed in the new settlement. The present inhabitants are largely descended from these Huguenots.

PABIANICE, a town of Russian Poland, in the government of Piotrkow, 30 m. N.W. of the town of Piotrkow, and 10 m. S.S.W. from Lodz-railway station. Pop. (1897), 18,251. It lies amidst extensive forests round the head-waters of the Nér, which were the hunting-grounds of the Polish kings. It has woollen, cloth and paper mills, and manufactures agricultural implements.

PABNA, or PUBNA, a town and district of British India, in the Rajshahi division of Eastern Bengal and Assam. The town is situated on the river Ichhamati, near the old bed of the Ganges. Pop. (1901), 18,424. The district of Pabna has an area of 1830 sq. m. Pop (1901), 1,420,461, showing an increase of 4·8% in the decade. It is bordered along its entire east face by the main stream of the Brahmaputra or Jamuna, and along its south-west

face by the Ganges or Padma. It is entirely of alluvial origin, the silt of the annual inundations overlying strata of clay on sand. Apart from the two great bordering rivers, it is intersected by countless water-channels of varying magnitude, so that during the rainy season every village is accessible by boat and by boat only. Almost the whole area is one green rice-field, the uniform level being broken only by clumps of bamboos and fruit-trees, which conceal the village sites. The district is a modern creation of British rule, being first formed out of Rajshahi district in 1832, and possesses no history of its own. The two staple crops are rice and jute. Sirajganj, on the Brahmaputra, is the largest mart for jute in Bengal. The Eastern Bengal railway cuts across the south-west corner of the district to Sara, where a bridge crosses the Ganges. The district was affected by the earthquake of the 12th of June 1897, which was most severely felt at Sirajganj.

PABST, FREDERICK (1836–1904), American brewer, was born at Nicholausreith, in Saxony, on the 28th of March 1836. In 1848 he emigrated with his parents to Chicago. There he became, first a waiter in an hotel, then a cabin-boy on a Lake Michigan steamer, and eventually captain of one of these vessels. In this last capacity he made the acquaintance of a German, Philip Best, the owner of a small but prosperous brewery at Milwaukee, and married his daughter. In 1862 Pabst was taken into partnership in his father-in-law's brewery, and set himself to work to study the details of the business. After obtaining a thorough mastery of the art of brewing, Pabst turned his attention to extending the market for the beer, and before long had raised the output of the Best brewery to 100,000 barrels a year. The brewery was eventually converted into a public company, and its capital repeatedly increased in order to cope with the continually increasing trade.

PACA, the Brazilian name for a large, heavily-built, short-tailed rodent mammal, easily recognized by its spotted fur. This rodent, *Coelogenys* (or *Agouti*) *paca*, together with one or two other tropical American species, represents a genus near akin to the agoutis and included in the family *Caviidae*. Pacas may be distinguished from agoutis by their heavier and more compact build, the longitudinal rows of light spots on the fur, the five-toed hind-feet, and the peculiar structure of the skull, in which the cheek-bones are expanded to form large capsules on the sides of the face, each enclosing a cavity opening on the side of the cheek. Their habits are very similar to those of agoutis, but when pursued they invariably take to the water. The young, of which seldom more than one is produced at a birth, remain in the burrows for several months. The flesh is eaten in Brazil. Males may be distinguished from females by the skull, in which the outer surface of the cheek-bones is roughened in the former and smooth in the latter sex. The paca-rana (*Dinomys branicki*), from the highlands of Peru, differs, among other features, by its well-developed tail and the arrangement of the spots. (See RODENTIA.)

PACATUS DREPANIUS, LATINUS (or LATINIUS), one of the Latin panegyrists, flourished at the end of the 4th century A.D. He probably came from Aginnum (Agen), in the south of France, in the territory of the Nitiobriges, and received his education in the rhetorical school of Burdigala (Bordeaux). He was the contemporary and intimate friend of Ausonius, who dedicated two of his minor works to Pacatus, and describes him as the greatest Latin poet after Virgil. Pacatus attained the rank of proconsul of Africa (A.D. 390) and held a confidential position at the imperial court. He is the author of an extant speech (ed. E. Bährens in *Panegyrici latini*, 1874, No. 12) delivered in the senate house at Rome (389) in honour of Theodosius I. It contains an account of the life and deeds of the emperor, the special subject of congratulation being the complete defeat of the usurper Maximus. The speech is one of the best of its kind. Though not altogether free from exaggeration and flattery, it is marked by considerable dignity and self-restraint, and is thus more important as an historical document than similar productions. The style is vivid, the language elegant but comparatively simple, exhibiting familiarity with the best classical literature. The writer of the panegyric must be distinguished from Drepanius Florus, deacon of Lyons (c. 850), author of some Christian poems and prose theological works.

See M. Schanz *Geschichte der römischen Litteratur* (1904), iv. I.

PACCHIA, GIROLAMO DEL, and PACCHIAROTTO (or PACCHIAROTTI), **JACOPO,** two painters of the Sienese school. One or other of them produced some good pictures, which used to pass as the performance of Perugino; reclaimed from Perugino, they were assigned to Pacchiarotto; now it is sufficiently settled that the good works are by G. del Pacchia, while nothing of Pacchiarotto's own doing transcends mediocrity. The mythical Pacchiarotto who worked actively at Fontainebleau has no authenticity.

Girolamo del Pacchia, son of a Hungarian cannon-founder, was born, probably in Siena, in 1477. Having joined a turbulent club named the Bardotti he disappeared from Siena in 1535, when the club was dispersed, and nothing of a later date is known about him. His most celebrated work is a fresco of the "Nativity of the Virgin," in the chapel of S Bernardino, Siena, graceful and tender, with a certain artificiality. Another renowned fresco, in the church of S Caterina, represents that saint on her visit to St Agnes of Montepulciano, who, having just expired, raises her foot by miracle. In the National Gallery of London there is a "Virgin and Child." The forms of G. del Pacchia are fuller than those of Perugino (his principal model of style appears to have been in reality Franciabigio); the drawing is not always unexceptionable; the female heads have sweetness and beauty of feature, and some of the colouring has noticeable force.

Pacchiarotto was born in Siena in 1474. In 1530 he took part in the conspiracy of the Libertini and Popolani, and in 1534 he joined the Bardotti. He had to hide for his life in 1535, and was concealed by the Observantine fathers in a tomb in the church of S Giovanni. He was stuffed in close to a new-buried corpse, and got covered with vermin and dreadfully exhausted by the close of the second day. After a while he resumed work; he was exiled in 1539, but recalled in the following year, and in that year or soon afterwards he died. Among the few extant works with which he is still credited is an "Assumption of the Virgin," in the Carmine of Siena. Other works rather dubiously attributed to him are in Siena, Buonconvento, Florence, Rome and London.

PACE, RICHARD (c. 1482–1536), English diplomatist, was educated at Winchester under Thomas Langton, at Padua, at Bologna, and probably at Oxford. In 1509 he went with Cardinal Christopher Bainbridge, archbishop of York, to Rome, where he won the esteem of Pope Leo X., who advised Henry VIII. to take him into his service. The English king did so, and in 1515 Pace became his secretary and in 1516 a secretary of state. In 1515 Wolsey sent him to urge the Swiss to attack France, and in 1519 he went to Germany to discuss with the electors the impending election to the imperial throne. He was made dean of St Paul's in 1519, and was also dean of Exeter and dean of Salisbury. He was present at the Field of the Cloth of Gold in 1520, and in 1521 he went to Venice with the object of winning the support of the republic for Wolsey, who was anxious at this time to become pope. At the end of 1526 he was recalled to England, and he died in 1536. His chief literary work was *De fructu* (Basel, 1517).

PACE (through O. Fr. *pas*, from Lat. *passus*, step, properly the stretch of the leg in walking, from *pandere*, to stretch), one movement of the leg in walking; hence used of the amount of ground covered by each single movement, or generally of the speed at which anything moves. The word is also used of a measure of distance, taken from the position of one foot to that of the other in making a single "pace," i.e. from 2½ ft. (the

military pace) to 1 yard. The Roman *passus* was reckoned from the position of the back foot at the beginning of the pace to the position of the same foot at the end of the movement, i.e. 5 Roman feet, 58·1 English inches, hence the Roman mile, *mille passus* = 1646 yards.

For pacing in horse-racing see HORSE-RACING.

PACHE, JEAN NICOLAS (1746–1823), French politician, was born in Paris, of Swiss parentage, the son of the *concierge* of the hôtel of Marshal de Castries. He became tutor to the marshal's children, and subsequently first secretary at the ministry of marine, head of supplies (*munitionnaire général des vivres*), and comptroller of the king's household. After spending several years in Switzerland with his family, he returned to France at the beginning of the Revolution. He was employed successively at the ministries of the interior and of war, and was appointed on the 20th of September 1793 third deputy *suppléant* of Paris by the Luxembourg section. Thus brought into notice, he was made minister of war in the following October. Pache was a Girondist himself, but aroused their hostility by his incompetence. He was supported, however, by Marat, and when he was superseded in the ministry of war by Beurnonville (Feb. 4, 1794) he was chosen mayor by the Parisians. In that capacity he contributed to the fall of the Girondists, but his relations with Hébert and Chaumette, and with the enemies of Robespierre led to his arrest on the 10th of May 1794. He owed his safety only to the amnesty of the 25th of October 1795. After acting as commissary to the civil hospitals of Paris in 1799, he retired from public life, and died at Thin-le-Moutier on the 18th of November 1823.

See L. Pierquin, *Mémoires sur Pache* ((Charleville, 1900).

PACHECO, FRANCISCO (1571–1654), Spanish painter and art historian, was born at Seville in 1571. Favourable specimens of his style are to be seen in the Madrid picture gallery, and also in two churches at Alcala de Guadaira near Seville. He attained great popularity, and about the beginning of the 17th century opened an academy of painting which was largely attended. Of his pupils by far the most distinguished was Velazquez, who afterwards became his son-in-law. From about 1625 he gave up painting and betook himself to literary society and pursuits; the most important of his works in this department is a treatise on the art of painting (*Arte de la pintura: su antiguedad y grandeza*, 1649), which is of considerable value for the information it contains on matters relating to Spanish art. He died in 1654.

PACHISI (Hindu *pachis*, twenty-five), the national table-game of India. In the palace of Akbar at Fatehpur Sikri the court of the zenana is divided into red and white squares, representing a pachisi-board, and here Akbar played the game with his courtiers, employing sixteen young slaves from his harem as living pieces. This was also done by the emperors of Delhi in their palace of Agra. A pachisi-board, which is usually embroidered on cloth, is marked with a cross of squares, each limb consisting of three rows of 8 squares, placed around a centre square. The outer rows each have ornaments on the fourth square from the end and the middle rows one on the end square, these ornamented squares forming "castles," in which pieces are safe from capture. The castles are so placed that from the centre square, or "home," whence all pieces start going down the middle row and back on the outside and then to the end of the next limb, will be exactly 25 squares, whence the name. Four players, generally two on a side, take part. The pieces, of which each player has four, are coloured yellow, green, red and black, and are entered, one at a time, from the centre and move down the middle row, then round the entire board and up the middle row again to the home square. The moves are regulated by six cowrie shells, which are thrown by hand down a slight incline. The throws indicate the number of squares a piece may move, as well as whether the player shall have a "grace," without which no piece, if taken, may be re-entered. A piece may be taken if another piece lands on the same square, unless the square be a castle. The object of each side is to get all eight pieces round and home before the opponents can do so.

See *Games, Ancient and Oriental*, by E. Falkner (London, 1892).

PACHMANN, VLADIMIR DE (1848-   ), Russian pianist, was born at Odessa, where his father was a professor at the university. He was educated in music at Vienna, and from 1869 to 1882 only rarely performed in public, being engaged in the meanwhile in assiduous study. He then obtained the greatest success, particularly as a player of Chopin, his brilliance of execution and rendering being no less remarkable than the playfulness of his platform manner.

PACHMARHI, a hill-station and sanatorium for British troops in the Central Provinces of India. Pop. (1901), 3020, rising to double that number in the season. It is situated at a height of 3500 ft. on a plateau of the Satpura hills in Hoshangabad district, 32 m. by road from Piparia station on the Great Indian Peninsula railway. Though not free from fever in the hot season, it affords the best available retreat for the Central Provinces.

PACHOMIUS, ST (292-346), Egyptian monk, the founder of Christian cenobitical life, was born, probably in 292, at Esna in Upper Egypt, of heathen parents. He served as a conscript in one of Constantine's campaigns, and on his return became a Christian (314); he at once went to live an eremitical life near Dendera by the Nile, putting himself under the guidance of an aged hermit. After three or four years he was called (by an angel, says the legend) to establish a monastery of cenobites, or monks living in common (see MONASTICISM, § 4). Pachomius spent his life in organizing and directing the great order he had created, which at his death included nine monasteries with some three thousand monks and a nunnery. The order was called Tabennesiot, from Tabennisi, near Dendera, the site of the first monastery. The most vivid account of the life and primitive rule is that given by Palladius in the Lausiac History, as witnessed by him (c. 410). Difficulties arose between Pachomius and the neighbouring bishops, which had to be composed at a synod at Esna. But St Athanasius was his firm friend and visited his monastery c. 330 and at a later period. Pachomius died (probably) in 346.

The best modern work on Pachomius is by P. Ladeuze, *Le Cénobitisme pakhomien* (1898). There have been differences of opinion in regard to the dates; those given above are Ladeuze's, now commonly accepted. The priority of the Greek *Life* of Pachomius over the Coptic may be said to be established; the historical character and value of this life are now fully recognized. A good analysis of all the literature is supplied in Herzog's *Realencyklopädie* (ed. 3). (E. C. B.)

PACHUCA, a city of Mexico and capital of the state of Hidalgo, 55 m. direct and 68 m. by rail N.N.E. of the city of Mexico. Pop. (1900), 37,487. Pachuca's railway connexions include the Mexican, the Hidalgo and the Mexican Oriental, besides which it has 5 m. of tramway line. The town stands in a valley of an inland range of the Sierra Madre Oriental, at an elevation over 8000 ft. above the sea, and in the midst of several very rich mineral districts—Atatonilco el Chico, Capula, Potosí, Real del Monte, Santa Rosa and Tepeneñé. It is said that some of these silver mines were known to the Indians before the discovery of America. Pachuca has some fine modern edifices, among which are the palace of justice, a scientific and literary institute, a school of mines and metallurgy, founded in 1877, a meteorological observatory and a public library. Mining is the chief occupation of its inhabitants, of whom about 7000 are employed underground. Electric power is derived from the Regla Falls, in the vicinity. The city's industrial establishments include smelting works and a large number of reduction works, among which are some of the largest and most important in the republic. It was here that Bartolomé de Medina discovered the "patio" process of reducing silver ores with quicksilver in 1557, and his old *hacienda de beneficio* is still to be seen. Pachuca was founded in 1534, some time after the mines were discovered. Here Pedro Romero de Terreros made the fortune in 1739 that enabled him to present a man-of-war to Spain and gain the title of Count of Regla. Pachuca was sacked in 1812, and so keen

xx. 8

was the desire to possess its sources of wealth, in common with other mining towns, that mining operations were partially suspended for a time and the mines were greatly damaged. In 1824 the Real del Monte mines were sold to an English company and became the centre of a remarkable mining speculation—the company ruining itself with lavish expenditures and discontinuing work in 1848. The mines in 1909 belonged to an American company.

PACHYMERES, GEORGIUS (1242-c. 1310), Byzantine historian and miscellaneous writer, was born at Nicaea, in Bithynia, where his father had taken refuge after the capture of Constantinople by the Latins in 1204. On their expulsion by Michael Palaeologus in 1261 Pachymeres settled in Constantinople, studied law, entered the church, and subsequently became chief advocate of the church (πρωτέκδικος) and chief justice of the imperial court (δικαιοφύλαξ). His literary activity was considerable, his most important work being a Byzantine history in 13 books, in continuation of that of Georgius Acropolita from 1261 (or rather 1255) to 1308, containing the history of the reigns of Michael and Andronicus Palaeologi. He was also the author of rhetorical exercises on hackneyed sophistical themes; of a *Quadrivium* (Arithmetic, Music, Geometry, Astronomy), valuable for the history of music and astronomy in the middle ages; a general sketch of Aristotelian philosophy; a paraphrase of the speeches and letters of Dionysius Areopagita; poems, including an autobiography; and a description of the Augusteum, the column erected by Justinian in the church of St Sophia to commemorate his victories over the Persians.

The *History* has been edited by I. Bekker (1835) in the *Corpus scriptorum hist. byzantinae*, also in J. P. Migne, *Patrologia graeca,* cxliii., cxliv.; for editions of the minor works see C. Krumbacher, *Geschichte der byzantinischen Litteratur* (1897).

PACIFIC BLOCKADE, a term invented by Hautefeuille, the French writer on International Maritime Law, to describe a blockade exercised by a great power for the purpose of bringing pressure to bear on a weaker state without actual war. That it is an act of violence, and therefore in the nature of war, is undeniable, seeing that it can only be employed as a measure of coercion by maritime powers able to bring into action such vastly superior forces to those the resisting state can dispose of that resistance is out of the question. In this respect it is an act of war, and any attempt to exercise it against a power strong enough to resist would be a commencement of hostilities, and at once bring into play the rights and duties affecting neutrals. On the other hand, the object and justification of a pacific blockade being to avoid war, that is general hostilities and disturbance of international traffic with the state against which the operation is carried on, rights of war cannot consistently be exercised against ships belonging to other states than those concerned. And yet, if neutrals were not to be affected by it, the coercive effect of such a blockade might be completely lost. Recent practice has been to limit interference with them to the extent barely necessary to carry out the purpose of the blockading powers.[1]

It is usual to refer to the intervention of France, England and Russia in Turkish affairs in 1827 as the first occasion on which the coercive value of pacific blockades was put to the test. Neutral vessels were not affected by it. This was followed by a number of other coercive measures described in the textbooks as pacific blockades. The first case, however, in which the operation was really a blockade, unaccompanied by hostilities, and which therefore can be properly called a "pacific blockade," was that which in 1837 Great Britain exercised against New Granada. A British subject and consul of the name of Russell was accused of stabbing a native of the country in a street brawl. He was arrested, and after being kept in detention for some months he was tried for the unlawful carrying of arms and

[1] There is always the alternative of making the blockade an act of war. This was done in 1902-3, when Great Britain, Germany and Italy proclaimed a blockade of certain ports of Venezuela and the mouths of the Orinoco. The blockade in this case was not pacific, but was war with all its consequences for belligerents and neutrals (see Foreign Office notice in *London Gazette* of December 20, 1902).

2a

sentenced to six years' imprisonment. The British government resented this treatment as "not only cruel and unjust towards Mr Russell, but disrespectful towards the British nation," and demanded the dismissal of the officials implicated and £1000 damages " as some compensation for the cruel injuries which had been inflicted upon Mr Russell" (State Papers, 1837–1838, p. 183). The New Granada government refused to comply with these demands, and the British representative, acting upon his instructions, called in the assistance of the West Indian fleet, but observed in his communication to the British naval officer in command that it was desirable to avoid hostilities, and to endeavour to bring about the desired result by a strict blockade only. This seems to be the first occasion on which it had occurred to anybody that a blockade without war might serve the purpose of war. This precedent was shortly afterwards followed by another somewhat similar case, in which from the 16th of April to the 28th of March 1838 to the 7th of November 1840 by the French the Mexican ports, to coerce the Mexican government into accept-ance of certain demands on behalf of French subjects who had suffered injury to their persons and damage to their property through insufficient protection by the Mexican authorities.

The blockade of Buenos Aires and the Argentine coast from the 28th of March 1838 to the 7th of November 1840 by the French fleet, a coercive measure consequent upon vexatious laws affect-ing foreign residents in the Argentine Republic, seems to have been the first case in which the operation was notified to the different representatives of foreign states. This notification was given in Paris, and at Buenos Aires, and to every ship approaching the blockaded places. This precedent of notifica-tion was, a few years later (1845), followed in another blockade against the same country by Great Britain and France, and in one in 1842 and 1844 by Great Britain against the port of Grey-town in Nicaragua. In 1850 Great Britain blockaded the ports of Greece in order to compel the Hellenic government to give satisfaction in the Don Pacifico case. Don Pacifico, a British subject, claimed £32,000 as damages for unprovoked pillage of his house by an Athenian mob. Greek vessels only were seized, and these were only sequestered. Greek vessels bona fide carry-ing cargoes belonging to foreigners were allowed to enter the blockaded ports.

Before the next case of blockade which can be described as "pacific" occurred came the Declaration of Paris (April 15, 1856), requiring that " blockades in order to be binding must be effective; that is to say, maintained by a force sufficient really to prevent access to the coast of the enemy."

Some ill-defined measures of blockade followed, such as that of 1860, when Victor Emmanuel, then king of Sardinia, joined the revolutionary government of Naples in blockading ports in Sicily, then held by the king of Naples, without any rupture of pacific relations between the two governments; that of 1861, in which Great Britain blockaded the port of Rio de Janeiro, to exact redress for pillage of an English vessel by the local popula-tion, at the same time declaring that she continued to be on friendly terms with the emperor of Brazil; and that in 1880, when a demonstration was made before the port of Dulcigno by a fleet of British, German, French, Austrian, Russian and Italian men-of-war, to compel the Turkish government to carry out the treaty conceding this town to Montenegro, and it was announced that if the town was not given up by the Turkish forces it would be blockaded.

The blockade which first gave rise to serious theoretical discussion on the subject was that instituted by France in 1884 in Chinese waters. On the 20th of October 1884 Admiral Courbet declared a blockade of all the ports and roadsteads between certain specified points of the island of Formosa. The British government protested that Admiral Coubert had not enough ships to render the blockade effective, and that it was therefore a violation of one of the articles of the Declaration of Paris of 1856; moreover, that the French government could only interfere with neutral vessels violating the blockade if there was a state of war. If a state of war existed, England as a neutral was bound to close her coaling stations to belligerents. The

British government held that in the circumstances France was waging war and not entitled to combine the rights of peace and warfare for her own benefit. Since then pacific blockades have only been exercised by the great powers as a joint measure in their common interest, which has also been that of peace; and in this respect the term is taking a new signification in accordance with the ordinary sense of the word " pacific."

In 1886 Greece was blockaded by Great Britain, Austria, Germany, Italy and Russia, to prevent her from engaging in war with Turkey, and thus forcing the powers to define their attitude towards the latter power. The instructions given to the British commander were to detain every ship under the Greek flag coming out of or entering any of the blockaded ports or harbours, or communicating with any ports within the limit blockaded; but if any parts of the cargo on board of such ships belonged to any subject or citizen of any foreign power other than Greece, and other than Austria, Germany, Italy and Russia, and had been shipped before notification of the blockade or after such notification, but under a charter made before the notifica-tion, such ship was not to be detained.

On the blockade of Crete in 1897 it was notified that " the admirals in command of the British, Austro-Hungarian, French, German, Italian, and Russian naval forces" had decided to put the island of Crete in a state of blockade, that " the blockade would be general for all ships under the Greek flag," and that " ships of the six powers or neutral powers may enter into the ports occupied by the powers and land their merchandise, but only if it is not for the Greek troops or the interior of the island," and that " these ships may be visited by the ships of the inter-national fleets."

Since the adoption of the Hague Convention of 1907 respecting the limitation of the employment of force for the recovery of contract debts, the contracting powers are under agreement " not to have recourse to armed force for the recovery of contract debts claimed from the government of one country by the govern-ment of another country as being due to its nationals," unless " the debtor state refuses or neglects to reply to an offer of arbitration, or after accepting the offer prevents any compromis from being agreed on, or after the arbitration fails to submit to the award " (Art. 1). Though this does not affect pacific blockades in principle, it supersedes them in practice by a new procedure for some of the cases in which they have hitherto been employed.   (T. Ba.)

PACIFIC OCEAN, the largest division of the hydrosphere, lying between Asia and Australia and North and South America. It is nearly landlocked to the N., communicating with the Arctic Ocean only by Bering Strait, which is 36 m. wide and of small depth. The southern boundary is generally regarded as the parallel of 40° S., but sometimes the part of the great Southern Ocean (40° to 66½° S.) between the meridians passing through South Cape in Tasmania and Cape Horn is included. The north to south distance from Bering Strait to the Antarctic circle is 9300 m., and the Pacific attains its greatest breadth, 10,000 m., at the equator. The coasts of the Pacific are of varied contour. The American coasts are for the most part mountainous and unbroken, the chief indentation being the Gulf of California; but the general type is departed from in the extreme north and south, the southern coast of South America consisting of bays and fjords with scattered islands, while the coast of Alaska is similarly broken in the south and becomes low and swampy towards the north. The coast of Australia is high and unbroken; there are no inlets of considerable size, although the small openings include some of the finest harbours in the world; as Moreton Bay and Port Jackson. The Asiatic coasts are for the most part low and irregular, and a number of seas are more or less completely enclosed and cut off from communi-cation with the open ocean. Bering Sea is bounded by the Alaskan Peninsula and the chain of the Aleutian Islands; the sea of Okhotsk is enclosed by the peninsula of Kamchatka and the Kurile Islands; the Sea of Japan is shut off by Sakhalin Island, the Japanese Islands and the peninsula of Korea; the Yellow Sea is an opening between the coast of China and Korea;

the China Sea lies between the Asiatic continent and the island of Formosa, the Philippine group, Palawan and Borneo. Amongst the islands of the Malay Archipelago are a number of enclosed areas—the Sulu, Celebes, Java, Banda and Arafura seas. The Arafura Sea extends eastwards to Torres Strait, and beyond the strait is the Coral Sea, bounded by New Guinea, the islands of Melanesia and north-eastern Australia.

The area and volume of the Pacific Ocean and its seas, with the mean depths calculated therefrom, are given in the article OCEAN.

Extent. The Pacific Ocean has one and three-quarter times the area of the Atlantic—the next largest division of the hydrosphere—and has more than double its volume of water. Its area is greater than the whole land surface of the globe, and the volume of its waters is six times that of all the land above sea-level. The total land area draining to the Pacific is estimated by Murray at 7,500,000 sq. m., or little more than one-fourth of the area draining to the Atlantic. The American rivers draining to the Pacific, except the Yukon, Columbia and Colorado, are unimportant. The chief Asiatic rivers are the Amur, the Hwang-ho and the Yangtsze-kiang: none of which enters the open Pacific directly. Hence the proportion of purely oceanic area to the total area is greater in the Pacific than in the Atlantic, the supply of detritus being smaller, and terrigenous deposits are not borne so far from land.

The bed of the Pacific is not naturally divided into physical regions, but for descriptive purposes the parts of the area lying *Relief of* east and west of 150° W. are conveniently dealt with *Bed.* separately. The eastern region is characterized by great uniformity of depth; the 2000-fathom line keeps close to the American coast except off the Isthmus of Panama, whence an ill-defined ridge of less than 2000 fathoms runs south-westwards, and again off the coast of South America in about 40° S., where a similar bank runs west and unites with the former. The bank then continues south to the Antarctic Ocean, in about 120° W. Practically the whole of the north-east Pacific is therefore more than 2000 fathoms deep, and the south-east has two roughly triangular spaces, including the greater part of the area, between 2000 and 3000 fathoms. Notwithstanding this great average depth, the " deeps " or areas over 3000 fathoms are small in number and extent. Five small deeps are recognized along a line close to the coast of South America and parallel to it, in the depression enclosed by the two banks mentioned—they extend from about 12° to 30° S.—and are named, from north to south, Milne-Edwards deep, Krümmel deep, Bartholomew deep, Richards deep and Haeckel deep. In the north-east the deeps are again few and small, but they are quite irregularly distributed, and not near the land. East of 150° W. the Pacific has few islands; the oceanic islands are volcanic, and coral formations are of course scanty. The most important group is the Galapagos Islands.

The western Pacific is in complete contrast to the part just described. Depths of less than 2000 fathoms occur continuously on a bank extending from south-eastern Asia, on which stands the Malay Archipelago. This bank continues southwards to the Antarctic Ocean, expanding into a plateau on which Australia stands, and a branch runs eastwards and then southwards from the north-east of Australia through New Zealand. The most considerable areas over 3000 fathoms are the Aldrich deep, an irregular triangle nearly as large as Australia, situated to the east of New Zealand, in which a sounding of 5155 fathoms was obtained by H.M.S. " Penguin," near the Tonga Islands: and the Tuscarora deep, a long, narrow trough running immediately to the east of Kamchatka, the Kurile Islands and Japan. A long strip within the Tuscarora deep forms the largest continuous area with a depth greater than 4000 fathoms. All the rest of the western Pacific is a region of quite irregular contour. The average depth varies from 1500 to 2500 fathoms, and from this level innumerable volcanic ridges and peaks rise almost or quite to the surface, their summits for the most part occupied by atolls and reefs of coral formation, while interspersed with these are depressions, mostly of small area, among which the deepest soundings recorded have been obtained. The United States telegraph ship " Nero," while surveying for a cable between Hawaii and the Philippines, sounded in 1900 the greatest depth yet known between Midway Islands and Guam (12° 43′ N., 145° 49′ E.) in 5269 fathoms, or almost exactly 6 m.

The following table, showing the area of the floor of the Pacific (to 40° S.) and the volume of water at different levels, is due to Sir J. Murray:—

Fathoms.	Areas. (sq. m.)	Volume. (cub. m.)
0–100	3,379,700	6,128,500
100–500	1,753,450	23,348,350
500–1000	1,707,650	28,323,700
1000–2000	6,902,550	52,628,500
2000–3000	39,621,550	32,545,400
3000–4000	2,164,150	1,357,900
over 4000	94,850	70,600
	55,623,900	144,402,950

So far as our knowledge goes, the present contours of the open Pacific Ocean are almost as they were in Palaeozoic times, and in the intervening ages changes of level and form have been slight. There is no reason to suppose that any considerable part of the vast area now covered by the waters of the Pacific has ever been exposed as dry land. Hence the Pacific basin may be regarded as a stable and homogeneous geographical unit, clearly marked off round nearly all its margin by steep abrupt slopes, extending in places through the whole known range of elevation above sea-level and of depression below it—from the Cordilleras of South America to the island chains of Siberia and Australia. (See OCEAN.)

The deeper parts of the bed of the Pacific are covered by deposits of red clay, which occupies an area estimated at no less than 105,672,000 sq. kilometres, or three-fifths of the *Deposits.* whole. Over a large part of the central Pacific, far removed from any possible land-influences or deposits of ooze, the red-clay region is characterized by the occurrence of manganese, which gives the clay a chocolate colour, and manganese nodules are found in vast numbers, along with sharks' teeth and the ear-bones and other bones of whales. Radiolarian ooze is found in the central Pacific in a region between 15° N. to 10° S. and 140° E. to 150° W., occurring in seven distinct localities, and covering an area of about 3,007,000 sq. kilometres. The " Challenger " discovered an area of radiolarian ooze between 7°-12° N. and 147°-152° W., and another in 2°-10° S., 152°-153° W. Between these two areas, almost on the equator, a strip of globigerina ooze was found, corresponding to the zone of globigerina in the equatorial region of the Atlantic. Globigerina ooze covers considerable areas in the intermediate depths of the west and south Pacific—west of New Zealand, and along the parallel of 40° S., between 80°-98° W. and 150°-118° W.—but this deposit is not known in the north-eastern part of the basin. The total area covered by it is estimated at 38,332,000 sq. kilometres—about two-thirds of that in the Atlantic. Pteropod ooze occurs only in the neighbourhood of Fiji and other islands of the western Pacific, passing up into fine coral sands and mud. Diatom ooze has been found in detached areas between the Philippine and Mariana islands, and near the Aleutian and Galapagos groups, forming an exception to the general rule of its occurrence only in high latitudes. All the enclosed seas are occupied by characteristic terrigenous deposits.

Partly on account of its great extent, and partly because there is no wide opening to the Arctic regions, the normal wind circulation is on the whole less modified in the North Pacific than in *Meteoro-* the Atlantic, except in the west, where the south-west *logy.* monsoon of southern Asia controls the prevailing winds. Its influence extending eastwards to 145° E., near the Ladrones, and southwards to the equator. In the South Pacific the north-west monsoon of Australia affects a belt running east of New Guinea to the Solomon Islands. In the east the north-east trade-belt extends between 5° and 25° N.; the south-east trade crosses the equator, and its mean southern limit is 25° S. The trade-winds are generally weaker and less persistent in the Pacific than in the Atlantic, and the intervening belt of equatorial calms is broader. Except in the east of the Pacific, the south-east trade is only fully developed during the southern winter; at other seasons the regular trade-belt is cut across from north-west to south-east by a band twenty to thirty degrees wide, in which the trades alternate with winds from north-east and north, and with calms, the calms prevailing chiefly at the boundary of the monsoon region (5° N.-15° S., 160°-185° E.). This area, in which the south-east trade is interrupted, includes the Fiji, Navigator and Society groups, and the Paumotus. In the Marquesas group the trade-wind is constant. Within the southern monsoon region there is a gradual transition to the north-west monsoon of New Guinea in low latitudes, and in higher latitudes to the north-east wind of the Queensland coast. The great warming and abundant rainfall of the island regions of the western Pacific, and the low temperature of the surface water in the east, cause a displacement of the southern tropical maximum of pressure to the east; hence we have a permanent " South Pacific anticyclone " close to the coast of South America. The characteristic feature of the south-western Pacific is therefore the relatively low pressure and the existence of a true monsoon region in the middle of the trade-wind belt. It is to be noted that the climate of the islands of the Pacific becomes more and more healthy the farther they are from the monsoon region. The island regions of the Pacific are everywhere characterized by uniform high air-temperatures; the mean annual range varies from 1° to 9° F., with extremes of 24° to 27°, and the diurnal range from 9° to 16°. In the monsoon region relative humidity is high, viz. 80 to 90 %. The rainfall is abundant; in the western island-groups there is no well-marked rainy season, but over the whole region the greater part of the rainfall takes place during the southern summer, even as far north as Hawaii. In the trade-wind region we find the characteristic heavy rainfall on the weather sides of the islands, and a shorter rainy season at the season of highest sun on the lee side. Buchan describes the island-studded portion of the western Pacific as the most extensive region of the globe characterized by an unusually heavy rainfall. Beyond the tropical high-pressure belt, the winds of the North Pacific are under the control of an area of low pressure, which, however, attains neither the size nor the intensity of the " Iceland " depression in the north

Atlantic. The result is that north-westerly winds, which in winter are exceedingly dry and cold, blow over the western or Asiatic area; westerly winds prevail in the centre, and south-westerly and southerly winds off the American coast. In the southern hemisphere there is a transition to the low-pressure belt encircling the Southern Ocean, in which westerly and north-westerly winds continue all the year round.

The distribution of temperature in the waters of the Pacific Ocean has been fully investigated, so far as is possible with the existing **Temperature.** observations, by G. Schott. At the surface an extensive area of maximum temperature (over 20° C.) occurs over 10° on each side of the equator to the west of the ocean. On the eastern side temperature falls to 22° on the equator and is slightly higher to N. and S. In the North Pacific, beyond lat. 40°, the surface is generally warmer on the E. than on the W., but this condition is, on the whole, reversed in corresponding southern latitudes. In the intermediate levels, down to depths not exceeding 1000 metres, a remarkable distribution appears. A narrow strip of cold water runs along the equator, widest to the east and narrowing westward, and separates two areas of maximum which have their greatest intensity in the western part of the ocean, and have their central portions in higher latitudes as depth increases, apparently tending constantly to a position in about latitude 30° to 35° N. and S. A comparison of this distribution with that of atmospheric pressure is of great interest. High temperature in the depth may be taken to mean descending water, just as high atmospheric pressure means descending air, and hence it would seem that the slow vertical movement of water in the Pacific reproduces to some extent the phenomena of the "doldrums" and "horse latitudes," with this difference, that the centres of maximum intensity lie off the east of the land instead of the west as in the case of the continents. The isothermal lines, in fact, suggest that in the vast area of the Pacific something corresponding to the "planetary circulation" is established, further investigation of which may be of extreme value in relation to current inquiries concerning the upper air. In the greater depths temperature is extraordinarily uniform, 80% of the existing observations falling within the limits of 1·6° C. and 1·9° C. In the enclosed seas of the western Pacific, temperature usually falls till a depth corresponding to that of the summit of the barriers which isolate them from the open ocean is reached, and below that point temperature is uniform to the bottom. In the Sulu Sea, for example, a temperature of 10·3° C. is reached at 400 fathoms, and this remains constant to the bottom in 2500 fathoms.

The surface waters of the North Pacific are relatively fresh, the salinity being on the whole much lower than in the other great **Salinity.** oceans. The saltest waters are found along a belt extending westwards from the American coast on the Tropic of Cancer to 160° E., then turning southwards to the equator. North of this salinity diminishes steadily, especially to the north-west, the Sea of Okhotsk showing the lowest salinity observed in any part of the globe. South and east of the axis mentioned salinity becomes less to just north of the equator, where it increases again, and the saltest waters of the whole Pacific are found, as we should expect, in the south-east trade-wind region, the maximum occurring in about 18° S. and 120° W. South of the Tropic of Capricorn the isohalines run nearly east and west, salinity diminishing quickly to the Southern Ocean. The bottom waters have almost uniformly a salinity of 34·8 per mille, corresponding closely with the bottom waters of the South Atlantic, but fresher than those of the North Atlantic.

The surface currents of the Pacific have not been studied in the same detail as those of the Atlantic, and their seasonal variations **Circulation.** are little known except in t e monsoon regions. Speaking generally, however, it may be said that they are for the most part under the direct control of the prevailing winds. The North Equatorial Current is due to the action of the north-east trades. It splits into two parts east of the Philippines, one division flowing northwards as the Kuro Siwo or Black Stream, the analogue of the Gulf Stream, to feed a drift circulation which follows the winds of the North Pacific, and finally forms the Californian Current flowing southwards along the American coast. Part of this rejoins the North Equatorial Current, and part probably forms the variable Mexican Current, which follows the coasts of Mexico and California close to the land. The Equatorial Counter-Current flowing eastwards is largely assisted during the latter half of the year by the south-west monsoon, and from July to October the south-west winds prevailing east of 150° E. further strengthen the current, but later in the year the easterly winds weaken or even destroy it. The South Equatorial Current is produced by the south-east trades, and is more vigorous than its northern counterpart. On reaching the western Pacific part of this current passes southwards, east of New Zealand, and again east of Australia, as the East Australian Current, part northwards to join the Equatorial Counter-Current, and during the north-east monsoon part makes its way through the China Sea towards the Indian Ocean. During the south-west monsoon this last branch is reversed, and the surface waters of the China Sea probably unite with the Kuro Siwo. Between the Kuro Siwo and the Asiatic coast a band of cold water, with a slight movement to the southward, known as the Oya Siwo, forms the analogue of the "Cold Wall" of the Atlantic. In the higher

latitudes of the South Pacific the surface movement forms part of the west wind-drift of the Roaring Forties. On the west coast of South America the cold waters of the Humboldt or Peruvian Current corresponding to the Benguela Current of the South Atlantic, make their way northwards, ultimately joining the South Equatorial Current. The surface circulation of the Pacific is, on the whole, less active than that of the Atlantic. The centres of the rotational movement are marked by "Sargasso Seas" in the north and south basins, but they are of small extent compared with the Sargasso Sea of the North Atlantic. From the known peculiarities of the distribution of temperature, it is probable that definite circulation of water is in the Pacific confined to levels very near the surface, except in the region of the Kuro Siwo, and possibly also in parts of the Peruvian Current. The only movement in the depths is the slow creep of ice-cold water northwards along the bottom from the Southern Ocean; but this is more marked, and apparently penetrates farther north, than in the Atlantic.

See *Reports* of expeditions of the U.S.S. "Albatross" and "Thetis," 1888–1891; A. Agassiz, *Expedition to the Tropical Pacific*, 1899–1900, 1904–1905; H.M.S. "Challenger," 1873–1876; "Egeria" 1888–1889 and 1899; "Elisabeth," 1877; "Gazelle," 1875–1876; "Planet," 1906; "Penguin," 1891–1903; "Tuscarora," 1873–1874; "Vettor Pisani," 1884; "Vitraz," 1887–1888; also observations of surveying and cable ships, and special papers in the *Annalen der Hydrographie* (for distribution of temperature see G. Schott, p. 2, 1910).

(H. N. D.)

ISLANDS OF THE PACIFIC OCEAN

Up to a certain point, the islands of the Pacific fall into an obvious classification, partly physical, partly political. In the west there is the great looped chain which fringes the east coast of Asia, and with it encloses the series of seas which form parts of the ocean. The north of the chain, from the Kuriles to Formosa, belongs to the empire of Japan; southward it is continued by the Philippines (belonging to the United States of America) which link it with the vast archipelago between the Pacific and Indian oceans, to which the name Malay Archipelago is commonly applied. As the loop of the Kuriles depends from the southern extremity of Kamchatka, so from the east of the same peninsula another loop extends across the northern part of the ocean to Alaska, and helps to demarcate the Bering Sea; this chain is distinctly broken to the east of the Commander Islands, but is practically continuous thereafter under the name of the Aleutian Islands. Islands form a much less important feature of the American Pacific coast than of the Asiatic; between 48° N. and 38° S. there are practically none, and to the north and south of these parallels respectively the islands, though large and numerous, are purely continental, lying close under the mainland, enclosing no seas, and forming no separate political units. South-eastward of the Malay Archipelago lies "the largest island and the smallest continent," Australia; eastward of the archipelago, New Guinea, the largest island if Australia be regarded as a continent only. With Australia may be associated the islands lying close under its coasts, including Tasmania. Next follow the two great islands and attendant islets of New Zealand.

There now remains a vast number of small islands which lie chiefly (but not entirely) within an area which may be defined as extending from the Philippines, New Guinea and Australia to 130° W., and from tropic to tropic. These islands fall principally into a number of groups clearly enough defined to be well seen on a map of small scale; they are moreover divided, as will be shown, into three main divisions; but whereas they have enough characteristics in common to render a general view of them desirable, there is no well-recognized name to cover them all. The name Polynesia was formerly taken to do so, but belongs properly to one of the three main divisions, to which the name Eastern Polynesia was otherwise given; Oceania and Oceanica are variants of another term which has been used for the same purpose, though by no means generally. Moreover usage varies slightly as regards the limits of the three main divisions, but the accompanying table shows the most usual classification, naming the principal groups within each, and distributing them according to the powers to which they are subject.

The following islands may be classified as oceanic, but not with any of the three main divisions: the Bonin Islands, north of the Marianas; belonging to Japan; Lord Howe and Norfolk Islands (to

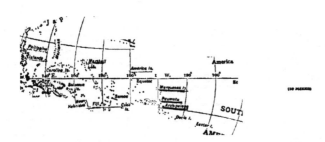

(10 MILES)

New South Wales); Easter Island (to Chile); the Galapagos islands (to Ecuador). In an area to be defined roughly as lying about the Tropic of Cancer, between Hawaii and the Bonin Islands, there are scattered a few small islands and reels, of most of which the position, if not the existence, is doubtful. Such are Patrocinio (about 28° 30′ N., 177° 18′ E.) and Ganges (30° 47′ N., 154° 15′ E.), among others which appear on most maps. Marcus Island, in 23° 10′ N., 154° E., was annexed by Japan in 1899 with a view to its becoming a cable station.

The following paragraphs review the oceanic islands generally, and are therefore concerned almost entirely with the central and mid-western parts of the ocean. It is impossible to estimate the total number of the islands; an atoll, for instance, which may

slate in the Marquesas, which afford a type of the extinct volcanic islands, as does Tahiti. In other areas, however, there is still volcanic activity, and in many cases volcanoes to which only tradition attributes eruptions can hardly be classified as extinct. Hawaii contains the celebrated active crater of Kilauea. In Tonga, in the New Hebrides, and in the long chain of the Solomons and the Bismarck Archipelago there is much activity. Submarine vents sometimes break forth, locally raising the level of the sea-bottom, or even forming temporary islands or shoals. Earthquakes are not uncommon in the volcanic areas. Most of the volcanic islands are lofty in proportion to their size. The peaks or sharp cones in which they

ISLANDS OF THE PACIFIC OCEAN

	MELANESIA.	Area, sq. m.	Pop.	MICRONESIA.	Area, sq. m.	Pop.	POLYNESIA.	Area, sq. m.	Pop.
To Great Britain.	Fiji	7,435	121,000	Gilbert Island	166	30,000	America Islands	260	300
	Louisiade Archip.	850	5,000				Cook Islands[1].	111	6,200
	Santa Cruz Island	380	5,000				Ellice Islands[1].	14	2,400
	Solomon Islands (part)	12,800	135,000				Manihiki Islands.	12	1,000
							Niué	36	4,000
							Phoenix Islands	16	60
							Pitcairn	2	170
							Tokelau Islands	7	500
							Tonga Islands.	385	19,000
Total, British		21,465	266,000		166	30,000		843	33,630
To United States of America				Guam	200	9,000	Hawaii	6,651	154,000
							Samoa (part).	95	6,000
Total, U.S.A.		—	—		200	9,000		6,746	160,000
To France	Loyalty Island	1,050	20,000				Marquesas Islands	490	4,300
	New Caledonia	6,450	52,000				Paumotu Archip.	364	5,000
							Society Islands	637	18,500
							Tubuai Islands	110	2,000
							Wallis Archip.	49	4,500
Total, French		7,500	72,000		—	—		1,641	34,300
To Germany.	Bismarck Archip.	20,000	188,000	Caroline Islands	380	36,000	Samoa (part).	985	33,000
	Solomon Islands (part)	4,200	45,000	Mariana Islands (excl. Guam)	245	2,500			
				Marshall Islands	160	15,000			
				Pelew Islands	175	3,100			
Total, German		24,200	233,000		960	56,600		985	33,000
	New Hebrides[2]	5,106	50,600						
TOTAL	Melanesia	58,271	621,600	Micronesia	1,326	95,600	Polynesia	10,215	260,930

The above figures give a total land area for the whole region of 69,561 sq. m., with a population of 978,130; but they are for the most part merely approximate.

be divided into a large number of islets, often bears a single name. The number of names of islands and separate groups in the *Index to the Islands of the Pacific* (W. T. Brigham), which covers the limited area under notice, is about 2650, exclusive of alternative names. Of these, it may be mentioned, there is a vast number, owing in some cases to divergence of spelling in the representation of native names, in others to European discoverers naming islands (sometimes twice or thrice successively) of which the native names subsequently came into use also.

The islands may be divided broadly into volcanic and coral islands, though the physiography of many islands is imperfectly known. There are ancient rocks, however, in New Caledonia, which has a geological affinity with New Zealand; old sedimentary rocks are known in New Pomerania, besides granite and porphyry, and slates, sandstone and chalk occur in Fiji, as well as young volcanic rocks. Along with these, similarly, hornblende and diabase occur in the Pelew Islands and gneiss and mica

[1] These are dependencies of New Zealand, as are also the following islands and groups which lie apart from the main Polynesian clusters, nearer New Zealand itself: Antipodes Islands, Auckland Islands, Bounty Islands, Campbell Islands, Chatham Islands, Kermadec Islands.
[2] Under British and French influence jointly.

frequently culminate, combined with the rich characteristic vegetation, are the principal features which have led all travellers to extol the beauty of the islands.

In the central and western Pacific the northern and southern limits of the reef-forming corals are approximately 30° N. and 30° S. It may be added that this belt narrows greatly towards the east, mainly from the south, in sympathy with the northward flow of cold water off the coast of South America. But apart from this the limits are seen to accord fairly closely with the geographical definition of the area under consideration. Here the broad distinction has been drawn between volcanic and coral islands; but this requires amplification, both because the coral islands follow more than one type, and because the volcanic islands in the form of fringing or barrier reefs. As to the distribution of coral reefs within the Pacific area, in Micronesia the northern Marianas (volcanic) are without reefs, which, however, are well developed in the south. The Pelew islands have extensive reefs, and the Caroline, Marshall and Gilbert islands are almost entirely coral. In Melanesia, as has been seen, the volcanic type predominates. Coral reefs occur round many of the islands (e.g. the Louisiade and Admiralty groups, New Caledonia and Fiji), but in some cases they are wholly absent or nearly so (e.g. the eastern Solomon Islands and the New Hebrides). Of the Polynesian Islands, the Hawaiian chain presents the type of a volcanic group through which coral reefs are not equally distributed. The main island of Hawaii and Maui at the east end are practically without reefs; which, however, are abundant farther west. Round the volcanic Marquesas Islands, again, coral is scanty, but the Society Islands, Samoa and Tonga have extensive reefs. The various minor groups to the north of these (Ellice, Phoenix, Union, Manihiki and the America Islands) are coral islands. Christmas, one of the last-named, is reputed to be the largest lagoon island in the Pacific. The Paumotu Archipelago is the most extensive of the coral groups.

The coral islands are generally of the form well known under the name of atoll, rising but slightly above sea-level, flat, and generally of annular form, enclosing a lagoon. Often, as has been said, the atoll is divided into a number of islets, but in some smaller atolls the ring is complete, and the sea-water gains access beneath the surface of the reef to the lagoon within, where it is sometimes seen to spout up at the rise of the tide. Besides the atolls there is a type of island which has been called the elevated coral island. The Loyalty Islands exhibit this type, in which former reefs appear as low cliffs, elevated above the sea, and separated from it by a level coastal tract. The island of Maré shows evidence of three such elevations, three distinct cliffs alternating with level tracts. For the much debated question as to the conditions under which atolls and reefs are formed, see CORAL REEFS. As to the local distribution of reefs, it has been maintained that in the case of active volcanic islands which have no reefs, their absence is due to subterranean heat. The contour of the sea-bed, however, has been shown to influence this distribution, the continuation of the slope of a steep shore beneath the sea being adverse to their formation, whereas on a gentler slope they may be formed.

Flora.—In considering the flora of the islands it is necessary to distinguish between the rich vegetation of the fertile volcanic islands and the poor vegetation of the coral islands. Those plants which are generally distributed are generally found to be propagated from seeds which can easily be carried by the wind or by ocean currents, or form the food of migratory birds. The tropical Asiatic element predominates on the low lands; the es characteristic of Australia and New Zealand occur principally on the upper parts of the high islands. In Hawaii there are instances of American elements. In the volcanic islands a distinction may be observed between the windward and leeward flanks, the moister windward slopes being the more richly clothed. But almost everywhere the vegetation serves to smooth the contours of the rugged hills, ferns, mosses and shrubs growing wherever their roots can cling, and leaving only the steepest crags uncovered to form, as in Tahiti, a striking contrast. The flora is estimated to include 15% of ferns, but they form only the most important group among many plants of beautiful foliage, such as dracaenas and crotons. Flowering plants are numerous, and the natives often (as in Hawaii) greatly appreciate flowers, which thus add a feature to the picturesqueness of island-life, though they do not usually grow in great profusion. Fruits are abundant, though indigenous fruits are few; the majority have been introduced by missionaries and others. Oranges are often plentiful, also pine-apples, guavas, custard-apples, mangoes and bananas. These last are of special importance, and the best kind, the Chinese banana, is said to have sprung from a plant given to the missionary John Williams, and cultivated in Samoa. The natives live very largely on vegetable food, among the most important plants which supply them being the taro, yam, banana, bread-fruit, arrow-root, pandanus and coco-nut. The last constitutes a valuable article of commerce in the form of copra, from which palm oil is expressed; the natives make use of this oil in made dishes, and also of the soft half-green kernel and the coco-nut "milk," the clear liquid within the nut. Their well-known drink, kava, is made from a variety of pepper-plant. The most characteristic trees are the coco-nut palm, pandanus and mangrove. The low coral islands suffer frequently from drought; their soil is sandy and unproductive, and in some cases the natives attempt cultivation by excavating trenches and fertilizing them with vegetable and other refuse.

Fauna.—The indigenous fauna of the islands is exceedingly poor in mammals, which are represented mainly by rats and bats. Pigs have been held to be indigenous on some islands, but were doubtless introduced by early navigators. Cattle and horses, where introduced, are found to degenerate rather rapidly unless the supply of fresh stock is kept up. Birds are more numerous than mammals,

among the most important kinds being the pigeons and doves, especially the fruit-eating pigeons. Megapodes are found in the Solomon Islands, the New Hebrides, Samoa, Tonga, the Carolines and the Marianas. The remarkable *didunculus* occurs in Samoa, and after the introduction of cats and rats, which preyed upon it, was compelled to change its habits dwelling in trees instead of on the ground. Insect life is rich in northern Melanesia; in southern Melanesia it is less so; in Fiji numerous kinds of insects occur, while individual numbers are small. In the rest of the islands the insect fauna is poor. But if this is true of the land fauna as a whole, especially on the atolls, where it consists mainly of a few birds, lizards and insects, the opposite is the case with the marine fauna. Fish are exceedingly abundant, especially in the lagoons of atolls, and form an important article of food supply for the natives, who are generally expert fishermen. The fish fauna of the islands is especially noted for the gorgeous colouring of many of the species. Among marine mammals, the dugong occurs in the parts about New Guinea and the Caroline Islands. Various sorts of whale are found, and the whaling industry reached the height of its importance about the middle of the 19th century. In considering the marine fauna the remarkable *palolo* or *balolo* should be mentioned. This annelid propagates its kind by rising to the surface and dividing itself. The occurrence of this process can be predicted exactly for one day, before sunrise, in October and November, and as both the worm and the fish which prey on it are appreciated by the natives as food the occasions of its appearance are of great importance to them.

History.—Not long after the death of Columbus, and when the Portuguese traders, working from the west, had hardly reached the confines of the Malay Archipelago, the Spaniard Vasco Nuñez de Balboa crossed America at its narrowest part and discovered the great ocean to the west of it (1513). The belief in the short and direct westward passage from Europe to the East Indies was thus shaken, but it was still held that some passage was to be found, and in 1519-1521 Fernão de Magalhães (Magellan) made the famous voyage in which he discovered the strait which bears his name. Sailing thence north-westward for many weeks, over a sea so calm that he named it *El Mar pacifico*, he sighted only two small islands. These may have been Puka Puka of the Tuamotu Archipelago and Flint Island; but it may be stated here that the identification of islands sighted by the early explorers is often a matter of conjecture, and that therefore some islands of which the definite discovery must be dated much later had in fact been seen by Europeans at this early period. In this narrative the familiar names of islands are used, irrespective of whether they were given by the first or later discoverers, or are native names. Magellan reached the "Ladrones" (MARIANAS) in 1521, and voyaged thence to the Philippines, where he was killed in a local war. In 1522-1524 various voyages of discovery were made on the west coast of America, partly in the hope of finding a strait connecting the two oceans to the region of the central isthmus. In 1525-1527 Garcia Jofre de Loaysa sailed to the Moluccas, but, like Magellan, missed the bulk of the oceanic islands. About this time, however, the Portuguese sighted the north coast of New Guinea. Fuller knowledge of this coast was acquired by Alvaro de Saavedra (1527-1529), and among later voyages those of Ruy Lopez de Villalobos (1542-1545) and Miguel Lopez de Legaspi (1564-1565) should be mentioned. These, however, like others of the period, did not greatly extend the knowledge of the Pacific islands, for the course between the Spanish American and Asiatic possessions did not lead voyagers among the more extensive archipelagoes. For the same reason the British and Dutch fleets which sailed with the object of harrying the Spaniards, under Sir Francis Drake (1577-1580), Thomas Cavendish (1586-1593) and Oliver van Noort (1598-1601), were not, as regards the Pacific, of prime geographical importance. But the theory of the existence of a great southern continent was now also attracting voyagers. Alvaro Mendaña de Neyra, after crossing a vast extent of ocean from Peru and sighting only one island, probably in the Ellice group, reached the Solomon Islands. In 1595-1596 he made a second voyage, and though he did not again reach these islands, the development of which was his objective, he discovered the Marquesas Islands, and afterwards Santa Cruz, where, having attempted to found a settlement, he died. Thereafter his pilot, Pedro Fernandez de Quiros, set out with the remainder of the company to make for the Philippines, and on the way discovered Ponape of the Caroline Islands, some of which group, however, had been known to the Portuguese as early as 1527. Quiros returned to Europe, and, obtaining command of a fleet, made a voyage in 1605-1607 during which he observed some of the Paumotu and Society Islands, and later discovered the small Duff group of the Santa Cruz Islands, passing thence to the main island of the New Hebrides, which he hailed as his objective, the southern continent. One of his commanders, Luis Vaes de Torres, struck off to the north-west, coasted along the south of the Louisiade Archipelago and New Guinea, traversed the strait which bears his name between New Guinea and Australia, and reached the Philippines. In 1615-1617 two Dutchmen, Jacob Lemaire and Willem Cornelis Schouten, having in view both the discovery of the southern continent and the possibility of establishing relations with the East Indies from the east, took a course which brought them to the north part of the Paumotu Archipelago, thence to part of the Tonga chain, and ultimately to New Pomerania, after which they reached the East Indies. In 1642-1643 Abel Tasman, working from the east, discovered Van Diemen's Land (Tasmania) and the west coast of New Zealand, subsequently reaching the Tonga Islands. Now for a while the tide of discovery slackened. Towards the close of the century the buccaneers extended their activity to the Pacific, but naturally added little to general knowledge. William Dampier, however, making various voyages in 1690-1705, explored the coasts of Australia and New Guinea, and at the opening of the century both the French and the Dutch showed some activity. The Dutchman Jacob Roggeveen, in the course of a voyage round the world in 1721-1722, crossed the Pacific from east to west, and discovered Easter Island, some of the northern islands of the Paumotu Archipelago, and (as is generally supposed) a part of the Samoan group. The voyage of Commodore George (afterwards Lord) Anson in 1740-1744 was for purposes rather of war than of exploration, and Commodore John Byron's voyage in 1765 had little result beyond gaining some additional knowledge of the Paumotu Archipelago.

It is about this time that what may be called the period of rediscovery set in fully. In the ensuing account a constant repetition of the names of the main archipelagoes will be found; it may of course be assumed that each successive voyager added something to the knowledge of them, but on the other hand, as has been said, islands were often rediscovered and renamed in cases where later voyagers took no account of the work of their predecessors, or where the earlier voyagers were unable clearly to define the positions of their discoveries. Moreover, rivalry between contemporary explorers of different nationalities sometimes caused them to ignore each other's work, and added to the confusion of nomenclature among the islands.

In 1767 Samuel Wallis worked through the central part of the Paumotus, and visited Tahiti and the Marianas, while his companion Philip Carteret discovered Pitcairn, and visited Santa Cruz, the Solomons and New Pomerania. The French were now taking a share in the work of discovery, and in 1768 Louis Antoine de Bougainville sailed by way of the central Paumotus, the Society Islands, Samoa, the northern New Hebrides, the south coast of New Guinea and the Louisiade and Bismarck archipelagoes. The next voyages in chronological order are those of the celebrated Captain James Cook (q.v.). Within the limits of the area under notice, his first voyage (1769) included visits to Tahiti and the Society group generally, to New Zealand and to the east coast of Australia, his second (1773-1774) to New Zealand, the Paumotu Archipelago, the Society Islands, Tonga and subsequently Easter Island, the Marquesas and the New Hebrides; and his third (1777-1778) to Tonga, the Cook or Norway group, and the Hawaiian Islands, of which, even if they were previously known to the Spaniards, he may be called the discoverer, and where he was subsequently killed. In 1786 Jean François Galoup de La Pérouse, in the course of the famous voyage from which he never returned, visited Easter Island, Samoa and Tonga. The still more famous voyage of William Bligh of the "Bounty" (1788) was followed by that of Captain Edwards of the "Pandora" (1791), who in the course of his

search for Bligh discovered Rotumah and other islands. The Hawaiian Islands came within the purview of George Vancouver, following the course of Cook in 1791. In 1792-1793 Joseph Antoine d'Entrecasteaux, searching for traces of La Pérouse, ranged the islands west of Tonga. In 1797 Captain J. Wilson of the missionary ship "Duff" visited the Society group, Fiji, Tonga and the Marquesas, and added to the knowledge of the Paumotu and Caroline Islands. Another power entered on the field of exploration when the Russians sent Adam Ivan Krusenstern to the Pacific (1803). He was followed by Otto von Kotzebue (1816) and Fabian Gottlieb von Bellingshausen (1819-1821). The work of these three was carried out principally in the easternmost part of Polynesia. In 1818-1819 the French navigator Louis Claude Desaulses de Freycinet ranged from New Guinea through the Marianas to Hawaii. Two of his countrymen followed him in 1823-1829—Louis Isidore Duperrey and Dumont d'Urville. Kotzebue made a second voyage, accompanied by scientists, in 1823-1826. In 1826-1828 Frederick William Beechey was at work in the middle parts of the ocean, and Feodor Petrovich Count Lütke, the Russian circumnavigator, in the northern. In 1834 Dr Debell Bennett made scientific researches in the Society, Hawaiian and Marquesas Islands, in 1835 Captain Robert Fitzroy was accompanied by Charles Darwin, and in 1836 sqq., Abel Aubert du Petit-Thouars was carrying on the work of the French in the Pacific. During his voyage of 1837-1840, Dumont d'Urville was again in Polynesia, working westward from the Paumotu and Marquesas Islands by Fiji and the Solomon, Loyalty and Louisiade groups to New Guinea. In 1839 sqq. the first important American expedition was made under Charles Wilkes, who covered a great extent of the ocean from Hawaii to Tonga, Fiji and New Zealand. Among later British explorers may be mentioned Captain J. Elphinstone Erskine (1849) and Captain H. M. Denham, and several important voyages for scientific research were made in the second half of the 19th century, including one from Austria under Captain Wüllerstorf Urbair (1858), and one from Italy in the vessel "Magenta" (1865-1868), which was accompanied by the scientist Dr Enrico Giglioli. The celebrated voyage of H.M.S. "Challenger" (1874-1875) and those of the American vessels "Tuscarora" (1873-1876) and "Albatross" (1888-1892) may complete the tale.

Whalers, sealers and traders followed in the wake of explorers, the traders dealing chiefly in copra, trepang, pearls, tortoiseshell, &c. The first actual settlers in the islands were largely men of bad character—deserting sailors, escapers from the penal settlements in Australia and others. It is not to be supposed that there were no orderly colonists, but that the natives suffered much at the hands of Europeans and Americans is only too clear. The class of traders who made a living by disreputable means and attempted to keep a monopoly of the island on which they settled, became notorious under the name of "beachcombers," and for each of the many dark chapters in Polynesian history there must have been many more unwritten. The kidnapping of natives for the South American and Australian labour markets was common. It cannot be denied that there has been actual deterioration of the native races, and elimination in their numbers, consequent upon contact with Europeans and Americans (see further, POLYNESIA). The romantic character of island-history has perhaps, however, tended to emphasize its dark side, and it is well to turn from it to recognize the work of the missionaries, who found in the Pacific one of their most extensive and important fields of labour, and have exercised not only a moral, but also a profound political influence in the islands since the London Missionary Society first established its agents in Tahiti in 1797. Many of them, moreover, have added greatly to the scientific knowledge of the islands and their inhabitants. The imposition of strict rules of life upon the natives was in some instances carried too far; in others their conversion to Christianity was little more than nominal, but cases of this sort are overshadowed by the fine work of William Ellis and John Williams (q. 1818) and many of their successors.

The discovery of sandalwood in Fiji in 1804, and the establishment of a trade therein, made that group a centre of interest in the early modern history of the Pacific islands. Moreover the London Missionary Society, having worked westward from its headquarters in Tahiti to Tonga as early as 1797, founded a settlement in Fiji in 1835. Meanwhile the white traders in Fiji had played an intimate part in the internal political affairs of the group, and in 1858 King Thakombau, being threatened with reprisals by the American consul on account of certain losses of property which he had sustained, asked for British protection, but did not obtain it. The British, however, were paramount among the white population, and as by 1870 not only American, but also German influence was extending through the islands (the first German government vessel visited Fiji in 1872), annexation was urged on Great Britain by Australia and New Zealand. Meanwhile the labour traffic, which had been initiated, so far as the Pacific islands were concerned, by an unsuccessful attempt in 1847 to employ New Hebridean labourers on a settlement near the present township of Eden in New South Wales, had attained considerable proportions, had been improperly exploited and, as already indicated, had led the natives to retaliation, sometimes without discernment, a notorious example of this (as was generally considered) being the murder of Bishop Patteson in 1871. In 1872 an act was passed by the British government to regulate the labour traffic; Fiji was annexed in 1874, and in 1875 another act established the post of the British high commissioner.

In 1842 the French had formally annexed the Marquesas Islands; and subsequently extended their sphere, as shown in the table at the outset of this article, both in the east of Polynesia and in the south of Melanesia. In some of the island-groups independent native states were recognized for some time by the powers, as in the case of Hawaii, which, after the deposition of the queen in 1893 and the proclamation of a republic in 1894, was annexed to the United States of America only in 1898; or, again, in the case of Tonga, which provided a curious example of the subordination of a native organization to unauthorized foreign influence. The partition of Polynesia was completed in 1899, when Samoa was divided between Germany and the United States. In Micronesia, since the discoveries of the early Spanish navigators, the Carolines, Mariana and Pelew Islands had been recognized as Spanish territory until 1885, when Germany began to establish herself in the first-named group. Spain had never occupied this group, but protested against the German action, and Pope Leo XIII. as arbitrator awarded the Carolines to her. Thereafter Spain made attempts at occupation, but serious conflicts with the natives ensued, and in 1899 the islands were sold to Germany, which thus became the predominating power in Micronesia. When Germany acquired the Bismarck Archipelago in Melanesia the introduction of German names (New Pomerania, *Neu Pommern,* for New Britain; *Neu Mecklenburg* for New Ireland; *Neu Langenburg* for the Duke of York Group, &c.) met with no little protest as contrary to precedent and international etiquette. The provision for the joint influence of Great Britain and France over the New Hebrides (1906) brought these islands into some prominence owing to the hostile criticism directed against the British government both in Australia and at home. The partition of the Pacific islands never led to any serious friction between the powers, though the acquisition of Hawaii was attempted by Britain, France and Japan before the United States annexed the group, and the negotiations as to Samoa threatened trouble for a while. There were occasional native risings, as in Samoa (where, however, the fighting was rather in the nature of civil warfare), the French possessions in eastern Polynesia, and the New Hebrides, apart from attacks on individual settlers or visitors, which have occurred here and there from the earliest period of exploration.

Administration.—Of the British possessions among the islands of the Pacific, Fiji is a colony, and its governor is also high commissioner for the western Pacific. In this capacity, assisted by deputies and resident commissioners, he exercises jurisdiction over all the islands except Fiji and those islands which are attached to New Zealand and New South Wales. Some of the islands (*e.g.* Tonga) are native states under British protection. Pitcairn, in accordance

with its peculiar conditions of settlement, has a peculiar system of local government. The New Hebrides are under a mixed British and French commission. The Hawaiian Islands form a territory of the United States of America and are administered as such; Guam is a naval station, as is Tutuila of the Samoan Islands, where the commandant exercises the functions of governor. New Caledonia is a French colony under a governor; the more easterly French islands are grouped together under the title of the French Establishments in Oceania, and are administered by a governor, privy council, administrative council, &c., Papeete in Tahiti being the capital. The seat of government of the German protectorate of Kaiser Wilhelm's Land (New Guinea) is Herbertshöhe in the Bismarck Archipelago. The administrative area includes the German Solomon Islands and the Caroline, Pelew and Mariana Islands, which are divided into three administrative groups—the eastern Carolines, western Carolines and Marianas. The Marshall Islands form a "district" (*Bezirk*) within the same administrative area. The German Samoan Islands are under an imperial governor.

Races.—In the oceanic islands of the Pacific three different peoples occur, who have been called Melanesians, Polynesians and Micronesians.[1] These form themselves naturally into two broad but very distinct divisions—the dark and brown races; the first division being represented by the Melanesians, and the Polynesians and Micronesians together forming the second. The Melanesians, sometimes called Papuans (*q.v.,* the Malay name for the natives of New Guinea, the headquarters of the race), are physically negroid in type, nearly black, with crisp curly hair, flat noses and thick lips. In all essentials they agree with the African type: such variations as there are, for example, in the more developed eyebrow ridges, narrower, often prominent nose, and somewhat higher narrower skull, obviously owing their existence to crossing with the Malay or the Polynesian races. The oceanic black peoples must thus be regarded as having a connexion more or less remote with the African negroes. Whether the two families have a common ancestor in the negritos of Malaysia and the Indian archipelago, or whether Papuan and Negrito are alike branches of an aboriginal African race, is a problem yet to be solved. But if their origin is unknown, there is little doubt that the Melanesians were the earliest occupants of the oceanic world, possibly reaching it from Malaysia. They undoubtedly constitute the oldest ethnic stock sometimes modified on the spot by crossings with migratory peoples (Malays, Polynesians); sometimes, as in the eastern Pacific, giving way entirely before the invaders. The traditions of many of the Polynesian islanders refer to a black indigenous race which occupied their islands when their ancestors arrived, and the black woolly-haired Papuan type is not only found to-day in Melanesia proper, but traces of it occur throughout Polynesia and Micronesia. That the oceanic blacks form one family there can be no doubt, and it is evidence of the immensely remote date at which their dispersion began that they have a multitude of languages often unintelligible except locally, and an extraordinary variety of insular customs; differentiations which must have needed centuries to be effected. Furthermore the Rev. R. H. Codrington (*Melanesian Languages*) has adduced evidence to prove that Melanesia is the most primitive form of the oceanic stock-language, and that both Malays and Polynesians speak later dialects of this archaic form of speech. The Melanesians then, must be regarded as the aborigines of Oceania. How they came to occupy the region it is impossible to say. Evidence exists as to the migrations of the brown races; but there is nothing to explain how the blacks came to inhabit the isolated Pacific islands. In this connexion it is a curious fact, and one which deepens the mystery, that, unlike the Polynesian peoples, who are all born sailors, the blacks are singularly unskilful seamen.

The second ethnic division, the Polynesian-Micronesian races, represents a far later migration and occupation of the Pacific islands. It has been urged that these brown peoples sprang from one stock with the Malays and the Malagasy of Madagascar; and that they represent this parent stock better than the Malays who have been much modified by crossings. But linguistic and physical evidence are against this theory. It is practically certain that the Polynesians at least are an older race than the Malays and their subfamilies. The view which has received most general acceptance is that they represent a branch of the Caucasic division of mankind who migrated at a remote period possibly in Neolithic times from the Asiatic mainland travelling by way of the Malay Archipelago and gradually colonizing the eastern Pacific. The Polynesians, who, as represented by such groups as the Samoans and Marquesas islanders, are the physical equal of Europeans, are of a light brown colour, tall, well-proportioned, with regular and often beautiful features. Such an explanation of the Polynesian's origin does not preclude a relationship with the Malays. It is most probable that the two stocks have Asiatic ancestors in common, though the Polynesians remain to-day, what they must have always been in remote times, a distinct race. Of their sub-division, the Micronesians, the same cannot be said. They are undoubtedly a very hybrid race, owing this characteristic to their geographical position in the area where the dominating races of the Pacific, Malays, Polynesians, Melanesians, Japanese

[1] From these the three main divisions of the islands are named POLYNESIA, MELANESIA, MICRONESIA (*q.v.*).

and Chinese, may be said to converge. Careful investigations have supported the theory that Micronesia was peopled largely from the Philippines or some portion of the Malay Archipelago at a much later period than the Polynesian migration. The Micronesians then are probably of Malay stock much modified by early Polynesian crossings, and probably, within historic times, by Papuan and even Japanese and Chinese migrations. While their general physique approximates to the Polynesian type, they are often characterized by a stunted form and a dark complexion.

In this review of the inhabitants of the Pacific islands an imaginary ethnological line has been drawn round it so as to include none but the branches of the two great divisions. But on the borders of the region, often without real boundary lines, are grouped other peoples, the true Malays, the Indonesians or pre-Malays with the Negritos to the westward and the Australians, who are generally admitted to be a distinct race. Of these races detailed information will be found under their several headings.

Prehistoric Remains.—One of the most obscure questions with which the ethnologist has to deal is that of the prehistoric remains which occur in different and widely separated parts of the oceanic region. The most remarkable of these are on Easter Island, where immense platforms built of dressed stone without mortar are found, together with stone images. Similar remains have been found on Pitcairn Island. On the island of Tongatabu in the Tonga group, there is a monument of great stone blocks which must have been brought thither by sea. In some of the Caroline Islands, again, there are extensive remains of stone buildings, and in the Marianas stone monuments occur. No native traditions assign origin to these remains, nor has any complete explanation of their existence been offered.

BIBLIOGRAPHY.—For the results of the various voyages of explorers see their narratives, especially those of Captain Cook, and among the earlier *Collections of voyages* see especially Captain James Burney, *Chronological History of the Discoveries in the South Sea or Pacific Ocean*—from the earliest navigators to 1764—(London, 1803-1817). Of general works (which are few) see C. E. Meinicke, *Die Inseln des Stillen Oceans* (Leipzig, 1875); F. H. H. Guillemard, *Australasia*, vol. ii., revised by A. H. Keane, in Stanford's *Compendium of Geography and Travel* (London, 1906); and W. T. Brigham, *Index to the Islands of the Pacific* (Honolulu, 1900). Among other works (the majority of which deal only with parts of the region known to the writers from travel), see J. A. Moerenhout, *Voyages aux Iles du Grand Océan* (1837); W. Ellis, *Polynesian Researches* (London, 1853); G. Turner, *Nineteen Years in Polynesia* (London, 1861); T. West, *Ten Years in South Central Polynesia* (London, 1865); J. Brenchley, *Cruise of the "Curaçoa" among the South Sea Islands during 1865* (London, 1873); W. Coote, *Western Pacific Islands* (London, 1883); H. H. Romilly, *The Western Pacific and New Guinea* (London, 1887); H. Stonehewer Cooper, *The Islands of the Pacific* (London, 1888; earlier editions, 1880, &c., were under the title *Coral Lands*); F. J. Moss, *Through Atolls and Islands* (London, 1889); W. T. Wawn, *The South Sea Islanders and the Queensland Labour Trade* (1889); G. Haurigot, *Les Établissements français en Océanie* (Paris, 1891); B. F. S. B. Powell, *In Savage Isles and Settled Lands* (London, 1892); "Sundowner," *Rambles in Polynesia* (London, 1897); M. M. Shoemaker, *Islands of the Southern Seas* (New York, 1808); Joachim Graf Pfeil, *Studien . . . aus der Südsee* (Brunswick, 1899); Robert Louis Stevenson, *In the South Seas* (London, 1900); A. R. Colquhoun, *The Mastery of the Pacific* (London, 1902); G. Wegener, *Deutschland in der Südsee* (Bielefeld, 1903); A. Krämer, *Hawaii, Ostmikronesien, und Samoa* (Stuttgart, 1906); J. D. Rogers, *Australasia*, vol. vi. of the *Historical Geography of the British Colonies*, edited by Sir C. P. Lucas (Oxford, 1907); T. A. Coghlan, *Statistical Account of the Seven Colonies of Australasia* (Sydney). With especial reference to the natives and their languages see Sir G. Grey, *Polynesian Mythology* (London, 1855); W. Gill, *Myths and Songs of the South Pacific* (London, 1876); J. D. Lang, *Origin and Migrations of the Polynesian Nation* (Sydney, 1877); A. Lesson, *Les Polynésiens* (Paris, 1880 seq.); R. H. Codrington, *The Melanesian Languages* (Oxford, 1885); E. Reeves, *Brown Men and Women* (London, 1898); J. Gaggin, *Among the Man-Eaters* (London, 1899); A. C. Haddon, *Head-hunters, Black, White and Brown* (London, 1902); D. Macdonald, *The Oceanic Languages: their Grammatical Structure, Vocabulary and Origin* (London, 1907); J. Macmillan Brown, *Maori and Polynesian* (London, 1907), and the articles POLYNESIA; MELANESIA. With especial reference to natural history, J. D. Hooker, *A Lecture on Insular Floras* (London, 1868); E. Drake del Castillo, *Remarques sur la flore de la Polynésie* (Paris, 1890); H. B. Guppy, *Observations of a Naturalist in the Pacific, 1896-1899* (London, 1903 seq.).

PACK, OTTO VON (c. 1480-1537), German conspirator, studied at the university of Leipzig, and obtained a responsible position under George, duke of Saxony, which he lost owing to his dishonesty. In 1528 he revealed to Philip, landgrave of Hesse, the details of a scheme agreed upon in Breslau by the archduke Ferdinand, afterwards the emperor Ferdinand I., and other influential princes, to conquer Hungary for Ferdinand and then to attack the reformers in Germany. Pack was sent

to Hungary to concert joint measures with John Zapolya, the opponent of Ferdinand in that country; but John, elector of Saxony, advised that the associates of Ferdinand should be asked to explain their conduct, and Pack's revelations were discovered to be false, the copy of the treaty which he had shown to Philip proving to be a forgery. For some time Pack lived the life of a fugitive, finally reaching the Netherlands, where he was seized at the request of Duke George. Examined under torture he admitted the forgery, and the government of the Netherlands passed sentence of death, which was carried out on the 8th of February 1537. This affair has given rise to an acute controversy as to whether Philip of Hesse was himself deceived by Pack, or was his assistant in concocting the scheme.

See W. Schomburgk, *Die Packschen Händel* (Leipzig, 1882); H. Schwarz, *Landgraf Philipp von Hessen und die Packschen Händel* (Leipzig, 1881); St Ehses, *Geschichte der Packschen Handel* (Freiburg, 1881) and *Landgraf Philipp von Hessen und Otto von Pack* (Freiburg, 1886); and L. von Ranke, *Deutsche Geschichte im Zeitalter der Reformation* (Leipzig, 1882).

PACK (apparently from the root *pak-, pag-*, seen in Lat. *pangere*, to fasten; cf. "compact"), primarily a bundle or parcel of goods securely wrapped and fastened for transport. The word, in this sense, is chiefly used of the bundles carried by pedlars. It was in early use, according to the *New English Dictionary*, in the wool trade, and may have been introduced from the Netherlands. As a measure of weight or quantity the term has been in use, chiefly locally, for various commodities, *e.g.* of wool, 240 lb, of gold-leaf 20 books of 25 leaves each. In a transferred sense, a "pack" is a collection or gathering of persons, animals or things; and the verb means generally to gather together in a compact body. "Pack-ice" is the floating ice which covers wide areas in the polar seas, broken into large pieces which are driven (packed) together by wind and current so as to form practically a continuous sheet. "Packet," a small parcel, a diminutive of "pack," was first confined in meaning to a parcel of despatches carried by a post, especially the state despatches or "mail"; and "packet" properly "packet-boat," was the name given to the vessels which carried these state despatches.

PACKER, ASA (1805-1879), American capitalist, was born in Mystic, Connecticut, on the 29th of December 1805. In 1822 he became a carpenter's apprentice at Brooklyn, Susquehanna county, Pennsylvania. He worked as a carpenter in New York City for a time and then in Springville, Pennsylvania, but in 1833 settled at Mauch Chunk, in the Lehigh Valley, where he became the owner of a canal-boat (carrying coal to Philadelphia), and then established the firm of A. & R. W. Packer, which built canal-boats and locks for the Lehigh Coal & Navigation Company, probably the first through shippers to New York. He urged upon the Coal & Navigation Company the advantage of a steam railway as a coal carrier, but the project was not then considered feasible. In 1851 the majority of the stock of the Delaware, Lehigh, Schuylkill & Susquehanna Railroad Company (incorporated in 1846), which became the Lehigh Valley Railroad Company in January 1853, came into his control, and between November 1852 and September 1855 a railway line was built for the Company, largely by Packer's personal credit, from Mauch Chunk to Easton. He built railways connecting the main line with coal-mines in Luzerne and Schuylkill counties; and he planned and built the extension (completed in 1868) of the line into the Susquehanna Valley and thence into New York state to connect at Waverly with the Erie railway. Packer also took an active part in politics. In 1841 and 1842 he was a member of the Pennsylvania House of Representatives; in 1843-1848 was county judge of Carbon county; in 1853-1857 was a Democratic member of the national House of Representatives; and in 1869 was the Democratic candidate for the governorship of Pennsylvania. In 1865 he gave $500,000 and 60 acres (afterwards increased to 115 acres) in South Bethlehem, Pennsylvania, for a technical school for the professions represented in the development of the Lehigh Valley; Lehigh University was chartered in 1866, and its main building, Packer Hall, was completed in 1869; he erected a library building in 1877 as a memorial to his daughter, Mrs Lucy Packer Linderman; and his will bequeathed $1,500,000 as an endowment for the university and $500,000 to the university library, and gave the university an interest (nearly one third) in his estate when finally distributed. He died in Philadelphia on the 17th of May 1879. The Packer Memorial Church (Protestant Episcopal) on the Lehigh University campus, given by his daughter, Mrs Mary Packer Cummings, was dedicated on the 13th of October 1887.

PACORUS, a Parthian name, borne by two Parthian princes.

1. PACORUS, son of Orodes I., was, after the battle of Carrhae, sent by his father into Syria at the head of an army in 52 B.C. The prince was still very young, and the real leader was Osaces. He was defeated and killed by C. Cassius, and soon after Pacorus was recalled by his father, because one of the satraps had rebelled and proclaimed him king (Dio Cass. xl. 28 sqq.; Justin xlii. 4; cf. Cicero, *ad Fam.* xv. 1; *ad Att.* vi. 1. 14). Father and son were reconciled, but the war against the Romans was always deferred. In the autumn of 45 Pacorus and the Arabic chieftain Alchaudonius came to the help of Q. Caecilius Bassus, who had rebelled against Caesar in Syria; but Pacorus soon returned, as his troops were unable to operate in the winter (Cic. *ad Att.* xiv. 9. 3; Dio Cass. xlvii. 27). At last in 40 B.C. the Roman fugitive Titus Labienus induced Orodes to send a great army under the command of Pacorus against the Roman provinces. Pacorus conquered the whole of Syria and Phoenicia with the exception of Tyre, and invaded Palestine, where he plundered Jerusalem, deposed Hyrcanus, and made his nephew Antigonus king (Dio Cass. xlviii. 24 sqq.; Joseph. *Ant.* xiv. 13; Tac. *Hist.* v. 9). Meanwhile Labienus occupied Cilicia and the southern parts of Asia Minor down to the Carian coast (Dio Cass. xlviii. 26; Strabo xiv. 660). But in 39 P. Ventidius Bassus, the general of Mark Antony, drove him back into Cilicia, where he was killed, defeated the Parthians in Syria (Dio Cass. xlviii. 39 sqq.) and at last beat Pacorus at Gindarus (in northern Syria), on the 9th of June 38, the anniversary of the battle of Carrhae. Pacorus himself was slain in the battle, which effectually stopped the Parthian conquests west of the Euphrates (Dio Cass. xlix. 19 seq.; Justin xlii. 4; Plut. *Anton.* 24; Strabo xvi. 751; Velleius ii. 78; cf. Horace, *Od.* iii. 6, 9).

2. PACORUS, Parthian king, only mentioned by Dio Cass. lxviii. 17; Arrian, *ap.* Suidas s.v. ἀνετή, according to whom he sold the kingdom of Osroëne to Abgar VII.; and Ammianus Marcellinus xxiii. 6. 23, who mentions that he enlarged Ctesiphon and built its walls. But from his numerous dated coins we learn that he was on the throne, with interruptions, from A.D. 78–95. He always calls himself Arsaces Pacorus. This mention of his proper name, together with the royal name Arsaces, shows that his kingdom was disputed by rivals. Two of them we know from coins—Vologaeses II., who appears from 77–79 and again from 111–146, and Artabanus III. in 80 and 81. Pacorus may have died about 105; he was succeeded by his brother Osroes.   (ED. M.)

PACUVIUS, MARCUS (c. 220–130 B.C.), Roman tragic poet, was the nephew and pupil of Ennius, by whom Roman tragedy was first raised to a position of influence and dignity. In the interval between the death of Ennius (169) and the advent of Accius, the youngest and most productive of the tragic poets, he alone maintained the continuity of the serious drama, and perpetuated the character first imparted to it by Ennius. Like Ennius he probably belonged to an Oscan stock, and was born at Brundusium, which had become a Roman colony in 244. Hence he never attained to that perfect idiomatic purity of style, which was the special glory of the early writers of comedy, Naevius and Plautus. Pacuvius obtained distinction also as a painter; and the elder Pliny (*Nat. Hist.* xxxv. 19) mentions a work of his in the temple of Hercules in the *Forum boarium*. He was less productive than either Ennius or Accius; and we hear of only about twelve of his plays, founded on Greek subjects (among them the *Antiope, Teucer, Armorum Judicium, Dulorestes, Chryses, Niptra,* &c., most founded on subjects connected with the Trojan cycle), and one *praetexta* (*Paulus*) written in connexion with the victory of Lucius Aemilius Paulus at Pydna

(168), as the *Clastidium* of Naevius and the *Ambracia* of Ennius were written in commemoration of great military successes. He continued to write tragedies till the age of eighty, when he exhibited a play in the same year as Accius, who was then thirty years of age. He retired to Tarentum for the last years of his life, and a story is told by Gellius (xiii. 2) of his being visited there by Accius on his way to Asia, who read his *Atreus* to him. The story is probably, like that of the visit of the young Terence to the veteran Caecilius, due to the invention of later grammarians; but it is invented in accordance with the traditionary criticism (Horace, *Epp.* ii. 1. 54–55) of the distinction between the two poets, the older being characterized rather by cultivated accomplishment (*doctus*), the younger by vigour and animation (*altus*). Pacuvius's epitaph, said to have been composed by himself, is quoted by Aulus Gellius (i. 24), with a tribute of admiration to its " modesty, simplicity and fine serious spirit "—

> Adulescens, tam etsi properas, te hoc saxum rogat
> Ut sese aspicias, deinde quod scriptum 'st legas.
> Hic sunt poetae Pacuvi Marci sita
> Ossa. Hoc volebam nescius ne esses. Vale.

Cicero, who frequently quotes from him with great admiration, appears (*De optimo genere oratorum,* l.) to rank him first among the Roman tragic poets, as Ennius among the epic, and Caecilius among the comic poets.

The fragments of Pacuvius quoted by Cicero in illustration or enforcement of his own ethical teaching appeal, by the fortitude, dignity, and magnanimity of the sentiment expressed in them, to what was noblest in the Roman temperament. They are inspired also by a fervid and steadfast glow of spirit and reveal a gentleness and humanity of sentiment blended with the severe gravity of the original Roman character. So far too as the Romans were capable of taking interest in speculative questions, the tragic poets contributed to stimulate curiosity on such subjects, and they anticipated Lucretius in using the conclusions of speculative philosophy as well as of common sense to assail some of the prevailing forms of superstition. Among the passages quoted from Pacuvius are several which indicate a taste both for physical and ethical speculation, and others which expose the pretensions of religious imposture. These poets aided also in developing that capacity which the Roman language subsequently displayed of being an organ of oratory, history and moral disquisition. The literary language of Rome was in process of formation during the 2nd century B.C., and it was in the latter part of this century that the series of great Roman orators, with whose spirit Roman tragedy has a strong affinity, begins. But the new creative effort in language was accompanied by considerable crudeness of execution, and the novel word-formations and varieties of inflexion introduced by Pacuvius exposed him to the ridicule of the satirist Lucilius, and, long afterwards, to that of his imitator Persius. But, notwithstanding the attempt to introduce an alien element into the Roman language, which proved incompatible with its natural genius, and his own failure to attain the idiomatic purity of Naevius, Plautus or Terence, the fragments of his dramas are sufficient to prove the service which he rendered to the formation of the literary language of Rome as well as to the culture and character of his contemporaries.

Fragments in O. Ribbeck, *Fragmenta scaenicae romanorum poesis* (1897), vol. I.; see also his *Römische Tragödie* (1875); L. Müller, *De Pacuvi fabulis* (1889); W. S. Teuffel, *Caecilius Statius, Pacuvius, Attius, Afranius* (1858); and Mommsen, *History of Rome,* bk. iv. c . 13.

PAD. (1) Probably from the same root as "pod," the husk or seed-covering in certain plants, a term used in various connexions, the sense being derived from that of a soft cushion, or cushion-like combination used either for protective purposes or as stuffing or stiffening. In zoology, it is particularly used of the fleshy elastic protuberances on the sole of the foot of many animals such as the cat and dog, the camel, &c.; and of the similar cushion beneath the toes of a bird's foot or of the tarsal cushion of an insect. In sporting phraseology the whole paw of a fox or other beast of chase is called the " pad." A special technical use, somewhat difficult to connect with the above meanings, is for the socket of a brace or for the handle of such tools as a key-hole saw. (2) The canting word "pad," now surviving in such words as "footpad," a highway robber, or "pad horse," a roadster riding-horse with an easy action, is the same as "path," adapted directly from the Low Ger. form *pad*, a track or road. (3) There is an old English dialect word for a frog (Scottish and North) or a toad, more familiar in the diminutive "paddock" (cf. *Hamlet*, iii. 4, 189; *Macbeth*, I. 1, 9). This is found in many Teutonic languages, cf. Dan. *padde*, Du. *pad;* &c. The diminutive is to be distinguished from "paddock," a small enclosed plot of pasture land, an altered form of "parrock," O. Eng. *pearroc*. (See PARK.)

PADDING, the term in textile manufacture used for the stiffening of various garments. The most useful and flexible material for this purpose is hair cloth, but this is too expensive to be used for the padding of cheap clothing. Hence many kinds of fibrous material are employed for the same purpose. Hair, cotton, flax, tow, jute and paper are used, alone and in combination. The fabrics are first woven, and then starched to obtain the necessary degree of stiffness and flexibility.

PADDINGTON, a municipality of Cumberland county, New South Wales, Australia, 3 m. S.E. of and suburban to Sydney. It is a busy industrial suburb, devoted to brewing, tanning, soap-boiling and various other manufactures. The town hall is one of the finest in the colony, and there is an excellent free library. Paddington returns one member to parliament. Pop. (1901), 22,034.

PADDINGTON, a north-western metropolitan borough of London, England, bounded E. by Hampstead and Marylebone, S. by the city of Westminster, and W. by Kensington, and extending N. to the boundary of the county of London. Pop. (1901), 143,976. The best houses are found in the streets and squares of Bayswater, in the south-west, neighbouring to Kensington Gardens (a small part of which is in the borough) and to Hyde Park, farther east, while in the north-east are broad avenues and "mansions" of residential flats. Bayswater Road, skirting the park and gardens, forms part of the southern boundary of the borough; Edgware Road forms the eastern; from this Harrow Road branches north-west, Bishop's Road and Westbourne Grove form a thoroughfare westward, and Queen's Road, Bayswater, leads south from there to Bayswater Road. The name of Paddington finds no place in Domesday—it may have been included in the manor of Tyburn—and the land belonged to the Abbey of Westminster at an early date. It was granted to the see of London by Edward VI. In the 18th century the picturesque rural scenery attracted artists, and even in the middle of the 19th the open country was reached within the confines of the present borough, which now contains no traces of antiquity. Bayswater is said to take its name from Baynard, a Norman, who after the Conquest held land here and had a castle by the Thames not far above the Tower of London, whence a ward of the city is called Castle Baynard. Many springs flowed forth here; the stream called Westbourne was near at hand, and water was formerly supplied hence to London. In the borough are the Paddington and the Queen's Park technical institutes; St. Mary's Hospital, Praed Street, with medical school; and Paddington Green children's hospital. The terminus of the Great Western railway, facing Praed Street, is called Paddington Station. The parliamentary borough of Paddington has north and south divisions, each returning one member. The borough council consists of a mayor, 10 aldermen and 60 councillors. Area, 2356·1 acres.

PADDLE. (1) A verb, meaning to splash, dabble or play about in water with the feet or hands. (2) A species of oar, with a broad flat blade and short handle, used without a rowlock for propelling canoes or other lightly-built craft (see CANOE). (3) A small spade-like implement, apparently first used to clear a ploughshare from clods of earth. The verb seems to be a frequentative form of "pad," to walk, cognate with "path," or of "pat," to strike gently, an onomatopoeic word; it may have been influenced by the Fr. *patrouiller*, in much the same sense. The verb may have given rise to "paddle," an oar, an easy transition in sense; but the *New English Dictionary* identifies this with the word for a small spade, which occurs earlier than the verb, and seems to have no connexion in sense with it. The implement was known in the 17th and 18th centuries also as "spaddle," a diminutive of "spade," but "paddle" occurs in this sense as early as 1407. The term "paddle" has been applied to many objects and implements resembling the oar in its broad-bladed end: *e.g.* a shovel used in mixing materials in glass-making, in brick-making, &c., and also to the float-boards in the paddle-wheel of a steamboat or the wheel of a water-mill.

PADERBORN (Lat. *Paderae Fontes*, *i.e.* the springs of the Pader), a town and episcopal see of Germany, in the Prussian province of Westphalia, 63 m. N.E. from Dortmund on the railway to Berlin via Altenbeken. Pop. (1905), 26,468, of whom about 80% are Roman Catholics. It derives its name from the springs of the Pader, a small affluent of the Lippe, which rise in the town under the cathedral to the number of nearly 200, and with such force as to drive several mills within a few yards of their source. A large part of the town has been rebuilt since a great fire of 1875. The most prominent of half-a-dozen churches is the Roman Catholic cathedral, the western part of which dates from the 11th, the central part from the 12th, and the eastern part from the 13th century; it was restored in 1891–1893. Among other treasures it contains the silver coffin of St Liborius, a substitute for one which was coined into dollars in 1622 by Christian of Brunswick, the celebrated freebooter. The chapel of St Bartholomew, although externally insignificant, dates from the earlier part of the 11th century, and is counted among the most interesting buildings in Westphalia; it was restored in 1852. The Jesuit church and the Protestant Abding-hofkirche are also interesting. The town hall is a picturesque edifice of the 13th century; it was partly rebuilt in the 16th, and was restored in the 19th century. Paderborn formerly possessed a university, founded in 1614, with faculties of theology and philosophy, but this was closed in 1819. The manufactures of the town include railway plant, glass, soap, tobacco and beer; and there is a trade in grain, cattle, fruit and wool.

Paderborn owes its early development to Charlemagne, who held a diet here in 777 and made it the seat of a bishop a few years later. The Saxon emperors also held diets in the city, which about the year 1000 was surrounded with walls. It joined the Hanseatic League, obtained many of the privileges of a free imperial town, and endeavoured to assert its independence of the bishop. The citizens gladly accepted the reformed doctrines, but the supremacy of the older faith was restored in 1604 by Bishop Theodore von Fürstenberg, who forcibly took possession of the city. It underwent the same fate at the hands of Christian of Brunswick during the Thirty Years' War. The bishopric of Paderborn formed part of the arch-diocese of Mainz, and its bishop became a prince of the empire about 1100. Some of the bishops were men of great activity, and the bishopric attained a certain measure of importance in North Germany, in spite of ravages during the Thirty Years' War and the Seven Years' War. It was secularized in 1803 and was given to Prussia, and after losing it for a few years that country regained it by the settlement of 1815. The last bishop was Franz Egon von Fürstenberg (d. 1825). The bishopric had an area of nearly 1000 sq. m. and a population of about 100,000. A new bishopric of Paderborn, with ecclesiastical authority only, was established in 1821.

See W. Richter, *Geschichte der Stadt Paderborn* (Paderborn, 1899–1903); A. Hübinger, *Die Verfassung der Stadt Paderborn im Mittelalter* (Münster, 1899); and J. Freisen, *Die Universität Paderborn* (Paderborn, 1898). For the history of the bishopric see W. F. Giefers, *Die Anfänge des Bistums Paderborn* (Paderborn, 1860); L. A. T. Holscher, *Die ältere Diozese Paderborn* (Paderborn, 1886); the *Urkunden des Bistums Paderborn*, edited by R. Wilmans (Münster 1874–1880): and W. Richter, *Studien und Quellen zur Paderborner Geschichte* (Paderborn, 1893).

PADEREWSKI, IGNACE JAN (1860–   ), Polish pianist and composer, was born in Podolia, a province of Russian Poland. He studied music chiefly at Warsaw, Berlin and

Vienna, where he was a pupil of Theodor Leschetizky (b. 1830), the pianist and composer. He made his first public appearance in Vienna in 1887, in Paris in 1889, and in London in 1890, his brilliant playing created a *furore* which went to almost extravagant lengths of admiration; and his triumphs were repeated in America in 1891. His name at once became synonymous with the highest pitch of pianoforte playing, and society was at his feet. In 1899 he married Baroness de Rosen, and after 1900 he appeared but little in public; but he became better known as a composer, chiefly of pieces for his own instrument. In 1901 his opera *Manru* was performed at Dresden.

PADIHAM, an urban district in the Clitheroe parliamentary division of Lancashire, England, 3 m. W. by N. of Burnley by the Lancashire and Yorkshire railway. Pop. (1901), 12,205. It lies in a wild and dreary district on the precipitous banks of the Calder. It possesses large cotton mills, and quarries and coal-mines are worked in the immediate neighbourhood. The church of St Leonard, founded before 1451, was frequently altered before it was rebuilt in 1866-1868 in the Perpendicular style. Padiham in 1251 was a manor in the possession of Edmund de Lacy.

PADILLA, JUAN LOPEZ DE, insurrectionary leader in the " guerra de las comunidades " in which the commons of Castile made a futile stand against the arbitrary policy of Charles V. and his Flemish ministers, was the eldest son of the commendator of Castile, and was born in Toledo towards the close of the 15th century. After the cities, by their deputies assembled at Avila, had vainly demanded the king's return, due regard for the rights of the cortes, and economical administration, to be entrusted to the hands of Spaniards, it was resolved to resort to force, and the " holy junta " was formed, with Padilla at its head. An attempt was first made to establish a national government in the name of the imbecile Joanna, who was then residing at Tordesillas; with this view they took possession of her person, seized upon the treasury books, archives, and seals of the kingdom, and stripped Adrian of his regency. But the junta soon alienated the nobility by the boldness with which it asserted democracy and total abolition of privilege, while it courted defeat in the field by assigning to the supreme command of its forces not Padilla but Don Pedro de Ciron, who had no recommendation but his high birth. After the army of the nobility had recaptured Tordesillas, Padilla did something to retrieve the loss by taking Torrelobaton and some other towns. But the junta, which was not fully in accord with its ablest leader, neutralized this advantage by granting an armistice; when hostilities were resumed the commons were completely defeated near Villalar (April 23, 1521), and Padilla, who had been taken prisoner, was publicly executed on the following day. His wife, Doña Maria Pacheco de Padilla, bravely defended Toledo against the royal troops for six months afterwards, but ultimately was compelled to take refuge in Portugal.

See Sandoval, *Historia de Carlos V.* (Pamplona, 1681); E. Armstrong, *The Emperor Charles V.* (1902); A. Rodriquez Villa, *Juana la Loca* (Madrid, 1892); and Pero Mejia, *Comunidades de Castilla*, in the *Biblioteca de autores españoles of Rivadeneyra*, vol. xxi.

PADISHAH, the Turkish form of the Persian *padshah*, a title —equivalent to "lord king"—of the reigning sovereign. Though strictly applied in the East to the shahs of Persia, it was also used of the Great Moguls or Tatar emperors of Delhi, and hence it is now used by the natives of British India of the British sovereign as emperor of India. In Europe it is applied to the sultan of Turkey. The Persian *padshah* is from *pati*, lord, master, and *shah*, king. It is now generally considered to have no etymological connexion with "pasha" (*q.v.*).

PADSTOW, a small seaport and market town in the St Austell parliamentary division of Cornwall, England, on a branch of the London & South Western railway. Pop. of urban district (1901), 1566. It lies near the north coast, on the west shore, and 2 m. from the mouth of the estuary of the river Camel, a picturesque inlet which from Padstow Bay penetrates 6 m. into the land. The church of St Petrock, with a massive roodstone in the churchyard, is mainly Perpendicular, with an Early

English tower. Within are an ancient font, a canopied piscina, and a fine timber roof over the nave and aisles. Other interesting churches in the locality are those of St Petrock Minor, St Minver, St Michael, St Constantine, and, most remarkable of all, St Enodock's. This building, erected in the 15th century amid the barren dunes bordering the east shore of the estuary near its mouth, in place of a more ancient oratory, was long buried beneath drifts of sand. From a little distance only the weather-beaten spire can be seen. A Norman font remains from the older foundation. A monastery formerly stood on the high ground west of Padstow, and according to tradition was founded by St Petrock in the 6th and razed by the Danes in the 10th century. Its site is occupied by Prideaux Place, an Elizabethan mansion, which contains among other valuable pictures Van Dyck's portrait of Queen Henrietta Maria. Pentire Point shelters Padstow Bay on the north-east, but the approach to the estuary is dangerous during north-westerly gales. Padstow, nevertheless, is a valuable harbour of refuge, although the river channel is narrow and much silted. Dredging, however, is prosecuted, the sand being sent inland, being useful as a manure through the carbonate of lime with which it is impregnated. The Padstow Harbour Association (1829) is devoted to the rescue of ships in distress, making no claims for salvage beyond the sums necessary for its maintenance. Padstow has fisheries and shipyards and some agricultural trade.

Padstow (Aldestowe 1273, Patrikstowe 1326, Patrestowe 1346) and St Ives are the only two tolerably safe harbours on the north coast of Cornwall. To this circumstance they both owed their selection for early settlement. St Petrock, who has been called the patron saint of Cornwall, is said to have landed here and also to have died here in the 6th century. At the time of the Domesday survey Bodmin, which treasured the saint's remains, had become the chief centre of religious influence. Padstow is not mentioned in that record. It was included in the bishop of Exeter's manor of Pawton, which had been annexed to the see of Crediton upon its formation by Edward the Elder in 909. Padstow was plundered by the Danes in 981. Until then it is said to have possessed a monastery, which thereupon was transferred to Bodmin. Two manors of Padstow are mentioned later—the prior of Bodmin's manor, which included the rectory, and a manor which passed from the Bonvilles to the Greys, marquesses of Dorset, both of which were eventually acquired by the family of Prideaux. From the letters patent addressed to the bailiffs of Padstow demanding the survey and delivery of ships for foreign service, the appointment of a king's butler for the port, and the frequent recourse which was had to the king's courts for the settlement of disputes of shipping, Padstow appears to have been a port of considerable repute in the 14th century. Its affairs were entrusted to a reeve or bailiff acting in conjunction with the principal men of the town. In 1540 Leland, without sufficient reason, credits Athelstan with the bestowal of such privileges as it then enjoyed, and describes it as a parish full of fishermen and Irishmen. Forty years later Norden describes it as an incorporation and market town. Carew in 1602 states that it had lately purchased a corporation and derived great profit from its trade with Ireland. Some steps towards incorporation were doubtless taken, but it is remarkable that no traces of its municipal character are discoverable in any subsequent records. A prescriptive market is held on Saturdays; two fairs of like nature have disappeared.

PADUA (Lat. *Patavium* ; Ital. *Padova*), a city of northern Italy, on the river Bacchiglione, 25 m. W. of Venice and 18 m. S.E. of Vicenza, with a population of 82,283. The city is picturesque, with arcaded streets, and many bridges crossing the various branches of the Bacchiglione, which once surrounded the ancient walls. The Palazzo della Ragione, with its great hall on the upper floor, is reputed to have the largest roof unsupported by columns in Europe; the hall is nearly rectangular, its length 267½ ft., its breadth 89 ft., and its height 78 ft.; the walls are covered with symbolical paintings in fresco; the building stands upon arches, and the upper storey is surrounded by an open loggia, not unlike that which surrounds the basilica of

Vicenza; the Palazzo was begun in 1172 and finished in 1219; in 1306 Fra Giovanni, an Augustinian friar, covered the whole with one roof; originally there were three roofs, spanning the three chambers into which the hall was at first divided; the internal partition walls remained till the fire of 1420, when the Venetian architects who undertook the restoration removed them, throwing all three compartments into one and forming the present great hall. In the Piazza dei Signori is the beautiful loggia called the Gran Guardia, begun in 1493. and finished in 1526, and close by is the Palazzo del Capitanio, the residence of the Venetian governors, with its great door, the work of Falconetto of Verona, 1532. The most famous of the Paduan churches is the basilica dedicated to Saint Anthony, commonly called Il Santo; the bones of the saint rest in a chapel richly ornamented with carved marbles, the work of various artists, among them of Sansovino and Falconetto; the basilica was begun about the year 1230 and completed in the following century; tradition says that the building was designed by Niccola Pisano; it is covered by seven cupolas, two of them pyramidal. On the piazza in front of the church is Donatello's magnificent equestrian statue of Erasmo da Narni, the Venetian general (1438–1441). The Eremitani is an Augustinian church of the 13th century, distinguished as containing the tombs of Jacopo (1324) and Ubertino (1345) da Carrara, lords of Padua, and for the chapel of SS James and Christopher, illustrated by Mantegna's frescoes. Close by the Eremitani is the small church of the Annunziata, known as the Madonna dell' Arena, whose inner walls are entirely covered with paintings by Giotto. Padua has long been famous for its university, founded by Frederick II. in 1238. Under the rule of Venice the university was governed by a board of three patricians, called the Riformatori dello Studio di Padova. The list of professors and alumni is long and illustrious, containing, among others, the names of Bembo, Sperone Speroni, Veselius, Acquapendente, Galileo, Pomponazzi, Pole, Scaliger, Tasso and Sobieski. The place of Padua in the history of art is nearly as important as its place in the history of learning. The presence of the university attracted many distinguished artists, as Giotto, Lippo Lippi and Donatello; and for native art there was the school of Squarcione (1394–1474), whence issued the great Mantegna (1431–1506). The industry of Padua has greatly developed in modern times. Corn and saw mills, distilleries, chemical factories, breweries, candle-works, ink-works, foundries, agricultural machine and automobile works, have been established and are flourishing. The trade of the district has grown to such an extent that Padua has become the central market for the whole of Venetia.

Padua claims to be the oldest city in north Italy; the inhabitants pretend to a fabulous descent from the Trojan Antenor, whose relics they recognized in a large stone sarcophagus exhumed in the year 1274. Their real origin is involved in that obscurity which conceals the ethnography of the earliest settlers in the Venetian plain. Padua early became a populous and thriving city, thanks to its excellent breed of horses and the wool of its sheep. Its men fought for the Romans at Cannae, and the city became so powerful that it was reported able to raise two hundred thousand fighting men. Abano in the neighbourhood was made illustrious by the birth of Livy, and Padua was the native place of Valerius Flaccus, Asconius Pedianus and Thrasea Paetus. Padua, in common with north-eastern Italy, suffered severely from the invasion of the Huns under Attila (452). It then passed under the Gothic kings Odoacer and Theodoric, but made submission to the Greeks in 540. The city was seized again by the Goths under Totila, and again restored to the Eastern Empire by Narses in 568. Following the course of events common to most cities of north-eastern Italy, the history of Padua falls under eight heads: (1) the Lombard rule, (2) the Frankish rule, (3) the period of the bishops, (4) the emergence of the commune, (5) the period of the despots, (6) the period of Venetian supremacy, (7) the period of Austrian supremacy, and finally (8) the period of united Italy. (1) Under the Lombards the city of Padua rose in revolt (601) against Agilulph, the Lombard king, and after suffering a long and bloody siege was stormed and burned by him. The city did not easily recover from this blow; and Padua was still weak when the Franks succeeded the Lombards as masters of north Italy. (2) At the Diet of Aix-la-Chapelle (828) the duchy and march of Friuli, in which Padua lay, was divided into four counties, one of which took its title from that city. (3) During the period of episcopal supremacy Padua does not appear to have been either very important or very active. The general tendency of its policy throughout the war of Investitures was Imperial and not Roman; and its bishops were, for the most part, Germans. (4) But under the surface two important movements were taking place. At the beginning of the 11th century the citizens established a constitution, composed of a general council or legislative assembly and a credenza or executive; and during the next century they were engaged in wars with Venice and Vicenza for the right of water-way on the Bacchiglione and the Brenta—so that, on the one hand, the city grew in power and self-reliance, while, on the other, the great families of Camposampiero, D'Este and Da Romano began to emerge and to divide the Paduan district between them. The citizens, in order to protect their liberties, were obliged to elect a podestà, and their choice fell first on one of the D'Este family (c. 1175). The temporary success of the Lombard league helped to strengthen the towns; but their ineradicable jealousy of one another soon reduced them to weakness again, so that in 1236 Frederick II. found little difficulty in establishing his vicar Ezzelino da Romano in Padua and the neighbouring cities, where he practised frightful cruelties on the inhabitants. When Ezzelino met his death, in 1259, Padua enjoyed a brief period of rest and prosperity; the university flourished; the basilica of the saint was begun; and the Paduans became masters of Vicenza. But this advance brought them into dangerous proximity to Can Grande della Scala, lord of Verona, to whom they had to yield in 1311. (5) As a reward for freeing the city from the Scalas, Jacopo da Carrara was elected lord of Padua in 1318. From that date till 1405, with the exception of two years (1388–1390) when Gian Galeazzo Visconti held the town, nine members of the Carrara family succeeded one another as lords of the city. It was a long period of restlessness, for the Carraresi were constantly at war; they were finally extinguished between the growing power of the Visconti and of Venice. (6) Padua passed under Venetian rule in 1405, and so remained, with a brief interval during the wars of the League of Cambray, till the fall of the republic in 1797. The city was governed by two Venetian nobles, a podestà for civil and a captain for military affairs; each of these was elected for sixteen months. Under these governors the great and small councils continued to discharge municipal business and to administer the Paduan law, contained in the statutes of 1276 and 1362. The treasury was managed by two chamberlains; and every five years the Paduans sent one of their nobles to reside as nuncio in Venice, and to watch the interests of his native town. (7 and 8) After the fall of the Venetian republic the history of Padua follows the history of Venice during the periods of French and Austrian supremacy. In 1866 the battle of Königgratz gave Italy the opportunity to shake off the last of the Austrian yoke, when Venetia, and with Venetia Padua, became part of the united Italian kingdom.

See "Chronicon patavinum," in L. A. Muratori's *Antiquitates italicae medii aevi*, vol. iv. (Milan, 1738); "Rolandino" and "Monaco padovano" (Muratori's *Annali d'Italia*, vol. viii., Venice, 1790; Corcusiorum historia," ibid. vol. xii.; Gattari, "Istoria padovana," ibid. vol. xvii.; Vergerius, "Vitae carrariensium principum," ibid. vol. xvi.); G. Verci, *Storia della Marca Trevigiana* (Venice, 1786); Abate G. Gennari, *Annali di Padova* (Padua); G. Cittadella, *Storia della dominazione carrarese* (Padua, 1842); P. Litta, *Famiglie celebri, s.v.* "Carraresi" (1825–1835); C.Cantu, *Illustrazione grande del Lombardo-Veneto* (Milan, 1857)); B. Gonzati, *La Basilica di Sant' Antonio di Padova* (Padua, 1853). (H. F. B.)

PADUCAH, a city and the county-seat of McCracken county, Kentucky, U.S.A., at the confluence of the Tennessee river with the Ohio, about 12 m. below the mouth of the Cumberland, and about 50 m. E. by N. of Cairo, Illinois. Pop. (1890), 12,797; (1900), 19,446, of whom 5814 were negroes and 516 were foreign-born; (1910 census) 22,760. It is served by three branches of the Illinois Central railroad by a branch of the Nashville Chattanooga & St Louis railway (of which it is the terminus), and by steamboat lines to Pittsburg, Louisville, St Louis, New Orleans, Nashville, Chattanooga, and other river ports. Paducah is in a rich agricultural region, and its wholesale trade is probably greater than that of any other city of the state except Louisville. Its trade is largely in groceries, whisky, tobacco, hardware, grain and live stock, vegetables and lumber. It is a large looseleaf tobacco market, and is a headquarters for tow boats carrying coal down the Mississippi. The Illinois Central and the Nashville, Chattanooga & St Louis railways have repair shops here; and there are numerous manufactures, the value of the factory products increasing from $2,976,931 in 1900 to $4,443,223 in 1905, or 49·3%. Paducah (said to have been named in honour of an Indian chief who lived in the vicinity and of whom there is a statue in the city) was settled in 1821, was laid out in 1827, was incorporated as a town in 1830, and was chartered as a city in 1856. The city was occupied by General U. S. Grant the 5th of September 1861; on the 25th of March 1864 it was entered by a Confederate force under General Nathan B. Forrest, who, however, was unable to capture the fortifications and immediately withdrew.

PAEAN (Gr. Παιάν, epic Παιήων), in Homer (*Il.* v. 401, 899), the physician of the gods. In other writers the word is a mere epithet of Apollo (*q.v.*) in his capacity as a god of healing (cf. *Ιατρόμαντις ούλιος*), but it is not known whether Paean was originally a separate deity or merely an aspect of Apollo. Homer leaves the question unanswered; Hesiod (cf. schol. Hom. *Od.* iv. 432) definitely separates the two, and in later poetry Paean is invoked independently as a health god. It is equally difficult to discover the relation between Paean or Paeon in the sense of " healer " and Paean in the sense of " song." Farnell refers to the ancient association between the healing craft and the singing of spells, and says that it is impossible to decide which is the original sense. At all events the meaning of "healer" gradually gave place to that of "hymn," from the phrase *Ιη Παιάν*. Such songs were originally addressed to Apollo (cf. the Homeric *Hymn to Apollo* 272, and notes in ed. by Sikes and Allen), and afterwards to other gods, Dionysus, Helios, Asclepius. About the 4th century the paean became merely a formula of adulation; its object was either to implore protection against disease and misfortune, or to offer thanks after such protection had been rendered. Its connexion with Apollo as the slayer of the python led to its association with battle and victory; hence it became the custom for a paean to be sung by an army on the march and before entering into battle, when a fleet left the harbour, and also after a victory had been won. The most famous paeans are those of Bacchylides (*q.v.*) and Pindar (*q.v.*). Paeans were sung at the festivals of Apollo (especially the Hyacinthia), at banquets, and later even at public funerals. In later times they were addressed not only to the gods, but to human beings. In this manner the Rhodians celebrated Ptolemy I. of Egypt, the Samians Lysander of Sparta, the Athenians Demetrius, the Delphians Craterus of Macedon. The word " paean " is now used in the sense of any song of joy or triumph.

See A. Fairbanks, " A Study of the Greek Paean," No. xii. of *Cornell Studies in Classical Philology* (New York, 1900); L. R. Farnell, *Cults of the Greek States.*

PAELIGNI, a people of ancient Italy, first mentioned as a member of a confederacy which included the Marsi, Marrucini and Vestini (*qq.v.*), with which the Romans came into conflict in the second Samnite War, 325 B.C. (Liv. viii. 29). On the submission of the Samnites they all came into alliance with Rome in 305-302 B.C. (Liv. ix. 45, x. 3, and Diod. xx. 101), the Paelignians having fought hard (Diod. xx. 90) against even this degree of subjection. Each of them was an independent unit, and in none was there any town or community politically separate from the tribe as a whole. Thus the Vestini issued coins in the 3rd century; each of them appears in the list of the allies in the Social War (Appian, *B.C.* i. 39, with J. Beloch, *Der italische Bund unter römischer Hegemonie*, p. 51). How purely Italic in sentiment these communities of the mountain country

remained appears from the choice of the mountain fortress of Corfinium as the rebel capital. It was renamed Vitellio, the Oscan form of Italia, a name which appears, written in Oscan alphabet, on the coins struck there in 90 B.C. (see R. S. Conway, *The Italic Dialects*, p. 216).

The inscriptions we possess are enough to show that the dialect spoken by these tribes was substantially the same from the northern boundary of the Frentani to some place in the upper Aternus valley not far from Amiternum (mod. Aquila), and that this dialect closely resembled the Oscan of Lucania and Samnium, though presenting some peculiarities of its own, which warrant, perhaps, the use of the name North Oscan. The clearest of these is the use of postpositions, as in Vestine *Poimunie-n*, " in templo Pomonali "; *pritrom-e*, *i.e. in proximum*, " on to what lies before you." Others are the sibilation of consonantal *i* and the assibilation of -*di-* to some sound like that of English *j* (denoted by *β* in the local variety of Latin alphabet), as in *vidadu*, " viamdō," *i.e.* " ad-viam "; *Musesa*=Lat. *Mussedia* ; and the loss of *d* (in pronunciation) in the ablative, as in *aetatu frata fertlid* (*i.e. aetate fertili finita*), where the contrast of the last with the other two forms shows that the -*d* was an archaism still occasionally used in writing. The last sentence of the interesting epitaph from which this phrase is taken may be quoted as a specimen of the dialect; the stone was found in Pentima, the ancient Corfinium, and the very perfect style of the Latin alphabet in which it is written shows that it cannot well be earlier than the last century B.C.: " Eite uus pritrome pacris, puus ecic lexe lifar," " ite vos porro pacati (cum bona pace), qui hoc scriptum (*libar*, 3rd decl. neut.) legistis." The form *lexe* (2nd plur. perf. indic.) is closely parallel to the inflection of the same person in Sanskrit and of quite unique linguistic interest.

The name *Paeigni* may belong to the NO-class of Ethnica (see SABINI), but the difference that it has no vowel before the suffix suggests that it may rather be parallel with the suffix of Lat. *privignus*. If it has any connexion with Lat. *paelex*, " concubine," it is conceivable that it meant " half-breeds," and was a name coined in contempt by the conquering Sabines, who turned the *Ionta Maronca* into the community of the *Marrucins* (*q.v.*). But, when unsupported by direct evidence, even the most tempting etymology is an unsafe guide. For the history of the Paeligni after 90 B.C. see the references given in *C. I. L.* ix. 290 (Sulmo, esp. Ovid, *e.g. Fasti*, iv. 79; *Amor.* ii. 16; Florus ii. 9; Caes., *B.C.*, i. 15) and 296 (Corfinium, *e.g.* Diod. Sic. xxxvii. 2, 4, Caes., *B.C.*, i. 15). None of the Latin inscriptions of the district need be older than Sulla, but some of them both in language and script show the style of his period (*e.g.* 3087, 3137); and, on the other hand, as several of the native inscriptions, which are all in the Latin alphabet, show the normal letters of the Ciceronian period, there is little doubt that, for religious and private purposes at least, the Paelignian dialect lasted down to the middle of the 1st century B.C.

Paelignian and this group of inscriptions generally form a most important link in the chain of the Italic dialects, as without them the transition from Oscan to Umbrian would be completely lost. The unique collection of inscriptions and antiquities of Pentima and the museum at Sulmona were both created by the late Professor Antonio de Nino whose brilliant gifts and unsparing devotion to the antiquities of his native district rescued every single Paelignian monument that we possess.

For further details and the text of the inscriptions, the place-names, &c., see R. S. Conway, *The Italic Dialects*, pp. 233 *seq.*, and the earlier authorities there cited. (R. S. C.)

PAEONIA, in ancient geography, the land of the Paeonians, the boundaries of which, like the early history of its inhabitants, are very obscure. The Paeonians are regarded as descendants of the Phrygians of Asia Minor, large numbers of whom in early times crossed over to Europe. According to the national legend (Herodotus v. 16), they were Teucrian colonists from Troy, and Homer (*Iliad*, ii. 848) speaks of Paeonians from the Axius fighting on the side of their Trojan kinsmen. Before the reign of Darius Hystaspes, they had made their way as far east as Perinthus in Thrace on the Propontis. At one time all Mygdonia, together with Crestonicè, was subject to them. When Xerxes crossed Chalcidicè on his way to Therma (Thessalonica) he is said to have marched "through Paeonian territory." They occupied the entire valley of the Axius (Vardar) as far inland as Stobi, the valleys to the east of it as far as the Strymon (Struma), and the country round Astibus and the river of the same name, with the water of which they anointed their kings. Emathia, the district between the Haliacmon (Bistritza) and Axius, was once called Paeonia; and Pieria and Pelagonia were inhabited by Paeonians. In consequence of the growth of Macedonian power, and under pressure from their Thracian neighbours, their territory was considerably diminished, and in historical times was limited to the N. of Macedonia from Illyria to the Strymon. The chief town and seat of the kings was Bylazora (Veles, Kuprolu on the Axius); in the Roman period, Stobi (Pusto-Gradsko). The Paeonians included several independent tribes, all later united under the rule of a single king. Little is known of their manners and customs. They adopted the cult of Dionysus, known amongst them as Dyalus or Dryalus, and Herodotus (iv. 33) mentions that the Thracian and Paeonian women offered sacrifice to Queen Artemis (probably Bendis). They worshipped the sun in the form of a small round disk fixed on the top of a pole. A passage in Athenaeus (ix. p. 398) seems to indicate the affinity of their language with Mysian. They drank barley beer and various decoctions made from plants and herbs. The country was rich in gold and a bituminous kind of wood (or stone, which burst into a blaze when in contact with water) called στύπη (or στύπος). The women were famous for their industry. In this connexion Herodotus (v. 12) tells the story that Darius, having seen at Sardis a beautiful Paeonian woman carrying a pitcher on her head, leading a horse to drink, and spinning flax, all at the same time, inquired who she was. Having been informed that she was a Paeonian, he sent instructions to Megabyzus, commander in Thrace, to deport two tribes of the nation without delay to Asia. At the time of the Persian invasion, the Paeonians on the lower Strymon had lost, while those in the north maintained, their independence. They frequently made inroads into Macedonian territory, until they were finally subdued by Philip, who permitted them to retain their government by kings. The daughter of Audoleon, one of these kings, was the wife of Pyrrhus, king of Epirus, and Alexander the Great wished to bestow the hand of his sister Cynane upon Langarus, who had shown himself loyal to Philip. An inscription, discovered in 1877 at Olympia on the base of a statue, states that it was set up by the community of the Paeonians in honour of their king and founder Dropion. Another king, whose name appears as Lyppeius on a fragment of an inscription found at Athens relating to a treaty of alliance is no doubt identical with the Lycceius or Lycpeius of Paeonian coins (see B. V. Head, *Historia numorum*, 1887, p. 207). In 280 the Gallic invaders under Brennus ravaged the land of the Paeonians, who, being further hard pressed by the Dardani, had no alternative but to join the Macedonians, whose downfall they shared. After the Roman conquest, Paeonia east and west of the Axius formed the second and third districts respectively of Macedonia (Livy xlv. 29). Under Diocletian Paeonia and Pelagonia formed a province called Macedonia *secunda* or *salutaris*, belonging to the prefecture of Illyricum.

See W. Tomaschek, " Die alten Thraker " in *Sitzungsberichte der k. Akad. der Wissenschaften*, xxviii. (Vienna, 1893); H. F. O. Abel, *Makedonien vor König Philipp* (Leipzig, 1847); C. O. Müller, *Über die Wohnsitze, die Abstammung und die ältere Geschichte des makedonischen Volkes* (Berlin, 1825); T. Desdevises-u-Dezert, *Géographie ancienne de la Macédoine* (Paris, 1863); see also MACEDONIA.

PAEONIUS, of Mende in Thrace, a Greek sculptor of the latter part of the 5th century. The statement of Pausanias that he executed one of the pediments of the temple of Zeus at Olympia is rejected by critics. But we possess an important work of Paeonius in the Victory found in the German excavations at Olympia, and set 'up, according to the most probable view, in memory of the battle of Sphacteria (see GREEK ART,

fig. 36). It bears the inscription " Dedicated to Olympian Zeus by the Messenians and Naupactians as a tithe of the spoil of their enemies. Paeonius of Mende made the statue, and was a successful competitor in the construction of the gable-figures for the temple." The gable figures last mentioned were doubtless gilt victories of bronze which stood *on* the gable, not *in* it. Pausanias seems to have misunderstood the phrase as implying that Paeonius made one of the pedimental groups.

PAEONY (botanically *Paeonia;* Nat. ord. Ranunculaceae *q.v.*) a genus of plants remarkable for their large and gorgeous flowers. There are two distinct sets, one the strong-growing herbaceous kind, with fleshy roots and annual stems, derived mainly from *Paeonia albiflora* and *P. officinalis;* the other called the tree paeony, stiff-growing plants with half-woody permanent stems, which have sprung from the Chinese *P. Moutan.*

The herbaceous paeonies usually grow from 2 to 3 ft. in height, and have large much-divided leaves, and ample flowers of varied and attractive colours, and of a globular form in the double varieties which are those most prized in gardens. They usually blossom in May and June, and as ornaments for large beds in pleasure grounds, and for the front parts of shrubberies, few flowers equal them in gorgeous effect. A good moist loamy soil suits them best, and a moderate supply of manure is beneficial. They are impatient of frequent transplantings or repeated divisions for purposes of propagation, but when necessary they may be multiplied by this means, early in autumn, care being taken that a sound bud is attached to each portion of the tuberous roots.

The older varieties of *P. albiflora* include *candida, festa, fragrans, Humei, Reevesii, rubescens, vestalis, Whitleyi,* &c.; those of *P. officinalis* embrace *albicans, anemoniflora, Baxteri, blanda, rosea, Sabini,* &c. The garden varieties of modern times are, however, still more beautiful, the flowers being in many instances delicately tinted with more than one colour, such as buff with bronzy centre, carmine with yellowish centre, rose with orange centre, white tinted with rose, &c.

The Siberian *P. tenuifolia,* with finely cut leaves and crimson flowers, is a graceful border plant, and its double-flowered variety is perhaps the most elegant of its race.

The Moutans or tree paeonies are remarkable for their subshrubby habit, forming vigorous plants sometimes attaining a height of 6 to 8 ft., and producing in May magnificent flowers which vary in colour from white to lilac, purple magenta, violet and rose. These are produced on the young shoots, which naturally burst forth early in the spring, and are in consequence liable in bleak localities, unless protected, to be cut off by spring frosts. They require to be thoroughly ripened in summer, and therefore a hot season and a dryish situation are desirable for their well-being; and they require rest during winter. Small plants with a single stem, if well matured so as to ensure their blossoming, make very attractive plants when forced. They are increased by grafting in late summer or autumn on the roots of the herbaceous paeonies.

The yellow-flowered tree paeony (*P. lutea*) was introduced from China in 1887, but is still very rare. There are hundreds of names given to the colour variations of both the herbaceous and tree paeonies, but as these have only a fleeting interest it is better to consult current catalogues for the latest types.

PAÈR, FERDINANDO (1771–1839), Italian musical composer, was born at Parma on the 1st of June 1771. He studied the theory of music under the violinist Ghiretti, a pupil of the Conservatoire della Pietà de' Turchini at Naples. His first opera, *La Locanda de' vagabondi,* was published when he was only sixteen; others rapidly followed, and his name was soon famous throughout Italy. In 1797 he went to Vienna, where his wife, the singer Riccardi, had obtained an engagement at the opera; here he produced a series of operas, including his *La Camilla ossia il Sotterraneo* (1799) and his *Achille* (1801). In 1803 he was appointed composer to the court theatre at Dresden, where his wife was also engaged as a singer, and in 1804 the life appointment of *Hofkapellmeister* was bestowed upon him by the elector. At Dresden he produced, *inter alia, Il Sargino* (1803).

an opera which obtained a wide popularity, and *Leonora* (1804), based on the same story as Beethoven's *Fidelio*. In 1807 Napoleon while in Dresden took a fancy to him, and took him with him to Warsaw and Paris at a salary of 28,000 francs. In 1812 he succeeded Spontini as conductor of the Italian opera in Paris. This post he retained at the Restoration, receiving also the posts of chamber composer to the king and conductor of the private orchestra of the duke of Orleans. In 1823 he retired from the Italian opera in favour of Rossini. In 1831 he was elected a member of the Academy, and in 1832 was appointed conductor of his orchestra by King Louis Philippe. He died on the 3rd of May 1839.

Paër wrote in all 43 operas, in the Italian style of Paesiello and Cimarosa. His other works, which include nine religious compositions, thirteen cantatas, and a short list of orchestral and chamber pieces, are of little importance; in any case the superficial quality of his compositions was such as to secure him popularity while he lived and after his death oblivion.

See R. Eitner, *Quellen-Lexikon* (Leipzig, 1902), vii. 277, sqq., where a list of his works is given.

PAESTUM (Gr. Ποσειδωνία; mod. Pesto), an ancient Greek city in Lucania, near the sea, with a railway station 24 m. S.E. of Salerno, 5 m. S. of the river Silarus (Salso). It is said by Strabo (v. 251) to have been founded by Troezenian and Achaean colonists from the still older colony of Sybaris, on the Gulf of Tarentum; this probably happened not later than about 600 B.C. Herodotus (i. 167) speaks of it as being already a flourishing city in about 540 B.C., when the neighbouring city of Velia was founded. For many years the city maintained its independence, though surrounded by the hostile native inhabitants of Lucania. Autonomous coins were struck, of which many specimens now exist (see NUMISMATICS). After long struggles the city fell into the hands of the Lucanians (who nevertheless did not expel the Greek colonists) and in 273 B.C. it became a Latin colony under the Roman rule, the name being changed to the Latin form Paestum. It successfully resisted the attacks of Hannibal; and it is noteworthy that it continued to strike copper coins even under Augustus and Tiberius. The neighbourhood was then healthy, highly cultivated, and celebrated for its flowers; the "twice blooming roses of Paestum" are mentioned by Virgil (*Geor.* iv. 118), Ovid (*Met.* xv. 708), Martial (iv. 41, 10; vi. 80, 6), and other Latin poets. Its present deserted and malarious state is probably owing to the silting up of the mouth of the Silarus, which has overflowed its bed, and converted the plain into unproductive marshy ground. Herds of buffaloes, and the few peasants who watch them, are now the only occupants of this once thickly populated and garden-like region. In 871 Paestum was sacked and partly destroyed by Saracen invaders; in the 11th century it was further dismantled by Robert Guiscard, and in the 16th century was finally deserted.

The ruins of Posidonia are among the most interesting of the Hellenic world. The earliest temple in Paestum, the so-called Basilica, must in point of style be associated with the temples D and F at Selinus, and is therefore to be dated about 570–554 B.C.[1] It is a building of unique plan, with nine columns in the front and eighteen at the sides, 4¾ ft. in diameter. A line of columns runs down the centre of the cella. The columns have marked entasis, and the flutings end in a semicircle, above which is generally a torus (always present in the so-called temple of Ceres). The capitals are remarkable, inasmuch as the necking immediately below the echinus is decorated with a band of leaves, the arrangement of which varies in different cases. The columns and the architraves upon them are well preserved, but there is nothing above the frieze existing, and the cella wall has entirely disappeared. Next in point of date comes the so-called temple of Ceres, a hexastyle peripteros, which may be dated after 540 B.C. The columns are all standing, and the west and part of the east pediment are still *in situ*; but of the cella, again, nothing is left. The capitals are like those of the Basilica, but the details are differently worked out. In front of this temple stood a sacrificial altar as long as the temple itself.

[1] The dating adopted in the present article, which is in absolute contradiction to that given in the previous edition of this work, is that given by R. Koldewey and O. Puchstein, *Die griechischen Tempel in Unteritalien und Sicilien* (Berlin, 1899), 11–35.

The most famous of the temples of Paestum, the so-called temple of Neptune, comes next in point of date (about 420 B.C.). It is a hexastyle peripteros with fourteen columns on each side, and is remarkably well-preserved, both pediments and the epistyle at the sides being still *in situ*. No traces of the decoration of the pediments and metopes have been preserved. The cella, the outer walls of which have to a great extent disappeared, has two internal rows of seven columns 4¾ ft. in diameter, upon which rests a simple epistyle, supporting a row of smaller columns, so that the interior of the cella was in two storeys.

The Temple of Peace is a building of the Roman period of the 2nd century B.C., with six Doric columns on the front, eight on the sides and none at the back; it was excavated in 1830 and is now entirely covered up. Traces of a Roman theatre and amphitheatre (?) have also been found. The circuit of the town walls, well built of squared blocks of travertine, and 16 ft. thick, of the Greek period, is almost entire; they are about 3 m. in circumference, enclosing an irregular, roughly rectangular area. There were four gates, that on the east with a single arched opening being well-preserved. Outside the north gate is a street of tombs, in some of which were found arms, vases and fine mural paintings (now in the Naples Museum).

The following table gives the chief dimensions of the four temples described above in feet:—

	Length without steps.	Breadth without steps.	Length of cella.	Breadth of cella.	Diameter of columns.	Height of columns.	Number of columns.
Basilica (so-called).	178	80¾	137¾	44½	4¾	21	50
Temple of Ceres (so-called).	108	47¾	78½	25½	6½	19½	34
Temple of Neptune (so-called).	197	80	149¾	44½	4¾	28	36
Temple of Peace (so-called).	84	44½	48½	28½	3	?	20

(T. As.)

PAEZ, JOSÉ ANTONIO (1790–1873), Venezuelan president, was born of Indian parents near Acarigua in the province of Barinas on the 13th of June 1790. He came to the front in the war of independence against Spain, and his military career, which began about 1810, was distinguished by the defeat of the Spanish forces at Mata de la Miel (1815), at Montecal and throughout the province of Apure (1816), and at Puerto Cabello (1823). In 1829 he furthered the secession of Venezuela from the republic of Colombia, and he became its first president (1830–1834). He was again president in 1839–1843, and dictator in 1846; but soon afterwards headed a revolution against his successor and was thrown into prison. In 1850 he was released and left the country, but in 1858 he returned, and in 1860 was made minister to the United States. A year afterwards he again returned and made himself dictator, but in 1863 was overthrown and exiled. He died in New York on the 6th of May 1873.

His autobiography was published at New York in 1867–1869, and his son Ramon Paez wrote *Public Life of J. A. Paez* (1864). An *Apoteosis* by Guzman Blanco was published at Paris in 1889.

PAEZ, PEDRO (1564–1622), Jesuit missionary to Abyssinia, was born at Olmedo in Old Castile in 1564. Having entered the Society of Jesus, he was set apart for foreign mission service, and sent to Goa in 1588. Within a year he and a fellow missionary were dispatched from that place to Abyssinia to act as spiritual directors to the Portuguese residents. On his way thither, he fell into the hands of pirates at Dhofar and was sent to Sanaa, capital of the Yemen, where he was detained for seven years by the pasha as a slave. Having been redeemed by his order in 1596, he spent some years in mission work on the west coast of India, and it was not until 1603 that he again set out for Abyssinia, and landed at the port of Massawa. At the headquarters of his order, in Fremona, he soon acquired the two chief dialects of the country, translated a catechism, and set about the education of some Abyssinian children. He also established a reputation as a preacher, and having been summoned to court, succeeded in vanquishing the native priests and in converting Za-Denghel, the negus, who wrote to the pope and the king of Spain for more missionaries, an act of zeal which involved him in civil war with the Abyssinian priests (who dreaded the influence of Paez) and ultimately cost him his life (Oct. 1604). Paez, who is said to have been the first European to visit the source of the Blue Nile, died of fever in 1622.

In addition to the translation of the Catechism, Paez is supposed to be the author of a treatise *De Abyssinorum erroribus* and a history of Ethiopia (ed. C. Beccari in *Rerum aethiopicarum scriptores occidentales inediti a saeculo XVI ad XIX* (1905).

See A. de Backer, *Bibliothèque de la Compagnie de Jésus* (ed C. Sommervogel) vi. (1895); W. D Cooley in *Bulletin de la société de géographie* (1872), 6th series, vol. iii.

PAGAN, a town and former capital, in Myingyan district, Upper Burma, 92 m. S.W. of Mandalay It was founded by King Pyinbya in 847, and remained the capital until the extinction of the dynasty in 1298. Pagan itself is now a mere village, but hundreds of pagodas in various stages of decay meet the eye in every direction. The majority of them were built by King Anawra-hta, who overcame the Peguan king, Manuha of Thaton It was Anawra-hta who introduced the Buddhist religion in Upper Burma, and who carried off nearly the whole Thaton population to build the pagodas at Pagan on the model of the Thaton originals. Many of these are of the highest architectural interest, besides being themselves most imposing structures. Pagan is still a popular place of Buddhist pilgrimage, and a museum has been built for the exhibition of antiquities found in the neighbourhood. The population in 1901 was 6254.

PAGAN (Lat. *paganus*, of or belonging to a *pagus*, a canton, country district, village, commune), a heathen, one who worships a false god or false gods, or one who belongs to a race or nation which practises idolatrous rites and professes polytheism. In its early application *paganus* was applied by the Christian Church to those who refused to believe in the one true God, and still followed the Greek, Roman and other ancient faiths. It thus of course excluded Jews. In the middle ages, at the time of the crusades and later, "pagan" and "paynim" (O Fr. *paenime*, Late Lat. *paganismus*, heathenism or heathen lands) were particularly applied to Mahommedans, and sometimes to Jews. A special significance attaches to the word when applied to one who adopts that attitude of cultured indifference to, or negation of, the various theistic systems of religion which was taken by so many of the educated and aristocratic classes in the ancient Hellenic and Roman world.

It has long been accepted that the application of the name *paganus*, villager, to non-Christians was due to the fact that it was in the rural districts that the old faiths lingered. This explanation assumes that the use of *paganus* in this sense arose after the establishment of Christianity as the religion generally accepted in the urban as opposed to the rural districts, and it is usually stated that an edict of the emperor Valentinian of 368 dealing with the *religio paganorum* (*Cod. Theod.* xvi. 2) contains the first documentary use of the word in this secondary sense. It has now been shown that the use can be traced much earlier. Tertullian (c. 202; *De corona militis*, xi.), says "*Apud hunc* (Christum) tam miles est' paganus fidelis quam paganus est miles infidelis." This gives the clue to the true explanation. In classical Latin *paganus* is frequently found in contradistinction to *miles* or *armatus* (cf. especially Tac. *Hist* i. 53; ii. 14, 88; iii. 24, 43, 77), where the opposition is between a regular enrolled soldier and the raw half-armed rustics who sometimes formed a rude militia in Roman wars, or, more widely, between a soldier and a civilian. Thus the Christians who prided themselves on being "soldiers of Christ" (*milites*) could rightly term

the non-Christians *pagani*. See also Gibbon, *Decline and Fall of the Roman Empire* (ed. Bury, 1896), ch. xxi. note *ad fin.*

PAGANINI, NICOLO (1784–1840), Italian virtuoso on the violin, was born at Genoa on the 18th of February 1784. His father Antonio, a clever amateur, who was in the shipping business, taught him the violin at a very early age, and he had further lessons from the *maestro di cappella* of the cathedral of San Lorenzo He first appeared in public at Genoa in 1793, with triumphant success. In 1795 he visited Parma for the purpose of taking lessons from Alessandro Rolla, who, however, said that he had nothing to teach him On returning home, he studied more diligently than ever, practising single passages for ten hours at a time, and publishing compositions so difficult that he alone could play them. His first professional tour, through the cities of Lombardy, was made with his father in 1797. For some years he led a chequered career; he gambled at cards, and had to pawn his violin; and between 1801 and 1804 he lived in retirement, in Tuscany, with a noble lady who was in love with him. In 1805 however he started on a tour through Europe, astonishing the world with his matchless performances, and especially with his unprecedented playing on the fourth string alone The princess of Lucca and Piombo, Napoleon's sister, made him her musical director, and he became a prominent figure at the court where his caprices and audacities were a byword He abandoned this in 1813, and visited Bologna, Milan, and other cities, gaining further fame by his extraordinary virtuosity In Venice, in 1815, he began a liaison with Antonia Bianchi, a dancer, which lasted till 1828; and by her he had a son Achillino, born in 1826. Meanwhile the world rang with his praises. In 1827 the pope honoured him with the Order of the Golden Spur; and, in the following year, he extended his travels to Germany, beginning with Vienna, where he created a profound sensation. He first appeared in Paris in 1831; and on the 3rd of June in that year his visit to England was preluded by the most romantic stories. He was described as a political victim who had been immured for twenty years in a dungeon, where he played all day long upon an old broken violin with one string, and thus gained his wonderful mechanical dexterity. The result of this and other foolish reports was that he could not walk the streets without being mobbed. He charged what for that time were enormous fees; and his net profits in England alone, during his six years of absence from his own country, amounted to some £17,000. In 1832 he returned to Italy, and bought a villa near Parma. In 1833 he spent the winter in Paris, and in 1834 Berlioz composed for him his beautiful symphony, *Harold en Italie*. He was then at the zenith of his fame; but his health, long since ruined by excessive study, declined rapidly. In 1838 he suffered serious losses in Paris through the failure of the "Casino Paganini," a gambling-house which was refused a licence. The disasters of this year increased his malady—laryngeal phthisis—and, after much suffering, he died at Nice on the 17th of May 1840. His will left a fortune of £80,000 to his son Achillino; and he bequeathed one of his violins, a fine Joseph Guarnerius, given him in early life by a kind French merchant, to the municipality of Genoa, who preserve it as one of their treasures. Paganini's style was impressive and passionate to the last degree. His *cantabile* passages moved his audience to tears, while his *tours de force* were so astonishing that a Viennese amateur publicly declared that he had seen the devil assisting him. His name stands in history as that of the most extraordinary executant ever known on the violin; and in spite of greater artists or no less remarkable later virtuosi, this reputation will remain with Paganini as the inaugurator of an epoch. He was the first to show what could be done by brilliance of technique, and his compositions were directed to that end. He was an undeniable genius, and it may be added that he behaved and looked like one, with his tall, emaciated figure and long black hair.

There are numerous lives of Paganini; see the article and bibliography in Grove's *Dictionary of Music*.

PAGE, THOMAS NELSON (1853-), American author, was born at Oakland Plantation, Hanover county, Virginia, on the 23rd of April 1853, the great-grandson of Thomas Nelson (1738-1789) and of John Page (1744-1808), both governors of Virginia, the former being a signer of the Declaration of Independence. After a course at Washington and Lee University (1869-1872) he graduated in law at the university of Virginia (1874), and practised, chiefly in Richmond, until 1893, when he removed to Washington, D. C., and devoted himself to writing and lecturing. In 1884 he had published in the *Century Magazine* "Marse Chan," a tale of life in Virginia during the Civil War, which immediately attracted attention. He wrote other stories of negro life and character ("Meh Lady," "Unc' Edinburg's Drowndia'," and "Ole 'Stracted "), which, with two others, were published in 1887 with the title *In Ole Virginia*, perhaps his most characteristic book. This was followed by *Befo' de War* (1888), dialect poems, written with Armistead Churchill Gordon (b. 1855); *On Newfound River* (1891), *The Old South* (1891), social and political essays; *Elsket and Other Stories* (1892), *The Burial of the Guns* (1894); *Pastime Stories* (1894), *The Old Gentleman of the Black Stock* (1897), *Social Life in Old Virginia before the War* (1897); *Two Prisoners* (1898), *Red Rock* (1898), a novel of the Reconstruction period; *Gordon Keith* (1903); *The Negro: the Southerner's Problem* (1904), *Bred in the Bone and Other Stories* (1904); *The Coast of Bohemia* (1906), poems; *The Old Dominion: Her Making and her Manners* (1907), a collection of essays; *Under the Crust* (1907), stories; *Robert E. Lee, the Southerner* (1908); *John Marvel, Assistant* (1909), a novel; and various books for children. He is at his best in those short stories in which, through negro character and dialect, he pictures the life of the Virginia gentry, especially as it centred about the mutual devotion of master and servant.

PAGE, WILLIAM (1811-1885), American artist, was born at Albany, New York, on the 3rd of January 1811. He studied for the ministry at the Andover Theological Seminary in 1828-1830 and in later life became a Swedenborgian. He received his training in art from S. F. B. Morse and in the schools of the National Academy of Design, and in 1836 became a National Academician. From 1849 to 1860, he lived in Rome, where he painted portraits of his friends Robert and Elizabeth Browning. The first collection of Lowell's *Poems* (1843) was dedicated to Page, who was also a friend of W. W. Story. In 1871-1873 he was president of the National Academy of Design. He died at Tottenville, Staten Island, New York, on the 1st of October 1885. Besides numerous portraits he painted "Farragut at the Battle of Mobile," belonging to the Tsar of Russia; a "Holy Family," in the Boston Athenaeum; and "The Young Merchants," at the Pennsylvania Academy of the Fine Arts, Philadelphia. He modelled and painted several portraits of Shakespeare, based on the Becker "death mask." He wrote *A New Geometrical Method of Measuring the Human Figure* (1860).

PAGE. (1) A term used of a boy, lad or young male person in various capacities, positions or offices. The etymology is doubtful; the word is common to the Romanic languages; cf. O. Fr. and Span. *page*, Port. *pagem*, Ital. *poggio* The Med. Lat. *pagius* has been commonly referred to Gr. *παιδίον*, diminutive of *παῖς*, boy, but the connexion is extremely doubtful. Others refer the word to the *pueri paedagogiani*, young slaves trained to become *paedagogi* (Gr. *παιδαγωγοί*), or tutors to young boys attending school. Under the empire, numbers of such youths were attached to the imperial household for the purposes of ceremonial attendance on state occasions, thus occupying much the same position as that of the pages of a royal or noble household in medieval and modern times. In fact the term *paedagogiani* became equivalent to *pueri honorarii, qui in palatio ministerio principis militabant* (so Du Cange, *Glossarium*, s.v.). Littré refers *pagius* to *pagensis*, i.e. rustic, belonging to the country districts (*pagus*), and adduces from this the fact that the *pagii* were not necessarily boys or youths; and quotes from Claude Fauchet (1530-1601) the statement (Lib. I. *Orig. milit.* cap. i.) that up to the time of

Charles VI. (1368-1403) and Charles VII. (1403-1461) "le mot de Page . . . . semblait être seulement donné à de viles personnes, comme à garçons de pied." Skeat (*Etym. Dict.*) points out that the form of the word in Portuguese, *pagem*, indicates the derivation from *pagensis*. The word "page" was applied in English to a boy or youth who was employed as an assistant to an older servant, acting as it were as an apprentice and learning his duties. In present usage the chief applications are: (a) to a boy or lad, generally wearing livery, and sometimes styled a "buttons," who is employed as a domestic servant; and (b) to a young boy who, dressed in fancy costume, forms part of the bridal procession at weddings. The word is also used (c) as the title of various officials of different rank in royal and other households; thus in the British royal household there are pages of honour, a page of the chambers, pages of the presence, and pages of the back stairs These, no doubt, descend from the *pueri paedagogiani* of the Roman imperial household through the young persons of noble or gentle birth, who, during the middle and later ages, served in the household of royal and noble persons, and received a training to fit them for their future position in society. In the times of chivalry the "page" was one who served a knight and was trained to knighthood, and ranked next to a squire. (See KNIGHTHOOD and VALET.)

(2) In the sense of one side of a leaf of printed or written matter, the word is *pagina*, pagina, and is derived through Fr. from Lat. *pagina* (*pangere*, to fasten).

PAGEANT, in its most general sense a show or spectacle; the more specific meanings are involved in the etymology of the word and its connexion with the history of the early mystery plays (see DRAMA). In its early forms, dating from the 14th century, the word is *pagyn* or *pagen*, the excrescent *t* or *d*, as in "tyrant," "ancient," not appearing till later. The Med. Lat. equivalent is *pagina*, and this, or at least the root from which it is formed, must be taken as the source. The senses, however, in which the word is used, viz. stage, platform, or scene played on a stage, are not those of the classical Lat. *pagina*, a page of a book, nor do they apparently occur in the medieval Latin of any language other than English. Further, it is not clear which meaning comes first, platform or scene. If the last, then "scene," i.e. a division of a play, might develop out of "page" of a book. If not, then *pagina* is a fresh formation from the root *pag* of *pangere*, to fix or fasten, the word meaning a fastened framework of wood forming a stage or platform; cf. the classical use of *compago*, structure. Others take *pagina* as a translation of Gr. *πήγμα*, platform, stage, a word from the same root *pag-*. Du Cange (*Glossarium*) quotes a use in Med. Lat. of *pegma* in this sense, *Machina lignea in qua statuae collocabantur*, and, Cotgrave gives " *Pegmate*, a stage or frame whereon pageants be set or carried."

As has been said, "pageant" is first found in the sense of a scene, a division or part of a play or of the platform on which such scene was played in the medieval drama. Thus we read of Queen Margaret in 1457 that at Coventry she saw "alle the pagentes pleyde save domesday which myght not be pleyde for lak of day," and in the accounts of the Smiths' gild at Coventry for 1450, five pence is paid "to bring the pageant into gosford-stret." A clear idea of what these stages were like when the mystery plays became processional (*processus*), that is, were acted on separate platforms moving along a street, is seen in Archdeacon Roger's contemporary account of the Chester plays about the end of the 16th century. "The maner of these playes were, every company had his pagiant, or parte, which pageants weare a high scafolde with 2 rowmes, a higher and a lower, upon 4 wheeles " (T. Sharp, *Dissertation on the Pageants or Mysteries at Coventry*, 1825, which contains most of the early references to the word). The movable platform, filled with emblematic or allegorical figures, naturally played an important part in processional shows with no dialogue or dramatic action. An instance (1432) of the practice and the use of the word is found in the *Munimenta gildhallae londiniensis* (ed. Riley), "Parabatur machina. . . . in cujus medio stabat gigas mirae magnitudinis .... ex utroque · latere . . . in eadem pagina erigebantur duo animalia vocata *antelops*." At Anne Boleyn's coronation, June 1, 1533, one "pageant" contained figures of Apollo and the Muses, another represented a castle, with "a heavenly roof and under it upon a green was a root or stock, whereout sprang a multitude of white and red roses" (Arber, *English Garner*, ii. 47, quoted in the *New English Dictionary*). Such "pageants" formed a feature, in a somewhat degraded shape, in the annual lord mayor's show in London. The development in meaning from "moving platform" to that of a "processional spectacle" or "show" is obvious.

The 20th century has seen in England what may in some respects be looked on as a revival but in general as a new departure in the shape of semi-dramatic spectacles illustrative of the history of a town or locality; to such spectacles the name of "Pageant" has been appropriately given. Coventry in its procession in commemoration of Lady Godiva's traditional exploit, has since 1678 illustrated an incident, however mythical, in the history of the town, and many of the ancient cities of the continent of Europe, as Siena, Bruges, Nuremberg, &c., have had, and still have, at intervals a procession of persons in the costumes of various periods, and of figures emblematical of the towns' associations and history. The modern pageant is far removed from a mere procession in dumb show, however bright with colour and interesting from an historical or artistic point of view such may be made. It consists of a series of scenes, representing historical events directly connected with the town or locality in which the pageant takes place. These are accompanied by appropriate dialogue, speeches, songs, &c., and with music and dances. The effect is naturally much heightened by the place of the performance, more particularly if this is the actual site of some of the scenes depicted, as at the Winchester Pageant (1908) where the background was formed by the ruins of Wolvesey Castle. The Sherborne pageant of 1905 was the first of the series of pageants. In 1907 and 1908 they became very numerous; of these the principal may be mentioned, those at Oxford, Bury St Edmunds in 1907; at Winchester, Chelsea, Dover and Pevensey in 1908; and that of the English Church at Fulham Palace 1909, a peculiarly interesting example of a pageant connected with an institution and not a locality.

The artistic success of a pageant depends on the beauty or historic interest of its site, the skilful choice of episodes and dramatic incidents, the grouping and massing of colour, and the appropriateness of the dialogue, speeches and incidental music. It is here that the skill and talent of the writer, designer or director of the pageant find scope. The name of the dramatist Louis N. Parker (b. 1852), the author of the Sherborne pageant, the earliest and one of the most successful, must always be associated with the movement, of which he was the originator."

More important, perhaps, than the aesthetic pleasure given is the educational effect produced not only on the spectators but also on the performers. The essence of the pageant is that all who take part are residents in the place and locality, that the costumes and accessories should be made locally, and that all classes and all ages should share in a common enthusiasm for the bringing back in the most vivid form the past history, often forgotten, in which all should feel they have an equal and common part.　　　　　　　　　　　　(C. We.)

PAGET, SIR JAMES, Bart. (1814–1899), British surgeon, born at Yarmouth on the 11th of January 1814, was the son of a brewer and shipowner. He was one of a large family, and his brother Sir George Paget (1809–1892), who became regius professor of physic at Cambridge in 1872, also had a distinguished career in medicine and was made a K.C.B. He attended a day-school in Yarmouth, and afterwards was destined for the navy; but this plan was given up, and at the age of sixteen he was apprenticed to a general practitioner, whom he served for four and a half years, during which time he gave his leisure hours to botanizing, and made a great collection of the flora of East Norfolk. At the end of his apprenticeship he published

with one of his brothers a very careful *Sketch of the Natural History of Yarmouth and its Neighbourhood*. In October 1834 he entered as a student at St Bartholomew's Hospital. Medical students in those days were left very much to themselves; there was no close supervision of their work, but it is probable that Paget gained rather than lost by having to fight his own way. He swept the board of prizes in 1835, and again in 1836; and in his first winter session he detected the presence of the *Trichina spiralis*, a minute parasite that infests the muscles of the human body.[1] In May 1836 he passed his examination at the Royal College of Surgeons, and became qualified to practise. The next seven years (1836–1843) were spent in London lodgings, and were a time of poverty, for he made only £15 a year by practice, and his father, having failed in business, could not give him any help. He managed to keep himself by writing for the medical journals, and preparing the catalogues of the hospital museum and of the pathological museum of the Royal College of Surgeons. In 1836 he had been made curator of the hospital museum, and in 1838 demonstrator of morbid anatomy at the hospital; but his advancement there was hindered by the privileges of the hospital apprentices, and by the fact that he had been too poor to afford a house-surgeoncy, or even a dressership. In 1841 he was made surgeon to the Finsbury Dispensary, but this appointment did not give him any experience in the graver operations of surgery. In 1843 he was appointed lecturer on general anatomy (microscopic anatomy) and physiology at the hospital, and warden of the hospital college then founded. For the next eight years he lived within the walls of the hospital, in charge of about thirty students resident in the little college. Besides his lectures and his superintendence of the resident students, he had to enter all new students, to advise them how to work, and to manage the finances and the general affairs of the school. Thus he was constantly occupied with the business of the school, and often passed a week, or more, without going outside the hospital gates. In 1844 he married Lydia, youngest daughter of the Rev. Henry North. In 1847 he was appointed an assistant-surgeon to the hospital, and Arris and Gale professor at the College of Surgeons. He held this professorship for six years and each year gave six lectures in surgical pathology. (The first edition of these lectures, which were the chief scientific work of his life, was published in 1853 as *Lectures on Surgical Pathology*.) In 1851 he was elected a Fellow of the Royal Society. In October 1851 he resigned the wardenship of the hospital. He had now become known as a great physiologist and pathologist: he had done for pathology in England what R. Virchow had done in Germany; but he had hardly begun to get into practice, and he had kept himself poor that he might pay his share of his father's debts—a task that it took him fourteen years to fulfil.

It is probable that no famous surgeon, not even John Hunter, ever founded his practice deeper in science than Paget did, or waited longer for his work to come back to him. In physiology he had mastered the chief English, French, German, Dutch and Italian literature of the subject, and by incessant study and microscope work had put himself level with the most advanced knowledge of his time; so that it was said of him by R. Owen, in 1851, that he had his choice, either to be the first physiologist in Europe, or to have the first surgical practice in London, with a baronetcy. His physiological lectures at St Bartholomew's Hospital were the chief cause of the rise in the fortunes of its school, which in 1843 had gone down to a low point. In pathology his work was even more important. He fills the place in pathology that had been left empty by Hunter's death in 1793—the time of transition from Hunter's teaching;

[1] This discovery is usually credited to R. Owen (q.v.). The facts appear to be as follows: Paget was a first-year's student, and, by means of a pocket lens, found in the dissecting-room that the specks in the infected muscles were parasitic worms and not, as previously thought, spicules of bone. Thomas Wormald, the senior demonstrator, who was no pathologist, sent a piece of the same muscle to Owen, who authoritatively pronounced the specks to be parasites and gave them their scientific name. It is probable that Owen did not realize that Paget had already made the discovery, and it was naturally associated with the name of the professor.

which for all its greatness was hindered by want of the modern microscope, to the pathology and bacteriology of the present day. It is Paget's greatest achievement that he made pathology dependent, in everything, on the use of the microscope—especially the pathology of tumours. He and Virchow may truly be called the founders of modern pathology; they stand together, Paget's *Lectures on Surgical Pathology* and Virchow's *Cellular-Pathologie*. When Paget, in 1851, began practice near Cavendish Square, he had still to wait a few years more for success in professional life. The "turn of the tide" came about 1854 or 1855; and in 1858 he was appointed surgeon extraordinary to Queen Victoria, and in 1863 surgeon in ordinary to the prince of Wales. He had for many years the largest and most arduous surgical practice in London. His day's work was seldom less than sixteen or seventeen hours. Cases sent to him for final judgment, with especial frequency, 'were those of tumours, and of all kinds of disease of the bones and joints, and all " neurotic " cases having symptoms of surgical disease. His supremacy lay rather in the science than in the art of surgery, but his name is associated also with certain great practical advances. He discovered the disease of the breast and the disease of the bones (osteitis deformans) which are called after his name; and he was the first at the hospital to urge enucleation of the tumour, instead of amputation of the limb, in cases of myeloid sarcoma.

In 1871 he nearly died from infection at a post mortem examination, and, to lighten the weight of his work, was obliged to resign his surgeoncy to the hospital. In this same year he received the honour of a baronetcy. In 1875 he was president of the Royal College of Surgeons, and in 1877 Hunterian orator. In 1878 he gave up operating, but for eight or ten years longer he still had a very heavy consulting practice. In 1881 he was president of the International Medical Congress held in London; in 1880 he gave, at Cambridge, a memorable address on " Elemental Pathology," setting forth the likeness of certain diseases of plants and trees to those of the human body. Besides shorter writings he also published *Clinical Lectures and Essays* (1st ed. 1875) and *Studies of Old Case-books* (1891). In 1883, on the death of Sir George Jessel, he was appointed vice-chancellor of the university of London. In 1889 he was appointed a member of the royal commission on vaccination. He died in London on the 30th of December 1899, in his eighty-fifth year. Sir James Paget had the gift of eloquence, and was one of the most careful and most delightful speakers of his time. He had a natural and unaffected pleasure in society, and he loved music. He possessed the rare gift of ability to turn swiftly from work to play; enjoying his holidays like a schoolboy, easily moved to laughter, keen to get the maximum of happiness out of very ordinary amusements, emotional in spite of incessant self-restraint, vigorous in spite of constant overwork. In him a certain light-hearted enjoyment was combined with the utmost reserve, unfailing religious faith, and the most scrupulous honour. He was all his life profoundly indifferent toward politics, both national and medical; his ideal was the unity of science and practice in the professional life. (S. P.)

PAGET OF BEAUDESERT, WILLIAM PAGET, 1ST BARON (1506-1563), English statesman, son of William Paget, one of the serjeants-at-mace of the city of London, was born in London in 1506, and was educated at St Paul's School, and at Trinity Hall, Cambridge, proceeding afterwards to the university of Paris. Probably through the influence of Stephen Gardiner, who had early befriended Paget, he was employed by Henry VIII. in several important diplomatic missions; in 1532 he was appointed clerk of the signet and soon afterwards of the privy council. He became secretary to Queen Anne of Cleves in 1539, and in 1543 he was sworn of the privy council and appointed secretary of state, in which position Henry VIII in his later years relied much on his advice, appointing him one of the council to act during the minority of Edward VI. Paget at first vigorously supported the protector Somerset, while counselling a moderation which Somerset did not always observe. In 1547 he was made comptroller of the king's house-

hold, chancellor of the duchy of Lancaster, and a knight of the Garter; and in 1549 he was summoned by writ to the House of Lords as Baron Paget de Beaudesert. About the same time he obtained extensive grants of lands, including Cannock Chase and Burton Abbey in Staffordshire; and in London the residence of the bishops of Exeter, afterwards known successively as Lincoln House and Essex House, on the site now occupied by the Outer Temple in the Strand. He also obtained Beaudesert in Staffordshire, which is still the chief seat of the Paget family. Paget shared Somerset's disgrace, being committed to the Tower in 1551 and degraded from the Order of the Garter in the following year, besides suffering a heavy fine by the Star Chamber for having profited at the expense of the Crown in his administration of the duchy of Lancaster. He was, however, restored to the king's favour in 1553, and was one of the twenty-six peers who signed Edward's settlement of the crown on Lady Jane Grey in June of that year. He made his peace with Queen Mary, who reinstated him as a knight of the Garter and in the privy council in 1553, and appointed him lord privy seal in 1556. On the accession of Elizabeth in 1558 Paget retired from public life, and died on the 9th of June 1563.

By his wife Anne Preston he had four sons, the two eldest of whom, Henry (d. 1568) and Thomas, succeeded in turn to the peerage. The youngest son, Charles Paget (d. 1612), was a well-known Catholic conspirator against Queen Elizabeth, in the position of secretary to Archbishop James Beaton, the ambassador of Mary Queen of Scots in Paris; although at times he also played the part of a spy and forwarded information to Walsingham and Cecil. Thomas, 3rd Baron Paget of Beaudesert (c. 1540-1589), a zealous Roman Catholic, was suspected of complicity in Charles's plots and was attainted in 1587. But the peerage was restored in 1604 to his son William (1572-1629), 4th Lord Paget, whose son William, the 5th lord (1609-1678), fought for Charles I. at Edgehill. William, the 6th lord (1637-1713), a supporter of the Revolution of 1688, was ambassador at Vienna from 1689 to 1693, and later at Constantinople, having much to do with bringing about the important treaty of Carlowitz in 1699. Henry, the 7th baron (c. 1665-1743), was raised to the peerage during his father's lifetime as Baron Burton in 1712, being one of the twelve peers created by the Tory ministry to secure a majority in the House of Lords, and was created earl of Uxbridge in 1714. His only son, Thomas Catesby Paget, the author of an *Essay on Human Life* (1734) and other writings, died in January 1742 before his father, leaving a son Henry (1719-1769), who became 2nd earl of Uxbridge. At the latter's death the earldom of Uxbridge and barony of Burton became extinct, the older barony of Paget of Beaudesert passing to his cousin Henry Bayly (1744-1812), heir general of the first baron, who in 1784 was created earl of Uxbridge. His second son, Sir Arthur Paget (1771-1840), was an eminent diplomatist during the Napoleonic wars, Sir Edward Paget (1775-1840), the fourth son, served under Sir John Moore in the Peninsula, and was afterwards second in command under Sir Arthur Wellesley; the fifth, Sir Charles Paget (1778-1839), served with distinction in the navy, and rose to the rank of vice-admiral. The eldest son Henry William, 2nd earl of Uxbridge (1768-1854), was in 1815 created marquess of Anglesey (q.v.).

PAGHMAN, a small district of Afghanistan to the west of Kabul, lying under the Paghman branch of the Hindu Kush range. It is exceedingly picturesque, the villages clinging to the sides of the mountain glens from which water is drawn for irrigation; and excellent fruit is grown.

PAGODA (Port. *pagode*, a word introduced in the 16th century by the early Portuguese adventurers in India, reproducing phonetically some native word, possibly Pers. *but-kodah*, a house for an idol, or some form of Sansk. *bhagavat*, divine, holy), an Eastern term for a temple, especially a building of a pyramid shape common in India and the Far East and devoted to sacred purposes; in Buddhist countries, notably China, the name of a many-sided tower in which are kept holy relics. More loosely " pagoda " is used in the East to signify any non-Christian or non-Mussulman place of worship. Pagoda or pagod was also the name given to a gold (occasionally also silver) coin, of about the value of seven shillings, at one time current in southern India. From this meaning is derived the expression "the pagoda tree," as synonymous with the "wealth of the Indies," whence the phrase to "shake the pagoda tree." There is a real tree, the *Plumieria acuminata*, bearing the name. It grows in India, and is of a small and graceful shape, and bears yellow and white flowers tinged with red.

PAHARI (properly Pahārī, the language of the mountains), a general name applied to the Indo-Aryan languages or dialects spoken in the lower ranges of the Himalaya from Nepal in the east, to Chamba of the Punjab in the west. These forms of speech fall into three groups—an eastern, consisting of the various dialects of Khas-kurā, the language of Nepal; a central, spoken in the north of the United Provinces, in Kumaon and Garhwal; and a western, spoken in the country round Simla and in Chamba. In Nepal, Khas-kura is the language only of the Aryan population, the mother tongue of most of the inhabitants being some form or. other of Tibeto-Burman speech (see TIBETO-BURMAN LANGUAGES), not Indo-Aryan. As may be expected, Khas-kura is mainly differentiated from Central Pahari through its being affected, both in grammar and vocabulary, by Tibeto-Burman idioms. The speakers of Central and Western Pahari have not been brought into close association with Tibeto-Burmans, and their language is therefore purely Aryan.

Khas-kurā, as its speakers themselves call it, passes under various names. The English generally call it Nēpālī or Naipālī (*i.e.* the language of Nepal), which is a misnomer, for it is not the principal form of speech used in that country. Moreover, the Nepalese employ a corruption of this very word to indicate what is really the main language of the country; viz. the Tibeto-Burman Nēwārī. Khas-kura is also called Gōrkhālī, or the language of the Gurkhas, and Pahārī or Parbatiyā, the language of the mountains. The number of speakers is not known, no census ever having been taken of Nepal; but in British India 143,721 were recorded in the census of 1901, most of whom were soldiers in, or others connected with, the British Gurkha regiments.

Central Pahari includes three dialects—Garhwālī, spoken mainly in Garhwal and the country round the hill station of Mussoorie; Jaunsārī, spoken in the Jaunsar tract of Dehra Dun; and Kumaunī, spoken in Kumaun, including the country round the hill station of Naini Tal. In 1901 the number of speakers was 1,270,931.

Western Pahari presents a great number of dialects. In the Simla Hill states alone no less than twenty-two, of which the most important are Sirmaurī and Keonṭhalī (the dialect of Simla itself), were recorded at the last census. To these may be added Chambiālī and Churāhī of the state of Chamba, Mandeālī of the state of Mandī, Gādī of Chamba and Kangra, Kuluhī of Kulu and others. In 1901 the total number of speakers was 1,710,029.

The southern face of the Himalaya has from time immemorial been occupied by two classes of people. In the first place there is an Indo-Chinese overflow from Tibet in the north. Most of these tribes speak Indo-Chinese languages of the Tibeto-Burman family, while a few have abandoned their ancestral speech and now employ broken half-Aryan dialects. The other class consists of the great tribe of Khasas or Khasiyās, Aryan in origin, the Κάσιοι of the Greek geographers. Who these people originally were, and how they entered India, are questions which have been more than once discussed without arriving at any very definite conclusion.[1] They are frequently mentioned in Sanskrit literature, were a thorn in the side of the rulers of Kashmir, and have occupied the lower Himalayas for many centuries. Nothing positive is known about their language, which they have long abandoned. Judging from the relics of it which appear in modern Pahari, it is probable that it belonged to the

same group as Kashmiri, Lahnda and Sindhi. They spread slowly from west to east, and are traditionally said to have reached Nepal in the early part of the 12th century A.D.

In the central and western Pahari tracts local traditions assert that from very early times there was constant communication with Rajputana and with the great kingdom of Kanauj in the Gangetic Doab. A succession of immigrants, the tide of which was materially increased at a later period by the pressure of the Mussulman invasion of India, entered the country, and founded several dynasties, some of which survive to the present day. These Rajputs intermarried with the Khasa inhabitants of their new home, and gave their rank to the descendants of these mixed unions. With the pride of birth these new-born Rajputs inherited the language of their fathers, and thus the tongue of the ruling class, and subsequently of the whole population of this portion of the Himalaya, became a form of Rajasthani, the language spoken in distant Rajputana.

The Rajput occupation of Nepal is of later date. In the early part of the 16th century a number of Rajputs of Udaipur in Rajputana, being oppressed by the Mussulmans, fled north and settled in Garhwal, Kumaon, and western Nepal. In A.D. 1559 a party of these conquered the small state of Gurkha, which lay about 70 m. north-west of Katmandu, the present capital of Nepal. In 1768 Prithwi Narayan Shah, the then Rajput ruler of Gurkha, made himself master of the whole of Nepal and founded the present Gurkhali dynasty of that country. His successors extended their rule westwards over Kumaon and Garhwal, and as far as the Simla Hill states. The inhabitants of Nepal included not only Aryan Khasas, but also, as has been said, a number of Tibeto-Burman tribes. The Rajputs of Gurkha could not impose their language upon these as they did upon the Khasas, but, owing to its being the tongue of the ruling race, it ultimately became generally understood and employed as the *lingua franca* of this polyglot country. Although the language of the Khasas has disappeared, the tribe is still numerically the most important Aryan one in this part of the Himalaya, and it hence gave its name to its newly adopted speech, which is at the present day locally known as "Khas-kura."

In the manner described above the Aryan language of the whole Pahari area is now a form of Rajasthani, exhibiting at the same time traces of the old Khasa language which it superseded, and also in Nepal of the Tibeto-Burman forms of speech by which it is surrounded. (For information regarding Rajasthani the reader is referred to the articles INDO-ARYAN LANGUAGES; PRAKRIT; and GUJARATI.)

Khas-kura shows most traces of Tibeto-Burman influence. The gender of nouns is purely sexual, and, although there is an oblique case derived from Rajasthani, it is so often confounded with the nominative, that in the singular number either can be employed for the other. Both these are due to Tibeto-Burman influence, but the non-Aryan idiom is most prominent in the use of the verb. There is an indefinite tense referring to present, past or future time according to the context, formed by suffixing the verb substantive to the root of the main verb, exactly as in some of the neighbouring Tibeto-Burman languages. There is a complete impersonal honorific conjugation which reminds one strongly of Tibetan. and, in colloquial speech, as in that tongue, the subject of any tense of a transitive verb, not only of a tense derived from the past participle, is put into the agent case.

In Eastern and Central Pahari the verb substantive is formed from the root *ach*, as in both Rajasthani and Kashmiri. In Rajasthani its present tense, being derived from the Sanskrit present *rcchāmi*, I go, does not change for gender. But in Pahari and Kashmiri it must be derived from the rare Sanskrit particle *rcchitas*, gone, for in these languages it is a participial tense and does change according to the gender of the subject. Thus, in the singular we have:—

	Khas-kura.		Kumauni.		Kashmiri.	
	Masc.	Fem.	Masc.	Fem.	Masc.	Fem.
I am . . .	chu	chu	chū	chū	chus	ches
Thou art . .	chas	ches	chai	chī	chukh	chekh
He is . . .	cha	cha	ch	chī	chuh	chĕh

Here we have a relic of the old Khasa language, which, as has been said, seems to have been related to Kashmiri. Other relics of Khasa,

[1] See ch. iv. of vol. ii. of R. T. Atkinson's *Himalayan Districts of the North-Western Provinces of India*, forming vol. xi of the "Gazetteer of the North-Western Provinces" (Allahabad, 1884), and the *Archaeological Survey of India*, xiv. 125 sqq. (Calcutta, 1882).

again agreeing with north-western India, are the tendency to shorten long vowels, the practice of epenthesis, or the modification of a vowel by the one which follows in the next syllable, and the frequent occurrence of disaspiration. Thus, Khas *sikhu*, Kumauni *sikhō*, but Hindi *sīkhnā*, to learn; Kumauni *yāsō*, plural *yāsā*, of this kind.

Regarding Western Pahari materials are not so complete. The speakers are not brought into contact with Tibeto-Burman languages, and hence we find no trace of these. But the signs of the influence of north-western languages are, as might be expected, still more apparent than farther east. In some dialects epenthesis is in full swing, as in (Churāhī) *khdid*, eating, fem. *khditi*. Very interesting is the mixed origin of the postpositions defining the various cases. Thus, while that of the genitive is generally the Rajasthani *rō*, that of the dative continually points to the west. Sometimes it is the Sindhi *kkā* (see SINDHĪ). At other times it is *jō*, where is here a locative of the base of the Sindhi genitive postposition *jō*. In all Indo-Aryan languages, the dative postposition is by origin the locative of some genitive one. In vocabulary, Western Pahari often employs, for the more common ideas, words which can most readily be connected with the north-western and Piśāca groups. (See INDO-ARYAN LANGUAGES.)

LITERATURE.—Khas-kura has a small literature which has grown up in recent years. We may mention the *Birsikhā*, an anonymous collection of folk-tales, and a *Rāmāyana* by Bhānu Bhaṭṭa. There are also several translations from Sanskrit. Of late years local scholars have done a good deal towards creating an interest in Central Pahari. Special mention may be made of Ganga Datt Upreti's *Proverbs and Folklore of Kumaun and Garhwal* (Lodiana, 1894); the same author's *Dialects of the Kumaun Division* (Almora, 1900); and Jwala Datt Joshi's translation of Daṇḍin's Sanskrit *Daśa Kumāra Carita* (Almora, 1892). A local poet who lived about a century ago, Gumānī Kavi by name, was the author of verses written in a peculiar style, and now much admired. Each verse consists of four lines, the first three being in Sanskrit, and the fourth a Hindi or Kumauni proverb. A collection of these, edited by Rewa Datt Upreti, was published in the *Indian Antiquary* for 1909 (pp. 177 seq.) under the title of *Gumānī-nīti*. Western Pahari has no literature. Portions of the Bible have been translated into Khas-kura (under the name of " Nepali "), Kumauni, Garhwali, Jaunsari and Chambiali.

AUTHORITIES.—S. H. Kellogg's *Hindi Grammar* (2nd ed., London, 1893) includes both Eastern and Central Pahari in its survey. For Khas see also A. Turnbull, *Nepali*, *i.e. Gorkhali or Parbate Grammar* (Darjeeling, 1904), and G. A. Grierson, " A Specimen of the Khas or Naipāli Language," in the *Zeitschrift der deutschen morgenländischen Gesellschaft* (1907), lxi. 659 seq. There is no authority dealing with Western Pahari as a whole. A. H. Diack's work, *The Kulu Dialect of Hindi* (Lahore, 1896), may be consulted for Kuluhi. See also T. Grahame Bailey's *Languages of the Northern Himalayas* (Royal Asiatic Society, London, 1908). Vol. ix., pt. iv., of the *Linguistic Survey of India* contains full particulars of all the Pahari dialects in great detail. (G. A. GR.)

PAHLAVĪ, or PEHLEVI, the name given by the followers of Zoroaster to the character in which are written the ancient translations of their sacred books and some other works which they preserve (see PERSIA: *Language*). The name can be traced back for many centuries; the great epic poet Firdousī (second half of the 10th Christian century) repeatedly speaks of Pahlavī books as the sources of his narratives, and he tells us among other things that in the time of the first Khosrau (Chosroes I., A.D. 531–579) the Pahlavī character alone was used in Persia.[1] The learned Ibn Mokaffa' (8th century) calls Pahlavī one of the languages of Persia, and seems to imply that it was an official language.[2] We cannot determine what characters, perhaps also dialects, were called Pahlavī before the Arab period. It is most suitable to confine the word, as is now generally done, to designate a kind of writing—not only that of the Pahlavī books, but of all inscriptions on stone and metal which use similar characters and are written on essentially the same principles as these books.

At first sight the Pahlavī books present the strangest spectacle of mixture of speech. Purely Semitic (Aramaic) words—and these not only nouns and verbs, but numerals, particles, demonstrative and even personal pronouns—stand side by side with Persian vocables. Often, however, the Semitic words are compounded in a way quite unsemitic, or have Persian terminations. As read by the modern Zoroastrians, there are also

many words which are neither Semitic nor Persian; but it is soon seen that this traditional pronunciation is untrustworthy. The character is cursive and very ambiguous, so that, for example, there is but one sign for *n*, *u*, and *r*, and one for *y*, *d*, and *g*, this has led to mistakes in the received pronunciation, which for many words can be shown to have been at one time more correct than it is now. But apart from such blunders there remain phenomena which could never have appeared in a real language; and the hot strife which raged till recently as to whether Pahlavī is Semitic or Persian has been closed by the discovery that it is merely a way of writing Persian in which the Persian words are partly represented—to the eye, not to the ear—by their Semitic equivalents. This view, the development of which began with Westergaard (*Zendavesta*, p. 20, note), is in full accordance with the true and ancient tradition. Thus Ibn Mokaffa', who translated many Pahlavī books into Arabic, tells us that the Persians had about one thousand words which they wrote otherwise than they were pronounced in Persian.[3] For *bread* he says they wrote LHMA, *i.e.* the Aramaic *lahmā*, but they pronounced *nān*, which is the common Persian word for bread. Similarly BSRA, the Aramaic *besrā*, flesh, was pronounced as the Persian *gōsht*. We still possess a glossary which actually gives the Pahlavī writing with its Persian pronunciation. This glossary, which besides Aramaic words contains also a variety of Persian words disguised in antique forms, or by errors due to the contracted style of writing, exists in various shapes, all of which, in spite of their corruptions, go back to the work which the statement of Ibn Mokaffa' had in view.[4] Thus the Persians did the same thing on a much larger scale, as when in English we write £ (libra) and pronounce " pound " or write & or & (et) and pronounce " and." No system was followed in the choice of Semitic forms. Sometimes a noun was written in its *status absolutus*, sometimes the emphatic *d* was added, and this was sometimes written as *n* sometimes as n. One verb was written in the perfect, another in the imperfect. Even various dialects were laid under contribution. The Semitic signs by which Persian synonyms were distinguished are sometimes quite arbitrary. Thus in Persian *khwēsh* and *khwat* both mean " self "; the former is written NFSHI (*nafshā* or *nafsheh*), the latter BNYSHE with the preposition *bê* prefixed. Personal pronouns are expressed in the dative (*i.e.* with prepositional *l* prefixed), thus LK (*lakh*) for *tu*, " thou," LNH (*lanā*) for *amā*, " we." Sometimes the same Semitic sign stands for two distinct Persian words that happen to agree in sound; thus because *hānā* is Aramaic for " this," HNA represents not only Persian *ē*, " this," but also the interjection *ē*, *i.e.* " O " as prefixed to a vocative. Sometimes for clearness a Persian termination is added to a Semitic word; thus, to distinguish between the two words for father, *pit* and *pitar*, the former is written AB and the latter ABITR. The Persian form is, however, not seldom used, even where there is a quite well-known Semitic ideogram.[5]

These difficulties of reading mostly disappear when the ideographic nature of the writing is recognized. We do not always know what Semitic word supplied some ambiguous group of letters (*e. g.* PUN for *pa*, " to," or HT for *agar*, " if "); but we always can tell the Persian word—which is the one important thing—though not always the exact pronunciation of it in that older stage of the language which the extant Pahlavī works belong to. In Pahlavī, for example, the word for " female " is written *mātak*, an ancient form which afterwards passed through *mādhak* into *mādha*. But it was a mistake of later ages to fancy that because this was so the sign T also meant D,

[1] We cannot assume, however, that the poet had a clear idea of what Pahlavī was.

[2] The passage, in which useful facts are mixed up with strange notions, is given abridged in *Fihrist*, p. 13. more fully by Yākūt, iii. 925. but most fully and accurately in the unprinted *Mafātīḥ al-ʿolūm*.

[3] *Fihrist*, p. 14, line 13 seq., cf. line 4 seq. The former passage was first cited by Quatremère, *Jour. As.* (1835), i. 256, and discussed by Clermont-Ganneau, ibid. (1866), i. 430. The expressions it uses are not always clear; perhaps the author of the *Fihrist* has condensed somewhat.

[4] Editions by Hoshangji, Jamaspji Asa and M. Haug (Bombay, 1870), and by C' Salemann (Leiden, 1878); See also J. Olshausen, " Zur Würdigung der Pahlavi-glossare " in Kuhn's *Zeit. f. vergl. Sprforsch.* N.F., vi. 521 seq.

[5] For examples of various peculiarities see the notes to Nöldeke's translation of the story of *Artakhshīr i Pāpakān* (Göttingen, 1879).

and so to write T for D in many cases, especially in foreign proper names. That a word is written in an older form than that which is pronounced is a phenomenon common to many languages whose literature covers a long period. So in English we still write, though we do not pronounce, the guttural in *through*, and write *laugh* when we pronounce *laf*.

Much graver difficulties arise from the cursive nature of the characters already alluded to. There are some groups which may theoretically be read in hundreds of ways; the same little sign may be *v̄*, *n̄*, *n*, *n̄*, *m̄*·*m*, *m*, and the *n* too may be either *h* or *hh*.

In older times there was still some little. distinction between letters that are now quite identical in form, but even the Egyptian fragments of Pahlavī writing of the 7th century show on the whole the same type as our MSS. The practical inconveniences to those who knew the language were not so great as they may seem; the Arabs also long used an equally ambiguous character without availing themselves of the diacritical points which had been devised long before.

Modern MSS., following Arabic models, introduce diacritical points from time to time, and often incorrectly. These give little help, however, in comparison with the so-called Pāzand or transcription of Pahlavī texts, as they are to be spoken, in the character in which the *Avestā* itself is written, and which is quite clear and has all vowels as well as consonants. The transcription is not philologically accurate; the language is often modernized, but not uniformly so. Pāzand MSS. present dialectical variations according to the taste or intelligence of authors and copyists, and all have many false readings. For us, however, they are of the greatest use. To get a conception of Pahlavī one cannot do better than read the *Mīnōi-Khiradh* in the Pahlavī with constant reference to the Pāzand.[1] Critical labour is still required to give an approximate reproduction of the author's own pronunciation of what he wrote.

The coins of the later Sassanid kings, of the princes of Tabaristan, and of some governors in the earlier Arab period, exhibit an alphabet very similar to Pahlavī MSS. On the older coins the several letters are more clearly distinguished, and in good specimens of well-struck coins of the oldest Sassanians almost every letter can be recognized with certainty. The same holds good for the inscriptions on gems and other small monuments of the early Sassanian period; but the clearest of all are the rock inscriptions of the Sassanians in the 3rd and 4th centuries, though in the 4th century a tendency to cursive forms begins to appear. Only *r* and *v* are always quite alike. The character of the language and the system of writing is essentially the same on coins, gems and rocks as in MSS.—pure Persian, in part strangely disguised in a Semitic garb. In details there are many differences between the Pahlavī of inscriptions and the books. Persian endings added to words written in Semitic form are much less common in the former, so that the person and number of a verb are often not to be made out. There are also orthographic variations; *e.g.* long *ā* in Persian forms is always expressed in book-Pahlavī, but not always in inscriptions. The unfamiliar contents of some of these inscriptions, their limited number, their bad preservation, and the imperfect way in which some of the most important of them have been published[2] leave many things still obscure in these monuments of Persian kings; but they have done much to clear up both great and small points in the history of Pahlavī.[3]

Some of the oldest Sassanian inscriptions are accompanied by a text belonging to the same system of writing, but with many variations in detail,[4] and an alphabet which, though derived

[1] *The Book of the Maīnyō-i-Khard in the Original Pahlavī*, ed. by Fr. Ch. Andreas (Kiel, 1882); idem, *The Pāzand and Sanskrit Texts*, by E. W. West (Stuttgart and London, 1871).

[2] See especially the great work of F. Stolze, *Persepolis* (2 vols., Berlin, 1882). It was De Sacy who began the decipherment of the inscriptions.

[3] Thus we now know that the ligature in book-Pahlavī which means " in," the original letters of which could not be made out, is for ʊ, " between." It is to be read *andar*.

[4] Thus *pus*, " son," is written ᴖ instead of ᴖᴖ; *pēsh*, " before," is written ᴖᴖ, but in the usual Pahlavī it is ᴖᴖᴖ = ᴖᴖᴖ.

from the same source with the other Pahlavī alphabets (the old Aramaic), has quite different forms. This character is also found on some gems and seals. It has been called Chaldaeo-Pahlavī, &c. Olshausen tries to make it probable that this was the writing of Media and the other that of Persia. The Persian dialect in both sets of inscriptions is identical or nearly so.[5]

The name Pahlavī means Parthian, Pahlav being the regular Persian transformation of the older Parthava.[6] This fact points to the conclusion that the system of writing was developed in Parthian times, when the great nobles, the Pahlavāns, ruled and Media was their main seat, "the Pahlav country." Other linguistic, graphical and historical indications point the same way; but it is still far from clear how the system was developed. We know, indeed, that even under the Achaemenids Aramaic writing and speech were employed far beyond the Aramaic lands, even in official documents and on coins. The Iranians had no convenient character, and might borrow the Aramaic letters as naturally as they subsequently borrowed those of the Arabs. But this does not explain the strange practice of writing Semitic words in place of so many Persian words which were to be read as Persian. It cannot be the invention of an individual, for in that case the system would have been more consistently worked out, and the appearance of two or more kinds of Pahlavī side by side at the beginning of the Sassanian period would be inexplicable. But we may remember that the Aramaic character first came to the Iranians from the region of the lower Euphrates and Tigris, where the complicated cuneiform character arose, and where it held its ground long after better ways of writing were known. In later antiquity probably very few Persians could read and write. All kinds of strange things are conceivable in an Eastern character confined to a narrow circle. Of the facts at least there is no doubt.

The Pahlavī literature embraces the translations of the holy books of the Zoroastrians, dating probably from the 6th century, and certain other religious books, especially the *Mīnōi-Khiradh* and the *Bundakish*.[7] The *Bundakish* dates from the Arab period. Zoroastrian priests continued to write the old language as a dead tongue and to use the old character long after the victory of a new empire, a new religion, a new form of the language (New Persian), and a new character. There was once a not quite inconsiderable profane literature, of which a good deal is preserved in Arabic or New Persian versions or reproductions, particularly in historical books about the time before Islam.[8] Very little profane literature still exists in Pahlavī; the romance of Ardashīr has been mentioned above.

See E. W. West's "Pahlavī Literature," in Geiger and Kuhn's *Grundriss der iranischen Philologie* (1896), vol. ii.; "The Extent, Language and Age of Pahlavī Literature" in *Sitzungsber. der k. Akad. der wiss. Phil. u. hist. Klasse* (Munich, 1888), pp. 399–443 and his *Pahlavī Texts* in *Sacred Books of the East* (1880–1897). The difficult study of Pahlavī is made more difficult by the corrupt state of our copies, due to ignorant and careless scribes.

Of glossaries, that of West (Bombay and London, 1874) is to be recommended; the large Pahlavī, Gujarati and English lexicon of Jamaspji Dastur Minocheherji (Bombay and London, 1877–1882) is very full, but has numerous false or uncertain forms, and must be used with much caution. (TH. N.)

PAIGNTON, a seaside resort in the Torquay parliamentary division of Devonshire, England, on Tor Bay, 2½ m. S.W. of Torquay, on the Great Western railway. Pop. of urban district (1901), 8385. The church of St John is mainly Perpendicular,

[5] What the *Fihrist* (p. 13 seq.) has about various forms of Persian writing certainly refers in part at least to the species of Pahlavī. But the statements are hardly all reliable, and in the lack of trustworthy specimens little can be made of them.

[6] This was finally proved by Olshausen, following earlier scholars; see J. Olshausen, *Parthava und Pahlav*, *Mâda* und *Mâh* (Berlin, 1877, and in the *Monatsb.* of the Academy).

[7] Translations ed. by F. Spiegel (1860), the *Bundakish* by N. L. Westergaard (Copenhagen, 1851) and F. Justi (Leipzig, 1868); other Pahlavī books by Spiegel and Haug, by Hoshangji, and other Indian Parsees.

[8] One other book, the stories of *Kalilag and Damnag*, in a Syriac version from the Pahlavī, the latter taken from the Sanskrit.

but has a late Norman doorway, and contains a carved and painted pulpit, and in the Kirkham chapel several interesting monuments of the Kirkham family, and a beautiful though damaged stone screen. Among other buildings and institutions are a novitiate of Marist Fathers, a science and art school, a pier with pavilion and concert rooms, and a yacht club. Little remains of an old palace of the bishops of Exeter apart from the 14th-century Bible Tower. Its last tenant was Bishop Miles Coverdale, who in 1535 published the first English translation of the whole Bible. The town owes its popularity to a firm expanse of sand, good bathing facilities, and a temperate climate.

PAIL, a bucket, a vessel for carrying water, milk or other liquids, made of wood or metal or other material, varying in size, and usually of a circular shape and somewhat wider at the top than the bottom. The word is of somewhat obscure origin. The present form points to the O. Eng. *pægel*, but the sense, that of a small wine-measure, a gill, is difficult to connect with the present one. The earlier forms of the word in Mid. Eng. spell the word *payle, paille*, and this rather points to a connexion with O. Fr. *poelle, payelle*, a small pan or flat dish, from Lat. *patella*, diminutive of *patera*, dish. The sense here also presents difficulties, " pail " in English being always a deep vessel.

PAILLERON, ÉDOUARD JULES HENRI (1834–1899), French poet and dramatist, was born in Paris on the 17th of September 1834. He was educated for the bar, but after pleading a single case he entered the first dragoon regiment and served for two years. With the artist J. A. Beaucé he travelled for some time in northern Africa, and soon after his return to Paris in 1860 he produced a volume of satires, *Les Parasites*, and a one-act piece, *La Parasite*, which was represented at the Odéon. He married in 1862 the daughter of François Buloz, thus obtaining a share in the proprietorship of the *Revue des deux mondes*. In 1869 he produced at the Gymnase theatre *Les Faux ménages*, a four-act comedy depending for its interest on the pathetic devotion of the Magdalene of the story. *L'Étincelle* (1879), a brilliant one-act comedy, secured another success, and in 1881 with *Le Monde où l'on s'ennuie* Pailleron produced one of the most strikingly successful pieces of the period. The play ridiculed contemporary academic society, and was filled with transparent allusions to well-known people. None of his subsequent efforts achieved so great a success. Pailleron was elected to the French Academy in 1882, and died on the 20th of April 1899.

PAIMPOL, a fishing port of western France, in the department of Côtes-du-Nord, 27½ m. N.N.W. of St Brieuc by road. Pop. (1906), 2340. Paimpol is well known for its association with the Icelandic cod-fisheries, for which it annually equips a large fleet. Steam sawing and boat-building are carried on; grain, &c., is exported; imports include coal and timber. A tribunal of commerce and a school of navigation are among the public institutions.

PAIN (from Lat. *poena*, Gr. ποινή, penalty, that which must be paid: O. Fr. *peine*), a term used loosely (1) for the psychological state, which may be generally described as " unpleasantness," arising, *e.g.* from the contemplation of a catastrophe or of moral turpitude, and (2) for physical (or psycho-physical) suffering, a specific sensation localized in a particular part of the body. The term is used in both senses as the opposite of " pleasure," though it is doubtful whether the antithesis between physical and psychical pleasure can be equally well attested. The investigation of the pleasure-pain phenomena of consciousness has taken a prominent place in psychological and ethical speculation, the terms " hedonics " and " algedonics " (ἀλγηδών, pain of body or mind) being coined to express different aspects of the subject. So in aesthetics attempts have been made to assign to pain a specific psychological function as tending to increase pleasure by contrast (so Fechner): pain, *e.g.* is a necessary element in the tragic. Scientists have experimented elaborately with a view to the precise localization of pain-sensations, and " pain-maps " can be drawn showing the exact situation of what are known as " pain-spots." For such experiments instruments known as " aesthesiometers " and " algometers " have been devised. The great variety of painful sensations—

throbbing, dull, acute, intermittent, stabbing—led to the conclusion among earlier investigators that pains differ in quality. It is, however, generally agreed that all pain is qualitatively the same, though subject to temporal and intensive modification. (See PSYCHOLOGY; AESTHETICS; NERVOUS SYSTEM; SYMPATHETIC SYSTEM.)

PAIN, BARRY (1867–   ), English humorous writer, was educated at Cambridge, and became a prominent contributor to *The Granta*. James Payn inserted his story, " The Hundred Gates," in the *Cornhill Magazine* in 1889, and shortly afterwards he became a contributor to *Punch* and the *Speaker*, and joined the staffs of the *Daily Chronicle* and *Black and White*. His works include: *In a Canadian Canoe* (1891); papers reprinted from *The Granta*; *Playthings and Parodies* (1892); *The Kindness of the Celestial* (1894); *The Octave of Claudius* (1897); *Eliza* (1900); *Another English Woman's Love Letters* (1901), &c. As a writer of parody and lightly humorous stories his name has become widely known.

PAINE, ROBERT TREAT (1731–1814), American politician, a signer of the Declaration of Independence, was born in Boston, Massachusetts, on the 11th of March 1731. He graduated at Harvard in 1749, and was admitted to the bar in 1750. In 1768 he was a delegate to the provincial convention which was called to meet in Boston, and conducted the prosecution of Captain Thomas Preston and his men for their share in the famous " Boston Massacre " of the 5th of March 1770. He served in the Massachusetts General Court in 1773–1774, in the Provincial Congress in 1774–1775, and in the Continental Congress in 1774–1778, and was speaker of the Massachusetts House of Representatives in 1777, a member of the executive council in 1779, a member of the committee which drafted the constitution of 1780, attorney-general of the state from 1777 to 1790, and a judge of the state supreme court from 1790 to 1804. He died in Boston on the 11th of May 1814.

See John Sanderson, *Biography of the Signers of the Declaration of Independence* (Philadelphia, 1823), vol. ii.

His son, ROBERT TREAT PAINE (1773–1811), who was christened Thomas but in 1801 took the name of his father and of an elder brother who died without issue in 1794, was a poet of some repute, but his verses have long been forgotten. His best known productions are *Adams and Liberty*, a once popular song written in 1798, *The Invention of Letters* (1795), and *The Ruling Passion*, the Harvard Phi Beta Kappa poem of 1797.

His *Works in Verse and Prose* (Boston, 1812) contains a biographical sketch.

PAINE, THOMAS (1737–1809), English author, was born at Thetford, Norfolk, on the 29th of January 1737, the son of a Quaker staymaker. After several years at sea and after trying various occupations on land, Paine took up his father's trade in London, where he supplemented his meagre grammar school education by attending science lectures. He succeeded in 1762 in gaining an appointment in the excise, but was discharged for neglect of duty in 1765. Three years later, however, he received another appointment, at Lewes in Sussex. He took a vigorous share in the debates of a local Whig club, and in 1772 he wrote a pamphlet embodying the grievances of excisemen and supporting their demands for an increase of pay. In 1774 he was dismissed the service for absence without leave—in order to escape his creditors.

A meeting with Benjamin Franklin in London was the turning point in his life. Franklin provided him with letters to his son-in-law, Richard Bache, and many of the leaders in the colonies' resistance to the mother country, then at an acute stage. Paine sailed for America in 1774. Bache introduced him to Robert Aitken, whose *Pennsylvania Magazine* he helped found and edited for eighteen months. On the 9th of January 1776 Paine published a pamphlet entitled *Common Sense*, a telling array of arguments for separation and for the establishment of a republic. His argument was that independence was the only consistent line to pursue, that " it must come to that some time or other "; that it would only be more difficult the more it was delayed, and that independence was the surest road to union. Written in simple convincing language, it was read everywhere, and the open movement to independence dates from its publication. Washington said that it "worked a powerful change in the minds of many men." Leaders in the New York Provincial Congress considered the advisability of answering it, but came to the conclusion that it was unanswerable. When war was declared, and fortune at first went against the colonists, Paine, who was then serving with General Greene as volunteer aide-de-camp, wrote the first of a series of influential tracts called *The Crisis*, of which the opening words, "These are the times that try men's souls," became a battle-cry. Paine's services were recognized by an appointment to be secretary of the commission sent by Congress to treat with the Indians, and a few months later to be secretary of the Congressional committee of foreign affairs. In 1779, however, he committed an indiscretion that brought him into trouble. He published information gained from his official position, and was compelled to resign. He was afterwards clerk of the Pennsylvania legislature, and accompanied John Laurens during his mission to France. His services were eventually recognized by the state of New York by a grant of an estate at New Rochelle, and from Pennsylvania and, at Washington's suggestion, from Congress he received considerable gifts of money.

In 1787 he sailed for Europe with the model of an iron bridge he had designed. This was publicly exhibited in Paris and London, and attracted great crowds. In England he determined to "open the eyes of the people to the madness and stupidity of the government." His first efforts in the *Prospects on the Rubicon* (1787) were directed against Pitt's war policy, and towards securing friendly relations with France. When Burke's *Reflections on the Revolution in France* appeared, in 1790, Paine at once wrote his answer, *The Rights of Man*. The first part appeared on the 13th of March 1791, and had an enormous circulation before the government took alarm and endeavoured to suppress it, thereby exciting intense curiosity to see it, even at the risk of heavy penalties. Those who know the book only by hearsay as the work of a furious incendiary will be surprised at the dignity, force and temperance of the style; it was the circumstances that made it inflammatory: Pitt "used to say," according to Lady Hester Stanhope, "that Tom Paine was quite in the right, but then he would add, 'What am I to do? As things are, if I were to encourage Tom Paine's opinions we should have a bloody revolution.'" Paine was indicted for treason in May 1792, but before the trial came off he was elected by the department of Calais to the French convention, and escaped into France, followed by a sentence of outlawry. The first years that he spent in France form a curious episode in his life. He was enthusiastically received, but as he knew little of the language translations of his speeches had to be read for him. He was bold enough to speak and vote for the "detention of Louis during the war and his perpetual banishment afterwards," and he pointed out that the execution of the king would alienate American sympathy. He incurred the suspicion of Robespierre; was thrown into prison, and escaped the guillotine by an accident. Before his arrest he had completed the first part of the *Age of Reason*, the publication of which made an instant change in his position on both sides of the Atlantic, the indignation in the United States being as strong as in England. The *Age of Reason* can now be estimated calmly. It was written from the point of view of a Quaker who did not believe in revealed religion, but who held that "all religions are in their nature mild and benign " when not associated with political systems. Intermixed with the coarse unceremonious ridicule of what he considered superstition and bad faith are many passages of earnest and even lofty eloquence in favour of a pure morality founded on natural religion. The work in short—a second part, written during his ten months' imprisonment, was published after his release—represents the deism of the 18th century in the hands of a rough, ready, passionate controversialist.

At the downfall of Robespierre Paine was restored to his seat in the convention, and served until it adjourned in October 1795. In 1796 he published a long letter to Washington,

attacking his military reputation and his presidential policy with inexcusable bitterness. In 1802 Paine sailed for America, but while his services in behalf of the colonies were gratefully remembered, his *Age of Reason* and his attack on Washington had alienated many of his friends. He died in New York on the 8th of June 1809, and was buried at New Rochelle, but his body was in 1819 removed to England by William Cobbett.

See the biography by Moncure D. Conway (1892).

PAINESVILLE, a city and the county-seat of Lake county, Ohio, U.S.A., on the Grand River, 3 m. S. of Lake Erie and about 30 m. N.E. of Cleveland. Pop. (1900) 5024, of whom 499 were foreign-born and 179 negroes; (1910) 5501. It is served by the Lake Shore & Michigan Southern, the New York, Chicago & St Louis and the Baltimore & Ohio railways, and by electric lines to Cleveland, Fairport and Ashtabula. It is the seat of Lake Erie College (non-sectarian, for women), the successor of Willoughby Seminary (1847), whose buildings at Willoughby, Ohio, were burned in 1856; the college was opened as the Lake Erie Female Seminary in 1859, and became Lake Erie College and Seminary in 1898 and Lake Erie College in 1908. Painesville is situated in a farming and fruit-growing country, and also has some manufactures. Three miles north, on Lake Erie, is the village of Fairport (pop. in 1900, 2073), with a good harbour and ore docks. The municipality owns and operates its waterworks and street-lighting plants. Painesville was founded in 1800-1802 by settlers from Connecticut and New York, conspicuous among whom was General Edward Paine (1746-1841), an officer from Connecticut in the War of Independence; it was incorporated as a village in 1832, and became a city in 1902 under the Ohio municipal code.

PAINTER-WORK, in the building trade. When work is painted one or both of two distinct ends is achieved, namely the preservation and the coloration of the material painted. The compounds used for painting—taking the word as meaning a thin protective or decorative coat—are very numerous, including oil-paint of many kinds, distemper, whitewash, tar; but the word "paint" is usually confined to a mixture of oil and pigment, together with other materials which possess properties necessary to enable the paint to dry hard and opaque. Oil paints are made up of four parts—the base, the vehicle, the solvent and the driers. Pigment may be added to these to obtain a paint of any desired colour.

There are several bases for oil paint, those most commonly used for building work being white lead, red lead, zinc white and oxide of iron. White lead is by far the commonest of bases for paint. When pure it consists of about 75% carbonate of lead and about 25% of lead hydrate. It is mixed with 6 or 7% by weight of pure linseed oil, and in this form is supplied to the painter. Sulphate of baryta is the chief adulterant used in the manufacture of white lead. White lead has greater covering properties and is more durable than the other bases. It should therefore always be used in external painting. Paints having white lead for a base darken with age, and become discoloured when exposed to the fumes of sulphuretted hydrogen, which exists to a greater or less extent in the air of all large towns. Zinc white, an oxide of zinc, is of a purer white colour than white lead. It is lighter, and does not possess the same durability or covering power. It is, however, useful in internal decoration, as it retains its colour well, even when subjected to the action of gases. Red lead is a lead oxide. It is used chiefly in the priming coat and as a base for some red paints. Like white lead, it is injured if exposed to acids or impure air, which cause discoloration and decay. Oxide of iron is used chiefly as a base in paints used for covering iron-work, the theory being that no destructive galvanic action can be set up, as might be the case with lead paint when used on iron. A variety of red pigments are made from oxide of iron, varying in hue from a pale to a deep brownish-red. They are quite permanent, and may be used under any conditions.

The vehicle is a liquid in which the particles of the base are held in suspension, enabling a thin coat of paint to be formed, uniform in colour and consistency, and which on drying forms a kind of skin over the surface to which it is applied. For oil paint the vehicles used are oils; for distemper water is employed.

The oils used as vehicles are chiefly linseed oil, raw and boiled, and poppy-seed oil. Nut oils are occasionally used for inferior work because they are much cheaper. Linseed oil, the one most commonly used, is obtained from the seeds of the flax by warming it and squeezing out the oil under hydraulic pressure. The resultant, which is of a transparent amber colour, is known as "raw" oil. It is used principally in interiors for light, bright colours, drying somewhat slowly and giving a firm elastic coat. The oil improves by keeping, and is sometimes "refined" with acids or alkalies. "Boiled" oil is the raw oil heated with driers, such as litharge or red lead, to a temperature from 350° to 500° F., at which it is maintained for three or four hours. It is thick and much darker in colour than the raw oil, drying much more quickly, with a coat hard and glossy but less elastic than that produced by raw oil. Poppy-seed oil is expressed from the seeds of the poppy plant. It does not possess the tenacity and quick-drying powers of boiled linseed oil, but being of a very light colour it is used for delicate colours.

Turpentine is used as a solvent, diluent, or "thinner," to bring the paint to a proper consistency so as to allow it to be spread in a thin even coat. When a flat dull surface is desired, turpentine alone is used with the base and the oil is omitted. The best turpentine comes from the pine forests of America. French turpentine is next in quality. Russian turpentine is the cheapest, and has usually a strong and unpleasant odour that renders it objectionable to work with. In consequence of the high price of turpentine of good quality, and the increasing difficulty of obtaining it, substitutes are coming into general use.

"Driers" are substances usually added to paint to hasten the process of oxidation, i.e. the drying, of the oil. Some pigments possess this quality, as red lead and white lead. The most notable driers are litharge, sugar of lead, patent driers, sulphate of zinc and manganese dioxide. Liquid driers, such as terebene, are also in use. Litharge, an oxide of lead, is in most general use. Sugar of lead is used, ground in oil, for light tints. Sulphate of zinc and manganese driers are used for paints in which zinc white is the base, which would be injured by lead driers.

"Pigments" are preparations of metallic, earthy or animal origin mixed into paint to give it colour. For oil paint they are usually ground in oil; for distemper they are sold as a finely ground powder. The ordinary pigments are white lead, zinc white, umbers, siennas, ochres, chromes, Venetian red, Indian red, lamp black, bone black, vegetable black, ultramarine, Prussian blue, vermilion, red lead, oxide of iron, lakes and Vandyke brown.

The term "enamel paint" was first given to a compound of zinc white, petrol and resin, which possessed on drying a hard glossy surface. The name is now applied to any coloured paint of this nature. Quick-drying enamels are spirit varnishes ground with the desired pigment. For slow-drying enamels oil varnishes form the vehicle.

Woodwork is often treated with a thin transparent-coloured liquid which changes the colour of the work without hiding the grain of the wood, and if the latter is good a very fine result is obtained. Sometimes the stain is produced by the combination of two or more chemicals applied separately, or soluble pigments may be mixed with a transparent vehicle and applied in the usual way. The vehicles for the pigments vary considerably, and include water, methylated spirit, size, turpentine and clear raw linseed oil.

Varnish is made by dissolving certain gums in linseed oil, turpentine, spirit or water. They give a transparent protective coat to painted and stained surfaces or to wall-paper or plain woodwork. Varnishes usually dry with a very smooth, hard and shiny surface, but "flat" or "dead" surfaces which are without gloss may be obtained with special varnish.

The gums used for hard-wearing or carriage varnishes, such as those to be exposed to the weather and frequently cleaned and polished, are amber, copal and gum animé. Amber is a yellow transparent or clouded gum found on the coasts of the Baltic, and particularly in Prussia. It makes a hard, durable and slow-drying varnish which does not darken with age. Copal gum is brought from the West India Islands and also from the East Indies. It makes the most durable varnish, and being tough and hard is generally used for external work. Gum animé, is a variety of copal found in the sandy soil of the East Indies. It is hard, durable and quick-drying, but unless the varnish is carefully made it is liable to crack. Varnishes for inside work, or cabinet varnishes, are made with a variety of resins dissolved in linseed oil and turpentine. The resultant gives a hard, lustrous surface, somewhat less durable than that of carriage varnishes. Turpentine varnishes are made from soft gums, such as dammar, common resin and mastic; they are light in colour, cheap and not very durable. Lacquers or spirit varnishes are made from very soft gums, such as shellac and sandarach, dissolved in methylated spirit. They are used for internal work, drying quickly, and becoming hard and very brilliant. Surfaces formed with such varnishes are liable to chip easily and scale off. Oil paint is very much improved by the addition of some varnish; it causes it to dry harder and more quickly and with a fine lustrous surface.

The driers used for varnish are generally acetate of lead or litharge. An excess of driers makes the varnish less durable and causes cracking.

There are many kinds of French polishes, mixed in different ways, but most are composed of shellac and sandarach dissolved in spirit. It is applied to the perfectly smooth surface of hard woods with a pad of flannel or wadding wrapped in linen, and well rubbed in with a circular motion.

A dull polish is procured by rubbing beeswax into the wood. It must be thoroughly rubbed in, a little turpentine being added as a lubricant when the rubber works stiffly.

If paint were applied over the bare knots of new wood it would be destroyed, or at least discoloured, by the exudation of resin from the knots. For the purpose of obviating this the knots are covered with two coats of a preparation called "knotting," made by dissolving shellac in methylated spirit.

Putty is required for stopping nail-holes and small crevices and irregularities in woodwork. It is made of powdered whiting and linseed oil mixed together and kneaded into a stiff paste. For light work "hard stopping," made of white lead and whiting, should be employed.

The tools and appliances of the painter are mixing pots, paint kettles to hold the colour for the painter at work, strainer, palette knife, scraping knife, hacking, stopping and chisel knives, the hammer, sponge, pumice, blow-lamp for burning off, and a variety of brushes, such as the duster, the ground brush, the tool, the distemper brush, the fitch and camel-hair pencil for picking out small parts and lines, the sable and flogger for gilding, the stippler; for grained work several steel graining combs with coarse and fine teeth, graining brush of hogs' hair, pencil over-grainer, and other special shaped brushes used to obtain the peculiar characteristics of different woods. It is absolutely necessary for good work to use brushes of a fine quality, and although expensive at first cost, they are undoubtedly cheapest in wear

Workmanship.—New woodwork requires to be knotted, primed, stopped, and in addition painted with three or four coats of oil colour. The priming coat is a thin coat of white lead, red lead and driers mixed with linseed oil and turpentine. Work should always be primed before the stopping is done. The second or "lead" coat is composed mainly of turpentine, linseed oil and white lead. The third coat is the ground for the finishing colour, and is made of white lead and linseed oil and turpentine, with enough pigment to bring it to a tint approaching the finishing colour. The remaining coat or coats is of similar composition. A "flatting" coat is made of white lead and turpentine with the desired pigment. One pound of colour will cover 4 sq. yds. in the first coat and 6 sq. yds. in the additional coat.

Graining.—Graining is understood among painters to be the imitating of the several different species of ornamental woods, as satinwood, rosewood, mahogany, oak and others. After the necessary coats of paint have been put on to the wood a ground is then laid of the required tint and left to dry. The painter then prepares small quantities of the same colour with a little brown, and boiled oil and turpentine, and, having mixed this, spreads it over some small part of his work. The flat hogs' hair brushes being dipped in the liquid and drawn down the newly-laid colour, the shades and grainings are produced. To obtain the mottled appearance the camels' hair pencils are applied, and when completed the work is left to dry, and afterwards covered by a coat or two of good copal varnish. Imitation wainscot requires the use of combs of various degrees of fineness to obtain the grain (whence the process is called *combing* by some persons), and the flower is got by wiping off the colour with a piece of rag. When dry it is over-grained to obtain a more complete representation of the natural wood, and then varnished. If the work be done in water-colour and not-in oil, beer grounds to act as a drier are mixed with the colour; this sets it ready for varnishing. A " patent graining machine," a sort of roller with a pattern upon it, is often used.

Marbling.—Marbling is the imitation of real marbles and granites, some of which are represented by splashing on the carefully prepared ground, which should have been painted and often rubbed and polished to obtain an even surface; others have to be painted in colours, and then well varnished.

Painting on Plaster Work.—Plastering should never be painted until it is thoroughly dry. Portland cement is best left for a year or two before being painted. Plaster work not previously painted will require four or five coats, Portland cement five or six. If plastered work is required to be painted immediately, it should be executed in Keene's or Parian cement (see PLASTER WORK). A great deal more paint is of course absorbed by plaster than by wood, just as wood absorbs more than iron.

Painting on Iron.—Iron and steel work should receive a coat of oxide paint at the manufacturer's works; additional coats are added after erection. All rust should be previously removed by means of wire brushes and paraffin or turpentine. The best paints for external iron work are composed of oxide of iron and red lead, mixed with linseed oil.

The following is an extract from the building by-laws of the municipality of Johannesburg:— '

" All structural metal work shall be thoroughly cleaned from scale and rust before painting. Faying surfaces in riveted work shall be painted before putting them together. All surfaces of steel or iron work inaccessible after erection shall be protected as far as possible either by coating them with ' Smith's ' or other approved bituminous composition, or by filling the spaces which they enclose with lime concrete."

Repainting Old Work.—Before beginning to repaint work of any description it must be thoroughly cleaned. If the surface is in good condition it will be sufficient to scrub down with good soap and water and afterwards sponge and wipe dry. If the work has become rough it will often be necessary to use pumice stone to facilitate the operation of cleaning. The pumice should be cut or rubbed to a flat surface and vigorously applied with plenty of clean water. It is essential that the work should be quite dry before any paint is applied. If the old surface is much cracked and blistered no amount of rubbing with pumice will enable the workman to obtain a good ground for the new coats, and it will be necessary to remove the old paint entirely. For this purpose painters most frequently use a paint burner or torch which burns paraffin oil under air pressure. This causes the paint to soften and blister under the heat, in which state it is readily scraped off by a blunt knife. The old-fashioned grate filled with charcoal held close to the surface by means of a long handle is now not often used. There has recently been a considerable increase in the use of chemical paint removers in paste or liquid form; as a rule these contain some alkali, such as lime or caustic soda. The preparation is brushed on to the paint required to be removed, and in the course of from ten minutes to half an hour the paint becomes so soft that it can readily be scraped off.

Blistering and Cracking.—The blistering of painted surfaces may be caused in several ways. If on iron, it may be the result of a particle of rust which, not having been removed in the process of cleaning, has increased in size and loosened the paint. If on plaster, a particle of unslaked lime may have " blown," with a similar result. On wood, blistering is usually caused by painting upon a wet surface or upon unseasoned wood. Blisters may also be caused by the use of too much oil in paint exposed to heat, or the application of one coat upon another before the latter is properly dry. To prevent blistering a method that has been tried with good results is to apply two coats of water paint (washable distemper) and follow by two coats of oil colour or varnish. Cracking is caused by the use of too much oil in the under coats and too little in the top coats.

Distemper.—New plaster-work must be quite dry before distemper is applied. The work should be stopped (that is, any irregularities filled up with plaster of Paris mixed with whiting and water to a paste) and then rubbed perfectly smooth with glass paper. Clairecole, a solution of thin size and whiting, is then applied to render the plaster non-absorbent, and this is followed by distemper of the desired colour. Distemper is made by soaking whiting in clean water to a creamy consistency. To this is added size which has been previously warmed, and the pigment required to colour the mixture; the whole is then well stirred and strained to remove any lumps. Many patent washable distempers under fancy names are now on the market in the form of paste or powder, which simply require to be mixed with water to be ready for use. If applied to woodwork distemper is apt to flake off.

The " one-knot " brush for cornices and other mouldings and the " two-knot " and " brass-bound " brushes for flat surfaces are usually employed for distempering and whitewashing.

A granular surface is produced by stippling or dabbing the surface with a stiff bristled brush specially made for this purpose.

Gilding, &c.—Very rich effects may be produced both in external and internal decorations by the judicious use of overlays of gold or silver. In their application, however, it must always be borne in mind that they are metals, not paints, and they should only be used in positions such as would be appropriate for the actual metals. " Dutch metal " and other imitations cost about one-third of the price of genuine gilding, and require to be protected from oxidization by a coat of lacquer. Gold leaf is affixed with gold size or other adhesive preparations. The best and most durable work is oil gilding, which involves less labour, and results in a richer appearance than other methods. The work is usually primed first of all with a solution of boiled linseed oil and white lead, and then covered with a fine glutinous composition called gold size, on which, when it is nearly dry, the gold leaf is laid in narrow strips with a fine brush, and pressed down with a pad of cotton-wool held in the fingers. As the slips must be made to overlap each other slightly to ensure the complete covering of the whole surface, the loose edges will remain unattached, to be afterwards struck off with a large sable or camel-hair brush. The joints, if the work be skilfully executed, will be invisible. For burnished gilding the work must be covered with various coats of gluten, plaster and bole, which last is mixed with gold size to secure the adhesion of the leaf.

AUTHORITIES.—A. C. Wright, M.A., B.Sc., *Simple Methods for Testing Painters' Materials*; Professor A. H. Church. *Colour*; Ellis A. Davidson, *House Painting, Graining, Marbling and Sign Writing*; W. J. Pearce, *Painting and Decorating*; A. S. Jennings, *Paint and Colour Mixing*; G. H. Hurst, F.C.S., *Painters, Colours, Oils and Varnishes*. (J. Bт.)

PAINTING, in art, the action of laying colour on a surface, or the representing of objects by the laying of colour on a surface It is with painting in the last sense, considered as one of the fine arts, that this article deals. In the first sense, in so far as painting is a part of the builder's and decorator's trade it is treated above under the heading PAINTER-WORK. The verb " to paint " is derived through Fr. *peindre* (*peint*, the past participle, was possibly the earliest part adopted, as is suggested in the *New English Dictionary*), from Lat. *pingere*, to paint. From the past participle *pictus* comes *pictura*, picture, and from the root *pig*, pigment. The ultimate meaning of the root is probably to decorate, adorn, and is seen in Gr. ποικίλος, many-coloured, variegated.

In Part I. of this article, after a brief notice of the general character of the art and an account of its earliest manifestations, a sketch is given of the course of its development from the ancient Egyptian period to modern times. (An account, by countries, of recent schools of painting will be found as an appendix at the end of Part III.) The point of view chosen is that of the relation of painting to nature, and it is shown how the art, beginning with the delineation of contour, passes on through stages when the effort is to render the truth of solid form, to the final period when, in the 17th century, the presentment of space, or nature in all her extent and variety, becomes the subject of representation. Certain special forms of painting characteristic of modern times, such as portraiture, genre painting, landscape, still-life, &c., are briefly discussed.

Part II. consists in tables of names and dates intended to afford a conspectus of the different historical schools of painting from the 12th century A.D. downwards.

Part III. is devoted to a comprehensive treatment of the different technical processes of painting in vogue in ancient and modern times.

AUTHORITIES.—There is one elaborate general treatise on the whole art of painting in all its branches and connexions. It is by Paillot de Montabert, and was published in Paris (1829–1850). It is entitled *Traité complet de la peinture*, and is in nine substantial volumes, with an additional volume of plates. It begins with establishing the value of rules for the art, and giving a dictionary of terms, lists of artists and works of art, &c. Vols. ii. and iii. give the history of the art in ancient, medieval and modern times. Vols. iv., v., vi. and vii. contain discussions on choice of subjects, design, composition, &c.; on proportions, anatomy, expression, drapery; on geometry, perspective, light and shade, and colour. In vol. viii., pp. 1–285 deal with colour, aerial perspective and execution; pp. 285–503 take up the different kinds of painting, history, portrait, landscape, genre, &c.; and pp. 503–661 are devoted to materials and processes, which subject is continued through vol. ix. To encaustic painting 125 pages are given, and 100 to painting in oil. A long discussion on painting grounds and pigments follows, while other processes of painting, in tempera, water-colour, enamel, mosaic, &c., are more briefly treated in about 200 pages, while the work ends with a notice of various artistic impediments. Vol. i. it should be said, contains on 70 pages a complete synopsis of the contents of the successive volumes. The best general *History of Painting* is that by Woltmann and Woermann (Eng. trans., London, 1880, &c.), but it does not go beyond the 16th century A.D. See also the separate articles on CHINA (*Art*), JAPAN (*Art*), EGYPT (*Art*), GREEK ART, ROMAN ART, &c.

For the Italian schools of painting may be consulted: Crowe and Cavalcaselle, *History of Painting in Italy* (2nd ed., London, 1902, &c.). The original edition was published in London under the titles *History of Painting in Italy* (3 vols., 1864–1866), and *History of Painting in North Italy* (2 vols., 1871), Venturi, *Storia dell' arte italiana* (Milan, 1901, &c.).

For the German: Janitschek, *Geschichte der deutschen Malerei* (Berlin, 1890).

For the Early Flemish: Crowe and Cavalcaselle, *The Early Flemish Painters* (2nd ed., London, 1872); Wurzbach, *Niederländisches Künstler-Lexicon* (Vienna and Leipzig, 1906, &c.); Weale, Hubert and John van Eyck (London, 1907).

For the Dutch: Wurzbach; Bode, *Studien zur Geschichte der Holländischen Malerei* (Braunschweig, 1883) and *Rembrandt und seine Zeitgenossen* (Leipzig, 1906); Havard, *The Dutch School of Painting* (trans., London, 1885).

For the French: Lady Dilke, *French Painters of the Eighteenth Century* (London, 1899); D. C. Thomson, *The Barbizon School*.

For the English: Redgrave, *A Century of Painters of the English School* (London, 1890).

For the Scottish: W. D. McKay, R.S.A., *The Scottish School of Painting* (London, 1906).

For the American: J. C. Van Dyke (ed.), *History of American Art* (New York, 1903, &c.); S. Isham, *A History of American Painting* (N. Y., 1905).

The modern schools generally are treated fully, with copious bibliographical references, by Richard Muther, *The History of Modern Painting* (2nd ed., Eng. trans., London, 1907).

PART I.—A SKETCH OF THE DEVELOPMENT OF THE ART

§ 1. *Constituents and General Character.*—If we trace back to the parent stock the various branches that support the luxuriant

modern growth of the graphic art; we see that this parent stock is in its origin twofold. Painting begins on the one side in outline delineation and on the other in the spreading of a coloured coating over a surface. In both cases the motive is at first utilitarian, or, at any rate, non-artistic. In the first the primary motive is to convey information. It has been noticed of certain savages that if one of them wants to convey to a companion the impression of a particular animal or object, he will draw with his finger in the air the outline of some characteristic feature by which it may be known, and if this do not avail he will sketch the same with a pointed stick upon the ground. It is but a step from this to delineation on some portable tablet that retains what is scratched or drawn upon it, and in this act a monument of the graphic art has come into being.

In the other case there are various motives of a non-aesthetic kind that lead to the covering of a surface with a coat of another substance. The human body, the first object of interest to man, is tender and is sensitive to cold. Wood, one of the earliest building materials and the one material for any sort of boat-building, is subject, especially when exposed to moisture, to decay. Again, the early vessel of clay, of neolithic date, because imperfectly burned, is porous. Now the properties of certain substances suitable for adhesive coatings on anything that needed protection or reinforcement would soon be noticed. Unctuous and oily substances like animal fat, mixed with ashes or some such material, are smeared by some savages on their bodies to keep them warm in cold regions and to defend them against insect bites in the tropics. Wax and resin and pitch, liquefied by the heat of the sun or by fire, would lend themselves readily for the coating of wood with a substance impervious to moisture. Vitreous glazes, first no doubt the result of accident, fused over the surface of the primitive clay vessel would give it the required impermeability. This is no more art than the mere delineation which is the other source of painting, but it begins to take on itself an aesthetic character when colour plays a part in it. There are physiological reasons why the colour red exercises an exciting influence, and strong colours generally, like glittering surfaces, make an aesthetic appeal. In prehistoric times the flesh was sometimes stripped from the skeleton of a corpse and the bones rubbed with red earth or ruddle, while the same easily procured colouring substance is used to decorate the person or the implement of the savage. In this sensibility to colour we find a second and distinct origin of the art of painting.

What a perspective does a glance back at the development of painting afford! Painting, an art that on a flat surface can suggest to illusion the presence of solid forms with length, breadth and thickness; that on the area of a few square inches can convey the impression of the vast spaces of the universe, and carry the eye from receding plane to plane till the persons or objects that people them grow too minute for the eye to discern; painting that can deck the world in Elysian brightness or veil it in the gloom of the Crucifixion, that intoxicates the senses with its revelation of beauty, or magician-like withdraws the veil from the mysterious complexity of nature; the art that can exhibit all this, and yet can suggest a hundredfold more than it can show, and by a line, a shade, a touch, can stir within us " thoughts that do often lie too deep for tears "—this Painting, the most fascinating, because most illusive in its nature, of all the arts of form, is in its first origin at one time a mere display to attract attention, as if one should cry out " See here!" and at another time a prosaic answer to a prosaic question about some natural object, " What is it like?" The coat or streak or dab of colour, the informing outline, are not in themselves aesthetic products. The former becomes artistic when the element of arrangement or pattern is introduced. There is arrangement when the shape and size of the mark or marks have a studied relation to those of the surface on which they are displayed; there is pattern when they are combined among themselves so that while distinct and contrasted they yet present the appearance of a unity. Again, the delineation, serving at first a purpose of use, is not in itself artistic, and it is a difficult question in aesthetic whether any representation of nature that aims only at resemblance really

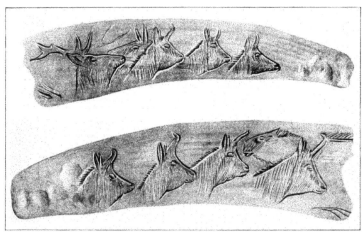

Figs. 1, 2.—Heads of Chamois, &c., Engraved on the Tines of an Antler.
(From the Cave of Gourdan, Haute-Garonne, France.)

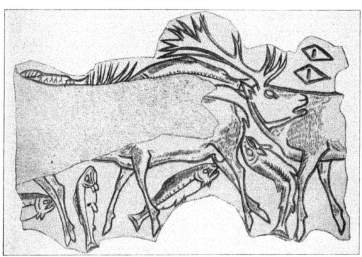

Fig. 3.—Stags and Salmon. The originals are engraved round an antler about an inch in diameter. (From the Grotto of Lortet, Hautes-Pyrénées, France.) Prehistoric incised drawings of animals.
Reproduced from Édouard Piette's *L'art pendant l'âge du renne* (Paris, 1907). By permission.

comes into the domain of art. It is of course acknowledged that a mere prosaically literal likeness of a natural object is not a work of art; but when the representation is of such a kind as to bring out the character of the object with discrimination and emphasis, to give the soul of it, as it were, and not the mere lineaments, then, logically or illogically, art claims it as its child. In the strict sense the delineation only becomes artistic when there is present the element of beauty in arrangement or composition. The insight and sympathy just referred to are qualities rather intellectual than artistic, and the really artistic element would be the tasteful fitting of the representation to the space within which it is displayed, and the harmonious relations of the lines or masses or tones or colours that it presents to the eye. In other words, in artistic delineation there will be united elements drawn from both the sources above indicated. The representation of nature will be present, and so will also a decorative effect produced by a pleasing combination of forms and lines.

§ 2. *Limitations of the Meaning of the word Painting.*—If delineation take on itself a decorative character, so too decoration, relying at first on a pleasing arrangement of mere lines or patches that have in themselves no significance, soon goes on to impart to these the similitude, more or less exact, of natural objects. Here we arrive at a distinction which must be drawn at the outset so as duly to limit the field which this survey of painting has to cover. The distinction is that between ornamental or, in a narrow sense, decorative painting on the one side, and painting proper on the other. In the first, the forms employed have either in themselves no significance or have a resemblance to nature that is only distant or conventional. In painting proper the imitation of nature is more advanced and is of greater importance than the decorative effect to the eye. It is not only present but preponderant, while in ornamental work the representative element is distinctly subordinate to the decorative effect. In Greek vase decoration the conventional floral forms, or the mannered animal figures that follow each other monotonously round vases of the "Oriental" style, belong to the domain of ornament, while the human forms, say, on the earliest red-figured vases, while displayed in pleasing patterns and in studied relation to the shape and structure of the vessel, exhibit so much variety and so great an effort on the part of the artist to achieve similitude to nature, that they claim a place for themselves in the annals of the painter's art.

A further limitation is also necessary at the outset. Pictorial designs may be produced without the equipment of the painter proper; that is to say, without the use of pigments or coloured substances in thin films rubbed on to or attached by a binding material upon a surface. They may be executed by setting together coloured pieces of some hard substance in the form of *Mosaic* (q.v.); by interweaving dyed threads of wool, linen or silk into a textile web to produce *Tapestry* (q.v.) or *Embroidery* (q.v.); by inlaying into each other strips of wood of different colours in the work called *Tarsia* or *Marquetry* (q.v.); by fusing different coloured vitreous pastes into contiguous cavities, as in *Enamelling* (see ENAMEL); or by framing together variously shaped pieces of transparent coloured glass into the stained glass window (see GLASS, STAINED).

These special methods of producing pictorial effects, in so far as the technical processes they involve are concerned, are excluded from view in this article and are dealt with under their own headings. Only at those periods when pictorial design was exclusively or especially represented by work in these forms will the results of these decorative processes be brought in to illustrate the general character of the painting of the time. For example, in the 5th and 6th Christian centuries the art of painting is mainly represented by the mosaics in the churches at Rome and Ravenna, and these must be included from the point of view of design in any review of painting, though as examples of mosaic technique and style they are treated in an article apart. Greek vase painting, again, is a special subject (see GREEK ART and CERAMICS), yet the designs on early Greek vases are the only extant monuments that illustrate for us the early stages of the development of classical painting as a whole. It will be

understood therefore that in this article the word "painting", means the spreading of thin films of colouring matter over surfaces to which they are made by different means to adhere, and it will only be taken in a wider sense in certain exceptional cases just indicated.

§ 3. *Importance in the Art of the Representation of Nature.*— If we regard painting as a whole, the imitation of nature may be established as its most distinctive characteristic and the guiding principle of its development. It must at the same time be understood that in the advanced criticism of painting, as it is formulated in modern times, no distinction is allowed among the different elements that go to make up a perfect production of the art: In such a production the idea, the form, the execution, the elements of representation and of beauty, and the individual expression of the artist in his handiwork, are essentially one, and none of them can be imagined as really existing without the others. It is not the case of a thought, envisaged pictorially, and deliberately clothed in an artistic dress, but of a thought that would have no existence save in so far as it is expressible in paint. This is the modern truth of the art, and the importance of the principle here involved will be illustrated in a later section, but it must be borne in mind that the painting to which this principle applies is a creation of comparatively modern times. As in music so in painting, it has been reserved for recent epochs to manifest the full capabilities of the art. Whereas the arts of architecture and sculpture, though they have found in the modern era new fields to conquer, yet grew to their full stature in ancient Hellas, those of music and painting remained almost in their infancy till the Renaissance. It was only in the 16th and 17th centuries that painters obtained such a mastery on the one hand over the forms of nature, and on the other over an adequate technique, that they were able to create works in which truth and beauty are one and the artistic speech exactly expresses the artistic idea. For this the painter had to command the whole resources of the science of perspective, linear and aerial, and all the technical capabilities of the many-sided processes of oil-paint. Till that stage in the development of the art was reached work was always on one side or another tentative and imperfect, but all through these long periods of endeavour there is one constant feature, and this is the effort of the artist to attain to truth in the representation of nature. No matter what was the character of his task or the material equipment of which he disposed, this ideal was for ever before his eyes, and hence it is that in the relation of the painter's work to nature we find that permanent feature which makes the development of the art from first to last a unity.

§ 4. *General Scheme of the Development of the Art.*—From this point of view, that of the relation of the work of the painter to nature, we may make a rough division of the whole history of the art into four main periods.

The first embraces the efforts of the older Oriental peoples, best represented by the painting of the Egyptians; the second includes the classical and medieval epochs up to the beginning of the 15th century; the third, the 15th and 16th centuries; and the fourth the time from the beginning of the 17th century onwards.

In the first period the endeavour is after truth of contour, in the second and third after truth of form, in the fourth after truth of space.

The Egyptian artist was satisfied if he could render with accuracy, and with proper emphasis on what is characteristic, the silhouettes of things in nature regarded as little more than flat objects cut out against a light background. The Greek and the medieval artist realized that objects had three dimensions, and that it was possible on a flat surface to give an indication of the thickness of anything, that is of its depth away from the spectator, as well as its length and breadth, but they cannot be said to have fully succeeded in the difficult task they set themselves. For this there was needful an efficient knowledge of perspective, and this the 15th century brought with it. During the 15th century the painter fully succeeds in mastering the representation of the third dimension, and during the next he exercises the power thus acquired in perfect freedom, producing some of the most-convincing and masterly presentments of solid forms upon a flat surface that the art has to show. During this period, however, and to a more partial extent even in the earlier classical epoch, efforts were being made to widen the horizon of the art and to embrace within the scope of its representations not only solid objects in themselves, but such objects as a whole in space, in due relation to each other and to the universe at large. It was reserved, however, for the masters of the 17th century perfectly to realize this ideal of the art, and in their hands painting as an art of representation is widened out to its fullest possible limits, and the whole of nature in all its aspects becomes for the first time the subject of the picture.

§ 5. *The Place of Classical Painting in the Development of the Art.*—This limitation of classical painting to the representation of form may be challenged, for some hold that Greek artists not only attempted but succeeded in the task of portraying objects in space in due relation to each other and to the system of things as a whole, and that the scope of their work was as extended as that of the Italian painter of the 16th century. The view taken in this article will presently be justified, but a word may be said here as to Greek painting in general and its relation to sculpture. The main arguments in favour of the more exalted view of this phase of the art are partly based on general cónsiderations, and partly on the existence of some examples which seem to show the artist grappling with the problems of space. The general argument, that because Greek sculptors achieved so much we must assume that the painters brought their art to the same level, is of no weight, because it has been already pointed out that painting and music are not in their development parallel to sculpture and architecture. Nothing, moreover, is really proved by the facts that painting was held by the ancients in higher estimation than its sister art, and that the painters gained great wealth and fame. Painting is a more attractive, more popular art than sculpture. It represents nature by a sort of trick or illusion, whereas sculpture with its three dimensions is more a matter of course. It is a puzzle how the object or scene, with its colours as well as its forms, can be made to appear on a few square inches of flat surface, and the artist who has the secret of the illusion is at once a man of mark. In Greece this was specially the case, because painting there made its appearance rather later than sculpture and so was from the first more conspicuous. Hence literary writers, when they refer to the arts generally, quote a painter rather than a sculptor. The people observed the painters, and these naturally made the most of themselves and of their art. The stories of the wealth and ostentation of some of these show that there was an atmosphere of *réclame* about the painters that must have affected the popular estimate, in an aesthetic sense, of their work. Then, too, popular criticism of painting has no standard. To the passer-by who watches the pavement artist, the result of his operations seems nature itself. "Better than I saw not who saw the truth," writes Dante (*Purg.* xii. 68) of incised outlines on a pavement, that cannot go very far in natural similitude. Vasari, though a trained artist, writes as if they "vied with nature" of certain works that, though excellent for their day, do not approach the modern type. We think ourselves that Raphael's babies are like nature till we see Correggio's, and that Venetian Venuses are "real flesh and blood" till that of Velazquez comes to prove them paint. The fact is that the expression "true to nature" is a relative one, and very little weight should be given to a merely popular or literary judgment on a question of the kind. Hence we must not assume that because ancient painting was extravagantly praised by those who knew no other, it therefore covered all the field of the art.

§ 6. *The Earliest Representative Art.*—Naturalistic design of a very effective kind appears at a very early stage of human development, and is practised among the most primitive races of the actual world, such as the Australians, the Bushmen of South Africa and the Eskimo. Of the existence of such art different explanations have been offered, some finding for the representations of natural objects motives of a religious or magical kind, while others are content to see in them the expression of a simple artistic delight in the imitation of objects of interest. The extraordinary merit, within certain limits, of

this early naturalistic work can be accounted for on sociological lines. As Grosse has put it (*The Beginnings of Art*, p. 198), "Power of observation and skill with the hand are the qualities demanded for primitive naturalistic pictorial art, and the faculty of observation and handiness of execution are at the same time the two indispensable requisites for the primitive hunter life. Primitive pictorial art, with its peculiar characteristics, thus appears fully comprehensible to us as an aesthetic exercise of two faculties which the struggle for existence has developed and improved among the primitive peoples." So far as concerns the power of seizing and rendering the characteristics of natural objects, some of the earliest examples of representative art in the world are among the best. The objects are animals, because these were the only ones that interested the early hunter, but tens of thousands of years ago the Palaeolithic cave-dwellers of western France drew and carved the mammoth, the reindeer, the antelope, and the horse, with astonishing skill and spirit.

Fig. 6, Plate III., shows the famous sketch of a mammoth made by a prehistoric hunter and artist of western France. The tusks, the trunk, the little eye, the forehead, and especially the shaggy fell of the long-haired elephant, are all effectively rendered.

Figs. 1, 2 and 3, Plate L, show three examples of the marvellous series of prehistoric carvings and incised drawings, from the caves of southern France, published by the late Édouard Piette. We note especially the remarkable effort to portray a stag turning its head, and the close observation displayed in the representation of the action of a running buck.

Even more striking are the Palaeolithic paintings discovered in the cave of Altamira at Santillane, near Santander in Spain. These are less ancient than the carvings and sketches mentioned above, but they date from a time when what is now Great Britain was not yet divided from the continent by the Channel, when the climate of southern Europe was still cold, and when animals now extinct—such as the European bison—were still common. These paintings, boldly sketched in three colours, may be reckoned as some 50,000 years old. They display the same power of correct observation and artistic skill as the earlier carvings. Notice in the remarkable examples given on Plate II. the black patches on the bison's winter coat and the red colour of the hide where, with the progress of the spring, he has got rid of the long hair from the more prominent parts of his body by rubbing himself against the rocks. The impressionist character of some of these sketches is doubtless partly due to the action of time; but note how, in the case of the great boar, the artist has represented the action of the legs in running as well as standing in much the same way as might be done in a rapid sketch by a modern painter. The mystery of these astounding paintings is increased by the fact that they are found in a cave to which no daylight has ever penetrated, sometimes in places almost inaccessible to sight or reach, and that they are surrounded by symbols of which none can read the meaning (see the two lozenges in fig. 3, Plate I.).

Palaeolithic art is, however, a phenomenon remote and isolated, and in the history of painting its main interest is to show how ancient is the striving of man after the accurate and spirited representation of nature. Modern savages on about the same plane of civilization do the same work, though not with equal artistic deftness, and Grosse reproduces (*loc.cit.*, ch. vii.) some characteristic designs of Australians and Bushmen. Some of these are of single figures, but there are also "large associated groups of men and animals with the landscapes around them." The pictures consist in outlines engraved or scratched on stone or wood or on previously blackened surfaces of hide, generally, though not always, giving prolife views, and are sometimes filled in with flat tints of colour. There is no perspective, except to this extent, that objects intended to appear distant are sometimes made smaller than near ones. In the extended scenes the figures and objects are dispersed over the field, without any arrangement on planes or artistic composition, but each is delineated with spirit and in essential features with accuracy.

It is a remarkable fact, but one easily explained, that when man advances from the hunter stage to a more settled agricultural life these spontaneous naturalistic drawings no 'longer appear. Neolithic man shows a marked advance on the capacity of his Palaeolithic predecessors in all the useful arts of life: his tools, his pottery, his weapons; but as an artist he was beyond comparison inferior. His attempts to draw men and beasts resulted in no more than conventional symbols, such as an intelligent child might scribble; of the Palaeolithic man's taste for design, as shown in the carved work of the caves, or of his power of reproducing nature, there is not a sign. Keenness of observation and deftness of hand are no longer developed because no longer needed for the purposes of existence, and representative art almost dies out, to be, however, revived at a further stage of civilization. At this further stage the sociological motive of art is commemoration. It is in connexion with the tomb, the temple and the palace that in early but still fully organized communities art finds its field of operations. Such communities we find in ancient Egypt and Babylonia, while similar phenomena showed themselves in old Oriental lands, such as India and China.

§ 7. *The Painting of Contour: Egypt and Babylonia.*—In ancient Egypt we find this graphic delineation of natural objects, so spontaneous and free among the hunter tribes, reduced to a system and carried out with certain well-established conventions. The chief of these was the almost universal envisagement in profile of the subject to be represented. Only in the case of subsidiary figures might a front or a back view or a three-quarter face be essayed. To bring the human figure into profile it was conventionalized, as fig. 7, Plate III., will show. The subject is an Egyptian of high rank, accompanied by his wife and son, fowling in the marshes of the Delta. It is part of a wall-painting from a tomb at Thebes dating about 1500 B.C. The head, it will be seen, is in profile, but the eye is drawn full-face. The shoulders are shown in front view, though by the outline of the breast, with its nipple, on the figure's right, and by the position far to the right of the navel, an indication is given that the view here is three-quarters. At the hips the figure is again in profile, and this is the position also of the legs. It will be observed that the two feet have the big toe on the same side, a device to escape the necessity of drawing the four toes as seen in the outside view of a foot. As a rule the action of these figures is made as clear as possible, and they are grouped in such a way that each is clearly seen, so that a crowd is shown either by a number of parallel outlines each a little in advance of the other suggesting a row seen in slight obliquity, or else by parallel rows of figures on lines one above the other. Animals are treated in the same way in profile, save that oxen will show the two horns, asses the two ears, as in front view, and the legs are arranged so that all are seen.

Within these narrow limits the Egyptian artist achieved extraordinary success in the truthful rendering of nature as expressed in the contours of figures and objects. If the human form be always conventionalized to the required flatness, the draughtsman is keen to seize every chance of securing variety. He fastens on the distinctive traits of different races with the zeal of a modern ethnologist, and in the case of royal personages he achieves success in individual portraiture. Though he could not render varieties of facial expression, he made the action of the limbs express all it could. The traditional Egyptian gravity did not exclude humour, and some good caricatures have been preserved. Egyptian drawing of animals, especially birds (see fig. 7, Plate III.), has in its way never been surpassed, and the specific points of beasts are as keenly noted as the racial characteristics of human beings. Animals, domestic or wild, are given with their particular gait or pose or expression, and the accent is always laid on those features that give the suggestion of strength or swiftness or lithe agility which marks the species. The precision of drawing is just as great in the case of lifeless objects, and any set of early, carefully-executed, hieroglyphic signs will give evidence of an eye and hand trained to perfection in the simpler tasks of the graphic art.

The representation of scenes, as distinct from single figures or groups, was not wholly beyond the Egyptian artist's horizon. His most ambitious attempts are the great battle-scenes of the period of the New Empire, when a Seti or a Rameses is seen

driving before him a host of routed foemen. The king in his chariot with the rearing horses is firmly rendered in the severe conventional style, but the crowd of fugitives, on a comparatively minute scale, are not arranged in the original clear fashion in parallel rows, but are tumbled about in extraordinary confusion all over the field, though always on the one flat plane. By another convention objects that cannot be given in profile are sometimes shown in ground plan. Thus a tank with trees round it will be drawn square in plan and the trees will be exhibited as if laid out flat on the ground, pointing on each side outwards from the tank.

In Babylonia and Assyria the mud-brick walls of palaces were coated with thin stucco, and this was in the interior sometimes painted, but few fragments of the work remain. On the exterior considerable use was made of decorative bands and panels of enamelled tiles, in which figure subjects were prominent, as we learn by the passage from Ezek. xxiii., about "men pourtrayed upon the wall, the images of the Chaldeans pourtrayed with vermilion." The best idea of Assyrian graphic design is gained from the slabs carved in very low relief, which contain annalistic records of the acts of the king and his people in war and peace. The human figure is treated here in a less conventional scheme, but at the same time with less variety and in a less spirited and interesting fashion than in Egypt. Of animals far fewer species are shown, but in the portrayal of the nobler beasts, notably the horse, the lion and the mastiff, there is an element of true grandeur that we seldom find in Egyptian design. Furthermore, the carver of the reliefs had a better idea of giving the impression of a scene than his brother of the Nileland, and in his representations of armies marching and fighting he introduces rivers, hills, trees, groups of buildings and the like, all of course delineated without perspective, but in far truer and more telling fashion than is the case with the scenes from the campaigns of Egyptian conquerors.

§ 8. *Painting in Pre-historic Greece.*—A new chapter in the history of ancient painting was opened by the discovery of relics of the art in the palaces and tombs of the Mycenaean period on the coasts and islands of the Aegean. The charming naturalistic representations of marine plants and animals on the painted vases are quite unlike anything which later Greek art has to offer, and exhibit a decorative taste that reminds us a little of the Japanese. What we are concerned with, however, are rather the examples of wall-painting in plaster found at Tiryns and Mycenae and in Crete. Of the former the first to attract notice was the well-known bull from Tiryns, represented in profile and in action, and accompanied by a human figure; but of far greater importance, because foreshadowing an advance in the pictorial art, are certain wall-paintings discovered more recently by Dr Evans at Cnossos in Crete. The question is not of the single figures in the usual profile view, like the already celebrated "Cup-bearer," however important these may be from the historical side, but of the so-called "miniature" wall-paintings that are now preserved in the museum at Candia, in which figures on a small scale are represented not singly but in crowds and in combination with buildings and landscape features that seem to carry us forward to far more advanced stages of the art of painting. To borrow a few sentences from Dr Arthur Evans's account of them on their first discovery (*Annual of British School at Athens,* vi. 46): " A special characteristic of these designs is the outline drawing in fine dark lines. This outline drawing is at the same time combined with a kind of artistic shorthand brought about by the simple process of introducing patches of reddish brown or of white on which groups belonging to one or other sex are thus delineated. In this way the respective flesh-tints of a series of men or women are given with a single sweep of the brush, their limbs and features being subsequently outlined on the background thus obtained." There is here, it is true, no perspective, but there is a distinct effort to give the general effect of objects in a mass, which corresponds curiously with the modern development of the art of painting called " impressionism."

§ 9. *The Painting of Form: Ancient Greece and Italy.*—As

is well-known, this early civilization in the Greek world of the second millenium B.C. was almost completely swept away, probably by the political cataclysm of about 1000 B.C. known as the Dorian Migration. Hellenic art proper, in its historical continuity, represents a new start altogether and the beginnings of it need not be sought earlier than about 800 to 700 B.C. The art of painting had then completely lost touch with the graceful naturalism and with the broad generalization of the "Aegean" period, and is represented by figure designs on the so-called "geometric" or "Dipylon" vases of the most primitive kind. For a long time Greek painting is chiefly represented by work on the vases, but that this may be regarded as in the strict sense painting is shown by the fact that tablets or panels (*pinakes*) that would certainly be called pictures were being painted at the same time by the same technical methods, and in some cases by the same craftsman, as the vases. As Klein remarks (*Euphronios*,[1] p. 252), "the most ancient material for Greek painting is clay in the form of the vase as well as of the pinax." Now we find in Pliny's account of the beginnings of Greek painting (*Nat. Hist.* xxxv. 15 seq.) certain stages indicated in the development of technique, and we are able to illustrate these stages from vases which correspond more or less in their chronological order with the succession of the stages in Pliny. The correspondence is not exact, and there are difficulties in the way of interpreting the statements from the monuments, but the two are certainly to be brought into connexion. According to Pliny the order of development seems to be (1) outlines; (2) [a] outlines filled in with flat tints, or [b] outlines with linear inner markings but no colour. Outline drawing is obviously always the first stage in the graphic art regarded as delineation, not decoration. The flat tints without inner markings are found on "Dipylon" vases of 800-700 B.C., and as for the inner markings, though there is a difficulty in the exact interpretation of Pliny's words, yet inner markings in the form of lines scratched on these silhouettes make their appearance very early. Two further stages are indicated by Pliny as the introduction of a red colour and the distinction between male and female figures by a painter named Eumarus of Athens. This would be by the use of white, which with red, an oxide of iron, appears on vases of about 600 B.C. Eumarus is also said to have "ventured to imitate all kinds of figures," and we cannot fail here to be reminded of the marvellous François vase at Florence (fig. 8, Plate III.) of the first half of the 6th century, which is of large size and is decorated with a wealth of figure designs from mythological sources that are among the most remarkable productions of the graphic art in existence. Human figures and animals are there displayed in an extraordinary variety of poses and illustrating all kinds of scenes, and the execution shows a firmness of hand and patience in the rendering of details to which no praise can do justice. The inner markings are rendered by lines with the most scrupulous care and finish. Cimon of Cleonae is said to have followed Eumarus with certain improvements which are of the utmost significance for the future of the art in Greece. He is said to have introduced four innovations: (a) "Catagrapha," which Pliny explains as "profile figures" but which must mean something more than this, seeing that profiles had been in use from the first. "Foreshortenings" is a possible and an intelligible rendering which moreover corresponds with what is further ascribed to him; (b) the representation of "countenances in different positions, looking backwards or upwards or downwards." The other improvements, in giving (c) the details of anatomy and (d) "the wrinkles and folds of drapery," are not of so much importance as such advance is normal and necessary. The introduction of foreshortened views is the matter of real moment, for this is the point at which Greek painting parts company with the older oriental traditions, and enters on a course of its own which leads directly to all the modern developments of the art.

The words of Pliny explaining the term "catagrapha" can be aptly illustrated from the vase paintings connected with the name of Epictetus. Epictetus was the leading figure among a company of Athenian vase decorators of the last decades of the 6th

century B.C. and the beginning of the 5th, who usher in the period of the most gifted and original masters of the craft. Their work is marked by efforts to give to the human figure a vigour and expressiveness it had never before attained, and to gain their end they essay all sorts of novel and difficult problems in drawing. In connexion with Pliny's words, Klein remarks (*Euphronios*, p. 47) that on their vases "the running figures look behind them; those that are jumping, revelling or fighting look up; the lifting or bending ones look down." Some of the best vases decorated by this set of artists, who are the first to use the so-called "red-figured" technique instead of painting as the older masters had done in black on red, are for qualities of strength, variety and animation unequalled by any of their successors of the later periods, yet it is significant of the whole character of this ancient painting that they are always conspicuously more successful with profiles and objects in an upright plane at right angles to the line of sight than with any forms which involve foreshortening or perspective. They are masters of contour but are still struggling for the full command over form, and it is noteworthy that the generation of these greatest of the vase-painters had passed away before these difficulties of foreshortening had been conquered.

We have now followed on the vases the development of Greek painting up to about the time of the Persian wars, and it must be noted that in other forms, as on terra-cotta tablets or pinakes, on the flat edges of sarcophagi in the same material, and occasionally on marble slabs or stelae, the same technical characteristics are to be observed. Of painting on a monumental scale Greece proper has hitherto shown no trace, yet at this very juncture, in the decades immediately after the Persian wars, there suddenly makes his appearance one of the greatest representatives of monumental wall-painting known to the annals of the art. This is Polygnotus, who, with some worthy associates, displayed on the walls of public buildings at Athens and at Delphi a series of noble compositions on a large scale that won the admiration of the whole Hellenic community.

To find any remains of mural painting that may seem to lead up to Polygnotus and his school we have to pass beyond the bounds of Greece proper into Italy, where, alike in the Greek and Etruscan cities and also at Rome, painting in this form was practised from an early date. Pliny mentions paintings at Ardea older than the city of Rome, and some very ancient ones at Caere. Two sets of early paintings, not actually on walls but on terra-cotta slabs meant for the coating of walls, have come to light in recent times at Cervetri, the ancient Caere, some of which, in the British Museum, were dated by the late A. S. Murray at about 600 B.C. (*Journal of Hellenic Studies*, x. 243), while others in the Louvre may be about half a century later. True wall-paintings, of possibly a still earlier date and certainly of more primitive design, were found in the Campana tomb at Veii (Dennis, *Etruria*, ch. i.). The paintings from Caere are executed on a white or yellowish "slip" in a few simple colours, and exhibit single figures in a frieze-like arrangement with little attempt at action and none at grouping. The flesh of the women is left the colour of the white ground, that of the men is painted a ruddy hue. To the 6th, and first half of the 5th century, belong wall-paintings in Italian tombs, which, whether in Greek cities or in Etruscan, show distinct signs of Hellenic influence. Some of these wall-paintings (*Antike Denkmäler*, ii., Taf. 41-43) show considerable liveliness in colouring and in action, and a freedom and gaiety in female costume that remind us of what we read about the painting of Polygnotus (*q.v.*). The place of this great painter in the general history of the graphic art is given to him for his ethical greatness and the austere beauty of his single figures, which ancient writers extol. All we have to do here is fix his place in the development of painting by noting the stage at which he had arrived in the representation of nature.

The wall-paintings of Polygnotus and his school must have exhibited a large number of figures powerfully characterized in action and expression, not in a confused mass nor summarized as at Cnossus, nor grouped together as in a modern composition, nor yet arranged in formal rows one above the other, but distributed at different levels on the one plane of the picture, the levels being distinguished by summary indications of a landscape setting. Parts of some of the figures were hidden by risings of the ground. The general effect is probably represented by the paintings on the vase in the Louvre shown in fig. 9, one side of which exhibits the destruction of the children of Niobe, and the other the Argonauts. Simplicity in design and ethical dignity in the single forms are here unmistakable.

It is probable that Polygnotus had not fully mastered the difficulties of foreshortening with which the early " red-figure " masters were struggling, but later designs both on vases and elsewhere do show that in the 4th century at any rate these had been

FIG. 9.—Vase painting in the Louvre, illustrating the style of Polygnotus.

overcome. The drawing on the so-called Ficoronian Cista, and on the best of the Greek mirror-backs, may be instanced. The ancients recognized that in the latter part of the 5th century B.C. painting made a great technical advance, so that all that had gone before seemed archaic, while for the first time " the gates of art " were opened and the perfect masters entered in. The advance is in the direction of the representation not of form only but of space, and seems from literary notices to have implied a considerable acquaintance with perspective science. The *locus classicus*, one of great importance, is in Vitruvius. In the preface to his seventh book he writes of Agatharcus, a painter who flourished at Athens in the middle and third quarter of the 5th century, that he executed a scene-painting for Aeschylus, and wrote a treatise upon it which inspired the philosophers Democritus and Anaxagoras to take up the subject, and to show scientifically from the constitution of the eye and the direction of rays of light how it was possible *in scenic paintings to give sure images of objects otherwise hard to fix correctly, so that when such objects were figured on an upright plane at right-angles to the line of sight some should appear to recede and others to come forwards.* It would not be easy to summarize more aptly the functions of perspective, and if philosophers of the eminence of those just mentioned worked out these rules and placed them at the disposal of the artists, the transition from ancient to modern painting should have been accomplished in the 5th century B.C.,

XX 8*

instead of just two thousand years afterwards! So far however as the existing evidence enables us to judge, this was not actually the case, and in spite of Agatharcus and the philosophers, painting pursued the even tenor of its way within the compara- lively narrow limits set for it by the genius of ancient art (see GREEK ART). It may be admitted that in many artistic qualities it was beyond praise. In beauty, in grace of line, in composition, we can imagine works of Apelles, of Zeuxis, of Protogenes, excelling even the efforts of the Italian painters, or only matched by the finest designs of a Raphael or a Leonardo. In the small encaustic pictures of a Pausias there may have been all the rich- ness and force we admire in a Chardin or a Monticelli. We may even concede that the Greek artist tried at times to transcend the natural limits of his art, and to represent various planes of space in perspective, as in the landscape scenes from the *Odyssey*, or in figure compositions such as the " Alexander and Darius at Issus," preserved to us in a mosaic, or the " Battle-piece " by Aristides that contained a hundred combatants. The facts, however, remain, first that the Greek pictures about which we chiefly read were of single figures, or subjects of a very limited and compact order with little variety of planes; and second, that the existing remains of ancient painting are so full of mistakes in perspective that the representation of distance cannot have been a matter to which the artists had really set themselves. The monumental evidence available on the last point is sufficient to override arguments to the contrary that may be built up on literary notices. No competent artist, or even teacher of drawing, who examines what is left of ancient painting, can fail to see that the problem of representing correctly the third dimension of space, though it may have been attacked, had certainly not been solved. It is of no avail to urge that these remains are not from the hands of the great artists but of mere decorators. In modern times the mere decora- tor, if he had passed through a school of art, would be as far above such childish blunders as a Royal Academician. We have only to consider dispassionately the photographic reproductions from ancient paintings (Herr- mann, *Denkmäler der Malerei des Altertums*, Munich, 1906, &c.) to see that the perspective researches of the philosophers had not resulted in a general comprehension among the artists of the science of receding planes. For example, in the famous wall-painting of " Zeus and Hera on Mount Ida " in the House of the Tragic Poet at Pompeii, the feet of the standing figure of the goddess are nearer to the spectator than the seat of her lord, but the upper part of her form is away on the farther side of him (see fig. 10, Plate III.). No one who could draw at all would be capable now of such a mistake. In interiors the perspective of the rafters of a roof, of a table, a stool, a throne, is in most cases faulty; and the scale of the figures seems often to be determined rather by their relative importance in the scene than by their position on the planes of the picture. In the Pompeian landscape-piece of " Paris on Mount Ida " (Herrmann, No. 8) there is no sense of the relative proportions of objects, and a cow in the foreground is much smaller than Paris, who is a long way back in the composition.

It is an additional confirmation of this view to find early Christian and early medieval painting confined to the representa- tion of the few near objects, which the older Oriental artists had all along envisaged. If classical painters had really revolu- tionized design, as it was actually revolutionized in the 15th century of our era, and had followed out to their logical conse- quence the innovations of Agatharcus, we may be sure that the influence of these innovations would not have been wholly lost even in the general decline of the arts at the break-up of the Roman Empire of the West. In any case, the influence would have survived in Byzantine art, where there was no such cataclysm. Yet we fail to see in the numerous pictorial miniatures from the 5th century onwards, or in the mosaics or the wall-paintings of the same epoch, any more effective grasp of the facts of the third dimension of space than was possessed by the pre-classical Egyptian.

All through the middle ages, therefore, the facts concerning painting with which we are here concerned remain the same, and the art appears almost exclusively concerned with the few selected objects and the single plane. The representation is at most of *form* and not of *space*.

§ 10. *Early Christian and Early Medieval Painting.*—The extant remains of early Christian painting may be considered under three heads: (1) the wall-paintings in the catacombs; (2) the pictorial decorations in books; (3) the mosaic pictures on the walls of the churches. (1) The first are in themselves of little importance, but are of historical interest as a link of connexion between the wall-painting of classical times and the more distinctively Christian forms of the art. They are slightly executed and on a small scale, the earliest, as being more near to classical models, are artistically the best. (2) That form of painting devoted to the decoration and illustration of books belongs more to the art of ornament than to painting proper (see ILLUMINATED MSS. and ILLUSTRATION). (3) Early Christian mosaics are noble monuments of the graphic art, and are its best representatives during the centuries from the 5th to the 8th. A dignified simplicity in design suits their large scale and architectural setting, and the aim of the artist is to present in forms of epic grandeur the personages of the sacred narratives. They are shown as in repose or engaged in some typical but simple action; the backgrounds being as a rule plain blue or gold and the accessories of the simplest possible description. The finest Christian mosaic is also the earliest. It is in the apse of S. Pudentiana, Rome, and displays Christ enthroned as teacher with the Apostles seated on each side of Him. It may date from the 4th century. Next to this the best examples are at Ravenna, in the tomb of Galla Placidia, the Baptistery, S. Apollinare Nuovo and S. Vitale, dating from the 5th and 6th centuries. The picture in the baptistery of the "Baptism of Christ" is the most artistic piece of composition and pictorial effect, and next to this comes the "Good Shepherd" of the tomb of Galla Placidia. The finest single figures are those of the white-robed saints between the windows of the nave of S. Apollinare Nuovo, and the most popular representations are the two processions of male and female saints lower down on the same walls. The famous mosaics in S. Vitale depicting Justinian and Theodora with courtiers in attendance, though historically interesting, are designed in a wooden fashion, and later mosaics at Palermo, Venice, Rome and other places are as a rule rather decorative than pictorial. Where the costly material of glass mosaic was not available, the churches of this period would show mural paintings on plaster of much the same design and artistic character, though comparatively ineffective.

In monumental painting the interval between the early Christian mosaics and mural pictures and the revival of the 13th century is filled by a series of wall and ceiling paintings of Carolingian, Romanesque and early Gothic date, in Italy, Germany and England. The earliest of which account need be taken are those in the recently excavated church of S. Maria Antiqua by the Forum at Rome (Rushworth, in *Papers of the British School at Rome*, vol. i., London, 1902), where there is a complete and, on the whole, well-preserved series consisting for the most part in single figures and simply composed scenes. Most of the work can be dated to the time of Pope John VII. at the beginning of the 8th century. Its style shows a mixture of Byzantine motives with elements that are native to Rome. It must be remembered that at the time Rome was strongly under Byzantine influence. Passing over some more fragmentary specimens, we may refer next to several series of mural

paintings in and near the island of Reichenau at the western end of the lake of Constance, where a school of painting flourished in the latter part of the 10th century. The work here is quite as good as anything Italy has to show, and represents a native German style, based on early Christian tradition, with very little dependence on Byzantine models. The most interesting piece is the "Last Judgment" in the church of St George at Oberzell on Reichenau, where, in a very simple but dignified and effective form, we find the earliest existing representation of this standard theme of later medieval monumental art (F. X. Kraus, *Wandgemälde der St Georgskirche zu Oberzell auf der Insel Reichenau,* Freiburg-i.-Br., 1884).

About a hundred years later, in the latter part of the 11th century, a mural painting of the same theme was executed in the church of S. Angelo in Formis near Capua in southern Italy, the style of which shows a mixture of Latin and Byzantine elements (F. X. Kraus, *Die Wandgemälde von S. Angelo in Formis,* Berlin, 1893).

To the middle of the 12th century belongs one of the most complete and interesting cycles of medieval wall-decoration, the display of a series of figures and scenes illustrating the eleventh chapter of Hebrews, in the chapter-house of the now secularized monastery of Brauweiler, near Cologne, in the Rhineland. Here the pictorial effect is simple, but the decorative treatment in regard to the filling of the spaces and the lines of composition is excellent. The design is Romanesque in its severity (E. Aus'm Weerth, *Wandmalereien des Mittelalters in den Rheinlanden,* Leipzig 1879). Romanesque also, but exhibiting an increase in animation and expressiveness, is the painting of the flat ceiling of the nave of the fine church of St Michael at Hildesheim. In the general decorative effect, the distribution of the subjects in the spaces, the blending of figures and ornament, the work, the main subject of which is the Tree of Jesse, is a masterpiece. Two nude figures of Adam and Eve are for the period remarkable productions. The date is the close of the 12th century.

Succeeding examples show unmistakable signs of the approach of the Gothic period. In the wall-paintings of the nuns' choir of the church of Gurk in Carinthia, a certain grace and tenderness begin to make themselves felt, and the same impression we gain from the extensive cycle in the choir of the cathedral of Brunswick, from the first decades of the 13th century. The picture of Herod's birthday feast is typical of the style of German painting of the time; there is nothing about it in the least rude or tentative. It is neither childish nor barbarous, but very accomplished in a conventional style that is exactly suited from the decorative point of view to a mural painting. The story is told effectively but in quaint fashion, and several incidents of it are shown in the same composition. There is no attempt to represent the third dimension of space, nor to give the perspective setting of the scene, but the drawing is easy and true and expressive. The studied grace in the bend of certain figures and the lively expressions of the faces are traits which prefigure Gothic art (see fig. 11, Plate III.).

Distinctively Gothic in their feeling were the wall-paintings in the chapel at Ramersdorf, opposite Bonn, dating from the beginning of the 14th century. They are only preserved in copies, but these enable us to see with what grace and feeling the slender figures were designed, how near to Angelico's came the tender angels making music where the virgin is receiving her celestial crown (E. Aus'm Weerth, *loc. cit.*). From the end of the 14th century, Castle Runkelstein, near Botzen in Tirol, has preserved an extensive cycle of secular wall-paintings, much repainted, but of unique interest as giving an idea how a medieval residence of the kind might be adorned. The style is of native growth and no influence from south of the Alps is to be discerned (Janitschek, *Geschichte der deutschen Malerei,* Berlin, 1890, 198 seq.). Technically speaking, all these mural paintings consist in little more than outlines filled in with flat tints, neither modelling of the forms nor perspective effect in the setting is attempted, but the work so far as it goes is wholly satisfactory. There is no coarseness of execution nor anything in the forms, gestures or expressions that offends the eye. The colours are bright and pure, the decorative effect often charming.

In the matter of panel paintings on wood, we have the interesting notice in Bede that Abbot Benedict of Wearmouth at the end of the 7th century brought from Italy portable pictures on wooden panels for the decoration of his church, part of which still remains. The style of the painting on these, it has recently been noticed, would resemble the existing wall-paintings of the beginning of the 8th century in S. Maria Antiqua in Rome, already referred to. Movable panel pictures in the form of representations of the Madonna and Child were produced in immense numbers at Byzantium and were imported largely into Italy, where they became of importance in connexion with the revival of painting in the 13th century. As a rule, however, paintings on panel were not movable but were attached to a screen, a door, or similar structure of wood consisting in framing and panels. This form of decoration is of special importance as it is really the origin of the modern picture. The painted panel, which at first forms an integral part of an architecturally designed structure of wood, gradually comes to attract to itself more and more importance, till it finally issues from its original setting and, emancipated from all relations to its surroundings, claims attention to itself as an independent work of art.

Painted panels in an architectural setting were used for the decoration of altar-fronts or *antependia*, of altar-backs or, as they are commonly called, altar-pieces, choir-screens, doors of presses and the like; or again for ceilings. There was painting also on the large wooden crucifixes displayed in churches, where a picture of Christ on the Cross might take the place of the more life-like carved image. In Italy painted panels were used as decoration of furniture, notably of the large carved chests or *cassoni* so common at the epoch of the Renaissance.

Examples of early medieval date do not appear to have survived. In Germany, where, as has been noticed, the arts in the 11th and 12th centuries stood at a higher level than in Italy or elsewhere in the west, certain *antependia* or altar-fronts from Soest in Westphalia of the 12th century are said to be the earliest known examples of German panel painting. One is preserved in the museum at Berlin. A little later the number of such panels introduced as part of the decoration of altar-backs, generally with folding doors, becomes very great. Painted panels as part of the decoration of screens are preserved in the choir at Cologne from the middle of the 14th century. In Italy the painted crucifix shared popular favour with the imported or imitated Byzantine Madonna-panels. A good example of the early painted altar-screen is preserved in Westminster Abbey.

Later, in the 15th century, the painted panel, generally with a single figure of a saint, becomes a common part of the carved, painted and gilded chancel screen in English churches, and many specimens are still to be seen, especially in East Anglia.

§ 11. *Beginnings of the Picture: German and Early Flemish Panel Painting.*—From the decorative panels introduced into wooden screen-work was developed in Germany and Flanders the picture proper, the mural painting passing out of use owing to the prevalence in the north of Gothic architecture, which does not admit of wall spaces for the display of pictures, but substitutes as a form of painting the stained-glass window. In Italy, where Gothic was treated as a plaything, the wall spaces were never sacrificed, and in the development of the art the mural picture took the lead, the painted panel remaining on the whole of secondary importance.

Priority in this development of the picture is claimed in Germany for the school of Prague, where a gild of painters was founded in 1348, but the first northern school of painting that influenced other schools and plays a part in the history of painting as a whole is the so-called school of Cologne, where painters such as Meister Wilhelm and Hermann Wynrich achieved reputation in the 14th century, and produced as their successor in the 15th Stephan Lochner, author of the so-called "Dombild" in the cathedral, and of the "Virgin of the Priests' Seminary." A little later than the earliest Cologne masters appears Hubert van Eyck, born near Maestricht at no great distance from the

Rhineland capital, who with his younger brother, Jan, heads the Early Flemish school of painting. Hubert is one of the great names in the history of the art, and is chiefly responsible for the altar-piece of the "Adoration of the Lamb" at Ghent, the most important masterpiece of the northern schools before the 17th century, and the earliest monument of the then newly developed art of oil painting. Table No. I. in Part II. of this article gives the names of the chief successors of the Van Eycks, and the school ends with the life and work of Quintin Matsys of Antwerp, in the first quarter of the 16th century. The spirit of the early Cologne school, and in the main of that of Flanders, is idyllic and devotional, but the artists of the latter school achieve extraordinary force and precision in their representation of the facts of nature. They are, moreover, the first painters of landscape, for in their hands the gold background of the medieval panels yields place to a rendering of natural scenery and of effects of distance, minute in details and fresh and delightful in feeling. The famous picture ascribed by some to Hubert van Eyck in the collection of Sir Francis Cook at Richmond is a good example. The subject is the "Three Maries at the Sepulchre," and the background is a wonderful view of a city intended for Jerusalem (see fig. 12, Plate IV.).

In Germany, on the other hand, the tendency of the 15th century was towards a rather crude realism in details, to which the higher artistic qualities of beauty and devotional sentiment were often sacrificed. This is a new phenomenon in the history of the art. In the older Oriental, the classical and the medieval phases of painting, though there is a constant effort to portray the truth of nature, yet the decorative instinct in the artist, his feeling for pattern, was a controlling element in the work, and the representation was conventionalized into a form that satisfied the ideal of beauty current at the time. Jan van Eyck was matter-of-fact in his realism, but avoided ugliness, whereas in Germany in the 15th and 16th centuries we find action and expression exaggerated to contortion and grimace, and all artistic qualities sacrificed to a mistaken idea of force. German art was, however, saved by the appearance of some artists of great genius who more than made up for the national insensibility to beauty by their earnestness and truth. Martin Schongauer of Colmar learnt his art from the painters of the Flemish Netherlands, and imbibed something of the feeling for beauty which the successors of Hubert van Eyck had never wholly lost. After Schongauer German art culminates at Nuremberg in the person of Albrecht Dürer, and a little later in that of Hans Holbein the younger. Contemporary with Dürer, Mathias Grunewald of Colmar exhibits a dramatic power in his creations that compensates for their exaggerated realism, and Bartholomäus Bruyn, of Cologne, prefigures the future success of the northern schools in portraiture. In Germany, however, the wars of religion in the 16th century checked the further growth of a national art. Holbein's migration to England is a significant sign of this, and German art in this phase of it may be said to come to an end in the person of Adam Elsheimer of Frankfort, who introduced German painting at Rome about the year 1600.

In the Netherlands the early religious school ends, as we have seen, with Quintin Matsys, and the next generation of Flemish painters for the most part practise their art in Italy, and import Italian fashions into the painting of their own country. From the ranks of these so-called Italianizers in the Flanders of the 16th century proceeds a little later the commanding personality of Rubens.

§ 12. *The Rise of Schools of Painting.*—The expression "school of painting" has more than once been used; what is the meaning of it? The history of painting has hitherto been treated in the article as a development that proceeded according to a natural law of evolution in independence of individuals. In painting, however, as in all the higher operations of the arts, the initiative of the individual counts for much, and the action and reaction on each other of individuals, and those groups of individuals whom common aims and practice draw together into schools, make up for us a good part of the interest of the historical study of painting. At certain periods this particular 'interest has been lacking.' In ancient Egypt, for example, and among the older Oriental peoples generally, schools of painting in the modern sense did not exist, for the arts were carried on on traditional lines and owed little, so far as records tell, to individual initiative.. In ancient Greece, on the contrary, we find ourselves at once in an atmosphere of names and achievements which give all the glamour of personal and biographical interest to the story of art. In the early Christian and early medieval periods, we return again to a time when the arts were practised in the same impersonal fashion as in the oldest days, but with the later medieval epoch we emerge once more into an era where the artist of genius, with his experiments and triumphs, his rivals and followers, is in the forefront of interest; when history is enlivened with anecdote, and takes light and shade from the changing fortunes of individuals.

There is a danger lest the human interest of such a period may lead us to forget the larger movements, impersonal and almost cosmic, which are all the time carrying these individuals and groups forward on their destined course. The history of painting cannot be understood if it be reduced to a notice, however full, of separate " schools " or to a series of biographies, fascinating as these may be made, of individual artists. Hence in what follows it is still the main course of the development of the art in its relation to nature that will be kept in view, while the information about names and dates and mutual relations of artists and schools, which is in its own way equally important, will be furnished in the tables constituting Part II. of this article.

What has just been said will prepare the reader for the fact that the first schools of painting here mentioned are those of Germany and Flanders, not those of Italy, though the latter are more important as well as actually prior. in point of time.

§ 13. *The Gothic Movement and the Proto-Renaissance, in their Influence on Painting north and south of the Alps.*—The revival of the arts of sculpture and painting in the Italy of the last part of the 13th century was an event of capital importance, not only for that country but for the west at large. Its importance has, however, been exaggerated, when it has been said to imply the rediscovery of the arts after a period in which they had suffered an entire eclipse. So far as Italy is concerned, both sculpture and painting had in the previous period sunk to a level so low that they could hardly be said to exist, but at the same epoch in lands north of the Alps they were producing works of considerable merit. Romanesque wall-painting of the 12th century, as represented in some Rhineland churches and cloisters, is immeasurably better than anything of the same period south of the Alps. In the arts of construction and ornament the lead remained for a long time with the northern peoples, and in every branch of decorative work with the exception of mosaic the craftsmanship of Germany and France surpassed anything that native Italian workmen could produce. By the middle of the 11th century the intellectual and social activity of the French people, was accompanied by an artistic movement that created the most complex and beautiful architectural monuments that the world has seen. The adornment of the great French Gothic cathedral was as.artistically perfect as its fabric was noble. For one, at any rate,-of the effects at which the painter aims, that of glowing and sumptuous colour, nothing can surpass the stained-glass windows of the Gothic churches, while the exteriors of the same buildings were enriched with hundreds of statues of monumental dignity endowed with a grace and expressiveness that reflect the spirit of the age.

The Gothic age in France was characterized by humanity, tenderness and the love of nature, and there are few epochs in human history the spirit of which is to us more congenial. The 11th century, which witnessed the growth of the various elements of culture that combined to give the age its ultimate character, saw also a movement of revival in another sphere. The reference is to what has been aptly termed a " Proto-Renaissance," the characteristic of which was a fresh interest in surviving remains of classical antiquity. In more than one region of 'the west, where these remains were specially in evidence, this interest

manifested itself, and the earliest sign of it was in Provence, the highly Romanized part of southern Gaul known *par excellence* as the " Provincia." To this is due the remarkable development of decorative sculpture in the first decades of the 12th century, which gave to that region the storied portals of St Gilles, and of St Trophime at Arles. Somewhat later, in the early part of the 13th, those portions of southern Italy under the direct rule of the emperor Frederick II. presented a similar phenomenon that has been fully discussed by M. Bertaux in his *L'Art dans l'Italie méridionale* (Paris, 1904). There were other centres of this same movement, and a recent writer enumerates no fewer than seven. The Gothic movement proper depended in no degree on the study of the antique, and in art the ornamental forms which express its spirit are naturalistic, not classical, while the fine figure sculpture above referred to is quite independent of ancient models, which hardly existed in the central regions of France where the Gothic movement had its being. Still the proto-Renaissance can be associated with it as another phase of the same awakening of intellectual life that marked the 12th century. Provence took the lead in the literary revival of the time, and the artistic movement that followed on this was influenced by the fact of the existence in those regions of abundant remains of classical art.

The Gothic movement was essentially northern in its origin, and its influence radiated from the Île de France.' What has been described as the idyllic grace, the tenderness, that mark the works of the early Cologne school, and to some extent those of the early Flemings, were Gothic in their origin, while the feeling for nature in landscape that characterises van Eyck, and the general tendency towards a realistic apprehension of the facts of things, may also be put down to the quickening of both thought and sympathy due to the Gothic movement. Hence, it is that, the northern schools of painting are noticed before the Italian because they were nearer to the source of the common inspiration. All the lands of the West, however, exhibit, each in its own special form, the same stir of a new intellectual, religious and artistic life. In Italy we meet with the same phenomena as in France, a proto-Renaissance, first in southern Italy and then, as we shall presently see, at Rome and at Pisa, and a religious and intellectual movement on Gothic lines that was embodied in the attractive personality of St Francis of Assisi. Francis was as perfect an embodiment of the Gothic temper as St Louis himself, and in his romantic enthusiasm, his tenderness, his humanity is in spirit more French than Italian.

§ 14. *The Rise of the Italian Schools of Painting.*—The revival of the arts in Italy in the latter part of the 13th century was the outcome of the two movements just noticed. The art of Niccola Pisano is now recognised as a phase of the proto-Renaissance of southern Italy, whence his family was derived. It represents a distinct advance on the revived classical sculpture of Provence or Campania because Niccola's artistic personality was a strong one, and he gives to his work the impress of the individual of genius. Throughout its history Italian art depends for its excellence on this personal element, and Niccola's achievement is epoch-making because of his personal vigour, not because he reinvented a lost art. Towards the end of the 13th century, painting began to show the results of the same renewed study of antique models, and here again the revival is connected with the names of gifted individuals. Among these the most noteworthy are the Roman Pietro Cavallini and Duccio di Buoninsegna of Siena. The condition of painting in Italy in late medieval days has already been indicated. Cavallini and Duccio now produce, in two standard forms of the art, the mural painting of the " Last Judgment " and the enthroned Madonna with angels—works characterized by good taste, by largeness and suavity of treatment, and by an execution which, if still somewhat primitive and laboured, at any rate aims at beauty of form and colour. The recently uncovered fresco of the Last Judgment by Cavallini, executed about 1293 on the western wall of S. Cecilia in Trastevere at Rome, is classical in feeling and represents an immense advance on the older rendering of the same subject in S. Angelo in Formis (see § 10). The vast

PLATE II

PAINTING

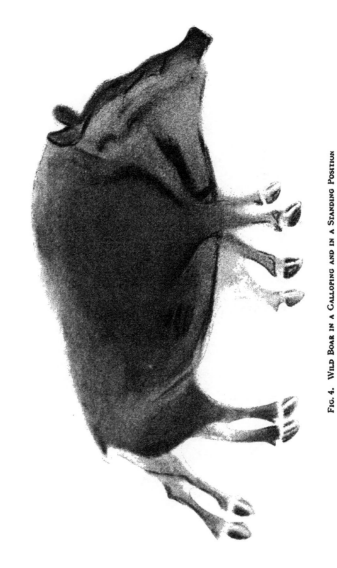

FIG. 4. WILD BOAR IN A GALLOPING AND IN A STANDING POSITION

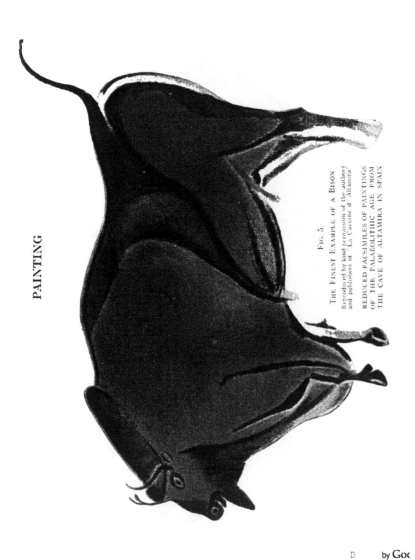

FIG. 5

THE FINEST EXAMPLE OF A BISON

Reproduced by kind permission of the authors
and publishers of "La Caverne d' Altamira"

REDUCED FACSIMILES OF PAINTINGS
OF THE PALAEOLITHIC AGE FROM
THE CAVE OF ALTAMIRA IN SPAIN

enthroned Madonna in the Rucellai chapel of S. Maria Novella at Florence, ascribed by Vasari to Cimabue, is now assigned by many to Duccio of Siena, and presents similar attractive qualities. Cimabue, a Florentine contemporary of Cavallini and Duccio, is famed in story as the chief representative of the painting of this period, but we possess no certain works from his hand except his mosaic at Pisa. His style would probably correspond to that of the painters just mentioned. His chief importance for our purpose resides in the fact that he was the teacher of the Florentine Giotto.

If the artists just referred to represent a revived classicism rather than a fresh and independent study of nature, Giotto is essentially a creation of the Gothic movement and his close association with the Franciscan cycle of ideas brings this fact into clearer relief. Giotto is in no way dependent on the study of the antique, but relies on his own steady and penetrating outlook upon man and upon nature. He is Gothic in his humanity, his sympathy, his love of truth, and he incorporates in his own person many of the most pleasing qualities of Gothic art as it had already manifested itself in France, while by the force of his own individual genius he raises these qualities to a higher level of artistic expression.

In the work of Giotto painting begins to enter on its modern era. The demonstrative element permanently takes the preeminence over the more decorative element we have called pattern-making. Though the pattern is always present, the elements of it become of increasing value in themselves as representations of nature, and the tendency henceforward for a couple of centuries is to exaggerate their importance so that the general decorative effect becomes subordinate. Giotto's greatness depends on the gift he possessed for holding the balance even among opposed artistic qualities. If he was interesting and convincing as a narrator, he had a fine eye at the same time for composition and balanced his masses with unerring tact. Neither he nor any of the Florentine frescoists had much sense of colour, and at this stage of the development of painting compositions of light and shade were not thought of, but in line and mass he pleases the eye as much as he satisfies the mind by his clear statement of the meaning and intention of his figures and groups.

In putting these together he is careful above all things to make them tell their story, and primitive as he is in technique he is as accomplished in this art as Raphael himself. Moreover, he holds the balance between the tendency, always so strong among his countrymen as among the Germans, to over-emphasis of action and expression, and the grace and self-restraint which are among the most precious of artistic qualities. He never sacrifices beauty to force, nor on the other hand does he allow his sense of grace of line to weaken the telling effect of action or grouping. A good example of his style, and one interesting also from the comparative standpoint, is his fresco of "Herod's Birthday Feast" in S. Croce at Florence (fig. 13, Plate IV.). We contrast it with the earlier wall-painting of the same subject in the cathedral at Brunswick (fig. 11, Plate III.). Giotto has reduced the number of actors to the minimum necessary for an effective presentation of the scene, but has charged each figure with meaning and presented the ensemble with a due regard for space as well as merely for form. The flatness of the older work has already been exchanged for an effective, if not yet fully correct, rendering of planes. The justice of the actions and expressions will at once strike the observer.

The Florentine school as a whole looks to Giotto as its head, because he embodies all the characteristics that made it great; but at the same time the artists that came after him in most cases failed by over-emphasis of the demonstrative element, and sacrificed beauty and sentiment to vigour and realism. The school as a whole is markedly intellectual, and as a result is at times prosaic, from which fault Giotto himself was saved by his Gothic tenderness and romance. His personality was so outstanding that it dominated the school for nearly a century. The "Giotteschi" is a name given to a number of Florentine painters whose labours cover the rest of the 14th century

among whom only one, Andrea di Cione, called Orcagna, lifted himself to any real eminence.

At Siena the Gothic movement made itself felt in the next artistic generation after that of Duccio. Its chief representative was Simone Martini. With him Sienese art takes upon itself a character contrasting markedly with the Florentine. It is on the demonstrative side less intellectual, less vigorous, less secular; and a dreamy melancholy, a tenderness that is a little sentimental, take the place of the alertness and force with which the personages in Florentine frescoes are endued. On the other hand, in decorative feeling, especially in regard to colour, Sienese painting surpasses that of the Florentines. Simone was followed by a number of artists who answered to the Florentine "Giotteschi" and carry on the style through the century, but as Florence produces an Orcagna, so at Siena about the middle of the 14th century there appear in the brothers Lorenzetti two artists of exceptional vigour, who carry art into new fields: Ambrogio Lorenzetti, the younger of the brothers, is specially represented by some frescoes in the Public Palace at Siena of a symbolical and didactic kind, representing Good and Bad Government, from which is selected a figure representing Peace (fig. 14, Plate V.). Sienese sentiment is here very apparent. Simone Martini's masterpiece had been a great religious fresco of an edifying kind on the wall of the chapel, and now in the rooms devoted to the secular business of the city Lorenzetti covers the walls with four large compositions on the subject named.

The painters of the Sienese school were on the whole faithful to the style indicated, and later on in the century they extend the boundaries of their school by spreading its influence into the hill country of Umbria. In the cities of this region Taddeo di Bartoli, one of the best of the followers of Simone, worked about the end of the century, and early Umbrian art in consequence exhibits the same devotional character, the same dreaminess, the same grace and decorative charm, that are at home in Siena.

Elsewhere in Italy the art of the 14th century represents a general advance beyond the old medieval standard, but no outstanding personality made its appearance and there was nothing that can be strictly termed a revival. At Rome, where on the foundation of the noble design of Cavallini there might have been reared a promising artistic structure, the removal early in the 14th century of the papal court to Avignon in France led to a cessation of all effort.

§ 15. *The Fifteenth Century, and its Influence on the Development of Painting at Florence.*—We come now to what was indicated in § 4 as the third of the main periods into which the history of painting may be divided. It is that in which, by the aid of the new agency of perspective, truth of form was for the first time perfectly mastered, and an advance was made in the rendering of the truth of space.

The opening of the 15th century in Italy is the most important epoch in the whole history of painting, for it was the real beginning of the modern era. Here Florence, the first home of Renaissance culture, unmistakably assumes the lead, and the new era is again opened by the agency of an individual of genius. The father of modern painting is the Florentine Masaccio. He not only advanced the art in those qualities in which Giotto had already made it great, but pointed the way towards the representation of the third dimension of objects and of space as a whole which had for so long been almost ignored. His short life course, for he died before he was thirty, only allowed him to execute one work of the first importance, the frescoes in the Brancacci chapel of the Carmine at Florence. There in the "Tribute Money" he told the story with all Giotto's force and directness, but with an added power in the creation of exalted types of human character, and in the presentation of solid shapes that seem to live before us. In the "Expulsion from Eden" he rose to greater heights. In the whole range of demonstrative art no more convincing, more moving, figures have ever been created than those of our first parents, Adam veiling his face in his hands, Eve throwing back her head and wailing aloud in agony, while in the foreshortened form of the angel that hovers above we discern the whole future development of the art for a century to come (see fig. 15, Plate V.). Above all qualities in Masaccio's work we are impressed with the simplicity and the ease of the work. The youthful artist possessed a reserve of power that, had he lived, would have carried him at one bound to heights that it took his actual successors in the school well nigh a century to climb.

The 15th century at Florence presents to us the picture of a progressive advance on the technical side of art, in the course of which various problems were attacked and one by one vanquished, till the form of painting in the style recognized in the school was finally perfected, and was then handed on to the great masters of expression, such as Raphael and Michelangelo, who used it as the obedient instrument of their wills. The efforts of the artists were inspired by a new intellectual and social movement of which this century was the scene. If the Gothic movement in the 14th century had inspired Giotto and Simone Martini, now it was the revived study of the antique, the true Renaissance, that was behind all the technical struggles of the artists. Painting was not, however, directly and immediately affected by the study of antique models. This was only one symptom of a general stir of intellectual life that is called by the apt term "humanism." In the early Gothic epoch the movement had been also in the direction of humanity, that is to say, of softness in manners and of the amenities and graces of life, but it was also a strictly religious movement. Now, in the 15th century, the inspiration of thought was rather pagan than Christian, and men were going back to the ideas and institutions of the antique world as a substitute for those which the Church had provided for thirty generations. The direct influence of these studies on art was chiefly felt in the case of architecture, which they practically transformed. Sculpture was influenced to a lesser degree, and painting least of all. It was not till the century was pretty far advanced that classical subjects of a mythological kind were adopted by artists like Botticelli and Piero di Cosimo, the first figures borrowed from the antique world being those of republican worthies displayed for purposes of public edification.

The elements which the humanistic movement contributed to Florentine art are the following: (1) The scientific study of perspective in all its branches, linear and aerial, including the science of shadows. (2) Anatomy, the study of the nude form both at rest and in action. (3) Truth of fact in details in animate and inanimate subjects. (4) The technique of oil painting. It must be observed that in this work the Florentines were joined by certain painters of Umbria, who were not satisfied with the Umbro-Sienese tradition already spoken of, but allied themselves with the leaders of the advance who were fighting under the banner of Masaccio.

Of the studies mentioned above by far the most important was that of perspective. Anatomy and realism in details only represented an advance along the lines painting had been already following. The new technique of oil painting, though of immense importance in connexion with the art as a whole, affected the Florentines comparatively little. Their favourite form of painting was the mural picture, not the self-contained panel or canvas for which the oil medium was specially designed, and for mural work fresco remained always supreme (see Part III., § 35). In this mural work the introduction of scientific perspective effected something like a transformation. The essence of the work from the decorative point of view had been its flatness. It was primarily pattern-making, and nature had been represented by contours which stood for objects without giving them their full dimensions. When the artist began to introduce varying planes of distance and to gain relief by light and shade, there was at once a change in the relation of the picture to the wall. It no longer agreed in its flatness with the facts of the surface of which it formed the enrichment, but opposed these by its suggestion of depth and distance. Hence while painting as a whole advanced enormously through this effort after the truth of space, yet decorative quality in this particular form of the art proportionately suffered.

The study of perspective owed much to the architect and scholar Brunellesco, one of the oldest as well as ablest of the men in whom the new movement of the 15th century was embodied. Brunellesco taught all he knew to Masaccio, for whose genius he felt strong admiration; but the artist in whom the result of the new study is most obvious is Paolo Uccello, a painter of much power, who was born as early as 1397. Uccello, as extant works testify, sometimes composed pictures mainly with a view to the perspective effects for which they furnished the opportunity. See fig. 16, Plate V., where in a fresco of a cavalry skirmish he has drawn in foreshortened view the figure of a warrior prone on the ground, as well as various weapons and other objects under the feet of the horses. A fresco of "The Flood" at Florence is even more naive in its parade of the painter's newly won skill in perspective science. The intarsists, or workers in inlaid woods, who were very numerous in Florence, also adopted perspective motives for their designs, and these testify to the fascination of the study during all the last part of the century and the beginning of the next.

The advance in anatomical studies may be illustrated in the person of Antonio Pollaiuolo. Masaccio had been as great in this department of the painter's craft as in any other; and in the Adam and Eve of the "Expulsion," and the famous nudes shown in the fresco of "Peter Baptizing," he had given the truth of action and expression as few have been able to render it; but in the matter of scientific accuracy in detail more anatomical study was needful, and to this men like Pollaiuolo now devoted themselves. Pollaiuolo's "Martyrdom of St Sebastian," in the London National Gallery, is a very notable illustration of the efforts which a conscientious and able Florentine of the period would make to master these problems of the scientific side of art. (See fig. 17, Plate V.)

On the whole, however, of the men of this group it was not a Florentine but the Umbrian Piero de' Franceschi that represents the greatest achievement on the formal side of art. His theoretical studies were profound. He wrote a treatise on perspective, representing an advance on the previous treatment of the science by Alberti; and to this study of linear perspective Piero united those of aerial perspective and the science of shadows. A fresco of his at Arezzo entitled the "Dream of Constantine" is epoch-making in presenting a night effect into the midst of which a bolt of celestial radiance is hurled, the incidence of which on the objects of the various planes of the picture has been carefully observed and accurately reproduced. (See fig. 18, Plate V.) Piero handed on his scientific accomplishments to a pupil, also an Umbrian of Florentine sympathies, Luca Signorelli of Cortona. He achieved still greater success than Pollaiuolo in the rendering of the nude form in action, but more conspicuously than any others of this group he sacrificed beauty to truth, and the nudes in his great series of frescoes on the Last Things at Orvieto are anatomized like écorchés, and are in colour and texture positively repellent. Luca's work is, however, of historical importance as leading on to that of Michelangelo.

A great power in the Florentine school of the 15th century was Andrea del Castagno, an artist with much of the vigour, the feeling for the monumental, of Masaccio, but without Masaccio's saving gift of suavity of treatment. He is best represented by some single figures representing Florentine worthies, whom he has painted as if they were statues in niches. They formed part of the decoration of a villa, and are noteworthy as wholly secular in subject. There is a massiveness about the forms which shows how thoroughly the 15th century Florentines were mastering the representation of solid objects in all their three dimensions. Other painters attracted attention at the time for their realistic treatment of details. Vasari singles out Alessio Baldovinetti.

The importance for art of the Florentine school of the 15th century resides in these efforts for the perfecting of painting on the formal side, which its representatives were themselves making and were inspiring in others. The general historian of the art will dwell rather on this aspect of the work of the school than on the numerous attractive features it offers to the superficial observer. The Fra Angelicos, the Filippo Lippis, the Benozzo Gozzolis, the Botticellis, the Filippino Lippis of the century express pleasantly in their work various phases of feeling, devotional, idyllic or pensive, and enjoy a proportionate popularity among the lovers of pictures. Exigencies of space preclude anything more than a mention of their names, but a sentence or two must be given to a painter of the last half of the century who represents better than any other the perfection of the monumental style in fresco painting. This painter is Ghirlandajo, to whom is ascribed a characteristic saying. When disturbed in hours of work about some domestic affair he exclaimed: " Trouble me not about these household matters; now that I begin to comprehend the method of this art I would fain they gave me to paint the whole circuit of the walls of Florence with stories." Ghirlandajo was entering into the heritage of technical knowledge and skill that had been laboriously acquired by his countrymen and their Umbrian comrades since the beginning of the century, and he spread himself upon the plastered walls of Tuscan churches with easy copiousness, in works which give us a better idea than any others of the time of how much can be accomplished in a form of art of the kind by sound tradition and a businesslike system of operation.

The mural painting of Ghirlandajo represents in its perfection one important phase of the art. It was still decorative in the sense that lime colour-washes were the natural finish of the lime plaster on the wall, and that these washes were arranged in a colour-pattern pleasing to the eye. The demonstrative element, that is, the significance of these patches of colour as representations of nature, was however in the eyes of both painter and public the matter of primary importance, and similitude was now carried as far as knowledge of anatomy and linear perspective rendered possible. Objects were rendered in their three dimensions and were properly set on their planes and surrounded with suitable accessories, while aerial perspective was only drawn on to give a general sense of space without the eye being attracted too far into the distance. As a specimen of the monumental style nothing can be better than Ghirlandajo's fresco of the " Burial of S. Fina " at S. Gimignano in Tuscany (see fig. 19, Plate V.). We note with what architectural feeling the composition is balanced, how simple and monumental is the effect.

§ 16. *The Fifteenth Century in the other Italian Schools.*—It has been already noticed that the painting of the 14th century in the Umbrian cities was inspired by that of Siena. Through the 15th century the Umbrian school developed on the same lines. Its artists were as a whole content to express the placid religious sentiment with which the Sienese had inspired them, and advanced in technical matters almost unconsciously, or at any rate without making the pronounced efforts of the Florentines. While Piero de' Franceschi and Luca Signorelli vied with the most ardent spirits among the Florentines in grappling with the formal problems of the art, their countrymen generally preserved the old flatness of effect, the quiet poses, the devout expressions of the older school. This Umbro-Sienese art produced in the latter part of the century the typical Umbrian painter Perugino, whose chief importance in the history of his art is the fact that he was the teacher of Raphael.

An Umbrian who united the suavity of style and feeling for beauty of the Peruginesques with a daring and scientific mastery that were Florentine was Piero de' Franceschi's pupil, Melozzo da Forlì. His historical importance largely resides in the fact that he was the first master of the so-called Roman school. As was noticed before in connexion with the early Roman master, Pietro Cavallini, the development of a native Roman school was checked by the departure of the papal court to France for the best part of a century. After the return, when affairs had been set in order, the popes began to gather round them artists to carry out various extensive commissions, such as the decoration of the walls of the newly-erected palace chapel of the Vatican, called from its founder the Sistine. These artists were not native Romans but Florentines and Umbrians, and among them was Melozzo da Forlì, who by taking up his

residence permanently at Rome became the founder of the Roman school, that was afterwards adorned by names like those of Raphael and Michelangelo.

In the story of the development of Italian painting Melozzo occupies an important place. He carried further the notion of a perspective treatment of the figure that was started by Masaccio's angel of the " Expulsion," and preceded Correggio in the device of representing a celestial event as it would appear to a spectator who was looking up at it from below.

On the whole, the three Umbrians, Piero de' Franceschi, with his two pupils Luca Signorelli and Melozzo, are the most important figures in the central Italian art of the formative period. There is one other artist in another part of Italy whose work more largely than even theirs, and who, like them a disciple of the Florentines, excelled the Florentines in science and power, and this is the Paduan Mantegna.

We are introduced now to the painters of north Italy. Their general character differs from that of the Umbro-Sienese school in that their work is somewhat hard and sombre, and wanting in the *naïveté* and tenderness of the masters who originally drew their inspiration from Simone Martini. Giotto had spent some time and accomplished some of his best work at Padua in the earliest years of the 14th century, but his influence had not lasted. Florentine art, in the more advanced form it wore in the first half of the 15th century, was again brought to it by Donatello and Paolo Uccello, who were at work there shortly before 1450. At that time Andrea Mantegna was receiving his first education from a painter, or rather *impresario*, named Francesco Squarcione, who directed his attention to antique models. Mantegna learnt from Donatello a statuesque feeling for form, and from Uccello a scientific interest in perspective, while, acting on the stimulus of his first teacher, he devoted himself to personal study of the remains of antique sculpture which were common in the Roman cities of north Italy. Mantegna built up his art on a scientific basis, but he knew how to inspire the form with a soul. His own personality was one of the strongest that we meet with in the annals of Italian art, and he stamped this on all he accomplished. No figures stand more firmly than Mantegna's, none have a more plastic fullness, in none are details of accoutrement or folds of drapery more clearly seen and rendered. The study of antique remains supplied him with a store of classical details that he uses with extraordinary accuracy and effectiveness in his representations of a Roman triumph, at Hampton Court. Ancient art invested, too, with a certain austere beauty his forms of women or children, and in classical nudes there is a firmness of modelling, a suppleness in movement, that we look for in vain among the Florentines. Fig. 20, Plate VI., which shows a dance of the Muses with Venus and Vulcan, is typical. Mantegna was not only a great personality, but he exercised a powerful and wide-reaching influence upon all the art of north Italy, including that of Venice. His perspective studies led him in the same direction as Melozzo da Forlì, and in some decorative paintings in the Camera degli Sposi at Mantua he pointed out the way that was afterwards to be followed by Correggio.

Mantegna's relations with the school of Venice introduce us to the most important and interesting of all the Italian schools save that of Florence. Venetian painting occupies a position by itself that corresponds with the place and history of the city that gave it birth. The connexions of Venice were not with the rest of Italy, but rather with the East and with Germany. Commercially speaking, she was the emporium of trade with both. Into her markets streamed the wealth of the Orient, and from her markets this was transferred across the Alps to cities like Nuremberg. From Germany had come a certain Gothic element into Venetian architecture in the 14th century, and a little later an influence of the same kind began to affect Venetian painting. Up to that time Venice had depended for her painters on the East, and had imported Byzantine Madonna pictures, and called in Byzantine mosaic-workers to adorn the walls and roof of her metropolitan church. The first sign of native activity is to be found at Murano, where, in the first half of the 15th century, a German, Justus of Allemagna, worked in partnership with a Muranese family. A little later a stranger from another quarter executes important commissions in the city of the lagoons. This was an Umbrian, Gentile da Fabriano, who possessed the suavity and tenderness of his school.

The natural tendency of Venetian taste, nourished for centuries on opulent Oriental stuffs, on gold and gems, ran in the direction of what was soft and pleasing to the sense. The northern Gothic and the Umbrian influences corresponded with this and flattered the natural tendency of the people. For the proper development of Venetian painting some element of Florentine strength and science was absolutely necessary, and this was imparted to the Venetian school by Mantegna through the medium of the Bellini.

The Bellini were a Venetian family of painters, of whom the father was originally an assistant to Gentile da Fabriano, but lived for a while at Padua, where his daughter Nicolosia became the wife of Mantegna. With the two Bellini sons, Gentile and Giovanni, Mantegna became very intimate, and a mutual influence was exercised that was greatly to the benefit of all. Mantegna softened a little what has been termed his " iron style," through the assimilation of some of the suavity and feeling for beauty and colour that were engrained in the Venetians, while on the other hand Mantegna imparted some of his own sternness and his Florentine science to his brothers-in-law, of whom the younger, Giovanni, was the formative master of the later Venetian school.

§ 17. *The Painting of the Sixteenth Century: the Mastery of Form.*—If we examine a drawing of the human figure by Raphael, Michelangelo, or Correggio, and compare it with the finest examples of Greek figure design on the vases, we note at once that to the ancient artist the form presented itself as a silhouette, and he had to put constraint on himself to realize its depth; whereas the moderns, so to say, think in the third dimension of space and every touch of their pencil presupposes it. The lovely " Aphrodite riding on a Swan," on the large Greek kylix in the British Museum, is posed in an impossible position between the wing of the creature and its body, where there would be no space for her to sit. The lines of her figure are exquisite, but she is pure contour, not form. In a Raphael nude the strokes of the chalk come forward from the back, bringing with them into relief the rounded limb which grows into plastic fullness before our eyes. Whether the parts recede or approach, or sway from side to side, the impression on the eye is equally clear and convincing. The lines do not merely limit a surface but caress the shape and model it by their very direction and comparative force into relief. In other words, these 16th-century masters for the first time perfectly realize the aim which was before the eyes of the Greeks; and Raphael, who in grace and truth and composition may have been only the peer of Apelles, probably surpassed his great predecessor in this easy and instinctive rendering of objects in their solidity.

In so far as the work of these masters of the culminating period, in its relation to nature, is of this character it needs no further analysis, and attention should rather be directed to those elements in Italian design of the 16th-century which have a special interest for the after development of the art.

Not only was form mastered as a matter of drawing, but relief was indicated by a subtle treatment of light and shade. Foreshortening as a matter of drawing requires to be accompanied by correct modulation of tone and colour, for as the form in question recedes from the eye, changes of the most delicate kind in the illumination and hue of the parts present themselves for record and reproduction. The artist who first achieved mastery in these refinements of chiaroscuro was Leonardo da Vinci, while Correggio as a colourist added to Leonardesque modelling an equally delicate rendering of the modulation of local colour in relation to the incidence of light, and the greater or less distance of each part from the eye. This represented a great advance in the rendering of natural truth, and prepared the way for the masters of the 17th century. It is not only by

linear perspective, or the progressive diminution in size of objects as they recede, that the effect of space and distance can be compassed. This depends more on what artists know as " tone " or " values," that is, on the gradual degradation of the intensity of light and shadow, and the diminishing saturation of colours, or, as we may express it in a word that is not however quite adequate, aerial perspective. That which Leonardo and Correggio had accomplished in the modelling, lighting and tinting of the single form in space had to be applied by succeeding artists to space as a whole, and this was the work not of the 16th but of the 17th century, and not of Italians but of the masters of the Netherlands and of Spain.

§ 18. *The Contribution of Venice.*—Before we enter upon this fourth period of the development of the art, something must be said of an all-important contribution that painting owes to the masters of Venice.

The reference is not only to Venetian colouring. This was partly, as we have seen, the result of the temperament and circumstances of the people, and we may ascribe also to the peculiar position of the city another Venetian characteristic. There is at Venice a sense of openness and space, and the artists seem anxious on their canvases to convey the same impression of a large entourage. The landscape background, which we have already found on early Flemish panels, becomes a feature of the pictures of the Venetians, but these avoid the meticulous detail of the Flemings and treat their spaces in a broader and simpler fashion. An indispensable condition however for the rich and varied effects of colour shown on Venetian canvases was the possession by the painters of an adequate technique. In the third part of this article an account is given of the change in technical methods due, not so much to the introduction of the oil medium by the Van Eycks, as to the exploitation at Venice of the unsuspected resources which that medium could be made to afford. Giovanni Bellini, not Hubert van Eyck, is really the primal painter in oil, because he was the first to manipulate it with freedom, and to play off against each other, the various effects of opaque and transparent pigment. His noble picture at Murano, representing the Doge Barbarigo adoring the Madonna, represents his art at its best (see fig. 21, Plate VI.).

Bellini rendered possible the painters of the culminating period of Venetian art, Giorgione, Titian, Tintoretto, with others hardly less great. Giorgione was the first who made the art, as an art of paint not merely of design, speak to the soul. His melting outlines and the crisp clean touches that wake the piece to life; his glowing hues and the pearly neutrals that give them repose and quality; the intimate appeal of his dreamy faces, his refined but voluptuous forms, and the large freedom of his spaces of sky and distance, all combine to impress us with a sense of the poetry and mystery of creation that we derive from the works of no other extant painter. The " Concert " of the Louvre, fig. 22, Plate VII. is typically Giorgionesque.

Tintoretto, more intellectually profound, more passionate, writes for us his message in his stormy brush-strokes, now shaking us with terror, now lifting our souls on the wings of his imagination; but with him as with the younger master it is always the painter who speaks, and always in the terms of colour and texture and handling. Lastly, between the two, unapproachable in his majestic calm, stands Titian. Combining the poetry of Giorgione with much of Tintoretto's depth and passion, he is the first, and still perhaps the greatest, of the supreme masters of the painter's art. His masterpiece is the great "Presentation" of the Venice Academy, fig. 23, Plate VII. Painting, it is true, has to advance in its development beyond the ideals of Titian's century, but it loses on the ethical side more than on the technical side it wins, and without the Venetians the world would have never known the full possibilities of the art that began so simply and at so early a stage of human civilization.

§ 19. *The Fourth Period: the Realization of the Truth of Space. Changed Relation of Painting to Nature.*—By the 17th century the development of painting had passed through all its stages, and the picture was no longer a mere silhouette or a transcript of objects against a flat background, but rather an enchanted mirror of the world, in which might be reflected space beyond space in infinite recession. With this transformation of the picture there was connected a complete change in the relation of the artist to nature. Throughout all the earlier epochs of the art that painter had concerned himself not with nature as a whole, but with certain selected aspects of nature that furnished him with his recognized subjects. These subjects were selected on account of their intrinsic beauty or importance, and as representing intrinsic worth they claimed to be delineated in the clearest and most substantial fashion. In the 17th century, not only was the world as a whole brought within the artist's view, but it presented itself as worthy in every part of his most reverent attention. In other words the art of the 17th century, and of the modern epoch in general, is democratic, and refuses to acknowledge that difference in artistic value among the aspects of nature which was at the basis of the essentially aristocratic art of the Greeks and Italians. It does not follow that selection is of any less importance in modern painting than it was of old; the change is that the basis of selection is not now a fixed intrinsic gradation amongst objects, but rather a variable difference dependent not on the object itself but on certain accidents of its position and lighting. The artist still demands that nature shall inspire him with her beauty, but he has learned that this beauty is so widely diffused that he may find it anywhere. It was a profound saying of John Constable that there is nothing ugly in nature, for, as he explained it, let the actual form and character of an object be what it would, the angle at which it might be viewed, and the effect upon it of light and colour, could always make it beautiful. It is when objects and groups of objects have taken on themselves this pictorial beauty, which only the artistically trained eye can discern, that the modern painter finds himself in the presence of his "subject," and he knows that this magical play of beauty may appear in the most casual and unlikely places, in mean and squalid corners, and upon the most ordinary objects of daily life. Sometimes it will be a heap of litter, sometimes a maiden's face, that will be touched with this pictorial charm. Things to the common eye most beautiful may be barren of it, while it may touch and glorify a clod.

The artist who was the first to demonstrate convincingly this principle of modern painting was Rembrandt. With Rembrandt the actual intrinsic character of the object before him was of small concern. Beauty was with him a matter of surface effect that depended on the combined influence of the actual local colour and superficial modelling of objects, with the passing condition of their lighting, and the greater or less clearness of the air through which they were seen. Behind the effect produced in this fortuitous fashion the object in itself vanished, so to say, from view. It was appearance that was important, not reality. Rembrandt's art was related essentially not to things as they were but as they seemed. The artists of the 15th century, whose careful delineation of objects gives them the title of the earliest realists, portrayed these objects in precise analytical fashion each for itself. More advanced painters regarded them not only in themselves but in their artistic relations as combining beauties of form and colour that together made up a pictorial effect. Rembrandt in his later work attended to the pictorial effect alone and practically annulled the objects, by reducing them to pure tone and colour. Things are not there at all, but only the semblance or effect or "impression" of things. Breadth is in this way combined with the most delicate unity, and a new form of painting, now called "impressionism," has come into being.

To give back nature just as she is seen, in a purely pictorial aspect, is the final achievement of the painter's craft, but as the differences of tone and colour on which pictorial beauty depends are extremely subtle, so it is only by a skill of touch that seems like the most accomplished sleight of hand that the required illusion can be produced, and in this way the actual handling of the brush assumes in modern painting an importance which in the old days it never possessed. The effect is produced not by definite statements of form and colour, but by what Sir Charles Eastlake termed "the judicious unfinish of a consummate workman," through which "the flat surface is transformed into space." Frans Hals of Haarlem, who was born in 1580, was perhaps the first to reveal the artistic possibilities of a free suggestive handling in oil paint, and Van Dyck is said to have marvelled how Hals was able to sketch in a portrait "with single strokes of the brush, each in the right place, without altering them and without fusing them together." In the wonderful late Velazquez at Vienna, the portrait of the Infant Philipp Prosper as a child of two years old, the white drapery, the minute fingers, the delicate baby face from which look out great eyes of darkest blue, are all indicated with touches so loosely thrown upon the canvas that seen near by they are all confusion—yet the life and truth are in them, and at the proper focal distance nature herself is before us. The touches combine to give the forms, the local colours, the depth, the solidity of nature, while at the same time the chief impression they convey is that of the opalescent play of changing tones and hues which, eluding the limitations of definite contours, make up to the painter's eye the chief beauty of the external world. Moreover it will be understood that this realization of the truth of space, which is the distinguishing quality of modern painting, does not mean that the artist is always to be rendering large views of sky and plain. The gift of setting objects in space, so that the atmosphere plays about them, and their relations of tone to their surroundings are absolutely correct and convincing, is shown just as well in a group of things close at hand as in a wide landscape. The backgrounds in the pictures by Velazquez of "The Surrender of Breda," and "Don Balthazar Carlos" at Madrid are magnificent in their limitless suggestion of the free spaces of earth and sky, but the artist's power in this respect is just as effectively shown in the creation of space in the interiors of "The Maids of Honour" and the "Spinners," and the skill with which he brings away the hand of the sitter from his white robe, in the "Innocent X." of the Doria Palace at Rome. The fact is that the scale on which the modern painter works, and the nature of his subjects, make no difference in the essential character of the result. A very few square feet of canvas were sufficient for Ruysdael to convey in his "Haarlem from the Dunes" the most sublime impression of infinity; and a Dutch Interior by De Hooch gives us just as much feeling of air and distance as one of the vast panoramic landscapes of De Koningk or Rubens.

§ 20. *Impressionism.*—The term "impressionism," much heard in artistic discussions of to-day, is said to date from a certain exhibition in Paris in 1871, in the catalogue of which the word was often used; a picture being called *Impression de mon pot-à-feu*, or *Impression d'un chat qui se promène*, &c. An influential critic summed up these impressions, and dubbed the exhibition "Salon des Impressionistes" (Muther, *Modern Painting*, 1896, ii. 718). It is a mistake however to suppose that the style of painting denoted by this term is an invention of the day, for, in so far as it is practised seriously and with adequate artistic powers, it is essentially the same style as that of some of the greatest 17th-century masters, such as Rembrandt and Velazquez. Modern investigation into the reasons of things has provided the system with a scientific basis and justification, and we can see that it really corresponds with the experimentally determined facts of human vision. The act of "seeing" may mean one or two different things. We may (1) allow our glance to travel leisurely over the field of vision, viewing the objects one by one, and forming a clear picture to ourselves of each in turn; or (2) we may try to take in the whole field of vision at a glance, ignoring the special objects and trying to frame before ourselves a sort of summary representation of the whole; or again, (3) we may choose a single point in the field of vision, and focus on that our attention, allowing the surrounding objects to group themselves in an indistinct general mass. We can look at nature in any one of these three ways; each is as legitimate as the others; but since in most ordinary cases we look at things in order to gain information about them, our vision is usually of the first or analytical kind, in which we fix the objects successively, noting each by each their individual characteristics. As the object of painting is to reproduce what is seen as we see it, so in the majority of cases painting corresponds to this, our usual way, of viewing nature. That is to say, all painters of the early schools, and the majority of painters at all times, represent nature in a way that answers to this analytical vision. The treatment of groups of objects in the mass, though, as we have seen, occasionally essayed even in ancient times (see §§ 8, 9), does not become the painter's ideal till the 17th century. We find then, and we find here and there through all the later periods of the art, efforts on the part of the artist to reproduce the effect of vision of the other two kinds, to show how objects look when regarded all together and not one by one, or how they look when we focus our attention on one of them but notice at the same time how all the others that are in the field of vision group themselves round in a penumbra, in which they are seen and yet not seen. The special developments of impressionistic art in recent times in France and England are dealt with in the article on IMPRESSIONISM (see also the appendix to this article on *Recent Schools of Painting*), but it is mentioned here as a style of painting that is the logical outcome of the evolution of the art which has been traced from the earliest times to the 17th century. For the particular pictorial beauty, on which the modern painter trains his eye, is largely a beauty of relation, and depends on the mutual effect on each other of the elements in a group. Unless these are looked at in the mass their pictorial quality will be entirely missed. This word on impressionism, as corresponding to certain ways of looking at nature, is accordingly a necessary adjunct to the critique of modern painting since the 17th century.

§ 21. *Painting in the Modern Schools.*—The history of the art has been presented here as an evolution, the ultimate outcome of which was the impressionist painting of 17th-century masters such as Rembrandt and Velazquez. In this form of painting the artist is only concerned with those aspects of nature which give him the sense of pictorial beauty in tone and colour, and these aspects he reproduces on his canvas, not as a mere mirror would, but touched, pervaded, transfigured by his own artistic personality. It does not follow however that these particular ideals of the art have inspired modern painters as a body. No one who visits the picture exhibitions of the day, or even our galleries of older art, will fail to note that a good deal of modern painting since the 17th century has been academic and conventional, or prosaically natural, or merely popular in its appeal. With work of this kind we are not concerned, and accordingly, in the table (VIII.) which follows in Part II. of the article, the names with few exceptions are those of artists who embody the maturer pictorial aims that have been under discussion.

Of the schools of the 17th century that of Spain, owing much to the so-called Italian "naturalists," produced the incomparable Velazquez with one or two notable contemporaries, and later on in the 18th century the interesting figure of Goya; while the influence of Velazquez on Whistler and other painters of to-day is a more important fact connected with the school than the recent appearance in it of brilliant technical executants such as Fortuny.

The schools of Flanders and of France are closely connected, and both owe much to Italian influence. The land of Italy, rather than any works of Italian painters, has been the inspiration of the so-called classical landscapists, among whom the Lorrainer Claude and the French Poussin take the rank of captains of a goodly band of followers. In figure painting the Venetians inspire Rubens, and Raphael stands at the head of the academic draughtsmen and composers of "historical" pieces who have been especially numerous in France. Rubens and Raphael together formed Le Brun in the days of Louis XIV., David and Delaroche in the two succeeding centuries, and the modern decorative figure painters, such as Baudry, whose works adorn the public buildings of France. Flemish influence is also strong in the French painting in a gallant vein of the 18th century

from the serious and beautiful art of Watteau (fig. 24, Plate VIII.) to the slighter productions of a Fragonard. Van Dyck, another Fleming of genius, is largely responsible for the British portraiture of the 18th century, which is affiliated to him through Kneller and Sir Peter Lely. There is something of the courtly elegance of Van Dyck in the beautiful Gainsborough at Edinburgh, representing the Hon. Mrs Graham (fig. 25, Plate VIII.). On the whole, though the representative masters of these two schools are original, or at any rate personal, in technique, they are in their attitude towards nature largely dependent on the traditions established in the great Italian schools of figure-painting of the 16th century. The contrast when we turn from France and Flanders to Holland is extraordinary. This country produced at the close of the 16th century and in the first half of the 17th a body of painters who owed no direct debt at all to Italy, and, so far as appears, would have been what they were had Titian and Raphael and Michelangelo never existed. They took advantage, it is true, of the mastery over nature and over the material apparatus of painting which had been won for the world by the Italians of the 15th and 16th centuries, but there their debt to the peninsula ended, and in their outlook upon nature they were entirely original.

The Dutch school is indeed an epitome of the art in its modern phase, and all that has been said of this applies with special force to the painting of Holland. Democratic in choice of subject, subtle in observation of tone and atmosphere, refined in colour, free and yet precise in execution, sensitive to every charm of texture and handling, the Dutch painter of the first half of the 17th century represents the most varied and the most finished accomplishment in paint that any school can show. Such work as he perfected could not fail to exercise a powerful effect on later art, and accordingly we find a current of influence flowing from Holland through the whole course of modern painting with the more copious tide that had its fountain-head in Italy. Hogarth and Chardin and Morland in the 18th century, the Norwich painters and Constable in the 19th, with the French Barbizon landscapists who look to the last as their head, all owe an incalculable debt to the sincere and simple but masterly art of the countrymen of Rembrandt.'

§ 22. *The Different Kinds of Painting represented in the Modern Schools.*—The fact that the Dutch painters have left us masterpieces in so many different walks of painting, makes it convenient that we should add here some brief notes on characteristic modern phases of the art on which they stamped the impress of their genius. The normal subject for the artist, as we have seen, up to the 17th century, was the figure-subject, generally in some connexion with religion. The Egyptian portrayed the men and women of his time, but the pictures, through their connexion with the sepulchre, had a quasi-religious significance. The Assyrian chronicled the acts of semi-divine kings. Greek artists, whether sculptors or painters, were in the majority of cases occupied with the doings of gods and heroes. Christian art, up to the 16th century, was almost exclusively devoted to religious themes. In all this art, as well as in the more secular figure-painting of the modern schools, the personages represented, with their doings and surroundings, were of intrinsic importance, and the portrayal of them was in a measure an act of service and of honour. *Portraiture* is differentiated from this kind of subject-picture through stages which it would be interesting to trace, but the portrait, though secular, is always treated in such a way as to exalt or dignify the sitter. Another kind of figure-piece, also differentiated by degrees from the subject-picture of the loftier kind, is the so-called *Genre Painting*, in which the human actors and their goings-on are in themselves indifferent, trivial, or mean and even repellent; and in which, accordingly, intrinsic interest of subject has disappeared to be replaced by an artistic interest of a different kind. *Landscape*, in modern times so important a branch of painting, is also an outcome of the traditional figure-piece, for at first it is nothing but a background to a scene in which human figures are prominent. *Marine Painting* is a branch of landscape art differentiated from this, but supplied at first in the same way with figure-interest.

The origin of *Animal Painting* is to be sought partly in figure-pieces, where, as in Egypt and Assyria, animals play a part in scenes of human life, and partly in landscapes, in which cattle, &c., are introduced to enliven the foreground. The *Hunting Picture*, combining a treatment of figures and animals in action with landscape of a picturesque character, gives an artist like Rubens a welcome opportunity, and the picture of *Dead Game* may be regarded as its offshoot. This brings us to the important class of *Still-Life Painting*, the relation of which to the figure-piece can be traced through the genre picture and the portrait. As a natural scene in the background, so on the nearer planes, a judiciously chosen group of accessory objects adds life and interest to the representation of a personage or scene from human life. Later on these objects, when regarded with the eyes of an artist fully opened to the beauty of the world, become in themselves fit for artistic, aye, even ideal, treatment; and a Volion will by the magic of his art make the interior of a huge and polished copper caldron look as grand as if it were the very vault of heaven itself.

§ 23. *Portraiture.*—Attention has already been called in § 7 to the skill of the Egyptian artist in marking differences of species and race in animals and men. In the case of personages of special distinction, notably kings, individual lineaments were portrayed with the same freshness, the same accent of truth. There is less of this power among the artists of Assyria. The naturalism of Cretan and Mycenaean art is so striking that we should expect to find portraiture represented among its remains, and this term may be fairly applied to the gold masks that covered the faces of bodies in the tombs opened by Dr Schliemann. In early (historical) Greek art some archaic vases show representations of named personages of the day, such as King Arkesilas of Cyrene, that may fall under the same heading, and portraiture was no doubt attempted in the early painted tombstones. The ideal character of Greek art however kept portraiture in the background till the later period after Alexander the Great, whose effigy limned by Apelles was one of the most famous pictures in antiquity. Our collections of works of classical art have been recently enriched by a series of actual painted portraits of men and women of the late classical period, executed on mummy cases in Egypt, and discovered in Graeco-Egyptian cemeteries. An attempt has been made by comparison with coins to identify some of the personages represented with members of the Ptolemaic house, including the famous Cleopatra, but it is safer to regard them, with Flinders Petrie, as portraits of ordinary men and women of the earliest centuries A.D. Technically they are of the highest interest, as will be noticed in § 42. From the artistic point of view one notes their variety, their lifelike character, and the pleasing impression of the human personality which some of them afford. There are specimens in the London National Gallery and British Museum.

During the early Christian and early medieval periods portraits always existed. The effigies of rulers appeared, for example, on their coins, and there are some creditable attempts at portraiture on Anglo-Saxon pieces of money. In painting we find the most continuous series in the illuminated MSS. where they occur in the so-called dedicatory pictures, in MSS. intended for royal or distinguished persons, where the patron is shown seated in state and perhaps receiving the volume. The object here, as Woltmann says, "always appears to be to give a true portrait of the exalted personage himself" (*Hist. of Painting*, Eng. trans., I. 212). Julia Anicia, granddaughter of Valentinus III., in the 6th century; the Carolingian emperor, Lothair, in the 9th; the Byzantine emperors, Basil II. in the 10th, and Nikephoros Botaniates in the 11th, &c., appear in this fashion. Some famous mosaic pictures in S. Vitale, Ravenna, contain effigies of Justinian, Theodora, and the Ravennese bishop, Maximian. In very many medieval works of art a small portrait of the donor or the artist makes its appearance as an accessory.

With the rise of schools of painting in the 14th and 15th centuries, especially in the north, the portrait begins to assume greater prominence. The living personage of the day not only

figures as donor, but takes his place in the picture itself as one of the actors in the sacred or historical scene which is portrayed. A good deal of misplaced ingenuity has been expended in older and more modern days in identifying by guess-work historical figures in old pictures, but there is no doubt that such were often introduced. Dante and some of his famous contemporaries make their appearance in a fresco ascribed to Giotto in the chapel of the Bargello at Florence. One is willing to see the face and form of the great Masaccio in the St Thomas with the red cloak, on the right of the group, in the fresco of the Tribute Money (see § 15). Dürer certainly paints himself as one of the Magi in his picture in the Uffizi. In Italy Ghirlandajo (see § 15) carried to an extreme this fashion, and thereby unduly secularized his biblical representations. The portrait proper, as an independent artistic creation, comes into vogue in the course of the 15th century both north and south of the Alps, and Jan van Eyck, Memlinc, and Dürer are in this department in advance of the Florentines, for whereas the latter almost confine themselves to flat profiles, Van Eyck introduces the three-quarter face view, which represents an improvement in the rendering of form. Mantegna and Antonello da Messina portray with great firmness, and to Uccello is ascribed an interesting series of heads of his contemporaries. It is Gentile and Giovanni Bellini however who may be regarded as the fathers of modern portrait painting. Venetian art was always more secular in spirit than that of the rest of Italy, and Venetian portraits were abundant. Those by Gentile Bellini of the Sultan Mahomet II., and by Giovanni of the Doge Loredano are specially famous. Vasari in his notice of the Bellini says that the Venetian palaces were full of family portraits going back sometimes to the fourth generation. Some of the finest portraits in the world are the work of the great Venetians of the 16th century, for they combine pictorial quality with an air of easy greatness which later painters find it hard to impart to their creations. Though greatly damaged, Titian's equestrian portrait of Charles V. at Madrid (fig. 26, Plate VIII.) is one of the very finest of existing works of the kind. It is somewhat remarkable that of the other Italian painters who executed portraits the most successful was the idealist Raphael, whose papal portraits of Julius II. and Leo X. are masterpieces of firm and accurate delineation. Leonardo's "Monna Lisa" is a study rather than a portrait proper.

The realistic vein, which, as we have seen, runs through northern painting, explains to some extent the extraordinary merit in portraiture of Holbein, who represents the culmination of the efforts in this direction of masters like Jan van Eyck and Dürer. Holbein is one of the greatest delineators that ever lived, and in many of his portraits he not only presents his sitter in life-like fashion, but he surrounds him with accessory objects, painted in an analytical spirit, but with a truthfulness that has seldom been equalled. The portrait of Georg Gysis at Berlin represents this side of Holbein's art at its best (fig. 27, Plate VIII.). Some fine portraits by Italianizing Flemings such as Antonio Moro (see Table I.) bring us to the notable masters in portraiture of the 17th century. All the schools of the period were great in this phase of the art, but it flourished more especially in Holland, where political events had developed in the people self-reliance and a strong sense of individuality. As a consequence the Dutch men and women of the period from about 1575 to 1675 were incessantly having their portraits painted, either singly or in groups. The so-called "corporation picture" was a feature of the times. This had for its subject some group of individuals associated as members of a company or board or military mess. Such works are almost incredibly numerous in Holland, and their artistic evolution is interesting to trace. The earlier ones of the 16th century are merely collections of single portraits each treated for itself, the link of connexion between the various members of the group being quite arbitrary. Later on efforts, that were ultimately successful, were made to group the portraits into a single composition so that the picture became an artistic whole. Frans Hals of Haarlem, one of the most brilliant painters of the impressionist school that he did much to found, achieved remarkable success in the artistic grouping of a number of portraits, so that each should have the desired prominence while yet the effect of the whole was that of a unity. His masterpieces in this department in the town-hall at Haarlem have never been equalled.

As portraitists the other great 17th-century masters fall into two sets, Rembrandt and Velasquez contrasting with Rubens and his pupil Van Dyck. The portraits of the two former are individualized studies in which the sitter has been envisaged in an artistic aspect, retaining his personality though sublimated to a harmonious display of tone and colour. The Flemings are more conventional, and representing rather the type than the individual, are disposed to sacrifice the individuality of the sitter to their predetermined scheme of beauty. Both Velasquez and Rubens have left portraits of Isabel de Bourbon, first wife of Philip IV. of Spain, but whereas the Spaniard's version gives us an uncomely face but one full of character, that of the Fleming shows us merely the big-eyed buxom wench we are accustomed to meet on all his canvases. Rembrandt was much less careful than Velasquez or Holbein or Hals to preserve the individuality of the sitter. He did not however, like the Flemings, convention-alize to a type, but worked each piece into an artistic study of tone, colour and texture, in the course of which he might deal somewhat cavalierly with the actual facts of the piece of nature before him. The result, though incomparable in its artistic strength, may sometimes, in comparison with a Velasquez, seem laboured, but there is one Rembrandt portrait, that of Jan Six at Amsterdam, that is painted as directly as a Hals, and with the subtilty of a Velasquez, while it possesses a richness of pictorial quality in which Rembrandt surpasses all his ancient or modern compeers (see fig. 28, Plate IX.).

In the 18th century, though France produced some good limners and Spain Goya, yet on the whole England was the home of the best portraiture. Van Dyck had been in the service of Charles I., and foreign representatives of his style carried on afterwards the tradition of his essentially courtly art, but there existed at the same time a line of native British portraitists of whom the latest and best was Hogarth. One special form of portraiture, the *miniature* (q.v.), has been characteristically English throughout. The greater English and Scottish portraitists of the latter part of the 18th century, headed by Reynolds, owed much to Van Dyck, and their work was of a pronounced pictorial character. Every portrait, that is to say, was before everything beautiful as a work of art. Detail, either of features or dress, was not insisted on; and the effort was rather to generalize than to accentuate characteristic points. In a word, while the artist recognized the claims of the facts before him to adequate portrayal, he endeavoured to fuse all the elements of the piece into one lovely artistic unity, and in so doing he secured in his work the predominant quality of breadth. This style, handed on to painters of less power, died out in the first half of the 19th century in attenuated produc-tions, in which harmony became emptiness. To this has suc-ceeded in Britain, still the home of the best European portraiture, a more modern style, the dominant notes of which have been truth and force. While the older school was seen at its best when dealing with the softer forms of the female sex and of youth, these moderns excelled in the delineation of character in strongly-marked male heads, and some of them could hardly succeed with a woman's portrait. The fine appreciation of character in portraiture shown by Sir John Watson Gordon about the middle of the 19th century marked the beginning of this forcible style of the later Victorian period, suited to an age of keen intellectual activity, of science and of matter-of-fact. More recently still, with the rapid development in certain circles of a taste for the life of fashion and pleasure, the portrait of the showily-dressed lady has come again into vogue, and if any special influence is here to be discerned it may be traced to Paris.

§ 24. *Genre Painting.* The term "genre" is elliptical—it stands for *genre bas*, and means the "low style," or the style in which there is no grandeur of subject or scale. A genre piece is a picture of a scene of ordinary human life without any religious or historical significance, and though it makes its appearance earlier, it was in the Netherland schools of the first half of the 17th century that it was established as a canonical form of the art. In Egypt we have seen that the subjects from human life have almost always a quasi-religious character, and the earliest examples of genre may be certain designs on early black-figured vases of the 6th century B.C. in Greece. Genre painting proper was introduced at a later period in Greece, and attracted special attention because of its contrast to the general spirit of classical art. It had a special name about which there is some difficulty but which seems to denote the same as *genre bas*. In early Christian and early medieval painting genre can hardly be recognized, but it makes its appearance in some of the later illuminated MSS. and becomes more common, especially north of the Alps, in the 15th century. It really begins in the treatment in a secular spirit of scenes from the sacred story. These scenes, in Italy, but still more among the prosaic artists of the north, were made more life-like and inter-esting when they were furnished with personages and accessories drawn from the present world. Real people of the day were as we have just seen introduced as actors in the scriptural events, and in the same way all the objects and accessories in the picture were portrayed from existing models. It was easy sometimes for the spectator to forget that he was looking at biblical characters and at saints and to take the scene from the standpoint of actuality. Rembrandt, one of whose chief titles to fame is derived from his religious pictures, often treats a Holy Family as if it were a mere domestic group of his own day. It was a change sure to come when the religious signifi-cance was abandoned, and the persons and objects reduced to the terms of ordinary life. This of course represented a break with a very long established tradition, and it was only by degrees, and in Germany and Flanders rather than in Italy, that the change was brought about. Thus for example, St. Eloi, the patron of goldsmiths, might be portrayed as saint, but also as artificer with the impediments of the craft about him. The next stage, represented by a charming picture by Quintin Matsys at Paris, shows us a goldsmith, no longer a saint, but busy with the same picturesque accessories (fig. 29, Plate IX.). He has however his wife by his side and she is reading a missal which preserves to the piece a faint religious odour. Afterwards all religious suggestion is dropped, and we have the familiar goldsmith or money changer in his everyday surround-ings, of which northern painting has furnished us with so many examples.

Genre painting, however, is something a little more special than is here implied. The term must not be made to cover all figure-pieces from ordinary life. There are pictures by the late Italian "naturalists" of this kind; Caravaggio's "Card Players" at Dresden is a familiar example. These are too large in scale to come under this heading, and the same applies to the *bodegones* or pictures of kitchens and shops full of pots and pans and eatables, which, largely influenced by the Italian pictures just noticed, were common in Spain in the early days of Velasquez. Nor again are the large and showy subject pictures, which constitute the popular items in the catalogues of Burlington House and the Salon, to be classed as "genre." The genre picture, as represented by its acknow-ledged masters, is small in scale, as suits the nature of its subject, but is studied in every part and finished with the most fastidious care. The particular incident or phase of life por-trayed is as a rule of little intrinsic importance, and only serves to bring figures together with some variety of pose and expression and to motive their surroundings. It is rarely that the masters of genre charge their pictures with satiric or didactic purpose. Jan Steen in Holland and Hogarth in England are the excep-tions that prove the rule. The interest is in the main an artistic one, and depends on the nice observance of relations of tone and colour, and a free and yet at the same time precise touch. All these qualities combine to lend to the typical genre picture an *intimité*, a sympathetic charm, that gives the masters of the style a firm hold on our affections. Probably the most excellent painters of genre are Terborch, Metsu and Brouwer, the two first painters of the life of the upper classes, the last of peasant existence in some of its mos. unlovely aspects. The pictures of Brouwer are among the most instructive documents of modern painting. They are all small pictures and nearly all exhibit nothing but two or three Loors drinking, fighting, or otherwise characteristically employed, but the artist's feeling for colour and tone; and above all his inimitable touch, has raised each to the rank of a masterpiece. He is best represented in the Munich Pinacotek, from which has been selected fig. 30, Plate IX. Hardly less admirable are Teniers in Flanders, De Hooch, Ver Meer of Delft, Jan Steen, A. van Ostade, in Holland, while in more modern times Hogarth, Chardin, Sir David Wilkie, Meissonier, and a host of others carry the tradition of the work down to our own day (see Table VIII.). Greuze may have the doubtful honour of having invented the sentimental figure-piece from ordinary life that delights the non-artistic spectator in our modern exhibitions.

§ 25. *Landscape and Marine Painting.* This is one of the most important and interesting of the forms of painting that belong especially to modern times. It is true that there is sufficient landscape in ancient art to furnish matter for a substantial book (Woermann, *Die Landschaft in der Kunst der alten Völker*, Munich, 1876), and the extant remains of Pompeian and Roman wall-painting contain a very fair proportion of works that may be brought under this heading. By far the most important examples are the half-dozen or so of pictures forming a series of illustrations of the *Odyssey*, that were found on the Esquiline at Rome in 1848, and are now in the Vatican library. As we shall see it to be the case with the landscapes of the late medieval period, these have all figure subjects on the nearer planes to which the landscape proper forms a background, but the latter is far more important than the figures. In some of these Odyssey landscapes there is a feeling after space and atmospheric effect, and in a few cases an almost modern treatment of light and shade, which give the works a prominent place among ancient productions which seem to prefigure the later developments of the art. In the rendering of landscape detail, especially in the matter of trees, nothing in antique art equals the pictures of a garden painted on the four walls of a room in the villa of Livia at Prima Porta near Rome. They are reproduced in *Antike Denkmäler* (Berlin, 1887, &c.). These may be the actual work of a painter of the Augustan age named Ludius or Studius, who is praised by Pliny (*Hist. Nat.* xxxv. 116) for having introduced a style of wall decoration in which "villas, harbours, landscape, gardens, sacred groves, woods, hills, fish-ponds, straits, streams and shores, any scene in short that took his fancy" were depicted in lively and facile fashion. Pompeian wall paintings exhibit many pieces of the kind, and we find the same style illustrated in the low reliefs in modelled stucco, of which the specimens found near the Villa Farnesina, and now in the Terme Museum at Rome, are the best known. In medieval painting landscape was practically reduced to a few typical objects, buildings, rocks, trees, clouds, &c., which stood for natural scenery. Occasionally however in the MSS. these objects are grouped in pictorial fashion, as in a Byzantine Psalter of the 10th century in the National Library at Paris. The beginning of the 15th century may be reckoned as the time when the modern development of landscape art had its origin, and Masaccio here, as in other walks of painting, takes the lead. Throughout the century the landscape background, always in strict subordination to the figure interest, is a common feature of Flemish and Italian pictures, but, in the latter especially, the forms of natural objects are very conventional, and the impression produced on the city-loving Tuscan or Paduan of the time by mountain scenery is shown by the fact that rocks are commonly shown not only as perpendicular but overhanging. Titian is the first painter who, as mountain-bred, depicts the soaring peaks with real knowledge and affection (see the distance in fig. 22, Plate VII.), and the Venetians are the first to paint landscape with some breadth and sense of spaciousness, while, as we have seen, the Flemings, from Hubert

van Eyck downwards, distinguish themselves by their minute rendering of details, in which they were followed later on by Dürer, who was fond of landscape, and by Altdorfer. Of Dürer indeed it has been said that some of his landscape sketches in water-colour are the first examples in which a natural scene is painted for its own sake alone. Some of the northern artists of the "Italianizing" school of the 16th century, such as Patinir, whom Dürer, about 1520, calls "Joachim the good landscape painter," Paul Bril later in the century, and Adam Elsheimer, who worked at Rome about 1600, with several of their contemporaries, must not be omitted in any sketch of the history of the art. South of the Alps, the late Italian Salvator Rosa treats the wilder aspects of nature with some imaginative power, and his work, as well as the scenery of his native land, had an influence in the rapid development of landscape art in the 17th century, which was in part worked out in the peninsula. What is known as "classical landscape" was perfected in the 17th century, and its most notable masters were the Lorrainer Claude Gelée and the French Poussin and Dughet, while the Italianizing Dutch painters Both and Berchem modify the style in accordance with the greater naturalism of their countrymen.

The landscapes of Claude are characteristic productions of the 17th century, because they convey as their primary impression that of space and atmosphere. The compositions, in which a few motives such as rounded masses of foliage are constantly repeated, are conventional; and there is little effort after naturalism or variety in detail; but the pictures are full of art, and reproduce in telling fashion some of the larger and grander aspects of the material creation. There are generally figures in the foreground, and these are often taken from classical fables or from scripture, but instead of the landscape, as in older Italian art, being a background to the figures, these last come in merely to enliven and give interest to the scenery. The style, in spite of a certain conventionality which offends some modern writers on art, has lived on, and was represented in our own country by Richard Wilson, the contemporary of Reynolds; and in some of his work, notably in the *Liber Studiorum*, by Turner. Even Corot, though so individual a painter, owes something to the tradition of classical landscape.

The prevailing tendency of modern landscape art, especially in more recent times, has been in the direction of naturalism. Here the masters of the Dutch school have produced the canonical works that exercise a perennial influence, and they were preceded by certain northern masters such as the elder Breughel, whose "Autumn" at Vienna has true poetry; Savary, Roghman, and Hercules Seghers. Several of the Dutch masters, even before the time of Rembrandt, excelled in the truthful rendering of the scenes and objects of their own simple but eminently paintable country; but it was Rembrandt, with his pupil de Koningk and his rival in this department Jacob Ruysdael, who were the first to show how a perfectly natural and unconventional rendering of a stretch of country under a broad expanse of sky might be raised by poetry and ideal feeling to the rank of one of the world's masterpieces of painting. Great as was Rembrandt in what Bode has called "the landscape of feeling," the "Haarlem from the Dunes" of Ruysdael (fig. 31, Plate IX.) with some others of this artist's acknowledged successes, surpass even his achievement.

Nearer our own time Constable caught the spirit of the best Dutch landscapists, and in robust naturalism, controlled by art and elevated to the ideal region by greatness of spirit, he became a worthy successor of the masters just named, while on the other side he furnished inspiration to the French painters of the so-called Barbizon school, and through them to many of the present-day painters in Holland and in Scotland.

To fix the place of J. M. W. Turner in landscape art is not easy, for the range of his powers was so vast that he covered the whole field of nature and united in his own person the classical and naturalistic schools. The special merits of each of these phases of the art are united in this artist's "Crossing the Brook" in the National Gallery, that is probably the most perfect landscape in the world (fig. 32, Plate IX.). In a good deal of Turner's later work there was a certain theatrical strain, and at times even a garishness in colour, while his intense idealism led him to strive after effects beyond the reach of human art. We may however put out of view everything in Turner's *œuvre* to which reasonable exception may on these grounds be taken, and there will still remain a body of work which for extent, variety, truth and artistic taste is like the British fleet among the navies of the world.

Among Turner's chief titles to honour is the fact that he portrayed the sea in all its moods with a knowledge and sympathy that give him a place alone among painters of marine. Marine painting began among the Greeks, who were fond of the sea, and the "Odyssey" and other classical landscapes are stronger on this side than the landscapes of the Tuscans or Umbrians, who cared as little for the ocean as for the mountains. The Venetians did less for the sea in their paintings than might have been expected, and in northern art not much was accomplished till the latter part of the 16th century, when the long line of the marine painters of Holland is opened by Hendrick Cornelius Vroom, who found a worthy theme for his art in the defeat of the Spanish Armada. Simon de Vlieger of Rotterdam, who was born about the beginning of the 17th century, was the master of W Vandevelde the younger (1633-1707), who has never been equalled for his truthful representation of calm seas and shipping. He painted innumerable pictures of the sea-fights of the time between the English and the Dutch, those representing the victories of the Dutch being in Holland, while at Hampton Court the English are triumphant. There are exquisite artistic qualities in the painting of Vandevelde, who is reckoned the canonical master in this branch of art; but the few sea-pieces by Ruysdael, especially the "Dykes" of the Louvre, and the "Stormy Sea" at Berlin, exhibit the element under far more imaginative aspects. Besides Turner there are many British artists of modern days who have won fame in this branch of art that is naturally attractive to islanders.

§ 26. *Animal Painting.*—In all early schools of representative art from the time of the cave-dwellers downwards, the artist has done better with animals than with the human figure, and there is no epoch of the art at which the portrayal of animals has not flourished. (On Egyptian and Assyrian animals see § 7.) In Greece the representations of animals on coins are so varied and so excellent that we may be sure that the praise given to the pictures of the same creatures by contemporary artists is not overdrawn. In northern art animals have always played an important part, and the motives of medieval decoration are largely drawn from this source, while beast symbolism brings them into vogue in connexion with religious themes. In Italian and early Flemish and German art animals are as a rule only accessories, though some artists in all these schools take special delight in them; and when, early in the 17th century, they begin to take the chief place, the motive is often found in Paradise, where Adam and Eve lord it over the animal creation. If De Vlieger and Ruysdael are the first to show the sea in agitation, Rubens may have the same credit for revealing the passion and power of the animal nature in the violent actions of the combat or the chase. In this his contemporary Frans Snyders (1579-1657), and after Snyders Jan Fyt, specialized, and the first named is generally placed at the head of animal painters proper.

In Holland, in the 17th century, the animal nature presented itself under the more contemplative aspect of the ruminants in the lush water-meadows. True to their principle of doing everything they attempt in the best possible way, the Dutch paint horses (Cuyp, Wouwerman) and cattle (Cuyp, Adrian Vandevelde, Paul Potter) with canonical perfection, while Hondekoeter delineates live cocks and hens, and Weenix dead hares and moor-fowl, in a way that makes us feel that the last word on such themes has been spoken. There is a large white turkey by Hondekoeter in which the truth of mass and of texture in the full soft plumage is combined with a delicacy in the detail of

the airy filaments, that is the despair of the most accomplished modern executant

But animals have been treated more nobly than when shown in Flemish agitation or in Dutch phlegmatic calm. Leonardo da Vinci was specially famed for his horses, which he may have treated with something of the majesty of Pheidias. Dürer has a magnificent horse in the "Knight and Death," but this is studied from the Colleoni monument Nearer our own time the painter of Napoleonic France, Géricault, gave a fine reading of the equine nature. Rembrandt's drawings of lions are notable features in his work, and in our own day in France and England the lion and other great beasts have been treated with true imaginative power.

§ 27. *Still-Life Painting.*—Like portraiture and landscape, the painting of objects on near planes, or as it is called still-life painting, is gradually differentiated from the figure-piece which was supreme in the early, and has been the staple product in all, the schools. Just as is the case with the other subsidiary branches of painting, it passes through only as a by-product, in the history of ancient classical painting, passes practically out of existence in medieval times, begins to come to a knowledge of itself in the 15th and 16th centuries, and attains canonicity in the Dutch school of the first half of the 17th century. Still-life may be called the characteristic form of painting of the modern world, because the intrinsic worth of the objects represented is a matter of complete indifference when compared with their artistic treatment in tone, colour and texture. By virtue of this treatment it has been noted (§§ 19, 20) that a study of a group of ordinary objects, when seen and depicted by a Rembrandt, may have all the essential qualities of the highest manifestations of the art. There is no finer Rembrandt for pictorial quality than the picture in the Louvre representing the carcase of a flayed ox in a flesher's booth. As illustrating the principle of modern painting this form of the graphic art has a value and importance which in itself it could hardly claim. It is needless to repeat in this connexion what has been said on modern painting in general, and it will suffice here to indicate briefly the history of this particular phase of the art.

The way was prepared for it as has been noticed by the minute and forcible rendering of accessory objects in the figure-pieces and portraits of the early Flemish masters, of Dürer, and above all of Holbein. The painting of flower and fruit pieces without figure interest by Jan Broughel the younger, who was born in 1601, represents a stage onward, and contemporary with him were several other Dutch and Flemish specialists in this department, among whom Jan David de Heem, born 1603, and the rather older Willem Klaasz Heda may be mentioned. Their subjects sometimes took the form of a luncheon table with vessels, plate, fruit and other eatables; at other times of groups of costly vessels of gold, silver and glass, or of articles used in art or science, such as musical instruments and the like; and it is especially to be noted that the handling stops always short of any illusive reproduction of the actual textures of the objects, while at the same time the differing surfaces of stuffs and metal and glass, of smooth-rinded apples and gnarled lemons, are all most justly rendered. In some of these pieces we realize the beauty of what Sir Charles Eastlake has called the "combination of solidity of execution with vivacity and grace of handling, the elasticity of surface which depends on the due balance of sharpness and softness, the vigorous touch and the delicate marking—all subservient to the truth of modelling." In this form of painting the French 18th-century artist Chardin, whose impasto was fuller, whose colouring more juicy than those of the Dutch, has achieved imperishable fame (see fig. 33, Plate X.), and the modern French, who understand better than others the technical business of painting, have carried on the fine tradition which has culminated in the work of Vollon. The Germans have also painted still-life to good result, and the comparative weakness in technique of British painters has kept them in this department rather in the background.

PART II., §28.—SCHOOLS OF PAINTING

[In the following Tables are included the main facts in the history of Painting since about A.D. 1000, with the artists of the first, second and third rank in their schools and periods. The relative importance of the artists is shown by the size of the capitals in which their names are printed. Facts and names of minor importance have in the interest of clearness been excluded. The names are given as commonly used, and where they differ from the headings of the separate biographical articles identification can be made by the Index. Words indicating localities are in italics.]

I.

Dates.	MEDIEVAL PAINTING & ITS OFFSHOOTS NORTH OF THE ALPS.			ITALY, (For Comparison.)	Dates.
	[From the Carolingian period till the XIIth century Germany is the chief European centre of artistic production. From about 1150 to 1300 France takes the lead. Italy is in the background till about 1250.]				
1000 to 1100	Romanesque Wall and Panel Painting, *Reichenau, Brauweiler, Brunswick, Hildesheim, Soest, &c.* Romanesque Sculpture, *Hildesheim, Brunswick, Wechselburg, Freiberg i. S., &c.*			*S. Angelo in Formis,* wall paintings of c.1100.	1000 to
1150 to	THE GOTHIC MOVEMENT IN CENTRAL FRANCE FROM 1150. Gothic decorative Sculpture, Stained Glass, Ivories, MS. Illuminations, &c. Qualities in the work:—Refinement, Tenderness of Feeling, Love of Nature. } 1150 to 1300			Byzantine panels imported. Proto-Renaissance, c. 1200–1300.	to 1200
c. 1350	GOTHIC INFLUENCE ON NORTHERN PAINTING. Wall and Panel Paintings at *Ramersdorf, Cologne, Westminster, &c.* THE EARLIEST NORTHERN SCHOOLS.			Gothic characteristics in GIOTTO, 1267–1337.	
	GERMANY. Early Religious Schools (Gothic). *Prague,* from c. 1348. *Cologne;* MEISTER WILHELM, fl. c. 1360.	**HOLLAND.**	**FLANDERS.** HUBERT & JAN VAN EYCK, fl. c. 1380–1440.		
1400	HERMANN WYNRICH, fl. c. 1400. STEPHAN LOCHNER (Dombild, c. 1440). German Realism begins. MARTIN SCHONGAUER (*Colmar*), c. 1450–1488. Influenced by Van der Weyden. BARTH. ZEITBLOM (*Ulm*), c. 1450–c. 1500. HANS HOLBEIN THE ELDER (*Augsburg*), d. 1526		Adoration of the Lamb, Ghent, 1432. ROGER VAN DER WEYDEN, 1399–1464 (in *Italy*, 1450). DIERICK BOUTS (*Haarlem*), 1400(?)–1475. (Perhaps author of the "*Lieversberg Passion.*") PETRUS CRISTUS, c. 1410–1472. HANS MEMLINC, c. 1430–1494. HUGO VAN DER GOES, c. 1435–1482. GERARD DAVID (*Oudewater*), c. 1450–1523.	MASACCIO, 1402–1429. Age of humanism begins.	1400
1500	**ALBRECHT DÜRER** (*Nuremberg*), 1471–1528. LUCAS CRANACH, 1472–1553. HANS BURGKMAIR, 1473–1531. MATHIAS GRUNEWALD, c. 1475–c. 1530. BARTH. BRUYN, c. 1493–c. 1555. Painter of Portraits. HANS HOLBEIN, 1497–1543. England his headquarters, 1526–1543. ADAM ELSHEIMER, 1578–1620. Influential at *Rome* c. 1600.	LUCAS VAN LEYDEN (*Leiden*), 1494–1533. JAN SCHOREEL, 1495–1562 (*Alkmaar*). MARTEN VAN HEEMSKERK (*Haarlem*), 1498–c. 1574.	QUINTIN MATSYS (*Antwerp*), c. 1466–1530. JOACHIM DE PATINIR, d. c. 1524. Landscape BREUGHEL THE ELDER, c. 1525–1570. and The BREUGHEL Family. Genre. MABUSE (JAN GOSSART), c. 1472–c. 1533. FRANS FLORIS (DE VRIENDT) c. 1520– 1570. Figures ANTONIO MORO, c. 1512–c. 1575. Portraits. PAUL BRIL, 1556–1626. Landscape.	RAPHAEL, d. 1520. The High Renaissance. TITIAN, d. 1576. TINTORETTO, 1528–1594.	1500
1600	German painting proper almost died out in the XVIIth and early XVIIIth centuries.	For the Dutch School of the XVIIth century, see Table VII.	PETER PAUL RUBENS, b. 1577. For the Flemish School as headed by Rubens, see Table VIII.	For later Italian Painting, see Table VI.	1600

II.

THE PROTO-RENAISSANCE AND THE REVIVAL OF ART IN *ITALY.*

1200	CONDITION OF THE ART OF PAINTING IN *ITALY* BEFORE THE REVIVAL. Wall Paintings of poor style, with hard black outlines, devoid of any feeling for beauty or truth to nature. Panel Paintings, chiefly in the form of Enthroned Madonnas of Byzantine type, heavy but dignified; and painted Crucifixes, repulsive in aspect, with exaggeration of physical suffering, black outlines, green shadows, hatched lights. [Best Italian Sculpture, e.g. by Antellami at *Parma,* c. 1200, greatly inferior to contemporary work in France.]	1200
1250	REVIVAL FIRST SEEN IN SCULPTURE. NICCOLA PISANO inspired by the Proto-Renaissance of *Southern Italy;* his pulpit at *Pisa,* 1260. REVIVAL OF PAINTING UNDER THE INFLUENCE OF THE PROTO-RENAISSANCE. At *ROME,* PIETRO CAVALLINI "Last Judgment" at S. Cecilia, *Rome,* c. 1293; at *SIENA,* DUCCIO DI BUONINSEGNA, c. 1255–c. 1315. (probably) Rucellai Madonna at *Florence,* and Madonna at *Siena;* at *FLORENCE,* CIMABUE, teacher of Giotto.	1250

III.

GOTHIC INFLUENCE ON THE ITALIAN REVIVAL.

[Gothic Naturalism, Expressiveness, and Feeling in the Sculpture of Giovanni Pisano and Andrea Pisano.]

FLORENCE.	SIENA.
GIOTTO, 1267–1337, great in composition and in natural and dramatic treatment of sacred themes.	SIMONE MARTINI, c. 1283–1344, exhibits the pensive sweetness that marks Sienese painting. At Siena painters' company founded 1355.
Painting carried on on traditional lines by the Giottesques, to the end of the century. 'At Florence painters' company founded 1349.	Sienese school preserves throughout its tender and devout feeling, and decorative charm.
TADDEO GADDI, STEFANO, MASO DI BANCO, BERNARDO DADDI, ANDREA ORCAGNA, AGNOLO GADDI, SPINELLO ARETINO, GIOVANNI DA MILANO, ANDREA DI FIRENZE, STARNINA, &c.	LIPPO MEMMI, BARTOLO DI FREDI, ANDREA VANNI. TADDEO BARTOLI, influences art in Umbria. THE LORENZETTI, d. c. 1348. Painters of dramatic power.

CONTEMPORARY PAINTING *IN OTHER PARTS OF ITALY.*

Revival hardly begins in XIVth century. Best work done by ALLEGRETTO DI NUZIO of *Fabriano* and ALTICHIERO of *Verona.*
FRA ANGELICO DA FIESOLE, 1387–1455, sums up the purely religious art of the Gothic period.

IV.

ITALIAN SCHOOLS OF THE FIFTEENTH CENTURY UNDER THE INFLUENCE OF THE RENAISSANCE.

Painting advances at *Florence*, declines at *Siena*. Other Italian schools begin to develop.

FLORENCE.	SIENA.	UMBRIA.	NORTH ITALY.	
MASOLINO DA PANICALE, 1383–c. 1440. Teacher of	TADDEO BARTOLI 1363–1422.	GENTILE DA FABRIANO, c. 1370–c. 1450. Visits *Venice* and *Florence*.	VERONA. VITTORE PISANO, d. 1456. Finest Italian medalist.	VENICE. [GENTILE da FABRIANO Works at *Venice*, c. 1422.]
MASACCIO, 1401–1429. Great as Giotto, with added knowledge and unique sense of the monumental in painting.	DOM. DI BARTOLO. SANO DI PIETRO.	NICCOLO ALUNNO. BENEDETTO BONFIGLI. FIORENZO DI LORENZO.		School of MURANO, influenced from Germany, and
FILIPPO LIPPI, 1406–1469. Idyllic charm. SANDRO BOTTICELLI, 1444–1510. Sentiment and beauty. Treats classical subjects.	MAT. DI GIOVANNI	B. CAPORALI, &c., &c.	PADUA. Native art begins with the school of FRANCESCO SQUARCIONE, 1394–1474.	THE VIVARINI flourish, c. 1440–c. 1500.
FILIPPINO LIPPI, 1460–1505. Grace, classical detail.	FRAN. DI GIORGIO, &c., &c.	Exhibit Umbrian naïvity on Sienese lines. No progress.	Classical remains studied. [DONATELLO & UCCELLO Work at *PADUA*, c. 1445.]	CARLO CRIVELLI, d. c. 1493.
BENOZZO GOZZOLI, 1424–1498. Copious in detail. COSIMO ROSSELLI, PIERO DI COSIMO.			From all these proceeds	ANTONELLO da MESSINA, c. 1430–1479. In *Venice*, 1473–6. Oil painting introduced, d. 1479.
PAOLO UCCELLO, 1397–1475, devotee of Perspective	carry art through the century on the same lines as in the XIVth cent.	PIERO DE' FRANCESCHI, c. 1416–1492, teacher of	AND. MANTEGNA, 1431–1506. Studies Tuscan Art and influences Venetian.	
AND. DEL CASTAGNO, c. 1390–1457. Vigour. DOM. VENEZIANO, c. 1400–(?) 1461, tries oil-paint? ALESSIO BALDOVINETTI, 1427–1499, realist.		MELOZZO da FORLI, 1438–1494. and of		CIMA DA CONEGLIANO, d. c. 1508.
ANT. POLLAIUOLO 1429–1498. Anatomy, nude, oil.		LUCA SIGNORELLI, 1441–1524. Realists of Florentine type. Progressive.	VICENZA. MONTAGNA, 1475–1523.	VITTORE CARPACCIO, d. c. 1522.
ANDREA DEL VERROCCHIO, 1435–1488. Great in sculpture. Teacher of Leonardo.			FERRARA. COSIMO TURA, d. c. 1496. LORENZO COSTA, 1460–1535.	THE BELLINI, Associated with Mantegna. JACOPO d. c. 1470.
DOM. DEL GHIRLANDAJO, 1449–1494. Master of monumental style in fresco.		GIOVANNI SANTIO, d. 1494. Father of Raphael.		
FRA BARTOLOMMEO, 1475–1517. } Perfection of art on the formal side. AND. DEL SARTO, 1487–1531. }	All these fore-runners of the great masters.	PIETRO PERUGINO, 1446–1524. Raphael's master.	BOLOGNA. FRANC. FRANCIA, 1490–1517.	GENTILE, c. 1429, 1507. GIOVANNI, c. 1430, 1516.
	Decline of Sienese Art.			

V.

THE GREAT ITALIAN MASTERS OF THE SIXTEENTH CENTURY.

FLORENCE.	UMBRIA.	NORTH ITALY. MILAN.	VENICE.
LEONARDO DA VINCI, 1452–1519. At Milan 1483–1500. "Last Supper" finished c. 1497.		BERNARDINO LUINI, c. 1461. Influenced by Leonardo 1549.	GIOVANNI BELLINI. GIORGIONE, c. 1477–1510.
	PERUGINO, SANZIO.		LORENZO LOTTO, c. 1480–c. 1556.
MICHELANGELO BUONARROTI, 1475–1564. Sistine Chapel ceiling painted 1508–1512. "Last Judgment," c. 1541. Dome of St. Peter's, c. 1560. SEBASTIANO DEL PIOMBO, 1485–1547.	RAFFAEL SANZIO, 1483–1520. Umbrian period to 1504. Florentine period, 1504–1508. Roman period, 1508–1520. GIOVANNI DA UDINE.	PARMA. CORREGGIO, 1494–1534. PARMIGIANO, 1504–1540. BRESCIA. MORETTO, c. 1498–1554.	PALMA VECCHIO, c. 1480–1528. TITIAN, died 1576, born 1477 (?) or some years later (?). — First dated work, 1507. "Tribute Money," c. 1508 (Dürer at *Venice*, 1506). "Peter Martyr," (?) 1530, influenced by Michelangelo "Presentation in Temple," 1510.
GIORGIO VASARI, 1511–1574. Writes lives of the artists. The Michelangelesque affects Italian design in general. Age of the mannerists.	GIULIO ROMANO, 1497–1546. IL PRADO DEL VAGA, &c., &c. Followers of Raphael.	BERGAMO. MORONI, c. 1510–1578.	PAUL VERONESE, 1528–1588. TINTORETTO, 1518–1594. "Paradise" begun, 1588.

VI.

THE LATER PHASES OF ITALIAN PAINTING.

			VENICE (continued).
Eclectics. *BOLOGNA SCHOOL.*		Naturalists.	PARIS BORDONE, SCHIAVONE, THE BASSANI, THE BONIFAZI, &c., all die before the end of XVIth century.
THE CARACCI, 1580–1609 LUDOVICO, AGOSTINO, ANNIBALE.		CARAVAGGIO, 1569–1609.	PADOVANINO, 1590–1650.
GUIDO RENI, 1575–1642; DOMENICHINO, 1581–1641.		RIBERA (Spaniard), 1588–1653. Strong light and shade.	G. B. TIEPOLO, 1692–1769. Decorative style. CANALETTO, 1697–1768. Views of Venice.
BARBIERI (GUERCINO), 1591–1666; SASSOFERRATO, 1605–1685.		SALVATOR ROSA, 1615–1673. Landscape.	LONGHI, 1702–1762; GUARDI, 1712–1793.

VII.

THE DUTCH SCHOOL OF THE SEVENTEENTH CENTURY.

Artists of native type.

Portraitists and Painters of Corporation Pictures.

Italianizers.

MIEREVELT, 1567–1641; RAVESTEYN, & 1570–1657; DE KEYSER, 1596–1667.

G. HONTHORST, 1590–1656.

PIETER LASTMAN, 1583–1633.

REMBRANDT, 1606–1669

FRANS HALS, 1580–1666.

VAN DER HELST, 1613–1670.

GERARD DOU, JAN VICTOR, GERBRANDT VAN DEN ECKHOUT, CAREL FABRITIUS, AART DE GELDER, FERD. BOL, GOVERT FLINCK, NICOLAS MAAS, Italianize after 1650.

(Poetic.)

DE HOOCH; VER MEER OF DELFT.

P. DE KONINCK.

(Aristocratic.) | (Rustic.)
G. TERBORCH. | A. VAN OSTADE.
O. METSU. | I. VAN OSTADE.
(Satiric.) | (Cavalier.)
JAN STEEN. | P. WOUWERMAN.

(Early landscapists, born before 1600.)
ESAJAS VAN DE VELDE, J. VAN GOYEN.
AERT VAN DER NEER. (Night scenes, moonlight.)
RUYSDAEL, HOBBEMA, WYNANTS.

JAN BOTH
NICOLAES BERCHEM

(Cattle and Landscape.)
A. CUYP; A. VAN DE VELDE; PAUL POTTER.

R. DU JARDIN

(Marine painters.)
SIMON DE VLIEGER; W. VAN DE VELDE;
L. BACKHUYSEN.

(Painters of the Decline.)
VAN MIERIS, C. NETSCHER, ADRIAN VAN DER WERFF.

DE HEEM; HEDA. (Still life.)
M. DE HONDEKOETER. (Poultry.)
JAN WEENIX. (Dead game.)
JAN VAN HUYSUM. (Flowers.)

(Architecture.)
JAN VAN DER HEYDEN.

VIII.

CONSPECTUS OF THE MODERN SCHOOLS SINCE 1600.

HOLLAND.	FLANDERS.	The Venetians.	*ITALY.*	Naturalists.	SPAIN.
			The Florentines. RAPHAEL Figure Painters.		
1580, HALS, 1666.	RUBENS, 1577–1640.	Landscapists.			RIBERA.
REMBRANDT, 1606–1669. Dutch School of Portrait, Landscape, Genre. See TABLE VII above.	VAN DYCK, 1599–1641. TENIERS, SNYDERS, BROUWER. FYT.	POUSSIN, 1594–1665. CLAUDE, 1600–1682. DUGHET, 1613–1675. (GASPAR POUSSIN.)	*FRANCE.* Age of LOUIS XIV. LE BRUN, 1619–1690.		VELAZQUEZ, 1599–1660. 1617, MURILLO, 1682.
		LI. V.			
GERMANY. CHODOWIECKI, 1726–1801. RAPHAEL MENGS, 1728–1779.	*BRITAIN.* HOGARTH, 1697–1764. KNELLER. 1723, REYNOLDS, GAINSBOROUGH, 1727–1788. 1792. ROMNEY. RAEBURN. 1765, WILKIE, 1841.	WATTEAU, 1684–1721. BOUCHER. PATER. FRAGONARD. CHARDIN, 1699–1779. GREUZE, 1725–1805.			GOYA, 1746–1828.
1784, CORNELIUS, 1867. 1789, OVERBECK, 1869. 1805, KAULBACH, 1874.	Norwich School. 1714, WILSON, 1782. 1776, CONSTABLE, 1837. TURNER, 1775–1851. Water Colour School.	1728, DAVID, 1825. INGRES. DELAROCHE. LAURENS, &c.			
Rom-anticists { RETHEL, 1816–1859. BÖCKLIN.	Pre-Raphaelites. WATTS.	COROT, 1796–1875. 1814, MILLET, 1875. Barbizon School. DIAZ. MONTICELLI.			AMERICA. 1828, DELACROIX, 1863. Rom-anti-cists 1700.
Modern Dutch, MARIS, &c.; Glasgow School.		Sentimental Genre.		Impressionists.	WHISTLER.

PART III.—THE TECHNIQUE OF PAINTING

§ 29. *The Materials of Painting.*—Painting begins, as we have seen, on the one side in outline delineation, on the other in the spreading of a coating of colour on a surface. For both these the material apparatus is ready at hand. Drawing may have begun merely with lines in the air, but lasting designs were soon produced either by indenting or marking any soft substance by a hard point, or by rubbing away a comparatively soft substance, such as a pointed piece of burnt wood, on a rough surface of harder grain. Almost all the materials in use for drawing are of primitive origin. Charcoal, coloured earths and soft stones are natural or easily procured. Our plumbago was known to Pliny (xxxiv. 18) and to Cennino (ch. 34), but it was not in common use till modern times. The black-lead pencil is first described as a novelty in 1565 (Quellenschriften edition of Cennino, p. 143). A metal point of ordinary lead or tin was used in medieval MSS. for drawing lines on parchment, or on a wooden surface previously whitened with chalk (Theophilus, II. ch. xvii.). Silver-point drawing is only a refinement on this. The metal point is dragged over a surface of wood or parchment that has been grounded with finely powdered bone-dust, or, as in modern times, with a wash of Chinese white (Cennino, ch. 6 seq.; Church, 292), and through the actual abrasion of the metal leaves a dark line in its track. Pliny knows the technique (xxxiii. 98). When a coloured fluid was at hand a pointed stick might be used to draw lines with it, but a primitive pen would soon be made from a split reed or the wing-feather of a bird.

The coating of one substance by another of which the colour is regarded from the aesthetic standpoint is the second source of the art of painting. To manipulate the coating substance so that it will lie evenly; to spread it by suitable mechanical means; and to secure its continued adherence when duly laid, are by no means difficult. Nature provides coloured juices of vegetable or of animal origin, and it has been suggested that the blood of the slain quarry or foeman smeared by the victor over his person was the first pigment. To imitate these by mixing powdered earths or other tinted substances in water is a very simple process. Certain reeds, the fibres of which spread out in water, were used as paint-brushes in ancient Egypt. A natural hare's-foot is still employed in theatrical circles to lay on a certain kind of pigment, and no great ingenuity would be required on the part of the hunter for the manufacture of a brush from the hair or bristles of the slain beast. In the matter of securing the adhesion of the coating thus spread, nature would again be the guide. Many animal and vegetable products are sticky and ultimately dry hard, while heat or moisture thins them to convenient fluidity. Great heat makes mineral substances liquid that harden when cold. Hence binding materials offer themselves in considerable abundance, and they are of so great importance in the painter's art that they form the basis of current classifications of the different kinds of painting.

§ 30. *The Surfaces covered by the Painter.*—Many important questions connected with the technique of painting depend on the nature of surfaces; for the covering coat—though from the present point of view only of interest aesthetically—may, as we have seen, originally serve a utilitarian purpose. The surface in question may be classed as follows: the human body; implements, vessels, weapons, articles of dress; objects of furniture, including books; boats and ships; walls and other parts of buildings; panels and other surfaces prepared especially or entirely to be painted on.

The differences among these from the present point of view are obvious. The body could not suitably be covered with a substance impervious to air and moisture; the coatings of a clay vessel and of a boat should on the other hand make them waterproof. The materials used in building often require protection from the weather. The painting on the prepared panel needs to resist time and any special influence due to location or climate. All such considerations are prior to the questions of colour, design, or aesthetic effect generally, in these coatings; and on them depend the binding materials, or media, with which the colouring substances are applied. The case of one particular surface much employed for pictorial display is exceptional. This is the wall-plaster so abundantly used for clothing an unsightly, rough, or perishable building material, like rubble or crude brick. This function it performs perfectly when left of its natural white or greyish hue, but its plain unbroken surface has seemed to demand some relief through colouring or a pattern, and the recognition of this led to one of the most important branches of the art, mural painting. Now lime-plaster, if painted on while it is still wet, retains upon its surface after it has dried the pigments used, although these have not been mixed with any binding material. On all other surfaces the pigments are mixed with some binding material, and on the character of this the kind of painting depends. There is thus a primary distinction between the process just referred to and all others. In the former, pigments, mixed only with water, are laid on while the plaster is wet, and from this " freshness " of the ground the process is called by an Italian term, painting " a fresco " or " on the fresh," though in ordinary parlance the word " fresco " has come to be used as a noun, as when we speak of the " frescoes " of Giotto. Furthermore, as " fresco " is the wall-painter's process *par excellence* the word is unfortunately often employed inaccurately for any mural picture, though this may have been executed by quite a different process. In contradistinction to painting " a fresco " all other processes are properly described by the Italian term " a tempera," meaning " with a mixture." The word is used as a noun in the sense of a substance mixed with another; but it is to be regarded as the imperative of the verb *temperare*, which both in Latin and Italian means " to divide or proportion duly," " to qualify by mixing," and generally " to regulate." *Tempera* means strictly " mix," just as " recipe," also employed as a substantive, is an imperative meaning " take." In ordinary parlance, however, the word tempera is confined to a certain class of binding materials to the exclusion of others, so that the more general term " media " is the best to employ in the present connexion. We go on, therefore, to consider these various media in relation to different surfaces and conditions.

§ 31. *Binding Materials or Media.*—The fundamental distinction among media is their solubility or non-solubility in water, though, as will be seen presently, some possess both these qualities. The non-soluble media are (1) of mineral, (2) of vegetable origin. (1) Of the former kind are all vitreous pastes or pottery glazes, with which imperishable coloured surfaces or designs are produced on glazed tiles used in the decoration of buildings, on ceramic products, and in all processes of enamelling. Silicate of potash, employed to fix pigments on to mural surfaces of plaster in the so-called " stereochrome " or " water-glass " processes of wall painting (see § 37), is another mineral medium, so too is paraffin wax. In the process called (unscientifically) " fresco secco," in which the painting is on dry plaster, lime is used as a binding material for the colours. Its action here is a chemical one (see § 36). (2) Non-soluble vegetable media are drying oils, resins, waxes (including paraffin wax, which is really mineral). In ancient times wax, and to some small extent also resins, were used as a protection against moisture, as in shipbuilding and some forms of wall-painting. Resins have always remained, but wax gradually went out of use in the earlier Christian centuries, and was replaced by the new medium, not used in classical times, of drying oil. In northern lands the desire to protect surfaces from the moisture of the air led to a more extensive use of oils and resins than in Italy; and it was in the Netherlands that in the 15th century oil media were for the first time adopted in the regular practice of painting, which they have dominated ever since.

The soluble media are of animal and vegetable origin. Egg, yolk or white, or both combined, is the chief of the former. Next in importance are size, gained by boiling down shreds of parchment, and fish glue. Egg is the chief medium in what is specially known as " tempera " painting, while for the painting commonly called distemper or "gouache," of which scene-painting is typical, size is used. Milk, ox-gall, casein and other substances are also employed. Of soluble vegetable media the most used are gums of various kinds. These are common "temperas" or tempera media, and, with glycerin or honey, form the usual binding material in what is called "water-colour" painting. Wine, vinegar, the milk of fig-shoots, &c., also occur in old recipes.

Attention must be drawn to the fact that substances can be prepared for use in painting that unite soluble and insoluble media, but can be diluted with water. These substances are known as "emulsions." A wax emulsion, which is also called "saponified wax," can be made by boiling wax in a solution of potash [in the proportions 100 bleached wax, 10 potash, 250 distilled water (Berger, *Beiträge*, i. 100)] till the wax is melted. When the solution has cooled it can be diluted with cold water. An admixture of oil is also possible. This, according to Berger, is what Pliny and Vitruvius (vii. 9, 3) call "Punic wax," a material of importance in ancient painting.

An oil emulsion can be made by mixing drying oil with water through the intermediary of gum or yolk of egg. An intimate mechanical compound, not a chemical one, is thus effected, and the mixture can be diluted with water. If gum arabic be used the result is a "lean" emulsion of a milky-white colour, if yolk of egg a "fat" emulsion of a yellowish tint. When these wax or oil emulsions are dry they have the waterproof character of their non-soluble constituents.

Lastly, it must be noticed that certain substances used in the graphic arts—some of which possess in themselves a certain unctuousness—can be, as it were, rubbed into a suitably roughened, and at the same time yielding, ground, to which they will adhere, though loosely, without binding material. This is the case with charcoal, chalks and pencil. The same property is imparted by a little gum or starch to soft coloured chalks, with which is executed the kind of work called "pastel." These are now also made up with an oleaginous medium and are known as "oil pastels." Pictures can be carried out in ordinary or in oil pastels, and the work should rank as a kind of painting. The coloured films, rubbed off from the sticks of soft chalk on a suitably rough and sometimes tinted paper, are artistic in their texture and capable of producing very beautiful effects of colour. Professor Church notes also that the colours laid on in this fashion seem peculiarly durable (*Chemistry*, p. 293).

§ 32. *The Processes of Painting: Preliminary Note.*—These will be discussed from the point of view of the media employed, but certain departures from strict logical arrangement will be convenient. Thus, different processes of monumental painting on walls may be brought together though distinct media are employed. Tempera and early oil practice cannot be separated.

Painting by the use of vitreous glazes fused by heat may be noticed first, as the process comes within the scope of the article, though it has generally been applied in a purely decorative spirit, so as to be a branch of the art of ornament rather than strictly speaking of painting (see § 2).

In painting processes proper fresco takes the lead. It is in its theory the simplest of all, and at the same time it has produced some of the most splendid results recorded in the annals of the art. With the fresco process may be grouped for the sake of convenience other methods of wall-painting, which share with it at any rate some of its characteristics.

One of these subsidiary methods of wall-painting is that known as the wax process or "encaustic," used in ancient times and revived in our own. Painting in wax, not specially on walls, was an important technique among the ancient Greeks, and the consideration of it introduces some difficult archaeological questions, at which space will not allow more than a glance. The wax used in the process, softened or melted by heat or driven by fire into the painting ground—whence the name "encaustic" or "burning in"—is really a tempera or binding material, and we are brought here to the important subject of tempera painting in general. It will have to be noticed in this connexion what were the chief binding materials used in the so-named

technique in different lands at the various stages of the art, and what conditions were imposed on the artist by the nature of his materials. Lastly, there is the all-important process in which the binding materials are oils and varnishes, a process to which attaches so much historical and artistic interest, while a form of tempera painting that has been specially developed in modern times, that known as water-colour, may claim a concluding word.

§ 33. *Historical Use of the Various Processes of Painting.*—The extent and nature of the employment of these processes at different periods may have here a brief notice.

Tempera painting has had a far longer history and more extended use than any other. The Spaniard Pacheco, the father-in-law and teacher of Velazquez, remarks on the veneration due to tempera because it had its birthday with art itself, and was the process in which the famous ancient artists accomplished such marvels. In the matter of antiquity, painting with vitreous glazes is its only rival: glazed tiles formed, in fact, the chief polychrome decoration for the exteriors of the palaces of Mesopotamia, and were used also in Egypt; but all the wall-paintings in ancient Egypt and Babylonia and Mycenaean Greece, all the mummy cases and papyrus rolls in the first-named country are executed in tempera, and the same is true of the wall-paintings in Italian tombs. In Greece Proper paintings on terra-cotta fixed by fire were very common in the period before the Persian wars. When monumental wall-painting came to the front just after that event it was almost certainly in tempera rather than in fresco that Polygnotus and his companions executed their masterpieces. It has been doubted whether these artists painted directly on plaster or on wooden panels fixed to the wall, but the discovery in Greece of genuine mural paintings of the Mycenaean period has set these doubts at rest. In Italy tomb-paintings actually on plaster exist from the 6th century B.C. The earlier panel painters of the 5th and 4th centuries B.C. also used tempera processes, though their exact media are not recorded. About the time of Alexander there seems to have been felt a demand for a style of painting in which could be obtained greater depth and brilliancy of colouring, with corresponding force in relief, than was possible in the traditional tempera; and this led to painting in a wax medium with which abundance of "body" could be secured. There are many puzzling questions connected with this ancient encaustic, but the discovery in recent years of actual specimens of the work, in the form of portraits on the late Egyptian mummy cases of the first centuries A.D. have assisted the study. Meanwhile a new technique to have been in process of evolution for use on walls, for the fresco process, in a complete or modified form, was certainly in use among the Romans.

The history of the fresco process, as will presently be seen, is somewhat puzzling. Vitruvius and Pliny know it, and it is mentioned in the *Mount Athos Handbook*, which incorporates the technical traditions of the art of the Eastern Empire; it appears also to have been in use in the Christian catacombs, but was not practised by the wall painters who adorned the early medieval churches south and north of the Alps. The difficulties of the process, and another reason to be noticed directly, may have led to its partial disuse in the West, but we find it again coming into vogue in Italy in the 13th and 14th centuries. In the early Christian centuries its place was taken in the monumental decoration of walls by marble inlays, and especially by glass mosaic, which is in itself an important form of wall-painting and may have put painting on plaster, and with it the fresco process, into the shade; notice will however presently be taken of a theory that seeks to establish a close technical connexion between mosaic work and the fresco painting, which, on the decline in the later medieval period of mosaic, came forward again into prominence.

The tempera processes were accordingly in vogue in early medieval times for wall-paintings (except to some extent in the East), for portable panels, and on parchment for the decoration and illustration of manuscripts. Meanwhile the use of drying oils as painting media was coming to be known, and both on plaster and on wood these were to some extent employed through the later medieval period, though without seriously challenging the supremacy of tempera. From the beginning of the 15th century, however, oil painting rose rapidly in estimation, and from the end of that century to our own time it has practically dominated the art. Wall-painting in fresco continued to be practised till the last part of the 18th century, and has been revived and supplemented by various other monumental processes in the 19th, but even for mural work the oil medium has proved itself a convenient substitute. Water-colour painting in its present form is essentially an art of the last hundred years. The old tempera processes have been partly revived in our own time for picture-painting, but the chief modern use of tempera is in scene-painting, where it is more commonly called " distemper."

§ 34. *Painting with Coloured Vitreous Pastes.*—There is no single work that deals with the whole subject of this material and its different uses in transparent or opaque form in the arts, but details will be found in the special articles where these uses are described. (See CERAMICS; MOSAIC; ENAMEL; GLASS, STAINED.) On the subject of the substances and processes employed in the colouring of the various vitreous pastes information will be found in H. H. Cunynghame's *Art Enamelling on Metals* (2nd ed., London, 1906, ch. vi.), but the subject is a large and highly technical one.

Coloured vitreous pastes are among the most valuable materials at the command of the decorative artists, and are employed in numerous techniques, as for example for the glazes of ceramic products including wall or floor tiles; for painted glass windows; for glass mosaic, and for all kinds of work in enamels. The vitreous paste is tinged in the mass with various metallic oxides, one of the finest colours being a ruby red obtained from gold. Silver gives yellow, copper a blue green, cobalt blue, chromium green, nickel brown, manganese violet, and so on. Tin in any form has the curious property of making the vitreous paste opaque. It should be understood that though the vitreous substance and the metallic oxides are essentially the same in all these processes, yet the preparation of the coloured pastes has to be specially conditioned in accordance with the particular technique in view. There are generally various ways of producing reds and blues and greens, &c., from oxides of different metals. The material is generally lustrous, and it admits of a great variety in colours, some of which are highly saturated and beautiful. It is on the lustre and colour of the substance, rather than on the pictorial designs that can be produced by its aid, that its artistic value depends; but though this implies that it comes under the heading " Ornament " rather than " Painting," yet in certain forms and at particular periods it has been the chief medium for the production of pictorial results, and must accordingly have here a brief notice.

The difference between opaque and transparent coloured glass is the basis of a division among the arts that employ the material. If it be kept *transparent* the finest possible effect is obtained in the stained-glass window, where the colours are seen by transmitted light. The stained-glass window came into general use in the early Gothic period, and was a substitute for the wall-paintings which had been common in the Romanesque churches of the 11th and 12th centuries. Hence it is a form, and a very sumptuous and beautiful form, of the art of mural painting, representing that art in the later medieval buildings north of the Alps. In Italy, where the practice of wall-painting continued without a break from early medieval to Renaissance times, the stained-glass window was not a national form of art.

The most effective use of *opaque* coloured vitreous pastes is in ceramics (pottery) and in glass mosaic. The terra-cotta plaque, or tile-painted with designs in glazes of the kind was, as we have seen (§ 7), one of the chief forms of exterior mural decoration in ancient Mesopotamia. The best existing examples were found not long ago on the site of the ancient Susa (" Shushan the palace " of Scripture) and are now in the Louvre. Human

figures, animals, and ornaments, are represented not only in lively colours but also in relief; that is to say, each separate glaze brick had its surface, measuring about 12 in. by 9 in., modelled as well as painted for the exact place it had to occupy in the design. On these bricks there are formed small ridges in relief intended to keep the different liquid glazes apart before they were fixed by vitrifaction in the kiln. Chemical analysis has shown that the yellow colour is an antimoniat of lead, the white is oxide of tin, similar to the well-known opaque white glaze used by the Della Robbia in Italy, the blues and greens are probably oxides of copper; the red a sub-oxide of copper (Semper, *Der Stil*, I. 332). This same region of the world has remained through all time a great centre for the production of coloured glazed tiles, but the use of " Persian," " Moresque," and other decorated plaques has been more ornamental than pictorial.

Glazed pottery only comes occasionally within the survey of the historian of painting. It does so in ancient Greece, because the earlier stages of the development of Greek painting can only be followed in this material; it does so, too, in a sense, in Italian faience and in some Oriental products, but these hardly fall within our view. The Greek vase was covered with a black glaze of extreme thinness and hardness, the composition of which is not known. Figure designs were painted in this on the natural clay of the vessel (see fig. 3, Plate IV.), or it was used for a background, the design being left the colour of the clay. Other colours, especially a red (oxide of iron) and white, were also employed to diversify the design and emphasize details, and these were also fixed by firing. A special kind of Greek vase was the so-called " polychrome lekuthos," a small upright vessel, the clay of which was covered with a white " slip " on which figure designs were painted in lively tints. The technique is not quite understood, but the colours were certainly fired. There is an article on " The Technical History of White Lecythi " in the *American Journal of Archaeology* for 1907; the processes are not, however, analysed.

In glass mosaic thin solid slabs of coloured vitreous pastes are broken up into little cubes of ½ in. to ½ in. in size and set in some suitable cement. The artist works from a coloured drawing and selects his cubes accordingly. Any number of shades of all hues can be obtained, and the modern mosaic workers of Italy boast that they dispose of some 25,000 different tints. As it is of the essence of the work to be simple and monumental in effect, a limited palette is all that is needed; and the mosaics recently executed in St Paul's in London are done in about thirty colours. The worker should have at hand appliances to cut to shape any particular cube wanted for a special detail.

The ancients used the art, and the finest existing ancient picture is in a mosaic, not indeed of glass pastes, but of coloured marbles. This is the famous " Battle of Issus " found at Pompeii. Glass mosaic came in under the early Roman Empire, but its chief use was in early Christian times, when it was the chief material for mural decoration of a pictorial kind. Ravenna is the place where this form of painting is most instructively represented, and the 5th and 6th centuries A.D. are the times of its greatest glory. At Rome and Constantinople there is fine early work, while that at Venice and Palermo is later. In the earliest and best examples the design is very simple, and a few monumental forms of epic dignity, against a flat background commonly of dark blue, represents the persons and scenes of the sacred narratives. The effect of colour is always sumptuous. Gold, especially for the backgrounds, is in later work freely employed.

The subject of *enamel* work forms the theme of a separate article. Here it need only be said that pictures can be produced by painting on a ground, generally of metal, with coloured vitreous pastes that are afterwards fixed by fusing. Limoges in France has been the great centre of the art, but enamelling loses in artistic value when a too exclusively pictorial result is aimed at.

§ 35. *Fresco Painting.*—Vitruvius (*De Architectura*, bk. vii. chs. 2, 3; age of Augustus), *Mount Athos Handbook* (*Hermeneia*, chs. 54 seq.; date uncertain but based on early tradition); Cennino

Cennini (*Trattato della pittura*, chs. 67 seq., ed. Milanesi, 1859; Eng. trans. by Christiana J. Herringham, Lond., 1899); Leon Battista Alberti (*De re aedificatoria*, bk. vi. ch. 9; early and middle 15th century); Vasari (*Opere*, ed. Milanesi, i. 181; middle of 16th century)—all refer in general terms to the fresco process, as one generally understood in their times. Armenini (*Dei veri precetti della pittura*; Ravenna, 1587), and Palomino (*El Museo pictorico*; Madrid, 1715-1724), give more detailed accounts of the actual technical procedure, of which they had preserved the tradition. Much information of the highest value and interest was collected at the time when, in the forties of the 19th century, the project for the decoration in fresco of the new English Houses of Parliament was under discussion. This is contained in various communications by Sir Charles Eastlake, Mr Charles Heath Wilson, and others, printed with the successive *Reports of the Commissioners on the Fine Arts* from 1842 onwards. The experience obtained in the revived modern work in fresco by Cornelius, Hess, and other German artists encouraged by King Ludwig I. of Bavaria, which began at Rome in the second decade of the 19th century, was also drawn upon for the purpose of these *Reports*. A useful compendium was issued at the time by W. B. Sarsfield Taylor, *A Manual of Fresco and Encaustic Painting* (Lond., 1843). F. G. Cremer's *Vollständige Anleitung zur Fresco-Malerei* (Düsseldorf, 1891), may also be mentioned as a recent manual. The chemistry of the process is well explained by Professor Church in his *Chemistry of Paints and Paintings*.

The fresco process is generally regarded as a method for the production of a picture. It is better to look upon it in the first place as a colour-finish to plaster-work. What it produces is a coloured surface of a certain quality of texture and a high degree of permanence, and it is a secondary matter that this coloured surface may be so diversified as to result in a pattern or a picture.

We do not know among what people the discovery was first made that a wash of liquid pigment over a freshly laid surface of lime plaster remained permanently incorporated with it when all was dry, and added to it great beauty of colour and texture. The Egyptians, the Assyrians, the Phoenicians, the Mycenaean and later Greeks, the ancient Italians—all made extensive use of plaster as a coating to brickwork or masonry, but when they coloured it this was done after it was dry and with the use of some binding material or tempera.

The earliest notice of the fresco technique that we have in extant literature is contained in the third chapter of the seventh book of Vitruvius, and it is there treated as a familiar, well-understood procedure, the last stage in the construction and finish of a wall. Pliny also in several passages of his *Natural History* treats the technique as a matter of common knowledge. In Vitruvius the processes of plastering *albaria opera* are first described (vii. 2, 3), and it is provided that after the rough cast, *trullissatio*, there are to follow three coats of plaster made of lime and sand, each one laid on when the one below is beginning to dry, and then three of plaster in which the place of the sand is taken by marble dust, at first coarse, then finer, and in the uppermost coat of all in finest powder. It might now be (1) finished with a plain face, but one brought up to such an exquisite surface that it would shine like a mirror (chs. 3, 9); or (2) with stamped ornaments in relief or figure designs modelled up by hand; or (3) it might be completed with a coat of colour, and this would be applied by the fresco process, for which Pliny uses the formula *udo illinere*, "to paint upon the wet." The reason why the pigments mixed with water only, without any gum or binding material, adhere when dry to the plaster is a chemical one. It was first clearly formulated by Otto Donner von Richter in connexion with researches he made on the Pompeian wall-paintings and published in 1868 as an appendix to Helbig's *Campanische Wandgemälde*. He demonstrated that when limestone is burnt into lime all the carbonic acid is driven out of it. When this lime is "slaked" by being drenched with water it drinks this in greedily and the resultant paste becomes saturated with an aqueous solution of hydrate of lime. When

this paste is mixed with sand and marble dust and laid on to the wall in the form of plaster this hydrate of lime in solution rises to the surface, and when the wet pigment is applied to this the liquid hydrate of lime or lime water, to use Professor Church's phrasing, "diffuses into the paint, soaks it through and through, and gradually takes up carbonic acid from the air, thus producing carbonate of lime, which acts as the binding material" (Church, p. 278). It is a mistake to speak of the pigment "sinking into the wet plaster." It remains as a fact upon the surface, but it is fixed there in a sort of crystalline skin of carbonate of lime—the element originally banished when the lime was burned—that has now re-formed on the surface of the plaster. This crystalline skin gives a certain metallic lustre to the surface of a fresco painting, and is sufficient to protect the colours from the action of external moisture, though on the other hand there are many causes chemical and physical that may contribute to their decay. If, however, proper care has been taken throughout, and conditions remain favourable, the fresco painting is quite permanent, and as Vitruvius says (vii. 3, 7), "the colours, when they have been carefully laid upon the wet plaster, do not lose their lustre but remain as they are in perpetuity . . . so that a plaster surface that has been properly finished does not become rough through time, nor can the colours be rubbed off, that is unless they have been carelessly applied or on a surface that has lost its moisture."

In the passage from which these words are taken Vitruvius gives useful hints as to the aesthetics of the fresco technique. Italian writers on the subject, such as Vasari, are generally so taken up with the pictorial design represented on the wall that the more essential characteristics of the process in itself are lost sight of. To Vitruvius the work is coloured plaster, not a picture on plaster, and he shows how important it is that the plaster should be finished with a fine surface of gleaming white so as to light up the transparent film of colour that clothes it. It is the result of such care in classical times that a surface of Pompeian plastering, self-tinted "a fresco," is beautiful without there being any question of pattern or design.

This beauty and polish of Pompeian, and generally of ancient Roman plaster, has recently been made the ground for calling in question the view accepted for a generation past that it was merely lime plaster painted on "a fresco," and for substituting a totally different technical hypothesis. The reference is to the treatment of ancient wall-painting generally in the first part of Berger's *Beiträge* (2nd ed., 1904, pp. 58 seq.). This writer denies that the well-known classical wall-paintings in question are frescoes, and evolves with great ingenuity a wholly new theory of this branch of ancient technique. It is his view that the plaster was prepared by a special process in which wax largely figured and which corresponds to, and indeed survives in, the so-called "stucco-lustro" of the modern Italians.

The process in question is described by L. B. Alberti (*De re aedificatoria*, vi. 9), who says that when the plaster wall surface has been carefully smoothed it must be anointed with a mixture of wax, resin and oil, which is to be driven in by heat, and then polished till the surface shines like a mirror. This is a classical process referred to by Vitruvius under the name "ganosis," as applied to the nude parts of marble statues, possibly to tone down the cold whiteness of the material. Now Vitruvius, and Pliny, who probably follows him, do as a fact prescribe this same process for use on plaster, but only in the one special case of a wall painted "a fresco" with vermilion, which was not supposed to resist the action of the light unless "locked up," in this way with a coating of this "Punic" or saponified wax. Neither writer gives any hint that the process was applied to plaster surfaces generally, or that the lustre of these was dependent on a wax polish, and Vitruvius's description is so clear that if wax had been in use he would certainly have said so.

Vitruvius prescribes so many successive coats of plaster, each one put on before the last was dry, and on the wet uppermost coat the colouring is laid. How can we with any reason substitute for this a method in which the plaster has to be made quite dry and then treated with quite a different material and process? Furthermore, Berger holds the astonishing theory that on the self-coloured surfaces of Pompeian and Roman plastered walls the colour was not applied, as in the fresco process, to the surface of the final coat, but was mixed up with the actual material of the *intonaco* so that this was a coat of coloured plaster. This is of course a matter susceptible of ocular proof, but the actual fragments of ancient coloured stucco referred to by Berger afford a very slender support to the hypothesis, whereas everyone who, like the present writer, possesses such fragments can satisfy himself that in almost every case the colour coat is confined to the surface. The writer has a fragment of such stucco from Rome, coloured with vermilion, and here there is clear evidence that some substance has soaked into the plaster to the depth of an eighth of an inch, as would be the case in the "ganosis" of Vitruvius. The part thus affected is yellowish and harder than the rest of the plaster. A careful chemical analysis, kindly made for the purpose of this article by Principal Laurie of Edinburgh shows that, although the small quantity of the material available makes it impossible to attain certainty, yet the substance may possibly be wax with the slight admixture of some greasy substance. On the other hand all the writer's other specimens show the colour laid on to all appearance "a fresco." The evidence of the coloured plaster in the house of about the 2nd century B.C. on Delos is wholly against Berger's view. The writer has many specimens of this, and they are all without exception coloured only on the surface. It is true that there are certain difficulties connected with Pompeian fresco practice, but the description of the process as a *wet* process in Vitruvius and Pliny is so absolutely unmistakable that Berger's theory must without hesitation be rejected.

The history of the fresco technique remains at the same time obscure. Here again Berger offers an interesting suggestion which cannot be passed over in silence. If the Pompeian technique, as he believes, be a wax process on dry plaster, followed by some form of tempera, how did the fresco technique, which is known both in East and West in the later medieval period, take its rise? The early medieval age was not a time when a difficult and monumental technique of the kind is likely to have been evolved, but Berger most ingeniously connects it with that of mosaic work. In mosaic the wall surface is at first rough plastered and a second and comparatively thin coat of cement is laid over it to receive and retain the cubes of coloured glass, only so much cement being laid each morning as the worker will cover with his tesserae before night. It was the practice sometimes to sketch in water-colours on the freshly laid patch of cement the design which was to be reproduced in mosaic, and Berger points to the incontestable fact if this sketch were allowed to remain without being covered with the cubes it would really be a painting in fresco. This is the way he thinks that the fresco practice actually began, and the period would be that of the decline of mosaic work in the West as the middle ages advanced.

In spite of the attractiveness of these suggestions, we must reaffirm the view of this article that the testimony of Vitruvius is conclusive for the knowledge by the Romans of the early empire of the fresco technique. Why we do not find evidence of it far earlier cannot be determined, but it is worth noting that the success of the process depends on the plaster holding the moisture for a sufficient time, and this it can only do if it be pretty thick. In ancient Egypt and Mesopotamia, for example, the plaster used as painting ground was very thin, and especially in those hot climates would never have lent itself to fresco treatment. On the other side, the decline, and perhaps temporary extinction, of the technique in the early middle ages may be reasonably explained by the general condition of the arts after the break-up of the Roman Empire of the West.

To return now to the technical questions from which this historical digression took its rise, it will be easily seen that the process of painting in fresco must be a rapid one, for it must be completed before the plaster has had time to dry. Hence only a certain portion of the work in hand is undertaken at a time, and only

so much of the final coat of plaster, called by the Italians *intonaco* is laid by the plasterer as will correspond to the amount the artist has laid out for himself in the time allowed him by the condition of the plaster. At the end of this time the plaster not painted on is cut away round the outline of the work already finished, and when operations are recommenced a fresh patch is laid on and joined up as neatly as possible to the old. In the making of these joints the ancient plasterer seems to have been more expert than the Italians of the Renaissance, and the seams are often pretty apparent in frescoes of the 15th and 16th centuries, so that they can be discerned in a good photograph. When they can be followed, they furnish information which it is often interesting to possess as to the amount that has been executed in a single day's work. Judging by this test, Mr Heath Wilson, in his *Life of Michelangelo*, computed that on the vault of the Sistine Michelangelo could paint a nude figure considerably above life size in two working days, the workmanship being perfect in every part. The colossal nude figures of young men on the cornice of the vault at most occupied four days each. The "Adam" (fig 34, Plate X.) was painted in four or perhaps in three. A day was generally occupied by the head of such figures, which were about 10 ft. high. Raphael, or rather his pupils, it is thus calculated, painted the *Incéndio del Borgo*, containing about 350 sq. ft., in about forty days, the group of the young man carrying his father occupying three. The group of the Three Graces in the Villa Farnesina took five days at most. Luini, a most accomplished executant, could paint "more than an entire figure, the size of life, in one day" (Second *Report*, p. 37). It has been noticed as one of the difficulties about the Pompeian frescoes, that joints hardly occur, or at any rate that larger surfaces of plaster were covered by the painter at a single time than was the case among Renaissance artists, and a conjectural explanation has been offered based on the fact that the ancient plaster ground, laid on in many successive coats while in each case the previous one was still humid, was thicker and would hold more moisture than the more modern intonaco, and would accordingly allow the artist longer time in which to carry out his work. Alberti, Armenini, and Palomino only contemplate one or two thin coats over the original rough cast, while Cornelius and his associates, who revived the process early in the 19th century, speak of an intonaco over the rough cast only about a quarter of an inch thick. A piece of plaster ground from Raphael's *Loggie* in the Vatican was found to be quite thin, and Donner calculated that the ancient grounds were on an average 3 in. thick, the modern only a little over 1 in. On such grounds work had necessarily to be finished within the day, and Cennino expressly says (ch. 67): "Consider how much you can paint in a day; for whatever you cover with plaster you must finish the same day." Hence almost invariably in Italian fresco practice every join means a new day's work. At Pompeii the plaster, it is thought, might have remained damp over night. In the *Mount Athos Handbook* tow was to be mixed with the plaster, undoubtedly to retard its drying.

This necessarily rapid execution gives to well-handled frescoes a simplicity and look of directness in technique that are of the essence of the aesthetic effect of this form of the art. Hence Vasari is right when he extols the process in the words, "of all the ways in which painters work, wall-painting is the finest and most masterly, since it consists in doing upon a single day that which in other methods may be accomplished in several by going over again what has been done. . . . there are many of our craft who do well enough in other kinds of work, as for example in oil or tempera, but fail in this, for this is in truth the most manly, the safest, and most solid of all ways of painting. Therefore let those who seek to work upon the wall, paint with a manly touch upon the fresh plaster, and avoid returning to it when it is dry " (*Opere*, ed. Milanesi, i. 181).

The process gives the artist another advantage in that his painting, being executed in the very material of the surface itself, seems essentially a part of the wall. It is lime painting on a lime ground, and fabric and enrichment are one. This can be noted in the *Sala del Constantino* in the Vatican at Rome, one of the *stanze* or suite of rooms decorated by Raphael and his associates. There are two figures here painted on the walls in oil, and though there is a certain depth and richness of effect secured in this medium, they are too obviously something added as an afterthought, while the figures in fresco seem an integral part of the wall.

Work of this kind, finished in each part at a sitting, is what the Italians call *buon fresco* or "true fresco," and it has always been, as it was with Vitruvius, the ideal of the art, but at many periods the painters have had to rely largely on retouches and reinforcements after the plaster was dry. Cennino devotes the 67th chapter of his *Trattato* to a description of the process, and expressly tells us that the method he recommends is the one traditional in the school of Giotto, of which he himself was a direct scion. He is fully alive to the importance of doing as much as possible while the ground is wet, for " to paint on the fresh—that is, a fixed portion on each day—is the best and most permanent way of laying on the colour, and the pleasantest method of painting "; but an ordinary artist of the early part of the 15th century had not sufficient skill to do all that was required at the one moment. Observations made on the works executed by various Italian masters from the 14th to the 16th century show great varieties in this matter of retouching, but the subject need not be dwelt on as it involves no principle. Every painter of worthy ambition, who had entered into the spirit of his craft, would desire to do all he could " on the fresh," and would be satisfied with, and indeed glory in, the conditions and limitations of the noble technique. Masaccio, even at the beginning of the 15th century, is remarkable for the amount of fine pictorial effect he secured without reliance on retouching. It was second-rate artists, like Pinturicchio, who delighted to furbish up their mural pictures with stucco reliefs and gilding and to add touches of more brilliant pigments than could be secured in the wet process. Giotto, Masaccio, Ghirlandajo, Michelangelo, Luini, are among the *frescanti* proper, who represent the true ideals of the craft.

The following notes upon the methods of the work are derived partly from observation of extant works and partly from the older treatises, but reference has also been made to modern practice in Germany and Italy, as information derived from this last source may be found useful by those who are disposed to-day to make essays in the process.

To avoid loss of time it is essential that the necessary drawing should all be accomplished beforehand. Pozzo, a painter and writer of the end of the 17th century says, " everyone knows that before beginning to paint it is necessary to prepare a drawing and well-studied coloured sketch, both of which are to be kept at hand in painting the fresco, so as not to have any other thought than that of the execution " (First *Report*, p. 35). In Cennino's time it seems to have been the practice to square out the work full size from the sketch on to the surface of the rough cast before the intonaco was laid. This at any rate enabled the artist to see how his work as a whole would come in relation to the space provided for it, but the actual intonaco had to be laid piece by piece over this general sketch and the drawing of each portion repeated on the new surface. In the palmy days of Italian painting, however, as well as in modern times, the design has been drawn out on a full-sized cartoon, and this cartoon, or a tracing from it, has been transferred piece by piece to the freshly laid intonaco on which the painting is about to be executed. The drawing may be nailed against the wall, and the outlines passed over with a blunt-pointed stylus of some hard material, that by dinting the paper impresses on the yielding plaster a line sufficient to guide the painter in his work; or the outlines of the cartoon may be pricked and "pounced " with a little bag of red or black powder that will leave a dotted outline on the wall.

The preparation of the intonaco itself is however a matter for much care. The lime should be prepared from a stone that is as far as possible pure carbonate of lime—the travertine of Tivoli, recommended by Vasari, is perfect for the purpose—and after it is burnt should be slaked with water and thoroughly macerated so that the lumps are all completely broken up. The slaked lime, of the consistency of a stiff paste, or as it is termed "putty," must be kept covered in from the air for a considerable period that varies according to different authorities from eight to twelve months to as many years. All experts, from Vitruvius downwards, are agreed on the necessity for this, but the exact scientific reason therefor does not seem to be quite clear. One advantage of the keeping is that the lime hydrate may take up a certain amount

of carbonic acid, though not too much, from the air. Church says that, " not more than one-third or at most two-fifths of the lime should be converted into the carbonate " (p. 191); but Faraday (Fifth *Report*, p. 25) was of opinion that through lapse of time there was brought about a molecular change that divided the particles more thoroughly and gave the lime a finer texture so as to mix better with the pigments. At any rate, when Cornelius and his associates started the modern fresco revival at Rome, in 1815, an old workman who had been employed under Raphael Mengs directed their attention to this tradition, and they used lime that had been kept in a slaked condition, but still caustic—that is, still deprived of most of its carbonic acid, for twelve years! For mixing the plaster the proportions of lime to sand or marble dust vary; Cennino gives two of sand to one of " rich " or caustic lime, but the Germans used three of sand to one of lime. Whatever its exact constitution, the intonaco has to be carefully laid each morning over that part of the rough cast, previously well wetted, that corresponds to the amount laid out for the day's work. Contrary to the prescription of Vitruvius and Pompeian practice, which favours a polished surface, the moderns prefer a slight roughness or "tooth " on the intonaco. Painting should not begin, so Cornelius advised (First *Report*, p. 24), till " the surface is in such a state that it will barely receive the impression of the finger, but not so wet as to be in danger of being stirred up by the brush."

The pigments are ready mixed in little pots, on a tin palette with a run round the edge, or on a table, and in old Italian practice each colour was compounded in three shades—dark, middle and light. The water should be boiled or distilled, or should be rainwater; for spring-water often contains carbonate of lime that would derange the chemistry of the process. Again, on account of the chemical action that takes place during the process, the pigments have to be carefully selected. The palette of the fresco painter is indeed a very restricted one, and this is another reason of the broad and simple effect of the work. Practically speaking only the earth colours, such as the ochres raw or burned, can be used with safety; even the white has to be pure white lime (in Italian, *bianco San-Giovanni*), since lead white used in oil painting (Italian, *biacca*) is inadmissible. Vegetable and animal pigments are as a rule excluded, " very few colours of organic origin withstanding the decomposing action of lime " (Church, p. 280). The brushes are of hog-bristles or otter-hair or sable, and have to be rather long in the hair. Round ones are recommended. According to early Italian practice, the painter would first outline the figures of objects, already drawn on the plaster, with a long-haired brush dipped in red ochre, and would then, *e.g.* in the case of the faces, lay in broadly with terre verte the shadows under the brows, below the nostrils, and round the chin, and bring down and fuse into these shadows the darkest of the three flesh-tints, with a dexterous blending of the wet pigments upon a surface that preserves their dampness. On the other side these half-tones are now modelled up into the lighter hues of the flesh. White may then be used in decided touches for the high lights, and the details of the eyes, mouth and other features put in without too much searching after accidents of local colour. Modern frescoists have found that " the tints first applied sink in and look faint, so that it is necessary sometimes to go over the surface repeatedly with the same colour before the full effect is gained " (First *Report*, p. 24), but it is well to allow in each case some minutes to elapse before touching any spot a second time. For the hair the Italians would make three tints suffice, the high lights again following with white. The draperies are broadly treated. After the whole has been laid in, in monochrome, with the green pigment, the folds would be marked out with the deepest of the three tints for shadow, and these shadows united by the middle tint. Lastly the lighter parts are painted up and finally reinforced with white. The work needs to be deftly touched, for too much handling of one spot may destroy the freshness of the tints and even rub up the ground. It is not necessary (as moderns have sometimes supposed) to put touch beside touch, never going twice over the same ground. So long as the pigments and the surface are wet the tints may be laid one over the other or fused at will, and may be " loaded " in some parts and in others thinly spread, the one essential being that a fresh and crisp effect shall not be lost. The wetness of the ground will always secure a certain softness in all touches, even those that give the strong high-lights, and so important is it that the plaster should not begin to dry, that it should be sprinkled if necessary with fresh water. The characteristic softness of the touches laid on " a fresco " is the more apparent when they are compared with those strokes of reinforcement which may be put on " a tempera " after the work is dry. Armenini says that the shadows may be finished and deepened by hatching, as in a drawing, with black and lake laid on with a soft brush with a medium of gum, size, or white and yolk of egg diluted with vinegar. Such retouches are always hard and " wiry," and are as much as possible to be avoided.

As examples of execution in fresco no works are better than those of Luini. He painted rapidly and thinly, securing thereby a transparency of effect that did not however preclude richness. Heath Wilson indeed says of his painting that " it may be compared to that of Rubens; it is juicy, transparent, and clear; . . . his execution is light and graceful." No sounder model could be taken for modern work. The high-water mark of achievement in fresco painting was however reached by a greater than Luini—by Michelangelo in his painting of the Sistine Chapel roof. Considering that since his boyhood he had had no practical experience of the fresco process, and refused the commission as long as he could because he was not a painter but a sculptor, Buonarroti's technical success in the manipulation of the difficult process is still more astounding than the aesthetic result of the work as a creation of imaginative genius. He had to paint for the most part lying on his back in a sort of cradle, and working with his arms above his head, and had no skilled assistants; yet there is no quality in the work that strikes us more than its freshness and air of easy mastery, as if the artist were playing with his task. The fusion of the lights and shadows through the most delicate half-tones is accomplished in that melting fashion for which the Italians used the term *sfumato* or "misty," while at the same time the touches are crisp and firm, the accent here and there decided; and the artist's incomparable mastery of form gives a massive solidity to the whole (see fig. 34, Plate X.)

In our own times and in English-speaking circles the fresco process has been discredited owing to the comparative failure of the experiments connected with the Houses of Parliament. On the condition of the frescoes there, as well as on that of the pictures in various other media, a series of *Memoranda* were made by Professor Church, and a select committee of the House of Lords took evidence on the subject as late as December 1906. Most of the frescoes executed in the forties and fifties of the 19th century had got into a deplorable state; but Church's belief was that the main cause of the decay was the sulphurous acid with which, owing to the consumption of coal and gas, the air of London is so highly charged. The action of this acid—a million tons of which are said to be belched out into the London atmosphere in every year—turns the carbonate of lime which forms the surface of the fresco into a sulphate, and it ceases to retain its binding power over the pigments. "The chemical change," he reports, "is accompanied by a mechanical expansion which causes a disruption of the ground and is the main cause of the destruction of the painting." It is a remarkable fact, however, that one of the frescoes in question, Sir John Tenniel's "St Cecilia," completed in 1850, painted very thinly and on a smooth surface, lasted well, and opposed "a considerable measure of successful resistance for nearly half a century on the part of a pure fresco to the hostile influence of the London atmosphere" (Church, *Memorandum*, iv. 1896).

Abroad, experience was more favourable. The earliest frescoes of the modern revival—those by Cornelius and his associates from the Casa Bartholdy at Rome—are in a fairly good state in the National Gallery at Berlin. Such too is the condition of Cornelius's large fresco in the Ludwigskirche at Munich. The best modern frescoes, from the artistic point of view, in all Europe are those of about 1850 by Alfred Rethel in the town-hall at Aix-la-Chapelle, and they are well preserved. The exterior frescoes on the Pinacotek at Munich have on the other hand mostly perished; but the climate of that city is severe in winter, and nothing else was really to be expected. We must not expect carbonate of lime to resist atmospheric influences which affect to a greater or less degree all mineral substances.

§ 36. *Fresco-Secco.*—(See Charles Heath Wilson, in appendix to Second *Report of the Commissioners on the Fine Arts*, London, 1843, p. 40; Church, *Chemistry of Paints and Painting*, 1901, p. 278).

The process called "fresco-secco" is a method of lime painting on a plaster surface that has been allowed to dry. It is described by Theophilus in the *Schedula* of about A.D. 1100; and Mr Charles Heath Wilson in 1843 wrote of it as "extensively used in Italy at present and with great success." It is of course obvious that paintings must often be executed on walls the plastering of which is already dry, and on which the true fresco process is imprac-

ticable. Some kind of painting in tempera is thus needful, and "fresco-secco" uses for this the lime that is the very constituent of the plaster. The process is thoroughly to drench the dry surface of the plaster the night before with water with which a little lime or baryta water has been mixed, and to renew the wetting the next morning. The artist then fixes up his cartoon, pounces the outlines, and sets to work to paint with the same pigments as used in *buon fresco* mixed with lime or baryta water or with a little slaked lime. If the wall become too dry a syringe is used to wet it. The directions given by Theophilus (i. 15) correspond with this modern practice. "When figures or representations of other things," he says, "are to be delineated on a dry wall, it must be forthwith moistened with water till it is thoroughly wet. On this wet ground all the colours must be laid that are required, and they must be all mixed with lime, and will dry with the wall so that they adhere to it." Mr C. H. Wilson praises the work for its convenience, economy, and ease of execution, and notes that "for ornament it is a better method than real fresco, as in the latter art it is quite impossible to make the joinings at outlines owing to the complicated forms of ornaments," but says that "it is in every important respect an inferior art to real fresco. Paintings executed in this mode are ever heavy and opaque, whereas fresco is light and transparent." He declares also for its durability, but Professor Church states what seems obvious, that "the fixation of the pigments . . . is less complete" than in real fresco though depending on the same chemical conditions(Second *Report*, 1843, p. 40; *Chemistry*, p. 279).

§ 37. *Stereochromy or Water-Glass Painting.*—(See *Chemisch-technische Bibliothek*, Band lxxviii., *Die Mineral-Malerei*, von A. Keim, Wien, &c., 1881; Rev. J. A. Rivington in *Journal of the Society of Arts*, No. 1630, Feb: 15, 1884; Mrs Lea Merritt and Professor Roberts Austin in *Journal of the Society of Arts*, No. 2246, Dec. 6, 1895; F. G. Cremer, *Beiträge zur Technik der Monumental-Malverfahren*, Düsseldorf, 1895).

Akin to "fresco-secco," in that a mineral agent is used to secure the adhesion of the colouring matter to the plaster, is the process known as stereochromy or water-glass painting. It is not a traditional process, but an outcome of comparatively modern chemical research, and is not yet a century old. It is based on the properties of the substance called water-glass, a silicate of potassium or of soda, perfected by the German chemist Von Fuchs about 1825. A process of painting called "stereochromy" was soon after evolved, in which pigments of the same kind as those used in fresco, mixed only with distilled water and laid on a prepared plaster ground, were afterwards fixed and securely locked up by being drenched with this substance, which is equivalent to a soluble glass. Some of the mural paintings in the Houses of Parliament, notably those by Maclise, were executed in this process. Improvements were more recently effected in the process with which the names of Keim and Recknagel of Munich are connected, and in this form it has been used a good deal in Germany in the last quarter of the 19th century both in interiors and in the open air. For example, in 1881 Professor Schraudolph of Munich painted in this process the front of the Hôtel Bellevue in that city. This improved water-glass painting was introduced to notice in England in a paper read before the Society of Arts by the Rev. J. A. Rivington on the 13th of February 1884, and printed in the *Journal* of the society, No. 1630. A more recent description is contained in F. G. Cremer's *Beiträge*.

The recipe for the preparation of the actual medium is as follows: 15 parts pounded quartzsand, 10 parts refined potash, 1 part powdered charcoal are mixed together and fused for 6 to 8 hours in a glass furnace. The resultant mass when cold is reduced to powder and boiled for 3 or 4 hours in an iron vessel with distilled water till it dissolves and yields a heavy syrupy liquor of strongly alkaline reaction. This can be diluted with water, and in the process is applied hot.

The ground is very carefully prepared, and over a thoroughly sound and dry backing a thin coat of plaster is laid, composed of only 1 part lime to 5 or 8 parts selected sand and pounded marble with a slight admixture of infusorial earth. The object is to obtain a homogeneous porous ground that can be thoroughly permeated with the solution, and to help to secure this the intonaco when dry is sprayed with hydrofluo-silicic acid to dissolve away the crystalline skin of carbonate of lime formed on the surface and to "open the pores" of the plaster. The surface of the painting ground, which is left with a decided "tooth" upon it, is then well soaked with the solution, and when dry will be found "hard but perfectly absorbent and ready for painting."

The pigments consist in the usual ochres and earths; chrome reds, greens, and yellows; Naples yellow (antimoniate of lead); cobalt blue and green; and artificial ultramarine; terre verte, &c., with zinc white or baryta white.

It is important however to note, that the pigments (which can be supplied by Messrs Schirmer, late Faulstich, of Munich, and many other firms) are mixed with various substances so as to render uniform the action upon them of the fixing solution and neutralize the action of its alkalies. The operations of painting, in which only distilled water is used with the colours, are easy and admit of considerable freedom. "Every variety of treatment is possible, and the method adapts itself to any individual style of painting." The work can be left and resumed at will. After the painting is dry there comes the all-important final process of fixing with the water-glass so ution. This is sprayed on in a hot state by means of a special apparatus, and the process is repeated till the wall can absorb no more, the idea being that the substance will penetrate right through to the wall, and when set will bind pigments, intonaco, rough plastering and wall into one hard mass of silicate that will be impervious to moisture or any injurious agencies. The last paragraph of the official account of the Keim process issued in 1883 for the guidance of those contemplating mural work runs as follows: "The fixing of the picture is accomplished by means of a hot solution of potash water-glass, thrown against the surface by means of a spray-producing machine in the form of a very fine spray. This fixing done, by several repetitions of the process, a solution of carbonate of ammonia is finally applied to the surface. The carbonate of potash, which is thus quickly formed, is removed by repeated washings with distilled water. Then the picture is dried by a moderate artificial heat. Finally a solution of paraffin in benzene may be used to enrich the colours and further preserve the painting from adverse influences."

§ 38. *Spirit Fresco or the "Gambier Parry" Process, with modifications by Professor Church.*—(See *Spirit Fresco Painting: an Account of the Process*, by T. Gambier Parry, London, 1883; Church, *Chemistry of Paints and Painting*, 288 seq.).

This process is also one of quite modern origin, but in Great Britain, at any rate, it is now very popular. Mr Gambier Parry, who invented and first put it into practice, claims for it that it "is not the mere addition of one or more medium to the many already known, but a system, complete from the first preparation of a wall to the last touch of the artist," and that the advantages it offers are " (1) durability (the principal materials being all but imperishable); (2) power to resist external damp and changes of temperature; (3) luminous effect; (4) a dead surface; (5) freedom from all chemical action on colours."

The theory of the process is much the same as that of stereochromy, the drenching of the ground with a solution that forms at the same time the medium of the pigments, so that the whole forms when dry a homogeneous mass. The solution or medium is however not a mineral one, but a combination of oils, varnishes and wax, the use of which makes the process nearly akin to that of oil painting. The objection to the use of oil painting proper on walls is the shininess of effect characteristic of that system, which is in mural work especially to be avoided, and "spirit fresco" aims at the elimination of the oleaginous element and the substitution of wax which gives the "matt" surface desired.

Mr Gambier Parry directs a carefully laid intonaco of ordinary plaster suitable for fresco on a dry backing, "the one primary necessity" being that the intonaco " should be left with its natural surface, its porous quality being absolutely essential. All smoothing process or 'floating ' with plaster of Paris destroys this quality. All cements must be avoided." When dry the surface of the wall must be well saturated with the medium, for which the following is the recipe: pure white wax 4 oz. by weight; elemi resin 2 oz. by weight dissolved in 2 oz. of rectified turpentine; oil of spike lavender 8 oz. by measure; copal varnish about 20 oz. by measure. These ingredients are melted and boiled together by a process described in his paper, and when used for the wall the medium is diluted in one and a half its bulk of good turpentine. With this diluted solution the wall is well soaked, and the directions continue, "after a few days left for evaporation, mix equal quantities of pure white lead in powder and of gilder's whitening in the medium slightly diluted with about a third of turpentine, and paint the surface thickly, and when sufficiently evaporated to bear a second coat, add it as thickly as a brush can lay it. This when dry, for

which two or three weeks may be required, produces a perfect surface " both white and absorbent.

The pigments, which are practically the same as those used in oil painting, must be ground in dry powder in the undiluted medium, and when prepared can be kept in tubes like oil colours. Solid painting with a good deal of body is recommended and pure oil of spike is freely used as painting medium. Pure spike oil may also be washed over the ground before painting " to melt the surface (hence the name Spirit *Fresco*) and prepare it to incorporate the colours painted *into* it." The spike oil is " the one common solvent of all the materials; . . . the moment the painter's brush touches the surface (already softened, *if necessary*, for the day's work) it opens to receive the colours, and on the rapid evaporation of the spike oil it closes them in, and thus the work is done." The oil of spike lavender, it may be noticed, is an essential oil prepared from *Lavandula spica*.

Professor Church has suggested improvement in the composition of the medium by eliminating the " doubtful constituents " elemi resin and bees'-wax and substituting paraffin wax, one of the safest of materials, dissolved in non-resinifiable oil of turpentine. This is mixed as before with copal varnish and used in the same way and with the same or better results as Mr Gambier Parry's medium.

§ 39. *Oil Processes of Wall Painting.*—The use of the oil medium for painting on plaster in medieval days opens up a much debated subject on which a word will be said in connexion with oil painting in general. In the later Renaissance period in Italy it came into limited use, and Leonardo essayed it in an imperfect form and with disastrous result in his " Last Supper " at Milan. Other artists, notably Sebastiano del Piombo, were more successful, and Vasari, who experimented in the technique, gives his readers recipes for the preparation of the plaster ground. This with Cennino (ch. 90) had consisted in a coat of size or diluted egg-tempera mixed with milk of fig-shoots, but later on there was substituted for this several coats of hot boiled linseed oil. This was still in common use in the 16th century, but Vasari himself had evolved a better recipe which he gives us in the 8th chapter of his " Introduction " to *Painting*. Over undercoatings of ordinary plaster he lays a stucco composed of equal parts of lime, pounded brick, and scales of iron mixed with white of egg and linseed oil. This is then grounded with white oil toned down with a mixture of red and yellow easily drying pigments, and on this the painting is executed.

In Edinburgh and other places Mrs Traquair has recently carried out wall paintings on dry plaster with oil colours much thinned with turpentine. The ground is prepared with several coats of white oil paint, and the finished work is finally varnished with the best copal carriage varnish.

In most cases oil painting intended for mural decoration has been executed on canvas, to be afterwards attached to the wall. This is the case more especially in France, and also in America at the Boston public library and other places. The effort here is to get rid of the shiny effect of oil painting proper by eliminating as far as practicable the oil. As this however serves as the binding material of the pigments the procedure is a risky one. To suppress the oil and to secure a " matt " surface Mr E. A. Abbey employed at Boston and elsewhere, as a medium for painting with ordinary oil colours, wax dissolved in spike oil and turpentine. In France Puvis de Chavannes used some preparation to secure a matt effect in his fine decorative oil painting on canvas.

§ 40. *Tempera Painting on Walls.*—This is a very ancient and widely diffused technique, but the processes of it do not differ in principle from those of panel painting in the same method. It is accordingly dealt with under tempera painting in general (§ 43).

§ 41. *Encaustic Painting on Walls.*—(See Schultze-Naumburg, *Die Technik der Malerei*, p. 122 seq.; Paillot de Montabert, *Traité complet de la peinture*, vol. ix.).

It has been already mentioned that wax is employed in modern mural painting in order to secure a matt surface. Many pictures have been carried out within the last century on walls in a regular wax medium that may or may not represent an ancient process. Hippolyte Flandrin executed his series of mural pictures in St Vincent de Paul and St Germain des Prés in Paris in a process worked out by Paillot de Montabert. Wax dissolved in turpentine or oil of spike is the main constituent of the medium with which the wall is saturated and the colours ground. Heat is used to drive the wax into the plaster.

A German recipe prepared by Andreas Müller in Düsseldorf has been used for mural paintings in the National Gallery, Berlin.

In this one part virgin wax is dissolved in two parts turpentine with a few drops of boiled linseed oil. The pigments are ground in boiled linseed oil with the addition of this medium. The plaster ground, well dried, is soaked with hot boiled linseed oil diluted with an equal quantity of turpentine. It is then grounded with several coats of oil paint for a priming and smoothed with pumice stone. The painting can be executed in a thin water colour technique or with a full body, and dries lighter than when wet and with a dead surface.

§ 42. *Encaustic Painting in general in Ancient and Modern Times.*—(See Cros and Henry, *L'Encoustique et les autres procédés de la peinture chez les anciens*, Paris, 1884; Flinders-Petrie, *Hawara*, &c., London, 1889; O. Donner v. Richter, *Über Technisches in die Malerei der Alten*, Munich, 1885; Berger, *Beiträge zur Entwickelungs-Geschichte der Maltechnik*, ii. 185 seq.; Munich, 1904).

Although in modern mural painting wax is employed to secure a matt surface, in ancient times it appears to have been valued rather from the depth and intensity it lent to colours when it was polished. It there represented an attempt to secure the same force and pictorial quality which in modern times are gained by the use of the oil medium. We are told of it by the ancients that it was a slow and troublesome process, and the name of it, meaning " burning in," shows that the inconvenience of á heating apparatus was inseparable from it; yet it seems at the same time to have been a generally accepted technique, and Greek writers from Anacreon to Procopius treat " wax " as the standard material for the painter. Nay more, hardly a day now passes without every one of us bearing testimony in the words he uses to the importance of the technique in antiquity. The *Etymologicum magnum* of the 12th century makes the process stand for painting generally (ἐγκαυμίνη-ἐζωγραφημένη), and the name " encaustic " came to be applied not only to painting but also to sumptuous calligraphy. Then it was applied to writing in general, and the name still survives in the Italian *inchiostro* and our own familiar " ink " (Eastlake, *Materials*, i. 151).

The technique of ancient encaustic has given rise to much discussion which till recently was carried on chiefly on a literary basis. Fresh material has been contributed by the discovery, in the eighties of the 19th century, in Egypt of a series of portraits on mummy cases, executed for the most part in a wax process, and dating probably from the first two or three centuries A.D. Previous to this discovery there was little material of a monumental kind, though what appears to be the painting apparatus of a Gallo-Roman artist in encaustic was found in 1847 at St Médard-des-Prés in La Vendée, and has been often figured. It should be stated at the outset that the modern process of dissolving wax in turpentine or an essential oil like oil of spike was not known to the ancients, who however knew how to mix resinous substances with it, as in the case of ship-painting (Pliny xi. 16; Dioscorides i. 98). They also saponified wax by boiling it with potash so as to form what was called " Punic wax " (Pliny xxi. 84 seq.), and this emulsion may be reduced with water, and at the same time combines with oil and with size, gum, egg and other temperas. Wax, Pliny says, may be coloured and used for painting—*ad edendas similitudines* (loc. cit.); but as the name " encaustic " implies, and as we gather from another of Pliny's phrases, *ceris pingere ac picturam inurere* (xxxv. 122), heat was an essential part of the process. Hence the material must have been employed as a rule in a more or less solid form and liquefied each time for use, and not in the form of a diluted solution or emulsion which could be made serviceable cold. It is true that Punic wax mixed with a little oil is prescribed by Vitruvius (vii. 9, 3) as a solution for covering and locking up from the air a coat of the changeable pigment vermilion laid on a wall (see § 35), but the solution is used hot and driven in by application of a heating apparatus.

The accounts of the technique furnished to us by Pliny can be brought into connexion with the actual remains, and Berger and others have succeeded fairly well in imitating these by processes evolved from the ancient notices. It is unfortunate that the most important passage of Pliny (xxxv. 149) appears corrupt. It runs in the received text as follows: *Encausto pingendi duo fuere antiquitus genera, cera et in ebore cestro, id est*

vericulo, donec classes pingi coepere. Hoc tertium accessit resolutis igni ceris penicillo utendi, quae pictura navibus nec sole nec sale ventive corrumpitur. Here three kinds of encaustic painting are mentioned, two old and one new (the comparative chronology of the processes need not come into question), and in the two last cases the distinction is that between two instruments of painting, the *cestrum* and the *penicillus* or brush. It is natural to suggest that instead of the word *cera*, which, as wax is the material common to all encaustic processes, need not have been introduced and on manuscript authority may be suspected, some word for a third instrument of painting should be restored. Berger, with some philological likelihood, conjectures the word *cauterio*, which means properly a "branding-iron," but which he believes to be a sort of hollowed spatula or spoon with a large and a small end by which melted waxes of different colours might be taken up, laid on a ground, such as a wooden panel, and manipulated in a soft state as pictorial effect required. Instruments of the kind were found in the Gallo-Roman tomb in La Vendée. The second kind of painting with the *cestrum* or *vericulum* was on ivory and must have been on a minute scale. The "cestrum" was certainly a tool of corresponding size, and some have seen in it a sort of point or graver, such as that with which the incised outlines were made on the figured ivory plaques in the Kertch room at St Petersburg (see below); others a small lancet-shaped spatula like the tools that sculptors employ for working on plaster. The brush, with which melted waxes could be laid on in washes, as was the case on ships, needs no explanation.

An examination of the portraits from the mummy cases (see fig. 35) makes it quite clear that the brush was used with coloured melted waxes to paint in, in sketchy fashion, the draperies and possibly to underpaint the flesh and hair, while the flesh was executed in a more *pastos* style, with waxes in a soft condition laid on and manipulated with some spatula-like instrument, which we may if we like call " cauterium " or " cestrum." The marks of such a tool are on several of the heads unmistakably in evidence, and may be seen on specimens in the London National Gallery. There is a difference of opinion however as to the constitution of the wax. Donner von Richter holds that the wax was " Punic," *i.e.* a kind of emulsion, and was blended with oil and resinous balsams so as to be transformed into a soft paste which could be manipulated cold with the spatula. Heat for " burning in " (*picturam inurere*) he thinks was afterwards applied, with the effect of slightly fusing and blending the coloured waxes that had been in this way worked into a picture. Berger, on the other hand, believes that the coloured wax pastes were manipulated hot with the " cauterium," which would be maintained in a heated condition, and that there was no subsequent process of " burning in." Flinders Petrie is of opinion that, even in the

Fig. 35.—Mummy of Artemidorus with painted portrait, inscribed " O Artemidorus, Farewell." About A.D. 200 (Brit. Mus.).

(From a photograph by W. A. Mansell & Co.)

case of the washes laid on with the brush, pure melted wax was employed and not a compound or emulsion, such as is generally assumed. Berger believes in a mixture of wax, oil and resin.

It is interesting to note that the distinguished modern painter, Arnold Böcklin, executed his picture of "Sappho" in coloured pastes composed of copal resin, turpentine and wax, manipulated with a curved spatula, and that he applied heat to fuse slightly the impasto. He believed he obtained in this way a brilliancy not to be compassed with oils.

The nature of the "cestron" technique on ivory is not known. The only existing artistic designs in ivory are executed by engraved lines, and these are sometimes filled in with coloured pastes. Exquisite work in this style exists in the Hermitage at St Petersburg, and there are examples in other museums, but this can hardly be termed encaustic painting. A better idea of the laboriously executed miniature portraits of which Pliny tells us can be gained from the small medallion portraits modelled in coloured wax that were common at the Renaissance period and are still executed to-day. In these however the smaller details are put in with the brush and pigment.

It is known from the evidence of the Erechtheum inscription that the encaustic process was employed for the painting of ornamental patterns on architectural features of marble buildings, but there is still considerable doubt as to the technique employed in such forms of decorative painting as the colouring of the white plaster that covered the surfaces of stonework on monumental buildings in inferior materials. Polychrome ornament on terracotta for architectural embellishment may have been fixed by the glaze as in ordinary vase painting, but Pliny says that Agrippa *figulinum opus encausto pinxit* in his Thermae. (xxxvi. 189). The technique of the polychrome lecuthi and of the polychrome terra-cotta statuary is not certain.

The later history of wax painting after the fall of the Western Empire is of interest in connexion with the evolution of the painter's technique as a whole. Its possible relation to oil painting will be noticed later on. Here it is enough to note that the so-called *Lucca MS.* of the 8th century mentions the mingling of wax with colours, and the Byzantine *Mount Athos Handbook*, recording probably the practice of the 11th century, gives a recipe for an emulsion of partly saponified wax with size as a painting medium. A recipe of the 15th century quoted by Mrs Merrifield from the MSS. of Le Begue gives a similar composition that can be thinned with water and used to temper all sorts of colours.

§ 43. *Tempera Painting.* [Cennino's *Trattato*, in the English edition with terminal essays by Mrs Herringham (London, 1899), is the best work to consult on the subject. The Society of Painters in Tempera published in 1907 a volume of *Papers* on the subject. F. Lloyd's *Practical Guide to Scene Painting and Painting in Distemper* (London, 1879), is chiefly about the painting of theatrical scenery, and this subject is also dealt with in articles by William Telbin in the *Magazine of Art* (1889), pp. 92, 195.]

The binding substances used in the tempera processes may be classed as follows: (1) Size, preferably that made from boiling down cuttings of parchment. Fish-glue, gum, especially gum tragacanth and gum arabic (the Senegal gum of commerce); glycerin, honey, milk, wine, beer, &c. (2) Eggs, in the form of (i) the yolk alone, (ii) the white alone, (iii) the whole contents of the egg beaten up, (iv) the same with the addition of the milk or sap of young shoots of the fig-tree, (v) the contents of the egg with the addition of about the same quantity of vinegar [(iv) was used in the south, (v) north of the Alps]. (3) Emulsions, in which wax or oil is mingled with substances which bring about the possibility of diluting the mixture with water. Thus oil can be made to unite mechanically (not chemically) with water by the interposition either of gum or of the yolk of egg.

Of these materials it may be noted that a size or gum tempera is always soluble in water, and is moreover always of a rather thin consistency. The latter applies also to white of egg. On the other hand the yolk of an egg makes a medium of greater body, and modern artists, especially in Germany, have painted in it with a full impasto. The yolk of egg or the whole egg slightly beaten up may be used to temper powdered pigments without any dilution by means of water, and the stiffest body can in this way be obtained. The medieval artists seem however always to have painted with egg thinly, diluting the yolk with about an equal quantity of water. Their panels show this, and we can argue the same from the number of successive coats of paint prescribed by Cennino and other writers. The former (ch. 165) mentions seven or eight or ten coats of colours tempered with yolk alone, that must have been well thinned with water. This point will be returned to later on. The yolk of egg is really itself an emulsion as it contains about 30% of oil or fatty matter, though in its fluid state it combines readily with water. "Egg yolk," writes Professor Church (*Chemistry*, p. 74), "must be regarded as essentially an oil medium. As it dries the oil hardens," and ultimately becomes a substance not unlike leather that is quite impervious to moisture. Hence while size tempera when dry yields to water egg tempera will resist it. Sir William Richmond gave a proof of this in evidence before a committee of the House of Lords in November 1906, describing how he had exposed a piece of plaster painted with yolk of egg medium to all weathers for six months on the roof of a church and found it at the end perfectly intact. As to the milk of young fig-shoots, it is interesting to know from Principal Laurie ("Pigments and Vehicles of the Old Masters," in *Journal of the Society of Arts*, Jan. 15, 1892, p. 172) that "fig-tree belongs to the same family as the india-rubber tree, and its juice contains caoutchouc." He says, "doubtless the mixture of albumen and caoutchouc would make a very tough and protective medium."

With regard to the historical use of these different media, the medieval Italians used almost exclusively the yolk of egg medium, and this is also the favourite tempera of the moderns. In fact in Italy the word "tempera," as used by Vasari and other writers, generally means the egg medium. On the other hand size or gum was more common north of the Alps. It is in most cases very difficult to decide what temperas were in vogue in different regions and at the various epochs of the art, and the following must not be taken for more than an approximate statement of the facts. As far as it is known, the binding material in ancient Egypt was for the most part size, while Greek influence from about 600 B.C. onwards may have led to the use of wax emulsion (Punic wax). For paintings on mummy cases, and on papyrus scrolls, the medium may have been size or gum. Professor Flinders Petrie says it was acacia gum. The wall paintings of ancient Mesopotamia as well as those of India and the farther East generally were all in tempera, and it is noteworthy that recipes and technical practices of the East and of the West seem to be curiously alike. The exact media used are doubtful. The same doubt exists with regard to the exact processes of wall and panel painting in tempera in ancient Greece and Italy, in the East, in Byzantine times, and in the early middle ages both north and south of the Alps. The materials and processes mentioned by Pliny or in the various technical handbooks are on the whole clearly established, but it is very difficult to say in particular cases what was the actual technique employed. Any certainty in this matter must be based on the results not only of superficial examination but of analysis, and the very small quantities of the materials that can be placed at the disposal of the chemist make it often impossible to arrive at a satisfactory diagnosis.

A story in Pliny (xxxv. 102) shows that the Greek panel painters, when not "encaustae," used a water tempera, but whether size or egg was its main constituent we do not know. Apelles is said to have covered his finished panels with a thin coat of what Pliny calls "atramentum," which may have been a white of egg varnish, for spirit varnishes were not known in antiquity (Berger i. and ii. 183), and the Greeks do not seem to have used drying oils nor varnishes made with these. Byzantine panel painting, according to the *Mount Athos Handbook*, was executed as a rule in an egg tempera (Berger iii. 75), and this technique was followed later on in Italy. For Greek and Etruscan (Italian) wall-paintings of the pagan period; for late Roman wall-paintings north of the Alps, and for Romanesque and Gothic wall-paintings, we have to choose amongst the theories of size or egg tempera, wax tempera (emulsion), and the lime painting in "fresco secco" described by Theophilus. When we come to the panel painting from the 12th to the 15th century we are on surer ground. For the north we have the technical directions of Theophilus, for the south those of Cennino. Theophilus (i. ch. xxvii.) prescribes a tempera of gum from the cherry tree, and, with some pigments, white of egg. The finished panel was to be covered with an oil varnish (vernition). Cennino prescribes a tempera of the yolk of egg alone, half and half with the pigments, which have been finely ground in water and are very liquid, so that there might be in the ultimate compound about as much water as egg. A tempera of the whole egg with the milk of fig-shoots he recommends, not for panels, but for retouching fresco-work on the wall when it is dry. Tempera panels painted with egg yolk are, like the gum tempera panels of Theophilus, to be varnished with *vernice liquida* (oil varnish). In these media were executed all the fine tempera panels of the early Italian and early German schools of the 15th century, and these represent a limited, but within its bounds a very perfect and interesting, form of the painter's art.

A word or two may be said here about the various subsidiary processes connected with 14th and 15th century panel painting, which are of great interest as showing the conscientious, and indeed devotional spirit in which the operations were carried out. At the outset of his *Trattato* Cennino gives a list of the processes the panel painter has to go through, and in subsequent chapters he describes minutely each of these. The artist must "know how to grind colours, to use glue, to fasten the linen on the panel, to prime with gesso, to scrape and smooth the gesso, to make reliefs in gesso, to put on bole, to gild, to burnish, to mix temperas, to lay on grounding colours, to transfer by pouncing through pricked lines, to sharpen lines with the stylus, to indent with little patterns, to carve, to colour, to ornament the panel, and finally to varnish it." The preliminary operations, before the artificer actually begins to "colour" or paint, will take him six years to learn, and it requires with Cennino half a hundred chapters to describe them. The wooden panel is carefully compacted and linen is glued down over its face, and over this is laid, in many successive coats, a gesso ground of slaked plaster of Paris mixed with size, with which composition raised ornaments, such as the nimbi of saints, &c., can be modelled. Both these and the flat parts of the panel are scraped and smoothed till they are like ivory. The design of the picture is then drawn out on the panel, and the outlines sharpened up with the utmost precision. The gilding of the background and of the carved woodwork in which the panel is set now follows. Armenian bole, ground finely with white of egg diluted with water, is spread over the gesso and carefully burnished as a ground for water gilding with white of egg. The gold is then burnished till it appears almost dark (in the shadow) from its own refulgence. The delicate indented patterns which are so charming on the gilded grounds of the painted panels on East Anglian screens, such as that at Southwold, are stamped with little punches, and Cennino says this is one of the most beautiful parts of the art. In the actual painting, which is on the non-gilded part of the panel, the utmost attention is paid to the ornamentation of brocaded draperies, in which gold is used as a ground and is made to show in parts, while glazes of pigment mixed with drying oil are also used. Directions for painting the flesh, which is to be done after the draperies and background, are precise. There is an under-painting in a monochrome of terra verte and white, and over this in successive coats of great thinness the flesh-tints are spread, every tint being laid in its right position on the face, the darkest flesh-tint being shaded down to the terra verte and softened off in a tender *sfumato* manner. Many coats are superimposed, but the green ground is still to remain slightly visible. At the last the lightest flesh-tint is used to obtain the reliefs and the high lights are touched in in white. The outlines are sharpened up with red mixed with black. The varnishing process should be delayed for at least a year, and the varnish, which was evidently thick, is to be spread by the fingers over the painted surfaces, care being taken not to let the varnish go over the gold ground. This should be done if possible in the sun, but Cennino says that if the varnish be boiled it will dry without being placed in the sun.

The process thus described is not what we should call, in the modern sense, painting, for the precision and conventionality of the work and the great importance given to subsidiary details are quite opposed to the spirit of the art since the 16th century. Nevertheless, the naïve simplicity of the design and the exquisite delicacy of the finish have an unfailing charm. We feel, as Cennino says, that the artist has loved and delighted in his work, and regarded his patient manipulation as a religious act. A modern artist in tempera specially praises the old work for its "breadth, transparency and purity of colour," qualities "owing to the gradual

bringing forward of the picture from a simple outline of extreme beauty." "This outline is never lost; its beautifully opposed and harmonising lines and masses are retained to the end, even strengthened and accentuated, giving great distinctness at a distance, even when not actually visible. A perfectly modulated monochrome of light and shade fills the outline, apparent through the overlaid glory of colour, over which again is thrown a veil of atmosphere, a refulgence of light, a suggestion of palpitating space" (Mrs Herringham's *Cennino*, p. 218). A difficulty in the technique is the rapid drying of the medium, that prevents the fusing of the colours together in the impasto, which is possible in oil painting. Woltmann (*History of Painting*, Eng. trans. i. 406) thought that in the north honey was mixed with the white of egg or size to prevent too rapid drying, and he wrote, "this method rendered possible a liquid and softly gradated handling, and though the Italian variety of tempera allowed greater depth in the shadows, the northern gave on the whole greater brightness." In Italy, owing to the rapid drying of the egg-yolk, modelling was often secured by hatching, which is not so pleasing in its effect as the other method of superimposing thin coats of paint one over the other till the proper effect of shading is secured. One notable quality of tempera is its transparency, which is referred to by Cennino when he says that the original under-painting of terra verte is never to be wholly obliterated.

The well-known group of the "Three Graces," from Botticelli's large panel of the "Allegory of Spring," at Florence, gives the quality of tempera painting very aptly (see fig. 36, Plate X.). There is a Society of Painters in Tempera in London, and some artists are enthusiastic in their admiration of the process for its purity, sincerity and permanence.

Under the heading "tempera" should be noticed another style of painting with a water-medium that is executed as a rule on a large scale and in a comparatively slight fashion. Painting for the purposes of temporary decoration on canvas or wood, so much used in the Italian cities of the Renaissance period, is of this kind. Large cartoons in colour for mural pictures or tapestry, of which Raphael's cartoons are the most famous examples, are other examples; while in modern times the technique is chiefly employed in theatrical scene painting. The pigments are tempered with size or gum, and body is given to them by whitening, pipe-clay or similar substance. Work executed in this medium dries much lighter than when it is put on, and to execute it effectively, as in the case of stage scenery, requires much skill and practice. "In the study of the art of distemper painting a source of considerable embarrassment to the inexperienced eye is that the colours when wet present such a different appearance to what they do when dry." So writes F. Lloyds, but W. Telbin, though he recognises this difficulty, extols the process. "A splendid material distemper! For atmosphere unequalled, and for strength as powerful as oil, in half an hour you can do with it that which in water or oil would take one or two days!" The English word "distemper" and the French "gouache" are commonly applied to this style of broad summary painting in body-colour. "Distemper" to English ears suggests house-decoration, "tempera" the work of the artist.

§ 44. *Oil Painting.*—(See Eastlake, *Materials for a History of Oil Painting* (London, 1847); Mérimée, *De la peinture à l'huile* (Paris, 1830); Berger, *Beiträge zur Entwicklungs-Geschichte der Maltechnik*, esp. iii. 221 sqq., and iv. (Munich, 1897), &c.; Dalbon, *Les Origines de la peinture à l'huile* (Paris, 1904); Ludwig, *Über die Grundsätze der Oelmalerei* (Leipzig, 1876); Lessing, *Über das Alter der Oelmalerei*, 1774.)

Oil painting is an art rather of the north than of the south and east, for its, development was undoubtedly furthered by the demand for moisture-resisting media in comparatively damp climates, and, moreover, the drying oils on which the technique depends were but sparingly prepared in lands where olive oil, which does not dry, was a staple product.

Certain vegetable oils dry naturally in the air by a process of oxydization, and this drying or hardening is not accompanied by any considerable shrinking, nor by any change of colour; so that oil and substances mixed with it do not alter in volume nor in appearance as a consequence of the drying process. There may be a slow subsequent alteration in the direction of darkening or becoming more yellow; but this is another matter. Among these oils the most important is linseed oil extracted from the seeds of the flax plant, poppy oil from the seeds of the opium poppy, and nut oil from the kernels of the common walnut. With these oils, generally linseed, ordinary tube colours used by painters in oil are prepared, and oil varnishes, also used by artists, are made by dissolving in them certain resins. Their natural drying qualities can be greatly aided by subjecting them to heat, and also by mingling with them chemical substances known as "dryers," of which certain salts of lead and zinc are the most familiar. How far back in antiquity such oils and their properties were known is doubtful. Certain varnishes are used in Egypt on mummy cases of the New Empire and on other surfaces, and, though some of these are soluble in water, others resist it, and may be made with drying oils or essential oils, though the art of distilling these last cannot be traced back in Egypt earlier than the Roman imperial period. (See Berthelot, *La Chimie au moyen âge*, i. 138 (Paris, 1893). When Pliny tells us (xiv. 123) that all resins are soluble in oil, we might think he was contemplating a varnish of the modern kind. Elsewhere, however (xxiv. 34), he prescribes such a solution as a sort of emollient ointment for wounds, so it is clear that the oil he has in view is non-drying olive oil that would not make a varnish. In two passages of his *Natural History* (xv. 24-32, xxiii. 79-96) Pliny discourses at length on various oils, but does not refer to their drying properties. There is really no direct evidence of the use among the Greeks and Romans of drying oils and oil varnishes, though a recent writer (Cremer, *Untersuchungen über den Beginn der Oelmalerei*, Düss., 1899) has searched for it with desperate eagerness. The chief purpose of painting for which such materials would have been in demand is the painting of ships, and this we know was carried out in the equally waterproof medium of wax, with which resin or pitch was commingled by heat. The earliest mention of the use of a drying oil in a process connected with painting is in the medical writer Aetius, of the beginning of the 6th century A.D., who says that nut oil dries and forms a protective varnish over gilding or encaustic painting. From this time onwards the use of drying oils and varnishes in painting processes is well established. The *Lucca* MS. of the 8th or 9th century A.D. gives a receipe for a transparent varnish composed of linseed oil and resin. In the *Mount Athos Handbook* "peseri," or boiled linseed oil, appears in common use, and with resin is made into a varnish. In the same treatise also we find a clear description of oil painting in the modern sense; but since the dates of the various portions of the *Handbook* are uncertain, we may refer rather to Theophilus (about A.D. 1100), who indicates the same process with equal clearness. The passages in Theophilus (i. chs. xx. and xxvi.-xxviii.) are of the first importance for the history of oil painting. He directs the artificer to take the colours he wishes to apply, to grind them carefully without water in oil of linseed prepared as he describes in ch. xx., and to paint therewith flesh and drapery, beasts or birds or foliage, just as he pleases. All kinds of pigments can be ground in the oil and used on wooden panels, for *the work must be put out in the sun to dry*. It is noteworthy that Theophilus (ch. xxvii.) seems to confine this method of painting to movable works (on panel, *in opere ligneo*, in his *tantum rebus quae sole siccari possunt*) that can be carried out into the sun, but in ch. xxv. of the more or less contemporary third book of Heraclius (Vienna *Quellenschriften*, No. iv.) oil-paint may be dried either in the sun or by artificial heat. Heraclius, moreover, knows how to mix dryers (oxide of lead) with his oil, a device with which Theophilus is not acquainted. Hence to the latter the defect of the medium was its slow drying, and Theophilus recommends as a quicker process the gum tempera already described. In any case, whether the painting be in oil or tempera, the finished panel must be varnished in the sun with " vernition " (ch. xxi.), a varnish compounded by heat of linseed oil and a gum, which is probably sandarac resin. The *Mount Athos Handbook*, § 53, describes practically the same technique, but indicates it as specially used for flesh, the inference being that the draperies were painted in tempera or with wax. It is worth noting that the well-known "black Madonnas," common in Italy as well as in the lands of the Greek Church, may be thus explained. They are Byzantine icons in which the flesh has been painted in oil and the draperies in another technique. The oil has darkened with age, while the tempera parts have remained in contrast comparatively fresh. Some of them are probably the earliest oil paintings extant.

Oil painting accordingly, though in an unsatisfactory form, is established at least as early as A.D. 1100. What had been its previous history? Here it is necessary to take note of the interesting suggestion of Berger, that it was gradually evolved in the early Christian centuries from the then declining encaustic technique of classical times. We learn from Dioscorides, who dates rather later than the time of Augustus, that resin was mixed with wax for the painting of ships, and when drying oils came into use they would make with wax and resin a medium requiring less heat to make it fluid than wax alone, and one therefore more convenient for the brush-form of encaustic. Berger suspects the presence of such a medium in some of the mummy-case portraits, and points for confirmation to the chemical analysis of some pigments found in the grave of a painter at Herne St Hubert in Belgium of about the time of Constantine the Great (i. and ii. 230 seq.). One part wax with two to three parts drying (nut) oil he finds by experiment a serviceable medium. Out of this changing wax-technique he thinks there proceeded the use of drying oils and resins as media in independence of wax. If we hesitate in the meantime to regard this as more than a hypothesis, it is yet worthy of attention, for any hypothesis that suggests a plausible connexion between phenomena the origin and relations of which are so obscure deserves a friendly reception.

The *Trattato* of Cennino Cennini represents two or three centuries of advance on the *Schedula* of Theophilus, and about contemporary with it is the so-called Strassburg MS., which gives a view of German practice just as the *Trattato* does of Italian. This MS., attention to which was first called by Eastlake (*Materials*, I. 126 seq.), contains a remarkable recipe for preparing "oil for the colours:" Linseed or hempseed or old nut oil is to be boiled with certain dryers, of which white copperas (sulphate of zinc) is one. This, when bleached in the sun, "will acquire a thick consistence, and also become as transparent as a fine crystal. And this oil dries very fast, and makes all colours beautifully clear and glossy besides. All painters are not acquainted with it: from its excellence it is called *oleum preciosum*, since half an ounce is well worth a shilling, and with this oil all colours are to be ground and tempered," while as a final process a few drops of varnish are to be added. The MS. probably dates rather before than after 1400.

Cennino's treatise, written a little later, gives avowedly the recipes and processes traditional in the school of Giotto throughout the 14th century. He begins his account of oil painting with the remark that it was an art much practised by the " Germans," thus bearing out what was said at the commencement of this section. He proceeds (chs. 90-94) to describe an oil technique for walls and for panels that sounds quite effective and modern. Linseed oil is to be bleached in the sun and mixed with liquid varnish in the proportion of an ounce of varnish to a pound of oil, and in this medium all colours are to be ground. " When you would paint a drapery with the three gradations," Cennino proceeds, " divide the tints and place them each in its position with your brush of squirrel hair, fusing one colour with another so that the pigments are thickly laid. Then wait certain days, come again and see how the paint covers, and repaint where needful. And in this way paint flesh or anything you please, and likewise mountains, trees and anything else." In other chapters Cennino recommends certain portions of a painting in tempera to be put in in oil, and nowhere does he give a hint that the work in oil gave any trouble through its unwillingness to dry. His medium appears, however, to have been thick, and perhaps somewhat viscous (ch. 92). This combination of oil paint and tempera on the same piece is a matter, as we shall presently see, of some significance.

In the *De re aedificatoria* of L. B. Alberti (written about 1450), vi. 9, there is a mention of " a new discovery of laying on colours with oil of linseed so that they resist for ever all injuries from weather and climate," which may have some reference to so-called " German " practice.

The next Italian writer who says anything to the purpose is

Filarete, who wrote a long treatise on architecture and the arts of design about 1464. It is published in the Vienna *Quellenschriften*, neue Folge, No. III. Like Cennino, Filarete (*loc. cit.* p. 41) speaks of oil painting as specially practised in " Germany," and says it is a fine art when anyone knows how to compass it. The medium is oil of linseed. " But is not this very thick?" he imagines some one objecting. " Yes, but there is a way of thinning it; I do not quite know how; but it will be stood out in a vessel and clarify itself. I understand however that there is a quicker way of managing this—but let this pass, and let us go on to the method of painting." Filarete's evident uncertainty about a process, which may be that of the Strassburg MS. for producing *oleum preciosum*, and his reference to " Germany," inclines us to look elsewhere than to Italy for knowledge about the oil technique. As a 'fact the evidence of the recipe books is borne out remarkably by that of other records which show that a great deal of oil painting of one kind or another went on in northern lands from the 13th century onwards. These records are partly in the form of accounts, showing large quantities of oil and resins furnished for the use of painters engaged in extensive works of decoration; and partly in the form of contracts for executing pictures " in good oil colours." It is true that oil might be merely employed in mordants for gilding or in varnishes, and for oil painting merely in house-decorator fashion over wood, or for colouring statues and reliefs in stone; nevertheless, with a use of proper critical methods, it has been possible for M. Dalbon and others to establish incontestably the employment in artistic wall and panel-painting of drying oils and varnishes before the 15th century, both north and, to a lesser extent, south of the Alps. These passages have been too often quoted to be cited here. (See Eastlake, *Materials*, p. 46 seq.; Berger, *Beiträge* iii. 206 seq., &c.) The earliest of the accounts, an English one, is dated 1239: " The king (Henry III.) to his treasurer and chamberlains. Pay from our treasury to Odo the goldsmith and Edward his son one hundred and seventeen shillings and tenpence for oil, sandarac resin, and colours bought, and for pictures executed in the Queen's Chamber at Westminster." Another, about 1275 (*temp.* Edward I.) runs: " To Robert King, for one cartload of charcoal for drying the painting in the King's Chamber, IIIs VIIId." In Flanders in 1304 there is an account (Dalbon, p. 43): " *Pour 10 los d'oile acatte pour faire destrempe as couleurs*," in 1373-1374 one for *XIII libvres d'olle de linnis à faire couleurs* " (p. 45). This was for the use of a certain painter Loys, who executed mural compositions of which some of the subjects are recorded. In the matter of contracts, Dalbon (p. 52) prints one of 1320 prescribing figure and landscape subjects, to be executed " *en la meilleur manière que il pourront estre faites en painture*," and concluding, " *et seront toutes ces choses faites à huille*," and he points convincingly to such wording as a proof that the work here under consideration must be regarded as artistic figure-painting and not mere house decoration. Lastly, just before 1400, the painter Jehan Malouel receives in 1399 oil with colours for " *la peinture de plusieurs tables et tableaux d'autel*," for the Carthusian convent of Champenol near Dijon, which proves the use of oil for panel as well as for mural painting.

The further question about the survival of actual remains of work of the class just noticed is a very difficult one. There seems no reason why all this mural and panel work in oil of the 14th century should have perished, unless the medium was faulty, and, as is natural, many attempts have been made to identify extant examples as representing these early phases of the oil technique. Mural work we need not perhaps expect to find, for we know from the later experience of the Italians of the 16th century that it was difficult even then to find a safe method for oil painting on plaster. With panels preservation would be more likely, and it is always possible that some datable work of the kind may be identified that will carry the monumental history of oil painting back into the 14th century. An exhibition of early English painted panels was held in 1896 in the rooms of the Society of Antiquaries of London, and some good judges believed at the time that certain 14th-century panels from St Michael at 'Plea, Norwich, were in oil, but this cannot be regarded as established.

If such then be the early history of oil painting, what attitude are we to adopt in face of the famous statement by Vasari that the technique was the invention of the Flemish painter Van Eyck in the year 1410? The statement was first made in the 21st chapter of Vasari's Introduction to his *Lives of the Artists* (1550), and runs as follows: " *Fu una bellissima inventione, ed un gran' commodità all' arte della pittura, il trovare il colorito a olio. Di che fu primo inventore in Fiandra Giovanni da Bruggia* (Jan van Eyck). In the life of Antonello da Messina, in the same edition, Vasari dresses up the bare fact he here relates, and gives it the personal anecdotal turn that accords with his literary methods. Here the " invention " follows on the incident of the splitting of a tempera panel varnished in oil, that according to traditional practice Van Eyck had put out in the sun to dry. This artist then turned his attention to devising some means for avoiding such mischances for the future, and, in Vasari's words, " being not less dissatisfied with the varnish than with the process of tempera painting, he began to devise means for preparing a kind of varnish which should dry in the shade, so as to avoid having to place his pictures in the sun. Having made experiments with many things both pure and mixed together, he at last found that linseed and nut oil, among the many which he had tested, were more drying than all the rest. These, therefore, boiled with other mixtures of his, made him the varnish which he had long desired." This varnish Vasari goes on to say he mixed with the colours and found that it " lit up the colours so powerfully that it gave a gloss of itself," without any after-coat of varnish.

Such is the famous passage in Vasari that has probably given rise to more controversy than any similar statement in the literature of the arts. The question is, in what did the " invention " of the Van Eycks, Hubert and Jan his younger brother, consist? and the first answer that would occur to anyone knowing alike the earlier history of the oil medium and Vasari's anecdotal predilections is the answer " There was no invention at all." The drying properties of linseed and nut oil and the way to increase these had long been known, as had also the preparation of sandarac oil-varnish, as well as a colourless (spirit?) varnish of which there is mention in accounts prior to the 15th century (Dalbon, p. 93). The mixing of varnish with oil for a medium was also known, and indeed the *oleum preciosum* may be the real " invention " of which Alberti and Filarete had only vaguely heard, and of which the Van Eycks later on received the credit. The epitaphs for the tombs of the two Van Eycks make no mention of such a feat as Vasari ascribes to them, and it is quite open to anyone to take up the position that it was no improvement in technique that brought to the Van Eycks their fame in connexion with oil painting, but rather an artistic improvement that consisted in using a traditional process to execute pictures which in design, finish, beauty and glow of colour far surpassed every-thing previously produced in the northern schools. Pliny writes of the works of a Greek painter of about 400 B.C. that they were the first that had the power " to rivet the gaze of the spectator," and in like manner we may say of the " Adoration of the Lamb " by the Van Eycks, the titular firstfruits of the oil painter's technique, that it impressed the world of its time so mightily through its artistic power and beauty as to elevate to a sort of mystic importance the very method in which the paints were mixed. There is much force in this view, but at the same time it is impossible to deny to the Van Eycks the credit of technical improvements. For one thing, an artist who has an exceptional feeling for colour, texture and delicacy of finish will certainly pay special attention to his technical media; for another, the Van Eycks had a reputation long before Vasari's time for researches into these media. In 1456, fifteen years after the death of the younger brother, Bartolommeo Facio, of Spezzia, wrote a tract *De viris illustribus* in which he speaks of a certain " Joannus Gallicus," who can be identified as Jan van Eyck, as specially " learned in those arts which contributed to the making of a picture, and was on that account credited with the discovery of many things in the properties of colours, which he had learned from ancient traditions recorded by Pliny and other writers." Filarete (c. 1464) also knew of the repute of Jan van Eyck in connexion with the oil technique. Hence we may credit the Van Eycks with certain technical improvements on traditional practices and preparations in the oil technique, though these can hardly be termed "inventions," while their artistic achievement was great enough to force into prominence whatever in the technical department they had accomplished.

Another and a more important question remains behind: What was, in fact, the practice in the matter of oil painting in vogue before the Van Eycks, altered or at any rate perfected by them and their successors, and in general use up to the time of Vasari; and how was it related to the older more widely diffused painting " a tempera "?

It is indisputable that the oil painting of the Van Eycks and the early Flemish school, together with that of the Florentines and Umbrians, and indeed of all the Italians up to Vasari's time, save the Venetians, Correggio, and some other north Italians, does not greatly differ in artistic effect, nor, as far as can be judged, in handling, from earlier or contemporary temperas. For example, at Venice in the 15th century, Crivelli paints always in tempera, Cima in oils, but the character of their surface is almost the same, and if anything the tempera is richer in effect than the oil. The contrary is no doubt the case with the tempera " Madonna with the Violet " in the Priests' Seminary at Cologne when compared with the somewhat later " Dombild," also by Stephan Lochner, which is believed to be painted in oils, but the two are still in technical character very nearly akin. The fact is that tempera panels were usually coated with an oil varnish, necessarily of a somewhat warm tint, and we could hardly expect to distinguish them from oil pictures painted in or covered by varnish, unless there were a difference in the handling of the pigments. The method of handling appears however to be on the whole the same, and there are many who believe that in all essentials it *is* the same. Tempera panels, as we have learned from Cennino, were not only varnished but in parts might be painted in oils (ch. 143), and it is one view of the technique of the early Flemings that it was only an over-painting in oils over a preparation in tempera. Berger is of the opinion that the process was something between the two, that is to say, that it was oil tempera, the medium being an emulsion of oil and water through the intermediary of a gum. Such a medium would, as he points out (*Beiträge*, iii. 247 seq.), combine the thinness and limpidity in manipulation characteristic of a water tempera with the property of drying hard and impervious to moisture. This is of course only a theory. Of far more weight is the suggestion made by Principal Laurie, of Edinburgh, who has carried on for years a series of careful experiments in the various pigments and media employed in oil painting. As one result of these experiments he has found that the ordinary drying oils and oil varnishes do not, as used to be assumed, " lock up " or completely cover and protect pigments so as to prevent the access of moisture and the gases of the atmosphere, but that this function is far more effectively performed by hard pine-balsams, such as Canada balsam, dissolved in an essential oil and so made into a varnish or painting medium. In pictures by Van Eyck Principal Laurie has detected what he believes to be the use of pigments of a notoriously fugitive character, and he is convinced that the most effectual medium for preserving these in the condition in which they have come down to us would be a natural pine-balsam, with probably a small proportion of drying oil; he suggests therefore that the introduction of these ingredients may be the real secret of the Van Eyck technique. There is as yet no proof that the Van Eycks really used such a medium, though it is a preparation possible at their time, and when thinned by a process of emulsification with egg. as Dr Laurie suggests, would be a serviceable one; but they and the other early oil painters certainly used a method, and in all probability media, that did not differ greatly as regards manipulation from those in vogue in tempera.

From the aesthetic point of view therefore we have to regard early oil painting as only another form of the older tempera,

expressing exactly the same artistic ideals and dominated by the same view of the relation of art to nature. To Vasari the artistic advantage of the oil medium was, first, its convenience, and, next, the depth and brilliancy it lent to the colours, which he says it " kindled," while at the same time it lent itself to a soft fusing of tints in manipulation, so that artists could give to their figures in this technique the greatest charm and beauty combined with a force that made them seem to stand out in relief from the panel. Such a description applies very justly to work like that of the Van Eycks in the " Adoration of the Lamb," or the later panels of Antonello da Messina, who, according to Vasari's often-repeated story, introduced the Flemish system of oil-painting into Venice. The description does not however apply to the freer, more sweeping, more passionate handling of the brush by the greatest of the Venetians such as Titian or Veronese, and still less to the oil painting of 17th-century masters like Rubens or Rembrandt or Velazquez. It is quite clear that whatever improvements in oil technique were due to the early Flemings, oil painting in the modern sense owes still more to the Venetians, who first taught the world the full artistic possibilities of the process. Giovanni Bellini, whose noble altarpiece in S. Pietro at Murano may be called, in a phrase once applied to another of his pictures, " the canon of Venetian art," is probably entitled to be called the father of modern oil painting. Beginning as a painter in tempera and adopting the new process about 1475, Bellini was able so far to master the new medium that he handed it on with all its possibilities indicated to Giorgione, Palma and Titian. That Venetian oil painting however, with all its brilliancy and freedom, was a child of the older tempera technique is shown by its characteristic method, which consisted in an under-painting in dead colour, over which were superimposed the transparent glazes that secured the characteristic Venetian richness of colouring. Now all the recent writers on the Van Eyck technique agree that, whatever were the exact media employed, the tempera tradition, and perhaps the tempera vehicles, were maintained for the underpainting. In the old tempera-panel technique of Cennino there was a monochrome underpainting in a greenish pigment, over which the flesh tints were spread in thin layers so as never completely to obliterate the ground. Such an underpainting in a few simple colours, black, white and red, was employed by Titian and others of the Venetians, and over it were laid the rich juicy transparent pigments, till " little by little he would have covered with real living flesh these first abstracts of his intention " (Boschini). There is some evidence that in many cases these underpaintings were in tempera, which would have the advantage of drying more quickly than under-paintings in oil, and Boschini (*Le Ricche minere della pittura veneziana*, 1674) expressly says that the blues in Venetian paintings, *e.g.* by Veronese, were painted often *a guazzo*. There was a reason, however, why the Venetians would alter the traditional practice of the Flemish forerunners. The latter were almost entirely panel painters, while the Venetians used canvas. Now certain media, like the hard pine-balsams which Dr Laurie thinks were the basis of the Van Eyck medium, are suitable for the immovable surfaces of a well-grounded panel, but would be liable to crack on canvas which is more or less yielding. Hence the tougher oil vehicles were in advanced Venetian painting exclusively employed.

This distinction between the thin transparent pigments and those of an opaque body, which is as old as oil painting in any form, becomes in the hands of Bellini and the later Venetians the fundamental principle of the technique. The full advantage of this thinness and transparency is gained by the use of the pigments in question as " glazes " over a previously laid solid impasto. This impasto may be modelled up in monochrome or in any desired tints chosen to work in with the colours of the superimposed glazes. Effects of colour of great depth and brilliancy may thus be obtained, and after the glaze has been floated over the surface a touch of the thumb, where the underpainting is loaded and lights are required, will so far thin it as to let the underlying colour show through and blend with the deeper tint of the glaze in the shadows. Thus in the noble Veronese in the London National Gallery, called the "Consecration of St Nicholas," the kneeling figure of the saint is robed in green with sleeves of golden orange. This latter colour is evidently carried through as underpainting over the whole draped portions of the figure, the green being then floated over and so manipulated that the golden tint shows through in parts and gives the high lights on the folds.

Again the relation of the two kinds of pigment may be reversed, and the full-bodied ones mixed with white may be struck into a previously laid transparent tint. The practice of painting into a wet glaze or rubbing is especially characteristic of the later Flemings, with Rubens at their head, and this again, though a polar opposite to that of the Venetians, is also derived from the earlier tempera, or modified tempera, techniques. The older tempera panels, when finished, were, as we have seen, covered with a coating of oil varnish generally of a warm golden hue, and in some parts they were, as Cennino tells us, glazed with transparent oil paint. Now Van Mander tells us in the introduction to his *Schilderboek* of 1604, verse 17, that the older Flemish and German oil painters, Van Eyck, Dürer and others, were accustomed, over a slightly painted monochrome of water-colour in which the drawing was carefully made out, to lay a thin coat of semi-transparent flesh tint in oil, through which the underpainting was still visible, and to use this as the ground for their subsequent operations. In the fully matured practice of Rubens this thin glaze became a complete painting of the shadows in rubbings of deep rich transparent oily pigment, into which the half-tones and the lights were painted while it was still wet. Descamps, in his *Vie des peintres flamands* (Paris, 1753),describes Rubens's method of laying in his shadows without any use of white, which he called the poison of this part of the picture, and then painting into them with solid pigment to secure modelling by touches laid boldly side by side, and afterwards tenderly fused by the brush. Over this preparation the artist would return with the few decided strokes which are the distinctive signs-manual of the great master. The characteristic advantages of this method of work are, first, breadth, and second, speed. The under tint, often of a rich soft umber or brown, being spread equally over the canvas makes its presence felt throughout, although all sorts of colours and textures may be painted into it. Hence the whole preserves a unity of effect that is highly pictorial. Further, as the whole beauty of the work depends on the skill of hand by which the solid pigment is partly sunk into the glaze at the shadow side, while it comes out drier and stronger in the lights, and as this must be done rightly at once or not at all, the process under a hand like that of Rubens is a singularly rapid one. Exquisite are the effects thus gained when the under tint is allowed to peep through here and there, blending with the solid touches to produce the subtlest effects of tone and colour.

Of these two distinct and indeed contrasted methods of handling oil pigment, with solid or with transparent underpainting, that of the Flemings has had most effect on later practice. The technique dominated on the whole the French school of the 18th century, and has had a good deal of influence on the painting of Scotland. In general, however, the oil painting of the 17th and succeeding centuries has not been bound by any distinctive rules and methods. Artists have felt themselves free, perhaps to an undue extent, in their choice of media, and it must be admitted that very good results have been achieved by the use of the simplest vehicles that have been known throughout the whole history of the art. If Rembrandt begins in the Flemish technique; Velasquez uses at first solid underpaintings of a somewhat heavy kind, but when these masters attain to full command of their media they paint apparently without any special system, obtaining the results they desired, now by one process and now again by another, but always working in a free untrammelled spirit, and treating the materials in the spirit of a master rather than of a slave. In modern painting generally we can no longer speak of established processes and methods of work, for every artist claims the right to experiment at his will, and to produce his result in the way that suits his own individuality and the special nature of the task before him.

§ 45. *Water-Colour Painting.*—(Cosmo Monkhouse, *The Earlier English Water-Colour Painters*, 2nd ed., London, 1897; Redgrave, *A Century of Painters*; and Hamerton, *The Graphic Arts*, contain chapters on this subject.)

Water-colour painting, as has been said, is only a particular form of tempera, in which the pigments are mixed with gum to make them adhere, and often with honey or glycerin to prevent them drying too fast. The surface operated on is for the most part paper, though "miniature" painting is in water-colour on ivory. The technique is in use for the illustrated papyrus rolls in ancient Egypt, and the illuminated MSS. of the medieval period. As a rule the pigments used in the MSS. were mixed with white and were opaque or "body" colours, while water-colour painting in the modern sense is mostly transparent, though the body-colour technique is also employed. There is no historical connexion between the water-colour painting on the vellum of medieval MSS. and the modern practice. Modern water-colour painting is a development rather from the drawings, which the painters from the 15th to the 17th century were constantly executing in the most varied media. Among the processes employed was the reinforcement of an outline drawing with the pen by means of a slight wash of the same colour, generally a brown. In these so-called pen-and-wash drawings artists like Rembrandt were fond of recording their impressions of nature, and the water-colour picture was evolved through the gradual development in importance of the wash as distinct from the line, and by the gradual addition to it of colour. It is true that we find some of the old masters occasionally executing fully-tinted water-colour drawings quite in a modern spirit. There are landscape studies in body-colour of this kind by Dürer and by Rubens. These are, however, of the nature of accidents, and the real development of the technique did not begin till the 18th century, when it was worked out, for the most part in England, by artists of whom the most important were Paul Sandby and John Robert Cozens, who flourished during the latter half of the 18th century. First the wash, which had been originally quite flat, and a mere adjunct to the pen outline, received a certain amount of modelling, and the advance was quickly made to a complete monochrome in which the firm outline still played an important part. The element of colour was first introduced in the form of neutral tints, a transparent wash of cool grey being used for the sky and distance, and a comparatively warm tint of brown for the foreground. "The progress of English water-colour," writes Mr Monkhouse, "was from monochrome through neutral tint to full colour." Cozens produced some beautiful atmospheric effects with these neutral tints, though the rendering of nature was only conventional, but it was reserved for the second generation of English water-colour artists to develop the full resources of the technique. This generation is represented centrally by Thomas Girtin (1775-1802) and J. M. W. Turner (1775-1851), the latter of whom is by far the greatest representative of the art that has hitherto appeared. To Girtin, who died young and whose genius, like that of Masaccio, developed early, is due the distinction of creating water-colour painting as an art dealing with the tones and colours of nature as they had been dealt with in the older media. W. H. Pyne, a contemporary water-colour artist who also wrote on the art, says of Girtin that he "prepared his drawings on the same principle which had hitherto been confined to painting in oil, namely, laying in the object upon his paper with the local colour, and shading the same with the individual tint of its own shadow. Previous to the practice of Turner and Girtin, drawings were shaded first entirely through, whatever their component parts—houses, cattle, trees, mountains, foregrounds, middle-ground and distances, all with black or grey, and these objects were afterwards stained or tinted, enriched or finished, as is now the custom to colour prints. It was the new practice, introduced by these distinguished artists, that acquired for designs in water-colours upon paper the title of paintings."

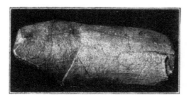

Fig. 6.—Prehistoric Drawing of a Mammoth.

Photo, W. A. Mansell & Co.
Fig. 7.—Egyptian Fowling in the Delta.

Photo, Alinari.
Fig. 10.—Zeus and Hera. Pompeian Wall Painting.

Photo, Alinari.
Fig. 8.—François Vase. Florence.

Photo, W. A. Mansell & Co.
Fig. 11.—Herod's Birthday Feast. Wall Painting in Cathedral at Brunswick.

Fig. 12.—The Maries at the Sepulchre, Hubert Van Eyck (?). (28x35.)

Fig. 13.—Herod's Birthday Feast, Giotto.

Fig. 14.—Peace, Lorenzetti. Siena.

Fig. 16.—Battle of S. Egidio, Uccello. (72x125.) National Gallery, London.

Fig. 17.—Martyrdom of S. Sebastian, Pollaiuolo. (114x79½.) National Gallery, London.

Fig. 18.—The Dream of Constantine, Piero Della Francesca. Arezzo.

Fig. 15.—The Expulsion from Eden, Masaccio.

Fig. 19.—Burial of S. Fina, Ghirlandajo. S. Gemignano.

PLATE VI.

PAINTING

By permission of Braun, Clément & Co., Dornach (Alsace) and Paris.
Fig. 20.—Dance of the Muses, Mantegna. (64 × 77.) Louvre.

Photo, Anderson.
Fig. 21.—Altarpiece at Murano, Bellini. Figures almost Life-size.

Photo, Neurdein.

Fig. 22.—The Concert, Giorgione (?). Louvre. (44 × 55.)

Photo, Anderson.

Fig. 23.—The Presentation in the Temple, Titian. (138 × 310.) Academy, Venice.

PLATE VIII   PAINTING

Photo, Hanfstaengl.
Fig. 24.—Fête Champêtre, Watteau. (22 × 18.)
Edinburgh.

Photo, Hanfstaengl.
Fig. 25.—Hon. Mrs. Graham, Gainsborough.
(93 × 60.) Edinburgh.

Photo, Anderson.
Fig. 26.—Charles V., Titian. (133 × 110.) Madrid.

Photo, Hanfstaengl.
Fig. 27.—George Gysis, Holbein. (38½ × 33.) Berlin.

Photo, Bruckmann.
Fig. 28.—Jan Six, Rembrandt. Six Collection, Amsterdam.

*By permission of Braun, Clément & Co.,
Dornach (Alsace) and Paris.*
**Fig. 29.—Le Banquier et sa Femme, Quintin Matsys.
(28½x27.) Louvre.**

Photo, Hanfstaengl.
Fig. 30.—A Singing Party, Brouwer. (16x21.) Munich.

Photo, Hanfstaengl.
**Fig. 32.—Crossing the Brook, Turner. (76x65.) National
Gallery, London.**

Photo, Hanfstaengl.
Fig. 31.—Haarlem, from the Dunes, Ruysdael. (20x24.) Hague.

PLATE X.   PAINTING

Photo, Anderson.

Fig. 36.—The Three Graces, Botticelli.   Florence.

By permission of Braun, Clement & Co., Dornach (Alsace) and Paris.

Fig. 33.—Still Life, Chardin. (74 x 50.) Louvre.

Photo, Anderson.

Fig. 34.—Figure of Adam, Michelangelo.   Rome.

Girtin " opened the gates of the art " and Turner entered in. If the palette of the former was still restricted, Turner exhausted all the resources of the colour box, and moreover enriched the art by adding to the traditional transparent washes the effects to be gained from the use of body colour. Body colours, however, were not only laid on by Turner with the solid impasto of the medieval illuminations. He was an adept at dragging thin films of them over a tinted ground so as to secure the subtle colour effects which can also be won in pastel. It would be useless to attempt any account of the technical methods of Turner or of the more modern practitioners in the art, for as in modern oil painting so here, each artist feels at liberty to adopt any media and processes which seem to promise the result he has in view. The varieties of paper used in modern water-colour practice are very numerous, and the idiosyncrasy of each artist expresses itself in the way he will manipulate his ground; superinduce one over the other his transparent washes; load with solid body colour; sponge or scratch the paper, or adopt any of the hundred devices in which modern practice of painting is so rife. (G. B. B.)

GENERAL AUTHORITIES ON TECHNIQUE.—Hamerton, *The Graphic Arts: A Treatise on the Varieties of Drawing, Painting and Engraving* (London, 1882), a work combining technical and artistic information, is the best single book on this subject. More archaeological is Berger, *Beiträge zur Entwickelungs-Geschichte der Maltechnik* (Munich, 1897-1904; partly in second editions. The last part is yet to come). The series *Quellenschriften für Kunstgeschichte und Kunsttechnik des Mittelalters und der Renaissance* (Vienna, various dates from 1871) contains many publications of much value, among them being, L, Cennino Cennini, *Das Buch von der Kunst*, German trans. of the *Trattato*, with note by Ilg; vii., Theophilus, *Schedula diversarum artium*, Ger. trans. by Ilg. Cennino's *Trattato* has also been edited in English by Mrs Herringham (London, 1899). Mrs Merrifield, *Ancient Practice of Painting* (2 vols., London, 1849), and Sir Charles Eastlake, *Materials for a History of Oil Painting* (2 vols., 1849 and 1869), are valuable standard works. Information as to Byzantine processes is to be found in the *Mount Athos Handbook* in " Manuel d'iconographie chrétienne grecque et latine," by Didron the elder (Paris, 1845). Church, *The Chemistry of Paints and Painting* (3rd ed., London, 1901), is by far the best book on its subject. *Vasari on Technique*, trans. by Miss Maclehose and edited with commentary by Baldwin Brown (London, 1907), contains a good deal of information. Paul Schultze-Naumburg, *Die Technik der Malerei* (Leipzig, no date); Vibert, *La Science de la peinture* (Paris, 1890), may also be mentioned.

RECENT SCHOOLS OF PAINTING

British.

At the beginning of the last quarter of the 19th century British art was held to be in a vigorous and authoritative position. During the years immediately preceding it had been developing with regularity and had displayed a vitality which seemed to be full of promise. It was supported by a large array of capable workers; it had gained the widest recognition from the public; and it was curiously free from those internal conflicts which diminish the strength of an appeal for popular appreciation. There were then few sharp divergences or subdivisions of an important kind. The leadership of the Royal Academy was generally conceded, and its relations with the mass of outside artists were little wanting in cordiality. One of the chief reasons for this understanding was that at this time an almost unprecedented approval was enjoyed by nearly all classes of painters. Picture-collecting had become a general fashion, and even the youngest workers received encouragement directly they gave evidence of a reasonable share of capacity. The demand was equal to the supply; and though the number of men who were adopting the artistic profession was rapidly increasing, there seemed little danger of over-production. Pictorial art had established upon all sorts of people a hold too strong, as it seemed, to be affected by change of fashion. All pointed in the direction of a permanent prosperity.

Subsequent events provided a curious commentary on the anticipations which were reasonable enough in 1875. That year is now seen to have been, not the beginning of an era of unexampled success for British pictorial art, but rather the culminating point of preceding activity. During the period which has succeeded we have witnessed a rapid decline in the popular interest in picture-painting and a marked alteration in the conditions under which artists have had to work. In the place of the former sympathy between the public and the producers, there grew up something which almost approached indifference to their best and sincerest efforts. Simultaneously there developed a great amount of internal dissension and of antagonism between different sections of the art community. As an effect of these two causes, a new set of circumstances came into existence, and the aspect of the British school underwent a radical change. Many art workers found other ways of using their energies. The slackening of the popular demand inclined them to experiment, and to test forms of practice which formerly were not accorded serious attention, and it led to the formation of detached hostile groups of artists always ready to contend over details of technical procedure. Restlessness became the dominant characteristic of the British school, along with some intolerance of the popular lack of sympathy.

The first sign of the coming change appeared very soon after 1875. The right of the Royal Academy to define and direct the policy of the British school was disputed in 1877, when the Grosvenor Gallery was started " with the intention of giving special advantages of exhibition to artists of established reputation, some of whom have previously been imperfectly known to the public." This exhibition gallery was designed not so much as a rival to the Academy, as to provide a place where could be collected the works of those men who did not care to make their appeal to the public through the medium of a large and heterogeneous exhibition. As a rallying place for the few unusual painters, standing apart from their fellows in conviction and method, it had good reason for existence; and that it was not regarded at Burlington House as a rival was proved by the fact that among the contributors to the first exhibition were included Sir Francis Grant, the President of the Royal Academy, and such artists as Leighton, Millais, G. F. Watts, Alma-Tadema, G. D. Leslie and E. J. Poynter, who were at the time Academicians or Associates. With them, however, appeared such men as Burne-Jones, Holman Hunt, Walter Crane, W. B. Richmond and J. McN. Whistler, who had not heretofore obtained the publicity to which they were entitled by the exceptional quality and intention of their work. There was doubtless some suggestion that the Academy was not keeping touch with the more important art movements, for shortly after the opening of the Grosvenor Gallery there began that attack upon the official art leaders which has been one of the most noteworthy incidents in recent art history in Great Britain. The initial stage of this conflict ended about 1886, when the vehemence of the attack had been weakened, partly by the withdrawal of some of the more prominent " outsiders," who had meanwhile been elected into the Academy, and partly by the formation of smaller societies, which afforded the more " advanced " of the younger men the opportunities which they desired for the exposition of their views. In a modified form, however, the antagonism between the Academy and the outsiders has continued. The various protesting art associations continue to work in most matters independently of one another, with the common belief that the dominant influence of Burlington House is not exercised entirely as it should be for the promotion of the best interests of British art, and that it maintains tradition as against the development of individualism and a " new style."

The agitation in all branches of art effort was not entirely without result even inside Burlington House. Some of the older academic views were modified, and changes seriously discussed, which formerly would have been rejected as opposed to all the traditions of the society. Its calmness under attack, and its ostentatious disregard of the demands made upon it by the younger and more strenuous outsiders, have veiled a great deal of shrewd observation of passing events. It may be said that the Academy has known when to break up an organization in which it recognized a possible source of danger, by selecting the ablest leaders of the opposition to fill vacancies in its own ranks; it has given places on its walls to the works of those

The Grosvenor Gallery and the Academy.

reformers who were not unwilling to be represented in the annual exhibitions; and it has, without seeming to yield to clamour, responded perceptibly to the pressure of professional opinion. In so doing, though it has not checked the progress of the changing fashion by which the popular liking for pictorial art has been diverted into other channels, it has kept its hold upon the public, and has not to any appreciable extent weakened its position of authority.

It is doubtful whether a more definite participation by the Academy in the controversies of the period would have been of *Changed* any use as a means of prolonging the former good *Conditions* relations between artists and the collectors of works *of British* of art. The change is the result of something more *Art.* than the failure of one art society to fulfil its entire mission. The steady falling off in the demand for modern pictures has been due to a combination of causes which have been powerful enough to alter nearly all the conditions under which British painters have to work. For example, the older collectors, who had for some years anterior to 1875 bought up eagerly most of the more important canvases which came within their reach, could find no more room in their galleries for further additions; again, artists, with the idea of profiting to the utmost by the keenness of the competition among the buyers, had forced up their prices to the highest limits. But the most active of all causes was that the younger generation of collectors did not show the same inclination that had swayed their predecessors to limit their attention to modern pictorial art. They turned more and more from pictures to other forms of artistic effort. They built themselves houses in which the possibility of hanging large canvases was not contemplated, and they began to call upon the craftsman and the decorator to supply them with what was necessary for the adornment of their homes. At first this modification in the popular taste was scarcely perceptible, but with every successive year it became more marked in its effect.

Latterly more money has been spent by one class of collectors upon pictures than was available even in the best of the times which have passed away; but this lavish expenditure has been devoted not to the acquisition of works by modern men, but to the purchase of examples of the old masters. Herein may often be recognized the wish to become possessed of objects which have a fictitious value in consequence of their rarity, or which are "sound investments." Evidence of the existence of this spirit among collectors is seen in the prevailing eagerness to acquire works which inadequately represent some famous master, or are even ascribed to him on grounds not always credible. The productions of minor men, such as Henry Morland, who had never been ranked among the masters, have received an amount of attention quite out of proportion to what merits they possess, if only they can be proved to be scarce examples, or historically notorious. All this implies in the creed of the art patron a change which has necessarily reacted on living painters and on the conditions of their art production.

These, then, are the conclusions to which we are led by a comparison of the movements which affected the British school *Portraiture.* between 1875 and the beginning of the 20th century. To a wide appreciation of all types of pictorial art succeeded a grudging and careless estimate of the value of the bulk of artistic endeavour. Only a few branches of production are still encouraged by anything approaching an efficient demand. Portraiture is the mainstay of the majority of the figure painters; it has never lost its popularity, and may be said to have maintained satisfactorily its hold upon all classes of society, for the desire to possess personal records is very general and is independent of any art fashion. It has persisted through all the changes of view which have been increasingly active in recent years. Episodical art, illustrating sentimental *Episodical* motives or incidents with some touch of dramatic *Art.* action, has remained popular, because it has some degree of literary interest; but imaginative works and pictures which have been produced chiefly as expressions of an

original regard for nature, or of some unusual conviction as to technical details, have found comparatively few admirers. The designers, however, and the workers in the decorative arts have found opportunities which formerly were denied to them. They have had more scope for the display *Decorative* of their ingenuity and more inducement to exercise *Art.* their powers of invention. A vigorous and influential school of design developed, which promised to evolve work of originality and excellence. British designers gained a hearing abroad, and earned emphatic approval in countries where a sound decorative tradition had been maintained for centuries.

The one dominant influence, that of the Pre-Raphaelite Brotherhood, which in the 'fifties was altering the whole complexion of British art, had begun to wane early in *Wane of* the 'seventies, and it was rapidly being replaced *pre-* by another scarcely less distinctive. The younger *Raphael-* generation of artists had wearied, even before 1875, *itism and* of the pre-Raphaelite precision, and were impatient *Rise of* of the restrictions imposed upon their freedom of *French* technical expression by a method of practice which required *Influence.* laborious application and unquestioning obedience to a rather formal code of regulations. They yearned for greater freedom and boldness, and for a better chance of asserting their individual capacities. So they gave way to a strong reaction against the creed of their immediate predecessors, and cut themselves deliberately adrift.

With the craving of young artists for new forms of technique came also the idea that the "old-master traditions" were opposed to the exact interpretation of nature, and were based too much upon convention to be adapted for the needs of men who believed that absolute realism was the one thing worth aiming at in picture-production. So Paris instead of Rome became the educational centre. There was to British students, dissatisfied with the half-hearted and imperfect systems of teaching with which they were tantalized at home, a peculiarly exhilarating atmosphere in the French studios—an amount of enthusiasm and a love of art for its own sake without parallel elsewhere. They saw in operation principles which led by the right sequence of stages to sure and certain results. In these circumstances they allowed their sympathies with French methods to become rather exaggerated, and were somewhat reckless in their adoption of both the good and bad qualities of so attractive a school.

At first the results of this breaking away from all the older educational customs were not wholly satisfactory. British students came back from France better craftsmen, stronger and sounder draughtsmen, more skilful manipulators, and with an infinitely more correct appreciation of refinements of tone-management than they had ever possessed before; but they brought back also a disproportionate amount of French mannerism and a number of affectations which sat awkwardly upon them. In the first flush of their conversion they went further than was wise or necessary, for they changed their motives as well as their methods. The quietness of subject and reserve of manner which had been hitherto eminently characteristic of the British school were abandoned for foreign sensationalism and exaggeration of effect. An affectation of extreme vivacity, a liking for theatrical suggestion, even an inclination towards coarse presentation of unpleasant incidents from modern life —all of which could be found in the paintings of the French artists who were then recognized as leaders—must be noted as importations from the Paris studios. They were the cause of a distinct degeneration in the artistic taste, and they introduced into British pictorial practice certain unnatural tendencies. Scarcely less evident was the depreciation in the instinctive colour-sense of British painters, which was brought about by the adoption of the French habit of regarding strict accuracy of tone-relation as the one important thing to aim at. Before this there had been a preference for rich and sumptuous harmonies and for chromatic effects which were rather compromises with, than exact renderings of, nature; but as the foreign influence grew more active, these pleasant adaptations, inspired by a sensuous love of colour for its own sake, were abandoned for more scientific statements. The colder and cruder tone-studies of the modern Frenchman became the models upon which the younger artists based themselves, and the standards against which they measured their own success. "Actuality" was gained, but much of the poetry, the delicacy, and the subtle charm which had distinguished British colourists were lost.

For some while there was a danger that the art of Great Britain might become hybrid, with the French strain predomi-*Danger of* nating. So many students had succumbed to the *the French* fascination of a system of training which seemed to *influence.* supply them with a perfect equipment on all points, that they were inclined to despise not only the educational methods of their own country, but also the inherent characteristics of British taste. The result was that the exhibitions were full of pictures which presented English people and English landscape in a purely arbitrary and artificial manner, strictly in accordance with a French convention which was out of sympathy with British instincts, and indeed, with British facts. Ultimately a discreet middle course was found between the extreme application of the science of the French art schools and the comparative irresponsibility in technical matters which had so long existed in the British Isles. In the careers of men like Stanhope Forbes, H. S. Tuke, Frank Bramley, and other prominent members of the school, many illustrations are provided of the way in which this readjustment has been effected. Their pictures, if taken in a sufficiently long sequence, summarize instructively the course of the movement which became active about 1875. They prove how valuable the interposition of France has been in the matter of artistic education, and how much Englishmen have improved in their understanding of the technique of painting.

One noteworthy outcome of the triumph of common sense over fanaticism must be mentioned. Now that the exact *Weakening* relation which French teaching should bear to British *of the* thought has been adjusted, an inclination to revive *French* the more typical of the forms of pictorial expression *influence.* which have had their vogue in the past is becoming increasingly evident. Picturesque domesticity is taking the place of theatrical sensation, the desire to select and represent what is more than ordinarily beautiful is ousting the former preference for what was brutal and ugly, the effort to please is once again stronger than the intention to surprise or shock the art lover. Even the Pre-Raphaelite theories and practices are being reconstructed, and quite a considerable group of young artists has sprung up who are avowed believers in the principles which were advocated so strenuously in 1850.

To French intervention can be ascribed the rise and progress of several movements which have had results of more than *Groups* ordinary moment. There was a few years ago much *within the* banding together of men who believed strongly in *British* the importance of asserting plainly their belief in *School.* the doctrines to which they had been converted abroad; and as a consequence of this desire for an offensive and defensive association, many detached groups were formed within the boundaries of the British school. Each of these groups had some peculiar tenet, and each one had a small orbit of its own in which it revolved, without concerning itself overmuch about what might be going on outside. Roughly, there were three classes into which the more thoughtful British artists could then be divided. One included those men who were in the main French in sympathy and manner; another consisted of those who were not insensible to the value of the foreign training, but yet did not wish to surrender entirely their faith in the British tradition; and the third, and smallest, was made up of a few individuals who were independent of all assistance from without, and had sufficient force of character to ignore what was going on in the art world. In this third class there was practically no common point of view: each man chose his own direction and followed it as he thought best, and each one was prepared to stand or fall by the opinion which he had formed as to the true

function of the painter. Necessarily, in such a gathering there were several notable personalities who may fairly be reckoned among the best of English modern masters.

Perhaps the most conspicuous of the groups was the gathering of painters who established themselves in the Cornish village of *The Newlyn* Newlyn (*q.v.*). This group—"The Newlyn School," as *School.* it was called—was afterwards much modified, and many of its most cherished beliefs were considerably altered. In its beginning it was essentially French in atmosphere, and advocated not only strict adherence to realism in choice and treatment of subject, but also the subordination of colour to tone-gradation, and the observance of certain technical details, such as the exclusive use of flat brushes and the laying on of pigments in square touches. The colony was formed, as it were, in stages; and as the school is to be reckoned in the future history of the British school, the order in which the adherents arrived may here be set on record. Edwin Harris came first, and was joined by Walter Langley. Then, in the following order, came Ralph Todd, L. Suthers, Fred Hall, Frank Bramley and T. C. Gotch, and Percy Craft and Stanhope Forbes together. H. Detmold and Chevallier Tayler next arrived; then Miss Elizabeth Armstrong (Mrs Stanhope Forbes), F. Bourdillon, W. Fortescue and Norman Garstin. Ayerst Ingram, H. S. Tuke, H. Martin and F. Millard were later visitors. Stanhope Forbes (b. 1857) was trained at the Lambeth School and at the Royal Academy, and afterwards in Bonnat's studio in Paris. His best known pictures are "A Fish Sale on a Cornish Beach" (1885), "Soldiers and Sailors" (1891), "Forging the Anchor" (1892), and "The Smithy" (1895). He was elected A.R.A. in 1892, and became full Member in 1910. Frank Bramley (b. 1867) studied art in the Lincoln School of Art and at Antwerp. He gained much popularity by his pictures, "A Hopeless Dawn" (1888), "For of such is the Kingdom of Heaven" (1891), and "After the Storm" (1896), and was elected an Associate in 1894. Of late years he had made a very definite departure from the technical methods which he followed in his earlier period. T. C. Gotch (b. 1854) had a varied art training, for he worked at the Slade School, then at Antwerp, and finally in Paris under Jean Paul Laurens. He did not long remain faithful to the Newlyn creed, but diverged about 1890 into a kind of decorative symbolism, and for some years devoted himself entirely to pictures of this type. The other men who must be ranked as supporters of the school adhered closely enough to the principles which were exemplified in the works of the leaders of the movement. They were faithful realists, sincere observers of the facts of the life with which they were brought in contact, and quite earnest in their efforts to paint what they saw, without modification or idealization.

Another group which received its inspiration directly from France was the Impressionist school (see IMPRESSIONISM). This *The Im-* group never had any distinct organization like that of *pressionist* the French Société des Impressionistes, but among the *School.* members of it there was a general agreement on points of procedure. They based themselves, more or less, upon prominent French artists like Manet, Renoir, Pissarro, and Claude Monet, and owed not a little to the example of J. A. M'N. Whistler, whose own art may be said to be in a great measure a product of Paris. One of the fundamental principles of their practice was the subdivision of colour masses into their component parts, and the rendering of gradated tints by the juxtaposition of touches of pure colour upon the canvas, rather than by attempting to match them by previously mixing them on the palette. In pictures so painted greater luminosity and more subtlety of aerial effects can be obtained. The works of the British Impressionists have been seen mostly in the exhibitions of the New English Art *The New* Club. This society was founded in 1885 by a number *English* of young artists who wished for facilities for exhibition *Art Club.* which they felt were denied to them in the other galleries. It drew the greater number of its earlier supporters from the men who had been trained in foreign schools, and a complete list of the contributors to its exhibitions includes the names of many of the best known of the younger painters. It was the meeting-place of numerous groups which advocated one or other of the new creeds, for among its members or exhibitors have been P. Wilson Steer, Fred Brown, J. S. Sargent (*q.v.*), Solomon J. Solomon, Stanhope Forbes, T. C. Gotch, Frank Bramley, Arthur Hacker, Francis Bate, Moffat Lindner, J. L. Henry, W. Russell, George Thomson, Arthur Tomson, Henry Tonks, C. W. Furse, R. Anning Bell, Walter Osborne, Laurence Housman, J. J. Shannon, W. L. Wyllie, H. S. Tuke, Maurice Greiffenhagen, G. P. Jacomb Hood, Alfred Parsons, Alfred East, J. Buxton Knight, C. H. Shannon, Mark Fisher, Walter Sickert, W. Strang, Frank Brangwyn, Edward Stott, Mortimer Menpes, Alfred Hartley, William Stott, J. R. Reid, Mouat Loudan, T. B. Kennington, H. Muhrman, A. D. Peppercorn, George Clausen and J. A. M'N. Whistler, and a number of the Scottish artists, like J. Lavery, J. Guthrie, George Henry, James Paterson, A. Roche, E. A. Walton, J. E. Christie and E. A. Hornel. A number of the men who have been more or less actively identified with it have been elected members of the Royal Academy, so that it may fairly claim to have exercised a definite influence upon the tendencies of modern art. It has certainly done much to prove the extent of the foreign influence upon the British school.

In its wider sense the Impressionist school may be said to include now all those students of nature who strive for the representation of broad effects rather than minute details, who look at the subject before them largely and comprehensively, and ignore all minor matters which would be likely to interfere with the simplicity of the pictorial rendering. To it can be assigned a number of artists who have never adopted, or have definitely abandoned, the prismatic analysis of colour advocated by the French Impressionists. These men were headed by J. A. M'N. Whistler (q.v.), born in America in 1834, and trained in Paris under Gleyre. His pictures have always been remarkable for their beauty of colour combination, and for their sensitive management of subtleties of tone. They gained for the artist a place among the chief modern executants, and have attracted to him a host of followers. Other notable painters who have places in the school are Mark Fisher, an American landscape painter who studied for a while in Gleyre's studio, one of the ablest interpreters in England of effects of sunlight and breezy atmosphere; A. D. Peppercorn, a pupil of Gérôme, who makes landscape a medium for the expression of a dignified sense of design and a carefully simplified appreciation of contrasts of tone; and P. Wilson Steer, an artist who began as a follower of Monet, and based upon his training in the Ecole des Beaux Arts a style of his own, which he displays effectively in both landscapes and figure pictures.

The International The International Society of Sculptors, Painters, and Gravers, inaugurated in 1898, although not by its nature confined to British art and artists, who compose little more than half of the electorate, has its home in London. It succeeds in its object of setting before the British public the most modern and eccentric expressions of the art of the chief European countries. Its exhibitions are striking and the contributions for the most part serious and interesting; but while the freedom of the artist is insisted on it is doubtful if the more exaggerated displays by rebellious painters and sculptors have had much influence on the native school. The presidents have been J. A. M'N. Whistler and Auguste Rodin, and the vice-presidents John Lavery and William Strang: these personalities, considered along with their views and their vigour, sufficiently indicate the spirit and the politics of the society.

Figure Painters. Generally speaking, the very large class of artists who fell only to a limited extent under the spell of French teaching includes most of the figure and landscape men and practically the whole of the portrait painters. In all sections of figure painting individual workers in improved technical methods have appeared, but most of them have gradually lost their distinguishing peculiarities of manner, and have year by year assimilated themselves more closely to their less advanced brethren. The section in which their energetic propagandism has been most effective is certainly that of imaginative composition. A definite mark has been made there by men like S.-J. Solomon (b. 1860; A.R.A. 1896; R.A. 1906), trained at the Royal Academy, the Munich Academy and the Ecole des Beaux Arts in Paris, and widely known by such pictures as "Samson" (1887), "The Judgment of Paris" (1890) and the "Birth of Love" (1895); and Arthur Hacker (b. 1858; A.R.A. 1894; R.A. 1910), educated at the Academy and in Bonnat's studio, and the painter of a considerable series of semi-historical and symbolical canvases. They exercised a considerable influence upon their contemporaries, and introduced some new elements into the later practice of the school. At the same time admirably effective work has been done in this section and others by many painters who have kept much more closely in touch with the older type of aesthetic belief, and have not associated themselves openly with any of the newer movements. Among the more prominent of these figure painters there are, or have been, some excellent craftsmen, whose contributions to the record of native British art can be accepted as full of permanent interest. In the school of historical incident good work was done by Sir John Gilbert (1817–1897; R.A. 1876), a robust and ingenious illustrator of romantic motives, with a never-failing capacity for picturesque invention; John Pettie (1839–1893; R.A. 1873), a fine colourist and a clever manipulator, whose scenes from the life of past centuries were full of rare vitality; P. H. Calderon (1833–1898; R.A. 1867), a graceful and sincere artist not wanting in originality; and H. Stacy Marks (1829–1898; R.A. 1879), who treated medieval motives with a touch of real humour. Besides these, there are Sir J. D. Linton (b. 1840), who has produced noteworthy compositions in oil and water colours; Frank Dicksee (b. 1853; A.R.A. 1881; R.A. 1891), who has gained wide popularity by pictures in which romance and sentiment are combined in equal proportions; A. C. Gow (b. 1848; R.A. 1881), whose "Cromwell at Dunbar" (1886), "Flight of James II. after the Battle of the Boyne" (1888), and "Crossing the Bidassoa" (1896) may be noted as typical examples of his performance; J. Seymour Lucas (b. 1849; A.R.A. 1886; R.A. 1898), trained at the Royal Academy Schools, and a brilliant painter of what may be called the by-play of history; W. Dendy Sadler (b. 1854), trained partly in London and partly at Düsseldorf, and well known by his quaintly humorous renderings

of the lighter side of life in the olden times; G. H. Boughton (born in England, but educated first in America and afterwards in Paris; A.R.A. 1879; R.A. 1896), a specialist in paintings of old and modern Dutch subjects; the Hon. John Collier (b. 1850), trained at the Slade School, at Munich, and in Paris, and a capable painter both of the nude figure and of costume; and Edwin A. Abbey, an American (b. 1852), educated at the Pennsylvania Academy of the Fine Arts. Abbey came to England in 1876 with a great reputation as an illustrator, and did not begin to exhibit oil pictures until 1890; he was elected an Academician in 1898. Then there are to be noted classicists like Lord Leighton, Sir L. Alma-Tadema, and Sir E. J. Poynter's students of the East like Frederick Goodall (b. 1822; A.R.A. 1853; R.A. 1863; d. 1904), and idealists like Sir W. B. Richmond, K.C.B.; R.A. 1895 —all of whom have done much to uphold the reputation of the British school for strength of accomplishment and variety of motive.

Painters of Sentiment. The painters of sentiment have in the main adhered closely to the tradition which has been handed down through successive generations. Among these may be noted Marcus Stone (b. 1840), elected an Academician in 1887, an original artist whose dainty fancies are familiar to students of modern art. His pictures nearly all appeared in the exhibitions of the Royal Academy. Another popular artist is G. D. Leslie (b. 1835), elected an Associate in 1868 and an Academician in 1876, who has been responsible for a number of domestic old-world subject-pictures remarkable for freshness of treatment and delicacy of feeling. The list may also be held to include Henry Woods (b. 1846; A.R.A. 1882; R.A. 1893), and since 1877 a painter of scenes from Venetian life; R. W. Macbeth (b. 1848; A.R.A. 1883; R.A. 1903), whose elegant treatment of rustic subjects displays a very attractive individuality. Among the painters of sentiment should also be included Sir Luke Fildes (b. 1844), educated at the South Kensington and Royal Academy Schools, elected an Academician in 1887, the painter of such famous pictures as "The Casual Ward" (1874), "The Widower" (1876), "The Return of the Penitent" (1879), and "The Doctor" (1892); and Sir Hubert von Herkomer, C.V.O. (b. 1849; A.R.A. 1879; R.A. 1890; knighted 1907), famous not only by his many memorable canvases and by his extraordinary versatility in the arts, but also as a teacher and a leader in a number of educational movements.

Military Painting. Not many military pictures of high merit have been produced during the period. The artists, indeed, who occupy themselves with this class of art are not numerous, and they mostly devote their energies to illustrative pictures rather than to large canvases. Lady Butler (née Elizabeth Thompson), whose "Roll Call," exhibited in 1874, brought her instant popularity, continued to paint subjects of the same type, among which "Quatre Bras" (1875), "The Defence of Rorke's Drift" (1881), "The Camel Corps" (1891) and "The Dawn of Waterloo" (1895) are perhaps the most worthy of record. Ernest Crofts (b. 1847; A.R.A. 1878; R.A. 1896), trained in London and Düsseldorf, has taken a prominent position by such pictures as "Napoleon at Ligny" (1875), "Napoleon leaving Moscow" (1887), "The Capture of a French Battery by the 53rd Regiment at Waterloo" (1896), and by many similar representations of historical battles. Occasional pictures have come also from A. C. Gow, R. Caton Woodville, W. B. Wollen, J. P. Beadle, John Charlton, and a few more men who are better known by their work in other directions.

Portraiture. The number of artists who have devoted the greater part of their energies to portraiture has been steadily on the increase. Most of the men who have taken definite rank among the figure painters have made reputations by their portraits also, but there are many others who have kept almost exclusively to this branch of practice. Into the first division come such noted artists as Sir John Millais, Sir E. J. Poynter, G. F. Watts, Sir Luke Fildes, Sir Hubert von Herkomer, Sir L. Alma-Tadema, Sir W. B. Richmond, Seymour Lucas, the Hon. John Collier, S. J. Solomon, Arthur Hacker, Sir W. Q. Orchardson, J. A. M'N. Whistler, Frank Dicksee, Stanhope Forbes, Frank Bramley, H. S. Tuke, T. C. Gotch, P. W. Steer, John Bacon and Frank Holl. In the second must be reckoned J. S. Sargent (A.R.A. 1894; R.A. 1897), an American citizen (b. 1856), a pupil of Carolus Duran, who after 1885 was recognized as one of the most brilliant painters of the day; J. J. Shannon, also an American (b. 1862), trained at the South Kensington School, and elected an Associate in 1897, a graceful and accomplished artist, with a sound technical method and a delightful sense of style; A. S. Cope (b. 1857), trained in Paris, and elected an Associate in 1899, who carries on soundly the better traditions of the British school; James Sant (b. 1820), elected an Academician in 1870, a strong favourite of the public throughout a long career; W. W. Ouless (b. 1848; A.R.A. 1877; R.A. 1881), trained in the Royal Academy Schools, an industrious and prolific worker; H. T. Wells (b. 1828; A.R.A. 1866; R.A. 1870), trained in London and Paris, who produced a long series of portraits and portrait groups, and many miniatures; W. Llewellyn (b. 1860), educated at the South Kensington Schools and in Cormon's studio in Paris, an able draughtsman and a thorough executant; C. W. Furse (q.v.), trained first in the Slade School under Professor Legros and afterwards in Paris, whose early death removed a master of his art; and others like Walter Osborne, Richard Jack, Glyn Philpot and Gerald Kelly.

In the class of figure painters, who are individual in their work, and owe little or nothing to the suggestions of foreign teachers, a number of artists can be enumerated who have in common little besides a sincere desire to express their personal conviction

Individual Figure Painters. in their own way. Among them are some of the most distinguished of modern artists, who stand out as the unquestioned chiefs of the school. Sir John Millais occupies a place in this group by virtue of his admirable pictorial work, and with him are W. Holman Hunt, Dante Gabriel Rossetti, G. F. Watts, Sir Edward Burne-Jones, Albert Moore and Ford Madox Brown, each one of whom may be regarded as a leader. There are also J. M. Strudwick (b. 1849), R. Spencer Stanhope (d. 1908) and Evelyn de Morgan, followers of Burne-Jones, and J. W. Waterhouse (A.R.A. 1885; R.A. 1895), in many ways the most original and inspired of English imaginative painters; and, again, M. Greiffenhagen, F. Cayley Robinson and Mrs Swynnerton. Into this class come also the decorative painters, Walter Crane

Decorative Painters. (b. 1845), a prolific illustrator and picture-painter and the producer of an extraordinary amount of work in all branches of decoration; Frank Brangwyn, whose pictures and designs are marked by fine qualities of execution and by much sumptuousness of colour; and several others, like H. J. Draper, Harold Speed, R. Anning Bell, Gerald Moira and G. Spencer Watson. As a branch of the decorative school, a small group of artists who have revived the practice of tempera-painting must also be noted. It includes Mrs Adrian Stokes, J. D. Batten, J. S. Southall, Arthur Gaskin, and a few others with well-marked decorative tendencies.

During recent years a movement has begun which apparently aims at the revival of Pre-Raphaelitism. It is headed by a few

The New Pre-Raphaelite School. young artists, whose methods show a mingling together of the precision of the 19th-century Pre-Raphaelites and a kind of decorative formality. The most influential of the artists concerned in the formation of this new school is J. Byam Shaw (b. 1872), whose originality and quaintness of fancy give to his pictures a more than ordinary degree of persuasiveness. A strong colourist and an able draughtsman, he possesses in a high degree the faculty of imaginative expression, allied with humour that never degenerates into farce. His strongest preference is for symbolical subjects which embody some moral lesson. Other prominent members of the group are F. Cadogan Cowper (A.R.A. 1907) and Miss Eleanor Fortescue-Brickdale, who is in manner much like Byam Shaw, but yet does not sink her individuality in mere imitative effort.

The painters of landscapes and sea-pictures have for the most part been little affected by the unrest which has caused so many

Landscape Painters. new departures in figure-work. A love of nature has always been one of the best British characteristics, and it has proved itself to be strong enough to keep those artists who seek their inspiration out of doors from falling to any great extent under the control of particular technical fashions. Therefore there is in the school of "open-air" painting little evidence of any change in point of view, or of the growth of any modern feeling at variance with that by which masters of landscape were swayed a century or more ago. Impressionism has gained a few adherents, and the French Barbizon school—itself created in response to a suggestion from England—has reacted upon a section of the younger artists. But, on the whole, in this branch of art the British school has gained in power and confidence, without surrendering that sturdy independence which in the past produced such momentous results. The absence of any common convention, or of any set pattern of landscape which would lead to uniformity of effort, has left the students of nature free to express themselves in a personal way. The most devout believers in the value of training, and in the infallibility of the dogmas which emanate from the Paris studios, have not, except in rare instances, demanded any radical remodelling of the British landscape school on French lines, as local conditions affecting the practice of this branch of art make impossible all drastic alterations. Most workers in the front rank can claim to be judged on individual merits, and not as members of a particular coterie. Still, it is convenient to divide the members of the landscape school into such classes as realists, romanticists and subjective painters of landscape.

Among the most notable of the first class are H. W. B. Davis (b. 1883; A.R.A. 1872; R.A. 1877), the painter of a long series of

Realistic Landscape. dainty scenes which suggest happily the charm of rural England; Peter Graham, elected an Academician in 1881, who has alternated for the greater part of his working life between Scottish moorland subjects, with cattle wandering on bare hillsides and pictures of coast scenery, with sea-gulls perched on dark rocks; David Murray (b. 1849; A.R.A. 1891; R.A. 1905), an artist whose career has been marked by consistent effort to interpret nature's suggestions with dignity and intelligence; Sir Ernest A. Waterlow (b. 1840; A.R.A. 1890; R.A. 1903), trained in the Royal Academy and afterwards President of the Royal Society of Painters in Water-Colours, a graceful painter, with a tender colour feeling and an excellent technical style; Yeend

King (b. 1855), trained partly in England, and partly in Paris under Bonnat and Cormon, a sound craftsman who made a reputation by landscapes in which are introduced groups of figures on a fairly important scale; Alfred Parsons (b. 1847), elected an Associate in 1897, who paints rich river scenery with careful regard for actuality and with much minuteness and exquisiteness of detail, especially in the rendering of flowers; and Frank Walton (b. 1840), who chooses, as a rule, landscape motives which enable him to display unusual powers of accurate draughtsmanship. To the same class of realists belonged Vicat Cole, R.A.; Birket Foster, J. W. Oakes, A.R.A.; Keeley Halswelle, and perhaps Alfred W. Hunt, though in his case realism was tempered by a delicate poetic imagination.

The romanticists and pastoral painters have in many cases been perceptibly affected by the example of the Barbizon school, but they owe much to such famous Englishmen as Cecil Lawson,

Romantic and Pastoral Painters. John Linnell (both of whom died in 1882), George Mason (A.R.A. 1868; d. 1872) and Frederick Walker (A.R.A. 1871; d. 1875). The most prominent later member of the group is, perhaps, Sir Alfred East (b. 1849), trained first in the Glasgow School of Art and afterwards in Paris, elected an Associate in 1899, a painter endowed with an exceptional faculty for suggesting the poetry of nature and with an admirable sense of decorative arrangement; but there are, besides, Leslie Thomson (b. 1851), whose art is especially sound and sincere; J. Aumonier, a pastoral painter with very refined appreciation of subtleties of aerial colour; C. W. Wyllie, a painter of delicate vision and charm of presentation; J. S. Hill, whose sombre landscapes are distinguished in design and impressive in their depth of tone; R. W. Allan (b. 1852), who uses a robust technical method with equal skill in landscape and coast subjects; J. Buxton Knight (b. 1842; d. 1908), a vigorous manipulator, with a liking for rich harmonies and low tones; Joseph Knight (b. 1838; d. 1909), whose well drawn and broadly painted pictures in oil and water-colour have been for many years appreciated by lovers of unaffected nature; Lionel P. Smythe (A.R.A. 1898), a colourist who handles exquisitely the most delicate atmospheric effects and is unusually successful in his rendering of diffused daylight; J. W. North (A.R.A. in 1893), a painter of fanciful landscapes in which definition of form is subordinated to modulations of decorative colour; Claude Hayes, who studied in the Royal Academy Schools, and carried on the tradition established by David Cox and his contemporaries; J. L. Pickering, a lover of dramatic light-and-shade contrasts and a student of romantic mountain scenery; A. D. Peppercorn, who gives breadth and dignity with sombre colour and delicate gradation of tone; Adrian Stokes (b. 1854; A.R.A. 1910) and M. Ridley Corbet (who died in 1902, only a few months after his election as an Associate of the Royal Academy), a classicist in landscape, in whose pictures can be perceived a definite reflection of the teaching of Professor Costa, the Italian master. There must also be noted, as leaders among the pastoral painters, George Clausen (b. 1852), trained first in the South Kensington School and afterwards in Paris under Bouguereau and Robert-Fleury, and elected an Associate in 1895 and R.A. in 1908, who began as a strict realist and afterwards developed into a rustic idealist; H. H. La Thangue, trained in the Royal Academy Schools and in Paris, elected an Associate in 1898, an artist of amazing technical vigour and an uncompromising interpreter of rural subjects; Edward Stott (A.R.A. 1906), trained in Paris under Carolus Duran and Cabanel, who paints delicately the more poetic aspects of the life of the fields; J. Arnesby Brown (b. 1866; A.R.A. 1903); Oliver Hall, Albert Goodwin, A. Friedenson and others.

The painters of landscape subjectively considered, who conventionalize nature with the idea of giving to their pictures a kind of sentimental as distinguished from emotional sug-

Subjective Landscape. gestion, are most strikingly represented by B. W. Leader (b. 1831), trained in the Worcester School of Design and in the Royal Academy Schools, and elected an Academician in 1898. He became a strong favourite of the public, and his academic and precise technical methods were widely admired by the many people who are not satisfied with unaffected transcriptions of natural scenes and of the passion of nature.

In marine painting no one has appeared to rival Henry Moore, perhaps the greatest student of wave-forms the world has seen; but good work has been done by the late Edwin

Marine Painting. Hayes, an Irish painter, whose powers showed no sign of failure up to his death in 1904, after some half-century of continuous labour; W. L. Wyllie (b. 1851; A.R.A. 1889; R.A. 1907), trained in the Royal Academy Schools, who paints sea and shipping with intelligent understanding; T. Somerscales, a self-taught artist, with an intimate knowledge of the ocean derived from long actual experience as a sailor; and especially C. Napier Hemy (b. 1841; A.R.A. 1898; R.A. 1910), trained at the Antwerp Academy and in the studio of Baron Leys, a powerful manipulator, with a preference for the dramatic aspects of his subject. J. C. Hook (d. 1907), retained into old age the subtle qualities which made his pictures notable among the best productions of the British school. Mention must be made of John Brett (1830–1902; A.R.A. 1881), the one Pre-Raphaelite sea painter, and Hamilton Macallum

(1841–1896), who painted rippling water in bright sunlight with delightful delicacy and charm of manner.

The school of animal painting is a small one, and includes only a few of marked ability. The chief members include Briton Riviere, (b. 1840; A.R.A. 1878; R.A. 1881), one of the most imaginative and inventive of living artists; J. M. Swan (1847–1910; A.R.A. 1894; R.A. 1905), trained first at Lambeth, and afterwards in Paris under Gérôme and Frémiet, a skilful manipulator and a **Animal** sensitive draughtsman, and especially remarkable for his **Painting.** intimate understanding of animal character, mainly of the *felidae* (see also SCULPTURE); J.T. Nettleship (1841–1902), trained chiefly in the Slade School, whose studies of the greater beasts of prey are admirably sincere and well painted; Miss Lucy Kemp-Welch (b. 1869), trained in the Herkomer School at Bushey, who paints horses with unusual power; and John Charlton (b. 1849), trained in the South Kensington School, also well known by his pictures of horses and dogs.

There are local schools which claim attention because of the value of their contributions to the aggregation of British art. **Scottish** The most notable of these belong to the Scottish school, **Schools.** the centres of Glasgow, Edinburgh, and Aberdeen, which have produced some of the most distinguished British artists. The Royal Academy of London, indeed, with most of the other leading art societies, has been largely recruited from Scotland. There have been added to its modern roll the names of W. Q. Orchardson, Peter Graham, J. MacWhirter, J. Pettie, Erskine Nichol, T. Faed, David Murray, Colin Hunter, R. W. Macbeth, D. Farquharson, J. Farquharson, George Henry: all of them painters of well-established reputation; and there are many other well-known Scottish artists who have made London their headquarters, like Arthur Melville, a portrait and subject-painter and a masterly water-colourist; E. A. Walton, who is equally successful with portraits, landscapes, and decorative compositions; J. Coutts-Michie, who alternates between portraiture and landscapes of admirable quality; John Lorimer, who has exhibited a number of excellent subject-pictures and many fine portraits; T. Graham, an unaffected painter of sentiment, and a good colourist; Grosvenor Thomas, known best by his freely handled and expressive landscapes; T. Austen Brown, who paints semi-decorative pastorals with unusual vigour of statement; John Lavery, who has taken rank amongst the best of recent portrait painters; and Robert Brough, another portrait painter of vigour, with a subtle sense of colour, whose early and tragic death cut short a promising career. The most notable of the men who remained in Scotland include Alexander Roche, whose remarkable capacity has brought him many successes in portraiture, figure compositions, and decorative paintings on a large scale; W. Y. MacGregor, a leader of the school of landscape painters, fine in style and a master of effect; D. Y. Cameron, an admirable oil-painter and a famous etcher; and Sir James Guthrie, P.R.S.A. well known for his excellent portraits; James Paterson, R. B. Nisbet and Robert Noble, all landscape painters of marked originality and sound technical method; W. McTaggart (d. 1910), the brilliant impressionist; E. A. Hornel and W. Hole, decorative painters who have produced many canvases remarkable for robust originality and rare breadth of treatment; W. Mouncey, a landscape painter who united the dignity of the Barbizon school with a typically Scottish freedom of expression; and Sir George Reid, ex-P.R.S.A., one of the ablest and most distinguished of portrait painters.

The water-colour painters can fairly be said to have kept unchanged the essential qualities of their particular form of picture. **Water-** They have departed scarcely at all from the executive **Colour.** methods which have been recognized as correct for nearly a century, but they have amplified them and have adapted them to a greater range of accomplishment, developing, it may be added, the "blottesque" or the accidental manner suggestive of summary decision. Latterly water-colour painting has come to rival oils in its application to all sorts of subjects; and it is used now with absolute freedom by a very large number of skilful artists. Many of the men who have done the best work in this medium are known as oil painters of the highest rank; and among living workers the same capacity to excel in either mode of expression is by no means uncommon. There have been in recent times such masters as Sir John Gilbert, Sir E. Burne-Jones, Ford Madox Brown, Dante Gabriel Rossetti, A. W. Hunt, H. G. Hine, Henry Moore, Albert Moore, C. E. Holloway, and perhaps should be included E. M. Wimperis, whose water-colours are at least as worthy of admiration as their oil pictures. As water-colourists, much credit is due to Sir E. J. Poynter for his landscapes, portraits, and figure drawings; Sir L. Alma-Tadema for his minutely detailed classic subjects; Sir J. D. Linton for his historical and romantic compositions; Sir E. A. Waterlow for his delicately expressive landscapes; Sir Hubert von Herkomer for his admirably handled figure subjects; George Clausen for pastorals charming in sentiment and distinguished by fine qualities of colour; J. Aumonier, A. D. Peppercorn, J. S. Hill, J. W. North, Leslie Thomson, Frank Walton and R. W. Allan for landscapes of special excellence; E. J. Gregory (d. 1909), and Cadogan Cowper, for figure compositions painted with amazing sureness of touch; Alfred Parsons for landscapes and flower studies; J. R. Reid, W. L. Wyllie, E. Hayes and

C. N. Hemy for sea and coast pictures; R. W. Macbeth, Claude Hayes and Lionel Smythe for rustic scenes with figures in the open air; J. M. Swan for paintings of animals; and G. H. Boughton for costume subjects and delicately poetic fancies. Besides, there is a long list of noteworthy painters whose reputations have been chiefly or entirely made by their successful management of water-colour, and into this list come Birket Foster, the head of the old-fashioned school of dainty rusticity; Carl Haag, a wonderful manipulator, who occupied himself almost exclusively with Eastern subjects; Thomas Collier, A. W. Weedon, H. B. Brabazon, G. A. Fripp, P. J. Naftel, G. P. Boyce, Albert Goodwin, R. Thorne-Waite, F. G. Cotman, Harry Hine, Clarence Whaite and Bernard Evans, whose landscapes show thorough understanding of nature and distinctive individuality of method; Mrs Allingham, an artist of exquisite refinement, whose idealizations of country life have a more than ordinary degree of merit; Clara Montalba, an able painter of impressions of Venice; Kate Greenaway, unrivalled as an interpreter of the graces of child-hood, and endowed with the rarest originality; Mrs Stanhope Forbes, an accomplished executant of well-imagined romantic motives; and J. R. Weguelin, one of the most facile and expressive painters of fantastic figure subjects. By the aid of these artists, and many others of at least equal ability, such as J. Crawhall, J. Paterson, R. Little, Edwin Alexander, Arthur Rackham and J. Walter West, traditions worthy of all respect have been maintained sincerely and with intelligent discrimination; and to their efforts has been accorded a larger measure of popular support than is bestowed upon any other form of pictorial production.

See Richard Muther, *History of Modern Painting* (Eng. ed., 1895); R. de la Sizeranne, *English Contemporary Art* (Eng. ed., 1898); Ernest Chesneau, *The English School of Painting* (2nd Eng. ed., 1885); Clement and Hutton, *Artists of the 19th Century* (Boston, U.S.A., 1885); David Martin and F. Newbery, *The Glasgow School of Painting* (1897); W. D. McKay, R.S.A., *The Scottish School of Painting* (London, 1906); E. Pinnington, *George Paul Chalmers and the Art of his Time* (1896); Gleeson White, *The Master Painters of Britain* (1897); E. T. Cook, *A Popular Handbook to the National Gallery*, vol. ii. (1901); J. E. Hodgson, R.A., *Fifty Years of British Art* (1887); A. G. Temple, *Painting in the Queen's Reign* (1897); Cosmo Monkhouse, *British Contemporary Artists* (1899); G. R. Redgrave, *History of Water-Colour Painting in England 1750–1889* (1889). Also the *Transactions* of the National Association for the Advancement of Art (Liverpool, 1888; Edinburgh, 1889; and Birmingham, 1890); the magazines devoted to the arts; and the principal reviews, such as "English Art in the Victorian Age" (*Quarterly Review*, January 1898). *The Year's Art* (1870–1910; ed. A. C. R. Carter) is an invaluable annual publication fully and accurately chronicling the art institutions and art movements in Great Britain. (M. H. S.)

FRANCE

The period between 1870 and the opening of the 20th century was singularly important in the history of France, and consequently of her art. The internal life of the people developed on new lines with a vigour that left a deep mark on the outcome of mental effort. Literature was foremost in this new movement. The novels of Balzac, Zola, Flaubert, the brothers de Goncourt, Daudet, Guy de Maupassant and the plays of Alexandre Dumas *fils*, filled as they are with the scientific spirit and social atmosphere of the time, opened the eyes of the young generation to appreciation of the visible beauty and the spiritual poetry of the world around them, and helped them to view it with more attentive eyes, more insight and more emotion. The aim of art was also to emancipate itself, by the growing efforts of independent artists, from the slavery of tradition, and to devote itself to a more personal contemplation and knowledge of contemporary life under every aspect. Modern French art tends to become more and more the art of the people—a mixture of naturalism and poetry, deriving its inspiration, by preference, from the world of the working man; no longer appealing only to a restricted and more or less fastidious public, but, on the contrary, adapting its aesthetic or moral teaching to popular apprehension. The whole past was not, of course, wiped out. The younger generation had to learn and profit by the lessons taught by their great precursors. To understand the true character of this recent development of French art it is needful, therefore, to glance at the past.

We need not dwell on the individual authorities who constitute the official hierarchy of the contemporary French school; these masters belong for the most part, by the date of their best work, to a former generation. Starting in many cases from very opposite points, but reconciled and united by time, they carried on, during the last quarter of the 19th century, with more or less distinction, the inevitable evolution of their personal gifts.

We still see the works of some of the staunch Romanticists: Jean Gigoux (d. 1892), Robert-Fleury (d. 1890), Jules Dupré (d. 1889), Lami (d. 1890), Cabat (d. 1893) and Isabey (d. 1886); and with these, though they did not follow quite the same road, may be named Français (d. 1897) and Charles Jacque (d. 1894). Next to them, Meissonier (d. 1891) crowded into the last twenty years of his life a mass of work which, for the most part, enhanced his fame; and Rosa Bonheur (d. 1899), working in retirement up to the age of seventy-seven, went on her accustomed way unmoved by external changes. Hébert, Harpignies, Ziem and Paul Flandrin survived. Among the generation which grew up under the Second Empire we find men of great intelligence and distinction; some, like Alexandre Cabanel (1824-1889), by pictures of historical genre, in a somewhat insipid and conventional style, but more particularly by female portraits, firm in flesh-painting and aristocratic in feeling; others, like Paul Baudry (1828-1886, q.v.), whose large decorative works, with their pure and lofty elegance, secured him lasting fame, and whose allegorical compositions were particularly remarkable; not less so his portraits, at first vivid, glowing and golden, but at the end of his life, under the influence of the new atmosphere, cooler in tone, but more eager, nervous and restless in feeling. Léon Gérôme (b. 1824, q.v.) was the originator, during the Second Empire, of the neo-Greek idea, an Orientalist and painter of historic genre, whose somewhat arid instinct for archaeological precision and finish developed to better ends in sculpture during later years. William Bouguereau (b. 1825, q.v.) painted symbolical and allegorical subjects in a sentimental style. Jules Lefebvre (b. 1836) had a brilliant career as a portrait painter, combined, in his earlier years, with admirable studies of the nude. These were followed by Benjamin Constant (d. 1902), a clever painter of past ages in the East and of modern Oriental life, who latterly directed his powers of vigorous and rapid brushwork to portrait-painting; Fernand Cormon, the inventive chronicler of primeval Gaul, and a solid and learned portrait painter; Aimé Morot, a man of versatile gifts, a painter of portraits full of life and ease. These formed the heart of the Institut. On the other hand, we find a group who betray a close affinity with the realist party—rejecting, like them, tradition at second-hand, though returning for direct teaching to some of the great masters: Léon Bonnat (b. 1833), educated in Spain, and preserving through a long series of official portraits an evident worship of the great realists of that nation; and again, under the same influence, Jean Paul Laurens (b. 1837), who has infused some return of vitality into historical painting by his clear and individual conceptions and realistic treatment. Jean Jacques Henner (b. 1829, q.v.), standing even more apart, lived in a Correggio-like dream of pale nude forms in dim landscape scenery; his love of exquisite texture, and his unvarying sense of beauty, with his refined dilettantism, link him on each side to the great groups of realists and idealists.

About the middle of the 19th century, after the vehement disputes between the partisans of line and the votaries of colour, otherwise the Classic and the Romantic schools, when a younger generation was resting from these follies, exhausted, weary, devoid even of any fine technique, two groups slowly formed on the opposite sides of the horizon—seers or dreamers, both protesting in different ways against the collapse of the French school, and against the alleged indifference and sceptical eclecticism of the painters who were regarded as the leaders. This was a revolt from the academic and conservative tradition. One was the group of original and nature-loving painters, keen and devoted observers of men and things, the realists, made illustrious by the three great personalities of Corot (q.v.), Millet (q.v.) and Courbet (q.v.), the real originators of French contemporary art. The other was the group of men of imagination, the idealists, who, in the pursuit of perfect beauty and an ideal moral standard, reverted to the dissimilar visions of Delacroix and Ingres, the ideals of rhythm as opposed to harmony, of style versus passion, which Théodore Chassériau had endeavoured to combine. Round Puvis de Chavannes (q.v.) and Gustave Moreau (q.v.) we find a group of artists who, in spite of the fascination exerted

of their intelligence by the great works of the old masters, especially the early Florentines and Venetians, would not accept the old technique, but strove to record in splendid imagery the wonders of the spiritual life, or claimed, by studying contemporary individuals, to reveal the psychology of modern minds. Among them were Gustave Ricard (1821-1873), whose portraits, suggesting the mystical charm sometimes of Leonardo and sometimes of Rembrandt, are full of deep unuttered vitality; Elie Delaunay (1828-1891), serious and expressive in his heroic compositions, keen and striking in his portraits; Eugène Fromentin (1820-1876), acute but subtle and silvery, a man of elegant mind, the writer of Les Maîtres d'autrefois, of Sahel and of Le Sahara, the discoverer—artistically—of Algeria. And round the loud and showy individuality of Courbet—healthy, nevertheless, and inspiring—a group, was gathered of men less judicious, but more stirring, more truculent, thoroughly original, but not less reverent to the old masters than they were defiant of contemporary authorities. They were even more ardent for a strong technique, but the masters who attracted them were the Dutch, the Flemish, the Venetians, who, like themselves, had aimed at recording the life of their day. Among these was François Bonvin (1817-1887), who, following Granet, carried on the evolution of a subdivision of genre, the study of domestic interiors. This Drolling, too, had done, early in the 19th century, his predecessors in France being Chardin and Le Nain. This class of subjects has not merely absorbed all genre-painting, but has become a very important factor in the presentment of modern life. Bonvin painted asylums, convent-life, studios, laboratories and schools. Alphonse Legros (q.v.), painter, sculptor and etcher, who settled in London, was of the same school, though independent in his individuality, celebrating with his brush and etching-needle the life of the poor and humble, and even of the vagabond and beggar. There were also Bracquemond, the reviver of the craft of etching; Fantin-Latour, the painter of highly romantic Wagnerian dreams, figure compositions grouped after the Dutch manner, and flower-pieces not surpassed in his day. Ribot, again, and Vollon, daring and dashing in their handling of the brush; Guillaume Régamey, one of the few military painters gifted with the epic sense; and even Carolus Duran, who, after painting "Murdered" (in the Lille Museum), combined with the professional duties of an official teacher a brilliant career as a portrait painter. A later member of this group, attracted to it by student friendship in the little drawing-school which under Lecoq de Boisbaudran competed in a modest way with the École des Beaux Arts, was J. C. Cazin, well known afterwards as a pronounced idealist. Finally, there was Manet, a connecting link between the realists and the impressionists. These two radiant focuses of imagination and of observation respectively were to be seen still intact during the later period, as represented by the most energetic of the masters who upheld them.

After the catastrophe of 1870, French art appeared to be reawakened by the disasters of the country; and at the great exhibition in Vienna in 1873 Count Andrassy exclaimed to Léon Bonnat, "After such a terrible crisis are up again, and victorious!" Immense energy prevailed in the studios, and money poured into France in consequence. The output increased rapidly, and at the same time study became more strenuous, and ambition grew bolder and more manly. Renewed activity stirred in the public academies, and a crowd of foreign students came to learn. Two great facts give a characteristic stamp to this new revival of French art: I. In the class of imaginative painting, the renewed impulse towards monumental or decorative work. II. In the class of nature studies, the growth of landscape painting, which developed along two parallel lines—Impressionism; and III. the "Open-air" school.

I. *Decoration.*—In decorative painting two men were the soul of the movement: Puvis de Chavannes and Philippe de Chennevières Pointel. As we look back on the last years of the Second Empire we see decorative painting sunk in profound lethargy. After Delacroix, Chassériau and Hippolyte Flandrin, and the completion of the great works in the Palais Bourbon, the Senate

House, the Cour des Comptes and a few churches—St Sulpice, St Vincent de Paul and St Germain des Prés—no serious attempts had been made in this direction. Excepting in the Hôtel de Ville, where Cabanel was winning his first laurels, and in the Opera House, a work that was progressing in silence, a few chapels only were decorated with paintings in the manner of easel pictures. But two famous exceptions led to a decorative revival: Puvis de Chavannes's splendid scheme of decoration at Amiens (all, with the exception of the last composition, which is dated 1882, executed without break between 1861 and 1867), and his work at Marseilles and at Poitiers; Baudry, with his ceiling in the Opera House, begun in 1866 but not shown to the public till 1874. There was also a movement for reviving French taste in the industrial arts by following the example of systematic teaching set by some foreign countries, more particularly by England. Decorative painting felt the same impulse. Philippe de Chennevières, curator of the Luxembourg Gallery and directeur des Beaux Arts (from 1874 till 1879), determined to encourage it by setting up a great rivalry between the most distinguished painters, like that which had stimulated the zeal of the artists of the Italian Renaissance. Taking up the task already attempted by Chenavard under the Republic of 1848, but abandoned in consequence of political changes, M. de Chennevières commissioned a select number of artists to decorate the walls of the Panthéon. The panels were to record certain events in the history of France, with due regard to the sacred character of the building. Twelve of the most noted painters were named, with a liberal breadth of selection so as to include the most dissimilar styles: Millet and Meissonier, of whom one refused and the other did not carry out the work; Cabanel and Puvis de Chavannes. The last-named was the first to begin, in 1878, and he too was the painter who put the crowning end to this great work in 1898. His pictures of the "Childhood of Ste Geneviève" (the patron saint of Paris), simple, full of feeling and of innocent charm, appropriate to a popular legend, with their airy Parisian landscape under a pallid sky, made a deep impression. Thenceforward Puvis de Chavannes had a constantly growing influence over younger men. His magnificent work at Amiens, "Ludus pro Patria" (1881-1882), at Lyons and at Rouen, in the Sorbonne and the Hôtel de Ville, for the Public Library at Boston, U.S.A., and on to his last composition, "The Old Age of Ste Geneviève," upheld to the end of the 19th century the sense of lofty purpose in decorative painting. Besides the Panthéon, which gave the first impetus to the movement, Philippe de Chennevières found other buildings to be decorated: the Luxembourg, the Palace of the Legion of Honour and that of the Council of State. The paintings in the Palais de Justice, the Sorbonne, the Hôtel de Ville, the College of Pharmacy, the Natural History Museum, the Opéra Comique, and many more, bear witness to this grand revival of mural painting. Every kind of talent was employed—historical painters, portrait painters, painters of allegory, of fancy scenes, of real life and of landscape. Among the most important were: J. P. Laurens and Benjamin Constant, Bonnat and Carolus Duran, Cormon, and Humbert, Joseph Blanc and L. Olivier Merson, Roll and Gervex, Besnard and Carrière, Harpignies and Pointelin, Raphaël Collin and Henri Martin.

II. *Impressionism.*—In 1874 common cause was made by a group of artists drawn together by sympathetic views and a craving for independence. Various in their tastes, they concentrated from every point of the compass to protest, like their precursors the realists, against the narrow views of academic teaching. Some had romantic proclivities, as the Dutchman Jongkindt, who played an important part in founding this group; others were followers of Daubigny, of Corot or of Millet; some came from the realistic party, whose influence and effort this new set was to carry on. Among these, Édouard Manet (1832-1883) holds a leading place; indeed, his influence, in spite of —or perhaps as a result of—much abuse, extended beyond his circle even so far as to affect academic teaching itself. He was first a pupil of Couture, and then, after Courbot, his real masters were the Spaniards—Velásques, El Greco and Goya—all of whom

he closely studied at the beginning of his career; but he soon felt the influence of Millet and of Corot. With a keen power of observation, he refined and lightened his style, striving for a subtle rendering of the exact relations of tone and values in light and atmosphere. With him, forming the original group, as represented by the Caillebotte collection in the Luxembourg, we find some landscape painters: Claude Monet, the painter of pure daylight, and the artist who by the title of one of his pictures, "An Impression," gave rise to the designation accepted by the group; Camille Pissarro, who at one time carried to an extreme the principle of dotting with pure tints, known as, *pointillisme*, or dotwork; Sisley, Cézanne and others. Among those who by preference studied the human figure were Edgard Degas (*q.v.*) and Auguste Renoir. After long and violent antagonism, such as had already greeted the earlier innovators, these painters, in spite of many protests, were officially recognized both at the Luxembourg and at the great Exhibition of 1900. Their aims have been various, some painting Man and some Nature. In the former case they claim to have gone back to the principle of the greatest artists and tried to record the life of their own time. Manet, Degas and Renoir have shown us aspects of city or vulgar life which had been left to genre-painting or caricature, but which they have represented with the charm of pathos, or with the bitter irony of their own mood, frank, transcripts of life with a feeling for style. For those who painted the scenery of nature there was an even wider field. They brought to their work a new visual sense, released from the clinging memories of past art; they endeavoured to fix the transient effects of moving life, changing under the subtlest and most fugitive effects of light and atmosphere, and the play of what may be called the elements of motion—sunshine, air and clouds— caring less for the exact transcript of motionless objects, which had hitherto been almost exclusively studied, such as the soil, trees and rocks, the inanimate features of the landscape. They introduced a fresh lightness of key, which had been too subservient to the relations of values; they discovered for their ends a new class of subjects essentially modern: towns, streets, railway stations, factories, coal-mines, ironworks and smoke, which they represent with an intelligent adaptation of Japanese art, taking new and audacious points of view, constantly varying the position of their horizon. This is indeed the very acme of naturalism, the last possible stage of modern landscape, covering the whole field of observation, doubling back to the starting-point of imagination. Notwithstanding—or because of—the outcry, of these views, peculiarities and tendencies, soon penetrated schools and studios. Three artists in particular became conspicuous among the most individual and most independent spirits: Besnard, who had taken the Grand Prix de Rome, and carried to the highest pitch his inexhaustible, and charming fancy in studies of the figure under the most unexpected play of light; Carrière, a pupil of Cabanel, who, sought and found in mysterious gloom the softened spirit of the humble, the warm caress of motherhood; and Raffaëlli, a pupil of Gérôme, who brought to light the unrecognized picturesqueness of the lowest depths of humanity.

III. *The "Plein-air", or Open-air, School.*—The same causes, explain the rise of the particular class of work thus commonly designated. Between Millet and Courbet, both redolent of the romantic and naturalistic influences of their time, though apart from them, stands an artist who had some share in establishing the continuity of the line of painters who combined figure-painting with landscape. This is Jules Breton (b. 1827, *q.v.*). More supple than his fellows, less harsh and less wilful, caring more for form and charm, he found it easier to treat "masses," and contributed to diffuse a taste for the artistic presentment and glorification of field labour. He was the chief link between a past style and Jules Bastien-Lepage (1848-1884, *q.v.*), who was in fact the founder of the school of open-air painting, a compromise between the academic manner and the new revolutionary ideas, a sort of academic continuation of the naturalistic evolution, which therefore exerted considerable influence on contemporary art. As a pupil of Cabanel and the Academy schools, enamoured of rustic life, he absorbed at an early stage, though not without hesitation, the love of atmospheric effects characteristic of Corot and of Manet. In his open-air heads and rural scenes he is seen as a conscientious nature worshipper, accurate and sincere, and, like Millet, imbued with a touch of mysticism which becomes even more evident in his immediate pupils. Round him there arose a little galaxy of painters, some more faithful to tradition, some followers of the best innovators, who firmly tread this path of light and modern life. These are Butin, Duez and Renouf, Roll and Gervex, Dagnan-Bouveret, Friant, Adolphe and Victor Binet and many more.

Immediately after the Exhibition of 1889 an event took place which was not without effect on the progress of French art. This was the schism in the Salon. The audacious work of the Société Nationale des Beaux Arts, which left anything that the Impressionists could do far behind, had accustomed the eyes of the public to the most daring attempts, while the numerous contributions of foreigners, especially from the north, where art aimed solely at a direct presentment of daily life, was a fresh encouragement to the study of modern conditions and of the lower classes. But, at the same time, the encroachment on space at the Exhibition (where no limit of number was imposed) by mere studies, hastened the reaction against the extravagances of the degenerate followers of Courbet, Manet and Bastien-Lepage. Remonstrances arose against their perverse and narrow-minded devotion to "truth," or rather to minute exactitude, their pedantry and affectation of documentation; sometimes derived from some old colourists who had not renounced their former ideal, sometimes from younger men impelled unconsciously by literature, which had as usual preceded art in the revolt. The protest was seen, too, in a modified treatment of landscape, which took on the warmer colours of sunset, and in a choice of religious subjects, such as a *pardon*, or a funeral, or a ceremonial benediction, and generally of more human and more pathetic scenes.

Bastien-Lepage, like his great precursor Millet, bore within him the germs of a reaction against the movement he had helped to promote. Dagnan-Bouveret, who began by painting "Sitting for a Photograph" (now at Lyons) and "An Accident," after painting "Le Pain bénit," ended with "The Pilgrims to Emmaus" and "The Last Supper." Friant, again, produced scenes of woe, "All Saints' Day" and "Grief"; and their younger successors, Henri Royer, Adler, Duvent and others, who adhered to this tradition, accommodated it to a more modern ideal, with more vivid colouring and more dramatic composition.

Still, this normal development could have no perceptible effect in modifying the purpose of painting. More was needed. A strong craving for imaginative work was very generally felt, and was revealing itself not merely in France but in Belgium, Scotland, America and Germany. This tendency ere long resulted in groups forming round certain well-known figures. Thus a group of refined dreamers, of poetic dilettanti and harmonious colourists, assembled under the leading of Henri Martin (a strange but attractive visionary, a pupil of Jean Paul Laurens and direct heir to Puvis de Chavannes, from whom he had much sound teaching) and of Aman-Jean, who had appeared at the same time, starting, but with more reserve, in the same direction. Some of this younger group affected no specific aim; the others, the larger number, leant towards contemporary life, which they endeavoured to depict, especially its aspirations and—according to the modern expression now in France of common usage—its "state of soul" typified by melody of line and the eloquent language of harmonies. Among them should he named, as exhibitors in the salons and in the great Exhibition of 1900, Ernest Laurent, Ridel and Hippolyte Fournier, M. and Mme H. Duhem, Le Sidaner, Paul Steck, &c. On the other hand, a second group had formed of sturdy and fervent naturalistic painters, in some ways resembling the school of 1855 of which mention has been made; young and bold, sometimes over-bold, enthusiastic and emotional, and bent on giving expression to the life of their own day; especially among the people, not merely

recording its exterior aspects but epitomizing its meaning by broad and strong synthetical compositions. At their head stood Cottet, who combined in himself the romantic fire and the feeling for orchestrated colour of Delacroix with the incisive realism and bold handling of Courbet; next, and very near to him, but more objective in his treatment, Lucien Simon, a manly painter and rich colourist. Both by preference painted heroic or pathetic scenes from the life of Breton mariners. After them came René Ménard, a more lyrical artist, whose classical themes and landscape carried us back to Poussin and Dauchez, Prinet, Wéry, &c.

Foreign influences had meanwhile proved stimulating to the new tendencies in art. Sympathy with the populace derived added impulse from the works of the Belgian painters Constantin Meunier, Léon Frédéric and Struys; a taste for strong and expressive colouring was diffused by certain American artists, pupils of Whistler, and yet more by a busy group of young Scotsmen favourably welcomed in Paris. But the most unforeseen result of this reactionary movement was a sudden reversion to tradition. The cry of the realists of every shade had been for "Nature!" The newcomers raised the opposition cry of "The Old Masters!" And in their name a protest was made against the narrowness of the documentary school of art, a demand for some loftier scheme of conventionality, and for a fuller expression of life, with its complex aspirations and visions. The spirit of English Pre-Raphaelitism made its way in France by the medium of translations from the English poets Shelley, Rossetti and Swinburne, and the work of their followers Stephane Mallarmé and Le Sâr Peladan; it gave rise to a little artificial impetus, which was furthered by the simultaneous but transient rage for the works of Burne-Jones, which were exhibited with his consent in some of the salons, and by the importation of William Morris's principles of decoration. The outcome was a few small groups of symbolists, the most famous being that of the Rose + Croix, organized by Le Sâr Peladan; then there was Henri Martin, and the little coterie of exhibitors attracted by a dealer, the late M. le Bare de Bouttiville, in which Cottet was for a short time entangled. But few interesting names are to be identified: Dulac (d. 1899), who became known chiefly for his mystical lithographs in colour; Maurice Denis and Bonnard, whose decorative compositions, with their refined and harmonious colouring, are not devoid of charm; Vuillard, &c. But it was in the school and studio of Gustave Moreau (1826-1898, q.v.) that the fire of idealism burned most hotly. This exceptional man and rare painter, locked up in his solitude, endeavoured, by a thorough and intelligent assimilation of all the traditions of the past, to find and create for himself a new tongue—rich, nervous, eloquent, strong and resplendent—in which to give utterance to the loftiest dreams that haunt the modern soul. He revived every old myth and rejuvenated every antique symbol, to represent in wonderful imagery all the serene magnificence and all the terrible struggles of the moral side of man, which he had explored to its lowest depths and most heroic heights in man and woman, in poetry and in death. Being appointed, towards the end of his life, to a professorship in the École des Beaux Arts, he regarded his duties as a real apostleship, and his teaching soon spread from his lecture-room and studio to those of the other masters. His own work, though hardly known to his pupils at the time, at first influenced their style; but, especially after his death, they were quickly disgusted with their own detestable imitation of subjects on which the master had set the stamp of his great individuality; they deserted the fabulous world of the Greek Olympus and the wonderful gardens of the Bible, to devote them to a passionate expression of modern life. Desvallières, indeed, remained conspicuous in his original manner; Sabatté, Maxence, Béronneau, Besson and many more happily worked out their way on other lines.

In trying to draw up the balance-sheet of French art at the beginning of the 20th century, it were vain to try to enter its work under the old-world headings of History, Genre, Portraits, Landscape. All the streams had burst their channels, all the currents mingled. Historical painting, reinstated for a time by Puvis de Chavannes and J. P. Laurens, in which Benjamin Constant and Cormon also distinguished themselves, had but a few adherents who tried to maintain its dignity, either in combination with landscape, like M. Tattegrain, or with the ineffectual aid of archaeology, like M. Rochegrosse. At certain times, especially just after 1870, the memory of the war gave birth to a special genre of military subjects, under the distinguished guidance of Meissonier (q.v.), and the peculiar talents of Alphonse de Neuville (q.v.), of Detaille (q.v.) and Protais. This phase of contemporary history being exhausted, gave way to pictures of military manœuvres, or colonial wars and incidents in recent history; it latterly went through a revival under a demand for subjects from the Empire and the Revolution, in consequence of the publication of many memoirs of those times. Side by side with "history," religious art formerly flourished greatly; indeed, next to mythology, it was always dear to the Academy. Apart from the subjects set for academical competitions, there was only one little revival of any interest in this kind. This was a sort of neo-evangelical offshoot, akin to the literature and stress of religious discussion; and its leader, a man of feeling rather than conviction, was J. C. Cazin (d. 1901). Like Puvis de Chavannes, and under the influence of Corot and Millet, of Hobbema, and yet more of Rembrandt, he attempted to renew the vitality of history and legend by the added charm of landscape and the introduction of more human, more living and more modern, elements into the figures and accessories. Following him, a little group developed this movement to extravagance. The recognized leader at the beginning of the 20th century was Dagnan-Bouveret.

Through mythology and allegory we are brought back to real life. No one now thinks in France of seeking any pretext for displaying the nude beauty of woman. Henner, perhaps, and Fantin-Latour, were the last to cherish a belief in Venus and Artemis, in naiads and nymphs. Painters go direct to the point nowadays; when they paint the nude, it is apart from abstract fancies, and under realistic aspects. They are content with the model. It is the living female. The whole motor force of the time lies in the expression, under various aspects, of real life. This it is which has given such a soaring flight to the two most primitive forms of the study of life, landscape and portraiture. Portraits have in fact adopted every style that can possibly be imagined: homely or fashionable, singly or in groups, by the fire or out of doors, in some familiar attitude and the surroundings of daily life, analytically precise, or synthetically broad, a literal transcript or a bold epitome of facts. As to landscape, no class of painting has been busier, more alive or more productive. It has overflowed into every other channel of art, giving them new spirit and a new life. It has led the van in every struggle and won every victory. Never was army more numerous or more various than that of the landscape painters, nor more independent. All the traditions find representatives among them, from Paul Flandrin to René Ménard. Naturalists, impressionists, open-air painters, learned in analysis or potent in invention. We need only name Harpignies, broadly decorative; Pointelin, thoughtful and austere; and Cazin, grave and tender, to give a general idea of the strength of the school.

Every quarter of the land has its painters: the north and the south, Provence and Auvergne, Brittany, dear to the young generation of colourists, the East, Algeria, Tunis—all contribute to form a French school of landscape, very living and daring, of which, as successors of Fromentin and Guillaumet, must be named Dinet, Marius Perret, Paul Leroy and Girardot. But it is more especially in the association of man and nature, in painting simple folk and their struggle for life amid their natural surroundings or by their homely hearth, in the glorification of humble toil, that the latest French art finds its most characteristic ideal life.　　　　　　　　　　　　　(L. Bɴ.)

BELGIUM

Belgium fills a great place in the realm of art; and while its painters show a preference for simple subjects, their technique is broad, rich and sound, the outcome of a fine tradition. Since 1855 international critics have been struck by the unity of effect produced by the works of the Belgian school, as expressed more especially by similarities of handling and colour. For the things which distinguish all Belgian painters, even in their most unpictorial divagations, are a strong sense of contrast or harmony of colouring, a free, bold style of brushwork, and a preference for rich and solid painting. It is the tradition of the old Flemish school. It would be more correct, indeed, to say traditions; for the modifications of each tendency, inevitably reviving when the success of another has exhausted itself, constantly show a reversion either to the domestic "Primitives" (or, as we might say, Pre-Raphaelites) of the Bruges school, or to the "decorative" painters of the later time at Antwerp, and no veneer of modern taste will ever succeed in masking this traditional perennial groundwork. In this way the prevailing authority of the French painter Louis David may be accounted for; as acknowledged at Brussels at the beginning of the 19th century, it was a reaction in antagonism to the heavy and flabby work of the late Antwerp school, an unconscious reversion perhaps to the finish and minuteness of the early painters of Bruges. Indeed, in France, himself David's most devoted disciple, was reproached with trying to revive the Gothic art of Jean de Bruges. Then, when David's followers produced only cold and feeble work, Wappers arose to restore the methods of another tradition, for which he secured a conspicuous triumph. Classical tinsel made way, indeed, for romantic tinsel. The new art was as conventional as the old, but it had the advantage of being adaptable to the taste for show and splendour which characterizes the nation, and it also admitted the presentment of certain historical personages who survived in the memory of the people. The inevitable reaction from this theatrical art, with its affectation of noble sentiments, was to brutal realism. Baron Henri Leys (q.v.) initiated it, and the crudity of his style gave rise to a belief in a systematic purpose of supplanting the Latin tradition by Germanic sentimentality. Leys's archaic realism was transformed at Brussels into a realism of observation and modern thought, in the painting of Charles de Groux. The influence of Leys on this artist was merely superficial; for though he, too, affected painful subjects, it was because they appealed to his compassion. The principle represented by de Groux was destined to pioneer the school in a better way; at the same time, from another side the authority of Courbet, the French realist, who had been for some time in Brussels, and that of the great landscape painters of the Fontainebleau school, had suggested to artists a more attentive study of nature and a remarkable reversion in technique to bolder and firmer handling. At this time, among other remarkable men, Alfred Stevens appeared on the scene, the finished artist of whom Camille Lemonnier truly said that he was "of the race of great painters, and, like them, careful of finish"—that in him "the eye, the hand and the brain all co-operated for the mysterious elaboration" of impasto, colour and chiaroscuro, and "the least touch was an operation of the mind." A brief period ensued during which the greater number of Belgian artists were carried away by the material charms of brushwork and paint. The striving after brilliant efforts of colour which had characterized the painters of the last generation then gave way to a devout study of values; and at the same time it is to be noted that in Belgium, as in France, landscape painters were the first to discover the possibility of giving new life to the interpretation of nature by simplicity and sincerity of expression. They tried to render their exact sensations; and we saw, as has been said, "an increasingly predominant revelation of instinctive feeling in all classes of painting." Artists took an impartial interest in all they saw, and the endeavour to paint well eliminated the hope of expressing a high ideal; they now sought only to utter in a work of art the impression made on them by an external fact; and, too often, the strength of the effort degenerated into brutality.

These new influences, which, in spite of the conservative school, had by degrees modified the aspect of Belgian art in general, led to the formation at Brussels of an association under the name of the Free Society of Fine Arts. This group of painters had a marked influence on the development of the school, and hand in hand with the pupils of Portaels—a teacher of sober methods, caring more for sound practice than for theories—it encouraged not merely the expression of deep and domestic feeling which we find in the works of Leys and de Groux; but also the endeavour to paint nature in the broad light of open air. The example of the Free Society found imitators; various artistic groups were formed to organise exhibitions where new works could be seen and studied irrespective of the influence of dealers, or of the conservatism of the authorities which was increasingly conspicuous in the official galleries; till what had at first been regarded as a mere audacious and fantastic demonstration assumed the dignity of respectable effort. The " Cercle des Vingt " (" The Twenty Club ") also exerted a marked influence. By introducing into its exhibitions works by the greatest foreign artists it released Belgian art from the uniformity which some too patriotic theorists would fain have imposed. The famous " principle of individuality in art " was asserted there in a really remarkable manner, for side by side with the experiments of painters bent on producing certain effects of light hung the works of men who clung to literary or abstract subjects. Other groups, again, were formed on the same lines; but then came the inevitable reaction. from these elaborations of quivering light and subtle expression, pushed, as it seemed, to an extreme. The youngest generation of Brussels painters, in revolt against the lights and ultra-refinements of their immediate predecessors, seem to take pleasure in a return to gums and bitumen, and to seek the violent effects so dear to the romantic painters of a past time.

Brussels is the real centre of art in Belgium. Antwerp, the home of Rubens, is resting on the memory of past glories, after vainly trying to uphold the .ideal formerly held in honour by Flemish painters. And yet, so great is the prestige of this ancient reputation, that Antwerp even now attracts artists from every land, and more especially the dealers who go thither to buy pictures as a common form of merchandise. At Ghent the wonderful energy of the authorities who get up the triennial exhibitions makes these the most interesting provincial shows of their kind; other towns, as Liége, Tournay, Namur, Mons and Spa also have periodical exhibitions.

From 1830, in the early days of the Belgian school of painting, we may observe a tendency to seek for the fullest qualities of colour, with delicate gradations of light and shade. In this Wappers led the way. At a time when his teachers in the Antwerp Academy would recognise nothing but the heavy brown tones of old paintings, he was already representing the transparent shadows of natural daylight. But heroic and sentimental romanticism was already making way for the serious expression of domestic and popular feeling, and thenceforward the prominence assumed by genre, and yet more by landscape, led to a deeper and more direct study of the various aspects of nature. At the same time a special sense of colour was the leading characteristic of the artists of the time, and it was truly said that " the ambition to be a fine painter was stronger than the desire for scrupulous exactitude." Artists evidently aimed, in the first place, at a solid impasto and glowing colour; an undertone, ruddy and golden, gleamed through the paler and more real hues of the over-painting. In this way we may certainly recognise the influence of the French colourists of Courbet's time; just as we may trace the influence of the grey tone prevalent in Manet's day in the effort to paint with more simple truth and fewer tricks of recipe, which became evident when the " Free Society " was founded at Brussels, and the pupils from Portaels's studio came to the front.

Among the artists who were then working the following must be named (with their best works in the Brussels Gallery): Alfred Stevens (q.v.), an incomparably charming painter, characterized by exquisite harmony of colour and marvellous dexterity with the brush. In the Brussels Gallery are his " The Lady in Pink," " The Studio," " The Widow," " A Painter and his Model," and " The Lady-Bird." Joseph Stevens, his brother, a master-painter of dogs, broad in his draughtsmanship, and painting in strong ·touches of colour, is represented by " The Dog-Market," " Brussels-Morning." " A Dog before a Mirror "; Henri de Braekeleer, the nephew and pupil of Leys, a fine painter of interiors, in warm and golden tones, by " The Geographer," " A Farm—Interior," " A Shop "; Lievin de Winne, portrait painter, sober in style and refined in execution, by " Leopold I. King of the Belgians "; Florent Willems, archaic and elegant, by " The Wedding Dress ";

Eugène Smits, a refined colourist, always working with the thought of Venice in his mind, by " The Procession of the Seasons "; Louis Dubois, a powerful colourist with a full brush, striving to resemble Courbet, by " Storks," " Fish "; Alfred Verwée, a fine animal painter, with special love for a sheeny silkiness of texture, by " The Estuary of the Scheldt," " The Fair Land of Flanders," " A Zeeland Team "; Alfred Verhaeren, a pupil of L. Dubois, by some " Interiors "; Félicien Rops, an extraordinary artist, precise in drawing, sensual and incisive, by " A Parisienne "; Félix ter Linden, a restless, refined nature, always trying new subtleties of the brush and palette-knife, by " Captives." Amongst other painters may be named Camille van Camp, Gustave de Jonghe, Franz Verhas, and his brother Jan Verhas, the painter of the popular " School Feast " in the Brussels Gallery; and Jan van Beers, the clever painter of female coquettishness, represented by pictures in the Antwerp Gallery.

As landscape painters, the chief are: Hippolyte Boulenger, a refined draughtsman and a delicate colourist, represented in the Brussels Gallery by " View of Dinant," " The Avenue of Old Hornbeams at Tervueren," " The Meuse at Hastière "; Alfred de Knyff, noble and elegant, by " The Marl Pit," " A Heath—Campine "; Joseph Coosemans, by " A Marsh—Campine "; Jules Montigny, by " Wet Weather "; Alph. Asselbergs, by " A Marsh—Campine." There are also Xavier and César de Cock, painters in light gay tones of colour; Gustave Den Duyts, a lover of melancholy twilight, represented in the same gallery by " A Winter Evening "; Mme Marie Collart, a seeker after the more melancholy and concentrated impressions of nature, by " The Old Orchard "; and Baron Jules Goethals.

Of the Antwerp school, François Lamorinière, archaic and minute, has in the Brussels Gallery his " View from Edeghem," and there is also Théodore Verstraete, sentimental, or frenzied.

As marine painters: Paul Jean Clays, who delights in vivid effects of colour, is represented at Brussels by " The Antwerp Roadstead," " Calm on the Scheldt "; Louis Artan, who prefers dark and powerful effects, by " The North Sea," besides Robert Mols, A. Bouvier, and Lemayeur.

As painters of town scenery may be named F. Stroobant, a draughtsman rather than a painter, who is represented in the Brussels Gallery by " The Grande Place at Brussels," and J. B. Van More, a colourist chiefly, by " The Cathedral at Belem."

The flower painter, Jean Robie, has in the Brussels Gallery " Flowers and Fruit."

Jean Portaels, the painter of " A Box at the Theatre," at Budapest, is represented in the Brussels Gallery by " The Daughter of Sion Insulted "; Emile Wauters, a master of free and solid brushwork, equally skilled in portraiture, historical composition and decorative portrait painting, by " The Madness of Hugo van der Goes "; Edouard Agneessens, a genuine painter, with breadth of vision and facile execution, by portraits; André Hennebicq, a painter of historical subjects, by " Labourers in the Campagna, Rome "; Isidore Verheyden, a landscapist and portrait painter, by " Woodcutters "; Eugène Verdyen and Emile Charlet should be mentioned, and the landscape painter Henri van der Hecht, whose " On the Sandhills " is in the Brussels Gallery.

The principal landscape painters of what is known as the " neutral tint " school (l'École du gris) are: Théodore Baron, faithful to the sterner features of Belgian scenery, represented in the Brussels Gallery by " A Winter Scene—Condroz "; Adrien Joseph Heymans, a careful student of singular effects of light, by " Springtime "; Jacques Rosseels, a painter of the cheerful rightness of the Flemish country, by " A Heath," besides Isidore Meyers and Florent Crabeels.

Some figure painters who may be added to this group are: Charles Hermans, whose picture " Dawn " (Brussels Gallery), exhibited in 1875, betrays the ascendancy of the principles upheld by the Free Society of Fine Arts; Jean de la Hoese, who has since made portraits his special line; Emile Sacré; Léon Philippet, represented in the Brussels Gallery by " The Murdered Man "; and Jan Stobbaerts, a masterly painter, powerful but coarse, by " A Farm—Interior."

Three more artists were destined to greater fame: Constantin Meunier, a highly respected artist, equally a painter and a sculptor, known as the Millet of the Flemish workman, who has depicted with noble feeling his admiration and pity for one contemporary state of the human race, and who is represented in the Brussels Gallery by " The Peasants' War "; Xavier Mellery, who tries to express in works of high artistic merit the inner life of men and things, and personifications of thought, by " A Drawing "; and Alexandre Struys, a strong and clever painter, expressing his sympathy with poverty and misfortune in works of remarkable ability.

Besides these, Charles Verlat, a powerful and skilled artist, painted a vast variety of subjects; his teaching was influential in the Antwerp Academy. In the Brussels Gallery he is represented by " Godfrey de Bouillon at the Siege of Jerusalem," " A Flock of Sheep attacked by an Eagle "; Alfred Cluysenaar, whose aim is to produce decorative work on an enormous scale, by " Canossa "; Albrecht de Vriendt, by " Homage done to Charles V. as a Child "; Juliaan de Vriendt, by " A Christmas Carol "; Victor Lagye, by

"The Witch." Franz Vinck, Wilhelm Geets, Karl Ooms, and P. van der Ouderaa, endeavour to perpetuate, while softening down, the style of historical painting so definitely formulated by Leys. Finally, Joseph Stallaert, a painter of classical subjects, is represented in the Brussels Gallery by "The Death of Dido." Eugène Devaux, a remarkable draughtsman, should also be named.

Works by all those artists were to be seen in the Historical Exhibition of Belgian Art at Brussels, 1880. Camille Lemonnier, in his *History of the Fine Arts in Belgium*, discussed this Exhibition very fully, pointing out three distinct periods in the history of the century. The first, romantic, literary and artificial, extended from 1830 till nearly 1850; the second was a period of transition, domestic in feeling, gradually developing to realism in the course of about twenty years; the third began in the 'seventies, a time of careful study, especially in landscape. This was followed by the beginning of a fourth period, characterized by a freer sense of light and atmosphere.

Apart from the exclusive tendency, inevitable under bureaucratic administration, the mere arrangement on an antiquated plan of the great academic salons was unsuited to the display of works intended to represent individual feeling or peculiarities of pictorial treatment. Hence it was that a great many painters came to prefer smaller and more eclectic shows, leading to the fashion, which still persists, of exhibitions by clubs or associations. The Fine Arts Club at Brussels had long since afforded opportunities for showing the pictures of the Société Libre, founded in 1868, which were condemned by the authorities as tending to "revolutionize" art. After this, two associations of young painters were formed at Brussels with a view to organizing their own exhibitions. The "Chrysalide" Club was founded in 1875, and the "Essor" (the "Soaring") Club in 1876. In 1882, however, the Essor obtained leave to open their exhibition in a room in the Palais des Beaux Arts at Brussels. This tolerance was all the more appreciated by the younger party because a new departure was in course of development, again a modification in the effort to represent light in painting. The "neutral tint" school had given way to the school of "whiteness"; a luminous effect was to be sought by a free use of brilliant colour with a very full brush. But ere long this method proved unsatisfactory, and attention was now turned towards a "sincerer and acuter perception of local values"; and again the influence of certain French painters was brought to bear—those of the group headed by C. Monet, preparing for that of the French painter G. Seurat, the first who carried into practice the systematic decomposition of colour by the process known as *pointillisme* (the intimate juxtaposition of dots of colour). In 1884, in consequence of a division in the Essor Club, the "XX" Club was founded, who, though thus limiting their number, reserved the right of "issuing yearly invitations, and thus testifying the sympathy they felt with the most independent artists of Belgium and with those foreign painters with whom they had the most pronounced affinity." For ten years the exhibitions of the "XX," whose careful and artistic arrangements were in themselves admirable, were the fount in Belgium of discussions on art. The limit of its existence to ten years was determined when the club was formed; but as it was desirable that the principle of liberty in art should still be held in honour, M. Octave Maus, the secretary of the "XX" Club, organized the exhibitions of the *Libre esthétique* in and since 1894. Other clubs have been formed in Brussels: the Fine Art Society in 1891 and the "Furrow" (*le Sillon*) in 1893. In 1894 another breach in the *Essor* Club, which, growing very weak, was soon to disappear—as the "Art Union" and the *Voornaerts* Club had done—led to the formation of the Society "for Art" (*pour l'art*); and in 1896 a party of that club established a salon of idealist art which favoured an exaggeration of the intellectual tendency already begun in the exhibitions of the "XX." Subsequently, in the exhibitions of the *Sillon* and of the *Labeur* Club (founded in 1898) a reaction set in, in favour of heavy brown tones and ponderous composition. At Antwerp the influence of the local societies—the "*Als Ik Kan*," the Independent Art Club, and the "XIII"—was less sensibly felt; it was, however, enough to confirm certain waverers in the direction of purely disinterested effort.

It would be impossible to classify into definite groups those painters whose first distinctive appearance was subsequent to the Historical Exhibition in 1880. Only an approximate grouping can be attempted by assigning each to the association in whose exhibitions he made the best display of what he aimed at expressing. Thus it was chiefly in the rooms of the *Essor* Club that works were shown by the following: L. Frédéric, a remarkable painter, combining wonderful facility of execution with a sincerely simple sentiment of homely pathos, represented at the Brussels Gallery by "Chalk Sellers"; E. Hoetarickx, a painter of crowds in the streets and parks; F. Seghers, a pleasing colourist, who had made flower-painting his speciality; two animal painters, F. van Leemputten, "Return from Work" (Brussels Gallery), and E. van Damme-Sylva, as well as the marine painter, A. Marcette. The landscape painters include J. de Greef, almost brutal in style, "The Pool at Rouge-Cloître" (Brussels Gallery), C. Wolles, and Hamesse. L. Houyoux, F. Halkett, L. Herbo are known for their portraits. And there are E. van Gelder, J. Mayné, A. Crespin, a learned decorative painter and E. Duyck, a graceful draughtsman, "A Dream" (Brussels Gallery). As designers may be named A. Heins, a clever illustrator, and A. Lynen, of a thoroughly Brussels type, keenly observant and satirical.

At the exhibitions of the "XX" were pictures by the following: Fernand Khnopff ("Memories," a pastel, in Brussels Gallery), an admirer of the refined domesticity of English contemporary art, and of mystical art, as represented by Gustave Moreau; H. van der Velde, a well-known exponent of the new methods in applied art; J. Ensor, a whimsical nature, loving strange combinations of colour and inconsequent fancies (Brussels Gallery: "The Lamp Man "); Th. van Rysselberghe, a clever painter, especially in the technique of dot painting (*pointillisme*); W. Schlobach, a remarkable colourist of uncertain tendencies; Henry de Groux, son of Ch. de Groux, a seer of visions represented in violent tones and workmanship; G. Vogels, a painter of thaw and rain; G. van Strydoneck, R. Wytsman, J. Delvin, F. Charlet, Mlle A. Boch, all of whom have striven to bring light into their pictures; W. Finch and G. Lemmen.

To the triennial salons, to the exhibitions of the "Artistic" clubs, to the House of Art (*Maison d'art*), at Brussels, and to the various Antwerp clubs, the following have contributed: F. Courtens, Roosels's brilliant pupil, an astonishing painter with a heavy impasto (Brussels Gallery: "Coming out of Church "); J. de Lalaing, full of lofty aims, but showing in his painting the qualities of a sculptor (Brussels Gallery: "A Prehistoric Hunter "); E. Claus, a lover of bright colour, and a genuine landscape painter (Brussels Gallery: "A Flock on the Road "); A. Baertsoen, who delights in the quiet corners of old Flemish towns; H. Evenepoel, a fine artist whose premature death deprived the Belgian school of a highly distinguished personality (Brussels Gallery: "Child at Play "); G. Vanaise, a painter of huge historical subjects; Ch. Mertens, a refined artist; E. Motte, an interesting painter with a love of archaic methods (Brussels Gallery: "A Girl's Head "); A. Lévêque, an accomplished draughtsman with a distinctive touch; L. Wolles, an admirable draughtsman; J. Leempoels, elaborate and minute; H. Richir, a portrait painter; J. van den Eeckhout, a clever pupil of Verheyden; J. Rosier, a skilful follower of Verlat; L. Abry, a painter of military subjects; E. Carpentier, E. Vanhove, Luyten and Desmeth.

Essentially of the Antwerp School are F. van Kuyck, P. Verhaert, de Jans, and Brunin of Ghent, Ch. Doudelet, C. Montald and van Biesbroeck.

There is a group of artists at Liège whose sincerity and high technical qualities have been recognized: A. Donnay, A. Rassenfosse, E. Berchmans, F. Maréchal, Dewitte. Of lady painters: Mmes E. Beernaert, L. Héger and J. Wytsman paint landscape; Mmes B. Art, A. Ronner, G. Meunier and M. De Bièvre paint flowers. Mmes A. d'Anethan, Lambert de Rothschild, M. Philippson, H. Calais and M. A. Marcotte paint figures and portraits.

The chief exhibitors at the *Société pour l'art* have been A. Clamberlani, a painter of large decorative compositions in subdued tones; H. Ottevaere, a painter of night or twilight landscapes; O. Coppens, R. Janssens and A. Hannotiau, who study old houses, deserted churches and dead cities; F. Baes, an excellent pupil of Frédéric Fabry; O. and J. Dierickx, painters of decorative figures; H. Meunier, an ingeniously decorative draughtsman; J. Delville, founder of the salons of idealist art.

Leading exhibitors at the *Voornaerts* Club have been E. Laermans, a strange artist, as it were a Daumier with anchylose joints, but a colourist (Brussels Gallery: "A Flemish Peasant "); V. Gilsoul, a clever pupil of Courtens (Brussels Gallery: "The Kennel "); J. du Jardin, the writer of *L'Art flamand*, an important critical work illustrated by J. Middeleer.

Contributors to the exhibitions of the *Sillon* Club comprise G. M. Stevens, P. Verdussen, P. Matthieu, J. Gouweloos, Bastien, Blieck, Wagemans and Smeers; and V. Mignot, ingenious in designing posters.

At the exhibitions of water-colours have been seen the works of Huberti, F. Bingé, V. Uytterschaut, Stacquet and H. Cassiers, who work with light washes or a clever use of body colour; Hagenaars, who paints with broad washes; Delaunois, the painter of mysterious interiors; Th. Lybaert, minute in his brushwork; M. Romberg and Titz, correct draughtsmen.

Since 1870 several important works of decorative painting in public buildings have been carried out in Belgium. Guffens, Swerts and Pauwels have succumbed to the influences of German art, often cold and stiff; A. and J. Dewriendt, V. Lagye, W. Geets and Van der Ouderaa have followed more or less in the footsteps of Leys. J. Stallaert has cleverly revived a classic style. Emile Wauters and A. Hennebicq have adopted the traditions of Historical Painting; and so too have L. CellaIt, A. Cluysenaar, J. de Lalaing and A. Bourland, though with a more decorative sense of conception and treatment. But of all these works, certainly the most remarkable is that artistic and intelligent fitness is that of M. Delbeke, in the market-hall at Ypres.

See Camille Lemonnier, *Histoire des arts en Belgique*; A. J. WautERs, *La Peinture flamande*; J. du Jardin, *L'Art flamand*.

(F. K.*)

HOLLAND

The entire Impressionist movement of the end of the 19th century failed to exercise the slightest influence upon the Dutch. They are only modern in so far as they again resort to the classics of their Fatherland. For a whole generation Josef Israels was at the head of Dutch art. Born in 1827 at Groningen, the son of a money-changer, he walked every day in his early years, with a linen money-bag under his arm, to the great banking house of Mesdag, a son of which became later the famous marine painter. During his student days in Amsterdam he lived in the Ghetto, in the house of a poor but orthodox Jewish family. He hungered in Paris, and was derided as a Jew in the Delaroche school there. Such were the experiences of life that formed his character. In Zantvoort, the little fishing village close to Haarlem, he made a similar discovery to that which Millet had already made at Barbizon. In the solitude of the remote village he discovered that not only in the pages of history, but also in everyday life, there are tragedies. Having at first only painted historical subjects, he now began to depict the hard struggle of the seafaring man, and the joys and griefs of the poor. He commenced the long series of pictures that for thirty years and more occupied the place of honour in all Dutch exhibitions. They do not contain a story that can be rendered into words; they only tell the tale of everyday life. Old women, with rough, toil-worn hands and good-natured wrinkled faces, sit comfortably at the stove. Weatherbeaten seamen wade through the water, splashed by the waves as they drag along the heavy anchors. A peasant child learns how to walk by the aid of a little cart. Again, the dawning light falls softly upon a peaceful deathbed, on which an old woman has just breathed her last. A sad and resigned melancholy characterizes and pervades all his works. His toilers do not stand up straight; they are broken, without hope, and humble, and accomplish their appointed task without pleasure and without interest. He paints human beings upon whom the oppressions of centuries are resting; eyes that neither gaze on the present nor into the future, but back on to the long, painful past. A Jew, bearing the Ghetto yet in his bosom, is talking to us; and in his painting of the lowly and oppressed he recounts the story of his own youth and the history of his own race.

The younger painters have divided Israels' subjects among them. Each has his own little field, which he tills and cultivates with industry and good sense; and paints one picture, to be repeated again and again during his lifetime. Christoph Birschop, born in Friesland, settled as an artist in the land of his birth, where the national costumes are so picturesque, with golden chains, lace caps and silver embroidered bodices. As in de Hoogh's pictures, the golden light streams through the window upon the floor, upon deep crimson table-covers; and upon a few silent human beings, whose lives are passed in dreamy monotony. Gerk Henkes paints the fogs of the canals, with boats gliding peacefully along. Albert Neuhuys selects simple family scenes, in cosy rooms with the sunlight peeping stealthily through the windows. Adolf Cortz, a pupil of Israels, loves the pale vapour of autumn, grey-green plains and dusty country roads, with silvery thistles and pale yellow flowers. The landscape painters, also, have more in common with the old Dutch classic masters than with the Parisian Impressionists. There, on the hill, Rembrandt's windmill slowly flaps its wings; there Potter's cows ruminate solemnly as they lie on the grass. There are no coruscation and dazzling brightness, only the grey-brownish mellowness that Van Goyen affected. Anton Mauve, Jacob Maris and Willem Maris (d. 1910), are the best known landscape men. Others are Mesdag, de Haas, Apol, Klinkenberg, Bastert, Blommers, de Kock, Bosboom, Ten Kate, du Chattel, Ter Meulen, Sande-Bakhuyzen. They all paint Dutch coast scenery, Dutch fields, and Dutch cattle, in excellent keeping with the old-master school, and with phlegmatic repose.

A few of the younger masters introduced a certain amount of movement into this distinguished, though somewhat somniferous, excellence. Breitner and Isak Israels seem to belong rather to Manet's school than to that of Holland. The "suburb" pictures of W. Tholen, the flat landscapes bathed in light by Paul Joseph Gabriel, and Jan Veth's and Havermann's impressionistic portraits prove that, even among the Dutch, there are artists who experiment. Jan Toorop has even attained

the proud distinction of being the *enfant terrible* of modern exhibitions, and his works appear to belong rather to the art of the old Assyrians than to the 19th century. But those who will endeavour to enter into their artistic spirit will soon discover that Toorop is deserving of more than a mere shrug of the shoulder; they will find that he is a great painter, who independently pursues original aims. At the present time all criticism of art is determined by the "line." All caprices and whims of the "line" are now ridden as much to death, and with the same enthusiasm, as were formerly those of "light." Toorop occupies one of the first places among those whose only aim consists in allowing the "line" to talk and make music. His astonishing power of physical expression may be noted. With what simple means, for example, he renders in his picture of the "Sphinx" all phases of hysterical desire; in that of "The Three Brides" nunlike resignation, chaste devotion and unbridled voluptuousness. If his mastery over gesture, the glance of the eye, be remarked—how each feature, each movement of the hand and head, each raising and closing of the eyelid, exactly expresses what it is intended to express—Toorop's pictures will no more be scoffed at than those of Giotto, but he will be recognized as one of the greatest masters of the "line" that the 19th century produced.

See Max Rooses, *Dutch Painters of the Nineteenth Century* (Eng. ed., London, 1898-1901).　　　　　　　　　　　　　(R. Mr.)

GERMANY

The German school of painting, like that of France, entered on a new phase after the Franco-German War of 1870. An empire had been built up of the agglomeration of separate states. Germany needed no longer to gaze back admiringly at older and greater epochs. The historical painter became neglected. Not the heroic deeds of the past, but the political glories of the new empire were to be immortalized. This transition is particularly noticeable in the work of Adolf von Menzel. At the time of political stagnation he had recorded on his canvas the glories of Prussia in the past. Now that the present had achieved an importance of its own, he painted "The Coronation of King William at Königsberg" and "King William's Departure for the Army"; and ultimately he became the painter of popular subjects. The motley throng in the streets had a special fascination for him, and he loved to draw the crowd pushing its eager way to listen to a band on the promenade, in the market, at the doors of a theatre, or the windows of a café. He discovered the poetry of the builder's yard and the workshop. In the "Moderne Cyklopen" (ironworks), painted in 1876, he left a monumental mark in the history of German art; for in this picture he depicts a simple incident in daily life, without any attempt at genre; and this was indeed the characteristic of his work for the next few years. Humorous anecdote, as represented by Knaus (b. 1829), Vautier (1829-1898), Defregger (b. 1835) and Grützner (b. 1846), found little acceptance. Serious representations of modern life were required; resort was made to all the expedients of the great painters, and the 'seventies were years of artistic study for Germany. Every great colourist in the past was thoroughly studied and his secrets discovered. In Germany, Wilhelm Leibl (b. 1844), holds the same prominent place that Courbet does in France. Leibl, like Courbet, (q.v.), showed that the task of painting is not to narrate, but to depict by the most convincing means at its disposal. He even went farther than Courbet in close scrutiny of nature. With loving patience he strove to translate into colour everything that his keen eye observed: he studied nature with the devotion of the medieval artist. No feeling, strictly speaking, is discernible in his work. His greatest pictures are only of quiet life, with human accessories, and his painful accuracy divests his pictures of poetry. But when he first appeared, he was necessary. His painting of "Three Peasant Women in Church" is a grand documentary work of that period, whose first aim was to conquer the picturesque. Leibl taught artists to study detail, to master the secrets of flower, leaf and stalk.

A great number of pupils were encouraged by him to gain such a thorough mastery of every detail of technique as to be enabled to paint pictures that were thoroughly good in workmanship, irrespective of genre or anecdote. Among these, W. Trübner (b. 1851) stands pre-eminently as a painter. His works during the 'seventies are among the best painting done at Munich during that period; they are full and rich in colour, broad and bold in their treatment of the subject. A contemporary of his was Bruno Piglhein (b. 1848), a German Chaplin in this Courbet group, not heavy and matter-of-fact, but bold and witty. He revived the art of pastel painting and pointed the way to a new style in panoramic and decorative painting, whilst infusing beauty and grace into all his works.

The movement in applied arts which began at this time is also important. The revival of the German Empire led to a renaissance in German taste. The "old German dwelling-rooms," which now became the fashion, could only be hung with pictures in keeping with the style of the old masters, and this entailed a closer study and imitation of their works than had hitherto been customary. Wilhelm Diez (b. 1839) at the head of the group, was as well acquainted with the epoch from Dürer and Holbein to Ostade and Rembrandt as any art historian. In Harburger (b. 1846) Adrian Brouwer lived once more; and in Löfftz (b. 1845) Quintin Matsys. Claus Meyer (b. 1846) imitated all the artistic tricks of Pieter de Hooch and Van der Neer of Delft. Holbein's costume studies were at first models for Fritz August Kaulbach (b. 1850). Later, he extended his studies to Dolci and Van Dyck, to Watteau and Gainsborough. Adolf Lier (1827-1882) applied the beauty of tone beloved by the old masters to landscape, Von Lenbach's works show the zenith of old-master talent in Germany. He had educated himself as a copyist of classical masterpieces, and passed through a schooling in the study of old masters such as none of his contemporaries had enjoyed. The copies which, as a young man, he made for Count Schack in Italy and Spain are among the best the brush has ever accomplished. Titian and Rubens, Velazquez and Giorgione, were imitated by him with equal success. In like manner he gave to his own works their distinguished old-master charm. More than all other painters of historical subjects, Lenbach enjoys the distinction of having been the historian of his epoch. He gave the great men of the era of the emperor William I. the form in which they will live in German history, and beauty of colour is blended in all these pictures with their brilliant evidence of thought. The aspirations of a whole generation to restore the technique of the old masters found their realization in Lenbach.

Such was the position of things when there was imported from France the desire to paint light and sun. It was argued that the views which the old masters held concerning colour were in glaring contradiction to what the eye actually saw. The old masters, it was said, paid particular attention to the conditions of light and shade under which they did their work. The golden character of the Italian Renaissance was traceable to the old cathedrals lighted by stained-glass windows. The light and shade of the Netherlands were in keeping with the light and shadow of the artists' studios lighted by little panes, and due partly to the fact that their pictures were intended to hang in dreamy, brown panelled chambers. But was this golden or brown light suitable for the 19th century? Were we not illogical, when for the sake of reproducing the tones of the old masters, we darkened our studios and shut out the daylight by coloured glass windows and heavy curtains? Was not light one of the greatest acquisitions of recent times? When the Dutch painted the world used only little panes of glass. Now the daylight streamed into our rooms through great white sheets of crystal. When our grandfathers lived there were only candles and oil lamps. Now we had gas and electric light. Instead of imitating the old masters, let us paint the colouristic charms that were unknown to them. Let us do honour to the new marvels of colour. With such arguments as were advanced in France, did artists in Germany adopt the *plein-air* and abandon older methods; and a development like that which took place in France after

the days of Manet ensued in Germany also. Daylight, which had so long been kept down, was now to be reproduced as clear and bright. After the art of painting strong effects full of daylight had been grappled with, other and more difficult problems of light effects were attempted. After the full blaze of sunshine had been successfully reproduced, such effects as the haze of early morning, the sultry vaporous atmosphere of the thunderstorm, the mysterious night, the blue-grey dawn, the delicate colours of variegated Chinese lanterns, the scintillation of gas and lamplight, and the dreamy twilight in the interior were dealt with.

Liebermann (b. 1849) was the first to join the new departure. In Paris he had learnt technique. Holland, the country of Max inspired him with the love for atmospheric effects, and the scenes of simple life provided him with many subjects. Perhaps the "Net Menders" in the Hamburg Kunsthalle is most typical of Liebermann's art. Frank Skarbina (b. 1849), who was the second to join the new movement in Berlin, proceeded to studies of twilight and artificial light effects.

Hans Herrman (b. 1858), who settled himself on quays and ports; Hugo Volgel, who endeavoured to utilize scenes from contemporary life for decorative pictures; and the two landscape painters, Ludwig Dettmann (b. 1865) and Walther Leistikow (b. 1865), are other representatives of modern Berlin art. Carlsruhe, in the 'eighties, produced some modern pictures of great merit, when Gustav Schönleber (b. 1851) and Herrmann Baisch (b. 1846) showed daintily conceived pictures of Dutch landscapes. In later years Count Leopold Kalckreuth (b. 1855), whose powerfully conceived representations of peasant life belong to the best productions of German realism, and Victor Weisshaupt (b. 1848), the animal painter, removed thence to Stuttgart, the residence also of Otto Reiniger (b. 1863), a landscape painter of great originality. At Dresden we find Gotthard Kuehl (b. 1850), long domiciled in Paris, who was one of the first to accept Manet's teaching. In North Germany, Worpswede became a German Barbizon; Ende (b. 1860), Vogeler, and Vinnen (b. 1863) also worked there. In Weimar, two landscape painters of great refinement must be mentioned—Theodor Hagen (b. 1842) and Gleichen-Russwurm (b. 1866). As far back as the 'seventies they rendered ploughed fields, hills enveloped in thin vapour at sunrise, waving fields of corn, and apple trees in full bloom trembling in the rays of the evening glow with a delicate understanding of natural effects.

But Munich still remains the headquarters of German art, which is there the first of all interests and pervades all circles. Almost all those who are working in other German towns receive in that city their inspirations and have indeed remained its citizens in heart. The international exhibitions have given a great European tone and impulse to creative work. Among the elders, Albert von Keller (b. 1841) has perhaps the greatest originality. He is one of those who practised the art of the brush as long ago as the 'seventies, and a painter, not for the sake of historical subjects or for genre, but for the sole love of his art. He painted everything, never restricted himself to any fixed programme, and never became trivial. He is perhaps in Germany the only painter of female portraits who has caught in his pictures a little of the charm that betrays itself in the expression and movements of the modern woman. In the works of Freiherr von Habermann (b. 1849) this refinement of sentiment, as expressed in colour, is combined with a still more decided shade of eccentricity. Already in his "Child of Sorrow," which hangs in the National Gallery at Berlin, he struck that painful chord that always remained his favourite. However different the subjects he has painted, a morbid note pervades them all.

In Heinrich Zügel (b. 1850), the Munich school possesses an animal painter who rivals the great Frenchmen in original power. Ludwig Dill (b. 1848), whom one must still count as "Dachauer," in spite of his migration to Carlsrube, had for some time past been famous as a painter of Venice, the lagoons and Chioggia, when the Impressionist movement became for him the starting-point of a new development. He strove for still brighter light, tried to realize the most subtle shades of colour, and raised himself from a painter of natural impressions to free and poetical lyricism. Arthur Langhammer (b. 1855), Ludwig Herterich, Leo Samberger (b. 1851), Hans von Bartels (b. 1856), Wilhelm Keller-Reutlinger (b. 1854), Beno Becker, Louis Corinth (b. 1858), Max Slevogt, are others that may be mentioned among the later Munich artists.

Fritz von Uhde (b. 1848) occupies a peculiar position as being the first to apply the principles of naturalism to religious art. Immediately before him, Eduard von Gebhardt (b. 1838) had gone back to the angular style of the old northern masters, that of Roger van der Weyden and Albert Dürer, believing he could draw the old Biblical events closer to present times by relating them in Luther's language and representing them as taking place in the most powerful epoch of German ecclesiastical history. Now that historical paintings had been dispossessed by modern and contemporary subjects, it followed also that scenes from the life of Christ had to be laid in modern times. "I do not assert that only the commonplace occurrences of everyday life can be painted. If the historical past be painted, it should be represented in human garb corresponding to the life we see about us, in the surroundings 'of our own country, peopled with the people moving before our very eyes, just as if the drama had only been enacted the previous evening." Thus wrote Bastien-Lepage in 1879, when creating his " Jeanne d'Arc," and in this sense did Uhde paint. But besides the charm of feeling expressed in the subtlest hues, there is also the charm of the noble line.

At the time when, in England, Rossetti and Burne-Jones, and, in France, Puvis de Chavannes and Gustave Moreau, stepped into the foreground, in Germany Feuerbach (1829-1880), Marées (1837-1887), Thoma (b. 1839), and Böcklin (1827-1901) were discovered. Feuerbach's life was one series of privations and disappointments. His " Banquet of Plato," " Song of Spring," " Iphigenia " and " Pietà," and his " Medea " and " Battle of the Amazons, " met with but scant recognition on their appearance. To some they appeared to lack sentiment, to others they were " not sufficiently German." When he died in Venice in 1880, he had become a stranger to his contemporaries. But posterity accorded him the laurel that his own age had denied him. Just those points in his pictures to which exception had been taken during his lifetime, the great solemn restfulness of his colouring and the calm dignity of his contours, made him appear contemporary.

Hans von Marées fulfilled a similar mission in the sphere of decorative art; his, likewise, was a talent that was not discovered until after his death. He is most in touch with Puvis de Chavannes. But the result was different. Puvis was recognized on his first appearance. Marées never had a chance of revealing his real strength. He was only 28 years of age when he first went to Rome; there in 1873, he was commissioned to paint some pictures for the walls of the Zoological Station at Naples. After that time, nothing more was heard of him until 1891, when four years after his death the works he had left behind him were exhibited and presented to the gallery of Schleissheim. The value of these works of art must not be sought in their technique. The art of Puvis rests on a firm realistic foundation, but Marées had finished his studies of nature too prematurely for the correctness of his drawing. In spite of this defect, they encourage as well as excite, owing to the principle which underlies them, and which they share in equal degree with those of Puvis. Like Puvis, Marées repudiated all illuminating efforts whereby forms might be brought into relief. He only retained what was intrinsically essential, the large lines in nature, as well as those of the human frame.

Next to these artists stands Hans Thoma, like one of the great masters of Dürer's time. In Marées and Feuerbach's works there is the solemn grandeur of the fresco; in those of Thoma there is nothing of Southern loveliness, but something of the homeliness of the old German art of woodcut; nay, something philistine, rustic, patriarchal—the simplicity of heart and childlike innocence that entrance us in German folklore,

in the paintings of Moritz von Schwind (1804-1871) and Ludwig Richter (1803-1884). He had grown up at Bernau, a small village of the Black Forest. Blossoming fruit-trees and silver brooks, green meadows and solitary peasants' cottages, silent valleys and warm summer evenings, grazing cattle and the cackle of the farmyard, all lived in his memory when he went to Weimar to study the painter's art. This pious faithfulness to the home of his birth and touching affection for the scenes of his childhood pervade all his art and are its leading feature. Even when depicting classical subjects, the mythological marvels of the ocean and centaurs, Thoma still remains the simple-hearted German, who, like Cranach, conceives antiquity as a romantic fairy tale, as the legendary period of chivalry.

Whether it be correct to place Böcklin (q.v.) in the same category with these painters, or whether he has a right to a separate place, posterity may decide. The great art of the old masters has weighed heavily upon the development of that of our own age. Even the idealists, who have been mentioned, trace their pedigree back to the old masters. However modern in conception, they are to all intents and purposes "old " as regards the form they employed to express their modern ideas. Böcklin has no ancestor in the history of art; no stroke of his brush reminds us of a leader. No one can think of tracing him back to the Academy of Düsseldorf, to Lessing, or Schorner, as his first teacher. Even less can he be called an imitator of the old masters. His works are the result of nature in her different aspects; they have not their origin in literary or historical suggestion. The catalogue of his conceptions, of landscape in varying moods, is inexhaustible. But landscape does not suffice to express his resources. Knights on the quest for adventure, Saracens storming flaming citadels, Tritons chasing the daughters of Neptune in the billowy waves; such were the subjects which appealed to him. He endowed all fanciful beings that people the atmosphere, that live in the trees, on lonely rocks, or that move and have their being in the slimy bottom of the sea, with body and soul, and placed a second world at the side of the world of actuality. Yet this universe of phantasy was too narrow for the master mind. If it be asked who created on the continent of Europe the most fervid religious paintings of the 19th century; who alone exhausted the entire scale of sensations, from the placidity of repose to the sublimity of heroism, from the gayest laughter to tragedy; who possessed the most solemn and most serious language of form and, at the same time, the greatest poetry of colour—the name of Böcklin will most probably form the answer.

These masters were for their younger brethren the pioneers into a new world of art. It was momentous for the painter's art that in Germany, no less than in England and France, a new movement at this time set in—the so-called " arts and crafts." Hitherto the various branches of art had followed different courses. The most beautiful paintings were often hung in surroundings grievously lacking in taste. Now arose the ambition to make the room itself a work of art. The picture, as such, now no more stands in the foreground, but the different arts strive together to form a single piece of art. The picture is regarded as merely a decorative accessory.

Among the younger painters still to be mentioned, Max Klinger (b. 1857) is perhaps the most brilliant. He had begun with the etching-needle, and by its aid gave us entire novels, crisp little dramas of everyday life. But this realism was only a preliminary phase enabling him to pass on to a great independent art of form. His great picture, " Christ in Olympus," combines beauty of form with deep philosophical meaning. Ibsen in 1873, in his Emperor and Galilean, talked of a "third realm," combining heathen beauty with Christian profundity. Klinger's " Christ in Olympus " strikes the beholder as the realization of this idea. Stuck (b. 1863) shares with him the Hellenic serenity of form, the classical simplicity. Apart from this, his pictures are thoroughly different. It might almost be said " Klinger is the Nazarene who stepped into Olympus "; the thoughtful, deep son of the North who carries profound physical problems into the beauty-loving Hellenic worship of the senses. Stuck's art is, also, almost classical in its insensibility and petrified coldness. In his first picture (1889) "The Guardian of Paradise" he painted a slim wiry angel, who, like Donatello's "St George," in calm confidence and self-assurance points the sword before him. And similar rigid figures standing erect in steadiness—always portraits of himself—recur again and again in his works. Even his religious pictures—the "Pietà" and "The Crucifixion"—are, in reality, antique. One would seek in vain in them for the piety of the old masters or the Germanic fervour of Uhde. Grand in style and line, firm, solemn, serious in arrangement, they are yet hard and cold in conception.

Ludwig von Hoffmann (b. 1861) stands next to him, a gentle, dreamy German. In Stuck's work everything is strong and rugged: here all is soft and round. There the massiveness of sculpture and stiff heraldic lines: here all dissolved into variegated fairy tales, glowing harmonies. However classical he may appear, yet it is only the old yearning of the German for Hesperia—the song of Mignon—that rings throughout his works; the longing to emerge from the mist and the fog into the light, from the humdrum of everyday life into the remote fabulous world of fairydom, the longing to escape from sin and attain perfect innocence.

There are numerous others deserving of mention besides those already discussed. Josef Sattler (d. 1867), Melchior Lechter (b. 1871), and Otto Greiner (b. 1869), and likewise those who, such as Von Berlepsch (b. 1852) and Otto Eckmann (b. 1865), devoted their energies again to "applied art."

See R. Muther, *The History of Modern Painting* (London, 1895); *Deutsches Künstler-Lexikon der Gegenwart in biographischen Skizzen* (Leipzig, 1898); Mrs de la Mazelière, *La Peinture allemande au XIX⁰ siècle* (Paris, 1900). (R. Mᴿ.)

AUSTRIA-HUNGARY

In Austria the influence of Makart (1840-1884) was predominant in the school of painting during the last quarter of the 19th century. He personified the classical expression of an epoch, when a long period of colour-blindness was followed by an intoxication of colour. Whilst Piloty's ambition stopped short at the presentation of correct historical pictures, his pupil, Makart felt himself a real painter. He does not interpret either deep thought or historical events, nor does he group his pictures together to suit the views of the art student. His work is essentially that of a colourist. Whatever his subject may be, whether he depicts "The Plague in Florence,"⁴ "The Nuptials of Caterina Cornaro," "The Triumphal Entry of Charles V.," "The Bark of Cleopatra," or "The Five Senses," "The Chase of Diana," or "The Chase of the Amazons," his pictures are romances of brilliant dresses and human flesh. A few studies of the nude and sketches of colour, in which he merely touched the notes that were to be combined into chords, were the sole preliminaries he required for his historical paintings. Draperies, jewels, and voluptuous female forms, flowers, fruit, fishes and marble—everything that is full of life and sensuous emotion, and shines and glitters, he heaps together into gorgeous still-life. And because by this picturesque sensuousness he restored to Austrian art a long-lost national peculiarity, his appearance on the scene was as epoch-making as if some strong power had shifted the centre of gravity of all current views and ideas.

In estimating Makart, however, we must not dwell on his pictures alone. He did more than merely paint—he lived them. Almost prematurely he dreamed the beautiful dream which in later days came nearer realization, that no art can exist apart from life—that life itself must be made an art. His studio, not without reason, was called his most beautiful work of art. Whithersoever his travels led him—to Granada, Algiers, or Cairo—he made extensive purchases, and refreshed his eye with the luscious splendour of rich silks and the soft lustrous hues of velvets. He made collections of carved ivory and Egyptian mummies, Gobelins, armour and weapons, old chests, antique sculpture, golden brocades with glittering embroideries, encrusted coverlets and the precious textures of the East,

columns, pictures, trophies of all ages and all climes. He scattered money broadcast in striving to realize his dream of beauty—to pass one night, one hour, in the world of Rubens, so bright in colour, so princely in splendour.

Uniting as he did these artistic qualities in his own person—not only because he was a painter, but because in no other besides did the great yearning for aesthetic culture find such powerful utterance—Makart exercised an influence in Austria far transcending the actual sphere of the painter's art. An intense fascination went forth from the little man with the black beard and penetrating glance. At that time Makart dominated not merely Viennese art, but likewise the whole cultured life of the capital. Not only the Makart hat and the Makart bouquet made their pilgrimage through the world, he became also the motive power in all intellectual spheres. When Charlotte Wolter acted Cleopatra or Messalina on the stage, she not only wore dresses specially sketched for her by Makart, but she also spoke in Makart's style, just as Hamerling wrote in it. A veritable Makart fever had, indeed, taken possession of Vienna. No other painter of the 19th century was so popular, the life of none other was surrounded by such princely sumptuousness. The scene when, during the festivals of 1879, he headed the procession of artists past the Imperial box, mounted on a white steed glittering with gold, the Rubens hat with white feathers on his head, amidst the boisterous acclamations of the populace, is unique in the modern history of art. It is the greatest homage that a Philistine century ever offered an artist.

The life of August von Pettenkofen (1821-1889), who should, after Makart, be accounted the greatest Austrian painter of the last quarter of the 19th century, was passed much more modestly and serenely. He had grown up on one of his father's estates in Galicia, and had been a cavalry officer before becoming a painter. His place in Austria is that of Menzel in Germany. With Pettenkofen a new style appeared. The representation of modern subjects now began to take the place of historical painting, which had for so long a time been the ruling taste; not in the sense of the old-fashioned genre picture, but in that of artistic refined painting. Here, again, the distinctive Austrian note can be easily recognized. Pettenkofen's people are lazy, and yawn. All is contemplative and peaceful, full of dreamy sleepy repose.

But neither Pettenkofen nor Makart has found followers. The great movement which, originating with Manet, took place in other centres of art, passed Austria by without leaving a trace. Hans Canon (b. 1829), who in his pictures transported the characters of the "Gründerzeit" to Venice of bygone days, and reproduced them as Venetian nobles and ladies of quality, is also a painter of note. So likewise is Rudolf Alt (b. 1812), still active with the brush in 1902, a refined painter in watercolours, who reproduces the beauties of Old Vienna in his subtle architectural sketches. Leopold Karl Müller (1834-1892), who had lived in Cairo with Makart, found his sphere of art in the variegated world of the Nile, and his ethnographical exactness, combined with his delicate colouring, made him for a long while much in request as a painter of Oriental scenes, and a popular illustrator of Egyptological works. Emil Schindler was a great landscape painter, who often rose from faithful interpretation of nature to an almost heroic height. Heinrich von Angeli (b. 1840), again, furnished—as he continued to do—the European courts with his representative pictures, combining refined conception with smooth elegant technique. These are the only artists who during the 'eighties rose above local mediocrity. After Makart died in 1884, the sun of Austrian art seemed to have set. Stagnation reigned supreme.

Only since the "Secession" from the old Society of Artists (*Künstlergenossenschaft*), which took place in 1896, has the former artistic life recommenced in Vienna. Theodor von Hermann, long domiciled in Paris, was the gifted initiator of the new movement, and succeeded in rousing a storm of discontent among the rising school of Viennese artists. They found a literary champion in their hero's father, who pleaded in eloquent language for a new Austrian culture. In November 1898 the

Secessionists opened their first exhibition in a building erected by Josef·Olbrück on the Wienerzeil. At first the importance of these exhibitions lay almost exclusively in the fact that the Viennese were thus given an opportunity of making acquaintance with the famous foreign masters. Puvis de Chavannes, Segantini, Besnard, Brangwyn, Meunier, Khnopff, Henri Martin, Vischer, who had until then been practically unknown in Austria, so that the public only then realized the inferiority of their country-men's artistic work. Thus while acquainting the Viennese public with the strivings of European art, the Secession endeavoured at the same time to produce, in rivalry with foreigners, works of equal artistic merit. Leading foreign masters now joined the movement, and Vienna, which had so long stood aside, through·inability to be represented worthily at interna-tional exhibitions, became once more a factor·in contemporary European art.

Among the painters of the Secession, Gustav Klint possesses, perhaps, the most powerful original talent. Refined portraits, subtle landscapes and decorative pictures, painted for the Tumba Palace and for the Vienna Hof Museum, first brought his name before the world. But he became famous in conse-quence of the controversy which arose around his picture " Philosophy." He had been commissioned to paint the large ceiling piece for the " aula " of the Vienna University, and instead of selecting a classical subject'he essayed an independent work. The heavens open; golden and silvery stars twinkle; sparks of light gleam; masses of green cloud and vapour form clusters; naked human forms float about; a fiery head, crowned with laurel, gazes on the scene with·large, serious eyes. Science climbs down to the sources of Truth; yet Truth always remains the inscrutable Sphinx. Klint paid the penalty of his bold originality by his work remaining dark and incomprehensible to most people. It has, notwithstanding, an historical importance for Austria corresponding to that which similar works of Besnard have for France. It embodies the first attempt·to place monu-mental painting upon a purely colouristic basis, and to portray allegorical subjects as pure visions of colour. After Klint, Josef Engelhart (b. 1864) is deserving of notice. He is the true painter of Viennese life. On his first appearance his art was centred in his native place, and was strong in local colour, which was lacking in refinement. To acquire subtlety, he studied the great foreign masters and became a clever juggler with the brush, showing as much dexterity as any of them. Yet this virtuosity meant, in his case, only a good schooling, which should enable him to return with improved means to those subjects best suited to his talent. His works are artistic, but at the same time distinctly local.

Carl Moll (b. 1861) understands how to render with equal skill the play of light in a room and that of the sunbeams upon the fresh green grass. The rural pictures of Rist produce a fresh, cool and sunny effect upon the eye; like a refreshing draught from a cool mountain spring—a piece of Norway on Austrian soil. Zettel's landscapes are almost too markedly Swiss in colour and conception. Julius von Kollmann worked a long time in Paris and London, and acquired, in intercourse with the great foreign painters—notably Carrière and Watts—an exquisitely refined taste, an almost hyperaesthetical sense for discreetly toned-down colour and for the music of the line. In Friedrich König, M. von Schwind's romantic vein is revived. Even the simplest scenes from nature appear under his hand as enchanted groves whispering secrets. Everything is true and, at the same time, dreamy and mysterious. The mythical beings of old German legends—dragons and enchanted princesses —peer through the forest thicket. Ernst Nowak (b. 1851), compared with him, is a sturdy painter, who knows his business well. He sings no delicate lyric. When one stands close by, his pictures appear like masonry—like reliefs. Seen from a distance, the blotches of colour unite into large powerful forms. Bernatzik understands how to interpret with great subtlety twilight moods—moonshine struggling with the light of street lamps, or with the dawn. Ticky followed Henri Martin in painting solemn forest pictures. Ferdinand André leans towards

the austere power of Millet. He tells us in his work of labour in the fields, of bronzed faces and hands callous with toil; and especially must his charcoal drawings be mentioned, in which the colour overlays the forms like light vapour, and which, small as they are, have a sculptural effect. Auchentaller—known for his female studies—and Hänisch and Otto Friedrich (b. 1862), refined and subtle as landscape painters, must also be mentioned.

In rivalry with the Secession, the " Künstlergenossenschaft " has taken a fresh upward flight. Among figure painters, Delug, Goltz (b. 1857), Hirschl and Veith are conspicuous, but still greater fascination is·exercised by landscape painters such as Amesadan, Charlemont, &c., whose works show Austrian art in its most amiable aspect. Apart from Austrians proper, there are also representatives of the other nationalities which compose " the monarchy of many tongues." Bohemia takes the lead with a celebrity of European reputation—Gabriel Max (b. 1840), who, although of Piloty's school and residing in Munich, never repudiated his Bohemian origin. The days of his youth were passed in Prague; and Prague, the medieval, with its narrow winding alleys, is the most mysterious of all Austrian cities, enveloped in the breath of old memories and bygone legends. From this soil Max drew the mysterious fragrance that char-acterises his pictures. His earliest work, the " Female Martyr on the Cross " (1867), struck that sweetly painful, half-torment-ing, half-enchanting keynote that has since remained ·distinc-tively his. Commonplace historical painting received at Max's hands an entirely new nuance. The morbidness of the mortuary and the lunatic asylum, interspersed with spectres—something perverse, unnatural and heartrending—this is the true note of his art. His martyrs are never men—only delicate girls and helpless women. His colouring corresponds to his subjects. The sensations his pictures produce are akin to those which the sight of a beautiful girl·lying in a mortuary, or the prison scene in Faust enacted in real life, might·be expected to excite. He even applies the results of hypnotism and ·spiritualism to Biblical characters. In many of his pictures refinement in the selection of effects is missing. By over-production Max has himself vulgarized his art. Yet, despite his manner of depicting the mysteries of the realms of shadows, and the intrusion of the 'spirit-world into realism, he remains' a modern master. A new province—the spectral—was opened up by him to art.

Hans Schwaiger is·the real raconteur of Bohemian legends. He, likewise, passed his youth in a small Bohemian village, over which old memories still brooded. In Hradec, places upon which the gallows had stood were still pointed out. The lonely corridors and passages of the ruined·castle were haunted by the shades of its old possessors. This is the mood that led Schwaiger to legend-painting. But underlying his fairy tales there are the gallows or the alchemy of Faust. The landscape with its gloomy skies, the wooden huts, turrets, dwarfed trees—such are ever the accompaniments of his figures.

Of the younger generation of painters, Emil Orlick (b. 1870) seems·to be the most versatile. Having acquired technique in Paris and Munich, he practically discovered Old Prague to the world of art. The dark little alleys of the ancient town, swarming with life compressed within their·narrow compass, fascinated him. In order to retain and convey all the impressions that crowded in upon him in·such superabundant plenitude, he learned how to use the knife of the wood-carver, the needle of the etcher, and the pencil of the lithographer. His studio more resembles the workshop of a printer than the atelier of a painter. In the field of lithography he has attained remarkable results. Orlick has also made his own everything that can be learned from the Japanese. Besides these masters, Albert Hynais, the creator of decorative pictures almost Parisian in conception, must be mentioned. The landscape painters Wickener, Jansa, Slavicek, and Hudecek relate, in gentle melancholy tones of colour, the atmosphere and solitude of the wide plains of Bohemia.

In Poland, painting has its home at·Cracow. Down to the year 1893 Johann Matejko was living there, in the capacity of director of the Academy. His pictures are remarkable for their originality and almost brutal force, and differ very widely from the conventional productions of historical painters. At the close of the 19th century Axentowicz, Olga Hojnauska, Meboffer, Stanislawski and Wyotkowski attracted attention. Although apparently laying much less stress on their Polish nationality than their Russian countrymen, their works proclaim the soul of the Polish nation, with its chivalrous gallantry and mute resigned grief, in a much purer form.

Hungary in the spring of 1900 lost him whom it revered as the greatest of its painters—Michael Munkacsy. Long before his death his brush had become idle. To the younger generation, which seeks different aims, his name has become almost synonymous with a wrongly-conceived old-masterly coloration, and with sensation painting and hollowness. " The Last Day of the Condemned Prisoner," his first youthful picture, contained the programme of his art. Then came " The Last Moments of Mozart," and " Milton dictating Paradise Lost." These titles summon up before our eyes a period of all that is false in eclectic art, dominated by Delaroche and Piloty. Even the simple subjects of the Gospel were treated by Munkacsy in Piloty's meretricious style. " Christ before Pilate," " Ecce Homo," " The Crucifixion "—all these are gala representations, costume get-up, and, to that extent, a pious lie. But when we condemn the faults of his period, his personal merit must not be forgotten. When he first came to the fore, ostentation of feeling was the fashion. Munkacsy is, in this respect, the genuine son of the period. He was not one of those who are strong enough to swim against the stream. Instead of raising others to his level, he descended to theirs. But he has the merit of having painted spectacular scenes, such as the period demanded, with genuine artistic power. Like Rahl, Ribot, Roybet and Makart, he was a maitre-peintre, a born genius with the brush. Von Uhde and Liebermann were disciples of his school. And if these two painters have left that period behind them, and if independent natural sight has followed upon the imitation of the old masters, it is Munkacsy who enabled them to take the leap.   (R. Mr.)

ITALY

Modern Italy has produced one artist who towers over all the others, Giovanni Segantini (q.v.). Segantini owes as little to his period of study in Milan as Millet did to his sojourn at Delaroche's school. Both derived from their teachers a complete mastery of technique, and as soon as they were in possession of all the aids to art, they discarded them in order to begin afresh. Each painted what he had painted as a youth. They dwelt far from the busy world—Millet in Barbizon, Segantini at Val d' Albola, 5000 feet above the sea-level. They are equally closely allied in art. Millet, who rejected all the artifice of embellishment and perceived only beauty in things as they are, learned to see in the human body a heroic grandeur, in the movements of peasants a majestic rhythm, which none before him had discovered. Although representing peasants, his works resemble sacred pictures, so grand are they in their sublime solemn simplicity. The same is true of Segantini's works. Like Millet, he found his vocation in observing the life of poor, humble people, and the rough grandeur of nature, at all seasons and all hours. As there is in Millet's, so also is there in Segantini's work a primitive, almost classical, simplicity of execution corresponding to the simplicity of the subjects treated. His pictures, with their cold silvery colouring, remind us of the wax-painting of old times and of the mosaic style of the middle ages. They are made up of small scintillating strokes; they are stony and look hard like steel. This technique alone, which touches in principle but not in effect, that of the pointillistes, permitted of his rendering what he wished to render, the stony crags of Alpine scenery, the thin scintillating air, the firm steel-like outlines. Finally, he passed from realistic subjects to thoughtful, Biblical and symbolical works. His "Annunciation," the " Divine Youth," and the " Massacre of the Innocents " were products of an art that had abandoned the firm ground

of naturalism and aimed at conquering supernatural worlds. This new aim he was unable to realise. He left the " Panorama of the Engadine," intended for the Paris Exhibition, in an unfinished state behind him. He died in his 42nd year, his head full of plans for the future. Modern Italy lost in him its greatest artist, and the history of art one of the rare geniuses.

Few words will suffice for the other Italian painters. The soil that had yielded down to Tiepolo's days such an abundant harvest was apparently in need of rest during the 19th century. At the Paris Exhibition of 1867 About called Italy " the tomb of art," and indeed until quite recent times Italian painting has had the character of mere pretty saleable goods. Francesco Vinea, Tito Conti, and Federigo Andreotti painted with tireless activity sleek drapery pictures, with Renaissance lords and smiling Renaissance ladies in them. Apart from such subjects, the comic, genre or anecdote ruled the fashion—somewhat coarse in colour and of a merrier tendency than is suitable for pictures of good taste. It was not until nearly the end of the 19th century that there was an increase in the number of painters who aim at real achievement. At the Paris Exhibition of 1900 only Detti's " Chest " and Signorini's " Cardinal " pictures reminded one of the comedy subjects formerly in vogue. The younger masters employ neither " drapery-mummeries " nor spicy anecdote. They paint the Italian country people with refined artistic discernment, though scarcely with the naturalism of northern nations. Apparently the calm, serious, ascetic, austere art initiated by Millet is foreign to the nature of this volatile, colour-loving people. Southern fire and delight in brilliant hues are especially characteristic of the Neapolitans. A tangle of baldacchinos, priests and choir boys, peasants making obeisance and kneeling during the passing of the Host, weddings, horse-races and country festivals, everything sparkling with colour and glowing in Neapolitan sunlight—such are the contents of Paolo Michetti's, Vincenzo Capri's; and Edoardo Dalbono's pictures. But Michetti, from being an adherent of this glittering art, has found his way to the monumental style. The Venetians acknowledge and honour as their leader Giacomo Favretto, who died very young. He painted drapery pictures, like most artists of the 'eighties, but they were never lackadaisical, never commonplace. The Venice of Canaletto and Goldoni, the magic city surrounded by the glamour of bygone splendour, rose again under Favretto's hands to fairylike radiance.

The older masters, Signorini, Tito Tommasi, Dall 'oca Branca, who depict the Piedmontese landscape, the light on the lagoons, and the colour charm of Venetian streets with so refined a touch, have numerous followers, whose pictures likewise testify to the seriousness that again took possession of Italian painters after a long period of purely commercial artistic industry. Side by side with these native Italians two others must be mentioned, who occupy an important place as interpreters of Parisian elegance and French art-history. Giuseppe de Nittis (born in Naples; died in Paris 1884) was principally known by his representations of French street life. The figures that enlivened his pictures were as full of charm as his rendering of atmospheric effects was refined. Giovanni Boldini, a Ferrarese living in Paris, also painted street scenes, full of throbbing life. But he excelled, besides, as a portrait-painter of ladies and children. He realized the aim of the Parisian Impressionists, which was to render life, and not merely mute repose. He understood in a masterly fashion how to catch the rapid movement of the head, the fleetest expression, the sparkling of the eye, a pretty gesture. From his pictures posterity will learn as much about the sensuous life of the 19th century as Greuze has told us about that of the 18th.

Among those who have been the leaders of modern Italian art, not already mentioned, are Domenico Morelli, Giovanni Costa, landscape painter; Sartorio, an Italian Pre-Raphaelite; Pasini, painter of the East; Muzzioli, a follower of Alma-Tadema; Barabino, historical painter; and most striking and original of all, Monticelli, whose glow of colours was often obtained, not only by palette-knife painting, but by squeezing the colour straight from the tubes on to the canvas.

See Ashton R. Willard, *History of Modern Italian Art* (London, 1898). (R. Mₑ.)

SPAIN AND PORTUGAL

Modern Spanish painting began with Mariano Fortuny (*q.v.*), who, dying as long ago as 1874, nevertheless left his mark even on the following generation of artists. During his residence in Paris in 1866 he had been strongly influenced by Meissonier, and subsequently selected similar subjects—scenes in 18th-century costume. In Fortuny, however, the French painter's elaborate finish is associated with something more intense and vivid, indicative of the southern Latin temperament. He collected in his studio in Rome the most artistic examples of medieval industry. The objects among which he lived he also painted with incisive spirit as a setting for elegant figures from the world of Watteau and of Goya, which are thrown into his pictures with amazing dash and sparkle; and this love of dazzling kaleidoscopic variety has animated his successors. Academic teaching tries to encourage historical painting. Hence, since the 'seventies, the chief paintings produced in Spain have been huge historical works, which have made the round of European exhibitions and then been collected in the Gallery of Modern Art at Madrid. There may be seen " The Mad Queen Juana," by Pradilla; " The Conversion of the Duke of Gandia," by Moreno Carbonero; " The Bell of Huesca," by Casado; " The Last Day of Numantia," by Vera; " Ines de Castro," by Cabello.

It is possible, of course, to discern in the love of the horrible displayed in these pictures an element of the national character, for in the land of bull-fights even painting turns to murder and sudden death, poison and the rope. However, at least we must admit the great power revealed, and recognise the audacious colouring. But in point of fact these works are only variants on those executed in France from the time of Delaroche to Jean Paul Laurens, and tell their story in the style that was current in Parisian studios in the 'sixties. What is called the national garb of Spain is mainly the cast-off fashion of Paris. After all this magniloquent work Fortuny's rococo became the rage. The same painters who had produced the great historical pictures were now content to take up a brilliant and dazzling miniature style; either, like Fortuny himself, using small and motley figures in baroque subjects, or adapting the modern national life of Spain to the rococo style.

Here again we observe the acrobatic dexterity with which the painters, Pradilla especially, use the brush. But here again there is nothing essentially new—only a repetition of what Fortuny had already done twenty years before. The Spanish school, therefore, presented a very old-fashioned aspect at the Paris Exhibition of 1900. The pictures shown there were mostly wild or emotional. Bedouins fighting, an antique quadriga flying past, the inhabitants of Pompeii hastily endeavouring to escape from the lava torrent, Don Quixote's Rosinante hanging to the sail of the windmill, and the terrors of the Day of Judgment were the subjects, Alvarez Dumont, Benlliure y Gil, Ulpiano Checa, Manuel Ramirez Ibañes and Moreno Carbonero were the painters. Among the huge canvases, a number of small pictures, things of no importance, were scattered, which showed only a genre-like wit. Spain is a somewhat barren land in modern art. There painting, although active, is blind to life and to the treasures of art which lie unheeded in the road. Only one artist, Agrasot, during the 'seventies painted pictures of Spanish low life of great sincerity, and much talent two young painters appeared who energetically threw themselves into the modern movement. One was Sorolla y Bastida, by whom there is a large fishing picture in the Luxembourg, which in its stern gravity might be the work of a Northern painter, the other was Ignacio Zuloaga, in whom Goya seems to live again. Old women, girls of the people, and *cocottes* especially, he has painted with admirable spirit and with breadth. Spain, which has taken so little part in the great movement since Manet's time, only repeating in old-fashioned guise things which are falsely regarded as national, seems at last to possess in Zuloaga an artist at once modern and genuinely national.

Portugal took an almost lower place in the Paris Exhibition. For whereas the historical Spanish school has endeavoured to be modern to some extent, at least in colour, the Portuguese cling to the blue-plush and red-velvet splendours of Delaroche in all their crudity. Weak pictures of monks and of visions are produced in numbers, together with genre pictures depicting the popular life of Portugal, spiced to the taste of the tourist. There are the younger men who aim at availing themselves of the efforts of the open-air painters; but even as followers of the Parisians they only say now what the French were saying long years ago through Bastien-Lepage, Puvis de Chavannes and Adrien Dumont. There is always a Frenchman behind the Portuguese, who guides his brush and sets his model. The only painter formed in the school is Carlos Reis, whose vast canvas " Sunset " has much in common with the first huge peasant pictures painted in Germany by Count Kalckreuth. One painter there is, however, who is quite independent and wholly Portuguese, a worthy successor of the great old masters of his native land, and this is Columbano, whose portraits of actors have a spark of the genius which inspired the works of Velasques and Goya.

See A. G. Temple, *Modern Spanish Painting* (1908). (R. Mₑ.)

DENMARK

Denmark resembles Holland in this: that in both, nature presents little luxury of emphasized colour or accentuated majesty of form. Broad flats are everywhere to be seen—vague, almost indefinable, in outline. Danish art is as demure and staid as the Danish landscape. As in Holland, the painters make no bold experiments, attempt no pretentious subjects, no rich colouring, nothing sportive or light. Like the Dutch, the Danes are somewhat sluggishly tranquil, loving dim twilight and the swirling mist. But Denmark is a leaner land than Holland, less moist and more thinly inhabited, so that its art lacks the comfortable self-satisfied character of Dutch art. It betrays rather a tremulous longing, a pleasing melancholy and delight in dreams, a trembling dread of contact with coarse and stern reality. It was only for a time, early in the 'seventies, that a touch of cosmopolitanism affected Danish art. The phase of grandiose historical painting and anecdotic genre was experienced there, as in every other country. In Karl Bloch (b. 1834), Denmark had a historical painter in some respects parallel with the German Piloty; in Axel Helsted (b. 1847), a genre painter reminding us of Ludwig Knaus. The two artists Laurits Tuzen (b. 1853) and Peter Kröyer (b. 1851), who are most nearly allied to Manet and Bastien-Lepage, have a sort of elegance that is almost Parisian. Kröyer, especially, has bold inventiveness and amazing skill. Open-air effects and twilight moods, the glare of sunshine and artificial light, he has painted with equal mastery. In portraiture, too, he stands alone. The two large pictures in which he recorded a " Meeting of the Committee of the Copenhagen Exhibition, 1887," and a " Meeting of the Copenhagen Academy of Sciences," are modern works which in power of expression may almost compare with those of Frans Hals. Such versatility and facile elegance are to be found in no other Danish painter. At the period of historic painting it was significant that next to Bloch, the 'cosmopolitan, came Kristian Zahrtmann (b. 1843), who painted scenes from the life of Eleonora Christina, a Danish heroine (daughter of Christian IV.), with the utmost simplicity, and without any emotional or theatrical pathos. This touching feeling for home and country is the keynote of Danish art. The Dane has now no sentiment but that of home; his country, once so powerful, has become but a small one, and has lost its political importance. Hence he clings to the little that is left to him with melancholy tenderness. Viggo Johansen (b. 1851), with his gentle dreaminess, is the best representative of modern Danish home-life. He shows us dark sitting-rooms, where a quiet party has met around the tea-table. " An Evening at Home," " The Christmas Tree," " Grandmother's Birthday," are typical subjects, and all have the same fresh and fragrant charm. He is also one of the best Danish landscape painters. The silvery atmosphere and sad, mysterious stillness of the island-realm rest on Johansen's pictures. Not less satisfactory in their little world are the rest: Holsöe (b. 1866), Lauritz Ring (b. 1854), Haslund, Syberg (b. 1862), Irminger (b. 1850), and Ilsted paint the pleasant life of Copenhagen. In Skagen, a fishing town at the extreme end of Jutland, we find painters of sea life: Michael Ancher (b. 1849), Anna Ancher (b. 1859), and C. Locher (b. 1851). The landscape painters Viggo Pederson (b. 1854), Philipsen (b. 1840), Julius Paulsen (b. 1860), Johan Rohde (b. 1856) have made their home in the villages round Copenhagen. Each has his own individuality and sees nature with his own eyes, and yet in all we find the same sober tone, the same gentle, tearful melancholy. The new Idealism has, however, been discernible in Denmark. Joakim Skovgaard (b. 1856), with his "Christ among the Dead" and "Pool of Bethesda," is trying to endow Denmark with a monumental type of art. Harald Slott-Möller (b. 1864) and J. F. Willumsen (b. 1863) affect a highly symbolical style. But even more than these painters, who aim at reproducing ancient folk-tales through the medium of modern mysticism, two others claim our attention, by the infusion into the old tradition of a very modern view of beauty approaching that of Whistler and of Carrière: one is Ejnar Nielsen, whose portraits have a peculiar, refined strain of gentle Danish melancholy; the other, V. Hammershöj, who has an exquisite sense of tone, and paints the magical effect of light in half-darkened rooms. Among the more noteworthy portrait painters, Aug. Jerndorff and Otto Bache should be included; and among the more decorative artists, L. Frölich; while Hans Tegner may be considered the greatest illustrator of his day. (R. Me.)

SWEDEN

There is as great a difference between Danish and Swedish art as between Copenhagen and Stockholm. Copenhagen is a homely provincial town and life is confined to home circles. In Stockholm we find the whirl of life and all the elegance of a capital. It has been styled the Paris of the North, and its art also wears this cosmopolitan aspect. Düsseldorf, where in the 'sixties most painters studied their art, appeared to latter-day artists too provincial. Munich and, to a still greater extent, Paris became their "Alma Mater," Salmson (1843-1894) and Hagborg (b. 1852), who were first initiated into naturalism in Paris, adopted this city for a domicile. They paint the fishermen of Brittany and the peasants of Picardy; and even when apparently interpreting Sweden, they only clothe their Parisian models in a Swedish garb. Those who returned to Stockholm turned their Parisian art into a Swedish art, but they have remained cosmopolitan until this day. Whilst there is something prosy and homely about Danish art, that of Sweden displays nervous elegance and cosmopolitan polish. Simplicity is in her eyes humdrum; she prefers light and brilliant notes. There, a naturalness and simplicity allows us to forget the difficulties of the brush: here, we chiefly receive the impression of a cleverly solved problem. There, the greatest moderation in colour, a soft all-pervading grey: here, a cunning play with delicate tones and gradations—a striving to render the most difficult effects of light with obedient hand. This tendency is particularly marked in the case of the landscape painters: Per Ekström (b. 1844), Nils Kreuger (b. 1858), Karl Nordström (b. 1865), Prince Eugen of Sweden (b. 1855), Axel Sjöberg Wallander (b. 1862), and Wahlberg (b. 1864). Nature in Sweden has not the idyllic softness, the veiled elegiac character, it displays in Denmark. It is more coquettish, southern and French, and the painters regard it also with French eyes.

As a painter of animals, Bruno Liljefors (b. 1860) created a sensation by his surprising pictures. Whatever his subjects —quails, capercailzies, dogs, hares, magpies or thrushes—he has caught the fleetest motions and the most transitory effects of light with the cleverness of a Japanese. With this exception, the Swedish painters cannot be classified according to "subjects." They are "virtuosi," calling every technical aspect of art their own—as well in fresco as in portrait painting. Oscar Björck

(b. 1860), Ernst Josephson (b. 1851), Georg Pauli (b. 1855), Richard Bergh (b. 1858), Hanna Hirsch now Pauli (b. 1864) are the best-known names. Carl Larsson's (b. 1853) decorative panneaux fascinate by their easy lightness and coquettish grace of execution. Ander Zorn (b. 1860), with his dazzling virtuosity, is as typical of Swedish as the prosaic simplicity of Johansen is of Danish art. His marine pictures, with their undulating waves and naked forms bathed in light, belong to the most surprising examples of the cleverness with which modern art can stereotype quivering motions; and the same boldness in handling his subjects, which triumphs over difficulties, makes his "interiors," his portraits and etchings, objects of admiration to every painter's eye. In his "Dance before the Window" all is vivacity and motion. His portrait of a "Peasant Woman" is a powerful harmony of sparkling yellow-red tones of colour. Besides these older masters, who cleave to the most dazzling light effects, there are the younger artists of the school of Carl Larsson, who aspire more to decorative effects on a grander scale. Gustav Fjälstad (b. 1868) exhibited a picture in the Paris Exhibition of 1900 that stood out like mosaic among its surroundings. And great similarity in method has Hermann Normann, who, as a landscape painter, also imitates the classic style. (R. Me.)

NORWAY

We enter a new world when in picture-galleries we pass to the Norwegian from the Swedish section. From the great city we are transported to nature, solemn and solitary, into a land of silence, where a rude, sparse population, a race of fishermen, snatches a scanty sustenance from the sea. The Norwegians also contributed for a time to the international market in works of art. They sent mainly genre pictures telling of the manners and customs of their country, or landscapes depicting the phenomena of Northern scenery. Adolf Tidemand (1814-1876) introduced his countrymen—the peasants and fishermen of the Northern coast—to the European public. We are introduced to Norwegian Christmas customs, accompany the Norseman on his nocturnal fishing expeditions, join the "Brudefaerd" across the Hardanger fjord, sit as disciples at the feet of the Norwegian sacristan. Ferdinand Fagerlin (b. 1825) and Hans Dahl are two other painters who, educated at Düsseldorf and settled in Germany, introduced the style of Knaus and Vautier to Norwegian art circles. Knud Badde (1808-1879), Hans Gude (b. 1825), Nils Björnsen Möller, Morten-Müller (b. 1828), Ludvig Munthe (1843-1896), and Adelsten Normann (b. 1848) are known as excellent landscape painters, who have faithfully portrayed the majestic mountain scenery and black pine forests of their native land, the cliffs that enclose the fjords, and the sparkling snowfields of the land of the midnight sun. But the time when actually had to be well seasoned, and every picture was bound to have a spice of genre or the attraction of something out of the common to make it palatable, is past and gone. As early as the 'sixties Björnson was president of a Norwegian society which made it its chief business to wage war against the shallow conventionalities of the Düsseldorf school. Ibsen was vice-president. In the works of the more modern artists there is not a single trace of Düsseldorf influence. Especially in the 'eighties, when naturalism was at its zenith, we find the Norwegians its boldest devotees. They portrayed life as they found it, without embellishment; they did not trouble about plastic elegance, but painted the land of their home and its people in a direct, rough-hewn style. Like the people we meet in the North, giants with stalwart iron frames, callous hands, and sunburnt faces, with their sou'-westers and blue blouses, who resemble sons of a bygone heroic age, have the painters themselves—notably Nils Gustav Wentzel (b. 1859), Svend Jörgensen (b. 1861), Kolstoe (b. 1860), Christian Krohg—something primitive in the directness, in, one might almost say, the barbarous brutality with which they approach their subjects. They preferred the most glaring effects of plein-air; they revelled in all the hues of the rainbow.

But these very uncouth fellows, who treated the figures in their pictures with such rough directness, painted even in those days landscapes with great refinement; not the midnight sun and the precipitous cliffs of the fjords, by which foreigners were sought to be impressed, but austere, simple nature, as it lies in deathlike and spectral repose—lonely meres, whose surface is unruffled by the keel of any boat, where no human being is visible, where no sound is audible; the hour of twilight, when the sun has disappeared behind the mountains, and all is chill and drear; the winter, when an icy blast sweeps over the crisp snow-fields; the spring, almost like winter, with its bare branches and its thin young shoots. Such were their themes, and painters like Amaldus Nilsen (b. 1838), Eilif Petersen (b. 1852), Christian Skredsvig (b. 1854), Fritz Thaulow (b. 1848), and Gerhard Munthe (b. 1849) arrested public attention by their exhibition of pictures of this character.

Latterly these painters have become more civilised, and have emancipated themselves from their early uncouthness. Jörgensen, Krohg, Kolstoe, Soot, Gustav Wentzel, no longer paint those herculean sailors and fishermen, those pictures of giants that formerly gave to Norwegian exhibitions their peculiar character. Elegance has taken possession of the Norwegian palette. This transformation began with Fritz Thaulow, and indeed his art threatened to relapse somewhat into routine, and even the ripples of his waters to sparkle somewhat coquettishly. Borgen (b. 1852), Hennig (b. 1871), Hjerlöw (b. 1863), and Stenersen (b. 1862) were gifted recruits of the ranks of Norwegian painters, whilst Halfdan Strom (b. 1863), who depicts rays of light issuing from silent windows and streaming and quivering over solitary landscapes, dark blue streams and ponds, nocturnal skies, variegated female dresses, contrasting as spots of colour with dark green meadows, has a delicacy in colouring that recalls Casin. Gerhard Munthe, who, as we have seen, first made a name by his delicate vernal scenery, has turned his attention to the classical side of art; and, finally Erik Werenskjold (b. 1855), who was also first known by his landscapes and scenes of country life, afterwards gained success as an illustrator of Norwegian folk-lore.   . (R. Mz.)

Russia

Until late in the 19th century modern Russian painting was unknown to western Europe. What had been seen of it in international exhibitions showed the traditions of primitive European art, with a distinct vein of barbarism. In the early 'fifties, painters were less bent on art than on political agitation; they used the brush as a means of propaganda in favour of some political idea. Peroff showed us the miserable condition of the serfs, the wastefulness and profligacy of the nobility. Vereschagin made himself the advocate of the soldier, painting the horrors of war long before the tsar's manifesto preached universal disarmament. Art suffered from this praiseworthy misapplication; many pictures were painted, but very few rose to the level of modern achievement in point of technique. It was only by the St Petersburg art journal Mir Iskustwo, and by a small exhibition arranged at Munich in 1892 by a group of Russian landscape painters, that it was realized that a younger Russian school had arisen, fully equipped with the methods of modern technique, and depicting Russian life with the stamp of individuality. At the Paris Exhibition of 1900 the productions of this young Russian school were seen with surprise. A florescence similiar to that which literature displayed in Pushkin, Dostoievsky and Tolstoy seemed to be beginning for Russian painting. Some of these young painters rushed into art with unbridled zest, painting with primitive force and boldness. They produced historical pictures, almost barbaric but of striking force; representations of the life of the people full of deep and hopeless gloom; the poor driven by the police and huddled together in dull indifference; the popes tramping across the lonely steppes, prayer-book in hand; peasants muttering prayers before a crucifix. There is great pathos in "The Karamasow Brothers," or "The Power of Darkness." At the same time we feel that a long-inherited tradition pervades all Russia. We find a characteristic ecclesiastical art, far removed from the productions of the fin de siècle, in which the rigid tradition of the Byzantines of the 3rd century still survives.

And, finally, there are landscapes almost Danish in their bloodless, dreamy tenderness. Among the historical painters Elias Repin is the most impressive. In his pictures, "Ivan the Cruel," "The Cossacks' Reply to the Sultan," and "The Miracle of Saint Nicholas," may be seen—what is so rare in historical painting—genuine purpose and style, Terror is rendered with Shakespearean power; the boldness with which he has reconstituted the past, and the power of pictorial psychology which has enabled him to give new life to his figures, are equally striking in "Sowing on the Volga" and "The Village Procession." He was the first to paint subjects of contemporary life, and the work, while thoroughly Russian, has high technical qualities—the sense of oppression, subjection and gloom is all-pervading. But he does not "point the moral," as Peroff did; he paints simply but sympathetically what he sees, and this lends his pictures something of the resigned melancholy of Russian songs. Even more impressive than Repin is Philippe Maliavine. He had rendered peasants, stalwart figures of powerful build; and, in a picture called "Laughter," Macbeth-like women, wrapped in rags of fiery red, are thrown on the canvas with astonishing power. Among religious painters Victor Vasnezov, the powerful decorator of the dome in the church of St Vladimir at Kiev, is the most distinguished figure. These paintings seem to have been executed in the very spirit of the Russian church; blazing with gold, they depend for much of their effect upon barbaric splendour. But Vasnezov has painted other things: "The Scythians," fighting with lance and battle-axe; horsemen making their way across the pathless steppe; and woods and landscapes pervaded by romantic charm, the home of the spirits of Russian legend. Next to Vasnezov is Michael Nesterov, a painter also of monks and saints, but as different from him as Zurbaran from the mosaic workers of Venice; and Valentin Serov, powerful in portraiture and fascinating in his landscape. It is to be remarked that although these artists are austere and unpolished in their figure-painting, they paint landscape with delicate refinement. Schischkin and Vassiliev were the first to paint their native land in all simplicity, and it is in landscape that Russian art at the present time still shows its most pleasing work. Savrassov depicts tender spring effects; Kuindshi light birch-copses full of quivering light; Sudkovski interprets the solemn majesty of the sea; Albert Benois paints in water-colour delicate Finnish scenery; Apollinaris Vasnezov has recorded the dismal wastes of Siberia, its dark plains and endless primeval forest, with powerful simplicity.

A special province in Russian art must be assigned to the Poles. It is difficult indeed to share to the full the admiration felt in Warsaw for the Polish painters. It is there firmly believed that Poland has a school of its own, owing nothing to Russia, Austria or Germany; an art which embodies all the chivalry and all the suffering of that land. The accessories are Polish, and so are the costumes. Jan Chelminski, Wojciech Gerson, Constantine Gorski; Apolonius Kendzierski, Joseph Rysszkievicz and Roman Szvoinicki are the principal artists. We see in their pictures a great deal of fighting, a great deal of weeping; but what there is peculiar to the Poles in the expression or technique of their works it is hard to discover.

Finland, on the other hand, is thoroughly modern. Belonging by descent to Sweden rather than to Russia, its painters' views of art also resemble those of the "Parisians of the North." They display no ungoverned power, but rather supple elegance. The play of light and the caprice of sunshine are rendered with much subtlety. Albert Edelfeldt is the most versatile artist of the group; Axel Gallen, at first naturalistic, developed into a decorative artist of fine style; Eero Jaernefelt charms with his airy studies and brilliant landscapes. Magnus Enckell, Pekka Halonen and Victor Vesterholm sustain the school with work remarkable for sober and tasteful feeling.   (R. Mz.)

Balkan States

Until quite recent times the Balkan States had no part at all in the history of art. But at the Paris Exhibition of 1900 it was noted with surprise that even in south-eastern Europe there was a certain pulsation of new life. And there were also signs that painting in the Balkans, which hitherto had appeared only as a reflex of Paris and Munich art, would ere long assume a definite national character. At this Exhibition Bulgaria seemed to be the most backward of all, its painters still representing the manners and customs of their country in the style of the illustrated papers. Market-places are seen, where women with golden chains, half-nude boys and old Jews are moving about; or cemeteries, with orthodox clergy praying and women sobbing; military pageants, wine harvests and horse fairs, old men performing the national dance, and topers jesting with brown-eyed girls. Such are the subjects that Anton Mittoff, Raymund Ulrich and Jaroslav Vesin paint. More original is Mvkuicka. In his most important work he represented the late princess of Bulgaria sitting on a throne, solemn and stately, in the background mosaics rich in gild, tall slim lilies at her side. In his other pictures he painted Biblical landscapes, battlefields wrapped in sulphurous smoke, and old Rabbis—all with a certain uncouth barbaric power. The Bulgarian painters have not as yet arrived at the aesthetic phase. One of the best among them, who paints delicate pale green landscapes, is Charalampi Ilieff; and Nicholas Michailoff, at Munich, has executed pictures, representing nymphs, that arrest attention by their delicate tone and their beautiful colouring.

Quite modern was the effect of the small Croatian-Slavonic Gallery in the Exhibition. Looking at the pictures there, the visitor might imagine himself on the banks of the Seine rather than in the East. The French saying, "*Faire des Whistler, faire des Dagnan, faire des Carrière,*" is eminently applicable to their work. Vlaho Bukovak, Nicola Masic, Csiks and Medovic all paint very modern pictures, and in excellent taste, only it is surprising to find upon them Croatian and not Parisian signatures.

Precisely the same judgment must be passed with regard to Rumania. Most of the painters live in Paris or Munich, have sought their inspiration at the feet of the advanced masters there, and paint, as pupils of these masters, pictures just as good in taste, just as cosmopolitan and equally devoid of character. Irène Deschly, a pupil of Carrière, illustrates the songs of François Coppée; Verona Gargouromin is devoted to the pale symbolism of Dagnan-Bouveret. Nicolas Grant paints bright landscapes, with apple trees with their pink blossoms, like Darnoye. Nicolas Gropeano appears as the double of Aman-Jean, with his female heads and pictures from fairy tales. Olga Koruca studied under Puvis de Chavannes, and painted Cleopatra quite in the tone of her master. A landscape by A. Segall was the only work that appeared to be really Rumanian, representing thatched huts.

Servia is in striking contrast to Rumania. No trace of modern influence has penetrated to her. There historical painting, such as was in vogue in France and Germany a generation ago, is the order of the day. Risto Voucanovitch paints his scenes from Servian history in brown; Paul Ivanovitch his in greyish *plein-air*. But in spite of this *passé* painting, the latter's works have no modern effect—as little as the sharply-drawn small landscapes of his brother Svatislav Ivanovitch. / (R. Mr.)

UNITED STATES

The history of painting in the United States practically began with the 19th century. The earlier years of the nation were devoted to establishing government, subduing the land and the aborigines, building a commonwealth out of primeval nature; and naturally enough the aesthetic things of life received not too much consideration. In Colonial times the graphic arts existed, to be sure, but in a feeble way. Painting was made up of portraits of prominent people; only an occasional artist was disposed towards historical pictures; but the total result added little to the sum of art or to the tale of history. The first artist of importance was J. S. Copley (1737–1815), with whom painting in America really began. Benjamin West (1738–1820) belongs in the same period, though he spent most of his life in England, and finally became President of the Royal Academy. As a painter he is not to be ranked so high as Copley. In the early part of the 19th century two men, John Trumbull (1756–

1843), a historical painter of importance, and Gilbert Stuart (1755–1828), a pre-eminent portrait painter, were the leaders; and after them came John Vanderlyn (1776–1852), Washington Allston (1779–1843), Rembrandt Peale (1787–1860), J. W. Jarvis (1780–1834), Thomas Sully (born in England, 1783–1872) —men of importance in their day. The style of all this early art was modelled upon that of the British school, and indeed most of the men had studied in England under the mastership of West, Lawrence and others. The middle or second period of painting in the United States began with the landscape work of Thomas Doughty (1793–1856) and Thomas Cole (1801–1848). It was not a refined or cultivated work, for the men were in great measure self-taught, but at least it was original and distinctly American. In subject and in spirit it was perhaps too panoramic and pompous; but in the hands of A. B. Durand (1796–1886), J. F. Kensett (1818–1872) and F. E. Church (1826–1900), it was modified in scale and improved in technique.

A group of painters called the Hudson River school finally emerged. To this school some of the strongest landscape painters in the United States owe their inspiration, though in almost every case there has been the modifying influence of foreign study. Contemporary with Cole came the portrait painters Chester Harding (1792–1866), C. L. Elliott (1812–1868), Henry Inman (1801–1846), William Page (1811–1885), G. P. A. Healy (1813–1894), Daniel Huntington and W. S. Mount (1807–1868), one of the earliest genre painters. Foreign art had been followed to good advantage by most of these painters, and as a result some excellent portraits were produced. The excellence of the work was not, however, appreciated by the public generally because art knowledge was not at that time a public possession. Little was required of the portrait painter beyond a recognizable likeness. A little later the teachings of the Düsseldorf school began to have an influence upon American art through Leutze (1816–1868), who was a German pupil of Lessing, and went to America to paint historical scenes from the War of Independence. But the foreign influence of the time to make the most impression came from France in 1855 with two American pupils of Couture —W. M. Hunt (1824–1879) and Thomas Hicks (1823–1890). Hunt had also been a pupil of Millet at Barbizon, and was the real introducer of the Barbizon painters to the American people. After his return to Boston his teaching and example had much weight in moulding artistic opinion. He, more than any other, turned the rising generation of painters towards the Paris schools. Contemporary with Hunt and following him were a number of painters, some self-taught and some schooled in Europe, who brought American art to a high standard of excellence. George Fuller (1822–1884), Eastman Johnson, Elihu Vedder, produced work of much merit; and John La Farge and Winslow Homer were unquestionably the foremost painters in the United States at the opening of the 20th century. In landscape the three strongest men have passed away—A. H. Wyant, George Inness, and Homer Martin. Swain Gifford, Edward Gay, Thomas Moran, Jervis McEntee, Albert Bierstadt, and other landscape painters of note who belonged to the middle period and reflected the traditions of the Hudson River school to some extent. With the Centennial Exhibition at Philadelphia in 1876 a widespread and momentous movement in American art began to shape itself. The display of pictures at Philadelphia, the national prosperity, and the sudden development of the wealth of the United States had doubtless much to do with it. Many young men from all parts of the country took up the study of art and began going abroad for instruction in the schools at Munich, and, later, at Paris. Before 1880 some of them had returned to the United States and founded schools and societies of art, like the Art Students' League and the Society of American Artists. The movement spread to the Western cities, and in a few years museums and art schools began to appear in all the prominent towns, and a national interest in art was awakened. After 1870 the predominant influence, as regards technical training, was French. Many students still go to Paris to complete their studies, though there is a large body of accomplished painters teaching in the home schools, with satisfactory results as regards the work of their pupils. From their French training, many of the American artists have been charged with echoing Parisian art; and the charge is partly true. They have accepted French methods because they think them the best, but their subjects and motives are sufficiently original.

Under separate biographical headings a number of modern American artists are noticed. Some of the greatest Americans however can hardly be said to belong to any American school. James McNeill Whistler, though American-born, is an example of the modern man without a country. E. A. Abbey, John S. Sargent, Mark Fisher and J. J. Shannon are American only by birth. They became resident in London and must be regarded as cosmopolitan in their methods and themes. This may be said with equal truth of many painters resident in Paris and elsewhere on the Continent. However good as art it may be, there is nothing distinctively American about the work of W. T. Dannat, Alexander Harrison, George Hitchcock, Garl Melchers, C. S. Pearce, E. L. Weeks, J. L. Stewart and Walter Gay. If they owe allegiance to any centre or city, it is to Paris rather than to New York.

During the last quarter of the 19th century much effort and money were devoted to the establishment of institutions like the Metropolitan Museum in New York, the Carnegie Museum at Pittsburg, and the Art Institute in Chicago. Every city of importance in the United States now has its gallery of paintings. Schools of technical training and societies of artists likewise exist wherever there are important galleries. Exhibitions during the winter season and at great national expositions give abundant opportunity for rising talent to display itself; and, in addition, there has been a growing public patronage of painting, as shown by the extensive mural decorations in the Congressional Library building at Washington, in the Boston Public Library, in many colleges and churches, in courts of justice, in the reception-rooms of large hotels, in theatres and elsewhere.

(J. C. van D.)

PAISIELLO (or **PAESIELLO**), **GIOVANNI** (1741–1816), Italian musical composer, was born at Tarento on the 9th of May 1741. The beauty of his voice attracted so much attention that in 1754 he was removed from the Jesuit college at Tarento to the Conservatorio di S. Onofrio at Naples, where he studied under Durante, and in process of time rose to the position of assistant master. For the theatre of the Conservatorio, which he left in 1763, he wrote some intermezzi, one of which attracted so much notice that he was invited to write two operas, *La Pupilla* and *Il Mondo al Rovescio*, for Bologna, and a third, *Il Marchese di Tulipano*, for Rome. His reputation being now firmly established, he settled for some years at Naples, where, notwithstanding the popularity of Piccini, Cimarosa and Guglielmi, of whose triumphs he was bitterly jealous, he produced a series of highly successful operas, one of which, *L'Idolo cinese*, made a deep impression upon the Neapolitan public. In 1772 he began to write church music, and composed a requiem for Gennara Borbone. In the same year he married Cecilia Pallini, with whom he lived in continued happiness. In 1776 Paisiello was invited by the empress Catherine II. to St Petersburg, where he remained for eight years, producing, among other charming works, his masterpiece, *Il Barbiere di Siviglia*, which soon attained a European reputation. The fate of this delightful opera marks an epoch in the history of Italian art; for with it the gentle suavity cultivated by the masters of the 18th century died out to make room for the dazzling brilliancy of a later period. When, in 1816, Rossini set the same libretto to music, under the title of *Almaviva*, it was hissed from the stage; but it made its way, nevertheless, and under its changed title, *Il Barbiere*, is now acknowledged as Rossini's greatest work, while Paisiello's opera is consigned to oblivion—a strange instance of poetical vengeance, since Paisiello himself had many years previously endeavoured to eclipse the fame of Pergolesi by resetting the libretto of his famous intermezzo, *La Serva padrona*.

Paisiello quitted Russia in 1784, and, after producing *Il Re Teodoro* at Vienna, entered the service of Ferdinand IV. at Naples, where he composed many of his best operas, including *Nina* and *La Molinara*. After many vicissitudes, resulting from political and dynastic changes, he was invited to Paris (1802) by Napoleon, whose favour he had won five years previously by a march composed for the funeral of General Hoche. Napoleon treated him munificently, while cruelly neglecting two far greater composers, Cherubini and Méhul, to whom the new favourite transferred the hatred he had formerly borne to Cimarosa, Guglielmi and Piccini. Paisiello conducted the music of the court in the Tuileries with a stipend of 10,000 francs and 4800 for lodging, but he entirely failed to conciliate the Parisian public, who received his opera *Proserpine* so coldly that, in 1803, he requested and with some difficulty obtained permission to return to Italy, upon the plea of his wife's ill health. On his arrival at Naples Paisiello was reinstated in his former appointments by Joseph Bonaparte and Murat, but he had taxed his genius beyond its strength, and was unable to meet the demands now made upon it for new ideas. His prospects, too, were precarious. The power of the Bonaparte family was tottering to its fall; and Paisiello's fortunes fell with it. The death of his wife in 1815 tried him severely. His health failed rapidly, and constitutional jealousy of the popularity of others was a source of worry and vexation. He died on the 5th of June 1816.

Paisiello's operas (of which he is known to have composed 94) abound with melodies, the graceful beauty of which is still warmly appreciated. Perhaps the best known of these airs is the famous "Nel cor più" from *La Molinara*, immortalized by Beethoven's delightful variations. His church music was very voluminous, comprising eight masses, besides many smaller works; he also produced fifty-one instrumental compositions and many detached pieces. MS. scores of many of his operas were presented to the library of the British Museum by Dragonetti.

The library of the Gerolamini at Naples possesses an interesting MS. compilation recording Paisiello's opinions on contemporary composers, and exhibiting him as a somewhat severe critic, especially of the work of Pergolesi. His *Life* has been written by F. Schizze (Milan, 1833).

PAISLEY, CLAUD HAMILTON, LORD (c. 1543–1622), Scottish politician, was a younger son of the 2nd earl of Arran. In 1553 he received the lands of the abbey of Paisley, and in 1568 he aided Mary Queen of Scots to escape from Lochleven castle, afterwards fighting for her at the battle of Langside. His estates having been forfeited on account of these proceedings, Hamilton was concerned in the murder of the regent Murray in 1570, and also in that of the regent Lennox in the following year; but in 1573 he recovered his estates. Then in 1579 the council decided to arrest Claud and his brother John (afterwards 1st marquess of Hamilton) and to punish them for their past misdeeds; but the brothers escaped to England, where Elizabeth used them as pawns in the diplomatic game, and later Claud lived for a short time in France. Returning to Scotland in 1586 and mixing again in politics, Hamilton sought to reconcile James VI. with his mother; he was in communication with Philip II. of Spain in the interests of Mary and the Roman Catholic religion, and neither the failure of Anthony Babington's plot nor even the defeat of the Spanish Armada put an end to these intrigues. In 1589 some of his letters were seized and he suffered a short imprisonment, after which he practically disappeared from public life. Hamilton, who was created a Scottish baron as Lord Paisley in 1587, was insane during his concluding years. His eldest son James was created earl of Abercorn (q.v.) in 1606.

PAISLEY, a municipal and police burgh of Renfrewshire, Scotland, on the White Cart, 3 m. from its junction with the Clyde, 7 m. W. by S. of Glasgow by the Glasgow & South-Western and Caledonian railways. Pop. (1891), 66,425; (1901) 79,363. In 1791 the river, which bisects the town, was made navigable for vessels of 50 tons and further deepened a century later. It is crossed by several bridges—including the Abercorn, St James's and the Abbey Bridges—and two railway viaducts. The old town, on the west bank of the stream, contains most of the principal warehouses and mills; the new town, begun towards the end of the 18th century, occupies much of the level ground that once formed the domains of the abbey. To the munificence of its citizens the town owes many of its finest public buildings. Opposite to the abbey church (see below) stands the town hall (1879-1882), which originated in a bequest by George Aitken Clark (1823-1873), and was completed by his relatives, the thread manufacturers of Anchor Mills. The new county buildings (1891) possess a handsome council hall, and the castellated municipal buildings (1818-1821) were the former county buildings; the sheriff court house (1885) in St James Street, and the free library and museum (including a picture gallery) at the head of High Street, were erected (1869-1872) by Sir Peter Coats (1808-1890). In Oakshaw Street stands the observatory (1883), the gift of Thomas Coats (1809-1883). Besides numerous board schools, the educational establishments include the John Neilson Endowed Institute (1852) on Oakshaw Hill, the grammar school (founded, 1576; rebuilt, 1864), and the academy for secondary education, and the technical college, in George Street. Among charitable institutions are the Royal Alexandra Infirmary, the Victoria Eye Infirmary (presented by Provost Mackenzie in 1899), the burgh asylum at Riccartsbar, the Abbey Poorhouse (including hospital and lunatic wards), the fever hospital and reception house, the Infectious Diseases Hospital and the Glenifier Home for Incurables. The Thomas Coats Memorial Church, belonging to the Baptist body, erected by the Coats family from designs by H. J. Blanc, R.S.A., is one of the finest modern ecclesiastical structures in Scotland. It is an Early English and Decorated cruciform building of red sandstone, with a tower surmounted by a beautiful open-work crown. Of parks and open spaces there are in the south, Brodie Park (22 acres), presented in 1871 by Robert Brodie; towards the north Fountain Gardens (7½ acres), the gift of Thomas Coats and named from the handsome iron fountain standing in the centre; in the north-west, St James Park (40 acres), with a racecourse (racing dates from 1620, when the earl of Abercorn and the Town Council gave silver bells for the prize); Dunn Square and the old quarry grounds converted and adorned; and Moss Plantation beyond the north-western boundary. There are the cemeteries at Hawkhead and at the west side of the town. Under the Reform Act of 1832 the burgh returns one member to Parliament. The town is governed by a council, with provost and bailies, and owns the gas and water supplies and the electric lighting. In the abbey precincts are statues to the poet Robert Tannahill (1774-1810) and Alexander Wilson (1766-1813), the American ornithologist, both of whom were born in Paisley, and, elsewhere, to Robert Burns, George Aitkin Clark, Thomas Coats and Sir Peter Coats.

Paisley has been an important manufacturing centre since the beginning of the 18th century, but the earlier linen, lawn and silk-gauze industries have become extinct, and even the famous Paisley shawls (imitation cashmere), the sale of which at one time exceeded £1,000,000 yearly in value, have ceased to be woven. The manufacture of linen thread, introduced about 1720 by Christian Shaw, daughter of the laird of Bargarran, gave way in 1812 to that of cotton thread, which has since grown to be the leading industry of the town. The Ferguslie mills (J. & P. Coats) and Anchor mills (Clark & Company) are now the dominant factors in the combination that controls the greater part of the thread trade of the world and together employ 10,000 hands. Other thriving industries include bleaching, dyeing, calico-printing, weaving (carpets, shawls, tartans), engineering, tanning, iron and brass founding, brewing, distilling, and the making of starch, cornflour, soap, marmalade and other preserves, besides some shipbuilding in the yards on the left bank of the White Cart.

The abbey was founded in 1163 as a Cluniac monastery by Walter Fitzalan, first High Steward of Scotland, the ancestor of the Scottish royal family of Stuart, and dedicated to the Virgin, St James, St Milburga of Much Wenlock in Shropshire (whence came the first monks) and St Mirinus (St Mirren), the patron-saint of Paisley, who is supposed to have been a contemporary of St Columba. The monastery became an abbey in 1219, was destroyed by the English under Aymer de Valence,

earl of Pembroke, in 1307, and rebuilt in the latter half of the 14th century, the Stuarts endowing it lavishly. At the Reformation (1561) the fabric was greatly injured by the 5th earl of Glencairn and the Protestants, who dismantled the altar, stripped the church of images and relics, and are even alleged to have burnt it. About the same date the central spire, 300 ft. high, built during the abbacy of John Hamilton (1511-1571), afterwards archbishop of St Andrews, collapsed, demolishing the choir and north transept. In 1553 Lord Claud Hamilton, then a boy of ten, was made abbot, and the abbey and monastery were erected into a temporal lordship in his favour in 1587. The abbey lands, after passing from his son the earl of Abercorn to the earl of Angus and then to Lord Dundonald, were purchased in 1764 by the 8th earl of Abercorn, who intended making the abbey his residence, but let the ground for building purposes. The abbey church originally consisted of a nave, choir without aisles, and transepts. The nave, in the Transitional and Decorated styles, with a rich mid-Pointed triforium of broad round arches, has been restored, and used as the parish church since 1862. The graceful west front has a deeply recessed Early Pointed doorway, surmounted by traceried windows and, above these, by a handsome Decorated stained-glass window of fire lights. Of the choir only the foundations remain to indicate its extent; at the east end stood the high altar before which Robert III. was interred in 1406. Over his grave a monument to the memory of the Royal House of Stuart was placed here by Queen Victoria (1888). The restored north transept has a window of remarkable beauty. The south transept contains St Mirren's chapel (founded in 1499), which is also called the "Sounding Aisle" from its echo. The chapel contains the tombs of abbot John Hamilton and of the children of the 1st lord Paisley, and the recumbent effigy of Marjory, daughter of Robert Bruce, who married Walter, the Steward, and was killed while hunting at Knock Hill between Renfrew and Paisley (1316).

About 3 m. S. of Paisley are the pleasant braes of Glenifier, sung by Tannahill, and 2½ m. S.E., occupying a hill on the left bank of the Leven, stand the ruins of Crookston Castle. The castle is at least as old as the 12th century and belonged to Robert de Croc, who witnessed the charter of the foundation of Paisley Abbey. In the following century it passed into the possession of a branch of the Stewarts, who retained it until the murder of Darnley (1567). Afterwards it changed hands several times, but was finally acquired from the Montrose family by Sir John Maxwell of Pollok.

The Romans effected a settlement in Paisley in A.D. 84, and built a fort called *Vanduara* on the high ground (Oakshaw Hill) to the west of the White Cart. The place seems to have been first known as Paslet or Passeleth, and was assigned along with certain lands in Renfrewshire to Walter Fitzalan, founder of the abbey. The village grew up round the abbey, and by the 15th century had become sufficiently important to excite the jealousy of the neighbouring burgh of Renfrew. To protect it from molestation Abbot Schaw (or Shaw) induced James IV., a frequent visitor, to erect it into a burgh of barony in 1488, a charter which gave it the right to return a member to the Scots parliament.

See *Chartulary of the Monastery of Paisley*, published by the Maitland Club (1832); J. Cameron Lees, *The Abbey of Paisley* (1878); Swan, *Description of the Town and Abbey of Paisley* (1835); and Robert Brown, *History of Paisley* (1886).

PAITA, or **PAYTA,** a seaport of northern Peru, chief town of the province of Paita in the department of Piura. Pop. (1906 estimate), 3800. The town has one of the best natural harbours of the Peruvian coast, is a port of call for the regular mail steamers between Valparaiso and Panama, and is the port of the departmental capital, Piura, with which it is connected by a railway 60 m. long. It is also the Pacific terminus of the railway across the Andes to Puerto Limon, on the Marañon, or upper Amazon. Paita faces on the bay of Paita, and is sheltered from southerly winds by a headland called Punta Paita and by a large hill called the Silla de Paita. The water supply is brought from the river Chira (17 m. distant). The exports include cotton, tobacco, petroleum, cattle, hides and straw hats. Paita dates from the early years of the Spanish Conquest, and was a prosperous port in colonial times. It was nearly destroyed by Lord Anson's fleet in 1741.

PAJOL, CLAUDE PIERRE, COUNT (1772–1844), French cavalry general, was born at Besançon. The son of an advocate, he was intended to follow his father's profession, but the events of 1789 turned his mind in another direction. Joining the battalion of Besançon, he took part in the political events of that year, and in 1791 went to the army of the Upper Rhine with a volunteer battalion. He took part in the campaign of 1792 and was one of the stormers at Hochheim (1793). From Custine's staff he was transferred to that of Kléber, with whom he took part in the Sambre and Rhine Campaigns (1794–96). After serving with Hoche and Masséna in Germany and Switzerland (1797–99), Pajol took a cavalry command under Moreau for the campaign on the upper Rhine. In the short years of peace Pajol, now colonel, was successively envoy to the Batavian Republic, and delegate at Napoleon's coronation. In 1805, the emperor employed him with the light cavalry. He distinguished himself at Austerlitz, and, after serving for a short time in Italy, he rejoined the *grande armée* as a general of brigade, in time to take part in the campaign of Friedland. Next year (1808) he was made a baron of the Empire. In 1809 he served on the Danube, and in the Russian War of 1812 led a division, and afterwards a corps, of cavalry. He survived the retreat, but his health was so broken that he retired to his native town of Besançon for a time. He was back again in active service, however, in time to be present at Dresden, at which battle he played a conspicuous part. In 1814 he commanded a corps of all arms in the Seine Valley. On the fall of Napoleon, Pajol gave in his adhesion to the Restoration government, but he rejoined his old master immediately upon his return to France. His (I) corps of cavalry played a prominent part in the campaign of 1815, both at Ligny and in the advance on the Wavre under Grouchy. On receiving the news of Waterloo, Pajol disengaged his command, and by a skilful retreat brought it safe and unbeaten to Paris. There he and his men played an active part in the actions which ended the war. The Bourbons, on their return, dismissed him, though this treatment was not, compared to that meted out to Ney and others, excessively harsh. In 1830 he took part in the overthrow of Charles X. He suppressed, sternly and vigorously, *émeutes* in Paris in 1831 and 1832, 1834 and 1839. A general, and a peer of France, he was put on the retired list in 1842, and died two years later.

His son, Count CHARLES PAUL VICTOR PAJOL (1821–1891), entered the army and had reached the rank of general of division when he was involved in the catastrophe of Metz (1870). He retired in 1877. Besides being a good soldier, he was a sculptor of some merit, who executed statues of his father and of Napoleon, and he wrote a life of his father and a history of the wars under Louis XV. (Paris 1881–1891).

See Count C. P. V. Pajol: *Pajol général en chef* (Paris, 1874); Thomas, *Les Grands cavaliers du premier empire* (Paris, 1892) and Choppin, in the *Journal des sciences militaires* (1890).

PAJOU, AUGUSTIN (1730–1809), French sculptor, was born in Paris on the 19th of September 1730. At eighteen he won the *Prix de Rome*; at thirty he exhibited his *Pluton tenant Cerbère enchiné* (now in the Louvre). His portrait busts of Buffon and of Madame Du Barry (1773), and his statuette of Bossuet (all in the Louvre), are amongst his best works. When B. Poyet constructed the Fontaine des Innocents from the earlier edifice of P. Lescot (see GOUJON) Pajou provided a number of new figures for the work. Mention should also be made of his bust of Carlin Bertinazzi (1763) at the Comédie Française, and the monument of Marie Leczinska, queen of Poland (in the Salon of 1769). Pajou died in Paris on the 8th of May 1809.

PAKHOI, or PEIHAI, a city and treaty port of China, in the west of the province of Kwang-tung, situated on a bay of the Gulf of Tong-king, formed by the peninsula running south-west from Lien-chow, in 21° 30′ N., 109° 10′ E. Pop. about 25,000.

Dating only from about 1820–1830, and at first little better than a nest of pirates, Pakhoi rapidly grew into commercial importance, owing partly to the complete freedom which it enjoyed from taxation, and partly to the diversion of trade produced by the T'ai-p'ing rebellion. The establishment of a Chinese customhouse and the opening of the ports of Hanoi and Haiphong for a time threatened to injure its prospects; but, foreign trade being permitted in 1876–1877, it began in 1879 to be regularly visited by foreign steamers. The Chinese town stands on the peninsula and faces due north. From the bluff, on which all the foreign community lives, a partly cultivated plain extends. Liquid indigo, sugar, aniseed and aniseed oil, cassia-lignea and cassia oil, cuttle-fish and hides are the chief exports. With Macao especially an extensive junk trade is carried on. A large number of the inhabitants engage in fishing and fish-curing. The preparation of dried fish is a speciality of Pakhoi, the fish being exported to Hong Kong.

PAKINGTON, the name of a famous English Worcestershire family, now represented by the barony of Hampton. Sir John Pakington (d. 1560) was a successful lawyer and a favourite at court, and Henry VIII. enriched him with estates, including that of Westwood in Worcestershire. His grandnephew and heir, Sir John Pakington (1549–1625), was another prominent courtier, Queen Elizabeth's "lusty Pakington," famous for his magnificence of living. His son John (1600–1624) was created a baronet in 1620. His son, Sir John, the second baronet (1620–1680), played an active part on the royalist side in the troubles of the Great Rebellion and the Commonwealth, and was taken prisoner at Worcester in 1651; Lady Dorothy, his wife (d. 1679), daughter of the lord keeper Thomas Coventry, was famous for her learning, and was long credited with the authorship of *The Whole Duty of Man* (1658), which has more recently been attributed to Richard Allestree (*q.v.*). Their grandson, Sir John, the 4th baronet (1671–1727) was a pronounced high Tory and was very prominent in political life; for long he was regarded as the original of Addison's Sir Roger de Coverley, but the reasons for this supposition are now regarded as inadequate. The baronetcy became extinct with the death of Sir John Pakington, the 8th baronet; in January 1830, but it was revived in 1846 for his maternal nephew and heir, John Somerset Pakington (1799–1880), whose name was originally Russell. Born on the 20th of February 1799 and educated at Eton and at Oriel College, Oxford, Pakington had a long career as an active and industrious Conservative politician, being member of parliament for Droitwich from 1837 to 1874. He was secretary for war and the colonies in 1852; first lord of the admiralty in 1858–1859 and again in 1866–1867; and secretary of state for war in 1867–1868. In 1874 he was created Baron Hampton, and he died in London on the 9th of April 1880. From 1875 until his death Hampton was chief civil service commissioner. In 1906 his grandson Herbert Stuart (b. 1883) became 4th baron Hampton. It is interesting to note that in 1329 Henry VIII. granted Sir John Pakington the right of wearing his hat in the royal presence.

PAKOKKU, a district in the Minbu division of Upper Burma, lying west of the Irrawaddy river and south of Mandalay, with the line of the Chin hills as a general boundary on the west. It has an area of 6210 sq. m. and a population (1901) of 356,480. The part of the district along the Irrawaddy and Chindwin rivers is alluvial. Beyond this, however, the country rises gradually to the low Shinmadaung and Tangyi ridges, where it is very arid. To the westward there is a rapid drop to the well-watered valley of the Yaw River, and then a rise over broken, dry country before the valleys of the Myit-tha and Mōn rivers are reached. The principal products are millet, sesamum and sugar produced from toddy-palms in the riverain districts, which also grow rice, grain, peas and beans. Tobacco and vegetables are also produced in some quantity, and maize is grown largely for the sake of the husk, which is used for native cheroot-wrappers, under the name of *yowpet*. The Yenangyat oil-fields, which produce quantities of petroleum, are in the south of the district, and iron used to be worked in a small way. There are 1151 sq. m. of reserved forests in the district. A good deal of teak and cutch is worked out. The cutch of the Yaw country is particularly esteemed. The average rainfall does not exceed 35 in. annually, and in many places water has to be carted for miles. West of the Pôndaung ridge, however, under the Chin hills, the rainfall exceeds 50 inches. The heat in May and June is very great, and the thermometer rises considerably above 100° F. in the shade.

The great majority of the population is Burmese, but in Yaw there is a peculiar race called Taungthas, who claim to be quite distinct from both Burmese and Chins. In 1901 the Taungthas numbered 5700.

The headquarters town, Pakokku, stands on the right bank of the Irrawaddy, and has grown into importance since the British occupation. It is the great boat-building centre of Upper Burma. The population in 1901 was 19,456. It may be described as the emporium of the trade of the Chindwin and Yaw river valleys. The steamers of the Irrawaddy Flotilla Company call here regularly, and it is the starting-point for the vessels plying on the Chindwin.

¹ **PAL, KRISTO DAS** (1839–1884), Indian publicist, was born in Calcutta in 1839, of the Teli or oil-man's caste, which ranks low in the Hindu social hierarchy. He received an English education at the Oriental Seminary and the Hindu Metropolitan College, and at an early age devoted himself to journalism. In 1861 he was appointed assistant secretary (and afterwards secretary) to the British Indian Association, a board of Bengal landlords, which numbered among its members some of the most cultured men of the day. At about the same time he became editor of the *Hindu Patriot*, originally started in 1853 and conducted with ability and zeal by Harish Chandra Mukerji until his death in 1861. This journal having been transferred by a trust deed to some members of the British Indian Association, it henceforth became to some extent an organ of that body. Thus Kristo Das Pal had rare opportunities for proving his abilities and independence during an eventful career of twenty-two years. In 1863 he was appointed justice of the peace and municipal commissioner of Calcutta. In 1872 he was made a member of the Bengal legislative council, where his practical good sense and moderation were much appreciated by successive lieutenant-governors. His opposition, however, to the Calcutta Municipal Bill of 1876, which first recognized the elective system, was attributed to his prejudice in favour of the "classes" against the "masses." In 1878 he received the decoration of C.I.E. In 1883 he was appointed a member of the viceroy's legislative council. In the discussions on the Rent Bill, which came up for consideration before the council, Kristo Das Pal, as secretary to the British Indian Association, necessarily took the side of the landlords. He died on the 24th of July 1884. Speaking after his death, Lord Ripon said: " By this melancholy event we have lost from among us a colleague of distinguished ability, from whom we had on all occasions received assistance, of which I readily acknowledge the value. . . . Mr Kristo Das Pal owed the honourable position to which he had attained to his own exertions. His intellectual attainments were of a high order, his rhetorical gifts were acknowledged by all who heard him, and were enhanced when addressing this council by his thorough mastery over the English language." A full length statue of him was unveiled by Lord Elgin at Calcutta in 1894.

See N. N. Ghose, *Kristo Das Pal, a Study* (Calcutta, 1887).

PALACE (Lat. *Palatium*, the name given by Augustus to his residence on the Palatine Hill), primarily the residence of a sovereign or prince, but in England, Spain and France extended to the residence of a bishop, and in the latter country to buildings appropriated to the public service, such as courts of justice, &c. In Italy the name is given to royal residences, to public buildings, and to such large mansions as in France are either known as *châteaux* if in the country, or *hôtels* if in Paris.

The earliest palaces in Egypt are those built in the rear of the Temple of Karnak by Thothmes III. and near the Temple of Medinet Habu, both in Thebes; the earliest in Greece are those at Cnossus and Phaestus in Crete (c. 1500 B.C.), and at Tiryns in the citadel (c. 1500 B.C.). The most remarkable series are those

erected by the Assyrians at Nimroud, Koyunjik and Khorsabad (859–667 B.C.), which were followed by the Persian palaces at Persepolis and Susa; the Parthian palaces at Al Hadhr and Diarbekr; and the Sassanian palaces of Serbistan, Firuzabad and Ctesiphon. The only palace known of the late Greek style is that found at Palatitza in Macedonia. Of the Roman period there are many examples, beginning with those on the Palatine Hill commenced by Augustus, continued and added to by his successors, Tiberius, Caligula, Domitian, Hadrian and Septimus Severus, which covered an area of over 1,000,000 sq. ft. The villa of Hadrian was virtually an immense palace, the buildings of which extended over 7 m. in length; of more modest proportions are the palace of Diocletian at Spalato and a fine example at Trèves in Germany. The palace of the Hebdomon at Constantinople, and a fragment at Ravenna of Theodoric's work, are all that remain of Byzantine palaces. Of Romanesque work the only examples are those at Gelnhausen built by Barbarossa, and the Wartburg in Germany. In the Gothic style in Italy, the best known examples are the ducal palace at Venice, and the Palazzi Vecchio and del Podesta (Bargello) at Florence; in France, the palace of the popes at Avignon, and the episcopal palaces of Beauvais, Laon, Poitiers and Lisieux; in England, the bishops' palaces of Wells, Norwich, Lincoln, portions of Edward the Confessor's palace at Westminster, and Wolsey's palace at Hampton Court; while such great country mansions as the "castles" of Alnwick, Kenilworth, Warwick, Rochester, Raglan and Stokesay, or Haddon Hall, come in the same category though the name is not employed. Belonging to the Mahommedan style are the palaces of the Alhambra and the Alcazar in Spain. Of the Renaissance period, numerous palaces exist in every country, the more important examples in Italy being those of the Vatican, the Quirinal and the Cancellaria, in Rome; the Caprarola near Rome; the palace of Caserta near Naples; the Pitti at Florence; the Palazzo del Te at Mantua; the court and eastern portion of the ducal palace of Venice, and the numerous examples of the Grand Canal; in France, the Louvre, the Tuileries (destroyed), and the Luxembourg, in Paris; Versailles and St Germain-en-Laye; and the châteaux of la Rochefoucauld, Fontainebleau, Chambord, Blois, Amboise, Chenonceaux and other palaces on the Loire; in Germany, the castle of Heidelberg, and the Zwinger palace at Dresden; in Spain, the palace of Charles V. at Grenada, the Escorial and the palace of Madrid; in England, the palace of Whitehall by Inigo Jones, of which only the banqueting hall was built, Windsor Castle, Blenheim, Chatsworth, Hampton Court; and in Scotland, the palaces of Holyrood and Linlithgow.

PALACIO VALDÉS, ARMANDO (1853–), Spanish novelist and critic, was born at Entralgo, in the province of Asturias, on the 4th of October 1853. His first writings were printed in the *Revista Europea*: These were pungent essays, remarkable for independent judgment and refined humour, and found so much favour with the public that the young beginner was soon appointed editor of the *Revista*. The best of his critical work is collected in *Los Oradores del Ateneo* (1878), *Los Novelistas españoles* (1878), *Nuevo viaje al Parnaso* and *La Literatura en 1881* (1882), this last being written in collaboration with Leopoldo Alas. In 1881 he published a novel, *El Señorito Octavio*, which shows an uncommon power of observation, and the promise of better things to come. In *Marta y María* (1883), a portrayal of the struggle between religious vocation and earthly passion, somewhat in the manner of Valera, Palacio Valdés achieved a very popular triumph which placed him in the first rank of contemporary Spanish novelists. *El Idilio de un enfermo* (1884), a most interesting fragment of autobiography, has scarcely met with the recognition which it deserves: perhaps because the pathos of the story is too unadorned. The publication of Pereda's *Sotileza* is doubtless responsible for the conception of *José* (1885), in which Palacio Valdés gives a realistic picture of the manners and customs of seafaring folk, creates the two convincing characters whom he names José and Leonarda, and embellishes the whole with passages of animated description barely inferior to the finest penned by Pereda himself. The emotional imagination of the writer expressed itself anew in the charming story *Riverita* (1886), one of whose attractive characters develops into the heroine of *Maximina* (1887); and from *Maximina*, in its turn, is taken the novice who figures as a professed nun among the personages of *La Hermana San Sulpicio* (1889), in which the love-passages between Zeferino Sanjurjo and Gloria Bermúdez are set off with elaborate, romantic descriptions of Seville. *El Cuarto poder* (1888) is, as its name implies, concerned with the details, not always edifying, of journalistic life. Two novels issued in 1892, *La Espuma* and *La Fe*, were enthusiastically praised in foreign countries, but in Spain their reception was cold. The explanation is to be found in the fact that the first of these books is an avowed satire on the Spanish aristocracy, and that the second was construed into an attack upon the Roman Catholic Church. During the acrimonious discussion which followed the publication of *La Espuma*, it was frequently asserted that the artist had improvised a fantastic caricature of originals whom he had never seen; yet as the characters in Coloma's *Pequeñeces* are painted in darker tones, and as the very critics who were foremost in charging Palacio Valdés with incompetence and ignorance are almost unanimous in praising Coloma's fidelity, it is manifest that the indictment against *La Espuma* cannot be maintained. Subsequently Palacio Valdés returned to his earlier and better manner in *Los Majos de Cádiz* (1896) and in *La Alegría del Capitán Ribot* (1899). In these novels, and still more in *Tristán, ó el pesimismo* (1906), he frees himself from the reproach of undue submission to French influences. In any case he takes a prominent place in modern Spanish literature as a keen analyst of emotion and a sympathetic, delicate, humorous observer. (J. F.-K.)

PALACKÝ, FRANTIŠEK [FRANCIS] (1798–1876), Czech historian and politician, was born on the 14th of June 1798 at Hodslavice (Hotzendorf) in Moravia. His ancestors had been members of the community of the Bohemian Brethren, and had secretly maintained their Protestant belief throughout the period of religious persecution, eventually giving their adherence to the Augsburg confession as approximate to their original faith. Palacký's father was a schoolmaster and a man of some learning. The son was sent in 1812 to the Protestant gymnasium at Pressburg, where he came in contact with the philologist Šafařík and became a zealous student of the Slav languages. After some years spent in private teaching Palacký settled in 1823 at Prague. Here he found a warm friend in Dobrovský, whose good relations with the Austrian authorities shielded him from the hostility shown by the government to students of Slav subjects. Dobrovský introduced him to Count Sternberg and his brother Francis, both of whom took an enthusiastic interest in Bohemian history. Count Francis was the principal founder of the Society of the Bohemian Museum, devoted to the collection of documents bearing on Bohemian history, with the object of reawakening national sentiment by the study of the national records. Public interest in the movement was stimulated in 1825 by the new *Journal of the Bohemian Museum (Časopis českého Musea)* of which Palacký was the first editor. The journal was at first published in Czech and German, and the Czech edition survived to become the most important literary organ of Bohemia. Palacký had received a modest appointment as archivist to Count Sternberg and in 1829 the Bohemian estates sought to confer on him the title of historiographer of Bohemia, with a small salary, but it was ten years before the consent of the Viennese authorities was obtained. Meanwhile the estates, with the tardy assent of Vienna, had undertaken to pay the expenses of publishing Palacký's capital work, *The History of the Bohemian People* (5 vols., 1836–1867). This book, which comes down to the year 1526 and the extinction of Czech independence, was founded on laborious research in the local archives of Bohemia and in the libraries of the chief cities of Europe, and remains the standard authority. The first volume was printed in German in 1836, and subsequently translated into Czech. The publication of the work was hindered by the police-censorship, which was especially active in criticizing his account of the Hussite movement. Palacký, though entirely national and Protestant in his sympathies, was careful to avoid an uncritical approbation of the Reformers' methods, but his statements were held by the authorities to be dangerous to the Catholic faith. He was therefore compelled to make excisions from his narrative and to accept as integral parts of his work passages interpolated by the censors. After the abolition of the police-censorship in 1848 he published a new edition, completed in 1876, restoring the original form of the work. The fairest and most considerable of Palacký's antagonists in the controversy aroused by his narrative of the early reformation in Bohemia was Baron Helfert, who received a brief from Vienna to write his *Hus und Hieronymus* (1853) to counteract the impression made by Palacký's *History*. K. A. K. Höfler, a German professor of history at Prague, edited the historical authorities for the period in a similar sense in his *Geschichte der hussitischen Bewegung in Böhmen*. Palacký replied in his *Geschichte des Hussitenthums und Professor Löffler* (Prague, 1868) and *Zur böhmischen Geschichtschreibung* (Prague, 1871).

The revolution of 1848 forced the historian into practical politics. He was deputed to the Reichstag which met at Kroměříž (Kremsier) in the autumn of that year, and was a member of the Slav congress at Prague. He refused to take part in the preliminary parliament consisting of 500 former deputies to the diet, which met at Frankfort, on the ground that as a Czech he had no interest in German affairs. He was at this time in favour of a strong Austrian empire, which should consist of a federation of the southern German and the Slav states, allowing of the retention of their individual rights. These views met with some degree of consideration at Vienna, and Palacký was even offered a portfolio in the Pillersdorf cabinet. The collapse of the federal idea and the definite triumph of the party of centralism in 1852 led to his retirement from politics. After the liberal concessions of 1860 and 1861, however, he became a life member of the Austrian senate. His views met with small support from the assembly, and with the exception of a short period after the decree of September 1871, by which the emperor raised hopes for Bohemian self-government, he ceased to appear in the senate from 1865 onwards. In the Bohemian Landtag he became the acknowledged leader of the nationalist-federal party. He sought the establishment of a Czech kingdom which should include Bohemia, Moravia and Silesia, and in his zeal for Czech autonomy he even entered into an alliance with the Conservative nobility and with the extreme Catholics. He attended the Panslavist congress at Moscow in 1867. He died at Prague on the 26th of May 1876.

Among his more important smaller historical works are: *Würdigung der alten böhmischen Geschichtschreiber* (Prague, 1830), dealing with authors of many of whose works were then inaccessible to Czech students; *Archiv český* (6 vols., Prague, 1840–1872); *Urkundliche Beiträge zur Gschichte des Hussitenkriegs* (2 vols., Prague, 1872–1874); *Documenta magistri Johannis Hus vitam, doctrinam, causam . . . illustrantia* (Prague, 1869). With Šafařík he wrote *Anfänge der böhmischen Dichtkunst* (Pressburg, 1818) and *Die ältesten Denkmäler der böhmischen Sprache* (Prague, 1840). Three volumes of his Czech articles and essays were published as *Radhost* (3 vols., Prague, 1871–1873). For accounts of Palacký see an article by Saint René Taillandier in the *Revue des deux mondes* (April, 1855); Count Lützow, *Lectures on the Historians of Bohemia* (London, 1905).

PALADIN (Lat. *palatinus*), strictly a courtier, a member of a royal household, one connected with a palace. From being applied to the famous twelve peers of Charlemagne, the word became a general term in romance for knights of great prowess.

PALAEMON, QUINTUS REMMIUS, Roman grammarian, a native of Vicentia, lived in the reigns of Tiberius and Claudius. From Suetonius (*De grammaticis*, 23) we learn that he was originally a slave who obtained his freedom and taught grammar at Roma. Though a man of profligate and arrogant character, he enjoyed a great reputation as a teacher; Quintilian and Persius are said to have been his pupils. His lost *Ars* (Juvenal, vii. 215), a system of grammar much used in his own time and largely drawn upon by later grammarians, contained rules for correct diction, illustrative quotations and treated of barbarisms and solecisms (Juvenal vi. 452). An extant *Ars grammatica* (discovered by Jovianus Pontanus in the 15th century) and other unimportant treatises on similar subjects have been wrongly ascribed to him.

See C. Marschall, *De Remmii Palaemonis libris grammaticis* (1887); "Latin Grammar in the First Century" by H. Nettleship in *Journal of Philology*, vol. xv. (1886); J. E. Sandys, *Hist. of Classical Scholarship* (2nd ed., 1906).

PALAEOBOTANY. In the present article the subject of vegetable palaeontology is treated from a botanical point of view. The science of botany is concerned with the vegetable kingdom as a whole, and not merely with the flora now living. The remains of the plants of former periods, which have come down to us in the fossilized state, are almost always fragmentary, and often imperfectly preserved; but their investigation is of the utmost importance to the botanist, as affording the only direct evidence of the past history of vegetable organisms. Since the publication of the *Origin of Species* the general acceptance of the doctrine of evolution has given a vastly increased significance to palaeontological data. The determination of the course of descent has now become the ultimate problem for the systematist; this is an historical question, and the historical documents available are the remains of the ancient organisms preserved in the rocks. The palaeobotanist thus endeavours to trace the history of plants in the past, with the hope of throwing light on their natural affinities and on the origin of the various groups. His investigations must embrace not only the comparative morphology and anatomy of fossil plants, but also their distribution over the earth's surface at different periods—a part of the subject which, besides its direct biological interest, has obvious bearings on ancient climatology and geography.

Preservation.—Before considering the results of palaeobotanical research, some account must be given of the way in which the evidence is presented, or, in other words, of the modes of preservation of vegetable remains. These fall under two main heads. On the one hand, there is the mode of preservation which gives rise to casts, moulds and generally impressions, exhibiting the *superficial* features of the specimen. The great majority of vegetable fossils are of this kind, and the term *incrustation* is used as a general term to cover all such methods of fossilization. On the other hand, there are specimens in which the tissues of the plant have been permeated by some mineral in solution, which, subsequently acting hard, has fixed and preserved the internal structure, often with astonishing perfection of detail. This second method of fossilization is termed *petrifaction.* In the case of incrustation the whole substance of the fossilized specimen—*e.g.*, a stem of *Sigillaria*—may be replaced by mineral matter, such as sandstone or shale, giving a cast of the whole, on the outer surface of which the external markings, such as the bases of leaves and the scars left by their fall, are visible in their natural form. Usually the original organic substance remains as a thin carbonaceous layer forming the surface of the cast, but sometimes it has entirely disappeared. The surrounding matrix will of course show the *mould* of the cast, with its elevations and depressions reversed. In the case of thin, flat organs such as leaves, the whole organ may be spread out in the plane of stratification, leaving its impress on the overlying and underlying layers. Here there has not necessarily been any replacement of organic by inorganic material; the whole leaf, for example, may remain, though reduced to a carbonaceous film. In such carbonaceous impression not only are the form and markings, such as venation, perfectly preserved, but something of the actual structure may remain. The cuticularized epidermis, especially, is often thus preserved, and may be removed by the use of appropriate reagents and examined microscopically. If sporangia and spores are present they also may persist in a perfectly recognizable form, and in fact much of our knowledge of the fructification of fossil Ferns and similar plants has been derived from specimens of this kind.

In many cases *internal* casts have been formed, some large cavity, such as a fistular pith, having become filled with mineral substance, which has taken the impress of the surrounding structures, such as the wood. The common casts of Calamites are of this nature, representing the form of the hollow medulla, and bearing on their surface the print of the nodal constrictions and of the ridges and furrows on the inner surface of the wood. The whole organic substance may have been removed, or may persist merely as a thin carbonaceous layer. Mistakes have often arisen from confusing these *medullary* casts with those of the stem as a whole.

Although some information as to minute structure may often be gleaned from the carbonaceous coating of impressions, the fossils preserved by *petrifaction* are the main source of our knowledge of the structural characters of ancient plants. The chemical bodies which have played the most important part as agents of petrifaction are silicic acid and calcium carbonate, though other substances, such as magnesium carbonate, calcium sulphate and ferric oxide have also been concerned, either as the chief constituents of petrifac-

tions, or mixed with other bodies. A large number of the most important remains of plants with structure preserved are silicious; this is the case, for example, with the famous French Permo-Carboniferous fossils of St Étienne, Autun, &c., which in the hands of Brongniart, Renault and others have yielded such brilliant scientific results. At a more recent horizon, the silicified specimens of the Mesozoic Gymnosperms from Great Britain, France, and especially North America, are no less important. Calcified specimens are especially characteristic of the British Carboniferous formation; their preservation is equally perfect with that of the silicified fossils, and their investigation by Witham, Binney, Williamson and others has proved no less fertile. In the Coal Measures of England and of certain German and Austrian districts (*e.g.* Langendreer in Westphalia; Ostrau in Moravia), calcareous nodules, crowded with vegetable fragments of every kind, occur in certain mines embedded in the substance of the coal and representing its raw material in a petrified condition. Even the most delicate tissues, such as cambium and phloem, the endosperm of seeds, or the formative tissue of the growing-point, are frequently preserved cell for cell, both in calcareous and silicious material. As a rule, the petrified remains, all-important for the revelation of structure, are fragmentary, and give little idea of the habit or external characters of the plants from which they were derived. Hence they must be brought into relation with the specimens preserved as casts or impressions, in order to gain a better conception of the plant as a whole. This is often a difficult task, and generally the fragmentary nature of practically all vegetable fossils is the chief hindrance to their investigation. Owing to this, it has become the common practice of palaeobotanists to give distinct generic names to detached parts of plants which may even have belonged to one and the same species. Thus the roots of *Sigillaria* are called *Stigmaria*, detached leaves *Sigillariophyllum*, and the fructifications *Sigillariostrobus*; the name *Sigillaria* applies to the stem, which, however, when old and partly decorticated has been called *Syringodendron*, while its woody cylinder has often been described under the name *Diploxylon*. This naming of portions of plants, however objectionable, is often not to be avoided; for detached organs constantly have to be described long before their relation to other parts is established—which, indeed, may never be accomplished. For example, the form and structure of *Stigmaria* have long been well known; but it is seldom possible to determine whether a given Stigmaria belonged to *Sigillaria*, *Lepidodendron* or some other genus. The correct piecing together of the fragmentary remains is one of the first problems of the palaeobotanist, and the gradual disappearance of superfluous names affords a fair measure of the progress of his science. The recent advance of fossil botany has depended in a very great degree on the study of petrified specimens with their structure preserved; so far, at least, as the older strata are concerned, it is, as a rule, only with the help of specimens showing structure that any safe conclusions as to the affinities of fossil plants can be arrived at.

The subject of coal (*q.v.*) is treated elsewhere. Here it need only be said that the masses of vegetable substance, more or less carbonized and chemically altered, of which coal is composed, frequently contain cells and fragments of tissue in a condition recognizable under the microscope, as for example spores (sometimes present in great quantities), elements of the wood, fibres of the bark, &c. These remnants, however, though interesting as revealing something of the sources of coal, are too fragmentary and imperfect to be of any botanical importance. In lignite, on the other hand, the organized structure is sometimes excellently preserved. In the Wealden of Belgium, for example, specimens of Ferns and Coniferae occur, in the form of lignite, which can be sectioned, like recent plants, with a razor, and exhibit an almost unaltered structure.

I.—PALAEOZOIC

The present section is concerned with the botany of the Palaeozoic age, from the oldest rocks in which vegetable remains have been found up to the close of the Permian period. The Glossopteris flora of India and the southern hemisphere, the age of which has been disputed, but is now regarded as for the most part Permo-Carboniferous, is, however, dealt with in the succeeding section, in connexion with the Mesozoic floras. The various groups of plants represented in the Palaeozoic rocks will first be considered in systematic order, after which some account will be given of the succession and distribution of the various floras during the period.

In dealing with the plants of such remote epochs, the relative importance of the various groups, so far as they are known to us, is naturally very different from that which they assume at the present day. There is no evidence that the Angiospermous flowering plants, now the dominant class, existed during the Palaeozoic period; they do not appear till far on in the Mesozoic epoch, and their earlier history is as yet entirely unknown. On the other hand, fern-like seed-plants, known as Pteridosperms, and Gymnosperms belonging almost entirely to families now extinct, were abundant, while the Pteridophyta attained a development exceeding anything that they can now show. Among the lower classes of plants we have scarcely any knowledge of Palaeozoic Bryophyta; Fungi were probably abundant, but their remains give us little information; while, even among the Algae, which are better represented, well characterized specimens are scanty.

With few exceptions, the remains of Palaeozoic Algae are of comparatively little botanical interest. A vast number of "species" **Algae.** have been described, but, as has been said, "by far the greater number of the supposed fossil Algae have no claim to be regarded as authentic records of this class of Thallophytes" (Seward, 1898). The investigations of Nathorst, Williamson and others have shown that a very large proportion of the casts and impressions attributed to Algae had in all probability a totally different origin. Some represent the tracks or burrows of worms, crustaceans or other animals; others, the course of rills of water on a sandy or muddy shore; others, again, the marks left on the bottom by bodies drifted along by the waves. In cases of doubt, evidence may be obtained from traces of organic structure, from the presence of carbonaceous matter, or, as Zeiller has pointed out, by the remains of animals such as Bryozoa being attached to the cast, showing that it represents a solid body and not a mere cavity or furrow. Evidence from traces of organization is alone conclusive; the presence of carbonaceous matter, though a useful indication, may be deceptive, for the organic substance may have been derived from other sources than the body which left the impression. The mere external form of the supposed Algae is rarely so characteristic as to afford satisfactory evidence of their nature. Some of the better-attested examples, among which are a few of considerable interest, may now be considered. Of Cyanophyceae, as we should expect, the Palaeozoic remains are very doubtful. *Gloiocaulis*, found by Renault in a coprolite of Permian age, was regarded by him as a Cyanophycean allied to *Gloeocapsa*; this may be so, but the argument drawn from the absence of nuclei, considering the extreme rarity of recognizable nuclei even in the best preserved fossil tissues, can hardly be taken seriously. *Girvanella*, found in Cambrian, Ordovician and Silurian rocks, as well as in later deposits, appears to have played a part in the origination of oölitic rock-structure. It consists of minute interwoven tubular filaments, and has been variously interpreted as possibly representing the sheaths of a Cyanophycean Alga, and as constituting a Siphoneous thallus of the type of the Codieae. The non-cellular order Siphoneae is fairly well represented in Palaeozoic strata, especially by calcareous verticillate forms referable to the family Dasycladeae; the separate tubular joints of the articulated thallus, bearing the prints of the whorled branches, are sometimes cylindrical (*Arthroporella*, *Vermiporella*, &c.), sometimes oval (*Sycidium*) or spherical (*Cyclocrinus*). These forms, and others like them, go back to the Silurian and Ordovician; while *Gyroporella*, from the Permian, is another fairly characteristic Siphoneous type. There can be no doubt that the verticillate Siphoneae, a group much isolated among recent organisms, are among the most ancient families of plants. The gigantic *Nematophycus*, to be described below, has been regarded as having Siphoneous affinities. Little trace of Confervaceae has been found; *Confervites chantransioides*, apparently consisting of branched cellular filaments, may perhaps represent a Cambrian Confervoid. *Cladiscothallus*, from the Culm of Russia, in which the filaments are united to form hemispherical or globular tufts, has been compared by Renault to a *Chaetophora*. This is one of the somewhat doubtful Algae occurring in boghead coal or torbanite, a carbonaceous rock the nature of which has been much disputed, in the law courts as well as in scientific literature. The boghead of Scotland, Autun and New South Wales is regarded by Renault and Bertrand as mainly composed of gelatinous Algae (*Pila* and *Reinschia*), having a hollow, saccate thallus formed of a single layer of cells. It may appear surprising that a body containing 65 % of carbon should be so largely made up of gelatinous Algae in a comparatively little altered condition, but the material is rich in bitumen, which seems to have replaced the water contained in the organisms when alive. It has recently been stated, however, that the supposed Algae are in reality the megaspores of Vascular Cryptogams. Scarcely anything is known of Palaeozoic Florideae; *Solenopora*, ranging from the Ordovician to the Jurassic, resembles, in the structure of its thallus, with definite zones of growth, Corallinaceae such as *Lithothamnion*, and may probably be of the same nature. A branched filamentous organism from the Lower Carboniferous of Scotland, described by Kidston under the name of *Bythotrephis worstoniensis*, shows some remains of cellular structure, and may probably be a true Alga, resembling some of the filamentous Florideae in habit.

Apart from the multitude of supposed fossil Algae described as "Fucoids" but usually not of Algal nature, and never presenting determinable characters, very little remains that can be referred to Palaeozoic Brown Algae. The most striking of all fossil Algae, however, *Nematophycus*, may possibly be a Phaeophycean. The first species of the genus, *Nematophycus Logani*, was discovered by Dawson in 1856 in the Lower and Middle Devonian of Canada, and was described by him as a Conifer under the name of *Prototaxites*. Carruthers, however, in 1872 established its Algal nature, and gave it the more appropriate name of *Nematophycus*. In *N. Logani* the stem, which is found in a silicified state, may be as much as 3 ft. in diameter. The tissue is made up of large, unseptate, occasionally branching tubes, with an undulating vertical course, among which much smaller tubes are irregularly interwoven. Radially placed gaps in the tissue (at first erroneously interpreted as medullary rays, but subsequently more aptly compared to the air-spaces of large Algae) contain very sparse hyphae, which here branch more freely than elsewhere. The concentric rings of growth, which form a characteristic feature, are due to periodic variations in the size of the larger tubes. Transverse septa have occasionally, but rarely, been detected in the smaller hyphae. Penhallow maintains that these smaller tubes arise as branches from the larger, but other observers have failed to confirm this. In *N. Storrsei*, from the Silurian (Wenlock) of South Wales, described by Barber, there is no sharp differentiation of the two kinds of tubes; they are rarely observed to branch, except in the gaps, which in this species are not radially directed. In *N. Ortoni* (Penhallow), from the Devonian of Canada, the tubes are quite uniform, and there are no spaces or concentric rings. The tubes have their cavity dilated at intervals, and Penhallow has therefore compared them with the trumpet-hyphae of Laminariaceae, but no transverse septa are anywhere visible. Several other species have been described. Carruthers compared the usually non-cellular structure of *Nematophycus* with that of Siphoneae such as *Halimeda*, while recognizing the points of resemblance to Laminariaceae (*e.g. Lessonia*) in the dimensions of the stem and its concentric rings of growth. Later writers, influenced by the occasional occurrence of transverse walls in the smaller hyphae, have laid more stress on Laminariaceous affinities. The existence of these gigantic Algae in Palaeozoic times, attested by such well-preserved specimens, is a fact of great interest, though their systematic position is still an open question. *Pachytheca*, a spherical organism, usually about the size of a small pea, found in rocks of Silurian and Devonian age, has been much investigated and discussed, without any decisive light having been thrown on its nature. It was once regarded as connected with *Nematophycus* (with which it sometimes occurs in association), possibly as its fructification. For this view however, there is no evidence, though the tissues of the two fossils are somewhat similar. *Pachytheca* is formed of cellular filaments resembling those of a *Cladophora*, irregularly interwoven in the central region, radiating towards the periphery, and often forked. In one case the spherical thallus was found seated in a cup-like receptacle. There can be little doubt of the Algal nature of the fossil, but beyond this it is impossible at present to carry its determination.

On the whole, it cannot be said that the Palaeozoic remains have as yet thrown much light on the evolution of the Algae, though we may not be prepared to maintain, with Zeiller, that plants of this class appear never to have assumed a form very different from that which they present at the present day.

The first evidence for the existence of Palaeozoic Bacteria was obtained in 1879 by Van Tieghem, who found that in silicified vegetable remains from the Coal Measures of St Étienne **Bacteria.** the cellulose membranes showed traces of subjection to butyric fermentation, such as is produced at the present day by *Bacillus Amylobacter*; he also claimed to have detected the organism itself. Since that time a number of fossil Bacteria, mainly from Palaeozoic strata, have been described by Renault, occurring in all kinds of fossilized vegetable and animal débris. The supposed *Micrococci* present little that is characteristic; the more definite, rod-like form of the *Bacilli* offers a better means of recognition, though far from an infallible one; in a few cases dark bodies, suggestive of endospores, have been found within the rods. On the whole, the occurrence of Bacteria in Palaeozoic times—so probable a priori—may be taken as established, though the attempt to discriminate species among them is probably futile.

Fungi were no doubt abundant among Palaeozoic vegetation. In examining the tissues of fossil plants of that epoch nothing is more common than to meet with mycelial hyphae in **Fungi.** and among the cells; in many cases the hyphae are septate, showing that the higher Fungi (Mycomycetes), as distinguished from the more algoid Phycomycetes, already existed. An endophytic Fungus referred to the latter group (*Peronosporeae antiquarius*, W. Smith) bears very definite terminal, or intercalary, spherical vesicles, which may probably be regarded as reproductive organs—either oögonia or sporangia. A minute Fungus bearing sporangia, found by Renault in the wood of a *Lepidodendron*, and named by him *Oöchytrium Lepidodendri*, is referred with much probability to the Chytridineae. Conceptacles containing Spores, so strongly suggesting the Chytridineous Fungus *Urophlyctis*, have recently been found, in petrified material, on the leaves of an *Alethopteris*, which appears to have undergone decay before fossilization set in. Small spores, almost certainly those of Fungi, are very common in the petrified tissues of Palaeozoic plants. Spherical sacs, bearing forked spines, described by Williamson under the name of *Zygosporites*, are frequent, usually in an isolated state.

Professor Seward, however, has found a *Zygosporites in situ*, terminating an apparently fungal hypha; he suggests a possible comparison with the mould *Mucor*. Bodies closely resembling the perithecia of Sphaeriaceous Fungi have often been observed on impressions of Palaeozoic plants, and may probably belong to the group indicated. Professor F. E. Weiss has obtained interesting evidence that the symbiotic association between roots and Fungi, known as " Mycorhiza," already occurred among Carboniferous plants. The few and incomplete data which we at present possess as to Palaeozoic Fungi do not as yet justify any inferences as to the evolution of these plants. The writer is not aware of any evidence for the occurrence of Palaeozoic Lichens.

The important class of the Bryophyta, which, on theoretical grounds, is commonly regarded as more primitive than the *Bryophyta.* Pteridophyta, is as yet scarcely represented among known fossils of Palaeozoic age. In the Lower Carboniferous of Scotland Mr Kidston has found several specimens of a large dichotomous thallus, with a very distinct midrib; the specimens, referred to the provisional genus *Thallites*, much resemble the larger thalloid Liverworts. Similar fossils have been described from still older rocks. In one or two cases Palaeozoic plants, resembling the true Mosses in habit, have been discovered; the best example is the *Muscites polytrichaceus* of Renault and Zeiller, from the Coal Measures of Commentry. In the absence, however, both of reproductive organs and of anatomical structure, it cannot be said that there is at present conclusive evidence for the existence of either Hepaticae or Musci in Palaeozoic times.

Our knowledge of the Vascular Cryptograms of the Palaeozoic period, though recent discoveries have somewhat reduced their *Pteridophyta.* relative importance, is still more extensive than of any other class of plants, and in fact it is here that the evidence of Palaeontology first becomes of essential importance to the botanist. They extend back through the Devonian, possibly to the Silurian system, but the systematic summary now to be given is based primarily on the rich materials afforded by the Carboniferous and Permian formations, from which our detailed knowledge of Palaeozoic plants has been chiefly derived.

In addition to the three classes, Equisetales, Lycopodiales and Filicales, under which recent Pteridophytes naturally group themselves, a fourth class, Sphenophyllales, existed in Palaeozoic times, clearly related to the Horsetails and more remotely to the Ferns and perhaps the Club-mosses, but with peculiarities of its own demanding an independent position. We further find that, whereas the Ferns of the present day form a well-defined and even isolated class, this was not the case at the time when the primary rocks were deposited. A great group of Palaeozoic fossils, showing evident affinity to Ferns, has proved to consist of seed-bearing plants allied to Gymnosperms, especially Cycads. This important class of plants will be described at the beginning of the Spermophyta under the name Pteridospermeae. The arrangement which we shall adopt for the Palaeozoic Pteridophyta is therefore as follows:—

     I. *Equisetales.*   II. *Sphenophyllales.*
    III. *Lycopodiales.*   IV. *Filicales.*

We must bear in mind that throughout the Palaeozoic period, and indeed far beyond it, vascular plants, so far as the existing evidence shows, were represented only by the Pteridophyta, Pteridosperms and Gymnosperms. Although the history of the Angiosperms may probably go much further back than present records show, there is no reason to suppose that they were present, as such, amongst the Palaeozoic vegetation. Consequently, the Pteridophytes, Gymnosperms and their allies had the field to themselves, so far as regards the higher plants, and filled places in nature which have now for the most part been seized on by families of more modern origin. Hence it is not surprising to find that the early Vascular Cryptograms were, beyond comparison, more varied and more highly organized than their displaced and often degraded successors. It is among the fossils of the Palaeozoic rocks that we first learn the possibilities of Pteridophytic organization.

I. *Equisetales.*—This class, represented in the recent flora by the single genus *Equisetum*, with about twenty species, was one of the dominant groups of plants in Carboniferous times. The Calamarieae, now known to have been the chief Palaeozoic representatives of the Horsetail stock, attained the dimensions of trees, reaching, according to Grand' Eury, a height of from 30 to 60 metres, and showed in all respects a higher and more varied organization than their recent successors.

Their remains occur in three principal forms of preservation: (1) carbonaceous impressions of the leafy branches, the fructifications and other parts; (2) casts of the stem; these are usually internal, or *medullary* casts, as described above. Around the cast the organic tissues may be represented by a carbonaceous layer, on the outer surface of which the external features, such as the remains of leaves, can sometimes be traced. More usually, however, the carbonaceous film is thin, and merely shows the impress of the medullary cast within; (3) petrified specimens of all parts—stem, roots, leaves and fructifications—showing the internal structure, more or less perfectly preserved. The correlation of these various remains presents considerable difficulties. Casts surrounded by wood, with its structure preserved, have sometimes been found, and have established their true relations. The position of the branches is shown both on casts and in petrified specimens, and has helped in their identification, while the petrified remains sometimes show enough of the external characters to allow of their correlation with impressions. Fructifications have often been found in connexion with leafy shoots, and the anatomical structure of the axis in sterile and fertile specimens has proved a valuable means of identification.

In *habit* the Calamarieae appear to have borne, on the whole, a general resemblance to the recent Equisetaceae, in spite of their enormously greater bulk. The leaves were constantly in whorls, and were usually of comparatively small size and of simple form. In the oldest known Calamarian, however, *Archaeocalamites* (Devonian and Lower Carboniferous), the leaves were repeatedly forked. There is evidence that in some, at least, of the Calamarieae the leaves of each verticil were united at the base to form a sheath. The free lamina, however, was always considerably more developed than in the recent family; in form it was usually linear or narrowly lanceolate. Different genera have been founded on leaf-bearing branches of Calamarieae; apart from *Archaeocalamites*, already mentioned, and *Autophyllites* (Grand' Eury), in both of which the leaves were dichotomous, we have *Annularia*, *Asterophyllites* and *Calamocladus* (in Grand' Eury's limited sense), with simple leaves. In some species of *Annularia* the extremely delicate ultimate twigs, bearing whorls of small lanceolate leaves, give a characteristic habit, suggesting that they may have belonged to herbaceous plants; other Annulariae, however, have been traced with certainty into connexion with the stems of large Calamites. In *Asterophyllites*, the generic distinction of which from *Annularia* is not always clear, the narrow linear leaves are in crowded whorls, and the ultimate branches distichously arranged; in the *Calamocladus* of Grand' Eury—characteristic of the Upper Coal Measures—the whorls are more remote, and the twigs polystichous in arrangement. In all these groups a leaf-sheath has been recognized.

The distribution of the branches on the main stem shows considerable variations, on which generic or sub-genera have been founded by C. E. Weiss. In *Archaeocalamites*, which certainly deserves generic rank, the branches may occur on every node, but only in certain parts of the stem; the ribs of successive internodes do not alternate, but are continuous, indicating that the leaves were superposed. Using *Calamites* as a generic name for all those Calamarian stems in which the ribs alternate at the nodes, we have, on Weiss's system, the following sub-genera: *Stylocalamites*, branches rare and irregularly arranged; *Calamitina*, branches in regular verticils, limited to certain nodes, which surmount specially short internodes; *Eucalamites*, branches present on every node. These distinctions can be recognized on petrified specimens, as well as on the casts, but their taxonomic value is somewhat doubtful. In many Calamites there is evidence that the aerial stem sprang from a horizontal rhizome, as in the common species *C. (Stylocalamites) Suckowi*; in other specimens the aerial stem has an independent, rooting base.

The *anatomical structure* of all parts of the plant is now known, in various Calamarieae, thanks more especially to the work of Williamson in England and of Renault in France. The stem has a structure which may be briefly characterized as that of an *Equisetum* with secondary growth in thickness (fig. 1, Plate). The usually fistular pith is surrounded by a ring of collateral vascular bundle, (see ANATOMY OF PLANTS, and PTERIDOPHYTA), each of which, with rare exceptions, has an intercellular canal at its inner edge, containing the disorganized spiral tracheae, just as in the recent genus. The cortex is often preserved; in certain cases it was strengthened by hypodermal strands of fibres, as in *Equisetum*. It is only in the rare cases where a very young twig is preserved that the primary structure of the stem is found unaltered. In all the larger specimens a broad zone of wood, with its elements in radial series, had been added. This secondary wood, in the true Calamites (*Arthropitys*, Goeppert), has a simple structure comparable to that of the simplest Coniferous woods; it is made up entirely of radial bands of tracheides interspersed with medullary rays. The pitting of the tracheides is more or less scalariform in character, and is limited to the radial walls. In favourable cases remains of the cambium are found on the outer border of the wood, and phloem is also present in the normal position, though it does not seem to have attained any considerable thickness. In the old stems the primary cortex was replaced by periderm, giving rise to a thick mass of bark. The above description applies to the stems of *Calamites* in the narrower sense (*Arthropitys* of the French authors), to which the specimens from the British Coal Measures mostly belong. *Archaeocalamites* appears to have had a similar structure, but in some specimens from the Lower Carboniferous of Burntisland, provisionally named *Protocalamites pettycurensis*, centripetal wood was present in the stem. In *Calamodendron* (Upper Coal Measures) the wood has a more complex structure than in *Calamites*, the principal rays including radial tracts of fibrous tissue, in addition to the usual parenchyma. *Arthrodendron* (Lower Coal Measures) approaches *Calamodendron* in this respect. The longitudinal course of the vascular bundles and their relation to the leaves in Calamarieae generally followed the *Equisetum* type, though more variable and sometimes more complex. The attachment of the branches was immediately above the node, and usually between two foliar traces, as in the recent genus. Where the structure of the leaves is preserved it proves to be of an extremely simple type; the narrow lamina is traversed by a single vascular bundle, separated by a sheath from the surrounding palisade-parenchyma. Stomata of the same structure as in *Equisetum* have been detected in the epidermis.

The roots (formerly described as a separate genus, *Astromyelon*) were borne directly on the nodes, not on short lateral branches as in *Equisetum*. They are of similar structure in all known Calamarieae, the main roots having a large pith, while the rootlets had little or none. The structure is in all respects that typical of roots, as shown by the centripetal primary wood, and the alternation of xylem and phloem groups observable in exceptionally favourable young specimens. A striking feature is the presence of large, radiating intercellular cavities in the cortex, suggesting an aquatic habit. The young roots show a double endoderms, just as in the recent *Equisetum*.

A considerable number of Calamarian *fructifications* are known, preserved, some as carbonaceous impressions, others as petrified specimens, exhibiting the internal structure. In many cases the cones have been found in connexion with branches bearing characteristic Calamarian foliage. Almost all strobili of the Calamarieae are constructed on the same general lines as those of *Equisetum*, with which some agree exactly; in most, however, the organization was more complex, the complexity consisting in the intercalation of whorls of sterile bracts, between those of the sporangiophores. In several cases heterospory, unknown among recent Equisetaceae, has been demonstrated in their Palaeozoic representatives.

Four main types of structure may be distinguished among Calamarian strobili.

1. *Calamostachys*, Schimper. Here the whorls of peltate sporangiophores alternate regularly with those of sterile bracts, the

FIG. 2.—*Calamostachys*. Diagrammatic longitudinal section of the cone, showing the axis (*ax*) bearing alternate whorls of bracts (*br*) and peltate sporangiophores (*sp*) with their sporangia (*sm*), the upturned tips of the bracts are only shown in every alternate verticil.

former being inserted on the axis midway between the latter (fig. 2). The sporangiophores, which are usually half as numerous in each verticil as the bracts, have the same form as in *Equisetum*, but each bears four sporangia only. The spores are frequently found to be still united in tetrads. In some species, *e.g.* the British *C. Binneyana*, numerous specimens have been examined and only one kind of spore observed; here, then, there is a strong presumption that the species was homosporous. In other cases, however, *e.g. C. Casheana*, Will., two kinds of spore occur, in different sporangia, but on the same strobilus and even on the same sporangiophore. The megaspores, of which there are many in the megasporangium, have a diameter about three times that of the microspores. The abortion of certain spores, which is known to have taken place both in the homosporous *C. Binneyana* and in the megasporangia of *C. Casheana*, may throw some light on the origin of the heterosporous condition. The bracts were sometimes coherent in their lower part (*e.g. C. Binneyana*), sometimes free (*e.g. C. Ludwigi*); in all cases their free extremities formed a protection to the fertile whorl above. In some continental species (*e.g. C. Grand' Eury*, Ren.) radial membranous plates hung down from each verticil of bracts, forming compartments in which the subjacent sporangio-

phores were enclosed. The anatomy of the axis is essentially similar to that of a young Calamarian twig, with some variations in detail. Strobili of the *Calamostachys* type occur in connexion both with *Annularia* and *Asterophyllites* foliage.

2. *Palaeostachya*, Weiss. Here, as in the previous genus, sterile and fertile verticils are ranged alternately on the axis of the cone. The main difference is that in *Palaeostachya* the sporangiophores, instead of standing midway between the whorls of bracts, are inserted immediately above them, springing, as it were, from the axil of the sterile verticil (fig. 3, A). This singular arrangement has suggested doubts as to the correctness of the current interpretation of the Equisetaceous **sporangiophore as a** modified leaf

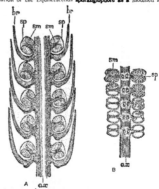

(After Renault. Scott, *Studies*.)

FIG. 3.

A, *Palaeostachya*. Diagrammatic longitudinal section of cone, showing the axis (*ax*) bearing the bracts (*br*) with peltate sporangiophores (*sp*) springing from their axils; *sm*, sporangia.

B, *Archaeocalamites*. Part of cone, showing the axis (*ax*) bearing peltate sporangiophores (*sp*) without bracts; *sm*, sporangia.

(cf. *Cheirostrobus* below). In most other respects the two genera agree; there is evidence for the occurrence of heterospory in some strobili referred to *Palaeostachya*. The anatomy of the axis is that of a young branch of a Calamite. According to Grand' Eury, the *Palaeostachya* fructification was most commonly associated with *Asterophyllites* foliage. The external aspect of a *Palaeostachya* is shown in fig. 4 (Plate).

3. *Equisetum* type of strobilus. In certain cases the strobili of Palaeozoic Calamarieae appear to have had essentially the same organization as in the recent genus, the axis bearing sporangiophores only, without intercalated bracts. It is remarkable that fructifications apparently of this kind have been found by Renault in close association with the most ancient of the Calamarieae—*Archaeocalamites*. In these strobili the peltate scales, like the vegetative leaves of the plant, are in superposed verticils; each appears to have borne four sporangia (fig. 3. B). Other cones, however, namely, those known as *Pothocites*, have also been attributed on good grounds to the genus *Archaeocalamites*; they are long strobili, constricted at intervals, and it is probable that the succession of fertile sporangiophores was interrupted here and there by the intercalation of sterile bracts, which may also have been present, at long intervals, in Renault's species. Cones from the Middle Coal Measures, described by Kidston under the name of *Equisetum Hemingwayi*, but probably belonging to one of the Calamarieae, bear a striking external resemblance to those of a recent *Equisetum*.

4. *Cingularia*, Weiss. This form of strobilus, from the Coal Measures of Germany, is imperfectly known, and its relation to Calamarieae not beyond doubt. In the lax strobili the sporangiophores, which are not peltate, but strap-shaped, were borne, as C. E. Weiss first showed, immediately *below* the verticils of bracts, the position thus being the reverse of that in *Palaeostachya*.

The Palaeozoic Calamarieae, though so far surpassing recent Equisetaceae, both in stature and complexity of organization, clearly belonged to the same class of Vascular Cryptogams. There is no satisfactory evidence for attributing Phanerogamic affinities to any members of the group, and the view, of which Williamson was the chief advocate, that they form a homogeneous Cryptogamic family, is now fully established.

II. *Sphenophyllales.*—The class of *Sphenophyllales*, as known to us at present, is of limited extent, embracing the two genera *Sphenophyllum* and *Cheirostrobus*, which may serve as types of two families within the class. The characters of *Sphenophyllum* are known with some completeness, while our knowledge of *Cheirostrobus* is confined to the fructification; the former will therefore be described first.

1. *Sphenophyllum.*—The genus *Sphenophyllum*, of which a number of species have been described, ranging probably from the Middle Devonian, through the Carboniferous, to the Permian or even the Lower Triassic, consisted of herbaceous plants of moderate dimensions. The long, slender stems, somewhat tumid at the nodes, were ribbed, the ribs running continuously through the nodes, a fact correlated with the superposition of the whorled leaves, the number of which in each verticil was some multiple of 3, and usually 6. In the species on which the genus was founded the leaves, as the generic name implies, are cuneate and entire, or toothed on their anterior margin;[1] in other cases they are deeply divided by dichotomy into narrow segments, or the whorl consists of a larger number (up to 30) of apparently simple, linear leaves, which may represent the segments of a smaller number. The different forms of leaf may occur on the same plant, the deeply divided foliage often characterizing the main stem, while the cuneate leaves were borne on lateral shoots. A comparison, formerly suggested, with the two forms of leaf in Batrachian Ranunculi has not proved to hold good; the idea of an aquatic habit is contradicted by the anatomical structure, and the hypothesis that the plants were of scandent growth is more probable. The species of *Sphenophyllum* have a graceful appearance, which has been compared with that of the trailing Galiums of hedgerows. Branches sprang from the nodes, though perhaps not truly axillary in position. The cones, more or less sharply differentiated, terminated certain of the branches.

The *anatomy* of the stem of *Sphenophyllum*, investigated by Renault, Williamson and others, is highly characteristic (fig. 5, Plate). The stem is traversed by a single stele, with solid wood, without pith; the primary xylem is triangular in section, the spiral elements forming one or two groups at each angle, while the phloem occupied the bays, so that the structure resembles that of a triarch root. Two leaf-trace bundles started from each angle of the stele, and forked, in passing through the nodes, to supply the veins of the leaf, or its subdivisions. The cortex was deeply furrowed on its outer surface. The primary structure is only found unaltered in the youngest stems; secondary growth by means of a cambium set in very early, xylem being formed internally and phloem externally in a perfectly normal manner. At the same time a deep-seated periderm arose, by which the primary cortex was soon entirely cut off. The secondary wood in the Lower Carboniferous species, *S. insigne*, has scalariform tracheides, and is traversed by regular medullary rays, but in the forms from later horizons the tracheides are reticulately pitted, and the rays are for the most part replaced by a network of xylem-parenchyma. There are no recent stems with a structure quite like that of *Sphenophyllum*; so far as the primary structure is concerned, the nearest approach is among the *Psiloteae*, with which other characters indicate some affinity; the base of the stem in *Psilotum* forms some secondary wood. The diarch roots of a *Sphenophyllum* have been described by Renault, who has also investigated the leaves; they were strongly constructed mechanically, and traversed by slender vascular bundles branching dichotomously.

Fructification.—Williamson thoroughly worked out, in petrified specimens, the organization of a cone which he named *Bowmanites Dawsoni*; it was subsequently demonstrated by Zeiller that this fructification belonged to a *Sphenophyllum*, the cones of the well-known species *S. cuneifolium* having a practically identical structure. The type of fructification described by Williamson and now named *Sphenophyllum Dawsoni* consists of long cylindrical cones, in external habit not unlike those of some Calamarieae. The axis,

which in structure resembles the vegetative stem in its primary condition, bears numerous verticils of bracts, those of each verticil being coherent in their lower part, so as to form a disc or cup, from the margin of which the free limbs of the bracts arise. The sporangia, which are about twice as numerous as the bracts, are seated singly on pedicels or sporangiophores springing from the upper surface of the bract-verticil, near its insertion on the axis (fig. 6). As a rule two sporangiophores belong to each bract. The sporangium is attached to the enlarged distal end of its pedicel, from which it hangs down, so as to suggest an anatropous ovule on its funiculus. Dehiscence appears to have taken place at the free end of the sporangium; the spores are numerous, and, so far as observed, of one kind only. Each sporangiophore is traversed throughout its length by a vascular bundle connected with that which supplies the subtending bract. This form of fructification appears, from Zeiller's researches, to have been common to several species of *Sphenophyllum*, but others show important differences. Thus *Bowmanites Römeri*, a fructification fully investigated by Solms-Laubach, differs from *S. Dawsoni* in the fact that each sporangiophore bears two sporangia, attached to a distal expansion approaching the peltate scale of the Equisetales. It is thus proved that the sporangiophore is not a mere sporangial stalk, but a distinct organ, in all probability representing a ventral lobe of the subtending bract. The recently discovered species, *Sphenophyllum fertile*, while resembling *Bowmanites Römeri* in its peltate, bisporangiate sporangiophores, is peculiar in the fact that both dorsal and ventral lobes of the sporophyll were fertile, dividing in a palmate manner into several branches, each of which constitutes a sporangiophore. Thus the sterile bracts of other species are here replaced by sporangium-bearing organs. In *Sphenophyllum majus*, where the cones are less sharply defined, the forked bract bears a group of four sporangia at the bifurcations, but their mode of insertion has not yet been made out.

2. *Cheirostrobeae.*—The family *Cheirostrobeae* is only known from the petrified fructification (*Cheirostrobus pettycurensis*) derived from the Lower Carboniferous of Burntisland in Scotland. The excellence of the preservation of the specimens has rendered it possible to investigate the complex structure in detail. The cone is of large size—3·5 cm. in diameter; the stout axis bears numerous whorls of compound sporophylls, the members of successive verticils being superposed. The sporophylls, of which there are eleven or

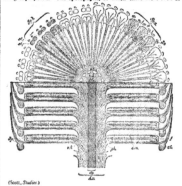

(Scott, *Studies*.)

FIG. 7.—*Cheirostrobus.* Diagram of cone, the upper part in transverse, the lower in longitudinal section. In the transverse section six sporophylls, each showing three segments, are represented.

Sp.s, Section through sterile segments.
Sp.b, Section through sporangio-phores.
st, Laminae of sterile segments.
f, Peltate expansions of sporangiophores.
v.b. Vascular bundles.
cy, Stele of axis (*Ax*).

In the longitudinal section the corresponding parts are shown.

In each sporophyll, in a whorl, are each composed of six segments, three being inferior or dorsal, and three superior or ventral. The dorsal segments are sterile, corresponding to the bracts of *Sphenophyllum Dawsoni,* while the ventral segments constitute peltate sporangiophores, each bearing four sporangia, just as in a

FIG. 6. — *Sphenophyllum Dawsoni.* Diagram of cone in longitudinal section.

ax, Axis.
br, Bracts.
sp, Sporangiophores, each bearing a sporangium, *sm.*
br', Whorl of bracts in surface view.

---

[1] In *S. speciosum* the leaves in a whorl were of unequal size.

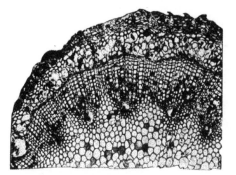

Fig. 1.—*Calamites*. Part of transverse section of a young stem, showing pith, vascular bundles with secondary wood, and cortex. *From a photograph (Scott, "Studies").*

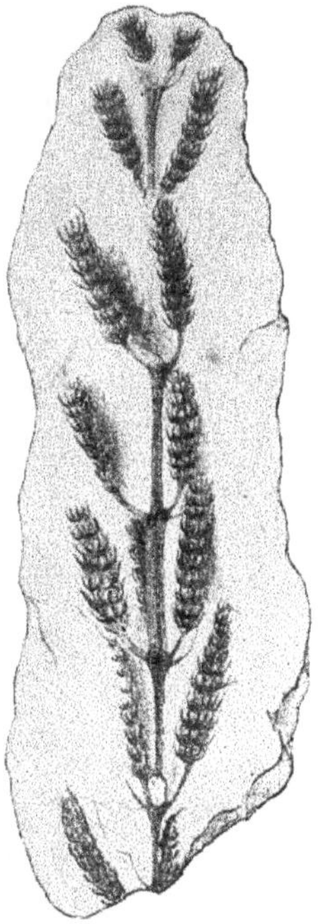

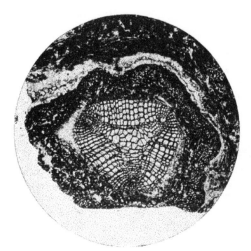

Fig. 4.—*Palaeostachya pedunculata*. Fertile shoot, bearing numerous cones and a few leaves. *After Williamson (Scott, "Studies").*

Fig. 5.—*Sphenophyllum insigne*. Transverse section of stem, showing triangular primary wood, secondary wood, remains of phloem, and primary cortex. *From a photograph (Scott, "Studies").*

PLATE II.   PALAEOBOTANY

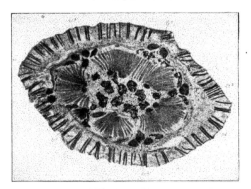

Fig. 22.—*Lyginodendron oldhamium.* Transverse section of stem, showing the pith containing groups of sclerotic cells, the primary xylem-strands, secondary wood and phloem, pericycle and cortex. *lt¹-lt⁵*, leaf-traces, numbered according to the phyllotaxis, *lt⁵* belonging to the lowest leaf of the five; *ph*, a group of primary phloem; *pd*, periderm, formed from pericycle.

A   B

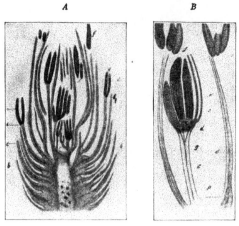

Fig. 31.—*Cordaianthus Penjoni.* *A*, Male catkin in longitudinal section: *a*, axis; *b*, bracts; *c, d*, filaments of stamens, bearing the pollen-sacs (*e* and *f*) at the top; *v*, apex of axis. *B*, Stamens more highly magnified: *g*, vascular bundle of filament; *e*, pollen-sac after dehiscence. *After Renault (Scott, "Studies").*

Calamarian fructification (fig. 7). The great length and slender proportions of the segments give the cone a peculiar character, but the relations of position appear to leave no doubt as to the homologies with the fructification of Sphenophyllene; as regards the sporangiophores, *Bowmanites Römeri* occupies exactly the middle place between *S. Dawsoni* and *Cheirostrobus*. The axis of the cone in *Cheirostrobus* contains a polyarch stele, with solid wood, from the angles of which vascular bundles pass out, dividing in the cortex, to supply the various segments of the sporophylls. In the peduncle of the strobilus secondary tissues are formed. While the anatomy has a somewhat Lycopodiaceous character, the arrangement of the appendages is altogether that of the Sphenophylleae; at the same time Calamarian affinities are indicated by the characters of the sporangiophores and sporangia.

The Sphenophyllales as a whole are best regarded as a synthetic group, combining certain characters of the Ferns and Lycopods with those of the Equisetales, while showing marked peculiarities of their own. Among existing plants their nearest affinities would appear to be with Psiloteae, as indicated not merely by the anatomy, but much more strongly by the way in which the sporangia are borne. There is good reason to believe that the ventral synangium of the Psiloteae corresponds to the ventral sporangiophore with its sporangia in the Sphenophyllales. Professor Thomas of Auckland, New Zealand, has brought forward some interesting variations in *Tmesipteris* which appear to afford additional support to this view.

Pseudobornia.—Professor Nathorst has described a remarkable Devonian plant, *Pseudobornia ursina* (from Bear Island, in the Arctic Ocean), which shows affinity both with the Equisetales and Sphenophyllales. The stem is articulated and branched, attaining a diameter of about 10 cm. The smaller branches bear the whorled leaves, probably four in each verticil. The leaves are highly compound, dividing dichotomously into several leaflets, each of which is deeply pinnatifid, with fine segments. When found detached these leaves were taken for the fronds of a Fern. The fructification consists of long, lax spikes, with whorled sporophylls; indications of megaspores have been detected in the sporangia. The discoverer makes this plant the type of a new class, the Pseudoborniales. At present only the external characters are known.

III. *Lycopodiales*.—In Palaeozoic ages the Lycopods formed one of the dominant groups of plants, remarkable alike for the number of species and for the great stature which many of them attained. The best known of the Palaeozoic Lycopods were trees, reaching 100 ft. or more in height, but side by side with these gigantic representatives of the class, small herbaceous Club-mosses, resembling those of the present day, also occurred. Broadly speaking, the Palaeozoic Lycopods, whatever their dimensions, show a general agreement in habit and structure with our living forms, though often attaining a much higher grade of organization. We will first take the arborescent Lycopods, as in every respect the more important group. They may all be classed under the one family Lepidodendreae, which is here taken to include *Sigillaria*.

Lepidodendreae.—The genus *Lepidodendron*, with very numerous species, ranging from the Devonian to the Permian, consisted of trees, with a tall upright shaft, bearing a dense crown of dichotomous branches, clothed with simple narrow leaves, ranged in some complex spiral phyllotaxis. In some cases the foliage is preserved *in situ*; more often, however, especially in the main stem and larger branches, the leaves had been shed, leaving behind them their scars and persistent bases, on which the characteristic sculpturing of the Lepidodendroid surface depends. The cones, often of large size, were either terminal on the smaller twigs, or, it is alleged, borne laterally on special branches of considerable dimensions. At its base the main stem terminated in dichotomous roots or rhizophores, bearing numerous rootlets. To these underground organs the name *Stigmaria* is applied; they are not clearly distinguishable from the corresponding parts of *Sigillaria*. The numerous described species of *Lepidodendron* are founded on the peculiarities of the leaf-cushions and scars, as shown on casts or impressions of the stem. The usually crowded leaf-cushions are spirally arranged, and present

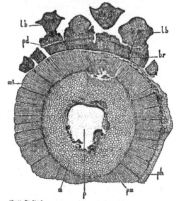

(After Stur. Scott, *Studies*.)

FIG. 8.—Leaf-base of a *Lepidodendron.*

r.c., Scar left by the leaf.
v.b., Print of vascular bundle.
p.p., Parichnos.
l, Ligule.
a,a, Superficial prints below scar.

XX 9*

no obvious orthostichies, thus differing from those of *Sigillaria*. Each leaf-cushion is slightly prominent; towards its upper end is the diamond-shaped or triangular scar left by the fall of the actual leaf (fig. 8). On the scar are three prints, the central one alone representing the vascular bundle, while the lateral prints (*parichnos*) mark the position of merely parenchymatous strands. In the median line, immediately above the leaf-scar, is a print representing the ligule, or rather the pit in which it was seated. On the flanks of the cushion, below the scar, are two superficial prints, perhaps comparable to lenticels. In the genus *Lepidophloios* the leaf-cushions are more prominent than in *Lepidodendron*, and their greatest diameter is in the transverse direction; on the older stems the leaf-scar lies towards the lower side of the cushion. The genus *Bothrodendron*, going back to the Upper Devonian, differs from *Lepidodendron* in its minute leaf-scars and the absence of leaf-cushions, the scars being flush with the smooth surface of the stem. In the Lower Carboniferous of central Russia beds of coal occur consisting of the cuticles of a *Bothrodendron*, which are not fossilized, but retain the consistency and chemical composition of similar tissues in recent plants.

The *anatomy* of *Lepidodendron* and its immediate allies is now well known in a number of species; the Carboniferous rocks of Great Britain are especially rich in petrified specimens, which formed the subject of Williamson's extensive investigations. The stem is in all cases monostelic; in most of the forms the central cylinder underwent secondary growth, and the distinction between primary and secondary wood is very sharply marked. In *L. Harcourtii*, however, the species earliest investigated (by Witham, 1833, and Brongniart, 1837), and in one or two other species, no secondary wood has yet been found. The primary wood of *Lepidodendron* forms a continuous cylinder, not broken up into distinct bundles; its development was clearly centripetal, the spiral elements forming more or less prominent peripheral groups. In the larger stems of most species there was a central pith, but in certain of the smaller branches, and throughout the stem in some species (*L. rhodumnense, L. selaginoides*), the wood was solid. A single leaf-trace, usually collateral in structure, passed out into each leaf. The primary structure of the stem was thus of a simple Lycopodiaceous type, resembling on a larger scale what we find in the upright stem of *Selaginella spinosa*. In most species (*e.g. L. selaginoides, L. Wunschianum, L. Veltheimianum*) secondary growth in thickness took place, and secondary wood was added,

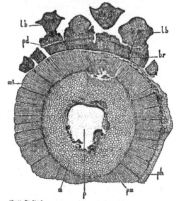

(Scott, *Studies*.)

FIG. 9.—*Lepidodendron Veltheimianum*. Transverse section of stem.

p, Pith, almost destroyed.
x, Zone of primary wood.
px, Protoxylem.
x², Secondary wood.

ph, Phloem and pericycle.
br, Stele of a branch.
pd, Periderm.
lb, Leaf-bases.

The primary cortex between stele and periderm has perished. (×4½.)

in the centrifugal direction, showing a regular radial arrangement, with medullary rays between the series of tracheides (fig. 9). The tissue thus formed often attained a considerable thickness. While primary phloem can be recognized with certainty in favourable cases, the question of the formation of secondary phloem by the cambium is not yet fully cleared up. In the *Lepidodendron fuliginosum* of Williamson, shown by its leaf-bases to have been a *Lepidophloios*, the secondary wood is very irregular, and consists largely of parenchyma. The same is the case in *Lepidodendron obovatum*, one of the few species in which both external and internal characters are known. The occurrence of secondary growth in these plants, demonstrated by Williamson's researches, is a point of great interest. Some analogy among recent Lycopods is afforded by the stem of *Isoetes*, and by the base of the stem in *Selaginella spinosa*; in the fossils the process was of a more normal type, but some of its details need further investigation. The cortex, often sharply differentiated into sclerotic and parenchymatous zones, is bordered externally by the persistent leaf-bases. The development of periderm was a constant feature, and this tissue attained a great thickness, consisting chiefly of a phelloderm, produced on the inner side of the formative layer, and no doubt subserving a mechanical function.

The structure of a *Bothrodendron* has recently been investigated and proves to be identical with that of the petrified stem which Williamson named *Lepidodendron mundum*. The anatomy is of the usual medullate Lepidodendroid type; no secondary growth has yet been detected in the stem.

The most interesting point in the structure of the leaf-base is the presence of a ligule, like that of *Isoetes* or *Selaginella*, which was seated in a deep pit, opening on the upper surface of the cushion, just above the insertion of the lamina. The latter shows marked xerophytic adaptations; the single vascular bundle was surrounded by a sheath of short tracheides, and the stomata were sheltered in two deep furrows of the lower surface.

The *cones* of *Lepidodendron* and its immediate allies are for the most part grouped under the name *Lepidostrobus*. These cones, varying from an inch to a foot in length, according to the species, were borne either on the ordinary twigs, or, as was conjectured, on the special branches (*Ulodendron* and *Halonia*) above referred to. In Ulodendron the large circular, distichously arranged prints were supposed to have been formed by the pressure of the bases of sessile cones, though this interpretation of the scars is open to doubt, and it is now more probable that they bore deciduous vegetative branches; in the Halonial branches characteristic of the genus *Lepidophloios* the tubercles may perhaps mark the points of insertion of pedunculate strobili. The organization of *Lepidostrobus* is essentially that of a Lycopodiaceous cone. The axis, which in anatomical structure resembles a vegetative twig, bears numerous spirally arranged sporophylls, each of which carries a single large sporangium on its upper surface (fig. 10). The sporophyll, usually almost horizontal in position, has an upturned lamina beyond the sporangium, and a shorter dorsal lobe, so that the form of the whole is somewhat peltate. A ligule is present immediately below the lamina, its position showing that the whole of the elongated horizontal pedicel on which the sporangium is seated corresponds to the short base of a vegetative leaf. The sporangia, usually of very large size compared with those of most recent Lycopods, have a palisade-like outer wall, and contain either an immense number of minute microspores, or a very small number of exceedingly large spores (fig. 10). It is very doubtful

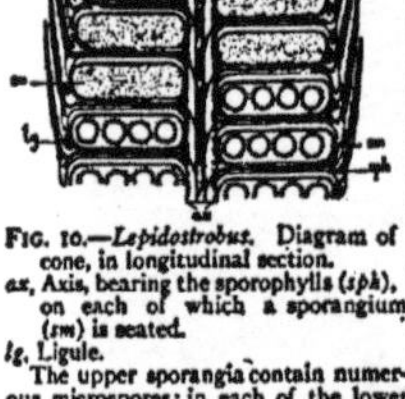

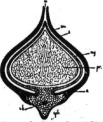

FIG. 10.—*Lepidostrobus*. Diagram of cone, in longitudinal section.
ax, Axis, bearing the sporophylls (*sph*), on each of which a sporangium (*sm*) is seated.
lg, Ligule.

The upper sporangia contain numerous microspores; in each of the lower spores or a very small number sporangia four megaspores are shown (fig. 10). It is very doubtful whether any homosporous *Lepidostrobi* existed, but there is reason to believe that here, as in the closely allied *Lepidocarpon*, microsporangia and megasporangia were in some cases borne on different strobili. In other species (*e.g.* in the cone attributed to the Lower Carboniferous *Lepidodendron Veltheimianum*) the arrangement was that usual in *Selaginella*, the microsporangia occurring above and the megasporangia below in the same strobilus (diagram, fig. 10). The genus *Spencerites* (Lower Coal Measures) differs from *Lepidostrobus* mainly in the insertion of the sporangium, which, instead of being attached along the whole upper surface of the sporophyll, was connected with an outgrowth on its upper surface by a small neck of tissue towards the distal end. The spores of this genus are curiously winged, and intermediate in size between the microspores and megaspores of *Lepidostrobus*; the question of homospory or heterospory is not yet decided. The cones of *Bothrodendron* and another form named *Mesostrobus* are in some respects intermediate between *Lepidostrobus* and *Spencerites*. A more important deviation from ordinary Lepidostroboid structure is shown by the

genus *Lepidocarpon*, from the English Coal Measures and the Lower Carboniferous of Scotland. In this fructification the organization is at first altogether that of a *Lepidostrobus*; in each megasporangium, however, only a single megaspore came to maturity, occupying almost the whole of the sporangial cavity (see fig. 12), but accompanied by the remains of its three abortive sister cells. As integument grew up from the superior surface of the sporophyll, completely enveloping the sporangium, except for a narrow crevice left open along the top. In favourable cases the prothallus is found preserved, within the functional megaspore or embryo-sac, and the whole appearance, especially as seen in a section tangential to the strobilus, is then remarkably seed-like (see diagram, fig. 11). The seed-like body was detached as a whole from the cone, and in this condition was known for many years under the name of *Cardiocarpon anomalum*, having been wrongly identified with a true Gymno-

FIG. 11.—*Lepidocarpon Lomaxii*. Diagrammatic section of "seed" in plane tangential to the parent strobilus.
sph, Sporophyll.
vb, Its vascular bundle.
i, Integument.
m, Micropylar crevice.
e, Base.
zm, Wall of sporangium.
mg, Membrane of functional megaspore, which is filled by the prothallus, *pr*.

spermous seed so named by Carruthers. The analogies with a seed are obvious; the chief difference is in the micropyle, which is not tubular, but forms a long crevice, running in a direction radial to the strobilus. *Lepidocarpon* affords a striking instance of homoplastic modification, for there is no reason to suppose that the Lycopods were on the line of descent of any existing Spermophyta. In a male cone, probably belonging to *Lepidocarpon Lomaxi*, the microsporangia are provided with incomplete integuments.

Another case of a "seed-bearing" Lycopod has lately been discovered by Miss Benson in *Miadesmia membranacea*, a slender Selaginella-like plant from the Lower Coal Measures of Lancashire. The female fructification is in the form of a rather lax strobilus. Each sporophyll bears a megasporangium, attached to its upper surface at the proximal end, containing a single large megaspore (fig. 13). The megasporangium is enclosed in an integument, which completely envelopes it, leaving only a narrow micropyle at the distal end (fig. 13). The long tentacles of the integument may have served to facilitate pollination. The seed-like character of the organ is even more striking in *Miadesmia* than in *Lepidocarpon*. There seems to be no near affinity between these genera, in which the seed-habit must have arisen independently.

Sigillaria.—The great genus *Sigillaria*, even richer in "species" than *Lepidodendron*, ranges throughout the Carboniferous, but has not yet been detected in earlier rocks. The Sigillariae, like the Lepidodendra, were large trees, but must have differed from those of the previous group in habit, for they appear to have branched sparingly or not at all, the lofty upright shaft terminating, like some modern *Xanthorrhoea*, in a great sheaf of long, grass-like leaves. The strobili were stalked, and borne on the main stem, among the leaves. The roots, or at least their functional representatives, resembled those of *Lepidodendron*. The chief distinctive character of *Sigillaria* lies in the arrangement of the leaf-scars, which form conspicuous vertical series on the surface of the stem.

(Scott, *Studies*.)

FIG. 12.—*Lepidocarpon Lomaxii*. Sporangium and sporophyll before development of integument. (× about 12.)
cu, Lateral cushions on sporophyll.
vb, Vascular bundle.
wp, Palisade layer of sporangium-wall.
a, Base of sporangium.
wi, Inner layer of wall.
mg, Membrane of megaspore or embryo-sac.

In one great division of the genus—the Eusigillariae—the stems are ribbed, each rib bearing a vertical row of leaf-scars: the ribbed Sigillariae were formerly divided into two sub-genera—*Rhytidolepis*,

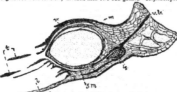

(From a drawing by Mrs D. H. Scott Scott, *Studies*.)

FIG. 13.—*Miadesmia membranacea*. Radial longitudinal section of seed-like organ. (× about 30.)

l, Lamina of sporophyll.
vb, Vascular bundle.
v, Velum or integument.
t, Tentacles.
lg, Ligules.
sm, Sporangium-wall.
m, Membrane of megaspore.

with the scars on each rib rather widely spaced, and *Favularia*, where they are approximated and separated by transverse furrows, each rib thus consisting of a series of contiguous leaf-bases. This distinction, however, has proved to have no constant taxonomic value, for both arrangements may occur on different parts of the same specimen. The species without ribs—Subsigillariae—were in like manner grouped under the two sub-genera *Clathraria* and *Leiodermaria*; in the former each scar is seated on a prominent cushion, while in the latter the surface of the stem (as in *Bothrodendron*) is perfectly smooth. Here also the distinction has proved not to hold good, *S. Brardi*, for example, showing both conditions on the same stem. All these names, however, are still in use as descriptive terms. Generally, the Eusigillariae are characteristic of the older Carboniferous strata, the Subsigillariae of the Upper Coal Measures and Permian. The leaf-scars throughout the genus show essentially the same prints as in *Lepidodendron*, differing only in details, and here also a ligule was present (fig. 14).

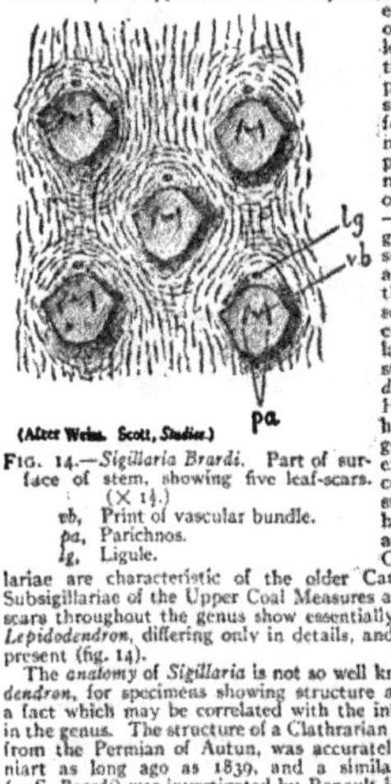

The *anatomy* of *Sigillaria* is not so well known as that of *Lepidodendron*, for specimens showing structure are comparatively rare, a fact which may be correlated with the infrequency of branching in the genus. The structure of a Clathrarian *Sigillaria* (*S. Menardi*), from the Permian of Autun, was accurately described by Brongniart as long ago as 1839, and a similar species, *S. spinulosa* (= *S. Brardi*) was investigated by Renault in 1875, but it was long before we had any trustworthy data for the anatomy of the ribbed forms. This gap in our knowledge has now been filled up, owing to Bertrand's investigation of a specimen referred by him to *S. elongata*, followed by the detailed researches of Kidston and Arber on *Sigillaria elegans*, *scutellata* and *mamillaris*. The structure of the ribbed Sigillariae, as at present known, essentially resembles that of a medullate *Lepidodendron*, though the ring of primary wood is narrower. Its outer margin is crenulated, the leaf-traces being given off from the middle of each bay. Secondary wood was formed in abundance, precisely as in most species of *Lepidodendron*. In the Subsigillarian species *S. Menardi* the primary wood is broken up into distinct bundles, while in *S. spinulosa* their separation is sometimes incomplete. The secondary cortex or periderm attained a great development, and in some cases shows considerable differentiation. On the whole, the anatomy of *Sigillaria* is closely related to that of the preceding group, and in fact a continuous series can be traced from the anatomically simplest species of *Lepidodendron* to the most modified *Sigillariae*. The leaves of *Sigillaria* are in some cases almost identical in structure with those of *Lepidodendron*,

(After Weiss. Scott, *Studies*.)

FIG. 14.—*Sigillaria Brardi*. Part of surface of stem, showing five leaf-scars. (× 1½.)

vb, Print of vascular bundle.
pa, Parichnos.
lg, Ligule.

but in certain species (*S. scutellata* and *S. mamillaris*) there is evidence that they were of the *Sigillariopsis* type, the leaf being traversed by two parallel vascular strands, derived from the bifurcation of the leaf-trace.

The nature of the *fructification* of *Sigillaria* was first satisfactorily determined in 1884 by Zeiller, who found the characteristic Sigillarian leaf-scars on the peduncles of certain large strobili (*Sigillariostrobus*). The cones, of which several species have been described, bear a strong general resemblance to *Lepidostrobus*, differing somewhat in the form of the sporophylls and some other details. The megaspores (reaching 2 mm. or more in diameter) were found lying loose on the sporophylls by Zeiller; the sporangia containing them were first observed by Kidston, in a species from the Coal Measures of Yorkshire. That the cones were heterosporous there can be no doubt, though little is known as yet of the microsporangia. The discovery of *Sigillariostrobus*, which was the fructification of Subsigillariae as well as of the ribbed species, has finally determined the question of the affinities of the genus, once keenly discussed: *Sigillaria* is now clearly proved to have been a genus of heterosporous Lycopods, with the closest affinities to *Lepidodendron*.

Stigmaria.—On present evidence there is no satisfactory distinction to be drawn between the subterranean organs of *Sigillaria* and those of *Lepidodendron* and its immediate allies, though some progress in the identification of special forms of *Stigmaria* has recently been made. These organs, to which the name *Stigmaria* was given by Brongniart, have been found in connexion with the upright stems both of *Sigillaria* and *Lepidodendron*. In the Coal Measures they commonly occur in the underclay beneath the coal-seams. Complete specimens of the stumps show that from the base of the aerial stem four Stigmarian branches were given off, which took a horizontal or obliquely descending course, forking at least twice. These main Stigmarian axes may be 2 to 3 ft. in diameter at the base, and 30 or 40 ft. in length. Their surface is studded with the characteristic scars of their appendages or rootlets, which radiated in all directions into the mud. Petrified specimens of the main *Stigmaria* are frequent, and those of its rootlets extraordinarily abundant. The two parts are very different in structure: in the main axis, as shown in the common Coal Measure form *Stigmaria ficoides*, the centre was occupied by the pith, which was surrounded by a zone of wood, centrifugally developed throughout. In other species, however, the centripetal primary xylem is represented. Phloem, surrounding the wood, is recognizable in good specimens; in the cortex the main feature is the great development of periderm. The rootlets, which branched by dichotomy, contain a slender monarch stele exactly like that in the roots of *Isoëtes* and some *Selaginellae* at the present day; they possessed, however, a complex absorptive apparatus, consisting of lateral strands of xylem, connecting the stele with tracheal plates in the outer cortex. The morphology of *Stigmaria* has been much discussed; the main axes, which do not agree perfectly either with rhizomes or roots, may best be regarded as comparable with the rhizophores of *Selaginellae*; they have also been compared with the embryonic stem, or protocorm, of certain species of *Lycopodium*; the homologies of the appendages with the roots of recent Lycopods appear manifest. It has been maintained by some palaeobotanists that the aerial stems of *Sigillaria* arose as buds on a creeping rhizome, but the evidence for this conclusion is as yet unconvincing.

Lycopodiëae.—Under this name are included the fossil Lycopods of herbaceous habit, which occur occasionally, from the Devonian onwards. One such plant, *Miadesmia*, has already been referred to, as one of the seed-bearing Lycopods. In some Lycopodiëae the leaves were all of one kind, while others were heterophyllous, like most species of *Selaginella*, Zeiller, is now used to include those forms in which the fructification has proved to be heterosporous. In *Selaginellites Suissei* there was a definite strobilus bearing both micro- and megasporangia; in each of the latter from 16 to 24 megaspores were developed; in *Selaginellites primaevus*, however, the number of megaspores was only 4, and the resemblance to a recent *Selaginella* was thus complete. *Selaginellites elongatus*, another heterosporous species, is remarkable for having no differentiated strobilus, a condition not known in the recent genus. The antiquity of the *Selaginella* type indicates that this group had no direct connexion with the Lepidodendreae, but sprang from a distinct and equally ancient herbaceous stock. There is, however, some evidence that *Isoëtes*, which in several respects agrees more nearly with the Lepidodendreae, may actually represent their last degenerate survivors (see *Pleuromeia*, in § 11. MESOZOIC). No homosporous Lycopoditeae have as yet been recognized.

IV. **Filicales.**—Of all Vascular Cryptogams the Ferns have best maintained their position down to the present day. Until recently it has been supposed that the class was well represented in the Palaeozoic period, and, indeed, that it was relatively, and perhaps absolutely far richer in species even than in the recent flora. Within the last few years, however, the position has completely changed, and the majority of the supposed Palaeozoic

Ferns are now commonly regarded as more probably seed-bearing plants, a conclusion for which, in certain cases, there is already convincing evidence. The great majority of specimens of fossil fern-like plants are preserved in the form of carbonaceous impressions of fronds, often of remarkable perfection and beauty. The characters shown by such specimens, however, when, as is usually the case, they are in the barren state, are notoriously unstable, or of small taxonomic value, among recent plants. Hence palaeobotanists have found it necessary to adopt a purely artificial system of classification, based on form and venation of the frond, in the absence of adequate data for a more natural grouping. The well-known form-genera *Pecopteris*, *Sphenopteris*, *Odontopteris*, &c., are of this provisional nature. The majority of these fronds have now fallen under suspicion and can no longer be accepted as those of Ferns; the indications often point to their having belonged to fern-like Spermophyta, as will be shown below.

It has thus become very difficult to decide what Palaeozoic plants should still be referred to the Filices. The fructifications by themselves are not necessarily decisive, for in certain cases the supposed sporangia of Marattiaceous Ferns have turned out to be in reality the microsporangia or pollen-sacs of seed-bearing plants (Pteridosperms). It is, however, probable that a considerable group of true Ferns, allied to Marattiaceae, existed in Palaeozoic times, side by side with simpler forms. In one respect the fronds of many Palaeozoic Ferns and Pteridosperms were peculiar, namely, in the presence on their rachis, and at the base of their pinnae, of anomalous leaflets, often totally different in form and venation from the ordinary pinnules. These curious appendages (*Aphlebiae*), at first regarded as parasitic growths, have been compared with the feathery outgrowths which occur on the rachis in the Cyatheaceous genus *Hemitelia*, and the anomalous pinnules found in certain species of *Gleichenia*, at the points of bifurcation of the frond.

Marattiaceae.—A considerable number of the Palaeozoic fern-like plants show indications—more or less decisive—of Marattiaceous affinities; some account of this group will first be given. The reference of these ferns to the family Marattiaceae, so restricted in the recent flora, rests, of course, primarily on evidence drawn from the fructifications. Typically Marattiaceous sori, consisting of exannulate sporangia united to form synangia, are frequent, and are almost always found on fronds with the character of *Pecopteris*, large, repeatedly pinnate leaves, resembling those of Cyatheaceae or some species of *Nephrodium*. In certain cases the anatomical structure of these leaves is known, and found to agree generally with that of recent coriaceous fern-fronds. The petiole was usually traversed by a single vascular bundle, hippocrepiform in section—a marked point of difference from the more complex petioles of recent Marattiaceae. There is evidence that in many cases these Pecopteroid fronds belonged to arborescent plants, the stems on which they were borne reaching a height of as much as 60 ft. These stems, known as *Megaphytum* when the leaves were in two rows, and as *Caulopteris* in the case of polystichous arrangement, are frequent, especially in the Permian of the Continent; when petrified, so that their internal structure is preserved, the name *Psaronius* is employed. The structure is often a complex one, the central region containing an elaborate system of numerous anastomosing steles, accompanied by sclerenchyma; the cortex is permeated or coated by a multitude of adventitious roots, forming a thick envelope to the stem. The whole structure bears a general resemblance to that of recent Marattiaceae, though differing in detail. We will now describe some of the fructifications, which are grouped under generic names of their own; these genera, as having a more natural basis, tend to supersede the artificial groups founded on vegetative characters. The genus *Asterotheca* includes a number of Ferns, chiefly of Coal Measure age, with fronds of the *Pecopteris* type. The sori, or synangia, ranged in two series on the under-side of the fertile pinnules, are circular, each consisting of 3 to 6 sporangia, attached to a central receptacle and partly united to each other (fig. 15, A); the sporangia separated when mature, dehiscing by a ventral slit. Stur's genus *Hawlea* (fig. 15, H), characterized by the separation of the sporangia, may only represent an advanced stage of an *Asterotheca*. In *Ptychocarpus* the fusion of the sporangia to form the synangium was much more complete; *Scolecopteris* resembles *Asterotheca*, but each synangium is stalked. In all these genera there is an obvious similarity to the synangia of *Kaulfussia*, while in some respects *Marattia* or *Danaea* is approached. In another Pecopteroid genus, *Sturiella*, the synangia resemble those of *Asterotheca*, but each sporangium is provided with a band of enlarged cells of the nature of an annulus (fig. 15, D). As a similar differentiation, though less marked,

appears in the recent genus *Angiopteris*, the presumption is in favour of the Marattiaceous affinities of *Sturiella*, which also shows some relation to the genus *Corynepteris* (see below, Botryopterideae). In the genus *Danaeites*, from the Coal Measures of the Saar, the synangia are much like those of the recent *Danaea*, each sporangium opening by an apical pore. In the *Grand' Eurya* of Stur the sporangia appear to have been free from each other, as in *Angiopteris*. On the whole there is thus good evidence for the frequency of Marattiaceae in the Palaeozoic period, though the possibility that the fructifications may really represent the microsporangia of fern-like spermophytes must always be borne in mind. In a certain number of genera the reference to Marattiaceae is much more doubtful. In *Dactylotheca*, for example (fig. 15, C), a Pecopteroid

(After various authors. *Scott, Studin*)

FIG. 15.—Group of Palaeozoic fructifications of Ferns or Pteridosperms.

A, *Asterotheca*. 1, Pinnule bearing 8 synangia. 2, Synangium in side view. 3, In section, magnified.
B, *Renaultia*. 1, Fertile pinnule, nat. size. 2, Sporangium, enlarged.
D, *Dactylotheca*, as in B.
D, *Sturiella*. Section of pinnule and synangium. *a*, Vascular bundle; *c*, hairs; *b*, *d*, annulus, magnified.
E, *Oligocarpia*. Sorus in surface-view, magnified.
F, *Crossotheca*. Fertile pinnule, bearing several tufts of microsporangia, magnified.
G, *Senftenbergia*. Group of annulate sporangia, magnified.
H, *Hawlea*. Synangium after dehiscence, magnified.
J, *Urnatopteris*. 1, Part of fertile pinna, nat. size. 2, Sporangia, showing apical pores, magnified.

Of the above, A, D, E, G and H, probably belong to true Ferns; F is the male fructification of a Pteridosperm (*Lyginodendron*); the rest are of doubtful nature.

genus, ranging throughout the Carboniferous, the elongated sporangia individually resemble those of Marattiaceae, but they are completely isolated, the characteristic grouping in sori being absent; the same remark applies to the Sphenopteroid *Renaultia* of Zeiller (fig. 15, B); the foliage of *Sphenopteris*, one of the most extensive of Palaeozoic frond-genera, with many different types of fructification, resembled that of various species of *Asplenium* or *Davallia*. In many fern-like plants of this period the fronds were dimorphic, the fertile leaves or pinnae having a form quite different from that of the vegetative portions. This was the case in *Urnatopteris* (Kidston), with Sphenopteroid sterile foliage; the sporangia, borne on the filiform pinnules of the fertile rachis, appear to have dehisced by an apical pore (fig 15, J). The magnificent Devonian Fern *Archaeopteris hibernica*, with a somewhat Adiantiform habit, bore special fertile pinnae; the fructification is still imperfectly understood, but the presence of stipules, observed by Kidston, has been adduced in support of Marattiaceous affinities. In all these cases there is reason to suspect that the plants may have been Pteridosperms, rather than Ferns.

Other Families.—The Marattiaceae are the only recent family of Ferns which can be supposed to have existed in anything like its present form in Palaeozoic times. Of other recent orders the indications are meagre and dubious, and there can be no doubt that a large proportion of Ferns from the older rocks (in so far as they were Ferns at all) belonged to families quite distinct from any which we recognise in the flora of our own day. Little or nothing is known of Palaeozoic Ophioglossaceae. Certain fructifications have been referred to Gleicheniaceae (*Oligocarpia*, fig. 15, E), Schizaeaceae (*Senftenbergia*, fig. 15, G), Hymenophyllaceae and Osmundaceae, and on good grounds, so far as the external characters of the sporangia are concerned; our knowledge of most of the Ferns in question is, however, far too incomplete to justify us in asserting that they actually belonged to the families indicated. In the case of the Osmundaceae there is good evidence, from anatomical characters, for tracing the family back to the Palaeozoic; their oldest members show a distinct relationship to the Botryopterideae, described in the next paragraph. Numerous more or less isolated fern-sporangia occur in the petrified material of the Carboniferous formation; the presence of an annulus is a frequent character among these specimens, while synangic sori are rare; it is thus certain that families remote from the Marattiaceae were abundantly represented during this period.

Botryopterideae.—The family *Botryopterideae*, first discovered by Renault, stands out with striking clearness among the Palaeozoic Ferns, and differs widely from any group now in existence. The *Botryopterideae* are chiefly known from petrified specimens; in the genus *Botryopteris* and certain species of *Zygopteris* we have a fairly complete knowledge of all parts of the plant. The type-genus *Botryopteris*, represented in the Permo-Carboniferous of France and in both the Lower and Upper Carboniferous of Great Britain, had a rhizome, with a very simple monostelic structure, bearing spirally arranged compound leaves, with lobed pinnules, probably of a somewhat fleshy texture. In the

(After Renault.)
FIG. 16.—*Zygopteris pinnata*.
A, Group of sporangia, in surface view.
B, Single sporangium, in transverse section, showing the annulus on both sides, magnified.

recent species, *B. forensis*, the plant was covered with characteristic jointed hairs, which have served to identify the various organs on which they occur. The sporangia were large pyriform sacs, shortly stalked, and borne in tufts on the branches of the fertile rachis, which developed no lamina. Each sporangium had, on one side only, a longitudinal or slightly oblique annulus, several cells in width; the numerous spores were all of the same size; certain differences among them, which have been interpreted as indicating heterospory, have now proved to depend merely on the state of preservation. The genus *Zygopteris*, of which numerous Carboniferous and Permian species are known, likewise had a monostelic stem, but the structure of its vascular cylinder was somewhat complex, resembling that of the most highly differentiated Hymenophyllaceae, with which some species of *Zygopteris* also agreed in the presence of axillary shoots. There is evidence that the stem in some species was a climbing one; the pinnate leaves, arranged on the stem in a two-fifths spiral, were dimorphic, the sterile fronds resembling some forms of

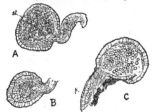

(From a drawing by Mrs D. H. Scott. *Scott, Studies.*)
FIG. 17.—*Stauropteris oldhamia*. Three sporangia borne on branchlets of the rachis. In A the atomium (*st*) or place of dehiscence is shown. B is cut tangentially. In C, *p* is the palisade tissue of the rachis. (× about 35.)

Sphenopteris. The petioles have a somewhat complex structure, the bundle often having, in transverse section, the form of an H; it has been proposed to subdivide the genus on the details of

the petiolar structure. It is characteristic of *Zygopteris* and its near allies that two rows of pinnae were borne on each side of the rachis, at least in the fertile fronds. On the fertile rachis the sporangia were borne in tufts, much as in the preceding genus; they were still larger, reaching 2·5 mm. in length, and had a multiseriate annulus, extending, however, to both sides of the sporangium (see fig. 16, A and B). In *Stauropteris*, a genus showing some affinity with *Zygopteris*, the branched rachis of the fertile frond terminates in fine branchlets, each bearing a single, spherical sporangium, without any differentiated annulus (fig. 17). The spores in the sporangia have been found in a germinating condition; the stages of germination correspond closely with those observed in recent homosporous ferns (fig. 18). This fact strongly confirms the conclusion, drawn from morphological and anatomical characters, that the Botryopterideae were true Ferns. The genus *Corynepteris* of Baily is interesting from the fact that its sporangia, while individually similar to those of *Zygopteris*, were grouped in sori or synangia, resembling those of an *Asterotheca*. The family Botryopterideae appears to have included a number of other genera, though in most cases the evidence from vegetative structure is alone available. The genus *Diplolabis* of Renault, shows much in common with *Zygopteris* as regards anatomical structure, but resembles *Corynepteris* in possessing a synangic fructification. The genus *Asterochlaena* of Corda with a deeply-lobed stele, goes back to the Devonian. The family as a whole is of great interest, as presenting points of contact with various recent orders, especially Hymenophyllaceae, Osmundaceae and Ophioglossaceae; the group appears to have been a synthetic one, belonging to a primitive stock (the Primofilices of Arber) from which the later Fern families may have sprung.

A number of genera of Palaeozoic "fern-fronds" have been described, of the fructification of which nothing is known. This is the case, for example, with *Diplotmema*, a genus only differing from *Sphenopteris* in the dichotomy of the primary pinnae, and with *Mariopteris*, which bears a similar relation to *Pecopteris*. The same holds good of the Pecopteroid Ferns included under *Callipteris* and *Callipteridium*. In such cases, as will be explained below, there is a strong presumption that the fronds were not those of Ferns, but of seed-bearing plants of the new class Pteridospermeae.

On the present evidence it appears that the class Filicales was well represented in the Palaeozoic flora, though by no means so dominant as was formerly supposed. The simpler Ferns (Primofilices) of the period are for the most part referred to the remarkable family Botryopterideae, a group very distinct from

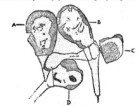

(From a drawing by Mr L. A. Boodle. *Scott, Studies.*)
FIG. 18.—*Stauropteris oldhamia*. Four germinating spores from the interior of a sporangium. All four are putting out rhizoids. In C, lying horizontally, an additional cell has been cut off between rhizoid and spore. (× 335.)

any of the more modern families, though showing analogies with them in various directions. On the other hand there was the far more complex Marattiaceous type, strikingly similar in both vegetative and reproductive characters to the recent members of the family. Although doubts have lately been cast on the authenticity of Palaeozoic Marattiaceae owing to the difficulty in distinguishing between their fructifications and the pollen-bearing organs of Pteridosperms, the anatomical evidence (stem of *Psaronius*) strongly confirms the opinion that a considerable group of these Ferns existed.

Spermophyta.—The Pteridospermeae, for which Potonié's name *Cycadofilices* is still sometimes used, include all the fern-like plants which, on the evidence available, appear to have been reproduced by means of seeds. The cases in which such evidence is decisive are but few, namely, *Lyginodendron oldhamium*, *Neuropteris heterophylla*, *Pecopteris Pluckenecii*, *Aneimites fertilis* and *Aneimites tenuifolius*. In the first-named plant the structure, both of the vegetative and reproductive organs, is known, and the evidence, from comparison and association, is sufficiently strong. In the other cases there is direct proof of continuity between seed and plant, but only the external characters are known. In a great number of forms, amounting to a majority of the Palaeozoic plants of fern-like habit, the indirect evidence is in favour of their having possessed seeds. We will begin with the Lyginodendreae, a group in which the anatomical characters indicated a systematic position between Ferns and Cycads, long before the reproductive organs were discovered.

Lyginodendreae.—Of the genus *Heterangium*, which still stands very near the true Ferns, several species are known, the oldest

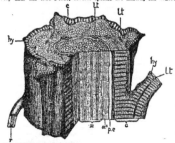

(After Williamson. Scott, *Studies*.)
FIG. 19.—*Heterangium Grievii.* Restoration of Stem, shown partly in transverse and longitudinal section, partly in surface view.

x, Primary wood.
x², Secondary wood.
p.c, Phloem and pericycle.
c, Cortex.
hy, Hypoderma.
lt, lt, Leaf-traces.
r, Adventitious root. Several leaf-bases are shown.

being *H. Grievii*, of Williamson, from the Lower Carboniferous of Scotland. This plant had a long, somewhat slender, ridged stem, the ridges corresponding to the decurrent bases of the spirally arranged leaves (fig. 19). The specimens on which the genus was founded are petrified, showing structure rather than habit, but conclusive evidence has now been obtained that the foliage of *H. Grievii* was of the type of *Sphenopteris* (*Diplotmema*) *elegans* (fig. 20), and was thus in appearance altogether that of a Fern, with somewhat the habit of an *Asplenium*. The stem has a single stele, resembling in general primary structure that of one of the simpler species of *Gleichenia*; there is no pith, the wood extending to the centre of the stele. The leaf-traces, where they traverse the cortex, have the structure of the foliar bundles in Cycads, for they are of the collateral type, and their xylem is mesarch, the spiral elements lying in the interior of the ligneous strand. The leaf-traces can be distinguished as distinct strands at the periphery of the stele, as shown in fig. 21. Most of the specimens had formed a zone of secondary wood and phloem resembling the corresponding tissues in a recent Cycad; the similarity extended to minute histological details, as is shown especially in *H. tiliaeoides*, a Coal Measures species, where the preservation is remarkably perfect. The cortex was strongly constructed mechanically; in addition to the strands of fibres at the periphery, horizontal plates of stone-cells were present in the inner cortex, giving both stem and petiole a transversely striated appearance, which has served to identify the different parts of the plant, even in the carbonized condition (cf. figs. 19 and 20). The single vascular bundle which traversed the petiole and its branches was concentric, the leaves resembling those of Ferns in structure as well as in habit. *Heterangium* shows, on the whole, a decided preponderance of Filicinean vegetative characters, though in the leaf-traces and the secondary tissues the Cycads are approached. The organs of reproduction are not yet known, though there is a probability that an associated seed allied to *Lagenostoma* (see below) belonged to *Heterangium*. In the Coal Measure genus *Megaloxylon*, of Seward, which in

structure bears a general resemblance to *Heterangium*, the primary wood consists for the most part of short wide tracheides; probably,

(After Stur. Scott, *Studies*.)
FIG. 20.—*Sphenopteris elegans* (foliage of *Heterangium Grievii*). Part of frond. (¾ nat. size.)

as the secondary tissues increased, it had become superfluous for conducting purposes, and was adapted rather for water-storage. In the genus *Lyginodendron*, of which *L. oldhamium*, from the

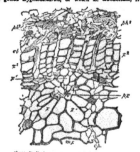

(Scott, *Studies*.)
FIG. 21.—*Heterangium Grievii.* Part of the stele of the stem in transverse section, showing a primary xylem-strand and adjacent tissues. (× 135.)

px, Protoxylem of strand.
x, Centripetal.
x¹, Centrifugal primary wood.
mx, Part of the internal wood.
c.p, Conjunctive tissue.
x², Secondary wood.
cb, Cambium.
ph², Phloem.

Coal Measures, is now the best-known of all Palaeozoic plants, the central wood has disappeared altogether and is replaced by pith; the primary wood is only represented in the leaf-trace strands, which form a ring of distinct collateral bundles around the pith:

(From a model after Oliver.)

FIG. 23.—*Lagenostoma Lomaxii* (the seed of *Lyginodendron*), Restoration of a seed, enclosed in the lobed cupule, which bears numerous glands. (× about 15.)

thus the "medullate-monostelic" structure characteristic of the higher plants was already attained. The individual bundles, however, have the same structure as in *Heterangium*, and agree

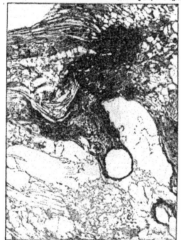

(From a photograph. Scott, *Studies.*)

FIG. 24.—Capitate gland on the cupule of *Lagenostoma Lomaxii.* (× 70.)

closely with the foliar bundles of Cycads. The secondary tissues, which are highly developed, are also of a Cycadean character (fig. 22, Plate). The vegetative organs of the plant are very completely known; the foliage has proved to be that of a *Sphenopteris*, identical with the species long known under the name of *S. Höninghausi*. Apart from the important advance shown in the anatomy of the stem, *Lyginodendron* agrees structurally with *Heterangium*. There is reason to believe that *Lyginodendron oldhamium* was a climbing plant comparable in some respects to such recent Ferns as *Davallia aculeata*. The roots were at first like those of Marattiaceae but grew in thickness like the roots of Gymnosperms.

The first definite evidence of the mode of reproduction of *Lyginodendron oldhamium* was due to F. W. Oliver, who in 1903 identified the seed, *Lagenostoma Lomaxii*, by means of the glands on its cupule, which agree exactly with those on the associated leaves and stems of the plant (cf. figs. 24 and 25). No similar glands are known on any other Palaeozoic plant. *Lagenostoma Lomaxii* is a small barrel-shaped seed (5·8 by 4·25 mm. when mature) enclosed in a husk or cupule, which completely enveloped it when young, but was ultimately open (figs. 23 and 26 and fig. 27 from another species). The seed was stalked, and there is an exact agreement in structure between the vascular strands of the stalk and cupule of the seed, and those of the rachis and leaflets of *Lyginodendron*, thus confirming the evidence from the glands. The seed itself is of a Cycadean type, and radially symmetrical. The single integument is united to the nucellus, except at the top, and is traversed by about nine vascular strands. In the apex of the nucellus, as in most Palaeozoic seeds and in recent Cycads, a pollen-chamber, for the reception of the pollen-grains or microspores, is excavated (fig. 26). In *Lagenostoma* the pollen-chamber has a peculiar

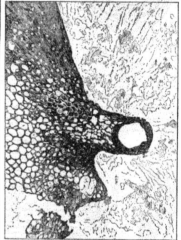

(From a photograph. Scott, *Studies.*)

FIG. 25.—Capitate Gland on the Petiole of *Lyginodendron oldhamium.* (× 70.)

structure, a solid column of tissue rising up in the middle, leaving only a narrow annular crevice, in which pollen-grains are found. The neck of the flask-shaped pollen-chamber projected a little from the micropyle and no doubt received the pollen directly. The seed, which need not be described in further detail, was a highly organized structure, showing little trace of the cryptogamic megasporangium from which we must suppose it to have been derived. From the structure of the seed-bearing stalk, and from the analogy of the similar form *Lagenostoma Sinclairi* (fig. 27) it appears that the seed was borne on a leaf, or part of a leaf, reduced to a branched rachis.

The male organs of *Lyginodendron* were discovered by Kidston, a year or two after the seeds were identified. They are of the type known as *Crossotheca*, formerly regarded as a Marattiaceous fructification. The genus is characterized by the arrangement of the sporangia, which hang down from the lower surface of the little oval fertile leaflets, the whole resembling an epaulet with its fringe (fig. 15, F; fig. 28). In the case of *Lyginodendron* the *Crossotheca* occurs in connexion with the vegetative parts of the frond. Each fertile pinnule bore six, or rarely seven fusiform microsporangia, described as bilocular; not improbably each may represent a synangium. The microspores are tetrahedral. This is the first case in which the pollen-bearing organs of a Pteridosperm have been identified with certainty.

It will be seen that, while the seeds of *Lyginodendron* were of an advanced Cycadean type, the microsporangiate organs were more like those of a Fern, the reproductive organs thus showing the same combination of characters which appears in the vegetative

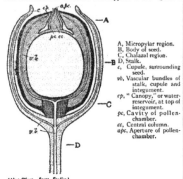

A, Micropylar region.
B, Body of seed.
C, Chalazal region.
D, Stalk.
c, Cupule, surrounding seed.
vb, Vascular bundles of stalk, cupule and integument.
cp, "Canopy," or water-reservoir, at top of integument.
pc, Cavity of pollen-chamber.
cc, Central column.
apc, Aperture of pollen-chamber.

(After Oliver. Scott, Studies.)
FIG. 26.—*Lagenostoma Lomaxii.* Diagram of seed in median longitudinal section.

to Lygino-

primary wood, together with an extensive development of anomalous wood and bast around the pith, a peculiarity which appears as an individual variation in some specimens of *Lyginodendron oldhamium.* It is probable that these stems belonged to plants with the fructification and foliage of Cycads, taking that group in the widest sense. It is only quite at the close of the Palaeozoic period that Cycads begin to appear. The Lygino-dendreae type of structure, however, appears to have formed the transition not only to the Cycadales, but also to the extinct family Cordaiteae, the characteristic Palaeozoic Gymnosperms (see p. 107).

Medulloseae.—In some respects the most remarkable family of the Cycad-fern alliance is that of the Medulloseae, seed-bearing plants often of great size, with a fern-like foliage, and a singularly complex anatomical structure without parallel among recent plants. Some of the Medulloseae must have had a habit not unlike that of tree-ferns, with compound leaves of enormous dimensions, belonging to various frond-genera—especially, as has now been proved, to *Alethopteris* and *Neuropteris*; these are among the most abundant of the Carboniferous fronds commonly attributed to Ferns, and extend back to the Devonian. In habit some species of *Alethopteris* resembled the recent *Angiopteris*, while the *Neuropteris* foliage may be compared with that of an *Osmunda.* The *Medullosa* stems have been found chiefly in the Permo-Carboniferous of France and Germany, but a Coal Measures species (*M. anglica*) has been discovered in Lancashire. The great anatomical characteristic of the stem of the Medulloseae is its polystelic structure with secondary development of wood and bast around each stele. In *M. anglica*, the simplest species known, the steles are uniform,

(After Arber.

(× 5.)

and usually only three in number; the structure of the stem is essentially that of a polystelic *Heterangium.* In the Permo-Carboniferous species, such as *M. stellata* and *M. Leuckarti*, the arrangement is more complicated, the steles showing a differentiation into a central and a peripheral system; the secondary growth was extensive and unequal, usually attaining its maximum on the outer side of the peripheral steles. In certain cases the structure was further complicated by the appearance of extrafascicular zones exterior to the whole stelar system. The spirally arranged petioles (*Myeloxylon*) were of great size, and their decurrent bases clothed the surface of the stem; their structure is closely similar to that of recent Cycadean petioles; in fact, the leaves generally, like those of *Stangeria* at the present day, while fern-like in habit, were Cycadean in structure. In the case of *Medullosa anglica* we have an a most complete knowledge of the vegetative organs—stem, leaf and root; Cycadean characters no doubt predominate, but the primary organization of the stem was that of a polystelic Fern. In the new genus *Sutcliffia*, also from the Coal Measures of Lancashire, the stem had a single, large central stele, from which smaller strands were given off, forming a kind of network, which gave rise to the numerous concentric leaf-traces which entered the

(From a sketch after Kidston. Scott, Studies.)
FIG. 28.—*Crossotheca Höninghaus*, the male fructification of *Lyginodendron.* Fertile leaflets bearing sporangia, and sterile leaflets on the rachis of the same leaf. (× 2.)

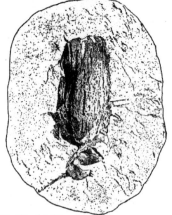

(After Kidston. Scott, Studies.)
FIG. 29.—*Neuropteris heterophylla.* Seed, attached to a branch of the rachis bearing two vegetative leaflets. (× 2.)

petioles. This plant may be regarded as anatomically the most primitive of the Medulloseae.

In one member of the Medulloseae, there is direct evidence of reproduction by seeds, for in *Neuropteris heterophylla* Kidston has demonstrated that large seeds, of the size of a hazel-nut, were borne on the frond (fig. 29). In this case the internal structure is not known, but another seed, *Trigonocarpus Parkinsoni*, associated with, and probably belonging to, the Alethopterid species, *Medullosa anglica*, occurs in the petrified condition and has been fully investigated. This is a large seed, with a very long micropyle; it has a beaked pollen-chamber, and a complex integument made up of hard and fleshy layers, closely resembling the seed of a modern Cycad; the nucellus, however, was free from the integument, each having its own vascular system. Various other seeds of the same type are known, and in a great number of instances Grand' Eury has found the fronds of Neuropterideae (Medulloseae) in close association with definite species of seeds, so there can be little doubt that the whole family was seed-bearing. Very little is known at present of the male organs. Some authors have been so much impressed by the similarity of this extinct family to the Cycads, that they have regarded them as being on the direct line of descent of the latter group; it is more probable, however, that they formed a short divergent phylum, distinct, though not remote, from the Cycadean stock.

Pecopterideae.—It has now been established that the form-genus *Pecopteris*, once regarded as representing the typical Marattiaceous foliage, was in part made up of seed-bearing plants. In 1905 Grand' Eury discovered the seeds of *Pecopteris Pluckeneti*, an Upper Coal Measure species, attached, in immense numbers, to the fronds, which are but little modified as compared with the ordinary vegetative foliage. The seeds are flat and winged, closely resembling those of some Cordaiteae (see below). Another form of fructification, compared with the sori of *Dicksonia*, appears to represent the male organs. There is reason to believe that other species of *Pecopteris* and similar genera, (*Callipteris* and *Mariopteris*) bore seeds, though the artificial group Pecopterideae probably also includes the fronds of true Marattiaceous Ferns.

Aneimiteae.—The genus *Aneimites*, resembling the Maidenhair Ferns in habit, has now been transferred to the Pteridosperms, the seeds having been discovered in 1904 by David White. In *A. fertilis*, from the Pottsville beds (Millstone Grit) of West Virginia, the rhomboidal seeds, flattened and winged like those of Cordaiteae, are borne terminally on the lateral pinnae of a frond, which elsewhere bears the characteristic cuneiform leaflets. Continuity between seeds and frond was also demonstrated in another species, *A. tenuifolius*. The allied genus *Eremopteris* occurs in association with seeds of a similar platyspermic type.

The Pteridosperms, of which only a few examples have been considered, evidently constituted a group of vast extent in Palaeozoic times. In a large majority of the Fern-like fossils of that period the evidence is in favour of reproduction by seeds, rather than by the cryptogamic methods of the true Ferns. The class, though clearly allied to the typical Gymnosperms, may be kept distinct for the present on account of the relatively primitive characters shown in the anatomy and morphology, and may be provisionally defined as follows: plants resembling Ferns in habit and in many anatomical characters, but bearing seeds of a Cycadean type; seeds and microsporangia borne on fronds only slightly modified as compared with the vegetative leaves.

Gymnospermous remains are common in Palaeozoic strata from the Devonian onwards. The investigations of the last quarter of the 19th century established that these early representatives of the class did not, as a rule, belong to any of its existing families, but formed for the most part a distinct group, that of the Cordaitales, which has long since died out. Specimens of true Cycads or Conifers are rare or doubtful until we come to the latest Palaeozoic rocks. Our knowledge of the Cordaiteae (the typical family of the class Cordaitales) is chiefly due to the French investigators, Grand' Eury and Renault, who successfully brought into connexion the various fragmentary remains, and made known their exact structure.

Cordaitales.—The discovery of the fossil trunks and of their rooted bases has shown that the Cordaiteae were large trees, reaching 30 metres or more in height; the lofty shaft bore a dense crown of branches, clothed with long simple leaves, spirally arranged. Fig. 30, founded on one of Grand' Eury's restorations, gives an idea of the habit of a tree of the genus *Cordaites*, characterized by its lanceolate acute leaves; in the typical *Cordaites* they were of a blunter shape, while in *Poacordaites* they were narrow and grasslike. The leaves as a rule far exceeded in size those of any of the Coniferae, attaining in some species a length of a metre. Of living genera, *Agathis* (to which the Kauri Pine of New Zealand belongs) probably comes nearest to the extinct family in habit, though at a long interval. The stem resembled that of Cycads in having a large pith, sometimes as much as 4 in. in diameter; the wood, however, was dense, and had the structure of that of an Araucarian Conifer; specimens of the wood have accordingly been commonly referred to the genus *Araucarioxylon*, and at one time the idea prevailed that the wood of this type indicated actual affinity with Araucarieae. Other characters, however, prove that the Cordaiteae were remote from that family, and the name *Araucarioxylon* is best limited to wood from later horizons, where a near relationship to Araucarieae is more probable.[1] In some cases the external

[1] Endlicher's name *Dadoxylon* is conveniently used for Palaeozoic specimens of the kind in question when nothing beyond the wood-structure is known.

tissues of the Cordaitean stem are well preserved; the cortex possessed a system of hypodermal strands of fibres, comparable to those found in the Lyginodendreae. In most cases the leaf-traces passed out from the stem in pairs, as in the recent *Ginkgo*; dividing up further as they entered the leaf-base. In many Cordaiteae the pith was *discoid*, i.e. fistular and partitioned by frequent diaphragms, as in some species of *Pinus* and other plants at the present day. The curious, transversely-ribbed fossils known as *Sternbergia* or *Artisia* have proved to be casts of the medullary cavity of Cordaiteae; their true nature was first demonstrated by Williamson in 1850. In those stems which have been referred with certainty to the Cordaiteae there is no centripetal wood; the spiral elements are adjacent to the pith, as in a recent Conifer or Cycad; certain stems, however, are known which connect this type of structure with that of the Lyginodendreae; this, for example, is the case in the Permian genus *Poroxylon*, investigated by Bertrand and Renault, which in general structure has much in common with Cordaiteae, but possesses strands of primary wood, mainly centripetal, at the

(After Grand' Eury, modified. Scott, *Studies.*)

FIG. 30.—*Dorycordaites*. Restoration, showing roots, trunk and branches bearing long lanceolate leaves and fructifications. The trunk is shown too short.

boundary of the pith, as in the case in *Lyginodendron*. Stems (*Mesoxylon*) intermediate in structure between *Poroxylon* and *Cordaites* have lately been discovered in the English Coal Measures. Corresponding strands of primary xylem have been observed in stems of the genus *Pitys* (Witham), of Lower Carboniferous age, which consisted of large trees, probably closely allied to *Cordaites*. There appears, in fact, so far as stem-structure is concerned, to have been no sharp break between the typical Palaeozoic Gymnosperms and pronounced Pteridosperms such as *Lyginodendron*.

The long, parallel-veined leaves of the Cordaiteae, which were commonly referred to Monocotyledons before their structure or connexion with other parts of the plant was known, have been shown by Renault to have essentially the same anatomy as a single leaflet of a Cycad such as *Zamia*. The vascular bundles, in particular, show precisely the characteristic collateral mesarch or exarch structure which is so constant in the recent family (see ANATOMY OF PLANTS). In fact, if the foliage alone were taken into account, the Cordaiteae might be described as simple-leaved Cycads. The reproductive organs, however, show that the two groups were in reality very distinct. Both male and female inflorescences have frequently been found in connexion with leaf-bearing branches (see restoration, fig. 30). The inflorescence is usually a spike bearing lateral cones or catkins, arranged sometimes distichously, sometimes in a spiral order. The investigation of silicified specimens has, in the hands of Renault, yielded striking results. A longitudinal section of a male *Cordaianthus* (the name applied to isolated fructifications) is shown in fig. 31, A, Plate. The organ figured is one of the catkins (about a centimetre in length) which were borne laterally on the spike. Some of the stamens are inserted between the bracts, in an apparently axillary position, while others are grouped about the apex of the axis. Each stamen consists of a long filament, bearing several erect, cylindrical pollen-sacs at its summit (cf. fig. 31, B, Plate). Some of the pollen-sacs had dehisced, while others still retained their pollen. The stamens are probably best compared with those of *Ginkgo*, but they have also been interpreted as corresponding to the male "flowers" of the Gnetaceae. In any case the morphology of the male Cordaitean fructification is clearly very remote from that of any of the Cycads or

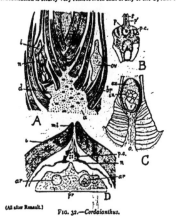

(All after Renault.)

FIG. 32.—*Cordaianthus.*

A, *C. Williamsoni.* Part of longitudinal section of ♀ catkin; *a*, axis, showing *v*, bundles in tangential section; *br*, bracts; *d*, short axillary shoot, bearing a bracteole and a terminal ovule; *i*, integument; *n*, nucellus of ovule; *ov*, another ovule seen from the outside. (× about 10.)

B, *C. Grand' Eury.* Nucellus of an ovule; *p.c*, pollen-chamber; *s*, canal leading to *p.c*; *p*, pollen-grains in *p.c*; *p'*, do. in canal. (× about 30.)

C, *C. Grand' Eury.* Lower part of canal, enlarged; *o*, cavity of canal, surrounded by a sheath of cells, dilated towards the bottom of canal, in which a large pollen-grain is caught; *ex*, exterior of pollen-grain; *in*, internal group of prothallial or antheridial cells. (× 150.)

D, *Cycadinocarpus augustodunensis.* Upper part of seed, in longitudinal section; *i*, integument; *mi*, micropyle; *n*, remains of nucellus; *p.c*, pollen-chamber (containing pollen-grains), with its canal extending up to the micropyle; *pr*, part of prothallus; *ar*, archegonia. All figures magnified.

true Coniferae, though some resemblance to the stamens of Araucarieae may be traced. The female inflorescences vary considerably in organization: in some species the axis of the spike bears solitary ovules, each accompanied by a few bracts, while in others the lateral appendages are catkins, each containing from two to several ovules. In the catkin shown in longitudinal section in fig. 32, A, it appears that each ovule was borne terminally, on an extremely short axillary shoot, as in *Taxus* among recent Gymnosperms. The ovule consists of an integument (regarded by some writers as double) enclosing the nucellus. In the upper part of the nucellus is a cavity or pollen-chamber, with a narrow canal leading into it, precisely as in the ovules of *Stangeria* or other Cycads at the present day (fig. 32, B). Within the pollen-chamber, and in the canal, pollen-grains are found, agreeing with those in the anthers, but usually of larger size (fig. 32, C). It was in this case that Renault first

made the exceedingly interesting discovery that each pollen-grain contains a group of cells, presumably representing an antheridium (fig. 32, C). Recent observations have completely confirmed Renault's interpretation of the facts, on which some doubt had been cast. In the isolated seeds of Cordaitales and Pteridosperms, pollen-grains are often found within the pollen-chamber, and the pluricellular structure of these pollen-grains has been repeatedly demonstrated. In the light of our present knowledge of *Ginkgo* and the Cycads, there can scarcely be a doubt that spermatozoids were formed in the cells of the antheridium of the Cordaitean pollen-grain and that of other Palaeozoic Spermophyta, the antheridium is much more developed than in any recent Gymnosperm, and it may be doubted whether any pollen-tube was formed. The morphology of the female inflorescence of Cordaiteae has not yet been cleared up, but *Taxus* and *Ginkgo* among recent plants appear to offer the nearest analogies. Much further investigation will be needed before the homologies between Cordaitean cones and the fructifications of the higher Cryptogams can be established. Anatomically the connexion of the family with the Pteridosperms (and through them, presumably, with some primitive group of Ferns) seems clear, but we have as yet no indications of the stages in the evolution of their reproductive organs. The class Cordaitales extends back to the Devonian, and it must be borne in mind that our knowledge of their fructifications is practically limited to representatives from the latest Palaeozoic horizons.

Isolated fossil seeds are common in the Carboniferous and Permian strata; in all cases they are of the orthotropous type, and resemble the seeds of Cycads or Ginkgo more nearly than those of any other living plants. Their internal structure is sometimes admirably preserved, so that the endosperm with its archegonia is clearly shown (fig. 32, D). It is a curious fact that in no case has an embryo been found in any of these seeds; probably fertilization took place after they were shed, and was followed immediately by germination. There is good evidence that many of the seeds belonged to Cordaitales, especially those seeds which had a flattened form, such as *Cardiocarpus*, *Cycadinocarpus*, *Samaropsis*, &c. Seeds of this kind have been found in connexion with the *Cordaianthus* inflorescences; the winged seeds of *Samaropsis*, borne on long pedicels, are attributed by Grand' Eury to the genus *Dorycordaites*. Many other forms of seed, and especially those which show radial symmetry, as for example *Trigonocarpus*, *Stephanospermum* and *Lagenostoma* belonged, as we have seen, to some of the plants grouped under Pteridospermeae, though other Pteridosperms had flattened seeds not as yet distinguishable from those of Cordaitales. The abundance and variety of Palaeozoic seeds, still so often of undetermined nature, indicate the vast extent of the spermophytic flora of that period.

The modern Gymnospermous orders have but few authentic representatives in Palaeozoic rocks. The history of the Ginkgoales will be found in the Mesozoic section of this article (see also GYMNOSPERMS); their nearest Palaeozoic representatives "were probably members of the Cordaitales, an extinct stock with which the Ginkgoaceae are closely connected" (Seward). Remains referable to Cycadophyta, so extraordinarily abundant in the succeeding period, are scanty. The curious genus *Dolerophyllum* (Saporta) may be mentioned in this connexion. This genus, from the Permo-Carboniferous of Autun, is represented by large, fleshy, reniform leaves or leaflets, with radiating dichotomous venation; the vascular bundles have in all respects the structure of those in the leaves of Cycads or Cordaiteae. The male sporophylls are similar in form to the vegetative leaves, but smaller; sunk in their parenchyma are numerous ovular loculi, containing large pollen-grains, which are pluricellular like those of *Cordaites*; the female fructification had not yet been identified with certainty. The curious male sporophylls may perhaps be remotely comparable to those recently discovered in Mesozoic Cycadophyta, of the group Bennettiteae. Some leaves of Cycadean habit (*e.g. Pterophyllum*, *Sphenozamites*) occur in the Coal Measures and Permian, and it is possible that the obscure Coal Measure genus *Norggerathia* may have Cycadean affinities. A fructification from the Permian of Autun, named *Cycadospadix milleryensis* by Renault, appears to belong to this family.

Now that the numerous specimens of wood formerly referred to Coniferae are known to have belonged to distinct orders, but few true Palaeozoic Conifers remain to be considered. The most important are the upper Coal Measure or Permian genera *Walchia*, *Ullmannia* and *Pagiophyllum*, all of which resembled certain Araucarieae in habit. In the case of *Walchia* there is some evidence as to the fructifications, which in one species (*W. filiciformis*) appear to be comparable to female Araucarian cones. There are also some anatomical points of agreement with this family. It is probable, however, that under the same generic name very heterogeneous plants have been confounded. In the case of *Ullmannia* the anatomical structure of the leaf, investigated by Solms-Laubach, proves at any rate that the tree was Coniferous.

There is no proof of the existence of Gnetaceae in Palaeozoic times. The very remarkable plumose seeds described by Renault under the name *Gnetopsis* are of uncertain affinity, but have much in common with *Lagenostoma*, the seed of *Lyginodendron*.

Succession of Floras.

Our knowledge of vegetation older than the Carboniferous is still far too scanty for any satisfactory history of the Palaeozoic Floras to be even attempted; a few, however, of the facts may be advantageously recapitulated in chronological order.

No recognizable plant-remains, if we accept one or two doubtful Algal specimens, have so far been yielded by the Cambrian. From the Ordovician and Silurian, however, a certain number of authentic remains of Algae (among many more that are questionable) have been investigated; they are for the most part either verticillate Siphonae, or the large—possibly Laminariaceous—Algae named *Nematophycus*, with the problematical but perhaps allied *Pachytheca*. The evidence for terrestrial Silurian vegetation is still dubious; apart from some obscure North American specimens, the true nature of which is not established. Potonié has described well-characterized Pteridophytes (such as the fern-like *Sphenopteridium* and *Bothrodendron* among Lycopods) from supposed Silurian strata in North Germany; the horizon, however, appears to be open to much doubt, and the specimens agree so nearly with some from the Lower Carboniferous as to render their Silurian age difficult of credence. The high development of the terrestrial flora in Devonian times renders it probable that land-plants existed far back in the Silurian ages, or still earlier. Even in the Lower Devonian, Ferns and Lepidodendreae have been recognized; the Middle and Upper Devonian beds contain a flora in which all the chief groups of Carboniferous plants are already represented. Considering the comparative meagreness of the Devonian record, we can scarcely doubt that the vegetation of that period, if adequately known, would prove to have been practically as rich as that of the succeeding age. Among Devonian plants, Equisetales, including not only *Archaeocalamites*, but forms referred to *Asterophyllites* and *Annularia*, occur; *Sphenophyllum* is known from Devonian strata in North America and Bear Island, and *Pseudobornia* from the latter; Lycopods are represented by *Bothrodendron* and *Lepidodendron*; a typical *Lepidostrobus*, with structure preserved, has lately been found in the Upper Devonian of Kentucky. Fern-like plants such as Sphenopterideae, *Archaeopteris* and *Aneimites*, with occasional arborescent Pecopterideae, are frequent; many of the genera, including *Alethopteris*, *Neuropteris* and *Megalopteris*, probably belonged, not to true Ferns, but to Pteridosperms; although our knowledge of internal structure is still comparatively scanty, there is evidence to prove that such plants were already present, as for example, the genus *Calamopitys*. The presence of Cordaitean leaves indicates that Gymnosperms of high organization already existed, a striking fact, showing the immense antiquity of this class compared with the angiospermous flowering plants.

Any detailed account of the horizons of Carboniferous plants would carry us much too far. For our present purpose we may divide the formation into Lower Carboniferous and Lower and Upper Coal Measures. In the Lower Carboniferous (Culm of Continental authors) many Devonian types survive—*e.g. Archaeocalamites*, *Bothrodendron*, *Archaeopteris*, *Megalopteris*, &c. Among fern-like fronds *Diplotmema* and *Rhacopteris* are characteristic. Some of the Lepidodendreae appear to approach *Sigillariae* in external characters. Sphenophylleae are still rare; it is to this horizon that the isolated type *Cheirostrobus* belongs. Many specimens with structure preserved are known from the Lower Carboniferous, and among them Pteridosperms (*Heterangium*, *Calamopitys*, *Cladoxylon*, *Protopitys*) are well represented, if we may judge by the anatomical characters. Of Gymnosperms we have Cordaitean leaves, and the stems known as *Pitys*, which probably belonged to the same family.

The Lower Coal Measures (Westphalian) have an enormously rich flora, embracing most of the types referred to in our systematic description. Calamarieae with the *Arthropitys* type of stem-structure abound, and Sphenophylleae are now well represented. *Bothrodendron* still survives, but *Lepidodendron*, *Lepidophloios*, and the ribbed Sigillariae are the characteristic Lycopods. The heterogeneous "Ferns" grouped under Spheno-

pterideae are especially abundant. Ferns of the genera referred to Marattiaceae are common, but arborescent stems of the *Psaronius* type are still comparatively rare. Numerous fronds such as *Alethopteris Neuropteris*, *Mariopteris*, &c., belonged to Pteridosperms, of which specimens showing structure are frequent in certain beds. *Cordaites*, *Dorycordaites* and many stems of the *Mesoxylon* type represent Gymnosperms; the seeds of Pteridosperms and Cordaiteae begin to be common. The Upper Coal Measures (Stephanian) are characterized among the Calamarieae, now more than ever abundant, by the prevalence of the Calamodendreae; new species of *Sphenophyllum* make their appearance; among the Lycopods, *Lepidodendron* and its immediate allies diminish, and smooth-barked Sigillariae are the characteristic representatives. "Ferns" and Pteridosperms are even more strongly represented than before, and this is the age in which the supposed Marattiaceous tree-ferns reached their maximum development. Among Pteridosperms it is the family Medullosese which is especially characteristic. Cordaiteae still increase, and Gymnospermous seeds become extraordinarily abundant. In the Upper Coal Measures the first Cycadophyta and Coniferae make their appearance. The Permian, so far at least as its lower beds are concerned, shows little change from the Stephanian; Conifers of the *Walchia* type are especially characteristic. The remarkable Permo-Carboniferous flora of India and the southern hemisphere is described in the next section of this article. During the earlier part of the Carboniferous epoch the vegetation of the world appears to have been remarkably uniform; while the deposition of the Coal Measures, however, was in progress, a differentiation of floral regions began. The sketch given above extends, for the later periods, to the vegetation of the northern hemisphere only.

AUTHORITIES.—Potonié, *Lehrbuch der Pflanzenpaläontologie* (Berlin, 1899); Renault, *Cours de botanique fossile*, vols. i.–iv. (Paris, 1881–1885); Scott, *Studies in Fossil Botany* (2nd ed., London, 1908–1909); "The present Position of Palaeozoic Botany," in *Progressus rei botanicae*, Band i. (Jena, 1907); Seward, *Fossil Plants* (in course of publication), vol. i. (Cambridge, 1898), vol. ii. (1910); Solms-Laubach, *Introduction to Fossil Botany* (Oxford, 1892); Zeiller, *Éléments de paléobotanique* (Paris, 1900). In these general works references to all important memoirs will be found.

(D. H. S.)

II.—MESOZOIC

The period dealt with in this section does not strictly correspond with that which it is customary to include within the limits of the Mesozoic system. The Mesozoic era, as defined in geological textbooks, includes the Triassic, Jurassic and Cretaceous epochs; but from the point of view of the evolution of plants and the succession of floras, this division is not the most natural or most convenient. Our aim is not simply to give a summary of the most striking botanical features of the several floras that have left traces in the sedimentary rocks, but rather to attempt to follow the different phases in the development of the vegetation of the world, as expressed in the contrasts exhibited by a comparison of the vegetation of the Coal period forests with that of the succeeding Mesozoic era up to the close of the Wealden period.

Towards the close of the Palaeozoic era, as represented by the Upper Carboniferous and Permian plant-bearing strata, the vegetation of the northern hemisphere and that of several regions in the southern hemisphere, consisted of numerous types of Vascular Cryptogams, with some members of the Gymnospermae, and several genera referred to the Pteridospermae and Cycadofilices (see section I. PALAEOZOIC). In the succeeding Permian period the vegetation retained for the most part the same general character; some of the Carboniferous genera died out, and a few new types made their appearance. The Upper Carboniferous and Permian plants may be grouped together as constituting a Permo-Carboniferous flora characterized by an abundance of arborescent Vascular Cryptogams and of an extinct class of plants to which the name Pteridosperms has recently been assigned—plants exhibiting a combination of Cycadean and filicinean characters and distinguished by the production of true gymnospermous seeds of a complex type. This flora had a wide distribution in North America, Europe and parts of

Asia; it extended to China and to the Zambesi region of tropical Africa (Map A, I. and II.).

On the other hand, the plant-beds of the Permo-Carboniferous age in South Africa, South America, India and Australia demonstrate the existence of a widely distributed vegetation *Glossopteris Flora.* which agrees in age with the Upper Carboniferous and Permian vegetation of the north, but differs from it to such an extent as to constitute a distinct flora. We must begin by briefly considering this southern Palaeozoic province if we would trace the Mesozoic floras to their origin, and obtain a connected view of the vegetation of the globe as it existed in late Palaeozoic times and at the beginning of the succeeding era.

In Australia, South America and South Africa a few plants have been found which agree closely with Lower Carboniferous types of the northern hemisphere. In New South Wales, for example, we have such genera as *Rhacopteris* and *Lepidodendron* represented by species very similar to those recorded from Lower Carboniferous or Culm rocks in Germany, Austria, England, Spitzbergen, North and South America and elsewhere. It is, in short, clear that the Culm flora, as we know it in the northern hemisphere, existed in the extreme south, and it is probable that during the earlier part of the Carboniferous period the vegetation of the world was uniform in character. We may possibly go a step farther, and assume that the climatic conditions under which the Culm plants of the Arctic regions flourished were not very different from those which prevailed in Europe, Asia, Chile and South Australia. From strata in New South Wales overlying Devonian and Lower Carboniferous rocks certain plants were discovered in the early part of the 19th century which were compared with European Jurassic genera, and for several years it was believed that these plant-beds belonged to the Mesozoic period. These supposed Mesozoic plants include certain genera which are of special interest. Foremost among these is the genus *Glossopteris* (fig. 1), applied by Brongniart in 1828 to sub-lanceolate or tongue-shaped leaves from India and Australia,

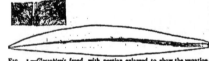

FIG. 1.—*Glossopteris* frond, with portion enlarged to show the venation. (Natural size = 36 cm. in length.) From Lower Gondwana rocks of India.

which have generally been regarded as the fronds of ferns characterised by a central midrib giving off lateral veins which repeatedly anastomose and form a network, like that in the leaves of *Antrophyum*, an existing member of the Polypodiaceae. The stems, long known from Australia and India as *Vertebraria*, have in recent years been proved to be the rhizomes of *Glossopteris*. It is only recently that undoubted sporangia have been found in close association with *Glossopteris* leaves. The genus possessed small broadly oval or triangular leaves in addition to the large fronds like that shown in fig. 1; it was with the smaller leaves that Mr Arber discovered sporangia exhibiting certain points of resemblance to the microsporangia of modern Cycads. We cannot as yet say whether these bodies represent a somewhat unusual type of fern sporangium or whether they are microsporangia; if the latter supposition is correct the plant must have been heterosporous; but we are still without evidence on this point. Associated with *Glossopteris* occurs another fern, *Gangamopteris*, usually recognised by the absence of a well marked midrib, though this character does not always afford a satisfactory distinguishing feature. In view of recent discoveries which have demonstrated the Pteridosperm nature of many supposed ferns of Palaeozoic age, we must admit the possibility that the term fern as applied to *Glossopteris* and *Gangamopteris* may be incorrect. An Equisetaceous plant, which Brongniart named *Phyllotheca* in 1828, is another member of the same flora; this type bears a close resemblance to *Equisetum* in the long internodes and the whorled leaves encircling the nodes, but differs in the looser leaf-sheaths and in the long spreading filiform leaf-segments, as also in the structure of the cones. *Phyllotheca* has been recognised in Europe in strata of Palaeozoic age, and Professor Zeiller has discovered a new species—*P. Rallii*—in Upper Carboniferous rocks in Asia Minor (Map A, VII.), which points to a close agreement between this genus and the well-known Palaeozoic *Annularia*. *Phyllotheca* occurs also in Jurassic rocks in Italy and in Siberian strata originally described as Jurassic, but which Zeiller has shown are no doubt of Permian age. Some examples of this genus, described by Etheridge from Permo-Carboniferous beds in New South Wales, differ in some respects from the ordinary form, and bear a superficial resemblance to the Equise-

taceous genus *Cingularia* from the Coal Measures of Germany. Other genera characteristic of this southern flora are mentioned later. The extraordinary abundance of *Glossopteris* in Permo-Carboniferous rocks of Australia, and in strata of the same age in India and South Africa, gave rise to the term " Glossopteris flora " for the assemblage of plants obtained from southern hemisphere rocks overlying beds containing Devonian and Lower Carboniferous fossils. The Glossopteris flora of Australia occurs in certain regions in association with deposits which are now recognised as true boulder-beds, formed during widespread glacial conditions. In India the same flora occurs in a thick series of fresh-water sediments, known as the Lower Gondwana system, including basal boulder-beds like those of Australia. Similar glacial deposits occur also in South America, and members of the Glossopteris flora have been discovered in Brazil and elsewhere. In South Africa, *Glossopteris, Gangamopteris* and other genera, identical with those from Australia and India, are abundantly represented, and here again, as in India and South America, the plants are found in association with extensive deposits of undoubted glacial origin. To state the case in a few words: there is in South Africa, South America, Australia and India an extensive series of sediments containing *Glossopteris, Gangamopteris* and other genera, and including beds full of ice-scratched boulders. These strata are homotaxial with Permo-Carboniferous rocks in Europe and North America, as determined by the order of succession of the rocks, and by the occurrence of typical Palaeozoic shells in associated marine deposits. The most important evidence on which this conclusion is based is afforded by the occurrence of European forms of Carboniferous shells in marine strata in New South Wales, which are intercalated between Coal Measures containing members of the Glossopteris flora, and by the discovery of similar shells, many of which are identical with the Australian species, in strata in the north-west of India and in Afghanistan, forming part of a thick series of marine beds known as the Salt Range group. This group of sediments in the extra-peninsular area of India includes a basal boulder-bed, referred on convincing evidence to the same geological horizon as the glacial deposits of the Indian peninsula (Talchir boulder-beds), South Africa (Ecca boulder-beds), Australia and Tasmania (Bacchus Marsh boulder-beds, &c.), and South America, which are associated with Glossopteris-bearing strata. We have a flora of wide distribution in South Africa, South America, Borneo, Australia, Tasmania and India which is clearly of Permo-Carboniferous age, but which differs in its composition from the flora of the same age in other parts of the world. This flora appears to have abruptly succeeded an older flora in Australia and elsewhere, which was precisely similar to that of Lower Carboniferous age in the northern hemisphere. The frequent occurrence of ice-formed deposits at the base of the beds in which *Glossopteris* and other genera make their appearance, almost necessitates the conclusion that the change in the character of the vegetation was connected with a lowering of temperature and the prevalence of glacial conditions over a wide area in India and the southern hemisphere. There can be little doubt that the Indian Lower Gondwana rocks, in which the boulder-beds and the Glossopteris flora occur, must be regarded as belonging to a vast continental area of which remnants are preserved in Australia, South Africa and South America. This continental area has been described as "Gondwana Land," a tract of enormous extent occupying an area part of which has since given place to a southern ocean, while detached masses persist as portions of more modern continents, which have enabled us to read in their fossil plants and ice-scratched boulders the records of a lost continent in which the Mesozoic vegetation of the northern hemisphere had its birth. Of the rocks of this southern continent those of the Indian Gondwana system are the richest in fossil plants; the most prominent types recorded from these, Permo-Carboniferous strata are *Glossopteris, Gangamopteris,* species referred to *Sphenopteris, Pecopteris, Macrotaeniopteris* and other Ferns; *Schizoneura* (fig. 2) and *Phyllotheca* among the Equisetales, *Naeggerathiopsis* and *Euryphyllum,* probably members of the Cordaitales (q.v. in section I. PALAEOZOIC); *Glossozamites* and *Pterophyllum* among the Cycadales, and various vegetative shoots recalling those of the coniferous genus *Voltzia,* a well-known Permian and Triassic plant of northern latitudes. The genera *Lepidodendron, Sigillaria, Stigmaria,* or *Calamites,* which played so great a share in the vegetation of the same age in the northern hemisphere, have not been recognized among the Palaeozoic forms of India, but examples of *Sigillaria, Lepidodendron* and *Bothrodendron* are known to have existed in South Africa in the Permo-Carboniferous era.

We may next inquire what types occur in the Glossopteris flora agreeing more or less closely with members of the rich Permo-Carboniferous vegetation of the north. The genus *Sphenophyllum,* abundant in the Coal Measures and Permian rocks of Europe and America, is represented by a single species recorded from India, *Sphenophyllum speciosum* (fig. 3), and a doubtful species from South Africa; *Annularia,* another common northern genus, is recorded from Australia, and the closely allied *Phyllotheca* constitutes another link between the two Permo-Carboniferous floras. The genus *Cordaites* may be compared, and indeed is probably identical with, certain forms recorded from India, South America, South Africa and Australia. While a few similar or even identical types may be recognized in both floras, there can be no doubt that, during a considerable period subsequent to that represented by the Lower Carboniferous or Culm rocks, there existed two distinct floras, one of which had its headquarters in the northern hemisphere, while the other flourished in a vast continental area in the south. Recent discoveries have shown that representatives of the two floras coexisted in certain regions; there was, in fact, a dovetailing between the northern and southern botanical provinces.

strata in Europe. In the Tongking area, therefore, a flora existed during the Rhaetic period consisting in part of genera which are abundant in the older Glossopteris beds of the south, and in part of well-known constituents of European Rhaetic floras. A characteristic member of the southern botanical province, *Schizoneura gondwanensis* (fig. 2) of India, is represented also by a closely allied if not an identical species—*S. paradoxa*—in the Lower Trias (Bunter) sandstones of the Vosges Mountains, associated with European

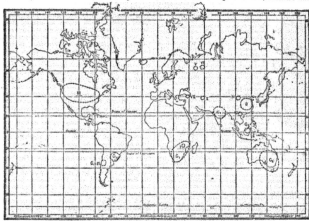

MAP A.—G₁-G₂. Glossopteris Flora.

I, II. Upper Carboniferous plants of the northern hemisphere facies, in the Zambesi district and in China.
III. Rhaetic flora of Tongking (*Glossopteris*, &c.; associated with northern types).
IV. Carboniferous plants (prov. Kansu).
V. *Glossopteris*, &c., in Permian rocks in prov. Vologda.

VI. Permian (Pechora valley).
VII. Permian (Pechora valley).
VIII. Upper Carboniferous (Herakleion).
VIII. Rhaetic (Honduras).
IX. Lower Jurassic, Upper Gondwana (Argentine).
X. Rhaetic (Persia).
XI. Triassic—Cretaceous.

In 1895 Professor Zeiller described several plants from the province of Rio Grande do Sul in South America (Map A, G₂), including a few typical members of the Glossopteris flora associated with a European species, *Lepidophloios laricinus*, one of the characteristic types of the Coal period, and with certain ferns resembling some species from European Permian rocks. A similar association was found also in Argentine rocks by Kurtz (Map A, G₂), and from South Africa *Sigillaria Brardi*, *Psygmophyllum*, *Bothrodendron* and other northern types are recorded in company with *Glossopteris*, *Glossamopteris* and *Naeggerathiopsis*.

The Coal-bearing strata which occupy a considerable area in China (Map A, II.), contain abundant samples of a vegetation which appears to have agreed in their main features with the Permo-Carboniferous floras of the northern hemisphere. In his account of some plants from the Coal Measures of Kansu (Map A. IV.) Dr Krasser has drawn attention to the apparent identity of certain leaf-fragments with those of *Naeggerathiopsis Hislopi*, a typical member of the Glossopteris flora; but this plant, so far as the evidence of vegetative leaves may be of value, differs in no essential respects from certain species of a European genus *Cordaites*. A comparatively rich fossil flora was described in 1882 from Tongking (Map A.III.) by Professor Zeiller—and this author has recently made important additions to his original account—which demonstrates an admixture of Glossopteris types with others which were recognized as identical with plants characteristic of Rhaetic

(After Feistmantel.)
FIG. 2.—*Schizoneura gondwanensis*, from Lower Gondwana rocks, India.

species which do not occur in the Glossopteris flora. Another plant found in the Vosges sandstones—*Neuropteridium grandifolium*—is also closely allied to species of the same "fern" recorded from the

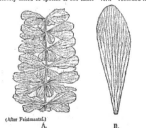

(After Feistmantel.)
A.
B.

FIG. 3.—*Sphenophyllum speciosum*, from Lower Gondwana rocks, India.
A. nat. size.   B. leaflet enlarged.

Lower Gondwana strata of India (fig. 4). South America and South Africa. These two instances—the Tongking beds of Rhaetic age and the Bunter sandstones of the Vosges—afford evidence of a northern extension of Glossopteris types and their association with European species. In 1898 an important discovery was made by Professor Amalitzky, which carries us a step further in our search for a connexion between the northern and southern floras. Amalitzky found in beds of Upper Permian age in the province of Vologda (Russia) (Map A, V.) species of *Glossopteris* and *Naeggerathiopsis* typical members of the Glossopteris flora, associated with species of the ferns *Taeniopteris*, *Callipteris* and *Sphenopteris*, a striking instance of a commingling in the far north of the northern hemisphere Permian species with migrants from "Gondwana Land." This association of types clearly points to a penetration of representatives of the Glossopteris flora to the north of Europe towards the close of the Permian period. Evidence of the same northern extension is supplied by floras described by Schmalhausen from Permian rocks in the Pechora valley (Map A, VI.), the Siberian genus *Rhipteramitet* being very similar to, and probably generically identical with, *Naeggerathiopsis* of the Glossopteris flora. The Permo-Carboniferous beds of South Africa, India and Australia are succeeded by other plant-bearing strata, containing numerous species agreeing closely with members of the Rhaetic and Jurassic floras of the northern hemisphere. These post-Permian floras, as represented by the Upper Gondwana beds of India and corresponding strata in Australia, South Africa, and South America, differ but slightly from the northern floras, and point to a uniformity in the Rhaetic and Jurassic vegetation which is in contrast to the existence of two botanical provinces during the latter part of the Palaeozoic period. A few plants described by Potonié from German and Portuguese East Africa demonstrate the occurrence of *Glossopteris* and a few other genera, referred to a Permo-Triassic horizon, in a region slightly to the north of Tete in the Zambesi district (Map A, I.), where typical European plants agreeing with Upper Carboniferous types were discovered several years ago, and described by Zeiller in 1883 and 1901. The existence of Upper Gondwana plants, resembling Jurassic species from the Rajmahal beds of India, has been demonstrated in the Argentine by Dr Kurtz.

(After Feistmantel.)
FIG. 4.— *Neuropteridium validum*. From Lower Gondwana rocks, India.

Having seen how the Glossopteris flora of the south gradually spread to the north in the Permian period, we may now take a brief survey of the succession of floras in the northern *Mesozoic Floras.* hemisphere, which have left traces in Mesozoic rocks of North America, Europe and Asia. Our knowledge of the Triassic vegetation is far from extensive; this is no doubt due in part to the fact that the conditions under which the Triassic rocks were deposited were not favourable to the existence of a luxuriant vegetation. The Triassic rocks of southern Europe and other regions are typical marine sediments. The Bunter sandstones of the Vosges have afforded several species of Lower Triassic plants; these include the Equisetaceous genus *Schizoneura*—a member also of the Glossopteris flora—bipinnate fern fronds referred to the genus *Anomopteris*, another fern, described originally as *Neuropteris grandifolia*, which agrees very closely with a southern hemisphere type (*Neuropteridium validum*, fig. 4), some large Equisetaceous stems apparently identical, except in size, with modern Horsetails. With these occur several Conifers, among others *Voltzia heterophylla* and some twigs referred to the genus *Albertia*, bearing large leaves like those of *Agathis australis* and some of the Araucarias, also a few representatives of the Cycadales. Among plants from Lower Triassic strata there are a few which form connecting links with the older Permo-Carboniferous flora; of these we have a species, described by Blanckenhon as *Sigillaria oculina*, which may be correctly referred to that genus, although an inspection of a plaster-cast of the type-specimen in the Berlin Bergakademi) left some doubt as to the sufficiency of the evidence for adopting the generic name *Sigillaria*. Another Triassic genus, *Pleuromeia*, is of interest as exhibiting, on the one hand, a striking resemblance to the recent genus *Isoetes*, from which it differs in its much larger stem, and on the other as

agreeing fairly closely with the Palaeozoic genera *Lepidodendron* and *Sigillaria*. There is, however, a marked difference, as regards the floras as a whole, between the uppermost Palaeozoic flora of the northern hemisphere and such species as have been recorded from Lower Triassic beds. There is evidence of a distinct break in the succession of the northern floras which is not apparent between the Permian and Trias floras of the south. Passing over the few known species of plants from the middle Trias (Muschelkalk) to the more abundant and more widely spread Upper Triassic species as recorded from Germany, Austria, Switzerland, North America and elsewhere, we find a vegetation characterized chiefly by an abundance of Ferns and Cycads, exhibiting the same general facies as that of the succeeding Rhaetic and Lower Jurassic floras. Among Cycads may be mentioned species of *Pterophyllum* (e.g. *P. Jaegeri*), represented by large pinnate fronds not unlike those of existing species of *Zamia*, some Equisetaceous plants and numerous Ferns which may be referred to such families as Gleicheniaceae, Dipteridinae and Matonineae. Representatives of the Gink-goales constitute characteristic members of the later Triassic floras, and these, with other types, carry us on without any break in continuity to the Rhaetic floras of Scania, Germany, Asia, Chile, Tonkin and Honduras (Map A, VIII.), and to the Jurassic and Wealden floras of many regions in both the north and south hemispheres. A comparative view of the plants found in various parts of the world, in beds ranging from the Upper Trias to the top of the Jurassic system, reveals a striking uniformity in the vegetation both in northern and southern latitudes during this long succession of ages. The Palaeozoic types are barely represented; the arborescent Vascular Cryptogams have been replaced by Cycads, Ginkgoales and Conifers as the dominant classes, while Ferns continue to hold their own. No undoubted Angiosperms have yet been found below the Cretaceous system. From the close of the Permian period, which marks the limit of the Upper Palaeozoic floras, to the period immediately preceding the apparently sudden appearance of Angiosperms, we have a succession of floras differing from one another in certain minor details, but linked together by the possession of many characters in common. It is impossible to consider in detail this long period in the history of plant-evolution, but we may briefly pass in review the most striking features of the vegetation as exhibited in the dominant types of the various classes of plants. Fragments of a Jurassic flora have recently been discovered by Dr Andersson, a member of Nordenskiold's Antarctic expedition, in Louis Philippe Land in lat. 64° 15′ S. Among other well-known Jurassic genera Nathorst has identified the following: *Equisetites*, *Cladophlebis*, *Todites*, *Thinnfeldia*, *Otozamites*, *Williamsonia pecten*, *Araucarites*. The discovery of this Antarctic flora is a further demonstration of the world-wide distribution of a uniform Jurassic flora.

Under the head of Algae there is little of primary importance to record, but it is of interest to notice the occurrence of certain forms which throw light on the antiquity of existing families *Algae.* of Algae. Species referred on good evidence to the Charophyta are represented by a few casts of oögonia and stem fragments, found in Jurassic and Wealden beds, which bear a striking resemblance to existing species. There is some evidence for the occurrence of similar *Chara* "fruits" in middle Triassic rocks; some doubtful fossils from the much older Devonian rocks have also been quoted as possible examples of the Charophyta. The oldest known Diatoms are represented by some specimens found entangled in the spicules of a Liassic sponge, and identified by Rothpletz as species of the recent genus *Pyxidicula*. The calcareous Siphoneae are represented by several forms, identified as species of *Diplopora*, *Triploporella*, *Neomeris* and other genera, from strata ranging from the lower Trias limestones of Tirol to the Cretaceous rocks of Mexico and elsewhere. It is probable that the Jurassic *Goniolina*, described from French localities, and other genera which need not be mentioned, may also be reckoned among the Mesozoic Siphoneae. A genus *Zonatrichites*, compared with species of Cyanophyceae, has been described as a Calcareous alga from Liassic limestones of Silesia. The geological history of Mosses and Liverworts is at present very incomplete, and founded on few and generally unsatisfactory fragments. It is hardly too much to say that no *Bryophyta.* absolutely trustworthy examples of Mosses have so far been found in Mesozoic strata. Of Liverworts there are a few species, such as *Palaeohepatica Rostafinskii* from the Lower Jurassic rocks of Cracow, *Marchantites erectus* from the Inferior Oolite rocks of Yorkshire, and *M. Zeilleri* from the Wealden beds of Sussex. These fossil Hepaticae are unfortunately founded only on sterile fragments, and placed in the Liverworts on the strength of their resemblance to the thallus of *Marchantia* and other recent genera.

The Palaeozoic Calamites were succeeded in the Triassic period by large *Equisetites*, differing, so far as we know, in no essential
Equise-
taceae.
respect from existing Equisetums. The large stems represented by casts of Triassic age, *Equisetites arenaceus* and other species, probably possessed the power of secondary growth in thickness; the cones were of the modern type, and the rhizomes occasionally formed large underground tubers like those frequently met with in *Equisetum arvense*, *E. sylvaticum* and other species. *Equisetites Muensteri* is a characteristic and fairly widely spread Rhaetic and Liassic species, having a comparatively slender stem, with leaf-sheaths consisting of a few broad and short leaf-segments. *Equisetites columnaris*, a common fossil in the Jurassic plant-beds of the Yorkshire coast, represents another type with relatively stout and occasionally branched vegetative shoots, bearing leaf-sheaths very like those of *Equisetum maximum* and other Horsetails. In the Wealden strata more slender forms have been found—*e.g. Equisetites Burchardti* and *E. Lyelli*—in England, Germany, Portugal, Japan and elsewhere, differing still less in dimensions from modern species. Of other Equisetales there are *Schizoneura* and *Phyllotheca*; the former first appears in Lower Gondwana rocks as a member of the Glossopteris flora, migrating at a later epoch into Europe, where it is represented by a Triassic species. The latter genus ranges from Upper Carboniferous to Jurassic rocks; it occurs in India, Australia, and elsewhere in the "Gondwana Land" vegetation, as well as in Palaeozoic rocks of Asia Minor, in Permian rocks of Siberia, and in Jurassic plant-beds of Italy. This genus, like the allied *Calamites*, appears to have possessed cones of more than one type; but we know little of the structure of these Mesozoic Equisetaceous genera as compared with our much more complete knowledge of *Calamites* and *Archaeocalamites*. (See section I., PALAEOZOIC.)

Reference has already been made to *Sigillaria oculina* and to the genus *Pleuromeia*. Palaeobotanical literature contains several
Lycopo-
diales.
records of species of *Lycopodites* and *Selaginellites*; nearly all of them are sterile fragments, bearing a more or less close resemblance to living Club-Mosses and Selaginellas, but lacking the more important reproductive organs. Nathorst has recently described a new type of lycopodiaceous cone, *Lycostrobus Scotti*, from Rhaetic rocks of Scania, from which he obtained both megaspores and microspores. An investigation by Miss Sollas of a plant long known from Rhaetic rocks in the Severn valley as *Naiadita acuminata* has shown that this genus is in all probability a small lycopodiaceous plant, and neither a Moss nor a Monocotyledon, as some writers have supposed. One of the best-known European species is *Lycopodites falcatus*, originally described by Lindley and Hutton from the Inferior Oolite of Yorkshire.

Among the large number of Mesozoic Ferns there are several species founded on sterile fronds which possess but little interest
Filicales.
from a botanical standpoint. Some plants, again, have been referred by certain authors to Ferns, while others have relegated them to the Cycads. As examples of these doubtful forms may be mentioned *Thinnfeldia*, characteristic of Rhaetic and Lower Jurassic rocks; *Dichopteris*, represented by some exceptionally fine Jurassic specimens, described by Zigno, from Italy; and *Ctenis*, a genus chiefly from Jurassic beds, founded on pinnate fronds like those of *Zamia* and other Cycads, with linear pinnae characterized by anastomosing veins. Plants referred to Schimper's genus *Lomatopteris* and to *Cycadopteris* of Zigno afford instances of the difficulty of distinguishing between the foliage of Ferns and Cycads. The close resemblance between specimens from Jurassic rocks placed in one or other of the genera *Thinnfeldia*, *Dichopteris*, *Cycadopteris*, &c., illustrates the unsatisfactory custom of founding new names on imperfect fronds. It is of interest to note that some leaf-fragments recently found in Permian rocks of Kansas, and placed in a new genus *Glenopteris*, are hardly distinguishable from specimens of Jurassic and Rhaetic age referred to *Thinnfeldia* and other Mesozoic genera. The difficulty of distinguishing between Ferns and Cycads is a necessary consequence of the common origin of these two classes; in Palaeozoic times the Cycadofilicies and Pteridospermae (see section I., PALAEOZOIC) played a prominent part, and even among recent Cycads and Ferns we will see a few indications of their close relationship. There is reason to believe that compound or generalized types—partly Ferns and partly

FIG. 5.
A, *Otozamites Beani*.
B, *O. Bunburyanus*.
Inferior Oolite, England.

Cycads—persisted into the Mesozoic era; but without more anatomical knowledge than we at present possess, it is impossible to do more than to point to a few indications afforded by external, and to a slight extent by internal structure, of the survival of Cycadofilicinean types. The genus *Otozamites*, which it is customary and probably correct to include in the Cycadales, is represented by certain species, such as *Otozamites Beani* (fig. 5, A), a characteristic Yorkshire fossil of Jurassic age, which in the form of the frond, bearing broad and relatively short pinnae, exhibits a striking agreement with the sterile portions of the fronds of *Aneimia rotundifolia*, a member of the fern family Schizaeaceae. Again, another species of the same genus, *O. Bunburyanus* (fig. 5, B), suggests a comparison with fern fronds like that of the recent species *Nephrolepis Duffi*. The scaly ramenta which occur in abundance on the leaf-stalk bases of fossil Cycads constitute another fern-character surviving in Mesozoic Cycadales. Without a fuller knowledge of internal structure and of the reproductive organs, we are compelled to speak of some of the Mesozoic plants as possibly Ferns or possibly Cycads, and not referable with certainty to one or other class. It has been found useful in some cases to examine microscopically the thin film of coal that often covers the pinnae of fossil fronds, in order to determine the form of the epidermal cells which may be preserved in the carbonized cuticle; rectilinear epidermal cell-walls are usually considered characteristic of Cycads, while cells with undulating walls are more likely to belong to Ferns. This distinction does not, however, afford a safe guide; the epidermal cells of some ferns, *e.g. Angiopteris*, have straight walls, and occasionally the surface cells of a Cycadean leaf-segment exhibit a fern-like character. Leaving out of account the numerous sterile fronds which cannot be certainly referred to particular families of Ferns, there are several genera which bear evidence in their sori, and to some extent in the form of the leaf, of their relationship to existing types.

The abundance of Palaeozoic plants with sporangia and sori of the Marattiaceous type is in striking contrast to the scarcity of Mesozoic ferns which can be reasonably included in the
Marat-
tiaceae.
Marattiaceae. One of the few forms so far recorded is that known as *Marattia Muensteri* from Rhaetic localities in Europe and Asia. Some species included in the genus *Danaeites* or *Danaeopsis* from Jurassic rocks of Poland, Austria and Switzerland may possibly be closely allied to the recent tropical genus *Danaea*. Of the Ophioglossaceae there are no satisfactory examples; one of the few fossils compared with a recent species, *Ophioglossum palmatum*, was described several years ago from Triassic rocks under the name *Cheiropteris*, but the resemblance is one of external form only, and practically valueless as a taxonomic criterion. It would appear that the eusporangiate Ferns suddenly sank to very subordinate position after the Palaeozoic era.

The Osmundaceae, represented by a few forms of Palaeozoic age, played a more prominent part in the Mesozoic floras. A species described by Schenk from Rhaetic rocks of Franconia as
Osmun-
daceae.
Acrostichies princeps is hardly distinguishable from *Todites Williamsoni*, a widely distributed species in Inferior Oolite strata. This Jurassic species bore bipinnate fronds not unlike those of the South African, Australian, and New Zealand Fern *Todea barbara*, which were characterized by a stout rachis and short broad pinnules bearing numerous large sporangia covering the under surface of the lamina. Specimens of *Todites* have been obtained from England, Poland, and elsewhere, sufficiently well preserved to afford good evidence of a correspondence in the structure of their sporangia with those of recent Osmundaceae. This Jurassic and Rhaetic type occurs in England, Germany, Poland, Italy, East Greenland, North America, Japan, China and Persia (Map A, X.). Bipinnate sterile fronds of *Todites* have in some instances been described under the designation *Pecopteris whitbiensis*. This and other names, such as *Asplenium whitbiense*, *A. nebbense*, *Asplenites Roesserti*,&c.,have been given to bipinnate fronds of a type frequently met with in different genera and families of recent Ferns, *e.g. Onoclea Struthiopteris*, species of *Cyathea*, *Asplenium*, *Gymnogramme*, &c. In most cases the Rhaetic, Jurassic andWealden Ferns included under one or other of these names are sterile, and cannot be assigned to a particular family, but some are undoubtedly

FIG. 6.—*Cladophlebis denticulata.*
Inferior Oolite, England.

the leaves of *Todites*, a genus which may often be recognized by the broad and relatively short bluntly-terminated pinnules. The Jurassic species *Cladophlebis denticulata* (fig. 6), recorded from several European localities, as well as from North America, Japan, China, Australia, India and Persia, affords an instance of a common type of bipinnate frond similar to *Todites Williamsoni*, which has been included in the Polypodiaceae; but such meagre evidence of the soral characters as we possess also points to a comparison with the recent fern *Todea barbara*. Our knowledge of the anatomy of fossil Osmundaceae has recently been considerably extended by Kidston and Gwynne-Vaughan. (For references, see Seward, *Fossil Plants*, vol. ii., 1910.)

Schizaeaceae. The Schizaeaceae include a widely spread species, originally named *Pecopteris exilis*, and subsequently placed in a new genus, *Klukia* (fig. 7), which is characterized by tripinnate fronds with short linear ultimate segments, bearing a single row of sporangia with an apical annulus ("monangic sori" of Prantl) on either side of the midrib. This type occurs in Rhaetic

FIG. 7.—*Klukia exilis.*
1-3, Sporangia enlarged.
4, Single fertile pinnule slightly enlarged.
5, Fragment of pinna.
Inferior Oolite, England.

and Lower Jurassic rocks of England, the Arctic regions, Japan and elsewhere. *Ruffordia Goepperti*, a Wealden type, and probably a member of the Schizaeaceae, has been recorded from England, Belgium, and other European countries, and Japan.

Gleicheniaceae. The Gleicheniaceae appear to have been represented by Triassic species in North America and Europe, and more abundantly in Jurassic, Wealden, or Lower Cretaceous rocks in Belgium, Greenland, Poland and elsewhere. Some exceptionally perfect fragments of rhizomes have been found by Dr C. Bommer of Brussels in some Wealden deposits at Hainaut in Belgium; but these have not yet been fully described. The dichotomously-branched fronds of the type represented by several recent species of *Gleichenia*, e.g. *G. dichotoma*, &c., are abundant in Lower Cretaceous plant-beds of Greenland, and suggest that in the latter part of the Mesozoic period the Gleicheniaceae held a position in the vegetation of the far north similar to that which they now occupy in the southern tropics of India and other regions.

Matoniaceae. The recent Malayan genus *Matonia* (Map B, Matonia), represented by two species, *M. pectinata* and *M. sarmentosa*, is clearly a survival in southern latitudes of a family which occupied an important place in the vegetation of the Rhaetic Jurassic and Wealden periods. The genera *Laccopteris* and *Matonidium* (fig. 8) may be cited as the two most important types, both as regards geographical and geological range, of this Mesozoic family; these ferns are recorded from England, France, Belgium, Germany, Austria, Portugal, Poland and Italy (Map B, M₁), also from Greenland (Map B, M₃), Spitsbergen (Map B, M³), and Persia (Map B, M⁴). From the southern Hemisphere, on the other hand, we know of one or two fragments only which can reasonably be referred to the Matonineae (Map B, M₂), a fact which may point to a northern origin for this family with its two surviving species almost confined to the Malayan region.

FIG. 8.—*Matonidium Goepperti.*
A, Summit of petiole.
B, Fertile pinnules.
Inferior Oolite, England.

Dipteridineae. The recent genus, *Dipteris*, with its four existing species, occurring chiefly in the Indo-Malayan region (Map B, Dipteris), is also a modern survival of several Mesozoic types represented by such genera as *Dictyophyllum* (fig. 9), *Hausmannia* and *Camptopteris*, which were abundant during the Rhaetic and Jurassic periods in England, Germany, Sweden and

elsewhere in Europe (Map B, D). Important additions to our knowledge of the fertile leaves and rhizomes of certain Rhaetic species of *Dictyophyllum* and other genera have recently been made by Professor Nathorst of Stockholm, and Professor Richter of Quedlinburg has made a thorough investigation of the vegetative organs of *Hausmannia*, a genus possibly identical with *Protorhipis*, which is abundant in Lower Cretaceous and other strata in various European localities. The Dipteridinae are represented also by species from Mesozoic rocks of Persia (Map B, D₁), Greenland (Map B, D₃), North America (D₄), South America (D₂) and China (D₅).

Cyatheaceae. The Cyatheaceae constitute another family of leptosporangiate Ferns which had several representatives in Mesozoic floras. The numerous species of fronds from Jurassic and Wealden rocks of North America and Europe referred to *Thyrsopteris*, a recent monotypic genus confined to Juan Fernandez, are in the majority of cases founded on sterile leaves, and of little or no botanical value. On the other hand, there are several fossil Ferns of Jurassic age possessing cup-like sori like those of *Thyrsopteris* and other Cyatheaceous Ferns,

(After Schenk.)
FIG. 9.—*Dictyophyllum.* Rhaetic rocks of Europe and Asia.

which indicate a wide Mesozoic distribution for this family. Among Jurassic species which should probably be classed as Cyatheaceae, *Coniopteris hymenophylloides* is recorded from England, France, Russia, Poland, Bornholm, Italy, the Arctic regions, North America, Japan, China, Australia and India. A few tree-ferns which may be included in this family—such as *Protopteris*—have been described from Wealden and Lower Cretaceous rocks of England, Germany and Austria. It is by no means easy in dealing with fossil ferns to distinguish between certain Polypodiaceae—such as species of *Davallia*—and members of the Cyatheaceae.

Polypodiaceae. It is a striking fact that among the numerous Mesozoic Ferns there are comparatively few that can with good reason be referred to the Polypodiaceae, a family which plays so dominant a rôle at the present day. The frequent occurrence of such names as *Asplenium*, *Adiantum*, *Davallia*, and other Polypodiaceous genera in lists of fossil ferns is thoroughly misleading. There are, indeed, a certain number of species which show traces of sori like those of modern species of *Asplenium* and other genera, but in most cases the names of recent ferns have been used on insufficient grounds. The Wealden and Jurassic genus *Onychiopsis* of England, Portugal, Belgium, Germany, Japan, South Africa and Australia, bears a close resemblance to the recent *Onychium (Cryptogramme)*. Other Jurassic Ferns described by Raciborski from Poland suggest a comparison with *Davallia*. The resemblance of the sporocarp-like bodies—discovered by Nathorst in association with Rhaetic *Sagenopteris* leaves, and more recently figured by Halle under a new generic name (*Hydropterangium*)—to the sporocarps of *Marsilia* is an argument in favour of including *Sagenopteris* in the Hydropterideae. The majority of the specimens included in the genus *Cladophlebis*, the Mesozoic representative of the Palaeozoic *Pecopteris* type of frond, are known only in a sterile condition, and cannot be assigned to their family position. A Wealden plant, *Weichselia Mantelli*, is worthy of mention as a species of very wide geographical distribution, and one of the most characteristic members of the Wealden flora. This type is distinguished by its large bipinnate fronds bearing long and narrow pinnae with close-set pinnules, characterized by the anastomosing secondary veins. No traces of sori have so far been found on the fronds. Similarly, the genus *Sagenopteris*, characterized by a habit like that of *Marsilia*, and represented by fronds consisting of a few spreading broadly oval or narrow segments, with anastomosing veins, borne on the apex of a common petiole, is abundant in rocks ranging from the Rhaetic to the Wealden, but has not so far been satisfactorily placed. The evidence adduced by Nathorst and some other writers is, however, not convincing; until we find well-preserved sporocarps in connection with vegetative fronds we prefer to keep an open mind as regards the position of *Sagenopteris*.

Cycadales. The abundance of Cycadean plants is one of the most striking features of Mesozoic floras. In most cases we have only the evidence of sterile fronds, and this is necessarily unsatisfactory; but the occurrence of numerous stems and fertile shoots demonstrates the wealth of Cycadean plants in many parts of the world, more particularly during the Jurassic and Wealden periods. From Palaeozoic rocks a few fronds have been described, such as *Pterophyllum Fayoli*, *P. Combrayi*, *Plagiozamites* and

Sphenozamites, chiefly from French localities, which are referred to the Cycads because of their similarity to the pinnate fronds of modern Cycadaceae. In the succeeding Triassic system Cycadean fronds, which there is good reason to refer to the Cycadales in Upper Triassic, Rhaetic, Jurassic and Wealden rocks in India, Australia, Japan, China and elsewhere in the southern hemisphere,

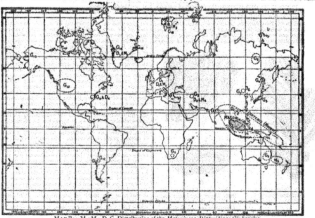

MAP B.—M₁–M₁₅, D. G. Distribution of the *Matonineae, Dipteridinae, Ginkgoales.*

D₁–D₄. Distribution of the *Dipteridinae.*
G₁–G₁₅. Distribution of the *Ginkgoales* during the Mesozoic and Tertiary Periods.
G₁ (Trias–Tertiary);
G₂, G₃ (Rhaetic–Jurassic);
G₄ (Tertiary, Sakhalin I.);

G₅ (Jurassic);
G₆ (Jurassic and Tertiary);
G₇ (Jurassic);
G₈ (Rhaetic–Jurassic);
G₉ (Trias–Rhaetic);
G₁₀ (Rhaetic, Chile);
G₁₁ (Trias);

G₁₂ (Cretaceous–Tertiary);
G₁₃ (Tertiary, Alaska);
G₁₄ (Cretaceous–Tertiary);
G₁₅ (Jurassic);
G₁₆ (Jurassic, Spitsbergen);
G₁₇ (Jurassic, Franz Josef Land).

plants become much more abundant, especially in the Keuper period; from Rhaetic rocks a still greater number of types have been recorded, among which may be mentioned *Nilssonia* (fig. 10), *Anomozamites*, *Pterophyllum*, *Otozamites*, *Cycadites* (fig. 11). The species of *Nilssonia* shown in fig. 10 (*N. compta*) is a characteristic member of the Jurassic flora, practically identical with a form from Rhaetic rocks described as *Nilssonia polymorpha*. The large frond of *Cycadites* represented in fig. 11 (*C. Saportae*) is from the Wealden strata of Sussex, and possibly identical with *Cycadites tenuisectus* from Portugal. In addition to these genera there are others, such as *Ctenozamites*, *Ctenis*, and *Podozamites*, the position of which is less certain. *Ctenozamites* occurs chiefly in the Rhaetic coal-bearing beds of Scania, and has been found also in the Liassic clays of

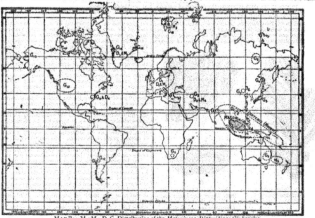

FIG. 10.—*Nilssonia compta.* Inferior Oolite, England.

Dorsetshire and in the Inferior Oolite beds of Yorkshire, as well as in Rhaetic strata in Persia and elsewhere; it is characterized by its bipinnate fronds, and may be compared with the recent Australian genus *Bowenia*—peculiar among living Cycads in having bipinnate fronds. *Ctenis* has been incorrectly placed among the ferns by some authors, on account of the occurrence of supposed sporangia on its pinnae; but there is reason to believe that these so-called sporangia are probably nothing more than prominent papillose cells of the epidermis. *Podozamites* (fig. 12) is usually considered to be a Cycad, but the broad pinnae (or leaves) and their arrangement on the axis suggests a possible relationship with the southern coniferous genus *Agathis*, represented by the Kauri pine and other recent species. The considerable variation in the size of the pinnae of *Podozamites*, as represented by species from the Jurassic rocks in the Arctic regions and various European localities, recalls the variation in length and breadth of the leaves of *Agathis*. With regard to the distinguishing features and the distribution of the numerous Cycadean leaves of Mesozoic age, the most striking fact is the abundance of

as well in North America, Greenland, and other Arctic lands and throughout Europe. It is noteworthy that Tertiary plant-beds have yielded hardly any specimens that can be recognized as Cycads.

A more important question is, What knowledge have we of the reproductive organs and stems of these fossil Cycads? Cycadean stems have recently been found in great abundance in Jurassic and possibly higher strata in Wyoming, South Dakota, and other parts of the United States. Cycadean stems have been found also in the uppermost Jurassic, Wealden and Lower Cretaceous rocks of England, India and other parts of the world. An example of an Indian Cycadean stem from Upper Gondwana rocks is represented in fig. 13; the surface of the trunk is covered with persistent bases (fig. 13, A) of the fronds known as *Ptilophyllum cutchense*, which are practically the same as the European species *Williamsonia pecten* (fig. 17). In a section of the stem (fig. 13, B) a large pith is seen to occupy the axial region, and this is surrounded by a zone of secondary wood, which appears to differ from the characteristic wood of modern Cycads (see GYMNOSPERMS) in having a more compact structure. It is interesting to find that G. R. Wieland of

FIG. 11.—*Cycadites Saportae.* Wealden, England.

Yale University has noticed in some of the Cycadean stems from the Black hills of Dakota and Wyoming that the wood appears to possess a similar structure, differing in its narrower medullary rays from the wood of modern Cycads. The lozenge-shaped areas external to the axis of the stem represent the sections of petioles, some of which are shown in fig. 13, A, attached to the stem. The majority of Mesozoic stems agree in external appearance with those of recent species of *Encephalartos*, *Macrozamia*, and some other genera; the trunk is encased in a mass of persistent petiole-bases separated from one another by a dense felt or packing of scaly ramenta. The structure of the leaf-stalks is like that of modern

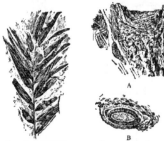

FIG. 12. — *Podozamites lanceolatus*. Inferior Oolite, England.

FIG. 13. — Cycadean stem, from Upper Gondwana rocks, India. A, Surface view; B, Transverse section of stem.

Cycads, but the ramenta, instead of having the form of long uni-cellular hairs like those on the petioles and bud-scales of existing species are exactly like the paleae or ramental scales characteristic of the majority of ferns. This fern-like character affords an interesting survival of the close relationship between Cycads and Ferns. Some examples of Jurassic Cycadean stems from Wyoming are characterized by an unusually rich development of ramental scales; the ramenta from the old leaf-bases form an almost complete covering over the surface of the trunk. Professor Lester Ward has instituted a new generic name, *Cycadella*, for these woolly forms. In a few cases the fossil stems show no trace of any lateral flowering shoots, and in that respect agree with modern forms: an instance of this is afforded by a large Cycadean trunk discovered some years ago in one of the Portland quarries, and named *Cycadeoidea gigantea* (fig 14). In this stem the flowers may have been terminal, as in existing Cycads. As a rule, however, the fossil stems show a marked difference from modern forms in the possession of lateral shoots given off from the axils of leaves, and terminating in a flower of complex structure containing numerous orthotropous seeds. These reproductive shoots differ in many important respects from the flowers of recent Cycads, and chiefly on this account it is customary to include the plants in a separate genus, *Bennettites*, and in a separate group—the Bennettitales—distinct from that of the Cycadales including the existing Cycads. The best preserved specimens of the true *Bennettites* type so far described are from the Lower Greensand and Wealden of England, and from Upper Mesozoic strata in North America, Italy and France. A study of the anatomical structure of the vegetative stem, which on the whole is very similar to that of recent Cycads (fig. 15, 1 and 2), reveals certain characters which are not met with in modern Cycads. The chief distinguishing feature is afforded by the leaf-traces in recent species (see GYMNOSPERMS)

FIG. 14. — *Cycadeoidea gigantea*. Portland rocks, England.

these pursue a somewhat complicated course as they pass from the petiole towards the vascular cylinder of the stem, but in *Bennettites* the vascular bundles from the leaves followed a more direct course through the cortex of the stem (fig 15, 3). Among existing types the genus *Macrozamia* appears to show the nearest approach to this simpler structure of the leaf-traces. In a Floridan species of *Zamia* the leaf-traces are described as characterized by a more direct course from the stele of the stem to the leaves than in most modern genera, thus agreeing more closely with the extinct *Bennettites*. The typical *Bennettites* female flower (fig 15, 4 and 7), as investigated in English, French, Italian, and American specimens, may be briefly described as a short lateral shoot or peduncle, arising in a leaf-axil and terminating in a bluntly rounded apex, bearing numerous linear bracts enclosing a central group of appendages, some of which consist of slender pedicels traversed by a vascular strand and bearing a single terminal ovule enclosed in an integument, which forms a distal canal or micropyle. Associated with these seminiferous pedicels occur sterile appendages consisting of slender stalks, terminating in distal expansions, which form a fleshy covering over the surface of the flower, leaving small apertures immediately above the micropyles for the entrance of the pollen-grains. It has been suggested by some authors that the almost complete investment of the small *Bennettites* seeds by the surrounding swollen ends of the interseminal scales (fig. 15, 7) represents an approach to the angiospermous ovary. In *Bennettites* the ovules are left exposed at the apex, but they are by no means so distinctly gymnospermous as in recent Cycads and Conifers. The seeds have in some cases been preserved in wonderful perfection, enabling one to make out the structure of the embryo, with its bluntly conical radicle and two fleshy cotyledons filling the exalbuminous seed (fig 15, 11).

Our knowledge of the reproductive organs of the Bennettitaceae has until recently been confined to the female flowers, as described by Carruthers, Solms-Laubach, Lignier, and others. The fortunate discovery of several hundred Cycadean stems in the United States, of Lower Cretaceous and Upper Jurassic age, has supplied abundant material which has lately been investigated and is still receiving attention at the hands of Mr Wieland. This investigator has already published a well-illustrated account of his discoveries, which give valuable information as to the morphology of the male organs, and lead us to expect additional results in the future of the greatest importance and interest. On some of the American stems flowers have been found, borne at the apex of lateral shoots, which possess fully developed male organs consisting of sporangia with spores (pollen-grains), surrounding a conical central receptacle bearing numerous small and probably functionless or immature ovules (fig. 15, 10). The structure of this type of flower may be briefly described as follows. In shape and size the flower is similar to that long known as the female flower of *Bennettites* and *Williamsonia*. A number of hairy linear bracts enclose the whole; internal to these occur 12 to 20 crowded pinnate leaves (sporophylls), with their apical portions bent over towards the axis of the flower, the bases of the petioles being fused together into a disk surrounding the base of the conical receptacle. Numerous pairs of pinnules are attached to the rachis of each sporophyll, and the larger pinnules bear 20 to 30 synangia (sori or plurilocular sporangia) (fig. 15, 8 and 9). The synangia consist of a stout wall composed of thick-walled cells, succeeded by a layer of more delicate and smaller elements; and internal to the wall occur two rows of sporangial loculi containing microspores. When the synangia are ripe dehiscence takes place along a median line between the two rows of loculi. The size, position, arrangement, and manner of dehiscence the sporangia bear a striking resemblance to those of *Marattia* and *Danaea* among recent Marattiaceae. The most important point elucidated by this discovery is the very close correspondence of the male organs of the *Bennettites* flower with the sporophylls and synangia of Marattiaceous ferns—a further relic of the common origin of Cycads and Ferns. It remains to be seen if the ovuliferous cone in the centre of the flower represents simply a functionless gynoecium, as in *Welwitschia* and abnormal cones of certain Coniferae, or if the flowers were hermaphrodite, with both male and female organs fully developed. We have a combination in the same flower of stalked ovules, the structure of which has already been described, and interseminal scales constituting a complex gynoecium, which exhibits in certain features an approach to the angiospermous type, and differs in structure from other Gymnosperm flowers, associated with male organs constructed on a plan almost identical with that of the sporophylls in Marattiaceae. In many of the flowers described by Mr Wieland the structure is identical in essential features with that of the female flowers of *Bennettites Gibsonianus* described by Carruthers and by Solms-Laubach, and with that of a French Liassic species described by Lignier: the whole consists of a convex receptacle bearing mature seeds at the tips of pedicels associated with interseminal scales (fig. 15, 7) as already described. Mr Wieland's researches have, however, demonstrated the existence in flowers of this type of the remains of a disk at the base of the receptacle, between the receptacle and the surrounding bracts, to which staminate leaves were originally attached. The flowers hitherto regarded as female were in some cases at least hermaphrodite, but the male organs had been thrown off before the complete development of the gynoecium. This fact suggests the possibility that the flowers described by Mr Wieland, in which the male organs are mature and the gynoecium is composed of very short and immature ovuliferous stalks and interseminal scales, are not essentially distinct from those which have lost the staminate leaves

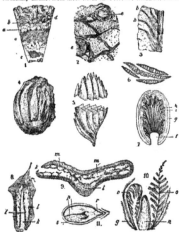

FIG. 15.

1, *Bennettites stem*: portion of transverse section of stem; *a*, vascular cylinder; *b*, leaf-traces; *c*, pith; *d*, cortex.
2, *Bennettites* stem, tangential section; *e*, flower-peduncles.
3, *Bennettites* stem, leaf-traces attached to the vascular cylinder and passing as simple strands through the cortex; *d*, cortex.
4, *Williamsonia*, Wealden, England.
5, Young leaf of *Bennettites*.
6, Ramenta of *Bennettites* in transverse section.
7, *Bennettites*, female flower in longitudinal section; *f*, apex of peduncle; *g*, bracts (shown in surface view in 4); *h*, seeds and seminiferous pedicels; *i*, interseminal scales.
8, *Bennettites*, synangium of male flower, showing line of dehiscence, *h*, and microspores, *l*.
9, Synangium, in transverse section, showing sporangial groups, *m*, and microspores, *l*.
10, *Bennettites* flower in vertical section, showing the central female portion, *n*, two sporophylls bearing synangia (male), *o*, and hairy bracts, *g*.
11, *Bennettites* seed in longitudinal section, showing the dicotyledonous embryo; *p*, cotyledons; *r*, radicle; *s*, testa.
(1–3, *after Carruthers*; 5, 8, 9 and 10, *after Wieland*; 7, *after Scott*; 11, *after Solms-Laubach*.)

and possess mature seeds. It is probable that the flowers of *Bennettites* were normally hermaphrodite, and they may have been markedly protandrous. We cannot decide at present whether the gynoecium in a flower, such as that represented in fig. 15, 7, has partially aborted or whether it would have matured later after the fall of the male organs.

It is clear that *Bennettites* differed in many essential respects from the few modern survivors of the Cycadophyta. Fossil flowers of a type more like that of modern Cycads are few in number, and it is not by any means certain that all of those described as Cycadean flowers and seeds were borne by plants which should be included in the Cycadophyta; a few female flowers have been described from Rhaetic rocks of Scania and elsewhere under the name *Zamiostrobus*—these consist of an axis with slender pedicels or carpophylls given off at a wide angle and bearing two ovules at the distal end; the structure is in fact similar to that of a *Zamia* female flower, in which the internodes of the peduncle have been elongated so as to give a looser arrangement to the carpels. It has been suggested

that one at least of the flowers, that originally described by Mr Carruthers from the Inferior Oolite of Yorkshire as *Beania gracilis*, may have been borne by a member of the Ginkgoales. From Jurassic rocks of France and Italy a few imperfect specimens have been described as carpels of Cycads, like those of the recent genus *Cycas* (see GYMNOSPERMS); while a few of these may have been correctly identified, an inspection of some of the original examples in the Paris collections leads one to express the opinion that others are too imperfect to determine. Pinnate fronds of the *Cycas* type, characterized by the presence of a midrib and no lateral veins in the linear pinnae, are recorded from Rhaetic rocks of Germany, from Wealden strata in England (fig. 11) and Portugal, and from Liassic beds in Dorsetshire. One large specimen is figured by Heer from Lower Cretaceous rocks of Greenland, and by the side of the frond is shown a carpel with lateral ovules, as in the female flower of *Cycas*; but an examination of the type-specimen in the Copenhagen Museum led the present writer to regard this supposed carpel as valueless. Professor Nathorst, as the result of a more recent examination of Heer's specimen, found that the segments of the frond are characterized by the presence of two parallel veins instead of a single midrib, with a row of stomata between them; for this type of Cycadean leaf he proposed the generic name *Pseudocycas*. Another well-known Cycadean genus is *Williamsonia*, so named by Mr Carruthers in 1870, and now applied to certain pinnate fronds—*e.g.* those previously described as *Zamites gigas* (fig. 16), and others known under such names as *Pterophyllum* or *Ptilophyllum pecten*, &c., both common Jurassic species—as well as to stems bearing peduncles with terminal oval flowers, similar in form to those of *Bennettites*. There is good evidence for supporting Professor Williamson's conclusions as to the organic connexion between the flowers, originally described from Inferior Oolite rocks of Yorkshire and subsequently named *Williamsonia* (fig. 15, 4), and the fronds of *Zamites gigas*, now known as *Williamsonia gigas* (fig. 16). There can be little doubt that the majority of the Cycadean fronds of Jurassic and Wealden age, which are nearly always found detached from the rest of

flowers known as *Williamsonia* were borne on the trunks which terminated in a centre of pinnate fronds of the type long known as *Zamites gigas*; this view was regarded by Saporta and others as incorrect, and the nature of the Bennettitean foliage was left an open question. A re-examination of the English material in the museums of Paris and elsewhere has confirmed Williamson's conclusions. Mr Wieland has also described young bipinnate fronds, very like those of recent species of *Zamia* and *Encephalartos*, attached to a *Bennettites* stem, and exhibiting the vernation characters of many recent Cycads (fig. 15, 5). In *Williamsonia* the stem bore comparatively long fertile shoots, which, in contrast to those of *Bennettites*, projected several inches beyond the surface of the main trunk, and terminated in a flower which appears to have resembled that of the true *Bennettites*. Nathorst has recently described specimens of *Williamsonia* from the Jurassic rocks of Whitby with micro-Sporophylls like those of Wieland's species. *Williamsonia* occurs in the Upper Gondwana rocks of India; it is recorded also from strata ranging from the Rhaetic to the Lower Cretaceous period in England, Portugal, Sweden, Bornholm, Greenland, Italy and North America. Professor Nathorst has described another type of stem from the Rhaetic beds of Scania. It consists of a comparatively small and repeatedly forked axis bearing in each fork a flower; the flowers, which are regarded as male and female, appear to be similar to those of *Bennettites*. The leaves, borne on the regions between the false dichotomies, are those of *Anomozamites minor*, a type of Cycadean frond originally determined by Brongniart. The flowers, or some of them, were originally described by Nathorst as *Williamsonia angustifolia*. This form of stem, of a habit entirely different from that of recent Cycads and extinct *Bennettites*, points to the existence in the Mesozoic era of another type of Gymnosperm allied to the Bennettitales of the Jurassic and Cretaceous periods by its flowers, but possessing a distinctive character in its vegetative organs. There is no doubt that the Cycadophyta, using the term suggested by Nathorst in 1902, was represented in the Mesozoic period by several distinct families or classes which played a dominant part in the floras of the world before the advent of the Angiosperms. In addition to the bisporangiate reproductive shoots of *Bennettites*, distinguished by many important features from the flowers of recent Cycads, a few specimens of flowers have been discovered exhibiting a much closer resemblance' to those of existing Cycads, *e.g. Androstrobus Balduini* from Bathonian rocks of France; *Zamites familiaris*, described many years ago by Corda, from Lower Cretaceous rocks of Bohemia, and *Androstrobus Nathorsti*, from Wealden beds in Sussex. The majority of the species were, however, characterized by flowers of a different type known as *Bennettites* and *Williamsonia*.

The living Maidenhair-tree (*Ginkgo biloba*) (see GYMNOSPERMS) remains, like *Matonia* and *Dipteris*, among the ferns, as an isolated relic in the midst *Ginkgoales.* of recent vegetation. In Rhaetic, Jurassic and Wealden floras, the Ginkgoales were exceedingly abundant (Map B, G_1–G_{11}); in addition to leaves agreeing almost exactly with those of the recent species (fig. 18), there are others separated as a distinct genus, *Baiera* (fig. 18, G), characterized by the greater number and narrower form of the segments, which may be best compared with such leaves as those of the recent fern *Actiniopteris* and of certain species of *Schizaea*. Male flowers, like those of *Ginkgo biloba*, but usually characterized by a rather larger number of oval pollen-sacs on the stamens, have been found in England, Germany, Siberia and elsewhere in association with *Ginkgo* and *Baiera* foliage. The occasional occurrence of three or even four pollen-sacs on the stamens of the recent species affords a still closer agreement between the extinct and living types. Seeds like those of *Ginkgo biloba* have also been recorded as fossils in Jurassic rocks, and it is possible that the type of flower known as *Beania*, from the Inferior Oolite rocks of Yorkshire, may have been borne by *Ginkgo* or *Baiera*.

FIG. 17.—Fronds of *Williamsonia pecten*.

The regions from which satisfactory examples of Ginkgoales (*Baiera* or *Ginkgo*) have been shown in Map B (G_1–G_{11}). Both Tertiary and Mesozoic localities are indicated in the map.

An adequate account of fossil Mesozoic Coniferae is impossible within the limits of this article. Coniferous twigs are very common in Mesozoic strata, but in most cases we are compelled **Coniferales.** to refer them to provisional genera, as the evidence of vegetative shoots alone is not sufficient to enable us to determine their position within the Coniferae. There are, however, several forms which it is reasonable to include in the Araucarineae; that this family was to the fore in the vegetation of the Jurassic period is unquestionable. We have not merely the striking resemblance of vegetative shoots to those of recent species of *Araucaria* and *Agathis*, *e.g.* species of *Nageiopsis*, abundantly represented in the Upper Jurassic beds of the Potomac area in North America, species of *Pagiophyllum* and other genera of Jurassic

and Wealden age, but an abundance of fossil wood (*Araucarioxylon*) from Jurassic and Cretaceous strata in Europe, North America, Madagascar and elsewhere agreeing with that of recent Araucarineae, in addition to several well-preserved female flowers.　C. A. Hollick

FIG. 18.—Leaves of Ginkgoales.

A, *Ginkgodium*, Japan (Jurassic).
B, C, D, E, F, H, *Ginkgo* leaves.—B, from Franz Josef Land (Jurassic);
　C, Greenland (Lower Cretaceous); D, Siberia (Jurassic); E, Germany
　(Wealden); F, England (Jurassic); H, China (Rhaetic).
G, *Baiera* leaf, Inferior Oolite, England.
(A, *after Yokoyama*; B, *after Nathorst*; C, D, *after Heer*; E. *after Schenk*;
　H, *after Krasser*. All the figures ½ nat. size.)

and E. C. Jeffrey have recently shown that some Lower Cretaceous specimens of the well-known genus *Brachyphyllum* obtained from Staten Island, N.Y., possess wood of the Araucarian type. This genus has long been known as a common and widely spread Jurassic and Cretaceous conifer, but owing to the absence of petrified specimens and of well-preserved cones, it has been impossible to refer it to a definite position in the Coniferales. It is now clear that some at least of the species of *Brachyphyllum* must be referred to the Araucarineae. In a recently published paper Seward and Ford have given a general account of the Araucarineae, recent and extinct, to which reference may be made for further details as to the geological history of this ancient section of the Coniferales. Some of the fossils referred to the genus *Kaidocarpon*, and originally described as monocotyledonous inflorescences, are undoubted Araucarian cones; other cones of the same type have been placed in the genus *Cycadeostrobus* and referred to Cycads. *Araucarites Hudlestoni*, described by Mr Carruthers from the Coralline Oolite rocks of Malton in Yorkshire; *Araucarites sphaerocarpa* from the Inferior Oolite of Somerset; also another cone found in the Northampton Sands, which is probably specifically identical with *A. Hudlestoni*, and named by Carruthers *Kaidocarpon ooliticum*, afford good illustrations of British Araucarian flowers. A flower of a rather different type, *Pseudaraucaria major*, exhibiting in the occurrence of two seeds in each scale an approach to the cones of Abietineae, has been described by Professor Fliche from Lower Cretaceous rocks of Argonne. The well-known Whitby jet of Upper Liassic age appears to have been formed to a large extent from Araucarian wood. Among the more abundant Conifers of Jurassic age may be mentioned such genera as *Thuytes* and *Cupressites*, which agree in their vegetative characters with members of the Cupressineae, but our knowledge of the cones is far from satisfactory. Many of the small female flowers borne on shoots with foliage of the *Cupressus* type consist of spirally disposed and not verticillate scales, *e.g. Thuytes expansus*, a common Jurassic species.

Fossil wood, described under the name *Cupressinoxylon*, has been recorded from several Mesozoic horizons in Europe and elsewhere, but this term has been employed in a wide sense as a designation for a type of structure met with not only in the Cupressineae, but in members of other families of Coniferae. The Abietineae do not appear to have played a prominent part before the Wealden period; various older species, *e.g.* Rhaetic specimens from Scania, are recorded, but it is not until we come to the Upper Jurassic and Wealden periods that this modern family was abundantly represented. Fossil wood of the *Pinites* type (*Pityoxylon*) has been described from England, France, Germany, Sweden, Spitsbergen, North America and elsewhere; some of the best British examples are obtained from the so-called Pine-raft, the remains of **water-logged and petrified wood of Lower Greensand age, seen at low water near Brook Point in the Isle of Wight. Well-preserved Abietineous female flowers have been obtained from the Wealden rocks of England and Belgium, *e.g. Pinites Dunkeri, P. Solmsi,* &c.; specimens of seeds and vegetative shoots are recorded also from Spitsbergen and other regions. Hollick and Jeffrey have recently added to our knowledge of the anatomy of Cretaceous** species of *Pinus*, and Miss Stopes and Dr Fujii have made important contributions on the structure of Cretaceous plants from Japan. Cones of Lower Cretaceous age have been described by Fliche from Argonne, which bear a close resemblance to the female flowers of recent species of *Cedrus*. The two surviving species of *Sequoia* afford an illustration of the persistence of an old type, but unfortunately most of the Mesozoic species referred to this genus do not possess sufficiently perfect cones to confirm their identification as examples of *Sequoia*. Some of the best examples of cones and twigs referred to *Sequoia* are those described by Heer from Cretaceous rocks of Greenland, and Professor D. P. Penhallow of Montreal has described the anatomical structure of the stem of *Sequoia Langsdorfi*, a Tertiary species occurring in Europe and North America.

There are a few points suggested by a general survey of the Mesozoic floras, which may be briefly touched on in conclusion. In following the progress of plant-life through those periods in the history of the earth of which records are left in ancient sediments, seams of coal or old land-surfaces, we recognise at certain stages a want of continuity between the floras of successive ages. The imperfection of the geological record, considered from the point of view of evolution, has been rendered familiar by Darwin's remarkable chapter in the *Origin of Species*. Breaks in the chain of life, as represented by gaps in the blurred and incomplete documents afforded by fragmentary fossils, are a necessary consequence of the general plan of geological evolution; they mark missing chapters rather than sudden breaks in an evolutionary series. On the other hand, a study of the plant-life of past ages tends to the conviction that too much stress may be laid on the imperfection of the geological record as a factor in the interpretation of palaeontological data. The doctrine of Uniformitarianism, as propounded by Lyell, served to establish geology on a firmer and more rational basis than it had previously possessed; but latterly the tendency has been to modify the Lyellian view by an admission of the probability of a more intense action of groups of forces at certain stages of the earth's history. As a definite instance a short review may be given of the evidence of palaeobotanical records as regards their bearing on plant-evolution. Starting with the Permo-Carboniferous vegetation, and omitting for the moment the Glossopteris flora, we find a comparatively homogeneous flora of wide geographical range, consisting to a large extent of arborescent lycopods, calamites, and other vascular cryptogams, plants which occupied a place comparable with that of Gymnosperms and Angiosperms in our modern forests; with these were other types of the greatest phylogenetic importance, which serve as finger-posts pointing to lines of evolution of which we have but the faintest signs among existing plants. Other types, again, which may be referred to the Gymnosperms, played a not unimportant part in the Palaeozoic vegetation. No conclusive proof has so far been adduced of the existence in those days of the Cycads, nor is there more than partial evidence of the occurrence of genera which can be placed with confidence in any of the existing families of Conifers. There are, moreover, no facts furnished by fossil plants in support of the view that Angiosperms were represented either in the low-lying forests or on the slopes of the mountains of the Coal period. Passing higher up the geological series, we find but scanty records of the vegetation that existed during the closing ages of the Permian period, and of the plants which witnessed the beginning of the Triassic period we have to be content with the most fragmentary relics. It is in rocks of Upper Triassic and Rhaetic age that abundant remains of rich floras are met with, and an examination of the general features of the vegetation reveals a striking contrast between the Lower Mesozoic plants and those of the Palaeozoic period. Arborescent Pteridophytes are barely represented, and such dominant types as *Lepidodendron*, *Sigillaria*, *Calamites* and *Sphenophyllum* have practically ceased to exist; Cycads and Conifers have assumed the leading rôle, and the still luxuriant fern vegetation has put on a different aspect. This description applies almost equally to the floras of the succeeding Jurassic and Wealden periods. The change to this newer type of vegetation was no doubt less sudden than it appears as read from palaeobotanical records, but the transition period between the Palaeozoic type of vegetation and that which flourished in the Lower Mesozoic

era, and continued to the close of the Wealden age, was probably characterised by rapid or almost sudden changes. In the southern hemisphere the Glossopteris flora succeeded a Lower Carboniferous vegetation with a rapidity similar to that which marked the passage in the north from Palaeozoic to Mesozoic floras. This apparently rapid alteration in the character of the southern vegetation took place at an earlier period than that which witnessed the transformation in the northern hemisphere. The appearance of a new type of vegetation in India and the southern hemisphere was probably connected with a widespread lowering of temperature, to which reference has already been made. It was from this Glossopteris flora that several types gradually migrated across the equator, where they formed part of the vegetation of more northern regions. The difference between the Glossopteris flora and those which have left traces in the Upper Gondwana rocks of India, in the Wianamatta and Hawkesbury beds of Australia, and in the Stormberg series of South Africa, is much less marked than that between the Permo-Carboniferous flora of the northern hemisphere and the succeeding Mesozoic vegetation. In other words, the change took place at an earlier period in the south than in the north. To return to the northern hemisphere, it is clear that the Wealden flora, as represented by plants recorded from England, France, Belgium, Portugal, Russia, Germany and other European regions, as also from Japan and elsewhere, carries on, with minor differences, the facies of the older Jurassic floras. It was at the close of the Wealden period that a second evolutionary wave swept over the vegetation of the world. This change is most strikingly illustrated by the inrush of Angiosperms, in the equally marked decrease in the Cycads, and in the altered character of the ferns. It would appear that in this case the new influence, supplied by the advent of Angiosperms, had its origin in the north. Unfortunately, our knowledge of the later floras in the southern hemisphere is very incomplete, but a similar transformation appears to have characterized the vegetation south of the equator. As to the nature of the chief factors concerned in the two revolutions in the vegetable kingdom, if it is admissible to use so strong a term, only a guess can be hazarded. Physical conditions no doubt played an important part, but whatever cause may have had the greatest share in disturbing the equilibrium of evolutionary forces, it would seem that the apparently sudden appearance of Cycads and other types at the close of the Palaeozoic period made a widespread and sudden impression on the whole character of the vegetation. At a later stage—in post-Wealden days—it was the appearance of Angiosperms, probably in northern latitudes, that formed the chief motive power in accelerating the transition in the facies of plant-life from that which marked what we have called the Mesozoic floras, to the vegetation of the Upper Cretaceous and Tertiary periods. With the advent of Angiosperms began, as the late marquis of Saporta expressed it, "Une révolution, ainsi rapide dans sa marche qu'universelle dans ses effets." From the floras of the Tertiary age we pass by gradual stages to those which characterize the present phase of evolutionary progress. Among modern floras we find here and there isolated types, such as *Ginkgo, Sequoia, Matonia, Dipteris* and the Cycads, persisting as more successful survivals which have held their own through the course of ages; these plants remain as vestiges from a remote past, and as links connecting the vegetation of to-day with that of the Mesozoic era.

AUTHORITIES.—*Glossopteris Flora*: Blanford, H. F., "On the age and correlation of the Plant-bearing Series of India, &c.," *Quarterly Journal Geol. Soc.* xxxi. (1875); Feistmantel, "Fossil Flora of the Gondwana System," *Mem. Geol. Surv. India*, vols. iii. &c. (1879, &c.); Seward, *Fossil Plants as Tests of Climate* (Cambridge, 1892), with bibliography; "The Glossopteris Flora," *Science Progress*, with bibliography; "On the Association of *Sigillaria* and *Glossopteris* in South Africa," *Q.J.G.S.*, vol. liii. (1897); E. A. N. Arber, *Catalogue of the Fossil Plants of the Glossopteris Flora in the Department of Geology* (British Museum), Nat. Hist., *Brit. Mus. Catalogue* (London, 1905), with full bibliography; Medlicott and Blanford, *Manual of the Geology of India* (2nd ed., Oldham, R., D., Calcutta, 1893); David, "Evidences of Glacial Action in Australia in Permo-Carboniferous time," *Q.J.G.S.*, vol. lii. (1896); Zeiller, *Éléments de paléobotanique* (Paris, 1900); Potonié, "Fossile Pflanzen aus deutsch und portugiesisch Ostafrika," *Deutsch-Ostafrika*, vii. (Berlin, 1900), with bibliography. *General* : Potonié, *Lehrbuch der Pflanzenpalaeontologie* (Berlin, 1899); Scott. *Studies in Fossil Botany* (1900); Seward, *Fossil Plants* (Cambridge: vol. i., 1898); vol. ii. 1910, with bibliography; Zeiller, " Revue des travaux de paléontologie végétale," *Rev. gén. bot.* (1903) et seq. Catalogue of the Mesozoic Plants in the British Museum, (*a*) " Wealden Flora," pts. i. and ii.; (*b*) " Jurassic Flora," pt. i. (1894–1901), pt. ii. (1904), with bibliography; " On the Structure and Affinities of *Matonia pectinata*, with Notes on the Geological History of the *Matonineae*," *Phil. Trans.* cxci. (1899); " On the Structure, &c., of *Dipteris*," ibid. cxciv. (1901, with bibliography; Seward and Ford, " The Araucarieae, recent and extinct," *Phil. Trans. R. Soc.* (London, 1906); G. R. Wieland, "American Fossil Cycads," *Publication Carnegie Instit.* (Washington, 1906); Nathorst, " Paläobotanische Mitteil.," *K. Svensk. Vetenskaps. Akad. Handl.* xlii., No. 5 (1907); *The Norwegian North-Polar Expedition*, iii. (1893–1896); " Fossil Plants from Franz Josef Land," L. F. Ward, " Status of the Mesozoic Floras of the United States," *Twentieth Ann. Rep. Geol. Survey* (Washington, 1900); Solms-Laubach, " Ueber das Genus *Pleuromeia*," *Bot. Zeit.* (1899); Newton and Teall, " Notes on a Collection of Rocks and Fossils from Franz Josef Land," *Q.J.G.S.* liii. (1897); Hollick and Jeffrey, " Studies of Cretaceous Coniferous remains," *Mem. New York Botanical Garden*, vol. iii. (1909); Stopes and Fujii, " Structure and Affinities of Cretaceous Plants," *Phil. Trans. R. Soc.* (1910). References to important papers on Mesozoic botany will be found in the bibliographies mentioned in the above list.   (A. C. Se.)

III.—Tertiary

After the Wealden period, and before the deposition of the lowest strata of the Chalk, so remarkable a change takes place in the character of the vegetation that this break *Lower Cretaceous.* must be taken as, botanically, the transition point from a Secondary to a Tertiary flora. A flora consisting entirely, with a single doubtful exception, of Gymnosperms and Cryptogams gives place to one containing many flowering plants; and these increase so rapidly that before long they seem to have crowded out many of the earlier types, and to have themselves become the dominant forms. Not only do Angiosperms suddenly become dominant in all known plant-bearing deposits of Upper Cretaceous age, but strangely enough the earliest found seem to belong to living orders, and commonly have been referred to existing genera. From Cretaceous times onwards local distribution may change; yet the successive floras can be analysed in the same way as, and compared with, the living floras of different regions. World-wide floras, such as seem to characterize some of the older periods, have ceased to be, and plants are distributed more markedly according to geographical provinces and in climatic zones. This being the case, it will be most convenient to discuss the Tertiary floras in successive order of appearance, since the main interest no longer lies in the occurrence of strange extinct plants or of transitional forms connecting orders now completely isolated.

The accurate correlation in time of the various scattered plant-bearing deposits is a matter of considerable difficulty, for plant-remains are preserved principally in lacustrine strata laid down in separate basins of small extent. This it is obvious must commonly be the case, as most leaves and fruits are not calculated to drift far in the sea without injury or in abundance; nor are they likely as a rule to be associated with marine organisms. Deposits containing marine fossils can be compared even when widely separated, for the ocean is continuous and many marine species are world-wide. Plants, on the other hand, like land and fresh-water animals, occupied areas which may or may not have been continuous. Therefore, without a knowledge of the physical geography of any particular period, we cannot know whether like or unlike floras might be expected in neighbouring areas during that period. If, however, we discover plant-bearing strata interstratified with deposits containing marine fossils, we can fix the period to which the plants belong, and may be able to correlate them in distinct areas, even though the floras be unlike. This clear stratigraphical evidence is, however, so rarely found that much uncertainty still remains as to the true age of several of the floras now to be described.

In rocks approximately equivalent to the Lower Greensand of England, or slightly earlier, Angiosperms make their first appearance; but as the only strata of this age in Britain are of marine origin, we have to turn to other countries for the evidence.

The earliest Angiosperm yet found in Europe is a single mono-cotyledonous leaf of doubtful affinities, named by Saporta *Alismacites primaevus* (fig. 1), and found in the Valenginian strata of Portugal. These deposits seem to be equivalent to British Wealden rocks, though in the latter, even in their upper part, no trace of Angiosperms has been discovered. No other undoubted Angiosperm has yet been discovered in Europe in strata of this age, but Heer records a poplar-like leaf from Urgonian strata, a stage newer than the Valenginian, in Greenland, and Saporta has described from strata of the same date in Portugal a Euphorbiaceous plant apparently closely allied to the living *Phyllanthus* and named by him *Choffatia Francheti* (fig. 2). We must turn to North America for a fuller knowledge of the earliest flowering-plants.

FIG. 1.—*Alismacites primaevus.*

In S. Dakota a remarkable series has been discovered, lying unmistakably between marine Upper Jurassic rocks below and Upper Cretaceous above. There has been a certain *American Cretaceous.* amount of confusion as to the exact strata in which the plants occur, but this has now been cleared up by the researches of Lester F. Ward, who has shown how the Secondary flora gives place to one of Tertiary character.

The lower strata—*i.e.* those most allied to the Jurassic—contain only Gymnosperms and Cryptogams. The next division (Dakota No. 2 of Meek and Hayden) contains Gymnosperms and Ferns of Neocomian types, or even of Neocomian species; but mingled with these occur a few dicotyledonous leaves belonging to four genera. The specimens are very fragmentary, and all that can be said is that one of the forms may be allied to oak, another to fig, a third to *Sapindus*, and the fourth may perhaps be near to elm. The " Potomac Formation " of Virginia and Maryland is doubtless also mainly of Neocomian age, for though it rests unconformably on much older strata, the successive floras found in it are so allied to those of S. Dakota as to leave little doubt as to the general homotaxis of the series. Lester Ward records no fewer than 737 distinct forms, consisting chiefly of Ferns, Cycads, Conifers and Dicotyledons, the Ferns and Cycads being confined mainly to the Older Potomac, while the Dicotyledons are principally represented in the Newer Potomac, though occurring more rarely even down to the base of the series. Six successive stages have been defined in the Potomac formation. The Mount Vernon beds, which occur about the middle of the series, have as yet yielded only a small number of species, though these include the most interesting early Angiosperms. Among them are recorded a *Cassuarina*, a leaf of *Sagittaria* (which however, as observed by Zeiller, may belong to *Smilax*), two species of poplar-like leaves with remarkably cordate bases, *Menispermites* (possibly a water-lily) and *Celastrophyllum* (perhaps allied to *Celastrus*). *Proteophyllum*, found in the same bed, and also in the Infra-Cretaceous of Portugal, seems to have belonged to a Proteaceous plant, though only leaves without fruits have yet been discovered in deposits of this early date. Whatever doubt may be left as to the exact botanical position of these early Lower Cretaceous Angiosperms, it is clear that both Monocotyledons and Dicotyledons are represented by several types of leaves, and that the flora extended over wide areas in North America and Greenland, and is found again at a few points in Europe. There is yet no clear evidence either of climatic zones or of the existence of geographical provinces during this period.

FIG. 2.—*Choffatia Francheti.*

The next strata, the Aquia Creek series, contain a well-marked dicotyledonous flora, in which both the form and nervation of the leaves begin to approximate to those of recent times. The leading characteristic of this Middle Potomac flora is the proportion of Dicotyledons. Notwithstanding this apparent passage-bed, there is a marked difference between the Older and the Newer Potomac floras, very few species passing from the one to the other. Only 15 out of 405 plants in the older series occur in the beds above though already more than 350 species have been determined from this newer series. The plants from the Amboy Clays, which form the most important division of the Newer Potomac series and were monographed in 1895 by J. S. Newberry, seem to belong to the commencement of the Upper Cretaceous period. It is remarkable that nearly 80% of the species are Dicotyledons, and that no Monocotyledons have been found. The mere enumeration of the genera will indicate how close the flowering plants are to living forms. Newberry records *Juglans*, *Myrica* (7 species), *Populus*, *Salix* (5 species), *Quercus*, *Planera*, *Ficus* (3 species), *Persoonia* and another extinct Proteaceous genus named *Proteoides*, *Magnolia* (7 species), *Liriodendron* (4 species), *Menispermites*, *Laurus* and allied plants, *Sassafras* (3 species), *Cinnamomum*, *Prunus*, *Hymenaea*, *Dalbergia*, *Bauhinia*, *Caesalpinia*, *Fontainea*, *Colutea* and other Leguminosae, *Ilex*, *Celastrus*, *Celastrophyllum* (10 species), *Acer*, *Rhamnites*, *Paliurus*, *Cissites*, *Tiliaephyllum*, *Passiflora*, *Eucalyptus* (5 species), *Hedera*, *Aralia* (8 species), *Cornophyllum*, *Andromeda* (4 species), *Myrsine*, *Sapotacites*, *Diospyros*, *Acerates*, *Viburnum* and various genera of uncertain affinities. The points that suggest themselves with regard to this flora are, that it includes a fair representation of the existing orders of warm-temperate deciduous trees; that the more primitive types—such as the *Amentaceae*—do not appear to preponderate to a greater extent than they do in the existing temperate flora; that the assemblage somewhat suggests American affinities; and that when we take into account deficient collecting, local conditions, and the non-preservation of succulent plants, there is no reason for saying that certain other orders must have been absent. The great rarity of Monocotyledons is a common characteristic of fossil floras known only, as this one is, from leaves principally belonging to deciduous trees. With regard to suggested American affinities, it must be borne in mind that the Neocomian Angiosperms are little known except in America and in Greenland, and that we therefore cannot yet say whether families now mainly American were not formerly of world-wide distribution. We know that this was the case with some, such as *Liriodendron*; and in *Eucalyptus* we see the converse, where a genus formerly American is now confined to a far distant region. The Neocomian flora has been collected from an area extending over about 30° of latitude; but there is little evidence of any corresponding climatic change. We cannot yet say, however, that the deposits are exactly contemporaneous, and the great climatic variations that have taken place in the northern hemisphere during the existence of our living flora should make us hesitate to correlate too nearly from the evidence of plants alone.

The highest division of the Dakota series (known as Dakota No. 1) which lies immediately beneath Upper Cretaceous strata with marine fossils, contains a flora so like that of the Tertiary deposits that only the clearest geological evidence has been considered sufficient to prove that Heer was wrong when he spoke of the plants as Miocene. These highest plant-bearing strata rest, according to Lester Ward, somewhat unconformably on the Dakota No. 2; they show also a marked difference in the included plants. The genera of Dicotyledons represented are *Quercus*, *Sassafras*, *Platanus*, *Celastrophyllum*, *Cissites*, *Viburnites*.

In the central parts of North America the lacustrine plant-bearing deposits are of enormous thickness, the Dakota series being followed by marine Cretaceous strata known as the Colorado and Montana groups, and these being succeeded conformably by a thousand feet or more of lacustrine shales, sandstones and coal-seams, belonging to the Laramie series. This also contains occasional marine Upper Cretaceous fossils, as well as reptiles of Cretaceous types. An extensive literature has grown up relating to these Laramie strata, for owing to the Tertiary aspect of the contained plants, geologists were slow to recognize that they could be truly contemporaneous and interbedded with others yielding Cretaceous animals. In addition to this, the earlier writers included in the Laramie series many deposits now known to be of later date and truly Tertiary, and the process of separation is even now only partially completed. It will be safest in these circumstances to accept as our guide to the true Laramie flora the carefully compiled "Catalogue" of F. H. Knowlton. According to this catalogue, the true Laramie flora includes about 250 species, more than half of which are deciduous forest trees, herbaceous Dicotyledons, Monocotyledons and Cryptogams, all being but poorly represented. Among the few Monocotyledons are leaves and fruits of palms, and traces of grasses and sedges. The Dicotyledons include several water-lilies, a somewhat doubtful *Trapa*, and many genera of forest trees still common in America. The genera best represented are *Ficus* (21 species), *Quercus* (16 species), *Populus* (11 species), *Rhamnus* (9 species), *Platanus* (8 species), *Viburnum* (7 species), *Magnolia* (6 species), *Cornus* (5 species), *Cinnamomum* (5 species), *Juglans* (4 species), *Acer* (4 species), *Salix* (4 species), *Aralia* (3 species), *Rhus* (3 species), *Sequoia* (3 species). Of trees now extinct in America, *Eucalyptus* and *Ginkgo* are perhaps the most noticeable. So large a proportion of the trees still belongs to the flora of North America that one is apt to overlook the fact that among the more specialized plants of one of the largest American orders, such as the *Compositae*, are still missing from strata belonging to the Cretaceous period.

The imperfection and want of continuity of the records in Europe have made it necessary in dealing with the Cretaceous floras for us to give the first place to America. But *European Cretaceous.* it is now advisable to return to Europe, where Upper Cretaceous plants are not uncommon, and the position of the deposits in the Cretaceous series can often be fixed accurately by their close association with marine strata belonging to definite subdivisions. As these divisions of Cretaceous time will have to be referred to more than once, it will be useful to tabulate them, thus showing which plant-beds seem to be referable to each, and what are the British strata of like age. It has not yet been found possible so closely to correlate the strata of Europe with those of America, where distance has allowed geographical differences in both fauna and flora to come into play; therefore, beyond the references to Lower or Upper Cretaceous, no classification of the American Cretaceous strata has here been given. In Europe the most commonly accepted divisions of the Cretaceous period are as follows:—

ENGLAND.	FRANCE, &c.
Wanting	Danian
Upper Chalk	Senonian
Middle Chalk	Turonian
Lower Chalk	
Upper Green-sand }	Cenomanian
Gault	Albian
	Aptian
Lower Green-sand	Valenginian
	Urgonian
Wealden	Neocomian

In the continental classification the deposits from the Gault downwards are grouped as Lower Cretaceous; but in Great Britain there is a strong break below the Gault and none above; and the Gault is therefore classed as Upper Cretaceous. The limits of the divisions in other places do not correspond, the British and continental strata often being so unlike that it is almost impossible to compare them. The doubt as to the exact British equivalent of the Valenginian strata of Portugal, which yield the earliest Dicotyledon, has already been alluded to. The plant-bearing deposits next in age, which have yielded Angiosperms, appear to belong to the Cenomanian, though from Westphalia a few species belonging to the Cryptogams and Gymnosperms, found in deposits correlated with the Gault, have been described by Hosius and von der Marck.

In Great Britain the whole of the Upper Cretaceous strata are of marine origin, and have yielded no land-plants beyond a few fir-cones, drift-wood and rare Dicotyledonous leaves in the Lower Chalk. Most of the deposits which have yielded Angiosperms of Cretaceous age in central Europe correspond in age with the English Upper Chalk (Senonian), but a small Cenomanian flora has been collected from the Unter Quader in Moravia. Heer described from this deposit at Moletein 13 genera, of which 7 are still living, containing 18 species, viz.: 1 fern, 4 Conifers, 1 palm, 2 figs, 1 *Credneria*, 2 laurels, 1 *Aralia*, 1 *Chondrophyllum* (of uncertain affinities), 2 magnolias, 2 species of *Myrtaceae* and a species of walnut. Saxony yields from strata of this period at Niederschoena 42 species, described by Ettingshausen. This small flora is most remarkable, for no fewer than 6 genera, containing 8 species, are referred to the *Proteaceae*. The Cenomanian flora of Bohemia is larger and equally peculiar. Among the Dicotyledons described by Velenovsky are the following: *Credneria* (5 species), *Araliaceae* (17 species), *Proteaceae* (8 species), *Myrica* (2 species), *Ficus* (5 species), *Quercus* (2 species), *Magnoliaceae* (5 species), *Bombaceae* (3 species), *Laurineae* (2 species), *Ebenaceae* (2 species), *Verbenaceae*, *Combretaceae*, *Sapindaceae* (2 species), *Camelliaceae*, *Ampelideae*, *Mimoseae*, *Caesalpineae* (5 species), *Eucalyptus* (2 species), *Pisonia*, *Phillyrea*, *Rhus*, *Prunus*, *Bignonia*,

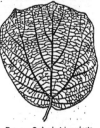

FIG. 3.—*Credneria triacuminata.*

Laurus, Salix, Benthamia. To this list Bayer adds *Aristolochia.*
The Cenomanian flora of central Europe appears to be a sub-
tropical one, with marked approaches to the living flora of Australia.
The majority of its Dicotyledons belong to existing genera, but
one of the most prolific and characteristic Cretaceous forms is *Credneria* (Fig. 3), a genus of doubtful affinities, which has been compared
by different authors to the poplars, planes, limes and other orders.

The Cretaceous plant-beds of Westphalia include both Upper
and Lower Senonian, the two floras being very distinct. Hosius
and von der Marck describe, for instance, 12 species of oak from
the Upper and 6 from the Lower strata, but no species is common
to the two. The same occurs with the figs, with 3 species above
and 8 below. The 6 species of *Credneria* are all confined to the older
deposits. In fact, not a single Dicotyledon is common to these
two closely allied divisions of the Cretaceous series; a circumstance
not easy to explain, when we see how well the oaks and figs are
represented in each. Four species of *Dewalquea*, a ranunculaceous
genus allied to the hellebore, make their appearance in the Upper
Senonian of Westphalia, other species occurring at Aix-la-Chapelle
in deposits of about the same age. The Senonian flora of the last-
named place, and that of Maestricht, are still only imperfectly
known. It is unnecessary to trace the variations of the Upper
Cretaceous flora from point to point; but the discoveries within
the Arctic circle have been so surprising that attention must again
be called to them. Besides the Lower Cretaceous plants already
mentioned, Heer has described from Greenland a flora of Cenomanian age, and another belonging to the Senonian. The Cenomanian strata have yielded already, 177 species, the different
groups being represented in these proportions: Cryptogams, 37, 30
of which are Ferns; Cycads, 8; Conifers, 27; Monocotyledons, 8; Ape-
talous Dicotyledons, 31; other Dicotyledons, 66. The Senonian strata
have yielded 118 species, 21 of which are Cryptogams, 12 Conifers,
5 Monocotyledons, 75 Dicotyledons. Forest trees, especially oaks,
are plentiful, and many of the species are identical with those found
in Cretaceous deposits in more southern latitudes. Both of these
floras suggest, however, that the climate of Greenland was somewhat colder than that of Westphalia, though scarcely colder than
warm-temperate.

The Cretaceous deposits just described are followed by a series
of Tertiary formations, but in Europe the continuity between
Cretaceous and Tertiary is not quite complete. The Tertiary
formations have been assigned to six periods; these are termed—
Paleocene, Eocene, Oligocene, Miocene, Pliocene, Pleistocene,
and each has its own botanical peculiarities.

During the Paleocene period the plants were not markedly
different from those of the Upper Cretaceous. Its flora is still
Paleocene but imperfectly known, for we are dependent on two
Plants. or three localities for the plants. There is found at
Sézanne, about 60 m. east of Paris, an isolated
deposit of calcareous tufa full of leaves, which gives a curious
insight into the vegetation which flourished in Paleocene times
around a waterfall. Sézanne yields Ferns in profusion, mingled
with other shade-loving plants such as would grow under the
trees in a moist ravine; its vegetation is comparable to that of
an island in the tropical seas. Monocotyledons are rare, the
only ones of much interest being some fragments of pandanaceous
leaves. The absence of Gymnosperms is noticeable. The
Proteaceae are also missing; but other Dicotyledons occur in
profusion, many of them being remarkable for the large size
of their deciduous leaves. Among the flowering plants are
Dewalquea, a ranunculaceous genus already mentioned as
occurring in the Upper Cretaceous, and numerous living genera
of forest-trees, such as occur throughout the Tertiary period,
and are readily comparable with living forms. Saporta has
described about seventy Dicotyledons, most of which are peculiar
to this locality.

The plant-bearing marls of Gelinden, near Liège, contain the
débris of a Paleocene forest. The trees seemed to have flourished
on neighbouring chalky heights. The most abundant species of
this forest were the oaks and chestnuts, of which a dozen have
been collected; laurels, *Viburnum*, ivy, several Aralias, *Dewalquea*,
a *Thuja* and several Ferns may be added. This flora is composed
by Saporta and Marion with that of southern Japan. Other deposits of this age in France have furnished plants of a more varied
aspect, including myrtles, araucarias, a bamboo and several fan-
leaved palms. Saporta points out the presence in these Paleocene
deposits of certain types common, on the one hand, to the American
Tertiary strata between the Missouri and the Rocky Mountains,
and on the other, to the Tertiary flora of Greenland. The Paleocene
deposits of Great Britain are of marine origin, and only yield pine-
cones and fragments of *Osmunda.*

The British Eocene and Oligocene strata yield so large a flora,
and contain plant-beds belonging to so many different stages,
that it is unfortunate we have still no monograph
on the subject, the one commenced by Ettingshausen *Eocene and*
and Gardner in 1879 having reached no farther than *Oligocene*
the Ferns and Gymnosperms. This deficiency *of Great*
makes it impossible to deal adequately with the *Britain.*
British Eocene plants, most of the material being either
unpublished or needing re-examination.

In the earliest Eocene plant-beds, in the Woolwich and Reading
series, a small but interesting flora is found, which suggests a temperate climate less warm than that of earlier or of later periods.
Leaves of planes are abundant, and among the plants recorded are
two figs, a laurel, a *Robinia*, a *Grevillea* and a palm. Ferns are scarce,
Ettingshausen and Gardner recording only *Anemia subcretacea* and
Pteris (?) *Prestwichii.* The only Gymnosperms determined are
Libocedrus adpressa, which is close to *L. decurrens* of the Yosemite,
and *Taxodium europaeum.* A few plants have been found in the
next stage, the Oldhaven beds, and among these are fig and
cinnamon. Gardner considers the plants to point to subtropical
conditions. The London Clay has yielded a large number of plants,
but most of the species are represented by fruits alone, not by
leaves. This circumstance makes it difficult to compare the flora
with that of other formations, for not only is it uncertain which
leaves and fruits belong to the same plant, but there is the additional
source of doubt, that different elements of the same flora may be
represented at different localities. Of some plants only the deciduous leaves are likely to be preserved, whilst other succulent-
leaved forms will only be known from their woody fruits. Among
the 200 plants of the London Clay are no Ferns, but 6 genera of
Gymnosperms—viz. *Callitris* (2 species), *Sequoia*, *Athrotaxis* (?)
Ginkgo, *Podocarpus*, *Pinus*; and several genera of palms, of which
the tropical *Nipa* is the most abundant and most characteristic,
among the others being fan-palms of the genera *Sabal* and *Chamaerops.* The Dicotyledons need further study. Among the fruits
Ettingshausen records *Quercus*, *Liquidambar*, *Laurus*, *Nyssa*,
Diospyros, *Symplocos*, *Magnolia*, *Victoria*, *Highlea*, *Sapindus*,
Cupania, *Eugenia*, *Eucalyptus*, *Amygdalus*; he suggests that the
fruits of the London Clay of Sheppey may belong to the same
plants as the leaves found at Alum Bay in the Isle of Wight.

The next stage is represented by the Lower Bagshot leaf-beds
of Alum Bay. These pipeclays yield a varied flora, Ettingshausen
recording 274 species, belonging to 116 genera and 63 families.
Gardner, however, is unable to reconcile this estimated richness
with our knowledge of the flora, and surmises that fossil plants
from other localities must have been inadvertently included. He
considers the flora to be the most tropical of any that has so far
been studied in the northern hemisphere. Its most conspicuous
plants are *Ficus Bowerbankii*, *Aralia primigenia*, *Comptonia
acutiloba*, *Dryandra Bunburyi*, *Cassia Ungeri* and the fruits of
Caesalpinia. The floras which it chiefly resembles are first, that
of Monte Bolca, and second, that of the Gres du Soissonais, which
latter Gardner thinks may be of the same age, and not earlier, as
is generally supposed. The total number of species found at Alum
Bay, according to this author, is only about 50 or 60.

To the Bagshot Sand succeeds the thick mass of sands with
intercalated plant-beds seen in Bournemouth cliffs. Each bed
yields peculiar forms, the total number of species amounting to
many hundred, most of them differing from those occurring in the
strata below. The plants suggest a comparison of the climate
and forests with those of the Malay Archipelago and tropical
America. At one place we find drifted fruits of *Nipa*, at another
Highlea and *Anona.* Other beds yield principally palms, willows,
laurels, *Eucalyptus* or Ferns; but there are no Cycads. As showing
the richness of this flora, we may mention that in the only orders
which have yet been monographed, Ferns are represented by 17
species and Gymnosperms by 10, though these are not the groups
best represented. Gardner speaks of the Bournemouth flora as
appearing to consist principally of trees or hard-wooded shrubs,
comparatively few remains of the herbaceous vegetation being
preserved. The higher Eocene strata of England—those above the
Bournemouth Beds—are of marine origin, and yield only drifted
fruits, principally fir-cones.

In the volcanic districts of the south-west of Scotland and the
north-east of Ireland plant-beds are found intercalated between
the lava-flows. These also, like the lignites of Bovey Tracey,
have been referred to the Miocene period, on the supposed evidence
of the plants; but more recent discoveries by Gardner tend to
throw doubt on this allocation, and suggest that, though of various
ages, the first-formed of these deposits may date back to early Eocene
times. The flora found in Mull points distinctly to temperate
conditions; but it is not yet certain whether this indicates a different
period from the subtropical flora of the south of England, or whether
the difference depends on latitude or local conditions. The plants
include a Fern, *Onoclea hebridica*, close to a living American form;
four Gymnosperms belonging to the genera *Cryptomeria*, *Ginkgo*,

Taxus and *Podocarpus*; Dicotyledons of about 30 species, several of which have been figured. Among the Dicotyledons may be mentioned *Platanus*, *Acer* (?), *Quercus* (?), *Viburnum*, *Alnus*, *Magnolia*, *Cordylus* (?), *Castanea* (?), *Zizyphus*, *Populus* and the nettle-like *Boehmeria antiqua*. The absence of the so-called cinnamon-leaves and the *Smilaceae*, which always enter into the composition of Middle Eocene and Oligocene floras, is noticeable. The Irish strata yield two ferns; 7 Gymnosperms, *Cupressus*, *Cryptomeria*, *Taxus*, *Podocarpus*, *Pinus* (2 species), *Tsuga*; and leaves of about 25 Dicotyledons. The most abundant leaf, according to Gardner, does not seem distinct from *Celastrophyllum Benedeni*, of the Palaeocene strata of Gelinden; a water-lily, *Nelumbium Buchii*, occurs also in Oligocene beds on the Continent; the species of *MacClintockia* (fig. 4) is found both in the Arctic floras and at Gelinden. Among the other plants are an alder, an oak and a doubtful cinnamon.

Leaving these Scottish and Irish deposits of doubtful age, we find in the Hampshire Basin a thick series of fluviatile, lacustrine and marine deposits undoubtedly of *Lower* and *Middle* Oligocene date. Their flora is still a singularly poor one, though plants have been obtained at many different levels; they perhaps indicate a somewhat cooler climate than that of the Bournemouth series. Among the more abundant plants are nucules of several species of *Chara*, and drifted fruits and seeds of water-lilies, of *Folliculites* (now generally referred to *Stratiotes*) and of *Limnocarpus* (allied to *Potamogeton*); there is little else mixed with these. Other seams are full of the twigs and cones of *Athrotaxis*, a Conifer now confined to Tasmania. Ferns are represented by *Gleichenia*, *Lygodium* and *Chrysodium Lanssdownum*, which last has a very wide range in time; Monocotyledons, by a Sabal

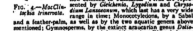

Fig. 4.—*MacClintockia trinervata*.

and a feather-palm, as well as by the two aquatic genera above mentioned; Gymnosperms, by the extinct araucarian genus *Doliostrobus*, by rare pine-cones, and by *Athrotaxis*. Dicotyledonous leaves are not plentiful, the genera recorded being *Andromeda*, *Cinnamomum*, *Zizyphus*, *Rhus*, *Viburnum*.

The lignite deposits and pipe-clays of Bovey Tracey in Devon, referred by Heer and Pengelly to the Miocene period, were considered by Gardner to be of the same age as the Bournemouth beds (Middle Eocene). Recent researches show, however, that Heer's view was more nearly correct. The flora of Bovey is like that of the lignite of the Wetterau, which is either highest Oligocene or lowest Miocene. Several species of *Nyssa* are common to the two districts, as are a climbing palm, two vines, a magnolia, &c. The common tree at Bovey is *Sequoia Couttsiae*, which probably grew in profusion in the sheltered valleys of Dartmoor, close to the lake. Above these strata in Great Britain there is a complete break, no species of plant ranging upwards into the next fossiliferous division.

Space will not allow us to deal with the numerous scattered deposits which have yielded Tertiary plants. It will be more to the purpose to take distant areas, where the order of the strata is clear, and compare the succession of the floras with *Central and Southern France.* that met with in other geographical regions and in other latitudes. For this study it will be most convenient to take next south and central France, for in that area can be found a series of plant-bearing strata in which is preserved a nearly continuous history of the vegetation from Upper Eocene down to Pliocene. The account is taken mainly from the writings of Saporta.

The gypsum-deposit of Upper Eocene date at Aix in Provence commences this series, and is remarkable for the variety and perfect preservation of its organic remains. Among its Gymnosperms are numerous *Cupressineae* of African affinity, belonging to the genera *Callitris* and *Widdringtonia*, and a juniper close to one indigenous in Greece. Fan-palms, several species of dragon-tree and a banana, like one living in Abyssinia, represent the more peculiar Monocotyledons. Among the noticeable Dicotyledons are the *Myricaceae*, *Proteaceae*, *Laurineae*, *Bombax*, the Judas-tree, *Acacia*, *Ailanthus*, while the most plentiful forms are the *Araliaceae*. Willows and poplars, with a few other plants of more temperate regions, are found rarely at Aix, and seemingly point to casual introduction from surrounding mountains. In a general way, spiny plants, with stiff branches and dry and coriaceous leaves, dominate the

flora, as they now do in Central Africa, to which region on the whole Saporta considers the flora to be most allied.

The succeeding Oligocene flora appears to be more characterized by a gradual replacement of the Eocene species by allied forms, than by any marked change in the assemblage or in the climatic conditions. It forms a perfectly gradual transition to the still newer Miocene period, the newer species slowly appearing and increasing in number. Saporta considers that in central and southern Europe the alternate dry and moist heat of the Eocene period gave place to a climate more equally and more universally humid, and that these conditions continued without material change into the succeeding Miocene stage. Among the types of vegetation which make their appearance in Europe during the Oligocene period may be mentioned the Conifers *Libocedrus salicornioides*, several species of *Chamaecyparis* and *Sequoia*, *Taxodium distichum* and *Glyptostrobus europaeus*. The palms include *Sabal haeringiana*, *S. major* and *Flabellaria*. Among the *Myricaceae* several species of *Comptonia* are common. These new-comers are all of American type. Aquatic plants, especially water-lilies, are abundant and varied; the soil-dry *Callitris* and *Widdringtonia* become scarce.

Though we do not propose to deal with the other European localities for Eocene and Oligocene plants, there is one district to which attention should be drawn, on account of *Plants in Amber.* the exceptional state of preservation of the specimens. On the Baltic shores of Prussia there is found a quantity of amber, containing remains of insects and plants. This is derived from strata of Oligocene age; and is particularly valuable because it preserves perfectly various soft parts of the plants, which are usually lost in fossil specimens. The tissues, in fact, are preserved just as they would be in Canada balsam. The amber yields such things as fallen flowers, perfect catkins of oak, pollen grains and fungi. It enables us to determine accurately orders and genera which otherwise are unknown in the fossil state, and it thus aids us in forming a truer idea of the flora of the period than can be formed at any locality where the harder parts alone are recognizable. No doubt this amber flora is still imperfectly known, but it is valuable as giving a good idea of the vegetation, during Oligocene times, of a mixed wood of pine and oak, in which there is a mixture of herbaceous and woody plants, such as would now be found under similar conditions.

The plants of which the floral organs or perfect fruits are preserved include the amber-bearing *Pinus succinifera*, *Smilax*, *Phoenix*, the spike of an aroid, 11 species of oak, 2 of chestnut, a beech, *Urticaceae*, 2 cinnamons and *Trianthera* among the *Lauraceae*, representatives of the *Cistaceae*, *Ternstroemiaceae*, *Dilleniaceae* (3 species of *Hibbertia*), *Geraniaceae* (*Geranium* and *Erodium*), *Oxalidaceae*, *Acer*, *Celastraceae*, *Olacaceae*, *Pittosporaceae*, *Ilex* (2 species), *Euphorbiaceae*, *Umbelliferae* (*Chaerophyllum*), *Saxifragaceae* (3 genera), *Hamamelidaceae*, *Rosaceae*, *Connaraceae*, *Ericaceae* (*Andromeda* and *Clethra*), *Myrsinaceae* (3 species), *Rubiaceae*, *Sambucus* (2 species), *Santalaceae*, *Loranthaceae* (3 species). We here discover for the first time various living families and genera, but there is still a noticeable absence of many of our most prolific existing groups. Whether this deficiency is accidental or real time will show.

The Miocene flora, which succeeds to that just described, is well represented in Europe; but till recently there has been an unfortunate tendency to refer Tertiary floras of all *Miocene.* dates to the Miocene period, unless the geological position of the strata was so clear as obviously to forbid this assignment. Thus plant-beds in the basalt of Scotland and Ireland were called Miocene; and in the Arctic regions and in North America even plant-beds of Upper Cretaceous age were referred to the same period. The reason for this was that some of the first Tertiary floras to be examined were certainly Miocene, and, when these plants had been studied, it was considered that somewhat similar assemblages found elsewhere in deposits of doubtful geological age must also be Miocene. For a long time it was not recognized that changes in the marine fauna, on which our geological classification mainly depends, correspond scarcely at all with changes in the land plants. It was not suspected, or the fact was ignored, that the break between Cretaceous and Tertiary—made so conspicuous by striking changes in the aquatic animals—had little or no importance in botanical history. It was not realized that an Upper Cretaceous flora needed critical examination to distinguish it from one of Miocene age, and that the two periods were not characterized by a sweeping change of generic type, such as took place among the marine invertebrates. It may appear absurd to a geologist that any one could mistake a Cretaceous flora for one of Miocene date, since the marine animals are completely different and the differences are striking. In the case of the plants, however, the Tertiary generic types in large part appeared in Upper Cretaceous times. Few or no extinct types are to be found in these older strata—there is nothing among the plants equivalent to the unmistakably extinct *Ammonites*, *Belemnites*, and a hundred other groups, and we only meet with constant variations in the same genus or family, these variations having seldom any obvious relation to phylogeny.

The Miocene period is unrepresented by any deposits in Great Britain, unless the Bovey lignite should belong to its earliest stage; we will therefore commence with the best known region—that of central Europe and especially of Switzerland, whence a prolific flora has been collected and described by Oswald Heer. The Miocene lacustrine deposits are contained in a number of silted-up lake-basins, which were successively formed and obliterated during the uprise of the Alps and the continuous folding and bending of the earth's crust which was so striking a feature of the period. These undulations tended to transform valleys into chains of lakes, into which the plants and animals of the surrounding area fell or were washed. We thus find preserved in the Upper Miocene lacustrine deposits of Switzerland a larger flora than is known from any other period of similar length; in fact, an analysis of its composition suggests that the Miocene flora of Switzerland must have been both larger and more varied than that now living in the same country. The best known locality for the Upper Miocene plants is Oeningen, on the Lake of Constance, where have been collected nearly 500 species of plants, the total number of Miocene plants found in Switzerland being stated to be now over 900. Among the characteristics of this Miocene flora are the large number of families represented, the marked increase in the deciduous-leaved plants, the gradual decrease in the number of palms and of tropical plants, and the replacement of these latter by Mediterranean or North American forms. According to Heer, the tropical forms in the Swiss Miocene agree rather with Asiatic types, while the subtropical and temperate plants are allied to forms now living in the temperate zone in North America. Of the 920 species described by Heer, 114 are Cryptogams and 806 flowering plants. Mosses are extremely rare, Heer only describing 3 species. Vascular Cryptogams still include one or two large horsetails with stems over an inch thick, and also 37 species of Fern; amongst the most interesting of which are 5 species belonging to the climbing *Lygodium*, a genus now living in Java. The number of Ferns is just equal to that now found in Switzerland. Cycads are only represented by fragments of two species, and this seems to be the last appearance of Cycads in Europe. The Coniferae include no fewer than 94 species of *Cupressineae* and 17 of *Abietineae*, including several species of *Sequoia*. Monocotyledons form one-sixth of the known Miocene flora, 25 of them being grasses and 39 sedges; but most of these need further study, and are very insufficiently characterized. Heer records one species of rice and four of millet. Most of the other Monocotyledons call for little remark, though among them is an *Iris*, a *Bromelia* and a ginger. *Smilax*, an earlier times, was common. Palms, referred to 11 species, are found, though they seem to have decreased in abundance; of them 7 are fan-palms, the others including *Phoeniciles*—form allied to the date—and a trailing palm, *Calamopsis*, allied to the canes and rattans. Among the Dicotyledons, the *Leguminosae* take the first place with 131 species, including *Acacia*, *Caesalpinia* and *Cassia*, each represented by several forms. The occurrence of 90 species of *Amentaceae* shows that; as the climate became less tropical, the relative proportion of this group to the total flora increased. Evergreen oaks are a marked characteristic of the period, more than half the Swiss species being allied to living American forms. Fig-trees referred to 17 species occur, all with undivided leathery leaves; one is close to the banyan, another to the indiarubber-tree. The *Laurineae* were plentiful, and include various true laurels, camphor-trees, cinnamon, *Persea* and *Sassafras*. The *Proteaceae*, according to Heer, are still common, the Australian genera *Hakea*, *Dryandra*, *Grevillea* and *Bankria*, being represented. Amongst gamopetalous plants several of our largest living families, including *Campanulaceae*, *Labiatae*, *Solanaceae* and *Primulaceae*, are still missing; and of *Borogineae*, *Scrophularineae*, *Gentianeae* and *Caprifoliaceae* there are only faint and doubtful indications. The *Compositae* are represented by isolated fruits of various species. Twining lianas met met with in a species of *Bignonia*; *Umbelliferae Ranunculaceae* and *Cruciferae*, are represented by a few fruits. These families, however, do not appear to have had anything like their present importance in the temperate flora, though, as they are mainly herbaceous plants with fruits of moderate hardness, they may have decayed and left no trace. The American *Liriodendron* still flourished in Europe. Water-lilies of the genera *Nymphaea* and *Nelumbium* occur. Maples were still plentiful, 20 species

having been described. *Rosaceae* are rare, *Crataegus*, *Prunus* and *Amygdalus*, being the only genera recorded. It is obvious that many of these Swiss Miocene plants will need more close study before their specific characters, or even their generic position, can be accepted as thoroughly made out; still, this will not affect the general composition of the flora, with its large proportion of deciduous trees and evergreens, and its noticeable deficiency in many of our largest living families.

From Europe it will be convenient to pass to a distant region of similar latitude, so that we may see to what extent botanical provinces existed in Eocene and Oligocene times. It so happens that the interior of temperate North America is almost the only region outside Europe in which a series of plant-bearing strata give a connected history of these periods, and in which the plants have been collected and studied. It is unfortunately still very difficult to correlate even approximately the strata on the two sides of the Atlantic, and there is great doubt as to what strata belong to each division of the Tertiary period even in different parts of North America. This difficulty will disappear as the strata become better known; but at present each of the silted-up lakes has to be studied separately, for we cannot expect so close a correspondence in their faunas and floras as is found in the more crowded and smaller basins in central Europe. *[marginal note: Tertiary of North America]*

Perhaps the most striking characteristic of the Tertiary floras of North America, as distinguished from those of Europe, is the greater continuity in their history and greater connexion with the existing flora of the same regions. This difference is readily explained when we remember that in Europe the main barriers which stop migration, such as the Alps and the Mediterranean, run east and west, while in America the only barriers of any importance run north and south. In consequence of this peculiarity, climatic or orographic changes in Europe tend to drive animals and plants into a cul de sac, from which there is no escape; but in America similar climatic waves merely cause the species alternately to retreat and advance. This difficulty in migration is probably the reason why the existing European flora is so poor in large-fruited trees compared with what it was in Miocene times or with the existing flora of North America. In America the contrast between the Eocene forests and those now living is much less striking, and this fact has led to the wrong assumption that the present American flora had its origin in the American continent. Such a conclusion is by no means warranted by the facts, for in Tertiary times, as we have seen, the European flora had a distinctly "American" facies. Therefore the so-called American forms may have originated in the Old World, or more probably, as Saporta suggests, in the polar regions, whence they were driven by the increase of cold southwards into Europe and into America. The American Tertiary flora is so large, and the geology of the deposits is so intricate, that it is out of the question to discuss them more fully within the limits of this article. We may point out, however, that the early Tertiary floras seem to indicate a much closer connexion and a greater community of species than is found between the existing plants of Europe and America. Or, rather, we should perhaps say that ancient floras suggest recent dispersal from the place of origin, and less time in which to vary and become modified by the loss of different groups in the two continents. Geographical provinces are certainly indicated by the Eocene flora of Europe and America, but these are less marked than those now existing.

If we turn to a more isolated region, like Australia, we find a Lower Eocene flora distinctly related to the existing flora of Australia and not to that of other continents. Australasia had then as now a peculiar flora of its own, though the former wide dispersal of the Proteaceae and Myrtaceae, and also the large number of Amentaceae then found in Australia, make the Eocene plants of Europe and Australia much less unlike than are the present floras. *[marginal note: Australia]*

Within the Arctic circle a large number of Tertiary plants have been collected. These were described by Heer, who referred them to the Miocene period; he recognized, in fact, two periods during which Angiosperms flourished within the Arctic regions, the one Upper Cretaceous, the other Miocene. To this view of the Miocene age of the plant-bearing strata in Greenland and Spitsbergen there are serious objections, which we will again refer to when the flora has been described. *[marginal note: Arctic Regions]*

The Tertiary flora of Greenland is of great interest, from the extremely high latitude at which the plants flourished, thirty of the species having been collected so far north as lat. 81°. Taking first this most northerly locality, in Grinnell Land, we find the flora to comprise 2 horsetails, 11 Conifers (including the living *Pinus Abies*), 2 grasses, a sedge, 2 poplars, a willow, 3 birches, 2 hazels, an elm, a *Viburnum*, a water-lily, and a lime. Such an assemblage at the present day would suggest a latitude quite 25° farther south; but it shows decidedly colder conditions than any of the European Eocene, Oligocene, or Miocene strata. From lat. 78° in Spitsbergen Heer records 136 species of fossil plants. More to the south, at Disco Island in lat. 70°, the Tertiary wood seem to have been principally composed of planes and Sequoias; but a large number of other genera occur, the total number of p ants already recorded being 137. From various parts of Greenland they now amount to at least 280. Among the plants from Disco, more than a quarter are also found in the Miocene of central Europe. The plants of Disco include, besides the plane and Sequoia, such warm-temperate trees as *Ginkgo*, oak, beech, poplar, maple, walnut, lime and magnolia. If these different deposits are contemporaneous, as is not improbable, there is a distinct change in the flora as we move farther from the pole, which suggests that difference of latitude then as now was accompanied by a difference in the flora. But if this process is continuous from latitude to latitude, then we ought not to look for a flora of equivalent age in the warm-temperate Miocene deposits of central Europe, but should rather expect to find that the temperate plants of Greenland were contemporaneous with a tropical flora in central Europe. As Mr Starkie Gardner has pointed out, it does not seem reasonable to assume that the same flora could have ranged then through 40° of latitude; it is more probable that an Eocene temperate flora found in the Arctic regions travelled southwards as the climate became cooler, till it became the Miocene temperate flora of central Europe. Mr Gardner suggests, therefore, that the plant-beds of Greenland and Spitsbergen represent the period of greatest heat, and are therefore wrongly referred to the Miocene. At present the evidence is scarcely sufficient to decide the question, for if this view is right, we ought to find within the Arctic circle truly Arctic floras equivalent to the cool Lower Eocene and Miocene periods; but these have not yet been met with.

A steady decrease of temperature marked the Pliocene period throughout Europe, and gradually brought the climatic conditions into correspondence with those now existing, *Pliocene.* till towards the end of the period neither climate nor physical geography differed greatly from those now existing. Concurrently with this change, the tropical and extinct forms disappeared, and the flora approached more and more nearly to that now existing in the districts where the fossil plants are found, though in the older deposits, at any rate, the geographical distribution still differed considerably from that now met with. At last, in the latest Pliocene strata (often called " pre-Glacial ") we find a flora consisting almost entirely of existing species belonging to the Palaearctic regions, and nearly all still living in the country where the fossils are found. This flora, however, is associated with a fauna of large mammals, the majority of which are extinct.

The plants of the Older Pliocene period are unknown in Great Britain, and little known throughout Europe except in central France and the Mediterranean region. The forests of central France during this epoch showed, according to Saporta, a singular admixture of living European species, with trees now characteristic of the Canary Isles and of North America. For instance, of the living species found at Meximieux, near Lyons, one is American, eight at least belong to the Canaries (six being characteristic of those islands), two are Asiatic, and ten still live in Europe. Taking into account, however, the closest living allies of the fossil plants, we find about equal affinities with the floras of Europe, America, and Asia. There is also a decided resemblance to the earlier Miocene flora. Among the more interesting plants of this deposit may be mentioned *Torreya nucifera*, now Japanese; an evergreen oak close to the common *Quercus Ilex*; *Laurus canariensis*, *Apollonias canariensis*, *Persea carolinensis*, and *Ilex canariensis*; *Daphne pontica* (a plant of Asia Minor); a species of box, scarcely differing from the English, and a bamboo. To this epoch, or perhaps to a stage slightly later, and not to the Newer Pliocene period, as is generally supposed, should probably be referred the lignite deposits of the Val d'Arno. This lignite and the accompanying leaf-bearing clays underlie and are apparently older than the strata with Newer Pliocene mammals and mollusca. The only mammal actually associated with the plants appears to be a species of tapir, a genus which in Europe seems to be characteristically Miocene and Older Pliocene. The plants of the Val d'Arno have been described by Ristori; they consist mainly of deciduous trees, a large proportion of which are known Miocene and early Pliocene forms, nearly all of them being extinct. A markedly upland character is given to the flora of this valley through the abundance of pines (9 species) and oaks (16 species) which it contains; but this peculiarity is readily accounted for by the steep slopes of the Apennines, which everywhere surround and dominate the old lake-basin. Among the other noticeable

plants may be mentioned *Betula* (3 species), *Alnus* (2 species), *Carpinus*, *Fagus* (4 species), *Salix* (4 species), *Populus* (2 species), *Platanus*, *Liquidambar*, *Planera*, *Ulmus* (2 species), *Ficus* (2 species), *Persoonia*, *Laurus* (5 species), *Persea*, *Sassafras*, *Cinnamomum* (5 species), *Oreodaphne*, *Diospyros* (2 species), *Andromeda*, *Magnolia*, *Acer* (3 species), *Sapindus*, *Celastrus* (2 species), *Ilex* (4 species), *Rhamnus* (3 species), *Juglans* (5 species), *Carya* (2 species), *Rhus*, *Myrica*, *Crataegus*, *Prunus*, *Cassia* (3 species). These plants suggest a colder climate than that indicated by the plants of Meximieux— they might, therefore, be thought to belong to a later period. The difference, however, is probably fully accounted for when we take into consideration the biting winds still felt in spring in the valley of the Arno, and the probable large admixture of plants washed down from the mountains above. Somewhat later Pliocene deposits in the Val d'Arno, as well as the tuffs associated with the Pliocene volcanoes in central France, yield plants of a more familiar type, a considerable proportion of them still living in the Mediterranean region, though some are only now found at distant localities, and others are extinct... The flora, however, is essentially Palaearctic, American and Australian types having disappeared.

A somewhat later Pliocene flora is represented by the plants found at Tegelen, near Venloo, on the borders of the Netherlands and Germany. This deposit is of especial interest for the light it throws on the origin of the existing flora of Britain. The Tegelen plants are mainly north European; but there occur others of central and south Europe, and various exotic and extinct forms, nearly all of which, however, belong to the Palaearctic region, though some may now be confined to widely separated parts of it. For instance, *Pterocarya caucasica* does not grow nearer than the Caucasus, where it is associated with the wild vine—also found at Tegelen; *Magnolia Kobus* is confined to the north island of Japan; another species of *Magnolia* cannot be identified and may be extinct. An extinct water-lily, *Euryale limburgensis*, belongs to a monotypic genus now confined to Assam and China; an extinct sedge, *Dulichium vespiforme*, belongs to a genus only living in America, though the only living species once flourished also in Denmark; an extinct species of water-aloe (*Stratiotes elegans*) makes a third genus, represented only by a single living species, which was evidently better represented in Pliocene times. A large proportion of the plants, however, may still be found living in Holland and Britain; but there is a singular scarcity of Composites, though this order is fairly well represented in British strata of slightly later date.

The latest Pliocene, or pre-Glacial, flora of northern Europe is best known from the Cromer Forest-bed of Norfolk and Suffolk, a fluvio-marine deposit which lies beneath the whole of the Glacial deposits of these counties, and passes downwards into the Crag, many of the animals actually associated with the plants being characteristic Pliocene species which seem immediately afterwards to have been exterminated by the increasing cold. The plants contained in the Cromer Forest-bed, of which about 150 species have now been determined, fall mainly into two groups—the forest-trees, and marsh and aquatic plants. We know little or nothing at present of the upland plants, or of those of dry or chalky soils. Forest trees are well represented; they are, in fact, better known than in any of the later English deposits. We find the living British species of *Rhamnus*, maple, aloe, hawthorn, apple, white-beam, guelder-rose, cornel, elm, birch, alder, hornbeam, hazel, oak, beech, willow, yew and pine, and also the spruce. This is an assemblage that could not well be found under conditions differing greatly from those now holding in Norfolk; there is an absence of both Arctic and south European plants. The variety of trees shows that the climate was mild and moist. Among the herbaceous plants we find, mingled with a number that still live in Norfolk, *Hypecoum procumbens*, the water-chestnut (*Trapa natans*), and *Najas minor*, none of which is now British.

On the Norfolk coast another thin plant-bed occurs locally above the Forest-bed and immediately beneath the Boulder Clay. This deposit shows no trace of forest-trees, but it is full of remains of Arctic mosses, and of the dwarf willow and birch; in short, it yields the flora now found within the Arctic circle.

The incoming of the Glacial epoch does not appear to have been accompanied by any acclimatization of the plants—the species belonging to temperate Europe were locally *Pleistocene.* exterminated, and Arctic forms took their places. The same Arctic flora reappears in deposits immediately above the highest Boulder Clay, deposits formed after the ice had passed away. These fossil Arctic plants have now been found as far south as Bovey Tracey in Devonshire, where Pengelly and Heer discovered the bear-berry and dwarf birch; London, where also *Betula nana* occurs; and at Deuben in Saxony, which lies nearly as far south as lat. 50°, but has yielded to Professor Nathorst's researches several Arctic species of willow and saxifrage. The cold period, however, was not continuous, for both in Great Britain and on the continent of Europe, as well as in Canada, it was broken by the recurrence of a milder climate and the reappearance of a flora almost identical with that now living in the same regions. This "inter-Glacial" flora, though so like that now found in the district, has interesting peculiarities. In England, for instance, it includes *Acer monspessulanum*, a southern maple which does not now extend nearer than central Europe, and *Cotoneaster Pyracantha*; also *Najas gramineo* and *N. minor*, both southern forms not now native of Britain. *Brassenia peltata*, a water-lily found in the warmer regions almost throughout the world, except in Europe, occurs abundantly in north Germany, but not in Great Britain. Similar inter-Glacial deposits in Tirol contain leaves of *Rhododendron ponticum*.

Space will not permit us to enter into any full discussion of the recurrence of Glacial and inter-Glacial periods and the influence they may have had on the flora. It is evident, however, that if climatic alternations, such as those just described, are part of the normal routine that has gone on through all geological periods, and are not merely confined to the latest, then such changes must evidently have had great influence on the evolution and geographical distribution both of species and of floras. Whether this was so is a question still to be decided, for in dealing with extinct floras it is difficult to decide, except in the most general way, to what climatic conditions they point. We seem to find indications of long-period climatic oscillations in Tertiary times, but none of the sudden invasion of an Arctic flora, like that which occurred during more recent times. It should not be forgotten, however, that an Arctic flora is mainly distinguishable from a temperate one by its poverty and dwarfed vegetation, its deciduous leaves and small fruits, rather than by the occurrence of any characteristic genera or families. Careful and long-continued study would therefore be needed before we could say of any extinct dwarfed flora that it included only plants which could withstand Arctic conditions.

Authorities.—H. Conwentz, *Monographie der baltischen Bernsteinbäume* (Danzig, 1890), *Die Flora des Bernsteins*, vol. ii. (1886); Sir W. Dawson, Papers on the Cretaceous Plants of British North America, *Trans. Roy. Soc. Canada* (1883–1896); C. von Ettingshausen, "Die Kreideflora von Niederschöna in Sachsen," *Sitz. k. Akad. Wiss. Wien*, math.-nat. Cl., vol. iv., Abth. i. (1867); "Report on . . . Fossil Flora of Sheppy," *Proc. Roy. Soc.* xxix. 388 (1879); "Report on . . . Fossil Flora of Alum Bay," ibid. xxx. 228 (1880); C. von Ettingshausen and J. S. Gardner, "Eocene Flora," vols. i. and ii., *Palaeont. Soc.* (1879–1886); W. M. Fontaine, "The Potomac or Younger Mesozoic Flora," *U.S. Geological Survey*, Monograph xv. (1889); J. S. Gardner, Flora of Alum Bay, in "Geology of the Isle of Wight," *Mem. Geol. Survey* (2nd ed., 1889); H. R. Goeppert and A. Menge, *Die Flora des Bernsteins und ihre Beziehungen zur Flora der Tertiärformation und der Gegenwart*, vol. i. (Danzig, 1883); O. Heer, *Flora tertiaria Helvetiae* (3 vols., Winterthur, 1855–1859); *Flora fossilis arctica* (7 vols., Zürich, 1868–1883), "Beiträge zur Kreideflora,—(1) Flora von Moletein in Mähren," *Neue Denkschr. allgem. schweiz. Gesell. Naturwiss.*, vol. xxiii. mém. 22 (Zürich, 1869–1873); *Primaeval World in Switzerland* (2 vols., 1876); F. H. Knowlton, "Catalogue of the Cretaceous and Tertiary Plants of North America," *Bull. U.S. Geol. Survey* (No. 152, 1898), "Flora of the Montana Formation," ibid., No. 163 (1900); Krasser, "Die fossile Kreideflora von Kunstadt in Mähren," *Beit. paleont. Geol. Oesterreich-Ungarns*, Bd. v. Hft. 3 (1896); Leo Lesquereux, "Contributions to the Fossil Flora of the Western Territories," *Rep. U.S. Geol. Survey of the Territories*; vols. vi., vii., viii. (1877–1883), "The Flora of the Dakota Group," *U.S. Geological Survey*, Monograph xvii. (1891); Meschinelli and Squinabol, *Flora tertiaria italica* (1892); this book contains a full bibliography relating to the Fossil Flora of Italy; J. S. Newberry, "The Flora of Amboy Clays," *U.S. Geological Survey*, Monograph xxvi. (1895); Hosius and von der Marck, "Die Flora der westphälischen Kreideformation," *Palaeontographica*, vol. xxvi. (1880), and supplement in ibid. vol. xxxi. (1883); A. G. Nathorst, "Glacialflora in Suchsen, am äussersten Rande des nordischen Diluviums," *Kongl. Vetenskaps-Akad. Forh.*, p. 519 (1894); Clement Reid, "Pliocene Deposits of Britain," *Mem. Geol. Survey* (1890), *Origin of the British Flora* (1899); C. and E. M. Reid, "The Fossil Flora of Tegelen-sur-Meuse, near Venloo, in the Province of Limburg," *Verh. Kon. Akad. Wetensch. Amsterdam*, 2e Sect. Dl. xiii. No. 6 (1907); "On the Pre-Glacial Flora of Britain," *Journ. Linn. Soc. (Botany)*, xxxviii. 206–227 (1908); C. de Saporta, "Prodrome d'une flore fossile des Travertins anciens de Sézanne," *Mém. soc. géol. France*, 2nd series, vol. viii. p. 289 (1868); "Recherches sur les végétaux fossiles de Meximieux," *Archiv. Mus. hist. nat. Lyon*, i. 131 (1876); *Monde des plantes avant l'apparition de l'homme* (1879); "Études sur la végétation du sud-est de la France à l'époque tertiaire," *Ann. sci. nat.* (1862–1888); *Flore fossile du*

Portugal (Lisbon, 1894); G. de Saporta and A. F. Marion, "Essai sur l'état de la végétation à l'époque des marnes heersiennes de Gelinden," *Mém. cour. acad. roy. belgique*, vol. xxxvii. No. 6 (1873), and vol. xii. No. 3 (1878); J. Velenovsky, "Die Flora der böhmischen Kreideformation," in *Beiträge zur Palaeontologie Oesterreich-Ungarns und des Orients*, vols. ii.-v. (1881–1885); Lester F. Ward, "Synopsis of the Flora of the Laramie Group," *6th Report U.S. Geological Survey*, pp. 399–558 (1885); "The Geographical Distribution of Fossil Plants," *8th Report U.S. Geological Survey*, pp. 663–960 (1889); "The Potomac Formation," *15th Report U.S. Geological Survey*, pp. 307–398 (1895); "Some Analogies in the Lower Cretaceous of Europe and America," *18th Report U.S. Geological Survey*, Pt. I., pp. 362–542 (1896); "The Cretaceous Formation of the Black Hills as indicated by the Fossil Plants," *19th Report U.S. Geological Survey*, Pt. II., pp. 521–946 (1899).   (C. K.).

PALAEOGRAPHY (Gr. παλαιός, ancient, and γράφειν, to write), the science of ancient handwriting acquired from study of surviving examples. While epigraphy is the science which deals with inscriptions (q.v.) engraved on stone or metal or other enduring material as memorials for future ages, palaeography takes cognisance of writings of a literary, economic, or legal nature written generally with stile, reed or pen, on tablets, rolls or codices. The boundary, however, between the two sciences is not always to be exactly defined. The fact that an inscription occurs upon a hard material in a fixed position does not necessarily bring it under the head of epigraphy. Such specimens of writing as the graffiti or wall-scribblings of Pompeii and ancient Rome belong as much to the one science as to the other; for they neither occupy the position of inscriptions set up with special design as epigraphical monuments, nor are they the movable written documents with which we connect the idea of palaeography. But such exceptions only slightly affect the broad distinction just specified.

The scope of this article is to trace the history of Greek and Latin palaeography from the earliest written documents in those languages which have survived. In Greek palaeography we have a subject which is self-contained. The Greek character, in its pure form, was used for one language only; but the universal study of that language throughout Europe and the wide diffusion of its literature have been the cause of the accumulation of Greek MSS. in every centre of learning. The field of Latin palaeography is much wider, for the Roman alphabet has made its way into every country of western Europe, and the study of its various developments and changes is essential for a proper understanding of the character which we write.

Handwriting, like every other art, has its different phases of growth, perfection and decay. A particular form of writing is gradually developed, then takes a finished or calligraphic style and becomes the hand of its period, then deteriorates, breaks up and disappears, or only drags on an artificial existence, being meanwhile superseded by another style which, either developed from the older hand or introduced independently, runs the same course, and in its turn is displaced by a younger rival. Thus in the history of Greek writing we see the literary uncial hand passing from early forms into the calligraphic stage; and then driven out by the minuscule, which again goes through a series of important changes. In Latin, the literary capital and uncial hands give place to the smaller character; and this, after running its course and developing national characteristics in the different countries of the West, deteriorates and is superseded almost universally by the Italian hand of the Renaissance.

Bearing in mind these natural changes, it is evident that a style of writing, once developed, is best at the period when it is in general use, and that the oldest examples of that period are the simplest, in which vigour and naturalness of handwriting are predominant. On the other hand, the fine execution of a MS. after the best period of the style has passed cannot conceal deterioration. The imitative nature of the calligraphy is detected both by the general impression on the eye, and by uncertainty and inconsistencies in the forms of letters. It is from a failure to keep in mind the natural laws of development and change that early dates, to which they have no title, have been given to imitative MSS.; and, on the other hand, even very ancient examples have been post-dated in an incredible manner.

Down to the time of the introduction of printing, writing ran in two lines—the natural cursive, and the set book-hand which was evolved from it. Cursive writing was essential for the ordinary business of life. MSS. written in the set book-hand filled the place now occupied by printed books, the writing being regular, the lines generally kept even by ruling or other guides, and the texts provided with regular margins. The set book-hand disappeared before the printing press; cursive writing necessarily remains.

In the study of handwriting it is difficult to exaggerate the great and enduring influence which the character of the material employed for receiving the script has had upon the formation of the written letters. The original use of clay by the Babylonians and Assyrians as their writing material was the primary cause of the wedge-shaped symbols which were produced by the natural process of puncturing so stiff and sluggish a substance. The clinging waxen surface of the tablets of the Greeks and Romans superinduced a broken and disconnected style of writing. The comparatively frail surface of papyrus called for a light touch and slenderly built characters. With the introduction of the smooth and hard-surfaced vellum, firmer and heavier letters, with marked contrasts of fine and thick strokes, became possible, and thence became the fashion. In the task which lies before us we shall have to deal mainly with MSS. written on the two very different materials, papyrus and vellum, and we shall find to how great an extent the general character and the detailed development of Greek and Latin writing, particularly for literary purposes, has been affected by the two materials.

The history of the ancient papyrus roll and of its successor, the medieval vellum codex, and the particulars of the mechanical arrangement of texts and other details appertaining to the evolution of the written book are described in the article MANUSCRIPT. In the present article our attention is confined to the history of the script.

The papyrus period of our subject, as regards literary works, ranges generally from the end of the 4th century B.C. to the 4th century of our era, when the papyrus roll as the vehicle for literature was superseded by the vellum codex. The vellum period extends from the 4th century to the 15th century, when the rise of the art of printing was the doom of the written book. Yet it must not be imagined that there is a hard and fast line separating the papyrus period from the vellum period. In the early centuries of our era there was a transitional period when the use of the two materials overlapped. The employment of vellum for literary purposes began tentatively quite at the beginning of that era; nor did the use of papyrus absolutely cease with the 4th century. But that century marks definitely the period when the change had become generally accepted.

In the case of non-literary documents, written in cursive hands, the papyrus period covers a still wider field. These documents range from the 3rd century B.C. down to the 7th century, and a certain number of examples even extend into the 8th century. The survival of cursive papyrus documents in large numbers is due to the fact that they are chiefly written in Egypt, where papyrus was the common writing material and where climatic conditions ensured their preservation. On the other hand, early cursive documents on vellum are scarce, for it must be borne in mind that, even allowing for the loss of such documents attributable to the perishable nature of that material in the moist climates of Europe, papyrus and waxen tablets were also the usual writing materials of the Greeks and Romans. The importance of the survival of Greek cursive papyri to so late a period is very great, for it enables us to trace the development of the Greek literary minuscule handwriting of the 9th century in a direct line from the cursive script of the papyri centuries earlier.

GREEK WRITING. I.—THE PAPYRI

In no branch of our subject has so great a development been

effected since about 1875 as in that of the palaeography of Greek papyri. Before that time our knowledge was very limited. The material was comparatively meagre; and, though its increase was certainly only a matter of time, yet the most sanguine would hardly have dared to foretell the remarkable abundance of documents which the excavations of a few years would bring to light.

The history of Greek writing on papyrus can now be followed with more or less fullness of material for a thousand years. Actual dated examples range from the late years of the 4th century B.C. to the 7th century A.D. We have a fair knowledge of the leading features of the writing of the 3rd and 2nd centuries B.C.; a less perfect acquaintance with those of the 1st century B.C. For the first four centuries of the Christian era there is a fairly continuous series of documents; of the 5th century only a few examples have as yet been recovered, but there is an abundance of material for the 6th and early 7th centuries. Thus it will be seen that, while for some periods we may be justified in drawing certain conclusions and laying down certain rules, for others we are still in an imperfect state of knowledge. But our knowledge will no doubt almost yearly become more exact, as fresh material is brought to light from the excavations which are now continually proceeding; and those periods in which the lack of papyri breaks the chain of evidence will sooner or later be as fully represented as the rest. The material certainly lies buried in the sands; it is our misfortune that the exact sites have not yet been struck.

The first discovery of Greek papyri was made in Europe in 1752, when the excavations on the site of Herculaneum yielded a number of charred rolls, which proved to be of a literary character. All subsequent discoveries we owe to Egypt; and it is to be observed that the papyri which are found in that country have come down to us under different conditions. Some, generally of a literary nature, were carefully deposited with the bodies of their owners in the tomb with the express intention of being preserved; hence such MSS. in several instances have come to our hands in fairly perfect condition. On the other hand, by far the larger number of those recently brought to light have been found on the sites of towns and villages, particularly in the district of the Fayûm, where they had been either accidentally lost or purposely thrown aside as of no value, or had even been used up as material for other purposes besides their original one. These are consequently for the most part in an imperfect and even fragmentary condition, although not a few of them have proved to be of the highest palaeographical and literary importance.

The date of the first find of Greek papyri in Egypt was in 1778, when some forty or fifty rolls were discovered by some native diggers, who, however, kept only one of them. After this scarcely anything appeared until the year 1820, when was found on the site of the Serapeum at Memphis, as it was reported, a group of documents of the 2nd century B.C. Then followed a fruitful period, when several important literary papyri were secured: in 1821, the Bankes Homer, containing the last book of the Iliad; in 1847, the roll containing the Lycophron and other orations of Hypereides; in 1849 and 1850, the Harris Homer, bk. xviii. of the Iliad, and a MS. of bks. ii.–iv.; and, in 1856, the Funeral Oration of Hypereides.

But the great bulk of the Greek papyri from Egypt is the result of excavations undertaken during the last quarter of the 19th century and down to the present day. Within this time four very important discoveries of documents in large quantities have taken place. In 1877 a great mass of papyri was found on the site of Arsinoë in the Fayûm, being chiefly of a non-literary nature, and unfortunately in a very fragmentary state; they are also late in date, being of the Byzantine period. The greater number passed into the possession of the Archduke Rainer, and are now at Vienna; the rest are divided between London, Oxford, Paris and Berlin. After an interval this find was followed by the recovery in 1892, in the same neighbourhood, and chiefly on the site of a village named Socnopaei Nesus, of an extensive series of documents of the Roman period;

ranging from the 1st century to the middle of the 3rd century. These papyri, being of an earlier date and in better condition than the Arsinoïte collection, are consequently of greater palaeographical value. Most of them are now in Berlin; many are in the British Museum; and some are at Vienna, Geneva and elsewhere. The third and fourth great finds, and the most important of all, were made by Messrs Grenfell and Hunt when excavating, in the seasons 1896-1897 and 1905-1906, for the Egypt Exploration Fund, at Behnesa, the ancient Oxyrhynchus. Thousands of papyri were here recovered, including, among the non-literary material, a number of rolls in good condition, and comprising also a great store of fragments of literary works, among which occur the now well-known " Logia," or " Sayings of Our Lord," and fragments of the Scriptures, and in some instances of not inconsiderable portions of the writings of various classical authors. This great collection ranges in date from the 2nd century B.C. to the 7th century A.D.; but in what proportion the documents fall to the several centuries cannot be determined until the series of volumes in which they are to be described for the Graeco-Roman branch of the Egypt Exploration Fund shall have made some substantial progress.

These four great collections of miscellaneous documents have been supplemented by finds of other groups, which fit into them and serve to make more complete the chronological series. Such are the correspondence of a Roman officer named Abinnaeus, of the middle of the 4th century, shared between the British Museum and the library of Geneva in the year 1892; a miscellaneous collection, ranging from the 2nd century B.C. to the 3rd or 4th century A.D., acquired for the Egypt Exploration Fund and published by that society (*Fayûm Towns and their Papyri*, 1900); another collection obtained for the same society from the cartonnage of mummy-cases dating back to the 3rd century B.C. (*The Hibeh Papyri*, 1906); and a series recovered from excavations at Tebtunis for the University of California (*The Tebtunis Papyri*, 1902, 1906), generally of the 2nd century B.C. But of these lesser groups by far the most interesting is that which Mr Flinders Petrie extracted, in 1889-1890, from a set of mummy-cases found in the necropolis of the village of Gurob in the Fayûm. In the manufacture of these coffins numbers of inscribed papyri had been employed. The fragments thus recovered proved to be some of the most valuable documents for the history of Greek palaeography hitherto found, supplying us with examples of writing of the 3rd century B.C. in fairly ample numbers, and thus carrying back our fuller knowledge of the subject to a period which up to that time had remained almost a blank. ; Besides miscellaneous documents, there are included the remains of registers of wills entered up from time to time by different scribes, and thus affording a variety of handwritings for study; and, further, the value of the collection is enhanced by the presence of fragments of the *Phaedo* and *Laches* of Plato, and of the lost *Antiope* of Euripides and of other classical works.

The last decade of the 19th century was also distinguished by the recovery of several literary works of the first importance, inscribed on papyri which had been deposited with the dead, and had thus remained in a fairly perfect condition. In 1889 the trustees of the British Museum acquired a copy of the lost 'Aθηναίων Πολιτεία of Aristotle—a papyrus of the mimes of the poet Herodas, and a portion of the oration of Hypereides against Philippides; and in 1896 they had the further good fortune to secure a papyrus containing considerable portions of the odes of Bacchylides, the contemporary of Pindar. And to the series of the orations of Hypereides the Louvre was enabled to add, in 1892, a MS. of the greater part of the oration against Athenogenes.

But the most valuable discovery, from a palaeographical point of view, took place in the present century. In 1902 a papyrus roll containing the greater portion of the *Persae*, a lyrical composition of Timotheus of Miletus, was found at Abusir, near Memphis, and is now at Berlin. It is written in a large hand of a style which had hitherto been known from a document at Vienna entitled the " Curse of Artemisia," and

assigned to the early part of the 3rd century B.C.; and from one or two other insignificant scraps. The new papyrus, however, appears to be even older, and may certainly be placed in the later years of the 4th century B.C.: the most ancient extant literary MS. in the Greek tongue. The ascription of this papyrus to the 4th century B.C. has received confirmation from the welcome discovery, in 1906, at Elephantine, of a document (a marriage contract) of the year 311-310 B.C., which is written in the same style of book-hand characters (*Aegypt. Urkunden d. kgl. Museen in Berlin, Elephantine Papyri*, 1907). Of quite recent date also is the recovery of a considerable part of a commentary on the *Theaetetus* of Plato, written in a fine uncial hand of the 2nd century, now in Berlin. Considerable fragments also of the *Paeans* of Pindar of the 1st or 2nd century; a papyrus containing an historical work attributed to Theopompus or Cratippus, perhaps of the early 3rd century; a copy of Plato's *Symposium* of the same period; and a portion of the *Panegyricus* of Isocrates, written in an uncial hand of the 2nd century, are printed in Part V. of the *Oxyrhynchus Papyri*. Further, many leaves of a papyrus codex containing fragments of four comedies of Menander were found in 1905 at Kom Ishkaou, the ancient Aphroditopolis. The recovery of so many great classical works within a few years may be accepted as an earnest of further finds of the same nature, now that excavations are being carried on systematically in Egypt.

From a study of the material thus placed at our disposal certain conclusions have been arrived at which satisfy us that the periodical changes which passed over the character of Greek writing as practised in Egypt coincide pretty nearly with the changes in the political administration of the country. The period of the rule of the Ptolemies from 323 to 30 B.C. has, in general, its own style of writing, which we recognize as the *Ptolemaic*; the period of Roman supremacy, beginning with the conquest of Augustus and ending with the reorganization of the empire by Diocletian in A.D. 284, is accompanied by a characteristic *Roman* hand; and with the change of administration which placed Egypt under the Byzantine division of the empire, and lasted down to the time of the Arab conquest in A.D. 640, there is a corresponding change to the *Byzantine* class of writing. These changes must obviously be attributed to the influence of the official handwritings of the time. A change of government naturally led to a change of the officials employed, and with the change of officials would naturally follow a change in the style of production of official documents. In illustration of this view, it is enough to call to mind the instances of such variations to be met with in the history of the palaeography of medieval Europe, due in the same way to political causes. It is interesting, too, to observe that in our own time the teaching in schools of a particular type of handwriting which finds favour in clerical examinations for the public service has not been without its influence on the general handwriting of the people.

Classifying, then, the writing of the papyri into the three groups—the Ptolemaic, the Roman, and the Byzantine—the next step is to determine, by a closer examination of the documents, the changes which characterize the several centuries traversed by those groups. In doing this, we cannot apply the exact terms which are employed in describing the MSS. of the middle ages. We have to do with writing which has not yet been cast into the formal literary moulds of the later times; and it has therefore been found necessary, as well as convenient, to divide the papyri simply into two series, representative of their contents and not of their style of production—namely literary papyri and non-literary papyri. Neither series, however, it is to be remembered, has a style of writing peculiar to itself. While the extant literary works are, as a rule, written with more or less formality, no doubt by professional scribes for the book-market, not a few of even the more valuable of them are copies in the ordinary cursive hands of the day. Conversely, while we find non-literary documents generally written in ordinary cursive hands, whether by official scribes or by private individuals yet occasionally we meet with one produced in the formal style more proper to literary examples. Again, while applying to particular letters in papyri such technical terms as capitals, or uncials, or minuscules, we cannot convey by those terms the exact ideas which we convey when thus describing the individual letters of · medieval manuscripts. For the letters of the papyrus period were not cast in finished moulds, while the uncial writing and the minuscule writing of the middle ages were settled literary hands. As will presently be seen, the early medieval uncial band of the vellum codices developed directly from the literary writing of the papyri; the minuscule book-hand of the 9th century was a new type moulded from the cursive into a fixed literary style.

Necessarily, the non-literary papyri are much more numerous than the literary documents, and present a much greater variety of handwriting, being in fact the result of the daily transactions of ordinary life; and how very widespread was the knowledge of writing among the Greek-speaking population of Egypt is sufficiently testified by the surviving examples, coming as they do from the hands of all sorts and conditions of men. We will first examine these specimens of the current handwriting of the day before passing to the review of the more or less artificial book-writing of the literary papyri.

Non-Literary, Cursive, Hands.—As already stated, the oldest material for the study of Greek cursive writing is chiefly contributed by the papyri discovered at Gurob. Among them are not only the fragments of official registers, which have been mentioned, but also a variety of miscellaneous documents relating to private affairs, and in various hands of the 3rd century and early 2nd century B.C. The non-literary cursive papyri bear actual dates ranging from 270 to 186 B.C. But the discovery (1906) of papyri at Elephantine takes our dated series of cursive documents back to 285-284 B.C.; and in this collection also is the oldest dated Greek document yet found—the marriage contract of the year 311-310 B.C., already mentioned. In this instance, however, the writing is not cursive, but of the literary type.

The leading characteristic of Greek cursive writing of the 3rd century B.C. is its strength and facility. While it may not compare with some later styles in the precise formation of particular letters, yet its freedom and spontaneous air lend it a particular charm and please the eye; very much in the same way that a scholar's practised and unconscious handwriting of a good type is more attractive than the more exact formality of a clerk's hand. The letters generally are widely spread and shallow, and, particularly in the official hands, they are linked together with horizontal connecting strokes to such an extent that the text has almost the appearance of depending from a continuous horizontal line. The extreme shallowness or flatness of many of the letters is very striking. A significant indication of the antiquity of Greek cursive writing is found in connexion with the letter *alpha*, which ·is, even at this early period, in one·of its forms reduced to a mere angle or wedge.

· A few lines from an official order (fig. 1) of the year 250 B.C. will serve to convey an idea of the trained cursive style of this century:—

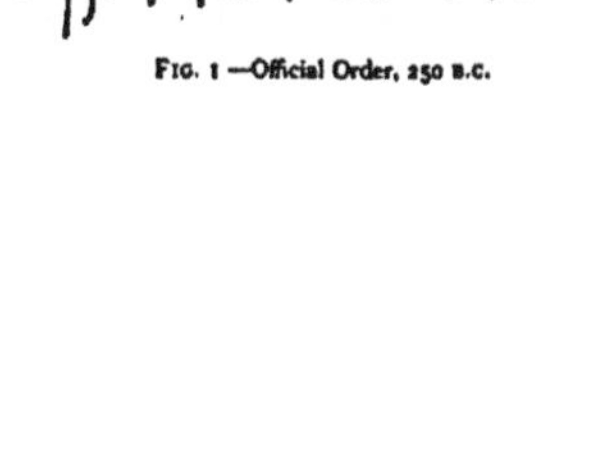

FIG. 1 —Official Order, 250 B.C.

(—ας τονούχου και της—
—τετρα και αλοστης—
—θεις τους θησαυρος εκ—
—τετρα και αλοστης—
—αυλων και τους εριμω—
—σφραγισμενος αποσ—)

As a contrast to this excellent hand, we give a facsimile of a section from a roughly written letter from a land steward to his employer, of about the same date:—

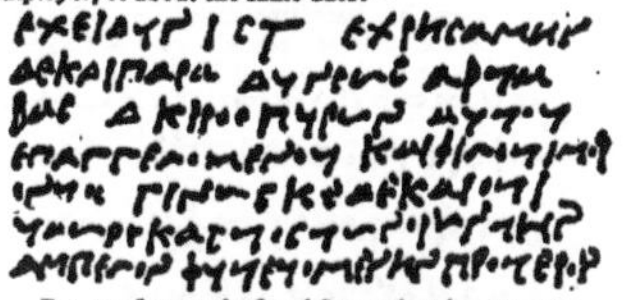

FIG. 2.—Letter of a Land Steward, 3rd century B.C.

(εχει δυνις γ εχρησαμην
δε και παρα δινως αρτα
βας δ κριθοτυρων αυτου
επαγγελομενου και φιλοτιμου
οντος γινωσκε δε και οτι
υδωρ εκαστος των ορων την
εμπελον φυτευομενην προτερος)

Here there is none of the linking of the letters which is seen in the other example: every letter stands distinct. But while the individual letters are clumsily written, the same laws govern their formation as in the other document. The shallow, wide-spread *mu*, the cursive *nu*, the small *theta*, *omikron*, and *rho*, are repeated. Here·also is seen the *iota*, with its horizontal stroke confined to the left of the vertical instead of crossing it, and the undeveloped *omega*, which has the appearance of being clipped—both forms being characteristic of the 3rd century B.C.

The trained clerical hands of the 2nd century B.C. (fig. 3) differ generally from those of the earlier century in a more perfect and less cursive formation, the older shallow type gradually disappearing, and the linking of letters by horizontal strokes being less continuous. But the Ptolemaic character marks the handwriting well through the century; and it is only towards the close of that period and as the next century is entered, that the hand begins to give way and to lose altogether its linked style and the peculiar crispness of the strokes which give it its distinctive appearance. The cursive hand in its best style (e.g. *N: et Extr.* pls. xxviii., xxix.) is very graceful and exact:—

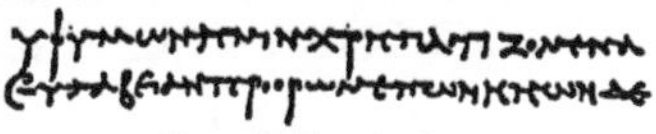

FIG. 3.—Petition, 163-160 B.C.

(υφ υμων ημιν χρηματιζομενα
ευλαβειαν προσρωμενων ημων δε)

Towards the end of the Ptolemaic period material greatly fails. There are very few extant cursive documents between the years 80 and 20 B.C. But marks of decadence already appear in the examples of the beginning of the 1st century B.C. The general character of the writing becomes slacker, and the forms of individual letters are less exact. These imperfections prepare us for the great change which was to follow.

With the Roman period comes roundness of style, in strong contrast to the stiffness and rigid linking of the Ptolemaic hand. Curves take the place of straight strokes in the individual letters, and even ligatures are formed in pliant sweeps of the pen. This transition from the stiff to the flexible finds something of a parallel in the development of the curving and flexible English charterhand of the 14th century from the rigid hand of the 13th century; following, it would seem, the natural law of relaxation. Roundness of style, then, is characteristic of Greek cursive writing in the papyri of the first three centuries of the Christian era, however much individual hands, or groups of hands, might vary among themselves.

A specimen (fig. 4) of cursive writing of the general Roman type is selected from a papyrus (Brit. Mus. No. cxxxi.) which is of more than usual interest, as it is on the verso side of the rolls of which it is composed that the text of Aristotle's *Constitution of Athens* has been transcribed. It contains the farming accounts of the bailiff of Epimachus, son of Polydeuces, the owner of an estate in the nome of Hermopolis in the 9th and 10th years of the reign of Vespasian, that is A.D. 78–79:—

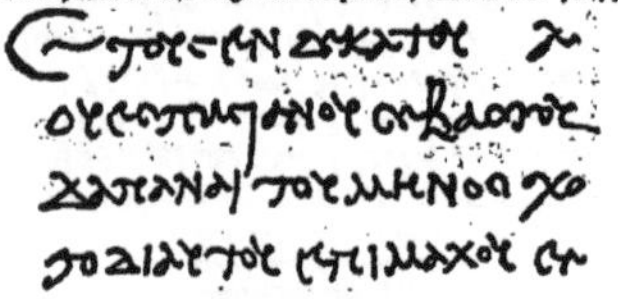

Fig. 4.—Farm Accounts, A.D. 78–79.

(ετους ενδεκατου α—
ουεσπασιανου ρεβαστου—
δαπαναι του μηνοσ χ—
το δι αυτου ετυμαχου ε—)

In the second half of the 1st century two styles of handwriting predominate in the cursive papyri. There is the clear and flowing hand, which may be termed the ordinary working hand; and there is also a small and very cursive style which appears in private correspondence and in legal contracts. The 2nd century follows on the same lines as the 1st century; but with the 3rd century decadence sets in; the writing begins to slope, and grows larger and rougher and tends to exaggeration.

This exaggeration of the writing of the later Roman period leads the way to the pedantic exaggeration and formalism characteristic of the Byzantine period. In this period the general style of writing is on a larger scale than in the Roman; exaggeration in the size of certain letters marks the progress of the 4th century. Material is wanting for full illustration of the changes effected in the 5th century; but the papyri of the 6th century show a further advance in formalism, the common style being upright and compressed and full of flourishes. In the 7th century the hand assumes a sloping style, which always seems to accompany decadence, and grows very irregular and straggling. A specimen of the fully developed Byzantine hand of a legal type is here shown in a few lines from a lease of a farm (fig. 5) in the 6th century (Brit. Mus. pap. cxiii 3):—

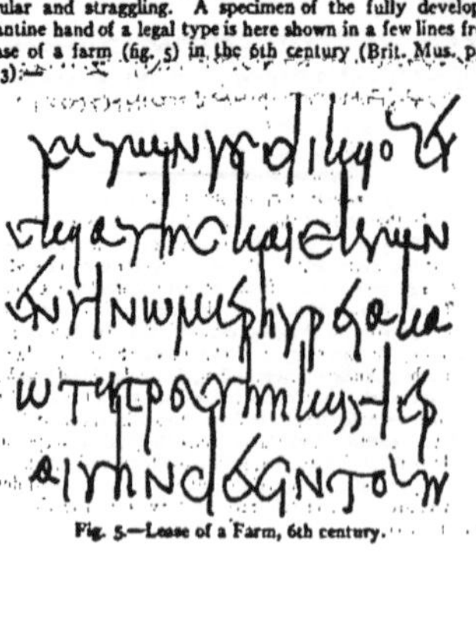

Fig. 5.—Lease of a Farm, 6th century.

In the long range covered by the Greek papyri the formation of individual letters necessarily varied under different influences; but in not a few instances the original shapes were remarkably maintained. From those which thus remained conservative it is rash to attempt to draw conclusions as to the precise age of the several documents in which they occur. On the other hand, there are some which at certain periods adopted shapes which were in vogue for a limited time and then disappeared, never to be resumed. Such forms can very properly be regarded as sure guides to the palaeographer in assigning dates. We may therefore take a brief survey of the Greek cursive alphabet of the papyri and note some of the peculiarities of individual letters. The incipient form of the *alpha* which gradually developed into the minuscule letter of the middle ages may be traced back to the Ptolemaic documents of the 2nd century B.C., but the more cursive letter, which was a simple acute angle, representing only two of the three strokes of which the primitive letter was composed, was characteristic of the 3rd century B.C., and seems to have gone out of use within the Ptolemaic period. The development of the cursive *beta* is interesting. At the very beginning we find two forms in use: the primitive capital letter and a cursive shape somewhat resembling a small *a*, being in fact an imperfectly written B in which the bows are slurred. This form lasted through the Ptolemaic period. Then arose the natural tendency to reverse the strokes and to form the letter on the principle of *u*; but still the capital letter also continued in use, so that through the Roman and Byzantine periods the *u*-shape and the B-shape run on side by side. Analogously the letter *kappa*, formed on somewhat the same lines as the *beta*, runs a similar course in developing a cursive *u*-shaped form by the side of the primitive capital. *Delta* remained fairly true to its primitive form until the Byzantine period, when the elongation of the head into a flourish led on to the minuscule letter which is familiar to us in the medieval and modern alphabet. *Epsilon*, the most frequently recurring letter in Greek texts, departs less from its original rounded uncial form that might have been expected. Frequent and varied as its cursive formations are, yet the original shape is seldom quite disguised, the variations almost in all instances arising from the devices of the scribe to dispose swiftly and conveniently the cross-bar by incorporating it with the rest of the letter. The tendency to curtail the second vertical limb of *eta*, leading eventually to the *h*-shape, is in evidence from the first. But in the development of this letter we have one of the instances of temporary forms which lasted only within a fixed period. In the 1st century, side by side with the more usual form, there appears a modification of it, somewhat resembling the contemporary *upsilon*, consisting of a shallow horizontal curve with a vertical limb slightly turned in at the foot, ꭒ. Its development from the original Η is evident: the first vertical limb is slurred, and survives only in the beginning of the horizontal curve, while the cross-bar and the second vertical are combined in the rest of the letter. This form was in general use from the middle of the 1st to the middle of the 2nd century, becoming less common after about A.D. 160, and practically disappearing about A.D. 200. The letters formed wholly or in part by circles or loops, *theta*, *omikron*, *rho*, *phi*, in the earlier centuries have such circles or loops of a small size. Just as there is an analogy between *beta* and *kappa* in their developments, as already noticed, so also do *mu* and *pi* advance on somewhat similar lines. From the earliest time there is a resemblance between the broad shallow forms of the two letters in the 3rd century B.C., and particularly when they adopt the form of a convex stroke the likeness is very close; and again, in both Roman and Byzantine periods an *n*-shaped development appears among the forms of both letters. There is also one phase in the development of *sigma* which affords a useful criterion for fixing the date of documents within a fixed limit of time. In the Ptolemaic period the letter, always of the C-form, is upright, with a flattened horizontal head; in the Roman period a tendency sets in to curve the head, and in the course of the 1st century, by the side of the old stiffer form of the letter, another more cursive one appears, in which the head is drawn down more and more in a curve, ℭ ℭ. This form is in common use from the latter part of the 1st century to the beginning of the 3rd century. The cursive form of *iou*, in which the horizontal stroke is kept to the left of the vertical limb, without crossing it, is one of the early shapes of the letter. The formation of the letter *Xi* in three distinct horizontal strokes is characteristic of the Ptolemaic period, as distinguished from the later type of letter in which the bars are more or less connected. Lastly, the early Ptolemaic form of the ω-shaped *omega* is noticeable from having its second curve undeveloped, the letter having the appearance of being clipped.

Literary Hands.—Literary papyri written in book-hands, distinct from the cursive writing which has been under consideration (and in which literary works were also occasionally written), may be divided into two classes: those which were produced by skilled scribes, and therefore presumably for the market, and those which were written less elegantly, but still in a literary hand, and were probably copied by or for scholars for their own use.

Standing at the head of all, and holding that rank as the only literary papyrus of any extent which may be placed in the 4th century B.C., is the famous lyrical work of Timotheus of Miletus, entitled the *Persae*, which has already been referred to and of which a section of a few lines is here reproduced:—

FIG. 6.—The *Persae* of Timotheus, late 4th century B.C..

(—μα φατο δε κυμαινω—
—ν σειριαι τε ναες ελλ—
—τε ηβαι πων πολυα—
—αξουσιμ πυρος δε αιθα—
—ς στοτοεντα δε αλγη—
—α·α μ ες ελλαδα γγαι—
—γνυτε μεσ τετραο—)

The hand, as will be seen, is rather heavy and irregular, but written with facility and strength, and, though the papyrus, perhaps, is not to be classed among the calligraphic productions for the book-market, it must rank as a well-written example of the literary script of the time. Capital forms of letters which afterwards assumed the rounded shapes known as uncial are here conspicuous.' The exactly formed *alpha*, the square *epsilon* with projecting head-stroke, the irregular *sigma*, the small *theta* and *omikron* are to be remarked. Indeed, the only letter which departs essentially from the lapidary character of the alphabet is the *omega*, here a half-cursive form but still retaining the principle of the structure of the old horse-shoe letter and quite distinct from the ω-shape which was soon to be developed. Of this type of writing are also the two non-literary documents already mentioned above, viz. the " Curse of Artemisia " at Vienna, and the marriage contract of the year 311-310 B.C., found at Elephantine. In the latter the *sigma* appears in the rounded uncial form.

By rare good fortune important literary fragments were recovered in the Gurob collection, which yielded the most

XX 10

ancient dated cursive documents of the 3rd century B.C., so that, almost from the beginning, we start with coeval specimens of both the cursive and of the book-hand, and we are in a position to compare the two styles on equal terms, and thus approximately to date the literary papyri. Palaeographically, this is a matter of the first importance; for while cursive documents, from their nature, in most instances bear actual dates, the periods of literary examples have chiefly to be decided by comparison, and often by conjecture.

The literary fragments from Gurob fall into the two groups just indicated, MSS. written for sale and scholars' copies. Of the former are some considerable portions of two works, the *Phaedo* of Plato and the lost *Antiope* of Euripides. Both are written in carefully formed characters of a small type, but of the two the *Phaedo* is the better executed. As the cursive fragments among which they were found date back to before the middle of the 3rd century B.C., it is reasonable to place these literary remains also about the same period. Their survival is a particularly interesting fact in the history of Greek palaeography, for in them we have specimens of literary rolls which may be fairly assumed to differ very little in appearance from the manuscripts contemporary with the great classical authors of Greece. Indeed, the *Phaedo* was probably written within a hundred years of the death of the author.

In the facsimile (fig. 7) of a few lines from this papyrus here placed before the reader, the characteristics of the Ptolemaic cursive hand are also to some extent to be observed in the formal book-hand:—

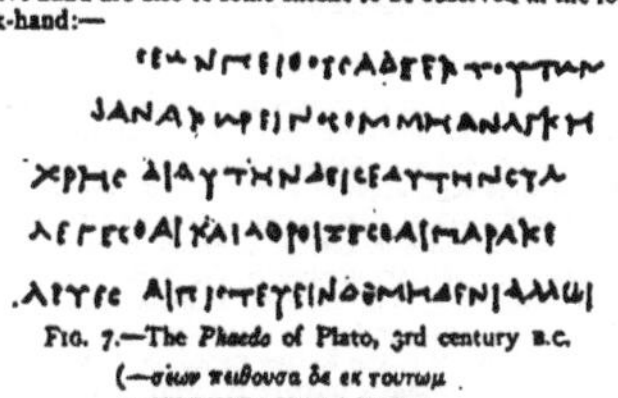

FIG. 7.—The *Phaedo* of Plato, 3rd century B.C.

(—σιων πειθουσα δε εκ τουτωμ
—αναπωρειν οσομ μη αναγκη
χρησ[θ]αι αυτην δ εις εαυτην συλ
λεγεσθαι και αθροιζεσθαι παρακε
λανεσ[θ]αι πιστευειν δε μηδενι αλλωι)

The general breadth of the square letters, the smallness of the letters composed of circles and loops, and the particular formation of such letters as *pi* and the clipped *omega*, are repeated. But the approach also of many of the letters to the lapidary capital forms, like those in the papyrus of Timotheus, is to be remarked, such as the precisely shaped *alpha*, and the *epsilon* in many instances made square with a long head-stroke. This mixture of forms seems to indicate an advance in the development of the book-hand of the 3rd century B.C., as contrasted with the archaic style of the older Timotheus.

Of the 2nd century B.C. there are extant only two papyri of literary works written in the formal book-hand, and both are now preserved in the Louvre. The one, a dialectical treatise containing quotations from classical authors, has long been known. The other is the oration of Hypereides against Athenogenes, which is an acquisition of comparatively recent date. The dialectical treatise must belong to the first half of the century, as there is on the verso side of the papyrus writing subsequently added in the year 160 B.C. The period of the Hypereides cannot be so closely defined; but the existence on the verso of later demotic writing, said to be of the Ptolemaic time, affords a limit, and the MS. has been accordingly placed in the second half of the century. While the writing of the earlier papyrus is of a light and rather sloping character, that of the Hypereides is firm and square and upright.

Passing to the 1st century B.C., the papyri which have been recovered from the ashes of Herculaneum come into account.

2a

Many of them, the texts of which are of a philosophical nature, are written in literary hands, and are conjectured to have possibly formed part of the library of their author, the philosopher Philodemus; they are therefore placed about the middle of the century. To the same time are assigned the remains of a roll containing the oration of Hypereides against Philippides and the third Epistle of Demosthenes (Brit. Mus. papp. cxxxiii., cxxxiv.). But the most important addition to the period is the handsomely written papyrus containing the poems of Bacchylides (fig. 8), which retains in the forms of the letters much of the character of the Ptolemaic style, although for other reasons it can hardly be placed earlier than about the middle of the century:—

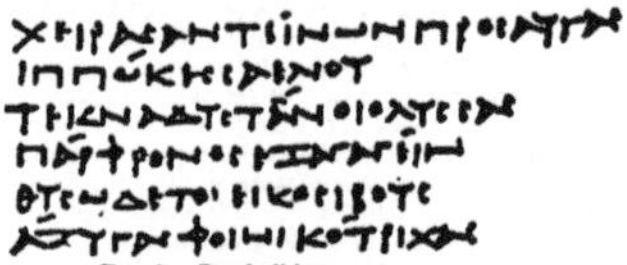

FIG. 8.—Bacchylides, 1st century B.C.

κυρας αντωνων προς αυγας
ετσκκει αελιου
τεκνα δυσταπου λυσσας ·
παρφρονος εξαγεγων
θυσω δε τοι εικοσι βους ·
αζυγας φοινικοτριχας)

With the latter half of the 1st century B.C. we quit the Ptolemaic period and pass to the consideration of the literary papyri of the Roman period; and it is especially in this latter period that our extended knowledge, acquired from recent discoveries, has led to the modification of views formerly held with regard to the dates to be attributed to certain important literary MSS. As in the case of non-literary documents, the literary writing of the Roman period differs from that of the Ptolemaic in adopting rounded forms and greater uniformity in the size of the letters.

Just on the threshold of the Roman period, near the end of the 1st century B.C., stands a fragmentary papyrus of the last two books of the *Iliad*, now in the British Museum (pap. cxxviii.), which is of sufficient extent to be noted. Then, emerging on the Christian era, we come upon a fine surviving specimen of literary writing, which we have satisfactory reason for placing near the beginning of the 1st century. It is a fragment of the third book of the *Odyssey* (fig. 9), the writing of which closely resembles that of an official document (Brit. Mus. pap. ccliv.) which happens to be written in a formal literary hand, and which from internal evidence can be dated within a few years of the close of the 1st century B.C. There can be no hesitation, therefore, in grouping the *Odyssey* with that document. The contrast between the round Roman style and the stiff and firm Ptolemaic hands is here well shown in the facsimiles from this papyrus (fig. 9) and the *Phaedo* and Bacchylides:—

ΠΑΙΔΕϹΕΜΟΙΑΓΕΤΗΛΕΜΑΧΩΙ
ΧΕΥΧΑΘΥΦΑΡΑΙΑΤΑΠΟΝΤΕϹΙΝΑ
ΩϹΕΦΙΘΟΙΔΑΡΑΤΟΥΜΑΛΛΜΕΝ
ΚΑΡΠΑΛΙΜΩϹΔΕΧΕΥΧΑΝΥΦΑΡ
ΑΝΛΕΓΝΗΤΑΜΙΗϹΙΤΟΝΚΑΙ
ΟΥΑΤΕΟΙΑΕΔΟΥϹΙΔΙΟΤΡΕΦΕ
ΛΝΔΑΡΑΠΗΛΕΜΑΧΟϹΠΕΡΙΚΑΛ
ΠΑΡΛΛΡΑΝΕϹΤΟΡΙΔΗϹΠΕΙϹΙϹ
ΕϹΛΙΦΡΟΝΛΛΝΕΒΑΙΝΕΚΑΙΗΝ

FIG. 9.—The *Odyssey*, beginning of 1st century.

ἱ παιδες εμοι αγε τηλεμαχον —
ζευξαθ υφ αρμει αγοντες ινα —
ωι εφαθ οι δ αρα του μαλα μεν —
περεαλμον δ εζευξαν υφ αρ —
αν δε γυνη ταμιη σιτον και —
οψα τε οια εδουσι διοτρεφε —
αν δ αρα τηλεμαχοι περικαλ —
παρ δ αρα νεστοριδη πεισιο
ες διφρον δ ανβαινε και ην —.

¹ In a similar style of writing are two fragments of Hesiodic poems recently published, with facsimiles, in the *Sitzungsberichte* (1900, p. 839) of the Berlin Academy. The earliest of the two, now at Strassburg, may be assigned to the first half of the 1st century; the other, at Berlin, appears to be of the 2nd century.

At this point two MSS. come into the series, in regard to which there is now held to be reason for revising views formerly entertained. The papyrus known as the Harris Homer (Brit. Mus. pap. cvii.), containing portions of the eighteenth book of the *Iliad*, which was formerly placed in the 1st century B.C., it is thought should be now brought down to a later date, and should be rather assigned to the 1st century of the Christian era. The great papyrus, too, of Hypereides, containing his orations against Demosthenes and for Lycophron and Euxenippus, which has been commonly placed also in the 1st century B.C., and by some even earlier, is now adjudged to belong to the latter part of the 1st century A.D.

Within the 1st century also is placed a papyrus of great literary interest, containing the mimes of the Alexandrian writer Herodas, which was discovered a few years ago and is now in the British Museum. The writing of this MS. differs from the usual type of literary hand, being a rough and ill-formed uncial, inscribed on narrow, and therefore inexpensive, papyrus; and if the roll were written for the market, it was a cheap copy, if indeed it was not made for private use. Of the same period is a papyrus of Isocrates, *De pace* (Brit. Mus. pap. cxxxii.), written in two hands, the one more clerical than the other; and two papyri of Homer, *Iliad*, iii.-iv. (Brit. Mus. pap. cxxxvi.), and *Iliad*, xiii.-xiv. (Brit. Mus. pap. dccxxii.), the first in a rough uneducated hand, but the latter a fine specimen of uncial writing. To about this period also is the Oxyrhynchus Pindar to be attributed, that is to the close of the 1st or beginning of the 2nd century. Then follows another famous papyrus, the Bankes Homer, containing the last book of the *Iliad*; which belongs to the 2nd century and is also written in a careful style of uncial writing. To these is to be added the beautiful papyrus at Berlin, containing a commentary on the *Theaetetus* of Plato, written in delicately formed uncials of excellent type of the 2nd century; and of the same age is the *Panegyricus* of Isocrates from Oxyrhynchus, in a round uncial hand. Three important papyri of the *Iliad*, written in large round uncials, of the 2nd century, are noticed below.

With regard to the later literary works on papyrus that have been recovered, the period which they occupy is somewhat uncertain. The following are, however, placed in the 3rd century, during which a sloping literary hand seems to have been developed, curiously anticipating a similar change which took place in the course of development of the uncial writing of the vellum MSS., the upright hand of the 4th to 6th centuries being followed by a sloping hand in the 7th and 8th centuries: a MS., now in the British Museum, of portions of bks. ii.-iv. of the *Iliad*, written on eighteen leaves of papyrus, put together in book-form, but inscribed on only one side; on the verso of some of the leaves is a short grammatical treatise attributed to Tryphon: portion of *Iliad* v., among the Oxyrhynchus papyri (No. cxxiii.): a fragment of Plato's *Laws* (Ox. pap. xxiii.): a papyrus of Isocrates, *in Nicoclem*, now at Marseilles: a fragment of Ezekiel, in book-form, in the Bodleian Library: a fragment of the "Shepherd" of Hermas at Berlin: and a fragment of Julius Africanus, the *Hellenica* of Theopompus or Cratippus, and the *Symposium* of Plato, all found at Oxyrhynchus.

Of the 3rd century also are some fragments which are palaeographically of interest, as they are written neither in the recognised literary hand nor in simple cursive, but in cursive characters moulded and adapted in a set form for literary use—thus anticipating the early stages of the development of the minuscule book-hand of the 9th century from the cursive writing of that time.

With the 3rd century the literary hand on papyrus appears to lose most of its importance. We are within measurable distance of the age of vellum, and of the formal uncial writing of the vellum MSS. which is found in some existing examples of the 4th century and in more abundant numbers of the 5th century. We have now to see how the connexion can be established between the literary handwriting of the papyri and the firmer and heavier literary uncial writing of the vellum codices. The literary hands on papyrus which have been reviewed above are distinctly of the style inscribed with a light touch most suitable to the comparatively frail material of papyrus. In the Bankes Homer, however, one may detect some indication of the fullness that characterizes the vellum uncial writing. But it now appears that a larger and rounder hand was also employed on papyrus at least as early as the 1st century. In proof of this we are able to cite a non-literary document (fig. 10) bearing an actual date, which happens to be written in characters that, exclusive of certain less formally-made letters, are of a large uncial literary type. This writing, though not actually of the finished style familiar to us in the early vellum MSS., yet resembles it so generally that it may be assumed, almost as a certainty, that there was in the 1st century a full literary uncial hand formed on this pattern, which was the direct ancestor of the vellum uncial. The tendency to employ at this period a calligraphic style, as seen in the fragments of the Odyssey and one of the Hesiodic poems mentioned above, supports this assumption. The document now referred to is a deed of sale written in the seventh year of Domitian, A.D. 88 (Brit. Mus. pap. cxli.). The letters still retaining a cursive element are *alpha*, *upsilon*, and in some instances *epsilon*.

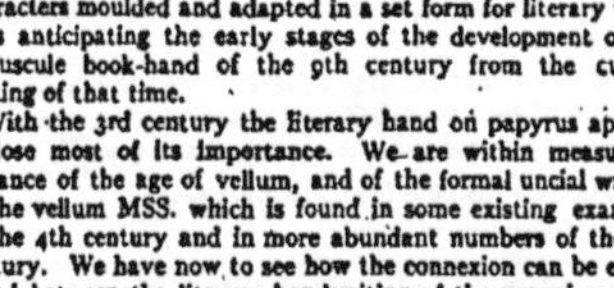

€ΝΠΠΟΛΕΜΑΙΔΙ ΕΥΕΓΓΕ
ΖΙΩΙ ΚΑΙ ΜΤΟΥΤΟΥΓΖΝ
ΥΤΟΥΠΕΘΕЄШCΩCEΤШ
ЄΓЄΠΙΓΑΦΗΝ ΑΠΟΤΗC
ΑΥΤΟΥΠЄΘЄ-ΕΛΑΙΩΝ

Fig. 10.—Deed of Sale, A.D. 88.

(—ψ πτολεμαιδι ευεργε—
—ξιωι και η τουτου γυ-
—υ του πεθεως εωι ετω—
—ετεπιγραφην απο της—
—αυτου πεθεα ελαιων—)

As evidence in support of this view that the uncial hand of the vellum MSS. is to be traced back to the period of the document just quoted, we have the important papyrus found by Mr Flinders Petrie at Hawara in Egypt, and now in the Bodleian Library, which contains a portion of the second book of the *Iliad*. The writing is of the large uncial type under consideration; and there is now full reason for assigning it to the 2nd century at latest. Before the discovery of the document of the year 88 there was nothing to give a clue to the real period of the Homer; and now the date which has been suggested is corroborated by a fragment of papyrus from Oxyrhynchus inscribed with some lines from the same book of the *Iliad* (fig. 11) in the same large uncial type (Ox. Pap. vol. i. no. 20, pl. v.). In this latter instance there can be no question of the early date of the writing as on the verso of the papyrus accounts of the end of the 2nd century or of the beginning of the 3rd century have been subsequently added. Yet a third example of the same character has more recently been found at Tebtunis (Tebt. Pap. vol. ii. no. 265,

pl. i.): again a considerable fragment of the second book of the *Iliad*.

Thus, then, in the 1st and 2nd centuries there was in use a large uncial hand which was evidently the forerunner of the literary uncial hand of the early vellum codices. It is also to be noted that the literary examples just mentioned are MSS. of Homer; and hence one is tempted to suggest that, as in the production of sumptuous copies on papyrus of a work of such universal popularity and veneration as the *Iliad* this large and handsome uncial was specially employed, so also the use of a

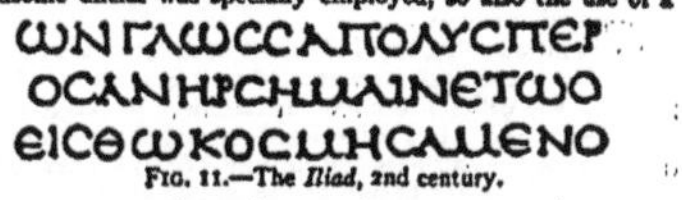

ШΝ ΓΛΩCCΑΠΟΛΥCΠΕΡ
ΟCΑΝ ΗΡCΗΜΑΙΝЄΤШΟ
ЄΙCЄ Ш ΚΟCΜΗCΑΜЄΝΟ

Fig. 11.—The *Iliad*, 2nd century.

(—ω γλωσσα πολυσπερ—
—ος απηρ σημ ινετω ο—
—ισθω κοσμησαμενο—)

similar type for the early vellum copies of the sacred text of the Scriptures naturally followed.

GREEK WRITING. II.—THE VELLUM CODICES

Uncial Writing.—It has been shown above how a round uncial hand had been developing in Greek writing on papyrus during the early centuries of the Christian era, and how even as early as the 2nd century a well-formed uncial script was in use, at least for sumptuous copies of so great and popular an author as Homer. We have now to describe the uncial hand as it appears in Greek MSS. written on vellum. This harder and firmer and smoother material afforded to the scribes better scope for a calligraphic style hardly possible on papyrus. With the ascendancy of the vellum codex as the vehicle for literature, the characters received the fixed and settled forms to which the name of uncial is more exactly attached than to the fluctuating letters of the early papyri. The term uncial has been borrowed from the nomenclature of Latin palaeography[1] and applied to Greek writing of the larger type, to distinguish it from the minuscule or smaller character which succeeded it in vellum MSS. of the 9th century. In Latin majuscule writing there exist both capitals and uncials, each class distinct. In Greek, MSS. pure capital-letter writing was never employed (except occasionally for ornamental titles at a late time). As distinguished from the square capitals of inscriptions, Greek uncial writing has certain rounded letters, as α, ε, ϲ, ω, modifications in others, and some letters extending above or below the line.

It is not probable that vellum codices were in ordinary use earlier than the 4th century; and it is in codices of that age that the handsome calligraphic uncial above referred to was developed. A few years ago the 4th century was the earliest limit to which palaeographers had dared to carry back any ancient vellum codex inscribed in uncials. But the recovery of the Homeric papyri written in the large uncials of the 2nd and 3rd century has led to a revision of former views on the date of one early vellum MS. in particular. This MS. is the fragmentary Homer of the Ambrosian Library at Milan, consisting of some fifty pieces of vellum cut out of the original codex for the sake of the pictures which they contain; and all of the text that has survived is that which happened to be on the back of the pictures. The Ambrosian Homer has hitherto been generally placed in the 5th century, and the difference of the style of the writing from that of the usual calligraphic type of uncial MSS. of that time, which had been remarked, was thought rather to indicate inferiority in age. But the similarity of the character of the writing (taller, and more slender than is usual in vellum codices) to that of the large uncials of the papyrus Homers of the 2nd and 3rd century from Hawara and Oxyrhynchus and Tebtunis is so striking that the

[1] St Jerome's often quoted words, "uncialibus, ut vulgo aiunt, litteris" in his preface to the book of Job, have never been explained satisfactorily. Of the character referred to as "uncial" there is no question; but the derivation of the term is not settled.

Ambrosian Homer must be classed with them. Hence it is now held that that MS. may certainly be as early as the 3rd century. But, as that century was still within the period when papyrus was the general vehicle for Greek literature, it may be asked why that material should not in this instance also have been used. The answer may fairly be ventured that vellum was certainly a better material to receive the illustrative paintings, and on that account was employed. The Ambrosian Homer may therefore be regarded as a most interesting link between the papyrus uncial of the 2nd century and the vellum uncial of the 4th and 5th centuries.

With the introduction, then, of vellum as the general writing material, the uncial characters entered on a new phase. The light touch and delicate forms so characteristic of calligraphy on papyrus gave place to a rounder and stronger hand, in which the contrast of fine hair-lines and thickened down-strokes adds so conspicuously to the beauty of the writing of early MSS. on vellum. And here it may be remarked, with respect to the attribution to particular periods of these early examples, that we are not altogether on firm ground. Internal evidence, such, for example, as the presence of the Eusebian Canons in a MS. of the Gospel, assists us in fixing a limit of age, but when there is no such support the dating of these early MSS. must be more or less conjectural. It is not till the beginning of the 6th century that we meet with an uncial MS. which can be approximately dated; and, taking this as a standard of comparison, we are enabled to distinguish those which undoubtedly have the appearance of greater age and to arrange them in some sort of chronological order. But these codices are too few in number to afford material in sufficient quantity for training the eye by familiarity with a variety of hands of any one period—the only method which can give entirely trustworthy results.

Among the earliest examples of vellum uncial MSS. are the three famous codices of the Bible. Of these, the most ancient, the Codex Vaticanus, is probably of the 4th century. The writing must, in its original condition, have been very perfect as a specimen of penmanship; but nearly the whole of the text has been traced over by a later hand, perhaps in the 10th or 11th century, and only such words or letters as were rejected as readings have been left untouched. Written in triple columns, in letters of uniform size, without enlarged initial letters to mark even the beginnings of books, the MS. has all the simplicity of extreme antiquity (*Pal. Soc.* pl. 104). The Codex Sinaiticus (*Pal. Soc.* pl. 105) has also the same marks of age, and is judged by its discoverer, Tischendorf, to be even more ancient than the Vatican MS. In this, however, a comparison of the writing of the two MSS. leads to the conclusion that he was mistaken. The writing of the Codex Sinaiticus is not so pure as that of the other MS., and, if that is a criterion of age, the Vatican MS. holds the first place. In one particular the Codex Sinaiticus has been thought to approach in form to its possible archetype on papyrus. It is written with four columns to a page, the open book thus presenting eight columns in sequence, and recalling the long line of columns on an open roll. With regard to such general outward resemblances between the later papyrus literary rolls and the early vellum uncial MSS., we may cite such papyri as the Berlin commentary on the *Theaetetus* of Plato of the 2nd century and the Oxyrhynchus fragment of Julius Africanus of the 3rd century as forerunners of the style in which the two great codices here mentioned were cast.

The Codex Alexandrinus (fig. 12) is placed in the middle of the 5th century. Here we have an advance on the style of the other two codices. The MS. is written in double columns only, and enlarged letters stand at the beginning of paragraphs. But yet the writing is generally more elegant than that of the Codex Sinaiticus. Examining these MSS. with a view to ascertain the rules which guided the scribes in their work, we find simplicity and regularity the leading features; the round letters formed in symmetrical curves; C and Ϲ, &c., finishing off in a hair-line sometimes thickened at the end into a dot; horizontal strokes fine, those of Є, Н, and Θ being either in the middle or high in the letter; the base of Δ and the cross-stroke

of Π also fine, and, as a rule, kept within the limits of the letters and not projecting beyond. Here also may be noticed the occurrence in the Codex Alexandrinus of Coptic forms of letters (*e.g.* Δ, Ц, *alpha* and *mu*) in the titles of books, &c., confirmatory of the tradition of the Egyptian origin of the MS.

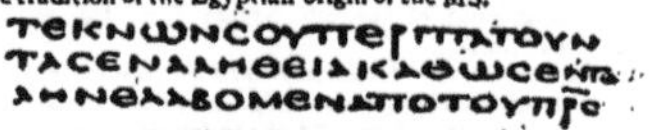

ΤΕΚΝΩΝϹΟΥΠΕΡΙΠΑΤΟΥΝ
ΤΑϹΕΝΑΛΗΘΕΙΑΚΑΘΩϹΕΝΤΑ
ΛΗΝΕΛΑΒΟΜΕΝΑΠΟΤΟΥΠΡϹ

FIG. 12.—The Bible (Cod. Alex.), 5th century.

(τεκνων σου περιπατουν
τας εν αληθεια καθως εντο
λην ελαβομεν απο του π[ατ]ρ[ο]ς).—2 John 4.

To the 5th century may also belong the palimpsest MS. of the Bible, known from the upper text as the Codex Ephraemi, at Paris (ed. Tischendorf, 1845), and the Octateuch (Codex Sarravianus), whose extant leaves are divided between Paris, Leiden and St Petersburg—both of which MSS. are probably of Egyptian origin. Perhaps of the end of the 5th or beginning of the 6th century is the illustrated Genesis of the Cottonian Library, now unfortunately reduced to fragments by fire, but once the finest example of its kind (*Cat. Anc. MSS.* i. pl. 8). And to about the same time belong the Dio Cassius of the Vatican (Silvestre, pl. 60) and the Pentateuch of the Bibliothèque Nationale (ibid. pl. 61).

In the writing of uncial MSS. of the 6th century there is a marked degeneration. The letters, though still round, are generally of a larger character, more heavily formed, and not so compactly written as in the preceding century. Horizontal strokes (*e.g.* in Δ, Π, Τ) are lengthened and finished off with heavy points or finials. The earliest example of this period which has to be noticed is the Dioscorides of Vienna (fig. 13), which is of particular value for the study of the palaeography of early vellum MSS. It is the first uncial example to which an approximate date can be given. There is good evidence to show that it was written early in the 6th century for Juliana Anicia, daughter of Flavius Anicius Olybrius, emperor of the West in 472. Here we already notice the characteristics of uncial writings of the 6th century, to which reference has been

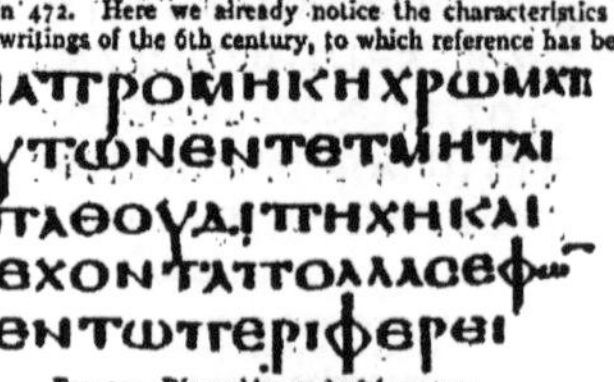

ΙΑΤΡΟΜΗΚΗΧΡΩΜΑΤΙ
ΥΤΩΝΕΝΤΕΤΜΗΤΑΙ
ΤΑΘΟΥΔΙΤΠΗΧΗΚΑΙ
ΕΧΟΝΤΑΤΤΟΛΛΑϹΕΦ·
ΕΝΤΩΠΕΡΙΦΕΡΕΙ

FIG. 13.—Dioscorides, early 6th century.

(—ια προμηκη χρωματι
—[α]ινεων υπερμηται
—[χα]ιραθου διτηχη και
—εχοντα πολλας εφ ω[ν]
—εν τω περιφερει)

made. To this century also belong the palimpsest Homer under a Syriac text in the British Museum (*Cat. Anc. MSS.* i. pl. 9); its companion volume, used by the same Syrian scribe, in which are fragments of St Luke's Gospel (ibid., pl. 10); the Dublin palimpsest fragments of St Matthew and Isaiah (T. K. Abbot, *Par Palimpsest*, Dubl.), written in Egypt; the fragments of the Pauline Epistles from Mount Athos, some of which are at Paris and others at Moscow (Silvestre, pls. 63, 64; Sabas, pl. A), of which, however, the writing has been disfigured by retracing at a later period; the Gospels (Cod. N) written in silver and gold on purple vellum, whose leaves are scattered in London (Cott. MS., Titus C. xv.), Rome, Vienna, St Petersburg, and its native home, Patmos; the fragmentary Eusebian Canons written on gilt vellum and highly ornamented, the sole remains, of some sumptuous volume (*Cat. Anc. MSS.* i. pl. 11), the Coislin Octateuch (Silvestre, pl. 65); the Genesis of Vienna, and the Codex Rossanensis, and the recently recovered Codex Sinopensis of the Gospels, instances of the very few early illustrated MSS. which have survived. Of the same period is the Codex Marchalianus of the Prophets, which, written in Egypt, follows in its style the Coptic form of uncial.

Reference may here be made to certain early bilingual Graeco-Latin uncial MSS., written in the 6th and 7th centuries, which, however, have rather to be studied apart, or in connexion with Latin palaeography; for the Greek letters of these MSS. run more or less upon the lines of the Latin forms. The best known of these examples are the Codex-Bezae of the New Testament, at Cambridge (*Pal. Soc.* pls. 14, 15), and the Codex Claromontanus of the Pauline Epistles, at Paris (*Pal. Soc.* pls. 63, 64), attributed to the 6th or 7th century; and the Laudian MS. of the Acts of the Apostles (*Pal. Soc* pl. 80) of the 7th century. To these may be added the Harleian Glossary (*Cat. Anc. MSS.* i. pl. 13), also of the 7th century. A later example, of the 8th century, is the Graeco-Latin Psalter, at Paris, MS. Coislin 186 (Omont, *Facs. des plus anciens MSS. grecs,* pl. vii.).

An offshoot of early Greek uncial writing on vellum is seen in the Moeso-Gothic alphabet which Ulfilas constructed for the use of his countrymen in the 4th century, mainly from the Greek letters. Of the few extant remains of Gothic MSS. the oldest and most perfect is the Codex Argenteus of the Gospels, at Upsala, of the 6th century (*Pal. Soc.* pl. 118), written in characters which compare with purely written Greek MSS. of the same period. Other Gothic fragments appear in the sloping uncial hand seen in Greek MSS. of the 7th and following centuries.

About the year 600 Greek uncial writing passes into a new stage. We leave the period of the round and enter on that of the oval character. The letters ϵ, ϴ, ϲ, ω, instead of being symmetrically formed on the lines of a circle, are made oval; and other letters are laterally compressed into a narrow shape. In the 7th century also the writing begins to slope to the right, and accents are introduced and afterwards systematically applied. This slanting style of uncials continues in use through the 8th and 9th and into the 10th centuries, becoming heavier as time goes on. In this class of writing there is again the same dearth of dated MSS. as in the round uncial, to serve as standards for the assignment of dates. We have to reach the 9th century before finding a single dated MS. in this kind of writing. It is true that sloping Greek uncial writing is found in a few scattered notes and glosses in Syriac MSS. which bear actual dates in the 7th century, and they are so far useful as showing that this hand was firmly established at that time; but they do not afford sufficient material in quantity to be of really practical use for comparison (see the tables of alphabets in Gardthausen's *Griech. Paläog.*). Of more value are a few palimpsest fragments of the *Elements* of Euclid and of Gospel Lectionaries which occur also in the Syriac collection in the British Museum, and are written in the 7th and 8th centuries. There is also in the Vatican a MS. (Reg. 886) of the Theodosian code, which can be assigned with fair accuracy to the close of the 7th century (Gardth. *Gr. Pal.* pl. 138), which, however, being calligraphically written, retains some of the earlier rounder forms. This MS. may be taken as an example of transitional style. In the fragment of a mathematical treatise (fig. 14) from Bobio, forming part of a MS. rewritten in the 8th century and assignable to the previous century, the slanting writing is fully developed. The formation of the letters is good, and conveys the impression that the scribe was writing a hand quite natural to him:—

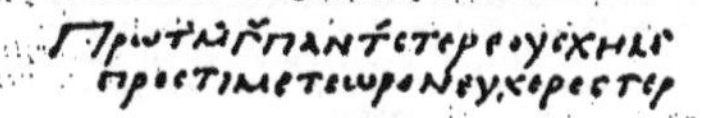

[Greek uncial facsimile]

FIG. 14.—Mathemat. Treatise, 7th century.

τχρωτ[ον] μ[εν] γ[αρ] ταντ[οι] ετεροου σχηματον]
προς τι μετεωρον ευχερεστερ—)

It should be also noticed that in this MS.—a secular one—

there are numerous abbreviations (Wattenbach, *Script. gr. specim.* tab. 8). An important document of this time is also the fragment of papyrus in the Imperial Library at Vienna, which bears the signatures of bishops and others to the acts of the Council of Constantinople of 680. Some of the signatures are in slanting uncials (Wattenb., *Script. gr. specim.,* tabb. 12, 13; Gardth., *Gr. Pal.* tab. 7). Of the 8th century is the collection of hymns (Brit. Mus., Add. MS. 26, 113) written without breathings or accents (*Cat. Anc. MSS.* i. pl. 14). To the same century belongs the Codex Marcianus, the Venetian MS. of the Old Testament, which is marked with breathings and accents. The plate reproduced from this MS. (Wattenb., *Script. gr. specim.,* tab. 9) contains in the second column a few lines written in round uncials, but in such a laboured style that nothing could more clearly prove the discontinuance of that form of writing as an ordinary hand. In the middle of the 9th century at length we find a MS. with a date in the Psalter of Bishop Uspensky of the year 862 (Wattenb. *Script. gr. specim.,* tab. 10). A little later in date is the MS. of Gregory of Nazianzus, written between 867 and 886 (Silvestre, pl. 71); and at the end of the 9th or beginning of the 10th century stands a lectionary in the Harleian collection (*Cat. Anc. MSS.* i. pl. 17). A valuable series of examples is also given by Omont (*Facsimiles des plus anc. MSS. grecs: de la Bibl. Nat.*). But by this time minuscule writing was well established, and the use of the more inconvenient uncial was henceforth almost entirely confined to church-service books. Owing to this limitation uncial writing now underwent a further calligraphic change. As the 10th century advances the sloping characters by degrees become more upright, and with this resumption of their old position they begin in the next century to cast off the compressed formation and again become rounder. All this is simply the result of calligraphic imitation. Bibles and service-books have always been the MSS. in particular on which finely formed writing has been lavished; and it was but natural that, when a style of writing fell into general disuse, its continuance, where it did continue, should become more and more traditional, and a work of copying rather than of writing. In the 10th century there are a few examples bearing dates. There are facsimiles from three of them, viz. a copy of the Gospels (fig. 15), in the Vatican, of 949 (*New Pal. Soc.* pl. 105), the Curzon Lectionary of 980, and the Harleian Lectionary of 995 (*Pal. Soc.* pls. 154, 26, 27). The Bodleian commentary on the Psalter (D. 4, 1) is likewise of great palaeographic value, being written partly in uncials and partly in minuscules of the middle of the 10th century (Gardth., *Gr. Pal.* p. 159, tab. 2, col. 4). This late form of uncial writing appears to have lasted to about the middle of the 11th century. (Omont. Facs. pl. xxii.). From it was formed the Slavonic writing in use at the present day:—

[Greek uncial facsimile]

ΛΕΓΩΝ·Η·ΚΕ·Ϊ·ΑΝ·Θ·ΕΛΗC·
ΔΥΝΑCΑΙ·ΜΕ·ΚΑ·Θ·Α
ΡΙCΑΙ·Η·ΚΑΙ·ΕΚ·ΤΕΙΝΑC·
ΤΗΝ·ΧΕΙΡΑ·ΗΨΑΤΟ
ΑΥΤΟΥ·Ο·ΙΗ·ΛΕΓΩΝ

FIG. 15.—The Gospels (Vatican), A.D. 949.

(λεγων + κυριε εαν θελης
δυνασαι με καθα
ρισαι + και εκτεινας
την χειρα ηψατο
αυτου ο ιησους λεγων)

Under the head of late uncial writing must be classed a few bilingual Graeco-Latin MSS. which have survived, written in a bastard kind of uncial in the west of Europe. This writing follows, wherever the shapes of the letters permit, the formation of corresponding Latin characters—the purely Greek forms being imitated in a clumsy fashion. Such MSS. are the Codex Augiensis of: Trinity College, Cambridge, of the end of the 9th century (*Pal. Soc.* pl. 127) and the Psalter of St Nicholas of Cusa (pl. 128) and the Codex Sangallensis and Boernerianus of the 10th century (pl. 179). The same imitative characters are used in quotations of Greek words in Latin MSS. of the same periods.

Minuscule Writing.—The beautifully formed minuscule book-hand, which practically superseded the uncial book-hand in the 9th century, did not spring into existence all at once. Its formation had been the work of centuries. It was the direct descendant of the cursive Greek writing of the papyri. It has been shown above, in tracing the progress of the non-literary, cursive writing on papyrus, how the original forms of the letters of the Greek alphabet went through various modifications, always tending towards the creation of the forms which eventually settled down into the recognized minuscules or small letters of the middle ages and modern times. The development of these modifications is apparent from the first; but it was in the Byzantine period especially that the changes became more marked and more rapid. All the minuscule forms, as we know them in medieval literature, had been practically evolved by the end of the 5th century, and in the course of the next two hundred years those forms became more and more confirmed. In the large formal cursive writing of the documents of the 6th and 7th centuries we can pick out the minuscule alphabet in the rough. It only needed to be cast in a calligraphic mould to become the book-hand minuscule, the later development of which we have now to trace. This calligraphic mould seems to have been found in the imperial chancery, from whence issued documents written in a fine round minuscule hand on an ample scale, as appears from one or two rare surviving examples attributed to the 8th and 9th centuries (see the facsimile of an imperial letter, dated variously A.D. 756 or 839, in Wattenbach, *Script. graec. specim.*, pls. xiv., xv., and in Omont, *Facs. des plus anc. MSS. grecs.* pls. xxvi., xxvii.; and Brit. Mus. papyrus xxxii.). The fine hand only needed to be reduced in scale to become the calligraphic minuscule book-hand of the vellum MSS.

Thus, then, in the 9th century, the minuscule book-hand came into general use for literature, and, with the finely prepared vellum of the time ready to receive it, it assumed under the pens of expert calligraphers the requisite cast, upright, regular and symmetrical, which renders it in its earliest stages one of the most beautiful forms of writing ever created.

Greek MSS. written in minuscules have been classed as follow: (1) *codices vetustissimi*, of the 9th century and to the middle of the 10th century; (2) *vetusti*, from the middle of the 10th to the middle of the 13th century; (3) *recentiores*, from the middle of the 13th century to the fall of Constantinople, 1453; (4) *novelli*, all after that date.

Of dated minuscule MSS. there is a not inconsiderable number scattered among the different libraries of Europe. Gardthausen (*Gr. Pal.* 344 seq.) gives a list of some thousand, ending at A.D. 1500. But, as might be expected, the majority belong to the later classes.[1] Of the 9th century there are not ten which actually bear dates and of these all but one belong to the latter half of the century. In the 10th century, however, the number rises to nearly fifty, in the 11th to more than a hundred.

In the period of *codices vetustissimi* the minuscule hand is distinguished by its simplicity and purity. The period has been well described as the classic age of minuscules. The letters are symmetrically formed; the writing is compact and upright, or has even a slight tendency to slope to the left. In a word, the beauty of this class of minuscule writing is unsurpassed. But in addition to these general characteristics there are special

[1] In Omont's *Facs. des MSS. grecs datés de la Bibl. Nat.* will be found a useful list of upwards of 300 facsimiles of dated Greek MSS. (including uncials).

distinctions which belong to it. The minuscule character is maintained intact, without intrusion of larger or uncial-formed letters. With its cessation as the ordinary literary hand the uncial character had not died out. We have seen that it was still used for liturgical books. It likewise continued to survive in a modified or half-uncial form for scholia, rubrics, titles, and special purposes—as, for example, in the Bodleian Euclid (fig. 16)—in minuscule written MSS. of the 9th and 10th centuries. These uses of the older character sufficed to keep it in remembrance, and it is therefore not a matter for surprise that some of its forms should reappear and commingle with the simple minuscule. This afterwards actually took place. But in the period now under consideration, when the minuscule had been cast into a new mould, and was, so to say, in the full vigour of youth, extraneous forms were rigorously excluded.

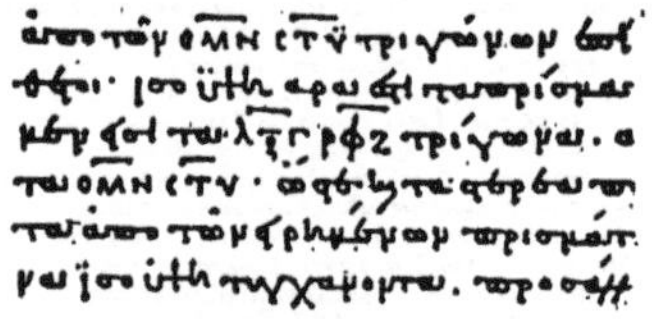

Fig. 16.—Euclid (Oxford), A.D. 888.

(ἀπὸ τῶν ὅΜΝ ΣΤΤ τριγώνων ἐπι-
θέτοι· ἰσούψη ἄρα ἐστὶ τὰ πρίσμα[τα]—
μεν ωσι τὰ ΑΞΤ ΡΦΖ τρίγωνα. α—
τὰ ὅΜΝ ΣΤΤ ὥστε [α]ίτα στερεα π—
τὰ ἀπὸ τῶν ευρημένων τριγμάτ[ων]—
να ἰσούψη τυγχάνοντα· πρὸς ἀλλ[ηλα]—)

The breathings also of this class are rectangular, in unison with the careful and deliberate character of the writing; and there is but slight, if any, separation of the words. In addition, as far as has hitherto been observed, the letters run above, or stand upon, the ruled lines, and do not depend from them as at a later period. The exact time at which this latter mechanical change took place cannot be named; like other changes it would naturally establish itself by usage. But at least in the middle of the 10th century it seems to have been in use. In the Bodleian MS. of Basil's homilies of 953 A.D. (*Pal. Soc.* pl. 82) the new method is followed; and if we are to accept the date of the 9th century ascribed to a MS. in the Ambrosian Library at Milan (Wattenb., *Script. gr. specim.*, tab. 17), in which the ruled lines run above the writing, the practice was yet earlier. Certain scribal peculiarities, however, about the MS. make us hesitate to place it so early. In the Laurentian Herodotus (W and V., *Exempla*, tab. 31), which belongs to the 10th century, sometimes the one, sometimes the other system is followed in different parts of the volume; and the same peculiarity happens in the MS. of Gregory of Nazianzus of A.D. 972 in the British Museum (*Pal. Soc.* pl. 25; *Exempla*, tab. 7). The second half of the 10th century therefore appears to be a period of transition in this respect.

The earliest dated example of *codices vetustissimi* is the copy of the Gospels belonging to Bishop Uspensky, written in the year 835. A facsimile is given by Gardthausen (*Beiträge*) and repeated in the *Exempla* (tab. 1). Better specimens have been photographed from the Oxford Euclid of A.D. 888 (*Pal. Soc.* pls. 65, 66; *Exempla*, tab. 2) from a MS. of Saints' Lives at Paris of A.D. 890 (Omont, *Facs. des MSS. gr. datés*, pl. 1), and from the Oxford Plato (fig. 17) of A.D. 895 (*Pal. Soc.* pl. 81; *Exempla*, tab. 3): Sabas (*Specim. Palaeograph.*), has also given two facsimiles from MSS. of 880 and 899.

Of dated examples of the first half of the 10th century about a dozen facsimiles are available.

After the middle of the 10th century we enter on the period of the *codices vetusti*, in which the writing becomes gradually less compact. The letters, so to say, open their ranks; and, from this circumstance alone, MSS. of the second half of the century may generally be distinguished from those fifty years earlier. But alterations also take place in the shapes of the letters. Side by side with the purely minuscule forms those of the uncial begin to reappear, the cause of which innovation has already been explained. These uncial forms first show

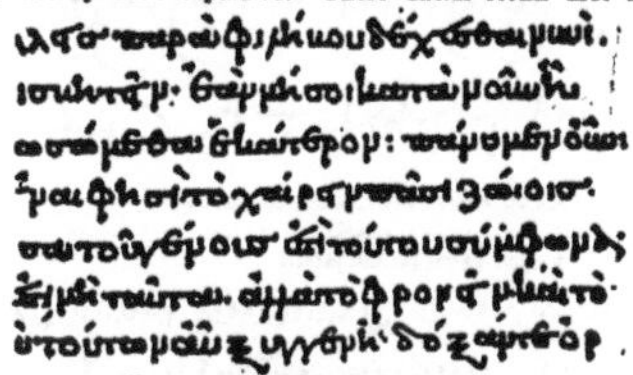

Fig. 17.—Plato (Oxford), A.D. 895.

(—[μιλ]λειs παρὰ φιλάβου δέχεσθαι νυνί.
—[αμφ]ισβητεῖν. ἐὰν μή σοι κατὰ νοῦν ᾖ.
—[συγκεφαλαι]ωσώμεθα ἑκάτερον· πάντ μεν οὖνι
—[εἶ]ναι φησί. τὸ χαίρειν πᾶσι ζῷοισι.
—[ὅ]σα τοῦ γένους ἐστὶ τούτου σύμφωνα
—ἐστι μὴ ταῦτα. ἀλλὰ τὸ φρονεῖν. καὶ τὸ
—[τὰ] τούτων αὖ ξυγγενῆ δόξάν τε ἀρ)

themselves at the end of the line, the point at which most changes first gained a footing, but by degrees they work back into the text, and at length become recognized members of the minuscule characters. In the 11th and 12th centuries they are well established, and become more and more prominent by the large or stilted forms which they assume. The change, however, in the general character of the writing of this class of *codices vetusti* is very gradual, uniformity and evenness being well maintained, especially in church books. On the other hand, a lighter and more cursive kind of minuscule is found contemporaneously in MSS. generally of a secular nature. In this hand many of the classical MSS. of the 10th or 11th centuries are written, as the MS. of Aeschylus and Sophocles, the Odyssey and the Apollonius Rhodius of the Laurentian Library at Florence, the Anthologia Palatina of Heidelberg and Paris, the Hippocrates of Venice (*Exempla*, tabb. 32-36, 38, 40), the Aristophanes of Ravenna (Wattenb., *Script. gr. specim.*, tab. 26), the Strabo of Paris (Omont, *Facs. des plus anc. MSS. grecs*, pl 40), a Demosthenes (fig. 18) at Florence (*Pal. Soc.* ii. pl. 88, 89), &c. In a facsimile from a Plutarch at Venice (*Exempla*, tab. 44), the scribe is seen to change from the formal to the more cursive hand. This style of writing is distinguishable by its light and graceful character from the current writing into which the minuscule degenerated at a later time.

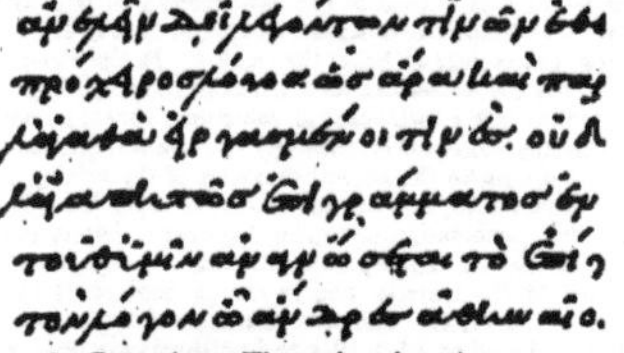

Fig. 18.—Demosthenes (Florence), early 11th century.

(ἀνελεῖν δεῖ λεγόντων τινῶν ἰσθ[ίλειν]—
πρόχειρος λόγος. ὡς ἄρα καὶ παρ'—
λ'ἀγαθὰ εἰργασμένοι τινές. οἰδ[ενὸς]—
λ'ἀγαπητὸς ἐπιγράμματος ἐν—
τοῦθ' ὑμῖν ἀναγνώσεται τὸ ἐπί[γραμμα]—
τὸν λόγον ὦ ἄνδρες ἀθηναῖοι)

The gradual rounding of the rectangular breathings takes place in this period. In the 11th century the smooth breathing, which would most readily lend itself to this modification, first appears in the new form. In the course of the 12th century both breathings have lost the old square shape; and about the same time contractions become more numerous, having been at first confined to the end of the line.

When the period of *codices recentiores* commences, the Greek

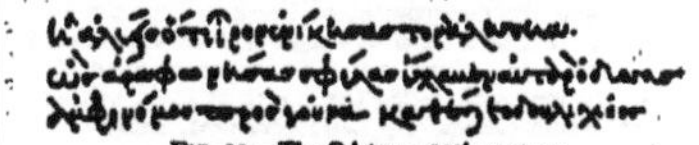

Fig. 19.—The Odyssey, 13th century.

(ἢ ἄλλαs ὅτι ἴρον ὑλίκησοι τὸν ἀλήτην
ὣς ἄρα φωνήσαs σφέλλας ἔλλαβεν αὐτὰρ ὀδύσσεὺs
ἀμφωνύμου πρὸς γοῦνα καθίζετο δουλιχ[ιῆ]οι)

minuscule hand undergoes extensive changes. The contrast between MSS. of the 13th century and those of a hundred years earlier is very marked. In the later examples the hand is generally more straggling, there is a greater number of exaggerated forms of letters, and marks of contraction and accents are dashed on more freely. There is altogether a sense of greater activity and haste. The increasing demand for books created a larger supply. Greater freedom and more variety appear in the examples of this class, together with an increasing use of ligatures and contractions. The general introduction of paper likewise assisted to break up the formal minuscule hand. To this rougher material a rougher style of writing was suited. Through the 14th and 15th centuries the decline of the set minuscule rapidly advances. The writing becomes even more involved and intricate, marks of contraction and accents are combined with the letters in a single action of the pen, and the general result is the production of a thoroughly cursive hand. In some respects, however, the change was not so rapid. Church books were still ordinarily written on vellum, which, as it became scarcer in the market (owing to the injury done to the trade by the competition of paper), was supplied from ancient codices which lay ready to hand on the shelves of libraries; and in these liturgical MSS. the more formal style of the minuscule was still maintained. In the 14th century there even appears a partial renaissance in the writing of Church MSS., modelled to some extent on the lines of the writing of the 12th century. The resemblance, however, is only superficial; for no writer can entirely disguise the character of the writing of his own time. And lastly there was yet another check upon the absolute disintegration of the minuscule book-hand in the 15th century exercised by the professional scribes who worked in Italy, and who in their calligraphical productions reverted again to the older style. The influence of the Renaissance is evident in many of the MSS. of the Italian Greeks, which served as models for the first Greek printing types.

The Greek minuscule book-hand had, then, by the end of the 15th century, become a cursive hand, from which the modern current hand is directly derived. We last saw the ancient cursive in use in the documents prior to the formation of the set minuscule book-hand, and no doubt it continued in use concurrently with the book-hand. But, as the latter passed through the transformations which have been traced, and gradually assumed a more current style, it may not unreasonably be supposed that it absorbed the cursive hand of the period, and with it whatever elements may have survived of the old cursive hand.

LATIN WRITING. I.—THE ROMAN CURSIVE

The course of Latin palaeography runs on the same lines as that of Greek palaeography. In regard to the former, as in regard to the latter, the documents fall into two main divisions. those which are written in the ordinary cursive hand of everyday life, and those which are written in the formal book-hand of literature. But Latin palaeography covers a wider ground than Greek. Greek writing being limited to the expression of the one language of a single people has a comparatively narrow and simple career. On the other hand, the Latin alphabet, having been adopted by the nations of western Europe, underwent many transformations in the course of development of the national handwritings of the different peoples, and consequently had a wide and varied career. But in one respect Latin palaeography is at a disadvantage as compared with the sister branch. As we have seen, Greek documents are extant dating back to the 4th century B.C., and the development of Greek writing can be fairly well illustrated by a series of examples of the succeeding centuries. There is no such series of Latin documents available to afford us the means of tracing the growth of Latin writing to the same remote period. No Latin document, either of a literary or of a non-literary character, has yet been recovered which can be placed with certainty earlier than the Christian era. Egypt, while giving up hundreds and thousands of documents in Greek, has hitherto yielded but little in Latin, even of the 1st century, and little too of the next following centuries. Indeed, for our knowledge of Latin writing of the 1st century we still have to depend chiefly upon the results of excavations at Pompeii and Herculaneum and in the Roman catacombs, upon the wall-scribblings which have been laid bare, and upon the waxen tablets and the few papyri which have thence been recovered.

At the time when we come into touch with the first extant examples of Roman writing, we find a few instances of a literary or book-hand as well as a fairly extensive variety of cursive hands. It will be convenient in the first place to examine the Roman cursive writing during the early centuries of our era. Then, for the moment suspending further research in this branch of our subject, we shall proceed to describe the literary script and to trace the development of the large form of book-hand, or majuscule writing, in its two divisions of capitals and uncials, and of the intermediate styles composed of a mixture of large and small letters, or consisting of a blend of the two classes of letters which has received the name of half-uncial. Then we shall turn to follow the development of the national hands, when it will be necessary to come into touch again with the Roman cursive, whence the western continental scripts were derived; and so we shall proceed to the formation of the minuscule writing of the middle ages.

The materials for the study of the early Roman cursive hand have been found in the wall-scribblings, or graffiti, of Pompeii and Herculaneum and Rome (collected in the *Corp. inscr. lat.* vol. iv.); in the series of 127 *libelli* or waxen tablets, consisting of *perscriptiones* and other deeds connected with sales by auction and tax receipts discovered in the house of the banker L. Caecilius Jucundus at Pompeii, and bearing dates of A.D. 15, 27, and 53-62 (published in *C.I.L.* iv., supplement); in a few scattered papyri from Egypt; and in a set of four-and-twenty waxen tablets bearing dates ranging from A.D. 131 to 167, which were found in ancient mining works in the neighbourhood of Alburnus Major (the modern Verespatak) in Dacia (*C. I. L.* iii.);

It will have been observed that in the case of the above documents there are three different kinds of material on which they have been inscribed: the plaster surface of walls, the waxen coatings of tablets, and the smooth surface of papyrus. The two former may be classed together as being of a nature which would offer a certain resistance to the free movement of the stilus, while in the case of papyrus the writing-reed or pen would run without impediment. Hence, in writing on the former materials there was a natural tendency to form the letters in disconnected strokes, to make them upright or even inclined to the left, and to employ vertical strokes in preference. The three following specimens from the graffiti and the two sets of tablets will demonstrate the conservative character of this kind of writing, covering as they do about a century and a half. This conservativeness may suggest the probability that the hand seen in the graffiti and the Pompeian tablets had not changed very materially from that practised a century or more earlier, and that it is practically the hand in which the Roman classical

writers composed their works. When examining the alphabet of this early Roman cursive hand, we find (as we found in the early Greek cursive) the first beginnings of the minuscule writing of the middle ages. The slurring of the strokes, whereby the bows of the capital letters were lost and their more exact forms

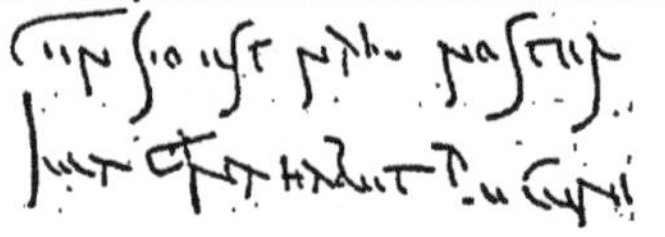

FIG. 20.—Wall inscription, 1st century.

(censio est nam noster
magna habet pecuni [am]).

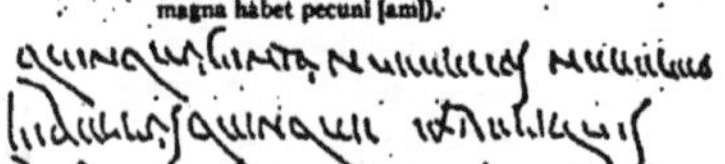

FIG. 21.—Pompeian Tablet, A.D. 59.

(quinquaginta nummos nummo
libellas quinque ex reliquis
ob fullonica ... anni L. Verani
Hupsaei et Albuci justi d.v.i.d. solut.)

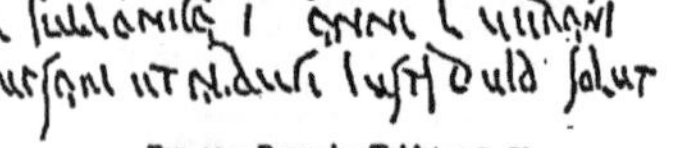

FIG. 22.—Dacian Tablet, A.D. 167.

(descriptum et recognitum factum ex libello—
erat Alb[urno] maiori ad statione Resculi in quo scri—
id quod i[nfra] s[criptum] est)

modified, led the way to the gradual development of the small letters. With regard to the particular forms of letters employed in the waxen tablets, compare the tables in *Corp. inscr. lat.*, vols. iii., iv. The letter A is formed by a main stroke supporting an oblique stroke above it and the cross bar is either omitted, or is indicated by a small vertical stroke dropping, as it were, out of the letter.

The main stroke of B dwindles to a slight curve, and the two bows are transformed into a long bent stroke so that the letter takes the shape of a stilted *a* or of a *d*. The D is chiefly like the uncial *ð*; the E is generally represented by the old form || found in inscriptions and in the Faliscan alphabet. In the modified form of G the first outline of the flat-headed *g* of later times appears; H, by losing half of its second upright limb in the haste of writing, comes near to being the small *h*. In the Pompeian tablets M has the four-stroke form ||||, as in the graffiti. In the Dacian tablets it is a rustic capital, sometimes almost an uncial ○. The hastily written O is formed by two strokes both convex, almost like *a*. As to the general character of the writing, it is close and compressed, and has an inclination to the left. There is also much combination or linking together of letters (*Corp. inscr. lat.* iii. tab. A). These peculiarities may, in some measure, be ascribed to the material and to the confined space at the command of the writer. The same character of cursive writing has also been found on a few tiles and potsherds inscribed with alphabets or short sentences—the exercises of children at school (*Corp. inscr. lat.* iii. 962).

In writing with the pen upon the smooth and unresisting surface of papyrus, the scribe would naturally write a more fluent hand. The disjointed writing of the graffiti and the tablets was changed for one which gradually became more consecutive and which naturally tended in course of time to slope to the right in the effort to be more current and to write letters in connexion without lifting the pen. One of the earliest available examples of Latin writing on papyrus to which an approximate date can be assigned is a fragment at Berlin containing portions of speeches delivered in the senate, said to be of the reign of Claudius, A.D. 41–54 (Steffens, *Lat. Pal.* taf. 101). The writing, though still somewhat restrained and admitting but little linking of the letters, is yet of a more flowing character than that of the contemporary tablets and graffiti.

We have to pass into the second century before finding the most perfect Latin document on papyrus, as yet discovered (fig. 23). This is now in the British Museum, and records the

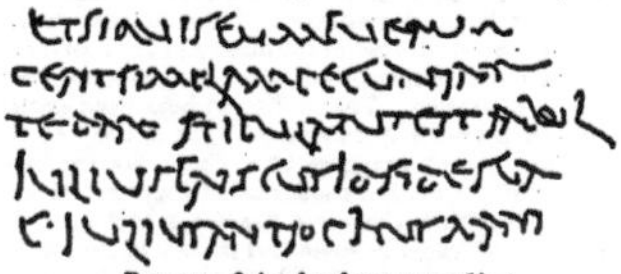

FIG. 23.—Sale of a slave, A.D. 166.

(—et si quis eum puerum
—cerit simplam pecuniam
—te dare stipulatus est Fabul
—Julius Priscus id fide sua
—C. Julius Antiochus mani—)

purchase of a slave-boy by an officer in the Roman fleet of Misenum stationed on the Syrian coast, A.D. 166 (*Pal. Soc.* i. 190; *Archaeologia* liv. p. 433). The writing of the body of the document is in a formal cursive, generally of the same formation as the inscriptions on the Dacian waxen tablets of the 2nd century, as will be seen from the accompanying facsimile of a few lines (fig. 23).

With this example of legal writing of the 2nd century it is interesting to compare two specimens of more ordinary cursive in different styles found in private letters of about the same time. The first (fig. 24) is taken from a fragmentary letter of the year 167 (Grenfell and Hunt, *Greek Papyri*, 2nd series, cviii.) and is a typical example of a hurried style.

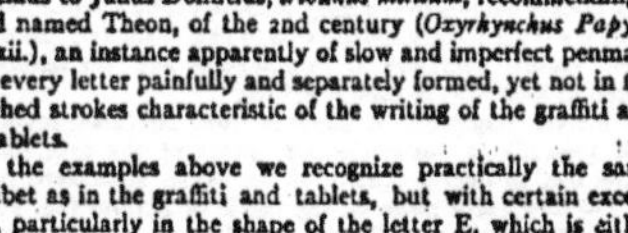

FIG. 24.—Letter, A.D. 167.

(Octobrium ad Puluinos ad—
interueniente Minucium—
et Apuleium nepotem scribam—
nonis Octobris imp. Uero ter—)

The second (fig. 25) is from a letter written by one Aurelius Archelaus to Julius Domitius, *tribunus militum*, recommending a friend named Theon, of the 2nd century (*Oxyrhynchus Papyri*, i., xxxii.), an instance apparently of slow and imperfect penmanship, every letter painfully and separately formed, yet not in the detached strokes characteristic of the writing of the graffiti and the tablets.

In the examples above we recognize practically the same alphabet as in the graffiti and tablets, but with certain exceptions, particularly in the shape of the letter E, which is either normal or written very cursively as an acute-angled tick, and in the reversion of other letters to the more normal capital forms.

There is not sufficient material to trace step by step the development of the Roman cursive hand between the 2nd and the 5th centuries; but still, with the few scattered examples at hand, there seems to be reason for conjecture that Latin writing on papyrus passed through phases not very dissimilar to those of Greek writing on the same material. For, when we emerge

from the 3rd century, we find an enlarged flowing hand, as in the Latin translation of the fables of Babrius in a fragmentary papyrus of the Amherst collection (No. xxvi.), ascribed to the 3rd or 4th century, and in a letter of recommendation from an

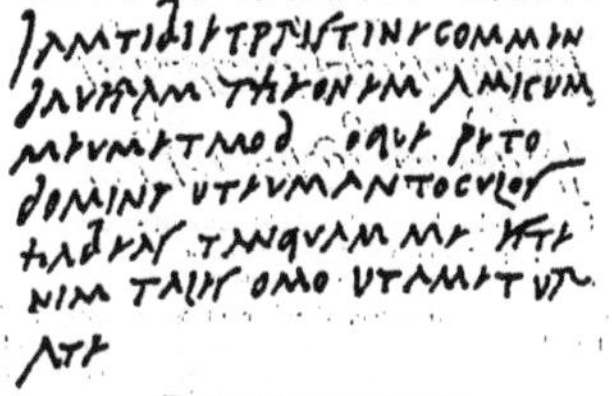

FIG. 25.—Letter, 2nd century.

(Jam ubi et pristine commen
dauerant Theonem amicum
meum et modio quioque puto
domine ut eum ant oculos
habeas tanquam me est e
nim tales omo ut ametur
a te)

Egyptian official of the 4th century, now at Strassburg (*Archiv. für Papyrusforschung*, iii. 2. 168); the handwriting of the latter recalling the large style of the Greek cursive of the Byzantine period (fig. 26). That there should be an affinity between the writing of Greek and that of Latin papyri emanating from Egypt is naturally to be expected.

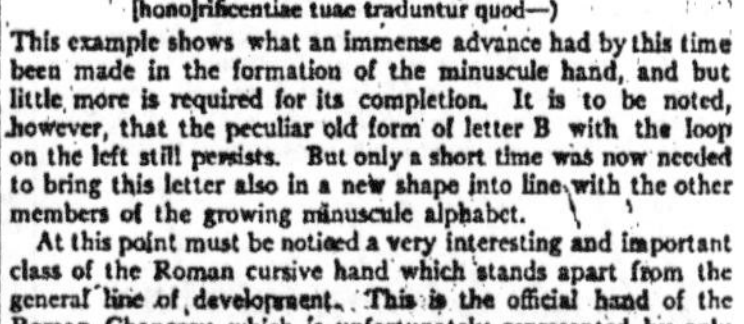

FIG. 26.—Letter of recommendation, 4th century.

(Cum in omnibus bonis benigni[tas]—
etiam scholasticos et maxime qui—
[hono]rificentiae tuae traduntur quod—)

This example shows what an immense advance had by this time been made in the formation of the minuscule hand, and but little more is required for its completion. It is to be noted, however, that the peculiar old form of letter B with the loop on the left still persists. But only a short time was now needed to bring this letter also in a new shape into line with the other members of the growing minuscule alphabet.

At this point must be noticed a very interesting and important class of the Roman cursive hand which stands apart from the general line of development. This is the official hand of the Roman Chancery, which is unfortunately represented by only two fragmentary papyri of the 5th century (fig. 27), and proves to be a curious moulding of the cursive in a calligraphic style, in which, however, the same characters appear as in other Roman cursive documents, if somewhat disguised. The papyri contain portions of two rescripts addressed to Egyptian officials, and are said to have been found at Phile and Elephantine. Both documents are in the same hand; and the fragments are divided between the libraries of Paris and Leiden. For a time the writing remained undeciphered, and Champollion-Figeac, while publishing a facsimile (*Chartes et MSS. sur papyrus*, 1840, pl. 14), had to confess that he was unable to read it. Massmann, however, with the experience gained in his work upon the waxed tablets, succeeded without much difficulty in reading the fragment at Leiden (*Libellus aurarius*, p. 147), and was followed by M. de Wailly, who published the whole of the fragments (*Mém. de l'Institut* (1842), xv. 399). Later, Mommsen and Jaffé have dealt with the text of the documents (*Jahrbuch des. gem. deut. Rechts* (1863), vi. 398), and compared in a table the forms of the letters with those of the Dacian tablets.

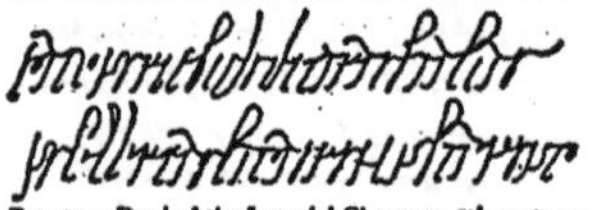

FIG. 27.—Deed of the Imperial Chancery, 5th century. (portionem ipsi debitam resarcire nec ullum precatorem ex instrumento)

The characters are large, the line of writing being about three-fourths of an inch deep, and the heads and tails of the long letters are flourished; but the even slope of the strokes imparts to the writing a certain uniform and graceful appearance. As to the actual shape of the letters, as will be seen from the reduced facsimile here given, there may be recognized in many of them only a more current form of those which have been described above. The A and R may be distinguished by noticing the different angle at which the top strokes are applied; the B, to suit the requirements of the more current style, is no longer the closed d-shaped letter of the tablets, but is open at the bow and more nearly resembles a reversed b; the tall letters f, h, l, and long s have developed loops; O and s-shaped U are very small, and written high in the line. The letters which seem to differ essentially from those of the tablets are E, M, N. The first of these is probably explained correctly by Jaffé as a development of the earlier ‖ quickly written and looped, and may be compared with the tick-shaped letter noticed above. The M and N have been compared with the minuscule forms of the Greek μω and πυ, as though the latter had been adopted; but they may with better reason be explained as merely cursive forms of the Latin capitals M and N. That this hand should have retained so much of the older formation of the Roman cursive is no doubt to be attributed to the fact of its being an official style of writing which would conform to tradition.

To continue the development which we saw attained in the letter of the 4th century above. (fig. 26) we turn to the documents on papyrus from Ravenna, Naples, and other places in Italy, which date from the 5th century and are written in a looser and more straggling hand (fig. 28). Examples of this hand will be found in largest numbers in Marini's work specially treating of these documents (*I papiri diplomatici*), and also in the publications of Mabillon (*De re diplomatica*) Champollion-Figeac (*Chartes et MSS. sur papyrus*), Massmann (*Urkunden in Neapel und Arezzo*), Gloria (*Paleografía*), as well as in *Facs. of Ancient Charters in the British Museum*, pt. iv., 1878, Nos. 45, 46, and in the *Facsimiles* of the Palaeographical Society.

FIG. 28.—Deed of Sale (Ravenna), A.D. 572. (huius splendediasimae urbis)

The letter a has now lost all trace of the capital; it is the open u-shaped minuscule, developed from the looped uncial (Ꙩ, Ꙫ); the b, throwing off the loop or curve on the left which gave it the appearance of d, has at length developed one on the right, and appears in the form familiar in modern writing; minuscule m, n, and u are fully formed (the last never joining a following letter, and thus always distinguishable from o); p, q, and r approach to the long minuscules, and s, having acquired an incipient tag, has taken the form γ which it keeps long after.

This form of writing was widely used, and was not confined to legal documents. It is found in grammatical works, as in

the second hand of the palimpsest MS. of Licinianus (*Cat. Anc. MSS.*, pt. ii., pls. 1, 2) of the 6th century, and in such volumes as the Josephus of the Ambrosian Library of the 7th century (*Pal. Soc.* pl. 59), and in the St Avitus of the 6th century and other MSS. written in France. It is indeed only natural to suppose that this, the most convenient, because cursive, hand, should have been employed for ordinary working MSS. which were in daily use. That so few of such MSS. should have survived is no doubt owing to the destruction of the greater number by the wear and tear to which they were subjected.

LATIN WRITING. II.—LITERARY HANDS

We have now to return to the 1st century, the date from which we started in the investigation of the Roman cursive writing, and take up the thread of the history of the book-hand of literature, a few rare examples of which have survived from the ruins of Herculaneum. That a Roman book-hand existed at a still earlier period is quite certain. The analogy of the survival of very ancient examples of a Greek literary hand is a sufficient proof; and it is a mere truism to say that as soon as there was a literature, there was likewise a book-hand for its vehicle. No work could be submitted for sale in the market that was not written in a style legible to all. Neatly written copies were essential, and the creation of a formal kind of writing fitted for the purpose naturally resulted. Such formal script must, however, be always more or less artificial as compared with the natural current hand of the time, and there must always be an antagonism between the two styles of script; and, as we have seen in Greek palaeography, the book-hand is always subject to the invading influence of the natural hand.

Capital Writing.—Among the Herculaneum fragmentary papyri, then, we find our earliest examples of the Roman literary hand, which must be earlier than A.D. 79, the year of the destruction of the city; and those examples prove to us that the usual literary hand was written in capital letters. Of these letters there are two kinds—the square and the rustic. Square capitals may be defined as those which have their horizontal lines at right angles with the vertical strokes; rustic letters are not less accurately formed, nor, as their title would seem to imply, are they rough in character, but, being without the exact finish of the square letters, and being more readily written, they have the appearance of greater simplicity. In capital writing the letters are not all of equal height; F and L, and in the rustic sometimes others, as B and R, overtop the rest. In the rustic alphabet the forms are generally lighter and more slender, with short horizontal strokes more or less oblique and wavy. Both styles of capital writing were obviously borrowed from the lapidary alphabets employed under the empire. Both styles were used for public notices inscribed on the walls of Pompeii and other places. But it has been observed that scribes with a natural conservatism would perpetuate a style some time longer in books than it might be used in inscriptions. We should therefore be prepared to allow for this in ascribing a date to a capital written MS., which might resemble an inscription older by a century or more. Rustic capitals, on account of their more convenient shape, came into more general use; and the greater number of the early MSS. in capitals which have survived are consequently found to be in this character. In the *Exempla codium latinorum* of Zangemeister and Wattenbach are collected specimens of capital writing.

The literary fragments of papyrus from Herculaneum are written generally in rustic capitals, either of the firm, solid character used in inscriptions, or of the lighter style employed in the fragments of a poem on the battle of Actium (fig. 29). As this poem is the earliest literary work in Latin, of any extent, written in the book-hand, a specimen of the writing is here given. Its period must necessarily lie between the year 31 B.C. the date of the battle and A.D. 79; and therefore we may place it at least early in the 1st century.

That the rustic capital hand was generally adopted for finely written literary MSS. from the period of our earliest examples onwards through the centuries immediately following may be assumed from the fact of that character being found so widely in favour when we come down to the period of the vellum MSS. Unfortunately no examples have survived to fill the gap between the first century and the oldest of the vellum codices written in rustic capitals of the 4th century. Of the three great MSS. of Virgil preserved in the Vatican Library, which are written in

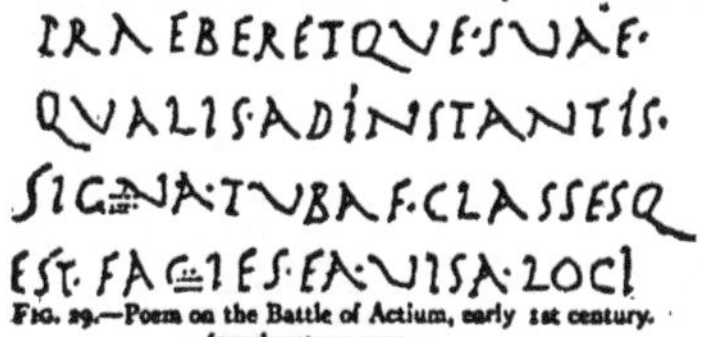

FIG. 29.—Poem on the Battle of Actium, early 1st century.

(praeberetque suae—
qualis ad instantis—
signa tubae classesq—
est facies ea visa loci—)

this character, the first in date is that known as the Schedae Vaticanae (*Exempla*, tab. 13; *Pal. Soc.* pl. 116, 117), a MS. famous for its series of well-finished illustrative paintings in classical style; it is ascribed to the 4th century. The other two MSS. are known as the Codex Romanus and the Codex Palatinus (*Exempla*, tab. 11, 12; *Pal. Soc.* pl. 113–115), and are now generally assigned to the 5th century. All three MSS. no doubt must always have been regarded as choice works; and the large scale of the writing employed, particularly in the case of the Romanus and the Palatinus, and the consequently magnificent size of the MSS. when complete, must indicate an unusual importance attaching to them. They were *éditions de luxe* of the great Roman poet. The writing of the Codex Palatinus (Fig. 30) especially is most exact, and is manifestly modelled on the best type of the rustic hand as seen in the inscriptions.

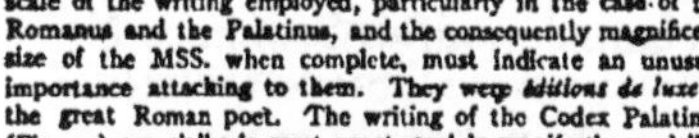

FIG. 30.—Virgil (Cod. Palatinus) 5th century.

(Testaturque deos iterum se ad proelia cogi
Bis iam Italos hostis haec altera foedera)

In assigning dates to the earliest MSS. of capital-writing, one feels the greatest hesitation, none of them bearing any internal evidence to assist the process. It is not indeed until the close of the 5th century that we reach firm ground—the Medicean Virgil of Florence having in it sufficient proof of having been written before the year 494. The writing is in delicately-formed letters, rather more spaced out than in the earlier examples (*Exempla*, tab. 10; *Pal. Soc.* pl. 86). Another ancient MS. in rustic capitals is the Codex Bembinus of Terence of the 4th or 5th century (*Exempla*, tab. 8, 9; *Pal. Soc.*, pl. 135), a volume which is also of particular interest on account of its marginal annotations, written in an early form of small hand. Among palimpsests the most notable is that of the Cicero *In Verrem* of the Vatican (*Exempla*, tab. 4).

Of vellum MSS. in square-capitals the examples are not so early as those in the rustic character. Portions of a MS. of Virgil in the square letter are preserved in the Vatican, and other leaves of the same are at Berlin (*Exempla*, tab. 14). Each page, however, begins with a large coloured initial, a style of ornamentation which is never found in the very earliest MSS. The date assigned to this MS. is therefore the end of the 4th century. In very similar writing, but not quite so exact, are some fragments of another MS. of Virgil in the library of St Gall, probably of a rather later time (*Exempla*, tab. 14c; *Pal. Soc.*, pl. 208).

In the 6th century capital-writing enters on its period of decadence, and the examples of it become imitative. Of this period is the Paris Prudentius (*Exempla*, tab. 15; *Pal. Soc.* pls. 29, 30) in rustic letters modelled on the old pattern of early

inscriptions, but with a very different result from that obtained by the early scribes. A comparison of this volume with such MSS. as the Codex Romanus and the Codex Palatinus shows the later date of the Prudentius in its widespread writing and in certain inconsistencies in forms. Of the 7th century is the Turin Sedulius (*Exemplo*, tab. 16), a MS. in which uncial writing also appears—the rough and misshapen letters being evidences of the cessation of capital writing as a hand in common use. The latest imitative example of an entire MS. in rustic capitals is in the Utrecht Psalter, written in triple columns and copied, to all appearance, from an ancient example, and illustrated with pen drawings. This MS. may be assigned to the beginning of the 9th century. If there were no other internal evidence of late date in the MS. the mixture of uncial letters with the capitals would decide it. In the Psalter of St Augustine's Canterbury, in the Cottonian Library (*Pal. Soc.* pl. 19; *Cat. Anc. MSS.* ii. pls. 12, 13), some leaves at the beginning are written in this imitative style early in the 8th century; and again it is found in the Benedictional of Bishop Aethelwold (*Pal. Soc.* pl. 143) of the 10th century. In the sumptuous MSS. of the Carlovingian school it was continually used; and it survived for such purposes as titles and colophons for some centur:es, usually in a degenerate form of the rustic letters.

Uncial Writing.—There was also another majuscule form of writing, besides capitals, employed as a literary book-hand at an early date, but not coeval with the early period of capital writing. This second book-hand was the so-called Uncial hand, a modification of the capital form of writing; in which the square angles of the original letters were rounded off and certain new curved shapes were introduced, the characteristic letters of the uncial alphabet being a, b, ϵ, ᴅ, ᴍ. The origin of some of these rounded letters may be traced in certain forms of the Roman cursive letters of the graffiti and the tablets. But a considerable length of time elapsed before the fully developed uncial alphabet was evolved from these incipient forms. In fact it is only in the vellum MSS. that we first find the firmly written literary uncial hand in perfect form. No doubt the new material, vellum, with its smooth hard surface, immediately afforded the means for the calligraphic perfection with which we find the uncial writing inscribed in these codices.

From the occurrence of isolated uncial forms in inscriptions, the actual period of growth of the finished literary hand has been determined to lie between the later part of the 2nd century and the 4th century. Uncial letters are especially prevalent in Roman-African inscriptions of the 3rd century; but certain letters of the uncial alphabet are not as yet therein matured; minuscule forms of a few letters, particularly *b* and *d*, are employed. The discovery also, at Oxyrhynchus, of a fragmentary papyrus of the 3rd century, containing a portion of an epitome of Livy, presents us with an example of the uncial hand in progress of formation for literary purposes, the text being composed mainly of letters of the uncial type, but including a certain proportion of letters, as *b*, *d*, *m*, *r*, of the minuscule or small character. At length in the 4th century, as already stated, the perfected uncial literary alphabet is found in the vellum codices.

There are still extant a very large number of Latin uncial MSS., a proof of the wide use of this form of literary writing in the early middle ages.

The *Exempla* of Zangemeister and Wattenbach, so often quoted above, contains a series of facsimiles which illustrate its progress through its career. The letter ᴍ has been adopted by the editors as a test letter, in the earlier forms of which the last limb is not curved or turned in. The letter ϵ also in its earlier and purer form has the cross stroke placed high. But, as in every style of writing, when once developed, the earliest examples are the best, being written with a free hand and natural stroke. The Gospels of Vercelli (*Exempla*, tab. 20), said to have been written by the hand of Eusebius himself, and which may indeed be of his time, is one of the most ancient uncial MSS. Its narrow columns and pure forms of letters have the stamp of antiquity. To the 4th century also is assigned the palimpsest Cicero *De republica* in the Vatican (*Exempla*, tab. 17; *Pal. Soc.*

pl. 160), a MS. written in fine large characters of the best type; and a very ancient fragment of a commentary on an ante-Hieronymian text, in three columns, has also survived at Fulda (*Exempla*, tab. 21). Among the most MSS. of the 5th century of which good photographic facsimiles are available are the two famous codices of Livy, at Vienna (fig. 31) and Paris (*Exempla*, tab. 18, 19; *Pal. Soc.* pl. 31, 32, 183)

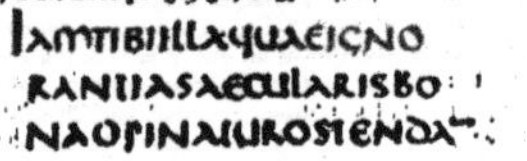

JAMTIBIHLAYUAEICNO
RANIIASAEQUIARISBO
NAOPINAIUROSIENDA

FIG. 31.—Livy (Vienna MS.), 5th century.
(Iam tibi illa quae igno
rantia saecularis bo
na opinatur ostendam)

To distinguish between uncial MSS. of the 5th and 6th centuries is not very easy, for the character of the writing changes but little, and is free from sign of weakness or wavering. It may, however, be noticed that in MSS. which are assigned to the latter century there is rather less compactness, and occasionally, as the century advances, there is a slight tendency to artificiality. When the 7th century is reached there is every evidence that uncial writing has entered on a new stage. The letters are more roughly and carelessly formed, and the compactness of the earlier style is altogether wanting. From this time down to the age of Charlemagne there is a continual deterioration, the writing of the 8th century being altogether misshapen. A more exact but imitative hand was, however, at the same time employed, when occasion required, for the production of calligraphic MSS., such as Biblical and liturgical books. Under the encouragement given by Charlemagne to such works, splendid uncial volumes were written in ornamental style, often in gold, several of which have survived to this day.

Mixed and Half-uncial Writing.—It is obvious that the majuscule styles of literary writing, viz. the square capital, the rustic capital and the uncial, were of too elaborate and too stately a character to serve all the many requirements of literature. The capital hands, as we have seen, appear to have been employed, at least in many instances, for codices produced on a grand scale, and presumably for special occasions; and if the uncial hand had a longer and wider career, yet in this case also there must often have been a sense that the employment of this fine character gave a special importance and value to the MS. It is not improbable that the survival of so large a number of uncial MSS. is due to the special care that they received at the hands of their owners. Other more manageable styles of writing were necessary, and concurrently with the majuscule hands other forms were developing. The hand which bears the name of Half-uncial was finally evolved, and had itself an important career as a book-hand as well as exercising a large influence on the medieval minuscule hand of literature.

From the first, as we have seen in the case of the graffiti and the tablets, a mingling of capital forms and minuscule forms was prevalent in the non-literary style of writing. There are indications that the same mingling of the two streams was allowed in writing of a literary character. It appears in a rudimentary state in a papyrus fragment from Herculaneum (*Exempla*, tab. 2 b); and it appears in the epitome of Livy of the 3rd century found at Oxyrhynchus, in which minuscule letters are interspersed among the uncial text. From the regularity and ease with which this MS. is written, it is to be assumed that the mixed hand was ordinarily practised at that time. It is often employed for marginal notes in the early vellum codices. It is used for the Verona Gaius (*Exempla*, tab. 24) of the 5th century, in which, besides the ordinary uncial shapes, *d* is also found as a minuscule, *r* as the transitional *r*, and *s* as the tall letter v. Again, in the uncial Florentine Pandects of the 6th century appears a hand which contains a large admixture of minuscule forms (*Exempla*, tab. 54). From these and other instances it is seen that in uncial MSS. of a secular nature,

as in works relating to law and grammar, the scribe did not feel himself restricted to a uniform use of the larger letters, as he would be in producing a church book or calligraphic MS.

But the mixed hand, although partaking something of the nature of the Half-uncial hand, was not actually that form of writing. The Half-uncial hand was not only a mingling of uncial and minuscule forms, but also a blending of them, the uncial element yielding more or less to the minuscule influence, while the minuscule element was reacted upon by the uncial sentiment of roundness and sweeping curves. In its full development the Half-uncial, or Roman Half-uncial as it is also called, were it not for a few lingering pure uncial forms, might equally well be described as a large-type minuscule hand. It has, in fact, been sometimes styled the pre-Carolingian minuscule. An early form of this writing is found in the papyrus fragment of Sallust's Catiline, perhaps of the early 5th century, recently recovered at Oxyrhynchus. In vellum codices of the 5th, 6th and 7th centuries Half-uncial writing of a very fine type is not uncommon. It is used for the marginal scholia of the Bembine Terence, of the 5th century. The MS. of the Fasti consulares, at Verona, brought down to 494 A.D. (*Exempla*, tab. 30), is also in this hand. But the earliest MS. of this class to which a more approximate date can be given is the Hilary of St Peter's at Rome (fig. 32), which was written in or before the year 509 or 510 (*Exempla*, tab. 52; *Pal. Soc.* pl. 136); the next is the Sulpicius Severus of Verona, of 517 (*Exempla*, tab. 31); and of the year 569 is a beautifully written MS. at Monte Cassino containing a Biblical commentary (*Exempla*, tab. 3).

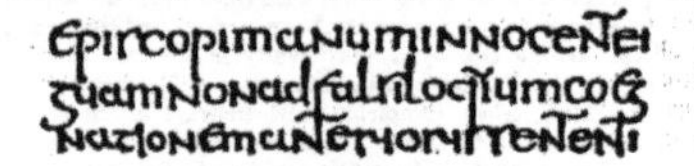

EPIRCOPIMANUMINNOCENTEI
QUAMNONADFALSILOQUIUMCOEG
NATIONEMANTERIORIPTENENTI

FIG. 32.—St Hilary. A.D. 509-510.
(episcopi manum innocente[m]—
[lin]guam non ad falsiloquium coeg [isti]—
nationem anterioris sententi[ae]—)

Other examples, of which good facsimiles may be consulted, are the Corbie MS. of Canons, at Paris (*Exempla*, tab, 41, 42), the St Severianus at Milan (*Pal. Soc.* pl. 161, 162), the Ashburnham St Augustine (*Pal. Soc.* ii. 9), and the Paris St Augustine (*New. Pal. Soc.* pl. 80), of the 6th century; and the Cologne MS. of Canons (*Exempla*, tab. 44), and the Josephus (*Pal. Soc.* pl. 138) and St Ambrose (*Pal. Soc.* pl. 137) of Milan, of the 6th or 7th century.

The influence which the Half-uncial literary hand exercised upon the minuscule book-writing of the 7th and 8th centuries may be traced in greater or less degree in the continental MSS. of that period. We shall find that it forms the basis for the beautiful national handwritings of Ireland and Britain; and it played an important part in the Carolingian reform of the book-hand of the Frankish Empire.

LATIN WRITING. III.—THE NATIONAL HANDS

We have now to follow the rise and development of the national handwritings of western Europe, all of which were derived from the Roman hand, but from different phases of it. While the Roman Empire was the central power controlling its colonies and conquests, the Roman handwriting, however far apart might be the several countries in which it was current, remained practically one and the same. But, when the empire was broken up and when independent nationalities arose upon its ruins and advanced upon independent paths of civilization, the handwriting inherited from Rome gradually assumed distinctive characters and took the complexions of the several countries, unless from some accident the continuity of the effects of the Roman occupation was disturbed, as it was in Britain by the Saxon invasion. On the continent of western Europe, in Italy, in Spain, in Gaul, the Roman cursive hand had become the common form of writing, and it remained the framework on which the national hands of those countries developed. Thus grow the Lombardic hand of Italy, the Visigothic hand of Spain, and the Merovingian and, later, the Carolingian hand of the Frankish Empire.[1] The earliest charters of the three national divisions, written in cursive hands directly descending from the Roman cursive, and dating generally from the 7th century, still remained related in their general style. It was in the book-hands, elaborated from the cursive character, that the lines of national demarcation became more clearly defined, although naturally there occur also many examples in mixed styles which it is difficult to assign to one or another country. ; ·

Lombardic Writing.—The national handwriting of Italy did not follow one and the same lines of development throughout the peninsula. In ordinary documents the cursive hand which is seen in the Ravenna deeds, the, direct descendant of the Roman cursive, continued in use, growing, in course of time, more and more intricate and difficult to read, the earliest examples, down to the middle of the 9th century, being in the large straggling character of their prototype. The illegible scrawl into which the hand finally degenerated in notarial instruments of southern Italy was at length suppressed by order of Frederick II. (A.D. 1210-1250). But at an early date the Lombardic book-hand was being formed out of this material. In northern Italy new influences were brought into action by Charlemagne's conquest, the independent growth of the native hand was checked, and a mixed style in which the Merovingian type was interwoven with the Italian was produced, to which the name of Franco-Lombardic has been given (see below, fig. 39). But in the Lombardic duchies of the south the native Lombardic book-hand had an unimpeded growth. In such centres as the monasteries of Monte Cassino near Naples and La Cava near Salerno, it took in the 9th century a very exact

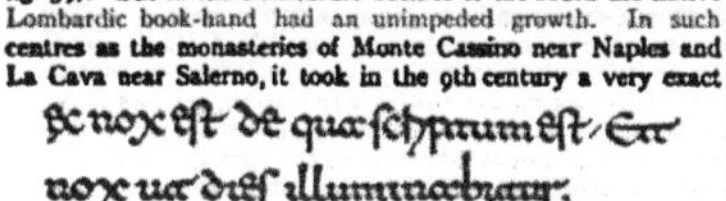

FIG. 33.—Exultat roll (Lombardic, 12th century).
([H]ec nox est de qua scriptum est Et
nox ut dies illuminabitur)

and uniform shape. From this date the attention which it received as a calligraphic form of writing, accompanied with accessory ornamentation of initial letters, brought it to a high state of perfection in the 11th century, when by the peculiar treatment of the letters, they assume that strong contrast of light and heavy strokes which when exaggerated, as it finally became, received the name of broken Lombardic. This style of hand lasted to the 13th century.

Papal Documents.—A word must be said in this place regarding the independent development of the hands used in the papal

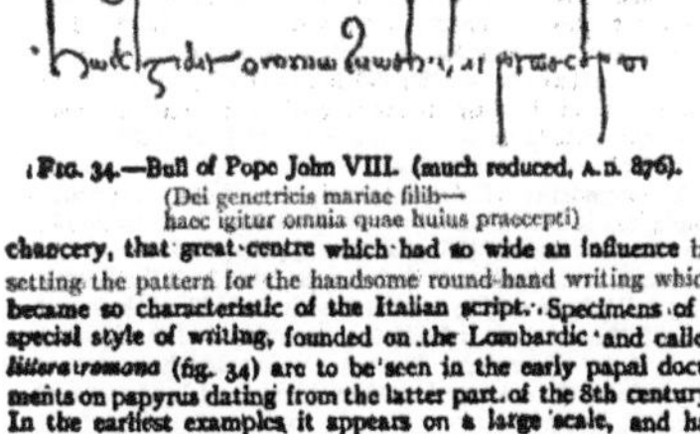

FIG. 34.—Bull of Pope John VIII. (much reduced, A.D. 876).
(Dei genetricis mariae filih—
haec igitur omnia quae huius praecepti)

chancery, that great centre which had so wide an influence by setting the pattern for the handsome round-hand writing which became so characteristic of the Italian script. Specimens of a special style of writing, founded on the Lombardic and called *littera romana* (fig. 34) are to be seen in the early papal documents on papyrus dating from the latter part of the 8th century. In the earliest examples, it appears on a large scale, and has rounded forms and sweeping strokes of a very bold character. Derived from the official Roman hand, it has certain letters

peculiar to itself, such as the letter *a* made almost like a Greek *ω*, *t* in the form of a loop, and *e* as a circle with a knot at the top.

This hand may be followed in examples from A.D. 788 through the 9th century (*Facs. de chartes et diplomes*, 1866; Ch. Figeac, *Chartes et doc. sur papyrus*, i-xii.; Letronne, *Diplom. mérov. etat.*, pl. 48. In a bull of Silvester II., dated in 999 (*Bibl. d'Ec. des chartes*, vol. xxxvii.), we find the hand becoming less round; and at the end of the next century, under Urban II., in 1097 (Mabillon, *De re dipl.* suppl. p. 115) and 1098 (Sickel, *Mon. graph.* v. 4), it is in a curious angular style, which, however, then disappears. During the 11th and 12th centuries the imperial chancery hand was also used for papal documents, and was in turn displaced by the exact and calligraphic papal Italian hand of the later middle ages.

Visigothic Writing.—The Visigothic writing of Spain ran a course of development not unlike that of the Lombardic. In the cursive hand attributed to the 7th century the Roman cursive has undergone little change in form; but another century developed a most distinctive character. In the 8th century appears the set book-hand in an even and not difficult character, marked by breadth of style and a good firm stroke. This style is maintained through the 9th century with little change, except that there is a growing tendency to calligraphy. In the 10th century the writing deteriorates; the letters are not so uniform, and, when calligraphically written, are generally thinner in stroke. The same changes which are discernible in all the hand-writings of western Europe in the 11th century are also to be traced in the Visigothic hand—particularly as regards the rather rigid character which it assumes. It continued in use down to the beginning of the 12th century. Perhaps the most characteristic letter of the book-hand is the *q*-shaped g. The following specimens (figs. 35, 36) illustrate the Visigothic as written in a large heavy hand of the 9th century (*Cat. Anc. MSS.* ii. Plate 37), and in a calligraphic example of 1109 (*Pal. Soc.* Plate 48).

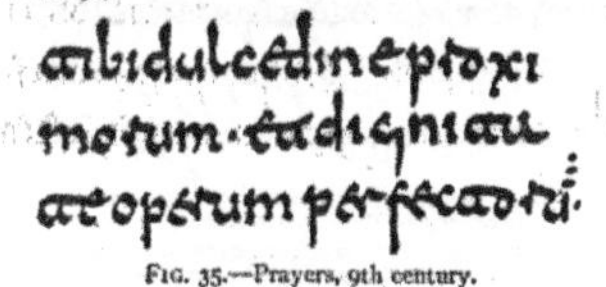

FIG. 35.—Prayers, 9th century.
(tibi dulcedine proxi
morum et dignita
te operum perfectorum)

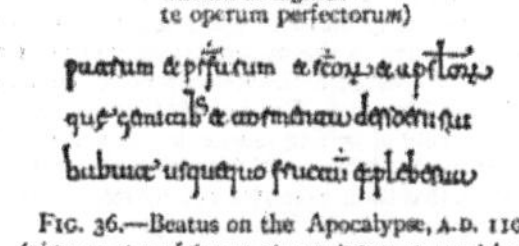

FIG. 36.—Beatus on the Apocalypse, A.D. 1109.
(patrum et profetarum et sanctorum et apostolorum
que gentilibus et tormenta desiderii sui
habuit usquequo fructum ex plebe sua)

Merovingian.—The early writing of the Frankish Empire, to which the title of Merovingian has been applied, had a wider range than the other two national hands already described. It had a long career both for diplomatic and literary purposes. In this writing, as it appears in documents, we see that the Roman cursive is subjected to a lateral pressure, so that the letters received a curiously cramped appearance, while the heads and tails are exaggerated to inordinate length.

Facsimiles of this hand, as used in the royal and imperial chanceries, are to be found scattered in various works; but a complete course of Merovingian diplomatic writing may be best studied in Letronne's *Diplomata*, and in the *Kaiserurkunden* of Professors Sybel and Sickel. In the earliest documents, commencing in the 7th century and continuing to the middle of the 8th century, the character is large and at first not so intricate as it becomes later in this period. The writing then grows into a more regular form, and in the 9th century a small hand is established, which, however, still retains the exaggerated heads and tails of letters. The direct course of this chancery hand may then be followed in the imperial documents, which from the

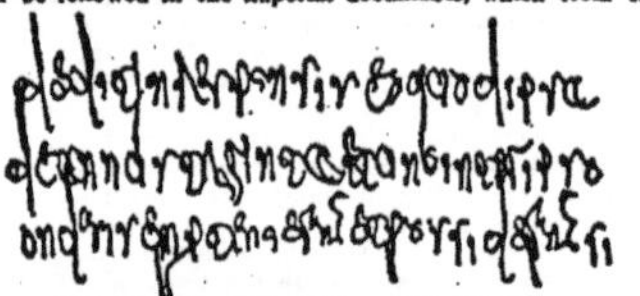

FIG. 37.—Merovingian diploma, A.D. 679–680.
(dedit in respunsis co quod ipsa—
de annus triginta et uno inter ipso—
—ondam semper tenuerant et possiderant si—)

second half of the 9th century are written in a hand more set and evidently influenced by the Carolingian minuscule. This form of writing, still accompanied by the lengthened strokes already referred to, continued in force, subject, however, to the varying changes which affected it in common with other hands, into the 12th century. Its influence was felt as well in France as in Germany and Italy; and certain of its characteristics also appear in the court-hand which the Normans brought with them into England.

The book-hand immediately derived from the early Merovingian diplomatic hand is seen in MSS. of the 7th and 8th centuries in a very neatly written but not very easy hand (*Cat. Anc. MSS.* ii. Plates 29, 30; Arndt, *Schriftsf.* 28).

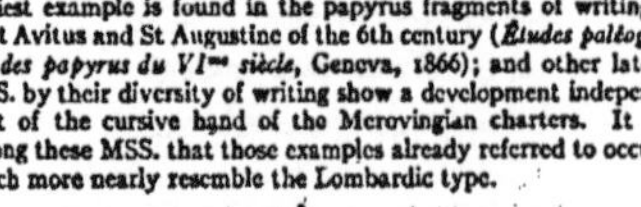

FIG. 38.—St Gregory's Moralia. 7th century.
Merovingian Writing, 7th century.
(—dam intra sinum sanctae eclesiae quasi uicinos ad—
positos increpant. Saepe uero arrogantes—
—dem quam tenent arrogantiam se fugire osten—)

But other varieties of the literary hand as written in France are seen to be more closely allied to the Roman cursive. The earliest example is found in the papyrus fragments of writings of St Avitus and St Augustine of the 6th century (*Études paléogr. sur des papyrus du VI™ siècle,* Geneva, 1866); and other later MSS. by their diversity of writing show a development independent of the cursive hand of the Merovingian charters. It is among these MSS. that those examples already referred to occur which more nearly resemble the Lombardic type.

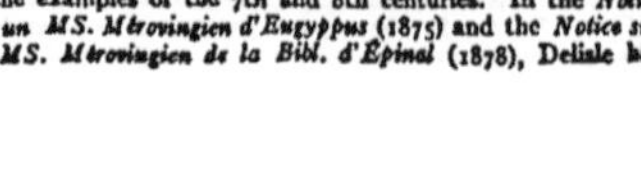

FIG. 39.—Ecclesiastical Canons (Franco-Lombardic), 8th century.
(propter unitatem salus propriaetate na—
non sub una substantia conuenientes, neque—
—itam sed unum eundem filium. Unicum deum)

The uncial and half-uncial hands had also their influence in the evolution of these Merovingian book-hands; and the mixture of so many different forms accounts for variety to be found in the examples of the 7th and 8th centuries. In the *Notice sur un MS. Mérovingien d'Eugyppius* (1875) and the *Notice sur un MS. Mérovingien de la Bibl. d'Épinal* (1878), Delisle has

given many valuable facsimiles in illustration of the different hands in these two MSS. of the early part of the 8th century. See also *Exempla Codd. Lat.* (tab. 37), and autotypes in *Cat. anc. MSS.* ii. There was, however, through all this period a general progress towards a settled minuscule writing which only required a master-hand to fix it in a purified and calligraphic form. How this was effected will be described below, after disposing of the early national writing of our own islands.

Irish Writing.—The early history of the palaeography of the British Isles stands apart from that of the continental schools. As was noticed above, the Roman handwriting which was used by the Roman settlers in Britain and was imparted by them to the native Britons was swept out of existence when the Saxon invasion abruptly destroyed the continuity of Roman civilization in these islands. Britain had to wait a long time for the reappearance of Roman writing in the country; but it was destined to reappear, though in a different phase, in book-form, not in cursive form; and not directly, but through another channel. That channel was Ireland.

It is evident that the civilization and learning which accompanied the establishment of an ancient Church in Ireland could not exist without a written literature. The Roman missionaries would certainly in the first place have imported copies of the Gospels and other books, and it cannot be doubted that through intercourse with England the Irish would obtain continental MSS. in sufficient numbers to serve as models for their scribes. From geographical and political conditions, however, no continuous intimacy with foreign countries was possible; and we are consequently prepared to find a form of writing borrowed in the first instance from a foreign school, but developed under an independent national system. In Ireland we have an instance how conservative writing may become, and how it will hand on old forms of letters from one generation to another when there is no exterior influence to act upon it. After once obtaining its models, the Irish school of writing was left to work out its own ideas, and continued to follow one direct line for centuries. The subsequent English conquest had no effect upon the national handwriting. Both peoples in the island pursued their own course. In MSS. in the Irish language the Irish character of writing was naturally employed; and the liturgical books produced in Irish monasteries by Irish monks were written in the same way. The grants and other deeds of the English settlers were, on the other hand, drawn up by English scribes in their then national writing. The Irish handwriting went on in its even uninterrupted course; and its consequent unchanging form makes it so difficult a matter to assign accurate dates to Irish MSS.

The early Irish handwriting is of two classes—the round and the pointed. The round hand is found in the earliest examples; the pointed hand, which also was developed at an early period became the general hand of the country, and survives in the native writing of the present day. Of the earliest surviving MSS. written in Ireland none are found to be in pure uncial letters. That uncial MSS. were introduced into the country by the early missionaries can hardly be doubted, if we consider that that character was so commonly employed as a bookhand, and especially for sacred texts. Nor is it impossible that Irish scribes may have practised this hand. The copy of the Gospels in uncials, found in the tomb of St Kilian, and preserved at Würzburg, has been quoted as an instance of Irish uncial. The writing, however, is the ordinary uncial, and bears no marks of Irish nationality (*Exempla*, tab. 58). The most ancient examples are in half-uncial letters, so similar in character to the continental half-uncial MSS. of Roman type noticed above, that there can be no hesitation in deriving the Irish from the Roman writing. We have only to compare the Irish MSS. of the round type with the continental MSS. to be convinced of the identity of their styles of writing. There are unfortunately no means of ascertaining the exact period when this style of hand was first adopted in Ireland. Among the very earliest surviving examples none bears a fixed date; and it is impossible to accept the traditional ascription of certain of them to particular saints of

Ireland, as St Patrick and St Columba. Such traditions are notoriously unstable ground upon which to take up a position. But an examination of certain examples will enable the palaeographer to arrive at certain conclusions. In Trinity College, Dublin, is preserved a fragmentary copy of the Gospels (*Nat. MSS. Ireland*, i. pl. ii.) vaguely assigned to a period from the 5th to the 7th century, and written in a round half-uncial hand closely resembling the continental hand, but bearing the general impress of its Irish origin. This MS. may perhaps be of the early part of the 7th century.

adillecientturrerpoxdar
limihmoldaurerrelamorti
ertdepuerincubiculomectum

Fic. 40.—Gospels, 7th century.
(ad ille deintus respondens [dicit, Noli mihi molestus esse, iam ostium clausum] est et pueri in cubiculo mecum [sunt])

Again, the Psalter (*Nat. MSS. Ireland*, i. pls. iii., iv.) traditionally ascribed to St Columba (d. 597), and perhaps of the 7th century, is a calligraphic specimen of the same kind of writing. The earliest examples of the continental half-uncial date back, as has been seen above, to the 5th century. Now the likeness between the earliest foreign and Irish MSS. forbids us to assume anything like collateral descent from a common and remote stock. Two different national hands, although derived from the same source, would not independently develop in the same way, and it may accordingly be granted that the point of contact, or the period at which the Irish scribes copied and adopted the Roman half-uncial, was not very long, comparatively, before the date of the now earliest surviving examples. This would take us back at least to the 6th century, in which period there is sufficient evidence of literary activity in Ireland. The beautiful Irish calligraphy, ornamented with designs of marvellous intricacy and brilliant colouring, which is seen in full vigour at the end of the 7th century, indicates no small amount of labour bestowed upon the cultivation of writing as an ornamental art. It is indeed surprising that such excellence was so quickly developed. The Book of Kells has been justly acknowledged as the culminating example of Irish calligraphy (*Nat. MSS. Ireland*, i. pls. vii.-xvii.; *Pal. Soc.* pls. 55, 56). The text is written in the large solid half-uncial hand which is again seen in the Gospels of St Chad at Lichfield (*Pal. Soc.* pls. 20, 21, 35), and, in a smaller form, in the English-written Lindisfarne Gospels (see below). Having arrived at the calligraphic excellence just referred to, the round hand appears to have been soon afterwards superseded, for general use, by the pointed; for the character of the large half-uncial writing of the Gospels of MacRegol, of about the year 800 (*Nat. MSS. Ireland*, i. pls. xxii.-xxiv.; *Pal. Soc.* pls. 90, 91), shows a very great deterioration from the vigorous writing of the Book of Kells, indicative of want of practice.

Traces of the existence of the pointed hand are early. It is found in a fully developed stage in the Book of Kells itself (*Pal. Soc.* pl. 88).' This form of writing, which may be termed the cursive hand of Ireland, differs in its origin from the national cursive hands of the Continent. In the latter the old Roman cursive has been shown to be the foundation. The Irish pointed hand, on the contrary, had nothing to do with the Roman cursive, but was simply a modification of the round hand, using the same forms of letters, but subjecting them to a lateral compression and drawing their limbs into points or hair-lines. As this process is found developed in the Book of Kells, its beginning may be fairly assigned to as early a time as the first half of the 7th century; but for positive date there is the same uncertainty as in regard to the first beginning of the round hand. The Book of Dimma (*Nat. MSS. Ireland*, i. pls. xviii., xix.) has been attributed to a scribe of about A.D. 650; but it appears rather to be of the 8th century, if we may judge by the analogy of English MSS. written in a similar hand. It is not in fact until we reach the period of the Book of Armagh (*Nat. MSS. Ireland*, pls. xxv.-xxix.), a MS. containing books of the New Testament and other matter, and written by Ferdomnach, a scribe who died in the year 844, that we are on safe ground. Here is clearly a pointed hand of the early part of the 9th century, very similar to the English pointed hand of Mercian charters of the same time. The MS. of the Gospels of MacDurnan, in the Lambeth Library (*Nat. MSS. Ireland*, i. pls. xxx., xxxi.) is an example of writing of the end of the 9th or beginning of the 10th century, showing a tendency to become more narrow and cramped. But coming down to the MSS. of the 11th or 12th centuries we find a change. The pointed hand by this time has become moulded into the angular and stereotyped form peculiar to Irish MSS. of the later middle ages. From the 12th to the 15th centuries there is a very gradual change. Indeed, a carefully written MS. of late date may very well pass for an example older by a century or more. A book of hymns of the 11th or 12th century (*Nat. MSS. Ireland*, i. pls. xxxii.-xxxvi.) may be referred to as a good typical specimen of the Irish hand of that period; and the Gospels of Maelbrighte, of A.D. 1138 (*Nat. MSS. Ireland*, i. pls. xl.-xlii.; *Pal. Soc.* pl. 212), as a calligraphic one.

In Irish MSS. of the later period, the ink is black, and the vellum, as a general rule, is coarse and discoloured, a defect which may be attributed to inexperience in the art of preparing the skins and to the effects of climate.

When a school of writing attained to the perfection which marked that of Ireland at an early date, so far in advance of other countries, it naturally followed that its influence should be felt beyond it own borders. How the influence of the Irish school asserted itself in England will be presently discussed. But on the Continent also Irish monks carried their civilizing power into different countries, and continued their native style of writing in the monasteries which they founded. At such centres as Luxeuil in France, Würzburg in Germany, St Gall in Switzerland, and Bobbio in Italy, they were as busy in the production of MSS. as they had been at home. At first such MSS. were no doubt as distinctly Irish in their character as if written in Ireland itself; but, after a time, as the bonds of connexion with that country were weakened, the form of writing would become rather traditional, and lose the elasticity of a native hand. As the national styles also which were practised around them became more perfected, the writing of the Irish houses would in turn be reacted on; and it is thus that the later MSS. produced in those houses can be distinguished. Archaic forms are traditionally retained, but the spirit of the hand dies and the writing becomes merely imitative.

English Writing.—In England there were two sources whence a national hand could be derived. From St Columba's foundation in Iona the Irish monks established monasteries in the northern parts of Britain; and in the year 635 the Irish missionary Aidan founded the see of Lindisfarne or Holy Isle, where there was established a school of writing destined to become famous. In the south of England the Roman missionaries had also brought into the country their own style of writing direct from Rome, and taught it in the newly founded monasteries. But their writing never became a national hand. Such a MS. as the Canterbury Psalter in the Cottonian Library (*Pal. Soc.* pl. 18) shows what could be done by English scribes in imitation of Roman uncials; and the existence of so few early charters in the same letters (*Facs. of Anc. Charters*, pt. i., Nos. 1, 2, 7), among the large number which have survived, goes to prove how limited was the influence of that form of writing. The famous MS. of the Bible known as the Codex Amiatinus, now at Florence, which was written in uncials at Jarrow in Northumbria, about the year 700, was almost certainly the work of foreign scribes. On the other hand, the Irish style made progress throughout England, and was adopted as the national hand, developing in course of time certain local peculiarities, and lasting as a distinct form of writing down to the time of the Norman Conquest. But, while English scribes at first copied their Irish models with faithful exactness, they soon learned to give to their writing the stamp of a national character, and imparted to it the elegance and strength which individualized the English hand for many centuries to come.

As in Ireland, so here we have to follow the course of the round hand as distinct from the pointed character. The earliest and most beautiful MS. of the former class is the Lindisfarne Gospels (fig. 41) or "Durham Book" in the Cottonian Library (*Pal. Soc.* pls. 3–6, 22; *Cat. Anc. MSS.* pt. ii. pls. 8–11), said to have been written by Eadfrith, bishop of Lindisfarne, about the year 700. The text is in very exactly formed half-uncials, differing but slightly from the same characters in Irish MSS., and is glossed in the Northumbrian dialect by Aldred, a writer of the 10th century.

FIG. 41.—Lindisfarne Gospels, c. A.D. 700.
(regnum caelorum. Beati mites quoniam ipsi possidebunt.
ric heofna eadge bidon ða milde fordon ða agnegad.)

MSS. in the same solid half-uncial hand are still to be seen in the Chapter Library of Durham; this style of writing having been practised more especially in the north of England. But in addition to this calligraphic book-writing, there was also a lighter form of the round letters which was used for less sumptuous MSS. or for more ordinary occasions. Specimens of this hand are found in the Durham Cassiodorus (*Pal. Soc.* pl. 164), in the Canterbury Gospels (*Pal. Soc.* pl. 7; *Cat. Anc. MSS.* pt. ii., pls. 17, 18), the Epinal Glossary (*E. Eng. Text Soc.*), and in a few charters (*Facs. Anc. Charters*, pt. i., 15; ii. 2, 3; *Pal. Soc.* 10), one of which, of A.D. 778, written in Wessex, is interesting as showing the extension of the round hand to the southern parts of England. The examples here enumerated are of the 8th and 9th centuries—the earlier ones being written in a free natural hand, and those of later date bearing evidence of decadence. Indeed the round hand was being rapidly displaced by the more convenient pointed hand, which was in full use in England in the middle of the 8th century. How late, however, the more calligraphic round hand could be continued under favouring circumstances is seen in the Liber Vitae or list of benefactors of Durham (*Cat. Anc. MSS.* pt. ii., pl. 25; *Pal. Soc.* pl. 238), the writing of which would, from its beautiful execution, be taken for that of the 8th century, did not internal evidence prove it to be of about the year 840.

The pointed hand ran its course through the 8th, 9th, and 10th centuries, until English writing came under the influence of the foreign minuscule. The leading characteristics of this hand in the 8th century are regularity and breadth in the formation of the letters and a calligraphic contrast of heavy and light strokes—the hand being then at its best. In the 9th century there is greater lateral compression, although regularity and correct formation are maintained. But in the 10th century there are signs of decadence. New forms are introduced, and there is a disposition to be imitative. A test letter of this latter century is found in the letter *a* with obliquely cut top, ꝏ.

The course of the progressive changes in the pointed hand may be followed in the *Facsimiles of Ancient Charters in the British Museum* and in the *Facsimiles of Anglo-Saxon MSS.* of the Rolls Series. The charters reproduced in these works have survived in sufficient numbers to enable us not only to form a fairly accurate knowledge of the criteria of their age, but also to recognize local peculiarities of writing. The Mercian scribes appear to have been very excellent penmen, writing a very graceful hand with much delicate play in the strokes. On the other hand the writing of Wessex was heavier and more straggling and is in such strong contrast to the Mercian hand that its examples may be easily detected with a little practice. Turning to books in which the pointed hand was employed, a very beautiful specimen, of the 8th century, is a copy of Bede's *Ecclesiastical History* (fig. 42) in the University Library at Cambridge (*Pal. Soc.* pls. 139, 140), which has in a marked degree that breadth of style which has been referred to. Not much later is another copy of the same work in the Cottonian Library (*Pal. Soc.* pl. 141; *Cat. Anc. MSS.* pt. ii., pl. 19), from which the following facsimile is taken.

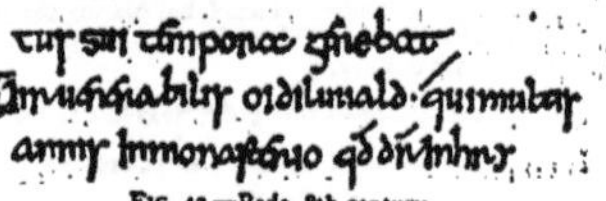

FIG. 42.—Bede, 8th century.
(tus sui tempora gerebat.
Uir uenerabilis oidiluuald, qui multis
annis in monasterio quod dicitur Inhry——)

For an example of the beginning of the 9th century, a MS. of miscellanea, of A.D. 811–814, also in the Cottonian Library, may be referred to (*Pal. Soc.* pl. 165; *Cat. Anc. MSS.* pt. ii. Plate 24); and a very interesting MS. written in the Wessex style is the Digby MS. 63 of the middle of the century (*Pal. Soc.* pl. 168). As seen in the charters, the pointed writing of the 10th century assumes generally a larger size, and is rather more artificial and calligraphic. A very beautiful example of the book-hand of this period is found in the volume known as the Durham Ritual (*Pal. Soc.* pl. 240), which, owing to the care bestowed on the writing and the archaism of the style, might at first sight pass for a MS. of higher antiquity.

In the latter part of the 10th century the foreign set minuscule hand began to make its way into England, consequent on increased intercourse with the Continent and political changes which followed. In the charters we find the foreign and native hands on the same page: the body of the document, in Latin, in Carolingian minuscules; the boundaries of the land conveyed, in the English hand. The same practice was followed in books. The charter (in book form) of King Eadgar to New Minster, Winchester, A.D. 966 (*Pal. Soc.* pls. 46, 47), the Benedictional of Bishop Æthelwold of Winchester (pls. 142, 144) before A.D. 984, and the MS. of the Office of the Cross, A.D. 1012–1020 (pl. 60), also written in Winchester, are all examples of the use of the foreign minuscule for Latin. The change also which the national hand underwent at this period may certainly be attributed to this foreign influence. The pointed hand, strictly so-called, is replaced by a rounder or rather square character, with lengthened strokes above and below the line.

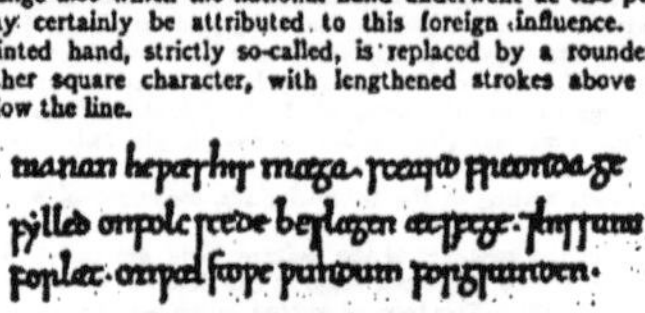

FIG. 43.—Chronicle, 11th century.
(manan he was his mæg. sceard freonda ge
fylled on folcstede beslagen æt secge. and his sunu
forlæt. on wælstowe wundum forgrunden.)

This style of writing becomes the ordinary English hand down to the time of the Norman Conquest. That event extinguished the national hand for official purposes—it disappears from charters; and the already established use of the Carolingian minuscule in Latin MSS. completed its exclusion as the hand-writing of the learned. It cannot, however, be doubted that it still lingered in those parts of the country where foreign influence did not at once penetrate, and that Englishmen still continued to write their own language in their own style of writing. But that the earlier distinctive national hand was soon overpowered by foreign teaching is evident in English MSS. of the 11th century, the writing of which is of the foreign type, although the English letter (thorn, Þ), survived and continued in use down to the 15th century, when it was transformed to y.

LATIN WRITING. IV.—THE CAROLINGIAN REFORM AND THE
MEDIEVAL MINUSCULE HAND

It has been stated above that in the Merovingian MSS. of the
8th century there was evident progress towards a settled minuscule book-hand which only required a master hand to fix it in
a purified and calligraphic form. This was effected under
Charlemagne, in whose reign the revival of learning naturally
led to a reform in handwriting. An ordinance of the year 789
required the revision of Church books; and a more correct
orthography and style of writing was the consequence. The
abbey of St Martin of Tours was one of the principal centres
from whence the reformation of the book-hand spread. Here,
from the year 796 to 804, Alcuin of York presided as abbot;
and it was specially under his direction that the Carolingian
minuscule writing took the simple and graceful form which was
gradually adopted to the exclusion of all other hands. In
carrying out this reformation we may well assume that Alcuin
brought to bear the results of the training which he had received
in his youth in the English school of writing, which had attained
to such proficiency, and that he was also beneficially influenced
by the fine examples of the Lombard school which he had seen
in Italy. In the new Carolingian minuscule all the uncouthness
of the later Merovingian hand disappears, and the simpler forms
of many of the letters found in the old Roman half-uncial and
minuscule hands are adopted. The character of Carolingian
writing through the 9th and early part of the 10th century
is one of general uniformity, with a contrast of light and
heavy strokes, the limbs of tall letters being clubbed or
thickened at the head by pressure on the pen. As to characteristic letters (fig. 44) the e, following the old type, is, in the
9th century, still frequently open, in the form of ei; the bows
of g are open, the letter somewhat resembling the numeral 3;
and there is little turning of the ends of letters, as m and n.

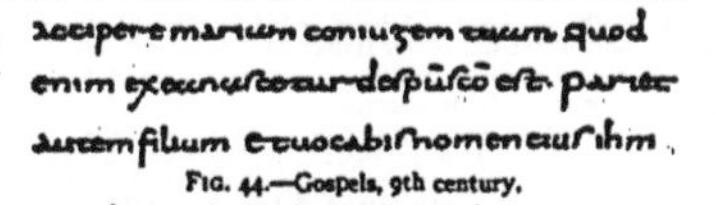

accipere mariam coniugem tuam quod
enim ex ea nascetur de spiritu sancto est. pariet
autem filium et uocabis nomen eius Iesum

FIG. 44.—Gospels, 9th century.

accipere mariam coniugem tuam quod
enim ex ea nascetur de spiritu sancio est. Pariet
autem filium et uocabis nomen eius Iesum)

In the 10th century the clubbing of the tall letters becomes
less pronounced, and the writing generally assumes, so to say, a
thinner appearance. But a great change is noticeable in the
writing of the 11th century. By this time the Carolingian
minuscule may be said to have put off its archaic form and to
develop into the more modern character of small letter. It
takes a more finished and accurate and more upright form, the
individual letters being drawn with much exactness, and generally on a rather larger scale than before. This style continues to
improve, and is reduced to a still more exact form of calligraphy
in the 12th century, which for absolute beauty of writing is
unsurpassed. In England especially (fig. 45) the writing of
this century is particularly fine.

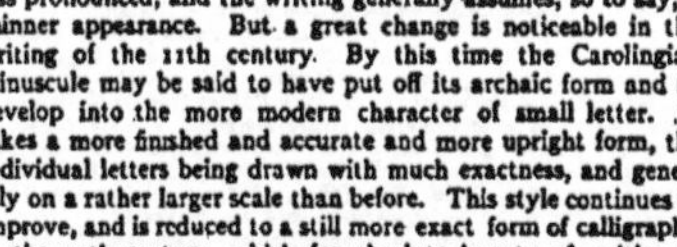

culof cu aruunulif sunt addeunt super
altare uitulum cu pelle et carnibus et
fimo cremat ext castra six propar dns.

FIG. 45.—Leviticus, A.D. 1176.

(—culos cum aruinulis suis adoleoit super
altare uitulum cum pelle et carnibus et
fimo cremans extra castra sicut praeoperat dominus).

As, however, the demand for written works increased, the fine
round-hand of the 12th century could not be maintained.
Economy of material became necessary, and a smaller hand
with more frequent contractions was the result. The larger and
more distinct writing of the 11th and 12th centuries is now
replaced by a more cramped though still distinct hand, in which
the letters are more linked together by connecting strokes,
and are more laterally compressed. This style of writing is
characteristic of the 13th century. But, while the book-hand
of this period is a great advance upon that of a hundred years
earlier, there is no tendency to a cursive style. Every letter is
clearly formed, and generally on the old shapes. The particular
letters which show weakness are those made of a succession of
vertical strokes, as m, n, u. The new method of connecting
these strokes, by turning the ends and running on, made the
distinction of such letters difficult, as, for example, in such a
word as minimi. The ambiguity thus arising was partly
obviated by the use of a small oblique stroke over the letter i,
which, to mark the double letter, had been introduced as early
as the 11th century. The dot on the letter came into fashion in
the 14th century.

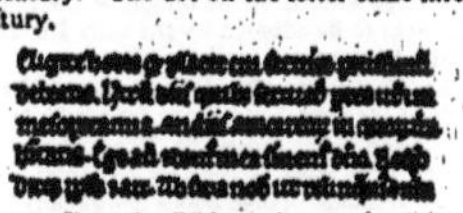

Eligite hodie quod placet cui seruire potissimum
debeatis. Utrum diis quibus seruierunt patres uestri in
mesopotamia, an diis amoreorum in quorum terra
habitatis. Ego autem et domus mea seruiemus domino Respon-
ditque populus ei ait, Absit a nobis ut relinquamus dominum)

FIG. 46.—Bible, 13th century.

(Eligite hodie quod placet cui seruire potissimum
debeatis. Utrum diis quibus seruierunt patres uestri in
mesopotamia, an diis amoreorum in quorum terra
habitatis. Ego autem et domus mea seruiemus domino. Respon-
ditque populus ei ait, Absit a nobis ut relinquamus dominum)

In MSS. of the 14th century minuscule writing becomes slacker,
and the consistency of formation of letters falters. There is a
tendency to write more cursively and without raising the pen,
as may be seen in the form of the letter a, of which the characteristic shape at this time is a, with both bows closed, in contrast
with the earlier a. In this century, however, the hand still
remains fairly stiff and upright. In the 15th century it becomes
very angular, and more and more cursive, but is at first kept
within bounds. In the course of the century, however, it grows
more slack and deformed, and the letters become continually
more cursive and misshapen. An exception, however, to this
disintegration of minuscule writing in the later centuries is to
be observed in church books. In these the old set hand of the
12th and 13th centuries was imitated and continued to be the
liturgical style of writing.

It is impossible to describe within limited space, and without
the aid of plentiful illustrations, all the varieties of handwriting
which were developed in the different countries of western
Europe, where the Carolingian minuscule was finally adopted
to the exclusion of the earlier national hands. In each country,
however, it acquired, in a greater or less degree, an individual
national stamp which can generally be recognized, and which
serves to distinguish MSS. written in different localities. A
broad line of distinction may be drawn between the writing of
northern and southern Europe from the 12th to the 15th century.
In the earlier part of this period the MSS. of England, northern
France and the Netherlands are closely connected. Indeed, in
the 12th and 13th centuries it is not always easy to decide as to
which of the three countries a particular MS. may belong. As
a rule, perhaps, English MSS. are written with more sense of
gracefulness; those of the Netherlands in darker ink. From the
latter part of the 13th century, however, national character
begins to assert itself more distinctly. In southern Europe the
influence of the Italian school of writing is manifest in the MSS.
of the south of France in the 13th and 14th centuries, and also,
though later, in those of Spain. That elegant roundness of
letter which the Italian scribes seem to have inherited from the
bold characters of the early papal chancery, and more recently
from Lombardic models, was generally adopted in the book-hand
of those districts. It is especially noticeable in calligraphic
specimens, as in church books—the writing of Spanish MSS. in
this style being distinguished by the blackness of the ink.
The medieval minuscule writing of Germany stands apart. It
never attained to the beauty of the hands of either the north or

the south which have been just noticed; and from its ruggedness and slow development German MSS. have the appearance of being older than they really are. The writing has also very commonly a certain slope in the letters which compares unfavourably with the upright and elegant hands of other countries. In western Europe generally the minuscule hand thus nationalized ran its course down to the time of the invention of printing, when the so-called black letter, or set hand of the 15th century in Germany and other countries, furnished models for the types. But in Italy, with the revival of learning, a more refined taste set in in the production of MSS., and scribes went back to an earlier time in search of a better standard of writing. Hence, in the first quarter of the 15th century, MSS. written on the lines of the Italian hand of the early 12th century begin to appear, and become continually more numerous. This revived hand was brought to perfection soon after the middle of the century, just at the right moment to be adopted by the early Italian printers, and to be perpetuated by them in their types.

English Cursive Charter-Hands.—It must also not be forgotten that by the side of the book-hand of the later middle ages there was the cursive hand of everyday use. This is represented in abundance in the large mass of charters and legal and domestic documents which remains. Some notice has already been taken of the development of the national cursive hands in the earliest times. From the 12th century downwards these hands settled into well defined and distinct styles peculiar to different countries, and passed through systematic changes which can be recognized as characteristic of particular periods. But, while the cursive hand thus followed out its own course, it was still subject to the same laws of change which governed the book-hand; and the letters of the two styles did not differ at any period in their organic formation. Confining our attention to the charter-hand, or court hand, practised in England, a few specimens may be taken to show the principal changes which it developed. In the 12th century the official hand which had been introduced after the Norman Conquest is characterized by exaggeration in the strokes above and below the line, a legacy of the old Roman cursive, as already noted. There is also a tendency to form the tops of tall vertical strokes, as in *b, h, l,* with a notch or cleft. The letters are well made and vigorous, though often rugged.

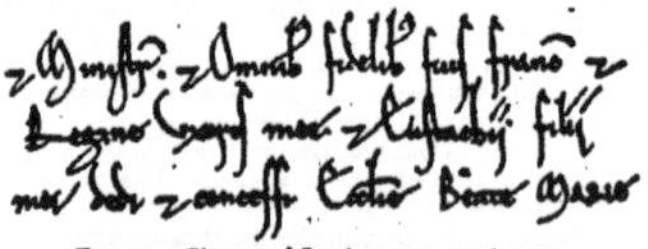

FIG. 47.—Charter of Stephen, A.D. 1136–1139.

(et ministris et omnibus fidelibus suis Francis et——Regine uxoris mee et Eustachii filii——mei dedi et concessi ecclesie Beate Marie)

As the century advances, the long limbs are brought into better proportion; and early in the 13th century a very delicate fine-stroked hand comes into use, the cleaving of the tops being now a regular system, and the branches formed by the cleft falling in a curve on either side. This style remains the writing of the reigns of John and Henry III.

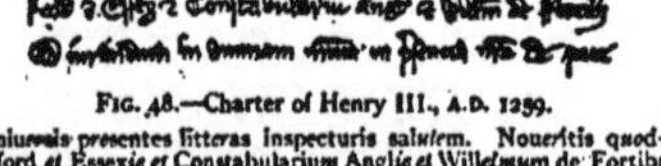

FIG. 48.—Charter of Henry III., A.D. 1299.

(uniuersis presentes litteras inspecturis salutem. Noueritis quod——ford et Essexie et Constabularium Anglie et Willelmum de Fortibus——ad iurandum in animam nostram in presencia nostra de pace)

Towards the latter part of the 13th century the letters grow rounder; there is generally more contrast of light and heavy

strokes; and the cleft tops begin, as it were, to shed the branch on the left.

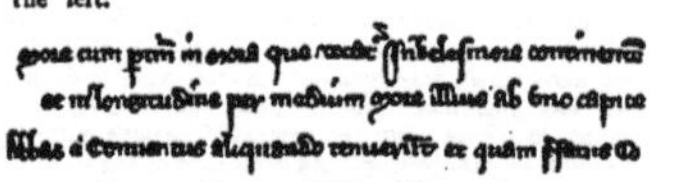

FIG. 49.—Charter of Edward I., A.D. 1303.

(More *cum pertinentiis* in mora que vocatur Inkelesmore continentem——se in longitudine per medium more illius ab uno capite——Abbas et Conuentus aliquando tenuerunt et quam prestatus Co—)

In the 14th century the changes thus introduced make further progress, and the round letters and single-branched vertical strokes become normal through the first half of the century. Then, however, the regular formation begins to give way and angularity sets in. Thus in the reign of Richard II. we have a hand presenting a mixture of round and angular elements—the letters retain their breadth but lose their curves. Hence, by further decadence, results the angular hand of the 15th century, at first compact, but afterwards straggling and ill-formed.

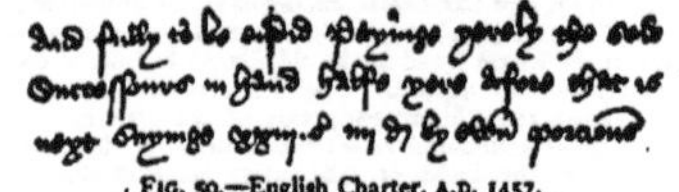

FIG. 50.—English Charter, A.D. 1457.

(and fully to be endid, payinge yerely the seid——successours in hand halfe yere afore that is——next suyinge xxiij. s. iiij. d. by evens porciouns.)

In concluding these remarks on the medieval cursive English writing, it is only necessary to remind the reader that the modern English cursive hand owes its origin to the general introduction into the west of the fine round Italian cursive hand of the 16th century—one of the notable legacies bequeathed to us by the wonderful age of the Renaissance.

BIBLIOGRAPHY.—General (*Greek and Latin*): J. Astle, *The Origin and Progress of Writing* (1803); E. M. Thompson, *Handbook of Greek and Roman Palaeography* (3rd ed., 1906); J. B. Silvestre, *Paléographie universelle* (1839–1841; and Eng. ed., 1850); Palaeographical Society, *Facsimiles of MSS. and Inscriptions* (two series, 1873–1883, 1884–1894); New Palaeographical Society, *Facsimiles of Ancient MSS., &c.* (1903, &c.); Vitelli and Paoli, *Collezione fiorentina di facsimili paleografici greci e latini* (1884–1897); Westwood, *Palaeographia sacra pictoria* (1843–1845); F. G. Kenyon, *Facsimiles of Biblical MSS. in the British Museum* (1900).

Greek Palaeography: B. de Montfaucon, *Palaeographia graeca* (1708); V. Gardthausen, *Griechische Palaeographie* (1879); W. Wattenbach, *Anleitung zur griechischen Palaeographie* (1895); F. G. Kenyon, *The Palaeography of Greek Papyri* (1899); N. Schow, *Charta papyracea graece scripta musei Borgiani Velitris* (1788); A. Peyron, *Papyri graeci regii taur. mus. Aegypti* (1826–1827); J. Forshall, *Greek Papyri in the British Museum* (1839); C. Leemans, *Papyri Graeci Mus. Lugd. Bat.* (1843, 1885); C. Babington, *Orations of Hyperides for Lycophron and for Euxenippus* (1853), and *The Funeral Oration of Hyperides over Leosthenes* (1858); W. Brunet de Presle, "Notices et textes des papyrus grecs du Musée du Louvre," &c. [tom. xviii. of *Notices et extraits des MSS. de la Bibl. Imp.*] (1865); J. Karabacek, *Mittheilungen aus der Sammlung der Papyrus Erzherzog Rainer* (1886), and *Führer durch die Ausstellung* (1894); C. Wessely, *Corpus papyrorum Raineri* (1895, &c.); J. P. Mahaffy, *On the Flinders-Petrie Papyri* (1891–1905); U. Wilcken, *Tafeln zur älteren griechischen Palaeographie* (1891), *Griechische Urkunden* (1892, &c.), *Griechische Ostraka* (1899), and *Archiv für Papyrusforschung* (1900, &c.); F. G. Kenyon, *Greek Papyri in the British Museum* (1893–1906), *Greek Classical Texts from Papyri in the British Museum* (1891, 1893), *Aristotle on the Constitution of Athens* (1892), and *The Poems of Bacchylides* (1898); E. Revillout, *Le Plaidoyer d'Hypéride contre Athénogène* (1892); Grenfell and Mahaffy, *The Revenue Laws of Ptolemy Philadelphus* (1896); J. Nicole, *Les Papyrus de Genève* (1896, &c.); Grenfell and Hunt, *The Oxyrhynchus Papyri* (1898, &c.), *Fayûm Towns* (1900), *The Amherst Papyri* (1900, 1901), and *The Tebtunis Papyri* (1902, &c.); C. Wessely, *Papyrorum scripturae graecae specimina* (1900); U. von Wilamowitz-Möllendorff, *Der Timotheus-Papyrus* (1903); H. Diels, *Berliner Klassikertexte* (1904, &c.); G. Vitelli, *Papiri fiorentini* (1905, &c.); T. Reinach, *Papyrus grecs et démotiques* (1905); Sabas, *Specim. palaeogr. codd. graec. et slav.* (1863); W. Wattenbach, *Schrifttafeln zur Geschichte der griech. Schrift* (1876), and *Scripturos graecae specimina* (1883); Wattenbach and von Velsen, *Exempla codd. graec. lill. minusc. scriptorum* (1878); H. Omont, *Facsim. des MSS. grecs datés de la bibl. nat.* (1891), *Facsim. des plus anciens MSS. de la bibl. nat.* (1892), and *Facsim. des MSS. grecs des xv. et xvi. siècles* (1887); A. Martin, *Facsim. des MSS. grecs d'Espagne* (1891); O. Lehmann, *Die tachygr. Abkürzungen der griech. Handschriften*; T. W. Allen, *Notes on Abbreviations in Greek MSS.* (1889).

Latin Palaeography: J. Mabillon, *De re diplomatica* (1709); Tassin and Toustain, *Nouveau traité de diplomatique* (1750–1765); T. Madox, *Formulare anglicanum* (1702); G. Hickes, *Linguarum septent. thesaurus* (1703–1705); F. S. Maffei, *Istoria diplomatica* (1727); G. Marini, *I Papiri diplomatici* (1805); G. Bessel, *Chronicon gotwicense* (1732); A. Fumagalli, *Delle Istituzioni diplomatiche* (1802); U. F. Kopp, *Palaeographia critica* (1817–1829); T. Sickel, *Schrifttaf. aus dem Nachlasse von U. F. von Kopp* (1870); C. T. G. Schönemann, *Versuch eines vollständ. Systems der all. Diplomatik* (1818); T. Sickel, *Lehre von den Urkunden der ersten Karolinger* (1867); J. Ficker, *Beiträge zur Urkundenlehre* (1877–1888); N. de Wailly, *Éléments de paléographie* (1838); A. Chassant, *Paléographie des chartes, &c.* (1885); L. Delisle, *Mélanges de paléographie, &c.* (1880), *Études paléographiques, &c.* (1886), *Mémoire sur l'école calligraphique de Tours* (1885); W. Wattenbach, *Anleitung zur latein. Palaeographie* (1886); A. Gloria, *Compendio di paleografia, &c.* (1870); C. Paoli, *Programma di paleografia lat. e di diplomatica* (1888–1900); H. Bresslau, *Handbuch der Urkundenlehre* (1889); M. Prou, *Manuel de paléographie* (1891); A. Giry, *Manuel de diplomatique* (1894); F. Leist, *Urkundenlehre* (1893); E. H. J. Reusens, *Éléments de paléographie* (1897–1899); W. Arndt, *Schrifttafeln zur Erlernung der latein. Palaeographie* (1887–1888); C. Wessely, *Schrifttaf. zur älteren latein. Palaeographie* (1898); F. Steffens, *Latein. Palaeographie-Tafeln* (1903, &c.); C. Zangemeister, *Inscriptiones pompeianae* [C.I.L. iv.] (1871), and *Tabulae ceratae Pompeis repertae* [C.I.L. iv.] (1898); Nicole and Morel, *Archives militaires du premier siècle* (1900); J. F. Massmann, *Libellus aurarius sive tabulae ceratae* (1841); T. Mommsen, *Instrumenta dacica in tab. cerat. conscripta* [C.I.L. iii.] (1873); A. Champollion-Figeac, *Chartes et MSS. sur papyrus* (1840); A. Letronne, *Diplômes et chartes de l'époque mérovingienne* (1845–1866); J. Tardif, *Facsim. de chartes et diplômes mérovingiens et carlovingiens* (1866); von Sybel and Sickel, *Kaiserurkunden in Abbildungen* (1880–1891); J. Pflugk-Harttung, *Specim. select. chart. pontif. roman.* (1885–1887); Zangemeister and Wattenbach, *Exempla codd. lat. litt. majusc. scriptorum* (1876–1879); E. Chatelain, *Uncialis scriptura codd. lat.* (1901–1902); A. Champollion-Figeac, *Paléographie des classiques latins* (1839); E. Chatelain, *Paléographie des classiques latins* (1884–1900); *Musée des archives nationales* (1872); *Musée des archives départementales* (1878); L. Delisle, *Album paléographique* (1887); T. Sickel, *Monumenta graphica ex archiv. et bibl. imp. austriacel collecta* (1858–1882); W. Schum, *Exempla codd. amplon. erfurtensium* (1882); A. Chroust, *Denkmäler der Schriftkunst des Mittelalters* (1899, &c.); Monaci and Paoli, *Archivio paleogr. italiano* (1882–1890); M. Monaci, *Facsimili di antichi manoscritti* (1881–1883); M. Morcaldi, *Codex diplom. cavensis* (1873, &c.); L. Tosti, *Bibliotheca casinensis* (1873–1880); *Paleografia artistica di Montecassino* (1876–1881); Ewald and Loewe, *Exempla scripturae visigoticae* (1883); C. Rodriguez, *Bibliotheca universal de la polygraphia española* (1738); A. Merino, *Escuela paleographica* (1780); J. Munos y Rivero, *Paleografia visigoda* (1881), *Manual de paleografia diplomatica española* (1890), and *Chrestomathia palaeographica* (1890); E. A. Bond, *Facsim. of Ancient Charters in the British Museum* (1873–1878); W. B. Sanders, *Facsim. of Anglo-Saxon MSS.* (charters) (1878–1884), and *Facsim. of National MSS. of England* (1865–1868); Varner and Ellis, *Facsim. of Royal and other Charters in the British Museum* (1903); C. Innes, *Facsim. of National MSS. of Scotland* (1867–1871); J. Anderson, *Selectus diplomatum et numismatum Scotiae thesaurus* (1739); J. T. Gilbert, *Facsim. of National MSS. of Ireland* (1874–1884); E. Chatelain, *Introduction à la lecture des notes tironiennes* (1900); J. L. Walther, *Lexicon Diplomaticum* (1747); A. Chassant, *Dictionnaire des abréviations latines et françaises* (1884); A. Cappelli, *Dizionario di abreviature latine et italiche* (1889); L. Traube, *Nomina sacra* (1907); A. Wright, *Court-Hand. restored* (1879); C. T. Martin, *The Record Interpreter* (1892).

The application of photographic processes to the reproduction of entire MSS. has received great impetus during the last few years, and will certainly be widely extended in the future. Many of the most ancient biblical and other MSS. have been thus reproduced, the librarians of the university of Leiden are issuing a great series comprising several of the oldest classical MSS.; and under the auspices of the pope and the Italian government famous MSS. in the Vatican and other libraries in Italy are being published by this method; not to mention the issue of various individual MSS. by other corporate bodies or private persons. (E. M. T.)

PALAEOLITHIC (Gr. παλαιός, old, and λίθος, stone), in anthropology, the characteristic epithet of the Drift or early Stone Age when Man shared the possession of Europe with the mammoth, the cave-bear, the woolly-haired rhinoceros and other extinct animals. The epoch is characterized by flint implements of the rudest type and never polished. The fully authenticated remains of palaeolithic man are few, and discoveries are confined to certain areas, e.g. France and north Italy. The reason is that interment appears not to have been practised by the river-drift hunters, and the only bones likely to be found would be those accidentally preserved in caves or rock-shelters. The first actual find of a palaeolithic implement was that of a rudely fashioned flint in a sandbank at Menchecourt in 1841 by Boucher de Perthes. Further discoveries have resulted in the division of the Palaeolithic Age into various epochs or sequences according to the faunas associated with the implements or the localities where found. One classification makes three divisions for the epoch, characterized respectively by the existence of the cave-bear, the mammoth and reindeer; another, two, marked by the prevalence of the mammoth and reindeer respectively. These divisions are, however, unsatisfactory, as the fauna relied on as characteristic must have existed synchronously. The four epochs or culture-sequences of G. de Mortillet have met with the most general acceptance. They are called from the places in France where the most typical finds of palaeolithic remains have been made—Chellian from Chelles, a few miles east of Paris; Mousterian from the cave of Moustier on the river Vézère, Dordogne; Solutrian from the cave at Solutré near Macon; and Madelenian from the rocky shelter of La Madeleine, Dordogne.

PALAEOLOGUS, a Byzantine family name which first appears in history about the middle of the 11th century, when George Palaeologus is mentioned among the prominent supporters of Nicephorus Botaniates, and afterwards as having helped to raise Alexius I. Comnenus to the throne in 1081; he is also noted for his brave defence of Durazzo against the Normans in that year. Michael Palaeologus, probably his son, was sent by Manuel II. Comnenus into Italy as ambassador to the court of Frederick I. in 1154; in the following year he took part in the campaign against William of Sicily, and died at Bari in 1155. A son or brother of Michael, named George, received from the emperor Manuel the title of *Sebastos*, and was entrusted with several important missions; it is uncertain whether he ought to be identified with the George Palaeologus who took part in the conspiracy which dethroned Isaac Angelus in favour of Alexius Angelus in 1195. Andronicus Palaeologus Comnenus was Great Domestic under Theodore Lascaris and John Vatatzes; his eldest son by Irene Palaeologina, Michael (q.v.), became the eighth emperor of that name in 1260, and was in turn followed by his son Andronicus II. (1282–1328). Michael, the son of Andronicus, and associated with him in the empire, died in 1320, but left a son, Andronicus III., who reigned from 1328 to 1341; John VI. (1355–1391), Manuel II. (1391–1425) and John VII. (1425–1448) then followed in lineal succession; Constantine XI. or XII., the last emperor of the East (1448–1453), was the younger brother of John VII. Other brothers were Demetrius, prince of the Morea until 1460, and Thomas, prince of Achaia, who died at Rome in 1465. A daughter of Thomas, Zoe by name, married Ivan III. of Russia. A younger branch of the Palaeologi held the principality of Monferrat from 1305 to 1533, when it became extinct.

See ROMAN EMPIRE, LATER, and articles on the separate rulers.

PALAEONTOLOGY (Gr. παλαιός, ancient, neut. pl. ὄντα, beings, and λογία, discourse, science), the science of extinct forms of life. Like many other natural sciences, this study dawned among the Greeks. It was retarded and took false directions until the revival of learning in Italy. It became established as a distinct branch in the beginning of the 19th century, and somewhat later received the appellation "palaeontology," which was given independently by De Blainville and by Fischer von Waldheim about 1834. In recent years the science of vegetable palaeontology has been given the distinct name of *Palaeobotany* (q.v.), so that "palaeontology" among biologists mainly refers to zoology; but historically the two cannot be disconnected.

Palaeontology both borrows from and sheds light upon geology and other branches of the physical history of the earth, each of which, such as palaeogeography or palaeometeorology, is the more fascinating because of the large element of the unknown, the need for constructive imagination, the appeal to other branches of biological and physical investigation for supplementary evidence, and the necessity of constant comparison with the present aspects of nature. The task of the palaeontologist thus begins with the appearance of life on the globe, and ends in close relation to the studies of the archaeologist and historian as well as of the zoologist and botanist. That wealth of evidence which the zoologist enjoys, including environment in all its aspects and anatomy in its perfection of organs and tissues, the palaeontologist finds partially or wholly destroyed, and his highest art is that of complete restoration of both the past forms and past environments of life (see Plates I. and II.; figs. 1, 2, 3, 4, 5). The degree of accuracy in such anatomical and physiographic restorations from relatively imperfect evidence will always represent the state of the science and the degree of its approach toward being exact or complete. Progress in the science also depends upon the pursuit of palaeontology as zoology and not as geology, because it was a mere accident of birth which connected palaeontology so closely with geology.

In order to illustrate the grateful services which palaeontology through restoration may render to the related earth sciences let us imagine a vast continent of the past wholly unknown in its physical features, elevation, climate, configuration, but richly represented by fossil remains. All the fossil plants and animals of every kind are brought from this continent into a great museum; the latitude, longitude and relative elevation of each specimen are precisely recorded; a corps of investigators, having the most exact and thorough training in zoology and botany, and gifted with imagination, will soon begin to restore the geographic and physiographic outlines of the continent, its fresh, brackish and salt-water confines, its seas, rivers and lakes, its forests, uplands, plains, meadows and swamps; also to a certain extent the cosmic relations of this continent, the amount and duration of its sunshine, as well as something of the chemical constitution of its atmosphere and the waters of its rivers and seas; they will trace the progressive changes which took place in the outlines of the continent and its surrounding oceans, following the invasions of the land by the sea and the re-emergence of the land and retreatal of the seashore; they will outline the shoals and deeps of its border seas, and trace the barriers which prevented intermingling of the inhabitants of the various provinces of the continent and the surrounding seas. From a study of remains of the mollusca, brachiopoda and other marine organisms they will determine the shallow water (littoral) and deep water (abyssal) regions of the surrounding oceans, and the clear or muddy, salt, brackish or fresh character of its inland and marginal seas; and even the physical conditions of the open sea at the time will be ascertained.

In such manner Johannes Walther (Die Fauna der Solnhofener Platten Kalke Bionomisch betrachtet. Festschrift zum 70ten Geburtstage von Ernst Haeckel, 1904) has restored the conditions existing in the lagoons and atoll reefs of the Jurassic sea of Solnhofen in Bavaria; he has traced the process of gradual accumulation of the coral mud now constituting the fine lithographic stones in the inter-reef region, and has recognized the periodic laying bare of the mud surfaces thus formed; he has determined the winds which carried the dust particles from the not far distant land and brought the insects from the adjacent Jurassic forests. Finally the presence of the flying lizards (Pterydactylus, Rhamphorhynchus) and the ancient birds (Archaeopteryx) is determined from remains in a most wonderful state of preservation in these ancient deposits.

Still another example of restoration, relating to the surface of a continent, may be cited. It has been discovered that at the beginning of the Eocene the lake of Rilly occupied a vast area east of the present site of Paris, a water-course fell there in cascades, and Munier-Chalmas has reconstructed all the details of that singular locality, plants which loved moist places, such as Marchantia, Asplenium, the covered banks overshadowed by

lindens, laurels, magnolias and palms; there also were found the vine and the ivy; mosses (Fontinalis) and Chara sheltered the crayfish (Astacus); insects and even flowers have left their delicate impressions in the travertine which formed the borders of this lake. The Oligocene lake basin of Florissant, Colorado, has been reconstructed similarly by Samuel Hubbard Scudder and T. D. A. Cockerell, including the plants of its shores, the insects which lived upon them, the fluctuations of its level, and many other characteristics of this extinct water body, now in the heart of the arid region of the Rocky Mountains.

Such restorations are possible because of the intimate fitness of animals and plants to their environment, and because such fitness has distinguished certain forms of life from the Cambrian to the present time; the species have altogether changed, but the laws governing the life of certain kinds of organisms have remained exactly the same for the whole period of time assigned to the duration of life; in fact, we read the conditions of the past in a mirror of adaptation, often sadly tarnished and incomplete owing to breaks in the palaeontological record, but constantly becoming more polished by discoveries which increase the understanding of life and its all-pervading relations to the non-life. Therefore adaptation is the central principle of modern palaeontology in its most comprehensive sense.

This conception of the science and its possibilities is the result of very gradual advances since the beginning of the 19th century in what is known as the method of palaeontology. The history of this science, like that of all physical sciences, covers two parallel lines of development which have acted and reacted upon each other—namely, progress in exploration, research and discovery, and progress in philosophic interpretation. Progress in these two lines is by no means uniform; while, for example, palaeontology enjoyed a sudden advance early in the 19th century through the discoveries and researches of Cuvier, guided by his genius as a comparative anatomist, it was checked by his failure as a natural philosopher. The great philosophical impulse was that given by Darwin in 1859 through his demonstration of the theory of descent, which gave tremendous zest to the search for pedigrees (phylogeny) of the existing and extinct types of animal and plant life. In future the philosophic method of palaeontology must continue to advance step by step with exploration; it would be a reproach to later generations if they did not progress as far beyond the philosophic status of Cuvier, Owen and even of Huxley and Cope, as the new materials represent an advance upon the material opportunities which came to them through exploration.

To set forth how best to do our thinking, rather than to follow the triumphs achieved in any particular line of exploration, and to present the point we have now reached in the method or principles of palaeontology, is the chief purpose of this article. The illustrations will be drawn both from vertebrate and invertebrate palaeontology. In the latter branch the author is wholly indebted to Professor Amadeus W. Grabau of Columbia University. The subject will be treated in its biological aspects, because the relations of palaeontology to historical and stratigraphic geology are more appropriately considered under the article GEOLOGY. See also, for botany, the article PALAEOBOTANY. We may first trace in outline the history of the birth of palaeontological ideas, from the time of their first adumbration. But for full details reference must be made to the treatises on the history of the science cited in the bibliography at the end of the article.

I.—FIRST HISTORIC PERIOD

The scientific recognition of fossils as connected with the past history of the earth, from Aristotle (384–322 B.C.) to the beginning of the 19th century, in connexion with the rise of comparative anatomy and geology.—The dawn of the science covers the first observation of facts and the rudiments of true interpretation. Among the Greeks, Aristotle (384–322 B.C.) Xenophon (430–357 B C) and Strabo (63 B.C.–A.D. 24) knew of the existence of fossils, and surmised in a crude way their relation to earth history. Similar prophetic views are found among certain Roman writers. The pioneers of the science in the 16th and 17th centuries put forth anticipations of some of the well-known modern principles, often followed by recantations, through deference to prevailing religious or traditional beliefs. There were the retarding influences of the Mosaic account of sudden creation, and the belief that fossils represented relics of a universal deluge. There were crude medieval notions that fossils were "freaks" or "sports" of nature (*lusus naturae*), or that they represented failures of a creative force within the earth (a notion of Greek and Arabic origin), or that larger and smaller fossils represented the remains of races of giants or of pygmies (the mythical idea).

As early as the middle of the 15th century Leonardo da Vinci (1452-1519) recognized in seashells as well as in the teeth of marine fishes proofs of ancient sea-levels on what are now the summits of the Apennines. Successive observers in Italy, notably Fracastoro (1483-1553), Fabio Colonna (1567-1640 or 1650) and Nicolaus Steno (1638-c. 1687), a Danish anatomist, professor in Padua, advanced the still embryonic science and set forth the principle of comparison of fossil with living forms. Near the end of the 17th century Martin Lister (1638-1712), examining the Mesozoic shell types of England, recognized the great similarity as well as the differences between these and modern species, and insisted on the need of close comparison of fossil and living shells, yet he clung to the old view that fossils were sports of nature. In Italy, where shells of the sub-Apennine formations were discovered in the extensive quarrying for the fortifications of cities, the close similarity between these Tertiary and the modern species soon led to the established recognition of their organic origin. In England Robert Hooke (1635-1703) held to the theory of extinction of fossil forms, and advanced the two most fertile ideas of deriving from fossils a chronology, or series of time intervals in the earth's history, and of primary changes of climate, to account for the former existence of tropical species in England.

The 18th century witnessed the development of these suggestions and the birth of many additional theories. Sir A. Geikie assigns high rank to Jean Étienne Guettard (1715-1786) for his treatises on fossils, although admitting that he had no clear idea of the sequence of formations. The theory of successive formations was soundly developing in the treatises of John Woodward (1665-1728) in England, of Antonio Vallisnieri (1661-1730) in Italy, and of Johann Gottlob Lehmann (d. 1767) in Germany, who distinguished between the primary, or unfossiliferous, and secondary or fossiliferous, formations. The beginnings of palaeogeography followed those of palaeometeorology. The Italian geologist Soldani distinguished (1758) between the fossil fauna of the deep sea and of the shore-lines. In the same year Johann Gesner (1709-1790) set forth the theory of a great period of time, which he estimated at 80,000 years, for the elevation of the shell-bearing levels of the Apennines to their present height above the sea. The brilliant French naturalist Georges Louis Leclerc, comte de Buffon (1707-1788), in *Les Époques de la nature*, included in his vast speculations the theory of alternate submergence and emergence of the continents. Abraham Gottlob Werner (1750-1817), the famous exponent of the aqueous theory of earth formation, observed in successive geological formations the gradual approach to the forms of existing species.

II.—SECOND HISTORIC PERIOD

Invertebrate palaeontology founded by Lamarck, vertebrate palaeontology by Cuvier. Palaeontology connected with comparative anatomy by Cuvier. Invertebrate fossils employed for the definite division of all the great periods of time.—Although pre-evolutionary, this was the heroic period of the science, extending from the close of the 18th century to the publication of Darwin's *Origin of Species* in 1859. Among the pioneers of this period were the vertebrate zoologists and comparative anatomists Peter Simon Pallas, Pieter Camper and Johann Friedrich Blumenbach. Pallas (1741-1811) in his great journey (1768-1774) through Siberia discovered the vast deposits of extinct mammoths and rhinoceroses. Camper (1722-1789) contrasted (1777) the

Pleistocene and recent species of elephants and Blumenbach (1752-1840) separated (1780) the mammoth from the existing species as *Elephas primigenius*. In 1793 Thomas Pennant (1726-1798) distinguished the American mastodon as *Elephas americanus*.

Political troubles and the dominating influence of Werner's speculations checked palaeontology in Germany, while under the leadership of Lamarck and Cuvier France came to the fore. J. B. Lamarck (1744-1829) was the founder of invertebrate palaeontology. The treatise which laid the foundation for all subsequent invertebrate palaeontology was his memoir, *Sur les fossiles des environs de Paris . . .* (1802-1806). Beginning in 1793 he boldly advocated evolution, and further elaborated five great principles—namely, the method of comparison of extinct and existing forms, the broad sequence of formations and succession of epochs, the correlation of geological horizons by means of fossils, the climatic or environmental changes as influencing the development of species, the inheritance of the bodily modifications caused by change of habit and habitat. As a natural philosopher he radically opposed Cuvier and was distinctly a precursor of uniformitarianism, advocating the hypothesis of slow changes and variations, both in living forms and in their environment. His speculations on phylogeny, of the descent of invertebrates and vertebrates, were, however, most fantastic and bore no relation to palaeontological evidence.

It is most interesting to note that William Smith (1769-1839), now known as the "father of historical geology," was born in the same year as Cuvier. Observing for himself (1794-1800) the stratigraphic value of fossils, he began to distinguish the great Mesozoic formations of England (1801). Cuvier (1769-1832) is famous as the founder of vertebrate palaeontology, and with Alexandre Brongniart (1770-1847) as the author of the first exact contribution to stratigraphic geology. Early trained as a comparative anatomist, the discovery of Upper Eocene mammals in the gypsum quarries of Montmartre found him fully prepared (1798), and in 1812 appeared his *Recherches sur les ossemens fossiles*, brilliantly written and constituting the foundation of the modern study of the extinct vertebrates. Invulnerable in exact anatomical description and comparison, he failed in all his philosophical generalizations, even in those strictly within the domain of anatomy. His famous "law of correlation," which by its apparent brilliancy added enormously to his prestige, is not supported by modern philosophical anatomy, and his services to stratigraphy were diminished by his generalizations as to a succession of sudden extinctions and renovations of life. His joint memoirs with Brongniart, *Essai sur la géographie minéralogique des environs de Paris avec une carte géognostique et des coupes de terrain* (1808) and *Description géologique des environs de Paris* (1835) were based on the wonderful succession of Tertiary faunas in the rocks of the Paris basin. In Cuvier's defence Charles Depéret maintains that the extreme theory of successive extinctions followed by a succession of creations is attributable to Cuvier's followers rather than to the master himself. Depéret points also that we owe to Cuvier the first clear expression of the idea of the increasing organic perfection of all forms of life from the lower to the higher horizons, and that, while he believed that extinctions were due to sudden revolutions on the surface of the earth, he also set forth the pregnant ideas that the renewals of animal life were by migration from other regions unknown, and that these migrations were favoured by alternate elevations and depressions which formed various land routes between great continents and islands. Thus Cuvier, following Buffon, clearly anticipated the modern doctrine of faunal migrations. His reactionary and retarding ideas as a special creationist and his advocacy of the cataclysmic theory of change exerted a baneful influence until overthrown by the uniformitarianism of James Hutton (1726-1797) and Charles Lyell (1797-1875) and the evolutionism of Darwin.

The chief contributions of Cuvier's great philosophical opponent, Étienne Geoffroy St Hilaire (1772-1844), are to be found in his maintenance with Lamarck of the doctrine of the mutability of species. In this connexion he developed his special theory of saltations, or of sudden modifications of structure through changes of environment, especially through the direct influences of temperature and atmosphere. He clearly set forth also the phenomena of analogous or parallel adaptation.

It was Alcide Dessalines d'Orbigny (1802–1857) who pushed to an extreme Cuvier's ideas of the fixity of species and of successive extinctions, and finally developed the wild hypothesis of twenty-seven distinct creations. While these views were current in France, exaggerating and surpassing the thought of Cuvier, they were strongly opposed in Germany by such authors as Ernst Friedrich von Schlotheim (1764–1832) and Heinrich Georg Bronn (1800–1862); and the latter demonstrated that certain species actually pass from one formation to another.

In the meantime the foundations of palaeobotany were being laid (1804) by Ernst Friedrich von Schlotheim (1764–1832), (1811) by Kaspar Maria Sternberg (1761–1838) and (1838) by Théophile Brongniart (1801–1876).

Following Cuvier's *Recherches sur les ossemens fossiles*, the rich succession of Tertiary mammalian life was gradually revealed to France through the explorations and descriptions of such authors as Croizet, Jobert, de Christol, Eymar, Pomel and Lartet, during a period of rather dry, systematic work, which included, however, the broader generalizations of Henri Marie Ducrotay de Blainville (1778–1850) and culminated in the comprehensive treatises on Tertiary palaeontology of Paul Gervais (1816–1879). Extending the knowledge of the extinct mammals of Germany, the principal contributors were Georg August Goldfuss (1782–1848), Georg Friedrich von Jaegar (1785–1866), Felix F. Plieninger (1807–1873) and Johann Jacob Kaup (1803–1873). As Cuvier founded the palaeontology of mammals and reptiles, so Louis Agassiz's epoch-making works *Recherches sur les poissons fossiles* (1833–1845) laid the secure foundations of palaeichthyology, and were followed by Christian Heinrich Pander's (1794–1865) classic memoirs on the fossil fishes of Russia. In philosophy Agassiz was distinctly a disciple of Cuvier and supporter of the doctrine of special creation, and to a more limited extent of cataclysmic extinctions. Animals of the next higher order, the amphibians of the coal measures and the Permian, were first comprehensively treated in the masterly memoirs of Christian Erich Hermann von Meyer (1801–1869) beginning in 1829, especially in his *Beiträge zur Petrefactenkunde* (1829–1830) and his *Zur Fauna der Vorwelt* (4 vols., 1845–1860). Successive discoveries gradually revealed the world of extinct Reptilia; in 1821 Charles König (1784–1851), the first keeper of the mineralogical collection in the British Museum, described *Ichthyosaurus* from the Jurassic; in the same year William Daniel Conybeare (1787–1857) described *Plesiosaurus*; and a year later (1822) *Masasaurus*; in 1822 William Buckland described the great carnivorous dinosaur *Megalosaurus*; while Gideon Algernon Mantell (1790–1852) in 1848 announced the discovery of *Iguanodon*. Some of the fossil Reptilia of France were made known through St Hilaire's researches on the Crocodilia (1831), and those of J. A. Deslongchamps (1794–1867) and his son on the teleosaurs, or long-snouted crocodiles. Materials accumulated far more rapidly, however, than the power of generalization and classification. Able as von Meyer was, his classification of the Reptilia failed because based upon the single adaptive characters of foot structure. The reptiles awaited a great classifier, and such a one appeared in England in the person of Sir Richard Owen (1804–1892), the direct successor of Cuvier and a comparative anatomist of the first rank. Non-committal as regards evolution, he vastly broadened the field of vertebrate palaeontology by his descriptions of the extinct fauna of England, of South America (including especially the great edentates revealed by the voyage of the "Beagle"), of Australia (the ancient and modern marsupials) and of New Zealand (the great struthious birds). His contributions on the Mesozoic reptiles of Great Britain culminated in his complete rearrangement and classification of this group, one of his greatest services to palaeontology. Meanwhile the researches of Hugh Falconer (1808–1865) and of Proby Thomas Cautley (1802–1871) in the sub-Himalayas

brought to light the marvellous fauna of the Siwalik hills of India, published in *Fauna antiqua Sivalensis* (London, 1845) and in the volumes of Falconer's individual researches. The ancient life of the Atlantic border of North America was also becoming known through the work of the pioneer vertebrate palaeontologists Thomas Jefferson (1743–1826), Richard Harlan (1796–1843), Jeffries Wyman (1814–1874) and Joseph Leidy (1823–1891). This was followed by the revelation of the vast ancient life of the western half of the American continent, which was destined to revolutionize the science. The master works of Joseph Leidy began with the first-fruits of western exploration in 1847 and extended through a series of grand memoirs, culminating in 1874. Leidy adhered strictly to Cuvier's exact descriptive methods, and while an evolutionist and recognizing clearly the genetic relationships of the horses and other groups, he never indulged in speculation.

The history of invertebrate palaeontology during the second period is more closely connected with the rise of historic geology and stratigraphy, especially with the settlement of the great and minor time divisions of the earth's history. The path-breaking works of Lamarck were soon followed by the monumental treatise of Gérard Paul Deshayes (1795–1875) entitled *Descriptions des coquilles fossiles des environs de Paris* (1824–1837), the first of a series of great contributions by this and other authors. These and other early monographs on the Tertiary shells of the Paris basin, of the environs of Bordeaux, and of the sub-Apennine formations of Italy, brought out the striking distinctness of these faunas from each other and from other molluscan faunas. Recognition of this threefold character led Deshayes to establish a threefold division of the Tertiary based on the percentage of molluscs belonging to types now living found in each. To these divisions Lyell gave in 1833 the names Eocene, Miocene and Pliocene.

James Hutton (1726–1797) had set forth (1788) the principle that during all geological time there has been no essential change in the character of events, and that uniformity of law is perfectly consistent with mutability in the results. Lyell marshalled all the observations he could collect in support of this principle, teaching that the present is the key to the past, and arraying all obtainable evidence against the cataclysmic theories of Cuvier. He thus exerted a potent influence on palaeontology through his persistent advocacy of uniformitarianism, a doctrine with which Lamarck should also be credited. As among the vertebrates, materials were accumulating rapidly for the great generalizations which were to follow in the third period. De Blainville added to the knowledge of the shells of the Paris basin; Giovanni Battista Brocchi (1772–1826) in 1814, and Luigi Bellardi (1818–1889) and Giovanni Michelotti (born 1812) in 1840, described the Pliocene molluscs of the sub-Apennine formation of Italy; from Germany and Austria appeared the epoch-making works of Heinrich Ernst Beyrich (1815–1896) and of Moritz Hoernes (1815–1868).

We shall pass over here the labours of Adam Sedgwick (1785–1873) and Sir Roderick Murchison (1792–1871) in the Palaeozoic of England, which because of their close relation to stratigraphy more properly concern geology; but must mention the grand contributions of Joachim Barrande (1799–1883), published in his *Système silurien du centre de la Bohème*, the first volume of which appeared in 1852. While establishing the historic divisions of the Silurian in Bohemia, Barrande also propounded his famous theory of "colonies," by which he attempted to explain the aberrant occurrence of strata containing animals of a more advanced stage among strata containing earlier and more primitive faunas; his assumption was that the second fauna had migrated from an unknown neighbouring region. It is proved that the specific instances on which Barrande's generalizations were founded were due to his misinterpretation of the overturned and faulted strata, but his conception of the simultaneous existence of two faunas, one of more ancient and one of more modern type, and of their alternation in a given area, was based on sound philosophical principles and has been confirmed by more recent work.

The greatest generalisation of this second period, however, was that partly prepared for by d'Orbigny, as will be more fully explained later in this article, and clearly expressed by Agassiz —namely, the law of repetition of ancestral stages of life in the course of the successive stages of individual development. This law of recapitulation, subsequently termed the "biogenetic law" by Ernest Haeckel, was the greatest philosophic contribution of this period, and proved to be not only one of the bulwarks of the evolution theory but one of the most important principles in the method of palaeontology.

On the whole, as in the case of vertebrate palaeontology, the pre-Darwinian period of invertebrate palaeontology was one of rather dry systematic description, in which, however, the applications of the science gradually extended to many regions of the world and to all divisions of the kingdom of invertebrates.

III.—THIRD HISTORIC PERIOD

Beginning with the publication of Darwin's great works, "Narrative of the Surveying Voyages of H.M.S. 'Adventure' and 'Beagle'" (1839), and "On the Origin of Species by Means of Natural Selection" (1859).—A review of the two first classic works of Charles Robert Darwin (1809–1882) and of their influence proves that he was the founder of modern palaeontology. Principles of descent and other applications of uniformitarianism which had been struggling for expression in the writings of Lamarck, St Hilaire and de Blainville here found their true interpretation, because the geological succession, the rise, the migrations, the extinctions, were all connected with the grand central idea of evolution from primordial forms.

A close study of the exact modes of evolution and of the philosophy of evolution is the distinguishing feature of this period. It appears from comparison of the work in the two great divisions of vertebrate and invertebrate palaeontology made for the first time in this article that in accuracy of observation and in close philosophical analysis of facts the students of invertebrate palaeontology led the way. This was due to the much greater completeness and abundance of material afforded among invertebrate fossils, and it was manifested in the demonstration of two great principles or laws: first, the law of recapitulation, which is found in its most ideal expression in the shells of invertebrates; second, in the law of direct genetic succession through very gradual modification. It is singular that the second law is still ignored by many zoologists. Both laws were of paramount importance, as direct evidence of Darwin's theory of descent, which, it will be remembered, was at the time regarded merely as an hypothesis. Nevertheless, the tracing of phylogeny, or direct lines of descent, suddenly began to attract far more interest than the naming and description of species.

The Law of Recapitulation. Acceleration: Retardation.—This law, that' in the stages of growth of individual development (ontogeny), an animal repeats the stages of its ancestral evolution (phylogeny) was, as we have stated, anticipated by d'Orbigny. He recognized the fact that the shells of molluscs, which grow by successive additions, preserve unchanged the whole series of stages of their individual development, so that each shell of a Cretaceous ammonite, for example, represents five stages of progressive modification as follows: the first is the *période embryonnaire*, during which the shell is smooth; the second and third represent periods of elaboration and ornamentation; the fourth is a period of initial degeneration; the fifth and last a period of degeneration when ornamentation becomes obsolete and the exterior smooth again, as in the young. D'Orbigny, being a special creationist, failed to recognize the bearing of these individual stages on evolution. Alpheus Hyatt (1838–1902) was the first to discover (1866) that these changes in the form of the ammonite shell agreed closely with those which had been 'passed through in the ancestral history of the species. In an epoch-making essay, *On the Parallelism between the Different stages of Life in the individual and those in the entire group of the Molluscous Order Tetrabranchiata* (1866), and in a number of subsequent memoirs, among which *Genesis of the Arietidae* (1889)

and *Phylogeny of an Acquired Characteristic* (1894) should be mentioned, he laid the foundations, by methods of the most exact analysis, for all future recapitulation work of invertebrate palaeontologists. He showed that from each individual shell of an ammonite the entire ancestral series may be reconstructed, and that, while the earlier shell-whorls retain the characters of the adults of preceding members of the series, a shell in its own adult stage adds a new character, which in turn becomes the pre-adult character of the types which will succeed it; finally, that this comparison between the revolutions of the life of an individual and the life of the entire order of ammonites is wonderfully harmonious and precise. Moreover, the last stages of individual life are prophetic not only of future rising and progressing derivatives, but in the case of senile individuals of future declining and degradational series.

Thus the recapitulation law, which had been built up independently from the observations and speculations on vertebrates by Lorenz Oken (1779–1851), Johann Friedrich Meckel (1781–1833), St Hilaire, Karl Ernst von Baer (1792–1876) and others, and had been applied (1842–1845) by Karl Vogt (1817–1895) and Agassiz, in their respective fields of observation, to comparison of individual stages with the adults of the same group in preceding geological periods, furnished the key to the determination of the ancestry of the invertebrates generally.

Hyatt went further and demonstrated that ancestral characters are passed through by successive descendants at a more and more accelerated rate in each generation, thus giving time for the appearance of new characters in the adult. His "law of acceleration" together with the complementary "law of retardation," or the slowing up in the development of certain characters (first propounded by E. D. Cope), was also a philo-

(From the *American Naturalist*.)

FIG. 6.

sophic contribution of the first importance (see fig. 6 and Plate III., fig. 7).

In the same year, 1866, Franz Martin Hilgendorf (1839–) studied the shells of *Planorbis* from the Miocene lake basin underlying the present village of Steinheim in Württemberg, and introduced the *method of examination of large numbers of individual specimens*, a method which has become of prime importance in the science. He discovered the actual transmutations in direct genetic series of species on the successive deposition levels of the old lake basin. This study of *direct genetic series* marked another great advance, and became possible in invertebrate palaeontology long before it was introduced among the vertebrates. Hyatt, in a re-examination of the Steinheim deposits, proved that successive modifications occur at the same level as well as in vertical succession. Melchior Neumayr (1845–1890) and C. M. Paul similarly demonstrated genetic series of *Paludina (Vivipara)* in the Pliocene lakes of Slavonia (1875).

The Mutations of Waagen. Orthogenesis.—In 1869 Wilhelm Heinrich Waagen (1841–1900) entered the field with the study of *Ammonites subradiatus*. He proposed the term "mutations" for the minute progressive changes of single characters in definite directions as observed in successive stratigraphic levels. Even when seen in minute features only he recognized them as constant progressive characters or "chronologic varieties" in contrast with contemporaneous or "geographic varieties," which he considered inconstant and of slight systematic value. More recent analysis has shown, however, that certain modifications observed within the same stratigraphic level are really grades of mutatiqns which show divergences comparable to those found in successive levels. The collective term "mutation," as now employed by palaeontologists, signifies a type modified to a slight degree in one or more of its characters along a progressive or definite line of phyletic development. The term "mutation" also applies to a single new character and for distinction[1] may be known as "the mutation of Waagen." This definitely directed evolution, or development in a few determinable directions, has since been termed "orthogenetic evolution," and is recognized by all workers in invertebrate palaeontology and phylogeny as fundamental because the facts of invertebrate palaeontology admit of no other interpretation.

Among the many who followed the method of attack first outlined by Hyatt, or who independently discovered his method, only a few can be mentioned here—namely, Waagen (1869), Neumayr (1871), Württemberger (1880), Branco (1880), Mojsisovics (1882), Buckman (1887), Karpinsky (1889), Jackson (1890), Beecher (1890), Perrin-Smith (1897), Clarke (1898) and Grabau (1904). Melchior Neumayr, the great Austrian palaeontologist, especially extended the philosophic foundations of modern invertebrate palaeontology, and traced a number of continuous genetic series (formenreihe) in successive horizons. He also demonstrated that mutations have this special or distinctive character, that they repeat in the same direction without oscillation or retrogression. He expressed great reserve as to the causes of these mutations. He was the first to attempt a comprehensive treatment of all invertebrates from the genetic point of view; but unfortunately his great work, entitled Die Stämme des Thierreichs (Vienna and Prague, 1889), was uncompleted.

The absolute agreement in the results independently obtained by these various investigators, the interpretation of individual development as the guide to phyletic development, the demonstration of continuous genetic series, each mutation falling into its proper place and all showing a definite direction, constitute contributions to biological philosophy of the first importance, which have been little known or appreciated by zoologists because of their publication in monographs of very special character.

Vertebrate Palaeontology after Darwin.—The impulse which Darwin gave to vertebrate palaeontology was immediate and unbounded, finding expression especially in the writings of Thomas Henry Huxley (1825-1895) in England, of Jean Albert Gaudry (b. 1827) in France, in America of Edward Drinker Cope (1840-1897) and Othniel Charles Marsh (1831-1899). Fine examples of the spirit of the period as applied to extinct Mammalia are Gaudry's Animaux fossiles et géologie de l'Attique (1862) on the Upper Miocene fauna of Pikermi near Athens, and the remarkable memoirs of Vladimir Onufrievich Kowalevsky (1842-1883), published in 1873. These works swept aside the dry traditional fossil lore which had been accumulating in France and Germany. They breathed the new spirit of the recognition of adaptation and descent. In 1867-1871 Milne Edwards published his memoirs on the Miocene birds of central France. Huxley's development of the method of palaeontology should be studied in his collected memoirs (Scientific Memoirs of Thomas Henry Huxley, 4 vols., 1898). In Kowalevsky's Versuch einer natürlichen Classification der Fossilen Huflhiere (1873) we find a model union of detailed inductive study with theory and working hypothesis. All these writers attacked the problem of descent, and published preliminary phylogenies of such animals as the horse, rhinoceros and elephant, which time has proved to be of only general value and not at all comparable to the exact phylogenetic series which were being established by invertebrate palaeontologists. Phyletic gaps began to be filled in this general way, however, by discovery, especially through remarkable

[1] The Dutch botanist, De Vries, has employed the term in another sense, to mean a slight jump or saltation.

discoveries in North America by Leidy, Cope and Marsh, and the ensuing phylogenies gave enormous prestige to palaeontology.

Cope's philosophic contributions to palaeontology began in 1868 (see essays in The Origin of the Fittest, New York, 1887, and The Primary Factors of Organic Evolution, Chicago, 1896) with the independent discovery and demonstration among vertebrates of the laws of acceleration and retardation. To the law of "recapitulation" he unfortunately applied Hyatt's term "parallelism," a term which is used now in another sense. He especially pointed out the laws of the "extinction of the specialised" and "survival of the non-specialized" forms of life, and challenged Darwin's principle of selection as an explanation of the origin of adaptations by saying that the "survival of the fittest" does not explain the "origin of the fittest." He personally sought to demonstrate such origin, first, in the existence of a specific internal growth force, which he termed bathmic force, and second in the direct inheritance of acquired mechanical modifications of the teeth and feet. He thus revived Lamarck's views and helped to found the so-called neo-Lamarckian school in America. To this school A. Hyatt, W. H. Dall and many other invertebrate palaeontologists subscribed.

History of Discovery. Vertebrates.—In discovery the theatre of interest has shifted from continent to continent, often in a sensational manner. After a long period of gradual revelation of the ancient life of Europe, extending eastward to Greece, eastern Asia and to Australia, attention became centred on North America, especially on Rocky Mountain exploration. New and unheard-of orders of amphibians, reptiles and mammals came to the surface of knowledge, revolutionizing thought, demonstrating the evolution theory, and solving some of the most important problems of descent. Especially noteworthy was the discovery of birds with teeth both in Europe (Archaeopteryx) and in North America (Hesperornis), of Eocene stages in the history of the horse, and of the giant dinosauria of the Jurassic and Cretaceous in North America. Then the stage of novelty suddenly shifted to South America, where after the pioneer labours of Darwin, Owen and Burmeister, the field of our knowledge was suddenly and vastly extended by explorations by the brothers Ameghino (Carlos and Florentino). We were in the midst of more thorough examination of the ancient world of Patagonia, of the Pampean region and of its submerged sister continent Antarctica, when the scene shifted to North Africa through the discoveries of Hugh J. L. Beadnell and Charles W. Andrews. These latter discoveries supply us with the ancestry of the elephants and many other forms. They round out our knowledge of Tertiary history, but leave the problems of the Cretaceous mammals and of their relations to Tertiary mammals still unsolved. Similarly, the Mesozoic reptiles have been traced successively to various parts of the world from France, Germany, England, to North America and South America, to Australia and New Zealand and to northern Russia, from Cretaceous times back into the Permian, and by latest reports into the Carboniferous.

Discovery of Invertebrates.—The most striking feature of exploration for invertebrates, next to the world-wide extent to which exploration has been carried on and results applied, is the early appearance of life. Until comparatively recent times the molluscs were considered as appearing on the limits of the Cambrian and Ordovician; but Charles D. Walcott has described a tiny lamellibranch (Modioloides) from the inferior Cambrian, and he reports the gastropod (?) genus Chuaria from the pre-Cambrian. Cephalopod molluscs have been traced back to the straight-shelled nautiloids of the genus Volborthella, while true ammonites have been found in the inferior Permian of the Continent and by American palaeontologists in the true coal measures. Similarly, early forms of the crustacean sub-class Merostomata have been traced to the pre-Cambrian of North America.

Recent discoveries of vertebrates are of the same significance, the most primitive fishes being traced to the Ordovician or base of the Silurian,[2] which proves that we shall discover more

[2] Professor Bashford Dean doubts the fish characters of these Ordovic Rocky Mountain forms. Froch admits their fish character but considers the rocks infaulted Devonic.

Fig. 1.—An ichthyosaur (*I. quadriscissus*) containing in the body cavity the partially preserved skeletons of seven young, proving that the young of the animal developed within the maternal body and were brought forth alive; *i. e.* that the ichthyosaur was a viviparous animal. (*Specimen presented to the American Museum of Natural History by the Royal Museum of Stuttgart through Professor Eberhard Fraas.*)

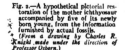 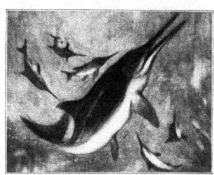

Fig. 2.—A hypothetical pictorial restoration of the mother ichthyosaur accompanied by five of its newly born young, from the information furnished by actual fossils. (*From a drawing by Charles R. Knight made under the direction of Professor Osborn.*)

Fig. 3.—One of the most perfect of the many specimens discovered and prepared by Herr Bernard Hauff, and showing the extraordinary preservation of the epidermis of the ichthyosaur, which gives the complete contour of the body in silhouette, the outlines of the paddles, of the remarkably fish-like tail, into the lower lobe of which the vertebral column extends, and the great integumentary dorsal fin.

Materials for the Restoration of Ichthyosaurs.—This plate illustrates the exceptional opportunity afforded the palaeontologist through the remarkably preserved remains of Ichthyosaurs in the quarries of Holzmaden near Stuttgart, Württemberg, excavated for many years by Herr Bernard Hauff. (*Illustrations reproduced by permission from specimens in the American Museum of Natural History, New York.*)

PLATE II.

PALAEONTOLOGY

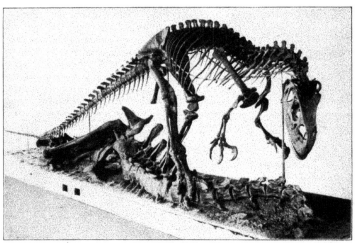

Fig. 4.—Skeleton of Allosaurus.

Fig. 5.—Restoration of Allosaurus.

Materials for the Restoration of Dinosaurs.—Carnivorous dinosaur (*Allosaurus*) of the Upper Jurassic period of North America, an animal closely related to the *Megalosaurus* type of England. The skeleton (fig. 4) was found nearly complete in the beds of the Morrison formation, Upper Jurassic of central Wyoming, U. S. A. Near it was discovered the posterior portion of the skeleton of a giant herbivorous dinosaur (*Brontosaurus Marsh*). It was observed that ten of the caudal vertebræ of the latter skeleton bore tooth marks and grooves corresponding exactly with the sharp pointed teeth in the jaw of the carnivorous dinosaur. This proved that the great herbivorous dinosaur had been preyed upon by its smaller carnivorous contemporary. Teeth of the carnivorous dinosaur scattered among the bones of the herbivorous dinosaur completed the line of circumstantial evidence. Upon this testimony the restoration (fig. 5) of the Megalosaur has been drawn by Charles R. Knight under the direction of Professor Osborn.

(*Originals reproduced by permission of the American Museum of Natural History.*)

This series of feet represents the evolutionary
succession from the Eocene *Hypohippus* (1) to the
modern *Equus* (6) seen in front and in side view.
The top bone is the *os calcis*, or hock bone, to which
the *tendon Achilles* is attached. The bottom bone
is the terminal phalanx which is inserted in the
heart of the hoof.

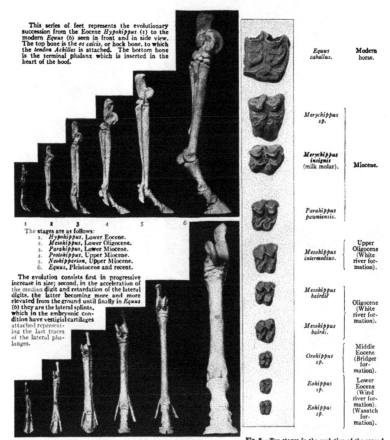

The stages are as follows:
1. *Hypohippus*, Lower Eocene.
2. *Mesohippus*, Lower Oligocene.
3. *Parahippus*, Lower Miocene.
4. *Protohippus*, Upper Miocene.
5. *Neohipparion*, Upper Miocene.
6. *Equus*, Pleistocene and recent.

The evolution consists first in progressive
increase in size; second, in the acceleration of
the median digit and retardation of the lateral
digits, the latter becoming more and more
elevated from the ground until finally in *Equus*
(6) they are the lateral splints,
which in the embryonic condition have vestigial cartilages
attached represent-
ing the last traces
of the lateral pha-
langes.

Equus caballus.	Modern horse.
Merychippus sp.	
Merychippus insignis (milk molar).	Miocene.
Parahippus pawniensis.	
Mesohippus intermedius.	Upper Oligocene (White river formation).
Mesohippus bairdii	
Mesohippus bairdi.	Oligocene (White river formation).
Orohippus sp.	Middle Eocene (Bridger formation).
Eohippus sp.	Lower Eocene (Wind river formation).
Eohippus sp.	(Wasatch formation).

Fig. 7.—Law of Acceleration and Retardation Illustrated in the Evolution of
the Hind Feet of the Horse.

(*From photos lent by the American Museum of Natural History.*)

Fig. 8.—Ten stages in the evolution of the second
upper molar tooth of the right side, arranged
according to geological level.

(*Nos. 1–9 from "American Equidae."*)

PLATE IV.   PALAEONTOLOGY

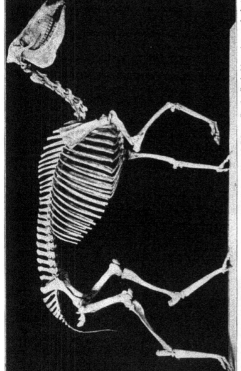

Fig. 12.—*Hypohippus*, a forest-living horse, rear view, showing large lateral digits on the fore and hind feet, adapted to prevent the animal from sinking into the soft soil.

Fig. 13.—*Neohipparion*, a plains-living horse with very slender limbs and lateral digits small and well raised from the ground, adapted to a dry, hard soil.

Laws of Local Adaptive Radiation and Polyphyletic Evolution, illustrated by two Upper Miocene Horses of the Plains Region of North America. These horses are of the same geologic age (Upper Miocene) and were found in the same geographic region (South Dakota, U.S.A.). One is supposed to have lived in the forests along the stream borders, and the other in the open plains.

(*Illustrations reproduced by permission of the American Museum of Natural History, New York.*)

Fig. 15.—Restoration of *Neohipparion*. (*From a drawing by Charles R. Knight, made under the direction of Professor Osborn.*)

Fig. 14.—Restoration of *Hypohippus*. (*From a drawing by Charles R. Knight, made under the direction of Professor Osborn.*)

ancient chordates in the Cambrian or even pre-Cambrian. Thus all recent discovery tends to carry the centres of origin and of dispersal of all animal types farther and farther back in geological time.

IV.—RELATIONS OF PALAEONTOLOGY TO OTHER PHYSICAL EARTH SCIENCES

Geology and Palaeophysiography.—Fossils are not absolute timekeepers, because we have little idea of the rate of evolution; they are only relative timekeepers, which enable us to check off the period of deposition of one formation with that of another. Huxley questioned the time value of fossils, but recent research has tended to show that identity of species and of mutations is, on the whole, a guide to synchroneity, though the general range of vertebrate and invertebrate life as well as of plant life is generally necessary for the establishment of approximate synchronism. Since fossils afford an immediate and generally a decisive clue to the mode of deposition of rocks, whether marine, lacustrine, fluviatile, flood plain or aeolian, they lead us naturally into palaeophysiography. Instances of marine and lacustrine analysis have been cited above. The analysis of continental faunas into those inhabiting rivers, lowlands, forests, plains or uplands, affords a key to physiographic conditions all through the Tertiary. For example, the famous bone-beds of the Oligocene of South Dakota have been analysed by W. D. Matthew, and are shown to contain fluviatile or channel beds with water and river-living forms, and neighbouring flood-plain sediments containing remains of plains-living forms. Thus we may complete the former physiographic picture of a vast flood plain east of the Rocky Mountains, traversed by slowly meandering streams.

As already intimated, our knowledge of *palaeometeorology*, or of past climates, is derivable chiefly from fossils. Suggested two centuries ago by Robert Hooke, this use of fossils has in the hands of Barrande, Neumayr, the marquis de Saporta (1895), Oswald Heer (1809–1883), and an army of followers developed into a sub-science of vast importance and interest. It is true that a great variety of evidence is afforded by the composition of the rocks, that glaciers have left their traces in glacial scratchings and transported boulders, also that proofs of arid or semi-arid conditions are found in the reddish colour of rocks in certain portions of the Palaeozoic, Trias and Eocene; but fossils afford the most precise and conclusive evidence as to the past history of climate, because of the fact that adaptations to temperature have remained constant for millions of years. All conclusions derived from the various forms of animal and plant life should be scrutinized closely and compared. The brilliant theories of the palaeobotanist, Oswald Heer, as to the extension of a sub-tropical climate to Europe and even to extreme northern latitudes in Tertiary time, which have appealed to the imagination and found their way so widely into literature, are now challenged by J. W. Gregory (*Climatic Variations, their Extent and Causes*, International Geological Congress, Mexico, 1906), who holds that the extent of climatic changes in past times has been greatly exaggerated.

It is to palaeogeography and zoogeography in their reciprocal relations that palaeontology has rendered the most unique services. Geographers are practically helpless as historians, and problems of the former elevation and distribution of the land and sea masses depend for their solution chiefly upon the palaeontologist. With good reason geographers have given reluctant consent to some of the bold restorations of ancient continental outlines by palaeontologists; one some of the greatest achievements of recent science have been in this field. The concurrence of botanical (Hooker, 1847); zoological; and finally of palaeontological evidence for the reconstruction of the continent of Antarctica, is one of the greatest triumphs of biological investigation. To the evidence advanced by a great number of authors comes the clinching testimony of the existence of a number of varieties of Australian marsupials in Patagonia, as originally discovered by Ameghino and more exactly described by members of the Princeton Patagonian expedition staff; while

the fossil shells of the Eocene of Patagonia as analysed by Ortmann give evidence of the existence of a continuous shore-line, or at least of shallow-water areas, between Australia, New Zealand and South America. This line of hypothesis and demonstration is typical of the palaeogeographic methods generally—namely, that vertebrate palaeontologists, impressed by the sudden appearance of extinct forms of continental life, demand land connexion or migration tracts from common centres of origin and dispersal, while the invertebrate palaeontologist alone is able to restore ancient coast-lines and determine the extent and width of these tracts. Thus has been built up a distinct and most important branch. The great contributors to the palaeogeography of Europe are Neumayr and Eduard Suess (b. 1831), followed by Frech, Canu, de Lapparent and others. Neumayr was the first to attempt to restore the grander earth outlines of the earth as a whole in Jurassic times. Suess outlined the ancient relations of Africa and Asia through his "Gondwana Land," a land mass practically identical with the "Lemuria" of zoologists. South American palaeogeography has been traced by von Ihring into a northern land mass, "Archelenia," and a southern mass, "Archiplata," the latter at times united with an antarctic continent. Following the pioneer studies of Dana, the American palaeontologists and stratographers Bailey Willis, John M. Clarke, Charles Schuchert and others have re-entered the study of the Palaeozoic geography of the North American continent with work of astonishing precision.

Zoogeography.—Closely connected with palaeogeography is zoogeography, the animal distribution of past periods. The science of zoogeography, founded by Humboldt, Edward Forbes, Huxley, P. L. Sclater, Alfred Russel Wallace and others, largely upon the present distribution of animal life, is now encountering through palaeontology a new and fascinating series of problems. In brief, it must connect living distribution with distribution in past time, and develop a system which will be in harmony with the main facts of zoology and palaeontology. The theory of past migrations from continent to continent, suggested by Cuvier to explain the replacement of the animal life which had become extinct through sudden geologic changes, was prophetic of one of the chief features of modern method—namely, the tracing of migrations. With this has been connected the theory of "centres of origin" or of the geographic regions where the chief characters of great groups have been established. Among invertebrates Barrande's doctrine of centres of origin was applied by Hyatt to the genesis of the Arietidae (1889); after studying thousands of individuals from the principal deposits of Europe he decided that the cradles of the various branches of this family were the basins of the Côte d'Or and southern Germany. Ortmann has traced the centre of dispersal of the fresh-water Crawfish genera *Cambarus, Potamobius* and *Cambaroides* to eastern Asia, where their common ancestors lived in Cretaceous time. Similarly, among vertebrates the method of restoring past centres of origin, largely originating with Edward Forbes, has developed into a most distinct and important branch of historical work. This branch of the science has reached the highest development in its application to the history of the extinct mammalia of the Tertiary through the original work of Cope and Henri Filhol, which has been brought to a much higher degree of exactness recently through the studies of H. F. Osborn, Charles Depéret, W. D. Matthew and H. G. Stehlin.

V.—RELATIONS OF PALAEONTOLOGY TO OTHER ZOOLOGICAL METHODS

Systematic Zoology.—It is obvious that the Linnaean binomial terminology and its subsequent trinomial refinement for species, sub-species, and varieties was adapted to express the differences between animals as they exist to-day, distributed contemporaneously over the surface of the earth, and that it is wholly inadapted to express either the minute gradations of successive generic series or the branchings of a genetically connected chain of life. Such gradations, termed "mutations" by Waagen, are distinguished, as observed, *in single characters*; they are the *nuances*, or grades of difference, which are the more gradual the more finely we dissect the geologic column, while the terms species, sub-species and variety are generally based upon a sum of changes in *several characters*. Thus palaeontology has brought to light an entirely new nomenclatural problem, which can only be solved by resolutely adopting an entirely different principle,

which is essentially, based on a theory of interrupted or, discontinuous characters, is inapplicable.

Embryology and Ontogeny.—In following the discovery of the law of recapitulation among palaeontologists we have clearly stated the chief contribution of palaeontology to the science of ontogeny—namely, the correspondences and differences between

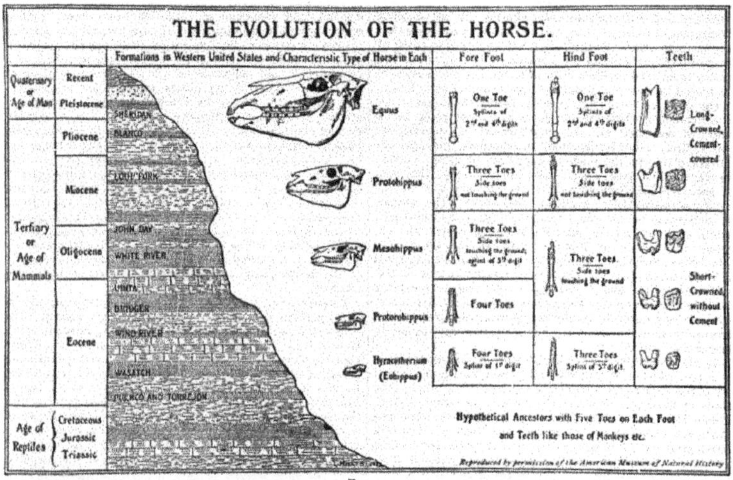

THE EVOLUTION OF THE HORSE.

		Formations in Western United States and Characteristic Type of Horse in Each	Fore Foot	Hind Foot	Teeth
Quaternary or Age of Man	Recent				
	Pleistocene	SHERIDAN — Equus	One Toe Splints of 2ⁿᵈ and 4ᵗʰ digits	One Toe Splints of 2ⁿᵈ and 4ᵗʰ digits	Long-Crowned, Cement-covered
	Pliocene	BLANCO			
Tertiary or Age of Mammals	Miocene	LOUP FORK — Protohippus	Three Toes Side toes not touching the ground	Three Toes Side toes not touching the ground	
	Oligocene	JOHN DAY — Mesohippus WHITE RIVER	Three Toes Side toes touching the ground, splint of 3ʳᵈ digit	Three Toes Side toes touching the ground	Short-Crowned without Cement
	Eocene	UINTA — Protorohippus BRIDGER WIND RIVER	Four Toes		
		WASATCH — Hyracotherium (Eohippus) PUERCO AND TORREJON	Four Toes Splint of 1ˢᵗ digit	Three Toes Splint of 5ᵗʰ digit	
Age of Reptiles	Cretaceous	Hypothetical Ancestors with Five Toes on Each Foot			
	Jurassic	and Teeth like those of Monkeys etc.			
	Triassic	*Reproduced by permission of the American Museum of Natural History*			

FIG. 9.

This révolution may be accomplished by adding the term " mutation ascending " or " mutation descending " for the minute steps of transformation, and the term *phylum*, as employed in Germany, for the minor and major branches of genetic series. Bit by bit mutations are added to each other in different single characters until a sum or degree of mutations is reached which no zoologist would hesitate to place in a separate species or in a separate genus.

The minute gradations observed by Hyatt, Waagen and all invertebrate palaeontologists, in the hard parts (shells) of molluscs, &c., are analogous to the equally minute gradations observed by vertebrate palaeontologists in the hard parts of reptiles and mammals. The mutations of Waagen may possibly, in fact, prove to be identical with the " definite variations " or " rectigradations " observed by Osborn in the teeth of mammals. For example, in the grinders of Eocene horses (see Plate III., fig. 8; also fig. 9) in a lower horizon a cusp is adumbrated in shadowy form, in a slightly higher horizon it is visible, in a still higher horizon it is full-grown; and we honour this final stage by assigning to the animal which bears it a new specific name. When a number of such characters accumulate, we further honour them by assigning a new generic name. This is exactly the nomenclature system laid down by Owen, Cope, Marsh and others, although established without any understanding of the law of mutation. But besides the innumerable characters which are visible and measurable, there are probably thousands which we cannot measure or which have not been discovered, since every part of the organism enjoys its gradual and independent evolution. In the face of the continuous series of characters and types revealed by palaeontology, the Linnaean terminology,

the individual order of development and the ancestral order of evolution. The mutual relations of palaeontology and embryology and comparative anatomy as means of determining the ancestry of animals are most interesting. In tracing the phylogeny, or ancestral history of organs, palaeontology affords the only absolute criterion on the successive evolution of organs *in time* as well as of (progressive) evolution *in form*. From comparative anatomy alone it is possible to arrange a series of living forms which, although structurally a convincing array because placed in a graded series, may be, nevertheless, in an order inverse to that of the actual historical succession. The most marked case of such inversion in comparative anatomy is that of Carl Gegenbaur (1826–1903), who in arranging the fins of fishes in support of his theory that the fin of the Australian lung-fish (*Ceratodus*) was the most primitive (or *Archipterygium*), placed as the primordial type a fin which palaeontology has proved to be one of the latest types if not the last. It is equally true that palaeontological evidence has frequently failed where we most sorely needed it. The student must therefore resort to what may be called a tripod of evidence, derived from the available facts of embryology, comparative anatomy and palaeontology.

VI.—THE PALAEONTOLOGIST AS HISTORIAN

The modes of change among animals, and methods of analysing them.—As historian the palaeontologist always has before him as one of his most fascinating problems phylogeny, or the restoration of the great tree of animal descent. Were the geologic record complete he would be able to trace the ancestry of man and of all other animals back to their very beginnings

In the primordial protoplasm. Dealing with interrupted evidence, however, it becomes necessary to exercise the closest analysis and synthesis as part of his general art as a restorer.

The most fundamental distinction in analysis is that which must be made between homogeny, or true *hereditary resemblance*, and those multiple forms of *adaptive resemblance* which are variously known as cases of " analogy," " parallelism," " convergence " and " homoplasy." Of these two kinds of genetic and adaptive resemblance, homogeny is the warp composed of the vertical, hereditary strands, which connect animals with their ancestors and their successors, while analogy is the woof, composed of the horizontal strands which tie animals together by their superficial resemblances. This wide distinction between similarity of descent and similarity of adaptation applies to every organ, to all groups of organs, to animals as a whole, and to all groups of animals. It is the old distinction between homology and analogy on a grand scale.

Analogy, in its power of transforming unlike and unrelated animals or unlike and unrelated parts of animals into likeness, has done such miracles that the inference of kinship is often almost irresistible. During the past century it was and even now is the very " will-o'-the-wisp " of evolution, always tending to lead the phylogenist astray. It is the first characteristic of analogy that it is superficial. Thus the shark, the ichthyosaur,

(After a drawing by Charles R. Knight, made under the direction of Professor Osborn.)

FIG. 10.—Analogous or convergent evolution in Fish, Reptile and Mammal.

The external similarity in the fore paddle and back fin of these three marine animals is absolute, although they are totally unrelated to each other, and have a totally different internal or skeletal structure. It is one of the most striking cases known of the law of analagous evolution.

A, Shark (*Lamna cornubica*), with long lobe of tail upturned.
B, Ichthyosaur (*Ichthyosaurus quadricissus*), with fin-like paddles, long lobe of tail down-turned.
C, Dolphin (*Sotalia fluviatilis*), with horizontal tail, fin or fluke.

and the dolphin (fig. 10) superficially resemble each other, but if the outer form be removed this resemblance proves to be a mere veneer of adaptation, because their internal skeletal parts are as radically different as are their genetic relations, founded on heredity. Analogy also produces equally remarkable internal or skeletal transformations. The ingenuity of nature, however, in adapting animals is not infinite, because the same devices are repeatedly employed by her to accomplish the same adaptive ends whether in fishes, reptiles, birds or mammals; thus she has repeated herself at least twenty-four times in the evolution of long-snouted rapacious swimming types of animals. The grandest application of analogy is that observed in the adaptations of groups of animals evolving on different continents, by which their various divisions tend to mimic those on other continents. Thus the collective fauna of ancient South America

mimics the independently evolved collective fauna of North America, the collective fauna of modern Australia mimics the collective fauna of the Lower Eocene of North America. Exactly the same principles have developed on a vaster scale among the Invertebrata. Among the ammonites of the Jurassic and Cretaceous periods types occur which in their external appearance so closely resemble each other that they could be taken for members of a single series, and not infrequently have been taken for species of the same genus and even for the same species; but their early stages of development and, in fact, their entire individual history prove them to be distinct and not infrequently to belong to widely separated genetic series.

Homogeny, in contrast, the " special homology " of Owen, is the supreme test of kinship or of hereditary relationship, and thus the basis of all sound reasoning in phylogeny. The two joints of the thumb, for example, are homogenous throughout the whole series of the pentadactylate, or five-fingered animals, from the most primitive amphibian to man.

The conclusion is that the sum of homogenous parts, which may be similar or dissimilar in external form according to their similarity or diversity of function, and the recognition of former similarities of adaptation (see below) are the true bases for the critical determination of kinship and phylogeny.

Adaptation and the Independent Evolution of Parts.—Step by step there have been established in palaeontology a number of laws relating to the evolution of the parts of animals which closely coincide with similar laws discovered by zoologists. All are contained in the broad generalization that every part of an animal, however minute, has its separate and independent basis in the hereditary substance of the germ cells from which it is derived and may enjoy consequently a separate and independent history. The consequences of this principle when applied to the adaptations of animals bring us to the very antithesis of Cuvier's supposed " law of correlation," for we find that, while the end results of adaptation are such that all parts of an animal conspire to make the whole adaptive, there is no fixed correlation either in the form or rate of development of parts, and that it is therefore impossible for the palaeontologist to predict the anatomy of an unknown animal from one of its parts only, unless the animal happens to belong to a type generally familiar. For example, among the land vertebrates the feet (associated with the structure of the limbs and trunk) may take one of many lines of adaptation to different media or habitat, either aquatic, terrestrial, arboreal or aerial; while the teeth (associated with the structure of the skull and jaws) also may take one of many lines of adaptation to different kinds of food, whether herbivorous, insectivorous or carnivorous. Through this independent adaptation of different parts to their specific ends there have arisen among vertebrates an almost unlimited number of combinations of foot and tooth structure, the possibilities of which are illustrated in the accompanying diagram (see fig. 11; also Plate III., fig. 8). As instances of such combinations, some of the (probably herbivorous) Eocene monkeys with arboreal limbs have teeth so difficult to distinguish from those of the herbivorous ground-living Eocene horses with cursorial limbs that at first in France and also in America they were both classed with the hoofed animals. Again, directly opposed to Cuvier's principle, we have discovered carnivores with hoofs, such as *Mesonyx*, and herbivores with sloth-like claws, such as *Chalicotherium*. This latter animal is closely related to one which Cuvier termed *Pangolin gigantesque*, and had he restored it according to his " law of correlation " he would have pictured a giant " scaly anteater," a type as wide as the poles from the actual form of *Chalicotherium*, which in body, limbs and teeth is a modified ungulate herbivore, related remotely to the tapirs. In its claws alone does it resemble the giant sloths.

This independence of adaptation applies to every detail of structure; the six cusps of a grinding tooth may all evolve alike, or each may evolve independently and differently. Independent evolution of parts is well shown among invertebrates, where the shell of an ammonite, for example, may change markedly in form without a corresponding change in suture, or vice versa.

Similarly, there is no correlation in the rate of evolution either of adjoining or of separated parts; the middle digit of the foot of the three-toed horse is accelerated in development, while the lateral digits on either side are retarded. Many examples might be cited among invertebrates also.

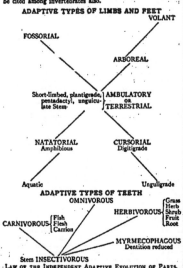

ADAPTIVE TYPES OF LIMBS AND FEET
VOLANT
FOSSORIAL
ARBOREAL
Short-limbed, plantigrade, pentadactyl, unguiculate Stem·   AMBULATORY OR TERRESTRIAL
NATATORIAL Amphibious
CURSORIAL Digitigrade
Aquatic   Unguligrade

ADAPTIVE TYPES OF TEETH
OMNIVOROUS
HERBIVOROUS {Grass Herb Shrub Fruit Root
CARNIVOROUS {Fish Flesh Carrion
MYRMECOPHAGOUS Dentition reduced
Stem INSECTIVOROUS

LAW OF THE INDEPENDENT ADAPTIVE EVOLUTION OF PARTS.

FIG. 11.—Diagram demonstrating that there are an indefinite number of combinations of various adaptive types of limbs and feet with various adaptive types of teeth, and that there is no fixed law of correlation between the two series of adaptations.

All these principles are consistent with Francis Galton's law of particulate inheritance in heredity, and with the modern doctrine of "unity of characters" held by students of Mendelian phenomena.

Sudden versus Gradual Evolution of Parts.—There is a broad and most interesting analogy between the evolution of parts of animals and of groups of animals studied as a whole. Thus we observe persistent organs and persistent types of animals, analogous organs and analogous types of animals, and this analogy applies still further to the rival and more or less contradictory hypotheses of the sudden as distinguished from the gradual appearance of new parts or organs of animals, and the sudden appearance of new types of animals. The first exponent of the theory of sudden appearance of new parts and new types, to our knowledge, was Geoffroy St Hilaire, who suggested saltatory evolution through the direct action of the environment on development, as explaining the abrupt transitions in the Mesozoic Crocodilia and the origin of the birds from the reptiles. Waagen's law of mutation, or the appearance of new parts or organs so gradually that they can be perceived only by following them through successive geologic time stages, appears to be directly contradictory to the saltation principle; it is certainly one of the most firmly established principles of palaeontology, and it constitutes the contribution *par excellence* of this branch of zoology to the law of evolution, since it is obvious that it could not possibly have been deduced from comparison of

living animals but only through the long perspective gained by comparison of animals succeeding each other in time. The essence of Waagen's law is orthogenesis, or evolution in a definite direction, and, if there does exist an internal hereditary principle controlling such orthogenetic evolution, there does not appear to be any essential contradiction between its gradual operation in the "mutations of Waagen" and its occasional hurried operation in the "mutations of de Vries," which are by their definition discontinuous or saltatory (Osborn, 1907).

VII.—MODES OF CHANGE IN ANIMALS AS A WHOLE OR IN GROUPS OF ANIMALS, AND METHODS OF ANALYSING THEM.

1. *Origin from Primitive or Stem Forms.*—As already observed, the same principles apply to groups of animals as to organs and groups of organs; an organ originates in a primitive and unspecialized stage, a group of animals originates in a primitive or stem form. It was early perceived by Huxley, Cope and many others that Cuvier's broad belief in a universal progression was erroneous, and there developed the distinction between "persistent primitive types" (Huxley) and "progressive types." The theoretical existence of primitive or stem forms was clearly perceived by Darwin, but the steps by which the stem form might be restored were first clearly enunciated by Huxley in 1880 (" On the Application of Evolution to the Arrangement of the Vertebrata and more particularly of the Mammalia," *Scient. Mem.* iv. 457) namely, by sharp separation of the primary or stem characters from the secondary or adaptive characters in all the known descendants or branches of a theoretical original form. The sum of the primitive characters approximately restores the primitive form; and the gaps in palaeontological evidence are supplied by analysis of the available zoological, embryological and anatomical evidence. Thus Huxley, with true prophetic instinct, found that the sum of primitive characters of all the higher placental mammals points to a stem form of a generalized insectivore type, a prophecy which has been fully confirmed by the latest research: On the other hand, Huxley's summation of the primitive characters of all the mammals led him to an amphibian stem type, a prophecy which has proved faulty because based on erroneous analysis and comparison. More or less independently, Huxley, Kowalevsky and Cope restored the stem ancestor of the hoofed animals, or ungulates, a restoration which has been nearly fulfilled by the discovery, in 1873, of the generalized type *Phenacodus* of northern Wyoming. Similar anticipations and verifications among the invertebrates have been made by Hyatt, Beecher, Jackson and others. In certain cases the character stem forms actually survive in unspecialized types. Thus the analysis of George Baur of the ancestral form of the lizards, mosasaurs, dinosaurs, crocodiles and phytosaurs led both to the generalized *Palaeohatteria* of the Permian and indirectly to the surviving Tuatara lizard of New Zealand.

2. *Adaptations to Alternations of Habitat. Law of Irreversibility of Evolution.*—In the long vicissitudes of time and procession of continental changes, animals have been subjected to alternations of habitat either through their own migrations or through the "migration of the environment itself," to employ Van den Broeck's epigrammatic description of the profound and sometimes sudden environmental changes which may take place in a single locality. The traces of alternations of adaptations corresponding to these alternations of habitat are recorded both in palaeontology and anatomy, although often after the obscure analogy of the earlier and later writings of a palimpsest. Huxley in 1880 briefly suggested the arboreal origin, or primordial tree-habitat of all the marsupials, a suggestion abundantly confirmed by the detailed studies of Dollo and of Bensley, according to which we may imagine the marsupials to have passed through (1) a former terrestrial phase, followed by (2) a primary arboreal phase—illustrated in the tree phalangers—followed by (3) a secondary terrestrial phase—illustrated in the kangaroos and wallabies—followed by (4) a secondary arboreal phase—illustrated in the tree kangaroos. Louis Dollo especially has

contributed most brilliant discussions of the theory of alternations of habitat as applied to the interpretation of the anatomy of the marsupials, of many kinds of fishes, of such reptiles as the herbivorous dinosaurs of the Upper Cretaceous. He has applied the theory with especial ingenuity to the interpretation of the circular bony plates in the carapace of the aberrant leather-back sea-turtles (Sphargidae) by prefacing an initial land phase, in which the typical armature of land tortoises was acquired, a first marine or pelagic phase, in which this armature was lost, a third littoral or seashore phase, in which a new polygonal armature was acquired, and a fourth resumed or secondary marine phase, in which this polygonal armature began to degenerate.

Each of these alternate life phases may leave some profound modification, which is partially obscured but seldom wholly lost; thus the tracing of the evidences of *former* adaptations is of great importance in phylogenetic study.

A very important evolutionary principle is that in such secondary returns to primary phases lost organs are never recovered, but new organs are acquired; hence the force of Dollo's dictum that evolution is *irreversible* from the point of view of structure, while frequently reversible, or recurrent, in point of view of the conditions of environment and adaptation.

3. *Adaptive Radiations of Groups, Continental and Local.*—Starting with the stem forms the descendants of which have passed through either persistent or changed habitats, we reach the underlying idea of the branching law of Lamarck or the law of divergence of Darwin, and find it perhaps most clearly expressed in the words "adaptive radiation" (Osborn), which convey the idea of radii in many directions. Among extinct Tertiary mammals we can actually trace the giving off of these radii in all directions, for taking advantage of every possibility to secure food, to escape enemies and to reproduce kind; further, among such well-known quadrupeds as the horses, rhinoceroses and titanotheres, the modifications involved in these radiations can be clearly traced. Thus the history of continental life presents a picture of contemporaneous radiations in different parts of the world and of a succession of radiations in the same parts. We observe the contemporaneous and largely independent radiations of the hoofed animals in South America, in Africa and in the great ancient continent comprising Europe, Asia and North America; we observe the Cretaceous radiation of hoofed animals in the northern hemisphere, followed by a second radiation of hoofed animals in the same region, in some cases one surviving spur of an old radiation becoming the centre of a new one. As a rule, the larger the geographic theatre the grander the radiation. Successive discoveries have revealed certain grand centres, such as (1) the marsupial radiation of Australia; (2) the little-known Cretaceous radiation of placental mammals in the northern hemisphere, which was probably connected in part with the peopling of South America, (3) the Tertiary placental radiation in the northern hemisphere, partly connected with Africa, (4) the main Tertiary radiation in South America. Each of these radiations produced a greater or less number of analogous groups, and while originally independent the animals thus evolving as autochthonous types finally mingled together as migrant or invading types. We are thus working out gradually the separate contributions of the land masses of North America, South America, Europe, Asia, Africa, and of Australia to the mammalian fauna of the world, a result which can be obtained through palaeontology only.

4. *Adaptive Local Radiation.*—On a smaller scale are the local adaptive radiations which occur through segregation of habit and local isolation in the same general geographic region wherever physiographic and climatic differences are sufficient to produce local differences in food supply or other local factors of change. This local divergence may proceed as rapidly as through wide geographical segregation or isolation. This principle has been demonstrated recently among Tertiary rhinoceroses and titanotheres, in which remains of four or five genetic series in the same geologic deposits have been discovered. We have proof that in the Upper Miocene of Colorado there existed a forest-living horse,

or more persistent primitive type, which was contemporaneous with and is found in the same deposits with the plains-living horse (*Neohipparion*) of the most advanced or specialized desert type (see Plate IV., figs. 12, 13, 14, 15). In times of drought these animals undoubtedly resorted to the same water-courses for drink, and thus their fossilized remains are found associated.

5. *The Law of Polyphyletic Evolution. The Sequence of Phyla or Genetic Series.*—There results from continental and local adaptive radiations the presence in the same geographical region of numerous distinct lines in a given group of animals. The polyphyletic law was early demonstrated among invertebrates by Neumayr (1889) when he showed that the ammonite genus *Phylloceras* follows not one but five distinct lines of evolution of unequal duration. The brachiopods, generally classed collectively as *Spirifer mucronatus*, follow at least five distinct lines of evolution in the Middle Devonian of North America, while more than twenty divergent lines have been observed by Grabau among the species of the gastropod genus *Fusus* in Tertiary and recent times. Vertebrate palaeontologists were slow to grasp this principle; while the early speculative phylogenies of the horse of Huxley and Marsh, for example, were mostly displayed monophyletically, or in single lines of descent, it is now recognized that the horses which were placed by Marsh in a single series are really to be ranged in a great number of contemporaneous but separate series, each but partially known, and that the direct phylum which leads to the modern horse has become a matter of far more difficult search. As early as 1862 Gaudry set forth this very polyphyletic principle in his tabular phylogenies, but failed to carry it to its logical application. It is now applied throughout the Vertebrata of both Mesozoic and Cenozoic times. Among marine Mesozoic reptiles, each of the groups broadly known as ichthyosaurs, plesiosaurs, mosasaurs and crocodiles were polyphyletic in a marked degree. Among land animals striking illustrations of this local polyphyletic law are found in the existence of seven or eight contemporary series of rhinoceroses, five or six contemporary series of horses, and an equally numerous contemporary series of American Miocene and Pliocene camels; in short, the polyphyletic condition is the rule rather than the exception. It is displayed to-day among the antelopes and to a limited degree among the zebras and rhinoceroses of Africa, a continent which exhibits a survival of the Miocene and Pliocene conditions of the northern hemisphere.

6. *Development of Analogous Progressive and Retrogressive Groups.*—Because of the repetition of analogous physiographic and climatic conditions in regions widely separated both in time and in space, we discover that continental and local adaptive radiations result in the creation of analogous groups of radii among all the vertebrates and invertebrates. Illustrations of this law were set forth by Cope as early as 1861 (see " Origin of Genera," reprinted in the *Origin of the Fittest*, pp. 95-106) in pointing out the extraordinary parallelisms between unrelated groups of amphibians, reptiles and mammals. In the Jurassic period there were no less than six orders of reptiles which independently abandoned terrestrial life and acquired more or less perfect adaptation to sea life. Nature, limited in her resources for adaptation, fashioned so many of these animals in like form that we have learned only recently to distinguish similarities of analogous habit from the similitudes of real kinship. From whatever order of Mammalia or Reptilia an animal may be derived, prolonged aquatic adaptation will model its outer, and finally its inner, structure according to certain advantageous designs. The requirements of an elongate body moving through the resistant medium of water are met by the evolution of similar entrant and exit curves, and the bodies of most swiftly moving aquatic animals evolve into forms resembling the hulls of modern sailing yachts (Bashford Dean). We owe especially to Willy Kükenthal, Eberhard Fraas, S.W. Williston and R. C. Osburn a summary of those modifications of form to which aquatic life invariably leads.

The law of analogy also operates in retrogression. A. Smith Woodward has observed that the decline of many groups of fishes is heralded by the tendency to assume elongate and finally eel-shaped forms, as seen independently, for example, among the declining Acanthodians or palaeozoic sharks, among the modern crossopterygian *Polypterus* and *Calamoichthys* of the Nile, in the modern dipneustan *Lepidosiren* and *Protopterus*, in the Triassic chondrostean *Belonorhynchus*, as well as in the bow-fin (*Amia*) and the garpike (*Lepidosteus*).

Among invertebrates similar analogous groups also develop. This is especially marked in retrogressive, though also well-known in progressive series. The loss of the power to coil, observed in the terminals of many declining series of gastropods from the Cambrian to the present time, and the similar loss of power among Nautiloidea and Ammonoidea of many genetic series, as well as the ostracean form assumed by various declining series of pelecypods and by some brachiopods, may be cited as examples.

7. *Periods of Gradual Evolution of Groups.*—It is certainly a very striking fact that wherever we have been able to trace genetic series, either of invertebrates or vertebrates, in closely sequent geological horizons, or life zones, we find strong proof of evolution through extremely gradual mutation simultaneously affecting many parts of each organism, as set forth above. This proof has been reached quite independently by a very large number of observers studying a still greater variety of animals. Such diverse organisms as brachiopods, ammonites, horses and rhinoceroses absolutely conform to this law in all those rare localities where we have been able to observe closely sequent stages. The inference is almost irresistible that the law of gradual transformation through minute continuous change is by far the most universal; but many palaeontologists as well as zoologists and botanists hold a contrary opinion.

8. *Periods of Rapid Evolution of Groups.*—The above law of gradual evolution is perfectly consistent with a second principle, namely, that at certain times evolution is much more rapid than at others, and that organisms are accelerated or retarded in development in a manner broadly analogous to the acceleration or retardation of separate organs. Thus H. S. Williams observes (*Geological Biology*, p. 268) that the evolution of those fundamental characters which mark differences between separate classes, orders, sub-orders, and even families of organisms, took place in relatively short periods of time. Among the brachiopods the chief expansion of each type is at a relatively early period in their life-history. Hyatt (1883) observed of the ammonites that each group originated suddenly and spread out with great rapidity. Depéret notes that the genus *Neumayria*, an ammonite of the Kimmeridgian, suddenly branches out into an "explosion" of forms. Depéret also observes the contrast between periods of quiescence and limited variability and periods of sudden efflorescence. A. Smith Woodward ("Relations of Palaeontology to Biology," *Annals and Mag. Natural Hist.*, 1906, p. 317) notes that the fundamental advances in the growth of fish life have always been sudden, beginning with excessive vigour at the end of long periods of apparent stagnation; while each advance has been marked by the fixed and definite acquisition of some new anatomical character or "expression point," a term first used by Cope. One of the causes of these sudden advances is undoubtedly to be found in the acquisition of a new and extremely useful character. Thus the perfect jaw and the perfect pair of lateral fins when first acquired among the fishes favoured a very rapid and for a time unchecked development. It by no means follows, however, from this incontrovertible evidence that the acquisition either of the jaw or of the lateral fins had not been in itself an extremely gradual process.

Thus both invertebrate and vertebrate palaeontologists have reached independently the conclusion that the evolution of groups is not continuously at a uniform rate, but that there are, especially in the beginnings of new phyla or at the time of acquisition of new organs, sudden variations in the rate of evolution which have been termed variously "rhythmic," "pulsating," "efflorescent," "intermittent" and even "explosive"! (Depéret).

This varying rate of evolution has (illogically, we believe) been compared with and advanced in support of the "mutation law of De Vries," or the theory of saltatory evolution, which we may next consider.

9. *Hypothesis of the Sudden Appearance of New Parts or Organs.*—The rarity of really continuous series has naturally led palaeontologists to support the hypothesis of brusque transitions of structure. As we have seen, this hypothesis was fathered by Geoffroy St Hilaire in 1830 from his studies of Mesozoic Crocodilia, was sustained by Haldemann, and quite recently has been revived by such eminent palaeontologists as Louis Dollo and A. Smith Woodward. The evidence for it is not to be confused with that for the law of rapid efflorescence of groups just considered. It should be remembered that palaeontology is the most unfavourable field of all for observation and demonstration of sudden saltations or mutations of character, because of the limited materials available for comparison and the rarity of genetic series. It should be borne in mind, first, that wherever a new animal suddenly appears or a new character suddenly arises in a fossil horizon we must consider whether such appearance may be due to the non-discovery of transitional links with older forms, or to the sudden invasion of a new type or new organ which has gradually evolved elsewhere. The rapid variation of certain groups of animals or the acceleration of certain organs is also not evidence of the sudden appearance of new adaptive characters. Such sudden appearances may be demonstrated possibly in zoology and embryology but never can be demonstrated by palaeontology, because of the incompleteness of the geological record.

10. *Decline or Senescence of Groups.*—Periods of gradual evolution and of efflorescence may be followed by stationary or senescent conditions. In his history of the *Arietidae* Hyatt points out that toward the close of the Cretaceous this entire group of ammonites appears to have been affected with some malady; the unrolled forms multiply, the septa are simplified, the ornamentation becomes heavy, thick, and finally disappears in the adult; the entire group ends by dying out and leaving no descendants. This is not due to environmental conditions solely, because senescent branches of normal progressive groups are found in all geologic horizons, beginning, for gastropods, in the Lower Cambrian. Among the ammonites the loss of power to coil the shell is one feature of racial old age, and in others old age is accompanied by closer coiling and loss of surface ornamentation, such as spines, ribs, spirals; while in other forms an arresting of variability precedes extinction. Thus Williams has observed that if we find a species breeding perfectly true we can conceive it to have reached the end of its racial life period. Brocchi and Daniel Rosa (1899) have developed the hypothesis of the progressive reduction of variability. Such decline is by no means a universal law of life, however, because among many of the continental vertebrates at least we observe extinctions repeatedly occurring during the expression of maximum variability. Whereas among many ammonites and gastropods smoothness of the shell, following upon an ornamental youthful condition, is generally a symptom of decline, among many other invertebrates and vertebrates, as C. E. Beecher (1856–1905) has pointed out (1898), many animals possessing hard parts tend toward the close of their racial history to produce a superfluity of dead matter, which accumulates in the form of spines among invertebrates, and of horns among the land vertebrates, reaching a maximum when the animals are really on the down-grade of development.

11. *The Extinction of Groups.*—We have seen that different lines vary in vitality and in longevity, that from the earliest times senescent branches are given off, that different lines vary in the rate of evolution, that extinction is often heralded by symptoms of racial old age, which, however, vary widely in different groups. In general we find an analogy between the development of groups and of organs; we discover that each phyletic branch of certain organisms traverses a geologic career comparable to the life of an individual, that we may often distinguish, especially among invertebrates, a phase of youth, a phase of maturity, a phase of senility or degeneration foreshadowing the extinction of a type.

Internal causes of extinction are to be found in exaggeration of body size, in the hypertrophy or over-specialization of certain organs, in the irreversibility of evolution, and possibly, although this has not been demonstrated, in a progressive reduction of variability. In a full analysis of this problem of internal and external causes in relation to the Tertiary Mammalia, H. F. Osborn (" Causes of Extinction of the Mammalia," *Amer. Naturalist*, 1906, pp. 769–795, 829–859) finds that foremost in the long series of causes which lead to extinction are the grander environmental changes, such as physiographic changes, diminished or contracted land areas, substitution of insular for continental conditions; changes of climate and secular lowering of temperature accompanied by deforestation and checking of the food supply; changes influencing the mating period as well as fertility; changes causing increased humidity, which in turn favours enemies among insect life. Similarly secular elevations of temperature, either accompanied by moisture or desiccation, by increasing droughts or by disturbance of the balance of nature, have been followed by great waves of extinction of the Mammalia. In the sphere of living environment, the varied evolution of plant life, the periods of forestation and deforestation, the introduction of deleterious plants simultaneously with harsh conditions of life and enforced migration, as well as of mechanically dangerous plants, are among the well-ascertained causes of diminution and extinction. The evolution of insect life in driving animals from feeding ranges and in the spread of disease probably has been a prime cause of extinction. Food competition among mammals, especially intensified on islands, and the introduction of Carnivores constitute another class of causes. Great waves of extinction have followed the long periods of the slow evolution of relatively inadaptive types of tooth and foot structure, as first demonstrated by Waldemar Kowalevsky; thus mammals are repeatedly observed in a *cul-de-sac* of structure from which there is no escape in an adaptive direction. Among still other causes are great bulk, which proves fatal under certain new conditions; relatively slow breeding; extreme specialization and development of dominant organs, such as horns and tusks, on which for a time selection centres to the detriment of more useful characters. Little proof is afforded among the mammals of extinction through arrested evolution or through the limiting of variation, although such laws undoubtedly exist. One of the chief deductions is that there are special dangers in numerical diminution of herds, which may arise from a chief or original cause and be followed by a conspiracy of other causes which are cumulative in effect. This survey of the phenomena of extinction in one great class of animals certainly establishes the existence of an almost infinite variety of causes, some of which are internal, some external in origin, operating on animals of different kinds.

VIII.—UNDERLYING BIOLOGICAL PRINCIPLES AS THEY APPEAR TO THE PALAEONTOLOGIST

It follows from the above brief summary that palaeontology affords a distinct and highly suggestive field of purely biological research; that is, of the causes of evolution underlying the observable modes which we have been describing. The net result of observation is not favourable to the essentially Darwinian view that the adaptive arises out of the fortuitous by selection, but is rather favourable to the hypothesis of the existence of some quite unknown intrinsic law of life which we are at present totally unable to comprehend or even conceive. We have shown that the direct observation of the origin of new characters in palaeontology brings them within that domain of natural law and order to which the evolution of the physical universe conforms. The nature of this law, which, upon the whole, appears to be purposive or teleological in its operations, is altogether a mystery which may or may not be illumined by future research. In other words, the origin, or first appearance of new characters, which is the essence of evolution, is an orderly process so far as the vertebrate and invertebrate palaeontologist observes it. The selection of organisms through the crucial test of fitness and the shaping of the organic world is an orderly process when contemplated on a grand scale, but of another kind; here the test of fitness is supreme. The only inkling of possible underlying principles in this orderly process is that there appears to be in respect to certain characters a potentiality or a predisposition through hereditary kinship to evolve in certain definite directions. Yet there is strong evidence against the existence of any law in the nature of an internal perfecting tendency which would operate independently of external conditions. In other words, a balance appears to be always sustained between the internal (hereditary and ontogenetic) and the external (environmental and sclectional) factors of evolution.

BIBLIOGRAPHY.—Among the older works on the history of palaeontology are the treatises of Giovanni Battista Brocchi (1772–1826), *Conchiologia fossile Subapennina ... Disc. sui progressi dello studio ...* 1843 (Milan); of Etienne Jules d'Archiac, *Histoire du progrès de la géologie de 1834 à 1860* (Paris, Soc. Géol. de France, 1847–1860); of Charles Lyell in his *Principles of Geology*. A clear narrative of the work of many of the earlier contributors is found in *Founders of Geology*, by Sir Archibald Geikie (London, 1897–1905). The most comprehensive and up-to-date reference work on the history of geology and palaeontology is *Geschichte der Geologie und Paläontologie*, by Karl Alfred von Zittel (Munich and Leipzig, 1899), the final life-work of this great authority, translated into English in part by Maria M. Ogilvie-Gordon, entitled " History of Geology and Palaeontology to the end of the 19th Century." The succession of life from the earliest times as it was known at the close of the last century was treated by the same author in his *Handbuch der Paläontologie* (5 vols., Munich and Leipzig, 1876–1893). Abbreviated editions of this work have appeared from the author, *Grundzüge der Paläontologie (Palaeozoologie)* (Munich and Leipzig, 1895, 2nd ed., 1903), and in English form in Charles R. Eastman's *Text-Book of Palaeontology* (1900–1902). A classic but unfinished work describing the methods of invertebrate palaeontology is *Die Stämme des Thierreichs* (Vienna, 1889), by Melchior Neumayr. In France admirable recent works are *Eléments de Paléontologie*, by Felix Bernard (Paris, 1895), and the still more recent philosophical treatise by Charles Depéret, *Les Transformations du monde animal* (Paris, 1907). Huxley's researches, and especially his share in the development of the philosophy of palaeontology, will be found in his essays, *The Scientific Memoirs of Thomas Henry Huxley* (4 vols., London, 1898–1902). The whole subject is treated systematically in Nicholson and Lydekker's *A Manual of Palaeontology* (2 vols., Edinburgh and London, 1889), and A. Smith Woodward's *Outlines of Vertebrate Palaeontology* (Cambridge, 1898).

Among American contributions to vertebrate palaeontology, the development of Cope's theories is to be found in the volumes of his collected essays, *The Origin of the Fittest* (New York, 1887), and *The Primary Factors of Organic Evolution* (Chicago, 1896). A brief summary of the rise of vertebrate palaeontology is found in the address of O. Marsh, entitled " History and Methods of Palaeontological Discovery " (American Association for the Advancement of Science, 1879). The chief presentations of the methods of the American school of invertebrate palaeontologists are to be found in A. Hyatt's great memoir " Genesis of the Arietidae " (*Smithsonian Contr. to Knowledge*, 673, 1889), in Hyatt's " Phylogeny of an Acquired Characteristic " (*Philosophical Soc. Proc.*, vol. xxxii. 1894), and in *Geological Biology*, by H. S. Williams (New York, 1895).

In preparing the present article the author has drawn freely on his own addresses: see H. F. Osborn, " The Rise of the Mammalia in North America " (*Proc. Amer. Assn. Adv. Science*, vol. xlii., 1893), " Ten Years' Progress in the Mammalian Palaeontology of North America " (*Comptes rendus du 6ᵉ Congrès intern. de zoologie*, session de Bern, 1904), " The Present Problems of Palaeontology " (Address before Section of Zool. International Congress of Arts and Science, St Louis, Sept. 1904), " The Causes of Extinction of Mammalia " (*Amer. Naturalist*, xl. 769–795, 829–859, 1906).

(H. F. O.)

PALAEOSPONDYLUS, a small fish-like organism, of which the skeleton is found fossil in the Middle Old Red Sandstone

Palaeospondylus gunni, restored by Dr R. H. Traquair.
(Nearly twice nat. size.)

of Achanarras, near Thurso, Caithness. It was thus named (Gr. ancient vertebra) by Dr R. H. Traquair in 1890, in allusion to its well-developed vertebral rings; and its structure was studied in detail in 1903 by Professor and Miss Sollas, who succeeded in making enlarged models of the fossil in wax. The skeleton as preserved is carbonized, and indicates an eel-shaped animal from 3 to 5 cm., in length: The skull, which must have consisted of hardened cartilage, exhibits pairs of nasal and auditory capsules, with a gill-apparatus below its hinder part, but no indications of ordinary jaws. The anterior opening of the brain-case is surrounded by a ring of hard cirri. A pair of " post-branchial plates " projects backwards from the head. The vertebral axis shows a series of broad rings, with distinct neural arches, but no ribs. Towards the end of the body both neural and haemal arches are continued into forked radial cartilages, which support a median fin. There are no traces either of paired fins or of dermal armour. The affinities of *Palaeospondylus* are doubtful, but it is probably related to the contemporaneous armoured Ostracoderms.

REFERENCES.—R. H. Traquair, paper in *Proc. Roy. Phys. Soc. Edin.*, xii. 312. (1894); W. J. Sollas and I. B. J. Sollas, paper in *Phil. Trans. Roy. Soc.* (1903 B.).   (A. S. Wo.)

PALAEOTHERIUM (*i.e.* ancient animal), a name applied by Cuvier to the remains of ungulate mammals recalling tapirs in general appearance, from the Lower Oligocene gypsum quarries of Paris. These were the first indications of the

(From the Paris gypsum.)
Restoration of *Palaeotherium magnum*. (About ¼ nat. size.)

occurrence in the fossil state of perissodactyle ungulates allied to the horse, although it was long before the relationship was recognized. The palaeotheres, which range in size from that of a pig to that of a small rhinoceros, are now regarded as representing a family, *Palaeotheriidae*, nearly related to the horse-tribe, and having, in fact, probably originated from the same ancestral stock, namely, *Hyracotherium* of the Lower Eocene (see EQUIDAE). The connecting line with *Hyracotherium* was formed by *Pachynolophus* (*Propalaeotherium*), and the line apparently terminated in *Paloplotherium*, which is also Oligocene. Representatives of the family occur in many parts of Europe, but the typical genus is unknown in North America, where, however, other forms occur.

Although palaeotheres resemble tapirs in general appearance, they differ in having only three toes on the fore as well as on the hind foot. The dentition normally comprises the typical series of 44 teeth, although in some instances the first premolar is wanting. The cheek-teeth are short-crowned, generally with no cement, the upper molars having a W-shaped outer wall, from which proceed two oblique transverse crests, while the lower ones carry two crescents. Unlike the early horses, the later premolars are as complex as the molars; and although there is a well-marked gap between the canine and the premolars, there is only a very short one between the former and the incisors. The orbit is completely open behind. In other respects the palaeotheres resemble the ancestral horses. They were, however, essentially marsh-dwelling animals, and exhibit no tendency to the cursorial type of limb so characteristic of the horse-line. They were, in fact, essentially inadaptive creatures, and hence rapidly died out.   (R. L.*)

PALAEOZOIC ERA, in geology, the oldest of the great time divisions in which organic remains have left any clear record. The three broad divisions—Palaeozoic, Mesozoic, Cainozoic—

which are employed by geologists to mark three stages in the development of life on the earth, are based primarily upon the fossil contents of the strata which, at one point or another, have been continuously forming since the very earliest times. The precise line in the " record of the rocks " where the chronicle of the Palaeozoic era closes and that of the Mesozoic era opens—as in more recent historical documents—is a matter for editorial caprice. The early geologists took the most natural dividing lines that came within their knowledge, namely, the line of change in general petrological characters, *e.g.* the " Transition Series " (*Übergangsgebirge*), the name given to rocks approximately of Palaeozoic age by A. G. Werner because they exhibited a transitional stage between the older crystalline rocks and the younger non-crystalline; later in Germany these same rocks were said to have been formed in the " Kohlenperiode " by H. G. Bronn and others, while in England H. T. de la Beche classed them as a Carbonaceous and Greywacke group. Finally, the divisional time separating the Palaeozoic record from that of the Mesozoic was made to coincide with a great natural break or unconformity of the strata. This was the most obvious course, for where such a break occurred there would be the most marked differences between the fossils found below and those found above the physical discordance. The divisions in the fossil record having been thus established, they must for convenience remain, but their artificiality cannot be too strongly emphasized, for the broad stratigraphical gaps and lithological groups which made the divisions sharp and clear to the earlier geologists are proved to be absent in other regions, and fossils which were formerly deemed characteristic of the Palaeozoic era are found in some places to commingle with forms of strongly marked Mesozoic type. In short, the record is more nearly complete than was originally supposed.

The Palaeozoic or Primary era is divided into the following periods or epochs: Cambrian, Ordovician, Silurian, Devonian, Carboniferous and Permian. The fact that fossils found in the rocks of the three earlier epochs—Cambrian, Ordovician, Silurian—have features in common, as distinguished from those in the three later epochs has led certain authors to divide this era into an earlier, Protozoic (Proterozoic) and a later Deuterozoic time. The rocks of Palaeozoic age are mainly sandy and muddy sediments with a considerable development of limestone in places. These sediments have been altered to shales, slates, quartzites, &c., and frequently they are found in a highly metamorphosed condition; in eastern North America, however, and in north-east Europe they still maintain their horizontality and primitive texture over large areas. The fossils of the earlier Palaeozoic rocks are characterized by the abundance of trilobites, graptolites, brachiopods, and the absence of all vertebrates except in the upper strata; the later rocks of the era are distinguished by the absence of graptolites, the gradual failing of the trilobites, the continued predominance of brachiopods and tabulate corals, the abundance of crinoids and the rapid development of placoderm and heterocercal ganoid fishes and amphibians. The land plants were all cryptogams, *Lepidodendron*, *Sigillaria*, followed by Conifers and Cycads. It is obvious from the advanced stage of development of the organisms found in the earliest of these Palaeozoic rocks that the beginnings of life must go much farther back, and indeed organic remains have been found in rocks older than the Cambrian; for convenience, therefore, the base of the Cambrian is usually placed at the zone of the trilobite *Olenellus*.   (J. A. H.)

PALAEPHATUS, the author of a small extant treatise, entitled Περὶ Ἀπίστων (On " Incredible Things "). It consists of a series of rationalizing explanations of Greek legends, without any attempt at arrangement or plan, and is probably an epitome, composed in the Byzantine age, of some larger work, perhaps the Ἄβεα τῶν μυθικῶν εἰρημένων, mentioned by Suidas as the work of a grammarian of Egypt or Athens. Suidas himself ascribes a Περὶ Ἀπίστων, in five books, to Palaephatus of Paros or Priene. The author was perhaps a contemporary of Euhemerus (3rd century B.C.). Suidas mentions two other writers of the name: (1) an epic poet of Athens, who lived before the time of

Homer; (2) an historian of Abydus, an intimate friend of Aristotle.

See edition by N. Festa, in *Mythographi graeci* (1902), in the Teubner series, with valuable prolegomena supplementary to *Intorno all' opuscolo di Palefato de incredibilibus* (1890), by the same writer.

PALAESTRA (Gr. παλαίστρα), the name apparently applied by the Greeks to two kinds of places used for gymnastic and athletic exercises. In the one case it seems confined to the places where boys and youths received a general gymnastic training, in the other to a part of a gymnasium where the *athletae*, the competitors in the public games, were trained in wrestling (παλαίω, to wrestle) and boxing. The boys' *palaestrae* were private institutions and generally bore the name of the manager or of the founder; thus at Athens there was a *palaestra* of Taureas (Plato, *Charmides*). The Romans used the terms *gymnasium* and *palaestra* indiscriminately for any place where gymnastic exercises were carried on.

PALAFOX DE MENDOZA, JUAN DE (1600–1659), Spanish bishop, was born in Aragon. He was appointed in 1639 bishop of Angelopolis (Puebla de los Angeles) in Mexico, and there honourably distinguished himself by his efforts to protect the natives from Spanish cruelty, forbidding any methods of conversion other than persuasion. In this he met with the uncompromising hostility of the Jesuits, whom in 1647 he laid under an interdict. He twice, in 1647 and 1649, laid a formal complaint against them at Rome. The pope, however, refused to approve his censures, and all he could obtain was a brief from Innocent X. (May 14, 1648), commanding the Jesuits to respect the episcopal jurisdiction. In 1653 the Jesuits succeeded in securing his translation to the little see of Osma in Old Castile. In 1694 Charles II. of Spain petitioned for his canonization; but though this passed through the preliminary stages, securing for Palafox the title of "Venerable," it was ultimately defeated, under Pius VI., by the intervention of the Jesuits.

See Antonio Gonzales de Resendo, *Vie de Palafox* (French trans., Paris, 1690).

PALAFOX Y MELZI, JOSE DE (1780–1847), duke of Saragossa, was the youngest son of an old Aragonese family. Brought up at the Spanish court, he entered the guards at an early age, and in 1808 as a sub-lieutenant accompanied Ferdinand to Bayonne; but after vainly attempting, in company with others, to secure Ferdinand's escape, he fled to Spain, and after a short period of retirement placed himself at the head of the patriot movement in Aragon. He was proclaimed by the populace governor of Saragossa and captain-general of Aragon (May 25, 1808). Despite the want of money and of regular troops, he lost no time in declaring war against the French, who had already overrun the neighbouring provinces of Catalonia and Navarre, and soon afterwards the attack he had provoked began. Saragossa as a fortress was both antiquated in design and scantily provided with munitions and supplies, and the defences resisted but a short time. But it was at that point that the real resistance began. A week's street fighting made the assailants masters of half the town, but Palafox's brother succeeded in forcing a passage into the city with 3000 troops. Stimulated by the appeals of Palafox and of the fierce and resolute demagogues who ruled the mob, the inhabitants resolved to contest possession of the remaining quarters of Saragossa inch by inch, and if necessary to retire to the suburb across the Ebro, destroying the bridge. The struggle, which was prolonged for nine days longer, resulted in the withdrawal of the French (Aug. 14), after a siege which had lasted 61 days in all. Palafox then attempted a short campaign in the open country, but when Napoleon's own army entered Spain, and destroyed one hostile army after another in a few weeks, Palafox was forced back into Saragossa, where he sustained a still more memorable second siege. This ended, after three months, in the fall of the town, or rather the cessation of resistance, for the town was in ruins and a pestilence had swept away many thousands of the defenders. Palafox himself, suffering from the epidemic, fell into the hands of the French and was kept

XX 10a

prisoner at Vincennes until December 1813. In June 1814 he was confirmed in the office of captain-general of Aragon, but soon afterwards withdrew from it, and ceased to take part in public affairs. From 1820 to 1823 he commanded the royal guard of King Ferdinand, but, taking the side of the Constitution in the civil troubles which followed, he was stripped of all his honours and offices by the king, whose restoration by French bayonets was the triumph of reaction and absolutism. Palafox remained in retirement for many years. He received the title of duke of Saragossa from Queen Maria Christine. From 1836 he took part in military and political affairs as captain-general of Aragon and a senator. He died at Madrid on the 15th of February 1847.

A biographical notice of Palafox appeared in the Spanish translation of Thiers's *Hist. des consulates de l'empire*, by F. de Madrago. For the two sieges of Saragossa, see C. W. C. Oman, *Peninsular War*, vol. i.; this account is both more accurate and more just than Napier's.

PALAMAS, GREGORIUS (c. 1296–1359), Greek mystic and chief apologist of the Hesychasts (*q.v.*), belonged to a distinguished Anatolian family, and his father held an important position at Constantinople. Palamas at an early age retired to Mt Athos, where he became acquainted with the mystical theories of the Hesychasts. In 1326 he went to Skëtê near Beroea, where he spent some years in isolation in a cell specially built for him. His health having broken down, he returned to Mt Athos, but, finding little relief, removed to Thessalonica. About this time Barlaam, the Calabrian monk, began his attacks upon the monks of Athos, and Palamas came forward as their champion. In 1341 and 1351 he took part in the two synods at Constantinople, which definitively secured the victory of the Palamites. During the civil war between John Cantacuzene and the Palaeologi, Palamas was imprisoned. After Cantacuzene's victory in 1347, Palamas was released and appointed archbishop of Thessalonica; being refused admittance by the inhabitants, he retired to the island of Lemnos, but subsequently obtained his see. Palamas endeavoured to justify the mysticism of the Hesychasts on dogmatic grounds. The chief objects of his attack were Barlaam, Gregorius Acindynus and Nicephorus Gregoras.

Palamas was a prolific writer, but only a few of his works have been published, most of which will be found in J. P. Migne, *Patrologia graeca* (cl., cli.). They consist of polemics against the Latins and their doctrine of the Procession of the Holy Ghost; Hesychastic writings; homilies; a life of St Peter (a monk of Athos); a rhetorical essay *Prosopopeia* (ed. A. Jahn, 1884), containing the accusations brought against the body by the soul, the defence made by the body, and the final pronouncement of the judges in favour of the body, on the ground that its sins are the result of inadequate teaching.

See the historical works of John Cantacuzene and Nicephorus Gregoras, the *Vita Palamae* by Philotheus, and the encomium by Nilus (both patriarchs of Constantinople); also C. Krumbacher, *Geschichte der byzantinischen Litteratur* (1897).

PALAMAU, a district of British India, in the Chota-Nagpur division of Bengal. It was formed out of Lohardaga, in 1894, and takes its name from a former state or chiefship. The administrative headquarters are at Daltonganj: pop. (1901), 5837. It consists of the lower spurs of the Chota-Nagpur plateau, sloping north to the valley of the Son. Area 4914 sq. m.; pop. (1901), 619,600, showing an increase of 3·8% in the decade; average density, 126 persons per sq. m., being the lowest in all Bengal. Palamau suffered severely from drought in 1897. A branch of the East Indian railway from the Son valley to the valuable coalfield near Daltonganj was opened in 1902. The only articles of export are jungle produce, such as lac and tussur silk. The forests are unprofitable.

See *Palamau District Gazetteer* (Calcutta, 1907).

PALAMCOTTAH, a town of British India, in the Tinnevelly district of Madras, on the opposite bank of the Tambraparni river to Tinnevelly town, with which it shares a station on the South Indian railway, 444 m. south of Madras. Pop. (1901), 39,545. It is the administrative headquarters of the district, and also the chief centre of Christian missions in south India. Among many educational institutions may be mentioned the Sarah Tucker College for Women, founded in 1895.

PALAMEDES, in Greek legend, son of Nauplius king of Euboea, one of the heroes of the Trojan War, belonging to the post-Homeric cycle of legends. During the siege of Troy, Agamemnon, Diomedes and Odysseus (who had been detected by Palamedes in an attempt to escape going to Troy by shamming madness) caused a letter containing money and purporting to come from Priam to be concealed in his tent. They then accused Palamedes of treasonable correspondence with the enemy, and he was ordered to be stoned to death. His father exacted a fearful vengeance from the Greeks on their way home, by placing false lights on the promontory of Caphareus. The story of Palamedes was first handled in the *Cypria* of Stasinus, and formed the subject of lost plays by Aeschylus (*Palamedes*), Sophocles (*Nauplius*), Euripides (*Palamedes*), of which some fragments remain. Sophists and rhetoricians, such as Gorgias and Alcidamas, amused themselves by writing declamations in favour of or against him. Palamedes was regarded as the inventor of the alphabet, lighthouses, weights and measures, dice, backgammon and the discus.

See Euripides, *Orestes*, 432 and schol.; Ovid, *Metam.* xiii. 56; Servius on Virgil, *Aeneid*, ii. 82, and Nettleship's note in Conington's edition; Philostratus, *Heroica*, 11; Euripides, *Frag.* 581; for different versions of his death see Dictys Cretensis ii. 15; Pausanias ii. 20, 31x. 31, 2; Dares Phrygius, 28; monograph by O. Jahn (Hamburg, 1836).

PALANPUR, a native state of India, in the Gujarat division of Bombay, on the southern border of Rajputana. Area, 1766 sq. m.; pop. (1901), 222,627, showing a decrease of 19 % in the decade. The country is mountainous, with much forest towards the north, but undulating and open in the south and east. The principal rivers are the Saraswati and Banas. The estimated gross revenue is £50,000; tribute to the gaekwar of Baroda, £2564. The chief, whose title is diwan, is an Afghan by descent. The state is traversed by the main line of the Rajputana-Malwa railway, and contains the British cantonment of Deesa. Wheat, rice and sugar-cane are the chief products. The state has suffered severely of recent years from plague. The town of PALANPUR is a railway junction for Deesa, 18 m. distant. Pop. (1901), 17,799.

Palanpur also gives its name to a political agency, or collection of native states; total area, 6303 sq. m.; pop. (1901), 467,271, showing a decrease of 28 % in the decade, due to the effects of famine.

PALANQUIN (pronounced *palankeen*, a form in which it is sometimes spelled), a covered litter used in India and other Eastern countries. It is usually some eight feet long by four feet in width and depth, fitted with movable blinds or shutters, and slung on poles carried by four bearers. Indian and Chinese women of rank always travelled in *palanquins*, and they were largely used by European residents in India before the railways. The *norimono* of Japan and the *kiaotsu* of China differ from the Indian palanquin only in the method of attaching the poles to the body of the conveyance. The word came into European use through Port. *palanquim*, which represents an East Indian word seen in several forms, *e.g.* Malay and Javanese *palangki*, Hindostani *palki*, Pali *pallanko*, &c., all in the sense of litter, couch, bed. The Sansk. *paryanka*, couch, bed, the source of all these words, is derived from *pari*, round, about, and *anka*, hook. The *New English Dictionary* points out the curious resemblance of these words with the Latin use of *phalanga* (Gr. φάλαγξ) for a bearing or carrying pole, whence the Span. *palanca* and *palanquino*, a bearer.

PALATE (Lat. *palatum*, possibly from the root of *pascere*, to feed), the roof of the mouth in man and vertebrate animals. The palate is divided into two parts, the anterior bony "hard palate" (see MOUTH), and the posterior fleshy "soft palate" (see PHARYNX). For the malformation consisting in a longitudinal fissure in the roof of the mouth, see CLEFT PALATE.

PALATINATE (Ger. *Pfalz*), a name given generally to any district ruled by a count palatine, but particularly to a district of Germany, a province of the kingdom of Bavaria, lying west of the Rhine. It is bounded on the N. by the Prussian Rhine province and the Hessian province of Rhein-Hessen; on the E.

by Baden, from which it is separated by the Rhine; on the S. by the imperial province of Alsace-Lorraine, from which it is divided by the Lauter; and on the W. by the administrative districts of Trier and Coblenz, belonging to the Prussian Rhine province. It has an area of 2288 sq. m., and a population (1905) of 885,280, showing a density of 386·9 to the square mile. As regards religion, the inhabitants are fairly equally distributed into Roman Catholics and Protestants.

The rivers in this fertile tract of country are the Rhine, Lauter, Queich, Speirbach, Glan and Blies. The Vosges, and their continuation the Hardt, run through the land from south to north and divide it into the fertile and mild plain of the Rhine, together with the slope of the Hardt range, on the east, and the rather inclement district on the west, which, running between the Saarbrück carboniferous mountains and the northern spurs of the Hardt range, ends in a porphyrous cluster of hills, the highest point of which is the Donnersberg (2254 ft.). The country on the east side and on the slopes of the Hardt yield a number of the most varied products, such as wine, fruit, corn, vegetables, flax and tobacco. Cattle are reared in great quantity and are of excellent quality. The mines yield iron, coal, quicksilver and salt. The industries are very active, especially in iron, machinery, paper, chemicals, shoes, woollen goods, beer, leather and tobacco. The province is well served by railway communication and, for purposes of administration, is divided into the following 16 districts: Bergzabern, Dürkheim, Frankenthal, Germersheim, Homburg, Kaisers-Jautern, Kirchheimbolanden, Kusel, Landau, Ludwigshafen, Neustadt, Pirmasens, Rockenhausen, St Ingbert, Spires and Zweibrücken. Spires (Speyer) is the seat of government, and the chief industrial centres are Ludwigshafen on the Rhine, which is the principal river port, Landau, and Neustadt, the seat of the wine trade.

See A. Becker, *Die Pfalz und die Pfälzer* (Leipzig, 1857); Mehlis, *Fahrten durch die Pfalz* (Augsburg, 1877); Kranz, *Handbuch der Pfalz* (Spires, 1902); Hensen, *Pfalzführer* (Neustadt, 1905); and Näher, *Die Burgen der rheinischen Pfalz* (Strassburg, 1887).

History.—The count palatine of the Rhine was a royal official who is first mentioned in the 10th century. The first count was Hermann I., who from 945 to 996, and although the office was not hereditary it appears to have been held mainly by his descendants until the death of Count Hermann III. in 1155. These counts had gradually extended their powers, had obtained the right of advocacy over the archbishop of Trier and the bishopric of Juliers, and ruled various isolated districts along the Rhine. In 1155 the German king, Frederick I., appointed his step-brother Conrad as count palatine. Conrad took up his residence at the castle of Juttenbuhel, near Heidelberg, which became the capital of the Palatinate. In 1195 Conrad was succeeded by his son-in-law Henry, son of Henry the Lion, duke of Saxony, who was a loyal supporter of the emperor Henry VI. After the latter's death in 1197 he assisted his own brother Otto, afterwards the emperor Otto IV., in his attempts to gain the German throne. Otto refused to reward Henry for this support, so in 1204 he assisted his rival, the German king Philip, but returned to Otto's side after Philip's murder in 1208. In 1211 Henry abdicated in favour of his son Henry, who died in 1214, when the Palatinate was given by the German king Frederick II. to Otto, the infant son of Louis I., duke of Bavaria, a member of the Wittelsbach family, who was betrothed to Agnes, sister of the late count, Henry. The break-up of the duchy of Franconia had increased the influence of the count palatine of the Rhine, and the importance of his position among the princes of the empire is shown by Roger of Hoveden, who, writing of the election to the German throne in 1198, singles out four princes as chief electors, among whom is the count palatine of the Rhine. In the *Sachsenspiegel*, a collection of German laws which was written before 1235, the count is given as the butler (dapifer) of the emperor, the first place among the lay electors.

The Palatinate was ruled by Louis of Bavaria on behalf of his son until 1228, when it passed to Otto who ruled until his death in 1253. Otto's possessions were soon afterwards divided, and his elder son Louis II. received the Palatinate and Upper Bavaria. Louis died in 1294 when these districts passed to his son Rudolph I. (d. 1319), and subsequently to his grandson Louis, afterwards the emperor Louis IV. By the Treaty of Pavia in 1329, Louis granted the Palatinate to his nephews Rudolph II. and Rupert I., who received from him at the same time a portion of the duchy of Upper Bavaria, which was called the upper Palatinate to distinguish it from the Rhenish, or lower Palatinate. Rudolph died in 1353, after which Rupert ruled alone until his death in 1390. In 1355 he had sold a portion of the upper Palatinate to the emperor Charles IV., but by various purchases he increased the area of the Rhenish Palatinate. His successor was his nephew Rupert II., who bought from the German king Wenceslaus a portion of the territory that his uncle had sold to Charles IV. He died in 1398 and was succeeded by his son Rupert III. In 1400 Rupert was elected German king, and when he died in 1410 his possessions were divided among his four sons: the eldest, Louis III., received the Rhenish Palatinate proper; the second son, John, obtained the upper Palatinate; while the outlying districts of Zweibrücken and Simmern passed to Stephen, and that of Mosbach to Otto.

When the possessions of the house of Wittelsbach were divided in 1255 and the branches of Bavaria and the Palatinate were founded, a dispute arose over the exercise of the electoral vote, and the question was not settled until in 1356 the Golden Bull bestowed the privilege upon the count palatine of the Rhine, who exercised it until 1623. The part played by Count Frederick V., titular king of Bohemia, during the Thirty Years' War induced the emperor Ferdinand II. to deprive him of his vote and to transfer it to the duke of Bavaria, Maximilian I. By the Peace of Westphalia in 1648 an eighth electorate was created for the count palatine, to which was added the office of treasurer. In 1777, however, the count resumed the ancient position of his family in the electoral college, and regained the office of steward which he retained until the formal dissolution of the empire in 1806.

To return to the history of the Palatinate as divided into four parts among the sons of the German king Rupert in 1410. John, the second of these brothers, died in 1443, and his son Christopher, having become king of Denmark in 1440, did not inherit the upper Palatinate, which was again united with the Rhenish Palatinate. Otto, the son of Otto (d. 1461), Rupert's fourth son, who had obtained Mosbach, died without sons in 1499, and this line became extinct, leaving only the two remaining lines with interests in the Rhenish Palatinate. After Rupert's death this was governed by his eldest son, the elector Louis III. (d. 1436), and then by the latter's sons, Louis IV. (d. 2449) and Frederick I. The elector Frederick, called the Victorious, was one of the foremost princes of his time. His nephew and successor, the elector Philip, carried on a war for the possession of the duchy of Bavaria-Landshut, which had been bequeathed to his son Rupert (d. 1504), but, when in 1507 an end was put to this struggle, Rupert's son, Otto Henry, only received Neuburg and Sulzbach. Louis V. and then Frederick II. succeeded Philip, but both died without sons and Otto Henry became elector. He, too, died without sons in 1559, when the senior branch became extinct, leaving only the branch descended from Rupert's third son, Stephen.

Already on Stephen's death in 1459 this family had been divided into two branches, those of Simmern and of Zweibrücken, and in 1514 the latter branch had been divided into the lines of Zweibrücken proper and of Veldentz. It was Frederick, count palatine of Simmern, who succeeded to the Palatinate on Otto Henry's death, becoming the elector Frederick III. The new elector, a keen but not a very bigoted Calvinist, was one of the most active of the Protestant princes. His son and successor, Louis VI. (d. 1583), was a Lutheran, but 'another son, John Casimir, who ruled the electorate on behalf of his young nephew, Frederick IV., from 1583 to 1592, gave every encouragement to the Calvinists. A similar line of action was followed by Frederick IV. himself after 1592.

He was the founder and head of the Evangelical Union established to combat the aggressive tendencies of the Roman Catholics. His son, the elector Frederick V., accepted the throne of Bohemia and thus brought on the Thirty Years' War. He was quickly driven from that country, and his own electorate was devastated by the Bavarians and Spaniards. At the peace of Westphalia in 1648 the Palatinate was restored to Frederick's son, Charles Louis, but it was shorn of the upper Palatinate, which Bavaria retained as the prize of war.

Scarcely had the Palatinate begun to recover when it was attacked by Louis XIV. For six years (1673-79) the electorate was devastated by the French troops, and even after the Treaty of Nijmwegen it suffered from the aggressive policy of Louis. In August 1680 the elector Charles Louis died, and when his son and successor, Charles, followed him to the grave five years later the ruling family became extinct in the senior line. Mention has already been made of a division of this family into two lines after 1459, and of a further division of the Zweibrücken line in 1514, when again two lines were founded. The junior of these, that of Veldentz, became extinct in 1694, but the senior, that of Zweibrücken proper, was still very flourishing. Under Count Wolfgang (d. 1569) it had purchased Sulzbach and Neuburg in 1557, and in the person of his grandson, Wolfgang William (d. 1653) it had secured the coveted duchies of Juliers and Berg. It was Philip William of Neuburg, the son of Wolfgang William, who became elector palatine in succession to Charles in 1685.

The French king's brother, Philip, duke of Orleans, had married Charlotte Elizabeth, a sister of the late elector Charles, and consequently the French king claimed a part of Charles's lands in 1680. His troops took Heidelberg and devastated the Palatinate, while Philip William took refuge in Vienna, where he died in 1690. Then in 1697, by the Treaty of Ryswick, Louis abandoned his claim in return for a sum of money. Just before this date the Palatinate began to be disturbed by troubles about religion. The great majority of the inhabitants were Protestants, but the family which succeeded in 1685 belonged to the Roman Catholic Church. Philip William, however, gave equal rights to all his subjects, but under his son and successor, the elector John William, the Protestants were deprived of various civil rights until the intervention of Prussia and of Brunswick in 1705 gave them some redress. The next elector, a brother of the last one, was Charles Philip, who removed his capital from Heidelberg to Mannheim in 1720. He died without male issue in December 1742. His successor was his kinsman, Charles Theodore, count palatine of Sulzbach, a cadet of the Zweibrücken-Neuburg line, and now with the exception of one or two small pieces the whole of the Palatinate was united under one ruler. Charles Theodore was a prince of refined and educated tastes and during his long reign his country enjoyed prosperity. In 1777 on the extinction of the other branch of the house of Wittelsbach, he became elector of Bavaria, and the Palatinate was henceforward united with Bavaria, the elector's capital being Munich. Charles Theodore died without legitimate sons in 1799, and his successor was Maximilian Joseph, a member of the Birkenfeld branch of the Zweibrücken family, who later became king of Bavaria as Maximilian I.

In 1802 the elector was obliged to cede the portion of the Palatinate lying on the left bank of the Rhine to France, and other portions to Baden and to Hesse-Darmstadt. Much of this, however, was regained in 1815, and since that date the Palatinate has formed part of the kingdom of Bavaria.

See Widder, *Versuch einer vollständigen geographisch-historischen Beschreibung der Kurfürstlichen Pfalz* (Frankfort, 1786–1788); L. Häusser, *Geschichte der Rheinischen Pfalz* (Heidelberg, 1845); Nebenius, *Geschichte der Pfalz* (Heidelberg, 1874); Gümbel, *Geschichte der protestanischen Kirche der Pfalz* (Kaiserslautern, 1885); the *Regesten der Pfalzgrafen am Rhein, 1214–1508*, edited by Koch and Wille (Innsbruck, 1894); and Wild, *Bilderatlas zur bodischpfälzischen Geschichte* (Heidelberg, 1904).

PALATINE (from Lat. *palatium*, a palace), pertaining to the palace and therefore to the emperor, king or other sovereign ruler. In the later Roman Empire certain officials attending on the emperor, or discharging other duties at his court, were called *palatini*; from the time of Constantine the Great the term was also applied to the soldiers stationed in or around the capital to distinguish them from those stationed on the frontier of the empire. In the East Roman Empire the word was used to designate officials concerned with the administration of the finances and the imperial lands.

This use of the word palatine was adopted by the Frankish kings of the Merovingian dynasty. They employed a high official, the *comes palatinus*, who at first assisted the king in his judicial duties and at a later date discharged many of these himself. Other counts palatine were employed on military and administrative work, and the system was maintained by the Carolingian sovereigns. The word paladin, used to describe the followers of Charlemagne, is a variant of palatine. A Frankish capitulary of 882 and Hincmar, archbishop of Reims, writing about the same time, testify to the extent to which the judicial work of the Frankish Empire had passed into their hands, and one grant of power was followed by another. Instead of remaining near the person of the king, some of the counts palatine were sent to various parts of his empire to act as judges and governors, the districts ruled by them being called palatinates. Being in a special sense the representatives of the sovereign they were entrusted with more extended power than the ordinary counts. Thus comes the later and more general use of the word palatine, its application as an adjective to persons entrusted with special powers and also to the districts over which these powers were exercised. By Henry the Fowler and especially by Otto the Great, they were sent into all parts of the country to support the royal authority by checking the independent tendencies of the great tribal dukes. We hear of a count palatine in Saxony, and of others in Lorraine, in Bavaria and in Swabia, their duties being to administer the royal estates in these duchies. The count palatine in Bavaria, an office held by the family of Wittelsbach, became duke of this land, the lower title being then merged in the higher one; and with one other exception the German counts palatine soon became insignificant, although, the office having become hereditary, Pfalzgrafen were in existence until the dissolution of the Holy Roman Empire in 1806. The exception was the count palatine of the Rhine, who became one of the four lay electors and the most important lay official of the empire. In the empire the word count palatine was also used to designate the officials who assisted the count palatine to exercise the rights which were reserved for his personal consideration. They were called *comites palatini caesarii*, or *comites sacri palatii*; in German, *Hofpfalzgrafen*.

From Germany the term palatine passed into England and Scotland, into Hungary and Poland. It appears in England about the end of the 11th century, being applied by Ordericus Vitalis, to Odo, bishop of Bayeux and earl of Kent. The word palatine came in England to be applied to the earls, or rulers, of certain counties, men who enjoyed exceptional powers. Their exceptional position is thus described by Stubbs (*Const. Hist.* vol. i.): They were "earldoms in which the earls were endowed with the superiority of whole counties, so that all the landholders held feudally of them, in which they received the whole profits of the courts and exercised all the regalia or royal rights, nominated the sheriffs, held their own councils and acted as independent princes except in the owing of homage and fealty to the king." The most important of the counties palatine were Durham and Chester, the bishop of the one and the earl of the other receiving special privileges from William I. Chester had its own parliament, consisting of barons of the county, and was not represented in the national assembly until 1541, while it retained some of its special privileges until 1830. The bishop of Durham retained temporal jurisdiction over the county until 1836. Lancashire was made a county, or duchy, palatine in 1351, and kept some of its special judicial privileges until 1873. Thus for several centuries the king's writs did not run in these three palatine counties, and at the present day Lancashire and Durham have their own courts of chancery. Owing to the ambiguous application of the word palatine to Odo of Bayeux, it is doubtful whether Kent was ever a palatine county; if so, it was one only for a few years during the 11th century. Other palatine counties, which only retained their exceptional position for a short time, were Shropshire, the Isle of Ely, Hexhamshire in Northumbria, and Pembrokeshire in Wales. In Ireland there were palatine districts, and the seven original earldoms of Scotland occupied positions somewhat analogous to that of the English palatine counties.

In Hungary the important office of palatine (Magyar *Nádor*) owes its inception to St Stephen. At first the head of the judicial system, the palatine undertook other duties, and became after the king the most important person in the realm. At one time he was chosen by the king from among four candidates named by the Diet. Under the later Habsburg rulers of Hungary the office was several times held by a member of this family, one of the palatines being the archduke Joseph. The office was abolished after the revolution of 1848.

In Poland the governors of the provinces of the kingdom were called palatines, and the provinces were sometimes called palatinates.

In America certain districts colonized by English settlers were treated as palatine provinces. In 1632 Cecilius Calvert, 2nd Lord Baltimore, received a charter from Charles I. giving him palatine rights in Maryland. In 1639 Sir Ferdinando Gorges, the lord of Maine, obtained one granting him as large and ample prerogatives as were enjoyed by the bishop of Durham. Carolina was another instance of a palatine province.

In addition to the authorities mentioned, see R. Schröder, *Lehrbuch der deutschen Rechtsgeschichte* (Leipzig, 1902); C. Pfaff, *Geschichte des Pfalzgrafenamtes* (Halle, 1847); G. T. Lapsley, *The County Palatine of Durham* (New York, 1900), and D. J. Medley, *English Constitutional History* (1907).   (A. W. H.*)

PALATKA, a city and the county-seat of Putnam county, Florida, U.S.A., in the N.E. part of the state, on the W. bank of the St John's river, about 100 m. from its mouth, and at the head of deep-water navigation. Pop. (1905) 3950; (1910) 3779. Palatka is served by the Georgia Southern & Florida (of which it is the southern terminal), the Atlantic Coast Line, and the Florida East Coast railways, and also has connexion by water with Baltimore, New York and Boston. Palatka is situated in a rich agricultural, orange-growing and timber region, for which it is the distributing centre. Large quantities of cypress lumber are shipped from Palatka. Palatka was incorporated as a town in 1853, and in 1872 was chartered as a city.

PALAVER (an adaptation of Port. *palavra*, a word or speech; Ital. *parola*; Fr. *parole*, from the Low Lat. *parabola*, a parable, story, talk; Gr. παραβολή, literally "comparison"; the Low Lat. *parabolare*, "to talk," gives Fr. *parler*, "to speak," whence "parley," "parliament," &c.), the name used by the Portuguese traders on the African coast for their conversations and bargaining with the natives. It was introduced into English in the 18th century through English sailors frequenting the Guinea coast. It has now passed into general use among the negroes of West and West Central Africa for any conference, either among themselves or with foreigners. From the amount of unnecessary talk characteristic of such meetings with natives, the word is used of any idle or cajoling talk.

PALAWARAM, a town of British India, in Chingleput district, Madras, 11 m. S. of Madras city, with a station on the South Indian railway; pop. (1901), 6416. Formerly called the presidency cantonment, as containing the native garrison for Madras city, it is now a dépôt for native infantry and the residence of European pensioners. There are several tanneries.

PALAZZOLO ACREIDE, a town of Sicily, in the province of Syracuse, 28 m. by road W. of it, 2285 ft. above sea-level. Pop. (1901), 14,840. The town occupies the site of the ancient *Acrae*, founded by Syracuse about 664 B.C. It followed in the main the fortunes of the mother city. In the treaty between the Romans and Hiero II. In 263 B.C. it was assigned to the latter. The ancient city lay on the hill above the modern town, the approach to it being defended by quarries, in which tombs of all periods have been discovered. The auditorium of the small theatre is well preserved, though nothing of the stage remains. Close to it are ruins of other buildings, which bear, without justification, the names Naumachia, Odeum (perhaps a bath establishment) and Palace of Hiero. The water supply was obtained by subterranean aqueducts. In the cliffs of the Monte Pineta to the south are other tomb chambers, and to the south again are the curious bas-reliefs called Santoni or Santicelli, mutilated in the 19th century by a peasant proprietor, which appear to be sepulchral also. Near here too is the necropolis of the Acrocoro della Torre, where many sarcophagi have been found. Five miles north lies Buscemi, near which a sacred grotto has been discovered, and also a church cut in the rock and surrounded by a cemetery.[1]

See C. Judica, *Antichità di Acre* (Messina, 1819). (Baron Judica's collection of antiquities was dispersed after his death.) J. Schubring, *Jahrbuch für Philologie*, Suppl. IV., 662–672.

PALE (through Fr. *pal*, from Lat. *palus*, a stake, for *paglus*, from the stem *pag-* of *pangere*, to fix; " pole " is from the same original source), a stake, particularly one of a closely set series driven into the ground to form the defensive work known as a " palisade "; also one of the lighter laths or strips of wood set vertically and fastened to a horizontal rail to form a " paling." Used as an historical term, a pale is a district marked off from the surrounding country by a different system of government and law or by definite boundaries. The best known of these districts was the " English Pale " in Ireland, dating from the reign of Henry II., although the word " pale " was not used in this connexion until the latter part of the 14th century. The Pale varied considerably, according to the strength or weakness of the English authorities, and in the time of Henry VIII. was bounded by a line drawn from Dundalk to Kells, thence to Naas, and from Naas E. to Dalkey, embracing, that is, part of the modern counties of Dublin, Louth, Meath, and Kildare. The Pale existed until the complete subjugation of Ireland under Elizabeth; the use of the word is frequent in Tudor times. There was an " English Pale " or " Calais Pale " also in France until 1558, extending from Gravelines to Wissant, and for a short time under the Tudors an English Pale in Scotland.

In heraldry a " pale " is a band placed vertically in the centre of a shield, hence " in pale " or " to impale " is used of the marshalling of two coats side by side on a shield divided vertically.

" Pale," in the sense of colourless, whitish, of a shade of colour lighter than the normal, is derived through O. Fr. *palle*, mod. *pâle*, from Lat. *pallidus*, *pallor*, *pallere*; and in that of a baker's shovel, or " peel " as it is sometimes called, from Lat. *pala*, spade, probably connected with the root of *pandere*, to spread out.

PALEARIO, AONIO (c. 1500–1570), Italian humanist and reformer, was born about 1500 at Veroli, in the Roman Campagna. Other forms of his name are Antonio Della Paglia, A. Degli Pagliaricci. In 1520 he went to Rome, where he entered the brilliant literary circle of Leo X. When Charles of Bourbon stormed Rome in 1527 Paleario went first to Perugia and then to Siena, where he settled as a teacher. In 1536 his didactic poem in Latin hexameters, *De immortalitate animarum*, was published at Lyons. It is divided into three books, the first containing his proofs of the divine existence, and the remaining two the theological and philosophical arguments for immortality based on that postulate. The whole concludes with a rhetorical description of the occurrences of the Second Advent. In 1542 a tract, written by him and entitled *Della Pienessa, sufficienza, et satisfazione della passione di Christo*, or *Libellus de morte Christi*, was made by the Inquisition the basis of a charge of heresy, from which, however, he successfully defended himself. In Siena he wrote his *Actio in pontifices romanos et eorum asseclas*, a vigorous indictment, in twenty "testimonia," against what he now believed to be the fundamental error of the Roman Church in subordinating Scripture to tradition, as well as against various particular doctrines, such as that of

[1] P. Orsi in *Notizie degli Scavi* (1899), 452–471; *Römische Quartalschrift* (1898), 624–631.

purgatory; it was not, however, printed until after his death (Leipzig, 1606). In 1546 he accepted a professorial chair at Lucca, which he exchanged in 1555 for that of Greek and Latin literature at Milan. Here about 1566 his enemies renewed their activity, and in 1567 he was formally accused by Fra Angelo the inquisitor of Milan. He was tried at Rome, condemned to death in October 1569, and executed in July 1570.

An edition of his works (*Ani. Palearii Veruloni Opera*), including four books of *Epistolae* and twelve *Orationes* besides the *De immortalitate*, was published at Lyons in 1552; this was followed by two others, at Basel, and several after his death, the fullest being that of Amsterdam, 1696. A work, entitled *Benefizio di Cristo* (" The Benefit of Christ's Death "), has been attributed to Paleario on insufficient grounds. Lives by Gurlitt (Hamburg, 1805); Young (2 vols., London, 1860); Bonnet (Paris, 1862).

PALENCIA, an inland province of Spain, one of the eight into which Old Castile was divided in 1833; bounded on the N. by Santander, E. by Burgos, S. by Valladolid, and W. by Valladolid and Leon. Pop. (1900), 192,473; area, 3256 sq. m. The surface of the province slopes gradually S. to the Duero (Douro) valley. The principal rivers are the Pisuerga and the Carrion, which unite at Dueñas and flow into the Duero at Valladolid. The chief tributaries of the Pisuerga within the province are the Arlanzon, the Burejo, the Cioza, and the united streams of the Buedo and Abanades; the Carrion is joined on the right by the Cueza. The north is traversed by the Cantabrian Mountains, the highest summit being the culminating point of the Sierra del Brezo (6355 ft.). There are extensive forests in this region and the valleys afford good pasturage. The remainder of Palencia, the " Tierra de Campos," belongs to the great Castilian table-land. In the south is a marsh or lake, known as La Laguna de la Nava. The mountainous district abounds in minerals, but only coal and small quantities of copper are worked. The province is crossed in the south-east by the trunk railway connecting Madrid with France via Irun, while the line to Santander traverses it throughout from north to south; there are also railways from the city of Palencia to Leon, and across the north from Mataporquera in Santander to La Robla in Leon. A branch of the Santander line gives access to the Orbo coal-fields. The main highways are good; the other roads often bad. The Canal de Castilla, begun in 1753, and completed in 1832, connects Alar del Rey with Valladolid. Wheat and other cereals, vegetables, hemp and flax are extensively grown, except in the mountainous districts. Flour and wine are made in large quantities, and there are manufactures of linen and woollen stuffs, oil, porcelain, leather, paper and rugs. Palencia rugs are in great demand throughout Spain. The only town with more than 5000 inhabitants is Palencia (*q.v.*).

For the history, inhabitants, &c., see CASTILE.

PALENCIA, an episcopal city, and the capital of the Spanish province of Palencia; on the left bank of the river Carrion, on the Canal de Castilla, at the junction of railways from Leon and Santander, and 7 m. N. by W. of Venta de Baños on the Madrid-Irun line. Pop. (1900), 15,940. Palencia is built in the midst of the level plains called the Tierra de Campos, 2690 ft. above sea-level. Three bridges across the Carrion afford access to the modern suburbs on the right bank. The older and by far the more important part of the city is protected on the west by the river; on the other sides the old machicolated walls, 36 ft. high by 9 ft. in thickness, are in fairly good preservation, and beautified by *alamedas* or promenades, which were laid out in 1778. The cathedral was begun in 1321, finished in 1504, and dedicated to St Antolin; it is a large building in the later and florid Gothic style of Spain. The site was previously occupied by a church erected by Sancho III. of Navarre and Castile (1026–1035) over the cave of St Antolin, which is still shown. The cathedral contains some valuable paintings, old Flemish tapestry, and beautiful carved woodwork and stonework. The church of San Miguel is a good and fairly well-preserved example of 13th-century work; that of San Francisco, of the same date, is inferior and has suffered more from modernization. The hospital of San Lazaro is said to date in part from the time of the Cid (q.v.), who here married Ximena in 1074.

Much has been done for education. Palencia has also hospitals, a foundling refuge, barracks and a bull-ring. Local industries include iron-founding, and the making of rugs, alcohol, leather, soap, porcelain, linen, cotton, wool, machinery and matches.

Palencia, the Pallantia of Strabo and Ptolemy, was the chief town of the Vaccaei. Its history during the Gothic and Moorish periods is obscure; but it was a Castilian town of some importance in the 12th and 13th centuries. The university founded here in 1208 by Alphonso IX. was removed in 1239 to Salamanca.

PALENQUE, the modern name of a deserted city in Mexico, in the narrow valley of the Otolum, in the north part of the state of Chiapas, 80 m. S. of the Gulf port of Carmen. About 30 m. away, on the left bank of the Usumacinta river, stand the ruins of Men-ché or Lorillard city. The original name of Palenque has been lost, and its present name is taken from the neighbouring village, Santo Domingo del Palenque. Unlike the dead cities of the Yucatán plains, Palenque is surrounded by wooded hills and overgrown by tropical vegetation.

There is less stone-carving on the exterior walls, door jambs and pillars of the buildings than on those of the Yucatán Peninsula; this is due to the harder and more uneven character of the limestone. Probably owing to the same cause, there is less cut stone in the walls, the Palenque builders using plaster to obtain smooth surfaces. There is, however, considerable carving on the interior walls, the best specimens being on the tablets, affixed to the walls with plaster. Modelling in stucco was extensively used. A few terra-cotta images have been found. Paint and coloured washes were liberally used to cover plastered surfaces and for ornamentation, and paints seem to have been used to bind plastered surfaces. The Palenque builders apparently used nothing but stone tools in their work.

The so-called Great Palace consists of a group of detached buildings, apparently ten in number, standing on two platforms of different elevations. Some of the interior structures and the detached one on the lower southern terrace are in a fair state of preservation. The plan of construction shows three parallel walls enclosing two corridors covered with the peculiar pointed arches or vaults characteristic of Palenque. The buildings appear to have been erected at different periods. A square tower rises from a central part of the platform to a height of about 40 ft., divided into a solid masonry base and three storeys connected by interior stairways. The Temple of Inscriptions, one of the largest and best preserved, is distinguished chiefly for its tablets, which contain only hieroglyphics. Sculptured slabs form balustrades to the steps leading up to the temple, and its exterior is ornamented with figures in stucco, the outer faces of the four pillars in front having life-size figures of women with children in their arms. The small Temple of Beau Relief stands on a narrow ledge of rock against the steep slope of the mountain. Its most important feature is a large stucco bas-relief, occupying a central position on the back wall of the sanctuary. It consists of a single figure, seated on a throne, beautifully modelled both in form, drapery and ornaments, with the face turned to one side and the arms outstretched, and is reproduced by H. H. Bancroft. The temples on the east side of the Otolum are distinguished by tall narrow vaults, perforated by numerous square openings giving the appearance of coarse lattice work. The Temple of the Sun stands upon a comparatively low pyramidal foundation. The interior consists of the usual pair of vaulted corridors. The sacred tablet on the back wall of the sanctuary is carved in low relief in limestone, and consists of two figures, apparently a priest and his assistant making offerings. There are rows of hieroglyphics on the sides and over the central design. The Temple of the Cross is a larger structure of similar design, and construction. The tablet belonging to this temple has excited controversy, because the design contains a representation of a Latin cross. The Temple of the Cerro, called that of the Cross No. 2, because its tablet is very similar to that just mentioned,

stands back against the slope of the mountain, and is in great part a ruin. (For history and further details see CENTRAL AMERICA; § *Archaeology*.)

PALERMO (Greek, Πάνορμος; Latin, *Panhormus*, *Panormus*), a city of Sicily, capital of a province of the same name, in the kingdom of Italy, and the see of an archbishop. Pop. (1906), town 264,036, commune 323,747. The city stands in the N.W. of the island, on a small bay looking E., the coast forming the chord of a semicircle of mountains which hem in the *campagna* of Palermo, called the Conca d'Oro. The most striking point is the mountain of Hiercte, now called Pellegrino (from the grotto of Santa Rosalia, a favourite place of pilgrimage) at the N. of this semicircle; at the S.E. is the promontory of Zaffarano, on which stood Soluntum (q.v.).

A neolithic settlement and necropolis were discovered in 1897 at the foot of Monte Pellegrino, on the N.E. side (E. Salinas in *Notizie degli Scavi*, 1907, 307). Palermo has been commonly thought to be an original Phoenician settlement of unknown date (though its true Phoenician name is unknown), but Holm (*Archivio storio siciliano*, 1888, iv. 421) has suggested that the settlement was originally Greek.[1] There is no record of any Greek colonies in that part of Sicily, and Panormus certainly was Phoenician as far back as history can carry us. According to Thucydides (vi. 2), as the Greeks colonised the E. of the island, the Phoenicians withdrew to the N.W., and concentrated themselves at Panormus, Motye, and Soluntum. Like the other Phoenician colonies in the west, Panormus came under the power of Carthage, and became the head of the Carthaginian dominion in Sicily. As such it became the centre of that strife between Europe and Africa, between Aryan and Semitic man, in its later stages between Christendom and Islam, which forms the great interest of Sicilian history. As the Semitic head of Sicily, it stands opposed to Syracuse, the Greek head. Under the Carthaginian it was the head of the Semitic part of Sicily; when, under the Saracen all Sicily came under Semitic rule, it was the chief seat of that rule. It was thrice won for Europe, by Greek, Roman and Norman conquerors—in 276 B.C. by the Epirot king Pyrrhus, in 254 B.C. by the Roman consuls Aulus Atilius and Gnaeus Cornelius Scipio, and in A.D. 1071 by Robert Guiscard and his brother Roger, the first count of Sicily. After the conquest by Pyrrhus the city was soon recovered by Carthage, but this first Greek occupation was the beginning of a connexion with western Greece and its islands which was revived under various forms in later times. After the Roman conquest an attempt to recover the city for Carthage was made in 250 B.C., which led only to a great Roman victory (see PUNIC WARS). Later, in the First Punic War, Hamilcar Barca was encamped for three years on Hiercte or Pellegrino, but the Roman possession of the city was not disturbed. Panormus received the privileges of autonomy and immunity from taxation. It seems probable that at the end of the republic the coinage for the west of Sicily was struck here (Mommsen, *Röm. Münzwesen*, 665). A colony was sent here by Augustus, and the place remained of considerable importance, though inferior to Catana. A fortunate chance has preserved to us a large number of the inscriptions set up in the Forum (Mommsen, *Corpus inscr. lat.* x. 752). The town was taken by the Vandal Genseric in A.D. 440. It afterwards became a part of the East-Gothic dominion, and was recovered for the empire by Belisarius in 535. It again remained a Roman possession for exactly three hundred years, till it was taken by the Saracens in 835. Panormus now became the Moslem capital. In 1062 the Pisan fleet broke through the chain of the harbour and carried off the bells of Pisa. After the Norman conquest the city remained for a short time in the hands of the dukes of Apulia. But in 1095 half the city was ceded to Count Roger, and in 1122 the rest was ceded to the second Roger. When he took the kingly title in 1130 it became "Prima sedes, corona regis, et regni caput."

[1] The coins bearing the name of מחנת are no longer assigned to Panormus; but certain coins with the name צץ (Ziz; about 410 B.C.) belong to it.

During the Norman reigns Palermo was the main centre of Sicilian history, especially during the disturbances in the reign of William the Bad (1154–1166). The emperor Henry VI. entered Palermo in 1194, and it was the chief scene of his cruelties. In 1198 his son Frederick, afterwards emperor, was crowned there. After his death Palermo was for a moment a commonwealth. It passed under the dominion of Charles of Anjou in 1266. In the next year, when the greater part of Sicily revolted on behalf of Conradin, Palermo was one of the few towns which was held for Charles; but the famous Vespers of 1282 put an

PALERMO

1. Marsovo
2. Cathedral
3. Palazzo Reale
4. La Martorana
5. San Cataldo
6. San Giovanni degli Eremiti
7. Palazzo Chiaramonti
8. S. Maria della Catena
9. Quattro Cantoni
10. Politeama Garibaldi
11. Teatro Massimo
12. University
13. Piazza Vittoria

end to the Angevin dominion. From that time Palermo shared in the many changes of the Sicilian kingdom. In 1535 Charles V. landed there on his return from Tunis. The last kings crowned at Palermo were Victor Amadeus of Savoy, in 1713, and Charles III. of Bourbon, in 1735. The loss of Naples by the Bourbons in 1798, and again in 1806, made Palermo once more the seat of a separate Sicilian kingdom. The city rose against Bourbon rule in 1820 and in 1848. In 1860 came the final deliverance, at the hands of Garibaldi; but with it came also the yet fuller loss of the position of Palermo as the capital of a kingdom of Sicily.

Site.—The original city was built on a tongue of land between two inlets of the sea. There is no doubt that the present main street, the Cassaro (Roman *castrum*, Arabic *Kasr*), Via Marmorea or Via Toledo (Via Vittorio Emmanuele), represents the line of the ancient town, with water on each side of it. Another

peninsula with one side to the open sea, meeting as it were the main city at right angles, formed in Polybius's time the *Neapolis*, or new town, in Saracen times Khalesa, a name which still survives in that of Calsa. But the two ancient harbours have been dried up; the two peninsulas have met; the long street has been extended to the present coast-line; a small inlet, called the Cala, alone represents the old haven. The city kept its ancient shape till after the time of the Norman kings. The old state of things fully explains the name Πάνορμος.

There are not many early remains in Palermo. The Phoenician and Greek antiquities in the museum do not belong to the city itself. The earliest existing buildings date from the time of the Norman kings, whose palaces and churches were built in the Saracenic and Byzantine styles prevalent in the island. Of Saracen works actually belonging to the time of Saracen occupation there are no whole buildings remaining, but many inscriptions and a good many columns, often inscribed with passages from the Koran, which have been used up again in later buildings, specially in the porch of the metropolitan church. This last was built by Archbishop Walter (*fl.* 1170)—an Englishman sent by Henry II. of England as tutor to William II. of Sicily—and consecrated in 1185, on the site of an ancient basilica, which on the Saracen conquest became a mosque, and on the Norman conquest became a church again, first of the Greek and then of the Latin rite. What remains of Walter's building is a rich example of the Christian-Saracen style, disfigured, unfortunately, by the addition of a totally unsuitable dome by Ferinando Fuga in 1781–1801. This church contains the tombs of the emperor Frederick II. and his parents—massive sarcophagi of red porphyry with canopies above them—and also the royal throne, higher than that of the archbishop; for the king of Sicily, as hereditary legate of the see of Rome, was the higher ecclesiastical officer of the two. But far the best example of the style is the chapel of the king's palace (cappella palatina), at the west end of the city. This is earlier than Walter's church, being the work of King Roger in 1143. The wonderful mosaics, the wooden roof, elaborately fretted and painted, and the marble incrustation of the lower part of the walls and the floor are very fine. Of the palace itself the greater part was rebuilt and added in Spanish times, but there are some other parts of Roger's work left, specially the hall called Sala Normanna.

Alongside of the churches of this Christian-Saracen type, there is another class which follows the Byzantine type. Of these the most perfect is the very small church of San Cataldo. But the best, much altered, but now largely restored to its former state, is the adjoining church of La Martorana, the work of George of Antioch, King Roger's admiral. This is rich with mosaics, among them the portraits of the king and the founder. Both these and the royal chapel have several small cupolas, and there is a still greater display in that way in the church of San Giovanni degli Eremiti, which it is hard to believe never was a mosque. It is the only church in Palermo with a bell-tower, itself crowned with a cupola.

Most of these buildings are witnesses in different ways to the peculiar position of Palermo in the 12th century as the "city of the threefold tongue," Greek, Arabic, and Latin. King Roger's sun dial in the palace is commemorated in all three, and it is to be noticed that the three inscriptions do not translate one another. In private inscriptions a fourth tongue, the Hebrew, is also often found. For in Palermo under the Norman kings Christians of both rites, Mahommedans and Jews were all allowed to flourish after their several fashions. In Saracen times there was a Slavonic quarter on the southern side of the city, and there is still a colony of United Greeks, or more strictly Albanians.

The series of Christian-Saracen buildings is continued in the country houses of the kings which surround the city, La Favara and Mimnerno, the works of Roger, and the better known Ziza and Cuba, the works severally of William the Bad and William the Good. The Saracenic architecture and Arabic inscriptions of these buildings have often caused them to be taken for works of the ancient ameers; but the inscriptions of themselves prove their date. All these buildings are the genuine work of Sicilian art, the art which had grown up in the island through the presence of the two most civilized races of the age, the Greek and the Saracen. Later in the 12th century the Cistercians brought in a type of church which, without any great change of mere style, has a very different effect, a high choir taking in some sort the place of the cupola. The greatest example of this is the neighbouring metropolitan church of Monreale (*q.v.*); more closely connected with Palermo is the church of San Spirito, outside the city on the south side, the scene of the Vespers.

Domestic and civil buildings from the 12th century to the 15th abound in Palermo, and they present several types of genuine national art, quite unlike anything in Italy. Of palaces the finest is perhaps the massive Palazzo Chiaramonte, now used as the courts of justice, erected subsequently to 1307. One of the halls has interesting paintings of 1377–1380 on its wooden ceiling; and in the upper storey of the court is a splendid three-light Gothic window. The later houses employ a very flat arch, the use of which goes on in some of the houses and smaller churches of the Renaissance. S. Maria della Catena may be taken as an especially good example. But the general aspect of the streets is later still, dating from mere Spanish times. Still many of the houses are stately in their way, with remarkable heavy balconies. The most striking point in the city is the central space at the crossing of the main streets, called the Quattro Cantoni. Two of the four are formed by the ancient Via Marmorea, but the Via Macqueda, which supplies the other two, was cut through a mass of small streets in Spanish times.

The city walls are now to a great extent removed. Of the gates only two remain, the Porta Nuova and the Porta Felice; both are fine examples of the baroque style, the former was erected in 1584 to commemorate the return of Charles V. fifty years earlier, the latter in 1582. Outside the walls new quarters have sprung up of recent years, and the Teatro Massimo and the Politeama Garibaldi; the former (begun by G. B. Basile and completed by his son in 1897) has room for 3200 spectators and is the largest in Italy.

The museum of Palermo, the richest in the island, has been transferred from the university to the former monastery of the Filippini. Among the most important are the objects from prehistoric tombs and the architectural fragments from Selinus, including several metopes with reliefs, which are of great importance as illustrating the development of Greek sculpture. None of the numerous Greek vases and terra-cottas is quite of the first class, though the collection is important. The bronzes are few, but include the famous ram from Syracuse. There is also the Casuccini collections of Etruscan sarcophagi, sepulchral urns and pottery. Almost the only classical antiquities from Palermo itself are Latin inscriptions of the imperial period, and two large coloured mosaics with figures found in the Piazza Vittoria in front of the royal palace in 1869: in 1906 excavations in the same square led to the discovery of a large private house, apparently of the 2nd or 3rd century A.D., to which these mosaics no doubt belonged. Of greater local interest are the medieval and Renaissance sculptures from Palermo itself, a large picture gallery, and an extensive collection of Sicilian majolica, &c.

The university, founded in 1779, rose to importance in recent years (from 300 students in 1872 to 1495 in 1897), but has slightly lost in numbers since. The city wears a prosperous and busy appearance. The Marina, or esplanade at the south of the town, affords a fine sea front with a view of the bay; near it are beautiful public gardens. In the immediate neighbourhood of the city are the oldest church in or near Palermo, the Lepers' church, founded by the first conqueror or deliverer, Count Roger, and the bridge over the forsaken stream of the Oreto, built in King Roger's day by the admiral George. There are also some later medieval houses and towers of some importance. These all lie on to the south of the city, towards the hill called Monte Griffone (Griffon-Greek), and the Giant's Cave, which has furnished rich stores for the palaeontologist. On

the other side, towards Pellegrino, is the new harbour of Palermo, round which a new quarter has sprung up, including a yard capable of building ships up to 475 ft. in length, and a dry dock for vessels up to 363 ft.

The steamship traffic at Palermo in 1906 amounted to 9035 vessels, with a total tonnage of 2,403,851 tons. Palermo is one of the two headquarters (the other being Genoa) of the Navigazione Generale Italiana, the chief Italian steamship company. The principal imports were 36,567 tons of timber (a large increase on the normal figures), 21,401[1] tons of wheat and 151,360 tons of coal; while the chief exports were 116,400 gallons of wine, 37,835 tons of sumach and 122,023 tons of oranges and lemons. Finding most of its valuable rates hypothecated to the meeting of old debts, the municipality of Palermo has embarked upon municipal ownership and trading in various directions.

The plain of Palermo is very fertile, and well watered by springs and streams, of the latter of which the Oreto is the chief. It is planted with orange and lemon groves, the products of which are largely exported, and with many palm-trees, the fruit of which, however, does not attain maturity. It also contains many villas of the wealthy inhabitants of Palermo, among the most beautiful of which is La Favorita, at the foot of Monte Pellegrino on the west, belonging to the Crown.

AUTHORITIES—Besides works dealing with Sicily generally, the established local work on Palermo is *Descrizione di Palermo antico*, by Salvatore Morso (2nd ed., Palermo, 1827). Modern research and criticism have been applied in *Die mittelalterliche Kunst in Palermo*, by Anton Springer (Bonn, 1869); *Historische Topographie von Panormus*, by Julius Schubring (Lübeck, 1870); *Studii di storia palermitana*, by Adolf Holm (Palermo, 1880). See also "The Normans in Palermo," in the third series of *Historical Essays*, by E. A. Freeman (London, 1879). The description of Palermo in the second volume of Gsell-Fel's guide-book, *Unter-Italien und Sicilien* (Leipzig), leaves nothing to wish for. Various articles in the *Archivio storico siciliano* and the series of *Documenti per servire alla storia della Sicilia*, both published by the Società siciliana per la storia patria, may also be consulted.   (E. A. F.; T. As.)

PALES, an old Italian goddess of flocks and shepherds. The festival called Parilia (less correctly Palilia) was celebrated in her honour at Rome and in the country on the 21st of April. In this festival Pales was invoked to grant protection and increase to flocks and herds; the shepherds entreated forgiveness for any unintentional profanation of holy places of which their flocks might have been guilty, and leaped three times across bonfires of hay and straw (Ovid, *Fasti*, iv. 731–805). The Parilia was not only a herdsmen's festival, but was regarded as the birthday celebration of Rome, which was supposed to have been founded on the same day. Pales plays a very subordinate part in the religion of Rome, even the sex of the divinity being uncertain. A male Pales was sometimes spoken of, corresponding in some respects to Pan; the female Pales was associated with Vesta and Anna Perenna.

PALESTINE, a geographical name of rather loose application. Etymological strictness would require it to denote exclusively the narrow strip of coast-land once occupied by the Philistines, from whose name it is derived. It is, however, conventionally used as a name for the territory which, in the Old Testament, is claimed as the inheritance of the pre-exilic Hebrews; thus it may be said generally to denote the southern third of the province of Syria. Except in the west, where the country is bordered by the Mediterranean Sea, the limit of this territory cannot be laid down on the map as a definite line. The modern subdivisions under the jurisdiction of the Ottoman Empire are in no sense conterminous with those of antiquity, and hence do not afford a boundary by which Palestine can be separated exactly from the rest of Syria in the north, or from the Sinaitic and Arabian deserts in the south and east; nor are the records of ancient boundaries sufficiently full and definite to make possible the complete demarcation of the country. Even the convention above referred to is inexact: it includes the Philistine territory, claimed but never settled by the Hebrews, and excludes the outlying parts of the large area claimed in Num. xxxiv. as the Hebrew possession (from the "River of Egypt" to Hamath). However, the Hebrews themselves have preserved, in the

[1] The figures for 1905 (40,005 tons, almost entirely from Russia) were abnormally high, while those for 1906 are correspondingly below the average.

proverbial expression "from Dan to Beersheba" (Judg. xx. 1, &c.), an indication of the normal north-and-south limits of their land; and in defining the area of the country under discussion it is this indication which is generally followed.

Taking as a guide the natural features most nearly corresponding to these outlying points, we may describe Palestine as the strip of land extending along the eastern shore of the Mediterranean Sea from the mouth of the Litany or Kasimiya River (33° 30' N.) southward to the mouth of the Wadi Ghuzza; the latter joins the sea in 31° 28' N., a short distance south of Gaza, and runs thence in a south-easterly direction so as to include on its northern side the site of Beersheba. Eastward there is no such definite border. The River Jordan, it is true, marks a line of delimitation between Western and Eastern Palestine; but it is practically impossible to say where the latter ends and the Arabian desert begins. Perhaps the line of the pilgrim road from Damascus to Mecca is the most convenient possible boundary. The total length of the region is about 140 m.; its breadth west of the Jordan ranges from about 23 m. in the north to about 80 m. in the south. According to the English engineers who surveyed the country on behalf of the Palestine Exploration Fund, the area of this part of the country is about 6040 sq. m. East of the Jordan, owing to the want of a proper survey, no figures so definite as these are available. The limits adopted are from the south border of Hermon to the mouth of the Mojib (Arnon), a distance of about 140 m.; the whole area has been calculated to be about 3800 sq. m. The territory of Palestine, Eastern and Western, is thus equal to rather more than one-sixth the size of England.

There is no ancient geographical term that covers all this area. Till the period of the Roman occupation it was subdivided into independent provinces or kingdoms, different at different times (such as Philistia, Canaan, Judah, Israel, Bashan, &c.), but never united under one collective designation. The extension of the name of Palestine beyond the limits of Philistia proper is not older than the Byzantine Period.

Physical Features.—Notwithstanding its small size, Palestine presents a variety of geographical detail so unusual as to be in itself sufficient to mark it out as a country of especial interest. The bordering regions, moreover, are as varied in character as is the country itself—sea to the west, a mountainous and sandy desert to the south, a lofty steppe plateau to the east, and the great masses of Lebanon to the north. In describing the general physical features of the country, the most significant point to notice is that (though it falls westward to the sea and rises eastward to an elevated plain) the rise from west to east is not continuous, but is sharply interrupted by the deep fissure of the Ghor or Jordan valley; which, running from north to south—for the greater part of its length depressed below sea-level—forms a division in the country of both physical and political importance. In this respect the function of the river Jordan in Palestine offers a strange contrast, often remarked upon, to that of the Nile in Egypt. The former is of no use for irrigation, except in the immediate neighbourhood of its banks, and is a barrier to cross which involves the labour of a considerable ascent at any point except its most northern section. The latter is at once the great fertilizer and the great highway of the country which it serves.

Western Palestine is a region intersected by groups of mountain peaks and ranges, forming a southern extension of the Lebanon system and running southward till they finally lose themselves in the desert. The watershed of this system is so placed that from two-thirds to three-fourths of the area lies on its western side. This fact, taken in connexion with the great depth of the depression of the Ghor below the Mediterranean—already 682 ft. at the Sea of Galilee—has a peculiar effect on the configuration of the country. On the west side the slope is gradual, especially in the broad plain that skirts the coast for the greater part of its length; on the east side it is steep—precipitous indeed, towards the southern end—and intersected by valleys worn to a tremendous depth by the force of the torrents that once ran down them.

This territory of Western Palestine divides naturally into two longitudinal strips—the maritime plain and the mountain region. These it will be convenient to consider separately.

I *The Maritime Plain*, which, with a few interruptions extends along the Mediterranean coast from Lebanon to Egypt, is a strip of land of remarkable fertility. It is formed of raised beaches and sea-beds, ranging from the Pliocene period downwards, and resting on Upper Eocene sandstone. It varies greatly in width. At the mouth of the Kasimiya it is some 4 m. across, and this breadth it maintains to a short distance south of Tyre, where it suddenly narrows; until, at Ras el-Abiad, it has been necessary to

cut a passage in the precipitous face of the cliff to allow the coast-road to be carried past it. This ancient work is the well-known "Ladder of Tyre." South of this promontory the plain begins to widen again; on the latitude of Acre (Akka), from which this part of the plain takes its name, it is from 4 to 5 m. across; while farther south, at Haifa, it is of still greater width, and opens into the extensive Merj Ibn 'Amir (Plain of Esdraelon) by which almost the whole of Western Palestine is intersected. South of Haifa the promontory of Carmel once more effaces the plain; here the passage along the coast is barely 200 yds. in width. At 'Athlit, 9 m. to the south, it is about 2 m.; from this point it expands uniformly to about 20 m., which is the breadth at the latitude of Ascalon. South of this it is shut in and broken up by groups of low hills. From the Kasimiya southwards the maritime plain is crossed by numerous river-beds, with a few exceptions winter torrents only. Among the perennial streams may be mentioned the Na'aman, south of Acre; the Mukatta' Kishon, at Haifa; the Nahr ez-Zerka, sometimes called the Crocodile River—so named from the crocodiles still occasionally to be seen in it; the Nahr el-Falik; the 'Aujeh a few miles north of Jaffa and the Nahr Rubin. The surface of the plain rises gradually from the coast inland to an altitude of about 200 ft. It is here and there diversified by small hills.

II. *The Mountain Region*, the great plain of Esdraelon, which forms what from the earliest times has been recognized to be the easiest entrance to the interior of the country, cuts abruptly through the mountain system, and so divides it into two groups. Each of these may be subdivided into two regions presenting their own special peculiarities.

a. The Galilean Mountains, north of the plain of Esdraelon, fall into two regions, divided by a line joining Acre with the north end of the Sea of Galilee. The northern region (Upper Galilee) is virtually an outlier of the Lebanon Mountains. At the south end is an elevated plateau, draining into the Kasimiya. The mountains are intersected by a complex system of valleys, of which some thirty run down into the Mediterranean. The face toward the Jordan valley is lofty and steep. The highest point is Jebel Jermak, 3934 ft. above the sea; about it, on the eastern and northern sides, are lofty plateaus. The region is fruitful, and in places well wooded; it is beyond question the most picturesque part of Palestine. The southern region (Lower Galilee) shows somewhat different characteristics. It consists of chains of comparatively low hills, for the greater part running east and west, enclosing a number of elevated plains. The principal of these plains is El-Buttauf, a tract 400 to 500 ft. above sea-level, enclosed within hills 1700 ft. high and measuring 9 m. east to west and 2 m. north to south. It is marshy at its eastern end and very fertile. This is the plain of Zebulun or Asochis, of antiquity. The plain of Tur'an, southeast of El-Buttauf, is smaller, but equally fertile. Among the principal mountains of this district may be named Jebel Tur'an, 1774 ft., and Jebel et-Tur (Tabor) 1843 ft.; the latter is an isolated mass of regular shape which commands the plain of Esdraelon. Eastward the country falls to the level of the Ghor by a succession of steps, among which the lava-covered Sahel el-Ahma may be mentioned, which lies west of the cliffs overhanging the Sea of Galilee. The chief valleys of this region are the Nahr Na'aman and its branches, which runs into the sea south of Acre, and the Wadi Mukatta', or Kishon, which joins the sea at Haifa. On the east may be mentioned the Wadi er-Rubadiya, Wadi el-Hamam and Wadi Fajjas, flowing into the Sea of Galilee or else into the Jordan.

b. The great plain of Esdraelon is one of the most important and striking of the natural features of Western Palestine. It is a large triangle, having its corners at Jenin, Jebel et-Tur, and the outlet of the Wadi Mukatta', by which last it communicates with the sea-coast. On the south-west it is bounded by the range of hills that terminates in the spur of Carmel. The modern name, as above-mentioned, is Merj Ibn 'Amir (" the meadow-land of the son of 'Amir"); in ancient times it was known as the Valley of Jezreel, of which name Esdraelon is a Greek corruption; and by another name (Har-Magedon) derived from that of the important town of Megiddo—it is referred to symbolically in Rev. xvi. 16. It is the great highway, and also the great battlefield, of Palestine. At the village of Afuleh its altitude is 260 ft. above the sea-level. In winter it is swampy, and in places almost impassable. The fertility of this region is proverbial. There are several small subsidiary plains that extend from it both north and south into the surrounding mountain region; of these we need only mention a broad valley running north-eastwards between Jebel Duhi, a range 15 m. long and 1690 ft. high, on the one side, and Mt Tabor and the hills of Nazareth on the other side. East of the watershed are a number of valleys running to the Ghor; the most remarkable of these are the Wadi el-Bireh and the Wadi Jalud, the latter containing the river that flows from the fine spring called 'Ain Jalud.

c. The second of the divisions into which we have grouped the mountain system lies south of the plain of Esdraelon. This is divisible into the districts of Samaria and Judaea. In the first of these the mountain ranges are complex, appearing to radiate from a centre at which lies Merj el-Ghuruk, a small plain about 4 m. east to west and 2 m. north to south. This plain has no outlet and is marshy in the rainy season. Connected with it are other small plains unnecessary to enumerate. For the greater part the principal mountains are near the watershed; they include Jebel Fuku'a (Gilboa), a range that forms the watershed at the eastern extremity of the plain of Esdraelon. The range of Carmel (highest point 1810 ft.) must also be included in this district; it runs from the central point above mentioned—though interrupted by many passes—to the end of the promontory which makes the harbour of Haifa, at its foot, the best on the Palestine coast. The highest mountains in the Samaria district are, however, in the neighbourhood of Nablus (Shechem). They include the rugged bare mass of Gerizim (2849 ft.), the smoother cactus-clad cone of Ebal (3077), and farther south Tell 'Asur (3318) at which point begins the

PALESTINE

Judaean range. On the eastern side of the watershed the most important feature is perhaps the great valley system that connects the Mukhnah (the plain south of Nablus) with the Ghor—beginning with the impressive Wadi Bilan and proceeding through the important and abundantly watered Wadi Far'a. Tell 'Asur stands a short distance north of Beitein (Bethel). South of it is the long zigzag range known as Jebel el-Kuds, named from Jerusalem (el-Kuds) the chief town built upon it. The highest point is Neby Samwil (Mizpah), 2935 ft. above the sea, north of Jerusalem. This city itself stands at an altitude of 2500 ft. To the south of it begins the subdivision of the Judaean mountains now known as Jebel el-Khalil, from Hebron (el-Khalil), which stands in an elevated basin some 500 ft. above the altitude of Jerusalem; it is here that the Judaean Mountains attain their greatest height. South of Hebron the ridge gradually becomes lower, and finally breaks up and loses itself in the southern desert.

On the west side of the watershed the mountainous district extends about half way to the sea, broken by deep valleys and passes. Among these the most important are the Wadi Selman (Valley of Aijalon) which seems to have been the principal route to Jerusalem in ancient times; the Wadi Isma'in south of this, along which runs the modern carriage road from Jaffa to Jerusalem; and the Wadi es-Surar, a higher section of the bed of the Nahr Rubin, along which now runs the railway line; farther to the south we may mention the Wadi es-Sunt, which opens up the country from Tell es-Safi (Gath?) eastward.

Between the mountainous country of Judaea and the maritime plain is an undulating region anciently known as the Shephelah. It is composed of horizontal strata of limestone, forming groups of hills intersected by a network of small and fertile valleys. In this region, which is of great historical importance, are the remains of many ancient cities. The adjacent part of the maritime plain is composed of a rich, light brown loamy soil. Although cultivated with most primitive appliances, and with little or no attempt at irrigation or artificial fertilization, the average yield is eight- to twelve-fold annually. This part of the plain is (in European nomenclature) divided into two at about the latitude of Jaffa, that to the north being the plain of Sarona (Sharon), the southern half being the plain of the Philistines.

On the east side of the watershed the ground slopes rapidly from its height of 2500 ft. above sea-level to a maximum depth of 1300 ft. below sea-level, within a distance of about 20 m. It is a waste, destitute of water and with but scanty vegetation. It has never been brought into cultivation; but in the first Christian centuries the caves in its valleys were the chosen refuge of Christian monasticism. It descends to the level of the Ghor by terraces, deeply cut through by profound ravines such as the Wadi es-Suweinit, Wadi Kelt, Wadi ed-Dahr, Wadi en-Nar (Kedron) and Wadi el 'Areijeh.

The southern district, which includes the white marl region of Beersheba, was in ancient times called the Negeb. It is a wide steppe region which (though it contains many remains of ancient towns and settlements, and was evidently at one time a territory of great importance) is now almost entirely inhabited by nomads. It should, however, be mentioned that the Turkish government has developed a town at Beersheba, under the jurisdiction of a Kaimmakam (lieutenant-governor), since the beginning of the 20th century.

The Ghor or Jordan valley is treated in a separate article (see JORDAN). There has been no systematic survey of Eastern Palestine such as was carried out in Western Palestine between 1873 and 1880 by the officers of the Palestine Exploration Fund. A good deal of work has been done by individual travellers, but the material for a full description of its physical character is as yet lacking. Two great rivers, the Yarmuk (Hieromax) and the Zerka (Jabbok), divide Eastern Palestine into three sections, namely Hauran (BASHAN, *q.v.*) with the Jaulan west of it; Jebel Ajlun (GILEAD, *q.v.*); and the Belk'a (the southern portion of Gilead and the ancient territory of the tribe of Reuben). The latter extends southward to the Mojib, which, as we have already seen, is the southern boundary of Eastern Palestine.

It is a matter of dispute whether Hauran should be included within Palestine proper, accepting its definition as the "ancient Hebrew territory." It is a large volcanic region, entirely covered with lava and other igneous rocks. Two remarkable rows of these run in lines from north to south, through the region of the Jaulan parallel to the Ghor, and from a long distance are conspicuous features in the landscape. The soil is fertile, and there are many remains of ancient wealth and civilization scattered over its surface. South of the Yarmuk the formation is Cretaceous, Hauran basalt being found only in the eastern portion. That region is much more mountainous than Hauran. South of the Zerka the country culminates in Jebel 'Osha, a peak of Jebel Jil'ad (" the mountain of Gilead "), 3596 ft. high. From this point southward the country assumes the appearance which is familiar to those who have visited Jerusalem—at elevated plateau, bounded on the west by the precipitous cliffs known as the mountains of Moab, with but a few peaks, such as Jebel Shihan (2781 ft.) and Jebel Neba (Nebo, 2643 ft.), conspicuous above the level of the ridge by reason of superior height.

Geology.—The oldest rocks consist of gneiss and schist, penetrated by dikes and bosses of granite, syenite, porphyry and other intrusive rocks. All of these are pre-Carboniferous in age and most of them probably belong to the Archean period. They are generally concealed by later deposits, but are exposed to view along the eastern margin of the Wadi Araba, at the foot of the plateau of Edom. Similar rocks occur also at one or two places in the desert of et-Tih, while towards the south they attain a greater extension, forming nearly the whole of Sinai and of the hills on the east side of the Gulf of Akaba. These ancient rocks, which form the foundation of the country, are overlaid unconformably by a series of conglomerates and sandstones, generally unfossiliferous and often red or purple in colour, very similar in character to the Nubian sandstone of Upper Egypt. In the midst of this series there is an inconstant band of fossiliferous limestone, which has been found in the Wadi Nasb and at other places on the southern border of et-Tih, and also along the western escarpment of the Edom plateau. The fossils include *Syringopora*, *Zaphrentis*, *Productus*, *Spirifer*, &c., and belong to the Carboniferous. The sandstone which lies below the limestone is also, no doubt, of Carboniferous age; but the sandstone above is conformably overlaid by Upper Cretaceous beds and is generally referred to the Lower Cretaceous. No unconformity, however, has yet been detected anywhere in the sandstone series, and in the absence of fossils the upper sandstone may represent any period from the Carboniferous to the Cretaceous. The Upper Cretaceous is represented by limestones with bands of chert, and contains Ammonites, Baculites, Hippurites and other fossils. It covers by far the greater part of Palestine, capping the table-lands of Moab and Edom, and forming most of the high land between the Jordan and the Mediterranean. It is overlaid towards the west by similar limestones, which contain nummulites and belong to the Eocene period; and these are followed near the coast by the calcareous sandstone of Philistia, which is referred by Hull to the Upper Eocene. Lava flows of basic character, belonging to the Tertiary period, cover extensive areas in Jaulan and Hauran; and smaller patches occur in the land of Moab and also west of the Jordan, especially near the Sea of Gennesareth Of Recent deposits the most interesting are the raised beaches near the coast and the terraces of the Jordan-Araba depression. The latter indicate that at one period nearly the whole of this depression was filled with water up to a level somewhat above that of the Mediterranean.

The geological structure of the country is very simple in its broad features, but of exceptional interest. In general the stratified deposits lie nearly flat and in regular conformable succession, the lowest resting upon the floor of ancient crystalline rocks. There is, however, a slight dip towards the west, so that the newest deposits lie near the coast. Moreover, along the eastern side of the Jordan-Araba valley there is a great fault, and on the eastern side of this fault the whole series of rocks stands at a much higher level than on the west. Consequently, west of the Jordan almost the whole country is formed of the newer beds (Upper Cretaceous and later), while east of the Jordan the older rocks, sometimes down to the Archean floor, are exposed at the foot of the plateau. The western margin of the valley is possibly defined by another fault which has not yet been detected; but in any case it is clear that the great depression owes its extraordinary depth to faulting. A line of depressions of similar character has been traced by E. Suess as far south as Lake Nyasa.[1]

Climate.—Palestine belongs to the sub-tropical zone: at the summer solstice the sun is ten degrees south of the zenith. The length of the day ranges from ten to fourteen hours. The great variety of altitude and of surface characteristics gives rise to a considerable number of local climatic peculiarities. On the maritime-plain the mean annual temperature is 70° F., the normal extremes being about 50° to about 90°. The harvest ripens about a fortnight earlier than among the mountains. Citrons and oranges flourish, as do melons and palms; the latter do not fruit abundantly, but this is less the fault of climate than of carelessness in fertilization. The rainfall is rather lower than among the mountains. In the mountainous regions the mean annual temperature is about 62°, but there is a great range of variation. In winter there are often several degrees of frost, though snow very rarely lies for more than a day or two. In summer the thermometer occasionally registers as much as 100° in the shade, or even a degree or two more: this however is exceptional, and 80°-90° is a more normal maximum for the year. The rainfall is about 28 in., sometimes less, and in exceptional years as much as 10 in. in excess of this figure has been registered. The vine, fig and olive grow well in this region. The climate of the Ghor, again, is different. Here the thermometer may rise as high as 130°. The rainfall is scanty, but as no civilized person inhabits the southern end of the Jordan valley throughout the year, and it has hitherto proved impossible to establish self-registering instruments, no systematic meteorological observations have been taken. In Eastern Palestine there is even a greater range of temperature; the loftier heights are covered in winter with snow. The thermometer may range within twenty-four hours from freezing-point to 80°.

The rainy season begins about the end of November, usually with a heavy thunderstorm: the rain at this part of the year is the "former rain " of the Old Testament. The earth, baked hard by the summer heat, is thus softened, and ploughing begins at once. The wettest month, as indicated by meteorological observation, is January; February is second to it, and December third; March is also a very wet month. In April the rains come to an end (the " latter rains ") and the winter crops receive their final fertilization. The winter crops (barley and wheat) are harvested from April to June. The summer crops (millet, sesame, figs, melons, grapes, olives, &c.) are fertilized by the heavy " dews " which are one of the most remarkable climatic features of the country and to a large extent atone for the total lack of rain for one half the year. These crops are harvested from August to October.

Water Supply.—Notwithstanding the long drought, it must not be supposed that Palestine is a waterless country, except in certain districts. There are very few spots from which a spring of some sort is not accessible. Perennial streams are, and in the recent geological ages always have been, rare in the country. The whole face of the land is pitted with ancient cisterns; indeed, many hillsides and fields are on that account most dangerous to walk over by night, except for those who are thoroughly familiar with the landmarks. These cisterns are bell-shaped or bottle-shaped excavations, with a narrow circular shaft in the top, hollowed in the rock and lined with cement. Besides these, more ambitious works are to be found, all now more or less ruined, in various parts of the country (see AQUEDUCTS: *Ancient*). Such are the aqueducts, of which remains exist at Jericho, Caesarea and other places east and west of the Jordan; but especially must be mentioned the enormous reservoirs known as Solomon's Pools, in a valley between Jerusalem and Hebron, by which the former city was supplied with water through an elaborate system of conduits. Many of these aqueducts, as well as countless numbers of now leaky cisterns, could with but little trouble be brought into use again, and would greatly enhance the fertility of the country. The most abundant springs in Palestine are the sources of the Jordan at Banias and at Tell el-Kadi. A considerable number of springs in the country are brackish, being impregnated with chemicals of various kinds or (when near a town) with sewage. The latter is the case of the Virgin's Fountain (Ain Umm ed-Daraj), which is the only natural source of water in the neighbourhood of Jerusalem.

Hot springs are found in various parts of the country, especially at El-Hamma, about 1 m. south of Tiberias, where the water has a temperature of 140° F. This is still used for curative purposes, as it was in the days of Herod, but it is neglected and dirty. The spring of the Zerka Ma'in (Callirrhoe) has a temperature of 142° F. There are also hot sulphur springs on the west side of the Dead Sea. Those of El-Hamma, below Gadara, are from 104° to 120° F. in temperature.

Fauna.—It has been calculated that about 595 different species of vertebrate animals are recorded or said to be found in Palestine—about 113 being mammals (including a few now extinct), 348 birds (including 30 species peculiar to the country), 91 reptiles and 43 fishes. Of the invertebrata the number is unknown, but it must be enormous. The most important domestic animals are the sheep and the goat; the breed of oxen is small and poor. The camel, the horse and the donkey are the draught animals; the flesh of the first

---

[1] See Lortet, *La Mer Morte* (Paris, 1877); E. Hull, *Mount Seir, Sinai and Western Palestine* (London, 1885); and *Memoir on the Geology and Geography of Arabia Petraea, Palestine and adjoining Districts* (London, 1886).

is eaten by the poorer classes, as is also occasionally that of the second. The dogs, which prowl in large numbers round the streets of towns and villages, are scarcely domesticated; much the same is true of the cats. Wild cats, cheetahs and leopards are found, but they are now rare, especially the latter. The lion, which inhabited the country in the time of the Hebrews, is now extinct. The most important wild animals are the hyena, wolf (now comparatively rare), fox and jackal. Bats, various species of rodents, and gazelles are very common, as is the ibex in the valleys of the Dead Sea. Among the most characteristic birds may be mentioned eagles, vultures, owls, partridges, bee-eaters and hoopoes; singing birds are on the whole uncommon. Snakes—many of them venomous—are numerous, and there are many varieties of lizards. The crocodile is seen (but now very rarely) in the Nahr ez-Zerka. Scorpions and large spiders are a universal pest.

Flora.—The flora of Palestine has a considerable range and variety, owing to the variation in local climatic conditions. In the Jordan valley the vegetation has a semi-tropical character, consonant with the great heat, which here is normal. The coast-plain has another type, *i.e.* the ordinary vegetation of the Mediterranean littoral. In the mountains the flora is, naturally, scantier than in these two more favoured regions, but even here there is a rich variety. In all parts of the country the contrast between the landscape in early spring and later, when the cessation of rains and the increase of heat has burnt up the vegetation, is very remarkable.

Population.—The inhabitants of Palestine are composed of a large number of elements, differing widely in ethnological affinities, language and religion. It may be interesting to mention, as an illustration of their heterogeneousness, that early in the 20th century a list of no less than fifty languages, spoken in Jerusalem as vernaculars, was there drawn up by a party of men whose various official positions enabled them to possess accurate information on the subject.[1] It is therefore no easy task to write concisely and at the same time with sufficient fullness on the ethnology of Palestine.

There are two classes into which the population of Palestine can be divided—the nomadic and the sedentary. The former is especially characteristic of Eastern Palestine, though Western Palestine also contains its full share. The pure Arab origin of the Bedouins is recognized in common conversation in the country, the word "Arab" being almost restricted to denote these wanderers, and seldom applied to the dwellers in towns and villages. It should be mentioned that there is another, entirely independent, nomad race, the despised Nowar, who correspond to the gipsies or tinkers of European countries. These people live under the poorest conditions, by doing smith's work; they speak among themselves a Romani dialect, much contaminated with Arabic in its vocabulary.

The sedentary population of the country villages—the fellahin, or agriculturists—is, on the whole, comparatively unmixed; but traces of various intrusive strains assert themselves. It is by no means unreasonable to suppose that there is a fundamental Canaanite element in this population: the "hewers of wood and drawers of water" often remain undisturbed through successive occupations of a land; and there is a remarkable correspondence of type between many of the modern fellahin and skeletons of ancient inhabitants which have been recovered in the course of excavation. New elements no doubt came in under the Assyrian, Persian and Roman dominations, and in more recent times there has been much contamination. The spread of Islam introduced a very considerable Neo-Arabian infusion. Those from southern Arabia were known as the Yaman tribe, those from northern Arabia the Kais (Qais). These two divisions absorbed the previous peasant population, and still nominally exist; down to the middle of the 19th century they were a fruitful source of quarrels and of bloodshed. The two great clans were further subdivided into families, but these minor divisions are also being gradually broken down. In the 19th century the short-lived Egyptian government introduced into the population an element from that country which still persists in the villages. These newcomers have not been completely assimilated with the villagers among whom they

[1] This list was intentionally made as exhaustive as possible, and included some languages (such as Welsh) spoken by one or two individual residents only. But even if, by omitting these accidental items, the list be reduced to thirty, a sufficient number will be left to indicate the cosmopolitan character of the city.

have found a home; the latter despise them, and discourage intermarriage.

Some of the larger villages—notably Bethlehem—which have always been leavened by Christianity, and with the development of industry have become comparatively prosperous, show tangible results of these happier circumstances in a higher standard of physique among the men and of personal appearance among the women. It is not uncommon in popular writings to attribute this superiority to a crusader strain—a theory which no one can possibly countenance who knows what miserable degenerates the half-breed descendants of the crusaders rapidly became, as a result of their immoral life and their ignorance of the sanitary precautions necessary in a trying climate.

The population of the larger towns is of a much more complex nature. In each there is primarily a large Arab element, consisting for the greater part of members of important and wealthy families. Thus, in Jerusalem, much of the local influence is in the hands of the families of El-Khalidi, El-Husseini and one or two others, who derive their descent from the heroes of the early days of Islam. The Turkish element is small, consisting exclusively of officials sent individually from Constantinople. There are very large contingents from the Mediterranean countries, especially Armenia, Greece and Italy, principally engaged in trade. The extraordinary development of Jewish colonization has since 1870 effected a revolution in the balance of population in some parts of the country, notably in Jerusalem. There are few residents in the country from the more eastern parts of Asia—if we except the Turkoman settlements in the Jaulan, a number of Persians, and a fairly large Afghan colony that since 1905 has established itself in Jaffa. The Mutăwileh (Motawila), who form the majority of the inhabitants of the villages north-west of Galilee, are probably long-settled immigrants from Persia. Some tribes of Kurds live in tents and huts near Lake Huleh. If the inmates of the countless monastic establishments be excluded, comparatively few from northern or western Europe will remain: the German "Templar" colonies being perhaps the most important. There must also be mentioned a Bosnian colony established at Caesarea Palestina, and the Circassian settlements placed in certain centres of Eastern Palestine by the Turkish government in order to keep a restraint on the Bedouin: the latter are also found in Galilee. There was formerly a large Sudanese and Algerian element in the population of some of the large towns, but these have been much reduced in numbers since the beginning of the 20th century: the Algerians however still maintain themselves in parts of Galilee.

The most interesting of all the non-Arab communities in the country, however, is without doubt the Samaritan sect in Nablus (Shechem); a gradually disappearing body, which has maintained an independent existence from the time when they were first settled by the Assyrians to occupy the land left waste by the captivity of the kingdom of Israel.

The total population of the country is roughly estimated at 650,000, but no authentic official census exists from which satisfactory information on this point is obtainable. Some two-thirds of this number are Moslems, the rest Christians of various sects, and Jews. The largest town in Palestine is Jerusalem, estimated to contain a population of about 60,000. The other towns of above 10,000 inhabitants are Jaffa (45,000), Gaza (35,000), Safed (30,000), Nablus (25,000), Kerak (20,000), Hebron (18,500), Es-Salt (15,000), Acre (11,000), Nazareth (11,000).

The above remarks apply to the permanent population. They would be incomplete without a passing word on the non-permanent elements which at certain seasons of the year are in the principal centres the most conspicuous. Especially in winter and early spring crowds of European and American tourists, Russian pilgrims and Bokharan devotees jostle, one another in the streets in picturesque incongruity.

Political Divisions.—Under the Ottoman jurisdiction Palestine has no independent existence. West of the Jordan, and to about half-way between Nablus and Jerusalem, is the southern portion of the vilayet or province of Beirut. South of this point is the sanjak[1] of Jerusalem, to which Nazareth with its immediate neighbourhood is added, so as to bring all the principal " Holy Places " under one jurisdiction. East of the Jordan the country forms part of the large vilayet of Syria, whose centre is at Damascus.

Communications.—Until 1892 communication through the country was entirely by caravan, and this primitive method is still followed over the greater part of its area. On the 26th of September of that year a railway between Jaffa and Jerusalem, with five intermediate stations, was opened, and has much facilitated transit between the coast and the mountains of Judaea. A railway from Haifa to Damascus was opened in 1905; it runs across the Plain of Esdraelon, enters the Ghor at Beisan, then, turning northwards, impinges on the Sea of Galilee at Samakh, and runs up the valley of the Yarmuk to join, at ed-Der'a, the line of the third railway. This was undertaken in 1901 to connect Damascus with Mecca; in 1906 it was finished as far as Ma'an, and in 1908 the section to Medina was completed. Carriage-roads also began to be constructed during the last decade of the 19th century. They are on the whole carelessly made and maintained, and are liable to go badly and more or less permanently out of repair in heavy rain. Of completed roads the most important are from Jaffa to Haifa, Jaffa to Nablus, Jaffa to Jerusalem, Jaffa to Gaza; Jerusalem to Jericho, Jerusalem to Bethlehem with a branch to Hebron, Jerusalem to Khan Lubban —ultimately to be extended to Nablus; and Gaza to Beersheba. Other roads have been begun in Galilee (*e.g.* Haifa to Tiberias and to Jenin); but in this respect the northern province is far behind the southern. For the rest there is a network of tracks, all practically impassable by wheeled vehicles, extending over the country and connecting the towns and villages one with another.

Industries.—There are no mines and few manufactures of importance in Palestine: the country is entirely agricultural. Although the processes are primitive and improvements are discouraged, both by the policy of the government and by an indolence and suspiciousness of innovation natural to the people themselves, fine crops of cereals are yielded, especially in the large wheat-lands of Hauran. Besides wheat, the following crops are to a greater or less extent cultivated—barley, millet, sesame, maize, beans, peas, lentils, kursenni (a species of vetch used as camel-food) and, in some parts of the country, tobacco. The agriculturist has many enemies to contend with, the tax-gatherer being perhaps the most deadly; and drought, earthquakes, rats and locusts have at all periods been responsible for barren years.

The fruit trade is very considerable. The value of the oranges exported from Jaffa in 1906 was £162,000; this amount increases annually, and of course in addition a considerable quantity is retained for home consumption. Besides these are grown melons, mulberries, bananas, apricots, quinces, walnuts, lemons and citron. The culture of the vine—formerly an important staple, as is proved by the countless ancient wine-presses scattered over the rocky hillsides of the whole country—fell to some extent into desuetude, no doubt owing to the Moslem prohibition of wine-drinking. It is, however, rapidly returning to favour, principally under Jewish auspices, and numerous vineyards now exist at different centres. All over the country are olive-trees, the fruit and oil of which are a staple product of the country; the trade is however hampered by an excessive tax on trees, which not only discourages plantation, but has the unfortunate effect of encouraging destruction. Other fruit trees are abundant, though less so than those we have mentioned: such are pomegranates, pears, almonds, peaches, and, in the warmer part of the country, palms. Apples are few and poor in quality. The *kharrub* (*carob*) is common and yields a fruit eaten by the poorer classes.[2] Of ordinary table vegetables a considerable quantity and variety are grown: such are the cabbage, cauliflower, *solanum* (egg-plant), cucumber, *hibiscus* (bamieh), lettuce, carrot, artichoke, &c. The potato is also grown in considerable quantities.

Beside the agricultural there is a considerable pastoral industry, though it is principally confined to production for home consumption. Sheep and goats are bred throughout the country; but the breeding of the beasts of burden (donkeys, horses, camels) is chiefly in the hands of the Bedouin.

Of the manufactures the following call for mention: pottery (at Gaza, Ramleh and Jerusalem); soap (from olive oil, principally at Nablus); we may perhaps also extend the term to include the collecting of salt (from the Dead Sea). This last is a government monopoly, but illicit manufacture and smuggling are highly organized. Some of the minor industries, such as bee-keeping, are practised with success by a few individuals. Other industries of less importance are basket-making, weaving, and silk and cotton

manufacture. Stone-quarrying has been fostered since 1900 by the great development of building at Jerusalem and other places. Wine is manufactured by several of the German and Jewish colonies, and by some of the monastic establishments. Regular industrial work is however handicapped by competition with the tourist trade in its several branches—acting as guides and camp servants, manufacture and sale of " souvenirs " (carved toys and trinkets in mother-of-pearl and olive-wood, forged antiquities and the like), and the analogous trade in *objets de piété* (rosaries, crosses, crude religious pictures, &c.) for pilgrims. Travellers in the country squander their money recklessly, and these trades, at once easy and lucrative, are thus fatally attractive to the indolent Syrian and prejudicial to the best interests of the country. (R. A. S. M.)

History

I.—*Old Testament History.*

Palestine is essentially a land of small divisions, and its configuration does not fit it to form a separate entity; it " has never belonged to one nation and probably never will."[3] Its position gives the key to its history. Along the west coast ran the great road for traders and for the campaigns which have made the land famous. The seaports (more especially in Syria, including Phoenicia), were well known to the pirates, traders and sea-powers of the Levant. The southernmost, Gaza, was joined by a road to the mixed peoples of the Egyptian Delta, and was also the port of the Arabian caravans. Arabia, in its turn, opens out into both Babylonia and Palestine, and a familiar route skirted the desert east of the Jordan into Syria to Damascus and Hamath. Damascus is closely connected with Galilee and Gilead, and has always been in contact with Mesopotamia, Assyria, Asia Minor and Armenia. Thus Palestine lay at the gate of Arabia and Egypt, and at the tail end of a number of small states stretching up into Asia Minor; it was encircled by the famous ancient civilizations of Babylonia, Assyria, South Arabia and Egypt, of the Hittites of Asia Minor, and of the Aegean peoples. Consequently its history cannot be isolated from that of the surrounding lands. Recent research in bringing to light considerable portions of long-forgotten ages is revolutionizing those impressions which were based upon the Old Testament—the sacred writings of a small fraction of this great area; and a broad survey of the vicissitudes of this area furnishes a truer perspective of the few centuries which concern the biblical student.[4] The history of the Israelites is only one aspect of the history of Palestine, and this is part of the history of a very closely interrelated portion of a world sharing many similar forms of thought and custom. It will be necessary here to approach the subject from a point of view which is less familiar to the biblical student, and to treat Palestine not merely as the land of the Bible, but as a land which has played a part in history for certainly more than 4000 years. The close of Old Testament history (the book of Nehemiah) in the Persian age forms a convenient division between ancient Palestine and the career of the land under non-oriental influence during the Greek and Roman ages. It also marks the culmination of a lengthy historical and religious development in the establishment of Judaism and its inveterate rival Samaritanism. The most important data bearing upon the first great period are given elsewhere in this work, and it is proposed to offer here a more general survey.[5]

To the prehistoric ages belong the palaeolithic and neolithic **Beginning** flints, from the distribution of which an attempt might be made **of history.** to give a synthetic sketch of early Palestinian man. A burial cave at Gezer has revealed the existence of a race of slight build and stature, muscular, with elongated crania, and thick and heavy skull-bones. The[6]

[1] A *sanjak* is usually a subordinate division of a *vilayet*, but that of Jerusalem has been independent ever since the Crimean War. This change was made on account of the trouble involved in referring all complications (arising from questions relating to the political standing of the holy places) to the superior officials of Beirut or Damascus, as had formerly been necessary.

[2] Sometimes imagined to be the " locusts " eaten by John the Baptist, on which account the tree is often called the locust-tree. But it was the insect which John used to eat; it is still eaten by the fellahin.

[3] G. A. Smith, *Hist. Geog. of the Holy Land*, p. 58. This and the author's art. " Trade and Commerce," *Ency. Bib.* vol. iv., and his *Jerusalem* (London, 1907), are invaluable for the relation between Palestinian geography and history. For the wider geographical relations, see especially D. G. Hogarth, *Nearer East* (London, 1902).

[4] See especially the writings of H. Winckler, in the 3rd ed. of Schrader's *Keilinschriften und das Alte Test.* (Berlin, 1903); his *Religionsgeschichtlicher u. geschichtlicher Orient* (1906), &c.

[5] See the articles on the surrounding countries and peoples, and, for the biblical traditions, art. JEWS.

[6] See H. Vincent, *Canaan d'après l'exploration récente* (Paris, 1907), pp. 374 sqq., also pp. 392-426.

people lived in caves or rude huts, and had domesticated animals (sheep, cow, pig, goat), the bones of which they fashioned into various implements. Physically they are quite distinct from the normal type, also found at Gezer, which was taller, of stronger build, with well-developed skulls, and is akin both to the Sinaitic and Palestinian type illustrated upon Egyptian monuments from c. 3000 B.C., and to the modern native.[1] The study of Oriental ethnology in the light of history is still very incomplete, but the regular trend of events points to a mixture of races from the south (the home of the Semites) and the north. At what period Palestine first became the " Semitic " land, which it has always remained, is uncertain; nor can one decide whether the characteristic megalithic monuments, especially to the east of the Jordan, are due to the first wave which introduced the Semitic (Canaanite) dialect and the place-names. At all events during the last centuries of the third millennium B.C., remarkable for the high state of civilization in Babylonia, Egypt and Crete, Palestine shares in the active life and intercourse of the age; and while its fertile fields are visited by Egypt, Babylonia (under Gimil-Sin, Gudea and Sargon) claims some supremacy over the west as far as the Mediterranean.

A more definite stage is reached in the period of the Hyksos (c. 1700), the invaders of Egypt, whose Asiatic origin is suggested *inter alia* by the proper-names which include "Jacob" and "Anath" as deities.[2] After their expulsion it is very significant to find that Egypt forthwith enters upon a series of campaigns in Palestine and Syria as far as the Euphrates, and its successes over a district whose political fate was bound up with Assyria and Asia Minor laid the foundation of a policy which became traditional. Apart from rather disconnected details which belong properly to the history of Babylonia and Egypt, it is not until about the 16th century B.C. that Palestine appears in the clear light of history, and henceforth its course can be traced with some sort of continuity. Of fundamental importance are the Amarna cuneiform tablets discovered in 1887, containing some of the political correspondence between Western Asia and Egypt for a few years of the reigns of Amenophis III. and IV. (c. 1414–1360).[3] The first Babylonian dynasty, now well known for its Khammurabi, belonged to the past, but the cuneiform script and language are still used among the Hittites of Asia Minor (centring at Boghaz-keui) and the kings of Syria and Palestine. Egypt itself was now passing from its greatness, and the Hittites (q.v.)—the term is open to some criticism—were its rivals for the possession of the intervening lands. Peoples (apparently Iranian) of Hittite connexion from the powerful state of Mitanni (Northern Syria and Mesopotamia) had already left their mark as far south as Jerusalem, as may be inferred from the personal names,[4] and to the intercourse with (apparently) Aegean culture revealed by excavation, the letters add references to mercenaries and bands from Meluḫḫa (viz. Arabia), Mesopotamia and the Levant. The diminutive cities of this cosmopolitan Palestine were ruled by kings, not necessarily of the native stock; some were appointed—and even anointed—by the Egyptian king, and the small extent of these city-states is obvious from the references to the kings of such near-lying sites as Jerusalem, Gezer, Ashkelon and Lachish. Torn by mutual jealousy and intrigue, and forming little confederations among

themselves, they were united by their common recognition of the Egyptian suzerain, their court of appeal, or in some short-lived attempt to withstand him. Apart from Jerusalem and a few towns on the coast, the real weight lay to the north, and especially in the state of Amor.[5] It is an age of internal disorganization and of heavy pressure by land and by sea from Northern Syria and Asia Minor. The land seethes with excitement, and Palestine, wavering between allegiance to Egypt and intrigues with the great movements at its north, is unable to take any independent line of action. The letters vividly describe the approach of the enemy, and, in appealing to Egypt, abound in protestations of loyalty, complaints of the disloyalty of other kings and excuses for the writers' suspicious conduct. Of exceptional interest are the letters from Jerusalem describing the hostility of the maritime coast and the disturbances of the Ḫabiru (" allies "), a name which, though often equated with that of the Hebrews, may have no ethnological or historical significance.[6] But Egypt was unable to help the loyalists, even ancient Mitanni lost its political independence, and the supremacy of the Hittites was assured. The history of the age illustrated by the Amarna letters is continued in the tablets found at Boghaz-keui, the capital of the old Hittite Empire.[7] Subsequent Egyptian evidence records that Seti I. (c. 1320) of the XIXth Dynasty led an expedition into Palestine, but struggles with the Hittites continued until Rameses II. (c. 1300) concluded with them an elaborate treaty which left him little more than Palestine. Even this province was with difficulty maintained: the disturbances in the Levant and in Asia Minor (which belong to Aegean and Hittite history) and the revival of Assyria were reshaping the political history of Western Asia.

Under Rameses III. (c. 1200–1169) we may recognize another age of disorganization in Palestine, in the movements with which the Philistines (q.v.) were concerned. Nevertheless, Egypt seems to have enjoyed a fresh spell of extended supremacy, and Rameses apparently succeeded in recovering Palestine and some part of Syria. But it was the close of a lengthy period during which Egypt had endeavoured to keep Palestine detached from Asia, and Palestine had realized the significance of a powerful empire at its south-western border. Somewhat later Tiglath-Pileser (c. 1100) pushed the limits of Assyrian suzerainty westwards over the lands formerly held by the great Hittite Empire. It is at this age, when the external evidence becomes extremely fragmentary, that new political movements were inaugurated and new confederations of states sprang into existence. Palestine had been politically part of Egypt or of the Hittite Empire; we now reach the stage where it becomes more closely identified with Israelite history.

Palestine had not as yet been absorbed by any of the great powers with whose history and culture it had been so closely bound up for so many centuries. In the " Amarna" age the little kings had a certain measure of independence, provided they guarded the royal caravan routes, paid tribute, refrained from conspiracy, and generally supported their suzerain and his agents. However profound the influence of Babylonia may have been, excavation has discovered comparatively few specific traces of it. Although cuneiform was used, the Palestinian letters show that the native language, as in the case of earlier proper-names, was most nearly akin to the later " Canaanite " (Hebrew, Moabite and Phoenician). In view of the relations subsisting among Palestine, Mitanni and the Hittites, it is evident that Babylonian *The Amarna period.*

---

[1] For fuller treatment of the data see R. A. S. Macalister's complete memoir of the Gezer excavations.

[2] Reference may be made to Ed. Meyer's admirable survey of Oriental history down to this age, *Gesch. d. Altertums* (Berlin, 1909), also to J. H. Breasted, *Hist. of Egypt* (London, 1906), bks. i.–iv.; and L. W. King, *Hist. of Bab. and Ass* vol. i. (London, 1910). Some knowledge of the culture, religion, history and interrelations over the area of which Palestine formed part is indispensable for any careful study of the ages upon which we now enter.

[3] See the admirable edition by J. A. Knudtzon, with full notes by O. Weber (Leipzig, 1907–1910). For their bearing on Palestine, see especially P. Dhorme, *Rev. biblique* (1908), pp. 500–519; (1909), pp. 50–73, 368–385.

[4] Dhorme, *op. cit.* (1909), pp. 60 sqq.; H. R. Hall, *Proc. Soc. Bibl. Arch.* (1909), xxxi. 233 seq.; Weber, *op. cit.*, p. 1088 seq.; cf. A. H. Sayce, *Arch. of Cuneiform Inscr.* (1907), pp. 193 sqq.

[5] Amor (Ass. *Amurru*, Bibl. *Amorite*), lay north of Lebanon and behind Phoenicia: but the term fluctuates (Weber, *op. cit.*, 1132 sqq.). See art. AMORITES, and A. T. Clay, *Amurru* (Philadelphia, 1909).

[6] See H. Winckler, *Alior. Forschung.* (1902), iii. 22; W. M. Müller in I. Benzinger, *Heb. Archäol.* (1907), p. 445; B. Eerdmans, *Alttest. Stud.* (1908), ii. 61 sqq.; Dhorme, *op. cit.* (1909), pp. 677 sqq. The movement of the Ḫabiru cannot be isolated from that represented in other letters (where the enemy are not described by this term), and their steps do not agree with those of the invading Israelites in the book of Joshua (q.v.).

[7] H. Winckler, *Mitteil. d. deutschen Orient-Gesell.* 2. Berlin (1907) No. 35; cf. J. Garstang, *Land of Hittites* (London, 1910), 326 sqq.

influence could have entered indirectly; and until one can determine how much is specifically Babylonian the analogies and parallels cannot be made the ground for sweeping assertions. The influence of a superior power upon the culture of a people cannot of course be denied; but history proves that it depends upon the resemblance between the two peoples and their respective levels of thought, and that it is not necessarily either deep or lasting. A better case might be made for Egypt; yet notwithstanding the presence of its colonies, the cult of its gods, the erection of temples or shrines, and the numerous traces of intercourse exposed by excavation, Palestine was Asiatic rather than Egyptian. Indeed Asiatic influence made itself felt in Egypt before the Hyksos age, and later, and more strongly, during the XVIIIth and following Dynasties, and deities of Syro-Palestinian fame (Resheph, Baal, Anath, the Baalath of Byblos, Kadesh, Astarte) found a hospitable welcome. On the whole, there was everywhere a common foundation of culture and thought, with local, tribal and national developments; and it is useful to observe the striking similarity of religious phraseology throughout the Semitic sources, and its similarity with the ideas in the Egyptian texts. And this becomes more instructive when comparison is made between cuneiform or Egyptian sources extending over many centuries and particular groups of evidence (Amarna letters, Canaanite and Aramaean inscriptions, the Old Testament and later Jewish literature to the Talmud), and pursued to the customs and beliefs of the same area to-day. The result is to emphasize (a) the inveterate and indissoluble connexion between religious, social and political life, (b) the differences between the ordinary current religious conceptions and specific positive developments of them, and (c) the vicissitudes of these particular growths in their relation to history.[1]

Religion. There is reason to believe that the religion of Palestine in the Amarna age was no inchoate or inarticulate belief; like the material culture it had passed through the elementary stages and was a fully established though not, perhaps, a very advanced organism. There were doubtless then, as later, numerous local deities, closely connected with local districts, differing perhaps in name, but the centre of similar ideas as regards their relations to their worshippers. Commercial and political intercourse had also brought a knowledge of other deities, who were worth venerating, or who were the survivors of a former supremacy, or whose recognition was enforced. It is particularly interesting to find in the Amarna letters that the supremacy of Egypt meant also that of the national god, and the loyal Palestinian kings acknowledge that their land belonged to Egypt's king and god. In accordance with what is now known to be a very widespread belief, the kingship was a semi-divine function, and the Pharaoh was the incarnation of Amon-Re. This would bring a greater coherence of worship among the chaos of local cults. The petty kings naturally recognize the identity of the Pharaoh, and they hail him as their god and identify him with the heads of their own pantheon. Thus he is called—in the cuneiform letters—their Shamash or their Addu. The former, the sun-deity, god of justice, &c., was already well known, to judge from Palestinian place-names (Beth-Shemesh, &c.). The latter, storm or weather god, or, in another aspect, god of rain and therefore of fertility, is specifically West Asiatic, and may be equated with Hadad and Ramman (see below). He is presumably *the* Baal who is associated with thunder and lightning, and with the bull, and who was familiar to the Egyptians of the XIXth and XXth Dynasties in the adulations of their divine king. He is probably also "the lord of the gods" (the head of a pantheon) invoked in a private cuneiform tablet unearthed at Taanach.[2] Besides these gods, and others whose fame may be inferred (Dagon,

Nebo, Nergal, &c.), there were the closely-related goddesses Ashira and Ishtar-Astarte (the Old Testament Asherah and Ashtoreth). Possibly the name Yahweh (see JEHOVAH) had already entered Palestine, but it is not prominent, and if, as in the case of certain other deities, the extension of the name and cult went hand-in-hand with political circumstances, these must be sought in the problems of the Hebrew monarchy.[3]

Rise of the Hebrew Monarchy. At an age when there were no great external empires to control Palestine the Hebrew monarchy arose and claimed a premier place amid its neighbours (c. 1000). How the small rival districts with their petty kings were united into a kingdom under a single head is a disputed question; the stages from the half-Hittite, half-Egyptian land to the independent Hebrew state with its national god are an unsolved problem. Biblical tradition quite plausibly represents a mighty invasion of tribes who had come from Southern Palestine and Northern Arabia (Elath, Ezion-geber)—but primarily from Egypt—and, after a series of national "judges," established the kingship. But no place can be found for this conquest, *as it is described,* either before the "Amarna" age (the date, following 1 Kings vi. 1) or about the time of Rameses II. and Mineptah (see Exod. I. 11); and if the latter king (c. 1244) records the subjugation of the people (? or land) "Israel," the complicated history of names does not guarantee the absolute identity of this "Israel" either with the pure Israelite tribes which invaded the land or with the intermixed people after this event (see JEWS: §§ 6-8). Whatever may have been the extent of this invasion and the sequel, the rise and persistence of an independent Palestinian kingdom was an event which concerned the neighbouring states. Its stability and the necessary furtherance of commerce, usual among Oriental kings, depended upon the attitude of the maritime coast (Philistia and Phoenicia), Edom, Moab, Ammon, Gilead and the Syrian states; and the biblical and external records for the next four centuries (to 586) frequently illustrate situations growing out of this interrelation. The evidence of the course of these crucial years is unequal and often sadly fragmentary, and is more conveniently noticed in connexion with the biblical history (see JEWS: §§ 9-17). A conspicuous feature is the difficulty of maintaining this single monarchy, which, however it originated, speedily became two rival states (Judah and Israel). These are separated by a very ambiguous frontier, and have their geographical and political links to the south and north respectively. The balance of power moves now to Israel and now to Judah, and tendencies to internal disintegration are illustrated by the dynastic changes in Israel and by the revolts and intrigues in both states. As the power of the surrounding empires revived, these entered again into Palestinian history. As regards Egypt, apart from a few references in biblical history (e.g. to its interference in Philistia and friendliness to Judah, see PHILISTINE), the chief event was the great invasion by Sheshonk (Shishak) in the latter part of the 10th century; but although it appears to be an isolated campaign, contact with Egypt, to judge from the archaeological results of the excavations, was never intermittent. The next definite stage is the dynasty of the Israelite Omri (*q.v.*), to whom is ascribed the founding of the city of Samaria. The dynasty lasted nearly half a century, and is contemporary with the expansion of Phoenicia, and presumably therefore with some prominence of the south maritime coast. The royal houses of Phoenicia, Israel and Judah were united by intermarriage, and the last two by joint undertakings in trade and war (note also 1 Kings ix. 26 seq.). Meanwhile Assyria was gradually establishing itself westwards, and a remarkable confederation of the heirs of the old Hittite kingdom, *Approach of Assyria.* "kings of the land of Ḥatti" (the Assyrian term for the Hittites) was formed to oppose it. Southern Asia Minor, Phoenicia, Ammon, the Syrian Desert and Israel (under Omri's son "Ahab the Israelite") sent their troops to support Damascus which, in spite of the repeated efforts of tendency to identify them—was perhaps known in Palestine, as it certainly was in Egypt and among the Hittites.[4]

---

[1] Much confusion can be and has been caused by disregarding (b) and by supposing that the appearance of similar elements of thought or custom implied the presence of similar more complete organisms (*e.g.* totemism, astral religion, jurisprudence). Cf. p. 182, n. 4.

[2] See, most recently, Ungnad's translation in H. Gressmann, *Ausgrabungen in Pal. u. d. A. T.* (Tübingen, 1908), p. 19 seq. The title "lord of heaven"—whether the Sun or Addu, there was a

[3] See S. A. Cook, *Expositor,* Aug. 1910, pp. 111-127.

Shalmaneser,[1] ·was·evidently able to hold its own from 854 to 839. The anti-Assyrian alliance was, as often in west Asia, a temporary one, and the inveterate rivalries of the small states are illustrated, in a striking manner, in the downfall of Omri's dynasty and the rise of that of Jehu (842–c. 745); in the bitter onslaughts ·of Damascus upon Israel, leading nearly to its annihilation; in an unsuccessful attack upon the king of Hamath by Damascus, Cilicia and small states in north Syria; in an Israelite expedition against Judah and Jerusalem (2 Kings xiv. 13. seq.); and finally in the recovery and extension of Israelite power—perhaps to Damascus—under Jeroboam II. In such vicissitudes as these· Palestinian history proceeds upon a much larger scale than the national biblical records relate, and the external evidence is of the greatest importance for the light it throws upon the varying.situations. Syria could control the situation, and it in turn was influenced by the ambitions of Assyria, to whose advantage it was when the small states were rent by mutual suspicion and hostility. It is possible, too, that, as the states did not scruple to take advantage of the difficulties of their rivals, Assyria played a more prominent part in keeping these jealousies alive than the evidence actually states. Moreover, in the light of these moves .and counter-moves one must interpret the isolated or incomplete narratives of Hebrew history.[2] The repeated blows of Assyria did not prevent the necessity of fresh expeditions, and later, Adad-Nirari III. (812–783) claims as tributary the land of Hatti, Amor, Tyre, Sidon, "the land of Omri" (Israel), Edom and Philistia. Israel at the death of Jeroboam was rent by divided factions, whereas Judah (under Uzziah) has now become a .powerful kingdom, controlling both Philistia and the Edomite port .of Elath on the gulf of 'Akaba. The dependence of Judaean sovereignty upon these districts was inevitable; the resources of Jerusalem obviously did not rely upon the small district of Judah alone. If Ammon also was tributary (2 Chron. xxvi. 8, xxvii.), dealings with Israel and perhaps Damascus could :probably be inferred.

A new period begins with Tiglath-Pileser IV. (745–728): pro- and anti-Assyrian parties now make themselves felt, and *Prodrou-* when north Syria was taken in 738, Tyre, Sidon, *sasss of* Damascus .(under .Rezin), "Samaria." (under *Assyria.* Menahem) and a queen of Aribi were among the tributaries. It is possible that Judah (under Uzziah and Jotham) had come to an understanding with Assyria; at all events Ahaz was at once encircled by fierce attacks, and was only saved by Tiglath-Pileser's campaign against. Philistia, north Israel and Damascus. With the ·siege and fall of Damascus (733–32) Assyria gained the north, and its supremacy was recognized by the tribes of the Syrian desert and Arabia (Aribi, Tema, Sheba). In 722 Samaria, though under an Assyrian vassal (Hoshea the last king), joined with Philistia in revolt; in 720 it was allied with Gaza and Damascus, and the persistence of unrest is evident when Sargon in 715 found it necessary to transport into Samaria various peoples of the desert. Judah itself was next involved in an anti-Assyrian league (with Edom, Moab and Philistia); but apparently submitted in time; nevertheless a .decade later (701), after the change of dynasty in Assyria, it .participated in a ·great but unsuccessful effort from Phoenicia to Philistia to shake off .the yoke, and suffered disastrously.[3] ·With the crushing blows upon Syria and Samaria the centre of interest moves southwards and the history is influenced by Assyria's rival Babylonia · (under Marduk-baladan and his successors), by north Arabia and by Egypt. Henceforth there is little Samarian history, and of Judah,. for nearly a century, few political events are :recorded (Jews: § 16). Judah was under Assyrian supremacy, and, although. it was involved with Arabians in the .revolt planned by Babylonia

·[1] Recently found to be the third of that name (H. W. Hogg, *The Interpreter,* 1910, p. 329).
· [2] So e.g. in references to Ammon: Damascus and Hamath, and in Judaean relations with Philistia, Moab and Edom. ·
[3] See art. HEZEKIAH.· A recently published inscription of Sennacherib (of 694 B.C.) mentions enslaved peoples from Philistia and Tyre, but does not name Judah.

(against 'Assurbanipal); it· appears ·to have been generally quiescent.

At this stage disturbances, now by Aramaean tribes, now by Arabia, combine with the new ·rise of Egypt and· the weakness of Assyria to mark ·a turning-point in the world's history. · Psammetichus (Psamtek) I.· (663–609) with *Revival of* his Greeks, Carians, Ionians and soldiers from Pales- *Egypt.* tine and Syria, re-established once more an Egyptian Empire, and ·replaced the. fluctuating relations between Palestine and the small dynasts of the Delta by a settled policy. ·Trading intercommunication in the Levant and the constant passage to and fro of merchants brought Egypt to the front, and, in an age of archaic revival, the'effort was made to re-establish the ancient supremacy over Palestine.and Syria. The precise meaning of these changes for Palestinian history and life can only incompletely be perceived, and even the significance of the great Scythian invasion and of the greater movements with which it was connected is uncertain (see SCYTHIA). At all events, Egypt (under Necho, 609–593) prepared to take advantage of the decay of Assyria, and marched into Asia. Judah (under Josiah) was overthrown at Megiddo, where about nine centuries previously the victory of Tethmoses (Thutmose) III. had made Egypt supreme over Palestine and Syria. But Egypt was now at once confronted by the Neo-Babylonian or Chaldean Empire (under Nabopolassar), which, after annihilating Assyria with the help of the .Medians, naturally claimed a right to. the Mediterranean coast-lands. The defeat of Necho by Nebuchadrezzar at. Carchemish (605) is one of the world-famous battles.

Although Syria and Palestine now became Babylonian, this revival of the Egyptian Empire aroused ·hopes in Judah of deliverance. and led to· revolts (under Jehoiachin *Babylonian* and Zedekiah), in which Judah was apparently not` *Empire.* alone.[4] They culminated in the fall of this kingdom in 586. Henceforth the history of Palestine is disconnected and fragmentary, and the few known events of political importance are isolated and can be supplemented only by inferences from the movements of Egypt, Philistia or Phoenicia, or ·from the Old ·Testament. According to the. Chaldean Nabonidus ·(553) .all .the .kings from Gaza ·to.the Euphrates assisted in .his buildings, and the Chaldean policy generally appears to have been favourable· towards faithful vassals. Cyrus meanwhile was rising to lead the Persians against Media. After a career of success he captured Babylonia (553) and forthwith claimed, in his famous inscription, the submission of Amor. For the next 200 years Palestine remained part of the new Persian Empire.which, with all its ramifications on land and on sea, embraced the civilized .world from .the Himalayas to the Levant, until the advent of Alexander the Great (see JEWS: § 10). Very gradually the face of history underwent a complete change. Egypt had resumed its earlier connexions with the Levantine heirs of the ancient Aegeans, the old. empires of the Nearer East had practically exhausted themselves, and Palestine passed into the fresh life and thought of the Greeks. (See below, p. 617.)

In any consideration of the internal conditions in Palestine it must be observed that there is a'continuity of thought, custom and culture which is independent of political changes *Internal* · and vicissitudes of names. With the establishment *Conditions.* of an .independent monarchy· Palestine· did not enter *Northern* into. a new world. ·Whatever internal changes *Influences.* ensued ·between the "Amarna" age and 1000 B.C., they have not left their mark upon the course of culture illustrated by the excavations. These still indicate communication with Egypt and the north (Syria, Asia. Minor; Assyria and the Levant not excluded), and even when a novel· culture presents itself, as in certain graves at Gezer, the affinities are with Cyprus and Asia Minor (Caria) of the 11th or 10th century.[5] The use of

[4] Cf. Jer. xxvii. 2 seq., and the history of the Egyptian Hophra (Apries, 588–569).
[5] At present it is difficult as regards Palestine to· distinguish Aegean influence (direct and indirect) from that of Asia Minor generally. Only after the old Cretan (Minoan) culture had passed its zenith and was already decadent does it suddenly appear in Cyprus (H. R. Hall, *Proc. Soc, Bibl. Arch.* xxxi. 227).

Iron came in about this time, perhaps from the north, and biblical history (1 Kings x. 28 seq., see the commentaries) even ascribes to Solomon the import of horses from Kue and Musri (Cilicia and Cappadocia). The cuneiform script, which continued in Egypt during the XIXth and XXth Dynasties, was perhaps still used in Palestine; it was doubtless familiar at least during the Assyrian supremacy. But in the meanwhile the "North Semitic" alphabet appears (from 850) with almost identical forms in extreme north Syria (e.g. Sam'al), in Cyprus, Gezer, *Alphabet.* and in Moab. The type is very closely related to the oldest European (Etruscan) forms, and, in a less degree, to the "South Semitic" (old Minaean and Sabaean); and since it at once begins (c. 700) to develop along separate paths (Canaanite and Aramaean), it may be inferred that the common ancestor was not of long derivation. This alphabet stands in contrast to the old varying types of the Aegean and Asia Minor area and can hardly be of local origin. Under what historical circumstances it was first distributed over Palestine and Syria is uncertain; it is a plausible conjecture that once more the north is responsible.[1] Too little is known of the north as a factor in Palestinian development to allow hasty inferences, but it is certainly noteworthy, at all events, that the names Amor and Ḫatti appear to move downwards, and that "Hittite" is applied to Palestine and Philistia by the Assyrians, and to Hebron in the Old Testament, and that Ezekiel (xvi. 3) calls Canaanite Jerusalem the offspring of an Amorite and a Hittite. It is to be observed, however, that the meaning of geographical and ethnical terms for culture in general must be properly tested—the term "Phoenician" is a conspicuous case in point. Thus, in north Syria the art has Assyrian and Hittite affinities, but is provincial and sometimes rough. Some of the personal names are foreign and find analogues in Asia Minor; but even as the Philistines appear in biblical history as a "Semitic" people, so inscriptions from north Syria (c. 800-700) are in Canaanite and early Aramaean dialects, and are in entire agreement with "Semitic" thought and ideas. The deities too generally hear familiar names. In Sam'al the kings Panammu and Q-r-l have non-Semitic names (Carian), but the gods include *The Gods.* Hadad, El (God *par excellence*), Resheph and the Sun-deity. In Hamath we meet with the Baal of Heaven, Sun and Moon deities, gods of heaven and earth, and others. A god "Most High" ('*elyōn*) was perhaps already known in Hamath.[2] The "Baal of Heaven," reminiscent of the Egyptian title "lord of heaven," given long before to Resheph, appears in the pantheon of Tyre (c. 677). The reference here is probably to the inveterate Hadad who, in his Aramaean form Ramman (Rimmon), is found in Palestine. Among the Hebrews, Yahweh, some of whose features associate him with thunder, lightning and storm, and with the gifts of the earth, has now become the national god, like the Moabite Chemosh or the Ammonite Milcom. (For the Edomite gods, see EDOM.) The name is known in the form Ya'u in north Syria (8th century), and, so far as the Israelite kings are concerned, appears first in the family of Ahab. No images of Yahweh or of earlier Canaanite deities have been unearthed; but images belong to a relatively advanced stage in the development of religion, and the aniconic stage may be represented by the sacred pillars and posts, by the small models of heads of bulls, and by the evidence for calf-cults in the Old Testament.[3] Yahweh was by no means the only god. Inter-

course and alliance introduced the cults of Chemosh, Milcom, the Baal of Tyre and the Astarte of Sidon. Excavation has brought to light figurines of the Egyptian Osiris, Isis, Ptah, Anubis and especially Bes. Assyrian conquest and domination influenced the cults at all events outside Judah and Israel, and when Sargon sent skilled men to teach "the fear of God and the king" (*cyl. inscr.* 72-74) the spread of Assyrian religious ideas among the Hebrews themselves is to be expected. Certainly about 600 the Queen of Heaven, who has Assyrian traits, was a favourite object of veneration (Jer. vii. 18, xliv. 17-19, 25); yet already a century earlier the goddess "Ishtar of heaven" was worshipped by a desert tribe (see ISHMAEL), and the titles "lady of heaven," "bride of the king of heaven," had been applied centuries before to west Asiatic goddesses (Anath, Kadesh, Ashira, &c.). Although no goddess is associated with the national god Yahweh, female deities abounded, as is amply shown by the numerous plaques of the great mother-goddess found in course of excavation. The picture which the evidence furnishes is as fundamental for our conception of Palestine during the monarchies as were the Amarna tablets for the age before they arose. The external evidence does not point to any intervening hiatus, and the archaeological data from the excavations do not reveal any dislocation of earlier conditions; earlier forms have simply developed and the evolution is a progressive one. Down to and at the time of the Assyrian supremacy, Palestine in religion and history was merely part of the greater area of mingled peoples sharing the same characteristics of custom and belief. This does not mean of course that the religion had no ethical traits—ethical motives are frequently found in the old Oriental religions—but they were bound up with certain naturalistic conceptions of the relation between deities and men, and herein lay their weakness.[4]

In the age of the Assyrian supremacy Palestine entered upon a series of changes, lasting for about three centuries (from about 740), which were of the greatest significance for *Sequel of* its internal development. The sweeping conquests *the Assyrian* of Assyria were "as critical for religious as for civil *Domination.* history."[5] The brutal methods of warfare, the cruel treatment of vanquished districts or cities, and the redistribution of bodies of inhabitants, broke the old bonds uniting deities, people and land. The framework of society was shattered, communal life and religion were disorganized. As the flood poured over Syria and flowed south, Israel (Samaria) suffered grievously, and the gaps caused by war and deportation were filled up by the introduction of new settlers by Sargon, and by his successors in the 7th century. Unfortunately, there is very little evidence in the biblical history for the subsequent career of Samaria, but it is clear that the old Israel of the dynasties of Omri and Jehu received crushing blows. The fact that among the new settlers were desert tribes, suggests the introduction, not merely of a simpler culture, but also of simpler groups of ideas. In the nature of the case, as time elapsed the new population must have taken root as securely as—one must conclude—the invading Israelites had done some centuries earlier. As a matter of fact the prophets Jeremiah and Ezekiel by no means regarded the population lying to the north of Judah as strangers, and the latter in turn were ready to share the Judaean distress at the fall of Jerusalem (Jer. xli. 5), and in later years offered to assist in rebuilding Yahweh's temple. Indeed, since the Samaritans subsequently accepted the Pentateuch, and claimed to inherit the ancestral traditions of the Israelite tribes, it is of no little value in the study of Palestinian history to observe the manner in which this people of singularly mixed origin so thoroughly assimilated itself to the land and at first was virtually a Jewish sect. But Samaria was not the only land to suffer. Judah, towards the close of the 8th century, was obviously very closely bound up with Philistia, Edom and Egypt; and this and Hezekiah's dealings with the anti-Assyrian party at Ekron do not indicate that any feeling of national exclusiveness, or any abhorrence of the

[1] On the points of contact with old Cretan and Anatolian scripts see A. J. Evans, *Scripta Minoa* (Oxford, 1909), p. 80 sqq. The persistence of evidence for the importance of Aegean and Asia Minor ("Hittite") peoples in the study of Palestine and surrounding lands is one of the most interesting features of recent discovery. Cf. H. Hogarth, *Ionia and the East* (Oxford, 1909), pp. 64 sqq.; E. Meyer, *Gesch. d. Altertums,* i. §§ 490, 523.
[2] So Dhorme interprets the place-name *Ur*(light of)-*bi-lc-o-ni* (*Rev. Bibl.* 1910, p. 67).
[3] See CALF, GOLDEN, and note the representation of a 'calf at er-Rummân (Ramman = Hadad) in east Jordan (Gressmann p. 35). It is obvious that the strict injunctions in Exod. xx. 4. Deut. iv. 16 sqq., 23, 25, and other references to idolatry, are the outcome of a reaction against images.
[4] W. R. Smith, *Rel. of the Semites* (London, 1894), p. 58.
[5] Ibid. p. 35; cf. pp. 65, 77 sqq., 358.

" uncircumcised Philistines " predominated. From the description of Sennacherib's invasion it is clear that social and economic conditions must have been seriously, perhaps radically disturbed,[1] and the quiescence of Judah during the next few decades implies an internal weakness and a submission to Assyrian supremacy. During the 7th century new movements were coming from Arabia, and tribes growing ever more restless made an invasion east of the Jordan through Edom, Moab and Ammon. Although they were repulsed, this awakening of a land which has so often fed Palestine and Syria, when viewed with the increasing weakness of Assyria, and subsequent vicissitudes in the history of the Edomites, Nabataeans and East Jordan tribes, forbids us to treat the invasion as an isolated raid.[2] Later, the fall of the Judaean kingdom and the deportation of the leading classes brought a new social upheaval. The land was not denuded, and the fact that " some scores of thousands of Jews remained in Judah through all the period of the exile,"[3] even though they were " the poorest of the land," revolutionizes ordinary notions of this period. (See Jews: § 18). But the Judaean historians have successfully concealed the course of events, although, as has long been recognized, there was some movement *Inaugura- upwards from the south of Judah of groups closely tion of related to Edomite and kindred peoples of South New Palestine and Northern Arabia. The immigrants, Conditions. like the new occupants of Samaria, gradually assimilated themselves to the new soil; but the circumstances can hardly be recovered, and even the relations between Judah and Samaria can only be inferred. In the latter part of the 6th century we find some restoration, some revival of the old monarchy in the person of Zerubbabel (520 B.C.); but again the course of events is problematical (Jews, § 20).[4] Not until the middle of the 5th century do the biblical records (book of Nehemiah) furnish a foundation for any reconstruction. Here Jerusalem is in sore distress and in urgent need of reorganization. Zerubbabel's age is of the past, and any attempt to revive political aspirations is considered detrimental to the interests of the surrounding peoples and of the Persian Empire. Scattered evidence suggests that the Edomites were responsible for a new catastrophe. Amid internal and external difficulties Nehemiah proceeds to repair religious and social abuses, and there is an important return of exiles from Babylonia. The ruling classes are related partly to the southern groups already mentioned and partly to Samaria; but the kingship of old is replaced by a high-priest, and, under the influence of Babylonian Jews of the strictest principles, a breach was made between Judah and Samaria which has never been healed (Jews: § 21 seq.). Biblical history itself recognises in the times of Artaxerxes, Nehemiah and Ezra the commencement of a new era, and although only too much remains obscure we have in these centuries a series of vicissitudes which separate the old Palestine of Egyptian, Hittite, Babylonian and Assyrian supremacy from the land which was about to enter the circle of Greek and Roman civilization. This division, it may be added, also seems to leave its mark upon the lengthy archaeological history of Palestine from the earliest times to the Byzantine age. There is a certain poverty and decadence of art, a certain simplicity of civilization and a decline in the shape and decoration of pottery which seems to exhibit signs of derivation from skin prototypes elsewhere associated with desert peoples. This phase comes at a stage which severs the earlier phases (including the " Amarna " age) from those which are very closely connected.

with Seleucid and later times. Its appearance has been associated with the invasion of the Israelites or with the establishment of the independent monarchy, but on very inadequate grounds; and since it has been independently placed at the latter part of the monarchy, its historical explanation may presumably be found in that break in the career of Palestine when peoples were changed and new organizations slowly grew up.[5] The great significance of these vicissitudes for the course of internal conditions in Palestine is evident when it is observed that the subsequent cleavage between Judah and Samaria, not earlier than the 5th century, presupposes an antecedent common foundation which, in view of the history of the monarchies, can hardly be earlier than the 7th century. These centuries represent an age which the Jewish historians have partly ignored (as regards Samaria) and partly obscured (as regards the return from exile and the reconstruction of Judah); but since this age stands at the head of an historical development which leads on to Christianity and Rabbinical Judaism, it is necessary to turn from Palestine as a land in order to notice more particularly certain features of the Old Testament upon which the foregoing evidence directly bears.

The Old Testament is essentially a Palestinian, an Oriental, work and is entirely in accord with Oriental thought and custom.[6] Yet, in its characteristic religion and *Biblical* legislation there are essential spiritual and ethical *Religion.* peculiarities which give it a uniqueness and a permanent value, the reality of which becomes more impressive when the Old Testament is viewed, not merely from a Christian or a Jewish teleology, but in the light of ancient, medieval and modern Palestine. The ideas which characterize the Old Testament are planted upon lower levels of thought, and they appear in different aspects (legal, prophetical, historical) and with certain developments both within its pages and in subsequent literature. To ignore or to obscure the features which are opposed to these ideas would be to ignore the witness of external evidence and to obscure the old Testament itself. The books were compiled and preserved for definite aims, and their teaching is directed now to the needs of the people as a whole—as in the ever popular stories of Genesis—now to the inculcation of the lessons of the past, and now to matters of ritual. They are addressed to a people whose mental processes and philosophy were primitive; and since teaching, in order to be communicable, must adapt itself to current beliefs of God, man and nature—and the inveterate conservatism of man must be born in mind—the trend of ideas must not be confused with the average standard of thought.[7] The teaching was not necessarily presented in the form of an over-elaborated moral lesson, but was associated with conceptions familiar to the land; and when these conceptions are examined from the anthropological standpoint, they are found to contain much that is strange and even abhorrent to modern convictions of a purely spiritual deity. There are moreover many traces of conflicting ideas and ideals, of cruder beliefs and customs, and of attempts to remove or elevate them. In Genesis and elsewhere there are examples of popular thought which have not the characteristic spirit of the prophets, and which, it is clear, could only gradually be purified. The notion of a Yahweh scarcely less limited in power than man, the naïve views of supernatural beings and their nearness to man, and the persistence of features which stand relatively low in the scale of mental culture, only serve to enhance the reality of the spirit which inspired the endeavour to reform. There were rites and customs which only after lapse of time were considered iniquitous. Magical practices and forms of sacred prostitution and human sacrifice were familiar, and the denunciations of the prophets and the

---

[1] See G. A. Smith, *Jerusalem*, ii. 160, 196 seq.
[2] See L. B. Paton, *Early Hist. of Syria and Pal.* (London, 1902), p. 269; Winckler, *Keilinschr. u. das A.T.*, p. 151.
[3] G. A. Smith, *Jerusalem*, ii. 269.
[4] On ordinary historical grounds it is probable that there was a political reorganization and a welding of the diverse elements throughout the land (J. A. Montgomery, *The Samaritans*, Philadelphia, 1907; p. 62 seq.). There is internal literary support for this in the criticism of Deuteronomy (which appears to have in view a comprehensive Israel and Judah at this period), and of various passages evidently earlier than Nehemiah's time (see R. H. Kennett, *Journ. of Theol. Stud.*, 1905, pp. 175–181; 1906, pp. 486, 498).

[5] For the late date, see F. Petrie, *Tell-el-Hesy* (1891), p. 47 seq., and Bliss and Macalister, *Excavations in Palestine* (1902), pp. 72, 74, 101, 124; and, for the suggestion in the text, S. A. Cook, *Expositor*, (Aug. 1909), pp. 104–114.
[6] See, e.g., E. Sellin, *Alttest. Relig. im Rahmen der andern altorientalischen* (Leipzig, 1908).
[7] On the characteristics of primitive thought, see G. F. Stout, *Manual of Psychology* (London, 1907), Bk. IV., especially pp. 574–579.

lawgivers show very· vividly the persistence of what was current religion but was hostile to their teaching.[1] There is an astonishing boisterousness (cf. Lam. ii. 7), joviality and sensualism, all in striking contrast to the austerity of nomad asceticism. There is a ferocity and fanaticism which manifests itself in the belief that war was a sacred campaign of deity against deity. Even if the account of the " ban " (utter destruction) at the Israelite conquest be unhistorical, it represents current ideas (cf. Josh. vi. 17 seq.; 1 Sam. xv. 3; 2 Kings xv. 16; 2 Chron. xxv. 12 seq.), and implies imperfect views of the Godhead at a more advanced stage of religion and morality.

There are conflicting ideas of death and the dead, and among them the belief in the very human feelings and needs of the dead and in their influence for good or evil.[2] Moreover, the proximity of burial-place and sanctuary and the belief in the kindly care of the famous dead for their descendants reflect

Holy Places. " primitive " and persisting ideas which find their parallel in the holy tombs of religious· or secular heroes in modern Palestine, and exemplify the firmness of the link uniting local groups with local *numens.* " The permanence of religion at holy places in the East "[3] is one of the most important features in the relation between popular and national religion. The local centres will survive political and historical vicissitudes and the changes of national cults and sects, and may outlive the national deities. The supernatural beings may change their name and may vary externally under Greek, Roman, Mahommedan or Christian influence; but their relation to the local groups remains essentially the same, although there is no regression to earlier organic connexions. The inveterate local, one may perhaps say immediate, powers are felt to be nearer at hand than the national deity, who is more closely bound up with the changing national fortunes and with current philosophy. These smaller deities are, as it were, telluric, and the territory of each is virtually henotheistic—as also its traditions—and even as to-day the saints or patrons enjoy a more real veneration among the peasants than does the Allah of the orthodox, the long-established worship of the ancient local beings always hampered the reformers of Yahwism (cf. Jer. ii. 28, xi. 13).[4] Whether they could be regarded as so many manifestations of a single deity or as really distinct entities, there were at all events similar and well understood relations between each and its group; and although the cult was nature-worship and was attended with a licentiousness which drew forth the denunciations of the prophets, this is only one aspect of the local deity's place in the religious conceptions of his circle. The excavations (at Gezer, Megiddo, Jericho, &c.) indicate a persisting gross and cruel idolatry, utterly opposed to the demands of the law and the prophets.[5] Jerusalem and the surrounding district have ominous heathen associations.[6] Jerusalem itself lay off

[1] See generally E. Meyer, *Gesch. d. Altertums* (Berlin, 1909), i. §§ 342 sqq. Ceremonial licentiousness was perhaps of northern origin (Meyer § 345). and as a preliminary to marriage seems to have been known not only in Assyria (Herod. i. 199), but also in Palestine ("a law of the Amorites"; *Test. of Judah,* ed. R. H. Charles, xii. 2); cf. E. S. Hartland, *Anthropol. Essays . . . E. B. Tylor* (Oxford, 1907), pp. 189–202. (For miscellaneous material see J. G. Frazer, ibid. pp. 101–174: " Folk-lore in the Old Testament.")
[2] See P. Torge, *Seelenglaube u. Unsterblichkeitshoffnung im Alten Test.* (Leipzig, 1909).
[3] The title of an instructive essay by Sir W. M. Ramsay in the *Expositor,* Nov. 1906, pp. 454 sqq. The whole subject involves also the various forms and developments of hero- and saint-cults, on which cf. E. Lucius, *Anfänge d. Heiligenkultus,* &c. (Tübingen, 1904); F. Saintyves, *Saints successeurs des dieux* (Paris, 1907)
[4] On the old Baals of Palestine, see H. P. Smith, in *O. T. and Semitic Studies in Memory of W. R. Harper* (Chicago, 1908), i. 35–64. For the persistence of the " high places," see G. F. Moore, *Ency. Bib.* arts. " High Place," " Idolatry and Primitive Religion."
[5] Vincent, *Canaan,* p. 204; cf. S. R. Driver, *Modern Research as illustrating the Bible* (London, 1909), pp. 60 sqq., 90.
[6] Viz. the shrines of Chemosh, Moloch, Baal of Tyre and Astarte of Sidon (1 Kings xi. 1–8; 2 Kings xi. 18, xxiii.); the valley of Hianom (see J. A. Montgomery, *Journ. Bibl. Lit.* xxvii. i. 24–47); and the place-names Anathoth (" Anaths "), Nob (Nebo?), Beth-nimb, Beth-shemesh. The name Jerusalem may be compounded

the main line of intercourse and one may look for a certain conservatism in its famous Temple. Temples, shrines and holy places were no novelty in Palestine, and the in-

Jerusalem and the Temple. auguration of the great centre of Judaism is ascribed to Solomon the son of the great conqueror David. Phoenician aid was enlisted to build it, and the Egyptian analogies to the construction accord with the known influence of Egypt upon Phoenician art. It is the dwelling-place of the deity, the centre of the nation and of the national hopes; the fall of the Temple follows after Yahweh left it, it is rebuilt and he returns (Zech. viii. 3). The Temple is merely part of the royal palace and the government buildings (cf. Ezek. xliii. 7 seq.), and this is as significant as the king's position in its management. It is in keeping with·the old conceptions of the divine kingship, which, though· they survive only in isolated biblical references, live on in the ideals of the Messianic king and his kingdom and in the post-exilic high priest.[7] The Temple is built, ornamented and furnished on lines ·which are quite incompatible with a· spiritual religion. Mythical features abound in the cherubim . and seraphim, the pillars of Jachin and Boaz,· the mysterious Nehushtan, the bronze-sea and the lavers. These agree with the more or less clear allusions in the Old Testament to myths of creation, Eden, deluge, mountain of gods, Titanic folk, world-dragons, heavenly hosts, &c., and also with the unearthed seals, tablets, altars, &c. representing mythical ideas. The ideas occur in varying forms from Egypt to Babylonia and point to a considerable body of thought, which is not less impressive when one takes into account the instances in the Old Testament where myths have been rationalized, elevated, or otherwise removed from their older forms (e.g. the story of the birth of Moses, accounts of creation and deluge, &c.), or when one observes the subsequent uncompromising objection to a display of artistic meaning, implying that it aroused definite conceptions. To reinterpret all these features as mere symbols, the lumber of ancient days, is to avoid the problem of their introduction into the Temple, and to assume an advance of popular thought which is not confirmed by the retention and fresh developments of the old ideas both in the pseudepigraphical literature and in the literature of Rabbinical Judaism.[8] The horses of the sun-god (2 Kings xxiii. 11), too, belong to a group of ideas which may perhaps be associated with the plan of the Temple and with the old hymn of dedication (1 Kings viii. 12 seq.). At all events, when one considers the Babylonian-Assyrian conceptions of Shamash as the supreme and righteous judge, god of truth and justice, or the monotheism of Amenophis IV. and his fine hymn to the sun-god, it is certain that a corresponding Palestinian deity would not necessarily be without ethical and elevated associations.[9] In short, the place·which the Temple held in with that of a deity (Winckler, *Keil. u. A.T.* 224·seq.; G. A. Smith, *Jerusalem,* ii. 25 seq.), and the deity Sedek is curiously associated with the names of the Jerusalem priests Zadok, Jehozadak (cf. Melchizedek of Salem, Gen. xiv.), and the kings Adonizedek and Zedekiah. The strange character of the names of the first kings in Israel and Judah (Saul, David and Solomon), noticed already by A. H. Sayce (*Modern Review,* 1884, pp. 158–169), cannot easily be explained.

[7] See A. B. Davidson, *Theol. of O. T.* (Edinburgh, 1904), p. 9; J. G. Frazer, *Adonis, Attis and Osiris* (London, 1907), pp. 12 sqq., 401. Cf. the title " The Anointed of Yahweh," the simile " as a messenger (angel) of Yahweh " (2 Sam. xiv. 17, xix. 27), and the idea of the king as the embodiment of his people's safety (2 Sam. xxi. 17; Lam. iv. 20). This absence of the deification of the king is characteristic of biblical religion which recognizes Yahweh as the only king; see H. Gressmann, *Ursprung d. israel.-jüd. Eschatologie* (Göttingen, 1905), pp. 250 sqq.
[8] For examples of the persistence of the interrelated ideas—whether of astral significance or not is another question—see A. Jeremias, *Babylon im Neuen Test.* (Leipzig, 1905), *Das Alte Test. im Lichte d. Alten Orients* (1906); E. Bischoff, *Bab. Astrales im Weltbilde d. Thalmud u. Midrasch* (1907).
[9] Cf. for an excellent example of Oriental religious thought, the fine Babylonian hymn to Ishtar (i.e. Astarte), L. W. King, *Seven Tablets of Creation* (London, 1907), pp. 222–237, and the specimens in R. W. Rogers, *Rel. of Bab. and Ass. in its Relations to Israel* (London 1908), pp. 142–184. On ethical conceptions of heathen deities, see L. King, *Development of Religion* (New York, 1910), pp. 268–286.

religious thought (cf. especially Isaiah), the character of the reforms ascribed to Josiah (2 Kings xxiii.), the pictures drawn by Jeremiah and Ezekiel, and the latter's condemnation of the half-Hittite, half-Amorite capital, combine with the events of later history to prove that the religion of the national sanctuary must not be too narrowly estimated from the denunciations of more spiritual minds or from a priori views of the inevitable concomitants of either henotheism or monotheism or of a lofty ethical teaching.

There is indeed a development, but it is none the less noteworthy that the post-exilic priestly ritual preserves in the *Post-exilic Develop-ments.* worship of the universal and only God Yahweh, rites, practices and ideas which can be understood only in the light of other nature-religions, especially that of Babylonia, with which there are striking parallels.[1] For example, the ephod, an object of divination, is still retained, but it is now restricted to the high-priest; and his position as head of a theocratic state, and his ceremonial dress with its heathenish associations presuppose a past monarchy.[2] Clad in almost barbaric splendour (cf. Ecclus. xlv., l., and Jos. Ant. iii. 7, &c.) he embodies the glory of the worshipping body like the kings of old, and sometimes plays as important a part in the later political history. The priestly system, as represented in the Pentateuch, is not fitted for the desert, where its initiation is ascribed, but on independent internal critical grounds belongs to the post-exilic age, where it stands at the head of further developments. It is the adaptation of the prophets' conceptions of Yahweh to old religious ideas, the building up of new conceptions upon an old basis, a fusion "between old heathen notions and prophetic ideas," and "this fusion is characteristic of the entire priestly law."[3] The priestly religion bound together the community in a way that alone preserved Jewish monotheism; it stands at the head of a long, unintermittent history, and it is to be viewed, not so much as the climax of Old Testament religion, but as one of a series of inseparable stages. In concentrating the religious observances of the people upon Jerusalem, its Temple and its priesthood, it became less spontaneous, and its services more remote from ordinary life. It left room for rival schools and sects, both within and without the priestly circles, and for continued development of the older and non-priestly thought. These reacted upon this institutional religion, which readapted and reinterpreted itself from time to time, and when they did not help to build up another theology (as in Christianity), they ended by assuming too rigid and unprogressive a shape (see QARAITES), or, breaking away from long-tried convention, became a mysticism with mixed results (see KABBALAH). While these vicissitudes take us away from Palestine, the course of native religious thought is very significant for its relation to the earlier stages. Although the national God was at once a transcendent ruler of the universe and also near at hand to man, the unconscious religious feeling found an outlet, not only in the splendid worship at Jerusalem, but in the more immediate intercessors, divine agencies, and the like; and when Judaism left its native soil the local supernatural beings revived—as characteristically as would the old place-names threw off their Greek dress—and they still survive, under a veneer of Mahommedanism, as the modern representatives of the Baals of the distant past.[4]

The uniqueness of the Old Testament religion is stamped upon the Mosaic legislation, which combines in archaic manner ritual, ethical and civil enactments. As a whole, *Biblical Law.* the economic conditions implied are pastoral and agricultural, and are relatively primitive; and the general rudimentary character of the legal ideas appears in the death penalty for the goring ox (Exod. xxi. 28), resort to ordeal (Num. v. 11-31), and in the treatment of murder, family, marriage, slaves and property. The use of writing is once contemplated (the "bill of divorce," Deut. xxiv. 3), but not in ordinary business; oaths and symbols are used instead of written contracts, and the commercial law is notably scanty. The simplicity of the legislation is also manifest in the land-system in Lev. xxv., which implies a fresh beginning and not a readjustment of earlier laws. In property succession there *Social Evolution.* is a feeling of tribal aloofness which would not be favourable to a central authority; and in fact the legal machinery is rude, and the carrying out of the law depends not so much upon courts and officials as upon religious considerations. If there is a supreme court, it is priestly (Deut. xvii. 8-13), and the legislation is bound up with the worship of Yahweh, who avenges wrong. This legislation appears as that of the Israelites, newly escaped from bondage in Egypt, joined by an *ethical* covenant-relation with Yahweh, and waiting in the desert to enter and conquer the land of their ancestors. But it is remarkable that, although within the Old Testament itself there are certain different backgrounds, important variations and developments of law, these are relatively insignificant when we consider the profound changes from the 15th-13th centuries (apparent by the period of the conquest) to the close of Old Testament history. Yet, the conditions in Palestine during the monarchies reveal grave and complex social problems, marked class distinctions, and constant intercourse and commercial enterprise.' There was no place for tribal exclusiveness, and the upkeep of a monarchy (including the Temple) and the occasional payment of tribute would require duly appointed officials and a central body. The pentateuchal laws relating to women belong to the country rather than to town life (note the picture of feminine luxury in Isa. iii. 16 sqq.; cf. Amos iv. 1-3). In general the pentateuchal legislation as a whole presupposes an undeveloped state of society, and would have been inadequate if not partly obsolete or unintelligible during the monarchies.[5] But more elaborate legal usages had long been known outside Palestine, and, to judge from the Talmud and the Syrian law-code (c. 5th century A.D.), long prevailed. Oriental law is primitive or advanced according to the social conditions, with the result that antiquity of ideas is no criterion of date, and modern desert custom is more archaic than the *Babylonian Law.* great code of the Babylonian king Khammurabi (c. 2000 B.C.). Common law is merely part of the national life, and where it is implicated with religion there is no uniformity over an area comprising different groups of people. In such a case there is resort to a controlling authority, whether self-imposed (like the divine Pharaoh of the Amarna age), or mutually agreed (as Mahomet and the Arabian clans).[6] It cannot be definitely said that the old Babylonian code was in force in Palestine. On the other hand, it is known that it was being diligently copied by Assur-bani-pal's scribes (7th century B.C.), and in view of the circumstances of the Assyrian domination, it is probable that, so far as Palestinian economic conditions permitted, a legislation more progressive than the Pentateuch

[1] The presence of parallels also in South Arabian and Phoenician cults suggests that the old Palestinian ritual was in general agreement with the Oriental religions. Specific influence on the part of Babylonia is not excluded; but the absence of striking points of agreement in other portions of the Old Testament may not be due to anything else than the particular character of the circles to which they belonged.
[2] See C. Westphal, *Jahwes Wohnstätten* (Giessen, 1908), pp. 137 sqq. A. Jeremias. *Hilprecht Anniversary Volume* (1910), pp. 223-242, and art. COSTUME: *Oriental.*
[3] C. G. Montefiore, in the *Hibbert Lectures,* 1892, p. 320, cf. p. 322 ("[the] marriage of heathen practice and monotheistic use is one of the oddest and saddest features of the whole priestly code"); cf. also p. 411, and, in general, Lectures vi.-ix.
[4] See Clermont-Canneau, *Pal. Explor. Fund, Quart. Statem.* (1875), pp. 209 sqq.; C. R. Conder, *Tent Work in Palestine* (London, 1878), ii. 218 sqq.; J. G. Frazer, *op. cit.,* p. 71, &c.; H. Gressmann,

Palästinas Erdgeruch in der israel. Relig. (Berlin, 1909), pp. 16 sqq. In the above, and in other respects also, a survey of the history of Palestine suggests the necessity of modifying that "biological" treatment of the development of thought which pays insufficient attention to the persistence of the representatives of different stages by the side of or after the disappearance of the higher stages; see I. King, *op. cit.,* pp. 204 sqq.
[5] Cf. J.-M. Lagrange, *Hist. Crit. and the O. T.* (London, 1905), p. 176; H. M. Wiener, *The Churchman* (1908), p. 23.
[6] See W. R. Smith, *Rel. of Semites,* p. 70, who compares the judicial authority of Moses. Note also the British Indian legislation imposed upon the various castes and creeds each with their peculiar rites and customs

was in use. The discovery at Gezer of Assyrian contract-tablets (651 and 648 B.C.)—one relating to the sale of land by a certain Nethaniah—at least suggests the prevalence of Assyrian custom, and this is confirmed by the technical business methods illustrated in Jer. xxxii. Moreover, among the Jewish families settled in the 5th century B.C. in Egypt (Elephantine) and Babylonia (Nippur), the Babylonian-Assyrian principles are in vogue, and the presumption that they were not unfamiliar in Palestine is strengthened further by the otherwise unaccountable appearance of Babylonian-Assyrian elements later in the Talmudic law. The denunciations in the prophetical writings of gross injustice, oppression and maladministration seem to presuppose definite laws, which either were ignored or which fell with severity upon the poor and unfortunate. They point to a considerable amount of written law, which was evidently class-legislation of an oppressive character.[1] The Babylonian code is essentially class-legislation, and from the point of view of the idealism of the Old Testament prophets, which raises the rights of humanity above everything else, the steps which the code takes to safeguard the rights of property (slaves included therein) would naturally seem harsh. The code also regulates wages and prices, and shows a certain humanity towards debtors; and here any failure to carry out these laws would obviously be denounced. While the code, according to its own lights, aims *Prophets* at strict justice rather than charity, the Old Testa-*and the Law.* ment has reforming aims, and the religious, legislative and social ideals are characterized by the insistence upon a lofty moral and ethical standard. These ideals are more religious than democratic. The appeal of the prophets, " is not for better institutions but for better men, not for the abolition of aristocratic privileges but for an honest and godly use of them."[2] The writers have in view a people with individual and collective rights and responsibilities, united by feelings of the deepest loyalty and kindliness and by common adherence to their only God. There is a marked growth of refinement and of ideas of morality, and a condemnation of the shameless vice and oppression which went on amid a punctilious and splendid worship. It is extremely significant that between the teaching of the prophetical writings and the spirit of the Mosaic legislation there is an unmistakable bond. The Mosaic law, in its reforming aspect, is characterized by the denunciation of heathenism and heathenish usages which belong to the old religion. There is an insistence upon individual responsibility (Deut. xxiv. 16; 2 Kings xiv. 6; cf. Jer. xxxi. 29 seq.; Ezek. xviii., xxxiii.), the more noteworthy when one considers the tenacity of the savage *talio* and its retention, though with some modifications, in the Babylonian code. There is a tendency to mitigate slavery, and the law of fugitive slaves is a particularly instructive innovation (Deut. xxiii. 15 seq., subsequently confined to the slave from outside). Corporal punishment is kept within limits (xxv. 3), but its very existence points to state-life rather than to the desert. Some attempt is made to diminish the destructiveness of war (xx. 10-20), but the passage is a remarkable illustration of a barbarous age. The endeavour is also made to improve the monarchy of the future (xvii. 14 sqq.), but mainly on religious grounds, in order to diminish foreign intercourse. Noteworthy, again, is the appeal to religious and ethical considerations in order to prevent injustice to the widow and fatherless and to unhappy debtors; statutory laws are either unknown, or, more probably, are presupposed. The pentateuchal legislation as a *Mosaic Codes* whole is placed at the very beginning of Israelite *Problems.* national history. Amid constant periods of apostasy two epoch-making events stand out: (a) the rediscovery of the Book of the Law (Deuteronomy is meant) in the time of Josiah (2 Kings xxii.) followed by a reform of sundry religious abuses dating from the foundation of the temple, and (b) the promulgation by Ezra of the Law of Yahweh, the law of Moses (Ezra. vii. 10, 14; Neh. viii. 1), in the age of Nehemiah, at the very close of biblical history. This legislation, endorsing

[1] O. C. Whitehouse, *Century Bible,* on Isa. x. 1 seq.
[2] See W. R. Smith, *Old Test. in the Jew. Church* (London, 1892), pp. 348, 350 seq.

(in certain well-defined portions) priestly authority, excludes a monarchy and stands at the head of a lengthy development in the way of expansion and interpretation. Its true place in biblical history has been the problem of generations of scholars,[3] and the discovery (Dec. 1901–Jan. 1902) of the Babylonian code has brought new problems of relationship and of external influences. Although on various grounds there is a strong probability that the code of Khammurabi must have been known in Palestine at some period, the Old Testament does not manifest such traces of the influence as might have been expected. Pentateuchal law is relatively unprogressive, it is marked by a characteristic simplicity, and by a spirit of reform, and the persisting primitive social conditions implied do not harmonize with other internal and external data. The existence of other laws, however, is to be presupposed, and there appear to be cases where the Babylonian code lies in the background. An independent authority concludes that " the co-existing likeness and differences argue for an independent recension of ancient custom deeply influenced by Babylonian law."[4] The questions are involved with the reforming spirit in biblical religion and history. On literary-historical grounds the Pentateuch in its present form is post-exilic, posterior to the old monarchies and to the ideals of the earlier prophetical writings. The laws are (a) partly contemporary collections (chiefly of a ritual and ceremonial character) and (b) partly collections of older and different origin, though now in post-exilic frames. The antiquity of certain principles and details is undeniable—as also in the Talmud—but since one must start from the organic connexions of the composite sources, the problems necessitate proper attention to the relation between the stages in the literary growth (working backwards) and the vicissitudes which culminate in the post-exilic age. The simplicity of the legislation (traditionally associated with Moab and Sinai and with Kadesh in South Palestine), the humanitarian and reforming spirit, the condemnation of abuses and customs are features which, in view of the background and scope of Deuteronomy, can hardly be severed from the internal events which connect Palestine of the Assyrian supremacy with the time of Nehemiah.[5]

The introduction, spread and prominence of the *name* Yahweh, the development of conceptions concerning his nature, his supremacy over other gods and the lofty monotheism *Character* which denied a plurality of gods, are questions *of O. T.* which, like the biblical legislative ideas, cannot be *History.* adequately examined within the narrow compass of the Old Testament alone.

The biblical history is a "canonical" history which looks back to the patriarchs, the exodus from Egypt, the law-giving and the covenant with Yahweh at Sinai, the conquest of Palestine by the Israelite tribes, the monarchy, the rival kingdoms, the fall and exile of the northern tribes, and, later, of the southern (Judah), and the reconstructions of Judah in the times of Cyrus, Darius and Artaxerxes. It is the first known example of continuous historical writing (Genesis to Kings, Chronicles-Ezra-Nehemiah), and represents a deliberate effort to go back from

[3] See BIBLE: *Old Test. Criticism*; JEWS, §§ 16, 23.
[4] C. H. W. Johns, Hastings's *Dict. Bible,* v. 611 seq., who points out that the intrusion of priestly power into the law courts is a recrudescence under changed conditions of a state of things from which the Babylonian code shows an emancipation nearly complete. The view formerly maintained by the present writer (*Laws of Moses and Code of Hammurabi,* 1903, pp. 204 sqq., 279 seq.,&c.) relied upon the difference between the exilic or post-exilic sources which unambiguously reflect Babylonian and related ideas, and the absence in other biblical sources of the features which an earlier comprehensive Babylonian influence would have produced, and it incorrectly assumed that the explanation might be found in the ordinary reconstructions of Israelite history. Cf. above, p. 182, n. 1.
[5] On the later history of the canonical law (Mishnah, Gemara, &c.) see TALMUD. The Talmud embodies law, which is related to the Babylonian code not only in content but also sometimes in spirit; see L. N. Dembitz, *Jew. Quart. Rev.* xix. (1906), pp. 109 seq. For the efforts of the Rabbis to improve the legal principles in Galilee in the 2nd and 3rd centuries A.D., see A. Büchler, Publication No. 1, Jews' College, London. With the removal of Judaism from Palestine and internal social changes the archaic primitive law reappeared, now influenced, however, by Mahommedan legislation.

the days when the Judaeans separated from the Samaritans to the very beginning of the world. A characteristic tone pervades the history, even of the antediluvian age, from the creation of Adam; or rather, the history of the earliest times has been written under its influence. It reveals itself in the days of the Patriarchs, before the "Amarna" age—or rather in the narratives relating to these remote ancestors. It will be perceived that an objective attitude to the subjective writings must be adopted, the starting-point is the writings themselves and not individual preconceptions of the authentic history which they embody. Although there are various points of contact with Palestinian external history, there is a failure to deal with some events of obvious importance, and an emphasis upon others which are less conspicuous in any broad survey of the land. There are numerous conflicting details which unite to prove that various sources have been used, and that the structure of the compilation is a very intricate one, the steps in its growth being extremely obscure.[1] In studying the internal peculiarities and the different circles of thought involved, it is found that they often imply written traditions which have a perspective different from that in which they are now placed. As regards the premonarchical period, some evidence points to a settlement *Pre-* (apparently from Aramaean localities) of the patri-*Mesorakhal* archs, and of Israel (Jacob) and his sons, *i.e.* the *Period.* "children of Israel." It ignores a descent into Egypt and the subsequent invasion.[2] The parallel account in the book of Joshua of the entrance of the "children of Israel" is, in its present form, the sequel to the journey of the people along the east of Edom and Moab after the escape from Egypt, and after a sojourn at Kadesh (Exodus-Deuteronomy). But other evidence also points to an entrance from Kadesh into Judah, and associates the kin of Moses, Kenites, Calebites and others. Thus, the tradition of a residence in Egypt, implied also in the stories of Joseph, has certainly become the "canonical" view, but the recollection was not shared by all the mixed peoples of Palestine; and to this difference of historical background in the traditions must be added divergent traditions of the earlier population. Traditions, oral and written, with widely differing standpoints have been brought together and merged. Moreover, the elaborate account of the vast invasion and conquest, the expulsion, extermination and subjugation of earlier inhabitants, and the occupation of cities and fields, combine to form a picture which cannot be placed in Palestine during the 15th–13th centuries. It must not be denied that the recollection of some invasion may have been greatly idealized by late writers, but it happens that there were important immigrations and internal movements in the 8th–6th centuries, that is to say, immediately preceding the post-exilic age, when this composite account in the Pentateuch and Joshua reached its present form. An enormous gap severs the pre-monarchical period from this age, and while the tribal schemes and tribal traditions can hardly be traced during the monarchies, the inclusion of Judah among the "sons" of Israel would not have originated when Judah and Israel were rival kingdoms. Yet the tribes survive in post-exilic literature and their traditions develop henceforth in *Jubilees, Testament of the XII Patriarchs,* &c. During the changes from the 8th century onwards a non-monarchical constitution naturally prevailed, first in the north and then in the north, and while in the north the mingled peoples of Samaria came to regard themselves as Israelite, the southern portion, the tribe of Judah, proves in 1 Chron. ii. & iv. to be largely of half-Edomite blood. A common ground previous to the Samaritan schism is ignored; it is found only in the period before the rival kingdoms. The political history of these

[1] In the art. JEWS, §§ 1–24, the biblical history is taken as the foundation, and the internal historical difficulties are noticed from stage to stage. In the present state of biblical historical criticism this plan seemed more advisable than any attempt to reconstruct the history; the necessity for some reconstruction will, however, be clear to the reader on the grounds of both the internal intricacies and the external evidence.

[2] See, in the first instance, E. Meyer (and B. Luther), *Die Israeliten und ihre Nachbarstämme* (Halle, 1906); also art. GENESIS.

monarchies in the book of Kings is singularly slight considering the extensive body of tradition which may be pre-supposed, *e.g.* for the reigns of Jeroboam II. and Uzziah, or which may be inferred from the evidence for different *The Monarchies.* sources dealing with other periods. The scanty *political* data in the annalistic notices of the north kingdom are supplemented by more detailed narratives of a few years leading up to the rise of the last dynasty, that of Jehu. The historical problems involved point to a loss of perspective (JEWS, § 11), and the particular interest in the stories of Elijah and Elisha in an historical work suggests that the political records passed through the hands of communities whose interest lay in these figures. Old tradition suggests the "schools of the prophets" at Jericho, Gilgal and Bethel, and in fact the proximity of these places, especially Bethel, to Judaean soil may be connected with the friendly and sometimes markedly favourable attitude to Judah in these narratives. The rise of the kingdom of Israel under Saul is treated at length, but more prominence is given to the influence of the prophet Samuel; and not only is Saul's history written from a didactic and prophetical standpoint (cf. similarly Ahab), but the great hero and ruler is handled locally as a petty king at Gibeah in Benjamin. The interest of the narratives clings around north Judah and Benjamin, and more attention is given to the rise of the Judaean dynasty, the hostility of Saul, and the romantic friendship between his son Jonathan and the young David of Bethlehem. The history of the northern and southern kingdoms is handled separately in Kings; but in Samuel the rise of each is closely interwoven, and to the greater glory of David. The account of his steps contains details touching Judah and its relation to Israel which cannot be reconciled with certain traditions of Saul and the Ephraimite Joshua. It combines amid diverse material a hero of Bethlehem and rival of Saul with the idea of a conqueror of this district; it introduces peculiar traditions of the ark and sanctuary, and it associates David with Hebron, Calebites and the wilderness of Paran.[3] The books of Samuel and Kings have become, in process of compilation, the natural sequel to the preceding books, but the conflicting features and the perplexing differences of standpoint recur elsewhere, and the relationship between them suggests that similar causes have been operative upon the compilation. The history of Judah is, broadly speaking, that of the Davidic dynasty and the Temple, and it begins at the time of the first king of the rival north. Care is taken to record the transference of secular power and of Yahweh's favour from Saul to David, and David accomplishes more successfully or on a larger scale the achievements ascribed to Saul. The religious superiority of Jerusalem over the idolatrous north and over the "high places" is the main theme, and with it is the supremacy of the native Zadokite priests of Jerusalem over others (*e.g.* of Shiloh), who are connected with the desert traditions. The political history is relatively slight and uneven, and the framework is rehandled in Chronicles upon more developed lines and from a later ecclesiastical standpoint, which suggests that many traditions of the monarchy were extant in a later dress. Both books represent the same general trend of political events, even where the "canonical" representation is most open to criticism. Chronicles, with the book of Ezra and Nehemiah, makes a continuity *Chronicles—* between the old Judah which fell in 586 and the *Ezra—* return (time of Cyrus), the rebuilding of the temple *Nehemiah.* (Darius), and the reorganization associated with Nehemiah and Ezra (Artaxerxes) Historical material after 586 is scanty in the extreme, and, apart from the records of Nehemiah and a few other passages, the interest lies in the religious history of the communities and reformers who returned from Babylonia. The late and composite book of Chronicles places at the head of the Israelite divisions, which ignore the exodus (1 Chron. vii.

[3] Whence the theory that David was of S. Judaean or S. Palestinian origin (Marquart, Winckler, Cheyne, *Ency. Bib.* cols. 1010, 2613 seq.), and, also, that he knit together the southern non-Judaean clans (see DAVID, JUDAH). But it is preferable to recognise different traditions of distinct origin and to inquire what genuine elements of history each may contain.

14, 20–24), a Judah consisting of fragments of an older stock replenished with families of South Palestinian, Edomite and North Arabian affinity. This half-Edomite population, recognizable also in Benjamin, manifests its presence in the official lists, and more especially in the ecclesiastical bodies inaugurated by David, from whose time the supremacy of this Judah is dated. The historical framework contains traditions of the reconstruction and repair of temple and cult, of the hostility of southern peoples and their allies, and of conflicts between king and priests. This retrospect of the Judaean kingdom must be taken with the following books, where the crucial features are (a) the presence (c. 444) of an aristocracy, partly (at all events) of half-Edomite affinity, before the return of any important body of exiles (Neh. iii.); (b) the gaps in the history between the fall of Samaria (722) and Jerusalem (586) to the rise of the hierocracy, and (c) the relation between the hints of renewed political activity in Zerubbabel's time, when the Temple was rebuilt (c. 520–516), and the mysterious catastrophe (with perhaps another disaster to the Temple), probably due to Edom, which is implied in the book of Nehemiah (c. 444). (See JEWS, § 22.) These data lead to the fundamental problem of Old Testament history. Since 1870 (Wellhausen's *De gentibus . . . Judaeis*) it has been recognized that 1 Chron. ii. and iv. accord with certain details in 1 Samuel, and appear to refer to a half-Edomite Judah in David's time (c. 1000 B.C.).[1] More recently E. Meyer, on the basis of a larger induction, has pointed out the relation of this Judah to a large group of Edomite or Edomite-Ishmaelite tribes.[2] The stories in Genesis represent a southern treatment of Palestinian tradition, with local and southern versions of legends and myths, and with interests which could only belong to the south.[3] It has long been perceived that Kadesh in South Palestine was connected with a law-giving and with some separate movement into Judah of clans associated with the family of Moses, Caleb, Kenites, &c. (see EXODUS, THE). With this it is natural to connect the transmission and *presence in the Old Testament* of specifically Kenite tradition, of the "southern" stories in Genesis, and of the stories of Levi.[4] The rise of this new Judah is generally attributed to David, but the southern clans remain independent for some five centuries, only moving a few miles nearer Jerusalem; and this vast interval severs the old half-Edomite or Arabian Judah from the sequel—the association of such names as Korah, Ethan and Heman with temple-psalms and psalmody.[5] It has long been agreed that biblical religion and history are indebted in some way to groups connected with Edom and North Arabia, and repeated endeavours have been made to explain the evidence in its bearing upon this lengthy period.[6] The problem, it is here suggested, is in the first instance a literary one—the literary treatment by southern groups, who have become Israelite, of a lengthy period of history. When the whole body of evidence is viewed comprehensively, it would seem that there was some movement northwards of semi-Edomite blood, tradition and literature, the date of which may be placed during the internal disorganization of Palestine, and presumably in the 6th century. Such a movement is in keeping with the course of Palestinian history from the traditional entrance of the Israelite tribes to the relatively recent migration of the tribe

[1] "The population of South Judah was of half-Arab origin" (W. R. Smith, *Old Test. Jew. Church*, p. 279).

[2] Meyer and Luther, *op. cit.*, p. 446, *et passim.*

[3] So especially Meyer and Luther, *op. cit.*; cf. also H. Gressmann, *Zeit. f. alt-test. Wissens.* (1910), p. 28 seq. Note also the view that the grand book of Job (q.v.) has an Edomite background.

[4] A. R. Gordon, *Early Trad. of Gen.* (London, 1907), pp. 74, 188; Meyer, *op. cit.*, pp. 83, 85 (on the Levites); Gressmann, *loc. cit.*; S. A. Cook, *Amer. Journ. of Theol.* (1909), pp. 382 seq. See GENESIS, LEVITES, and JEWS, § 20.

[5] On the names, see GENEALOGY: *Biblical*; LEVITES, § 2, end, and *Ency. Bib.* col. 1665 seq.

[6] W. R. Harper (*Amos and Hosea*, 1905, p. liv.) observes: "Every year since the work of W. R. Smith brings Israel into closer relationship with Arabia"; cf. also N. Schmidt's conclusions (*Hibbert Journal*, 1908, p. 342), and the Jerahmeelite theory of T. K. Cheyne, who writes (*Decline and Fall of the Kingdom of Judah*, London, 1908, p. xxxvii.) ". . . by far the greater part of the extant literary monuments of ancient Israel are precisely those monuments whose producers were most preoccupied by N. Arabia."

of 'Amr.' In the Old Testament popular feeling knows of two phases: Edom, the more powerful brother of Jacob (or Israel) —both could share in the traditions of Abraham, Isaac and Jacob—and the hatred of the treacherous Edom in the prophetical writings. Earlier phases have not survived, and the last-mentioned is relatively late,[1] after the southern influence had left itself upon history, legend, the Temple and the ecclesiastical bodies. On these grounds, then, it would seem that among the vicissitudes of the 8th and following centuries may be placed a movement of the greatest importance for Israelite history and for the growth of the Old Testament, one, however, which has been reshaped and supplemented (in the account of the Exodus and Invasion) and deliberately suppressed or ignored in the history of the age (viz. in Ezra-Nehemiah).

The unanimous recognition on the part of all biblical scholars that the Old Testament cannot be taken as it stands as a trustworthy account of the history with which it deals, necessitates a hypothesis or, it may be, a series of *Trend of Criticism.* hypotheses, which shall enable one to approach the more detailed study of its history and religion. The curious and popular tradition that Ezra rewrote the Old Testament (2 Esd. xiv.), the concessions of conservative scholars, and even the view that the Hebrew text is too uncertain for literary criticism, indicate that the starting-point of inquiry must be the present form of the writings. The necessary work of literary analysis reached its most definite stage in the now famous hypothesis of Graf (1865–1866) and especially Wellhausen (1878), which was made more widely known to English readers, directly and indirectly through W. Robertson Smith, in the 9th edition of this Encyclopaedia.[2] The work of literary criticism and its application to biblical history and religion passed into a new stage as external evidence accumulated, and, more particularly since 1900, the problems have assumed new shapes. The tendency has been to assign more of the Old Testament, in its present form, to the Persian age and later; and also to work upon lines which are influenced sometimes by the close agreement with Oriental conditions generally and sometimes by the very striking divergences. It is the merit of Hugo Winckler especially to have lifted biblical study out of the somewhat narrow lines upon which it had usually proceeded, but, at the time of writing (1910), Old Testament criticism still awaits a sound reconciliation of the admitted internal intricacies and of the external evidence for Palestine and that larger area of which it forms part. Upon the convergence of the manifold lines of investigation rest all reconstructions, all methodical studies of biblical religion, law and prophecy, and all endeavours to place the various developments in an adequate historical framework.

The preliminary hypotheses, it would seem, must be both literary and historical. The varied standpoints (historical, social, legal, religious, &c.) combine with the fragmentary character *Preliminary* of much of the evidence to suggest that the literature *Hypotheses.* has passed through different circles, with excision or revision of older material, and with the incorporation of other material, sometimes of older origin and of independent literary growth. Consequently, one is restricted in the first instance to such literature as survives and in the form which the last editors or compilers gave it. Different views as regards history (e.g. invasions, tribal movements, rival kingdoms) and religion (e.g. the Yahweh of Kadesh, Sinai, Jerusalem, &c.), and different priestly, prophetical and popular ideas are only to be expected, considering the character of Palestinian population. Hence to weave the data into a single historical outline or into an orderly evolution of thought is to overlook the probability of bona

[1] J. Dissard, *Rev. Bibl.*, 1905, pp. 410–425. Some S. Pal. revolt is also reflected shortly before the rise of the Jehu dynasty (JEWS, § 11). A few centuries later, the Edomites (Idumaeans) were again closely connected with the Jews; an Idumaean dynasty—that of the Herods—ruled in Judah, and once more there must have been a considerable amount of intermixture.

[2] Cf. R. H. Kennett, *Journ. Theol. Stud.* (1906), p. 487; *Camb. Bibl. Essays* (ed. Swete), p. 117. For an Edomite invasion between 586 and the Greek period, see also H. Winckler, *Altor. Forsch.* (1900), pp. 428 sqq., 455.

[3] Especially Wellhausen's articles, "Pentateuch," "Israel," "Moab," and W. R. Smith's large series including" Bible," "David," "Decalogue," "Judges," "Kings," "Levites," "Messiah," "Priest," "Prophet," "Psalms," &c.

side divergences of tradition and to assume that more rudimentary or primitive thought was excluded by the admitted development of religious-social ideals. The oldest nucleus of historical tradition appears to belong to Samaria, but it has been adjusted to other standpoints or interests, which are apparently connected partly with the half-Edomite and partly with the old indigenous Judaean stock.[1] Genesis–Kings (incomplete; some further material in Jeremiah) and the later Chronicles—Nehemiah are in their present form posterior to Nehemiah's time. Unfortunately the 'events of his age are shrouded in obscurity, but one can recognize the return of exiles from Babylon to Jerusalem and its environs—now half-Edomite—and various internal rivalries which culminate in the Samaritan schism.[2] The ecclesiastical rivalries have left their mark in the Pentateuch and (the later) Chronicles, and the Samaritan secession appears to have coloured even the book of Kings. These sources then are "post-exilic," and the elimination of material first composed in that age leaves historical, legal and other material which was obviously in circulation (so, e.g., the non-priestly portions of Genesis).[3] The relatively earlier group of books is now the result of two complicated and continuous redactions, "Deuteronomic" (Deut.–Kings) and "Priestly" (Genesis–Joshua, with traces in the following books). The former is exceptionally intricate, being in its various aspects distinctly earlier, and in parts even later than the "priestly." Its standpoint, too, varies, the phases being now northern or wider Israelite, now half-Edomite or Judaean, and now anti-Samarian.

Moreover, there is a late incorporation of literature, sometimes untouched by and sometimes merely approximating to "Deuteronomic" language or thought. How very late the historical books are in their present text or form may be seen from the Septuagint version of Joshua, Samuel and Kings, and from their internal literary structure, which suggests that only at the last stages of compilation were they brought into their present shape.[4] The result as a whole tends to show that the "canonical" history belongs to the last literary vicissitudes, and that similar influences (which have not affected every book in the same manner) have been at work throughout.

The history of the past is viewed from rather different positions which, on the whole, are subsequent to the relatively recent changes that gave birth to new organizations in Samaria and Judah. Consequently, in addition to the ordinary requirements of historical criticism, biblical study has to take into account the intricate composite character of the sources and the background of these positions. It is the criticism of sources which have both a literary and an historical compositeness. Not only are the standpoints of local interest (Samaria, Benjamin, Judah and the half-Edomite Judah being involved), but there are remarkable developments in the ecclesiastical bodies (Zadokites of Jerusalem, country and half-Edomite priests, Aaronites) which have influenced both the writing and the revision of the sources (see LEVITES). Yet it is noteworthy that the traditions are usually reshaped, readjusted or reinterpreted, and are not replaced by entirely new ones. Thus, the Samaritans claim the traditions of the land; the Chronicler traces the connexion between "pre-exilic" and "post-exilic" Judaeans, ignoring and obscuring intervening events; the south Palestinian cycle of tradition is adapted to the history of a descent and an exodus from Egypt; Zadokite priests are enrolled as Aaronites, and the hierarchical traditions

Reshaping of Tradition.

reveal stages of orderly and active development in order to authorize the changing standpoints of different periods and circles.[5] This feature recurs in later Palestinian literature (see MIDRASH, TALMUD) where there are *later* forms of thought and tradition, some elements of which although often of older origin, are almost or entirely wanting in the Old Testament. Much that would otherwise be unintelligible becomes more clear when one realizes the readiness with which settlers adopt the traditional belief and custom of a land, and the psychological fact that teaching must be relevant and must satisfy the primary religious feelings and aspirations, that it must not be at entire variance with current beliefs, but must represent the older beliefs in a new form. Any comparison of the treatment of biblical figures or events in the later literature will illustrate the retention of certain old details, the appearance of new ones, and an organic connexion which is everywhere in accordance with contemporary thought and teaching. If this raises the presumption that even the oldest and most isolated biblical evidence may rest upon still older authority, it shows also that the fuller details and context cannot be confidently recovered; and that earlier forms would accord with earlier Palestinian belief.[6] Hence, although records may be most untrustworthy in their present form or connexion, one cannot necessarily deny that a romance may presuppose a reality of history or that it may preserve the fact of an event even at the period to which it is ascribed (e.g. Abraham and Amraphel in Gen. xiv.; the invasions before 1000 B.C., &c.). But in all such cases the *present* form of the material may be more profitably used for the study of the historical or religious conceptions of *its* age. At the same time, the complexity of the vicissitudes of traditions, exemplified in modern Palestine itself, cannot be ignored.[7] Finally, biblical history is an intentional and reasoned arrangement of material, based upon composite sources, for religious and didactic purposes. Regarded as an historical work there is a remarkable absence of proportion, and a loss of perspective in the relation between antediluvian, patriarchal, Mosaic and later periods. From the literary-critical results, however, it is not so much the history of consecutive periods as the account of consecutive periods by compilers who are not far removed from one another. Investigation may concern itself not so much with what was possibly or probably known, but with what is actually presented. The fact remains that when accepted tradition conflicts with more reliable evidence it stands upon a level by itself;[8] and it is certain that a compilation based upon the knowledge which modern research—whether in the exact sciences or in history—has gained would have neither meaning for nor influence upon the people whom it was desired to instruct. A considerable amount of earlier history and literature has been lost, and it is probable that the traditions of the origins of the composite Israelites, as they are now preserved, embody evidence belonging to the nearer events of the 8th–6th centuries. The history of these centuries is of fundamental importance in any attempt to "reconstruct" biblical history.[9] The fall of Samaria and Judah was a literary as well as a political catastrophe, and precisely how much earlier material has been

[1] A Samarian (or Ephraimite or N. Israelite) nucleus may be recognized in the books of Joshua–Kings; see the articles on these books, JEWS, § 6; cf. Meyer, pp. 478 n. 2, 486 seq., and K. Lincke, *Samaria u. seine Propheten* (1903), p. 24. These preserve old poetical literature (Judg. v., 2 Sam. i.), stories of conquest and settlement, and they connect with the liturgy in Deut. xxvii. Joshua's covenant at Shechem and the Shechemite covenant-god (cf. Kennett, *Journ. Theol. Stud.*, 1906, pp. 493 seq.; Lincke, *op. cit.*, p. 89. W. Erbt, *Die Hebräer* (1906), pp. 27 seq.; Meyer and Luther, pp. 542 seq., 550 seq.).

[2] There seems to be both political and religious animosity, but it is not certain that Josephus is wrong in placing the schism at the close of the Persian period; see, on this point, J. Marquart, *Isr. u. Jüd. Gesch.* (1896), p. 57 seq.; C. Steuernagel, *Theolog. Stud. u. Krit.* (1909), p. 5; G. Jahn, *Bücher Ezra u. Nehemia* (Leiden, 1909), pp. 173–176; C. C. Torrey, *Ezra Studies* (Chicago, 1910), pp. 321 sqq. Old priestly rivalries between Cutha and Babylon may explain why the mixed Samaritans became known as Cuthaeans; according to the prevailing theory their predecessors, the "ten tribes" had been exiled in the 8th century.

[3] The term "post-exilic" is applied to literature and history after the return of exiles and the religious reconstruction of Judah. This, on the traditional view, would be in 537, if there were then any prominent return. Failing this, one must descend to the time of Nehemiah, which the biblical history itself regards as epoch-making. The tendency to make the exile an abrupt and complete change in life is based upon the theory underlying Chronicles–Nehemiah and is misleading (see Torrey, *op. cit.* pp. 287 sqq., &c.).

[4] Cf. the "Deuteronomic" form of Samuel, and the dependence of the literary growth of Genesis and the account of the exodus and invasion of Palestine upon the "southern" cycle of tradition.

[5] Cf. S. A. Cook, *Critical Notes on Old Testament History* (1907), pp. 62 seq., 67 75 sqq., 112 seq.

[6] This applies also to the prophetical writings, the study of which is complicated by their use of past history to give point to *later* ideas and by the recurrence in history of somewhat similar events. As regards the situations which presuppose the ruin of Jerusalem and a return of exiles, the obscure events after the time of Zerubbabel cannot be left out of account. (See JEWS, §§ 14, 17 [p. 282], 22 n. 5, and art. ZEPHANIAH.)

[7] Note the rapid growth and embellishment of tradition, the inextricable interweaving of fact and fiction, the circumstantial or rationalized stories of imaginary beings, the supernatural or mythical stories of thoroughly historical persons, the absolute loss of perspective, and a reliance not upon the merits of a tradition but upon the authority with which it is associated.

[8] Cf. the remarkable Arabian stories of their predecessors, and the mingling of accurate and inaccurate data in Manetho and Ctesias.

[9] The evidence for Jewish colonies at Elephantine in Upper Egypt (5th century B.C.) has opened up new paths for inquiry. According to some scholars it is probable that they were descended from the soldiers settled by Psamtek I. (7th century), and not only are they in touch with Judah and Samaria, but in Psamtek's time an effort was made by the Asiatic and other mercenaries to escape into Ethiopia (J. H. Breasted, *Eg. hist. doc.* iv. 506 seq.). It is already suggested that allusions to a sojourn in Egypt may refer, not to the remote times of Jacob and Moses but to the circumstances of the 7th century; see C. Steuernagel, *op. cit.* pp. 7–12; E. Meyer, *Sitzungsberichte* of the Berlin Academy, June 1908, p. 655, n. 1.

preserved is a problem in itself. It is very noteworthy, however, that, while no care was taken to preserve the history of the Chaldean and Persian Empires—and consequently the most confused ideas subsequently arose—the days of the Assyrian supremacy leave a much clearer imprint (cf. even the apocryphal book of Tobit). It may perhaps be no mere chance that with the dynasties of Omri and Jehu the historical continuity is more firm, that older forms of prophetical narrative are preserved (the times from Ahab to Jehu), and that to the reign of the great Jeroboam (first half of the 8th century), the canonical writers have ascribed the earliest of the extant prophetical writings (Amos and Hosea).

External evidence for Palestine, in emphasizing the necessity for a reconsideration of the serious difficulties in the Old Testament, *Summary.* and in illustrating at once its agreement and still more perplexing disagreement with contemporary conditions, furnishes a more striking proof of its uniqueness and of its permanent value. The Old Testament preserves traces of forgotten history and legend, of strange Oriental mythology, and the remains of a semi-heathenish past. "Canonical" history, legislation and religion assumed their present forms, and, while the earlier stages can only incompletely be traced, the book stands at the head of subsequent literature, paving the way for Christianity and Rabbinical Judaism, and influencing the growth of Mahommedanism. In leaving the land of its birth it has been taken as a whole, and for many centuries has been regarded as an infallible record of divinely granted knowledge and of divinely shaped history. During what is relatively a very brief period deeper inquiry and newer knowledge have forced a slow, painful but steady readjustment of religious convictions. While the ideals and teaching of the Old Testament have always struck a responsive chord, scientific knowledge of the evolution of man, of the world's history and of man's place in the universe, constantly reveals the difference between the value of the old Oriental legacy for its influence upon the development of mankind and the unessential character of that which has had inevitably to be relinquished. Yet, wonderful as the Old Testament has ever seemed to past generations, it becomes far more profound a phenomenon when it is viewed, not in its own perspective of the unity of history—from the time of Adam, but in the history of Palestine and of the old Oriental area. It enshrines the result of certain influences, the teaching of certain truths, and the acquisition of new conceptions of the relations between man and man, and man and God. Man's primary religious feeling seeks to bring him into association with the events and persons of his race, and that which in the Old Testament appears most perishable, most defective, and which suffers most under critical inquiry, was necessary in order to adapt new teaching to the commonly accepted beliefs of a bygone and primitive people.[3] The place of the Old Testament in the general education of the world is at the close of one era and at the beginning of another. After a lengthy development in the history of the human race a definite stage seems to have been reached about 5000 B.C., which step by step led on to those great ancient cultures (Egyptian, Aegean, Babylonian) which surrounded Palestine.[3] These have influenced all subsequent civilization, and it was impossible that ancient Palestine could have been isolated from contemporary thought and history. After reaching an astonishing height (roughly 2500–1500 B.C.) these civilizing powers slowly decayed, and we reach the middle of the first millennium B.C.—the age which is associated with the "Deutero-Isaiah" (Isa. xl.–lv.), with Cyrus and Zoroaster, with Buddha and Confucius, and with Phocylides and Socrates.[3] This age, which comes midway between the second Egyptian dynasty (c. 3000 B.C.) and the present day, connects the decline of the old Oriental empires with the rise of the Persians, Greeks and Romans. In both Babylonia and Egypt it was an age of revival, but there was no longer any vitality in the old soil. In Palestine, on the other hand, the downfall of the old monarchies and the infusion of new blood gave fresh life to the land. There had indeed been previous immigrations, but the passage from the desert into the midst of Palestinian culture led to the adoption of the old semi-heathenism of the land, a declension, and a descent from the relative simplicity of tribal life.[4] Now, however, the political conditions were favourable, and for a time Palestine could work out its own development. In these vicissitudes which led to the growth of the Old Testament, in its preservation among a devoted people, and in the results which have ensued down to to-day, it is impossible not to believe that the history of the past, with its manifold evolutions of thought and action, points the way to the religion of the future.   (S. A. C.)

---

[1] Cf. P. Gardner, *Hist. View of New Test.* (1904) 26, 44. sqq.
[2] See Meyer's interesting remarks, *Gesch. d. Alt.* i. §§ 592 sqq.
[3] Cf. A. P. Stanley, *Jewish Church* (1865), Lectures xlv. seq.; A. Jeremias, *Monoth. Strömungen* (Leipzig, 1904), p. 43 seq. Among the developments in Greek thought of this period, especially interesting for the Old Testament is the teaching associated with Phocylides of Miletus; see Lincke, *Samaria*, pp. 47 seq.
[4] Cf. G. A. Smith, *Hist. Geog.* pp. 85 sqq., also the Arab historian Ibn Khaldūn (on the effects of civilization upon Arab tribes (see *e.g.* R. A. Nicholson, *Lit. Hist. of the Arabs* [London, 1907], pp. 439 sqq.)

II.—*From Alexander-the-Great to A.D. 70.*

After the taking of Tyre Alexander decided to advance upon Egypt. With the exception of Gaza, the whole of *Syria Palaestina* (as it was called) had made its submission. *Alexander* That—in summary form—is the narrative of the *the Great.* Greek historian Arrian (*Anabasis*, ii. 25). Apart from the facts contained in this statement, the phraseology is of some importance, as the district of "Palestinian Syria" clearly includes more than the territory of the Philistines, which the adjective properly denotes (Josephus, *Antiquities*, i. 6, 2, xiii. v. 10). From the military point of view—and Arrian drew upon the memoirs of two of Alexander's lieutenants—the significant thing was that not merely was the coast route from Tyre to Gaza open, but also there was no danger of a flank attack as the expeditionary force proceeded. Palestinian Syria, in fact, is here synonymous with what is commonly called Palestine. Similarly Josephus quotes from Herodotus the statement that the Syrians *in Palestine* are circumcised and profess to have learned the practice from the Egyptians (C. *Apionem*, i. 22, §§ 169, 171, Niese); and he comments that the Jews are the only inhabitants of Palestine who do so. These two examples of the wider use of the adjective and noun seem to testify to the forgotten predominance of the Philistines in the land of Canaan.

But, in spite of the statement and silence of Arrian, Jewish tradition, as reported by Josephus (*Ant.* xi. 8, 3 sqq.), represents the high priest at Jerusalem as refusing Alexander's offered alliance and request for supplies. The Samaritans—the Jews ignored in their records all other inhabitants of Palestine—courted his favour, but the Jews kept faith with Darius so long as he lived. Consequently a visit to Jerusalem is interpolated in the journey from Tyre to Gaza; and, Alexander, contrary to all expectation, is made to respect the high priest's passive resistance. He had seen his figure in a dream; and so he sacrificed to God according to his direction, inspected the book of Daniel, and gave them—and at their request the Jews of Babylon and Media—leave to follow their own laws. The Samaritans were prompt to claim like privileges, but were forced to confess that, though they were Hebrews, they were called the Sidonians of Shechem and were not Jews. The whole story seems to be merely a dramatic setting of the fact that in the new age inaugurated by Alexander the Jews enjoyed religious liberty. The Samaritans are the villains of the piece. But it is possible that Palestinian Jews accompanied the expedition as guides or exerted their influence with Jews of the Dispersion on behalf of Alexander.

It appears from this tradition that the Jews of Palestine occupied little more than Jerusalem. There were kings of Syria in the train of Alexander who thought he was mad when he bowed before the high priest. We may draw the inference that they formed an insignificant item in the population of a small province of the Persian Empire, and yet doubt whether they did actually refuse—alone of all the inhabitants of Palestine—to submit to the conqueror of the whole. At any rate they came into line with the rest of Syria and were included in the province of Coele-Syria, which extended from the Taurus and Lebanon range to Egypt. The province was entrusted first of all to Parmenio (Curtius iv. 1, 4) and by him handed over to Andromachus (Curtius iv. 5, 9). In 331 B.C. the Samaritans rebelled and burned Andromachus alive (Curtius iv. 8, 9): Alexander came up from Egypt, punished the rebels, and settled Macedonians in their city. The loyalty of the Jews he rewarded by granting them Samaritan territory free of tribute—according to a statement attributed by Josephus (c. *Apionem*, ii. § 43, Niese) to Hecataeus.

After the death of Alexander (323 B.C.) Ptolemy Lagi, who became satrap and then king of Egypt by right of conquest (Diodorus xviii. 39), invaded Coele-Syria in 320 B.C. *Ptolemy I.* Then or after the battle of Gaza in 312 B.C. Ptolemy was opposed by the Jews and entered Jerusalem by taking advantage of the Sabbath rest (Agatharchides *ap. Jos. c. Apionem* i. 22, §§ 209 seq.; cf. *Ant.* xii. 1, 1). Whenever this occupation took place, Ptolemy became master of Palestine in 312 B.C., and though, as Josephus complains, he may have disgraced his title, *Soter*, by momentary severity at the outset, later he created in the minds of the Jews the impression that in Palestine or in Egypt he was—in deed as well as in name—their preserver. Since 315 B.C. Palestine had been occupied by the forces of Antigonus. Ptolemy's successful forward movement was undertaken by the advice of Seleucus (Diodorus xix. 80 sqq.), who followed it up by regaining possession of Babylonia. So the Seleucid era began in 312 B.C. (cf. *Maccabees*, i. 10) and the dynasty of Seleucus justified the "prophecy" of Daniel (xi. 5): "And the king of the south (Ptolemy) shall be strong, but one of his captains (Seleucus) shall be strong above him and have dominion" (see SELEUCID DYNASTY).

Abandoned by his captain and future rival, Seleucus, Ptolemy retired and left Palestine to Antigonus for ten years. In 302 B.C., by terms of his alliance with Seleucus, Lysimachus and Cassander, he set out with a considerable force and subdued all the cities of Coele-Syria (Diodorus xx. 113). A rumour of the defeat of his allies sent him back from the siege of Sidon into Egypt, and in the partition of the empire, which followed their victory over Antigonus at Issus, he was ignored. But when Seleucus came to claim Palestine as part of his share, he found his old chief Ptolemy in possession and retired under protest. From 301 B.C.–198 B.C. Palestine remained, with short interruptions, in the hands of the Ptolemies.

Of Palestine, as it was during this century of Egyptian domination, there is much to be learned from the traditions, reported by Josephus (*Ant.* xii. 4), in which the career of Joseph, the son of Tobiah, is glorified as the means whereby the Jews of Palestine misfortunes were rectified. This Joseph was the nephew of Onias, son of Simon the Righteous, and high priest. Onias is described—in order to enhance the glory of Joseph—as a man of small intelligence and deficient in wealth. In consequence of this deficiency he failed to pay the tribute due from the people to Ptolemy, as his fathers had done, and is set down by Josephus as a miser who cared nothing for the protest of Ptolemy's special ambassador. Considering the character of Joseph as it was revealed by prosperity, one is tempted to find other explanations of his conduct than avarice. It is clearly indicated that the Jews as a whole were poor, and it is admitted that Onias was not wealthy. Perhaps it was the Sabbatical year, when no tribute was due. Perhaps Onias would not draw upon the sacred treasure in order to pay tribute to Ptolemy. In any case Joseph borrowed money from his friends in Samaria; and this point in the story proves that the Jews were supposed to have dealings with the Samaritans at the time and could require of them the last proof of friendship. Armed with his borrowed money, Joseph betook himself to Egypt; and there outbid the magnates of Syria when the taxes of the province were put up to auction. He had gained the ear of the king by entertaining his ambassador, and the representatives of the cities—the Greek cities of Syria—were discomfited. The king gave him troops and he borrowed more money from the king's friends. When he began to collect taxes he was met with refusal and insult at Ascalon and at Scythopolis, but he executed the chief men of each city and sent their goods to the king. Warned by these examples, the Syrians opened their gates to him and paid their taxes. For twenty-two years he held his office and was to all intents and purposes governor of Syria, Phoenicia and Samaria—"A good man" (Josephus calls him) "and a man of mind, who rescued the people of the Jews from poverty and weakness, and set them on the way to comparative splendour" (*Ant.* xii. 4, 10).

The story illustrates the rise of a wealthy class among the Jews of Palestine, to whom the tolerant and distant rule of the Ptolemies afforded wider opportunities. At the beginning it is said that the Samaritans were prosperous and persecuted the Jews, but this Jewish hero embracing his opportunities reversed the situation and presumably paid the tribute due from the Jews by exacting more from the non-Jewish inhabitants of his province. He is a type of the Jews who embraced the Greek way of life

as it was lived at Alexandria; but his influence in Palestine was insidious rather than actively subversive of Judaism. It was different when the Jews who wished to be men of the world took their Hellenism from the Seleucid court and courted the favour of Antiochus Epiphanes.

Halfway through this century (249 B.C.) the desultory warfare between Egypt and the Seleucid power came to a temporary end (Dan. xi. 6). Ptolemy II. Philadelphus gave his daughter Berenice with a great dowry to Antiochus II. Theos. When Ptolemy died (247 B.C.), Antiochus' divorced wife Laodice was restored to favour, and Antiochus died suddenly in order that she might regain her power. Berenice and her son were likewise removed from the path of her son Seleucus. In the vain hope of protecting his sister Berenice, the new king of Egypt, Ptolemy III. Eugeretes L, invaded the Seleucid territory, "entered the fortress of the king of the north" (Dan. xi. 7 sqq.), and only returned—laden with spoils, images captured from Egypt by Cambyses, and captives (Jerome on Daniel *loc. cit.*)—to put down a domestic rebellion. Seleucis reconquered northern Syria without much difficulty (Justin xxxvii. 2, 1), but on an attempt to seize Palestine he was signally defeated by Ptolemy (Justin xxvii. 2, 4).

In 223 B.C. Antiochus III. the Great came to the throne of the Seleucid Empire and set about extending its boundaries in different directions. His first attempt on Palestine (221 B.C.) failed; the second succeeded by the   *Antiochus III.* treachery of Ptolemy's lieutenant, who had been recalled to Alexandria in consequence of his successful resistance to the earlier invasion. But in spite of this assistance the conquest of Coele-Syria was not quickly achieved; and when Antiochus advanced in 218 B.C. he was opposed by the Egyptians on land and sea. Nevertheless he made his way into Palestine, planted garrisons at Philoteria on the Sea of Galilee and Scythopolis, and finally stormed Rabbath-ammon (Philadelphia) which was held by partisans of Egypt. Early in 217 B.C. Ptolemy Philopater led his forces towards Raphia, which with Gaza was now in the hands of Antiochus, and drove the invaders back. The great multitude was given into his hand, but he was not to be strengthened permanently by his triumph (Dan. xi. 11 sqq.). Polybius describes his triumphal progress (v. 86): "All the cities vied with one another in returning to their allegiance. The inhabitants of those parts are always ready to accommodate themselves to the situation of the moment and prompt to pay the courtesies required by the occasion. And in this case it was natural enough because of their deep-seated affection for the royal house of Alexandria."

When Ptolemy Philopater died in 205 B.C., Antiochus and Philip of Macedon, his nominal friends, made a secret compact for the division of his possessions outside Egypt. The time had come of which Daniel (xi. 13 sqq.) says: "The king of the north shall return after certain years with a great army and with much riches. And in those times there shall many stand up against the king of the south; also the robbers of thy people shall exalt themselves to establish the vision; but they shall fall." Palestine was apparently allotted to Antiochus and he came to take it, while Philip created a diversion in Thrace and Asia Minor. Already he had allies among the Jews, and, if Daniel is to be trusted, there were other Jews who rose up to shake off the yoke of foreign supremacy, Seleucid or Egyptian, and succeeded only in rendering the triumph of Antiochus easier of achievement. But in the year 200 B.C. Rome intervened with an embassy, which declared war upon Philip and directed Antiochus and Ptolemy to make peace (Polyb. xvi. 27). And in 198 B.C. Antiochus heard that Scopas, Ptolemy's hired commander-in-chief had retaken Coele-Syria (Polyb. xvi. 39) and had subdued the nation of the Jews in the winter. For these sufficient reasons Antiochus hurried back and defeated Scopas at Paneas, which was known later as Caesarea Philippi (Polyb. xvi. 18 seq.). After his victory he took formal possession of Batanaea, Samaria, Abila and Gadara; "and after a little the Jews who dwelt round about the shrine called Jerusalem came over to him" (Polyb. xvi. 39). Only Gaza withstood him, as it withstood Alexander; and Polybius (xvi. 40) pauses to praise their fidelity to Ptolemy. The siege of Gaza was famous; but in the end the city was taken by storm, and Antiochus, secure at last of the province, which his ancestors had so long coveted, was at peace with Ptolemy, as the Roman embassy directed. From Palestine Antiochus turned to the Greek cities of Asia Minor, and by 196 B.C. he was in Thrace. There he was confronted by the ambassadors of Rome, who expressed their surprise at his actions. Antiochus replied that he was recovering the territory won by Seleucus his ancestor, and inquired by what right did the Romans dispute with him about the free cities in

Antiochus and Rome. Asia (Polyb. xviii. 33 seq.). The conference was broken off by a false report of Ptolemy's death, but war between Rome and Antiochus was clearly inevitable—and Antiochus was joined by Hannibal. After much diplomacy, Antiochus advanced into Greece and Rome declared war upon him in 191 B.C. (Livy xxxvi. 1). He was defeated on the seas and driven first out of Greece and then out of Asia Minor. His army was practically destroyed at Magnesia, and he was forced to accept the terms of peace, which the Romans had offered and he had refused before the battle. By the peace of Apamea (188 B.C.) he abandoned all territory beyond the Taurus and agreed to pay the whole cost of the war. He had stood in the beauteous land—the land of Israel—with destruction in his hand. He had made agreement with Ptolemy. He had turned his face unto the isles and had taken many. But now a commander had put an end to his defiance and had even returned his reproach unto him (Dan. xi. 16-18). After Magnesia men said " King Antiochus the Great *was* " (Appian, *Syr.* 37); and the by-word was soon .justified in fact, for he plundered a temple of Bel at Elymais to replenish his exhausted treasury and met the fitting punishment from the gods at the hands of the inhabitants (Diodorus xxix. 15). He stumbled and fell and was not found (Dan. xi. 19).

The need which drove Antiochus to this sacrilege rested heavily upon his successor Seleucus IV. (reigned 187-175 B.C.).

Seleucus IV. The indemnity had still to be paid and Daniel designates Seleucus as " one that shall cause an exactor to pass through the glory of the kingdom " (xi. 20). A tradition preserved in 2 Macc. iii. describes the attempt of Heliodorus, the Seleucid prime minister, to plunder the temple at Jerusalem. The holy city lay in perfect peace and the laws were very well kept because of the piety of Onias the high priest. But one Simon, a Benjamite, who had become guardian of the temple, quarrelled with Onias about the city market, and reported to the governor of Coele-Syria and Phoenicia that the treasury was full of untold sums of money. The priests and people besought Heliodorus to leave this sacred treasure untouched, but he persisted and—in answer to their prayers—was overthrown by a horse with a terrible rider and scourged by two youths. Onias, fearful of the consequences, offered a sacrifice for his restoration, and the two youths appeared to him with the message that he was restored for the sake of Onias. The description of the previous tranquillity may be exaggerated, though it is clear that the Jews, like the other inhabitants of Palestine, must have been left very much to themselves; but the enmity between the adherents of Simon and the pious Jews, who supported and venerated Onias, seems to be a necessary precondition of the state of affairs soon to be revealed. There were already Jews who wished to make terms with their overlord at all costs.

When Antiochus IV. Epiphanes (175-164 B.C.) succeeded to the throne, Jason—whose name betrays a leaning towards

Antiochus IV. and Jason. Hellenism—the brother of Onias, offered the king a bribe for the high-priesthood and another for leave to convert Jerusalem into a Greek city (2 Macc. iv. 7 sqq.). Antiochus had spent his youth at Rome as a hostage, and the death of Seleucus found him filling the office of war minister at Athens. The Hellenistic Jews were, therefore, his natural allies, and allies were very necessary to him if he was to establish himself in Syria. Onias had proceeded to Antioch to explain the disorder and bloodshed due to Jason's followers, ·and so Jason, high priest of the Jews by grace. of Antiochus,

had his way. The existing privileges, which the Jews owed to their ambassador to Rome, were thrust aside. In defiance of the law a gymnasium was set up under the shadow of the citadel. The young men of the upper classes assumed the Greek hat, and were banded together into a gild of *ephebi* on the Greek model. In fact Jason established in Jerusalem the institutions which Strabo expressly describes as visible signs of the Greek way of life—" gymnasia and associations of *ephebi* and clans and Greek names borne by Romans " (v. p. 264, referring to Neapolis)—and that on his own initiative. The party who wished to make a covenant with the heathen (1 Macc. i. 11 sqq.) were in the majority; and so far and so long as they were in the ascendant Antiochus was rid of his chief danger in Palestine, the debatable land between Syria and Egypt. At first Egypt was well disposed to him, as Cleopatra his sister was regent. But she died in 173 B.C.

The struggle for the possession of Palestine began in 170 B.C., when Rome was preoccupied with the war against Perseus of Macedonia. Antiochus sent an ambassador to Rome to protest that Ptolemy, contrary to all law and equity, was attacking him (Polyb. xxvii. 17). In self defence, therefore, Antiochus .advanced through Palestine and defeated the Egyptian army near Pelusium on the frontier. At the news the young king, Ptolemy Philometor, fled by sea, only to fall into his uncle's hands; but his younger brother, Ptolemy Euergetes II., was proclaimed king by the people of Alexandria (Polyb. xxix. 8). Thus Antiochus entered Egypt as the champion of the rightful king and laid siege to Alexandria, which was held by the usurper. When he abandoned the siege and returned to Syria, Philometor, whom he had established at Memphis, was reconciled with his brother, being convinced of his protector's duplicity by the fact that he left a Syrian garrison in Pelusium. In 168 B.C. Antiochus returned and found that the pretext for his presence there was gone. Moreover the defeat of Perseus at Pydna set Rome free to take a strong line in Egypt. As he approached Alexandria Antiochus met the Roman ambassador, and, after a brief attempt at evasion, accepted his ultimatum on the spot. He evacuated Egypt and returned home cowed (Dan. xi. 30; cf. Polyb. xxix. 11). Later he could attend the celebration of the Roman triumph over Macedonia, and surpass it by a festival at Antioch in honour of his conquest of Egypt (Polyb. xxxi. 3-5); but the loss of Pelusium made it imperative that he should be sure of Palestine. His friends, the Hellenizing Jews had split up into factions. Menelaus, the brother of Simon the Benjamite, had bought the high-priesthood over the head of Jason, who fled into the country of the Ammonites, in 172 B.C. (2 Macc. iv. 23 sqq.). To secure his position (for he was not even of the priestly tribe) Menelaus persuaded the deputy of Antiochus, who was dealing with a revolt at Tarsus, to put Onias to death. Antiochus, on his return, had his deputy executed and wept for the dead Onias. But Menelaus managed to retain his position, and his accusers were put to death. Antiochus could pity Onias, who had been tempted from the sanctuary at Daphne, but he needed an ally in Jerusalem—and money. Then, during the first or second invasion of Egypt, Jason, hearing· that Antiochus was dead, returned suddenly and massacred all the followers of Menelaus, who did not take refuge in the citadel. He had some claim to the loyalty of such pious Jews as remained, because he was of the tribe of Levi—in spite of the means he, like Menelaus, had employed to get the high-priesthood. His temporary success reveals the strength of the party who wished to adopt the Greek way of life without consenting to the complete substitution of the authority of.Antiochus for the prescriptions of the Mosaic Law. · It was also a warning to.Antiochus, who returned to exact a bloody vengeance and to loot the Temple, (169 or 168 B.C.). After the evacuation of Egypt, Antiochus· followed out the policy which Jason had suggested to him at the first. Jerusalem was suddenly occupied by one of his captains, and a garrison was planted in a new fortress on *Hellenism.* Mount Zion. Then to coerce the Jews into conformity, the Law was outraged in the Holy Place. The worship of Zeus Olympius replaced the worship of Yahweb, and swine·

were offered as in the Eleusinian mysteries. At the same time the Samaritan temple at Shechem was made over to Zeus Xenius: it is probable that the Samaritans were, like the Jews, divided into two parties. The practice of Judaism was prohibited by a royal edict (1 Macc. i. 41–63; 2 Macc. vi.–vii. 42), and some of the Jews died rather than disobey the law of Moses. It is legitimate to suppose that this attitude would have surprised Antiochus if he had heard of it. His Jewish friends, first Jeson and then Menelaus, had been enlightened enough to throw off their prejudices, and, so far as he could know, they represented the majority of the Jews. Zeus was for him the supreme god of the Greek pantheon, and the syncretism, which he suggested for the sake of uniformity in his empire, assuredly involved no indignity to the only God of the Jews. At Athens Antiochus began to build a vast temple of Zeus Olympius, in place of one begun by Peisistratus; but it was only finished by Hadrian in A.D. 130. Zeus Olympius was figured on his coins, and he erected a statue of Zeus Olympius in the Temple of Apollo at Daphne. More, he identified himself—Epiphanes, *God Manifest* —with Zeus, when he magnified himself above all other gods (Dan. xi. 37). To the minority of strict Jews he was therefore "the abomination of desolation standing where *he* ought not "; but the majority he carried with him and, when he was dying (165 B.C.) during his eastern campaigns, he wrote to the loyal Jews as their fellow citizen and general, exhorting them to preserve their present goodwill towards him and his son, on the ground that his son would continue his policy in gentleness and kindness, and so maintain friendly relations with them (2 Macc. ix.).

For the Jews who still deserved the name the policy of Antiochus wore a very different aspect. Many of them became

Jewish Revolt.   martyrs for the Law, and for a time none would raise his hand to defend himself on the Sabbath if at all. No record remains of the success of the Athenian missionary whom Antiochus sent to preach the new Catholicism; but the soldiers at any rate did their work thoroughly. At last a priestly family at a village called Modein committed themselves to active resistance; and, when they suspended the Sabbath law for purposes of self defence, they were joined by the Hasidacans (Assidaeans), who seem to have been the spiritual ancestors of the Pharisees. The situation was plain enough: unless the particular law of the Sabbath was suspended there would soon have been none to keep the Law at all in Palestine. Jerusalem had apostatized, but the country so far as it was populated by Jews was faithful. Under Judas Maccabeus the outlaws wandered up and down re-establishing by force their proscribed religion. In 165 B.C. they attained their end, the regent of Syria conceded the measure of toleration they required with the approval of Rome; and in 164 B.C. the temple was purged of its desecration. But Judas did not lay down his arms, and added to his resources by rescuing the Jews of Galilee and Gilead and settling them in Judaea (1 Macc. v.). The Nabataean Arabs and the Greeks of Scythopolis befriended them, but the province generally was hostile. In spite of their hostility Judas more than held his own until the regent defeated him at Bethzachariah. The rebels were driven back on Mount Zion and were besieged (163 B.C.). The rumour of a pretender to the throne saved them from destruction, and they capitulated, exchanging the strongholds they had for their lives. At any rate the time of compulsory fusion with the Greeks was ended once for all. In 162 B.C. Demetrius, the son of Seleucus, escaped from Rome and was proclaimed king. Like Antiochus Epiphanes, who also had spent his youth as a hostage in Rome, he was inclined to listen to the Hellenizing Jews, whom he found assembled in full force at Antioch, and to support them against Judas, who was now supreme in Judaea. But he dealt more

Alcimus.   subtly with them: instead of a pagan missionary he sent them Alcimus, a legitimate high-priest, who detached the Hasidaeans from Judas. Indeed, Alcimus and his company did more mischief among the Israelites than the heathen (1 Macc. vii. 13) and Judas took vengeance upon those who deserted from him. Nicanor was appointed governor and prevailed upon

Judas to settle down like an ordinary citizen. But Alcimus complained to the king and Judas fled just in time to escape being sent to Antioch as a prisoner. In the battle of Adasa, which soon followed, Nicanor was defeated and his forces annihilated, thanks to the Jews who came out from all the villages of Judaea (1 Macc. vii. 46). At this point (161 B.C.) Judas sent an embassy to Rome and an alliance was concluded (1 Macc. viii.), too late to save Judas from the determined and victorious attack of Demetrius. The death of Judas at Elasa left the field open to the apostates, and his followers were reduced to the level of roving brigands. The Syrian general made fruitless attempts to capture them, and build forts in Judaea whose garrisons should harass Israel (1 Macc. ix. 50–53), but Jonathan and Simon, brothers of Judas, found their power increase until Jonathan ruled at Michmash as judge and destroyed the godless out of Israel (1 Macc. ix. 73).

In 153 B.C. there appeared another of the series of pretenders to the Syrian throne, to whose rivalry Jonathan, and Simon after him, owed the position they acquired for

Jonathan and Simon.   themselves and their nation. Jonathan was recognized as the head of the Jews, and his prestige and power were such that the charges of the Hellenizing Jews received scant attention. As the years went on he became Strategus and the Syrian garrisons were withdrawn from all the strongholds except Jerusalem and Bethzur. In 147 B.C. he defeated the governor of Coele-Syria in another civil war and received Ekron as his personal reward—as it was said in the name of the prophet Zachariah (ix. 7), "and Ekron shall be as a Jebusite." The king for whom he fought was defeated; but his successor acceded to the demands of Jonathan, added three districts of Samaria to Judaea and freed the whole from tribute. The next king confirmed this and appointed Simon military commander of the district stretching from Tyre to Egypt. So with Syrian as well as Jewish troops the brothers set about subduing Palestine; and Jonathan sent ambassadors in the name of the high-priest and people of the Jews to Rome and Sparta. In spite of the treacherous murder of Jonathan by the Syrian general, the prosperity of the Jews was more than maintained by Simon. The port of Joppa, which was already occupied by a Jewish garrison, was cleared of its inhabitants and populated by Jews. Finally, in 141 B.C., the new era began: the yoke of the heathen was taken away from Israel and Simon was declared high-priest and general and ruler of the Jews for ever until there should arise a faithful prophet (1 Macc. xiii. 41, xiv. 41).

In 135 B.C. the political ambitions of the Jews were rudely checked: a new king of Syria, Antiochus Sidetes, resented their encroachments at Joppa and Gazara and drove them

John Hyrcanus.   back into Jerusalem. In 134 famine compelled John Hyrcanus, who had succeeded his father Simon, to a belated compliance with the king's demands. The Jews laid down their arms, dismantled Jerusalem, and agreed to pay rent for Joppa and Cazara. But in 129 B.C. Antiochus died fighting in the East and for sixty-five years the Jews enjoyed independence. John Hyrcanus was not slow to take advantage of his opportunities. He conquered the Samaritans and destroyed the temple on Mount Gerizim. He subdued the Edomites and compelled them to become Jews. Soon after his death his sons stormed Samaria, which Alexander the Great had colonized with Macedonian soldiers, and razed it to the ground. Judas Aristobulus, who succeeded and was the first of the Hasmonaeans, called himself king and followed his father's example by compelling the Ituraeans to become Jews, and so creating the Galilee of New Testament times. In this case, as in that of the Edomites, it is natural to suppose that there existed already a nucleus of professing Jews which made the wholesale conversion possible. By this time (103 B.C.) it was clear that the Hasmonaeans were —from the point of view of a purist—practically indistinguishable from the Hellenizers whom Judas had opposed so keenly, except that they did not abandon the formal observances of Judaism, and even enforced them upon foreigners. Consequently the Jews were divided into two parties—Pharisees and Sadducees—of whom the Pharisees cared only for doing or enduring the will of God as revealed in Scripture or in the events of history. This division bore bitter fruit in the reign of *Pharisees* Alexander Jannaeus (104–78 B.C.), who by a standing *and* army achieved a territorial expansion which was little *Sadducees.* to the mind of the Pharisees. At first his attack upon Ptolemais brought him into conflict with Egypt, in which he was worsted, but the Jewish general who commanded the Egyptian army persuaded the queen to evacuate Palestine. Then he turned to the country east of the Jordan, and then to Philistia. Later he was utterly defeated by a king of Arabians and fled to Jerusalem, only to find that the Pharisees had raised his people against him and would only be satisfied by his death. The rebels' appeal to the Seleucid governor of part of Syria (88 B.C.) caused a revulsion in his favour, and finally he made peace by more than Roman methods. Aretas, the Arabian king, pressed him hard on the south and the east, but he was able to make some conquests still on the east of the Jordan. In spite of his quarrel with the Pharisees, he seems to have offered the cities he conquered the choice between Judaism and destruction (Jos. *Ant.* xiii. 15, 4). Under Alexandra, his widow (78–69 B.C.), the Pharisees ruled the Jews and no expansion of the kingdom was attempted. It was threatened by Tigranes, king of Armenia, who then held the Syrian Empire, but a bribe and the imminence of the Romans (Jos. *Ant.* xiii. 16, 4; *War* I. 5, 3) saved it. At her death a civil war began between her sons, which left the *Pompey.* way open for Rome. Pompey's lieutenant Scaurus entered Syria in 65 B.C., after the final defeat of Mithradates, and Pompey soon followed to take command of the situation. Three parties pleaded before him, the representatives of the rival kings and a deputation from the people who wished to obey no king, but only the priests of their God (Jos. *Ant.* xiv. 3, 2.) Pompey finally decided in favour of Hyrcanus, and entered Jerusalem by the aid of his party. The adherents of Aristobulus seized and held the temple mount against the Romans, but on the Day of Atonement of the year 63 B.C. their position was stormed and the priests were cut down at the altars (Jos. *Ant.* xiv. 4, 2—4; *War* I. 7). Hyrcanus was left as high-priest—*not* king of the Jews—and his territory was curtailed. The coast towns and the Decapolis, together with Samaria and Scythopolis, were incorporated in the new Roman province of Syria.

In 61 B.C. Pompey celebrated the third of a series of triumphs over Africa, Europe and Asia, and in his train, among the prisoners of war, was Aristobulus, king of Judaea. Palestine meanwhile remained quiet until 57 B.C., when Alexander, the son of Aristobulus, escaped from his Roman captivity and attempted to make himself master of his father's kingdom. Aulus Gabinius, the new proconsul of Syria, defeated his hastily gathered forces, besieged him in one of the fortresses he had managed to acquire, and induced him to abandon his attempt in return for his life. The impotence of Hyrcanus was so obvious that Gabinius proceeded to deprive him of all political power by dividing the country into five cantons, having Jerusalem, Gazara, Amathus, Jericho, and Sepphoris, as their capitals. Other raids, headed by Aristobulus, or his son, or his adherent Peitholaus, disturbed Palestine during the interval between 57 and 51 B.C. and served to create a prejudice against the Jews in the mind of their masters. But with the civil wars which began in 49 B.C. there came opportunities which Hyrcanus, at the instance of Antipater, used to ingratiate himself with Caesar. Once more, as in the days of Simon, the suzerain power was divided against itself, and, though Rome was as strong as the Seleucids had been weak, Caesar was grateful. For timely help in the Egyptian War of 47 B.C. Hyrcanus was rewarded by the title of Ethnarch, and Antipater with the Roman citizenship and the office of procurator of Judaea. The sons of Antipater became deputies for their father; and it appears that Galilee, which was entrusted to Herod, fell within his jurisdiction.

The The power of this Idumaean family provoked popular *Herods.* risings and Antipater was poisoned. But Herod held his ground as governor of Coele-Syria and retained the favour of Cassius and Mark Antony in turn, despite the complaints of the Jewish nobility. In 42 B.C., however, the tyrant of Tyre encroached upon Galilean territory and in 40 B.C. Herod had to fly for his life before the Parthians. Even as a landless fugitive Herod could count upon Roman support. At the instance of Mark Antony; and with the assent of Octavian, the senate declared him king of Judaea, and after two years' fighting he made his title good. Antigonus, whom the Parthians had set upon his throne, was beheaded by his Roman allies (37 B.C.). As king of the Jews (37–4 B.C.) Herod was completely subject and eagerly subservient to his Roman masters. In 36 B.C. (for example) or earlier, Mark Antony gave Cleopatra the whole of Phoenicia and the coast of the Philistines south of Eleuthesus, with the exception only of Tyre and Sidon, part of the Arabian territory and the district of Jericho. Herod acquiesced and leased Jericho, the most fertile part of his kingdom, from Cleopatra. In the war between Antony and Octavian Cleopatra prevented Herod from joining Antony and so left him free to pay court to Octavian after Actium (31 B.C.). A year later Octavian restored to the Jewish kingdom Jericho, Gadara, Hippos, Samaria, Gaza, Anthedon, Joppa and Straton's Tower (Caesarea). Secure of his position, Herod began to build temples and palaces and whole cities up and down Palestine as visible embodiments of the Greek civilization which was to distinguish the Roman Empire from barbarian lands. A sedulous courtier, he was rewarded with the confidence of Augustus, who ordered the procurators of Syria to do nothing without taking his advice. But with the establishment of (relatively) universal peace Palestine ceased to be a factor in general history. Herod the Great enlarged his borders and fostered the Greek civilization of the cities under his sway. After his death his kingdom was dismembered and gradually came under the direct rule of Rome. Herod Agrippa (A.D. 41–44) revived the glories of the reign of Alexandra and won the favour of the Pharisees; but his attempt to form a confederacy of client-princes was nipped in the bud. Even the war which ended with the destruction of Jerusalem in A.D. 70, and the rebellion under Hadrian, which led to the edict forbidding the Jews to enter Jerusalem, are matters proper to the history of the Jews.

References to authorities other than Josephus are given in the course of the article; his *Antiquities* and *War* are the chief source for the period. All modern authorities are given by Schürer.

(J. H. A. H.)

III.—From A.D. 70 to the Present Day.

Owing to the peculiar conditions of the land and the varied interests involved in it, the later history may best be treated in four sections. In the first the general political history will be set forth; in the second a sketch will be given of the cult of the " holy places "; the third will contain some particulars regarding the history of modern colonization by foreigners, which, while it has not affected the political status of the country, has produced very considerable modifications in its population and life; and the fourth will consist of a brief notice of the progress of exploration and scientific research whereby our knowledge of the past and the present of the land has been systematized.

1. *Political History from* A.D. 70.—The destruction of Jerusalem was followed by the dispersal of the Jews, of whom till then it had been the religious and political centre. The *The* first seat of the sanhedrin was at Jamnia (Yebna), *Dispersion.* where the Rabbinic system began to be formulated. This extraordinary spiritual tyranny, for it seems little else, acquired a wonderful hold and exercised a singularly uniting power over the scattered nation. The sharp contrasts between its compulsory religious observances and those of the rest of the world prevented such an absorption of the Jewish people into the Roman Empire as had caused the disappearance of the ten tribes of Israel by their merging with the Assyrians.

It would appear that at first, after the destruction of the city, no specially repressive measures were contemplated by the conquering Romans, who rather attempted to reconcile the Jews to their subject state by a leniency which had proved successful in the case of other tribes brought by conquest within the empire,

But they had reckoned without the isolating influence of Rabbinism. Here and there small insurrections took place, in themselves easily suppressed, but showing the Romans that they had a turbulent and troublesome people to deal with. At last Hadrian determined to stamp out this aggressive Jewish nationalism. He issued an edict forbidding the reading of the law, the observance of the Sabbath, and the rite of circumcision; and determined to convert the still half-ruined Jerusalem into a Roman colony.

The consequence of this edict was the meteor-like outbreak of Bar-Cochebas (*q.v.*) A.D. 132–135. The origin of this person *Bar-Cochebas.* and the history of his rise to power are unknown. Nor is it certain whether he himself at first made a personal claim to be the promised Messiah; but it was his recognition as such by the distinguished Rabbi Akiba, then the most influential Jew alive, which placed him in the command of the insurrection, with 200,000 men at his command. Jerusalem was captured, as well as a large number of strongholds and villages throughout the country. Julius Severus, sent with an immense army by Hadrian, came to quell the insurrection. He recaptured Jerusalem, at the siege of which Bar-Cochebas himself was slain. The rebels fled to Bether—the modern Bittir, near Jerusalem, where the fortress garrisoned by them still remains, under the name Khurbet el-Yahud, or " Ruin of the Jews "—and were there defeated and slaughtered in a sanguinary encounter. It is said that as many as 580,000 men were slain! Hadrian then turned Jerusalem into a Roman colony, changed its name to Aelia Capitolina, built a temple of Jupiter on the site of the Jewish temple and (it is alleged) a temple of Venus on the site of the Holy Sepulchre, and forbade any Jew, on pain of death, to appear within sight of the city.

This disaster was the death-blow to hopes of a Jewish national independence, and the leaders of the people devoted *Rabbinic Schools.* themselves thenceforth to legal and religious study in the Rabbinical schools, which from A.D. 135 (the year of the suppression of the revolt) onwards developed in various towns in the hitherto despised province of Galilee. Shefa'Amr (Shafram), Sha'arah (Shaaraim) and especially Tubariya (Tiberias) became centres of this learning; and the remains of synagogues of the 2nd or 3rd century which still exist in Galilee attest the strength of Judaism in that district during the years following the abortive attempt of Bar-Cochebas.

Palestine thus continued directly under Roman rule. In A.D. 105, under Trajan, Cornelius Palma added Gilead and Moab to the empire. In 295 Auranitis, Batanea and Trachonitis, were added to the province.

The pilgrimage of the Empress Helena properly belongs to the second section into which we have divided this history; we therefore pass it over for the present. The conversion of Constantine to Christianity—or rather the profession of Christianity by Constantine—seemed likely to result in another Jewish persecution, foreshadowed by severe repressive edicts. This, however, was averted by the emperor's death.

The progress of the corrupt Christianity of the empire of Byzantium was checked for a while under Julian the Apostate, who, among other indications of his opposition to Christianity, rescinded the edicts against the Jews on his coming to the throne in 361, and gave orders for the restoration of the Jewish temple. The latter work was interrupted almost as soon as begun by an extraordinary phenomenon—the outburst of flames and loud detonations, easily explained at the time as a divine judgment on this direct attempt to falsify the prophecy of Christ. It has been ingeniously suggested in this more scientific generation that the explosion was due to the ignition of some forgotten store of oil or naphtha, such as was said to have been stored in the temple (2 Macc. i. 19–23, 36), and similar to a store discovered, with less disastrous consequences, in another part of the city early in the 19th century.[1]

On the partition of the empire in A.D. 395 Palestine naturally fell to the share of the emperor of the East. From this onward for more than two hundred years there is a period

[1] See *Palestine Expl. Fund Quarterly Statement*, 1902, p. 389.

of comparative quiet in Palestine, with no external political interference. The country was nominally Christian; the only history it displays being that of the development *The later Empire.* of pilgrimage and of the cult of holy places and of relics, varied by occasional persecutions of the Jews. The elaborate building operations of Justinian (527–565) must not be forgotten. The " Golden Gate " of the Temple area and part of the church which is now the El-Aksa Mosque at Jerusalem, are due to him.

Not till 611 do we find any event of importance in the uninteresting record of Byzantine sovereignty. But this and the following years were signalized by a series of *Chosroes II.* catastrophes of the first magnitude. Chosroes II. (*q.v.*), king of Persia, made an inroad into Syria; joined by the Jews, anxious to revenge their misfortunes, he swept over the country, carrying plunder and destruction wherever he went. Monasteries and churches were burnt and sacked, and Jerusalem was taken; the Holy Sepulchre church was destroyed and its treasures carried off; the other churches were likewise razed to the ground; the patriarch was taken prisoner. It is alleged that 90,000 persons were massacred. Thus for a time the province of Syria with Palestine was lost to the empire of Byzantium.

The Emperor Heraclius reconquered the lost territory in 629. But his triumph was short-lived. A more formidable enemy was already on the way, and the final wresting of Syria from the feeble relics of the Roman Empire was imminent.

The separate tribal units of Arabia, more or less impotent when divided and at war with one another, received for the first time an indissoluble bond of union from the *Rise of Islam.* prophet Mahomet, whose perfect knowledge of human nature (at least of Arab human nature) enabled him to formulate a religious system that was calculated to command an enthusiastic acceptance by the tribes to which it was primarily addressed. His successor, Abu Bekr, called on the tribes of Arabia to unite and to capture the fertile province of Syria from the Christians. Heraclius had not sufficient time to prepare to meet this new foe, and was defeated in his first engagement with Abu Bekr. (For the general history of this period see CALIPHATE.) The latter seized Bostra and proceeded to march to Damascus. He died, however, before carrying out his design (A.D. 634), and was succeeded by Omar, who, after a siege of seventy days entered the city. Other towns fell in turn, such as Caesarea, Sebusteh (Samaria), Nablus (Shechem), Lydd, Jaffa.

Meanwhile Heraclius was not idle. He collected a huge army and in 636 marched against the Arabs. The latter retreated to the Yarmuk River, where the Byzantines met them. Betrayed, it is said, by a Christian who had suffered personal wrongs at the hands of certain of the Byzantine generals, the army of Heraclius was utterly defeated, and with it fell the Byzantine Empire in Syria and Palestine.

After this victory Omar's army marched against Jerusalem, which after a feeble resistance capitulated. The terms of peace, though on the whole moderate, were of a *Omar.* galling and humiliating nature, being ingeniously contrived to make the Christians ever conscious of their own inferiority. Restrictions in church-building, in dress, in the use of beasts of burden, in social intercourse with Moslems, and in the use of bells and of the sign of the cross were enforced. When these terms were agreed upon and signed Omar, under the leadership of the Christian patriarch Sophronius, visited the Holy Rock (the prayer-place of David and the site of the Jewish temple). This he found to be defiled with filth, spread upon it by the Christians in despite of the Jews. Omar and his followers in person cleaned it, and established the place of prayer which, though later rebuilt, has borne his name ever since.

Dissensions and rivalries soon broke out among the Moslem leaders, and in 661 Moawiya, the first caliph of the Omayyad dynasty, transferred the seat of the caliphate from *Abdalmalik.* Mecca to Damascus, where it remained till the Abbasids seized the sovereignty and transferred it to Bagdad

(730). Rivals sprang up from time to time. In 684 Caliph Abdalmalik ('Abd el-Melek), in order to weaken the prestige of Mecca, set himself to beautify the holy shrine of Jerusalem, and built the *Kubbet es-Sakhrah*, or Dome of the Rock, which still remains one of the most beautiful buildings in the world (CALIPHATE: B 5). In 831 the Church of the Holy Sepulchre was restored; but about a hundred years later it was again destroyed as a result of the revolt of the Carmathians (q.v.), who in 929 pillaged Mecca. This produced a Moslem exodus to Jerusalem, with the consequence mentioned. The Carmathian revolt, one of the first of the great splits in the Moslem world, was followed by others: in 936 Egypt declared its independence, under a line of caliphs which claimed descent from Fatima, daughter of the prophet (see FATIMITES); and in 996 Hakim Bi-amrillah mounted the Egyptian throne. This madman caused the church of the Holy Sepulchre to be entirely destroyed: and giving himself out to be the incarnation of Deity, his cult was founded by two Persians, Darazi and Hamza ibn Ali, in the Lebanon; where among the Druses it still persists (see DRUSES).

The contentions between the Abbasid and Fatimite caliphs continued till 1072, when Palestine suffered its next invasion. This was that of the Seljuk Turkomans from Khorasan. On behalf of their king, the Khwarizmian general Atsiz invaded Palestine and captured Jerusalem and Damascus, and then marched on Egypt to carry out his original purpose of destroying the Fatimites. The Egyptians, however, repulsed the invaders and drove them back, retaking the captured Syrian cities.

The sufferings of the Christians and the desecrations of their sacred buildings during these troubled times created wide-spread indignation through the west: and this indignation was inflamed into fury by Peter the Hermit, a native of Picardy, *The Crusades.* who in early life had been a soldier. In 1093 he went in pilgrimage to Jerusalem, and in his wrath at the miseries of the pilgrims he returned to Europe and preached the duty of the Church to rescue the "holy places" from the infidel. The Church responded, and under Peter's leadership a motley crowd, principally of French origin, set out in 1096 for the Holy Land. Others, under better generalship, followed; but of the 600,000 that started from their homes only about 40,000 succeeded in reaching Jerusalem, ill-discipline, famine and battles by the way having reduced their ranks. They captured Jerusalem, however, in July 1099, and the leader of the assault, Godfrey of Boulogne, was made king of Jerusalem.

So was founded the Latin kingdom of Jerusalem, whose history is one of the most painful ever penned (see CRUSADES). *Frankish Kingdom.* It is a record of almost unredeemed "envy, hatred, and malice," and of vice with its consequent diseases, all rendered the more repulsive in that its transactions were carried on in the name of religion. For 88 turbulent years this feudal kingdom was imposed on the country, and then it disappeared as suddenly as it came, leaving no trace but the ruins of castles and churches, a few place-names, and an undying hereditary hatred of Christianity among the native population.

The abortive Second Crusade (1147), led by the kings of France and Germany, came to aid the rapidly weakening Latin kingdom after their failure to hold Edessa against Nureddin, the ruler of northern Syria.

In 1173 Nureddin died, and his kingdom was seized by Saladin (Salah ed-Din), a man of Kurdish origin, who had previously distinguished himself by capturing Egypt in company with Shirkuh, the general of Nureddin. Saladin almost immediately set himself to drive the Franks from the country. The Frankish king was the boy Baldwin IV., who had paid for the errors of his fathers by being afflicted with leprosy. After being defeated by Saladin at Banias, the Franks were compelled to make a treaty with the Moslem leader. The treaty was broken, and Saladin proceeded to take action. The wretched leper king meanwhile died, his successor, Baldwin V. also a young boy,

was poisoned, and the kingdom passed to the worthless Guy de Lusignan, who in the following year (1187) was crushed by Saladin at the battle of Hattin, which restored the whole of Palestine to the Moslems.

The Third Crusade (1189) to recover Jerusalem was led by Frederick I. of Germany. Acre was captured, but quarrels among the chiefs of the expedition made the enterprise ineffective. It was in this crusade that Richard Coeur-de-lion was especially distinguished among the Frankish warriors.

Saladin died in 1193. In 1198 and 1204 took place the Fourth and Fifth Crusades—mere expeditions, as abortive as the third. And as though it were foreordained that no element of horror should be wanting from the history of the crusades, in 1212 there took place one of the most ghastly tragedies that has ever happened in the world—the Crusade of the Children. Fifty thousand boys and girls were persuaded by some pestilent dreamers that their childish innocence would effect what their immoral fathers had failed to accomplish, and so left their homes on an expedition to capture the Holy Land. The vast majority never returned; the happiest of them were shipwrecked and drowned in the Mediterranean. This event is of some historical importance in that it indicates how obvious to their contemporaries was the evil character of those engaged in the more serious expeditions.[1]

The other four crusades which took place from time to time down to 1272 are of no special importance, though there is a certain amount of interest in the fact that after the sixth crusade, in 1229, emperor Frederick II. was permitted to occupy Jerusalem for ten years. But a new element, the Mongolians of Central Asia, now bursts in on the scene. The tribes from east of the Caspian had conquered Persia in 1218. They were driven westward by pressure of the Tatars, and in 1228 had been called by the ruler of Damascus to his aid. In 1240, however, they transferred their alliance to the sultan of Egypt, and pillaged Northern Syria. Driven downward through Galilee they seized Jerusalem, massacred its inhabitants and plundered its churches. They then marched on to Gaza, where the Egyptians joined them, and together inflicted a crushing defeat on the Christians and Moslems of Syria, for once compelled to unite by the common danger. The Khwarizmians and Egyptians afterwards quarrelled, and the former were compelled to retire, leaving Palestine under the rule of the Mameluke[2] sultans of Egypt. Shortly afterwards however, another Central Asiatic invasion—that of the Tatar tribes, took place. Under their leader Hulagu these tribes came by way of Bagdad, which they captured in 1258, and in 1260 they attacked and captured Damascus and ravaged Syria. Bibars (Beibars, Baibars), general of the Egyptian sultan Kotuz, met and drove them back; and having murdered his master, became sultan in his stead. He then proceeded to attack and destroy the relics of Christian possession in Palestine. One after another—Caesarea, Safed, Jaffa, Antioch—they fell, leaving at last Acre (Akka) only. Bibars died in 1277, and in 1291 Acre itself was captured by Khatel son of Kala'un, who thus put a final end to Frankish domination.

During the 14th century there is little of interest in the history of Palestine. The Christians made efforts to creep back to their former possessions and churches were rebuilt in Jerusalem, Bethlehem and Nazareth; but another devastation was the result of the ferocious inroads of the Mongolian Timur (Tamerlane) in 1400.

The last stage of the history of Palestine was reached in 1516, when the war between the Ottoman sultan and the Mamelukes of Egypt resulted in the transference of the country *Turkish Dominion.* to the dominion of the Turks. This change of rulers did not produce much change in the administration or condition of the country. Local governors were appointed from headquarters: revenues were annually sent to Constantinople: various public works were undertaken, such as the

[1] This story is probably the historic basis of the legend of the "Pied Piper of Hamelin."
[2] The Mamelukes were originally military slaves, who in Egypt succeeded in seizing the supreme power. See EGYPT: *History* (*Moslem period*).

rebuilding of the walls of Jerusalem by Suleiman the Magnificent (1537): but on the whole Palestine ceases for nearly three hundred years from this point to have a history, save the dreary record of the sanguinary quarrels of local sheiks and of oppression of the peasants by the various government officials. Few names or events stand out in the history of this period: perhaps the most interesting personality is that of the Druse prince Fakhr ud-Din (1595–1634), whose expulsion of the Arabs from the coast as far south as Acre and establishment of his own kingdom, in defiance of Ottoman authority—to say nothing of his dilettante cultivation of art, the result of a temporary sojourn in Italy—make him worth a passing notice. The German botanist, Leonhard Rauwolf (d. 1596 or 1606), who visited Palestine in 1575, has left a vivid description of the difficulties that then beset even so simple a journey as that from Jaffa to Jerusalem. The former town he found in ruins. A safe conduct had to be obtained from the governor of Ramleh before the party could proceed. At Yazur they were stopped by an official who extorted heavy blackmail on the ground that the sultan had given him charge of the "holy places" and had forbidden him to admit anyone to them without payment (!). Further on they had a scuffle with certain "Arabians"; and at last, after successfully accomplishing the passage of the "rough and stony" road that led to Jerusalem, they were obliged to dismount before the gate of the city till they should receive license from the governor to enter.

Towards the close of the 18th century a chief of the family of Zaidan, named Dhaher el-Amir, rose to power in Acre. To *El-Jazzar.* him fled from Egypt an Albanian slave named Ahmed, who (from the expertness with which he had been wont to carry out his master's orders to get rid of inconvenient rivals) bore the surname *el-Jazzar*, "the butcher." He had, however, incurred punishment for refusing to obey a command of his master, Mahommed Bey, and so took refuge with the Palestinian sheik. After five years Mahommed Bey died and el-Jazzar returned to Egypt. Dhaher revolted against the Turkish government and el-Jazzar was commissioned to quell the rising; his long residence with Dhaher having given him knowledge which marked him out as the most suitable for the purpose. He was successful in his enterprise, and was installed as governor in Dhaher's place. He was a man of barbaric aesthetic taste, and Acre owes some of its public buildings to him: but he was also capricious and tyrannical, and well lived up to his surname. Till 1791 the French had had factories and business establishments at Acre;[1] el-Jazzar ordered them in that year summarily to leave the town. In 1798 Napoleon, returning from his unsuccessful attempt at founding an empire on the Nile, came to stir up a Syrian rising against the Turkish authorities. He attacked el-Jazzar in Acre, after capturing Jaffa, Ramleh and Lydd. A detachment of troops was sent under General Jean Baptiste Kléber across the plain of Esdraelon to take Nazareth and Tiberias, and defeated the Arabs between Fuleh and Afuleh. Napoleon was however compelled by the English to raise the siege. El-Jazzar died in 1806 and was succeeded by his milder adopted son, Suleiman, who on his death in 1814 was followed by the fanatic Abdullah. This bigoted Moslem caused the Jewish secretary of his office to be murdered. The Jew had anticipated just such an event, and had secretly arranged that after his death an inventory of Abdullah's property should fall into the hands of the government—knowing that the latter had claims on the estates of el-Jazzar and Suleiman. The government accordingly pressed their claims: Abdullah refused to pay and was besieged in Acre. He called for the intervention of Mehemet Ali, governor of Egypt; the latter settled the dispute, but Abdullah then refused to discharge the claims of Mehemet Ali. The latter accordingly sent 20,000 men under the command of his son Ibrahim Pasha, who besieged Acre in 1831 and entered and plundered it. So began the short-lived Egyptian domination of Palestine. Mehemet Ali proved

[1] When this French colony was established is uncertain; Maundrell found them there at the end of the 17th century.

no less a tyrannical master than the Turks and the sheiks; the country revolted in 1834, but the insurrection was quelled. In 1840 Lebanon revolted; and in the same year the Turks, with the aid of France, England and Austria, regained Palestine and expelled the Egyptian governor.

From 1840 onwards the Ottoman government gradually strengthened its hold on Palestine. The power of the local *Recent history.* sheiks was step by step reduced, till it at last became evanescent—to the unmixed advantage of the whole country; and the increase of European interests has led to the establishment of consulates and vice-consulates of the great powers in Jerusalem and in the ports.

The battle of religions still continued. In 1847 the dispute in the Church of the Nativity at Bethlehem about the right to mark with a star the birthplace of Christ became one of the prime causes of the Crimean war. In 1860 occurred a sudden anti-Christian outbreak in Damascus and the Lebanon, in which 14,000 Christians were massacred. On the other hand it may be mentioned that on the 30th of June 1855 the cross was for the first time since the crusades borne aloft through the streets of Jerusalem on the occasion of the visit of a European prince; and that in 1858 the sacred area of the Haramesh-Sherif—the mosque on the site of the Temple of Jerusalem—was for the first time thrown open to Christian visitors. The latter half of the 19th century is mainly occupied with the record of a very remarkable process of colonisation and settlement—French and Russian monastic and other establishments, some of them semi-religious and semi-political; German colonies; fanatical American communities; Jewish agricultural settlements—all, so to speak, "nibbling" at the country, and each so intent upon gaining a step on its rivals as to be forgetful of the gathering storm. For in the background of all is the vast peninsula of Arabia, which at long intervals fills with its wild, untamable humanity to a point beyond which it cannot support them. This has been the origin of the long succession of Semitic waves—Babylonian, Assyrian, Canaanite, Hebrew, Nabataean, Moslem—that have flowed over Mesopotamia and Palestine; there is every reason to suppose that they will be followed by others, and that the Arab will remain master at the end, as he was in the beginning.

In 1896 Herzl (*q.v.*) issued his proposal for the establishment of a Jewish state in Palestine and in 1898 he came to the country to investigate its possibilities. The same year was signalised by the picturesque visit of the German emperor, William II.; which gave a great stimulus to German interests in the Holy Land.

In 1902 Palestine was devastated by a severe epidemic of cholera. In 1906 arose a dispute between the British and Turkish governments about the boundary between Turkish and Egyptian territory, as the Turks had interfered with some of the landmarks. A joint commission was appointed, which marked out the boundary from Rafah, about midway between Gaza and El-Arish, in an almost straight line S.S.W. to Tabah in 29° 30′ on the west side of the gulf of Akaba. A map of the boundary will be found in the *Geographical Journal* (1907), xxix. 88.

2. The Holy Places.—To the vast majority of civilised humanity, Jewish, Christian and Moslem, the religious interest of the associations of Palestine predominates over every other, and at all ages has attracted pilgrims to its shrines. We need not here do more than allude to the centralization of Jewish ideas and aspirations in Jerusalem, especially in the holy rock on which tradition (and probably textual corruption) have placed the scene of Abraham's sacrifice of Isaac, and over which the Most Holy Place of the Temple stood. The same associations are those of the Moslem, whose religion has so strangely absorbed the prophets and traditions of the older faiths. Other shrines, such as the alleged tomb of Moses, and the mosque of Hebron over the cave of Machpelah, are the centres of Moslem pilgrimage. Christianity is however responsible for the greatest development of the cult of holy-places, and it is to the sacred shrines of christendom that we propose to confine our attention.

There is no evidence that the earliest Christians were imbued with the archaeological spirit that interested itself in sites which the Risen Lord had vacated. The site of Golgotha and of the the Holy Sepulchre, of the manger or of the home at Bethany, were to them of no special moment in comparison with the one all-important fact that "Christ was risen." It was not till the clear-cut impress of the events of Christ's life, death and resurrection had with the lapse of years faded from human recollection, that there arose a desire to "seek the living among the dead." The story begins with Helena, mother of Constantine the Great, who became fired with zeal to fix definitely the spots where the great events of Christianity had taken place, and in A.D. 326 visited Palestine for the purpose.

The Holy Sepulchre. Helena's pilgrimage was, as might be expected, attended with complete success. The True Cross was discovered; and by excavation conducted under Constantine's auspices, the Holy Sepulchre, "contrary to all expectation" as Eusebius naïvely says, was discovered also (see JERUSALEM; and SEPULCHRE, THE HOLY). The seed thus sown rapidly germinated and multiplied. The stream of pilgrimage to the Holy Land began immediately, and has been flowing ever since. Onwards from A.D. 333, when an anonymous pilgrim from Bordeaux visited the "holy places" and left a succinct account of his route and of the sights which came under his notice, we possess a continuous chain of testimony written by pilgrims relating what they heard and saw.

It is a pathetic record. No site, no legend, is too impossible for the unquestioning faith of these simple-minded men and women. And by comparing one record with another, we can follow the multiplication of "holy places," and sometimes can even see them being shifted from one spot to another, as the centuries pass. Not one of these devout souls had any shadow of suspicion that, except natural features (such as the Mount of Olives, the Jordan, Ebal, Gerizim, &c.) and *possibly* a very few individual sites (such as Jacob's well at Shechem), there was not a single spot in the whole elaborate system that could show even the flimsiest evidence of authenticity! The growth and development of "holy sites" can best be illustrated, in an article like the present, by a few figures. The account of the "holy places" seen in Palestine by the Bordeaux pilgrim, just mentioned, occupies twelve pages in the translation of the *Palestine Pilgrims' Text Society* (in whose publications the records of these early travellers can most conveniently be studied): and those twelve pages may be reduced to seven or eight as they are printed with wide margins, and have many footnotes added by the editor. On the other hand the experiences and observations of Felix Fabri, a Dominican monk who came to Palestine about A.D. 1480, occupies in the same series two large volumes of over 600 pages each![1]

This process of development has been illustrated in our own time—a single instance will suffice. In the so-called "Via Dolorosa" is a cave which was opened and planned about 1870. It subsequently became closed and forgotten, houses covering its entrance. In 1906 it was re-opened, the houses being cleared away, and a hospice for Greek pilgrims erected in place of them. During these works some local archaeologists attempted to penetrate the cave but were driven away by the labourers with curses. At last the hospice was finished and the cave opened for inspection. A pair of stocks was then shown beautifully cut in the rock, where no stocks appeared in the plan of 1870; with a crude painting suspended on the wall above, blasphemously representing the Messiah confined in them![2]

The Franciscans were nominated custodians of the "holy places" by Pope Gregory IX. in 1230. Certain sites have, however, always been held by the Oriental sects, and since 1808, when the Holy Sepulchre church was destroyed by fire, the number of these has greatly increased. Indeed the 19th

[1] This comparison is made in full realization of the fact that the Bordeaux record is a dry catalogue, and that Fabri's work is swelled by the miscellaneous gossip and "padding" which makes it one of the most delightful books ever written in the middle ages.
[2] See the exposure in the *Revue Biblique* (the organ of the Dominican school of St Stephen at Jerusalem) for 1907.

XX. II

century was disgraced, in Palestine, by a feverish "scramble" for sacred sites, in which the most rudimentary ethics of Christianity were forgotten in the all-mastering desire to oust rival sects and orders. Bribery, fraud, even violence, have in turn been employed to serve the end in view: and churches, chapels and monasteries, most of them in the worst architectural taste, have sprung up like mushrooms over the surface of the country, and are perpetuating the memory of pseudo-sanctuaries which from every point of view were best relegated to oblivion. The zeal and self-sacrificing devotion which some of these establishments, and their inmates, display, and their noble labours on behalf of the country, its people and its history throw into yet more painful relief the actions and attitudes of some of their fellow-Christians.

The authenticity of the "holy places" was first attacked seriously in the 18th century by a bookseller of Altona named Korte; and since he led the way, a steady fire of criticism has been poured at this huge mass of invention. The process of manufacturing new sites, however, continues unchecked. Even the Protestant churches are not exempt from blame in the matter; a small tomb near the Damascus Gate of Jerusalem has been fixed upon by a number of English enthusiasts as the true "Holy Sepulchre," an identification for which there is nothing to be said.

The monasteries of the Roman communion and their residents were under French protection until the disturbance between Greek and Franciscan monks in the Holy Sepulchre church (Nov. 4, 1901), which arose over the question as to the right to sweep a certain flight of stairs. Stones and other weapons were freely used, and several of the combatants and bystanders were seriously injured. As one result of the subsequent investigations, Latin monks of other countries were assigned to the protection of the consuls of those countries.

3. Colonization.—Down to the time of Mehemet Ali the only foreigners permanently resident in the country were the members of various monastic orders, and a few traders, such as the French merchants of Acre. The first protestant missionaries (those under the London Society for the Promotion of Christianity among the Jews), settled in Jerusalem in 1823; to them is due the inception of the trade in olive-wood articles, invented for the support of their converts. In 1846-1848 a remarkable religious brotherhood (the *Brüderhaus,* founded by Spittler of Basel) settled in Jerusalem: it was originally intended to be a settlement of celibate mechanics that would form a nucleus of mission work to evangelize the world. One of this community was Dr C. Schick, who lived over 50 years in Jerusalem, and made many valuable contributions to its archaeology. In 1849 came the first of several examples that have appeared in Palestine from time to time of that curious product of American religious life—a community of dupes or visionaries led by a prophet or prophetess with claims to divine guidance. The leader in this case was one Mrs Minor, who came to prepare the land for the expected Second Advent. Her followers quarrelled and separated in 1853. This event is of importance, as it had much to do with the remarkable development of Jewish colonization which is a special feature of the latter part of the history of the 19th century in Palestine. For Mrs Minor, having an interest in the Jewish people, was befriended by Sir Moses Montefiore; after her death her property was placed in charge of a Jew, and later passed into the hands of the Alliance Israélite Universelle. This body in 1870 established an agricultural colony for Jews on the road from Jaffa to Jerusalem ("Mikweh Israel").

Another visionary American colony, led by a certain Adams, came in 1866. They brought with them framed houses from America, which are still standing at Jaffa. But the Adamsites suffered from disease and poverty, and lost heart in a couple of years: returning to America, they sold their property to a German community, the *Tempelgemeinde,* a Unitarian sect led by Messrs Hoffmann and Hardegg who established themselves in Jaffa in 1868. Unlike the ill-fated American communities, these hardy Württemberg peasants have flourished in Palestine, and their three colonies—at Jaffa, Haifa, and Jerusalem—are the most important European communities now in the country

2d

Since 1870 there has been a steady development of Jewish immigration, consisting principally of refugees from countries where anti-Semitism is an important element in politics. Baron de Rothschild has invested large sums in Jewish colonies, but at the commencement of the present century he handed over their administration to the Jewish Colonization Association. Time alone can show how far these colonies are likely to be permanently successful, or how the subtly enervating influence of the climate will affect later generations.

4. *Exploration.*—Previous to the 19th century the turbulent condition of the country made exploration difficult, and, off the beaten track, impossible. There are many books written by early pilgrims and by more secular travellers who visited the country, which—when they are not devoted to the setting forth of valueless traditions, as is too often the case—give very useful and interesting pictures of the conditions of life and of travel in the country. Scientific exploration does not begin before Edward Robinson, an American clergyman, who, after devoting many years to study to fit himself for the work, made a series of journeys through the country, and under the title of *Biblical Researches in Palestine* (1841–1856) published his itineraries and observations. His work is marred by the hastiness of his visits and consequent superficiality of his descriptions of sites, and by some rash and untenable identifications: but it is at once a standard and the foundation of all subsequent topographical work in the country. He was worthily followed by Titus Tobler, who in 1853 and later years published volumes abounding in exact observation; and by V. Guerin, whose *Description géographique, historique, et archéologique de la Palestine*, in 7 vols. (1868–1880), contains an extraordinary mass of material collected in personal travel through the country.

In 1864 was founded the Palestine Exploration Fund, under the auspices of which an ordnance survey map of the country was completed (published 1881), and accompanied by volumes containing memoirs on the topography, orography, hydrography, archaeology, fauna and flora, and other details. A similar work east of the Jordan was begun but (1882) stopped by the Ottoman government. The same society initiated the scientific exploration of the mounds of Palestine. In 1891 it excavated Tell el-Hesi (Lachish); in 1896–1898 the south wall of Jerusalem; in 1898–1900 Tell es-Safi (Gath) and some smaller mounds in the Shephelah; all under the direction of Dr F. J. Bliss. In 1902 it began the excavation of Gezer under the direction of R. A. S. Macalister (see GEZER).

The example thus set has been followed by French, German and American explorers. The *Deutscher Palästina-Verein* was founded in 1878, and under its auspices important surveys have been carried out, especially those of G. Schumacher east of the Jordan; Tell el-Mutesellim (Megiddo) has also been excavated. The Austrian Dr E. Sellin, working independently, has excavated Tell Ta'nuk (Taanach), and in 1907 began work upon the mount of Jericho. An admirable biblical and archaeological school, under the control of the Dominican order, exists at Jerusalem; and German and American archaeological institutions, educational in purpose, are also there established. Valuable work in exploration is annually done by the directors of these schools and by their pupils. Under this head we must not omit to mention A. Musil's investigations of some remote parts of Eastern Palestine, and R. E. Brünnow's great survey of Petra, with part of Moab and Edom.

BIBLIOGRAPHY.—The literature relating to Palestine is very abundant; see especially, P. Thomsen, *Systemat. Bibliog. f. Palästina-Literatur*, i., 1895–1904 (Leipzig, 1908). A large collection of names of works will be found in R. Röhricht, *Bibliotheca geographica Palaestinae* (1890). Older bibliographies are T. Tobler, *Bibliographia Geographica Palaestinae* (1869), with a supplement in Petzholdt's *Neuer Anzeiger für Bibliographie und Bibliothekswissenschaft* (1875).
TOPOGRAPHY.—C. Ritter, *Vergleichende Erdkunde*, xv.–xvii. (1848–1855); E. Robinson, *Biblical Researches in Palestine* (1841). *Later Biblical Researches* (1856); *Physical Geography* (1865); A. Reland, *Palaestina monumentis veteribus illustrata* (1714); H. B. Tristram, *Land of Israel* (1865), *Land of Moab* (1873); *The Palestine*

Exploration Fund; map and companion volumes (Memoirs of the Survey of Western Palestine), 7 vols.; S. Merrill, *East of the Jordan* (1881); T. Tobler, *Bethlehem* (1849), *Nazareth* (1868), *Dritte Wanderung* (1859); C. R. Conder, *Tent Work in Palestine* (1878); G. Schumacher, *Across the Jordan* (1885); *The Jaulan* (1888), *Abila* (1889), *Pella* (1888), and *Northern Ajlun* (1890); C. R. Conder, *Heth and Moab* (1883); C. Baedeker, *Palestine and Syria* (1906); Victor Guérin, *Description géographique, historique, et archéologique de la Palestine* (1868–1880); G. A. Smith, *Historical Geography of the Holy Land* (1897); F. J. Bliss, *The Development of Palestine Exploration* (1906).
HISTORY.—L. B. Paton, *Early History of Syria and Palestine* (1902); H. Winckler in 3rd ed. of Schrader's *Keilinschriften u. d. Alte Test.* (1903); G. Cormack, *Egypt in Asia* (1908); see further art. JEWS, § 45; J. A. Montgomery, *The Samaritans* (1907), E. Schürer, *Geschichte des jüdischen Volkes im Zeitalter Jesu Christi* (3rd ed., 1898); S. Merrill, *Galilee in the time of Christ* (1885); W. Besant and E. H. Palmer, *Jerusalem* (4th ed., 1899); *Regesta regni hierosolymitani, 1097–1291* (ed. R. Röhricht, 1893, 1904); R. Röhricht, *Geschichte der Kreuzzüge* (1898); B. von Kugler, *Geschichte der Kreuzzüge* (1880); C. R. Conder, *Latin Kingdom of Jerusalem, 1099–1291* (1897); E. G. Rey, *Les Colonies franques de Syrie* (1883); J. Finn, *Stirring Times or Records from Jerusalem* (1878); C. H. Churchill, *Mount Lebanon* (1853, for modern history).
RELIGION, FOLKLORE, CUSTOM.—H. J. van Lennep, *Bible Lands, their Modern Customs and Manners* (1875); W. M. Thomson, *The Land and the Book* (1881–1883); W. R. Smith, *Lectures on the Religion of the Semites* (1894); G. A. Barton, *Sketch of Semitic Origins* (1902); S. I. Curtiss, *Primitive Semitic Religion To-day* (1902); W. R. Smith, *Kinship and Marriage* (1903); J. E. Hanauer, *Tales Told in Palestine* (1904); J. Lagrange, *Études sur les religions sémitiques* (1905); J. E. Hanauer, *Folklore of the Holy Land* (1907); J. G. Frazer, *Adonis, Attis and Osiris: Studies in the History of Oriental Religion* (1907); A. Jaussen, *Coutumes des Arabes au Pays de Moab* (1908); S. A. Cook, *Religion of Ancient Palestine* (1908).
EXCAVATIONS AND ARCHAEOLOGY.—C. Clermont-Ganneau, *Recueil d'archéologie orientale* (from 1885), *Archaeological Researches in Palestine, 1873–1874* (2 vols., 1899, 1896); W. M. F. Petrie, *Tell el-Hesy* (1891); F. J. Bliss, *A Mound of Many Cities* (1894), *Excavations at Jerusalem, 1894–1897* (1898); F. J. Bliss and R. A. S. Macalister, *Excavations in Palestine, 1898–1900* (1902); E. Sellin, *Tell Ta'annek* (Denkschriften of the Vienna Academy, 1904); J. P. Peters and H. Thiersch, *Painted Tombs in the Necropolis of Marissa* (1905); G. Schumacher, *Tell el-Mutesellim*, vol. i. (1908); E. Sellin, *Excav. of Jericho*, in *Mitteil. d. deutschen orient. Gesellschaft zu Berlin*, No. 39 (1908); G. Perrot and C. Chipiez, *History of Art in Sardinia, Judaea, &c.* (1890); I. Benzinger, *Hebräische Archäologie* (2nd ed., 1907); H. Vincent, *Canaan d'après l'exploration récente* (1907); H. Gressmann, *Ausgrab. in Pal. u. d. Alte Test.* (1908), *Pal. Erdgeruch in der israel. Relig.* (1909); S. R. Driver, *Modern Research as illustrating the Bible* (1909); P. Thomsen, *Palästina u. seine Kultur* (1909).
EPIGRAPHY AND NUMISMATICS.—F. de Saulcy, *Numismatique de la Terre Sainte* (1875); F. W. Madden, *Coins of the Jews* (1881); T. Reinach, *Jewish Coins* (1903). See further, SEMITIC LANGUAGES and NUMISMATICS.
THE "HOLY PLACES."—Liévin de Hamme, *Guide de la Terre Sainte* (1876).
EARLY PILGRIMS AND GEOGRAPHERS.—A. Neubauer, *La géographie du Talmud* (1868); P. de Lagarde, *Onomastica sacra* (1870); E. Carmoly, *Itinéraires de la Terre Sainte* (1847); P. Geyer, *Itinera hierosolymitana, saec.*, iv.–viii. (1898). Publications of the Société de l'orient Latin, and of the Palestine Pilgrims Text Society.
FAUNA AND FLORA.—H. B. Tristram, *Natural History of the Bible* (1867); G. E. Post, *Flora of Syria, Palestine and Sinai* (1896).
CLIMATE.—J. Glaisher, *Meteorological Observations at Jerusalem* (1903).
JOURNALS.—*Quarterly Statement, Palestine Exploration Fund* (from 1869); *Zeitschrift des deutschen Palästina-Vereins* (from 1878); *Revue biblique* (from 1892); *Revue de l'orient Latin* (from 1893); *Mitteilungen der vorderasiatischen Gesellschaft* (from 1897).

(R. A. S. M.)

PALESTINE, a city and the county-seat of Anderson county, Texas, U.S.A., about 90 m. E. by N. of Waco. Pop. (1910 census) 10,482. It is served by two lines of the International & Great Northern railway, and by the Texas State railway. Palestine is the trade centre of a district which produces cotton, timber; fruit (especially peaches), an excellent grade of wrapper tobacco, petroleum, iron-ore and salt. It has various manufactures, including cotton gins, cotton-seed oil, cigars, lumber and brick. Its factory products were valued at $735,162 in 1905. About 2 m. south-west of Palestine a settlement (the first in the present Anderson county) was made in 1837, and there Fort Houston, a stockade fort, was built to protect the settlers from the Indians. Palestine was laid out and was made the county-seat in 1846; it was chartered as a city in 1875, and rechartered in 1905. In 1909 it adopted a commission government.

PALESTRINA, GIOVANNI PIERLUIGI DA (1526–1594), Italian composer, was born in Palestrina (the ancient Praeneste) at the foot of the Sabine mountains, in 1526. The various versions of his name make an interesting record. He appears as Palestina, Pellestrino, Gio. Palestina, Gianetto Palestrina, Gianetto da Palestrina, Gian Pierl. de Palestrina, Joh. Petrus Aloisius, Jo. Petraloys, Gianetto, Giov. Prenestini, Joannes Praenestinus, Joannes Petraloysius Prenestinus.

Palestrina seems to have been at Rome from 1540 to 1544, when he studied possibly under Gaudio Mell, but not under Goudimel as has erroneously been assumed. On the 12th of June 1547 he married Lucrezia de Goria. In 1551, by favour of Pope Julius III., he was elected Magister Cappellae and Magister Puerorum at the Cappella Giulia, S. Pietro in Vaticano, with a salary of six scudi per month, and a house. Three years later he published his *First Book of Masses*, dedicated to Pope Julius III., and beginning with the missa "Ecce sacerdos magnus." On the 13th of January 1555, Palestrina was enrolled, by command of Pope Julius III., among the singers of the Cappella Sistina. This honour involved the resignation of his office at the Cappella Giulia, which was accordingly bestowed upon his friend Animuccia. But the legality of the new appointment was disputed on the ground that Palestrina was married, and the father of four children, his wife, Lucrezia, being still alive; and, though, for the moment, the pope's will was law, the case assumed a different complexion after his death, which took place only five weeks afterwards. The next pope, Marcellus II., was succeeded after a reign of 23 days, by Paul IV.; and within less than a year (July 30, 1555) that stern reformer dismissed Palestrina, together with two other married singers, A. Ferrabosco and Bari, with a consolatory pension of six scudi per month to each. This cruel disappointment caused Palestrina a dangerous illness; but in October 1555 he was appointed maestro di cappella at the Lateran, without forfeiting his pension; and in February 1561 he exchanged this preferment for a similar one, with an allowance of 16 scudi per month, at Santa Maria Maggiore.

Palestrina remained in office at this celebrated basilica for ten years, and to this period is assigned an important chapter in the history of music. Many circumstantial details of this chapter are undoubtedly legends, due to the pious imagination of Baini and others. In 1562 the council of Trent censured the prevalent style of ecclesiastical music with extreme severity. In 1564 Pope Pius IV. commissioned eight cardinals to investigate the causes of complaint; and these proved to be so well founded that it was seriously proposed to forbid the use of all music in the services of the Church, except unisonous and unaccompanied plain-chant. In these circumstances Palestrina is said to have been invited by two of the most active members of the commission to come to the rescue. He accordingly submitted three masses to Cardinal Carlo Borromeo for approval. These were privately rehearsed, in presence of the commissioners, at the palace of Cardinal Vitellozzi; and the judges were unanimous in deciding that the third mass fulfilled, in the highest possible degree, all the conditions demanded. The private trial took place in June 1565, and on the 19th of that month the mass was publicly sung at the Sistine Chapel, in presence of Pope Pius IV., who compared its music to that heard by St John in his vision of the New Jerusalem. Parvi transcribed it, for the library of the choir, in characters of extraordinary size and beauty; and Palestrina was appointed by the pope composer to the Sistine Chapel, an office created expressly in his honour and confirmed to him by seven later pontiffs, though with the very insufficient honorarium of three scudi per month, in addition to the six which formed his pension.

In 1567 this mass was printed in Palestrina's *Liber secundus missarum*. The volume was dedicated to Philip II. of Spain, but the mass was called the *Missa Papae Marcelli*. This title, clearly given in honour of the short-lived pope Marcellus II.,

has given rise to an absurd story, told by Pellegrini and others, to the effect that the mass was composed by Pope Marcellus I., martyred early in the 4th century, and was only discovered by Palestrina. Of course in the 4th century such music was inconceivable. The *Missa Papae Marcelli* is now almost certainly known to have been composed in 1562, two years before Paul IV.'s commission. Its ineffable beauty had often been described in glowing terms by those who heard it in the Sistine Chapel, but it was only first heard in England in 1882, when the Bach choir, consisting of 200 unaccompanied voices, sang it at St James's Hall, under the direction of Mr Otto Goldschmidt.

Upon the death of Animuccia in 1571 Palestrina was re-elected to his appointment at the Cappella Giulia. He also succeeded Animuccia as maestro di cappella at the oratory of Philip Neri; but these appointments were far from lucrative, and he still remained a very poor man. A letter of thanks for 100 scudi, written on the 21st of March 1570 to the duke of Mantua, illustrates this situation. In 1580 he was much distressed by the death of his wife; and the loss of three promising sons, Angelo, Ridolfo and Silla, left him with one child only—Igino—a very unworthy descendant. In February 1581 he married the rich widow Virginia Dormuli. In 1586 Pope Sixtus V. wished to appoint him maestro to the pontifical choir, as successor to Antonio Boccapadule, then about to resign, and commissioned Boccapadule to prepare the choir for the change. Boccapadule, however, managed so clumsily that Palestrina was accused of having meanly plotted for his own advancement. The Pope was very angry, and punished the calumniators very severely; but Palestrina lost the appointment. These troubles, however, did not hinder his work, which he continued without intermission until the 2nd of February 1594, when he breathed his last in the arms of his friend, Filippo Neri. (W. S. R.)

In the articles, MUSIC, COUNTERPOINT, CONTRAPUNTAL FORMS, HARMONY, MASS, MOTET, and that portion of INSTRUMENTATION which deals with vocal music, the reader will find information as to many features of Palestrina's style and its relation to that of the 16th century in general. So simple are the materials of 16th-century music, and so close its limitations, that the difference between great and small artists, and still more the difference between one great artist and another, can be detected only by long and familiar experience. A great artist, working within limits so narrow and yet so natural, is fortunately apt to give us exceptional opportunities for acquiring the right kind of experience of his art, since his genius becomes far more prolific than a genius with a wider field for its energies. Yet all 16th-century masters seem to be illuminated by the infallibility of the normal musical technique of their time. This technique is no longer so familiar to us that its euphony and vivid tone can fail to impress us wherever we meet it. There is probably no respectable school piece of the 16th century, which, if properly performed in a Roman Catholic church, would be quickly distinguishable by ear from the style of Palestrina. But when we find that every addition to our acquaintance with Palestrina's works is an acquisition, not to our notions of the progressive possibilities of 16th-century music, but to our whole sense of style, we may then recognise that we are in the presence of one of the greatest artists of all time.

Palestrina's work has many styles. Within its narrow range there can be no such glaring contrasts as those of the "three styles" of Beethoven; yet the distinctions are as real as they are delicate. His early, or Flemish style, was apt to lead him into the notorious Flemish disregard of proportion. Yet in some of his greatest works, such as the *Missa brevis*, we find unmistakably Flemish features so idealized as to produce breadth of phrase (*Missa brevis*, Agnus Dei), remarkably modern firmness of form (ibid. second Kyrie), and close canonic sequence carried to surprising length resulting in natural unexpectedness of harmony and subtle swing of cross rhythm (*Amen* of Credo).

If we find it convenient to divide Palestrina's work roughly into three types, we shall be able to take the *Missa Papae Marcelli* as the crowning representative of his second style. It probably is his greatest work; at all events it continues to make that impression whenever it is read after a long course of his other works; yet there are many masses, too numerous to mention, which cannot easily be considered inferior to it. Indeed F. X. Haberl, the editor of the complete critical edition of Palestrina's works, prefers the *Missa Ecce ego Joannes*, first published by him in the 24th volume of that edition in 1887.

Palestrina-scholars will hardly think us singular for placing on the same plane as the *Missa Papae Marcelli* at least 16 out of Palestrina's 94 extant masses: *Missa brevis*, bk. 3, no. 3; *Dies sanctificatus*, bk. 6, no. 1; *Dilexi quoniam*, bk. 6, no. 5; *O admirabile commercium*, bk. 8, no. 3; *Dum complerentur*, bk. 8, no. 5; *Veni sponsa Christi*, bk. 9, no. 2; *Quinti toni*, bk. 10, no. 5; *Octavi toni*, bk. 11, no. 4; *Alma Redemptoris*, bk. 11, no. 5; *Ascendo ad Patrem*, bk. 12, no. 3; *Tu es Petrus*, bk. 12, no. 5; *Hodie Christus natus est*, bk. 13, no. 2; *Beatus Laurentius*, bk. 14, vol. 3; *Assumpta est Maria*, bk. 14, no. 5; *Tu es Petrus*, bk. 15, no. 5; *Ecce ego Joannes*, bk. 15, no. 6.

The third and most distinctive phase of Palestrina's style is that in which he relies entirely upon the beauty of simple masses of harmony without any polyphonic elaboration whatever. Sometimes, as in his four-part litanies, this simplicity is mainly a practical necessity; but it is more often used for the purpose of his profoundest expressions of sacramental or penitential devotion, as for instance in the motet *Fratres ego enim accepi*, the *Stabat Mater* and the first, really the latest, book of *Lamentations*.

Besides these three main styles there are numerous cross-currents. There is the interaction between the madrigal and ecclesiastical style, which Palestrina sometimes contrives to show without confusion or degradation, as in the mass *Vestiva i colli*. There is the style of the *madrigali spirituali*, including *Le Vergine* of Petrarca; which again distinguishes itself into a broader and a slighter manner. And there is lastly an astounding absorption of the wildest freaks of Flemish ingenuity into the loftiest polyphonic ecclesiastical style; the great example of which is the *Missa L'Homme armé*, a work much maligned by writers who know only its title and the part played by its secular theme in medieval music.

The works published in Palestrina's lifetime naturally contain a large proportion of his earlier compositions. After his death the publication of his works continued for some years. We are apt to read the musical history of the 17th century in the light of the works of its composers. But a somewhat different view of that time is suggested by the continual pouring out by influential publishers of posthumous works of Palestrina, in far greater quantities than Palestrina had either the influence or resource to publish in his lifetime. We regard the 17th-century monodists as triumphant iconoclasts; but it was not until their primitive efforts had been buried beneath the entirely new arts to which they led, that the style of Palestrina ceased to be upheld as the one artistic ideal. Moreover the posthumous works of Palestrina belong almost entirely to his latest and finest period; so that a study of Palestrina confined to the works which he himself was able to publish gives no adequate idea of the proportion which his greater works bear to the rest. It was not, then, the rise of monody that crowded 16th-century art out into a long oblivion. On the contrary, the Palestrina tradition was the one thing which gave 17th-century composers a practical basis for their technical training. Only in the 18th century did the new art, before coming to maturity under Bach and Handel, reduce the Palestrina style to a dead language.

In the middle of the 19th century that dead language revived in a renascence which has steadily spread throughout Europe. The *Musica divina* of Canon K. Proske of Regensburg, begun in 1853, was perhaps the first decisive step towards the restoration of Roman Catholic church music. The St Cecilia Verein, with Dr F. X. Haberl as its president, has carried on the publication and use of such music with the greatest energy in every civilized country. The difficulties of reintroducing it in its native home, Italy, were so enormous that it is arguable that they might not yet have been surmounted but for the adoption of less purely artistic methods by Don Lorenzo Perosi, who succeeded in crowding the Italian churches by the performance of compositions written in an artless manner which, by its mere negation of display, was fitted to produce upon unsophisticated listeners such devout impressions as might gradually wean them from the taste for theatrical modern church music. The pope's fiat has now inculcated the use of Gregorian and 16th-century church music as far as possible in all Roman Catholic churches, and the effect has been astonishing. Within eighteen months of Pius X.'s decree on church music, the choir of Cologne Cathedral, previously far less accustomed to a pure polyphonic style than most German Protestant choirs, at Easter of 1905 gave a very satisfactory performance of the *Missa Papae Marcelli*. The influence of what is henceforth an inevitable and continual familiarity with Palestrina's style, at least among Roman Catholics, cannot fail to have the profoundest effect upon modern musical culture.

Palestrina's works, as contained in the complete edition published by Breitkopf and Härtel, comprise 256 motets in 7 vols., the last two consisting largely of pieces hitherto unpublished, with one or two wrongly or doubtfully ascribed to Palestrina; 15 books of masses, of which only 6 were published in Palestrina's lifetime, the 7th being incompletely projected by him, and the 14th and 15th first collected by Haberl in 1887 and 1888; 3 books of *magnificats*, on all the customary tones; 1 vol. of hymns; 1 vol. (2 books) of offertories for the whole year; a volume containing 3 books of litanies and several 12-part motets; 3 books of lamentations; a very large volume of madrigals containing 2 early books and 30 later madrigals collected from mixed publications; 2 books of *Madrigali spirituali*, and 4 vols. of miscellaneous works, newly discovered, imperfectly preserved and doubtful. The fourth book of motets is not, like the first three, a collection of works written at different times, but a single scheme, being a setting of the Song of Solomon; and the fifth volume is, like the offertories, designed for use throughout the church year.

(D. F. T.)

PALETTE (the Fr. diminutive of *pale*, spade, blade of an oar, from Lat. *pala*, spade, baker's shovel or peel; cf. *pandere*, to spread), a term applied to many objects which are flat and thin, and specifically to a thin tablet made of wood, porcelain, or other material on which artists place their colours. The term is also used of the shallow box, with partitions for the different coloured *tesserae*, used by mosaic workers. By transference the colours which an individual artist employs are known as his "palette." The "palette-knife" is a thin flexible knife used for arranging the colours on the palette, &c., and also for the application of colour on the canvas in large masses.

PALEY, FREDERICK APTHORP (1815-1888), English classical scholar, was born at Easingwold in Yorkshire on the 14th of January 1815. He was the grandson of William Paley, and was educated at Shrewsbury school and St John's College, Cambridge (B.A. 1838). His conversion to Roman Catholicism forced him to leave Cambridge in 1846, but he returned in 1860 and resumed his work as "coach," until in 1874 he was appointed professor of classical literature at the newly founded Roman Catholic University at Kensington. This institution was closed in 1877 for lack of funds, and Paley removed to Boscombe, where he died on the 8th of December 1888. His most important editions are: Aeschylus, with Latin notes (1844-1847), the work by which he first attracted attention; Aeschylus (4th ed., 1879), Euripides (2nd ed., 1872), Hesiod (2nd ed., 1883), Homer's *Iliad* (2nd ed., 1884), Sophocles, *Philoctetes, Electra, Trachiniae, Ajax* (1880)—all with English commentary and forming part of the *Bibliotheca classica*; select private orations of Demosthenes (3rd ed., 1896-1898); Theocritus (2nd ed., 1869), with brief Latin notes, one of the best of his minor works. He possessed considerable knowledge of architecture, and published a *Manual of Gothic Architecture* (1846) and *Manual of Gothic Mouldings* (6th ed., 1902).

PALEY, WILLIAM (1743-1805), English divine and philosopher, was born at Peterborough. He was educated at Giggleswick school, of which his father was head master, and at Christ's College, Cambridge. He graduated in 1763 as senior wrangler, became fellow in 1766, and in 1768 tutor of his college. He lectured on Clarke, Butler and Locke, and also delivered a systematic course on moral philosophy, which subsequently formed the basis of his well-known treatise. The subscription controversy was then agitating the university, and Paley published an anonymous *Defence* of a pamphlet in which Bishop Law had advocated the retrenchment and simplification of the Thirty-nine Articles; he did not, however, sign the petition (called the "Feathers" petition from being drawn up at a meeting at the Feathers tavern) for a relaxation of the terms of subscription. In 1776 Paley was presented to the rectory of Musgrave in Westmorland, supplemented at the end of the year by the vicarage of Dalston, and presently exchanged for that of Appleby. In 1782 he became archdeacon of Carlisle. At the suggestion of his friend John Law (son of Edward Law, bishop of Carlisle and formerly his colleague at Cambridge), Paley published (1785) his lectures, revised and enlarged, under the title of *The Principles of Moral and Political Philosophy*. The book at once became the ethical text-book of the University of Cambridge, and passed through fifteen editions in the author's lifetime. He strenuously supported the abolition of the slave trade, and in 1789 wrote a paper on the subject. *The Principles* was followed in 1790 by his first essay in The field of Christian apologetics, *Horae Paulinae, or the Truth of the Scripture History of St Paul evinced by a Comparison of the Epistles which bear his Name with the Acts of the Apostles and with one another*, probably the most original of its author's works. It was followed in 1794 by the celebrated *View of the Evidences of Christianity*. Paley's latitudinarian views are said to have debarred him from the highest positions in the Church. But for his services in defence of the faith the bishop of London gave him a stall in St Paul's; the bishop of Lincoln made him subdean of that cathedral, and the bishop of Durham conferred upon him the rectory of Bishopwearmouth. During the remainder of his life his time was divided between Bishopwearmouth and Lincoln. In 1802 he published *Natural Theology, or Evidences of the Existence and Attributes of the Deity collected from the Appearances of Nature*, his last, and, in some respects, his most remarkable book. In this he endeavoured, as he says in the dedication to the bishop of Durham, to repair in the study his deficiencies in the church. He died on the 25th of May 1805.

In the dedication just referred to, Paley claims a systematic unity for his works. It is true that "they have been written in an order the very reverse of that in which they ought to be read"; nevertheless the *Natural Theology* forms "the completion of a regular and comprehensive design." The truth of this will be apparent if it is considered that the *Moral and Political Philosophy* admittedly embodies two presuppositions: (1) that "God Almighty wills and wishes the happiness of His creatures," and (2) that adequate motives must be supplied to virtue by a system of future rewards and punishments. Now the second presupposition depends, according to Paley, on the credibility of the Christian religion (which he treats almost exclusively as the revelation of these "new sanctions" of morality). The *Evidences* and the *Horae Paulinae* were intended as a demonstration of this credibility. The argument of these books, however, depends in turn upon the assumption of a benevolent Creator desirous of communicating with His creatures for their good; and the *Natural Theology*, by applying the argument from design to prove the existence of such a Deity, becomes the foundation of the argumentative edifice.

In his *Natural Theology* Paley has adapted with consummate skill the argument which Ray (1691) and Derham (1711) and Nieuwentyt[1] (1730) had already made familiar to Englishmen. "For my part," he says, "I take my stand in human anatomy"; and what he everywhere insists upon is "the necessity, in each particular case, of an intelligent designing mind for the contriving and determining of the forms which organized bodies bear." This is the whole argument, and the book consists of a mass of well-

[1] Bernard Nieuwentyt (1654–1718) was a Dutch disciple of Descartes, whose *Regt gebruik der Werelt Beschouwingen*, published in 1716, was translated into English in 1730 by J. Chamberlayne under the title of *The Religious Philosopher*. A charge of wholesale plagiarism from this book was brought against Paley in the *Athenaeum* for 1848. Paley refers several times to Nieuwentyt, who uses the famous illustration of the watch. But the illustration is not peculiar to Nieuwentyt, and had been appropriated by many others before Paley. The germ of the idea is to be found in Cicero, *De natura deorum*, ii. 34 (see Hallam, *Literature of Europe*, ii. 385, note.) In the case of a writer whose chief merit is the way in which he has worked up existing material, a general charge of plagiarism is almost irrelevant.

chosen instances marshalled in support of it. But by placing Paley's facts in a new light, the theory of evolution has deprived his argument of its force, so far as it applies the idea of special contrivance to individual organs or to species.

The *Evidences of Christianity* is mainly a condensation of Bishop Douglas's *Criterion* and Lardner's *Credibility of the Gospel History*. But the task is so judiciously performed that it would probably be difficult to get a more effective statement of the external evidences of Christianity than Paley has here presented. His idea of revelation depends upon the same mechanical conception of the relation of God to the world which dominates his *Natural Theology*; and he seeks to prove the divine origin of Christianity by isolating it from the general history of mankind, whereas later writers find their chief argument in the continuity of the process of revelation.

The face of the world has changed so greatly since Paley's day that we are apt to do less than justice to his undoubted merits. He is nowhere original, and nowhere profound, but his strong reasoning power, his faculty of clear arrangement and forcible statement, place him in the first rank of expositors and advocates. He masses his arguments, it has been said, with a general's eye. His style is perfectly perspicuous, and its "strong home-touch" compensates for what is lacking in elasticity and grace. Paley displays little or no spirituality of feeling; but this is a matter in which one age is apt to misjudge another, and Paley was at least practically benevolent and conscientiously attentive to his parish duties. The active part he took in advocating the abolition of the slave-trade is evidence of a wider power of sympathy. His unconquerable cheerfulness becomes itself almost religious in the last chapters of the *Natural Theology*, considering that they were written during the intervals of relief from the painful complaint which finally proved fatal to him.

For his life, see *Public Characters*(1802):Aikin's *General Biography*, vii. (1808); Lives, by G. W. Meadley (1809) and his son Edmund Paley, prefixed to the 1825 edition of his works; Leslie Stephen in *Dictionary of National Biography*; *Quarterly Review*, ii. (Aug. 1809); ix. (July 1813). On Paley as a theologian and philosopher, see Leslie Stephen, *English Thought in the Eighteenth Century*, i. 405 seq., ii. 121 seq.; R. Buddensieg, in Herzog-Hauck's *Realencyklopädie für protestantische Theologie*, xiv. (1904). See also ETHICS.

PALFREY, JOHN GORHAM (1796–1881), American historian, was born in Boston, Massachusetts, on the 2nd of May 1796. He graduated at Harvard, 1815, and became a Unitarian minister, being pastor of the Brattle Square church, Boston, 1818–1831. He was professor of sacred literature in the Harvard divinity school, 1830–1839. Entering politics, he was secretary of state of Massachusetts, 1844–1847; a representative in Congress, 1847–1849; and postmaster of Boston, 1861–1867. He was editor of the *North American Review*, 1835–1843. As a writer he is best known by his *History of New England* to the revolutionary war, in five volumes, of which the first appeared in 1859 and the last posthumously in 1890. He died at Cambridge, Massachusetts, on the 26th of April 1881.

PALFREY, a riding-horse, particularly one of smaller and lighter type than the war-horse, the "destrier" (Med. Lat. *dextrarius*, because led by the right hand till used), which was only ridden in battle or tournament. The palfrey was thus used on the march, &c., and also as a lady's riding-horse. "Palfrey" came into English through the O. Fr. *palefrei*, one of the numerous forms which the word took in its descent from the Late Lat. *paraveredus*, a hybrid word from Gr. παρά, in the sense of extra, and *veredus*, a post-horse, probably a Celtic word, for one who draws a *rheda* or carriage. The form *parefredus* gives the Mod. Ger. *Pferd*, horse, through the O.H.G. *pfarifrid*.

PALGHAT, a town of British India, in the Malabar district of Madras, on the Madras railway. Pop. (1901), 44,177. As the key to Travancore and Malabar from the East, it was formerly of considerable strategic importance. The fort fell into British hands in 1768, and subsequently formed the basis of many of the operations against Tippoo, which terminated in the storming of Seringapatam. The easy ascent by the Palghat Pass, formerly covered with teak forests, supplies the great route from the west coast to the interior. The municipality manages the Victoria college.

PALGRAVE, SIR FRANCIS (1788–1861), English historian, was the son of Meyer Cohen, a Jewish stockbroker, and was born in London in July 1788. He was educated privately and was so precocious a boy as to translate a Latin version of the *Battle of the Frogs and Mice* into French in 1796, which was published by his father in 1797. In 1803 Palgrave was articled to a firm of solicitors, but was called to the bar at the Middle Temple in 1827. On his marriage in 1823 with Elizabeth, daughter of Dawson Turner of Great Yarmouth, he had become a Christian, and had changed his name to Palgrave, the maiden name of his wife's mother. His work as a barrister was chiefly concerned with pedigree cases before the House of Lords. He edited for the Record Commission *Parliamentary Writs* (London, 1827–1834); *Rotuli curiae regis* (London, 1835); *The antient kalendars and inventories of the treasury of his majesty's exchequer* (London, 1836); and *Documents and records illustrating the history of Scotland* (London, 1837), which contains an elaborate introduction. In 1831 he published his *History of England, Anglo-Saxon Period,* later editions of which were published as *History of the Anglo-Saxons;* in 1832, his *Rise and Progress of the English Commonwealth,* pronounced by Freeman a "memorable book"; and in 1834 his *Essay upon the original authority of the king's council.* In 1832 he was knighted, and after serving as one of the municipal corporations commissioners, became deputy-keeper of the public records in 1838, holding this office until his death at Hampstead on the 6th of July 1861. Palgrave's most important work is his *History of Normandy and England,* which appeared in four volumes (London 1851–1864), and deals with the history of the two countries down to 1101.

He also wrote *Truths and Fictions of the Middle Ages* (London, 1837, and again 1844); *The Lord and the Vassal* (London, 1844); and *Handbook for Travellers in Northern Italy* (London, 1842, and subsequent editions).

Palgrave's four sons were: Francis Turner Palgrave (*q.v.*), sometime professor of poetry at Oxford; William Gifford Palgrave; Sir Robert Harry Inglis Palgrave (b. 1827), an authority upon banking and economics generally; and Sir Reginald Francis Douce Palgrave.

WILLIAM GIFFORD PALGRAVE (1826–1888) went to India as a soldier after a brilliant career at Charterhouse School and Trinity College, Oxford; but, having become a Roman Catholic, he was ordained priest and served as a Jesuit missionary in India, Syria, and Arabia. Forsaking the priesthood, about 1864, he was employed as a diplomatist by the British government in Egypt, Asia Minor, the West Indies, and Bulgaria, being appointed resident minister in Uruguay in 1884; he died at Montevideo on the 30th of September 1888. He wrote a romance, *Hermann Agha* (London, 1872), *A Narrative of a Year's Journey through Central and Eastern Arabia* (London, 1865), *Essays on Eastern Questions* (London, 1872), and other works.

SIR REGINALD PALGRAVE (1829–1904) became a solicitor in 1851; but two years later was appointed a clerk in the House of Commons, becoming clerk of the House on the retirement of Sir Erskine May in 1886. He was made a K.C.B. in 1892, retired from his office in 1900, and died at Salisbury on the 13th of July 1904. Sir Reginald wrote *The Chairman's Handbook; The House of Commons: Illustrations of its History and Practice* (London, 1869); and *Cromwell; an appreciation based on contemporary evidence* (London, 1890). He also assisted to edit the tenth edition of Erskine May's *Law, Privileges, Proceedings and Usage of Parliament* (London, 1896).

PALGRAVE, FRANCIS TURNER (1824–1897), English critic and poet, eldest son of Sir Francis Palgrave, the historian, was born at Great Yarmouth, on the 28th of September 1824. His childhood was spent at Yarmouth and at his father's house in Hampstead. At fourteen he was sent as a day-boy to Charterhouse; and in 1843, having in the meanwhile travelled extensively in Italy and other parts of the continent, he proceeded to Oxford, having won a scholarship at Balliol. In 1846 he interrupted his university career to serve as assistant private secretary to Gladstone, but returned to Oxford the next year, and took a first class in Literae Humaniores. From 1847 to 1862 he was fellow of Exeter College, and in 1849 entered the Education Department at Whitehall. In 1850 he accepted the vice-principalship of Kneller Hall Training College at Twickenham. There he came into contact with Tennyson, and laid the foundation of a lifelong friendship. When the training college was abandoned, Palgrave returned to Whitehall in 1855, becoming

examiner in the Education Department, and eventually assistant secretary. He married, in 1862, Cecil Grenville Milnes, daughter of James Milnes-Gaskell. In 1884 he resigned his position at the Education Department, and in the following year succeeded John Campbell Shairp as professor of poetry at Oxford. He died in London on the 24th of October 1897, and was buried in the cemetery on Barnes Common. Palgrave published both criticism and poetry, but his work as a critic was by far the more important. His *Visions of England* (1880–1881) has dignity and lucidity, but little of the "natural magic" which the greatest of his predecessors in the Oxford chair considered rightly to be the test of inspiration. His last volume of poetry, *Amenophis,* appeared in 1892. On the other hand, his criticism was always marked by fine and sensitive tact, quick intuitive perception, and generally sound judgment. His *Handbook to the Fine Arts Collection, International Exhibition, 1862,* and his *Essays on Art* (1866), though not free from dogmatism and over-emphasis, were sincere contributions to art criticism, full of striking judgments strikingly expressed. His *Landscape in Poetry* (1897) showed wide knowledge and critical appreciation of one of the most attractive aspects of poetic interpretation. But Palgrave's principal contribution to the development of literary taste was contained in his *Golden Treasury of English Songs and Lyrics* (1861), an anthology of the best poetry in the language constructed upon a plan sound and spacious, and followed out with a delicacy of feeling which could scarcely be surpassed. Palgrave followed it with a *Treasury of Sacred Song* (1889), and a second series of the *Golden Treasury* (1897), including the work of later poets, but in neither of these was quite the same exquisiteness of judgment preserved. Among his other works were *The Passionate Pilgrim* (1858), a volume of selections from Herrick entitled *Chrysomela* (1877), a memoir of Clough (1862) and a critical essay on Scott (1866) prefixed to an edition of his poems.

See Gwenllian F. Palgrave, *F. T. Palgrave* (1899).

PALI, the language used in daily intercourse between cultured people in the north of India from the 7th century B.C. It continued to be used throughout India and its confines as a literary language for about a thousand years, and is still, though in a continually decreasing degree, the literary language of Burma, Siam, and Ceylon. Two factors combined to give Pali its importance as one of the few great literary languages of the world: the one political, the other religious. The political factor was the rise during the 7th century B.C. of the Kosala power. Previous to this the Aryan settlements, along the three routes they followed in their penetration into India, had remained isolated, independent and small communities. Their language bore the same relation to the Vedic speech as the various Italian dialects bore to Latin. The welding together of the great Kosala kingdom, more than twice the size of England, in the very centre of the settled country, led insensibly but irresistibly to the establishment of a standard of speech, and the standard followed was the language used at the court at Sāvatthi in the Nepalese hills, the capital of Kosala. When Cotama the Buddha, himself a Kosalan by birth, determined on the use, for the propagation of his religious reforms, of the living tongue of the people, he and his followers naturally made full use of the advantages already gained by the form of speech current through the wide extent of his own country. A result followed somewhat similar to the effect, on the German language, of the Lutheran reformation. When, in the generations after the Buddha's death, his disciples compiled the documents of the faith, the form they adopted became dominant. But local varieties of speech continued to exist.

The etymology of the word Pali is uncertain. It probably means "row, line, canon," and is used, in its exact technical sense, of the language of the canon, containing the documents of the Buddhist faith. But when Pali first became known to Europeans it was already used also, by those who wrote in Pali, of the language of the later writings, which bear the same relation to the standard literary Pali of the canonical texts as medieval does to classical Latin. A further extension of the meaning in which the word Pali was used followed in a very suggestive way. The first book edited by a European in Pali was the *Mahāvaṃsa*, or Great Chronicle of Ceylon, published there in 1837 by Turnour, then colonial secretary in the island. James Prinsep was then devoting his rare genius to the decipherment of the early inscriptions of northern India, especially those of Asoka in the 3rd century B.C. He derived the greatest assistance from Turnour's work not only in historical information, but also as regards the forms of words and grammatical inflexions. The resemblance was so close that Prinsep called the alphabet he was deciphering the Pali alphabet, and the language expressed in it he called the Pali language. This was so nearly correct that the usage has been followed by other European scholars, and is being increasingly adopted. It receives the support of Mahānāma, the author of the Great Chronicle, who wrote in Ceylon in the 5th century A.D. He says (p. 253, ed. Turnour) that Buddhaghosa translated the commentaries, then existing only in Sinhalese, into Pali. The name here used by the chronicler for Pali is " the Māgadhī tongue," by which expression is meant, not exactly the language spoken in Māgadha, but the language in use at the court of Asoka, king of Kosala and Māgadha. With this use of the word, philologically inexact, but historically quite defensible, may be compared the use of the word English, which is not exactly the language of the Angles, or of the word French, which is not exactly the language of the Franks. The question of Pali becomes therefore three-fold: Pali before the canon, the canon, and the writings subsequent to the canon. The present writer has suggested that the word Pali should be reserved for the language of the canon, and other words used for the earlier and later forms of it;[1] but the usage generally followed is so convenient that there is little likelihood of the suggestion being followed. The threefold division will therefore be here adhered to.

For the history of Pali before the canonical books were composed we have no direct evidence. None of the pre-Buddhistic sites have as yet been excavated; and, with one doubtful exception, no inscriptions older than the texts have as yet been found. We have to argue back from the state of things revealed in the texts, of various dates from 450-250 B.C., and in the inscriptions from that date onwards. The inscriptions have now been subjected to a very full critical and philological analysis in Professor Otto Franke's *Pali und Sanskrit* (Strassburg, 1902). He shows that in the 3rd century B.C. the language used throughout northern India was practically one, and that it was derived directly from the speech of the Vedic Aryans, retaining many Vedic forms lost in the later classical Sanskrit. His list of such forms is much more complete than that given by Childers in the introduction to his *Dictionary of the Pali Language*. The particular form of this general speech which was used as the *lingua franca*, the Hindustani of the period, was the form in use in Kosala. Franke also shows that there were local peculiarities in small matters of spelling and inflexion, and that the particular form of the language used in and about the Avanti district, of which the capital was Ujjeni (a celebrated pre-Buddhistic city), was the basis of the language used in the sacred texts as we now have them. Long ago Westergaard, Rhys Davids and Ernst Kuhn,[2] had made the same suggestion, mainly on historical grounds. Mahinda, who took the texts to Ceylon, having been born at Vedisa in that district. The careful and complete collection, by Franke, of the philological evidence at present available, has raised this hypothesis into a practical certainty. The inscriptions are at present scattered through a number of learned periodicals; a complete list of all those that can be approximately dated between the 3rd century B.C. and the 2nd century A.D. is given in the first chapter of Franke's book. M. E. Senart has collected in his *Inscriptions de Piyadasi* (Paris, 1881-1886) those inscriptions of Asoka which were known up to the date of his work, subjecting them to a careful analysis, and providing an index to the words occurring in them. What is greatly needed is a new edition of this work including the Asoka inscriptions discovered during the last twenty years, and a similar edition of the other inscriptions. The whole of the Pali inscriptions so far discovered might fill somewhat more than a hundred pages of text. An outline of the history of the Pali alphabet has been given, with illustrations and references to the authorities, in Rhys Davids's *Buddhist India*, pp. 107-140.

The canonical texts are divided into three collections called Piṭakas, *i.e.* baskets. This figure of speech refers, not to a basket or box in which things can be stored, but to the baskets, used in India in excavations, as a means of handing on the earth from one worker to another. The first Piṭaka contains the *Vinaya*—that is, Rules of the Order; the second the *Suttas*, giving the doctrine, and the third the *Abhidhamma*, analytical exercises in the psychological system on which the doctrine is based. These have now nearly all, mainly through the work of the Pali Text Society, been published in Pali.

The Vinaya was edited in 5 vols. by H. Oldenberg; and the more important parts of it have been translated into English by Rhys Davids and Oldenberg in their *Vinaya Texts*.

The Sutta Piṭaka consists of five *Nikāyas*, four principal and one supplementary. The four principal ones have been published for the Pali Text Society, and some volumes have been translated into English or German. These four Nikāyas, sixteen volumes in all, are the main authorities for the doctrines of early Buddhism. The fifth Nikāya is a miscellaneous collection of treatises, mostly very short, on a variety of subjects. It contains lyrical and ballad poetry, specimens of early exegesis and commentary, lives of the saints, collections of edifying anecdotes and of the now well-known *Jātakas* or Birth Stories. Of these, eleven volumes had by 1910 been edited for the Pali Text Society by various scholars, the Jātakas and two other treatises had appeared elsewhere, and two works (one a selection of lives of distinguished early Buddhists, and the other an ancient commentary), were still in MS.

Of the seven treatises contained in the Abhidhamma Piṭaka five, and one-third of the sixth, had by 1910 been published by the Pali Text Society; and one, the *Dhamma Sangaṇi*, had been translated by Mrs Rhys Davids. A description of the contents of all these books in the canon is given in Rhys Davids's *American Lectures*, pp. 44-86.

A certain amount of progress has been made in the historical criticism of these books. Out of the twenty-nine works contained in the three Piṭakas only one claims to have an author. That one is the *Kathā Vatthu*, ascribed to Tissa the son of Moggali,[3] who presided over the third council held under Asoka. It is the latest book of the third Piṭaka. All the rest of the canonical works grew up in the schools of the Order, and most of them appear to contain documents, or passages, of different dates. In his masterly analysis of the Vinaya, in the introduction to his edition of the text, Professor Oldenberg has shown that there are at least three strata in the existing presentation of the Rules of the Order, the oldest portions going back probably to the time of the Buddha himself. Professor Rhys Davids has put forward similar views with respect to the Jātakas and the Sutta Nipāta in his *Buddhist India*, and with respect to the Nikāyas in general in the introduction to his *Dialogues of the Buddha*. And Professor Windisch has discussed the legends of the temptation in his *Māra und Buddha*, and those relating to the Buddha's birth in his *Buddha's Geburt*. It seems probable that the Vinaya and the four Nikāyas were put substantially into the shape in which we now have them before the council at Vesāli, a hundred years after the Buddha's death; that slight alterations and additions were made in them, and the miscellaneous Nikāya and the Abhidhamma books completed, at various times down to the third council under Asoka; and that the canon was then considered closed. No evidence has yet been found of any alterations made, after that time, in Ceylon; but there were probably before that time, in India, other books, now lost, and other recensions of some of the above.

Of classical Pali in northern India subsequent to the canon there is but little evidence. Three works only have survived. These are the *Milinda-pañha*, edited by V. Trenckner, and translated by Rhys Davids under the title *Questions of King Milinda*; the *Netti Paharaṇa*, edited by E. Hardy for the Pali Text Society in 1902; and the *Petaka Upadesa*. The former belongs to the north-west, the others to the centre of India, and all three may be dated vaguely in the first or second centuries A.D. The first, a religious romance of remarkable interest, may owe its preservation to the charm of its style, the others to the accident that they were attributed by mistake to a famous apostle. In any-case they are the sole survivors of what must

[1] *Journal* of the Royal Asiatic Society (1903), p. 398.
[2] Westergaard, *Über den ältesten Zeitraum der indischen Geschichte*, p. 87; Rhys Davids, *Transactions of the Philological Society* (1875), p. 70; Kuhn, *Beiträge zur Pali Grammatik*, 7-9.
[3] No doubt identical with Upagupta, the teacher of Asoka (cf. Vincent Smith, *Early History of India*, 2nd ed., 1908, and refs.).

have been a vast and varied literature. Professor Takakusu has shown the possibility of several complete books belonging to it being still extant in Chinese translations,[1] and we may yet hope to recover original fragments in central Asia, Tibet, or Nepal.

At p. 66 of the *Gandha Vaṃsa*, a modern catalogue of Pali books and authors, written in Pali, there is given a list of ten authors who wrote Pali books in India, probably southern India. We may conclude that these books are still extant in Burma, where the catalogue was drawn up. Two only of these ten authors are otherwise known. The first is Dhammapāla, who wrote in Kāñcipura, the modern Conjevaram in south India, in the 5th century of our era. His principal work is a series of commentaries on five of the lyrical anthologies included in the miscellaneous Nikāya. Three of these have been published by the Pali Text Society; and Professor E. Hardy has discussed in the *Zeitschrift der deutschen morgenländischen Gesellschaft* (1897), pp. 105-127, all that is known about him. Dhammapāla wrote also a commentary on the Netti mentioned above. The second is Buddhadatta, who wrote the *Jinālaṅkāra* in the 5th century A.D. It has been edited and translated by Professor J. Gray. It is a poem, of no great interest, on the life of the Buddha.

The whole of these Pali books composed in India have been lost there. They have been preserved for us by the unbroken succession of Pali scholars in Ceylon and Burma. These scholars (most of them members of the Buddhist Order, but many of them laymen) not only copied and recopied the Indian Pali books, but wrote a very large number themselves. We are thus beginning to know something of the history of this literature. Two departments have been subjected to critical study: the Ceylon chronicles by Professor W. Geiger in his *Mahāvaṃsa und Dīpavaṃsa*, and the earlier grammatical works by Professor O. Franke in two articles in the *Journal of the Pali Text Society* for 1903, and in his *Geschichte und Kritik der einheimischen Pali Grammatik*. Dr Forchhammer in his *Jardine Prize Essay*, and Dr Mabel Bode in the introduction to her edition of the *Sāsana-vaṃsa*, have collected many details as to the Pali literature in Burma.

The results of these investigations show that in Ceylon from the 3rd century B.C. onwards there has been a continuous succession of teachers and scholars. Many of them lived in the various *vihāras* or residences situate throughout the island; but the main centre of intellectual effort, down to the 8th century, was the Mahā Vihāra, the Great Minster, at Anurādhapura. This was, in fact, a great university. Authors refer, in the prefaces to their books, to the Great Minster as the source of their knowledge. And to it students flocked from all parts of India. The most famous of these was Buddhaghosa, from Behar in North India, who studied at the Minster in the 5th century A.D., and wrote there all his well-known works. Two volumes only of these, out of about twenty still extant in MS., have been edited for the Pali Text Society. About a century before this the *Dīpa-vaṃsa*, or Island Chronicle, had been composed in Pali verse by so indifferent that it is apparently the work of a beginner in Pali composition. No work written in Pali in Ceylon at a date older than this has been discovered yet. It would seem that up to the 4th century of our era the Sinhalese had written exclusively in their own tongue; that is to say that for six centuries they had studied and understood Pali as a dead language without using it as a means of literary expression. In Burma, on the other hand, where Pali was probably introduced from Ceylon, no writings in Pali can be dated before the 11th century of our era. Of the history of Pali in Siam very little is known. There have been good Pali scholars there since late medieval times. A very excellent edition of the twenty-seven canonical books has been recently printed there, and there exist in our European libraries a number of Pali MSS. written in Siam.

It would be too early to attempt any estimate of the value of this secondary Pali literature. Only a few volumes, out of several hundreds known to be extant in MS. have yet been published. But the department of the chronicles, the only

[1] *Journal* of the Pali Text Society (1905), pp. 72, 86.

one so far, at all adequately treated, has thrown so much light on many points of the history of India that we may reasonably expect results equally valuable from the publication and study of the remainder. The works on religion and philosophy especially will be of as much service for the history of ideas in these later periods as the publication of the canonical books has already been for the earlier period to which they refer. The Pali books written in Ceylon, Burma and Siam will be our best and oldest, and in many respects our only, authorities for the sociology and politics, the literature and the religion, of their respective countries.

SELECTED AUTHORITIES.—*Texts*: Pali Text Society (63 vols., 1882-1908); H. Oldenberg, *The Vinaya Piṭakam* (5 vols., London, 1879-1883); V. Fausböll, *The Jātaka* (7 vols., London, 1877-1897); G. Turnour, *The Mahāvaṃsa* (Colombo, 1837); H. Oldenberg, *The Dīpavaṃsa* (London, 1879); V. Trenckner, *Milinda* (London, 1880). *Translations*: Rhys Davids and H. Oldenberg, *Vinaya Texts* (3 vols., Oxford, 1881-1885); Rhys Davids, *Milinda* (2 vols., Oxford, 1890-1894), *Dialogues of the Buddha* (Oxford, 1899); H. C. Warren, *Buddhism in Translations* (Cambridge, Mass. 1896); Mrs Rhys Davids, *Buddhist Psychology* (London, 1900); K. E. Neumann, *Reden des Gotamo Buddho* (3 vols., Leipzig, 1896-1898); *Lieder der Mönche und Nonnen* (Berlin, 1899); Max Müller and V. Fausböll, *Dhammapada and Sutta Nipāta* (Oxford, 1881). *Philology*: R. C. Childers, *Dictionary of the Pali Language* (London, 1872-1875); Ernst Kuhn, *Beiträge zur Pali Grammatik* (Berlin, 1875); E. Müller, *Pali Grammar* (London, 1884); R. O. Franke, *Geschichte und Kritik der einheimischen Pali-Grammatik und Lexicographie*, and *Pali und Sanskrit* (Strasburg, 1902); D. Andersen, *Pali Reader* (London, 1904-1907); *History* (of the alphabet, language and texts): Rhys Davids, *American Lectures* (London, 3rd ed., 1908); *Buddhist India* (London, 1903); E. Windisch, *Māra und Buddha* (Leipzig, 1895), and *Buddha's Geburt* (Leipzig, 1908); W. Geiger, *Mahāvaṃsa und Dīpavaṃsa* (Leipzig, 1905); E. Forchhammer, *Jardine Prize Essay* (Rangoon, 1885); Dr Mabel Bode, *Sāsana-vaṃsa* (London, 1897). (T. W. R. D.)

PALIKAO, CHARLES GUILLAUME MARIE APPOLLINAIRE ANTOINE COUSIN MONTAUBAN, COMTE DE (1796-1878), French general and statesman, was born in Paris on the 24th of June 1796. As a cavalry officer young Montauban saw much service in Algeria, but he was still only a colonel when in 1847 he effected the capture of Abd-el-Kader. After rising to the rank of general of division and commanding the province of Constantine, he was appointed in 1858 to a command at home, and at the close of 1859 was selected to lead the French troops in the joint French and British expedition to China. His conduct of the operations did not escape criticism, but in 1862 he received from Napoleon III. the title of comte de Palikao (from the action of that name); he had already been made a senator. The allegation that he had acquired a vast fortune by the plunder of the Pekin summer palace seems to have been without foundation. In 1865 he was appointed to the command of the IV. army corps at Lyons, in the training of which he displayed exceptional energy and administrative capacity. In 1870 he was not given a command in the field, but after the opening disasters had shaken the Ollivier ministry he was entrusted by the empress-regent with the portfolio of war, and became president of the council (Aug. 10). He at once, with great success, reorganized the military resources of the nation. He claimed to have raised Marshal MacMahon's force at Châlons to 140,000 men, to have created three new army corps, 35 new regiments and 100,000 *gardes mobiles*, and to have brought the defences of the capital to a state of efficiency—all this in twenty-four days. He conceived the idea of sending the army of Châlons to raise the blockade of Metz. The scheme depended on a precision and rapidity of which the army of Châlons was no longer capable, and ended with the disaster of Sedan. After the capitulation of the emperor the dictatorship was offered to Palikao, but he refused to desert the empire, and proposed to establish a council of national defence, with himself as "lieutenant-general of government." Before a decision was made, the chamber was invaded by the mob, and Palikao fled to Belgium. In 1871 he appeared before the parliamentary commission of inquiry, and in the same year established *Un Ministère de la guerre de vingt-quatre jours*. He died at Versailles on the 8th of January 1878.

PALIMPSEST. The custom of removing writing from the surface of the material on which it had been inscribed, and thus preparing that surface for the reception of another text, has been practised from early times. The term palimpsest (from Gr. πάλιν, again, and ψάω, I scrape) is used by Catullus, apparently with reference to papyrus; by Cicero, in a passage wherein he is evidently speaking of waxen tablets; and by Plutarch, when he narrates that Plato compared Dionysius to a βιβλίον παλίμψηστον, in that his tyrant nature, being δυσέκπλυτος, showed itself like the imperfectly erased writing of a palimpsest MS. In this passage reference is clearly made to the washing off of writing from papyrus. The word παλίμψηστος can only in its first use have been applied to MSS. which were actually scraped or rubbed, and which were, therefore, composed of a material of sufficient strength to bear the process. In the first instance, then, it might be applied to waxen tablets; secondly, to vellum books. There are still to be seen, among the surviving waxen tablets, some which contain traces of an earlier writing under a fresh layer of wax. Papyrus could not be scraped or rubbed; the writing was washed from it with the sponge. This, however, could not be so thoroughly done as to leave a perfectly clean surface, and the material was accordingly only used a second time for documents of an ephemeral or common nature. To apply, therefore, the title of palimpsest to a MS. of this substance was not strictly correct; the fact that it was so applied proves that the term was a common expression. Traces of earlier writing are very rarely to be detected in extant papyri. Indeed, the supply of that material must have been so abundant that it was hardly necessary to go to the trouble of preparing a papyrus, already used, for a second writing.

In the early period of palimpsests, vellum MSS. were no doubt also washed rather than scraped. The original surface of the material, at all events, was not so thoroughly defaced as was afterwards the case. In course of time, by atmospheric action or other chemical causes, the original writing would to some extent reappear; and it is thus that so many of the capital and uncial palimpsests have been successfully deciphered. In the later middle ages the surface of the vellum was scraped away and the writing with it. The reading of the later examples is therefore very difficult or altogether impossible. Besides actual rasure, various recipes for effacing the writing have been found, such as to soften the surface with milk and meal, and then to rub with pumice. In the case of such a process being used, total obliteration must almost inevitably have been the result. To intensify the traces of the original writing, when such exist, various chemical reagents have been tried with more or less success. The old method of smearing the vellum with tincture of gall restored the writing, but did irreparable damage by blackening the surface, and, as the stain grew darker in course of time, by rendering the text altogether illegible. Of modern reagents the most harmless appears to be hydrosulphate of ammonia; but this also must be used with caution.

The primary cause of the destruction of vellum MSS. by wilful obliteration was, it need hardly be said, the dearth of material. In the case of Greek MSS., so great was the consumption of old codices for the sake of the material, that a synodal decree of the year 691 forbade the destruction of MSS. of the Scriptures or the church fathers—imperfect or injured volumes excepted. The decline of the vellum trade also on the introduction of paper caused a scarcity which was only to be made good by recourse to material already once used. Vast destruction of the broad quartos of the early centuries of our era took place in the period which followed the fall of the Roman Empire. The most valuable Latin palimpsests are accordingly found in the volumes which were remade from the 7th to the 9th centuries, a period during which the large volumes referred to must have been still fairly numerous. Late Latin palimpsests rarely yield anything of value. It has been remarked that no entire work has been found in any instance in the original text of a palimpsest, but that portions of many works have been taken to make up a single volume. These facts prove that scribes were indis-

criminate in supplying themselves with material from any old volumes that happened to be at hand.

An enumeration of the different palimpsests of value is not here possible (see Wattenbach, *Schriftwesen*, 3rd ed., pp. 299-317); but a few may be mentioned of which facsimiles are accessible. The MS. in the Bibliothèque Nationale, Paris, known as the Codex Ephraemi, containing portions of the Old and New Testaments in Greek, attributed to the 5th century, is covered with works of Ephraem Syrus in a hand of the 12th century (ed. Tischendorf, 1843, 1845). Among the Syriac MSS. obtained from the Nitrian desert in Egypt, and now deposited in the British Museum, some important Greek texts have been recovered. A volume containing a work of Severus of Antioch of the beginning of the 9th century is written on palimpsest leaves taken from MSS. of the *Iliad* of Homer and the Gospel of St Luke, both of the 6th century (*Cat. Anc. MSS.* vol. i., pls. 9, 10), and the *Elements* of Euclid of the 7th or 8th century. To the same collection belongs the double palimpsest, in which a text of St John Chrysostom, in Syriac, of the 9th or 10th century, covers a Latin grammatical treatise in a cursive hand of the 6th century, which in its turn has displaced the Latin annals of the historian Granius Licinianus, of the 5th century (*Cat. Anc. MSS.* ii., pls. 1, 2). Among Latin palimpsests also may be noticed those which have been reproduced in the *Exempla* of Zangemeister and Wattenbach. These are—the Ambrosian Plautus, in rustic capitals, of the 4th or 5th century, re-written with portions of the Bible in the 9th century (pl. 6); the Cicero *De republica* of the Vatican, in uncials, of the 4th century, covered by St Augustine on the Psalms, of the 7th century (pl. 17; *Pal. Soc.*, pl. 160); the Codex Theodosianus of Turin, of the 5th or 6th century (pl. 23); the Fasti Consulares of Verona, of A.D. 486 (pl. 29); and the Arian fragment of the Vatican, of the 5th century (pl. 31). Most of these originally belonged to the monastery of Bobbio, a fact which gives some indication of the great literary wealth of that house. By using skill and judgment, with a favouring light, photography may be often made a useful agent in the decipherment of obscure palimpsest texts. (E. M. T.)

PALINDROME (Gr. πάλιν, again, and δρόμος, a course), a verse or sentence which runs the same when read either backwards or forwards. Such is the verse—

Roma tibi subito motibus ibit amor;

or

Signa te, signa, temere me tangis et angis;

or

νίψον ἀνομήματα μὴ μόναν ὄψιν.

Some have refined upon the palindrome, and composed verses each word of which is the same read backwards as forwards; for instance, that of Camden—

Odo tenet mulum, madidam mappam tenet Anna,
Anna tenet mappam madidam, mulum tenet Odo.

The following is still more complicated, as reading in four ways—upwards and downwards as well as backwards and forwards:—

```
S A T O R
A R E P O
T E N E T
O P E R A
R O T A S
```

PALINGENESIS (Gr. πάλιν, again, γένεσις, becoming, birth), a term used in philosophy, theology and biology. In philosophy it denotes in its broadest sense the theory (e.g. of the Pythagoreans) that the human soul does not die with the body but is " born again " in new incarnations. It is thus the equivalent of metempsychosis (q.v.). The term has a narrower and more specific use in the system of Schopenhauer, who applies it to his doctrine that the will does not die but manifests itself afresh in new individuals. He thus repudiates the primitive metempsychosis doctrine which maintains the reincarnation of the particular soul. The word " palingenesis " or rather " palingenesia " may be traced back to the Stoics, who used the term for the continual re-creation of the universe by the Demiurgus (Creator) after its absorption into himself. Similarly Philo speaks of Noah and his sons as leaders of a " renovation " or " re-birth " of the earth. Josephus uses the term of the national restoration of the Jews, Plutarch of the transmigration of souls, and Cicero of his own return from exile. In the New Testament the properly theological sense of spiritual regeneration is used, though the word itself occurs only twice; and it is used by the church fathers, e.g. for the rite of baptism or for the state of repentance. In modern biology (e.g. Haeckel and Fritz Müller)

" palingenesis " has been used for the exact reproduction of ancestral features by inheritance, as opposed to " kenogenesis " (Gr. καινός new), in which the inherited characteristics are modified by environment.

PALISSY, BERNARD (1510–1589), French potter (see CERAMICS), is said to have been born about 1510, either at Saintes or Agen, but both date and locality are uncertain. It has been stated, on insufficient authority, that his father was a glass-painter and that he served as his father's apprentice. He tells us that he was apprenticed to a glass-painter and that he also acquired in his youth the elements of land-surveying. At the end of his apprenticeship he followed the general custom and became a travelling workman; acquiring fresh knowledge in many parts of France and the Low Countries, perhaps even in the Rhine Provinces of Germany and in Italy.

About 1539 it appears that he returned to his native district and, having married, took up his abode at Saintes. How he lived during the first years of his married life we have little record except when he tells us, in his autobiography, that he practised the arts of a portrait-painter, glass-painter and land-surveyor as a means of livelihood. It is known for instance that he was commissioned to survey and prepare a plan of the salt marshes in the neighbourhood of Saintes when the council of Francis I. determined to establish a salt tax in the Saintonge. It is not quite clear, from his own account, whether it was during his *Wanderjahr* or after he settled at Saintes that he was shown a white enamelled cup which caused him such surprise that he determined to spend his life—to use his own expressive phrase " like a man who gropes in the dark "—in order to discover the secrets of its manufacture. Most writers have supposed that this piece of fine white pottery was a piece of the enamelled majolica of Italy, but such a theory is hardly bear examination. In Palissy's time pottery covered with beautiful white tin-enamel was manufactured at many centres in Italy, Spain, Germany and the South of France, and it is inconceivable that a man so travelled and so acute should not have been well acquainted with its appearance and properties. What is much more likely is that Palissy saw, among the treasures of some nobleman, a specimen of Chinese porcelain, then one of the wonders of the European world, and, knowing nothing of its nature, substance or manufacture, he set himself to work to discover the secrets for himself. At the neighbouring village of La Chapelle-des-Pots he mastered the rudiments of peasant pottery as it was practised in the 16th century. Other equipment he had none, except such indefinite information as he presumably had acquired during his travels of the manufacture of European tin-enamelled pottery.

For nearly sixteen years Palissy laboured on in these wild endeavours, through a succession of utter failures, working with the utmost diligence and constancy·but, for the most part, without a gleam of hope. The story is a most tragic one; for at times he and his family were reduced to the bitterest poverty; he burned his furniture and even, it is said, the floor boards of his house to feed the fires of his furnaces; sustaining meanwhile the reproaches of his wife, who, with her little family clamouring for food, evidently regarded these proceedings as little short of insanity. All these struggles and failures are most faithfully recorded by Palissy himself in one of the simplest and most interesting pieces of autobiography ever written. The tragedy of it all is that Palissy not only failed to discover the secret of Chinese porcelain, which we assume him to have been searching for, but that when he did succeed in making the special type of pottery that will always be associated with his name it should have been inferior in artistic merit to the contemporary productions of Spain and Italy. His first successes can only have been a superior kind of " peasant pottery " decorated with modelled or applied reliefs coloured naturalistically with glazes and enamels. These works had already attracted attention locally when, in 1548, the constable de Montmorency was sent into the Saintonge to suppress the revolution there. Montmorency protected the potter and found him employment in decorating with his glazed terra-cottas the château d'Ecouen. The

patronage of such an influential noble soon brought Palissy into fame at the French court, and although he was an avowed Protestant, he was protected by these nobles from the ordinances of the parliament of Bordeaux when, in 1562, the property of all the Protestants in this district was seized. Palissy's workshops and kilns were destroyed, but he himself was saved, and, by the interposition of the all-powerful constable, he was appointed " inventor of rustic pottery to the king and the queen-mother "; about 1563, under royal protection, he was allowed to establish a fresh pottery works in Paris in the vicinity of the royal palace of the Louvre. The site of his kilns indeed became afterwards a portion of the gardens of the Tuileries. For about twenty-five years from this date Palissy lived ·and worked in Paris. He appears to have been a personal favourite of Catherine de' Medicis, and of her sons, in spite of his profession of the reformed religion.

Working for the court, his productions passed through many phases, for besides continuing his " rustic figulines " he made a large number of dishes and plaques ornamented with scriptural or mythological subjects in relief, and in many cases he appears' to have made reproductions of the pewter dishes of François Briot and other metal workers of the period. During this period too he gave several series of public lectures ·on natural history—the entrance fee being one crown, a large fee for those days—in which he poured forth all the ideas of his fecund mind. His ideas of springs and underground waters were far in advance of the general knowledge of his time, and he was one of the first men in Europe to enunciate the correct theory of fossils.

The close of Palissy's life was quite in keeping with his · active and stormy youth. Like Ambroise Paré, and some other notable men of his time, he was protected against ecclesiastical persecution by the court and some of the great nobles, but in the fanatical outburst of 1588 he was thrown into the Bastille, and although Henry III. offered him his freedom if he would recant, Palissy refused to save his life on any such terms. He was condemned to death when nearly eighty years of age, but he died in one of the dungeons of the Bastille in 1589.

Palissy's Pottery.—The technique of the various wares he made shows their derivation from the ordinary peasant pottery of the period, though Palissy's productions are, of course, vastly superior to anything of their kind previously made in Europe. It appears almost certain that he never used the potter's wheel, as all his best known pieces have evidently been pressed into a mould and then finished by modelling or by the application of ornament moulded in relief. His most characteristic productions are the large plates, ewers, oval dishes and vases to which he applied realistic figures of reptiles, fish, shells, plants and other objects. This is, however, not the work of an artist, but

Rustic Plate by Palissy.

that of a highly gifted naturalist at the dawn of modern science, who delighted to copy, with faithful accuracy, all the details of reptiles, fishes, plants or shells. We may be sure that his fossil shells were not forgotten, and it has been suggested, with great probability, that these pieces of Palissy's were only manufactured after his removal to Paris, as the shells are always well-known forms from the Eocene deposits of the Paris basin. Casts from these objects were fixed on to a metal dish or vase of the shape required, and a fresh cast of the whole formed a mould from which Palissy could reproduce many articles of the same kind. The various parts of each piece were painted in realistic colours, or as nearly so as could be reached by the pigments Palissy was able to discover and prepare. These colours were mostly various shades of blue from indigo to ultramarine, some rather vivid greens, several tints of browns and greys, and, more rarely, yellow. A careful examination of the most authentic Palissy productions shows that they excel in the sharpness of their modelling, in a perfect neatness of manufacture and, above all, in the subdued richness of their general tone of colour. The crude greens, bright purples and yellows are only found in the works of his imitators; whilst in the marbled colours on the backs of the dishes Palissy's work is soft and well fused, in the imitations it is generally dry, even harsh and uneven. Other pieces, such as dishes and plaques, were ornamented by figure subjects treated after the same fashion, generally scriptural scenes or subjects from classical mythology, copied, in many cases, from works in sculpture by contemporary artists.

Another class of designs used by Palissy were plates, tasse and the like, with geometrical patterns moulded in relief and pierced through, forming a sort of open network. Perhaps the most successful, as works of art, were those plates and ewers which Palissy moulded in exact facsimile of the rich and delicate works in pewter for which François Briot and other Swiss metal-workers were so celebrated. These are in very slight relief, executed with cameo-like finish, and are mostly of good design belonging to the school of metal-working developed by the Italian goldsmiths of the 16th century. Palissy's ceramic reproductions of these metal plates were not improved by the colours with which he picked out the designs.

Some few enamelled earthenware statuettes, full of vigour and expression, have been attributed to Palissy; but it is doubtful whether he ever worked in the round. On the whole his productions cannot be assigned a high rank as works of art, though they have always been highly valued, and in the 17th century attempts were made, both at Delft and Lambeth, to adapt his " rustic " dishes with the reliefs of animals and human figures. These imitations are very blunt in modelling and coarsely painted. They are generally marked on the back in blue with initials and a date—showing them to be honest adaptations to a different medium, not attempts at forgery such as have been produced during the last fifty years or so. One of the first signs of the revival of old French faience, a movement that was in great activity between 1840 and 1870, was the appearance of copies of Palissy's " Bestiole " dishes, made with great skill and success by Avisseau of Tours, and afterwards by Pull of Paris. Though both these men produced original works of their own, collectors have had great cause to regret the excellence of their copies, for many of the best, being unmarked, have found their way into good collections. The well-known potter, Barbizet, who set out to make " Palissys " for the million, flooded France for a time with rude copies that ought never to have deceived anyone.

The best collections of Palissy's ware are those in the museums of the Louvre, the Hôtel Cluny, and Sèvres; and in England that in the Victoria and Albert Museum, together with a few choice specimens in the British Museum and in the Wallace Collection.

As an author, Palissy was undoubtedly more successful than as a potter. A very high position amongst French writers is assigned to him by Lamartine (B. Palissy, 8vo., Paris, 1852). He wrote with vigour and simplicity on a great variety of subjects, such as agriculture, natural philosophy, religion, and especially in his L'Art de terre, where he gives an account of his processes and how he discovered them.

See Morley, Life of Palissy (1855); Marryat, Pottery (1850, pp. 31 seq.); A. Dumesnil, B. Palissy, le potier de terre (1851); A. Tainturier, Terres émaillées de Palissy (1863); Delecluze, B. Palissy (1838); Enjubault, L'Art céramique de B. Palissy (1858); Audiat, Étude sur la vie . . . de B. Palissy (1868); H. Delange, Monographie de l'œuvre de B. Palissy (1862). For Palissy as a Huguenot, see Rossignol, Des Protestantes illustres, No. iv. (1861). The best English account of Palissy as a potter is that given by M. L. Solon, the most distinguished pottery-artist of the 19th century, in his History and Description of the Old French Faience (1903). (W. B.°)

PALITANA, a native state of India in the Kathiawar agency of the Bombay presidency. Area, 289 sq. m.; pop. (1901),

51,856, showing a decrease of 15% in the decade. The chief is a Gohel Rajput, with the title of Thakur Sahib. Gross revenue, £42,000; tribute jointly to the gaekwar of Baroda and the nawab of Junagarh, £700. The capital of the state is Palitana; pop. 12,800. Above the town to the west rises the hill of Satrunja, sacred to the Jains. On this hill, which is truly a city of temples, all the peculiarities of Jain architecture are found in a marked degree. Some of the temples are as old as the 11th century, and they are spread over the intervening period down to the present. The hill is visited by crowds of pilgrims every year.

See J. Burgess, Notes of a Visit to Satrunjaya Hill (Bombay, 1869).

PALK STRAITS, the channel lying between the mainland of India and the island of Ceylon. It is named after Robert Palk, governor of Madras (1755-1763). The straits lie north of the line of reefs called Adam's Bridge, while the Gulf of Manaar lies south of it. The two channels are connected by the Pamban passage.

PALL, a word the various meanings of which can be traced to the Latin word pallium, that is, a piece of cloth used either as a covering or as a garment. In the last sense the pallium was the ludarus, the square or oblong-shaped outer garment of the Greeks. In the sense of a garment the English usage of " pall " is confined to the ecclesiastical vestment (see PALLIUM) and to the supertunica or dalmatic, the pallium regale or imperial mantle, one of the principal coronation vestments of British sovereigns. The heraldic bearing known as a " pall " takes the form of the Y of the ecclesiastical vestment. The chief applications of the word, in the sense of a covering, are to an altar frontal, to a linen cloth used to veil the chalice in the Catholic service of the Eucharist, and to a heavy black, purple or white covering for a coffin or hearse. The livery companies of London possessed sumptuous state palls for the funerals of their members, of which some are still in existence. The Merchant Taylors' company have two examples of Italian workmanship. The so-called " Walworth pall " of the Fishmongers' company probably dates from the 16th century. The Vintners' pall is of cloth of gold and purple velvet, with a figure of St Martin of Tours, the company's patron saint.

An entirely different word is " to pall," to become or make stale, insipid or tasteless, hence to cease to interest from constant repetition; this is a shortened form of " appal " (O. Fr. apallir, to become pale; Lat. pallidus).

PALLA, PALA, or IMPALA, the native name of a red South African antelope of the size of a fallow-deer, characterized by the large black lyrate horns of the bucks, and the presence in both sexes of a pair of glands on the back of the hind feet bearing a tuft of black hairs. On the east side the palla (Aepyceros melampus) ranges as far north as the southern Sudan; but in Angola it is replaced by a species or race (Ae. petersi) with a black " blaze " down the face. Pallas associate in large herds on open country in the neighbourhood of water. (See ANTELOPE.)

PALLADIAN, the term given in English architecture to one of the phases of the Italian Renaissance, introduced into England in 1620 by Inigo Jones, a great admirer of the works of Andrea Palladio (q.v.). In 1716, Richard Boyle, 3rd earl of Burlington, who also admired the works of Palladio, copied some of them, the front of old Burlington House being more or less a reproduction of the Palazzo Porto at Vicenza, and the villa at Chiswick a copy of the Villa Capua near Vicenza. It is probably due to Lord Burlington that the title Palladian is the designation for the Italian style as practised in England. In 1862 Sir Gilbert Scott's Gothic design for the new government offices was rejected and Lord Palmerston selected in preference the Palladian style. In France and America, Barozzi Vignole (1507-1573), another Italian architect, holds a similar position as the chief authority on the Italian Renaissance.

PALLADIO, ANDREA (1518-1580), Italian architect, was born in Vicenza on the 30th of November 1518. The works of Vitruvius and Alberti were studied by him at an early period, and his student life was spent in Rome, where he was taken by his patron Count Trissino. In 1547 he returned to Vicenza, where he designed a very large number of fine buildings—among the chief being the Palazzo della Ragione, with two storeys of open arcades of the Tuscan and Ionic orders, and the Barbarano, Porti and Chieregati palaces. Most of these buildings look better on paper than in reality, as they are mainly built of brick, covered with stucco, now in a very dilapidated condition; but this does not affect the merit of their design, as Palladio intended them to have been executed in stone. Pope Paul III. sent for him to Rome to report upon the state of St Peter's. In Venice, too, Palladio built many stately churches and palaces, such as S. Giorgio Maggiore, the Capuchin church, and some large palaces on the Grand Canal. His last great work was the Teatro Olimpico at Vicenza, which was finished, though not altogether after the original design, by his pupil and fellow citizen Scamozzi.

In addition to his town buildings Palladio designed many country villas in various parts of northern Italy. The villa of Capra is perhaps the finest of these, and has frequently been imitated. Palladio was a great student of classical literature, and published in 1575 an edition of Caesar's *Commentaries* with notes. His *I quattro libri dell' architettura*, first published at Venice in 1570, has passed into countless editions, and been translated into every European language. The original edition is a small folio, richly illustrated with well-executed full-page woodcuts of plans, elevations, and details of buildings—chiefly either ancient Roman temples or else palaces designed and built by himself. Among many others, an edition with notes was published in England by Inigo Jones, most of whose works, and especially the palace of Whitehall, of which only the banqueting room remains, owed much to Palladio's inspiration. The style adopted and partially invented by Palladio expressed a kind of revolt against the extreme licence both of composition and ornament into which the architecture of his time had fallen. He was fascinated by the stateliness and proportion of the buildings of ancient Rome, and did not reflect that reproductions of these, however great their archaeological accuracy, could not but be lifeless and unsuited to the wants of the 16th century. Palladio's carefully measured drawings of ancient buildings are now of great value, as in many cases the buildings have altogether or in part ceased to exist.

AUTHORITIES.—Montanari, *Vita di Andrea Palladio* (1749); Rigato, *Osservazioni sopra Andrea Palladio* (1811); Magrini, *Memorie intorno la vita di Andrea Palladio* (1845); Milizia, *Memorie degli architetti*, ii. 35–54 (1781); Symonds, *Renaissance in Italy—Fine Arts*, pp. 94–99; Zanella, *Vita di Andrea Palladio* (Milan, 1880); Barichella, *Vita di Andrea Palladio* (Lonigo, 1880).

PALLADIUM (Gr. παλλάδιον), an archaic wooden image (ξόανον) of Pallas Athena, preserved in the citadel of Troy as a pledge of the safety of the city. It represented the goddess, standing in the stiff archaic style, holding a spear in her right hand, in her left a distaff and spindle or a shield. According to Apollodorus (iii, 12, 3) it was made by order of Athena, and was intended as an image of Pallas, the daughter of Triton, whom she had accidentally slain, Pallas and Athena being thus regarded as two distinct beings. It was said that Zeus threw it down from heaven when Ilus was founding the city of Ilium, Odysseus and Diomedes carried it off from the temple of Athena, and thus made the capture of Troy possible. According to some accounts, there was a second Palladium at Troy, which was taken to Italy by Aeneas and kept in the temple of Vesta at Rome. Many cities in Greece and Italy claimed to possess the genuine Trojan Palladium. Its theft is a frequent subject in Greek art, especially of the earlier time.

PALLADIUM [symbol Pd, atomic weight 106·7 (O=16)], in chemistry, a metallic element associated with the platinum group. It is found in platinum ores, and also in the native condition and associated with gold and silver in Brazilian gold-bearing sand. Many methods have been devised for the isolation of the metal from platinum ore. R. Bunsen (*Ann.*, 1868, 146, p. 265), after removing most of the platinum as ammonium platinochloride, precipitates the residual metals of the group by iron; the resulting precipitate is then heated with ammonium chloride and evaporated with fuming nitric acid, the residue taken up in water, and the palladium precipitated as potassium palladium chloride. This is purified by dissolving it in hot water and evaporating the solution with oxalic acid, taking up the residue in potassium chloride, and filtering off any potassium platinochloride formed. The filtrate deposits potassium palladium chloride, which on heating in a current of hydrogen leaves a residue of the metal. Roessler (*Zeit. f. chemie*, 1866, p. 175) precipitates both platinum and palladium as double chlorides, the resulting mixed chlorides being reduced to the metals by ignition in hydrogen, taken up in aqua regia, the solution neutralized, and the palladium precipitated by mercuric cyanide. See also T. Wilm (*Ber.*, 1880, 13, p. 1198; 1881, 14, p. 629; 1882, 15, p. 241) on its separation as palladosammine chloride, and Cox (*Phil. Mag.*, 1843, 23, p. 16) on the separation of palladium from Brazilian gold sand. Pure palladium may be obtained by the reduction of the double chloride (NH$_4$)$_2$ PdCl$_4$ in a current of hydrogen, or of palladious chloride with formic acid.

It is a ductile metal of silvery lustre, with a specific gravity of 11·97 (0°C.). It is the most easily fusible of the metals of the platinum group, its melting-point being about 1530–1550° C. (L. Holborn and F. Henning, *Sitsb. Akad. Berlin*, 1905, p. 311). It readily distils when heated in the electric furnace. Its mean specific heat between 0° and t°C. is 0·0582 + 0·000010t (J. Violle, *Comptes rendus*, 1879, 89, p. 702). Palladium finds application in the form of alloys for astronomical instruments, in dentistry, and in the construction of springs and movements of clocks. Native palladium is dimorphous. It is soluble in nitric acid, more especially if the acid contains oxides of nitrogen, and when obtained in the finely divided condition by reduction of its salts, it is to some extent soluble in hydrochloric acid. It also dissolves in boiling concentrated sulphuric acid and in hydriodic acid. It oxidises when fused with caustic alkalis. It combines with fluorine and with chlorine at a dull red heat, but not with iodine, whilst bromine has scarcely any action on the metal. It combines with sulphur directly, and according to T. Wilm (*Ber.*, 1882, 15, p. 2225) forms the oxide Pd$_2$O, when heated in a current of air.

Two series of salts are known, namely, palladious salts and palladic salts, corresponding to the two oxides PdO and PdO$_2$. Of these the palladious salts only are stable, the palladic salts readily passing into the palladious form on boiling with water. The palladium compounds show a complete analogy with the corresponding platinum salts. All the salts of the metal when heated decompose and leave a residue of the metal; the metal may also be obtained from solutions of the salts by the addition of zinc, iron, formic acid, phosphorus and hot alcohol. Sulphuretted hydrogen gives with palladium salts a precipitate of palladium sulphide which is insoluble in ammonium sulphide; mercuric chloride gives the characteristic yellowish precipitate of palladious chloride, and potassium iodide the black palladious iodide which dissolves on addition of excess of the precipitant. These two latter reactions may be used for the recognition of palladium, as may also the behaviour of the salts with ammonia, this reagent giving a brown precipitate, which turns to a red shade, and is soluble in a large excess of the precipitant to a clear solution, from which by adding hydrochloric acid a yellow precipitate of palladosammine chloride, Pd(NH$_3$)$_2$Cl$_2$ is obtained. Palladium is permeable to hydrogen at a temperature of 240° C. and upwards. It absorbs hydrogen and other gases, the heat of occlusion being 4640 calories per gram of hydrogen. The occluded hydrogen is strongly bound to the metal, only traces of the gas being given off on standing *in vacuo*, but it is easily removed when heated to 100° C. T. Graham (*Phil. Mag.*, 1866–1869) was of the opinion that the occluded hydrogen underwent great condensation and behaved as a quasi-metal (to which he gave the name "hydrogenium"), forming an alloy with the palladium; but L. Troost and P. Hautefeuille (*Ann. chim. phys.*, 1874, (5) 2, p. 279) considered that a definite compound of composition Pd$_2$H was formed. The more recent work of C. Hoitsema (*Zeit. phys. chim.*, 1895, 17, p. 1) however, appears to disprove the formation of a definite compound (see also J. Dewar, *Phil. Mag.*, 1874, (4) 47, pp. 324, 342). A palladium hydride was obtained by Graham by the reduction of palladious sulphate with sodium hypophosphite. It is an unstable black powder, which readily loses hydrogen at 0° C. C. Paal and J. Gerum (*Ber.*, 1908, 41, p. 818) have shown that when palladium black is suspended in water one volume of the metal combines with 1204 volumes of hydrogen, or in the atomic proportion Pd/H = 1/1·98.

Palladious oxide, PdO, is a black powder formed by heating spongy palladium to a dull red heat in a current of oxygen or by gentle ignition of the nitrate. It is insoluble in acids, is easily reduced, and decomposes when heated. Palladic oxide, PdO₂, is obtained in the hydrated condition, PdO₂·nH₂O, by the action of ozone on palladious chloride; by the electrolytic oxidation of palladious nitrate in slightly acid solution (L. Wöhler); and by the action of caustic potash on potassium palladio-chloride; the liquid being neutralized with acetic acid (I. Bellucci, *Zeit. anorg. Chem.*, 1905, 47, p. 287). It is a dark red or brown coloured powder, which loses oxygen on heating. When boiled with water it passes into the lower oxide. It is an energetic oxidizing agent, and when freshly prepared is soluble in dilute mineral acids. A hydrated form of the monoxide, PdO·nH₂O, is obtained by hydrolyzing a faintly acid solution of the nitrate (L. Wöhler, *Zeit. anorg. Chem.*, 1905, 46, p. 323), or by the action of a slight excess of caustic soda on the double chloride K₂PdCl₄. It is a dark brown powder which loses its water of hydration when dried in air, and in the dry condition is difficultly soluble in acids. By the electrolytic oxidation of palladious nitrate L. Wöhler and F. Martin (Ib., 1908, 57, p. 398), obtained a hydrated oxide, Pd₂O₃·nH₂O, as a dark brown powder which dissolves in hydrochloric acid, forming an unstable chloride.

Palladious chloride, PdCl₂, is obtained as a deliquescent crystalline mass when spongy palladium is heated to dull redness in a current of dry chlorine. A hydrated form, of composition PdCl₂·2H₂O, results on dissolving palladium in aqua regia, containing only a small proportion of nitric acid. It crystallizes from water as a reddish-brown solid. It absorbs hydrogen and is easily reduced. It combines with carbon monoxide to form compounds of composition PdCl₂·2CO; 2PdCl₂·3CO; PdCl₂·CO (E. Fink, *Comptes Rendus*, 1898, 126, p. 646), and can be used for the determination of the amount of carbon monoxide in air (Potain and R. Drouin, Ib., 1898, 126, p. 938). On treatment with dry ammonia gas it yields palladiodiammine chloride, Pd(NH₃)₂Cl₂. Palladious chloride combines with hydroxylamine to form the compounds Pd(NH₂O)₂Cl₂ and Pd(NH₂O)₄Cl₂. The first results from the action of hydroxylamine on the chloride in the presence of sodium carbonate, and may be isolated as the free base. The other is thrown down as a yellow granular precipitate when a small quantity of dilute hydrochloric acid is added to the base, Pd(NH₂O)₄(OH)₂ (S. Feisel and A. Nowak, *Ann.*, 1907, 351, p. 439). The chloride PdCl₂ is only known in acid solution, and is obtained when palladium is dissolved in aqua regia or when palladic oxide is dissolved in concentrated hydrochloric acid. The solution is brown in colour and gradually loses chlorine, being converted into palladious chloride. Both chlorides combine with many other metallic chlorides to form characteristic double salts, the double potassium salts having the formulae K₄PdCl₆ and K₂PdCl₄. The former may be prepared by adding an excess of potassium chloride to palladious chloride, or by boiling K₂PdCl₄ with a large excess of water. It crystallizes in prisms which are readily soluble in water but are practically insoluble in absolute alcohol. It is decomposed by direct heating, and also by heating in a current of hydrogen. The latter compound is formed when chlorine is passed into a warm aqueous solution of the former or by dissolving palladium in aqua regia and saturating the solution with potassium chloride. It crystallizes in scarlet octahedra which darken on heating, and decompose when strongly heated. It is slightly soluble in cold water, but dissolves in warm dilute hydrochloric acid. When boiled with alcohol it is reduced to the metallic condition.

The *subsulphide*, Pd₄S, is obtained as a hard, green coloured mass when palladosammine chloride is fused with sulphur or when the sulphide PdS is fused with sulphur and ammonium chloride. It loses sulphur slowly when heated and is insoluble in acids. *Palladious sulphide*, PdS, is obtained by precipitation of the corresponding salts with sulphuretted hydrogen, or by the action of dry sulphuretted hydrogen gas on palladosammine chloride. As prepared in the dry way it is a hard, blue coloured, insoluble mass, but if obtained by precipitation is of a brownish-black colour and is soluble in nitric acid. When heated in air it oxidizes to a basic sulphate. The *disulphide*, PdS₂, is a brownish-black crystalline powder which is formed when the double ammonium palladium chloride (NH₄)₂PdCl₆ is heated to redness with caustic soda and sulphur. It combines with the alkaline sulphides. It gradually loses sulphur on heating, and is easily soluble in aqua regia. A sulphide of composition Pd₃S₄ has been described (R. Schneider, *Pogg. Ann.*, 1873, 148, p. 625).

Palladium sulphate, PdSO₄·2H₂O, is obtained by dissolving the oxide in sulphuric acid, or by the action of nitric and sulphuric acids on the metal. It forms a reddish-brown, deliquescent, crystalline mass, and is easily soluble in water, but in the presence of a large excess of water yields a basic sulphate. *Palladium nitrate*, Pd(NO₃)₂, crystallizes in brownish-yellow deliquescent prisms and is obtained by dissolving the metal in nitric acid. It is very soluble in water, and its aqueous solution decomposes on boiling, with precipitation of a basic nitrate. *Palladious cyanide*, Pd(CN)₂, is obtained as a yellowish precipitate when palladium chloride is precipitated by mercuric cyanide. It is insoluble in water, and on heating decomposes into palladium and cyanogen. It is soluble in solutions of the alkaline cyanides, with formation

of double cyanides of the type K₂Pd(CN)₄. On account of its insolubility and its stability it is useful for the separation of palladium from the other metals of the platinum group.

The palladium salts combine with ammonia to form characteristic compounds, which may be grouped into two main divisions: (1) the palladammines (palladosammines) of type [Pd(NH₃)₄]X₂, and (2) the palladiodiammines [Pd(NH₃)₂]X₂. The palladosammines are obtained by adding a large excess of ammonia to the palladious salts, the resulting clear solution being then precipitated by the mineral acid corresponding to the salt used. This method of preparation serves well for the chloride, from which other salts may be obtained by double decomposition. These salts are fairly stable, and are red, yellow or orange in colour. The palladiodiammine salts are mostly colourless, and are not very stable; acids convert them into the palladosammines, and they lose two molecules of ammonia very easily. They are formed by the action of a large excess of ammonia on the palladious salts or on the corresponding palladosammine salts in the presence of water.

Numerous determinations of the atomic weight of palladium have been made, the values obtained varying from 105·7 to 107·249 (see *Amer. Chem. Jour.*, 1899, 21, p. 943; *Ann.*, 1905, 341, p. 235; *Jour. Chem. Soc.*, 1894, 65, p. 20). The International Commission on Atomic Weights, 1909, recount several new determinations: Haas (*Dissertation*, Erlangen, 1908) from reduction of palladosammine bromide obtained the value 106·7; Kemmerer (*Thesis*, Pennsylvania, 1908), from reduction of the corresponding chloride and cyanide obtains a mean value of 106·434; whilst A. Gutbier and his collaborators, from analyses of palladosammine chloride and bromide, obtained the values 106·64 ±0·03 and 106·65 ±0·02 from the chloride, and 106·655 from the bromide (*Jour. pr. chem.*, 1909, ii. 79, pp. 235, 457).

PALLADIUS, RUTILIUS TAURUS AEMILIANUS, a Roman author of the 4th century A.D. He wrote a poem on agriculture (*De re rustica*) in fourteen books, the material being derived from Columella and other earlier writers. The work is conveniently arranged, but far inferior in every other respect to that of Columella.

There is a modern German edition by Schmitt (Leipzig, 1898).

PALLANZA, a small industrial town and summer and winter resort of the province of Novara, Piedmont, Italy, 659 ft. above sea-level. Pop. (1901), 4619 (town); 7207 (commune). It occupies a position of great natural beauty, on a promontory on the W. of Lago Maggiore, with a semicircle of mountains behind and the lake and Borromean Islands in front, 62 m. N. of Novara direct. The annual mean temperature is 55° Fahr.; January, 37·1°, July, 74°. There is a fine botanical garden.

PALLAS, PETER SIMON (1741–1811), German naturalist and traveller, was born in Berlin on the 22nd of September 1741, the son of Simon Pallas, surgeon in the Prussian army and professor of surgery in Berlin. He was intended for the medical profession, and studied at the universities of Berlin, Halle, Göttingen and Leiden. He early displayed a strong leaning towards natural history. In 1761 he went to England, where for a year he devoted himself to a thorough study of the collections and to a geological investigation of part of the coast; and at the age of twenty-three he was elected a foreign member of the Royal Society. He then spent some time in Holland, and the results of his investigations appeared at the Hague in 1766 in his *Elenchus Zoophytorum* and *Miscellanea Zoologica*, and in 1767–1804 in his *Spicilegia Zoologica* (Berlin). In 1768 he accepted the invitation of the empress Catharine II. to fill the professorship of natural history in the Imperial Academy of Science, St Petersburg, and in the same year he was appointed naturalist to a scientific expedition through Russia and Siberia, the immediate object of which was the observation of the transit of Venus in 1769. In this leisurely journey Pallas went by Kasan to the Caspian, spent some time among the Kalmucks, crossed the Urals to Tobolsk, visited the Altai mountains, traced the Irtish to Kolyvan, went on to Tomsk and the Yenisei, crossed Lake Baikal, and extended his journey to the frontiers of China. Few explorations have been so fruitful as this six years' journey. The leading results were given in his *Reisen durch verschiedene Provinzen des russischen Reichs* (3 vols., St Petersburg, 1771–1776), richly illustrated with coloured plates. A French translation in 1788–1793, in 8 vols., with 9 vols. of plates, contained, in addition to the narrative, the natural history results of the expedition; and an English translation in three volumes appeared in 1812. As special results of this great journey may be mentioned *Sammlungen historischer Nachrichten über die mongolischen Völkerschaften* (2 vols., St Petersburg, 1776–1802); *Novae species quadrupedum*, 1778–1779; Pallas's contributions to the dictionary of languages of the Russian empire, 1786–1789; *Icones insectorum, praesertim Rossiae Sibericeque peculiarium*, 1781–1806; *Zoographia rosso-asiatica* (3 vols., 1831); besides many special papers in the *Transactions* of the academies of St Petersburg and Berlin. The empress bought Pallas's natural history collections for 20,000 roubles, 5000 more than he asked for them, and allowed him to keep them for life. He spent a considerable time in 1793–1794 in visiting the southern provinces of Russia, and was so greatly attracted by the Crimea that he determined to take up his residence there. The empress gave him a large estate at Simpheropol and 10,000 roubles to assist in equipping a house. Though disappointed with the Crimea as a place of residence, Pallas continued to live there, devoted to constant research, especially in botany, till the death of his second wife in 1810, when he removed to Berlin, where he died on the 8th of September 1811. The results of his journey in southern Russia were given in his *Bemerkungen auf einer Reise durch die südlichen Statthalterschaften des russischen Reichs* (Leipzig, 1799–1801; English translation by Blagdon, vols. v.–viii. of *Modern Discoveries*, 1802, and another in 2 vols., 1812). Pallas also edited and contributed to *Neue nordische Beiträge zur physikalischen Erd- und Völkerbeschreibung, Naturgeschichte, und Oekonomie* (1781–1796), published *Illustrationes plantarum imperfecte vel nondum cognitarum* (Leipzig, 1803), and contributed to Buffon's *Natural History* a paper on the formation of mountains.

See the essay of Rudolphi in the *Transactions* of the Berlin Academy for 1812; Cuvier's *Éloge* in his *Recueil des éloges historiques*, vol. ii.; and the Life in Jardine's *Naturalists' Library*, vol. iv. (Edin., 1843).

PALLAVICINO, FERRANTE (1618–1644), Italian writer of pasquinades, a member of the old Italian family of the Pallavicini, was born at Piacenza in 1618. He received a good education at Padua and elsewhere, and early in life entered the Augustinian order, residing chiefly in Venice. For a year he accompanied Ottavio Piccolomini, duke of Amalfi, in his German campaigns as field chaplain, and shortly after his return he published a number of clever but exceedingly scurrilous satires on the Roman curia and on the powerful house of the Barberini, which was so keenly resented at Rome that a price was set on his head. A Frenchman, Charles de Breche, decoyed him from Venice to the neighbourhood of Avignon, and there betrayed him. After fourteen months' imprisonment he was beheaded at Avignon on the 6th of March, 1644.

His *Opere permesse* was published at Venice in 1655, but being, as may be imagined, inferior in scurrility and grossness (Pallavicino's specialities), are much less prized by the curious than the *Opere scelte* (Geneva, 1660), which were more than once reprinted in Holland, and were translated into German in 1663.

PALLAVICINO (or PALLAVICINI), **PIETRO SFORZA** (1607–1667), Italian cardinal and historian, son of the Marquis Alessandro Pallavicino of Parma, was born at Rome in 1607. Having taken holy orders in 1630, and joined the Society of Jesus in 1638, he successively taught philosophy and theology in the Collegium Romanum; as professor of theology he was a member of the congregation appointed by Innocent X. to investigate the Jansenist heresy. In 1659 he was made a cardinal by Alexander VII. He died at Rome on the 5th of June 1667. Pallavicino is chiefly known by his history of the council of Trent, written

in Italian, and published at Rome in two folio volumes in 1656–1657 (2nd ed., considerably modified, in 1666). In this he continued the task begun by Terenzio Alciati, who had been commissioned by Urban VIII. to correct and supersede the very damaging work of Sarpi on the same subject. Alciati and Pallavicino had access to many important sources from the use of which Sarpi had been precluded; the contending parties, however, are far from agreed as to the completeness of the refutation. The work was translated into Latin by a Jesuit named Giattinus (Antwerp, 1670–1673). There is a good edition of the original by Zaccharia (6 vols., Faenza, 1792–1799). It was translated into German by Klitsche in 1835–1837. He also wrote a life of Alexander VII. and a tragedy (*Ermenegildo*, 1644), &c.

His collected *Opere* were published in Rome in 1844–1848.

PALLIUM or **PALL** (derived, so far as the name is concerned, from the Roman *pallium* or *palla*, a woollen cloak), an ecclesiastical vestment in the Roman Catholic Church, originally peculiar to the pope, but for many centuries past bestowed by him on all metropolitans, primates and archbishops as a symbol of the jurisdiction delegated to them by the Holy See. The pallium, in its present form, is a narrow band, "three fingers broad," woven of white lamb's wool, with a loop in the centre resting on the shoulders over the chasuble, and two dependent lappets, before and behind; so that when seen from front or back the ornament resembles the letter Y. It is decorated with six purple crosses, one on each tail and four on the loop, is doubled on the left shoulder, and is garnished, back and front, with three jewelled gold pins. The two latter characteristics seem to be survivals of the time when the Roman *pallium*, like the Greek ὠμοφόριον was a simple scarf doubled and pinned on the left shoulder.

The origin of the pallium as an ecclesiastical vestment is lost in antiquity. The theory that explains it in connexion with the figure of the Good Shepherd carrying the lamb on his shoulders, so common in early Christian art, is obviously an explanation a posteriori. The ceremonial connected with the preparation of the pallium and its bestowal upon the pope at his coronation, however, suggests some such symbolism. The lambs whose wool is destined for the making of the *pallia* are solemnly presented at the altar by the nuns of the convent of St Agnes at

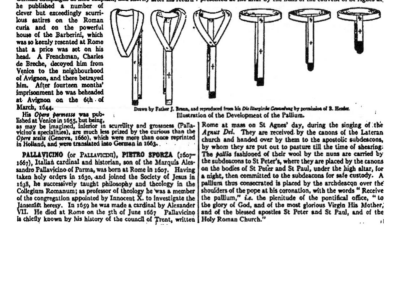

Drawn by Father J. Braun, and reproduced from his *Die liturgische Gewandung* by permission of B. Herder.
Illustration of the Development of the Pallium.

Rome at mass on St Agnes' day, during the singing of the *Agnus Dei*. They are received by the canons of the Lateran church and handed over by them to the apostolic subdeacons, by whom they are put out to pasture till the time of shearing. The *pallia* fashioned of their wool by the nuns are carried by the subdeacons to St Peter's, where they are placed by the canons on the bodies of St Peter and St Paul, under the high altar, for a night, then committed to the subdeacons for safe custody. A pallium thus consecrated is placed by the archdeacon over the shoulders of the pope at his coronation, with the words "Receive the pallium," *i.e.* the plenitude of the pontifical office, "to the glory of God, and of the most glorious Virgin His Mother, and of the blessed apostles St Peter and St Paul, and of the Holy Roman Church."

The elaborate ceremonial might suggest an effort to symbolize the command "Feed My lambs!" given to St Peter, and its transference to Peter's successors. Some such idea underlies the developed ceremonial; but the pallium itself was in its origin no more than an ensign of the episcopal dignity, as it remains in the East, where—under the name of ὠμοφόριον (ὦμος, shoulder, φέρειν, to carry)—it is worn by all bishops. Moreover, whatever symbolism may be evolved from the lambs' wool is vitiated, so far as origins are concerned, by the fact that the papal *pallia* were at one time made of white linen (see Johannes Diaconus, *Vita S. Gregorii M. lib. IV.* cap. 8, *pallium ejus bysso candente contextum*).[1]

The right to wear the pallium seems, in the first instance, to have been conceded by the popes merely as a mark of honour. The first recorded example of the bestowal of the pallium by the popes is the grant of Pope Symmachus in 513 to Caesarius of Arles, as papal vicar. By the time of Gregory I. it was given not only to vicars but as a mark of honour to distinguish bishops, and it is still conferred on the bishops of Autun, Bamberg, Dol, Lucca, Ostia, Pavia and Verona. St Boniface caused a reforming synod, between 840 and 850, to decree that in future all metropolitans must seek their pallium at Rome (see Boniface's letter to Cuthbert, 78, *Monumenta Germaniae, epistolae,* III.); and though this rule was not universally followed even until the 13th century, it is now uncanonical for an archbishop to exercise the functions proper to his office until the pallium has been received. Every archbishop must apply for it, personally or by deputy, within three months after his consecration, and it is buried with him at his death (see ARCHBISHOP). The pallium is never granted until after payment of considerable dues. This payment, originally supposed to be voluntary, became one of the great abuses of the papacy, especially during the period of the Renaissance, and it was the large amount (raised largely by indulgences) which was paid by Albert, archbishop of Mainz, to the papacy that roused Luther to protest. Though the pallium is thus a vestment distinctive of bishops having metropolitan jurisdiction, it may only be worn by them within their jurisdiction, and then only on certain solemn occasions. The pope alone has the right to wear everywhere and at all times a vestment which is held to symbolize the plenitude of ecclesiastical power.

See P. Hinschius, *Kirchenrecht,* II. 23 sqq.; Gresar, "Das römische Pallium und die ältesten liturgischen Scharpen " (in *Festschrift zum elfhundertjährigen Jubiläum des campo santo in Rom,* Freiburg, 1897); Du Cange, *Glossarium* s.v. "Pallium "; Joseph Braun, *Die liturgische Gewandung im Occident und Orient* (Freiburg-i-B., 1907).

PALL-MALL, an obsolete English game of French origin, called in France *paille-maille* (from *palla,* ball, and *malleus,* mallet). Sir Robert Dallington, in his *Method for Travel* (1598), says: " Among all the exercises of France, I prefer none before the Paille-Maille." James I., in his *Basilikon doron,* recommended it as a proper game for Prince Henry, and it was actually introduced into England in the reign of Charles I., or perhaps a few years earlier. Thomas Blount's *Glossographia* (ed. 1670) describes it as follows: " Pale Maille, a game wherein a round bowle is with a mallet struck through a high arch of iron (standing at either end of an alley), which he that can do at the fewest blows, or at the number agreed on, wins. This game was heretofore used in the long alley near St James's, and vulgarly called Pell-Mell." The pronunciation here described as " vulgar " afterwards became classic. A mallet and balls used in the game were found in 1845 and are now in the British Museum. The mallet resembles that used in croquet, but its head is curved and its ends sloped towards the shaft. The balls are of boxwood and about one foot in circumference. Pepys describes the alley as of hard sand " dressed with powdered cockle-shells." The length of the alley varied, that at St James's being about 800 yds. Some alleys had side walls.

[1] Father Joseph Braun, S.J., holds that the pallium, unlike other vestments, had a liturgical origin, and that it was akin to the scarves of office worn by priests and priestesses in pagan rites. See *Die pontificalen Gewänder des Abendlandes,* p. 174 (Freiburg-i-B. 1898).

PALLONE (Italian for "large ball," from *palla,* ball), the national ball game of Italy. It is descended, as are all other court games, such as tennis and pelota, from the two ball games played by the Romans, in one of which a large inflated ball, called *follis,* was used. The other, probably the immediate ancestor of pallone, was played with a smaller ball, the *pila.* Pallone was played in Tuscany as early as the 14th century, and is still very popular in northern and central Italy. It is played in a court (*sferisterio*), usually 100 yds. long and 17 yds. wide. A white line crosses the middle of the court, which is bounded on one side by a high wall, the spectators sitting round the other three sides, usually protected by wire screens. One end of the court is called the *battuta* and the other the *ribattuta.* At the end of the *battuta* is placed a spring-board, upon which stands the player who receives the service. The implements of the game are the *pallone* (ball) and the *bracciale* (bat). The *pallone* is an inflated ball covered with leather, about 4½ in. in diameter. The *bracciale* is an oak gauntlet, tubular in shape, and covered with long spike-like protuberances. It weighs between five and six pounds and is provided with a grip for the hand. The game is played by two-sides—blues and reds—of three men each, the *battitore* (batter), *spalla* (back) and *terzino* (third). At the beginning of a game the *battitore* stands on the spring-board and receives the ball thrown to him on the bound by a seventh player, the *mandarino,* who does duty for both sides. The batter may ignore the ball until it comes to him to his liking, when he runs down the spring-board and strikes it with his *bracciale* over the centre line towards his opponents. The game then proceeds until a player fails to return the ball correctly, or hits it out of bounds, or it touches his person. This counts a point for the adversary. Four points make a game, counting 15, 30, 40 and 50.

See *Il Giuoco del pallone,* by G. Franceschini (Milan, 1903).

PALM, JOHANN PHILIPP (1768-1806), German bookseller, a victim of Napoleonic tyranny in Germany, was born at Schorndorf, in Württemberg, on the 17th of November 1768. Having been apprenticed to his uncle, the publisher Johann Jakob Palm (1750-1826), in Erlangen, he married the daughter of the bookseller Stein in Nuremberg, and in course of time became proprietor of his father-in-law's business. In the spring of 1806 the firm of Stein sent to the bookselling establishment of Stage in Augsburg a pamphlet (presumably written by Philipp Christian Yelin in Ansbach) entitled *Deutschland in seiner tiefen Erniedrigung* (" Germany in her deep humiliation "), which strongly attacked Napoleon and the behaviour of the French troops in Bavaria. Napoleon, on being apprised of the violent attack made upon his régime and failing to discover the actual author, had Palm arrested and handed over to a military commission at Braunau on the Bavarian-Austrian frontier, with peremptory instructions to try and execute the prisoner within twenty-four hours. Palm was denied the right of defence, and after a mock trial on the 25th of August 1806 he was shot on the following day. A life-size bronze statue was erected to his memory in Braunau in 1866, and on the centenary of his death numerous patriotic meetings were held in Bavaria.

See F. Schultheis, *Johann Philipp Palm* (Nuremberg, 1860); and J. Rackl, *Der nürnberger Buchhändler Johann Philipp Palm* (Nuremberg, 1906).

PALM (Lat. *palma,* Gr. παλάμη), originally the flat of the hand, in which sense it is still used; from this sense the word was transferred as a name of the trees described below. The emblematic use of the word (= prize, honour) represents a further transference from the employment of the palm-leaves as symbols of victory.

The Palms (*Palmaceae*) have been termed the princes of the vegetable kingdom. Neither the anatomy of their stems nor the conformation of their flowers, however, entitles them to any such high position in the vegetable hierarchy. Their stems are not more complicated in structure than those of the common butcher's broom (*Ruscus*); their flowers are for the most part as simple as those of a rush (*Juncus*). The order Palmaceae is characterized among monocotyledonous plants by the presence of an unbranched stem bearing a tuft of leaves at the extremity only, or with the leaves scattered; these leaves, often gigantic in size, being usually firm in texture and branching in a pinnate or palmate fashion. The flowers are borne on simple or branching spikes, very generally protected by a spathe or spathes, and each consists typically of a perianth of six greenish, somewhat inconspicuous segments in two rows, with six stamens, or pistil of 1–3 carpels, each with a single ovule and a succulent or dry fruit, never dehiscent (fig. 1, A and B). The seed consists almost exclusively of endosperm, or albumen in a cavity in which is lodged the relatively very minute embryo

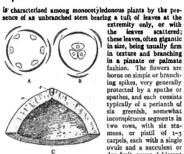

FIG. 1, A,B.—Floral diagrams of a Palm (*Chamaerops humilis*).
A, male flower. B, female-flower.
C, Upper portion of Coco-nut seed, showing *e*, embryo, embedded in *a*, endosperm.

(fig. 1, C). These are the general characteristics by which this very well-defined order may be discriminated, but, in a group containing considerably more than a thousand species, deviations from the general plan of structure occur with some frequency. As the characteristic appearances of palms depend to a large extent upon these modifications, some of the more important among them may briefly be noticed.

Taking the stem first, we may mention that it is in very many palms relatively tall, erect, unbranched, regularly cylindrical,

marked with circular scars indicating the position of those leaves which have now fallen away. It, varies in diameter from the thickness of a reed (as in *Chamaedorea*) to a sturdy pillar-like structure as seen in the date-palm, Palmyra palm (fig. 7) or Talipot. In other cases the very slender stem is prostrate, or

FIG. 2.—*Daemonorops Draco* (a Rattan Palm).
1, Young shoot much reduced. 2, Part of stem bearing male inflorescence. 3, Part of female inflorescence. 4, The same bearing ripe fruits.

or dilated below so as to form an elongated cone, either smooth, or covered with the projecting remnants of the former leaves, or

(After Bentley and Trimen, *Medicinal Plants*, by permission of Messrs J. & A. Churchill.)

FIG. 3.—Areca Palm (*Areca Catechu*).
1, Tree, very much reduced.
2, Part of leaf.
3, Portion of inflorescence with male flowers above, female (larger) below.
4, Petal of a male flower.
5, Male flower opened by removal of a petal.
6, Fruit.
7, 8, Same cut across, and lengthwise. 9, Fibrous pericarp; *en*, ruminated endosperm; *e*, embryo.

scandent by means of formidable hooked prickles which, by enabling the plant to support itself on the branches of neighbouring trees, also permit the stem to grow to a very great length and so to expose the foliage to the light and air above the tree-tops of the dense forests these palms grow in, as in the genus *Calamus*, the Rattan or Cane palms. In some few instances the trunk, or that portion of it which is above ground, is so short that the plant is in a loose way called "stemless" or "acaulescent," as in *Geonoma*, and as happens sometimes in the only species found in a wild state in Europe, *Chamaerops humilis*. The vegetable ivory (*Phytelephas*) of equatorial America has a very short thick stem bearing a tall cluster of leaves which appears to rise from the ground. In many species the trunk is covered with a dense network of stiff fibres, often compacted together at the free ends into spines. This fibrous material, which is so valuable for cordage, consists of the fibrous tissue of the leaf-stalk, which in these cases persists after the decay of the softer portions. It is very characteristic of some palms to produce from the base of the stem a series of adventitious roots which gradually thrust themselves into the soil and serve to steady the tree and prevent its overthrow by the wind. The underground stem of some species, e.g. of *Calamus*, is a rhizome, or root-stock, lengthening in a more or less horizontal manner by the development of the terminal bud, and sending up lateral branches like suckers from the root-stock, which form dense thickets of cane-like stems. The branching of the stem above ground is unusual, except in the case of the Doum palm of Egypt (*Hyphaene*), where the stem forks, often repeatedly; this is due to the development of a branch to an equal strength with the main stem. In other cases branching, when present, is probably the result of some injury to the terminal bud at the top of the stem, in consequence of which buds sprout out from below the apex.

The internal structure of the stem does not differ fundamentally from that of a typical monocotyledonous stem, the taller, harder trunks owing their hardness not only to the fibrous or woody skeleton but also to the fact that, as growth goes on, the originally soft cellular ground tissue through which the fibres run becomes hardened by the deposit of woody matter within the cells, so that ultimately the cellular portions become as hard as the woody fibrous tissue.

The leaves of palms are either arranged at more or less distant intervals along the stem, as in the canes (*Calamus, Daemonorops*, fig. 2, &c.), or are approximated in tufts at the end of the stem, thus forming those noble crowns of foliage (figs. 5, 6, 7) which are so closely associated with the general idea of a palm. In the young condition, while still unfolded, these leaves, with the succulent end of the stem from which they arise, form "the cabbage," which in some species is highly esteemed as an article of food.

The adult leaf very generally presents a sheathing base tapering upwards into the stalk or petiole, and this again bearing the lamina or blade. The sheath and the petiole very often bear stout spines, as in the rattan palms (see fig. 2); and when, in course of time, the upper parts of the leaf decay and fall off, the base of the leaf-stalk and sheath often remain, either entirely or in their fibrous portions only, which latter constitute the investment to the stem already mentioned. In size the leaves vary within very wide limits, some being only a few inches in extent, while those of the noble *Caryota* may be measured in tens of feet. In form the leaves of palms are very rarely simple; usually they are more or less divided, sometimes, as in *Caryota*, extremely so. In species of *Geonoma, Verschaffeltia* and some others, the leaf splits into two divisions at the apex and not elsewhere; but more usually the leaves branch regularly in a palmate fashion as in the fan-palms *Latania, Borassus* (fig. 7), *Chamaerops, Sabal,* &c., or in a pinnate fashion as in the feather-palms, *Areca* (fig. 3), *Kentia, Calamus, Daemonorops* (fig. 2), &c. The form of the segments is generally more or less linear, but a very distinct appearance is given by the broad wedge-shaped leaflets of such palms as *Caryota, Martinezia* or *Mauritia*. These forms run one into another by transitional gradations; and even in the same palm the form of the leaf is often very different at different stages of its growth, so that it is a difficult matter to name correctly seedling or juvenile palms in the condition in which we generally meet with them in the nurseries, or even to foresee what the future development of the plant is likely to be. Like the other parts of the plant, the leaves are sometimes invested with hairs or spines; and, in some instances, as in the magnificent *Ceroxylon andicola*, the under surface is of a glaucous white or bluish colour, from a coating of wax.

The inflorescence of palms consists generally of a fleshy spike, either simple or much branched, studded with numerous, sometimes extremely numerous, flowers, and enveloped by one or more sheathing bracts called "spathes" (fig. 5). These parts may be small, or they may attain relatively enormous dimensions, hanging down from amid the crown of foliage like huge tresses, and adding greatly to the noble effect of the leaves. In some cases, as in the Talipot palm, the tree only flowers once; it grows for many years until it has become a large tree then develops a huge inflorescence, and after the fruit has ripened, dies.

The individual flowers are usually small (figs. 3, 6), greenish and insignificant; their general structure has been mentioned already. Modifications from the typical structure arise from difference of

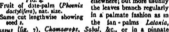

FIG. 4.
1, Fruit of date-palm (*Phoenix dactylifera*), nat. size.
2, Same cut lengthwise showing seed s.

texture, and especially from suppression of parts, in consequence of which the flowers are very generally unisexual (figs. 1, 3, 6), though the flowers of the two sexes are generally produced on the same tree (monoecious), not indeed always in the same season, for a tree in

FIG. 5.—*Acrocomia sclerocarpa*, much reduced.
sp, Spathe enveloping the fruits, shown on a larger scale in 1.
2, A fruit.
3, The same cut lengthwise.
m, Fibrous mesocarp; en, hard endocarp; s, seed.

one year may produce all male flowers and in the next all female flowers. Sometimes the flowers are modified by an increase in the number of parts; thus the usually six stamens may be represented by 12 to 24 or even by hundreds. The carpels are usually three in number, and more or less combined; but they may be free, and their number may be reduced to two or even one. In any case each carpel contains but a single ovule.

Owing to the sexual arrangements before mentioned, the pollen has to be transported by the agency of the wind or of insects to the female flowers. This is facilitated sometimes by the elastic movements of the stamens and anthers, which liberate the pollen so freely at certain times that travellers speak of the date-palms of Egypt (*Phoenix dactylifera*) being at daybreak hidden in a mist of pollen grains. In other cases fertilization is effected by the agency of man, who removes the male flowers and scatters the pollen over the fruit-bearing trees. This practice has been followed in the case of the date from time immemorial; and it afforded one of the earliest and most irrefragable proofs by means of which the sexuality of plants was finally established. In the course of ripening of the fruit two of the carpels with their ovules may become absorbed, as in the coco-nut, the fruit of which contains only one seed though the three carpels are indicated by the three longitudinal sutures and by the presence of three germ-pores on the hard endocarp.

The fruit is various in form, size and character; sometimes, as in the common date (fig. 4) it is a berry with a fleshy rind enclosing a hard stony kernel, the true seed, the fruit of *Areca* (fig. 3) is similar; sometimes it is a kind of drupe as in *Acrocomia* (fig. 5), or the coco-nut, *Cocos nucifera*, where the fibrous central portion investing the hard shell corresponds to the fleshy portion of a plum or cherry, while the shell or nut corresponds to the stone of stone-fruits, the seed being the kernel. In *Borassus* the three seeds are each enclosed in a separate chamber formed by the stony endocarp (fig 7). Sometimes, as in the species of *Metroxylon* (fig. 6), *Raphia, Daemonorops* (fig. 2), &c., the fruit is covered with hard, pointed, reflexed shining scales, which give it a very remarkable appearance.

The seeds show a corresponding variety in size and shape, but always consist of a mass of endosperm, in which is embedded a relatively very minute embryo (figs. 1, 4, 6). The hard stone of the date is the endosperm, the white oily flesh of the coco-nut is the same substance in a softer condition; the so-called " vegetable ivory " is derived from the endosperm of *Phytelephas*. In some genera the inner seed coat becomes thickened along **the course of** the vascular bundles and growing into the endosperm **produces the** characteristic appearance in section known as *ruminate*—this is well shown in the Areca nut (fig. 3).

sticks, fibre, paper, starch, sugar, oil, wax, wine, tannin, dyeing materials, resin and a host of minor products, which render them most valuable to the natives and to tropical agriculturists The Coco-nut palm, *Cocos nucifera*, and the Date palm, *Phoenix dactylifera*, have been treated under separate headings. Sugar and liquids capable of becoming fermented are produced by *Caryota urens*.

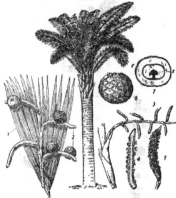

FIG 6.—Sago Palm (*Metroxylon Sagus*).

1, Apex of leaf 6, Fruit.
2, Branchlet of fruiting spadix. 7, Fruit cut lengthwise, showing
3, Branchlet of male inflorescence.   seed s and the minute em-
4, Spike of male flowers.   bryo c which is embedded in
5, Same cut lengthwise.   a horny endosperm.

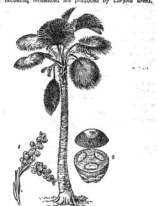

FIG. 7.—Palmyra Palm (*Borassus flabellifer*), a female tree.
1, Portion of female inflorescence showing young fruits.
2, Fruit cut across showing the three seeds, all much reduced.

The order contains 132 genera with about 1100 species mainly tropical, but with some representatives in warm temperate regions. *Chamaerops humilis* is a native of the Mediterranean region, and the date-palm yields fruit in southern Europe as far north as 38° N latitude. In eastern Asia the Palms, like other tropical families, extend along the coast reaching Korea and the south of Japan. In America a few small genera occur in the southern United States and California; and in South America the southern limit is reached in the Chilean genus *Jubaea* (the Chile coco-nut) at 37° S. latitude. The great centres of distribution are tropical America and tropical Asia; tropical Africa contains only 11 genera, though some of the species, like the Doum palm (*Hyphaene thebaica*) and the Deleb or Palmyra palm (*Borassus flabellifer*) have a wide distribution. With three exceptions Old and New World forms are distinct—the coco-nut (*Cocos nucifera*) is widely distributed on the coasts of tropical Africa, in India and the South Seas, the other species of the genus are confined to the western hemisphere. The oil palm (*Elaeis guineensis*) is a native of west tropical Africa, the other species of the genus is tropical American. *Raphia* has also species in both tropical Africa and tropical America.

The 132 genera of the order are ranged under seven tribes, distinguished by the nature of the foliage, the sexual conditions of the flower, the character of the seed, the position of the raphe, &c. Other characters serving to distinguish the minor groups are afforded by the habit, the position of the spathes, the " aestivation " of the flower, the nature of the stigma, the ovary, fruit, &c.

It is impossible to overestimate the utility of palms. They furnish food, shelter, clothing, timber, fuel, building materials,

Cocos nucifera, Borassus flabellifer, Rhapis vinifera, Arenga saccharifera, Phoenix silvestris, Mauritia vinifera, &c. Starch is procured in abundance from the stem of the Sago palm, *Metroxylon* (fig 6) and others. The fleshy mesocarp of the fruit of *Elaeis guineensis* of western tropical Africa yields, when crushed and boiled, " palm oil." Coco-nut oil is extracted from the oily endosperm of the coco-nut. Wax is exuded from the stem of *Ceroxylon andicola* and *Copernicia cerifera*. A variety of " dragon's blood," a resin, is procured from *Daemonorops Draco* and other species. Edible fruits are yielded by the date, the staple food of some districts of northern Africa. The coco-nut is a source of wealth to its possessors; and many of the species, e.g *Areca sapida* (Cabbage-palm and others), are valued for their " cabbage "; but, as this is the terminal bud whose removal causes the destruction of the tree, this is a wasteful article of diet unless care be taken by judicious planting to avert the annihilation of the supplies. The famous " coco de mer," or double coco-nut, whose floating nuts are the objects of so many legends and superstitions, is known to science as *Lodoicea seychellarum*. The tree is peculiar to the Seychelles, where it is used for many useful purposes. Its fruit is like a huge plum, containing a stone or nut like two coco-nuts (in their husks) united together. These illustrations must suffice to indicate the numerous economic uses of palms.

The only species that can be cultivated in the open air in England and then only under exceptionally favourable circumstances, are the European Fan palm, *Chamaerops humilis*, the Chusan palm, *Trachycarpus Fortunei*, &c., and the Chilean *Jubaea spectabilis*. The date palm is commonly planted along the Mediterranean coast. There are several low growing palms, such as *Rhapis flabelliformis*, *Chamaerops humilis*, &c., which are suited for ordinary green-house culture, and many of which, from the thick texture of their leaves, are enabled to resist the dry and often gas-laden atmosphere of living rooms.

PALMA, JACOPO (c. 1480–1528), Italian painter of the Venetian school, was born at Serinalta near Bergamo, towards 1480, and died at the age of forty-eight in July 1528. He is currently named Palma Vecchio (Old Palma) to distinguish him from Palma Giovine, his grand-nephew, a much inferior painter. His grandfather's name was Negretto He is reputed to have been a companion and competitor of Lorenzo Lotto, and to some extent a pupil of Titian, after arriving in Venice early in the

16th century; he may also have been the master of Bonifazio. His earlier works betray the influence of the Bellini; but modifying his style from the study of Giorgione and Titian, Palma took high rank among those painters of the distinctively Venetian type who remain a little below the leading masters. For richness of colour he is hardly to be surpassed; but neither in invention nor vigorous draughtsmanship does he often attain any peculiar excellence. A face frequently seen in his pictures is that of his (so-called) daughter Violante, of whom Titian was said to be enamoured. Two works by Palma are more particularly celebrated. The first is a composition of six paintings in the Venetian church of S. Maria Formosa, with St Barbara in the centre, under the dead Christ, and to right and left SS. Dominic, Sebastian, John Baptist and Anthony. The second work is in the Dresden Gallery, representing three sisters seated in the open air; it is frequently named "The Three Graces." A third fine work, discovered in Venice in 1900, is a portrait supposed to represent Violante. Other leading examples are: the "Last Supper," in S. Maria Mater Domini; a "Madonna," in the church of S. Stefano in Vicenza; the "Epiphany," in the Brera of Milan; the "Holy Family, with a young shepherd adoring," in the Louvre; "St Stephen and other Saints," "Christ and the Widow of Nain," and the "Assumption of the Virgin," in the Academy of Venice; and "Christ at Emmaus," in the Pitti Gallery. The beautiful portrait of the National Gallery, London, with a background of foliage, originally described as "Ariosto" and as by Titian, and now reascribed to that master, was for some years assumed to be an unknown poet by Palma Vecchio. It is certainly much more like the work of Titian than of Palma. In 1907 the Staedel Institute in Frankfort acquired an important work by Palma Vecchio, identified by its director as an illustration of Ovid's second *Metamorphosis*, and named "Jupiter and Calisto."

Palma's grand-nephew, Palma Giovane, was also named Jacopo (1544 to about 1626). His works belong to the decline of Venetian art. (W. M R.)

PALMA, or PALMA DE MALLORCA, the capital of the Spanish province of the Balearic Islands, the residence of a captain-general, an episcopal see, and a flourishing seaport, situated 135 m. S.S.E. of Barcelona, on the south-west coast of Majorca, at the head of the fine Bay of Palma, which stretches inland for about 10 m. between Capes Cala Figuera and Regana. Pop. (1900), 63,937, including a colony of Jews converted to Christianity (*Chuetas*). Palma is the meeting place of all the highways in the island, and the terminus of the railway to Inca, Manacor, and Alcudia. The ramparts, which enclose the city on all sides except towards the port (where they were demolished in 1872), have a circuit of a little more than 4 m. Though begun in 1562, they were not finished till 1836. Palma underwent considerable change in the 19th century, and the fine old-world Moorish character of the place suffered accordingly. The more conspicuous buildings are the cathedral, the exchange, the royal palace, now occupied by the captain-general, and the law courts, the episcopal palace, a handsome late Renaissance building (1616), the general hospital (1456), the town-house (end of the 16th century), the picture gallery, and the college. The church of San Francisco is interesting for the tomb of Raimon Lull, a native of Palma. The cathedral was erected and dedicated to the Virgin by King James I. of Aragon as he sailed to the conquest of Majorca; but, though founded in 1230, it was not finished till 1601. The older and more interesting portions are the royal chapel (1232), with the marble sarcophagus of James II. (d. 1311) which was erected here in 1779; and the south front with the elaborately-sculptured doorway known as *del mirador* (1389). The exchange (*lonja*), a Gothic building begun in 1426, excited the admiration of the emperor Charles V. Palma has a seminary founded in 1700, a collection of archives dating from the 14th century, a school and museum of fine arts, a nautical school and an institute founded in 1836 to replace the old university (1503).

The harbour, formed by a mole constructed to a length of 387 yds. in the 14th century and afterwards extended to more than 650 yds., has been greatly improved since 1875 by dredging and a further addition to the mole of 136 yds. Previously it was not accessible to vessels drawing more than 18 ft. Palma has frequent and regular communication by steamer with Barcelona, Valencia and Alicante. Puertopí, about 2 m. south-west of the city, was once a good harbour, but is now fit only for small craft. Palma has a thriving trade in grain, wine, oil, almonds, fruit, vegetables, silk, foodstuffs and livestock. There are manufactures of alcohol, liqueurs, chocolate, starch, sugar, preserves, flour, soap, leather, earthenware, glass, matches, paper, linen, woollen goods and rugs.

Palma probably owes, if not its existence, at least its name (symbolized on the Roman coins by a palm branch), to Metellus Balearicus, who in 123 B.C. settled three thousand Roman and Spanish colonists on the island. The bishopric dates from the 14th century. About 1 m. south-west of Palma is the castle of Bellver or Belbez, the ancient residence of the kings of Majorca. Miramar, the beautiful country seat of the archduke Ludwig Salvator of Austria, is 12 m. north of Palma.

PALMA, or SAN MIGUEL DE LA PALMA, a Spanish island in the Atlantic Ocean, forming part of the Canary Islands (*q.v.*). Pop. (1900), 41,994; area 280 sq. m. Palma is 26 m. long, with an extreme breadth of 16 m. It lies 67 m. W.N.W. of Teneriffe. It is traversed from north to south by a chain of mountains, the highest of which is 7900 ft. above sea-level. At the broadest part is a crater 9 m. in diameter, known as the Caldera (*i.e.* cauldron). The bottom of the crater has an elevation of 2300 ft., and it is overhung by peaks that rise more than 5000 ft. above it. Palma contains several mineral springs, but there is great want of fresh water. The only stream which is never dried up is that which issues from the Caldera. In 1677 an eruption, preceded by an earthquake, took place from a volcano at the southern extremity of the island, and much damage was done. Santa Cruz de la Palma (pop 7024) on the eastern coast is the principal town. The anchorage is good.

PALM BEACH, a winter resort on the east coast of Florida, U.S.A., in Palm Beach county, about 264 m. S. of St Augustine; served by the Florida East Coast railway. It is situated on a peninsula (about 30 m. long and 1 m. wide) separated from the mainland by Lake Worth, an arm of the Atlantic Ocean, and derives its name from the groves of coco-nut palms which fringe the lake. The coco-nut was introduced here by chance, through the wrecking, off the coast, in January 1879, of a coco-nut-laden Spanish vessel. The Gulf Stream is within about 1 m. of the above, and the climate is mild and equable, the winter temperature normally ranging between 70° and 75° F. On the Atlantic is the Breakers, a large hotel, and facing Lake Worth is the Royal Poinciana, the largest hotel in the southern states. Palm Beach has few permanent residents and is not incorporated. On the mainland just across the lake is the city of West Palm Beach (pop. in 1905, 1280; 1910, 1743), a pleasure resort and the county-seat of Palm Beach county (created in 1909).

PALM-CIVET, or PARADOXURE, the name of the members of the civet-like genus *Paradoxurus*, represented by several species mainly from south-east Asia. (See CARNIVORA.) Palm-civets are mostly about the size of the domestic cat, or rather larger, chiefly arboreal in habits, with dark uniform, spotted or striped fur. The common Indian palm-civet (*P. niger*) ranges throughout India, wherever there are trees, frequently taking up its abodes in roof-thatch. Its diet consists of small mammals and reptiles, birds and their eggs, fruit and vegetables. From four to six young are brought forth at a litter, and are easily tamed. Other species are the Ceylonese *P. aureus*, the brown *P. jerdoni*, the Himalayan *P. grayi* and the Malayan *P. Hermaphroditus*. The small-toothed palm-civets, from the Malay Archipelago, Sumatra and Java, have been separated from the typical group to form the genus *Arctogale*. In Africa the group is represented by two species of *Nandinia*, which show several primitive characters.

PALMELLA, a town of Portugal, in the district of Lisbon (formerly included in the province of Estremadura), at the north-eastern extremity of the Serra da Arrabida, and on the Lisbon-Setubal railway. Pop. (1900), inclusive of the neighbouring village of Marateca, 11,478. Palmella is an ancient 'and picturesque town, still surrounded by massive but ruined walls and dominated by a medieval castle. Viticulture, market-gardening and fruit-farming are important local industries. Palmella was taken from the Moors in 1147 by Alphonso I. (Affonso Henriques), and entrusted in 1186 to the knights of Santiago. The title "duke of Palmella" dates from 1834, when it was conferred on the statesman Pedro de Sousa-Holstein, count of Palmella (1781–1850).

PALMER, SIR CHARLES MARK, BART. (1822–1907), English shipbuilder, was born at South Shields on the 3rd of November 1822. His father, originally the captain of a whaler, removed in 1828 to Newcastle-on-Tyne, where he conducted a ship-owning and ship-broking business. Charles Palmer at the age of fifteen entered a shipping business in that town, whence, after six months, he went to Marseilles, where his father had procured him a post in a large commercial house, at the same time entrust-ing him with the local agency of his own business. After two years' experience at Marseilles he entered his father's business at Newcastle, and in 1842 he became a partner. His business capacity attracted the attention of a leading local colliery owner, and he was appointed manager of the Marley Hill colliery in which he became a partner in 1846. Subsequently he was made one of the managers of the associated collieries north and south of the Tyne owned by Lord Ravensworth, Lord Wharncliffe, the marquess of Bute, and Lord Strathmore, and in due course he gradually purchased these properties out of the profits of the Marley Hill colliery. Simultaneously he greatly developed the then recently-established coke trade, obtaining the coke contracts for several of the large English and continental railways. About 1850 the question of coal-transport to the London market became a serious question for north country colliery proprietors. Palmer therefore built, largely according to his own plans, the "John Bowes," the first iron screw-collier, and several other steam-colliers, in a yard established by him at Jarrow, then a small Tyneside village. He then purchased iron-mines in York-shire, and erected along the Tyne at Jarrow large shipbuilding yards, blast-furnaces, steel-works, rolling-mills and engine-works, fitted on the most elaborate scale. The firm produced war-ships as well as merchant vessels, and their system of rolling armour plates, introduced in 1856, was generally adopted by other builders. In 1865 he turned the business into Palmer's Shipbuilding and Iron Company, Limited. In 1886 his services in connexion with the settlement of the costly dispute between British ship-owners and the Suez Canal Company (of which he was then a director) were rewarded with a baronetcy. He died in London on the 4th of June 1907.

PALMER, EDWARD HENRY (1840–1882), English orientalist, the son of a private schoolmaster, was born at Cambridge, on the 7th of August 1840. He was educated at the Perse School, and as a schoolboy showed the characteristic bent of his mind by picking up the Romany tongue and a great familiarity with the life of the gipsies. From school he was sent to London as a clerk in the city. Palmer disliked this life, and varied it by learning French and Italian, mainly by frequenting the society of foreigners wherever he could find it. In 1859 he returned to Cambridge, apparently dying of consumption. He had an almost miraculous recovery, and in 1860, while he was thinking of a new start in life, fell in with Sayyid Abdallah, teacher of Hindustani at Cambridge, under whose influence he began his Oriental studies. He matriculated at St John's College in November 1863, and in 1867 was elected a fellow on account of his attainments as an orientalist, especially in Persian and Hindustani. During his residence at St John's he catalogued the Persian, Arabic and Turkish manuscripts in the university library, and in the libraries of King's and Trinity. In 1867 he published a treatise on *Oriental Mysticism*, based on the *Maksad-i-Aksá* of Aziz ibn Mohammad Nafasi. He was engaged in 1869 to join the survey of Sinai, undertaken by the Palestine Exploration Fund, and followed up this work in the next year by exploring the desert of El-Tih in company with Charles Drake (1840–1874). They completed this journey on foot and without escort, making friends among the Bedouin, to whom Palmer was known as "Abdallah Effendi." After a visit to the Lebanon and to Damascus, where he made the acquaintance of Sir Richard Burton, then consul there, he returned to England in 1870 by way of Constanti-nople and Vienna. At Vienna he met Arminius Vambéry. The results of this expedition appeared in the *Desert of the Exodus* (1871); in a report published in the journal of the Palestine Exploration Fund (1871); and in an article on the *Secret Sects of Syria* in the *Quarterly Review* (1873). In the close of the year 1871 he became Lord Almoner's Professor of Arabic at Cambridge; married, and settled down to teaching. His salary was small, and his affairs were further complicated by the long illness of his wife, who died in 1878. In 1881, two years after his second marriage, he left Cambridge, and joined the staff of the *Standard* newspaper to write on non-political subjects. He was called to the English bar in 1874, and early in 1882 he was asked by the government to go to the East and assist the Egyptian expedition by his influence over the Arabs of the desert El-Tih. He was instructed, apparently, to prevent the Arab sheikhs from joining the Egyptian rebels and to secure their non-interference with the Suez Canal. He went to Gaza, without an escort made his way safely through the desert to Suez—an exploit of singular boldness —and was highly successful in his negotiations with the Bedouin. He was appointed interpreter-in-chief to the force in Egypt, and from Suez he was again sent into the desert with Captain William John Gill and Flag-Lieutenant Harold Charrington to procure camels and gain the allegiance of the sheikhs by considerable presents of money. On this journey he and his companions were led into an ambush and murdered (August 1882). Their remains, recovered after the war by the efforts of Sir Charles (then Colonel) Warren, now lie in St Paul's Cathedral.

Palmer's highest qualities appeared in his travels, especially in the heroic adventures of his last journeys. His brilliant scholarship is displayed rather in the works he wrote in Persian and other Eastern languages than in his English books, which were generally written under pressure. His scholarship was wholly Eastern in character, and lacked the critical qualities of the modern school of Oriental learning in Europe. All his works show a great linguistic range and very versatile talent; but he left no permanent literary monument worthy of his powers. His chief writings are *The Desert of the Exodus* (1871), *Poems of Behá ed Din* (Ar. and Eng., 1876–1877), *Arabic Grammar* (1874), *History of Jerusalem* (1871), by Besant and Palmer—the latter wrote the part taken from Arabic sources; *Persian Dictionary* (1876) and *English and Persian Dictionary* (posthumous, 1883); translation of the Koran (1880) for the *Sacred Books of the East* series, a spirited but not very accurate rendering. He also did good service in editing the *Name Lists* of the Palestine Exploration.

PALMER, ERASTUS DOW (1817–1904), American sculptor, was born at Pompey, New York, on the 2nd of April 1817. In his leisure moments as a carpenter he started by carving portraits in cameo, and then began to model in clay with much success. Among his works are: "The White Captive" (1858) in the Metropolitan Museum of Art, New York; "Peace in Bondage" (1863); "Angel at the Sepulchre" (1865), Albany, New York; a bronze statue of Chancellor Robert R. Livingston (1874), in Statuary Hall, Capitol, Washington; and many portrait busts. He died in Albany on the 9th of March 1904. His son, Walter Launt Palmer (b. 1854), who studied art under Carolus-Duran in Paris, became a member of the National Academy of Design (1897), and is best known for his painting of snow scenes.

PALMER, GEORGE (1818–1897), British biscuit-manufacturer, was born on the 18th of January 1818, at Long Sutton, Somerset-shire, where his family had been yeomen-farmers for several generations. The Palmers were Quakers, and George Palmer was educated at the school of the Society of Friends at Sidcot, Somersetshire. About 1832 he was apprenticed to a miller and confectioner at Taunton, and in 1841, in conjunction with Thomas Huntley, set up as a biscuit-manufacturer at Reading. By the application of steam-machinery to biscuit-manufacture the firm of Huntley & Palmer in a comparatively short time built up a very large business, of which on the death of Huntley in 1857 George Palmer and his two brothers, Samuel and William Isaac Palmer, became proprietors. In the same year George

Palmer was elected mayor of Reading, and from 1878-1885 he was Liberal member of Parliament for the town. He died at Reading, to which he had been a most generous benefactor, on the 19th of August 1897. His sons, George William Palmer (b. 1851) and Sir Walter Palmer (b. 1858), displayed a like munificence, particularly in connexion with University College, Reading. George William Palmer, besides being mayor of Reading, represented the town in Parliament as a Liberal. Sir Walter Palmer, who was created a baronet in 1904, became Conservative member for Salisbury in 1900.

PALMER, JOHN McAULEY (1817-1900), American soldier and political leader, was born at Eagle Creek, Kentucky, on the 13th of September 1817. In 1831 his family removed to Illinois, and in 1839 he was admitted to the bar in that state. He was a member of the state constitutional convention of 1847. In 1852-1855 he was a Democratic member of the state Senate, but joined the Republican party upon its organization and became one of its leaders in Illinois. He was a delegate to the Republican national convention in 1856 and a Republican presidential elector in 1860. In 1861 he was a delegate to the peace convention in Washington. During the Civil War he served in the Union army, rising from the rank of colonel to that of major-general in the volunteer service and taking part in the capture of New Madrid and Island No. 10, in the battles of Stone River and Chickamauga, and, under Thomas, in the Atlanta campaign. He was governor of Illinois from 1869 to 1873. In 1872 he joined the Liberal-Republicans, and eventually returned to the Democratic party. In 1891-1897 he was a Democratic member of the United States Senate. In 1896 he was nominated for the presidency, by the "Gold-Democrats," but received no electoral votes. He died at Springfield, Illinois, on the 25th of September 1900.

See *The Personal Recollections of John M. Palmer—The Story of an Earnest Life*, published posthumously in 1901.

PALMER, RAY (1808-1887), American clergyman and hymn-writer, was born in Little Compton, Rhode Island, on the 12th of November 1808. He graduated at Yale College in 1830, and in 1832 was licensed to preach by the New Haven West Association of Congregational Ministers. In 1835-1850 he was pastor of the Central Congregational Church of Bath, Maine, and in 1850-1866 of the First Congregational Church of Albany, New York; and from 1866 to 1878 was corresponding secretary of the American Congregational Union. He died on the 29th of March 1887 in Newark, New Jersey, where, from 1881 to 1884 he had been assistant pastor of the Belleville Avenue Congregational Church. His most widely known hymn, beginning "My faith looks up to Thee, Thou Lamb of Calvary," was written in 1830, was set to the tune "Olivet" by Lowell Mason, and has been translated into many languages; his hymn beginning "Jesus, these eyes have never seen" (1858) is also well-known.

Among the hymns translated by him are those beginning: "O Christ, our King, Creator, Lord" (by Gregory the Great); "Come Holy Ghost in love" (by Robert II. of France); "Jesus, thou Joy of loving hearts" (by Bernard of Clairvaux); and "O, Bread to pilgrims given" (from the Latin). Other hymns(some of them translations from Latin) and poems were collected in his *Complete Poetical Works* (1876), followed in 1880 by *Voices of Hope and Gladness*. He also wrote *Spiritual Improvement* (1839), republished in 1851 as *Closet Hours; Hints on the Formation of Religious Opinions* (1860), and *Earnest Words on True Success in Life* (1873).

PALMER, SAMUEL (1805-1881), English landscape painter and etcher, was born in London on the 27th of January 1805. He was delicate as a child, but in 1819 he exhibited both at the Royal Academy and the British Institution; and shortly afterwards he became intimate with John Linnell, who introduced him to Varley, Mulready, and, above all, to William Blake, whose strange and mystic genius had the most powerful effect on Palmer's art. An illness led to a residence of seven years at Shoreham in Kent, and the characteristics of the scenery of the district are constantly recurrent in his works. Among the more important productions of this time are the "Bright Cloud" and the "Skylark," paintings in oil, which was Palmer's usual medium in earlier life. In 1839 he married a daughter of Linnell. The

wedding tour was to Italy, where he spent over two years in study. Returning to London, he was in 1843 elected an associate and in 1854 a full member of the Society of Painters in Water Colours, a method to which he afterwards adhered in his painted work. His productions are distinguished by an excellent command over the forms of landscape, and by mastery of rich, glowing and potent colouring. Among the best and most important paintings executed by Palmer during his later years was a noble series of illustrations to Milton's *L'Allegro* and *Il Penseroso*. In 1853 the artist was elected a member of the English Etching Club. Considering his reputation and success in this department of art, his plates are few in number. Their virtues are not those of a rapid and vivid sketch; they aim rather at truth and completeness of tonality, and embody many of the characteristics of other modes of engraving—of mezzotint, of line, and of woodcut. Readily accessible and sufficiently representative plates may be studied in the "Early Ploughman," in *Etching and Etchers* (1st ed.), and the "Herdsman's Cottage," in the third edition of the same work. In 1861 Palmer removed to Reigate, where he died on the 24th of May 1881. One of his latest efforts was the production of a series of etchings to illustrate his English metrical version of Virgil's *Eclogues*, which was published in 1883, illustrated with reproductions of the artist's water-colours and with etchings, of which most were completed by his son, A. H. Palmer.

PALMER, a township of Hampden county, Massachusetts, U.S.A. Pop. (1910 U.S. census) 8610. It has an area of about 31 sq. m. of broken hill country. Its chief village, also named Palmer, about 15 m. east of Springfield, is on the Chicopee river, is served by the Boston & Albany and the Central Vermont railways, and by an electric line to Springfield, and has varied manufactures; the other villages are Thorndike, Bondsville, and Three Rivers. The principal manufactures are cotton goods, carpets and wire goods. Palmer was originally settled in 1716, but received a notable accession of population from a large Scotch-Irish colony which went from Ulster to Boston in 1718. Their settlement was followed, apparently, by immigration from Ireland in 1727. In 1752 the plantation was incorporated as a "district," and under a general state law of 1775 gained the legal rights of a township. Palmer was a centre of disaffection in the time of the Shays Rebellion.

See T. H. Temple, *History of the Town of Palmer ... 1716-1889* (Palmer, 1889).

PALMER, a pilgrim who as a sign or token that he had made pilgrimage to Palestine carried a palm-branch attached to his staff, or more frequently a cross made of two strips of palm-leaf fastened to his hat. The word is frequently used as synonymous with "pilgrim" (see PILGRIMAGE). The name "palmer" or "palmer-worm" is often given to many kinds of hairy caterpillars, specifically to that of the destructive tineid moth, *Ypsilophus pomicella*. The name is either due to the English use of "palm" for the blossom or catkin of the willow-tree, to which the caterpillars bear some resemblance, or to the wandering pilgrim-like habits of such caterpillars. Artificial flies used in angling, covered with bristling hairs, are known also as "palmers" or "hackles."

PALMERSTON, HENRY JOHN TEMPLE, 3RD VISCOUNT (1784-1865), English statesman, was born at Broadlands, near Romsey, Hants, on the 20th of October 1784. The Irish branch of the Temple family, from which Lord Palmerston descended, was very distantly related to the great English house of the same name, but these Irish Temples were not without distinction. In the reign of Elizabeth they had furnished a secretary to Sir Philip Sidney and to Essex in Sir William Temple (1555-1627), afterwards provost of Trinity College, Dublin, whose son, Sir John Temple (1600-1677), was master of the rolls in Ireland. The latter's son, Sir William Temple (*q.v.*), figured as one of the ablest diplomatists of the age. From his younger brother, Sir John Temple (1632-1704), who was speaker of the Irish House of Commons, Lord Palmerston descended. The eldest son of the speaker, Henry, 1st Viscount Palmerston (*c.* 1673-1757), was created a peer of Ireland on the 12th of March 1723, and was succeeded by his grandson, Henry the second viscount (1739–1802), who married Miss Mary Mee (d. 1805), a lady celebrated for her beauty.

The 2nd viscount's eldest son, Henry John, is mentioned by Lady Elliot in her correspondence as a boy of singular vivacity and energy. These qualities adhered to him through life, and he had scarcely left Harrow, at the age of eighteen, when the death of his father (April 17, 1802) raised him to the Irish peerage. It was no doubt owing to his birth and connexions, but still more to his own talents and character, that Lord Palmerston was thrown at a very early age into the full stream of political and official life. Before he was four-and-twenty he had stood two contested elections for the university of Cambridge, at which he was defeated, and he entered parliament for a pocket-borough, Newtown, Isle of Wight, in June 1807. Through the interest of his guardians Lord Malmesbury and Lord Chichester, the duke of Portland made him one of the junior lords of the Admiralty on the formation of his administration in 1807. A few months later he delivered his maiden speech in the House of Commons in defence of the expedition against Copenhagen, which he conceived to be justified by the known designs of Napoleon on the Danish court. This speech was so successful that when Perceval formed his government in 1809, he proposed to this young man of five-and-twenty to take the chancellorship of the exchequer. Lord Palmerston, however, preferred the less important office of secretary-at-war, charged exclusively with the financial business of the army, without a seat in the cabinet, and in this position he remained, without any signs of an ambitious temperament or of great political abilities, for twenty years (1809–1828). During the whole of that period Lord Palmerston was chiefly known as a man of fashion, and a subordinate minister without influence on the general policy of the cabinets he served. Some of the most humorous poetical pieces in the *New Whig Guide* were from his pen, and he was entirely devoted, like his friends Peel and Croker, to the Tory party of that day. Lord Palmerston never was a Whig, still less a Radical; he was a statesman of the old English aristocratic type, liberal in his sentiments, favourable to the march of progress, but entirely opposed to the claims of democratic government.

In the later years of Lord Liverpool's administration, after the death of Lord Londonderry in 1822, strong dissensions existed in the cabinet. The Liberal section of the government was gaining ground. Canning became foreign minister and leader of the House of Commons. Huskisson began to advocate and apply the doctrines of free trade. Roman Catholic emancipation was made an open question. Although Lord Palmerston was not in the cabinet, he cordially supported the measures of Canning and his friends. Upon the death of Lord Liverpool, Canning was called to the head of affairs; the Tories, including Peel, withdrew their support, and an alliance was formed between the Liberal members of the late ministry and the Whigs. In this combination the chancellorship of the exchequer was first offered to Lord Palmerston, who accepted it, but this appointment was frustrated by the king's intrigue with Herries, and Palmerston was content to remain secretary-at-war with a seat in the cabinet, which he now entered for the first time. The Canning administration ended in four months by the death of its illustrious chief, and was succeeded by the feeble ministry of Lord Goderich, which barely survived the year. But the " Canningites," as they were termed, remained, and the duke of Wellington hastened to include Palmerston, Huskisson, Charles Grant, Lamb (Lord Melbourne) and Dudley in his government. A dispute between the duke and Huskisson soon led to the resignation of that minister, and his friends felt bound to share his fate. In the spring of 1828 Palmerston found himself in opposition. From that moment he appears to have directed his attention closely to foreign affairs; indeed he had already urged on the duke of Wellington a more active interference in the affairs of Greece; he had made several visits to Paris, where he foresaw with great accuracy the impending revolution; and on the 1st of June 1829 he made his first great speech on foreign affairs. Lord Palmerston was no orator; his language was unstudied, and his delivery somewhat embarrassed; but he generally found words to say the right thing at the right time, and to address the House of Commons in the language best adapted to the capacity and the temper of his audience. An attempt was made by the duke of Wellington in September 1830 to induce Palmerston to re-enter the cabinet, which he refused to do without Lord Lansdowne and Lord Grey, and from that time forward he may be said to have associated his political fortunes with those of the Whig party. It was therefore natural that Lord Grey should place the department of foreign affairs in his hands upon the formation of the great ministry of 1830, and Palmerston entered with zeal on the duties of an office over which he continued to exert his powerful influence, both in and out of office, for twenty years.

The revolution of July 1830 had just given a strong shock to the existing settlement of Europe. The kingdom of the Netherlands was rent asunder by the Belgian revolution; Portugal was the scene of civil war; the Spanish succession was about to open and place an infant princess on the throne. Poland was in arms against Russia, and the northern powers formed a closer alliance, threatening to the peace and the liberties of Europe. In presence of these varied dangers, Lord Palmerston was prepared to act with spirit and resolution, and the result was a notable achievement of his diplomacy. The king of the Netherlands had appealed to the powers who had placed him on the throne to maintain his rights; and a conference assembled accordingly in London to settle the question, which involved the independence of Belgium and the security of England. On the one hand, the northern powers were anxious to defend the king of Holland; on the other hand a party in France aspired to annex the Belgian provinces. The policy of the British government was a close alliance with France, but an alliance based on the principle that no interests were to be promoted at variance with the just rights of others, or which could give to any other nation well-founded cause of jealousy. If the northern powers supported the king of Holland by force, they would encounter the resistance of France and England united in arms, if France sought to annex Belgium she would forfeit the alliance of England, and find herself opposed by the whole continent of Europe. In the end the policy of England prevailed; numerous difficulties, both great and small, were overcome by the conference, although on the verge of war, peace was maintained; and Prince Leopold of Saxe-Coburg was placed upon the throne of Belgium.

In 1833 and 1834 the youthful queens Donna Maria of Portugal and Isabella of Spain were the representatives and the hope of the constitutional party in those countries—assailed and hard pressed by their absolutist kinsmen Don Miguel and Don Carlos, who were the representatives of the male line of succession. Lord Palmerston conceived and executed the plan of a quadruple alliance of the constitutional states of the West to serve as a counterpoise to the northern alliance. A treaty for the pacification of the Peninsula was signed in London on the 22nd of April 1834; and, although the struggle was somewhat prolonged in Spain, it accomplished its object. France, however, had been a reluctant party to this treaty. She never executed her share in it with zeal or fidelity. Louis Philippe was accused of secretly favouring the Carlists, and he positively refused to be a party to direct interference in Spain. It is probable that the hesitation of the French court on this question was one of the causes of the extreme personal hostility Lord Palmerston never ceased to show towards the king of the French down to the end of his life, if indeed that sentiment had not taken its origin at a much earlier period. Nevertheless, at this same time (June 1834) Lord Palmerston wrote that " Paris is the pivot of my foreign policy." M. Thiers was at that time in office. Unfortunately these differences, growing out of the opposite policies of the two countries at the court of Madrid, increased in each succeeding year; and a constant but sterile rivalry was kept up, which ended in results more or less humiliating and injurious to both nations.

The affairs of the East interested Lord Palmerston in the highest degree. During the Greek War of Independence he had strenuously supported the claims of the Hellenes against the

"Turks and the execution of the Treaty of London. But from 1830 the defence of the Ottoman Empire became one of the cardinal objects of his policy. He believed in the regeneration of Turkey. "All that we hear," he wrote to Bulwer (Lord Dalling), "about the decay of the Turkish Empire, and its being a dead body or a sapless trunk, and so forth, is pure unadulterated nonsense." The two great aims he had in view were to prevent the establishment of Russia on the Bosporus and of France on the Nile, and he regarded the maintenance of the authority of the Porte as the chief barrier against both these aggressions. Against Russia he had long maintained a suspicious and hostile attitude. He was a party to the publication of the "Portfolio" in 1834, and to the mission of the "Vixen" to force the blockade of Circassia about the same time. He regarded the treaty of Unkiar Skelessi which Russia extorted from the Porte in 1832, when she came to the relief of the sultan after the battle of Konieh, with great jealousy; and, when the power of Mehemet Ali in Egypt appeared to threaten the existence of the Ottoman dynasty, he succeeded in effecting a combination of all the powers, who signed the celebrated collective note of the 27th of July 1839, pledging them to maintain the independence and integrity of the Turkish Empire as a security for the peace of Europe. On two former occasions, in 1833 and in 1835, the policy of Lord Palmerston, who proposed to afford material aid to the Porte against the pasha of Egypt, was overruled by the cabinet; and again, in 1839, when Baron Brunnow first proposed the active interference of Russia and England, the offer was rejected. But in 1840 Lord Palmerston returned to the charge and prevailed. The moment was critical, for Mehemet Ali had occupied Syria and won the battle of Nezib against the Turkish forces, and on the 1st of July 1839 the sultan Mohammed expired. The Egyptian forces occupied Syria, and threatened Turkey; and Lord Ponsonby, then British ambassador at Constantinople, vehemently urged the necessity of crushing so formidable a rebellion against the Ottoman power. But France, though her ambassador had signed the collective note in the previous year, declined to be a party to measures of coercion against the pasha of Egypt. Palmerston, irritated at her Egyptian policy, flung himself into the arms of the northern powers, and the treaty of the 15th of July 1840 was signed in London without the knowledge or concurrence of France. This measure was not taken without great hesitation, and strong opposition on the part of several members of the British cabinet. Lord Palmerston himself declared in a letter to Lord Melbourne that he should quit the ministry if his policy was not adopted; and he carried his point. The bombardment of Beirût, the fall of Acre, and the total collapse of the boasted power of Mehemet Ali followed in rapid succession, and before the close of the year Lord Palmerston's policy, which had convulsed and terrified Europe, was triumphant, and the author of it was regarded as one of the most powerful statesmen of the age. At the same time, though acting with Russia in the Levant, the British government engaged in the affairs of Afghanistan to defeat her intrigues in Central Asia, and a contest with China was terminated by the conquest of Chusan, afterwards exchanged for the island of Hong-Kong.

Within a few months Lord Melbourne's administration came to an end (1841), and Lord Palmerston remained for five years out of office. The crisis was past, but the change which took place by the substitution of M. Guizot for M. Thiers in France, and of Lord Aberdeen for Lord Palmerston in England, was a fortunate event for the peace of the world. Lord Palmerston had adopted the opinion that peace with France was not to be relied on, and indeed that war between the two countries was sooner or later inevitable. Lord Aberdeen and M. Guizot inaugurated a different policy; by mutual confidence and friendly offices they entirely succeeded in restoring the most cordial understanding between the two governments, and the irritation which Lord Palmerston had inflamed gradually subsided. During the administration of Sir Robert Peel, Lord Palmerston led a retired life, but he attacked with characteristic bitterness the Ashburton treaty with the United States, which closed successfully some other questions he had long kept open. In all these transactions, whilst full justice must be done to the force and patriotic vigour which Lord Palmerston brought to bear on the questions he took in hand, it was but too apparent that he imported into them an amount of passion, of personal animosity, and imperious language which rendered him in the eyes of the queen and of his colleagues a dangerous minister. On this ground, when Lord John Russell attempted, in December 1845, to form a ministry, the combination failed because Lord Grey refused to join a government in which Lord Palmerston should resume the direction of foreign affairs. A few months later, however, this difficulty was surmounted; the Whigs returned to power, and Palmerston to the foreign office (July 1846), with a strong assurance that Lord John Russell should exercise a strict control over his proceedings. A few days sufficed to show how vain was this expectation. The French government regarded the appointment of Palmerston as a certain sign of renewed hostilities, and they availed themselves of a despatch in which Palmerston had put forward the name of a Coburg prince as a candidate for the hand of the young queen of Spain, as a justification for a departure from the engagements entered into between M. Guizot and Lord Aberdeen. However little the conduct of the French government in this transaction of the Spanish marriages can be vindicated, it is certain that it originated in the belief that in Palmerston France had a restless and subtle enemy. The efforts of the British minister to defeat the French marriages of the Spanish princesses, by an appeal to the treaty of Utrecht and the other powers of Europe, were wholly unsuccessful; France won the game, though with no small loss of honourable reputation.

The revolution of 1848 spread like a conflagration through Europe, and shook every throne on the Continent except those of Russia, Spain, and Belgium. Palmerston sympathised, or was supposed to sympathise, openly with the revolutionary party abroad. No state was regarded by him with more aversion than Austria. Yet his opposition to Austria was chiefly based upon her occupation of great part of Italy and her Italian policy, for Palmerston maintained that the existence of Austria as a great power north of the Alps was an essential element in the system of Europe. Antipathies and sympathies had a large share in the political views of Lord Palmerston, and his sympathies had ever been passionately awakened by the cause of Italian independence. He supported the Sicilians against the king of Naples, and even allowed arms to be sent them from the arsenal at Woolwich; and, although he had endeavoured to restrain the king of Sardinia from his rash attack on the superior forces of Austria, he obtained for him a reduction of the penalty of defeat. Austria, weakened by the revolution, sent an envoy to London to request the mediation of England, based on a large cession of Italian territory; Lord Palmerston rejected the terms he might have obtained for Piedmont. Ere long the reaction came; this straw-fire of revolution burnt itself out in a couple of years. In Hungary the civil war, which had thundered at the gates of Vienna, was brought to a close by Russian intervention. Prince Schwarzenberg assumed the government of the empire with dictatorial power; and, in spite of what Palmerston termed his "judicious bottle-holding," the movement he had encouraged and applauded, but to which he could give no material aid, was everywhere subdued. The British government, or at least Palmerston as its representative, was regarded with suspicion and resentment by every power in Europe, except the French republic; and even that was shortly afterwards to be alienated by Palmerston's attack on Greece.

This state of things was regarded with the utmost annoyance by the British court and by most of the British ministers. Palmerston had on many occasions taken important steps without their knowledge, which they disapproved. Over the Foreign Office he asserted and exercised an arbitrary dominion, which the feeble efforts of the premier could not control. The queen and the prince consort (see VICTORIA, QUEEN) did not conceal their indignation at the position in which he had placed them with all the other courts of Europe. When Kossuth, the

Hungarian leader, landed in England, Palmerston proposed to receive him at Broadlands, a design which was only prevented by a peremptory vote of the cabinet; and in 1850 he took advantage of Don Pacifico's very questionable claims on the Hellenic government to organize an attack on the little kingdom of Greece.[1] Greece being a state under the joint protection of three powers, Russia and France protested against its coercion by the British fleet, and the French ambassador temporarily left London, which promptly led to the termination of the affair. But it was taken up in parliament with great warmth. After a memorable debate (June 17), Palmerston's policy was condemned by a vote of the House of Lords. The House of Commons was moved by Roebuck to reverse the sentence, which it did (June 29) by a majority of 46, after having heard from Palmerston the most eloquent and powerful speech ever delivered by him, in which he sought to vindicate, not only his claims on the Greek government for Don Pacifico, but his entire administration of foreign affairs. It was in this speech, which lasted five hours, that Palmerston made the well-known declaration that a British subject—" Civis Romanus sum "—ought everywhere to be protected by the strong arm of the British government against injustice and wrong. Yet, notwithstanding this parliamentary triumph, there were not a few of his own colleagues and supporters who condemned the spirit in which the foreign relations of the Crown were carried on; and in that same year the queen addressed a minute to the prime minister in which she recorded her dissatisfaction at the manner in which Lord Palmerston evaded the obligation to submit his measures for the royal sanction as failing in sincerity to the Crown. This minute was communicated to Palmerston, who did not resign upon it. These various circumstances, and many more, had given rise to distrust and uneasiness in the cabinet, and these feelings reached their climax when Palmerston, on the occurrence of the coup d'état by which Louis Napoleon made himself master of France, expressed to the French ambassador in London, without the concurrence of his colleagues, his personal approval of that act. Upon this Lord John Russell advised his dismissal from office (Dec. 1851). Palmerston speedily avenged himself by turning out the government on a militia bill; but although he survived for many years, and twice filled the highest office in the state, his career as foreign minister ended for ever, and he returned to the foreign office no more. Indeed, he assured Lord Aberdeen, in 1853, that he did not wish to resume the seals of that department. Notwithstanding the zeal and ability which he had invariably displayed as foreign minister, it had long been felt by his colleagues that his eager and frequent interference in the affairs of foreign countries, his imperious temper, the extreme acerbity of his language abroad, of which there are ample proofs in his published correspondence, and the evasions and artifices he employed to carry his points at home, rendered him a dangerous representative of the foreign interests of the country. But the lesson of his dismissal was not altogether lost on him. Although his great reputation was chiefly earned as a foreign minister, it may be said that the last ten years of his life, in which he filled other offices, were not the least useful or dignified portion of his career.

Upon the formation of the cabinet of 1853, which was composed by the junction of the surviving followers of Sir Robert Peel with the Whigs, under the earl of Aberdeen, Lord Palmerston accepted with the best possible grace the office of secretary of state for the home office, nor was he ever chargeable with the slightest attempt to undermine that government. At one moment he withdrew from it, because Lord John Russell persisted in presenting a project of reform which appeared to him entirely out of season; and he advocated, with reason, measures

[1] David Pacifico (1784–1854) was a Portuguese Jew, born a British subject at Gibraltar. He became a merchant at Athens, and in 1847 his house was burnt down in an anti-Semitic riot. Pacifico brought an action, laying the damages at £26,000. At the same time George Finlay, the historian, was urging his own grievances against the Greek government, and as both claims were repudiated Palmerston took them up. Eventually Pacifico received a substantial sum.

of greater energy on the approach of war, which might possibly, if they had been adopted, have averted the contest with Russia. As the difficulties of the Crimean campaign increased, it was not Lord Palmerston but Lord John Russell who broke up the government by refusing to meet Roebuck's motion of inquiry. Palmerston remained faithful and loyal to his colleagues in the hour of danger. Upon the resignation of Lord Aberdeen and the duke of Newcastle, the general sentiment of the House of Commons and the country called Palmerston to the head of affairs, and he entered, on the 5th of February 1855, upon the high office, which he retained, with one short interval, to the day of his death. Palmerston was in the seventy-first year of his life when he became prime minister of England.

A series of fortunate events followed his accession to power. In March 1855 the death of the emperor Nicholas removed his chief antagonist. In September Sevastopol was taken. The administration of the British army was reformed by a consolidation of offices. In the following spring peace was signed in Paris. Never since Pitt had a minister enjoyed a greater share of popularity and power, and, unlike Pitt, Palmerston had the prestige of victory in war. He was assailed in parliament by the eloquence of Gladstone, the sarcasms of Disraeli, and the animosity of the Manchester Radicals, but the country was with him. Defeated by a hostile combination of parties in the House of Commons on the question of the Chinese war in 1857 and the alleged insult to the British flag in the seizure of the lorcha " Arrow," he dissolved parliament and appealed to the nation. The result was the utter defeat of the extreme Radical party and the return of a more compact Liberal majority. The great events of the succeeding years, the Indian Mutiny, and the invasion of Italy by Napoleon III., belong rather to the general history of the times than to the life of Palmerston; but it was fortunate that a strong and able government was at the head of affairs. Lord Derby's second administration of 1858 lasted but a single year, Palmerston having casually been defeated on a measure for removing conspiracies to murder abroad from the class of misdemeanour to that of felony, which was introduced in consequence of Orsini's attempt on the life of the emperor of the French. But in June 1859 Palmerston returned to power, and it was on this occasion that he proposed to Cobden, one of his most constant opponents, to take office, and on the refusal of that gentleman Milner Gibson was appointed to the board of trade, although he had been the prime mover of the defeat of the government on the Conspiracy Bill. Palmerston had learnt by experience that it was wiser to conciliate an opponent than to attempt to crush him, and that the imperious tone he had sometimes adopted in the House of Commons, and his supposed obsequiousness to the emperor of the French, were the causes of the temporary reverse he had sustained. Although Palmerston approved the objects of the French invasion of Italy in so far as they went to establish Italian independence, the annexation of Savoy and Nice to France was an incident which revived his old suspicions of the good faith of the French emperor. About this time he expressed to the duke of Somerset his conviction that Napoleon III. " had at the bottom of his heart a deep and unextinguishable desire to humble and punish England," and that war with France was a contingency to be provided against. The unprotected condition of the principal British fortresses and arsenals had long attracted his attention, and he succeeded in inducing the House of Commons to vote nine millions for the fortification of those important points.

In 1856 the projects for cutting a navigable canal through the Isthmus of Suez was brought forward by M. de Lesseps, and resisted by Palmerston with all the weight he could bring to bear against it. He did not foresee the advantages to be derived by British commerce from this great work, and he was strongly opposed to the establishment of a powerful French company on the soil of Egypt. The concession of land to the company was reduced by his intervention, but in other respects the work proceeded and was accomplished. It may here be mentioned, as a remarkable instance of his foresight, that

Palmerston told Lord Malmesbury, on his accession to the foreign office in 1858, that the chief reason of his opposition to the canal was this: he believed that, if the canal was made and proved successful, Great Britain, as the first mercantile state, and that most closely connected with the would be the power most interested in it; that England East erefore be drawn irresistibly into a more direct interference Egypt, which it was desirable to avoid because England had already enough upon her hands, and because intervention might lead to a rupture with France. He therefore preferred that no such line of communication should be opened.

Upon the outbreak of the American Civil War in 1861, Lord Palmerston acknowledged that it was the duty of the British government to stand aloof from the fray; but his own opinion led him rather to desire than to avert the rupture of the Union, which might have been the result of a refusal on the part of England and France, to recognize a blockade of the Southern ports, which was notoriously imperfect, and extremely prejudicial to the interests of Europe. The cabinet was not of this opinion, and, although the belligerent rights of the South were promptly recognised, the neutrality of the Government was strictly observed. When, however, the Southern envoys were taken by force from the " Trent," a British packet, Palmerston did not hesitate a moment to insist upon a full and complete reparation for so gross an infraction of international law. But the difficulty with the American government over the " Alabama " and other vessels, fitted out in British ports to help the Southern cause, was only settled at last (see ALABAMA ARBITRATION) by an award extremely onerous to England.

The last transaction in which Palmerston engaged arose out of the attack by the Germanic Confederation, and its leading states Austria and Prussia, on the kingdom of Denmark and the duchies of Schleswig and Holstein. There was but one feeling in the British public and the nation as to the dishonest character of that unprovoked aggression, and it was foreseen that Austria would ere long have reason to repent her share in it. Palmerston endeavoured to induce France and Russia to concur with England in maintaining the Treaty of London, which had guaranteed the integrity of the Danish dominions. But those powers, for reasons of their own, stood aloof, and the conference held in London in 1864 was without effect. A proposal to send the British fleet into the Baltic was overruled, and the result was that Denmark was left to her own resources against her formidable enemies. In the following year, on the 18th of October 1865, Lord Palmerston died at Brocket Hall, after a short illness, in the eighty-first year of his age. His remains were laid in Westminster Abbey.

Although there was much in the official life of Lord Palmerston which inspired distrust and alarm to men of a less ardent and contentious temperament, he had a lofty conception of the strength and the duties of England, he was the irreconcilable enemy of slavery, injustice and oppression, and he laboured with inexhaustible energy for the dignity and security of the Empire. In private life his gaiety, his buoyancy, his high breeding, made even his political opponents forget their differences; and even the warmest altercations on public affairs were merged in his large hospitality and cordial social relations. In this respect he was aided with consummate ability by the tact and grace of Lady Palmerston, the widow of the 5th Earl Cowper, whom he married at the close of 1839, and who died in 1869. She devoted herself with enthusiasm to all her husband's interests and pursuits, and she made his house the most attractive centre of society in London, if not in Europe. They had no children, and the title became extinct, the property descending to Lady Palmerston's second son by Earl Cowper, W. F. Cowper-Temple, afterwards Baron Mount Temple, and then to her grandson Evelyn Ashley (1836–1907) son of her daughter, who married the 7th earl of Shaftesbury—who was Lord Palmerston's private secretary from 1858 to 1865.

The *Life of Lord Palmerston*, by Lord Dalling (2 vols., 1870), with valuable selections from the minister's autobiographical diaries and private correspondence, only came down to 1847, and was completed by Evelyn Ashley (vol. iii.; 1874; iv., v., 1876). The whole was re-edited by Mr Ashley, in two volumes (1879), the standard biography. The *Life* by Lloyd Sanders (1888) is an excellent shorter work.

PALMERSTON, the chief town of the Northern Territory of South Australia, in Palmerston county, on the E. shore of Port Darwin, 2000 m. direct N.N.W. of Adelaide. The town stands 60 ft. above the level of the sea, by which it is almost surrounded. There are a government house, a town hall, and an experimental nursery garden. Palmerston has a magnificent harbour, accessible to ocean-going vessels, and the jetty is connected by rail with Playford, 146 m. distant. Cool breezes blow almost continuously throughout the year. The mean annual rainfall is 62·21 in. Pop. (1901), 1973, mostly Chinese.

PALMETTO, in botany, a popular name for *Sabal Palmetto,* the Palmetto palm, a native of the southern United States, especially in Florida. It has an erect stem, 70 to 80 ft. high and deeply cut fan-shaped leaves, 5 to 8 ft. long; the fruit is a black drupe ⅓ to ½ in. long. The trunks make good piles for wharves, &c., as the wood resists the attacks of borers; the leaves are used for thatching. The palm is grown as a pot-plant in greenhouses.

PALMISTRY, (from "palmist," one who studies the palm, and the Teutonic affix *ry* signifying "art "; also called CHIROMANCY, from χείρ, the hand, and μαντεία, divination). The desire to learn what the future has in store is nearly as old as the sense of responsibility in mankind, and has been the parent of many empirical systems of fortune-telling, which profess to afford positive knowledge whereby the affairs of life may be regulated, and the dangers of failure foretold. Most of these systems come into the category of occult pursuits, as they are the interpretations of phenomena on the ground of fanciful presumptions, by an appeal to unreal or at least unverifiable influences and relations.

One of the oldest of this large family of predictive systems is that of palmistry, whereby the various irregularities and flexion-folds of the skin of the hand are interpreted as being associated with mental or moral dispositions and powers, as well as with the current of future events in the life of the individual. How far back in prehistoric times this system has been practised it is impossible to say, but in China it is said to have existed 3000 years before Christ,[1] and in Greek literature it is treated even in the most ancient writings as well-known belief. Thomas Blackwell[2] has collected some Homeric references: a work by Melampus of Alexandria is extant in several versions. Polemon, Aristotle and Adamantius may also be named as having dealt with the subject; as also have the medical writers of Greece and Rome—Hippocrates, Galen and Paulus Aegineta, and in later times the Arabian commentators on these authors. From references which can be gathered from patristic writings it is abundantly evident that the belief in the mystical meaning of marks on the "organ of organs" was a part of the popular philosophy of their times.

After the invention of printing a very considerable mass of literature concerning this subject was produced during the 16th and 17th centuries. Praetorius, in his *Ludicrum chiromanticum* (Jena, 1661)[3] has collected the titles of 77. Other works are quoted by Fulleborn and Hörst, and by writers on the history of philosophy and magic; altogether about 98 books on the subject published before 1700 are at present accessible. There is not very much variety among these treatises, one of the earliest, valuable on account of its rarity, is the block-book by Hartlieb, *Die Kunst Ciromantia,*[4] published at Augsburg about 1470 (probably, but it bears no imprint of place or date). In this there are colossal figures of hands, each of which has its regions marked out by inscriptions. Few of these works are of sufficient interest to require mention.

[1] Giles, in *Contemporary Review* (1905).
[2] *Proofs of the Inquiry into the Life and Writings of Homer,* p. 330 (London, 1736).
[3] This book is worthy of note on account of the quaint and sarcastic humour of its numerous acrostic verses.
[4] There is a copy in the Rylands Library, Manchester. See also Dibdin's *Bibliographical Decameron* (1817), i. 143.

The best are those by Pompeius,Robert Fludd, John de Indagine, Taisnierus, Baptista dalla Porta, S. Cardan, Goclenius, Cocles, Frölich, Summer, Rothmann, Ingebert, Pomponius Gauricus, and Tricassus Mantuanus. There are also early Hebrew works, of which one by Gedaliah is extant. An Indian literature is also said to exist. Some of these authors attempt to separate the physiognomical part of the subject (Chirognomia) from the astrological (Chiromantia); see especially Caspar Schott in *Magia naturalis universalis*, Bamberg, 1677. Since the middle of the 19th century, in spite of the enactments of laws in Britain and elsewhere against the practice, there has been a recrudescence of belief in palmistry, and a new literature has grown up differing little in essence from the older. The more important books of this series are K. G. Carus, *Über Grund u. Bedeutung der verschiedenen Formen der Hand*, 1846; Landsberg, *Die Handteller* (Posen,1861); Adolf Desbarolles, *Les Mystères de la main* (1859); C. S. D'Arpentigny, *Chirognomie, la science de la main* (1865), of which an English version has been published by Heron Allen in 1886; G. Z. Gessmann, *Katechismus der Handlesekunst* (Berlin, 1889); Czynszi, *Die Deutung der Handlinien* (Dresden, 1893); R. Beamish, *The Psychonomy of the Hand* (1865); Frith. and Allen, *The Science of Palmistry* (1883); Cotton, *Palmistry* and its practical uses (1890). Some of the older writers appealed to Scripture as supporting their systems, especially the texts Exod. xiii. 16; Job xxxvii. 7; and Prov. iii. 16. A considerable amount of literature *pro* and *con* was devoted to this controversy in the 17th and 18th centuries.

At the present day palmistry is practised in nearly all parts of China. The criteria of judgment used there are referred to in the article by Professor H. A. Giles, already quoted. It is also extensively practised in India, especially by one caste of Brahmins, the Joshi. In Syria and Egypt the palmist can be seen plying his trade at the cafés; and among the Arabs there are chiromantists who are consulted as to the probable success of enterprises. It is probably from their original Indian home that the traditional *dukkeripen* (fortune-telling) of the gipsies has been derived.

This system of divination has the charm of simplicity and definiteness, as an application of the " doctrine of signatures " which formed so extensive an element in the occult writings of the past six centuries. In the course of ages every detail has been brought under a formal set of rules, which only need mechanical application. There have been in past times considerable divergences in the practice, but at present there is a fairly uniform system in vogue. One school lays special stress on the general shape and outline of the hand. Corvacus enumerates 70 varieties, Pamphilus cuts them down to 6, John de Indagine to 27, and Tricassus Mantuanus raises them to 80. The characters of softness or hardness, dryness or moisture, &c., are taken account of in these classifications. The lines of cardinal importance are (1) the rasceta or cross sulci, which isolate the hand from the forearm at the wrist, and which are the flexion folds between the looser forearm skin and that tied down to the fascia above the level of the anterior annular ligament. (2) The line which isolates the ball of the thumb, where the skin ceases to be tied to the front of the palmar fascia, is called the line of life. (3) A line starting above the head of the second metacarpal bone and crossing the hand to the middle of its ulnar border is the line of the head. (4) The transverse line below this which passes from the ulnar border a little above the level of the head of the fifth metacarpal and ends somewhere about the root of the index finger is the line of the heart. (5) The vertical line descending from the middle of the wrist to end about the base of the middle finger is the line of fortune. (6) The oblique line which begins at the wrist end of the line of life and descends towards the ulnar end of the line of the head is the line of the liver.

These lines isolate certain swellings or monticuli, the largest of which is (1) the ball of the thumb, called the mountain of Venus; (2) that at the base of the index finger is the mountain of Jupiter; (3) at the root of the middle finger is the mountain of Saturn, while those at the bases of ring and little finger are respectively the mountains of the (4) Sun and (5) of Mercury. Above the mountain of Mercury, and between the lines of head and heart is (6) the mountain of Mars, and above the line of the heart is (7) the mountain of the Moon. The relative sizes of these mountains have assigned to them their definite correlations with characters: the 1st with charity, love, libertinage; the 2nd with religiosity, ambition, love of honour, pride, superstition; the 3rd with wisdom, good fortune, prudence, or when deficient improvidence, ignorance, failure; the 4th when large makes for success, celebrity, intelligence, audacity, when small meanness or love of obscurity; the 5th indicates love of knowledge, industry, aptitude for commerce, and in its extreme forms on the one hand love of gain and dishonesty, on the other slackness and laziness. The 6th is related to degrees of courage, resolution, rashness or timidity; the 7th indicates sensitiveness, morality, good conduct, or immorality, overbearing temper and self-will.

The swellings on the palmar faces of the phalanges of the several fingers are also indicative, the 1st and 2nd of the thumb respectively, of the logical faculty and of the will; the 1st, 2nd and 3rd of the index finger, of materialism, law and order, idealism; those of the middle finger, humanity, system, intelligence; of the ring finger, truth, economy, energy; and of the little finger, goodness, prudence, reflectiveness.

Over and above these there are other marks, crosses, triangles, &c., of which more than a hundred have been described and figured by different authors, each with its interpretation; and in addition the back of the hand has its ridges. The Chinese combine podoscopy with chiromancy.

To the anatomist the roughnesses of the palm are of considerable interest. The folds are so disposed that the thick skin shall be capable of bending in grasping, while at the same time it requires to be tightly bound down to the skeleton of the hand, else the slipping of the skin would lead to insecurity of prehension, as the quilting or buttoning down of the covers of furniture by upholsterers keeps them from slipping. For this purpose the skin is tied by connecting fibres of white fibrillar tissue to the deep layer of the dermis along the lateral and lower edges of the palmar fascia and to the sheaths of the flexor tendons. The folds, therefore, which are disposed for the purpose of making the grasp secure, vary with the relative lengths of the metacarpal bones, with the mutual relations of the sheaths of the tendons, and the edge of the palmar fascia, somewhat also with the insertion of the palmaris brevis muscle. The sulci are emphasized because the subcutaneous fat, which is copious in order to pad the skin for the purpose of firmness of holding, being restricted to the intervals between the lines along which the skin is tied down, makes these intervals project, and these are the monticuli. The swelling of the mountain of Venus is simply the indication of the size of the muscles of the ball of the thumb, and can be increased by their exercise. Similarly the hypothenar muscles for the little finger underlie the three ulnar marginal mountains, the sizes of which depend on their development and on the prominence of the pisiform bone.

That these purely mechanical arrangements have any psychic, occult or predictive meaning is a fantastic imagination, which seems to have a peculiar attraction for certain types of mind, and as there can be no fundamental hypothesis of correlation, its discussion does not lie within the province of reason.

(A. Ma.)

PALMITIC ACID, *n*-HEXADECYLIC ACID, $CH_3(CH_2)_{14}CO_2H$, an organic acid found as a glyceride, palmitin, in all animal fats, and partly as glyceride and partly uncombined in palm oil. The cetyl ester is spermaceti, and the myricyl ester is largely present in beeswax. It is most conveniently obtained from olive oil, after removal of the oleic acid (*q.v.*), or from Japanese beeswax, which is its glyceride. Artificially it may be prepared by heating cetyl alcohol with soda lime to 270° or by fusing oleic acid with potassium hydrate.

PALM SUNDAY (*Dominica palmarum*), the Sunday before Easter, so called from the custom, still observed in the Roman Catholic Church, of blessing palm branches and carrying them in procession in commemoration of Christ's triumphal entry into Jerusalem. In the Western Church, Palm Sunday is counted as the first day of Holy Week, and its ceremonies usher in the series of services, culminating in those of Good Friday, which commemorate the Passion of the Lord.

The ceremonies on Palm Sunday as celebrated now in the Roman Catholic Church are divided in three distinct parts: (1) The solemn blessing of the palms, (2) the procession, (3) the mass.

Branches of palm, olive or sprouting willow (hence in England known as " palm ") having been placed before the altar, or at the Epistle side, after Terce and the sprinkling of holy water, the priest, either in a purple cope or an alb without chasuble, proceeds to bless them. The ceremony begins with the singing by the choir of the anthem *Hosanna Filio David*; the collect follows; then the singing of a lesson from Exodus xv. by the subdeacon; then the Gradual, reciting antiphonally the conspiracy of the chief priests and Pharisees, and concluding with Christ's prayer on Mt Olivet; then the Gospel, sung by the deacon in the ordinary way, followed by a " continuation of the Holy Gospel " (Matt. xxi. and sqq.). After this the priest blesses the palms in a series of prayers, that those who receive them " may be protected in soul and body," and that " into whatever place they may be brought the inhabitants of that place may obtain Thy benediction; and all adversity being removed, &c." The priest then sprinkles the palms thrice with holy water, saying the prayer *Asperges me*, &c., and also incenses them thrice. The principal of the clergy present then approaches and gives a palm to the celebrant, who then, in his turn, distributes the branches, first to the principal of the clergy, then to the deacon and subdeacon, and to the other clergy in order of rank, and lastly to the laity, all of whom receive the palms kneeling, and kiss the palm and the hand of the celebrant. During the distribution antiphons are sung.

The deacon now turns to the people and says *Procedamus in pace*, and the procession begins. It is headed by a thurifer carrying a smoking thurible; then comes the sub-deacon carrying the cross between two acolytes with lighted tapers: the clergy next in order, the celebrant coming last with the deacon on his left, all carrying branches and singing antiphonally, so long as the procession lasts, the account of the entry into Jerusalem, ending with " *Benedictus qui venit in nomine Domini: Hosanna in excelsis*." On returning to the church, two or four singers enter first and close the doors, then, turning towards the procession outside, sing the first two verses of the hymn " *Gloria, laus et honor*," those outside repeating them, and so on till the hymn is finished. This done, the subdeacon strikes the door with the staff of the cross, when it is immediately opened, and the procession enters singing. The mass that follows, characterised by all the outward signs of sorrow proper to Passion Week, is in striking contrast with the joyous triumph of the procession.

In the Orthodox Eastern Church Palm Sunday (κυριακή or ἑορτή τῶν βαίων, ἑορτή βαιοφόρος, or ἡ βαιοφόρος) is not included in Holy Week, but is regarded as a joyous festival commemorating Christ's triumphal entry into Jerusalem. There is no longer a procession; but the palms (in Russia willow twigs) are blessed, and are held by the worshippers during the service.

The earliest extant account of a liturgical celebration of Palm Sunday is that given in the *Peregrinatio Silviae* (*Eleutheriae*),[1] which dates from the 4th century and contains a detailed account of the Holy Week ceremonies at Jerusalem by a Spanish lady of rank:—

The actual festival began at one o'clock with a service in the church on the Mount of Olives; at three o'clock clergy and people went in procession, singing hymns, to the scene of the Ascension; two hours of prayer, singing and reading of appropriate Scriptures followed, until, at five o'clock the reading of the passage from the Gospel telling how " the children with olive branches and palms go to meet the Lord, and cry: ' Blessed is he that cometh in the name of the Lord ' " gave the signal for the crowd to break up, and, carrying branches of olive and palm, to conduct the bishop, *in eo typo quo tunc Dominus deductus est*,[2] with cries of " Blessed is he that cometh in the name of the Lord!" to the Church of the Resurrection in Jerusalem, where a further service was held.

This celebration would seem to have been long established at Jerusalem, and there is evidence that in the 4th and 5th centuries it had already been copied in other parts of the East. In the West, however, it was not introduced until much later. To Pope Leo I. (d. 461) the present *Dominica palmarum* was

[1] The text is published among the appendices to Duchesne's *Origines du culte Chrétien* (2nd ed., 1898), p. 486, " Procession du soir."

[2] Drews takes this to mean " riding on an ass."

known as *Dominica passionis*, Passion Sunday, and the Western Church treated it as a day, not of rejoicing, but of mourning. The earliest record in the West of the blessing of the palms and the subsequent procession is the *liber ordinum* of the West Gothic Church (published by Férotin, Paris, 1904, pp. 178 sqq.), which dates from the 6th century; this shows plainly that the ceremonial of the procession had been borrowed from Jerusalem. As to how far, and at what period, it became common there is very little evidence. For England, the earliest record is the mention by Aldhelm, bishop of Sherborne (d. 709), in his *De laudibus virginitatis* (cap. 30, Migne *Patrol. Lat.* 89, p. 128), of a *sacrosancta palmarum solemnitas*, which probably means a procession, since he speaks of the *Benedictus qui venit*, &c., being sung antiphonally. As the middle ages advanced the procession became more and more popular and increasingly a dramatic representation of the triumphal progress of Christ, the bishop riding on an ass or horse, as in the East.[2] Flowers, too, were blessed, as well as palms and willow, and carried in the procession (hence the names *pascha floridum, dominica florum et ramorum, les pâques fleuries*).

The origin of the ceremony of blessing the palms is more obscure. It is not essential to the dramatic character of the celebration and for centuries seems to have formed no usual part of it. Herr Drews (*Realencyklop.* XXI. p. 417, 40-60) ascribes to it an entirely separate and pagan origin. It is significant that olive and willow should have been chosen for benediction together with, or as substitutes for palm, and that an exorcizing power should have been ascribed to the consecrated branches: they were to heal disease, ward off devils, protect the houses where they were set up against lightning and fire, and the fields where they were planted against hail and storms. But healing power had been ascribed to the olive in pagan antiquity, and in the same way the willow had from time immemorial been credited by the Teutonic peoples with the possession of protective qualities. It was natural that olive and willow should have been chosen for the Palm Sunday ceremony, for they are the earliest trees to bud in the spring; their consecration, however, may be explained by the intention to Christianize a pagan belief, and it is easy to see how their mystic virtues came in this way to be ascribed to the palm also. When and where the custom first arose is unknown.

Of the reformed churches, the Church of England alone includes Palm Sunday in the Holy Week celebrations. The blessing of the palms and the procession were, however, abolished at the Reformation, and the name " Palm Sunday," though it survives in popular usage, is not mentioned in the Book of Common Prayer. The intention of the compilers of the Prayer-book seems to have been to restore the " Sunday next before Easter," as it is styled, to its earlier Western character of Passion Sunday, the second lesson at matins (Matt. xxvi. 5) and the special collect, Epistle (Phil. II. 5) and Gospel (Matt. xxvii. 1) at the celebration of Holy Communion all dwelling on the humiliation and passion of Christ, with no reference to the triumphal entry into Jerusalem. The modern revival, in certain churches of an " advanced " type, of the ceremonies of blessing the palms and carrying them in procession has no official warrant, and is therefore without any significance as illustrating the authoritative point of view of the Church of England.

Of the Lutheran churches only that of Brandenburg seems to have kept the Palm Sunday procession for a while. This was prescribed by the Church order (*Kirchenordnung*) of 1540, but without the ceremony of blessing the palms; it was abolished by the revised Church order of 1572.

See the article "*Palmsonntag*" in Wetzer und Welte, *Kirchenlexikon* (2nd ed.), ix. 1319 sqq.: article " *Woche, grosse*," by Drews in Herzog-Hauck, *Realencyklopädie* (3rd ed., Leipzig, 1908), xxi. 415; Wiepen, *Palmsonntagsprozessionen und Palmesel* (Bonn, 1903); L. Duchesne, *Origines du culte Chrétien* (2nd ed., Paris, 1898), p. 237. For ceremonies anciently observed in England on Palm Sunday see M. E. C. Walcott, *Sacred Archaeology* (1868) and J. Brand, *Popular antiquities* (ed. 1870).

PALMYRA, the Greek and Latin name of a famous city of the East, now a mere collection of Arab hovels, but still an object of interest on account of its wonderful ruins. In 2 Chron.

[2] For curious instances of the part played by the ass in medieval church festivals see the article FOOLS, FEAST OF,

viii. 4, and in the native inscriptions, it is called Tadmor, and this is the name by which it is known among the Arabs at the present day (Tadmur, Tudmur).[1] The site of Palmyra lies 150 m. N.E. of Damascus and five days' camel journey from the Euphrates, in an oasis of the Syrian desert, 1,300 ft. above sea-level. At this point the great trade routes met in ancient times, the one crossing from the Phoenician ports to the Persian Gulf, the other coming up from Petra and south Arabia.

The earliest mention of Palmyra is in 2 Chron. viii. 4, where Solomon is said to have built "Tadmor in the wilderness"; 1 Kings ix. 18, however, from which the Chronicler derived his statement, reads "Tamar" in the Hebrew text, with "Tadmor" in the Hebrew margin; there can be no doubt that the text is right and refers to Tamar in the land of Judah (Ezek. xlvii. 19; xlviii. 28). The Chronicler, we must suppose, altered the name because Tadmor was a city more familiar and renowned in his day, or possibly because he wished to increase the extent of Solomon's kingdom. The date of the Chronicler may be placed about 300 B.C., so Palmyra must have been in existence long before that. There is reason to believe that before the 6th century B.C. the caravans reached Damascus without coming near the oasis of Tadmor; probably, therefore, we may connect the origin of the city with the gradual forward movement of the nomad Arabs which followed on the overthrow of the ancient nationalities of Syria by the Babylonian Empire (6th century B.C.). The Arabian tribes began to take possession of the partly cultivated lands east of Canaan, became masters of the Eastern trade, gradually acquired settled habits, and learned to speak and write in Aramaic, the language which was most widely current throughout the region west of the Euphrates in the time of the Persian Empire (6th-4th century B.C.). It is not till much later that Palmyra first appears in Western literature. We learn from Appian (Bell. civ. v. 9) that in 42-41 B.C. the city was rich enough to excite the cupidity of M. Antonius (Mark Antony), while the population was not too large to save itself by timely flight. The series of native inscriptions, written in Aramaic, begins a few years after; the earliest bears the date 304 of the Seleucid era, i.e. 9 B.C. (Cooke, North-Semitic Inscriptions No. 141 = Vogüé, Syrie Centrale No. 30a); by this time Palmyra had become an important trade-post between the Roman and the Parthian states. Its characteristic civilization grew out of a mixture of various elements, Arabic, Aramaic, Greek and Roman. The bulk of the population was of Arab race, and though Aramaic was used as the written language, in common intercourse Arabic had by no means disappeared. The proper names and the names of deities, while partly Aramaic, are also in part unmistakably Arabic: it is suggestive that a purely Arabic term (faḫd, NSI. No. 136) was used for the septs into which the citizens were divided.

Originally an Arab settlement, the oasis was transformed in the course of time from a mere halting-place for caravans to a city of the first rank. The true Arab despises agriculture; but the pursuit of commerce, the organization and conduct of trading caravans, cannot be carried on without widespread connexions of blood and hospitality between the merchant and the leading sheiks on the route. An Arabian merchant city is thus necessarily aristocratic, and its chiefs can hardly be other than pure Arabs of good blood. Palmyra also possessed the character of a religious centre, with the worship of the Sun-god dominating that of inferior deities.

The chief luxuries of the ancient world, silks, jewels, pearls, perfumes, incense and the like, were drawn from India, China and southern Arabia. Pliny (N. H. xii. 41) reckons the yearly import of these wares into Rome at not less than three-quarters of a million of English money. The trade followed two routes:

one by the Red Sea, Egypt and Alexandria, the other from the Persian Gulf through the Syro-Arabian desert. The latter, when the Nabataean kingdom of Petra (q.v.) came to an end (A.D. 105), passed into the hands of the Palmyrene merchants. Their caravans (συνοδίαι) travelled right across the desert to the great entrepôts on the Euphrates, Vologesias, about 55 m. south-east of Babylon, or Forath or Charax close to the Persian Gulf (NSI. Nos. 113-115). The trade was enormously profitable, not only to the merchants but to the town, which levied a rigorous duty on all exports and imports; at the same time formidable risks had to be faced both from the desert-tribes and from the Parthians, and successfully to plan or convoy a great caravan came to be looked upon as a distinguished service to the state, often recognized by public monuments erected by "council and people" or by the merchants interested in the venture. These monuments, a conspicuous feature of Palmyrene architecture, took the form of statues placed on brackets projecting from the upper part of the pillars which lined the principal thoroughfares. Thus arose, beside minor streets, the imposing central avenue which, starting from a triumphal arch near the great temple of the Sun, formed the main axis of the city from south-east to north-west for a length of 1240 yards, and at one time consisted of not less than 750 columns of rosy-white limestone, each 55 ft. high.

Local industries do not seem to have been important. One of the chief of them was the production of salt from the deposits of the desert;[2] another was no doubt the manufacture of leather; the inscriptions mention also a powerful gild of workers in gold and silver (NSI. No. 126); but Palmyra was not an industrial town, and the exacting fiscal system which drew profit even out of the bare necessaries of life—such as water, oil, wheat, salt, wine, straw, wool, skins (see Tariff ii. b, NSI. pp. 315 sqq.)—must have weighed heavily upon the artisan class. The prominent townsmen were engaged in the organization and even the personal conduct of caravans, the discharge of public offices such as those of strategos, secretary, guardian of the wells, president of the banquets of Bel, chief of the market (see NSI. Nos. 114, 115, 121, 122), sometimes the victualling of a Roman expedition. The capable performance of these functions, which often involved considerable pecuniary sacrifices, ensured public esteem, honorary inscriptions and statues; and to these honours the head of a great house was careful to add the glory of a splendid tomb, consecrated as the "long home" (lit. "house of eternity," cf. Eccles. xii. 5) of himself, his sons and his sons' sons for ever. These tombs, which lie outside the city and overlook it from the surrounding hills, a feature characteristically Arabic, remain the most interesting monuments of Palmyra. Some are lofty towers containing sepulchral chambers in stories;[3] others are house-like buildings with a single chamber and a richly ornamented portico; the sides of these chambers within are adorned with the names and sculptured portraits of the dead. As a rule the buildings of Palmyra do not possess any architectural individuality, but these tombs are an exception. The style of all the ruins is late classic and highly ornate, but without refinement.

The rise of Palmyra to a position of political importance may be dated from the time when the Romans established themselves on the Syrian coast. As early as the first imperial period the city must have admitted the suzerainty of Rome, for decrees respecting its custom-dues were issued by Germanicus (A.D. 17-19) and Cn. Domitius Corbulo (A.D. 57-66). At the same time the city had by no means surrendered its independence, for even in the days of Vespasian (A.D. 69-79) the distinctive

· ¹ How the name Palmyra arose is obscure. The Greek for a palm is φοῖνιξ, and the Greek ending -yra could not have been affixed to the Latin palma. Schultens (Vita Sal., Index geogr.) cites Tatmur as a variant of the Arabic name; this might mean "abounding in palms" (from the root tamar); otherwise Tadmor may have been originally an Assyrian name. See Lagarde, Bildung der Nomina, p. 125 a.

² "The soil of this marsh [east of Palmyra] is so impregnated with salt that a trench or pit sunk in it becomes filled in a short time with concentrated brine, the water of which evaporates in the intense sunshine and leaves an incrustation of excellent salt." Post, Narrative of a Second Journey to Palmyra in Pal. Expl. Fund's Qtly. St. (1892), p. 324.

³ One of these tomb-towers, called Kaṣr eth-Thuniyeh, is 111 ft. high, 33½ ft. square at the base, 25 ft. 8 in. square above the basement; it contains six stories and places for 480 bodies. Opposite the entrance within is a hall with recesses for coffins and a richly panelled ceiling; underneath is an immense vault.

position of Palmyra as an intermediate state between the two great powers of Rome and Parthia was recognized and carefully watched. The splendid period of Palmyra (A.D. 130-270), to which the greater part of the inscribed monuments belong, started from the overthrow of Petra (A.D. 105), which left Palmyra without a competitor for the Eastern trade. Hadrian treated the city with special favour, and on the occasion of his visit in A.D. 130, granted it the name of Hadriana Palmyra (ורא בבחרא NSI. p. 322).' Under the same emperor the customs were revised and a new tariff promulgated (April, A.D. 137), cancelling the loose system of taxation "by custom" which formerly had prevailed.[1] The great fiscal inscription, which still remains where it was set up, gives the fullest picture of the life and commerce of the city. The government was vested in the council (βουλή) and people (δῆμος), and administered by civil officers with Greek titles, the *proedros* (president), the *grammateus* (secretary), the archons, syndics and *dekaprôtoi* (a fiscal council of ten), following the model of a Greek municipality under the Roman Empire. At a later date, probably under Septimius Severus or Caracalla (beginning of 3rd century), Palmyra received the *Jus italicum* and the status of a colony; the executive officials of the council and people were called *strattêgoi*, equivalent to the Roman *duumviri* (NSI. Nos. 121, 127); and Palmyrenes who became Roman citizens began to take Roman names, usually Septimius or Julius Aurelius, in addition to their native names.

' It was the Parthian wars of the 3rd century which brought Palmyra to the front, and for a brief period raised her to an almost dazzling position as mistress of the Roman East. A new career of ambition was opened to her citizens in the Roman honours that rewarded services to the imperial armies during their frequent expeditions in the East. One house which was thus distinguished had risen to a leading place in the city and before long played no small part in the world's history. Its members, as we learn from the inscriptions, prefixed to their Semitic names the Roman *gentilicium* of Septimius, which shows that they received the citizenship under Septimius Severus (A.D. 193-211), presumably in recognition of their services in connexion with his Parthian expedition. In the next generation Septimius Odainath or Odenathus, son of Hairan, had attained the rank of Roman senator (συγκλητικόs, Vogüé No. 21, NSI. p. 285 *n*). conferred no doubt when Alexander Severus visited Palmyra in A.D. 230-231; his son again, Septimius Hairan, seems to have been the first of the family to receive the title of Rās Tadmor ("chief of Tadmor") in addition to his Roman rank (NSI. No. 125); while his son—the relationship, though nowhere stated, is practically certain—the famous Septimius Odainath, commonly known as Odenathus (q.v.), the husband of Zenobia, received even higher rank, the consular dignity (ὑπατικός) which is given him in an inscription dated A.D. 258, in the reign of Valerian (NSI. No. 126). The East was then agitated by the advance of the Parthian Empire under the Sassanidae, and the Palmyrenes, in spite of their Roman honours and their Roman civilization, which did not really go much below the surface, were by no means prepared to commit themselves altogether to the Roman side.[2] But Parthian ambitions made it necessary for the Palmyrenes to choose one side or other, and their choice leaned towards Rome, both because they dreaded interference with their religious freedom and because the Roman emperor was further off than the Persian king. In the contests which followed there can be no doubt that the Palmyrene princes cherished the idea of an independent empire of their own, though they never threw over their allegiance to the Roman suzerain until the closing act of the drama. Their opportunity came with the disaster which befell the Roman army under Valerian (q.v.) at Edessa, a disaster, says

[1] The full text, both Greek and Palmyrene, with an English translation, is given in NSI, pp. 313-340. The tariff should be compared with the Greek Tariff of Coptos A.D. 90 (Flinders Petrie, *Koptos*, pp. 27 sqq.) and the Latin Tariff of Zarai (*Corp. inscr. lat.* viii. 4508).
[2] For the general history of the Period see PERSIA: *History*, A. § viii., "The Sassanian Empire."

Mommsen, which had nearly the same significance for the Roman East as the victory of the Goths at the mouth of the Danube and the fall of Decius; the emperor was captured (A.D. 260) and died in captivity. The Persians swept victoriously over Asia Minor and North Syria; not however without resistance on the part of Odenathus, who inflicted considerable losses on the bands returning home from the pillage of Antioch. It was probably not long after this that Odenathus, with a keen eye for his advantage, made an attempt to attach himself to Shapur I. (q.v.) the Persian king;[3] his gifts and letters, however, were contemptuously rejected, and from that time, as it seems, he threw himself warmly into the Roman cause. After the captivity and death of Valerian, Gallienus succeeded to a merely nominal rule in the East, and was too careless and self-indulgent to take any active measures to recover the lost provinces. Thereupon the two leading generals of the Roman army, Macrianus and Callistus, renounced their allegiance and proclaimed the two sons of the former as emperors (A.D. 261). During the crisis Odenathus remained loyal to Gallienus, and was rewarded for his fidelity by the grant of a position without parallel under ordinary circumstances; as hereditary prince of Palmyra he was appointed *dux Orientis*, a sort of vice-emperor for the East (A.D. 262). He started promptly upon the work of recovery. With his Palmyrene troops,[4] strengthened by what was left of the Roman army corps, he took the offensive against Shapur, defeated him at Ctesiphon, and in a series of brilliant engagements won back the East for Rome. During his absence at the wars, we learn from the inscriptions (A.D. 262-267) that Palmyra was administered by his deputy Septimius Worod, "procurator ducenarius of Caesar our lord," also styled "commandant," as being Odenathus' viceroy (ἀργαπίτης, NSI. Nos. 127-129). Then in the zenith of his success Odenathus was assassinated at Ḥoms (Emesa) along with his eldest son Herodes (A.D. 266-267). The fortunes of Palmyra now passed into the vigorous hands of ZENOBIA (q.v.), who had been actively supporting her husband in his policy. Zenobia seems to have ruled on behalf of her young son Wahab-allath or Athenodōrus as the name is Graecized, who counts the years of his reign from the date of his father's death. Under Odenathus Palmyra had extended her sway over Syria and Arabia, perhaps also over Armenia, Cilicia and Cappadocia; but now the troops of Zenobia, numbering it is said 70,000, proceeded to occupy Egypt; the Romans under Probus resisted vigorously but without avail, and by the beginning of A.D. 270, when Aurelian succeeded Claudius as emperor, Wahab-allath was governing Egypt with the title of "king." His coins of 270 struck at Alexandria bear the legend v(ir) c(onsularis) R(omanorum) im(perator) d(ux) R(omanorum) and display his head beside that of Aurelian, but the latter alone is styled *Augustus*. Meanwhile the Palmyrenes were pushing their influence not only in Egypt but in Asia Minor; they contrived to establish garrisons as far west as Ancyra and even Chalcedon opposite Byzantium, while still professing to act under the terms of the joint rule conferred by Gallienus. Then in the course of the year A.D. 270-271 came the inevitable and open breach. In Palmyra Zenobia is still called "queen" (βασίλισσα, NSI. No. 131; cf. Wadd. 2628), but in distant quarters, such as Egypt, she and her son claim the dignity of Augustus;

[3] Petrus Patricius. *Fragm. hist. graec.* iv. 187.
[4] The Palmyrene archers were especially famous. Appian mentions them in connexion with M. Antony's raid in 41 B.C. (*Bell. civ.* v. 9). Later on a contingent served with the Roman army in Africa, Britain, Italy, Hungary, where grave-stones with Palmyrene and Latin inscriptions have been found; see Lidzbarski, *Nordsem. epigr.* p. 481 seq.; *Ephemeris*, ii. 92 (a Latin inscription of the time of Marcus Aurelius), and NSI. p. 312. The South Shields inscription, now in the Free Library of the town, was found in the neighbouring Roman camp; it is given in NSI. p. 250. The Palmyrene soldier who set it up was no doubt an archer. Jewish tradition had reason to remember these formidable Palmyrenes in the Roman armies; according to the Talmud 80,000 of them assisted at the destruction of the first temple, 8000 at that of the second! Talm. Jerus. *Taanith*, fol. 68 a, Midrash *Ekha*, ii. 2. For other references to Palmyra (called Tarmod) in the Talmud see Neubauer *Géogr. du Talm.* 301 sqq.

Wahab-allath(5th year)begins to issue coins at Alexandria without the head of Aurelian and bearing the imperial title; and Zenobia's coins bear the same. It was at this time (A.D. 271) that the two chief Palmyrene generals Zabdā and Zabbai, set up a statue to the deceased Odenathus and gave him the sounding designation of " king of kings and restorer of the whole city " (NSI. No. 130). These assumptions marked a definite rejection of all allegiance to Rome. Aurelian, the true Augustus, quickly grasped the situation, and took strenuous measures to deal with it. At the close of A.D. 270 Probus brought back Egypt into the empire, not without a considerable struggle; then in 271 Aurelian made preparations for a great campaign against the seat of the mischief itself. He approached by way of Cappadocia, where he reduced the Palmyrene garrisons, and thence through Cilicia he entered Syria. At Antioch the Palmyrene forces under Zabdā attempted to resist his advances, but they were compelled to fall back upon the great route which leads from Antioch through Emesa (mod. Ḥoms) to their native city. At Emesa the Palmyrenes were defeated in a stiffly contested battle. At length Aurelian arrived before the walls of Palmyra, which was captured probably in the spring of A.D. 272. In accordance with the judicious policy which he had observed in Asia Minor and at Antioch, he granted full pardon to the citizens; only the chief officials and advisers were put to death; Zenobia and her son were captured and reserved for his triumph when he returned to Rome. But the final stage in the conquest of the city was yet to come. A few months later, in the autumn of 272—the latest inscription is dated August 272 (Vogüé, No. 116)—the Palmyrenes revolted, killed the Roman garrison quartered in the city, and proclaimed one Antiochus as their chief. Aurelian heard of it just when he had crossed the Hellespont on his way home. He returned instantly before any one expected him, and took the city by surprise. Palmyra was destroyed and the population put to the sword. Aurelian restored the walls and the great Temple of the Sun (A.D. 273); but the city never recovered its splendour or importance.

Language.—The language spoken at Palmyra was a dialect of western Aramaic, and belongs to the same group as Nabataean and the Aramaic spoken in Egypt. In some important points, however, the dialect was related to the eastern Aramaic or Syrian (e.g. the plur. ending in *ē*; the dropping of the final ǐ of the pronominal suffix third pers. sing. with nouns, and of the final ǔ of the third pers. pl. of the verb; the infin. ending *ā*, &c). But the relation to western Aramaic is closer; specially characteristic are the following features: the imperf. beginning with *y*, not as in Syriac and the eastern dialects with *n* or *l*; the plur. ending *-ayyā*; the forms of the demonstrative pronouns, &c. On the bulk of the population was of Arab race, it is not surprising that many of the proper names are Arabic and that several Arabic words occur in the inscriptions. The technical terms of municipal government are mostly Greek, transliterated into Palmyrene; a few Latin words occur, of course in Aramaic forms. For further characteristics of the dialect see Nöldeke, ZDMG. xxiv. 85–109. The writing is a modified form of the old Aramaic character, and especially interesting because it represents almost the last stage through which the ancient alphabet passed before it developed into the Hebrew square character.

The names of the months were the same as those used by the Nabataeans, Syrians and later Jews, viz. the Babylonian. The calendar was the Syro-Macedonian, a solar, as distinct from the primitive lunar, calendar, which Roman influence disseminated throughout Syria; it was practically a reproduction of the Julian calendar. Dates were reckoned by the Seleucid era, which began in October 312 B.C.

Religion.—The religion of Palmyra did not differ in essentials from that of the north Syrians and the Arab tribes of the eastern desert. The chief god of the Palmyrenes was a solar deity; called Samas or Shamash (" sun "), or Bel, or Malak-bel,[1] whose great temple is still the most imposing feature among the ruins of Palmyra. Both Bel and Malak-bel were of Babylonian origin. Sometimes associated with the Sun-god was 'Aglī-bol the Moon-god who is represented as a young Roman warrior with a large crescent attached to his shoulders (Rom. 1, and Vogüé pl. xii. No. 141). The great goddess of the Aramaeans, 'Athar-'atheh, in Greek Atargatis

[1] Transcribed Μαλαχβῆλος, Malagbelus, &c., and in the Palm. inscr. given in *NSI.*, p. 268, translated Sol sanctissimus; he was further identified with *Zaîs*. Malak-bel has been explained as " messenger of Bel "; but more probably *Malak* is the common Babylonian epithet *malik* given to various gods, and means " counsellor "; Malak-bel will then be the sun as the visible representative of Bel.

(q.v.), and Allath, the chief goddess of the ancient Arabs, were also worshipped at Palmyra. Another deity whose name occurs in votive inscriptions, is Baal-shamim, *i.e.* " B of the heavens," = Zeùs μέγιστος ὕψιστος, sometimes called " lord of eternity," but he was not included among the national gods of Palmyra, so far as we know, though he probably had a temple there. Another interesting divine name, lately discovered, is that of a distinctly Arabic deity " Sha'a-alqūm the good and bountiful god who does not drink wine " (NSI. No. 140 B); the name means " he who accompanies, the protector of, the people "—the divine patron of the caravan. A common formula in Palmyrene dedications runs " To him whose name is blessed for ever, the good and the compassionate "; out of reverence the name of the deity was not pronounced; was it Bel or Malak-bel? It is worth noticing that this epithet like " lord of eternity " (or, " of the world "), has a distinctly Jewish character. Altogether about 22 names of gods are found in Palmyrene; some of them, however, only occur in compound proper names.

After its overthrow by Aurelian, Palm ra was partially revived as a military station by Diocletian (endyof 3rd century A.D.), as we learn from a Latin inscription found on the site. Before this time Christianity had made its way into the oasis, for among the fathers present at the Council of Nicaea (A.D. 325) was Marinus bishop of Palmyra. The names of two other bishops of the 5th and 6th centuries have come down to us. About A.D. 400, Palmyra was the station of the first Illyrian legion (*Not. dign.* i. 85, ed. Böcking); Justinian in 527 furnished it with an aqueduct, and built the wall of which the ruins still remain (Procopius, *De aedif.* ii. 11). At the Moslem conquest of Syria, Palmyra capitulated to Khālid (see CALIPHATE) without embracing Islam (Balādsorī [Balâdhurî], 111 seq.; Yâqūt, i. 831). The town became a Moslem fortress and received a considerable Arab colony; for in the reign of Merwān II. (A.H. 127–132) it sent a thousand Kalbite horsemen to aid the revolt of Emesa, to the district of which it is reckoned by the Arabic geographers. The rebellion was sternly suppressed and the walls of the city destroyed (Ibn al-Athîr, A.H. 127, ed. Tornberg V., 249; cf. *Frag. hist. ar.* 139, Ibn Wâdih, ii. 330). In this connexion Yâqūt tells a curious story of the opening of one of the tombs by the caliph, which in spite of fabulous incidents, recalling the legend of Roderic the Goth, shows some traces of local knowledge. The ruins of Palmyra greatly interested the Arabs, and are commemorated in several poems quoted by Yâqūt and others; they are referred to by the early poet Nābigha as proofs of the might of Solomon and his sovereignty over their builders the Jinn (Derenbourg, *Journ. As.* xii. 209)—a legend which must have come from the Jews, who either clung to the ruins after the great overthrow or returned in the time of Diocletian. References to Palmyra in later times have been collected by Quatremère, *Sultans Mamlouks*, ii. pt. 1. p. 255 seq. All but annihilated by earthquake in the 11th century, it recovered considerable prosperity; when Benjamin of Tudela visited the city, which was still called Tadmor, he found 2000 Jews within the walls (12th century). It was still a wealthy place as late as the 14th century; but in the general decline of the East, and owing to changes in the trade routes, it sunk at length to a poor group of hovels gathered in the courtyard of the Temple of the Sun. The ruins first became known to Europe through the visit of Dr William Halifax of Aleppo in 1691; his *Relation of a voyage to Tadmor* has been printed from his autograph in the Pal. Explor. Fund's Quarterly Statement for 1890. Halifax not only took measurements, but copied 18 Greek and 4 Palmyrene texts. The architecture was carefully studied by Wood and Dawkins in 1751, whose splendid folio (*The Ruins of Palmyra*, London, 1753) also gave copies of inscriptions. But the epigraphic wealth of Palmyra was first opened to study by the collections of Waddington (vol. iii.) and De Vogüé (*La Syria centrale*) made in 1864–1862. Since that time the most valuable document which has come to light is the great fiscal inscription discovered in 1882 by Prince Abamelek Lazarew.

See also A. D. Mordtmann, *Sitzungsb.* of the Munich Acad. (1875); Sachau, ZDMG. xxxv. 728 sqq.; D. H. Müller, *Palm. Inschr.* (1898); J. Mordtmann *Palmyrenisches* (1899); Clermont-Ganneau, *Études d'arch. or.* i, *Recueil. d'arch. or.* iii., v., vi.; Lidzbarski, *Ephemeric,* i.I and ii.; Sobernheim, *Palm. Inschr.* (1905).: The *Répertoire d'épigrsém.* contains the new texts which have been published since 1900. For the coins von Sallet's *Fürsten von Palmyra* (1866) must be read with his later essay in the *Num. Zeitschr.* ü. 31 seq. (1870). Critical discussions of the history will be found in Schiller, *Gesch. d. Römischen Kaiserzeit,* i. 2 Teil (1883), pp. 823 sqq. and 857 sqq., and Mommsen, *Provinces of the Roman Empire,* (Eng. trans., 1886), pp. 92 sqq. (G. A. C.)

PALNI HILLS, a range of hills in south India, in the Madura district of Madras. They are an offshoot from the Western Ghats, and, while distinct from the adjacent Anamalai Hills, form part of the same system. They contain the hill station of Kodaikanal (7200 ft.), which has a milder and more equable climate than Ootacamund in the Nilgiri Hills. There is some coffee cultivation on the lower slopes.

PALO ALTO, a city of Santa Clara county, California, U.S.A., between two of the coast ranges, about 28 m. S. of San Francisco,

and about 18 m. from the sea. Pop. (1910) 4486. It is served by the coast division of the Southern Pacific railway, and is the railway station for Leland Stanford Jr. University (q.v.), which is about 1 m. south-west of the city. At Menlo Park is St Patrick's Theological Seminary (Roman Catholic). By all real estate deeds the sale of intoxicating liquors is for ever prohibited in the city; and an act of the state legislature in 1909 prohibited the sale of intoxicating liquor within 1½ m. of the grounds of the university. The name (Sp. "tall tree") was derived from a solitary redwood-tree standing in the outskirts of the city. Palo Alto was laid out in 1892, but had no real existence before 1893. It was incorporated as a town in 1894, having previously been a part of Mayfield township; in 1909 it was chartered as a city. Palo Alto suffered severely in the earthquake of 1906.

PALOMINO DE CASTRO Y VELASCO, ACISCLO ANTONIO (1653–1726), Spanish painter and writer on art, was born of good family at Bujalance, near Cordoba, in 1653, and studied philosophy, theology and law at that capital, receiving also lessons in painting from Valdes Leal, who visited Cordoba in 1672, and afterwards from Alfaro (1675). After taking minor orders he removed to Madrid in 1678, where he associated with Alfaro, Coello and Careño, and executed some indifferent frescoes. He soon afterwards married a lady of rank, and, having been appointed alcalde of the mesta, was himself ennobled; and in 1688 he was appointed painter to the king. He visited Valencia in 1697, and remained there three or four years, again devoting himself with but poor success to fresco painting. Between 1705 and 1715 he resided for considerable periods at Salamanca, Granada and Cordoba; in the latter year the first volume of his work on art appeared in Madrid. After the death of his wife in 1725 Palomino took priest's orders. He died on the 13th of August 1726.

His work in 3 vols. folio (1715–1724), entitled *El Museo pictorico y escala optica*, consists of three parts, of which the first two, on the theory and practice of the art of painting, are without interest or value; the third, with the subtitle *El Parnaso español pintoresco laureado*, is a mine of important biographical material relating to Spanish artists, which, notwithstanding its faulty style, has procured for the author the not altogether undeserved honour of being called the "Spanish Vasari." It was partially translated into English in 1739; an abridgment of the original (*Las Vidas de los pintores y estatuarios españoles*) was published in London in 1742, and afterwards appeared in a French translation in 1749. A German version was published at Dresden in 1781, and a reprint of the entire work at Madrid in 1797.

PALTOCK, ROBERT (1697–1767), English writer, the only son of Thomas Paltock of St James's, Westminster, was born in 1697. He became an attorney and lived for some time in Clement's Inn, whence he removed, before 1750, to Back Lane, Lambeth. He married Anna Skinner, through whom his son, also named Skinner, inherited a small property at Ryme Intrinseca, Dorset. There Robert Paltock, who died in London on the 20th of March 1767, was buried. Paltock owes his fame to his romantic *Life and Adventures of Peter Wilkins* (1751), which excited the admiration of men like Coleridge, Southey, Charles Lamb, Sir Walter Scott and Leigh Hunt. It has been several times reprinted, notably with an introduction by Mr A. H. Bullen in 1884. It was translated into French (1763) and into German (1767).

PALUDAN-MÜLLER, FREDERIK (1809–1876), Danish poet, was the third son of Jens Paludan-Müller, from 1830 to 1845 bishop of Aarhus, and born at Kjerteminde in Fünen, on the 7th of February 1809. In 1819 his father was transferred to Odense, and Frederik began to attend the Latin school there. In 1828 he passed to the university of Copenhagen. In 1832 he opened his poetical career with *Four Romances*, and a romantic comedy entitled *Kjærlighed ved hoffet* ("Love at Court"). This enjoyed a considerable success, and was succeeded in 1833 by *Dandserinden* ("The Dancing Girl"). Paludan-Müller was accepted by criticism without a struggle, and few writers have excited less hostility than he. He was not, however, well inspired in his lyrical drama of *Amor and Psyche* in 1834 nor in his Oriental tale of *Zuleimas flugt* ("Zuleima's Flight") in 1835, in each of which he was too vividly influenced by Byron. But he

regained all that he had lost by his two volumes of poems in 1836 and 1838. From 1838 to 1840 Paludan-Müller was making the grand tour in Europe and his genius greatly expanded; in Italy he wrote *Venus*, a lyrical poem of extreme beauty. In the same year, 1841, he began to publish a great work on which he had long been engaged, and which he did not conclude until 1848; this was *Adam Homo*, a narrative epic, satirical, modern and descriptive,into which Paludan-Müller wove all his variegated impressions of Denmark and of love. This remains the typical classic of Danish poetical literature. In 1844 he composed three enchanting idylls, *Dryadens bryllup* ("The Dryad's Wedding") *Tithon* ("Tithonus") and *Abels død* ("The Death of Abel"). From 1850 a certain decline in the poet's physical energy became manifest and he wrote less. His majestic drama of *Kalanus* belongs to 1854. Then for seven years he kept silence. *Paradiset* ("Paradise") 1861; and *Benedikt fra Nurcia* ("Benedict of Nurcia") 1861; bear evidence of malady, both physical and mental. Paludan-Müller wrote considerably after this, but never recovered his early raptures, except in the very latest of all his poems, the enchanting welcome to death, entitled *Adonis*. The poet lived a very retired life, first in Copenhagen, then for many years in a cottage on the outskirts of the royal park of Fredensborg, and finally in a house in Ny Adelgade, Copenhagen, where he died on the 27th of December 1876. (E. G.)

PALWAL, a town of British India, in Gurgaon district, Punjab. Pop. (1901), 12,830. It is a place of great antiquity, supposed to figure in the earliest Aryan traditions under the name of Apelava, part of the Pandavs kingdom of Indraprastha. Its importance is mainly historical, but it is a centre for the cotton trade of the neighbourhood, having a station on the Delhi-Agra branch of the Great Indian Peninsula railway.

PAMIERS, a town of south-western France, capital of an arrondissement in the department of Ariège, 40 m. S. by E. of Toulouse on the railway to Foix. Pop. (1906), town, 7728; commune, 10,449. Pamiers is the seat of a bishopric dating from the end of the 13th century. The cathedral (chiefly of the 17th century) with an octagonal Gothic tower, is a bizarre mixture of the Graeco-Roman and Gothic styles; the church of Notre-Dame du Camp (17th and 18th centuries) has its choir crenelated and machicolated façade of the 14th century. Pamiers has a sub-prefecture, a tribunal of first instance, a communal college and a school of commerce and industry. Iron and steel of excellent quality, chains and carriage-springs are among its products. It has also tanneries and wool, flour, paper and saw mills, brickworks and lime-kilns; and commerce in grain, flour, fodder, fruit and vegetables.; There are stone quarries and nursery gardens in the vicinity, and the white wine of the district is well known.

Pamiers was originally a castle built in the beginning of the 11th century by Roger II., count of Foix, on lands belonging to the abbey of St Antonin de Frédelas. The abbots of St Antonin, and afterwards the bishops, shared the authority over the town with the counts. This gave rise to numerous disputes between monks, counts, sovereigns, bishops and the consuls of the town. Pamiers was sacked by Jean de Foix in 1486, again during the religious wars, when the abbey of St Antonin was destroyed, and finally, in 1628, by Henry II. of Bourbon prince of Condé.

PAMIRS, a mountainous region of central Asia, lying on the north-west border of India. Since 1875 the Pamirs have probably been the best explored region in High Asia. Not only have many travellers of many nationalities directed their steps towards the Bam-i-dunya ("the Roof of the World ") in search of adventure or of scientific information, but the government surveys of Russia and India have met in these high altitudes, and there effected a connexion which will help to solve many of the geodetic problems which beset the superficial survey of Asia. Since Wood first discovered a source of the Oxus in Lake Victoria in 1837, and left us a somewhat erroneous conception of the physiography of the Pamirs, the gradual approach of Russia from the north stimulated the processes of exploration from the side of India. Native explorers from India first began to be busy in the Pamirs about 1860, and continued their investigations for the following fifteen years. In 1874 the mission of Sir D. Forsyth to Yarkand led to the first systematic geographical exploitation of the Pamir country. In 1885 Ney Elias made his famous journey across the Pamirs from east to west, identifying the Rang Kul as the Dragon Lake of Chinese geographers—a distinction which has also been claimed by some geographers for Lake Victoria. Then Lockhart and Woodthorpe in 1886 passed along the Wakhan tributary of the Oxus from its head to Ishkashim in Badakshan, and completed an enduring record of most excellent geographical research. Bonvalot in 1887, Littledale in 1888, Cumberland, Bower and Dauvergne, followed by Younghusband in succeeding years, extending to 1890; Dunmore in 1892 and Sven Hedin in 1894-1895, have all contributed more or less to Pamir geography; but the honours of successful inquiry in those high altitudes still fall to Lord Curzon, whose researches in 1894 led to a singularly clear and comprehensive description of Pamir geography, as well as to the best map compilation that till then had existed. Meanwhile Russian explorers and Russian topographers had been equally busy from the north. The famous soldier Skobelev was probably the first European to visit the Great Kara Kul. He was followed by scientific missions systematically organized by the Russian government. In 1883 Putiata's mission started south. Gromchevsky was hard at work from 1888 to 1892. Yanov began again in 1891, after a short spell of rest, and has left his mark as a permanent record in the valley of Sarhad (or Wakhan), between the Baroghil pass and Bozai Gumbas. Finally, in 1895, the Russian mission under General Shvelkovsky met the British mission under General Gerard on the banks of Lake Victoria, and from that point to the Chinese frontier eastward demarcated the line which thereafter was to divide Russian from British interests in highest Asia. Since then other travellers have visited the Pamirs, but the junction of the Russian and British surveys (the latter based on triangulation carried across the Hindu Kush from India) disposes of any further claim to the honours of geographical exploration.

Our estimate of the extent of Pamir conformation depends much on the significance of the word Pamir. If we accept the *Pamir Conformation* Persian derivation of the term (which is advanced by Curzon as being perhaps the most plausible), *pai-mir*, or "the foot of mountain peaks," we have a definition which is by no means an inapt illustration of the actual facts of configuration. It has been too often assumed that the plateau of Tibet and the uplands of the Pamirs are analogous in physiography, and that they merge into each other. This is hardly the case. Littledale points out (*R. G. S. Journ.*, vol. vii.) that the high-level valleys of glacial formation which distinguish the Pamirs have no real counterpart in the Chang or plains of Tibet. The latter are 2000 ft. higher; they are intersected by narrow ranges, and are drained by no rivers of importance. They form a region of salt lakes and stagnant marshes, relieved by wide flat spaces of open plateau country. The absence of any vegetation beyond grass or scrub is a striking feature common to both Pamir and Chang, but there the resemblance ceases, and the physical conformation of mountain and valley to the east and to the west of the upper sources of the Zarafshan is radically distinct.

The axis, or backbone, of Pamir formation is the great meridional mountain chain of Sarikol—the ancient Taurus of *The Pamirs* tradition and history—on which stands the highest peak north of the Himalaya, the Mustagh Ata (25,000 ft.). This chain divides off the high-level sources of the Oxus on the west from the streams which sweep downwards into the Turkestan depression of Kashgar on the east. There are the true Pamirs (*i.e.* valleys reaching up in long slopes to the foot of mountain peaks) on either side, and the Pamirs on the west differ in some essential respects from those on the east. On the west the following are generally recognized as distinct Pamirs: (1) the Great Pamir, of which the dominant feature is Lake Victoria; (2) the Little Pamir, separated from the Great Pamir on the north by what is now known as the Nicolas

range; (3) the Pamir-i-Wakhan, which is the narrow trough of the Wakhan tributary of the Oxus, the term Pamir applying to its upper reaches only; (4) the Alichur—the Pamir of the Yeshil Kul and Ghund—immediately to the north of the Great Pamir; (5) the Sarez Pamir, which forms the valley of the Murghab river, which has here found its way round the east of the Great Pamir and the Alichur from the Little Pamir, and now makes westwards for the Oxus. This branch was considered by many geographers as the main Oxus stream, and Lake Chakmaktin, at its head, was by them regarded as the Oxus source. At the foot of the Sares Pamir stands the most advanced Russian outpost of Murghabi. To the north-east of the Alichur are the Rang Kul and the Kara Kul (or Kargosh) Pamirs. Rang Kul Lake occupies a central basin or depression; but the Kara Kul drains away north-eastwards through the Sarikol (as the latter, bending westwards, merges into the Trans-Alai) to Kashgar and the Turkestan plains. Similar characteristics distinguish all these Pamirs. They are hemmed in and separated by snow-capped mountain peaks and ridges, which are seamed with glaciers terminating in moraines and shingle slopes at the base of the foot-hills. Long sweeps of grassy upland bestrewn with boulders lead from the stream beds up to the snowfields, yellow, grey or vivid green, according to the season and the measure of sunlight, fold upon fold in interminable succession, their bleak monotony being only relieved by the grace of flowers for a short space during the summer months.

To the east of the Sarikol chain is the Taghdumbash Pamir, which claims many of the characteristics of the western Pamirs at its upper or western extremity, where the Karachukar, which drains it, is a comparatively small stream. But where the Karachukar, joining forces with the Khunjerab, stretches out northwards for a comparatively straight run to Tashkurghan, dividing asunder the two parallel ranges of Sarikol and Kandar, which together form the Sarikol chain, the appellation Pamir can hardly be maintained. This is the richest portion of the Sarikol province. Here are stone-built houses collected in scattered detachments, with a spread of cultivation reaching down to the river. Here are water-mills and many permanent appliances of civilization suited to the lower altitude (11,500 ft., the average height of the upper Pamirs being about 13,000), and here we are no longer near the sources of the river at the foot of the mountain peaks. One other so-called Pamir exists to the east of the Sarikol, separated therefrom by the eastern range (the Kandar) of the Sarikol, which is known as Mariom or Mariong. But this Pamir is situated nowhere near the sources of the Zarafshan or Raskam river, which it borders, and possesses little in common with the Pamirs of the west. The Mariom Pamir defines the western extremity of the Kuen Lun, which stretches eastwards for 250 m. before it becomes the political boundary of northern Tibet.

The Mustagh chain, which holds within its grasp the mightiest system of glaciers in the world, forms a junction with the Sarikol at the head of the Taghdumbash, where also another great system *The Mustagh Chain and Karakoram Extension* (that of the Hindu Kush) has its eastern roots. The political boundary between the extreme north of the Kashmir dependencies and the extreme south of Chinese Turkestan is carried by the Zarafshan or Raskam river which runs parallel to the Mustagh at its northern foot (its valley dividing the Muztagh from the Kuen Lun), to a point in about 79° 20′ E., where it is transferred to the watershed of the Kuen Lun. Within the limits of these partially explored highlands, lying between the Pamirs and the Tibetan table-land, exact geographical definition is impossible. But we may follow Godwin-Austen in accepting the main chain of the Muztagh as merging into the head of the Taghdumbash, where also another system, its axis being defined and divided by the transverse stream of the Shyok at its westward bend, whilst the Karakoram range, in which the Shyok rises, is a subsidiary northern branch. The pass over the Karakoram (18,500 ft.) is the most formidable obstacle on the main trade route between Leh and Kashgar.

The Taghdumbash Pamir occupies a geographical position of some political significance. One important pass (the Beyik, 15,100 ft.) leads from the Russian Pamirs into Sarikol across its *The Taghdumbash Pamir* northern border. A second pass (the Wakhjir, 16,150 ft.) connects the head of the Wakhan valley of Afghanistan with the Sarikol province across its western head, whilst a third (the Kilik, 15,600 ft.) leads into the head of the Hunza river and opens a difficult and dangerous route to Gilgit. The Tagh-dumbash is claimed both by China and Kanjut (or Hunza), and there is consequently an open boundary question at this corner of the Pamirs.

From Lake Victoria of the Great Pamir the northern boundary of that extended strip of Afghanistan which reaches out to the head of the Taghdumbash from Badakshan north of the Hindu Kush is to be traced: westwards, in the Lake Victoria affluent of the Oxus; and eastwards, on the Nicolas range, dividing the Great and Little Pamirs, till it over-looks a point on the Aksu (or Murghab) river in about 74° 40′ E. Here it diverges southwards to the Sarikol chain, north of Taghdumbash. This eastward extension was laid down by the Pamir Boundary Commission of 1895. All the head of the Little Pamir, with the Wakhan valley, is consequently Afghan territory, but no military posts have been established so far. The Alichur, Rang Kul, Kargosh (Kara Kul) and Sarez are Russian Pamirs. The Mariom Pamir is Chinese.

Boundary between Russia and Afghan-istan.

The Wakhan glaciers under the Wakhjir water-parting, Lake Chakmaktin near the sources of the Aksu, and Lake Victoria of the Great Pamir have all been claimed as indicating the true source of the Oxus. But detailed examination of their hydrographical conditions proves that neither of the two lakes, Victoria (13,400 ft.) or Chakmaktin (13,020 ft.), can justly be regarded as sources, both of them being derived from the same mighty system of glacial snowfields on the summit of the Nicolas range. Both may be regarded as incidents in the course of glacial streams (incidents which are diminishing in volume day by day), rather than original springs or sources. The same glacial beds of the Nicolas range send down tributary waters to the Panja or Wakhan river, below its junction with the ice stream from Wakhjir, and thus it becomes impossible to decide whether the glaciers of the Wakhjir or the glaciers of Nicolas should be regarded as effecting the most important contribution to the main stream. There is evidence also that glacial moraine formations from time to time may have largely affected the catchment area of these tribu-tary streams. It would be as rash to assert that from Lake Victoria no waters could ever have issued with an eastward flow as it would be to state that from Chakmaktin none ever flow westwards. The measure of the veracity of Chinese pilgrims and geographers in the early centuries of our era must not be balanced on such points as these.

Glacial Sources of the Oxus.

There is no evidence that the Pamirs were ever the support of permanent settlements. The few mud-built buildings which once existed at Chakmaktin and at Langar only decide recent occupation which could hardly have possessed a permanent character, and the few shrines and domed tombs which are scattered here and there about the empty desolation of the Pamir slopes are all of them of recent construction. The nomadic population which seeks pasturage during the summer months in these dreary altitudes is entirely Kirghiz, and we may take it for granted that it will soon be entirely Russian. The non-Russian population during the summer of 1895 could not have amounted to more than a few hundred souls—occupying a few encampments in the Little Pamir and in the Tagh-dumbash. The total population of the Russian Pamirs has been reckoned at 250 "kibitkas," or 1500 souls. There is no ethno-graphical distinction to be traced between the Kirghiz of the Alichur Pamir and the Kirghiz of the Taghdumbash.

Population and Ethno-graphy.

The Kirghiz are Sunni Mahommedans by faith, but amongst them there are curious survivals of an ancient ritual of which the origin is to be traced to those Nestorian Christian communities of Central Asia which existed in the middle ages. A Christian bishopric existed at Yarkand in Marco Polo's time, and is supposed to have survived for another century (1350). The last Gurkhan of the Kara Khitai Empire in the early part of the 13th century (the legendary Prester John) was a member of a Christian tribe called Naiman, which is one of the four chief tribal divisions mentioned by Ney Elias. The Naiman tribe claim kinship with the Kipchaks. It is curious that the same survival of Christian ceremonial should be found amongst the Sarikoli, a Shiah people of Aryan descent akin to the Tajiks of Badakshan, as may be traced amongst the Kirghiz. Christian symbols have been discovered in the southern towns of Chinese Turkestan by Sven Hedin.

Evidences of the Survival of Christian Symbols.

The total area of the Pamir country may be estimated as about 150 m. long by 150 m. broad, of which about one-tenth is grass pasture land and the rest mountainous. All of it once formed part of the ancient kingdom of Bolor, itself a survival of the yet more ancient empire of the Yue-chi, Tokharistan; and across it, in spite of its bleak inhospitality, there have been one or two recognized trade routes from east to west throughout all ages. The most important commercially was that which passed north-west via Tashkurghan and Rang Kul, from Chinese Turkestan to the khanates north of the Oxus; but the route via Tashkurghan and Lake Victoria to Badakshan was also well trodden. The great pilgrim route of Buddhist days was that which connects the ancient Buddhist cities of the Takla Makan in Chinese Turkestan with Chitral (Kashkar), by the Baroghil Pass across the Hindu Kush. This was but one link in a chain of devout peregrination

Area of the Pamirs.

Trade Routes.

which stretched from China to India, and which included every intervening Buddhist centre of note which existed in the early centuries of our era.

For six or seven months of the year (November to April) the Pamirs are covered with snow, the lakes are frozen, and the passes nearly impracticable. The mean temperature during the month of January recorded by Russian observers at the Murghabi—or Pamiraki—post is −13° F. In July this rises to 62° F., the elevation of the station being 13,150 ft. During the spring and summer months the prevalence of fierce cutting winds, which are shaped by the conformation of the valleys into blasts as through a funnel, following the strike of the valleys either up or down, makes travelling painful and existence in camp most unpleasant. In the absence of wind the summer atmosphere is often bright and exhilarating, but there is a constant tendency to sudden squalls of wind and rain, which pass as quickly as they gather. The most settled record of the Pamir Boundary Commission of 1895 lasted from the 19th of August to the 11th of September, the maximum temperature being recorded at 77° on the 21st of August at Kizil Rabat (12,570 ft.); and yet on the 16th of August snow had fallen to the depth of 6 in. and the Beyik Pass was blocked. There were indications that monsoon influences extended as far north at least as the Great Pamir, and a definite analogy was established between the record of barometric pressure on the Pamirs and that of the outer ranges of the Himalaya.

Climate of the Pamirs.

AUTHORITIES.—Captain J. Wood, *A Journey to the Source of the Oxus* (new ed., London, 1872); *Report of the Forsyth Mission* (Cal-cutta, 1875); Colonel T. E. Gordon, *The Roof of the World* (London, 1876); Pitman (trans.), *Through the Heart of Asia* (London, 1889); Earl of Dunmore, *The Pamirs* (London, 1893); Major Cumberland, *Sport on the Pamirs* (London, 1895); Hon. G. N. Curzon, "The Pamirs and the Source of the Oxus," *R. G. S. Journ.*, vol. viii.; *Report of the Proceedings of the Pamir Boundary Commission* (Cal-cutta, 1897). (T. H. H.*)

PAMPA, LA, a territory of the southern pampa region of Argentina, bounded N. by Mendoza, San Luis and Cordoba, E. by Buenos Aires, S. by the territory of Rio Negro, from which it is separated by the river Colorado, and W. by Mendoza. Pop. (1904, official estimate), 52,150. It belongs geographically to the southern part of the great Argentine pampas, from which its name is derived, but in reality only a part of its surface belongs to the plain region. The western and southern part (perhaps the larger) is much broken by hills, swamps and sandy wastes, with occasional stretches of wooded country. The western half is crossed by a broad depression, extending from Mendoza south-east to an intersection with the valley of the Colorado, which was once the outlet of the closed drainage basin occupied by the provinces of Mendoza, San Juan and San Luis. This depression is partially filled with swamps and lakes, into which flow the rivers Atuel and Salado. An obscure continuation of these rivers, called the Chadi-leubu, flows south-east from the great swamps into the large lake of Urrelauquen, about 60 m. north of the Colorado. There are a great number of lakes in La Pampa, especially in the south-east. The eastern half is described as fertile and well adapted for grazing, although the rainfall is very light. Since the closing years of the 19th century there has been a large emigration of stock-raisers and agriculturists into La Pampa, and the territory has become an important producer of cattle and sheep, wheat, Indian corn, linseed, barley and alfalfa. The climate is excessively dry, and the temperature ranges from the severe frosts of winter to an extreme of 104° F. in summer. Strong, constant winds are characteristic of this region. Railways have been extended into the territory from Buenos Aires and Bahia Blanca, the latter being the nearest seaport. There is connexion also with the Transandine railway line on the north. The capital is General Acha (pop. about 3000 in 1905), and the only other places of importance are Santa Rosa de Toay and Victorica, both small, uninteresting "camp" villages.

PAMPAS (Span. *La Pampa*, from a Quichua word signifying a level open space or terrace), an extensive plain of Argentina, extending from the Rio Colorado north to the Gran Chaco, and from the foothills of the Andes east to the Paraná and Atlantic coast.[1] It consists of a great calcareo-argillaceous sheet, once

[1] There are other pampas in South America, such as the Pampas de Aullagas, in Bolivia, the Pampas del Sacramento between the Huallaga and Ucayali rivers in eastern Peru, and others less well known, but when the word Pampas is used alone the great Argentine plain is meant.

the bed of an ancient sea, covered on the west by shingle and sand, and on the east by deposits of estuary silt of irregular thickness brought down from the northern highlands. Its western and northern limits, formed by the foothills and talus slopes of the Andes, and by the south of the great forested depression of the Gran Chaco, cannot be accurately defined, but its area is estimated at 200,000 to 300,000 sq. m. Its greatest breadth is across the south, between the 36th and 37th parallels, and its least in the north, where the eastern ranges of the Andes project deeply into its north-western angle. Its surface is broken in the north-west by the *sierras* of Tucuman, Catamarca, San Luis and Cordoba, the latter rising from the midst of the plain, and by some small isolated *sierras* and hills on the south. It has a gradual slope from north-west to south-east, from an elevation above sea-level of 2320 ft. at Mendoza to 20 ft. at Buenos Aires on the La Plata—the distance across (between Mendoza and Buenos Aires) being about 635 m. There are other slight irregularities in its surface, such as the longitudinal depression on the west, the saline, arid depression west of the Cordoba *sierras*, the Mar de Chiquita depression N.E. of Cordoba, and some smaller areas elsewhere. Apart from these the plain appears perfectly level. The east, which is humid, fertile and grassy, has no natural arboreal growth, except in the vicinity of Cordoba and in the north, where algarrobas and some of the Chaco species are to be found. In the extreme south some species of low, thorny bushes cover considerable areas in the vicinity of the hill-ranges, otherwise the plain is destitute of native trees. Since the arrival of Europeans several species have been introduced successfully, such as the eucalyptus, poplar, *paraiso* (*Melia Azedarach*), peach, willow, *ombú* (*Pircunia*) and others.

The distinctive vegetation of the grassy pampas is the tall, coarse-leaved "pampas grass" (*Cynerium argenteum*) whose feathery spikes often reach a height of eight or nine feet. It covers large areas to the exclusion of all other species except the trefoils and herbs that grow between its tussocks. The natural grasses of the pampas are popularly divided into *pasto dura* (hard pasturage), which includes the large, tussock-forming species, and *pasto molle* (soft pasturage), the tender undergrowth. Since the advent of Europeans other forage plants have been introduced, the most successful and profitable being alfalfa or lucerne (*Medicago sativa*), which is widely cultivated both for hay and for green pasturage for the fattening of market stock.

West of this region is a dry, sandy, semi-barren plain, called the "sterile pampas." It has large saline areas, brackish streams and lakes, and immense sandy deserts, and in singular contrast to the fertile, treeless region of the east it supports large areas of stunted trees and thorny bushes. Most prominent in this hardy but unattractive growth is the "chañar" (*Gurliaca* or *Gourliaca decorticans*), which is characteristic of the whole area, and led Professor Griesbach to suggest the substitution of "formacion del chañar" for "formacion del monte," the designation adopted by botanists for this particular region. The chañar is thorny and of low, irregular growth, and furnishes a strong durable wood and a sweet fruit.

The grassy plains are well watered by streams flowing to the Paraná, La Plata and coast, though some of these are brackish. There are large saline areas in northern Santa Fé, Santiago del Estero and Cordoba provinces, and throughout the greater part of the pampean plain wells cannot be sunk lower than 18 or 20 ft. without encountering brackish water. On the sterile pampas these conditions are still more common, and the drainage southward through the Desaguadero and Salado being charged with saline matter. There are many saline lakes scattered over this pampas, the largest being the Mar de Chiquita, and Lake Porongos in Cordoba, the great swamps and lagoon on the lower Salado in Mendoza, and Lake Bebedero in San Juan.

The fauna of the pampas is limited to comparatively few species, all of which are found beyond its limits, also. These include the viscacha (*Lagostomus trichodactylus*), Patagonian hare (*Dolichotis patogonica*), coypú (*Myopotamus coypú*), cui (*Cavia australis*), tucotuco (*Ctenomys magellanica*), jaguar (*Felis onça*), puma (*Felis concolor*), grass-cat (resembling *Felis catus*), wood-cat (*Felis geoffroyi*),

a fox-like dog (*Felis bajeros*, Azara), aguará (akin to *Canis jubatus*), skunk, weasel (*Galictis barbara*), deer (*Cervus campestris*), four species of armadillo, and two of the opossum. Hudson considers the burrowing viscacha, or biscacha, the most characteristic denizen of the pampas, though the large yellow opossum (*Didelphys crassicaudata*) seems to be singularly adapted to life on the level grassy plain. The avifauna is apparently richer, owing to migration. Hudson enumerates 18 species of storks, ibises, herons, spoon-bills and flamingoes, 20 species of ducks, geese and swans, 10 or 12 of the rallines, including the graceful ypicaha or dancing bird, and 25 of the Limicolae (13 of which are visitors from North America). Land birds are not numerous. Vultures and hawks are common, and there are a few owls, the best known of which is the "minera" (*Geositta cunicularia*), which inhabits the burrow of the viscacha. Among other species of land birds, some 40 in number, are the military starling (*Sturnella*), whose red breast makes it a conspicuous object on the pampas, the white-banded mocking-bird, the *chañar* or "crested screamer" (*Chauna chavarria*), the tinamou, and the rhea, or South American ostrich. There are two species of the tinamou—the rufous and spotted—which are called partridges and are often hunted with snares by horsemen. The rhea, once very numerous, is now found farther inland than formerly, and is steadily diminishing in number.

Civilized occupation is working many changes in the character and appearance of the pampas. The first change was in the introduction of cattle and horses. Cattle were pastured on the open pampas and were guarded by men called *gauchos* or *mestizos*, who became celebrated for their horsemanship, their hardihood and their lawlessness. Attention was then turned to sheep-breeding, which developed another and better type of plainsmen—the Irish and Scotch shepherds. Then followed the extensive cultivation of cereals, forage crops, &c., which led to the general use of fences, the employment of immigrant labourers, largely Italian and Spanish, the building of railways and the growth of "camp" towns. The picturesque gaucho is slowly disappearing in the eastern provinces, and the herds and flocks are being driven farther inland. The rural population of the pampas is still sparse and the estancias are very large.

See W. H. Hudson, *The Naturalist in La Plata* (London, 1895); Charles Darwin, *Voyage of the Beagle* (London, 1839 and 1869); and Richardo Napp, *La republica argentina* (Buenos Aires, 1876; also in German).

PAMPERO, the cold south-west wind which blows over the great plains of southern Argentina. The term is somewhat loosely applied to any strong south-west wind in that region, but more strictly to a rain squall or thunderstorm arising suddenly in the prevailing currents from north and north-east. Pamperos are experienced at Buenos Aires on an average about a dozen times in the year, chiefly during October, November and January.

PAMPHILUS (1st century A.D.), a Greek grammarian, of the school of Aristarchus. He was the author of a comprehensive lexicon, in 95 books, of foreign or obscure words (γλῶσσαι ἥτοι λέξεις), the idea of which was credited to another grammarian, Zopyrion, himself the compiler of the first four books. The work itself is lost, but an epitome by Diogenianus (2nd century) formed the basis of the lexicon of Hesychius. A similar compilation, called Λειμών ("meadow"; cf. the *Praia* of Suetonius) from its varied contents, dealing chiefly with mythological marvels, was probably a supplement to the lexicon, although some scholars identify them. Pamphilus was one of the chief authorities used by Athenaeus in the *Deipnosophists*. Suidas assigns to another Pamphilus, simply described as "a philosopher," a number of works, some of which were probably by Pamphilus the grammarian.

See G. Thilo in Ersch and Gruber's *Allgemeine Encyclopädie*, M. Schmidt, appendix to his edition of Hesychius, (1862) vol. iv.; A. Westermann in Pauly's *Real-encyclopädie* (1848).

PAMPHILUS, an eminent promoter of learning in the early church, is said to have been born, of good family, in Phoenicia (Berytus?) in the latter half of the 3rd century. After studying at Alexandria under Pierius, the disciple of Origen, he was ordained presbyter at Caesarea in Palestine. There he established a theological school, and warmly encouraged students; he also founded, or at least largely extended, the great library to which Eusebius and Jerome were afterwards so much indebted. He was very zealous in the transcription and distribution of copies of Scripture and of the works of various Christian writers, especially of Origen; the copy of the complete works of the last-named in the library of Caesarea was chiefly in the handwriting of Pamphilus himself. At the outbreak of the persecution under Maximin, Pamphilus was thrown into prison (A.D. 307) and there, along with his attached friend and pupil Eusebius (sometimes distinguished as Eusebius Pamphili), he composed an *Apology for Origen*, in five books, to which a sixth was afterwards added by Eusebius. He was put to death in 309 by Firmilian, prefect of Caesarea.

Only the first book of the *Apology* of Pamphilus is extant, and that but in an imperfect Latin translation by Rufinus. It is printed in Lommatzsch's edition of Origen, vol. xxiv., and in Routh, *Rel. soc.* iv. 339 (cf. iii. 487,500, fragments). Photius (Codex 118) gives a short survey of the whole. Jerome mentions *Letters* to friends, and there may have been other works. Eusebius' memoir of Pamphilus has not survived. See E. Preuschen in Herzog-Hauck's *Realencyklopädie*, and A. Harnack, *Altchristl. Litteraturgesch.* i. 543.

PAMPHILUS, a Greek painter of the 4th century, of the school of Sicyon. He was an academic artist, noted for accurate drawing, and obtained such a reputation that not only could he charge his pupils great sums, but he was also successful in introducing drawing in Greece as a necessary part of liberal education.

PAMPHLETS. The earliest appearance of the word is in the *Philobiblon* (1344) of Richard de Bury, who speaks of " panfletos exiguos " (ch. viii.). In English we have " this leud pamflet " (*Test. of Love*, bk. iii.), Occleve's " Though that this pamfilet " (*Reg. of Pr.* 2060), Lydgate's " Whiche is a paunflet " (*Minor Poems*, 180) and Caxton's " paunflettis and bookys " (*Book of Eneydos*, 1490, Prologue). In all these examples pamphlet is used to indicate the extent of the production, and in contradistinction to book. A short codicil in a will of 1495 is called "this pampelet" (*Test. Ebor.* iv. 26). In the 17th century the word was used for single plays, poems, newspapers and news letters (Murray's *New English Dict.* vii. 410).

Not till the 18th century did pamphlet begin to assume its modern meaning of prose controversial tract. " Pamphlet " and " pamphlétaire " are of comparatively recent introduction into French from the English, and generally indicate fugitive criticism of a more severe, not to say libellous, character than with us. The derivation of the word is a subject of contention among etymologists. The supposed origin from the amatory poem of " Pamphilus," and a certain Pamphila, an author of the 1st century, may be dismissed as fanciful. The experts are also undecided as to what is actually understood by a pamphlet. Some bibliographers apply the term to everything, except periodicals, of quarto size and under, if not more than fifty pages, while others would limit its application to two or three sheets of printed matter which have first appeared in an unbound condition. These are merely physical peculiarities, and include academical dissertations, chap-books and broadsides, which from their special subjects belong to a separate class from the pamphlet proper. As regards its literary characteristics, the chief notes of a pamphlet are brevity and spontaneity. It has a distinct aim, and relates to some matter of current interest, whether personal, religious, political or literary. Usually intended to support a particular line of argument, it may be descriptive, controversial, didactic or satirical. It is not so much a class, as a form of literature, and from its ephemeral character represents the changeful currents of public opinion more closely than the bulky volume published after the formation of that opinion. The history of pamphlets being the entire record of popular feeling, all that is necessary here is to briefly indicate the chief families of political and religious pamphlets which have exercised marked influence, and more particularly in those countries—England and France—where pamphlets have made so large a figure in influencing thoughts and events. It is difficult to point out much in ancient literature which precisely answers to our modern view of the pamphlet. The *libelli famosi* of the Romans were simply abusive pasquinades. Some of the small treatises of Lucian, the lost *Anti-Cato* of Caesar, Seneca's *Apocolocyntosis* written against Claudius, Julian's Καίσαρες ἢ συμπόσιον and 'Αντιοχικὸς ἢ μισοπώγων, from their general application, just escape the charge of being mere satires, and may therefore claim to rank as early specimens of the pamphlet.

At the end of the 14th century the Lollard doctrines were widely circulated by means of the tracts and leaflets of Wyclif and his followers. The *Ploughman's Prayer* and *Lanthorne of Light*, which appeared about the time of Oldcastle's martyrdom, were extremely popular, and similar brief vernacular pieces became so common that it was thought necessary in 1418 to enact that persons in authority should search out and apprehend all persons owning English books. The printers of the 15th century produced many controversial tractates, and Caxton and Wynkin de Worde printed in the lesser form. It was in France that the printing-press first began to supply reading for the common people. During the last twenty years of the 15th century there arose an extensive popular literature of farces, tales in verse and prose, satires, almanacs, &c., extending to a few leaves apiece, and circulated by the itinerant booksellers still known as colporteurs. These folk-books soon spread from France to Italy and Spain, and were introduced into England at the beginning of the 16th century, doubtless from the same quarter, as most of our early chap-books are translations or adaptations from the French. Another form of literature even more transient was the broadside, or single sheet printed on one side only, which appears to have flourished principally in England, but which had been in use from the first invention of printing for papal indulgences, royal proclamations and similar documents. Throughout western Europe, about the middle of the 16th century, the broadside made a considerable figure in times of political agitation. In England it was chiefly used for ballads, which soon became so extremely popular that during the first ten years of the reign of Elizabeth the names of no less than forty ballad printers appear in the Stationers' registers.

The humanist movement at the beginning of the 16th century produced the famous *Epistolae obscurorum virorum*, and the leading spirits of the Reformation period—Erasmus, Hutten, Luther, Melanchthon, Frascowitz, Vergerio, Curio and Calvin—found in tracts a ready method of widely circulating their opinions. The course of ecclesiastical events was precipitated in England by the *Supplicacyon for the Beggars* (1528) of Simon Fish, answered by Sir Thomas More's *Supplycacion of Poor Soulys*. In the time of Edward VI. brief tracts were largely used as a propagandist instrument in favour of the Reformed religion. The licensing of the press by Mary greatly hindered the production of this kind of literature. From about 1570 there came an unceasing flow of Puritan pamphlets, of which more than forty were reprinted under the title of *A parte of a register* (London, Waldegrave, 4to). In 1584 was published a tract entitled *A briefe and plaine Declaration concerning the desires of all those faithful ministers that have and do seeke for the discipline and reformation of the Church of Englande*, believed to have been written by W. Fulke D.D. Against this John Bridges, dean of Sarum, preached at Paul's Cross, and expanded his sermon into what be called *A defence of the government established in the church of England* (1587), which gave rise to *Oh read over D. John Bridges . . . . Printed at the cost and charges of M. Marprelate gentleman* (1588), which first gave the name to the famous Martin Marprelate tracts, whose titles sufficiently indicate their opposition to priestly orders and episcopacy. Bishop Cooper's *Admonition to the People of England* (1589) came next, followed on the other side by *Hay any worke for Cooper . . . by Martin the Metropolitane*, and by others from both parties to the number of about thirty-two. The controversy lasted ten years, and ended in the discomfiture of the Puritans and the seizure of their secret press. The writers on the Marprelate side are generally supposed to have been Penry, Throgmorton, Udal and Fenner, and their opponents Bishop Cooper, John Lilly and Nash.

As early as the middle of the 16th century we find ballads of news; and in the reigns of Elizabeth and James I. small pamphlets, translated from the German and French, and known as "newsbooks," were circulated by the so-called " Mercury-women." These were the immediate predecessors of weekly newspapers, and continued to the end of the 17th century. A proclamation was issued by Charles II., on the 17th of May 1680, " for suppressing the printing and publishing of unlicensed news-books and pamphlets of news."

In the 17th century pamphlets began to contribute more than ever to the formation of public opinion. Nearly one hundred were written by or about the restless John Lilburne, but still more numerous were those of the undaunted Prynne, who himself published above one hundred and sixty, besides many weighty folios and quartos. Charles I. found energetic supporters in Peter Heylin and Sir Roger L'Estrange, the latter noted for the coarseness of his pen. The most distinguished pamphleteer of the period was John Milton, who began his career in this direction by five anti-episcopal tracts (1641-1642) during the Smectymnuus quarrel. In 1643 his wife's desertion caused him to publish anonymously *Doctrine and discipline of divorce*, followed by several others on the same subject. He printed *Of Education; to Mr. Samuel Hartlib* in 1644, and, unlicensed and unregistered, his famous *Areopagitica—a speech for the liberty of unlicensed printing*. He defended the trial and execution of the king in *Tenure of kings and magistrates* (1648). The *Eikon Basilike* dispute was conducted with more ponderous weapons than the kind we are now discussing. When Monk held supreme power Milton addressed to him *The present means of a free commonwealth* and *Readie and easie way* (1660), both pleading for a commonwealth in preference to a monarchy. John Goodwin, the author of *Obstructors of Justice* (1649), John Phillipps, the nephew of Milton, and Abiezer Coppe were violent and prolific partisan writers, the last-named specially known for his extreme Presbyterian principles. The tract *Killing no murder* (1657), aimed at Cromwell, and attributed to Colonel Titus or Colonel Sexby, excited more attention than any other political effusion of the time. The history of the Civil War period is told day by day in the well-known collection made by George Thomason the bookseller, now preserved in the British Museum. It includes pamphlets, books, newspapers and MSS. relating to the Civil War, the Commonwealth and Restoration, and numbers 22,255 pieces ranging from 1640 to 1661, and is bound in 2008 volumes. Each article was dated by Thomason at the time of acquisition. William Miller was another bookseller famous for his collection of pamphlets (1600-1710), which were catalogued by Tooker. William Laycock printed a *Proposal for raising a fund* for buying them up for the nation.

The Catholic controversy during the reign of James II. gave rise to a multitude of books and pamphlets,-which have been described by Peck (*Catalogue*, 1735) and by Jones (*Catalogue*, Chetham Society, 2 vols., 1859-1865). Politics were naturally the chief feature of the floating literature connected with the Revolution of 1688. The political tracts of Lord Halifax are interesting both in matter and manner. He wrote *The character of a trimmer* (1688), circulated in MS. as early as 1685. About the middle of the reign Defoe was introduced to William III., and produced the first of his pamphlets on occasional conformity. He issued in 1697 his two defences of standing armies in support of the government, and published sets of tracts on the partition treaty, the union with Scotland, and many other subjects. His *Shortest Way with the Dissenters* (1702) placed him in the pillory.

Under Queen Anne pamphlets arrived at a remarkable degree of importance. Never before or since has this method of publication been used by such masters of thought and language. Political writing of any degree of authority was almost entirely confined to pamphlets. If the Whigs were able to command the services of Addison and Steele, the Tories fought with the terrible pen of Swift. Second in power if not in literary ability were Bolingbroke, Somers, Atterbury, Prior and Pulteney. The government viewed with a jealous eye the free use of this powerful instrument, and St John seized upon fourteen booksellers and publishers in one day for " libels " upon the administration (see *Annals of Queen Anne*, Oct. 23, 1711). In 1712 a duty was laid upon newspapers and pamphlets, displeasing all parties, and soon falling into disuse. Bishop Hoadly's

sermon on the kingdom of Christ (1717), denying that there was any such thing as a visible Church of Christ, occasioned the Bangorian controversy, which produced nearly two hundred pamphlets. Soon after this period party-writing declined from its comparatively high standard and fell into meaner and venal hands. Under George III. Bute took Dr Shebbeare from Newgate in order to employ his pen. The court party received the support of a few able pamphlets, among which may be mentioned *The consideration of the German War* against the policy of Pitt, and *The prerogative droit de Roy* (1764) vindicating the prerogative. We must not forget that although Samuel Johnson was a pensioned scribe he has for an excuse that his political tracts are his worst performances. Edmund Burke, on the other hand, has produced in this form some of his most valued writings. The troubles in America and the union between Ireland and Great Britain are subjects which are abundantly illustrated in pamphlet literature.

Early in the 19th century the rise of the quarterly reviews threw open a new channel of publicity to those who had previously used pamphlets to spread their opinions, and later on the rapid growth of monthly magazines and weekly reviews afforded controversialists a much more certain and extensive circulation than they could ensure by an isolated publication. Although pamphlets are no longer the sole or most important factor of public opinion, the minor literature of great events is never likely to be entirely confined to periodicals. The following topics, which might be largely increased in number, have each been discussed by a multitude of pamphlets, most of which, however, are likely to have been hopeless aspirants for a more certain means of preservation: the Bullion Question (1810), the Poor Laws (1828-1834), *Tracts for the Times* and the ensuing controversy (1833-1845), Dr Hampden (1836), the Canadian Revolt (1837-1838), the Corn Laws (1841-1848), Gorham Controversy (1849-1850), Crimean War and Indian Mutiny (1854-1859), Schleswig-Holstein (1863-1864), Ireland (1868-1869), the Franco-German War, with *Dame Europa's School* and its imitators (1870-1871), Vaticanism, occasioned by Mr Gladstone's *Vatican Decrees* (1874), the Eastern Question (1877-1880), the Irish Land Laws (1880-1882), Ireland and Home Rule (1885-1886), South African War (1899-1902) and Tariff Reform (1903).

France.—The activity of the French press in putting forth small tracts in favour of the Reformed religion caused the Sorbonne in 1523 to petition the king to abolish the diabolical art of printing. Even one or two sheets of printed matter were found too cumbersome, and single leaves or placards were issued in such numbers that they were the subject of a special edict on the 28th of September 1553. An *ordonnance* of February 1566 was specially directed against libellous pamphlets and those who wrote, printed or even possessed them. The rivalry between Francis I. and Charles V. gave rise to many political pamphlets, and under Francis II. the Guises were attacked by similar means. Fr. Hotman directed his *Epistre envoiée au lygre de France* against the Cardinal de Lorraine. The Valois and Henry III. in particular were severely handled in *Les Hermaphrodites* (c. 1605), which was followed by a long series of imitations. Between Francis I. and Charles IX. the general tone of the pamphlet-literature was grave and pedantic. From the latter period to the death of Henry IV. it became more cruel and dangerous.

The *Satyre Ménippée* (1594), one of the most perfect models of the pamphlet in the language, did infinite harm to the League. The pamphlets against the Jesuits were many and violent. Père Richeome defended the order in *Chasse du renard Pasquier* (1603), the latter person being their vigorous opponent Étienne Pasquier. On the death of the king the country was filled with appeals for revenge against the Jesuits for his murder; the best known of them was the *Anti-Coton* (1611), generally attributed to César de Plaix. During the regency of Mary de' Medici the pamphlet changed its severer form to a more facetious type. In spite of the danger of such proceeding under the uncompromising ministry of Richelieu, there was no lack of libels upon him, which were even in most instances printed in France. These largely increased during the Fronde, but it was Mazarin who was the subject of more of this literature than any other historical personage. It has been calculated that from the Parisian press alone there came sufficient *Mazarinades* to fill 150 quarto volumes each of 400 pages. Eight hundred were published during the siege of Paris (Feb. 8 to March 11, 1649). A collection of satirical pieces was entitled *Tableau du gouvernement de Richelieu, Mazarin, Fouquet, et Colbert* (1693). Pamphlets dealing with the amours of the king and his courtiers were in vogue in the time of Louis XIV., the most caustic of them being the *Carte géographique de la cour* (1668) of Busny-Rabutin. The presses of Holland and the Low Countries teemed with tracts against Colbert, Le Tellier, Louvois and Père Lachaise. The first of the ever-memorable *Provinciales* appeared on the 23rd of January 1656, under the title of *Lettre de Louis de Montalte à un provincial de ses amis*, and the remaining eighteen came out at regular intervals during the next fifteen months. They excited extraordinary attention throughout Europe. The Jesuit replies were feeble and ineffectual. John Law and the schemes of the bubble period caused much popular raillery. During the long reign of Louis XV., the distinguished names of Voltaire, Rousseau, Montesquieu, Diderot, D'Alembert, D'Holbach, Helvétius and Beaumarchais must be added to the list of writers in this class.

The preliminary struggle between the parliament and the Crown gave rise to hundreds of pamphlets, which grew still more numerous as the Revolution approached. Linguet and Mirabeau began their appeals to the people. Camille Desmoulins came into notice as a publicist during the elections for the states-general; but perhaps the piece which caused the most sensation was the *Qu'est ce que le Tiers État* (1789) of the Abbé Sieyès. The *Domine salvum fac regem* and *Pange lingua* (1789) were two royalist brochures of unsavoury memory. The queen was the subject of vile attack and indiscreet defence (see H. d'Almeras, *Marie Antoinette et les pamphlets*, 1907). The financial disorders of 1790 occasioned the *Effets des assignats sur le prix du pain* of Dupont de Nemours; Necker was attacked in the *Criminelle Nechrologie* of Marat; and the *Vrai miroir de la noblesse* dragged the titled names of France through the mire. The massacre of the Champ de Mars, the death of Mirabeau, and the flight of the king in 1791, the noyades of Lyons and the crime of Charlotte Corday in 1793, and the terrible winter of 1794 have each their respective pamphlet literature, more or less violent in tone. Perhaps the most complete collection of French revolutionary pamphlets is that in the Bibliothèque Nationale: the British Museum possesses a wonderful collection formed by John Wilson Croker. Under the consulate and the empire the only writers of note who ventured to seek this method of appealing to the world were Mme de Staël, B. Constant and Chateaubriand. The royalist reaction in 1816 was the cause of the *Pétition* of Paul Louis Courier, the first of those brilliant productions of a master of the art. He gained the distinction of judicial procedure with his *Simple Discours* in 1821, and published in 1824 his last political work, *Le Pamphlet des pamphlets*, the most eloquent justification of the pamphlet ever penned. The *Mémoire à consulter* of Montlosier attacked the growing power of the Congregation. The year 1827 saw an augmentation of severity in the press laws and the establishment of the censure. The opposition also increased in power and activity, but found its greatest support in the songs of Béranger and the journalism of Mignet, Thiers and Carrel. M. de Cormenin was the chief pamphleteer of the reign of Louis Philippe. The events of 1848 gave birth to a number of pamphlets, chiefly pale copies of the more virile writings of the first revolution. Among the few men of power Louis Veuillot was the Père Duchesne of the Clericals and Victor Hugo the Camille Desmoulins or Marat of the Republicans. After 1852 there was no lack of venal apologies of the *coup d'état*. The second empire suffered from many bitter attacks, among which may be mentioned the *Lettre sur l'histoire de France* (1861) of the Duc d'Aumale, *Propos de Labiénus* (1865) of Rogeard, *Dialogue aux enfers* (1864) of Maurice Joly and Ferry's *Comples fantastiques d'Haussmann* (1868). In more recent times the Panama prosecutions and the Dreyfus case gave occasion to an immense pamphlet literature.

Germany.—In Germany, the cradle of printing, the pamphlet (*Flugschrift*) was soon a recognized and popular vehicle of thought, and the fierce religious controversies of the Reformation period afforded a unique opportunity for its use. The employment of the pamphlet in this connexion was characteristic of the new age. In coarse and violent language the pamphlets appealed directly to the people, whose sympathy the leaders of the opposing parties were most anxious to secure, and their issue on an enormous scale was undoubtedly one of the most potent influences in rousing the German people against the pope and the Roman Catholic Church. In general their tone was extremely intemperate, and they formed, as one authority has described those of a century later, " a mass of panegyric, admonition, invective, controversy and scurrility." Luther was one of the earliest and most effective writers of the polemical pamphlet. His adherents quickly followed his example, and his opponents also were not slow to avail themselves of a weapon which was

proving itself so powerful. So intense at this time did this pamphlet war become that Erasmus wrote " apud Germanos, vix quicquam vendibile est praeter Lutherana ae anti Lutherana."

A remarkable feature was the coarseness of many of these pamphlets. No sense of decency or propriety restrained their writers in dealing either with sacred or with secular subjects, and this attracted the notice of the imperial authorities, who were also alarmed by the remarkable growth of disorder, attributable in part at least to the wide circulation of pamphlet literature. Accordingly the issue of libellous pamphlets was forbidden by order of the diet of Nuremberg in 1524, and again by the diets of Spires in 1529, of Augsburg in 1530 and of Regensburg in 1541, while in 1589 the emperor Rudolph II. fulminated against them.

The usual method of selling these pamphlets was by means of hawkers. J. Janssen (*History of the German People*, Eng. trans., vol. iii.) says these men " went about in swarms offering pamphlets, caricatures and lampoons for sale; in the larger towns vendors of every description of printed matter jostled each other in the street."

The controversies of the earlier period of the Thirty Years' War, when this struggle was German rather than international, produced a second flood of pamphlets, which possessed the same characteristics as the earlier one. In the disturbed years also which preceded the actual outbreak of war attempts were made in pamphlets to justify almost every action, however unjust or dishonourable, while at the same time those who held different opinions were mercilessly and scurrilously attacked. The leading German princes were among the foremost to use pamphlets in this connexion, especially perhaps Maximilian of Bavaria and Christian of Anhalt.

LITERATURE.—An excellent catalogue by W. Oldys of the pamphlets in the Harleian Library is added to the 10th volume of the edition of the *Miscellany* by T. Park; and in the *Biblioteca volante* di G. Cinelli (2nd ed., 4 vols. 4to, 1734–1747) there may be seen a bibliography of pamphlet-literature, chiefly Italian and Latin, with notes. See also *Cat. of the three collections of books, pamphlets, &c., in the British Museum on the French Rev.*, 1899; *Cat. of the Thomason books, pamphlets &c.*, 1908, 2 vols. A few of the more representative collections of pamphlets in English may be mentioned. These are: *The Phenix* (2 vols. 8vo. 1707); Morgan's *Phoenix britannicus* (4to, 1732); Bishop Edmund Gibson's *Preservative against Popery* (3 vols. folio, 1738, new ed., 18 vols. sm. 8vo, 1848–1849), consisting chiefly of the anti-Catholic discourses of James II.'s time; *The Harleian Miscellany* (8 vols. 4to, 1744–1753; new ed. by T. Park, 10 vols. 4to, 1808–1813, containing 600 to 700 pieces illustrative of English history, from the library of Edward Harley, earl of Oxford); *Collection of scarce and valuable tracts [known as Lord Somers' Tracts]* (16 parts 4to, 1748–1752, 2nd ed. by Sir W. Scott, 13 vols. 4to, 1809–1815), also full of matter for English history; *The Pamphleteer* (29 vols. 8vo, 1813–1828), containing the best pamphlets of that day; and Arthur Waugh, *The Pamphlet Library* (4 vols. 8vo, 1897–1898), giving examples of political, religious and literary pamphlets from Wycliff to Newman, with historical essays.

For the derivation of the word pamphlet consult Skeat's *Etymological Dict.*; Pegge's *Anonymiana*; *Notes and Queries*, 3rd series, vol. iv. pp. 315, 379, 462, 482, vol. v. pp. 167, 290; 6th series, vol. ii. p. 156; 7th series, vol. vi. pp. 261, 431; Murray's *New English Dict.* vol. vii. The general history of the subject may be traced in M. Davies, *Icon libellorum* (1715); W. Oldys, " History of the Origin of Pamphlets," in Morgan's *Phoenix Brit.* and Nichols's *Lit. Anecdotes*; Dr Johnson's Introduction to the *Harleian Miscellany*; D'Israeli, *Amenities of Literature*; *Revue des deux mondes* (April 1, 1846); *Irish Quart. Review*, vii. 267; *Edinburgh Review* (Oct. 1855); *Quarterly Review* (April 1908); *The Library*, new series, vol. I. 298; Huth's *Ancient Ballads and Broadsides* (Philobiblon Soc.); W. Maskell, *Martin-Marprelate Controversy* (1845); E. Arber, *Sketch of Marprelate Controversy* (1895); W. Pierce, *Hist. Introd. to the Marprelate Tracts* (1908); T. Jones, *Cat. of collection of tracts for and against Popery—the whole of Peck's tracts and his references* (Chetham Soc., 1856–1865); Blakey's *Hist. of Political Literature*; Andrews, *Hist. of British Journalism*; Larousse, *Grand Dict. Universel*; Nodier, *Sur la liberté de la presse*; Leber, *De L'état réel de la presse* (1834); Moreau, *Bibliographie des mazarinades* (1850–1851); Bulletin du *Bibliophile Belge* (1859–1863); Nisard, *Hist. des livres populaires* (1854); A. Germond de Lavigne, *Des Pamphlets de la fin de l'empire*, &c. 1814–1817, Catalogue (Paris, 1879); Paris, *Bibl. nationale, catalogue des Factums, etc., antérieurs à 1790*, by A. Corda, Paris, 1890; A. Maire, *Répertoire des thèses de doctorale lettres des universités françaises 1810–1900* (Paris, 1903); and the annual *Catalogue des Thèses et Écrits Académiques* (Hachette) 1885–1910. For German academical dissertations see G. Fock, *Catalogus dissertationum philologicorum classicarum* (Leipzig, 1894), and many special catalogues by Klussmann (1889–1903), Kukula (1892–1893), Milkau (for Bonn, 1818–1885), Pretzsch (for Breslau, 1811–1885) and others. For Dutch pamphlets see L. D. Petit, *Bibliotheek van nederlandsche Pamfletten* (2 vols. 4to, Hague, 1882–1884); and W. P. C. Knuttel, *Catalogus van de Pamfletten Verzameling berustende in de K. Bibliotheek 1486–1795* (5 parts 4to, Hague, 1889–1905). For methods of dealing with pamphlets in libraries, see various articles in *Library Journal* (1880, 1887, 1889, 1894). (H. R. T.)

PAMPHYLIA, in ancient geography, the region in the south of Asia Minor, between Lycia and Cilicia, extending from the Mediterranean to Mt Taurus. It was bounded on the N. by Pisidia and was therefore a country of small extent, having a coast-line of only about 75 m. with a breadth of about 30 m. There can be little doubt that the Pamphylians and Pisidians were the same people, though the former had received colonies from Greece and other lands, and from this cause, combined with the greater fertility of their territory, had become more civilized than their neighbours in the interior. But the distinction between the two seems to have been established at an early period. Herodotus, who does not mention the Pisidians, enumerates the Pamphylians among the nations of Asia Minor, while Ephorus mentions them both, correctly including the one among the nations on the coast, the other among those of the interior. The early Pamphylians, like the Lycians, had an alphabet of their own, partly Greek, partly " Aslanic," which a few inscriptions on marble and coins preserve. Under the Roman administration the term Pamphylia was extended so as to include Pisidia and the whole tract up to the frontiers of Phrygia and Lycaonia, and in this wider sense it is employed by Ptolemy.

Pamphylia consists almost entirely of a plain, extending from the slopes of Taurus to the sea, but this plain, though presenting an unbroken level to the eye, does not all consist of alluvial deposits, but is formed in part of travertine. " The rivers pouring out of the caverns at the base of the Lycian and Pisidian ranges of the Taurus come forth from their subterranean courses charged with carbonate of lime, and are continually adding to the Pamphylian plain. They build up natural aqueducts of limestone, and after flowing for a time on these elevated beds burst their walls and take a new course. Consequently it is very difficult to reconcile the accounts of this district, as transmitted by ancient authors, with its present aspect and the distribution of the streams which water it. By the sea-side in the west of the district the travertine forms cliffs from 20 to 80 ft. high " (Forbes's *Lycia*, ii. 188). Strabo describes a river which he terms Catarractes as a large stream falling with a great noise over a lofty cliff. This is the cataract near Adalia. East of Adalia is the Cestrus, and beyond that again the Eurymedon, both of which were considerable streams, navigable in antiquity for some little distance from the sea. Near the mouth of the latter was a lake called Caprias, mentioned by Strabo; but it is now a mere salt marsh.

The chief towns on the coast are: Olbia, the first town in Pamphylia, near the Lycian frontier; Attalia (q.v.); and Side (q.v.). On a hill above the Eurymedon stood Aspendus (q.v.) and above the river Cestrus was Perga (q.v.). Between the two rivers, but somewhat farther inland, stood Sylleum, a strong fortress, which even ventured to defy the arms of Alexander. These towns are not known to have been Greek colonies; but the foundation of Aspendus was traditionally ascribed to the Argives, and Side was said to be a colony from Cyme in Aeolis. The legend related by Herodotus and Strabo, which ascribed the origin of the Pamphylians to a colony led into their country by Amphilochus and Calchas after the Trojan War, is merely a characteristic myth. The coins of Aspendus, though of Greek character, bear legends in a barbarous dialect; and probably the Pamphylians were of Asiatic origin and mixed race. They became largely hellenized in Roman times, and have left magnificent memorials of their civilization at Perga, Aspendus and Side. The district is now largely peopled with recent settlers from Greece, Crete and the Balkans.

The Pamphylians are first mentioned among the nations subdued by the Mermnad kings of Lydia, and afterwards passed in succession under the dominion of the Persian and Macedonian monarchs. After the defeat of Antiochus III. in 190 B.C. they were included among the provinces annexed by the Romans to the dominions of Eumenes of Pergamum; but somewhat later they joined with the Pisidians and Cilicians in piratical ravages, and Side became the chief centre and slave mart of these freebooters. Pamphylia was for a short time included in the dominions of Amyntas, king of Galatia, but after his death lapsed into a district of a Roman province, and its name is not again mentioned in history.

    See C. Lanckoronski, *Les Villes de la Pamphylie et de la Pisidie* (1890).   (D. G. H.)

PAMPLONA, or **PAMPELUNA,** the capital of the Spanish province of Navarre, and an episcopal see; situated 1378 ft. above sea-level, on the left bank of the Arga, a tributary of the Ebro. Pop. (1900), 28,886. Pamplona has a station on the Ebro railway connecting Alsasua with Saragossa. From its position it has always been the principal fortress of Navarre. The old outworks have been partly demolished and replaced by modern forts, while suburbs have grown up round the inner walls and bastions. The citadel, south-west of the city, was constructed by order of Philip II. (1556-1598), and was modelled on that of Antwerp. The streets of the city are regular and broad; there are three fine squares or plazas. The most attractive of these is the arcaded Plaza del Castillo, flanked by the hall of the provincial council and by the theatre. The cathedral is a late Gothic structure begun in 1397 by Charles III. (El Noble) of Navarre, who is buried within its walls; of the older Romanesque cathedral only a small portion of the cloisters remains. The fine interior is remarkable for the peculiar structure of its apse, and for the choir-stalls carved in English oak by Miguel Ancheta, a native artist (1530). The principal façade is Corinthian, from designs of Ventura Rodriguez (1783). The same architect designed the superb aqueduct by which the city is supplied with water from Monte Francoa, some nine miles off. The beautiful cloisters on the south side of the cathedral, and the chapter-house beyond them, as well as the old churches of San Saturnino (Gothic) and San Nicolas (Romanesque), are also of interest to the student of architecture. There are also the bull-ring, capable of accommodating 8000 spectators, the *pelota* court (el *Trinquete*) and several parks or gardens. The city is well provided with schools for both sexes; it has also a large hospital.

Pamplona has a flourishing agricultural trade, besides manufactures of cloth, linen stuffs, flour, soap, leather, cards, paper, earthenware, iron and nails. The yearly fair in connexion with the feast of San Fermín (July 7), the patron saint of the city, attracts a large concourse from all parts of northern Spain.

Originally a town of the Vascones, Pamplona was rebuilt in 68 B.C. by Pompey the Great, whence the name Pompaelo or Pompelo (Strabo). It was captured by Euric the Goth in 466 and by the Franks under Childebert in 542; it was dismantled by Charlemagne in 778, but repulsed the emir of Saragossa in 907. In the 14th century it was greatly strengthened and beautified by Charles III., who built a citadel on the site now occupied by the Plaza de Toros and by the Basilica de S. Ignacio, the church marking the spot where Ignatius de Loyola received his wound in defending the place against André de Foix in 1521. From 1808 it was occupied by the French until taken by Wellington in 1813. In the Carlist War of 1836-40 it was held by the Cristinos, and in 1875-76 it was more than once attacked, but never taken, by the Carlists.

PAN (" pasturer "), in Greek mythology, son of Hermes and one of the daughters of Dryops (" oak-man "), or of Zeus and the nymph Callisto, god of shepherds, flocks and forests. He is not mentioned in Homer or Hesiod. The most poetical account of his birth and life is given in the so-called Homeric hymn *To Pan*. He was born with horns, a goat's beard and feet and a tall, his person being completely covered with hair. His mother was so alarmed at his appearance that she fled; but Hermes took him to Olympus, where he became the favourite of the gods, especially Dionysus. His life and characteristics were typical of the old shepherds and goatherds. He was essentially a rustic god," a wood-spirit conceived in the form of a goat," living in woods and caves, and traversing the tops of the mountains; he protected and gave fertility to flocks; he hunted and fished; of music, he invented the shepherd's pipe, said to have been made from the reed into which the nymph Syrinx was transformed when fleeing from his embraces (Ovid, *Metam.* i. 691 sqq.). With a kind of trumpet formed out of a shell he terrified the Titans in their fight with the Olympian gods. By his unexpected appearance he sometimes inspires men with sudden terror—hence the expression " panic " fear. Like other spirits of the woods and fields, he possesses the power of inspiration and prophecy, in which he is said to have instructed Apollo. As a nature-god he was brought into connexion with Cybele and Dionysus, the latter of whom he accompanied on his Indian expedition. Associated with Pan is a number of Panisci, male and female forest imps, his wives and children, who send evil dreams and apparitions to terrify mankind. His original home was Arcadia; his cult was introduced into Athens at the time of the battle of Marathon, when he promised his assistance against the Persians if the Athenians in return would worship him. A cave was consecrated to him on the north side of the Acropolis, where he was annually honoured with a sacrifice and a torch-race (Herodotus vi. 105). In later times, by a misinterpretation of his name (or from the identification of the Greek god with the ram-headed Egyptian god Chnum, the creator of the world), he was pantheistically conceived as the universal god (τὸ πᾶν). The pine and oak were sacred to him, and his offerings were goats, lambs, cows, new wine, honey and milk. The Romans identified him with Inuus and Faunus.

In art Pan is represented in two different aspects. Sometimes he has goat's feet and horns, curly hair and a long beard, half animal, half man; sometimes he is a handsome youth, with long flowing hair, only characterized by horns just beginning to grow, the shepherd's crook and pipe. In bas-reliefs he is often shown presiding over the dances of nymphs, whom he is sometimes pursuing in a state of intoxication. He has furnished some of the attributes of the ordinary conception of the devil. The story (alluded to by Milton, Rabelais, Mrs Browning and Schiller) of the pilot Thamus, who, sailing near the island of Paxi in the time of Tiberius, was commanded by a mighty voice to proclaim that " Pan is dead," is found in Plutarch (*De orac. defectu*, 17). As this story coincided with the birth (or crucifixion) of Christ it was thought to herald the end of the old world and the beginning of the new. According to Roscher (in *Neue Jahrbücher für Philologie*, 1892) it was of Egyptian origin, the name Thamus being connected with Thmouis, a town in the neighbourhood of Mendes, distinguished for the worship of the ram; according to Herodotus (ii. 46), in Egyptian the goat and Pan were both called Mendes. S. Reinach suggests that the words uttered by the "voice" were Θαμοῦς, Θαμοῦς, πάνμεγας, τέθνηκε (" Tammuz, Tammuz, the all-great, is dead "), and that it was merely the lament for the " great Tammuz " or Adonis (see L. R. Farnell in *The Year's Work in Classical Studies*, 1907).

See W. Gebhard, *Pankultus* (Brunswick, 1872); P. Wetzel, *De Jove et Pane dis arcadicis* (Breslau, 1873); W. Immerwahr, *Kulte et Mythen Arkadiens* (1891), vol. i., and V. Bérard, *De l'Origine des cultes arcadiens* (1894), who endeavour to show that Pan is a sun-god (σαν, θαίω); articles by W. H. Roscher in *Lexikon der Mythologie* and by J. A. Hild in Daremberg and Saglio's *Dictionnaire des Antiquités*; E. E. Sikes in *Classical Review* (1895), ix. 70; O. Gruppe, *Griechische Mythologie* (1906), vol. ii.

PAN (common in various forms to many Teutonic languages, cf. Ger. *Pfanne*; it is generally taken to be an early adaptation in a shortened form of Lat. *patina*, shallow bowl or dish, from *patere*, to lie open), a term applied to various sorts of open, flat, shallow vessels. Its application has been greatly extended by analogy, *e.g.* to the upper part of the skull; to variously shaped objects capable of retaining substances, such as that part of the lock in early firearms which held the priming (whence the expression " flash in the pan," for a premature and futile effort); or the circular metal dish in which gold is separated from gravel, earth, &c., by shaking or washing (whence the phrase " to pan out," to obtain a good result). Small ice-floes are also called " pans," and the name is given to a hard substratum of soil which acts as a floor to the surface soil and is usually impervious to water. For " pan " or " pane " in architecture see HALF-TIMBER WORK.

The Hindostani *pān* is the betel-leaf, which, mixed with areca-nut, lime, &c., is chewed by the natives of the East Indies.

The common prefix " pan," signifying universal, all-embracing (Gr. πᾶς, all), is often combined with the names of races, nationalities and religions, conveying an aspiration for the political or spiritual union of all the units of the nation or creed; familiar examples are Pan-Slavonic, Pan-German, Pan-Islamism, Pan-Anglican, Pan-American.

PANA, a city of Christian county, Illinois, U.S.A., in the central part of the state. Pop. (1900) 5530 (727 being foreign-born); (1910) 6055. It is served by the Baltimore & Ohio Southwestern, the Cleveland, Cincinnati, Chicago & St Louis, the Illinois Central and the Chicago & Eastern Illinois railways. It is in the Illinois coal region, and coal-mining is the most important industry; the city is also a shipping point for hay and grain grown in the vicinity. Pana was incorporated in 1857, and was reincorporated in 1877. Its name is said to be a corrupted form of " Pani." (Pawnee), the name of a tribe of Indians.

PANACEA (Gr. πανάκεια, all-healing, from πᾶς, all, and ἀκέομαι, to heal), a universal remedy, or cure for all diseases, a term applied in the middle ages to a mythical herb supposed to possess this quality. Many herbs have had the power of curing all diseases attributed to them, and have hence had the name of " all-heal "; such have been, among others, the mistletoe, the woundwort (*Stachys palustris*), the yarrow or milfoil, and the great valerian.

PANACHE, a French word adapted from Ital. *pennachio*, Lat. *penna*, feather, for a plume of feathers on a helmet or hat; the " panache " should be properly distinguished from the " plume," as being a large cluster of feathers fixed on the top of the helmet and flowing over it, the " plume " being a single feather at the side or front. The word " panache " is often used figuratively in French of a flamboyant piece of ornamentation, a " purple patch " in literature, or any exaggerated form of decoration.

PANAENUS, brother of Pheidias, a Greek painter who worked in conjunction with Polygnotus and Micon at Athens. He also painted the marble sides of the throne of the statue of Zeus erected by his brother at Olympia.

PANAETIUS (c. 185–180 to 110–108 B.C.), Greek Stoic philosopher, belonged to a Rhodian family, but was probably educated partly in Pergamum under Crates of Mallus and afterwards in Athens, where he attended the lectures of Diogenes the Babylonian, Critolaus and Carneades. He subsequently went to Rome, where he became the friend of Laelius and of Scipio the Younger. He lived as a guest in the house of the latter, and accompanied him on his mission to Egypt and Asia (143 or 141). He returned with Scipio to Rome, where he did much to introduce Stoic doctrines and Greek philosophy. He had a number of distinguished Romans as pupils, amongst them Q. Mucius Scaevola the augur and Q. Aelius Tubero. After the murder of Scipio in 129, he resided by turns in Athens and Rome, but chiefly in Athens, where he succeeded Antipater of Tarsus as head of the Stoic school. The right of citizenship was offered him by the Athenians, but he refused it. His chief pupil in philosophy was Posidonius of Apamea. In his teaching he laid stress on ethics; and his most important works, of which only insignificant fragments are preserved, were on this subject. They are as follow: Περὶ τοῦ καθήκοντος (On Duty), in three books, the original of the first two books of Cicero's *De officiis*; Περὶ προνοίας (On Providence), used by Cicero in his *De divinatione* (ii.) and probably in part of the second book of the *De Deorum natura*; a political treatise (perhaps called Περὶ πολιτείας), used by Cicero in his *De republica*; Περὶ εὐθυμίας (On Cheerfulness); Περὶ αἱρέσεων (On Philosophical Schools); a letter to Q. Aelius Tubero, *De dolore patiendo* (Cicero, *De finibus*, iv. 9, 23).

Edition of the fragments by H. N. Fowler (Bonn, 1885), and in F. van Lynden's monograph (Leiden, 1802). See also A. Schmekel, *Die Philosophie der mittleren Stoa* (1892); F. Susemihl, *Geschichte der griechischen Litteratur in der Alexandrinerzeit* (1892), ii. 63–80; E. Zeller, " Beiträge zur Kenntniss des Stoikers Panätius " in *Commentationes philologae in honorem Th. Mommseni* (1877); on the use made of him by Cicero, R. Hirzel, *Untersuchungen zu Ciceros philosophischen Schriften* (1877-1883). For his importance in the Stoic succession and his philosophy generally, see STOICS.

PANAMA, a Central American republic, occupying the Isthmus of Panama, and lying approximately between 7° 15′ and 9° 30′ N. and between 77° 15′ and 83° 30′ W. It is bounded N. by the Caribbean Sea, E. by Colombia, of which it was formerly a part, S. by the Gulf (or Bay) of Panama, an arm of the Pacific, and W. by Costa Rica. Its area is estimated at from 31,500 to 33,800 sq. m.; its greatest width is 118 m. and its greatest length 430 m.; its land frontier is only about 350 m., but on the Caribbean it has a coast of 478 m. and on the Pacific a coast of 767 m.

Physical Features.—The Isthmus of Panama, coextensive with the republic, is the whole neck of land between the American continents; in another use the term " Isthmus of Panama " is applied to the narrow crossing between the cities of Colon and Panama, the other narrow crossings, further east, being the Isthmus of San Blas (31 m.) and the Isthmus of Darien (46 m.). The use of the term " Isthmus of Panama " to include the whole country is becoming more common. The Caribbean coast-line is concave, the Pacific deeply convex. The Mosquito Gulf is to the N.W., the Gulf of Darien to the N.E., and on the N. coast are several bays. Almirante Bay, near the Costa Rican boundary, is 2–13 m. wide, with many islands and good anchorage, protected by Columbus Island, about 8 m. long; immediately east of it, and connected with it, is Chiriqui lagoon (area about 320 sq. m.), 32 m. long, 12 m. wide at the widest point, with a maximum depth of 120 ft., protected on the sea side by Chiriqui Archipelago; immediately east of Colon, at the narrowest part of the isthmus, is the Gulf of San Blas, 20 m. long and 10 m. wide, protected by a peninsula and by the Mulatas Archipelago—low, sandy islands stretching about 80 m. along the coast—and having the excellent harbour of Mandinga in the south-west; still farther east is Caledonia Bay with another good harbour. On the north coast there are about 630 islands with a total area of about 150 sq. m. The Pacific coast is deeply indented by the Gulf of Panama, which is 100 m. wide between Cape Garachine and Cape Malo, and has the Bay of Parita (20 m. wide at its mouth) on its west side, north of Cape Malo, and the Gulf of San Miguel (15 m. wide at its mouth) on its east side, north of Cape Garachine. Darien Harbour, formed by the Tuira and Savannah rivers, is a part of the Gulf of San Miguel and is 11 m. long, 2–4 m. wide, and nearly landlocked. In the Gulf of Panama there are 16 large and about 100 smaller islands (the Pearl Islands), with a total area of 450 sq. m., the largest being Rey or San Miguel (15 m. long and 7 m. wide), and San José (15 sq. m.); both are well wooded. West of the Gulf of Panama and separated from it by Azuero Peninsula is the Gulf of Montijo, 20 m. long and 14 m. wide at its mouth, across which stretches Cebaco Island, 13½ m. long and 3 m. wide; west of Cebaco is Coiba, the largest island of the republic, 21 m. long and 4–12 m. wide.

The country has no lakes; the apparent exceptions are the artificial lakes, Bohio (or Gatun) and Sova, of the Canal Zone. There are a few swamps, especially on the northern shore. But the drainage is good; about 150 streams empty into the Caribbean and some 325 into the Pacific. In the eastern part are three complicated drainage systems of rivers very largely tidal. The largest is that of the Tuira (formerly called Rio Darien), whose headwaters are near the Caribbean and which empties into the Pacific in the Gulf of San Miguel. The Chepo (or Bayano) also is a digitate system with a drainage area reaching from the Caribbean to the Pacific; it is navigable for about 120 m. by small boats. The Chagres flows from a source near the Pacific south-west and then north to the Caribbean; is a little more than 100 m. long and is navigable for about half that distance; it varies greatly in depth, sometimes rising 35 ft. in 24 hours (at Gamboa), and drains about 1000 sq. m. West of these three rivers are simpler and comparatively unimportant river systems, rising near the centre of the isthmus. Orographically the country is remarkable. The " exceedingly irregularly rounded, low-pointed mountains and hills covered by dense forests " (Hill) are Antillean, not Andean, and lie at right angles to the axes of the systems of North and South America. The only regular ranges in Panama are in the extreme western part where the Costa Rica divide continues into Panama, and, immediately south of this and parallel to it, the Cordillera of San Blas, or Sierra de Chiriqui, where the highest peaks are Chiriqui (11,265 ft.) and, on the Costa Rican

boundary, Pico Blanco (11,740 ft.) and Rovalo (7020 ft.); there are two passes, 3600 and 4000 ft. high respectively. On the eastern boundary of the republic is the Serrania del Darien, an Andean range, partly in Colombia. The rough country between contains the following so-called " Sierras," which are not really ranges: in Veragua province, Sierra de Veragua, with Santiago (9275 ft.) near the Chiriqui range, and Santa Maria (4600 ft.), immediately north of the city of Santa Fé; in Los Santos province (Azuero Peninsula), bold hills rising 3000 ft., and in Panama province, the much-broken Sierra de Panama, which has a maximum height of 1700 ft. and a minimum, at the Culebra Pass, of 290 ft., the lowest point, except the interoceanic water-parting in Nicaragua, which is 153 ft., in the western continental system. There have been no active volcanoes since the Pliocene Tertiary time, but the country is still subject to dangerous earthquakes. There are a few plains, like that of David, in Chiriqui province, but irregular surface is normal; and this irregularity is the result of very heavy rains with a consequent extremely developed drainage system cutting river valleys down nearly to the sea-level, and of marine erosion, as may be seen by the bold and rugged islands, notably those in the Gulf of Panama. It is improbable that there has been any connexion by water between the two oceans here since Tertiary time.

Climate.—The mean temperature varies little throughout the republic, being about 80° F.: at Colon, where 68° is a low and 95° a high temperature, the mean is 79·1°; at Panama the mean is 80·6°. But this difference is not the usual one: normally the Caribbean coast is a degree or two warmer than the Pacific coast. There is a wet and a dry season; in the former, from the middle of April to the middle of December, there falls (in heavy, short rains) about 85 % of the total annual precipitation, and south-east winds prevail. The north-east wind prevails in the dry season, which is dusty and bracing. The rainfall at Colon on the north coast varies from 85 to 155 in., with 125 as the mean; at Gamboa in the interior it varies from 75 to 140 in., with 92 as the mean; and at Panama on the south coast it varies between 47 and 90 (rarely 104 in.), the mean being 67 in.

Natural Resources.—Gold is mined to a small extent; the most productive mines are about Darien and in Cocle province. Copper has been found between the Plain of David and Bocas del Toro. There are valuable deposits of coal near Bocas del Toro and Golfo Dulce. There are important salt mines near Agua Dulce on Parita Bay. Iron is found in several parts of the Isthmus. Mineral springs are common, especially near former volcanoes.

There are valuable vegetable dye-stuffs, medicinal plants (especially sarsaparilla, copaiba and ipecacuanha), cabinet and building timber (mahogany, &c.), india-rubber, tropical fruits (especially bananas), and various palms; fish are economically important—the name Panama is said to have meant in an Indian dialect " rich in fish "—and on the Pacific coast, oysters and pearl " oysters " (*Meleagrina californica*)—the headquarters of the pearl fishery is the city of San Miguel on the largest of the Pearl Islands, and Coiba Island. There is little agriculture, though the soil is rich and fertile; bananas (occupying about one-half the area under cultivation and grown especially in the north-west), coffee (also grown especially on the Costa Rican border in Chiriqui province), cacao (growing wild in Bocas del Toro province), tobacco, and cereals are the largest crops. Stock-raising is favoured by the excellent grazing lands; blooded cattle are imported for breeding.

Soap and chocolate are manufactured in Panama City. Tobacco and salt manufactures are government monopolies. Sugar refineries are projected. In the canal zone there are great shops for the manufacture and repair of machinery.

Commerce and Communications.—The principal ports are Colon, Panama[1] and Bocas del Toro, the last being a banana-shipping port. In 1908 the country's imports were valued at $7,806,811 (vegetable products, $1,879,297; agricultural products, $1,258,900; textiles, $1,187,802; mineral products, $788,069; and wines and liquors, $675,703); the textiles mainly from Great Britain, all other imports largely from the United States); and the exports were valued at $1,757,135 (including vegetable products, mostly bananas, $1,539,395, animal products, $135,207, and mineral products, $79,620), of which $1,587,217 was the value of goods shipped to the United States. $113,038 of goods to Great Britain, and $34,495 to Germany. Besides bananas the largest exports are hides, rubber, coco-nuts, limes, native curios and guaquä bark. Transportation along the rivers from point to point on either coast is easy. The Panama railway, the only one in the country, is 47¼ m. long, and runs between Colon and Panama; it was made possible by the rush of gold-miners across the isthmus in the years immediately after 1849; was financed by the New York house of Howland & Aspinwall—Aspinwall (later Colon) was named in honour of the junior member, William Henry Aspinwall, (1807–1875)—and was completed in February 1855, at an expense of $7,500,000. It was purchased by De Lesseps's Compagnie Universelle de Canal Interocéanique de Panama for $25,500,000; and, with the other holdings of the French company, 68,869 shares (more than 97 % of the total) passed to the

[1] Christobal, the port of Colon, and Balboa, the port of Panama, lie within the Canal Zone and are under the jurisdiction of the United States.

United States government. The line of railway is very nearly that of the canal, and the work of the railway engineers was of great value to the French engineers of the canal. There are several telegraphic and telephone systems; a wireless telegraph station at Colon; and telegraphic cables from Colon and Panama which, with a connecting cable across the isthmus, give an "all-cable" service to South America, to the United States and to Europe. There are two old wagon roads from Panama City, one, now little used, north to Porto Bello, and the other (called the royal road) 17 m. north-west to Cruces at the head of navigation on the Chagres River. Other roads are mere rough trails.

Inhabitants and Towns.—The population in 1909 was about 361,000. The inhabitants exhibit various degrees of admixture of Indian, negro and Spanish blood, with an increasing proportion of foreigners. The Indians are most numerous in the western part. The negroes, largely from Jamaica and the other West Indies, came in large numbers to work on the canal. The Spanish was the race that stood for civilization before North American influence became strong. Many Spanish peasants, Italians and Greeks came in to work on the canal, but this is not a permanent population. As elsewhere in Spanish America, there has been German colonization, notably in Cocle province, where a large tropical estate was established in 1894.

The principal cities in Panama are: Colon (*q.v.*), at the Caribbean end of the canal; Panama (*q.v.*), at the Pacific end of the canal, and near it, in the Canal Zone, the cities of Balboa and Ancon; Bocas del Toro (pop. about 4000), capital of the province of the same name, in the north-western corner of the country, with a large trade in bananas and good fishing in the bay; Porto Bello (pop. about 3000), formerly an important commercial city, in Colon province, on Porto Bello Bay, where Columbus established the colony of Nombre de Dios in 1502—the present city was founded in 1584, was often captured by the English (notably by Admiral Edward Vernon in 1753), and by buccaneers, and is the terminus of an old paved road to Panama, whence gold was brought to Porto Bello for shipment; Chagres (pop. about 2500), also in Colon province, formerly an important port, and now a fishing place; Agua Dulce, formerly called Trinidad (pop. about 2000), in Cocle province, on Parita Bay, the centre of the salt industry; and San Miguel, on an island of the same name in the Gulf of Panama, the principal pearl fishery. The larger inland cities are: Ciudad de David (pop. about 8000), the capital of Chiriqui, 12 m. from the Pacific, 60 m. east of the Costa Rican boundary, with a trade in cattle; Las Santos (pop. about 7200), the capital of Los Santos province; Santiago de Veragua (pop. about 7000), 300 ft. above the sea, with various manufactories, gold, silver and copper mines, and mineral springs and baths near the city; Las Tablas (pop. about 6500) and Pese (pop. about 5600) in Los Santos province; Penonome (pop. about 3000), on the river of that name in Cocle province (of which it is the capital), with a trade in straw hats, tobacco, cacao, coffee, cotton, rubber, cedar and cattle; and the Canal Zone Gorgona (3000) and Obispo (2500), each with an American colony.

Administration.—By the constitution promulgated on the 13th of February 1904 the government is a highly centralized republic. All male citizens over 21 years of age have the right to vote, except those under judicial interdiction and those judicially inhabilitated by reason of crime. The president, who must be at least 35 years old, is elected by popular vote for four years, is ineligible to succeed himself and appoints cabinet members (secretaries of foreign affairs, government and justice, treasury, interior ["fomento"] and public instruction); five supreme court judges (who decide on the constitutionality of a bill vetoed by the president on constitutional grounds—their action, if favourable to the constitutionality of such a bill, makes the president's signature mandatory); diplomatic representatives; and the governors (annually) of the provinces, who are responsible only to him. The president's salary is $18,000 a year. There is no vice-president, but the National Assembly elects every two years three *designados*, the first of whom would succeed the president if he should die. The National Assembly is a single chamber, whose deputies (each at least 25 years old) are elected for four years by popular vote on the basis of 1 to every 10,000 inhabitants (or fraction over 5000); it meets biennially; by a two-thirds vote it may pass any bill over the president's veto—the president has five or ten days, according to the length of the bill, in which to veto any act of the legislature. At the head of the judiciary is the Supreme Court already referred to; the superior court and the circuit courts are composed of judges appointed for four years by the members of

the Supreme Court. The municipal court justices are appointed by the Supreme Court judges for one year.

The seven provinces, restoring an old administrative division, are: Panama, with most of the territory east of the canal and a little (on the Pacific side) west of the canal; Colon, on either side of the canal, along the Caribbean; Cocle, west and south; Los Santos, farther west and south, on the Azuero Peninsula, west of the Gulf; Veragua, to the north-west, crossing to the Mosquito Gulf; and Chiriqui, farthest west, on the Pacific, and Bocas del Toro on the Caribbean. The provinces are divided into municipal districts (*distritos municipales*), each of which has a municipal legislature (*consejo municipal*), popularly elected for two years, and an *alcalde*, who is the agent of the governor of the province and is appointed annually. By the treaty of the 18th of November 1908 Panama ceded to the United States the "Canal Zone," a strip of land reaching 5 m. on either side of the canal and including certain islands in the Gulf of Panama; from this cession were excluded the cities of Colon and Panama, over which the United States received jurisdiction only as regards sanitation and water-supply.

Education.—The system of public education dates from the independence of Panama only and has not been developed. But primary instruction has been greatly improved; there is a school of arts and trades at the capital, in which there are endowed scholarships for pupils from different provinces; a normal school has been established to train teachers for the Indians; high schools and training schools have been opened; and the government pays the expenses of several students in Europe.

Coinage and Finance.—In June 1904, under the terms of an agreement with the American Secretary of War, Panama adopted the gold standard with the balboa, equivalent to an American gold dollar, as the unit; and promised to keep in a bank in the United States a deposit of American money equal to 15 % of its issue of fractional silver currency, which is limited to four and a half million balboas. This agreement put an end to the fluctuations of the paper currency previously used. Currency of Panama is legal tender in the Canal Zone, and that of the United States in the Republic of Panama. The republic has no debt: it refused to accept responsibility for a part of the Colombian debt; and it has no standing army. On the 30th of June 1908 the total cash assets of the government were $7,860,607, of which $6,000,000 was invested in New York City real estate, and more than $1,500,000 was in deposits in New York. In the six months ending with that date the receipts were $1,239,574 (largely from import and export duties, and taxes on liquors, tobacco, matches, coffee, opium, salt, steamship companies and money changers), and the cash balance for the six months was $105,307.

History.—The Isthmus of Panama was probably visited by Alonso de Ojeda in 1499. In 1501 Rodrigo Bastidas coasted along from the Gulf of Venezuela to the present Porto Bello. Columbus in 1502 coasted along from Almirante Bay to Porto Bello Bay, where he planted a colony (Nombre de Dios) in November; the Indians destroyed it almost immediately; it was re-established in 1510, by Diego de Nicuesaa, governor of the newly established province of Castilla del Oro, which included what is now Nicaragua, Costa Rica and Panama. In 1510 Martin Fernandez de Enciso, following Alonso de Ojeda to the New World, took the survivors of Ojeda's colony of Nueva Andalucia (near the present Cartagena and east of Panama) and founded on the Tuira river the colony of Santa Maria la Antigua del Darien (commonly called Darien). An insurrection against Enciso in December 1510 put in command Vasco Nuñez de Balboa, who had accompanied Rodrigo de Bastidas in the voyage of 1501. In September 1513 Nuñez crossed the isthmus and (on the 25th or 26th) discovered the Pacific. Immediately afterwards he was succeeded by Pedro Arias de Avila, by whom Nueva Andalucia and Castilla del Oro were united in 1514 under the name of Tierra Firma, and who founded in 1519 the city of Panama, now the oldest European settlement on the mainland in America. The portage between the two oceans was of great commercial importance, especially in the 16th century, when treasure from Peru (and treasure was the *raison d'être* of the Spanish settlements in Panama) was carried across the isthmus from Panama City. A Scotch settlement under letters patent from the Scotch Parliament was made by William Paterson (*q.v.*) in 1698 on the site of the present Porto Escoces (in the north-eastern part of the republic), but in 1700 the Spanish authorities expelled the few settlers still there. Panama was a part of the viceroyalty of New Granada created in 1718, and in 1819 became a part of the independent nation of Colombia and in 1831 of New Granada, from which in 1841 Panama and Veragua provinces seceded as the state (short-lived) of the Isthmus of Panama.

The constitution of the Granadine Confederation of 1853 gave the states the right to withdraw, and in 1857 Panama[1] again seceded, soon to return. When Nuñez in 1885 disregarded the constitution of 1863, which made the component states severally sovereign, he was strongly opposed by the people of Panama, who had no actual representation in the convention which made the constitution of 1886, an instrument allowing Panama (which it made a department and not a state) no local government. The large expenditures of the French canal company made the department singularly alluring to corrupt officials of the central government, and Panama suffered severely before the liquidation of the company in 1889. There were risings in 1895 and in 1898-1902, the latter ceasing with American interposition. The treaty of the United States in 1846 with New Granada, granting transportation facilities on the Isthmus to the United States, then preparing for war with Mexico, and guaranteeing on the part of the United States the sovereignty of New Granada in the Isthmus, has been considered the first step toward the establishment of an American protectorate over the Isthmus. In 1901 by the negotiation of the Hay-Pauncefote Treaty it became possible for the United States alone to build and control an interoceanic canal. The Hay-Herran Treaty of January 1903, providing that the United States take over the Panama Canal was not ratified by the Colombian Congress, possibly because it was hoped that settlement might be delayed until the concession to the company expired, and that then the payment from the United States would come directly to the Colombian government; and the Congress, which had been specially called for the purpose—there was no regular legislative government in Bogotá in 1898-1903—adjourned on the 31st of October. Three days later, on the 3rd of November, the independence of Panama was declared. Commander John F. Hubbard of the United States gunboat "Nashville" at Colon forbade the transportation of Colombian troops across the Isthmus, and landed 42 marines to prevent the occupation of Colon by the Colombian force; the diplomatic excuse for his action was that by the treaty of 1846 the United States had promised to keep the Isthmus open, and that a civil war would have closed it. On the 7th of November Panama was virtually recognized by the United States, when her diplomatic representative was received; and on the 18th of November a treaty was signed between the United States and Panama, ceding to the United States the "Canal Zone," for which and for the canal concession the United States promised to pay $10,000,000 immediately and $250,000 annually as rental, the first payment to be made nine years after the ratification of the treaty. On the 4th of January 1904, two months after the declaration of independence, a constitutional assembly was elected, which met on the 15th of January, adopted the constitution described above, and chose as president Manuel Amador Guerrero (1834-1909). He was succeeded in October 1908 by Domingo de Obaldia. In 1905 a treaty was made with Costa Rica for the demarcation of the boundary line between the two countries.

See Henri Pensa, *La République et le Canal de Panama* (Paris, 1906), devoted mainly to the question of international law; Valdés, *Geografía del istmo de Panama* (New York, 1905); R. T. Hill, "The Geological History of the Isthmus of Panama and Portions of Porto Rico" (1898), vol. 28, pp. 151-285, of the *Bulletin of the Museum of Comparative Zoology* of Harvard College; E. J. Cattell (ed.), *Panama* (Philadelphia, 1905), being pt. i, § 27 of the Foreign Commercial Guide of the Philadelphia Commercial Museum; and the publications on Panama of the International Bureau of American Republics.

PANAMA, the capital and the chief Pacific port of the republic of Panama, the capital of the province of the same name, in the south-central part of the country, at the head of the Gulf of Panama, and at the south terminus of the Panama railway, 47½ m. from Colon, and of the Panama Canal. Pop. (1910) about 30,000, of whom nearly one-half were foreign-born or of foreign parentage. Panama is served by regular steamers to San Francisco, Yokohama and other Pacific ports. The city

[1] The state of Panama, with boundaries nearly corresponding to those of the present republic, and including the province of Panama and other provinces, was created in 1855 by legislative enactment.

is built on a rocky peninsula jutting out to the east, near the mouth of the Rio Grande and at the foot of Mt Ancon (560 ft.). The harbour is good and is enclosed at the south by several rugged islands, the largest being Perico and Flamenco (belonging to the United States) and Taboga (935 ft.), which is a place of country residence for wealthy citizens. The main streets run north and south and are cut by the Avenida Central; nearly all the streets are narrow and crooked. The principal squares are Cathedral, Santa Ana, Bolivar and Lesseps. The city proper is almost entirely enclosed by the remains of a great granite wall (built in 1673, when the new city was established), on the top of which on the side facing the sea is Las Bovedas promenade. The public buildings include the cathedral (1760), the government palace, the municipal palace, the episcopal palace, the church of Santa Ana, a national theatre, a school of arts and trades, a foreign hospital, the former administration building of the Canal Company, Santo Tomas Hospital, the pesthouse of Punta Mala and various asylums. The houses are mostly of stone, with red tile roofs, two or three storeys high, built in the Spanish style around central patios, or courts, and with balconies projecting far over the narrow streets; in such houses the lowest floor is often rented to a poorer family. There are dwellings above most of the shops. The streets are lighted with electricity; and there are electric street railways and telephones in the city. The water supply and drainage systems were introduced by the United States government, which controls the sanitation of the city, but has no other jurisdiction over it. Two miles inland is Ancon, in the Canal Zone, in which are the hospitals of the Isthmian Canal Commission and the largest hotel on the Isthmus. The city of Panama was formerly a stronghold of yellow fever and malaria, which American sanitary measures have practically eradicated. Panama has had an important trade: its imports, about twice as valuable as its exports, include cotton goods, haberdashery, coal, flour, silk goods and rice; the most valuable exports are gold, india-rubber, mother of pearl and cocobolo wood. At Balboa (3 m. west of the city, connected with it by railway, and formerly called La Boca), the port of Panama and the actual terminus of the canal, is in the Canal Zone and is a port under the jurisdiction of the United States, the commercial future of Panama is dependent upon American tariffs and the degree to which Panama and Balboa may be identified. At Balboa there are three wharves, one 985 ft. long and another 1000 ft. long, but their capacity is so insufficient that lighterage is still necessary. In the city there is one small dock which can be used only at full tide. Small vessels may coal at Naos, an island in the Gulf of Panama, which is owned by the United States. Soap and chocolate are manufactured. Founded in 1519 by Pedro Arias de Avila, Panama is the oldest European town on the mainland of America. In the 16th century the city was the strongest Spanish fortress in the New World, excepting Cartagena, and gold and silver were brought hither by ship from Peru and were carried across the Isthmus to Chagres, but as Spain's fleets even in the Pacific were more and more often attacked in the 17th century, Panama became less important, though it was still the chief Spanish port on the Pacific. In 1671 the city was destroyed by Henry Morgan, the buccaneer; it was rebuilt in 1673 by Alfonso Mercado de Villacorta about five miles west of the old site and nearer the roadstead. The city has often been visited by earthquakes. In the city in June 1826 the Panama Congress met (see PAN-AMERICAN CONFERENCES).

PANAMA CANAL. When he crossed the Atlantic, the object Columbus had in view was to find a western passage from Europe to Cathay. It was with the greatest reluctance; and only after a generation of unremitting toil that the explorers who succeeded him became convinced that the American continent was continuous, and formed a barrier of enormous extent to the passage of vessels. The question of cutting a canal through this barrier at some suitable point was immediately raised. In 1550 the Portuguese navigator Antonio Galvao published a book to demonstrate that a canal could be cut at Tehuantepec,

Nicaragua, Panama or Darien, and in 1551 the Spanish historian F. L. de Gomara submitted a memorial to Philip II. urging in forcible language that the work be undertaken without delay. But the project was opposed by the Spanish Government, who had now concluded that a monopoly of communication with their possessions in the New World was of more importance than a passage by sea to Cathay. It even discouraged the improvement of the communications by land. To seek or make known any better route than the one from Porto Bello to Panama was forbidden under penalty of death. For more than two centuries no serious steps were taken towards the construction of the canal, if exception be made of William Paterson's disastrous Darien scheme in 1698. In 1771 the Spanish government, having changed its policy, ordered a survey for a canal at Tehuantepec, and finding that line impracticable, ordered surveys in 1779 at Nicaragua; but political disturbances in Europe soon prevented further action. In 1808 the isthmus was examined by Alexander von Humboldt, who pointed out the lines which he considered worthy of study. After the Central American republics acquired their independence in 1823, there was a decided increase of interest in the canal question. In 1825 the Republic of the Centre, having received applications for concessions from citizens of Great Britain, and also from citizens of the United States, made overtures to the United States for aid in constructing a canal, but they resulted in nothing. In 1830 a concession was granted to a Dutch corporation under the special patronage of the king of the Netherlands to construct a canal through Nicaragua, but the revolution and the separation of Belgium from Holland followed, and the scheme fell through. Subsequently numerous concessions were granted to citizens of the United States, France and Belgium, both for the Nicaragua and the Panama lines, but with the exception of the concession of 1878 for Panama and that of 1887 for Nicaragua, no work of construction was done under any of them.

Knowledge of the topography of the isthmus was extremely vague until the great increase of travel due to the discovery of gold in California in 1848 rendered improved communications a necessity. A railroad at Panama and a canal at Nicaragua were both projected. Instrumental surveys for the former in 1849, and for the latter in 1850, were made by American engineers, and, with some small exceptions, were the first accurate surveys made up to that time. The work done resulted in geographical knowledge sufficient to eliminate from consideration all but the following routes: (1) Nicaragua; (2) Panama; (3) San Blas; (4) Caledonia Bay; (5) Darien; (6) Atrato river, of which last there were four variants, the Tuyra, the Truando, the Napipi and the Bojaya. In 1866, in response to an inquiry from Congress, Admiral Charles H. Davis, U.S. Navy, reported that " there does not exist in the libraries of the world the means of determining even approximately the most practicable route for a ship canal across the American isthmus." To clear up the subject, the United States government sent out, between 1870 and 1875, a series of expeditions under officers of the navy, by whom all of the above routes were examined. The result was to show that the only lines by which a tunnel could be avoided were the Panama and the Nicaragua lines; and in 1876 a United States Commission reported that the Nicaragua route possessed greater advantages and offered fewer difficulties than any other. At Panama the isthmus is narrower than at any other point except San Blas, its width in a straight line being only 35 m. and the height of the continental divide is only 300 ft., which is higher than the Nicaragua summit, but less than half the height on any other route. At Nicaragua the distance is greater, being about 156 m. in a straight line, but more than one third is covered by Lake Nicaragua, a sheet of fresh water with an area of about 3000 sq. m. and a maximum depth of over 200 ft., the surface being about 105 ft. above sea-level. Lake Nicaragua is connected with the Atlantic by a navigable river, the San Juan, and is separated from the Pacific by the continental divide, which is about 160 ft. above sea-level. At Nicaragua only a canal with locks is feasible, but at Panama a sea-level canal is a physical possibility.

By the Clayton-Bulwer Treaty of 1850 with Great Britain, by the treaty of 1846 with New Granada (Colombia), Article XXXV., and by the treaty of 1867 with Nicaragua, Article XV., the United States guaranteed that the projected canal, whether the Panama or the Nicaraguan, should be neutral, and, furthermore, that it be used and enjoyed upon equal terms by the citizens of both countries in each case. A modification of the Clayton-Bulwer Treaty being necessary to enable the United States to build the canal, a treaty making such modifications, but preserving the principle of neutrality, known as the Hay-Pauncefote Treaty, was negotiated with Great Britain in 1900; it was amended by the United States Senate, and the amendments not proving acceptable to Great Britain, the treaty lapsed in March 1901. A new treaty, however, was negotiated in the autumn, and accepted in December by the U.S. Senate.

The completion of the Suez Canal in 1869, and its subsequent success as a commercial enterprise, drew attention more forcibly than ever to the American isthmus. In 1876 an association entitled " Société Civile Internationale du Canal Interocéanique " was organized in Paris to make surveys and explorations for a ship canal. An expedition under the direction of Lieut. L. N. B. Wyse, an officer of the French navy, was sent to the isthmus to examine the Panama line. In May 1878 Lieut. Wyse, in the name of the association, obtained a concession from the Colombian government, commonly known as the Wyse Concession. This is the concession under which work upon the Panama Canal has been prosecuted. Its first holders did no work of construction.

In May 1879 an International Congress composed of 135 delegates from various nations—some from Great Britain, United States and Germany, but the majority came from France—was convened in Paris under the *Panama* auspices of Ferdinand de Lesseps, to consider the *Company* best situation for, and the plan of, a canal. After a session of two weeks the Congress decided that the canal should be at the sea-level, and at Panama. Immediately after the adjournment of the Congress the Panama Canal Company was organized under a general law of France, with Lesseps as president, and it purchased the Wyse Concession at the price of 10,000,000 francs. An attempt to float this company in August 1879 failed, but a second attempt, made in December 1880, was fully successful, 6,000,000 shares of 500 francs each being sold. The next two years were devoted to surveys and examinations and preliminary work upon the canal. The plan adopted was for a sea-level canal having a depth of 29½ ft. and bottom width of 72 ft., involving excavation estimated at 157,000,000 cub. yds. The cost was estimated by Lesseps in 1880 at 658,000,000 francs, and the time required at eight years. The terminus on the Atlantic side was fixed by the anchorage at Colon, and that on the Pacific side by the anchorage at Panama. Leaving Colon, the canal was to pass through low ground by a direct line for a distance of 6 m. to Gatun, where it intersected the valley of the Chagres river; pass up that valley for a distance of 21 m. to Obispo, where it left the Chagres and ascended the valley of a tributary, the Cumacho; cut through the watershed at Culebra, and thence descend by the valley of the Rio Grande to Panama Bay. Its total length from deep water in the Atlantic to deep water in the Pacific was about 47 m. It was laid out in such a way as to give easy curvature everywhere; the sharpest curve, of which there was but one, had a radius of 6200 ft., four others had a radius of 8200 ft., and all others had a radius of 9800 ft. or more. To secure this it was necessary to select a point for crossing the watershed where the height was somewhat greater than that of the lowest pass. The line was essentially the same as that followed by the Panama railroad, the concession for which granted a monopoly of that route; the Wyse Concession, therefore, was applicable only upon condition that the canal company could come to an amicable agreement with the railroad company.

The principal difficulties to be encountered in carrying out this plan consisted in the enormous dimensions of the cut to be made at Culebra, and in the control of the Chagres river, the valley of which is occupied by the canal for a large part of its length. This stream is of torrential character, its discharge varying from a minimum of about 350 cub. ft. to a maximum of over 100,000 cub. ft. per second. It rose at Gamboa on the 1st of December 1890, 18⅓ ft. in twelve hours, its volume increasing from 15,600 cub. ft. to 57,800 cub. ft. per second at the same time; and similar violent changes are not uncommon. To admit a stream of this character to the canal would be an intolerable nuisance to navigation unless space could be provided for its waters to spread out. For a canal with locks the remedy is simple, but for a sea-level canal the problem is much more difficult, and no satisfactory solution of the question was ever reached under the Lesseps plan.

Work under this plan continued until the latter part of 1887, the management being characterized by a degree of extravagance and corruption rarely if ever equalled in the history of the world. By that time it had become evident that the canal could not be completed at the sea-level with the resources of time and money then available. The plan was accordingly changed to one including locks, and work was pushed on with vigour until 1883, when the company, becoming bankrupt, was dissolved by a judgment of the Tribunal Civil de la Seine, dated the 4th of February 1889, a liquidator being appointed by the court to take charge of its affairs. One of the more important duties assigned to this official was to keep the property together and the concession alive, with a view to the formation of a new company for the completion of the canal. He gradually reduced the number of men employed, and finally suspended the works on the 15th of May 1889. He then proceeded to satisfy himself that the canal project was feasible, a question about which the failure of the company had caused grave doubts, and to this end caused an inquiry to be held by a commission of French and foreign engineers. This commission reported on the 9th of May 1890 that a canal with locks, for which they submitted a plan, could be built in eight years at a cost of 580,000,000 francs for the works, which sum should be increased to 900,000,000 francs to include administration and financing. They reported that the plant in hand was in good condition and would probably suffice for finishing the canal, and they estimated the value of the work done and of the plant in hand at 450,000,000 francs.

The time within which the canal was to be completed under the Wyse Concession having nearly expired, the liquidator sought and obtained from the Colombian government an extension of ten years. Twice subsequently the time was extended by the Colombian government, the date ultimately fixed for the completion of the canal being the 31st of October 1910. For each of these extensions the Colombian government exacted heavy subsidies.

The liquidator finally secured the organization of a new company on the 20th of October 1894. The old company and the liquidator had raised by the sale of stock and bonds the sum of 1,271,682,637 francs. The securities issued to raise this money had a par value of 2,245,151,200 francs, held by about 200,000 persons. In all about 72,000,000 cub. yds. had been excavated, and an enormous quantity of machinery and other plant had been purchased and transported to the isthmus at an estimated cost of 150,000,000 francs. Nearly all of the stock of the Panama railroad—68,534 of the 70,000 shares existing—also had been purchased, at a cost of 93,268,186 francs.

The new company was regularly organized under French law, and was recognized by the Colombian government. It Second was technically a private corporation, but the great Panama number of persons interested in the securities of the Company. old company, and the special legislation of the French Chambers, gave it a semi-national character. By the law of the 8th of June 1888, all machinery and tools used in the work must be of French manufacture, and raw material must be of French origin. Its capital stock consisted of 650,000 shares of 100 francs each, of which 50,000 shares belonged to Colombia. It succeeded to all the rights of the old company in the concessions, lands, buildings, plant, maps, drawings, &c., and shares of the Panama railroad. For the contingency that the canal should not be completed, special conditions were made as to the Panama railroad shares. These were to revert to the liquidator, but the company had the privilege of purchasing them for 20,000,000 francs in cash and half the net annual profits of the road. The Panama railroad retained its separate organization as an American corporation.

Immediately after its organization in 1894 the new company took possession of the property (except the Panama railroad shares, which were held in trust for its benefit), and proceeded to make a new study of the entire subject of the canal in its engineering and commercial aspects. It resumed the work of excavation, with a moderate number of men sufficient to comply with the terms of the concession, in a part of the line—the Emperador and Culebra cuts—where such excavation must contribute to the enterprise if completed under any plan. By the middle of 1895, about 2000 men had been collected, and since that time the work progressed continuously, the number of workmen varying between 1900 and 3600. The amount of material excavated to the end of 1899 was about 5,000,000 cubic yards. The amount expended to the 30th of June 1899 was about 35,000,000 francs, besides about 6,500,000 francs advanced to the Panama Railroad Company for building a pier at La Boca.

The charter provided for the appointment by the company and the liquidator of a special engineering commission of five members, to report upon the work done and the conclusions to be drawn therefrom, this report to be rendered when the amounts expended by the new company should have reached a out one-half its capital. The report was to be made public, and a special meeting of the stockholders was then to be held to determine whether or not the canal should be completed, and to provide ways and means. The time for this report and special meeting arrived in 1898. In the meanwhile the company had called to its aid a technical committee composed of fourteen engineers, European and American, some of them among the most eminent in their profession. After a study of all the data available, and of such additional surveys and examinations as it considered should be made, this committee rendered an elaborate report dated the 16th of November 1898. This report was referred to the statutory commission of five, who reported in 1899 that the canal could be built according to that project within the limits of time and money estimated. The special meeting of stockholders was called immediately after the regular annual meeting of the 30th of December 1899. It is understood that the liquidator (who held about one-fourth the stock) refused to take part in it, and that no conclusions were reached as to the expediency of completing the canal or as to providing ways and means. The engineering questions had been solved to the satisfaction of the company, but the financial questions had been made extremely difficult, if not insoluble, by the appearance of the United States government in the field as a probable builder of an isthmian canal. The company continued to conduct its operations in a provisional way, without appealing to the public for capital.

The plan adopted by the company involved two levels above the sea-level—one of them an artificial lake to be created by a dam at Bohio, to be reached from the Atlantic by a flight of two locks, and the other, the summit-level, to be reached by another flight of two locks from the preceding. The summit-level was to have its surface at high water 102 ft. above the sea, and to be supplied with water by a feeder leading from an artificial reservoir to be constructed at Alajuela in the upper Chagres valley; the ascent on the Pacific side to be likewise by four locks. The canal was to have a depth of 29⅓ ft. and a bottom width of about 98 ft., with an increased width in certain specified parts. Its general plan was the same as that adopted by the old company. The locks were to be double, or twin locks, the chambers to have a serviceable length in the clear of 738 ft. with a width of 82 ft. and a depth of 32 ft. 10 in., with lifts varying from 20 to 33 ft., according to situation and stage of water. The time required to build the canal was estimated at ten years; and its cost at 525,000,000 francs for the works, not including administration and financing.

The occupation of the Panama route by Europeans, and the prospect of a canal there under foreign control, was not a pleasing spectacle to the people of the United Nicaragua States. The favour with which the Nicaragua Scheme. route had been considered since 1876 began to assume a partisan character, and the movement to construct a canal on that line to assume a practical shape. In 1884 a treaty, known as the Frelinghuysen-Zarala Treaty, was negotiated with Nicaragua, by the terms of which the United States Government was to build the canal without cost to Nicaragua, and after completion it was to be owned and managed jointly by the two governments. The treaty was submitted to the United States Senate, and in the vote for ratification, on the 29th of January 1885, received thirty-two votes in its favour against twenty-three. The necessary two-thirds vote not having been obtained, the treaty was not ratified, and a change of administration occurring soon afterwards, it was withdrawn from further consideration. This failure led to the formation in New York by private citizens in 1886 of the Nicaragua Canal Association, for the purpose of obtaining the necessary concessions, making surveys, laying out the route, and organizing such corporations as should be required to construct the canal. They obtained a concession from Nicaragua in April 1887, and one from Costa Rica in August 1888, and sent parties to survey the canal. An act for the incorporation of an association to be known as the Maritime Canal Company of Nicaragua passed Congress and was approved on the 20th of February 1889, and on the 4th of May 1889 the company was organized. It took over the concessions and, acting through a construction company, began work upon the canal in June 1889. Operations upon a moderate scale and mainly of a preliminary character were continued until 1893, when the financial disturbances of that period drove the construction company into bankruptcy and compelled a suspension of the work. It has not since been resumed. At that time the canal had been excavated to a depth of 17 ft. and a width of 280 ft. for a distance of about 3000 ft. inland from Greytown; the canal line had been cleared of timber for a distance of about 20 m.; a railroad had been constructed for a distance of about 11 m. inland from Greytown; a pier had been built for the improvement of Greytown harbour and other works undertaken. In all, about $4,500,000 had been expended.

Congress continued to take an interest in the enterprise, and in 1895 provided for a board of engineers to inquire into the possibility, permanence, and cost of the canal as projected by the Maritime Canal Company. The report of this board, dated April 1895, severely criticized the plans and estimates of the company, and led to the appointment in 1897 of another board, to make additional surveys and examinations, and to prepare new plans and estimates. The second board recommended some radical changes in the plans, and especially in the estimates, but its report was not completed when the revival of the Panama scheme attracted the attention of Congress, and led to the creation in 1899 of the Isthmian Canal Commission. In the meanwhile the property of the Maritime Canal Company has become nearly worthless through decay, and its concession has been declared forfeited by the Nicaraguan government.

The interest of the United States in an isthmian canal was not essentially different from that of other maritime nations *Isthmian* down to about the middle of the 19th century, but *Canal Com-* it assumed great strength when California was *mission.* acquired, and it has steadily grown as the importance of the Pacific States has developed. In 1848 and again in 1884, treaties were negotiated with Nicaragua authorising the United States to build the canal, but in neither case was the treaty ratified. The Spanish War of 1898 gave a tremendous impetus to popular interest in the matter, and it seemed an article of the national faith that the canal must be built, and, furthermore, that it must be under American control. To the American people the canal appears to be not merely a business enterprise from which a direct revenue is to be obtained, but rather a means of unifying and strengthening their national political interests, and of developing their industries, particularly in the Pacific States; in short, a means essential to their national growth. The Isthmian Canal Commission created by Congress in 1899 to examine all practicable routes, and to report which was the most practicable and most feasible for a canal under the control, management and ownership of the United States, reported that there was no route which did not present greater disadvantages than those of Panama and Nicaragua. It recommended that the canal at Panama have a depth of 35 ft. and a bottom width 150 ft., the locks to be double, the lock chambers to have a length 740 ft., width 84 ft. and depth 35 ft. in the clear. The cost of a canal with these dimensions, built essentially upon the French plans, was estimated at $156,378,258. A plan, however, was recommended in which the height of the Bohio dam was increased about 20 ft., the level of Lake Bohio raised by that amount, the lake made the summit-level, and the Alajuela dam omitted. The cost upon this plan was estimated at $143,071,127.

According to the plan recommended by the Commission for Nicaragua the line began at Greytown on the Caribbean Sea, where an artificial harbour was to be constructed and follow the valley of the San Juan for 100 m. to Lake Nicaragua; thence across the lake about 70 m. to the mouth of Las Lajas river; then up the valley of that stream through the watershed, and down the valley of the Rio Grande, 17 m. to Brito on the Pacific, where also an artificial harbour was to be constructed. The distance from ocean to ocean is 187 m. About midway between the lake and the Caribbean the San Juan receives its most important affluent, the San Carlos, and undergoes a radical change in character. Above the junction it is a clear water stream, capable of improvement by locks and dams. Below, it is choked with sand, and not available for slack-water navigation. A dam across the San Juan above the mouth of the San Carlos was to maintain the water of the river above that point on a level with the lake. The line of the canal occupied essentially the bed of the river from the lake to the dam; from the dam to the Caribbean it followed the left bank of the river, keeping at a safe distance from it, and occasionally cutting through a high projecting ridge. The lake and the river above the dam constitute the summit-level, which would have varied in height at different seasons from 104 to 110 ft. above mean sea-level. It would have been reached from the Caribbean side by five locks, the first having a lift of 36½ ft., and the others a uniform lift of 18½ ft. each, making a total lift of 110½ ft. from low tide in the Caribbean to high tide in the lake. From the Pacific side the summit would have been reached by four locks having a uniform lift of 28½ ft. each, or a total lift of 114 ft. from low tide in the Pacific to high tide in the lake. The time required to build the canal was estimated at ten years, and its cost at $200,540,000.

The report of the commission, transmitted to Congress at the end of 1900, ended thus:—

The Panama Canal, after completion, would be shorter, have fewer locks and less curvature than the Nicaragua Canal. The measure of these advantages is the time required for a vessel to pass through, which is estimated for an average ship at 12 hours for Panama and 33 hours for Nicaragua. On the other hand, the distance from San Francisco to New York is 377 m. to New Orleans 579 m. and to Liverpool 386 m. greater via Panama than via Nicaragua. The time required to pass over these distances being greater than the difference in the time of transit through the canals, the Nicaragua line, after completion, would be somewhat the more advantageous of the two to the United States, notwithstanding the greater cost of maintaining the longer canal.

The government of Colombia, in which lies the Panama Canal, has granted an exclusive concession, which still has many years to run. It is not free to grant the necessary rights to the United States, except upon condition that an agreement be reached with the New Panama Canal Company. The Commission believes that such agreement is impracticable. So far as can be ascertained, the company is not willing to sell its franchise, but will allow the United States to become the owner of part of its stock. The Commission considers such an arrangement inadmissible. The Governments of Nicaragua and Costa Rica, on the other hand, are untrammelled by concessions, and are free to grant to the United States such privileges as may be mutually agreed upon.

In view of all the facts, and particularly in view of all the difficulties of obtaining the necessary rights, privileges and franchises on the Panama route, and assuming that Nicaragua and Costa Rica recognize the value of the canal to themselves, and are prepared to grant concessions on terms which are reasonable and acceptable to the United States, the Commission is of the opinion that " the most practicable and feasible route for " an isthmian canal, to be " under the control, management and ownership of the United States," is that known as the Nicaragua route.

This report caused the New Panama Canal Company to view the question of selling its property in a new light, and in the spring of 1901 it obtained permission from the *Panama* Colombian government to dispose of it to the United *Route* States. It showed itself, however, somewhat reluc- *adopted.* tant to name a price to the Canal Commission, and it was not till January 1902 that it definitely offered to accept $40,000,000. In consequence of this offer, the commission in a supplementary report issued on the 18th of January 1902 reversed the conclusion it had stated in its main report, and advised the adoption of the Panama route, with purchase of the works, &c., of the French company. A few days previous to this report the Hepburn bill authorizing the Nicaragua canal at a cost of $180,000,000 had been carried in the House of Representatives by a large majority, but when it reached the Senate an amendment—the so-called Spooner bill—was moved and finally became law on the 28th of June 1902. This authorized the president to acquire all the property of the Panama Canal Company, including not less than 68,869 shares of the Panama Railroad Company, for a sum not exceeding $40,000,000, and· to obtain from Colombia perpetual control of a strip of land 6 m. wide; while if he failed to come to terms with the company and with Colombia in a reasonable time and on reasonable terms, he was by treaty to obtain from Costa Rica and Nicaragua the territory necessary for the Nicaragua canal.

Negotiations were forthwith opened with Colombia, and ultimately. a treaty (the Hay-Herran treaty) was signed in January 1903. The Colombian Senate, however, refused ratification, and it seemed as if the Panama scheme would have to be abandoned when the complexion of affairs was changed by Panama revolting from Colombia and declaring itself independent in November 1903. Within a month the new republic, by the Hay-Bunau-Varilla treaty, granted the United States the, use, occupation and control of a strip of land 10 m. wide for the purposes of the canal. A few days after the ratification of this treaty by the United States Senate in February 1904—the concession of the French company having been purchased —a commission was appointed to undertake the organization and management of the enterprise, and in June Mr J. F. Wallace was chosen chief engineer. Work was begun without delay, but the commission's methods of administration and control soon proved unsatisfactory, and in April 1905 it was reorganized, three of its members being constituted an executive committee which was to be at Panama continuously. Shortly afterwards, at the end of June, Mr Wallace resigned his position as chief engineer and was succeeded by Mr John F. Stevens.

In connexion with the reorganization of the commission a board of consulting engineers, five being nominated by European governments, was appointed in June 1905 to consider the question, which so far had not .been settled, whether the canal should be made at sea-level, without locks (at· least except tidal regulating locks at or near the Pacific terminus), or should rise to some elevation above sea-level, with locks. The board reported in January 1906. The majority (eight members out of thirteen) declared in favour of a sea-level canal as the only plan " giving reasonable assurance of safe and uninterrupted navigation "; and they considered that such a canal could be constructed in twelve or thirteen years' time, that the cost would be less than $250,000,000, and that it would endure for all time. The minority recommended a lock canal, rising to an elevation of 85 ft. above mean sea-level, on the grounds that it would cost about $100,000,000 less than the proposed sea-level canal, that it could be built in much less time, that it would afford a better navigation, that it would be adequate for all its uses for a longer time, and that it could be enlarged if need should arise with greater facility and less cost. The chief engineer, Mr Stevens, also favoured the lock or high-level scheme for the reasons, among others, that it would provide as safe and a quicker passage for ships, and, therefore would be of greater capacity; that it would provide; beyond question, the best solution of the vital problem.how safely to care for the flood waters of the Chagres and other streams, that provision was made for enlarging its capacity to almost any extent at very much less expense of time and money than could be provided for by any· sea-level plan; that its cost of operation, maintenance and fixed charges would be very much less than those of any sea-level canal; and that the time and cost of its construction would be not more than one-half that of a canal of the sea-level type. These conflicting reports were then submitted to the Isthmian Canal Commission for consideration, with the result that on the 5th of February, it reported, one member only dissenting, in favour of the lock canal recommended by· the minority.of the board of consulting engineers. Finally this plan was adopted by Congress in June 1906. Later in the same year tenders were invited from contractors who were prepared to undertake the construction of the canal. These were opened in January 1907, but .none of .them was regarded as entirely satisfactory, and

English Miles

President Roosevelt decided that it would be best for the government to continue the work, which was placed under the more immediate control of the U.S.A. Corps of Engineers. At the same time the Isthmian Canal Commission was reorganized, Major G. W. Goethals, of the Corps of Engineers, becoming engineer in chief and chairman, in succession to Mr J. F. Stevens who, after succeeding Mr T. P. Shonts as chairman, himself resigned on the 1st of April.

The following are the leading particulars of the canal, the course of which is shown on the accompanying map. The length from deep water in the Atlantic to deep water in the Pacific will be about 50 m., or, since the distance from deep water to the shore-line is about 4½ m. in Limon Bay and about 5 m. at Panama, approximately 40½ m. from shore to shore. The summit level, regulated between 82 and 87 ft. above sea-level, will extend for 31½ m. from a large earth dam at Gatun to a smaller one at Pedro Miguel, and is to be reached by a flight of 3 locks at the former point. The Gatun dam will be 7200 ft. long along the crest including the spillway, will have a maximum width at its base of 2000 ft., and will be uniformly 100 ft. wide at its top, which will rise 115 ft. above sea-level. The lake (Lake Gatun) enclosed by these dams will be 164½ sq. m. in area, and will constitute a reservoir for receiving the floods of the Chagres and other rivers as well as for supplying water for lockage. A smaller lake (Lake Miraflores), with a surface elevation of 55 ft. and an area of about 2 sq. m. will extend from a lock at Pedro Miguel to Miraflores, where the valley of the Rio Grande is to be closed by an earth dam on the west and a concrete dam with spillway on the east, and the canal is to descend to sea-level by a flight of two locks. All the locks are to be in duplicate, each being 110 ft. wide with a usable length of 1000 ft. divided by a middle gate. The channel leading from deep water in the Caribbean sea to Gatun will be about 7 m. long and 500 ft. broad, increasing to 1000 ft. from a point 4000 ft. north of the locks in order to form a waiting basin for ships. From Gatun locks, 0·6 m. in length, the channel is to be 1000 ft. or more in width for a distance of nearly 16 m. to San Pablo. Thence it narrows first to 800 ft., and then for a short distance to 700 ft., for 3½ m. to mile 27 near Juan Grande, and to 500 ft. for 4½ m. from Juan Grande to Obispo (mile 31½). From this point through the Culebra cut to Pedro Miguel lock, it will be only 300 ft. wide, but will widen again to 500 ft. through Miraflores lake, 1½ m. long, to Miraflores locks, the total length of which including approaches will be nearly a mile, and will thence maintain the same width for the remaining 8 m. to deep water on the Pacific. The minimum bottom width of the canal will thus be 300 ft., the average being 649 ft., while the minimum depth will be 41 ft.

In 1909 it was estimated that the construction of the canal would be completed by the 1st of January 1915, and that the total cost to the United States would not exceed $375,000,000 including $50,000,000 paid to the French Canal Company and the Republic of Panama, $7,382,000 for civil administration, and $20,053,000 for sanitation. The last was one of the most necessary expenditures of all, since without it disease would have greatly retarded the work or perhaps prevented it altogether.

See W. F. Johnson, *Four Centuries of the Panama Canal* (New York, 1906); *Report of the Board of Consulting Engineers for the Panama Canal* (Washington, 1906); *Annual Reports of the Isthmian Canal Commission* (Washington); Vaughan Cornish, *The Panama Canal and its Makers* (London, 1909).

PAN-AMERICAN CONFERENCES. At intervals delegates from the independent countries of North, Central and South America have met in the interests of peace and for the improvement of commercial relations and for the discussion of various other matters of common interest. A movement for some form of union among the Spanish colonies of Central and South America was inaugurated by Simon Bolivar while those colonies were still fighting for independence from Spain, and in 1815 the United States, which in May 1822 had recognized their independence and in December 1823 had promulgated the Monroe Doctrine, was invited by the governments of Mexico and Colombia to send commissioners to a congress to be held at Panama in the following year. Henry Clay, the secretary of state, hoped the congress might be the means of establishing a league of American republics under the hegemony of the United States, and under his influence President J. Q. Adams accepted the invitation, giving notice however that the commissioners from the United States would not be authorized to act in any way inconsistent with the neutral attitude of their country toward Spain and her revolting colonies. The principal objects of the Spanish-Americans in calling the congress were, in fact, to form a league of states to resist Spain or any other

European power that might attempt to interfere in America and to consider the expediency of freeing Cuba and Porto Rico from Spanish rule; but in his message to the Senate asking that body to approve his appointment of commissioners Adams declared that his object in appointing them was to manifest a friendly interest in the young republics, give them some advice, promote commercial reciprocity, obtain from the congress satisfactory definitions of the terms "blockade" and "neutral rights" and encourage religious liberty. In the Senate the proposed mission provoked a spirited attack on the administration. Some senators feared that it might be the means of dragging the United States into entangling alliances; others charged that the President had construed the Monroe Doctrine as a pledge to the southern republics that if the powers of Europe joined Spain against them the United States would come to their assistance with arms and men; and a few from the slaveholding states wished to have nothing to do with the republics because they proposed to make Cuba and Porto Rico independent and liberate the slaves on those islands. The Senate finally, after a delay of more than ten weeks, confirmed the appointments. There was further delay in the House of Representatives, which was asked to make an appropriation for the mission; one of the commissioners, Richard C. Anderson (1788–1826), died on the way (at Cartagena, July 24), and when the other, John Sergeant (1779–1852), reached Panama the congress, consisting of representatives from Colombia, Guatemala, Mexico and Peru, had met (June 22), concluded and signed a "treaty of union, league and perpetual confederation" and adjourned to meet again at Tacubaya, near the City of Mexico. The governments of Guatemala, Mexico and Peru refused to ratify the treaty and the Panama congress or conference was a failure. The meeting at Tacubaya was never held.

Mexico proposed another conference in 1831, and repeated the proposal in 1838, 1839 and 1840, but each time without result. In December 1847, while Mexico and the United States were at war, a conference of representatives from Bolivia, Chile, Ecuador, New Granada and Peru met at Lima, gave the other American republics the privilege of joining in its deliberations or becoming parties to its agreements, continued to deliberate until the 1st of March 1848, and concluded a treaty of confederation, a treaty of commerce and navigation, a postal treaty and a consular convention; but with the exception of the ratification of the consular convention by New Granada its work was rejected. Representatives from Peru, Chile and Ecuador met at Santiago in September 1856 and signed the "Continental Treaty" designed to promote the union of the Latin-American republics, but expressing hostility toward the United States as a consequence of the filibustering expeditions of William Walker (1824–1860); it never became effective. In response to an invitation from the government of Peru to each of the Latin-American countries, representatives from Guatemala, Colombia, Venezuela, Ecuador, Peru, Bolivia and Argentina met in a conference at Lima in November 1864 to form a "Union." Colombia was opposed to extending the invitation to the United States lest that country should "embarrass the action of the Congress"; the conference itself accomplished little. In 1877–1878 jurists from Peru, Bolivia, Cuba, Chile, Ecuador, Honduras, Argentina, Venezuela and Costa Rica met at Lima and concluded a treaty of extradition and a treaty on private international law, and Uruguay and Guatemala agreed to adhere to them. War among the South American states prevented the holding of a conference which had been called by the government of Colombia to meet at Panama in September 1881 and of another which had been called by the government of the United States to meet at Washington in November 1882. In 1888–1889 jurists from Argentina, Bolivia, Brazil, Chile, Paraguay, Peru and Uruguay met at Montevideo and concluded treaties on international civil law, international commercial law, international penal law, international law of procedure, literary and artistic property, trade-marks and patents, several of which were subsequently ratified by the South American countries.

In May 1888 the Congress of the United States had passed an Act authorizing the President to invite the several Latin-American governments to a conference in Washington to consider measures for preserving the peace, the formation of a customs union, the establishment of better communication between ports, the adoption of a common silver coin, a uniform system of weights, measures, patent-rights, copyrights and trade-marks, the subject of sanitation of ships and quarantine, &c. All the governments except Santo Domingo accepted the invitation and this conference is commonly known as the first Pan-American Conference. It met on the 2nd of October 1889, was presided over by James G. Blaine, the American secretary of state, who had been instrumental in having the conference called, and continued its sessions until the 19th of April 1890. A majority of its members voted for compulsory arbitration, and recommendations were made relating to reciprocity treaties, customs regulations, port duties, the free navigation of American rivers, sanitary regulations, a monetary union, weights and measures, patents and trade-marks, an international American bank, an intercontinental railway, the extradition of criminals, and several other matters. Nothing came of its recommendations, however, except the establishment in Washington of an International Bureau of American Republics for the collection and publication of information relating to the commerce, products, laws and customs of the countries represented. At the suggestion of President McKinley the government of Mexico called the second Pan-American Conference to meet at the. City of Mexico on the 22nd of October 1901. There was a full representation and the sessions were continued until the 31st of January 1902. The chief subject of discussion was arbitration, and after much wrangling between those who insisted upon compulsory arbitration and those opposed to it a majority of the delegations signed a project whereby their countries should become parties to the Hague conventions of 1899, which provide for voluntary arbitration. At the same time ten delegations signed a project for a treaty providing for compulsory arbitration. The conference also approved a project for a treaty whereby controversies arising from pecuniary claims of individuals of one country against the government of another should be submitted to the arbitration court established by the Hague convention. The conference ratified a resolution of the first conference recommending the construction of complementary lines of the proposed Pan-American railway.

At this conference, too, the International Bureau of American Republics was organized under a governing board of diplomatists with the secretary of state of the United States as chairman; it was directed to publish a monthly bulletin, and in several other respects was made a more important institution. Its governing board was directed to arrange for the third Pan-American Conference, and this body was in session at Rio de Janeiro from the 21st of July to the 26th of August 1906. Delegates attended from the United States, Argentina, Bolivia, Brazil, Chile, Colombia, Costa Rica, Cuba, San Domingo, Ecuador, Guatemala, Honduras, Mexico, Nicaragua, Panama, Paraguay, Peru, Salvador and Uruguay; Haiti and Venezuela were not represented. The secretary of state of the United States, Elihu Root, though not a delegate, addressed the conference. The subjects considered were much the same as those at the two preceding conferences. With respect to arbitration this conference passed a resolution that the delegates from the American republics to the second conference at the Hague be instructed to endeavour to secure there " the celebration of a general arbitration convention so effective and definite that, meriting the approval of the civilized world, it shall be accepted and put in force by every nation." With respect to copyrights, patents and trademarks this conference re-affirmed the conventions of the second conference, with some modifications, with respect to naturalization it recommended that whenever a native of one country who has been naturalized in another again takes up his residence in his native country without intending to return to his adopted country he should be considered as having reassumed his original citizenship; and with

respect to the forcible collection of public debts to which the " Drago Doctrine " [1] is opposed, the conference recommended that " the Governments represented therein consider the point of inviting the Second Peace Conference at the Hague to consider the question of the compulsory collection of public debts, and, in general, means tending to diminish between nations conflicts having an exclusively pecuniary origin." The fourth Conference met in Buenos Aires in July–August 1910, agreed to submit to arbitration such money claims as cannot be amicably settled by diplomacy, and renamed the Bureau the Bureau of Pan-American Union.[2]

The first Pan-American scientific congress met at Santiago, Chile, on the 25th of December 1908 for the consideration of distinctly American problems. It continued in session until the 5th of January 1909, and resolved that a second congress for the same purpose should meet at Washington in 1912.

See *International American Conference, Reports and Recommendations* (Washington, 1890), and especially the Historical Appendix.

PANATHENAEA, the oldest and most important of the Athenian festivals. It was originally a religious celebration, founded by Erechtheus (Erichthonius), in honour of Athena Polias, the patron goddess of the city. It is said that when Theseus united the whole land under one government he made the festival of the city-goddess common to the entire country, and changed the older name Athenaea to Panathenaea (Plutarch, *Theseus*, 24). The union (Synoecism) itself was celebrated by a distinct festival, called Synoecia or Synoecesia, which had no connexion with the Panathenaea. In addition to the religious rites there is said to have been a chariot race from the earliest times, in which Erechtheus himself won the prize. Considerable alterations were introduced into the proceedings by Peisistratus (q.v.) and his sons. It is probable that the distinction of Greater and Lesser Panathenaea dates from this period, the latter being a shorter and simpler festival held every year. Every fourth year the festival was celebrated with peculiar magnificence; gymnastic sports were added to the horse races; and there is little doubt that Peisistratus aimed at making the penteteric Panathenaea the great Ionian festival in rivalry to the Dorian Olympia. The penteteric festival was celebrated in the third year of each Olympiad. The annual festival, probably held on the 28th and 29th of Hecatombaeon (about the middle of August), consisted solely of the sacrifices and rites proper to this season in the cult of Athena. One of these rites originally consisted in carrying a new peplus (the state robe of Athena) through the streets to the Acropolis to clothe the ancient carved image of the goddess, a ceremonial known in other cities and represented by the writer of the *Iliad* (vi. 87) as being in use at Troy; but it is probable that this rite was afterwards restricted to the great penteteric festival. The peplus was a costly, saffron-coloured garment, embroidered with scenes from the battle between the gods and giants, in which Athena had taken part. At least as early as the 3rd century B.C. the custom was introduced of spreading the peplus like a sail on the mast of a ship, which was rolled on a machine in the procession. Even the religious rites were celebrated with much greater splendour at the Greater Panathenaea. The whole empire shared in the great sacrifice; every colony and every subject state sent a deputation and sacrificial animals. On the great day of the feast there was a procession of the priests, the sacrificial assistants of every kind, the representatives of every part of the empire with their victims, of the cavalry, in short of the population of Attica and

[1] So named from a note (1902) directed by Dr Don Louis Maria Drago, the Argentine minister of foreign affairs, to the Argentine diplomatic representative at Washington at the time of the difficulties of Venezuela incident to the collection of debts owed to foreigners by that country.

[2] The Bureau is supported by contributions, varying in amount according to population, of the twenty-one American republics. Andrew Carnegie contributed $750,000 and the various republics $250,000 for the erection of a permanent home for the Bureau in Washington. The Bureau has a library of some 15,000 volumes, and publishes numerous handbooks, pamphlets and maps, in addition to its monthly *Bulletins*. Its executive head is a director, chosen by the Governing Board.

great part of its dependencies. After the presentation of the peplus, the hecatomb was sacrificed. The subject of the frieze of the Parthenon is an idealized treatment of this great procession. The festival which had been beautified by Peisistratus was made still more imposing under the rule of Pericles. He introduced a regular musical contest in place of the old recitations of the rhapsodes, which were an old standing accompaniment of the festival. This contest took place in the Odeum, originally built for this purpose by Pericles himself. The order of the *agones* from this time onwards was—first the musical, then the gymnastic, then the equestrian contest. Many kinds of contest, such as the chariot race of the *apobatai* (said to have been introduced by Erechtheus), which were not in use at Olympia, were practised in Athens. *Apobates* was the name given to the companion of the charioteer, who showed his skill by leaping out of the chariot and up again while the horses were going at full speed. There were in addition several minor contests: the *Pyrrhic*, or war dance, celebrating the victory of Athena over the giants; the *Euandria*, whereby a certain number of men, distinguished for height, strength and beauty, were chosen as leaders of the procession; the *Lampadedromia*, or torch-race; the *Naumachia* (Regatta), which took place on the last day of the festival. The proceedings were under the superintendence of ten *athlothetae*, one from each tribe, the lesser Panathenaea being managed by *hieropoei*. In the musical contests, a golden crown was given as first prize; in the sports, a garland of leaves from the sacred olive trees of Athena, and vases filled with oil from the same. Many specimens of these Panathenaic vases have been found; on one side is the figure of Athena, on the other a design showing the nature of the competition in which they were given as prizes. The season of the festival was the 24th to the 29th of Hecatombaeon, and the great day was the 28th.

See A. Mommsen, *Feste der Stadt Athen* (1898); A. Michaelis, *Der Parthenon* (1871), with full bibliography; P. Stengel, *Die griechischen Kultusaltertümer* (1898); L. C. Purser in Smith's *Dictionary of Antiquities* (3rd ed., 1891); L. R. Farnell, *Cults of the Greek States*; also article ATHENA and works quoted.

PANCH MAHALS (= Five Districts), a district of British India, in the northern division of Bombay. Area, 1606 sq. m., pop. (1901), 261,020, showing a decrease of 17 % in the decade, owing to famine. The administrative headquarters are at Godhra, pop. (1901), 20,915. Though including Champaner, the old Hindu capital of Gujarat, now a ruin, this tract has no history of its own. It became British territory as recently as 1861, by a transfer from Sindhia; and it is the only district of Bombay proper that is administered on the non-regulation system, the collector being also political agent for Rewa Kantha. It consists of two separate parts, divided by the territory of a native state. The south-western portion is for the most part a level plain of rich soil; while the northern, although it comprises some fertile valleys, is generally rugged, undulating and barren, with but little cultivation. The mineral products comprise sandstone, granite and other kinds of building stone. Mining for manganese on a large scale has been begun by a European firm, and the iron and lead ores may possibly become profitable. Only recently has any attempt been made to conserve the extensive forest tracts, and consequently little timber of any size is to be found. The principal crops are maize, millets, rice, pulse and oilseeds; there are manufactures of lac bracelets and lacquered toys; the chief export is timber. Both portions of the district are crossed by the branch of the Bombay and Baroda railway from Anand, (through Godhra and Dohad, to Ratlam; and a chord line, opened in 1904, runs from Godhra to Baroda city. The district suffered very severely from the famine of 1899–1900.

PANCREAS (Gr. πᾶν, all; κρέας, flesh), or sweetbread, in anatomy, the elongated, tongue-shaped, digestive gland, of a pinkish colour, which lies across the posterior wall of the abdomen about the level of the first lumbar vertebra behind, and of the transpyloric plane in front (see ANATOMY: *Superficial and Artistic*). Its right end is only a little to the right of the mid line

of the abdomen and is curved down, round the superior mesenteric vessels, into the form of a ⊂. This hook-like right end is known as the head of the pancreas, and its curvature is adapted to the concavity of the duodenum (see fig.) The first inch of the straight limb is narrower from above downward than the rest and forms the neck. This part lies just in front of the beginning of the portal vein, just below the pyloric opening of the stomach and just above the superior mesenteric vessels. The next three or four inches of the pancreas, to the left of the neck, form the body and this part lies in front of the left kidney and adrenal body, while it helps to form the posterior wall of the "stomach chamber" (see ALIMENTARY CANAL). At its left extremity the body tapers to form the tail, which usually touches the spleen (see DUCTLESS GLANDS) just below the hilum, and above the basal triangle of that viscus where the splenic flexure of the colon is situated. On the upper border of the body, a little to the left of the mid line of the abdomen, is a convexity or hump, which is known as the tuber omentale of the pancreas, and touches the elevation (bearing the same name) on the liver.

The pancreas is altogether behind the peritoneum. In its greater part it is covered in front by the lesser sac (see COELOM AND SEROUS MEMBRANES), but the lower part of the front of the head and the very narrow lower surface of the body are in contact with the greater sac. There is one main duct of the pancreas, which is sometimes known as the duct of Wirsung; it is thin-walled and white, and runs the whole length of the organ nearer the back than the front. As it reaches the head it turns downward and opens into the second part of the duodenum, joining the common bile duct while they are both piercing the walls of the gut. A smaller accessory pancreatic duct is found, which communicates with the main duct and usually opens into the duodenum about three-quarters of an inch above the papilla of the latter. It drains the lower part of the head, and either crosses or communicates with the duct of Wirsung to reach its opening (see A. M. Schirmer, *Beitrag zur Geschichte und Anat. des Pancreas*, Basel, 1893).

The pancreas has no real capsule, but is divided up into lobules, which are merely held together by their ducts and by loose areolar tissue; the glands of which these lobules are made up are of the acino-tubular variety (see EPITHELIAL TISSUES). Small groups of epithelium-like cells without ducts (Islets of Langerhans) occur among the glandular tissue and are characteristic of the pancreas. In cases of diabetes they sometimes degenerate. In the centre of each acinus of the main glandular tissue of the pancreas are often found small spindle-shaped cells (centro-acinar cells of Langerhans). For details of microscopic structure see *Essentials of Histology*, by E. A. Schäfer (London, 1907).

Embryology.—The pancreas is developed, by three diverticula, from that part of the foregut which will later form the duodenum. Of these diverticula the left ventral disappears early,[1] but the right ventral, which is really an outgrowth from the lower part of the common bile duct, forms the head of the pancreas. The body and tail are formed from the dorsal diverticulum, and the two parts, at first separate, join one another so that the ducts communicate, and eventually the ventral one takes almost all the secretion of the gland to the intestine, while that part of the dorsal one which is nearest the duodenum atrophies and forms the duct of Santorini. The main pancreatic duct (of Wirsung) is therefore formed partly by the ventral and partly by the dorsal diverticulum. As the diverticula grow they give off lateral branches, which branch again and again until the terminal buds form the acini of the gland. At first the pancreas grows upward, between the stomach, and between the two layers of the dorsal mesogastrium (see COELOM AND SEROUS MEMBRANES), but when the stomach and duodenum turn over to the right, the gland becomes horizontal and the opening of the right ventral diverticulum becomes more dorsal. Later, by the unequal growth of the duodenal walls, it comes to enter the gut on its left side where the papilla is permanently situated. After the turning over of the pancreas to the right the peritoneum is absorbed from its dorsal aspect. The islets of Langerhans are now regarded as portions of the glandular epithelium which have been isolated by the invasion and growth round them of mesenchyme (see Quain's *Anatomy*, vol. L, 1908).

Comparative Anatomy.—In the Acrania (Amphioxus) no representative of a pancreas has been found, but in the Cyclostomata (hags and lampreys) there is a small lobular gland opening into the bile duct which probably represents it. In the Elasmobranchs (sharks and rays) there is a definite compact pancreas of considerable size. In the Teleostomi, which include the true bony fish (Teleostei), the sturgeon and Polyterus, the pancreas is sometimes

---

[1] N. W. Ingalls has shown (*Archiv. f. mik. Anat. und Entwickl.* Bd. 70, 1907), that in a human embryo of 4·9 mm. the two ventral buds persist and join one another below the liver bud.

a compact gland and sometimes diffuse between the layers of the mesentery; at other times it is so surrounded by the liver as to be difficult to find.

Among the Dipnoi (mud fish), Protopterus has it embedded in the walls of the stomach and intestine.

The Amphibia have a definite compact pancreas which lies in the U-shaped loop between the stomach and duodenum, and is massed round the bile duct. In the Reptilia there are sometimes several ducts, as in the crocodile and the water tortoise (Emys), and this arrangement is also found in birds (the pigeon, for instance, has three ducts opening into the duodenum at very different levels). In mammals the gland is usually compact, though

into the pancreas is of some medico-legal importance as being a cause of death. The condition is rarely recognized in time for operative interference. *Acute haemorrhagic pancreatitis* is a combination of inflammation with haemorrhage in which the pancreas is found enlarged and infiltrated with blood. Violent pain, vomiting and collapse, are the chief features as is also the case in *pancreatic abscess* in which the abscess may be single or multiple. In the latter case operation has been followed by recovery. Haemorrhagic inflammation has been followed by *gangrene of the pancreas*, which usually terminates fatally. In two remarkable cases, however, reported by Chiari recovery followed on the discharge per rectum of the necrosed pancreas. *Chronic pancreatitis* is said by

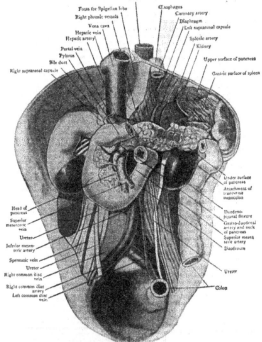

From Ambrose Birmingham, *Cunningham's Text Book of Anatomy.*

- FIG. 1.—The Viscera and Vessels on the Posterior Abdominal Wall.

The stomach, liver and most of the intestines have been removed. The peritoneum has been preserved on the right kidney, and the fossa for the Spigelian lobe. In taking out the liver, the vena cava was left behind. The stomach-bed is well shown. (From a body hardened by chromic-acid injections.)

sometimes, as in the rabbit, it is diffuse. It usually has two ducts, as in man, though in many animals, such as the ox, sheep and goat, only one persists. When there is only one duct it may open with the common bile duct, e.g. sheep and cat, or may be very far away as in the ox and rabbit. (F. G. P.)

Diseases of the pancreas.—As the pancreas plays an important part in the physiology of digestion much attention has of late been paid to the question of its secretions. In sclerosis, atrophy, acute and chronic inflammatory changes and new growths in the pancreas an absence or lessening of its secretion may be evident. *Haemorrhage*

Mayo Robson to occur in connexion with the symptoms of catarrhal jaundice, which he suggests is due to the pressure on the common duct by the swollen pancreatic tissue. The organ is enlarged and very hard, and the symptoms are pain, dyspepsia, jaundice, loss of weight and the presence of fat in the stools. This latter sign is common to all forms of pancreatic disease. In connexion with all pancreatic diseases small yellowish patches are found in the pancreatic tissue, mesentery, omentum and abdominal fatty tissue generally, and the tissues appear to be studded with whitish areas often not larger than a pin's head. The condition, which was first observed by Balser, has been termed "fat-necrosis." The pancreas like other organs, is subject to the occurrence of new growths, tumours and cysts, syphilis and tuberculosis.

PANDA (*Aelurus fulgens*), a carnivorous mammal of the family Procyonidae (see CARNIVORA). This animal, rather larger than a cat, ranges from the eastern Himalaya to north-west China. In the former area it is found at heights of from 7000 to 12,000 ft. above the sea, among rocks and trees, and chiefly feeds on fruits and other vegetable substances. Its fur is of a remarkably rich reddish-brown colour, darker below; the face is white, with the exception of a vertical stripe of red from just above the eye to the gape; there are several pale rings on the tail, the tip of which is black.

PANDARUS, in Greek legend, son of Lycaon, a Lycian, one of the heroes of the Trojan war. He is not an important figure in Homer. He breaks the truce between the Trojans and the Greeks by treacherously wounding Menelaus with an arrow, and finally he is slain by Diomedes (Homer, *Iliad*, ii. 827, iv. 88, v. 290). In medieval romance he became a prominent figure in the tale of Troilus and Cressida. He encouraged the amour between the Trojan prince and his niece Cressida; and the word "pander" has passed into modern language as the common title of a lovers' go-between in the worst sense.

PANDECTS (Lat. *pandecta*, adapted from Gr. πανδέκτης, all-containing), a name given to a compendium or digest of Roman law compiled by order of the emperor Justinian in the 6th century (A.D. 530-533). The pandects were divided into fifty books, each book containing several titles, divided into laws, and the laws into several parts or paragraphs. The number of jurists from whose works extracts were made is thirty-nine, but the writings of Ulpian and Paulus make up quite half the work. The work was declared to be the sole source of non-statute law: commentaries on the compilation were forbidden, or even the citing of the original works of the jurists for the explaining of ambiguities in the text. See JUSTINIAN; and ROMAN LAW.

PANDERMA (Gr. *Panormus*), a town of Asia Minor, on the south shore of the Sea of Marmora, near the site of Cyzicus. It has a trade in cereals, cotton, opium,avalonia and boracite and is connected by a carriage road with Balikisri. Pop. 10,000 (7000 Moslems).

PANDHARPUR, a town of British India, in Sholapur district of Bombay, on the right bank of the river Bhima, 38 m. W. of Sholapur town. Pop. (1901), 32,405. Pandharpur is the most popular place of pilgrimage in the Deccan, its celebrated temple being dedicated to Vithoba, a form of Vishnu. Three assemblages are held annually. In 1906 a light railway was opened to Pandharpur from Barsi Road on the Great Indian Peninsula railway.

PANDORA (the "All-giving") in Greek mythology, according to Hesiod (*Theog.* 570-612) the first woman. After Prometheus had stolen fire from heaven and bestowed it upon mortals Zeus determined to counteract this blessing. He accordingly commissioned Hephaestus to fashion a woman out of earth, upon whom the gods bestowed their choicest gifts. Hephaestus gave her a human voice, Aphrodite beauty and powers of seduction, Hermes cunning and the art of flattery. Zeus gave her a jar (πίθος), the so-called "Pandora's box" (see below), containing all kinds of misery and evil, and sent her, thus equipped, to Epimetheus, who, forgetting the warning of his brother Prometheus to accept no present from Zeus, made her his wife. Pandora afterwards opened the jar, from which all manner of evils flew out over the earth (for parallels in other countries, see Frazer's *Pausanias*, ii. 320). Hope alone remained at the bottom, the lid having been shut down before she escaped. (Hesiod, *W. and D.* 54-105). According to a later story, the jar contained, not evils, but blessings, which would have been preserved for the human race, had they not been lost through the opening of the jar out of curiosity by man himself (Babrius, *Fab.* 58).

See J. E. Harrison, "Pandora's Box," in *Journal of Hellenic Studies*, xx. (1900), in which the opening of the jar is explained as

an aetiological myth based on the Athenian festival of the Pithoigia (part of the Anthesteria, *q.v.*), and P. Gardner, "A new Pandora vase" (xxi., ibid., 1901). Pandora is only another form of the Earth goddess, who is conceived as releasing evil spirits from the πίθοι, which served the purpose of a grave (cf. the removal of the *lapis manalis* from the *mundus*, a circular pit at Rome supposed to be the opening to the world below, on three days in the year, whereby an opportunity of revisiting earth was afforded the dead). See also O. Gruppe, *Griechische Mythologie* (1906), i. 94.

PANDUA, a ruined city in Malda district of Eastern Bengal and Assam, once a Mahommedan capital. It is situated 7 m. N.E. of Malda, and about 20 m. from the other great ruined city of Gaur (*q.v.*), from which it was largely built. It was probably originally an outpost of Gaur, and grew in importance as Gaur became unhealthy. In A.D. 1353 Haji Shamsuddin Ilyas, the first independent king of Bengal, transferred his capital from Gaur to Pandua; but the time of its prosperity was short, and in A.D. 1453 the capital was transferred back to Gaur. Its only celebrated building is the Adina Mosque, which was described by James Fergusson as the finest example of Pathan architecture in existence. This great mosque was built by Sikandar Shah in 1369 (see INDIAN ARCHITECTURE). Pandua now, like Gaur, is almost entirely given over to the jungle.

PANDULPH [PANDOLFO] (d. 1226), Roman ecclesiastical politician, papal legate to England and bishop of Norwich, was born in Rome, and first came to England in 1211, when he was commissioned by Innocent III. to negotiate with King John. Obtaining no satisfactory concessions, he is said to have produced the papal sentence of excommunication in the very presence of the king. In May 1213 he again visited England to receive the king's submission. The ceremony took place at Dover, and on the following day John, of his own motion, formally surrendered England to the representative of Rome to receive it again as a papal fief. Pandulph repaid this act of humility by using every means to avert the threatened French invasion of England. For nearly a year he was superseded by the cardinal-legate Nicholas of Tusculum; but returning in 1215 was present at the conference of Runnymede, when the great charter was signed. He rendered valuable aid to John who rewarded him with the see of Norwich. The arrival of the cardinal-legate Gualo (1216) relegated Pandulph to a secondary position; but after Gualo's departure (1218) he came forward once more. As representing the pope he claimed a control over Hubert de Burgh and the other ministers of the young Henry III.; and his correspondence shows that he interfered in every department of the administration. His arrogance was tolerated while the regency was still in need of papal assistance; but in 1221 Hubert de Burgh and the primate Stephen Langton successfully moved the pope to recall Pandulph and to send no other legate *a latere* in his place. Pandulph retained the see of Norwich, but from this time drops out of English politics. He died in Rome on the 16th of September 1226 but his body was taken to Norwich for burial.

See W. Shirley, *Royal and Other Historical Letters* ("Rolls series"), vol. i.; Miss K. Norgate, *John Lackland* (1902); W. Stubbs, *Constitutional History* (1897) vol. i.

PANDURA (*tanboura, tanbur, tambora, mandore, pandore, bandora, bandoer*, &c.), an ancient oriental stringed instrument, a member of the lute family, having a long neck, a highly-vaulted back, and originally two or three strings plucked by the fingers. There were in antiquity at least two distinct varieties of pandura, or tanbur. (1) The more or less pear-shaped type used in Assyria and Persia and introduced by way of Asia Minor into Greece, whence it passed to the Roman Empire. In this type the body, when the graceful inward curves which led up gradually from base to neck were replaced by a more sloping outline, approximated to an elongated triangle with the corners rounded off. (2) The oval type, a favourite instrument of the Egyptians, also found in ancient Persia and among the Arabs of North Africa, who introduced it into Spain. Our definite knowledge of the pandura is derived from the treatise on music by Fārābi,[1] the Arab scholar who flourished

[1] See Michael Casiri, *Bibl. Arab. Hisp.*, i. 347.

in the 10th century. He mentions two kinds of *tanburs*, devoting to each a chapter, *i.e.* the tanbur of Khorasan, the Persian type, and the tanbur of Bagdad, the Assyrian variety; these differ in form, in length, and in the arrangement of the frets. Unfortunately, Farabi does not describe the shape of the body, being more concerned with the musical scale and compass of the instrument; but means of identification are supplied by ancient monuments. There is a tanbur on an Assyrian bas-relief of the reign of Assur-nasir-pal, *c.* 880 B.C. (British Museum), on a slab illustrating camp life; the musician is playing on a pear-shaped tanbur with a very long slender neck, which would have served for two strings at the most, while two men, disguised in the skins of wild beasts, are dancing in front of him.

There were in Farabi's day five frets at least, whereas on the tanbur of Khorasan there were no fewer than eighteen, which extended for half the length of the instrument. Five of these frets were fixed or invariable in position, the thirteen others being interpolated between them. The fixed frets, counting from the nut, gave an interval of one tone to the first, of a fourth to the second, of a fifth to the third, of an octave to the fourth, and of a major ninth to the fifth, thus providing a succession of fourths and fifths. The additional frets were placed between these, so that the octaves generally contained seventeen intervals of one-third tone each. The two principal accordances for the tanbur of Khorasan were the *marriage* when the strings were in unison, and the *lute* or accordance in fourths. Farabi mentions a tail-piece or *zobalba*, to which the strings, generally two in number but sometimes three, were attached; they rested on a bridge provided with as many notches as there were strings. In the tanbur of Khorasan they were wound round pegs placed opposite each other in the two sides of the head, as in the modern violin. [1]

Pollux[2] states that the pandura was invented by the Assyrians or Egyptians, and had three strings. Theodore Reinach[3] is of opinion that pandura was a generic term for instruments of the lute type during the Roman and Alexandrine periods. This may be the case, but from the modern standpoint we cannot in our classification afford to disregard the invariable characteristics observed in the modern, no less than in the ancient and medieval, tanburs or panduras.

To be able to identify the pandura it is as well to bear in mind the distinctive features of other instruments with which it might be confounded. The tanbur had a long neck resembling a section of a cylinder and a highly vaulted back, and its strings were plucked. In the rebab the neck was wanting or at best rudimentary, consisting of the gradual narrowing of the body towards the head, and during the middle ages in Europe, as rebec, it was always a bowed instrument. The early lutes had larger bodies than tanburs, the neck was short compared to the length of the body, the head was generally bent back at right angles, and the convex was not so deeply vaulted as that of the tanbur. The barbiton or bass lute had a long neck also, but wider, to take six, seven, or even nine strings, and from the back or profile view the general appearance was what is known as boat-shaped.

Under the Romans the pandura had become somewhat modified: the long neck was preserved but was made wider to take four strings, and the body was either oval[4] or slightly broader at the base, but without the inward curves of the pear-shaped instruments. A striking example of the former is to be seen among the marbles of the Townley Collection at the British Museum on a bas-relief illustrating the marriage feast of Eros and Psyche, a Roman sculpture assigned to c. 150 B.C. This example is of great value to the archaeology of music, for the instrument can be studied in full and in profile. The arrangement of the four pegs in the back of the head is Oriental.

The Persians had a six-stringed tanbur,[4] which they distinguished

as the *scheschta*,[5] whereas a three-stringed variety was known as the *schrud*.

The tanbur survived during the middle ages and as late as the 18th century; it may be traced in the musical documents of several countries. In England the name of pandura or bandoer was given to an instrument with wire strings having no characteristic structural feature in common with the ancient tanbur but resembling the cittern (q.v.). The bandoer had a flat back and sound-board joined by ribs having a wavy outline. A smaller size of the same instrument was called *orpheoreon*, and a larger and wider *penorcon*; these are described and figured by Praetorius,[6] who suggests that this instrument, invented in England as bandoer, is probably similar to the Greek *πανδοῦρα*. This bandora, we learn from an entry in Sir Philip Leycester's[7] index to his commonplace book of 1575, was invented by "John Rose dwellinge in Bridewell anno 4to Elizabeth, who left a sonne farre exceedinge himself in makinge instruments."

A 17th-century French MS. (Add. 30342, fol. 144) in the British Museum, containing drawings of musical instruments, gives the tambora, not the English hybrid, but a true descendant of the ancient Oriental tanbur, with nine strings, a rose sound-hole and seven frets; the French writer erroneously states that it is similar to the cistre (cittern). Filippo Bonanni[8] gives an illustration of the same kind of instrument, with ten strings in five pairs of unisons, and calls it pandura. (K. S.)

PANE (Fr. *pan*, Lat. *pannus*, a cloth, garment), originally a piece of cloth, especially one of a number of pieces of cloth or other material joined to form one piece for a garment; the word is thus also applied to the "slashes" in the material of a dress made to show a rich lining or the colour of a lining when different from the outer side of the garment. In this sense the word only survives in English in "counterpane," an outer coverlet for a bed. "Pane" is used frequently for the flat side of anything, especially in diamond-cutting of the sides to the "table" of a brilliant, or to the faces of a bolt nut or hammer-head. The most common use of the word now is that of a piece of glass filling a compartment in a window. In architecture the word is also applied to a bay of a window, compartment of a partition, side of a tower, turret, &c. (See BAY and HALF-TIMBER WORK.)

PANEGYRIC, strictly a formal public speech delivered in high praise of a person or thing, and generally high studied or undiscriminating eulogy. It is derived from *πανηγυρικός* (a speech) "fit for a general assembly" (*πανήγυρις, panegyris*). In Athens such speeches were delivered at national festivals or games, with the object of rousing the citizens to emulate the glorious deeds of their ancestors. The most famous are the *Olympiacus* of Gorgias, the *Olympiacus* of Lysias, and the *Panegyricus* and *Panathenaicus* (neither of them, however, actually delivered) of Isocrates. Funeral orations, such as the famous speech put into the mouth of Pericles by Thucydides, also partook of the nature of panegyrics. The Romans confined the panegyric to the living, and reserved the funeral oration exclusively for the dead. The most celebrated example of a Latin panegyric (*panegyricus*) is that delivered by the younger Pliny (A.D. 100) in the senate on the occasion of his assumption of the consulship, containing a somewhat fulsome eulogy of Trajan. Towards the end of the 3rd and during the 4th century, as a result of the orientalizing of the Imperial court by Diocletian, it became customary to celebrate as a matter of course the superhuman virtues and achievements of the reigning emperor. Twelve speeches of the kind (Pliny's included), eight of them by famous Gallic rhetoricians (Claudius Mamertinus, Eumenius, Nazarius, Drepanius Pacatus) and three of anonymous authorship, have been collected under the title of *Panegyrici veteres latini* (ed. E. Bährens, 1874). Speaking generally, they are characterized by a stilted, affected style and a tone of gross adulation. There are extant similar orations by Ausonius,

[1] *Onomasticon,* iv. 60.
[2] See Daremberg and Saglio, "*Dict. des antiquités grecques et romaines,* article "Lyre," p. 1450; also *Revue des études grecques,* viii. 371, &c., with illustrations, some of which the present writer would prefer to classify as early lutes, owing to the absence of the characteristic long neck of the tanburs.
[3] This instrument resembles the oval tanburs represented in the miniatures of musicians in the Cantigas di Santa Maria (13th century) having two strings, and on each side a group of three very small, round sound-holes, probably of Moorish origin. The MS. is numbered J. b. 2 in the Escorial; the miniatures are reproduced in J. F. Riaño's *Critical and Biogr. Notes on early Spanish Music* (London, 1887).
[4] In the miniatures of the Cantigas there are oval tanburs with

six or seven strings, one played by a Moor; both have the tail-piece in the form of a crescent.
[5] See Hammer von Purgstall on the "Seven Seas," in '*Jahrbücher der Literatur,* xxxvi. 290 (Vienna, 1826).
[6] *Syntagma musicum* (Wolfenbüttel, 1618), pl. xvii. and ch. 28, 63; reprint in *Publik. d. Ges. f. Musikforschung* (Berlin, 1884), Jahrgang XII.
[7] See Dr F. J. Furnivall's edition of *Captain Cox or Robert Laneham's letter,* Ballad Society (London, 1871), p. 67.
[8] See *Gabinetto armonico,* ch. 49, pl. 97 (Rome, 1722).

Symmachus and Ennodius, and panegyrics in verse by Claudian, Merobaudes, Priscian, Corippus and others.

See C. G. Heyne, " Censura xii. panegyricorum veterum," in his *Opuscula academica* (1812), vi. 80–118; H. Rühl, *De xii panegyricis latinis* (progr. Greifswald, 1868); R. Pichin, *Les Derniers écrivains profanes* (Paris, 1906).

PANEL (O. Fr. *panel*, mod. *panneau*, piece of cloth, from Med. Lat. *pannellus*, diminutive of *pannus*, cloth), a piece of cloth, slip of parchment, or portion of a surface of wood or stone enclosed in a compartment. In the first sense the word survives in the use of "panel" or "pannel" for the cloth-stuffed lining of a saddle. From the slip of parchment on which the list of jurymen is drawn up by the sheriff, "panel" in English law is applied to a jury, who are thus said to be "empanelled." In Scots law the word is used of the indictment, and of the person or persons named in the indictment; "panel" is thus the equivalent of the English "prisoner at the bar." In building and architecture (Fr. *panneau*; Ital. *quadretto, formello*; Ger. *Feld*) "panel" is properly used of the piece of wood framed within the stiles and rails of a door, filling up the aperture; but it is often applied both to the whole square frame and the sinking itself, and also to the ranges of sunken compartments in cornices, corbel tables, groined vaults, ceilings, &c. In Norman work these recesses are generally shallow, and more of the nature of *arcades*. In Early English work the square panels are ornamented with quatrefoils, cusped circles, &c., and the larger panels are often deeply recessed, and form niches with trefoil heads and sometimes canopies. In the Decorated style the cusping and other enrichments of panels become more elaborate, and they are often filled with shields, foliages, and sometimes figures. Towards the end of this period the walls of important buildings were often entirely covered with long or square panels, the former frequently forming niches with statues. The use of panels in this way became very common in Perpendicular work, the wall frequently being entirely covered with long, short and square panels, which latter are frequently richly cusped, and filled with every species of ornament, as shields, bosses of foliage, portcullis, lilies, Tudor roses, &c. Wooden panellings very much resembled those of stone, except in the Tudor period, when the panels were enriched by a varied design, imitating the plaits of a piece of linen or a napkin folded in a great number of parallel lines. This is generally called the *linen pattern*. Wooden ceilings, which are very common, are composed of thin oak boards nailed to the rafters, collars, &c., and divided into panels by oak mouldings fixed on them, with carved bosses at the intersections.

PANENTHEISM, the name given by K. C. F. Krause (*q.v.*) to his philosophic theory. Krause held that all existence is one great unity, which he called *Wesen* (Essence). This Essence is God, and includes within itself the finite unities of man, reason and nature. God therefore includes the world in Himself and extends beyond it. The theory is a conciliation of Theism and Pantheism.

PANGOLIN, the Malay name for one of the species of the scaly anteaters, which belong to the order *Edentata* (*q.v.*), and typify the family *Manidae* and the genus *Manis*. These animals, which might be taken for reptiles rather than mammals, are found in the warmer parts of Asia and throughout Africa. Pangolins range from 1 to 3 ft. in length, exclusive of the tail, which may be much shorter than or nearly twice the length of the rest of the animal. Their legs are short, so that the body is only a few inches off the ground; the ears are very small; and the tongue is long and worm-like, and used to capture ants. Their most striking character, however, is the coat of broad overlapping horny scales, which cover the whole animal, with the exception of the under surface of the body, and in some species the lower part of the tip of the tail. Besides the scales there are generally, especially in the Indian species, a number of isolated hairs, which grow between the scales, and are scattered over the soft and flexible skin of the belly. There are five toes on each foot, the claws on the first toe rudimentary, but the others, especially the third of the forefoot, long, curved, and

laterally compressed. In walking the fore-claws are turned backwards and inwards, so that the weight of the animal rests on the back and outer surfaces, and the points are thus kept from becoming blunted. The skull is long, smooth and rounded, with imperfect zygomatic arches, no teeth of any sort, and, as in other ant-eating mammals, with the bony palate extending unusually far backwards towards the throat. The lower jaw consists of a pair of thin rod-like bones, welded to each other at the chin, and rather loosely attached to the skull by a joint which, instead of being horizontal, is tilted up at an angle of 45°, the outwardly-twisted condyles articulating with the inner surfaces of the long glenoid processes in a manner unique among mammals.

The genus *Manis*, which contains all the pangolins, may be

White-bellied Pangolin (*Manis tricuspis*).

conveniently divided into two groups, distinguished by geographical distribution and certain convenient, though not highly important, external characters. The Asiatic pangolins are characterized by having the central series of body-scales continued to the extreme end of the tail, by having many isolated hairs growing between the scales of the back, and by their small external ears. They all have a small naked spot beneath the tip of the tail, which is said to be of service as an organ of touch. There are three species: viz. *Manis javanica*, ranging from Burma, through the Malay Peninsula and Java, to Borneo; *M. macrura*, found in China, Formosa and Nepal; and the Indian Pangolin, *M. pentadactyla*, distributed over the whole of India and Ceylon. The African species have the central series of scales suddenly interrupted and breaking into two at a point about 2 or 3 in. from the tip of the tail; they have no hair between the scales, and no external ears. The following four species belong to this group: the long-tailed pangolin (*M. macrura*), with a tail nearly twice as long as its body, and containing as many as forty-six caudal vertebrae, nearly the largest number known among Mammals; the white-bellied pangolin (*M. tricuspis*), closely allied to the last, but with longer three-lobed scales, and white belly hairs; and the short-tailed and giant pangolins (*M. temmincki* and *gigantea*), both of which have the tail covered entirely with scales. Those species with a naked patch on the under side of the tail can climb trees. The four species of the second group are found in West Africa, although some extend into south and eastern equatorial Africa.

(O. T.; R. L.*)

PANIN, NIKITA IVANOVICH, COUNT (1718–1783), Russian statesman, was born at Danzig on the 18th of September 1718. He passed his childhood at Pernau, where his father was commandant. In 1740 he entered the army, and rumour had it that he was one of the favourites of the empress Elizabeth. In 1747 he was accredited to Copenhagen as Russian minister, but a few months later was transferred to Stockholm, where for the next twelve years he played a conspicuous part as the chief opponent of the French party. It is said that during his residence in Sweden Panin, who certainly had a strong speculative bent, conceived a fondness for constitutional forms of government. Politically he was a pupil of Alexis Bestuzhev; consequently, when in the middle 'fifties Russia suddenly turned Francophil instead of Francophobe, Panin's position became extremely difficult. However, he found a friend in Bestuzhev's supplanter, Michael Vorontsov, and when in 1760 he was unexpectedly appointed the governor of the little grand duke Paul, his influence was assured. He was on Catherine's side during the revolution of 1762, but his jealousy of the influence which the Orlovs seemed likely to obtain over the new empress predisposed him to favour the proclamation of his ward the grand duke Paul as emperor, with Catherine as regent only.

To circumscribe the influence of the ruling favourites he next suggested the formation of a cabinet council of six or eight ministers, through whom all the business of the state was to be transacted; but Catherine, suspecting in the skilfully presented novelty a subtle attempt to limit her power, rejected it after some hesitation. Nevertheless Panin continued to be indispensable. He owed his influence partly to the fact that he was the governor of Paul, who was greatly attached to him; partly to the peculiar circumstances in which Catherine had mounted the throne; and partly to his knowledge of foreign affairs. Although acting as minister of foreign affairs he was never made chancellor; but he was the political mentor of Catherine during the first eighteen years of her reign. Panin was the inventor of the famous "Northern Accord," which aimed at opposing a combination of Russia, Prussia, Poland, Sweden, and perhaps Great Britain, against the Bourbon-Habsburg League. Such an attempt to bind together nations with such different aims and characters was doomed to failure. Great Britain, for instance, could never be persuaded that it was as much in her interests as in the interests of Russia to subsidize the anti-French party in Sweden. Yet the idea of the "Northern Accord," though never quite realized, had important political consequences and influenced the policy of Russia for many years. It explains, too, Panin's strange tenderness towards Poland. For a long time he could not endure the thought of destroying her, because he regarded her as an indispensable member of his "Accord," wherein she was to supply the place of Austria, whom circumstances had temporarily detached from the Russian alliance. Poland, Panin opined, would be especially useful in case of Oriental combinations. All the diplomatic questions concerning Russia from 1762 to 1783 are intimately associated with the name of Panin. It was only when the impossibility of realizing the "Northern Accord" became patent that his influence began to wane, and Russia sacrificed millions of roubles fruitlessly in the endeavour to carry out his pet scheme.

After 1772, when Gustavus III. upset Panin's plans in Sweden, Panin, whose policy hitherto had been at least original and independent, became more and more subservient to Frederick II. of Prussia. As to Poland, his views differed widely from the views of both Frederick and Catherine. He seriously guaranteed the integrity of Polish territory, after placing Stanislaus II. on the throne, in order that Poland, undivided and as strong as circumstances would permit, might be drawn wholly within the orbit of Russia. But he did not foresee the complications which were likely to arise from Russia's interference in the domestic affairs of Poland. Thus the confederation of Bar, and the Turkish War thereupon ensuing, took him completely by surprise and considerably weakened his position. He was forced to acquiesce in the first partition of Poland, and when Russia came off third best, Gregory Orlov declared in the council that the minister who had signed such a partition treaty was worthy of death. Panin further incensed Catherine by meddling with the marriage arrangements of the grand duke Paul and by advocating a closer alliance with Prussia, whereas the empress was beginning to incline more and more towards

Austria. Nevertheless, even after the second marriage of Paul Panin maintained all his old influence over his pupil, who, like himself, was now a warm admirer of the king of Prussia. There are even traditions from this period of an actual conspiracy of Panin and Paul against the empress. As the Austrian influence increased Panin found a fresh enemy in Joseph II., and the efforts of the old statesman to prevent a matrimonial alliance between the Russian and Austrian courts determined Catherine to get rid of a counsellor of whom, for some mysterious reason, she was secretly afraid. The circumstances of his disgrace are complicated and obscure. The final rupture seems to have arisen on the question of the declaration of " the armed neutrality of the North;" but we know that Potemkin and the English ambassador, James Harris (afterwards 1st earl of Malmesbury), were both working against him some time before that. In May 1781 Panin was dismissed. He died in Italy on the 31st of March 1783. Panin was one of the most learned, accomplished and courteous Russians of his day. Catherine called him " her encyclopaedia." The earl of Buckinghamshire declared him to be the most amiable negotiator he had ever met. He was also of a most humane disposition and a friend of Liberal institutions. As to his honesty and kindness of heart there were never two opinions. By nature a sybarite, he took care to have the best cook in the capital, and women had for him an irresistible attraction, though he was never married.

See anonymous *Life of Count N. I. Panin* (Rus.; St Petersburg, 1787); *Political correspondence* (Rus. and Fr.), Collections of Russian Histor. Society, vol. ix. (St Petersburg, 1873); V. A. Bilbasov, *Geschichte Katharina II.* (Berlin, 1891–1893); A. Brückner, *Materials for the Biography of Count Panin* (Rus.; St Petersburg, 1888).

(R. N. B.)

PANIPAT, a town of British India, in Karnal district of the Punjab, 53 m. N. of Delhi by rail. Pop. (1901), 26,914. The town is of great antiquity, dating back to the great war of the *Mahábhárata* between the Pándavas and Kaurava brethren, when it formed one of the tracts demanded by Yudisthira from Duryodhana as the price of peace. In modern times, the plains of Panipat thrice formed the scene of decisive battles which sealed the fate of upper India—in 1526, when Báber completely defeated the imperial forces; in 1556, when his grandson, Akbar, on the same battlefield, conquered Himu, the Hindu general of the Afghán Adil Sháh, thus a second time establishing the Mogul power; and finally, on the 7th of January 1761, when Ahmad Sháh Durání shattered the Mahratta confederacy. The neighbourhood is a favourite manœuvring ground for British camps of instruction. The modern town stands near the old bank of the Jumna, on high ground composed of the débris of earlier buildings. It is a centre of trade, and has manufactures of cotton cloth, metal-ware and glass. There are factories for ginning and pressing cotton.

PANIZZI, SIR ANTHONY (1797–1879), English librarian, was born at Brescello, in the duchy of Modena, Italy, on the 16th of September 1797. After taking his degree at the university of Parma, Antonio Panizzi became an advocate. A fervent patriot, he was implicated in the movement set on foot in 1821 to overturn the government of his native duchy, and in October of that year barely escaped arrest by a precipitate flight. He first established himself at Lugano, where he published an anonymous and now excessively rare pamphlet, generally known as *I Processi di Rubiera*, an exposure of the monstrous injustice and illegalities of the Modenese government's proceedings against suspected persons. Expelled from Switzerland at the joint instance of Austria, France and Sardinia, he came to England in May 1823, in a state bordering upon destitution. His countryman, Ugo Foscolo, provided him with introductions to William Roscoe and Dr William Shepherd, a Unitarian minister in Liverpool, and he earned a living for some time by giving Italian lessons. Roscoe introduced him to Brougham, by whose influence he was made, in 1828, professor of Italian at University College, London. His chair was almost a sinecure; but his abilities rapidly gained him a footing in London; and in 1831 Brougham, then lord chancellor, used his *ex officio* position as a principal trustee of the British Museum to obtain for Panizzi the post of an extra assistant librarian of the Printed Book department. At the same time he was working at his edition of Boiardo's *Orlando innamorato*. Boiardo's fame had been eclipsed for three centuries by the adaptation of Berni; and it is highly to the honour of Panizzi to have redeemed him from oblivion and restored to Italy one of the very best of her narrative poets. His edition of the *Orlando innamorato* and the *Orlando furioso* was published between 1830 and 1834, prefaced by a valuable essay on the influence of Celtic legends on medieval romance. In 1835 he edited Boiardo's minor poems, and was about the same time engaged in preparing a catalogue of the library of the Royal Society.

The unsatisfactory condition and illiberal management of the British Museum had long excited discontent, and at length a trivial circumstance led to the appointment of a parliamentary committee, which sat throughout the sessions of 1835-1836, and probed the condition of the institution very thoroughly. Panizzi's principal contributions to its inquiries with regard to the library were an enormous mass of statistics respecting foreign libraries, and some admirable evidence on the catalogue of printed books then in contemplation. In 1837 he was appointed keeper of printed books. The entire collection, except the King's Library, had to be removed from Montague House to the new building, the reading-room service had to be reorganized, rules for the new printed catalogue had to be prepared, and the catalogue itself undertaken. All these tasks were successfully accomplished; but, although the rules of cataloguing devised by Panizzi and his assistants have become the basis of subsequent work, progress of the catalogue itself was slow. The first volume, comprising letter A, was published in 1841, and from that time, although the catalogue was continued and completed in MS., no attempt was made to print any more until 1881. The chief cause of this comparative failure was injudicious interference with Panizzi, occasioned by the impatience of the trustees and the public. Panizzi's appointment, as that of a foreigner, had from the first been highly unpopular. He gradually broke down opposition, partly by his social influence, but far more by the sterling merits of his administration and his constant efforts to improve the library. The most remarkable of these was his report, printed in 1845, upon the museum's extraordinary deficiencies in general literature, which ultimately procured the increase of the annual grant for the purchase of books to £10,000. His friendship with Thomas Grenville (1755-1846) led to the nation being enriched by the bequest of the unique Grenville library, valued even then at £50,000. In 1847-1849 a royal commission sat to inquire into the general state of the museum, and Panizzi was the centre of the proceedings. His administration, fiercely attacked from many quarters, was triumphantly vindicated in every point. Panizzi immediately became by far the most influential official in the museum, though he did not actually succeed to the principal librarianship until 1856. It was thus as merely keeper of printed books that he conceived and carried out the achievement by which he is probably best remembered—the erection of the new library and reading-room. Purchases had been discouraged from lack of room in which to deposit the books. Panizzi cast his eye on the empty quadrangle enclosed by the museum buildings, and conceived the daring idea of occupying it with a central cupola too distant, and adjacent galleries too low, to obstruct the inner windows of the original edifice. The cupola was to cover three hundred readers, the galleries to provide storage for a million of books. The original design, sketched by Panizzi's own hand on the 18th of April 1852, was submitted to the trustees on the 5th of May; in May 1854 the necessary expenditure was sanctioned by parliament, and the building was opened in May 1857. Its construction had involved a multitude of ingenious arrangements, all of which had been contrived or inspected by Panizzi, who had a genius for minute detail and a gift for mechanical invention.

Panizzi succeeded Sir Henry Ellis as principal librarian in March 1856. During his tenure of this post a great improvement was effected in the condition of the museum

staff by the recognition of the institution as a branch of the civil service, and the decision was taken to remove the natural history collections to Kensington. Of this questionable measure Panizzi was a warm advocate; he was heartily glad to be rid of the naturalists. He had small love for science and its professors, and, as his friend Macaulay said; "would at any time have given three mammoths for one Aldus." Many important additions to the collections were made during his administration, especially the Temple bequest of antiquities, and the Halicarnassean sculptures discovered at Budrun (Halicarnassus) by C. T. Newton. Panizzi retired in July 1866, but continued to interest himself actively in the affairs of the museum until his death, on the 8th of April 1879. He had been created a K.C.B. in 1869.

Panizzi had become a naturalized Englishman, but his devotion to the British Museum was rivalled by his devotion to his native land, and his personal influence with English Liberal statesmen enabled him often to promote her cause. Throughout the revolutionary movements of 1848-1849, and again during the campaign of 1859 and the subsequent transactions due to the union of Naples to the kingdom of upper Italy, Panizzi was in constant communication with the Italian patriots and their confidential representative with the English ministers. He laboured, according to circumstances, now to excite, now to mitigate, the English jealousy of France; now to moderate their apprehensions of revolutionary excesses; now to secure encouragement or connivance for Garibaldi. The letters addressed to him by patriotic Italians, edited by his literary executor and biographer, L. Fagan, alone compose a thick volume. He was charitable to his exiled countrymen in England, and, chiefly at his own expense, equipped a steamer, which was lost at sea, to rescue the Neapolitan prisoners of state on the island of Santo Stefano. His services were recognized by the offer of a senatorship and of the direction of public instruction in Italy; these offers he declined, though in his latter years he frequently visited the land of his birth.

His administrative faculty was extraordinary: to the widest grasp he united the minutest attention to matters of detail. By introducing great ideas into the management of the museum he not only redeemed it from being a mere show-place, but raised the standard of library administration all over England. His moral character was the counterpart of his intellectual: he was warm-hearted and magnanimous; extreme in love and hate—a formidable enemy, but a devoted friend. His intimate friends included Lord Palmerston, Gladstone, Roscoe, Grenville, Macaulay, Lord Langdale and his family, Rutherfurd (lord advocate), and, above all perhaps, Francis Haywood, the translator of Kant. His most celebrated friendship, however, is that with Prosper Mérimée, who, having begun by seeking to enlist his influence with the English government on behalf of Napoleon III., discovered a congeniality of tastes which produced a delightful correspondence. Mérimée's part has been published by Fagan; Panizzi's perished in the conflagration kindled by the Paris commune.

See Fagan, *Life of Sir Anthony Panizzi* (Lon., 1880). (R. G.)

PANJABI (properly PAÑJABĪ), the language of the Central Punjab (properly Panjab). It is spoken by over 71,000,000 people between (approximately speaking) the 77th and 74th degrees of east longitude. The vernacular of this tract was originally an old form of the modern Lahndā, a member of the outer group of Indo-Aryan languages (q.v.), but it has been overlaid by the expansion of the midland Saurasēnī Prakrit (see PRAKRIT) to its east, and now belongs to the intermediate group, possessing most of the characteristics of the midland language, with occasional traces of the old outer basis which become more and more prominent as we go westwards. At the 74th degree of east longitude we find it merging into the modern Lahndā. The language is fully described in the article HINDOSTANI.

PANJDEH, or PENJDEH, a village of Russian Turkestan, rendered famous by "the Panjdeh scare" of 1885. It is situated on the east side of the Kushk river near its junction with the

Murghab at Pul-i-Khishti. In March 1885 when the Russo-Afghan Boundary Commission should have been engaged in settling the boundary-line, this portion of it was in dispute between the Afghans and the Russians. A part of the Afghan force was encamped on the west bank of the Kushk, and on the 29th of March General Komarov sent an ultimatum demanding their withdrawal. On their refusal the Russians attacked them at 3 a.m. on the 30th of March and drove them across the Pul-i-Khishti Bridge with a loss of some 600 men. The incident nearly give rise to war between England and Russia; but the amir Abdur-Rahman, who was present at the Rawalpindi conference with Lord Dufferin at the time, affected to regard the matter as a mere frontier scuffle. The border-line subsequently laid down gives to Russia the corner between the Kushk and Murghab rivers as far as Maruchak on the Murghab, and the Kushk post has now become the frontier post of the Russian army of occupation.

PANNA, or PUNNA, a native state of Central India, in the Bundelkhand agency. Area, 2402 sq. m.; pop. (1901), 192,986, showing a decrease of 19% in the preceding decade due to famine; tribute £13,000. The chief, whose title is maharaja, is a rajput of the Bundela clan, descended from Chhatar Sal, the champion of the independence of Bundelkhand in the 18th century. The maharaja Lokpal Singh died in 1898, leaving an only son, Madho Singh, who, in 1902, was found guilty by a special commission on the charge of poisoning his uncle, and was deposed. The diamond mines, for which the state was formerly famous, are now scarcely profitable. There are no railways, but one or two good roads. The town of PANNA is 62 m. S. of Banda. Pop. (1901), 11,346. It has a fine modern palace and several handsome temples and shrines.

PANNAGE (O. Fr. *pasnage*, from Med. Lat. *pasnagium*, *pasnaticum* for *pastionaticum*, *pascio*; *pascere*, to feed), an English legal term for the feeding of swine in a wood or forest, hence used of a right or privilege to do this. The word is also used generally of the food, such as acorns, beech-mast, &c., on which the swine feed.

PANNIER (Fr. *panier*, Lat. *panarium*, a basket for carrying bread, *panis*), a basket for carrying bread or other provisions; more especially a broad, flat basket, generally slung in pairs across a mule, pony or ass for transport. The term has also been applied to an overskirt in a woman's dress attached to the back of the bodice and draped so as to give a "pannier" appearance. At various times in the history of costume this appearance has been produced by a framework of padded whalebone, steel, &c., used to support the dress, such frameworks being known as "panniers." At the Inns of Court, London, there was formerly an official known as a "pannier man," whose duties were concerned with procuring provisions at market, blowing the horn before meals, &c. The office has been in many of the inns long obsolete, and was formally abolished at the Inner Temple in 1900. At the Inner Temple the robed waiters in hall have been called "panniers," and apparently were in some way connected with the officer above mentioned, but the proper duties of the two were in no way identical.

PANNONIA, in ancient geography a country bounded north and east by the Danube, conterminous westward with Noricum and upper Italy, and southward with Dalmatia and upper Moesia. It thus corresponds to the south-western part of Hungary, with portions of lower Austria, Styria, Carniola, Croatia, and Slavonia. Its original inhabitants (Pannonii, sometimes called Paeonii by the Greeks) were probably of Illyrian race. From the 4th century B.C. it was invaded by various Celtic tribes, probably survivors of the hosts of Brennus, the chief of whom were the Carni, Scordisci and Taurisci. Little is heard of Pannonia until 35 B.C., when its inhabitants, having taken up arms in support of the Dalmatians, were attacked by Augustus, who conquered and occupied Siscia (Sissek). The country was not, however, definitely subdued until 9 B.C., when it was incorporated with Illyria, the frontier of which was thus extended as far as the Danube. In A.D. 7 the Pannonians, with the Dalmatians and other Illyrian tribes, revolted, and were overcome by Tiberius and Germanicus, after a hard-fought campaign which lasted for two years. In A.D. 10 Pannonia was organized as a separate province—according to A. W. Zumpt (*Studia romana*), not till A.D. 20; at least, when the three legions stationed there mutinied after the death of Augustus (A.D. 14), Junius Blaesus is spoken of by Tacitus (*Annals*, i. 16) as legate of Pannonia and commander of the legions. The proximity of dangerous barbarian tribes (Quadi, Marcomanni) necessitated the presence of a large number of troops (seven legions in later times), and numerous fortresses were built on the bank of the Danube. Some time between the years 102 and 107, which marked the termination of the first and second Dacian wars, Trajan divided the province into Pannonia *superior* (ἡ ἄνω), the western, and *inferior* (ἡ κάτω), the eastern portion. According to Ptolemy, these divisions were separated by a line drawn from Arrabona (Raab) in the north to Servitium (Gradiska) in the south; later, the boundary was placed farther east. The whole country was sometimes called the Pannonias (*Pannoniae*). Pannonia *superior* was under the consular legate, who had formerly administered the single province, and had three legions under his control: Pannonia *inferior* at first under a praetorian legate with a single legion as garrison, after Marcus Aurelius under a consular legate, still with only one legion. The frontier on the Danube was protected by the establishment of the two colonies Aelia Mursia (Esse) and Aelia Aquincum (Alt-Ofen, modern Buda) by Hadrian.

Under Diocletian a fourfold division of the country was made. Pannonia *inferior* was divided into (1) Valeria (so called from Diocletian's daughter, the wife of Galerius), extending along the Danube from Altinum (Mohacs) to Brigetio (Ó-Szőny), and (2) Pannonia *secunda*, round about Sirmium (Mitrovitz) at the meeting of the valleys of the Save, Drave, and Danube. Pannonia *superior* was divided into (3) Pannonia *prima*, its northern, and (4) Savia (also called Pannonia *ripariensis*), its southern part. Valeria and Pannonia *prima* were under a *praeses* and a *dux*; Pannonia *secunda* under a *consularis* and a *dux*; Savia under a *dux* and, later a *corrector*. In the middle of the 5th century Pannonia was ceded to the Huns by Theodosius II., and after the death of Attila successively passed into the hands of the Ostrogoths, Longobards (Lombards), and Avars.

The inhabitants of Pannonia are described as brave and warlike, but cruel and treacherous. Except in the mountainous districts, the country was fairly productive, especially after the great forests had been cleared by Probus and Galerius. Before that time timber had been one of its most important exports. Its chief agricultural products were oats and barley, from which the inhabitants brewed a kind of beer named *sabaea*. Vines and olive-trees were little cultivated, the former having been first introduced in the neighbourhood of Sirmium by Probus. *Saliunca* (Celtic, *nard*) was a common growth, as in Noricum. Pannonia was also famous for its breed of hunting-dogs. Although no mention is made of its mineral wealth by the ancients, it is probable that it contained iron and silver mines. Its chief rivers were the Dravus (Drave), Savus (Save), and Arrabo (Raab), in addition to the Danuvius (less correctly, Danubius), into which the first three rivers flow.

The native settlements consisted of *pagi* (cantons) containing a number of *vici* (villages), the majority of the large towns being of Roman origin. In Upper Pannonia were Vindobona (Vienna), probably founded by Vespasian; Carnuntum (*q.v.*, Petronell); Arrabona (Raab), a considerable military station; Brigetio; Savaria or Sabaria (Stein-am-Anger), founded by Claudius, a frequent residence of the later emperors, and capital of Pannonia *prima*; Poetovio (Pettau); Siscia, a place of great importance down to the end of the empire; Emona (Laibach), later assigned to Italy; Nauportus (Ober-Laibach). In Lower Pannonia were Sirmium, first mentioned in A.D. 6, also a frequent residence of the later emperors; Sopianae (Fünfkirchen), seat of the *praeses* of Valeria, and an important place at the meeting of five roads; Aquincum, the residence of the *dux* of Valeria, the seat of *legio ii adiutrix*.

See J. Marquardt, *Römische Staatsverwaltung*, i. (2nd ed., 1881), 291; *Corpus inscriptionum latinarum*, iii. 415; G. Zippel, *Die römische Herrschaft in Illyrien* (Leipzig, 1877); Mommsen, *Provinces of the Roman Empire* (Eng. trans.), i. 22, 38; A. Forbiger, *Handbuch der alten Geographie von Europa* (Hamburg, 1877); article in Smith's *Dictionary of Greek and Roman Geography*, ii. (1873); Ptolemy, ii. 15, 16; Pliny, *Nat. Hist.* ii. 28; Strabo vii. 313; Dio Cassius xlix. 34–38, liv. 31–34, lv. 28–32; Vell Pat. ii. 110.

PANOPLY, a complete suit of armour. The word represents the Gr. πανοπλία (πᾶς, all, and ὅπλα, arms), the full armour of a hoplite or heavy-armed soldier, *i.e.* the shield, breastplate, helmet and greaves, together with the sword and lance. As applied to armour of a later date, " panoply " did not come into use till the end of the 16th century and beginning of the 17th century, and was then used of the complete suits of plate-armour covering the whole body. The figurative use of the word is chiefly due to the phrase ἡ πανοπλία τοῦ Θεοῦ, "the whole armour of God" (Eph. vi. 11).

PANORAMA (Gr. πᾶν, all, and ὅραμα, view), the name given originally to a pictorial representation of the whole view visible from one point by an observer who in turning round looks successively to all points of the horizon. In an ordinary picture only a small part of the objects visible from one point is included, far less being generally given than the eye of the observer can take in whilst stationary. The drawing is in this case made by projecting the objects to be represented from the point occupied by the eye on a plane. If a greater part of a landscape has to be represented, it becomes more convenient for the artist to suppose himself surrounded by a cylindrical surface in whose centre he stands, and to project the landscape from this position on the cylinder. In a panorama such a cylinder, originally of about 60 ft., but now extending to upwards of 130 ft. diameter, is covered with an accurate representation in colours of a landscape, so that an observer standing in the centre of the cylinder sees the picture like an actual landscape in nature completely surround him in all directions. This gives an effect of great reality to the picture, which is skilfully aided in various ways. The observer stands on a platform representing, say, the flat roof of a house, and the space between this platform and the picture is covered with real objects which gradually blend into the picture itself. The picture is lighted from above, but a roof is spread over the central platform so that no light but that reflected from the picture reaches the eye. To make this light appear the more brilliant, the passages and staircase which lead the spectator to the platform are kept nearly dark. These panoramas, suggested by a German architectural painter named Breisig, were first executed by Robert Barker, an Edinburgh artist, who exhibited one in Edinburgh in 1788, representing a view of that city. A view of London and views of sea fights and battles of the Napoleonic wars followed. Panoramas gained less favour on the continent of Europe, until, after the Franco-German War, a panorama of the siege of Paris was exhibited in Paris. Since then some notable panoramas have been on view in the cities of Europe and America.

The name panorama, or panoramic view, is also given to drawings of views from mountain peaks or other points of view, such as are found in many hotels in the Alps, or, on a smaller scale, in guide-books to Switzerland and other mountainous districts. In photography a panoramic camera is one which enables a wide picture to be taken.

PANPSYCHISM (Gr. πᾶν, all; ψυχή, soul), a philosophical term applied to any theory of nature which recognizes the existence of a psychical element throughout the objective world. In such theories not only animals and plants but even the smallest particles of matter are regarded as having some rudimentary kind of sensation or " soul," which plays the same part in relation to their objective activities or modifications as the soul does in the case of human beings. Such theories are the modern scientific or semi-scientific counterparts of the primitive animism of savage races, and may be compared with the hylozoism of the Greek physicists. In modern times the chief exponents of panpsychist views are Thomas Carlyle,

Fechner and Paulsen: a similar idea lay at the root of the physical theories of the Stoics.

PANSY, or **HEARTSEASE.** This flower has been so long cultivated that its source is a matter of uncertainty. As we now see it, it is a purely artificial production, differing considerably from any wild plant known. It is generally supposed to be merely a cultivated form of *Viola tricolor* (see VIOLET), a cornfield weed, while others assert it to be the result of hybridization between *V. tricolor* and other species such as *V. altaica*, *V. grandiflora*, &c. Some experiments of M. Carrière go to show that seeds of the wild *V. tricolor* will produce forms so like those of the cultivated pansy that it is reasonable to assume that that flower has originated from the wild plant by continuous selection. The changes that have been effected from the wild type are,

Wild Pansy (*Viola tricolor*), about half nat. size.
1, Stamen, with spur.   3. Transverse section of same.
2, Pistil, after fertilization, cut   1–3 enlarged.
lengthwise, showing the numerous parietally attached ovules.

however, more striking to the eye than really fundamental. Increase in size, an alteration in form, by virtue of which the narrow oblong petals are converted into circular ones, and variations in the intensity and distribution of the colour—these are the changes that have been wrought by continued selection, while the more essential parts of the flower have been relatively unaffected. The modern varieties of the pansy consist of the show varieties, and the fancy varieties, obtained from Belgium, and now very much improved. Show varieties are subdivided according to the colour of the flowers into selfs, white grounds and yellow grounds. The fancy or Belgian pansies have various colours blended, and the petals are blotched, streaked or edged. The bedding varieties, known as violas or tufted pansies, have been raised by crossing the pale-blue *Viola cornuta*, and also *V. lutea*, with the show pansies. They are hardier than the true pansies and are free-blooming sorts marked rather by effectiveness of colour in the mass than by quality in the individual flower; they are extremely useful in spring and summer flower-gardening.

The pansy flourishes in well enriched garden soil, in an open but cool situation, a loamy soil being preferable. Cow-dung is the best manure on a light soil. The established sorts are increased by cuttings, whilst seeds are sown to procure novelties. The cuttings, which should consist by preference of the smaller, non-flowering growths from the base of the plant, may be inserted early in September, in sandy soil, under a hand-light or in boxes under glass, and as soon as rooted should be removed to a fresh bed of fine sandy soil. The seeds may be sown in July, August or September. The bed may be prepared early in September, to be in readiness for planting, by being well manured with cow-dung and trenched up to a depth of 2 ft. The plants should be planted in rows at about a foot apart. In spring they should be mulched with half-rotten manure, and the shoots as they lengthen should be pegged down into this enriched surface to induce the formation of new roots. If the blooms show signs of exhaustion by the inconstancy of their colour or marking, all the flowers should be picked off, and this top-dressing and pegging-down process performed in a thorough manner, watering in dry weather, and keeping as cool as possible. Successional beds may be put in about February, the young plants being struck later, and wintered in cold frames. The fancy pansies require similar treatment, but are generally of a more vigorous constitution.

When grown in pots in a cold frame, about half a dozen shoots filling out a 6-in. pot, pansies are very handsome decorative objects. The cuttings should be struck early in August, and the plants shifted into their blooming-pots by the middle of October; a rich open loamy compost is necessary to success, and they must be kept free of aphides. Both the potted plants and those grown in the open beds benefit by the use of liquid manure.

PANTAENUS, head of the catechetical school at Alexandria, c. A.D. 180–200, known chiefly as having been the master of Clement, who succeeded him, and of Alexander, bishop of Jerusalem. Clement speaks of him as the " Sicilian bee," but of his birth and death nothing is known. Eusebius and Jerome speak of him as having been, originally at least, a Stoic, and as having been sent, on account of his zeal and learning, as a missionary to " India." There is some reason to think that this means the Malabar coast. There was a considerable intercourse between south India and the east Mediterranean at the time, and Christian thought possibly did something to mould the great system of Tamil philosophy known as the *Saiva Siddhanta*. Pantaenus " expounded the treasures of divine doctrine both orally and in writing," but only a few brief reminiscences of his teaching are extant (see Routh, *Rel. sac.* i. 375–383). Lightfoot suggests that the conclusion of the well-known Epistle to Diognetus, chs. 11, 12, may be the work of Pantaenus. Clement thought highly of his abilities, and Origen appeals to his authority in connexion with the inclusion of philosophy in the theological course.

PANTALOON (Ital. *pantalone*), a character in the old Italian popular comedy, said to represent a Venetian, from the favourite Venetian saint San Pantaleone, and transferred from it to pantomime (*q.v.*). The Italian pantaloon was always a silly old man with spectacles and wearing slippers, and his character was maintained in pantomime and has also made his name a synonym for a tottering dotard, as in Shakespeare's *As You Like It* (ii. vii. 158). From the Venetian usage the word " pantaloon " (whence " pants ") has also been used to certain forms of garment for the legs, the exact meaning varying at different times.

PANTECHNICON, an invented word, from Gr. πᾶς, all, and τεχνικόν, of or belonging to the arts (τέχναι), originally used as the name of a bazaar in which all kinds of artistic work was sold; it was established in Motcomb Street, Belgrave Square, London, early in the 19th century, but failed and was turned into a furniture depository, in which sense the word has now passed into general usage. The large vans used for removing furniture are hence known as pantechnicon vans or pantechnicons simply.

PANTELLERIA, or PANTALARIA (ancient *Cossyra*[1]), an island in the Mediterranean, 62 m. S. by W. of the south-western extremity of Sicily, and 44 m. E. of the African coast, belonging to the Sicilian province of Trapani. Pop. (1901), 8683. It is entirely of volcanic origin, and about 45 sq. m. in area; the highest point, an extinct crater, is 2743 ft. above sea-level. Hot mineral springs and ebullitions of steam still testify to the presence of volcanic activity. The island is fertile, but lacks fresh water. The principal town (pop. about 3000) is on the north-west, upon the only harbour (only fit for small steamers), which is fortified. There is also a penal colony here. The island can be reached by steamer from Trapani, and lies close to the main route from east to west through the Mediterranean. In 1905 about 300,000

[1] The name is Semitic, but its meaning is uncertain.

gallons of wine (mostly sweet wine), and 1900 tons of dried raisins, to the value of £34,720, were exported.

On the west coast, 2 m. south-east of the harbour, a neolithic village was situated, with a rampart of small blocks of obsidian, about 25 ft. high, 33 ft. wide at the base, and 16 at the top, upon the undefended eastern side: within it remains of huts were found, with pottery, tools of obsidian, &c. The objects discovered are in the museum at Syracuse. To the south-east, in the district known as the Cunelie, are a large number of tombs, known as *sesi*, similar in character to the *nuraghi* of Sardinia, though of smaller size, consisting of round or elliptical towers with sepulchral chambers in them, built of rough blocks of lava. Fifty-seven of them can still be traced. The largest is an ellipse of about 60 by 66 ft., but most of the *sesi* have a diameter of 20–25 ft. only. The identical character of the pottery found in the *sesi* with that found in the prehistoric village proves that the former are the tombs of the inhabitants of the latter. This population came from Africa, not from Sicily, and was of Iberian or Ibero-Ligurian stock. After a considerable interval, during which the island probably remained uninhabited, the Carthaginians took possession of it (no doubt owing to its importance as a station on the way to Sicily) probably about the beginning of the 7th century B.C., occupying as their acropolis the twin hill of San Marco and Sta Teresa, 1 m. south of the town of Pantelleria, where there are considerable remains of walls in rectangular blocks of masonry, and also of a number of cisterns. Punic tombs have also been discovered, and the votive terra-cottas of a small sanctuary of the Punic period were found near the north coast.

The Romans occupied the island as the Fasti Triumphales record in 255 B.C., lost it again the next year, and recovered it in 217 B.C. Under the Empire it served as a place of banishment for prominent persons and members of the imperial family. The town enjoyed municipal rights. In 700 the Christian population was annihilated by the Arabs, from whom the island was taken in 1123 by Roger of Sicily. In 1311 a Spanish fleet, under the command of Requesens, won a considerable victory here, and his family became princes of Pantelleria until 1553, when the town was sacked by the Turks.

See Orsi, " Pantelleria " (in *Monumenti dei Lincei* 1899, ix. 193–284). (T. As.)

PANTHEISM (Gr. πᾶν, all, θεός, god), the doctrine which identifies the universe with God, or God with the universe. The term " pantheist " was apparently first used by John Toland in 1705, and it was at once adopted by French and English writers. Though the term is thus of recent origin, the system of thought or attitude of mind for which it stands may be traced back both in European and in Eastern philosophy to a very early stage. At the same time pantheism almost necessarily presupposes a more concrete and less sophisticated conception of God and the universe. It presents itself historically as an intellectual revolt against the difficulties involved in the presupposition of theistic and polytheistic systems, and in philosophy as an attempt to solve the dualism of the one and the many, unity and difference, thought and extension. Thus the pious Hindu, confronted by the impossibility of obtaining perfect knowledge by the senses or by reason, finds his sole perfection in the contemplation of the infinite (Brahma). In Greece the idea of a fundamental unity behind the plurality of phenomena was present, though vaguely, in the minds of the early physicists (see IONIAN SCHOOL), but the first thinker who focussed the problem clearly was Xenophanes. Unlike the Hindu, Xenophanes inclined to pantheism as a protest against the anthropomorphic polytheism of the time, which seemed to him improperly to exalt one of the many modes of finite existence into the place of the Infinite. Thus Xenophanes for the first time postulates a supreme God whose

[2] Strictly, pantheism is to identify the universe with God, while the term " pancosmism " (πᾶν, κόσμος, the universe) has frequently been used for the identification of God with the universe. For practical purposes this refinement is of small value, the two ideas being aspects of the same thing; cf. 'A. M. Fairbairn, *Studies in Philos. Relig. Hist.* (1877), p. 392. Both " Atheism " (*q.v.*) and " Acosmism " are used as contradictories.

characteristic is primarily the negation of the Finite. A similar metaphysic from a different starting-point is found in Heraclitus, who postulates behind the perpetually changing universe of phenomena a One which remains. This attitude towards existence, expressing itself in different phraseology, has been prominent to a greater or less degree since Xenophanes and Heraclitus. Thus the metaphysic of Plato finds reality only in the "Idea," of which all phenomena are merely imperfect copies. Neoplatonism (and especially Plotinus) adopted a similar attitude. The Stoics, with the supreme object of giving to human life a definite unity and purpose, made the individual a part of the universe and sought to obliterate all differences. The universe to them is a manifestation of divine reason, while all things come from and return to (the ὁδὸς ἄνω κάτω) the πνεῦμα διάπυρον, the ultimate matter. The same problems in a different context confronted the monotheistic religions of Judaism and Christianity. We find Philo Judaeus endeavouring to free the concept of the Old Testament Yahweh from anthropomorphic characteristics and finite determinations. But though Philo sees the difficulties of the orthodox Judaism he cannot accept pantheism or mysticism so far as to give up the personality of God (see Logos).

With Neoplatonism we enter upon a somewhat different though closely allied attitude of mind. To Plotinus God lies beyond sense and imagination: all the theologian can do is to point the way in which the thinker must travel. Though the spirit and the language of Plotinus is closely allied to that of pantheism, the result of his thinking is not pantheism but mysticism. This may be briefly illustrated by a comparison with the greatest of modern pantheists, Spinoza. To him God is the immanent principle of the universe—"Deus sive Natura." On the principle that everything which is determined (finite) is "negated" ("determinatio est negatio"), God, the ultimate reality must be entirely undetermined. To explain the universe Spinoza proceeds to argue that God, though undetermined ab extra, is capable of infinite self-determination. Thus God, the causa sui, manifests himself in an infinite multiplicity of particular modes. Spinoza is, therefore, both pantheist and pancosmist: God exists only as realized in the cosmos: the cosmos exists only as a manifestation of God. Plotinus, on the other hand, cannot admit any realization or manifestation of the Infinite: God is necessarily above the world—he has no attributes, and is unthinkable. Such a view is not pantheism but mysticism (q.v.), and should be compared with the theology of Oriental races.

The semi-Oriental mysticism of the Neoplatonists and the Logos doctrines of the Stoics alike influence early Christian doctrine, and the pantheistic view is found frequently in medieval theology (e.g. in Erigena, Meister Eckhardt, Jakob Boehme). The Arabic scholar Averroes gave Aristotle to western Europe in a pantheistic garb, and thus influenced medieval scientists. So Bruno constructed a personified nature, and the scientific and humanistic era began. The pantheism of Spinoza, combining as it did the religious and the scientific points of view, had a wide influence upon thought and culture. Schelling (in his Identity-philosophy) and Hegel both carried on the pantheistic tradition, though after Hegel broke up into two lines of thought, the one pantheistic the other atheistic.

From the religious point of view there are two main problems. The first is to establish any real relation between the individual and God without destroying personality and with it the whole idea of human responsibility and free will: the second is to explain the infinity of God without destroying his personality. In what sense can God be outside the world (see Deism): in what sense in it (pantheism)? The great objection to pantheism is that, though ostensibly it magnifies the Creator and gets rid of the difficult dualism of Creator and Creation, it tends practically to deny his existence in any practical intelligible sense.

See, further, Theism; Deism; Atheism; Absolute.

PANTHEON (Lat. pantheum or pantheon; Gr. πάνθειον, all-holy, from πᾶς, all, and θεός god), the name of two buildings in Rome and Paris respectively; more generally, the name of any building in which as a mark of honour the bodies of the nation's famous men are buried, or "memorials" or monuments to them are placed. Thus Westminster Abbey is sometimes styled the British "Pantheon," and the rotunda in the Escorial where the kings of Spain are buried also bears the name. Near Regensburg (q.v.) is the pantheon of German worthies, known as the Valhalla. The first building to which the name was given was that built in Rome in 27 B.C. by Agrippa; it was burned later and the existing building was erected in the reign of Hadrian; since A.D. 609 it has been a Christian church, S Maria Rotunda. It was the Paris building that gave rise to the generic use of the term for a building where a nation's illustrious dead rest. The Pantheon in Paris was the church built in the classical style by Soufflot; it was begun in 1764 and consecrated to the patroness of the city, Sainte Geneviève. At the Revolution it was secularized under the name of Le Panthéon, and dedicated to the great men of the nation. It was reconsecrated in 1828 for worship, was again secularized in 1830, was once more a place of worship from 1851 to 1870, and was then a third time secularized. On the entablature is inscribed the words Aux Grandes Hommes La Patrie Reconnaissante. The decree of 1885 finally established the building for the purpose for which the name now stands.

PANTHER, another name for the leopard (q.v.), also used in America as the name of the puma (q.v.). The word is an adaptation of Lat. panthera; Gr. πάνθηρ, the supposed derivation of which from πᾶς, all, and θήρ, animal, gave rise to many tales and fables in medieval bestiaries and later scientific works. The panther was supposed to be a distinct animal from the pardus, pard, the leopard, to which also many legends were attached. In modern times a distinction had been unscientifically drawn between a larger type of leopard to which the name panther was given, and a smaller and more graceful specimen.

PANTIN, a town of northern France in the department of Seine, on the Canal d'Ourcq, adjoining the fortifications of Paris on the north-east. Pop. (1906), 32,604. The manufacture of boilers, railway wagons, machinery, oil, glass, chemicals, polish and perfumery, and the operations of dye-works, foundries and distilleries, represent some of the varied branches of its industrial activity. There is also a state-manufactory of tobacco.

PANTOGRAPH, or Pantagraph (from the Greek πάντα, all, and γράφειν, to write), an instrument for making a reduced, an enlarged, or an exact copy of a plane figure.

In its commonest form it consists of two long arms, AB and AC (fig. 1), jointed together at A, and two short arms, FD and FE, jointed together at F and with the long arms at D and E; FD is made exactly equal to AB and FE to AD, so that ADFE is a parallelogram whatever the angle at A. The instrument is supported parallel to the paper on castors, on which it moves freely. A tube is usually fixed vertically at c, near the extremity of the long arm AC, and similar tubes are mounted on plates which slide along the short arms BD and FD; they are intended to hold either the axle pin on a weighted fulcrum round which the instrument turns, or a steel pointer, or a pencil, interchangeably. When the centres of the tubes are exactly in a straight line, as on the dotted line bfc, the small triangle bfD will always be similar to the large triangle bcA; and then, if the fulcrum is placed under b, the pencil at f, and the pointer at c, when the instrument is moved round the fulcrum as a pivot, the pencil and the pointer will move parallel to each other through distances which will be respectively in the proportion of bf to bc; thus the pencil at f draws a reduced copy of the map under the pointer at c; if the pencil and the pointer were interchanged an enlarged copy would be drawn; if the fulcrum and pencil were interchanged, and the sliders set for f to bisect bc, the map would be copied exactly. Lines are engraved on the arms BD and FD, to indicate the positions to which the sliders must be set for the ratios ⅓, ⅔ . ., which are commonly required.

FIG. 1.

The square pantograph of Adrian Gavard consists of two graduated arms which are pivoted on a plain bar and connected by a graduated bar sliding between them throughout their entire length, to be set at any required distance from the plain bar; a sliding plate carrying a vertical tube, to hold either the axle of the fulcrum, the pencil, or the pointer, is mounted on one of the arms and on a prolongation of the plain bar beyond the other arm, and also on the graduated connecting bar; and an additional arm is provided by means of which reductions below or enlargements above the scales given on the instrument can be readily effected.

The *eidograph* (Gr. εἶδος, form) is designed to supersede the pantograph, which is somewhat unsteady, having several supports and joints. It is composed of three graduated bars, one of which is held over a fulcrum and carries the others, which are lighter, one at each extremity. The three bars are movable from end to end in box-sockets, each having an index and a vernier in contact with the graduated scale. The box-socket of the principal bar turns round the vertical axle of the fulcrum; that of each side bar is attached to a vertical axle, which also carries a grooved wheel of large diameter and turns in a collar at either end of the principal bar. The two wheels are of exactly the same diameter and are connected by a steel band fitting tightly into the grooves, so that they always turn together through identical arcs; thus the side bars over which they are respectively mounted, when once set parallel, turn with them and always remain parallel. A pointer is held at the end of one of the side bars and a pencil at the diagonally opposite end of the other. The bars may be readily set by their graduated scales to positions in which the distances of the pencil and the pointer from the fulcrum will always be in the ratio of the given and the required map scales.

Numerous other modifications have been proposed from time to time; many forms are described in G. Pellehn's *Der Pantograph* (Berlin, 1903).

PANTOMIME, a term which has been employed in different senses at different times in the history of the drama. Of the Roman *pantomimus*, a spectacular kind of play in which the functions of the actor were confined to gesticulation and dancing, while occasional music was sung by a chorus or behind the scenes, some account is given under DRAMA. In Roman usage the term was applied both to the actor of this kind of play and to the play itself; less logically, we also use the term to signify the method of the actor when confined to gesticulation. Historically speaking, so far as the Western drama is concerned there is no intrinsic difference between the Roman *pantomimus* and the modern "ballet of action," except that the latter is accompanied by instrumental music only, and that the personages appearing in it are not usually masked. The English "dumb-show," though fulfilling a special purpose of its own, was likewise in the true sense of the word pantomimic. The modern pantomime, as the word is still used, more especially in connexion with the English stage, signifies a dramatic entertainment in which the action is carried on with the help of spectacle, music and dancing, and in which the performance of that action or of its adjuncts is conducted by certain conventional characters, originally derived from Italian "masked comedy," itself an adaptation of the *fabulae Atellanae* of ancient Italy. Were it not for this addition, it would be difficult to define modern pantomime so as to distinguish it from the masque; and the least rational of English dramatic species would have to be regarded as essentially identical with another to which English literature owes some of its choicest fruit.

The contributory elements which modern pantomime contains very speedily, though in varying proportions and manifold combinations, introduced themselves into the modern drama as it had been called into life by the Renaissance. In Italy the transition was almost imperceptible from the pastoral drama to the opera; on the Spanish stage ballets with allegorical figures and military spectacles were known towards the close of the 16th century; in France ballets were introduced in the days of Marie de' Medici, and the popularity of the opera was fully established in the earlier part of the reign of Louis XIV. The history of these elements need not be pursued here, but there is a special ingredient in modern pantomime of which something more has to be said. From the latter part of the 16th century (Henry III. in 1596, sought to divert the dreaded states-general at Blois by means of the celebrated Italian company of the *Gelosi*) professional Italian comedy (*commedia dell' arte*, called *commedia all' improviso* only because of the skill with which the schemes of its plays were filled up by improvisation) had found its way to Paris with its merry company of characters,

partly corresponding to the favourite types of regular comedy both ancient and modern, but largely borrowed from the new species of masked comedy—so called from its action being carried on by certain typical figures in masks—said to have been invented earlier in the same century by Angelo Beolco (Ruzzante) of Padua. These types, local in origin, included *Pantalone* the Venetian merchant, who survives in the uncommercial *Pantaloon*, the Bolognese *Dottore*. The *Zannis* (*Giovannis*) were the domestic servants in this species of comedy, and included among other varieties the *Arlecchino*. This is by far the most interesting of these types, and by far the best discussed. The *Arlecchino* was formerly supposed to have been, like the rest, of Italian origin. The very remarkable contribution (cited below) of Dr Otto Driesen to the literature of folk-lore as well as to that of the stage seems however to establish the conclusion (to which earlier conjectures pointed) that the word *Harlequin* or *Herlequin* is of French origin, and that the dramatic figure of Harlequin is an evolution from the popular tradition of the harlekin-folk, mentioned about the end of the 11th century by the Norman Ordericus Vitalis. The "damned souls" of legend became the comic demons of later centuries, the *croque-sots* with the devil's mask; they left the impress of their likeness on the hell-mouth of the religious drama, but were gradually humanized as a favourite type of the Parisian popular street-masques (*charivaris*) of the 14th and 15th centuries. Italian literature contains only a single passage before the end of the 16th century which can be brought into any connexion with this type—the *alichino* (cat's back) of canto xxi. of the *Inferno*. The French harlequin was, however, easily adopted into the family of Italian comedy, where he may, like his costume,[1] have been associated with early national traditions, and where he continued to diverge from his fellow *Zannis* of the stolid sort, the *Scapin* of French comedy-farce. From the time of the performances in France of the celebrated *Fedeli* company, which played there at intervals from the beginning to the middle of the 17th century onwards, performing in a court ballet in 1636, Tristan Martinelli had been its harlequin, and the character thus preceded that of the Parisian favourite Trivelin, whose name Cardinal de Retz was fond of applying to Cardinal Mazarin. There can be no pretence here of pursuing the French harlequin through his later developments in the various species of the comic drama, including that of the marionettes, or of examining the history of his supersession by Pierrot and of his ultimate extinction.

Students of French comedy, and of Molière in particular, are aware of the influence of the Italian players upon the progress of French comedy, and upon the works of its incomparable master. In other countries, where the favourite types of Italian popular comedy had been less generally seen or were unknown, popular comic figures such as the English fools and clowns, the German *Hanswurst*, or the Dutch *Pickelhering*, were ready to renew themselves in any and every fashion which preserved to them the gross salt favoured by their patrons. Indeed, in Germany, where the term pantomime was not used, a rude form of dramatic buffoonery, corresponding to the coarser sides of the modern English species so-called, long flourished, and threw back for centuries the progress of the regular drama. The banishment of *Hanswurst* from the German stage was formally proclaimed by the famous actress Caroline Neuber at Leipzig in a play composed for the purpose in 1737. After being at last suppressed, it found a commendable substitute in the modern *Zauberposse*, the more genial Vienna counterpart of the Paris *féerie* and the modern English extravaganza.

In England, where the masque was only quite exceptionally revived after the Restoration, the love of spectacle and other frivolous allurements was at first mainly met by the various forms of dramatic entertainment which went by the name of "opera." In the preface to *Albion and Albanius* (1685), Dryden gives a definition of opera which would fairly apply to modern extravaganza, or to modern pantomime with the harlequinade

[1] The traditional costume of the ancient Roman *mimi* included the *centunculus* or variegated (harlequin's) jacket, the shaven head, the sooty face and the unshod feet.

left out. Character-dancing was, however, at the same time largely introduced into regular comedy; and, as the theatres vied with one another in seeking *quocunque modo* to gain the favour of the public, the English stage was fully prepared for the innovation which awaited it. Curiously enough, the long-lived but cumbrous growth called pantomime in England owes its immediate origin to the beginnings of a dramatic species which has artistically furnished congenial delight to nearly two centuries of Frenchmen. Of the early history it must here suffice to say that the unprivileged actors, at the fairs, who had borrowed some of the favourite character-types of Italian popular comedy, after eluding prohibitions against the use by them of dialogue and song, were at last allowed to set up a comic opera of their own. About the second quarter of the 18th century, before these performers were incorporated with the Italians, the light kind of dramatic entertainment combining pantomime proper with dialogue and song enjoyed high favour with the French and their visitors during this period of peace. The *vaudeville* was cultivated by Le Sage and other writers of mark, though it did not conquer an enduring place in dramatic literature till rather later, when it had, moreover, been completely nationalized by the extension of the Italian types.

· It was this popular species of entertainment which, under the name of pantomime, was transplanted to England before in France it had attained to any fixed form, or could claim for its productions any place in dramatic literature. Colley Cibber mentions as the first example, followed by " that Succession of monstrous Medlies," a piece on the story of Mars and Venus, which was still in dumb-show; for he describes it as " form'd into a connected Presentation of Dances in Character, wherein the Passions were so happily expressed, and the whole Story so intelligibly told, by a mute Narration of Gesture only, that even thinking Spectators allow'd it both a pleasing and a rational Entertainment." There is nothing to show that Harlequin and his companions figured in this piece. Genest, who has no record of it, dates the period when such entertainments first came into vogue in England about 1723. In that year the pantomime of *Harlequin Dr Faustus* had been produced at Drury Lane—its author being John Thurmond, a dancing master, who afterwards (in 1727) published a grotesque entertainment called *The Miser, or Wagner and Abericock* (a copy of this is in the Dyce Library). Hereupon, in December 1723, John Rich (1692–1761), then lessee of the theatre in Lincoln's Inn Fields, produced there as a rival pantomime *The Necromancer, or History of Dr Faustus*, no doubt, says Genest, " gotten up with superior splendour." He had as early as 1717 been connected with the production of a piece called *Harlequin Executed*, and there seem traces of similar entertainments as far back as the year 1700. But it was the inspiriting influence of French example and the keen rivalry between the London houses, which in 1723 really established pantomime on the English stage. Rich was at the time fighting a difficult battle against Drury Lane, and his pantomimes at Lincoln's Inn Fields, and afterwards at Covent Garden, were extraordinarily successful. He was himself an inimitable harlequin, and from Garrick's lines in his honour it appears that his acting consisted of " frolic gestures " without words. The favourite Drury Lane harlequin was Pinkethman (Pope's " poor Pinky "); readers of the *Tatler* (No. 188) will remember the ironical nicety with which his merits are weighed against those of his competitor Rich at the other house. Colley Cibber, when described by Pope as " mounting the wind on grinning dragons " briskly denied having in his own person or otherwise encouraged such fooleries; in his *Apology*, however, he enters into an elaborate defence of himself for having allowed himself to be forced into countenancing the " gin-shops of the stage," pleading that he was justified by necessity, as Henry IV. was in changing his religion. Another butt of Pope's, Lewis Theobald, was himself the author of more than one pantomime; their titles already run in the familiar fashion, e.g. A *Dramatick Entertainment, call'd Harlequin a Sorcerer, with the Loves of Pluto and Proserpine* (1725; the " book of the words," as it may be called, is in the Dyce Library). In

another early pantomime (also in the Dyce Library) called *Perseus and Andromeda, with the Rape of Colombine, or The Flying Lovers*, there are five " interludes, three serious and two comic." This is precisely in the manner of Fielding's dramatic squib against pantomimes, *Tumble-down Dick, or Phaeton in the Suds*, first acted in 1744, and ironically dedicated to " Mr John Lun," the name that Rich chose to assume as harlequin. It is a capital bit of burlesque, which seems to have been directly suggested by Pritchard's *Fall of Phaeton*, produced in 1736.

There seems no need to pursue further the history of English pantomime in detail. "Things of this nature are above criticism," as Mr Machine, the " composer " of *Phaeton*, says in Fielding's piece. The attempt was made more than once to free the stage from the incubus of entertainments to which the public persisted in flocking; in vain Colley Cibber at first laid down the rule of never giving a pantomime together with a good play; in vain his son Theophilus after him advised the return of part of the entrance money to those who would leave the house before the pantomime began. "It may be questioned," says the chronicler, " if there was a demand for the return of £20 in ten years." Pantomime carried everything before it when there were several theatres in London, and a dearth of high dramatic talent prevailed in all; and, allowing for occasional counter-attractions of a not very dissimilar nature, pantomime continued to flourish after the Licensing Act of 1737 had restricted the number of London play-houses, and after Garrick's star had risen on the theatrical horizon. He was himself obliged to satisfy the public appetite, and to disoblige the admirers of his art, in deference to the drama's most imperious patrons—the public at large.

In France an attempt was made by Noverre (q.v.) to restore pantomime proper to the stage as an independent species, by treating mythological subjects seriously in artificial ballets. This attempt, which of course could not prove permanently successful, met in England also with great applause. In an anonymous tract of the year 1789 in the Dyce Library, attributed by Dyce to Archdeacon Nares (the author of the *Glossary*), Noverre's pantomime or ballet *Cupid and Psyche* is commended as of very extraordinary merit in the choice and execution of the subject. It seems to have been without words. The writer of the tract states that " very lately the serious pantomime has made a new advance in this country, and has gained establishment in an English theatre "; but he leaves it an open question whether the grand ballet of *Medea and Jason* (apparently produced a few years earlier, for a burlesque on the subject came out in 1781) was the first complete performance of the kind produced in England. He also notes *The Death of Captain Cook*, adapted from the Parisian stage, as possessing considerable dramatic merit, and exhibiting " a pleasing picture of savage customs and manners."

To conclude, the chief difference between the earlier and later forms of English pantomime seems to lie in the fact that in the earlier Harlequin pervaded the action, appearing in the comic scenes which alternated throughout the piece with the serious which formed the backbone of the story. Columbine (originally in Italian comedy Harlequin's daughter) was generally a village maiden courted by her adventurous lover, whom village constables pursued, thus performing the laborious part of the policeman of the modern harlequinade. The brilliant scenic effects were of course accumulated, instead of upon the transformation scene, upon the last scene of all, which in modern pantomime follows upon the shadowy chase of the characters called the *rally*. The commanding influence of the clown, to whom pantaloon is attached as friend, flatterer and foil, seems to be of comparatively modern growth; the most famous of his craft was undoubtedly Joseph Grimaldi (1779–1837). His memory is above all connected with the famous pantomime of *Mother Goose*, produced at Covent Garden in 1806. The older British type of Christmas pantomime, which kept its place in London till the 'seventies, has been preserved from oblivion in Thackeray's *Sketches and Travels in London*. The species is not yet wholly extinct; but, by degrees, the rise of the music-halls and the popularity of a new type of music-hall performer influenced the character of the show which was given under the name of a Christmas pantomime at the theatres, and it became more of a burlesque "variety entertainment," dovetailed into a fairy play and with the "harlequinade" part (which had formed the closing scene of the older sort) sometimes omitted. The word had really lost its meaning. The thing itself survived rather in such occasional appearances of the Pierrot "drama without words" as charmed London playgoers in the early 'nineties in such pieces as L'Enfant prodigue.

AUTHORITIES.—For a general survey see K. F. F. Flögel, Geschichte des Grotesk-Komischen, revised ed. by F. W. Eveling (1867); A. Pougin, Dictionnaire historique et pittoresque du théâtre (Paris, 1885). As to the commedia dell'arte, masked, comedy, in Italy and France, and their influence on French regular comedy, see L. Moland, Molière et la comédie italienne (2nd ed., Paris, 1867), and O. Driesen's remarkable study, Der Ursprung des Harlekin (Berlin, 1904). As to the German Hanswurst and Hanswurstiaden, see G. Gervinus, Geschichte der deutschen Dichtung, vol. iii. (Leipzig, 1853); E. Devrient, Gesch. der deutschen Schauspielkunst, vol. ii. (Leipzig, 1848), and as to the German Harlequin, Lessing's Hamburgische Dramaturgie, no. 18 (1767), and the reference there to Julius Möser's Harlekin oder Vertheidigung des Grotesk-Komischen (1761). As to English pantomime, see Genest, Account of the English Stage (10 vols., Bath, 1832), especially vol. iii.; Dibdin, Complete History of the Stage (5 vols., London, 1800), especially vols. ii., iv., and v.; Apology for the Life of Colley Cibber, ed. R. W. Lowe (2 vols., London, 1889); P. Fitzgerald, Life of Garrick (2 vols., London, 1868).

(A. W. W.)

PANTÓN, a town of north-western Spain, in the province of Lugo; in a mountainous district, watered by the rivers Miño and Cabe. Pop. (1900), 12,988. Livestock is extensively reared, and large quantities of wheat, wine, oats and potatoes are produced. The other industries are distilling and linen manufacture. The nearest railway station is 6 m. east, at Monforte.

PANTRY (O. Fr. paneterie; Med. Lat. panetaria, a bread-shop, from panis, bread), originally a room in a house used for the storage of bread, hence "panter" or "pantler," an officer of a household in charge of the bread and stores. In the royal household of England the office was merged in that of butler. At coronations the office of "panneter" was held by the lord of the manor of Kibworth Beauchamp; it was his duty to carry the salt-cellar and carving-knives to the royal table, and he kept these as his fee. The last holder of the office was Ambrose Dudley, son of John, duke of Northumberland, at Elizabeth's coronation. At his death the manor reverted to the Crown. "Pantry" was early widened in meaning to include a room in a house used for the storing of all kinds of food, and is now restricted to the butler's or parlourmaid's room, where plate, china, glass, &c., for the use of the table is kept, and duties in connexion with the serving of the table are performed.

PANTUN (PANTOUM), a form of verse of Malay origin. An imitation of the form has been adopted in French and also in English verse, where it is known as "pantoum." The Malay pantun is a quatrain, the first and third and the second and fourth lines of which rhyme. The peculiarity of the verse-form resides in the fact that the first two lines have as a rule no actual connexion, in so far as meaning is concerned, with the two last, or with one another, and have for their raison d'être a sense of supplying rhymes for the concluding lines. For instance:—

Sěnŭdoh kāyu di-rimba
Bĕnang kārap bĕr-simpul pŭleh:
Sŭnggoh dŭdok bĕr-tindek riba,
Jāngan di-hārap kato-kan bŭleh.

The rhododendron is a wood of the jungle,
The strings within the frame-work of the loom are in a tangled
   knot.
It is true that I sit on thy lap,
But do not therefore cherish the hope that thou canst take any other liberty.

Here, it will be seen, the first two lines have no meaning, though according to the Malayan mind, on occasion, these "rhyme-making" lines are held to contain some obscure, symbolical reference to those which follow them. The Malay is not exacting with regard to the correctness of his rhymes,

and to his ear rimba and riba rhyme as exactly as pŭleh and bŭleh. It should also be noted that in the above example, as is not infrequently the case with the Malay pantun, there is a similar attempt at rhyme between the initial words of the lines as well as between the word with which they conclude, sěnŭdoh and sŭnggoh, bĕnang and jāngan, and kārap and hārap all rhyming to the Malayan ear. There are large numbers of well-known pantun with which practically all Malays are acquainted, as are the commoner proverbs are familiar to us all, and it is not an infrequent practice in conversation for the first line of a pantun—viz.: one of the two lines to which no real meaning attaches—to be quoted alone, the audience being supposed to possess the necessary knowledge to fit on the remaining lines for himself and thus to discover the significance of the allusion. Among cultured Malays, more especially those living in the neighbourhood of the raja's court, new pantun are constantly being composed, many of them being of a highly topical character, and these improvisations are quoted from man to man until they become current like the old, well-known verses, though within a far more restricted area. Often too, the pantun is used in love-making, but they are then usually composed for the exclusive use of the author and for the delectation of his lady-loves, and do not find their way into the public stock of verses. "Capping" pantun is also a not uncommon pastime, and many Malays will continue such contests for hours without once repeating the same verse, and often improvising quatrains when their stock threatens to become exhausted. When this game is played by skilled versifiers, the pantun last quoted, and very frequently the second line thereof, is used as the tag on to which to hang the succeeding verse.

The "pantoum" as a form of verse was introduced into French by Victor Hugo in Les Orientales (1829). It was also practised by Théodore de Banville and Leconte de Lisle. Austin Dobson's In Town is an example of its use, in a lighter manner, in English. In the French and English imitation the verse form is in four-line stanzas, the second and fourth line of each verse forming the first and third of the next, and so on to the last stanza, where the first and third line of the first stanza form the second and fourth line.

(H. CL.)

PANYASIS (more correctly, PANYASSIS), of Halicarnassus, Greek epic poet, uncle or cousin of Herodotus, flourished about 470 B.C. He was put to death by the tyrant Lygdamis (c. 454). His chief poems were the Heracleias in 14 books, describing the adventures of Heracles in various parts of the world, and the Ionica in elegiacs, giving an account of the founding and settlement of the Ionic colonies in Asia Minor. Although not much esteemed in his own time, which was unfavourable to epic poetry, he was highly thought of by later critics, some of whom assigned him the next place to Homer (see Quintilian, Inst. orat. x. 1. 54). The few extant fragments show beauty and fullness of expression, and harmonious rhythm.

Fragments in G. Kinkel, Epic. poet. fragmenta (1877), ed. separately by J. P Tzschirner (1842); F. P Funcke, De Panyasidis vita (1837); R. Krausse, De Panyaside (1891).

PAOLI, CESARE (1840–1902), Italian historian and palaeographer, son of senator Baldassare Paoli, was born and educated in Florence. At the age of twenty-one he was given an appointment in the record office of his native city; from 1865 to 1871 he was attached to the Archives of Sienna, but eventually returned to Florence. In 1874 he was appointed first professor of palaeography and diplomatics at the Istituto di Studii Superiori in Florence, where he continued to work at the interpretation of MSS. In 1887 he became editor of the Archivio storico italiano, to which he himself contributed numerous articles. His works consist of a large number of historical essays, studies on palaeography, transcriptions of state and other papers, reviews, &c.

See C. Lupi, "Cesare Paoli," in the Archivio storico italiano, vol. xxix. (1902), with a complete list of his works.

PAOLI, PASQUALE (1725–1807), Corsican general and patriot, was born at Stretta in the parish of Rostino He was the son of Giacinto Paoli, who had led the Corsican rebels against Genoese tyranny. Pasquale followed his father into exile, serving with distinction in the Neapolitan army; on his return to Corsica (q.v.) he was chosen commander-in-chief of the rebel forces, and after a series of successful actions he drove the Genoese from the whole island except a few coast towns. He then set to work to reorganize the government, introducing many useful reforms, and he founded a university at Corte. In 1767 he wrested the island of Capraia from the Genoese, who, despairing of ever being able to subjugate Corsica, again sold their rights over it to France. For two years Paoli fought desperately against the new invaders, until in 1769 he was defeated by vastly superior forces under Count de Vaux, and obliged to take refuge in England. In 1789 he went to Paris with the permission of the constituent assembly, and was afterwards sent back to Corsica with the rank of lieutenant-general. Disgusted with the excesses of the revolutionary government and having been accused of treason by the Convention, he summoned a consulta, or assembly, at Corte in 1793, with himself as president and formally seceded from France. He then offered the suzerainty of the island to the British government, but finding no support in that quarter, he was forced to go into exile once more, and Corsica became a French department. He retired to London in 1796, when he obtained a pension; he died on the 5th of February 1807.

See Boswell's *Life of Johnson*, and his *Account of Corsica and Memoirs of P. Paoli* (1768); N. Tommaseo, "Lettered Pasquale de Paoli" (in *Archivio storico italiano*, 1st series, vol. xi.), and *Della Corsica, &c.* (ibid., nuova serie, vol. xi., parte ii.); Pompei, *De L'état de la Corse* (Paris, 1821); Giovanni Livi, "Lettere inedite di Pasquale Paoli" (in *Arch. stor. ital.*, 5th series, vols. v. and vi.); Bartoli, *Historia di Pascal Paoli* (Bastia, 1891); Lencisa, *P. Paoli e la guerra d'indipendenza della Corsica* (Milano, 1890); and Comte de Buttafuoco, *Fragments pour servir à l'histoire de la Corse de 1764 à 1769* (Bastia, 1859).

PAPACY[1] (a term formed on the analogy of "abbacy" from Lat. *papa*, pope; cf. Fr. *papauté* on the analogy of *royauté*. Florence of Worcester, A.D. 1044, quoted by Du Cange *s.v. Papa*, has the Latin form *papatia*; the *New Eng. Dict.* quotes Gower, *Conf.* i. 258, as the earliest instance of the word *Papacie*), the name most commonly applied to the office and position of the bishop or pope of Rome, in respect both of the ecclesiastical and temporal authority claimed by him, *i.e.* as successor of St Peter and Vicar of Christ, over the Catholic Church, and as sovereign of the former papal states. (See POPE and ROMAN CATHOLIC CHURCH.)

I.—From the Origins to 1087.

The Christian community at Rome, founded, apparently, in the time of the emperor Claudius (41–54), at once assumed great importance, as is clearly attested by the Epistle to *The Primitive Roman Church*. the Romans (58). It received later the visit of Paul while a prisoner, and, according to a tradition which is now but little disputed, that of the apostle Peter. Peter died there, in 64, without doubt, among the Christians whom Nero had put to death as guilty of the burning of Rome. Paul's career was also terminated at Rome by martyrdom. Other places had been honoured by the presence and preaching of these great leaders of new-born Christianity; but it is at Rome that they had borne witness to the Gospel by the shedding of their blood; there they were buried, and their tombs were known and honoured. These facts rendered the Roman Church in the highest degree sacred. About the time that Peter and Paul died in Rome the primitive centre of Christianity—that is to say, Jerusalem—was disappearing amidst the disaster of the war of the Roman Empire with the Jews. Moreover, the Church of Jerusalem, narrowed by Jewish Christian particularism, was hardly qualified to remain the metropolis of Christianity, which was gradually gaining ground in the Graeco-Roman world. The true centre of this world was the capital of the Empire; the transference was consequently accepted as natural at an early

[1] This article is a general history in outline of the papacy itself. Special periods, or aspects are dealt with in fuller detail elsewhere, *e.g.* in the biographical notices of the various popes, or in such articles as CHURCH HISTORY; ROMAN CATHOLIC CHURCH; INVESTITURES; CANON LAW; ECCLESIASTICAL JURISDICTION; ULTRAMONTANISM; or the articles on the various ecclesiastical councils.

date. The idea that the Roman Church is at the head of the other Churches, and has towards them certain duties consequent on this position, is expressed in various ways, with more or less clearness, in writings such as those of Clemens Romanus, Ignatius of Antioch and Hermas. In the 2nd century all Christendom flocked to Rome; there was a constant stream of people—bishops from distant parts, apologists or heresiarchs. All that was done or taught in Rome was immediately echoed through all the other Churches; Irenaeus and Tertullian constantly lay stress upon the tradition of the Roman Church, which in those very early days was almost without rivals, save in Asia, where there were a number of flourishing Churches, also apostolic in origin, forming a compact group and conscious of their dignity. The great reception given to Polycarp on his visit to Rome in A.D. 155 and the attitude of St Irenaeus show that on the whole the traditions of Rome and of Asia harmonized quite well. They came into conflict, however (c. A.D. 190), on the question of the celebration of the festival of Easter. The bishop of Rome, Victor, desired his colleagues in the various parts of the Empire to form themselves into councils to inquire into this matter. *Early Authority of the Roman Bishops.* The invitation was accepted by all; and, the consultation resulting in favour of the Roman usage, Victor thought fit to exclude the recalcitrant Churches of Asia from the Catholic communion. His conduct in this dispute, though its severity may have been open to criticism,[2] indicates a very definite conception on his part of his authority over the universal Church. In the 3rd century the same position was maintained, and the heads of the Roman Church continued to speak with the greatest authority. We find cases of their intervention in the ecclesiastical affairs of Alexandria, of the East, of Africa, Gaul and Spain. Though the manner in which they wielded their authority sometimes meets with criticism (Irenaeus, Cyprian, Firmilianus), the principle of it is never questioned. However, as time went on, certain Churches became powerful centres of Christianity, and even when they did not come into conflict with her, their very existence tended to diminish the prestige of the Roman Church.

After the period of the persecutions had passed by, the great ecclesiastical capitals Carthage, Alexandria, Antioch and Constantinople, as secondary centres of organization *Centrifugal Forces in the Catholic Church.* and administration, drew to themselves and kept in their hands a share in ecclesiastical affairs. It was only under quite exceptional circumstances that any need was felt for oecumenical decisions. Further, the direction of affairs, both ordinary and extraordinary, tended to pass from the bishops to the state, which was now christianized. The Eastern Church had soon *de facto* as its head the Eastern emperors. Henceforth it receded more and more from the influence of the Roman Church, and this centrifugal movement was greatly helped by the fact that the Roman Church, having ceased to know the Greek language, found herself practically excluded from the world of Greek Christianity.

In the West also centrifugal forces made themselves felt. After Cyprian the African episcopate, in proportion as it perfected its organization, seemed to feel less and less the need for close relations with the apostolic see. In the 4th century the Donatist party was in open schism; the orthodox party had the upper hand in the time of Aurelius and Augustine; the regular meeting of the councils further increased the corporate cohesion of the African Episcopal body. From them sprang a code of ecclesiastical laws and a whole judicial organization. With this organization, under the popes Zosimus, Boniface and Celestine the Roman Church came into conflict on somewhat trivial grounds, and was, on the whole, being worsted in the struggle, when the Vandal invasion of Africa took place, and for nearly a century to come the Catholic communities were subjected to very hard treatment. The revival which took place under Byzantine rule (6th and 7th centuries) was of little importance;

[2] Victor's conduct in this matter was not approved by a number of bishops (including Irenaeus), who protested against it (*derusepaschdebortes*) in the interests of peace and Christian love (Eusebius, *Hist. eccl.* v. 24).—[ED.]

but the autonomy which had been denied them under Aurelius was maintained to the end, that is to say, up till the Mahommedan conquest.

During the 4th century it is to be noticed that, generally speaking, the Roman Church played a comparatively insignificant *The Roman* part in the West. From the time of popes Damasus *Church in* and Siricius various affairs were referred to Rome *the 4th* from Africa, Spain or Gaul. The popes were asked *Century.* to give decisions, and in answer to those demands drew up their first decretals. However, side by side with the Roman see was that of Milan, which was also the capital of the Western Empire. From time to time it seemed as if Milan would become to Rome what Constantinople was to Alexandria. However, any danger that menaced the prestige of Rome disappeared when the emperor Honorius removed the imperial residence to Ravenna, and still more so when the Western emperors were replaced in the north of Italy by barbarian sovereigns, who were Arians.

In Spain, Gaul, Brittany and the provinces of the Danube, similar political changes took place. When orthodox Christianity *The Church* had gained the upper hand beyond the Alps and the *in the* Pyrenees, the episcopate of those countries grouped *Teutonic* itself, as it had done in the East, around the *Kingdoms.* sovereigns. In Spain was produced a fairly strong religious centralization around the Visigothic king and the metropolitan of Toledo. In Gaul there was no chief metropolitan; but the king's court became, even sooner than that of Spain, the centre of episcopal affairs. The Britons and Irish, whose remoteness made them free from restriction, developed still more decided individuality. In short, the workings of all the Western episcopates, from Africa to the ocean, the Rhine and the Danube, lay outside the ordinary influence of the Roman see. All of them, *Restriction* even down to the metropolitan sees of Milan and *of the* Aquileia, practised a certain degree of autonomy, and *Papal* in the 6th century this developed into what is called *Authority.* the Schism of the Three Chapters. With the exception of this schism, these episcopates were by no means in opposition to the Holy See. They always kept up relations of some kind, especially by means of pilgrimages, and it was admitted that in any disputes which might arise with the Eastern Church, the pope had the right to speak as representative of the whole of the Western Church. He was, moreover, the only bishop of a great see—for Carthage had practically ceased to count—who was at that time a subject of the Roman emperor.

This was the situation when St Gregory was elected pope in 590. We may add that in peninsular Italy, which was most clearly under his ecclesiastical jurisdiction, the Lombards had spread havoc and ruin; so that nearly ninety bishoprics had been suppressed, either temporarily or definitively. The pope could act directly only on the bishoprics of the coast districts or the islands. Beyond this limited circle he had to act by means of diplomatic channels, through the governments of the Lombards, Franks and Visigoths. On the Byzantine side his hands were less tied; but here he had to reckon with the theory of the five patriarchates which had been a force since Justinian. According to Byzantine ideas, the Church was governed—under the supreme authority, of course, of the emperor—by the five patriarchs of Rome, Constantinople, Alexandria, Antioch and Jerusalem: Rome had for a long time opposed this division, but, since some kind of division was necessary, had put forward the idea of the three sees of St Peter—Rome, Alexandria and Antioch—those of Constantinople and Jerusalem being set aside, as resulting from later usurpations. But the last named were just the most important; in fact the only ones which counted at all, since the monophysite secession had reduced the number of the orthodox in Syria and Egypt practically to nothing. This dissidence Islam was to complete, and by actually suppressing the patriarchate of Jerusalem to reduce Byzantine Christendom to the two patriarchates of Rome and Constantinople.

There was no comparison between the two from the point of view of the East. The new Rome, where the emperor reigned, prevailed over the old, which was practically abandoned to the barbarians. She was still by courtesy given the precedence, but that was all; the council in Trullo (692) even claimed to impose reforms on her. When Rome, abandoned by the *Rome and* distant emperors, was placed under the protection of *Constan-* the Franks (754), relations between her and the Greek *tinople.* Church became gradually more rare, the chief occasions being the question of the images in the 8th century, the quarrel between Photius and Ignatius in the 9th, the affairs of the four marriages of the emperor Leo VI. and of the patriarch Theophylact in the 10th. On these different occasions the pope, ignored in ordinary times, was made use of by the Byzantine government to ratify measures which it had found necessary to adopt in opposition to the opinion of the Greek episcopate.

These relations were obviously very different from those which had been observed originally, and it would be an injustice to the Roman Church to take them as typical of her relations with other Christian bodies. She had done all she could to defend her former position. Towards the end of the 4th century, when southern Illyricum (Macedonia, Greece, Crete) was passing under the authority of the Eastern emperor, she tried to keep him within her ecclesiastical obedience by creating the vicariate of Thessalonica. Pope Zosimus (417) made trial of a similar organization in the hope of attaching the churches of the Gauls more closely to himself. It was also he who began the struggle against the autonomy of Africa. But it was all without effect. From the 6th century onwards the apostolic vicars of Arles and Thessalonica were merely the titular holders of pontifical honours, with no real authority over those who were nominally under their jurisdiction.

It was Gregory I. who, though with no premeditated intention, was the first to break this circle of autonomous or dissident Churches which was restricting the influences of the *Gregory* apostolic see. As the result of the missions sent to the *Great,* England by him and his successors there arose a *590-604.* church which, in spite of certain Irish elements, was and remained Roman in origin, and, above all, spirit and tendency. In it the traditions of old culture and religious learning imported from Rome, where they had almost ceased to bear any fruit, found a new soil, in which they flourished. Theodore, Wilfrid, Benedict Biscop, Bede, Boniface, Ecgbert, Alcuin, revived the fire of learning, which was almost extinct, and by their aid enlightenment was carried to the Continent, to decadent Gaul and barbarian Germany. The Churches of England and Germany, founded, far from all traditions of autonomy, by Roman legates, tendered their obedience voluntarily. In Gaul there was no hostility to the Holy See, but on the contrary a profound veneration for the great Christian sanctuary of the West. The Carolingian princes, when Boniface pointed them towards Rome, followed him without their clergy offering any resistance on grounds of principle. The question of reform having arisen, from the apostolic see alone could its fulfilment be expected, since in it, with the succession of St Peter, were preserved the most august traditions of Christianity.

The surprising thing is that, although Rome was then included within the empire of the Franks, so that the popes were afforded special opportunities for activity, they showed for the most part no eagerness to strengthen their authority over the clergy beyond the Alps. Appeals and other matters of detail were referred to them more often than under the Merovingians. They gave answers to such questions as were submitted to them; but the machinery moved when set in motion from outside; but the popes did not attempt to interfere on their own initiative. The Frankish Church was directed, in fact, by the government of Charlemagne and Louis the Pious. When this failed, as happened during the wars and partitions which followed the death of Louis, the fate of this Church, with no effective head and under no regular direction, was very uncertain. It was then that a clerk who saw that there was but an uncertain prospect of help from the pope of his time, conceived *The False* the shrewd idea of appealing to the popes of the past, *Decretals.* so as to exhort the contemporary generation through the mouth of former popes, from Clement to Gregory. This design was realized in the celebrated forgery known as the " False Decretals " (see DECRETALS).

Hardly were they in circulation throughout the Frankish Empire when it happened that a pope, Nicholas I., was elected *Nicholas I., 858-867.* who was animated by the same spirit as that which had inspired them. There was no lack of opportunities for intervening in the affairs not only of the Western but of the Eastern Church, and he seized upon them with great decision. He staunchly supported the patriarch Ignatius against his rival, Photius, at Constantinople; he upheld the rights of Teutberga, who had been repudiated by her husband, Lothair II.of Lorraine, against that prince and his brother, the emperor Louis II.; and he combated Hincmar, the powerful metropolitan of Reims. It was in the course of this last dispute that the False Decretals found their way to Rome. Nicholas received them with some reserve; he refrained from giving them his sanction, and only borrowed from them what they had already borrowed from authentic texts, but in general he took up the same attitude as the forger had ascribed to his remote predecessors. The language of his successors, Andrian II. and John VIII., still shows some trace of the energy and pride of Nicholas. But the circumstances were becoming difficult. Europe was being split up under the influence of feudalism; Christendom was assailed by the barbarians, Norsemen, Saracens and Huns; at Rome the papacy was passing into the power of the local aristocracy, with whom after Otto I. it was disputed from time to time by the sovereigns of Germany. It was still being held in strict subjection by the latter when, towards the end of the 11th century, Hildebrand (Gregory VII.) undertook its enfranchisement and began the war of the investitures (q.v.), from which the papacy was to issue with such an extraordinary renewal of its vitality.

In Eastern Christendom the papacy was at this period an almost forgotten institution, whose pretensions were always *Schism of East and West.* met by the combined opposition of the imperial authority, which was still preponderant in the Byzantine Church, and the authority of the patriarchate of Constantinople, around which centred all that survived of Christianity in those regions. To complete the situation, a formal rupture had occurred in 1054 between the patriarch Michael Cerularius and Pope Leo IX.

In the West, Rome and her sanctuaries had always been held in the highest veneration, and the pilgrimage to Rome was *General Position of the Papacy in Theory.* still the most important in the West. The pope, as officiating in these holiest of all sanctuaries, as guardian of the tombs of St Peter and St Paul and the inheritor of their rank, their rights, and their traditions, was the greatest ecclesiastical figure and the highest religious authority in the West. The greatest princes bowed before him; it was he who consecrated the emperor. In virtue of the spurious donation of Constantine, forged at Rome in the time of Charlemagne, which was at first circulated in obscurity, but ended by gaining universal credit, it was believed that the first Christian emperor, in withdrawing to Constantinople, had bestowed on the pope all the provinces of the Western Empire, and that in consequence all sovereignty in the West, even that of the emperor, was derived from pontifical concessions. From all points of view, both religious and political, the pope was thus the greatest man of the West, the ideal head of all Christendom.

When it was necessary to account for this position, theologians quoted the text of the Gospels, where St Peter is represented as the rock on which the Church is built, the pastor of the sheep and lambs of the Lord, the doorkeeper of the kingdom of heaven. The statements made in the New Testament about St Peter were applied without hesitation to all the popes, considered as his successors, the inheritors of his see (*Petri-sedes*) and of all his prerogatives. This idea, moreover, that the bishops of Rome were the successors of St Peter was expressed very early —as far back as the 2nd century. Whatever may be said as to its historical value, it symbolizes very well the great authority of the Roman Church in the early days of Christianity; an

authority which was then administered by the bishops of Rome, and came to be more and more identified with them. The councils were also quoted, and especially that of Nicaea, which does not itself mention the question, but certain texts of which contained the famous gloss: *Ecclesia romana semper habuit primatum*. But this proof was rather insufficient, as indeed it was felt to be, and, in any case, nothing could be deduced from it save a kind of precedence in honour, which was never contested even by the Greeks. The Gospel and unbroken tradition offered a better argument.

In his capacity as head of the church, " and president of the Christian agape," as St Ignatius of Antioch would have said, the pope was considered to be the supreme president and moderator of the oecumenical assemblies. When the episcopate met in council the bishop of Rome had to be at its head. No decisions of a general nature, whether dogmatic or disciplinary, could be made without his consent. The appeal from all patriarchal or conciliary judgments was to him; and on those occasions when he had to depose bishops of the highest standing, notably those of Alexandria and Constantinople, his judgments were carried into effect. During the religious struggles between the East and West he was on a few occasions condemned (by the Eastern council of Sardica, by Dioscorus, by Photius); but the sentences were not carried out, and were even, as in the case of Dioscorus, considered and punished as sacrilegious attacks. In the West the principle, " prima sedes a nemine judicatur," was always recognized and applied.

In ordinary practice this theoretically wide authority had only a limited application. The apostolic see hardly ever interfered in the government of the local Churches. *Practical Ideas of the Papacy.* Save in its own metropolitan province, it took no part in the nomination of bishops; the provincial or regional councils were held without its authorization; their judgments and regulations were carried out without any suggestion that they should be ratified by Rome. It is only after the False Decretals that we meet with the idea that a bishop cannot be deposed and his place filled without the consent of the pope. And it should be noticed that this idea was put forward, not by the pope with the object of increasing his power, but by the opinion of the Church with a view to defending the bishops against unjust sentences, and especially those inspired by the secular authority.

It was admitted, however, throughout the whole Church that the Holy See had an appellate jurisdiction, and recourse was had to it on occasion. At the council of Sardica (343) an attempt had been made to regulate the procedure in these appeals, by recognizing as the right of the pope the reversing of judgments, and the appointment of fresh judges. In practice, appeals to the pope, when they involved the annulling of a judgment, were judged by the pope in person.

But the intervention of the Holy See in the ecclesiastical affairs of the West, which resulted from these appeals, was only of a limited, sporadic and occasional nature. Nothing could have been more removed from a centralized administration than the condition in which matters stood with regard to this point. The pope was the head of the Church, but he exercised his authority only intermittently. When he did exercise it, it was far more frequently at the request of bishops or princes, or of the faithful, than of his own initiative. Nor had any administrative body for the supreme government of the Church ever been organized. The old Roman clergy, the deacons and priests of the church at Rome (*presbyteri incardinati, cardinales*) formed the pope's council, and when necessary his tribunal; to them were usually added the bishops of the neighbourhood. The body of ecclesiastical notaries served as the staff of the chancery.

The Roman Church had from a very early date possessed considerable wealth. Long before Constantine we find her employing it in aid of the most distant churches, *Territorial Possessions of the Holy See.* as far afield as Cappadocia and Arabia. Her real property, confiscated under Diocletian, was restored by Constantine, and since then had been continually increased by gifts and bequests. In the 4th and 5th centuries, the Roman Church possessed property in all parts of the empire; but gradually, whether because the confiscations of the barbarian emperors had curtailed its extent, or because the popes had made efforts to concentrate it nearer to themselves, the property of the Holy See came to be confined almost entirely to Italy. In the time of St Gregory there subsisted only what lay in Byzantine Italy, the Lombards having confiscated the property of the Church as well as the imperial domains. During the quarrels between the papacy and the Byzantine Empire her domains in lower Italy and Sicily also disappeared as time went on, and the territorial possessions of the Roman Church were concentrated in the neighbourhood of Rome.

It was then, towards the middle of the 8th century, that the pope, who already exercised a great influence over the *Beginnings of the* government of the city and province of Rome, *Temporal Power.* defending her peacefully and with difficulty against the advancing Lombard conquests, saw that he was forced, short of the protection of the Greek Empire, to put himself under the protection of the Frankish princes. Thus there arose a kind of sovereignty, disputed, it is true, by Constantinople, but which succeeded in maintaining itself. Rome, together with such of the Byzantine territories as still subsisted in her neighbourhood, was considered as a domain sacred to the apostle Peter, and entrusted to the administration of his successor, the pope. To it were added the exarchate of Ravenna and a few other districts of central Italy, which had been recently conquered by the Lombards and retaken by the Frankish kings Pippin and Charlemagne. Such was the foundation of the papal state.

The higher places in the government were occupied by the clergy, who for matters of detail made use of the civil and military officials who had carried on the administration under the Byzantine rule. But these lay officials could not long be content with a subordinate position, and hence arose incessant friction, which called for constant intervention on the part of the Frankish sovereigns. In 824 a kind of protectorate was organized, and serious guarantees were conceded to the lay aristocracy.

Shortly afterwards, in the partition of the Carolingian Empire, Italy passed under the rule of a prince of its own, Louis II., who, with the title of emperor, made his authority felt in political matters. Shortly after his death (875) fresh upheavals reduced to nothing the power of the Carolingian princes; the clergy of Rome found itself without a protector, exposed to the animosity of the lay aristocracy. The authority of the pontificate was seriously impaired by these circumstances. One of the great families of Rome, that of the *vestararius* Theophylact, took possession of the temporal authority, and succeeded in influencing the papal elections. After Theophylact the power passed to his daughter Marozia, a woman of the most debased character; then to her son Alberic, a serious-minded prince; and then to Alberic's son Octavius, who from " prince of the Romans" became pope (John XII.) when yet a mere boy. After Marozia and Alberic and the rest another branch of the same family, the Crescentii, exercised the temporal powers of the Holy See; and after them the same régime was continued by the counts of Tusculum, who were sprung from the same stock, which sometimes provided the Roman Church with the most unlikely and least honourable pontiffs.

The pope, like all the bishops, was chosen by means of election, in which both the clergy and the laity took part. The latter *Election of* were represented in the most essential functions *the Popes.* of the election by the aristocracy: at first by the senate, and later by the *exercitus romanus,* or rather of its staff, composed of Byzantine officers. It was the latter which gave rise to the feudal aristocracy which we see appearing under the Carolingians. The new pope was chosen by the principal members of the clergy and nobles, and then set before the assembled people, who gave their decision by acclamation; and this acclamation was accepted as the vote of the assembly of the faithful. The pope-elect was then put in possession of the episcopal house, and after waiting till the next Sunday his consecration was proceeded with. This ceremony was at first celebrated in the Lateran, but from Byzantine times onwards it took place at St Peter's. It was also under the Byzantine régime that the condition was imposed that the pope should not be consecrated until the emperor had ratified his election. This had not been required under the old Latin emperors nor under the Gothic kings, and it disappeared of its own accord with the Byzantine régime. It was revived, however, by the emperor Louis the Pious, much to the disgust of the Romans, who resisted on several occasions. The Roman " princes " or " senators " in the 10th century went still further: it was they who actually nominated the pope. The same was the case with the Saxon emperors (Otto I., II. and III.), and in the 11th century of the lords of Tusculum, the latter nominating themselves and choosing members of their own family for the pontificate. When the emperor Henry III. (1046) put an end to this oppression it was only to substitute another. The popes of Tusculum did, at least, belong to the country, while the German kings chose bishops from the other side of the Alps. Such was the state of affairs up to the time of Hildebrand.

The entry of Hildebrand into the counsels of the papacy marks the beginning of a great change in this institution. He cannot, however, claim the honour of having opened *The Hildebrandine* the way which he impelled his predecessors to follow *Reform.* even before following it himself. All good Christians were calling for reform; bishops, princes, and monks were in agreement on this point when they spoke or acted according to their convictions. Many of them had tried to effect something; but these isolated efforts were often countermined by incompatible aims, and had produced no serious results. It is in the supreme head of the Church that the movement ought to have found its origin and inspiration. There was no dispute as to his possessing the authority in spiritual matters necessary to impose reform and overbear the resistance which might arise; no one was better qualified than he to treat with the holders of the temporal power and obtain the support which was necessary from them. The Fathers of the Church had repeated times without number that the priesthood stands above even the supreme secular authority; the Bible was full of stories most aptly illustrating this theory; nobody questioned that, within the Church, the pope was the Vicar of Christ, and that, as such, his powers were unlimited; as proof positive could be cited councils and decretals—whether authentic or spurious; at any rate all authorized by long usage and taken as received authorities. It only remained to take possession of this incontestable power and use it with firmness and consistency. The example of Nicholas I., two centuries before, had shown the position which a pope could occupy in Christendom; but for a long time past the man had come short of the institution, the workman of his tool. Under Leo IX. (1048-1054) the pope suddenly came forward as the active and indefatigable champion of reform; simony and incontinence of the clergy were attacked by the one most qualified to purify the Church of them. Henceforth the way was open, and it became clear that, given good popes, the reform movement might be carried into effect. The choice of the pope was then subject to the pleasure of the sovereign of Germany, against whom the Roman feudal lords, devoted as they were to the old abuses, were in constant revolt. In the midst of the frequent changes of pope which went on during these years, and the political vicissitudes of Italy, Hildebrand took such measures as enabled him to checkmate the opposition of the Roman barons by turning against them, now the armed force of the Normans, now the influence of the German king.[1]

[1] On the 9th of April 1058, six days after the death of Pope Stephen X., John, bishop of Velletri, the nominee of the Roman nobles, was enthroned as Pope Benedict X. Hildebrand set up Gerard, bishop of Florence, as a rival candidate, won over a part of the Romans to his cause, and secured the support of the empress regent Agnes at the Diet of Augsburg in June. Gerard was elected pope at Siena (as Nicholas II., q.v.) by those cardinals who had fled from Rome on the elevation of Benedict X. A synod was held at Sutri, at which the powerful Godfrey, duke of Lorraine and Spoleto, and margrave of Tuscany, and the chancellor Wibert were present. Measures were here concerted against Pope Benedict, who was driven out of Rome in January 1059, Nicholas II. being

Side by side with the general movement towards reform, he had set before himself the object of freeing the papacy, not only from its temporal oppressors but also from its protectors. He was successful at the council of 1059, the pontifical election was placed out of reach of the schemes of the local feudal lords and restored to the heads of the clergy; certain reservations were made with regard to those rights which the Holy See was considered to have conceded personally to Henry of Germany (the young king Henry IV., son of the emperor Henry III.), but nothing more. At the election of Alexander II. (1061–1073)—a rival to whom was for a long time supported by the German king—and even at the election of Hildebrand, this rule had its effect. Henceforth the elections remained entirely free from those secular influences which had hitherto been so oppressive. In 1073 Hildebrand was raised to the pontifical throne by the acclamation of the people of Rome, under the name of Gregory VII.

The work of reform was now in a good way; the freedom of the pontifical elections had been assured, which gave some *Gregory VII., 1085–1085.* promise that the struggle against abuses would be conducted successfully. All that now remained was to go on following wisely and firmly the way that had already been opened. But this attitude was not likely to appeal to the exuberant energy of the new pope. Hitherto he had had to reckon with obstacles more powerful than those which were now left for him to conquer, and, what was more, with the fact that his authority depended upon the will of others. But now that his hands were no longer tied, he could act freely. The choice of the pope had been almost entirely removed from the sphere of secular influence, and especially from that of the German king. Gregory claimed that the same condition should apply to bishops, and these were the grounds of the dispute about investitures—a dispute which could find no solution, for it was impossible for the Teutonic sovereigns to renounce all interest in a matter of such importance in the workings of their state. Since the time of Clovis the German sovereigns had never ceased to intervene in such matters. But this question soon fell into the background. Gregory's contention was that the secular sovereigns should be entirely in the power of the head of the Church, and that he should be able to advance them or dispossess them at will, according to the estimate which he formed of their conduct. A terrible struggle arose between these obviously exorbitant demands and the resistance which they provoked. Its details cannot be described in this place (see INVESTITURES); we need only say that this ill-fated quarrel was not calculated to advance the reform movement, but rather to impede it, and, further, that it ended in failure. Gregory died far away from Rome, upon which he had brought incalculable evils; and not only Rome, but the papacy itself had to pay the penalty for the want of moderation of the pope. Great indeed was the difference between the state in which he received it and that in which he left it. We must not, however, let this mislead us. This struggle between spiritual and secular powers, owing to the tremendous sensation which it created throughout Christendom, showed the nations that at the head of the Church there was a great force for justice, always able to combat iniquity and oppression, and sometimes to defeat them, however powerful the evil and the tyrants might seem. The scene at Canossa, which had at the moment a merely relative importance, remained in the memories of men as a symbol which was hateful or comforting, according to the point of view from which it was considered. As to Gregory's political pretensions, zealous theorists were quick to transform them into legal principles; and though his immediate successors, somewhat deafened by the disturbance which they had aroused, seem to have neglected them at first, they were handed on to more distant heirs and reappeared in future struggles.

Gregory himself, in his last moments, seems to have felt that it was impossible to maintain them, for Didier, abbot of Monte-regularly enthroned on the 24th of the same month. A synod assembled at the Lateran in April passed the famous new regulations for the elections to the papacy. (See CONCLAVE and LATERAN COUNCILS.)—[ED.]

Cassino (Victor III., 1086–1087), whom he nominated as his successor, was well known for his moderation. It was no longer a question of continuing the policy of Gregory VII., but of saving the work of Hildebrand.   (L. D.*)

II.—Period from 1087 to 1305.

Gregory VII. had clearly revealed to the world the broad lines of the religious and political programme of the medieval papacy, and had begun to put it into execution. *The Work of Gregory VII.* To reform the Church in every grade and purge the priesthood in order to shield it from feudal influences and from the domination of lay sovereignties; to convert the Church thus regenerated, spiritualized, and detached from the world, into an organism which would be submissive to the absolute authority of the papal see, and to concentrate at Rome all its energies and jurisdictions; to establish the supremacy of the Roman see over all the Christian Churches, and win over to the Roman Church the Churches of the Byzantine Empire, Africa and Asia; to establish the temporal domain of St Peter, not only by taking possession of Rome and Italy, but also by placing all the crowns of Europe under the supreme sovereignty of the popes, or even in direct vassalage to them; and, finally, to maintain unity of faith in Christendom and defend it against the attacks of unbelievers, Mussulmans, heretics and pagans—these were the main features of his scheme. The task, however, was so gigantic that after 150 years of strenuous effort, at the period which may be considered as the apogee of its power, that is, in the first half of the 13th century, the papacy had attained only incomplete results. At several points the work remained unfinished, for decadence followed close upon the moment of extreme greatness. It is more particularly in the part of this programme that relates to the internal policy of the papacy, to the subjection of the Church to the Curia, and to the intensive concentration of the ecclesiastical forces in the hands of the leader of Christendom, that Gregory went farthest in the execution of his plan and approached nearest the goal. For the rest, so formidable were the external obstacles that, without theoretically renouncing his claims, he was unable to realize them in practice in a manner satisfactory to himself.

In order to give a clear idea of the vicissitudes through which the papal institution passed between the years 1087 and 1305 and to show the measure of its success or failure at different stages in its course, it is convenient to divide this section into four periods.

1. *Period from Urban II. to Calixtus II.* (1087–1124).— Gregory VII.'s immediate successors accomplished the most pressing work by liberating the Church from feudal subjection, either by force or by diplomacy. This *Urban II., 1088–1099.* was, indeed, the indispensable condition of its internal and external progress. The great figure of this period is unquestionably the French Cluniac Urban II., who led the Hildebrandine reformation with more vehemence than Gregory himself and was the originator of the crusades. Never throughout the middle ages was pope more energetic, impetuous or uncompromising. His inflexible will informed the movement directed against the enemy within, against the simoniacal prelate and the princely usurper of the rights of the Church, and prescribed the movement against the enemy without, against the infidel who held the Holy Sepulchre. Urban set his hand to reforms from which his predecessor Gregory had recoiled. He simultaneously excommunicated several sovereigns and mercilessly persecuted the archbishops and bishops who were hostile to reform. He took no pains to temper the zeal of his legates, but incited them to the struggle, and, not content with prohibiting lay investiture and simony, expressly forbade prelates and even priests to pay homage to the civil power. Distrusting the secular clergy, who were wholly sunk in the *Reform of the Church.* world, he looked to the regular clergy for support, and thus led the papacy into that course which it continued to pursue after his death. Henceforth the monk was to be the docile instrument of the wishes of Rome, to be

opposed to the official priesthood according to Rome's needs. Urban was the first to proclaim with emphasis the necessity of a close association of the Curia with the religious orders, and this he made the essential basis of the theocratic government. As the originator of the first crusade, Urban is entitled to the honour of the idea and its execution. There is no doubt that he wished to satisfy the complaints that emanated from the Christians dwelling in Jerusalem and from the pilgrims to the Holy Sepulchre, but it is no less certain that he was disturbed by the fears aroused throughout the Latin world by the recrudescence of Mussulman invasions, and particularly by the victory won by the Almoravides over the Christian army at Zalaca (1086). The progress of these African Mussulmans into Spain and their incessant piracies in Italy were perhaps the occasional cause that determined Urban II. to work upon the imagination of the infidels by an expedition into Syria. The papacy of that time believed in the political unity of Islam, in a solidarity —which did not exist—among the Mussulmans of Asia Minor, Syria, Egypt and the Barbary coasts; and if it waited until the year 1095 to carry out this project, it was because the conflict with the Germanic Empire prevented the earlier realization of its dream. The essential reason of Urban II.'s action, and consequently the true cause of the crusade, was the ambition of the pope to unite with Rome and the Roman Church the Churches of Jerusalem, Antioch, Alexandria and even Constantinople, which the Greek schism had rendered independent. This thought had already crossed the minds of Leo IX. and Gregory VII., but circumstances had never allowed them to put it into execution. Armed by the reformation with a moral authority which made it possible to concentrate the forces of the West under the supreme direction of the Church and its leaders, Urban II. addressed himself with his customary decision to the execution of this enormous enterprise. With him, as with all his successors, the idea of a collective expedition of Europe for the recovery of the Holy Places was always associated with the sanguine hope of extinguishing the schism at Constantinople, its very centre, by the substitution of a Latin for a Byzantine domination. Of these two objects, he was only to realize the former; but the crusade may well be said to have been his own work. He created it and preached it; he organized it, dominated it, and constantly supervised it. He was ever ready to act, either personally or through his delegates, and never ceased to be the effective leader of all the feudal soldiers he enrolled under the banner of the Holy See. He corresponded perpetually with his legates and with the military leaders, who kept him accurately informed of the position of the troops and the progress of the operations. He acted as intermediary between the soldiers of Christ and their brothers who remained in Europe, announcing successes, organizing fresh expeditions, and spurring the laggards to take the road to Jerusalem.

The vast conflict aroused by the Hildebrandine reformation, and particularly the investiture conflict, continued under the three successors of Urban II.; but with them it assumed a different character, and a tendency arose to terminate it by other means. The violence and disorders provoked by the struggle brought about a reaction, which was organized by certain prelates who advocated a policy of conciliation, such as the Frenchman Ivo, bishop of Chartres (c. 1040-1116). These conciliatory prelates were sincere supporters of the reformation, and combated simony, the marriage or concubinage of priests, and the immorality of sovereigns with the same conviction as the most ardent followers of Gregory VII. and Urban II.; but they held that the intimate union of Church and State was indispensable to the social order, and that the rights of kings should be respected as well as the rights of priests. The text they preached was harmony between the priesthood and the state. Dividing what the irreconcilables of the Hildebrandine party considered as an indissoluble whole, they made a sharp distinction between the property of the Church and the Church itself, between the political and territorial power of the bishops and their religious authority,

and between the feudal investiture which confers lands and jurisdiction and the spiritual investiture which confers ecclesiastical rights. This doctrine gradually rallied all moderate minds, and finally inspired the directors of Christendom in Rome itself. It explains the new attitude of Paschal II. and Calixtus II., who were both sincere reformers, but who sought in a policy of compromise the solution of the difficult problem of the relations of Church and State.

History has not done sufficient justice to the Italian monk Paschal II., who was the equal of Urban in private virtues, personal disinterestedness, and religious conviction, but was surpassed by him in ardour and rigidity of conduct. Altered circumstances and tendencies of opinion called for a policy of conciliation. In France, Paschal granted absolution to Philip I.—who had many times been anathematized by his predecessors—and reconciled him solemnly with the Church, on the sole condition that he should swear to renounce his adulterous marriage. The pope could be under no delusion as to the value of this oath, which indeed was not kept; he merely regularized formally a state of affairs which the intractable Urban II. himself had never been able to prevent. As for the French question of the investitures, it was settled apparently without any treaty being expressly drawn up between the parties. The kings of France contemporary with Paschal II. ceased to practice spiritual investiture, or even to receive feudal homage from the bishops. They did not, however, renounce all intervention or all profit in the nominations to prelacies, but their intervention was no longer exhibited under the forms which the Hildebrandine party held to be illegal. In England, Paschal II. put an end to the long quarrel between the royal government and Anselm of Canterbury by accepting the Concordat of London (1107). The crown in England also abandoned investiture by the pastoral staff and ring, but, more fortunate than in France, retained the right of receiving feudal homage from the episcopate. As for Germany, the Emperor Henry V. wrung from the pope, by a display of force at Rome, concessions which provoked the indignant clamours of the most ardent reformers in France and Italy. It must not, however, be forgotten that, in the negotiations at Sutri, Paschal had pride and independence enough to propose to the emperor the only solution of the conflict that was entirely logical and essentially Christian, namely, the renunciation by the Church of its temporal power and the renunciation by the lay lords of all intervention in elections and investitures—in other words, the absolute separation of the priesthood and the state. The idea was contrary to the whole evolution of medieval Catholicism, and the German bishops were the first to repudiate it. At all events, it is certain that Paschal II. prepared the way for the Concordat of Worms. On the other hand, with more acuteness than his predecessors, he realized that the papacy could not sustain the struggle against Germany unless it could rely upon the support of another Christian kingdom of the West; and he concluded with Philip I. of France and Louis the Fat, at the Council of Troyes (1107), an alliance which was for more than a century the salvation of the court of Rome. It is from this time that we find the popes in moments of crisis transporting themselves to Capetian territory, installing their governments and convening their councils there, and from that place of refuge fulminating with impunity against the internal and external foe. Without sacrificing the essential principles of the reformation, Paschal II. practised a policy of peace and reaction in every way contrary to that of the two preceding popes, and it was which him that the struggle was once more placed upon the religious basis. He refused to retain Hugo, bishop of Die (d. 1106), as legate; like Urban and Gregory, he gave or confirmed monastic privileges without the protection he granted to the monks assuming a character of hostility towards the episcopate; and, finally, he gave an impulse to the reformation of the chapters, and, unlike Urban II., maintained the rights of the canons against the claims of the abbots.

Guy, the archbishop of Vienne, who had been one of the

keenest to disavow the policy of Paschal II., was obliged to continue it when he assumed the tiara under the name of **Calixtus II.** By the Concordat of Worms, which he signed with the Emperor Henry V. in 1122, the investiture was divided between the ecclesiastical and the lay powers, the emperor investing with the sceptre, the pope with the pastoral staff and ring. The work did honour to the perseverance and ability of Calixtus, but it was merely the application of the ideas of Paschal II. and Ivo of Chartres. The understanding, however, between the two contracting parties was very far from being clear and complete, as each party still sought to attain its own aim by spreading in the Christian world divergent interpretations of the concordat and widely-differing plans for reducing it to its final form. And, again, if this transaction settled the investiture question, it did not solve the problem of the reconciliation of the universal power of the popes with the claims of the emperors to the government of Europe; and the conflict subsisted—slumbering, it is true, but ever ready to awake under other forms. Nevertheless, the two great Christian agitations directed by the papacy at the end of the 11th century and the beginning of the 12th—the reformation and the crusade—were of capital importance for the foundation of the immense religious monarchy that had its centre in Rome; and it is from this period that the papal monarchy actually dates.

The entry of the Christians into Jerusalem produced an extraordinary effect upon the faithful of the West. In it they *Effect of the* saw the most manifest sign of the divine protection *Latin* and of the supernatural power of the pope, the *Conquest of* supreme director of the expedition. At its inception *Jerusalem.* the Latin kingdom of the Holy Land was within a little of becoming an ecclesiastical principality, ruled by a patriarch under the authority of the pope. Daimbert, the first patriarch of Jerusalem, was convinced that the Roman Church alone could be sovereign of the new state, and attempted to compel Godfrey of Bouillon to hand over to him by a solemn agreement the town and citadel of Jerusalem, and also Jaffa. The clergy, indeed, received a large share; but the government of the Latin principality remained lay and military, the only form of government possible for a colony surrounded by perils and camped in a hostile country. Not only was the result of the crusade extremely favourable to the extension of the Roman power, but throughout the middle ages the papacy never ceased to derive almost incalculable political and financial advantages from the agitation produced by the preachers and the crusading expeditions. The mere fact of the crusaders being placed under the special protection of the Church and the pope, and loaded with privileges, freed them from the jurisdiction, and even, up to a certain point, from the lordship of their natural masters, to become the almost direct subjects of the papacy; and the common law was then practically suspended for the benefit of the Church and the leader who represented it.

As for the reformation, which under Urban II. and his immediate successors was aimed not only at the episcopate *Subordina-* but also at the capitulary bodies and monastic *tion of the* clergy, it, too, could but tend to a consider- *Episcopate* able extension of the authority of the successors of *to the Papal* St Peter, for it struck an irremediable blow at *Monarchy.* the ancient Christian hierarchy. The first manifest result of the change was the weakening of the metropolitans. The visible symptom of this decadence of the archiepiscopal power was the growing frequency during the Hildebrandine conflict of episcopal confirmations and consecrations made by the popes themselves or their legates. From an active instrument of the religious society, the archiepiscopate degenerated into a purely formal power; while the episcopate itself, which the sincere reformers wished to liberate and purge in order to strengthen it, emerged from the crisis sensibly weakened as well as ameliorated. The episcopate, while it gained in intelligence and morality, lost a part of its independence. It was raised above feudalism only to be abased before the two directing forces of the reformation, the papacy and the religious orders.

To place itself in a better posture for combating the simoniacal and concubinary prelates, the court of Rome had had to multiply exemptions and accelerate the movement which impelled the monks to make themselves independent of the bishops. Even in the cities, the seats of the episcopal power, the reformation encouraged the attempts at revolt or autonomy which tended everywhere to diminish that power. The cathedral chapters took advantage of this situation to oppose their jurisdiction to that of the bishops, and to encroach on their prerogatives. When war was declared on the schismatic prelates, the reforming popes supported the canons, and, unconsciously or not, helped them to form themselves into privileged bodies living their own lives and affecting to recognize the court of Rome as their only superior authority. Other adversaries of the episcopate, the burgesses and the petty nobles dwelling in the city, also profited by these frequent changes of bishops, and the disorders that ensued. It was the monarchy of the bishops of Rome that naturally benefited by these attacks on the aristocratic principle represented by the high prelacies in the Church. By drawing to their side all the forces of the ecclesiastical body to combat feudalism, Urban II. and his successors, with their monks and legates, changed the constitution of that body, and changed it to their own advantage. The new situation of these popes and the growth of their authority were also manifested in the material organization of their administration and chancery. Under Urban II. the formulary of the papal bulls began to crystallize, and the letters amassed in the papal offices were differentiated clearly into great and little bulls, according to their style, arrangement and signs of validation. Under Paschal II. the type of the leaden seal affixed to the bulls (representing the heads of the apostles Peter and Paul) was fixed, and the use of Roman minuscule finally substituted for that of the Lombard script.

2. *Period from Honorius II. to Celestine III. (1124-1198).*— After the reformation and the crusade the papal monarchy existed, and the next step was to consolidate and extend it. This task fell to the popes of the 12th century. Two of them in particular—the two who had the longest reigns—viz. Innocent II. and Alexander III., achieved the widest extension of the power entrusted to them, and in many respects their pontificates may be regarded as a preparation for and adumbration of the pontificate of Innocent III. This period, however, is characterized not only by the thoroughgoing development of the authority of the Holy See, but also by the severe struggle the popes had to sustain against the hostile forces that were opposed to their conquests or to the mere exercise of what they regarded as their right.

In the secular contest, Germany and the imperialist pretensions of its leaders were invariably the principal *The Papacy* obstacle. Until the accession of Adrian IV., how- *and the* ever, there had been considerable periods of tran- *German* quillity; years even of unbroken peace and alliance *Emperors.* with the Germanic power. Under Honorius II. the empire, represented by Lothair III. of Supplinburg, yielded to the papacy, and Lothair, who was elected by the clergy *Honorius II.* and protected by the legates, begged the pope to *1124-1130.* confirm his election. Before his coronation he had renounced the right, so jealously guarded by Henry V., of assisting in the election of bishops and abbots, and he even undertook to refrain from exacting homage from the prelates and to content himself with fealty. This undertaking, however, did not prevent him from bringing all his influence to bear upon the ecclesiastical nominations. When the schism of 1130 broke out he endeavoured to procure the cancellation of the clauses of the Concordat of Worms and to recover lay investiture by way of compensation for the support he had given to Innocent II., one of the competing popes. This scheme, however, was frustrated by the firmness of Innocent and St Bernard, and Lothair had to resign himself to the zealous conservation of the privileges granted to the Empire by the terms of the concordat. The ardour he had displayed in securing the recognition of Innocent and defending him against his enemies, particularly the anti-pope

Anacletus and the kingdom of the Two Sicilies, involved him in a course which was not precisely favourable to the imperial rights. Innocent II. was the virtual master of this *Innocent II.* monarch, whose championship of the papacy brought *1130-1143.* not the smallest advantage, not even that of being crowned emperor with the habitual ceremonial at the place consecrated by tradition. It may even be maintained that his elevation was due solely to his personal claims. This was a victory for Rome, and it was repeated in the case of the first Hohenstaufen, Conrad III., who owed his elevation (1138) mainly to the princes of the Church and the legate of Innocent II., by whom he was crowned. He also had to submit to the consequences of his origin on the occasion of a double election not foreseen by the Concordat of Worms, when he was forced to admit the necessity of appeal to Rome and to acknowledge the supremacy of the papal decision. The situation changed *Eugenius* In 1152, under Eugenius III., when Frederick *III.* Barbarossa was elected German king. He notified *1145-1153.* his election to the pope, but did not seek the pope's approval. None the less, Eugenius III. felicitated the new sovereign on his election, and even signed the treaty of Constance with him (1153). The pope had need of Frederick to defend him against the revolted Romans and to help him to recover his temporal power, which had been gravely compromised. Anastasius IV. pursued the same policy, and *Anasta-* summoned the German to Rome (1154). Frederick, *sius IV.,* however, was determined to keep the seat of the *1153-1154.* Empire for himself, to dispute Italy with the pope, and to oppose the divine right of kings to the divine right of priests. When he had taken Lombardy (1158) and had had the principles of the imperial supremacy proclaimed by his jurists at the diet of Roncaglia, the court of Rome realized that war was inevitable, and two ener- *Adrian IV.,* getic popes, Adrian IV. and Alexander III., reso- *1154-1189.* lutely sustained the struggle, the latter for nearly twenty years. Victims of the communal claims at Rome, they constituted themselves the champions of similar claims in northern Italy, and their alliance with the Lombard communes ultimately led to success. In his duel with Barba- *Alexan-* rossa, Alexander III., one of the greatest of medieval *der III.,* popes, displayed extraordinary courage, address and *1159-1181.* perseverance. Although it must be admitted that the tenacity of the Lombard republics contributed powerfully to the pope's victory, and that the triumph of the Milanese at Legnano (1176) was the determining cause of Frederick's submission at Venice, yet we must not exaggerate the importance of the solemn act by which Barbarossa, kneeling before his conqueror, recognized the spiritual supremacy of the Holy See, and swore fidelity and respect to it. In its final form, the truce of Venice was not only not unfavourable secularly to the Empire, but even granted it very extensive advantages. Nor must it be forgotten that, in the eyes of contemporaries, the scene at Venice had none of that humiliating character which later historians have attributed to it.

This was not the only success gained by Alexander III. over lay sovereigns. The conflict of the priesthood with the kingdoms *Alexander* and nations that were tending to aggrandize them- *III. and* selves by transcending the religious limits of the *Henry II.* medieval theocracy took place on another theatre. *of England.* The affair of Thomas Becket (q.v.) involved the papacy in a quarrel with the powerful monarchy of the Angevins, whose representative, Henry II., was master of England and of the half of France. Alexander's diplomatic skill and moral authority, reinforced by the Capetian alliance and the revulsion of feeling caused by the murder of Becket, enabled him to force the despotic Henry to yield, and even to do penance at the tomb of the martyr. The Plantagenet abjured the Constitutions of Clarendon, recognized the rights of the pope over the Church of England, and augmented the privileges and domains of the archbishopric of Canterbury. Although Becket was a man of narrow sympathies and by no means of liberal views, he had died for the liberties of his caste, and the aureole

that surrounded him enhanced the prestige and ascendancy of the papacy.

Unfortunately for the papacy, the successors of Alexander III. lacked vigour, and their pontificates were too brief to allow them to pursue a strong policy against the Germanic *The Papacy* imperialism. Never were the leaders of the Church *and the* in such jeopardy as during the reign of Barbarossa's *Emperor* son, Henry VI. This vigorous despot, whose ambi- *Henry VI.* tions were not all chimerical, had succeeded where his predecessors, including Frederick, had failed. His marriage with the heiress of the old Norman kings had made him master of Sicily and the duchy of Apulia and Calabria, and he succeeded in conquering and retaining almost all the remainder of the peninsula. Under Celestine III. the papal state was surrounded on every side by German soldiers, and but for the premature death of the emperor, whom Abbot Joachim of Floris called the "hammer of the world," the temporal power of the popes might perhaps have been annihilated.

The Norman kingdom, which had conquered Sicily and southern Italy at the end of the 11th century, was almost as grave a source of anxiety to the popes of this period. *The Papacy* Not only was its very existence an obstacle to the *and the* spread of their temporal power in the peninsula, *Norman* but it frequently acted in concert with the pope's *Kingdom* enemies and thwarted the papal policy. The *in South* attempts of Honorius II. (1128) and Innocent II. *Italy.* (1130) to wrest Apulia and Calabria from King Roger II., and Adrian IV.'s war with William I. (1156), were one and all unsuccessful; and the papacy had to content itself with the vassalage and tribute of the Normans, and allowed them to organize the ecclesiastical government of their domains in their own fashion, to limit the right of appeal to Rome, and to curtail the power of the Roman legates. At this period, moreover, the "Norman Question" was intimately connected with the "Eastern Question." The Norman adventurers in possession of Palermo and Naples perpetually tended to look for their aggrandizement to the Byzantine Empire. In the interests of their temporal dominion, the 12th-century popes could not suffer an Italian power to dominate on the other side of the Adriatic and instal itself at Constantinople. This contingency explains the vacillating and illogical character of the papal diplomacy with regard to the Byzantine problem, and, *inter alia*, the opposition of Eugenius III. in 1150 to Roger II.'s projected crusade, which was directed towards the conquest of the Greek state. The popes were under the constant sway of two contrary influences—on the one hand, the seducing prospect of subduing the Eastern Church and triumphing over the schism, and, on the other, the apprehension of seeing the Normans of Sicily, their competitors in Italy, increasing their already formidable power by successful expeditions into the Balkan Peninsula. Dread of the Normans, too, explains the singular attitude of the Curia towards the Comneni, of whom it was alternately the enemy and the protector or ally.

But, as regards its temporal aims on Italy, the most inconvenient and tenacious, if not the most dangerous, adversary of the 12th-century papacy was the Roman commune. *The Papacy* Since the middle of the 11th century the party of *and the* municipal autonomy and, indeed, the whole of the *Commune* European middle classes, who wished to shake off *of Rome.* the feudal yoke and secure independence, had been ranged against the successor of St Peter. The first symptoms of resistance were exhibited under Innocent II. (1142), who was unable to stem the growing revolution or prevent the establishment of a Roman senate sitting in the Capitol. The strength of classical reminiscence and the instinct of liberty were reinforced by the support given to communal aspirations by the popular agitator and dangerous tribune, Arnold of *Arnold of* Brescia (q.v.), whose theories arrived at an opportune *Brescia.* moment to encourage the revolted commons. He denied the power of clerks to possess fiefs, and allowed them only religious authority and tithes. The successors of Innocent II. were even less successful in maintaining their supremacy in

Rome. Lucius II., when called upon to renounce all his regalian rights, fell mortally wounded in an attempt to drive the autonomists by force from the Capitol (1145). Under Eugenius III. the Romans sacked and destroyed the houses of the clerks and cardinals, besieged St Peter's and the Lateran, and massacred the pilgrims. The pope was forced to fly with the Sacred College, to escape the necessity of recognizing the commune, and thus left the field free to Arnold of Brescia (1145). On his return to Rome, Eugenius had to treat with his rebel subjects and to acknowledge the senate they had elected, but he was unable to procure the expulsion of the agitator. The more energetic Adrian IV. refused to truckle to the municipality, placed it under an interdict (1155), and allied himself with Frederick Barbarossa to quell an insurrection which respected the rights of emperors no more than the rights of popes. From the moment that Arnold of Brescia, absorbed in his chimerical project of reviving the ancient Roman republic, disregarded the imperial power and neglected to shelter himself behind the German in his conflict with the priesthood, his failure was certain and his fate foredoomed. He was hanged and burned, probably in pursuance of the secret agreement between the pope and the emperor; and Adrian IV. was reconciled with the Romans (1156). The commune, however, subsisted, and was on several occasions strong enough to eject the masters who were distasteful to it. Unfortunately for Alexander III. the Roman question was complicated during his pontificate with the desperate struggle with the Empire. The populace of the Tiber welcomed and expelled him with equal enthusiasm, and when his body was brought back from exile, the mob went before the cortège and threw mud and stones upon the funeral litter. All obeyed the pontiff of Rome—save Rome itself. Lucius III., who was pope for four years (1181–1185), remained in Rome four months, while Urban III. and Gregory VIII. never entered the city. At length the two parties grew weary of this state of revolution, and a régime of conciliation, the fruit of mutual concessions, was established under Clement III. By the act of 1188, the fundamental charter of the Roman commune, the people recognized the supremacy of the pope over the senate and the town, while the pope on his part sanctioned the legal existence of the commune and of its government and assemblies. Inasmuch as Clement was compelled to make terms with this new power which had established itself against him in the very centre of his dominion, the victory may fairly be said to have rested with the commune.

Although, among other obstacles, the popes of the 12th century had experienced some difficulty in subduing the inhabitants of the city, which was the seat and centre of the Christian world, their monarchy did not cease to gain in authority, solidity and prestige, and the work of centralization, which was gradually making them masters of the whole ecclesiastical organism, was accomplished steadily and without serious interruption. If Rome expelled them, they always found a sure refuge in France, where Alexander III. carried on his government for several years; and the whole of Europe acknowledged their immense power. Under Honorius II. the custom prevailed of substituting legates a latere, simple priests or deacons of the Curia, for the regionary delegates, who had grown too independent; and that excellent instrument of rule, the Roman legate, carried the papal will into the remotest courts of Europe. The episcopate and the great monastic prelacies continued to lose their independence, as was shown by Honorius II. deputing a cardinal to Monte Cassino to elect an abbot of his choosing. The progress of the Roman power was especially manifested under Innocent II., who had triumphed over the schism, and was supported by the Empire and by Bernard of Clairvaux, the first moral authority of his time. He suspended an archbishop of Sens (1136) who had neglected to take into consideration the appeal to Rome, summoned an archbishop of Milan to Rome to receive the pallium from the pope's hands, lavished exemptions, and extended the right of appeal to such abnormal lengths that a Byzantine ambassador is reported to have exclaimed to Lothair III.,

Develop-ment of the Centralized Organization.

"Your Pope Innocent is not a bishop, but an emperor." When the universal Church assembled at the second Lateran Council (1139), this leader of religion declared to the bishops that he was the absolute master of Christendom. "Ye know," he said, "that Rome is the capital of the world, that ye hold your dignities of the Roman pontiff as a vassal holds his fiefs of his sovereign, and that ye cannot retain them without his assent." Under Eugenius III., a Cistercian monk who was scarcely equal to his task, the papal absolutism grew sensibly weaker, and if we may credit the testimony of the usually well-informed German chronicler, Otto of Freising, there arose in the college of cardinals a kind of fermentation which was exceedingly disquieting for the personal power of the leader of the Church. In the case of a difference of opinion between Eugenius and the Sacred College, Otto relates that the cardinals addressed to the pope this astounding protest: "Thou must know that it is by us thou hast been raised to the supreme dignity. We are the hinges (cardines) upon which the universal Church rests and moves. It is through us that from a private person thou hast become the father of all Christians. It is, then, no longer to thyself but rather to us that thou belongest henceforth. Thou must not sacrifice to private and recent friendships the traditional affections of the papacy. Perforce thou must consult before everything the general interest of Christendom, and must consider it an obligation of thine office to respect the opinions of the highest dignitaries of the court of Rome." If we admit that the cardinals of Eugenius III. succeeded in restricting the omnipotence of their master for their own ends, it must invariably have been the Curia that dictated its wishes to the Church and to Europe. The papacy, however, recovered its ascendancy during the pontificate of Alexander III., and seemed more powerful than ever. The recently created royalties sought from the papacy the conservation of their titles and the benediction of their crowns, and placed themselves voluntarily in its vassalage. The practice of the nomination of bishops by the Curia and of papal recommendation to prebends and benefices of every kind grew daily more general, and the number of appeals to Rome and exemptions granted to abbeys and even to simple churches increased continually. The third Lateran Council (1179) was a triumph for the leader of the Church. At that council wise and urgent measures were taken against the abuses that discredited the priesthood, but the principle of appeals and exemptions and the question of the increasing abuse of the power wielded by the Roman legates remained untouched. The treatise on canon law known as the Decretum Gratiani, which was compiled towards the middle of the 12th century and had an enduring and far-reaching effect (see CANON LAW), merely gave theoretical sanction to the existing situation in the Church. It propagated doctrines in favour of the power of the Holy See, established the superiority of the popes over the councils, and gave legal force to their decretals. According to its author, "they (the popes) are above all the laws of the Church, and can use them according to their wish; they alone judge and cannot be judged."

It was by its constant reliance on monachism that the papacy of the 12th century had attained this result, and the popes of that period were especially fortunate in having for their champion the monk St Bernard, whose admirable qualities enabled him to dominate public opinion. St Bernard completed the reformation, combated heresy, and by his immense moral ascendancy gained victories by which Rome benefited. As instances of his more direct services, he put an end to the schism of 1130 and attached Italy and the world to the side of Innocent III. Although he had saved the papal institution from one of the gravest perils it had ever encountered, the cardinals, the court of Rome and Innocent himself could not easily pardon him for being what he had become—a private person more powerful in the Church than the pope and the bishops, and holding that power by his personal prestige. He incurred their special reproaches by his condemnation of the irresistible evolution which impelled Rome to desire exclusive dominion over Catholic Europe and to devote

Influence of Bernard of Clairvaux.

her attention to earthly things. He did not condemn the temporal power of the popes in plain terms, but both his writings and his conduct proved that that power was in his opinion difficult to reconcile with the spiritual mission of the papacy, and was, moreover, a menace to the future of the institution. (See BERNARD, SAINT.)

At the very moment when the papacy thus attained omnipotence, symptoms of discontent and opposition arose. The bishops resisted centralization. Archbishop Hildebert of Tours protested to Honorius II. against the appeals to Rome, while others complained of the exactions of the legates, or, like John of Salisbury, animadverted upon the excessive powers of the bureaucracy at the Lateran. In the councils strange speeches were heard from the mouths of laymen, who were beginning to carry to extreme lengths the spirit of independence with regard to Rome. When a question arose at Toulouse in 1160 as to the best means of settling the papal schism, this audacious statement was made before the kings of France and England: " That the best course was to side with neither of the two popes; that the apostolic see had been ever a burden to the princes; that advantage must be taken of the schism to throw off the yoke; and that, while awaiting the death of one of the competitors, the authority of the bishops was sufficient in France and England alike for the government of the churches." The ecclesiastics themselves, however, were the first to denounce the abuses at Rome. The treatises of Gerboh of Reichersberg (1093-1160) abound in trenchant attacks upon the greed and venality of the Curia, the arrogance and extortion of the legates, the abuse of exemptions and appeals, and the German policy of Adrian IV. and Alexander III. In his efforts to make the papal institution entirely worthy of its mission St Bernard himself did not shrink from presenting to the papacy " the mirror in which it could recognize its deformities." In common with all enlightened opinion, he complained bitterly of the excessive multiplication of exemptions, of the exaggerated extension of appeals to Rome, of the luxury of the Roman court, of the venality of the cardinals, and of the injury done to the traditional hierarchy by the very extent of the papal power, which was calculated to turn the strongest head. In St Bernard's treatise De considerationc, addressed to Pope Eugenius III., the papacy receives as many reprimands and attacks as it does marks of affection and friendly counsel. To warn Eugenius against pride, Bernard reminds him in biblical terms that an insensate sovereign on a throne resembles " an ape upon a housetop," and that the dignity with which he is invested does not prevent him from being a man, that is, " a being, naked, poor, miserable, made for toil and not for honours." To his thinking, poison and the dagger were less to be feared by the pope than the lust of power. Ambition and cupidity were the source of the most deplorable abuses in the Roman Church,. The cardinals, said Bernard, were satraps who put pomp before the truth. He was at a loss to justify the unheard-of luxury of the Roman court. " I do not find," he said, " that St Peter ever appeared in public loaded with gold and jewels, clad in silk, mounted on a white mule, surrounded by soldiers and followed by a brilliant retinue. In the glitter that environs thee, rather wouldst thou be taken for the successor of Constantine than for the successor of Peter,"

Rome, however, had greater dangers to cope with than the indignant reproofs of her friends the monks, and the opposition of the bishops, who were displeased at the spectacle of their authority waning day by day. It was at this period that the Catholic edifice of the middle ages began to be shaken by the boldness of philosophical speculation as applied to theological studies and also by the growth of heresy. Hitherto more tolerant of heresy than the local authorities, the papacy no felt compelled to take defensive measures against it, and especially against Albigensianism, which had made great strides in the south of France since the middle of the 12th century. Innocent II., Eugenius III. and Alexander III. excommunicated the sectaries of Languedoc and their abettors, Alexander even sending armed missions to

hunt them down and punish them. But the preaching of the papal legates, even when supported by military demonstrations, had no effect; and the Albigensian question, together with other questions vital for the future of the papacy, remained unsettled and more formidable than ever when Innocent III. was elected.

3. Period from Innocent III. to Alexander IV. (1198-1261).— Under the pontificates of Innocent III. and his five immediate successors the Roman monarchy seemed to have reached the pinnacle of its moral prestige, religious authority and temporal power, and this development was due in great measure to Innocent III. himself. Between the perhaps excessive admiration of Innocent's biographer, Friedrich von Hurter, and the cooler estimate of a later historian, Félix Rocquain, who, after taking into consideration Innocent's political mistakes, lack of foresight and numerous disappointments and failures, concludes that his reputation has been much exaggerated, it is possible to steer a middle course and form a judgment that is at once impartial and conformable to the historical facts. Innocent was an eminent jurist and canonist,' and never ceased to use his immense power in the service of the law. Indeed, a great part of his life was passed in hearing pleadings and pronouncing judgments, and few sovereigns have ever worked so industriously or shown such solicitude for the impartial exercise of their judicial functions. It is difficult to comprehend Innocent's extraordinary activity. Over and above the weight of political affairs, he bore resolutely for eighteen years the overwhelming burden of the presidency of a tribunal before which the whole of Europe came to plead. To him, also, in his capacity of theologian, the whole of Europe submitted every obscure, delicate or controverted question, whether legal problem or case of conscience. This, undoubtedly, was the part of his task that Innocent preferred, and it was to this, as well as to his much overrated moral and theological treatises, that he owed his enormous contemporary prestige. As a statesman, he certainly committed grave faults—through excess of diplomatic subtlety, lack of forethought, and sometimes even through ingenuousness; but it must with justice be admitted that, in spite of his reputation for pugnacity and obstinacy, he never failed, either by temperament or on principle, to exhaust every peaceful expedient in settling questions. He was averse from violence, and never resorted to bellicose acts or to the employment of force save in the last extremity. If his policy miscarried in several quarters it was eminently successful in others; and if we consider the sum of his efforts to achieve the programme of the medieval papacy, it cannot be denied that the extent of his rule and the profound influence he exerted on his times entitle him to be regarded as the most perfect type of medieval pope and one of the most powerful figures in history. .

A superficial glance at Innocent's correspondence is sufficient to convince us that he was pre-eminently concerned for the reformation and moral welfare of the Church, and was animated by the best intentions for the re-establishment in the ecclesiastical body of order, peace and respect for the hierarchy. This was one of the principal objects of his activity, and this important side of his work received decisive sanction by the promulgation of the decrees of the fourth Lateran Council (1215). At this council almost all the questions at issue related to reform, and many give evidence of great breadth of mind, as well as of a very acute sense of contemporary necessities. Innocent's letters, however, not only reveal that superior wisdom which can take into account practical needs and relax severity of principle at the right moment, as well as that spirit of tolerance and equity which is opposed to the excess of zeal and intellectual narrowness of subordinates, but they also prove that, in the internal government of the Church, he was bent on gathering into his hands all .the. motive threads, and that he stretched the absolutist tradition to its furthest limits, intervening in the most trifling acts in the lives of the clergy, and regarding it as an obligation of his office to act and think for all. The heretic peril, which increased during his pontificate, forced him to take decisive measures against the Albigenses in the south of France, but before proscribing them he spent ten years (1198-1208) in endeavouring to convert the misbelievers, and history should not forget the pacific character of these early efforts. It *The Albigensian Crusade* was because they did not succeed that necessity and the violence of human passions subsequently forced him into a course of action which he had not chosen and which led him further than he wished to go. When he was compelled to decree the Albigensian crusade he endeavoured more than once to discontinue the work, which had become perverted, and to curb the crusading ardour of Simon de Montfort. Failing in his attempt to maintain the religious character of the crusade, he wished to prevent it from ending secularly in its extreme consequence and logical outcome. On several occasions he defended the cause of moderation and justice against the fanatical crusaders, but he never had the energy to make it prevail. It is very doubtful whether this was possible, and an impartial historian must take into account the insuperable difficulties encountered by the medieval popes in their efforts to stem the flood of fanaticism.

It was more particularly in the definitive constitution of the temporal and political power of the papacy, in the extension of *Papal Imperialism under Innocent III.* what may be called Roman imperialism, that chance favoured his efforts and enabled him to pursue his conquests farthest. This imperialism was undoubtedly of a special nature; it rested on moral authority and political and financial power rather than on material and military strength. But it is no less certain that Innocent attempted to subject the kings of Europe by making them his tributaries and vassals. He wished to acquire the mastery of souls by unifying the faith and centralizing the priesthood, but he also aspired to possess temporal supremacy, if not as direct owner, at least as suzerain, over all the national crowns, and thus to realize the idea with which he was penetrated and which he himself expressed clearly. He wished to be at once pope and emperor, leader of religion and universal sovereign. And, in fact, he exercised or claimed suzerain rights, together with the political and pecuniary advantages accruing, over the greater number of the lay sovereigns of his time. He was more or less effectively the supreme temporal chief of the kingdom of Sicily and Naples, Sardinia, the states of the Iberian peninsula (Castile, Leon, Navarre and Portugal), Aragon (which, under Peter II., was the type of vassal and tributary kingdom of the Roman power), the Scandinavian states, the kingdom of Hungary, the Slav states of Bohemia, Poland, Servia, Bosnia and Bulgaria, and the Christian states founded in Syria by the crusaders of the 13th century. The success of Roman imperialism was particularly remarkable in England, where Innocent was confronted by one of the principal potentates of the West, by the heir of the power that had been founded by two statesmen of the first rank, William the Conqueror and Henry II. In Richard I. and John he had exceptionally authoritative adversaries, but after one of the fiercest wars ever waged by the civil power against the Church, Innocent at length gained over John the most complete victory that has ever been won by a religious potentate over a temporal sovereign, and constrained him to *Innocent III.* make complete submission. In 1213 the pope *and John of England.* became not only the nominal suzerain but, *de facto* and *de jure*, the veritable sovereign of England, and during the last years of John and the first years of Henry III. he governed England effectively by his legates. This was the most striking success of Innocent's diplomacy and the culminating point of his secular work.

The papacy, however, encountered serious obstacles, at first at the very centre of the papal empire, at Rome, where the pope had to contend with the party of communal autonomy for ten years before being able to secure the mastery at Rome. His *Innocent III.* immense authority narrowly escaped destruction *Rome and Italy.* but a stone's-throw from the Lateran palace; but the victory finally rested with him, since the Roman people could not dispense with the Roman Church, to which it owed its existence. Reared in the nurture of the pope, the populace of the Tiber renounced its stormy liberty in 1209,

and accepted the peace and order that a beneficent master gave; but when Innocent attempted to extend to the whole of Italy the régime of paternal subjection that had been so successful at Rome, the difficulties of the enterprise surpassed the powers even of a leader of religion. He succeeded in imposing his will on the nobles and communes in the patrimony of St Peter, and, as guardian of Henry VI.'s son Frederick, was for some time able to conduct the government of the kingdom of the Two Sicilies, but in his claims on the rest of Italy the failure of the temporal power was manifest. He was unable, either by diplomacy or force of arms, to make Italian unity redound to the exclusive benefit of the Holy See. Nor was his failure due to lack of activity or energy, but rather to the insuperable obstacles in his path—the physical configuration of Italy, and, above all, the invincible repugnance of the Italian municipalities to submit to the mastery of a religious power.

As far as the Empire was concerned, chance at first favoured Innocent. For ten years a Germany weakened and divided by the rivalry of Philip of Swabia and Otto of Brunswick *Innocent III.* left his hands free to act in Italy, and his pontificate *and the Empire.* marks a period of comparative quiet in the ardent conflict between pope and emperor which continued throughout the middle ages. Not until 1210, when Otto of Brunswick turned against the pope to whom he owed his crown, was Innocent compelled to open hostilities; and the struggle ended in a victory for the Curia. Frederick II., the new emperor created by Innocent, began by handing over his country to Rome and sacrificing the rights of the Empire to the union of the two great authorities of the Christian world. In his dealings with Frederick, Innocent experienced grievous vicissitudes and disappointments, but finally became master of the situation. One nation only—the France of Philip Augustus—was able to remain outside the Roman vassalage. There is not a word, in the documents concerning the relations of Philip Augustus with Rome, from which we may conclude that the Capetian crown submitted, or that the papacy wished to impose upon it the effective suzerainty of the Holy See. Innocent III. had been able to encroach on France at one point only, when the Albigensian crusade had enabled him to exercise over the southern fiefs conquered by Simon de Montfort a political and secular supremacy in the form of collections of moneys. Finally, Innocent III. was more fortunate than his predecessors, and, if he did not succeed in carrying out his projected crusade and recovering the Holy Places, he at least benefited by the Franco-Venetian expedition of 1202. Europe refused to take any direct action against the Mussulman, but Latin feudalism, assembled at Venice, diverted the crusade by an act *question of Constantinople.* of formal disobedience, marched on Constantinople, seized the Greek Empire and founded a Latin Empire in its place; and Innocent had to accept the *fait accompli*. Though condemning it on principle, he turned it to the interests of the Roman Church as well as of the universal Church. With joy and pride he welcomed the Byzantine East into the circle of vassal peoples and kingdoms of Rome bound politically to the see of St Peter, and with the same emotions beheld the patriarchate of Constantinople at last recognize Roman supremacy. But from this enormous increase of territory and influence arose a whole series of new and difficult problems. The court of Rome had to substitute for the old Greek hierarchy a hierarchy of Latin bishops; to force the remaining Greek clergy to practise the beliefs and rites of the Roman religion and bow to the supremacy of the pope; to maintain in the Greco-Latin Eastern Church the necessary order, morality and subordination; to defend it against the greed and violence of the nobles and barons who had founded the Latin Empire; and to compel the leaders of the new empire to submit to the apostolic power and execute its commands. In his endeavours to carry out the whole of this programme, Innocent III. met with insuperable obstacles and many disappointments. On the one hand, the Greeks were unwilling to abandon their religion and national cult, and scarcely recognized the ecclesiastical supremacy of the papacy. On the other hand, the upstart Latin emperors, far from proving submissive and humble tools, assumed with the purple the habits and pretensions of the sovereigns they had dispossessed. Nevertheless, Innocent left his successors a much vaster and more stable political dominion than that which he had received from his predecessors, since it comprised both East and West; and his five immediate successors were able to preserve this ascendancy. They even extended the limits of Roman imperialism by converting the pagans of the Baltic to Christianity, and further reinforced the work of ecclesiastical centralization by enlisting in their service a force which had recently come into existence and was rapidly becoming popular—the mendicant orders, and notably the Dominicans and Franciscans. The *The Friars* Roman power was also increased by the formation *and the* of the universities—privileged corporations of *Universities.* masters and students, which escaped the local power of the bishop and his chancellor only to place themselves under the direction and supervision of the Holy See. Mistress of the entire Christian organism, Rome thus gained control of international education, and the mendicant monks who formed her devoted militia lost no time in monopolizing the professorial chairs. Although the ecclesiastical monarchy continued to gain strength, the successors of Innocent III. made less use than he of their immense power. Under Gregory IX. (1227-1241) and Innocent IV. (1243-1254) the conflict between the priesthood and the Empire was revived by the enigmatic Frederick II., the polyglot and lettered emperor, the friend of Saracens, the despot who, in youth styled "king of priests," in later years personified ideas that were directly opposed to the medieval theocracy; and the struggle lasted nearly thirty years. The Hohenstaufen succumbed to it, and the papacy itself received a terrible shock, which shook its vast empire to the foundations.

Nevertheless, the first half of the 13th century may be regarded as the grand epoch of medieval papal history. Supreme in *Culmination* Europe, the papacy gathered into a body of doctrine *of the Papal* the decisions given in virtue of its enormous *de facto* *Power.* power, and promulgated its collected decrees and *orscula* to form the immutable law of the Christian world. Innocent III., Honorius III. and Gregory IX. employed their jurists to collect the most important of their rulings, and Gregory's decrees became the definitive repository of the canon law. Besides making laws for the Christendom of the present and the future, these popes employed themselves in giving a more regular form to their principal administrative organ, the offices of the Curia. The development of the Roman chancery is also a characteristic sign of the evolution that was taking place. From the time of Innocent III. the usages of the apostolic scribes become transformed into precise rules, which for the most part remained in force until the 15th century.

4. *Period from Urban IV. to Benedict XI. (1261-1305).*— This period comprises 13 pontificates, all of short duration (three or four years at the most, and some only a few months), with the exception of that of Boniface VIII., who was pope for nine years. This accidental fact constitutes a prime difference in favour of the preceding period, in which there were only five pontiffs during the first sixty years of the 13th century. Towards the end of the 13th century the directors of the Christian world occupied the throne of St Peter for too short a time to be able to make their personal views prevail or to execute their political projects at leisure after ripe meditation. Whatever the merit of a Gregory X. or a Nicholas III., the brevity of their pontificates prevented any one of these ephemeral sovereigns from being a great pope.

But other and far more important differences characterize this period. Although there was no theoretical restriction to *Influence of* the temporal supremacy and religious power of the *the Power* papacy, certain historical facts of great importance *of France.* contributed to the fatal diminution of their extent. The first of these was the preponderance of the French monarchy and nation in Europe. Founded by the conquests of Philip Augustus and Louis VIII. and legitimated and extended by the policy and moral influence of the crowned saint, Louis IX.,

the French monarchy enjoyed undisputed supremacy at the end of the 13th century and the beginning of the 14th; and this hegemony of France was manifested, not only by the extension of the direct power exercised by the French kings over all the neighbouring nationalities, but also by the establishment of Capetian dynasties in the kingdom of the Two Sicilies and in Hungary. From this time the sovereign of Rome, like other sovereigns, had to submit to French influence. But, whereas the pope was sometimes compelled to become the instrument of the policy of the kings of France or the adventurers of their race, he was often able to utilize this new and pervading force for the realization of his own designs, although he endeavoured from time to time, but without enduring success, to shake off the overwhelming yoke of the French. In short, it was in the sphere of French interests much more than in that of the general interests of Latin Christendom that the activities of these popes were exerted. The fact of many of the popes being of French birth and France the field of their diplomacy shows that the supreme pontificate was already becoming French in character. This change was a prelude to the more or less complete subjection of the papacy to French influence which took place in the following century at the period of the "Babylonish Captivity," the violent reaction personified by Boniface VIII. affording but a brief respite in this irresistible evolution. It was the Frenchman Urban IV. (1261-1264) who called Charles of Anjou into Italy to combat the last heirs of Frederick II. and thus paved the way for the establishment of the Angevin dynasty on the throne of Naples. Under Clement IV. (1265-1268) an agreement was concluded by which Sicily was handed over to the brother of St Louis, and the victories of Benevento (1266) and Tagliacozzo (1267) assured the triumph of the Guelph party and enabled the Angevins to plant themselves definitely on Neapolitan soil. Conradin's tragic and inevitable end closed the last act of the secular struggle between the Holy See and the Empire. Haunted by the recollection of that formidable conflict and lulled in the security of the Great Interregnum, which was to render Germany long powerless, the papacy thought merely of the support that France could give, and paid no heed to the dangers threatened by the extension of Charles of Anjou's monarchy in central and northern Italy. The Visconti Gregory X. (1271-1276) made an attempt to bring about a reaction against the tendency which had influenced his two immediate predecessors. He placed himself outside the theatre of French influence, and occupied himself solely with the task of giving to the papal monarchy that character of universality and political superiority which had made the greatness of an Alexander III. or an Innocent III. He opposed the aggrandizing projects of the Angevins, intervened in Germany with a view to terminating the Great Interregnum, and sought a necessary counterpoise to Capetian predominance in an alliance with Rudolph of Habsburg, who had become an emperor without imperilling the papacy. The Orsini Nicholas III. pursued the same policy with regard to the independence and greatness of the Roman See, but died too soon for the cause he upheld, and, at his death in 1280, the inevitable current revived with overpowering force. His successor, Martin IV. (1281-1285), a prelate of Champagne, brother of several councillors of the king of France, prebendary at Rouen and Tours, and one of the most zealous in favour of the canonization of Louis IX., ascended the papal throne under the auspices of Charles of Anjou, and undertook the government of the Church with the sole intention of furthering in every way the interests of the country of his birth. A Frenchman before everything, he abased the papal power to such an extent as to excite the indignation of his contemporaries, often slavishly subordinating it to the exigencies of the domestic and foreign policy of the Angevins at Naples and the reigning house at Paris. But he was prevented from carrying out this policy by an unforeseen blow, the Sicilian Vespers (March 1282), an event important both in itself and in its results. By rejecting the Capetian sovereign that Rome wished to thrust upon it to deliver it from the dynasty of Aragon, the little island of Sicily arrested the progress of French imperialism, ruined the vast projects of Charles of Anjou, and liberated the papacy in its own despite from a subjection that perverted and shook its power. Honorius IV. (1285-1287) and Nicholas IV. (1288-1292) were able to act with greater dignity and independence than their predecessors. Though remaining leagued with the Angevins, in southern Italy, they dared to look to Germany and Rudolph of Habsburg to help them in their efforts to add to the papal dominion a part of northern Italy and, in particular, Tuscany. But they still continued to desire the restoration of the Angevin dynasty in Sicily and to assist the designs of France on Aragon by preaching a crusade against the masters of Barcelona and Palermo. The hopes of the Curia were frustrated by the resistance of the Aragonese and Sicilians, and Charles of Valois, to whom the Curia eventually destined the crown of Aragon, had to resign it for that of Constantinople, which they also failed to secure.

Boniface VIII. himself at the beginning of his pontificate yielded to the current, and, like his predecessors, adapted his external policy to the pretensions and interests of the great Capetian house, which, like all his predecessors, he at first countenanced. In spite of his instincts for dominion and the ardour of his temperament, he made no attempt to shake off the French yoke, and did not decide on hostilities with France until Philip the Fair and his legists attempted to change the character of the kingship, emphasized its lay tendencies, and exerted themselves to gratify the desire for political and financial independence which was shared by the French nation and many other European peoples. The war which ensued between the pope and the king of France ended in the complete defeat of the papacy, which was reduced to impotence (1303), and though the storm ceased during the nine months' pontificate of Benedict XI., the See of St Peter recovered neither its normal equilibrium nor its traditional character. The accession of the first Avignon pope, Clement V., marks the final subjection of the papal power to the Capetian government, the inevitable result of the European situation created in the preceding century.

Boniface VIII. 1294-1303.

Subjection of the Papacy to France.

In other respects the papacy of this period found itself in a very inferior situation to that which it had occupied under Innocent III. and the popes of the first half of the 13th century. The fall of the Latin Empire and the retaking of Constantinople by the Palaeologi freed a great part of the Eastern world from the political and religious direction of Rome, and this fact necessarily engaged the diplomacy of Urban IV. and his successors in an entirely different direction. To them the Eastern problem presented a less complex aspect. There could no longer be any serious question of a collective expedition of Europe for the recovery of the Holy Places. The ingenuous faith of a Louis IX. was alone capable of giving rise to two crusades organized privately and without the influence or even the approval of the pope. Although all these popes, and Gregory X. especially, never ceased theoretically to urge the Christian world to the crusade, they were actuated by the desire of remaining faithful to tradition, and more particularly by the political and financial advantages accruing to the Holy See from the preaching and the crusading 'expeditions. The European state of mind no longer lent itself to such enterprises, and, moreover, under such brief pontificates, the attenuated Roman power could not expect to succeed where Innocent III. himself had failed. The main preoccupation of all these popes was how best to repair the injury done to orthodox Europe and to Rome by the destruction of the Latin Empire. Several of them thought of restoring the lost empire by force, and thus giving a pendant to the fourth crusade; but the Curia finally realized the enormous difficulties of such a project, and convinced themselves that the only practical solution of the difficulty was to come to an understanding with the Palaeologi and realize pacifically the long-dreamed union of the Greek and Latin Churches. The negotiations begun by Urban IV. and continued more or less actively by his successors were at last concluded in 1274 by Gregory X.

Council of Lyons, 1274. Relations with the Eastern Church.

The Council of Lyons proclaimed the union, which was destined to be effective for a few years at least and to be prolonged precariously in the midst of unfavourable circumstances. The Greek mind was opposed to the union; the acquiescence of the Byzantine emperors was but an ephemeral expedient of their foreign policy; and the peace between the Latins and Greeks settled on Byzantine soil could not endure for long. The principal obstacle, however, was the incompatibility of the popes' Byzantine and Italian policies. The popes were in favour of Charles of Anjou and his dynasty, but Charles was hostile to the union of the two Churches, since it was his intention to seize the Byzantine Empire and substitute himself for the Palaeologi. Almost all the successors of Urban IV. were compelled to exert their diplomacy against the aggrandizing aims of the man they had themselves installed in southern Italy, and to protect the Greek emperor, with whom they were negotiating the religious question. On several occasions between the years 1271 and 1273 the Angevins of Naples, who had great influence in Achaea and Albania and were solidly supported by their allies in the Balkan Peninsula, nearly carried out their project; and in 1274 the opposition of Charles of Anjou came near to compromising the operations of the council of Lyons and ruining the work of Gregory X. The papacy, however, held its ground, and Nicholas III., the worthy continuer of Gregory, succeeded in preserving the union and triumphing over the Angevin power. The Angevins took their revenge under Martin IV., who was a stanch supporter of the French. Three weeks after his coronation Martin excommunicated the Greek emperor and all his subjects, and allied himself with Charles of Anjou and the Venetians to compass his downfall. In this case, too, the Sicilian Vespers was the rock on which the hopes and pretensions of the sovereign of Naples suffered shipwreck. After Martin's death the last popes of the 13th century, and notably Boniface VIII., in vain thought to find in another Capetian, Charles of Valois, the man who was to re-establish the Latin dominion at Byzantium. But the East was lost; the union of 1274 was quickly dissolved; and the reconciliation of the two Churches again entered into the category of chimeras.

During this period the papal institution, considered in its internal development, already showed symptoms of decadence. The diminution of religious faith and sacerdotal prestige shook it to its very foundations. The growth of the lay spirit continued to manifest itself among the burgesses of the towns as well as among the feudal princes and sovereigns. The social factors of communism and nationalism, against which Innocent III. and his successors had struggled, became more powerful and more hostile to theocratic domination. That a sovereign like St Louis should be able to associate himself officially with the feudalism of his realm to repress abuses of church jurisdiction; that a contemporary of Philip the Fair, the lawyer Pierre Dubois, should dare to suggest the secularization of ecclesiastical property and the conversion of the clergy into a class of functionaries paid out of the royal treasury; and that Philip the Fair, the adversary of Boniface VIII., should be able to rely in his conflict with the leader of the Church on the popular consent obtained at a meeting of the Three Estates of France—all point to a singular demoralization of the sentiments and principles on which were based the whole power of the pontiff of Rome and the entire organization of medieval Catholicism. Both by its attitude and by its governmental acts, the papacy of the later 13th century itself contributed to increase the discredit and disaffection from which it suffered. Under Urban IV. and his successors the great moral and religious sovereignty of former times became a purely bureaucratic monarchy, in which the main preoccupation of the governors appeared to be the financial exploitation of Christendom. In the registers of these popes, which are now being actively investigated and published, dispensations (licences to violate the laws of the Church); indulgences, imposts levied with increasing regularity on universal Christendom and, in particular, on the clerks; the

Decay of the Papacy.

settlement of questions relating to church debts; the granting of lucrative benefices to Roman functionaries; the divers processes by which the Curia acquired the immediate disposal of monastic, capitulary and episcopal revenues—in short, all financial matters are of the first importance. It was in the 14th century more especially that the Apostolic Chamber spread the net of its fiscal administration wider and wider over Christian Europe; but at the close of the 13th century all the preliminary measures had been taken to procure for the papal treasury its enormous and permanent resources. The continued efforts of the popes to drain Christian gold to Rome were limited only by the fiscal pretensions of the lay sovereigns, and it was this financial rivalry that gave rise to the inevitable conflict between Boniface VIII. and Philip the Fair.

By thus devoting itself to material interests, the papacy contemporary with the last Capetians lost its moral greatness *Abuse of* and fell in the opinion of the peoples; and it did *the Papal* itself no less injury by the abnormal extension of *Power.* the bounds of its absolutism. By its exaggerated methods of centralization the papal monarchy had absorbed within itself all the living forces of the religious world and suppressed all the liberties in which the Church of old had lived. The subjection of the secular clergy was complete, while the episcopate retained no shadow of its independence. The decree of Clement IV. (1266), empowering the papacy to dispose of all vacant bishoprics at the court of Rome, merely sanctioned a usage that had long been established. But the control exercised by the Roman Curia over the episcopate had been realized by many other means. It was seldom that an episcopal election took place without a division in the chapter, in which resided the electoral right. In such an event, the competitors appealed to the Holy See and abdicated their right, either voluntarily or under coercion, *in manibus papae*, while the pope took possession of the vacant see. Nominations directly made by the court of Rome, especially in the case of dioceses long vacant, became increasingly numerous. The principle of election by canons was repeatedly violated, and threatened to disappear; and at the end of the 13th century the spectacle was common of prelates, whether nominated or confirmed by the pope, entitling themselves " bishops by the grace of the Holy See." The custom in force required bishops established by papal authority to take an oath of fidelity to the pope and the Roman Church, and this oath bound them in a particular fashion to the Curia. Those bishops, however, who had been elected under normal conditions, conformably to the old law, were deprived of the essential parts of their legitimate authority. They lost, for example, their jurisdiction, which they were seldom able to exercise in their own names, but in almost every case as commissaries delegated by the apostolic authority.

The regular clergy, who were almost wholly sheltered from the power of the diocesan bishops, found themselves, even more than the secular priesthood, in a state of complete dependence on the Curia. The papacy of this period continually intervened in the internal affairs of the monasteries. Not only did the monks continue to seek from the papacy the confirmation of their privileges and property, but they also referred almost all their disputes to the arbitration of the pope. Their elections gave rise to innumerable lawsuits, which all terminated at the court of Rome, and in most cases it was the pope himself who designated the monks to fill vacant posts in the abbeys. Thus the pope became the great ecclesiastical elector as well as the universal judge and supreme legislator. On this extreme concentration of the Christian power was employed throughout Europe an army of official agents or officious adherents of the Holy See, who were animated by an irrepressible zeal for the aggrandizement of the papacy. These officials originally consisted of an obedient and devoted militia of mendicant friars, both Franciscans and Dominicans, who took their orders from Rome alone, and whose efforts the papacy stimulated by lavishing exemptions, privileges, and full sacerdotal powers. Subsequently they were represented by the

apostolic notaries, who were charged to exercise throughout Christendom the gracious jurisdiction of the leaders of the Church and to preside over the most important acts in the private lives of the faithful. These tools of Rome, both clerks and laymen, continued to increase in every diocese. They were not invested with their office until they had been examined by a papal chaplain, or sometimes even by the vice-chancellor of the Curia.

The sovereign direction of this enormous monarchy belonged to the pope alone, who was assisted in important affairs by the advice and collaboration of the College of Cardinals, who had become the sole electors to the papacy. Towards the close of the 13th century the necessity arose for an express ruling on the question of the exercise of this electoral right. In 1274 Gregory X., completing the measures taken by Alexander III. in the 12th century, promulgated the celebrated constitution by which the cardinal-electors were shut up in conclave and, in the event of their not having designated the new pope within three days, were constrained to perform their duty by a progressive reduction of their food-allowance (see CONCLAVE). But at the head of this vast body there existed a constant tendency which was opposed to the absorption of all the power by a single and unbridled will. In the last years of this period fresh signs appeared of a reaction that emanated from the Sacred College itself. The cardinal-electors endeavoured to derive from their electoral power a right of control over the acts of the pope elect. In 1294, and again in 1303, they laid themselves under an obligation, previously to the election, to subscribe to the political engagements which each promised rigorously to observe in the event of his becoming pope. In general, these engagements bore upon the limitation of the number of cardinals, the prohibition to nominate new ones without previous notification to the Sacred College, the sharing between the cardinals and the pope of certain revenues specified by a bull of Nicholas IV., and the obligatory consultation of the consistories for the principal acts of the temporal and spiritual government. It is conceivable that a pope of Boniface VIII.'s temperament would not submit kindly to any restriction of the discretionary power with which he was invested by tradition, and he endeavoured to make the cardinals dependent on him and even to dispense with their services as far as possible, only assembling them in consistory in cases of extreme necessity. This tendency of the Sacred College to convert the Roman Church into a constitutional monarchy, in which it should itself play the part of parliament, was a sufficiently grave symptom of the progress of the new spirit. But throughout the ecclesiastical society traditional bonds were loosened and anarchy was rife, and this at the very moment when the enemies of the priesthood and its leaders redoubled their attack. In fine, the decadence of the papal institution manifested itself in an irremediable manner when it had accomplished no more than the half of its task. The growth of national kingdoms, the anti-clerical tendencies of the emancipated middle classes, the competition of lay imperialisms, and all the other elements of resistance which had been encountered by the papacy in its progress and had at first tended only to shackle it, now presented an insurmountable barrier. The papacy was weakened by its contest with these adverse elements, and it was through its failure to triumph over them that its dream of European dominion, both temporal and spiritual, entered but very incompletely into the field of realities. (A. Lu.)

III.—*Period from 1305 to 1590.*

The accession of the Gascon Clement V. in 1305 marks the beginning of a new era in the history of the papacy; for this pope, formerly archbishop of Bordeaux, remained *Clement V.* in France, without once crossing the threshold of *1305-1314.* the Eternal City. Clement's motive for this reso- *Settlement* lution was his fear that the independence of the *at Avignon.* ecclesiastical government might be endangered among the frightful dissensions and party conflicts by which Italy was then convulsed; while at the same time he yielded to the pressure exercised on him by the French king Philip the Fair. In March 1309, Clement V. transferred his residence to Avignon, a town which at that time belonged to the king of Naples, but was surrounded by the countship of Venaissin, which as early as 1228 had passed into the possession of the Roman See. Clement V. remained at Avignon till the day of his death, so that with him begins the so-called Babylonian Exile of the popes. Through this, and his excessive subservience to Philip the Fair, his reign proved the reverse of salutary to the Church. The pope's subservience was above all conspicuous in his attitude towards the proceedings brought against the order of the Temple, which was dissolved by the council of Vienne (see TEMPLARS). His possession of Ferrara involved Clement in a violent struggle with the republic of Venice, in which he was ultimately victorious.

His successor John XXII. a native of Cahors, was elected as the result of very stormy negotiations, after a two years' *John XXII.* vacancy of the see (1316). Like his predecessor *1316-1334.* he fixed his permanent residence at Avignon, where he had formerly been bishop. But while Clement V. had contented himself with the hospitality of the Dominican monastery at Avignon, John XXII. installed himself with great state in the episcopal palace, hard by the cathedral. *Character of* The essential features of this new epoch in the *the Avignon* history of the papacy, beginning with the two popes *Papacy.* mentioned, are intimately connected with this lasting separation from the traditional seat of the papacy, and from Italian soil in general: a separation which reduced the head of the Church to a fatal dependence on the French kings. Themselves Frenchmen, and surrounded by a College of Cardinals in which the French element predominated, the popes gave to their ecclesiastical administration a certain French character, till they stood in more and more danger of serving purely national interests, in cases where the obligations of their office demanded complete impartiality. And thus the prestige of the papacy was sensibly diminished by the view, to which the jealousy of the nations soon gave currency, that the supreme dignity of the Church was simply a convenient tool for French statecraft. The accusation might not always be supported by facts, but it tended to shake popular confidence in the head of the universal Church, and to inspire other countries with the feeling of a national opposition to an ecclesiastical régime now entirely Gallicized. The consequent loosening of the ties between the individual provinces of the Church and the Apostolic See, combined with the capricious policy of the court at Avignon, which often regarded nothing but personal and family interests, accelerated the decay of the ecclesiastical organism, and justified the most dismal forebodings for the future. To crown all, the feud between Church and Empire broke out again with unprecedented violence. The most prominent leaders of the opposition to the papacy, whether ecclesiastical or political, joined forces with the German king, Louis of Bavaria, and offered him their aid against John XXII. *Opposition to* The clerical opposition was led by the very popular *the Papacy.* and influential Minorites who were at that time engaged in a remarkably bitter controversy with the pope as to the practical interpretation of the idea of evangelical poverty. Their influence can be clearly traced in the appeal to a general council, issued by Louis in 1324 at Sachsenhausen near Frankfort-on-the-Main. This document, which confused the political problem with the theological, was bound to envenom the quarrel between emperor and pope beyond all remedy. Side by side with the Minorites, the spokesmen of the specifically political opposition to the papacy were the Parisian professors, Marsilius of Padua and John of Jandun, the composers of the "Defender of the Peace" (*defensor pacis*). In conjunction with the Minorites and the Ghibellines of Italy, Marsilius succeeded in enticing Louis to the fateful expedition to Rome and the revolutionary actions of 1328. The conferring of the imperial crown by the Roman populace, the deposition of the pope by the same body, and the election of an anti-pope in the person of the Minorite Pietro

da Corvara, translated into acts the doctrines of the *defensor pacis.* The struggle, which still further aggravated the dependence of the pope on France, was waged on both sides with the utmost bitterness, and the end was not in sight when John XXII. died, full of years, on the 4th of December 1334.

Even the following pope, Benedict XII., a man of the strictest morality, failed, in spite of his mild and pacific disposition, to adjust the conflict with Louis of Bavaria and the eccentric Fraticelli. King Philip VI. and the car- *Benedict XII.* dinals of the French party worked energetically *1334-1342.* against the projected peace with Louis; and Benedict was not endowed with sufficient strength of will to carry through his designs in the teeth of their opposition. He failed, equally, to stifle the first beginnings of the war between France and England; but it is at least to his honour that he exerted his whole influence in the cause of peace.

His efforts in the direction of reform, moreover, deserve recognition. In Avignon he began to erect himself a suitable residence, which, with considerable additions by later popes, developed into the celebrated papal castle of Avignon. This enormous edifice, founded on the cathedral rock, is an extraordinary mixture of castle and convent, palace and fortress. It was Benedict XII. also who elevated the doctrine of the beatific vision of the saints into a dogma.

Benedict XII. was again succeeded, in 1342, by a Frenchman from the south, Pierre Roger de Beaufort, who was born in the castle of Maumont, in the diocese of Limóges. He *Clement VI.* assumed the title of Clement VI. In contrast with *1342-1352.* his peace-loving predecessor, and in accordance with his own more energetic character, he pursued with decision and success the traditions of John XXII. in his dealings with Louis of Bavaria. With great dexterity he turned the feud between the houses of Luxemburg and Wittelsbach to the destruction of Louis; and the death-struggle between the two seemed about to break out, when Louis met his untimely end. To all appearances the victory of the papacy was decisive; but it was a Pyrrhic victory, as events were quickly to prove. In Rome there ensued, during the pontificate of Clement, the revolutions of the visionary Cola di Rienzo (*q.v.*) who restored the old republic, though not for long. By his purchase of Avignon, and the creation of numerous French cardinals, the pope consolidated the close connexion of the Roman Church with France: but the interests of that Church suffered severely through the riches and patronage which Clement lavished on his relatives, and through the princely luxury of his court. His generosity—which degenerated into prodigality—compelled him to open fresh sources of revenue; and in this he succeeded, though not without serious detriment to the interests of the Church.

It was fortunate for the Church that Clement VI. was followed by a man of an entirely different temperament—Innocent VI. This strict and upright pope appears to have taken Benedict XII. for his example. He undertook, *Innocent VI.* though not with complete success, a reformation of *1352-1362.* ecclesiastical abuses; and it was he who assisted in restoring the Empire at last to some measure of stability. But the culminating glory of his reign was the restoration of the almost ruined papal dominion in Italy, by means of the highly-gifted Cardinal Albornoz. The restoration of the Apostolic See to its original and proper seat was now possible; and the need for such a step was the more pressing, since residence in the castle at Avignon had become extremely precarious, owing to the ever-increasing confusion of French affairs. Innocent VI., in fact, entertained the thought of visiting Rome; but age and illness prevented his doing so.

The intention of Innocent was put into execution by his successor—the learned and pious Urban V. Two events of the first magnitude make his reign one of the most *Urban V.* memorable in the century. The first of these was *1362-1370.* the return to Rome. This was an object which the emperor Charles IV. had prosecuted with all his energies; which alone could revive the languishing reputation of the papacy, by withdrawing it from the turmoils of the Anglo-French War, and bring within the bounds of possibility the much-needed *Temporary* reformation in ecclesiastical affairs. In 1367 it *Return to Rome* became an accomplished fact. Turning a deaf ear to the remonstrances of the French king and the French cardinals, the pope quitted Avignon on the 13th of April 1367; and on the 16th of October he entered Rome, now completely fallen to ruin. The ensuing year, after his return to the Eternal City, witnessed the second great landmark in the reign of Urban V.—the Roman expedition of Charles IV., and the renewal of amicable relations between the Empire and the Church. Unfortunately, the pope failed to deal satisfactorily with the highly complicated situation in Italy; and the result was that, on the 27th of September 1370, he returned to Avignon, where he died on the following 19th of December.

It was the opinion of Petrarch that, had Urban remained in Rome, he would have been entitled to rank with the most distinguished men of his era; and, if we discount this single act of weakness, he must be classed as one of the noblest and best of popes. Especial credit is due to his struggles against the moral corruptions of the day, though they proved inadequate to eliminate all traces of the prevalent disorders.

Gregory XI., though equally distinguished for his erudition and pure morals, his piety, modesty and wisdom, was fated to *Gregory XI., 1370-1378.* pay dearly for the weakness of his predecessor in abandoning Rome so early. He lived to see the national spirit of Italy thoroughly aroused against a papacy turned French. The disastrous error of almost exclusively appointing Provençals, foreigners ignorant of both the country and the people, to the government of the Papal States, now found a terrible Nemesis: and there came a national upheaval, such as Italy had not yet witnessed. The feud between Italian and Frenchman broke out in a violent form; and it was in vain that St Catherine of Siena proffered her mediation in the bloody strife betwixt the pope and the Florentine republic. The letters that she addressed to the pontiff, on this and other occasions, are documents, which are, perhaps, unique in their kind, and of great literary beauty. It was also St Catherine who prevailed on Gregory XI. to return to *Definite Return to Rome.* Rome. On the 13th of September 1376 he left Avignon; on the 17th of January 1377 he made his entry into the city of St Peter. Thus ended the exile in France; but it left an evil legacy in the schism under Gregory's successor. Gregory, the last pope whom France has given to the Church, died on the 27th of March 1378, after taking measures to ensure a speedy and unanimous election for his successor.

The conclave, which took place in Rome, for the first time for 75 years, resulted in the election of Bartolomeo Prignano *Urban VI., 1378-1389.* (April 8, 1378); who took the name of Pope Urban VI. Canonically the election was perfectly valid;[1] so that the only popes, to be regarded as legitimate, are the successors of Urban. It is true that his election was immediately impugned by the cardinals on frivolous grounds; but the responsibility for this rests, partially at least, with the pope himself, whose reckless and inconsiderate zeal for reform was bound to excite a revolution among the worldly cardinals still yearning for the fleshpots of Avignon. This revolution could already be foreseen with tolerable certainty, when Urban embroiled himself even with his political friends—the queen of Naples and her husband, Duke Otto of Brunswick. Similarly, he quarrelled with Count Onorato Gaetano of Fondi. The cardinals, excited to the highest pitch of irritation, now knew where they could look for support. Thirteen of them assembled at Anagni, and thence, on the 9th of August, issued a passionate manifesto, announcing the invalidity of Urban's election, on *Election of Anti-pope Clement VII.* the ground that it had been forced upon the conclave by the Roman populace. As soon as the rebellious cardinals were further assured of the protection of the French king, Charles V., they elected, with the tacit consent of the three Italian cardinals, Robert of Geneva as anti-pope

[1] See Pastor, *Geschichte der Päpste*, I., 121.

(Fondi, Sept. 20). Robert assumed the style of Clement VII.; and thus Christendom was brought face to face with the worst misfortune conceivable—the Great Schism (1378-1417).

The chief responsibility for this rests with the worldly College of Cardinals, who were longing to return to France, and thence drew their inspiration. This college *The Great Schism.* was a creation of the Avignon period; which must therefore, in the last resort, be considered responsible for this appalling calamity. Severe censure, moreover, attaches to Charles V., of France. There may be room for dispute, as to the extent to which the king's share in the schism was due to the instigation of the revolted cardinals; there can be not the slightest doubt that his attitude was the decisive factor in perpetuating and widening the breach. The anti-pope was recognized not only by Charles of France, but by the princes of the Empire dependent on him, by Scotland and Savoy, and finally by the Spanish dominions and Portugal. On the other hand, the emperor Charles IV. and his son Wenceslaus, the greater part of the Empire, England, Hungary, Poland, Denmark, Norway and Sweden, together with the majority of the Italian states—Naples excepted—remained loyal to the pope. Urban, in fact—who meanwhile had created a new College of Cardinals with members of different nationalities—enjoyed one great advantage; his rival failed to hold his own in Italy, with which country the actual decision virtually lay. Unfortunately, in the time that followed, Urban was guilty of the grossest errors, pursuing his personal interests, and sacrificing, all too soon, that universal point of view which ought to have governed his policy. The struggle against his powerful neighbour on the frontier, Queen Joanna of Naples, rapidly became his one guiding motive; and thus he was led into a perfect labyrinth of blunders. He excommunicated the queen as a stiff-necked adherent of the French anti-pope, and in 1381 conferred Naples on the ambitious Charles of Durazzo, with whom he was soon inextricably embroiled; while, a little later, he fell out with his new College of Cardinals. On the 15th of October 1389, he died, with few to lament him.

After the death of Urban VI., fourteen cardinals of his obedience assembled, and after long negotiations elected the scion of a noble Neapolitan family; Cardinal Pietro *Boniface IX., 1389-1404.* Tomacelli (Nov. 2, 1389). The title which he took was that of Boniface IX. The new pope—a man of high moral character, great sagacity, eloquence, and of a kindly disposition—at once instituted an entirely different policy from that pursued by his predecessor. This was especially the case in his treatment of Naples. In May 1390 Ladislaus, the son of Charles of Durazzo, who had been assassinated in the February of 1386, received the royal crown at the hands of a papal legate. To his cause Boniface IX. closely attached himself; and his support of the king against the Angevins cost him enormous sums, without which Ladislaus could not have secured his victory over the French claimant. By these means, the schism was averted from Italy, and Naples won for the Roman obedience. The situation in the papal state, which Boniface found in the greatest confusion, was at the outset far more difficult to deal with. But here also he attained in time a considerable measure of success, although the methods employed were scarcely above criticism. His greatest success, however, was gained in the Eternal City itself; for he contrived, after many vicissitudes, to induce the Romans to annul their republican constitution and acknowledge the papal supremacy, even in municipal matters.

To give this supremacy a firmer basis, Boniface fortified the Vatican and the Capitol, and restored the castle of St Angelo—which had previously been used as a quarry—providing it with walls and battlements, and erecting a tower in the centre. This castle, indeed, yielded a safe shelter to the pope in January 1400, when the Colonnas made their attempt to surprise Rome. However, the adventure failed; and by the aid of Ladislaus, the castles of the Colonnas in the vicinity of Rome were destroyed. In 1401 this powerful family made its submission, accepting the favourable terms which the pope had had the good sense to offer. Henceforward quiet prevailed, and Boniface ruled as a stern master in Rome. But he was soon confronted with an extremely dangerous enemy, in the person of Duke Gian Galeazzo Visconti of Milan, who was aiming at the sovereignty of all Italy.[*] In July 1402 he made himself master of Bologna; and his death in September of the same year was a stroke of good fortune for the pope. Bologna was now recovered for the Church (Sept. 2, 1403), and soon afterwards Perugia also surrendered.

Thus Boniface IX., as a secular prince, occupies an important position; but as pope his activity must be unfavourably judged. Even if Dietrich of Niem frequently painted him too black, there is no question that the means which Boniface employed to fill the papal treasury seriously impaired the prestige of the highest spiritual office and the reverence due to it. His nepotism, again, casts a dark shadow over his memory; but most regrettable of all was his indifference towards the ending of the schism. Yet it should be borne in mind, that, when Clement VII. died suddenly on the 16th of September 1394, and the Avignon cardinals immediately elected the Spaniard Pedro de Luna as anti-pope (under the title of Benedict XIII.), Boniface IX. was left face to face with an extraordinarily skilful, adroit, and unscrupulous antagonist.

On the death of Boniface (Oct. 1, 1404), the Roman cardinals once more elected a Neapolitan, Cosimo dei Migliorati, who, at the age of 65, assumed the name of Innocent VII. *Innocent VII., 1404-1406.* Innocent, who was animated by a great love for the sciences and all the arts of peace, enjoyed only a brief pontificate, but his reign is not without importance, if only as an example of the generous patronage which the papacy—even in its darkest days—has lavished on literature and science. Significant also is the foothold gained at this time in the Curia itself by the humanists—Poggio, Bruni and others. The appointment of these skilled humanist writers to the Chancery was a consequence of the difficult conditions of the time. The crisis which the Catholic Church underwent, during this terrible epoch, was the greatest in all her history: for while everything was thrown into the utmost confusion by the life and death struggles of the rival popes, while the ecclesiastical revenues and emoluments were used almost exclusively for the reward of partisan service, while everywhere the worldliness of the clergy had reached its highest pitch, heretical movements, by which the whole order of the Church was threatened with overthrow, were gaining strength in England, France, Italy, Germany and especially in Bohemia.

The crisis came to a head in the pontificate of Gregory XII. This pope, so distinguished in many respects, owed his election *Gregory XII., 1406-1415.* mainly to the circumstance that he was considered a zealous champion of the restoration of unity within the Church: and he displayed, in fact, during the earlier portion of his reign, an exalted enthusiasm for this great task. Later his attitude changed; and the protracted negotiations for a conference with Benedict XIII. remained fruitless. The result of this change in the attitude of Gregory was the formation of a strong malcontent party in the College of Cardinals; to counteract whose influence, the pope—faithless to the conditions attached to his election—resorted to the plan of creating new members. Stormy discussions at Lucca followed; but they failed to prevent Gregory from nominating four fresh cardinals (May 9, 1408). The sequel was that seven of the cardinals attached to Gregory's Roman Curia withdrew to Pisa.

At the same period, the relations of Benedict XIII. with France suffered a significant modification. In that country, *Benedict XIII. and France.* it became more and more manifest that Benedict had no genuine desire to heal the schism in the Church, in spite of the ardent zeal for union which he had displayed immediately before and after his election. In May 1408 France withdrew from his obedience; and it was not long before French policy succeeded in effecting a reconciliation and understanding between the cardinals of Benedict XIII. and those who had seceded from Gregory XII. Precisely as

if the Holy See were vacant, the cardinals began to act as the actual rulers of the Church, and issued formal invitations to a council to be opened at Pisa on the Feast *Council of Pisa.* of the Annunciation (March 25) 1409. Both popes attempted to foil the disaffected cardinals by convening councils of their own; but their efforts were doomed to failure.

On the other hand, the council of the cardinals—though, by the strict rules of canonical law, its convocation was absolutely illegal—attained the utmost importance. But these rules, and, in fact, the whole Catholic doctrine of the primacy were almost entirely obscured by the schism. Scholars like Langenstein, Gerson and Zabarella, evolved a new theory as to ecumenical councils, which from the point of view of Roman Catholic principles must be described as revolutionary. At the synod of the dissident cardinals, assembled at Pisa, views of this type were in the ascendant; and, although protests were not lacking, the necessities of the time served as a pretext for ignoring all objections.

That the council was merely a tool in the hands of the ambitious and adroit Baldassare Cossa, was a fact unsuspected by its members who were animated by a fiery enthusiasm for the re-establishment of ecclesiastical unity; nor did they pause to reflect that an action against *both* popes could not possibly be lawful. Since whole universities and numerous scholars had pronounced in favour of the new theories, the Pisan synod dismissed all canonical scruples, and unhesitatingly laid claim to authority over both popes, one of whom was necessarily the legitimate pope. It was in vain that Carlo di Malatesta, a stanch adherent of Gregory, sought at the eleventh hour to negotiate a compromise between Gregory and the synod: It was in vain that this cultured prince, imbued with the principles of humanism, represented to the cardinals that this new path would lead quickly to the goal, but that this goal could not be unity but a triple schism. The council declared that it was canonically convened, ecumenical, and representative of the whole Catholic Church; then proceeded immediately to the trial and deposition of Benedict XIII. and Gregory XII. The synod grounded its procedure against the rival popes on a fact, ostensibly patent to all, but actually believed by none—that they were both supporters of the schism, and not merely this, but *heretics* in the truest and fullest sense of the word, since their attitude had impugned and subverted the article of faith concerning the one Holy, Catholic and Apostolic Church. On the ground of this extremely dubious declaration, designed to compensate for the absence of any authentic and firm foundation in ecclesiastical law, the Pisan assembly on the 5th of June announced the deposition of Gregory XII. and Benedict XIII., as manifest heretics and partisans of the schism. *Alexander V., 1409-1410.* The next step was to elect a new pope; and on the 26th of June 1409 the choice fell on the venerable cardinal-archbishop of Milan, the Greek Petros Filargis, who assumed the title of Alexander V.

The premature and futile character of these drastic and violent proceedings at Pisa was only too speedily evident. The powerful following which Gregory enjoyed in Italy and Germany, and Benedict in Spain and Scotland, ought to have shown from the very first that a simple decree of deposition could never suffice to overthrow the two popes. Thus, as the sentence of Pisa found recognition in France and England, as well as in many parts of Germany and Italy, the synod, which was to secure the restoration of unity, proved only the cause for worse confusion—instead of two, there were now three popes.

Alexander V., the pope of the council, died on the 3rd of May 1410. The cardinals at once elected his successor—Baldassare Cossa, who took the name of John XXIII. Of all *John XXIII., 1410-1415.* the consequences of the disastrous Pisan council, the election of this man was the most unfortunate. True, it cannot be demonstrated that all the fearful accusations afterwards levelled at John XXIII. were based on fact: but it is certain that this cunning politician was so far infected with the corruption of his age that he was not in the least degree fitted to fulfil the requirements of the supreme ecclesiastical dignity. From him the welfare of the Church had nothing to hope. All eyes were consequently turned to the energetic German king, Sigismund, who was inspired by the best motives, and who succeeded in surmounting the formidable obstacles which barred the way to an ecumenical council. It was mainly due to Sigismund's indefatigable and magnificent activity, that the council of Constance met and was so numerously attended. It is remarkable how fortune seemed to assist his efforts. The capture of Rome by King Ladislaus of Naples had compelled John XXIII. to take refuge in Florence (June 1413), where that dangerous guest received a not very friendly welcome. Since John's most immediate need was now protection and assistance against his terrible opponent Ladislaus, he sent, towards the close of August 1413, Cardinals Chalant and Francesco Zabarella, together with the celebrated Greek Manuel Chrysoloras, to King Sigismund, and commissioned them to determine the time and place of the forthcoming council. The agreement was soon concluded. On the 9th of December John XXIII. signed the bull convening the council at Constance, and pledged his word to appear there in person. He might have hoped that his share in convening the synod would give him a certain right to regulate its proceedings, and that, by the aid of his numerous Italian prelates, he would be able to influence it more or less according to his views. But in this he was greatly deceived. So soon as he realized the true position of affairs he attempted to break up the council by his flight to Schaffhausen (March 20-21, 1415)—a project in which he would doubtless have succeeded but for the sagacity and energy of Sigismund.

In spite of everything, the excitement in Constance was unbounded. In the midst of the confusion, which reigned supreme in the council, the upper hand was gained by that party which held that the only method by which the schism could be ended and a reformation of ecclesiastical discipline ensured was a drastic limitation of the papal privileges. The limitation was to be effected by the general council: consequently, the pope must be brought under the jurisdiction of that council, and—in the opinion of many—remain under its jurisdiction for all time. Thus, in the third, fourth and fifth general sessions it was enacted, with characteristic precipitation, that an ecumenical council could not be dissolved or set aside by the pope, without its consent: the corollary to which was, that the present council, notwithstanding the flight of John XXIII., continued to exist in the full possession of its powers, and that, in matters pertaining to belief and the eradication of schism, all men—even the pope—were bound to obey the general council, whose authority extended over all Christians, including the pope himself.

By these decrees—which created as the supreme authority within the Church a power which had not been appointed as such by Christ[1]—the members of the council of Constance sought to give their position a theoretical basis before proceeding to independent action against the pope. But these declarations as to the superiority of an ecumenical council never attained legal validity, in spite of their defence by Pierre d'Ailly and Gerson. Emanating from an assembly without a head, which could not possibly be an ecumenical council without the assent of one of the popes (of whom one was necessarily the legitimate pope)—enacted, in opposition to the cardinals, by a majority of persons for the most part unqualified, and in a fashion which *Deposition* was thus distinctly different from that of the old *of John* councils—they can only be regarded as a *coup de XXIII. main*, a last resort in the universal confusion. On the 29th of May the council deposed John XXIII.

The legitimate pope, Gregory XII., now consented to resign, but under strict reservation of the legality of his pontificate.

[1] Here of course the author speaks of the papal supremacy and not of papal infallibility in matters of faith and morals—a doctrine which was formally declared a dogma of the Church only at the Vatican council in 1870.—[ED.]

By consenting to this, the synod indirectly acknowledged that its previous sessions had not possessed an ecumenical character, and also that Gregory's predecessors, up to *Resignation* Urban VI., had been legitimate popes. In presence *of Gregory* of the council, reconstituted by Gregory, Malatesta *XII.* announced the resignation of the latter; and the grateful assembly appointed Gregory *legatus a latere* to the marches of Ancona—a dignity which he was not destined to enjoy for long, as he died on the 18th of October 1417. (See CONSTANCE, COUNCIL OF.)

From the abdication of Gregory XII. to the election of Martin V., the Apostolic See was vacant; and the council, newly convened and authorized by the legitimate pope *Vacancy of* before his resignation, conducted the government of *the Holy* the Church. After the condemnation and burning of *See.* John Huss (*q.v.*), the reformation of the Church, both in its head and members, claimed the main attention of the fathers of the council. Among the many difficulties which beset the question, not the least obvious was the length of time during which the Church must remain without a ruler, if—as Sigismund and the German nation demanded—the papal election were deferred till the completion of the internal reforms. The result was decided by the policy of the cardinals, who since May 1417 had openly devoted their whole energies to the acceleration of that election; and union was preserved by means of a compromise arranged by Bishop Henry of Winchester, the uncle of the English king. The terms of the agreement were that a synodal decree should give an absolute assurance that the work of reformation would be taken in hand immediately after the election; reforms, on which all the nations were already united, were to be published *before* the election; and the mode of the papal election itself was to be determined by deputies. When the last-named condition had been fulfilled on the 28th of October the conclave began, on the 8th of November 1417, in the *Kaufhaus* of Constance; and, no later than St Martin's day, the cardinal-deacon Oddo Colonna was elected Pope Martin V.

With the accession of Martin V. unity was at last restored to the Church, and contemporary Christendom gave *Martin V.,* way to transports of joy. Any secular power—a *1417-1431.* bitter opponent of the papacy admits—would have succumbed in the schism: but so wonderful was the organization of the spiritual empire, and so indestructible the conception of the papacy itself, that this (the deepest of all cleavages) served only to prove its indivisibility (Gregorovius, *Geschichte Roms* vi.). Martin V. appeared to possess every quality which could enable him to represent the universal Church with strength and dignity. In order to maintain his independence, he energetically repudiated all proposals that he should establish his residence in France or Germany, and once more took up his abode in Rome. On the 30th of September 1420 he made his entry into the almost completely ruinous town. To repair the ravages of neglect, and, more especially, to restore the decayed churches, Martin at once expended large sums; while, later, he engaged famous artists, like Gentile da Fabriano and Masaccio, and encouraged all forms of art by every means within his power. Numerous humanists were appointed to the Chancery, and the Romans were loud in their praise of the papal régime. But he was not content with laying the foundations for the renovation of the Eternal City: he was the architect who rebuilt the papal monarchy, which the schism had reduced to the verge of dissolution. To this difficult problem he brought remarkable skill and aptness, energy and ability. His temporal sovereignty he attempted to strengthen through his family connexions, and magnificent provision in general was made for the members of his house.

Nor was the activity of Martin V. less successful in political than in ecclesiastical reform, which latter included the combating of the Fraticelli, the amendment of the clergy, the encouragement of piety by the regulation of feast-days, the recommendation of increased devotion to the sacrament of the altar, and the strengthening of the conception of the Church by the great jubilee of 1423. At the same time the crowning reward of his labours was the effacing of the last traces of the schism. He prosecuted successfully the conflict with the adherents of Benedict XIII, who, till the day of his death[1] clung to the remnants of his usurped authority (see BENEDICT XIII.). An attempt on the part of Alphonso V. of Aragon to renew the schism failed; and, in 1429, the Spaniard was compelled to give up his anti-pope, Clement VIII. Count John of Armagnac, whom Martin had excommunicated as a protector of schismatics, was also driven to make submission. Martin rendered the greatest service by his admission of a whole series of distinguished men into the College of Cardinals; but he was less fortunate in his struggles against Hussitism. His death took place on the 20th of February 1431, and the inscription on his grave—still preserved in the Lateran church—styles him "the felicity of his age" (temporum suorum felicitas).

The Colonna pope was followed by the strict, moral and pious Gabriel Condulmaro, under the title of Eugenius IV. Eugenius IV. His pontificate was not altogether happy. At the very 1431-1447 first, his violent and premature measures against the and the Colonna family, which had received such unbounded Council of favour from his predecessor, embroiled him in a Basel. sanguinary feud. Far worse, however, were the conflicts which Eugenius had to support against the Council of Basel—already dissolved on the 18th of December 1431. At the beginning, indeed, a reconciliation between the pope and council was effected by Sigismund who, on the 31st of May 1433, was crowned emperor at Rome. But, as early as the 29th of May 1434 a revolution broke out in Rome, which, on the 4th of June, drove the pope in flight to Florence; where he was obliged to remain, while Giovanni Vitelleschi restored order in the papal state.

The migration of Eugenius IV. to Florence was of extreme importance; for this town was the real home of the new art, and the intellectual focus of all the humanistic movements in Italy. At Florence the pope came into closer contact with the humanists, and to this circumstance is due the gradual dominance which they attained in the Roman Curia—a dominance which, both in itself, and even more because of the frankly pagan leanings of many in that party, was bound to awaken serious misgivings.

The Italian troubles, which had entailed the exile of Eugenius IV., were still insignificant in comparison with those conjured up by the fanatics of the Council in Basel. The decrees enacted by that body made deep inroads on the rights of the Holy See; and the conflict increased in violence. On the 31st of July 1437 the fathers of Basel summoned Eugenius IV. to appear before their tribunal. The pope retorted on the 18th of September by transferring the scene of the council to Ferrara—afterwards to Florence. There, in July 1439, the union with the Greeks was effected: but it remained simply a paper agreement. On the 25th of June 1439 the synod—which had already pronounced sentence of heresy on Eugenius IV., by reason of his obstinate disobedience to the assembly of the Church—formally deposed him; and, on the 5th of November, a rival pontiff was elected in the person of the Felix V. ambitious Amadeus of Savoy, who now took the Anti-pope. title of Felix V. (See BASEL, COUNCIL OF, and FELIX V.) Thus the assembly of Christendom at Basel had resulted, not in the reformation of the Church, but in a new schism! This, in fact, was an inevitable sequel to the attempt to overthrow the monarchical constitution of the Church. The anti-pope—the last in the history of the papacy—made no headway, although the council invested him with the power of levying annates to a greater extent than had ever been claimed by the Roman Curia.

The crime of this new schism was soon to be expiated by its perpetrators. The disinclination of sovereigns and peoples to a division, of the disastrous consequences of which the West had only lately had plentiful experiences, was so pronounced that

[1] May 23, 1423: vide the Chronicle of Martin de Alpartil, edited by Ehrle (1906).

the violent proceeding of the Basel fathers alienated from them the sympathies of nearly all who, till then, had leaned to their side. While the prestige of the schismatics waned, Eugenius IV. gained new friends; and on the 28th of September 1443 his reconciliation with Alphonso of Naples enabled him to return to Rome. In consequence of the absence of the pope, the Eternal City was once more little better than a ruin; and the work of restoration was immediately begun by Eugenius.

During the chaos of the schism, France and Germany had adopted a semi-schismatic attitude: the former by the Pragmatic Sanction of Bourges (June 7, 1438); the latter by a declaration of neutrality in March 1438. The efforts of Aeneas Silvius Piccolomini brought matters into a channel more favourable to the Holy See; and an understanding with Germany was reached. This consummation was soon followed by the death of Eugenius (Feb. 23, 1447). No apter estimate of his character can be found than the words of Aeneas Silvius himself: "He was a great-hearted man; but his chief error was that he was a stranger to moderation, and regulated his actions, not by his ability, but by his wishes." From the charge of nepotism he was entirely exempt; and, to the present day, the purity of his life has never been impugned even by the voice of faction. He was a father to the poor and sick, in the highest sense of the word; and he left behind him an enduring monument in his amendment and regeneration, first of the religious orders, then of the clergy. Again, the patronage which he showed to art and artists was of the greatest importance. All that could be done in that cause, during this stormy epoch, was done by Eugenius. It was by his commission that Filarete prepared the still-extant bronzework of St Peter's, and the Chapel of the Holy Sacrament in the Vatican was painted by Fiesole.

On the death of Eugenius IV. the situation was menacing enough, but, to the surprise and joy of all, Tomaso Parentucelli, cardinal of Bologna, was elected without disturbance, as Pope Nicholas V. With him the Christian Renaissance Nicholas V. ascended the papal throne. He was the son of a 1447-1455. physician from Sarzana, who was not too well endowed with the gifts of fortune; and the boy, with all his talents, could only prosecute his studies at great personal sacrifices. He was possessed of a deep-seated enthusiasm for science and art, of a sincerely pious and idealistic temperament, and of an ardent love for the Church. After his ordination, his great learning and stainless life led him to office after office in the Church, each higher and more influential than the last. Not only did he love the studies of the humanist, but he himself was a Christian humanist. Yet among all his far-reaching plans for the encouragement of art and science, Nicholas V. had always the well-being of the Church primarily in view; and the highest goal of his pontificate, which inaugurated the Maecenatian era of the popedom, was to ennoble that Church by the works of intellect and art. It is astonishing to contemplate how much he achieved, during his brief reign, in the cause of the Renaissance in both art and literature. True, his designs were even greater, but his term of government was too short to allow of their actual execution. A simply gigantic plan was drawn out, with the assistance of the celebrated Alberti, for the reconstruction of the Leonine City, the Vatican and St Peter's. The rebuilding of the last-named was rendered advisable by the precarious condition of the structure, but stopped short in the early stages. In the Vatican, however, Fiesole completed the noble frescoes, from the lives of St Stephen and St Lawrence, which are still preserved to us. Nicholas, again, lent the protection and encouragement of his powerful arm to science as well as art, till the papal court became a veritable domain of the Muses. He supported all scientific enterprises with unlimited generosity, and the most famous savants of all countries flocked to Rome. Yet it is surprising—and scarcely excusable—that Nicholas, while selecting the men whom he considered necessary for his literary work, passed over much which ought to have aroused grave suspicion in his mind. Thus the active humanistic life, called into existence by the enthusiasm of the pope, was not without its dark side. Quite apart from the fact that

Rome became the scene of a *chronique scandaleuse* among these scholars, there was something unnatural in the predominance of the humanists in the Curia.

The fostering care of the science-loving pope extended also to the field of ecclesiastical literature; and the greatest importance attaches to the energy he developed as a collector of manuscripts and books. His agents travelled as far as Prussia, and even into the East. All this activity served to enrich the Vatican library, the foundation of which is for Nicholas V. an abiding title to fame. In political and ecclesiastical affairs he similarly manifested great vigour; and his extraordinarily pacific disposition did more than anything else towards diminishing the difficulties with which he had to contend on his entry upon office. An agreement was very quickly concluded with King Alphonso of Naples. In the Empire the affairs of the Church were ameliorated—though not so quickly—by the Concordat of Vienna (1448). The Council of Basel was compelled to dissolve, and the anti-pope Felix V. to abdicate: and, though even after the termination of the synod men like Jacob of Jüterbogk (*q.s.*) were found to champion ecclesiastical parliamentarianism and the more advanced ideas of Basel, they were confronted, on the other hand, by an array of redoubtable controversialists, who entered the lists to defend, both in speech and writing, the privileges of the Apostolic See. Among these, Torquemada, Rodericus Sancius de Arevalo, Capistrano and Piero del Monte were especially active for the restoration of the papacy. Fortunate as Nicholas was in the *haute politique* of the Church, he was equally so in his efforts to re-establish and maintain peace in Rome and the papal state. In Poland, Bohemia, Hungary, Bosnia and Croatia—even in Cyprus itself —he was zealous for the peace of the Church.

The long-hoped cessation of civil war within the Church had now come, and Nicholas considered that the event could not better be celebrated than by the proclamation of a universal jubilee—an announcement which evoked a thrill of joy in the whole of Christendom. A special point of attraction in this jubilee of 1450 was the canonization of Bernardino of Siena; and, in spite of the plague which broke out in Rome, the celebrations ran a brilliant course.

Jubilee of 1450.

It was the wish of the pope that the jubilee should be followed by a revival of religious life in all Christian countries. To put this project into execution, the Church opened her " treasuries of grace," connected with the jubilee dispensation, for the peculiar benefit of those nations that had suffered most from the turmoils of the last few decades, or were prevented from visiting the Eternal City. Nicholas of Cusa was nominated legate for Germany, and began the work of reformation by travelling through every province in Germany dispensing blessings. It was under Nicholas V. that the last imperial coronation was solemnized at Rome. There is a touch of tragedy in the fact that, in the following year, the pope saw his temporal sovereignty—even his life—threatened by a conspiracy hatched among the adherents of the pseudo-humanism. The prime mover in the plot, Stefano Porcaro, was executed. Nicholas had scarcely recovered from the shock, when news came of the capture of Constantinople by the Turks; and his efforts to unite the Christian powers against the Moslem failed. This darkened the evening of his life, and he died in the night of the 24-25th of March 1455. From the universal standpoint of history the significance of Nicholas's pontificate lies in the fact that he put himself at the head of the artistic and literary Renaissance. By this means he introduced a new epoch in the history of the papacy and of civilization: Rome, the centre of ecclesiastical life, was now to become the centre of literature and art.

The short reign of the Spaniard, Alphonso de Borgia, as Pope Calixtus III., is almost completely filled by his heroic efforts to arm Christendom for the common defence against Islam. Unfortunately all the warnings and admonitions of the old man fell on deaf ears, though he himself parted with his mitre and plate in order to equip a fleet against the Turks. The Mahommedans, indeed, were severely punished at Belgrade (1456), and in the sea-

Calixtus III., 1455-1458.

fight of Metelino (1457): but the indolence of the European princes, who failed to push home the victory, rendered the success abortive. Bitterly disillusioned, Calixtus died on the 14th of August 1458. His memory would be stainless but for the deep shadow cast on it by the advancement which he conferred upon his relatives.

When Aeneas Sylvius Piccolomini was elected pope as Pius II. the papal throne was ascended by a man whose name was famous as poet, historian, humanist and statesman, and whose far-seeing eye and exact knowledge of affairs seemed peculiarly to fit him for his position. On the other hand, the troubled and not impeccable past of the new pontiff was bound to excite some misgiving; while, at the same time, severe bodily suffering had brought old age on a man of but 53 years. In spite of his infirmity and the brief duration of his reign, Pius II. accomplished much for the restoration of the prestige and authority of the Holy See. His indefatigable activity on behalf of Western civilization, now threatened with extinction by the Ottomans, excites admiration and adds an undying lustre to his memory. If we except the Eastern question, Pius II. was principally exercised by the opposition to papal authority which was gaining ground in Germany and France. In the former country the movement was headed by the worldly archbishop-elector Diether of Mainz;[1] in the latter by Louis XI., who played the autocrat in ecclesiastical matters. In full consciousness of his high-priestly dignity he set his face against these and all similar attempts; and his zeal and firmness in defending the authority and rights of the Holy See against the attacks of the conciliar and national parties within the Church deserve double recognition, in view of the eminently difficult circumstances of that period. Nor did he shrink from excursions in the direction of reform, now become an imperative necessity. His attempt to reunite Bohemia with the Church was destined to failure; but the one great aim of the pope during his whole reign was the organization of a gigantic crusade—a project which showed a correct appreciation of the danger with which the Church and the West in general were menaced by the Crescent. It is profoundly affecting to contemplate this man, a mere wreck from gout, shrinking from no fatigue, no labour, and no personal sacrifices; disregarding the obstacles and difficulties thrown in his way by cardinals and temporal princes, whose fatal infatuation refused to see the peril which hung above them all; recurring time after time, with all his intellect and energy, to the realization of his scheme; and finally adopting the high-hearted resolve of placing himself at the head of the crusade. Tortured by bodily, and still more by mental suffering, the old pope reached Ancona. There he was struck down by fever; and on the 15th of August 1464 death had released him from all his afflictions—a tragic close which has thrown a halo round his memory. In the sphere of art he left an enduring monument in the Renaissance town of Pienza.

Pius II., 1458-1464.

The humanist Pius II. was succeeded by a splendour-loving Venetian, Pietro Barbo, the nephew of Eugenius IV., who is known as Pope Paul II. With his accession the situation altered; for he no longer made the Turkish War the centre of his whole activity, as both his immediate predecessors had done. Nevertheless, he was far from indifferent to the Ottoman danger. Paul took energetic measures against the principle of the absolute supremacy of the state as maintained by the Venetians and by Louis XI. of France; while in Bohemia he ordered the deposition of George Podebrad (Dec. 1466). The widely diffused view that this pope was an enemy of science and culture is unfounded. It may be traced back to Platina, who, resenting his arrest, avenged himself by a biographical caricature. What the pope actually sought to combat by his dissolution of the Roman Academy

Paul II., 1464-1471.

[1] Diether von Isenburg (1412-1463), second son of Count Diether of Isenburg-Büdingen; rector of the university of Erfurt, 1434; archbishop of Mainz, 1459. He led the movement for a reform of the Empire and the opposition to the papal encroachments, supporting the theory of church government enunciated at Constance and Basel and condemned in Pius II.'s bull *Execrabilis*.—[ED.]

was simply the non-Christian tendency of the Renaissance, standing as it did on a purely pagan basis—"the stench of heathendom," as Dante described it. In other respects Paul II. encouraged men of learning and the art of printing, and built the magnificent palace of San Marco, in which he established a noble collection of artistic treasures.

The long pontificate of the Franciscan Francesco della Rovere, under the title of Pope Sixtus IV., displays striking contrasts of light and shade; and with him begins *Sixtus IV.* the series of the so-called "political popes." It *1471-1484.* remains a lamentable fact that Sixtus IV. frequently subordinated the Father of Christendom to the Italian prince, that he passed all bounds in the preferment of his own family, and in many ways deviated into all too worldly courses. The decay of ecclesiastical discipline grew to alarming proportions under Sixtus. During his reign crying abuses continued and grew in spite of certain reforms.

The nepotism in which the pope indulged is especially inexcusable. His feud with Lorenzo de' Medici culminated in the Pazzi conspiracy, the tragic sequel to which was the assassination of Giuliano de' Medici (April 26, 1478). That the pope himself was guiltless of any share in that atrocious deed is beyond dispute; but it is deeply to be regretted that his name plays a part in the history of this conspiracy. Sixtus was far from blind to the Turkish peril, but here also he was hampered by the indifference of the secular powers. Again, the close of his reign was marked by the wars against Ferrara and Naples, and subsequently against Venice and the Colonnas; and these drove the question of a crusade completely into the background. In the affairs of the Church he favoured the mendicant orders, and declared against the cruel and unjust proceedings of the Spanish Inquisition. His nominations to the cardinalate were not happy. The College of Cardinals, and the Curia in general, grew more and more infected with worldliness during his pontificate. On the other side, however, the pope did splendid service to art and science, while to men of letters he allowed incredible freedom. The Vatican library was enriched and thrown open for public use, Platina—the historian of the popes—receiving the post of librarian. The city of Rome was transfigured. At the papal order there arose the Ponte Sisto, the hospital of San Spirito, Santa Maria del popolo, Santa Maria della pace, and finally the Sistine Chapel, for the decoration of which the most famous Tuscan and Umbrian artists were summoned to Rome. This fresco-cycle, with its numerous allusions to contemporary history, is still preserved, and forms the noblest monument of the Rovere pope.

The reign of Innocent VIII. is mainly occupied by his troubles with the faithless Ferdinand of Naples. These sprang from his *Innocent* participation in the War of the Barons; but to this *VIII., 1484-* the pope was absolutely compelled. Innocent's bull *1492.* concerning witchcraft (Dec. 5, 1484) has brought upon him many attacks. But this bull contains no sort of dogmatic decision on the nature of sorcery. The very form of the bull, which merely sums up the various items of information that had reached the pope, is enough to prove that the decree was not intended to bind anyone to belief in such things. Moreover the bull contained no essentially new regulations as to witchcraft. It is absurd to make this document responsible for the introduction of the bloody persecution of witches, for, according to the *Sachsenspiegel,* the civil law already punished sorcery with death. The action of Innocent VIII was simply limited to defining the jurisdiction of the inquisitors with regard to magic. The bull merely authorized, in cases of sorcery, the procedure of the canonical inquisition, which was conducted exclusively by spiritual judges and differed entirely from that of the later witch-trials. Even if the bull encouraged the persecution of witches, in so far as it encouraged the inquisitors to take earnest action, there is still no valid ground for the accusation that Innocent VIII. introduced the trial of witches and must bear the responsibility for the terrible misery which was afterwards brought on humanity by that institution.

During the last three decades of the 15th century the Roman Curia, and the College of Cardinals in particular, became increasingly worldly. This explains how on the *Alexander* death of Innocent VIII. (July 25, 1492), simonical *VI., 1492-* intrigues succeeded in procuring the election of *1503.* Cardinal Rodrigo Borgia, a man of the most abandoned morals, who did not change his mode of life when he ascended the throne as Pope Alexander VI. The beginning of his reign was not unpromising; but all too soon that nepotism began which attained its height under this Spanish pope, and dominated his whole pontificate. A long series of scandals resulted. The cardinals opposed to Alexander, headed by Giuliano della Rovere, found protection and support with Charles VIII. of France, who laid claim to Naples. In prosecution of this design the king appeared in Italy in the autumn of 1494, pursued his triumphant march through Lombardy and Tuscany, and, on the 31st of December, entered Rome. Charles had the word *reform* perpetually on his lips; but it could deceive none who were acquainted with the man. At first he threatened Alexander with deposition: but on the 15th of January 1495 an agreement was concluded between pope and king.

While the French were marching on Naples there arose a hostile coalition which compelled them to beat a hasty retreat —the Holy League of March 1495. All their conquests were lost; and the pope now determined to chastise the Orsini family, whose treachery had thrown him into the hands of the French. The project miscarried, and on the 25th of January 1497 the papal forces were defeated.

In June occurred the mysterious assassination of the duke of Gandia, which appeared for a while to mark the turning-point in Alexander's life. For some time he entertained serious thoughts of reformation; but the matter was first postponed and then forgotten. The last state now became worse than the first, as Alexander fell more and more under the spell of the infamous Cesare Borgia. One scandal followed hard on the other, and opposition naturally sprang up. Unfortunately, Savonarola, the head of that opposition, transgressed all bounds in his well-meant zeal. He refused to yield the pope that obedience to which he was doubly pledged as a priest and the member of an order. Even after his excommunication (May 12, 1497) he continued to exercise the functions of his office, under the shelter of the secular arm. In the end he demanded a council for the deposition of the pope. His fall soon followed, when he had lost all ground in Florence; and his execution on the 23rd of May 1498 freed Alexander from a formidable enemy (see SAVONAROLA). From the Catholic standpoint Savonarola must certainly be condemned: mainly because he completely forgot the doctrine of the Church that the sinful and vicious life of superiors, including the pope, is not competent to abrogate their jurisdiction.

After the death of Charles VIII. Alexander entered into an agreement and alliance with his successor Louis XII. The fruits of this compact were reaped by Cesare Borgia, who resigned his cardinal's hat, became duke of Valentinois, annihilated the minor nobles of the papal state, and made himself the true dictator of Rome. His soaring plans were destroyed by the death of Alexander VI., who met his end on the 18th of August 1503 by the Roman fever—not by poison.

The only bright pages in the dark chapter of Alexander's *popedom* are his efforts on behalf of the Turkish War (1499-1502), his activity for the diffusion of Christianity in America, and his judicial awards (May 3-4, 1493) on the question of the colonial empires of Spain and Portugal, by which he avoided a bloody war. It is folly to speak of a donation of lands which did not belong to the pope, or to maintain that the freedom of the Americans was extinguished by the decision of Alexander VI. The expression "donation" simply referred to what had already been won *under just title*: the decree contained a deed of gift, but it was an adjustment between the powers concerned and the other European princes, not a parcelling out of the New World and its inhabitants. The monarchs on whom the *privilegium* was conferred, received a right of priority with respect to the provinces first discovered by them. Precisely as to-day inventions are guarded by patents, and literary and arthtic creations by the law of copyright, so, at that period, the papal bull and the protection of the Roman Church were an effective means for ensuring that a country should reap where she had sown and should maintain the territory she had discovered and conquered by arduous efforts; while other claimants, with predatory designs, were warned back ·by the ecclesiastical censorship. In the Vatican the memory of Alexander VI. is still perpetuated by the Appartamenta Borgia, decorated by Pinturicchio with magnificent frescoes, and since restored by Leo XIII.

The short reign of the noble Pius III. (Sept. 22–Oct. 18, 1503) witnessed the violent end of Cesare Borgia's dominion. As *Pius III.,* early as the 1st of November Cardinal Giuliano *1503.* della Rovere was elected by the conclave as Julius II. He was one of those personalities in which everything transcends the ordinary scale. He was endowed with great force of will, indomitable courage, extra-*Julius II.,* ordinary acumen, heroic constancy and a discrimi-*1503-1513.* nating instinct for everything beautiful. A nature formed on great broad lines—a man of spontaneous impulses carrying away others as he himself was carried away, a genuine Latin in the whole of his being—he belongs to those imposing figures of the Italian Renaissance whose character is summarized in contemporary literature by the word *terribile*, which is best translated "extraordinary" or "magnificent."

As cardinal Julius II. had been the adversary of Alexander VI., as pope he stood equally in diametrical opposition to his predecessor. The Borgia's foremost thought had been for his family; Julius devoted his effort to the Church and the papacy. His chief idea was to revive the world-dominion of the popedom, but first to secure the independence and prestige of the Holy See on the basis of a firmly established and independent territorial sovereignty. Thus two problems presented themselves: the restoration of the papal state, which had been reduced to chaos by the Borgias; and the liberation of the Holy See from the onerous dependence on France—in other words, the expulsion of the French "barbarians" from Italy. His solution of the first problem entitles Julius II. to rank with Innocent III. and Cardinal Albornos as the third founder of the papal state. His active prosecution of the second task made the Rovere pope, in the eyes of Italian patriots, the hero of the century. At the beginning of the struggle Julius had to endure many a hard blow; but his courage never failed—or, at most, but for a moment—even after the French victory at Ravenna, on Easter Sunday 1512. In the end the Swiss saved the Holy See; and, when Julius died the power of France had been broken in Italy, although the power of Spain had taken its place.

The conflict with France led to a schism in the College of Cardinals, which resulted in the *conciliabulum* of Pisa. Julius adroitly checkmated the cardinals by convening a general council, which was held in the Lateran. This assembly was also designed to deal with the question of reform, when the pope was summoned from this world (Feb. 20–21, 1513). Of his ecclesiastical achievements the bull against simony at papal elections deserves the most honourable mention. Again, by his restoration of the papal state, after the frightful era of the Borgias, Julius became the saviour of the papal power. But this does not exhaust his significance; he was, at the same time, the renewer of the papal Maecenate in the domain of art. It is to his lasting praise that he took into his service the three greatest artistic geniuses of the time—Bramante, Michelangelo and Raphael—and entrusted them with congenial tasks. Bramante drew out the plan for the new cathedral of St Peter and the reconstruction of the Vatican. On the 18th of April 1506 the foundation-stone of the new St Peter's was laid; 120 years later,· on the 18th of November 1626, Urban VIII. consecrated the new cathedral · of the world, on which twenty popes had laboured, in conjunction with the first architects of the day, modifying in many points the grandiose

original design of Bramante, and receiving the contributions of every Christian land.

St Peter's, indeed, is a monument of the history of art, not merely within these 120 years from the zenith of the Renaissance till the transition into Baroque—from Bramante, *The new* Raphael, Michelangelo, to Maderna and Bernini—*St Peter's* but down to the 19th century, in which Canova *and the* and Thorwaldsen erected there the last great papal *Vatican.* monuments. But a still more striking period of art is represented by the Vatican, with its antique collections, the Sistine and the Stanze. Here, too, we are everywhere confronted with the name of Julius II. It was he who inaugurated the collection of ancient statues in the Belvedere, and caused the wonderful roof of the Sistine Chapel to be painted by Michelangelo (cf. Steinmann, *Die sixtin. Kapelle II.*, 1905). Simultaneously, on the commission of the pope, Raphael decorated the Vatican with frescoes glorifying the Church and the papacy. In the Camera della Segnatura he depicted the four intellectual powers—theology, philosophy, poetry and law. In the Stanza d'Eliodoro Julius II. was visibly extolled as the Head of the Church, sure at all times of the aid of Heaven.[1]

As so often occurs in the history of the papacy, Julius II. was followed by a man of an entirely different type—Leo X. Though not yet 37 years of age, Giovanni de' Medici, distinguished for his generosity, mildness and *Leo X.,* courtesy, was elevated to the pontifical chair by *1513-1521.* the adroit manoeuvres of the younger cardinals. His policy—though officially he declared his intention of following in the steps of his predecessor—was at first extremely reserved. His ambition was to play the rôle of peacemaker, and his conciliatory policy achieved many successes. Thus, in the very first year of his reign, he removed the schism which had broken out under Julius II. As a statesman Leo X. often walked by very crooked paths; but the reproach that he allowed his policy to be swayed exclusively by his family interests is unjustified. It may be admitted that he clung to his native Florence and to his family with warm affection; but the" really decisive factor which governed his attitude throughout was his anxiety for the temporal and spiritual independence of the Holy See. The conquest of Milan by the French led to a personal interview at Bologna, where the " Concordat " with France was concluded. This document annulled the Pragmatic Sanction of Bourges, with its schismatic tendencies, but at the same time confirmed the preponderating influence of the king upon the Gallican Church—a concession which in spite of its many dubious aspects at least made the sovereign the natural defender of the Church and gave him the strongest motive for remaining Catholic. The war for the duchy of Urbino (1516-17) entailed disastrous consequences, as from it dates the complete disorganization of papal finance. It was, moreover, a contributing cause of the conspiracy of Cardinal Petrucci,[2] the suppression of which was followed (July, 1517) by the creation of 31 new cardinals in one day. This—the greatest of recorded creations—turned the scale once and for all in favour of the papal authority and against the cardinals. The efforts of Leo to promote a crusade, which fall mainly in the years 1517 and 1518, deserve all recognition, but very various opinions have been held as to the attitude of the pope towards the Imperial election consequent on the death of Maximilian I. The fundamental motive for his proceedings at that period was not nepotistic tendencies—which doubtless played their part, but only a secondary one—but his anxiety for the moral and temporal independence of the Holy See. For this reason Leo, from the very first, entertained no genuine desire for the selection either of Charles V. or Francis I. of France. By playing off one against the other he succeeded in holding both in suspense, and induced them to conclude agreements safeguarding the pope and the Medici. Of the two,

[1] The closer connexion of these frescoes with contemporary history was first elucidated by Pastor, in his *Geschichte der Päpste*, vol. iii., which also contains the most complete account of the reign of this the second Rovere pope.—[ED.]

[2] Alfonso Petrucci (d. 1517), a Sienese. He was degraded from the cardinalate by Leo X.—[ED.]

the French king appeared the less dangerous, and the result was that Leo championed his cause with all his energies. Not till the eleventh hour, when the election of the Habsburg, to whom he was entirely opposed, was seen to be certain did he give way. He thus at least avoided an open rupture with the new emperor—a rupture which would have been all the more perilous on account of the religious revolution now imminent in Germany. There the great secession from Rome was brought about by Martin Luther; but, in spite of his striking personality, the upheaval which was destined to shatter the unity of the Western Church was not his undivided work. True, he was the most powerful agent in the destruction of the existing order; but, in reality, he merely put the match to a pile of inflammable materials which had been collecting for centuries (see REFORMATION). A main cause of the cleavage in Germany was the position of ecclesiastical affairs, which—though by no means hopeless—yet stood in urgent need of emendation, and, combined with this, the deeply resented financial system of the Curia. Thus Luther assumed the leadership of a national opposition, and appeared as the champion who was to undertake the much-needed reform of abuses which clamoured for redress. The occasion for the schism was given by the conflict with regard to indulgences, in the course of which Luther was not content to attack actual grievances, but assailed the Catholic doctrine itself. In June 1518 the canonical proceedings against Luther were begun in Rome; but, owing to political influences, only slow progress was made. It was not till the 15th of June 1520 that his new theology was condemned by the bull *Exsurge*, and Luther himself threatened with excommunication—a penalty which was only enforced owing to his refusal to submit, on the 3rd of January 1521.

The state of Germany, together with the unwise behaviour of Francis I., compelled Leo X. to side with Charles V. against the French king; and the united forces of the empire and papacy had achieved the most brilliant success in upper Italy, when Leo died unexpectedly, on the 1st of December 1521. The character of the first Medician pope shows a peculiar mixture of noble and ignoble qualities. With an insatiable love of pleasure he combined a certain external piety and a magnificent generosity in his charities. His financial administration was disastrous, and led simply to bankruptcy. On music, hunting, expensive feasts and theatrical performances money was squandered, while, with unexampled optimism the pope was blind to the deadly earnestness of the times.

Leo's name is generally associated with the idea of the Medician era as a golden age of science and art. This conception is only partially justified. The reputation of a greater Maecenas—ascribed to him by his eulogists—dwindles before a sober, critical contemplation, and his undeniable merits are by no means equal to those which fame has assigned to him. The love of science and literature, which animated the son of Lorenzo the Magnificent, frequently took the shape of literary dilettantism. In many respects the brilliance of this long and often vaunted Maecenate of Leo X. is more apparent than real. There are times when it irresistibly conveys the impression of dazzling fireworks of which nothing remains but the memory. The genuine significance of Leo lies rather in the stimulus which he gave. From this point of view his deserts are undoubtedly great; and for that reason he possesses an indefeasible right to a certain share in the renown of the papacy as a civilizing agent of the highest rank.

As a patron of art Leo occupies a more exalted plane. In this domain the first place must be assigned to the splendid achievements of Raphael, whom the pope entrusted with new and comprehensive commissions—the *Stanza dell' incendio*, the Logge, and the tapestry-cartoons, the originals of the last named being now in London. But, though illuminated by the rays of art, and loaded with the exuberant panegyrics of humanists and poets, the reign of the first Medicean pontiff, by its unbounded devotion to purely secular tendencies and its comparative neglect of the Church herself proved disastrous for the See of St Peter.

By a wonderful dispensation the successor to this scion of the Medici was Adrian VI.—a man who saw his noblest task, not in an artistic Maecenate, nor in the prosecution of political designs, but in the reform of the Church in all its members. Careless of the glories of Renaissance art, a stranger to all worldly instincts, the earnest Netherlander inscribed on his banner the healing of the moral ulcers, the restoration of unity to the Church—especially in Germany—and the preservation of the West from the Turkish danger. How clearly he read the causes of religious decadence, how deeply he himself was convinced of the need of trenchant reform, is best shown by his instructions to Chieregati, his nuncio to Germany, in which he laid the axe to the root of the tree with unheard-of freedom. Unfortunately, it was all in vain. Luther and his adherents overwhelmed the noble pope with unmeasured abuse. The two great rivals, Francis I. and Charles V., were deaf to his admonitions to make common cause against the Turks. The intrigues of Cardinal Soderini led to a breach with France and drove Adrian into the arms of the Imperial league. Soon afterwards, on the 14th of September 1523, he died. Long misunderstood and slandered, Adrian VI., the last German pope, is now by all parties ranked among the most revered and most worthy of the popes. No one now denies that he was one of those exceptional men, who without self-seeking spend their lives in the service of a cause and fight bravely against the stream of corruption. Even though, in his all too brief pontificate, he failed to attain any definite results, he at least fulfilled the first condition of any cure by laying bare the seat of disease, gave an important impetus to the cause of the reform of the Church, and laid down the principles on which this was afterwards carried through. His activity, in fact, will always remain one of the brightest chapters in the history of the papacy.

Under Leo X. Cardinal Giulio de' Medici, the cousin of that pope, had already exercised a decisive influence upon Catholic policy; and the tiara now fell to his lot. Clement VII.—so the new pontiff styled himself—was soon to discover the weight of the crown which he had gained. The international situation was the most difficult imaginable, and altogether beyond the powers of the timorous, vacillating and irresolute Medician pope. His determination to stand aloof from the great duel between Francis I. and Charles V. failed him at the first trial. He had not enough courage and perspicacity to await in patience the result of the race between France and Germany for the duchy of Milan—a contest which was decided at Pavia (Feb. 24, 1525). The haughty victors found Clement on the side of their opponent, and he was forced into an alliance with the emperor (April 1, 1525). The overweening arrogance of the Spaniards soon drove the pope back into the ranks of their enemies. On the 22nd of May 1526 Clement acceded to the League of Cognac, and joined the Italians in their struggle against the Spanish supremacy. This step he was destined bitterly to repent. The tempest descended on the pope and on Rome with a violence which cannot be paralleled, even in the days of Alaric and Genseric, or of the Norman Robert Guiscard. On the 6th of May 1527 the Eternal City was stormed by the Imperial troops and subjected to appalling devastation in the famous sack. Clement was detained for seven months a prisoner in the castle of St Angelo. He then went into exile at Orvieto and Viterbo, and only on the 6th of October 1528 returned to his desolate residence. After the fall of the French dominion in Italy he made his peace with the emperor at Barcelona (June 29, 1529); in return for which he received the assistance of Charles in re-establishing the rule of the Medici in Florence. During the Italian turmoil the schism in Germany had made such alarming progress that it now proved impossible to bridge the chasm. With regard to the question of a council the pope was so obsessed by doubts and fears that he was unable to advance a single step; nor, till the day of his death could he break off his pitiful vacillation between Charles V. and Francis I. While large portions of Germany were lost to the Church the revolt from Rome proceeded apace in Switzerland

and the Scandinavian countries. To add to the disasters, the divorce of Henry VIII. led to the English schism. Whether another head of the Church could have prevented the defection of England is of course an idle question. But Clement VII. was far from possessing the qualities which would have enabled him to show a bold front to the ambitious Cardinal Wolsey and the masterful and passionate Henry VIII. At the death of Clement (Sept. 25, 1534), the complete disruption of the Church seemed inevitable.

When all seemed lost salvation was near. Even in the reign of the two Medici popes the way which was to lead to better things had been silently paved within the Church. Under Leo X. himself there had been formed in Rome, in the Oratory of the Divine Love, a body of excellent men of strictly Catholic sentiments. It was by members of this Oratory—especially St Caetano di Tiene, Carafa (later Paul IV.), and the great bishop of Verona, Giberti—that the foundations of the Catholic reformation were laid. Under Clement VII. the establishment of new religious orders—Theatines, Somascians, Barnabites and Capuchins—had sown the seeds of a new life in the ancient Church. The harvest was reaped during the long pontificate of the Farnese pope, Paul III. With his accession *Paul III., 1534-1549.* devotion to religion and the Church began to regain their old mastery. True, Paul III. was not a representative of the Catholic reformation, in the full sense of the words. In many points, especially his great nepotism— witness the promotion of the worthless Pier Luigi Farnese— he remained, even as pope, a true child of the Renaissance period in which he had risen to greatness. Nevertheless he possessed the necessary adaptability and acumen to enable him to do justice to the demands of the new age, which imperatively demanded that the interests of the Church should be the first consideration. Thus, in the course of his long reign he did valuable work in the cause of the Catholic reformation and prepared the way for the Catholic restoration. It was he who regenerated the College of Cardinals by leavening it with men of ability, who took in hand the reform of the Curia, confirmed the Jesuit Order, and finally brought the Council of Trent into existence (Sessions I.–X. of the council, first period, 1545–1549). In order to check the progress of Protestantism in Italy Paul III. founded the Congregation of the Inquisition (1542). Political differences, and the transference of the council to Bologna in 1547, brought the pope into sharp collision with the emperor, who now attempted by means of the *Interim* to regulate the religious affairs of Germany according to his wishes —but in vain. The disobedience of his favourite Ottavio hastened the death of the old pope (Nov. 10, 1549).

Under the Farnese pope art enjoyed an Indian summer. The most important work for which he was responsible is the "Last Judgment" of Michelangelo in the Sistine Chapel. In 1547 Michelangelo was further entrusted with the superintendence of the reconstruction of St Peter's. He utilized his power by rejecting the innovations of Antonio da Sangallo, saved the plan of Bramante, and left behind him sufficient drawings to serve the completion of the famous cupola. Titian painted Paul's portrait, and Guglielmo della Porta cast the bronze statue which now adorns his grave in St Peter's.

After a protracted conclave Giovanni Maria del Monte was elected, on the 7th of February 1550, as Pope Julius III. He *Julius III., 1550-1555.* submitted to the emperor's demands and again convened the council (Sessions XL–XVI., second period), but was obliged to suspend it on the 22nd of April 1552, in consequence of the war between Charles V. and Maurice of Saxony. From this time onwards the pope failed to exhibit requisite energy. In his beautiful villa before the Porta del Popolo he sought to banish political and ecclesiastical anxieties from his mind. Yet even now he was not wholly inactive. The religious affairs of England especially engaged his attention; and the nomination of Cardinal Pole as his legate to that country, on the death of Edward VI. (1553), was an extremely adroit step. That the measure was fruitless was not the fault of Julius III., who died on the 23rd of March 1555.

The feeble régime of Julius had made it evident that a pope of another type was necessary if the papal see were to preserve the moral and political influence which it had regained under Paul III. On the 10th of April 1555, after a conclave which lasted five days, the reform party secured *Marcellus II., 1555.* the election of the distinguished Marcellus II. Unfortunately, on the 1st of May, an attack of apoplexy cut short the life of this pope, who seemed peculiarly adapted for the reformation of the Church.

On the 23rd of May 1555 Gian Pietro Carafa, the strictest of the strict, was elected as his successor, under the title of Paul IV. Though already 79 years of age, he was animated by the fiery zeal of youth, and he employed the most drastic methods for executing the necessary reforms and combating the advance of Protestantism. Always an opponent *Paul IV., 1555-1559.* of the Spaniards, Paul IV., in the most violent and impolitic fashion, declared against the Habsburgs. The conflict with the Colonna was soon followed by the war with Spain, which, in spite of the French alliance, ended so disastrously, in 1557, that the pope henceforward devoted himself exclusively to ecclesiastical affairs. The sequel was the end of the nepotism and the relentless prosecution of reform within the Church. Protestantism was successfully eradicated in Italy; but the pope failed to prevent the secession of England. After his death the rigour of the Inquisition gave rise to an insurrection in Rome. The Venetian ambassador says of Paul IV. that, although all feared his strictness, all venerated his learning and wisdom.

The reaction against the iron administration of Paul IV. explains the fact that, after his decease, a more worldly-minded pope was again elected in the person of Cardinal Giovanni Angelo de' Medici—Pius IV. *Pius IV., 1559-1565.* In striking contrast to his predecessor he favoured the Habsburgs. A suit was instituted against the Carafa, and Cardinal Carafa was even executed. To his own relatives, however, Pius IV. accorded no great influence, the advancement of his distinguished nephew, Carlo Borromeo (q.v.), being singularly fortunate for the Church. The most important act of his reign was the reassembling of the Council of Trent (Sessions XVII.–XXV., third period, 1562–1563). It was an impressive moment, when, on the 4th of December 1563, the great ecumenical synod of the Church came to a close. Till the last it was obliged to contend with the most formidable difficulties: yet it succeeded in effecting many notable reforms and in illuminating and crystallizing the distinctive doctrines of Catholicism. The breach with the Protestant Reformation was now final, and all Catholics felt themselves once more united and brought into intimate connexion with the centre of unity at Rome (see TRENT, COUNCIL OF).

The three great successors of Pius IV. inaugurate the heroic age of the Catholic reformation and restoration. All three were of humble extraction, and sprang from the people in the full sense of the phrase. Pius V., *Pius V., 1566-1572.* formerly Michele Ghisleri and a member of the Dominican Order observed even as pope the strictest rules of the brotherhood, and was already regarded as a saint by his contemporaries. For Rome, in especial, he completed the task of reform. The Curia, once so corrupt, was completely metamorphosed, and once more became a rallying point for men of stainless character, so that it produced a profound impression even on non-Catholics; while the original methods of St Philip Neri had a profound influence on the reform of popular morals. In the rest of Italy also Pius V. put into execution the reformatory decrees of Trent. In 1566 he gave publicity to the Tridentine catechism; in 1568 he introduced the amended Roman breviary; everywhere he insisted on strict monastic discipline, and the compulsory residence of bishops within their sees. At the same period Carlo Borromeo made his diocese of Milan the model of a reformed bishopric. The pope supported Mary Stuart with money; his troops assisted Charles IX. of France against the Huguenots; and he lent his aid to Philip II. against the Calvinists of the Netherlands. But his greatest joy was that he succeeded where Pius II. had failed, despite all his efforts, by bringing to a head an enterprise against the Turks—then masters of the Mediterranean. He negotiated an alliance between the Venetians and Spaniards, contributed ships and soldiers, and secured the election of Don John of Austria to the supreme command. He was privileged to survive the victory of the Christians at Lepanto; but on the 1st of May in the following year he died, as piously as he had lived. The last pope to be canonized, his pontificate marks the zenith of the Catholic reformation.

The renewed vigour which this internal reformation had infused into the Church was now manifest in its external effects; and Pius V., the pope of reform, was followed by the popes of the Catholic restoration. These, without intermitting the work of reformation, endeavoured by every means to further the outward expansion of Catholicism. On the one hand missions were despatched to America, India, China and Japan; on the other, a strenuous attempt was made to reannex the conquests of Protestantism. In a word, the age of the Catholic restoration was beginning—a movement which has been misnamed the counter Reformation. In this period, the newly created religious orders were the right arm of the papacy, especially the Jesuits and the Capuchins. In place of the earlier supineness, the battle was now joined all along the line. Everywhere, in Germany and France, in Switzerland and the Low Countries, in Poland and Hungary, efforts were made to check the current of Protestantism and to re-establish the orthodox faith. This activity extended to wider and wider areas, and enterprises were even set on foot to regain England, Sweden and Russia for the Church. This universal outburst of energy for the restoration of Catholicism, which only came to a standstill in the middle of the 17th century, found one of its most zealous promotors in Ugo Boncompagni—*Gregory XIII., 1572-1585.* Pope Gregory XIII. Though not of an ascetic nature, he followed unswervingly in the path of his predecessors by consecrating his energies to the translation of the reformatory decrees into practice. At the same time he showed himself anxious to further the cause of ecclesiastical instruction and Catholic science. He created a special Congregation to deal with episcopal affairs, and organized the Congregation of the Index, instituted by Pius V. On behalf of the diffusion of Catholicism throughout the world he spared no efforts; and wherever he was able he supported the great restoration. He was especially active in the erection and encouragement of educational institutions. In Rome he founded the splendid College of the Jesuits; and he patronized the Collegium Germanicum of St Ignatius; while, at the same time, he found means for the endowment of English and Irish colleges. In fact, his generosity for the cause of education was so unbounded that he found himself in financial difficulties. Gregory did good service, moreover, by his reform of the calendar which bears his name, by his emended edition of the *Corpus juris canonici* and by the creation of nunciatures. That he celebrated the night of St Bartholomew was due to the fact that, according to his information, the step was a last resort to ensure the preservation of the royal family and the Catholic religion from the attacks of the revolutionary Huguenots. In his political enterprises he was less fortunate. He proved unable to devise a common plan of action on the part of the Catholic princes against Elizabeth of England and the Turks; while he was also powerless to check the spread of brigandage in the papal state.

On the death of Gregory XIII., Felice Peretti, cardinal of Montalto, a member of the Franciscan order, ascended the Apostolic throne as Sixtus V. (April 1585–August *Sixtus V., 1585-1590.* 1590). His first task was the extirpation of the bandits and the restoration of order within the papal state. In the course of a year the drastic measures of this born ruler made this state the safest country in Europe. He introduced a strictly ordered administration, encouraged the sciences, and enlarged the Vatican library, housing it in a splendid building erected for the purpose in the Vatican itself. He was an active patron of agriculture and commerce: he even

interested himself in the draining of the Pontine marshes. The financial system he almost completely reorganized. With a boldness worthy of Julius II., he devised the most gigantic schemes for the annihilation of the Turkish Empire and the conquest of Egypt and Palestine. Elizabeth of England he wished to restore to the Roman obedience either by conversion or by force; but these projects were shattered by the destruction of the Spanish Armada. Down to his death the pope kept a vigilant eye on the troubles in France. Here his great object was to save France for the Catholic religion, and, as far as possible, to secure her position as a power of the first rank. To this fundamental axiom of his policy he remained faithful throughout all vicissitudes.

In Rome itself Sixtus displayed extraordinary activity. The Pincian, the Esquiline, and the south-easterly part of the Caelian hills received essentially their present form by the creation of the Via Sistina, Felice, delle Quattro Fontane, di Sta Croce in Gerusalemme, &c.; by the buildings at Sta Maria Maggiore, the Villa Montalto, the reconstruction of the Lateran, and the aqueduct of the Felice, which partially utilized the Alexandrina and cost upwards of 300,000 scudi. The erection of the obelisks of the Vatican, the Lateran, the Piazza del Popolo and the square behind the tribune of Sta Maria Maggiore lent a lustre to Rome which no other city in the world could rival. The columns of Trajan and Antoninus were restored and bedecked with gilded statues of the Apostles; nor was this the only case in which the high-minded pope made the monuments of antiquity subservient to Christian ideas. His principal architect was Domenico Fontana, who, in conjunction with Guglielmo della Porta, completed the uniquely beautiful cupola of St Peter's which had already been designed by Michelangelo in a detailed model. In Santa Maria Maggiore the pope erected the noble Sistine Chapel, in which he was laid to rest. Indeed, the monumental character of Rome dates from this era. The organizing activity of Sixtus V. was not, however, restricted to the Eternal City, but extended to the whole administration of the Church. The number of cardinals was fixed at seventy—six bishops, fifty priests and fourteen deacons. In 1588 followed the new regulations with respect to the Roman Congregations, which henceforth were to be fifteen in number. Thus the pope laid the foundations of that wonderful and silent engine of universal government by which Rome still rules the Catholics of every land on the face of the globe.

When we reflect that all this was achieved in a single pontificate of but five years' duration, the energy of Sixtus V. appears simply astounding. He was, without doubt, by far the most important of the post-Tridentine popes, and his latest biographer might well say that he died overweighted with services to the Church and to humanity. (L. v. P.)

IV.—*Period from 1590 to 1870.*

The history of the papacy from 1590 to 1870 falls into four main periods: (1) 1590–1648; territorial expansion, definitely checked by the peace of Westphalia; (2) 1648–1789; waning prestige, financial embarrassments, futile reforms; (3) 1789–1814; revolution and Napoleonic reorganization; (4) 1814–1870; restoration and centralization.

1. 1590–1648. The keynote of the counter Reformation had been struck by the popes who immediately preceded this period. They sought to reconquer Europe for the Roman Catholic Church. In the overthrow of the Spanish Armada they had already received a great defeat; with the peace of Westphalia the Catholic advance was baffled. Sixtus V. was succeeded in rapid succession by three popes: Urban VII., who died on the 27th of September 1590, after a papacy of only 12 days; Gregory XIV. (Dec. 1590 to Oct. 1591); Innocent IX. (Oct. to Dec. 1591).

The first noteworthy pontiff of the period was Clement VIII., who gained a vast advantage by allying the papacy with the rising power of France. Since 1559 the popes had *Clement VIII., 1592-1605.* been without exception in favour of Spain, which firmly possessed of Milan on the north and of Naples 1592-1605.

on the south, held the States of the Church as in a vice, and thereby dominated the politics of the peninsula. After Henry IV. had taken Paris at the price of a mass, it became possible for the popes to play off the Bourbons against the Habsburgs; but the transfer of favour was made so gradually that the opposition of the papacy to Spain did not become open till just before Clement VIII. passed off the stage. His successor, Leo XI., undisguisedly French in sympathy, reigned but twenty-seven days—a sorry return for the 300,000 ducats which his election is rumoured to have cost.

Leo XI., 1605.

Henry IV. Under Paul V. Rome was successful in some minor negotiations with Savoy, Genoa, Tuscany and Naples; but Venice, under the leadership of Paolo Sarpi (*q.v.*), proved unbending under ban and interdict; the state defiantly upheld its sovereign rights, kept most of the clergy at their posts, and expelled the recalcitrant Jesuits. When peace was arranged through French mediation in 1607 the papacy had lost greatly in prestige: it was evident that the once terrible interdict was antiquated, wherefore it has never since been employed against the entire territory of a state.

Paul V., 1605-1621.

During the second and third decades of the 17th century the most coveted bit of Italian soil was the Valtelline. If Spain could gain this Alpine valley her territories would touch those of Austria, so that the Habsburgs north of the Alps could send troops to the aid of their Spanish cousins against Venice, and Spain in turn could help to subdue the Protestant princes of Germany in the Thirty Years' War (1618-1648). From the Grisons, who favoured France and Venice, Spain seized the Valtelline in 1620, incidentally uprooting heresy there by the massacre of six hundred Protestants. Paul V. repeatedly lamented that he was unable to oppose such Spanish aggressions without extending protection to heretics. This scruple was, however, not shared by his successor, Gregory XV., who secured the consent of the powers to the occupation of the Valtelline by papal troops, a diplomatic victory destined, however, to lead ere long to humiliation. Gregory's brief but notable pontificate marks nevertheless the high-tide of the counter-Reformation. Not for generations had the prospects for the ultimate annihilation of Protestantism been brighter. In the Empire the collapse of the Bohemian revolt led ultimately to the merciless repression of the Evangelicals in Bohemia (1627), and in the hereditary lands of Austria (1628), as well as to the transference of the electoral dignity from the Calvinistic elector of the Palatinate to the staunchly Catholic Max.milian of Bavaria. In France the Huguenots were shorn of almost all their military power, a process completed by the fall of La Rochelle in 1628. In Holland the expiration of the Twelve Years' Truce in 1621 forced the Dutch Protestants once more to gird on the sword. England, meanwhile, was isolated from her co-religionists. King James I., who had coquetted twenty years previously with Clement VIII., and then had avenged the Gunpowder Plot (1605) by the most stringent regulation of his Roman Catholic subjects, was now dazzled by the project of the Spanish marriage. The royal dupe was the last man in the world to check the advance of the papacy. That service to Protestantism was performed by Catholic powers jealous of the preponderance of the Habsburgs. In view of these antipathies the treaty of 1627 between France, Spain and the pope is but an episode: instructive, however, in that the project, originated apparently by the pope, provided that England should be dismembered, and that Ireland should be treated as a papal fief. The true tendency of affairs manifested itself in 1629, when the emperor Ferdinand II. (1619-1637), at the zenith of his fortunes, forced the Protestant princes of Germany to restore to the Roman hierarchy all the ecclesiastical territories they had secularized during the past seventy-four years. Then France, freed from the fear of domestic enemies, arose to help the heretics to harry the house of Habsburg. Arranging a truce between Poland and Sweden, she unleashed Gustavus Adolphus. Thus by diplomacy as well as by force of arms Catholic France made possible the continued

Gregory XV., 1621-1623.

The Counter-Reformation.

existence of a Protestant Germany, and helped to create the balance of power between Catholic, Lutheran and Reformed within the Empire, that, crystallized in the Peace of Westphalia, fixed the religious boundaries of central Europe for upwards of two centuries.

If it was Richelieu and not the pope who was the real arbiter of destinies from 1624 to 1642, Urban VIII. was usually content. In Italy he supported France against Spain in the controversy over the succession to Mantua (1627-1631). In the Empire he manifested his antipathy to the overshadowing Habsburgs by plotting for a time to carry the next imperial election in favour of Bavaria. He is said to have rejoiced privately over Swedish victories, and certainly it was unerring instinct which told him that the great European conflict was no longer religious but dynastic. Anti-Spanish to the core, he became the greatest papal militarist since Julius II.; but Tuscany, Modena and Venice checkmated him in his ambitious attempt to conquer the duchy of Parma. Like most of the papal armies of the last three centuries, Urban's troops distinguished themselves by wretched strategy, cowardice ·in rank and file, and a Fabian avoidance of fighting which, discreet as it may be in the field of diplomacy, has invariably failed to save Rome on the field of battle.

Urban VIII., 1623-1644.

The States of the Church were enlarged during this period by the reversion of two important fiefs—namely, Ferrara (1598) and Urbino (1631). Increase of territory, so far from filling the papal treasury, was postponed for the moment the progressive pauperization of the people. After annexation, the city of Ferrara sank rapidly from her perhaps artificial prosperity to the dead level, losing two-thirds of her population in the process. The financial difficulties of Italy were due to many causes, notably to a shifting of ·trade routes; but those of the papal states seem caused chiefly by misgovernment. .Militarism may account for much of the tremendous deficit under Urban VIII.; but the real cancer was nepotism. The disease was inherent in the body politic. Each pope, confronted by the spectre of feudal anarchy, felt he could rely truly only on those utterly dependent on himself; consequently he raised his own relations to wealth and influence. This method had helped the House of Valois to consolidate its power; but what was tonic for a dynasty was death to a state whose headship was elective. The relations of one pope became the enemies of the next; and each pontiff governed at the expense of his successors. Under Clement VIII. the Aldobrandini, more splendidly under Paul V. the Borghesi, with canny haste under the short-lived Gregory XV. the Lodovisi, with unparalleled rapacity Urban's Barberini enriched themselves from a chronically depleted treasury. To raise money offices were systematically sold, and issue after issue of the two kinds of *monti*-securities, which may be roughly described as government · bonds and as life annuities, was marketed at ruinous rates. More than a score of years after the Barberini had dropped the reins of power Alexander VII. said they alone had burdened the state with the payment of 483,000 scudi of annual interest, a tremendous item in a budget where the income was perhaps but 2,000,000. For a while interest charges consumed 85% of the income of the government. Skilful refunding postponed the day of evil, but cash on hand was too often a temptation to plunder. The financial woes of the next period, which is one of decline, were largely the legacy of this age of glory.

The Papal States.

Nepotism.

The common people, as always, had to pay. The farming of exorbitant taxes, coupled as it was too often with dishonest concessions to the tax farmer, made the over-burdened peasantry drink the doubly bitter cup of exploitation and injustice. Economic distress increased the number of highway robberies, these in turn lamed commercial intercourse.

The tale of these glories, with their attendant woes, does not exhaust the history of the papacy. Not as diplomatists, not as governors, but as successive heads of a spiritual kingdom, did the popes win their grandest triumphs. At a time when the non-Catholic theologians were chiefly small fry, bent on

petty or sulphurous polemics; great Jesuit teachers like Bellarmine (d. 1621) laid siege to the very foundations of the
Controversialist and Missionary Triumphs. Protestant citadel. These thinkers performed for
the unity of the faith in France and in the
Catholic states of Germany services of transcendent
merit, exceeding far in importance those of their
flourishing allies, the Inquisitions of Spain, Italy, and of the
Spanish Netherlands (see INQUISITION). But the most fundamental spiritual progress of the papacy was made by its devoted
missionaries. While the majority of Protestant leaders left
the conversion of the heathen to some remote and inscrutable
interposition of Providence, the Jesuits, Franciscans, Dominicans
and kindred orders were busily engaged in making Roman
Catholics of the nations brought by Oriental commerce or
American colonial enterprise into contact with Spain, Portugal
and France. Though many of the spectacular triumphs of the
cross in Asia and Africa proved to be evanescent, nevertheless
South America stands the impressive memorial of the greatest
forward movement in the history of the papacy: a solidly
Roman continent.

2. *1648-1789.* From the close of the Thirty Years' War
to the outbreak of the French Revolution the papacy suffered
abroad waning political prestige; at home, progressive financial
embarrassment accompanied by a series of inadequate governmental reforms; and in the world at large, gradual diminution of
reverence for spiritual authority. From slow beginnings these
factors kept gaining momentum until they compassed the
overthrow of the mighty order of the Jesuits, and culminated
in the revolutionary spoliation of the Church.

At the election of Innocent X. (1644–1655) the favour of the
Curia was transferred from France, where it had rested for over
Foreign Relations. forty years, to the House of Habsburg, where it
remained, save for the brief reign of Clement IX.
(1667–1669), for half a century. The era of tension
with France coincides with the earlier years of Louis XIV.
(1643–1715); its main causes were the Jansenist and the Gallican
controversies (see JANSENISM and GALLICANISM). The French
crown was willing to sacrifice the Jansenists, who disturbed
that dead level of uniformity so grateful to autocrats; but
Jansenism and Gallicanism. Gallicanism touched its very prerogatives, and was
a point of honour which could never be abandoned
outright. The regalia controversy, which broke
out in 1673, led up to the classic declaration of the
Gallican clergy of 1682; and, when aggravated by a conflict
over the immunity of the palace of the French ambassador at
Rome, resulted in 1688 in the suspension of diplomatic relations
with Innocent XI., the imprisonment of the papal nuncio, and
the seizure of Avignon and the Venaissin. So pronounced an
enemy of French preponderance did Innocent become that he
approved the League of Augsburg, and was not sorry to see the
Catholic James II., whom he considered a tool of Louis, thrust
from the throne of England by the Protestant William of Orange.
Fear of the coalition, however, led the Grand Monarch to make
peace with Innocent XII. (1691–1700). The good relations
with France were but a truce, for the Bourbon powers became
so mighty in the 18th century that they practically ignored the
territorial interests of the papacy. Thus Clement XI. (1700–
1721), who espoused the losing Habsburg side in the War of the
Spanish Succession, saw his nuncio excluded from the negotiations leading to the Peace of Utrecht, while the lay signatories
disposed of Sicily in defiance of his alleged overlordship. Similarly Clement XII. (1730–1740) looked on impotently when the
sudden Bourbon conquest of Naples in the War of the Polish
Succession set at nought his claims to feudal sovereignty, and
established Tannucci as minister of justice, a position in which
for forty-three years he regulated the relations of church and
state after a method most repugnant to Rome. No better
fared Clement's medieval rights to Parma; nor could the sagacious and popular Benedict XIV. (1740–1758), who refused to
press obsolete claims, either keep the foreign armies in the War
of the Austrian Succession from trespassing on the States of
the Church or prevent the ignoring at the Peace of Aix-la-

Chapelle of the papal overlordship over Parma and Piacenza.
In fact, since the doctrinaire protest of Innocent X. against the
Peace of Westphalia, at almost every important settlement
of European boundaries the popes had been ignored or otherwise snubbed. Not for two centuries had the political prestige
of the papacy been lower. Moreover, a feeling of revulsion
against the Jesuits was sweeping over western Europe: they
were accused of being the incarnation of the most baneful principles, political, intellectual, moral; and though Clement XIII.
(1758–1769) protected them against the pressure
Suppression of the Jesuits. of the Bourbon courts, his successor Clement XIV.
(1769–1774) was forced in 1773 to disband the
army of the Black Pope (see JESUITS). The sacri-
fice of these trusted soldiers failed however to sate the thirst
of the new age. Pius VI. (1775–1799), was treated with
scant respect by his neighbours. Naples refused him tribute;
Joseph II. of Austria politely but resolutely introduced fundamental Gallican reforms ("Josephism"); in 1786 at the Synod
of Pistoia (q.v.) Joseph's brother Leopold urged similar principles on Tuscany, while in Germany the very archbishops were
conspiring by the Punctation of Ems to aggrandize themselves
like true Febronians, at the expense of the pope (see FEBRONIAN-
ISM). These aggressions of monarchy and the episcopate were
rendered vain, outside the Habsburg dominions, by the revolution; and to the Habsburg dominions the clerical revolution
of 1790 caused the loss of what is to-day Belgium. However,
the deluge which shattered the opposition to Rome in the
great national churches submerged for a time the papacy
itself.

In the States of the Church, during the first part of the period the outstanding feature in the history of the Temporal Power
is the overthrow of nepotism; in the second, a dull
The States of the Church. conflict with debt. The chief enemies of nepotism
were Alexander VII. (1655–1667), who dignified
the secretaryship of state and gave it its present
pre-eminence by refusing to deliver it up to one of his relations;
and Innocent XII. (1691–1700), whose bull *Romanum decet ponti-
ficem* ordered that no pope should make more than one nephew
cardinal, and should not grant him an income over twelve
thousand scudi. Thus by 1700 nepotistic plunder had practically ceased, and with the exception of the magnificent pecula-
tions of Cardinal Coscia under Benedict XIII. (1724–1730), the
central administration of finance has been usually considered
honest. Nepotism, however, still left its scars upon the body
politic, shown in the progressive decay of agriculture in the
Campagna, causing Rome to starve in the midst of fertile but
untilled nepotistic *latifundia*. The fight against the legacy
of debt was slower and more dreary. One pope, Innocent XI.
(1676–1780), threatened at first with bankruptcy, managed to
leave a surplus; but this condition, the product of severe economy
and oppressive taxation, could not be maintained. In the
18th century it became necessary to resort to fiscal measures
which were often harmful. Thus Clement XI., at war with
Austria in 1708, debased the currency; Clement XII. (1730–1740)
issued paper money and set up a government lottery, excommunicating all subjects who put their money into the lotteries
of Genoa or Naples; Benedict XIV. (1740–1758) found stamped
paper a failure; and Clement XIII. (1758–1769) made a forced
loan. The stoppage of payments from Bourbon countries
during the Jesuit struggle brought the annual deficit to nearly
500,000 scudi. Under Pius VI. (1775–1799) the emission of
paper money, followed by an unsuccessful attempt to market
government securities, produced a panic. By 1783 the taxes
had been farmed for years in advance and the treasury was in
desperate straits. Retrenchment often cut to the bone; wise
reforms shattered on the inexperience or corruption of officials.
Grand attempts to increase the national wealth usually cost
the government more in fixed charges of interest than they
yielded in rentals or taxes. The States of the Church, like
France, were on the brink of bankruptcy. From this disgrace they were saved by a more imminent catastrophe—the
Revolution.

The revolt against spiritual authority belongs rather to the history of modern thought than to that of the papacy. The *Intellectual Renaissance* and Protestantism had their effect in *Movement* producing that Enlightenment which swept over *against the* western Europe in the 18th century. Although *Papacy.* Descartes died in 1650 in the communion of the Church, his philosophy contained seeds of revolt; and the sensualism of Locke, popularized in Italy by Genovesi, prepared the way for revolution. In an age when Voltaire preached toleration and the great penologist Beccaria attacked the death-penalty and torture, in the States of the Church heretics were still liable to torture, the relapsed to capital punishment; and in a backward country like Spain the single reign of Philip V. (1700-1746) had witnessed the burning of over a thousand heretics. If ecclesiastical authority fostered what was commonly regarded as intolerant obscurantism, to be enlightened meant to be prepared in spirit for that reform which soon developed into the Revolution.

3. 1789-1814. In the decade previous to the outbreak of the French Revolution the foreign policy of Pius VI. had been *The Papacy* directed chiefly against decentralization, while his *and the* chief aim at home was to avoid bankruptcy by in-*Revolution.* creasing his income. From 1789 on the French situation absorbed his attention. France, like the States of the Church, was facing financial ruin; but France did what the government of priests could not: namely, saved the day by the confiscation and sale of ecclesiastical property. It was not the aim of the Constituent Assembly to pauperize or annihilate the Church; it purposed to reorganize it on a juster basis. These reforms, embodied in the Civil Constitution of the Clergy, were part of the new Fundamental Law of the kingdom. The majority of the priests and bishops refused to swear assent to what they held to be an invasion of the divine right of the hierarchy, and after some months of unfortunate indecision Pius VI. (1775-1799) formally condemned it. Thenceforward France treated the papacy as an inimical power. The sullen toleration of the non-juring priests changed into sanguinary persecution. The harrying was halted in 1795; and soon after the directory had been succeeded by the consulate, the Catholic religion was re-established by the concordat of 1801. From 1790 on, however, the rising power of France had been directed against Rome. In September 1791 France annexed Avignon and the Venaissin, thus removing for ever that territorial pawn with whose threatened loss the French monarchs had for centuries disciplined their popes. In 1793 Hugon de Basseville (q.v.), a diplomatic agent of France, was murdered at Rome, a deed not avenged until the Italian victories of Bonaparte. In the peace of Tolentino (Feb. 1797) the pope surrendered his claims to Avignon, the Venaissin, Bologna, Ferrara and the Romagna; he also promised to disband his worthless army, to yield up certain treasures of art, and to pay a large indemnity. Bonaparte believed that after these losses the temporal power would collapse of its own weight; but so peaceful a solution was not to be. During republican agitation at Rome the French general Duphot was killed, a French army advanced on the city, and *Pius VII.* carried the aged pontiff a prisoner of war to Valence in *1800-1823.* Dauphiné, where he died on the 29th of August 1799.

His successor Pius VII., elected at Venice on the 14th of the following March, soon entered Rome and began his reign auspiciously by appointing as secretary of state Ercole Consalvi (q.v.), the greatest papal diplomatist of the 19th century. The political juncture was favourable for a reconciliation with *Concordat* France. In the concordat of 1801 the papacy *of 1801.* recognized the validity of the sales of Church property, and still further reduced the number of dioceses; it provided that the government should appoint and support the archbishops and bishops, but that the pope should confirm them; and France recognized the temporal power, though shorn of Ferrara, Bologna and the Romagna. The supplementary Organic Articles of April 1802, however, centralized the administration of the Church in the hands of the First Consul; and some of these one-sided regulations

were considered by Rome to be minute and oppressive; nevertheless, the Napoleonic arrangements remained in force, with but brief exceptions, till the year 1905. The indignation of the pope and his advisers was not deep enough to prevent the ratification in 1803 of a somewhat similar concordat for the Italian Republic. In 1804 Pius consented to anoint Napoleon emperor, thus casting over a conquered crown the halo of legitimacy. The era of good feeling was, however, soon ended by friction, which arose at a number of points. At length, in 1809, Napoleon annexed the papal states; and Pius, who excommunicated the invaders of his territory, was removed to France. The captive was, however, by no means powerless; by refusing canonical institution to the French bishops he involved the ecclesiastical system of Napoleon in inextricable confusion. After the return from Moscow the emperor negotiated with his prisoner a new and more exacting concordat, but two months later the repentant pope abrogated this treaty and declared all the official acts of the new French bishops to be invalid. By this time Napoleon was tottering to his fall; shortly before the catastrophe of Elba he allowed the pope to return to the States of the Church. Pius entered Rome amid great rejoicing on the 24th of May 1814, a day which marks the beginning of a new era in the history of the papacy. In September of the same year, by the bull *Sollicitudo omnium ecclesiarum*, he reconstituted the Society of Jesus.

Though the relations with France dominated the papal policy during the revolutionary period, the affairs of Germany received no small share of attention. The peace of Lunéville (1801) established the French boundary at the Rhine; and the German princes who thereby lost lands west of the river were indemnified by the secularization of ecclesiastical *Secularization* territories to the east. The scheme of readjust-*tions of* ment, known as the Enactment of the Delegates of *1803.* the Empire (*Reichsdeputationshauptschluss*) of 1803, secularized practically all the ecclesiastical states of Germany. Thus at one stroke there was broken the age-long direct political power of the hierarchy in the Holy Roman Empire; and the ultimate heir of the bulk of these lands was Protestant Prussia.

4. 1814-1870. The foreign policy of the papacy so long as conducted by Consalvi, or in his spirit, was supremely successful. From 1814 to 1830 Europe witnessed the restoration *The Papacy* of legitimate monarchy. The once exiled dynasties *and the* conscientiously re-established the legitimate Church, *Restoration.* and both conservative powers made common cause against revolutionary tendencies. Throughout Europe the governing classes regarded this "union of throne and altar" as axiomatic. For the pope, as eldest legitimate sovereign and protagonist against the Revolution, Consalvi obtained from the Congress of Vienna the restitution of the States of the Church in practically their full extent. By concluding concordats with all the important Catholic powers save Austria he made it possible to crush Jansenism, Febronianism and Gallicanism. By bulls of circumscription, issued after consultation with various Protestant states of Germany, he rearranged their Catholic dioceses and readjusted ecclesiastical incomes. By unfailing tact he gained the good will of Great Britain, where before him no cardinal had set foot for two centuries, and secured that friendly understanding between the British government and the Vatican which has since proved so valuable to Rome. After Consalvi's retirement, Leo XII. (1823-1829) continued his policy and secured further advantageous concordats. In the sixteen months' reign of Pius VIII. (1829-1830) came the achievement of Catholic emancipation in England and the Revolution of 1830; and the pope departed from the principle of legitimacy by recognizing Louis Philippe as king of the French. The pontificate of Gregory XVI. (1831-1846) was singularly infelicitous. The controversy with Prussia about the education of children of whose parents but one was Roman Catholic led to the imprisonment of Droste-Vischering, archbishop of Cologne, and later of Dunin, archbishop of Gnesen-Posen; but the accession of the royal romanticist Frederick William IV. in 1840 brought a pacific reversal of the Prussian policy, sometimes

judged more benevolent than wise. In France agitation was directed chiefly against the Jesuits, active in the movement to displace ancient local catechisms and liturgies by the Roman texts, to enroll the laity in Roman confraternities, and to induce the bishops to visit Rome more frequently. To check this ultramontane propaganda the government secured from the papacy in 1845 the promise to close the Jesuit houses and novitiates in France.

In Italy, however, lay the chief obstacles to the success of all papal undertakings. The revolution of 1830, though somewhat tardily felt in the States of the Church, compelled Gregory to rest his rule on foreign bayonets. In return he was obliged to lend an ear to the proposals of France, and above all to those of Austria. This meant opposition to all schemes for the unification of Italy. In 1815 the Italian peninsula had been divided into seven small states. Besides the government of the pope there were three kingdoms: Sardinia, Lombardo-Venetia and Naples; and three duchies: Parma, Modena, Tuscany. To these regions the Napoleonic régime had given a certain measure of unity; but Metternich, dominant after 1815, held Italy to be merely a geographical term. To its unification Austria was the chief obstacle; she owned Lombardo-Venetia; she controlled the three duchies, whose rulers were Austrian princes; and she upheld the autocracy of the king of Naples and that of the pope against all revolutionary movements. To the Italian patriot the papacy seemed in league with the oppressor. The pope sacrificed the national aspirations of his subjects to his international relations as head of the Church; and he sacrificed their craving for liberty to the alliance with autocracy on which rested the continued existence of the temporal power. The dual position of the pope, as supreme head of the Church on earth and as a minor Italian prince, was destined to break down through its inherent contradiction; it was the task of Pius IX. to postpone the catastrophe.

The reign of Pius IX. falls into three distinct parts. Until driven from Rome by the republican agitation of 1848 he was a popular idol, open to liberal political views. From his return in 1850 to 1870 he was the reactionary ruler of territories menaced by the movement for Italian unity, and sustained only by French bayonets; yet he was interested primarily in pointing out to an often incredulous world that most of the vaunted, intellectual and religious progress of the 19th century was but pestilent error, properly to be condemned by himself as the infallible vicegerent of God. The third division of his career, from the loss of the temporal power to his death, inaugurates a new period for the papacy.

Pius IX., 1846-1878.

At the outset of his reign he faced a crisis. It was clear that he could not continue the repressive tactics of his predecessor. Italy and Europe were astir with the Liberal agitation, which in 1848 culminated in the series of revolutions by which the settlement of 1815 was destined to be profoundly modified. Liberal churchmen in Italy, while rejecting Mazzini's dream of a republic, had evolved projects for attaining national unity while preserving the temporal power. The exiled abbé Vincenzo Gioberti championed an Italian confederacy under the presidency of the pope; based in hand with the unity of the nation should go the unity of the faith. In allusion to medieval partisans of the papacy this theory was dubbed Neo-Guelphism. Towards such a solution Pius IX. was at first not unfavourably inclined, but the revolution of 1848 cured him of his Liberal leanings. In November of that year he fled in disguise from his capital to Gaeta, in the kingdom of Naples, and when French arms had made feasible his restoration to Rome in April 1850 he returned in a temper of stubborn resistance to all reform; henceforth he was no longer open to the influence of men of the type of Rossi or Rosmini, but took the inspiration of his policy from Cardinal Antonelli and the Jesuits. The same pope who had signalized his accession by carrying out a certain number of Liberal reforms set his name in 1864 to the famous *Syllabus*, which was in effect a declaration of war by the papacy against the leading principles of modern civilization (see SYLLABUS).

The Papacy and Italian Unity.

As from 1849 to 1870 the fate of the papacy was determined not so much by domestic conditions, which, save for certain slight ameliorations, were those of the preceding reigns, as by foreign politics, it is necessary to consider the relations of Rome with each of the powers in turn; and in so doing one must trace not merely the negotiations of kings and popes, but must seek to understand also the aims of parliamentary parties, which from 1848 on increasingly determine ecclesiastical legislation.

The chief ally of the papacy from 1849 to 1870 was France. The policy which made Louis Napoleon dictator forced him into mortal conflict with the republican parties; and the price of the parliamentary support of the Catholic majority was high. Even before Napoleon's election as president, Falloux, the Catholic leader, had promised to secure intervention in favour of the dispossessed pope. Napoleon, however, could not forget that as a young man he himself had vainly fought to obtain from Gregory XVI. those liberties which Pius IX. still refused to grant; he therefore essayed diplomacy, not arms. Nevertheless, to forestall the rescue of the pope by Austrian troops, he sent, in August 1849, an army corps under Oudinot to Civita Vecchia. By heading off reactionary Austria Napoleon hoped to conciliate the French Liberals; by helping the pope, to satisfy the Catholics; by concessions to be wrung both from Pius and from the Roman triumvirs, to achieve a bloodless victory. As neither party yielded, Oudinot listened to his Catholic advisers, attacked Rome, with which the French Republic was technically at peace—and was roundly repulsed by Garibaldi. To relieve their inglorious predicament the ministry hurried the Liberal diplomatist, Ferdinand de Lesseps, to Rome to prevent further conflict. At the moment when Lesseps had secured the signing of a treaty with the Roman Republic permitting peaceful occupation of the city by the French army, he was peremptorily recalled and Oudinot was as unexpectedly ordered to take the city by storm. This amazing reversal of policy was procured by the intrigues of Catholic diplomatists and German Jesuits, conveyed to Paris by Prince de la Tour d'Auvergne. For the honour of the army and the Church republican France thereupon destroyed the Roman republic. Napoleon lost 1200 in dead and wounded, actually secured not a single reform on which he had insisted, and drew upon himself the fateful obligation to mount perpetual guard over the Vatican. As the catspaw of clerical reaction he had also to acquiesce in that "Roman campaign at home" that resulted in the Falloux Act of 1850, which in the name of liberty of education put the university in bondage to the archbishops, militated against lay teachers and set them in secondary and primary schools, and set them under clerical control, made it ominously easy for members of religious congregations to become instructors of youth, and cut the nerve of the communal school system. That education was delivered up to the Church was partly the result of the terror inspired in the middle classes by the socialistic upheavals of 1848. The bourgeoisie sought the support of the clergy, and irreligion became as unfashionable among them as it had been among the nobility after 1793. Religion was thought to be part of a fashionable education, and the training of girls came almost exclusively into the hands of the religious orders and congregations. So long as the alliance of the autocratic empire and the clergy lasted (1852-1860), intellectual reaction reigned; the university professorships of history and philosophy were suppressed. This alliance of the empire with the clergy was shaken by the Italian War of 1859, which resulted in the loss by the pope of two-thirds of his territories. Napoleon was evidently returning to the traditions of his youth, and in the September Convention of 1864 it looked as if he would abandon Rome to its manifest destiny. This solution was spoiled by the impatience of Garibaldi and the supineness of the Romans themselves. In 1867 Napoleon made himself once more guardian of the Holy See; but the wonders wrought by the new French chassepots at the battle of Mentana cost the friendship of Italy. Thereafter Napoleon was blindly staggering to his fall. He

Prince Cameron of Papacy.

Napoleon III.

Papacy.

aimed at honour-in upholding the pope, in driving the Austrian tyrant from Italy; in attacking Prussia. The Austrian support on which he relied confidently in 1870 proved delusive, for he could obtain nothing from Austria unless he had Italy with him, and nothing from Italy without the evacuation of Rome. Even after the war with Prussia had actually broken out he refused Italian aid at the price of the abandonment of the city, a step which he nevertheless reversed hurriedly twenty days too late. With Napoleon fell the temporal power; but the French hierarchy still kept his gifts in the shape of the congregations, the pro-Catholic colonial policy, and a certain control of education. Of these privileges the Church was to be deprived a generation later. The Third Republic can never forget that it was to the support of the temporal sovereignty of the pope that Napoleon III. owed his empire and France her deepest humiliation.

On the withdrawal of the French garrison Rome was occupied by the troops of Victor Emmanuel. This monarch had always *Italian Oc-* been a thorn in the side of the papacy. Under him *cupation of* Sardinia had adopted the Siccardi Laws of 1850, *Rome.* which had taken away the right of asylum and the jurisdiction of the Church over its own clergy. His reputation for sacrilege, increased five years later by the abolition of many monasteries, became notorious when the formation of the kingdom of Italy (1861) took away all the dominions of the pope except the patrimony of Peter, thereby reducing the papal provinces from twenty to five, and their population from over 3,000,000 to about 685,000. This act was followed in 1867 by the confiscation of church property, and on the 20th of September 1870 by the triumphant seizure of Rome.

If France was the right arm and Italy the scourge of the papacy under Pius IX., the Spanish-speaking countries were its *The Papacy* obedient tools. Torn by civil wars, their harassed *and the* rulers sought papal recognition at a cost which *Spanish* more experienced governments would have refused. *States.* Thus Isabella II. of Spain in the concordat of 1851 confirmed the exclusive privileges of the Roman religion and gave the control of all education to the Church; but after the Revolution of 1868 Spain departed for the first time from the principle of the unity of the faith by establishing liberty of worship, which was, however, a dead letter. On the Spanish model concordats were arranged with various Central and South American republics, perhaps the most ironclad being that concluded with Ecuador in 1862 (abrogated 1878).

Among the more stable governments of Europe reaction in favour of conservatism and religion after 1848 was used by *Concordat* clerical parties to obtain concordats more systematic *with* and thoroughgoing than had been concluded even *Austria,* after 1814. Austria, for instance, although long *1855.* the political mainstay of the papacy, had never abandoned the broad lines of ecclesiastical policy laid down by Joseph II.; but the young Francis Joseph, seeking the aid of Rome in curbing heterogeneous nationalities, in 1855 negotiated a concordat whose paragraphs regarding the censorship, education and marriage were far-reaching. It was, moreover, the first document of the sort in which a first-class power recognized that the rights of the Church are based upon " divine institution and canon law," not upon governmental concession. Violated by the Liberal constitution of 1867, which granted religious liberty, depotentiated by laws setting up lay jurisdiction over matrimonial cases and state control of education, it was abrogated in 1870 by Austria, who alleged that the proclamation of papal infallibility had so altered the status of one of the contracting parties that the agreement was void.

Passing over Portugal, the remaining European state which is Roman Catholic is Belgium. Torn from Austria by the *Belgium.* clerical revolution of 1790, after many vicissitudes it was united in 1815 with Holland and placed under the rule of the Protestant William I., king of the United Netherlands. The constitutional guarantee of religious liberty had from the outset been resisted by the powerful and resolute priesthood, supported by numerous sympathizers among the nobility. As the arbitrary king alienated the Liberal Catholics, who were

still more or less under the spell of the French Revolution, the Catholic provinces took advantage of the upheavals of 1830 to form the independent kingdom of Belgium. Its Fundamental Law of 1831, conceived in the spirit of the English Whigs, and later imitated in the European countries, granted liberty of worship and of education. Strangely enough, this liberty meant increase of power for the Clericals; for besides putting an end to stringent state interference in the education of future priests, it made possible a free and far-reaching Catholic school system whose crown was the episcopally controlled university of Louvain (1834). The Education Act of 1842 led to the formation of the Liberal party, whose bond of union was resistance to clericalism, whose watchword was the "independence of the civil power." The Catholics and Liberals were alternately in control until 1894, when the tenfold enlargement of the electorate broke down the Liberal party completely. The chief theme of contention, developed through many a noteworthy phase, has been the question of schools. In the half-century from 1830 to 1880 the cloisters likewise prospered and multiplied fivefold. The result of this evolution is that Belgium is to-day the most staunchly Catholic land north of the Alps.

In Holland, as in Belgium, the education question has been uppermost. Here, even after 1831 the Roman Catholics constituted three-eighths of the population. Allied with *Holland.* the Liberals against the orthodox Protestants, who were threatening religious liberty, the Catholics assisted in 1857 to establish a system of non-sectarian state schools, where attendance is not obligatory nor instruction gratuitous. Changing front, in 1868, in league with the orthodox, they tried to make these denominational; but as the Liberals defeated their attempt, they founded schools of their own.

In the non-Catholic countries of Europe during the reign of Pius IX., and in fact during the whole 19th century, the important gains of Rome were in strategic position rather *Other non-* than in numbers. The spread of toleration, which *Catholic* always favours minorities, broke down between 1845 *Countries.* and 1873 the Lutheran exclusiveness of Norway, Denmark and Sweden; but as yet the Catholics form a disappearing fraction of the population. In European Russia, as a result of the partitions of Poland under Catherine II. (1762-1796), about one-tenth of the people are Roman Catholics. The Ruthenians had united with Rome at Brest in 1596, forming a group of Uniates distinct from the Poles, who belonged to the Latin rite. In spite of the assurances of Catherine, Russia has repeatedly persecuted the Ruthenian Uniates, in order to incorporate them into the Holy Orthodox Church; and she has occasionally taken drastic measures against the Poles, particularly after the revolts of 1830 and 1863. After more than a century of repression in 1905 the Edict of Toleration brought some relief.

The remarkable extension of the Catholic hierarchy by Pius IX. into Protestant lands, legally possible because of toleration, was in some cases made practicable because of immigration. Though this factor was perhaps not prominent in the case of Holland (1853) or Scotland (1878) it was Irish immigration which made it feasible in England (1850). For a time the Roman propaganda in England, which drew to itself High Churchmen like Newman and Manning, was viewed with apprehension; but though the Roman Catholic Church has grown greatly in influence in the country, the number of its adherents, in proportion to the growth of population, has not very greatly increased.

In the United States of America, however, the Catholic population has increased by leaps and bounds through immigration. The famines of the 'forties, with their subsequent political and economic difficulties, transferred to America millions of the Irish, whose genius for organization in politics has not fallen short of their zeal for religion. The German-speaking immigrants have also had a creditable share in the work of church extension, but the Italians have manifested no marked ardour for their faith. The losses in transplantation have been huge, but it is impossible to estimate them accurately, for even the current figures for the Catholic population are based on detailed estimates rather than on an actual count.

: Summing up the history of the papacy from the Congress of Vienna to the fall of the temporal power, one finds statistical gains in Protestant countries offset perhaps by relative losses in Catholic lands, both largely due to the closely related forces of toleration and immigration. While the hold of the popes on the States of the Church was constantly weakening, their power over the domestic policies of foreign governments was increasing; and the transition from autocracy to parliamentary rule accelerated this process, at least in non-Catholic territories. The unparalleled spread of ultramontane ideas (see ULTRA-MONTANISM) brought about a centralization of authority at Rome such as would have appalled the 18th century. This centralization was, however, for the time not so much legal as doctrinal. In 1854 Pius IX. by his sole authority established a dogma (see IMMACULATE CONCEPTION); and the infallibility implied in this act was openly acknowledged in 1870 by the Council of the Vatican (see VATICAN COUNCIL and INFALLIBILITY). Thus were the spiritual prerogatives of the papacy exalted in the very summer that the temporal power was brought low.   (W. W. R.*)

V.—Period from 1870 to 1900.

The few months that elapsed between the 18th of July 1870 and the 18th of January 1871 witnessed four events that have been fraught with more consequence to the papacy than anything else that had affected that institution for the past three centuries. They were as follows: (1) The proclamation of the Infallibility of the Pope on the 18th of July 1870; (2) the fall of the Napoleonic empire and the establishment of the third French republic on the 4th of September 1870; (3) the occupation of Rome by the Italian forces on the 20th of September 1870, resulting in the incorporation of the remaining states of the Church in the kingdom of Italy; and (4) the foundation of the German Empire by the proclamation, on the 18th of January 1871, of the king of Prussia as hereditary German emperor. These changes, which so greatly disturbed the current of all European relations, could not fail to react upon the papal policy in various ways. They brought its existing tendencies into greater relief, set before it new aims and diverted it into new channels. Essential modifications could not, of course, be at once effected or even indicated in a power whose life-blood is tradition, and whose main strength has always lain in calmly abiding the issue of events and in temporizing. The eight years that Pius IX. was permitted to see after the loss of his temporalities entirely harmonize with this character. The veil that hides the negotiations which, during the closing months of the Franco-German War, were carried on between Bismarck and the pope, through the agency of Cardinal Bonnhose, has not yet been lifted, and perhaps never will be. According to Prince Bismarck's own account of the matter, as given in his *Gedanken und Erinnerungen*, these negotiations were initiated by the chancellor, who, between the 5th and 9th of November 1870, entertained *pourparlers* with Archbishop Ledochowski on the question of the territorial interests of the pope. The chancellor, acting, as he himself says, in the spirit of the adage, " one hand washes the other," proposed to that prelate that the pope should give earnest of the relations subsisting between him and Germany by influencing the French clergy in the direction of the conclusion of peace. The cool reception his endeavours met with, both at the hands of the French ecclesiastics as well as in Rome, satisfied Bismarck " that the papal hierarchy lacked either the power or the good will to afford Germany assistance of sufficient value to make it worth while giving umbrage to both the German Protestants and the Italian national party, and risking a reaction of the latter upon the future relations between the two countries, which would be the inevitable result were Germany openly to espouse the papal cause in Rome." These utterances are eminently characteristic. They show how far Bismarck was (even at the close of 1870) from

Bismarck and the Temporal Power.

comprehending the traditional policy of the papacy towards Germany and German interests, and how little he conceived it possible to employ the relations between the future empire and the Vatican as a point of departure for a successful and consistent ecclesiastical policy. Rome, in a certain sense, showed itself possessed of far greater foresight. The German politicians and the Prussian diplomatists accredited to Rome had worked too openly at undermining the papal hierarchy, and had veiled their sympathies for Piedmont far too lightly to lead the Vatican to expect, after the 20th of September 1870, a genuine and firm intervention on the part of Prussia on behalf of the temporal power of the Holy See. To satisfy the demands of Bismarck in November 1870 would have cost the Vatican more than it would ever have gained. It could neither afford to trifle with the sympathies of the French Catholics nor to interrupt the progress of those elements, which would naturally be a thorn in the side of the young German Empire, thus undo Bismarck's work, and restore the Vatican policy to its pristine strength and vigour. It was soon to be perceived how carefully the Curia had made its calculations.

The address of the Catholic deputies to the emperor William in Versailles on the 18th of February 1871, pleading for the restoration of the States of the Church and the temporal sovereignty of the pope, and for the reconstitution of the Catholic group formed in the Prussian Landtag in 1860 as the *Centrum* or Centre Party in the new Reichstag (April 1871), must not be regarded as the origin but rather the immediate occasion of the *Kulturkampf*. The congratulations which the pope sent to the emperor William on receiving the announcement of the establishment of the German Empire (March 6, 1871) were a last exchange of civilities, and the abolition of the Catholic department in the Prussian ministry of public worship (July 8, 1871) quickly followed, together with the appointment of Falk as *Kultusminister* (Jan. 22, 1872), and the School Inspection Law of the 9th of February 1872.

On the 30th of January Bismarck took the opportunity of inveighing against the formation of the sectarian Centrum as being " one of the most monstrous phenomena in the world of politics," and he left no room for doubt in the minds of his hearers that he regarded the leadership of Windthorst as constituting, in his eyes, a peril to the national unity. In his *Memoirs* (ii. 126) he declares that the *Kulturkampf* was mainly initiated by him as a Polish question. This declaration, in view of the development of affairs, must appear as strange as the chancellor's confession (*Memoirs*, ii. 129 seq.) that he endeavoured to persuade the emperor of the advantage of having a nuncio accredited to Berlin (in lieu of the Catholic department of public worship). The refusal of the emperor William to entertain this project shows that in such matters his judgment was more correct than that of his counsellor, and the incident proves that the latter had anything but a clear insight into the historical position. He was drifting about with no higher aim than a " hand-to-mouth " policy, whilst the Holy See could feel the superiority with which the consciousness of centuries of tradition had endowed it, and took full advantage of the mistakes of its opponent. The chancellor never realised the gravity of the onslaught which, with his *Kulturkampf*, he was making upon the conscience and liberty of his Catholic fellow citizens. He dealt with the great question at issue from the standpoint of the diplomatist, rather than from that of the statesman well versed in ecclesiastical history and possessing an insight into what it implies; and by his violent, inconsiderate action he unwittingly drove into the ranks of Ultramontanism the moderate elements of the Catholic population. This conflict, moreover, brought Ultramontanism the enormous advantage that, even after the abolition of the May Laws, it had still left to it a well-disciplined press, an admirable organization, and a network of interests and interested parties; and all these combined to make the Centrum the strongest and the most influential political party in Germany for the remainder of the 19th century. Owing to these circumstances, the rise and further development of the

The Kulturkampf.

Kulturkampf were viewed in Jesuit and Vatican circles with feelings of the utmost complacency.

The purely ecclesiastical policy of Pius IX. was guided by the earnest desire to see the doctrine of Papal Infallibility brought to universal recognition. The definition of the Immaculate Conception (1854) and the proclamation of the Syllabus (1864) were finger-posts pointing the way to the Council of 1870. The pope had been persuaded that the proclamation of the new dogma would be effected without difficulty and without discussion; and when the pronouncement actually met with opposition, he was both surprised and embittered. For a moment the idea was entertained of giving way to the opposition and deferring a decision in the matter, or, in the manner of the fathers in the Council of Trent, adjourning it to the Greek kalends. But the party that needed for its purposes an infallible pope readily persuaded Pius IX. that if the council broke up without arriving at a decision favourable to the papacy, this would be tantamount to a serious defeat of the Holy See and an open victory for the Gallican system. The consequence was the bull *Pastor aeternus*, which Pius IX. issued on the 15th of July. This did not by any means represent all the demands of the Jesuits, and it was couched in terms which appeared not unacceptable to the majority of the Catholics. The fact that the bishops were prepared to forego their opposition was not unknown in Rome. It was anticipated by the authorities. But in Germany, as also in France, the waves of anti-Infallibility were rolling so high, that the further development of events was viewed with no small concern. Under normal conditions, the situation could not fail to terminate favourably for the Vatican. That the *Kulturkampf* had followed so rapidly upon the war was the greatest piece of good fortune that could have befallen the Holy See. The war demanded both in Germany and France the sacrifice of all available energy and public spirit; while the *Kulturkampf*, by bringing into relief the question of the external existence of the Church, thrust all internal dogmatic interests and problems completely into the background. The egregious blunder in the May Laws was the punitive clauses directed against the inferior clergy. Instead of enlisting them as friends, the Prussian government contrived by wild and wanton persecution to make them its enemies. The open protection it accorded to the Old Catholic movement contributed in no small measure to estrange those influential elements which, whilst favouring the suppression of Ultramontane tendencies, desired no schism in the Church, and viewed with horror the idea of a National Church in Bismarck's sense (see OLD CATHOLICS). Thus we find that the bitter years of the *Kulturkampf* extricated the Vatican from one of the most difficult situations in which it had ever been placed. Pius IX. could now fold his hands, so far as the future was concerned. It is well known that he fed on inspirations, and expected each day the advent of some supernatural occurrence which should bring about the triumph of the Church. In this frame of mind, on the 24th of June 1872, he addressed the German *Lesenerein*, and referred to the stone that would soon fall from on high and crush the feet of the Colossus. Yet the stone has not fallen from the summit of the holy hill, and the Colossus of the German Empire has not crumbled into dust, which is more than can be said for the pope's inspirations, which led him to expect the sudden withdrawal of the Italians from Rome, and a solution of the Roman question in the sense inspired by his visionary policy. The Holy See directed all its energies towards the solution of the problem; in the event of its proving to be insoluble, it would take care that it should remain a festering sore in the body of the monarchy. (For the *Kulturkampf* see further GERMANY: *History*.)

The documents of the Vatican Council which have been published since 1870 leave no room for doubt that the proclamation of Papal Infallibility was intended to be followed by a further declaration, to the effect that the doctrine of the temporal power of the pope should be regarded as a revealed article of faith; yet the advantage and necessity of the temporal power were not to be regarded as a revealed dogma properly speaking, but as a truth guaranteed by the doctrinal body of the Holy Church. These articles, contained in the 5th Scheme, and zealously championed by the sectaries of the Jesuit order, reveal the immediate object for which the council of 1869–1870 was convened. The resolutions were devised to save the situation, in view of the impending loss of the temporalities. No one could expect that Pius IX. would recognize the annexation of Rome by Italy. Rome, even in the 19th century, had been a spectator of many changes in the political world. It had seen more than one kingdom rise and fall. No wonder, then, that the Vatican, confronted by a new Italy, observed *The Papacy* a passive and expectant attitude, and sanctioned no *and the new* jot or tittle that could infringe its rights or be *Italian* interpreted as a renunciation of its temporal sove- *Kingdom.* reignty. It was quite in keeping that Pius IX. availed himself to the full of the (for him) convenient clauses of the Italian Law of Guarantees (May 13, 1871), while refusing the civil list of three and a quarter million lire provided for his use, and inhibiting Italian Catholics from participating in the elections to the House of Deputies (*nè elettori nè eletti*).[1] This step was regarded in Italy as a natural one. Although the Liberal record of the pope was a thing of the past, and his policy had, since Gaeta, become firmly identified with the reactionary policy of Antonelli, yet the early years of his pontificate were in such lively recollection as to allow of Pius IX.'s appearing to some extent in the light of a national hero. And rightly; for he had always had a warm heart for Italy; and had it not been for the anti-ecclesiastical policy of the house of Piedmont, he would not, in the 'sixties, have been wholly averse from reconciliation. The hitherto unpublished correspondence of the pope with Victor Emmanuel contains remarkable proofs in support of this contention, and a further corroboration can also be preceived in the conciliatory attitude of Pius IX. on the death of the king.

Pius died on the 7th of February 1878, only a few weeks later than his opponent. He had long passed the traditional years of Peter's pontificate, had reigned longer than any previous wearer of the tiara, and had seen some brilliant days—days of illusory glory. On his death he left the Church shaken to its very foundations, and in feud with almost every government. In Italy the Holy See was surrounded by a hostile force, whose "prisoner" the lord of the Vatican declared himself to be. In Spain and Portugal, and also in Belgium, a Liberalism inimical to the Church was in power. Prussia, together with other German states, was in arms against pope and episcopate. In France the Conservative Monarchical party had just shown its inability to preserve the Crown, whilst the Republic had anchored itself firmly by denouncing the clergy as its enemy. There was hardly a sovereign or a government in Christendom against which Pius IX. had not either protested or against which he had not openly declared war. Such was the heritage that devolved upon Leo XIII. on his election on the 20th of February 1878.

Leo XIII. brought to his new dignity many qualities that caused his election to be sympathetically received. In contrast to his predecessor, he was a man of slow and calm deliberation, and it was natural to suppose that he *Leo XIII.* was little, if at all, accessible to impulses of the *1878–1903.* moment or to the persuasions of his entourage. He was endowed with a certain scholastic erudition, and enjoyed the reputation of being a good Latinist. As nuncio in Brussels he had become acquainted with the trans-Alpine world, and had been initiated into the working of the machinery of modern politics and modern parliamentary government. The fact that he had for so long been absent from Rome afforded ground for the belief that he was not inclined to identify himself with any of the parties at the Vatican court. These were the considerations that had caused

[1] By the Law of Guarantees the pope was recognized as an independent sovereign, with jurisdiction over his own palaces and their extensive precincts and the right to receive diplomatic representatives accredited to him. He also received the right to appoint bishops, who—except in Rome and the suburbicarian districts—were to be Italian subjects; and, with a significant exception, the *exequatur*, *placet regium*, and every form of government permission for the publication and execution of acts of ecclesiastical authority were abolished. (See also ITALY: *History*.)

the Moderates in the Sacred College to fix their eyes upon him. The appointment of Franchi as secretary of state was a bid for peace that was viewed by the Irreconcilables with ill-disguised vexation. The following years of Leo XIII.'s pontificate only tended to increase their dissatisfaction. The first care of the new pope was to pave the way for the restoration of peace with Russia and the German Empire, and it was owing to his patience, persistence and energy that these efforts for peace were crowned with success. In the case of Germany he made many concessions which appeared to the *Zelanti* to be excessive, and made even still greater ones to France and Russia, to the great distress of the Poles. But at last Leo XIII. could
Leo XIII. as Diplomatist. boast not only of having re-established diplomatic relations with most of the powers, but also of having entered into a convention with the great powers of the North, which accorded him, in conjunction with the three emperors, a leading position as champion of the conservative interests of humanity. How proud Leo XIII. was of his importance in this position is shown by the beautiful encyclical, *De civitatum constitutione christiana* ("Immortale Dei" of Nov. 1, 1885), in which he adopted the strongest attitude against the principle of the sovereignty of the people (*ex iis autem Pontificum praescriptis illud omnino intelligi necesse est, ortum publicae potestatis a Deo ipso, non a multitudine repeti posse*), refuting the notion that the principle of public power emanates from the will of the people alone (*principatum non esse nisi populi voluntatem*), and absolutely rejecting the sovereignty of the people as such. But this attitude was adopted by Leo XIII. not as an end but as a means. The real aims of his rule were disclosed in the second phase of his pontificate.

At its very commencement, the pope in his first encyclical (Easter 1878) proclaimed the necessity of a temporal hierarchy. This was at the time regarded merely as a formality imposed by circumstances, and was not to be seriously entertained; but it became more and more evident that the recovery of the temporalities was the real mainspring of Leo's whole policy. In the negotiations with Germany, it was clearly seen that it was from that side that the pope expected intervention in favour of restitution; and, according to all appearances, Bismarck did for a while keep alive these representations, though with more tact than candour. After peace had been concluded, Leo, by the agency of Galimberti, reminded the chancellor of the settlement of the Roman question. Bismarck replied that he was "unaware of the existence of any such question." The two visits paid by Emperor William II. to the Vatican could not fail to remove any doubts in the mind of the pope as to the fact that Germany did not dream of giving him back Rome. The Austro-German-Italian triple alliance was a dire blow to his expectations, and Crispi's policy with its irritating and galling pin-pricks caused the cup to overflow.

Thus slowly, but yet deliberately, between 1887 and 1893, a transformation took place in Leo's spirit and policy, and with
Leo XIII. and the French Republic. it was brought about one of the most momentous changes in the attitude of the Church towards the problems of the times and their impelling forces. A *rapprochement* with France inevitably entailed not only an alliance with modern democracy, but also a recognition of its principles and aims. In Rome there was no room for both pope and king. The note of the pope to Rampolla of the 8th of October 1895, in consequence of the celebrations on the 20th of September, declared, in terms more decided than any that had until then been uttered, that the papacy required a territorial sovereignty in order to ensure its full independence, and that its interests were therefore incompatible with the existence of the kingdom of Italy as then constituted. The inevitable consequences ensued. Italy regarded the pope more than ever as a foe within its walls; and the policy of the pope, as regards Italy, aimed at replacing the kingdom by one or more republics, in which the temporal power should, in some form or other, find a place. But the continuance of the Republic in Paris was a condition precedent to the establishment of a republic in Rome, and the first had no chance of existence if the democracy in France did not remain

in power. The result was the policy of the *Ralliement*. Instructions were given to the French Catholics to break with monarchical principles, and both externally and internally to cleave to the Republic as representing the best form of constitutional government. In carrying out the régime of Rampolla, which was, in every respect, a bad imitation of that of Antonelli, the Vatican left no stone unturned in its attempt to coerce the conscience of the French royalist¹; it did not even stop at dishonour, as was evidenced by the case of the unhappy Mgr d'Hulst, who, in order to evade the censorship of his pamphlet on Old Testament criticism, had to abandon both his king and his principles, only to die in exile of a broken heart. The case was characteristic of the whole Catholic monarchical party, which, owing to the pope's interference in French politics, became disintegrated and dissolved, a fate that was all the more painful seeing that the *Ralliement* failed to influence the course of events. The "atheistic" Republic did not for one moment think of putting on sackcloth, or even of giving the Church a single proof of esteem and sympathy.

In one respect it was impossible for the papacy to continue on the path it had taken. In his first encyclical, Leo XIII. had sounded the clarion for battle against the Social *The Pope* Democracy; his encyclical *Novarum rerum* en- *and Social* deavoured to show the means to be employed, *Democracy.* mainly in view of the condition of things in Belgium, for solving the social question on Christian lines. But the Christian Democracy, which, starting in Belgium and France, had now extended its activity to Italy, Austria and Germany, and was striving to arrive at this solution, degenerated everywhere into a political party. The leaders of this party came into close contact with the Social Democrats, and their relations became so cordial that Social Democracy everywhere declared the "Démocratie Chrétienne" to be its forerunner and pioneer. The electioneering alliances, which were everywhere in vogue, but particularly in Germany, between the Catholics and popular party and the Social Democrats, throw a lurid light upon the character of a movement that certainly went far beyond the intentions of the pope, but which it was now difficult to undo or to hold in check. For it is the essence of the matter that there were further considerations going far beyond the Roman question and forcing the Curia to adhere to the sovereignty of the people.

The external rehabilitation of the Church had become, in many points, a *fait accompli*, but, internally, events had not kept pace with it. Catholic romanticism had withered- *Alienation* away in France, as it had in Germany. "Liberal *of the* Catholicism," which was its offspring, had died with *Educated* Montalembert, after being placed under a ban by *Middle* Rome. The national religious movement, associated *Class.* in Italy with the great names of Rosmini and Gioberti, had similarly been disavowed and crushed. The development of the last decade of the 19th century had clearly shown that the educated *bourgeoisie*, the *tiers état*, in whose hands the supreme power had since 1848 become vested throughout Europe, was either entirely lost to the Church or, at all events, indifferent to what were called Ultramontane tendencies. The educated *bourgeoisie*, which controls the fields of politics, science, finance, administration, art and literature, does not trouble itself about that great spiritual universal monarchy which Rome, as heir of the Caesars, claimed for the Vatican, and to which the Curia of to-day still clings. This *bourgeoisie* and the modern state that it upholds stand and fall with the motion of a constitutional state, whose magna carta is municipal and spiritual liberty, institutions with which the ideas of the Curia are in direct conflict. The more the hope of being able to regain these middle classes of society disappeared, the more decidedly did the Curia perceive that it must seek the support and the regeneration of its power in the steadily growing democracy, and endeavour through the medium of universal suffrage to secure the influence which this new alliance was able to offer.

The pontificate of Leo XIII. in its first phase aimed at preserving a certain balance of power. Whilst not openly repelling the tendencies of the Jesuits, Leo yet showed himself well disposed towards, and even amenable to, views of a diametri-*The Papacy* cally opposite kind; and as soon as the Vatican *and the* threw itself into the arms of France, and bade fare-*Modern* well to the idea of a national Italy, the policy of *Democracy.* equilibrium had to be abandoned. The second phase in Leo's policy could only be accomplished with the aid of the Jesuits, or rather, it required the submission of the ecclesiastical hierarchy to the mandates of the Society of Jesus. The further consequence was that all aspirations were subjected to the thraldom of the Church. The pontificate of Leo XIII. is distinguished by the great number of persecutions, prosecutions and injuries inflicted upon Catholic *savants*, from the prosecution of Antonio Rosmini down to the proscription directed against the heads of the American Church. Episodes, such as the protection so long extended to the Leo Taxil affair, and to the revelations of Diana Vaughan (the object of which last was to bring Italian freemasonry and its ostensible work, the unity of Italy, into discredit), together with the attitude of the Ultra-montanes press in the Dreyfus affair, and later towards England, the invigoration of political agitation by the Lourdes celebration and by anti-Semitism, were all manifestations that could not raise the " system " in the estimation of the cultured and civilised world. Perhaps even more dangerous was the employment of the whole ecclesiastical organization, and of Catholicism generally, for political purposes.

No one will be so foolish or so unjust as to hold Leo XIII. responsible for the excesses committed by the subordinate departments of his government, in disclosing prosecuting and sometimes even fraudulently misrepresenting his aims and ends. But all these details, upon which it is not necessary to dwell, are overshadowed beyond all doubt by the one great fact that the ecclesiastical régime had not only taken under its wing the solution of social questions, but also claimed that political action was within the proper scope of the Church, and, moreover, arrogated to itself the right of interfering by means of " Direc-tives " with the political life of nations. This was nothing new, for as early as 1215 the English barons protested against it. But the weakening of the papacy had allowed this claim to lapse for centuries. To have revived it, and to have carried it out as far as is possible, was the work of Leo XIII.

It would be both presumptuous and premature to pass a final verdict upon the value and success of a policy to which, whatever else be said, must be accorded a certain meed of praise for its daring. Even in 1892 Spüller, in his essay upon Lamennais, pointed out how the latest evolution of Catholicism was taking the course indicated by Lamennais in his *Livre du peuple* (1837), and how the hermit of " La Chênaie," who departed this life in bitter strife with Rome, declared himself to be the actual precursor of modern Christian Socialism. He hinted that the work of Leo XIII. was, in his eyes, merely a new attempt to build up afresh the theocracy of the middle ages upon the ruins of the old monarchies, utilizing to this end the inexperience of the young and easily beguiled democracies of the dawning 20th century. To comprehend these views aright, we must first remember that what in the first half of the 19th century, and also in the days of Lamennais, was understood by Democracy was not coincident with the meaning of this expression as it was afterwards used, and as the Christian Socialists understood it. Down to 1848, and even still later, " Democracy " was used to cover the whole mass of the people, pre-eminently represented by the broad strata of the *bourgeoisie*; in 1900 the Democratic party itself meant by this term the rule of the labouring class organised as a nation, which, by its numerical superiority, thrust aside all other classes, including the *bourgeoisie*, and excluded them from participation in its rule. In like manner it would be erroneous to confuse the sense of the expression as it obtains on the continent of Europe with what is under-stood under this term in England and America. In this latter case the term " Democracy,". as applied to the historical development of Great Britain and the United States, denotes a constitutional state in which every citizen has rights

proportionate to his energy and intelligence. The socialistic idea, with which the " Démocratie Chrétienne " had identified itself both in France and Belgium; regards numbers as the centre of gravity of the whole state organism. As a matter of fact it recognizes as actual citizens only the labourer, or, in other words, the proletariat.

On surveying the situation, certain weak points in the policy of the Vatican under Leo XIII. were manifest even to a con-temporary observer. They might be summed up as follows: (1) An unmistakable decline of religious fervour in church life. (2) The intensifying and nurturing of all the passions and questionable practices which are so easily encouraged by practical politics, and are incompatible in almost all points with the priestly office. (3) An ever-increasing displacement of all the refined, educated and nobler elements of society by such as are rude and uncultured, by what, in fact, may be styled the ecclesi-astical " Trottori." (4) The naturally resulting paralysis of intelligence and scientific research, which the Church either proscribed or only sullenly tolerated. (5) The increasing decay and waxing corruption of the Romance nations, and the fostering of that diseased state of things which displayed itself in France in so many instances, such as the Dreyfus case, the anti-Semitic movement, and the campaign for and against the Assumptionists and their newspaper, the *Croix*. (6) The increasing estrange-ment of German and Anglo-Saxon feeling. As against these, noteworthy reasons might be urged in favour of the new development. It might well be maintained that the faults just enumerated were only cankers inseparable from every new and great movement, and that these excrescences would disappear in course of time, and the whole movement enter upon a more tranquil path. Moreover, in the industrial districts of Germany, for example, the Christian industrial movement, supported by Protestants and Catholics alike, had achieved considerable results, and proved a serviceable means of combating the seductions of Socialism. Finally, the Church had reminded the wealthy classes of their duties to the sick and toilers, and by making the social question its own it had gone a long way towards permeating all social and political conditions with the spirit of Christianity.   (F. X. K.)

VI.—*Period from 1900 to 1910.*

On the 3rd of March 1903 Leo XIII. celebrated his Jubilee with more than ordinary splendour, the occasion bringing him rich tributes of respect from all parts of the world, Catholic and non-Catholic; on the 20th of July following he died. The succession was expected to fall to Leo's secretary of state, Cardinal Rampolla; but he was credited with having inspired the French sympathies of the late pope; Austria exercised its right of veto (see CONCLAVE, *ad fin.*), and on the 8th of August, Giuseppe Sarto, who as cardinal patriarch of Venice had shown a friendly disposition towards the Italian government, was elected pope. He took as his secretary of state Cardinal Raphael Merry del Val, a Spaniard of English birth and educa- *Pius X.* tion, well versed in diplomacy, but of well-known ultramontane tendencies. The new pope was known to be no politician, but a simple and saintly priest, and in some quarters there were hopes that the attitude of the papacy towards the Italian kingdom might now be changed. But the name he assumed, Pius X., was significant; and, even had he had the will, it was soon clear that he had not the power to make any material departure from the policy of the first " prisoner of the Vatican." What was even more important, the new régime at the Vatican soon made itself felt in the relations of the Holy See with the world of modern thought and with the modern conception of the state.

The new pope's motto, it is said, was " to establish all things in Christ " (*instaurare omnia in Christo*); and since, *ex hypothesi*, he himself was Christ's vicar on earth, the working out of this principle meant in effect the extension and consolidation of the papal authority and, as far as possible, an end to the com-promises by means of which the papacy had sought to make friends of the Mammon of unrighteousness. It was this spirit which informed such decrees as that on " mixed marriages "

(*Ne temere*) of 1907, which widened still further the social gulf between Catholics and Protestants (see MARRIAGE: *Canon Law*), or the refusal to allow the French bishops to accept the Associations Law passed by the French government after the denunciation of the concordat and the separation of Church and State (see FRANCE: *History*): better that the Church in France should sink into more than apostolic poverty than that a tittle of the rights of the Holy See should be surrendered. Above all it was this spirit that breathed through every line of the famous encyclical, *Pascendi gregis*, directed against the "Modernists" (see ROMAN CATHOLIC CHURCH: *History*), which denounced with bitter scorn and irony those so-called Catholics who dared to attempt to reconcile the doctrine of the Church with the results of modern science, and who, presumptuously disregarding the authority of the Holy See, maintained "the absurd doctrine that would make of the laity the factor of progress in the Church." That under Pius X. the papacy had abandoned none of its pretensions to dominate consciences, not of Catholics only, was again proved in 1910 when, at the very moment when the pope was praising the English people for their spirit of tolerance which led the British government to introduce a bill to alter the form of the Declaration made by the sovereign on his accession into a form inoffensive to Roman Catholics, he was remonstrating with the government of Spain for abrogating the law forbidding the Spanish dissident churches to display publicly the symbols of the Christian faith or to conduct their services otherwise than semi-privately.

In pursuance of the task of strengthening the Holy See, the Vatican policy under Pius X. was not merely one of defiance *Church Reforms.* towards supposed hostile forces within and without the Church; it was also strenuous in pushing on the work of internal organization and reform. In 1904 a commission of cardinals was appointed to undertake the stupendous task of codifying the canon law (see CANON LAW), and in *Reforms of Pius X.* 1908 an extensive reorganization of the Curia was carried out, in order to conform its machinery more nearly to present-day needs (see CURIA ROMANA). In taking England, the United States and other non-Catholic states from under the care of the Congregation of the Propaganda, the pope raised the status of the Roman Catholic Church in those countries. All these changes tended to consolidating the centralized authority of the papacy. Other reforms were of a different character. One of the earliest acts of the new pontificate was to forbid the use in the services of the Church of any music later than Palestrina, a drastic order justified by the extreme degradation into which church music had fallen in Italy, but in general honoured rather in the spirit than in the letter. More important was the appointment in 1907 of a commission, under the presidency of Abbot Gasquet, to attempt the restoration of the pure text of the Vulgate as St Jerome wrote it.

Such activities might well be taken as proof that the papacy at the outset of the 20th century possessed a vigour which it was *Causes of the Revival of the Papacy.* far from possessing a hundred years earlier. Under Pius VI. and Pius VII. the papacy had reached the lowest depths of spiritual and political impotence since the Reformation, and the belief was even widespread that the prisoner of Fontainebleau would be the last of the long line of St Peter's successors. This weakness was due not to attacks from without—for orthodox Protestantism had long since lost its aggressive force—but to disruptive tendencies within the Church; the Enlightenment of the 18th century had sapped the foundations of the faith among the world of intellect and fashion; the development of Gallicanism and Febronianism threatened to leave the Holy See but a shadowy pre-eminence over a series of national churches, and even to obliterate the frontier line between Catholicism and Protestantism. It was the Revolution, which at one moment seemed finally to have engulfed the papacy, which in fact preserved it; Febronianism, as a force to be seriously reckoned with, perished in the downfall of the ecclesiastical principalities of the old Empire; Gallicanism perished with the constitutional Church in France, and its

XX 12*

principles fell into discredit with a generation which associated it with the Revolution and its excesses. In the reaction that followed the chaos of the Revolutionary epoch men turned to the papacy as alone giving a foothold of authority in a confused and quaking world. The Romantic movement helped, with its idealization of a past but vaguely realized and imperfectly understood, and Chateaubriand heralded in the Catholic reaction with his *Génie du Christianisme* (1801) a brilliant if superficial attack on the encyclopaedists and their neo-Paganism, and a glorification of the Christian Church as supreme not only in the regions of faith and morals, but also in those of intellect and art. More weighty was the *Du Pape* of Joseph de Maistre (1819), closely reasoned and fortified with a wealth of learning, which had an enormous influence upon all those who thought that they saw in the union of "altar and throne" the palladium of society. The Holy Empire was dead, in spite of the pope's protest at Vienna against the failure to restore "the centre of political unity"; Joseph de Maistre's idea was to set up the Holy See in its place. To many minds the papacy thus came to represent a unifying principle, as opposed to the disruptive tendencies of Liberalism and Nationalism, and the papal monarchy came to be surrounded with a new halo, as in some sort realizing that ideal of a "federation of the world" after which the age was dimly feeling.

So far as politics are concerned this sentiment was practically confined to certain classes, which saw their traditional advantages threatened by the revolutionary tendencies of the *The Papacy and Modern Thought.* times; and the alliance between the throne and the altar, by confusing the interests of the papacy with those of political parties, tended—as Leo XIII. had the wit to realize—to involve the fate of the one with that of the other, as in France. Far stronger was the appeal made by the authoritative attitude of the papacy to all those who were disturbed by the scientific spirit of the age: the ceaseless questioning of all the foundations on which faith and morality had been supposed to rest. Biblical criticism, by throwing doubt on the infallibility of the Scriptures, was undermining the traditional foundation of orthodox Protestantism, and most of the Protestant Churches, divided between antagonistic tendencies, were ceasing to speak with a certain voice. To logical but timid minds, like that of J. H. Newman, which could not be content with a compromise with truth, but feared to face ultimate realities, the rigidly authoritative attitude of Rome made an irresistible appeal. The process, maybe, from the point of view of those outside, was to make a mental wilderness and call it peace; but from the papal point of view it had a double advantage: it attracted those in search of religious certainty, it facilitated the maintenance of its hold over the Catholic democracy. The methods by which it has sought to maintain this hold are criticized in the article ULTRAMONTANISM.

There can also be little doubt—though the Curia itself would not admit it—that the spiritual power of the papacy has been greatly increased by the loss of the temporal power. *The Loss of Temporal Power.* The pope is no longer a petty Italian prince who, in the order to preserve his dominions, was necessarily involved in the tangle of European diplomacy; he is the monarch of a vast, admirably organized, spiritual world-empire, and when —as must needs happen—the overlapping of the spiritual and temporal spheres brings him into conflict with a secular power, his diplomacy is backed, wherever Catholic sentiment is strong, by a force which the secular power has much difficulty in resisting; for in spiritual matters (and the term covers a wide field) the Catholic, however loyal to his country he may be, must obey God, whose vicegerent is the pope, rather than man. Even Bismarck, in the end, had to "go to Canossa."

It is, indeed, possible to exaggerate this power. The fact that the Vatican presents a great force hostile to and obstructive of certain characteristic tendencies of modern life and thought has necessarily raised up a powerful opposition even in countries traditionally Catholic. France no longer deserves the title of eldest daughter of the Church; the Catholicism of Italy is largely superficial; even Spain has shown signs of restiveness. On the other hand, the great opportunity now open to the papacy on its spiritual side, is proved by the growing respect in which it has been held since 1870 in the English-speaking countries, where Roman Catholics are in a minority and their Church is in no sense established. Without doubt, opinion has been influenced in these countries by the fact that Rome has not been sufficiently strong to exercise any disturbing influence on the general course of national affairs, while in both its conspicuous members set a high example of private and civic conduct.

(W. A. P.)

List of the Pontiffs of the Roman Church.[1]

Date of Election or Consecration.		Date of Death.
c. 41	B. Petrus	29 vi, c. 65–67
c. 67	S. Linus	23 ix, c. 79
c. 79	S. Cletus (*Anencletus*)	26 iv, c. 91
c. 91	S. Clemens I	23 xi, c. 100
c. 100	S. Evaristus	26 x, c. 109
c. 109	S. Alexander	3 v, c. 119
c. 119	S. Sixtus (*Xystus*)	3 iv, c. 126
? 128	S. Telesphorus	5 i, 137
c. 138	S. Hyginus	11 i, 142
c. 142	S. Pius	11 vii, c. 156
c. 157	S. Anicetus	17 iv, 167
168	S. Soter	22 iv, c. 176
177	S. Eleutherus	26 v, 189
c. 190	S. Victor I.	20 iv, c. 202
c. 202	S. Zephyrinus	26 viii, 217
218	S. Calixtus I.	14 x, 222
222	S. Urbanus I.	25 v, 230
230	S. Pontianus	res. 28 ix, 235
235 (21 xi, ord.)	S. Anterus	3 i, 236
236	S. Fabianus	20 i, 250
251 (iii. el.)	S. Cornelius	14 ix, 253
253 el.	S. Lucius	5 iii, 254
254 (12 v ?, el.)	S. Stephanus I.	2 viii, 257
257 viii	S. Sixtus (*Xystus*) II.	6 viii, 258
259 22 vii, el.	S. Dionysius	26 xii, 268
269 5 i, el.	S. Felix	30 xii, 274
275 c. 5 i	S. Eutychianus	8 xii, 283
283 17 xii	S. Gaius	22 iv, 296
296 30 vi	S. Marcellinus	(? 25 x), 304
307 el.	S. Marcellus	15 i, 309
309 iv, el.	S. Eusebius	17 viii, 309
310 2 vii	S. Melchiades (*Miltiades*)	11 i, 314
314 31 i	S. Sylvester	31 xii, 335
336 18 i	S. Marcus	7 x, 336
337 6 ii, el.	S. Julius	12 iv, 352
352 22 v	S. Liberius	24 ix, 366
366 ix	S. Damasus	10 xii, 384
384 xii	S. Siricius	26 xi, 398
398 xi–xii	S. Anastasius I.	† vert. anno 401–2
402	S. Innocentius I.	12 iii, 417
417 18 iii, cs.	S. Zosimus	26 xii, 418
418 28 xii	S. Bonifacius I.	4 ix, 422
422 c. 10 ix	S. Coelestinus I.	† c. 26 vii, 432
432 31 vii	S. Sixtus III.	18 viii, 440
440 viii, el.	S. Leo I.	10 xi, 461
461 12 xi, cs.	S. Hilarus	21 ii, 468
468 25 ii, cs.	S. Simplicius	2 iii, 483
483	S. Felix III.	25 ii, 492
492 1 iii, cs.	S. Gelasius	19 xi, 496
496 c. 24 xi, cs.	S. Anastasius II.	† at cap. 19 xi, 498
498 22 xi	S. Symmachus	† at sepult. 19 vii, 514
514 20 vii, cs.	S. Hormisdas	sepult. 7 viii, 523
523 13 viii	S. Joannes I.	18 v, 526
526 12 vii, cs.	S. Felix IV.	† sepel. 12 x (?), 530
530 17 ix, el.	Bonifacius II.	sepel. 17 x, 532
532 31 xii, cs.	Joannes II.	† sepel. 27 v, 535
533 3 vi, cs.	S. Agapetus I.	22 iv, 536
536 8 vi, cs.	S. Silverius, *exul*	† sepel. 20 vi, c. 538
537 29 iii, cs.	Vigilius	7 vi, 555
555 p. 7 vi, cs.	Pelagius I.	3 iii, 560
560 14 vii, cs.	Joannes III.	† sepel. 13 vii, 573
574 3 vi, cs.	Benedictus I.	31 vii, 578
578 27 xi, cs.	Pelagius II.	† sepel. 6 ii, 590
590 3 ix, cs.	S. Gregorius I.	† sepel. 12 iii, 604
604 13 ix, cs.	Sabinianus	† 22 ii, 606
607 19 ii, cs.	Bonifacius III.	† sepel. 12 xi, 607
608 15 ix, cs.	S. Bonifacius IV.	† sepel. 25 v, 615
615 19 x, cs.	S. Deusdedit	sepel. 8 xi, 618
619 23 xii, cs.	Bonifacius V.	† sepel. 25 x, 625
625 3 xi, cs.	Honorius	† sepel. 12 x, 638

Date of Election or Consecration.			Date of Death.
640 28 v, cs.	Severinus	sepel. 2 viii,	640
640 25 xii, cs.	Joannes IV.	sepel. 12 x,	642
642 24 xi, cs.	Theodorus I.	sepel. 14 v,	649
649 vi–vii, cs.	S. Martinus	† exul 16 ix,	655
654 10 viii, cs.	S. Eugenius I.	sepel. 3 vi,	657
657 30 vii, cs.	S. Vitalianus	sepel. 27 i,	672
672 11 iv, cs.	Adeodatus	† sepel. 16 vi,	676
676 2 xi, cs.	Donus	† sep. 11 iv,	678
678 vi–vii, cs.	S. Agatho	sep. 10 i,	681
682 17 viii, cs.	S. Leo II.	sep. 3 vii,	683
684 26 vi, cs.	S. Benedictus II.	sep. 8 v,	685
685 23 vii, cs.	Joannes V.	sep. 2 viii,	686
686 21 x, cs.	Conon	† sepel. 22 ix,	687
687 x–xii, el.	S. Sergius I.	sepel. 8 ix,	701
701 30 x, cs.	Joannes VI.	sepel. 10–11 i,	705
705 1 iii, cs.	Joannes VII.	† sep. 18 x,	707
708 18 i (?)	Sisinnius	† sep. 7 ii,	708
708 25 iii, cs.	Constantinus I.	9 iv,	715
715 19 v, cs.	S. Gregorius II.	† sepel. 11 ii,	731
731 11 ii, el.	S. Gregorius III.	† sep. 29 xi,	741
741 3 xii, cs.	S. Zacharias	† 15 iii,	752
752 iii, el.	Stephanus II.	† ex.	752
752 26 iii, cs.	Stephanus III.	† sep. 26 iv,	757
757 29 v, cs.	S. Paulus I.	28 vi,	767
767 5 vii, cs.	Constantinus II.	depos. 6 viii,	768
768 7 viii, cs.	Stephanus IV	1 ii,	772
772 1 ii, el.	Hadrianus I.	25 xii,	795
795 26 xii, el.	S. Leo III.	† sep. 12 vi,	816
816 vi, el.	Stephanus V.	† 24 i,	817
817 25 i, cs.	S. Paschalis I.	† c. 14 v,	824
824 v–vi	Eugenius II.	† viii,	827
827	Valentinus.	† ex. ann.	827
827 ex. ann.	Gregorius IV.		844
844	Sergius II.	27 i,	847
847 10 iv, cs.	S. Leo IV.	17 vii,	855
855 29 ix, cs.	Benedictus III.	7 iv,	858
858 25 iv, cs.	S. Nicolaus I.	13 xi,	867
867 14 xii, cs.	Hadrianus II.	† c. 1 xii,	872
872 14 xii	Joannes VIII.	15 xii,	882
882 c. xii	Marinus I.	c. v,	884
884 c. v, el.	Hadrianus III.	c. viii–ix,	885
885 c. ix, el.	Stephanus VI.	c. ix,	891
891 c. ix	Formosus	4 iv,	896
896 c. 23 v, el.	Bonifacius VI.	c. 6 vi,	896
896 c. 11 vi, intrus	Stephanus VI.=(VII.)	*amot.* † vii,	897
897 viii, cs.	Romanus	c. xi,	897
897 c. xi	Theodorus II.	† post 20 dies	
898 c. vi, cs.	Joannes IX.	vii,	900
900 6–26 vii	Benedictus IV.	vii,	903
903 c. viii	Leo V.	† c. ix,	903
903 c. x	Christophorus	*amot.*	904
904 29 i, cs.	Sergius III.	† p. 4 ix,	911
911 c. ix, cs.	Anastasius III.	† c. xi,	913
913 c. xi, cs.	Lando	c. v,	914
913 15 v, cs.	Joannes X.	† in carcere	929
929 c. vii, cs.	Leo VI.	c. ii,	929
929 c. ii, cs.	Stephanus VIII	† 13 iii,	931
931 c. iii, cs.	Joannes XI.	c. i,	936
936 c. 9 i, cs.	Leo VI. (VII.)	† vii,	939
939 2. 19 vii, cons.	Stephanus IX.	x,	942
942 c. 11 xi, cons.	Marinus II.	c. iv,	946
946 c. iv	Agapetus II.	c. 8 xi,	955
	Joannes XII.	(*amot.* 4 xii, 963) † 14 v,	964
963 6 xii	Leo VIII.	c. iii,	965
964 v, el.	Benedict V.	*exul*	965
965 1 x, cs.	Joannes XIII.	6 ix,	972
973 19 i, cs.	Benedict VI.	† *occis.* vii,	974
974 x	Benedictus VII.	x,	983
983 ex. ann.	Joannes XIV.	† *occis.* 20 vii,	984
984	Bonifacius VII.	vii,	985
985 1 ix, cs.	Joannes XV.	† in. iv,	996
996 3 v, cs.	Gregorius V.		999
999 in. iv, cs.	Sylvester II. (*Gerbert*)	12 v,	1003
1003 13 vi, cs.	Joannes XVII. (*Sicco*)	7 xii,	1003
1003 25 xii, cs.	Joannes XVIII.	vi,	1009
1009 p. 20 vi, cs.	Sergius IV.	16–22 vi,	1012
1012 22 vi, cs.	Benedict VIII.	7 iv,	1024
1024 24 vi–15 vii, cs.	Joannes XIX.		1033
1033 i, cs.	Benedictus IX.	resignat. i,	1045
1045 i v, intr.	Gregorius VI.	resignat. 20 xii,	1046
1046 25 xii, cs.	Clemens II.	9 x,	1047
1048 17 vii, cs.	Damasus II.	9 viii,	1048
1049 12 ii, cs.	S. Leo IX.	19 iv,	1054
1055 13 iv, cs.	Victor II.	28 vii,	1057
1057 2 viii, cs.	Stephanus X.	29 iii,	1058
1058 5 iv, el.	Benedict X.	*expuls.* c. i,	1059

[1] As recorded in the registers of the Roman Church (from P. B. Gams, *Series episcoporum Romanae ecclesiae*).

Date of Election or Consecration		Date of Death
1059 24 i, cs.	Nicolaus II.	† 27 vii, 1061
1061 1 x, el.	Alexander II.	† 21 iv, 1073
1073 22 iv, el.	S. Gregorius VII.	25 v, 1085
1086 24 v, el.	Victor III.	16 ix, 1087
1088 12 iii, el.	Urbanus II.	29 vii, 1099
1099 13 viii, el.	Paschalis II.	21 i, 1118
1118 24 i, el.	Gelasius II.	29 i, 1119
1119 2 ii, el.	Calixtus II.	13-14 xii,1124
1124 15-16 xii, el.	Honorius II.	14 ii, 1130
1130 14 ii, el.	Innocentius II.	24 ix, 1143
1143 26 ix, el.	Coelestinus II.	8 iii, 1144
1144 12 iii, el.	Lucius II.	15 ii, 1145
1145 15 ii, el.	Eugenius III.	8 vii, 1153
1153 12 vii, cs.	Anastasius IV.	3 xii, 1154
1154 4 xii, el.	Hadrianus IV.	1 ix, 1159
1159 7 ix, el.	Alexander III.	30 viii, 1181
1181 1 ix	Lucius III.	25 xi, 1185
1185 25 xi	Urbanus III.	20 x, 1187
1187 21 x, el.	Gregorius VIII.	17 xii, 1187
1187 19 xii, el.	Clemens III.	iii, 1191
1191 30 iii, el.	Coelestinus III.	8 i, 1198
1198 8 i	Innocentius III.	16 vii, 1216
1216 18 vii	Honorius III.	18 iii, 1227
1227 19 iii	Gregorius IX.	21 viii, 1241
1241 x	Coelestinus IV.	17-18 xi, 1241
1243 25 vi	Innocentius IV.	13 xii, 1254
1254 25 xii	Alexander IV.	25 v, 1261
1261 29 viii	Urbanus IV.	2 x, 1264
1265 5 ii	Clemens IV.	29 xi, 1268
1271 1 ix	Gregorius X.	11 i, 1276
1276 23 ii cs.	Innocentius V.	22 vi, 1276
1276 12 vii, el.	Hadrianus V.	17 viii, 1276
1276 13 ix	Joannes XXI.	16 v, 1277
1277 25 xi	Nicolaus III.	22 viii, 1280
1281 22 ii	Martinus IV.	28 iii, 1285
1285 2 iv	Honorius IV.	3 iv, 1287
1288 15 ii	Nicolaus IV.	4 iv, 1292
1294 5 vii	S. Coelestinus V. († 19 v, 1296) res. 13 xii,	1294
1294 24 xii	Bonifacius VIII.	11 x, 1303
1303 22 x	Benedictus XI.	7 vii, 1304
1305 5 vi	Clemens V.	20 iv, 1314
1316 7 viii	Joannes XXII.	4 xii, 1334
1334 20 xii	Benedictus XII.	25 iv, 1342
1342 7 v, el.	Clemens VI.	6 xii, 1352
1352 18 xii	Innocentius VI.	12 ix, 1362
1362 28 x	Urbanus V.	19 xii, 1370
1370 30 xii	Gregorius XI.	27 iii, 1378
1378 8 iv	Urbanus VI.	15 x, 1389
1378 20 ix	Clemens VII. antipapa Aven.	16 ix, 1394
1394 28 ix	Benedict XIII. (amot 26 vii) 1417	23 v, 1423
1389 2 xi	Bonifacius IX.	1 x, 1404
1404 17 x	Innocentius VII.	6 xi, 1406
1406 2 xii	Gregorius XII. († 1419) resignat. 4 vii,	1415
1409 26 vi	Alexander V.	† 3 v, 1410
1410 17 v	Joannes XXIII. († 22 xi, 1419) amot. 24 v,	1415
1417 11 xi	Martinus V.	20 ii, 1431
1431 3 iii	Eugenius IV.	23 ii, 1447
1447 6 iii	Nicolaus V.	24 iii, 1455
1458 8 iv	Calixtus III.	6 viii, 1458
1458 19 viii	Pius II.	15 viii, 1464
1464 31 viii	Paulus II.	28 vii, 1471
1471 9 viii	Sixtus IV.	12 viii, 1484
1484 24 viii	Innocentius VIII.	25 vii, 1492
1492 11 viii	Alexander VI.	18 viii, 1503
1503 22 ix	Pius III.	18 x, 1503
1503 1 xi	Julius II.	21 ii, 1513
1513 15 iii	Leo X.	1 xii, 1521
1522 9 i	Hadrianus VI.	14 ix, 1523
1523 19 xi	Clemens VII.	25 ix, 1534
1534 13 x	Paulus III.	10 xi, 1549
1550 8 ii	Julius III.	23 iii, 1555
1555 9 iv	Marcellus II.	30 iv, 1555
1555 23 v	Paulus IV.	18 viii, 1559
1559 25 xii	Pius IV.	9 xii, 1565
1566 17 i, cs.	S. Pius V.	1 v, 1572
1572 26 v	Gregorius XIII.	10 iv, 1585
1585 1 v, cs.	Sixtus V.	27 viii, 1590
1590 15 ix, el.	Urbanus VII.	27 ix, 1590
1590 5 xii	Gregorius XIV.	15 x, 1591
1591 29 x, el.	Innocentius IX.	30 xii, 1591
1592 30 i, el.	Clemens VIII.	5 iii, 1605
1605 1 iv, el.	Leo XI.	27 iv, 1605

Date of Election or Consecration		Date of Death
1605 16 v, el.	Paulus V.	28 i, 1621
1621 9 ii	Gregorius XV.	8 vii, 1623
1623 6 viii, el.	Urbanus VIII.	29 vii, 1644
1644 15 ix	Innocentius X.	7 i, 1655
1655 7 iv	Alexander VII.	22 v, 1667
1667 20 vi	Clemens IX.	9 xii, 1669
1670 29 iv	Clemens X.	22 vii, 1676
1676 21 ix	Innocentius XI.	12 viii, 1689
1689 6 x	Alexander VIII.	1 ii, 1691
1691 12 vii	Innocentius XII.	27 ix, 1700
1700 23 xi, el.	Clemens XI.	19 iii, 1721
1721 8 v	Innocentius XIII.	7 iii, 1724
1724 29 v	Benedictus XIII.	21 ii, 1730
1730 12 vii	Clemens XII.	6 ii, 1740
1740 17 viii	Benedictus XIV.	3 v, 1758
1758 6 vii	Clemens XIII.	2 ii, 1769
1769 19 v	Clemens XIV.	22 ix, 1774
1775 15 ii	Pius VI.	29 viii, 1799
1800 14 iii	Pius VII.	20 viii, 1823
1823 28 ix	Leo XII.	10 ii, 1829
1829 31 iii	Pius VIII.	30 xi, 1830
1831 2 ii	Gregorius XVI.	1 vi, 1846
1846 16 vi, el.	Pius IX.	3 vii, 1877
1877 vii, el.	Leo XIII.	20 vii, 1903
1903 4 viii, el.	Pius X.	

BIBLIOGRAPHY.—The works mentioned below are for the most part those not included in the separate bibliographies to the articles on the individual popes (qq.v.).

General.—Of encyclopaedias may be mentioned the New Schaff-Herzog Encyclopaedia of Religious Knowledge (New York, 1908 sqq.); the Catholic Encyclopaedia (New York, 1907 sqq.); Herzog-Hauck, Realencyklopädie (3rd ed., Leipzig, 1896 sqq.); Wetzer and Welte, Kirchenlexikon (2nd ed., Freiburg-im-Breisgau, 1882–1901); C. Moroni, Dizionario di erudizione storico-ecclesiastica (Venice, 1840 sqq.), all of which contain articles on individual popes and subjects connected with the papacy, with bibliographies. For chronological detail, see Z. V. Lobkowitz, Statistik der Päpste (Freiburg i. B., 1905). Carefully indexed source materials in the original languages are given by C. Mirbt, Quellen zur Geschichte des Papsttums und des römischen Katholizismus (2nd enlarged ed., Tübingen, 1901); many fragments in translation under "Papacy" in History for Ready Reference, ed. by J. N. Larned (vols. iv., vi., vii. Springfield, 1895-1910). Helpful Church histories are F. X. Funk, Lehrbuch der Kirchengeschichte (5th ed., Paderborn, 1907); A. Knöpfler, Lehrbuch der Kirchengeschichte (4th ed., Freiburg i. B., 1906), both Roman Catholic; also the Lutheran work of J. H. Kurtz, Lehrbuch der Kirchengeschichte, ed. N. Bonwetsch and P. Tschackert (14th ed., Leipzig, 1906). (W. W. R.*)

Period I. To 1087.—A bibliography of the history of the papacy during the first eleven centuries would embrace all the vast number of works on the history of the Church during this period. Of these a selected list will be found in the bibliography to the article CHURCH HISTORY. Here it must suffice to mention certain modern works bearing more particularly on this period. Harnack, Lehrbuch der Dogmengeschichte, 3rd ed. i. 400 et seq.; Hinschius, Kirchenrecht, vol. i. §§ 22-25, 74; Sohm, Kirchenrecht, vol. i. § 29 et seq.; Löning, Geschichte des deutschen Kirchenrechts (1878); Duchesne, Églises séparées (1905), Les Premiers temps de l'état pontifical (1904).

Period II: (a) From 1087 to 1124.—L. Paulot's Un Pape français: Urbain II. (Paris, 1903), which is written with a Catholic bias, is the only biography of Urban II. that is at all full. Cf. M. F. Stern, Zur Biographie des Papstes Urbans II. (Berlin, 1883). On Paschal II., see E. Franz, Papst Paschalis II. (Breslau, 1877); W. Schum, Die Politik Papst Paschals II. gegen Kaiser Heinrich V. im Jahre 1112 (Erfurt, 1877); and the excellent "Étude des relations entre le Saint-Siège et le royaume de France de 1099 à 1108," published by Bernard Monod in the Positions des thèses des élèves de l'École des Chartes (1904). The Bullarium of Calixtus II. and the History (Paris, 1891) of his pontificate have been published by Ulysse Robert. Cf. M. Maurer, Papst Calixt II. (Munich, 1889). Besides these monographs, useful information on the history of the popes of this period will be found in the following: R. Röhricht, Geschichte des Königreichs Jerusalem (Innsbruck, 1898) and Geschichte des ersten Kreuzzuges (Innsbruck, 1901); H. von Sybel, Geschichte des ersten Kreuzzugs (2nd ed., Leipzig, 1881); H. Hagenmeyer, Peter der Eremit (Leipzig, 1879); F. Chalandon, Essai sur le règne d'Alexis I. Comnène (Paris, 1900); G. Meyer von Knonau, Jahrbücher des deutschen Reiches unter Heinrich IV. und Heinrich V. (Leipzig, 1890 et seq.); Carl Mirbt, Die Publizistik im Zeitalter Gregors VII. (Leipzig, 1894); Ernst Bernheim, Zur Geschichte des Wormser Konkordates (Göttingen, 1878); Martin Rule, The Life and Times of St Anselm (2 vols., London, 1883); and Klemm, Der Investiturstreit unter Heinrich I.

(b) From 1124 to 1198.—Monographs dealing expressly with the pontificates of this period are scarce. Mention, however, must be made of H. Reuter's *Geschichte Alexanders III. und der Kirche seiner Zeit* (3 vols., Berlin, 1860–1864). Much information on the policy of these popes will be found in the works on the great personages of the time: W. Bernhardi, *Lothar von Supplinburg* (Leipzig, 1879), and *Konrad III.* (Leipzig, 1883); H. Prutz, *Kaiser Friedrich I.* (3 vols., Danzig, 1871–1874); P. Scheffer-Boichorst, *Kaiser Friedrichs I. letzter Streit mit der Kurie* (Berlin, 1866); Julius Ficker, *Reinald von Dassel* (Cologne, 1850); Th. Toeche, *Kaiser Heinrich VI.* (Leipzig, 1867); J. Jastrow and G. Winter, *Deutsche Geschichte im Zeitalter der Hohenstaufen* (2 vols., Berlin, 1897–1901); F. von Raumer, *Geschichte der Hohenstaufen und ihrer Zeit* (5th ed., 6 vols., Leipzig, 1878); A. Hausrath, *Arnold von Brescia* (Leipzig, 1891); Dietr. Hirsch, *Studien zur Geschichte König Ludwigs VII. von Frankreich* (Leipzig, 1892); O. Cartellieri, *Abt Suger von Saint-Denis* (Berlin, 1898); F. Vacandard, *Vie de S. Bernard* (2 vols., Paris, 1895); J. Thiel, *Die politische Thätigkeit des Abtes Bernhard von Clairvaux* (Königsberg, 1885); A. Luchaire, *Louis VII., Philippe-Auguste, Louis VIII.* (vol. iii. pt. i. of Lavisse's *Histoire de France*); H. Böhmer, *Kirche und Staat in England und in der Normandie im XI. und XII. Jahrhundert*, (Leipzig, 1899); Kate Norgate, *England under the Angevin kings* (London, 1887); and P. Scheffer-Boichorst, "Hat Papst Hadrian IV. zu Gunsten des englischen Königs über Irland verfügt?" in *Mitteilungendes Instituts für österr. Geschichtsforschung* (supplementary vol. iv., 1893).

(c) *From 1198 to 1261.*—On the pontificate of Innocent III. in general, see F. von Hurter, *Geschichte Papst Innocens III.* (3rd and 2nd ed., 4 vols., Hamburg, 1841–1844); and A. Luchaire, *Innocent III., Rome et l'Italie* (2nd ed., Paris, 1905), *Innocent III. la croisade des albigeois* (Paris, 1905), *Innocent III., la papauté et l'empire* (Paris, 1906), *Innocent III., la question d'orient* (Paris, 1906), and *Innocent III., les royautés vassales du Saint-Siège* (Paris, 1908). Cf. E. Winkelmann, *Philipp von Schwaben und Otto IV, von Braunschweig* (2 vols., Leipzig, 1873–1878); W. Norden, *Das Papsttum und Byzans* (Berlin, 1903), a considerable part of which is devoted to Innocent III.; E. Gerland, *Geschichte des lateinischen Kaiserreiches von Konstantinopel* (Homburg, 1905); R. Davidsohn, *Philipp II. August von Frankreich und Ingebord* (Stuttgart, 1888); R. Schwemer, *Innocens III. und die deutsche Kirche während des Thronstreites von 1198–1208* (Strasburg, 1882); Else Gütschow, *Innocens III. und England* (Munich, 1904); and many other detailed monographs. The pontificate of Honorius III. is dealt with by J. Clausen in his *Papst Honorius III.* (Bonn, 1895), and his registers have been published by P. Pressutti (2 vols., Rome, 1884 and 1888–1895). On Gregory IX., see J. Felten, *Papst Gregor IX.* (Freiburg i. Br., 1886); P. Balan, *Storia di Gregorio IX. e dei suoi tempi* (3 vols., Modena, 1872–1873); and J. Marx, *Die vita Gregorii IX.* (Berlin, 1889). The publication of the registers of this pope was begun by L. Auvray in the *Bibliothèque des écoles de Rome et d'Athènes* (Paris, 1890 et seq.). On Innocent IV., see E. Berger, *St Louis et Innocent IV.* (Paris, 1893); E. Winkelmann, *Kaiser Friedrich II.* (2 vols., Leipzig, 1889–1897); P. Aldinger, *Die Neubesetzung der deutschen Bistümer unter Papst Innocens IV.* (Leipzig, 1901); and C. Rodenberg, *Innocens IV. und das Königreich Sicilien* (Halle, 1892). The publication of the registers of Innocent IV. was undertaken by Elie Berger (1881 et seq.), and those of Alexander IV. by J. de Loye, A. Coulon and C. Bourel de la Roncière (1895 et seq.). As the history of the later Hohenstaufens is intimately bound up with that of the contemporary popes, mention must be made of F. W. Schirrmacher, *Die letzten Hohenstaufen* (Göttingen, 1871); A. Karst, *Geschichte Manfreds vom Ende Friedrichs II. bis su seiner Krönung* (Berlin, 1897); and K. Hampe, *Geschichte Konradins von Hohenstaufen* (Innsbruck, 1894).

(d) *From 1261 to 1305.*—L. Dorez and J. Guiraud, members of the French school at Rome, began the publication of the registers of Urban IV. (1892 et seq.); E. Jordan, those of Clement IV. (1893 et seq.); and J. Guiraud and L. Cadier, those of Gregory X. (1893 et seq.). On Gregory X., see F. Walter, *Die Politik der Kurie unter Gregor X.* (Berlin, 1894). The pontificate of John XXI. has been dealt with by R. Stapper, *Papst Johannes XXI.* (Münster i. W., 1898), and that of Nicholas III. by A. Demski, *Papst Nikolaus III.* (Münster i. W., 1903), in vol. vi. of the *Kirchengeschichtliche Studien*, ed. by Knöpfler, Schrörs and Sdralek. The publication of the registers of Nicholas III. was undertaken by J. Gay (1898 et seq.). Much information on the policy of these popes will be found in the following: R. Sternfeld, *Ludwigs des Heiligen Kreuzzug nach Tunis und die Politik Karls I. von Sizilien* (Berlin, 1896); Ch. V. Langlois, *Le Règne de Philippe III. le Hardi* (Paris, 1887); L. Leclère, *Les Rapports de la papauté et de la France sous Philippe III.* (Brussels, 1889); C. Minieri-Riccio, *Alcuni fatti riguardanti Carlo I. d'Angiò . . .* (Naples, 1874), and *Il Regno di Carlo I. d'Angiò, in the Archivio storico italiano* (3rd series, vols. xxiii., xxiv., xxv., xxvi.; 4th series, vols. ii., iii., iv., v., vii., 1875–1881); A. Busson, *Die Idee des deutschen Erbreichs und die ersten Habsburger* (Vienna, 1878); G. del Giudice, *La Famiglia di re Manfredi* (Naples, 1880); and H. Otto, *Die Beziehungen Rudolfs von Habsburg zu Papst Gregor X.* (Innsbruck, 1895). There is a good account of the policy of Martin IV. in O. Cartellieri, *Peter von Aragon und die sizilianischen Vesper* (Heidelberg, 1904). On Honorius IV., see introduction to the complete edition of his registers by Maurice Prou (1886–1888).

E. Langlois has published the registers of Nicholas IV. (1886–1893), and Otto Schiff deals with his pontificate in his *Studien zur Geschichte Papst Nikolaus IV.* (1897). On Celestine V., see H. Schulz, *Peter von Murrhone (Papst Coelestin V.)*, Berlin, 1894. The publication of the registers of Boniface VIII. was begun by G. Digard, M. Faucon and A. Thomas (1884 et seq.). Of the vast literature on this pontificate we must content ourselves with citing: Heinrich Finke, *Aus den Tagen Bonifaz' VIII.* (Münster i. W., 1902); Ch. V. Langlois, "St. Louis, Philippe le Bel, Les Derniers capétiens directs" (vol. iii., pt. ii. of Lavisse's *Histoire de France*); Ernest Renan, *Études sur la politique religieuse du règne de Philippe le Bel* (1899); A. Baudrillart, "Des Idées qu'on se faisait au XIVe siècle sur le droit d'intervention du souverain pontife en matière politique," in the *Revue d'histoire et de littérature religieuses* (vol. iii., 1898); and R. Holtzmann, *Wilhelm von Nogaret* (Freiburg i. Br., 1898). The pontificate of Benedict XI. is dealt with by F. Funke in his *Papst Benedikt XI.* (Münster i. W., 1891). Cf. Ch. Grandjean, "Recherches sur l'administration financière du pape Benoît XI," in the *Mélanges d'archéologie et d'histoire* (vol. iii., 1883), published by the French School at Rome. Grandjean has published the registers of Benedict XI. (1883 et seq.).

Among works of a more general character that throw light on the history of the papacy during the 12th and 13th centuries, the first place must be given to Walter Norden's *Das Papsttum und Bysans. Die Trennung der beiden Mächte und das Problem ihrer Wiedervereinigung bis zum Untergange des byzantinischen Reichs* (Berlin, 1903), which contains an account of the question of the East in its relations with the papal policy, from the rise of the schism down to the end of the middle ages. See also Félix Rocquain, *La Papauté au moyen âge* (Paris, 1881) and *La Cour de Rome et l'esprit de réforme avant Luther* (3 vols., Paris, 1893–1897); J. B. Sägmüller, *Die Thätigkeit und Stellung der Cardinäle bis Papst Bonifaz VIII.* (Freiburg i. Br., 1896); and A. Gottlob, *Die päpstlichen Kreuzzugssteuern des 13. Jahrhunderts* (Heiligenstadt, 1892) and *Kreuzablass und Almosenablass* (Stuttgart, 1906). (A. Lu.)

Period III. 1305–1590.—Baluze, *Vitae paparum avenionensium* (1305–1394), 2 t. (Paris, 1693); Raynaldus, *Annales eccles. ab anno 1198* (to 1565), annotated and added to by J. D. Mansi (15 vols., Lucca, 1747–1756); J. Mansi, *Concil. collectio*; Theodoricus of Niem, *De schismate*, ed. Erler (1890); Christophe, *Histoire de la papauté* (1873); Hefele, *Conciliengeschichte* (Freiburg i. B., 1855, seq.); Höfler, *Die avignonesischen Päpsta* (1871); Creighton, *History of the Papacy* (1882, seq.); L. Pastor, *Geschichte der Päpste* (Freiburg i. B., 1886, seq.; Eng. trans. by F. I. Antrobus, 1891, seq.); Pastor, *Acta pontific.* (1904); N. Valois, *La France et le grand schisme*, 4 t. (1896, seq.); Haller, *Papsttum und Kirchenreform* (1903). For the Papacy in connexion with the Renaissance, see E. Müntz, *Les Arts* (1892); Voigt, *Wiederbelebung des klassischen Altertums* (1893); J. Burckhardt, *Cultur der Renaissance in Italien*, 2 B. (ed. L. Geiger, 1907). For the palace at Avignon, see Ehrle, *Bibl. rom. pontif.* I. (1890).

To the authorities for the lives of individual popes attached to the biographies under their several headings, and to the articles on the councils of Basel, Constance, Trent, may be added: Clement V.—Boutaric, *Philippe le Bel* (1861); König, *Papst. Kammer unter Clemens' v. in. Johann XXII.* (1894); Finke, *Acta Aragonen.* (1908). John XXII.—Böhmer, *Regest. Ludwigs des Baiers* (1839); *Vatikanische Acten* (1891); Riezler, *Literarische Widersacher* (1874); Müller, *Kampf Ludwigs mit der Curie* (1879–1880); Coulon, *Lettres secrètes de Jean XXII., relat. à la France*, I. (1907); Mollat, *Lettres commun. de Jean XXII.*, i.–iv. (1907). Clement VI.—Werunsky, *Kaiser Karl IV.*, I. (1800), ii. (1882–1886); Papencordt, *Cola di Rienzo* (1841); Déprez, *Lett. closes* 1901 seq. Innocent VI.—Werunsky, *Ital. Politik Innoc. VI. u. Karl IV.* (1878); id., *Karl IV.* ii. (1882–1886), iii. (1892); Cerasoli, *Archivio napolit.* 22–23; Kirsch, *Kollectorien* (1892); Daumet, *Innocent VI. et Blanche de Bourbon* (1899). Urban V.—Magnan, *Urbain V.* (1863); Werunsky, *Karl IV.* iii. (1892); Prou, *Relat. polit. avec les rois de France* (1888); Wurm, *Albornos* (1892); Kirsch, *Rückkehr der Päpste Urban V. und Gregor XI. nach Rom* (1898); Lecacheux, *Lettres secrètes* (1902, seq.). Gregory XI.—Mirot, *Retour de St Siège à Rome* (1899); Tommaseo, *Lettere de S. Caterina* (1860); M. A. Mignaty, *Catherine de Sienne* (1886). Boniface IX.—Vita, ap. Muratori, *Script.* iii. 2; *Cosmodromium*, Gobelini Persona, ed. Jansen (1900); Jansen, *Bonifacius IX. u. die deutsche Kirche* (1904). Innocent VII.—Gregory XII., schismatic popes, council of Constance, &c. *Monum. concil. gen. saec. XV.* (1857–1896); Alpartils, *Chronica*, ed. Ehrle (1906); Pliemetfrieder, *Literarische Polemik* (1909). Martin V.—*Vitae*, ap. Muratori, iii. 2; Ottenthal, *Bullenregister Martins V. u. Eugens IV.* (1885). Eugenius IV.—*Vita*, ap. Muratori, *Script.* iii. 2; *Repert. germanic.* I. (1897) Müntz, *Les Arts* (1878–1879); Valois, *Pragmatique sanction* (1907). Nicholas V.—Manetti, *Vita Nicolai V.*, ap. Muratori, *Script.* iii. 2; Vespasiano da Bisticci, *Vite* (1839); Georgius (1742); Müntz, *Les Arts* (1878–1879); Creighton, *Papacy* ii. (1882). Paul II.—Ammanati, *Epistolae et commentarii* (1506); Gaspar Veronensis, *Vita*, ap. Marini, Archiatri ii. and Muratori iii. 2 new ed. by Zippel (1903); Canensius, *Vita*, ed. Quirini (1740); Creighton, *Papacy* iii. (1887); Müntz, *Les Arts* ii. (1879). Sixtus IV.—Infessura, *Diario*, ed. Tommasini (1890); Notajo di Nantiporto, *Diarii*, ap. Muratori,

Script. iii. 2; Jacobus Volaterranus, Diarium, ap. Muratori, Script. xxiii.; Schmarzow, Melozzo da Forlì (1886); Steinmann, Sixtinische Capelle i. (1901); Schlecht, Andrea Zamometić i. (1893). INNOCENT VIII.—Infessura, op. cit.; Burchardi, Diarium i.-ii. ed. cit. (also for Alexander VI.); Burchardi, Diarium, ed. Thuasne, i. (1883). JULIUS II.—Brosch, Julius II. u. d. Kirchenstaat (1878); Geymüller, Entwürfe für St Peter (1875-1880); Schulte, Maximilian als Candidat für den päpstlichen Stuhl (1906). LEO X.—Hergenröther, Reg. Leonis X. (1884-1891); Jovius, Vita (1548); Roscoe, Leone X. ed. Bossi (1816); Janssen, Gesch. d. deutschen Volks i. ii.-iii. 18 (1897); Schulte, Fugger in Rom (1904); Kalkoff, Luthers römischer Prozess (1906). ADRIAN VI.—Burmann, Adrianus VI. (1727). CLEMENT VII.—Friedensburg, Nuntiaturberichte i. (1892); Ehses, Documente zur Geschichte der Ehescheidung Heinrichs VIII. (1893); Ehses, Conc. trident. iv. (1904); Fraikin, Nonciatures de France i. (1906). PAUL III.—Friedensburg, Nuntiaturberichte ii. sqq. (1892-1908); Venetianische Depeschen vom Kaiserhof i. (1889); Ehses, Concil. trident. iv. (1904); Merkle, Concil. trident. diaria i.; Maurenbrecher, Karl V. (1865); de Leva, Carlo V. iii.-v. (1867 seq.); Pastor, Reunionsbestrebungen Karls V. (1879); Janssen, Deutsche Geschichte iii. 18. (1899). JULIUS III.—Massarelli, ap. Döllinger, Concil. v. Trient (1876); de Leva, Carlo V. v. (1890). MARCELLUS II.—Pollidorus, Vita (1744). PIUS IV.—Pallavicini, Concilio di Trento (1656); Duruy, Cardinal Carafa (1888); Susta, Curie und Concil. i.-ii. (1904-1909); Steinherr, Nuntiaturberichte i. and iii. (1877-1903). PIUS V.—Guglielmotti, Marcantonio Colonna (1862). GREGORY XIII.—Theiner, Annales ecclesiastici (1856); Maffei, Annali (1746); Brosch, Kirchenstaat i. (1880); Nuntiaturberichte, ed. Hansen, and Schellhass, i. (1892); Steinhuber, Collegium germanicum i. 2-ii. 2 (1907); Duhr, Jesuiten in Deutschland i. (1907); Astrain, Comp. de Jesus de España (3 vols., 1902). SIXTUS V.—Memorie autografe, ed. Cugnoni, Archivio d. Soc. Rom. (1882); Nuntiaturberichte, i. seq. (1895); Balzani, in Cambridge Modern History; Hübner, Sixte-Quinte (1870).

(L. DE P.)

Periods IV., V., VI. 1590 onwards.—In addition to the general works already mentioned, see M. Brosch, Geschichte des Kirchenstaates (Gotha, 1880-1882), utilizing Venetian archives; L. Ranke, History of the Papacy in the 16th and 17th centuries (1840 and frequently); A. R. Pennington, Epochs of the Papacy (London, 1881); F. Nippold, The Papacy in the Nineteenth Century (New York, 1900); B. Labanca, Il Papato (Torino, 1905), with Italian bibliography; F. Nielsen, The History of the Papacy in the Nineteenth Century (London, 1906), the scholarly and fascinating work of a Danish Lutheran bishop; A. Galton, Church and State in France, 1300-1907 (London, 1907); E. Bourgeois and E. Clermont, Rome et Napoléon III. (Paris, 1907), exposing secret negotiations; A. Debidour, L'Église catholique et l'état sous la troisième république (Paris, 1906-1909), valuable though strongly anti-clerical; R. de Cesare, Roma e lo stato del papa dal ritorno di Pio IX. (2 vols. Rome, 1907); in abridged translation, The Last Days of Papal Rome (Boston, 1909). (W. W. R.*)

PAPEETE, the capital of the Pacific island of Tahiti, and the chief port and trading centre, and the seat of government of the French establishments in Oceania. Pop. 4280 (1500 French). The town, lying on the north-west coast of the island, on a beautiful harbour entered by two passages through the protecting reef, and backed by five mountains, is French in character as far as concerns the richer quarters. It has a cathedral, barracks and arsenal, government buildings and a botanical garden. The Chinese quarter and the picturesque native market contrast strongly with the European settlement. Of the entrances to the harbour, which is of fair extent and depth, that of Papeete has about seven fathoms depth; that of Taunoa is shallower, though wider and more convenient.

PAPENBURG, a town in the Prussian province of Hanover, 27 m. by rail S. by W. of Emden, and near the right bank of the Ems, with which it is connected by a canal 3 m. long. Pop. (1905), 7673. It lies in the centre of extensive moors and in appearance resembles a Dutch town. The industries include shipbuilding, oil and glass mills, and manufactures of chemicals, cement, nickel goods and machinery. It is a very prosperous port and its trade, carried on mainly by water, is mostly in the agricultural produce of the extensive moors and pasture lands which lie around it. Papenburg was founded in 1675 and became a town in 1860.

PAPER (Fr. *papier*, from Lat. *papyrus*), the general name for the substance commonly used for writing upon, or for wrapping things in. The origin and early history of paper as a writing material are involved in much obscurity. The art of making it from fibrous matter appears to have been practised by the Chinese at a very distant period. Different writers have traced

it back to the 2nd century B.C. But, however remote its age may have been in eastern Asia, paper first became available for the rest of the world in the middle of the 8th century. In 751 the Arabs, who had occupied Samarkand early in the century, were attacked there by Chinese. The invasion was repelled by the Arab governor, who in the pursuit, it is related, captured certain prisoners who were skilled in paper-making and who imparted their knowledge to their new masters. Hence began the Arabian manufacture, which rapidly spread to all parts of the Arab dominions. The extent to which it was adopted for literary purposes is proved by the comparatively large number of early Arabic MSS. on paper which have been preserved dating from the 9th century.[1]

There has existed a not inconsiderable difficulty in regard to the material of which the Arab paper was composed. In Europe it has been referred to by old writers as *charta bombycina, gossypina, cuttunea, xylina, damascena* and *serica*. The last title seems to have been derived from its glossy and silken appearance; the title *damascena* merely points to its great central emporium, Damascus. But the other terms indicate an idea, which has been persistent, that the paper manufactured by the Arabs was composed of the wool from the cotton-plant, reduced to a pulp according to the method attributed to the Chinese; and it had been generally accepted that the distinction between Oriental paper and European paper lay in the fact that the former was a cotton-paper and the latter a rag-paper. But this theory has been disturbed by recent investigations, which have shown that the material of the Arab paper was itself substantially linen. It seems that the Arabs, and the skilled Persian workmen whom they employed, at once resorted to flax, which grows abundantly in Khorasan, as their principal material, afterwards also making use of rags, supplemented, as the demand grew, with any vegetable fibre that would serve; and that cotton, if used at all, was used very sparingly. Still there remain the old titles *charta bombycina*, &c., to be explained; and an ingenious solution has been offered that the term *charta bombycina*, or χάρτη βομβύκινος, is an erroneous reading of *charta bambycina*, or χάρτη βαμβύκινος, paper manufactured at the Syrian town of Bambyce or βαμβύκη, the Arab Mambidsch (Karabacek in *Mittheilungen aus der Sammlung der Papyrus Erzherzog Rainer*, ii.-iii. 87, iv. 117). Without accepting this as an altogether sufficient explanation of so widely used a term as the-medieval *charta bombycina*, and passing from the question of material to other differences, paper of Oriental manufacture in the middle ages was usually distinguished by its stout substance and glossy surface, and was devoid of water-marks, the employment of which became universal in the European factories. Besides the titles referred to above, paper also received the names of *charta* and *papyrus*, transferred to it from the Egyptian writing material manufactured from the papyrus plant (see PAPYRUS).

It was probably first brought into Greece through trade with Asia, and thence transmitted to neighbouring countries. Theophilus presbyter, writing in the 12th century (*Schedula diversarum artium*, i. 23), refers to it under the name of Greek parchment, *pergamena graeca*. There is a record of the use of

[1] A few of the earliest dated examples may be instanced. The *Gharíbu 'l-Hadíth*, a treatise on the rare and curious words in the sayings of Mahomet and his companions, written in the year 866, is probably one of the oldest paper MSS. in existence (*Pal. Soc.* Orient. Ser. pl. 6). It is preserved in the University Library of Leiden. A treatise by an Arabian physician on the nourishment of the different members of the body, of the year 960, is the oldest dated Arabic MS. on paper in the British Museum (Or. MS. 2600; *Pal. Soc.,* pl. 96). The Bodleian Library possesses a MS. of the *Díwanu 'l-Adab*, a grammatical work of A.D. 974, of particular interest as having been written at Samarkand on paper presumably made at that seat of the first Arab manufacture (*Pal. Soc.* pl. 60). Other early examples are two MSS. at Paris, of the years 969 (*Fonds arabe, suppl.,* 952) and 980 (*Fonds arabe,* 55): a volume of poems written at Baghdad, A.D. 990, now at Leipzig, and the Gospel of St Luke, A.D. 993, in the Vatican Library (*Pal. Soc.,* pls. 7, 21). In the great collection of Syriac MSS., which were obtained from the Nitrian desert in Egypt and are now in the British Museum, there are many volumes written on paper of the 10th century. The two oldest dated examples, however, are not earlier than A.D. 1075 and 1084.

paper by the empress Irene at the end of the 11th or beginning of the 12th century, in her rules for the nuns of Constantinople. It does not appear, however, to have been very extensively used in Greece before the middle of the 13th century, for, with one doubtful exception, there are no extant Greek MSS. on paper which bear date prior to that period.

The manufacture of paper in Europe was first established by the Moors in Spain in the middle of the 12th century, the head-quarters of the industry being Xativa, Valencia and Toledo. But on the fall of the Moorish power the manufacture, passing into the hands of the less skilled Christians, declined in the quality of its production. In Italy also the art of paper-making was no doubt established through the Arab occupation of Sicily. But the paper which was made both there and in Spain, was in the first instance of the Oriental quality. In the laws of Alphonso of 1263 it is referred to as cloth parchment, a term which well describes its stout substance. The first mention of rag-paper occurs in the tract of Peter, abbot of Cluny (A.D. 1122–1150), *adversus Judaeos*, cap. 5, where, among the various kinds of books, he refers to such as are written on material made "ex rasuris veterum pannorum."

A few words may here be said respecting MSS. written in European countries on Oriental paper or paper made in the Oriental fashion. Several which have been quoted as early instances have proved, on further examination, to be nothing but vellum. The ancient fragments of the Gospel of St Mark, preserved at Venice, which were stated by Maffei to be of paper, by Mont-faucon of papyrus, and by the Benedictines of bark, are in fact written on skin. The oldest recorded document on paper was a deed of King Roger of Sicily, of the year 1102; and there are others of Sicilian kings, of the 12th century. A Visigothic paper MS. of the 12th century from Silos near Burgos is now in the Bibliothèque Nationale, Paris. A notarial register on paper, at Geneva, dates from 1154. The oldest known imperial deed on the same material is a charter of Frederick II. to the nuns of Goess in Styria, of the year 1228, now at Vienna. In 1231, however, the same emperor forbade further use of paper for public documents, which were in future to be inscribed on vellum. Transcripts of imperial acts of Frederick II. about A.D. 1241 are at Naples. In Venice the *Liber plegiorum*, the entries in which begin with the year 1223, is made of rough paper; and similarly the registers of the Council of Ten, beginning in 1325, and the register of the emperor Henry VII. (1308–1313) preserved at Turin, are also written on a like substance. In the British Museum there is an older example in a MS. (Arundel 268) which contains some astronomical treatises written on an excellent paper in an Italian hand of the first half of the 13th century. The autograph MS. of Albert de Beham, 1238–1255, at Munich, is on paper. In the Public Record Office there is a letter on paper from Raymond, son of Raymond, duke of Narbonne and count of Toulouse, to Henry III. of England, written within the years 1216–1222. The letters addressed from Castile to Edward I., in 1279 and following years (Pauli in *Bericht, Berl. Abad.*, 1854), are instances of Spanish-made paper; and other specimens in existence prove that in this latter country a rough kind of *charta bombycina* was manufactured to a comparatively late date.

In Italy the first place which appears to have become a great centre of the paper-making industry was Fabriano in the marquisate of Ancona, where mills were first set up in 1276, and which rose into importance on the decline of the manufacture in Spain. The earliest known water-marks in paper from this factory are of the years 1293 and 1294. The jurist Bartolo, in his treatise *De insigniis et armis*, refers to the excellent paper made there in the middle of the 14th century, an encomium which will be supported by those who have had occasion to examine the extant MSS. on Italian paper of that period. In 1340 a factory was established at Padua; another arose later at Treviso; and others followed in the territories of Florence, Bologna, Parma, Milan, Venice and other districts. From the factories of northern Italy the wants of southern Germany were supplied as late as the 15th century. As an instance the case of Görlitz

has been cited, which drew its paper from Milan and Venice for the half century between 1376 and 1426. But in Germany also factories were rapidly founded. The earliest are said to have been set up between Cologne and Mainz, and in Mainz itself about 1320. At Nuremberg Ulman Stromer established a mill in 1390, with the aid of Italian workmen. Other places of early manufacture were Ratisbon and Augsburg. Western Germany, as well as the Netherlands and England, is said to have obtained paper at first from France and Burgundy through the markets of Bruges, Antwerp and Cologne. France owed the establishment of her first paper-mills to Spain, whence we are told the art of paper-making was introduced, as early as the year 1189, into the district of Hérault. At a later period, in 1406, among the accounts of the church of Troyes, paper-mills appear as *molins à toile*. The development of the trade in France must have been very rapid. And with the progress of manufacture in France that of the Netherlands also grew.

In the second half of the 14th century the use of paper for all literary purposes had become well established in all western Europe; and in the course of the 15th century it gradually superseded vellum. In MSS. of this latter period it is not unusual to find a mixture of vellum and paper, a vellum sheet forming the outer, or the outer and inner, leaves of a quire while the rest are of paper.

With regard to the early use of paper in England, there is evidence that at the beginning of the 14th century it was a not uncommon material, particularly for registers and accounts. Under the year 1310, the records of Merton College, Oxford, show that paper was purchased "pro registro," which Professor Rogers (*Hist. Agricul. and Prices*, i. 644) is of opinion was probably paper of the same character as that of the Bordeaux customs register in the Public Record Office, which date from the first year of Edward II. The college register referred to, which was probably used for entering the books that the fellows borrowed from the library, has perished. There is, however, in the British Museum a paper MS. (Add. 31,223), written in England, of even earlier date than the one recorded in the Merton archives. This is a register of the hustings court of Lyme Regis, the entries in which begin in the year 1309. The paper, of a rough manufacture, is similar to the kind which was used in Spain. It may have been imported direct from that country or from Bordeaux; and a seaport town on the south coast of England is exactly the place where such early relics might be looked for. Professor Rogers also mentions an early specimen of paper in the archives of Merton College, on which is written a bill of the year 1332; and some leaves of water-marked paper of 1333 exist in the Harleian collection. Only a few years later in date is the first of the registers of the King's Hall at Cambridge, a series of which, on paper, is preserved in the library of Trinity College. Of the middle of the 14th century also are many municipal books and records. The knowledge, however, which we have of the history of paper-making in England is extremely scanty. The first maker whose name is known is John Tate, who is said to have set up a mill in Hertford early in the 16th century; and Sir John Spilman, Queen Elizabeth's jeweller, erected a paper-mill at Dartford, and in 1589 obtained a licence for ten years to make all sorts of white writing-paper and to gather, for the purpose, all manner of linen rags, scrolls or scraps of parchment, old fishing nets, &c. (Dunkin, *Hist. of Dartford*, 305; Harl. MS. 2296, f. 124 b). But it is incredible that no paper was made in the country before the time of the Tudors. The comparatively cheap rates at which it was sold in the 15th century in inland towns seem to afford ground for assuming that there was at that time a native industry in this commodity.

As far as the prices have been observed at which different kinds of paper were sold in England, it has been found that in 1355–1356 the price of a quire of small folio paper was 5d., both in Oxford and London. In the 15th century the average price seems to have ranged from 3d. to 4d. for the quire, and from 3s. 4d. to 4s. for the ream. At the beginning of the 16th century the price fell to 2d. or 3d. the quire, and to 3s. or 3s. 6d. the ream; but in the second half of the century, owing to the debasement of the coinage, it rose, in common with all other commodities, to nearly 4d. the quire, and to rather more than 5s. the ream. The relatively higher price of the ream in this last period, as compared with that of the quire, seems to imply a more extensive use of the material which enabled the trader to dispose of broken bulk more quickly than formerly, and so to sell by the quire at a comparatively cheap rate.

Brown paper appears in entries of 1570-1572, and was sold in bundles at 2s. to 2s. 4d. Blotting paper is apparently of even earlier date, being mentioned under the year 1465. It was a coarse, grey, unsized paper, fragments of which have been found among the leaves of 15th-century accounts, where it had been left after being used for blotting. Early in the 16th century blotting-paper must have been in ordinary use, for it is referred to in W. Horman's *Vulgaria*, 1519 (p. 80 b): "Blottyng papyr serveth to drye weete wryitynge, lest there be made blottis or blurris"; and early in the next century "charta bibula" is mentioned in the *Pinacotheca* (i. 175) of Nicius Erythraeus. It is remarkable that, in spite of the comparatively early date of this invention, sand continued generally in use, and even at the present day continues in several countries in fairly common use as an ink absorbent.

A study of the various water-marks has yielded some results in tracing the different channels in which the paper trade of different countries . flowed. Experience also of the different kinds of paper and a knowledge of the water-marks (the earliest of which is of about the year 1282) aid the student in fixing nearly exact periods of undated documents. European paper of the 14th century may generally be recognized by its firm texture, its stoutness, and the large size of its wires. The water-marks are usually simple in design; and, being the result of the impress of thick wires, they are therefore strongly marked. In the course of the 15th century the texture gradually becomes finer and the water-marks more elaborate. While the old subjects of the latter are still continued in use, they are more neatly outlined, and, particularly in Italian paper, they are frequently enclosed in circles. The practice of inserting the full name of the maker in the water-mark came into fashion early in the 16th century. But it is interesting to know that for a very brief period in the 14th century, from about 1307 to 1320, the practice actually obtained at Fabriano, but was then abandoned in favour of simple initial letters, which had already been used even in the 13th century. The date of manufacture appears first in the water-marks of paper made in 1545. The variety of subjects of water-marks is most extensive. Animals, birds, fishes, heads, flowers, domestic and warlike implements, armorial bearings, &c., are found from the earliest times. Some of these, such as armorial bearings and national, provincial or personal cognizances, as the imperial crown, the crossed keys or the cardinal's hat, can be attributed to particular countries or districts; and the wide dissemination of the paper bearing these marks in different countries serves to prove how large and international was the paper trade in the 14th and 15th centuries.

AUTHORITIES.—G. *Meerman et doctorum virorum od eum epistolae alque observationes de chartas vulgaris seu lineas origine* (the Hague, 1767); J. G. Schwandner, *Charta linea* (Vienna, 1788); G. F. Wehrs, *Vom Papier* (Halle, 1789); J. G. J. Breitkopf, *Ursprung der Spielkarten und Einführung des Leinenpapieres* (Leipzig, 1784-1801); M. Koops, *Historical Account*, &c. (London, 1801); Sotzmann, "Über die ältere Papierfabrikation," in *Serapeum* (Leipzig, 1846); C. M. Briquet, "Recherches sur les premiers papiers, du x⁰ au xiv⁰ siècle," in *Mém. antiquaires de France*, xlvi. (Paris, 1886), and *Le Papier arabe au moyen âge* (Bern, 1888); C. Paoli, "Carta di cotone e carta di lino," in *Archivio storico italiano*, ser. 4, tom. xv. (1885); J. Karabacek, *Mittheilungen aus der Sammlung der Papyrus Erzherzog Rainer*, ii.-iii. 87 (1887), iv. 117 (1897); Midoux and Matton, *Etude sur les Filigranes* (Paris, 1868); C. M. Briquet, *Les Filigranes: Dictionnaire historique des marques du papier dès leur apparition vers 1282 jusqu'en 1600* (Paris, 1907), with a bibliography of works on water-marks; W. Wattenbach, *Das Schriftwesen im Mittelalter* (Leipzig, 1896); J. E. T. Rogers, *History of Agriculture and Prices in England* (Oxford, 1866-1882).   (E. M. T.)

PAPER MANUFACTURE

In the modern sense " paper " may best be described as a more or less thin tissue composed of any fibrous material, whose individual fibres, first separated by mechanical action, are then deposited and felted together on wire cloth while suspended in water (see FIBRES). The main constituent in the structure of all plants is the fibre or cellulose which forms the casing or walls of the different cells; it is the woody portion of the plant freed from all foreign substances, and forms, so to speak, the skeleton of vegetable fibre to the amount of 75 to 78%. Its forms and combinations are extremely varied, but it always consists of the same chemical elements, carbon, hydrogen and oxygen, and in the same proportions. It is the object of the paper-maker to eliminate the glutinous, resinous, siliceous and other intercellular matters and to produce the fibre as pure and as strong as possible. Linen and cotton rags, having already undergone a process of manufacture, consist of almost pure fibres with the addition of fatty and colouring matters which can be got rid of by simple boiling under a low pressure of steam with a weak alkaline solution; but the substitutes for rags, esparto, wood, straw, &c., being used as they come from the soil, contain all the intercellular matter in its original form, which has to be dissolved by strong chemical treatment under a high temperature. The vegetable fibre or cellulose, being of a tougher and stronger nature, is untouched by the action of caustic soda (which is the chemical generally employed for the purpose), unless the treatment be carried too far, whilst animal fibres or other organic matters are rendered soluble or destroyed by it. The cellulose, after its resolution by chemical treatment, is still impregnated with insoluble colouring matters, which have to be eliminated or destroyed by treatment with a solution of chlorine or bleaching-powder. The object of the paper-maker in treating any one particular fibre is to carry the action of the dissolving and bleaching agents just so far as to obtain the fibre as free from impurities and as white in colour as is desired. The usefulness of a plant for a good white paper depends upon the strength and elasticity of its fibres, upon the proportion of cellular tissue contained in them, and upon the ease with which this can be freed from the encrusting and intercellular matters. Although experiments had previously been made with many fibrous materials, paper was made in Europe, until the middle of the 19th century, almost entirely from rags, either linen or cotton. At that period other fibres began to be adopted as substitutes, due in part, no doubt, to insufficient supply of rags for the increasing consumption of paper, and to the consequent rise in price. The most important of these substitutes are esparto-grass, wood and straw, and these, together with flax (linen), hemp, jute and cotton rags, form the principal raw material for the manufacture of paper.

Paper was first entirely made by hand, sheet by sheet, but in 1798 the invention of the paper machine by Louis Robert, a clerk in the employ of Messrs Didot, of the Essonne Paper Mills in France, gave a new impetus to the industry. The invention was introduced into England by Henry Fourdrinier (1766-1854), the proprietor of a mill at Dartford in Kent. He secured the assistance of Bryan Donkin (1768-1855), and after much toil and perseverance, attended with great expense, for which he received no recompense, succeeded in 1803 in erecting a machine at Frogmore, Herts, which worked comparatively well. This machine, by the subsequent improvements of Dickinson, Causon, Crompton and others, has been brought to the state of perfection in which it now stands. It embraces a multitude of most ingenious and delicate operations, and produces in a few minutes, and in one continuous process from the prepared pulp, sheets of paper ready for use. Machine-made paper has now gradually supplanted that made by hand for all except special purposes, such as bank-note, ledger, drawing and other high-class papers—in one word, in cases where great durability is the chief requisite.

The various uses to which paper is put in the present day are multitudinous, but the main classes may be grouped into four: (1) writing and drawing papers; (2) printing and news-papers; (3) wrapping papers; (4) tissue and cigarette papers.

The process of paper manufacture consists of two main divisions: (1) the treatment of the raw material, including cleansing, dusting, boiling, washing, bleaching and reducing to pulp;

(2) the methods by which the prepared pulp or fibres are converted into paper ready for the market; this is paper-making proper, and includes the operations of beating, sizing, colouring, making the sheet or web, surfacing, cutting, &c.

Rags. Rags arrive at the mill from the rag merchants, either roughly sorted into grades or mixed in quality and material, and the first process is to free them from sand, dust and other impurities. To effect this they are usually passed in bulk through an ordinary revolving duster. They are then sorted into grades, and cut to a workable size about four inches square. For the best work, hand-cutting, done by women, is still preferred, but it is expensive and good machines have now been designed for this purpose. After further thrashing and dusting, the rags are ready for boiling, the object of which is not only to get rid of the dirt still remaining in them and to remove some of the colouring matter, but also to decompose a particular glutinous substance which would impair the flexibility of the fibres and render them too harsh and stiff for readily making into paper. Various forms of vessels are used for boiling, but usually they are made to revolve by means of suitable gearing, and are either cylindrical or spherical (fig. 1).

FIG. 1.—Revolving Spherical Rag Boiler.

In these the rags are boiled with an alkaline solution under a low steam pressure for six to twelve hours. The next step is that of washing and "breaking in," which takes place in an engine called the "breaker." This (fig. 2) is an oblong shallow vessel or trough with rounded ends and dished bottom, usually about 13 ft. long by 6 ft. wide, by about 2 ft. 6 in. in depth, but the size varies greatly. It is partly divided along the centre by a partition or "mid-feather," and furnished with a heavy cast-iron roll fitted round its circumference with knives or bars of steel in bunches or clumps. Underneath the roll and fixed in the bottom of the trough is the "plate," consisting of a number of parallel steel bars bedded in a wooden frame. The roll can be raised or lowered on the plate so as to increase or diminish, as desired, the cutting action of the bars and plate on the material. The duty of the roll is to cut and tease out the rags, and also to act as a lifter to cause the stuff to circulate round the trough. The breaker is half filled with water and packed with the boiled rags; an ample supply of clean water is run into the engine for washing the rags, the dirty water being withdrawn by the "drum-washer," a hollow cylinder fitted with buckets and covered with fine wire-cloth. During the washing process the roll is gradually lowered on the plate to tease out the rags into their original fibres; this operation takes from two to four hours. As soon as all signs of the textile nature of the material are destroyed, the washing water is turned off, the drum-washer lifted, and a solution of chlorine or bleach is run in to bring the pulp up to the degree of whiteness desired, after which the rag "half-stuff," as it is now called, is emptied into steeps or drainers, where it is stored ready for use.

In treating esparto (the use of which for paper-making is almost confined to Great Britain) the object is to free it from all encrusting **Esparto.** and intercellular matter. To effect this it is digested with a strong solution of caustic soda under a high temperature, in boilers which are almost invariably stationary. The most usual form is that known as Sinclair's patent (fig. 3). This boiler is constructed of wrought-iron or steel plates, and holds from 2½ to 3 tons of grass. It is charged through the opening at the top A, and the boiled material taken out from a door B at the side; the grass rests on a false bottom of perforated plates C, through which the liquor drains, and by means of two "vomiting" pipes,

D, D, at the sides of the boiler, connecting the space at the bottom with a similar space at the top, a continuous circulation of steam and liquor is maintained through the grass. The steam pressure is kept up to 30 to 40 lb per sq. in. for three or four hours; then the strong liquor or lye, which contains all the resinous and intercellular matters dissolved by the action of the caustic soda, is run off and stored in tanks for subsequent recovery of the soda, while the grass is taken to the "potcher" or washing engine. In construction and working this is similar to the breaking engine used for rags; in it the grass is reduced to pulp, and washed for about twenty minutes to free it from the traces of soda liquor remaining

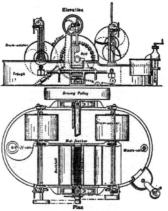

FIG. 2.—Rag-breaking Engine.

after the partial washing in the boiler. As soon as the wash water is running clear it is shut off, and the necessary quantity of a solution of bleaching powder or chlorine (averaging about 6 to 8 % on the raw material) is run into the potcher, and the contents are heated by steam to a temperature of about 90° F. After about four to six hours the bleaching is complete, the drum-washer is let down, fresh water run into the potcher, and the grass washed to free it from all traces of chlorine, an operation generally assisted by the use of a little antichlor or hyposulphite of soda. The esparto, as shipped in bales from the Spanish or African fields, is mixed with roots, weeds and other impurities; and as most of these do not boil or bleach as rapidly as the esparto they would, if not taken out of the pulp, show up in the finished paper as specks and spots. To get rid of them the esparto pulp when washed and bleached is run from the potcher into storage chests, from which it is pumped over a long, narrow serpentine settling table or "sand-table," made of wood and fitted with divisions, or "weirs," behind which the heavy impurities or weeds fall to the bottom and are caught. The pulp is next passed over what is known as a "presse-pâte" (fig. 4) or "half-stuff" machine, very similar to the wet end of a paper machine, consisting of strainers fitted with coarse-cut strainer plates, a short wire and a pair of couch and press rolls. The pulp is drawn by suction through the strainers, which keep back the finer impurities that have passed the sand-table, and then flows on to the wire-cloth in the form of a thick web of pulp. After passing through the couch and press rolls, the pulp leaves the machine with about 70 % of moisture, and is ready for the beating engine, the first operation of paper-making proper. This is the usual process, though various modifications are introduced in different mills and for different purposes.

Most kinds of straw can be utilized for making into paper, the varieties generally used being rye, oat, wheat and barley; of these, **Straw.** the two former are the most important, as they give the largest yield in fibres. Germany and France are the two principal users of straw, which closely resembles esparto in its chemical constitution, and is reduced to a pulp by a somewhat similar process.

Scandinavia, Germany, the United States and Canada are the countries which mainly use wood as a material for paper-making, owing to their possession of large forest areas. They also export large quantities of wood-pulp to other countries. In Europe the

Wood. Scotch fir (*Pinus sylvestris*), the spruce (*Picea excelsa*), the poplar (*Populus alba*) and the aspen (*Populus tremula*), are the timbers principally employed; and in America the black spruce (*Picea nigra*), the hemlock (*Tsuga canadensis*), the poplar (*Populus grandidentata*) and the aspen (*Populus tremuloides*). Two kinds of wood-pulp are used for paper manufacture, one prepared mechanically and the other chemically. The former is obtained by disintegrating the wood entirely by machinery, without the use of chemicals, and is, as may readily be understood, a very inferior pulp. In the manufacture of chemical wood-pulp, very great

about seven or eight hours, in a similar manner to esparto and straw, though it requires much severer treatment. The steam pressure varies from 90 ℔ to as much as 150 ℔ per sq. in., and the amount of soda required is about 16% of Na_2O, estimated on the barked and cleaned wood. The essential feature of the sulphite process is the employment of a solution of sulphurous acid combined with a certain amount of base, either magnesia or lime. As the acid reaction of the bisulphite solution would attack any exposed ironwork with which it comes in contact, the boilers in all cases should be lined with lead. The type of boiler employed varies according to the process adopted. The principal patents connected with the sulphite process are those of Tilghman, Ekman,

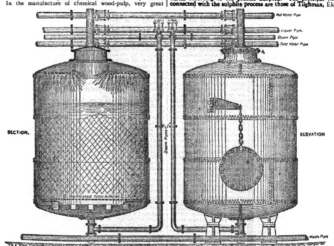

SECTION.   *Hot Water Pipe*   *Liquor Pipe.*   *Steam Pipe*   *Cold Water Pipe*   **ELEVATION**   *Waste Pipe*

FIG. 3.—Sinclair Esparto Boiler.

advances have been made since 1880; and wood-pulp has grown to be one of the most important fibres for paper-making purposes. Two methods are in use, known respectively as the soda or alkaline process, and the sulphite or acid process, according as soda or sulphur (or rather sulphurous acid) forms the base of the reagent employed. Trees of medium age are usually selected, varying from seventy to eighty years' growth and running from 8 to 12 in. in diameter. They are felled in winter, and reach the mill in logs about 4 ft. long. After being freed from bark and the knots taken out by machinery, the logs are cut into small cubical chips about ¼ to ½ in. in size by a revolving cutter. The chips are then bruised by being passed between two heavy iron rolls to allow the boiling solution thoroughly to penetrate them, and are conveyed to the boilers over a screen of coarse wire-cloth, which separates out the fine sawdust as well as any dirt or sand. In the soda process the wood is boiled in large revolving or upright stationary boilers for

Francke, Ritter-Kellner, Mitscherlich, and Partington. The subsequent operations, in both the acid and alkaline processes of washing, bleaching and straining the pulp, are all very similar to those described for esparto. Wood-pulp produced by the sulphite process differs in a marked degree from that made by the soda process; the fibre in the former case is harsher and stronger, and papers made from it are characterized by their hardness and transparency, whereas those made from soda pulp are softer and more mellow, corresponding in some way to the difference between linen and cotton fibres. Each class of pulp is largely used, both alone and mixed with other materials.

Within recent years important modifications and improvements have been adopted in the preparation of esparto and wood halfstuff with a view to reduce the cost of manufacture and save waste of material. From the boiler to the beater the process becomes a continuous one, so that the prepared pulp requires practically no

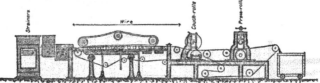

Strainers   *Wire*   *Couch-rolls*   *Press-rolls*

FIG. 4.—"Press-Pâte," or Half-stuff Machine.

handling till it is made into finished paper at the end of the machine; this effects a considerable saving in cost of labour and reduces the waste of material incidental to a series of disconnected operations.

From the potcher or breaking engine the esparto or wood pulp is discharged, by means of a patent circulator or pump, into the first of a series of upright bleaching towers. These towers (fig. 5) are built up of wrought-iron rods and a special kind of cement. They are usually about 16 ft. high in the parallel by 8½ ft. in diameter; the bottom of the tower is conical and connected to a powerful circulator or pump, which discharges the pulp into the top of the tower and causes thereby a continuous circulation and a thorough mixing of the

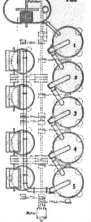

pulp and bleach. A special form of concentrator is fixed on the top of the first tower, which reduces the water in the pulp as it leaves the potcher to the minimum quantity necessary for perfect circulation in the tower; by this means a considerable saving is effected in the quantity of bleach required. After the necessary concentration of the pulp in No. 1 tower, the bleaching liquor is added and the circulator at the foot of the tower put in motion. A two-way valve in the discharge pipe allows the pulp to pass on to tower No. 2, and so on through the series. The circulator in each tower is only put in working for a short time once in every hour and there is never more than one circulator working in the series at one time. There is no manual labour in working the process, perfect cleanliness, and a great saving in power over the old process. Each tower will hold about two tons of dry pulp. When the pulp is fully bleached in the last tower of the series, fresh water is run into it, and a

to the one on the first tower, is put in motion and washes out all traces of the bleach in about 25 to 30 minutes. These concentrators effect also another purpose, taking to some extent the place of the presse-pâte machine for removing roots, weeds and other impurities.

From the last tower and concentrator the bleached pulp is pumped through a line of pipes to the beaters, valves being fixed in the line of pipes to discharge into whichever beater is desired. These beaters are constructed in tower-form like the bleachers, the roll and plate being fixed on the top of the tower and the circulation effected in the same way as in the bleachers. Fig. 5 shows plan and elevation of such an arrangement of beaters and bleachers arranged in series.

The beaters are made to hold each about 1500 lb of dry paper and a series of four of these can make from 55 to 60 tons of paper per week.

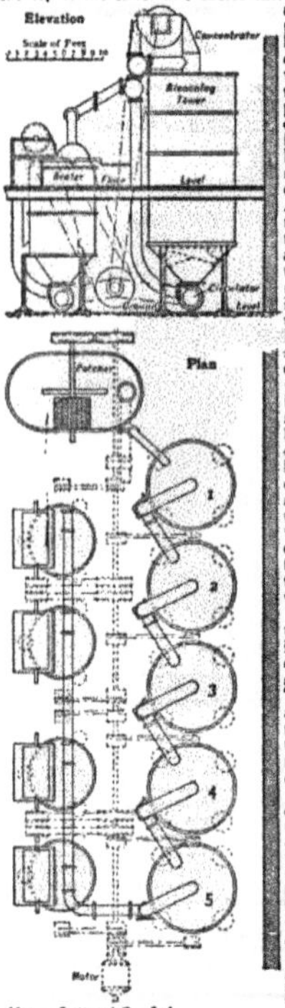

Masson, Scott and Co., Ltd.

FIG. 5.—Esparto Bleaching and Beating Plant.

Fibres like jute, hemp, manila, &c., are chiefly used for the manufacture of coarse papers where strength is of more importance than appearance, such as wrapping-papers, paper for telegraph-forms, &c. The boiling processes for them are similar to those used for esparto and straw.

The alkaline liquors in which rags, esparto and other paper-making materials had been boiled were formerly run into the nearest water-course; but now, partly because it is insisted upon in England by the Rivers Pollution Acts, **Soda Recovery.** and partly because the recovery of the soda can be made remunerative, all these liquors are preserved and the soda they contain utilised. One of the best and most economical of the simple recovery plants is that invented by Porion, a French distiller, and named after him. This consists of an evaporating chamber A, on the floor of which a few inches of the liquid to be evaporated rest. By the action of fanners B, B revolving at a high speed and dipping into the liquid, it is thrown up in a fine spray through which the heated gases pass to the chimney. After being concentrated in the evaporating chamber the liquid flows into the incinerating furnaces C,C, where the remaining water is driven off by the heat of the fire D, and the mass afterwards ignited to drive off the carbonaceous matter. A considerable feature in this evaporator is Menzies and Davis's patent smell chamber E, a chamber filled with masonry in which the strongly-smelling gases from the incinerating furnace are allowed to remain at a red heat for a short time. After being recovered, the soda, in the form of crude carbonate, is lixiviated and re-causticised by boiling with milk of lime.

Porion's method is open, however, to the objection that the whole of the sulphur in the coal employed for the furnaces finds its way into the recovered soda, and forms sulphur compounds, thus reducing the value of the ash for boiling purposes; in addition, a considerable amount of soda is volatilised during the evaporation. By the application of the system of multiple-effect evaporation to the recovery of waste liquors these drawbacks disappear, and an important change has been made in the soda-recovery plant of the paper-mill. This system of multiple-effect evaporation, originally introduced by M. Rillieux, was perfected by the invention of Homer T. Yaryan, of Toledo, Ohio, U.S.A. This type may here be taken for description, though other types of evaporator are now also employed, notably the ordinary vertical tube multiple effect evaporator as used for concentrating sugar liquors. The Yaryan evaporator was originally applied in the United States to the concentration of the waste alkaline liquors of paper-mills; it then came into extensive use for the manufacture and refining of sugar, the production of glucose and a variety of other purposes. The principle of multiple-effect evaporation is to utilise the latent heat of a vapour given off from a liquid under a certain pressure to vaporize a further quantity of the liquid under a pressure maintained by mechanical means below that of the first. The essential feature which distinguishes the Yaryan evaporator consists in the boiling of the liquor to be treated while it is passing through a series of tubes, which constitute a coil and are heated externally by steam or vapour. The quantity of liquor entering the coil is so controlled that it is only permitted partially to fill the tubes, and thus leaves room for the instantaneous liberation of the vapour and its free escape.[1] As the liquor descends from tube to tube it becomes concentrated and reduced in volume until it ultimately passes into a "separator," where it impinges on a plate or disk, which causes a complete separation of the vapour and liquid; each then passes on to the next "effect," the liquid through the second coil of tubes and the vapour to the chamber enclosing them. This combination of a series of tubes, or coil, and separator constitutes a vessel or "effect," and the evaporator consists of a series, usually three or more, of these vessels, one above the other (fig. 7). The vital feature, it will be understood, is therefore that the latent heat of the original steam, after performing its function in the first effect, is passed on to the second and then to the third or more effects, in each of which an equal amount of work is done before passing to the final condenser, where a vacuum is maintained. Thus, if the total temperature be divided three times, the result is a triple-effect. If four times, a quadruple-effect. Taking an evaporation of 10 lb of water per pound of coal, a single-effect apparatus will evaporate 10 lb of water, a

[1] In England, it should be stated, it is found that both for paper liquors and other liquors equally good evaporation results are obtained and the tubes kept cleaner by keeping them under a head of liquor, i.e. the liquor is fed into the bottom row of tubes and has to ascend row by row to the top row, from which it flows to the separator.

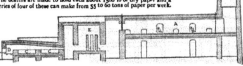

FIG. 6.—Porion Evaporator.

double-effect 20 ℔, a triple-effect 30 ℔, and so on.[1] The liquor to be concentrated is pumped from the storage tanks to the top or first effect of the Yaryan apparatus through a series of multiple-effect heaters, corresponding to the number of effects in the machine, by means of which the liquor is heated to as near the boiling point as possible of the liquor in the tubes of the first effect.

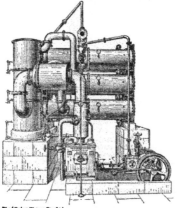

The Mirrlees Watson Co., Ltd.
FIG. 7.—The Yaryan Patent Multiple Effect Evaporator.

Live steam is introduced into the chamber surrounding the tubes of the first effect, and from the separator of the last effect the concentrated liquor is pumped to the incinerator.

Any form of incinerating hearth can be used in conjunction with the multiple-effect evaporator, but one very suitable to the continuous work of, and the high degree of concentration produced by, the Yaryan machine is that known as the Warren rotary furnace. This consists of a revolving iron cylinder lined with brick, about 12 ft. long by 10 ft. in diameter. The lining being 6 in. thicker at the inlet[2] than at the discharge, the interior of the furnace is conical in form so that the ash gradually works forward and is eventually discharged fully burnt into trucks for storage, or on a travelling band, and so carried automatically to the dissolving or lixiviating tanks. The strong liquor runs in at one end in a slow continuous stream; by the rotation of the hearth the burning mass is carried up the sides and drops through the flame again to the bottom, much in the same manner as rags do in a revolving duster. In this way all the labour required to stir the ash of the ordinary hearth is dispensed with, and the burning material comes continuously in close contact with the flame, a complete and thorough combustion being the result. The fire-box is situated at the delivery end of the furnace, and is mounted on trucks[3] so that it can be run back when cleaning or repairing the brickwork. The waste heat is utilized in raising steam in a steam boiler set behind the furnace, and often in keeping the thick liquor hot after leaving the evaporator and before entering the rotary furnace.

Paper-making proper from prepared pulp, whether of rags, esparto, wood or other raw material, may be said to begin with the operation technically known as "beating" which is

[1] The figures given here are theoretical rather than actual. In practice a double effect is not capable of evaporating twice as much with 1 ℔ of coal as a single-effect, owing to loss of efficiency through radiation, &c.

[2] This was the original Warren principle, but has largely been abandoned in favour of a parallel brick lining throughout; the ash gradually works forward and is discharged as described.

[3] A later method is to build the fire-box on the descending side of the rotary furnace, while a specially constructed door and ash discharge shoot are provided at the ascending side, which gives access to the inside of the furnace and provides all the other essentials without the loss of heat which resulted from the portable fire-box, due to leakage between the box and the rotary furnace proper.

carried out in one of the various forms of beating engine or "Hollander." The object of the beater is to reduce the fibres to suitable lengths and also to beat or bruise them into a stiff pulp of sufficient consistency to absorb **Beating.** and carry the water necessary to felt them together on the wires

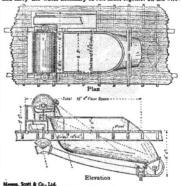

Plan

Elevation

Masson, Scott & Co., Ltd.
FIG. 8.—Taylor's Patent Beater.

cloth of the paper-machine. This operation is one of the most important and most delicate processes in the manufacture, requiring experience, skill and careful manipulation. Not only does every class of fibre demand its own special treatment, but this treatment has to be modified and varied in each case to suit the qualities and substances of the papers to be made from it.

Although there are now in use a great many forms of beating engine, they are all, more or less, modifications of the original Hollander, which in its essential details differs little from the breaking engine already described. There are usually more bars in the roll and plate than in the breaker; the bars of the plate are set at a slight angle to the fly-bars of the roll to act as shears in a similar manner to a pair of scissors. Bars and plates of bronze are frequently used for the higher grades of paper to avoid rust and dirt and to produce a softer and less violent action on the fibres. The time required for the beating process varies from 3 to 4 hours up to 10 and 12 and even more. Beating engines fitted with mechanical circulation by pumps or otherwise have been extensively adopted, more particularly for working esparto and the other substitutes for rags. Fig. 8 shows one of these beaters, known as the Taylor beater; the roll and plate are fixed above the trough of the beater, which has no partition or mid-feather, and from the lower end a powerful circulator or pump circulates the pulp through the beater and discharges it through a pipe in a continuous stream in front of the roll. In the pipe is fixed a two-way valve, so that when the beating operation is complete the finished pulp can be run into the stuff-chests of the paper machine. The advantages of this form of beater are that a quicker and more thorough circulation of the pulp takes place than when the roll has to do the double duty of making the pulp travel and beating it up at the same time, and thus tends to reduce the time of the operation. Also more bars can be fixed in the roll, increasing its effect on the pulp, and less power is required than when the roll revolves in the middle of the stuff as in the ordinary form of beater.

Beating engines of quite a different construction are now largely used in American mills, and also to some extent in Great Britain. These are known as "refiners," and the most important forms are the Jordan and Kingsland beaters (so called from the names of the inventors), or modifications of them.

The first (fig. 9) consists of a conical plug or roll fixed on a shaft and revolving at a high rate of speed within an outer casing of corresponding shape; both the plug and the casing are furnished with steel bars parallel with the shaft, but set at slightly different angles, taking the place of the bars in the roll and plate of the ordinary beater. This conical plug or roll can be moved in either direction parallel to its axis and by this means the cutting action of the two sets of bars can be increased or reduced. The pulp flows into the top of the beater at the smaller end of the cone through a box provided with an arrangement for regulating the flow and passes out through an opening in the casing at the other end. The roll or plug revolves at from 350 to 400 revolutions per minute, and requires a power to drive it of from 25 to 40 h.p.,

FIG. 9.—Jordan Beater.

according to the work to be done, and one engine is capable of passing as much as 1000 lb weight of dry pulp per hour. The Kingsland beater consists of a circular box or casing, on both inside faces of which are fixed a number of knives or bars of steel or bronze; inside the case is a revolving disk of metal fitted on both sides with corresponding and similar bars. The contact between the revolving and stationary bars can be regulated, as in the Jordan engine, to give the required amount of beating action on the pulp. The refiner is essentially a finishing process as an adjunct to the beating process proper. The advantages to be derived from its use are a considerable saving in the time occupied in beating and the production of a more uniform and evenly divided pulp, particularly where a mixture of different fibres is used. By the use of the refiner the time occupied in the beater can be reduced by nearly one-half, the half-beaten pulp passing through the refiner from the beater on its way to the paper-machine. It is not, however, generally employed for the best kinds of paper.

During the operation of beating various materials and chemicals are added to the pulp for the purposes of sizing, loading, colouring, &c. Papers for writing and most of those for printing purposes must be rendered non-absorbent of ink or other liquid applied to them. To effect this some form of animal or vegetable size or glue must be applied to the paper, either as a coating on the finished web or sheet, or mixed with the pulp in the beating engine. The former, called "tub-sizing" will be described later; the latter which is known as "engine-sizing" consists in filling up the interstices of the fibres with a chemical precipitate of finely-divided resin, which, when dried and heated on the cylinders of the paper-machine, possesses the property of being with difficulty wetted with water. Except in the very best qualities of paper, it is usual to add to the pulp a certain quantity of cheap loading material; such as china-clay or kaolin, or pearl-hardening, a chemically precipitated form of sulphate of lime. The addition of such loading material to a moderate extent, say 10 to 15%, is not entirely in the nature of an adulterant, as it serves to close up the pores of the paper, and for ordinary writing, printing and lithographic papers renders the material softer, enabling it to take a much better and more even surface or glaze. But if added in excess it is detrimental to the strength and hardness of the sheet. Most materials however well bleached, have a more or less yellowish tinge; to produce the desired white shade in the paper certain quantities of red and blue in the form of pigments or dyes must be added to the pulp. The blues usually employed are ultramarine, smalts and the aniline blues, while the red dyes are generally preparations of either cochineal or the aniline dyes. Other colours are required in the manufacture of papers of different tints, and with one or two exceptions they must be mixed with the pulp in the beater.

There are two distinct processes of producing the finished paper from the pulp, known respectively as "hand-made" *Paper* and "machine-made." The expense of manu-*Machine.* facture of hand-made paper and the consequent high price render it too costly for ordinary use; the entire process on the machine occupies a few minutes, while in the ordinary state of the weather it could not be done by hand in less than a week.

A brief description of the hand-made process will suffice and it will at the same time facilitate the right comprehension of

the machine process. Only the finest qualities of rags are used for hand-made paper; and the preparation of the half-stuff is the same as that already described under treatment of rags. The pulp after being prepared in the beating engine is run into

FIG. 10.

large chests from which the vat is supplied; before reaching this it is strained as on the paper-machine (see below). The sheet of paper is made on a mould of fine wire-cloth with a removable frame of wood to keep the pulp from running off, extending slightly above the surface of the mould, called the "deckel." To form the sheet, the paper-maker dips the mould into a vat (see fig. 10) containing the prepared pulp, lifting up just so much as will make a sheet of the required thickness; as soon as the

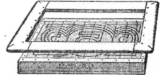

FIG. 11.—Mould and Deckel for hand-made paper.

mould is removed from the vat, the water begins to drain through the wire-cloth and to leave the fibres on the surface in the form of a coherent sheet, the felting or intertwining being assisted by a lateral motion or "shake" given to the mould by the workman; the movable deckel is then taken off, and the mould is given to another workman, called the "coucher," who turns it over and presses it against a felt, by this means transferring or "couching" the sheet from the wire to the felt. A number of the sheets thus formed are piled one above another alternately with pieces of felt, and the whole is subjected to strong pressure to expel the water; the felts are then removed and the sheets are again pressed and dried, when they are ready for sizing. Any pattern or name required in the sheet is obtained by making the wire-cloth mould in such a way that it is slightly raised in those parts where the pattern is needed (fig. 11); consequently less pulp lodges there and the paper is proportionately thinner, thus showing the exact counterpart of the pattern on the mould; such are known as "watermarks." The expense of manufacturing paper in this way is very much greater than by machinery; but the gain in strength, partly owing to the time allowed to the fibres to knit together, and partly to the free expansion and contraction permitted them in drying, still maintains a steady demand for this class of paper.

The paper-machine (fig. 12) consists essentially of an endless mould of fine wire-cloth on which the pulp flows and on which a continuous sheet of paper is formed; the sheet then passes through a series of press rolls and over a number of steam-heated cylinders until it is dry. From the beating engines, the pulp is emptied into storage tanks or stuff-chests, fitted with revolving arms or agitators; from these the pulp is pumped into a long upright supply box at a higher level, called the stuff box, which communicates with the sand trap or table by means of a regulating valve. With the pulp a certain amount of water is allowed to flow on to the sand trap so as to dilute it sufficiently to form on the wire-cloth of face of a rapidly-revolving disk driven by a pair of speed-cones, so that the speed of the shake can be altered. The object of this shake is to interlace the fibres together, but it also assists in keeping the water from passing through the wire too rapidly before the paper has been properly formed. Most machines have two suction-boxes with the "dandy-roll" revolving between them on the top

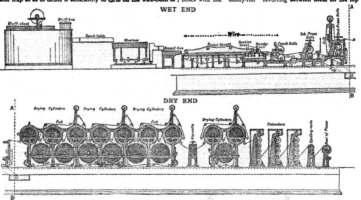

FIG. 12.—Paper-Making Machine.

the paper-machine. The sand trap consists of an elevated table in which is sunk a shallow serpentine channel lined on the bottom with rough felt and divided throughout its length by a number of small strips of wood, behind which the impurities collect as the pulp flows over them on its way to the strainers.

The strainers are made of plates of brass or some hard and durable composition with fine parallel slits cut in them, through which the fibres pass, all knots and improperly divided portions *Straining.* remaining behind; the pulp is made to pass through them by the rapid vibration of the plates themselves or by a strong suction underneath them, or sometimes by a combination of the two. From the strainers the pulp flows into a long wooden box or trough, of the same width as the paper machine, called the "breast-box," and thence on to the wire-cloth. The wire consists of a continuous woven brass cloth, supported horizontally by small brass rolls, called 'tube-rolls,' carried on a *Forming the Sheet.* frame; it is usually 40 to 50 ft. long and is stretched tight over two rolls, one at each end of the frame, called respectively the "breast-roll" and the "lower-couch roll." The ordinary gauge for the wire-cloth is 66 meshes to the inch for writings and printings; finer wires are sometimes used, however, up to 80 to the inch; for lower grades the mesh is coarser. The water, mixed with the pulp, flows from the wire-cloth by gravitation along the lines of contact between it and the tube-rolls; this water, which contains a considerable percentage of fibre, especially from finely beaten pulps, drops into a flat copper or wooden tray, from which it flows into a tank and is pumped up with the water for diluting the pulp so that none of it shall be wasted. From the tube-rolls the wire conveys the pulp over a pair of suction-boxes for extracting the remaining water from the web. The width of the web of paper is determined by two continuous straps of vulcanized rubber about 1½ in. square, one on each side of the wire, called the "deckel-straps"; the distance between these straps can be increased or diminished; they serve to guide the pulp from the

FIG. 13.—Dandy-roll.

moment it spreads on the wire until it arrives at the first suction-box, where the web is sufficiently dry to retain its edges. The *Shake.* frame of the machine from the breast-roll to the first suction-box is hung on a pair of strong hinges, and is capable of a slight horizontal motion imparted by a horizontal connecting-rod, one end of which is eccentrically keyed on to the

of the pulp (so called because it can be made to give to the paper any desired water-marking). The "dandy-roll" (fig. 13) is a light skeleton cylinder covered with wire-cloth on which small *Water-* pieces of wire are soldered representing the watermark *marking* to be reproduced in the paper. From the last suction- *and* box the half-dried sheet of pulp passes between the *Couching.* "couch-rolls," so called from the corresponding operation of couching in hand-made paper, which, by pressing out most of the remaining moisture, impart sufficient consistency to the paper to enable it to leave the wire; both rolls are covered with a felt jacket, and the top one is provided with levers and weights to increase or diminish the pressure on the web. The paper is now fully formed, and is next carried by means of endless felts *Pressing* between two and sometimes three pairs of press-rolls *and Drying.* to extract the remaining moisture, and to obliterate as much as possible the impression of the wire-cloth from the under-side of the web. The web of paper is finally dried by passing it over a series of hollow steam-heated drying cylinders driven one from the other by gearing. The slower and more gradual the drying process the better, as the change on the fibres of the web due to the rapid contraction in drying is thereby not so excessive, and the heat required at one time is not so great nor so likely to damage the quality of the paper; the heating surface should therefore be as large as possible, and a great number of cylinders is required now that the machines are driven at high speeds. The cylinders are so placed that both surfaces of the web are alternately in contact with the heating surface. All the cylinders, except the first two or three with which the moist paper comes in contact and where the greatest evaporation occurs, are encased by continuous travelling felts. The drying cylinders are generally divided into two sets between which is placed a pair of highly polished chilled iron rolls heated by steam, called "nip-rolls," or "smoothers," the purpose of which is to flatten or smooth the surface of the paper while in a partially dry condition. Before being reeled up at the end of the machine the web of paper is passed through two *Surfacing.* or more sets of "calenders," according to the degree of surface or smoothness required. These calenders consist of a vertical stack of chilled iron rolls, generally five in number, revolving one upon another, and one or more of which are bored and heated by steam; pressure can be applied to the stack as required by means of levers and screws. The web of paper is now wound up in long reels at the end of the machine.

Paper-machines are now usually driven by two separate steam engines. The first, running at a constant speed, drives the strainers, pumps, shake motion, &c., while the second, working the paper-machine, varies in speed according to the rate at which it requires to be driven. The power consumed by the two engines will average from 40 to 100 h.p. The drying cylinders of the paper-machine form a convenient and economical condenser for the two steam-engines, and it is customary to exhaust the driving engine into the drying cylinders and utilize the latent heat in the steam for drying the paper, supplementing the supply when necessary with live steam. The speed of the machine has frequently to be altered while in motion. An alteration of a few feet per minute can be effected by changing the driving-speed of the steam-engine governor; for a greater change the machine must be stopped and other driving-wheels substituted. Arrangements are made in the driving-gear by which the various parts of the machine can be slightly altered in speed relatively to one another, to allow for the varying contraction or expansion of the paper web for different kinds and thicknesses of paper. The average speed of a paper-machine on fine writing-papers of medium weight is from 60 to 90 ft. per minute, but for printing-papers, newspapers, &c., the machine is driven from 130 up to as much as 300 and 400 ft. per minute. The width of machines varies greatly in different mills, from about 60 in. to as much as 150 in. wide. Mills running on higher classes of papers as a rule use narrow machines, as these make a closer and more even sheet of paper than wider ones. On fine writing-papers an average machine will make from 20 to 40 tons per week, while for common printing and newspapers the weekly output will amount to 50 to 70 tons.

All hand-made papers, and many of the best classes of machine-made papers, instead of being sized in the beater with a preparation *Tub-sizing.* of resin are what is called " tub-sized," that is, coated with a solution of gelatin. Such papers, when machine-made, are reeled off the machine straight from the drying cylinders in the rough state. The web is then led slowly through a tub or vat containing a heated solution of animal glue or gelatin mixed with a certain amount of alum; after passing through a pair of brass rolls to squeeze out the superfluous size, the web is reeled up again and allowed to remain for some time for the size to set. The paper is then led by means of continuous travelling tapes over a long series of open skeleton drums, about 4 ft. in diameter, inside

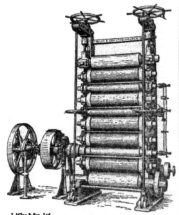

J. Milne & Son, Ltd.

Fig. 14.—Super-calender.

The bottom roll and the 3rd, 6th, 8th and 10th rolls, all reckoned from the bottom, are made of highly polished chilled cast-iron; the others of highly compressed paper.

which revolve fans for creating a circulation of hot air; rows of steam-pipes underneath the line of drums furnish the heat for drying. Slow and gradual drying is essential to this process to get the full benefit of the sizing properties of the gelatin. In hand-made papers, the sheets are passed by handfuls of three or five on an endless felt through the gelatin solution and between a pair of rolls, and then slowly dried on rope lines or " tribbles " in a steam-heated and well-ventilated loft.

The cheaper kinds of paper are glazed on the paper-machine in the calenders as before described. For the better class or very highly-glazed papers and those that are tub-sized, *Glazing or* subsequent glazing process is required; this is effected *Surfacing.* by sheet or plate-glazing and by super-calendering or web-glazing. The plate-glazing process is adopted mainly for the best grades of writing-papers, as it gives a smoother, higher and more permanent gloss than has yet been imitated by the roll-calender. In this method each sheet is placed by hand between two zinc or copper plates until a pile of sheets and plates has been formed sufficient to make a handful for passing through the glazing-rolls; this handful of about two quires or 48 sheets of paper, is then passed backwards and forwards between two chilled-iron rolls gearing together. A considerable pressure can be brought to bear upon the top roll by levers and weights, or by a pair of screws; the pressure on the rolls, and the number of times the handful is passed through, are varied according to the amount of gloss required on the paper. The super-calender (see fig. 14) is used to imitate the plate-glazed surface, partly as a matter of economy in cost, but principally for the high surfaces required on papers for books and periodicals to show up wood-cuts and photographic illustrations. It usually consists of a stack of chilled cast-iron rolls, alternating with rolls of compressed cotton or paper so that the web at each nip is between cotton and iron; it will be seen from the illustration that there are two cotton rolls together in the stack for the purpose of reversing the action on the paper and so making both sides alike; pressure is applied to the rolls at the top by compound levers and weights or screws. A very high surface can be quickly given to paper by friction with the assistance of heat; the process is known as " burnishing," and is used mostly for envelope papers and wrappings where one surface only of the web is required to be glazed. It is produced by the friction of a chilled-iron roll on one of cotton or paper, the ratio of the revolutions being as 4 to 5; steam is admitted to the burnishing iron roll.

At the end of the 19th century a large and increasing demand sprang up for papers embossed with a special pattern, such as linen-finish, &c.; these are used principally for fancy writing-papers, programmes, menu-cards, &c. This embossing is effected usually on the plate-glazing machine, in the case of linen and similar finishes by enclosing each sheet of paper between two pieces of linen or other suitable material to give the desired texture or pattern on the surface of the sheet. Each sheet of paper with its two pieces of cloth is placed between zinc plates and passed backwards and forwards between the rolls of the machine as in plate-glazing.

Except for special purposes, such for example as for use in a continuous printing-machine, paper is usually sent from the mill in the form of sheets. A number of reels of paper is *Cutting.* hung on spindles between two upright frames to feed the cutting-machine (see fig. 15); the various webs of paper are drawn forward together through two small rollers, and ripped into widths of the required size by means of a number of pairs of circular knives or " slitters "; they then pass between another pair of rollers, and over a long dead-knife fixed across the cutting-machine, on which they are cut into sheets by another transverse knife fastened to a revolving drum and acting with the dead-knife like a large pair of shears. The cut sheets then fall upon an endless travelling felt, from which they are stacked in piles by boys. It is often necessary, as in the case of water-marked papers, that the sheets should be cut with great exactness so that the designs shall appear

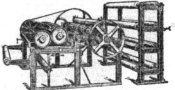

James Bertram & Son, Ltd.

Fig. 15.—Reel Paper Cutter.

in the centre of the sheet; the ordinary cutter cannot be relied upon for this purpose and in its place a machine called a " single-sheet cutter " is used. In this cutter only one web of paper is cut at a time; between the circular slitters and the transverse knives is placed a measuring-drum, which receives an oscillating motion and can be adjusted by suitable mechanism to draw the exact amount of paper forward for the length of sheet required.

All that now remains to be done before the paper is ready for the market is overhauling or sheeting. This operation consists in sorting out all speckled, spotted or damaged sheets, or sheets of different shades of colour, &c.; this entails considerable time and expense as each sheet has to be passed in review separately.

Sheeting. This sorting is usually performed by women. Papers are as a rule sorted into three different qualities, known in the trade respectively as "perfect," "retree" and "broke"; the best of the defective sheets form the second quality "retree," a term derived from the French word *retirer* (to draw out), and are sold at a reduced price; sheets that are torn or damaged or too badly marked to pass for the third quality "broke," are returned to the mill to be repulped as waste paper.

Sizes of Paper. Paper is sold in sheets of different sizes and is made up into reams containing from 480 to 516 sheets; these sizes correspond to different trade names, such for example as foolscap, post, demy, royal, &c.; the following are the ordinary sizes:—

Writing Papers.		Drawing and Book Papers.		Printing Papers.	
	Inches.		Inches.		Inches.
Pott	12½ × 15	Demy	15½ × 20	Demy	17½ × 22½
Foolscap	13¼ × 16½	Medium	17½ × 22½	Double demy	22½ × 35
Double foolscap	16½ × 26½	Royal	19 × 24	Quad demy	35 × 45
Foolscap and third	13¼ × 22	Super-royal	19¼ × 27	Double foolscap	17 × 27
Foolscap and half	13¼ × 24¾	Imperial	22 × 30	Royal	20 × 25
Pinched post	14½ × 18½	Elephant	23 × 28	Double royal	25 × 40
Small post	15¼ × 19	Double elephant	26½ × 40	Double crown	20 × 30
Large post	16½ × 21	Colombier	23½ × 34½	Quad crown	30 × 40
Double large post	21 × 33	Atlas	26 × 34	Imperial	22 × 30
Medium	18 × 23	Antiquarian	31 × 53		

Standards of Quality. With the enormously increased production of paper and the great reduction in price within recent years, it has been found that the "science" of paper-making has scarcely advanced with the same rapid strides as the art itself. Although a sheet of paper made to-day differs little as a fabric from the papers of earlier epochs, the introduction of new and cheaper forms of vegetable fibres and the auxiliary methods of treating them have caused a great change in the quality, strength and lasting power of the manufactured article. The undue introduction of excessive quantities of mechanical or ground wood-pulp in the period 1870–1880 into the cheaper qualities of printing-papers, particularly in Germany, first drew attention to this matter, since it was noticed that books printed on paper in which much of this material had been used soon began to discolour and turn brown where exposed to the air or light, and after a time the paper became brittle. This important question began to be scientifically investigated in Germany about the year 1885 by the Imperial Testing Institution in Berlin. A scheme of testing papers has been formulated and officially adopted by which the chemical and physical properties of different papers are compared and brought to numerical expression. The result of these investigations has been the fixing of certain standards of quality for papers intended for different purposes. These qualities are grouped and defined under such heads as the following:—

Strength, expressed in terms of the weight or strain which the paper will support.

Elasticity and texture, measured by elongation under strain and resistance to crumpling or rubbing.

Bulk, expressed in the precise terms of specific gravity or weight per unit of volume.

Of not less importance are the qualities which belong to paper as a chemical substance or mixture, which are: (1) its actual composition; (2) the liability to change under whatever conditions of storage and use it may be subjected to. For all papers to be used for any permanent purpose these physical and chemical qualities must ultimately rank as regulating the consumption and production of papers.

In England and Wales in 1907 there were 207 mills, using 409 machines and 99 vats for hand-made paper; in Scotland, 59 mills and 111 machines; in Ireland, 7 mills and 11 machines. A rough estimate of the amount of capital embarked in the industry may be formed on the basis that average mills would represent from £20,000 to £30,000 and upwards per machine.

The table at foot of page shows the amounts and values of the British imports and exports of paper and paper-making materials in 1907.

Article.	Imports.		Exports.	
	Weight.	Value.	Weight.	Value.
	Tons.	£	Tons.	£
Paper, unprinted	268,036	3,917,954	87,055 (Paper, unprinted; Paper, printed; Straw- and millboards)	2,342,420
Paper, printed	11,494	621,293		
Straw- and millboards	164,381	1,134,568		
	443,911	5,673,815		
Rags, linen and cotton	20,039	206,151	122,909 (including other paper making materials.)	752,739
Esparto and other vegetable fibres	202,523	738,834		
Wood-pulp—				
Chemical	282,098	2,396,856		
Mechanical	192,756	915,491		
	697,416	4,257,332		

AUTHORITIES.—Arnot, "Technology of the Paper-trade," Cantor Lectures, Society of Arts (London, 1877); Clapperton, *Practical Paper-Making* (London, 1894); Cross and Bevan, *Report on Indian Fibres and Fibrous Substances* (London, 1887); id., *Cellulose* (London, 1895–1905); id., *A Text-Book of Paper-Making* (London, 1888); Clayton Beadle, *Chapters on Paper-Making* (London); Davis, *The Manufacture of Paper* (Philadelphia, 1886); Dropisch, *Die Papier Machine* (Brunswick, 1878); id., *Papierfabrikation* (with atlas) (Weimar, 1881); Griffin and Little, *The Chemistry of Paper-making* (New York, 1894); Herzberg, *Papierprüfung* (Berlin, 1888; Eng. trans. by P. N. Evans, London); id., *Mikroskopische Untersuchung des Papiers* (Berlin, 1887); Hofmann, *Handbuch der Papier-fabrikation* (Berlin, 1897); Hoyer, *Fabrikation des Papiers* (Brunswick, 1886); Indian government, *Report on the Manufacture of Paper and Paper Pulp in Burmah* (London, 1906); Schubert, *Die Cellulose-fabrikation* (Berlin, 1897); id., *Die Praxis der Papierfabrikation* (Berlin, 1898); id., *Die Holzstoff-oder Holzschliff-fabrikation* (Berlin, 1898); Sindall, *Paper Technology* (London, 1904–1905); "Report of the Committee on the Deterioration of Paper," Society of Arts (London, 1898); Wyatt, "Paper-making," *Proc. Inst. C. E.*, lxxix. (London, 1885); id., "Sizing Paper with Rosin," *Proc. Inst. C.E.*, xci. (London, 1887); *Paper-Makers' Monthly Journal* (London, since 1872); *Paper-Trade Journal* (New York, since 1872); *Papier-Zeitung* (Berlin, since 1876). (J. W. W.)

India Paper.—This name is given to a very thin and light but tough and opaque kind of paper, sometimes used for printing books—especially Bibles—of which it is desirable to reduce the bulk and weight as far as possible without impairing their durability or diminishing their type. The name was originally given in England, about the middle of the 18th century, to a soft absorbent paper of a pale buff shade, imported from China, where it was made by hand on a paper-making frame generally similar to that used in Europe. The name probably originated in the prevailing tendency, down to the end of the 18th century, to describe as "Indian" anything which came from the Far East (cf. Indian ink). This so-called India paper was used for printing the earliest and finest impressions of engravings, hence known as "India proofs."

The name of India paper is now chiefly associated with European (especially British) machine-made, thin, opaque printing papers used in the highest class of book-printing. In 1841 an Oxford graduate brought home from the Far East a small quantity of extremely thin paper, which was manifestly more opaque and tough, for its weight, than any paper then made in Europe. He presented it to the Oxford University Press, and in 1842 Thomas Combe, printer to the University, used it for 24 copies of the smallest Bible then in existence—Diamond 24mo. These books were scarcely a third of the usual thickness, and were regarded with great interest; one was presented to Queen Victoria, and the rest to other persons. Combe tried

In vain to trace the source of this Bible. In 1874 a copy of this Bible fell into the hands of Henry Frowde, and experiments were instituted at the Oxford University paper-mills at Wolvercote with the object of producing similar paper. On the 24th of August 1875 an impression of the Bible, similar in all respects to that of 1842, was placed on sale by the Oxford University Press. The feat of compression was regarded as astounding, the demand was enormous, and in a very short time 250,000 copies of this "Oxford India paper Bible" had been sold. Many other editions of the Bible, besides other books, were printed on the Oxford India paper, and the marvels of compression accomplished by its use created great interest at the Paris Exhibition of 1900. Its strength was as remarkable as its lightness; volumes of 1500 pages were suspended for several months by a single leaf, as thin as tissue, and when they were examined at the close of the exhibition, it was found that the leaf had not started, the paper had not stretched, and the volume closed as well as ever. The paper, when subjected to severe rubbing, instead of breaking into holes like ordinary printing paper, assumed a texture resembling chamois leather, and a strip 3 in. wide was found able to support a weight of 28 ℔ without yielding.

The success of the Oxford India paper led to similar experiments by other manufacturers, and there were in 1910 nine mills (two each in England, Germany and Italy, one each in France, Holland and Belgium) in which India paper was being produced. India paper is mostly made upon a Fourdrinier machine in continuous lengths, in contradistinction to a hand-made paper, which cannot be made of a greater size than the frame employed in its production. The material used in its manufacture is chiefly rag, with entire freedom from mechanical wood pulp. The opacity of modern India paper, so remarkable in view of the thinness of the sheet, is mainly due to the admixture of a large proportion of mineral matter which is retained by the fibres. The extraordinary properties of this paper are due, not to the use of special ingredients, but to the peculiar care necessary in the treatment of the fibres, which are specially "beaten" in the beating engine, so as to give strength to the paper, and a capacity for retaining a large percentage of mineral matter. The advantage gained by the use of India paper is the diminution of the weight and bulk of a volume—usually to about one-third of those involved by the use of good ordinary printing paper—without any alteration in the size and legibility of its type and without any loss of opacity, which is an absolute necessity in all papers used for high-class book printing to prevent the type showing through. . (W. E. G. F.)

PAPHLAGONIA, an ancient district of Asia Minor, situated on the Euxine Sea between Bithynia and Pontus, separated from Galatia by a prolongation to the east of the Bithynian Olympus. According to Strabo, the river Parthenius formed the western limit of the region, which was bounded on the east by the Halys. Although the Paphlagonians play scarcely any part in history, they were one of the most ancient nations of Asia Minor (*Iliad*, ii. 851). They are mentioned by Herodotus among the races conquered by Croesus, and sent an important contingent to the army of Xerxes in 480 B.C. Xenophon speaks of them as being governed by a prince of their own, without any reference to the neighbouring satraps, a freedom due, perhaps, to the nature of the country, with its lofty mountain ranges and difficult passes. At a later period Paphlagonia passed under the Macedonian kings, and after the death of Alexander the Great it was assigned, together with Cappadocia and Mysia to Eumenes. It continued, however, to be governed by native princes until it was absorbed by the encroaching power of Pontus. The rulers of that dynasty became masters of the greater part of Paphlagonia as early as the reign of Mithradates III. (302–266 B.C.), but it was not till that of Pharnaces I. that Sinope fell into their hands (183 B.C.). From this time the whole province was incorporated with the kingdom of Pontus until the fall of the great Mithradates (65 B.C.). Pompey united the coast districts of Paphlagonia with the province of Bithynia, but left the interior of the country under the native princes, until the dynasty became extinct and the whole country was incorporated in the Roman empire. All these rulers appear to have borne the name of Pylaemenes, as a token that they claimed descent from the chieftain of that name who figures in the *Iliad* as leader of the Paphlagonians. Under the Roman Empire Paphlagonia, with the greater part of Pontus, was united into one province with Bithynia, as we find to have been the case in the time of the younger Pliny; but the name was still retained by geographers, though its boundaries are not distinctly defined by Ptolemy. It reappears as a separate province in the 5th century (Hierocles, *Synecd.* c. 33).

The ethnic relations of the Paphlagonians are very uncertain. It seems perhaps most probable that they belonged to the same race as the Cappadocians, who held the adjoining province of Pontus, and were undoubtedly a Semitic race. Their language, however, would appear from Strabo to have been distinct. Equally obscure is the relation between the Paphlagonians and the Eneti or Heneti (mentioned in connexion with them in the Homeric catalogue) who were supposed in antiquity to be the ancestors of the Veneti, who dwelt at the head of the Adriatic. But no trace is found in historical times of any tribe of that name in Asia Minor.

The greater part of Paphlagonia is a rugged mountainous country, but it contains fertile valleys, and produces great abundance of fruit. The mountains are clothed with dense forests, which are conspicuous for the quantity of boxwood which they furnish. Hence its coasts were from an early period occupied by Greek colonies, among which the flourishing city of Sinope, founded from Miletus about 630 B.C., stood pre-eminent. Amastris, a few miles east of the Parthenius, became important under the Macedonian monarchs; while Amisus, a colony of Sinope, situated a short distance east of the Halys, and therefore not strictly in Paphlagonia as defined by Strabo, rose to be almost a rival of its parent city. The most considerable towns of the interior were Gangra, in ancient times the capital of the Paphlagonian kings, afterwards called Germanicopolis, situated near the frontier of Galatia, and Pompeiopolis, in the valley of the Amnias (a tributary of the Halys), near which were extensive mines of the mineral called by Strabo *sandarake* (red arsenic), which was largely exported from Sinope.

See Hommaire de Hell, *Voyage en Turquie* (Paris, 1854–1860); W. J. Hamilton, *Researches* (London, 1842); W. M. Ramsay, *Hist. Geog. of Asia Minor* (London, 1890).

PAPHOS, an ancient city and sanctuary on the west coast of Cyprus. The sanctuary and older town (Palaepaphos) lie at Kouklia, about 10 m. west of Limasol, about a mile inland on the left bank of the Diorizo River (anc. Bocarus), the mouth of which formed its harbour. New Paphos (Papho or Baffo), which had already superseded Old Paphos in Roman times, lies 10 m. farther west, and 1 m. south of modern Ktima, at the other end of a fertile coast-plain. Paphos was believed to have been founded either by the Arcadian Agapenor, returning from the Trojan War (c. 1180 B.C.), or by his reputed contemporary Cinyras, whose clan retained royal privileges down to the Ptolemaic conquest of Cyprus in 295 B.C., and held the Paphian priesthood till the Roman occupation in 58 B.C. The town certainly dates back to the close of the Mycenaean Bronze age, and had a king Eteandros among the allies of Assur-bani-pal of Assyria in 668 B.C.[1] A later king of the same name is commemorated by two inscribed bracelets of gold now in the Metropolitan Museum of New York. In Hellenic times the kingdom of Paphos was only second to Salamis in extent and influence, and bordered on those of Soli and Curium.

Paphos owes its ancient fame to the cult of the "Paphian goddess" (ἡ Παφία Ἀφροσσα, or ἡ Παφία, in inscriptions, or simply ἡ θεά), a nature-worship of the same type as the cults of Phoenician Astarte, maintained by a college of orgiastic ministers, practising sensual excess and self-mutilation.[2] The Greeks identified both this and a similar cult at Ascalon with their own worship of Aphrodite,[3] and localized at Paphos the legend of her birth from the sea foam, which is in fact accumulated here, on certain winds, in masses more than a foot deep.[4] Her grave also was

[1] E. Schrader, *Abh. k. Preuss. Ak. Wiss.* (1879), pp. 31-36; *Sitzb. k. Preuss. Ak. Wiss.* (1890), pp. 337-344.
[2] Athan. c. *graecos*, 10. On all these cults see J. G. Frazer, *Adonis, Attis, Osiris* (London, 1906).
[3] Herod. i. 105; see further ASTARTE, APHRODITE.
[4] Oberhummer, *Die Insel Cypern* (Munich, 1903), pp. 108-110.

shown in this city. She was worshipped, under the form of a conical stone, in an open-air sanctuary of the usual Cypriote type (not unlike those of Mycenaean Greece), the general form of which is known from representations on late gems, and on Roman imperial coins;[1] its ground plan was discovered by excavations in 1888.[2] It suffered repeatedly from earthquakes, and was rebuilt more than once; in Roman times it consisted of an open court, irregularly quadrangular, with porticos and chambers on three sides, and a gateway through them on the east. The position of the sacred stone, and the interpretation of many details shown on the gems and coins, remain uncertain. South of the main court lie the remains of what may be either an earlier temple, or the traditional tomb of Cinyras, almost wholly destroyed except its west wall of gigantic stone slabs.

After the foundation of New Paphos and the extinction of the Cinyrad and Ptolemaic dynasties, the importance of the Old Town declined rapidly. Though restored by Augustus and renamed Sebastê, after the great earthquake of 15 B.C., and visited in state by Titus before his Jewish War in 70 B.C., it was ruinous and desolate by Jerome's time[3]; but the prestige of its priest-kings partly lingers in the exceptional privileges of the patriarch of the Cypriote Church (see CYPRUS, CHURCH OF).

New Paphos became the administrative capital of the whole island in Ptolemaic and Roman days, as well as the head of one of the four Roman districts; it was also a flourishing commercial city in the time of Strabo, and famous for its oil, and for "diamonds" of medicinal power. There was a festal procession thence annually to the ancient temple. In A.D. 960 it was attacked and destroyed by the Saracens. The site shows a Roman theatre, amphitheatre, temple and other ruins, with part of the city wall, and the moles of the Roman harbour, with a ruined Greek cathedral and other medieval buildings. Outside the walls lies another columnar building. Some rock tombs hard by may be of earlier than Roman date.

See W. H. Engel, *Kypros* (Berlin, 1841) (classical allusions); M. R. James and others, *Journ. Hellenic Studies*, ix. 147 sqq. (history and archaeology); G. F. Hill, *Brit. Mus. Cat. Coins of Cyprus* (London, 1904) (coins); art. "Aphrodite" in Roscher's *Lexicon der gr. u. röm. Mythologie*; also works cited in footnotes, and article CYPRUS.

(J. L. M.)

PAPIAS, of Hierapolis in Phrygia, one of the "Apostolic Fathers" (*q.v.*). His *Exposition of the Lord's Oracles*, the prime early authority as to the Gospels of Matthew and Mark (see GOSPELS), is known only through fragments in later writers, chiefly Eusebius of Caesarea (*H. E.* iii. 39). The latter had a bias against Papias on account of the influence which his work had in perpetuating, through Irenaeus and others, belief in a millennial reign of Christ upon earth. He calls him a man of small mental capacity, who took the figurative language of apostolic traditions for literal fact. This may have been so to some degree; but Papias (whose name itself denotes that he was of the native Phrygian stock, and who shared the enthusiastic religious temper characteristic of Phrygia, see MONTANISM) was nearer in spirit to the actual Christianity of the sub-apostolic age, especially in western Asia, than Eusebius realized. In Papias's circle the exceptional in connexion with Christianity seemed quite normal. Eusebius quotes from him the resurrection of a dead person[4] in the experience of "Philip the Apostle" —who had resided in Hierapolis, and from whose daughters Papias derived the story—and also the drinking of poison ("when put to the test by the unbelievers," says Philip of Sidê, by "Justus, surnamed Barsabbas") without ill effect.[5] Papias

[1] G. F. Hill, *Brit. Mus. Cat. Coins of Cyprus* (London, 1904), pls. xv.–xviii. (coins of Paphos), pl. xxvi. (other coins and gems).
[2] M. R. James, E. A. Gardner, and others, *Journ. Hellenic Studies*, ix. 134, 147 sqq.
[3] Dio Cass., liv. 23, 7; Strabo 683; Tac. *Hist.* 2, 2 sqq.; Jerome, *Vit. Hilarionis.* For the "Paphian Diamonds" (Pliny, *Nat. Hist.* xxxvii. 58); see E. Oberhummer, *loc. cit.*, p. 185. For the fame of Paphian oil see Hom. *Od.* viii. 362 sqq.; *Hymn Aphr.* 58 sqq.; Isidore, *Origines*, xvii. 7, 64.
[4] "The mother of Manaim" (cf. Acts xiii. 1), according to the citation in Philip of Sidê.
[5] Perhaps this is the basis of a clause in the secondary ending to Mark's Gospel (xvi. 18).

also believed a revolting story as to the supernatural swelling of the body of Judas Iscariot. But if he was credulous of marvels, he was careful to insist on good evidence for what he accepted as Christ's own teaching, in the face of current unauthorized views. Papias was also a pioneer in the habit, later so general, of taking the work of the Six Days (*Hexaemeron*) and the account of Paradise as referring mystically to Christ and His Church (so says Anastasius of Sinai).

About his date, which is important in connexion with his witness, there is some doubt. Setting aside the exploded tradition that he was martyred along with Polycarp (*c.* A.D. 155), we have the witness of Irenaeus that he was "a companion (*ἑταῖρος*) of Polycarp," who was born not later than A.D. ·69.· We may waive his other statement that Papias was "a hearer of John," owing to the possibility of a false inference in this case. But the fact that Irenaeus thought of him as Polycarp's contemporary and "a man of the old time" (*ἀρχαῖος ἀνήρ*), together with the affinity between the religious tendencies described in Papias's Preface (as quoted by Eusebius) and those reflected in the Epistles of Polycarp and Ignatius, all point to his having flourished in the first quarter of the 2nd century. Indeed, Eusebius, who deals with him along with Clement and Ignatius (rather than Polycarp) under the reign of Trajan, and before referring at all to Hadrian's reign (A.D. 117–138), suggests that he wrote[6] about A.D. 115. It has been usual, however, to assign to his work a date *c.* 130–140, or even later. No fact is known inconsistent with *c.* 60–135 as the period of Papias's life. Eusebius (iii. 36) calls him "bishop" of Hierapolis, but whether with good ground is uncertain.

Papias uses the term "the Elders," or Fathers of the Christian community, to describe the original witnesses to Christ's teaching, *i.e.* his personal disciples in particular. It was their traditions as to the purport of that teaching which he·was concerned to preserve. But to Irenaeus the term came to mean the primitive custodians of tradition derived from these, such as Papias and his contemporaries, whose traditions Papias committed to writing. Not a few such traditions Irenaeus has embodied in his work *Against Heresies*, so preserving in some cases the substance of Papias's *Exposition* (see Lightfoot, *Apostolic Fathers*, 1891, for these, as for all texts bearing on Papias).

See articles in the *Dict. of Christian Biog.*, *Dict. of Christ and the Gospels*, and Hauck's *Realencyklopädie*, xiv., in all of which further references will be found.

(J. V. B.)

PAPIER MÂCHÉ (French for mashed or pulped paper), a term embracing numerous manufactures in which paper pulp is employed, pressed and moulded into various forms other than uniform sheets. The art has long been practised in the East. Persian papier mâché has long been noted, and in Kashmir under the name of *kar-i-halamdani*, or pen-tray work, the manufacture of small painted boxes, trays and cases of papier mâché is a characteristic industry. In Japan articles are made by gluing together a number of sheets of paper, when in a damp condition, upon moulds. China also produces elegant papier mâché articles. About the middle of the 18th century papier mâché work came into prominence in Europe in the form of trays, boxes and other small domestic articles, japanned and ornamented in imitation of Oriental manufactures of the same class, or of lacquered wood; and contemporaneously papier mâché snuff-boxes ornamented in vernis Martin came into favour. In 1772 Henry Clay of Birmingham patented a method of preparing this material, which he used for coach-building, for door and other panels, and for many furniture and structural purposes. In 1845 the application of the material to internal architectural decoration was patented by C. F. Bielefeld of London, and for this purpose it has come into extensive use. Under the name of carton pierre a substance which is essentially papier mâché is also largely employed as a substitute

[6] See further *Dict. of Christ and the Gospels*, &c. The supposition that Philip of Sidê implies a date under Hadrian is a mistake. For the later date, see J. B. Lightfoot, *Essays on "Supernatural Religion"* (1889), pp. 142–216.

for plaster in the moulded ornaments of roofs and walls, and the ordinary roofing felts, too, are very closely allied in their composition to papier mâché. Under the name of ceramic papier mâché, architectural enrichments are also made of a composition derived from paper pulp, resin, glue, a drying oil and acetate of lead. Among the other articles for which the substance is used may be enumerated masks, dolls' heads and other toys, anatomical and botanical models, artists' lay figures, milliners' and clothiers' blocks, mirror and picture-frames, tubes, &c.

The materials for the commoner classes of work are old waste and scrap paper, repulped and mixed with a strong size of glue and paste. To this very often are added large quantities of ground chalk, clay and fine sand, so that the preparation is little more than a plaster held together by the fibrous pulp. Wood pulp (from Sweden) is now largely used for making papier mâché. For the finest class of work Clay's original method is retained. It consists of soaking several sheets of a specially made paper in a strong size of paste and glue, pasting these together, and pressing them in the mould of the article to be made. The moulded mass is dried in a stove, and, if necessary, further similar layers of paper are added, till the required thickness is attained. The dried object is hardened by dipping in oil, after which it is variously trimmed and prepared for japanning and ornamentation. For very delicate relief ornaments, a pulp of scrap paper is prepared, which after drying is ground to powder mixed with paste and a proportion of potash, all of which are thoroughly incorporated into a fine smooth stiff paste. The numerous processes by which surface decoration is applied to papier mâché differ in no way from the application of like ornamentation to other surfaces. Papier mâché for its weight is an exceedingly tough, strong, durable substance, possessed of some elasticity, little subject to warp or fracture, and unaffected by damp.

See L. E. Andés, *Die Fabrikation der Papiermaché- und Papierstoff-Waaren* (Vienna, 1900); A. Winzer, *Die Bereitung und Benützung der Papiermaché und ähnlicher Kompositionen* (4th ed., Weimar, 1907).

PAPIN, DENIS (1647–c. 1712), French physicist, one of the inventors of the steam-engine, was a native of Blois, where he was born on the 22nd of August 1647. In 1661 or 1662 he entered upon the study of medicine at the university of Angers, where he graduated in 1669. Some time prior to 1674 he removed to Paris and assisted Christiaan Huygens in his experiments with the air-pump, the results of which (*Expériences du Vuide*) were published at Paris in that year, and also in the form of five papers by Huygens and Papin jointly, in the *Philosophical Transactions* for 1675. Shortly after the publication of the *Expériences*, Papin, who had crossed to London, was hospitably received by Robert Boyle, whom he assisted in his laboratory and with his writings. About this time also he introduced into the air-pump the improvement of making it with double barrels, and replacing by the two valves the turncock hitherto used; he is said, moreover, to have been the first to use the plate and receiver. Subsequently he invented the condensing-pump, and in 1680 he was admitted, on Boyle's nomination, to the Royal Society. In the previous year he had exhibited to the society his famous "steam digester, or engine for softening bones," afterwards described in a tract published at Paris and entitled *La Manière d'amollir les os et de faire couire toutes sortes de viandes en fort peu de tems et à peu de frais, avec une description de la marmite, ses propriétés et ses usages*. This device consisted of a vessel provided with a tightly fitting lid, so that under pressure its contents could be raised to a high temperature; a safety valve was used, for the first time, to guard against an excessive rise in the pressure. After further experiments with the digester he accepted an invitation to Venice to take part in the work of the recently founded Academy of the Philosophical and Mathematical Sciences; here he remained until 1684, when he returned to London and received from the Royal Society an appointment as "temporary curator of experiments," with a small salary. In this capacity he carried on numerous and varied investigations. He discovered a siphon acting in the same manner as the "sipho wirtembergicus" (*Phil. Tr.*, 1685), and also constructed a model of an engine for raising water from a river by means of pumps worked by a water-wheel driven by the current. In November 1687 he was appointed to the chair of mathematics in the university of Marburg, and here he remained until 1696, when he removed to Cassel. From the

time of his settlement in Germany he carried on an active correspondence with Huygens and Leibnitz, which is still preserved, and in one of his letters to Leibnitz, in 1698, he mentions that he is engaged on a machine for raising water to a great height by the force of fire; in a later communication he speaks also of a little carriage he had constructed to be propelled by this force. Again in 1702 he wrote about a steam "ballista," which he anticipated would "promptly compel France to make an enduring peace." In 1705 Leibnitz sent Papin a sketch of Thomas Savery's engine for raising water, and this stimulated him to further exertions, which resulted two years afterwards in the publication of the *Ars nova ad aquam ignis adminiculo efficacissime elevandam* (Cassel, 1707), in which his high-pressure boiler and its applications are described (see STEAM ENGINE). In 1707 he resolved to quit Cassel for London, and on the 24th of September of that year he sailed with his family from Cassel in an ingeniously constructed boat, propelled by paddle-wheels, to be worked by the crew, with which he apparently expected to reach the mouth of the Weser. At Münden, however, the vessel was confiscated at the instance of the boatmen, who objected to the invasion of their exclusive privileges in the Weser navigation. Papin, on his arrival in London, found himself without resources and almost without friends; applications through Sir Hans Sloane to the Royal Society for grants of money were made in vain, and he died in total obscurity, probably about the beginning of 1712. His name is attached to the principal street of his native town, Blois, where also he is commemorated by a bronze statue.

The published writings of Papin, besides those already referred to, consist for the most part of a large number of papers, principally on hydraulics and pneumatics, contributed to the *Journal des savans*, the *Nouvelles de la république des lettres*, the *Philosophical Transactions*, and the *Acta eruditorum*; many of them were collected by himself into a *Fasciculus dissertationum* (Marburg, 1695), of which he published also a translation into French, *Recueil de diverses pièces touchant quelques nouvelles machines* (Cassel, 1695). His correspondence with Leibnitz and Huygens, along with a biography, was published by Dr Ernst Gerland (*Leibnizens und Huygens Briefwechsel mit Papin, nebst der Biographie Papins* (Berlin, 1881). See also L. de la Saussaye and E. Péan, *La Vie et les ouvrages de Denis Papin* (Paris, 1869); and Baron Ernoul, *Denis Papin, sa vie et ses ouvrages* (4th ed., 1888).

PAPINEAU, LOUIS JOSEPH (1786–1871), Canadian rebel and politician, son of Joseph Papineau, royal notary and member of the house of Assembly of Lower Canada, was born at Montreal on the 7th of October 1786. He was educated at the seminary of Quebec, where he developed the gift of declamatory and persuasive oratory. He was called to the bar of Lower Canada on the 19th of May 1810. On the 18th of June 1808 he was elected a member of the House of Assembly of the province of Lower Canada, for the county of Kent. In 1815 he became speaker of the house, being already recognized as the leader of the French Canadian party. At this time there were many grievances in the country which demanded redress; but each faction was more inclined to insist upon the exercise of its special rights than to fulfil its common responsibilities. In December 1820 Lord Dalhousie, governor of Lower Canada, appointed Papineau a member of the executive council; but Papineau, finding himself without real influence on the council, resigned in January 1823. In that year he went to England to protest on behalf of the French Canadians against the projected union of Upper and Lower Canada, a mission in which he was unsuccessful. Nevertheless his opposition to the government became more and more pronounced, till in 1827 Lord Dalhousie refused to confirm his appointment to the speakership, and resigned his governorship when the house persisted in its choice. The aim of the French Canadian opposition at this time was to obtain financial and also constitutional reforms. Matters came to a head when the legislative assembly of Lower Canada refused supplies and Papineau arranged for concerted action with William Lyon Mackenzie, the leader of the reform party in Upper Canada. In 1835 Lord Gosford, the new governor of Lower Canada, was instructed by the cabinet in London to inquire into the alleged grievances of the French Canadians. But the attitude of the opposition remained no less hostile than before, and in March 1837 the governor was authorized to reject the demand for constitutional reform and to apply public funds in his control to the purposes of government. In June a warning proclamation by the governor was answered by a series of violent speeches by Papineau, who in August was deprived of his commission in the militia.

Papineau had formerly professed a deep reverence for British institutions, and he had acquired a theoretical knowledge of the constitution, but he did not possess the qualities of a statesman, and consequently in his determination to apply the strict letter of the constitution he overlooked those elements and compensating forces and powers which through custom and usage had been incorporated in British institutions, and had given them permanence. In his earlier career he had voiced the aspirations of a section of the people at a time when it appeared to them that their national existence was threatened. In the course of time party strife became more bitter; real issues were lost sight of; and Papineau, falling in with the views of one O'Callaghan, who distrusted everything British, became an annexationist. Realizing that his cause was not advanced by persuasive eloquence, he adopted a threatening attitude which caused men of sober judgment to waver in their allegiance. These men he denounced as traitors; but a band of youthful enthusiasts encouraged their leader in his revolutionary course. The bishop of Montreal and of Quebec, and a large number of the citizens, protested, but nothing less than bloodshed would satisfy the misguided patriots. On the 23rd of October 1837 a meeting of delegates from the six counties of Lower Canada was held at St Charles, at which resistance to the government by force of arms was decided upon, and in which Papineau took part. In November preparations were made for a general stampede at Montreal, and on the 7th of the month Papineau's house was sacked and a fight took place between the "constitutionals" and the "sons of liberty." Towards the middle of November Colonel Gore was commanded to effect the arrest of Papineau and his principal adherents on a charge of high treason. A few hundred armed men had assembled at Saint Denis to resist the troops, and early on the morning of the 22nd of November hostilities commenced, which were maintained for several hours and resulted in many casualties. On the eve of the fray Papineau sought safety in flight, followed by the leading spirits of the movement. On the 1st of December 1837 a proclamation was issued, declaring Papineau a rebel, and placing a price upon his head. He had found shelter in the United States, where he remained in safety throughout the whole period of the fighting. The rebellion broke out afresh in the autumn of 1838, but it was soon repressed. Those taken in open rebellion were deported by Lord Durham to save them from the scaffold; and although 90 were condemned to death only 12 were executed.

Attempts have been made to transfer the responsibility for the act of violence to O'Callaghan and other prominent leaders in the revolt; but Papineau's own words, "The patriots of this city would have avenged the massacre but they were so poor and so badly organized that they were not fit to meet the regular troops," prove that he did not discountenance recourse to arms. Writing of the events of 1837 in the year 1848 he said: "The smallest success at Montreal or Toronto would have induced the American government, in spite of its president, to support the movement." It would thus seem that he was intriguing to bring about intervention by the United States with a view to annexation; and as the independence of the French Canadian race, which he professed to desire, could not have been achieved under the constitution of the American republic, it is inconsistent to regard his services to his fellow-countrymen as those of a true patriot. Papineau, in pursuing towards the end a policy of blind passion, overlooked real grievances, and prevented remedial action. After the rebellion relief was accorded because the obstacle was removed, and it is evident that a broad-minded statesman, or a skilful diplomat, would have accomplished more for French

Canada than the fiery eloquence and dubious methods of a leader who plunged his followers into the throes of war, and deserted them at the supreme moment. From 1839 till 1847 Papineau lived in Paris. In the latter year an amnesty was granted to those who had participated in the rebellion in Canada; and, although in June 1838 Lord Durham had issued a proclamation threatening Papineau with death if he returned to Canada, he was now admitted to the benefit of the amnesty. On his return to Canada, when the two provinces were now united, he became a member of the lower house and continued to take part in public life, demanding " the independence of Canada, for the Canadians need never expect justice from England, and to submit to her would be an eternal disgrace." He unsuccessfully agitated for the re-division of upper and lower Canada, and in 1854 retired into private life. He died at Montebello, in the province of Quebec, on the 24th of September 1871.

See L. O. David, *Les Deux Papineau*; Fenning Taylor, *Louis Joseph Papineau* (Montreal, 1865); Alfred De Celles, *Papineau-Cartier* (Toronto, 1906); H. J. Morgan, *Sketches of Celebrated Canadians* (Quebec, 1862); Rose's *Cyclopaedia of Canadian Biography*; *Annual Register*, 1836–1837; Sir Spencer Walpole, *History of England* (5 vols., London, 1878–1886), vol. iii. (A. G. D.)

PAPINIAN (AEMILIUS PAPINIANUS), Roman jurist, was *magister libellorum* and afterwards praetorian prefect under Septimius Severus. He was an intimate friend of the emperor, whom he accompanied to Britain, and before his death Severus specially commended his two sons to his charge. Papinian tried to keep peace between the brothers, but with no better result than to excite the hatred of Caracalla, to which he fell a victim in the general slaughter of Geta's friends which followed the fratricide of A.D. 212. The details are variously related, and have undergone legendary embellishment, but the murder of Papinian, which took place under Caracalla's own eyes, was one of the most disgraceful crimes of that tyrant. Little more is known about Papinian. He was perhaps a Syrian by birth, for he is said to have been a kinsman of Severus's second wife, Julia Domna; that he studied law with Severus under Scaevola is asserted in an interpolated passage in Spartian (*Caracal.* c. 8). Papinian's place and work as a jurist are discussed under ROMAN LAW.

PAPPENHEIM, GOTTFRIED HEINRICH, COUNT OF (1594–1632), imperial field marshal in the Thirty Years' War, was born on the 29th of May 1594 at the little town of Pappenheim on the Altmühl, now in Bavaria, the seat of a free lordship of the empire, from which the ancient family to which he belonged derived its name.[1] He was educated at Altdorf and at Tübingen, and subsequently travelled in southern and central Europe, mastering the various languages, and seeking knightly adventures. His stay in these countries led him eventually to adopt the Roman Catholic faith (1614), to which he devoted the rest of his life. At the outbreak of the great war he abandoned the legal and diplomatic career on which he had embarked, and in his zeal for the Catholic service in Poland and afterwards under the Catholic League. He soon became a lieutenant-colonel, and displayed brilliant courage at the battle of the White Hill near Prague (Nov. 8, 1620), where he was left for dead on the field. In the following year he fought against Mansfeld in western

[1] The family of Pappenheim is of great antiquity. In the 12th century they were known as the "marshals of Kalatin (Kalden)"; in the 13th they first appear as counts and marshals of Pappenheim, their right to the hereditary marshalship of the empire being confirmed to them by the emperor Louis IV. in 1334. After the Golden Bull of 1355 they held both marshalship and castle of Pappenheim as fiefs of the Saxon electorate. In the 17th century the family was represented by several lines: those of Pappenheim (which held the margraviate of Stühlingen till 1635), Treutlingen and Aletzheim, and the older branches (dating from the 13th and 14th centuries) of the marshals of Biberach and of Rechberg-Wertingen-Hohenreichen. Gottfried Heinrich, who belonged to the Treutlingen branch, was the only one of this ancient and widely-ramified family to attain great distinction, though many other members of it played a strenuous, if subordinate, part in the history of Germany. The family, mediatized under Bavaria in 1806, survives now only in the descendants of the Aletzheim branch.

Germany, and in 1623 became colonel of a regiment of cuirassiers, afterwards the famous "Pappenheimers." In the same year, as an ardent friend of Spain, the ally of his sovereign and the champion of his faith, he raised troops for the Italian war and served with the Spaniards in Lombardy and the Grisons. It was his long and heroic defence of the post of Riva on the Lake of Garda which first brought him conspicuously to the front. In 1626 Maximilian of Bavaria, the head of the League, recalled him to Germany and entrusted him with the suppression of a dangerous insurrection which had broken out in Upper Austria. Pappenheim swiftly carried out his task, encountering a most desperate resistance, but always successful; and in a few weeks he had crushed the rebellion with ruthless severity (actions of Efferdingen, Gmünden, Vöcklabruck and Wolfsegg, 15th–30th November 1626). After this he served with Tilly against King Christian IV. of Denmark, and besieged and took Wolfenbüttel. His hope of obtaining the sovereignty and possessions of the evicted prince was, after a long intrigue, definitely disappointed. In 1628 he was made a count of the empire. The siege and storm of Magdeburg followed, and Pappenheim, like Tilly, has been accused of the most savage cruelty in this transaction. But it is known that, disappointed of Wolfenbüttel, Pappenheim desired the profitable sovereignty of Magdeburg, and it can hardly be maintained that he deliberately destroyed a prospective source of wealth. At any rate, the sack of Magdeburg was not more discreditable than that of most other towns taken by storm in the 17th century. From the military point of view Pappenheim's conduct was excellent; his measures were skilful, and his personal valour, as always, conspicuous. So much could not be said of his tactics at the battle of Breitenfeld, the loss of which was not a little due to the impetuous cavalry general, who was never so happy as when leading a great charge of horse. The retreat of the imperialists from the lost field he covered, however, with care and skill, and subsequently he won great glory by his operations on the lower Rhine and the Weser in rear of the victorious army of Gustavus Adolphus. Much-needed reinforcements for the king of Sweden were thus detained in front of Pappenheim's small and newly-raised force in the north. His operations were far-ranging and his restless activity dominated the country from Stade to Cassel, and from Hildes-heim to Maastricht. Being now a field marshal in the imperial service, he was recalled to join Wallenstein, and assisted the generalissimo in Saxony against the Swedes; but was again despatched towards Cologne and the lower Rhine. In his absence a great battle became imminent, and Pappenheim was hurriedly recalled. He appeared with his horsemen in the midst of the battle of Lützen (Nov. 6th–16th, 1632). His furious attack was for the moment successful. As Rupert at Marston Moor sought Cromwell as his worthiest opponent, so now Pappenheim sought Gustavus. At about the same time as the king was killed, Pappenheim received a mortal wound in another part of the field. He died on the following day in the Pleissenburg at Leipzig.

See *Kriegsschriften von baierischen Officieren* I. II, V. (Munich, 1820); Hess, *Gottfried Heinrich Graf zu Pappenheim* (Leipzig, 1855); Ersch and Gruber, *Allgem. Encyklopädie*, III. 11 (Leipzig, 1838); Wittich, in *Allgem. deutsche Biographie*, Band 25 (Leipzig, 1887), and works there quoted.

PAPPUS OF ALEXANDRIA, Greek geometer, flourished about the end of the 3rd century A.D. In a period of general stagnation in mathematical studies, he stands out as a remarkable exception. How far he was above his contemporaries, how little appreciated or understood by them, is shown by the absence of references to him in other Greek writers, and by the fact that his work had no effect in arresting the decay of mathematical science. In this respect the fate of Pappus strikingly resembles that of Diophantus. In his *Collection*, Pappus gives no indication of the date of the authors whose treatises he makes use of, or of the time at which he himself wrote. If we had no other information than can be derived from his work, we should only know that he was later than Claudius Ptolemy whom he often quotes. Suidas states that he was of the same

age as Theon of Alexandria, who wrote commentaries on Ptolemy's great work, the *Syntaxis mathematica*, and flourished in the reign of Theodosius I. (A.D. 379–395). Suidas says also that Pappus wrote a commentary upon the same work of Ptolemy. But it would seem incredible that two contemporaries should have at the same time and in the same style composed commentaries upon one and the same work, and yet neither should have been mentioned by the other, whether as friend or opponent. It is more probable that Pappus's commentary was written long before Theon's, but was largely assimilated by the latter, and that Suidas, through failure to disconnect the two commentaries, assigned a like date to both. A different date is given by the marginal notes to a 10th-century MS., where it is stated, in connexion with the reign of Diocletian (A.D. 284–305), that Pappus wrote during that period; and in the absence of any other testimony it seems best to accept the date indicated by the scholiast.

The great work of Pappus, in eight books and entitled συναγωγή or *Collection*, we possess only in an incomplete form, the first book being lost, and the rest having suffered considerably. Suidas enumerates other works of Pappus as follows: Χωρογραφία οἰκουμενική, εἰς τὰ τέσσαρα βιβλία τῆς Πτολεμαίου μεγάλης συντάξεως ὑπόμνημα, ποταμοὺς τοὺς ἐν Λιβύῃ, ὀνειροκριτικά. The question of Pappus's commentary on Ptolemy's work is discussed by Hultsch, *Pappi collectio* (Berlin, 1878), vol. iii. p. xiii. seq. Pappus himself refers to another commentary of his own on the Ἀνάλημμα of Diodorus, of whom nothing is known. He also wrote commentaries on Euclid's *Elements* (of which fragments are preserved in Proclus and the Scholia, while that on the tenth Book has been found in an Arabic MS.), and on Ptolemy's Ἁρμονικά.

The characteristics of Pappus's *Collection* are that it contains an account, systematically arranged, of the most important results obtained by his predecessors, and, secondly, notes explanatory of, or extending, previous discoveries. These discoveries form, in fact, a text upon which Pappus enlarges discursively. Very valuable are the systematic introductions to the various books which set forth clearly in outline the contents and the general scope of the subjects to be treated. From these introductions we are able to judge of the style of Pappus's writing, which is excellent and even elegant the moment he is free from the shackles of mathematical formulae and expressions. At the same time, his characteristic exactness makes his collection a most admirable substitute for the texts of the many valuable treatises of earlier mathematicians which time has deprived us. We proceed to summarize briefly the contents of that portion of the *Collection* which has survived, mentioning separately certain propositions which seem to be among the most important.

We can only conjecture that the lost book i., as well as book ii., was concerned with arithmetic, book iii. being clearly introduced as beginning a new subject.

The whole of book ii. (the former part of which is lost, the existing fragment beginning in the middle of the 14th proposition) related to a system of multiplication due to Apollonius of Perga. On this subject see Nesselmann, *Algebra der Griechen* (Berlin, 1842), pp. 125–134; and M. Cantor, *Gesch. d. Math.* i.[3] 331.

Book iii. contains geometrical problems, plane and solid. It may be divided into five sections: (1) On the famous problem of finding two mean proportionals between two given lines, which arose from that of duplicating the cube, reduced by Hippocrates to the former. Pappus gives several solutions of this problem, including a method of making successive approximations to the solution, the significance of which he apparently failed to appreciate; he adds his own solution of the more general problem of finding geometrically the side of a cube whose content is in any given ratio to that of a given one. (2) On the arithmetic, geometric and harmonic means between two straight lines, and the problem of representing all three in one and the same geometrical figure. This serves as an introduction to a general theory of means, of which Pappus distinguishes ten kinds, and gives a table representing examples of each in whole numbers. (3) On a curious problem suggested by Eucl. i. 21. (4) On the inscribing of each of the five regular polyhedra in a sphere. (5) An addition by a later writer on another solution of the first problem of the book.

Of book iv. the title and preface have been lost, so that the programme has to be gathered from the book itself. At the beginning is the well-known generalization of Eucl. i. 47, then follow various theorems on the circle, leading up to the problem of the construction of a circle which shall circumscribe three given circles, touching each other two and two. This and several other propositions on contact, e.g. cases of circles touching one another and inscribed in the figure made of three semicircles and known as ἄρβηλος (shoemaker's knife) form the first division of the book. Pappus turns then to a consideration of certain properties of Archimedes's spiral, the conchoid of Nicomedes (already mentioned in book i. as supplying a method of doubling the cube), and the curve discovered most probably by Hippias of Elis about 420 B.C., and known by the name ἡ τετραγωνίζουσα, or quadratrix. Proposition 30 describes the construction of a curve of double curvature called by Pappus the helix on a sphere; it is described by a point moving uniformly along the arc of a great circle, which itself turns about its diameter uniformly, the point describing a quadrant and the great circle a complete revolution in the same time. The area of the surface included between this curve and its base is found—the first known instance of a quadrature of a curved surface. The rest of the book treats of the trisection of an angle, and the solution of more general problems of the same kind by means of the quadratrix and spiral. In one solution of the former problem is the first recorded use of the property of a conic (a hyperbola) with reference to the focus and directrix.

In book v., after an interesting preface concerning regular polygons, and containing remarks upon the hexagonal form of the cells of honeycombs, Pappus addresses himself to the comparison of the areas of different plane figures which have all the same perimeter (following Zenodorus's treatise on this subject), and of the volumes of different solid figures which have all the same superficial area, and, lastly, a comparison of the five regular solids of Plato. Incidentally Pappus describes the thirteen other polyhedra bounded by equilateral and equiangular but not similar polygons, discovered by Archimedes, and finds, by a method recalling that of Archimedes, the surface and volume of a sphere.

According to the preface, book vi. is intended to resolve difficulties occurring in the so-called μικρὸς ἀστρονομούμενος. It accordingly comments on the *Sphaerica* of Theodosius, the *Moving Sphere* of Autolycus, Theodosius's book on *Day and Night*, the treatise of Aristarchus *On the Size and Distances of the Sun and Moon*, and Euclid's *Optics* and *Phaenomena*.

The preface of book vii. explains the terms analysis and synthesis, and the distinction between theorem and problem. Pappus then enumerates works of Euclid, Apollonius, Aristaeus and Eratosthenes, thirty-three books in all, the substance of which he intends to give, with the lemmas necessary for their elucidation. With the mention of the *Porisms* of Euclid we have an account of the relation of porism to theorem and problem. In the same preface is included (a) the famous problem known by Pappus's name, often enunciated thus: *Having given a number of straight lines, to find the geometric locus of a point such that the lengths of the perpendiculars upon, or (more generally) the lines drawn from it obliquely at given inclinations to, the given lines satisfy the condition that the product of certain of them may bear a constant ratio to the product of the remaining ones*; (Pappus does not express it in this form but by means of composition of ratios, saying that if the ratio is *given* which is compounded of the ratios of pairs—one of one set and one of another—of the lines so drawn, and of the ratio of the odd one, if any, to a given straight line, the point will lie on a curve *given in position*); (b) the theorems which were rediscovered and named after Paul Guldin, but appear to have been discovered by Pappus himself. Book vii. contains also (1), under the head of the *de determinata sectione* of Apollonius, lemmas which, closely examined, are seen to be cases of the involution of six points; (2) important lemmas on the *Porisms* of Euclid (see PORISM); (3) a lemma upon the *Surface Loci* of Euclid which states that the locus of a point such that its distance from a given point bears a constant ratio to its distance from a given straight line is a conic, and is followed by proofs that the conic is a parabola, ellipse, or hyperbola according as the constant ratio is equal to, less than or greater than 1 (the first recorded proofs of the properties, which do not appear in Apollonius).

Lastly, book viii. treats principally of mechanics, the properties of the centre of gravity, and some mechanical powers. Interspersed are some questions of pure geometry. Proposition 14 shows how to draw an ellipse through five given points, and Prop. 15 gives a simple construction for the axes of an ellipse when a pair of conjugate diameters are given.

AUTHORITIES.—Of the whole work of Pappus the best edition is that of Hultsch, bearing the title *Pappi alexandrini collectionis quae supersunt e libris manuscriptis edidit latina interpretatione et commentariis instruxit Fridericus Hultsch* (Berlin, 1876–1878). Previously the entire collection had been published only in a Latin translation, *Pappi alexandrini mathematicae collectiones a Federico Commandino Urbinate in latinum conversae et commentariis illustratae* (Pesaro, 1588) [reprinted at Venice, 1589, and Pesaro, 1602). A second (inferior) edition of this work was published by Carolus Manolessius.

Of books which contain parts of Pappus's work, or treat incidentally of it, we may mention the following titles: (1) *Pappi alexandrini collectiones mathematicae nunc primum graece edidit Herm. Jos. Eisen-*mann, libri quinti pars altera (Parisiis, 1824). (2) *Pappi alexandrini secundi libri mathematicas collectionis fragmentum e codice MS. edidit latinum fecit notisque illustravit Johannes Wallis* (Oxonii, 1688). (3) *Apollonii pergaei de sectione rationis libri duo ex arabico MSo. latine versi, accedunt eiusdem de sectione spatii libri duo restituti, praemittitur Pappi alexandrini praefatio ad VIImum collectionis mathematicae, nunc primum graece edita: cum lemmatibus eiusdem Pappi ad hos Apollonii libros, opera et studio Edmundi Halley* (Oxonii. 1706). (4) *Der Sammlung des Pappus von Alexandrien siebentes und achtes Buch griechisch und deutsch*, published by C. I. Gerhardt, Halle, 1871. (5) The portions relating to Apollonius are reprinted in Heiberg's *Apollonius*, ii. 101 sqq. (T. L. H.)

PAPUANS (Malay *papuwah* or *puwak-puwak*, "frizzled," "woolly-haired," in reference to their characteristic hairdressing), the name given to the people of New Guinea and the other islands of Melanesia. The pure Papuan seems to be confined to the north-western part of New Guinea, and possibly the interior. But Papuans of mixed blood are found throughout the island (unless the Karons be of Negrito stock), and from Flores in the west to Fiji in the east. The ethnological affinities of the Papuans have not been satisfactorily settled. Physically they are negroid in type, and while tribes allied to the Papuans have been traced through Timor, Flores and the highlands of the Malay Peninsula to the Deccan of India, these "Oriental negroes," as they have been called, have many curious resemblances with some East African tribes. Besides the appearance of the hair, the raised cicatrices, the belief in omens and sorcery, the practices for testing the courage of youths, &c., they are equally rude, merry and boisterous, but amenable to discipline, and with decided artistic tastes and faculty. Several of the above practices are common to the Australians, who, though generally inferior, have many points of resemblance (osteological and other) with Papuans, to whom the extinct Tasmanians were still more closely allied. It may be that from an indigenous Negrito stock of the Indian archipelago both negroes and Papuans sprang, and that the latter are an original cross between the Negrito and the immigrating Caucasian who passed eastward to found the great Polynesian race.[1]

The typical Papuan is distinctly tall, far exceeding the average Malay height, and is seldom shorter, often taller, than the European. He is strongly built, somewhat "spur-heeled." He varies in colour from a sooty-brown to a black, little less intense than that of the darkest negro. He has a small dolichocephalous head, prominent nose somewhat curved and high but depressed at the tip, high narrow forehead with projecting brows, oval face and dark eyes. The jaw projects and the lips are full. His hair is black and frizzly, worn generally in a mop, often of large dimensions, but sometimes worked into plaits with grease or mud. On some islands the men collect their hair into small bunches, and carefully bind each bunch round with fine vegetable fibre from the roots up to within about two inches from the end. Dr Turner[2] gives a good description of this process. He once counted the bunches on a young man's head, and found nearly seven hundred. There is a usually little hair on the face, but chest, legs and fore-arms are generally hirsute, the hair short and crisp.

The constitution of society is everywhere simple. The

[1] Huxley believed that the Papuans were more closely allied to the negroes of Africa than any other race. Later scientists have endeavoured to identify the Papuans with the Negritos of the Philippines and the Semangs of the Malay Peninsula. Alfred Russel Wallace pronounced against this hypothesis in an appendix to his *Malay Archipelago* (1883 ed., p. 602), where he observes that "the black, woolly-haired races of the Philippines and the Malay Peninsula . . . have little affinity or resemblance to the Papuans." Dr A. B. Meyer, who spent several years in the Malay Archipelago and New Guinea, developed a contrary conclusion in his *Die Negritos der Philippinen* (1878), holding that the Negritos and Papuans are identical, and that possibly, or even probably, the former are an offshoot of the latter, like some other Polynesian islanders. A. C. Haddon, discussing, in *Nature* (September 1899), a later paper by Dr Meyer in English on the same subject (*The Distribution of the Negritos*, Dresden, 1899), practically adopted Meyer's views, after an independent examination of numerous skulls. As to how the Papuans, who are the aborigines of New Guinea, may have peopled other and much more distant islands, information is lacking.
[2] *Nineteen Years in Polynesia*, pp. 77, 78.

people live in village communities whose members appear to be more or less inter-related. There are no priests and no hereditary chiefs, though among the more advanced tribes rank is hereditary. Totemistic clans have been observed in Torres strait, and on the Finsch and west coasts. Chiefship is quite unrecognized, except on the Keriwina Islands. Possessions, such as gardens, houses, pigs, &c., belong to individuals and not to the community, and pass to the owner's heirs, who differ in relationship in different districts. The land within certain boundaries belongs to the tribe, but a member may take possession of any unappropriated portion. There are certain degrees of relationship within which a man may not marry. In some districts he may not marry into his own village, or into his mother's tribe; in others he may select a wife from certain tribes only. Payment, or a present, is always made for a wife to her father, brother or guardian (who is generally her maternal uncle). Presents are also often made to the bride. Polygamy is practised, but not frequently, and from the wife (or wives) there comes no opposition. The child belongs sometimes to the mother's, sometimes to the father's tribe. The Papuan woman, who is, as a rule, more modest than the Polynesian, is the household drudge, and does the greater part of the outdoor work, but the man assists in clearing new gardens and in digging and planting the soil.

In western New Guinea, according to the Dutch missionaries, there is a vague notion of a universal spirit, practically represented by several malevolent powers, as *Manoin*, the most *Spirit-worship.* powerful, who resides in the woods; *Narwoje*, in the clouds, above the trees, a sort of Erl-Konig who carries off children; *Faknik*, in the rocks by the sea, who raises storms. As a protection against these the people construct—having first with much ceremony chosen a tree for the purpose—certain rude images called karwars, each representing a recently dead progenitor, whose spirit is then invoked to occupy the image and protect them against their enemies and give success to their undertakings. The karwar is about a foot high, with head disproportionately large; the male figures are sometimes represented with a spear and shield, the female holding a snake. They observe omens, have magicians and rain-makers, and sometimes resort to ordeal to discover a crime. Temples (so called) are found in the north and west, built like the houses, but larger, the piles being carved into figures, and the roof-beams and other prominent points decorated with representations of crocodiles or lizards, coarse human figures, and other grotesque ornamentation; but their use is not clear. Neither temples nor images (except small figures worn as amulets) occur among the people of the south-east; but they have a great dread of departed spirits, especially those of the hostile inland tribes, and of a being called Vata, who causes disease and death.

All Papuans believe that within them resides an invisible other self, or spirit, which may occasionally leave the body in the hours of sleep and after death hovers for some period at least round the scenes of its embodied life. This ghost acquires supernatural powers, which at any time it may return to exercise inimically to relations or acquaintances who offend it. In the dark, and in the depths of forests or mountains, malevolent—never embodied—spirits love to be abroad. These are the spirits which, taking up their abode in a village, cause disease and death; and to escape from such attacks the inhabitants may fly the village for good, and, by dwelling scattered in the recesses of the forest for a time before choosing a new site, they hope to throw their enemy off their trail. Spirits of evil, but not of good, therefore require to be propitiated. The powers of nature—thunder, lightning and storm, all supposed to be caused by evil and angry spirits—are held in the greatest dread. Under the category of religious observances may perhaps come those held previously to the departure of the great trading or *lakatoi* fleet; their taboo-proclaiming customs, their ceremonial and sacred initiation ceremonies for boys and girls on reaching puberty, when masks are worn and the "bull-roarer" swung, as also the harvest festivals, at which great trophies of the produce of field and forest are erected, preparatory to a big feast enlivened with music and dancing. In the north and north-east of New Guinea ancestor-worship is widely practised. Amulets are worn to ensure success in buying, selling, hunting, fishing and in war, as well as for protection against evil. Circumcision is practised in some regions. Although some of the coast peoples are nominally Mahommedans, and some few converts to Christianity have been made, the vast majority of Papuans remain pagan.

The dead are disposed of in various ways. The spirit is supposed not to leave the body immediately, and a corpse is either buried for a time, and then disinterred and the bones cleaned and deposited in or near the deceased's dwelling or in some distant cave; or the body is exposed on a platform or dried over a fire, and the mummy kept for a few years. Sometimes the head, oftener the jaw-bone

and portions of the skeleton are preserved as relics. Little houses are frequently erected over the grave as a habitation for the spirit. Soon after death food is offered to the departed—with an infant a calabash of its mother's milk—and that he may have no wants, his earthly possessions, after being broken, are laid near his resting-place. A path through the jungle from the grave to the sea is often made so that the spirit may bathe. A widow must shave her head, smear her body with black and the exudations of the corpse, and wear mourning for a long time. The dead are referred to by some roundabout phrase, never by name, for this might have the dangerous result of bringing back the spirit. These dwell chiefly in the moon, and are particularly active at full moon. The houses which they haunt, and beneath or near which their bodies are buried, are deserted from time to time, especially by a newly-married couple or by women before child-birth.

Yams, taro and sweet potatoes constitute in some districts the main food of the people, while in others sago is the staple diet. Forest fruits and vegetables are also eaten. Maize *Food.* and rice—which are not indigenous—are eagerly sought after. The Papuan varies his vegetable diet with the flesh of the wild pig, wallabi and other small animals, which are hunted with dogs. Birds are snared or limed. Fish abound at many parts of the coast, and are taken by lines, or speared at night by torch-light, or netted, or a river is dammed and the fish stupefied with the root of a milletia. Turtle and dugong are caught. The kima, a great mussel weighing (without shell) 20 to 30 lb, and other shell-fish, are eaten, as are also dogs, flying foxes, lizards, beetles and all kinds of insects. Food is cooked in various ways. Cooking-pots, made at various parts of the coast, form one of the great exchanges for sago; but where such vessels do not reach, food is cooked by the women on the embers, done up in leaves, or in holes in the ground over heated stones. The sexes eat apart. In the interior salt is difficult to get, and sea-water, which is carried inland in hollow bamboos, is used in cooking in place of it. Salt, too, is obtained from the ashes of wood saturated by sea-water. In the Fly River region, kava, prepared from *Piper methysticum*, is drunk without any of the ceremonial importance associated with it in Polynesia. As a rule the Papuans have no intoxicating drink and do not know the art of fermenting palm-sap or cane-juice. Tobacco is indigenous in some parts, and is smoked everywhere, except on the north-east coast and on the islands, where its use is quite unknown. In some few districts a species of clay is eaten.

The male Papuan is usually naked save for a loin-cloth made of the bark of the Hibiscus, Broussonetia and other plants, or a girdle of leaves. In the more civilized parts cotton garments *Clothing* are used. Papuans have usually a great dislike to *and* rain and carry a mat of pandanus leaves as a protection *Ornaments.* against it. Except in one or two localities (on the north-east and west), the women are invariably decently clothed. The Papuan loves personal adornment and loses no chance of dressing himself up. His chief home-made ornaments are necklaces, armlets and ear-rings of shells, teeth or fibre, and cassowary, cockatoo, or bird of paradise feathers—the last two, or a flower, are worn through the septum of the nose. With his head encircled by a coronet of dogs' teeth, and covered with a network cap or piece of bark-cloth, the septum of the nose transfixed by a pencil of bone or shell, and perhaps a shell or fibre armlet or two, the Papuan is in complete everyday attire. On festal occasions he decks his well-forked-out and dyed hair with feathers and flowers, and sticks others in his ear-lobe holes and under his armlets; while a warrior will have *oula* shells and various bones of his victims dangling from ringlets of his hair, or fixed to his armbands or girdle. The Papuan comb is characteristic. This is a long piece of bamboo split at one end into prongs, while the other projects beyond the forehead sometimes two feet or more, and into it are stuck the bright feathers of parrots and other birds. The fairer tribes at the east end tattoo, no definite meaning apparently being attached to the pattern, for they welcome suggestions from Manchester. For the women it is simply a decoration. Men are not tattooed till they have killed some one. Raised cicatrices usually take the place of tattooing with the darker races. Rosenberg says the scars on the breast and arms register the number of sea-voyages made.

The Papuans build excellent canoes and other boats, and in some districts there are professional boat-builders of great skill, the best craft coming from East Cape and the Louisiades. These *Boat-building.* boats are either plain dug-outs, with or without out- *and* riggers, or regularly built by planks tightly laced and *building.* well caulked to an excavated keel. The most remarkable of their vessels is the "lakatoi," composed of several capacious dug-outs, each nearly 50 ft. long, which are strongly lashed together to a width of some 24 ft., decked and fitted with two masts, each carrying a huge mat sail picturesquely fashioned. On the deck high crates are built for the reception of some thousands of pieces of pottery for conveyance annually to the Fly River district to exchange for sago.

Papuans are very fond of music, using Pan-pipes, a Jew's harp of the Papuans' own fabrication, and the flute; on occasions *Music.* of ceremony the drum only is used—this instrument being always open at one end and tapped by the fingers. To the accompaniment of the drum, dancing—as a rhythmic but stationary movement of the feet or an evolutionary march—almost invariably goes, but rarely singing. All sorts of jingling sounds also are music to the ear, especially the clattering in time of strings of beans in their dry shells, and so these and other rattles are found attached to the drum, leg-bands and many of the utensils, implements and weapons.

Nearly all Papuan houses are built in Malay fashion on piles, and this not only on the coast but on the hillsides. In the north, the **Houses.** east and south-west of the island immense communal houses (*morong*) are met with. Some of these are between 500 and 700 ft. in length, with a rounded, boat-shaped roof thatched with palm-branches, and looking inside, when undivided, like dark tunnels. In some districts the natives live together in one of these giant structures, which are divided into compartments. Communal dwellings on a much smaller scale occur at Meroka, east of the Astrolabe mountains. As a rule elsewhere each family has its independent dwelling. On the north coast the houses are not built on piles; the walls, of bamboo or palm branches, are very low, and the projecting roof nearly reaches the ground; a barrier at the entrance keeps out pigs and dogs. A sort of table or bench stands outside, used by the men only, for meals and for the subsequent siesta. In east New Guinea sometimes the houses are two-storeyed, the lower part being used for stores. The ordinary house is 60 to 70 ft. long with a passage down the centre, and stands on a platform or veranda raised on piles, with the ridge-pole projecting considerably at the gables so that the roof may cover it at each end. Under this shade the inmates spend much of their time; here their meals, which are cooked on the ground beneath the house, are served. The furniture consists of earthen bowls, drinking-cups, wooden neck-rests, spoons, &c., artistically carved, mats, plaited baskets and boxes. The pottery is moulded and fire-baked. In a few districts villages are built at a short distance off the shore, as a protection against raids by the inland tribes. The interior villages are frequently situated on hill crests, or on top of steep-faced rocks as difficult of access as possible, whence a clear view all round can be had. Where such natural defences are wanting the village is protected by high palisades and by fighting platforms on trees commanding its approaches. The "dobbos," or tree-houses, built in high trees, are more or less peculiar to British New Guinea. On the north-east coast many of the villages are tastefully kept, their whole area being clean swept, nicely sanded, and planted with ornamental shrubs, and have in their centre little square palaver places laid with flat stones, each with an erect stone pillar as a back-rest. Excellent suspension bridges span some of the larger rivers, made of interlaced rattan ropes secured to trees on opposite banks, so very similar to those seen in Sumatra as to suggest some Malay influence.

Papuan weapons are the bow and arrow (in the Fly River region, the north and north-east coasts); a beheading knife of a sharp seg-**Weapons.** ment of bamboo; a shafted stone club—rayed, disk-shaped or ball-headed (in use all over the island); spears of various forms, pointed and barbed; the spear-thrower (on the Finsch coast); and hardwood clubs and shields, widely differing in pattern and ornamentation with the district of their manufacture. The Papuan bow is rather short, the arrows barbed and tipped with cassowary or human bone. The Papuans are mostly ignorant of iron, but work skilfully with axes of stone or tridacna shell and bone chisels, cutting down trees 20 in. in diameter. Two men working on a tree trunk, one making a cut with the adze lengthwise and the other chopping off the piece across, will soon hollow out a large canoe. Every man has a stone axe, each village generally owning a large one. Their knives are of bamboo hardened by fire. In digging they use the pointed stick. In British New Guinea alone is the man-catcher (a rattan loop at the end of a handle with a pith spike projecting into it) met with. In the D'Entrecasteaux Islands the sling is in use. For war the natives smear themselves in grotesque fashion with lime or ochres, and in some parts hold in their teeth against the chin a face-like mask, supposed to strike terror into the foe, against whom they advance warily (if not timidly), yelling and blowing their war-trumpets. The war canoe (which is a long, narrow dug-out outrigger, capable of holding twenty-eight men) is only a transport, for they never fight in it. The conch-shell is the trumpet of alarm and call to arms. The vendetta—resulting, when successful, in the bringing back the head of the slain as a trophy to be set up, as a house ornament—is widely practised. The eastern tribes salute by squeezing simultaneously the nose and stomach, and both there and on the north coast friendship is ratified by sacrificing a dog. In other places they wave green branches, and on the south coast, pour water over their heads, a custom noticed by Cook at Mallicolo (New Hebrides). A mother often pets they keep little pigs, which the women suckle.

The Papuan numerals extend usually to 5 only. In Astrolabe Bay the limit is 6; with the more degraded tribes it is 3, or, as in Torres straits, they have names only for 1 and 2; 3 is 2+1.

Language.—The Papuan languages or dialects are very numerous, owing, doubtless, to the perpetual intertribal hostility which has fostered isolation. In grammatical structure there is considerable resemblance between these dialects, but the verbal differences have become great. Several dialects are sometimes found on one island. The following are some broad characteristics of the Papuan

languages. Consonants are freely used; some of the consonantal sounds being difficult to represent by Roman characters. Many of the syllables are closed. There does not appear to be any difference between the definite and the indefinite article, except in Fiji. Nouns are divided into two classes, one of which takes a pronominal suffix, while the other never takes such a suffix. The principle of this division appears to be a near or remote connexion between the possessor and the thing possessed. Those things which belong to a person, as the parts of his body, &c., take the pronominal suffix; a thing possessed merely for use would not take it. Thus, in Fijian the word *luwe* means either a son or a daughter—one's own child, and it takes the possessive pronoun suffixed, as *luwena*; but the word *ngone*, a child, but not necessarily one's own child, takes the possessive pronoun before it, as *nona ngone*, his child, *i.e.* his to look after or bring up. Gender is only sexual. Many words are used indiscriminately, as nouns, adjectives or verbs, without change; but sometimes a noun is indicated by its termination. In most of the languages there are no changes in nouns to form the plural, but an added numeral indicates number. Case is shown by particles, which precede the nouns. Adjectives follow their substantives. Pronouns are numerous, and the personal pronoun includes four numbers—singular, dual, trinal and general plural, also inclusive and exclusive. Almost any word may be made into a verb by using with it a verbal particle. The difference in the verbal particles in the different languages is very great. In the verbs there are causative, intensive or frequentative, and reciprocal forms.

See R. H. Codrington, *The Melanesians* (1891), *Melanesian Languages* (1885); B. Hagen, *Unter den Papuas* (Wiesbaden, 1899); G. von der Gabelentz and A. B. Meyer, *Beiträge zur Kenniniss der melanesischen, &c., Sprachen* (Leipzig, 1882); A. B. Meyer and R. Parkinson, *Album von Papúa Typen* (Dresden, 1894); F. S. A. de Clercq, *Ethnographische Beschrijving van de West-en Noordkust van N. N. G.* (Leiden, 1893); A. C. Haddon, *Decorative Art of British New Guinea* (Dublin, 1894).

PAPYRUS, the paper reed, the *Cyperus Papyrus* of Linnaeus, in ancient times widely cultivated in the Delta of Egypt, where it was used for various purposes, and especially as a writing material. The plant is now extinct in Lower Egypt, but is found in the Upper Nile regions and in Abyssinia. Theophrastus (*Hist. plant.* iv. 10) states that it likewise grew in Syria; and, according to Pliny, it was also a native plant of the Niger and Euphrates. Its Greek title *πάπυρος*, Lat. *papyrus*, appears to be of Egyptian origin. By Herodotus it is always called *βίβλος*. The first accurate description of the plant is given by Theophrastus, from whom we learn that it grew in shallows of 2 cubits (about 3 ft.) or less, its main root being of the thickness of a man's wrist and 10 cubits in length. From this root, which lay horizontally, smaller roots pushed down into the mud, and the stem of the plant sprang up to the height of 4 cubits, being triangular and tapering in form. The tufted head or umbel is likened by Pliny to a thyrsus.

The various uses to which the papyrus plant was applied are also enumerated by Theophrastus. Of the head nothing could be made but garlands for the shrines of the gods; but the wood of the root was employed in the manufacture of different utensils as well as for fuel. Of the stem of the plant were made boats, sails, mats, cloth, cords, and, above all, writing materials. Its pith was also a common article of food, and was eaten both cooked and in its natural state. Herodotus, too, notices its consumption as food (ii. 92), and incidentally mentions that it provided the material of which the priests' sandals were made (ii. 37). He likewise refers to the use of byblus as tow for caulking the seams of ships; and the statement of Theophrastus that King Antigonus made the rigging of his fleet of the same material is illustrated by the ship's cable, *ὅπλον βίβλινον*, wherewith the doors were fastened when Ulysses slew the suitors in his hall (*Odyss.* xxi. 390). That the plant was itself used also as the principal material in the construction of light skiffs suitable for the navigation of the pools and shallows of the Nile, and even of the river itself, is shown by sculptures of the fourth dynasty, in which men are represented building a boat with stems cut from a neighbouring plantation of papyrus (Lepsius, *Denkm.* ii. 12). It is to boats of this description that Isaiah probably refers in the "vessels of bulrushes upon the waters" (xviii. 2). If the Hebrew *gômer* (גמא) also is to be identified with the Egyptian papyrus, something may be said in favour of the tradition that the bulrushes of which the ark was composed in which the infant Moses was laid were in fact papyrus. But it seems hardly credible that the *Cyperus papyrus* could have sufficed for the many uses to which it is said to have been applied and we may conclude that several plants of the genus *Cyperus* were comprehended under the head of byblus or papyrus—an opinion which is supported by the words of Strabo, who mentions both inferior and superior qualities. The *Cyperus dives* is still

grown in Egypt, and is used to this day for many of the purposes named by ancient writers.

The widespread use throughout the ancient world of the writing material manufactured from the papyrus plant is attested by early writers, and by documents and sculptures. Papyrus rolls are represented in ancient Egyptian wall-paintings; and extant examples of the rolls themselves are sufficiently numerous. The most ancient Egyptian papyrus now known contains accounts of the reign of King Assa (3580-3536 B.C.). The earliest literary papyrus is that known, from the name of its former owner, as the Prisse papyrus, and now preserved at Paris, containing a work composed in the reign of a king of the fifth dynasty, and computed to be itself of the age of upwards of 2500 years B.C. The papyri discovered in Egypt have often been found in tombs, and in the hands, or swathed with the bodies, of mummies. The ritual of the dead is most frequently the subject. Besides the ritual and religious rolls, there are the hieratic, civil and literary documents, and the demotic and enchorial papyri, relating generally to sales of property. Coptic papyri mainly contain Biblical or religious texts or monastic deeds. Papyrus was also known to the Assyrians, who called it " the reed of Egypt."

The early use of Papyrus among the Greeks is proved by the reference of Herodotus (v. 58) to its introduction among the Ionian Greeks, who gave it the name of διφθέραι, " skins," the material to which they had already been accustomed. In Athens it was doubtless in use for literary as well as for other purposes as early as the 5th century B.C. An inscription relating to the rebuilding of the Erechtheum in 407 B.C. records the purchase of two papyrus rolls, to be used for the fair copy of the rough accounts. The very large number of classical and other Greek papyri, of the Ptolemaic and later periods, which have been recovered in Egypt, are noticed in the article on PALAEOGRAPHY. The rolls found in the ruins of Herculaneum contain generally the less interesting works of writers of the Epicurean school.

Papyrus also made its way into Italy, but at how early a period there is nothing to show. It may be presumed, however, that from the very first it was employed as the vehicle for Roman literature. Under the Empire its use must have been extensive, for not only was it required for the production of books, but it was universally employed for domestic purposes, correspondence and legal documents. So indispensable did it

become that it is reported that in the reign of Tiberius, owing to the scarcity and dearness of the material caused by a failure of the papyrus crop, there was a danger of the ordinary business of life being deranged (Pliny, *N.H.* xiii. 13).

The account which Pliny (*N.H.* xiii. 11-13) has transmitted to us of the manufacture of the writing material from the papyrus plant should be taken strictly to refer to the process followed in his own time; but, with some differences in details, the same general method of treatment had doubtlessly been practised from time immemorial. His text, however, is so confused, both from obscurity of style and from corruptions in the MSS., that there is much difference of opinion as to the meaning of many words and phrases employed in his narrative, and their application in particular points of detail. In one important particular, however, affecting the primary construction of the material, there can no longer be any doubt. The old idea that it was made from layers or pellicules growing between the rind and a central stalk has been abandoned, as it has been proved that the plant, like other reeds, contains only a cellular pith within the rind. The stem was in fact cut into longitudinal strips for the purpose of being converted into the writing material, those from the centre of the plant being the broadest and most valuable. The strips (*inae, philyrae*), which were cut with a sharp knife or some such instrument, were laid on a board side by side to the required width, thus forming a layer (*scheda*), across which another layer of shorter strips was laid at right angles. The two layers thus " woven."—Pliny uses the word *texere* in describing this part of the process—formed a sheet (*plagula* or *net*), which was then soaked in water of the Nile. The mention of a particular water has caused trouble to the commentators. Some have supposed that certain chemical properties of which the Nile water was possessed acted as a glue or cement to cause the two layers to adhere; others, with more reason, that glutinous matter contained in the material itself was solved by the action of water, whether from the Nile or any other source; and others again read in Pliny's words an implication that a paste was actually used. The sheet was finally hammered and dried in the sun. Any roughness was levelled by polishing with ivory or a smooth shell. But the material was also subject to other defects, such as moisture lurking between the layers, which might be detected by strokes of the mallet; spots or stains; and spongy strips (*taeniae*), in which the ink would run and spoil the sheet. When such faults occurred, the papyrus must be re-made. To form a roll the several sheets *κολλήσεις* were joined together with paste (glue being too hard), but not more than twenty sheets in a roll (*scapus*). As, however, there are still extant rolls consisting of more than the prescribed number of sheets, either the reading of *vicenae* is corrupt, or the number was not constant in all times. The *scapus* seems to have been a standard length of papyrus, as sold by the stationers. The best sheet formed the first or outside sheet of the roll, and the others were joined on in order of quality, so that the worst sheets were in the centre of the roll. This arrangement was adopted, not for the purpose of fraudulently selling bad material under cover of the better exterior, but in order that the outside of the roll should be composed of that which would best stand wear and tear. Besides, in case of the entire roll not being filled with the text, the unused and inferior sheets at the end could be better spared, and so might be cut off.

The different kinds of papyrus writing material and their dimensions are also enumerated by Pliny. The best quality, formed from the middle and broadest strips of the plant, was originally named *hieratica*, but afterwards, in flattery of the emperor Augustus, it was called, after him, *Augusta*; and the *charta Livia*, or second quality, was so named in honour of his wife. The *hieratica* thus descended to the third rank. The first two were 13 digiti, or about 9½ in. in width; the *hieratica*, 11 digiti or 8 in. Next came the *charta amphitheatrica*, named after the principal place of its manufacture, the amphitheatre of Alexandria, of 9 digiti or 6½ in. wide. The *charta Fanniana* appears to have been a kind of papyrus worked up from the *amphitheatrica*, which by flattening and other methods was increased in width by an inch, in the factory of a certain Fannius at Rome. The *Saitica*, which took its name from the city of Sais, and was probably of 8 digiti or 5½ in., was of a common description. The *Taeniotica*, named apparently from the place of its manufacture, a tongue of land (*ταινία*) near Alexandria, was sold by weight, and was of uncertain width, perhaps from 4½ to 5 in. And lastly there was the common packing-paper, the *charta emporetica*, of 6 digiti or 4½ in. Isidore (*Etymol.* vi. 10) mentions yet another kind, the *Corneliana*, first made under C. Cornelius Gallus, prefect of Egypt, which, however, may have been the same as the *amphitheatrica* or *Fanniana*. The name of the man who had incurred the anger of Augustus may have been suppressed by the same influence that expunged the episode of Gallus from the Fourth Georgic (Birt, *Antik. Buchwesen*, p. 250). In the reign of the emperor Claudius also another kind was introduced and entitled *Claudia*. It had been found by experience that the *charta Augusta* was, from its fineness and porous nature, ill suited for literary use; it was accordingly reserved for correspondence only, and for other purposes was replaced by the new paper.

The *charta Claudia* was made from a composition of the first and second qualities, the *Augusta* and the *Livia*, a layer of the former being backed with one of the latter; and the sheet was increased to nearly a foot in width. The largest of all, however, was the *macrocollon*, probably of good quality and equal to the hieratic, and a cubit or nearly 18 in. wide. It was used by Cicero (*Ep. ad Attic.* xiii. 25, xvi. 3). The width, however, proved inconvenient, and the broad sheet was liable to injury by tearing.

An examination of extant papyri has had the result of proving that sheets of large size, measuring about 12 in., were sometimes used. A large class of examples run to 10 in., others to 8 in., while the smaller sizes range from 4 to 6 in.

An interesting question arises as to the accuracy of the different measurements given by Pliny. His figures regarding the width of the different kinds of papyri have generally been understood to concern the width (or height) of the rolls, as distinguished from their length. It has, however, been observed that in practice the width of extant rolls does not tally in any satisfactory degree with Pliny's measurements; and a more plausible explanation has been offered (Birt, *Antik. Buchwesen*, pp. 251 seq.) that the breadth (not height) of the individual sheets of which the rolls are composed is referred to.

The first sheet of a roll was named πρωτόκολλον; the last, ἐσχατόκολλιον. Under the Romans, the former bore the name of the *comes largitionum*, who had control of the manufacture, with the date and name of place. It was the practice to cut away the portion thus marked; but in case of legal documents this mutilation was forbidden by the laws of Justinian. On the Arab conquest of Egypt in the 7th century, the manufacture was continued, and the protocols were marked at first, as it appears, with inscriptions in both Greek and Arabic, and later in the latter language alone. There are several examples extant, some being in the British Museum, ranging between the years 670 and 715 (see facsimiles in C. H. Becker, *Papyri Schott-Reinhardt*, i. (Heidelberg, 1906); and cf. "Arabische Papyri des Aphroditofundes," in *Zeitsch. für Assyriologie*, xx. (1906), 68–104. The Arab inscriptions are accompanied by curious scrawls on each side, which may be imitated from words used in the Latin inscriptions of the Roman period.

Papyrus was cultivated and manufactured for writing material by the Arabs in Egypt down to the time when the growing industry of paper in the 8th and 9th centuries rendered it no longer a necessity (see PAPER). It seems to have entirely given place to paper in the 10th century. Varro's statement, repeated by Pliny, that papyrus was first made in Alexander's time, should probably be taken to mean that its manufacture, which till then had been a government monopoly, was relieved from all restrictions. It is not probable, however, that it was ever manufactured from the native plant anywhere but in Egypt. At Rome there was certainly some kind of industry in papyrus, the *charta Fanniana*, already referred to, being an instance in illustration. But it seems probable that this industry was confined to the re-making of material imported into Italy, as in the case of the *charta Claudia*. This second manufacture, however, is thought to have been detrimental to the papyrus, as it would then have been in a dried condition requiring artificial aids, such as a more liberal use of gum or paste, in the process. The more brittle condition of the Latin papyri found at Herculaneum has been instanced as the evil result of this re-making of the material.

As to cultivation of the plant in Europe, according to Strabo the Romans obtained the papyrus plant from Lake Trasimene and other lakes of Etruria, but this statement is unsupported by any other ancient authority. At a later period, however, a papyrus was cultivated in Sicily, which has been identified by Parlatore with the Syrian variety (*Cyperus syriacus*), far exceeding in height the Egyptian plant, and having a more drooping head. It grew in the east and south of the island, where it was introduced during the Arab occupation. It was seen in the 10th century, by the Arab traveller Ibn-Haukal, in the neighbourhood of Palermo, where it throve luxuriantly in the pools of the Papireto, a stream to which it lent its name. From it paper was made for the sultan's use. But in the 13th century it began to fail, and in 1591 the drying up of the Papireto caused the extinction of the plant in that district. It is still to be seen at Syracuse, but it was probably transplanted thither at a later time, and reared only as a curiosity, as there is no notice of it to be found previous to 1674. It is with this Syracusan plant that some attempts have been made in modern times to manufacture a writing material similar to ancient papyrus.

Even after the introduction of vellum as the ordinary vehicle for literature papyrus still continued to some extent in use outside Egypt, and was not entirely superseded until a late date. It ceased, however, to be used for books sooner than for documents. In the 5th century St Augustine apologizes for sending a letter written on vellum instead of the more usual substance, papyrus (*Ep.* xv.); and Cassiodorus (*Varr.* xi. 38); writing in the 6th century, indulges in a high-flown panegyric on the plant and its value. Of medieval literary Greek papyri very few relics have survived, but of documents coming down to the 8th and 9th centuries an increasing number is being brought to light among the discoveries in Egypt.

Medieval Latin MSS. on papyrus in book form are still extant in different libraries of Europe, viz.: the Homilies of St Avitus, of the 6th century, at Paris; Sermons and Epistles of St Augustine, of the 6th or 7th century, at Paris and Geneva; works of Hilary, of the 6th century, at Vienna; fragments of the Digests, of the 6th century, at Pommersfeld; the Antiquities of Josephus, of the 7th century, at Milan; Isidore, *De contemptu mundi*, of the 7th century, at St Gall; and the Register of the Church of Ravenna, of the 10th century, at Munich. The employment of this material in Italy for legal purposes is sufficiently illustrated by the large number of documents in Latin which were preserved at Ravenna, and date from the 5th to the 10th century. In the papal chancery it was used at an early date, evidence of its presence there being found in the biography of Gregory I. But of the extant papal deeds the earliest to which an authentic date can be attached is a bull of Adrian I. of the year 788, while the latest appears to be one of 1022. There is evidence to show that in the 10th century papyrus was used, to the exclusion of other materials, in papal deeds. In France it was a common writing substance in the 6th century (Gregory of Tours, *Hist. Franc.* v. 5). Of the Merovingian period there are still extant several papyrus deeds, the earliest of the year 625, the latest of 692. Under Charlemagne and his successors it was not used. By the 12th century the manufacture of papyrus had entirely ceased, as appears from a note by Eustathius in his commentary on the *Odyssey*, xxi. 390.

AUTHORITIES.—Melch. Guilandino's commentary on the chapters of Pliny relating to papyrus, *Papyrus, hoc est commentarius, &c.* (Venice, 1572); Montfaucon, "Dissertation sur la plante appellée Papyrus," in the *Mémoires de l'académie des inscriptions* (1729), pp. 592–608; T. C. Tychsen, "De chartae papyraceae in Europa per medium aevum usu," in the *Comment. Soc. Reg. Scient. Gottingensis* (1820), pp. 141–208; Dureau de la Malle, "Mémoire sur le papyrus," in the *Mém. de l'Institut* (1851), pp. 140–183; P. Parlatore, "Mémoire sur le papyrus des anciens," in the *Mém. à l'Acad. des sciences* (1854), pp. 469–502; Blümner, *Technologie und Terminologie der Gewerbe und Künste bei Griechen und Römern*, i. 308–327 (Leipzig, 1875); C. Paoli, *Del Papiro* (Florence, 1878); G. Cosentino, "La Carta di papiro," in *Archivio storico siciliano* (1889), pp. 134–164. See also W. Wattenbach, *Das Schriftwesen im Mittelalter* (Leipzig, 1896); T. Birt, *Das antike Buchwesen* (Berlin, 1882); F. G. Kenyon, *The Palaeography of Greek Papyri* (Oxford, 1899); and W. Schubart, *Das Buch bei den Griechen und Römern* (Berlin, 1907). (E. M. T.)

PAR (Lat. *par*, equal), technically a commercial and banking term. When stocks, shares, &c., are purchasable at the price originally paid for them or at their nominal or face value they are said to be *at par*. When the purchase price is higher than the face value, they are *above par*, or *at a premium*; when below face value, they are *below par*, or *at a discount. Par of exchange* is the amount of money in the currency of one country which is equivalent to the same amount in the terms of another, both currencies being of the same metal and of a fixed standard of weight and purity. (See EXCHANGE.)

PARÁ, or GRÃO PARÁ, a northern state of Brazil, bounded N. by the three Guianas and the Atlantic, E. by the Atlantic and the states of Maranhão and Goyaz,[1] S. by Goyaz and Matto Grosso and W. by Amazonas. It is the third largest state of the republic, having an area of 443,922 sq. m.; pop. (1890), 328,455, (1900), 445,356. The Amazon valley has its outlet to the ocean through the central part of the state, the outlet, or neck, being comparatively narrow and the territory on both sides rising to the level of the ancient plateau that covered this part of the continent. In the north is the Guiana plateau, sometimes called Brazilian Guiana, which is "blanketed" and made semiarid by the mountain ranges on the Brazil-Guiana frontier. In the south the country rises in forested terraces and is broken by escarpments caused by the erosion of the northern slope of the great central plateau of Brazil. With the exception of the

Guiana highlands, and some grassy plains on the island of Marajó and in some other places, the state is densely forested, and its lowest levels are covered with a network of rivers, lakes and connecting channels.

The rivers of the state may be grouped under three general systems: the Amazon and its tributaries, the Tocantins and its tributaries and the rivers flowing direct to the Atlantic. The Amazon crosses the state in a general E.N.E. direction for about 500 m. Its channels, tributaries, *furos* (arms), *igarapés* (creeks, or literally, " canoe paths "), by-channels and reservoir lakes form an extremely complicated hydrographic system. From the north seven large tributaries are received—the Jamundá (which forms the boundary line with Amazonas), Trombetas, Maecurú, Jauary, Parú, Jary and Anauera-pucú. The first is, strictly speaking, a tributary of the Trombetas, though several *furos* connect with the Amazon before its main channel opens into the Trombetas. All these rivers have their sources on the Guiana highlands within the limits of the state, and flow southward to the Amazon over numerous rapids and falls, with comparatively short navigable channels before entering the great river. From the south two great tributaries are received—the Tapajos and Xingú—both having · their sources outside the state (see AMAZON). The Pará estuary, usually called the Pará river, belongs to the Tocantins, although popularly described as a mouth of the Amazon. The Amazon water passes through it except in times of flood. It is connected with the Amazon by navigable tidal *furos*, in which the current is hardly perceptible. The estuary is about 200 m. long and 5 to 30 m. wide, and receives the waters of a large number of streams, the largest of which is the Guamá and its chief tributary, the Capim. A number of small rivers discharge into the Atlantic north and south of the Amazon, the largest of which are the Gurupy, which forms the boundary line with Maranhão, the Araguary, which drains a large area of the eastern slope of the Guiana highlands, and the Oyapok, which forms the boundary line with French Guiana.

Lying across the mouth of the Amazon and dividing it into three channels are the islands of Caviana and Mexiana, the first 47 m. and the second 27 m. in length, north-west to south-east, both traversed by the equator, and both devoted to cattle-raising. Somewhat different in character is the island of Marajó, or Joannes, which lies between the Amazon and Pará estuary. It is 163 m. long by 99 m. wide, and its area is about 15,000 sq. m. This island is only partly alluvial in character, a considerable area on its eastern and southern sides having the same geological formation as the neighbouring mainland.· The larger part, the north-western, belongs to the flood-plains of the Amazon, being covered with swamps, forests and open meadows, and subject to annual inundations. There are several towns and villages on the island, and stock-raising, now in a state of decadence, has long been its principal industry. Of interest to archaeologists is the largest of its several lakes, called Arary, in the centre of which is a small island celebrated for its Indian antiquities, chiefly pottery. On the Atlantic coast the principal island is Maracá (lat. 2° N.), 26 m. long by 20 m. wide, which lies, in part, off the entrance to the Amapa river.

Pará is crossed by the equator, and its climate is wholly tropical, but there is a wide variation in temperature and rainfall. In general, it is hot and dry on the Guiana plateau, and hot and humid throughout the forested region. In the latter, there are two recognized seasons, wet and dry, which differ only in the amount of rainfall, a strictly dry season being unknown. The trade winds, which blow up the Amazon with much force, moderate the heat and make healthy most of the settlements on the great river itself; but the settlements along its tributaries, which are not swept by these winds, are afflicted with malaria. The population is concentrated at widely separated points on the coast and navigable rivers, except on Marajó island, where open country and pastoral pursuits have opened up inland districts. The principal occupation is the collecting and marketing of forest products such as rubber (from *Hevea brasiliensis*), gutta-percha, or *bolata* (*Mimusops elata*), Brazil nuts (*Bertholetia excelsis*), sarsaparilla (*Smilax*), cumaru or tonka beans (*Dipterix odorata*), copaiba (*Copaifera officinarum*), guaraná (*Paulinia sorbilis*), *cravo* (an aromatic· bark of *Dicypellium caryophillatum*) and many others. In earlier days cotton, sugar-cane, rice, tobacco, cacao and even coffee were cultivated, but the demand for rubber caused their abandonment in most places. Cacao (*Theobroma cacao*) is still widely cultivated, as also *mandioca* (*Manihot utilissima*) in some localities. Pará produces many kinds of fruits—the orange, banana, abrico, cajú, abacate (alligator pear), mango, sapotilha, fructa de Conde, grape, &c., besides a large number hardly known beyond the Amazon valley. The pastoral industries were once important in Pará, especially on the islands of Marajó, Caviana and Mexiana, and included the rearing of horses, cattle, and sheep. At present little is done in these industries, and the people depend upon importation for draft animals and fresh meat. There remain a few cattle ranges on Marajó and other islands, but the industry is apparently losing ground. Mining receives some attention on the Atlantic slope of the Guiana plateau, where gold washings of no great importance have been found in the Counani and other streams. There are no manufactures in the state outside the city of Pará (*q.v.*).

Transportation depends wholly on river craft, the one railway of the state, the Pará & Bragança, not being able to meet expenses from its traffic receipts. The capital of the state is Pará, or Belem do Pará, and its history is largely that of this city. Other important towns are Alemaquer (pop. about 1500; of the municipio in 1890, 7539), on a by-channel of the Amazon; Breves (mun. 12,593 in 1890), a river port in the south-west part of Marajó, on a channel connecting the Amazon with the Pará estuary; Bragança (mun. 16,046 in 1890), a small town in one of the few agricultural districts of the state, 147 m. by rail north-east of Pará, on the river Cæté, near the coast; Obidos (about 1000; mun. 12,666 in 1890), on the north bank of the Amazon at a point called the Pauxis narrows, a little over 1 m. wide, attractively situated on a hillside in a healthful locality; and Santarem (12,062 in 1890), on the right bank of the Tapajos, 2½ m. from the Amazon, dating from 1661, and the most prosperous and populous town between Pará and Manáos.

PARÁ (officially BELEM; sometimes BELEM DO PARÁ), a city and port of Brazil, capital of the state of Pará, and the see of a bishop, on a point of land formed by the entrance of the Guamá river into the Pará (86 m. from the Atlantic), in 1° 28' S., 48° 28' W. Pop. of the city and rural districts of the municipality (1890), 50,064; (1900, estimate), 100,000. There is a large Portuguese contingent in the population, and the foreign element, engaged in trade and transportation, is also important. The Indian admixture is strongly apparent in the Amazon valley and is noticeable in Pará. A small railway, built by the state, runs north-eastward in the direction of Bragança (112 m.), on the sea-coast. The Guamá river is enlarged at its mouth to form an estuary called the bay of Guajará, partially shut off from the Pará by several islands and forming the anchorage of the port, and the Pará is the estuary mouth of the Tocantins river. The Pará is about 20 m. wide here.

The city is built on an alluvial forested plain only a few feet above the level of the river, and its streets usually end at the margin of the impenetrable forest. The climate is hot and humid, but the temperature and diurnal changes are remarkably uniform throughout the year. The annual rainfall, according to Professor M. F. Draenert, is 70 in. (Reclus says 120 in.), of which 56 in. are credited to the rainy season (January to June). H. W. Bates gives the average temperature at 81° F., the minimum at 73°, and the maximum (2 p.m.) at 89° to 94°. These favourable climatic conditions tend to make the city healthy, but through defective drainage, insanitary habits and surroundings, and improper diet the death-rate is high. The plan of the city is regular and, owing to the density of the forest, it has no outlying suburbs. The streets are usually narrow, straight and well paved. Among the many public squares and gardens the largest are the Praça Caetano Brandão, with a statue of the bishop of that name; the Praça da Independencia, surrounded by government buildings and having an elaborate monument to General Gurjão; the Praça Visconde do Rio Branço, with a statue of José da Gama Melchior; the Praça de Baptista Campos, with artificial cascades, lake, island and winding paths; the Praça da Republica, with a monument representing the Republic; and the Praça de Prudente Moraes, named in honour of the first civilian president of Brazil. Another public outdoor resort is the Bosque, a tract of forest on the outskirts of the city. The public buildings and institutions are in great part relics of an older régime. The great cruciform cathedral, on the Praça Caetano Brandão, dates from the middle of the 18th century. In the vicinity, facing on the Praça da Independencia, are the government and municipal palaces—built by order of Pombal (c. 1760), when Portugal contemplated the creation of a great empire on the Amazon. The bishop's palace and episcopal seminary, near the cathedral, were once the Jesuits' college, and the custom-house on the water-front was once the convent and church of the Mercenarios. One of the most notable buildings of the city is the Theatro da Paz (Peace Theatre), which faces upon the Praça da Republica and was built by the government during the second empire. Other noteworthy buildings are the Caridade hospital, the Misericordia hospital (known as the "Santa Casa"), the military barracks occupying another old convent, and the Castello fort, a relic of colonial days. Pará has a number of schools and colleges, public and private, of secondary grade, such as the Ateneo Paranense, Instituto Lauro Sodré and Lyceu Benjamin Constant. There is an exceptionally fine museum (Museu Goeldi), with important collections in anthropology; ethnology, zoology and botany, drawn from the Amazon valley. The private dwellings are chiefly of the Portuguese one storey type, with red tile roofs and thick walls of broken stone and mortar, generally plastered outside but sometimes covered with blue and white Lisbon tiles.

Pará is the entrepôt for the Amazon valley and the principal commercial city of northern Brazil. It is the headquarters of the Amazon Navigation Company, which owns a fleet of 40 river steamers, of 500 to 900 tons, and sends them up the Amazon to the Peruvian frontier, and up all the large tributaries where trading settlements have been established. Two or three coastwise companies also make regular calls at this port, and several transatlantic lines afford regular communication with Lisbon, Liverpool, Hamburg and New York. The port is accessible to large steamers, but those of light draft only can lie alongside the quays, the larger being obliged to anchor some distance out. Extensive port improvements have been undertaken. The exports of Pará include rubber, cacao, Brazil nuts and a large number of minor products, such as isinglass, palm fibre, fine woods, tonka beans, deerskins, balsam copaiba, annatto, and other forest products.

Pará was founded in 1615 by Francisco Caldeira de Castello-Branco, who commanded a small expedition from Maranhão sent thither to secure possession of the country for Portugal and drive out the Dutch and English traders. The settlement, which he named Nossa Senhora de Belem (Our Lady of Bethlehem), grew to be one of the most turbulent and ungovernable towns of Brazil. Rivalry with Maranhão, the capital of the Amazon dependencies, slave-hunting, and bitter controversies with the Jesuits who sought to protect the Indians from this traffic, combined to cause agitation. In 1641 it had a population of only 400, but it had four monasteries and was already largely interested in the Indian slave traffic. In 1652 the Pará territory was made a separate capitania, with the town of Pará as the capital, but it was reannexed to Maranhão in 1654. The final separation occurred in 1772, and Pará again became the capital, continuing as such through all the political changes that have since occurred. The bishopric of Pará dates from 1723. The popular movement in Portugal in 1820 in favour of a constitution and parliament (Cortes) had its echo in Pará, where in 1821 the populace and garrison joined in creating a government of their own and in sending a deputation to Lisbon. The declaration of Brazilian independence of 1822 and creation of an empire

under Dom Pedro I. was not accepted by Pará, partly because of its influential Portuguese population, and partly through jealousy of Rio de Janeiro as the centre of political power. In 1823 a naval expedition under Lord Cochrane, then in the service of Brazil, took possession of Maranhão, from which place the small brig "Dom Miguel" under the command of Captain John Grenfell was sent to Pará. This officer conveyed the impression that the whole fleet was behind him, and on the 15th of August the junta governativa organized in the preceding year surrendered its authority and Pará became part of the newly created Brazilian empire. An uprising against the new government soon occurred, which resulted in the arrest of the insurgents, the execution of their leaders, and the incarceration of 253 prisoners in the hold of a small vessel, where all but four died from suffocation before morning. Conspiracies and revolts followed, and in 1835 an outbreak of the worse elements, made up chiefly of Indians and half-breeds, occurred, known as the "Revolução da Cabanagem," which was chiefly directed against the Portuguese, and then against the Freemasons. All whites were compelled to leave the city and take refuge on neighbouring islands. The Indians and half-breeds obtained the mastery, under the leadership of Antonio and Francisco Vinagres and Eduardo Angelim, and plunged the city and neighbouring towns into a state of anarchy, the population being reduced from 25,000 to 15,000. The revolt was overcome in 1836, but the city did not recover from its effects until 1848. But the opening of the Amazon to foreign trade in 1867 greatly increased the importance of the city, and its growth has gone forward steadily since that event. (A. J. L.)

PARABLE (Gr. παραβολή, a comparison or similitude), originally the name given by Greek rhetoricians to a literary illustration avowedly introduced as such. In late Greek it came to mean a fictitious narrative or allegory (generally something that might naturally occur) by which moral or spiritual relations are typically set forth, as in the New Testament. The parable differs from the apologue in the inherent probability of the story itself, and in excluding animals or inanimate creatures from passing out of their natural sphere and assuming the powers of man, but it resembles it in the essential qualities of brevity and definiteness, and also in its Eastern origin. There are many beautiful examples of the parable in the Old Testament, that of Nathan, for instance, in 2 Sam. xii. 1-9, that of the woman of Tekoah in 2 Sam. xiv. 1-13, and others in the Prophets.

PARABOLA, a plane curve of the second degree. It may be defined as a section of a right circular cone by a plane parallel to a tangent plane to the cone, or as the locus of a point which moves so that its distances from a fixed point and a fixed line are equal. It is therefore a conic section having its eccentricity equal to unity. The parabola is the curve described by a projectile which moves in a non-resisting medium under the influence of gravity. (see MECHANICS). The general relations between the parabola, ellipse and hyperbola are treated in the articles GEOMETRY, ANALYTICAL, and CONIC SECTIONS; and various projective properties are demonstrated in the article GEOMETRY, PROJECTIVE. Here only the specific properties of the parabola will be given.

The form of the curve is shown in fig. 1, where P is a point on the curve equidistant from the fixed line AB, known as the directrix, and the fixed point F known as the focus. The line CD passing through the focus and perpendicular to the directrix is the axis or principal diameter, and meets the curve in the vertex G. The line FL perpendicular to the axis, and passing through the focus, is the semilatus rectum, the latus rectum being the focal chord parallel to the directrix. Any line parallel to the axis is a diameter, and the parameter of any diameter is measured by the focal chord drawn parallel to the tangent at the vertex of the diameter and is equal

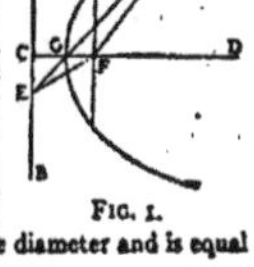

FIG. 1.

to four times the focal distance of the vertex. To construct the parabola when the focus and directrix are given, draw the axis CD and bisect CF at G, which gives the vertex. Any number of points on the parabola are obtained by taking any point E on the directrix, joining EG and EF and drawing FP so that the angles PFE and DFE are equal. Then EG produced meets FP in a point on the curve. By joining the points so obtained the parabola may be described. A mechanical construction, when the same conditions are given, consists in taking a rigid bar ABC bent at right angles at B (fig. 2),

and fastening a string of length BC to C and F. Then if a pencil be placed along BC so as to keep the string taut, and the limb AB be slid along the directrix, the pencil will trace out the parabola.

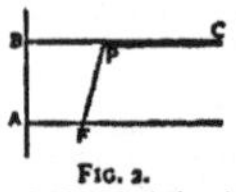

FIG. 2.

Properties which may be readily deduced by euclidian methods from the definition include the following: the tangent at any point bisects the angle between the focal distance and the perpendicular on the directrix and is equally inclined to the focal distance and the axis; tangents at the extremities of a focal chord intersect at right angles on the directrix, and as a corollary we have that the locus of the intersection of tangents at right angles is the directrix; the circumcircle of a triangle circumscribing a parabola passes through the focus; the subtangent is equal to twice the abscissa of the point of contact; the subnormal is constant and equals the semilatus rectum; and the radius of curvature at a point P is $2 (FP)^{1/2}/a^{1}$ where a is the semilatus rectum and FP the focal distance of P.

A fundamental property of the curve is that the *line at infinity* is a tangent (see GEOMETRY, PROJECTIVE), and it follows that the centre and the second real focus and directrix are at infinity. It also follows that a line half-way between a point and its polar and parallel to the latter touches the parabola, and therefore the lines joining the middle points of the sides of a self-conjugate triangle form a circumscribing triangle, and also that the nine-point circle of a self-conjugate triangle passes through the focus. The orthocentre of a triangle circumscribing a parabola is on the directrix; a deduction from this theorem is that the centre of the circumcircle of a self-conjugate triangle is on the directrix ("Steiner's Theorem").

In the article GEOMETRY, ANALYTICAL, it is shown that the general equation of the second degree represents a parabola when the highest terms form a perfect square. **Analytic Geometry.** This is the analytical expression of the projective property that the line at infinity is a tangent. The simplest equation to the parabola is that which is referred to its axis and the tangent at the vertex as the axes of co-ordinates, when it assumes the form $y^2 = 4ax$ where $2a =$ semilatus rectum; this may be deduced directly from the definition. An equation of similar form is obtained when the axes of co-ordinates are any diameter and the tangent at the vertex. The equations to the tangent and normal at the point $x'y'$ are $yy' = 2a(x+x')$ and $2a(y-y')+y'(x-x')=0$, and may be obtained by general methods (see GEOMETRY, ANALYTICAL, and INFINITESIMAL CALCULUS). More convenient forms in terms of a single parameter are deduced by substituting $x'=am^2$, $y'=2am$ (for on eliminating m between these relations the equation to the parabola is obtained). The tangent then becomes $my=x+am^2$ and the normal $y=mx+2am-am^3$. The envelope of this last equation is $27ay^2=4(x-2a)^3$, which shows that the evolute of a parabola is a *semi-cubical parabola* (see below *Higher Orders*). The cartesian equation to a parabola which touches the co-ordinate axes is $\sqrt{ax}+\sqrt{by}=1$, and the polar equation when the focus is the pole and the axis the initial line is $r \cos^2\theta/2 = a$.

The equation to a parabola in triangular co-ordinates is generally derived by expressing the condition that the line at infinity is a tangent in the equation to the general conic. For example, in trilinear co-ordinates, the equation to the general conic circumscribing the triangle of reference is $l\beta\gamma+m\gamma\alpha+n\alpha\beta=0$; for this to be a parabola the line $a\alpha + b\beta + c\gamma=0$ must be a tangent. Expressing this condition we obtain

$\sqrt{la} = \sqrt{mb} = \sqrt{nc} = o$ as the relation which must hold between the co-efficients of the above equation and the sides of the triangle of reference for the equation to represent a parabola. Similarly, the conditions for the inscribed conic $\sqrt{l\alpha}+\sqrt{m\beta}+\sqrt{n\gamma}=o$ to be a parabola is $lbc+mca+nab=o$, and the conic for which the triangle of reference is self-conjugate is $la^1+mβ^1+ny^2=c$ is $a^2mn+b^2nl+c^2lm=o$. The various forms in areal co-ordinates may be derived from the above by substituting λa for l, μb for m and νc for n, or directly by expressing the condition for tangency of the line $x+y+z=o$ to the conic expressed in areal co-ordinates. In tangential (p, q, r) co-ordinates the inscribed and circumscribed conics take the forms $\lambda qr+\mu rp+\nu pq=o$ and $\sqrt{\lambda p}+\sqrt{\mu q}+\sqrt{\nu r}=o$; these are parabolas when $\lambda+\mu+\nu=o$ and $\sqrt{\lambda}=\sqrt{\mu}=\sqrt{\nu}=o$ respectively.

The length of a parabolic arc can be obtained by the methods of the infinitesimal calculus; the curve is directly quadrable, the area of any portion between two ordinates being two thirds of the circumscribing parallelogram. The pedal equation with the focus as origin is $p^2=ar$; the first positive pedal for the vertex is the cissoid (q.v.) and for the focus the directrix. (See INFINITESIMAL CALCULUS.)

REFERENCES.—Geometrical constructions of the parabola are to be found in T. H. Eagles' *Plane Curves* (1885). See the bibliography to the articles CONIC SECTIONS; GEOMETRY, ANALYTICAL; and GEOMETRY, PROJECTIVE.

In the geometry of plane curves, the term parabola is often used to denote the curves given by the general equation $a^mx^2=y^{m+2}$, thus $ax=y^2$ is the quadratic or Apollonian parabola; $a^2x=y^3$ is the cubic parabola, $a^3x=y^4$ is **Higher** the biquadratic parabola; *semi parabolas* have the **Orders.** general equation $ax^{m-1}=y^m$, thus $ax^2=y^3$ is the semicubical parabola and $ax^3=y^4$ the semibiquadratic parabola. These curves were investigated by René Descartes, Sir Isaac Newton, Colin Maclaurin and others. Here we shall treat only the more important forms.

The *cartesian parabola* is a cubic curve which is also known as the trident of Newton on account of its three-pronged form. Its equation is $xy=ax^3+bx^2+cx+d$, and it consists of two legs asymptotic to the axis of y and two parabolic legs (fig. 3). The simplest form is $axy=x^4-a^4$, in this case the serpentine position shown in the figure degenerates into a point of inflexion. Descartes used the curve to solve sextic equations by determining its intersections with a circle; mechanical constructions were given by Descartes (*Geometry*, lib. 3) and Maclaurin (*Organica geometrica*).

The *cubic parabola* (fig. 4) is a cubic curve having the equation $y=ax^3+bx^2+cx+d$. It consists of two parabolic branches tending in opposite directions. John Wallis utilized the intersections of this curve with a right line to solve cubic equations, and Edmund Halley solved sextic equations with the aid of a circle.

Diverging parabolas are cubic curves given by the equation $y^2=ax^3+bx^2+cx+d$. Newton discussed the five forms which arise from the relations of the roots of the cubic equation. When all the

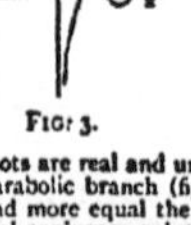

FIG. 3. 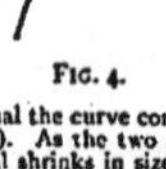   FIG. 4. 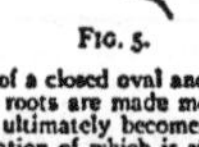   FIG. 5.

roots are real and unequal the curve consists of a closed oval and a parabolic branch (fig. 5). As the two lesser roots are made more and more equal the oval shrinks in size and ultimately becomes a real conjugate point, and the curve, the equation of which is $y^2=(x-a)^2(x-b)$ (in which $a>b$) consists of this point and a bell-like branch resembling the right-hand member of fig. 5. If two roots are imaginary the equation is $y^2=(x^2+a^2)(x-b)$ and the curve resembles the parabolic branch, as in the preceding case. This is sometimes termed the *campaniform* (or bell-shaped) parabola. If the two greater roots are equal the equation is $y^2=(x-a)(x-b)^2$ (in which $a<b$) and the curve assumes the form shown in fig. 6, and is known as the *nodated* parabola. Finally, if all the roots are equal, in which case the equation becomes $y^2=(x-a)^3$; this curve is the *cuspidal* or *semicubical* parabola (fig. 7). This curve, which is sometimes termed the Neilian parabola after William Neil (1637-1670), is the evolute of the ordinary parabola, and is especially interesting as being the first

curve to be rectified. This was accomplished in 1657 by Neil in England, and in 1659 by Heinrich van Heuraet in Holland. Newton showed that all the five varieties of the diverging parabolas may be exhibited as plane sections of the solid of revolution of the semi-cubical parabola. A plane oblique to the axis and passing below the vertex gives the first variety; if it passes through the vertex,

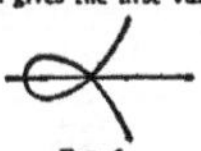

FIG. 6. 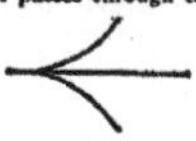   FIG. 7.

the second form; if above the vertex and oblique or parallel to the axis, the third form; if below the vertex and touching the surface, the fourth form, and if the plane contains the axis, the fifth form results (see CURVE).

The biquadratic parabola has, in its most general form, the equation $y = ax^4 + bx^3 + cx^2 + dx + e$, and consists of a serpentinous and two parabolic branches (fig. 8). If all the roots of the quartic in

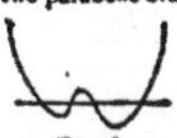

FIG. 8. 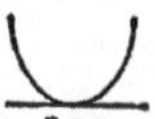   FIG. 9. 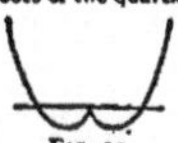   FIG. 10.

x are equal the curve assumes the form shown in fig. 9, the axis of x being a double tangent. If the two middle roots are equal, fig. 1 results. Other forms which correspond to other relations between the roots can be readily deduced from the most general form. (See CURVE; and GEOMETRY, ANALYTICAL.)

PARACELSUS (c. 1490–1541), the famous German physician of the 16th century, was probably born near Einsiedeln, in the canton Schwyz, in 1490 or 1491 according to some, or 1493 according to others. His father, the natural son of a grand-master of the Teutonic order, was Wilhelm Bombast von Hohenheim, who had a hard struggle to make a subsistence as a physician. His mother was superintendent of the hospital at Einsiedeln, a post she relinquished upon her marriage. Paracelsus's name was Theophrastus Bombast von Hohenheim; for the names Philippus and Aureolus which are sometimes added good authority is wanting, and the epithet Paracelsus, like some similar compounds, was probably one of his own making, and was meant to denote his superiority to Celsus.

Of the early years of Paracelsus's life hardly anything is known. His father was his first teacher, and took pains to instruct him in all the learning of the time, especially in medicine. Doubtless Paracelsus learned rapidly what was put before him, but he seems at a comparatively early age to have questioned the value of what he was expected to acquire, and to have soon struck out ways for himself. At the age of sixteen he entered the university of Basel, but probably soon abandoned the studies therein pursued. He next went to J. Trithemius, the abbot of Sponheim and afterwards of Würzburg, under whom he prosecuted chemical researches. Trithemius is the reputed author of some obscure tracts on the great elixir, and as there was no other chemistry going Paracelsus would have to devote himself to the reiterated operations so characteristic of the notions of that time. But the confection of the stone of the philosophers was too remote a possibility to gratify the fiery spirit of a youth like Paracelsus, eager to make what he knew, or could learn, at once available for practical medicine. So he left school chemistry as he had forsaken university culture, and started for the mines in Tirol owned by the wealthy family of the Fuggers. The sort of knowledge he got there pleased him much more. There at least he was in contact with reality. The struggle with nature before the precious metals could be made of use impressed upon him more and more the importance of actual personal observation. He saw all the mechanical difficulties that had to be overcome in mining; he learned the nature and succession of rocks, the physical properties of minerals, ores and metals; he got a notion of mineral waters; he was an eyewitness of the accidents which befel the miners, and studied the diseases which attacked them; he had proof that positive knowledge of nature was not to be got in schools and universities, but only by going to nature herself, and to those who were constantly engaged with her. Hence came Paracelsus's peculiar mode of study. He attached no value to mere scholarship; scholastic disputations he utterly ignored and despised—and especially the discussions on medical topics, which turned more upon theories and definitions than upon actual practice. He therefore went wandering over a great part of Europe to learn all that he could. In so doing he was one of the first physicians of modern times to profit by a mode of study which is now reckoned indispensable. The book of nature, he affirmed, is that which the physician must read, and to do so he must walk over the leaves. The humours and passions and diseases of different nations are different, and the physician must go among the nations if he will be master of his art; the more he knows of other nations, the better he will understand his own. And the commentary of his own and succeeding centuries upon these very extreme views is that Paracelsus was no scholar, but an ignorant vagabond. He himself, however, valued his method and his knowledge very differently, and argued that he knew what his predecessors were ignorant of, because he had been taught in no human school. "Whence have I all my secrets, out of what writers and authors? Ask rather how the beasts have learned their arts. If nature can instruct irrational animals, can it not much more men?" In this new school discovered by Paracelsus, and since attended with the happiest results by many others, he remained for about ten years. He had acquired great stores of facts, which it was impossible for him to have reduced to order, but which gave him an unquestionable superiority to his contemporaries. So in 1526 or 1527, on his return to Basel, he was appointed town physician, and shortly afterwards he gave a course of lectures on medicine in the university. Unfortunately for him, the lectures broke away from tradition. They were in German, not in Latin; they were expositions of his own experience, of his own views, of his own methods of curing, adapted to the diseases which afflicted the Germans in the year 1527, and they were not commentaries on the text of Galen or Avicenna. They attacked, not only these great authorities, but the German graduates who followed them and disputed about them in 1527. They criticised in no measured terms the current medicine of the time, and exposed the practical ignorance, the pomposity, and the greed of those who practised it.

The truth of Paracelsus's doctrines was apparently confirmed by his success in curing or mitigating diseases for which the regular physicians could do nothing. For about a couple of years his reputation and practice increased to a surprising extent. But at the end of that time people began to recover themselves. Paracelsus had burst upon the schools with such novel views and methods, with such irresistible criticism, that all opposition was at first crushed flat. Gradually the sea began to rise. His enemies watched for slips and failures; the physicians maintained that he had no degree, and insisted that he should give proof of his qualifications. Moreover, he had a pharmaceutical system of his own which did not harmonize with the commercial arrangements of the apothecaries, and he not only did not use up their drugs like the Galenists, but, in the exercise of his functions as town physician, he urged the authorities to keep a sharp eye on the purity of their wares, upon their knowledge of their art, and upon their transactions with their friends the physicians. The growing jealousy and enmity culminated in a dispute with Canon Cornelius von Lichtenfels, who, having called in Paracelsus after other physicians had given up his case, refused to pay the fee he had promised in the event of cure; and, as the judges, to their discredit, sided with the canon, Paracelsus had no alternative but to tell them his opinion of the whole case and of their notions of justice. So little doubt left he on the subject that his friends judged it prudent for him to leave Basel at once, as it had been resolved to punish him for the attack on the authorities of which he had been guilty. He departed in such haste that he carried nothing with him, and some chemical apparatus and other property were taken charge of by J. Oporinus (1507–1568), his pupil and amanuensis. He went first to Esslingen, where he remained for a brief period, but had soon to leave from absolute want. Then began his wandering life, the course of which can be traced by the dates of his various writings. He thus visited in succession Colmar, Nuremberg, Appenzell, Zurich, Pfäffers, Augsburg, Villach, Meran, Middelheim and other places, seldom staying a twelvemonth in any of them. In this way he spent some dozen years, till 1541, when he was invited by Archbishop Ernst to settle at Salzburg, under his protection. After his endless tossing about, this seemed a promise and place of repose. It proved, however, to be the complete and final rest that he found, for after a few months he died, on the 24th of September. The cause of his death, like most other details in his history, is uncertain. His enemies asserted that he died in a low tavern in consequence of a drunken debauch of some days' duration. Others maintain that he was thrown down a steep place by some emissaries either of the physicians or of the apothecaries, both of whom he had during his life most grievously harassed. He was buried in the churchyard of St Sebastian, but in 1752 his bones were removed to the porch of the church, and a monument of reddish-white marble was erected to his memory.

The first book by Paracelsus was printed at Augsburg in 1529. It is entitled *Practica D. Theophrasti Paracelsi, gemacht auff Europen*, and forms a small quarto pamphlet of five leaves. Prior to this, in 1526–1527, appeared a programme of the lectures he intended to deliver at Basel, but this can hardly be reckoned a specific work. During his lifetime fourteen works and editions were published, and thereafter, between 1542 and 1845, there were at least two hundred and thirty-four separate publications according to Mook's enumeration. The first collected edition was made by Johann Huser in German. It was printed at Basel in 1589–1591, in eleven volumes quarto, and is the best of all the editions. Huser did not employ the early printed copies only, but collected all the manuscripts which he could procure, and used them also in forming his text. The only drawback is that rather than omit anything which Paracelsus may have composed, he has gone to the opposite extreme and included writings with which it is pretty certain Paracelsus had nothing to do. The second collected German edition is in four volumes folio, 1603–1605. Parallel with it in 1603 the first collected Latin edition was made by Palthenius. It is in eleven volumes quarto, and was completed in 1605. Again, in 1616–1618 appeared a reissue of the folio German edition of 1603, and finally in 1658 came the Geneva Latin version, in three volumes folio, edited by Bitiskius.

The works were originally composed in Swiss-German, a vigorous speech which Paracelsus wielded with unmistakable power. The Latin versions were made or edited by Adam von Bodenstein, Gerard Dorn, Michael Toxites and Oporinus, about the middle of the 16th century. A few translations into other languages exist, as of the *Chirurgia magna*, and some other works into French, and of one or two into Dutch, Italian and even Arabic. The translations into English amount to about a dozen, dating mostly from the middle of the 17th century. The original editions of Paracelsus's works are getting less and less common; even the English versions are among the rarest of their class. Over and above the numerous editions, there is a bulky literature of an explanatory and controversial character, for which the world is indebted to Paracelsus's followers and enemies. A good deal of it is taken up with a defence of chemical, or, they were called, "spagyric," medicines against the attacks of the supporters of the Galenic pharmacopoeia.

The aim of all Paracelsus's writing is to promote the progress of medicine, and he endeavours to put before physicians a grand ideal of their profession. In his attempts he takes the widest view of medicine. He bases it on the general relationship which man bears to nature as a whole; he cannot divorce the life of man from that of the universe; he cannot think of disease otherwise than as a phase of life. He is compelled, therefore, to rest his medical practice upon general theories of the present state of things; his medical system—if there is such a thing—is an adaptation of his cosmogony. It is this latter which has been the stumbling-block to many past critics of Paracelsus, and unless its character is remembered it will be the same to others in the future. Dissatisfied with the Aristotelianism of his time, Paracelsus turned with greater expectation to the Neoplatonism which was reviving. His eagerness to understand the relationship of man to the universe led him to the Kabbala, where these mysteries seemed to be explained, and from these unsubstantial materials he constructed, so far as it can be understood, his visionary philosophy. Interwoven with it, however, were the results of his own personal experience and work in natural history and chemical pharmacy and practical medicine, unfettered by any speculative generalizations, and so shrewd an observer as Paracelsus was must have often felt that his philosophy and his experience did not agree with one another.

Some of his doctrines are alluded to in the article MEDICINE (q.v.), and it would serve no purpose to give even a brief sketch of his views, seeing that their influence has passed entirely away, and that they are of interest only in their place in a general history of medicine and philosophy. Defective, however, as they may have

been, and unfounded in fact, his kabbalistic doctrines led him to trace the dependence of the human body upon outer nature for its sustenance and cure. The doctrine of signatures, the supposed connexion of every part of the little world of man with a corresponding part of the great world of nature, was a fanciful and false exaggeration of this doctrine, but the idea carried in its train that of specifics. This led to the search for these, which were not to be found in the bewildering and untested mixtures of the Galenic prescriptions. Paracelsus had seen how bodies were purified and intensified by chemical operations, and he thought if plants and minerals could be made to yield their active principles it would surely be better to employ these than the crude and unprepared originals. He had besides arrived by some kind of intuition at the conclusion that the operations in the body were of a chemical character, and that when disordered they were to be put right by counter operations of the same kind. It may be claimed for Paracelsus that he embraced within the idea of chemical action something more than the alchemists did. Whether or not he believed in the philosopher's elixir is of very little consequence. If he did, he was like the rest of his age; but he troubled himself very little, if at all, about it. He did believe in the immediate use for therapeutics of the salts and other preparations which his practical skill enabled him to make. Technically he was not a chemist; he did not concern himself either with the composition of his compounds or with an explanation of what occurred in their making. If he could get potent drugs to cure disease he was content, and he worked very hard in an empirical way to make them. That he found out some new compounds is certain; but not one great and marked discovery can be ascribed to him. Probably, therefore, his positive services are to be summed up in this wide application of chemical ideas to pharmacy and therapeutics; his indirect and possibly greater services are to be found in the stimulus, the revolutionary stimulus, of his ideas about method and general theory. It is most difficult to appreciate aright this man of fervid imagination, of powerful and persistent convictions, of unbased honesty and love of truth, of keen insight into the errors (as he thought them) of his time, of a merciless will to lay bare these errors and to reform the abuses to which they gave rise, who in an instant offends us by his boasting, his grossness, his want of self-respect. It is a problem how to reconcile his ignorance, his weakness, his superstition, his crude notions, his erroneous observations, his ridiculous influences and theories, with his grasp of method, his lofty views of the true scope of medicine, his lucid statements, his incisive and epigrammatic criticisms of men and motives.

See Marx, *Zur Würdigung des Theophrastus von Hohenheim* (Göttingen, 1842); Mook, *Theophrastus Paracelsus, eine kritische Studie* (Würzburg, 1876); Hartman, *Life of P. T. Paracelsus* (London, 1887); Schubert und Sudhoff, *Paracelsus-Forschungen* (Frankfurt a.M., 1887–1889); Sudhoff, *Versuch einer Kritik der Echtheit der Paracelsischen Schriften* (Berlin, 1894); Waite, *The Hermetic and Alchemical Writings of Paracelsus* (London, 1894).

PARACHUTE (from Ital. *parare*, to shield, protect; cf. "parasol," "parapet," and Fr. *chute*, a fall), an instrument more or less resembling a large umbrella, which by the resistance it offers to the air enables an aeronaut attached to it to descend safely from a balloon or flying machine in the air. The principle of the parachute is so simple that the idea must have occurred to persons in all ages. Simon de la Loubère (1642–1729), in his *History of Siam* (Paris, 1691), tells of a person who frequently diverted the court by the prodigious leaps he used to take, having two parachutes or umbrellas fastened to his girdle. In 1783 Sébastien Lenormand practically demonstrated the efficiency of a parachute by descending from the tower of Montpellier observatory; but he merely regarded it as a useful means whereby to escape from fire. To J. P. Blanchard (1753–1809) is due the idea of using it as an adjunct to the balloon. As early as 1785 he had constructed a parachute to which was attached a basket. In this he placed a dog, which descended safely to the ground when the parachute was released from a balloon at a considerable elevation. It is stated that he descended himself from a balloon in a parachute in 1793; but, owing to some defect in its construction he fell too rapidly, and broke his leg. André Jacques Garnerin (1769–1823) was the first person who successfully descended from a balloon in a parachute, and he repeated this experiment so often that he may be said to have first demonstrated the practicability of using the machine, though his elder brother, J. B. O. Garnerin (1766–1849), also claimed a share in the merit of perfecting it. In 1793 he was taken prisoner at Marchiennes, and while in captivity at Bude (Budapest) thought out the means of descending from a balloon by means of a parachute. His first public experiment was made on the 22nd of October 1797. He ascended from the park of Monceau, at Paris, and at the height of about 1½ m. he released the parachute, which was attached to the balloon in place of a car; the balloon, relieved suddenly of so great a weight, rose very rapidly till it burst, while the parachute descended very fast, making violent oscillations all the way. Garnerin, however, reached the earth in safety. He repeated his parachute experiment in England on the 21st of September 1802. The parachute was dome-shaped, and bore a resemblance to a large

umbrella (fig. 1). The case or dome was made of white canvas, about 23 ft. in diameter. At the top was a truck or round piece of wood 10 in. In diameter, with a hole in its centre, fastened to the canvas by 32 short pieces of tape. The parachute was suspended from a hoop attached to the netting of the balloon, and below it was placed a cylindrical basket, 4 ft. high and 2½ ft. in diameter, which contained the aeronaut. The ascent took place at about six o'clock from North Audley Street, London; and at a height of about (it is believed) 8000 ft. Garnerin separated the parachute from the balloon. For a few seconds his fate seemed certain, as the parachute retained the collapsed state in which it had originally ascended and fell very rapidly. It suddenly, however, expanded, and the rapidity of its descent was at once checked, though oscillations were so violent that the car, which was suspended 20 ft. below, was sometimes on a level with the rest of the apparatus. Some accounts state that these oscillations increased, others that they decreased as the parachute descended; the latter seems the more probable. It came to the ground in a field at the back of St Pancras Church, the descent having occupied rather more than ten minutes. Garnerin was hurt a little by the violence with which the basket containing him struck the earth; but a few cuts and a slight nausea represented all the ill effects of his fall. A few years later, Jordaki Kuparento, a Polish aeronaut, made real use of a parachute. He ascended from Warsaw on the 24th of July 1808, in a fire-balloon, which, at a considerable elevation, took fire; but he was able to effect his descent in safety by means of his parachute.

The next experiment made with a parachute resulted in the death of Robert Cocking, who as early as 1814 had become interested in the subject. The great defect of Garnerin's umbrella-shaped parachute had been its violent oscillation during descent, and Cocking considered that if the parachute were made of a conical form (vertex downwards) the whole of this oscillation would be avoided; and if it were made of sufficient size there would be resistance enough to check too rapid a descent. He therefore constructed a parachute on this

principle (fig. 2), the radius of which at its widest part was about 17 ft. It was stated in the public announcements previous to the experiment that the whole weighed 223 ℔; but from the evidence at the inquest it appeared that the weight must have been over 400 ℔ exclusive of Cocking's weight, which was 177 ℔. On the 24th of July 1837, the Nassau balloon, with Charles Green, the aeronaut, and Edward Spencer, a solici-

FIG. 2.—Cocking's Parachute.

tor, in the car, and having suspended below it the parachute,

in the car of which was Cocking, rose from Vauxhall Gardens, London, at twenty-five minutes to eight in the evening. A good deal of difficulty was experienced in rising to a suitable height, partly in consequence of the resistance to the air offered by the expanded parachute, and partly owing to its weight. Cocking wished the height to be 8000 ft.; but when the balloon reached the height of 5000 ft., nearly over Greenwich, Green called out to Cocking that he should be unable to ascend to the requisite height if the parachute was to descend in daylight. Cocking accordingly let slip the catch which was to liberate him from the balloon. The parachute for a few seconds descended very rapidly, but still evenly, until suddenly the upper rim seemed to give way and the whole apparatus collapsed (taking a form resembling an umbrella turned inside out, and nearly closed), and the machine descended with great rapidity, oscillating very much. When about 200 or 300 ft. from the ground the basket became disengaged from the remnant of the parachute, and Cocking was found in a field at Lee, literally dashed to pieces.

Many objections were made to the form of Cocking's parachute; but there is little doubt that had it been constructed of sufficient strength, and perhaps of somewhat larger size, it would have answered its purpose. John Wise (1808–1879), the American aeronaut, made some experiments on parachutes of both forms (Garnerin's and Cocking's), and found that the latter always were much more steady, descending generally in a spiral curve.

A descending balloon half-full of gas either does rise, or can with a little management be made to rise, to the top of the netting and take the form of a parachute, thus materially lessening the rapidity of descent. Wise, in fact, having noticed this, once purposely exploded his balloon when at a considerable altitude, and the resistance offered to the air by the envelope of the balloon was sufficient to enable him to reach the ground without injury. In more recent times the use of the parachute has become fairly common, but a good many serious accidents have occurred.

PARADE (Fr. *parade*, an adaptation from Ital. *parata*; cf. Span. *parada*, from Lat. *parare*, to prepare, equip, furnish), a word of which the principal meanings are display, show, a military gathering of troops for a specific purpose, an assembly of people for a promenade, the place where the troops assemble, and a road or street where people may walk. In the military sense, a "parade" is a mustering of troops on the parade-ground for drill, for inspection, for the delivery of special orders, or for other purposes, either at regular stated hours or on special occasions.

PARADISE (Gr. παράδεισος), the name of a supernatural locality reserved for God and for chosen men, which occurs in the Greek Bible, both for the earthly "garden" of Eden (see EDEN), and for the heavenly "garden," where true Israelites after death see the face of God (4 Esdras viii. 52; Luke xxiii. 43; 2 Cor. xii. 4; Rev. ii. 7). The Hebrew *pardes* (פרדס), to which *παράδεισος* corresponds, occurs thrice in the Old Testament in late books, in the general sense of "park, grove"; it is derived somewhat hazardously from the Zend *pairidaēza*, an enclosure (once only in the *Avesta*), though another word (*Vara*) is used in the account of the mythical enclosure of Yima (see DELUGE). But what interests us most is not the name, but the conception and its imaginative vehicle. The conception is the original godlikeness of human nature, and the necessity of expecting a closer union between God and man in the future than is possible at present. The imaginative form which this conception takes is that before the present condition arose man dwelt near to God in God's own mountain home, and that when the mischief wrought by "the serpent" has been undone, man—or more strictly the true Israel—shall once more be admitted to his old privilege. According to the fullest Old Testament account (Ezek. xxviii. 12–19; see ADAM), the holy mountain was in a definite earthly region, and certainly it was appropriate for worshippers of Yahweh that it should be so (1 Kings xx. 23, 28). But there are traces in that account itself as well as in Gen. ii. that an earlier belief placed the divine home in heaven. Similarly the Zoroastrians speak of their Paradise-mountain Alburz both as heavenly and as earthly (*Bundahish*, xx. 1, with West's note). It appears that originally the Hebrew Paradise-mountain was placed in heaven, but that afterwards it was transferred to earth. It was of stupendous size; indeed, properly it was the earth itself.[1] Later on each Semitic people may have chosen its own mountain, recognizing, however, perhaps, that in primeval times it was of vaster dimensions than at present, just as the Jews believed that in the next age the "mountain of Yahweh's house" would become far larger (Isa. ii. 2= Mic. iv. 1; Ezek. xl. 2; Zech. xiv. 10; Rev. xxi. 10); compare the idealisation of the earthly Alburz of the Iranians " in revelation " (*Bund.* v. 3, viii. 2, xii. 1–8).

We now return to the accounts in Ezek. xxviii. and Gen. ii. The references in the former to the precious stones and to the "stones of fire" may be grouped with the references in Enoch (xviii. 6–8, xxiv.) to seven supernatural mountains each composed of a different beautiful stone, and with the throne of God on the seventh. These mountains are to be connected with the seven planets, each of which was symbolized by a different metal, or at least colour.[2] Ezekiel's mountain therefore has come to earth from heaven. And a similar result follows if we group the four rivers of Paradise in Gen. ii. with the phrase so often applied to Canaan, "flowing with milk and honey" (Exod. iii. 8; Num. xiii. 27, &c.). For this descriptive phrase is evidently mythical,[3] and refers to the belief in the four rivers of the heavenly Paradise which "poured honey and milk, oil and wine" (*Slavonic Enoch*, viii. 5; cf. *Vision of Paul*, xxiii.). In fact, the four rivers originally flowed in heavenly soil, and only when the mountain of Elohim was transferred to this lower earth could mythological geographers think of determining their earthly course, and whether Havilah, or Cush, or Canaan, or Babylonia, was irrigated by one or another of them. But what happened to Paradise when the affrighted human pair left it? One view (see *Eth. Enoch*, xxxii. 2, 3, 1x. 8, lxxvii. 3, 4, &c.) was that its site was in some nameless, inaccessible region, still guarded by " the serpents and the cherubim " (*Eth. Enoch*, xx. 7), and that in the next age its gates would be opened, and the threatening sword (Gen. iii. 24) put away by the Messianic priest-king (*Testaments of the Twelve Patriarchs*, Levi, 18). This agrees with the story in Gen. ii., iii., except that the original narrator knew the site of the garden. It is a sufficiently reasonable view, for if Paradise lay in some definite earthly region, and if no one knows " the paths of Paradise " (4 Esdras iv. 7), it would seem that it must have ceased to exist visibly. This idea appears to be implied by those Jewish writers, who, especially after the fall of Jerusalem (A.D. 70), dwelt so much on the hope of the heavenly Paradise, reviving, partly under emotional pressure and partly as the result of a fresh influx of mythology, the old myth of a celestial garden of God. To notice only a few leading passages. In *Apoc. Bar.* iv. 3 it appears to be stated that when Adam transgressed, the vision of the city of God and the possession of Paradise were removed from him, and similarly the stress laid in 4 Esdras iv. 7, vi. 2, vii. (36), 53, viii. 52, on the heavenly Paradise seems to show that no earthly one was supposed to exist.[4] Beautiful, indeed, is the use made of that form of belief in these passages, with which we may group Rev. xxi. 1; xxii. 5, where, as in 4 Esdras viii. 52, Paradise and the city of God are combined.

Some strange disclosures on this subject are made by the *Slavonic Enoch* (c. viii.; cf. xlii. 3), according to which there are two Paradises. The former is in the third heaven, which explains the well-known saying of St Paul in 2 Cor. xii. 2, 4;

[1] It was the Babylonian " mountain of the lands," which meant not only mother earth, but the earth imagined to exist within the heaven; cf. Jeremias, *Atao*, pp. 11, 12, 28, and Jastrow, *Religion of Bab. and Ass.*, p. 558.
[2] See Zimmern, *K.A.T.* (3), pp. 616 sqq.
[3] See also 1 Esdras ii. 19. This explains Joel iv. 18; Isa. lv. 1 (wine and milk). See also *Varna*, xlix. 5 (*Zendavesta*); and cf. Cheyne, *Ency. Bib.*, col. 2104, and especially Uscner, *Rheinisches Museum*, lvii. 177–192.
[4] The statement in Gen. iii. 24 comes from a form of the story in which the " garden " was not geographically localized.

the latter is conventionally called the Paradise of Eden. In fact, the belief in an earthly Paradise never wholly died. Medieval writers loved it. The mountain of Purgatory in Dante's poem is "crowned by the delicious shades of the terrestrial Paradise."

See further *The Apocalypse of Baruch* and *The Ethiopic and the Slavonic Enoch*, both edited by R. H. Charles; also Kautzsch's *Apocrypha*, and Volz, *Jüdische Eschatologie* (1903), pp. 374–8, whose full references are most useful. On the Biblical references, cf. Gunkel, *Genesis* (2), pp. 21–35; Cheyne, *Ency. Bib.*, " Paradise "; and on Babylonian views, Jeremias, " Hölle und Paradies " (in *Der alte Orient*). The Mahommedan's Paradise is a sensuous transformation of the Jewish; see especially *Koran*, Sura iv., and note the phrase " gardens of Firdaus," *Koran*, xviii. 107. For the Koran and the Zoroastrian books see the *Sacred Books of the East* (Oxford Series). The doorkeeper of the mountain-Paradise of the Parsees is the Amshaspand Vohu-manō (*Vendidad*, xix. 31). (T. K. C.)

PARADOS (Fr. = back cover), a term used in fortification, expressing a work the purpose of which is to cover the defenders of a line of trenches or parapet from reverse fire, *i.e.* fire from the rear.

PARADOX (Gr. παρά, beyond, contrary to, δόξα, opinion), a proposition or statement which appears to be at variance with generally-received opinion, or which apparently is self-contradictory, absurd or untrue, but either contains a concealed truth or may on examination be proved to be true. A "paradox" has been compared with a "paralogism" (παρά, λόγος, reason), as that which is contrary to opinion only and not contrary to reason, but it is frequently used in the sense of that which is really absurd or untrue.

PARAFFIN, the name given to a mineral wax and oil, and also used as a generic name of a particular series of hydrocarbons.

Commercial Paraffin.—Refined commercial paraffin is a white or bluish-white, translucent, waxy solid substance, of laminocrystalline structure, devoid of taste and smell, and characterized by chemical indifference. It consists of about 85% of carbon and 15% of hydrogen. Although the credit of having first (in 1830) investigated the properties of solid paraffin, obtained from wood-tar, belongs to Karl Reichenbach, the existence of paraffin in petroleum had been more or less hazily known for some time previous. In 1809 Fuchs found solid hydrocarbons in the Tegernsee oils, and in 1819 Buchner separated them from these oils in comparative purity. By the latter they were described as " mountain-fats," and they were identified with paraffin in 1835 by von Kobel. Reichenbach described the results of a series of experiments on the reactions between various substances and paraffin, and on account of the inert nature of the material gave to it its present name (from the Lat. *parum*, too little, and *affinitas*, affinity); he expressly stated that the accent should fall on the second " a," but usage has transferred it to the first.

Paraffin was obtained by Laurent in 1830 by the distillation of bituminous schist, and in 1835 by Dumas from coal-tar; but the product appears to have been regarded only as a curiosity, and Lord Playfair has stated that prior to 1850 he never saw a piece of more than one ounce in weight. Paraffin is asserted to have been made for sale by Reichenbach's process from wood-tar by John Thom, of Birkacre, before 1835. In 1833 Laurent suggested the working of the Autun shale, and products manufactured from this material were exhibited by Selligue in 1839.

According to F. H. Storer, the credit of having first placed the manufacture of paraffin on a commercial basis is deservedly given to Selligue, whose patent specifications, both in France and England, sufficiently clearly show that his processes of distilling bituminous schist, &c., and of purifying the distillate, had reached considerable perfection prior to 1845. In its present form, however, the paraffin or shale-oil industry owes its existence to Dr James Young. In 1850 he applied for his celebrated patent (No. 13,292) " for obtaining paraffine oil, or an oil containing paraffine, and paraffine from bituminous coals " by slow distillation. The process was extensively carried out in the United States under licence from Young, until crude petroleum was produced in that country in such abundance, and at so low a cost, that the distillation of bituminous minerals became unprofitable. The highly bituminous Boghead coal, or Torbanehill mineral, which yielded 120 to 130 gallons of crude oil per ton, was worked out in 1862, and since then the Scottish mineral oils and paraffin have been obtained from the bituminous shales of the coal-measures, the amount of such shale raised in Great Britain in 1907 being 2,590,028 tons.

The following list represents an attempt to assign a geological age to the various occurrences of oil-shale and similar substances throughout the world:—

OIL-SHALES.

Geological System.							Locality.
Miocene	.	.	.	.	.	.	France (Vagnas), Servia.
Eocene	.	.	.	.	.	.	Brazil.
Cretaceous	.	.	.	.	.	.	Syria, Montana, New Zealand.
Neocomian	.	.	.	.	.	.	Spain.
Jurassic	.	.	.	.	.	.	Dorset, Württemberg.
Permian	.	.	.	.	.	.	France (Autun, &c.).
Carboniferous	.	.	.	.	.	.	Scotland, Yorkshire, Stafford, Flint, France, Nova Scotia.

KEROSENE-SHALE

Permo-Carboniferous	.	.	Queensland, New South Wales, Tasmania.

TAR-LIGNITE

Miocene	.	.	.	.	.	.	Moravia, Lower Austria, Bavaria. Rhenish Prussia, Hesse, Saxony.
Oligocene	.	.	.	.	.	.	Bohemia, Tirol.

Oil-Shale.—The oil-shale of Scotland is dark grey or black, and has a laminated or horny fracture. Its specific gravity is about 1·75, and 20 cub. ft. of it weigh rather less than a ton. The richer kinds yield about 30 gallons of oil per ton of shale, and in some cases as much as 40 gallons, but the higher yield is usually obtained at the expense of the solid paraffin and of the quality of the heavy oils. The inferior shales yield about 18 gallons of oil, but a much larger amount of sulphate of ammonia. The oil consists chiefly of members of the paraffin and olefine series, and thus differs essentially from that obtained from true coal-shales, in which the hydrocarbons of the benzene group are largely represented.

A full account of the Scotch shale-oil industry, as the most important and typical, will be given later, the corresponding industries in other countries and districts being dealt with first.

In addition to the Carboniferous oil-shales of Flint and Stafford, the Kimmeridge shale, a bluish-grey slaty clay, containing thin beds of highly bituminous shale, occurs in Dorsetshire, and has from time to time attracted attention as a possible source of shale-oil products. The so-called "Kerosene-shale" of New South Wales has been extensively mined, and the industry is now being developed by the Commonwealth Oil Corporation, Ltd. The French shale-oil industry is much older than that of Scotland, but has made far less progress, the amount of shale distilled in 1897 being 200,000 tons, as compared with 2,259,000 tons in Scotland. The shales of New Zealand have never been extensively worked, the production having decreased instead of increased. Oil-shale of good quality occurs in Servia, and has been found to yield from 43½ to 54½ gallons of oil per ton. The production of mineral oils and paraffin by the distillation of lignite is carried on in Saxony, the mineral worked being a peculiar earthy lignite, occurring within a small portion of the Saxon-Thuringian brown-coal formation. Other occurrences of this mineral have been indicated in the list of localities above.

The Shale-Oil Industry of Scotland.—The modern development of the shale-oil industry of Scotland dates from the commencement of Robert Bell's works at Broxburn in 1862.

The oil-shales are found in the Calciferous Sandstone series, lying between the Carboniferous Limestone and the Old Red Sandstone. They occur at several points in the belt of Carboniferous rocks across the centre of Scotland, for the most part in small synclinal basins, the largest of which is that at Pentland, where the levels are 2 m. long, without important faults. Mining is carried on, where the seams are over 4 ft. thick, by the "pillar and stall" system; seams under 4 ft. are

XX 13

worked by the "longwall" system. The shale is blasted down by gunpowder, and passed over a 1-in. riddle, the smalls being left underground. Before being retorted the shale is passed through a toothed breaker, which reduces it to flat pieces 6 in. square. These fall into a shoot, and thence into iron tubs of 10 to 25 cwt. capacity, which run on rails to the tops of the retorts.

The retorts in which the shale is distilled have undergone considerable variation and improvement since the foundation of the industry. Originally horizontal retorts, like those used in the manufacture of coal-gas, were employed, and the heavy oils and paraffin were burned as fuel. When the latter product became valuable vertical retorts were adopted, as the solid hydrocarbons undergo less dissociation under these conditions. Steam was employed to carry the oil vapours from the retort. The earliest form of vertical retort was circular (2 ft. in diameter) or oval (2 ft. by 1 ft. 4 in.) and 8 or 10 ft. long. Six or eight of these were grouped together, and the heating was so effected that the bottoms of the retorts were at the highest temperature. They were charged by means of hoppers at the top, the exhausted shale being withdrawn through a water-seal every hour and fresh added, whence this is known as the "continuous system."

In the first Henderson retort (1873) the spent shale was used as fuel. The retorts, which were oblong in cross-section, were arranged in groups of four, and had a capacity of 18 cwt. They were charged in rotation, as follows: when a sufficient temperature had been attained in the chamber containing them, one retort was charged from the top, and in four hours the one diagonally opposite to it was charged. After eight hours the one next to the first was charged, and after twelve hours the fourth. Up to the sixteenth hour only ordinary fuel was used in the furnace, but the spent shale from the first retort was then discharged into it. The other retorts were similarly discharged in the above order at intervals of four hours, each being at once recharged. The shale was black when discharged, but soon glowed brightly. Owing to the small amount of carbon in the spent shale, only a slow draught was kept up. The outlet for the oil vapours was at the lower and less heated end of the retorts, and steam, which had been superheated by passage through pipes arranged along one side of the retort chamber, was blown in copiously through pipes to aid in the uniform heating of the shale and to continuously remove the oil vapours, dissociation from overheating being thus minimized. It was believed that a temperature of about 800° F. produced the best results. This retort was worked on what is known as the "intermittent system."

The Pentland Composite retort (1882) and the later Henderson type (1889) were both continuous-working and gas-heated, the second being a modification of the first, designed with a view to obtaining a larger yield of sulphate of ammonia without detriment to the crude oil. In both the upper part of the retort was of cast iron and the lower of fire-clay. The upper portion was heated to a temperature of about 900° F. whilst the lower was maintained at about 1300° F. The charge in the retort gradually travelled down, owing to the periodical removal of spent shale at the bottom, and the descent was so regulated that no shale passed into the highly-heated part until it had parted with the oil it was capable of yielding. The shale, however, still contained nitrogen, which in the presence of steam produced ammonia at the higher temperature.

The three classes of retorts now employed in the distillation of shale in the Scottish oil-works are covered by the following patents:—

1. *In use at Pumpherston, Dalmeny and Oakbank*—No. 8371 of 1894; No. 7113 of 1895; No. 4249 of 1897.
2. *In use by Young's Paraffin Light and Mineral Oil Company, Ltd.*—No. 13,665 of 1897; No. 15,238 of 1899.
3. *In use by the Broxburn Oil Company, Ltd.*—No. 26,647 of 1901.

The objects of the invention for which patent No. 8371 of 1894 was granted to Bryson (of Pumpherston Oil Works), Jones (of Dalmeny Oil Works), and Fraser (of Pumpherston Oil Company, Ltd.), are described in the specification as "to so construct the retorts and provide them with means whereby fluxing or dandering of the substance being heated is prevented in the retorts; also to effect an intermittent, continuous, or nearly so, movement within the retort." In order to carry out these objects, the bottom of the

2a

retort is provided with a disk or table to support the material within the retort. Above the table there is a revolving arm or scraper, by the action of which a portion of the material is continuously swept off the table and discharged into the hopper below. The column of material within the retort is thus caused to move downwards, and the tendency of the material to flux or dander is thereby prevented or reduced. In order to pulverize the material before reaching the hopper, teeth may be formed upon the lower part of the retort and upon the table, and the revolving scraper may be similarly toothed. A short revolving worm or screw may be substituted for the table or scraper. As a modification, the table may be made convex and provided on each side with rocking-arms connected together above the table by a cross-arm or scraper.

The principal object of the invention for which patent No. 7113 of 1895 was granted to the same applicants is stated to be such arrangement of the parts of the retort as results in the retort, after being heated and started, requiring "practically no fuel to keep it going, owing to the great amount of heat generated in the retort by means of the effectual decomposition of the carbon contained in the waste material by means of one or more jets of steam (which may be superheated) being passed into the retort as near the outlet or discharge-door of the retort as possible, thus utilizing all, or nearly all, the heat contained in the waste material within the retort, thus saving labour, time and expense, as well as wear and tear of the retort."

The object of the invention for which patent No. 4249 of 1897 was granted to Bryson is stated to be " to so construct the hoppers of the retorts that one or more retorts can be drawn for discharge through one door, and also to provide simple and efficient means for operating the said door."

Patent No. 13,665 of 1897 was granted to William Young and John Fyfe for an invention the objects of which are described in the specification in the following words: "To reduce labour, save fuel, and increase the products, and to enable existing but worn-out retorts that have been erected in accordance with the above invention to be economically replaced upon existing foundations by similar retorts, provided with improved and enlarged multiple hoppers for the reception of the shale to pass through the retorts, and also enlarged chambers for the reception of the ash or exhausted shale; the retorts being provided with mechanical arrangements for the continuous passage of the fresh shale into them from the multiple hopper, and the continuous discharge of the ash or spent shale into the receiving chamber. Those improved mechanical alterations in the structure of the retorts greatly reduce the manual labour, enabling most of the work to be done during the day, the multiple hopper and spent-shale chamber being of such dimensions as will supply fresh shale and receive the spent shale during the night-shift, the only labour then required being the supervision, regulating temperature of the retorts, and seeing that the mechanical arrangements are working properly."

The multiple hoppers are constructed of mild steel plates with flat bottoms to which the retorts are bolted by flanges, the steel bottoms admitting of the differential expansion, to which the retorts are subject, taking place without damage to the retorts or hoppers. To ensure the shale regularly passing from the hoppers to the retorts, each hopper is provided with a rocking-shaft to which are attached rods or chains hanging into the mouths of the retorts, these rods or chains being thus made to rise or fall. The spent shale receiving-chambers at the lower end of each retort are of greatly enlarged size, and the lower end of each retort is provided with a mechanical device for the continuous discharge of the spent shale into these chambers. The improvements are stated to be specially applicable to retorts of the Young and Beilby (Pentland) type.

Patent No. 15,238 of 1899 was obtained by the same inventors for improvements designed to obviate objections found to attach to retorts constructed on the ordinary Young and Beilby system. In the use of such retorts, composed of an upper metallic section and a lower fire-brick section, with chambers or hoppers at their upper ends, these upper ends became gradually filled up with hard carbonaceous matter, and this necessitated the periodical stopping of the working to have such matter removed. Moreover, the shale residues became fluxed and fixed to the walls of the lower section of the retorts. The residues were further liable to pass through the retort in an imperfectly exhausted condition, and to pass more quickly down the front or side of the retort next the discharging door. It was also found that when air and steam were used difficulties arose in regulating the quantities and proportions of steam and air used to burn the carbon out of the shale residues while preventing obstructions due to fluxing of the residues. To overcome these drawbacks each retort is composed of four sections, viz. a hopper, redistillation chamber at the top, a metallic section, a fire-brick chamber, and a combustion chamber of large capacity at the bottom. The combustion chamber is not externally heated, but receives the spent shale from the retort in a red-hot condition, and the further supply of heat in this chamber is wholly due to the burning of the carbon by the introduced air and steam, the danger of the fluxing and fixing of the shale residue to the walls of the chamber being thus minimized. To successfully burn the carbon remaining in the shale residue when it reaches the combustion chamber, so as to obtain the maximum yield of ammonia, careful regulation of the quantity and proportions of the air and steam is necessary, and a special device is provided for this.

The important construction of retorts for which patent No. 26,647 of 1901 was granted to N. M. Henderson of the Broxburn Oil Works, relates to such retorts as are described in the same inventor's previous patent, No. 6726 of 1889. The patentee dispenses with the chamber or space between the upper and lower retorts, the upper cast-iron retorts being carried direct on the upper end of the lower brick retorts, thus forming practically one continuous retort from top to bottom; and instead of one toothed roller being employed for the purpose of withdrawing the exhausted residue, a pair of toothed rollers is used for each retort. This improved construction is stated to give "better and larger results with less labour and expense in working and for repairs."

The vapour from these retorts, amounting to about 3000 cub. ft. per ton, is partially condensed by being passed through 70 to 100 vertical 4-in. pipes, whose lower ends fit into a chest. About one-third of the vapour is condensed, the liquid, consisting of about 75% of ammoniacal liquor and 25% of crude oil, flowing into a separating tank, whence the two products are separately withdrawn for further treatment. Part of the uncondensed gas is sometimes purified and used for illuminating purposes, when it gives a light of about 25 candle-power. The remainder is used as fuel, usually after compression or scrubbing to remove all condensable vapours.

Crude shale-oil is of dark green colour, has a specific gravity 0·860 to 0·890, and as at present manufactured, with the newer forms of retorts, has a setting point of about 90° F. It contains from 70 to 80% of members of the paraffin and olefine series, together with bases of the pyridine series, and some cresols and phenols. Beilby states that average Scotch shale-oil contains from 1·16 to 1·45% of nitrogen, mainly removable by sulphuric acid of specific gravity 1·220, and mostly remaining in the pitchy residues left on distillation. The lightest distillate, known as naphtha, contains from 60 to 70% of olefines and other hydrocarbons acted upon by fuming nitric acid, and the lubricating oils consist mainly of olefines. The paraffin wax chiefly distils over with the oil of specific gravity above 0·840.

In the refining of crude shale-oil, the greatest care is exercised to prevent dissociation of the paraffin, large volumes of super-heated steam being passed into the still, through a perforated pipe, at a pressure of from 10 to 40 ℔, to facilitate distillation at the lowest possible temperature. The original system of intermittent distillation is now employed only at the works of Young's Company. The stills have cast-iron bottoms and malleable-iron upper parts, their former capacity being 1200 to 1400 gallons, but those now made usually holding 2000 to 2500 gallons. Each still has its own water-condenser, the flow of water being regulated according to the nature of the distillate. The usual condensing surface is 230 ft. of 4-in. pipe. The process now in general practice is, with slight variations, the Henderson system of continuous distillation (patent No. 13,014 of 1885). It consists of a primary wagon-still, connected with two side-stills, which are further connected with pot-shaped coking-stills. The oil is heated in feed-heaters by the gases evolved from the hottest still before passing into the first still, where the temperature is so regulated as to drive off only naphtha up to about 0·760 specific gravity. The heavier portion of the oil passes to the other stills, the outermost receiving the heaviest only.

In both these systems the naphtha is collected separately, while the remainder of the distillate, known as "once-run oil," is condensed without fractionation. This "once-run oil" is treated with sulphuric acid and alkali at a temperature of 100° F. In agitators of varying construction—some being horizontal cylinders with a shaft carrying paddles, while others take the form of vertical cylindrical tanks with egg-shaped bottoms—in which agitation is produced by means of compressed air. The loss of oil during the agitation is estimated at 1·5 to 2·0 %.

The oil is next fractionated, either by the intermittent or the continuous system. After the most volatile fractions have distilled off, steam is blown in through a pipe at the bottom of the still. In many cases the distillate, with a density up to

0·770, constitutes the crude naphtha, and that up to a density of 0·850 the burning oil. The remainder of the distillate, which solidifies at common temperatures; consists chiefly of lubricating oils and paraffin. These three fractions are delivered from the condensers into separate tanks. Although the crude-oil stills of Henderson may be employed for the continuous distillation of the once-run or other oils obtained in the process of refining, the inventor prefers another form of apparatus which he patented in 1883 (No. 540), and this is now generally used. This consists of three horizontal cylindrical stills, 7 ft. in diameter and 19 ft. in length. The oil enters through a pipe which passes through one end of the still and discharges at the opposite end, while the outlet-pipe is fitted below the inlet-pipe at the bottom of the end through which the latter passes, inlet and discharge being thus as far as possible from each other. The oil circulates as in the crude-oil stills. The burning oil is next treated with acid and alkali, and subsequently again fractionally distilled, the heavier portion yielding paraffin scale, while the residues are redistilled. The final chemical purification of the burning oil resembles that last referred to, but only half the quantity of acid is employed. The lighter products of these distillations form the crude shale naphtha, which is treated with acid and alkali, and redistilled, when the lightest fractions constitute the Scotch " gasoline " of commerce, and the remainder is known as " naphtha."

The solid paraffin, which is known in its crude state as paraffin scale, was formerly produced from the heavy oil obtained in the first, second and third distillations, that from the first giving " hard scale," while those from the second and third gave " soft scale." The hard scale was crystallized out in shallow tanks, and the contained oil driven out by compression of the paraffin in filter bags. Soft scale was obtained by refrigeration, cooled revolving drums being caused to dip into trays containing the oil, when the paraffin adhered to the drums and was scraped off by a mechanical contrivance. Later improved appliances have aimed at the slow cooling of oil in bulk, whereby large crystals of paraffin are produced. Several processes have been invented, the most generally used being that patented by Henderson (No. 9557 of 1884). His cooler consists of a jacketed trough having a curved bottom, and divided into a series of transverse casings by metal disks, each consisting of two thin plates bolted together, but with a space between, in which, as also in the jacket surrounding the trough, cold brine is circulated. The paraffin crystallizes on the cold surfaces, from which it is constantly removed by scrapers, so that successive portions of the oil are cooled. The solid paraffin accumulates in a well or channel, where it is stirred up by rotary arms, so that it may be readily drawn away by a pump to the filter-press, whereby the solid paraffin is freed from oil. In the improved process of cooling employed at the works of the Oakbank Oil Company the oil to be cooled is pumped through coils submerged in the expressed oil from the filter-presses into the inner space of vertical coolers formed of two cast-iron tubes, and thence direct to the filter-presses. In the inner chamber of the coolers are fitted revolving scrapers, while in the outer annular space compressed ammonia is expanded.

The crude paraffin is then refined, for which purpose the " naphtha treatment " was formerly employed, but this has now given place almost entirely to the " sweating process." In the former the paraffin is dissolved in naphtha and then crystallized out. The sweating process consists in heating the crude wax to such a temperature that the softer portions are melted and flow away with the oil. In the process patented by N. M. Henderson (Nos. 1292 of 1887 and 11,799 of 1891), a chamber, 52 ft. by 13 ft. by 10 ft. high, heated by steam-pipes, and provided with large doors and ventilators for cooling, is fitted with a number of superimposed trays, 21 ft. by 6 ft. by 6 in. deep. These rest on transverse heating pipes, and each tray has a diaphragm of wire gauze. The bottoms communicate with short pipes fitted with swivel nozzles, worked on a vertical shaft. The diaphragms are covered with ½ in. of water, and the crude paraffin is melted and pumped through charging-pipes on to its surface. When the paraffin has solidified, the water is drawn off, leaving the cake resting on the gauze. Doors and ventilators are then closed, and the chamber is heated, whereupon the liquefied impurities are drained off until the outflowing paraffin sets on a thermometer bulb at 130° F. The remainder is melted and decolorized by agitation with finely powdered charcoal. The charcoal is mainly separated by subsidence, and the paraffin drawn off into filters, whence, freed from the suspended charcoal, it runs into moulds, and is thus formed into cakes of suitable size for packing. The lubricating oils are refined by the use of sulphuric acid and alkali, substantially in the same manner as the burning oils.

The following table shows the average yield, in 1895, of the various commercial products from crude shale-oil at two of the principal Scottish refineries. The percentages are, however, often varied to suit market requirements:—

Young's Paraffin Light and Mineral Oil Co.

	%
Gasoline and naphtha	6·09
Burning oils	31·84
Intermediate and heavy oils	23·97
Paraffin scale	13·53
Total	75·43
Loss	24·57
	100·00

Broxburn Oil Co.

	%	
Naphtha		3·0
Burning oil	30·0	
Gas oil	9·0	
		39·0
Lubricating oil		18·0
Paraffin		10·0
Loss		30·0
		100·0

From the ammoniacal liquor the ammonia is driven off by the application of heat in stills, the evolved vapour being conducted into " cracker-boxes," which are now usually of circular form, from 5 to 8 in. in diameter, and 6 to 12 in. in depth. In these boxes the ammonia is brought into contact with sulphuric acid of about 50° Tw., and is thus converted into sulphate. Wilton's form of cracker-box, which is now generally in use, is provided with an arrangement for the automatic discharge on to a drying table of the sulphate of ammonia as it is deposited in the well of the box, and the process is worked continuously. For the heating of the ammoniacal liquor the ordinary horizontal boiler-stills formerly used have been superseded by " column-" stills, in which the liquor is exposed over a large area, as it passes from top to bottom of the still, to the action of a current of steam. (B. R.)

PARAFFIN, in chemistry, the generic name given to the hydrocarbons of the general formula C_nH_{2n+2}. Many of these hydrocarbons exist as naturally occurring products, the lower (gaseous) members of the series being met with as exhalations from decaying organic matter, or issuing from fissures in the earth; and the higher members of the series occur in petroleum (chiefly American) and ozokerite. They may be synthetized by reducing the alkyl halides (preferably the iodides) with nascent hydrogen, using either sodium amalgam, zinc and hydrochloric acid, concentrated hydriodic acid (Berthelot, Jour. Pharm. 1868, 104, p. 103), aluminium amalgam (H. Wislicenus, ibid., 1896 (2), 54) or the zinc-copper couple (J. H. Gladstone and A. Tribe, Ber., 1873, 6, p. 202 seq.) as reducing agents.

They may also be derived from alkyl halides by heating to 120–140° with aluminium chloride in the proportion of three molecules of alkyl halide to one molecule of aluminium chloride (B. Köhnlein, Ber., 1883, 16, p. 560); by heating with zinc and water to 150–160° C. (E. Frankland, Ann., 1849, 71, p. 203; 1850, 74, p. 41), $2RI+2Zn+2H_2O = 2RH+ZnI_2+Zn(OH)_2$; by conversion into zinc alkyls, which are then decomposed by water, $ZnR_2+2H_2O=2RH+Zn(OH)_2$; by conversion into the Grignard reagent with metallic magnesium and decomposition of this either by water, dilute acids or preferably ammonium chloride (J. Houben, Ber., 1903, 38, p. 3019), $RMgI+H_2O = RH + MgI(OH)$; by the action of potassium hydride (H. Moissan, Comptes rendus, 1902, 134, p. 389); and by the action of sodium, in absolute ether solution (A. Wurtz, *Ann. chim. phys.*, 1855, (3), 44, p. 275). $2RI+2Na=R\cdot R+2NaI$. They may also be obtained by the reduction of the higher fatty acids with hydriodic acid (F. Krafft, *Ber.*, 1882, 15, pp. 1687, 1711), $C_nH_{2n}O_2+6HI = C_nH_{2n+2}+2H_2O+3I_2$; by the conversion of ketones into ketone chlorides by the action of phosphorus pentachloride, these being then reduced by hydriodic acid,

$$(C_nH_{2n+1})_2 CO \rightarrow (C_nH_{2n+1})_2CCl_2 \rightarrow (C_nH_{2n+1})_2CH_2;$$

by the reduction of unsaturated hydrocarbons with hydrogen in the presence of a " contact " substance, such, for example, as reduced nickel, copper, iron or cobalt (P. Sabatier and J. B. Senderens, *Ann. chim. phys.*, 1905 [8], 4, pp. 319, 433); by the elimination of carbon dioxide from the fatty acids on heating their salts with soda-lime or baryta, $CH_3CO_2Na+NaOH = CH_4+Na_2CO_3$, or by heating their barium salts with sodium methylate *in vacuo* (I. Mai, *Ber.*, 1889, 22, p. 2133); by the electrolysis of the fatty acids (H. Kolbe, *Ann.*, 1849, 69, p. 257), $2C_2H_5O_2 = C_2H_6+2CO_2+H_2O$; and by the action of the zinc alkyls on the ketone chlorides, $(CH_3)_2CCl_2+Zn(CH_3)_2=C_5H_{12}+ZnCl_2$.

The principal members of the series are shown in the following table:—

Name.	Formula.	Melting-point.	Boiling-point.
Methane	CH_4	-184°	-164° (760 mm.)
Ethane	C_2H_6	-172·1°	-84·1° (749 „)
Propane	C_3H_8	-45°	-44·5°
Normal Butane	C_4H_{10}	—	+1°
Isobutane	C_4H_{10}	—	-17°
Normal Pentane	C_5H_{12}	—	+36·3°
Secondary Pentane	„	—	+30·4°
Tertiary Pentane	„	—	+9·5°
Hexane	C_6H_{14}	—	+69°
Heptane	C_7H_{16}	—	98-99°
Octane	C_8H_{18}	—	125-126°
Nonane	C_9H_{20}	-51°	150°
Decane	$C_{10}H_{22}$	-31°	173·4°
Undecane	$C_{11}H_{24}$	-26·5°	196°
Dodecane	$C_{12}H_{26}$	-12°	214-216°
Tridecane	$C_{13}H_{28}$	-6·2°	234°
Tetradecane	$C_{14}H_{30}$	+4°	252°
Pentadecane	$C_{15}H_{32}$	+10°	270°
Hexadecane	$C_{16}H_{34}$	+18°	287°
Heptadecane	$C_{17}H_{36}$	+22°	170° (15 mm.)
Octadecane	$C_{18}H_{38}$	+28°	317°
Nonadecane	$C_{19}H_{40}$	+32°	330°
Eicosane	$C_{20}H_{42}$	+37°	205° (15 mm.)
Heneicosane	$C_{21}H_{44}$	+40°	215° („ „)
Docosane	$C_{22}H_{46}$	+44°	224° („ „)
Tricosane	$C_{23}H_{48}$	+48°	234° („ „)
Tetracosane	$C_{24}H_{50}$	+51°	243° („ „)
Hexacosane	$C_{26}H_{54}$	—	—
Hentriacontane	$C_{31}H_{64}$	-68°	302° (15 mm.)
Dotriacontane	$C_{32}H_{66}$	-70·5°	331° („ „)
Pentatriacontane	$C_{35}H_{72}$	+75°	331° („ „)
Dimyricyl	$C_{60}H_{122}$	+102°	—

The lowest members of the series are gases at ordinary temperature; those of carbon content C_5 to C_{15} are colourless liquids, and the higher members from C_{16} onwards are crystalline solids. The highest members only volatilize without decomposition when distilled under diminished pressure. They are not soluble in water, although the lower and middle members of the series are readily soluble in alcohol and ether, the solubility, however, decreasing with increase of molecular weight, so that the highest members of the series are almost insoluble in these solvents. The specific gravity increases with the molecular weight but always remains below that of water. The paraffins are characterized by their great inertness towards most chemical reagents. Fuming sulphuric acid converts the middle and higher members of the series into sulphonic acids and dissolves the lower members (R. A. Worstall, *Amer. Chem. Journ.*, 1898, 20, p. 664). Dilute nitric acid, when heated with the paraffins in a tube, converts them into secondary and tertiary nitro-derivatives (M. Konowalow, *Ber.*, 1895, 28, p. 1852), whilst long boiling with strong nitric acid or nitro-sulphuric acid converts the middle and higher members of the series partly into primary mono- and di-nitro compounds and partly oxidizes them to carbonic, acetic, oxalic and succinic acids (Worstall, *ibid.*, 20, p. 202; 21, p. 211). Fuming nitric acid only reacts slowly with the normal paraffins at ordinary temperature, but with those containing a tertiary carbon atom the reaction is very energetic, oxidation products (fatty acids and dibasic acids) and a small quantity of polynitro compounds are obtained (W. Markownikow, *Centralblatt*, 1899, 1, p. 1064; *Ber.*, 1899, 32, p. 1441). Chlorine reacts with the paraffins, readily substituting hydrogen. Isomeric hydrocarbons in this series first appear with butane, the number increasing rapidly as the complexity of the molecule increases. For a means of determining the number of isomers see E. Cayley, *Ber.*, 1875, 8, p.1056; F. Hermann, *Ber.*, 1898, 31, p. 91.

For *Methane* see MARSH GAS. *Ethane*, C_2H_6, occurs in crude petroleum. It may be prepared by the general methods given above; by heating mercury ethyl with concentrated sulphuric acid (C. Schorlemmer, *Ann.*, 1864, 132, p. 234); or by heating acetic anhydride with barium peroxide (F. Schützenberger, *Zeit. für Chemie*, 1865, p. 703). $2(CH_3CO)_2O+BaO_2=C_2H_6+Ba(C_2H_3O_2)_2+2CO_2$. It is a colourless gas which can be liquefied at 4° C. by a pressure of 46 atmospheres. By slow combustion it yields first water and acetaldehyde, which then oxidizes to oxides of carbon and water (W. A. Bone; see FLAME), whilst in ozonized air at 100° it gives ethyl alcohol, together with acetaldehyde and traces of formaldehyde (Bone, *Proc. Chem. Soc.*, 1904, 20, p. 127).

Dimyricyl (hexacontane), $C_{60}H_{122}$, is prepared by fusing myricyl iodide with sodium (C. Hell and C. Hägele, *Ber.*, 1889, 22, p. 502). It is only very slightly soluble in alcohol and ether.

PARAGON, a term for that which is a model of excellence or pattern of perfection, hence some person or thing which has no equal. The word was adopted from the O. Fr. *paragon*, Mod. *parangon*, Ital. *paragone* and Span. *paragon*. The Spanish has usually been taken as the source, and the word explained as from the prepositional phrase *para con*, in comparison with. But the word first appears in Italian, meaning a " touchstone." The Italian word may be connected with the Gr. παρακονᾶν, to sharpen by the use of a whetstone (ἀκονή). The term has been used in several technical applications, *e.g.* in printing, of a large style of type between " great primer " and " double pica," now usually called " two-line long primer "; of a diamond weighing more than 100 carats; and formerly of a fabric used for hangings in the 17th and 18th centuries.

PARAGRAPH, a term for a section or division of written or printed matter, which, as beginning a new subject, marking a break in the subject, &c., is signified by beginning the section on a new line set back or indented; also by the symbol, now ¶, a reversed P, formerly ℂ or D, to mark such a division. The Gr. παραγραφή (παρά and γράφειν, to write alongside or beside) was used of the short horizontal line or stroke which marked a line in a MS. where such a division occurs; and παραγραφή of a marginal note, also the division so marked. The word " paragraph," besides these technical typographical meanings, is also applied to the separate numbered sections in an affidavit or other legal document, or in a statute, &c., and in journalism to a short item of news or brief notice of events.

PARAGUAY, an inland republic of South America, between 20° 16' 14" and 26° 31' S. and 54° 37' and 62° W. It is bounded on the N.W. by Bolivia, N. and E. by Brazil, S.E., S. and W. by Argentina. Pop. (1905 estimate), 631,347, including 50,000 Iguassú Indians; area, about 97,700 sq. m.

By the treaty of 1872 the Brazilian frontier was drawn up the Paraná from the mouth of the Iguassú or Y-Guazú (25° 30' S.) to the Salto Grande or Great Cataract of La Guayra (24° 7'), thence west along the watershed of the Sierra de Maracayú, north along the Sierra de Ambaya to the sources of the Apá, and down that stream to its junction with the Paraguay. The Buenos Aires treaty of the 3rd of February 1876 fixed the frontier between Argentina and Paraguay, and assigned to Paraguay the portion of the Gran Chaco between Rio Verde and Bahia Negra; the appropriation of the portion between Rio Verde and the Pilcomayo was submitted to the arbitration of the president of the United States, who in 1878 assigned it to Paraguay. The frontier line towards Bolivia has long been in dispute.

Physical Features.—The river Paraguay, running from north to south, divides the republic into two sections, the eastern section, or Paraguay Oriental, being the most important. The western section forms part of the great plain called the Gran Chaco (see ARGENTINA), and is to a large extent unexplored. Paraguay proper, or the country between the Paraguay and the Paraná, is traversed from north to south by a broad irregular belt of highlands, which are known as the Cordillera Ambaya, Cordillera Urucury, &c., but partake rather of the character of plateaus, and form a continuation and outwork of the great interior plateau of Brazil. The elevation nowhere much exceeds 2200 ft. On the western side these highlands terminate with a more or less sharply defined edge, the country sloping gradually up to their bases in gentle undulations with open, ill-defined valleys; on the eastern side they send out broad spurs enclosing deep-cut valleys, and the whole country retains more of an upland character. The tributaries that flow westward to the Paraguay are consequently to some extent navigable, while those that run eastward to the Paraná are interrupted by rapids and falls, often of a formidable description. The Pilcomayo, the largest western tributary of the Paraguay, and an important frontier river, is only navigable in its upper and lower reaches. From the Asuncion plateau southwards, near the confluence of the Paraguay and Paraná, there is a vast stretch of marshy country, draining partly into the Ypoa lagoon, and smaller tracts of the same character are found in other parts of the lowlands, especially in the valley of the Paraguay. Many parts of the country sloping to the Paraná are nearly covered with dense forest, and have been left in possession of the sparsely scattered native tribes. But the country sloping to the Paraguay, and comprising the greater part of the settled districts, is, in keeping with its proximity to the vast plains of Argentina, grassy and open, though the hills are usually covered with forest and clumps of trees are frequent in the lowlands. Except in the marshy regions and along the rivers, the soil is dry, porous and sandy.

Geology.—Little is known of the geology of Paraguay. A large part of the area is covered by Quaternary deposits, which completely conceal the solid foundation on which they rest. The hills and plateaus appear to be composed chiefly of the same sandstone series which in the Brazilian province of Rio Grande do Sul contains seams of coal, with plant remains similar to those of the Karharbári series of India (Permian or Upper Carboniferous). It is probable, also, that the Palaeozoic rocks of Matto Grosso extend into the northern part of the country.

Minerals.—The gold mines said to have been concealed by the Jesuits may have had no existence; and though iron was worked by F. S. Lopez at Ibicuy (70 m. south-east of Asuncion), and native copper, oxide of manganese, marbles, lime and salt have been found, the real wealth of the country consists rather in the variety and value of its vegetable products.

Climate and Fauna.—The year in Paraguay is divided into two seasons—"summer," lasting from October to March, and "winter," from April to September. December, January and February are generally the hottest months, and May, June, July and August the coldest. The mean temperature for the year seems to be about 75° or 76°; for summer 81°, for winter 71°. The annual rainfall is about 46 in., fairly well distributed throughout the year, though the heaviest precipitation occurs in August, September and October. The prevailing winds blow from the north or south. The south wind is dry, cool and invigorating, and banishes mosquitoes for a time; the north wind is hot, moist and relaxing. Violent wind storms generally come from the south.

The fauna of Paraguay proper is practically the same as that of Brazil. Caymans, water-hogs (*capinchos*), several kinds of deer (*Cervus paludosus* the largest), ounces, opossums, armadillos, vampires, the American ostrich, the ibis, the jabiru, various species popularly called partridges, the *pato real* or royal duck, the *Palamedes cornuta*, parrots and parakeets, are among the more notable forms. Insect life is peculiarly abundant; the red stump-like ant-hills are a feature in every landscape, and bees used to be kept in all the mission villages.

Population.—The great majority of the inhabitants are of Indian (Guarani) descent, with very slight traces of foreign blood. Civilization has not made much progress, and the habits of the people are more primitive than those in the more advanced neighbouring republics. As a general rule the Paraguayans are indolent, especially the men. Climatic conditions obviate the necessity of any superfluity of clothing. A cotton chemise, and a white *manta* wrapped in Moorish fashion over

head and body, constitute the dress of the women; a cotton shirt and trousers that of the men. Boots and shoes are worn only by the upper classes. Goitre and leprosy are the only endemic diseases; but the natives, being underfed, are prone to diarrhoea and dyspepsia. The common language of the country is Guarani, although in a few districts Tupi is spoken. The country people as a rule understand a little Spanish, if living near any trading centre. "New Australia" is a pastoral and agricultural settlement, originally founded in 1893 by immigrants from Australia as an experiment in communism. The colony failed at first, and was reconstituted in 1894. The settlers numbered 161 in 1908. Immigration is on a small scale (1024 in 1908), but tends to increase; it is encouraged by the government, which seeks to divert to Paraguay some portion of the Italian labour immigrant into Brazil and Argentina. In 1908 the total foreign population numbered about 18,000, half of whom were natives of Argentina. The principal towns are Asuncion, the capital (pop. 1905, 60,250), Villa Rica (25,000), Concepcion (15,000) and Villa del Pilar (10,000); these are described in separate articles. Encarnacion on the Paraná has a large transit trade.

Government.—The constitution of the republic was voted by a constituent assembly on the 25th of November 1870. Legislative power is vested in a Congress consisting of a Senate and a Chamber of Deputies, elected by universal manhood suffrage in the proportion of one senator for every 12,000 inhabitants and one deputy for every 6000. Every member of Congress receives a salary of about £200. The head of the executive is the president, chosen by an electoral college for four years, and only re-eligible after eight consecutive years. He is aided by a cabinet of five ministers, responsible to Congress. Should he die during his term, or otherwise become unable to fulfil his duties, the president is succeeded by the vice-president (similarly elected), who is *ex officio* chairman of the Senate. The highest judicial authority is the Supreme Court, which is empowered to decide upon the constitutional validity of acts passed by Congress; its three members are appointed for four years by Congress, subject to the approval of the president. There are five courts of appeal, and inferior tribunals in all the large towns. The civil and criminal codes at Argentina have been adopted, almost without change. For purposes of local administration the republic is divided into 23 counties (*partidos*), which are subdivided into communes.

Religion and Instruction.—Roman Catholicism is the established religion, but the constitution guarantees full liberty to all other creeds. Asuncion, the only bishopric in the state, is in the archiepiscopal province of Buenos Aires. Education is backward and was long neglected. By law it is free and compulsory, but in some districts the attendance of many children is impossible. In 1907 there were 554 primary schools with 41,000 pupils.

Defence.—In 1908 the standing army, including cavalry, infantry and artillery, numbered about 1150 men; and there were five government steamers used for transport and revenue purposes.

Finance.—The financial situation of Paraguay has been a source of anxiety for many years. In 1885, after interest had been unpaid for 11 years on bonds amounting to £1,505,400, an agreement was made for the issue of new scrip to the value of £850,000 in quittance of all claims for capital and arrears of interest, certain public lands being also ceded to the bondholders as compensation. In 1895 an arrangement was made for a reduction of the rate of interest, for the funding of the arrears, and for the creation of a sinking fund. The government were unable to meet their obligations under the new contract, and in 1898 the outstanding amount had risen to £994,600. Provision has now been made for the service of this foreign debt, and the authorities have been able regularly to meet the service of the coupons. The total outstanding on the 31st of December 1908 was £831,850. Besides the London debt, there are many other claims on Paraguay, including (1908) about £1,050,000 due to Brazil, about £2,500,000 due to Argentina, and an internal debt of £850,000. The guarantee debt due to the Paraguay Central railway exceeds £1,500,000; and the total indebtedness of the republic on the 31st of December 1908 may be estimated at £7,650,000.

The revenue is derived mainly from import duties, and the most important branches of expenditure are the salaries of public officials, the army, public instruction and debt. The estimated revenue and expenditure for the three years 1906–1908 are shown in the following table:—

	1906	1907	1908
Revenue Expenditure	£452,812 454,564	£635,000 677,982	£599,828 506,502

The budget for 1906 remained in force in 1907 and 1908.

Industry.—The principal industries are the cultivation and preparation of *yerba maté* (Paraguayan tea), cattle-farming, fruit-growing, tobacco-planting and timber-cutting. *Yerba maté*, classified as *Ilex paraguayensis*, is a shrub. The leaves are stripped, withered, rolled and sorted, then packed in sacks and exported, chiefly to Argentina. Paraguayan tea is used in place of the ordinary tea or coffee in many parts of South America. Medical experts state that the beverage infused from the leaves has a stimulating effect, and is also slightly diuretic. The total amount exported from Paraguay in 1908 was 4133 tons. The majority of the *yerbales* (tea plantations) were formerly the property of the government, but have been acquired by private enterprise. An important feature about *yerba maté* is the small expense necessary for its production, and the cheap rate, notwithstanding the high tariff on its importation, at which it can be placed on the Argentine market as compared with ordinary tea or Brazilian coffee.

The cattle industry comes next in importance. The number of animals was estimated at 5,500,000 on the 31st of December 1908; an increase of about 45% since the census of 1899. The animals are small, but Durham and Hereford bulls have been introduced from Argentina to improve the breed. The increase in the herds has caused the owners of *saladero* establishments in Argentina and Uruguay to try the working of factories in Paraguay for the preparation of *tasajo* (jerked beef) and the manufacture of extract of meat. Both grasses and climate are against sheep-farming on a large scale.

Oranges are exported to Buenos Aires, Rosario and Montevideo, and are largely used for fattening hogs. The orange groves are often uncultivated, but yield abundantly; 10,700,000 dozens of oranges were exported in 1908. Pineapples are also exported, and sugar-cane, cotton, coffee and ramie are cultivated. Tobacco, although of inferior quality, is grown to a considerable extent; the quantity exported rose from about 35 tons in 1900 to 5014 tons in 1908. Tobacco is chiefly exported to Germany. The staple diet of the Paraguayans is still, as when the Spaniards first came, maize and mandioca (the chief ingredient in the excellent *chipa* or Paraguayan bread), varied, it may be, with the seeds of the *Victoria regia*, whose magnificent blossoms are the great feature of several of the lakes and rivers.

The forests abound in such timber as quebracho, cedar, curupey, lapacho and urundey. Some of these, such as the lapacho and quebracho, are of rare excellence and durability, as is shown by the wonderful state of preservation in which the woodwork of early Jesuit churches still remains. Fifteen plants are known to furnish dyes, and eight are sources of fibre—the caraguatay especially being employed in the manufacture of the exquisite *ñanduty* or spider web lace of the natives. Rum, sugar, bricks, leather, furniture and extract of meat are manufactured.

Commerce.—The commercial situation of Paraguay has improved in consequence of the investment of foreign capital in industrial enterprise. The principal articles imported are textiles, hardware, wines, rice, flour, canned goods and general provisions; the exports are *yerba maté*, hides, hair, dried meat, wood, oranges, tobacco. Most of the export trade is with Buenos Aires or Montevideo. The values for the five years 1904–1908 were:—

	1904	1905	1906	1907	1908
Imports Exports	£713,146 639,252	£935,703 566,602	£1,253,439 539,028	£1,572,255 647,222	£814,591 773,419

Of the imports into Paraguay, 29% came from Germany in 1908, 21% from the United Kingdom and 19% from Argentina.

Communications.—Numerous ocean-going liners, most of which fly the Brazilian or the Argentine flag, ply on the Paraguay and the Paraná, smaller vessels ascend the tributary streams, which are also utilized for floating lumber down to the ports. Out of 1320 ships which entered Asuncion in 1908 and 1184 which cleared, none was of British or United States nationality. The Brazilian Lloyd S.S. Co. provides direct and regular communication between Asuncion and New York. The only railway in the republic is the Paraguay Central which was open in 1906 between Asuncion and Pirapó (154 m.). The completion of the line to Encarnacion was then undertaken (1906–1911), a train-ferry across the Paraná affording connexion with Posadas. These extensions, and the alteration of gauge to that of the Argentine North-Eastern, were carried out mainly at the cost of the Argentine government, which acquired a controlling interest in the Paraguay Central. They were intended to shorten the journey between Buenos Aires and Asuncion from 5 days to 36 hours. There are some fairly good wagon roads, and the government appropriates annually a considerable sum for their extension.

Post and Telegraph.—Paraguay entered the Universal Postal Union in 1884. Telegraph lines connect Asuncion with other towns, and two cables put the republic in communication with the rest of the world by way of Corrientes and Posadas.

Money and Credit.—The banks open for business in 1904 were the Mercantile Bank, the Territorial Bank, the Bank of Los Rios & Co., and the Agricultural Bank: the last named has a capital of £207,590, advanced by the government, and lends money to the agricultural and industrial classes. The Paraguayan Bank, with a capital of £600,000, was opened in 1905, and the state bank (Banco de la República), with a total authorized capital of £4,000,000, was opened on the 30th of June 1908. The Conversion Office, which is authorized to sell or lend gold, receives a fixed revenue of £30,000 from certain import and export dues; it was reorganized in 1903 for the administration of the public debt. In the same year the gold and silver coinage of Paraguay were legally standardized as identical with those of Argentina (5 gold dollars or pesos = £1); but paper money is about the only circulating medium, and gold commands a high premium (1600% in December 1908). The normal value of the paper or currency dollar is about 4s. 8d. (For purposes of conversion the gold dollar has been taken at 5 = £1 throughout this article, and the currency dollar at 50 = £1.)

Weights and Measures.—The metric system is officially adopted, but the weights in common use are the *tonelada* (2025 lb), the *quintal* (101·4 lb), the *arroba* (25·35 lb), the *libra* (1·014 lb) and the *onza* (·0616 lb). The unit for liquid measure is the *cuarta* (·1665 gallon); for dry measure the *almud* (·66 bushel) and *fanega* (1½ bushels). The land measures are the *legua* (2·689 m.), the *sino* (69½ sq. yds.), and the *legua cuadrada* (12½ sq. m.).

History.—In 1527 Sebastian Cabot reached Paraguay and built a fort called Santo Espiritu. Asuncion was founded on the 15th of August 1535 by Juan de Ayolas, and his successor, Martinez de Irala, determined to make it the capital of the Spanish possessions east of the Andes. From this centre Spanish adventurers pushed east to La Guayra, beyond the Paraná, and west into the Gran Chaco; and before long vast numbers of the less warlike natives were reduced to serfdom. The name Paraguay was applied not only to the country between the Paraguay and the Paraná, but to the whole Spanish territory, which now comprises parts of Brazil, Uruguay and the Argentine provinces of Buenos Aires, Entre Rios, Corrientes, Misiones, and part of Santa Fé. It was not till 1620 that Paraguay proper and Rio de la Plata or Buenos Aires were separated as distinct governments, and they were both dependent on the vice-royalty of Peru till 1776, when Buenos Aires was erected into a vice-royalty, and Paraguay placed under its jurisdiction. The first Christian missions in Paraguay were established by the Franciscans—Armenta, Lebron, Solano (who was afterwards canonized as the "Apostle of Paraguay") and Bolanos—between 1542 and 1560; but neither they nor the first Jesuit missionaries, Salonio, Field and Ortega, were allowed to make their enterprise a permanent success. This fell to the lot of the second band of Jesuits, Cataldino, Mazeta and Lorenzana, who began work in 1605. Though they succeeded in establishing a kind of *imperium in imperio*, and were allowed to drill the natives to the use of arms, the Jesuits never controlled the government of Paraguay; indeed they had nearly as often to defend themselves from the hostility of the governor and bishop at Asuncion as from the invasions of the Paulistas or Portuguese settlers of São Paulo. It was only by the powerful assistance of Zabala, governor of Buenos Aires, that the anti-Jesuit and quasi-national party which had been formed under Antequera was crushed in 1735. In 1750, however, Ferdinand VI. of Spain ceded to the Portuguese, in exchange for the fortified village of Colonia del Sacramento (Uruguay), both the district of La Guayra and a territory of some 20,000 sq. m. east of the Uruguay. The Jesuits resisted the transference, and it was only after several engagements that they were defeated by the combined forces of Spain and Portugal. The treaty was revoked by Spain in 1761, but the missions never recovered their prosperity, and the Jesuits were finally expelled in 1769. In 1811 Paraguay declared itself independent of Spain; by 1814 it was a despotism in the hands of Dr J. G. R. Francia (*q.v.*). On Francia's death, in 1840, the chief power passed to his nephew, Carlos Antonio Lopez (*q.v.*), who in 1862 was succeeded by his son Francisco Sólano Lopez. In 1864 a dispute arose between the younger Lopez and the Brazilian government, and Lopez marched an army through Argentine territory to invade southern Brazil.

This act induced the governments of Brazil, Uruguay and Argentina to combine for the purpose of suppressing Lopez. The invasion of Paraguay then took place, and a struggle involving an enormous sacrifice of life and treasure lasted for five years, only coming to a close when the Paraguayan forces were totally defeated and Lopez was killed at the battle of Aquidaban on the 1st of March 1870. During this warfare every male Paraguayan capable of bearing arms was forced to fight, whole regiments being formed of boys of from 12 to 15 years of age. Even women were used as beasts of burden to carry ammunition and stores, and when no longer capable of work were left to die by the roadside or murdered to avoid any ill consequences occurring from their capture. When the war broke out the population of Paraguay was 1,337,439; when hostilities ceased it consisted of 28,746 men, 106,254 women above 15 years of age, and 86,079 children. During the retreat of the Paraguayans the dictator ordered every town and village passed through to be razed to the ground, and every living animal for which no use could be found to be slaughtered. When the end came the country and people were in a state of absolute prostration.

After the death of Lopez the government was administered by a triumvirate consisting of Cirilo Rivarola, Carlos Loizaga and José Diaz de Bedoza, until, in November 1870, the present constitution was formulated. The policy of Brazil was for a time directed towards the annexation of Paraguay; the debt due to Brazil on account of the war was assessed at £40,000,000, a sum which Paraguay could never hope to pay; and it was not until 1876 that the Brazilian army of occupation was wholly withdrawn. But the rivalry between Brazil and Argentina, and the necessity of maintaining the balance of power among the South American republics, enabled Paraguay to remain independent. No violent constitutional change took place after 1870, though there have been spasmodic outbreaks of revolution, as in 1881, in 1894, in 1898, in December 1904—when a somewhat serious civil war was ended by the peace of Pilcomayo—in July 1908 and in September 1909. None of these disturbances deeply or permanently affected the welfare of the republic, nor were all of them accompanied by bloodshed. Under the presidency of J. B. Egusquiza (1894-1898) the boundary dispute with Bolivia became acute; but war was averted, largely owing to the success of the revolution, which forced the president to resign. The main interest of recent Paraguayan history is economic rather than political. In that history the gradual development of commerce, the financial reforms in 1895, and the extension of the Paraguay Central railway after 1906, were events of far greater importance than any political movement which took place between 1870 and 1910.

BIBLIOGRAPHY.—For an account of physical features, inhabitants, products, &c., see H. Decoud, Geografía de la república del Paraguay (5th ed., Leipzig, 1906); E. de B. La Dardye, Paraguay: the Land and its People, ed. E. G. Ravenstein (London, 1892); W. Vallentin, Paraguay: das Land der Guaranis (Berlin, 1907); R. V. F. Trevenfeld, Paraguay in Wort und Bild (Berlin, 1904); H. Mangels, Wirtschaftliche, naturgeschichtliche und klimaiologische Abhandlungen aus Paraguay (Munich, 1904); W. B. Grubb, Among the Indians of the Paraguayan Chaco (London, 1904); E. Bolland, Exploraciones practicadas en el Alto Paraguay y en la Laguna Gaiba (Buenos Aires, 1901). Commerce and Finance: British consular reports (London, annual); Report of the Council of the Corporation of Foreign Bondholders (London, annual); statistical publications of the Paraguay government and presidential messages, in Spanish (Asuncion, annual); Revue du Paraguay (Asuncion, monthly); Paraguay (Washington, Bureau of Amer. Republics, 2nd ed. 1902). History: P. de Angelis, Colección de documentos, &c. (1835); H. Charlevoix, Histoire de Paraguay (1835); G. Funes, Ensayo de la história civil del Paraguay, &c. (1816); Lozano, História de la conquista del Paraguay (Buenos Aires, 1873-1874); R. B. Cunninghame Graham, A Vanished Arcadia (London, 1901); C. A. Washburn, The History of Paraguay (New York, 1871); E. C. Jourdan, Guerra do Paraguay (Rio de Janeiro, 1890); R. F. Burton, Letters from the Battlefields of Paraguay (London, 1870); A. Audibert, Question de limites entre el Paraguay y Bolivia (Asuncion, 1901); H. Decoud, List of Books . . . relating to Paraguay (Washington, 1905).

PARAHYBA (PARAHIBA or PARAHYBA DO NORTE), a state of north-eastern Brazil, bounded N. by Rio Grande do Norte, E. by the Atlantic, S. by Pernambuco, and W. by Ceará. Pop.

(1890), 457,232; (1900), 490,784. Area, 28,854 sq. m. It consists of a narrow coastal zone, 30 to 40 m. wide, along the seaboard, behind which the country rises sharply to a highland region forming part of the great central plateau of Brazil. The long, dry season (April to October), together with occasional devastating droughts (sêccas) lasting two or more years, prevents the development of forests and damages the agricultural and pastoral industries of the state. There is only one river of importance, the Parahyba do Norte, which crosses the southern part of the state from west to east with a course of about 240 m. The state is poorly watered and covered with a scanty vegetation suitable for pasturage only. Stock-raising is favoured by the existence of a bromeliaceous plant, called macambira, which is sufficiently juicy to satisfy the thirst of the animals. On the low lands and along some of the river valleys agriculture is the chief occupation of the people; cotton and sugar are largely produced and some tobacco is grown. The exports include hides, skins, cotton, sugar and tobacco. Rubber of the Ceará type is also found and forms an item among the smaller exports. The eastern extremity of the state is served by a railway originally called the Conde d'Eu railway but now forming part of the Great Western of Brazil system, which runs westward and northward from Parahyba to Independencia (71 m.), where it connects with the extension of the Natal and Nova Cruz line, and a branch runs southward to Pilar, 15 m. from its junction and 46 m. from Parahyba. Another small branch runs westward from the station of Mulungú to Alagôa Grande (14 m.). The capital is Parahyba (q.v.), and other important towns, with the populations (in 1890) of their municipalities, which include large rural districts and sometimes several other towns, are: Arcia (26,590); Bananeiras (20,058); Campina Grande (21,475); Guarabira (26,625); Manānguape (20,754); Pilar (10,133, town); Pombal (12,804); and Souza (11,135).

Parahyba formed part of the original grant, known as the capitania of Itamaracá, from the Portuguese crown to Pero Lopes de Souza. It was not settled until 1584, when a fort was erected near the present port of Cabedello under the name of São Filippe.

PARAHYBA (PARAHYBA DO NORTE), a city and port of Brazil, capital of Parahyba state, on the right bank of the Parahyba do Norte river, 11 m. above its mouth and 65 m. N. of Recife. Pop. (1890), 18,645, including several suburbs and Cabedello; (1908, estimate), 30,000. Parahyba is the starting-point of the Conde d'Eu railway, now a part of the Great Western of Brazil system, which includes a main line to Independencia, where it connects with the Natal & Nova Cruz line of Rio Grande do Norte, and a branch to Cabedello. The entrance to the Parahyba do Norte River being obstructed by a stone reef and sand bars, only vessels drawing less than 14 ft. can effect an entrance. The "Varadouro," as the lower part of the city is called, is built on the margin of the river and is devoted principally to commerce. Behind this is a low hill on whose northern slope and broad summit the upper city is built, and a tramway line runs to the suburb of Trincheira. There are some good public buildings, including the parish church (matris) of N.S. das Neves, the old Franciscan convent and church, the government palace, and the treasury. There are a normal school, a lyceum, a national gymnasium, and a school for marine apprentices. Parahyba was founded in 1585. It was called Frederickstadt by the Dutch, who occupied the Franciscan convent as a government house, and Felippéa in honour of the king of Spain when the Dutch were expelled. Its original name was resumed on the separation (1640) of Portugal and her colonies from Spanish rule.

PARAHYBA DO SUL, a river of Brazil, having its source on the campos of Bocaina, on the northern slope of the Serra do Mar in the western part of the state of São Paulo, and flowing at first south-westerly and then after a horse-shoe curve in the vicinity of Jacarehy in a general E.N.E. direction to the Atlantic in lat. 21° 38' S. Its upper course for a distance of 80 m., or to the confluence of the Parahybuna, is known as the Parahytinga. The navigable channel from São Fidelis to the

Atlantic is 54 m. long, and the total length of the river, including the Parahytinga, is 540 m. Its source is about 4920 ft. above sea-level. The Parahyba passes through a fertile, long-settled country, a part of which was for many years the principal coffee-producing region of Brazil. Its lower course passes through the rich alluvial sugar-producing district of Campos. Among the towns on the Parahyba are Campos, São Fidelis, Parahyba do Sul, Juiz de Fora, Barra do Pirahy (railway junction), Rezende, Queluz and Lorena.

PARALDEHYDE, in medicine, a clear colourless liquid (for the chemistry see ALDEHYDES), soluble in 1 in 10 of water and freely in alcohol. Paraldehyde is a powerful hypnotic, giving a refreshing quiet sleep which is not followed by unpleasant after effects. As it does not depress the heart when used in medicinal doses, it may be given to patients suffering from cardiac disease. It is much used to produce sleep in the insane. As it is largely excreted by the lungs it may be found useful in bronchial asthma. When taken continuously the drug soon loses its power as a hypnotic. Its unpleasant taste usually prevents the formation of a paraldehyde habit, but it occasionally occurs with symptoms resembling delirium tremens. When taken in an overdose paraldehyde kills by producing respiratory failure.

PARALLAX (Gr. παραλλάξ, alternately), in astronomy, the apparent change in the direction of a heavenly body when viewed from two different points. Geocentric parallax is the angle between the direction of the body as seen from the surface of the earth and the direction in which it appears from the centre of the earth. Annual parallax is the angle between the direction in which a star appears from the earth and the direction in which it appears from the centre of the sun. For stellar parallaxes see STAR; the solar parallax is discussed below.

SOLAR PARALLAX.—The problem of the distance of the sun has always been regarded as the fundamental one of celestial measurement. The difficulties in the way of solving it are very great, and up to the present time the best authorities are not agreed as to the result, the effect of half a century of research having been merely to reduce the uncertainty within continually narrower limits. The mutations of opinion on the subject during the last fifty years have been remarkable. Up to about the middle of the 19th century it was supposed that transits of Venus across the disk of the sun afforded the most trustworthy method of making the determination in question; and when Encke in 1824 published his classic discussion of the transits of 1761 and 1769, it was supposed that we must wait until the transits of 1874 and 1882 had been observed and discussed before any further light would be thrown on the subject. The parallax 8·5776″ found by Encke was therefore accepted without question, and was employed in the *Nautical Almanac* from 1834 to 1869. Doubt was first thrown on the accuracy of this number by an announcement from Hansen in 1862 that the observed parallactic inequality of the moon was irreconcilable with the accepted value of the solar parallax, and indicated the much larger value 8·97″. This result was soon apparently confirmed by several other researches founded both on theory and observation, and so strong did the evidence appear to be that the value 8·95″ was used in the *Nautical Almanac* from 1870 to 1881. The most remarkable feature of the discussion since 1862 is that the successive examinations of the subject have led to a continually diminishing value, so that at the present time it seems possible that the actual parallax of the sun is almost as near to the old value of Encke as to that which first replaced it. The value of 8·848″, determined by S. Newcomb, was used from 1882 to 1900; and since then the value 8·80″ has been employed, having been adopted at a Paris conference in 1896.[1]

Five fundamentally different methods of determining the distance of the sun have been worked out and applied. They are as follows:—

I. That of direct measurement.—From the measures of the parallax of either Venus or Mars the parallax of the sun can be immediately derived, because the ratios of distances in the solar system are known with the last degree of precision. Transits of Venus and observations of various kinds on Mars are all to be included in this class. *(Methods of Determining the ...)*

II. The second method is in principle extremely simple, consisting merely in multiplying the observed velocity of light by the time which it takes light to travel from the sun to the earth. The velocity is now well determined; the difficulty is to determine the time of passage.

III. The third method is through the determination of the mass of the earth relative to that of the sun. In astronomical practice the masses of the planets are commonly expressed as fractions of the mass of the sun, the latter being taken as unity. When we know the mass of the earth in gravitational measure, its product by the denominator of the fraction just mentioned gives the mass of the sun in gravitational measure. From this the distance of the sun can be at once determined by a fundamental equation of planetary motion.

IV. The fourth method is through the parallactic inequality in the moon's motion. For the relation of this inequality to the solar parallax see MOON.

V. The fifth method consists in observing the displacement in the direction of the sun, or of one of the nearer planets, due to the motion of the earth round the common centre of gravity of the earth and moon. It requires a precise knowledge of the moon's mass. The uncertainty of this mass impairs the accuracy of the method.

I. To begin with the results of the first method. The transits of Venus observed in 1874 and 1882 might be expected to hold a leading place in the discussion. No purely astronomical enterprise was ever carried out on so large a scale or at so great an expenditure of money *(Transits of Venus)* and labour as was devoted to the observations of these transits, and for several years before their occurrence the astronomers of every leading nation were busy in discussing methods of observation and working out the multifarious details necessary to their successful application. In the preceding century reliance was placed entirely on the observed moments at which Venus entered upon or left the limb of the sun, but in 1874 it was possible to determine the relative positions of Venus and the sun during the whole course of the transit. Two methods were devised. One was to use a heliometer to measure the distance between the limbs of Venus and the sun during the whole time that she was seen projected on the solar disk, and the other was to take photographs of the sun during the period of the transit and subsequently measure the negatives. The Germans laid the greatest stress on measures with the heliometer; the Americans, English, and French on the photographic method. These four nations sent out well-equipped expeditions to various quarters of the globe, both in 1874 and 1882, to make the required observations; but when the results were discussed they were found to be extremely unsatisfactory. It had been supposed that, with the greatly improved telescopes of modern times, contact observations could be made with much greater precision than in 1761 and 1769, yet, for some reason which it is not easy to explain completely, the modern observations were but little better than the older ones. Discrepancies difficult to account for were found among the estimates of even the best observers. The photographs led to no more definite result than the observations of contacts, except perhaps those taken by the Americans, who had adopted a more complete system than the Europeans; but even these were by no means satisfactory. Nor did the measures made by the Germans with heliometers come out any better. By the American photographs the distances between the centres of Venus and the sun, and the angles between the line adjoining the centres and the meridian, could be separately measured and a separate result for the parallax derived from each. The results were:—

Transit of 1874:	Distances; par.	=8·888″,
	Pos. angles; „	=8·873″,
Transit of 1882:	Distances; „	=8·873″,
	Pos. angles; „	=8·772″,

[1] R. S. Ball, *Spherical Astronomy*, p. 303.

The German measures with the heliometer gave apparently concordant results, as follows:—

Transit of 1874: par. = 8·876″.
Transit of 1882: „ = 8·879″.

The combined result from both these methods is 8·857″, while the combination of all the contact observations made by all the parties gave the much smaller result, 8·794″. Had the internal contacts alone been used, which many astronomers would have considered the proper course, the result would have been 8·776″.

In 1877 Sir David Gill organized an expedition to the island of Ascension to observe the parallax of Mars with the heliometer. **Planetary** By measurements giving the position of Mars among **Parallaxes.** the neighbouring stars in the morning and evening, the effect of parallax could be obtained as well as by observing from two different stations; in fact the rotation of the earth carried the observer himself round a parallel of latitude, so that the comparison of his own morning and evening observations could be used as if they had been made at different stations. The result was 8·78″. The failure of the method based on transits of Venus led to an international effort carried out on the initiative of Sir David Gill to measure the parallax by observations on those minor planets which approach nearest the earth. The scheme of observations was organized on an extended scale. The three bodies chosen for observation were: Victoria (June 10 to Aug. 26, 1889); Iris (Oct. 12 to Dec. 10, 1888); and Sappho (Sept. 18 to Oct. 25, 1888). The distances of these bodies at the times of opposition were somewhat less than unity, though more than twice as great as that of Mars in 1877. The drawback of greater distance was, however, in Gill's opinion, more than compensated by the accuracy with which the observations could be made. The instruments used were heliometers, the construction and use of which had been greatly improved, largely through the efforts of Gill himself. The planets in question appeared in the telescope as star-like objects which could be compared with the stars with much greater accuracy than a planetary disk like that of Mars, the apparent form of which was changed by its varying phase, due to the different directions of the sun's illumination. These observations were worked up and discussed by Gill with great elaboration in the *Annals of the Cape Observatory*, vols. vi. and vii. The results were for the solar parallax π:—

From Victoria, $\pi = 8\cdot801″ \pm 0\cdot006″$,
„ Sappho, $\pi = 8\cdot798″ \pm 0\cdot011″$,
„ Iris, $\pi = 8\cdot812″ \pm 0\cdot009″$.

The general mean result was 8·802″. From the meridian observations of the same planets made for the purpose of controlling the elements of motion of the planets Auwers found $\pi = 8\cdot806″$.

In 1898 the remarkable minor planet Eros was discovered, which, on those rare occasions when in opposition near perihelion, would approach the earth to a distance of 0·16. On these occasions the actual parallax would be six times greater than that of the sun, and could therefore be measured with much greater precision than in the case of any other planet. Such an approach had occurred in 1894, but the planet was not then discovered. At the opposition of 1900–1901 the minimum distance was 0·32, much less than that of any other planet. Advantage was taken of the occasion to make photographic measures for parallax at various points of the earth on a very large scale. Owing to the difficulties inherent in determining the position of so faint an object among a great number of stars, the results have taken about ten years to work out. The photographic right ascensions gave the values 8·80″ + 0·007″ ± 0·0027″ (Hinks) and 8·80″ + 0·0067″ ± 0·0025″ (Perrine); the micrometric observations gave the value 8·806″ ± 0·004 (Hinks).[1]

II. The velocity of light (q.v.) has been measured with all the precision necessary for the purpose. The latest result is 299,860 kilometres per second, with a probable error of perhaps 30 kilometres—that is, about the ten-thousandth part of the quantity itself. This degree of precision is far beyond any we

[1] *Mon. Not. R.A.S.* (May 1909,) p. 544; ibid. (June 1910), p. 588.

can hope to reach in the solar parallax. The other element which enters into consideration is the time required for light to pass from the sun to the earth. Here no such precision can be attained. Both direct and indirect methods are available. The direct method consists in observing the times of some momentary or rapidly varying celestial phenomenon, as it appears when seen from opposite points of the earth's orbit. The only phenomena of the sort available are eclipses of Jupiter's satellites, especially of the first. Unfortunately these eclipses cannot be observed without an error of at least several seconds, and not infrequently important fractions of a minute. As the entire time required for light to pass over the radius of the earth's orbit is only about 500 seconds, this error is fatal to the method. The indirect method is based upon the observed constant of aberration or the displacement of the stars due to the earth's motion. The minuteness of this displacement, about 20·50″, makes its precise determination an extremely difficult matter. The most careful determinations are affected by systematic errors arising from those diurnal and annual changes of temperature, the effect of which cannot be wholly eliminated in astronomical observation; and the recently discovered variation of latitude has introduced a new element of uncertainty into the determination. In consequence of it, the values formerly found were systematically too small by an amount which even now it is difficult to estimate with precision. Struve's classic number, universally accepted during the second half of the 19th century, was 20·445″. Serious doubt was first cast upon its accuracy by the observations of Nyrén with the same instrument during the years 1880–1882, but on a much larger number of stars. His result, from his observations alone, was 20·52″; and taking into account the other Pulkowa results, he concluded the most probable value to be 20·492″. In 1895 Chandler, from a general discussion of all the observations, derived the value of 20·50″. Since then, two elaborate series of observations made with the zenith telescope for the purpose of determining the variation of latitude and the constant of aberration have been carried on by Professor C. L. Doolittle at the Flower Observatory near Philadelphia, and Professor J. K. Rees and his assistants at the observatory of Columbia University, New York. Each of these works is self-consistent and seemingly trustworthy, but there is a difference between the two which it is difficult to account for. Rees's result is 20·47″; Doolittle's, from 20·46″ to 20·56″. This last value agrees very closely with a determination made by Gill at the Cape of Good Hope, and most other recent determinations give values exceeding 20·50″. On the whole it is probable that the value exceeds 20·50″; and so far as the results of direct observation are concerned may, for the present, be fixed at 20·52″. The corresponding value of the solar parallax is 8·782″. In addition to the doubt thrown on this result by the discrepancy between various determinations of the constant of aberration, it is sometimes doubted whether the latter constant necessarily expresses with entire precision the ratio of the velocity of the earth to the velocity of light. While the theory that it does seems highly probable, it cannot be regarded as absolutely certain.

III. The combined mass of the earth and moon admits of being determined by its effect in changing the position of the plane of the orbit of Venus. The motion of the node of **Mass of the** this plane is found with great exactness from observa- **Earth.** tions of the transits of Venus. So exact is the latter determination that, were there no weak point in the subsequent parts of the process, this method would give far the most certain result for the solar parallax. Its weak point is that the apparent motion of the node depends partly upon the motion of the ecliptic, which cannot be determined with equal precision. The derivation of the distance of the sun by it is of such interest from its simplicity that we shall show the computation.

From the observed motion of the node of Venus, as shown by the four transits of 1761, 1769, 1874 and 1882, is found

$$\text{Mass of (earth + moon)} = \frac{\text{Mass of sun}}{332600}.$$

In gravitational units of mass, based on the metre and second as units of length and time,

Log. earth's mass = 14·60052
„ moon's „   = 12·6895.

The sum of the corresponding numbers multiplied by 332600 gives

Log. sun's mass = 20·12773.

Putting a for the mean distance of the earth from the sun, and n for its mean motion in one second, we use the fundamental equation

$$a^3 n^2 = M_1 + M',$$

M_1 being the sun's mass, and M' the combined masses of the earth and moon, which are, however, too small to affect the result. For the mean motion of the earth in one second in circular measure, we have

$$n = \frac{2\pi}{31558149}; \log. n = 7\cdot29907$$

the denominator of the fraction being the number of seconds in the sidereal year. Then, from the formula

$$a^3 = \frac{M_1}{n^2} = \frac{[20\cdot12773]}{13\cdot59814}$$

we find

Log. a in metres =   11·17653
Log. equat. rad. ⊕ =   6·80470

Sine ☉'s eq. hor. par.   3·62817
Sun's eq. hor. par.   8·762".

IV. The determination of the solar parallax through the parallactic inequality of the moon's motion also involves two elements—one of observation, the other of purely mathematical theory. The inequality in question has its greatest negative value near the time of the moon's first quarter, and the greatest positive value near the third quarter. Meridian observations of the moon have been heretofore made by observing the transit of its illuminated limb. At first quarter its first limb is illuminated; at third quarter, its second limb. In each case the results of the observations may be systematically in error, not only from the uncertain diameter of the moon, but in a still greater degree from the varying effect of irradiation and the personal equation of the observers. The theoretical element is the ratio of the parallactic inequality to the solar parallax. The determination of this ratio is one of the most difficult problems in the lunar theory. Accepting the definitive result of the researches of E. W. Brown the value of the solar parallax derived by this method is about 8·773".

V. The fifth method is, as we have said, the most uncertain of all; it will therefore suffice to quote the result. which is

$$\pi = 8\cdot818".$$

The following may be taken as the most probable values of the solar parallax, as derived independently by the five methods we have described:—

From measures of parallax . 8·802"
„   velocity of light   . 8·781"
„   mass of the earth   . 8·762"
„   par. ineq. of moon   . 8·773"
„   lunar equation   . 8·818"

The question of the possible or probable error of these results is one on which there is a marked divergence of opinion among investigators. Probably no general agreement could now be reached on a statement more definite than this; the last result may be left out of consideration, and the value of the solar parallax is probably contained between the limits 8·77" and 8·80." The most likely distance of the sun may be stated in round numbers as 93,000,000 miles.   (S. N.)

PARALLELISM, PSYCHOPHYSICAL, in pyschology, the theory that the conscious and nervous processes vary concomitantly whether or not there be any causal connexion between them; in other words " that modifications of consciousness emerge contemporaneously with corresponding modifications of nervous process " (Stout). The theory is the third possible alternative in considering the relation between mind and body, the others being interaction and one-sided action (e.g. materialism). It should be observed that this theory is merely a statement, not an explanation. (See PSYCHOLOGY.)

PARALLEL MOTION, a form of link-work invented by James Watt, and used in steam-engines (see STEAM-ENGINE, § 88), to connect the head of the piston rod, moving up and down in a vertical path, with the end of the beam, moving in the arc of a circle. An ordinary form is shown diagrammatically in figure. MN is the path in which the piston-rod head, or crosshead, as it is often called, is to be guided. ABC is the middle line of half the beam, C being the fixed centre about which the beam oscillates. A link BD connects a point in the beam with a radius link ED, which

Watt's Parallel Motion.

oscillates about a fixed centre at E. A point P in BD, taken so that BP : DP :: EN : CM, move in a path which coincides very closely with the straight line MPN, Any other point F in the line CP or CP produced is made to copy this motion by means of the links AF and FG, parallel to ,BD and AC, In the ordinary application of .the parallel motion a point. such as F is the point of attachment of the piston-rod, and P is used to drive a pump-rod. Other points in the line CP produced are occasionally made use of by adding other links parallel to AC and BD,

Watt's linkage gives no more than an approximation to straight-line motion, but in a well-designed example the amount of deviation need not exceed one four-thousandth of the length of stroke. It was for long believed that the production of an exact straight-line motion by pure linkage was impossible, until the problem was solved by the invention of the Peaucellier cell. (See also MECHANICS; *Applied Mechanics*, §§ 77, 78.)

PARALLELS, in siegecraft, a term used to express the trenches drawn by besiegers in a generally parallel direction to the front of a fortress chosen for attack. Parallels are employed along with " zigzag approaches " in the " formal attack " or siege proper. They are traced in short zigzag lengths (the prolongation of each length falling clear of the hostile works), in order to avoid enfilade; but their obliquity is of course made as slight as is consistent with due protection in order to save time and labour. The " first parallel " is opened at a convenient distance from the fortress, by numerous working parties, who dig (under cover of night) a continuous line of entrenchments facing the point or points of attack. Zigzags are next dug to the rear (when necessary) to give sheltered access to the parallel, and from this new zigzags are pushed out towards the defenders, to be connected by a " second parallel," and so on until finally a parallel is made sufficiently close to the fortress to permit of an assault over the open, the parallels becoming stronger and more solid as they approach to closer range. This system of parallels provides, within range of the defenders' weapons, shelter in which the besieger can safely mass men and material for the prosecution of the attack. Parallels and approaches are constructed either by ordinary " trench work," executed simultaneously by a large number of men strung out along the intended line, or by " sapping " in which one trained " sapper," as it were, burrows a trench in the required direction, others following him to widen and improve the work.

PARALUS and **SALAMINIA,** the name of two ancient Athenian triremes used for sacred embassies, the conveyance of despatches and tribute money, the transportation of state criminals, and as flagships in time of war. It is probable that a third vessel of the same kind (called Delia) was used exclusively for Delian embassies, although it has been identified by some with the Salaminia.

PARALYSIS, or **PALSY** (from Gr. παράλυσις, to relax; Wycliffe has *palsy*, and another old form of the word is *parlesy*), a term which in its wider acceptation indicates abolition of motor, sensory, sensorial or vaso-motor functions, but in medical nomenclature is usually restricted to the loss or impairment of voluntary muscular power. Paralysis is to be regarded rather as a symptom than a disease *per se*; it may arise (1) from injury or disease of nervous and muscular structures, and is then termed *organic paralysis*; or (2) from purely dynamic disturbances in the nervous structures of the brain which preside over voluntary movement. The latter is *functional motor paralysis*, a symptom common in certain neuroses, especially hysteria. For *general paralysis of the insane*, see INSANITY.

Whether the loss of motor power be functional or organic in origin, it may be generalised in all the muscles of the body, or localized to one or many. The different forms of paralysis of the voluntary muscles which may arise from organic disease can be understood by a consideration of the motor path of voluntary impulses from brain to muscle. There are two neural segments in this path, an upper cerebral and a lower spinal; the former has its departure platform in the brain and its terminus in the whole of the anterior grey matter of the spinal cord, whence issues the lower spinal segment of the motor path to the muscles. The nerve fibres of the upper cerebral segment are prolongations of the large psycho-motor cells; the nerve fibres of the lower segment are prolongations by the anterior roots and motor nerves of the large cells in the grey matter of the cord. Disease or destruction of any part of the upper cerebral segment will give rise to loss of voluntary power, for the influence of the mind on the muscles is removed in proportion to the destruction of this efferent path (see diagram in NEUROPATHOLOGY). Disease or destruction of the lower spinal segment causes not only loss of voluntary power but an atrophy of the muscles themselves. Paralysis may therefore be divided into three great groups: (1) loss of voluntary power without muscular wasting except from disuse, and without electrical changes in the muscles due to injury or disease of the upper cerebral segment of the motor path of volition; (2) loss of muscular power with wasting and electrical changes in the muscles due to disease or injury of the lower spinal segment formed by the cells of the grey matter of the spinal cord, the anterior roots and the peripheral motor nerves; (3) primary wasting of the muscles.

The more common forms of paralysis will now be described.

1. *Hemiplegia*, or paralysis affecting one side of the body, is a frequent result of apoplexy (*q.v.*); there is loss of motion of the tongue, face, trunk and extremities on the side of the body opposite the lesion in the brain. In a case of severe complete hemiplegia both arm and leg are powerless; the face is paralysed chiefly in the lower part, while the upper part moves almost as well as on the unparalysed side, and the eye can be shut at will, unlike peripheral facial paralysis (Bell's palsy). The tongue when protruded deviates towards the paralysed side, and the muscles of mastication contract equally in ordinary action, although difficulty arises in eating, from food accumulating between the cheek and gums on the paralysed side. Speech is thick and indistinct, and when there is right-sided hemiplegia in a right-handed person, there may be associated various forms of aphasia (*q.v.*), because the speech centres are in the left hemisphere of the brain. Some muscles are completely paralysed, others are merely weakened, while others, *e.g.* the trunk muscles, are *apparently* unaffected. In many cases of even complete hemiplegia, improvement, especially in children, takes place after a few weeks or months, and is generally first indicated by return of movement in the muscles which are habitually associated in their action with those of the opposite unparalysed side; thus, movement of the leg returns first at the hip and knee joints, and of the arm at the shoulder and elbow, although the hand may remain motionless. The recovery however in the majority of cases is only partial, and the sufferer of hemiplegia is left with a permanent weakness of one side of the body, often associated with contracture and rigidity, giving rise to a characteristic gait and attitude. The patient in walking leans to the sound side and swings round the affected leg from the hip, the inner side of the toe of the boot scraping the ground as it is raised and advanced. The arm is adducted at the shoulder, flexed at the elbow, wrist and fingers, and resists all attempts at extension. According to the part of the brain damaged variations of paralytic symptoms may arise; thus occasionally

the paralysis may be limited more or less to the face, the arm or the leg. In such case it is termed a *monoplegia*, a condition sometimes arising from cerebral tumour. Occasionally the face is paralysed on one side and the arm and leg on the other side; this condition is termed *alternate hemiplegia*, which is due to the fact that the disease has damaged the motor path from the brain to the leg and arm before it has crossed over to the opposite side, whereas the path to the face muscles is damaged after it has crossed. In rare cases both leg, arm and face on one side may be paralysed—*triplegia*; or all four limbs—*bilateral hemiplegia*. Infantile spastic paralysis, *infantile diplegia*, or as it is sometimes called Little's disease, is a *birth palsy* caused by injury from protracted labour, the use of forceps or other causes. The symptoms are generally not observed until long after birth. Convulsions are common, and the child is unable to sit up or walk long after the age at which it should do so.

Paraplegia is a term applied to paralysis of the lower extremities; there are many causes, but in the great majority of instances it arises from a local or general disease or injury of the spinal cord. A localized transverse myelitis will interrupt the motor and sensory paths which connect the brain with the spinal grey matter below the lesion, and when the destruction is complete, motor and sensory paralysis in all the structures below the injury results; thus fracture, dislocation and disease of the spinal column (*e.g.* tubercular caries, syphilitic disease of the membranes, localized tumours and haemorrhages) may cause compression and inflammatory softening, and the result is paralysis of the voluntary muscles, loss of sensation, loss of control over the bowel and bladder, and a great tendency to the development of bed-sores. The muscles do not waste except from disuse, nor undergo electrical changes unless the disease affects extensively the spinal grey matter or roots as well as the cerebral path. When it does so, as in the case of *acute spreading myelitis*, the symptoms are usually more severe and the outlook is more grave.

In cases of *focal myelitis* from injury or disease, recovery may take place and the return of power and sensation may occur to such an extent that the patient is able to walk long distances; this happy termination in cases of localized disease or injury of the spinal cord often takes place by keeping the patient on his back in bed, daily practising massage and passive movements, and so managing the case as to avoid bedsores and septic inflammation of the bladder—the two dangerous complications which are liable to arise.

2. Paralysis may result from acute inflammatory affections of the spinal cord involving the grey and white matter—*myelitis* (see NEUROPATHOLOGY).

Infantile or Essential Paralysis.—This is a form of spinal paralysis occurring with frequency in young children; in Scandinavian countries the disease is prevalent and sometimes assumes an epidemic form, whereby one is led to believe that it is due to an infective organism. The names *infantile* and *essential* paralysis were given before the true nature of the disease in the spinal cord was known; precisely the same affection may occasionally occur, however, in adults, and then it is termed *adult spinal paralysis*. The medical name for this disease is *acute anterior poliomyelitis* (Gr. πολιός, grey, and μυελός, marrow), because the anterior grey matter of the spinal cord is the seat of acute inflammation, and destruction of the spinal motor nerve path to the muscles. The extent of the spinal grey matter affected and the degree of destruction of the motor nerve elements which ensues determine the extent and permanency of the paralysis. The term *atrophic spinal paralysis* is sometimes employed as indicating the permanent wasting of muscles that results.

Infantile paralysis often commences suddenly, and the paralysis may not be observed until a few days have elapsed; the earliest symptoms noticeable are fever, convulsions and sometimes vomiting; and, if the child is old enough, it may complain of pains or numbness or tingling in the limb or limbs which are subsequently found to be paralysed. It is characteristic, however, of the disease that there is no loss of sensation in the paralysed limb. The whole of the limb is not necessarily paralysed, often it is only a group of muscles, and even if the paralysis affects both legs or the arm and leg on one side, it generally fails in the uniform distribution of the previously described paraplegia or hemiplegia. The affected muscles rapidly waste and become flaccid, the electrical reactions change, and finally the muscles may cease to respond to electrical stimulation whether of the continuous or interrupted current. In the less severe cases (and they are the most common) only a group of muscles undergo complete paralysis and atrophy, and there is always hope of some return of power in a paralysed limb. Associated with the withered condition of the limb due to the muscular atrophy is an enfeebled circulation, rendering the limb cold, blue and livid; the nutrition of the bones and other parts is involved, so that a limb paralysed in early infancy does not grow and is shorter than its fellow. Deformities arise, some the result of simply failing muscular support; others due to permanent changes in the position of the limbs, for example clubfoot. There is absence of bladder and bowel troubles, and bedsores do not occur; the disease itself is rarely, if ever, fatal. About a month after the onset of the disease local treatment of the atrophied muscles should be commenced, and every effort should be made by massage, by suitable positions and passive movements to promote the circulation and prevent deformities in the affected limbs. Should these measures fail, surgical aid should be sought.

Sub-acute and chronic forms of atrophic and spinal paralysis have been described, but some of them were undoubtedly cases of peripheral neuritis.

Wasting Palsy. Progressive Muscular Atrophy.—This is a chronic disease characterized by slow and insidious weakness and wasting of groups of muscles due to disease of the anterior spinal grey matter. It begins mostly in adult life between 25 and 45 years of age, and affects males more than females. In the majority of cases it commences in the upper extremities, and the small muscles of the hand are especially liable to be affected. The palmar eminences of the thumb and little finger, owing to the wasting of the muscles, gradually disappear, and a flat ape-like hand is the result; in extreme cases all the small muscles of the hand are atrophied, and a claw-like hand is the result. The muscles which are next most liable to atrophy are those of the shoulder and upper arm, and the atrophy may thence spread to the muscles of the neck and trunk, and the intercostals and even the diaphragm may be affected, causing serious difficulties of respiration. The lower extremities are less often and later affected by wasting. This disease generally runs a slow and progressive course; it may however be years before it spreads from the hand to the arm, and a period of arrest may occur before other muscles become involved. A characteristic feature of the disease is fibrillary twitching of the wasting muscles. The electrical excitability of the muscles is diminished rather than changed, except where the wasting is very extreme, when a partial reaction of degeneration may be obtained. Sensation is unaffected, as the disease is limited to the motor cells of the anterior grey matter (see NEUROPATHOLOGY). There is no affection of the bowel or bladder. Death usually occurs from intercurrent diseases, *e.g.* bronchitis, pneumonia, or broncho-pneumonia. Some patients die owing to failure of the respiratory muscles; others from the disease spreading to the medulla oblongata (the bulb of the brain) and causing bulbar paralysis. The chronic morbid process leading to decay and destruction of the spinal motor cells which is the essential pathological feature of this disease is generally accompanied, and sometimes preceded, by degeneration of the path of voluntary impulses from the brain. It is then called *amyotrophic lateral sclerosis*, a rapid form of progressive muscular atrophy.

Bulbar Paralysis.—A number of different morbid conditions may give rise to a group of symptoms, the principal features of which are paralysis of the muscles concerned in speech, swallowing, phonation and mastication. These symptoms may arise suddenly from vascular lesions or inflammatory processes, which involve the nuclei of origin of the cranial nerves supplying the muscles of the tongue, lips, pharynx and larynx. But there is also a slow degenerative insidious *progressive bulbar paralysis* affecting both sexes pretty equally; it came on between 40 to 60 years of age, and the cause is unknown. Slight indistinctness of speech, especially in the utterance of consonants requiring the elevation of the tip of the tongue to the dental arch and palate, is usually the first symptom. Later the explosive lip sounds are indistinctly uttered; simultaneously, owing to paralysis of the soft palate, the speech becomes nasal in character and sooner or later, associated with this difficulty of speech, there is a difficulty of swallowing, partly because the tongue is unable to convey the food to the back of the mouth, and it accumulates between the cheeks and gums. Moreover the pharyngeal muscles are unable to seize the food and start the process of swallowing on account of the paralysis of the soft palate; liquids are apt to regurgitate through the nostrils, the patient must therefore be nourished with soft semi-solid food. As the disease proceeds, the difficulty of speech and swallowing is increased by the affection of the laryngeal muscles; the pitch of the voice is lowered and the glottis is imperfectly closed during deglutition; there is consequently a tendency for liquids and food to pass into the larynx and set up fits of coughing, which, however, are ineffectual. Later the muscles of mastication are affected and the disease may extend to the respiratory centre, giving rise to attacks of dyspnoea. The intellectual faculties are as a rule unimpaired, although the facial expression and the curious emotional mobility of the countenance, with a tendency of the patient to burst into tears or laughter, would suggest weak-mindedness. Whilst the lower half of the face is strikingly affected, the upper half retains its normal expression and power of movement. This disease is usually rapidly fatal, since it affects the vital centres, and liability to broncho-pneumonia excited by the entrance of food into the air passages is also a constant danger in the later stages.

Bulbar Paralysis without Anatomical Change.—This condition is also termed "myasthenia gravis"; it differs from acute and chronic bulbar disease by the absence of muscular atrophy, by normal electrical excitability of the muscles, by a marked development of the paralysis by fatigue, and by considerable remissions of the symptoms. The bulbar symptoms are the most prominent, but all voluntary muscles are more or less affected, especially the eye-muscles. It is a rare disease affecting both sexes equally at almost any age, the causes and pathology of which are unknown.

3. Paralysis resulting from disease or injury of the motor path to the muscles in the peripheral nervous system.

Neuritis.—Paralysis may arise in a muscle, a group of muscles, a whole limb, the lower extremities, or there may be a generalized paralysis of voluntary muscles as a result of neuritis. A typical example of neuritis giving rise to paralysis owing to inflammatory swelling and compression is afforded by the facial nerve; this purely motor nerve as it passes out of the skull through a narrow bony passage is easily compressed and its function interfered with, causing a paralysis of the whole of one side of the face and *Bell's Palsy*. Exposure to a cold draught in a person with rheumatic diathesis is a frequent cause. As an example of simple mechanical compression producing paralysis, *crutch palsy* may be cited; it is the result of continuous compression of the musculo-spiral nerve as it winds round the bone of the upper arm.

Lead poisoning may give rise to a localized neuritis affecting the posterior inter-osseous nerve, especially in painters and in those whose occupations necessitate excessive use of the extensors of the forearm; the result is *wrist drop* or *lead palsy*.

Sciatica is a painful inflammatory condition of the sciatic nerve, in which there may be weakness of the muscles; but inability to move the limb is more on account of the pain it causes than on account of paralysis of the muscles. Exposure to cold and wet, *e.g.* sitting on a damp seat, may lead to sciatica in a gouty or rheumatic person.

Multiple neuritis is a painful generalized inflammation of the peripheral nervous system and arises in many toxic conditions of the blood; among the most important are lead, arsenic and chronic alcohol poisoning. It also occurs in diabetes, diphtheria, beri-beri and other conditions (see NEUROPATHOLOGY). A short description of the commonest form will be given. It occurs in chronic alcoholism and especially in women, and is most frequently due to a combination of a septic absorption from some internal disease and the abuse of alcohol. In a marked case the patient may suffer from *paraplegia*, but it is distinguished from the paraplegia of spinal disease by the fact that there is loss of control of the sphincters only when there is associated dementia, and that instead of the limbs being insensible they are extremely painful on deep pressure. There is wasting of the muscles, and electrical changes in them; frequently there is anaesthesia and analgesia of the skin, which takes a stocking-like distribution. In severe cases the upper limbs may be affected, and all the muscles of the body are more or less liable to be paralysed—even the heart may· suffer. The mental condition in such a severe case is usually quite characteristic; there is delirium, the patient is the subject of hallucinations and delusions; there is loss of knowledge of time and place, and illusions of personal identity. A constant symptom is the loss of memory of recent events, while those of early life are easily recollected.

Paralyses—termed medically muscular dystrophies—may arise from a primary atrophy of muscle apparently independent of any discoverable change in the nervous system, but due to a *congenital* developmental defect of the muscles. Heredity plays an important part in the incidence of these diseases, members of the same family being affected with the same type of disease, and at the same period of life. There may be a tendency in a family to the affection of one sex and not the other; on the other hand, children of both sexes may suffer in the same family. It is curious that the majority of cases are males, and that it is transmitted by women who are not themselves its subjects. Many different clinical types have been described based upon the age of onset, the groups of muscles first affected, and the presence or absence of apparent hypertrophy; they are however all varieties of one affection, and in a case where there is an apparent enlargement of muscles there is really atrophy of the contractile muscle fibres and overgrowth of fat and interstitial fibrous tissue; consequently this form of the disease is called *pseudo-hypertrophic paralysis*.

The muscular dystrophies may be divided into two groups according to the period of life in which the malady manifests itself: (1) Those occurring in childhood; (2) those occurring in youth or adult life. In the first group the muscles may be atrophied or *apparently* hypertrophied. A progressive atrophy of muscles associated with progressive weakness and various disabilities of movement is soon recognized in the relation of cause and effect; but the parents whose first child looks like an infant Hercules, with abnormally large calves and buttocks, cannot for some time appreciate any connexion of this condition with a muscular weakness which is manifested in various ways. The child stands with its feet widely separated; it waddles along rather than walks; it falls easily and rises with difficulty, having to use the hands to push against the floor; it then rests one hand on the knee, and then the other hand on the other knee, and climbs, as it were, up its own thighs in order to assume the erect posture. In this pseudo-hypertrophic form of paralysis the outlook is very grave, and there is little hope of the patient reaching adult life.

Paralysis agitans, Shaking Palsy or Parkinson's Disease is a chronic progressive disease of the nervous system occurring late in life, and characterized by weakness, tremors and stiffness of the muscles associated with a peculiar attitude and gait. The first sign of the disease is weakness followed by tremor of one hand; this consists of continuous movements of the thumb and forefinger as in rolling a pill, or of movements of the hand like beating a tom-tom; then the hand is affected, and later there is tremor at the ankle. In some cases there is a continual nodding movement of the head. These tremors are at the rate of five per second and cease during sleep. The

attitude and gait are very characteristic; the head is bent forward, and the patient in beginning to walk takes slow steps, which soon become short and quick as if he were running after his centre of gravity. The intellect is clear and in marked contrast to the mask-like expression. This disease lasts for years, and but little can be done in the way of treatment, except passive movements of the limb to prevent contracture.

Treatment.—There are certain general principles in the treatment of all forms of paralysis which may be summarized as follows. 1. Rest in bed and attention to the vital functions of the body, the heart's action, the respiratory functions, nutrition and excretion. The pulse is the best guide to the administration of drugs and stimulants. As regards the respiratory function, one of the dangers of paralysis is an intercurrent pneumonia—sometimes unavoidable, often due, however, to attempts to give nourishment to a patient in an insensible state, with the result that some of the fluid enters the bronchial tubes, when either the reflex protective coughing is not excited or is ineffectual. Attention to the bowels and bladder is most important. A purge at the onset of paralysis is indicated when the pulse is full and of high tension, and the regular action of the bowels is necessary in all conditions. Retention of urine should be carefully avoided, if necessary by the passing of a catheter, but too much emphasis cannot be laid upon the importance of adopting aseptic precautions to avoid infection of the bladder. Daily inspection of the back should be made of all paralysed patients, and precautions taken to keep the skin of all parts exposed to pressure clean; the back should be laved with eau-de-Cologne or spirit to harden the skin. Any sign of a red spot on the back or buttock of the paralysed side should be a warning note of the possibility of a bedsore; zinc powder or ointment should be applied and the effect of pressure on the part be removed if possible by change of posture and by the use of a water-bed. It is important to cover all warm bottles with flannel, for owing to insensibility large blisters, which heal with difficulty, may result. In cases of paraplegia the legs should be covered with warm woollen hand-knitted stockings, and a cradle employed to protect the feet from the continuous weight of the bed-clothes, a fruitful source of foot drop. 2. As soon as the acute symptoms have passed off passive movement and massage may be employed with advantage; in some cases electrical treatment is indicated; but as a rule, especially in children, electrical treatment offers the disadvantage of being painful and not accomplishing more than can be effected by massage and passive movements. When the passive movements are being made the patient should be instructed by the operator to will the movement which he is performing, and thus try to re-establish the connexion of the brain with the muscles through the point of interruption or by a new path if that is not possible.

(F. W. MO.)

PARAMARIBO, the capital of Dutch Guiana or Surinam (see GUIANA), in 5° 44' 30" N., 55° 12' 54" W., 20 m. from the sea on the right bank of the Surinam, here a tidal river nearly a mile broad and 18 ft. deep. Pop. (1905), 33,821. Built on a plateau about 16 ft. above low-water level, Paramaribo is well-drained, clean and in general healthy. The straight canals running at right angles to the river, the broad, straight tree-planted streets, the spacious squares, and the solid plain public buildings would not be unworthy of a town in the Netherlands.

The Indian village of Paramaribo became the site of a French settlement probably in 1640, and in 1650 it was made the capital of the colony by Lord Willoughby of Parham. In 1683 it was still only a " cluster of twenty-seven dwellings, more than half of them grog-shops," but by 1790 it counted more than a thousand houses. The town was partly burned down in 1821, and again in 1832.

PARAMECIUM, O. F. Müller, (often misspelt Paramaecium, Paramoecium), a genus of aspirotrochous ciliate Infusoria (*q.v.*), characterized by its slipper-like shape, common in infusions, especially when they contain a little animal matter. It has two dorsal contractile vacuoles, each receiving the mouths of five radiating canals from the inner layer of the ectosarc, and a large ovoid meganucleus, and one or two micronuclei. From its abundance, the ease with which it can be cultivated and observed, its relatively simple structure and adequately large size ($\frac{1}{75}$ in.), it is most frequently selected for elementary study and demonstration, as well as for purposes of research.

PARAMENT (Fr. *parement*, from Late Lat. *paramentum*, adornment, *parare*, to prepare, equip), a term applied by ancient writers to the hangings or ornaments of a room of state.

PARAMOUNT (Anglo-Fr. *paramont*, up above, *par à mont*, up or on top of the mountain), superior, supreme, holding the highest authority, or being of the greatest importance. The word was first used, as a term of feudal law, of the lord, the "lord paramount," who held his fief from no superior lord, and was thus opposed to "mesne lord," one who held from a superior. To those who held their fiefs from one who was not a "lord paramount" was given the correlative term "paravail," *par à val*, in the valley. The word was confused by English lawyers with "avail," help, assistance, profit, and applied to the actual working tenant of the land, the lowest tenant or occupier.

PARANÁ, a state of southern Brazil, bounded N. by São Paulo, E. by the Atlantic, S. by Santa Catharina and the republic of Argentina, and W. by Matto Grosso and the republic of Paraguay, with the Paraná river as its western boundary line. Area, 85,451 sq. m.; pop. (1890), 249,491; (1900), 327,136. It includes two dissimilar regions—a narrow coastal zone, thickly wooded, swampy, and semi-tropical in character, and a high plateau (2500 to 3000 ft.) whose precipitous, deeply eroded eastern escarpments are known as the Serra do Mar, or Serra do Cubatão. The southern part of the state is densely forested and has large tracts of Paraguay tea (*Ilex paraguayensis*), known in Brazil as *herva maté*, or *matte*. The plateau slopes westward to the Paraná river, is well watered and moderately fertile, and has a remarkably uniform climate of a mild temperate character. The larger rivers of the state comprise the Parana-panema and its tributaries the Cinza-and Tibagy, the Ivahy, Piquiry, Jejuy-guassú, and the Iguassú with its principal tributary the Rio Negro. The Paranapanema and a small tributary, the Itararé, form the boundary line with São Paulo west of the Serra do Mar, and the Iguassú and Negro, the boundary line with Santa Catharina and Argentina—both streams having their sources in the Serra do Mar and flowing westward to the Paraná. The other streams have shorter courses, and all are obstructed by falls and rapids. Twenty miles above the mouth of the Iguassu are the Iguassú Falls, 215 ft. high, broken into twenty or more falls separated by rocks and islands, and surrounded by a wild, unsettled and wooded country. The falls are reached by occasional light-draught steamers on the Paraná between Posadas (Argentina) and the mouth of the Iguassú, and thence by canoe to the vicinity of the falls. The surface of the plateau is undulating and the greater part is adapted to agricultural and pastoral purposes. There are two railway systems—the Paranagua to Curityba (69 m.) with an extension to Ponta Grossa (118 m.) and branches to Rio Negro (55 m.), Porto Amazonas (6 m.) and Antonina (10 m.); and the São Paulo & Rio Grande, which crosses the state from northeast to south-west from Porto União da Victoria, on the Iguassú, to a junction with the Sorocabana line of São Paulo at Itararé. The upper Paraná is navigable between the Guayrá, or Sete Quedas, and the Urubu-punga Falls. The chief export of Paraná is Paraguay tea (a forest product). There is a large foreign element in the population owing to the immigrant colonies established on the uplands, and considerable progress has been made in small farming and education. Besides the capital, Curityba, the principal towns are Paranaguá; Antonina, at the head of the Bay of Paranaguá, with a population of 7739 in 1890; Campo Largo, 20 m. west of Curityba (pop. 10,642 in 1890); Castro, N.N.W. of the capital on the São Paulo & Rio Grande line (pop. of the municipio, 10,319 in 1890); and Ponta Grossa (pop. of municipio, 4774 in 1890), north-west of Curityba at the junction of the two railway systems of the state.

Paraná was settled by gold prospectors from São Paulo and formed part of that captaincy and province down to 1853, when it was made an independent province. The first missions of the Jesuits on the Paraná were situated just above the Guayrá Falls in this state and had reached a highly prosperous condition when the Indian slave hunters of São Paulo (called Mamelucos) compelled them to leave their settlements and emigrate in mass to what is now the Argentine territory of Misiones. The ruins of their principal mission, known as Ciudad Real, are overgrown with forest.

PARANÁ, a city and port of Argentina, capital of the province of Entre Rios, and the see of a bishopric, situated on the left bank of the Paraná river, 410 m. by navigable channels (about 240 m. direct) N.W. of Buenos Aires. Pop. (1895), 24,261; (1904, estimate), 27,000. The city occupies a gently rolling site 120 ft. above the river and about 2 m. from its riverside port of Bajada Grande, with which it is connected by railway, tramway and highway. It is classed as a seaport, and ocean-going vessels of not over 12 ft. draught can ascend to Bajada. There is also a daily ferry service across the river to Santa Fé (7 m. distant), which is connected by railway with Rosario and Buenos Aires. Paraná is also the western terminus of a provincial railway system, which connects with Concepción and Concordia, on the Uruguay river, and with other important towns of the province. The mean annual temperature is about 66° F. and the climate is bracing and healthful. Its port of Bajada Grande, on the river shore below the bluffs, has the custom-house and a fine wharf for the accommodation of the Entre Rios railway and river craft. Paraná was founded in 1730 by colonists from Santa Fé and was at first known as Bajada (a landing place). It was made the capital of the province by General Mansilla in 1821 (Concepción had previously been the capital), but in 1861 General Urquiza restored the seat of government to Concepción, where it remained until 1882, when Paraná again became the capital. Paraná was also the capital of the Argentine Confederation from 1852 to 1861.

PARANAGUÁ, a seaport of the state of Paraná, Brazil, on the southern shore of the Bay of Paranaguá, about 9 m. from the bar of the main channel. Pop. of the municipality (1890), 11,794, of which a little more than one half belonged to the town. Paranaguá is the principal port of the state, and is a port of call for steamers in the coastwise trade. It is the coastal terminus of a railway running to Curityba, the capital (69 m.), with extensions to other inland towns and a branch to Antonina, at the head of the bay, 10½ m. west of Paranaguá by water. Its exports consist chiefly of *maté*, or Paraguay tea. The town was founded in 1560.

The Bay of Paranaguá opens into the Atlantic in lat. 25° 32′ S. through three channels and extends westward from the bar about 19 m. It is irregular in outline, receives the waters of a large number of small streams, and is comparatively shallow. Light-draught steamers can ascend to Antonina at the head of the bay. The broad entrance to the bay, which is the gateway to the state of Paraná is nearly filled by the large Ilha do Mel (Honey Island) on which stands an antiquated fort commanding the only practicable channel.

PARANDHAR, a hill fort of British India, in Poona district, Bombay, 4472 ft. above the sea, 20 m. S.E. of Poona: pop. (1901), 944. It figures repeatedly in the rising of Sivaji against the Mahommedans, and was the favourite stronghold of the Peshwas whenever the unwalled city of Poona was threatened. It gave its name to a treaty with the Mahrattas, signed in 1776 but never carried into effect. It is now utilized as a sanatorium for British soldiers.

PARANOIA (Gr. παρά, beyond, and νοῦς, to understand), a chronic mental disease, of which systematized delusions with or without hallucinations of the senses are the prominent characteristics. The delusions may take the form of ideas of persecution or of grandeur and ambition; these may exist separately or run concurrently in the same individual, or they may become transformed in the course of the patient's life from a persecutory to an ambitious character. The disease may begin during adolescence, but the great majority of the subjects manifest no symptoms of the affection until full adult life.

The prominent and distinguishing symptom of paranoia is the delusion which is gradually organized out of a mass of original but erroneous beliefs or convictions until it forms an integral part of the ordinary mental processes of the subject and becomes fused with his personality. This slow process of the growth of a false idea is technically known as "systematization," and the resulting delusion is then said to be "systematized." As such delusions are coherently formed there is no manifest mental confusion in their expression. Notwithstanding the fixity of the delusion it is subject in some cases to transformation which permits of the gradual substitution of delusions of grandeur for delusions of persecution. It happens also that periods of remission from the influence of the delusion may occur from time to time in individual cases, and it may even happen, though very rarely, that the delusion may permanently disappear.

It is necessary to point out that there is undoubtedly what may be called a paranoiac mental constitution, in which delusions may appear without becoming fixed or in which they may never appear. The characteristics of this type of mind are credulity, a tendency to mysticism and a certain aloofness from reality, combined, as the case may be, with timidity and suspicion or with vanity and pride. On such a soil it is easy to understand that, given the necessary circumstances, a systematized delusional insanity may develop.

The term paranoia appears to have been first applied by R. von Krafft-Ebing in 1879 to all forms of systematized delusional insanity. Werner in 1889 suggested its generic use to supplant *Wahnsinn* and *Verrücktheit*, the German equivalents of mental states which originally meant, respectively, the delusional insanity of ambition and the delusional insanity of persecution—terms which had become hopelessly confused owing to divergences in the published descriptions of various authors.

The rapid development of clinical study has now resulted in the isolation of a comparatively small group of diseases to which the term is applied and the relegation of other groups bearing more or less marked resemblances to it to their proper categories. Thus, for example, it had formerly been held that acute paranoia was frequently a curable disease. It is now proved that the so-called acute forms were not true paranoias, many of them being transitory phases of E. Kraepelin's dementia praecox, others being terminal conditions of acute melancholia, or acute confusional insanity, or even protracted cases of delirium tremens. While it removes from the paranoia group innumerable phases of delusional insanity met with in patients labouring under secondary dementia as a result of alcoholism or acute insanity, such a statement does not exclude patients who may have had, during their previous life, one or more attacks of some acute mental disease, such as mania, for the paranoiac mental constitution may be, though rarely, subject to other forms of neurosis. Attempts have been made to base a differential diagnosis of paranoia upon the presence or absence of a morbid emotional element in the mind of the subjects, with the object of referring to the group only such cases as manifest a purely intellectual disorder of mind. Though in some cases of the disease the mental symptoms may, at the time of observation, be of a purely intellectual nature, the further back the history of any case is traced the greater is the evidence of the influence of preceding emotional disturbances in moulding the intellectual peculiarities. Indeed it may be said that the fundamental emotions of vanity or pride and of fear or suspicion are the groundwork of the disease. We are justified therefore in ascribing the intellectual aberrations which are manifested by delusions, in part at least, to the preponderating influence of morbid emotions which alter the perceptive and aperceptive processes upon which depend the normal relation of the human mind to its environment. Although, generally speaking, paranoiacs manifest marked intellectual clearness and a certain amount of determination of character in the exposition of their symptoms and in their manner of reacting under the influence of their delusions, there is, without any doubt, an element of original abnormality in their mental constitution. Such a mental constitution is particularly subject to emotional disturbances which find a favourable field of operation in an innate mysticism allied with credulity which is impervious to the rational appeal of the intellect. In those respects the paranoiac presents an exaggeration of, and a departure from, the psychical constitution of normal individuals, who, while subject both to emotion and to mystic thought, retain the power of correcting any tendency to the predominance of these mental qualities by an appeal to reality. It is just here that the paranoiac fails, and in this failure lies the key to the pathological condition. For the present the question as to whether this defect is congenital or acquired owing to some superimposed pathological condition cannot be answered. However that may be, it is frequently ascertained from the testimony of friends and relatives that the patients have always been regarded as "queer," strange, and different from other people in their modes of thought. It is usually stated that nervous or mental diseases occur in the family histories of over 50% of the subjects of this affection.

Paranoia is classified for clinical purposes according to the form of delusion which the patients exhibit. Thus there are described the Persecutory, the Litigious, the Ambitious and the Amatory types. It will be observed that these divisions depend upon the prevalence of the primary emotions of fear or suspicion, pride or vanity and love.

. According to V. Magnan, the course of paranoia is progressive, and each individual passes through the stages of persecution and ambition successively. Many authorities accept Magnan's description, which has now attained to the distinction of a classic, but it is objected to by others on the ground that many cases commence with delusions of ambition and manifest the same symptoms unchanged during their whole life, while other patients suffering from delusions of persecution never develop the ambitious form of the disease. Against these arguments Magnan and his disciples assert that the relative duration of the stages and the relative intensity of the symptoms vary widely; that in the first instance the persecutory stage may be so short or so indefinite in its symptoms as to escape observation; and that in the second instance the persecutory stage may be so prolonged as within the short compass of a human life to preclude the possibility of the development of an ambitious stage. As however there exist types of the disease which, admittedly, do not conform to Magnan's progressive form it will be more convenient to adopt the ordinary description here.

1. *Persecutory Paranoia.*—This form is characterized by delusions of persecution with hallucinations of a painful and distressing character. In predisposed persons there is often observed an anomaly of character dating from early life. The subjects are of a retiring disposition, generally studious, though not brilliant or successful workers. They prefer solitude to the society of their fellows and are apt to be introspective, self-analytical or given to unusual modes of thought or literary pursuits. Towards the commencement of the insanity the patients become gloomy, preoccupied and irritable. Suspicions regarding the attitude of others take possession of their minds, and they ultimately come to suspect the conduct of their nearest relatives. The conversations of friends are supposed by the patient to be interlarded with phrases which, on examination, he believes to contain hidden meanings, and the newspapers appear to abound in veiled references to him. A stray word, a look, a gesture, a smile, a cough, a shrug of the shoulders on the part of a stranger are apt to be misinterpreted and brooded over. The extraordinary prevalence of this imagined conspiracy may lead the patient to regard himself as a person of great importance, and may result in the formation of delusions of ambition which intermingle themselves with the general conceptions of persecution, or which may wholly supplant the persecutory insanity.

At this juncture, however, it generally happens that hallucinations begin to appear. These, in the great majority of instances, are auditory and usually commence with indefinite noises in the ears, such as ringing sounds, hissing or whistling. Gradually they assume a more definite form until isolated words and ultimately formed sentence are distinctly heard. There is great diversity in the completeness of the verbal hallucinations in different patients. Some patients never experience more than the subjective annoyance of isolated words generally of an insulting character, while others are compelled to listen to regular dialogues carried on by unknown voices concerning themselves. A not uncommon form of verbal hallucination is formulated in the complaint of the patients that "all their thoughts are read and proclaimed aloud." Even more than the enforced listening to verbal hallucinations this "thought reading" distresses the patient and often leads him to acts of violence, for the privacy of his inmost thoughts is, he believes, desecrated, and he often feels helpless and desperate at a condition from which there is no possible escape.

Though some of the subjects do not develop any other form of hallucination, it is unfortunately the lot of others to suffer, in addition, from hallucinations of taste, smell or touch. The misinterpretation of subjective sensations in these sense organs leads to the formulation of delusions of poisoning, of being subjected to the influence of noxious gases or powders, or of being acted on by agencies such as electricity. Such are the persons who take their food to chemists for analysis; who complain to the police that people are acting upon them injuriously; who hermetically seal every crevice that admits air to their bedrooms to prevent the entrance of poisonous fumes; or who place glass castors between the feet of their beds and the floor with the object of insulating electric currents. Such patients obtain little sleep; some of them indeed remain awake all night—for the symptoms are usually worse at night—and have to be content with such snatches of sleep as they are able to obtain at odd times during the day. It is obvious that a person tormented and distracted in the way described may at any moment lose self-control and become a danger to the community. But perhaps the most distressing and most distracting of all hallucinations are those which for want of a better name are termed "sexual." The subjects of these hallucinations, both male and female, under the belief that improper liberties are taken with them, are more clamant and threatening than any other class of paranoiac.

During the course of a disease so distressing in its symptoms the patient's suspicions as to the authors of his persecution vary much in indefiniteness. He often never fixes the direct blame upon any individual, but refers to his persecutors as "they" or a "society," or some corporate body such as "lawyers," "priests" or "freemasons." It not infrequently happens however, that suspicions gradually converge upon some individual or that from an early stage of the disease the patient has, generally under the influence of hallucinations, fixed the origin of his trouble upon one or two persons. When this takes place the matter is always serious from the point of view of physical danger to the inculpated person, especially if the patient is of a violent or vindictive disposition.

The persecutory type of the disease may persist for an indefinite period—even for twenty or thirty years—without any change except for the important fact that remissions in the intensity of the symptoms occur from time to time. These remissions may be so marked as to give rise to the belief that the patient has recovered, but in true paranoia this is hardly ever the case, and sooner or later the persecution begins again in all its former intensity.

2. *Ambitious Paranoia.*—After a long period of persecution a change in the symptoms may set in, in some cases, and the intensity of the hallucinations may become modified. At the same time delusions of grandeur begin to appear, at first faintly, but gradually they increase in force until they ultimately supplant the delusions of persecution. At the same time the hallucinations of a disagreeable nature fade away and are replaced by auditory hallucinations conformable to the new delusions of grandeur. Undoubtedly, however, this form of paranoia may commence, so far as can be observed, with delusions of grandeur, in which case there is seldom or never a transformation of the personality or of the delusions from grandeur to persecution, although delusions of persecution may engraft themselves or run side by side with the predominant ambitious delusions.

The emotional basis of ambitious paranoia is pride, and every phase of human vanity and aspiration is represented in the delusions of the patients. There is moreover considerably less logical acumen displayed in the explanations of their beliefs by such patients than in the case of the subjects of persecution. Many of them affect to be the descendants of historical personages without any regard for accurate genealogical detail. They have no compunction in disowning their natural parents or explaining that they have been "changed in their cradles" in order to account for the fact that they are of exalted or even of royal birth. Dominated by such beliefs paranoiacs have been known to travel all over the world in search of confirmation of their delusions. It is people of this kind who drop into the ears of confiding strangers vague hints as to their exalted origin and kindred, and who make desperate and occasionally alarming attempts to force their way into the presence of princes and rulers. The sphere of religion affords an endless field for the ambitious paranoiacs and some of them may even aspire to divine authority, but as a rule the true paranoiac does not lose touch with earth. The more extravagant delusions of persons who call themselves by divine names and assume omnipotent attributes are usually found in patients who have passed through acute attacks of insanity such as mania or dementia praecox and are mentally enfeebled.

A not uncommon form of paranoia combining both ambition and persecution is where the subject believes that he is a man of unbounded wealth or power, of the rights to which he is, however, deprived by the machinations of his enemies. These patients frequently obtain the knowledge on which they base their delusions through auditory hallucinations. They are often so troublesome, threatening and persistent in their determination to obtain redress for their imagined wrongs, that they have to be forcibly detained in asylums in the public interest.

On the whole, however, the ambitious paranoiac is not troublesome, but calm, dignified, self-possessed, and reserved on the subject of his delusions. He is usually capable of reasoning as correctly and of performing work as efficiently as ordinary people. Many of them, however, while living in society are liable to give expression to their delusions under the influence of excitement, or to behave so strangely and unconventionally on unsuitable occasions as to render their seclusion either necessary or highly desirable.

3. *Amatory Paranoia.*—A distinguishing feature of this form of paranoia is that the subjects are chivalrous and idealistic in their love. Some of them believe that they have been "mystically" married to a person of the opposite sex usually in a prominent social position. The fact that they may have never spoken to or perhaps never seen the person in question is immaterial. The conviction that their love is reciprocated and the relationship understood by the other party is unshakable, and is usually based upon suppositions that to a normal mind would appear either trivial or wholly unreal. The object of affection, if not mythical or of too exalted a position to be approached, is not infrequently persecuted by the admirer, who takes every opportunity of obtruding personally or by letter the evidences of an ardent adoration. The situation thus created can easily become complicated and embarrassing before it is realized that the persistent wooer is insane.

The failure of their schemes or repeated repulses may, in the case of some patients, originate delusions of persecution directed, not against the object of affection, but against those who are supposed to have conspired to prevent the success of the patient's desires. Under the influence of these delusions of persecution the patient may lose self-control and resort to violence against his supposed persecutors.

The subjects of this form of paranoia are in the majority of instances unmarried women well advanced in years who have led irreproachable lives, or men of a romantic disposition who have lived their mental lives more in the realm of chimeras than in the region of real facts. The delusions in this form of paranoia are never accompanied by hallucinations.

Closely allied, if not identical with amatory paranoia, is the form in which jealousy forms the basis of morbid suspicions with or without definite delusions. The subject is usually poor in mental resource, but proud, vindictive and suspicious. It is eminently a condition which arises spontaneously in certain persons whose mental constitution is of the paranoiac type, i.e. persons who are naturally credulous, mystical and suspicious. The subjects are extraordinarily assiduous in watching the objects of their jealousy, whether husbands, wives or sweethearts. Their conduct in this respect is fertile in producing domestic dispeace and unhappiness, and in the case of unmarried persons in creating complicated or delicate situations. It not infrequently happens, just as in the case of the class of amatory paranoiacs, that delusions of persecution establish themselves, usually directed towards persons who are believed to have secured the affections of the object of jealousy. The disease then follows the ordinary course of the insanity of persecution but usually without hallucinations of the senses. The subjects are highly dangerous and violent. Under the influence of their delusions murder and even mutilation may be resorted to by the male, and poisoning or vitriol-throwing by the female subjects.

4. *Litigious Paranoia (paranoia querulans)*.—The clinical form of litigious paranoia presents uniform characteristic features which are recognized in every civilized community. The basic emotion is vanity, but added to that is a strong element both of acquisitiveness and avarice. Moreover the subjects are, as regards character, persistent, opinionative and stubborn. When these qualities are superadded to a mind of the paranoiac type, which as has been pointed out, is more influenced by the passions or emotions than by ordinary rational considerations, it can readily be appreciated that the subjects are capable of creating difficulties and anxieties which sooner or later may lead to their forcible seclusion in the interests of social order.

It is important to observe that the rights such people lay claim to or the wrongs they complain of may not necessarily be imaginary. But, whether imaginary or real, the statement of their case is always made to rest upon some foundation of fact, and is moreover presented, if not with ability, at any rate with forensic skill and plausibility. As the litigants are persons of one idea, and only capable of seeing one side of the case—their own—and as they are actuated by convictions which preclude feelings of delicacy or diffidence, they ultimately succeed in obtaining a hearing in a court of law under circumstances which would have discouraged any normal individual. Once in the law courts their doom is sealed. Neither the loss of the case nor the payment of heavy expenses have any effect in disheartening the litigant, who carries his suit from court to court until the methods of legal appeal are exhausted. The suit may be raised again and again on some side issue, or some different legal action may be initiated. In spite of the alienation of the sympathy of his relations and the advice of his friends and lawyers the paranoiac continues his futile litigation in the firm belief that he is only defending himself from fraud or seeking to regain his just rights. After exhausting his means and perhaps those of his family and finding himself unable to continue to litigate to the same advantage as formerly, delusions of persecution begin to establish themselves. He accuses the judges of corruption, the lawyers of being in the pay of his enemies and imagines the existence of a conspiracy to prevent him from obtaining justice. One of two things usually happens at this stage. Though well versed in legal procedure he may one day lose self-control and resort to threats of violence. He is then probably arrested and may on examination be found insane and committed to an asylum. Another not uncommon result is that finding himself non-suited in a court of law he commits a technical assault upon, it may be, some high legal functionary, or on some person in a prominent social position, with the object of securing an opportunity of directing public attention to his grievances. The only result is, as in the former instance, his medical certification and incarceration.

Paranoia is generally a hopeless affection from the point of view of recovery. From what has been stated regarding its genesis and slow development it is apparent that no form of

ordinary medical treatment can be of the least avail in modifying its symptoms. The best that can be done in the interests of the patients is to place them in surroundings where they can be shielded from influences which aggravate their delusions and in other respects to make their unfortunate lot as pleasant and as easy to endure as possible.

As has been frequently stated, the subjects of most forms of paranoia are liable to commit crime, usually of violence, which may lead to their being tried for assault or murder. The question of their responsibility before the law is therefore one of the first importance (see also INSANITY: *Law*). The famous case of McNaghten, tried in 1843 for the murder of Mr Drummond, private secretary to Sir Robert Peel, is, in this connexion, highly important, for McNaghten was a typical paranoiac labouring under delusions of persecution, and his case formed the basis of the famous deliverance of the judges in the House of Lords, in the same year, on the general question of criminal responsibility in insanity. Answer 4 of the judges' deliverance contains the following statement of law: If "he labours under such *partial* delusion only and is not *in other respects insane* we think he must be considered in the same situation as to responsibility as if the facts to which the delusion exists were real. For example, if under the influence of his delusion he supposes another man to be in the act of attempting to take away his life, and he kills that man, as he supposes, in self-defence, he would be exempt from punishment. If his delusion was that the deceased had inflicted a serious injury to his character and fortune, and he killed him in revenge for such supposed injury, he would be liable to punishment."

In considering this deliverance it must be remembered that it was given under the influence of the enormous public interest created by the McNaghten trial. It has also to be remembered that in a criminal court the term responsibility means liability to legal punishment. The dictum laid down in answer 4 is open to several objections. (1) It is based upon the erroneous assumption that a person may be insane on one point and sane on every other. This is a loose popular fallacy for which there is no foundation in clinical medicine. The systematization of a delusion involves, as has been pointed out, the whole personality and affects emotion, intellect and conduct. The human mind is not divided into mutually exclusive compartments, but is one indivisible whole liable to be profoundly modified in its relation to its environment according to the emotional strength of the predominant morbid concepts. (2) It does not take into account the pathological diminution of the power of self-control. The influence of continued delusions of persecution, especially if accompanied by painful hallucinations, undermines the power of self-control and tends ultimately to reduce the subject towards the condition of an automaton which reacts reflexly and blindly to the impulse of the moment. (3) The opinion is further at fault in so far as it assumes that the test of responsibility rests upon the knowledge of right and wrong, which implies the power to do right and to avoid wrong, an assumption which is very far from the truth when applied to the insane. The number of insane criminals who possess no theoretical knowledge of right and wrong is very few indeed, so few that for practical purposes they may be disregarded.

The true paranoiac is a person of an anomalous mental constitution apart from his insanity; although he may to outward appearances be able, on occasion, to converse or to act rationally, the moment he is dominated by his delusions he becomes not partially but wholly insane; when in addition his mind is distracted by ideas of persecution or hallucinations, or both, he becomes potentially capable of committing crime, not because of any inherent vicious propensity but in virtue of his insanity. There is therefore no middle course, from the medical point of view, in respect to the criminal responsibility of the subjects of paranoia; they are all insane wholly, not partially, and should only be dealt with as persons of unsound mind.

See Bianchi, *Textbook of Insanity* (Eng. trans., 1906); Clouston, *Mental Diseases* (6th ed.); Krafft-Ebing, *Textbook of Insanity* (American trans., 1904); Kraepelin, *Psychiatrie* (6th ed., Leipzig,

1890); Magnan, *Le Délire chronique* (Paris, 1890); Stewart Paton, *Psychiatry* (Philadelphia, 1905); Percy Smith, "Paranoia," in *Journ. of Mental Science* (1904), p. 607.   (J. Mn.)

PARAPET (Ital. *parapetto*, Fr. *parapet*, from *para*, imperative of Ital. *parare*, to cover, defend, and *petto*, breast, Lat. *pectus*; the German word is *Brustwehr*), a dwarf wall along the edge of a roof, or round a lead flat, terrace walk, &c., to prevent persons from falling over, and as a protection to the defenders in case of a siege. Parapets are either plain, embattled, perforated or panelled. The last two are found in all styles except the Romanesque. Plain parapets are simply portions of the wall generally overhanging a little, with a *coping* at the top and *corbel* table below. Embattled parapets are sometimes panelled, but oftener pierced for the discharge of arrows, &c. Perforated parapets are pierced in various devices—as circles, trefoils, quatrefoils and other designs—so that the light is seen through. Panelled parapets are those ornamented by a series of panels, either oblong or square, and more or less enriched, but are not perforated. These are common in the Decorated and Perpendicular periods.

PARAPHERNALIA (Lat. *paraphernalia,* sc. *bona*, from Gr. παράφερνα; παρά, beside, and φερνή, dower), a term originally of Roman law, signifying all the property which a married woman who was *sui juris* held apart from her dower (*dos*). A husband could not deal with such except with his wife's consent. Modern systems of law, which are based on the Roman, mainly follow the same principle, and the word preserves its old meaning. In English and Scottish law the term is confined to articles of jewelry, dress and other purely personal things, for the law relating to which see HUSBAND AND WIFE. The word is also used in a general sense of accessories, external equipment, cumbersome or showy trappings.

PARAPHRASE (Gr. παράφρασις, from παραφράζειν, to relate something in different words, παρά, beside, and φράζειν, speak, tell), a rendering into other words of a passage in prose or verse, giving the sense in a fuller, simpler or clearer fashion, also a free translation or adaptation of a passage in a foreign language. The term is specifically used in the Scottish and other Presbyterian churches of metrical versions for singing of certain passages of the Bible.

PARASCENIUM (Gr. παρασκήνιον), in a Greek theatre, the wall on either side of the stage, reaching from the back wall (σκηνή) to the orchestra.

PARASITE (From Gr. παρά, beside, σῖτος food), literally "mess-mate," a term originally conveying no idea of reproach or contempt, as in later times. The early parasites may be divided into two classes, religious and civil. The former were assistants of the priests, their chief duty being to collect the corn dues which were contributed by the farmers of the temple lands or which came in from other sources (Athenaeus vi. 235; Pollux vi. 35). Considerable obscurity exists as to their other functions, but they seem to have been charged with providing food for the visitors to the temples, with the care of certain offerings, and with the arrangement of the sacrificial banquets. In Attica the parasites appear to have been confined to certain demes (Acharnae, Diomeia), and were appointed by the demes to which the temples belonged. The "civil" parasites were a class of persons who received invitations to dine in the *prytaneum* and subsequently in the *tholos*) as distinguished from those who had the right to dine there *ex officio*. An entirely different meaning (" sponger ") became attached to the word from the character introduced into the Middle and New Comedy, first by Alexis, and firmly established by Diphilus. The chief object of this class of parasites was a good dinner, for which they were ready to submit to almost any humiliation. Numerous examples occur in the comedies of Plautus; and Alciphron and Athenaeus (vi. 236 sqq.) give instances of the insults they had to put up with at the hands of both host and guests. Some of them played the part of professional jesters (like the later buffoons and court fools), and kept collections of witticisms ready for use at their patrons' table; others relied upon flattery, others again condescended to the most degrading devices (Plutarch, *De adulatore*, 23; *De educatione puerorum*, 17). The

term parasite; from meaning a " hanger-on," has been transferred to any living creature which lives on another one.

See Juvenal v. 170 with J. E. B. Mayor's note, and the exhaustive article by M. H. Meier in Ersch and Gruber's *Allgemeine Encyclopädie.*

PARASITIC DISEASES. It has long been recognized that various specific pathological conditions are due to the presence and action of parasites (see PARASITISM) in the human body, but in recent years the part played in the causation of the so-called infective diseases by various members of the Schizomycetes—fission fungi—and by Protozoan and other animal parasites has been more widely and more thoroughly investigated (see BACTERIOLOGY). The knowledge gained has not only modified our conception of the pathology of these diseases, but has had a most important influence upon our methods of treatment of sufferers, both as individuals and as members of communities. For clinical and other details of the diseases mentioned in the following classification, see the separate articles on them; the present article is concerned mainly with important modern discoveries as regards aetiology and pathology. In certain cases indeed the aetiology is still obscure. Thus, according to Guarnieri, and Councilman & Calkins, there is associated with vaccinia and with small-pox a Protozoan parasite, *Cytoryctes variolae*, Guar. This parasite is described as present in the cytoplasm of the stratified epithelium of the skin and mucous membranes in cases of vaccinia, but in the nuclei of the same cells in cases of variola or small-pox, whilst it is suggested that there may be a third phase of existence, not yet demonstrated, in which it occurs as minute spores or germs which are very readily carried in dust and by air currents from point to point. In certain other conditions, such as mumps, dengue, epidemic dropsy, oriental sore—with which the Leishman-Donovan bodies (*Helcosoma tropicum*, Wright) are supposed to be closely associated (see also *Kála-ázar* below)—verruga, framboesia or yaws—with which is commonly associated a spirochaete (Castellani) and a special micrococcus (Pierez, Nichols)—and beri-beri, the disease may be the result of the action of specific micro-organisms, though as yet it has not been possible to *demonstrate* any aetiologica relationship between any micro-organisms found and the special disease. Such diseases as haemoglobinuric fever or black-water fever, which are also presumably parasitic diseases, are probably associated directly with malaria; this supposition is the more probable in that both of these are recognized as occurring specially in those patients who have been weakened by malaria.

The following classification is based partly upon the biological relations of the parasites and partly on the pathological phenomena of individual diseases:—

A.—Diseases due to Vegetable Parasites.

I.—To SCHIZOMYCETES, BACTERIA OR FISSION FUNGI.

1. *Caused by the Pyogenetic Micrococci.*

Suppuration and Septicaemia.	Erysipelas.
Infective Endocarditis.	Gonorrhoea.

2. *Caused by Specific Bacilli.*

(a) Acute Infective Fevers.

Cholera.	Infective Meningitis.
Typhoid Fever	Influenza.
Malta Fever.	Yellow Fever and Weil's Disease.
Relapsing Fever.	Diphtheria.
Plague.	Tetanus.
Pneumonia.	

(b) More Chronic Infective Diseases (tissue parasites).

Tuberculosis.	Glanders. Leprosy

II.—To HIGHER VEGETABLE PARASITES.

Actinomycosis, Madura Foot, Aspergillosis and other Mycoses.

B.—Diseases due to Animal Parasites.

I.—To PROTOZOA.

Malaria.	Kála-ázar.
Amoebic Dysentery.	Tsetse-fly Disease.
Haemoglobinuric Fever.	Sleeping Sickness.
Syphilis.	

II.—To OTHER ANIMAL PARASITES.

Filariasis, &c.

C.—Infective Diseases in which an organism has been found, but has not finally been connected with the disease.

Hydrophobia.   Scarlet Fever.

D.—Infective Diseases not yet proved to be due to micro-organisms.

Small-pox.   Mumps.
Typhus Fever.   Whooping Cough, &c.
Measles

A.—Diseases due to Vegetable Parasites.

I.—To Schizomycetes, Bacteria or Fission Fungi.

1. Caused by the Pyogenetic Microcci.

Suppuration and Septicaemia.—It is now recognized that although nitrate of silver, turpentine, castor oil, perchloride of mercury and certain other chemical substances are capable of producing suppuration, the most common causes of this condition are undoubtedly the so-called pus-producing bacteria. Of these perhaps the most important are the staphylococci (cocci arranged like bunches of grapes), streptococci (cocci arranged in chains), and pneumococci, though certain other organisms not usually associated with pus-formation are undoubtedly capable of setting up this condition, *e.g. Bacillus pyocyaneus, Bacillus coli communis*, and the typhoid bacillus. These organisms (the products of which, by chemical irritation, stimulate the leucocytes to emigration) bring about the death and digestion of the tissues and fluids (which no longer " clot ") with which they come in contact, pus (matter) being thus formed: this accumulates in the tissues, in the serous cavities, or even on mucous surfaces; septicaemia or blood-poisoning, secondary infection of tissues and organs at a distance from the original site of infection, or pyaemia, with the formation of secondary abscesses, may thus be set up.

In septicaemia the pus-forming organisms grow at the seat of introduction, and produce special poisons or toxins, which, absorbed into the blood, give rise to symptoms of fever. From the point of introduction, however, the organisms may be swept away either by the lymph or by the blood, and carried to positions in which they set up further inflammatory or suppurative changes. In the streptococcal inflammations spreading by the lymph channels appears to be specially prevalent. In the blood the organisms, if in small numbers, are usually destroyed by the plasma, which has a powerful bactericidal action; should they escape, however, they are carried without multiplication into the capillaries of the general circulation, of the lung, or of the liver, where, being stopped, they may give rise to a second focus of infection, especially if at the point of impaction the vitality of the tissues is in any way lowered. Unless the blood is very much impoverished, its bactericidal action is usually sufficiently powerful to bring about the destruction of anything but comparatively large masses of pyogenetic organisms. This bactericidal power, however, may be lost; in such case the pus-forming organisms may actually multiply, a general haemic infection resulting. Should micro-organisms be conveyed by the veins to the heart, and there be deposited on an injured valve, an *infective endocarditis* is the result; from such a deposit numerous organisms may be continuously poured into the circulation. Simple thrombi or clots may also become infected with micro-organisms. Fragments of these, washed away, may form septic plugs in the vessels and give rise to abscesses at the points where they become impacted. A distinction must be drawn between sapraemia and septicaemia. In sapraemia the toxic products of saprophytic organisms are absorbed from a gangrenous or necrotic mass, from an ulcerating surface, or from a large surface on which saprophytic organisms are living and feeding on dead tissues: for example, we may have such a condition in the clots that sometimes remain after childbirth on the inner surface of the wall of the womb. So long as no micro-organisms follow the toxins, the condition is purely sapraemic, but should any organisms make their way into and multiply in the blood, the condition becomes one of septicaemia. The term pyaemia is usually associated with the formation of fresh secondary foci of suppuration in distant parts of the body. If the primary abscess occurs in the lungs, the secondary or metastatic abscesses usually occur in the vessels of the general or systemic circulation, and less frequently in other vessels of the lung. When the primary abscess occurs in the systemic area, the secondary abscess occurs first in the lung, and less frequently in the systemic vessels; whilst if the primary abscess be in the portal area (the veins of the digestive tract), the secondary abscesses are usually distributed over the same area, the lungs and systemic vessels being more rarely affected.

Infective Endocarditis.—Acute malignant or ulcerative endocarditis occurs in certain forms of septicaemia or of pyaemia. It is brought about by the Streptococcus pyogenes (see Plate II. fig. 2), the pneumococcus, or the *Staphylococcus pyogenes aureus* (see Plate I. fig. 4), or, more rarely, by the gonococcus, the typhoid bacillus or the tubercle bacillus, as they gain access to acute or chronic valvular lesions of the heart. The aortic and mitral valves are usually affected, the pulmonary and tricuspid valves much more rarely, though Washbourn states that the infective form occurs on the right side more frequently than does simple endocarditis. A rapid necrosis of the surface of the valve is early followed by a deposition of fibrin and leucocytes on the necrosed tissue; the bacteria, though not present in the circulating blood during life, are found in these vegetations which break down very rapidly; ulcerative lesions are thus formed, and fragments of the septic clot (*i.e.* the fibrinous vegetations with their enclosed bacteria) are carried in the circulating blood to different parts of the body, and, becoming impacted in the smaller vessels, give rise to septic infarcts and abscesses. The ulceration of the valves, or in the first part of the aorta, may be so extensive that aneurysm, or even perforation, may ensue.

In certain cases of streptococcic endocarditis the use of antistreptococcic serum appears to have been attended with good results. Sir A. Wright found that the introduction of vaccines prepared from the pus-producing organisms after first lowering the opsonic index almost invariably, after a very short interval, causes it to rise. He found, too, that the vaccine is specially efficacious when it is prepared from the organisms associated with the special form of suppuration to be treated. Whenever the opsonic index becomes higher under this treatment the suppurative process gradually subsides: boils, acne, pustules, carbuncles all giving way to the vaccine treatment. The immunity so obtained is attributed to the increased activity of the serum as the result of the presence of an increased amount of opsonins. Further, Bier maintains that a passive congestion and oedema induced by constriction of a part by means of a ligature or by a modification of the old method of cupping without breaking the skin appears to have a similar effect in modifying localized suppurative processes, that is processes set up by pus-producing organisms. Wright holds that this treatment is always more effective when the opsonic index is high and that the mere accumulation of oedematous fluid in the part is sufficient to raise the opsonic index of that fluid and therefore to bring about a greater phagocytic activity of the leucocytes that are found in such enormous numbers in the neighbourhood of suppurative organisms and their products.

Erysipelas.—In 1883 Fehleisen demonstrated that in all cases of active erysipelatous inflammation a streptococcus or chain of micrococci (similar to those met with in certain forms of suppuration) may be found in the lymph spaces in the skin. The multiplying streptococci found in the lymph spaces form an active poison, which, acting on the blood-vessels, causes them to dilate; it also " attracts " leucocytes, and usually induces proliferation of the endothelial cells lining the lymphatics. These cells—perhaps by using up all available oxygen—interfere with the growth of the streptococcus and act as phagocytes, taking up or devouring the dead or weakened micro-organisms. Both mild and severe phlegmonous cases of erysipelas are the result of the action of this special coccus, alone, or in combination with other organisms. It has been observed that cancerous and other malignant tumours appear to recede under an attack of erysipelas, and certain cases have been recorded by both Fehleisen and Coley in which complete cessation of growth and degeneration of the tumour have followed such an attack. As the streptococcus of erysipelas can be isolated and grown in pure culture in broth, it was thought by these observers that a subcutaneous injection of such a cultivation might be of value in the treatment of cancerous tumours. No difficulty was experienced in setting up erysipelas by inoculation, but in some cases the process was so acute that the remedy was more fatal than the disease. The virulence of the streptococcus of erysipelas, as pointed out by Fehleisen and Coley, is greatly exalted when the coccus is grown alongside the *Bacillus prodigiosus* and certain other saprophytic organisms which flourish at the body-temperature. It is an easier matter to control the action of a non-multiplying poison, even though exceedingly active, than of one capable, under favourable conditions, of producing an indefinite amount of even a weaker poison. The erysipelatous virus having been raised to as high a degree of activity as possible by cultivating it along with the *Bacillus prodigiosus*—the bacillus of " bleeding " bread—in broth, is killed by heat, and the resulting fluid, which contains a quantity of the toxic substances that set up the characteristic erysipelatous changes, is utilised for the production of an inflammatory process—which can now be accurately controlled, and which is said to be very beneficial in the treatment of certain malignant tumours. The accurate determination of the aetiology of erysipelas has led to the adoption of a scientific method of treatment of the disease. The *Streptococcus erysipelatis* is found, not specially in the zone in which inflammation has become evident, but in the tissues outside this zone; in fact, the streptococci appear to be most numerous in the lymphatics of the tissues in which there is little change. Before the appearance of any redness there is a dilatation of the lymph spaces with fluid, and the tissues become slightly oedematous. As soon, however, as the distension of vessels and the emigration of leucocytes, with the accompanying swelling and redness, become marked, the streptococci disappear or are imperfectly stained—they are undergoing degenerative changes—the inflammatory " reaction " apparently being sufficient to bring about this result.

If it were possible to set up the same reaction outside the advancing streptococci might not a barrier be raised against their advance? This theory was tested on animals, and it was found that the application of iodine, oil of mustard, cantharides and similar rubefacients would prevent the advance of certain micro-organisms. This treatment was applied to erysipelatous patients with the most satisfactory result, the spread of the disease being prevented whenever the zone of inflammation was extended over a sufficiently wide area. The mere " ringing " of the red patch by nitrate of silver or some other similar irritant, as at one time recommended, is not sufficient: it is necessary that the reaction should extend for some little distance beyond the zone to which the streptococci have already advanced.

Gonorrhoea.—A micro-organism, the gonococcus, is the cause of gonorrhoea. It is found in the pus of the urethra and in the conjunctiva lying between the epithelial cells, where it sets up considerable irritation and exudation; it occurs in the fluid of joints of patients affected with gonorrhoeal arthritis; also in the pleuritic effusion and in the vegetations of gonorrhoeal endocarditis. It is a small diplococcus, the elements of which are flattened or slightly concave disks apposed to one another; these, dividing transversely, sometimes form tetrads. They are found in large numbers, usually in the leucocytes, adherent to the epithelial cells or lying free. They stain readily with the basic aniline dyes, but lose this stain when treated by Gram's method. The gonococcus is best grown on human blood-serum mixed with agar (Wertheim), though it grows on ordinary solidified blood-serum or on blood-agar. Like the pneumococcus, it soon dies out, usually before the eighth or ninth day, unless reinoculations are made. It forms a semi-transparent disk-like growth, with somewhat irregular margins, or with small processes running out beyond the main colony. It acts by means of toxins, which have been found to set up irritative

changes when injected, without the gonococci, into the anterior chamber of the eye of the rabbit.

2. Caused by Specific Bacilli.
(a) Acute Infective Fevers.

Cholera.—In 1884 Koch, in the report of the German Cholera Commission in Egypt and India, brought forward overwhelming evidence in proof of his contention that a special bacterium is the causal agent of cholera; subsequent observers in all countries in which cholera has been met with have confirmed Koch's observation. The organism described is the " comma " bacillus or vibrio, one of the spirilla, which usually occurs as a slightly curved rod 1 to 2μ in length and 0.5 to 0.6μ in thickness. These comma-shaped rods occur singly or in pairs; they may be joined together to form circles, half-circles, or " S "-shaped curves (see Plate II. fig. 3).

In cultivations in specially prepared media they may be so grouped as to form long wavy or spiral threads, each of which may be made up of ten, twenty, or even thirty, of the short curved vibrios; in the stools of cholera patients, especially during the earlier stages of the disease, they are found in considerable numbers; they may also be found in the contents of the lower bowel and in the substance of the mucous membrane of the lower part of the small intestine, especially in the crypts and in and around the epithelium lining the follicles. It is sometimes difficult, in the later stages of the disease, to obtain these organisms in sufficiently large numbers to be able to distinguish them by direct microscopic examination, but by using the Dunbar-Schottelius method they can be detected even when present in small numbers. A quantity of faintly alkaline meat broth, with 2 % of peptone and 1 % common salt, is inoculated with some of the contents of the intestine, and is placed in an incubator at a temperature of 35° C. for about twelve hours, when, if any cholera bacilli are present, a delicate pellicle, consisting almost entirely of short " comma " bacilli, appears on the surface. If the growth be allowed to continue, the bacilli increase in length, but after a time the pellicle is gradually lost, the cholera organisms being overgrown, as it were, by the other organisms. In order to obtain a pure culture of the cholera bacillus, remove a small fragment of the young film, shake it up thoroughly in a little broth, and then make gelatine-plate cultivations, when most characteristic colonies appear as small greyish or white points. Each of these, when examined under a low-power lens, has a yellow tinge; the margins are wavy or crenated; the surface is granular and has a peculiar ground-glass appearance; around the growing colony liquefaction takes place, and the colony gradually sinks to the bottom of the liquefying area, which now appears as a clear ring. The organism grows very luxuriantly in milk, in which, however, it gives rise to no very noticeable alteration; its presence can only be recognized by a faint aromatic and sweetish smell, which can scarcely be distinguished from the aromatic smell of the milk itself, except by the most practised nose.

The cholera bacillus may remain alive in water for some time, but it appears to be less resistant than many of the putrefactive and saprophytic organisms. It grows better in a saline solution (brackish water) than in perfectly fresh water; it flourishes in serum and other albuminous fluids, especially when peptones are present. Its power of forming poisonous substances appears to vary directly with the amount and nature of the albumen present in the nutrient medium; and though it grows most readily in the presence of peptone, it appears to form the most virulent poison when grown in some form or other of crude albumen to which there is not too free access of oxygen. From the experiments carried out by Koch, Nicati and Rietsch, and Macleod, there appears to be no doubt that the healthy stomach and intestine are not favourable breeding-grounds for the cholera bacillus. In the first place, it requires an alkaline medium for its full and active development, and the acid found in a healthy stomach seems to exert an exceedingly deleterious influence upon it. Secondly, it appears to be incapable of developing except when left at rest, so that the active peristaltic movement of the intestine interferes with its development. Moreover, it forms its poison most easily in the presence of crude albumen. It is interesting to note what an important bearing these facts have on the personal and general spread of cholera. Large quantities of the cholera bacillus may be injected into the stomach of a guinea-pig without any intoxicative or other symptoms of cholera making their appearance. Further, healthy individuals have swallowed, without any ill effect, pills containing the dejecta from cholera cases, although cases are recorded in which "artificial" infection of the human subject has undoubtedly taken place, whilst, as Metchnikoff demonstrated, very young rabbits, deriving milk from mothers whose mammary glands have been smeared with a culture of the cholera vibrio, soon succumbed, suffering from the classical symptoms of this disease.

If, however, previous to the injection of the cholera bacillus the acidity of the stomach be neutralised by an alkaline fluid, especially if at the same time the peristaltic action of the intestine be paralysed by an injection of morphia, a characteristic attack of cholera is developed, the animal is poisoned, and in the large intestine a considerable quantity of fluid faeces containing numerous cholera bacilli may be found. There appear to be slight differences in the cholera organisms found in connexion with different outbreaks, but the main characteristics are preserved throughout, and are sufficiently distinctive to mark out all these organisms as belonging to the cholera group. Amongst the known predisposing causes of cholera are the incautious use of purgative medicines, the use of unripe fruit, insufficient food and intemperance. These may be all looked upon as playing the part of the alkaline solution in altering the composition of the gastric juices, and especially as setting up alkaline fermentation in the stomach and small intestine; beyond this, however, the irritation set up may bring about an accumulation of inflammatory serous fluid, from the albumens of which, as we have seen, the cholera organism has the power of producing very active toxins.

The part played by want of personal cleanliness, overcrowding and unfavourable hygienic conditions may be readily understood if it be remembered that the cholera bacillus may grow outside the body. The number of cases in which epidemics of cholera have been traced to the use of drinking-water contaminated with the discharges from cholera patients is now considerable. The more organic matter present the greater is the virulence of water so contaminated; and the addition of such water to milk has, in one instance at least, led to an outbreak. If cholera dejecta be sprinkled on moist soil or damp linen, and kept at blood-heat, the bacillus multiplies at an enormous rate in the first twenty-four or thirty-six hours; but, as seen in the Dunbar-Schottelius method, at the end of three or four days it is gradually overcome by the other bacteria present, which, growing strongly and asserting themselves, cause it to die out. The importance of this saprophytic growth in the propagation of the disease can scarcely be over-estimated. Water which contains an ordinary amount of organic and inorganic matter in solution does not allow of the multiplication of this organism, which may soon die out; but when organic matter is present in excess, as at the margin of stagnant pools and tanks, development occurs, especially on the floating solid particles. This bacillus grows at a temperature of 30° C. on meat, eggs, vegetables and moistened bread; also on cheese, coffee, chocolate and dilute sugar solutions. In some experiments carried out by Cartwright Wood and the writer in connexion with the passage of the cholera organism through filters it remained alive in the charcoal filtering medium for a period of at least forty-two days, and probably for a couple of months. It must be remembered that cholera bacilli are gradually overcome or overgrown by other organisms, as only on this supposition can the immunity enjoyed by certain regions, even after the water and soil have been contaminated, provided that no fresh supply is brought in "to relight the torch," be explained. In most of the regions in which cholera remains endemic the wells are merely dug-out pits beneath the slightly raised houses, and are open for the reception of sewage and excreta at all times. These dejecta contain organic material which serves as a nutriment on which infective organisms, derived from the soil and ground-water, may flourish. Not only dejecta, but also the rinsings from soiled linen and utensils used by cholera patients should be removed as soon as possible, "without allowing them to come into contact with the surface of the soil, with wells," or with vegetables and the like. The discovery of Koch's comma bacillus has so

altered our conceptions of the aetiology of this disease that we now study the conditions under which the bacillus can multiply and be disseminated, instead of concerning ourselves with the cholera itself as some definite entity. Telluric agencies become merely secondary factors, the dissemination of the disease by winds from country to country is no longer regarded as being possible, whilst the spread of cholera epidemics along the lines of human intercourse and travel is now recognized. The virulent bacillus requires the human organism to carry it from those localities in which it is endemic to those in which epidemics occur. The epidemiologist has come to look upon the study of the cholera organism and the conditions under which it exists as of more importance than mere local conditions, which are only important in so far as they contribute to the propagation and distribution of the cholera bacillus, and he knows that the only means of preventing its spread is the careful inspection of everything coming from cholera-stricken regions. He also recognizes that the herding together of people of depressed vitality, under unhygienic and often filthy conditions, in quarantine stations or ships, is one of the surest means of promoting an epidemic of the disease; that attention should be confined to the careful isolation of all patients, and to the disinfection of articles of clothing, feeding utensils, and the like; that the comma bacillus can only be driven out of rooms by means of light and fresh air; that thorough personal, culinary and household cleanliness is necessary; that all water except that known to be pure should be carefully boiled; and that all excess, both in eating and drinking, should be avoided. The object of the physician in such cases must be first to isolate as completely as possible all his cholera patients, and then to get rid of all predisposing causes in the patients themselves, causes which have already been indicated in connexion with the aetiology of the disease.

Attention has frequently been drawn to the fact that patients who have lived for some time in a cholera region, or who have already suffered from an attack of cholera, appear to enjoy a partial immunity against the disease. Haffkine, working on the assumption that the symptoms of cholera are produced by a toxin formed by the cholera organism, came to the conclusion that, by introducing first a modified and then a more virulent poison directly into the tissues under the skin, and not into the alimentary canal, it would be possible to obtain a certain insusceptibility to the action of this poison. He found that for this purpose the cholera bacillus, as ordinarily obtained in pure culture from the intestinal canal, is too potent for the preliminary inoculation, but is not sufficiently active for the second, if any marked protection is to be obtained. By allowing the organism to grow in a well-aerated culture the virulence is gradually diminished, and this virulence, once abolished, does not return even when numerous successive cultures are made on agar or other nutrient media. On the other hand, by passing the cholera bacillus successively through the peritoneal cavities of a series of about thirty guinea-pigs, he obtains a virus of great activity; this activity is soon lost on agar cultivations, and it is necessary, from time to time, again to pass the bacillus through guinea-pigs, three or four passages now being sufficient to reinforce the activity.

From these two cultures the vaccines are prepared as follows: The surface of a slant agar tube is smeared with the modified cholera organism. After this has been allowed to grow for twenty-four hours, a small quantity of sterile water is poured into the tube, and the surface-growth is carefully scraped off and made into an emulsion in the water; this is then poured off, and the process is repeated until the whole of the growth has been removed. The mixture is made up with water to a bulk of 8 c.c., so that if 1 c.c. is injected the patient receives ⅛ of a surface-growth; it is found that this quantity, when injected subcutaneously into a guinea-pig, gives a distinct reaction, but does not cause necrosis of the tissues. If the vaccine is to be kept for any length of time, the emulsion is made with 0·5 % carbolic acid solution, prepared with carefully sterilised water, and the mixture is made up to 6 c.c. instead of 8 c.c., since the carbolic acid appears to interfere slightly with the activity of the virus. The stronger virus is prepared in exactly the same way. The preliminary injection, which is made in the left flank, is followed by a rise in temperature and by local reaction.

After three or four hours there is noticeable swelling and some pain; and after ten hours a rise in temperature, usually not very marked, occurs. These signs soon disappear, and at the end of three or four days the second injection is made, usually on the opposite side. This is also followed by a rise of temperature, by swelling, pain and local redness; these, however, as before, soon pass off, and leave no ill effects behind. A guinea-pig treated in this fashion is now immune against some eight or ten times the lethal dose of cholera poison, and, from all statistics that can be obtained, a similar protection is conferred upon the human being.

Pfeiffer found that when a small quantity of the cholera vibrio is injected into the peritoneal cavity of a guinea-pig highly immunized against cholera by Haffkine's or a similar method, these vibrios rapidly become motionless and granular, then very much swollen and finally "dissolve." This is known as Pfeiffer's reaction. A similar reaction may be obtained when a quantity of a culture of the cholera vibrio mixed with the serum derived from a guinea-pig immunized against the cholera vibrio, or from a patient convalescent from the disease, is injected into the peritoneal cavity of a guinea pig not subjected to any preliminary treatment; and, going a step further, it was found that the dissolution of the cholera vibrio is brought about even when the mixture of vibrio and serum is made in a test tube. On this series of experiments as a foundation, the theory of acquired immunity has been reared.

† Evidence has been collected that spirilla, almost identical in appearance with the cholera bacillus, may be present in water and in healthy stools, and that it is in many cases almost impossible to diagnose between these and the cholera bacillus; but although these spirilla may interfere with the diagnosis, they do not invalidate Koch's main contention, that a special form of the comma bacillus, which gives a *complete group* of reactions, is the cause of this disease, especially when these reactions are met with in an organism *that comes from the human intestine.*

Typhoid Fever.—Our information concerning the aetiology of typhoid fever was largely increased during the last twenty years of the 19th century. In 1880 Eberth and Klebs independently, and in 1882 Coats, described a bacillus which has since been found to be intimately associated with typhoid fever. This organism (Plate II. fig. 4) usually appears in the form of a short bacillus from 2 to 3μ in length and 0·3 to 0·5μ in breadth; it has slightly rounded ends and is stained at the poles; it may also occur as a somewhat longer rod more equally stained throughout. Surrounding the young organism are numerous long and well-formed flagella, which give it a very characteristic appearance under the microscope. At present there is no evidence that the typhoid bacillus forms spores. These bacilli are found in the adenoid follicles or lymphatic tissues of the intestine, in the mesenteric glands, in the spleen, liver and kidneys, and may also be detected even in the small lymphoid masses in the lung and in the post-typhoid abscesses formed in the bones, kidneys, or other parts of the body; indeed, it is probable that they were first seen by von Recklinghausen in 1871 in such abscesses. They undoubtedly occur in the deject of patients suffering from typhoid fever, whilst in recent years it has been demonstrated that they may also be found in the urine. It is evident, therefore, that the urine, as well as the faeces, may be the vehicle by means of which the disease has been unwittingly spread in certain otherwise inexplicable outbreaks of typhoid fever, especially as the bacillus may be present in the urine when the acute stage of the disease has gone by, and when it has been assumed that, as the patient is convalescent, he is no longer a focus from which the infection may be spread. Easton and Knox found typhoid bacilli in the urine of 21 % of a series of their typhoid patients.

In 1906 Kayser demonstrated what had previously been suspected, that the typhoid bacilli may persist for considerable periods in the bile duct and gall bladder, whence they pass into the intestinal tract and are discharged with the evacuations. Patients in whom this occurs are spoken of as "typhoid carriers." They become convalescent and except that now and again they suffer from slight attacks of diarrhoea they appear to be perfectly healthy. It has been observed, however, especially during these attacks of diarrhoea, that typhoid bacilli may be found in the faeces. Curiously enough the bacilli are as virulent as are those isolated when the disease is at its height. Hence these typhoid carriers are exceedingly dangerous centres of infection, and as women act as "carriers" much more frequently than do men, although, as is well known, typhoid fever attacks men much more frequently than women, the facilities

for the distribution of the disease are great, as women so frequently act as laundresses, cooks, housemaids, nurses and the like. Frosch states that out of 6708 typhoid patients 310 excreted bacilli for more than 10 weeks after convalescence; 144 of these were no longer infective at the end of three months; 64 had ceased to be infective at the end of a year, and 102 at the end of three and a-half years; further back than this no authentic records could be obtained, but from a critical examination of the histories of 25 such carrier cases he was convinced that 14 had been continuously infective for from four to nine years. Dr Donald Greig, in 1908, reported a case in which the patient appears to have been a typhoid carrier for fifty-two years from the time of convalescence. Frosch pointed out, what has now been fully confirmed, that the bacilli in these cases though often present in the faeces in enormous numbers may disappear and again reappear from time to time and that a continuous series of examinations is necessary before a convalescent patient can be acquitted of being a "typhoid carrier." In this connexion it is interesting to note that Blumenthal and Kayser have discovered typhoid bacilli in the interior of gall-stones. Drs Alexander and J. C. G. Ledingham, examining the 90 female patients and attendants in a Scottish asylum in which, during some four or five years, 31 cases of typhoid had occurred in small groups in which the source of infection could not be traced to any recognized channel, found amongst them three "typhoid carriers." The importance of such a discovery amongst asylum patients may be readily understood when the careless and uncleanly habits of insane patients are borne in mind. As it has been demonstrated that the typhoid bacillus is found, not merely in the lymphatic tissue but, in 75 % of the cases, actually circulating in the blood, the appearance of the bacillus in the secretions and excretions may be readily understood.

There can be little doubt that typhoid bacilli are not, as is very frequently assumed, present merely in the lymphatic glands and in the spleen (see Plate II. fig. 5): they may be found in almost any part of the lymphatic system, in lymph spaces, in the connective tissues, where they appear to give rise to marked proliferation of the endothelial cells, and especially in the various secreting organs. It is probable that the proliferation often noticed in the minute portal spaces in the liver, in cases of typhoid fever, is simply a type of a similar proliferation going on in other parts and tissues of the body. It was for long assumed that the typhoid bacillus could multiply freely in water, but recent experiments appear to indicate that this is not the case, unless a much larger quantity of soluble organic matter is present than is usually met with in water. The fact, however, that the organism may remain alive in water is of great importance; and, as in the case of cholera, it must be recognized that certain of the great epidemics of typhoid or enteric fever have been the result of "water-borne infection." The bacillus, a facultative parasite, grows outside the body, with somewhat characteristic appearances and reactions: it flourishes specially well on a slightly acid medium; in the presence of putrefactive organisms which develop strongly alkaline products it may gradually die out, but it appears to retain its vitality longer in the presence of acid-forming organisms. It may, however, be stated generally that after a time the typhoid bacillus becomes weakened, and may even die out, in the presence of rapidly growing putrefactive organisms. In distilled water it may remain alive for a considerable period—five or six weeks, or even longer. It grows on all the ordinary nutrient media. It does not coagulate milk; hence it may grow luxuriantly in that medium without giving rise to any alteration in its physical characters; contaminated milk, therefore, is specially dangerous affording as it does an excellent vehicle for the dissemination of the typhoid bacillus which may also be conveyed by food and even by water. To food the bacillus is readily conveyed by flies, on their limbs or by the proboscis, which become infected by the excrement on which they crawl and feed. The observations of physicians working amongst the British troops in South Africa afford abundant evidence that the typhoid bacillus may also be carried along with dust from excreta to fresh patients, for although these bacilli die very rapidly when they are desiccated, they remain alive sufficiently long to enable them to multiply and flourish when again brought into contact with moist food, milk, &c.

When inoculated on potato, careful examination will reveal the fact that certain almost invisible moist patches are present; these are made up of rapidly multiplying typhoid bacilli. The typhoid bacillus grows in gelatin, especially on the surface, somewhat like the bacillus coli communis, but with a less luxuriant growth. This organism, when taken from young broth cultures twelve to twenty-four hours old—during the period at which flagella are best seen—and examined microscopically, exhibits very lively movements. When, as pointed out by Gruber and Durham, blood-serum, in certain dilutions, from a case of typhoid fever is added to such a culture, the broth, at first turbid, owing to the suspended and moving microorganisms, gradually becomes clear, and a deposit is formed which is found to be made up of masses or clumps of typhoid bacilli which have lost their motility. This reaction is so characteristic and definite, that when the mixture is kept under examination under the microscope, it is quite possible to follow the slowing-down movement and massing together of the organisms. It is found, moreover, that normal diluted blood-serum has no such effect on the bacilli. This property of the blood-serum is acquired at such an early date of the disease—sometimes even at the end of the first week—and occurs with such regularity, that typhoid fever may now actually be diagnosed by the presence or absence of this " agglutinating " property in the blood. If serum taken from a patient supposed to be suffering from typhoid fever, and diluted with saline solution to 1 in 10, to 1 in 50, or in still greater dilution, causes the bacilli to lose their motility and to become aggregated into clumps within an hour, it may be concluded that the patient is suffering from typhoid fever; if this agglutination be not obtained with a dilution of 1 in 10, in from 15 to 30 minutes, experience has shown that the patient is not suffering from this disease. Certain other diseases, such as cholera, give a similar specific serum reaction with their specific organisms. These sera have, in addition, a slight common action—a general agglutinating power—which, however, is not manifested except in concentrated solutions, the higher dilutions failing to give any clumping action at all, except with the specific bacillus associated with the disease from which the patient, from whom the serum is taken, is suffering.

Wright and Semple, working on Haffkine's lines, introduced a method of vaccination against typhoid, corresponding somewhat to that devised by Haffkine to protect against cholera. They first obtained a typhoid bacillus of fairly constant virulence and of such strength and power of multiplication that an agar culture of 24 hours' growth when divided into four, and injected hypodermically, will kill four fairly large guinea-pigs, each weighing 350 to 400 grammes. A similar culture emulsified in bouillon or saline solution and killed by heating for five minutes at 60° C. is a vaccine sufficient for from four to twenty doses. In place of the agar culture a bouillon culture heated for the same period may be used as the vaccine. In either case the vaccine is injected under the skin of the loin well above the crest of the ileum. This injection is usually followed by local tenderness and swelling within three or four hours, and swelling and tenderness in the position of the nearest lymphatic glands, marked malaise, headache, a general feeling of restlessness and discomfort and a rise of temperature. The blood of a patient so treated early causes agglutination of typhoid bacilli and acts on these bacilli much as does cholera serum in Pfeiffer's reaction. At the end of ten days a second and stronger dose is given. After each injection there is, according to Wright, a " negative phase " during which the patient is somewhat more susceptible to the attacks of the typhoid bacillus. This negative phase soon passes off and a distinct positive or protected phase appears. The practical outcome of this is that wherever possible a patient who is going into a typhoid infected area should be vaccinated some little time before he sets out. There seems to be no doubt that if this be done a very marked, though not complete, protection is conferred. For a time the agglutinative and lytic powers of the serum continue to rise and the patient so vaccinated is far less susceptible to the action of the typhoid bacillus. It is recorded in favour of this method of treatment that of 4502 soldiers of the Indian army inoculated 0·98 % contracted typhoid, while of 25,851 soldiers of the same army who were not inoculated over 2⅖ % (2·54) contracted typhoid. Similarly, at Ladysmith, of the whole of the besieged soldiers only 1705 had been inoculated, but of these only 2 % contracted typhoid, whilst of 10,529 uninoculated men 14 % were attacked. Wright, who has been indefatigable in carrying out and watching this method of treatment, has been able to accumulate statistics dealing with 49,600 individuals —of these 8600 were inoculated, and 2¼ % contracted typhoid, 12 % of these succumbing to the disease. Of the 41,000 uninoculated men 51 % contracted the disease, 21 % of those attacked succumbing.

Mediterranean or Malta Fever.—Until comparatively recently, Mediterranean fever was looked upon as a form of typhoid fever, which in certain respects it resembles; the temperature curve, however, has a more undulatory character, except in the malignant type, where the temperature remains high throughout the course of the attack. According to Hughes, this disease is widely distributed in the countries bordering upon the Mediterranean south of latitude 46° N., and along the Red Sea littoral. Analogous forms of fever giving a " specific " serum reaction with the micrococcus of this disease are also met with in parts of India, China, Africa and America.

The *Micrococcus melitensis vel Brucei* (1887), which is found most abundantly in the enlarged spleen of the patient suffering from Malta fever, is a very minute organism (0·33μ in diameter), ovoid or nearly round, arranged in pairs or in very short chains. If a drop of the blood taken directly from the spleen be smeared over the surface of agar nutrient medium, minute transparent colourless colonies appear; in thirty-six hours these have a slight amber tinge, and in four or five days from their first appearance they become opaque. These colonies, which flourish at the temperature of the human blood, cease to grow at the room-temperature except in summer, and if kept moist, soon die at anything below 60° F., though when dried they retain their vitality for some time. As the organism grows and multiplies in broth there is opacity of the medium at the end of five or six days, this being followed by precipitation, so that a comparatively clear supernatant fluid remains. It grows best on media slightly less alkaline than human blood; it is very vigorous and may resist desiccation for several weeks.

This organism is distinctly pathogenetic to monkeys, and its virulence may be so increased that other animals may be affected by it. Though unable to live in clean or virgin soil, it may lead a saprophytic existence in soil polluted with faecal matter. Hughes maintains that the " virus " leaves the body of goats and of man along with the faeces and urine. The importance of this in ambulatory cases is very evident, especially when it is remembered that goats feeding on grass, &c. which has come in contact with such urine are readily infected. It seldom appears to be carried for any considerable distance. Infection is not conveyed by the sputum, sweat, breath or scraping of the skin of patients, and infected dust does not seem to play a very important part in producing the disease. Hughes divides the fever into three types. In the malignant form the onset is sudden, there are headache, racking pain over the whole body, nausea and sometimes vomiting; the tongue is foul, coated and swollen, and the breath very offensive; the temperature may continue for some time at 103° to 105° F. The stools in the diarrhoea which is sometimes present may be most offensive. At the end of a few days the lungs become congested and pneumonic, the pulse weak, hyperpyrexia appears, and death ensues. A second type, by far the most common, is the " undulatory " type, in which there is remittent pyrexia, separated by periods in which the patient appears to be improving. These pyrexial curves, from one to seven in number, average about ten days each, the first being the longest,—eighteen to twenty-three days. In an intermittent type, in which the temperature-curve closely resembles the hectic pyrexial curve of phthisis or suppuration, the " undulatory " character is also marked. A considerable number of toxic symptoms make their appearance—localized neuritis, synovitis, anaemia, emaciation, bronchial catarrh, weakness of the heart, neuralgia, profuse night-sweats and similar conditions. Patients otherwise healthy usually recover, even after prolonged attacks of the disease, but the mortality amongst patients suffering from organic mischief of any kind may be comparatively high. The diagnosis from malaria, phthisis, rheumatic affections and pneumonia may, in most cases, be made fairly easily, but the serum agglutinating reaction (first demonstrated by Wright in 1897) with cultures of the *Micrococcus melitensis*, corresponding to the typhoid reaction with the typhoid bacillus, is sometimes the only trustworthy feature by which a diagnosis may be made between this fever and the above-mentioned diseases. About 50 % of the goats in Malta give a positive agglutinative reaction and about 10 % excrete milk which contains the micrococcus.

Sir David Bruce, in his investigations on the tsetse fly disease, pointed out that certain wild animals although apparently in good health might serve as reservoirs for, or storehouses of, the N'gana parasite. He was therefore quite prepared to find that the *Micrococcus melitensis* might similarly be "stored" in an animal which might show but slight, if any, manifestations of Malta fever. Indications as to the direction in which to look were given in the following fashion. There was a strike amongst' the dairymen supplying the barracks in Malta and it became necessary to replace the goat's milk in the dietary of the troops by condensed milk. What followed ? In the first half of the year 1906 there had been 144 cases (in 1905 there had been 750 cases), in the second half after the alteration of the milk supply, only 32 cases were recorded and in 1907, 7 cases during the whole year. In the navy during the same period there were, in 1905, 498 cases, in 1906, 248 cases and, from January to September 1907, not a single case.

The most common method of infection is by the ingestion of milk, but the milk when handled may also give rise to infection through finding its way into cuts, bruises, &c. In the goat the disease is of an extremely mild character, the clinical symptoms, which are present for two or three days only, being easily overlooked. In spite of this the goat is highly susceptible to the infection either by the various methods of inoculation or as the result of feeding with contaminated or infected material. The micrococcus is often found in the circulating blood from which it may be excreted along with the urine and faeces. In time, however, it disappears, first from the general circulation and most of the viscera, persisting longest in the spleen, kidneys and lymphatic glands. In the later stages of the disease the micrococcus is found in the milk even after it has disappeared from the above glands. It is during this stage that the milk of the goat is so dangerous, as now and again it may contain an enormous number of the specific micrococcus varying "within wide limits from day to day," although bearing "no relationship to the severity of the infection, air temperature, &c.; the presence of the *Micrococcus melitensis* in the milk appears to be merely the result of a mechanical flushing of the mammary glands by means of which the cocci multiplying therein are removed." As pointed out by the Mediterranean Fever Commission the micrococcus of Malta fever from its vantage ground in the milk may make its way to ordinary ice-creams and to native cheeses, in which it appears to retain its full virulence. Monkeys are especially susceptible to this disease, contracting it readily when they are fed with milk from an infected goat. In 1905 an interesting experiment was, unintentionally, carried out. An official of the United States Bureau of Animal Industry visiting Malta in the summer of that year purchased a herd of 61 milch-goats and four billy goats. These were shipped via Antwerp to the United States. On arrival at Antwerp the goats were transferred to a quarantine station, where they remained for five days and were then consigned by steamer to New York. On board the SS. "Joshua Nicholson," which took the goats from Malta to Antwerp, were twenty-three officers and men; ten out of the twenty-three were afterwards traced. One was found to have been infected by *M. melitensis* at an unknown date, and eight had subsequently suffered from febrile attacks, five yielding conclusive evidence of infection by *M. melitensis*. It is interesting to note, however, that two men who boiled the milk before drinking it, and an officer and a cabin-boy who disliked the milk and did not drink it at all, came off scot free.

These cases leave by themselves might leave the question somewhat open, as there was a possibility that the men attacked might have been in contact with infected patients in Malta. A far more conclusive case was the following. A woman at the quarantine station at Athenia, N. J., U.S.A., who partook freely of the mixed milk from several goats, over a considerable period, suffered from a typical attack of Mediterranean fever some nine or ten weeks after the goats had been landed in America. In this case "contact" with and other modes of exposure to infection by human patients could all be eliminated.

It may be held then that the *M. melitensis* leads a more or less passive existence in the body of the Maltese goat, only exercising its full pathogenic action when it gains entrance to the human body. There is some slight evidence that the *Micrococcus melitensis* may remain alive with its virulence unimpaired even when taken up by the mosquitoes Acartomyia and Stegomyia, and again in the common blood-sucking fly, Stomoxys, for a short period, four or five days. It can be recovered for a longer period and still in a fairly virulent condition from the excreta of these insects. In spite of this, transmission of the disease by these insects, though apparently possible, does not appear to be of very frequent occurrence. Inoculation with a vaccine prepared from the *Micrococcus melitensis* appears to exert a protective influence for a period of about four months, after which time there is a marked diminution in the immunity conferred by this vaccination.

Relapsing Fever.—The specific cause of relapsing fever (famine fever) appears to be the *Spirillum Obermeieri*, an organism which occurs in the blood (during the febrile stages) of patients suffering from this disease. Between the febrile stages are periods of intermission, during which the spirillum disappears from the blood and, apparently, retires to the spleen. This disease, in epidemic form, follows in the footsteps of famine and destitution, specially affecting young people between the ages of fifteen and twenty; it seldom attacks children under five years of age, but when it attacks patients over thirty it assumes a very virulent form. In monkeys inoculated with blood containing the *Spirillum Obermeieri* the first symptoms appear between the second and sixth days. In the human subject this incubation period may last as long as three weeks; then comes an attack of fever, which continues for about a week, and is followed by a similar period of apparent convalescence, on which ensues a pyrexial relapse, continuing about half as long as the first. The spirilla, the cause of this disease, are fine spirals with pointed ends, three or four times as long as the diameter of a red blood corpuscle. Although it has as yet been found impossible to cultivate these spirilla outside the body, human beings, and monkeys injected with blood containing them, contract the disease; and in monkeys it has been found that during the period before the relapse the spirilla have made their way into the cells of the spleen. As yet little is known as to the mode of development of these organisms, and of the method of their transmission from one patient to another, but it is thought that, as in the case of malaria and the tsetse-fly disease, they may be carried by bloodsucking insects. Relapsing fever is distinguished from typhoid fever by its sudden onset, and by the distinct intermissions; and from influenza by the enlargement of the spleen and liver. The most satisfactory method of diagnosis is the examination of the blood for the presence of the spirillum during the febrile stage. The *post-mortem* appearances are those of a toxic (bacterial) poisoning. Curious infarction-like masses, in which are numerous spirilla, are found in the spleen; in the liver there is evidence of acute interstitial hepatitis, with cloudy swelling of the liver cells; and similar changes occur in the kidney. Fatty degeneration of the heart and voluntary muscles may also be met with.

Plague.—During recent years opportunities for the study of plague have unfortunately been only too numerous. In patients suffering from this disease, a micro-organism, capable of leading either a saprophytic life or a parasitic existence in the human body, and in some of the lower animals, was described independently by Kitasato and Lowson and by Yersin, 1894, in Hong-Kong. It is a short moderately thick oval bacillus, with rounded ends, which stain deeply, leaving a clear band in the centre (see Plate II., fig. 7). It thus resembles the short diphtheria bacillus and the influenza bacillus. Certain other forms are met with—long rods and "large oval bacilli, pear-shaped or round, imperfectly stained pale involution forms "—but the above is the most characteristic. It grows readily on most media at the temperature of the body, but, like the glanders bacillus, soon loses its virulence in cultivations. It may be obtained in pure cultures from the lymph glands, and from the abscesses that are formed in the groin or other positions in which the glands become enlarged and softened. It may also be found in the spleen and in the blood, and, in the case of patients suffering from the pneumonic form of the disease, even in the lungs and in the sputum. It has also been found in the faeces and urine. (It is very important that these excretions from plague patients should always be most carefully disinfected.) This organism, when obtained in pure culture and inoculated into rats, mice, guinea-pigs or rabbits, produces exactly the same symptoms as does material taken fresh from the softened glands. The symptoms are local swelling, enlargement and softening of the lymphatic glands, and high fever.

The difficulty of explaining the spread of plague, at one time apparently almost insuperable, has at last been overcome, as it has been found that although the acute pneumonic plague is undoubtedly highly contagious, the spread of the bubonic and septicaemic forms could not be explained on the same hypothesis. As the pneumonic form is met with in only about 2·5 % of the whole of the cases, transmission by direct contagion seems to be an utterly inadequate explanation. In the autumn of 1896, when the plague broke out in India, and those dealing

PARASITIC DISEASES

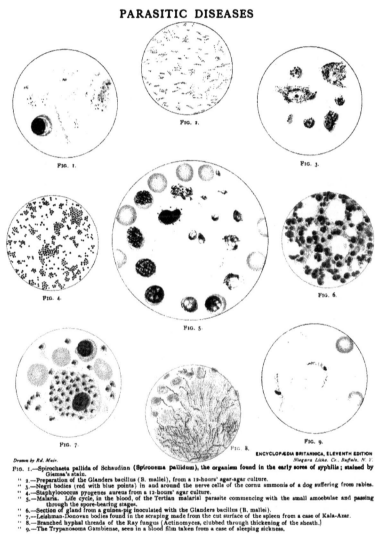

Drawn by Rd. Muir.

Fig. 1.—Spirochaeta pallida of Schaudinn (Spironema pallidum), the organism found in the early sores of syphilis; stained by Giemsa's stain.

" 2.—Preparation of the Glanders bacillus (B. mallei), from a 12-hours' agar-agar culture.

" 3.—Negri bodies (red with blue points) in and around the nerve cells of the cornu ammonis of a dog suffering from rabies.

" 4.—Staphylococcus pyogenes aureus from a 12-hours' agar culture.

" 5.—Malaria. Life cycle, in the blood, of the Tertian malarial parasite commencing with the small amoebulae and passing through the spore-bearing stages.

" 6.—Section of gland from a guinea-pig inoculated with the Glanders bacillus (B. mallei).

" 7.—Leishman-Donovan bodies found in the scraping made from the cut surface of the spleen from a case of Kala-Azar.

" 8.—Branched hyphal threads of the Ray fungus (Actinomyces, clubbed through thickening of the sheath.)

" 9.—The Trypanosoma Gambiense, seen in a blood film taken from a case of sleeping sickness.

with the outbreak came to the conclusion that certain houses were centres of infection, it was noticed that these houses were most infective at night, and that they might actually be centres of infection although uninhabited; indeed the infection seemed to spread to houses between which and the infected house there appeared to be no intercommunication of any kind. This seemed to be inexplicable except on the assumption that the infective agent, the *Bacillus pestis*, was, in some way or other, carried by animals. It had already been noted that rats disappeared from plague-stricken houses, many dying before the appearance of the plague in the human population. Simond, noting these conditions, suggested that the plague bacillus might be transmitted by the flea from rat to rat and from rat to man. Although he was not able to demonstrate this connexion he indicated a line of research to other observers, who, as knowledge accumulated, were able to complete each link in the chain of infection. The plague bacillus having been found in the rat, the next step was to demonstrate its presence in the flea, and living plague germs were found in the stomachs of fleas inhabiting plague-infected houses. Several species seem to be able to transmit this germ, but in none of them does the plague bacillus appear to undergo any special development —alternation of generations or the like—as in the case of the protozoon of malaria in its passage from and to the mosquito and the human subject —it simply passes unchanged through the alimentary canal of the flea, is excreted in the faeces, and is carried into the wound made by the epipharynx-mandibles of the flea.

At least three species of animals, two rats and the human subject, and three species of fleas are involved in this chain. The rat fleas are *Pulex cheopis* found in India, and *Ceratophyllus fasciatus*, the rat flea of northern Europe, and *Pulex irritans*, the common flea, all of which have the power of transmitting the disease. In India of course the *Pulex cheopis*, usually solely associated with rats, seems to play the most prominent part. The two rats involved are the *Mus decumanus*, or brown rat, which is found in the sewers and develops the plague first, and the *Mus rattus*, the common black house-rat. From the sewer-rat the house-rat is infected, and from the house-rat man. Under ordinary conditions rat fleas do not attack the human subject, but, as the rats are attacked by plague and die, the infected fleas, starve out as it were, leave them and transfer their attentions to other animals and the human subject, infecting many of those they bite. Colonel Bannerman maintains that this infection takes place in the majority of cases, by this chain of transmission, and that there is no evidence that the excreta of these rats infect food or contaminate the soil. Colonel Lamb, summarizing the experimental evidence on this question, writes:—

" 1. Close contact of plague-infected animals with healthy animals, if fleas are excluded, does not give rise to an epizootic among the latter. As the godowns (experimental huts) were never cleaned out, close contact includes contact with faeces and urine of infected animals, and contact with and eating of food contaminated with faeces and urine of infected animals as well as with pus from open plague ulcers; (2) close contact of young, even when suckled by plague-infected mothers, did not give the disease to the former; (3) if fleas are present, then the epizootic, once started, spreads from animal to animal, the rate of progress being in direct proportion to the number of fleas present; (4) an epizootic of plague may start without direct contact of healthy animal and infected animal; (5) the rat flea can convey plague from rat to rat; (6) infection can take place without any contact with contaminated soil; (7) aerial infection is excluded."

The experiments lead to the conclusion that fleas and fleas alone, are the transmitting agents of infection. Bannerman gives in concise form similar evidence in relation to naturally infected native houses. Infection is carried from place to place by fleas, usually on the body or in the clothing of the human being. Such fleas, fed on infected blood, may remain alive for three weeks, and of this period, we are told, may remain infective for fifteen days. At the first opportunity these fleas forsake the human host and return to their natural host the rat. In most of the epidemics there is a definite sequence of events. First the brown rats are attacked, then the black rats,

then the human subject, and Colonel Lamb suggests that after the rat disappears the flea starves for about three days and then attacks the human subject. Then comes the incubation period of plague, three days. Following this is the period of average duration of the disease, five or six days. This time-table, he says, corresponds to the period—when the epidemics are at their height—that intervenes between the maximum death-rate in rats and the maximum death-rate in man, about ten to fourteen days. This history of the connexion between the flea, the rat, and the human subject reads almost like a fairy tale, but it is now one of the well-authenticated and sober facts of modern medicine.

In India, where the notions of cleanliness are somewhat different from those recognized in Great Britain, most of the conditions favourable to the spread of the plague bacillus are of the most perfect character. This organism may pass into the soil with faeces; it may there remain for some time, and then be taken into the body of one of the lower animals, or of man, and give rise to a fresh outbreak. Kitasato and Yersin were both able to prove that soil and dust from infected houses contain the bacillus, that such bacillus is capable of inducing an attack of plague in the lower animals, and that flies fed on the dejecta or other bacillus-containing material, die, and in turn contain bacilli which are capable of setting up infection. Hankin claims that ants may carry the plague to and from rats, and so to the human being. It has already been mentioned that the organism rapidly loses its virulence when cultivated outside the body; on the other hand, on being passed through a series of animals its virulence gradually increases. Thus may be explained the fact that in most outbreaks of plague there is an early period during which the death-rate is very low; after a time the percentage mortality is enormously increased, the virulence of the disease being very great and its course rapid. There seem to be notable differences in the degree of susceptibility of different races and different individuals, and those who have passed safely through an attack appear to have acquired a marked degree of immunity.

Two methods of treatment, both of which seem to have been attended with a certain degree of success, are now being tried. Haffkine, who was the first to produce a vaccine for the treatment of cholera, prepared a vaccine of a somewhat similar type for the treatment of plague. For this the *Bacillus pestis* is cultivated in flasks of bouillon; to this small drops or particles of ghee (Indian butter) are added; these form centres around which the organisms may develop. As the organisms multiply they grow down into the broth, but gradually becoming fewer in number as the floating mass on the surface is left, they fine down to a point and so come to resemble stalactites. These are broken off, from time to time, by shaking, others immediately beginning to form in their place. This may go on for six weeks. The flask with its contents is then well shaken and heated in a water bath to 70° C. for from one to three hours. On testing by culture the fluid should now be sterile, *i.e.* no bacilli should remain alive, and the fluid, ready for use, may be injected into the subcutaneous tissues of the arm in a dose of from 3 cc. for a man and 2 to 2½ cc. for a woman, children receiving relatively small amounts. A rise of temperature, followed by malaise and headache, which pass off in about 24 hours, is soon noted, and some local swelling and redness appear at the seat of injection. The Indian Plague Commission were satisfied that the use of this vaccine diminishes the incidence of attacks of plague, and that, although it does not confer a complete immunity against the disease, the case mortality is lowered. They are of opinion also that protection is not conferred at once, but Lieut.-Colonel Bannerman states that the protection is immediate and lasts for six or even twelve months. In the official report (Annual Report of the Sanitary Commissioner with the Government of India) for 1904 occurs the following: " That its value is great is certain, not only does it largely diminish the danger of plague being contracted, but, if it fails to prevent the attack, the probability of a fatal event is reduced by one-half."

This method of treatment, however, is of no avail in the case of patients already attacked; for such cases Yersin's serum treatment must be called in. Various other vaccines have been described, but all consist of some form of killed or attenuated bacilli, and the results attained do not vary very greatly. Yersin, who first demonstrated the plague bacillus also devised the method of preparing an "antipest serum." A horse was inoculated repeatedly, at intervals, and with gradually increasing doses of living plague bacilli. It was afterwards found that cultures sterilized by heat served equally well for this inoculation of the horse and of course were much more easily worked with. This process of preparation may have to be continued for from six months to a year. The horse is then bled and from the clot the serum is separated, care being taken to determine by injection of the blood into mice that no living bacilli have by accident made their way into, and remained in, the horse's blood. The serum is not considered to be sufficiently active until a drop and a half will protect the mouse against a dose of living bacilli fatal to a control mouse in from 48 to 60 hours. When this serum is injected in sufficiently large doses subcutaneously in mild cases, and subcutaneously and intravenously (*Lancet*, 1903, i. 1287) in more severe cases in doses of 150 to 300 cc, the results seem to be excellent, especially when the serum is injected into the tissues around the bubo or swellings formed in this disease. Calmette and Salimbeni used the serum in 142 cases in the Oporto outbreak. Amongst these they had a mortality of under 15 %, whilst amongst 72 patients not so treated the death-rate was over 63 %. This serum kills the bacilli and at the same time neutralizes the toxin formed during the course of the disease. The best results are obtained when large doses are given, and when the serum injected subcutaneously is thrown into the area in which the lymph flows towards the bubo. As in the case of the diphtheria antitoxic serum joint pains and rashes may follow its exhibition, but no other ill effects have been noted.

Pneumonia.—The case in favour of acute lobar pneumonia being an infective disease was a very strong one, even before it was possible to show that a special organism bore any aetiological relation to it. In 1880, Friedländer claimed that he had isolated such an organism, but the pneumo-bacillus then described appears to be inactive as compared with the pneumococcus isolated by Fraenkel and Talamon. This latter organism which is usually found in the sputum, is an encapsuled diplococcus. Grown on serum or agar over which sterile blood has been smeared, it occurs as minute, glistening, rather prominent points, almost like a fine spray of water or dew. When the organism is cultivated in broth the capsule disappears, and chains of diplococci are seen. It resembles the influenza bacillus in a most remarkable manner. It may be found, in almost every case of pneumonia, in the "rusty" or "prune-juice" sputum. Injected into rabbits, it produces death with very great certainty; and by passing the organism through these animals its virulence may be markedly increased. Like the influenza bacillus and even the diphtheria bacillus, this organism may be present in the mouth and lungs of perfectly healthy individuals, and it is only when the vitality of the system is lowered by cold or other depressing influences that pneumonia is induced; two factors, the presence of the bacillus and the lowered vitality, being both necessary for the production of this disease in the human subject. It is quite possible, however, that, as in the case of cholera, a slight inflammatory exudation may supply a nutrient medium in which the bacillus rapidly acquires greatly increased virulence, and so becomes a much more active agent of infection.

It is claimed by the brothers Klemperer, by Washbourn and by others, that they have been able to produce an anti-pneumococcic serum, by means of which they are able to treat successfully severe cases of pneumonia. The catarrhal pneumonia so frequently met with during the course of whooping-cough, measles and other specific infective fevers, is also in all probability due to the action of some organism of which the influenza bacillus and the *Diplococcus pneumoniae* are types.

Infective meningitis is, in most of the recent works on medicine, divided into four forms: (1) the acute epidemic cerebro-spinal form; (2) a posterior basic form, which, however, is closely allied to the first; (3) suppurative meningitis, usually associated with pneumonia, erysipelas, and pyaemia; and (4) tubercular meningitis, due to the specific tubercle bacillus.

1. The first form, acute infective or epidemic cerebro-spinal meningitis, is usually associated with Weichselbaum's *Diplococcus intracellularis meningitidis* (two closely apposed disks), which is found in the exudate, especially in the leucocytes, of the meninges of the brain and cord. It grows, as transparent colonies, on blood-agar at the temperature of the body, but dies out very rapidly unless reinoculated, and has little pathogenetic effect on any of the lower animals, though under certain conditions it has been found to produce meningitis when injected under the dura mater.

More or less successful attempts have been made to treat acute epidemic cerebro-spinal meningitis by means of antisera obtained from different sources. Flexner uses the serum of horses that have been highly immunized against numerous strains of the meningococcus, the process of immunization extending over four or five months. Meister, Lucius and Brüning supply Ruppel's antibacterial serum derived from animals immunized against several strains of meningococcus of high pathogenic activity. Both these sera may be looked upon as polyvalent sera. Ivy Mackenzie and Martin, pointing out that the cerebro-spinal fluid, even of patients who have recovered from this form of meningitis, contains no antibodies, tried and recommended injections of the patient's own blood serum into the spinal canal. In all cases the action seems to be much the same. These sera contain immune body and complement, and are distinctly bactericidal, acting on the meningococcus and rendering it much more easily taken up and digested by the white blood corpuscles. It is possible that these sera may also exert some slight antitoxic action. The serum is injected directly into the spinal canal, a corresponding quantity of the cerebro-spinal fluid having first been withdrawn by lumbar puncture. The treatment thus resembles the treatment of lockjaw, where the antitetanus serum is brought as directly as possible into contact with the nerve centres. The dose of these sera ranges from 15 to 40 cc. according to the severity of the disease. Although the general mortality of the disease is from 50 to 80 %, it is stated that where Flexner's serum is used the mortality falls to 33 %. The result corresponds somewhat closely to those obtained with antidiphtheria serum in diphtheria. In patients injected on the first day of the disease the mortality was only about 15 %, on and from the fourth to the seventh day 22 %, but after the seventh day 36 %. From this it is evident that although the serum has a distinct effect in bringing about the phagocytosis of the meningococcus and the neutralization of the toxins produced, it cannot make good any damage already done to the tissues. Mackenzie and Martin treated 20 cases with the blood taken from patients suffering, or convalescent, from meningitis. Of 16 acute cases treated 14 received serum from patients who had already recovered from the disease, 8 of the patients recovered, 6 died, and 2 cases which received their own serum both recovered. In the presence of an anti-cerebro-spinal-fever sera the meningeal cocci become diminished in number and do not stain so readily, whilst, simultaneously, the polymorpho-nuclear leucocytes seem to be diminished in number. The serum should be given until the temperature becomes normal. Mackenzie and Martin assert that even normal human blood contains substances which are bactericidal to the meningeal coccus, but that these substances increase "in amount and activity in the blood serum of patients suffering from an acute or chronic meningococcic infection, and the serum of a patient recently recovered from an infection shows the evidence of the presence of these substances in a still greater degree." They were able to demonstrate, moreover, that the destructive action on the cocci depends on an immune body which requires the presence of a complement to complete the process. The cerebro-spinal fluid differs from the serum in that it does not contain substances which kill this meningeal coccus *in vitro*, nor are the immune body and complement present in the blood, found in this cerebro-spinal fluid. Hence the efficacy of the blood when it is called upon to replace the fluid in the cerebro-spinal canal.

2. *Posterior basic meningitis*, according to Dr Still, "is frequently seen during the first six months of life, a period at which tuberculous and epidemic cerebro-spinal meningitis are quite uncommon." The organism found in this disease resembles the *diplococcus intracellularis meningitidis* very closely, but differs from it in that it remains alive without recultivation for a considerably longer period. It is less pathogenetic than that organism, of which possibly it is simply a more highly saprophytic form. This is a somewhat important point, as it would account for the great resemblance that exists between the sporadic and the epidemic forms of meningitis.

3. In *suppurative meningitis* these two organisms may still be found in a certain proportion of the cases, but their place may be taken by the pneumococcus or *Diplococcus pneumoniae* or Fraenkel's pneumococcus—*Diplococcus lanceolatus*—which appears to grow in two forms. In the first it is an encapsulated organism, consisting of small oval cocci arranged in pairs or in short chains; the capsule is unstained. When the pneumococcus grows in chains—the second form—as when cultivated outside the body, on blood-serum or on agar over the surface of which a small quantity of sterile blood has been smeared, it produces very minute translucent colonies. Like Weichselbaum's bacillus, it must be recultivated every three or four days, otherwise it soon dies out. Unlike the other forms previously described, it may, when passed through animals, become extremely virulent, very small quantities being sufficient to kill a rabbit. Although the pneumococcus is found in the majority of these cases, especially in children, suppurative

meningitis may also accompany or follow the various diseases that are set up by the *Streptococcus pyogenes* and *Streptococcus erysipelotis*; whilst along with it staphylococci and the *Bacillus coli communis* have sometimes been found. In other cases, again, there is a mixed infection of the pneumococcus and the *Streptococcus pyogenes*, especially in cases of disease of the middle ear. As might be expected in meningitis occurring in connexion with the specific infective diseases, *e.g.* influenza and typhoid fever, the presence of the specific bacilli of these diseases may usually be demonstrated in the meningeal pus or fluid.

4. The fourth form, *tubercular meningitis* (acute hydrocephalus), is met with most frequently in young children. It is now generally accepted that this condition is the result of the introduction of the tubercle bacillus into the blood-vessels and lymph spaces of the meninges at the base of the brain, and along the fissures of Sylvius.

Influenza.—From 1889 up to the present time, influenza has every year with unfailing regularity broken out in epidemic form in some part of the United Kingdom, and often has swept over the whole country. The fact that the period of incubation is short, and that the infective agent is extremely active at a very early stage of the disease, renders it one of the most rapidly-spreading maladies with which we have to deal. The infective agent, first observed by Pfeiffer and Canon, is a minute bacillus or diplococcus less that 1μ in length and 0·5μ in thickness; it is found in little groups or in pairs. Each diplococcus is stained at the poles, a clear band remaining in the middle; in this respect it resembles the plague bacillus. It is found in the blood—though here it seems to be comparatively inactive—and in enormous numbers in the bronchial mucus. It is not easily stained in a solution of carbol-fuchsin, but in some cases such numbers are present that a cover-glass preparation may show practically no other organisms. Agar, smeared with blood, and inoculated, gives an almost pure cultivation of very minute transparent colonies, similar to those of the *Diplococcus pneumoniae*, but as a rule somewhat smaller. This organism, found only in cases of influenza, appears to have the power of forming toxins which continue to act for some time after recovery seems to have taken place; it appears to exert such a general devitalizing effect on the tissues that micro-organisms which ordinarily are held in check are allowed to run riot, with the result that catarrh, pneumonia and similar conditions are developed, especially when cold and other lowering conditions co-operate with the poison. This toxin produces special results in those organs which, through over-use, impaired nutrition or disease, are already only just able to carry on their work. Hence in cases of influenza the cause of death is usually associated with the failure of some organ that had already been working up to its full capacity, and in which the margin of reserve power had been reduced to a minimum. It is for this reason that rest, nutrition, warmth and tonics are such important and successful factors in the treatment of this condition.

Yellow Fever, endemic in the West Indies and the north-eastern coast of South America, may become epidemic wherever the temperature and humidity are high, especially along the seashore in the tropical Atlantic coast of North America. It appears to be one of the specific infective fevers in which the liver, ine , and gastro-intestinal systems, and especially their blood-vessels, are affected. In 1897 Sanarelli reported, in the *Annales de l'Institut Pasteur*, that he had found a bacillus in the blood-vessels of the liver and kidneys, and in the cells of the peritoneal fluid, but never in the alimentary tract, of yellow fever patients. These, he maintained, were perfectly distinct from the putrefactive microbes occurring in the tissues in the later stages, their colonies not growing like those of the bacillus coli communis. They grow readily on all the ordinary artificial nutrient media, as short rods with rounded ends, usually about 2 to 4μ in length and about half as broad as they are long. They are stained by Gram's method and readily by most of the aniline dyes, are ciliated, and do not liquefy gelatine. They flourish specially well alongside moulds, in the dark, in badly-ventilated, warm, moist places, and remain alive for some time in sea-water:

these facts, as Sanarelli points out, may afford an explanation of the special persistence of yellow fever in old, badly-ventilated ships, and in dark, dirty and insanitary sea-coast towns. Once the organism, whatever it may be, finds its way into the system, it soon makes its presence felt, and toxic symptoms are developed. The temperature rises; the pulse, at first rapid, gradually slows down; and after some time persistent vomiting of bile comes on. At the end of three or four days the temperature and pulse fall, and there is a period during which the patient appears comparatively well; this is followed in a few hours by icterus and scanty secretion of urine. There may be actual anuria, or the small quantity of urine passed may be loaded with casts and albumen; delirium, convulsions and haemorrhages from all the mucous surfaces may now occur, or secondary infections of various kinds, boils, abscesses, suppurations and septicaemia, may result. These often prove fatal when the patient appears to be almost convalescent from the original disease. As regards prognosis, it has been found that the "lower the initial temperature the milder will the case be" (Macpherson). An initial temperature of 106° F. is an exceedingly unfavourable sign. Patients addicted to the use of alcohol are, as a rule, much more severely affected than are others. Treatment is principally directed towards prevention and towards the alleviation of symptoms, though Sanarelli has hopes that an "anti"-serum may be useful. More recently S. Flexner, working with the American Commission, isolated another organism, which, he maintains, is the pathogenetic agent in the production of yellow fever; whilst Durham and Myers maintain that a small bacillus previously observed by G. M. Sternberg and others is the true cause of this disease.

Professor Boyce, enumerating the hypotheses as to the cause of yellow fever, points out that as in the case of malaria, suspicion turned to "that form of Miasm which was supposed to arise from the mixture, in a marsh or on a mud flat, of salt with fresh water." It was early recognized that yellow fever was not carried directly from person to person, but little of definite character was known as to the poison and the method of its dissemination, and Fergusson states that "it is a terrestrial poison which high atmospheric heat generates amongst the newly arrived, and without that heat it cannot exist." The following passage from Beauperthuy (see his collected papers published in 1891) is quoted by Boyce: "But rubbish! the small amount of sulphuretted hydrogen or marsh gas which might arise from a marsh could not possibly hurt a fly, much less a man. It is not that, it is a mosquito called in Cumana the 'Zancudo bobo,' the striped or domestic mosquito." Beauperthuy, recently as he wrote, then stood almost alone in this opinion. Now we know that yellow fever, in common with other specific diseases, is caused by the action of an organized virus. The search for a vegetable parasite, bacillus or micrococcus, as above indicated, has been very close and strenuous, but it may now be held that up to the present no bacillus or micrococcus, well authenticated as capable of causing yellow fever, has been discovered. Latterly a search has been made for protozoal organisms, organisms similar to those present in the blood of malarious patients and like conditions, or for spirochaetes similar to those associated with relapsing fever, and Boyce drew attention to the fact that a spirochaete has recently been identified in the tissues taken from cases of yellow fever. It has however been demonstrated that the virus, whatever it may be, is carried by a species of mosquito; this seems to favour the protozoan hypothesis, especially as it is found that the *Stegomyia fasciata*, Fab. (or *S. calopus*, Meig.), after taking the blood from an infected patient is not infective immediately but only becomes capable of infecting by its bite at the end of twelve days. It would appear therefore that residence in this mosquito is necessary for the material to become fully infective. During this period some special metamorphosis may occur, and metamorphosis essential to the development of the parasite, or, on the other hand, the time may be required for it to make its way to some position from which it may emerge from the mosquito when that insect "strikes." In the interval between the bite of an infected Stegomyia and the appearance of the disease (5 or 6 days) the blood of the patient contains a virus which, when taken into the mosquito, may develop into the infective material; moreover, this virus persists alive and active for three days after the disease is fully developed, but at the end of this time it disappears, so far, at any rate, as its infective power is concerned, from the blood, secretions and tissues of the patient. Further, there is no evidence that the infective virus is ever transmitted directly from the patient in secretions or in fact in anything but blood or blood-serum. The infective material, then, is present in the human subject for about eight days, during which the blood and even the blood-serum may serve as a vehicle for the infective agent. If during this period the patient is bitten by the Stegomyia the mosquito cannot distribute the infection for twelve days, but after this the power of transmitting reinfection persists for weeks and even months during cold weather when the insect is torpid. As soon, however, as the warm weather comes round and the mosquito becomes active and again begins to bite there is evidence that it still maintains its power of transmitting infection; indeed Boyce states that mosquitos infected in one year are capable of transmitting infection and starting a fresh epidemic in the following warm season. When it is remembered that a mosquito by a single bite is capable of setting up an attack of the disease, we see how important is this question.

The Stegomyia, known as the domestic or house mosquito, is spoken of as the "Tiger" mosquito, "Scots' Grey," or "Black and White Mosquito," from the fact that there is "a lyre-shaped pattern in white on the back of the thorax, transverse white bands on the abdomen, and white spots on the sides of the thorax; while the legs have white bands with the last hind tarsal joint also white" (Boyce). It is also spoken of as the "cistern mosquito," as it breeds in the cisterns, barrels, water butts, &c., containing the only water-supply of many houses. It may pass through its various stages of development in any small vessels, but the larvae are not usually found in natural collections of water, such as gutters, pools or wells, if the ovipositing insect can gain access to cleaner and purer water.

The egg of the Stegomyia deposited on the water develops in from 10 to 20 hours into the larval form, the so-called "wiggle-waggle." It remains in this stage for from 1 to 8 days, then becomes a pupa, and within 48 hours becomes a fully developed mosquito. The larvae can only develop if they are left in water, though a very small amount of water will serve to keep them alive. The eggs on the other hand are very resistant, and even when removed from water may continue viable for as long a period as three months. The Stegomyia affects clean water-butts and cisterns by preference. Consequently its presence is not confined to unhygienic districts; they may, however, "seek refuge for breeding purposes in the shallow street drains and wells in the town." The Stegomyia does not announce its advent and attack by a "ping" such as that made by the Anopheles, it works perfectly noiselessly and almost ceaselessly (from 3 p.m. to early morning) so that any human beings in its neighbourhood are not safe from its attacks either afternoon or night.

The most important prophylactic measures against the Stegomyia are ample mosquito nets "with a gauge of eighteen meshes to the inch" (Boyce), so arranged that the person sleeping may not come near the net; these nets should be used not only at night but at the afternoon siesta. Then the living room should be screened against the entrance of these pests, thorough ventilation should be secured; and all pools and stagnant waters, especially in the neighbourhood of houses, should be drained, water-butts and cisterns should be screened and all stagnant waters oiled with kerosene or petroleum, where drainage is impossible. What has been done through the carrying out of these and similar measures may be gathered from the record of the Panama Canal. In 1884 the French Panama Canal Company, employing from 15,000 to 18,000 men, lost by death 60 per 1000 annually (in 1885 over 70 per 1000). In 1904, when the Americans had taken over the work of construction, Col. W. C. Gorgas undertook to clear the country of the Stegomyia, and within two or three years yellow fever had been eradicated. The death-rate from malaria was also greatly diminished, and by the end of 1907 the death-rate per annum amongst 45,000 workers was only 18 per 1000, a lower death-rate than is met with in many large English towns. Similar examples might be cited from other places, but the above is sufficiently striking to carry conviction that the methods employed in carrying on the warfare against tropical diseases have been attended with unexampled success. These diseases, at one time so greatly feared, are now so much under control that some one has said "ere long we shall be sending our patients to the tropics in search of a health resort."

Weil's disease, a disease which may be considered along with acute yellow atrophy and yellow fever, is one in which there is an acute febrile condition, associated with jaundice, inflammation of the kidney and enlargement of the spleen. It appears to be a toxic condition of a less acute character, however, than the other two, in which the functions and structure of the liver and kidney are specially interfered with. There is a marked affection of the gastro-intestinal system, and the nervous system is also in some cases profoundly involved. Haemorrhage into the mucous and serous membranes is a marked feature. The liver cells and kidney epithelium undergo fatty changes, though in the earlier stages there is a cloudy swelling, probably also toxic in origin. Organisms of the Proteus group, which appear to have the power, in certain circumstances, of forming toxic substances in larger quantities than can be readily destroyed by the liver, and which then make their appearance in the kidney and spleen, are supposed to be the cause of this condition.

Diphtheria.—In regard to no disease has medical opinion undergone greater modification than it has in respect of diphtheria. Accurately applied, bacteriology has here gained one of its greatest triumphs. Not only have the aetiology and diagnosis of this disease been made clear, but knowledge acquired in connexion with the production of the disease has been applied to a most successful method of treatment. In 1875 Klebs described a small bacillus with rounded ends, and with, here and there, small clear unstained spaces in its substance. He, however, also described streptococci as present in certain cases of diphtheria, and concluded that there must be two kinds of diphtheria, one associated with each of these organisms. In 1883 he again took up the question; and in the following year Loeffler gave a systematic description of what is now known as the Klebs-Loeffler bacillus, which was afterwards proved by Roux and Yersin and many other observers to be the *causa causans* of diphtheria. This bacillus is a slightly-curved rod with rounded, pointed, or club-shaped end or ends (see Plate II. fig 9). It is usually from 1·2 to 5μ or more in length and from 0·3 to 0·5μ in breadth; rarely it may be considerably larger in both dimensions. It is non-motile, and may exhibit great variety of form, according to the age of the culture and the nature of the medium upon which it is growing. It is stained by Gram's method if the decolorizing process be not too prolonged, and also by Loeffler's methylene-blue method. Except in the very young forms, it is readily recognizable by a series of transverse alternate stained and unstained bands. The bacillus may be wedge-shaped, spindle-shaped, comma-shaped or ovoid. In the shorter forms the polar staining is usually well marked; in the longer bacilli, the transverse striation. Very characteristic club-shaped forms or branching filaments are met with in old cultures, or where there is a superabundance of nutritive material. In what may be called the handle of the club the banded appearance is specially well marked. These specific bacilli are found in large numbers on the surface of the diphtheritic membrane (Plate II. fig. 10), and may easily be detached for bacteriological examination. In certain cases they may be found by direct microscopic examination, especially when they are stained by Gram's method, but it is far more easy to demonstrate their presence by the culture method. On Loeffler's special medium the bacilli flourish so well at body-temperature—about 37° C.—that, like the cholera bacillus, they outgrow the other organisms present, and may be obtained in comparatively pure culture. Distinct colonies may often be found as early as the eighth or twelfth hour of incubation; in from eighteen to twenty-four hours they appear as rounded, elevated, moderately translucent, greyish white colonies, with a yellow tinge, the surface moist and the margins slightly irregular or scalloped. They are thicker and somewhat more opaque in the centre. When the colonies are few and widely separated, each may grow to a considerable size, 4 to 5 mm.; but when more numerous and closer together, they remain small and almost invariably discrete, with distinct intervals between them. In older, growths the central opacity becomes more marked and the crenation more distinct, the moist, shiny appearance being lost. When the surface of the serum is dry, the growth, as a rule, does not attain any very large size.

These " pure " colonies, when sown in slightly alkaline broth, grow with great vigour; and if a small amount of such a 48 hours' culture be injected under the skin of a guinea-pig, the animal succumbs, with a marked local reaction and distinct symptoms of toxic poisoning very similar to those met with in cases of diphtheria of the human subject. Roux and Yersin demonstrated that the poison was not contained in the bodies of the bacilli, but that it was formed and thrown out by them from and into the nutrient medium. Moreover, they could produce all the toxic symptoms, the local reactions, and even the paralysis which often follows the disease in the human subject, by injecting the culture from which they had previously removed the whole of the diphtheria bacilli by filtration. This cultivation, then, contains a poisonous material, which, incapable of multiplying in the tissues, may be given in carefully graduated doses. If, therefore, there is anything in the theory that tissues may be gradually "acclimatized" to the poisons of these toxic substances, they saw that it should be possible to prove it in connexion with this disease. Behring, going still further, found that the tissues so acclimatized have the power of producing a substance capable of neutralizing the toxin, a substance which, at first confined to the cells, when formed in large quantities overflows into the fluids of the blood, with which it is distributed throughout the body. The bulk of this toxin-neutralizing substance remains in the blood-serum after separation of the clot. In proof of this he showed that (1) if this serum be injected into an animal before it is inoculated with even more than a lethal dose of the diphtheria bacillus or its products, the animal remains perfectly well; (2) a certain quantity of this serum, mixed with diphtheria toxin and injected into a guinea-pig, gives rise to no ill effects; and (3) that even when injected some hours after the bacillus or its toxins, the serum is still capable of neutralizing the action of these substances. In these experiments we have the germ of the present antitoxic treatment which has so materially diminished the percentage mortality in diphtheria. This serum may also be used as a prophylactic agent.

The antitoxic serum as now used is prepared by injecting into the subcutaneous tissues of a horse the products of the diphtheria bacillus. The bacillus, grown in broth containing peptone and blood-serum or blood-plasma, is filtered and heated to a temperature of 68° or 70° C. for one hour. It then contains only a small amount of active toxin, but injected into the horse it renders that animal highly insusceptible to the action of strong diphtheria toxins, and even induces the production of a considerable amount of antitoxin. This production of antitoxin, however, may be accelerated by subsequent repeated injections, with increasing doses of strong diphtheria toxin, which may be so powerful that ⅓ to ½ of a drop, or even less, is a fatal dose for a medium-sized guinea-pig. The antitoxic serum so prepared may contain 200, 400, 600 or even more " units " of antitoxin per c.c.—the unit being that quantity of antitoxin that will so far neutralize 100 lethal doses (a lethal dose is the smallest quantity that will kill a 250-gramme guinea-pig on the fifth day) of toxin for a 250-gramme guinea-pig, that the animal continues alive on the fifth day from the injection. This, however, is a purely arbitrary standard of neutralizing power, as it is found that, owing to the complicated structure of the toxin, the neutralizing and the lethal powers do not always go hand in hand; but as the toxin used in testing the antitoxin is always compared with the original standard, accurate results are easily obtained.

Diphtheria, though still prevalent in cities, has now lost many of its terrors. In the large hospitals under the Metropolitan Asylums Board the death-rate fell from nearly 40% in 1889 to under 10% in 1903; and if antitoxin be given as soon as the disease manifests itself, the mortality is brought down to a very insignificant figure. It has been maintained that 'as soon as antitoxin came into use the number of cases of paralysis increased rather than diminished. This may be readily understood when it is borne in mind that many patients recover under the use of antitoxin who would undoubtedly have succumbed in the pre-antitoxin days; and it cannot be too strongly insisted that although the antitoxin introduced neutralizes the free toxin and prevents its further action on the tissues, it cannot entirely neutralize that which is already acting on the cells, nor can it make good damage already done before it is injected. Even allowing that antitoxin is not accountable for the whole of the improvement in the percentage mortality statistics since 1896, it has undoubtedly accounted for a very large proportion of recoveries. Antitoxin often cuts short functional albuminuria, but it cannot repair damage already done to the renal epithelium before the antitoxin was given. The clinical evidence of the value of antitoxin in the relief that it affords to the patient is even more important than that derived from the consideration of statistics.

The diphtheria bacillus or its poison acts locally as a caustic and irritant, and generally or constitutionally as a protoplasmic poison, the most evident lesions produced by it being degeneration of nerves and muscles, and, in acute cases, changes in the walls of the blood-vessels. Other organisms, streptococci or staphylococci, when present, may undoubtedly increase the mortality by producing secondary complications, which end in suppuration. Diphtheria bacilli may also be found in pus, as in the discharges from cases of otorrhoea.

Tetanus (Lockjaw).—Although tetanus was one of the later diseases to which a definite micro-organismal origin could be assigned, it has long been looked upon as a disease typical of the "septic" group. In 1885 Nicolaier described an organism multiplying outside the body and capable of setting up tetanus, but this was only obtained in pure culture by Kitasato, a Japanese, and by the Italians in 1889. It has a very characteristic series of appearances at different stages of its development. First it grows as long, very slender threads, which rapidly break up into shorter sections from 4 to 5μ in length (see Plate II. fig. 11). In these shorter rods spores may appear on the second or up to the seventh day, according to the temperature at which the growth occurs. The rods then assume a very characteristic pin or drumstick form; they are non-motile, are somewhat rounded at the ends, and at one end the spore, which is of greater diameter than the rod, causes a very considerable expansion. Before sporulation the organisms are distinctly motile, occurring in rods of different lengths, in most cases surrounded by bundles of beautiful flagella, which at a later stage are thrown off, the presence of flagella corresponding very closely with the "motile" period. The bacillus grows best at the temperature of the body; it becomes inactive at 14° C. at the one extreme, and at from 42° to 43° C. at the other; in the latter case involution forms, clubs and branching and degenerated forms, often make their appearance. It is killed by exposure for an hour to a temperature of from 60° to 65° C.; the spores however are very resistant to the action of heat, as they withstand the temperature of boiling water for several minutes. The organism has been found in garden earth, in the excrement of animals—horses—and in dust taken from the streets or from living-rooms, especially when it has been allowed to remain at rest for a considerable period. It has also been demonstrated in, and separated from the pus of wounds (see Plate II. fig. 12) in patients suffering from lockjaw, but it is then invariably found associated with the micro-organisms that give rise to suppuration.

It is important to remember that this bacillus is a strict anaerobe, and can only grow when free oxygen has been removed from the cultivation medium. It may be cultivated in gelatine to which has been added from 2 to 3% of grape-sugar, when, along the line of the stab culture, it forms a delicate growth, almost like a fir-tree, the tip of which never comes quite to the surface of the gelatine. The most luxuriant growth—evidenced by the longest branches—occurs in the depth of the gelatine away from free oxygen. After a time the gelatine becomes sticky, and then undergoes slow liquefaction, the growth sinking and leaving the upper layers comparatively clear. This organism is not an obligate parasite, but a facultative; it may grow outside the body and remain alive for long periods.

Lockjaw is most common amongst agricultural labourers, gardeners, soldiers on campaign, in those who go about with bare feet, or who, like young children, are liable to get their 'knees or hands accidentally wounded by rough contact with the ground. Anything which devitalizes the tissues—such as cold, bruising, malnutrition, the action of other organisms and their products—may all be predisposing factors, in so far as they place the tissue at a disadvantage and allow of the multiplication and development of the specific bacillus of tetanus. In order to produce the disease, it is not sufficient merely to inoculate tetanus bacilli, especially where resistant animals are concerned: they must be injected along with some of their toxins or with other organisms, the presence of which seems to increase the power of, or assist, the tetanus organism, by diverting the activity of the cells and so allowing the bacillus to develop. The poison formed by this organism resembles the enzymes and diphtheria poison, in that it is destroyed at a temperature of 65° C. in about five minutes, and even at the temperature of the body soon loses its strength, although, when kept on ice and protected from the action of light, it retains its specific properties for months. Though slowly formed, it is tremendously potent, 1½½½es part of a drop (the five-millionth part of a c.c.) of the broth in which an active culture has been allowed to grow for three weeks or a month being sufficient to kill a mouse in twenty-four hours, ½½ of a drop killing a rabbit, ½ a dog, or ½ of a drop a fowl or a pigeon; it is from 100 to 400 times as active as strychnine, and 400 times as poisonous as atropine. It has been observed that, quite apart from size, animals exhibit different degrees of susceptibility. Frogs kept at their ordinary temperature are exceedingly insusceptible, but when they are kept warm it is possible to tetanize them, though only after a prolonged incubation period, such as is met with in very chronic cases of tetanus in the human subject. In experimentally-produced tetanus the spasms usually commence and are most pronounced in the muscles near the site of inoculation. It was at one time supposed that this was because the poison acted directly upon the nerve terminations, or possibly upon the muscles; but as it is now known that it acts directly on the cells of the central nervous system, it may, as in the case of rabies, find its way along the lymphatic channels of the nerves to those points of the central nervous system with which these nerves are directly connected, spasms occurring in the course of the muscular distribution of the nerves that receive their impulses from the cells of that area. As the amount of toxin introduced may be contained in a very small quantity of fluid and still be very dilute, the local reaction of the connective-tissue cells may be exceedingly slight; consequently a very small wound may allow of the introduction of a strong poisonous dose. Many of the cases of so-called idiopathic tetanus are only idiopathic because the wound is trifling in character, and, unless suppuration has taken place, has healed rapidly after the poison has been introduced. In tetanus, as in diphtheria, the organisms producing the poison, if found in the body at all, are developed only at the seat of inoculation; they do not make their way into the surrounding tissues. In this we have an explanation of the fact that all the earlier experiments with the blood from tetanus patients gave absolutely negative results. It is sometimes stated that the production of tetanus toxin in a wound soon ceases, owing to the arrest of the development of the bacillus, even in cases that ultimately succumb to the disease. Roux and Vaillard, however, maintain that no case of tetanus can be treated with any prospect of success unless the focus into which the bacilli have been introduced is freely removed. The antitetanus serum was the first antitoxic serum produced. It is found, however, that though the anti-tetanic serum is capable of acting as a prophylactic, and of preventing the appearance of tetanic symptoms in animals that are afterwards, or simultaneously, injected with tetanus toxin,

it does not give very satisfactory results when it is injected after tetanic symptoms have made their appearance. It would appear that in such cases the tetanus poison has become too firmly bound up with the protoplasm of the nerve cells, and has already done a considerable amount of damage.

(b) More Chronic Infective Diseases (Tissue Parasites).

Tuberculosis.—In no quarter of the field of preventive medicine have more important results accrued from the discovery of a specific infective organism than in the case of Koch's demonstration and separation in pure culture of the tubercle bacillus and the association of this bacillus with the transmission of tuberculosis. In connexion with diagnosis—both directly from observation of the organism in the sputum and urine of tuberculous patients, and indirectly through the tuberculin test, especially on animals—this discovery has been of very great importance; and through a study of the life-history of the bacillus and its relation to animal tissues much has been learned as to the prevention of tuberculosis, and something even as to methods of treatment. One of the great difficulties met with in the earlier periods of the study of this organism was its slow, though persistent, growth. At first cultivations in fluid media were not kept sufficiently long under observation to allow of its growth; it was exceedingly difficult to obtain pure cultures, and then to keep them, and in impure cultures the tubercle bacilli were rapidly overgrown. Taken directly from the body, they do not grow on most of the ordinary media, and it was only when Koch used solidified blood-serum that he succeeded in obtaining pure cultures. Though they may now be demonstrated by what appear to be very simple methods, before these methods were devised it was practically impossible to obtain any satisfactory results.

The principle involved in the staining of the tubercle bacillus is that when once it has taken up fuchsin, or gentian violet, it retains the stain much more firmly than do most organisms and tissues, so that if a specimen be thoroughly stained with fuchsin and then decolorized by a mineral acid—25% of sulphuric acid, say—although the colour is washed out of the tissues and most other organisms, the tubercle bacilli retain it; and even after the section has been stained with methylene-blue, to bring the other tissues and organisms into view, these bacilli still remain bright red, and stand out prominently on a blue background. If a small fragment of tuberculous tissue be pounded in a sterile mortar and smeared over the surface of inspissated blood-serum solidified at a comparatively low temperature, and if evaporation be prevented, dry scaly growths make their appearance at the end of some fourteen days. If these be reinoculated through several generations, they ultimately assume a more saprophytic character, and will grow in broth containing 5% of glycerin, or on a peptone beef-agar to which a similar quantity of glycerin has been added. On these media the tubercle bacillus grows more luxuriantly, though after a time its virulence appears to be diminished. On blood-serum its virulence is preserved for long periods if successive cultivations be made. It occurs in the tissues or in cultivations as a delicate rod or thread 1·5 to 3·5μ in length and about 0·2 to 0·5μ in thickness (see Plate I., fig. 15). It is usually slightly curved, and two rods may be arranged end to end at an open angle. There is some doubt as to whether tubercle bacilli contain spores, but little masses of deeply-stained protoplasm can be seen, alternating with clear spaces within the sheath; these clear spaces have been held to be spores. This organism is found in the lungs and sputum in various forms of consumption; it is met with in tuberculous ulcers of the intestine, in the lymph spaces around the vessels in tuberculous meningitis, in tuberculous nodules in all parts of the body, and in tuberculous disease of the skin—lupus. It is found also in the tuberculous lesions of animals; in the throat-glands, tonsils, spleen and bones of the pig; in the spleen of the horse; and in the lungs and pleura of the cow. Tuberculosis may be produced artificially by injecting the tubercle bacillus into animals, some being much more susceptible than others. Milk drawn from an udder in which there are breaking-down tuberculous foci, may contain an enormous number of active tubercle bacilli; and pigs fed upon this milk develop a typical tuberculosis, commencing in the glands of the throat, which can be traced from point to point, with the utmost precision. It must be assumed that what takes place in the pig may also take place in the human subject; and a sufficient number of cases are now on record to show that the swallowing of tuberculous material is a cause of tuberculosis, especially amongst children and adolescents. Inhaled tubercle bacilli from the recently-dried sputum of phthisical patients, like milk derived from tuberculous udders, may set up tuberculosis of the lungs or of the alimentary tract, especially when the epithelial layer is unhealthy or imperfect. The two main causes of the prevalence of tuberculosis in the human subject are: (1) tubercle bacilli may become so modified that they can flourish saprophytically; as yet it has not been possible to trace the exact conditions under which they live, but we are gradually coming to recognize that, although when they come from the body they are almost obligate parasites, they may gradually acquire saprophytic characters. (2) Many of the domestic animals are readily infected with tuberculosis, and in turn may become additional centres from which infection may radiate.

Koch's tuberculin has been of inestimable value in the early diagnosis of tuberculosis, especially in animals.

Tuberculin, from which the tuberculin test derives its name, consists of the products of the tubercle bacillus when grown for a month or six weeks in peptone meat-broth to which a small proportion, say 5 or 6%, of glycerin has been added. The tubercle bacilli are then killed at boiling temperature, and are partially removed by sedimentation, and completely by filtration through a Berkfeld or Pasteur-Chamberland filter. If a large dose of this filtered fluid be injected under the skin of a healthy man or brute, it is possible to produce some local swelling and to induce a rise of temperature; but in a similar patient suffering from tuberculosis a very much smaller dose (one which does not affect the healthy individual in the slightest degree) is sufficient to bring about the characteristic swelling and rise of temperature. To obtain trustworthy results the dosage must always be carefully attended to. The reaction is only obtained under certain well-defined conditions. Driven animals seldom, if ever, react properly. Cattle to be tested should be allowed to remain at rest for some time; they should be well fed, and be carefully protected from cold or draughts. After an injection of tuberculin into the subcutaneous tissues (usually in front of the shoulder or on the chest-wall) they should be kept under the same conditions and should be watched very carefully; the temperature should be taken at the sixth hour, and every three hours afterwards up to the twenty-first or even twenty-fourth hour. If during this time the temperature rises to 103° F., there can be little doubt that the animal is tuberculous; but if it remains under 103°, the animal must be considered free from disease: if the temperature remains between these points the case is a doubtful one, and, according to Sir John M'Fadyean, should be retested at the end of a month. It is interesting to note that the test is not trustworthy in the case of animals in which tuberculosis is far advanced, especially when the temperature is already high—103° F. In such cases, however, it is an easy matter to diagnose the disease by the ordinary clinical methods. At first objections were raised to this test on two grounds: (1) that mistakes in diagnosis are sometimes made; (2) that tuberculin may affect the milk of healthy animals into which it is injected. As the methods of using the tuberculin have been perfected, and as the conditions under which the reaction is obtained have become better known, mistakes have rapidly become fewer; whilst it has been amply proved that tuberculin has not the slightest deteriorating effect on the quality of the milk.

Tuberculin and similar substances are sometimes used as specific reagents in the diagnosis of tuberculosis in the human subject. When small quantities of old tuberculin are injected subcutaneously into a tuberculous patient in whom, however, no tubercle bacilli may be demonstrable, the temperature begins to rise in six or eight hours and continues to rise for twelve hours or, in rare cases, for an even longer period, a rise of a single degree being considered sufficient to indicate the presence of the disease. Along with this there is usually some swelling and tenderness, with perhaps redness at the seat of injection, whilst there is also some evidence of a vascular congestion in the neighbourhood of any tuberculous lesion. A second method of applying tuberculin as a diagnostic reagent is that of Pirquet, who, after diluting old tuberculin with two parts of normal saline solution and one part of 5% carbolic glycerin, places a drop of the mixture on the skin and scrapes away the epidermis in lines with " a small dental burr." The skin is similarly treated with normal saline some 2 or 3 in. away from that at which the tuberculin is used In the tuberculin area a little papule develops; this may become a vesicle, surrounded by slight redness and swelling (in the " saline " area nothing of the kind appears). The swelling begins about six hours after the scarification is made and continues to increase for

24 hours. Reactions, however, are obtained by this test in patients who are not suffering from any active tubercular lesion, whilst on the other hand in certain cases it fails to indicate the presence of tubercle when it is undoubtedly there. Calmette's or Wolff-Eisner's ophthalmic reaction test, a third method of using tuberculin, consists in dropping a weak solution of tuberculin into the conjunctival sac of one eye; this is followed by a mild attack of conjunctivitis or inflammation of the eye in the tuberculous patient, whilst in the normal patient no such inflammation should appear. Although this test appears to be of considerable value, it fails to give any information in cases of advanced tuberculosis, of general miliary tuberculosis and of tuberculous meningitis. It certainly possesses one great advantage over the others—it does not give any reaction in the presence of dormant tubercle in persons clinically sound and healthy. The inflammation of the eye may, however, be so acute, especially where strong solutions of tuberculin are used, that considerable damage may be done, more especially should there be any dormant disease of the eye. It must be remembered that in all these tests the exhibition of tuberculin increases for a time the sensitiveness of the patient each time it is administered. It sets up a negative phase, as already described, and renders the patient more susceptible to the action of a fresh dose. It is evident, therefore, that the careful worker wishing to obtain minimal effects will give small doses and gradually repeat these as he may find necessary.

In 1890 Koch, whose brilliant researches on tuberculosis had opened up a new field of investigation and had inspired new hope in the breasts of patients and physicians alike, followed up his method of diagnosis with a method of vaccination with the products of the tubercle bacillus separated from glycerinated broth culture after the vitality of the bacilli had been destroyed. As is frequently the case with new remedies, this was used so indiscriminately that it soon fell into disrepute. The results in certain cases, however, were so successful that careful investigations into the character and action of tuberculin and into the conditions under which it may be used with advantage were undertaken. Tuberculins composed of the triturated bodies of tubercle bacilli, of the external secretions of these bacilli, and of their various constituents in different combinations, were experimented with, but at the present time Koch's two tuberculins—especially his new tuberculin—hold the field. The "old tuberculin" consists of the glycerin broth culture of the tubercle bacilli mentioned above. The new tuberculin consists of the centrifugalized deposit from a saline solution of the extract of the triturated dead tubercle bacilli; this is stored in small tubes, each containing two milligrammes of solid substance. This is diluted with distilled water containing 20% of glycerin, great care being taken to maintain the sterility of the solution. The dose is usually from $\frac{1}{1000}$ to $\frac{1}{500}$ of a milligramme for an adult, increasing to $\frac{1}{10}$; according to Sir A. Wright it should not go beyond this.

Perhaps no one has done more to rehabilitate the tuberculin treatment than Sir Almroth Wright, who after a long series of experiments devised what he called the tuberculo-opsonic index, about which a few words may be of interest. It is well-known that certain cells in the human blood have the power of taking bacteria into their substance and there digesting them. This, the so-called " phagocytic power " of Metchnikoff, was found to vary somewhat under different conditions, and Wright set himself to determine, if possible, what were the factors that modified this variability. He found that the white blood corpuscles, the polymorphonuclear cells, whether from healthy or tuberculous patients, always showed practically the same phagocytic activity when mixed with a fine emulsion of tubercle bacilli and the serum from a healthy patient. If, however, corpuscles from the same individuals, whether healthy or tuberculous, were allowed to act upon the bacilli in the presence of serum drawn from a tuberculous patient, one of three things might happen: (1) the bacilli might be taken up in smaller numbers than in the above series of experiments; (2) they might be taken up in larger numbers; or (3) they might be taken up in what might be called normal numbers. In (1) and (2) Wright holds there is evidence of a tuberculous condition, in (3) of course the evidence is negative. He found, however, that when a dose of tuberculin was injected into a tuberculous patient there was a distinct fall in the number of tubercle bacilli taken up by the leucocytes treated with the serum of the patient. This condition Wright speaks of as the " negative phase." Increased phagocytic activity of the cells is associated with what is spoken of as the positive phase. The theory is that the blood serum has the power of preparing bacteria to be eaten by the phagocytes in the same sense that boiling, say, prepares food for ready digestion by the human subject, and Wright applied the term opsonin to the unknown constituent or complex of constituents of the serum that exerts this action upon the bacteria. The opsonic index is obtained by comparing the average number of bacilli taken up by, say, 100 leucocytes, to which the serum from a tuberculous patient has been added, with the number of bacteria taken up by a hundred similar corpuscles to which normal serum has been added, the ratio between the two giving the opsonic index. Wright maintains that after the injection of small doses of tuberculin during a negative phase which first appears, i.e. whilst there is a fall in the number of bacilli taken up by the leucocytes of the blood, the patient is more susceptible than before to the attacks of the tubercle bacillus. Following this, however, there is a gradual rise in the opsonic index until it passes the normal and the patient enters a positive phase, during which the susceptibility to the attacks of the tubercle bacillus is considerably diminished. When the effects of this dose are passing off a fresh injection should be made; this again induces a negative phase, but one that should not be so marked as in the first instance, whilst the positive phase which succeeds should be still more marked than that first obtained. If this can be repeated systematically and regularly the patient should begin, and continue, to improve. The difficulties involved in the determination of the opsonic index are, however, exceedingly great, and the personal factor enters so largely into the question that some observers are very doubtful as to the practical utility of this method. In Wright's hands, however, and in the hands of those who work with him, very satisfactory results are obtained. The tuberculin treatment, fortunately, does not stand or fall by the success of the opsonic index determination, especially as most valuable information as to the course of the disease and the effects of the tuberculin may be obtained by a study of the daily temperature chart and of the general condition of the patient.

Tuberculin should not be injected more frequently than about once in 10 or 14 days, and it is well not to increase the dose too rapidly. Wherever the temperature continues high, even a degree beyond normal, and where the pulse is over 100, it is not wise to give tuberculin, nor does it seem to be of any great value where the disease is making rapid headway or has become generalized, especially where there is meningitis or bleeding from the lungs.

It is interesting to note, in connexion with the diagnostic significance of the opsonic index, that in non-tuberculous subjects the administration of a small dose of tuberculin is followed by no negative phase such as is met with in the tuberculous subject. The phagocytic power of the white blood corpuscles is determined by noting the number of organisms taken up by the leucocytes when mixed with equal parts of a standard emulsion of tubercle bacilli and blood serum incubated in fine glass tubes for 15 minutes at a temperature of 37° C. If the period of incubation is much shorter than this the results are irregular, whilst if the period is longer so many organisms are taken up that it becomes impossible to differentiate two sets of sera.

As an example we might adduce the following. Taking a tuberculous patient's serum + leucocytes + tubercle bacilli, let us say we have an average of 1·8 bacilli per leucocyte in 50 or 100 leucocytes counted; with normal serum + corpuscles + tubercle bacilli the average number of bacilli per leucocyte in the same number of cells counted is 3. From these figures the opsonic index obtained is 1·8 ÷ 3 = 0·6. = opsonic index.

Leprosy.—Armauer Hansen in 1871, and Neisser in 1881, described a "leprosy bacillus" corresponding in size and in certain points of staining reaction to the tubercle bacillus, and it is now generally accepted that this bacillus is the direct and specific causal agent of leprosy. The discovery of this organism paved the way for the proof that the tubercular and anaesthetic forms of leprosy are essentially the same disease, or rather are the manifestations of the action of a common organism attacking different series of tissues.

To demonstrate the presence of the leprosy bacillus, tie an indiarubber ring firmly around the base of one of the leprosy tubercles. As soon as the blood is driven out, leaving the nodule pale, make a puncture with the point of a sharp knife. From this puncture a clear fluid exudes; this, dried on a cover-glass, stained with carbol-fuchsin, and rapidly decolorized with a weak mineral acid, shows bacilli stained red and very like tubercle bacilli; they differ from that organism, however, in that they are somewhat shorter, and that if the acid be too strong or be allowed to act on them for too long a time, the colour is discharged from them much more readily. These organisms, which are from 4 to 6µ in length and 0·3µ in breadth, are as a rule more rigid and more pointed than are the tubercle bacilli (see Plate II., fig. 16). It is doubtful whether they form spores. They are found in large numbers lying embedded in a kind of gelatinous substance in the lymphatics of the skin, in certain cells of which they appear to be taken up.

It is curious that these bacilli affect specially the skin and nerves, but rarely the lungs and serous membranes, thus being in sharp contrast to the tubercle bacillus, which affects the latter very frequently and the former more rarely. They are seldom found in the blood, though they have been described as occuring there in the later stages of the disease. It is stated that leprosy has been inoculated directly into the human subject, the patient dying some five or six years after inoculation; but up to the present no pure culture of the leprosy bacillus has been obtained; it has therefore been impossible to produce the disease by the inoculation of the bacillus only. What evidence we have at our disposal, however, is all in favour of the transmissibility of the disease from patient to patient and through the agency of the leprosy bacillus. None of the numerous non-bacillary theories of leprosy account at all satisfactorily for this transmissibility of the disease, for its progressive nature, and for the peculiar series of histological changes that are met with in various parts and organs of the leprous body. Leprosy occurs in all climates. It is found where no fish diet can be obtained, and where pork and rice are never used, though to these substances has been assigned the power of giving rise to the disease. Locality appears to influence it but little, and with improved sanitation and increased cleanliness it is being gradually eradicated. The only factor that is common in all forms of leprosy, and is met with in every case, is the specific bacillus; and in spite of the fact that it has yet been found impossible to trace the method of transmission, we must from what is known of the presence and action of bacilli, in other diseases, especially in tuberculosis, assign to the leprosy bacillus the rôle of leprosy-producer, until much stronger evidence than has yet been obtained can be brought forward in favour of any of the numerous other causes that have been assigned. Two cases are recorded in which people have contracted leprosy from pricking their fingers with needles whilst sewing a leper's clothes; and a man who had never been out of Dublin is said to have contracted the disease by sleeping with his brother, a soldier who had returned from India suffering from leprosy.

Glanders.—Farcy in the human subject resembles the same disease experimentally produced in animals with material from a glandered animal, and as there is no pathological distinction between the two, from the aetiological standpoint, they may be considered together. If the pus from a glanders abscess be mixed with a little sterile saline solution and spread over the cut surface of a boiled potato kept at the body-temperature, bright yellow or honey-coloured, thick, moist-looking colonies grow very rapidly and luxuriantly. These colonies gradually become darker in colour, until they assume a café-au-lait, or even a chocolate, tint. On examining one of them microscopically, it is found to be made up of bacilli 2 to 5µ long and ⅓ to ⅓ of their own length broad (see Plate I, fig. 2 and fig. 6). The bacillus is usually straight or slightly curved and rounded at one end; it appears to be non-motile. As first pointed out by Loeffler and Schütz, when a portion of a culture is inoculated subcutaneously, typical farcy, with the acute septicaemia or blood-poisoning so characteristic of certain cases of glanders and farcy, is the result. The human subject is usually inoculated through wounds or scratches, or through the application of the nasal discharge of a glandered animal to the mucous membrane of the nose or mouth. Man is not specially susceptible to the glanders virus, but as he frequently comes into contact with glandered horses a considerable number of cases of farcy in man are met with, although amongst knackers it is a comparatively rare disease. Cattle never contract it by the ordinary channels, and even when inoculated exhibit nothing more than localized ulceration. The goat appears to occupy an intermediate position between cattle and the horse in this respect; in sheep, which are fairly susceptible the disease runs its course slowly, and appears to resemble chronic farcy in man. In rabbits and the dog the disease runs a very slow and modified course. Although field-mice are extraordinarily susceptible, white mice and house mice, unless previously fed on sugar or with phloridzin, are unaffected by inoculation of the glanders bacillus. The pigeon is the only bird in which glanders has been produced. Lions and tigers are said to contract the disease, and to take it in a very severe and

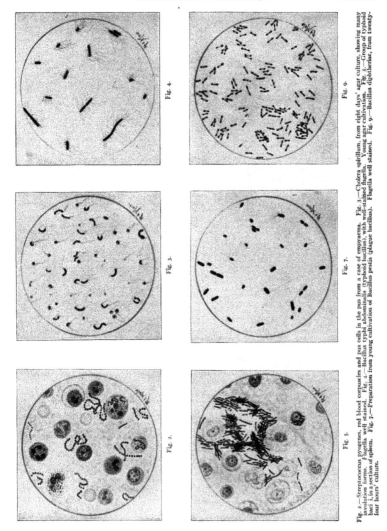

Fig. 2.—Streptococcus pyogenes, red blood corpuscles and pus cells in the pus from a case of empyaema. Fig. 3.—Cholera spirillum, from eight days' agar culture, showing many involution forms. Flagella well stained. Fig. 4.—Bacillus typhi abdominalis (typhoid bacillus), with well-stained flagella. Young agar cultivation. Fig. 5.—Group of typhoid baci l, in a section of spleen. Fig. 7.—Preparation from young cultivation of Bacillus pestis (plague bacillus). Flagella well stained. Fig. 9.—Bacillus diphtheriae, from twenty-four hours' culture.

PLATE III.

PARASITIC DISEASES

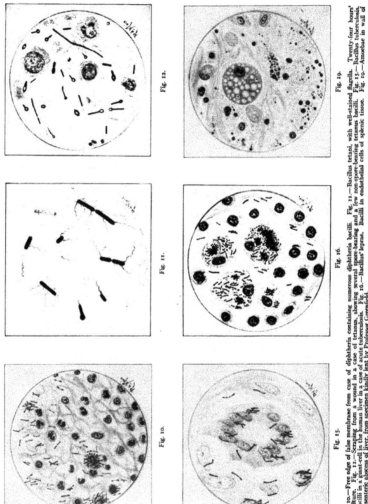

Fig. 12.

Fig. 19.

Fig. 11.

Fig. 16.

Fig. 10.

Fig. 15.

Fig. 10.—Free edge of false membrane from case of diphtheria containing numerous diphtheria bacilli. **Fig. 11.**—Bacillus tetani, with well-stained flagella. Twenty-four hours' culture. **Fig. 12.**—Scraping from a wound in a case of tetanus, showing several spore-bearing and a few non-spore-bearing tetanus bacilli. **Fig. 15.**—Bacillus tuberculosis. Bacilli in a giant-cell in the human liver in a case of acute tuberculosis. **Fig. 16.**—Bacillus leprae. Bacilli in endothelial cells of splenic tissue. **Fig. 19.**—Amoebae in wall of dysenteric abscess of liver, from specimen kindly lent by Professor Greenfield.

rapidly fatal form. The glanders organism soon loses its virulence and even its vitality. Dry, it dies in about ten days; placed in distilled water, in about five days; but kept moist, or on culture media, it retains its vitality for about a month, although its activity soon becomes considerably lessened. These bacilli are readily killed at a temperature of 55°C.; they can pass through the kidneys, even when there is no lesion to be made out either with the naked eye or under the microscope (Sherrington and Bonome).

The glanders bacillus grows best in the presence of oxygen, but it may grow anaërobically; it then appears to have the power of forming toxin, either more in quantity or of greater activity than when it has access to a free supply of oxygen. This poison (mallein) is used for the purpose of diagnosing the presence of glanders. A cultivation is made in peptonized bouillon to which a small portion of glycerin has been added. The bacillus is allowed to grow and multiply at the temperature of the body for a month or six weeks; the organisms are then killed by heat and o·5 % carbolic acid is added. The cultivation is then filtered through a porcelain filter in order to remove the bodies of the bacilli, and the resulting fluid, clear and amber-coloured, should have the power, when injected in quantities of 1 c.c., of giving the specific reaction in an animal suffering from glanders; in a healthy animal 6 c.c. will give no reaction. The suspected animal should be kept at rest and in a warm stable for twenty-four to forty-eight hours before the test is applied. The temperature should be normal, as no proper reaction is obtained in an animal in which the temperature is high. This reaction, which is a very definite one, consists in a rise of temperature of from 2° to 4° F., and the appearance of a swelling of from 3 to 4 in. in diameter and from 1 to 1½ in. in height, before the sixteenth or eighteenth hour; this swelling should continue to increase for some hours. It has been suggested that the injection of $\frac{1}{10}$ to $\frac{1}{5}$ c.c. of mallein, at intervals of two or three days, may be used with advantage in the treatment of glanders. Glandered horses seem to improve under this treatment, and then certainly do not react even to much larger doses of mallein. The mallein test has revealed the fact that glanders is a far more common and more widespread disease than was at one time supposed.

II.—To Higher Vegetable Parasites

Actinomycosis.—This disease is very prevalent in certain low-lying districts, especially amongst cattle, giving rise to the condition known as "sarcoma," "wooden tongue," "wens," "bony growths on the jaw," &c. It is characterized by the presence of a fungus, which, at first growing in the form of long slender threads that may be broken up into short rods and cocci, ultimately, as the result of a degenerative process, assumes the form of a "ray-fungus," in which a series of club-like rays are arranged around a common centre (see Plate I., fig. 8). It is probably a streptothrix—*Streptothrix Försteri.* Numerous cases have been observed in the human subject. Suppuration and the formation of fistulous openings, surrounded by exuberant granulations, "proud flesh," usually supervene where it is growing and multiplying in the tissues of the human body, and in the pus discharged are yellowish green or reddish brown points, each made up of a central irregular mycelium composed of short rods and spores, along with the clubs already mentioned. The mycelial threads may reach a considerable length (20 to 100μ); some of them become thicker, and are thus differentiated from the rest; the peripheral club is the result of swelling of the sheath; the filaments nearer the centre of the mycelial mass contain spores, which measure from 1 to 2μ in diameter. This fungus appears to lead a saprophytic existence, but it has the power of living in the tissues of the animal body, to which it makes its way through or around curious or loose teeth, or through abrasions of the tongue or tonsils. After the above positions, the abdomen, especially near the vermiform appendix, is a special seat of election, or in some cases the thorax, the lesions being traceable downwards from the neck. Any of the abdominal or thoracic organs may thus be affected. The process spreads somewhat slowly, but once started may extend in any direction,

XX 13*

its track being marked by the formation of a large qua tity of fibrous tissue, often around a long fistula. In the more recent growths, and in solid organs, cavities of some size, containing a soft semi-purulent cheesy-looking material, may be found, this mass in some cases being surrounded by dense fibrous tissue. When once a sinus is formed the diagnosis is easy, but before this the disease, where tumours of considerable size are rapidly formed, may readily be mistaken for sarcoma, or when the lungs are affected, for tuberculosis, especially as bronchitis and pleuritic effusion are frequently associated with both actinomycosis and tuberculosis.

Mycetoma, the Madura foot of India, is a disease very similar to actinomycosis, and, like that disease, is produced by a somewhat characteristic streptothrix. It usually attacks the feet and legs, however, and appears to be the result of infection through injured tissues. Under certain conditions and in long-standing cases the fungus appears to become pigmented (black) and degenerated.

Other forms of fungus disease or *Mycoses* are described. Aspergillosis, or pigeon-breeders' disease, is the result of infection with the *Aspergillus fumigatus.* Certain tumours appear to be the result of the action of a yeast, Blastomycosis or Saccharomycosis. The spores of the *Penicillium glaucum,* and of some of the Mucors, are also said to have the power of setting up irritation, which may end in the formation of a so-called granuloma or granulation tissue tumour. These, however, are comparatively rare.

B.—Diseases due to Animal Parasites.

I.—To Protozoa

Malaria.—Following Laveran's discovery, in 1880, of a parasite in the blood of patients suffering from malaria, our knowledge of this and similar diseases has increased by leaps and bounds, and most important questions concerning tropical diseases have now been cleared up. Numerous observations have been carried out with the object of determining the parasitic forms found in different forms of malaria—the tertian, quartan, and aestivo-autumnal fever—in each of which, in the red blood corpuscles, a series of developmental stages of the parasite from a small pale translucent amoebiform body may be followed. This small body first becomes lobulated, nucleated and pigmented; it then, after assuming a more or less marked rosette-shape with a deeply pigmented centre, breaks up into a series of small, rounded, hyaline masses of protoplasm, each of which has a central bright point. The number of these, contained in a kind of capsule, varies from 8 to 10 in the quartan, and from 11 to 20 in the tertian and aestivo-autumnal forms. There are certain differences in the arrangement of the pigment, which is present in larger quantities and distributed over a wider area in the somewhat larger parasites that are found in the tertian and quartan fevers. In the parasite of the aestivo-autumnal fever the pigment is usually found in minute dots, dividing near the pole at the point of division of the organism, along with it in the earlier stages (see Plate I., fig. 5). Here, too, the rosette form is not so distinct as in the parasite of tertian fever, and in the latter is not so distinct as in the quartan parasites. These dividing forms make their appearance immediately before the onset of a malarial paroxysm, and their presence is diagnostic. The process of division goes on especially in the blood-forming organs, and is therefore met with more frequently in the spleen and in bone-marrow than in any other situation. The parasites, at certain stages of their development, may escape from the red blood corpuscles, in which case (especially when exposed to the air for a few minutes) they send out long processes of protoplasm and become very active, moving about in the plasma and between the corpuscles, sometimes losing their processes, which, however, continue in active movement. In the aestivo-autumnal fever curious crescent-shaped or ovoid bodies were amongst the first of the parasitic organisms described as occurring in the blood, in the red corpuscles of which they develop. Manson maintains that from these arise the flagellate forms, all of which, he thinks, are developed in order that the life of the malarial parasite may be continued outside the human body. It is probable that most of the pigment found in the organs taken from malarial patients is derived from red blood corpuscles broken down by the malarial parasites; many of these, in turn, are devoured by leucocytes, which in malarial blood are usually greatly increased in number, and frequently contain much pigment, which they have obtained either directly from the fluid plasma or from the pigmented parasitic organism. The work recently carried out by Bruce on the tsetse-fly parasite, by A. J. Smith on Texas fever, and by W. S. Thayer and Hewitson on the blood parasites of birds, has opened up the way for the further study of the malarial parasites outside the human body. There can be no doubt as to the close relation of the multiplication and sporulation of the malarial parasite with the ague paroxysm: the anaemia results from the breaking down of blood corpuscles. Toxic substances are present in the blood during the setting free of the spores; of this we have proof in the increased toxicity of the urine during the paroxysmal stages of the disease; moreover necrotic areas, similar to those found in acute toxic fevers produced by other micro-organisms, are met with. It is well to bear in mind that the accumulation of débris of parasites and corpuscles in the capillaries may be an additional factor in this necrosis, especially when to this is added the impairment of nutrition necessarily involved by the impoverished condition of the malarial blood. It is interesting to note that, although, as pointed out by Nuttall, the Italian and Tirolese peasantry have long been firmly of the opinion that malaria is transmitted through the mosquito, and although the American, Dr Josiah Nott, in 1848 referred to malaria as if the mosquito theory had already been advanced, little attention was given to this question by most observers. Still earlier, Rasori (in 1846) had stated that "for many years I have held the opinion that intermittent fevers are produced by parasites, which renew the paroxysm by the act of their reproduction, which recurs more or less rapidly according to the variety of the species"; and this appears to be the first well-authenticated reference to this subject. Nuttall, who gives an excellent summary of the literature on the mosquito hypothesis of malaria, assigns to King the honour of again drawing attention to this question. Laveran in 1891, Koch in 1892, Manson in 1894, Bignami and Mendini in 1896, and Grassi in 1898, all turned their attention to this hypothesis. Manson, basing his hypothesis upon what he had observed as regards the transmission of Filaria by the mosquito, suggested a series of experiments to Major Ronald Ross. These were carried out in 1895, when it was found that in mosquitoes that had taken up blood containing amoeboid parasites, crescents, which were first described as cells, appeared in the stomach-wall after four or five days; these contained a number of stationary vacuoles and pigment granules, ten to twenty in number, bunched together or distributed in lines. Grassi, Bignami and Bastianelli confirm and supplement Ross's observations; they find that *Anopheles claviger*, taking the blood from a patient suffering from malaria, soon develops haemosporidia in the intestine. These parasites are then found between the muscular fibres of the stomach; they increase in size, become pigmented, and more and more vacuolated, until they project into the body-cavity. On the sixth day these large spheres contain an enormous number of minute bodies, refractive droplets like fat, and a diminishing amount of pigment. On the seventh day numerous filaments, arranged in rows around several foci, are seen. They are very delicate, are stained with difficulty, and appear to be perfectly independent of each other, though grouped within a capsule. After the capsule has ruptured, these thread-like "sporozooites," escaping into the body-cavity, gradually make their way to and accumulate in the cells or tubules of the salivary glands, whence their passage through the proboscis into the human blood is easily understood.

Thus two phases or cycles of existence have been demonstrated—one within the human body, the second in the mosquito. *Development of the Malarial Parasite.* That within the human body appears to be capable of going on almost indefinitely as long as the patient lives, but that in the mosquito appears to be an offshoot or an intermediate stage. The minute specks of protoplasm, the amoebulae, which have already been described as occurring in the red blood corpuscles of the higher animals, increase in size, take up blood pigment, probably from the red corpuscles, and then become developed into sporocytes or gametocytes. The sporocyte is the form which, remaining in the body, ultimately breaks up, as already seen, into a series of minute spores or amoebulae, which in turn go through the same cycle again, increasing in size and forming spores, and so on indefinitely. Gametocytes (the true sexual form) are in certain species, to outward appearance, very similar to the sporocyte, but in others they assume the crescentic shape, and can thus be recognised. The male cell resembles the female cell very closely, except that the protoplasm is hyaline and homogeneous-looking, whilst that of the female cell is granular. It has already been noted that when the blood is withdrawn from the body certain of the malarial parasites become flagellated. These flagella may be looked upon as sperm elements, which, forming in the male gametocyte, are extruded from that cell, and, once set free, seek out the granular female gametocytes. A single flagellum becomes attached to a small projection that appears on the female cell; it then makes its way into the protoplasm of the female cell, in which rapid streaming movements are then developed. In certain species the female cell is somewhat elongated, and may be peculiarly constricted. It becomes motile, and appears to have the power of piercing the tissues. In this way the first stages of development in the mosquito are passed. The gametocytes, taken along with the blood into the stomach of this insect, pass through the various phases above mentioned, though the zygote form of the human malarial parasite has not yet been traced. In the blood of a patient bitten by an infected mosquito the ordinary malarial parasite may be demonstrated without any difficulty at the end of a week or ten days, and the cycle recommences.

This theory, now no longer a hypothesis, in which the mosquito acts as an intermediary host for one stage of the parasite and transmits the parasite to man, affords an explanation of many apparently anomalous conditions associated with the transmission of malaria, whilst it harmonizes with many facts which, though frequently observed, were very difficult of explanation. Malaria was supposed to be associated with watery exhalations and with the fall of dew, but a wall or a row of trees was seemingly quite sufficient to prevent the passage of infection. It was met with on wet soils, on broken ground, in marshes, swamps and jungles; on the other hand, it was supposed to be due to the poisonous exhalations from rocks. All this is now explained by the fact that these are the positions in which mosquitoes occur: wherever there are stagnant pools, even of a temporary nature, mosquitoes may breed. It has been observed that although the malarial "miasma" never produces any ill effects in patients living at more than a few feet from the surface of the ground, malaria may be found at a height of from 7000 to 9000 ft. above sea-level; and the fact that a belt of trees or a wall will stop the passage of the poison is readily explicable on the mosquito theory. These insects are incapable, owing to their limited power of flight, of rising more than a few feet from the ground, and cannot make their way through a belt of trees of even moderate thickness. Broken ground, such as is found in connexion with railway cuttings and canals, may be a focus from which malaria may spread. In such broken ground pools are of common occurrence, and afford the conditions for the development of the mosquito, and infected tools used in one area may easily convey the ova to another. All these facts afford further support of this theory. The conditions of climate under which malaria is most rife are those which are most suitable for the development of the mosquito. The protection afforded by fires, the recognized value of mosquito curtains, the simultaneous disappearance of Anopheles and malaria on the complete draining of a neighbourhood, the coincidence of malaria and mosquitoes, and the protection afforded by large expanses of water near walls and trees are also important in this connexion.

The mosquitoes specially associated with the transmission of malaria in the human subject belong apparently to the genus

Anopheles. *Anopheles claviger (maculipennis)* and *Anopheles bifurcatus* both are found in Great Britain; *Anopheles pictus* is **Species of Mosquito Concerned.** another species found in Europe, but so far not in Great Britain. A member of the genus Culex, the grey mosquito or *Culex fatigans*, is the intermediate host of the proteosoma of birds, on which many of the intermediate phases of the life-history of these parasites have been studied. Ross describes a dappled-wing mosquito as the one with which he performed his experiments on birds in India. *Anopheles claviger* is interesting in view of the former prevalence of malaria in Great Britain.

The remedy for malaria appears to be the removal or spoiling of the breeding grounds of the mosquito, thorough drainage of pools and puddles, or, where this cannot be easily effected, the throwing of a certain amount " of kerosene on the surface of these pools " (Nuttall).

Amoebic Dysentery.—In addition to the dysentery set up by bacteria, a form—amoebic dysentery or amoebic enteritis—has been described which is said to be due to an animal parasite, and it has been proposed to separate the various types of dysentery according to their aetiology, in which case the amoebic group is probably more specific than any other. The amoeba (*Amoeba dysenteriae, Entamoeba histolytica,* of Schaudinn) supposed to give rise to this condition was first described by Lösch in 1875. Since then this amoeba has been described either as a harmless parasite or as a cause of dysentery in Europe, Africa, the United States and in Brazil, and more recently in India. This organism, which is usually placed amongst the rhizopods, consists of a small rounded, ovoid or pear-shaped globule of protoplasm, varying in size from 6 to 40μ, though, as Lafleur points out, these limits are seldom reached, the organism being usually from one and a half to three times the diameter of a leucocyte—from 12 to 26μ (see Plate II., fig. 19). Its margins are well defined, and the body appears to consist of a granular inner portion and a homogeneous outer portion, the latter being somewhat lighter in colour than the inner; in the resting stage this division cannot be made out. The organism appears to pass through at least two phases, one corresponding to a cystic, the other to an amoeboid, stage. In the latter stage, if the organism be examined on a warm stage, it is seen to send out processes, and, as in other amoebae, vacuoles may be seen as clear spaces lying in the granular and darker-coloured inner protoplasm. In the small vacuoles a deeply stained point may be seen. These vacuoles may be extruded through the ectoplasm. In some cases the vacuoles are so numerous that they occupy the whole of the space usually occupied by the granular protoplasm, and are merely surrounded by a zone of variable thickness, which " has the appearance of finely granular glass of a distinctly pale green tint" (Lafleur). In the cystic stage a nucleus which appears amongst the vacuoles may be made out, usually towards one side of the amoeba. This nucleus is of considerable size, i.e. nearly as large as a red blood corpuscle, and is readily distinguishable from the surrounding protoplasm. When stained by the Benda method (safranin and light green) a more deeply staining nucleolus may be seen in the nucleus. The nucleus is perhaps best seen when stained by this method, but it is always difficult to obtain well-stained specimens of this organism. If these amoebae can be kept under observation for some time evidence of amitotic division may sometimes be seen. Red blood corpuscles are often engulfed by this amoeba, as are also micrococci and bacilli. The movements of the amoebae are most active at a temperature of about 90° to 98° F. From the fact that pigment is contained in these organisms, it is supposed that they take in the red blood corpuscles as nutritive material, and that other substances may be taken in to serve a similar purpose. Nothing is known of the method of multiplication of the amoeba, but it is supposed that it may be both by fission and by spore formation. These organisms are present in the early stage of the acute disease, and disappear at the later stages. Perhaps of some importance is the fact that the abscesses found in the liver and lung, which occur so frequently in cases of dysentery, usually contain, especially in the portions immediately adjoining the suppurating mass, a considerable number of these amoebae. In the very small abscesses the amoebae are numerous and active, and occupy the capillaries in the tissues. It is quite possible that this plugging of the capillaries with amoebae is the cause both of the haemorrhages and of the small areas of necrosed tissue, the supply of nutriment being cut off from the liver cells and from the lung tissues, and that suppuration occurs only as a secondary process, though Councilman and Lafleur maintain that the amoeba itself is the primary cause of suppuration. It is possible, of course, that the suppuration is due to the action of pus-forming organisms conveyed along with, or following, the amoeba, as we know that the growth of suppurating organisms can go on in dead tissues when these organisms have no chance of surviving in the healthy tissues and fluids of the body. Lafleur holds that the amoeba forms a toxic substance which exerts a direct devitalizing effect on the liver cells, and that the amoeba itself causes suppuration. The abscesses in the lung, which invariably extend directly from the liver and occur at the base of the right lung, also contain these amoebae. For these reasons this organism is looked upon as the cause of dysentery and of certain forms of dysenteric abscess.

They differ from the *Entamoeba coli*—often met with in the intestine—which has a more distinct nucleus containing larger chromatin masses and is surrounded by a highly refractile nuclear membrane. Further, in the *Entamoeba coli* the cytoplasm is of the same character throughout, there being no differentiation into ectoplasm and endoplasm. The *Amoeba histolytica* is often met with in a " resting phase," in which the nucleus is less distinctly marked, and may consist of small masses of chromatin distributed throughout the cell or penetrating small buds formed on the surface. Around each of these buds, three, four or more, a highly refractile cyst wall is formed, the cysts becoming separated from the rest of the cell, the remnant of which undergoes disintegration. These cysts are extremely resistant, and probably maintain the continuity of the species outside the body.

In the active phase, the amoeboid form appears able by its tough membranous pseudopodia to push its way into the mucous membrane of the large intestine, especially the rectum, the lower part of the ileum and the flexures. Once it is ensconced in these tissues, small soft oedematous looking swellings soon appear on the mucous surface. Marshall points out that the amoebae probably reach the liver by the portal circulation from the dysenteric lesions in which the amoebae are found. Other observers maintain that the amoebae may pass through the walls of the intestine, through the peritoneal cavity, and so on to the liver where they give rise to typical abscesses.

Syphilis.—It has long been recognized that syphilis is a specific infective disease, but although characterized by fever, anaemia, and increased growths of tissue followed by rapid degeneration and ulceration of tissue, it is only within quite recent years that a definite parasitic organism, present in all cases of typical syphilis, has been isolated and studied. Schaudinn and Hoffmann, followed by Metchnikoff and others, have described as of constant occurrence a spiral or screw-shaped organism in which are seen from half a dozen to a dozen well-defined, short, regular, almost semicircular curves. This organism, when examined fresh, in normal or physiological salt solution, exhibits active screw-like movements as it rotates along its long axis; from time to time it becomes more or less bow-shaped and then straightens out, the while moving about from point to point in the field of the microscope. It is not very strongly refractile, and can only be examined properly with the aid of special central illumination and in the presence of minute particles, by the movements of which the organism is more readily traced.

In order to obtain this organism for demonstration it is a good plan to wash the primary or secondary syphilitic sore thoroughly with alcohol; some of the clear fluid is then collected on a coverglass; or, perhaps better still, the lymphatic gland nearest to one of these sores may be punctured with a hypodermic needle, the fluid being driven out on to a slide on which some normal saline solution has been placed. When the organism has been examined alive the film may be carefully dried and then stained by Giemsa's modification of the Romanowsky stain (see Plate I., fig. 1). This stain, which may be obtained ready prepared from Grübler, of Leipzig, under the name of "Giemsa'sche Lösung für die Romanowsky Färbung," is made as follows: Azur II.-eosin compound, 3 grms. and Azur II. 0·8 grm. are mixed and dried thoroughly in the desiccator over sulphuric acid; this mixture is then *very finely pulverised*, passed through a fine-meshed silk sieve and dissolved at 60° C. in Merck's glycerin, 250 grms., the mixture being well shaken; 250 grms. of methyl-alcohol (Kahlbaum I.), which has been previously heated to 60 C., is then added. The whole, after being well shaken, is allowed to stand for twenty-four hours and filtered. The solution, now ready for use, should be kept in a yellow glass bottle. To 1 c.c. of ammonia-free distilled water add 1 drop of this stain. Stain for from a quarter to three-quarters of an hour. Wash in running water, blot, dry, and mount in Canada balsam. Longer exposure to the action of a more dilute Giemsa fluid often gives excellent results.

The stained organisms may be seen as delicate, reddish, regular spirals with pointed extremities. They usually measure from 4 to 14μ in length, though they may reach 18 or 22μ; the breadth is about 0·25μ. In a section of the liver from a case of congenital syphilis an enormous number of these spirochaetes may be found.

Stain by Levaditi's method as follows: Fix fragments of tissue not more than 1 mm. thick in 10% formol solution for twenty-four hours. Rinse in distilled water and harden in 96% alcohol for twenty-four hours. Then wash in distilled water for some minutes, *i.e.* until the pieces fall to the bottom of the vessel, and transfer to a 1·5–3% solution of nitrate of silver (3% is preferable when the tissues have been obtained from the living patient). This impregnation should be carried on at a temperature of 38° C. for from three to five days, according to the nature of the tissue. "Reduce" the silver in the following solution: Pyrogallic acid, 2·4%, Formol, 5c.c., Aq. dest., 100 c.c. Allow this solution to act on the tissues for from twenty-four to forty-eight hours at room temperature. Again wash in distilled water, dehydrate with alcohol, clear with xylol and cedar-oil, and embed in paraffin. The sections should not be more than 5μ thick. In a section so stained the spirochaetes are seen as dark spirals standing out against a pale yellow background. On staining with a weak counterstain many of the spirals may be seen actually within the liver cells.

This organism may be found in the lung, spleen and other visceral organs, and even in the heart of a patient suffering from syphilis. It has also been found in syphilitic lesions produced experimentally in the higher apes, especially the chimpanzee. As a result of these observations it is now generally accepted as being the primary cause of syphilitic lesions in the human subject. It is certainly present in the lesions usually met with in cases of primary and secondary syphilis of the human subject, and by its action on the blood and tissues of the body produces an antigen, a specific (?) substance, the presence of which has been utilized by Wassermann in the diagnosis of syphilis. He uses the method of deviation of complement by the antigen substances contained in the syphilitic fluid blood or cerebro spinal fluid—by which the lytic action of a haemolysing fluid is prevented.

Kála-ásar.—The non-malarial remittent fever, met with in China, known as dum-dum fever in India and as kála-ázar in Assam, is associated with peculiar parasitic bodies described by Donovan and Leishman (*Herpetomonas Donovani*) (? *Helcosoma tropicum*, Wright). This fever is characterized by its great chronicity, associated with very profound, and ultimately fatal, bloodlessness, in which there is not only a fall in the number of red blood corpuscles, but a marked diminution in the number of white blood corpuscles. Ulceration of the skin and mucous membrane, especially of the lower parts of the small intestine and of the first part of the colon is often present, this being accompanied by dropsy and by distinct enlargement of the liver and spleen. Leonard Rogers, who has given an excellent account of this condition, points out that there is a marked increase in the number of cells in the bone-marrow.

The Leishman-Donovan bodies have been found in large numbers, especially in the spleen (see Plate I., fig. 7); they may also be found in the ulcerating surfaces and wherever the cellular proliferation is marked. These organisms may be found in sections, or they may be demonstrated in film preparations made from the material scraped from the freshly-cut surface of the spleen.

The films are best stained by Leishman's method: Solution A.—Medicinal methylene-blue (Grübler), 1 part; distilled water, 100 parts; sodium carbonate, 1·5 parts. This mixture is heated to 65° C. for twelve hours and then allowed to stand at room temperature for ten days. Solution B.—Eosin extra B.A. (Grübler), 1 part; distilled water, 1000 parts. Mix equal parts of solutions A and B in a large open vessel and allow to stand for from six to twelve hours, stirring from time to time with a glass rod. Filter, and wash

the precipitate which remains on the paper with a large volume of distilled water until the washings are colourless or only tinged a pale blue. Collect the insoluble residue, dry and pulverize.

Make a 0·15% solution of the powder (which may also be obtained from Grübler & Co., Leipzig) in absolute methyl alcohol (Merck's "for analysis"), and transfer to a clean, dry, well stoppered bottle. Pour three or four drops of this stain on to the prepared film (blood, bone, marrow, &c.) and run from side to side. After about half a minute add six or eight drops of distilled water, and mix thoroughly by moving the slide or cover-glass. Allow the stain to act for five minutes longer or, if the film be thick, for ten. Wash with distilled water, leaving a drop or two on the glass for about a minute. Examine at once or after drying without heat and mounting in xylol balsam.

These peculiar parasitic bodies appear as deeply stained points, rounded, oval or cockle-shaped, lying free or grouped in the large endothelial cells of the spleen. Examined under a magnification of 1000 diameters they are found to measure from 3·5 to 2·5μ, or even less, in diameter. Their protoplasm is stained, somewhat unequally, light blue; and from this light blue background two very deeply stained violet corpuscles of unequal size stand out prominently; the smaller of these is more deeply stained than the larger, is thinner, somewhat more elongated or rod-shaped, and parallel or running at right angles to the large corpuscle or obliquely from it. The larger corpuscle is rounded of oval, conical, or sometimes almost dumb-bell shaped. These bodies may appear to touch one another, though usually they are disconnected. Most of these Donovan-Leishman bodies are embedded in the protoplasm of the large endothelial or mononuclear splenic cells, of similar cells in the bone marrow, or of certain lymphatic glands. They may also be seen lying in the protoplasm of the endothelial cells lining the capillary vessels and lymphatics. They are considered by Leishman and Leonard Rogers to be organisms in an intermediate stage of development of either a Trypanosome or some form of Herpetomonas. Rogers, who succeeded in cultivating them outside the body, described changes which he considers are associated with this latter germ. Patton goes further than this, and states that the *Leishmania donovani* Lav. et Mesn. taken up by the bed bug closely resembles in its life cycle that of the Herpetomonas of the common housefly. It is thought that the Leishman-Donovan bodies are the tissue parasite stage, and that the herpetomonas stage is probably to be sought for in the blood of the patient.

Tsetse-Fly Disease (Trypanosomiasis).—The interesting observations carried out by Sir David Bruce have invested the tsetse-fly with an entirely new significance and importance. In 1895 Bruce first observed that in the tsetse disease—*n'gana*—there may be found a flagellated haematozoon closely resembling the *Trypanosoma Evansii* found in Surra. This, like the Surra organism, is very similar in appearance to, but considerably smaller than, the haematozoon often found in the blood of the healthy rat. It has, however, as a rule a single flagellum only. A small quantity of blood, taken from an affected buffalo, wildebeest, koodoo, bushbuck or hyaena—in all of which animals it was found by Bruce—when inoculated into a horse, mule, donkey, cow, dog, cat, rabbit, guinea-pig, rat or mouse, produces a similar disease, the organisms being found sometimes in enormous numbers in the blood of the inoculated animal, especially in the dog and in the rat. He then found that the tsetse-fly can produce the disease in a healthy animal only when it has first charged itself with blood from a diseased animal, and be produced evidence that *Glossina morsitans* is not capable of producing the disease except by carrying the parasites from one animal to another in the blood that it takes through its proboscis into its stomach. The parasites taken in along with such blood may remain in the stomach and alive for a period of 118 hours, but shortly after that the stomach is found to be empty, and the parasites contained in the excrement no longer retain their vitality. The mode of multiplication of these organisms has been studied by Rose-Bradford and Plimmer, who maintain that the multiplication takes place principally in the spleen and lymphatic glands. The tsetse-fly parasite, however, is still imperfectly understood, though much attention is now being paid to its life-history and development.

Sleeping Sickness (Trypanosomiasis).—To the group of diseases caused by Trypanosomes must now be added sleeping sickness. This disease is due to the presence and action in the human body of a form known as *T. gambiense* (Dutton).

In order to demonstrate the parasite in the blood of a case of sleeping sickness, where they are very scanty and difficult to find, the best method is repeated centrifugalization of the blood (Bruce), 10 c.c. being treated at a time; then the sediment in a number of these tubes is collected and again centrifugalised. The living trypanosome may, as a rule, be distinguished in this final sediment, even under a low power of the microscope. The organism may be found in greater numbers in the cerebro-spinal fluid of a case in which the symptoms of sleeping sickness have been developed, though centrifugalization of from 10 to 15 c.c. of the cerebro-spinal fluid for half an hour may be necessary before they can be demonstrated. Greig and Gray, at Mott's suggestion, were able to find the organism in the fluid removed by means of a hypodermic syringe from the swollen lymph glands that appear as one of the earliest signs of infection. Examined fresh and in its native fluid or in normal saline solution it is seen as an actively motile, highly refractile, somewhat spindle-shaped organism (see Plate I., fig. 9). The anterior end is prolonged into a pointed flagellum, the posterior end being slightly blunted or rounded. This organism darts about rapidly between the red blood corpuscles or other corpuscles or particles, and shows rapid undulations, the flagellum beating quickly and the body following the flagellum. In this body a couple of very bright points may be seen. On staining by Leishman's stain (see under *Kāla-āzar*) the general protoplasm of the body is stained blue and is somewhat granular. This trypanosome is from 15 to 25μ in length (without the flagellum, which is from 5 to 6μ) and from 1·5 to 2·5μ broad. In the centre of the spindle-shaped mass is a very distinct reddish purple oval corpuscle corresponding to the larger of the two bright points seen in the unstained specimen; this, the nucleus or macronucleus, is slightly granular. Near the posterior or blunt end of the organism is a second, but much smaller, deeply stained reddish purple point, the second of the bright spots seen in the unstained specimen; this is known as the micro-nucleus or centrosome. Around the micro-nucleus is a kind of court or area of less deeply stained protoplasm, arising from or near which and running along the margin of the body is a narrow band with a very sharply defined wavy free margin. This thin band of protoplasm seems to be continuous with the large spindle-shaped body of the trypanosome, but at the free margin it takes on the red tint of the micro-nucleus instead of the blue tint of the protoplasm. The undulatory membrane, as this band is called, is narrowest at the posterior end, getting broader and broader until the micro-nucleus is reached, beyond which it tapers off irregularly until finally it merges in the flagellum. In sleeping sickness the presence of this organism is usually associated with distinct anaemia, the red cells being diminished in number and the haemoglobin in quantity. Along with this there is an increase in the number of mononuclear leucocytes.

The trypanosome is carried to the human patient by the *Glossina palpalis*, in the proboscis of which the organisms may be seen for some short time after the insect has sucked blood from an infected patient. These trypanosomes have been found living and active in the stomach of this insect up to 118 hours, but after 149 hours no living parasites can be demonstrated. They undergo no metamorphoses in this intermediate host and are simply discharged in the intestinal excreta. It may be readily understood that the trypanosome under these conditions soon loses its virulence, and an animal cannot be infected through the bite of the Glossina for more than 48 hours after the infected blood has been ingested by the fly. The organism may remain latent in the human body for a considerable period. It certainly sets up very tardily any changes by which its presence can be detected. The first symptoms of its presence and activity are enlargement of the lymphatic glands, especially those behind the neck, a condition often accompanied by irregular and intermittent fever.

After a time, in from three months to three years, according to Bruce, the organism gains access to the fluid in the cerebro-spinal canal. Accompanying this latter migration are languor, lassitude, a gradually increasing apathy, and finally profound somnolence.

The incubation period, or that between the time of infection and the appearance of the symptoms associated with trypanosomiasis may be as short as four weeks, or it may extend over several years. The inhabitants of the island of Senegal who have lived in Casamance do not consider themselves safe from the disease until at least seven years after they have left an infected area. At first, amongst negroes, according to Dutton and Todd, there is no external clinical sign of disease except glandular enlargement; in mulattoes and whites an irregular and intermittent fever may be the chief sign of infection, "the temperature being raised for two to four days, then falling to normal or below normal for four or five days." In other cases the fever is of the septic type, the temperature being normal in the morning but rising in the evening to 101·3° or 102·2° F., rarely to 104° F., the curve differing from that characteristic of malaria in which the rise usually takes place in the morning. Moreover, in sleeping sickness there are no rigors before the rise of temperature and but slight sweating, such as there is usually occurring at the end of the rise. Here again we have a distinction between the malarial condition and that of sleeping sickness. The respiration and the pulse rate are increased both during the febrile and the non-febrile attacks; the respiration is from 29 to 30 a minute, and the pulse rises to 90, and even up to 140, a minute, according to the degree of cardiac excitability which appears to be constantly present. The localized swelling and redness are seen as puffiness of the face, oedema of the eyelids and ankles and feet, congested erythematous patches on the face, trunk or limbs. Anaemia, general weakness and wasting, at first very slightly marked, gradually become prominent features, and headache is often present. The enlargement of the spleen appears to go on concurrently with enlargement of the lymphatic glands. Manson points out that trypanosomiasis may terminate fatally without the appearance of any characteristic symptoms of sleeping sickness, but as a rule the "sleeping" or second stage supervenes. The temperature now becomes of the hectic type, rising to 101·2° F. in the evening and falling to 98·6° F. in the morning. Here again there are no rigors or sweating. During the last stages of the disease the rectal temperature may fall as low as 95° and for the last day or two to 92° F., the pulse and respiration falling with the temperature. The irritability of the heart is still marked. Headache in the supraorbital region, and pain in the back, and even in the feet, have been described. Activity and intelligence give place to laziness, apathy and dullness; the face loses its brightness, the eyelids approximate, and the muscles around the mouth and nose become flabby and flaccid, the patient becomes drowsy, and when questioned replies only after a marked interval. Fibrillary tremors of the tongue and shaking of the hands and arms, distinct even during rest, become increased when any voluntary movement is attempted. These tremors may extend to the lower limbs and trunk. Epileptiform convulsions, general weakness and progressive emaciation come on, and shortly before death there is incontinence of urine and faeces. "The intellectual faculties gradually become impaired, the patient has a certain amount of difficulty in understanding what is said to him, and becomes emotional, often crying for no reason whatever; delirium is usually absent, the drowsiness increases and the patient's attitude becomes characteristic, the head falls forward on the chest and the eyelids are closed. At first the patient is easily aroused from this drowsy condition, but soon he reaches a stage in which he falls sound asleep almost in any attitude and under any conditions, especially after meals. These periods of sleep, which become gradually longer and more profound, lead eventually to a comatose condition from which the patient can be aroused only with the greatest difficulty. It is at this stage that the temperature becomes normal and death occurs." Nabarro points out, however, that this condition of drowsiness and sleep leading eventually to coma, is by no means invariably present

In the early part of the sleeping-sickness stage patients often sleep more than usual, but later do not sleep excessively. They become lethargic and indifferent to their surroundings, however, and often lie with their eyes closed. When spoken to they bear and understand what is said to them and after a longer or shorter interval give a very brief reply.

The leucocytosis that occurs during the course of this form of trypanosomiasis is due, apparently, to secondary or terminal bacterial infections so frequently associated with the disease in its later stages. The first stage of the disease, that of fever, may last for several years; the second or nervous stage with tremors, &c., for from four to eight months. It is quite exceptional for the disease to be prolonged for more than a year from the time that the nervous symptoms become manifest, though a European who contracted trypanosomiasis in Uganda, having delusions and becoming drowsy within the year, did not die of sleeping sickness until more than eighteen months from the onset of the nervous symptoms.

The *Glossina palpalis* is not found in swamps. It affects a belt of from ten to thirty yards broad along banks bounding water shaded by scrub and underwood. It may, however, follow or be carried by the animal or human subject it is attacking for a distance of, say, three hundred yards, but unless carried it will not cross an artificial clearing of more than thirty yards made in the natural fly belt. The authorities in the plague-stricken areas recommend, therefore, the clearance of belts thirty yards in width along portions of the lake side, at fords and in such other places as are frequented by natives. No infected person should be allowed to enter a "fly area," so that they may not act as centres from which the flies, acting as carriers, may convey infection. The provision of clothing for natives who are compelled to work in fly areas is an important precautionary measure.

There seems to be some doubt as to whether *Trypanosoma gambiense* of Dutton is the same organism and produces the same conditions as the Trypanosoma of Bruce and Nabarro from Uganda, but most observers seem to think that the two species are the same and yield the same results when inoculated into animals. It is supposed that this trypanosome may pass through certain stages of metamorphosis in the human or animal body, and different drugs have been recommended as trypanocides during these various stages, an arsenic preparation (atoxyl) first being given, and then, when the organisms have disappeared, injections of bichloride of mercury, this salt appearing to prevent the relapses which occur when atoxyl only is given over a prolonged period. Ehrlich, treating animals suffering from trypanosomiasis with parafuchsin, found that although the parasites disappeared from the blood they soon recurred. On the exhibition of another dose of parafuchsin they again disappeared. This was repeated for a considerable number of times, but after a time the parafuchsin lost its effect, the trypanosome having acquired an immunity against this substance; they had in fact become "fuchsin-fast." Such fuchsin-fast organisms injected into animals still retain their immunity against parafuchsin and may transmit it through more than 100 generations. Nevertheless, they cannot withstand the action of other trypanocidal drugs. The outcome of all this is that large doses of the trypanocidal drug should be given at once, and that the same drug should never be given over too long a period, a fresh drug often being effective even when the first drug has lost action.

II.—To other Animal Parasites.

Filariasis.—Since Bancroft and Manson first described *Filaria nocturna* and its relation to the common form of filariasis, the most important contribution to our knowledge has been made, at the suggestion of the younger Bancroft, by Dr G. C. Low, who has demonstrated that the embryos of the filaria may be found in the proboscis of the mosquito (*Culex ciliaris*), whence they probably find their way into the circulating blood of the human subject. It appears that the filaria 'embryo after being taken, with the blood of the patient, into the stomach of the mosquito, loses its sheath; after which, leaving the stomach, it passes into the thoracic muscles of its intermediate host, and becomes more fully developed, increasing considerably in size and attaining a mouth, an alimentary canal, and the characteristic trilobed caudal appendage. It now leaves the thoracic muscles, and, passing towards the head, makes its way "into the loose cellular tissue which abounds in the prothorax in the neighbourhood of the salivary glands." Most of them then "pass along the neck, enter the lower part of the head," whence they may pass into the proboscis. Although it has never been demonstrated that the filaria is directly inoculated into the human subject from the proboscis of the mosquito, it seems impossible to doubt that when the mosquito "strikes," the filaria makes its way into the circulation directly from the proboscis. It is important to note that the mosquito, when fed on banana pulp, does not eject the filaria from its proboscis. This, however, is not to be wondered at, as the filaria is apparently unable to live on the juices of the banana; moreover, the consistence of the banana is very different from that of the human skin. The importance of this observation, as affording an additional reason for taking measures to get rid of the mosquito in districts in which filariasis is rife, can scarcely be over-estimated.

C.—Infective Diseases in which an Organism has been found, but has not finally been connected with the Disease.

Hydrophobia is usually contracted by man through inoculation of an abraded surface with the saliva of an animal affected with rabies—through the bite of a dog, the animal in which the so-called rabies of the streets occurs. The puppy is specially dangerous, as, although it may be suffering from rabies when the saliva contains an extremely exalted virus, the animal may exhibit no signs of the disease almost up to the time of its death. The other animals that may be affected "naturally" are wolves, cats, foxes, horses, cows and deer; but all warm-blooded animals may be successfully inoculated with the disease. The principal changes met with are found in the nervous system, and include distension of the perivascular lymphatic sheaths, congestion and oedema of the brain and spinal cord and of the meninges. Haemorrhages occur into the cerebral ventricles of the brain, especially in the floor of the fourth, and on the surface and in the substance of the medulla oblongata, and the spinal cord.

In addition to these small haemorrhages, collections of leucocytes are met with in hyperaemic areas in the medulla oblongata and pons, sometimes in the cortical cerebral tissue and in the spinal cord, in the perivascular lymphatics of the grey matter of the anterior horns and in the white matter of the postero-internal and postero-external columns. Here also the nerve cells are seen to be vacuolated, hyaline and granular, and often pigmented; thrombi may be present in some of the smaller vessels, and the collections of leucocytes may be so prominent, especially in the medulla, that they have been described as miliary abscesses. Haemorrhages are also common in the various mucous and serous membranes; hyaline changes in and around the walls of blood-vessels; proliferation of the endothelium; swelling and vacuolation of nerve cells; pericellular infiltration with leucocytes, and infiltration of the salivary glands with leucocytes (Coats). An increased number of leucocytes and microcytes in the blood has also been made out. The virus, whatever it may be, has a power of multiplying in the tissues, and of producing a toxic substance which, as in the case of tetanus toxin, appears to act specially on the central nervous system.

In recent years fresh interest has been aroused in the morbid histology of the brain and cord in hydrophobia by the appearance of Negri's description of "bodies" which he claims are found in the central nervous system only in hydrophobia or rabies (see Plate I., fig. 3). These bodies, which are rounded, oval, triangular, or slightly spindle- or sausage-shaped, when specially stained consist of a red (acidophile) basis in which stand out small blue (basophile) granules, rods and circles, often situated within vacuoles. A small central point which is surrounded by no clear space is supposed to correspond to the nucleus of a protozoan. But this can be little more than a suggestion. The Negri bodies are certainly present in the central nervous system in cases of hydrophobia, and have not been found in similar positions in any other disease. They are present in large numbers, even at an early stage of the disease, although they are then so small that they may easily escape detection, so small indeed that they may pass through the pores of a Berkefeld filter, the filtrate in such cases being capable of acting as a rabic virus. In the more chronic cases and in the later stages of the disease the Negri bodies may attain a considerable size and may be easily seen under the microscope. They are from 0·5μ to 10μ in diameter—the longer the course of the disease the larger the bodies, these larger forms seldom if ever being met with in specially susceptible animals, which soon succumb to the disease. The Negri bodies may be constricted in the middle, or, if somewhat elongated, there may be two or three constrictions which give it the appearance of a string of sausages. They may be met with in almost all the nerve cells of the central nervous system in well-developed cases of hydrophobia, but they are most numerous and are found most readily in the cells of the cornu ammonis, and then in the Purkinje cells of the cerebellum.

Although there are several methods of preparing these organisms for microscopical examination, the following is perhaps the simplest. A fragment of the grey substance, say from the cornu ammonis, is taken from a section made at right angles to the surface and placed on a slide about one inch from the end. A coverslip is now " pressed upon it until it is spread out in a moderately thin layer; then the coverslip is moved slowly and evenly over the slide," leaving the first three-quarters of an inch of the slide clear. In making the smear only slight pressure is used, the pressure beginning on the edge of the coverslip away from the end of the slide towards which the coverslip is travelling, thus driving more of the nerve tissues along the smear " and producing more well-spread nerve cells." The smears are then air-dried, placed in methyl-alcohol for one minute, and then in a freshly-prepared mixture of 10 c.c. of distilled water, three drops of a saturated alcoholic solution of rose anilin violet, and six drops of Loeffler's alkaline methylene blue, which is warmed until steam rises; the stain is then poured from the specimen, which after being rinsed in water is allowed to dry and is then mounted in Canada balsam.

The nature of the disease produced by the inoculation of saliva from a rabid animal appears to depend upon (1) the quantity of the rabic virus introduced; (2) the point of its introduction; (3) the activity of the virus. Thus by diluting the poison with distilled water or saline solution and injecting small quantities, the period of incubation may be prolonged. Slight wounds of the skin, of the limbs and of the back are followed by a long incubation period; but when the inoculation takes place in the tips of the fingers or in the skin of the face, where nerves are numerous, and especially where the wound is lacerated or deep, the incubation period is much shorter and the attack usually more severe. This, as in tetanus, is accounted for by the fact that the lymphatics of the nerves are much more directly continuous with the central nervous system than are any other set of lymphatics. The poison appears to act directly upon the cells of the central nervous system.

Arising out of recent researches on hydrophobia, two methods of treatment—one of which, at any rate, has been attended by conspicuous success—have been put into practice. The first of these, Pasteur's, is based upon the fact that rabic virus may be intensified or attenuated at will. Pasteur found that although the virus taken from the cerebrospinal fluid of the dog always produces death in the same period when inoculated into the same animal, virus taken from other animals has not the same activity. If passed through a succession of monkeys it may become so attenuated that it is no longer lethal. If either the " monkey virus," which is not fatal to the rabbit, or the " dog virus," which kills in twelve to fourteen days, be passed through a series of rabbits, the virulence may be so exalted that it may kill in about six days: its activity cannot be increased beyond this point by any means at present at our disposal. This intensified virus was therefore named *virus fixe* by Pasteur, and it forms a standard from which to work. He found, too, that under certain conditions of temperature the virus may be readily attenuated, one hour at 50° or half an hour at 60° C. completely destroying it. A 5 % solution of carbolic acid acting for half an hour, or a 1 per 1000 solution of bichloride of mercury or acetic acid or permanganate of potash, brings about the same result, as do also exposure to air and sunlight. The poison contained in the spinal cord of the rabbit exposed to dry air and not allowed to undergo putrefactive changes gradually loses its activity, and at the end of fourteen to fifteen days is incapable of setting up rabic symp-

toms. A series of cords from rabbits inoculated with the *virus fixe* are cut into short segments, which, held in series by the dura mater, are suspended in sterile glass flasks plugged with cotton-wool and containing a quantity of potassium hydrate—a powerful absorbent of water. At the end of twenty-four hours the activity of the virus is found to have fallen but slightly; at the end of forty-eight hours there is a still further falling off, until on the fourteenth or fifteenth day the virus is no longer lethal. With material so prepared Pasteur treated patients who had been bitten by mad dogs. On the first day of treatment small quantities of an emulsion of the cord exposed for thirteen or fourteen days in saline solution are injected subcutaneously, and the treatment is continued for from fifteen to twenty-one days, according to the severity of the bite, a stronger emulsion—i.e. an emulsion made of a cord that has been desiccated for a shorter period—being used for each succeeding injection, until at last the patient is injected with an emulsion which has been exposed to the air for only three days. In the human subject the period of incubation of the disease is comparatively prolonged, owing to the insusceptibility of the tissues to the action of this poison; there is therefore some chance of obtaining a complete protection or acclimatization of the tissues before the incubation period is completed. The virus introduced at the bite has then no more chance of affecting the nerve centres than has the strong virus injected in the late stages of the protective inoculation: the nerve centres, having become gradually acclimatized to the poisons of the rabic virus, are able to carry on their proper functions in its presence, until in time, as in the case of microbial poisons, the virus is gradually neutralized and eliminated from the body. Various modifications and improvements of this method have from time to time been devised, but all are based on, and are merely extensions of, Pasteur's original work and method. As soon as it was found that antitoxins were formed in the tissues in the case of an attack of tetanus, attention was drawn to the necessity of determining whether something similar might not be done in the production of an antirabic serum for the treatment of rabies. Babes and Lepp, and then Tizzoni and his colleagues Schwarz and Centanni, starting from *virus fixe*, obtained a series of weaker inoculating materials by submitting it for different periods to the action of gastric juice. Beginning with a weak virus so prepared, and from time to time injecting successively stronger emulsions (seventeen injections in twenty days) into a sheep, they succeeded in obtaining a serum of such antirabic power that if injected in the proportion of 1 to 25,000 of body-weight, an animal is protected against a lethal dose of *virus fixe*. The activity of this serum is still further reinforced if a fresh series of injections is made at intervals varying from two to five months, occupying twelve days. This antirabic substance stored in the blood has not only the power of anticipating (neutralizing?) the action of the poison, but also of acting as a direct curative agent; as a prophylactic agent, readily kept in stock and easily and rapidly exhibited, it possesses very great advantages over the inoculation method. It must be borne in mind that the longer the period after the infection the greater must be the amount of serum used to obtain a successful result.

As regards the necessity for any treatment it may be pointed out that although the saliva of a rabid dog may be infective three days before the manifestation of any symptoms of the disease death takes place almost invariably within six days of the first symptom. If therefore the animal remains alive for ten days after the patient is bitten, there is no necessity for the antirabic treatment to be applied and the patient need fear no evil results from the bite.

There can be little doubt that hydrophobia is a specific disease due to a multiplication of some virus in the nervous system, in the elements of which it is ultimately fixed; that it passes from the wound to the central nervous system by the lymphatics; and that, as in tetanus, the muscular spasms are the result of the action of some special poison on the central nervous system.

Scarlet Fever.—In scarlet fever recent observations have been comparatively few and unimportant. Crooke, and later Klein, and others have, however, shown that in the glands and throats of scarlet fever patients a streptococcus, to which is assigned the chief aetiological rôle in connexion with this disease, is present. On the other hand, it is maintained by many observers that these streptococci are nothing more than the streptococci found in puerperal fever, erysipelas, and similar infective conditions, and certainly the organisms described closely resemble *Streptococcus pyogenes*. In 1904 Mallory described certain "bodies" which he considers may be associated with scarlet fever, and which were sufficiently distinctive to justify him in suggesting that he was dealing with the "various stages in the developmental cycle of a protozoan." These bodies, which were demonstrated in four cases of scarlet fever, "occur in and between the epithelial cells of the epidermis and free in the superficial lymph vessels and spaces of the corium." They are small, varying from the size of a blood platelet to that of a red blood corpuscle, and "stained delicately but sharply with methylene blue." Well formed rosettes with numerous segments may be seen, forms which Mallory thinks may correspond to the phase of asexual development of the malarial parasite. He also describes "coarsely reticulated forms which may represent stages in sporogony or be due to degeneration of the other forms." He gives beautiful illustrations, both drawings and photographs, of these organisms, and without claiming that he has proved any aetiological relation between these bodies and scarlet fever, states that his personal opinion is that such relation exists.

D.—Infective Diseases not yet proved to be due to Micro-organisms.

Small-pox.—There have been few recent additions to our knowledge of the aetiology of small-pox, though Dr Monckton Copeman now holds that the small-pox organism, like that of vaccine, is probably a very minute bacillus, which, from its behaviour in the presence of glycerin, is possessed of the power of forming spores. If vaccine lymph, taken from the calf, be protected from all extraneous sporebearing organisms and treated with 50 % solution of glycerin, it, in time, becomes absolutely sterile as regards ordinary non-sporebearing organisms. Even the staphylococci and streptococci, usually found in calf lymph, cannot withstand the prolonged action of this substance, but sporebearing organisms still remain alive and active. Moreover, the lymph still retains its power of producing vaccine vesicles, so that the vaccine organism, in its powers of resistance, resembles the sporebearing, and not the non-sporebearing, organisms with which we are acquainted. This vaccine organism must be very minute; it is stated that it can be cultivated only on special media, though it multiplies freely in the superficial cutaneous tissues of the calf, the monkey and the human subject. Perhaps the most important outcome of Dr Monckton Copeman's work on this subject is that he has obtained a vaccine lymph from which are eliminated all streptococci and staphylococci, and, if the lymph be taken with reasonable care, any other organisms which could possibly give rise to untoward results.

Typhus Fever.—Although it is fully recognized that typhus must be one of the specific infective fevers brought about by the action of a special micro-organism, no definite information as to the bacterial aetiology of this condition has been obtained. It is always looked upon as a " filth " disease; and from the frequency of minute haemorrhages, and from the resemblance to the haemorrhagic septicaemias in other respects, it appears probable that the bacillus of typhus is the organism described by Mott in 1883 as an actively motile dumb-bell coccus, and ten years later by Dubieff and Bruhl as the *Diplococcus typhosus exanthematicus*; the polar staining and general resemblance to the diplococcus of fowl cholera, the plague bacillus, the diplococcus of " Wildseuche,",certain forms of swine fever and hog cholera, and others of the haemorrhagic septicaemias, are sufficient to suggest the generic affinity of this organism to this septicaemic group. We have as yet, however (1910), no absolute proof of the aetiological relation of the bacillus to this disease.

Measles.—In measles, as in scarlet fever, micrococci have had ascribed to them the power of setting up the specific disease.

Canon and Pielicke have, however, described minute bacilli somewhat resembling those described as occurring in vaccine lymph. These are found in the blood in the early stages of the disease, and also in the profuse catarrhal secretions so characteristic of this condition. There are no records of the successful inoculation of this minute bacillus, and until such evidence is forthcoming this organism must be looked upon as being an accessory, possibly, but not the prime cause, of measles.

Mumps.—It is generally accepted that mumps is probably caused by a specific micro-organism, the infective material making its way in the first instance through the ducts to the parotid and other salivary glands. It appears to bring about a peculiar oedematous inflammation of the interstitial tissue of the glands, but slight parenchymatous changes may also be observed. The virus is present in the tissues for some days before there is any manifestation of parotid swelling, but during this period it is extremely active, and the disease may be readily transmitted from patient to patient. The infectivity continues for some time, probably for nearly a week after naked-eye manifestations of the diseased condition have disappeared.

Whooping-Cough.—A diplococcus, a streptococcus, and various higher fungi have in turn been put down as the cause of this disease. It must, from its resemblance to the other specific infective fevers, be considered as an infective disease of microbic origin, which goes through a regular period of incubation and invasion, and in which true nervous lesions, especially of the pneumogastric and superior laryngeal nerves, are somewhat common.

Affanassieff, and later Köplick, have described a minute bacillus, with rounded ends and bi-polar staining, which occurs in the mucus discharged at the end of a paroxysm of whooping-cough. Köplick examined sixteen cases, and found this organism in thirteen of them. There can be little doubt that the infective material is contained in the expectoration. It may remain active for a considerable period, but is then usually attached to solid particles. It is not readily carried by the breath, and multiplies specially in the mucous membranes, setting up inflammation, probably through its toxic products, which appear to be absorbed, and, as in the case of the tetanus poison, to travel specially along the lymphatics of the local nerves. Affections of the lung—bronchitis and broncho-pneumonia—may be directly associated with the disease, but it is much more likely that these affections are the result of secondary infection of tissues already in a weakened condition.

AUTHORITIES.—General: Allbutt and Rolleston, *System of Medicine* (2nd ed., London, 1905 et seq.); Castellani and Chalmers, *Manual of Tropical Medicine* (London, 1910); Fischer, *The Structure and Functions of Bacteria*, trans. by K. Coppen Jones (Oxford, 1900); Manson, Sir P., *Tropical Diseases* (3rd ed., London, 1903); Nuttall, " On the Rôle of Insects, &c., as carriers in the spread of bacterial and parasitic diseases of man and animals " (*Johns Hopkins Hospital Reports*, viii., 1899); Schneidemühl, *Lehrb. d. vergleich. Path. u. Therapie d. Menschen u. d. Hausthiere* (Leipzig, 1898); Woodhead, *Bacteria and their Products* (London, 1891). Actinomycosis: Boström, *Ziegler's Beitr. z. pathol. Anatomie*, Bd. ix. (1891); Illich, *Beitrag z. Klinik d. Actinomykose* (Vienna, 1892); M'Fadyean, *Journ. Compar. Path. and Therap.*, vol. ii. (1899). Cerebro-Spinal Meningitis: Councilman, Mallory and Wright, *Rep. Bd. Health, Mass.* (Boston, 1898); Davis, *Journ. Infect. Diseases*, iv. 558 (1907); Mackenzie and Martin, *Journ. Path. and Bacteriol.* xii. 539 (1908); Ruppel, *Deutsche med. Wochenschr.*, S. 1366 (1906); Shennan and Ritchie, *Journ. Path. and Bacteriol.* xii. 456 (1908); Symmers and others, *Brit. Med. Journ.* ii. 1334 (1906). Cholera: Dunbar, in Lubarsch u. Ostertag's *Ergebn. d. allg. Pathologie*, vol. i. (1896). Diphtheria: Behring, " Die Geschichte d. Diphtherie (Leipzig, 1895), and various other papers, principally in *Zeits. f. Hygiene*, Bd. xii. (1892) onwards; Ehrlich, " Die Werthbemessung d. Diphtherieheilserums u. d. theoret. Grundlagen," *Klinisches Jahrb.* Bd. vi. (1897); Klebs, " Ueber Diphtherie," *Verh. d. II. Congr. f. inn. Med. in Wiesbaden* (1883); Loeffler, " Unters. ü. d. Bedeut. d. Mikro-org. f. d. Entst. d. Diphtheritis b. Menschen, &c.," *Mitth. a. d. k. Gesundheitsamte*, Bd. ii. (1884); Martin, Sidney, Goulstonian Lectures, *Brit. Med. Journ.* vol. i. (1892); Nuttall and Graham Smith, *The Bacteriology of Diphtheria* (Cambridge, 1908); Roux and Yersin, " Contrib. à l'étude d. l. Diphtérie," *Annales de l'Inst. Pasteur*, t. ii.–iv. (1888–1890). Dysentery: Kartulis, " Die Amoeben-dysenterie," in Kolle and Wassermann's *Handb. d. path. Mikro-org. Ergänz. Bd.* p. 347 (1906); Osler, " On the Amoeba coli in Dysentery

and in Dysenteric Liver Abscess," *Johns Hopkins Hosp. Bull.* vol. i.
(1890). **Erysipelas:** Coley, *Proc. Roy. Soc. Med.* (London, 1909), vol. iii.
(Surg. Sect.), p. 1; Fehleisen, *Aetiologie der Erysipels* (Berlin, 1883).
Filariasis: Low, " On Filaria Nocturna in ' Culex,' " *Brit. Med.
Journ.* vol. i. (1900); Manson, *Tropical Diseases* (3rd ed., London,
1903). **Gonorrhoea:** Bumm, *Der Mikro-organismus d. gonorrh.
Schleimhaut-Erkrankungen* (Wiesbaden, 1885); 'see, *Le Gonocoque*
(Paris, 1896). **Glanders:** Korányi, in Nothnagel's *Specielle Patho-
logie*, Bd. v. (1897); Loeffler and Schütz, *Deutsche med. Wochenschr.*
(1882, Eng. trans., 1886); M'Fadyean, " Pulmonary Lesions of
Glanders," *Journ. Comp. Path. and Therap.* vol. viii. (1895); *Journ.
State Medicine*, pp. 1, 65, 73, 125 (1905). **Hydrophobia:** Babes and
Lepp, " Rech. s. l. vaccination antirabique," *Ann. de l'inst. Pasteur*,
t. iii. (1889); Högyes, in Nothnagel's *Specielle Pathologie*, Bd. v.
(1897); Negri, *Boll. soc. med. chir. di Pavia*, No. 2, 4 (1903);
Ztschr. f. Hyg., Bd. xliii. S. 507, Bd. xliv. S. 519 (1903); Pasteur,
Traitement de la rage (Paris, 1886), and numerous papers in the
Compt. rend. acad. d. sc. (Paris, from 1881 onwards); and in *Ann.
de l'inst. Pasteur*, t. i. (1887) and t. ii. (1888); Tizzoni and Centanni,
Lancet, vol. ii. (1895). **Influenza:** Canon, " Ueber einen Mikro-org. i.,
Blute v. Influenzakranken," *Deutsche med. Wochenschr.* (1892);
Pfeiffer, " Vorl. Mitth. ü. d. Erreger d. Influenza," *Deutsche med.
Wochenschr.* (1892). **Kala-azar:** Laveran et Mesnil, *Compt. rend.
acad. d. sc.* cxxxvii. p. 957 (Paris, 1903); Leishman, in Allbutt and
Rolleston's *Syst. Med.* vol. ii., pt. ii. p. 226 (2nd ed., London, 1907);
Patton, *Scientific Memoirs Gov. India*, No. 27 (1907), No. 31 (1907);
Rogers, *Brit. Med. Journ.* t. i. 427, 490, 557 (1907). **Leprosy:** Hansen
and Looft, *Leprosy in its Clin. and Path. Aspects*, trans. by N. Walker
(Bristol, 1895); *Mitth. u. Verhandl. d.3 internat. wissensch. Lepra-
Conferenz z. Berlin* (1897); Rake, *Reports of the Trinidad Asylum*
(1886–1893); *Report of the Leprosy Commission to India* (1893).
Mycetoma or Madura Foot: Bocarro, " Analysis of 100 Cases of
Mycetoma," *Lancet*, vol. ii. (1893); Boyce and Surveyor, *Proc. Path.
Soc. Lond.* vol. liii. (1893); Vandyke Carter, *Trans. Path. Soc. Lond.*
vol. xxiv. (1873), and " On Mycetoma or the Fungus Disease of India "
(London, 1874); Kanthack, *Journ. Path. and Bact.* vol. i. (1892);
Lewis and Cunningham, *Physiol. and Pathol. Researches* (1875);
" Fungus Disease of India," *Quain's Dict. of Medicine*, vol. i.
(1894); Unna and Delbanco, *Monats. f. prakt. Derm.* Bd. xxx.,
S. 545 (1900); Vincent, " Et. s. l. parasite d. pied Madure,"
Ann. de l'inst. Pasteur, t. viii. (1894). **Malaria:** Celli, *Malaria*,
trans. by Eyre (London, 1900); Nuttall, " Neuere Forsch. ü. d. Rolle
d. Mosquitos, &c.," *Centralbl. f. Bact. u. Parasitenk.* Abt. I. (1900),
and in *Journ. Trop. Med.* vols. ii. iii. (1900), and *Journ. Hyg.* vols.
i., ii. (1901); Nuttall and Shipley, *Journ. Hyg.* i. 4, 45, 269, 451
(1901), ii. 58 (1902); Ruge in Kolle and Wassermann's *Handb. d.
path. Mikro-org.* Ergäns. Bd. (Jena, 1907). **Malta Fever:** Bruce,
" Note on the Discovery of a Micro-organism in Malta Fever,"
Practitioner (1887); " Obs. on Malta Fever," *Brit. Med. Journ.* vol. i.
(1889); " Malta Fever," in Davidson's *Hygiene of Warm Climates*
(Edinburgh, 1893); Eyre, *Quart. Journ. Med.* i. 209 (1908); Hughes,
" Investig. into the Etiology of Mediterranean Fevers," *Lancet*, ii.
(1892); and in *Ann. de l'inst. Pasteur*, t. viii. (1893); *Reports of
Commission on Mediterranean Fever* (London, 1905 et seq.). **Infective
Meningitis:** Neumann and Schäffer, *Z. Actiol. d. eiterig. Meningitis*;
Virch. *Archiv.* Bd. cix. (1887); Weichselbaum, *Fortschritte d.
Medicin*, Bd. v. (1887). **Plague:** Bannerman, *Journ. Hyg.* v. 179
(1906); and *Edin. Med. Journ.* n.s., xxiii. 417 (1908); Bitter, " Ueb.
d. Haffkine'schen Schutzimpfungen gegen Pest," *Zeits. f. Hygiene*,
Bd. xxx. (1899); Calmette et Salimbeni, *Ann. de l'inst. Pasteur*,
xiii. 865 (1899); Haffkine, " Further Papers relating to the
Outbreak of Plague in India, No. III." (London, 1898), and *Brit.
Med. Journ.*, i. 1461 (1897); Kitasato, *The Lancet*, ii. 375, 428
(1894), and *Brit. Med. Journ.* ii. 369 (1894); Klein, *Studies in the
Bacteriology and Etiology of Oriental Plague* (London, 1906); Lamb,
" Summary of Work of the Plague Commission " (Calcutta, 1908);
Lowson, *Lancet*, ii. 325 (1894), see also *Brit. Med. Journ.* ii. 369
(1894); *Reports on Plague Investigations in India*, in *Journ. Hyg.*
vii. 421 (1906), viii. 323, 693 (1907–1908); Simond, *Ann. de l'inst.
Pasteur*, xii. 625 (1898); Yersin, " La Peste bubonique à Hong-
Kong," *Ann. de l'inst. Pasteur*, t. viii. (1894); also Yersin, Calmette
and Borrel, *op. cit.*, t. ix. (1895). **Relapsing Fever:** Koch, *Deutsche
med. Wochenschr.* (1879); Soudakewitch, " Recherches s. l. fièvre
recurrente," *Ann. de l'inst. Pasteur*, t. v. (1891). **Sleeping Sickness:**
Browning, *Journ. Path. and Bacteriol.* xii. 166 (1908); *Bulletin of
the Sleeping Sickness Bureau* (No. 1, London, Oct. 1908 onwards);
Dutton and Todd, " First Report of the Trypanosomiasis Expedition
to Senegal, 1902 " (Liverpool, 1903); Dutton, Todd and Christy,
Brit. Med. Journ., i. 186 (1904); Eärlich, *Berl. klin. Wochenschr.*
S.S. 233, 280, 310, 341 (1907); Laveran and Mesnil, *Trypanosomes and
Trypanosomiases*, trans. by Nabarro (London, 1907); Royal Society,
Reports of the Sleeping Sickness Commission, No. 1 (London, Aug.
1903 onwards). **Suppuration and Septicæmia:** Watson Cheyne,
Suppuration and Septic Diseases (Edinburgh and London, 1889).
Surra: Evans, *Report on " Surra " Disease* (Bombay, 1880);
Lewis, *Appendix*, 14th *Ann. Rep. of Sanit. Commission with the
Govt. of India* (1878); Lingard, *Report on Surra in Equines, Bovines,
Buffaloes and Canines* (2 vols., Bombay, 1893 and 1899); Steel,
*Investig. into an Obscure and Fatal Disease among Transport Mules
in British Burma* (1885). **Syphilis:** Metchnikoff, *Lancet*, i. 1553,

1629 (1906); *The New Hygiene* (Harben Lectures, London, 1906);
Ann. de l'inst. Pasteur, xxi. 753 (1907); Metchnikoff and Roux,
Ann. de l'inst. Pasteur, t. xvii.–xx. (1903–1906); Schaudinn and
Hoffmann, *Arb. a. d. Kaiserl Gesundheitsamte*, xxii. 527 (1905);
Berl. klin. Wochenschr. S. 673 (1905); Wassermann, *Berl. klin.
Wochenschr.* S.S. 1599, 1634 (1907); Wassermann, Neisser and
Bruck, *Deutsche med. Wochenschr.* S. 745 (1906). **Tetanus:** Behring,
" Die Blutserumtherapie," *Zeits. f. Hygiene*, Bd. xii. (1892); Knud
Faber, *Om Tatanos som Infektionssygdom* (Copenhagen, 1890);
Kitasato, *Zeits. f. Hygiene*, Bd. vii. (1889), and Bd. xii. (1892);
Nicolaier, *Beitr. s. Actiol. d. Wundstarrkrampfes* (Göttingen, 1885);
Rose, *Der Starrkrampf b. Menschen* (Stuttgart, 1897); Roux and
Borrel, " Tetanos cérébral et immunité contre le tétanos," *Ann. de
l'inst. Pasteur*, t. xii. (1898); Vaillard, Vaillard and Rouget, Vaillard
and Vincent, various articles in the *Ann. de l'inst. Pasteur*, t. v.
(1891), and t. vi. (1892); Wassermann and Takaki, " Ueb. tetanus-
antitox. Eigenschaften d. normalen Centralnervensystems," *Berl.
klin. Wochenschr.* (1898). **Tsetse-fly Disease:** Bradford and Plimmer, *Proc. Roy. Soc. Lond.* lxv. 274 (1899); Bruce, *Tsetse-fly
Disease or Nagana, in Zululand* (Durban, 1895); and London, 1897;
Kanthack, Durham and Blandford, *Proc. Roy. Soc. Lond.* lxiv. 100
(1898). **Tuberculosis** Bosanquet and Eyre, *Serums, Vaccines and
Toxines* (2nd ed., London, 1909); Calmette, *Compt. rend. acad. d.
sc.* cxliv. 1324 (Paris, 1907); Fortescue-Brickdale, *Bristol Med.
Chir. Journ.* xxvi. 112 (1908); Koch, *Deutsche med. Wochenschr.*
S. 1029 (1890); S. 209 (1897); *Mitth. a. d. kaiserl. Gesundheitsamte*,
Bd. ii. (1884); von Pirquet, *Deutsch. med. Wochenschr.* S. 865 (1907);
Report, with Appendices, of the Royal Commission on Tuberculosis
(London, 1895); *Reports*, Royal Commission on Tuberculosis
(London, 1901–1907); Wolff-Eisner, *The Ophthalmic and Cutaneous
Diagnosis of Tuberculosis* (Eng. trans., New York, 1908); Wright,
Lancet, ii. 1598, 1674 (1905). **Typhoid Fever:** Chantemesse, in
Charcot's *Traité de médecine*, t. i. (1891); Chantemesse and Widal,
" Étude expér. a. l'exaltation, l'immuns. et l. thérap. d. l'infection
typhique," *Ann. de l'inst. Pasteur*, t. vi. (1892); Davies and Walker
Hall, *Proc. Roy. Soc. Med.* vol. i. (London, 1908), (Epidem. Section),
p. 175; Durham, " On a Special Action of the Serum of highly
Immunized Animals," *Journ. Path. and Bact.* vol. iv. (1896–1907);
Easton, *Boston Med. and Surg. Journ.* cliii. 195 (1905); Förster,
Münch. med. Wochenschr. S. (1908); Frosch, *Klin. Jahrb.* xix.
537 (Jena, 1908); Max Grüber, " Z. Theorie d. Agglutination,"
Münch. med. Wochenschr. (1890); Gründaum, *Lancet*, vol. ii. (1896);
Kayser, *Arb. a. d. kaiserl. Gesundheitsamte*, Bd. 25, S.S. 173, 176
(Berlin, 1906); Bd. 25, S. 223 (1907); Ledingham and Ledingham, *Brit.
Med. Journ.* i. 15 (London, 1908); Sanarelli, " Études a. l. Fièvre
typhoïde expérimentale," *Ann. de l'inst. Pasteur*, t. vi. (1892), and
t. viii. (1894); Thomson and Ledingham, *38th Annual Report, Local
Government Board*, p. 369 (London, 1909); Wright and Semple,
British Med. Journ. (1897), i. 256; **Variola:** Calkins, *Journ. Med.
Research* (1904), xi. 136; Councilman, Magrath and Brinckerhoff,
Journ. Med. Research (1903), ix. 373, (1904), xi. 12; Guarnieri, *Arch.
per le sci.med.* (1892) xxvi. 403; *Centralbl. f. Bact. u. Parasitenk.*,
Bd. xvi. (1894); 339. **Yellow Fever:** Weil's Disease Weil, " Ueb. eine eigenthüml.
m. Milztumor, Ikterus . . . akute Infectionskrankheit," *Deutsche
Arch. f. klin. Med.* (1886), Bd. xxxix. **Yellow Fever:** Beauperthuy,
Travaux scientifiques (Bordeaux, 1891); Boyce, *Yellow Fever Prophylaxis in New Orleans* (1905; being Memoir XIX, Liverpool School
of Tropical Medicine, London, 1906); *Health Progress and Administration in the West Indies* (London, 1910); Sanarelli, " Etiol. et
Path. d. l. Fièvre jaune," and other papers in *Ann. de l'inst. Pasteur*,
(1897) t. xi., and (1898) t. xii.; Durham and Myers, " Interim
Report on Yellow Fever," *Brit. Med. Journ.* (1901), i. 450.

(G. S. W.)

PARASITISM, in biology, the condition of an organism which
obtains its nourishment wholly or partially from the body of
another living organism, and which usually brings about extensive modifications in both guest and host, a phenomenon
widespread amongst animals and plants. The term has been
appropriated by biologists as a metaphor from the Greek (see
PARASITE). The lives of organisms are so closely intermeshed
that if dependence on other organisms for food be the criterion
of parasitism it is doubtful if any escape the taint. Green
plants, it is true, build up their food from the inorganic elements
of the air and the soil, and are farthest removed from the suspicion of dependence; but most, if not all, thrive only by the aid
of living microbes either actually attached to their roots or
swarming in the nutrient soil. Saprophytes, organisms that
live on organic matter, are merely parasites of the dead, whilst
all animals derive their nourishment from the bodies of plants,
either directly or indirectly through one or more sets of other
animals. It is plain, therefore, that if parasitism is to be employed as a scientific term it must connote something more
than mere dependence on another living organism for nutrition.
The necessary additional conceptions are two: the bodies of

host and parasite must be in temporary or permanent physical contact other than the mere preying of the latter on the former; and the presence of the parasite must not be beneficial, and is usually detrimental to the host.

It is obvious that within the limits of the strictest definition of parasitism that will cover the facts many degrees occur. The terms *symbiosis* and *commensalism* have been applied to conditions really outside the definition of parasitism, but closely related and usually described in the same connexion. Both terms cover the physical consorting of organisms in such a fashion that mutual service is rendered.

The name symbiosis was invented by the botanist A. de Bary in 1879, and is applied to such an extraordinary community as the thallus of a lichen, which is composed of a fungus and an alga so intimately associated, physically and physiologically, that it was not until 1868 that the dual nature of the whole was discovered. The presence of chlorophyll, which had always been associated only with vegetable organisms, was detected by Max Schultze in 1851 in the animals *Hydra* and *Vortex*, and later on by Ray Lankester in *Spongilla* and by P. Geddes in some Turbellarian worms. On the theory that the chlorophyll occurs in independent vegetable cells embedded in the animal tissues, such cases form other instances of symbiosis, for the oxygen liberated by the green cells enables their animal hosts to live in fouler water, whilst the hosts provide shelter and possibly nitrogenous food to their guests.

The term commensalism was introduced in 1876 by P. J. Van Beneden to cover a large number of cases in which "animals have established themselves on each other, and live together on a good understanding and without injury." The most familiar instance is that of fishes of the genus *Fierasfer* which live in the digestive tube of sea-cucumbers (*Holuthuria*; see ECHINO-DERMA). A variety of commensalism was termed mutualism by Van Beneden and applied to cases where there appeared to be an exchange of benefits. A well-known instance of mutualism is the relation between sea-anemones and hermit crabs. The hermit crab occupies the discarded shell of a mollusc, and anemones such as *Sagartia* or *Adamsia* are attached to the outside of the shell. The bright colours of the anemone advertise its distasteful capacity for stinging, and secure protection for the crab, whilst the anemone gains by vicarious locomotion and possibly has the benefit of floating fragments from the food of the crab.

It is plain that such terms as symbiosis, commensalism and mutualism cannot be sharply marked off from each other or from true parasitism, and must be taken as descriptive terms rather than as definite categories into which each particular association between organisms can be fitted.

R. Leuckart has made the most useful attempt to classify true parasites. Occasional, or temporary, parasites are to be distinguished from permanent, or stationary, parasites. The former seek their host chiefly to obtain food or shelter and are comparatively little modified by their habits when compared with their nearest unparasitic relatives. They may infest either animals or plants, and as they attack only the superficial surfaces of their hosts, or cavities easy of access from the exterior, they correspond closely with another useful term introduced by Leuckart. They are Epizoa or Ectoparasites, as distinguished from Entozoa or Endoparasites. They include such organisms as plant-lice, and caterpillars which feed on the green parts of plants, and animals such as the flea, the bed-bug and the leech, which usually abandon their hosts when they have obtained their object. Many ectoparasites, however, pass their whole lives attached to their hosts; lice, for instance, lay their eggs on the hairs or feathers or in rugosities of the skin of birds and mammals; the development of the egg, the larval stages and the adult life are all parasitic. Permanent or stationary parasites arrive in most cases endoparasitic, inhabiting the internal organs; bacteria, gregarines, nematodes and tapeworms are familiar instances. But here also there are no sharp lines of demarcation. Leuckart divided endoparasites according to the nature and duration of their strictly parasitic life: (1) Some have free-living and self-supporting embryos that do not become sexually mature until they have reached their host; (2) others have embryos which are parasitic but migratory, moving either to another part of their host, to another host, or to a free life before becoming mature; (3) others again are parasitic in every stage of their lives, remaining in the same host, and being without a migratory stage.

Origin of Parasitism.—Now that the theory of spontaneous generation has been disproved, the problem of parasitism is no more than detection of the various causes which may have led organisms to change their environment. Every kind of parasite has relations more or less closely akin which have not acquired the parasitic habit, and every gradation exists between temporary and permanent parasites, between creatures that have been only slightly modified and those that have been profoundly modified in relation to this habit. There are many opportunities for an animal or plant in its adult or embryonic stage to be swallowed accidentally by an animal, or to gain entrance to the tissues of a plant, whilst in the case of ectoparasites there is no fundamental difference between an organism selecting a dead or a living environment for food or shelter. If the living environment in the latter case prove to have special advantages, or if the interior of the body first reached accidentally in the former case prove not too different from the normal environment and provide a better shelter, a more convenient temperature, or an easier food supply, the accident may pass into a habit. From the extent to which parasitism exists amongst animals and plants it is clear that it must have arisen independently in an enormous number of cases, and it may be supposed that there must be many cases in which it has been of recent occurrence; E. Metchnikoff, indeed, has suggested that amongst parasites we are to look for the latest products of evolution. In any case it is impossible to suppose that parasites form a natural group; no doubt in many cases the whole of a group, as for instance the group of tapeworms, is parasitic, but indications point clearly to the tapeworms having had free-living ancestors. Parasitism is in short a physiological habit, which theoretically may be assumed by any organism, and which actually has been assumed by members of nearly every living group.

LIST OF PARASITES

A.—Animals.

Vertebrata.—These are rarely parasitic, and cases are unknown amongst mammals, birds, reptiles and amphibia. Amongst fish and cyclostomes, *Myxine* burrows into codfish, *Remora* attaches itself to the external surface of sharks; *Rhodeus amarus*, the bitterling, a small, carp-like fresh-water fish, injects its eggs into the mantle-cavity of pond-mussels, where the fry develop, whilst the mollusc reciprocates by throwing off its embryos on the parent fish; *Stegophilus insidiosus*, a small colourless fish from Brazil and the Argentine, lives parasitically in the gill-cavity of large cat-fishes and sucks the blood in the gills of a large Silurid; *Vandellia cirrhosa*, the candiru of Brazil, a minute fish 60 mm. in length, enters and ascends the urethra of people bathing, being attracted by the urine; it cannot be withdrawn, owing to the erectile spines on its gill-covers. The natives in some parts of the Amazon protect themselves whilst in the water by wearing a sheath of minutely perforated coco-nut shell.

Mollusca.—Few if any are true parasites. The Gasteropods, *Eulimae*, *Styliferae* and *Entoconchae* lodge in Echinoderms, the latter at least being truly parasitic.

Protochorda and *Hemichorda.*—Most of these are sessile and may lodge on other animals, but are not parasitic.

Arachnida.—*Mites* and *Ticks* are Arachnids, the vast majority of which are parasitic, and species of which infest almost every vertebrate group, but there are some free-living forms. Pycno-gonids are parasitic in their youthful stages on Hydroids, whilst the Pentastomids have been so much modified by parasitism that they were long regarded as worms; they may occur in most vertebrates.

Crustacea.—These contain an immense number of forms in all stages of parasitism. Some Copepods are amongst the most degenerate parasites known, the so-called fish-lice being for the most part Copepods with piercing mouth-organs, elaborate clinging apparatus, and degenerate organs of locomotion. In *Lernea*, the female, after becoming attached to its host, undergoes a retrogressive metamorphosis, losing almost completely the segmentation of the body and discarding the appendages and sense-organs, whilst the male, although not so degenerate in structure, is dwarfed in size and itself becomes a parasite of the female. The *Cirripeds* are all sessile in the adult condition. The *Lepadidae* are the least modified and are rarely parasitic; the *Balanidae* are more modified and frequently become embedded in the skin of whales. The *Abdominalia* live as parasites buried in the shells of other Cirripeds and of molluscs. The *Apoda* live as parasites in the mantle of other Cirripeds, whilst the *Rhizocephala* live chiefly on the abdomen of Decapod Crustacea, sending burrowing root-like nutritive processes into their tissues.

Insecta.—A very large number of insects are temporary or permanent parasites of animals or plants, the adult stages being chiefly ectoparasitic, the larval stages endoparasitic. The *Hemimeridae*, allies of the earwigs, are ectoparasites on rats. The *Mallophaga* or bird-lice are degenerate wingless insects spending their whole lives as ectoparasites on birds and mammals. The larvae of *Hemerobiinae* are parasitic on Aphides. The saw-flies are parasitic on plants. There are over 200,000 species known of the *Hymenoptera parasitica* or *Terebrantia*. The adults deposit their eggs in the eggs, caterpillars or adults of other insects, particularly Lepidoptera. The clothes-moth, for instance, is known to be subject to the attack of over sixty species of Hymenoptera. To such an extent has parasitism been developed in this group, that the parasites themselves are attacked by other parasites, giving rise to the phenomenon known as hyperparasitism. The gall-flies (see GALLS) are included amongst the Terebrantia, but in their case the early stages are passed in vegetable galls more frequently than in the bodies of other insects. The ruby-flies (*Hymenoptera Tubulifera*), in the larval condition are parasitic on the larvae of wasps and bees. The *Denudatae* are bees that in the larval stage are parasitic on other bees, the larvae of the parasites being deposited in the food-cells prepared for their own larvae by other bees. Many of the fossorial Hymenoptera form no special nests for their young, but take advantage of the abodes and food-stores prepared by other insects. The very large number of Hymenopterous insects that collect living larvae to be shut up as provender for their developing young are in a sense parasitic. The complex relations of ants with other insects must be referred to in this connexion. The nests of many species are inhabited by foreign insects of various orders, such insects being termed myrmecophilous or ants'-nest insects. The relations between the ants and their guests are very complex, and the guests migrate with their hosts. *Aphidae*, *Coccidae* and other bugs that secrete sugary matter are cherished and tended by ants; so also the caterpillars of some Lycaenid butterflies are kept as a kind of domesticated animal for some useful purpose. There are also many Orthoptera, Hemiptera, and other insects, as well as some acarids and wood-lice found only in ants'-nests as cherished or tolerated guests. The relations between ants and plants is also interesting; the ants live as parasites on the plants or trees, but in return protect them from more harmful intruders. Such phenomena are on the border-line between symbiosis and true parasitism. Although most beetles live on decaying animal or vegetable matter, a large number are parasitic in the adult or larval condition on animals or plants. The curious beetle known as *Platypsyllus castoris* is known only as an ectoparasite of the beaver, whilst the *Leptinidae* are parasites of several species of mammals. The minute beetles of the families *Mordellidae* and *Rhipiphoridae* are endoparasites of wasps and cockroaches, whilst the larvae of many of the *Cantharidae* are parasites of locusts. The *Strepsiptera* are endoparasites of Hymenoptera and Hemiptera. The habits of the Diptera easily pass over into parasitism, and a very large number are temporary or permanent parasites in the adult or larval stages. Most of the larvae of the *Cecidomyiidae* live in plants and form galls or other deformities. The blood-sucking habits of mosquitoes and gnats and sand-flies have not led to any special development in the direction of parasitism. The larvae of *Bombyliidae* are endoparasites of the larvae of mason-bees, and some of the *Cyrtidae* similarly infest spiders, whilst the *Tachinidae* deposit their larvae in other living insects, caterpillars being especially selected. The larvae of some of the *Sarcophagidae* may be deposited in the nostrils of man and other animals, where they may cause death, whilst those of the South American genus *Lucilia* infest the nasal fossae and frontal sinuses of man, producing great suffering, and the larvae of the numerous kinds of bot-fly attack man and many animals. The very large group of Pupipara live by sucking the blood of mammals and birds, and many of them are reduced to wingless permanent parasites. The single member of the family *Braulidae* is a parasite of the bee. The well-known fleas (Aphaniptera or Siphonaptera) are ectoparasites in the adult condition; the larval stages are usually to be found in organic refuse. The larvae of most Lepidoptera are temporary ectoparasites of plants, but a few attack other insects, such as coccids and aphids. All the Hemiptera (bugs) have sucking-mouth organs and the majority of them are temporary parasites of plants or other animals. Some, such as the bed-bug, have been so modified by parasitism as to be found only in human dwellings, others, such as the aphids or plant-lice, are permanent parasites of plants, many of them producing galls. The coccids, or scale insects, have been still further modified as plant ectoparasites. The *Pediculidae*, or lice, are the most completely parasitic of insects, and are degraded wingless insects found on almost any kind of bird or mammal,

but in most cases so highly modified as to be capable of existence only on the particular species with which they are associated.

Lower Invertebrates.—No true Chaetopods are parasitic, but a few are commensal. The leeches are probably Chaetopods modified by parasitism; and Myzostomes are still more highly modified relatives of the group, very degenerate and parasitic on Crinoids. A few rotifers are ecto- and endo-parasites. No Brachiopods, Polyzoa or Echinoderms are true parasites. The flat-worms and round-worms contain the most characteristic endoparasites, and parasitism is so characteristic a feature of most of the groups that it is discussed in the separate articles dealing with the various natural assemblages of such worms. All the Cestodes (see TAPEWORM), most of the Trematodes (*q.v.*), and a few of the Planarians (*q.v.*) are parasites of animals. Most Nemertines are free-living, but *Cephalothrix galatheae* is endoparasitic in the ovaries of the Crustacean *Galathea strigosa*, whilst *Eunemertes* and *Tetrastemma* occur in Ascidians, and *Malacobdella* in lamellibranch Molluscs. The degraded Mesozoa (*q.v.*) are endoparasites of Planarians, Nemertines and Ophiurids. The Nematoda (*q.v.*) or typical round-worms, exhibit every degree from absolute free-life to absolute parasitism in animals and plants. The Echiuroidea (*q.v.*) are mostly free-living, but the male of *Bonellia* lives as a very degenerate parasite in the uterus and pharynx of the female. Although Coelentera and Porifera are usually sessile, very few are true parasites; young stages of the *Narcomedusae* are parasitic in the mouth of adults of different species, whilst *Mnestra parasites* is a degenerate medusa living on the pelagic mollusc *Phyllirhoe*. The Protozoa, from their minute size and capacity to live in fluids, naturally include an enormous number of parasitic forms, the importance of which in producing disease in their hosts is so great that a very large special literature on parasitic protozoology is being formed (see PATHOLOGY). Of the *Sarcodina* (*q.v.*) many forms of Amoeba such as *Amoeba coli* are associated with dysentery and kindred diseases. A very large number of the *Mastigophora* (*q.v.*), including such forms as the trypanosome of sleeping-sickness, are parasitic; in fact, observation by adequate means of the juices of almost any animal reveals the occasional presence of some kind of mobile protozoon, provided with a whip-like process. The enormous group of *Sporozoa* (*q.v.*) are entirely parasitic, and have been found in every group of animals except the Protozoa and Coelentera. *Infusoria* (*q.v.*) contain a considerable number of parasitic forms, some endoparasitic; others like the Suctoria, ectoparasitic.

B.—Plants.

Bacteria.—Every degree of adaptation to parasitism occurs amongst bacteria, a majority of which pass at least some stage of their lives in a parasitic condition.

Fungi.—As in the case of Bacteria, the absence of chlorophyll from the tissues of fungi makes it necessary that they should take up carbon compounds already assimilated by other organisms, and accordingly they are either saprophytes or parasites. The mycelium is, so to say, the parasitic organ of the fungus, ramifying in the tissues of the host. The plant may obtain access to its host by means of spores which enter usually by wounds in the case of animal and plant hosts, but occasionally by natural apertures such as the stomata of plants. The fungi that develop in the organs of warm-blooded animals reach the blood-stream through wounds, and thence spread to the tissues where germination takes place. Many fungi, especially those that are epiphytic, reach the tissues of their host by germ-tubes which emerge from the spore and penetrate either by a natural or artificial aperture, whilst in other cases the germ-tubes or hyphae actually penetrate uninjured tissues or membranes.

The fungi parasitic on animals are in most cases little known, and additions to the list, of which the pathological rather than the botanical features have been worked out, are constantly being made. A number of species of *Eurotium* and *Aspergillus*, usually saprophytic, may migrate to the bodies of animals, spreading in the tissues and exciting a disease known as mycosis or aspergillosis. They were first discussed in the disease of the human ear known as otomycosis, but they occur also in lungs and air-passages of mammals and birds. Recent pathological investigations conducted at the Prosectorium of the Zoological Society of London, show that mycosis is extremely frequent and fatal in birds and reptiles, and rather less frequent in mammals. Almost any organ of the body is liable to attack. The *Laboulbenieae* are probably Ascomycetes restricted to parasitism on insects, chiefly beetles and flies, sometimes forming a thick fur on the bodies and spreading by spores. The *Entomophthoreae*, possibly *Mucorini*, are also restricted to insects, the fungus that kills the common house-fly being the most familiar example. *Cordyceps militaris* and *Botrytis bassii* are familiar examples of Ascomycete fungi that attack the caterpillars of insects, the latter producing the fatal disease " muscardine " of the silkworm. The group of *Saprolegnieae* usually vegetate as saprophytes but readily settle on aquatic animals such as goldfish, salmon, salamanders and frogs, with fatal results. It is not yet entirely certain if diseases of this kind, of which the salmon disease is the most notorious, are produced on healthy animals, by the attacks of the fungi, or if some antecedent predisposing condition be necessary. There are a number of well-known fungi that produce diseases of the skin in man and other vertebrates. *Achorion Schoenleinii* produces favus in man, rabbits, cats, fowls and other birds and mammals. *Trichophyton tonsurans* (Malmsten), is the fungus of tinea or ringworm in man, oxen, horses, dogs and rabbits. *Saccharomyces albicans* (Reess), produces thrush of the mouth in young herbivora and birds. *Actinomyces bovis* (Harz) is associated with swellings on the jaw-bone of cattle and kangaroos, but has been found in pigs and human beings.

The fungi parasitic on plants are much better known and are responsible for a large number of diseases. They display every gradation from occasional to complete parasitism. Amongst the *Pyrenomycetes*, the group *Erysipheae* contain a large number of common parasites; the main body of the fungus is usually epiphytic as in various mildews (q.v.). Ergot (q.v.) is the most familiar example of the group. The *Discomycetes* are chiefly saprophytic, being common on dead fruits, roots and so forth, but many of them kill living plants: *Exoascus* on plums, peaches and cherries. *Sclerotinia* is most common on dead juicy fruits, but will destroy turnips in store, and has been known to attack living *Phaseolus* and *Petunia*. The *Hymenocytes* are naturally saprophytes, but when they gain access through wounds are the most destructive parasites of living timber. The *Ustilagineae* are endoparasites in Phanerogams, and are especially notorious for their attacks on grain-crops and grasses. The species of *Ustilago* set up hypertrophy in the tissues of their hosts, and the enlarged spaces thus formed become filled with the spores of the parasite. The *Uredineae* are also endoparasites of the higher plants and produce the diseases known as rusts which specially affect cultivated plants. The *Peronosporeae* are all parasites of plants and are the most destructive enemies of agriculture and horticulture. *Phytophthora infestans* (de Bary), the potato-disease fungus, is a typical example.

Algae.—The chlorophyll-containing green and yellow cells found in Hydroids and Planarians referred to in connexion with symbiosis and the small green algae that infest the hairs of sloths are on the border-line of parasitism. A species of *Nostoc* occurs in the intercellular spaces of other plants; *Chlorochytrium* is found in the tissues of *Lemna*, and *Phyllosiphon arisari* (Kühn) infests the parenchyma of *Arum arisarum*.

The flowering plants have a considerable number of representatives which have become epiphytes and which exhibit various degrees of parasitic degeneration. The Monotropeae allied to the heaths, are degenerate, with no chlorophyll and with scale-like leaves but the evidence as to their parasitism is more than doubtful; they are possibly only saprophytic. The allied Lennoaceae, a small group also devoid of chlorophyll and with scale-leaves, are true root-parasites. The genus *Cuscuta* of the Convolvulaceae consists of the true parasites known as dodders. They are destitute of chlorophyll and attach themselves to other plants by twining stems on which occur haustoria that penetrate the tissues of the host and absorb nutritive material. *Cuscuta europaea*, the great dodder, is a parasite of nettles and hops; *Cuscuta epilinum* is the flax dodder; *Cuscuta epithymum* attacks a number of low-growing plants; and *Cuscutum trifolii* is very destructive to clover., Several genera of Scrophulariaceae are partially parasitic; they contain chlorophyll but have degenerate roots with haustoria. *Euphrasia*, the eye-bright, attacks the roots of grasses; *Pedicularis*, the lousewort, *Rhinanthus*, the rattle, *Melampyrum*, the cow-wheat and *Bartsia* are all partly parasitic on the roots of other plants. The Orobanchaceae or broomworts, are all destitute of chlorophyll and have scale-leaves; they are parasitic on the roots of other plants, species attacking various Leguminosae, ivy, hemp and hazel. The *Cytinaceae* are true parasites devoid of chlorophyll and leaves, with deformed bodies and conspicuous flowers or inflorescences. Most of them are tropical, and the group is widely scattered throughout the world. The *Santalales* are all parasitic; some members like *Thesium linophyllum* (the bastard toad-flax), a root parasite, and *Viscum album* (the mistletoe), parasitic on branches, have chlorophyll, but rather degenerate leaves; others like the tropical Balanophoraceae are devoid of chlorophyll and foliage leaves and have deformed bodies. Of the Lauraceae, a few genera such as *Cassytha* (the tropical "dodder-laurels,") are true parasites, without chlorophyll and with twining stems.

Effect of Parasitism on Parasites.—The phenomena of parasitism occur so generally in the animal and vegetable kingdoms and are repeated in degrees so varying that no categorical statements can be laid down as to the effects produced on the organisms concerned. All living creatures have a certain degree of correspondence with the conditions of their environment, and parasitism is only a special case of such adaptation. The widest generalization that can be made regarding it is that parasitism tends towards a rigid adaptation to a relatively limited and stable environment, whilst free life tends towards a looser correspondence with a more varying environment. The *summum bonum* of a parasite is to reach and maintain existence in the limited conditions afforded by its host; the goal of the free-living organism is a varying or experimental fitness for varying surrounding conditions. And, if the metaphor be continued, the danger of parasitism for the parasite, is that if it become too nicely adjusted to the special conditions of its host, and fail to attain these, it will inevitably perish. The degeneration of parasites is merely a more precise adaptation; in the favourable environment the degenerate, or specialized parasite is best equipped for successful existence, but the smallest change of environment is fatal. Such a generalization as has been formulated covers nearly all the peculiarities of parasitism. Organs of prehension are notably developed; parasitic plants have twining stems, boring roots and special clinging organs; parasitic animals display hooks, suckers and boring apparatus. The normal organs of locomotion tend to disappear, whether these be wings or walking legs. Organs of sense, the chief purpose of which is to make animals react quickly to changes in the environment, become degenerate in proportion as the changes which the parasite may have to encounter are diminished. The changes correlated with nutrition equally conform with the generalization. The chlorophyll of the plant becomes unnecessary and tends to disappear; the stem has no longer to thrust a spreading crown of leaves into the tenuous air or groping rootlets into the soil, but absorbs already prepared nourishment from the tissues of its host through compact conduits. And so the parasitic higher plant tends to lose its division into stem and leaves and roots, and to acquire a compact and amorphous body. The animal has no longer to seek its food, and the lithe segmentation of a body adapted for locomotion becomes replaced by a squat or insinuating form. Jaws give place to sucking and piercing tubes, the alimentary canal becomes simplified, or may disappear altogether, the parasite living in the juices of its host, and absorbing them through the skin. So, also, parasites obtaining protection from the tissues of their host lose their intrinsic protective mechanisms.

The reproduction of parasites offers many peculiarities, all of which are readily correlated with our generalization. A creature rigidly adapted to a special environment fails if it does not reach that environment, and hence species most successful in reproduction are able to afford the largest number of misses to secure a few hits and so to maintain existence. High reproductive capacity is still more urgent when the parasites tend to bring to an end their own environment by killing their hosts. Reproduction in parasites, so far from being degenerate, displays an exuberance of activity, and an extraordinary efficiency. In parasitic flowering plants the flowers tend to be highly conspicuous, the seeds to be numerous, and specially adapted to ready diffusion. Amongst the fungi, the reproductive processes are most prolific, spores are produced by myriads, and very many special adaptations exist for the protection of the latter during their transference from host to host. It is notorious that the spores of bacteria and the higher fungi resist changes of temperature, desiccation, and the action of physical and chemical agents, to an astonishing extent. Vegetative reproduction is extremely active under favourable conditions, and resting reproductive bodies of varying morphological character are produced in great abundance. Amongst fungi, a phenomenon known as heteroecism is developed as a special adaptation to parasitic conditions, and recalls the similar adaptations in many animal parasites. At one stage of its existence, the fungus is adapted to one host, at another stage to another host. *Puccinia graminis*, the fungoid rust affecting many grasses, is a typical instance. It inhabits wheat, rye and other grasses, developing a mycelium in the tissues of young plants. During the summer, the mycelium gives rise to large numbers of simple processes which break through the tissues of the host and bud off orange-coloured *uredogonidia*. These small bodies are scattered by the wind, and reach other plants on which they germinate, enter the new host through the stomata and give rise to new mycelia. Towards autumn, when the tissues of the host are becoming hard and dry, darker-coloured *teleutogonidia* are produced, and these remain quiescent during the winter. In spring they germinate, produce small free-living mycelia on which in due course *sporidia* are formed. When these, scattered by the wind, fall on the leaf of the barberry-plant, they germinate, and entering the leaf-tissue of the new host by the stomata produce a mycelium bearing reproductive organs so different from those of the phase on the grass-plant, that it was described as a distinct fungus (*Aecidium berberidis*), before its relation with the rust of grasses was known. The spores of the *Aecidium* when they reach grasses give rise to the *Puccinia* stage again.

The reproductive processes of animal parasites are equally exuberant. In the first place, hermaphroditism is very common, and the animals in many cases are capable of self-fertilization. Parthenogenetic reproduction and various forms of vegetative budding are found in all stages of the life-history of animal parasites. The prolificness of many parasites is almost incredible. R. Leuckart pointed out that a human tapeworm has an average life of two years, and produces in that time about 1500 proglottides, each containing between fifty and sixty thousand eggs, so that the single tapeworm has over eighty million chances of successfully reproducing its kind. The devices for nourishing and protecting the eggs and embryos are numerous and elaborate, and many complex cases of larval migration and complicated cases of heteroecism occur. (See TREMATODE and TAPEWORM.)

The physiological adaptations of parasites are notable, especially in cases where the hosts are warm-blooded. The parasites tend to become so specialized as to be peculiar to particular hosts; ectoparasites frequently differ from species to species of host, and the flea of one mammal, for instance, may rapidly die if it be transferred to another although similar host. The larval and adult stages of endoparasites become similarly specialized, and although there are many cases in which the parasites that excite a disease in one kind of animal are able to infect animals of different species, the general tendency is in the direction of absolute limitation of one parasite, and indeed one stage of one parasite to one kind of host. The series of events seems to be a gradual progression from temporary or occasional parasitism to obligatory parasitism and to a further restriction of the obligatory parasite to a particular kind of host.

Effect of Parasitism on Hosts.—The intensity of the effect of parasitism on the hosts of the parasites ranges from the slightest local injury to complete destruction. Most animals and plants harbour a number of parasites, and seem to be unaffected by them. On the other hand, as special knowledge increases, the range of the direct and indirect effect of parasites is seen to be greater. It is probable that in a majority of cases, the tissues of animals and plants resist the entrance of microbes unless there is some abrasion or wound. In the case of plants the actual local damage caused by animal or vegetable ectoparasites may be insignificant, but the wounds afford a ready entrance to the spores or hyphae of destructive endoparasites. So also in the case of animals, it is probable that few microbes can enter the skin or penetrate the walls of the alimentary canal if these be undamaged. But as knowledge advances the indirect effect of parasites is seen to be of more and more importance. Through the wounds caused by biting-insects the microbes of various skin diseases and inflammations may gain entrance subsequently, or the insects may themselves be the carriers of the dangerous endoparasites, as in the cases of mosquitoes and malaria, fleas and plague, tsetse flies and sleeping sickness. Similarly the wounds caused by small intestinal worms may be in themselves trifling, but afford a means of entrance to microbes. It has been shown, for instance, that there is an association between appendicitis and the presence of small nematodes. The latter wound the coecum and allow the microbes that set up the subsequent inflammation to reach their nidus. It has been suggested that the presence of similar wounding parasites precedes tubercular infection of the gut.

The parasites themselves may cause direct mechanical injury, and such injury is greatly aggravated where active reproduction takes place on or in the host, with larval migrations.

A tangled mass of Ascarid worms may occlude the gut; masses of eggs, larvae or adults may block bloodvessels or cause pressure on important nerves. The irritation caused by the movements or the secretions of the parasites may set up a reaction in the tissues of the host leading to abnormal growths (*e.g.* galls and pearls) or hypertrophies. Migrations of the parasites or larvae may cause serious or fatal damage. The abstraction of food-substances from the tissues of the host may be insignificant even if the parasites are numerous, but it is notable that in many cases the effect is not merely that of causing an extra drain on the food-supply of the host which might be met by increased appetite. The action is frequently selective; particular substances, such as glycogen, are absorbed in quantities, or particular organs are specially attacked, with a consequent overthrow of the metabolic balance. Serious anaemia out of all proportion to the mass of parasites present is frequently produced, and the hosts become weak and fail to thrive. A. Giard has worked out the special case which he has designated as "parasitic castration" and shown to be frequent amongst animal hosts. Sometimes by direct attacks on the primary sexual organs, and sometimes by secondary disturbance of metabolism, the presence of the parasites retards or inhibits sexual maturity, with the result that the secondary sexual characters fail to appear. The most usual and serious effect on their hosts of parasites is, however, the result of toxins liberated by them. (See PARASITIC DISEASES.)

Finally, the attacks of parasites have led to the development by the hosts of a great series of protective mechanisms. Such adaptations range from the presence of thickened cuticles, and hairs or spines, the discharge of waxy, sticky or slimy secretions, to the most elaborate reactions of the tissues of the host to the toxins liberated by the parasites.

History and Literature of Parasitism.—The history and literature of parasitism are inextricably involved with the history and literature of zoology, botany, medicine and pathology. Pliny recognized the mistletoe as a distinct parasitic plant and gave an account of its reproduction by seed. Until the 18th century little more was done. In 1755 Pfeiffer in his treatise on *Fungus melitensis* (in Linnaeus's *amoenitat. acad.* Dissert. LXV. vol. iv.) made a group of parasitic flowering plants, but included epiphytes like the ivy. In 1832 A. de Candolle (*Physiol. végétale*, vol. iii.) attempted to divide and classify flowering parasites on morphological and physiological grounds, and since then, the study of parasitism has been a part of all botanical treatises. With regard to Fungi, A. de Bary's treatise on the *Comparative Morphology and Biology of the Fungi, Mycetozoa and Bacteria* (Eng. ed., 1887) remains the standard work. There is in addition a large special literature on bacteriology. With regard to animal parasites, the first real steps in knowledge were the refutation of spontaneous generation (see BIOGENESIS). Linnaeus traced the descent of the liver fluke of sheep from a free-living stage, and although his particular observations were erroneous, they laid the foundation on which later observers worked, and pointed the way towards discovery of larval migrations and heteroecism. O. Fr. Müller in 1773. and L. H. Bojanus in the beginning of the 19th century reached more nearly to a correct interpretation. J. J. Steenstrup in his famous monograph of which an English edition was published by the Ray Society in 1845 (*On the Alternation of Generations, or the Propagation and Development of Animals through Alternate Generations*) interpreted many scattered observations by a clear and coherent theory. Thereafter there was a steady and consistent progress, and the literature of animal parasites merges in that of general zoology. The two best-known names are those of T. S. Cobbold (*Entozoa: an Introduction to the Study of Helminthology*, 1869) and R. Leuckart (*The Parasites of Man*, Eng. trans., 1886), the former describing a very large number of types, and the latter adding enormously to scientific knowledge of the structure and life-history. Of more modern books, G. Fleming's Eng. ed. of L. G. Neumann's *Parasites and Parasitic Diseases of the Domesticated Animals*, and the Eng. ed. of Max Braun's *Animal Parasites of Man* (1906), are the most comprehensive. (P. C. M.)

PARASNATH, a hill and place of Jain pilgrimage in British India, in Hazaribagh district, Bengal; 4480 ft. above the sea; 18 m. from Giridih station on the East Indian railway. It derives its name from the last of the twenty-four Jain saints, who is believed to have attained *nirvana* or beatific annihilation. It is crowded with temples, some of recent date; and the scruples of the Jains have prevented it from being utilized as a sanatorium, for which purpose it is otherwise well adapted.

PARASOL (Fr., from Ital. *parasole*: *parare*, to shield, and *sole*, sun), a sunshade, a light or small form of umbrella, covered with coloured silk or other material. In Japan and China gaily coloured parasols of paper stretched on bamboo frames are used by all classes. The parasol of an elaborate and highly ornamented type has been the symbol of high honour and office in the East, being borne over rulers, princes and nobles. The negro chiefs of West Africa reserve to themselves the privilege of bearing parasols of considerable size and substantial construction, the size varying and denoting gradations in rank

PARAVICINO Y ARTEAGA, HORTENSIO FELIX (1580–1633), Spanish preacher and poet, was born at Madrid on the 12th of October 1580, was educated at the Jesuit college in Ocaña, and on the 18th of April 1600 joined the Trinitarian order. A sermon pronounced before Philip III. at Salamanca in 1605 brought Paravicino into notice; he rose to high posts in his order, was entrusted with important foreign missions, became royal preacher in 1616, and on the death of Philip III. in 1621 delivered a famous funeral oration which was the subject of acute controversy. He died at Madrid on the 12th of December 1633. His *Oraciones evangélicas* (1638–1641) show that he was not without a vein of genuine eloquence, but he often degenerates into vapid declamation, and indulges in far-fetched tropes and metaphors. His *Obras pósthumas, divinas y humanas* (1641) include his devout and secular poems, as well as a play entitled *Gridonia*; his verse, like his prose, exaggerates the characteristic defects of Gongorism.

PARAY-LE-MONIAL, a town of east-central France in the department of Saone-et-Loire, 58 m. W.N.W. of Mâcon by the Paris-Lyon railway, on which it is a junction for Moulins, Lozanne, Clermont and Roanne. Pop. (1906), 3382. It lies on the slope of a hill on the right bank of the Bourbince and has a port on the Canal du Centre. The chief building in the town is the priory church of St Pierre. Erected in the 12th century in the Romanesque style of Burgundy, it closely resembles the abbey church of Cluny in the length of the transepts, the height of the vaulting and the general plan. The town is the centre of a district important for its horse-raising; bricks, tiles and mosaics are the chief manufactures of the town. In the 10th century a Benedictine priory was founded at Paray-le-Monial. In the 16th century the town was an industrial centre, but its prosperity was retarded by the wars of religion and still more by the revocation of the edict of Nantes. In 1685 the visions of Marguerite Marie Alacoque, a nun of the convent of the Visitation, who believed herself to possess the Sacred Heart of Jesus, attracted religious gatherings to the town, and yearly pilgrimages to Paray-le-Monial still take place.

PARCEL (Fr. *parcelle*, Ital. *particella*, Lat. *particula*, diminutive of *pars*, part), a small part or division of anything; particularly, in the law of real property and conveyancing, a portion of a manor or estate, and so the name of that portion of a legal document, such as a conveyance or lease relating to lands, which contains a description of the estate dealt with. The word is also used of a package of goods contained in a wrapping or cover for transmission by carriage, &c., or by post; hence the term "parcel-post" for the branch of the post-office service which deals with the transmission of such packages. "Parcel" was formerly used in an adverbial or quasi-adverbial sense, meaning "partly," "to some extent," thus "parcel-Protestant," "parcel-lawyer," &c. This use survives in "parcel-gilt," *i.e.* partly gilt, a term applied to articles made of silver with a gilt lining.

PARCHIM (PARCHEM), a town of Germany, in the grand duchy of Mecklenburg-Schwerin, on the Elde, which flows through it in two arms, 23 m. S.E. of Schwerin, on the railway from Ludwigslust to Neubrandenburg. Pop. (1905), 10,397. It was the birthplace of Moltke, to whom a monument was erected in 1876. It is an ancient place surrounded with walls, and contains a Gothic town hall and two interesting churches. Founded about 1210, Parchim was during part of the 14th century the residence of one branch of the family of the dukes of Mecklenburg. It became a prosperous industrial town during

the 16th century, but this prosperity was destroyed by the Thirty Years' War. A revival, however, set in during the 19th century.

See Hübbe, *Zur topographischen Entwickelung der Stadt Parchim* (Parchim, 1899); and Weltzien, *Zur Geschichte Parchims* (Parchim, 1903).

PARCHMENT. Skins of certain animals, prepared after particular methods, have supplied writing material on which has been inscribed the literature of centuries. Such a durable substance, in most cases easily obtainable in fair abundance, would naturally suggest itself for the purpose, and we are therefore prepared for evidence of its use, and also for the survival of actual specimens, from very ancient times. The tradition of the employment of skins as writing material by the ancient Egyptians is to be traced back to the period of the Pharaohs of the IVth Dynasty, and in the British Museum and elsewhere there exist skin-rolls which date back to some 1500 years B.C. But the country which not only manufactured but also exported in abundance the writing material made from the papyrus plant (see PAPYRUS) hardly needed to make use of any other material, and the instances of skin-rolls inscribed in Egypt must at all times have been rare. But in western Asia the practice of using skins as writing material must have been widespread even at a very early period. The Jews made use of them for their sacred books, and it may be presumed for other literature also; and the old tradition has been maintained by this conservative race down to our own day, requiring the synagogue rolls to be inscribed on this time-honoured material. No doubt their neighbours the Phoenicians, so ready to adapt the customs of other nations to their own advantage, would also have followed the same practice. The Persians inscribed their annals on skins; and skins were employed by the Ionian Greeks, as proved by the words of Herodotus (v. 58). There is no evidence forthcoming that the same usage was followed by the western Greeks and by the Italic tribes; but it is difficult to suppose that at a remote period, before the importation of papyrus, such an obviously convenient writing material as skin was not used among the early civilized races of Greece and Italy.

The method of preparation of skins for the service of literature in those distant ages is unknown to us; but it may be assumed that it was more or less imperfect, and that the material was rather of the character of tanned leather than of the thinner and better prepared substance which was to follow at a later time. The improvement of the manufacture to which we refer was to be of a nature so thorough as to endow the material with a new name destined to last down to the present day.

The new manufacture was traditionally attributed to Eumenes II. of Pergamum, 197–158 B.C. The common story, as told by Pliny on the authority of Varro, is that Eumenes, when seeking to enlarge the library of his capital, was opposed by the jealousy of the Ptolemies, who forbade the export of papyrus from Egypt, thus hoping to check the growth of the rival library; and that the Pergamene king was thus compelled to revert to the old custom of using skins as writing material. It is needless to regard this story as literally true, or as other than a popular explanation of a great development of the manufacture of skin material for books in the reign of Eumenes. In former times the prepared skins had been known by the natural titles διφθέραι, μεμβράναι, the Latin *membranae*, and these were at first also attached to the new manufacture; but the latter soon received a special name after the place of its origin, and became known as περγαμηνή, *charta pergamena*, from which descends our English term parchment, through the French *parchemin*. The title of *pergamena* actually appears first in the edict *De pretiis rerum* of Diocletian (A.D. 301), and in a passage in one of St Jerome's Epistles.

The principal improvement in the new manufacture was the dressing of the skins in such a way as to render them capable of receiving writing on both sides, the older methods probably treating only one side for the purpose, a practice which was sufficient in times when the roll was the ordinary form of book and when it was not customary to write on the back as well as on the face of the material. The invention of parchment with its two surfaces, recto and verso, equally available for the scribe, ensured the development of the codex. (See MANUSCRIPT.)

The animals whose skins were found appropriate for the manufacture of the new parchment were chiefly sheep, goats and calves. But in course of time there has arisen a distinction between the coarser and finer qualities of the material; and, while parchment made from ordinary skins of sheep and goats continued to bear the name, the finer kinds of manufacture produced from the more delicate skins of the calf or kid, or of still-born or newly-born calves or lambs, came to be generally known as vellum (Fr. *velin*). The skin codices of the early and middle ages being for the most part composed of the finer kinds of material, it has become the custom to describe them as of vellum, although in some instances it would be more correct to call the material parchment.

The ordinary modern process of preparing the skins is by washing, liming, unhairing, scraping, washing a second time, stretching evenly on a frame, scraping a second time and paring down inequalities, dusting with sifted chalk and rubbing with pumice. Somewhat similar methods, no doubt varying in details, must have been employed from the first.

The comparatively large number of ancient and medieval MSS. that have survived enables us to gather some knowledge of the varieties of the material in different periods and in different countries. We know from references in Roman authors that parchment or vellum was entering into competition with papyrus as a writing material at least as early as the 2nd century of our era (see MANUSCRIPT), though at that time it was probably not so skilfully prepared as to be a dangerous rival. But the surviving examples of the 3rd and 4th centuries show that a rapid improvement must almost at once have been effected, for the vellum of that age is generally of a thin and delicate texture, firm and crisp, with a smooth and glossy surface. Here it should be noticed that there was always, and in some periods and in some countries more than in others, a difference in colour between the surface of the skin from which the hair had been removed and the inner surface next to the flesh of the animal, the latter being whiter than the other. This difference is generally more noticeable in the older examples, those of a later period having usually been treated more thoroughly with chalk and pumice. To obviate any unsightly contrast, it was customary, when making up the quires for a volume, to lay hair-side next to hair-side and flesh-side to flesh-side, so that, at whatever place the codex was opened, the tint of the open pages should be uniform.

As a rule, the vellum of early MSS., down to and including the 6th century, is of good quality and well prepared. After this, the demand increasing, a greater amount of inferior material came into the market. The manufacture necessarily varied in different countries. In Ireland and England the vellum of the early MSS. is usually of stouter quality than that of foreign examples. In Italy and Greece and in the European countries generally bordering on the Mediterranean, a highly polished surface came into favour in the middle ages, with the ill effect that the hardness of the material resisted absorption, and that there was always a tendency for ink and paint to flake off. On the other hand, in western Europe a soft pliant vellum was in vogue for the better classes of MSS. from the 12th century onwards. In the period of the Italian Renaissance a material of extreme whiteness and purity was affected.

Examples of uterine vellum, prepared from still-born or newly-born young, are met with in choice volumes. A remarkable instance of a codex composed of this delicate substance is the Additional MS. 23035, of the 13th and 14th centuries, in the British Museum, which is made up of as many as 579 leaves, without being a volume of abnormal bulk.

In conclusion, we must briefly notice the employment of vellum of a sumptuous character to add splendour to specially choice codices of the early middle ages. The art of dyeing the material with a rich purple colour was practised both in Constantinople and in Rome; and, at least as far back as the 3rd century, MSS., generally of the Scriptures, were produced written in silver and gold on the precious stained vellum: a useless luxury, denounced by St Jerome in a well-known passage in his preface to the Book of Job. A certain number of early examples still survive, in a more or less perfect condition: such as the MS. of the Gospels in the Old Latin version at Verona, of the 4th or 5th century; the celebrated codex of Genesis in the Imperial Library at Vienna; the Rossano MS. and the Patmos MS. of the Gospels in Greek; the Gothic Gospels of Ulfilas at Upsala, and others, of the 6th century, besides a few somewhat later specimens. In the revival of learning under Charlemagne a further encouragement was given to the production of such codices; but soon afterwards the art of purple-staining appears to have been lost or abandoned. A last trace of it is found in a few isolated instances of stained vellum leaves inserted for ornament in MSS. of the period of the Renaissance.

AUTHORITIES.—Particulars of the early manufacture and use of parchment and vellum are to be found in most of the handbooks on palaeography and book-development, such as W. Wattenbach, *Das Schriftwesen im Mittelalter* (3rd ed., 1896); G. Birt, *Das antike Buchwesen* (1882); Sir E. M. Thompson, *Handbook of Greek and Latin Palaeography* (3rd ed., 1906). See also La Lande, *Art de faire le parchemin* (1762); G. Peignot, *Essai sur l'histoire du parchemin et du velin* (1812); A. Watt, *The Art of Leather Manufacture* (1885).

(E. M. T.)

PARCLOSE (from the O. Fr. *parclore*, to close thoroughly; Lat. *claudere*), an architectural term for a screen or railing used to enclose a chantry, tomb, chapel, &c., in a church, and for the space thus enclosed.

PARDAILLAN, the name of an old French family of Armagnac, of which several members distinguished themselves in the service of the kings of France in the 16th and 17th centuries. Antoine Arnaud de Pardaillan, *maréchal de camp*, served Henry IV. in Franche-Comté, Picardy and Savoy; and was created marquis de Montespan in 1612 and marquis d'Antin in 1615 under Louis XIII. His grandson Louis Henri, marquis de Montespan, was the husband of Mme de Montespan, the mistress of Louis XIV. Louis Antoine de Pardaillan de Gondrin (1665–1736), legitimate son of the famous marquise, became lieutenant-general of the armies of the king in 1702, governor of the Orléanais, director-general of buildings in 1708, lieutenant-general in Alsace, member of the council of regency, and minister of state. He was created duc d'Antin in 1711. The last duc d'Antin, Louis, died in 1757.

PARDESSUS, JEAN MARIE (1772–1853), French lawyer, was born at Blois on the 11th of August 1772. He was educated by the Oratorians, and then studied law, at first under his father, a lawyer at the *Présidial*, who was a pupil of Robert J. Pothier. In 1796, after the Terror, he married, but his wife died at the end of three years. He was thus a widower at the age of twenty-seven, but refused to remarry and so gave his children a step-mother. He wrote a *Traité des servitudes* (1806), which went through eight editions, then a *Traité du contrat et des lettres de change* (1809), which pointed him out as fitted for the chair of commercial law recently formed at the faculty of law at Paris. The emperor, however, had insisted that the position should be open to competition. Pardessus entered (1810) and was successful over two other candidates, André M. J. J. Dupin and Persil, who afterwards became brilliant lawyers. His lectures were published under the title *Cours de droit commercial* (4 vols., 1813–1817). In 1815 Pardessus was elected deputy for the department of Loir-et-Cher, and from 1820 to 1830 was constantly re-elected; then, however, he refused to take the oath of allegiance to Louis Philippe, and was deprived of his office. After the publication of the first volume of his *Collection des lois maritimes antérieures au xviii* *siècle* (1828) he was elected a member of the Académie des Inscriptions et Belles Lettres. He continued his collection of maritime laws (4 vols., 1828–1845), and published *Les Us et coutumes de la mer* (2 vols., 1847). He also brought out two volumes of Merovingian diplomas (*Diplomata, chartae, epistolae, leges*, 1843–1849); vols. iv.–vi. of the *Table chronologique des diplomes*; and vol. xxi. of *Ordonnances des rois de France* (1849), preceded by an *Essai sur l'ancienne organisation judiciaire*, which was reprinted in part in 1851. In 1843 Pardessus published a critical edition of the *Loi salique*, followed by 14 dissertations, which greatly advanced the knowledge of the subject. He died at Pimpeneau near Blois on the 27th of May 1853.

See notices in *Journal général de l'instruction publique* (July 27, 1853), in the *Bibliothèque de l'école des chartes* (3rd series, 1854, v. 453), and in the "Histoire de l'académie des inscriptions et belles lettres" (vol. xx. of the *Mémoires de l'académie*, 1861).

PARDO BAZÁN, EMILIA (1851–   ), Spanish author, was born at Corunna, Spain, on the 16th of September 1851. Married in her eighteenth year to Sr D. José Quiroga, a Galician country gentleman, she interested herself in politics, and is believed to have taken an active part in the subterranean campaign against Amadeo of Savoy and, later, against the republic. In 1876 she came into notice as the successful competitor for a literary prize offered by the municipality of Oviedo, the subject of her essay being the Benedictine monk, Benito Jerónimo Feijóo. This was followed by a series of articles inserted in *La Ciencia cristiana*, a magazine of the purest orthodoxy, edited by Juan M. Ortí y Lara. Her first novel, *Pascual López* (1879), is a simple exercise in fantasy of no remarkable promise, though it contains good descriptive passages of the romantic type. It was followed by a more striking story, *Un Viaje de novios* (1881), in which a discreet attempt was made to introduce into Spain the methods of French realism. The book caused a sensation among the literary cliques, and this sensation was increased by the appearance of another naturalistic tale, *La Tribuna* (1885), wherein the influence of Zola is unmistakable. Meanwhile, the writer's reply to her critics was issued under the title of *La Cuestión palpitante* (1883), a clever piece of rhetoric, but of no special value as regards criticism or dialectics. The naturalistic scenes of *El Cisne de Vilamorta* (1885) are more numerous, more pronounced, than in any of its predecessors, though the authoress shrinks from the logical application of her theories by supplying a romantic and inappropriate ending. Probably the best of Sra Pardo Bazán's work is embodied in *Los Pazos de Ulloa* (1886), the painfully exact history of a decadent aristocratic family, as notable for its portraits of types like Nucha and Julián as for its creation of characters like those of the political bravos, Barbacana and Trampeta. Yet perhaps its most abiding merit lies in its pictures of country life, its poetic realization of Galician scenery set down in an elaborate, highly-coloured style, which, if not always academically correct, is invariably effective. A sequel, with the significant title of *La Madre naturaleza* (1887), marks a further advance in the path of naturalism, and henceforward Sra Pardo Bazán was universally recognized as one of the chiefs of the new naturalistic movement in Spain. The title was confirmed by the publication of *Insolación* and *Morriña*, both issued in 1889. In this year her reputation as a novelist reached its highest point. Her later stories, *La Cristiana* (1890), *Cuentos de amor* (1894), *Arco Iris* (1895), *Misterio* (1903) and *La Quimera* (1905), though not wanting in charm, awakened less interest. In 1905 she published a la, entitled *Verdad*, remarkable for its boldness rather than for its dramatic qualities.   (J. F.-K.)

PARDOE, JULIA (1806–1862), English writer, was born at Beverley, Yorkshire, in 1806. When fourteen years old she published a volume of poems. In 1835 she went to Constantinople and her experiences there furnished her with material for vivid pictures of Eastern life in the *City of the Sultan* (1837), *Romance of the Harem* (1839) and *Beauties of the Bosphorus* (1839). Her other works, not always historically accurate, include *Louis XIV. and the Court of France in the Seventeenth Century* (1847); *The Court and Reign of Francis I.*(1849); *The Life and Memoirs of Marie de Médici* (1852); *Episodes of French History during the Consulate and the First Empire* (1859); and several sprightly and pleasant novels. In 1860 she was granted a civil list pension. She died on the 26th of November 1862.

PARDON (through the Fr. from Late Lat. *perdonare*, to remit a debt or other obligation on a penalty), the remission, by the power entrusted with the execution of the laws, of the penalty attached to a crime. The right of pardoning is coextensive with the right of punishing. In a perfect legal system, says Beccaria, pardons should be excluded, for the clemency of the prince seems a tacit disapprobation of the laws (*Dei Delitti e delle pene*, ch. xx.).[1] In practice the prerogative is extremely valuable, when used with discretion, as a means of adjusting the different degrees of moral guilt in crimes or of rectifying a miscarriage of justice. By the law of England pardon is the sole prerogative of the king, and it is declared by 27 Hen. VIII. c. 24 that no other person has power to pardon or remit any treasons or felonies whatsoever. This position follows logically from the theory of English law that all offences are breaches of the king's peace. Indictments still conclude with a statement that the offence was committed "against the peace of our lord king, his crown and dignity." The Crown by pardon only remits the penalty for an attack upon itself. The prerogative is in modern times exercised by delegation, the Crown acting upon the representation of the secretary of state for the home department in Great Britain, or of the lord lieutenant in Ireland. The prerogative of the Crown is subject to some restrictions : (1) The committing of a subject of the realm to a prison out of the realm is by the Habeas Corpus Act a *praemunire*, unpardonable even by the king (31 Car. II. c. 2, § 12). (2) The king cannot pardon an offence in a matter of private rather than of public wrong, so as to prejudice the person injured by the offence. Thus a common nuisance cannot be pardoned while it remains unredressed, or so as to prevent an abatement of it. A fine or penalty imposed for the offence may, however, be remitted. By an act of 1859 (22 Vict. c. 32) his majesty is enabled to remit wholly or in part any sum of money imposed upon conviction, and, if the offender has been imprisoned in default of payment, to extend to him the royal mercy. There are other statutes dealing with special offences, *e.g.* by the Remission of Penalties Act 1875 his majesty may remit any penalty imposed under 21 Geo. III. c. 49 (an act for preventing certain abuses and profanations on the Lord's Day called Sunday). (3) The king's pardon cannot be pleaded in bar of an impeachment. This principle, first asserted by a resolution of the House of Commons in the earl of Danby's case (May 5, 1679), forms one of the provisions of the Act of Settlement, 12 & 13 Will. III. c. 2. It is there enacted " that no pardon under the great seal of England shall be pleadable to an impeachment by the Commons in parliament," § 3. This provision does not extend to abridging the prerogative after the impeachment has been heard and determined. Thus three of the rebel lords were pardoned after impeachment and attainder in 1715. (4) In the case of treason, murder or rape a pardon is ineffectual unless the offence be particularly specified therein (13 Rich. II. c. 1, § 2). Before the Bill of Rights, 1 Will. & M. c. 2, § 2, this statute seems to have been frequently evaded by a *non obstante* clause. But, since by the Bill of Rights no dispensation by *non obstante* is allowed, general words contrary to the statute of Richard II. would seem to be ineffectual.

Pardon may be actual or constructive. Actual pardon is by warrant under the great seal, or under the sign-manual countersigned by a secretary of state (7 & 8 Geo. IV. c. 28, § 13). Constructive pardon is obtained by endurance of the punishment. By 9 Geo. IV. c. 32, § 3, the endurance of a punishment on conviction of a felony not capital has the same effect as a pardon under the great seal. This principle is reaffirmed in the Larceny Act 1861, § 100, and in the Malicious Injuries to Property Act 1861, § 67. Further, pardon may be free or conditional. A conditional pardon most commonly occurs where an offender sentenced to death has his sentence commuted to penal servitude or any less punishment. The condition of his pardon is the endurance by him of the substituted punishment. The effect of pardon, whether actual or constructive, is to put the person pardoned in the position of an innocent man, so that he may have

[1] See further, on the ethical aspect, Montesquieu, *Esprit des lois*, bk. vi. ch. 21; Bentham, *Principles of Penal Law*, bk. vi. ch. 4.

an action against any one thenceforth calling him traitor or felon. He cannot refuse to give evidence respecting the offence pardoned on the ground that his answer would tend to criminate him. A pardon may be pleaded on arraignment in bar of an indictment (though not of an impeachment), or after verdict in arrest of judgment. No doubt it would generally be advantageous to plead it as early as possible.

It is obvious that, though the Crowd is invested with the right to pardon, this does not prevent pardon being granted by the higher authority of an act of parliament. Acts of indemnity have frequently been passed, the effect of which is the same as pardon or remission by the Crown. Examples of acts of indemnity are two private acts passed in 1880 to relieve Lords Byron and Plunket from the disabilities and penalties to which they were liable for sitting and voting in the House of Peers without taking the oath.

Civil rights are not divested by pardon. The person injured may have a right of action against the offender in spite of the pardon of the latter, if the right of action has once vested, for the Crown cannot affect private rights. In Scotland this civil right is specially preserved by various statutes. Thus 1503, c. 174, provides that, if any respite or remission happen to be granted before the party grieved be first satisfied, the same is to be null and of none avail. The assythment, or indemnification due to the heirs of the person murdered from the murderer, is due if the murderer has received pardon, though not if he has suffered the penalty of the law. The pardon transmitted by the secretary of state is applied by the supreme court, who grant the necessary orders to the magistrates in whose custody the convict is.

In the United States the president is empowered to pardon offences against the United States, except in cases of impeachments (U. S. Constitution, art. ii. § 2). The power of pardon is also vested in the executive authority of the different states, with or without the concurrence of the legislative authority, although in some states there are boards of pardon of which the governor is a member *ex officio*. Thus by the New York Code of Criminal Procedure the governor of the state of New York has power to grant reprieves, commutations and pardons, except in the case of treason, where he can only suspend the execution of the sentence until the case can be reported to the legislature, with whom the power of pardon in this case rests. The usual form of pardon in the United States is by deed under seal of the executive.

PARDUBITZ (Czech, *Pardubic*), a town of Bohemia, Austria, 65 m. E. of Prague by rail. Pop. (1900), 17,029, mostly Czech. The most interesting buildings are the old fortified château of the 16th century, with its Gothic chapel restored in 1880; the church of St Bartholomew, dating in its present form from 1538; the new town hall (1894); the Grünes Tor, also built in 1538; and the handsome new synagogue. Pardubitz has a tolerably active trade in grain and timber, and the horse-fairs attract numerous customers.

PARÉ, AMBROISE (1510–1590), French surgeon, was born at Laval, in the province of Maine, and died at Paris in 1590. His professional career and services to his art are described in the article SURGERY. A collection of his works was published at Paris in 1575 and they were afterwards frequently reprinted. Several editions have appeared in German and Dutch, and among the English translations was that of Thomas Johnson (1665).

See J. F. Malgaigne, *Œuvres complètes* (Paris, 1840); Le Paulmier, *Ambroise Paré d'après de nouveaux documents découverts aux archives nationales et de papiers de famille* (Paris, 1885); Stephen Paget, *Ambroise Paré and his Times* (London, 1897).

PAREJA, JUAN DE (1606–1670), Spanish painter, was born a slave in the West Indies about 1606, and in early life passed into the service of Velasquez, who employed him in colour-grinding and other menial work of the studio. By day he closely watched his master's methods, and by night stealthily practised with his brushes until he had attained considerable manipulative skill. The story goes that, having succeeded in producing a picture satisfactory to himself, he contrived furtively to place it among those on which Velasquez had been working, immediately before an expected visit of King Philip IV. The performance was duly discovered and praised, and Pareja forthwith received his freedom, which, however, he continued to devote to his former employer's service. His extant works are not very numerous; the best known, the "Calling of St Matthew," now in the Prado, Madrid, has considerable merit as regards technique, but does not reveal much originality, insight or devotional feeling. He died in 1670.

PARENT, SIMON NAPOLEON (1855–), Canadian politician, son of Simon Polycarpe Parent, merchant, was born in the village of Beauport, in the province of Quebec, on the 12th of September 1855. He was educated at Laval University, where he graduated in 1881. In the same year he was called to the bar of the province of Quebec. He married in 1877 Marie Louise Clara Gendron, of Beauport. In 1890 Parent was elected a member of the municipal council of Quebec, and served as mayor of the city from 1894 to 1906. From the year 1890 to 1905 he represented the county of Saint-Sauveur as a Liberal in the legislative assembly of his native province, and on the formation of the Marchand administration in 1897 he accepted the portfolio of minister of lands, forests and fisheries. After Marchand's death in September 1900 he was called by the lieutenant-governor to form a cabinet, and continued in office as prime minister until his retirement from public life in August 1905. Parent proved a capable administrator of provincial and municipal affairs. Under his administration the finances of the city of Quebec were improved, an electric car service was provided, public parks were opened, a system of electric light was established and the streets were well paved. In 1905 he became chairman of the Transcontinental railway of Canada.

PARENTHESIS (from Gr. παρενθεσις, put in alongside), the grammatical term denoting the insertion (and so also the signs for such insertion) of a word, phrase or sentence between other words or in another sentence, without interfering with the construction, and serving a qualifying, explanatory or supplementary purpose. In writing or printing such parenthetical words or sentences are marked off by commas, dashes, or, more usually, by square or semi-circular brackets.

PARENZO, a seaport of Austria, in Istria, 95 m. S. by W. of Trieste by rail. Pop. (1900), 9962, mostly Italian. It is situated on the west coast of Istria, and is built on a peninsula nowhere more than 5 ft. above the sea-level; and from the fact that the pavements of the Roman period are 3 ft. below the present surface it is inferred that this part of the coast is slowly subsiding. Parenzo has considerable historic and architectural interest, and its well-preserved cathedral of St Maurus, erected probably between 535 and 543, is one of the most interesting buildings in the whole of Austria. The basilican type is very pure; there are three naves; the apse is hexagonal without and round within. The total length of the church proper is only 110 ft.; but in front of the west entrance is a square atrium with three arches on each side; to the west of the atrium is a now roofless baptistery, and to the west of that rises the campanile; so that the total length from campanile to apse is about 230 ft. Mosaics, now greatly spoiled, form the chief decoration of both outside and inside. The high altar is covered with a noble baldachin, dating from 1277. The basilica is one of those churches in which the priest when celebrating mass stands behind the altar with his face to the west. An older church is referred to in the inscription of Euphrasius in the mosaic of the apse of the cathedral, and remains of its mosaic pavement and of its apse have been found under the floor of the present church; it belongs perhaps to the 5th century A.D.; while at a still lower level another pavement, perhaps of the 4th century A.D., has been discovered, belonging to the first church, which lay to the north of the present. Several inscriptions mention the name of donors of parts of it. The mosaic pavement of the present church was almost entirely destroyed in 1880, when the floor-level was raised. Small portions of two temples and an inscribed stone are the only remains of the ancient Roman city that readily catch the eye. Parenzo is the seat of the Provincial Diet of Istria, and is also an episcopal see.

Parenzo (Lat. *Parentium*), conquered by the Romans in 178 B.C., was made a colony probably by Augustus after the battle of Actium, for its title in inscriptions is Colonia Julia and not, as it has often been given, Colonia Ulpia. It grew to be a place of some note with about 6000 inhabitants within its walls and 10,000 in its suburbs. The bishopric, founded in 524, gradually acquired ecclesiastical authority over a large number of abbeys and other foundations in the surrounding country. The city, which had long been under the influence of Venice, formally recognized Venetian supremacy in 1267, and as a Venetian town it was in 1354 attacked and plundered by Paganino Doria of Genoa. The bishoprics of Pola and Parenzo were united in 1827.

See John Mason Neale, *Notes on Dalmatia, Istria, &c.* (London, 1861), with ground plan of cathedral; E. A. Freeman, *Sketches from the Subject and Neighbour Lands of Venice* (London, 1881); and Neumann, *Der Dom von Parenzo* (Vienna, 1902).

PARGA, a seaport of Albania, European Turkey, in the vilayet of Iannina, and on the Ionian Sea. Pop. (1905), about 5000, of whom the majority are Greeks. Parga has a rock-built citadel and a harbour formed by a mole which the Venetians constructed in 1572. It exports citrons, wool, oak, bark and skins. Originally occupying the site of the ancient Toryne (or Palaeo-Parga), a short distance to the west, Parga was removed to its present position after the Turkish invasion in the 15th century. Under Venetian protection, freely accepted in 1401, the inhabitants maintained their municipal independence and commercial prosperity down to the destruction of the Venetian republic in 1797, though on two occasions, in 1500 and 1560, their city was burned by the Turks. The attempts of Ali Pasha of Iannina to make himself master of the place were thwarted partly by the presence of a French garrison in the citadel and partly by the heroic attitude of the Pargiotes themselves, who were anxious to have their city incorporated with the Ionian Republic. To secure their purpose they in 1814 expelled the French garrison and accepted British protection; but the British Government in 1815 determined to go back to the convention of 1800 by which Parga was to be surrendered to Turkey, though no mosque was to be built or Mussulman to settle within its territory. Rather than subject themselves to the tyranny of Ali Pasha, the Pargiotes decided to forsake their country; and accordingly in 1819, having previously exhumed and burned the remains of their ancestors, they emigrated to the Ionian Islands. The Turkish government was constrained to pay them £142,425 by way of compensation.

PARGETTING (from O. Fr. *pargeter* or *parjeter*; *par*, all over, and *jeter*, to throw, i.e. " rough cast "; other derivations suggested have been from Lat. *spargere*, to sprinkle, and from *paries*, a wall, the last due to writing the *parjet* in the form *pariet*), a term applied to the decoration in relief of the plastering between the studwork on the outside of half-timber houses, or sometimes covering the whole wall. The devices were stamped on the wet plaster. This seems generally to have been done by sticking a number of pins in a board in certain lines or curves, and then pressing on the wet plaster in various directions, so as to form geometrical figures. Sometimes these devices are in relief, and in the time of Elizabeth represent figures, birds, foliages, &c.; fine examples are to be seen at Ipswich, Maidstone, Newark, &c. (See PLASTER-WORK.) The term is also applied to the lining of the inside of smoke flues to form an even surface for the passage of the smoke.

PARIAH, a name long adopted in European usage for the " outcastes " of India. Strictly speaking the Paraiyans are the agricultural labourer caste of the Tamil country in Madras, and are by no means the lowest of the low. The majority are ploughmen, formerly *adscripti glebae*, but some of them are weavers, and no less than 350 subdivisions have been distinguished. The name can be traced back to inscriptions of the 11th century, and the " Pariah poet," Tiruvalluvar, author of the famous Tamil poem, the *Kurral*, probably lived at about that

time. The accepted derivation of the word is from the Tamil *parai*, the large drum of which the Paraiyans are the hereditary beaters at festivals, &c. In 1901 the total number of Paraiyans in all India was 2½ millions, almost confined to the south of Madras. In the Telugu country their place is taken by the Malas, in the Kanarese country by the Holeyas and in the Deccan by the Mahars. Some of their privileges and duties seem to show that they represent the original owners of the land, subjected by a conquering race. The Pariahs supplied a notable proportion of Clive's sepoys, and are still enlisted in the Madras sappers and miners. They have always acted as domestic servants to Europeans. That they are not deficient in intelligence is proved by the high position which some of them, when converted to Christianity, have occupied in the professions. In modern official usage the " outcastes " generally are termed Panchamas in Madras, and special efforts are made for their education.

See Caldwell, *Comparative Grammar of the Dravidian Languages* (pp. 540-554), and the Madras *Census Reports* for 1891 and 1901.

PARIAH DOG, a dog of a domesticated breed that has reverted, in a greater or less degree, to a half-wild condition. Troops of such dogs are found in the towns and villages of Eastern Europe, Asia and Africa; and they probably interbreed with wolves, jackals and wild dogs. The Indian breed is near akin to the Australian dingo.

PARIAN CHRONICLE (*Chronicon* or *Marmor Parium*), a marble tablet found in the island of Paros in 1627, now among the Arundel Marbles at Oxford. It originally embraced an outline of Greek history from the reign of Cecrops, legendary king of Athens, down to the archonship of Diognetus at Athens (264 B.C.). The Chronicle seems to have been set up by a private person, but, as the opening of the inscription has perished, we do not know the occasion or motives which prompted the step. The author of the Chronicle has given much attention to the festivals, and to poetry and music; thus he has recorded the dates of the establishment of festivals, of the introduction of various kinds of poetry, the births and deaths of the poets, and their victories in contests of poetical skill. On the other hand, important political and military events are often entirely omitted; thus the return of the Heraclidae, Lycurgus, the wars of Messene, Draco, Solon, Cleisthenes, Pericles, the Peloponnesian War and the Thirty Tyrants are not even mentioned. The years are reckoned backwards from the archonship of Diognetus, and the dates are further specified by the kings and archons of Athens. The reckoning by Olympiads is not employed. The Chronicle consists of 93 lines, written chiefly in the Attic dialect.

The Parian Chronicle (first published by Selden in 1628) is printed by A. Böckh in the *Corpus inscriptionum graecarum*, vol. ii., No. 2374, and by C. W. Müller in the *Fragmenta historicorum graecorum*, vol. i.; there are separate editions by J. Flach (1883) and F. Jacoby (1904). A new fragment was discovered in 1897, bringing the Chronicle down to the year 299 (ed. Crispi and Wilhelm in *Mittheilungen des archaeologischen Instituts, athenische Abtheilung*, vol. xxii., 1897). See also " Notes on the Text of the Parian Marble " and review of Jacoby's edition by J. A. R. Munro in *Classical Review* (March and October, 1901 and June 1905).

PARINI, GIUSEPPE (1729-1799), Italian poet, was born at Bosio in the Milanese, on the 22nd of May 1729. His parents, who possessed a small farm on the shore of Lake Pusiano, sent him to Milan, where he studied under the Barnabites in the Academy Arcimboldi, maintaining himself latterly by copying manuscripts. In 1752 he published at Lugano, under the pseudonym of Ripano Eupilino, a small volume of *sciolto* verse which secured his election to the Accademia dei Trasformati at Milan and to that of the Arcadi at Rome. His poem, *Il Mattino*, which was published in 1763, and which marked a distinct advance in Italian blank verse, consisted of ironical instructions to a young nobleman as to the best method of spending his mornings. It at once established Parini's popularity and influence, and two years later a continuation of the same theme was published under the title of *Il Mezzogiorno*. The Austrian plenipotentiary, Count Firmian, interested himself in procuring the poet's advancement, appointing him. in the first place, editor of the Milan *Gazette*, and in 1760, in despite of the Jesuits, to a specially created chair of belles lettres in the Palatine School. On the French occupation of Milan he was appointed magistrate by Napoleon and Saliceti, but almost immediately retired to resume his literary work and to complete *Il Vespro* and *La Notte* (published after his death), which with the two other poems already mentioned compose what is collectively entitled *Il Giorno*. Among his other poems his rather artificial *Odi*, composed between 1757 and 1795, have appeared in various editions. He died on the 15th of August 1799.

His works, edited by Reina, were published in 6 vols. 8vo (Milan, 1801-1804); and an excellent critical edition by G. Mazzoni appeared at Florence in 1897.

PARIS (also called ALEXANDROS), in Greek legend, the son of Priam, king of Troy and Hecuba. Before he was born his mother dreamed that she was delivered of a firebrand. The dream was interpreted that her child would ruin his country, and when Paris was born he was exposed on Mt Ida. His life was saved by the herdsmen, and he grew up among them, distinguished for beauty and strength, till he was recognized and received by his parents. He was said to have been called Alexandros from his bravery in defending the herds against raids. When the strife arose at the marriage of Peleus and Thetis between Hera, Athena and Aphrodite, each claiming the apple that should belong to the most beautiful, Paris was selected as the judge. The three rivals unveiled their divine charms before a mortal judge on Mt Ida. Each tried to bribe the judge, Hera by promising power, Athena wisdom, Aphrodite the most beautiful woman in the world. Paris decided in favour of Aphrodite, and thus made Hera and Athena bitter enemies of his country (Homer, *Iliad*, xxiv. 25; Euripides, *Troades*, 925. *Andromache*, 284; *Helena*, 23). To gain the woman whom Aphrodite had promised, Paris set sail for Lacedaemon, deserting his old love Oenone, daughter of the river-god Cebren, who in vain warned him of the consequences. He was hospitably received by Menelaus, whose kindness he repaid by persuading his wife Helen to flee with him to Troy (*Iliad*, vi. 290). The siege of Troy by the united Greeks followed. Paris proved a lazy and backward fighter, though not wanting in actual courage when he could be roused to exert himself. Before the capture of the city he was mortally wounded by Philoctetes with an arrow (Sophocles, *Philoctetes*, 1426). He then bethought him of the slighted nymph Oenone, who he knew could heal the wound. He was carried into her presence, but she refused to save him. Afterwards, when she found he was dead, she committed suicide (Apollodorus iii. 12). The judgment of Paris became a favourite subject in Greek art. Paris is represented as a beautiful young man, beardless, wearing the pointed Phrygian cap, and often holding the apple in his hand.

PARIS, ALEXIS PAULIN (1800-1881), French *savant*, was born at Avenay (Marne) on the 25th of March 1800. He published in 1824 an *Apologie pour l'école romantique*, and took an active part in Parisian journalism. His appointment, in 1828, to the department of manuscripts in the Bibliothèque royale left him leisure to pursue his studies in medieval French literature. Paulin Paris lived before minute methods of research had been generally adopted in modern literature, and his chief merit is that by his numerous editions of early French poems he continued the work begun by Dominique Méon in arousing general interest in the then little-known epics of chivalry. Admitted to the Académie des Inscriptions et Belles Lettres in 1837, he was shortly afterwards appointed on the commission entrusted with the continuation of the *Histoire littéraire de la France*. In 1853 a chair of medieval literature was founded at the Collège de France, and Paulin Paris became the first occupant. He retired in 1872 with the title of honorary professor, and was promoted officer of the Legion of Honour in the next year. He died on the 13th of February 1881 in Paris.

His works include: *Manuscrits français de la bibliothèque du roi* (7 vols., 1836-1848); *Li Romans di Garin le Loherain, précédé d'un examen des romans carlovingiens* (1883-1885); *Li Romans de Berte aux grans piés* (1832); *Le Romancero français, histoire de quelques*

anciens trouvères et choix de leurs chansons (1833); an edition of the *Grandes chroniques de France* (1836-1840); *La Chanson d'Antioche* (1848); *Les Aventures de maître Renart et d'Ysengrin* (1861) and *Les Romans de la table ronde* (1868-1877), both put into modern French.

His son Gaston Paris contributed a biographical notice to vol. xxix. of the *Histoire littéraire*.

PARIS, BRUNO PAULIN GASTON (1839-1903), French scholar, son of Paulin Paris, was born at Avenay (Marne) on the 9th of August 1839. In his childhood Gaston Paris learned to appreciate the Old French romances as poems and stories, and this early impulse to the study of Romance literature was placed on a solid basis by courses of study at Bonn (1856-1857) under Friedrich Diez, at Göttingen (1857-1858) and finally at the École des Chartes (1858-1861). His first important work was an *Étude sur le rôle de l'accent latin dans la langue française* (1862). The subject was developed later in his *Lettre à M. Léon Gautier sur la versification latine rhythmique* (1866). Gaston Paris maintained that French versification was a natural development of popular Latin methods which depended on accent rather than quantity, and were as widely different from classical rules as the Low Latin was from the classical idiom. For his degree as doctor he presented a thesis on the *Histoire poétique de Charlemagne* (1865). He succeeded his father as professor of medieval French literature at the Collège de France in 1872; in 1876 he was admitted to the Academy of Inscriptions and in 1896 to the French Academy; and in 1895 he was appointed director of the Collège de France. Gaston Paris won a European reputation as a Romance scholar. He had learnt German methods of exact research, but besides being an accurate philologist he was a literary critic of great acumen and breadth of view, and brought a singularly clear mind to bear on his favourite study of medieval French literature. His *Vie de Saint-Alexis* (1872) broke new ground and provided a model for future editors of medieval texts. It included the original text and the variations of it dating from the 11th, 13th and 14th centuries. Gaston Paris contributed largely to the *Histoire littéraire de la France*, and with Paul Meyer published *Romania*, a journal devoted to the study of Romance literature. Among his other numerous works are *Les Plus anciens monuments de la langue française* (1875); a *Manuel d'ancien Français* (1888); an edition of the *Mystère de la passion d'Arnoul Greban* (1878), in collaboration with M. Gaston Raynaud; *Deux rédactions du roman des sept sages de Rome* (1876); a translation of the *Grammaire des langues romanes* (1874-1878) of Friedrich Diez, in collaboration with MM. Brachet and Morel-Fatio. Among his works of a more popular nature are *La Poésie du moyen âge* (1885 and 1895); *Penseurs et poètes* (1897); *Poèmes et légendes du moyen âge* (1900); *François Villon* (1901), an admirable monograph contributed to the "Grands Écrivains Français" series; *Légendes du moyen âge* (1903). His excellent summary of medieval French literature forms a volume of the Temple Primers. Gaston Paris endeared himself to a wide circle of scholars outside his own country by his unfailing urbanity and generosity. In France itself he trained at the École des Chartes and the Collège de France a band of disciples who continued the traditions of exact research that he established. Among them were: Léopold Pannier; Marius Sepet, the author of *Le Drame chrétien au moyen âge* (1878) and of the *Origines catholiques du théâtre moderne* (1901); Charles Joret, Alfred Morel-Fatio; Gaston Raynaud, who is responsible for various volumes of the excellent editions published by the *Société des anciens textes français*, Arsène Darmesteter and others. Gaston Paris died in Paris on the 6th of March 1903.

See "Hommage à Gaston Paris" (1903), the opening lecture of his successor, Joseph Bédier, in the chair of medieval literature at the Collège de France; A. Thomas, *Essais de philologie française* (1897); W. P. Ker, in the *Fortnightly Review* (July, 1904); M. Croiset, *Notice sur Gaston Paris* (1904); J Bédier et M Roques, *Bibliographie des travaux de Gaston Paris* (1904).

PARIS, FRANÇOIS DE (1690-1727), French theologian, was born in Paris on the 3rd of June 1690. He zealously opposed the bull *Unigenitus* (1713), which condemned P. Quesnel's annotated translation of the Bible. He gave further support to the Jansenists, and when he died (May 1, 1727) his grave in the cemetery of St Médard became a place of fanatical pilgrimage and wonder-working. The king ordered the churchyard to be closed in 1732, but earth which had been taken from the grave proved equally efficacious and helped to encourage the disorder which marked the close of the Jansenist struggle (see JANSENISM).

Lives by B. de la Bruyère and B. Doyen (1731). See also P. F. Matthieu, *Histoire des miracles et des convulsionnaires de St Médard*; M. Tollemache, *French Jansenists* (London, 1893).

PARIS,.LOUIS PHILIPPE ALBERT D'ORLÉANS, COMTE DE (1838–1894), son of the duc d'Orléans, the eldest son of King Louis Philippe, was born on the 24th of August 1838. His mother was the princess Helen of Mecklenburg-Schwerin, a Protestant. By the death of his father through a carriage accident in 1842, the count, who was then only four years of age, became heir-apparent to the French throne. On the deposition of Louis Philippe in 1848, the duchess of Orléans struggled to secure the succession to her son, and bore him through an excited populace to the chamber of deputies. The chamber itself was soon invaded, however, and the Republic proclaimed. The Orleanists were driven into exile, and the duchess proceeded with her two sons, the comte de Paris and the duc de Chartres, first to Eisenach in Saxony, and then to Claremont in Surrey. After his mother's death in 1858 the count made a long foreign tour. In 1861 he and his brother accompanied their uncle, the prince de Joinville, to the United States. The brothers were attached to the staff of General McClellan, commanding the "Army of the Potomac." In April 1862 the count took part in the siege of Yorktown, and was present at the action of Williamsburg on the 5th of May. He was also with McClellan at the battle of Fair Oaks, and was personally engaged in the sanguinary battle at Gaines Mill on the 27th of June. When difficulties arose between France and the United States with regard to the affairs of Mexico, the Orléans princes withdrew from the American army and returned to Europe. During the winter of 1862–1863 the count took a special interest in the organization of the Lancashire Cotton Famine Fund, and contributed an article to the *Revue des deux mondes* entitled "Christmas Week in Lancashire." On the 30th of May 1864 he married his cousin, the princess Marie Isabelle, daughter of the duc de Montpensier; and his son and heir, the duc d'Orléans, was born at York House, Twickenham, in 1869. The count was refused permission to serve in the Franco-Prussian War, but after the fall of Napoleon III. he returned to France. Abstaining from putting himself forward, he lived quietly on his estates, which had been restored to him by a vote of the Assembly. In August 1873 there was an important political conference at Frohsdorf, the result of which was that a fusion was effected, by which the comte de Paris agreed to waive his claims to the throne in favour of those of the comte de Chambord. By the death of the latter in 1883 the count became undisputed head of the house of Bourbon; but he did not show any disposition to push his claims. The popularity of the Orléans family, however, was shown on the occasion of the marriage of the comte de Paris's eldest daughter with the duke of Braganza, son of the king of Portugal, in May 1886. This so alarmed the French government that it led to a new law of expulsion, by which direct claimants to the French throne and their heirs were banished from France (June 11, 1886). The comte de Paris again retired to England, taking up his abode at Sheen House, near Richmond Park. Here he devoted his leisure to his favourite studies. In addition to his work *Les Associations ouvrières en Angleterre*, which was published in 1869 and translated into English, the count edited the letters of his father, and published at intervals in eight volumes his *Histoire de la guerre civile en Amérique*. In his later years the count seriously compromised the prospects of the Royalist party by the relations into which he entered with General Boulanger. He died on the 8th of September 1894.

PARIS, the capital of France and the department of Seine, situated on both banks of the Seine, 233 m. from its mouth and 285 m. S.S.E. of London by rail and steamer via Dover and Calais, in 48° 50′ 14″ N., 2° 20′ 14″ E. (observatory). It occupies the centre of the so-called Paris basin, which is traversed by the Seine from south-east to north-west, open towards the west, and surrounded by a line of Jurassic heights. The granitic substratum is covered by Jurassic, Cretaceous and Tertiary formations; and at several points building materials—freestone, limestone or gypsum—have been laid bare by erosion. It is partly, indeed, to the existence of such quarries in its neighbourhood, and to the vicinity of the grain-bearing regions of the Beauce and Brie that the city owes its development. Still more important is its position at the meeting-place of the great natural highways leading from the Mediterranean to the ocean by way of the Rhone valley and from Spain northwards over the lowlands of western France. The altitude of Paris varies between 80 ft. (at the Point du Jour, the exit of the Seine from the fortifications) and 420 ft. at the hill of Montmartre in the north of the city; the other chief eminence is the hill of Ste Geneviève, on the left bank. Since 1840 Paris has been completely surrounded by a wall, which since 1860 has served also as the limit for the collection of municipal customs dues (*octroi*). Proposals are constantly being brought forward to demolish this wall—which, with its talus, is encircled by a broad and deep ditch—either entirely or at least from the Point du Jour, where the Seine intersects the wall below the city, to Pantin, so as to extend the limits of the city as far as the Seine, which runs almost parallel with the wall for that distance. Within the wall the area of the city is 19,279 acres; the river runs through it from east to west in a broad curve for a distance of nearly 8 m.

Climate.—Paris has a fairly uniform climate. The mean temperature, calculated from observations extending over fifty years (1841–1890), is 49°·8 F. The highest reading (observed in July 1874 and again in July 1881) is 101° F., the lowest (in December 1879) is −14°. The monthly means for the fifty years 1841–1890 were: January 35°·9, February 38°·3, March 42°·3, April 49°·5, May 55°·6, June 61°·7, July 64°·6, August 63°·5, September 58°·2, October 49°·8, November 40°·2, December 36°·6. The Seine freezes when the temperature falls below 18°. It was frozen in nearly its whole extent from Bercy to Auteuil in the winters of 1819–1820, 1829–1830, 1879–1880 and 1890–1891. Rain falls, on an average, on about 200 days, the average quantity in a year being between 22 and 23 in. The rainfall from December to April inclusive is less than the average, while the rainfall from May to November exceeds the average for the whole year. The driest month is February, the rainiest June—the rainfall for these months being respectively 1·3 in. and 2·3 in. The prevailing winds are those from the south, south-west and west. The general character of the climate, somewhat continental in winter and oceanic in summer, has been more closely observed since the three observatories at different heights on the Eiffel Tower were added in 1889 to the old-established ones of the parks of St Maur and Montsouris.[1] The observatory at the old church-tower St Jacques (16th century) in the centre of the city, and since 1896 a municipal establishment, is of special interest on account of the study made there of the transparency and purity of the air. There are barely 100 days in the year when the air is very clear. Generally the city is covered by floating mists, possibly 1500 ft. in thickness. During the prevalence of north-easterly winds the sky is most obscured, since on that side lies the greatest number of factories with smoking chimneys.

Defences.—Paris, described in a recent German account as the greatest fortress in the world, possesses three perfectly distinct rings of defences. The two inner, the enceinte and the circle of detached forts around it, are of the bastioned type which French engineers of the Noizet school favoured; they were built in the time of Louis Philippe, and with very few additions sustained the siege of 1870–71. The outer works, of more modern type, forming an entrenched camp which in area is rivalled only by the Antwerp system of defences, were built after the Franco-German War.

The enceinte ("the fortifications" of the guide-books) is of plain bastion trace, without ravelins but with a deep dry ditch (escarp, but not counterscarp revetted). It is nearly 22 m. in perimeter and has 93 bastions, 67 gates and 9 railway passages. The greater part of the enceinte has, however, been given up, and a larger one projected—as at Antwerp—by connecting up the old detached forts.

[1] The observatories of the Tour St Jacques and of Montsouris belong to the municipality of Paris: that of St Maur depends on the Central Bureau of Meteorology, a national institution.

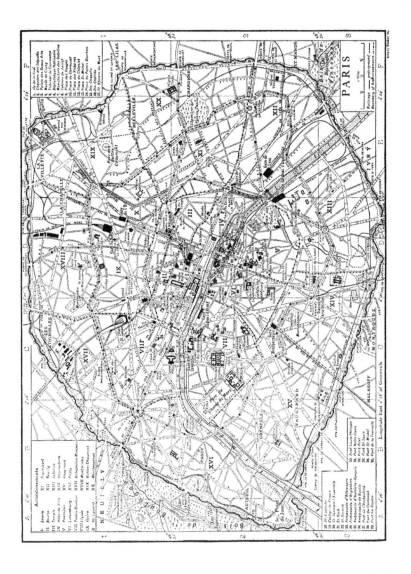

PARIS

These forts, which endured the siege in. 1870-71, have a perimeter of about 34 m. Each is designed as a miniature fortress with ample casemates and high cavaliers, the tenailles and ravelins, however, being as a rule omitted. On the north side there are three forts (connected by a plain parapet) around St Denis, one of these being arranged to control an inundation. Next, to the right, or eastward, comes Fort Aubervillers, which commands the approaches north of the wood of Bondy. These four works lie in relatively low ground. The eastern works are situated on higher ground (500–350 ft.); they consist of four forts and various small redoubts, and command the approaches from the great wood of Bondy. In low ground again at the narrowest point of the great loop of the Marne (near St Maur-les-Fosses) there are two redoubts connected by a parapet, and between the Seine and the Marne, in advance of their confluence, Fort Charenton. On the south side of the city, hardly more than a mile from the enceinte, is a row of forts, Ivry, Bicêtre, Montrouge, Vanves and Issy, solidly constructed works in themselves but, as was shown in 1870, nearly useless for the defences of the city against rifled guns, as (with the exception of Bicêtre) they are overlooked by the plateau of Châtillon. On the west side of Paris is the famous fortress of Mont Valérien, standing 536 ft. above the sea and about 450 above the river. This completes the catalogue of the inner fort-line. It is strengthened by two groups of works which were erected in " provisional " form during the siege,[1] and afterwards reconstructed as permanent forts—Hautes Bruyères on the plateau of Villejuif, 2 m. south of Fort Bicêtre, and the Châtillon fort and batteries which now prevent access to the celebrated plateau that overlooks Paris from a height of 600 ft., and of which the rear batteries sweep almost the whole of the ground between Bicêtre and Mont Valérien.

The new works are 11 m. from the Louvre and 8 from the enceinte. They form a circle of 75 m. circumference, and an army which attempted to invest Paris to-day would have to be at least 500,000 strong, irrespective of all field and covering forces. The actual defence of the works, apart from troops temporarily collected in the fortified area, would need some 170,000 men only.

The entrenched camp falls into three sections—the north, the east and the south-west.. The forts of the general 1874–1875 French type, see FORTIFICATION AND SIEGECRAFT) have from 24 to 60 heavy guns and 600 to 1200 men each, the redoubts, batteries and annexe-batteries generally 200 men and 6 guns. In the northern section a ridge crosses the northern extremities of the St Germain-Argenteuil loop of the Seine after the fashion of the armature of a horse-shoe magnet; on this ridge (about 560 ft.) is a group of works, named after the village of Cormeilles, commanding the lower Seine, the Argenteuil peninsula and the lower ground towards the Oise. At an average distance of 5 m. from St Denis lie the works of the Montlignon-Domont position (about 600–670 ft.), which sweep all ground to the north, cross their fire with the Cormeilles works, and deny the plateau of Montmorency-Méry-sur-Oise to an enemy. At Écouen, on an isolated hill, are a fort and a redoubt, and to the right near these Fort Stains and two batteries on the ceinture railway. The important eastern section consists of the Vaujours position, the salient of the whole fortress, which commands the countryside to the north as far as Dammartin and Claye, crosses its fire with Stains on the one hand and Villiers on the other, and itself lies on a steep hill at the outer edge of the forest of Bondy which allows free and concealed communication between the fort and the inner line of works. The Vaujours works are armoured. Three miles to the right of Vaujours is Fort Chelles, which bars the roads and railways of the Marne valley. On the other side of the Marne, on ground made historic by the events of 1870, are forts Villiers and Champigny, designed as a bridgehead to enable the defenders to assemble in front of the Marne. To the right of these is a fort near Boissy-St-Leger, and on the right of the whole section are the armoured works of the

[1] The plateau of Mont Avron on the east side, which was provisionally fortified in 1870, is not now defended.

Villeneuve-St-Georges position, which command the Seine and Yères country as far as Brie and Corbeil. The left of the southwestern section is formed by the powerful Fort Palaiseau and its annexe-batteries, which command the Yvette valley. Behind Fort Palaiseau, midway between it and Fort Châtillon, is the Verrières, group, overlooking the valley of the Bièvre. To the right of Palaiseau on the high ground towards Versailles are other works, and around Versailles itself is a semi-circle of batteries right and left of the armoured Fort St Cyr. In various positions around Marly there are some seven or eight batteries.

Topography.—The development of Paris can be traced outwards in approximately concentric rings from the Gallo-Roman town on the Île de la Cité to the fortifications which now form its boundary. A line of boulevards known as the Grands Boulevards,[2] coinciding in great part with ramparts of the 14th, 16th and 17th centuries, encloses most of old Paris, a portion of which extends southwards beyond the Boulevard St Germain. Outside the Grands Boulevards lie the *faubourgs* or old suburbs, round which runs another enceinte of boulevards—*boulevards extérieurs*—corresponding to ramparts of the 18th century. Beyond them other and more modern suburbs incorporated with the city after 1860 stretch to the boulevards which line the present fortifications. On the north, east and south these are commercial or industrial in character, inhabited by the working classes and *petite bourgeoisie*, while here and there there are still areas devoted to market gardening; those on the west are residential centres for the upper classes (Auteuil and Passy). Of the *faubourgs* of Paris those to the north and east are mainly commercial (Faubourgs St Denis, St Martin, Poissonnière) or industrial (Faubourgs du Temple and St Antoine) in character, while to the west the Faubourg St Honoré, the Champs Élysées and the Faubourg St Germain are occupied by the residences of the upper classes of the population. The chief resorts of business and pleasure are concentrated within the Grands Boulevards, and more especially on the north bank of the Seine. No uniformity marks the street-plan of this or the other quarters of the city. One broad and almost straight thoroughfare bisects it under various names from Neuilly (W.N.W.) to Vincennes (E.S.E.). Within the limits of the Grands Boulevards it is known as the Rue de Rivoli (over 2 m. in length) and the Rue St Antoine and runs parallel with and close to the Seine from the Place de la Concorde to the Place de la Bastille. From the Eastern station to the observatory Paris is traversed N.N.E. and S.S.W. for 2½ m. by another important thoroughfare—the Boulevard de Strasbourg continued as the Boulevard de Sébastopol, as the Boulevard du Palais on the Île de la Cité, and on the south bank as the Boulevard St Michel. The line of the Grands Boulevards from the Madeleine to the Bastille, by way of the Place de l'Opéra, the Porte-St Denis and the Porte St Martin (two triumphal arches erected in the latter half of the 17th century in honour of Louis XIV.) and the Place de la République stretches for nearly 3 m. It contains most of the large cafés and several of the chief theatres, and though its gaiety and animation are concentrated at the western end—in the Boulevards des Italiens, des Capucines and de la Madeleine—it is as a whole one of the most celebrated avenues in the world. On the right side of the river may also be mentioned the Rue Royale, from the Madeleine to the Place de la Concorde; the Malesherbes and Haussmann boulevards, the first stretching from the Place Madeleine north-west to the fortifications, the second from the Grands Boulevards near the Place de l'Opéra nearly to the Place de l'Étoile; the Avenue de l'Opéra, which unites the Place du Palais Royal, approximately the central point of Paris, with the Place de l'Opéra; the Rue de la Paix, connecting the Place Vendôme with the Place de l'Opéra, and noted for its fashionable dress-making establishments, and the Rue Auber and Rue du Quatre Septembre, also terminating in the Place de l'Opéra, in the vicinity of which are found some

[2] The word *boulevard* means " bulwark " or fortification and thus has direct reference to the old ramparts. But since the middle of the 19th century the title has been applied to new thoroughfares not traced on the site of an old enceinte.

of the finest shops in Paris; the Rue St Honoré running parallel with the Rue de Rivoli, from the Rue Royale to the Central Markets; the Rue de Lafayette, one of the longest streets of Paris, traversing the town from the Opera to the Bassin de la Villette; the Boulevard Magenta, from Montmartre to the Place de la République; and the Rue de Turbigo, from this place to the Halles Centrales. On the left side of the river the main thoroughfare is the Boulevard St Germain, beginning at the Pont Sully, skirting the Quartier Latin, the educational quarter on the north, and terminating at the Pont de la Concorde after traversing a quarter mainly devoted to ministries, embassies and other official buildings and to the residences of the *noblesse*.

Squares.—Some of the chief squares have already been mentioned. The finest is the Place de la Concorde, laid out under Louis XV. by J. A. Gabriel and noted as the scene of the execution of Louis XVI., Marie Antoinette and many other victims of the Revolution. The central decoration consists of an obelisk from the great temple at Luxor in Upper Egypt, presented to Louis Philippe in 1831 by Mehemet Ali, and flanked by two monumental fountains. The formation of the Place Vendôme was begun towards the end of the 17th century. In the middle there is a column surmounted by a statue of Napoleon I. and decorated with plates of bronze on which are depicted scenes from the campaign of 1805. The Place de l'Étoile is the centre of twelve avenues radiating from it in all directions. The chief of these is the fashionable Avenue des Champs Élysées which connects it with the Place de la Concorde; while on the other side the Avenue de la Grande Armée leads to the fortifications, the two forming a section of the main artery of Paris; the well-wooded Avenue du Bois de Boulogne forms the threshold of the celebrated park of that name. In the centre of the Place, the Arc de Triomphe de l'Étoile, the largest triumphal arch in the world (162 ft. high by 147 ft. wide), commemorates the military triumphs of the Revolutionary and Napoleonic troops. The finest of the sculptures on its façades is that representing the departure of the volunteers in 1792 by François Rude. The Place de la République, in which stands a huge statue of the Republic, did not receive its present form till 1879. The Place de la Bastille stands a little to the east of the site of the famous state prison. It contains the Colonne de Juillet erected in memory of those who fell in the revolution of July 1830. The Place du Carrousel, enclosed within the western wings of the Louvre and so named from a revel given there by Louis XIV., was enlarged about the middle of the 19th century. The triumphal arch on its west side commemorates the victories of 1805 and formed the main entrance to the Tuileries palace (see below). Facing the arch there is a stone pyramid forming the background to a statue of Gambetta. Other squares are the Place des Victoires, dating from 1685, with the equestrian statue of Louis XIV.; the Place des Vosges, formerly Place Royale, formed by Henry IV. on the site of the old Tournelles Palace and containing the equestrian statue of Louis XIII.; the Place de l'Hôtel de Ville, once the Place de Grève and the scene of many state executions from the beginning of the 14th century till 1830; the Place du Châtelet, on the site of the prison of the Grand Châtelet, pulled down in 1802, with a fountain and a column commemorative of victories of Napoleon, and the Place de la Nation decorated with a fountain and a bronze group representing the Triumph of the Republic, and with two columns of 1788 surmounted by statues of St Louis and Philip Augustus, corresponding to the east of the city to the Place de l'Étoile at the west.

South of the Seine are the Place St Michel, adorned with a monumental fountain, and one of the great centres of traffic in Paris; the Carrefour de l'Observatoire, with the monument to Francis Jarnier, the explorer, and the statue of General Ney standing on the spot where he was shot; the Place du Panthéon; the Place Denfert Rochereau, adorned with a colossal lion symbolizing the defence of Belfort in 1871; the Place St Sulpice, with a modern fountain embellished with the statues of the preachers Bossuet, Fénelon, Massillon and Fléchier; the Place Vauban, behind the Invalides; and the Place du Palais Bourbon, in front of the Chamber of Deputies. On the Île de la Cité in front of the cathedral is the Place du Parvis-Notre-Dame, with the equestrian statue of Charlemagne.

Besides those already mentioned, Paris possesses other monumental fountains of artistic value. The Fontaine des Innocents in the Square des Innocents belonged to the church of that name demolished in 1786. It is a graceful work of the Renaissance designed by Pierre Lescot and retains sculptures by Jean Goujon. On its reconstruction on the present site other carvings were added by Augustin Pajou. A fountain of the first half of the 18th century in the Rue de Grenelle is remarkable for its rich decoration, while another in the Avenue de l'Observatoire is an elaborate modern work, the central group of which by J. B. Carpeaux represents the four quarters of the globe supporting the terrestrial sphere. The Fontaine de Medicis (17th century) in the Luxembourg garden is a work of Salomon Debrosse in the Doric style; the fountain in the Place Louvois (1844) representing the rivers of France is by Louis Visconti. In 1872 Sir Richard Wallace gave the municipality fifty drinking-fountains which are placed in different parts of the city.

The Seine.—The Seine flows for nearly 8 m. through Paris. As it enters and as it leaves the city it is crossed by a viaduct used by the circular railway and for ordinary traffic; that of Point du Jour has two storeys of arches. Three bridges—the Passerelle de l'Estacade, between the Île St Louis and the right bank, the Pont des Arts and the Passerelle Debilly (close to the Trocadéro)—are for foot passengers only; all the others are for carriages as well. The most famous, and in its actual state the oldest, is the Pont Neuf, begun in 1578, the two portions of which rest on the extremity of the island called La Cité, the point at which the river is at its widest (863 ft.). On the embankment below the Pont Neuf stands the equestrian statue of Henry IV. Between La Cité and the left bank the width of the lesser channel is reduced to 95 ft. The river has a width of 540 ft. as it enters Paris and of 446 ft. as it leaves it. After its entrance to the city it passes under the bridges of Tolbiac, Bercy and Austerlitz, that of Sully, those of Marie and Louis Philippe between the Île St Louis and the right bank; that of La Tournelle between the Île St Louis and the left bank; that of St Louis between the Île St Louis and La Cité. The Cité communicates with the right bank by the Pont d'Arcole, the Pont Notre-Dame, built on foundations of the 15th century, and the Pont-au Change, owing its name to the shops of the money-changers and goldsmiths which bordered its medieval predecessor; with the left bank by that of the Archevéché, the so-called Pont au Double, the Petit Pont and the Pont St Michel, the original of which was built towards the end of the 14th century. Below the Pont Neuf come the Pont des Arts, Pont du Carrousel, Pont Royal (a fine stone structure leading to the Tuileries), and those of Solférino, la Concorde, Alexandre III. (the finest and most modern bridge in Paris, its foundation-stone having been laid by the czar Nicholas II. in 1896), Invalides, Alma, Iéna (opposite the Champ de Mars), Passy, Grenelle and Mirabeau. The Seine has at times caused disastrous floods in the city, as in January 1910. (See SEINE.)

The houses of Paris nowhere abut directly on the river banks, which in their whole extent from the bridge of Austerlitz to Passy are protected by broad embankments or "quais." At the foot of these lie several ports for the unloading and loading of goods, &c.,—on the right side Bercy for wines, La Rapée for timber, Port Mazas, the Port de l'Arsenal at the mouth of the St Martin canal,[1] the Port Henry IV., des Celestins, St Paul, des Ormes, de l'Hôtel de Ville (the two latter for fruit) and the Port St Nicolas (foreign vessels); on the left bank the Port de la Gare for petroleum, St Bernard for wines and the embarcation of sewage, and the ports of La Tournelle (old iron), Orsay (building material), the Invalides, Gros Caillou, the Cygnes, Grenelle and Javel (refuse). Besides the river ports, the port of Paris also includes the canals of St Martin and the portions of the canals of St Denis and the Ourcq within the walls. All three debouch in the busy and extensive basin of La Villette in the north-east of the city. The traffic of the port is chiefly in coal, building materials and stone, manure and fertilizers, agricultural produce and food-stuffs.

Promenades and Parks.—In the heart of Paris are situated the gardens of the Tuileries[2] (56 acres), designed by André Le Notre under Louis XIV. Though added to and altered afterwards they retain the main outlines of the original plan. They are laid out in parterres and bosquets, planted with chestnut trees, lindens and plane trees, and adorned with playing fountains and basins, and numerous statues mostly antique in subject. From the terrace along the river-side a fine view is to be had over the Seine to the park and palace of the Trocadéro; and

---

[1] This canal (3 m. long) leaving the Seine below Austerlitz bridge, passes by a tunnel under the Place de la Bastille and Boulevard Richard Lenoir, and rises by sluices to the La Villette basin, from which the St Denis canal (4 m. long) descends to the Seine at St Denis. In this way boats going up or down the river can avoid passing through Paris. The canal de l'Ourcq, which supplies the two canals mentioned, contributes to the water-supply of Paris as well as to its transport facilities.

[2] These gardens are the property of the state, the other areas mentioned being the property of the town.

from the terraces along the Place de la Concorde the eye takes in the Place and the Avenue of the Champs Élysées. The gardens of the Luxembourg,[1] planned by S. Debrosse (17th century) and situated in front of the palace occupied by the senate, are about the same size as those of the Tuileries; with less regularity of form they present greater variety of appearance. In the line of the main entrance extends the beautiful Observatory Walk, terminating in the monumental fountain mentioned above. Besides these gardens laid out in the French taste, with straight walks and regular beds, there are several in what the French designate the English style. The finest and most extensive of these, the Buttes-Chaumont Gardens, in the north-east of the city, occupy 57 acres of very irregular ground, which up to 1866 was occupied by plaster-quarries, limekilns and brickworks. The "buttes" or knolls are now covered with turf, flowers and shrubbery. Advantage has been taken of the varying relief of the site to form a fine lake and a cascade with picturesque rocks. The Montsouris Park, in the south of the city, 38 acres in extent, also consists of broken ground; in the middle stands the meteorological observatory, built after the model of the Tunisian palace of Bardo, and it also contains a monument in memory of the Flatters expedition to the Sahara in 1881. The small Monceau Park, in the aristocratic quarter to the north of the Boulevard Haussmann, is a portion of the old park belonging to King Louis Philippe, and contains monuments to Chopin, Gounod, Guy de Maupassant and others.

The Jardin des Plantes[1] (founded in the first half of the 17th century), about 58 acres in extent, combines both styles. Its museum of natural history (1793), with its zoological gardens, its hothouses and greenhouses, its nursery and naturalization gardens, its museums of zoology, anatomy, anthropology, botany, mineralogy and geology, its laboratories, and its courses of lectures by the most distinguished professors in all branches of natural science, make it an institution of universally acknowledged eminence.

Other open spaces worthy of mention are the Champs Élysées (west of the Place de la Concorde), begun at the end of the 17th century but only established in their present form since 1858; the Trocadéro Park, laid out for the exhibition of 1878, with its lakes, cascade and aquarium; the Champ de Mars (laid out about 1770 as a manœuvring ground for the École Militaire), containing the Eiffel Tower (q.v.), the gardens of the Palais Royal, surrounded by galleries; and the Ranelagh in Passy.

The Bois de Boulogne and Bois de Vincennes situated outside the fortifications are on a far larger scale than the parks within them. The Bois de Boulogne, commonly called the "Bois," is reached by the wide avenue of the Champs Élysées as far as the Arc de Triomphe and thence by the avenue of the Bois de Boulogne or that of the Grande Armée. The first of these, with its side walks for foot passengers and equestrians, grass-plots, flower-beds and elegant buildings, affords a wide prospect over the Bois and the hills of St Cloud and Mont Valérien. The Bois de Boulogne covers an area of 2100 acres, is occupied by turf, clumps of trees, sheets of water or running streams. Here are the two race-courses of Longchamp (flat races) and Auteuil (steeplechases), the park of the small château of Bagatelle, 1777, the grounds of the Polo Club and the Racing Club and the gardens of the Acclimatization Society, which, with their menageries, conservatories and aquarium, are largely visited by pleasure-seekers. Trees for the public parks and squares are grown in the municipal nurseries situated on the south border of the Bois. On the east it is adjoined by the Park of La Muette, with the old royal château. The Bois de Vincennes (see VINCENNES) is 2300 acres in area and is similarly adorned with streams, lakes and cascades.

Churches.—The most important church in Paris is the cathedral of Notre-Dame, founded in 1163, completed about 1240. Measuring 130 yds. in length and 52 yds. in breadth, the church consists of a choir and apse, a short transept, and a nave with double aisles which are continued round the choir and are flanked by square chapels added after the completion of the rest of the church. The central spire, 148 ft. in height, was erected in the course of a restoration carried out between 1846 and 1879 under the direction of Viollet le Duc. Two massive square towers crown the principal façade. Its three doors are decorated with fine early Gothic carving and surmounted by a row of figures representing twenty-eight kings of Israel and Judah. Above the central door is a rose window, above which is a third storey consisting of a graceful gallery of pointed arches supported

[1] These gardens are the property of the state, the other areas mentioned being the property of the town.

on slender columns. The transept has two façades, also richly decorated with chiselled work and containing rose windows. Of the elaborate decoration of the interior all that is medieval is a part of the screen of the choir (the first half of the 14th century), with sculptures representing scenes from the life of Christ, and the stained glass of the rose windows (13th century). The woodwork in the choir (early 18th century), and a marble group called the "Vow of Louis XIII." (17th century) by Couston and Coysevox, are other noticeable works of art. The church possesses the Crown of Thorns and a fragment of the Cross, which attract numerous pilgrims.

Paris is poor in Romanesque architecture, which is represented chiefly in the nave and transept of St Germain-des-Prés, the choir of which is Gothic in tendency. The church, which once belonged to the celebrated abbey of St Germain founded in the 6th century, contains fine modern frescoes by Hippolyte Flandrin. The Transition style is also exemplified in St Pierre-de-Montmartre (12th century). Besides the cathedral there are several churches of the Gothic period, the most important being St Julien-le-Pauvre, now serving as a Greek church, which is contemporary with Notre-Dame; St Germain-l'Auxerrois (13th to 16th centuries), whose projecting porch is a graceful work of 1435; St Séverin (mainly of the 13th and 16th centuries); St Gervais, largely in the Flamboyant Gothic style with an interesting façade by S. Debrosse in the classical manner; and St Merry (1520-1612), almost wholly Gothic in architecture. St Gervais, St Merry and St Germain all contain valuable works of art, the stained glass of the two former being especially noteworthy.

St Étienne-du-Mont combines the Gothic and Renaissance styles in its nave and transept, while its choir is of Gothic, its façade of pure Renaissance architecture. In the interior, one of the most beautiful in the city, there is a fine rood-loft (1600-1605) by Pierre Biard and a splendid collection of stained windows of the 16th and early 17th centuries; a chapel contains part of the sarcophagus of Ste Geneviève, which is the object of a pilgrimage. St Eustache (1532-c. 1650), though its construction displays many Gothic characteristics, belongs wholly, with the exception of a Classical façade of the 18th century, to the Renaissance period, being unique in this respect among the more important of French churches. The church contains the sarcophagus and statue (by A. Coysevox) of Colbert and the tombs of other eminent men.

Of churches in the Classical style the principal are St Sulpice (1655-1777), almost equalling Notre-Dame in dimensions and possessing a façade by J. N. Servandoni rank among the finest of its period; St Roch (1653-1740), which contains numerous works of art of the 17th and 18th centuries; St Paul-St Louis (1627-1641); and the church (1645-1665) of the former nunnery of Val-de-Grace (now a military hospital and medical school), which has a dome built after the model of St Peter's at Rome. All these churches are in the old city.

Of the churches of the 19th century, the most remarkable is that of the Sacré Cœur, an important resort of pilgrims, begun in 1876 and overlooking Paris from the heights of Montmartre. The Sacré Cœur is in the Romanesque style, but is surmounted by a Byzantine dome behind which rises a lofty belfry. The bell presented by the dioceses of Savoy and known as "la Savoyarde" weighs between 17 and 18 tons. Of the other modern churches the oldest is the Madeleine, built under Napoleon I. by Pierre Vignon on the foundations of a church of the 18th century and finished in 1842. It was intended by the emperor as a "temple of glory" and is built on the lines of a Roman temple with a fine colonnade surrounding it. The interior, consisting of a single nave bordered by chapels and roofed with cupolas, is decorated with sculptures and painting by eminent modern artists. Notre-Dame-de-Lorette (1823-1836) and St Vincent-de-Paul (1824-1844) are in the style of early Christian basilicas. Both contain good frescoes, the frieze of the nave in St Vincent-de-Paul being an elaborate work by Hippolyte Flandrin, Ste Clotilde, the most important representation of modern Gothic in Paris, dates from the middle of the century. St Augustin and La Trinité in the Renaissance style were both built between 1860 and 1870. With the exception of Ste Clotilde in the St Germain quarter and the Madeleine, the modern churches above mentioned are all in the northern quarters of Paris.

Civil Buildings.—The most important of the civil buildings of Paris is the palace of the Louvre (*Lupora*), the south front of which extends along the Seine for about half a mile. It owes its origin to Philip Augustus, who erected a huge keep defended by a rectangle of fortifications in what is now the south-west corner of the quadrangle, where its plan is traced on the pavement. The fortress was demolished by Francis I. and under that monarch and his successors Pierre Lescot built the portions of the wings to the south and west of the courtyard, which rank among the finest examples of Renaissance architecture. The rest of the buildings surrounding the courtyard date from the reigns of Louis XIII. and XIV., the most noteworthy feature being the colonnade (1666–1670) of the east façade designed by Claude Perrault. The two wings projecting westwards from the corners of the quadrangle, each consisting of two parallel galleries with pavilions at intervals, were built under Napoleon III., with the exception of the Grande Galerie and at right angles to it the Pavillon Henry IV., containing the Apollo gallery, which were erected on the river front by Cathérine de Medici and Henry IV. Of these two wings that on the north is occupied by the ministry of finance. The history of the palace of the Tuileries (so called in allusion to the tile kilns which occupied its site) is intimately connected with that of the Louvre, its origin being due to Cathérine de Medici and Henry IV. The latter built the wing, rebuilt under Napoleon III., which united it with the Grande Galerie, the corresponding wing on the north side dating from various periods of the 19th century. The palace itself was burnt by the Communists in 1871, with the exception of the terminal pavilion on the south (Pavillon de Flore); only the northern terminal pavilion (Pavillon de Marsan, now occupied by the museum of decorative arts) was rebuilt.

Next in importance to the Louvre is the Palais de Justice (law courts), a huge assemblage of buildings covering the greater part of the Ile de la Cité to the west of the Boulevard du Palais. During the Gallo-Roman period the site was occupied by a citadel which became the palace of the Merovingian kings and afterwards of the Capetian kings. In the 12th and 13th centuries it was altered and enlarged by the latter, and during part of that period was also occupied by the parlement of Paris, to which it was entirely made over under Charles V. In 1618, 1737 and 1776 the building was ravaged by fire, and in its present state is in great part the outcome of a systematic reconstruction begun in 1840. In the interior the only medieval remains are the Sainte-Chapelle, the Conciergerie, an old prison where Marie Antoinette and other illustrious victims of the Revolution were confined, and some halls and kitchens of the 13th century. All these are on the ground floor, a portion of which is assigned to the police. The courts, which include the Cour de Cassation, the supreme tribunal in France, the Court of Appeal and the Court of First Instance, are on the first floor, the chief feature of which is the fine Salle des Pas Perdus, the successor of the Grand' Salle, a hall originally built by Philip the Fair and rebuilt after fires in 1618 and 1871. The Sainte-Chapelle, one of the most perfect specimens of Gothic art, was erected from 1245 to 1248 by St Louis as a shrine for the crown of thorns and other relics now at Notre-Dame, and was restored in the 19th century. It comprises a lower portion for the use of the servants and retainers and the upper portion or royal chapel, the latter richly decorated and lighted by lofty windows set close together and filled with beautiful stained glass. The Palais de Justice presents towards the west a Greek façade by J. L. Duc (d. 1879), which is reckoned among the finest achievements of modern art. The façade towards the Seine embodies four towers which date in parts from the reconstruction under the Capetian dynasty. That at the east angle (the Tour de l'Horloge) contains a clock of 1370, said to be the oldest public clock in France. A handsome iron railing of 1787 separates the courtyard on the east side from the Boulevard du Palais.

About a quarter of a mile south of the Palais de Justice adjoining the Jardin de Cluny lies the Hôtel de Cluny, acquired in 1833 by the antiquarian A. du Sommerard as a repository for his collections and now belonging to the state. It is a graceful and well-preserved building in late Gothic style distinguished for the beautiful carving of the doors, dormer windows and open-work parapet. The mansion, which contains a rich Gothic chapel, was erected at the end of the 15th century by Jacques d'Amboise, abbot of Cluny. It stands on the site of a Roman palace said to have been built by the emperor Constantius Chlorus (d. 306), and ruins of the baths are still to be seen adjoining it.

The other civil buildings of Paris are inferior in interest and attraction. The Hôtel des Invalides on the left bank of the Seine opposite the Champs Elysées dates from the reign of Louis XIV.; by whom it was founded as a retreat for wounded and infirm soldiers, its inmates are few in number, and the building also serves as headquarters of the military governor of Paris. A garden and a spacious esplanade stretching to the Quai d'Orsay precede the north façade; the entrance to this opens into the Cour d'Honneur, a courtyard enclosed by a moat above which is a battery of cannon used for salutes on important occasions. On either side of the Cour d'Honneur lie the museums of military history and of artillery (weapons and armour). The parish church of St Louis, decorated with flags captured in the wars of the Second Empire, closes the south side of the Cour d'Honneur, while behind all rises a magnificent gilded dome sheltering another church, the Eglise royale, built by J. H. Mansart from 1693 to 1706. The central crypt of this church contains a fine sarcophagus of red porphyry in which lie

the remains of Napoleon I., brought from St Helena in 1840, while close by are the tombs of his friends Duroc and Bertrand.

The Panthéon, on the left bank near the Luxembourg garden, was built to the plans of J. G. Soufflot in the last half of the 18th century under the name of Ste Geneviève, whose previous sanctuary it replaced. In 1791 the Constituent Assembly decreed that it should be no longer a church but a pantheon for great Frenchmen. Voltaire and Mirabeau were the first to be entombed in the Panthéon as it then came to be called. Reconsecrated and resecularized more than once during the 19th century, the building finally regained its present name in 1885, when Victor Hugo was buried there. The Panthéon is an imposing domed building in the form of a Greek cross. The tympanum above the portico by David d'Angers and, in the interior, paintings of the life of Ste Geneviève by Puvis de Chavannes are features of its artistic decoration.

Various public bodies occupy mansions and palaces built under the ancient régime. The Palais Royal, built by Richelieu about 1630 and afterwards inhabited by Anne of Austria, the regent Philip II. of Orleans and Philippe Egalité, is now occupied by the Council of State and the Théâtre Français. The Palace of the Luxembourg stands on the site of a mansion belonging to Duke Francis of Luxembourg, which was rebuilt by Marie de Medici, wife of Henry IV. The architect, Salomon Debrosse, was ordered to take the Pitti Palace at Florence as his model, but notwithstanding the general plan of the building is French. The south façade facing the Luxembourg garden was rebuilt in the original style under Louis Philippe. The residence of various royal personages during the 17th and 18th centuries, the Luxembourg became during the revolutionary period the palace of the Directory and later of the Consulate. In the 19th century it was occupied by the senate of Napoleon I., by the chamber of peers under Louis Philippe, by the senate under Napoleon III., and since 1879 by the republican senate. The chamber of deputies meets in the Palais Bourbon, built in the 18th century for members of the Bourbon-Condé family. The façade, which faces the Pont de la Concorde, is in the style of an ancient temple and dates from the early years of the 19th century, when the corps législatif held their sittings in the building. The Palais de l'Elysée, the residence of the president of the republic, was built in 1718 for Louis d'Auvergne, count of Evreux, and was afterwards acquired by Madame de Pompadour; during the 19th century Napoleon I., Napoleon III., and other illustrious persons resided there. The building has been often altered and enlarged. The hôtel-de-ville (1873–1882), on the right bank of the Seine opposite the Ile de la Cité, stands on the site of a town hall built from 1535 to 1628, much enlarged towards 1840, and destroyed by the Communists in 1871. It is an isolated building in the French Renaissance style, the west façade with its statuary, pilasters, high-pitched roofs and dormer windows being specially elaborate. The interior has been decorated by many prominent artists.

Certain of the schools and museums of Paris occupy buildings of architectural interest. The Conservatoire des Arts et Métiers, a technical school and museum of machinery, &c., founded by the engineer Vaucanson in 1775, is established in the old Cluniac priory of St Martin-des-Champs, enlarged in the 19th century. The refectory is a fine hall of the 13th century; the church with an interesting choir in the Transition style dates from the 11th to the 13th centuries. The Musée Carnavalet was built in the 16th century for François de Kernevenoy, whence its present name, and enlarged in 1660; Mme de Sévigné afterwards resided there. The national archives are stored in the Hôtel Soubise, a mansion of the early 18th century with 19th-century additions, standing on the site of a house built by Olivier de Clisson in 1370. It was afterwards added to by the family of Guise and rebuilt by François de Rohan, duke of Soubise. The palace of Cardinal Mazarin, augmented in modern times, contains the Bibliothèque Nationale. The Palais de l'Institut, formerly the Collège Mazarin, dates from the last half of the 17th century; it is the seat of the academies (except the Academy of Medicine, which occupies a modern building close to the Ecole des Beaux-Arts) and of the Bureau des Longitudes, the great national astronomical council. The Military School overlooking the Champ de Mars is a fine building of the 18th century. The huge Sorbonne buildings date from the latter years of the 19th century with the exception of the church, which belonged to the college as reconstructed by Richelieu. The astronomical observatory, through the centre of which runs the meridian of Paris, is a splendidly equipped building erected under Louis XIV., according to the designs of Claude Perrault. The Ecole des Beaux-Arts (facing the Louvre on the left bank of the Seine), with its interesting collections, partly occupies the site of an Augustine convent and comprises the old Hôtel Chimay. It was erected from 1820 to 1838 and added to later. The most striking feature is the façade of the principal building designed by F. L. J. Duban. The courtyard contains part of the façade of the Norman château of Gaillon (16th century), which was destroyed at the Revolution, and the portal of the château of Anet (erected by Philibert Delorme in 1548) has been adapted as one of the entrances. The Grand Palais des Beaux-Arts, where horse-shows, &c., as well as annual exhibitions of paintings and sculptures are held, and the Petit Palais des Beaux-Arts, which contains art collections belonging to the city, date from 1897–

1900. Both buildings stand close to the north end of the Pont Alexandre III.

The Bourse, built in imitation of an ancient temple, dates from the first half of the 19th century; the Tribunal of Commerce and the Palais du Trocadéro, built for the exhibition of 1878, are both imposing buildings of the latter half of that period, to which also belongs the Hôtel des Postes et Télégraphes.

Among the numerous historic mansions of Paris a few demand special mention. The so-called Maison de François I. (on the Cours la Reine overlooking the Seine) is a small but beautifully decorated building erected at Moret in 1527 and re-erected in Paris in 1826. In the St Gervais quarter are the Hôtel de Beauvais of the latter half of the 17th century and the Hôtel Lamoignon, built after 1580 for Diane de France, duchess of Angoulême, both of which have handsome courtyards; in the same quarter is the Hôtel de Sens, of the 15th century, residence of the archbishops of Sens, whose province then included the diocese of Paris. The Hôtel Lambert on the Ile St Louis, built by L. Levau in the 17th century for Nicholas Lambert and afterwards inhabited by Mme du Châtelet and Voltaire and George Sand, has a magnificent staircase and many works of art. The Hôtel de Sully, built for the duke of Sully from 1624 to 1630, is in the Rue St Antoine and has an interesting courtyard. Of the fine mansion of the dukes of Burgundy the only relic is a tower of the early 15th century built by Jean Sans Peur.

Theatres, &c.—Of the theatres of Paris four—the Opéra, the Opéra-Comique, the Théâtre Français and the Odéon—receive state subventions, amounting in all to £51,000 per annum. The Opéra (entitled the National Academy of Music) was originally founded in 1671 by Pierre Perrin, from whom the management was taken over by J. B. Lully. After several changes of locale, it was eventually transferred from the Rue Le Peletier to the present opera-house. The building, which covers 2¾ acres, is one of the finest theatres in the world. The process of erection, directed by Charles Garnier, lasted from 1861 to 1875 and cost nearly 1¼ million sterling. The front is decorated on the ground storey with allegorical groups (Music by Guillaume; Lyrical Poetry by Jouffroy; Lyrical Drama by Perraud; and Dancing by Carpeaux) and allegorical statues. Surmounting its angles are huge gilded groups representing music and poetry, and above it appears the dome which covers the auditorium. Behind that rises the vast pediment above the stage decorated at the corners with Pegasi by Lequesne. On the summit of the pediment an Apollo, raising aloft his lyre, is seen against the sky. The interior is decorated throughout with massive gilding, flamboyant scroll-work, statues, paintings, &c. The grand vestibule, with statues of Lully, Rameau, Gluck and Handel, the grand staircase, the *avant-foyer* or corridor leading to the *foyer*, and the *foyer* or crush-room itself are especially noteworthy. The last is a majestic apartment with a ceiling decorated with fine painting by Paul Baudry. The auditorium is seated for 2156; its ceiling is painted by J. E. Lenepveu. Behind the stage is the *foyer de la danse* or green-room for the ballet, adorned with large allegorical panels and portraits of the most eminent danseuses.

The Théâtre Français or Comédie Française was formed in 1681 under the latter name by the union of Molière's company with two other theatrical companies of the time. The name Théâtre Français dates from 1791, when part of the company headed by the tragedian Talma migrated to the south-west wing of the Palais Royal, which the company, reunified in 1799, has since occupied. Both the Théâtre Français and the less important Odéon, a building of 1782 twice rebuilt, close to the Luxembourg garden, represent the works of the classical dramatists and modern dramas both tragic and comic. The Opéra-Comique, founded in the early 18th century, occupies a building in the Boulevard des Italiens reconstructed after a fire in 1887. Serious as well as light opera is performed there.

Other theatres well known and long established are the Gymnase (chiefly comedy), the Vaudeville and the Porte St Martin (serious drama and comedy), the Variétés and the Palais Royal (farce and vaudeville); and the theatres named after and managed by Sarah Bernhardt and Réjane, the Théâtre Antoine, the Gaîté and the Ambigu may also be mentioned. The finest concerts in Paris are those of the Conservatoire de Musique et de Déclamation (Rue du Faubourg Poissonnière), while the Concerts Lamoureux and the Concerts Colonne are also of a high order. Musical and local performances of a more popular kind are given at the music halls, *cafés concerts* and *cabarets artistiques*, with which the city abounds.

Paris is the chief centre for sport in France, and the principal societies for the encouragement of sport have their headquarters in the city. Among these may be mentioned the *Société d'encouragement pour l'amélioration des races de chevaux en France* (associated with the Jockey Club), which is the chief authority in the country as regards racing, and the *Union des sociétés françaises de sports athlétiques,* which comprises committees for the organization of athletics, football, lawn tennis and amateur sport generally. The *Racing Club de France,* the *Stade français* and the *Union athlétique du premier arrondissement* are the chief Parisian athletic clubs. Race meetings are held at Longchamp and Auteuil in the Bois de Boulogne, and at Chantilly, Vincennes, St Cloud, St Ouen, Maisons-Laffitte and other places in the vicinity.

Museums.—Some of the more important museums of Paris require

notice. The richest and most celebrated occupies the Louvre. On the ground floor are museums (1) of ancient sculpture, containing such treasures as the Venus of Milo, the Pallas of Velletri (the most beautiful of all statues of Minerva), the colossal group of the Tiber, discovered at Rome in the 14th century, &c.; (2) of Medieval and Renaissance sculpture, comprising works of Michelangelo, Jean Goujon, Germain Pilon, &c., and rooms devoted to early Christian antiquities and works by the Della Robbia and their school; (3) of modern French sculpture, with works by Puget, the brothers Coustou Coysevox, Chaude, Houdin, Rude, David of Angers, Carpeaux, &c.; (4) of Egyptian sculpture and inscriptions; (5) of antiquities from Assyria, Palestine, Phoenicia and other parts of Asia; (6) of engravings.

On the first floor are (1) the picture galleries, rich in works of the Italian painters, especially of Leonardo da Vinci (including his Mona Lisa), Raphael, Titian and Paolo Veronese; of the Spanish masters Murillo is best represented; and there are numerous works by Rubens, Van Dyck and Teniers, and by Rembrandt and Holbein. The examples of French art form about one-third of the collection, and include (1) the collection bequeathed in 1869 by Dr La Caze (chiefly works of the 18th century); (2) a collection of ancient bronzes; (3) a collection of furniture of the 17th and 18th centuries; (4) a rich museum of drawings by great masters; (5) a museum of Medieval, Renaissance and modern art pottery, objects in bronze, glass and ivory, &c.; (6) the Rothschild collection of objects of art; (7) smaller antiquities from Susiana, Chaldaea and Egypt; (8) a collection of ancient pottery embodying the Campana collection purchased from the Papal government in 1861; (9) the royal jewels and a splendid collection of enamels in the spacious Apollo gallery designed by Charles Lebrun. On the second floor are French pictures of the 19th century, the Thomy-Théry art-collection bequeathed in 1903, and the marine, ethnographical and Chinese museums. The Pavilion de La Trémoille contains a continuation of the Egyptian museum and antiquities brought from Susiana by Augustus De Morgan between 1897 and 1905. A museum of decorative art occupies the Pavillon de Marsan.

The museum of the Luxembourg, installed in a building near the palace occupied by the senate, is devoted to works of living painters and sculptors acquired by the state. They remain there for ten years after the death of the artists, that the finest may be selected for the Louvre.

The Cluny museum occupies the old mansion of the abbots of that order (see above). It contains about 11,000 examples of Medieval and Renaissance art-sculptures in marble, wood and stone, ivories, enamels and mosaics, pottery and porcelain, tapestries, bronzes, specimens of goldsmith's work, both religious and civil, including nine gold crowns of the 7th century found near Toledo, Venetian glass, furniture, iron-work, state carriages, ancient boots and shoes and pictures.

The Carnavalet museum comprises a collection illustrating the history of Paris. The Petit Palais des Beaux-Arts contains art-collections belonging to the city (especially the Dutuit collection). The house of Gustave Moreau, Rue Rochefoucauld, is now a museum of his paintings, and that of Victor Hugo, Place des Vosges, contains a collection of objects relating to the poet.

The Trocadéro Palace contains a museum of casts illustrating the progress of sculpture, chiefly that of France, from the 11th to the 18th century, it also possesses a collection of Khmer antiquities from Cambodia and an ethnographical museum. In the same neighbourhood are the Guimet museum, containing the collections of Oriental pottery, of objects relating to the Oriental religions and of antiquities presented to the state in 1885 by Emile Guimet of Lyons; and the Galliéra museum, erected by the duchess of Galliéra and containing a collection of tapestries and other works of art belonging to the city. The Cernuschi Oriental museum, close to the Monceau Park, was bequeathed to the city in 1895 by M. Cernuschi.

The collection of MSS., engravings, medals and antiques in the Bibliothèque Nationale are important, as also are the industrial and machinery exhibits of the Conservatoire des Arts et Métiers.

For libraries see LIBRARIES.

Population.—Paris is divided into twenty arrondissements. Only the first twelve belonged to it previous to 1860; the others correspond to the old suburban communes then annexed. The first four arrondissements occupy the space on the right of the river, extending from the Place de la Concorde to the Bastille, and from the Seine to the line of the Grands Boulevards; the 5th, 6th and 7th arrondissements lie opposite them on the left side; the 8th, 9th, 10th, 11th and 12th surround the first four arrondissements on the north; the 13th, 14th and 15th are formed out of the old suburban communes of the left side; and the 16th, 17th, 18th, 19th and 20th out of the old suburban communes of the right side.

The growth of the population during the 19th century is shown in the following table, which gives the population present on the census day, including the *population comptée à part, i.e.* troops, inmates of hospitals, prisons, schools, &c.

Years.	Population.	Years.	Population.
1801	547,756	1866	1,825,274
1817	713,966	1872	1,851,792
1831	785,862	1876	1,988,806
1836	899,313	1881	2,239,928
1841	935,261	1886	2,260,945
1846	1,053,897	1891	2,424,705
1851	1,053,262	1896	2,511,629
1856	1,174,346	1901	2,660,559
1861	1,696,141	1906	2,722,731

Below is shown the population of the arrondissements separately (in 1906), together with the comparative density of population therein. The most thickly populated region of Paris comprises a zone stretching northwards frcm the Île de la Cité and the Île St Louis to the fortifications, and including the central quarters of St Gervais with 400 inhabitants to the acre, Ste Avoie with 391 inhabitants to the acre, and Bonne-Nouvelle with 406 inhabitants to the acre. The central arrondissements on the north bank, which (with the exception of L, the Louvre) are among the most densely populated, tended in the latter part of the 19th century to decrease in density, while the outlying arrondissements (XII.-XX.), which with the exception of Batignolles and Montmartre are comparatively thinly populated, increased in density, and this tendency continued in the early years of the 20th century.

Quarters.	Population.	Inhabitants per acre.
I. Louvre . .	St Germain l'Auxerrois, Halles, Palais Royal, Place Vendôme.	60,906	130
II. Bourse .	Gaillon, Vivienne, Mail, Bonne-Nouvelle.	61,116	253
III. Temple . .	Arts-et-Métiers, Enfants-Rouges, Archives, Ste Avoie.	86,152	300
IV. Hôtel-de-Ville	St Merri, St Gervais, Arsenal, Notre-Dame.	96,490	249
V. Panthéon . .	St Victor, Jardin des Plantes, Val de Grace, Sorbonne.	117,666	191
VI. Luxembourg.	Monnaie, Odéon, Notre-Dame des Champs, St Germain des Prés.	97,055	186
VII. Palais Bourbon	St Thomas d'Aquin, Invalides, Ecole-Militaire, Gros-Caillou.	97,375	98
VIII. Elysée . .	Champs Elysées, Faubourg-du-Roule, Madeleine, Europe.	99,769	101
IX. Opéra . .	St Georges, Chaussée d'Antin, Faubourg Montmartre, Rochechouart.	118,818	226
X. St Laurent .	St Vincent de Paul, Porte St Denis, Porte St Martin, Hôpital St Louis.	151,697	215
XI. Popincourt .	Folie-Méricourt, St Ambroise, Roquette, Ste Marguerite.	232,050	260
XII. Reuilly . .	Bel-Air, Picpus, Bercy, Quinze-Vingts.	138,648	99
XIII. Gobelins .	Salpêtrière, Gare, Maison-Blanche, Croulebarbe.	133,133	86
XIV. Observatoire	Montparnasse,Santé,Petit-Montrouge, Plaisance.	150,136	131
XV. Vaugirard .	St Lambert, Necker, Grenelle, Javel.	168,190	94
XVI. Passy . .	Auteuil, Muette, Porte-Dauphine, Chaillot.	130,719	75
XVII. Batignolles-Monceau	Ternes, Plaine-Monceau, Batignolles, Epinette.	207,127	188
XVIII. Montmartre .	Grandes-Carrières, Clignancourt, Goutte-d'Or, Chapelle.	258,174	201
XIX. Buttes-Chaumont	Villette, Pont-de-Flandre, Amérique, Combat.	148,081	101
XX. Ménilmontant	Belleville,St Fargeau,Père-Lachaise, Charonne.	169,429	132

The birth-rate, which diminished steadily in the 19th century, is low—on an average 54,000 births per annum (1901-1905) or 20·2 per 1000 inhabitants as compared with 31·8 in 1851-1855. The death-rate also is low, 48,000 deaths per annum (1901-1905), averaging 17·9 deaths per 1000 inhabitants. This is accounted for by the fact that Paris is pre-eminently a town of adults, as the following figures, referring to the year 1908, show:—

Inhabitants under 1 year of age	41,107
„ „ from 1 to 19 years of age	676,993
„ „ „ 20 „ 39 „ „	1,108,340
„ „ „ 40 „ 59 „ „	663,435
„ „ of 60 years and over	223,836
„ „ unknown age	9,018

In these circumstances there is nothing remarkable in the annual number of marriages in Paris (26,000), a high marriage rate (9·8 per 1000) for the total number of inhabitants, but a low one (28·4 per 1000) compared with the number of marriageable persons.

A large number of the inhabitants (on an average 636 out of every 1000) are not Parisians by birth. The foreign nationalities chiefly represented are Belgians, Germans, Swiss, Italians, Luxembourgers, English, Russians, Americans, Austrians, Dutch, Spaniards. The Belgians, Germans and Italians, mostly artisans, live chiefly in the industrial districts in the north and east of the city. The English and Americans, on the other hand, congregate in the wealthy districts of the Champs Elysées and Passy.

Municipal Administration.—Each arrondissement is divided into four quarters, each of which nominates a member of the municipal council. These 80 councillors, together with 21 additional councillors elected by the cantons of the rest of the department, form the departmental council. The chief functionaries of the arrondissement are a mayor (*maire*) and three deputies (*adjoints*) appointed by the president. The mayors act as registrars, draw up electoral and recruiting lists and superintend the poor-relief of their arrondissement. There is a justice of the peace (*juge de paix*) nominated by the government in each arrondissement. There is no elective mayor of Paris: the president of the municipal council, who is nominated by his colleagues, merely acts as chairman of their meetings. When occasion requires, the function of mayor of Paris is discharged by the prefect of Seine. The municipal council discusses and votes the budget of the city, scrutinizes the administrative measures of the two prefects and deliberates on municipal affairs in general. The prefect of Seine and the prefect of police (both magistrates named by the government, but each with a quite distinct sphere of action) represent the executive authority as opposed to the municipal council, which latter has no power, by refusing a vote of credit, to stop any public service the maintenance of which legally devolves on the city: in case of such refusal the minister of the interior may officially insert the credit in the budget. In like manner he may appeal to the head of the state to cancel any decision in which the council has exceeded its legal functions.

The prefecture of Seine comprises the following departments (*directions*), subdivided into *bureaux*:—

1. Municipal affairs, including bureaux for the supervision of city property, of provisioning, of cemeteries, of public buildings, &c.
2. Departmental affairs (including the bureau concerned with the care of lunatics and foundlings).
3. Primary education.
4. Streets and public works, including the bureau of water, canals and sewers, and the bureau of public thoroughfares, promenades and lighting.
5. Finance.

The administrative functions of the prefect necessitate a large technical staff of engineers, inspectors, &c., who are divided among the various *services* attached to the departments. There are also a number of councils and committees on special branches of public work attached to the prefecture (*commission des logements insalubres, de statistique municipale*, &c.). The administration of the three important departments of the *octroi*, poor-relief (*assistance publique*) and pawnbroking (the *mont-de-piété*) is also under the control of the prefect.

The prefecture of police includes the whole department of Seine and the neighbouring communes of the department of Seine-et-Oise—Meudon, St Cloud, Sèvres and Enghien. Its sphere embraces the apprehension and punishment of criminals (*police judiciaire*), general police-work (including political service) and municipal policing. The state, in view of the non-municipal functions of the Paris police, repays a proportion of the annual budget which this prefecture receives from the city. The budget of the prefect of police is voted *en bloc* by the municipal council.

Besides numerous duties consequent on the maintenance of order, the inspection of weights and measures, authority over public spectacles, surveillance of markets and a wide hygienic and sanitary authority belong to the sphere of this prefect. In the last connexion mention may be made of an important body attached to the prefecture of police—the Conseil d'Hygiène Publique et de Salubrité of the department of the Seine, composed of 24 members nominated by the prefect of police and 17 members called to it in virtue of their office. To it are referred such questions as the sources from which to obtain drinking-water for the town, the sanitary measures to be taken during important works, the work connected with the main sewers for the cleaning of the Seine and the utilization of the sewage water, the health of workpeople employed in factories, the sanitary condition of the occupants of schools and prisons, questions relating to the disinfection of infected districts, the heating of public vehicles and dwellings, the conveyance of infected persons, night shelters, &c. Board of health (*commissions d'hygiène*) in each of the twenty arrondissements act in co-operation with this control council. The municipal police, consisting of brigades of *gardiens de la paix*, are divided among the arrondissements in each of which there is an *officier de paix* in command. There are besides six brigades in reserve, one attached to the central markets, another entrusted with the surveillance of cabs, while the others are held in readiness for exceptional duties, *e.g.* to reinforce the arrondissement brigades at public ceremonies or in times of disorder. In nearly every quarter there is a *commissaire de police*, whose duties are of a semi-legal nature; the police require his sanction before they can commit an arrested individual to prison, and he also fulfils magisterial functions in minor disputes, &c.

Finance.—The chief item of ordinary expenditure is the service of the municipal debt, the total of which in 1905 was nearly £125,000,000. Its annual cost rose from £722,000 in 1860 to £3,583,000 in 1875 and £4,826,000 in 1905. In the latter year the other chief items of expenditure were:—

Poor relief	£1,490,000
Prefecture of police	1,448,000
Primary instruction	1,206,000
Streets and roads	916,000
Water and drainage	579,000
Collection of octroi	471,000

The general total of ordinary expenditure was £14,192,000, and of ordinary and extraordinary expenditure £16,995,000.

The chief of the ordinary sources of revenue are:—

Octroi (municipal customs)	£4,351,000
Communal centimes, dog tax and other special taxes	3,268,000
Revenue from gas company	969,000
Water rate and income from canals	943,000
Public vehicles	614,000
State contribution to, and receipts of prefecture of police	514,000
Revenue from public markets	367,000

The total of ordinary revenue was £14,365,000, and of all revenue, ordinary and extraordinary, £25,426,000.

Communications.—Passenger-transport is in the hands of companies. The ordinary omnibuses are the property of the Compagnie Générale des Omnibus, founded in 1855, which has a charter conferring a monopoly until 1910 in return for a payment of £80 per annum for each vehicle. The organization of the omnibus service is under the supervision of the prefect of the Seine. Since 1906 motor-driven omnibuses have been in use. The Compagnie Générale owns a number of tramways, and there are several other tramway companies. The cab companies, the chief of which are the Compagnie Générale des Voitures and the *compagnie* Urbaine, have no monopoly. The use of the taximeter is general and motor-cabs are numerous. Cabs pay a license fee and are under the surveillance of the prefect of the Seine as regards tariff and the concession of stands. The steamers (*bateaux-omnibus*) ply on the Seine between Charenton and Suresnes.

The great railways of France, with the exception of the Midi railway, have terminal stations in Paris. The principal stations of the northern, eastern and western systems (that of the latter known as the Gare St Lazare) lie near the outer boulevards in the north-centre of the city; the terminus of the Paris-Lyon-Méditerranée railway is in the south-east, close to the right bank of the Seine; opposite to it, on the left bank, is the station du Quai d'Austerlitz,

and on the Quai d'Orsay the Gare du Quai d'Orsay, both belonging to the Orléans railway. The Gare Montparnasse, to the south-west of the Luxembourg, is used by the western and the state railways. Other less important stations are the Gare de Vincennes (line of the eastern railway to Vincennes), the Gares du Luxembourg and de Paris-Denfert (line of the Orleans railway to Sceaux and Limours), and the Gare des Invalides (line of western railway to Versailles). Railway communication round Paris is afforded by the Chemin de Fer de Ceinture, which has some thirty stations along the line of ramparts or near it. The Métropolitain, an electric railway begun in 1898, and running chiefly underground, has a line traversing Paris from east to west (Porte Maillot to the Cours de Vincennes) and a line following the outer boulevards; within the ring formed by the latter there are transverse lines.

Streets.—The total length of the thoroughfares of Paris exceeds 600 m. For the most part, and especially in the business and industrial quarters where traffic is heavy and incessant, they are paved with stone, Yvette sandstone from the neighbourhood of Paris being the chief material. Wood and macadam come next in importance to stone, and there is a small proportion of asphalte roadway. The upkeep and cleansing is under the supervision of a branch of the department of public works (*service technique de la voie publique et de l'éclairage*), and for this purpose the city is divided into sections, each comprising two or three arrondissements. All streets having a width of 25 ft. or more are planted with rows of trees, chestnuts and planes being chiefly used for this purpose, and in many of the wide thoroughfares there are planted strips down the middle.

The upkeep (exclusive of cleansing) of the thoroughfares cost about £500,000, towards which the state, as usual, contributed £120,000 and the department £16,000. In the same year the cleansing cost about £450,000. The original cost of paving a street is borne by the owners of the property bordering it; but in the case of avenues of exceptional width they bear only a proportion of the outlay. Payments are exacted in return for the right to erect newspaper kiosks, &c., to place chairs and tables on the footways and similar concessions.

Water.—The water and sewage system of Paris is supervised by a branch of the public works department (*bureau des eaux, canaux et assainissement*). The water supply comprises a domestic supply of spring water and a supply for industrial and street cleansing purposes, derived from rivers and artesian wells. The domestic supply, which averaged 55,000,000 gallons daily in 1905, has three sources of origin:—

1. The springs of the Dhuis, to the east of Paris, whence the water is conveyed by an aqueduct 82 m. in length to a reservoir in the quarter of Ménilmontant.

2. The springs of the Vanne, south-east of Paris, whence the water comes by an aqueduct 108 m. in length to a reservoir near Montsouris Park. The springs of the Loing and Lunain, south-east of Paris, also supply the Montsouris reservoir.

3. The springs of the Avre, near Verneuil, to the west of the city, the aqueduct from which is 63 m. in length and ends at the St Cloud reservoir.

In addition, filtering installations at the pumping station of Ivry, St Maur and elsewhere make it possible to supplement the domestic supp with river water in hot summers.

Water for public and industrial purposes is obtained (1) from pumping stations at Ivry and other points on the banks of the Seine, and at St Maur on the Marne; (2) from the Ourcq canal, which starts at Mareuil on the Ourcq and ends in the Villette basin; (3) from artesian wells and the aqueduct of Arcueil from Rungis, the latter being of trifling importance. The water is stored in reservoirs in the higher localities of the city, which for the purposes of distribution is divided into zones of altitude; thus the water from the Vanne, stored at the Montsouris reservoir at an altitude of 260 ft., is supplied to the central and lowest part of the city. The upper parts of the quarters of Montmartre, Belleville and Montrouge being too high to benefit by the supply from the ordinary reservoirs, are supplied from elevated reservoirs, to which the water is pumped by special works.

The water is distributed throughout the city by two systems: the low or variable pressure, carrying the river water for use in the streets, courts and industrial premises; the high pressure, taking the spring water to the various floors of buildings, and supplying hydraulic lifts, drinking fountains and fire-plugs. The total length of pipes is nearly 1600 m. The water arrives in all cases from two different directions, so that in case of accident the interruptions of the supply may be reduced to a minimum. Consumers are supplied by meter (*compteur*) at a price of 35 centimes the cubic metre (domestic supply) and at a minimum charge of 16 centimes for river water. In its dealings with individuals the municipality is represented by a company (*Compagnie générale des eaux*), which acts as a collecting agent and receives a commission on the takings. Its charter expires at the end of 1910. In 1905, for the first time, the gross takings reached £800,000.

Drainage.—The drainage system of Paris comprises four main collectors, with a length in all of nearly 20 m.; 27 m. of secondary collectors and several hundred miles of ordinary sewers. Its capacity is such that the Seine (except in certain cases of exceptional pressure, such as sudden and violent storms) is kept free from sewage water, which is utilized on sewage farms. The larger sewers, which vary between 9 and 20 ft. in width, are bordered by ledges, between which the water runs, and are cleansed by means of slides exactly fitting the channel and mounted on wagons or boats propelled by the force of the stream. Of the main collectors, that serving the north-eastern quarters of the city and debouching in the Seine at St Denis is the longest (7½ m.). The other main sewers converge at Clichy, on the right bank of the Seine, where a powerful elevator forces the sewage partly across the bridge, partly through a tunnel acting as a syphon below the river-level, to the left bank. Thence part of it is distributed over the estate of Gennevilliers, from which it returns purified, after having fertilized the plots, to the Seine. At Colombes a second elevator drives the surplus unused sewage to the hills above Argenteuil (right bank), where begins a conduit extending westwards. This conveys a portion of the sewage to a third elevator at Pierrelaye, whence it is distributed on the hills of Méry and the remainder to the Parc d'Achères (left bank), the irrigation fields of Carrières-sous-Poissy (right bank), and finally those of Mureaux, opposite Meulan. Certain parts of Paris lie too low for their drains to run into the main sewers, and special elevators are required to raise the sewage of the districts of Bercy, Javel and the Cité. The sewers are used as conduits for water-pipes, gas-pipes, telegraph and telephone wires and pneumatic tubes.

Lighting.—Gas-lighting in Paris is in the hands of a company whose operations are supervised and directed by municipal engineers. The company pays to the municipality an annual sum of £8000 for the privilege of laying pipes in the streets and 2 centimes for every cubic metre of gas consumed; in addition, the profits of the company, after a fixed dividend has been paid on the stock, are divided with the municipality. The company is bound to supply gas at 30 centimes per cubic metre to private consumers and at half that price for public services. In 1905 the total sum paid by the company amounted to nearly £1,000,000. It was provided that on the expiration of its charter the plant should be made over to the municipality. Electric light is supplied by a number of companies, to each of which in return for certain payments a segment (*secteur électrique*) of the city is assigned, though the concession carries with it no monopoly; the municipality has an electrical station of its own beneath the central markets.

Law and Justice (see FRANCE: *Justice*, for an account of the judicial system of the country as a whole).—Paris is the seat of four courts having jurisdiction over all France: (1) the Tribunal des Conflits, for settling disputes between the judicial and administrative authorities on questions as to their respective jurisdiction; (2) the Council of State, which includes a section for cases of litigation between private persons and public departments; (3) the Cour des Comptes; and (4) the Cour de Cassation. The first three sit in the Palais Royal, the fourth in the Palais de Justice, which is also the seat of (1) a *cour d'appel* for seven departments (seven civil chambers, one chamber of appeal for the correctional police, one chamber for preliminary proceedings); (2) a *cour d'assises* ; (3) a tribunal of first instance for the department of Seine, comprising seven chambers for civil affairs, four chambers of correctional police; (4) a police court where each *juge de paix* presides in his turn assisted by a *commissaire de police*. Litigations between the departmental or municipal administrations and private persons are decided by the *conseil de préfecture*. Besides these courts there are *conseils de prud'hommes* and a tribunal of commerce. The *conseils de prud'hommes* settle differences between workmen and workmen, or between workmen and masters; the whole initiative, however, rests with the parties. There are four of these bodies in Paris (for the metal trades, the chemical trades, the textile trades and building industries), composed of an equal number of masters and men. The tribunal of commerce, sitting in a building opposite the Palais de Justice, is composed of business men elected by the "notables" of their order, and deals with cases arising out of commercial transactions; declarations of bankruptcy are made before it; it also acts as registrar of trademarks and of articles of association of companies; and as court of appeal to the *conseils de prud'hommes*.

Prisons.—There are three places of detention in Paris—the Dépot of the prefecture of police (in the Palais de Justice), where persons arrested and not released by the commissaries of police are temporarily confined, the Conciergerie or *maison de justice*, for the reception of prisoners accused of crimes, who are there submitted to a preliminary examination before the president of the court of assizes, and the Santé (near the Place Denfert-Rochereau), for prisoners awaiting trial and for remanded prisoners. The old prisons of Mazas, Ste Pélagie and La Grande-Roquette, the demolition of which was ordered in 1894, have been replaced by the prison of Fresnes-lès-Rungis for condemned prisoners. The prisoners, kept in solitary confinement, are divided into three groups: those undergoing short sentence, those sentenced to hard labour while awaiting transference to their final place of detention or to sentences over a year, and sick prisoners occupying the central infirmary of the prison. The Petit Roquette (occupied by children) was replaced by the agricultural and horticultural colony of Montesson, inaugurated in 1896.

Education (see also FRANCE).—In 1905 there were 170 public *écoles maternelles* (kindergartens) with 57,000 pupils, and 48 private schools of the kind with 7800 pupils, besides a certain number of *écoles enfantines*, exclusively managed, as are the *écoles maternelles*,

by women, and serving as a link between the latter and the *écoles primaires*, for timid and backward children of from 6 to 8 years of age. There were 374 public primary schools with 173,000 pupils, while over 63,000 children were educated in private primary schools. Subsidiary to the primary schools are the *caisses des écoles* (school treasuries), which give clothing, &c., to indigent children and maintain the *cantines scolaires* for the provision of hot mid-day meals; the *classes de garde* and the *garderies*, which look after children beyond the ordinary school hours; the *classes de vacances*, school camps and school colonies for children during the holidays; and the *internats primaires*, which for a small payment board and lodge children whose parents or guardians are unable to do so satisfactorily.

The higher primary schools (*écoles primaires supérieures*), which give a course of 3 or 4 years, number 66 for boys (Collège Chaptal,[1] *écoles*, J. B. Say, Turgot, Colbert, Lavoisier, Arago) and two for girls (Sophie Germain and Edgar Quinet). Supplementary courses take the place of these schools for children who can afford two years at most for schooling after leaving the primary school. Side by side with the higher primary school, the teaching in which has a commercial rather than an industrial bias, are the *écoles professionelles*, technical schools for the training of craftsmen. The Ecole Diderot trains pupils in wood- and iron-working; the Ecole Germain Pilon teaches practical drawing, and the Ecole Barnard Palissy teaches applied art; the Ecole Boulle trains cabinet-makers, and the Ecole Estienne teaches all the processes connected with book-production. The school of physics and chemistry imparts both theoretical and practical knowledge of these sciences. The Ecole Dorian is a school of the same type as the Ecole Diderot, but is intended for very poor children, who are received from the age of seven and boarded and lodged. Six *écoles ménagères* train girls in the duties and employments of their sex. The municipality also provides gratuitous popular courses in scientific and historical subjects at the Hôtel de Ville, and there are numerous private associations giving courses of instruction (the Philotechnic Association, the Polytechnic Association, the *Union française de la jeunesse*, &c.). Teachers for the elementary primary schools are recruited from two training colleges in the city.

Secondary and Higher Education.—There are 13 lycées for boys and a municipal college—the Collège Rollin. These give classical and modern courses, and usually have classes preparing pupils for one or more of the government schools. For girls there are five lycées.

The five faculties of medicine, law, science, literature and Protestant theology, and the higher school of pharmacy, form the body of faculties, the association of which is known as the *University of Paris*. The faculties of science and literature, together with their library, are established at the Sorbonne, which is also the seat of the *académie*, of which Paris is the centre, and of the *Ecole des chartes*. The faculty of medicine with its laboratories (*école pratique*) occupies separate buildings near the Sorbonne. The law school is also close to the Sorbonne. Of the 12,600 students at the university in 1905-1906 some 1260 were foreigners, Russians and Rumanians being most numerous among the latter. The faculty of law is the most largely attended, some 6000 students being enrolled therein. The Collège de France, founded by Francis I. and situated opposite the Sorbonne, gives instruction of a popular kind to adults of the general public; the various branches of learning are represented by over 40 chairs. The *Muséum d'histoire naturelle* gives instruction in the natural sciences; the *Ecole pratique des hautes études*, whose students are instructed at the Sorbonne and other scientific establishments in the city, has for its object the encouragement of scientific research. In addition, there are several great national schools attached to various ministries. Dependent on the ministry of education are the *Ecole normale supérieure*, for the training of teachers in lycées; the *Ecole des chartes* (palaeography and the use of archives); the *Ecole spéciale des langues orientales*, for the training of interpreters; the *Ecole nationale et spéciale des beaux-arts* (painting, sculpture, architecture, &c.), in the various departments of which are conferred the *prix de Rome*, entitling their winners to a four years' period of study in Italy; the *Conservatoire national de musique et de déclamation* (music and acting), which also confers a *grand prix* and possesses a fine library and collection of musical instruments; the *Ecole nationale des arts décoratifs* (art applied to the artistic industries); the *Ecole du Louvre*, for the instruction of directors of museums. Depending on the ministry of war are the *Ecole polytechnique*, which trains military, governmental and civil engineers; the *Ecole supérieure de guerre* (successor of the officers' training school, founded in 1751) for advanced military studies. Attached to the ministry of commerce and industry are the *Ecole centrale des arts et manufactures* for the training of industrial engineers, works managers, &c.; the *Conservatoire des arts et métiers*, which has a rich museum of industrial inventions and provides courses in science as applied to the arts. The *Institut national agronomique*, a higher school of scientific agriculture, is dependent on the ministry of agriculture, and the *Ecole coloniale* for the instruction

[1] The Collège Chaptal has a wider scope than the higher primary schools; it has in view general culture rather than commercial aptitude, and also prepares students for the great scientific schools (*école des mines*, *école polytechnique*, &c.).　. .

both of natives of French colonies and of colonial functionaries, on the ministry of the colonies. The *École nationale des ponts et chaussées* for the training of government engineers, and the *École nationale supérieure des mines* for mining engineers, are under the minister of public works. Of free institutions of higher education the most prominent are the *Catholic institute*, with faculties of law and theology and schools of advanced literary and scientific studies, the *Pasteur institute*, founded by Pasteur in 1886 and famous for the treatment of hydrophobia and for its research-laboratories, and the school of political science which prepares candidates for political and governmental careers. The two latter receive state subvention. There are numerous private associations giving courses of instruction, the more important being the Philotechnic Association, the Polytechnic Association and the *Union française de la jeunesse*.

Among the numerous learned societies of Paris the first in importance is the Institut de France (see ACADEMIES). The French Association for the advancement of the sciences, founded in 1872, is based on the model of the older British society, and, like it, meets every year in a different town.

In art Paris has long held a leading place. The Société des Artistes français holds an annual *salon* or exhibition in May and June at the Palais d'Industrie. It is open to artists of all nationalities. Works are selected and awards (including the *Prix de Rome*) made by a jury of experts selected by the exhibitors. The society was founded in 1872, but the *salon* takes its name from the academy exhibitions, which, first held in the Palais Royal in 1667, were transferred to the Salon Carré in the Louvre in 1669. As a result of dissension over the awards of 1889, the society of fine arts (Société Nationale des Beaux-Arts) established a separate *salon*, in the Champ de Mars, in May, June and July. There is also a Société du Salon d'Automne.

Charity.—The administration of public charity is entrusted to a responsible director, under the authority of the Seine prefect, and assisted by a board of supervision, the members of which are nominated by the president. The funds at his disposal are derived (1) from the revenue of certain estates, houses, farms, woods, stocks, shares, (2) from taxes on seats in the theatres (one-tenth of the price), balls, concerts, the mont de piété, and allotments in the cemeteries; (3) from the municipal subsidy; (4) from other sources (including voluntary donations). The charges on the administration consist of (1) the treatment of the sick in the hospitals; (2) the lodging of old men and of incurables in the *hospices*; (3) the support of charity children; (4) the distribution of out-door relief (*secours à domicile*) by the *bureaux de bienfaisance*; (5) the dispensation of medical assistance *à domicile*.

The doctors, surgeons, chemists, both resident and non-resident, connected with the numerous hospitals, are all admitted by competitive examination. They are assisted by three grades of students, *internes* (who receive a salary), *externes* and *stagiaires* (probationers).

Of the *hospices* and similar institutions, the following are the chief: Bicêtre (men), less than a mile south of the fortifications; La Salpêtrière (women), Ivry (both sexes); *maisons de retraite* (for persons not without resources) Issy, La Rochefoucauld, Ste Pérines *fondations* (privately endowed institutions)—Brézins at Garches (for ironworkers), Devillas, Chardon-Lagache, Lenoir-Jousseran, Galignani (booksellers, printers, &c.), Alquier-Debrousse; and sections for the insane—Bicêtre (men), Salpêtrière (women), these being distinct from the ordinary departmental asylums controlled by the prefect.

Foundlings and orphans are sent to the *Hospice des enfants assistés*, which also receives children whose parents are patients in the hospitals or undergoing imprisonment. This institution is not intended as a permanent home. Infants are not kept in the institution, but are boarded out with nurses in the country; the older ones are boarded out with families or placed in technical schools. Up to thirteen years of age the children are kept at the expense of the department of Seine, after which they are apprenticed.

The following establishments in or near Paris belong to the nation and are dependent on the ministry of the interior: The Quinze-Vingts gives shelter to the 300 blind for whom it was founded by St Louis, and gives outdoor assistance besides. The blind asylum for the young (*Institution des jeunes aveugles*) has 250 pupils of both sexes. The deaf-mute institution (*Institution nationale des sourds-muets*) is for boys only, and they are generally paid for by the state, the departments and the communes. The Charenton asylum is for the insane. Those of Vincennes (for male patients) and Le Vesinet (for female patients) take in convalescents from the hospitals. The Vacassy asylum at Charenton is for workmen incapacitated by accident. The *Hôtel des invalides* is for old and infirm soldiers. Private bodies also maintain a great number of institutions.

Religion.—Some 75% of the population of Paris is Roman Catholic. The department of Seine forms the diocese of the archbishop of Paris, and the city is divided into 70 parishes. It has the important higher ecclesiastical seminary of St Sulpice, two lower seminaries and others for training the clergy for missionary and colonial work. Paris is also the seat of the central council of the Reformed Church and of the executive committee of the General Synod of the Lutheran Church, and forms a consistory of both these churches, whose adherents together number about 90,000. There are also some 50,000 Jews, Paris being the seat of the Grand Rabbinate of France and of the central consistory.

Industries.—The larger manufacturing establishments of Paris comprise engineering and repairing works connected with the railways, similar private works, foundries and sugar refineries. Government works are the tobacco factories of Gros Caillou and Reuilly, depending on the ministry of finance; the national printing establishment, under the ministry of justice; the mint (with a collection of medals and coins), established in an 18th century building close to the Pont Neuf and under the control of the ministry of finance; and the famous tapestry factory and dye-works (with a tapestry museum) of the Gobelins, under the minister of education. The list of minor establishments is varied, most of them being devoted to the production of the so-called *articles de Paris* (feathers, artificial flowers, dolls, toys and fancy goods in general), and carrying the principle of, the division of labour to an extreme. The establishments which rank next to those above mentioned in the number of workmen are the pharmaceutical factories, the gasworks, the printing-offices, cabinet-makers' workshops, tailoring and dress-making establishments (very numerous) and hat factories.

The textile industries hardly exist in Paris; there are a few tanneries on the Bièvre, but the leather industry is chiefly represented by the production of morocco leather goods classed as *articles de Paris*. Mention may be made here of the *bureaux de placement gratuit*, maintained by the municipality, where those in search of work or workers are put in touch with one another.

Markets.—The slaughter-houses, cattle-yards, and with few exceptions the markets of Paris, belong to the municipality. The chief slaughter-house is the *abattoir général* of La Villette, covering a space of 47 acres in the extreme north-east of the city on the bank of the Canal de l'Ourcq; adjoining it, with an area of about 55 acres, on the opposite bank of the canal, are the municipal cattle-yards and markets, which have accommodation for many thousands of animals, and are connected with the Ceinture railway so that the cattle-trucks are brought straight into the market. Cattle-traders and butchers pay dues for the use of these establishments. There are other less extensive slaughter-yards at Vaugirard. Most of the cattle come from Calvados, Maine-et-Loire, Vaucluse, Nièvre, Loire-Inférieure and Orne; sheep from Seine-et-Marne, Aveyron, Aisne, Seine-et-Oise, Lot and Cantal; pigs from Loire-Inférieure and other western departments; calves from Loiret, Eure-et-Loir and others of the northern departments. Dead meat, game, poultry, fruit, vegetables, fish and the other food-supplies have their centre of wholesale distribution at the Halles Centrales, close to the Louvre, which comprise besides a large uncovered space a number of pavilions of iron and glass covering some 10 acres. Close to the Halles is the Bourse de Commerce, which is a centre for transactions in alcohol, wheat, rye and oats, flour, oil and sugar; and a market for flour, the trade in which is more important than that in wheat, is held in the Place St Germain l'Auxerrois, sales being effected chiefly by the medium of samples. Most of the wines and spirits consumed in Paris pass through the entrepôts of Bercy and the wine-market on the Quai St Bernard, the first specially connected with the wine-trade, the second with the brandy-trade. In addition, there are other provision markets in various quarters of the city, owned and supervised by the municipality, as well as numerous flower-markets, bird-markets, a market for horses, carriages, bicycles and dogs, &c. Two fairs are still held in Paris—the *foire aux jambons* in the Boulevard Richard Lenoir during Holy week, and the *foire au pain d'épices* in the Place de la Nation and its vicinity at Easter time. Market and market-places are placed under the double supervision of the prefect of Seine and the prefect of police. The former official has to do with the authorization, removal, suppression, and holding of the markets, the fixing and collecting of the dues, the choice of sites, the erection and maintenance of buildings, and the location of vehicles. The latter maintains order, keeps the roads clear, and watches against fraud. There is a municipal laboratory, where any purchaser can have the provisions he has bought analysed, and can obtain precise information as to their quality. Spoiled provisions are seized by the agents of the prefecture.

The Chamber of Commerce occupies a building close to the Bourse.

BIBLIOGRAPHY.—P. Joanne, *Dictionnaire géographique et administratif de la France*, vol. v. (Paris, 1899), s.v. " Paris," a comprehensive and detailed account from the topographical, administrative and historical points of view; M. Block, *Dictionnaire de l'administration française*, vol. ii. (Paris, 1905), s.v. " Paris "; *Annuaire statistique de la ville de Paris*, issued by the *Service de la statistique municipale*; Baedeker's *Paris*; T. Okey, *The Story of Paris* (London, 1906); W. F. Lonergen, *Historic Churches of Paris* (London, 1896); G. Pessard, *Nouveau dictionnaire historique de Paris* (Paris, 1904); E. Fournier, *Paris à travers les âges* (Paris, 1876–1882); C. Normand, *Nouvel itinéraire-guide artistique et archéologique de Paris* (Paris, 1889), &c.   (R. Tr.)

History.—At its first appearance in history there was nothing to foreshow the important part which Paris was to play in Europe and in the world. An island in the Seine, now almost lost in the modern city, and then much smaller than at present, was for centuries the entire site. The sole importance of the town lay in its being the capital of a similarly insignificant Gallic people, which navigated the lower course of the Seine, and doubtless from time to time visited the coasts of Britain. So few were its inhabitants that they early put themselves under the protection of their powerful neighbours, the Senones, and this vassalship was the source of the political dependence of Paris on Sens throughout the Roman period, and of a religious subordination which lasted till the 17th century. The capital did not at once take the name of the Parisii, whose centre it was, but long kept that of Lucetia, Lucotetia or Lutetia, of which Lutèce is the generally recognized French form.

During the War of Gallic Independence, after being subjugated by Caesar, who even in 53 B.C. made their territory the meeting-place of deputies from all Gaul, the Parisii took part in the great rising of the year 52, at the same time separating their cause from that of the Senones, who were held in check by Caesar's lieutenant, Labienus. They joined their forces to the army commanded by an Aulercian, the old Camulogenus, which in turn was to unite with the Bellovaci to crush Labienus advancing from Sens to attack the Parisians. Having marched along the right bank of the river till opposite Lutetia, Labienus learned that the Bellovaci were in arms, and, fearing to find himself between two armies at a distance from his headquarters, he sought to get rid of Camulogenus, who, posted on the left bank, endeavoured to bar his way. The bridges had been cut and the town burned by order of the Gallic chief. By means of a stratagem Labienus drew his opponent up the river to the district now occupied by the Jardin des Plantes, and quietly by night crossed the Seine lower down in the neighbourhood of Grenelle, near a place which Caesar calls Metiosedum, identified, but not conclusively, with Meudon. The Gauls, retracing their steps a little, met the Romans and allowed themselves to be routed and dispersed; their leader fell in the fore-front of the battle. Still unsubdued, the Parisii were called upon by the general council assembled in Alesia to furnish eight thousand men to help in raising the siege of that city. It is doubtful whether they were able to contribute the whole of this contingent, when their powerful neighbours the Bellovaci managed to send only two thousand of the ten thousand demanded of them. This was their last effort, and after the check at Alesia they took no part in the desperate resistance offered by the Bellovaci.

Lutetia was somewhat neglected under the Roman emperors of the first centuries. Its inhabitants continued quietly carrying on their river traffic, and devoted part of their wealth to the maintenance of a great temple to Jupiter built on the site of the present cathedral of Notre Dame. It is not known at what date Christianity was introduced into the future capital of France; but it is probable, judging by the use of the title "city," that Lutetia was the see of one of the earliest of the bishoprics of Gallia Celtica. The name of the founder of the church is known, but a keen controversy, not yet settled, has recently been raised with regard to the date when the first Roman missionary, St Dionysius or Denis, reached the banks of the Seine, along with his two deacons, Rusticus and Eleutherius. A pious belief, which, in spite of its antiquity, has its origin in nothing better than parochial vanity, identifies the first-named with Dionysius the Areopagite, who was converted by St Paul at Athens, and thus takes us back to the middle of the 1st century of the Christian era. Better founded in the opinion which dates the evangelization of the city two centuries later; the regular list of bishops, of whom, after Denis, the most famous was St Marcel, begins about 250.

Lutetia was in some sort the cradle of Christian liberty, having been the capital, from 292 to 306, of the mild Constantius Chlorus, who put an end to persecution in Brittany, Gaul and Spain, over which he ruled. This emperor fixed his residence on the banks of the Seine, doubtless for the purpose of watching the Germans without losing sight of Brittany, where the Roman authority was always unstable; perhaps he also felt something of the same fancy for Lutetia which Julian afterwards expressed in his works and his letters. Be that as it may, the fact that these two princes chose to live there naturally drew attention to the city, where several buildings now rose on the left side of the river which could not have been reared within the narrow

boundaries of the island. There was the imperial palace, the remains of which, a magnificent vaulted chamber, beside the Hôtel de Cluny, are now known, probably correctly, as Julian's Baths. At some distance up the river, in the quarter of St Victor, excavations in 1870 and in 1883 laid bare the foundations of the amphitheatre, which was capable of holding about 10,000 spectators, and thus suggests the existence of a population of 20,000 to 25,000 souls. Dwelling-houses, villas, and probably also an extensive cemetery, occupied the slope of the hill of St Geneviève.

It was at Lutetia that, in 360, Julian, already Caesar, was in spite of himself proclaimed Augustus by the legions he had more than once led to victory in Germany. The troops invaded his palace, which, to judge by various circumstances of the mutiny, must have been of great extent. As for the city itself, it was as yet but a little town (πολίχνη) according to the imperial author in his Misopogon. The successive sojourns of Valentinian I. and Gratian scarcely increased its importance. The latest emperors preferred Trèves, Arles, and Vienne in Gaul, and, besides, allowed Paris, about 410, to be absorbed by the powerful Armorican league. When the patricians, Aetius, Aegidius and Syagrius, held almost independent sway over the small portion of Gaul which still held together, they dwelt at Soissons, and it was there that Clovis fixed himself during the ten or eleven years between the defeat of Syagrius (486) and the surrender of Paris (497), which opened its gates, at the advice of St Geneviève, only after the conversion of the Frankish king. In 508, at the return of his victorious expedition against the south, Clovis made Paris the official capital of his realm—*Cathedram regni constituit*, says Gregory of Tours. He chose as his residence the palace of the Thermae, and lost no time in erecting on the summit of the hill, as his future place of interment, the basilica of St Peter and St Paul, which became not long afterwards the church and abbey of St Geneviève. After the death of Clovis, in spite of the supremacy granted to the kingdom of Austrasia, or Metz, Paris remained the true political centre of the various Frankish states, insomuch that the four sons of Clothaire, fearing the prestige which would attach to whoever of them might possess it, made it a sort of neutral town, though after all it was seized by Sigebert, king of Austrasia, Chilperic, king of Neustria (who managed to keep possession for some time, and repaired the amphitheatre), and Guntram, king of Burgundy. The last sovereign had to defend himself in 585 against the pretender Gondovald, whose ambition aspired to uniting the whole of Gaul under his dominion, and marching on Paris to make it the seat of the half-barbarian half-Roman administration of the kingdom of which he had dreamed.

Numerous calamities befell Paris from 586, when a terrible conflagration took place, to the close of the Merovingian dynasty. During a severe famine Bishop Landry sold the church plate to alleviate the distress of the people, and it was probably he who, in company with St Eloi (Eligius), founded the Hôtel Dieu. The kings in the long run almost abandoned the town, especially when the Austrasian influence under the mayors of the palace tended to shift the centre of the Frankish power towards the Rhine.

Though the Merovingian period was for art a time of the deepest decadence, Paris was nevertheless adorned and enriched by pious foundations. Mention has already been made of the abbey of St Peter, which became after the death of Clovis the abbey of St Geneviève. On the same side of the river, but in the valley, Childebert, with the assistance of Bishop St Germain, founded St Vincent, known a little later as St Germain-des-Prés, which was the necropolis of the Frankish kings before St Denis. On the right bank the same king built St Vincent le Rond (afterwards St Germain l'Auxerrois), and in La Cité, beside the cathedral of St Etienne, the basilica of Notre Dame, which excited the admiration of his contemporaries, and in the 12th century obtained the title of cathedral. Various monasteries were erected on both sides of the river, and served to group in thickly-peopled suburbs the population, which had grown too large for the island.

The first Carolingian, Pippin the Short, occasionally lived at Paris, sometimes in the palace of Julian, sometimes in the old palace of the Roman governors of the town, at the lower end of the island: the latter ultimately became the usual residence. Under Charlemagne Paris ceased to be capital; and under Charles the Bald it became the seat of mere counts. But the invasions of the Northmen attracted general attention to the town, and showed that its political importance could no longer be neglected. When the suburbs were pillaged and burned by the pirates, and the city regularly besieged in 885, Paris was heroically defended by its "lords," and the emperor Charles the Fat felt bound to hasten from Germany to its relief. The pusillanimity which he showed in purchasing the retreat of the Normans was the main cause of his deposition in 887, while the courage displayed by Count Odo, or Eudes, procured him the crown of France; Robert, Odo's brother, succeeded him; and, although Robert's son, Hugh the Great, was only duke of France and count of Paris, his power counterbalanced that of the last of the Carolingians, shut up in Laon as their capital.

With Hugh Capet in 987 the capital of the duchy of France definitively became the capital of the kingdom, and in spite of the frequent absence of the kings, several of whom preferred to reside at Orleans, the town continued to increase in size and population, and saw the development of those institutions which were destined to secure its greatness. Henry I. founded the abbey of St Martin-des-Champs, Louis VI. that of St Victor, the mother-house of an order, and a nursery of literature and theology. Under Louis VII. the royal domain was the scene of one of the greatest artistic revolutions recorded in history: the Romanesque style of architecture was exchanged for the Pointed or Gothic, of which Suger, in his reconstruction of the basilica of St Denis, exhibited the earliest type. The capital could not remain aloof from this movement; several sumptuous buildings were erected; the Romanesque choir of St Germain-des-Prés was thrown down to give place to another more spacious and elegant; and when, in 1163, Pope Alexander III. had solemnly consecrated it, he was invited by Bishop Maurice de Sully to lay the first stone of Notre Dame de Paris, a cathedral on a grander scale than any previously undertaken. Paris still possesses the Romanesque nave of St Germain-des-Prés, preserved when the building was rebuilt in the 12th century; the Pointed choir, consecrated in 1163; and the entire cathedral of Notre Dame, which, completed sixty years later, underwent various modifications down to the beginning of the 14th century. The sacristy is modern; the site previous to 1831 was occupied by the episcopal palace, also built by Maurice de Sully, who by a new street had opened up this part of the island. It was Louis VII. also who granted to the Templars the piece of marshland on the left bank of the Seine on which the Paris Temple,[1] the headquarters of the order in Europe, was built (see TEMPLARS).

Philip Augustus may be considered the second founder of Paris. He seldom quitted it save for his military expeditions, and he there built for himself, near St Germain l'Auxerrois, the Louvre, the royal dwelling *par excellence*, whose keep was the official centre of feudalism. He created or organized a regular system of administration, with its headquarters at Paris; and under his patronage the public lectures delivered at Pré-aux-Clercs were regulated and grouped under the title of a university in 1200.

This university, the most famous and flourishing in Christendom, considerably augmented the local population, and formed as it were a new town on the left side of the river, where the great fortified precincts of the Templars, the important abbeys of Ste Geneviève, St Germain-des-Prés and St Victor, and a vast

[1] After the suppression of the Templars in 1312 the Temple was assigned to the Knights of St John. It was used as a state prison in the 14th century, and as barracks in the 16th. The church and the greater part of the other buildings survived in the 17th century. At the Revolution the keep (1265 or 1270) alone survived of the Templars' buildings. It was here that Louis XVI. and the royal family were imprisoned. It became a place of pilgrimage for the Royalists, and was, in consequence, pulled down under the Empire in 1811. Its site is occupied by the Place du Temple.

Carthusian monastery already stood. Colleges were erected to receive the students of the different countries, and became the great meeting-place of the studious youth of all Europe.

The right side of the river, where commerce and industry had taken up their abode, and where the Louvre, the abbey of St Martin, and a large number of secondary religious establishments were already erected, became a centre of activity at least as important as that on the left. The old suburbs, too, were now incorporated with the town and enclosed in the new line of fortifications constructed by Philip Augustus, which, however, did not take in the great abbeys on the left side of the river, and thus obliged them to build defensive works of their own.

Philip Augustus issued from the Louvre a celebrated order, that the streets of the town should be paved. Not far from his palace, on the site of the present Halles Centrales, he laid out an extensive cemetery and a market-place, which both took their name from the Church of the Innocents, a building of the same reign, destroyed at the Revolution. Fountains were placed in all the quarters. As for the lighting of the town, till the close of the 16th century the only lamps were those in front of the madonnas at the street corners. But the first "illumination" of Paris occurred under Philip Augustus: on his return from a victorious expedition to Flanders in 1214 he was welcomed by the Parisians as a conqueror; and the public rejoicings lasted for seven days, "interrupted by no night," says the chronicler, alluding to the torches and lamps with which the citizens lighted up the fronts of their houses. Ferrand, count of Flanders, the traitor vassal, was dragged behind the king to the dungeons of the Louvre.

In 1226 there was held at Paris a council which, by excommunicating Raymond VII., count of Toulouse, helped to prepare the way for the most important treaty which had as yet been signed in the capital. By this treaty (April 12, 1229) the regent, Blanche of Castile, the widow of Louis VIII., obtained from Raymond VII. a great part of his possessions, while the remainder was secured to the house of Capet through the marriage of Alphonse of Poitiers, brother of St Louis, with Jeanne, the heiress of Languedoc.

In affection for his capital St Louis equalled, or even surpassed, his grandfather Philip, and Paris reciprocated his goodwill. The head of the administration was at that time the provost of Paris, a judiciary magistrate and police functionary whose extensive powers had given rise to the most flagrant abuses. Louis IX. reformed this office and filled it with the judge of greatest integrity to be found in his kingdom. This was the famous Étienne Boileau, who showed such vigilance and uprightness that the capital was completely purged of evildoers; the sense of security thus produced attracted a certain number of new inhabitants, and, to the advantage of the public revenue, increased the value of the trade. It was Étienne Boileau who, by the king's express command, drew up those statutes of the commercial and industrial gilds of Paris which, modified by the necessities of new times and the caprice of princes, remained in force till the Revolution.

St Louis caused a partial restoration of St Germain l'Auxerrois, his parish church (completed in the 15th century, and deplorably altered under Louis XV.); and besides preferring the palace of La Cité to the Louvre, he entirely rebuilt it, and rendered it one of the most comfortable residences of his time. Of this edifice there still remain, among the buildings of the present Palais de Justice, the great guard-room, the kitchens with their four enormous chimneys, three round towers on the quay, and, one of the marvels of the middle ages, the Sainte Chapelle, erected in 1248 to receive the crown of thorns sent from Constantinople. This church, often imitated during the 13th and 14th centuries, is like an immense shrine in open work; its large windows contain admirable stained glass of its own date, and its paintings and sculptures (restored in the 19th century by Viollet-le-Duc) give a vivid picture of the religious beliefs of the middle ages. It has a lower storey ingeniously arranged, which served as a chapel for the palace servants. The Sainte Chapelle was designed by Pierre de Montereau, one of the most celebrated architects of his time, to whom is attributed another marvel still extant, the refectory of the abbey of St Martin, now occupied by the library of the Conservatoire des Arts et des Métiers. This incomparable artist was buried in the abbey of St Germain-des-Prés, where, too, he had raised magnificent buildings now no longer existing. Under St Louis, Robert de Sorbon, a common priest, founded in 1253 an unpretending theological college which afterwards became the celebrated faculty of the Sorbonne, whose decisions were wellnigh as authoritative as those of Rome.

The capital of France had but a feeble share in the communal movement which in the north characterizes the 11th, 12th and 13th centuries. Placed directly under the central power, it was never strong enough to force concessions; and in truth it did not claim them, satisfied with the advantages of all kinds secured for it by its political position and its university And, besides, the privileges which it did enjoy, while they could be revoked at the king's pleasure, were of considerable extent. Its inhabitants were not subjected to forced labour or arbitrary imposts, and the liberty of the citizens and their commerce and industry were protected by wise regulations. The university and all those closely connected with it possessed the fullest rights and liberties. There was a municipal or bourgeois militia, which rendered the greatest service to Philip Augustus and St Louis, but afterwards became an instrument of revolt. The communal administration devolved on *échevins* or *jurés*, who, in conjunction with the notables, chose a nominal mayor called provost of the merchants (*prévôt des marchands*). The powers of this official had been grievously curtailed in favour of the provost of Paris and his lieutenants, named by the sovereign. His main duties were to regulate the price of provisions and to control the incidence of taxation on merchandise. He was the chief inspector of bridges and public wells, superintendent of the river police, and commander of the guard of the city walls, which it was also his duty to keep in repair. And, finally, he had jurisdiction in commercial affairs until the creation of the consular tribunals by the chancellor Michel L'Hôpital. The violent attempts made by Étienne Marcel in the 14th century, and those of the communes of 1793 and 1871, showed what reason royalty had to fear too great an expansion of the municipal power at Paris.

The town council met in the 13th and 14th centuries in an unpretending house on Ste Geneviève, near the city walls on the left side of the river. The municipal assemblies were afterwards held near the Place de Crève, on the right side of the river, in the "Maison aux Piliers," which Francis I. allowed to be replaced by an imposing hôtel de ville.

The last of the direct descendants of Capet, and the first two Valois kings did little for their capital. Philip the Fair, however, increased its political importance by making it the seat of the highest court in the kingdom, the parlement, which he organized between 1302 and 1304, and to which he surrendered a part of his cité palace. Under the three sons of Philip the Fair, the Tour de Nesle, which stood opposite, on the site now occupied by the buildings of the Institute, was the scene of frightful orgies, equally celebrated in history and romance. One of the queens, who, if the chronicles are to be trusted, took part in these expiated her crimes in Château-Gaillard, where she was strangled in 1315 by order of her husband, Louis X. During the first part of the War of the Hundred Years, Paris escaped being taken by the English, but felt the effects of the national misfortunes. Whilst destitution excited in the country the revolt of the Jacquerie, in the city the miseries of the time were attributed to the vices of the feudal system, and the citizens seemed ready for insurrection. The provost of the merchants, Étienne Marcel, equally endowed with courage and intellect, sought to turn this double movement to account in the interest of the municipal liberties of Paris and of constitutional guarantees. The cause which he supported was lost through the violence of his own acts. Not content with having massacred two ministers under the very eyes of the dauphin Charles, who was regent whilst his father John lay captive in London, he joined the Jacquerie, and was not afraid to call into Paris the king of Navarre, Charles the Bad, a notorious firebrand, who at that time was making common cause with the English. Public sentiment, at first favourable to Marcel's schemes, shrank from open treason. A watch was set on him, and, at the moment when, having the keys of the town in his possession in virtue of his office, he was preparing to open one of the gates, he was assassinated by order of Jean Maillard, one of the heads of the *milice*, on the night of the 31st of July 1358. Marcel had enlarged Philip Augustus's line of fortifications on the right side of the river, and had begun a new one.

When he became king in 1364, Charles V. forgot the outrages he had suffered at the hands of the Parisians during his regency. He robbed the Louvre to some extent of its military equipment, in order to make it a convenient and sumptuous residence; its open-work staircases and his galleries are mentioned in terms of the highest praise by writers of the time. This did not, however, remain always his favourite palace; having built or rebuilt in the St Antoine quarter the mansion of St Paul or St Pol, he was particularly fond of living in it during the latter part of his life, and it was there that he died in 1380. It was Charles V. who, in conjunction with the provost of Paris, Hugues Aubriot, erected the famous Bastille to protect the St Antoine gate as part of an enlarged scheme of fortification. A library which he founded—a rich one for the times—became the nucleus of the national library. With the exception of some of the upper portions of the Sainte Chapelle, which were altered or reconstructed by this prince or his son Charles VI., there are no remains of the buildings of Charles V.

The reign of Charles VI. was as disastrous for the city as that of his father had been prosperous. From the very accession of the new king, the citizens, who had for some time been relieved by a great reduction of the taxes, and had received a promise of further alleviation, found themselves subjected to the most odious fiscal exactions on the part of the king's uncle, who was not satisfied with the well-stored treasury of Charles V., which he had unscrupulously pillaged. In March 1382 occurred what is called the revolt of the "Maillotins" (*i.e.* men with mallets): Preoccupied with his expedition against the Flemings, Charles VI. delayed putting down the revolt, and for the moment remitted the new taxes. On his victorious return on the 10th of January 1383, the Parisians in alarm drew up their forces in front of the town gates under the pretext of showing their sovereign what aid he might derive from them, but really in order to intimidate him. They were ordered to retire within the walls and to lay down their arms, and they obeyed. The king and his uncles, having destroyed the gates, made their way into Paris as into a besieged city; and with the decapitation of Desmarets, one of the most faithful servants of the Crown, began a series of bloody executions. Ostensibly through the intercession of the regents an end was put to that species of severities, a heavy fine being substituted, much larger in amount than the annual value of the abolished taxes. The municipal administration was suspended for several years, and its functions bestowed on the provost of Paris, a magistrate nominated by the Crown.

The calamities which followed were due to the weakness and incapacity of the government, given over, because of the madness of Charles VI., to the intrigues of a wicked queen and of princes who brought the most bloodthirsty passions to the service of their boundless ambition. First came the rivalry between the dukes of Orleans and Burgundy, brought to an end in 1407 by assassination of the former. Next followed the relentless struggle for supremacy between two hostile parties: the Armagnacs on one side, commanded by Count Bernard of Armagnac (who for a brief period had the title of constable), and supported by the nobles and burgesses; and on the other side the Burgundians, depending on the common people, and recognizing John the Fearless, duke of Burgundy, as their head. The mob was headed by a skinner at the Hôtel Dieu called Simon Caboche, and hence the name *Cabochiens* was given to the Burgundian party in Paris. They became masters of Paris in' 1412 and 1413; but so violent were their excesses that the most timid rose in revolt, and the decimated bourgeoisie managed by a bold stroke to recover possession of the town. The Armagnacs again entered Paris, but their intrigues with England and their tyranny rendered them odious in their turn; the Burgundians were recalled in 1418, and returned with Caboche and a formidable band of pillagers and' assassins. Perrinet Leclerc, son of a bourgeois guard, secretly opened the gates to them one night in May. The king resided in the Hôtel St Paul, an unconscious spectator of those savage scenes which the princes Louis and John, successively dauphins, were helpless to prevent.

The third dauphin, Charles, afterwards Charles VII., managed to put an end to the civil war, but it was by a crime as base as it was impolitic—the assassination of John the Fearless on the bridge of Montereau in 1419. Next year a treaty, from the ignominy of which Paris happily escaped, gave a daughter of Charles VI. to Henry V. of England, and along with her, in spite of the Salic law, the crown of France. The king of England made his entry into Paris in December 1420, and was there received with a solemnity which ill concealed the misery and real consternation of the poor people crushed by fifteen years of murders, pillage and famine. Charles VI. remained almost abandoned at the Hôtel St Paul, where he died in 1422, whilst his son-in-law went to hold a brilliant court at the Louvre and Vincennes. Henry V. of England also died in 1422. His son Henry VI., then one year old, came to Paris nine years later to be crowned at Notre Dame, and the city continued under the government of the duke of Bedford till his death in 1435.

The English rule was a mild one, but it was not signalized by the execution of any of those works of utility or ornament so characteristic of the kings of France. The choir of St Severin, however, shows a style of architecture peculiarly English, and Sauval relates that the duke of Bedford erected in the Louvre a 'fine gallery decorated with paintings. Without assuming the mission of delivering Paris, Joan of Arc, remaining with Charles VII. after his coronation at Reims, led him towards the capital; but the badly conducted and abortive enterprise almost proved fatal to the Maid of Orleans, who was severely wounded at the assault of the gate of St Honoré on the 8th of September 1429. The siege having been raised, Charles awaited the invitation of the Parisians themselves upon the defection of the Burgundians and the surrender of St Denis. The St Jacques gate was opened by the citizens of the guard to the constable de Richemont[1] on the 13th of April 1436; but the solemn entry of the king did not take place till November of the following year; subsequently occupied by his various expeditions or attracted by his residences in Berry or Touraine, he spent but little time in Paris, where he retired either to the Hôtel St Paul or to a neighbouring palace, Les Tournelles, which had been acquired by his father.

Louis XI. made equal use of St Paul and Les Tournelles, but towards the close of his life he immured himself at Plessis-les-Tours: It was in his reign, in 1469, that the first French printing-press was set up in the Sorbonne. Charles VIII. scarcely left Plessis-les-Tours and Amboise except to go to Italy; Louis XII. alternated between the castle at Blois and the palace of Les Tournelles, where he died on the 1st of January 1515.

Francis I. lived at Chambord, at Fontainebleau, at St Germain, and at Villers-Cotterets; but he proposed to form at Paris a residence in keeping with the taste of the Renaissance. Paris had remained for more than thirty years almost a stranger to the artistic movement begun between 1498 and 1500, after the Italian expedition. Previous to 1533, the date of the commencement of the Hôtel de Ville and the church of St Eustache, Paris did not possess, apart from the "Court of Accounts," any important building in the new style. Between 1527 and 1540 Francis I. demolished the old Louvre, and in 1541 Pierre Lescot began a new palace four times as large, which was

[1] Arthur, earl of Richmond, afterwards Arthur III. (q.v.), duke of Brittany.

XX 14

not finished till the reign of Louis XIV. The buildings were not sufficiently advanced under Henry II. to allow of his leaving Les Tournelles, where in 1559 he died from a wound received at a tournament. His widow, Catherine de' Medici, immediately caused this palace to be demolished, and sent her three sons—Francis II., Charles IX. and Henry III.—to the unfinished Louvre. Outside the line of the fortifications she laid the foundations of the Château des Tuileries as a residence for herself.

Of the three brothers, it was Charles IX. who resided most at the Louvre; it was there that' in 1572 he signed the order for the massacre of St Bartholomew. Henry III. remained for the most part at Blois, and hardly came to Paris except to be witness of the power of his enemies, the Guises.

Taking advantage of the absence of the kings, the League had made Paris a centre of opposition. The municipal militia were restored and reorganized; each of the 16 quarters or arrondissements had to elect a deputy for the central council, which became the council, or rather faction, of The Sixteen, and for four years, from 1587 to 1591, held the city under a yoke of iron. Henry III., having come to the Louvre in 1588, unwillingly received there the duke of Guise, and while endeavouring to take measures for his own protection provoked a riot known as the Day of the Barricades (May 12). It was with difficulty that he escaped from his palace, which at that time had no communication with the country, and which Henry IV. afterwards proposed to unite with the Tuileries in order to provide a sure means of escape in case of need.

When, after the murder of the duke of Guise at Blois at the close of 1588, Henry III. desired to return to Paris, he was not yet master of the city, and was obliged to besiege it in concert with his presumptive heir, the king of Navarre. The operations were suddenly interrupted on the 1st of August 1589, by the assassination of the king, and Henry IV. carried his arms elsewhere. He returned with his victorious forces in 1590. This second siege lasted more than four years, and was marked by terrible suffering, produced by famine and the tyranny of The Sixteen, who were supported by the intrigues of the king of Spain and the violent harangues of the preachers. Even the conversion of the king did not allay the spirit of fanaticism, for the king's sincerity was suspected, and the words (which history, however, fails to substantiate), "Paris is surely worth a mass," were attributed to him. But after the coronation of the king at Chartres the commonalty of Paris, weary of intriguing with strangers and Leaguers, gave such decided expression to its feelings that those of its leaders who had kept aloof, or broken off from the faction of The Sixteen attached themselves to the parlement, which had already evaded the ambitious designs of the king of Spain; and after various negotiations the provost of the merchants, L'Huillier, offered the keys of the city to Henry IV. on the 22nd of March 1594. The king met no resistance except on the part of a company of German landsknechts, which was cut in pieces, and the students of the university, who, steeped in the doctrines of the League, tried to hold their quarter against the royal troops, but were dispersed. The Spanish soldiers who had remained in the town decamped next da .

Henry IV., who carried on the building of the Louvre, was the last monarch who occupied it as a regular residence. Attempts on his life were made from time to time, and at last, on the 14th of May 1610, he fell under Ravaillac's knife near the market-house in Rue de la Ferronnerie.

Whether royalty gave it the benefit of its presence or not, Paris continued all the same to increase in political importance and in population. Here is the picture of the city presented about 1560 by Michel de Castelnau, one of the most celebrated chroniclers of the 16th century:—

"Paris is the capital of all the kingdom, and one of the most famous in the world, as well for the splendour of its parlement (which is an illustrious company of thirty judges attended by three hundred advocates and more, who have reputation in all Christendom of being the best seen in human laws and acquainted with justice) as for its faculty of theology and for the other tongues and sciences,

2a

which shine more in this town than in any other in the world, besides the mechanic arts and the marvellous traffic which render it very populous, rich and opulent; in such sort that the other towns of France and all the magistrates and subjects have their eyes directed thither as to the model of their decisions and their political administrations."

Castelnau spoke rather as a statesman and a magistrate, and did not look close enough to see that the university was beginning to decline. The progress of the sciences somewhat lessened the importance of its classes, too specially devoted to theology and literature; the eyes of men were turned towards Italy, which was then considered the great centre of intellectual advance; the colleges of the Jesuits were formidable rivals; the triumphs of Protestantism deprived it of most of the students, who used to flock to it from England, Germany and Scandinavia; and finally the unfortunate part it played in political affairs weakened its influence so much that, after the reign of Henry IV. it no longer sent its deputies to the states-general.

If the city on the left side of the river neither extended its circuit nor increased its population, it began in the 16th century to be filled with large mansions (hôtels), and its communications with the right bank were rendered easier and more direct when Henry IV. constructed across the lower end of the island of La Cité the Pont Neuf, which, though retaining its original name, is now the oldest bridge in Paris. On the right side of the river commerce and the progress of centralization continued to attract new inhabitants, and old villages become suburbs were enclosed within the line of a bastioned first enceinte, the ramparts of Étienne Marcel being, however, still left untouched. Although Louis XIII., except during his minority, rarely stayed much in Paris, he was seldom long absent from it. His mother, Mary de' Medici, built the palace of the Luxembourg, which, after being extended under Louis Philippe, became the seat of the senate.

Louis XIII. finished, with the exception of the eastern front, the buildings enclosing the square court of the Louvre, and carried on the wing which was to join the palace to the Tuileries. Queen Anne of Austria founded the Val de Grâce, the dome of which, afterwards painted on the interior by Mignard, remains one of the finest in Paris. Richelieu built for himself the Palais Royal, since restored, and rebuilt the Sorbonne, where now stands his magnificent tomb by Girardon. The island of St Louis above La Cité, till then occupied by gardens and meadows, became a populous parish, whose streets were laid out in straight lines, and whose finest houses still date from the 17th century. Building also went on in the Quartier du Marais (quarter of the marsh); and the whole of the Place Royale (now Place des Vosges), with its curious arcaded galleries, belongs to this period. The church of St Paul and St Louis was built by the Jesuits beside the ruins of the old Hôtel St Paul; the church of St Gervais received a façade which has become in our time too famous. St Étienne du Mont and St Eustache were completed (in the latter case with the exception of the front). The beautiful Salle des Pas-Perdus (Hall of Lost Footsteps) was added to the Palais de Justice. Besides these buildings and extensions Paris was indebted to Louis XIII. and his minister Richelieu for three important institutions—the royal printing press in 1620, the Jardin des Plantes in 1626, and the French Academy in 1635. The bishopric of Paris was separated from that of Sens and erected into an archbishopric in 1623.

As memorials of Mazarin Paris still possesses the Collège des Quatre-Nations, erected with one of his legacies immediately after his death, and since appropriated to the Institute, and the palace which, enlarged in the 19th century, now accommodates the national library.

The stormy minority of Louis XIV. was spent at St Germain and Paris, where the court was held at the Palais Royal. The intrigues of the prince of Condé, Cardinal de Retz, and (for a brief space) Turenne resulted in a siege of Paris, during which more epigrams than balls were fired off; but the cannon of the Bastille, discharged by order of Mademoiselle de Montpensier, enabled Condé to enter the city. Bloody riots followed, and came to an end only with the exhaustion of the populace and

its voluntary submission to the king. Though Louis XIV. ceased to stay in Paris after he grew up, he did not neglect the work of embellishment. On the site of the fortifications of Étienne Marcel, which during the previous hundred years had been gradually disappearing, he laid out the line of boulevards connecting the quarter of the Bastille with that of the Madeleine. Though he no longer inhabited the Louvre (and it never was again the seat of royalty), he caused the great colonnade to be constructed after the plans of Claude Perrault. This immense and imposing façade, 548 ft. long, has the defect of being quite out of harmony with the rest of the building, which it hides instead of introducing. The same desire for effect, altogether irrespective of congruity, appears again in the observatory erected by the same Perrault, without the smallest consideration of the wise suggestions made by Cassini. The Place Vendôme, the Place des Victoires, the triumphal gates of St Denis and St Martin and several fountains, are also productions of the reign of Louis XIV. The hospital of La Salpêtrière, with its majestically simple dome, was finished by Libéral Bruant. The Hôtel des Invalides, one of the finest institutions of the grand monarque, was also erected, with its chapel, between 1671 and 1675, by Bruant; but it was reserved for the architect Hardouin Mansart to give to this imposing edifice a complement worthy of itself: it was he who raised the dome, admirable alike for its proportions, for the excellent distribution of its ornaments, and for its gilded lantern, which rises 344 ft. above the ground. "Private persons," says Voltaire, "in imitation of their king, raised a thousand splendid edifices. The number increased so greatly that from the neighbourhood of the Palais Royal and of St Sulpice there were formed in Paris two new towns much finer than the old one." All the aristocracy had not thought fit to take up their residence at Versailles, and the great geniuses of the century, Corneille, Racine, La Fontaine, Molière, Madame de Sévigné, had their houses in Paris; there also was the Hôtel de Rambouillet, so famous in the literary history of the 17th century.

The halls of the Palais Royal during the minority of Louis XV. were the scene of the excesses of the regency; later on the king from time to time resided at the Tuileries, which henceforward came to be customarily regarded as the official seat of the monarchy. To the reign of Louis XV. are due the rebuilding of the Palais Royal, the "Place" now called De la Concorde, the military school, the greater part of the church of Ste Geneviève, or Panthéon (a masterpiece of the architect Soufflot), the church of St Roch, the palace of the Élysée (now the residence of the president of the republic), the Palais Bourbon (with the exception of the façade), now occupied by the chamber of deputies, and the mint, a majestic and scholarly work by the architect Antoine, as well as the rebuilding of the Collège de France.

Louis XVI. finished or vigorously carried on the works begun by his grandfather. He did not come to live in Paris till compelled by the Revolution. That historical movement began indeed at Versailles on the 17th of June 1789, when the states-general were transformed into a constituent assembly; but the first act of violence which proved the starting-point of all its excesses was performed in Paris on the 14th of July 1789 when Paris inaugurated, with the capture of the Bastille, its "national guard," organized and then commanded by the celebrated La Fayette. At the same time the assassination of the last provost of the merchants, Jacques de Flesselles, gave the opportunity of establishing, with more extended powers, the mairie (mayoralty) of Paris, which was first occupied by Bailly, and soon became, under the title of commune, a political power capable of effectively counterbalancing the central authority.[1]

Paris had at that time once more outgrown its limits. The quarter on the left side of the river had more than doubled its extent by the accession of the great monasteries, the faubourgs of St Germain and St Marceau, the Jardin des Plantes, and

[1] Owing to the armed and organized revolutionary elements in the assemblies of the Sections, which enabled the revolutionary commune to direct and control popular émeutes.

the whole of Mont Ste Geneviève. The line of the new enceinte is still marked by a circuit of boulevards passing from the Champs de Mars at Pont d'Austerlitz by Place de l'Enfer and Place d'Italie. Similar enlargements, also marked out by a series of boulevards, incorporated with the town on the right side of the faubourgs of St Antoine and Poissonnière and the quarters of La Chaussée d'Antin and Chaillot. In 1784 was begun, instead of a line of fortifications, a simple customs-wall, with sixty propylaea or pavilions in a heavy but characteristic style, of which the finest are adorned with columns or pilasters like those of Paestum. In front of the Place du Trône (now Place de la Nation), which formed as it were a façade for Paris on the east side, there were erected two lofty rostral columns bearing the statues of Philip Augustus and St Louis. Towards the west, the city front was the Place Louis XV. (Place de la Concorde), preceded by the magnificent avenue of the Champs Élysées. Between the barriers of La Villette and Pantin, where the highways for Flanders and Germany terminated, was built a monumental rotunda flanked on the ground floor by four peristyles arranged as a Greek cross, and in the second storey lighted by low arcades supported by columns of the Paestum type. None of these works were completed till the time of the empire. It was also in the latter part of the reign of Louis XIV., and under the first republic, that the quarter of La Chaussée d'Antin was built.

The history of Paris during the Revolutionary period is the history rather of France, and to a certain extent of the whole world (see FRANCE: *History*; FRENCH REVOLUTION; and the articles on the JACOBINS and other clubs). During the Consulate hardly anything of note took place at Paris except the explosion of the infernal machine directed against Bonaparte on the 24th of December 1800.

The coronation of Napoleon by Pope Pius VII. was celebrated in Notre Dame on the 2nd of December 1804. Eight years later, during the Russian campaign, the conspiracy of General Malet, happily suppressed, was on the point of letting loose on all France a dreadful civil war. The empire, however, was then on the wane, and Paris was witness of its fall when, after a battle on the heights of Montmartre and at the *barrière de Clichy*, the city was obliged to surrender to the allies on the 30th of March 1814.

For the next two months the city was in the occupation of the allies and witnessed a hitherto unique assembly of sovereigns and statesmen. Their deliberations issued on the 30th of May 1814 in the first treaty of Paris (see PARIS, *Treaties of*, below). So far as the city itself was concerned, the only permanent loss that it suffered through the occupation was that of the art treasures with which Napoleon had enriched it at the expense of other capitals; among these were many paintings and pieces of statuary from the Louvre, and the famous bronze horses from Venice, which were taken down from the triumphal arch of the Carrousel and restored to the façade of St Mark's. The expressed determination of Blücher and his Prussians to blow up the Pont de Jéna, built to commemorate Napoleon's crushing victory of 1806, was frustrated by the vigorous intervention of Wellington and of the emperor Alexander I.

Paris under the Restoration witnessed the revival of religious ceremonials to which it had long been unaccustomed, notably the great Corpus Christi procession, in which the king himself carried a candle. Then came Napoleon's return from Elba (March 1815) and the interlude of the Hundred Days. After Waterloo, though there was fighting round Paris, there was no effort to defend the city against the allied armies; for the Parisians had grown thoroughly weary of Napoleon, and Louis XVIII., though he returned "in the baggage train of the enemy," was received by the populace with rapturous acclamation (see LOUIS XVIII.). The second treaty of Paris was signed on the 20th of November of the same year (see below). It left France in the occupation of 150,000 foreign troops, and the crown and government under the tutelage of a committee of representatives of the foreign great powers in Paris.

Paris now became the centre of the royalist reaction, and of

a political proscription which reflected, though without its popular excesses, the White Terror of the South. The most conspicuous event of this time was the tragedy of the trial and execution of Marshal Ney (*q.v.*). For the rest, the only event of note that occurred in Paris under Louis XVIII. was the assassination of the duke of Berry by Louvel on the 13th of February 1820. Ten years later the revolution of 1830,[1] splendidly commemorated by the Column of July in Place de la Bastile, put Charles X. to flight and inaugurated the reign of Louis Philippe, a troublous period which was closed by the revolution of 1848 and a new republic. It was this reign, however, that surrounded Paris with bastioned fortifications with ditches and detached forts, the outcome of the warlike fever aroused by the exclusion of France from the treaty of London of 1840 (see MEHEMET ALI). The republic of 1848 brought no greater quiet to the city than did the reign of Louis Philippe. The most terrible insurrection was that of the 23rd-26th of June 1848, distinguished by the devotion and heroic death of the Archbishop Affre. It was quelled by General Cavaignac, who then for some months held the executive power. Prince Louis Napoleon next became president of the republic, and after dissolving the chamber of deputies on the 2nd of December 1851, caused himself to be proclaimed emperor just a year later.

The second empire completed that material transformation of Paris which had already been begun at the fall of the ancient monarchy. First came numerous cases of destruction and demolition caused by the suppression of the old monasteries and of many parish churches. A number of medieval buildings, civil or military, were cleared away for the sake of regularity of plan and improvements in the public streets, or to satisfy the taste of the owners, who thought more of their comfort or profit than of the historic interest of their old mansions or houses.

It was under the first empire that the new series of improvements were inaugurated which have made Paris a modern city. Napoleon began the Rue de Rivoli, built along this street the wing intended to connect the Tuileries with the Louvre, erected in front of the court of the Tuileries the triumphal arch of the Carrousel, in imitation of that of Septimius Severus at Rome. In the middle of the Place Vendôme was reared, on the model of Trajan's column, the column of the Grand Army, surmounted by the statue of the emperor. To immortalize this same Grand Army he ordered from the architect Pierre Vignon a Temple of Victory, which without changing the form of its Corinthian peristyle has become the church of the Madeleine; the entrance to the avenue of the Champs Élysées was spanned by the vast triumphal arch De l'Étoile (of the star), which owes its celebrity not only to its colossal dimensions and its magnificent situation, but also to one of the four subjects sculptured upon its faces —the *Chant du départ* or *Marseillaise*, one of the masterpieces of Rude and of modern sculpture. Another masterpiece was executed by David of Angers—the pediment of the Panthéon, not less famous than Soufflot's dome. The museum of the Louvre, founded by decree of the Convention on the 27th of July 1793, was organized and considerably enlarged; that of the Luxembourg was created in 1805, but was not appropriated exclusively to modern artists till under the Restoration. The Conservatoire des Arts et Métiers, due to the Convention, received also considerable additions in the old priory or abbey of St Martin des Champs, where the council of the Five Hundred had installed it in 1798.

Under the Restoration and under the government of July many new buildings were erected; but, with the exception of the Bourse, constructed by the architects Brongniart and Labarre, and the colonnade of the Chamber of Deputies, these are of interest not so much for their size as for the new artistic tendencies affected in their architecture. People had grown weary of the eternal Graeco-Roman compilations rendered

[1] Notable in the history of the city for the discovery by the populace of the effectiveness of barricades against regular troops. These had been last used in the Fronde.

2a

fashionable by the Renaissance, and reduced under the empire to mere imitations, in producing which all inspiration was repressed. The necessity of being rational in architecture, and of taking full account of practical wants, was recognized; and more suggestive and plastic models were sought in the past. These were to be found, it was believed, in Greece; and in consequence the government under Louis Philippe saw itself obliged to found the French school at Athens, in order to allow young artists to study their favourite types on the spot. In the case of churches it was deemed judicious to revive the Christian basilicas of the first centuries, as at Notre Dame de Lorette and St Vincent de Paul; and a little later to bring in again the styles of the middle ages, as in the ogival church of St Clotilde.

Old buildings were also the object of labours more or less important. The Place de la Concorde was altered in various ways, and adorned with eight statues of towns and with two fountains; on the 25th of October 1836 the Egyptian obelisk, brought at great expense from Luxor, was erected in the centre. The general restoration of the cathedral of Notre Dame was voted by the Chamber in 1845, and entrusted to Viollet-le-Duc; and the palace of the Luxembourg and the Hôtel de Ville were considerably ·enlarged at the same time, in the style of the existing edifices.

But the great transformer of Paris in modern times was Napoleon III. To him or to his reign we owe the Grand Opéra, the masterpiece of the architect Garnier; the new Hôtel-Dieu; the finishing of the galleries which complete the Louvre and connect it with the Tuileries; the extension of the Palais de Justice and its new front on the old Place Dauphine; the tribunal of commerce; the central markets; several of the finest railway stations; the viaduct at Auteuil; the churches of La Trinité, St Augustin, St Ambroise, St François Xavier, Belleville, Ménilmontant, &c. For the first international Paris exhibition (that of 1855) was constructed the " palace of industry "; the enlargement of the national library was commenced; the museum of French antiquities was created by the savant Du Sommerard, and installed in the old "hôtel" built at the end of the 15th century for the abbots of Cluny.

All this is but the smallest part of the memorials which Napoleon III. left of his presence. Not only was the city traversed in all directions by new thoroughfares, and sumptuous houses raised or restored in every quarter, but the line of the fortifications was made in 1859 the limit of the city. The area was thus doubled, extending to 7450 hectares or 18,410 acres, instead of 3402 hectares or 8407 acres. It was otherwise with the population; to the 1,200,000 inhabitants which Paris possessed in 1858 the incorporation of the suburban zone only added 600,000.

Paris had to pay dear for its growth and prosperity under the second empire. This government, which, by straightening and widening the streets, thought it had effectually guarded against the attempts of its internal enemies, had not sufficiently defended itself from external attack, and at the first reverses of 1870 Paris found itself prepared to overthrow the empire, but by no means able to hold out against the approaching Prussians.

The two sieges of Paris in 1870-71 are among the most dramatic episodes of its history. The first siege began on the 19th of September 1870, with the occupation by the Germans of the heights on the left side of the river and the capture of the unfinished redoubt of Châtillon. Two days later the investment was complete. General Trochu, head of the French Government and governor of the city, had under his command 400,000 men—a force which ought to have been able to hold out against the 240,000 Germans by whom it was besieged, had it not been composed for the most part of hurried levies of raw soldiers with inexperienced officers, and of national guards who, never having been subjected to strict military discipline, were a source of weakness rather than of strength. The guards, it is true, displayed a certain warlike spirit, but it was for the sole purpose of exciting disorder. Open revolt broke out on the 31st of October; it was suppressed, but increased the

demoralization of the besieged and the demands of the Prussians. The partial successes which the French obtained in engagements on both sides of the river were rendered useless by the Germans recapturing all the best positions; the severity of winter told heavily on the garrison, and the armies in the provinces which were to have co-operated with it were held in check by the Germans in the west and south. In obedience to public opinion a great sortie was undertaken; this, in fact, was the only alternative to a surrender; for, the empire having organized everything in expectation of victory and not of disaster, Paris, insufficiently provisioned for the increase of population caused by the influx of refugees, was already suffering the horrors of famine. Accidental circumstances combined with the indecision of the leaders to render the enterprise a failure. Despatches sent by balloon to the army of the Loire instructing it to make a diversion reached their destination too late; the bridge of Champigny over the Marne could not be constructed in time; the most advantageous positions remained in the hands of the Germans; and on the 2nd and 3rd of December the French abandoned the positions they had seized on the 29th and 30th of November. Another sortie made towards the north on the 21st of December was repulsed, and the besieged lost the Avron plateau, the key to the positions which they still held on that side. The bombardment began on the 17th of December, and great damage was done to the forts on the left of the Seine, especially those of Vanves and Issy, directly commanded by the Châtillon battery. A third and last sortie (which proved fatal to Regnault the painter) was attempted in January 1871, but resulted in hopeless retreat. An armistice was signed on the 27th of January, the capitulation on the 28th. The revictualling of the city was not accomplished without much difficulty, in spite of the generous rivalry of foreign nations (London alone sending provisions to the value of £80,000).

On the 1st of March the Germans entered Paris. This event, which marked the close of the siege, was at the same time the first preparation for the "commune;" for the national guard, taking advantage of the general confusion and the powerlessness of the regular army, carried a number of cannon to the heights of Montmartre and Belleville under pretext of saving them. President Thiers, appreciating the danger, attempted on the 18th of March to remove the ordnance; his action was the signal of an insurrection which, successful from the first, initiated a series of terrible outrages by the murder of the two generals, Lecomte and Thomas. The government, afraid of the defection of the troops, who were demoralized by failure and suffering, had evacuated the forts on the left side of the river and concentrated the army at Versailles (the forts on the right side were still to be held for some time by the Germans). Mont Valérien happily remained in the hands of the government and became the pivot of the attack during the second siege. All the sorties made by the insurgents in the direction of Versailles (where the National Assembly was in session from the 20th of March) proved unsuccessful, and cost them two of their improvised leaders—Generals Flourens and Duval. The incapacity and mutual hatred of their chiefs rendered all organization and durable resistance impossible. On Sunday the 21st of May the government forces, commanded by Marshal MacMahon, having already captured the forts on the right side of the river, made their way within the walls; but they had still to fight hard from barricade to barricade before they were masters of the city; Belleville, the special Red Republican quarter, was not assaulted and taken till Friday. Meanwhile the communists were committing the most horrible excesses: the archbishop of Paris (Georges Darboy, q.v.), President Bonjean, priests, magistrates, journalists and private individuals, whom they had seized as hostages, were shot in batches in the prisons; and a scheme of destruction was ruthlessly carried into effect by men and women with cases of petroleum (pétroleurs and pétroleuses). The Hôtel de Ville, the Palais de Justice, the Tuileries, the Ministry of Finance, the palace of the Legion of Honour, that of the Council of State, part of the Rue de Rivoli, &c., were ravaged by the flames; barrels of gunpowder were placed in Notre Dame and the Pantheon, ready to blow up the buildings; and the whole city would have been involved in ruin if the national troops had not gained a last and crowning victory in the neighbourhood of La Roquette and Père-la-Chaise on the 28th of May. Besides the large number of insurgents who, taken in arms, were pitilessly shot, others were afterwards condemned to death, to penal servitude, to transportation; and the survivors only obtained their liberty by the decree of 1879.

From this double trial Paris emerged diminished and almost robbed of its dignity as capital; for the parliamentary assemblies and the government went to sit at Versailles. For a little it was thought that the city would not recover from the blow which had fallen on it. All came back, however—confidence, prosperity, and, along with that, increasing growth of population and the execution of great public works. The Hôtel de Ville was rebuilt, the school of medicine adorned with an imposing façade, a vast school of pharmacy established in the old gardens of the Luxembourg, and boulevards completed. The exhibition of 1878 was more marvellous than those of 1855 and 1867, and left a lasting memorial—the palace of the Trocadéro. And the chambers in 1879 considered quiet sufficiently restored to take possession of their customary quarters in the Palais Bourbon and the Luxembourg.　　　　　　　　　(A. S.-P.; W. A. P.)

The Universal Exhibition of 1878, destined to show Europe that France had recovered her material prosperity and moral power, attracted a large concourse. The number of admissions was about 13,000,000. A grand fête, full of gaiety and enthusiasm, was held on the 30th of June. This was the first public rejoicing since the war. The terrible winter of 1879–1880 was the severest of the century; the Seine, entirely frozen, resembled a sea of ice. The 14th of July, the anniversary of the taking of the Bastille, was adopted as the French national holiday and celebrated for the first time in 1880. A grand military review was held in the Bois de Boulogne, at which President Grévy distributed flags to all the regiments of the army. On the 17th of March 1881 a national loan of a thousand million francs was issued for the purpose of executing important public works. This loan was covered fifteen times, Paris alone subscribing for ten thousand millions. At the time of the legislative elections, on the 21st of August and the 4th of September 1881, several tumults occurred in the Belleville district, Gambetta, who was a candidate in the two wards of that district vainly tried to address the electors. The great orator died in the following year, on the 31st of December, from the effects of an accident, and his funeral, celebrated in Paris at the expense of the State, was attended by an immense gathering. A slight Legitimist agitation followed Gambetta's death. An unfortunate event occurred on the 29th of September 1883, the day when the king of Spain, Alphonso XII., returned from his visit to Berlin, where he had reviewed the 15th regiment of Prussian Uhlans, of which he was the honorary colonel. The cries of "Down with the Uhlan!" with which he was greeted by the Paris crowd, gave rise to serious diplomatic incidents. On the 26th of May 1885 the following decree was rendered: "The Pantheon is restored to its primitive and legal destination. The remains of the great men who have merited national recognition will be disposed therein." But it was only on the 4th of August 1899 that the ashes of Lazare Carnot, Hoche, Marceau, Latour d'Auvergne and Baudin were solemnly transported to the Pantheon. Victor Hugo's funeral was celebrated on the 1st of June 1885, and by an urgency vote they were made national obsequies. It was decided that the corpse should be exposed one day and one night under the Arc de Triomphe, veiled with an immense crape. A few days before, upon the occasion of the anniversary of the fall of the Commune, a tumultuous political manifestation had been made in front of the tomb of the Communists buried in Père Lachaise cemetery.

In 1886 the Monarchists renewed their political demonstrations; the most important one was the reception given by the Count of Paris at the Galliera mansion on the occasion of the marriage of his daughter with the King of Portugal. The Count of Paris had invited to this reception all the foreign ambassadors, and some disturbance having taken place, the Chamber of Deputies, on the 11th of June 1886, voted a law interdicting sojourn upon French territory to the Orleanist and Bonapartist pretenders to the throne of France, and also to their direct heirs. At that epoch Paris was in a state of agitation and discontent, and various catastrophes occurred. First of all came the disastrous bankruptcy of a large financial concern called the Union Générale; then the scandal concerning the traffic in decorations, in which M. Wilson, son-in-law of M. Jules Grévy, was compromised, and which eventually led to the resignation of the President; finally the deplorable Panama affair profoundly enervated the Parisians, and made them feel the necessity of shouting for a military master, some adventurer who would promise them a revenge. All this led to Boulangism. It was by wild acclamations and frantic shouts that General Boulanger was greeted, first at the review of the army on the 14th of July, then two days later at the opening of the Military Club, afterwards at the Winter Circus, where the Patriots' League held a mass meeting under the presidency of Paul Déroulède, and finally, on the 8th of July, at an immense demonstration at the Lyons railway station, when "le brav' Général" left Paris to take command of the 13th army corps at Clermont Ferrand. Popular refrains were sung in the streets in the midst of immense excitement on the 27th of January 1889 at the time of the election of General Boulanger as deputy for the Seine department. A majority of 80,000 votes had invested him with an immense moral authority, and he appeared as though elected as the candidate of the entire country; but he lacked the necessary audacity to complete his triumph, and the Government having decided to prosecute him for conspiracy against the security of the state, before the Senate acting as a High Court of Justice, he fled with his accomplices, Rochefort and Dillon. All three were condemned by default, on the 14th of August, to imprisonment in a fortified enclosure.

Other events had also troubled this astonishing interlude of Boulangism. On the 23rd of February 1887 a terrible fire destroyed the Opéra Comique during a performance, and a great many of the audience perished in the flames. The first performance of *Lohengrin*, which took place at the Eden Theatre on the 1st of May 1887, was also the cause of street rioting. In 1888 there were several strikes. That of the day labourers, which lasted more than a month, occasioned violent scenes, owing to the sudden death of Émile Eudes, a Communist, while he was speaking in favour of the strike at a public meeting. On the 2nd of December there were manifestations in memory of Baudin, a representative of the people, killed upon the barricades in 1851 while fighting in the defence of the Republic. But a calm finally came, and then the Parisians thought only of celebrating the centenary of the Revolution of 1789 by a universal exhibition. This exhibition contained a profusion of marvels such as had never before been seen, and indicated what enormous industrial progress had been accomplished. Sadi Carnot, who had succeeded M Jules Grévy as President of the Republic on the 3rd of December 1887, officially opened the exhibition on the 6th of May 1889. Numerous fêtes were held in the grounds while the exhibition lasted. The Eiffel Tower and the illuminated fountains enraptured the crowd of visitors, while the Rue du Caire, with its Egyptian donkey-drivers, obtained a prodigious success. Most of the nations were represented at this exhibition. Germany alone confined her co-operation to the display of some paintings. The Shah of Persia, in honour of whom splendid fêtes were organized, and the King of Greece, the Prince of Wales, the Lord Mayor of London, several Russian grand dukes, Annamite, Tunisian, Moorish, Egyptian and African princes successively visited the Exhibition. There were 30,000,000 visitors. On the 18th of August a banquet was given in the Palais de l'Industrie by the Paris Municipal Council to all the mayors in France, and 15,000 of these officials were present.

In 1890 the duke of Orleans, having attained his majority, came to Paris to draw for military service with the youngest conscripts of his class. He was arrested, and placed, first in the Conciergerie, and later in the prison at Clairvaux, but was released after a few months' incarceration. The following years were remarkable for more strikes and several demonstrations by the students, which led in 1893 to conflicts with the police, in one of which a student was killed. On the 17th of October an enthusiastic welcome was extended to Admiral Avellan and the Russian sailors upon their arrival in Paris. It was about this time that dynamite began to be used by the Anarchists. After Ravachol, who commenced the sinister exploits of the "propaganda by acts," it was Vaillant who threw a bomb into the "Temple of the Laws" on the 9th of December 1893, and wounded forty-six deputies. Then there was a succession of these attacks during the two following months, for Ravachol and Vaillant had found emulators. Henry scattered fright and death among the peaceable customers of a brasserie, while bombs were thrown into the doorways and staircases of houses inhabited by wealthy people. Upon the steps of the Madeleine Church, Parvels, who was already the author of two dynamite plots, was struck down by the destructive machine that he was about to throw into the body of the church. Laurent Tailhade himself, who had celebrated with his pen the beauty of Vaillant's gesture, was subsequently wounded by dynamite thrown into the Café Foy, where he was lunching.

The visit of the emperor and empress of Russia, on the 5th, 6th and 7th of October 1896, was celebrated by incomparable fêtes. The Rue de la Paix was decorated with ropes and sails, stretched across the street like the rigging of a vast vessel, in honour of the Russian sailors. Nothing could be seen anywhere except flags, cockades and badges formed of the colours of the two friendly nations. In the evening there were open-air balls, with farandoles and orchestras at all the street corners. Popular enthusiasm was again manifested on the 31st of August, when President Faure returned from his visit to the Russian court. On the 4th of May 1897 the terrible conflagration at the Charity Bazaar in the Rue Jean Goujon threw into mourning one hundred and forty families of the nobility or the aristocracy of Paris, and spread sorrow among the class always considerate in its benevolence. Then all minds were again troubled and disturbances occurred in the streets for more than two years over the Dreyfus case, dividing the French people into two camps.

President Faure died suddenly on the 18th of February 1899. The very day of his funeral, Paul Déroulède and Marcel Habert tried to make a *coup d'état* by urging General Roget to lead his troops, which had formed part of the guard of honour at the obsequies, against the Elysée. Immediately arrested and put on trial, Déroulède and Habert were acquitted by a timorous jury.

M. Émile Loubet, President of the Senate, was chosen successor to M. Félix Faure. Upon his return to Paris from the Versailles Congress, where he had been elected President of the French Republic, he was greeted by hisses and cries of "Panama!" cries in no wise justifiable. Some time afterwards, Jules Guérin, by a desperate resistance against a summons of the police to give himself up, made the public believe for two months in the existence of an impregnable fortress in the Rue Chabrol, in the very centre of Paris. On the 4th of June there was a great scandal at the Auteuil Races, which President Loubet had been, according to custom, invited to attend. He was insulted and struck by Baron de Christiani, who was encouraged by the young royalists of the "Œillets Blancs" Association. A week later, the extraordinary and excessive police measures taken to prevent a disturbance at the Grand Prix occasioned the downfall of the Dupuy ministry. M. Waldeck-Rousseau then formed a cabinet, himself becoming president of the council. The new premier immediately took energetic measures against the enemies of the Republic. Compromising documents found in various domiciliary searches made among the Monarchists and Nationalists formed the basis of prosecutions before the High Court of Justice. The trial resulted in the condemnation of Jules Guérin to a term of imprisonment, and the banishment of Paul Déroulède, Marcel Habert, André Buffet and the Marquis de Lur Saluces, thereby ridding France of all these promoters of disorder, and opening a new era of peace, which lasted throughout the Universal Exhibition of 1900.

This exhibition covered an enormous space, including the slope of the Trocadéro, the Champ de Mars, the Esplanade of the Invalides and both sides of the Seine bordered by the Rue de Paris and the Rue des Nations. Seen from the new Alexandre III. bridge, the spectacle was as fairy-like as a stage setting. Close beside, at the left, were the palaces of the different nations, each one showing its characteristic architecture, and all being of an astonishing diversity. To the right were the pavilion of the city of Paris and the enormous greenhouses, and in the distance Old Paris, so picturesquely constructed by Robida. In short, exotic edifices and scintillating cupolas arose with unparalleled profusion, creating in the heart of Paris a veritable city of dreams and illusion. The most distant countries sent their art treasures or the marvels of their industry. The number of visitors was 51,000,000, and the personages of mark included the Shah of Persia, the King of Sweden, the King of the Belgians and the King of Greece, all of whom were successively the guests of France. On the 22nd of September 22,000 mayors accepted the invitation to the banquet offered in their honour by President Loubet, and thus solemnly affirmed their Republican faith. This admirably organized banquet was spread in the Tuileries Gardens. The exhibition of 1900, a brilliant epilogue of the closing century, was a grand manifestation of universal concord, of the union of peoples by art, science, industry, all branches of human genius.   (DE B.)

The bibliography of the history of Paris is immense, and it must suffice here, so far as authorities on the medieval period are concerned, to refer to the long list of works, &c., given by Ulysse Chevalier in his *Répertoire des sources historiques du moyen âge, topo-bibliographs* (Montbéliard, 1903), pp. 2267-2290. See also Lacombe, *Bibliographie parisienne, tableaux de mœurs, 1600-1880* (Paris, 1886), and Pessard, *Nouveau dict. hist. de Paris* (1904). Of general works may be mentioned specially J. C. Dulaure, *Hist. Physique, civile et morale de Paris* (1821; new ed. continued by Leynadier and Roquette, 1874; Paul Robiquet, *Hist. municipale de Paris*, up to Henry IV. (1880-1904); J. Lebeul, *Hist. de la ville et de tout le diocèse de Paris* (Paris, 1754-1758, new ed. revised and enlarged, by H. Cocheris, 1863-1867); and the *Hist. générale de Paris*, published under the authority of the municipality, of which vol. xxxix. was issued in 1906. Important special works on later periods are W. A. Schmidt, *Pariser Zustände während der Revolutionszeit, 1789-1800* (Jena, 1874-1876. French trans., *Paris pendant la révolution*, by P. Viollet, 1880-1894), and *Tableaux de la révolution française* (Leipzig, 1867-1870); F. Aulard, *Collection de documents relatifs à l'hist. de Paris pendant la révolution* (1899-1903); Lanzac de Labone, *Paris sous Napoléon* (1905); Simond, *Paris de 1800 à 1900* (1902); Cilleuls, *Hist. de l'administration parisienne au xixme siècle* (1900)

PARIS, TREATIES OF (1814–1815). Among the very many treaties and conventions signed at Paris those which bear the title of "treaties of Paris" *par excellence* are the two sets of treaties, both of the highest importance in the history of the international politics of Europe and the formation of its public law, signed in Paris on the 30th of May 1814 and the 20th of November 1815. The first embodied the abortive attempt made by the Allies and Louis XVIII. of France to re-establish lasting peace in Europe after the first abdication of Napoleon at Fontainebleau on the 11th of April 1814. The second contained the penal and cautionary measures which the Allies found it necessary to impose when the practically unopposed return of Napoleon from Elba, and his resumption of power, had proved the weakness of the Bourbon monarchy. (See EUROPE: *History*.)

The treaty of the 30th of May 1814 and the secret treaty which accompanied it, were signed by Talleyrand for France; by Lords Castlereagh, Aberdeen and Cathcart for Great Britain; by Counts Rasumovski and Nesselrode for Russia; by Prince Metternich and Count Stadion for Austria; and by Baron Hardenberg and W. von Humboldt for Prussia. Sweden and Portugal adhered later, and Spain adhered on the 20th of July to the public treaty, to which there were in all eight signatories. It is this public treaty which is known as the first treaty of Paris.

It was signed in eight instruments identical in substance. The Allies, who appear as acting in the most friendly co-operation with Louis XVIII., declare that their aim is to establish a lasting peace based on a just distribution of forces among the powers, and that as France has returned to "the paternal government of her kings" they no longer think it necessary to exact those guarantees which they had been regretfully compelled to insist on from her late government. The preamble is more than a flourish of diplomatic humanity; for the treaty is extraordinarily favourable to France. Putting aside as much of the treaty as is common form, and minute details for which the text must be consulted, it secured her in the possession of all the territory she held in Europe on the 1st of January 1792 (Art. II.); it restored her colonies, except Tobago, Santa Lucia, Île de France (Mauritius), Rodriguez, and the Seychelles, surrendered to England and the part of San Domingo formerly Spanish, which was to return to Spain (Art. VIII.). Sweden resigned her claim on Guadaloupe (Art. IX.); Portugal resigned French Guiana (Art. X.). The rectifications of the European frontier of France are detailed in the eight subsections of Art. III. They were valuable. France obtained (1) a piece of territory south of Mons; (2 and 3) a larger piece around Philippeville, on the Sambre and Meuse; (4) a rectification including Sarrelouis, (5) a piece of land to connect the formerly isolated fortress of Landau with her own dominions; (6) a better frontier on the east at Doubes; (7) a better frontier as against Geneva, (8) the subprefectures of Annecy and Chambéry (Savoy). By the same article she secured all the German enclaves in Alsace, Avignon, the Venaissin and Montbéliard. Art. VI. secured Holland to the house of Nassau, with an addition of territory, not defined in this instrument; asserted the independence, and right to federate of the German states, and the full sovereignty of all the states of Italy outside of the Italian dominions of Austria. Art. VII. gave Malta to Great Britain. By Art. XV. France was to retain two-thirds of all warships and naval stores existing in ports which had belonged to the empire of Napoleon, but were outside the borders of France, with exception of the Dutch ships. Arts. XVIII. to XXXI. dealt with pecuniary claims, return of documents, renunciation of all claims for compensation, &c. By Art. XXXII. the powers bind themselves to meet at Vienna within two months to arrange a final settlement of Europe. Additional articles provided for the settlement of pecuniary claims in the late grand-duchy of Warsaw, for the abrogation of treaties signed with Prussia since the Peace of Basel. By her additional article with Great Britain, France undertook to suppress the slave trade within five years, and to help to bring about its general suppression.

The separate and secret articles of the treaty (or "Secret Treaty" as they are commonly called), were meant to bind France to agree in principle to the readjustments and allotments of territory and population to be made at the approaching Congress of Vienna (q.v.).

The treaties of the 20th of November 1815 and their dependent instruments, were signed in very different circumstances. The representative of France was the duc de Richelieu; Great Britain was represented by Castlereagh and Wellington; Austria by Metternich and Count Wessenberg; Prussia by Hardenberg and W. von Humboldt; Russia by Rasumovski and Capo d'Istria. The preamble stated the altered spirit and purpose of the Allies. It insisted that, as the powers had saved France and Europe from Napoleon's last adventure, they were entitled to compensation and security for the future. They had decided to exact indemnities, partly pecuniary and partly territorial, such as could be exacted without injuring the essential interest of France. The territorial penalty imposed was moderate. France retained the enclaves she had secured by the previous treaty She had to resign her gains on the north and eastern frontier, to surrender Philippeville, Marienbourg, Bouillon, Sarrelouis and Landau, to cede certain territories to Geneva, and she lost Annecy and Chambéry The standard taken was the frontier of 1790 (Art. L). By Art III. she agreed to dismantle the fortress of Huningen near Basel. The most grievous articles

of the treaty are those which imposed the payment of an indemnity, and the occupation of a part of French territory as security for payment. Art. IV. fixed the indemnity at 700,000,000 frs. Art. V. fixed the strength of the army of occupation at 150,000 under a commander-in-chief to be named by the powers, and specified the fortresses it was to hold in the north and north-east of France. The period of occupation was limited to five years, but might be reduced to three. All provisions of the treaty of the 30th of May 1814, and of the Final Act of the Congress of Vienna not expressly revoked were to remain in force. By an additional article the powers agreed to join Great Britain in suppressing the slave trade. Certain complimentary instruments were attached to the treaty. (1) A separate article with Russia in regard to pecuniary claims in Poland. (2) A convention as to payment of indemnity under Art. IV. (3) Convention as to the occupation and the rationing of the foreign troops. (4) A convention as to settlement of claims of British bondholders. The retrocession of the colonies was made dependent on the partial settlement of these claims. (5) A convention to arrange for settlement of claims under Art. XIX., &c., of the treaty of the 30th of May 1814.

On the day of the signing of the second treaty of Paris, a treaty of alliance, commonly spoken of as the treaty of the 20th of November 1815, was signed in Paris by Great Britain, Austria, Russia and Prussia. It contained six articles. The first declared the determination of the Allies to enforce the treaty signed with France; the second, third and fourth reaffirmed their determination to exclude the Bonaparte family from the throne, and specified the measures they were prepared to take to support one another The fifth declared that the alliance for the purposes stated would continue when the five years' occupation of France was ended. The sixth article stated that in order to facilitate and assure the execution of the present treaty, the High Contracting Parties had decided to hold periodical meetings of the sovereigns or their ministers, for the examination of such measures as appeared to be salutary for the repose and prosperity of their peoples and the maintenance of the peace of Europe. It was in accordance with this last article that the congresses of Aix-la-Chapelle (1818), Troppau (1820), Laibach (1821), and Verona (1822) were held (see EUROPE: History).

BIBLIOGRAPHY.—See Sir E. Hertslet, The Map of Europe by Treaty, i. (London, 1875), and Martens, Nouveau recueil de traités, &c., ii. (Göttingen, 1818).

PARIS, a city and the county seat of Edgar county, Illinois, U.S.A., in the E. part of the state, about 19 m. N.W. of Terre Haute, Ind. Pop. (1890), 4996; (1900), 6105, of whom 179 were foreign-born and 277 negroes; (1910) 7664. Paris is served by the Vandalia, and the Cleveland, Cincinnati, Chicago & St Louis (New York Central system) railways; the main line and the Cairo division of the latter intersect here, and the city is the transfer point for traffic from the E. and W. to the N. and S., and vice versa. It is in a rich farming region, of which Indian corn and oats are important products, and has a large trade. Paris was founded about 1825, was incorporated in 1853, and was re-incorporated in 1873.

PARIS, a city and the county-seat of Lamar county, Texas, U.S.A., about 93 m. N.E. of Dallas. Pop. (1890), 8254; (1900), 9358, of whom 3061 were negroes; (1910 census), 11,269. It is served by the St Louis & San Francisco (of which it is a terminus), the Gulf, Colorado & Santa Fé, the Texas & Pacific, and the Texas Midland railways. The city has cotton gins and a cotton compress, and various manufactures. In 1905 its factory products were valued at $854,930. Paris was settled in 1841, incorporated as a town in 1874, and chartered as a city in 1905.

PARISH (Gr. παροικία, district, neighbourhood; πάροικος, one dwelling near or beside, from παρά, οἶκος, house; Lat. parochia, Late Lat. parochia; cf. Fr. paroisse), originally an episcopal district or diocese. In the early Christian Church each district was administered by a bishop and his attendant presbyters and deacons, and the word parochia was frequently applied to such a district (Du Cange, sub. tit.). Scattered congregations or churches within the *parochia* were served by itinerant presbyters. Towards the close of the 4th century it had become usual for the bishop to appoint resident presbyters to defined districts or territories, to which the term "parish" came gradually to be applied (see also DIOCESE). Parish, in English ecclesiastical law, may be defined as the township or cluster of townships which was assigned to the ministration of a single priest, to whom its tithes and other ecclesiastical dues were paid; but the word has now acquired several distinct meanings.

The Old Ecclesiastical Parish.—In the absence of evidence to the contrary, the ecclesiastical parish is presumed to be composed of a single township or vill, and to be conterminous with the manor within the ambit of which it is comprised. Before the process of subinfeudation became prevalent, the most ancient manors were the districts which we call by that name when speaking of the tenants, or "townships" when we regard the inhabitants, or "parishes" as to matters ecclesiastical. The parish as an institution is in reality later in date than the township. The latter has been in fact the unit of local administration ever since England was settled in its several states and kingdoms, the beginnings of the parochial system in England are attributed to Theodore of Tarsus, who was archbishop of Canterbury towards the close of the 7th century. The system was extended in the reign of Edgar, and it appears not to have been complete until the reign of Edward III. It has been considered that the intimate connexion of church and state militates against the view that the parochial system was founded as a national institution, since any legislation on the subject of the township and parochial systems would probably have resulted in the merging of the one into the other. "The fact that the two systems, the parish and the township, have existed for more than a thousand years side by side, identical in area and administered by the same persons, and yet separate in character and machinery, is a sufficient proof that no legislative act could have been needed in the first place; nor was there any lay council of the whole nation which could have sanctioned such a measure" (Stubbs, *Const. Hist.* i. 227). The boundaries of the old ecclesiastical parishes are usually identical with those of the township or townships comprised within its precinct; they are determined by usage, in the absence of charters or records, and are evidenced by perambulations, which formerly took place on the "gang-days" in Rogation week, but are now, where they still survive, for the most part held triennially, the Poor-Law Act of 1844 permitting the parish officers to charge the expense on the poor-rate, "provided the perambulations do not occur more than once in three years." The expense of preserving the boundary by land-marks or bound-stones is chargeable to the same rate. Many parishes contain more than one township, and this is especially the case in the northern counties, where the separate townships are organized for administrative purposes under an act passed in 1662. In the southern and midland districts the parishes are for the most part subdivided into hamlets or other local divisions known as "tythings," "boroughs," and the like; the distinction between a parish and a subordinate district lies chiefly in the fact that the latter will be found to have never had a church or a constable to itself. The select committee of 1873, appointed to inquire into parochial boundaries, reported to the effect that the parish bears no definite relation to any other administrative area, except indeed to the poor-law union. It may be situated in different counties or hundreds, and in many instances it contains, in addition to its principal district, several outlying portions intermixed with the lands in other parishes.

After the abolition of compulsory church rates in 1868 the old ecclesiastical parish ceased to be of importance as an instrument of local government. Its officers, however, have still important duties to perform. The rector, vicar or incumbent is a corporation-sole, in whom is vested the freehold of the church and churchyard, subject to the parishioners' rights of user; their rights of burial have been enlarged by various acts. The churchwardens are the principal lay officers. Their duties consist in keeping the church and churchyard in repair and in raising

a voluntary rate for the purpose to the best of their power; they have also the duty of keeping order in church during divine service. The other officials are the parish clerk and sexton. They have freeholds in their offices and are paid by customary fees. The office of the clerk is regulated by an act of 1844, enabling a curate to undertake its duties, and providing facilities for vacating the office in case of misconduct. The only civil function of the parish clerk remaining in 1894 was the custody of maps and documents, required to be deposited with him under standing orders of parliament before certain public works were begun. By the Local Government Act 1894 they are now deposited with the chairman or clerk of a parish council.

The New Ecclesiastical Parish.—Under the powers given by the Church Building Acts, and acts for making new parishes, many populous parishes have been subdivided into smaller ecclesiastical parishes. This division has not affected the parish in its civil aspect.

The Civil Parish.—For purposes of civil government the term "parish" means a district for which a separate poor-rate is or can be made, or for which a separate overseer is or can be appointed; and by the Interpretation Act 1889 this definition is to be used in interpreting all statutes subsequent to 1866, except where the context is inconsistent therewith. This district may of itself constitute a poor law union; but in the great majority of cases the unions, or areas under the jurisdiction of boards of guardians according to the Poor-Law Amendment Act of 1834, are made up of aggregated poor-law parishes. Each of these poor-law parishes may represent the extent of an old ecclesiastical parish, or a township separately rated by custom before the practice was stayed in 1819 or separated from a large parish under the act of 1662, or it may represent a chapelry, tything, borough, ward, quarter or hamlet, or other subdivision of the ancient parish, or, under various acts, an area formed by the merger of an extra-parochial place with an adjoining district by the union of detached portions with adjoining parishes, or by the subdivision of a large parish for the better administration of the relief of the poor. The civil importance of the poor-law parishes may be dated from the introduction of the poor law by the statute of 43 Elizabeth, which directed overseers of the poor to be appointed in every parish, and made the churchwardens into *ex-officio* overseers. The statute was preceded by tentative provisions of the same kind enacted in the reigns of Edward VI. and Mary and in the fifth year of Elizabeth, and after several renewals was made perpetual in the reign of Charles I. The chief part of the parochial organization was the vestry-meeting. It derived its name from the old place of assembly, the vestry room attached to the church or chapel. The vestry represented the old assembly of the township, and retained so much of its business as had not been insensibly transferred to the court-baron and court-leet. The freemen, now appearing as the ratepayers, elected the "parish officers," as the churchwardens and way-wardens, the assessors, the overseers, and (if required) paid assistant-overseers, a secretary or vestry-clerk, and a collector of rates if the guardians applied for his appointment. Common vestries were meetings of all the ratepayers assembled on a three days' notice; select vestries were regulated by local custom, or derived their power from the Vestries Act 1831 (Hobhouse's Act). The vestries could adopt various acts, and appoint persons to carry those acts into execution. The Local Government Act 1894 restored the parish to its position as the unit of local government by establishing parish councils. (See ENGLAND: *Local Government.*)

The Parish in Scotland.—There can be little doubt that about the beginning of the 13th century the whole, or almost the whole, of the kingdom of Scotland was parochially divided. It seems probable (though the point is obscure) that the bishops presided at the first formation of the parishes—the parish being a subdivision of the diocese—and at any rate down to the date of the Reformation they exercised the power of creating new parishes within their respective dioceses (Duncan, *Parochial Law*, p. 4). After the Reformation the power of altering parishes was assumed by the legislature. The existing parochial districts being found unsuited to the ecclesiastical requirements of the time, a general act was passed in 1581, which made provision for the parochial clergy, and, *inter alia*, directed that "a sufficient and competent" district should be appropriated to each church as a parish (1581, cap. 100). Thereafter, by a series of special acts in the first place, and, subsequent to the year 1617, by the decrees of parliamentary commissions, the creation of suitable parochial districts was proceeded with. In the year 1707 the powers exercised by the commissioners were permanently transferred to the court of session, whose judges were appointed to act in future as "commissioners for the Plantation of Kirks and Valuation of Teinds" (Act, 1707, cap. 9). Under this statute the areas of parishes continued to be altered and defined down to 1844, when the act commonly known as Graham's Act was passed (7 & 8 Vict. c. 44). This act, which applied to the disjunction and erection of parishes, introduced a simpler form of procedure, and to some extent dispensed with the consent of the heritors, which had been required under the earlier statute.

The main division of parishes in Scotland was into civil and ecclesiastical, or, to speak more accurately, into parishes proper (*i.e.* for all purposes, civil and ecclesiastical) and ecclesiastical parishes. This division is expressed in legal language by the terms parishes *quoad omnia* (*i.e. quoad civilia et sacra*) and parishes *quoad sacra—civilia* being such matters as church rates, education, poor law and sanitary purposes, and *sacra* being such as concern the administration of church ordinances, and fall under the cognizance of the church courts. There are other minor divisions which will be noticed below. (1) *The Parish Proper.*—In a number of instances it is difficult to determine the exact areas of such parishes at the present day. The boundaries of the old ecclesiastical parish were nowhere recorded, and the descriptions in the titles of private properties which appear to lie in the parish have sometimes to be taken as evidence, and sometimes the fact that the inhabitants attended a particular church or made payments in favour of a particular minister. Where there has been a union or disjunction and erection of parishes the evidence of the relative statute, order in council, or decree of commission or of court of teinds. The parishes proper vary to a great degree both in size and population. For ecclesiastical purposes, the minister and kirk-session constitute the parochial authority. The minister is vested with the manse and glebe, to be held by him for himself and his successors in office, and along with the kirk-session he administers church ordinances and exercises church discipline. The oldest governing authority was the meeting of the heritors or landowners of the parish. Though gradually shorn of much of its old importance, the heritors' meeting retained the power of imposing an assessment for the purpose of providing and maintaining a church and churchyard and a manse and glebe for the minister. It also possessed power to assess under the Parochial Buildings Acts of 1862 and 1866. Kirk-session and heritors were the educational authority until the establishment of school boards in 1872. (2) *Quoad Sacra Parishes.*—The ecclesiastical or *quoad sacra* parish is a modern creation. Under Graham's Act, above mentioned, a parish may be disjoined and erected *quoad sacra tantum* on the application of persons who have built and endowed a church, and who offer securities for its proper maintenance. By the Education Act of 1872 the *quoad sacra* parish was adopted as a separate school district. (3) *Extra-Burghal Parishes.*—For sanitary purposes, highways and some others, certain classes of burghs were made separate areas from the parishes in which they lay. This fact created a set of incomplete parishes, called extra-burghal. (4) *Burghal, Landward and Burghal-Landward (or Mixed) Parishes.*—This division of parishes depends, as the names imply, upon local character and situation of the parochial districts. · The importance of the distinction arose in connexion with the rule of assessment adopted for various parochial burdens, and the nature of the rights of the minister and corresponding obligations of the parishioners. (5) *Combined Parishes.*—Under the Poor-Law, Education and Registration Acts power was given to the central authority to combine parishes for purposes of local administration. The Local Government (Scotland) Act 1894 reformed parish government, although not to the same extent as the corresponding English act. It established a local government board for Scotland, with a parish council in every parish, and abolished all parochial boards. The number of councillors for a parish council was fixed at not less than five nor more than thirty-one, the number being determined, in the case of landward parishes, by the county council; in the case of burghal parishes by the town council and, in the case of mixed parishes, by county and town councils jointly.

The Parish in the United States.—The term "parish" is not in use as a territorial designation except in Louisiana, the sixty parishes of which correspond to the counties of the other states of the Union. In the American Episcopal Church the word is frequently used to denote an ecclesiastical district.

AUTHORITIES.—The principal records from which information may be gained as to the oldest parochial system in England are the records called *Nomina villarum*, the *Taxatio papae Nicholai* made in 1291, the *Nonarum inquisitiones* relating to assessments made upon the clergy, the *Valor ecclesiasticus* of Henry VIII., the lay subsidies from the reign of Edward III. to that of Charles II., the hearth-tax assessments and the land-tax accounts. On the subject of the parish generally see Stubbs's *Constitutional History*; Glen's *Parish Law*; Steer's *Parish Law*; Toulmin Smith's work on the *Parish*; S. and B. Webb, *English Local Government*, vol. i.; Redlich and Hirst, *Local Government in England*; O. J. Reichel. *Rise of the Parochial System in England* (1905). For fuller information regarding the Scottish parish see Connell on *Teinds*; Duncan's *Parochial Ecclesiastical Law*; the Cobden Club essays on *Local Government and Taxation in the United Kingdom* (1882); Goudy and Smith's *Local Government in Scotland*; Atkinson, *Local Government in Scotland*.

PARISITE, a rare mineral, consisting of cerium, lanthanum, didymium and calcium fluo-carbonate, $(CeF)_2Ca(CO_3)_3$. It is found only as crystals, which belong to the hexagonal system and usually have the form of acute double pyramids terminated by the basal planes; the faces of the hexagonal pyramids are striated horizontally, and parallel to the basal plane there is a perfect cleavage. The crystals are hair-brown in colour and are translucent. The hardness is 4½ and the specific gravity 4·36. Light which has traversed a crystal of parisite exhibits a characteristic absorption spectrum. Until recently the only known occurrence of this mineral was in the famous emerald mine at Muzo in Colombia, South America, where it was found by J. J. Paris, who re-discovered and worked the mine in the early part of the 19th century; here it is associated with emerald in a bituminous limestone of Cretaceous age (see EMERALD).

Closely allied to parisite, and indeed first described as such, is a mineral from the nepheline-syenite district of Julianehaab in south Greenland. To this the name synchysite (from Gr. συγχυσις, confounding) has been given. The crystals are rhombohedral (as distinct from hexagonal; they have the composition $CeFCa(CO_3)_2$, and specific gravity 3·90. At the same locality there is also found a barium-parisite, which differs from the Colombian parisite in containing barium in place of calcium, the formula being $(CeF)_2Ba(CO_3)_3$; this is named cordylite on account of the club-shaped form (κορδύλη, a club) of its hexagonal crystals. Bastnäsite is a cerium lanthanum and didymium fluo-carbonate $(CeF)CO_3$, from Bastnäs, near Riddarhyttan, in Vestmanland, Sweden, and the Pike's Peak region in Colorado, U.S.A. (L. J. S.)

PARK, EDWARDS AMASA (1808–1900), American Congregational theologian, was born in Providence, Rhode Island, on the 29th of December 1808, the son of Calvin Park (1774–1847), a Congregational minister, professor from 1804 to 1825 at Brown University, and pastor at Stoughton, Massachusetts, in 1826–1840. The son graduated at Brown University in 1826, was a teacher at Braintree for two years, and in 1831 graduated from Andover theological seminary. He was co-pastor (with R. S. Storrs) of the orthodox Congregational church of Braintree in 1831–1833; professor of mental and moral philosophy at Amherst in 1835; and Bartlett professor of sacred rhetoric (1836–1847), and Abbot professor of Christian theology (1847–1881) at Andover. He died at Andover on the 4th of June 1900. An ardent admirer of Jonathan Edwards, whose great-grand-daughter he married, Park was one of the most notable American theologians and orators. He was the most prominent leader of the "new school" of of "New England Theology." He left his theological impress on the *Bibliotheca sacra* which he and Bela B. Edwards took over in 1844 from Edward Robinson, who had founded it in 1843, and of which Park was assistant editor until 1851 and editor-in-chief from 1851 to 1884. As a general statement of the position of orthodox Congregationalism he drew up and annotated the "Associate Creed of Andover Theological Seminary" (1883), and the anonymously published "Worcester Creed" of 1884 was his popularized and simplified statement. He edited in 1860 *The Atonement*, a collection of essays by various hands, prefaced by his study of the "Rise of the Edwardean Theory of the Atonement." Dr Park's sermon, "The Theology of the Intellect and that of the Feelings," delivered in 1850 before the convention of the Congregational ministers of Massachusetts, and published in the *Bibliotheca sacra* of July 1850, was the cause of a long and bitter controversy, metaphysical rather than doctrinal, with Charles Hodge. Some of Park's sermons were published in 1885, under the title *Discourses on Some Theological Doctrines as Related to the Religious Character.* With Austin Phelps and Lowell Mason he prepared *The Sabbath Hymn Book* (1858).

See *Professor Park and His Pupils* (Boston, 1899), a memorial of his 90th birthday, with articles by R. S. Storrs, G. R. W. Scott, Joseph Cook, G. Frederick Wright and others.

PARK, MUNGO (1771–1806?), Scottish explorer of the Niger, was born in Selkirkshire, Scotland, on the 10th of September 1771, at Foulshiels on the Yarrow—the farm which his father rented from the duke of Buccleuch. He was the seventh in a family of thirteen. Having received a good education, he was apprenticed to a surgeon named Thomas Anderson in Selkirk, and then attended the university of Edinburgh for three sessions (1789–1791), obtaining the surgical diploma. By his brother-in-law, James Dickson, a botanist of repute, he was introduced to Sir Joseph Banks, then president of the Royal Society, and through his good offices obtained the post of assistant-surgeon on board the " Worcester " East Indiaman. In this capacity he made the voyage in 1792 to Benkulen, in Sumatra, and on his return in 1793 he contributed a description of eight new Sumatran fishes to the *Transactions* of the Linnean Society.

Park in 1794 offered his services to the African Association, then looking out for a successor to Major Daniel Houghton, who had been sent out in 1790 to discover the course of the Niger and had perished in the Sahara. Supported by the influence of Sir Joseph Banks, Park was successful in his application. On the 21st of June 1795 he reached the Gambia and ascended that river 200 miles to a British trading station named Pisania. On the 2nd of December, accompanied by two negro servants, he started for the unknown interior. He chose the route crossing the upper Senegal basin and through the semi-desert region of Kaarta. The journey was full of difficulties, and at Ludamar he was imprisoned by a Moorish chief for four months. He escaped, alone and with nothing save his horse and a pocket compass, on the 1st of July 1796, and on the 21st of the same month reached the long-sought Niger at Segu, being the first European to gaze on its waters. He followed the river down stream 80 m. to Silla, where he was obliged to turn back, being without means and utterly exhausted. On his return journey, begun on the 30th of July, he took a route more to the south than that originally followed, keeping close to the Niger as far as Bamako, thus tracing the course of that stream in all for some 300 miles. At Kamalia he fell ill, and owed his life to the kindness of a negro in whose house he lived for seven months. Eventually he reached Pisania again on the 10th of June 1797, returning to England by way of America on the 22nd of December. He had been thought to be dead, and his return home with the news of the discovery of the Niger evoked great public enthusiasm. An account of his journey was at once drawn up for the African Association by Bryan Edwards, and a detailed narrative from his own pen appeared in 1799 (*Travels in the Interior of Africa*). Abundance of incident and an unaffected style rendered the work extremely popular, and it still holds its place as an acknowledged classic in this department of literature.

Settling at Foulshiels, Park in August 1799 married a daughter of his old master, Thomas Anderson. Two offers made to him to go to New South Wales in some official capacity came to nothing, and in October 1801 Park removed to Peebles, where he practised as a doctor. In the autumn of 1803 he was invited by the government to lead another expedition to the Niger. Park, who chafed at the hardness and monotony of life at Peebles, accepted the offer, but the starting of the expedition was delayed. Part of the waiting time was occupied in the perfecting of his Arabic—his teacher being Sidi Ambak Bubi, a native of Mogador; whose vagaries both amused and alarmed the people of Peebles. In May 1804 Park went back to Foulshiels, where he made the acquaintance of Sir Walter Scott,

then living near by at Ashesteil, with whom he soon became on terms of warm friendship. In September he was summoned to London to leave on the new expedition; he parted from Sir Walter with the hopeful proverb on his lips, " Freits (omens) follow those that look to them." Park had at that time adopted the theory that the Niger and the Congo were one, and in a memorandum drawn up before he left England he wrote: " My hopes of returning by the Congo are not altogether fanciful." He sailed from Portsmouth for the Gambia on the 31st of January 1805, having been given a captain's commission as head of the government expedition. Alexander Anderson, his brother-in-law, was second in command, and on him was bestowed a lieutenancy. George Scott, a fellow Borderer, was draughtsman, and the party included four or five artificers. At Gorée (then in British occupation) Park was joined by Lieutenant Martyn, R.A., thirty-five privates and two seamen. The expedition did not reach the Niger until the middle of August, when only eleven Europeans were left alive; the rest had succumbed to fever or dysentery. From Bamako the journey to Segu was made by canoe. Having received permission from the ruler of that town to proceed, at Sansandig, a little below Segu, Park made ready for his journey down the still unknown part of the river. Park, helped by one soldier, the only one left capable of work, converted two canoes into one tolerably good boat, 40 ft. long and 6 ft. broad. This he christened H.M. schooner "Joliba " (the native name for the Niger), and in it, with the surviving members of his party, he set sail down stream on the 19th of November. At Sansandig, on the 28th of October, Anderson had died, and in him Park lost the only member of the party—except Scott, already dead—who had been of real use. Those who embarked in the " Joliba " were Park, Martyn, three European soldiers (one mad), a guide and three slaves. Before his departure Park gave to Isaaco, a Mandingo guide who had been with him thus far, letters to take back to the Gambia for transmission to England. The spirit with which Park began the final stage of his enterprise is well illustrated by his letter to the head of the Colonial Office:—

" I shall," he wrote, " set sail for the east with the fixed resolution to discover the termination of the Niger or perish in the attempt . . . though all the Europeans who are with me should die, and though I were myself half dead, I would still persevere, and if I could not succeed in the object of my journey, I would at least die on the Niger."

To his wife he wrote stating his intention not to stop nor land anywhere till he reached the coast, where he expected to arrive about the end of January 1806. These were the last communications received from Park, and nothing more was heard of the party until reports of disaster reached the settlements on the Gambia. At length the British government engaged Isaaco to go to the Niger to ascertain the fate of the explorer. At Sansandig Isaaco found the guide who had gone down stream with Park, and the substantial accuracy of the story he told was later confirmed by the investigations of Hugh Clapperton and Richard Lander. This guide (Amadi) stated that Park's canoe descended the river to Yauri, where he (the guide) landed. In this long journey of about 1000 miles Park, who had plenty of provisions, stuck to his resolution of keeping aloof from the natives. Below Jenné, came Timbuktu, and at various other places the natives came out in canoes and attacked his boat. These attacks were all repulsed, Park and his party having plenty of firearms and ammunition and the natives having none. The boat also escaped the many perils attendant on the navigation of an unknown stream strewn with many rapids—Park had built the " Joliba " so that it drew only a foot of water. But at the Bussa rapids, not far below Yauri, the boat struck on a rock and remained fast. On the bank were gathered hostile natives, who attacked the party with bow and arrow and throwing spears. Their position being untenable, Park, Martyn, and the two soldiers who still survived, sprang into the river and were drowned. The sole survivor was one of the slaves, from whom was obtained the story of the final scene. Isaaco, and later Lander, obtained some of Park's effects, but his journal was never recovered. In 1827 his second son, Thomas, landed on the Guinea coast, intending to make his way to Bussa, where he thought his father might be detained a prisoner, but after penetrating some little distance inland he died of fever. Park's widow died in 1840.

J. Thomson's *Mungo Park and the Niger* (London, 1890) contains the best critical estimate of the explorer and his work. See also the Life (by Wishaw) prefixed to *Journal of a Mission into the Interior of Africa in 1805* (London, 1815); H. B., *Life of Mungo Park* (Edinburgh, 1835); and an interesting passage in Lockhart's *Life of Sir Walter Scott*, vol. ii.

PARK (Fr. *parc*; Ital. *parco*; Sp. *parque*; O.Eng. *pearroc*; connected with Ger. *pferch*, fold, and *pfarrei*, district, translating med. Lat. *parochia*, parish), a word ordinarily used in two senses: (a) an enclosed tract of ground, consisting of grass-land, planted with trees and shrubs, and surrounding a large country house; (b) a similar space in or near a town, laid out ornamentally, and used by the public as an "open space" for health or recreation. The term "park" first occurs in English as a term of the forest law of England for a tract of ground enclosed and privileged for beasts of the chase, the distinguishing characteristics of which were "vert," i.e. the green leaves of trees, "venison," i.e. deer, and "enclosure." A "park" was a franchise obtained by prescription or by grant from the crown (see FOREST LAW; also DEER PARK).

The word has had a technical military significance since the early part of the 17th century. Originally meaning the space occupied by the artillery, baggage and supply vehicles of an army when at rest, it came to be used of the mass of vehicles itself. From this mass first of all the artillery, becoming more mobile, separated itself; then as the mobility of armies in general became greater they outpaced their heavy vehicles, with the result that faster moving transport units had to be created to keep up communication. A "park" is thus at the present day a large unit consisting of several hundred vehicles carrying stores; it moves several days' marches in rear of the army, and forms a reservoir from "whence the mobile ammunition and supply columns" draw the supplies and stores required for the army's needs. "Parking" vehicles is massing them for a halt. The word "park" is still used to mean that portion of an artillery or administrative troops' camp or bivouac in which the vehicles are placed.

PARKER, SIR GILBERT (1862–   ), British novelist and politician, was born at Camden East, Addington, Ontario, on the 23rd of November 1862, the son of Captain J. Parker, R.A. He was educated at Ottawa and at Trinity University, Toronto. In 1886 he went to Australia, and became for a while associate-editor of the *Sydney Morning Herald*. He also travelled extensively in the Pacific, and subsequently in northern Canada; and in the early 'nineties he began to make a growing reputation in London as a writer of romantic fiction. The best of his novels are those in which he first took for his subject the history and life of the French Canadians; and his permanent literary reputation rests on the fine quality, descriptive and dramatic, of his Canadian stories. *Pierre and his People* (1892) was followed by *Mrs Falchion* (1893), *The Trail of the Sword* (1894), *When Valmond came to Pontiac* (1895), *An Adventurer of the North* (1895), and *The Seats of the Mighty* (1896, dramatized in 1897). *The Lane that had no Turning* (1900) contains some of his best work. In *The Battle of the Strong* (1898) he broke new ground, laying his scene in the Channel Islands. His chief later books were *The Right of Way* (1901), *Donovan Pasha* (1902), *The Ladder of Swords* (1904), *The Weavers* (1907) and *Northern Lights* (1909). In 1895 he married Miss Van Tine of New York, a wealthy heiress. His Canadian connexion and his experience in Australia and elsewhere had made him a strong Imperialist in politics, and from that time he began to devote himself in large measure to a political career. He still kept up his literary work, but some of the books last mentioned cannot compare with those by which he made his name. He was elected to parliament in 1900 (re-elected 1906 and 1910) as Conservative member for Gravesend and soon made his mark in the House of Commons. He was

knighted in 1902, and in succeeding years continually strengthened his position in the party, particularly by his energetic work on behalf of Tariff Reform and Imperial Preference. If he had given up to public life what at one time seemed to be due to literature, he gave it for enthusiasm in the Imperialist movement; and with the progress of that cause he came to rank by 1910 as one of the foremost men in the Unionist party outside those who had held office.

PARKER, SIR HYDE, BART. (1714–1782), British vice-admiral, was born at Tredington, Worcestershire, on the 25th of February, 1714, his father, a clergyman, being a son of Sir Henry Parker, Bart. His paternal grandfather had married a daughter of Bishop Alexander Hyde, of Salisbury. He began his career at sea in the merchant service. Entering the royal navy at the age of twenty-four, he was made lieutenant in 1744, and in 1748 he was made post-captain. During the latter part of the Seven Years' War he served in the East Indies, taking part in the capture of Pondicherry (1761) and of Manila (1762). In the latter year Parker with two ships captured one of the valuable Spanish plate ships in her voyage between Acapulco and Manila. In 1778 he became rear-admiral, and went to North American waters as second-in-command. For some time before Rodney's arrival he was in command on the Leeward Islands station, and conducted a skilful campaign against the French at Martinique. In 1781, having returned home and become vice-admiral, he fell in with a Dutch fleet of about his own force, though far better equipped, near the Dogger Bank (Aug. 5). After a fiercely contested battle, in which neither combatant gained any advantage, both sides drew off. Parker considered that he had not been properly equipped for his task, and insisted on resigning his command. In 1782 he accepted the East Indies command, though he had just succeeded to the family baronetcy. On the outward voyage his flagship, the "Cato" (60), was lost with all on board.

His second son, Admiral SIR HYDE PARKER (1739–1807), entered the navy at an early age, and became lieutenant in 1758, having passed most of his early service in his father's ships. Five years later he became a post-captain, and from 1766 onwards for many years he served in the West Indies and in North American waters, particularly distinguishing himself in breaking the defences of the North river (New York) in 1776. His services on this occasion earned him a knighthood in 1779. In 1778 he was engaged in the Savannah expedition, and in the following year his ship was wrecked on the hostile Cuban coast. His men, however, entrenched themselves, and were in the end brought off safely. Parker was with his father at the Dogger Bank, and with Howe in the two actions in the Straits of Gibraltar. In 1793, having just become rear-admiral, he served under Lord Hood at Toulon and in Corsica, and two years later, now a vice-admiral, he took part, under Hotham, in the indecisive fleet actions of the 13th of March and the 13th of July 1795. From 1796 to 1800 he was in command at Jamaica and ably conducted the operations in the West Indies. In 1801 he was appointed to command the fleet destined to break up the northern armed neutrality, with Nelson as his second-in-command. Copenhagen, the first objective of the expedition, fell on the 2nd of April to the fierce attack of Nelson's squadron, Parker with the heavier ships taking little part. Subsequently Parker hesitated to advance up the Baltic after his victory, a decision which was severely criticised. Soon afterwards he was recalled and Nelson succeeded him. He died in 1807.

The family name was continued in the navy in his eldest son, who became vice-admiral and was First Sea Lord of the Admiralty in 1853 (dying in 1854); and also in that son's son, who as a captain in the Black Sea was killed in 1854 when storming a Russian fort.

PARKER, JOHN HENRY (1806–1884), English writer on architecture, the son of a London merchant, was born on the 1st of March 1806. He was educated at Manor House School, Chiswick, and in 1821 entered business as a bookseller. Succeeding his uncle, Joseph Parker, as a bookseller at Oxford in 1832, he conducted the business with great success, the most important of the firm's publications being perhaps the series of the " Oxford Pocket Classics." In 1836 he brought out his *Glossary of Architecture*, which, published in the earlier years of the Gothic revival in England, had considerable influence in extending the movement, and supplied a valuable help to young architects. In 1848 he edited the fifth edition of Rickman's *Gothic Architecture*, and in 1849 he published a handbook based on his earlier volume and entitled *Introduction to the Study of Gothic Architecture*. The completion of Hudson Turner's *Domestic Architecture of the Middle Ages* next engaged his attention, three volumes being published (1853–1860). In 1858 he published *Mediaeval Architecture of Chester*. Parker was one of the chief advocates of the " restoration " of ecclesiastical buildings, and published in 1866 *Architectural Antiquities of the City of Wells*. Latterly he devoted much attention to explorations of the history of Rome by means of excavations, and succeeded in satisfying himself of the historical truth of much usually regarded as legendary. Two volumes of his *Archaeology of Rome* were published at Oxford in 1874 and 1876. In recognition of his labours he was decorated by the king of Italy, and received a medal from Pope Pius IX. In 1869 he endowed the keepership of the Ashmolean Museum with a sum yielding £250 a year, and under the new arrangement he was appointed the first keeper. In 1871 he was nominated C.B. He died at Oxford on the 31st of January 1884.

PARKER, JOSEPH (1830–1902), English Nonconformist divine, was born at Hexham-on-Tyne on the 9th of April 1830, his father being a stonemason. He managed to pick up a fair education, which in after-life he constantly supplemented. In the revolutionary years from 1845 to 1850 young Parker as a local preacher and temperance orator gained a reputation for vigorous utterance. He was influenced by Thomas Cooper, the Chartist, and Edward Miall, the Liberationist, and was much associated with Joseph Cowen, afterwards M. P. for Newcastle. In the spring of 1852 he wrote to Dr John Campbell, minister of Whitefield Tabernacle, Moorfields, London, for advice as to entering the Congregational ministry, and after a short probation he became Campbell's assistant. He also attended lectures in logic and philosophy at University College, London. From 1853 to 1858 he was pastor at Banbury. His next charge was at Cavendish Street, Manchester, where he rapidly made himself felt as a power in English Nonconformity. While here he published a volume of lectures entitled *Church Questions*, and, anonymously, *Ecce Deus* (1868), a work provoked by Seeley's *Ecce Homo*. The university of Chicago conferred on him the degree of D.D. In 1869 he returned to London as minister of the Poultry church, founded by Thomas Goodwin. Almost at once he began the scheme which resulted in the erection of the great City Temple in Holborn Viaduct. It cost £70,000, and was opened on the 19th of May 1874. From this centre his influence spread far and wide. His stimulating and original sermons, with their notable leaning towards the use of a racy vernacular, made him one of the best known personalities of his time. Dr Parker was twice chairman of the London Congregational Board and twice of the Congregational Union of England and Wales. The death of his second wife in 1899 was a blow from which he never fully recovered, and he died on the 28th of November 1902.

Parker was pre-eminently a preacher, and his published works are chiefly sermons and expositions, chief among them being *City Temple Sermons* (1869–1870) and *The People's Bible*, in 25 vols. (1885–1895). Other volumes include the autobiographical *Springdale Abbey* (1869), *The Inner Life of Christ* (1881), *Apostolic Life* (1884), *Tyne Chylde: My Life and Teaching* (1883; new ed., 1889), *A Preacher's Life* (1899).

See E. C. Pike, *Dr Parker and his Friends* (1905); *Congregational Year-Book* (1904).

PARKER, MARTIN (c. 1600–c. 1656), English ballad writer, was probably a London tavern-keeper. About 1625 he seems to have begun publishing ballads, a large number of which bearing his signature or his initials, "M.P.," are preserved in the British Museum. Dryden considered him the best ballad writer of his time. His sympathies were with the Royalist cause during the Civil War, and it was in support of the declining fortunes of Charles I. that he wrote the best known of his ballads, " When the King enjoys his own again," which he first published in 1643, and which, after enjoying great popularity at the Restoration, became a favourite Jacobite song in the 18th century. Parker also wrote a nautical ballad, " Sailors for my Money," which in a revised version survives as " When the stormy winds do blow." It is not known when he died, but the appearance in 1656 of a " funeral elegy," in which the ballad writer was satirically celebrated is perhaps a correct indication of the date of his death.

See *The Roxburghe Ballads*, vol. iii. (Ballad Soc., 9 vols., 1871–1899); Joseph Ritson, *Bibliographia Poetica* (London, 1802); *Ancient Songs and Ballads from Henry II. to the Revolution*, ed. by W. C. Hazlitt (London, 1877); Sir S. E. Brydges and J. Haslewood, *The British Bibliographer*, vol. ii. (London, 1810); Thomas Corser, *Collectanea Anglo-poetica* (London, 1860–1883).

PARKER, MATTHEW (1504–1575), archbishop of Canterbury, was the eldest son of William Parker, a citizen of Norwich, where he was born, in St Saviour's parish, on the 6th of August 1504. His mother's maiden name was Alice Monins, and a John Monins married Cranmer's sister Jane, but no definite relationship between the two archbishops has been traced. William Parker died about 1516, and his widow married a certain John Baker. Matthew was sent in 1522 to Corpus Christi College, Cambridge, where he is said by most of his biographers, including the latest, to have been contemporary with Cecil; but Cecil was only two years old when Parker went to Cambridge. He graduated B.A. in 1525, was ordained deacon in April and priest in June 1527, and was elected fellow of Corpus in the following September. He commenced M.A. in 1528, and was one of the Cambridge scholars whom Wolsey wished to transplant to his newly founded Cardinal College at Oxford. Parker, like Cranmer, declined the invitation. He had come under the influence of the Cambridge reformers, and after Anne Boleyn's recognition as queen he was made her chaplain. Through her he was appointed dean of the college of secular canons at Stoke-by-Clare in 1535. Latimer wrote to him in that year urging him not to fall short of the expectations which had been formed of his ability. In 1537 he was appointed chaplain to Henry VIII., and in 1538 he was threatened with prosecution by the reactionary party. The bishop of Dover, however, reported to Cromwell that Parker "hath ever been of a good judgment and set forth the Word of God after a good manner. For this he suffers some grudge." He graduated D.D. in that year, and in 1541 he was appointed to the second prebend in the reconstituted cathedral church of Ely. In 1544 on Henry VIII.'s recommendation he was elected master of Corpus Christi College, and in 1545 vice-chancellor of the university. He got into some trouble with the chancellor, Gardiner, over a ribald play, "Pammachius," performed by the students, deriding the old ecclesiastical system, though Bonner wrote to Parker of the assured affection he bore him. On the passing of the act of parliament in 1545 enabling the king to dissolve chantries and colleges, Parker was appointed one of the commissioners for Cambridge, and their report saved its colleges, if there had ever been any intention to destroy them. Stoke, however, was dissolved in the following reign, and Parker received a pension equivalent to £400 a year in modern currency. He took advantage of the new reign to marry in June, 1547, before clerical marriages had been legalized by parliament and convocation, Margaret, daughter of Robert Harlestone, a Norfolk squire. During Kett's rebellion he was allowed to preach in the rebels' camp on Mousehold Hill, but without much effect; and later on he encouraged his chaplain, Alexander Neville, to write his history of the rising. His Protestantism advanced with the times, and he received higher promotion under Northumberland than under the moderate Somerset. Bucer was his friend at Cambridge, and he preached Bucer's funeral sermon in 1551. In 1552 he was promoted to the rich deanery of Lincoln, and in July 1553 he supped with Northumberland at Cambridge, when the duke marched north on his hopeless campaign against Mary.

As a supporter of Northumberland and a married man, Parker was naturally deprived of his deanery, his mastership of Corpus, and his other preferments. But he found means to live in England throughout Mary's reign without further molestation. He was not cast in a heroic mould, and he had no desire to figure at the stake; like Cecil, and Elizabeth herself, he had a great respect for authority, and when his time came he could consistently impose authority on others. He was not eager to assume this task, and he made great efforts to avoid promotion to the archbishopric of Canterbury, which Elizabeth designed for him as soon as she had succeeded to the throne. He was elected on the 1st of August 1559; but it was difficult to find the requisite four bishops willing and qualified to consecrate him, and not until the 17th of December did Barlow, Scory, Coverdale and Hodgkins perform that ceremony at Lambeth. The legend of an indecent consecration at the Nag's Head tavern in Fleet Street seems first to have been printed by the Jesuit, Christopher Holywood, in 1604; and it has long been abandoned by reputable controversialists. Parker's consecration was, however, only made legally valid by the plenitude of the royal supremacy; for the Edwardine Ordinal, which was used, had been repealed by Mary and not re-enacted by the parliament of 1559.

Parker owes his fame to circumstances rather than to personal qualifications. This wise moderation of the Elizabethan settlement, which had been effected before his appointment, was obviously not due to him; and Elizabeth could have placed Knox or Bonner in the chair of St Augustine had she been so minded. But she wanted a moderate man, and so she chose Parker. He possessed all the qualifications she expected from an archbishop except celibacy. He distrusted popular enthusiasm, and he wrote in horror of the idea that " the people "should be the reformers of the Church. He was not inspiring as a leader of religion; and no dogma, no original theory of church government, no prayer-book, not even a tract or a hymn is associated with his name. The 56 volumes published by the Parker Society include only one by its eponymous hero, and that is a volume of correspondence. He was a disciplinarian, a scholar, a modest and moderate man of genuine piety and irreproachable morals. His historical research was exemplified in his De antiquitate ecclesiae, and his editions of Asser, Matthew Paris, Walsingham, and the compiler known as Matthew of Westminster; his liturgical skill was shown in his version of the psalter and in the occasional prayers and thanksgivings which he was called upon to compose; and he left a priceless collection of manuscripts to his college at Cambridge.

He was happier in these pursuits than in the exercise of his jurisdiction. With secular politics he had little to do, and he was never admitted to Elizabeth's privy council. But ecclesiastical politics gave him an infinity of trouble. Many of the reformers wanted no bishops at all, while the Catholics wanted those of the old dispensation, and the queen herself grudged episcopal privilege until she discovered in it one of the chief bulwarks of the royal supremacy. Parker was therefore left to stem the rising tide of Puritan feeling with little support from parliament, convocation or the Crown. The bishops' Interpretations and Further Considerations, issued in 1560, tolerated a lower vestiarian standard than was prescribed by the rubric of 1559; the Advertisements, which Parker published in 1566, to check the Puritan descent, had to appear without specific royal sanction; and the Reformatio legum ecclesiasticarum, which Foxe published with Parker's approval, received neither royal, parliamentary nor synodical authorization. Parliament even contested the claim of the bishops to determine matters of faith. " Surely," said Parker to Peter Wentworth, " you will refer yourselves wholly to us therein. " " No, by the faith I bear to God," retorted Wentworth," we will pass nothing before we understand what it is; for that were but to ,make you popes. Make you popes who list, for we will make you none." Disputes about vestments had expanded into a controversy over the whole field of Church government and authority, and Parker died on the 17th of May, 1575, lamenting that Puritan

ideas of "governance" would " in conclusion undo the queen and all others that depended upon her." By his personal conduct he had set an ideal example for Anglican priests, and it was not his fault that national authority failed to crush the individualistic tendencies of the Protestant Reformation.

John Strype's Life of Parker, originally published in 1711, and re-edited for the Clarendon Press in 1821 (3 vols.), is the principal source for Parker's life. A biographical sketch written from a different point of view was published by W. M. Kennedy in 1908. See also J. Bass Mullinger's scholarly life in Dict. Nat. Biog.; W. H. Frere's volume in Stephens and Hunt's Church History; Strype's Works (General Index); Gough's Index to Parker Soc. Publ. Fuller, Burnet, Collier and R. W. Dixon's Histories of the Church; Birt's Elizabethan Settlement; H. Gee's Elizabethan Clergy (1898); Froude's Hist. of England; and vol. vi. in Longman's Political History.   (A. F. P.)

PARKER, SAMUEL (1640–1688), English bishop, was born at Northampton, and educated at Wadham College, Oxford. His Presbyterian views caused him to move to Trinity College, where, however, the influence of the senior fellow induced him to join the Church of England, and he was ordained in 1664. In 1665 he published an essay entitled Tentamina physico-theologica de Deo, dedicated to Archbishop Sheldon, who in 1667 appointed him one of his chaplains. He became rector of Chartham, Kent, in the same year. In 1670 he became archdeacon of Canterbury, and two years after he was appointed rector of Ickham, Kent. In 1673 he was elected master of Edenbridge Hospital. His Discourse of Ecclesiastical Politie (London, 1670), advocating state regulation of religious affairs, led him into controversy with Andrew Marvell (1621–1675). James II. appointed him to the bishopric of Oxford in 1686, and he in turn forwarded the king's policy, especially by defending the royal right to appoint Roman Catholics to office. In 1687 the ecclesiastical commission forcibly installed him as president of Magdalen College, Oxford, the fellows having refused to elect any of the king's nominees. He was commonly regarded as a Roman Catholic, but he would appear to have been no more than an extreme exponent of the High Church doctrine of passive obedience. After he became president the action of the king in replacing the expelled fellows with Roman Catholics agitated him to such a degree as to hasten his end; to the priests sent to persuade him on his death-bed to be received into the Roman Church he declared that he " never had been and never would be of that religion," and he died in the communion of the Church of England.

Parker's second son, SAMUEL PARKER (1681–1730), was the author of Bibliotheca biblica, or Patristic Commentary on the Scriptures (1720–1735), an abridged translation of Eusebius, and other works. He was also responsible during 1708 and 1709 for a monthly periodical entitled Censura temporum, or Good and Ill Tendencies of Books. He passed most of his life in retirement at Oxford. His younger son Richard founded the well-known publishing firm in Oxford.

See Magdalen College and James II. 1686–1688, by the Rev. J. R. Bloxam (Oxford Historical Society, 1886).

PARKER, THEODORE (1810–1860), American preacher and social reformer, was born at Lexington, Massachusetts, on the 24th of August 1810, the youngest of eleven children. His father, John Parker, a small farmer and skilful mechanic, was a typical New England yeoman. His mother took great pains with the religious education of her children, " caring, however, but little for doctrines," and making religion to consist of love and good works. His paternal grand-father, Captain John Parker (1729–1775), was the leader of the Lexington minute-men in the skirmish at Lexington. Theodore obtained the elements of knowledge in the schools of the district, which were open during the winter months only. During the rest of the year he worked on his father's farm.. At the age of seventeen he became himself a winter schoolmaster, working on the farm as usual (until 1831) while he followed his studies and going over to Cambridge for the examinations only. For the theological course he took up in 1834 his residence in the college, meeting his expenses by a small sum amassed by school-keeping and by help from a poor students' fund, and graduating in 1836. At the close of his college career he began his translation (published in 1843) of Wilhelm M. L. De Wette's *Beiträge zur Einleitung in das Alte Testament*. His journal and letters show that he had made acquaintance with a large number of languages, including Hebrew, Chaldee, Syriac, Arabic, Coptic, Ethiopic, as well as the classical and the principal modern European languages. When he entered the divinity school he was an orthodox Unitarian; when he left it, he entertained strong doubts about the infallibility of the Bible, the possibility of miracles, and the exclusive claims of Christianity and the Church. Emerson's transcendentalism greatly influenced him, and Strauss's *Leben Jesu* left its mark upon his thought. His first ministerial charge was over a small village parish, West Roxbury, a few miles from Boston; here he was ordained as a Unitarian clergyman in June 1837 and here he preached until January 1846. His views were slowly assuming the form which subsequently found such strong expression in his writing; but the progress was slow, and the cautious reserve of his first rationalistic utterances was in striking contrast with his subsequent rashness. But on the 19th of May 1841 he preached at Boston a sermon on "the transient and permanent in Christianity," which presented in embryo the main principles and ideas of his final theological position, and the preaching of which determined his subsequent relations to the churches with which he was connected and to the whole ecclesiastical world. The Boston Unitarian clergy denounced the preacher, and declared that the "young man must be silenced." No Unitarian publisher could be found for his sermon, and nearly all the pulpits of the city were closed against him. A number of gentlemen in Boston, however, invited him to give a series of lectures there. The result was that he delivered in the Masonic Hall, in the winter of 1841–1842, as lectures, substantially the volume afterwards published as the *Discourse of Matters pertaining to Religion*. The lectures in their published form made his name famous throughout America and Europe, and confirmed the stricter Unitarians in America in their attitude towards him and his supporters. His friends, however, resolved that he should be heard in Boston, and there, beginning with 1845, he preached regularly for fourteen years. Previous to his removal from West Roxbury to Boston Parker spent a year in Europe, calling in Germany upon Paulus, Gervinus, De Wette and Ewald, and preaching in Liverpool in the pulpits of James Martineau and J. H. Thom. After January 1846 he devoted himself exclusively to his work in Boston. In addition to his Sunday labours he lectured throughout the States, and prosecuted his wide studies, collecting particularly the materials for an *opus magnum* on the development of religion in mankind. Above all he took up the question of the emancipation of the slaves, and fearlessly advocated in Boston and elsewhere, from the platform and through the press, the cause of the negroes. He made his influence felt also by correspondence with political leaders and by able political speeches, one of which, delivered in 1858, contained the sentence, " Democracy is direct self-government, over all the people, by all the people, for all the people," which probably suggested Abraham Lincoln's oft-quoted variant. Parker assisted actively in the escape of fugitive slaves, and for trying to prevent the rendition of perhaps the most famous of them, Anthony Burns, was indicted, but the indictment was quashed. He also gave his aid to John Brown (q.v.). By his voice, his pen, and his utterly fearless action in social and political matters he became a great power in Boston and America generally. But his days were numbered. His mother had suffered from phthisis; and he himself now fell a victim to the same disease. In January 1859 he suffered a violent haemorrhage of the lungs, and sought relief by retreating first to the West Indies and afterwards to Europe. He died at Florence on the 10th of May 1860.

The fundamental articles of Parker's religious faith were the three "instinctive intuitions" of God, of a moral law, and of immortality. His own mind, heart and life were undoubtedly pervaded, sustained and ruled by the feelings, convictions and hopes which he formulated in these three articles; and he rationalized his own religious conceptions in a number of expositions which do credit to his sincerity and courage. But he was a preacher rather than a thinker, a reformer rather than a philosopher.

Parker's principal works are: *A Discourse of Matters pertaining to Religion* (1842); *Ten Sermons of Religion* (1853); and *Sermons of Theism, Atheism and the Popular Theology* (1853). A collected edition of his works was published in England by Frances Power Cobbe (14 vols., 1863–1870), and another—the Centenary edition—in Boston, Mass., by the American Unitarian Association (14 vols., 1907–1911); a volume of *Theodore Parker's Prayers*, edited by Rufus Leighton and Matilda Goddard, was published in America in 1861, and a volume of Parker's *West Roxbury Sermons*, with a biographical sketch by Frank B. Sanborn, was published in Boston, Mass., in 1892. A German translation of part of his works was made by Ziethen (Leipzig 1854–1857).

The best biographies are John Weiss's *Life and Correspondence of Theodore Parker* (New York, 1864); O. B. Frothingham's *Theodore Parker: a Biography* (Boston, 1874); and John White Chadwick's *Theodore Parker, Preacher and Reformer* (Boston, 1900), the last containing a good bibliography. Valuable reviews of Parker's theological position and of his character and work have appeared—by James Martineau, in the *National Review* (April 1860), and J. H. Thom, in the *Theological Review* (March 1864).

PARKERSBURG, a city and the county-seat of Wood county, West Virginia, U.S.A., on the Ohio river, at the mouth of the Little Kanawha, about 95 m. below Wheeling. Pop. (1890), 8408; (1900), 11,703, of whom 515 were foreign-born and 783 were negroes; (1910 census), 17,842. Parkersburg is served by the Baltimore & Ohio, the Baltimore & Ohio Southwestern, and the Little Kanawha railways, by electric railway to Marietta, Ohio, and by passenger and freight boats to Pittsburg, Cincinnati, intermediate ports, and ports on the Little Kanawha. Parkersburg is the see of a Protestant Episcopal bishop. Oil, coal, natural gas and fire-clay abound in the neighbouring region, and the city is engaged in the refining of oil and the manufacture of pottery, brick and tile, glass, lumber, furniture, flour, steel, and foundry and machine-shop products. In 1905 the value of the factory products was $3,778,139 (21.9% more than in 1900). Parkersburg was settled in 1789, was incorporated in 1820, and received a new charter in 1903, when its boundaries were enlarged. About 2 m. below the city is the island which was the home of Harman Blennerhassett (q.v.) and bears his name.

PARKES, SIR HARRY SMITH (1828–1885), English diplomatist, son of Harry Parkes, founder of the firm of Parkes, Otway & Co., ironmasters, was born at Birchills Hall, near Walsall in Staffordshire, in 1828. When but four years old his mother died and in the following year his father was killed in a carriage accident. Being thus left an orphan, he found a home with his uncle, a retired naval officer, at Birmingham. He received his education at King Edward's Grammar School. In 1837 his uncle died, and in 1841 he sailed for Macao in China, to take up his residence at the house of his cousin, Mrs Gutzlaff. At this time what was known as the " Opium War " had broken out, and Parkes eagerly prepared himself to take part in the events which were passing around him by diligently applying himself to the study of Chinese. In 1842 he received his first appointment in the consular service. Fortunately for him, he was privileged to accompany Sir Henry Pottinger in his expedition up the Yangtsze-kiang to Nanking, and after having taken part in the capture of Chinkiang and the surrender of Nanking, he witnessed the signing of the treaty on board the " Cornwallis " in August 1842. By this treaty the five ports of Canton, Amoy, Fuchow, Ningpo and Shanghai were opened to trade. After short residences at Canton and the newly opened Amoy, Parkes was appointed to the consulate at Fuchow. Here he served under Mr (afterwards Sir) Rutherford Alcock, who was one of the few Englishmen who knew how to manage the Chinese. In 1849 he returned to England on leave, and after visiting the Continent and doing some hard work for the foreign office he returned to China in 1851. After a short stay at Amoy as interpreter he was transferred in the same capacity to Canton. In May 1854 he was promoted to be consul at Amoy, and in 1855 was chosen as secretary to the mission to Bangkok, being largely instrumental in negotiating the first European treaty with Siam. In June 1856 he returned to Canton as acting consul, a position which brought him into renewed contact with Commissioner Yeh, whose insolence and obstinacy led to the second China War. Yeh had now met a man of even greater power and determination than himself, and when, in October 1856, as a climax to many outrages, Yeh seized the British lorcha " Arrow " and made prisoners of her crew, Parkes at once closed with his enemy. In response to a strongly worded despatch from Parkes, Sir John Bowring, governor of Hong-Kong, placed matters in the hands of Admiral Sir M. Seymour, who took Canton at the close of the same month but had not a sufficient force to hold it. In December 1857 Canton was again bombarded by Admiral Seymour. Parkes, who was attached to the admiral's staff, was the first man to enter the city, and himself tracked down and arrested Commissioner Yeh. As the city was to be held, an allied commission was appointed to govern it, consisting of two Englishmen, of whom one was Parkes, and a French naval officer. Parkes virtually governed this city of a million inhabitants for three years. Meanwhile the treacherous attack at Taku upon Sir Frederick Bruce led to a renewal of hostilities in the north, and Parkes was ordered up to serve as interpreter and adviser to Lord Elgin (July,1860). In pursuance of these duties he went in advance of the army to the city of Tungchow, near Peking, to arrange a meeting between Lord Elgin and the Chinese commissioners who had been appointed to draw up the preliminaries of peace. While thus engaged he, Mr (afterwards Lord) Loch, Mr de Norman, Lord Elgin's secretary of legation, Mr Bowlby, the *Times* correspondent, and others, were treacherously taken prisoners (Sept. 18, 1860). Parkes and Loch were carried off to the prison of the board of punishments at Peking, where they were separately herded with the lowest class of criminals. After ten days' confinement in this den of iniquity they were removed to a temple in the city, where they were comfortably housed and fed, and from which, after a further detention, they were granted their liberty. For this signal instance of treachery Lord Elgin burned down the Summer Palace of the emperor. Towards the end of 1860 Parkes returned to his post at Canton. On the restoration (Oct. 1861) of the city to the Chinese he returned to England on leave, when he was made K.C.B. for his services; he had received the companionship of the order in 1860. On his return to China he served for a short time as consul at Shanghai, and was then appointed minister to Japan (1865). For eighteen years he held this post, and throughout that time he strenuously used his influence in support of the Liberal party of Japan. So earnestly did he throw in his lot with these reformers that he became a marked man, and incurred the bitter hostility of the reactionaries, who on three separate occasions attempted to assassinate him. In 1882 he was transferred to Peking. While in Peking his health failed, and he died of malarial fever on the 21st of March 1885. In 1856 Sir H. (then Mr) Parkes married Miss Fanny Plumer, who died in 1879. The standard *Life* is by Stanley Lane-Poole (1894). (R. K. D.)

PARKES, SIR HENRY (1815–1896), Australian statesman, was born at Stoneleigh, in Warwickshire, on the 27th of May 1815. The son of parents in very humble circumstances, he received only a rudimentary education, and at an early age was obliged to earn his living as a common labourer. Failing to make his way in England, he emigrated to Australia in 1839, and after a time settled in Sydney as an ivory-turner. Conscious of his great powers, he worked unremittingly to repair the deficiencies of his education, and developed a genuine taste for literature, and a gift for versification which won the approval of so severe a judge as Tennyson. His first volume of poems was published in 1842, under the title of *Stolen Moments*. He now began to take an active part in politics, and soon showed himself the wielder of an incisive style as a leader-writer, and a popular orator of unrivalled influence. He took a prominent

part in the movement against the transportation of convicts, and in 1849 started the *Empire* newspaper to inculcate his policy of attacking abuses while remaining loyal to the Crown. The paper at once made its mark, but owing to financial difficulties ceased to appear in 1858. One of the reforms for which Parkes fought most strenuously was the full introduction of responsible government. He was returned to the legislative council under the old constitution as member for Sydney, and on the establishment of a legislative assembly in 1856 was elected for East Sydney. His parliamentary career was twice interrupted by pecuniary embarrassments; indeed, he never acquired the art of making money, and in spite of a public subscription raised in 1887 died in absolute penury. He was elected for East Sydney in 1859 at the first general election under the new electoral act, and sat till 1861, when he was sent to England as a commissioner for promoting emigration. He made a prolonged stay in England, and described his impressions in a series of letters to the *Sydney Morning Herald*, some of which were reprinted in 1869 under the title of *Australian Views of England*. He returned to Australia in 1863, and, re-entering the Assembly, became colonial secretary in the Martin ministry from 1866 to 1868. He succeeded in passing the Public Schools Act of 1866, which for the first time instituted an efficient system of primary education in the colony. His great chance came in 1872, when the Martin ministry resigned on the question of the sum payable by Victoria in lieu of border duties. Parkes had for several years persistently advocated free imports as a remedy for the financial distress of the colony. He now became prime minister and colonial secretary; and rising to the height of his opportunity, he removed the cause of dispute by throwing the colony open to trade. He held office till 1875, and on the fall of the Robertson ministry again became premier and colonial secretary from March till August 1877. At the end of this year he was made K.C.M.G. Finding that the state of parties did not allow of the existence of a stable ministry, he formed a coalition with Sir John Robertson, and became premier and colonial secretary for the third time from December 1878 to January 1883. In 1882 and in 1883–1884 he paid prolonged visits to England. Already distinguished among Australian statesmen for breadth of outlook and passionate devotion to the Empire, he returned with those qualities enhanced. For a time he found himself almost in a position of isolation, but in 1887 the policy of protection adopted by his successors brought him again into office. His free trade policy was once more successful. Other important measures of his administration were the reform of the civil service, the prohibition of Chinese immigration, and the railways and public works acts. He fell from office in January 1889, but in the following March became for the fifth time premier and colonial secretary. The remainder of his life was chiefly devoted to the question of Australian federation. The Federal Convention at Melbourne in 1890 was mainly his work; and he presided over the convention at Sydney in 1891, and was chiefly responsible for the draft constitution there carried. Defeated in October 1891 on his refusal to accept an eight hours' day for coal-miners, he remained in opposition for the rest of his career, sacrificing even free trade in the hope of smoothing the path of federation. He died at Sydney on the 27th of April 1896; but though he did not live to see the realization of his efforts, he may justly be called the Father of the Australian Commonwealth.

He published, in addition to the works already named and numerous volumes of verse, a collection of speeches on the *Federal Government of Australia* (1890), and an autobiography, *Fifty Years in the making of Australian History* (1892).

PARKIN, GEORGE ROBERT (1846–   ), British Canadian educationist, was born at Salisbury, New Brunswick, on the 8th of February 1846. His father had gone to Canada from Yorkshire. Parkin was the youngest of a family of thirteen, and after attending the local schools he started at an early age as a teacher. Bent on improving his own education, he then entered the university of New Brunswick, where he carried off high honours in 1866–1868. From 1868 to 1872 he was head master of Bathurst grammar school; but he was not content with the opportunities for study open to him in Canada, and he went to England and entered Oxford. Here the enthusiastic young Canadian was not only profoundly affected himself by entering strenuously into the life of the ancient university (he was secretary of the Union when H. H. Asquith was president), but in his turn was instrumental in bringing the possibilities of British Imperialism to the minds of some of the ablest among his contemporaries—his juniors by six or eight years. It is hardly too much to say that in his intercourse at Oxford in the early 'seventies with men of influence who were then undergraduates the imperialist movement in England substantially began. On returning to Canada he became principal of the chief New Brunswick school at Fredericton (where in 1878 he married), and for fifteen years he did excellent work in this capacity. But in 1889 he was again drawn more directly into the imperialist cause. The federation movement had gone ahead in the meanwhile, and Parkin had always been associated with it; and now he became a missionary speaker for the Imperial Federation League, travelling for several years about the empire for that purpose. He also became Canadian correspondent of *The Times*, and in that capacity helped to make Canada better known in the mother country. In 1894 he was given the honorary degree of LL.D. by Oxford. In 1895 he returned to scholastic work as principal of Upper Canada College, Toronto, and retained this post till 1902; but he continued in the meanwhile to support the imperialist movement by voice and pen. When in 1902 an organizer was required for the Rhodes Scholarship Trust (see RHODES, CECIL), in order to create the machinery for working it in the countries to which it applied, he accepted the appointment; and his devotion to this task was largely responsible for the success with which Rhodes's idea was carried out at Oxford. His publications include *Reorganization of the British Empire* (1882), *Imperial Federation* (1892), *Round the Empire* (1892), *Life of Edward Thring* (1897), *Life of Sir John Macdonald* (1907).

PARKINSON, JAMES (d. 1824), English palaeontologist, was educated for the medical profession, and practised in Hoxton, from about the year 1785. He was a Fellow of the Royal College of Surgeons, and one of the original members of the Geological Society of London (1807). He was author of numerous chemical and medical books, the most important of which were *Organic Remains of a Former World* (3 vols., 1804, 1808, 1811), and *Outlines of Oryctology* (1822). Parkinson died in London, on the 21st of December 1824.

See *Hist. of Collections in Brit. Mus. Nat. Hist. Dep.* (1904), pp. 315–316.

PARKMAN, FRANCIS (1823–1893), American historian, was born in Boston on the 16th of September 1823. His great-grandfather, Ebenezer Parkman, a graduate of Harvard in 1721, was for nearly sixty years minister of the Congregational Church in Westborough, and was noted for his devotion to the study of history. One of this good clergyman's sons, Samuel Parkman, became an eminent merchant in Boston, and exhibited much skill in horticulture. Samuel's son, Francis Parkman, a graduate of Harvard in 1807, was one of the most eminent of the Boston clergymen, a pupil and friend of Channing, and noted among Unitarians for a broadly tolerant disposition. This Dr Parkman, a man of rare sagacity and exquisite humour, was the father of Francis Parkman, the historian. His mother was a descendant of the celebrated John Cotton. She was the daughter of Nathaniel Hall of Medford, member of a family which was represented in the convention that framed the constitution of Massachusetts in 1780.

Francis Parkman was the eldest of her six children. As a boy his health was delicate, so that it was thought best for him to spend much of his time at his grandfather Hall's home in Medford rather than in the city. That home was situated on the border of the Middlesex Fells, a rough and rocky woodland, 4000 acres in extent, as wild and savage in many places as the primeval forest. The place is within 8 m. of Boston, and it may be doubted if anywhere else can be found another

such magnificent piece of wilderness so near to a great city. There young Parkman spent his leisure hours in collecting eggs, insects and reptiles, trapping squirrels and woodchucks, and shooting birds with arrows. This breezy life saved him from the artificial stupidity which is too often superinduced in boys by their school training. At the age of fourteen Parkman began to show a strong taste for literary composition. In 1841, while a student at Harvard, he made a rough journey of exploration in the woods of northern New Hampshire, where he had a taste of adventure slightly spiced with hardship. About this time he made up his mind to write a history of the last French war in America, which ended in the conquest of Canada, and some time afterwards he enlarged the plan so as to include the whole course of the American conflict between France and Great Britain; or, to use his own words, "The history of the American forest; for this was the light in which I regarded it. My theme fascinated me, and I was haunted with wilderness images day and night." The way in which true genius works could not be more happily described. In the course of 1842 an attack of illness led to his making a journey in Italy, where he spent some time in a monastery belonging to one of the strictest of all the monastic orders, the Passionists, brethren addicted to wearing hair shirts and scourging themselves without mercy. In the young historian's eyes these good brethren were of much value as living and breathing historic material. In 1844 he graduated at Harvard with high rank.

He now made up his mind to study the real wilderness in its gloom and vastness, and to meet face to face the dusky warriors of the Stone Age. To-day such a thing can hardly be done within the United States, for nowhere does the primitive wilderness exist save here and there in shreds and patches. So recently as the middle of the 19th century, however, it covered the western half of the continent, and could be reached by a journey of 1600 or 1700 miles from Boston to the plains of Nebraska. Parkman had become an adept in woodcraft and a dead shot with the rifle, and could do such things with horses, tame or wild, as civilized people never see done except in a circus. In company with his friend and classmate, Mr Quincy Shaw, he passed several months with the Ogillalah band of Sioux. Knowledge, intrepidity and tact carried Parkman through these experiences unscathed, and good luck kept him clear of encounters with hostile Indians, in which these qualities might not have sufficed to avert destruction. It was a very important experience in relation to his life-work. This outdoor life, however, did not suffice to recruit Parkman's health, and by 1848, when he began writing *The Conspiracy of Pontiac*, he had reached a truly pitiable condition. The trouble seems to have been some form of nervous exhaustion, accompanied with such hypersensitiveness of the eyes that it was impossible to keep them open except in a dark room. Against these difficulties he struggled with characteristic obstinacy. He invented a machine which so supported his hand that he could write legibly with closed eyes. Books and documents were read aloud to him, while notes were made by him with eyes shut, and were afterwards deciphered and read aloud to him till he had mastered them. After half an hour his strength would give out, and in these circumstances his rate of composition for a long time averaged scarcely six lines a day. The superb historical monograph composed under such difficulties was published in 1851. It had but a small sale, as the American public was then too ignorant to feel much interest in American history.

Undeterred by this inhospitable reception, Parkman took up at the beginning his great work on *France and England in the New World*, to which the book just mentioned was in reality the sequel. This work obliged him to trace out, collect, arrange, and digest a great mass of incongruous material scattered on both sides of the Atlantic, a large portion of which was in manuscript, and required much tedious exploration and the employment of trained copyists. This work involved several journeys to Europe, and was performed with a thoroughness approaching finality. In 1865 the first volume of the great work appeared, under the title of *Pioneers of France in the New World*; and then seven-and-twenty years more elapsed before the final volumes came out in 1892. Nowhere can we find a better illustration of the French critic's definition of a great life—a thought conceived in youth, and realized in later years. After the *Pioneers*, the sequence is *The Jesuits in North America, La Salle and the Discovery of the Great West, The Old Régime in Canada, Frontenac and New France and Louis XIV., Montcalm and Wolfe, A Half Century of Conflict.* As one obstacle after another was surmounted, as one grand division of the work after another became an accomplished fact, the effect upon Parkman's condition seems to have been bracing, and he acquired fresh impetus as he approached the goal. There can be little doubt that his physical condition was much improved by his habit of cultivating plants in garden and conservatory. He was a horticulturist of profound attainments, and himself originated several new varieties of flowers. His work in this department made him an enthusiastic adherent of the views of Darwin. He was professor of horticulture in the agricultural school of Harvard in 1871-1872, and published a few books on the subject of gardening. He died at Jamaica Plain, near Boston, on the 8th of November 1893.

The significance of Parkman's work consists partly in the success with which he has depicted the North-American Indians, those belated children of the Stone Age, who have been so persistently misunderstood alike by romancers, such as Cooper, and by detractors like Dr Palfrey. Parkman was the first great literary author who really understood the Indian's character and motives. Against this savage background of the forest Parkman shows the rise, progress and dramatic termination of the colossal struggle between France and Great Britain for colonial empire. With true philosophic insight he shows that France failed in the struggle not because of any inferiority in the ability and character of the men to whom the work was entrusted, but chiefly by reason of her despotic and protective régime. There is no more eloquent commentary upon the wholesome results of British self-government than is to be found in Parkman's book. But while the author deals with history philosophically, he does not, like Buckle, hurl at the reader's head huge generalizations, or, like Carlyle, preach him into somnolence. With all its manifold instructiveness, his book is a narrative as entertaining as those of Macaulay or Froude. In judicial impartiality Parkman may be compared with Gardiner, and for accuracy of learning with Stubbs.

There is a good *Life* by G. H. Farnham (Boston, 1900). (J. Fī.)

PARLA KIMEDI, a town of British India, in Ganjam district of Madras. Pop. (1901), 17,336. It is the residence of a rája, who claims descent from the ancient kings of Orissa. His estate covers an area of 614 sq. m., and pays a revenue of £7000 out of an estimated income of £36,000. He maintains a college, and has constructed a light railway (25 m.) to the station of Naupada on the East Coast railway. There is a trade in rice, and mats and other articles are woven of reeds.

PARLEMENT (see PARLIAMENT), in O. Fr. the name given to any meeting for discussion or debate (*parler*, to speak), a sense in which it was still used by Joinville, but from the latter half of the 13th century employed in France in a special sense to designate the sessions of the royal court (*curia regis*). Finally, when the Parlement of Paris had become a permanent court of justice, having the supreme authority in cases brought before it, and especially in appeals against the sentences of the *baillis* and seneschals, it retained this name, which was also given to the other supreme courts of the same nature which were created after its model in the provinces.

The early Capetians had a custom, based upon ancient precedents, of summoning periodically to their court their principal vassals and the prelates of their kingdom. These gatherings took place on the occasion of one of the great festivals of the year, in the town in which the king was then in residence. Here they deliberated upon political matters and the vassals and prelates gave the king their advice. But the monarch also gave judgment here in those cases which were brought before him. These were few in number during the early days of the

Capetian dynasty; for though the king always maintained the principle that he was judge, and even that his competence in this respect was general and unlimited, this competence was at the same time undefined and it was not compulsory to submit cases to the king. At this period, too, appeals, strictly so called, did not exist. Nevertheless when a suit was brought before the king he judged it with the assistance of his prelates and vassals assembled around him, who formed his council. This was the *curia regis*. But in law the king was sole judge, the vassals and prelates being only advisers. During the 12th and at the beginning of the 13th centuries the *curia regis* continued to discharge these functions, except that its importance and actual competence continued to increase, and that we frequently find in it, in addition to the vassals and prelates who formed the council, *consiliarii*, who are evidently men whom the king had in his entourage, as his ordinary and professional councillors. Under the reign of St Louis (which was also the period at which the name parlement began to be applied to these judicial sessions) the aspect of affairs changed. The judicial competence of the Parlement developed and became more clearly defined; the system of appeals came into existence, and appeals against the judgments of the *baillis* and seneschals were brought before it; cases concerning the royal towns, the *bonnes villes*, were also decided by it. Again, in the old registers of the Parlement at this period, the first *Olim* books, we see the names of the same councillors recurring from session to session. This suggests that a sufficient number of councillors was assured beforehand, and a list drawn up for each session; the vassals and prelates still figuring as a complementary body at the council.

Next came the series of ordinances regulating the tenure of the Parlement, those of 1278, 1291, 1296 and 1308, and the institution was regularized. Not only were the persons who were to constitute each Parlement named in advance, but those who were not placed on this list, even though vassals or prelates, were excluded from judging cases. The royal *baillis* had to attend the Parlement, in order to answer for their judgments, and at an early date was fixed the order of the different *bailliages*, in which the cases coming from them were heard. The *baillis*, when not interested in the case, formed part of the council, but were afterwards excluded from it. Before the middle of the 14th century the personnel of the Parlement, both presidents and councillors, became fixed *de facto* if not *de jure*. Every year a list was drawn up of those who were to hold the session, and although this list was annual, it contains the same names year after year; they are as yet, however, only annual commissaries (*commissaires*). In 1344 they became officials (*officiers*) fixed but not yet irremovable. At the same time the Parlement had become permanent, the number of the sessions had diminished, but their length had increased. In the course of the 14th century it became the rule for the Parlement to sit from Martinmas (Nov. 11) till the end of May; later the session was prolonged till the middle of August, the rest of the year forming the vacation. The Parlement had also become fixed at Paris, and, by a development which goes back to fairly early times, the presidents and councillors, instead of being merely the king's advisers, had acquired certain powers, though these were conferred by the monarch; they were, in fact, true magistrates. The king held his court in person less and less often, and it pronounced its decrees in his absence; we even find him pleading his cause before it as plaintiff or defendant. In the 14th century, however, we still find the Parlement referring delicate affairs to the king; but in the 15th century it had acquired a jurisdiction independent in principle. As to its composition, it continued to preserve one notable feature which recalled its origin. It had originally been an assembly of lay vassals and prelates; when its composition became fixed and consisted of councillor-magistrates, a certain number of these offices were necessarily occupied by laymen, and others by ecclesiastics, the *conseillers lais* and the *conseillers clercs*.

The Parlement was at the same time the court of peers (*cour des pairs*). This had as its origin the old principle according to which every vassal had the right to be tried by his peers, i.e. by the vassals holding fiefs from the same lord, who sat in judgment with that lord as their president. This, it is well known, resulted in the formation of the ancient college of the peers of France, which consisted of six laymen and six ecclesiastics. But although in strict logic the feudal causes concerning them should have been judged by them alone, they could not maintain this right in the *curia regis*; the other persons sitting in it could also take part in judging causes which concerned the peers. Finally the peers of France, the number of whom was increased in course of time by fresh royal creations of peerages, became *ex officio* members of the Parlement; they were the hereditary councillors, taking the oath as official magistrates, and, if they wished, sitting and having a deliberative function in the Parlement. In suits brought against them personally or involving the rights of their peerage they had the right of being judged by the Parlement, the other peers being present, or having been duly summoned.

While maintaining its unity, the Parlement had been sub-divided into several *chambres* or sections. In the first place there was the *Grand Chambre*, which represented the primitive Parlement. To it was reserved the judgment in certain important cases, and in it a peculiar procedure was followed, known as *oral*, though it admitted certain written documents. Even after the offices of the Parlement had become legally saleable the councillors could only pass from the other chambers into the *Chambre* by order of seniority. The *Chambres des enquêtes* and *des requêtes* originated at the time when it became customary to draw up lists for each session of the Parlement. The *enquêteurs* or *auditeurs* of the Parlement had at first been an auxiliary staff of clerks to whom were entrusted the inquests ordered by the Parlement. But later, when the institution of the appeal was fully developed, and the procedure before the various jurisdictions became a highly technical matter, above all when it admitted written evidence, the documents connected with other inquests also came before the Parlement. A new form of appeal grew up side by side with the older form, which had been mainly an oral procedure, namely the appeal by writing (*appel par écrit*). In order to judge these new appeals the Parlement had above all to study written documents, the inquests which had been made and written down under the jurisdiction of the court of first instance. The duty of the *enquêteurs* was to make an abstract of the written documents and report on them. Later the reporters (*rapporteurs*) were admitted to judge these questions together with a certain number of members of the Parlement, and from 1316 onwards these two kinds of member formed together a *chambre des enquêtes*. As yet, no doubt, the *rapporteur* only gave his opinion on the case which he had prepared, but after 1336 all those who formed part of the chamber were put on the same footing, taking it in turn to report and giving judgment as a whole. For a long time, however, the *Grand Chambre* received all cases, then sent them to the *Chambre des enquêtes* with directions; before it too were argued questions arising out of the inquiry made by the *Chambre des enquêtes*, to the decisions of which it gave effect and which it had the power to revise. But one by one it lost all these rights, and in the 16th century they are no longer heard of. Several *Chambres des enquêtes* were created after the first one, and it was they who had the greater part of the work.

The *Chambre des requêtes* was of an entirely different nature. At the beginning of the 14th century a certain number of those who were to hold the session of the Parlement were set apart to receive and judge the petitions (*requêtes*) on judicial questions which had been presented to the king and not yet dealt with. This eventually led to the formation of a chamber, in the strict sense of the word, the *Requêtes du palais*. But this became purely a jurisdiction for privileged persons; before it (or before the *Requêtes de l'hôtel*, as the case might be) were brought the civil suits of those who enjoyed the right of *Committimus*. The *Chambre des requêtes* had not supreme jurisdiction, but appeals from its decisions could be made to the Parlement proper.

The Parlement had also a criminal chamber, that of *La Tournelle*, which was not legally created until the 16th century, but was active long before then. It had no definite membership, but the *conseillers lois* served in it in turn.

Originally there was only one Parlement, that of Paris; as was indeed logical, considering that the Parlement was simply a continuation of the *curia regis*, which, like the king, could only be one. But the exigencies of the administration of justice led to the successive creation of a certain number of provincial parlements. Their creation, moreover, was generally dictated by political circumstances, after the incorporation of a province in the domain of the Crown. Sometimes it was a question of a province which, before its annexation, possessed a superior and sovereign jurisdiction of its own, and to which it was desired to preserve this advantage. Or else it might be a province forming part of feudal France, which before the annexation had had a superior jurisdiction from which the Crown had endeavoured to institute an appeal to the Parlement of Paris, but for which after the annexation it was no longer necessary to maintain this appeal, so that the province might now be given a supreme court, a parlement. Sometimes an intermediate régime was set up between the annexation of the province and the creation of its provincial parlement, under which delegates from the Parlement of Paris went and held assizes there. Thus were created successively the parlements of Toulouse, Grenoble, Bordeaux, Dijon, Rouen, Aix, Rennes, Pau, Metz, Douai, Besançon and Nancy. From 1762 to 1771 there was even a parlement for the principality of Dombes. The provincial parlements reproduced in a smaller scale the organization of that of Paris; but they did not combine the functions of a court of peers. They each claimed to possess equal powers within their own province. There were also great judicial bodies exercising the same functions as the parlements, though without bearing the name, such as the *Conseil souverain* of Alsace at Colmar, the *Conseil supérieur* of Roussillon at Perpignan; the provincial council of Artois had not the supreme jurisdiction in all respects.

The parlements, besides their judicial functions, also possessed political rights; they claimed a share in the higher policy of the realm, and the position of guardians of its fundamental laws. In general the laws did not come into effect within their province until they had been registered by the parlements. This was the method of promulgation admitted by the ancient law of France, but the parlements verified the laws before registering them, i.e. they examined them to see whether they were in conformity with the principles of law and justice, and with the interests of the king and his subjects; if they considered that this was not the case they refused their registration and addressed remonstrances (*remontrances*) to the king. In acting thus they were merely conforming to the duty of counselling (*devoir de conseil*) which all the superior authorities had towards the king, and the text of the ordinances (*ordonnances*) had often invited them to do so. It was natural, however, that in the end the royal will should seek to impose itself. In order to enforce the registration of edicts the king would send *lettres de cachet*, known as *lettres de jussion*, which were not, however, always obeyed. Or he could come in person to hold the parlement, and have the law registered in his presence in a *lit de justice*. This was explained in theory by the principle that if the king himself held his court, it lost, by the fact of his presence, all the authority which he had delegated to it; for the moment the only authority existing in it was that of the king, just as in the ancient *curia regis* there was the principle that *apparente rege cessat magistratus*.[1] But, principally in the 18th century, the parlements maintained that only a voluntary registration, by the consent of the parlement, was valid.

The parlements had also a wide power of administration. They could make regulations (*pouvoir réglementaire*) having the force of law within their province, upon all points not settled by law, when the matter with which they dealt fell within their judicial competence, and for this it was only necessary that their interference in the matter was not forbidden by law. These were what were called *arrêts de règlement*.

By this means the parlements took part in the administration, except in matters the cognisance of which was attributed to another supreme court as that of taxation was to the *cours des aides*. They could also, within the same limits, address injunctions (*injonctions*) to officials and individuals.

See La Roche-Flavin, *Treize livres des parlements de France* (1617); Felix Aubert, *Histoire du parlement de Paris, des origines à François I.* (2 vols., 1894); Ch. V. Langlois, *Textes relatifs à l'histoire du parlement depuis les origines jusqu'en 1314* (1888); Guilhiermoz, *Enquêtes et procès* (1892); Glasson, *Le Parlement de Paris, son rôle politique depuis le règne de Charles VII. jusqu'à la révolution* (2 vols., 1901). (J. F. E.)

PARLIAMENT (Anglo-Lat. *parliamentum*, Fr. *parlement*, from *parler*, to speak), the name given to the supreme legislature of the United Kingdom of Great Britain and Ireland. (For the old French *parlement*, see PARLEMENT; and for analogous foreign assemblies see the articles on their respective countries.) The word is found in English from the 13th century, first for a debate, then for a formal conference, and for the great councils of the Plantagenet kings; and the modern sense has come to be applied retrospectively. William the Conqueror is said in the Chronicle to have had " very deep speech with his Witan "; this " deep speech " (in Latin *colloquium*, in French *parlement*) was the distinguishing feature of a meeting between king and people, and thus gave its name to the national assembly itself. The Statute of Westminster (1275) first uses " parlement " of the great council in England.

The British Parliament consists of the King (or Queen regnant), the Lords spiritual and temporal, and the Commons; and it meets in two houses, the House of Lords (the Upper or Second chamber) and the House of Commons.

1. The Crown, pre-eminent in rank and dignity, is the legal source of parliamentary authority. The sovereign virtually appoints the lords spiritual, and all the peerages of the lords temporal have been created by the Crown. The king summons parliament to meet, and prescribes the time and place of its meeting, prorogues and dissolves it, and commands the issue of writs for the election of members of the House of Commons. By several statutes, beginning with the 4 Edward III. c. 14, the annual meeting of parliament had been ordained; but these statutes, continually disregarded, were virtually repealed in the reigns of Charles II. and William and Mary (16 Ch. II. 31; 6 & 7 Will. & Mary, 32). The present statute law merely exacts the meeting of parliament once in three years; but the annual voting of supplies has long since superseded obsolete statutes. When parliament is assembled it cannot proceed to business until the king has declared the causes of summons, in person or by commission; and though the veto of the Crown on legislation has long been obsolete, bills passed by the two houses only become law on receiving the royal assent.

2. The House of Lords is distinguished by peculiar dignities, privileges and jurisdictions. Peers individually enjoy the rank and precedence of their several dignities, and are hereditary councillors of the Crown. Collectively with the lords spiritual they form a permanent council of the Crown; and, when assembled in parliament, they form the highest court of judicature in the realm, and are (in constitutional theory at all events) a co-equal branch of the legislature, without whose consent no laws can be made (see below, *House of Lords Question*). Their judicature is of various kinds, viz. for the trial of peers; for determining claims of peerage and offices of honour, under references from the Crown; for the trial of controverted elections of Scotch and Irish peers; for the final determination of appeals from courts in England, Scotland and Ireland; and lastly, for the trial of impeachments.

The House of Commons also has its own peculiar privileges and jurisdictions. Above all, it has the paramount right of originating the imposition of all taxes, and the granting of supplies for the service of the state. It has also enjoyed, from early times, the right of determining all matters concerning the

Or rather, the representatives of the Commons (see REPRESENTATION); but the term has long been used for the deputies themselves collectively.

election of its own members, and their right to sit and vote in parliament. This right, however, has been greatly abridged, as, in 1868, the trial of controverted elections was transferred to the courts of law; but its jurisdiction in matters of election, not otherwise provided for by statute, is still retained intact. As part of this jurisdiction the house directs the Speaker to issue warrants to the clerk of the Crown to make out new writs for the election of members to fill up such vacancies as occur during the sitting of parliament.

Privileges of Parliament.—Both houses are in the enjoyment of certain privileges, designed to maintain their authority, independence and dignity. These privileges are founded mainly upon the law and custom of parliament, while some have been confirmed, and others abridged or abrogated by statute. The Lords rely entirely upon their inherent right, as having " a place and voice in parliament "; but, by a custom dating from the 6th Henry VIII., the Commons lay claim, by humble petition to the Crown at the commencement of every parliament, " to their ancient and undoubted rights and privileges." Each house has its separate rights and jurisdictions; but privileges properly so-called, being founded upon the law and custom of parliament, are common to both houses. Each house adjudges whether any breach of privilege has been committed, and punishes offenders by censure or commitment. This right of commitment is incontestably established, and it extends to the protection of officers of the house, lawfully and properly executing its orders, who are also empowered to call in the assistance of the civil power. The causes of such commitments cannot be inquired into by courts of law, nor can prisoners be admitted to bail. Breaches of privilege may be summarized as disobedience to any orders or rules of the house, indignities offered to its character or proceedings, assaults, insults, or libels upon members, or interference with officers of the house in discharge of their duty, or tampering with witnesses. Such offences are dealt with as contempts, according to the circumstances of the respective cases, of which numerous precedents are to be found in the journals of both houses. The Lords may imprison for a fixed period, and impose fines; the Commons can only imprison generally, the commitment being concluded by the prorogation, and have long discontinued the imposition of fines.

Freedom of speech has been one of the most cherished privileges of parliament from early times. Constantly asserted, and often violated, it was finally declared by the Bill of Rights " that the freedom of speech, and debates and proceedings in parliament, ought not to be impeached or questioned in any court or place out of parliament." Such a privilege is essential to the independence of parliament, and to the protection of members in discharge of their duties. But, while it protects members from molestation elsewhere, it leaves them open to censure or other punishment by the house itself, whenever they abuse their privilege and transgress the rules of orderly debate.

Freedom from arrest is a privilege of the highest antiquity. It was formerly of extended scope, but has been reduced, by later legislation, within very narrow limits. Formerly not only the persons of members but their goods were protected, and their privilege extended to their servants. At present members are themselves free from arrest, but otherwise they are liable to all the processes of the courts. If arrested, they will be immediately discharged, upon motion in the court whence the process issued. Peers and peeresses are, by the privilege of peerage, free from arrest at all times. Members of the House of Commons are free only for forty days after prorogation and forty days before the next appointed meeting; but prorogations are so arranged as to ensure a continuance of the privilege. Formerly, even suits against members were stayed, but this offensive privilege has been abolished by statute. Exemption from attending as witnesses upon subpoena, once an acknowledged privilege, is no longer insisted upon; but immunity from service upon juries is at once an ancient privilege and a statutory right. The privilege of freedom from arrest is limited to civil causes, and has not been suffered to exempt members from the operation of the criminal law, nor even from commitments for contempt by other courts. But, whenever the freedom of a member is so interfered with, the courts are required immediately to inform the house of the causes of his commitment. Witnesses, suitors, counsel and agents in attendance upon parliament are protected from arrest and molestation, and from the consequences of statements made by them, or other proceedings in the conduct of their cases.

As both houses, in enforcing their privileges, are obliged to commit offenders or otherwise interfere with the liberty of the subject, the exercise of these privileges has naturally been called in question before the courts. Each house is the sole judge of its own privileges; but the courts are bound to administer the law, and, where law and privilege have seemed to be at variance, a conflict of jurisdiction has arisen between parliament and the courts. Many interesting controversies have arisen upon such occasions; but of late years privilege has been carefully restrained within the proper limits of the law, and the courts have amply recognized the authority of parliament.

Parliamentary Procedure.—It will be convenient here to sketch the general lines of procedure. On the day appointed by royal proclamation for the meeting of a new parliament both houses assemble in their respective chambers, when the Lords Commissioners for opening the parliament summon the Commons to the bar of the House of Lords, by the mouth of Black Rod, to hear the commission read. The lord chancellor states that, when the members of both houses shall be sworn, the king will declare the causes of his calling this parliament; and, it being necessary that a Speaker of the House of Commons shall be first chosen, the Commons are directed to proceed to the appointment of a Speaker, and to present him, on the following day, for His Majesty's royal approbation. The Commons at once withdraw to their own house and proceed to the election of their Speaker The next day the Speaker-elect proceeds, with the house, to the House of Lords, and, on receiving the royal approbation, lays claim, in the accustomed form, on behalf of the Commons, "to their ancient and undoubted rights and privileges." The Speaker, now fully confirmed, returns to the House of Commons, and, after repeating his acknowledgments, reminds the house that the first thing to be done is to take and subscribe the oath required by law. Having first taken the oath himself, he is followed by other members, who come to the table to be sworn. The swearing of members in both houses proceeds from day to day, until the greater number have taken the oath, or affirmation, when the causes of summons are declared by His Majesty in person, or by commission, in "the King's speech." This speech being considered in both houses, an Address (q.v.) in answer is agreed to, which is presented to His Majesty by the whole house, or by "the lords with white staves" in one house and privy councillors in the other.

The debate on the Address being over, the real business of the session now commences: the committees of supply and ways and means are set up; bills are introduced; motions are made; committees are appointed; and both houses are, at once, in full activity. The Lord Chancellor presides over the deliberations of the Lords, and the Speaker over those of the Commons. A quorum of the House of Lords, including the chancellor, is three (thirty for divisions); that of the House of Commons, including the Speaker, is forty.

Every matter is determined, in both houses, upon questions put from the chair, and resolved in the affirmative or negative, or otherwise disposed of by the withdrawal of the motion, by amendments, by the adjournment of the house, by reading the orders of the day, or by the previous question. Notices are required to be given of original motions; and the different stages of bills, and other matters appointed for consideration by the house, stand as orders of the day. Questions of privilege are allowed precedence of all the business on any day; but this rule, being liable to grave abuses, is guarded by strict limitations. Debates arise when a question has been proposed from the chair; and at the close of the debate (for the "closure" in the House of Commons, see below, *House of Commons, Internal Reforms*) the question is put, with or without amendment, as the case may be, and is determined, when necessary, by a division. No question or bill, substantially the same as one upon which the judgment of the house has already been given, may be again proposed during the same session.

Members claim to be heard in debate by rising in their places. When more than one member rises at the same time, in the Lords the member who is to speak is called by the house, in the Commons by the Speaker. Every member, when called, is bound to speak to the question before the house; and calls to order are very frequent. A member may speak once only to any question, except to explain, or upon a point of order, or to reply when a member has himself submitted a motion to the house, or when an amendment has been moved which constitutes a new question. He may not refer to past debates, nor to debates in the other house; nor may he refer to any other member by name, or use offensive and disorderly language against the king, either House of Parliament, or other members. Members offending against any of the rules of debate are called to order by

the Speaker, or the attention of the chair is directed to the breach of order by another member. Order is generally enforced by the authority of the chair; but in extreme cases, and especially when obstruction is being practised, the offending member is named by the Speaker, and suspended by an order of the house, or otherwise punished at the discretion of the house.

At the conclusion of a debate, unless the motion be withdrawn, or the question (on being put from the chair) be agreed to or negatived, the house proceeds to a division, which effects the twofold purpose of ascertaining the numbers supporting and opposing the question, and of recording the names of members voting on either side. On each side of the house is a division lobby; and in the Lords the "contents" and in the Commons the "ayes" are directed to go to the right, and the "not contents" or "noes" to the left. The former pass into the right lobby, at the back of the Speaker's chair, and return to the house through the bar; the latter pass into the left lobby, at the bar, and return at the back of the chair. The opposing parties are thus kept entirely clear of one another. In each lobby there are two members acting as tellers, who count the members as they pass, and two division clerks who take down their names. After the division the four tellers advance to the table, and the numbers are reported by one of the tellers for the majority. In case of an equality of numbers, in the Lords the question is negatived in virtue of the ancient rule "semper praesumitur pro negante"; in the Commons the Speaker gives the casting vote.

Committees of the Whole House.—For the sake of convenience in the transaction of business there are several kinds of committees. Of these the most important is a committee of the whole house, which, as it consists of the entire body of members, can scarcely be accounted a committee. It is presided over by a chairman, who sits in the clerk's chair at the table, the mace, which represents the authority of the house itself, being for the time placed under the table. In this committee are discussed the several provisions of bills, resolutions and other matters requiring the consideration of details. To facilitate discussion, members are allowed to speak any number of times to the same question; otherwise the proceedings are similar to those of the house itself. In the Lords the chair is taken by the chairman of committees; and in the Commons by the chairman of the committee of ways and means, or in his absence by any other member. The quorum of such a committee is the same as that of the house itself. It reports from time to time to the house, but has no power of adjournment.

Grand and Standing Committees.—In the House of Commons there were formerly four grand committees, viz. for religion, for grievances, for courts of justice, and for trade. They were founded upon the valuable principle of a distribution of labours among several bodies of members; but, having fallen into disuse, they were discontinued in 1832. The ancient committee of privileges, in which "all who come are to have voices," is still appointed at the commencement of every session, but is rarely called into action, as it has been found more convenient to appoint a select committee to inquire into any question of privilege as it arises. In 1882 a partial revival of grand committees was effected by the appointment of two standing committees for the consideration of bills relating to law and courts of justice and to trade; and grand committees have since been considerably extended.

Select Committees.—In select committees both houses find the means of delegating inquiries, and the consideration of other matters, which could not be undertaken by the whole house. The reports of such committees have formed the groundwork of many important measures; and bills are often referred to them which receive a fuller examination than could be expected in a committee of the whole house. Power is given to such committees, when required, to send for persons, papers and records. In the Lords the power of examining witnesses upon oath has always been exercised, but it was not until 1871 that the same power was extended to the Commons, by statute.

Communications between the Two Houses.—In the course of the proceedings of parliament, frequent communications between the two houses become necessary. Of these the most usual and convenient form is that of a message. Formerly the Lords sent a message by two judges or two masters in chancery, and the Commons by a deputation of their own members; but since 1855 messages have been taken from one house to the other by one of the clerks at the table. A more formal communication is effected by a conference, in reference to amendments to bills or other matters; but this proceeding has been in great measure superseded by the more simple form of a message. The two houses are also occasionally brought into communication by means of joint committees and of select committees communicating with each other.

Communications between the Crown and Parliament.—Communications, in various forms, are also conducted between the Crown

PARLIAMENT

and both Houses of Parliament. Of these the most important are those in which the king, in person or by commission, is present in the House of Lords to open or prorogue parliament, or to give the royal assent to bills. His Majesty is then in direct communication with the three estates of the realm, assembled in the same chamber. The king also sends messages to both houses under the royal sign manual, when all the members are uncovered. Verbal messages are also sent, and the king's pleasure, or royal recommendation or consent to bills or other matters, signified through a minister of the Crown or a privy councillor. Messages under the sign manual are acknowledged by addresses, except where grants of money are proposed, in which case no address is presented by the Commons, who acknowledge them by making provision accordingly.

Both houses approach the Crown, sometimes by joint addresses, but usually by separate addresses from each house. Such addresses are presented to His Majesty, either by the whole house, or by the lords with white staves in one house and by privy councillors in the other. His Majesty answers, in person, addresses presented by the whole house; but, when presented otherwise, an answer is brought by one of the lords with white staves, or by one of the privy councillors, by whom the address has been presented. Resolutions of either house are also sometimes directed to be laid before His Majesty; and messages of congratulation or condolence are sent to other members of the royal family.

The Passing of Public Bills.—The passing of bills forms the most considerable part of the business of parliament; but a brief notice will suffice to explain the methods of procedure. These are substantially the same in both houses; but the privileges of the Commons, in regard to supply and taxation, require that all bills imposing a charge upon the people should originate in that house. On the other hand, the Lords claim that bills for restoration of honours or in blood, or relating to their own privileges and jurisdiction, should commence in their house. An act of grace, or general pardon, originates with the Crown, and is read once only in both houses. Bills are divided into public and private; but here the former only are referred to. In the Lords any peer is entitled to present a bill, but in the Commons a member is required to obtain the previous leave of the house to bring in the bill; and, in the case of bills relating to religion, trade, grants of public money, or charges upon the subject, a preliminary committee is necessary before such leave will be given. A bill, when presented, is read a first time, and ordered to be printed; and a day is appointed for the second reading. At this latter stage the principle of the bill is discussed; and, if disapproved of by an adverse vote, the bill is lost and cannot be renewed during the same session. If approved of, it is usually committed to a committee of the whole house where every provision is open to debate and amendment. When the bill has been fully considered it is reported to the house, with or without amendments, and is ready to pass through its remaining stages. Sometimes, however, the bill is first referred to a select committee; or to a grand committee and not to committee of the whole house.

When a bill has been reported from a committee of the whole house, or from a standing committee, with amendments, the bill, as amended, is ordered to be considered on a future day, when further amendments may be made, or the bill may be recommitted. The next and last stage is the third reading, when the principle of the measure, and its amended provisions, are open to review. Even at this stage the bill may be lost; but if the third reading be agreed to, it is at once passed and sent to the other house. There it is open to the like discussions and amendments, and may be rejected. If returned without amendment, the bill merely awaits the royal assent; but if returned with amendments, such amendments must be agreed to, or otherwise adjusted by the two houses, before it can be submitted for the royal assent. The royal assent consummates the work of legislation, and converts the bill into an act of parliament.

Petitions.—Both houses are approached by the people by means of petitions, of which prodigious numbers are presented to the House of Commons every session. They are referred to the committee on public petitions, under whose directions they are classified, analysed, and the number of signatures counted; and, when necessary, the petitions are printed *in extenso.*

Parliamentary Papers.—Another source of information is found in parliamentary papers. These are of various kinds. The greater part are obtained either by a direct order of the house itself, or by an address to the Crown for documents relating to matters in which the prerogatives of the Crown are concerned. Other papers, relating to foreign and colonial affairs and other public matters, are presented to both houses by command of His Majesty. Again, many papers are annually presented in pursuance of acts of parliament.

The Granting of Supplies.—The exclusive right of the Commons to grant supplies, and to originate all measures of taxation, imposes a very onerous service upon that house. This is mainly performed by two committees of the whole house—the committee of supply, and the committee of ways and means. The former deals with all the estimates for the public service presented to the house by command of His Majesty; and the latter votes out of the Consolidated Fund such sums as are necessary to meet the supplies already

granted, and originates all taxes for the service of the year. It is here that the annual financial statement of the chancellor of the exchequer, commonly known as "the Budget," is delivered. The resolutions of these committees are reported to the house, and, when agreed to, form the foundation of bills, to be passed by both houses, and submitted for the royal assent; and towards the close of the session an Appropriation Act is passed, applying all the grants for the service of the year.

Elections.—The extensive jurisdiction of the Commons in matters of election, already referred to, formerly occupied a considerable share of their time, but its exercise has now been contracted within narrow limits. Whenever a vacancy occurs during the continuance of a parliament, a warrant for a new writ is issued by the Speaker, by order of the house during the session, and in pursuance of statutes during the recess. The causes of vacancies are the death of a member, his being called to the House of Peers, his acceptance of an office from the Crown, or his bankruptcy. When any doubt arises as to the issue of a writ, it is usual to appoint a committee to inquire into the circumstances of the case; and during the recess the Speaker may reserve doubtful cases for the determination of the house.

Controverted elections had been originally tried by select committees, afterwards by the committee of privileges and elections, and ultimately by the whole house, with scandalous partiality, but under the Grenville Act of 1770, and other later acts, by select committees, so constituted as to form a more judicial tribunal. The influence of party bias, however, too obviously prevailed until 1839, when Sir Robert Peel introduced an improved system of nomination, which distinctly raised the character of election committees; but a tribunal constituted of political partisans, however chosen, was still open to jealousy and suspicion, and at length, in 1868, the trial of election petitions was transferred to judges of the superior courts, to whose determination the house gives effect, by the issue of new writs or otherwise. The house, however, still retains and exercises its jurisdiction in all cases not relegated, by statute, to the judges.

Impeachments and Trial of Peers.—Other forms of parliamentary judicature still remain to be mentioned. Upon impeachments by the Commons, the Lords exercise the highest criminal judicature known to the law; but the occasions upon which it has been brought into action have been very rare in modern times. Another judicature is that of the trial of peers by the House of Lords. And, lastly, by a bill of attainder, the entire parliament may be called to sit in judgment upon offenders.

Private Bill Legislation.—One other important function of parliament remains to be noticed—that of private bill legislation. Here the duties of parliament are partly legislative and partly judicial. Public interests are promoted, and private rights secured. This whole jurisdiction has been regulated by special standing orders, and by elaborate arrangements for the nomination of capable and impartial committees. A prodigious legislative work has been accomplished—but under conditions most costly to the promoters and opponents of private bills, and involving a serious addition to the onerous labours of members of parliament.

HISTORY OF THE BRITISH PARLIAMENT

The Anglo-Saxon Polity.—The origin of parliament is to be traced to Anglo-Saxon times. The Angles, Saxons and other Teutonic races who conquered Britain brought to their new homes their own laws and customs, their settled framework of society, their kinship, their village communities, and a certain rude representation in local affairs. And we find in the Anglo-Saxon polity, as developed during their rule in England, all the constituent parts of parliament. In their own lands they had chiefs and leaders, but no kings. But conquest and territorial settlement were followed by the assumption of royal dignities; and the victorious chiefs were accepted by their followers as kings. They were quick to assume the traditional attributes of royalty. A direct descent from their god Woden, and hereditary right, at once clothed them with a halo of glory and with supreme power; and, when the pagan deity was deposed, the king received consecration from a Christian archbishop, and was invested with sacred attributes as "the Lord's anointed." But the Saxon monarch was a patriarchal king of limited authority, who acted in concert with his people; and, though his succession was hereditary, in his own family, his direct descendant was liable to be passed over in favour of a worthier heir. Such a ruler was a fitting precursor of a line of constitutional kings, who in later times were to govern with the advice and consent of a free parliament.

Meanwhile any council approaching the constitution of a House of Lords was of slow growth. Anglo-Saxon society, indeed, was not without an aristocracy. The highest in rank were æthelings—generally; if not exclusively, sons and brothers of the king. The ealdorman, originally a high officer, having the executive government of a shire, and a seat in the king's witan, became hereditary in certain families, and eventually attained the dignity of an earl. But centuries were to pass before the English nobility was to assume its modern character and denominations. At the head of each village was an eorl, the chief of the freemen, or ceorls—their leader in war and patron in peace. The king's gesiths and thegns formed another privileged class. Admitted to offices in the king's household and councils, and enriched by grants of land, they gradually formed a feudal nobility.

The revival of the Christian Church, under the Anglo-Saxon rule, created another order of rulers and councillors, destined to take a leading part in the government of the state. The archbishops and bishops, having spiritual authority in their own dioceses, and exercising much local influence in temporal affairs, were also members of the national council, or witenagemót, and by their greater learning and capacity were not long in acquiring a leading part in the councils of the realm. Ecclesiastical councils were also held, comprising bishops, abbots, and clergy, in which we observe the origin of convocation. The abbots, thus associated with the bishops, also found a place with them in the witenagemót. By these several orders, summoned to advise the king in affairs of state, was formed a council of magnates—to be developed, in course of time, into an upper chamber, or House of Lords.

The rise of the Commons (see REPRESENTATION) as a political power in the national councils, was of yet slower development: but in the Anglo-Saxon moots may be discerned the first germs of popular government in England. In the town-moot the assembled freemen and cultivators of the "folk-lands" regulated the civil affairs of their own township, tithing, village or parish. In the burgh-moot the inhabitants administered their municipal business, under the presidency of a reeve. The hundred-moot assumed a more representative character, comprising the reeve and a selected number of freemen from the several townships and burghs within the hundred. The shire-moot, or shire-gemót, was an assembly yet more important. An ealdorman was its president, and exercised a jurisdiction over a shire, or district comprising several hundreds. Attended by a reeve and four freemen from every hundred, it assumed a distinctly representative character. Its members, if not *elected* (in the modern sense) by the popular voice, were, in some fashion, *deputed* to act on behalf of those whose interests they had come to guard. The shire-moot was also the general folk-moot of the tribe, assembled in arms, to whom their leaders referred the decision of questions of peace and war.

Superior to these local institutions was the witenagemót, or assembly of wise men, with whom the king took counsel in legislation and the government of the state. This national council was the true beginning of the parliament of England. Such a council was originally held in each of the kingdoms commonly known as the Heptarchy; and after their union in a single realm, under King Edgar, the witenagemót became the deliberative and legislative assembly, or parliament, of the extended estate. The witenagemót made laws, imposed taxes, concluded treaties, advised the king as to the disposal of public lands and the appointment and removal of officers of state, and even assumed to elect and depose the king himself. The king had now attained to greater power, and more royal dignities and prerogatives. He was unquestionably the chief power in the witenagemót; but the laws were already promulgated, as in later times, as having been agreed to with the advice and consent of the witan. The witan also exercised jurisdiction as a supreme court. These ancient customs present further examples of the continuity of English constitutional forms.

The constitution of the witenagemót, however, was necessarily less popular than that of the local moots in the hundred or the shire. The king himself was generally present; and at his summons came prelates, abbots, ealdormen, the king's gesiths and thegns, officers of state and of the royal household, and leading tenants in chief of lands held from the crown. Crowds sometimes attended the meetings of the witan, and shouted their acclamations of approval or dissent; and, so far, the popular voice was associated with its deliberations; but it was at a distance from all but the inhabitants of the place in which it was assembled, and until a system of representation (q.s.) had slowly grown up there could be no further admission of the people to its deliberations. In the town-moot the whole body of freemen and cultivators of the folk-lands met freely under a spreading oak, or on the village green; in the hundred-moot, or shire-gemót, deputies from neighbouring communities could readily find a place; but all was changed in the wider council of a kingdom. When there were many kingdoms, distance obstructed any general gathering of the Commons; and in the wider area of England such a gathering became impossible. Centuries were yet to pass before this obstacle was to be overcome by representation; but, in the meantime, the local institutions of the Anglo-Saxons were not without their influence upon the central council. The self-government of a free people informed the bishops, ealdormen, ceorls and thegns who dwelt among them of their interests and needs, their sufferings and their wrongs; and, while the popular forces were increasing with an advancing society, they grew more powerful in the councils of their rulers.

Another circumstance must not be overlooked in estimating the political influence of the people in Anglo-Saxon times. For five centuries the country was convulsed with incessant wars —wars with the Britons, whom the invaders were driving from their homes, wars between the several kingdoms, wars with the Welsh, wars with the Picts, wars with the Danes. How could the people continue to assert their civil rights amid the clash of arms and a frequent change of masters? The warrior-kings and their armed followers were rulers in the land which they had conquered. At the same time the unsettled condition of the country repressed the social advancement of its people. Agriculture could not prosper when the farm of the husbandman too often became a battlefield. Trade could not be extended without security to property and industry. Under such conditions the great body of the people continued as peasants, handicraftsmen and slaves. The time had not yet come when they could make their voice heard in the councils of the state.

The Norman Conquest.—The Anglo-Saxon polity was suddenly overthrown by the Norman Conquest. A stern foreign king had seized the crown, and was prepared to rule his conquered realm by the sword. He brought with him the absolutist principles of continental rulers, and the advanced feudal system of France and Normandy. Feudalism had been slowly gaining ground under the Saxon kings, and now it was firmly established as a military organization. William the Conqueror at once rewarded his warlike barons and followers with enormous grants of land. The Saxon landowners and peasants were despoiled, and the invaders settled in their homesteads. The king claimed the broad lands of England as his own, by right of conquest; and when he allowed his warriors to share the spoil he attached the strict condition of military service in return for every grant of land. An effective army of occupation of all ranks was thus quartered upon every province throughout the realm. England was held by the sword; a foreign king, foreign nobles, and a foreign soldiery were in possession of the soil, and swore fealty to their master, from whom they held it. Saxon bishops were deposed, and foreign prelates appointed to rule over the English Church. Instead of calling a national witenagemót, the king took counsel with the officers of his state and household, the bishops, abbots, earls, barons and knights by whom he was pleased to surround himself. Some of the forms of a national council were indeed maintained, and its counsel and consent were proclaimed in the making of laws; but, in truth, the king was absolute.

Such a revolution seemed fatal to the liberties and ancient customs of Saxon England. What power could withstand the harsh conqueror? But the indestructible elements of English society prevailed over the sword. The king grasped, in his own hands, the higher administration and judicature of the realm;

but he continued the old local courts of the hundred and the shire, which had been the basis of Saxon freedom. The Norman polity was otherwise destined to favour the liberties of the people, through agencies which had been designed to crush them. The powerful nobles, whom William and his successors exalted, became formidable rivals of the Crown itself; while ambitious barons were in their turn held in check by a jealous and exacting church. The ruling powers, if combined, would have reduced the people to slavery; but their divisions proved a continual source of weakness. In the meantime the strong rule of the Normans, bitter as it was to Englishmen, repressed intestine wars and the disorders of a divided realm. Civil justice was fairly administered. When the spoils of the conquerors had been secured, the rights of property were protected, industry and trade were left free, and the occupation of the soil by foreigners drove numbers of landowners and freemen into the towns, where they prospered as merchants, traders and artificers, and collected thriving populations of townsmen. Meanwhile, foreign rulers having brought England into closer relations with the Continent, its commerce was extended to distant lands, ports and shipping were encouraged, and English traders were at once enriched and enlightened. Hence new classes of society were growing, who were eventually to become the Commons of England.

The Crown, the Barons, the Church and the People.—While these social changes were steadily advancing, the barons were already preparing the way for the assertion of popular rights. Ambitious, turbulent and grasping, they were constantly at issue with the Crown. Enjoying vast estates and great commands, and sharing with the prelates the government of the state, as members of the king's council, they were ever ready to raise the standard of revolt. The king could always count upon barons faithful to his cause, but he also appealed for aid to the Church and the people. The baronage was thus broken by insurrections, and decimated by civil wars, while the value of popular alliances was revealed. The power of the people was ever increasing, while their oppressors were being struck down. The population of the country was still Saxon; they had been subdued, but had not been driven forth from the land, like the Britons in former invasions. The English language was still the common speech of the people; and Norman blood was being mingled with the broader stream of Saxon life. A continuous nationality was thus preserved, and was outgrowing the foreign element.

The Crown was weakened by disputed successions and foreign wars, and the baronage by the blood-stained fields of civil warfare; while both in turn looked to the people in their troubles. Meanwhile the Church was struggling, alike against the Crown and the barons, in defence of its ecclesiastical privileges and temporal possessions. Its clergy were brought by their spiritual ministrations into close relations with the people, and their culture contributed to the intellectual growth of English society. When William Rufus was threatened by his armed barons he took counsel with Archbishop Lanfranc, and promised good laws and justice to the people. His promises were broken; but, like later charters, as lightly set aside, they were a recognition of the political rights of the people. By the charter of Henry I. restoring to the people the laws of Edward the Confessor, the continuity of English institutions was acknowledged; and this concession was also proclaimed through Archbishop Anselm, the church and the people being again associated with the Crown against the barons. And throughout his reign the clergy and the English people were cordially united in support of the Crown. In the anarchic reign of Stephen—also distinguished by its futile charters—the clergy were driven into opposition to the king, while his oppressions alienated the people. Henry II. commenced his reign with another charter, which may be taken as a profession of good intentions on the part of the new king. So strong-willed a king, who could cripple his too powerful nobles, and forge shackles for the Church, was not predisposed to extend the liberties of his people; but they supported him loyally in his critical struggles; and his vigorous reforms in the

administrative, judicial and financial organization of his realm promoted the prosperity and political influence of the Commons. At the same time the barons created in this and the two previous reigns, being no longer exclusively Norman in blood and connexion, associated themselves more readily with the interests and sympathies of the people. Under Richard I. the principle of representation was somewhat advanced, but it was confined to the assessment and collection of taxes in the different shires.

Magna Carta (q.v.).—It was under King John that the greatest progress was made in national liberties. The loss of Normandy served to draw the baronage closer to the English people; and the king soon united all the forces of the realm against him. He outraged the Church, the barons and the people. He could no longer play one class against another; and they combined to extort the Great Charter of their liberties at Runnymede (1215). It was there ordained that no scutage or aid, except the three regular feudal aids, should be imposed, save by the common council of the realm. To this council the archbishops, bishops, abbots, earls and greater barons were to be summoned personally by the king's letters, and tenants in chief by a general writ through the sheriff. The summons was required to appoint a certain place, to give 40 days' notice at least, and to state the cause of meeting. At length we seem to reach some approach to modern usage.

Growth of the Commons.—The improved administration of successive kings had tended to enlarge the powers of the Crown. But one hundred and fifty years had now passed since the Conquest, and great advances had been made in the condition of the people, and more particularly in the population, wealth and self-government of towns. Many had obtained royal charters, elected their own magistrates, and enjoyed various commercial privileges. They were already a power in the state, which was soon to be more distinctly recognised.

The charter of King John was again promulgated under Henry III., for the sake of a subsidy; and henceforth the Commons learned to insist upon the redress of grievances in return for a grant of money. This reign was memorable in the history of parliament.[1] Again the king was in conflict with his barons, who rebelled against his gross misgovernment of the realm. Simon de Montfort, earl of Leicester, was a patriot in advance of his age and fought for the English people as well as for his own order. The barons, indeed, were doubtful allies of the popular cause, and leaned to the king rather than to Simon. But the towns, the clergy, the universities and large bodies of the commonalty rallied round him, and he overthrew the king and his followers at Lewes. He was now master of the realm, and proclaimed a new constitution. Kings had made promises, and granted illusory charters; but the rebel earl called an English parliament (1265) into being. Churchmen were on his side, and a few barons; but his main reliance was upon the Commons. He summoned to a national council, or parliament, bishops, abbots, earls and barons, together with two knights from every shire and two burgesses from every borough. Knights had indeed been summoned to former councils; but never until now had delegates from the towns been invited to sit with bishops, barons and knights of the shire.

In the reign of Edward I. parliament assumed substantially its present form of king, lords and commons. The irregular and unauthorized scheme of Simon de Montfort was fully adopted; and in 1295 the king summoned to a parliament two knights from

[1] In 1254 we have a distinct case of two knights summoned from each shire by royal writ. A war was going on in Gascony, and the king wanted money. He called the barons and asked if they would provide the necessary funds. The barons said that unfortunately the minor gentry were exceedingly unwilling to contribute, and the king sent to ask that two knights from each shire might be sent up to consult with him. In the result, the Commons refused to grant a subsidy, and the king had to fall back on the Church; but though the summoning of the knights of the shire was in form a small change from the previous practice of sending some one down to the counties to put pressure on them, the innovation is important as the first occasion on which their representatives met in a central assembly.—[H. Ch.]

every shire chosen by the freeholders at the shire court, and two burgesses from every city, borough and leading town.[1] The rebel earl had enlarged the basis of the national council; and, to secure popular support, the politic king accepted it as a convenient instrument of taxation. The knights and freeholders had increased in numbers and wealth; and the towns, continually advancing in population,' trade and commerce, had become valuable contributors to the revenue of the state. The grant of subsidies to the Crown, by the assembled baronage and representatives of the shires and towns, was a legal and comprehensive impost upon the entire realm.

Secession of the Clergy.—It formed part of Edward's policy to embrace the clergy in his scheme for the representation of all orders and classes of his subjects. They were summoned to attend the parliament of 1295 and succeeding parliaments of his reign, and their form of summons has been continued until the present time; but the clergy resolutely held aloof from the national council, and insisted upon voting their subsidies in their own convocations of Canterbury and York. The bishops retained their high place among the earls and barons, but the clergy sacrificed to ecclesiastical jealousies the privilege of sharing in the political councils of the state. As yet, indeed, this privilege seemed little more than the voting of subsidies, but it was soon to embrace the redress of grievances and the framing of laws for the general welfare of the realm. This great power they forfeited; and who shall say how it might have been wielded, in the interests of the Church, and in the legislation of their country? They could not have withstood the Reformation; they would have been forced to yield to the power of the Crown and the heated resolution of the laity; but they might have saved a large share of the endowments of the Church, and perhaps have modified the doctrines and formularies of the reformed establishment.

Reluctance of the Commons to Attend.—Meanwhile the Commons, unconscious of their future power, took their humble place in the great council of the realm. The knights of the shire, as lesser barons, or landowners of good social standing, could sit beside the magnates of the land without constraint; but modest traders from the towns were overawed by the power and dignity of their new associates. They knew that they were summoned for no other purpose than the taxing of themselves and their fellow townsmen; their attendance was irksome; it interrupted their own business; and their journeys exposed them to many hardships and dangers. It is not surprising that they should have shrunk from the exercise of so doubtful a privilege. Considerable numbers absented themselves from a thankless service; and their constituents, far from exacting the attendance of their members, as in modern times, begrudged the sorry stipend of 2s. a day, paid to their representatives while on duty, and strove to evade the burden imposed upon them by the Crown. Some even purchased charters, withdrawing franchises which they had not yet learned to value. Nor, in truth, did the representation of towns at this period afford much protection to the rights and interests of the people. Towns were enfranchised at the will or caprice of the Crown and the sheriffs; they could be excluded at pleasure; and the least show of independence would be followed by the omission of another writ of

[1] It now appears that substantially this was effected as early as 1275. The transition period between Simon de Montfort's parliament of 1265 and the " model parliament " of 1295 was long a puzzle to historical students, since, except for two provincial councils in 1283, no trace was found in the records, between 1265 and 1295, of the representation—of cities or boroughs, or of representation of the counties between 1275 and 1290. But in 1910 Mr C. Hilary Jenkinson (see *English Historical Review*, for April) found in the Record Office some old documents which proved to be fragments of three writs and of returns of members for the Easter parliament of 1275. They make it certain that knights of the shire were then present, and that burgesses and citizens were summoned (not as in 1265 through the mayors, but as since 1295 through the sheriffs). The importance of the 1295 parliament thus appears to be smaller in English constitutional history, the full reforms appearing to have been adopted 20 years earlier. It is noteworthy, however, that in the writs of 1275 the instruction to the sheriff is "venire facias," not " eligi facias."—[H. Ch.]

summons. But the principle of representation (*q.v.*), once established, was to be developed with the expansion of society; and the despised burgesses of Edward I., not having seceded, like the clergy, were destined to become a potential class in the parliaments of England.

Sitting of Parliament at Westminster.—Another constitutional change during this reign was the summoning of parliament to Westminster instead of to various towns in different parts of the country. This custom invested parliament with the character of a settled institution, and constituted it a high court for the hearing of petitions and the redress of grievances. The growth of its judicature, as a court of appeal, was also favoured by the fixity of its place of meeting.

Authority of Parliament recognized by Law.—Great was the power of the Crown, and the king himself was bold and statesmanlike; but the union of classes against him proved too strong for prerogative. In 1297, having outraged the Church, the barons, and the Commons, by illegal exactions, he was forced to confirm the Great Charter and the Charter of Forests, with further securities against the taxation of the people without their consent and, in return, obtained timely subsidies from the parliament. Henceforth the financial necessities of a succession of kings ensured the frequent assembling of parliaments. Nor were they long contented with the humble function of voting subsidies, but boldly insisted on the redress of grievances and further securities for national liberties. In 1322 it was declared by statute 15 Edw. II. that " the matters to be established for the estate of the king and of his heirs, and for the estate of the realm and of the people, should be treated, accorded, and established in parliament, by the king, and by the assent of the prelates, earls and barons, and the commonalty of the realm, according as had been before accustomed." The constitutional powers of parliament as a legislature were here amply recognized —not by royal charter, or by the occasional exercise of prerogative, but by an authoritative statute. And these powers were soon to be exercised in a striking form. Already parliament had deliberated the principle that the redress of grievances should have precedence of the grant of subsidies; it had maintained the right of approving councillors of the Crown, and punishing them for the abuse of their powers; and in 1327 the king himself was finally deposed, and the succession of his son, Edward III., declared by parliament.

Union of Knights of the Shire and Burgesses.—At this period the constitution of parliament was also settling down to its later and permanent shape. Hitherto the different orders or estates had deliberated separately, and agreed upon their several grants to the Crown. The knights of the shire were naturally drawn, by social ties and class interests, into alliance with the barons; but at length they joined the citizens and burgesses, and in the first parliament of Edward III. they are found sitting together as " the Commons."

This may be taken as the turning point in the political history of England. If all the landowners of the country had become united as an order of nobles, they might have proved too strong for the development of national liberties, while the union of the country gentlemen with the burgesses formed an estate of the realm which was destined to prevail over all other powers. The withdrawal of the clergy, who would probably have been led by the bishops to take part with themselves and the barons, further strengthened the united Commons.

Increasing Influence of Parliament.—The reign of Edward III. witnessed further advances in the authority of parliament, and changes in its constitution. The king, being in continual need of subsidies, was forced to summon parliament every year, and in order to encourage its liberality he frequently sought its advice upon the most important issues of peace or war, and readily entertained the petitions of the Commons praying for the redress of grievances. During this reign also, the advice and consent of the Commons, as well as of the Lords spiritual and temporal, was regularly recorded in the enacting part of every statute.

Separation of the Two Houses.—But a more important event is to be assigned to this reign,—the formal separation of parliament into the two houses of Lords and Commons. There is no evidence—nor is it probable—that the different estates ever voted together as a single assembly. It appears from the rolls of parliament that in the early part of this reign, the causes of summons having been declared to the assembled estates, the three estates deliberated separately, but afterwards delivered a collective answer to the king. While their deliberations were short they could be conducted apart, in the same chamber; but, in course of time, it was found convenient for the Commons to have a chamber of their own, and they adjourned their sittings to the chapter-house of the abbot of Westminster, where they continued to be held after the more formal and permanent separation had taken place. The date of this event is generally assigned to the 17th Edward III.

The Commons as Petitioners.—Parliament had now assumed its present outward form. But it was far from enjoying the authority which it acquired in later times. The Crown was still paramount; the small body of earls and barons—not exceeding 40—were connected with the royal family, or in the service of the king, or under his influence; the prelates, once distinguished by their independence, were now seekers of royal favour; and the Commons, though often able to extort concessions in return for their contributions to the royal exchequer, as yet held an inferior position among the estates of the realm. Instead of enjoying an equal share in the framing of laws, they appeared before the king in the humble guise of petitioners. Their petitions, together with the king's answers, were recorded in the rolls of parliament; but it was not until the parliament had been discharged from attendance that statutes were framed by the judges and entered on the statute rolls. Under such conditions legislation was, in truth, the prerogative of the Crown rather than of parliament. Enactments were often found in the statutes at variance with the petitions and royal answers, and neither prayed for by the Commons nor assented to by the Lords. In vain the Commons protested against so grave an abuse of royal authority; but the same practice was continued during this and succeeding reigns. Henry V., in the second year of his reign, promised " that nothing should be enacted to the petitions of the Commons, contrary to their asking, whereby they should be bound without their assent;" but, so long as the old method of framing laws was adhered to, there could be no security against abuse; and it was not until the reign of Henry VI. that the introduction of the more regular system of legislating by bill and statute ensured the thorough agreement of all the estates in the several provisions of every statute.

Increasing Boldness of the Commons.—The Commons, however, notwithstanding these and other discouragements, were constantly growing bolder in the assertion of their rights. They now ventured to brave the displeasure of the king, without seeking to shelter themselves behind powerful barons, upon whose forwardness in the national cause they could not reckon. Notably in 1376 their stout Speaker, Peter de la Mare, inveighed, in their name, against the gross mismanagement of the war, impeached ministers of the realm, complained of the heavy burdens under which the people suffered, and even demanded that a true account should be rendered of the public expenditure. The brave Speaker was cast into prison, and a new parliament was summoned which speedily reversed the resolutions of the last. But the death of the king changed the aspect of affairs. Another parliament was called, when it was found that the spirit of the Commons was not subdued. Peter de la Mare was released from prison, and again elected to the chair. The demands of the former parliament were reiterated with greater boldness and persistence, the evil councillors of the late reign were driven out, and it was conceded that the principal officers of state should be appointed and removed, during the minority of Richard II., upon the advice of the lords. The Commons also insisted upon the annual assembling of parliament under the stringent provisions of a binding law. They claimed the right, not only of voting subsidies, but of appropriating them, and of examining public accounts. They inquired into public abuses, and impeached ministers of the Crown. Even the king himself was deposed by the parliament. Thus during this reign all the great powers of parliament were asserted and exercised. The foreign wars of Henry IV. and Henry V., by continuing the financial necessities of the Crown, maintained for a while the powers which parliament had acquired by the struggles of centuries.

Relapse of Parliamentary Influence.—But a period of civil wars and disputed successions was now at hand, which checked the further development of parliamentary liberties. The effective power of a political institution is determined, not by assertions of authority, nor even by its legal recognition, but by the external forces by which it is supported, controlled or overborne. With the close of the Wars of the Roses the life of parliament seems to have well-nigh expired.

To this constitutional relapse various causes contributed at the same period. The Crown had recovered its absolute supremacy. The powerful baronage had been decimated on the battlefield and the scaffold; and vast estates had been confiscated to the Crown. Kings had no longer any dread of their prowess as defenders of their own order or party, or as leaders of the people. The royal treasury had been enriched by their ruin; while the close of a long succession of wars with France and Scotland relieved it of that continual drain which had reduced the Crown to an unwelcome dependence upon parliament. Not only were the fortunes of the baronage laid low, but feudalism was also dying out in England as on the continent. It was no longer a force which could control the Crown; and it was being further weakened by changes in the art of war. The mailed horseman, the battle-axe and cross-bow of the burgher and yeoman, could not cope with the cannon and arquebus of the royal army.

In earlier times the Church had often stood forth against the domination of kings, but now it was in passive submission to the Throne. The prelates were attracted to the court, and sought the highest offices of state; the inferior clergy had long been losing their influence over the laity by their ignorance and want of moral elevation at a period of increasing enlightenment; while the Church at large was weakened by schisms and a wider freedom of thought. Hence the Church, like the baronage, had ceased to be a check upon the Crown.

Meanwhile what had become of the ever-growing power of the Commons? It is true they had lost their stalwart leaders, the armed barons and outspoken prelates, but they had themselves advanced in numbers, riches and enlightenment; they had overspread the land as knights and freeholders, or dwelt in populous towns enriched by merchandise. Why could they not find leaders of their own? Because they had lost the liberal franchises of an early age. All freeholders, or suitors present at the county court, were formerly entitled to vote for a knight of the shire; but in the eighth year of Henry VI. (1430) an act was passed (c. 37) by which this right was confined to 40s. freeholders, resident in the county. Large numbers of electors were thus disfranchised. In the view of parliament they were " of no value," and complaints had been made that they were under the influence of the nobles and greater landowners; but a popular element had been withdrawn from the county representation, and the restricted franchise cannot have impaired the influence of the nobles.

As for the cities and boroughs, they had virtually renounced their electoral privileges. As we have seen, they had never valued them very highly; and now by royal charters, or by the usurpation of small self-elected bodies of burgesses, the choice of members had fallen into the hands of town councils and neighbouring landowners. The anomalous system of close and nomination boroughs, which had arisen thus early in English history, was suffered to continue without a check for four centuries, as a notorious blot upon a free constitution.

All these changes exalted the prerogatives of the Crown. Amid the clash of arms and the strife of hostile parties the voice of parliament had been stifled; and, when peace was restored, a powerful king could dispense with an assembly which might prove troublesome, and from whom he rarely needed help. Hence for a period of two hundred years, from the reign of Henry VI. to that of Elizabeth, the free parliaments of England were in abeyance. The institution retained its form and constituent parts; its rights and privileges were theoretically recognized, but its freedom and national character were little more than shadows.

The Three Estates of the Realm.—This check in the fortunes of parliament affords a fitting occasion for examining the composition of each of the three estates of the realm.

Lords Spiritual and Temporal.—The archbishops and bishops had held an eminent position in the councils of Saxon and Norman kings, and many priors and abbots were from time to time associated with them as lords spiritual, until the suppression of the monasteries by Henry VIII. They generally outnumbered their brethren, the temporal peers, who sat with them in the same assembly.

The lords temporal comprised several dignities. Of these the baron, though now the lowest in rank, was the most ancient. The title was familiar in Saxon times, but it was not until after the Norman Conquest that it was invested with a distinct feudal dignity. Next in antiquity was the earl, whose official title was known to Danes and Saxons, and who after the Conquest obtained a dignity equivalent to that of count in foreign states. The highest dignity, that of duke, was not created until Edward III. conferred it upon his son, Edward the Black Prince. The rank of marquess was first created by Richard II., with precedence after a duke. It was in the reign of Henry VI. that the rank of viscount was created, to be placed between the earl and the baron. Thus the peerage consisted of the five dignities of duke, marquess, earl, viscount and baron. During the 15th century the number of temporal peers summoned to parliament rarely exceeded fifty, and no more than twenty-nine received writs of summons to the first parliament of Henry VII. There were only fifty-nine at the death of Queen Elizabeth. At the accession of William III. this number had been increased to about one hundred and fifty.

Life Peerages.—The several orders of the peerage are alike distinguished by the hereditary character of their dignities. Some life peerages, indeed, were created between the reigns of Richard II. and Henry VI., and several ladies had received life peerages between the reigns of Charles II. and George II. The highest authorities had also held that the creation of life peerages was within the prerogative of the Crown. But four hundred years had elapsed since the creation of a life peer, entitled to sit in parliament, when Queen Victoria was advised to create Sir James Parke, an eminent judge, a baron for life, under the title of Lord Wensleydale. The object of this deviation from the accustomed practice was to strengthen the judicature of the House of Lords, without unduly enlarging the numbers of the peerage. But the Lords at once took exception to this act of the Crown, and, holding that a prerogative so long disused could not be revived, in derogation of the hereditary character of the peerage, resolved that Lord Wensleydale was not entitled by his letters patent and writ of summons to sit and vote in parliament. His lordship accordingly received a new patent, and took his seat as an hereditary peer. But the necessity of some such expedient for improving the appellate jurisdiction of the House of Lords could not be contested; and in 1876 three lords of appeal in ordinary were constituted by statute, enjoying the rank of baron for life, and the right of sitting and voting in the House of Lords so long as they continue in office.

The Commons.—The Commons formed a more numerous body. In the reign of Edward I. there were about 275 members, in that of Edward III. 250, and in that of Henry VI. 300. In the reign of Henry VIII. parliament added 27 members for Wales and four for the county and city of Chester, and in the reign of Charles II. 4 for the county and city of Durham. Between the reigns of Henry VIII. and Charles II. 130 members were also added by royal charter.

Parliament under Henry VIII.—To resume the history of parliament at a later period, let us glance at the reign of Henry VIII. Never had the power of the Crown been greater than when this king succeeded to the throne, and never had a more imperious will been displayed by any king of England. Parliament was at his feet to do his bidding, and the Reformation enormously increased his power. He had become a pope to the bishops; the old nobles who had resisted his will had perished in the field or on the scaffold; the new nobles were his creatures; and he had the vast wealth of the Church in his hands as largesses to his adherents. Such was the dependence of parliament upon the Crown and its advisers during the Reformation period that in less than thirty years four vital changes were decreed in the national faith. Each of the successive reigns inaugurated a new religion.

Queen Elisabeth and her Parliaments.—With the reign of Elizabeth commenced a new era in the life of parliament. She had received the royal prerogatives unimpaired, and her hand was strong enough to wield them. But in the long interval since Edward IV. the entire framework of English society had been changed; it was a new England that the queen was called upon to govern. The coarse barons of feudal times had been succeeded by English country gentlemen, beyond the influence of the court, and identified with all the interests and sympathies of their country neighbours. From this class were chosen nearly all the knights of the shire, and a considerable proportion of the members for cities and boroughs. They were generally distinguished by a manly independence, and were prepared to uphold the rights and privileges of parliament and the interests of their constituents. A change no less remarkable had occurred in other classes of society. The country was peopled with yeomen and farmers, far superior to the cultivators of the soil in feudal times; and the towns and seaports had grown into important centres of commerce and manufactures. Advances not less striking had been made in the enlightenment and culture of society. But, above all, recent religious revolutions had awakened a spirit of thought and inquiry by no means confined to questions of faith. The Puritans, hostile to the Church, and jealous of every semblance of Catholic revival, were embittered against the state, which was identified, in their eyes, with many ecclesiastical enormities; and stubborn temper was destined to become a strong motive force in restoring the authority of parliament.

The parliaments of Elizabeth, though rarely summoned, displayed an unaccustomed spirit. They discussed the succession to the Crown, the marriage of the queen, and ecclesiastical abuses; they upheld the privileges of the Commons and their right to advise the Crown upon all matters of state; and they condemned the grant of monopolies. The bold words of the Wentworths and Yelvertons were such as had not been heard before in parliament. The conflicts between Elizabeth and the Commons marked the revival of the independence of parliament, and foreshadowed graver troubles at no distant period.

Conflicts of James I. with the Commons.—James I., with short-sighted pedantry, provoked a succession of conflicts with the Commons, in which abuses of prerogative were stoutly resisted and the rights and privileges of parliament resolutely asserted. The "remonstrance" of 1610 and the "protestation" of 1621 would have taught a politic ruler that the Commons could no longer be trifled with; but those lessons were lost upon James and upon his ill-fated son.

Charles I. and the Commonwealth.—The momentous struggles between Charles I. and his parliaments cannot be followed in this place. The earlier parliaments of this reign fairly represented the earnest and temperate judgment of the country. They were determined to obtain the redress of grievances and to restrain undue prerogatives; but there was no taint of disloyalty to the Crown; there were no dreams of revolution. But the contest at length became embittered, until there was no issue but the arbitrament of the sword. The period of the Great Rebellion and the Commonwealth proved the supreme power of the Commons, when supported by popular forces. Everything gave way before them. They raised victorious armies in the field, they overthrew the Church and the House of Lords, and they brought the king himself to the scaffold. It also displayed the impotence of a parliament which has lost the confidence of the country, or is overborne by mobs, by an army, or by the strong will of a dictator.

Political Agitation of this Period.—It is to this time of fierce political passions that we trace the origin of political agitation as an organized method of influencing the deliberations of parliament. The whole country was then aroused by passionate exhortations from the pulpit and in the press. No less than thirty thousand political tracts and newspapers during this period have been preserved. Petitions to parliament were multiplied in order to strengthen the hands of the popular leaders. Clamorous meetings were held to stimulate or overawe parliament. Such methods, restrained after the Restoration, have been revived in later times, and now form part of the acknowledged system of parliamentary government.

Parliament after the Restoration.—On the restoration of Charles II. parliament was at once restored to its old constitution, and its sittings were revived as if they had suffered no interruption. No outward change had been effected by the late revolution; but that a stronger spirit of resistance to abuses of prerogative had been aroused was soon to be disclosed in the deposition of James II. and "the glorious revolution" of 1688. At this time the full rights of parliament were explicitly declared, and securities taken for the maintenance of public liberties. The theory of a constitutional monarchy and a free parliament was established; but after two revolutions it is curious to observe the indirect methods by which the Commons were henceforth kept in subjection to the Crown and the territorial aristocracy. The representation had long become an illusion. The knights of the shire were the nominees of nobles and great landowners; the borough members were returned by the Crown, by noble patrons or close corporations; even the representation of cities, with greater pretensions to independence, was controlled by bribery. Nor were rulers content with their control of the representation, but, after the Restoration, the infamous system of bribing the members themselves became a recognized instrument of administration. The country gentlemen were not less attached to the principles of rational liberty than their fathers, and would have resisted further encroachments of prerogatives; but they were satisfied with the Revolution settlement and the remedial laws of William III., and no new issue had yet arisen to awaken opposition. Accordingly, they ranged themselves with one or other of the political parties into which parliament was now beginning to be divided, and bore their part in the more measured strifes of the 18th century. From the Revolution till the reign of George III. the effective power of the state was wielded by the Crown, the Church and the territorial aristocracy; but the influence of public opinion since the stirring events of the 17th century had greatly increased. Both parties were constrained to defer to it; and, notwithstanding the flagrant defects in the representation, parliament generally kept itself in accord with the general sentiments of the country.

Union of Scotland.—On the union of Scotland in 1707 important changes were made in the constitution of parliament. The House of Lords was reinforced by the addition of sixteen peers, representing the peerage of Scotland, and elected every parliament; and the Scottish peers, as a body, were admitted to all the privileges of peerage, except the right of sitting in parliament or upon the trial of peers. No prerogative, however, was given to the Crown to create new peerages after the union; and, while they are distinguished by their antiquity, their number is consequently decreasing. To the House of Commons were assigned forty-five members, representing the shires and burghs of Scotland.

Parliament under George III.—With the reign of George III. there opened a new period in the history of parliament. Agitation in its various forms, an active and aggressive press, public meetings and political associations, the free use of the right of petition, and a turbulent spirit among the people seriously changed the relations of parliament to the country. And the publication of debates, which was fully established in 1771, at once increased the direct responsibility of parliament to the people, and ultimately brought about other results, to which we shall presently advert.

Union of Ireland.—In this reign another important change was effected in the constitution of parliament. Upon the union with Ireland, in 1801, four Irish bishops were added to the lords spiritual, who sat by rotation of sessions, and represented the episcopal body of the Church of Ireland. But those bishops were deprived of their seats in parliament in 1869, on the disestablishment of the Church of Ireland. Twenty-eight representative peers, elected for life by the peerage of Ireland, were admitted to the House of Lords. All the Irish peers were

also entitled to the privilege of peerage. In two particulars the Irish peerage was treated in a different manner from the peerage of Scotland. The Crown was empowered to create a new Irish peerage whenever three Irish peerages in existence at the time of the Union have become extinct, or when the number of Irish peers, exclusive of those holding peerages of the United Kingdom, has been reduced to one hundred. And, further, Irish peers were permitted to sit in the House of Commons for any place in Great Britain, forfeiting, however, the privilege of peerage while sitting in the lower house.

At the same time one hundred representatives of Ireland were added to the House of Commons. This addition raised the number of members to six hundred and fifty-eight. Parliament now became the parliament of the United Kingdom.

Schemes for Improving the Representation.—By the union of Scotland and Ireland the electoral abuses of those countries were combined with those of England. Notwithstanding a defective representation, however, parliament generally sustained its position as fairly embodying the political sentiments of its time. Public opinion had been awakened, and could not safely be ignored by any party in the state. Under a narrow and corrupt electoral system the ablest men in the country found an entrance into the House of Commons; and their rivalry and ambition ensured the acceptance of popular principles and the passing of many remedial measures. As society expanded, and new classes were called into existence, the pressure of public opinion upon the legislature was assuming a more decisive character. The grave defects of the representation were notorious, and some minor electoral abuses had been from time to time corrected. But the fundamental evils—nomination boroughs, limited rights of election, the sale of seats in parliament, the prevalence of bribery, and the enormous expense of elections—though constantly exposed, long held their ground against all assailants. So far back as 1770 Lord Chatham had denounced these flagrant abuses. "Before the end of this century," he said, "either the parliament will reform itself from within, or be reformed with a vengeance from without." In 1782, and again in 1783 and 1785, his distinguished son, William Pitt, condemned the abuses of the representation, and proposed schemes of parliamentary reform. In 1793 Mr Grey (afterwards Earl Grey) submitted a motion on the same subject; but the excesses of the French Revolution, political troubles at home, and exhausting wars abroad discouraged the supporters of reform for many years. Under more favourable conditions the question assumed greater proportions. Lord John Russell especially distinguished himself in 1820, and in several succeeding years, by the able exposure of abuses and by temperate schemes of reform. His efforts were assisted by the scandalous disclosures of bribery at Grampound, Penryn and East Retford. All moderate proposals were rejected; but the concurrence of a dissolution, on the death of George IV., with the French Revolution in 1830, and an ill-timed declaration of the duke of Wellington that the representation was perfect and could not be improved, suddenly precipitated the memorable crisis of parliamentary reform. It now fell to the lot of Earl Grey, as premier, to be the leader in a cause which he had espoused in his early youth.

The Reform Acts of 1832.—The result of the memorable struggle which ensued may be briefly told. By the Reform Acts of 1832 the representation of the United Kingdom was reconstructed. In England, fifty-six nomination boroughs returning one hundred and eleven members were disfranchised; thirty boroughs were each deprived of one member, and Weymouth and Melcombe Regis, which had returned four members, were now reduced to two. Means were thus found for the enfranchisement of populous places. Twenty-two large towns, including metropolitan districts, became entitled to return two members, and twenty less considerable towns acquired the right of returning one member each. The number of county members was increased from ninety-four to one hundred and fifty-nine, the larger counties being divided for the purposes of representation.

The elective franchise was also placed upon a new basis. In the boroughs a £10 household suffrage was substituted for the narrow and unequal franchises which had sprung up—the rights of freemen, in corporate towns, being alone respected. In the counties, copyholders and leaseholders for terms of years, and tenants at will paying a rent of £50 a year, were added to the 40s. freeholders.

By the Scottish Reform Act the number of members representing Scotland was increased from forty-five, as arranged at the union, to fifty-three, of whom thirty were assigned to counties and twenty-three to cities and burghs. In counties the franchise was conferred upon owners of property of £10 a year, and certain classes of leaseholders; in burghs, upon £10 householders, as in England.

By the Irish Reform Act, no boroughs, however small, were disfranchised; but the franchise was given to £10 householders, and county constituencies were enlarged. These franchises, however, were extended in 1850, when an £8 household suffrage was given to the boroughs, and additions were made to the county franchises. The hundred members assigned to that country at the union were increased to one hundred and five. Notwithstanding these various changes, however, the total number of the House of Commons was still maintained at six hundred and fifty-eight.

The legislature was now brought into closer relations with the people, and became more sensitive to the pressure of popular forces. The immediate effects of this new spirit were perceptible in the increased legislative activity of the reformed parliament, its vigorous grappling with old abuses, and its preference of the public welfare to the narrower interests of classes. But, signal as was the regeneration of parliament, several electoral evils still needed correction. Strenuous efforts were made, with indifferent success, to overcome bribery and corruption, and proposals were often ineffectually made to restrain the undue influence of landlords and employers of labour by the ballot; improvements were made in the registration and polling of electors, and the property qualification of members was abolished. Complaints were also urged that the middle classes had been admitted to power, while the working classes were excluded from the late scheme of enfranchisement. It was not till 1867 however that any substantial advance was made.

Increased Power of the Commons.—Prior to the reign of Charles I. the condition of society had been such as naturally to subordinate the Commons to the Crown and the Lords. After the Revolution of 1688 society had so far advanced that, under a free representation, the Commons might have striven with both upon equal terms. But, as by far the greater part of the representation was in the hands of the king and the territorial nobles, the large constitutional powers of the Commons were held safely in check. After 1832, when the representation became a reality, a corresponding authority was asserted by the Commons. For several years, indeed, by reason of the weakness of the Liberal party, the Lords were able successfully to resist the Commons upon many important occasions; but it was soon acknowledged that they must yield whenever a decisive majority of the Commons, supported by public opinion, insisted upon the passing of any measure, however repugnant to the sentiments of the upper house. And it became a political axiom that the Commons alone determined the fate of ministries.

Later Measures of Reform.—In 1852, and again in 1854, Lord John Russell introduced measures of parliamentary reform; but constitutional changes were discouraged by the Crimean War. In 1859 Lord Derby's Conservative government proposed another scheme of reform, which was defeated; and in 1860 Lord John Russell brought in another bill, which was not proceeded with; and the question of reform continued in abeyance until after the death of Lord Palmerston. Earl Russell, who succeeded him as premier, was prompt to redeem former pledges, and hastened to submit to a new parliament, in 1866, another scheme of reform. This measure, and the

ministry by whom it was promoted, were overthrown by a combination of the Conservative opposition and the memorable "cave" of members of the Liberal party. But the popular sentiment in favour of reform, which had for some years been inert, was suddenly aroused by the defeat of a Liberal ministry and the triumph of the party opposed to reform. Lord Derby and his colleagues were now constrained to undertake the settlement of this embarrassing question; and by a strange concurrence of political events and party tactics a scheme far more democratic than that of the Liberal government was accepted by the same parliament, under the auspices of a Conservative ministry.

The Reform Acts of 1867-1868.—By the English Reform Act of 1867 four corrupt boroughs were disfranchised, and thirty-eight boroughs returning two members were henceforth to return one only. A third member was given to Manchester, Liverpool, Birmingham and Leeds; a second member to Merthyr Tydfil and Salford; the Tower Hamlets was divided into two boroughs, each returning two members; and ten new boroughs were created, returning one member each, with the exception of Chelsea, to which two were assigned. By these changes twenty-six seats were taken from boroughs, while a member was given to the university of London. But before this act came into operation seven other English boroughs were disfranchised by the Scottish Reform Act of 1868, these seats being given to Scotland. Thirteen new divisions of counties were erected, to which twenty-five members were assigned. In counties the franchise of copyholders and leaseholders was reduced from £10 to £5, and the occupation franchise from £50 to £12. In boroughs the franchise was extended to all occupiers of dwelling-houses rated to the poor-rates, and to lodgers occupying lodgings of the annual value of £10 unfurnished.

By the Scottish Reform Act of 1868, the number of members representing Scotland was increased from fifty-three to sixty—three new members being given to the shires, two to the universities, and two to cities and burghs. The county franchise was extended to owners of lands and heritages of £5 yearly value, and to occupiers of the rateable value of £14; and the burgh franchise to all occupiers of dwelling-houses paying rates, and to tenants of lodgings of £10 annual value unfurnished.

By the Irish Reform Act of 1868 no change was made in the number of members nor in the distribution of seats; but the boroughs of Sligo and Cashel, already disfranchised, were still left without representation. The county franchise was left unchanged; but the borough franchise was extended to occupiers of houses rated at £4, and of lodgings of the annual value of £10 unfurnished.

That these changes in the representation—especially the household suffrage in boroughs—were a notable advance upon the reforms of 1832, in the direction of democracy, cannot be questioned. The enlarged constituencies speedily overthrew the ministry to whom these measures were due; and the new parliament further extended the recent scheme of reform by granting to electors the protection of the ballot (q.v.), for which advanced reformers had contended since 1832. Nor was the existing representation long suffered to continue without question. First, it was proposed, in 1872, to extend the household franchise to counties, and this proposal found favour in the country and in the House of Commons; but, the Conservative party having been restored to power in 1874, no measure of that character could be promoted with any prospect of success. At the dissolution of 1880 a more general revision of the representation was advocated by leading members of the Liberal party, who were soon restored to power.

(T. E. M.; H. Ch.)

Acts of 1884-1885.—The Reform Act of 1884 was ultimately carried with the goodwill of both of the great political parties. The Conservatives resisted Mr Gladstone's attempt to carry a great extension of the franchise before he had disclosed his scheme of redistribution, and the bill was thrown out by the House of Lords in August 1884. But after a conference of Mr Gladstone with Lord Salisbury, to whom the whole scheme was confided, an agreement was reached, and the bill was passed in the autumn session. In the following session (1885) the Redistribution Act was passed.

A uniform household and lodger franchise was established in counties and boroughs. If a dwelling was held as part payment for service, the occupier was not deprived of his vote because his home was the property of his master. The obligation was thrown on the overseers of ascertaining whether any other man besides the owner was entitled to be registered as an inhabitant occupier, and the owner was bound to supply the overseers with information. The Registration Acts were otherwise widely amended. Polling-places were multiplied, so that little time need be lost in recording a vote. These and other beneficial changes went a long way towards giving a vote to every one who had a decent home. By the Redistribution of Seats Act 1885 all boroughs with less than 15,000 inhabitants ceased to return a member. These small towns were merged into their counties, and the counties were subdivided into a great number of single-member constituencies, so that the inhabitants of the disfranchised boroughs voted for the member for the division of the county in which they were situated. Boroughs with less than 50,000 inhabitants returning two members were in future to return only one, and towns of over 100,000 were divided into separate constituencies, and received additional members in proportion to their population. The members for the City of London were reduced to two, but Greater London, including Croydon, returned sixty. Divided Liverpool returned nine, Glasgow seven, Edinburgh, Dublin and Belfast each four, and so on. Six additional seats were given to England and twelve to Scotland, so that, allowing for a diminution by disfranchisement for corruption, the numbers of the House of Commons were raised to 670 members.

Results of Reform since 1832.—From a constitutional standpoint it is important to recognize the results of the successive Reform Acts on the working of parliament as regards the position of the executive on the one hand and the electorate on the other. Before 1832 the functions of ministers were mainly administrative, and parliament was able to deal much as it pleased with their rare legislative proposals without thereby depriving them of office. Moreover, since before that date ministers were, generally speaking, in fact as well as in theory appointed by the king, while the general confidence of the majority in the House of Commons followed the confidence not so much of the electorate as of the Crown, that house was able on occasions to exercise an effective control over foreign policy. Pitt, after 1784, was defeated several times on foreign and domestic issues, yet his resignation was neither expected nor desired. In 1788, when the regency of the prince of Wales appeared probable, and again in 1812, it was generally assumed that it would be in his power to dismiss his father's ministers and to maintain the Whigs in office without dissolving parliament. This system, while it gave to ministers security of tenure, left much effective freedom of action to the House of Commons. But the Reform Act of 1832 introduced a new order of things. In 1835 the result of a general election was for the first time the direct cause of a change of ministry, and in 1841 a House of Commons was elected for the express purpose of bringing a particular statesman into power. The electorate voted for Sir Robert Peel, and it would have been as impossible for the house then elected to deny him their support as it would be for the college of electors in the United States to exercise their private judgment in the selection of a president. As time went on, and the party system became more closely organized in the enlarged electorate, the voting power throughout the country came to exercise an influence in the House. The premier was now a party leader who derived his power in reality neither from the Crown nor from parliament, but from the electorate, and to the electorate he could appeal if deserted by his parliamentary majority. Unless it was proposed to drive him from the office in which it was elected to support him, that majority would not venture to defeat, or even seriously to modify, his legislative proposals, or to pass any censure on his foreign policy,

for all such action would now be held to be equivalent to a vote of no confidence. From the passing of the Reform Act of 1867 down to 1900 (with a single exception due to the lowering of the franchise and the redistribution of seats) the electorate voted alternately for the rival party leaders, and it was the function of the houses elected for that purpose to pass the measures and to endorse the general policy with which those leaders were respectively identified. The cabinet (q.v.), composed of colleagues selected by the prime minister, had practically, though indirectly, become an executive committee acting on behalf of the electorate, that is to say, the majority which returned their party to office; and the House of Commons practically ceased to exercise control over ministers except in so far as a revolt in the party forming the majority could influence the prime minister, or force him to resign or dissolve. Meanwhile, the virtual identification of the electorate with the nation by the successive extensions of the franchise added immensely to its power, the chief limitation being supplied by the Septennial Act. The House of Lords, whatever its nominal rights, came henceforth in practice to exercise restriction rather on the House of Commons than on the will of the electorate, for the acquiescence of the upper house in the decision of the electors, when appealed to on a specific point of issue between the two houses, was gradually accepted by its leaders as a constitutional convention.

The history of parliament, as an institution, centres in this later period round two points, (A) the friction between Lords and Commons, resulting in proposals for the remodelling of the upper house, and (B) the changes in procedure within the House of Commons, necessitated by new conditions of work and the desire to make it a more business-like assembly. These two movements will be discussed separately.

A. House of Lords Question.—In the altered position of the House of Lords, the occasional checks given by it to the House of Commons were bound to cause friction with the representatives of the people. In the nature of things this was a matter of importance only when the Liberal party was in power and measures were proposed by the Liberal leaders which involved such extreme changes that the preponderantly Conservative upper house could amend or reject them with some confidence in its action being supported by the electorate. The frequent differences between the two houses during the parliament of 1880–1885, culminating in the postponement by the upper house of the Reform Bill, caused the status of that house to be much discussed during the general election of 1885, and proposals for its "mending or ending" to be freely canvassed on Radical platforms. On the 5th of March 1886 Mr Labouchere moved a resolution in the House of Commons condemning the hereditary principle. This was resisted by Mr Gladstone, then prime minister, on the ground that he had never supported an abstract resolution unless he was prepared to follow it up by action, and that the time for this had not arrived. On a division the motion was negatived by 202 votes against 166. The question of the constitution of the House of Lords was much agitated in 1888. The Conservatives were again in power, but many of them thought that it would be prudent to forestall by a moderate reform the more drastic remedies now openly advocated by their opponents. On the other hand, Radicals were disposed to resist all changes involving the maintenance of the hereditary principle, lest they should thereby strengthen the House of Lords. On the 9th of March Mr Labouchere again moved his resolution in the House of Commons. Mr W. H. Smith, the leader of the house, in resisting the motion, admitted that some changes were desirable, and agreed with a previous speaker that it was by the Conservatives that such changes ought to be effected. On the 19th of March in the same year Lord Rosebery, in the House of Lords, moved for a select committee to inquire into the subject. He took the opportunity to explain his own plan of reform. While he did not wish to abolish the hereditary principle, he desired that no peer, outside the Royal family, should be a member of the house by right of birth alone. To the representatives of the peers he proposed to add other men who had achieved distinction in a public career. He attached a high importance to the existence of a second chamber. His motion was negatived by 97 votes against 50. On the 26th of April Lord Dunraven withdrew a bill for the reform of the House of Lords on the promise of the government to deal with the matter, and on the 18th of June Lord Salisbury fulfilled this pledge. He introduced a bill on that day to provide for the creation of a limited number of life peers and for the exclusion of unworthy members from the house. Under this measure a maximum of five life-peerages in any one year might be created, but the total number was never to exceed fifty. In respect of three out of these five life-peers the choice of the Crown was restricted to judges, generals, admirals, ambassadors, privy councillors and ex-governors of colonies. The two additional life-peers were to be appointed in regard to some special qualification to be stated in the message to the house announcing the intention of the Crown to make the appointment. Power was also to be given to the house to expel members for the period of the current parliament by an address to the Crown praying that their writs of summons might be cancelled. The bill was read a second time on the 10th of July, but it met with a cold reception and was dropped. The only outcome of all that was written and said in this year was that in 1889, after the report of a select committee set up in 1888, the Lords made a few changes in their standing orders, among which the order establishing a quorum of thirty in divisions and those for the constitution of standing committees were the most important.

The parliament which met at Westminster in August 1892 was more democratic in its tendencies than any of its predecessors. At the beginning of the session of 1893, in the course of which the Home Rule Bill was passed by the House of Commons, government bills were introduced for quinquennial parliaments, for the amendment of registration, and for the limitation of each elector to a single vote. The introduction of these bills served merely as a declaration of government policy, and they were not further pressed. On the 24th of March a resolution in favour of payment of members was carried by 276 votes against 229, and again in 1895 by 176 to 158. But the rejection of the Home Rule Bill by the House of Lords, with the apparent acquiescence of the country, combined with the retirement of Mr Gladstone to weaken the influence of this House of Commons, and small importance was attached to its abstract resolutions. In the ensuing session of 1894 an amendment to the Address condemning the hereditary principle was moved by Mr Labouchere, and carried by 147 to 145. The government, however, holding that this was not the way in which a great question should be raised, withdrew the Address, and carried another without the insertion. In his last public utterance Mr Gladstone directed the attention of his party to the reform of the House of Lords, and Lord Rosebery endeavoured to concentrate on such a policy the energies of his supporters at the general election. But the result of the dissolution of 1895, showing, as it did, that on the chief political issue of the day the electorate had agreed with the House of Lords and had disagreed with the House of Commons, greatly strengthened the upper house, and after that date the subject was but little discussed until the Liberal party again came into power ten years later. The House of Lords claimed the right to resist changes made by the House of Commons until the will of the people had been definitely declared, and its defenders contended that its ultimate dependence on the electorate, now generally acknowledged, rendered the freedom from ministerial control secured to it by its constitution a national safeguard.

In 1907, under the Radical government of Sir H. Campbell-Bannerman (q.v.), the conflict between the Commons and the Lords again became more acute. And the prime minister in May obtained a large majority in the lower house for a resolution, on which a bill was to be founded, involving a complicated method of overriding the will of the Lords when the Commons had three times passed a bill. But no further immediate step was taken. In 1908 a strong committee of the House of Lords

with Lord Rosebery as chairman, which had been appointed in consequence of the introduction by Lord Newton of a bill for reforming the constitution of the upper house, presented an interesting report in favour of largely restricting the hereditary element and adopting a method of selection.

So the question stood when in 1909 matters came to a head through the introduction of Mr Lloyd George's budget. It had always been accepted as the constitutional right of the House of Lords to reject a financial measure sent up by the Commons but not to amend it, but the rejection of the budget (which was, in point of form, referred to the judgment of the electorate) now precipitated a struggle with the Liberal party, who had persistently denied any right on the part of the upper house to force a dissolution. The Liberal leaders contended that, even if constitutional, the claim of the House of Lords to reject a budget was practically obsolete, and having been revived must now be formally abolished; and they went to the country for a mandate to carry their view into law. The elections of January 1910 gave an unsatisfactory answer, since the two principal parties, the Liberals and the Unionists, returned practically equal; but the Liberal government had also on their side the Irish Nationalist and the Labour parties, which gave them a majority in the House of Commons if they could concentrate the combined forces on the House of Lords question. This Mr Asquith contrived to do; and having introduced and carried through the House of Commons a series of resolutions defining his proposals, he had also tabled a bill which was to be sent up to the House of Lords, when the death of the king suddenly interrupted the course of this constitutional conflict, and gave a breathing-space for both sides to consider the possibility of coming to terms. In June Mr Asquith took the initiative in inviting the leaders of the Opposition to a conference with closed doors, and a series of meetings between four representatives of each side were begun. The government were represented by Mr Asquith, Mr Lloyd George, Mr Birrell and Lord Crewe. The Unionists were represented by Mr Balfour, Lord Lansdowne, Mr Austin Chamberlain and Lord Cawdor.

The situation on the Radical side at this juncture may be best understood by setting out the resolutions passed in the House of Commons, and the text of the parliament bill of which Mr Asquith had given notice:—

The Resolutions.—" 1. That it is expedient that the House of Lords be disabled by law from rejecting or amending a money bill, but that any such limitation by law shall not be taken to diminish or qualify the existing rights and privileges of the House of Commons.

"For the purpose of this resolution, a bill shall be considered a money bill if in the opinion of the Speaker it contains only provisions dealing with all or any of the following subjects—namely, the imposition, repeal, remission, alteration or regulation of taxation; charges on the Consolidated Fund or the provision of money by parliament; supply; the appropriation, control or regulation of public money; the raising or guarantee of any loan or the repayment thereof; or matters incidental to those subjects or any of them.

" 2. That it is expedient that the powers of the House of Lords, as respects bills other than money bills, be restricted by law, so that any such bill which has passed the House of Commons in three successive sessions and, having been sent up to the House of Lords at least one month before the end of the session, has been rejected by that house in each of those sessions, shall become law without the consent of the House of Lords, on the royal assent being declared: provided that at least two years shall have elapsed between the date of the first introduction of the bill in the House of Commons and the date on which it passes the House of Commons for the third time.

"For the purpose of this resolution a bill shall be treated as rejected by the House of Lords if it has not been passed by the House of Lords either without amendment or with such amendments only as may be agreed upon by both houses.

" 3. That it is expedient to limit the duration of parliament to five years."

The Parliament Bill, 1910.—" Whereas it is expedient that provision should be made for regulating the relations between the two Houses of Parliament: And whereas it is intended to substitute for the House of Lords as it at present exists a second chamber constituted on a popular instead of hereditary basis, but such substitution cannot be immediately brought into operation: And whereas provision will require hereafter to be made by parliament in a measure effecting such substitution for limiting and defining the powers of the new second-chamber, but it is expedient to make such provision as in this act appears for restricting the existing powers of the House of Lords: Be it therefore enacted by the king's most excellent majesty, by and with the advice and consent of the Lords spiritual and temporal, and Commons, in this present parliament assembled, and by the authority of the same, as follows:—

" 1. (1) If a money bill, having been passed by the House of Commons, and sent up to the House of Lords at least one month before the end of the session, is not passed by the House of Lords without amendment within one month after it is so sent up to that house, the bill shall, unless the House of Commons direct to the contrary, be presented to His Majesty and become an act of parliament on the royal assent being signified, notwithstanding that the House of Lords have not consented to the bill.

" (2) A money bill means a bill which in the opinion of the Speaker of the House of Commons contains only provisions dealing with all or any of the following subjects—namely, the imposition, repeal, remission, alteration or regulation of taxation; charges on the consolidated fund or the provision of money by parliament; supply; the appropriation, control or regulation of public money; the raising or guarantee of any loan or the repayment thereof; or matters incidental to those subjects or any of them.

" (3) When a bill to which the House of Lords has not consented is presented to His Majesty for assent as a money bill, the bill shall be accompanied by a certificate of the Speaker of the House of Commons that it is a money bill.

" (4) No amendment shall be allowed to a money bill which, in the opinion of the Speaker of the House of Commons, is such as to prevent the bill retaining the character of a money bill.

" 2. (1) If any bill other than a money bill is passed by the House of Commons in three successive sessions (whether of the same parliament or not), and, having been sent up to the House of Lords at least one month before the end of the session, is rejected by the House of Lords in each of those sessions, that bill shall, on its rejection for the third time by the House of Lords, unless the House of Commons direct to the contrary, be presented to His Majesty and become an act of parliament on the royal assent being signified thereto, notwithstanding that the House of Lords has not consented to the bill: provided that this provision shall not take effect unless two years have elapsed between the date of the first introduction of the bill in the House of Commons and the date on which it passes the House of Commons for the third time.

" (2) A bill shall be deemed to be rejected by the House of Lords if it is not passed by the House of Lords either without amendment or with such amendments only as may be agreed to by both houses.

" (3) A bill shall be deemed to be the same bill as a former bill sent up to the House of Lords in the preceding session if, when it is sent up to the House of Lords, it is identical with the former bill or contains only such alterations as are certified by the Speaker of the House of Commons to be necessary owing to the time which has elapsed since the date of the former bill, or to represent amendments which have been made by the House of Lords in the former bill in the preceding session.

" Provided that the House of Commons may, if they think fit, on the passage of such a bill through the house in the second or third session, suggest any further amendments without inserting the amendments in the bill, and any such suggested amendments shall be considered by the House of Lords, and if agreed to by that house, shall be treated as amendments made by the House of Lords and agreed to by the House of Commons; but the exercise of this power by the House of Commons shall not affect the operation of this section in the event of the bill being rejected by the House of Lords.

" 3. Any certificate of the Speaker of the House of Commons given under this act shall be conclusive for all purposes, and shall not be questioned in any court of law.

" 4. Nothing in this act shall diminish or qualify the existing rights and privileges of the House of Commons.

" 5. Five years shall be substituted for seven years as the time fixed for the maximum duration of parliament under the Septennial Act 1715."

Meanwhile, in the House of Lords, Lord Rosebery had carried three resolutions declaring certain principles for the reform of the second chamber, which were assented to by, the Unionist leaders; the policy opposed to that of the government thus became that of willingness for reform of the constitution of the Upper Chamber, but not for abolition of its powers.

Lord Rosebery's Resolutions.—(1) " That a strong and efficient Second Chamber is not merely an integral part of the British Constitution, but is necessary to the well-being of the State and to the balance of Parliament." (2) " Such a Chamber can best be obtained by the reform and reconstitution of the House of Lords." (3) " That a necessary preliminary to such reform and reconstitution is the acceptance of the principle that the possession of a peerage should no longer of itself give the right to sit and vote in the House of Lords."

During the summer and autumn the private meetings between the eight leaders were continued, until twenty had been held. But on the 10th of November Mr Asquith issued a brief statement that the conference on the constitutional question had come to an end, without arriving at an agreement. Within a few days he announced that another appeal would at once be made to the electorate. The Parliament Bill was hurriedly introduced into the House of Lords, with a statement by Lord Crewe that no amendments would be accepted. The dissolution was fixed for the 28th of November. Time was short for any declaration of policy by the Unionist peers, but it was given shape at once, first by the adoption of a further resolution moved by Lord Rosebery for the remodelling of the Upper House, and secondly by Lord Lansdowne's shelving the Parliament Bill by coupling the adjournment of the debate on it with the adoption of resolutions providing for the settlement of differences between a reconstituted Upper House and the House of Commons.

Lord Rosebery's additional resolution provided that " in future the House of Lords shall consist of Lords of Parliament: (a) chosen by the whole body of hereditary peers from among themselves and by nomination by the Crown; (b) sitting by virtue of offices and of qualifications held by them; (c) chosen from outside." The Lansdowne resolutions provided in effect that, when the House of Lords had been " reconstituted and reduced in numbers " in accordance with Lord Rosebery's plan, (1) any differences arising between the two houses with regard to a Bill other than a Money Bill, in two successive sessions, and within an interval of not less than one year, should be settled, if not adjustable otherwise, in a joint sitting composed of members of both houses, except in the case of " a matter which is of great gravity and has not been adequately submitted to the judgment of the people," which should then be " submitted for decision to the electors by Referendum "; (2) and as to Money Bills, the Lords were prepared to forgo their constitutional right of rejection or amendment, if effectual provision were made against " tacking," the decision whether other than financial matters were dealt with in the Bill resting with a joint committee of both Houses, with the Speaker of the House of Commons as chairman, having a casting vote only.

The general election took place in December, and resulted practically in no change from the previous situation. Both sides won and lost seats, and the eventual numbers were: Liberals 272, Labour 42, Irish Nationalists 84 (8 being " Independents " following Mr William O'Brien), Unionists 272. Thus, including the doubtful votes of the 8 Independent Nationalists, Mr Asquith retained an apparent majority of 126 for the ministerial policy, resting as it did on the determination of the Irish Nationalists to pave the way for Home Rule by destroying the veto of the House of Lords.

B. *House of Commons Internal Reforms.*—We have already sketched the main lines of English parliamentary procedure. Until the forms of the House of Commons were openly utilized to delay the progress of government business by what became known as " obstruction " the changes made in the years following 1832 were comparatively insignificant. They consisted in (1) the discontinuance of superfluous forms, questions and amendments; (2) restrictions of debates upon questions of form; (3) improved arrangements for the distribution of business; (4) the delegation of some of the minor functions of the house to committees and officers of the house; and (5) increased publicity in the proceedings of the house. But with the entry of Mr Parnell and his Irish Nationalist followers into parliament (1875-1880) a new era began in the history of the House of Commons. Their tactics were to oppose all business of whatever kind, and at all hours.

It was not until February 1880 that the house so far overcame its reluctance to restrict liberty of discussion as to pass, in its earliest form, the rule dealing with " order in debate." It provided that whenever a member was named by the Speaker or chairman as " disregarding the authority of the chair, or abusing the rules of the house by persistently and wilfully obstructing the rules of the house," a motion might be made, to be decided without amendment or debate, for his suspension from the service of the house during the remainder of the sitting; and that if the same member should be suspended three times

In one session, his suspension on the third occasion should continue for a week, and until a motion had been made upon which it should be decided, at one sitting, by the house, whether the suspension should then cease or not. The general election, which took place two months later, restored Mr Gladstone to power and to the leadership of the house. Mr Parnell returned to parliament with a more numerous following, and resumed his former tactics. In January 1881 the Protection of Persons and Property (Ireland) Bill was introduced. For twenty-two hours Parnell fought the motion giving precedence to the bill, and for four sittings its introduction. The fourth sitting lasted forty-one hours. Then Mr Speaker Brand intervened, and declined to call on any other member who might rise to address the house, because repeated dilatory motions had been supported by small minorities in opposition to the general sense of the house. He added: " A crisis has thus arisen which demands the prompt interposition of the chair and of the house. The usual rules have proved powerless to ensure orderly and effective debate. An important measure, recommended by Her Majesty nearly a month since, and declared to be urgent in the interests of the state by a decisive majority, is being arrested by the action of an inconsiderable minority, the members of which have resorted to those modes of obstruction which have been recognized by the house as a parliamentary offence. The dignity, the credit, and the authority of this house are seriously threatened, and it is necessary they should be vindicated. . . . Future measures for ensuring orderly debate I must leave to the judgment of the house. But the house must either assume more effectual control over its debates, or entrust greater powers to the chair." The Speaker then put the question, which was carried by an overwhelming majority. Then followed the decisive struggle. Mr Gladstone gave notice for the next day (Feb. 3) of an urgency rule, which ordered, " That if the house shall resolve by a majority of three to one that the state of public business is urgent, the whole power of the house to make rules shall be and remain with the Speaker until he shall declare that the state of public business is no longer urgent." On the next day a scene of great disorder ended in the suspension of the Nationalist members, at first singly, and afterwards in groups. The urgency rule was then passed without further difficulty, and the house proceeded to resolve, " That the state of public business is urgent." The Speaker laid upon the table rules of sufficient stringency, and while they remained in force progress in public business was possible. During this session the Speaker had to intervene on points of order 935 times, and the chairman of committees 930 times; so that, allowing only five minutes on each occasion, the wrangling between the chair and members occupied 150 hours.

The events of the session of 1881 and the direct appeal of the Speaker to the house proved the necessity of changes in the rules of procedure more drastic than had hitherto been *The Closure.* proposed. Accordingly, in the first week of the session of 1882 Mr Gladstone laid his proposals on the table, and in moving the first resolution on 20th February, he reviewed, in an eloquent speech, the history of the standing orders. It was his opinion, on general grounds, that the house should settle its own procedure, but he showed that the numerous committees which, since 1832, had sat on the subject, had failed for the most part to carry their recommendations into effect from the lack of the requisite " propelling power," and he expressed his regret that the concentration of this power in the hands of the government had rendered it necessary that they should undertake a task not properly theirs. He noted two main features in the history of the case: (1) the constantly increasing labours of the house, and (2) its constantly decreasing power to despatch its duties; and while he declared that " the fundamental change which has occurred is owing to the passing of the first great Reform Bill," he pointed out that the strain had not become intolerable till the development in recent years of obstructive tactics. He defined obstruction as " the disposition either of the minority of the house, or of individuals, to resist the prevailing will of the house otherwise than by argument," and

reached the conclusion that the only remedy for a state of things by which the dignity and efficiency of the house were alike compromised, was the adoption in a carefully guarded form of the process known on the Continent as the " clôture." He explained that in his early years the house was virtually possessed of a closing power, because it was possessed of a means of sufficiently making known its inclinations; and to those inclinations uniform deference was paid by members, but that since this moral sanction had ceased to be operative, it was necessary to substitute for it a written law. The power to close debate had been of necessity assumed by almost all the European and American assemblies, the conduct of whose members was shaped by no traditional considerations; and the entry into parliament of a body of men to whom the traditions of the house were as nothing made it necessary for the House of Commons to follow this example. He proposed, therefore, that when it appeared to the Speaker, or to the chairman of committees, during any debate to be the evident sense of the house, or of the committee, that the question be now put, he might so inform the house, and that thereupon on a motion being made, " That the question be now put," the question under discussion should be forthwith put from the chair, and decided in the affirmative if supported by more than 200 members, or, when less than 40 members had voted against it, by more than 100 members. This resolution was vehemently contested by the opposition, who denounced it as an unprecedented interference with the liberty of debate, but was eventually carried in the autumn session of the same year, after a discussion extending over nineteen sittings.

On the 20th of November the standing order of the 28th of February 1880, providing for the suspension of members who persistently and wilfully obstructed the business of the house or disregarded the authority of the chair, was amended by the increase of the penalty to suspension on the first occasion for one week, on the second occasion for a fortnight, and on the third, or any subsequent occasion, for a month. The other rules, framed with a view to freeing the wheels of the parliamentary machine, and for the most part identical with the regulations adopted by Mr Speaker Brand under the urgency resolution of 1881, were carried in the course of the autumn session, and became standing orders on the 27th of November.

Mr Gladstone's closure rule verified neither the hopes of its supporters nor the fears of its opponents. It was not put into operation until the 20th of February 1885, when the Speaker's declaration of the evident sense of the house was ratified by a majority of 207—a margin of but seven votes over the necessary quorum. It was clear that no Speaker was likely to run the risk of a rebuff by again assuming the initiative unless in the face of extreme urgency, and, in fact, the rule was enforced twice only during the five years of its existence.

In 1887 the Conservative government, before the introduction of a new Crimes Act for Ireland, gave efficiency to the rule by an important amendment. They proposed that any member during a debate might claim to move, " That the question be now put," and that with the consent of the chair this question should be put forthwith, and decided without amendment or debate. Thus the initiative was transferred from the Speaker to the house. Mr Gladstone objected strongly to this alteration, chiefly on the ground that it would throw an unfair burden of responsibility upon the Speaker, who would now have to decide on a question of opinion, whereas under the old rule he was only called upon to determine a question of evident fact. The alternative most generally advocated by the opposition was the automatic closure by a bare majority at the end of each sitting, an arrangement by which the chair would be relieved from an invidious responsibility; but it was pointed out that under such a system the length of debates would not vary with the importance of the questions debated. After fourteen sittings the closure rule was passed on the 18th of March and made a standing order.

In the next session, on the 28th of February 1888, the rule was yet further strengthened by the reduction of the majority necessary for its enforcement from 200 to 100, the closure rule remaining as follows:—

That, after a question has been proposed, a member rising in his place may claim to move, "That the question be now put," and, unless it shall appear to the chair that such motion is an abuse of the rules of the house or an infringement of the rights of the minority, the question, "That the question be now put," shall be put forthwith, and decided without amendment or debate.

When the motion "That the question be now put" has been carried, and the question consequent thereon has been decided, any further motion may be made (the assent of the chair as aforesaid not having been withheld), which may be requisite to bring to a decision any question already proposed from the chair; and also if a clause be then under consideration, a motion may be made (the assent of the chair as aforesaid not having been withheld), "That the question 'That certain words of the clause defined in the motion stand part of the clause,' or 'That the clause stand part of, or be added to, the bill,' be now put." Such motions shall be put forthwith, and decided without amendment or debate.

That questions for the closure of debate shall be decided in the affirmative, if, when a division be taken, it appears by the numbers declared from the chair that not less than one hundred members voted in the majority in support of the motion.

The closure, originally brought into being to defeat the tactics of obstruction in special emergencies, thus became a part of parliamentary routine. And, the principle being *The Guillotine.* once accepted, its operation was soon extended.

The practice of retarding the progress of government measures by amendments moved to every line, adopted by both the great political parties when in opposition, led to the use of what became known as the "guillotine," for forcing through parliament important bills, most of the clauses in which were thus undiscussed. The "guillotine," means that the house decides how much time shall be devoted to certain stages of a measure, definite dates being laid down at which the closure shall be enforced and division taken. On the 17th of June 1887, after prolonged debates on the Crimes Bill in committee, clause 6 only having been reached, the remaining 14 clauses were put without discussion, and the bill was reported in accordance with previous notice. This was the first use of the "guillotine," but the precedent was followed by Mr Gladstone in 1893, when many of the clauses of the Home Rule Bill were carried through committee and on report by the same machinery. To the Conservatives must be imputed the invention of this method of legislation, to their opponents the use of it for attempting to carry a great constitutional innovation to which the majority of English and Scottish representatives were opposed, and subsequently its extension and development (1906–1909) as a regular part of the legislative machinery.

The principle of closure has been extended even to the debates on supply. The old rule, that the redress of grievances should *Supply Rules.* precede the granting of money, dating from a time when the minister of the Crown was so far from commanding the confidence of the majority in the House of Commons that he was the chief object of their attacks, nevertheless continued to govern the proceedings of the house in relation to supply without much resultant inconvenience, until the period when the new methods adopted by the Irish Nationalist party created a new situation. Until 1872 it continued to be possible to discuss any subject by an amendment to the motion for going into supply. In that year a resolution was passed limiting the amendments to matters relevant to the class of estimates about to be considered, and these relevant amendments were further restricted to the first day on which it was proposed to go into committee. This resolution was continued in 1873, but was allowed to drop in 1874. It was revived in a modified form in 1876, but was again allowed to drop in 1877. In 1879, on the recommendation of the Northcote committee, it was provided in a sessional order that whenever the committees of supply or of ways and means stood as the first order on a Monday, the Speaker should leave the chair without question put, except on first going into committee on the army, navy and civil service estimates respectively. In 1882 Thursday was added to Monday for the purposes of the order, and, some further exceptions having been made to the operation of the rule, it became a standing order. The conditions, however, under which the estimates were voted remained unsatisfactory. The most useful function of the opposition is the exposure of abuses in the various departments of administration, and this can best be performed upon the estimates. But ministers, occupied with their legislative proposals, were irresistibly tempted to postpone the consideration of the estimates until the last weeks of the session, when they were hurried through thin houses, the members of which were impatient to be gone. To meet this abuse, and to distribute the time with some regard to the comparative importance of the subjects discussed, Mr Balfour in 1896 proposed and carried a sessional order for the closure of supply, a maximum of twenty-three days being given to its consideration, of which the last three alone might be taken after the 5th of August. On the last but one of the allotted days at 10 o'clock the chairman was to put the outstanding votes, and on the last day the Speaker was to put the remaining questions necessary to complete the reports of supply. In 1901 Mr Balfour so altered the resolution that the question was put, not with respect to each vote, but to each class of votes in the Civil Service estimates, and to the total amounts of the outstanding votes in the army, navy and revenue estimates.

It is only possible here to refer briefly to some other changes in the procedure of the house which altered in various respects *Other Changes in Methods.* its character as a business-like assembly. The chief of these is as regards the hours. On Mondays, Tuesdays, Wednesdays and Thursdays the house meets at 2.45 p.m., "questions" beginning at 3 and ending (apart from urgency) at 3.45; and opposed business ends at 11. On Fridays the house meets at 12 noon, and opposed business is suspended at 5 p.m.; this is the only day when government business has not precedence, and private members' bills have the first call, though at 8.15 p.m. on Tuesdays and Wednesdays up to Easter and on Wednesdays up to Whitsuntide the business is interrupted in order that private members' motions may be taken. These arrangements, which only date from 1906, represent a considerable change from the old days before 1879 when the standing order was formed that no opposed business, with certain exceptions, should be taken after 12.30 a.m., or 1888 when the closing hour was fixed at midnight. In fact the hours of the house have become generally earlier. Another important change has been made as regards motions for the adjournment of the house, which used to afford an opportunity to the private members at any time to discuss matters of urgent importance. Since 1902 no motion for the adjournment of the house can be made until all "questions" have been disposed of, and then, if forty members support it, the debate takes place at 8.15 p.m. This alteration has much modified the character of the debates on such motions, which used to be taken when feelings were hot, whereas now there is time for reflection. In other respects the most noticeable thing in the recent evolution of the House of Commons has been its steady loss of power, as an assembly, in face of the control of the government and party leaders. In former times the private members had far larger opportunities for introducing and carrying bills, which now have no chance, unless the government affords "facilities "; and the great function of debating "supply " has largely been restricted by the closure, under which millions of money are voted without debate. The house is still ruled by technical rules of procedure which are, in the main, dilatory and obstructive, and hamper the expression of views which are distasteful to the Whips or to the government, who can by them arrange the business so as to suit their convenience. It is true indeed that this dilatory character of the proceedings assists to encourage debate, within limits; but with the influx of a new class of representatives, especially the Labour members, there has been in recent years a rather pronounced feeling that the procedure of the house might well be drastically revised with the object of making it a more business-like assembly. Reform of the House of Commons has been postponed to some extent because reform of the House of Lords has, to professed reformers, been a better "cry "; but when reform is once "in the air " in parliament it is not likely to stop, with so large a field of antiquated procedure before it as is represented by many of the traditional methods of the House of Commons. (H. CH.)

PARMA, a town and episcopal see of Emilia, Italy, capital of the province of Parma, situated on the Parma, a tributary of the Po, 55 m. N.W. of Bologna by rail. Pop. (1906), 48,523. Parma, one of the finest cities of northern Italy, lies in a fertile tract of the Lombard plain, within view of the Alps and sheltered by the Apennines, 170 ft. above sea-level. From south to north it is traversed by the channel of the Parma, crossed here by three bridges; and from east to west runs the line of the Via Aemilia, by which ancient Parma was connected on the one hand with *Ariminum* (Rimini), and on the other with *Placentia* (Piacenza). The old ramparts and bastions (excluding the circuit of the citadel of 1591, now in great part demolished, in the south-east) make an enceinte of about 4½ m., but the enclosed area is not all occupied by streets and houses.

In the centre of the city the Via Aemilia widens out into the Piazza Garibaldi, a large square which contains the Palazzo del Governo and the Palazzo Municipale, both dating from 1627. The cathedral of the Assumption (originally S. Herculanus), erected between 1064 and 1074, and consecrated in 1106 by Pope Paschal II., is a Lombardo-Romanesque building in the form of a Latin cross. The severe west front is relieved by three rows of semicircular arches, and has a central porch (there were at one time three) supported by huge red marble lions, sculptured no doubt with the rest of the façade by Giovanni Bono da Bissone in 1281. On the south side of the façade is a large brick campanile, and the foundations of another may be seen on the north. The walls and ceiling of the fine Romanesque interior are covered with frescoes of 1570, subdued in colour and well suited to the character of the building; those of the octagonal cupola representing the Assumption of the Virgin are by Correggio, but much restored. The crypt contains the shrine of the bishop S. Bernardino degli Uberti and the tomb of Bartolommeo Prato—the former by Prospero Clementi of Reggio. In the sacristy are fine intarsias. To the south-west of the cathedral stands the baptistery, designed by Benedetto Antelami; it was begun in 1196 and not completed till 1281. The whole structure is composed of red and grey Verona marble. Externally it is an irregular octagon, each face consisting of a lower storey with a semicircular arch (in three cases occupied by a portal), with sculptures by Antelami, four tiers of small columns supporting as many continuous architraves, and forming open galleries, and above these (an addition of the Gothic period) a row of five engaged columns supporting a series of pointed arches and a cornice. Internally it is a polygon of sixteen unequal sides, and the cupola is supported by sixteen ribs, springing from the same number of columns. The frescoes are interesting works of the early 13th century. In the centre is an octagonal font bearing date 1294. The episcopal palace shows traces of the building of 1232. To the east of the cathedral, and at no great distance, stands the church of S. Giovanni Evangelista, which was founded along with the Benedictine monastery in 981, but as a building dates from 1510, and has a façade erected by Simone Moschino early in the 17th century. The interior is an extremely fine early Renaissance work. The frescoes on the cupola representing the vision of S. John are by Correggio, and the arabesques on the vault of the nave by Anselmi. The Madonna della Steccata (Our Lady of the Palisade), a fine church in the form of a Greek cross, erected between 1521 and 1539 after Zaccagni's designs, contains the tombs and monuments of many of the Bourbon and Farnese dukes of Parma, and preserves its pictures, Parmigiano's "Moses Breaking the Tables of the Law" and Anselmi's "Coronation of the Virgin." S. Francesco, probably the earliest Franciscan church in northern Italy (1230-1298; now a prison), is a Gothic building in brick with a fine rose-window. The Palazzo della Pilotta is a vast and irregular group of buildings dating mainly from the 16th and 17th centuries; it now comprises the academy of fine arts (1752) and its valuable picture gallery. Among the most celebrated pictures here are Correggio's "Madonna di San Girolamo" and "Madonna della Scodella." The Teatro Farnese, a remarkable wooden structure erected in 1618-1619 from Aleotti d'Argenta's designs, and capable of containing 4500 persons, is also in this palace. There are other beautiful ceiling frescoes by Correggio in the former Benedictine nunnery of S. Paolo, executed in 1518-1519; in an adjoining chamber are fine arabesques by Araldi (d. 1528); thence come also some fine majolica tiles (1471-1482), now in the museum. The royal university of Parma, founded in 1601 by Ranuccio I., and reconstituted by Philip of Bourbon in 1768, has faculties in law, medicine and natural science, and possesses an observatory, and natural science collections, among which is the Eritrean Zoological Museum. A very considerable trade is carried on at Parma in grain, cattle and the dairy produce of the district. The *grana* cheese known as Parmesan is not now so well made at Parma as in some other parts of Italy—Lodi, for example.

From archaeological discoveries it would appear that the ancient town was preceded by a prehistoric settlement of the Bronze Age, the dwellings of which rested upon piles—one, indeed, of the so-called *terremare*, which are especially frequent in the neighbourhood of Parma. Parma became a Roman colony of 2000 colonists in 183 B.C., four years after the construction of the Via Aemilia, on which it lay. The bridge by which the Via Aemilia crossed the river Parma, from which it probably takes its name, is still preserved, but has been much altered. A bishop of Parma is mentioned in the acts of the council of Rome of A.D. 378. It fell into the power of Alboin in 569 and became the seat of a Lombard duchy; it was still one of the wealthiest cities of Aemilia in the Lombard period. During the 11th, 12th and 13th centuries Parma had its full share of the Guelph and Ghibelline struggles, in which it mainly took the part of the former, and also carried on repeated hostilities with Borgo San Donnino and Piacenza. Its bishop Cadalus (1046-1071) was elected to the papacy by the Lombard and German bishops in 1061, and marched on Rome, but was driven back by the partisans of Alexander III. To him is due the building of the cathedral. As a republic its government was mainly in the hands of the Rossi, Pallavicino, Correggio and Sanvitale families. The fruitless siege of Parma in 1248 was the last effort of Frederick II. In the cathedral flags captured in this siege are preserved. In 1307 the city became a lordship under Giberto da Correggio, who laid the basis of its territorial power by conquering Reggio, Brescello and Guastalla, and was made commander-in-chief of the Guelphs by Robert of Apulia. The Correggio family never managed to keep possession of it for long, and in 1346 they sold it to the Visconti (who constructed a citadel, La Rocchetta, in 1356, of which some remains exist on the east bank of the river, while the later * this du pont* may be seen on the west bank), and from them it passed to the Sforza. Becoming subject to Pope Julius II. in 1512, Parma remained (in spite of the French occupation from 1515 to 1521) a papal possession till 1545, when Paul III. (Alexander Farnese) invested his son Pierluigi with the duchies of Parma and Piacenza. There were eight dukes of Parma of the Farnese line—Pierluigi (d. 1547), Ottavio (1586), Alessandro (1592), Ranuccio I. (1622), Odoardo (1646), Ranuccio II. (1694), Francesco (1727), Antonio (1731). Antonio and Francesco both having died childless, the duchy passed to Charles of Bourbon (Don Carlos), infante of Spain, who, becoming king of Naples in 1734, surrendered Parma and Piacenza to Austria, but retained the artistic treasures of the Farnese dynasty which he had removed from Parma to Naples. Spain reconquered the duchies in the war of succession (1745); they were recovered by Austria in 1746; and Maria Theresa again surrendered them to Don Philip, infante of Spain, in 1748. Ferdinand, Philip's son, who succeeded under Dutillot's regency in 1765, saw his states occupied by the revolutionary forces of France in 1796, and had to purchase his life-interest with 6,000,000 lire and 25 of the best paintings in Parma. On his death in 1802 the duchies were incorporated with the French republic and his son Louis became "king of Etruria." Parma was thus governed for several years by Moreau de Saint-Méry and by Junot. At the congress of Vienna, Parma, Piacenza and Guastalla were assigned to Marie Louise (daughter of Francis I. of Austria and Napoleon's second consort), and on her death they passed in 1847 to Charles II. (son of Louis of Etruria and Marie Louise, daughter of Charles IV., king of Spain). The new duke, unwilling to yield to the wishes of his people for greater political liberty, was soon compelled to take flight, and the duchy was for a time ruled by a provisional government and by Charles Albert of Sardinia; but in April 1849 Baron d'Aspre with 15,000 Austrians took possession of Parma, and the ducal government was restored under Austrian protection. Charles II. (who had in 1820 married Theresa, daughter of Victor Emmanuel of Sardinia) abdicated in favour of his son Charles III., on the 14th of March, 1849. On the assassination of Charles III. in 1854, his widow, Marie Louise (daughter of Ferdinand, prince of Artois and duke of Berry), became regent for her son Robert. In 1860 his possessions were formally incorporated with the new kingdom of Italy.

The duchy of Parma in 1849 had an area of 2376 sq. m. divided into five provinces—Borgo San Donnino, Valditaro, Parma, Lunigiana Parmense and Piacenza. Its population in 1851 was 497,343. Under Marie Louise (1815-1847) the territory of Guastalla (50 sq. m.) formed part of the duchy, but it was transferred in 1847 to Modena in exchange for the communes of Bagnone, Filattiera, &c., which went to constitute the Lunigiana Parmense.

See Affò, *Storia di Parma* (1792-1795); Scarabelli, *Storia dei ducati di Parma, Piacenza, e Guastalla* (1858); Buttafuoco, *Dizion. corogr. dei ducati,* &c. (1853); *Mon. hist. ad provincias parmensem at placentinam pertinentia* (1855, &c.); L. Testi, *Parma* (Bergamo, 1905).

PARMENIDES OF ELEA (Velia) in Italy, Greek philosopher. According to Diogenes Laertius he was " in his prime " 504-500 B.C., and would thus seem to have been born about 539. Plato indeed (*Parmenides,* 127 B) makes Socrates see and hear Parmenides when the latter was about sixty-five years of age, in which case he cannot have been born before 519; but in the absence of evidence that any such meeting took place this may be regarded as one of Plato's anachronisms. However this may be, Parmenides was a contemporary, probably a younger contemporary, of Heraclitus, with whom the first succession of physicists ended, while Empedocles and Anaxagoras, with whom the second succession of physicists began, were very much his juniors. Belonging, it is said, to a rich and distinguished family, Parmenides attached himself, at any rate for a time, to the aristocratic society or brotherhood which Pythagoras had established at Croton; and accordingly one part of his system, the physical part, is apparently Pythagorean. To Xenophanes, the founder of Eleaticism—whom he must have known, even if he was never in any strict sense of the word his disciple—Parmenides was, perhaps, more deeply indebted, as the theological speculations of that thinker unquestionably suggested to him the theory of Being and Not-Being, of the One and the Many, by which he sought to reconcile Ionian " monism," or rather " henism," with Italiote dualism. Tradition relates that Parmenides framed laws for the Eleates, who each year took an oath to observe them.

Parmenides embodied his tenets in a short poem, called *Nature,* of which fragments, amounting in all to about 160 lines, have been preserved in the writings of Sextus Empiricus, Simplicius and others. It is traditionally divided into three parts—the " Proem," " Truth " (τὰ πρὸς ἀλήθειαν), and " Opinion " (τὰ πρὸς δόξαν). In " Truth," starting from the formula " the Ent (or existent) is, the Nonent(or non-existent) is not," Parmenides attempted to distinguish between the unity or universal element of nature and its variety or particularity, insisting upon the reality of its unity, which is therefore the object of knowledge, and upon the unreality of its variety, which is therefore the object, not of knowledge, but of opinion. In " Opinion " he propounded a theory of the world of seeming and its development, pointing out however that, in accordance with the principles already laid down, these cosmological speculations do not pretend to anything more than probability. In spite of the contemptuous remarks of Cicero and Plutarch about Parmenides's versification, *Nature* is not without literary merit. The introduction, though rugged, is forcible and picturesque; and the rest of the poem is written in a simple and effective style suitable to the subject.

Proem.—In the " Proem " the poet describes his journey from darkness to light. Borne in a whirling chariot, and attended by the daughters of the sun, he reaches a temple sacred to an unnamed goddess (variously identified by the commentators with Nature, Wisdom or Themis), by whom the rest of the poem is spoken. He must learn all things, she tells him, both truth, which is certain, and human opinions; for, though in human opinions there can be no " true faith," they must be studied notwithstanding for what they are worth.

Truth.—" Truth " begins with the declaration of Parmenides's principle in opposition to the principles of his predecessors. There are three ways of research, and three ways only. Of these, one asserts the non-existence of the existent and the existence of the non-existent [*i.e.* Thales, Anaximander and Anaximenes suppose the single element which they respectively postulate to be transformed into the various sorts of matter which they discover in the world around them, thus assuming the non-existence of that which is elemental and the existence of that which is non-elemental]; another, pursued by " restless " persons, whose " road returns upon itself," assumes that 'a thing " is and is not," " is the same and not the same " [an obvious reference, as Bernays points out in the *Rheinisches Museum,* vii. 114 seq., to Heraclitus, the philosopher of flux]. These are ways of error, because they confound existence and non-existence. In contrast to them the way of truth starts from the proposition that " the Ent is, the Nonent is not."

On the strength of the fundamental distinction between the Ent and the Nonent, the goddess next announces certain characteristics of the former. The Ent is uncreated, for it cannot be derived either from the Ent or from the Nonent; it is imperishable, for it cannot pass into the Nonent; it is whole, indivisible, continuous, for nothing exists to break its continuity in space; it is unchangeable [for nothing exists to break its continuity in time]; it is perfect, for there is nothing which it can want; it never was, nor will be, but only is; it is evenly extended in every direction, and therefore a sphere, exactly balanced; it is identical with thought [*i.e.* it is the object, and the sole object, of thought as opposed to sensation; sensation being concerned with variety and change].

As then the Ent is one, invariable and immutable, all plurality, variety and mutation belong to the Nonent. Whence it follows that all things to which men attribute reality, generation and destruction, being and not-being, change of place, alteration of colour are no more than empty words.

Opinion.—The investigation of the Ent [*i.e.* the existent unity, extended throughout space and enduring throughout time, which reason discovers beneath the variety and the mutability of things] being now complete, it remains in " Opinion " to describe the plurality of things, not as they are, for they are not, but as they seem to be. In the phenomenal world then, there are, it has been thought and Parmenides accepts the theory, which appears to be of Pythagorean origin], two primary elements—namely, fire, which is gentle, thin, homogeneous, and night, which is dark, thick, heavy. Of these elements [which, according to Aristotle, were, or rather were analogous to, the Ent and the Nonent respectively] all things consist, and from them they derive their several characteristics. The foundation for a cosmology having thus been laid in dualism, the poem went on to describe the generation of " earth and sun, and moon and air that is common to all, and th° milky way, and furthest Olympus, and the glowing stars "; but the scanty fragments which have survived suffice only to show that Parmenides regarded the universe as a series of concentric rings or spheres composed of the two primary elements and of combinations of them, the whole system being directed by an unnamed goddess established at its centre. Next came a theory of animal development. This again was followed by a psychology, which made thought [as well as sensation, which was conceived to differ from thought only in respect of its object] depend upon the excess of the one or the other of the two constituent elements, fire and night. " Such, opinion tells us, was the generation, such is the present existence, such will be the end, of those things to which men have given distinguishing names."

In the truism " the Ent is, the Nonent is not," ὃν ἔστι, μὴ ὃν οὐκ ἔστι, Parmenides breaks with his predecessors, the physicists of the Ionian succession. Asking themselves—What is the material universe, they had replied respectively—It is water, It is μετα ξύ τι, It is air, It is fire. Thus, while their question meant, or ought to have meant, What is the single element which underlies the apparent plurality of the material world? their answers, Parmenides conceived, by attributing to the selected element various and varying qualities, reintroduced the plurality which the question sought to eliminate. If we would discover that which is common to all things at all times, we must, he submitted, exclude the differences of things, whether simultaneous or successive. Hence, whereas his predecessors had confounded that which is universally existent with that which is not universally existent, he proposed to distinguish carefully between that which is universally existent and that which is not universally existent, between ὄν and μὴ ὄν. The fundamental truism is the epigrammatic assertion of this distinction.

In short, the single corporeal element of the Ionian physicists was, to borrow a phrase from Aristotle, a permanent οὐσία having πάθη which change; but they either neglected the πάθη or confounded them with the οὐσία. Parmenides sought to reduce the variety of nature to a single material element; but he strictly discriminated the inconstant πάθη from the constant οὐσία, and, understanding by "existence" universal, invariable, immutable being, refused to attribute to the πάθη anything more than the semblance of existence.

Having thus discriminated between the permanent unity of nature and its superficial plurality, Parmenides proceeded to the separate investigation of the Ent and the Nonent. The universality of the Ent, he conceived, necessarily carries with it certain characteristics. It is one; it is eternal; it is whole and continuous, both in time and in space; it is immovable and immutable; it is limited, but limited only by itself; it is evenly extended in every direction, and therefore spherical. These propositions having been reached, apart from particular experience, by reflection upon the fundamental principle, we have in them, Parmenides conceived, a body of information resting upon a firm basis and entitled to be called "truth." Further, the information thus obtained is the sum total of "truth"; for, as "existence" in the strict sense of the word cannot be attributed to anything besides the universal element, so nothing besides the universal element can properly be said to be "known."

If Parmenides's poem had had "Being" for its subject it would doubtless have ended at this point. Its subject is, however, "Nature"; and nature, besides its unity, has also the semblance, if no more than the semblance, of plurality. Hence the theory of the unity of nature is necessarily followed by a theory of its seeming plurality, that is to say, of the variety and mutation of things. The theory of plurality cannot indeed pretend to the certainty of the theory of unity, being of necessity untrustworthy, because it is the partial and inconstant representation of that which is partial and inconstant in nature. But, as the material world includes, together with a real unity, the semblance of plurality, so the theory of the material world includes, together with the certain theory of the former, a probable theory of the latter. "Opinion" is then no mere excrescence; it is the necessary sequel to "Truth."

Thus, whereas the Ionians, confounding the unity and the plurality of the universe, had neglected plurality, and the Pythagoreans, contenting themselves with the reduction of the variety of nature to a duality or a series of dualities, had neglected unity, Parmenides, taking a hint from Xenophanes, made the antagonistic doctrines supply one another's deficiencies; for, as Xenophanes in his theological system had recognized at once the unity of God and the plurality of things, so Parmenides in his system of nature recognized at once the rational unity of the Ent and the phenomenal plurality of the Nonent:

The foregoing statement of Parmenides's position differs from Zeller's account of it in two important particulars. First, whereas it has been assumed above that Xenophanes was theologian rather than philosopher, whence it would seem to follow that the philosophical doctrine of unity originated, not with him, but with Parmenides, Zeller, supposing Xenophanes to have taught, not merely the unity of God, but also the unity of Being, assigns to Parmenides no more than an exacter conception of the doctrine of the unity of Being, the justification of that doctrine, and the denial of the plurality and the mutability of things. This view of the relations of Xenophanes and Parmenides is not borne out by their writings; and, though ancient authorities may be quoted in its favour, it would seem that in this case as in others, they have fallen into the easy mistake of confounding successive phases of doctrine, "construing the utterances of the master in accordance with the principles of his scholar—the vague by the more definite, the simpler by the more finished and elaborate theory" (W. H. Thompson). Secondly, whereas it has been argued above that "Opinion" is necessarily included in the system, Zeller, supposing Parmenides

to deny the Nonent even as a matter of opinion, regards that part of the poem which has opinion for its subject as no more than a revised and improved statement of the views of opponents, introduced in order that the reader, having before him the false doctrine as well as the true one, may be led the more certainly to embrace the latter. In the judgment of the present writer, Parmenides, while he denied the real existence of plurality, recognized its apparent existence, and consequently, however little value he might attach to opinion, was bound to take account of it : "pour celui même qui nie l'existence réelle de la nature," says Renouvier, "il reste encore à faire une histoire naturelle de l'apparence et de l'illusion."

The teaching of Parmenides variously influenced both his immediate successors and subsequent thinkers. By his recognition of an apparent plurality supplementary to the real unity, he effected the transition from the "monism" or "henism" of the first physical succession to the "pluralism" of the second. While Empedocles and Democritus are careful to emphasise their dissent from "Truth," it is obvious that "Opinion" is the basis of their cosmologies. The doctrine of the deceitfulness of "the undiscerning eye and the echoing ear" soon established itself, though the grounds upon which Empedocles, Anaxagoras and Democritus maintained it were not those which were alleged by Parmenides. Indirectly, through the dialectic of his pupil and friend Zeno and otherwise, the doctrine of the inadequacy of sensation led to the humanist movement, which for a time threatened to put an end to philosophical and scientific speculation. But the positive influence of Parmenides's teaching was not yet exhausted. To say that the Platonism of Plato's later years, the Platonism of the Parmenides, the Philebus and the Timaeus, is the philosophy of Parmenides enlarged and reconstituted, may perhaps seem paradoxical in the face of the severe criticism to which Eleaticism is subjected, not only in the Parmenides, but also in the Sophist. The criticism was, however, preparatory to a reconstruction. Thus may be explained the selection of an Eleatic stranger to be the chief speaker in the latter, and of Parmenides himself to take the lead in the former. In the Sophist criticism predominates over reconstruction, the Zenonian logic being turned against the Parmenides metaphysic in such a way as to show that both the one and the other need revision: see 241 D, 244 B seq., 257 B seq., 258 D. In particular, Plato taxes Parmenides with his inconsistency in attributing (as he certainly did) to the fundamental unity extension and sphericity, so that "the worshipped ὄν is after all a pitiful μὴ ὄν" (W. H. Thompson). In the Parmenides reconstruction predominates over criticism—the letter of Eleaticism being here represented by Zeno, its spirit, as Plato conceived it, by Parmenides. Not the least important of the results obtained in this dialogue is the discovery that, whereas the doctrine of the "one" and the "many" is suicidal and barren so long as the "solitary one" and the "indefinitely many" are absolutely separated (137 C seq. and 163 B seq.), it becomes consistent and fruitful as soon as a "definite plurality" is interpolated between them (142 B seq., 157 B seq., 160 B seq.). In short, Parmenides was no idealist, but Plato recognized in him, and rightly, the precursor of idealism.

BIBLIOGRAPHY.—The fragments have been skilfully edited by H. Diels, in Parmenides Lehrgedicht, griechisch u. deutsch (Berlin, 1897), with commentary; in Poetarum philosophorum fragmenta with brief Latin notes, critical and interpretative (Berlin, 1901); and in Die Fragmente d. Vorsokratiker (Berlin, 2nd ed., 1906), with German translation); and Diels' text is reproduced with a helpful Latin commentary in Ritter and Preller's Historia philosophiae graecae (8th ed., revised by E. Wellmann, Gotha, 1898). The philosophical system is expounded and discussed by E. Zeller, D. Philosophie d. Griechen (5th ed., Leipzig, 1892; Eng. trans., London, 1881); by T. Gomperz, Griechische Denker (Leipzig, 1896; Eng. trans., London, 1901); and by J. Burnet, Early Greek Philosophy (London, 1908). For the cosmology, see A. B. Krische, D. theologischen Lehren d. griechischen Denker (Göttingen, 1840). On the relations of Eleaticism and Platonism, see W. H. Thompson, "On Plato's Sophist," in the Journal of Philology viii. 303 seq. For other texts, translations, commentaries and monographs see the excellent bibliography contained in the Grundriss d. Geschichte d. Philosophie of Überweg and Heinze (10th ed., Berlin, 1909; Eng. Trans., London, 1880). (H JA.)

PARMENIO (c. 400–330 B.C.), Macedonian general in the service of Philip II. and Alexander the Great. During the reign of Philip Parmenio obtained a great victory over the Illyrians (356); he was one of the Macedonian delegates appointed to conclude peace with Athens (346), and was sent with an army to uphold Macedonian influence in Euboea (342). In 336 he was sent with Amyntas and Attalus to make preparations for the reduction of Asia. He led the left wing in the battles of the Granicus, Issus and Gaugamela. After the conquest of Drangiana, Alexander was informed that Philotas, son of Parmenio, was involved in a conspiracy against his life. Philotas was condemned by the army and put to death. Alexander, thinking it dangerous to allow the father to live, sent orders to Media for the assassination of Parmenio. There was no proof that Parmenio was in any way implicated in the conspiracy, but he was not even afforded the opportunity of defending himself.

See Arrian, *Anabasis*; Plutarch, *Alexander*; Diod. Sic. xvii.; Curtius vii. 2, 11; Justin xii. 5; for modern authorities see under ALEXANDER III., THE GREAT.

PARMIGIANO (1504–1540). The name of this celebrated painter of the Lombard school was, in full, Girolamo Francesco Maria Mazzuoli, or Mazzola; he dropped the name Girolamo, and was only known as Francesco. He has been more commonly named Il Parmigiano (or its diminutive, Il Parmigianino), from his native city, Parma. Francesco, born on the 11th of January 1504, was the son of a painter. Losing his father in early childhood, he was brought up by two uncles, also painters, Michele and Pier-Ilario Mazzola. His faculty for the art developed at a very boyish age, and he addicted himself to the style of Correggio, who visited Parma in 1519. He did not, however, become an imitator of Correggio; his style in its maturity may be regarded as a fusion of Correggio with Raphael and Giulio Romano, and thus fairly original. Even at the age of fourteen (Vasari says sixteen) he had painted a "Baptism of Christ," surprisingly mature. Before the age of nineteen, when he migrated to Rome, he had covered with frescoes seven chapels in the church of S. Giovanni Evangelista, Parma. Prior to starting for the city of the popes in 1523 he deemed it expedient to execute some specimen pictures. One of these was a portrait of himself as seen in a convex mirror, with all the details of divergent perspective, &c., wonderfully exact—a work which both from this curiosity of treatment and from the beauty of the sitter—for Parmigiano was then "more like an angel than a man" —could not fail to attract. Arrived in Rome, he presented his specimen pictures to the pope, Clement VII., who gladly and admiringly accepted them, and assigned to the youthful genius the painting of the Sala de' Pontefici, the ceilings of which had been already decorated by Giovanni da Udine. But while fortune was winning him with her most insinuating smiles, the utter ruin of the sack by the Constable de Bourbon and his German and other soldiers overtook both Rome and Parmigiano. At the date of this hideous catastrophe he was engaged in painting that large picture which now figures in the National Gallery, the "Vision of St Jerome" (with the Baptist pointing upward and backward to the Madonna and infant Jesus in the sky). It is said that through all the crash and peril of this barbarian irruption Parmigiano sat quietly before his vast panel, painting as if nothing had happened. A band of German soldiery burst into his apartment, breathing fire and slaughter; but, struck with amazement at the sight, and with some reverence for art and her votary (the other events of the siege forbid us to suppose that reverence for religion had any part in it), they calmed down, and afforded the painter all the protection that he needed at the moment. Their captain, being something of a connoisseur, exacted his tribute, however—a large number of designs. Rome was now no place for Parmigiano. He left with his uncle, intending apparently to return to Parma; but, staying in Bologna he settled down there for a while, and was induced to remain three or four years. Here he painted for the nuns of St Margaret his most celebrated altarpiece (now in the Academy of Bologna), the "Madonna and Child, with Margaret and other saints."

X.X 15

Spite of the great disaster of Rome, the life of Mazzola had hitherto been fairly prosperous—the admiration which he excited being proportionate to his charm of person and manner, and to the precocity and brilliancy (rather than depth) of his genius; but from this time forward he became an unfortunate, and it would appear a soured and self-neglected, man. In 1531 he returned to Parma, and was commissioned to execute an extensive series of frescoes in the choir of the church of S. Maria della Steccata. These were to be completed in November 1532; and half-payment, 200 golden scudi, was made to him in advance. A ceiling was allotted to him, and an arch in front of the ceiling; on the arch he painted six figures—two of them in full colour, and four in monochrome—Adam, Eve, some Virtues, and the famous figure (monochrome) of Moses about to shatter the tables of the law. But, after five or six years from the date of the contract, Parmigiano had barely made a good beginning with his stipulated work. According to Vasari, he neglected painting in favour of alchemy—he laboured over futile attempts to "congeal mercury," being in a hurry to get rich anyhow. It is rather difficult to believe that the various graphic and caustic phrases which Vasari bestows upon this theory of the facts of Mazzola's life are altogether gratuitous and wide of the mark; nevertheless the painter's principal biographer, the Padre Affò, undertook to refute Vasari's statements, and most subsequent writers have accepted Affò's conclusions. Whatever the cause, Parmigiano failed to fulfil his contract, and was imprisoned in default. Promising to amend, he was released; but instead of redeeming his pledge he decamped to Casal Maggiore, in the territory of Cremona. Here, according even to Vasari, he relinquished alchemy and resumed painting; yet he still hankered (or is said by Vasari to have hankered) after his retorts and furnaces, lost all his brightness, and presented a dim, poverty-stricken, hirsute and uncivilized aspect. He died of a fever on the 24th of August 1540, before he had completed his thirty-seventh year. By his own desire he was buried naked in the church of the Servites called La Fontana, near Casal Maggiore.

Grace has always and rightly been regarded as the chief artistic endowment of Parmigiano—grace which is graceful as an expression of the painter's nature, but partakes partly of the artificial and affected in its developments. "Un po' di grazia del Parmigianino" (a little, or, as we might say, just a spice, of Parmigianino's grace) was among the ingredients which Agostino Caracci's famed sonnet desiderates for a perfect picture. Mazzola constantly made many studies of the same figure, in order to get the most graceful attainable form, movement and drapery—the last being a point in which he was very successful. The proportions of his figures are over-long for the truth of nature—the stature, fingers and neck; one of his Madonnas, now in the Pitti Gallery, is currently named "La Madonna del collo lungo." Neither expression nor colour is a strong point in his works; the figures in his compositions are generally few—the chief exception being the picture of "Christ Preaching to the Multitude." He etched a few plates, being apparently the earliest Italian painter who was also an etcher; but the statement that he produced several woodcuts is not correct—he overlooked the production of them by other hands.

The most admired easel-picture of Parmigiano is the "Cupid Making a Bow," with two children at his feet, one crying, and the other laughing. This was painted in 1536 for Francesco Boiardi of Parma, and is now in the gallery of Vienna. There are various replicas of it, and some of these may perhaps be from Mazzola's own hand. Of his portrait-painting, two interesting examples are the likeness of Amerigo Vespucci (after whom America is named) in the Studj Gallery of Naples, and the painter's own portrait in the Uffizi of Florence. One of Parmigiano's principal pupils was his cousin, Girolamo di Michele Mazzola; probably some of the works attributed to Francesco are really by Girolamo.

See B. Bossi, *Disegni originali di Francesco Mazzuoli* (1789); A. S. Mortara, *Della Vita di Francesco Mazzuoli* (1846); Toschi, *Affreschi*, &c. (1846).
(W. M. R.)

2a

PARNAHYBA, or **PARNAHIBA,** a port of the state of Piauhy, Brazil, on the right bank of the Parnahyba river, 230 m. below the c pital, Therezina. Pop. of the municipality (1890), 4415. Parnahyba is situated at the point where the most easterly of the delta outlets, or channels, called the Rio Iguarassú, branches off from the main stream. All the outlet channels of the river are obstructed by bars built up by the strong current along the Atlantic coast, and only vessels of light draught can enter. The town has some well-constructed buildings of the old Portuguese type, including two churches and a fine hospital. Parnahyba is the commercial entrepôt of the state. It exports hides, goat-skins, cotton and tobacco, chiefly through the small port of Amarração, at the mouth of the Rio Iguarassú, 11 m. distant.

PARNASSUS (mod. *Liakoura or Likeri*), a mountain of Greece, 8070 ft., in the south of Phocis, rising over the town of Delphi. It had several prominent peaks, the chief known as Tithorea and Lycoreia (whence the modern name). Parnassus was one of the most holy mountains in Greece, hallowed by the worship of Apollo, of the Muses, and of the Corycian nymphs, and by the orgies of the Bacchantes. Two projecting cliffs, named the Phaedriadae, frame the gorge in which the Castalian spring flows out, and just to the west of this, on a shelf above the ravine of the Pleistus, is the site of the Pythian shrine of Apollo and the Delphic oracle. The Corycian cave is on the plateau between Delphi and the summit.

PARNASSUS PLAYS, a series of three scholastic entertainments performed at St John's College, Cambridge, between 1597 and 1603. They are satirical in character and aim at setting forth the wretched state of scholars and the small respect paid to learning by the world at large, as exemplified in the adventures of two university men, Philomusus and Studioso. The first part, *The Pilgrimage to Parnassus*, describes allegorically their four year's journey to Parnassus, *i.e.* their progress through the university course of logic, rhetoric, &c., and the temptations set before them by their meeting with Madido, a drunkard, Stupido, a puritan who hates learning, Amoretto, a lover, and Ingenioso, a disappointed student. The play was doubtless originally intended to stand alone, but the favour with which it was received led to the writing of a sequel, *The Return from Parnassus*, which deals with the adventures of the two students after the completion of their studies at the university, and shows them discovering by bitter experience of how little pecuniary value their learning is. They again meet Ingenioso, who is making a scanty living by the press, but is on the search for a patron, as well as a new character, Luxurioso. All four now leave the university for London, while a draper, a tailor and a tapster lament their unpaid bills. Philomusus and Studioso find work respectively as a sexton and a tutor in a merchant's family, while Luxurioso becomes a writer and singer of ballads. In the meanwhile Ingenioso has met with a patron, a coxcombical fellow named Gullio, for whom he composes amorous verses in the style of Chaucer, Spenser and Shakespeare, the last alone being to the patron's satisfaction. Gullio is indeed a great admirer of Shakespeare, and in his conversations with Ingenioso we have some of the most interesting of the early allusions to him.

A further sequel, *The Second Part of the Return from Parnassus, or the Scourge of Simony*, is a more ambitious, and from every point of view more interesting, production than the two earlier pieces. In it we again meet with Ingenioso, now become a satirist, who on pretence of discussing a recently published collection of extracts from contemporary poetry, John Bodenham's *Belvedere*, briefly criticizes, or rather characterizes, a number of writers of the day, among them being Spenser, Constable, Drayton, John Davies, Marston, Marlowe, Jonson, Shakespeare and Nashe—the last of whom is referred to as dead. It is impossible here to detail the plot of the play, and it can only be said that Philomusus and Studioso, having tried all means of earning a living, abandon any further attempt to turn their learning to account and determine to become shepherds. Several

new characters are introduced in this part, real persons such as Danter, the printer, Richard Burbage and William Kemp, the actors, as well as such abstractions as Furor Poeticus and Phantasma. The second title of the piece, " The Scourge of Simony," is justified by a sub-plot dealing with the attempts of one, Academico, to obtain a living from an ignorant country patron, Sir Roderick, who, however, presents it, on the recommendation of his son Amoretto, who has been bribed, to a non-university man Immerito.

The three pieces have but small literary and dramatic value, their importance consisting almost wholly in the allusions to, and criticisms of contemporary literature. Their author is unknown, but it is fairly certain, from the evidence of general style, as well as some peculiarities of language, that they are the work of the same writer. The only name which has been put forward with any reasonable probability is that of John Day, whose claim has been supported with much ingenuity by Professor I. Gollancz (see full discussion in Dr A. W. Ward's *Eng. Dram. Lit.* ii. 640, note 2), but the question still awaits definitive solution.

As to the date there is more evidence. The three pieces were evidently performed at Christmas of different years, the last being not later than Christmas 1602, as is shown by the references to Queen Elizabeth, while the *Pilgrimage* mentions books not printed until 1598, and hence can hardly have been earlier than that year. The prologue of 2 *Return* states that that play had been written for the preceding year, and also, in a passage of which the reading is somewhat doubtful, implies that the whole series had extended over four years. Thus we arrive at either 1599, 1600 and 1602, or 1598, 1599 and 1601, as, on the whole, the most likely dates of performance. Mr Fleay, on grounds which do not seem conclusive, dates them 1598, 1601 and 1602.

The question of how far the characters are meant to represent actual persons has been much discussed. Mr Fleay maintains that the whole is a personal satire, his identifications of the chief characters in 2 *Return* being (1) Ingenioso, Thomas Nashe, (2) Furor Poeticus, J. Marston, (3) Phantasma, Sir John Davies, (4) Philomusus, T. Lodge, (5) Studioso, Drayton. Professor Gollancz identifies Judicio with Henry Chettle (*Proc. of Brit. Acad.*, 1903–1904, p. 202). Dr Ward, while rejecting Mr Fleay's identifications as a whole, considers that by the time the final part was written the author may have more or less identified Ingenioso with Nashe, though the character was not originally conceived with this intention. This is of course possible, and the fact that Ingenioso himself speaks in praise of Nashe, who is regarded as dead, is not an insuperable objection. We must not, however, overlook the fact that the author was evidently very familiar with Nashe's works, and that all three parts, not only in the speeches of Ingenioso, but throughout, are full of reminiscences of his writings.

BIBLIOGRAPHY.—The only part of the trilogy which was in print at an early date was 2 *Return*, called simply *The Return from Parnassus, or the Scourge of Simony* (1606), two editions bearing the same date. This has been several times reprinted, the best separate edition being that of Professor Arber in the "English Scholars' Library" (1879). Manuscript copies of all three plays were found among T. Hearne's papers in the Bodleian by the Rev. W. D. Macray and were printed by him in 1886 (the last from one of the editions of 1606, collated with the MS.). A recent edition in modern spelling by Mr O. Smeaton in the "Temple Dramatists" is of little value. All questions connected with the play have been elaborately discussed by Dr W. Lühr in a dissertation entitled *Die drei cambridger Spiele vom Parnass* (Kiel, 1900). See also, Dr Ward's *English Dramatic Literature*, ii. 633–643; F. G. Fleay's *Biog. Chron. of the Eng. Drama*, ii. 347–355.   (R. B. McK.)

PARNELL, CHARLES STEWART (1846–1891), Irish Nationalist leader, was born at Avondale, Co. Wicklow, on the 27th of June 1846. His father was John Henry Parnell, a country gentleman of strong Nationalist and Liberal sympathies, who married in 1834 Delia Tudor, daughter of Commodore Charles Stewart of the United States navy. The Parnell family was of English origin, and more than one of its members attained civic note at Congleton in Cheshire under the Stuarts and during the

Commonwealth. Among them was Thomas Parnell, who migrated to Ireland after the Restoration. He had two sons, Thomas Parnell the poet and John Parnell, who became an Irish judge. From the latter Charles Stewart Parnell was lineally descended in the fifth generation. Sir John Parnell, chancellor of the exchequer in Grattan's parliament, and one of O'Connell's lieutenants in the parliament of the United Kingdom, was the grandson of Parnell the judge. The estate of Avondale was settled on him by a friend and bequeathed by him to his youngest son William (grandfather of Charles Stewart Parnell). His eldest son was imbecile. His second son was Sir Henry Parnell, a noted politician and financier in the early part of the 19th century, who held office under Grey and Melbourne, and after being raised to the peerage as Baron Congleton, died by his own hand in 1842. William Parnell was a keen student of Irish politics, with a strong leaning towards the popular side, and in 1805 he published a pamphlet entitled "Thoughts on the Causes of Popular Discontents," which was favourably noticed by Sydney Smith in the *Edinburgh Review*. Thus by birth and ancestry, and especially by the influence of his mother, who inherited a hatred of England from her father, Charles Stewart Parnell was, as it were, dedicated to the Irish national cause. He was of English extraction, a landowner, and a Protestant. Educated at private schools in England and at Magdalen College, Cambridge, his temperament and demeanour were singularly un-Irish on the surface—reserved, cold, repellent and unemotional. He appears to have been rather turbulent as a school-boy, contentious, insubordinate, and not over-scrupulous. He was fond of cricket and devoted to mathematics, but had little taste for other studies or other games. He was subject to somnambulism, and liable to severe fits of depression—facts which, taken in connexion with the existence of mental affliction among his ancestors, with his love of solitude and mystery, and his invincible superstitions about omens, numbers and the like, may perhaps suggest that his own mental equilibrium was not always stable. He was as little at home in an English school or an English university as he was afterwards in the House of Commons. "These English," he said to his brother at school, "despise us because we are Irish; but we must stand up to them. That's the way to treat an Englishman—stand up to him."

Parnell was not an active politician in his early years. He found salvation as a Nationalist and even as a potential rebel over the execution of the "Manchester Martyrs" in 1867, but it was not until some years afterwards that he resolved to enter parliament. In the meanwhile he paid a lengthened visit to the United States. At the general election of 1874 he desired to stand for the county of Wicklow, of which he was high sheriff at the time. The lord-lieutenant declined to relieve him of his disqualifying office, and his brother John stood in his place, but was unsuccessful at the poll. Shortly afterwards a bye-election occurred in Dublin, owing to Colonel Taylor having accepted office in the Disraeli government, and Parnell resolved to oppose him as a supporter of Isaac Butt, but was heavily beaten. He was, however, elected for Meath in the spring of 1875.

Butt had scrupulously respected the dignity of parliament and the traditions and courtesy of debate. He looked very coldly on the method of "obstruction"—a method invented by certain members of the Conservative party in opposition to the first Gladstone Administration. Parnell, however, entered parliament as a virtual rebel who knew that physical force was of no avail, but believed that political exasperation might attain the desired results. He resolved to make obstruction in parliament do the work of outrage in the country, to set the church-bell ringing—to borrow Mr Gladstone's metaphor—and to keep it ringing in season and out of season in the ears of the House of Commons. He did not choose to condemn outrages to gratify the Pharisaism of English members of parliament. He courted the alliance of the physical force party, and he had to pay the price for it. He invented and encouraged "boycotting," and did not discourage outrage. When a supporter in America offered him twenty-five dollars, "five for bread and twenty for lead," he accepted the gift, and he subsequently told the story on at least one Irish platform. In the course of the negotiations in 1882, which resulted in what was known as the Kilmainham Treaty, he wrote to Captain O'Shea: "If the arrears question be settled upon the lines indicated by us, I have every confidence that the exertions we should be able to make strenuously and unremittingly would be effective in stopping outrages and intimidation of all kinds." This is at least an admission that he had, or could place, his hand on the stop-valve, even if it be not open to the gloss placed on it by Captain O'Shea in a conversation repeated in the House of Commons by Mr Forster, "that the conspiracy which has been used to get up boycotting and outrage will now be used to put them down."

In 1877 Parnell entered on an organized course of obstruction. He and Mr Joseph Gillis Biggar, one of his henchmen, were gradually joined by a small band of the more advanced Home Rulers, and occasionally assisted up to a certain point by one or two English members. Butt was practically deposed and worried into his grave. William Shaw, a "transient and embarrassed phantom," was elected in his place, but Parnell became the real leader of a Nationalist party. The original Home Rule party was split in twain, and after the general election of 1880 the more moderate section of it ceased to exist. Obstruction in Parnell's hands was no mere weapon of delay and exasperation; it was a calculated policy, the initial stage of a campaign designed to show the malcontents in Ireland and their kinsmen in other lands that Butt's strictly constitutional methods were quite helpless, but that the parliamentary armoury still contained weapons which he could so handle as to convince the Irish people and even the Fenian and other physical force societies that the way to Irish legislative independence lay through the House of Commons. The Fenians were hard to convince, but in the autumn of 1877 Parnell persuaded the Home Rule Confederation of Great Britain (an association founded by Butt, but largely supported by Fenians) to depose Butt from its presidency and to elect himself in his place. He defined his attitude quite clearly in a speech delivered in New York early in 1880: "A true revolutionary movement in Ireland should, in my opinion, partake both of a constitutional and illegal character. It should be both an open and a secret organization, using the constitution for its own purposes, but also taking advantage of its secret combination." Parnell's opportunity came with the general election of 1880, which displaced the Conservative government of Lord Beaconsfield and restored Mr Gladstone to power with a majority strong enough at the outset to overpower the Opposition, even should the latter be reinforced by the whole of Parnell's contingent. Distress was acute in Ireland, and famine was imminent. Ministers had taken measures to relieve the situation before the dissolution was announced, but Lord Beaconsfield had warned the country that there was a danger ahead in Ireland "in its ultimate results scarcely less disastrous than pestilence and famine. . . . A portion of its population is attempting to sever the constitutional tie which unites it to Great Britain in that bond which has favoured the power and prosperity of both. It is to be hoped that all men of light and leading will resist this destructive doctrine." The Liberal party and its leaders retorted that they were as strongly opposed to Home Rule as their opponents, but Lord Beaconsfield's manifesto undoubtedly had the effect of alienating the Irish vote in the English constituencies from the Tory party and throwing it on the side of the Liberal candidates. This was Parnell's deliberate policy. He would have no alliance with either English party. He would support each in turn with a sole regard to the balance of political power in parliament and a fixed determination to hold it in his own hands if he could. From the time that he became its leader the Home Rule party sat together in the House of Commons and always on the Opposition side.

In the government formed by Mr Gladstone in 1880 Lord Cowper became viceroy and Mr W. E. Forster chief secretary for Ireland. The outlook was gloomy enough, but the Gladstone government do not seem to have anticipated, as Peel anticipated in 1841, that Ireland would be their difficulty. Yet the Land League had been formed by Michael Davitt and others in the autumn of 1879 for the purpose of agrarian agitation, and Parnell after some hesitation had given it his sanction. He visited the United States at the close of 1879. It was then and there that the "new departure"—the alliance of the open and the secret organizations—was confirmed and consolidated. Parnell obtained the countenance and support of the Clan-na-Gael, a revolutionary organization of the American-Irish, and the Land League began to absorb all the more violent spirits in Ireland, though the Fenian brotherhood still held officially aloof from it. As soon as the general election was announced Parnell returned to Ireland in order to direct the campaign in person. Though he had supported the Liberals at the election, he soon found himself in conflict with a government which could neither tolerate disturbance nor countenance a Nationalist agitation, and he entered on the struggle with forces organised, with money in his chest, and with a definite but still undeveloped plan of action. The prevailing distress increased and outrages began to multiply. A fresh Relief Bill was introduced by the government, and in order to stave off a measure to prevent evictions introduced by the Irish party, Mr Forster consented to add a clause to the Relief Bill for giving compensation in certain circumstances to tenants evicted for non-payment of rent. This clause was afterwards embodied in a separate measure known as the Compensation for Disturbance Bill, which after a stormy career in the House of Commons was summarily rejected by the House of Lords.

The whole Irish question was once more opened up in its more dangerous and more exasperating form. It became clear that the land question—supposed to have been settled by Mr Gladstone's Act of 1870—would have to be reconsidered in all its bearings, and a commission was appointed for the purpose. In Ireland things went from bad to worse. Evictions increased and outrages were multiplied. As the winter wore on, Mr Forster persuaded his colleagues that exceptional measures were needed. An abortive prosecution of Parnell and some of his leading colleagues had by this time intensified the situation. Parliament was summoned early, and a Coercion Bill for one year, practically suspending the Habeas Corpus Act and allowing the arrest of suspects at the discretion of the government, was introduced, to be followed shortly by an Arms Bill. Parnell regarded the measure as a declaration of war, and met it in that spirit. Its discussion was doggedly obstructed at every stage, and on one occasion the debate was only brought to a close, after lasting for forty-one hours, by the Speaker's claiming to interpret the general sense of the house and resolving to put the question without further discussion. The rules of procedure were then amended afresh in a very drastic sense, and as soon as the bill was passed Mr Gladstone introduced a new Land Bill, which occupied the greater part of the session. Parnell accepted it with many reserves. He could not ignore its concessions, and was not disposed to undervalue them, but he had to make it clear to the revolutionary party, whose support was indispensable, that he regarded it only as a payment on account, even from the agrarian point of view, and no payment at all from the national point of view. Accordingly the Land League at his instigation determined to "test" the act by advising tenants in general to refrain from taking their cases into court until certain cases selected by the Land League had been decided. The government treated this policy, which was certainly not designed to make the act work freely and beneficially, as a deliberate attempt to intercept its benefits and to keep the Irish people in subjection to the Land League; and on this and other grounds—notably their attitude of the League and its leaders towards crime and outrage—Parnell was arrested under the Coercion Act and lodged in Kilmainham gaol (October 17, 1881).

Parnell in prison at once became more powerful for evil than he had ever been, either for good or for evil, outside. He may have known that the policy of Mr Forster was little favoured by several of his colleagues, and he probably calculated that the detention of large numbers of suspects without cause assigned and without trial would sooner or later create opposition in England. Mr Forster had assured his colleagues and the House of Commons that the power of arbitrary arrest would enable the police to lay their hands on the chief agents of disturbance, and it was Parnell's policy to show that so long as the grievances of the Irish tenants remained unredressed no number of arrests could either check the tide of outrage or restore the country to tranquillity. Several of his leading colleagues followed him into captivity at Kilmainham, and the Land League was dissolved, its treasurer, Patrick Egan, escaping to Paris and carrying with him its books and accounts. Before it was formally suppressed the League had issued a manifesto, signed by Parnell and several of his fellow-prisoners, calling upon the tenants to pay no rents until the government had restored the constitutional rights of the people. Discouraged by the priests, the No-Rent manifesto had little effect, but it embittered the struggle and exasperated the temper of the people on both sides of the Irish Channel.

Lord Cowper and Mr Forster were compelled to ask for a renewal of the Coercion Act with enlarged powers. But there were members of the cabinet who had only accepted it with reluctance, and were now convinced not only that it had failed, but that it could never succeed. A modus vivendi was desired on both sides. Negotiations were set on foot through the agency of Captain O'Shea—at that time and for long afterwards a firm political and personal friend of Parnell, but ultimately his accuser in the divorce court—and after a somewhat intricate course they resulted in what was known as the Kilmainham Treaty. As a consequence of this informal agreement, Parnell and two of his friends were to be released at once, the understanding being, as Mr Gladstone stated in a letter to Lord Cowper, "that Parnell and his friends are ready to abandon 'No Rent' formally, and to declare against outrage energetically, intimidation included, if and when the government announce a satisfactory plan for dealing with arrears." Parnell's own version of the understanding has been quoted above. It also included a hope that the government would allow the Coercion Act to lapse and govern the country by the same laws as in England. Parnell and his friends were released, and Lord Cowper and Mr Forster at once resigned.

The Phoenix Park murders (May 6, 1882) followed (see IRELAND: History). Parnell was prostrated by this catastrophe. In a public manifesto to the Irish people he declared that "no act has ever been perpetrated in our country, during the exciting struggle for social and political rights of the past fifty years, that has so stained the name of hospitable Ireland as this cowardly and unprovoked assassination of a friendly stranger." Privately to his own friends and to Mr Gladstone he expressed his desire to withdraw from public life. There were those who believed that nevertheless he was privy to the Invincible conspiracy. There is some prima facie foundation for this belief in the indifference he had always displayed towards crime and outrage when crime and outrage could be made to serve his purpose; in his equivocal relation to the more violent and unscrupulous forms of Irish sedition, and in the fact that Byrne, an official of the Land League, was in collusion with the Invincibles, that the knives with which the murder was done had been concealed at the offices of the Land League in London, and had been conveyed to Dublin by Byrne's wife. But the maxim is fecit cui prodest disallows these suspicions. Parnell gained nothing by the murders, and seemed for a time to have lost everything. A new Crimes Bill was introduced and made operative for a period of three years. A régime of renewed coercion was maintained by Lord Spencer and Mr (afterwards Sir George) Trevelyan, who had succeeded Lord Frederick Cavendish in the office of chief secretary; Ireland was tortured for three years by the necessary severity of its administration, and England was exasperated by a succession of dynamite outrages organized chiefly in America, which Parnell was powerless to prevent. The Phoenix Park murders did more than any other incident of his time and career to frustrate Parnell's policy and render Home Rule impossible.

For more than two years after the Phoenix Park murders Parnell's influence in parliament, and even in Ireland, was only intermittently and not very energetically exerted. His health was indifferent, his absences from the House of Commons were frequent and mysterious, and he had already formed those relations with Mrs O'Shea which were ultimately to bring him to the divorce court. The Phoenix Park murderers were arrested and brought to justice early in 1883. Mr Forster seized the opportunity to deliver a scathing indictment of Parnell in the House of Commons. In an almost contemptuous reply Parnell repudiated the charges in general terms, disavowed all sympathy with dynamite outrages, their authors and abettors—the only occasion on which he ever did so—declined to plead in detail before an English tribunal, and declared that he sought only the approbation of the Irish people. This last was shortly afterwards manifested in the form of a subscription known as the "Parnell Tribute," which quickly reached the amount of £37,000, and was presented to Parnell, partly for the liquidation of debts he was known to have contracted, but mainly in recognition of his public services. The Irish National League, a successor to the suppressed Land League, was founded in the autumn of 1882 at a meeting over which Parnell presided, but he looked on it at first with little favour, and its action was largely paralysed by the operation of the Crimes Act and the vigorous administration of Lord Spencer.

The Crimes Act, passed in 1882, was to expire in 1885, but the government of Mr Gladstone was in no position to renew it as it stood. In May notice was given for its partial renewal, subject to changes more of form than of substance. The second reading was fixed for the 10th of June. On the 8th of June Parnell, with thirty-nine of his followers, voted with the Opposition against the budget, and defeated the government by a majority of 264 votes to 252. Mr Gladstone forthwith resigned. Lord Salisbury undertook to form a government, and Lord Carnarvon became viceroy. The session was rapidly brought to an end with a view to the dissolution rendered necessary by the Franchise Act passed in 1884—a measure which was certain to increase the number of Parnell's adherents in parliament. It seems probable that Parnell had convinced himself before he resolved to join forces with the Opposition that a Conservative government would not renew the Crimes Act. At any rate, no attempt to renew it was made by the new government. Moreover, Lord Carnarvon, the new viceroy, was known to Parnell and to some others among the Irish leaders to be not unfavourable to some form of Home Rule if due regard were paid to imperial unity and security. He sought and obtained a personal interview with Parnell, explicitly declared that he was speaking for himself alone, heard Parnell's views, expounded his own, and forthwith reported what had taken place to the Prime Minister. In the result the new cabinet refused to move in the direction apparently desired by Lord Carnarvon.

Parnell opened the electoral campaign with a speech in Dublin, in which he pronounced unequivocally in favour of self-government for Ireland, and expressed his confident hope " that it may not be necessary for us in the new parliament to devote our attention to subsidiary measures, and that it may be possible for us to have a programme and a platform with only one plank, and that one plank National Independence." This was startling to English ears. The press denounced Parnell; Lord Hartington (afterwards the duke of Devonshire) protested against so fatal and mischievous a programme; Mr Chamberlain repudiated it with even greater emphasis. Meanwhile Mr Gladstone was slowly convincing himself that the passing of the Franchise Act had made it the duty of English statesmen and English party leaders to give a respectful hearing to the Irish National demand, and to consider how far it could be satisfied subject to the governing principle of " maintaining the supremacy of the crown, the unity of the Empire, and all the authority of parliament necessary for the conservation of the unity." This was the position he took up in the Hawarden manifesto issued in September before the general election of 1885. Speaking later at Newport in October, Lord Salisbury treated the Irish leader with unwonted deference and respect. Parnell, however, took no notice of the Newport speech, and waited for Mr Gladstone to declare himself more fully in Midlothian. But in this he was disappointed.

Mr Gladstone went no farther than he had done at Hawarden, and he implored the electorate to give him a majority independent of the Irish vote. Subsequently Parnell invited him in a public speech to declare his policy and to sketch the constitution he would give to Ireland subject to the limitations he had insisted on. To this Mr Gladstone replied, " through the same confidential channel," that he could not consider the Irish demand before it had been constitutionally formulated, and that, not being in an official position, he could not usurp the functions of a government. The reply to this was the issue of a manifesto to the Irish electors of Great Britain violently denouncing the Liberal party and directing all Irish Nationalists to give their votes to the Tories. In these circumstances the general election was fought, and resulted in the return of 335 Liberals, four of whom were classed as " independent," 249 Conservatives and 86 followers of Parnell.

Mr Gladstone had now ascertained the strength of the Irish demand, but was left absolutely dependent on the votes of those who represented it. Through Mr Arthur Balfour he made informal overtures to Lord Salisbury proffering his own support in case the Prime Minister should be disposed to consider the Irish demand in a " just and liberal spirit "; but he received no encouragement. Towards the close of the year it became known through various channels that he himself was considering the matter and had advanced as far as accepting the principle of an Irish parliament in Dublin for the transaction of Irish affairs. Before the end of January Lord Salisbury's government was defeated on the Address, the Opposition including the full strength of the Irish party. Mr Gladstone once more became prime minister, with Mr John Morley (an old Home Ruler) as chief secretary, and Mr Chamberlain provisionally included in the cabinet. Lord Hartington, Mr Bright and some other Liberal chiefs, however, declined to join him.

Mr Gladstone's return to power at the head of an administration conditionally committed to Home Rule marks the culminating point of Parnell's influence on English politics and English parties. And after the defeat of the Home Rule ministry in 1886, Parnell was naturally associated closely with the Liberal Opposition. At the same time he withdrew himself largely from active interposition in current parliamentary affairs, and relaxed his control over the action and policy of his followers in Ireland. He entered occasionally into London society—where in certain quarters he was now a welcome guest—but in general he lived apart, often concealing his whereabouts and giving no address but the House of Commons, answering no letters, and seldom fulfilling engagements. He seems to have thought that Home Rule being now in the keeping of an English party, it was time to show that he had in him the qualities of a statesman as well as those of a revolutionary and a rebel. His influence on the remedial legislation proposed by the Unionist government for Ireland was considerable, but he seldom missed an opportunity of making it felt. It more than once happened to him to find measures, which had been contemptuously rejected when he had proposed them, ultimately adopted by the government; and it may be that the comparative tranquillity which Ireland enjoyed at the close of the 19th century was due quite as much to legislation inspired and recommended by himself as to the disintegration of his following which ensued upon his appearance in the divorce court and long survived his death. No sooner was Lord Salisbury's new government installed in office in 1886, than Parnell introduced a comprehensive Tenants' Relief Bill. The government would have none of it, though in the following session they adopted and carried many of its leading provisions. Its rejection was followed by renewed agitation in Ireland, in which Parnell took no part. He was ill—" dangerously ill," he said himself at the time—and some of his more hot-headed followers devised the famous " Plan of Campaign," on which he was never consulted and which never had his approval. Ireland was once more thrown into a turmoil of agitation, turbulence and crime, and the Unionist government, which had hoped to be able to govern the country by means of the ordinary law, was compelled to resort to severe repressive measures and fresh coercive legislation. Mr Balfour became chief secretary, and early in the session of 1887 the new measure was introduced and carried. Parnell took no very prominent part in resisting it. In the course of the spring *The Times* had begun publishing a series of articles entitled "Parnellism and Crime," on lines following Mr Forster's indictment of Parnell in 1883, though with much greater detail of circumstance and accusation. Some of the charges were undoubtedly well founded, some were exaggerated, some were merely the colourable fictions of political prepossession, pronounced to be not proven by the special commission which ultimately inquired into them. One of the articles, which appeared on the 18th of April, was accompanied by the facsimile of a letter purporting to be signed but not written by Parnell, in which he apologized for his attitude on the Phoenix Park murders, and specially excused the murder of Mr Burke. On the same evening, in the House of Commons, Parnell declared the letter to be a forgery, and denied that he had ever written any letter to that effect. He was not believed, and the second reading of the Crimes Act followed. Later in the session the attention of the house was again called to the subject, and it was invited by Sir Charles Lewis, an Ulster member and a bitter antagonist of the Nationalists, to declare the charges of *The Times* a breach of privilege. The government met this proposal by an offer to pay the expenses of a libel action against *The Times* on behalf of the Irish members incriminated. This offer was refused. Mr Gladstone then proposed that a select committee should inquire into the charges, and to this Parnell assented. But the government rejected the proposal. For the rest, Parnell continued to maintain for the most part an attitude of moderation, reserve and retreat, though he more than once came forward to protest against the harshness of the Irish administration and to plead for further remedial legislation. In July 1888 he announced that Mr Cecil Rhodes had sent him a sum of £10,000 in support of the Home Rule movement, subject to the condition that the Irish representation should be retained in the House of Commons in any future measure dealing with the question. About the same time the question of "Parnellism and Crime" again became acute. Mr F. H. O'Donnell, an ex-M.P. and former member of the Irish party, brought an action against *The Times* for libel. His case was a weak one, and a verdict was obtained by the defendants. But in the course of the proceedings the attorney-general, counsel for *The Times*, affirmed the readiness of his clients to establish all the charges advanced, including the genuineness of the letter which Parnell had declared to be a forgery. Parnell once more invited the House of Commons to refer this particular issue—that of the letter—to a select committee. This was again refused; but after some hesitation the government resolved to appoint by act of parliament a special commission, composed of three judges of the High Court, to inquire into all the charges advanced by *The Times*. This led to what was in substance, though not perhaps in judicial form, the most remarkable state trial of the 19th century. The commission began to sit in September 1888, and issued its report in February 1890. It heard evidence of immense volume and variety, and the speech of Sir Charles Russell in defence was afterwards published in a bulky volume. Parnell gave evidence at great length, with much composure and some cynicism. On the whole he produced a not unfavourable impression, though some of his statements might seem to justify Mr Gladstone's opinion that he was not a man of exact veracity. The report of the commission was a very voluminous document, and was variously interpreted by different parties to the controversy. Their conclusions may be left to speak for themselves:—

" I. We find that the respondent members of parliament collectively were not members of a conspiracy having for its object to establish the absolute independence of Ireland, but we find that some of them, together with Mr Davitt, established and joined in the Land League organization with the intention, by its means, to bring about the absolute independence of Ireland as a separate nation.

" II. We find that the respondents did enter into a conspiracy, by a system of coercion and intimidation, to promote an agrarian agitation against the payment of agricultural rents, for the purpose of impoverishing and expelling from the country the Irish landlords, who were styled ' the English garrison.'

" III. We find that the charge that ' when on certain occasions they thought it politic to denounce, and did denounce, certain crimes in public, they afterwards led their supporters to believe such denunciations were not sincere,' is not established. We entirely acquit Mr Parnell and the other respondents of the charge of insincerity in their denunciation of the Phoenix Park murders, and find that the 'facsimile' letter, on which this charge was chiefly based as against Mr Parnell, is a forgery.

" IV. We find that the respondents did disseminate the *Irish World* and other newspapers tending to incite to sedition and the commission of other crime.

" V. We find that the respondents did not directly incite persons to the commission of crime other than intimidation, but that they did incite to intimidation, and that the consequence of that incitement was that crime and outrage were committed by the persons incited. We find that it has not been proved that the respondents made payments for the purpose of inciting persons to commit crime.

" VI. We find, as to the allegation that the respondents did nothing to prevent crime, and expressed no *bona fide* disapproval, that some of the respondents, and in particular Mr Davitt, did express *bona fide* disapproval of crime and outrage, but that the respondents did not denounce the system of intimidation that led to crime and outrage, but persisted in it with knowledge of its effect.

" VII. We find that the respondents did defend persons charged with agrarian crime, and supported their families; but that it has not been proved that they subscribed to testimonials for, or were intimately associated with, notorious criminals, or that they made payments to procure the escape of criminals from justice.

" VIII. We find, as to the allegation that the respondents made payments to compensate persons who had been injured in the commission of crime, that they did make such payments.

" IX. As to the allegation that the respondents invited the assistance and co-operation of, and accepted subscriptions of money from, known advocates of crime and the use of dynamite, we find that the respondents did invite the assistance and co-operation of, and accepted subscriptions of money from, Patrick Ford, a known advocate of crime and the use of dynamite; but that it has not been proved that the respondents, or any of them, knew that the Clan-na-Gael controlled the League, or was collecting money for the Parliamentary Fund. It has been proved that the respondents invited and obtained the assistance and co-operation of the Physical Force Party in America, including the Clan-na-Gael, in order to obtain that assistance abstained from repudiating or condemning the action of that party."

The specific charges brought against Parnell personally were thus dealt with by the commissioners:—

" (a) That at the time of the Kilmainham negotiations Mr Parnell knew that Sheridan and Boyton had been organizing outrage, and therefore wished to use them to put down outrage.

" We find that this charge has not been proved.

" (b) That Mr Parnell was intimate with the leading Invincibles; that he probably learned from them what they were about when he was released on *parole* in April 1882; and that he recognized the Phoenix Park murders as their handiwork.

" We find that there is no foundation for this charge. We have already stated that the Invincibles were not a branch of the Land League.

" (c) That Mr Parnell on 23rd January 1883, by an opportune remittance, enabled F. Byrne to escape from justice to France.

" We find that Mr Parnell did not make any remittance to enable F. Byrne to escape from justice."

The case of the facsimile letter alleged to have been written by Parnell broke down altogether. It was proved to be a forgery. It had been purchased with other documents from one Richard Pigott, a needy and disreputable Irish journalist, who afterwards tried to blackmail Archbishop Walsh by offering, in a letter which was produced in court, to confess its forgery. Mercilessly cross-examined by Sir Charles Russell on this letter to the archbishop, Pigott broke down utterly. Before the commission sat again he fled to Madrid, and there blew his brains out. He had confessed the forgery to Mr Labouchere in the presence of Mr G. A. Sala, but did not stay to be cross-examined on his confession. The attorney-general withdrew the letter on behalf of *The Times*, and the commission pronounced it to be a forgery. Shortly after the letter had been withdrawn, Parnell filed an action against *The Times* for libel, claiming damages to the amount of £100,000. The action was compromised without going into court by a payment of £5000.

Practically, the damaging effect of some of the findings of the commission was neutralized by Parnell's triumphant vindication in the matter of the facsimile letter and of the darker charges levelled at him. Parties remained of the same opinion as before: the Unionists still holding that Parnell was steeped to the lips in treason, if not in crime; while the Home Rulers made abundance of capital out of his personal vindication, and sought to excuse the incriminating findings of the commission by the historic antecedents of the Nationalist cause and party. The failure to produce the books and papers of the Land League was overlooked, and little importance was attached by partisans to the fact that in spite of this default (leaving unexplained the manner in which over £100,000 had been expended), the commissioners " found that the respondents did make payments to compensate persons who had been injured in the commission of crime." Parnell and his colleagues were accepted as allies worthy of the confidence of an English party; they were made much of in Gladstonian Liberal society; and towards the close of 1889, before the commission had reported, but some months after the forged letter had been withdrawn, Parnell visited Hawarden to confer with Mr Gladstone on the measure of Home Rule to be introduced by the latter should he again be restored to power. What occurred at this conference was afterwards disclosed by Parnell, but Mr Gladstone vehemently denied the accuracy of his statements on the subject.

But Parnell's fall was at hand. In December 1889 Captain O'Shea filed a petition for divorce on the ground of his wife's adultery with Parnell. Parnell's intimacy with Mrs O'Shea had begun in 1881, though at what date it became a guilty one is not in evidence. Captain O'Shea had in that year challenged him to a duel, but was pacified by the explanations of Mrs O'Shea. It is known that Captain O'Shea had been Parnell's confidential agent in the negotiation of the Kilmainham Treaty, and in 1885 Parnell had strained his personal authority to the utmost to secure Captain O'Shea's return for Galway, and had quelled a formidable revolt among some of his most influential followers in doing so. It is not known why Captain O'Shea, who, if not blind to a matter of notoriety, must have been complaisant in 1885, became vindictive in 1889. No defence being offered, a decree of divorce was pronounced, and in June 1891 Parnell and Mrs O'Shea were married.

At first the Irish party determined to stand by Parnell. The decree was pronounced on the 17th of November 1890. On the 20th a great meeting of his political friends and supporters was held in Dublin, and a resolution that in all political matters Parnell possessed the confidence of the Irish nation was carried by acclamation. But the Irish party reckoned without its English allies. The "Nonconformist conscience," which had swallowed the report of the commission, was shocked by the decree of the divorce court. At a meeting of the National Liberal Federation held at Sheffield on the 21st of November, Mr John Morley was privately but firmly given to understand that the Nonconformists would insist on Parnell's resignation. Parliament was to meet on the 25th. Mr Gladstone tried to convey to Parnell privately his conviction that unless Parnell retired the cause of Home Rule was lost. But the message never reached Parnell. Mr Gladstone then requested Mr John Morley to see Parnell; but he could not be found. Finally, on the 24th, Mr Gladstone wrote to Mr Morley the famous and fatal letter, in which he declared his conviction " that, notwithstanding the splendid services rendered by Mr Parnell to his country, his continuance at the present moment in the leadership would be disastrous in the highest degree to the cause of Ireland," and that " the continuance I speak of would not only place many hearty and effective friends of the Irish cause in a position of great embarrassment, but would render my retention of the leadership of the Liberal party, based as it has been mainly upon the presentation of the Irish cause, almost a nullity." This letter was not published until after the Irish parliamentary party had met in the House of Commons and re-elected Parnell as its chairman

without a dissentient voice. But its publication was a thunderclap. A few days later Parnell was requested by a majority of the party to convene a fresh meeting. It took place in Committee Room No. 15, which became historic by the occasion, and after several days of angry recrimination and passionate discussion, during which Parnell, who occupied the chair, scornfully refused to put to the vote a resolution for his own deposition, 45 members retired to another room and there declared his leadership at an end. The remainder, 26 in number, stood by him. The party was thus divided into Parnellites and anti-Parnellites, and the schism was not healed until several years after Parnell's death.

This was practically the end of Parnell's political career in England. The scene of operations was transferred to Ireland, and there Parnell fought incessantly a bitter and a losing fight, which ended only with his death. He declared that Ireland could never achieve her emancipation by force, and that if she was to achieve it by constitutional methods, it could only be through the agency of a united Nationalist party rigidly eschewing alliance with any English party. This was the policy he proclaimed in a manifesto issued before the opening of the sittings in Committee Room No. 15, and with this policy, when deserted by the bulk of his former followers, he appealed to the Fenians in Ireland—" the hillside men," as Mr Davitt, who had abandoned him early in the crisis, contemptuously called them. The Fenians rallied to his side, giving him their votes and their support, but they were no match for the Church, which had declared against him. An attempt at reconciliation was made in the spring, at what was known as " the Boulogne negotiations," where Mr William O'Brien endeavoured to arrange an understanding; but it came to nothing in the end. Probably Parnell was never very anxious for its success. He seems to have regarded the situation as fatally compromised by the extent to which his former followers were committed to an English alliance, and he probably saw that the only way to recover his lost position was to build up a new independent party. He knew well enough that this would take time—five years was the shortest period he allowed himself—but before many months were passed he was dead. The life he led, the agonies he endured, at times, unwilling to be alone, strange in his ways and demeanour. He visited Ireland for the last time in September, and the last public meeting he attended was on the 27th of that month. The next day he sent for his friend Dr Kenny, who found him suffering from acute rheumatism and general debility. He left Ireland on the 30th, promising to return on the following Saturday week. He did return on that day, but it was in his coffin. He took to his bed shortly after his return to his home at Brighton, and on the 6th of October he died. His remains were conveyed to Dublin, and on Sunday, the 11th of October, they were laid to rest in the presence of a vast assemblage of the Irish people in Glasnevin Cemetery, not far from the grave of O'Connell.

The principal materials for a biography of Parnell and the history of the Parnellite movement are to be found in *Hansard's Parliamentary Debates* (1875–1891); in the *Annual Register* for the same period; in the *Report of the Special Commission* issued in 1890; in *The Life of Charles Stewart Parnell*, by R. Barry O'Brien; in *The Parnellite Movement*, by T. P. O'Connor, M.P.; and in a copious biography of Parnell contributed by an anonymous but well-informed writer to the *Dict. of Nat. Biog.*, vol. xliii.

(J. R. T.)

PARNELL, THOMAS (1679–1718), English poet, was born in Dublin in 1679. His father, Thomas Parnell, belonged to a family (see above) which had been long settled at Congleton, Cheshire, but being a partisan of the Commonwealth, he removed with his children to Ireland after the Restoration, and purchased an estate in Tipperary which descended to his son. In 1693 the son entered Trinity College, Cambridge, and in 1700 took his

M.A. degree, being ordained deacon in the same year in spite of his youth. In 1704 he became minor canon of St Patrick's Cathedral and in 1706 archdeacon of Clogher. Shortly after receiving this preferment he married Anne Minchin, to whom he was sincerely attached. Swift says that nearly a year after her death (1711) he was still ill with grief. His visits to London are said to have begun as early as 1706. He was intimate with Richard Steele and Joseph Addison, and although in 1711 he abandoned his Whig politics, there was no change in the friendship. Parnell was introduced to Lord Bolingbroke in 1712 by Swift, and subsequently to the earl of Oxford. In 1713 he contributed to the *Poetical Miscellanies* edited for Tonson by Steele, and published his *Essay on the Different Styles of Poetry.* He was a member of the Scriblerus Club, and, Pope says that he had a hand in "An Essay of the learned Martinus Scriblerus concerning the Origin of Sciences." He wrote the "Essay on the Life and writings and learning of Homer"[1] prefixed to Pope's translations, and in the autumn of 1714 both were at Bath together. In 1716 Parnell was presented to the vicarage of Finglass, when he resigned his archdeaconry. In the same year he published *Homer's Battle of the Frogs and Mice. With the remarks of Zoilus. To which is prefixed, the Life of the said Zoilus.* Parnell was in London again in 1718, and, on the way back to Ireland, was taken ill and died at Chester, where he was buried on the 24th of October.

Parnell's best known poem is "The Hermit," an admirably executed moral *conte* written in the heroic couplet. It is based on an old story to be found in the *Gesta Romanorum* and other sources. He cannot in any sense be said to have been a disciple of Pope, though his verse may owe something to his friend's revision. But this and other of his pieces, "The Hymn to Contentment," "The Night Piece on Death," "The Fairy Tale," were original in treatment, and exercised some influence on the work of Goldsmith, Gray and Collins. Pope's selection of his poems was justified by the publication in 1758 of *Posthumous Works of Dr Thomas Parnell, containing Poems Moral and Divine, and on various other subjects,* which in no way added to his fame. They were contemptuously dismissed as unauthentic by Thomas Gray and Samuel Johnson, but there seems no reason to doubt the authorship.

In 1770 *Poems on Several Occasions* was printed with a life of the author by Oliver Goldsmith. His *Poetical Works* were printed in Anderson's and other collections of the British Poets. See *The Poetical Works* (1894) edited by George A. Aitken for the Aldine Edition of the British Poets. An edition by the Rev. John Mitford for the same series (1833) was reprinted in 1866. His correspondence with Pope is published in Pope's *Works* (ed. Elwin and Courthorpe, vii. 451–467).

PARNON (mod. Malevo), the mountain ridge on the east of the Laconian plain. Height 6365 ft. It is visible from Athens above the top of the Argive mountains.

PARNY, ÉVARISTE DÉSIRÉ DE FORGES, VICOMTE DE (1753–1814), was born in the Isle of Bourbon on the 6th of February 1753. He was sent to France at nine years old, was educated at Rennes, and in 1771 entered the army. He was, however, shortly recalled to the Isle of Bourbon, where he fell in love with a young lady whom he addresses as Éléonore. Her father refused to consent to her marriage with Parny, and she married some one else. Parny returned to France, and published his *Poésies érotiques* in 1778. He also published about the same time his *Voyage de Bourgogne* (1777), written in collaboration with his friend Antoine de Bertin (1752–1790); *Épître aux insurgents de Boston* (1777), and *Opuscules poétiques* (1779). In 1796 appeared the *Guerre des dieux,* a poem in the style of Voltaire's *Pucelle,* directed against Christianity. Parny devoted himself in his later years almost entirely to the religious and political-burlesque. He was elected to the Academy in 1803, and in 1813 received a pension from Napoleon. In 1805 he produced an extraordinary allegoric poem attacking George III.,

[1] Pope acknowledged the essay with affectionate praise, but in 1729 he said it was written "upon such memoirs as I had collected," and later he complained of its defects, saying it had cost him more pains to revise than it would have done to write it.

his family and his subjects, under the eccentric title of "Goddam! Goddam! par un French-dog." Parny's early love poems and elegies, however, show a remarkable grace and ease, a good deal of tenderness, and considerable fancy and wit. One famous piece, the *Elegy on a Young Girl,* is scarcely to be excelled in its kind. Parny died in 1814.

His *Œuvres choisies* were published in 1827. There is a sketch of Parny in Sainte-Beuve's *Portraits contemporains.*

PARODY (Gr. παρῳδία, literally a song sung beside, a comic parallel), an imitation of the form or style of a serious writing in matter of a meaner kind so as to produce a ludicrous effect. Parody is almost as old in European literature as serious writing. The *Batrachomyomachia,* or "Battle of the Frogs and Mice," a travesty of the heroic epos, was ascribed at one time to Homer himself; and it is probably at least as old as the 5th century B.C. The great tragic poetry of Greece very soon provoked the parodist. Aristophanes parodied the style of Euripides in the *Acharnians* with a comic power that has never been surpassed. The debased grand style of medieval romance was parodied in *Don Quixote.* Shakespeare parodied the extravagant heroics of an earlier stage, and was himself parodied by Marston, incidentally in his plays and elaborately in a roughly humorous burlesque of *Venus and Adonis.* The most celebrated parody of the Restoration was Buckingham's *Rehearsal* (1672), in which the tragedies of Dryden were inimitably ridiculed. At the beginning of the 18th century *The Splendid Shilling* of John Philips (1676–1709), which Addison said was "the finest burlesque poem in the English language," brilliantly introduced a fashion for using the solemn movement of Milton's blank verse to celebrate ridiculous incidents. In 1736, Isaac Hawkins Browne (1705–1760) published a volume, *A Pipe of Tobacco,* in which the poetical styles of Colley Cibber, Ambrose Philips, James Thomson, Edward Young and Jonathan Swift were delightfully reproduced. In the following century, Shelley and John Hamilton Reynolds almost simultaneously produced cruel imitations of the naïveté and baldness of Wordsworth's *Peter Bell* (1819). But in that generation the most celebrated parodists were the brothers Smith, whose *Rejected Addresses* may be regarded as classic in this kind of artificial production. The Victorian age has produced a plentiful crop of parodists in prose and in verse, in dramatic poetry and in lyric poetry. By common consent, the most subtle and dexterous of these was C. S. Calverley, who succeeded in reproducing not merely tricks of phrase and metre, but even manneristic turns of thought. In a later day, Mr Owen Seaman has repeated, and sometimes surpassed, the agile feats of Calverley.

PAROLE (shortened from the Fr. *parole d'honneur,* word of honour), a military term signifying the engagement given by a prisoner of war that if released he will not again take up arms against his captors during the term of the engagement or the war, unless previously relieved of the obligation by exchange. "Parole" is also used in the same sense as "word" to imply a watchword or password. The French word, formed from the Late Lat. *paraula, parabola,* Gr. παραβολή, story, parable, was also adopted into English as "parol," *i.e.* verbal, oral, by word of mouth, now only used in the legal term "parol evidence," *i.e.* oral as opposed to documentary evidence.

PAROPAMISUS, the name given by the Greeks to the parts of the Hindu Kush bordering Kohistan to the north-west of Kabul. It is now applied in a restricted sense to the water-parting between Herat and the Russian frontier on the Kushk river, which possesses no local name of its own. From Herat city to the crest of the Paropamisus, which is crossed by several easy passes, is a distance of about 36 m., involving a rise of 1000 ft.

PAROS, or PARO, an island in the Aegean Sea, one of the largest of the group of the Cyclades, with a population of 8000. It lies to the west of Naxos, from which it is separated by a channel about 6 m. broad, and with which it is now grouped together, in popular language, under the common name of Paronaxia. It is in 37° N. lat. and 25° 10' E. long. Its greatest length from N.E. to S.W. is 13 m., and its greatest breadth

10 m. It is formed of a single mountain about 2500 ft. high, sloping evenly down on all sides to a maritime plain, which is broadest on the north-east and south-west sides. The island is composed of marble, though gneiss and mica-schist are to be found in a few places. The capital, Paroekia or Parikia (Italian, *Parechia*), situated on a bay on the north-west side of the island, occupies the site of the ancient capital Paros. Its harbour admits small vessels; the entrance is dangerous on account of rocks. Houses built in the Italian style with terraced roofs, shadowed by luxuriant vines, and surrounded by gardens of oranges and pomegranates, give to the town a picturesque and pleasing aspect. Here on a rock beside the sea are the remains of a medieval castle built almost entirely of ancient marble remains. Similar traces of antiquity in the shape of bas-reliefs, inscriptions, columns, &c., are numerous in the town, and on a terrace to the south of it is a precinct of Asclepius. Outside the town is the church of Katapoliani ('Η 'Εκατονταπυλιανή), said to have been founded by the empress Helena; there are two adjoining churches, one of very early form, and also a baptistery with a cruciform font.

On the north side of the island is the bay of Naoussa (Naussa) or Agoussa, forming a safe and roomy harbour. In ancient times it was closed by a chain or boom. Another good harbour is that of Drios on the south-east side, where the Turkish fleet used to anchor on its annual voyage through the Aegean. The three villages of Tragoulas, Marmora and Kepidi (Κηπίδι, pronounced Tschipidi), situated on an open plain on the eastern side of the island, and rich in remains of antiquity, probably occupy the site of an ancient town. They are known together as the " villages of Kephalos," from the steep and lofty headland of Kephalos. On this headland stands an abandoned monastery of St Anthony, amidst the ruins of a medieval castle, which belonged to the Venetian family of the Venieri, and was gallantly though fruitlessly defended against the Turkish general Barbarossa in 1537.

Parian marble, which is white and semi-transparent, with a coarse grain and a very beautiful texture, was the chief source of wealth to the island. The celebrated marble quarries lie on the northern side of the mountain anciently known as Marpessa (afterwards Capresso), a little below a former convent of St Mina. The marble, which was exported from the 6th century B.C., and used by Praxiteles and other great Greek sculptors, was obtained by means of subterranean quarries driven horizontally or at a descending angle into the rock, and the marble thus quarried by lamplight got the name of Lychnites, Lychneus (from *lychnos*, a lamp), or Lygdos (Plin. *H. N.* xxxvi. 5, 14; Plato, *Eryxias*, 400 D; Athen. v. 2050; Diod. Sic. 2, 52). Several of these tunnels are still to be seen. At the entrance to one of them is a bas-relief dedicated to Pan and the Nymphs. Several attempts to work the marble have been made in modern times, but it has not been exported in any great quantities.

History.—The story that Paros was colonized by one Paros of Parrhasia, who brought with him a colony of Arcadians to the island (Heraclides, *De rubus publicis*, 8; Steph. Byz. *s.v.* Πάρος), is one of those etymologizing fictions in which Greek legend abounds. Ancient names of the island are said to have been Plateia (or Pactia), Demetrias, Zacynthus, Hyria, Hyleessa, Minoa and Cabarnis (Steph. Byz.). From Athens the island afterwards received a colony of Ionians (Schol. Dionys. *Per.* 525; cf. Herod. i. 171), under whom it attained a high degree of prosperity. It sent out colonies to Thasos (Thuc. iv. 104; Strabo, 487) and Parium on the Hellespont. In the former colony, which was planted in the 15th or 18th Olympiad, the poet Archilochus, native of Paros, is said to have taken part. As late as 385 B.C. the Parians, in conjunction with Dionysius of Syracuse, founded a colony on the Illyrian island of Pharos (Diod. Sic. xv. 13). So high was the reputation of the Parians that they were chosen by the people of Miletus to arbitrate in a party dispute (Herod. v. 28 seq.). Shortly before the Persian War Paros seems to have been a dependency of Naxos (Herod. v. 31). In the Persian War Paros sided with the Persians and sent a trireme to Marathon to support them.

In retaliation, the capital Paros was besieged by an Athenian fleet under Miltiades, who demanded a fine of 100 talents. But the town offered a vigorous resistance, and the Athenians were obliged to sail away after a siege of twenty-six days, during which they had laid the island waste. It was at a temple of Demeter Thesmophorus in Paros that Miltiades received the wound of which he afterwards died (Herod. vi. 133–136). By means of an inscription Ross was enabled to identify the site of the temple; it lies, in agreement with the description of Herodotus, on a low hill beyond the boundaries of the town. Paros also sided with Xerxes against Greece, but after the battle of Artemisium the Parian contingent remained in Cythnos watching the progress of events (Herod. viii. 67). For this unpatriotic conduct the islanders were punished by Themistocles, who exacted a heavy fine (Herod. viii. 112). Under the Athenian naval confederacy, Paros paid the highest tribute of all the islands subject to Athens —30 talents annually, according to the assessment of Olymp. 88, 4 (429 B.C.). Little is known of the constitution of Paros, but inscriptions seem to show that it was democratic, with a senate (*Boule*) at the head of affairs (*Corpus inscript.* 2376–2383; Ross, *Inscr. ined.* ii. 147, 148). In 410 B.C. the Athenian general Theramenes found an oligarchy at Paros; he deposed it and restored the democracy (Diod. Sic. xiii. 47). Paros was included in the new Athenian confederacy of 378 B.C., but afterwards, along with Chios, it renounced its connexion with Athens, probably about 357 B.C. Thenceforward the island lost its political importance. From the inscription of Adule we learn that the Cyclades, and consequently Paros, were subject to the Ptolemies of Egypt. Afterwards they passed under the rule of Rome. When the Latins made themselves masters of Constantinople, Paros, like the rest, became subject to Venice. In 1537 it was conquered by the Turks. The island now belongs to the kingdom of Greece. Among the most interesting discoveries made in the island is the Parian Chronicle (*q.v.*).

See Tournefort, *Voyage du Levant*, i. 232 seq. (Lyons, 1717); Clarke, *Travels*, iii. (London, 1814); Leake, *Travels in Northern Greece*, iii. 84 seq. (London, 1835); Prokesch, *Denkwürdigkeiten*, ii. 19 seq. (Stuttgart, 1836); Ross, *Reisen auf den griechischen Inseln*, i. 44 seq. (Stuttgart, and Tübingen, 1840); Fiedler, *Reise durch alle Theile des Königreiches Griechenland*, ii. 179 seq. (Leipzig, 1841); Bursian, *Geographie von Griechenland*, ii. 483 seq. (Leipzig, 1872). For the Parian Chronicle, *Inscriptiones graecae*, xii. 100 sqq.

PAROXYSM (Med. Lat. *paroxysmus*, from the Gr. παροξύνειν, to make sharp, ὀξύς), a violent outbreak or display of emotion or feeling. The term is used of a fit of laughter, pain, anger or fear, and particularly an acute stage in a disease is the earliest sense of the word.

PARQUETRY (Fr. *parqueterie*, from *parquet*, flooring, originally a small compartment), a term applied to a kind of mosaic of wood used for ornamental flooring. Materials contrasting in colour and grain, such as oak, walnut, cherry, lime, pine, &c. are employed; and in the more expensive kinds the richly coloured tropical woods are also used. The patterns of parquet flooring are entirely geometrical and angular (squares, triangles, lozenges, &c.), curved and irregular forms being avoided on account of the expense and difficulty of fitting. There are two classes of parquetry in use—veneers and solid parquet. The veneers are usually about a quarter of an inch in thickness, and are laid over already existing floors. Solid parquet of an inch or more in thickness consists of single pieces of wood grooved and tongued together, having consequently the pattern alike on both sides.

PARR, CATHERINE (1512–1548), the sixth queen of Henry VIII., was a daughter of Sir Thomas Parr (d. 1517), of Kendal, an official of the royal household. When only a girl she was married to Edward Borough, and after his death in or before 1529 to John Neville, Lord Latimer, who died in 1542 or 1543. Latimer had only been dead a few months when, on the 12th of July 1543, Catherine was married to Henry VIII. at Hampton Court. The new queen, who was regent of England during the king's absence in 1544, acted in a very kindly fashion towards her stepchildren; but her patience with the king did not prevent a charge of heresy from being brought against her. Henry, however, would not permit her arrest, and she became a widow for the third time on his death in January 1547. In the same year she married a former lover, Sir Thomas Seymour, now Lord Seymour of Sudeley. Soon after this event, on the 7th of September 1548, she died at Sudeley castle. Catherine was a pious and charitable woman and a friend of learning; she wrote *The Lamentation or Complaint of a Sinner*, which was published after her death.

See A. Strickland, *Lives of the Queens of England*, vol. III. (1877).

PARR, SAMUEL (1747-1825), English schoolmaster, son of Samuel Parr, surgeon at Harrow-on-the-Hill, was born there on the 26th of January 1747. At Easter 1752 he was sent to Harrow School as a free scholar, and when left in 1761 he began to help his father in his practice, but the old surgeon realized that his son's talents lay elsewhere, and Samuel was sent (1765) to Emmanuel College, Cambridge. From February 1767 to the close of 1771 he served under Robert Sumner as head assistant at Harrow, where he had Sheridan among his pupils. When the head master died in September 1771 Parr, after vainly applying for the position, started a school at Stanmore, which he conducted for five years. Then he became head master of Colchester Grammar School (1776-1778) and subsequently of Norwich School (1778-1786). He had taken priest's orders at Colchester, and in 1780 was presented to the small rectory of Asterby in Lincolnshire, and three years later to the vicarage of Hatton near Warwick. He exchanged this latter benefice for Wadenhoe, Northamptonshire, in 1789, stipulating to be allowed to reside, as assistant curate, in the parsonage of Hatton, where he took a limited number of pupils. Here he spent the rest of his days, enjoying his excellent library, described by H. G. Bohn in *Bibliotheca Parriana* (1827), and here his friends, Porson and E. H. Barker, passed many months in his company. The degree of LL.D. was conferred on him by the university of Cambridge in 1781. Parr died at Hatton vicarage on the 6th of March 1825.

Dr Parr's writings fill several volumes, but they are all beneath the reputation which he acquired through the variety of his knowledge and dogmatism of his conversation. The chief of them are his *Characters of Charles James Fox* (1809); and his unjustifiable reprint of the *Tracts of Warburton and a Warburtonian, not admitted into their works*, a scathing exposure of Warburton and Hurd. Even amid the terrors of the French Revolution he adhered to Whiggism, and his correspondence included every man of eminence, either literary or political, who adopted the same creed. In private life his model was Johnson. He succeeded in copying his uncouthness and pompous manner, but had neither his humour nor his real authority. He was famous as a writer of epitaphs and wrote inscriptions for the tombs of Burke, Charles Burney, Johnson, Fox and Gibbon.

There are two memoirs of his life, one by the Rev. William Field (1828), the other, with his works and his letters, by John Johnstone (1828); and E. H. Barker published in 1828-1829 two volumes of *Parriana*, a confused mass of information on Parr and his friends. An essay on his life is included in De Quincey's works, vol. v., and a little volume of the *Aphorisms, Opinions and Reflections of the late Dr Parr* appeared in 1826.

PARR, THOMAS (c. 1483-1635), English centenarian, known as "Old Parr," is reputed to have been born in 1483, at Winnington, Shropshire, the son of a farmer. In 1500 he is said to have left his home and entered domestic service, and in 1518 to have returned to Winnington to occupy the small holding he then inherited on the death of his father. In 1563, at the age of eighty, he married his first wife, by whom he had a son and a daughter, both of whom died in infancy. At the age of 122, his first wife having died, he married again. His vigour seems to have been unimpaired, and when 130 years old he is said to have threshed corn. In 1635 the news reached the ears of Thomas Howard, 2nd earl of Arundel, who resolved to exhibit him at court, and had him conveyed to London in a specially constructed litter. Here he was presented to King Charles I.,

but the change of air and diet soon affected him, and the old man died at Lord Arundel's house in London, on the 14th of November 1635. He was buried in the south transept of Westminster Abbey where the inscription over his grave reads: " Tho: Parr of ye county of Salopp Born in Ao 1483. He lived in ye reignes of Ten Princes viz. K. Edw. 4, K. Ed. V. K. Rich. 3. K. Hen. 7. K. Hen. 8. K. Edw. 6. Q. Ma. Q. Eliz. K. Ja. and K. Charles, aged 152 yeares and was buried here Nov: 15. 1635." A post-mortem examination made by the king's orders by Dr William Harvey, revealed the fact that his internal organs were in an unusually perfect state, and his cartilages unossified.

PARR, a name originally applied to the small Salmonoids abundant in British rivers, which were for a long time considered to constitute a distinct species of fish (*Salmo salmulus*). They possess the broad head, short snout and large eye characteristic of young Salmonoida, and are ornamented on the sides of the body and tail with about eleven or more broad dark cross-bars, the so-called parr-marks. However, John Shaw proved, by experiment, that these fishes represent merely the first stage of growth of the salmon, before it assumes, at an age of one or two years, and when about six inches long, the silvery smolt-dress preparatory to its first migration to the sea. The parr-marks are produced by a deposit of black pigment in the skin, and appear very soon after the exclusion of the fish from the egg; they are still visible for some time below the new coat of scales of the smolt-stage, but have entirely disappeared on the first return of the young salmon from the sea. Although the juvenile condition of the parr is now universally admitted, it is a remarkable fact that many male parr, from 7 to 8 inches long, have their sexual organs fully developed, and that their milt has all the fertilizing properties of the seminal fluid of a full-grown and sexually matured salmon. Not only the salmon, but also the other species of *Salmo*, the grayling, and probably also the *Coregoni*, pass through a parr-stage of growth. The young of all these fishes are barred, the salmon having generally eleven or more bars, and the parr of the migratory trout from nine to ten, or two or three more than the river-trout. In some of the small races or species of river-trout the parr-marks are retained throughout life, but subject to changes in intensity of colour.

PARRAMATTA, a town of Cumberland county, New South Wales, Australia, 14 m. by rail N.W. of Sydney. Pop. (1901) 12,568. It is situated on the Parramatta River, an arm of Port Jackson, and was one of the earliest inland settlements (1788), the seat of many of the public establishments connected with the working of the convict system. Many of these still remain in another form (the district hospital, the lunatic asylum, the gaol, two asylums for the infirm and destitute, the Protestant and Catholic orphan schools), involving a government expenditure which partly sustains the business of the town. Parramatta was one of the earliest seats of the tweed manufacture, but its principal industrial dependence has been on the fruit trade. With the exception of Pennant and Pennant Hills, there is an outburst of trap rock, the surface soil is the disintegration of the Wainamatta shale, which is well suited for orangeries and orchards. The first grain grown in the colony was harvested at Parramatta, then called Roschill. The earlier governors had their country residence near the town, and the domain is now a public park in the hands of the municipality. An early observatory, where in 1822 were made the observations for the *Parramatta Catalogue*, numbering 7385 stars, has long been abandoned. Parramatta was incorporated in 1861. It has one of the finest race-courses in Australia, and in the King's School, founded in 1832, the oldest grammar school in the colony.

PARRHASIUS, of Ephesus, one of the greatest painters of Greece. He settled in Athens, and may be ranked among the Attic artists. The period of his activity is fixed by the anecdote which Xenophon records of the conversation between him and Socrates on the subject of art; he was therefore distinguished as a painter before 399 B.C. Seneca relates a tale that Parrhasius bought one of the Olynthians whom Philip sold into slavery, 346 B.C., and tortured him in order to have a model for his picture of Prometheus; but the story, which is similar to one told of Michelangelo, is chronologically impossible. Another tale recorded of him describes his contest with Zeuxis. The latter painted some grapes so perfectly that birds came to peck at them. He then called on Parrhasius to draw aside the curtain and show his picture, but, finding that his rival's picture was the curtain itself, he acknowledged himself to be surpassed, for Zeuxis had deceived birds, but Parrhasius had deceived Zeuxis. He was universally placed in the very first rank among painters. His skilful drawing of outlines is especially praised, and many of his drawings on wood and parchment were preserved and highly valued by later painters for purposes of study. He first attained skill in making his figures appear to stand out from the background. His picture of Theseus adorned the Capitol in Rome. His other works, besides the obscene subjects with which he is said to have amused his leisure, are chiefly mythological groups. A picture of the Demos, the personified People of Athens, is famous; according to the story, which is probably based upon epigrams, the twelve prominent character-istics of the people, though apparently quite inconsistent with each other, were distinctly expressed in this figure.

PARRICIDE (probably for Lat. *parricidia*, from *pater*, father, and *caedere*, to slay), strictly the murder of a parent; the term however has been extended to include the murder of any relative or of an ascendant by a descendant. The first Roman law against parricide was that of the *Lex Cornelia de sicariis et veneficis* (c. 81 B.C.), which enacted that the murderer of a parent should be sewed up in a sack and thrown into the sea, and provided other punishments for the killing of near relatives. The *Lex Pompeia de parricidiis* (52 B.C.) re-enacted the principal provisions of the Lex Cornelia and defined parricide as the deliberate and wrongful slaying of ascendants, husbands, wives, cousins, brothers and sisters, uncles and aunts, stepfathers and mothers, fathers and mothers-in-law, patrons and descendants. For the murder of a father, mother, grandfather or grandmother, the Lex Pompeia ordained that the guilty person should be whipped till he bled, sewn up in a sack with a dog, a cock, a viper and an ape, and thrown into the sea. Failing water, he was either to be torn in pieces by wild beasts or burned.

English law has never made any legal distinction between killing a parent or other relative and simple murder, and the Netherlands and Germany follow in the same direction. French law has been exceptionally severe in its treatment of parricide. Before the Revolution, the parricide if a male, had to make a recantation of his crime, and then suffered the loss of his right hand; his body was afterwards burned and the ashes scattered to the winds. If the parricide was a female she was burned or hanged. After the Revolution the penalty became simply one of death, but the compilers of the penal code adjudged this insufficient and reintroduced some of the previous provisions: the parricide was brought to the place of execution clad in a shirt, bare-footed, and the head enveloped in a black veil. While he was exposed on the scaffold, an officer read aloud the decree of condemnation; the culprit then had his right hand cut off, and was immediately afterwards executed. On the revision of the penal code in 1832 the cutting off of the right hand was omitted, but the other details remained. Other continental European countries, following the example of France, treat the crime of parricide with exceptional severity.

PARROT (according to Skeat, from Fr. *Perrot* or *Pierrot*, the diminutive of the proper name *Pierre*[1]), the name given [2] "Parakeet" (in Shakespeare, I *Hen. IV.* ii. 3. 88, "Para-quito") is said by the same authority to be from the Spanish *Peri-quito* or *Perroquito*, a small Parrot, diminutive of *Perico*, a Parrot, which again may be a diminutive from *Pedro*, the proper name. Parakeet (spelt in various ways in English) is usually applied to the smaller kinds of Parrots, especially those which have long tails, not as *Perroquet* in French, which is used as a general term for all Parrots, *Perruche*, or sometimes *Perriche*, being the ordinary name for what we call Parakeet. The old English "Popinjay" and the old French *Papegaut* have almost passed out of use, but the German *Papagei* and

generally to a large and very natural group of birds, which for more than a score of centuries have attracted attention, not only from their gaudy plumage, but, at first and chiefly, it would seem, from the readiness with which many of them learn to imitate the sounds they hear, repeating the words and even phrases of human speech with a fidelity that is often astonishing. It is said that no representation of any parrot appears in Egyptian art, nor does any reference to a bird of the kind occur in the Bible, whence it has been concluded that neither painters nor writers had any knowledge of it. Aristotle is commonly supposed to be the first author who mentions a parrot; but this is an error, for nearly a century earlier Ctesias in his *Indica* (cap. 3),[1] under the name of βίττακος (*Bittacus*), so neatly described a bird which could speak an "Indian" language—naturally, as he seems thought—or Greek—if it had been taught so to do—about as big as a sparrow-hawk (*Hierax*), with a purple face and a black beard, otherwise blue-green (*cyaneus*) and vermilion in colour, so that there cannot be much risk in declaring that he must have had before him a male example of what is now commonly known as the Blossom-headed parakeet, and to ornithologists as *Palaeornis cyanocephalus*, an inhabitant of many parts of India. After Ctesias comes Aristotle's ψιττάκη (*Psittace*), which Sundevall supposes him to have described, only from hearsay. There can be no doubt that the Indian conquests of Alexander were the means of making the parrot better known in Europe, and it is in reference to this fact that another Eastern species of *Palaeornis* now bears the name of *P. alexandri*, though from the localities it inhabits it could hardly have had anything to do with the Macedonian hero. That Africa had parrots does not seem to have been discovered by the ancients till long after, as Pliny tells us (vi. 29) that they were first met with beyond the limits of Upper Egypt by explorers employed by Nero. These birds, highly prized from the first, reprobated by the moralist, and celebrated by more than one classical poet, in the course of time were brought in great numbers to Rome, and ministered in various ways to the luxury of the age. Not only were they lodged in cages of tortoise-shell and ivory, with silver wires, but they were professedly esteemed as delicacies for the table, and one emperor is said to have fed his lions upon them! With the decline of the Roman Empire the demand for parrots in Europe lessened, and so the supply dwindled, yet all knowledge of them was not wholly lost, and they are occasionally mentioned by one writer or another until in the 13th century began that career of geographical discovery which has since proceeded uninterruptedly. This immediately brought with it the knowledge of many more forms of these birds than had ever before been seen. Yet so numerous is the group that even now new species of parrots are not uncommonly recognized.

The home of the vast majority of parrot-forms is unquestion-ably within the tropics, but the popular belief that parrots are tropical birds only is a great mistake. In North America the Carolina parakeet, *Conurus carolinensis*, at the beginning of the 19th century used to range in summer as high as the shores of lakes Erie and Ontario—a latitude equal to the south of France; and even much later it reached, according to trust-worthy information, the junction of the Ohio and the Mississippi, though now its limits have been so much curtailed that its occurrence in any but the Gulf States is doubtful. In South America, at least four species are found in Chile or the La Plata region, and one, *Conurus patagonus*, is pretty common on the bleak coast of the Strait of Magellan. In Africa it is true that no species is known to extend to within some ten degrees of the tropic of Cancer; but *Pionias robustus* inhabits territories

Italian *Papagaio* still continue in vogue. These names can be traced to the Arabic *Babaghâ*; but the source of that word is unknown. The Anglo-Saxon name of the Parret, a river in Somerset, is Pedreda or Pedrida, which at first sight looks as if it had to do with the proper name, Petrus: but Skeat believes there is no connexion between them—the latter portion of the word being *rîð*, a stream.

[1] The passage seems to have escaped the notice of all naturalists except W. J. Broderip, who mentioned it in his article "Psittacidae," in the *Penny Cyclopaedia* (xix. 83).

lying quite as far to the southward of the tropic of Capricorn. In India the northern range of the group is only bounded by the slopes of the Himalaya, and farther to the eastward parrots are not only abundant over the whole of the Malay Archipelago, as well as Australia and Tasmania, but two very well-defined families are peculiar to New Zealand and its adjacent islands (see KAKAPO and NESTOR). No parrot has recently inhabited the Palaearctic Region,[1] and but one (the *Conurus carolinensis*, just mentioned) probably belongs to the Nearctic; nor are parrots represented by many different forms in either the Ethiopian or the Indian Regions. In continental Asia the distribution of parrots is rather remarkable. None extend farther to the westward than the valley of the Indus,[2] which, considering the nature of the country in Baluchistan and Afghanistan, is perhaps intelligible enough; but it is not so easy to understand why none are found either in Cochin China or China proper; and they are also wanting in the Philippine Islands, which is the more remarkable and instructive when we find how abundant they are in the groups a little farther to the southward. Indeed, A. R. Wallace has well remarked that the portion of the earth's surface which contains the largest number of parrots, in proportion to its area, is undoubtedly that covered by the islands extending from Celebes to the Solomon group. "The area of these islands is probably not one-fifteenth of that of the four tropical regions, yet they contain from one-fifth to one-fourth of all the known parrots" (*Geogr. Distr. Animals*, ii. 330). He goes on to observe also that in this area are found many of the most remarkable forms—all the red Lories, the great cockatoos, the pigmy *Nasiternae* and other singularities. In South America the species of parrots, though numerically nearly as abundant, are far less diversified in form, and all of them seem capable of being referred to two, or, at most, three sections. The species that has the widest range, and that by far, is the common Ring-necked Parakeet, *Palaeornis torquatus*, a well-known cage-bird which is found from the mouth of the Gambia across Africa to the coast of the Red Sea, as well as throughout the whole of India, Ceylon and Burmah to Tenasserim.[3] On the other hand, there are plenty of cases of parrots which are restricted to an extremely small area—often an island of insignificant size, as *Conurus xantholaemus*, confined to the island of St Thomas in the Antilles, and *Palaeornis exsul* to that of Rodrigues in the Indian Ocean—to say nothing of the remarkable instance of *Nestor productus* (see NESTOR).

The systematic treatment of this very natural group of birds has long been a subject of much difficulty. A few systematists, among whom C. L. Bonaparte was chief, placed them at the top of the class, conceiving that they were the analogues of the *Primates* among mammals. T. H. Huxley recognised the *Psittacomorphae* as forming one of the principal groups of Carinate birds, and they are now generally regarded as forming a suborder *Psittaci* of the Cuculiform birds (see NESTOR). Owing to the erroneous number of forms and the close similarities of structure, the subdivision of the group has presented great difficulties. Buffon was unaware of the existence of some of the most remarkable forms of the group, in particular of

[1] A few remains of a Parrot have been recognized from the Miocene of the Allier in France, by A. Milne-Edwards (*Ois. Foss. France*, vol. ii. p. 525, pl. cc.), and are said by him to show the greatest resemblance to the common Grey Parrot of Africa, *Psittacus erithacus*, through having also some affinity to the Ring-necked Parakeet of the same country, *Palaeornis torquatus*. He refers them, however, to the same genus as the former, under the name of *Psittacus verreauxi*.

[2] The statements that have been made, and even repeated by writers of authority, as to the occurrence of "a green parrot" in Syria (Chesney, *Exped. Survey Euphrates and Tigris*, ii. 443, 537) and of a parrot in Turkestan (*Jour. As. Soc. Bengal*, viii. 1007) originated with gentlemen who had no ornithological knowledge, and are evidently erroneous.

[3] It is right to state, however, that the African examples of this bird are said to be distinguishable from the Asiatic by their somewhat shorter wings and weaker bill, and hence they are considered by some authorities to form a distinct species or subspecies, *P. docilis*; but in thus regarding them the difference of locality seems to have influenced opinion, and without that difference they would scarcely have been separated, for in many other groups of birds distinctions so slight are regarded as barely evidence of local races.

Strigops and *Nestor*; but he began by making two great divisions of those that he did know, separating the parrots of the Old World from the parrots of the New, and subdividing each of these divisions into various sections somewhat in accordance with the names they had received in popular language—a practice he followed on many other occasions, for it seems to have been with him a belief that there is more truth in the discrimination of the unlearned than the scientific are apt to allow. In 1867-1868 Dr O. Finsch published at Leiden an elaborate monograph of the parrots,[4] regarding them as a family, in which he admitted 26 genera, forming 5 subfamilies: (1) that composed of *Strigops* (KAKAPO), only; (2) that containing the crested forms or cockatoos; (3) one which he named *Sittacinae*, comprising all the long-tailed species—a somewhat heterogeneous assemblage, made up of MACAWS (*q.v.*) and what are commonly known as parakeets; (4) the parrots proper with short tails; and (5) the so-called "brush-tongued" parrots, consisting of the LORIES (*q.v.*) and NESTORS (*q.v.*). In 1874 A. H. Garrod communicated to the Zoological Society the results of his dissection of examples of 82 species of parrots, which had lived in its gardens, and these results were published in its *Proceedings* for that year (pp. 586-598, pls. 70, 71). Summarily expressed, Garrod's scheme was to divide the parrots into two families, *Palaeornithidae* and *Psittacidae*, assigning to the former three subfamilies, *Palaeornithinae*, *Cacatuinae* and *Stringopinae*, and to the latter four, *Arinae*, *Pyrrhurinae*, *Platycercinae* and *Chrysotinae*. That each of these sections, except the *Cacatuinae*, is artificial any regard to osteology would show. In the *Journal für Ornithologie* for 1881 A. Reichenow published a *Conspectus Psittacorum*, founded, as several others [5] have been, on external characters only. He makes 9 families of the group, and recognizes 45 genera, and 442 species, besides subspecies. His grouping is generally very different from Garrod's, but displays as much artificiality: for instance, *Nestor* is referred to the family which is otherwise composed of the cockatoos.

The system now generally accepted is based on a combination of external and anatomical characters, and is due to Count T. Salvadori (*Cat. Birds, Brit. Mus.* XX., 1891), and H. F. Gadow (Bronn's *Thier-Reich, Aves*, 1893). About 80 genera with more than 500 species are recognized, divided into the family *Psittacidae* with the subfamilies *Stringopinae*, *Psittacinae* and *Cacatuinae*, and the family *Trichoglossidae* with the subfamilies *Cyclopsittacinae*, *Loriinae* and *Nestorinae*.

The headquarters of parrots are in the Australian Region and the Malay countries; they are abundant in South America; in Africa and India the number of forms is relatively small; in Europe and North Asia there are none now alive, in North America only one. Parrots are gregarious and usually feed and roost in companies, but are at least temporarily monogamous. Most climb and walk well; the flight is powerful but low and undulating in most. The food is varied but chiefly vegetable, whilst parrots are alone amongst birds in holding the food in the claws. The usual cry is harsh and discordant, but many softer notes are employed. A large number of forms learn in captivity to talk and whistle, the well-known red-tailed grey parrot (*Psittacus erithacus*) of tropical Africa being pre-eminent. The eggs are laid usually in holes in trees, rocks, or the ground, no lining being formed. The larger species produce one to three, the smaller as many as twelve, the colour being dull white. The young when hatched are naked and helpless. (A. N.)

PARROT-FISHES, more correctly called PARROT-WRASSES, marine fishes of the family *Scaridae* closely allied to the wrasses or *Labridae*. The family contains eight genera of which the principal are *Scarus*, *Pseudoscarus*, *Odax* and *Sparisoma*. They are easily recognized by their large scales, of which there are from twenty-one to twenty-five in the lateral line, by having invariably nine spines and ten rays in the dorsal fin and two spines with eight rays in the anal, and especially by their singular

[4] *Die Papageien, monographisch bearbeitet.*

[5] Such, for instance, as Kuhl's treatise with the same title, which appeared in 1820, and Wagler's *Monographia Psittacorum*, published in 1832—both good of their kind and time.

dentition, of jaws as well as pharynx. The teeth of the jaws are soldered together, and form a sharp-edged beak similar to that of a parrot, but without a middle projecting point, and the upper and lower beak are divided into two lateral halves by a median suture. In a few species the single teeth can be still distinguished, but in the majority (*Pseudoscarus*) they are united into a homogeneous substance with polished surface. By this sharp and hard beak parrot-fishes are enabled to bite or scrape off those parts of coral-stocks which contain the polypes or to cut off branches of tough fucus, which in some of the species forms the principal portion of their diet. The process of triturating the food is performed by the pharyngeal teeth, which likewise are united, and form plates with broad masticatory surfaces, not unlike the grinding surface of the molars of the elephant. Of these plates there is one pair above, opposed to and fitting into the single one which is coalesced to the lower pharyngeal bone. The contents of the alimentary canal, which are always found to be finely divided and reduced to a pulp, prove the efficiency of this triturating apparatus; in fact, ever since the time of Aristotle it has been maintained that the *Scarus* ruminates. Nearly one hundred species of parrot-fishes are known from the tropical and sub-tropical parts of the Indo-Pacific and Atlantic Oceans; like other coral-feeding fishes, they are absent on the Pacific coasts of tropical America and on the coast of tropical West Africa. The most celebrated is the *Scarus* of the Mediterranean. Beautiful colours prevail in this group of wrasses, but are subject to great changes and variations in the same species, almost all are evanescent and cannot be preserved after death. The majority of parrot-fishes are eatable, some even esteemed; but they (especially the carnivorous kinds) not unfrequently acquire poisonous properties after they have fed on corals or medusae containing an acrid poison. Many attain to a considerable size, upwards of 3 ft. in length.

PARRY, SIR CHARLES HUBERT HASTINGS, BART., English musical composer (1848–   ), second son of Thomas Gambier Parry, of Highnam Court, Gloucester, was born at Bournemouth on the 27th of February 1848. He was educated at Malvern, Twyford, near Winchester, Eton (from 1861), and Exeter College, Oxford. While still at Eton he wrote music, two anthems being published in 1865; a service in D was dedicated to Sir John Stainer. He took the degree of Mus.B. at Oxford at the age of eighteen, and that of B.A. in 1870; he then left Oxford for London, where in the following year he entered Lloyd's, abandoning business for art soon afterwards. He studied successively with H. H. Pierson (at Stuttgart), Sterndale Bennett and Macfarren; but the most important part of his artistic development was due to Edward Dannreuther. Among the larger works of this early period must be mentioned an overture, *Guillem da Cabestanh* (Crystal Palace, 1879), a pianoforte concerto in F sharp minor, played by Dannreuther at the Crystal Palace and Richter concerts in 1880, and his first choral work, the *Scenes from Prometheus Unbound*, produced at the Gloucester Festival, 1880. These, like a symphony in G given at the Birmingham Festival of 1882, seemed strange even to educated hearers, who were confused by the novelty of treatment. It was not until his setting of Shirley's ode, *The Glories of our Blood and State*, was brought out at Gloucester, 1883, and the *Partita* for violin and pianoforte was published about the same time, that Parry's importance came to be realized. With his sublime eight-part setting of Milton's *Blest Pair of Sirens* (Bach Choir, 1887) began a fine series of compositions to sacred or semi-sacred words. In *Judith* (Birmingham, 1888), the *Ode on St Cecilia's Day* (Leeds, 1889), *L'Allegro ed il penseroso* (Norwich, 1890), *De Profundis* (Hereford, 1891), *The Lotus Eaters* (Cambridge, 1892), *Job* (Gloucester, 1892), *King Saul* (Birmingham, 1894), *Invocation to Music* (Leeds, 1895), *Magnificat* (Hereford, 1897), *A Song of Darkness and Light* (Gloucester, 1898), and *Te Deum* (Hereford, 1900), are revealed the highest qualities of music. Skill in piling up climax after climax, and command of every choral resource, are the technical qualities most prominent in these works; but in his orchestral compositions, such as the three later symphonies, in F, C and E minor,

in two suites, one for strings alone, and above all in his *Symphonic Variations* (1897), he shows himself a master of the orchestra, and his experiments in modification of the conventional classical forms, such as appear in the work last named, or in the *Nineteen Variations for Pianoforte Solo*, are always successful. His music to *The Birds* of Aristophanes (Cambridge, 1883) and *The Frogs* (Oxford, 1892) are striking examples of humour in music; and that to *Agamemnon* (Cambridge, 1900) is among the most impressive compositions of the kind. His chamber music, exquisite part-songs and solo songs maintain the high standard of his greater works. At the opening of the Royal College of Music in 1883 he was appointed professor of composition and of musical history, and in 1894, on the retirement of Sir George Grove, Parry succeeded him as principal. He was appointed Choragus of Oxford University in 1883, succeeding Stainer in the professorship of the university in 1900. He received the honorary degree of Mus.D. at Cambridge 1883, Oxford 1884, Dublin 1891; and was knighted in 1898. Outside the domain of creative music, Parry's work for music was of the greatest importance: as a contributor of many of the most important articles on musical forms, &c., in Grove's dictionary, his literary work first attracted attention; in his *Studies of Great Composers* musical biography was treated, almost for the first time, in a really enlightened and enlightening way; and his *Art of Music* is a splendid monument of musical literature, in which the theory of evolution is applied to musical history with wonderful skill and success.

PARRY, SIR WILLIAM EDWARD (1790–1855), English rear-admiral and Arctic explorer, was born in Bath on the 19th of December 1790, the son of a doctor. At the age of thirteen he joined the flag-ship of Admiral Cornwallis in the Channel fleet as a first-class volunteer; in 1806 became a midshipman, and in 1810 was promoted to the rank of lieutenant in the "Alexander" frigate, which was employed for the next three years in the protection of the Spitzbergen whale-fishery. He took advantage of this opportunity for the study and practice of astronomical observations in northern latitudes, and afterwards published the results of his studies in a small volume on *Nautical Astronomy by Night* (1816). From 1813–1817 he served on the North American station. In 1818 he was given the command of the "Alexander" brig in the Arctic expedition under Captain (afterwards Sir) John Ross. This expedition returned to England without having made any new discoveries but Parry, confident, as he expressed it, "that attempts at Polar discovery had been hitherto relinquished just at a time when there was the greatest chance of succeeding," in the following year obtained the chief command of a new Arctic expedition, consisting of the two ships "Griper" and "Hecla." This expedition returned to England in November 1820 after a voyage of almost unprecedented Arctic success (see POLAR REGIONS), having accomplished more than half the journey from Greenland to Bering Strait, the completion of which solved the ancient problem of a North-west Passage. A narrative of the expedition, entitled *Journal of a Voyage to discover a North-west Passage*, appeared in 1821. Upon his return Lieutenant Parry was promoted to the rank of commander. In May 1821 he set sail with the "Fury" and "Hecla" on a second expedition to discover a North-west Passage, but was compelled to return to England in October 1823 without achieving his purpose. During his absence he had in November 1821 been promoted to post rank, and shortly after his return he was appointed acting hydrographer to the navy. His *Journal of a Second Voyage*, &c., appeared in 1824. With the same ships he undertook a third expedition on the same quest in 1824, but was again unsuccessful, and the "Fury" being wrecked, he returned home in October 1825 with a double ship's company. Of this voyage he published an account in 1826. In the following year he obtained the sanction of the Admiralty for an attempt up the North Pole from the northern shores of Spitzbergen, and his extreme latitude of 82° 45′ N. lat. remained for 49 years the highest latitude attained. He published an account of this journey under the title of *Narrative of the Attempt to reach the*

North Pole, &c. (1827). In April 1829 he was knighted. He was subsequently selected for the post of comptroller of the newly created department of steam machinery of the Navy, and held this office until his retirement from active service in 1846, when he was appointed captain-superintendent of Haslar Hospital. He attained the rank of rear-admiral in 1852, and in the following year became a governor of Greenwich Hospital, and retained this post till his death on the 8th of July 1855. The religious side of Sir Edward Parry's character was strongly marked, and besides the journals of his different voyages he was also the author of a *Lecture to Seamen*, and *Thoughts on the Parental Character of God.*

See *Memoirs of Rear-Admiral Sir W. E. Parry*, by his son, Rev. Edward Parry (3rd ed., 1857).

PARRY (from Fr. *parer*, to ward off), to turn aside a blow from a weapon. The term is used especially of a defensive movement of the sword or foil in fencing, hence, by transference, to ward off any attack, to turn aside an objectionable question. (See FENCING, &c.)

PARSEES, or PARSIS, the followers in India of Zoroaster (Zarathustra), being the descendants of the ancient Persians who emigrated to India on the conquest of their country by the Arabs in the 8th century. They first landed at Sanjan on the coast of Gujarat, where the Hindu rulers received them hospitably. To this day their vernacular language is Gujarati, which they have cultivated in literature and journalism. Their settlement in Bombay dates only from the British occupation of that island. In 1901 the total number of Parsees in all India was 94,000, of whom all but 7000 were found in the Bombay presidency and the adjoining state of Baroda, the rest being widely scattered as traders in the large towns.

Among Parsees the men are well formed, active, handsome and intelligent. They have light olive complexions, a fine aquiline nose, bright black eyes, a well-turned chin, heavy arched eyebrows, thick sensual lips, and usually wear a light curling moustache. The women are delicate in frame, with small hands and feet, fair complexions, beautiful black eyes, finely arched eyebrows, and a profusion of long black hair, which they dress to perfection, and ornament with pearls and gems. The Parsees are much more liberal in their treatment of women than any other Asiatic race; they allow them to appear freely in public, and leave them the entire management of household affairs.

The characteristic costume of the Parsees (now frequently abandoned) is loose and flowing, very picturesque in appearance, and admirably adapted to the climate in which he lives. The head is covered with a turban, or a cap of a fashion peculiar to the Parsees; it is made of stiff material, something like the European hat, without any rim, and has an angle from the top of the forehead backwards. It would not be respectful to uncover in presence of an equal, much less of a superior. The colour is chocolate or maroon, except with the priests, who wear a white turban.

A Parsee must be born upon the ground floor of the house, as the teachings of their religion require life to be commenced in humility, and by " good thoughts, words and actions " alone can an elevated position be attained either in this world or the next. The mother is not seen by any member of the family for forty days. Upon the seventh day after the birth an astrologer is invited to cast the nativity of the child. He has first to enumerate the names which the child may bear, so that the parents may make choice of one of them. Then he draws on a wooden board a set of hieroglyphs in chalk, and his dexterity in counting or recounting the stars under whose region or influence the child is declared to be born is marvelled at by the superstitious creatures thronging around him. This document is preserved in the family archives as a guidance and encouragement to the child through life. At the age of seven or thereabouts, according to the judgment of the priest, the first religious ceremony is performed upon the young Parsee. He is first subjected to the process of purification, which consists of an ablution with *nirang* (cow-urine). The ceremony consists in investing him with the *kusti*, or girdle of his faith. This is a cord,

woven by women of the priestly class, composed of seventy-two threads, representing the seventy-two chapters of the *Yasna*, a portion of the Zend-Avesta, in the sacredness of which the young neophyte is figuratively bound. The priest ties the cord around the waist as he pronounces the benediction upon the child, throwing upon his head at each sentence slices of fruit, seeds, perfumes and spices. He is thus received into the religion of Zoroaster, and is henceforth considered morally accountable for his acts. If a child die before the performance of this ceremony he is considered to have gone back to Ahura-Mazda, who gave him, as pure as he entered into this world, having not reached the age of accountability.

The marriages of children engage the earliest attention of the parents. The wedding day having been fixed by an astrologer, who consults the stars for a happy season, a Parsee priest goes from house to house with a list of the guests to be invited, and delivers the invitations with much ceremony. The father of the bride waits upon near relatives and distinguished personages, soliciting the honour of their attendance. A little before sunset a procession is formed at the house of the bridegroom, and proceeds with a band of music, amid great pomp and ceremony, to the house of the bride's father. Here a number of relatives and friends are collected at the door to receive the bridegroom with due honour. Presents are sent before, according to the time-honoured custom of the East. Upon the arrival of the procession at the house of the bride the gentlemen gallantly remain outside, leaving room for the ladies to enter the house as the escort of the bridegroom. As he passes the threshold his future mother-in-law meets him with a tray filled with fruits and rice, which she strews at his feet. The fathers of the young couple are seated side by side, and between them stands the priest ready to perform the ceremony. The young couple are seated in two chairs opposite each other, their right hands tied together by a silken cord, which is gradually wound around them as the ceremony progresses, the bride in the meantime being concealed with a veil of silk or muslin. The priest lights a lamp of incense, and repeats the nuptial benediction first in Zend and then in Sanskrit. At the conclusion of the ceremony they each throw upon the other some grains of rice, and the most expeditious in performing this feat is considered to have got the start of the other in the future control of the household, and receives the applause of the male or female part of the congregation as the case may be. The priest now throws some grains of rice upon the heads of the married pair in token of wishing them abundance; bouquets of flowers are handed to the assembled guests, and rose-water is showered upon them. The bride and bridegroom now break some sweetmeats, and, after they have served each other, the company are invited to partake of refreshments. At the termination of this feast the procession re-forms, and with lanterns and music escorts the bridegroom back to his own house, where they feast until midnight. As midnight approaches they return to the house of the bride, and escort her, with her dowry, to the house of the bridegroom, and, having delivered her safely to her future lord and master, disperse to their respective homes. Eight days afterwards a wedding feast is given by the newly-married couple, to which only near relatives and particular friends are invited. This feast is composed entirely of vegetables, but at each course the wine is served, and toasts are proposed, as " happiness to the young couple," &c.

The funeral ceremonies of the Parsees are solemn and imposing. When the medical attendant declares the case hopeless a priest advances to the bed of the dying man, repeats sundry texts of the Zend-Avesta, the substance of which tends to afford him consolation, and breathes a prayer for the forgiveness of his sins. After life is extinct a funeral sermon is delivered by the priest, in which the deceased is made the subject of an exhortation to his relatives and friends to live pure, holy and righteous lives, so that they may hope to meet again in paradise. The body is then taken to the ground floor where it was born, and, after being washed and perfumed, is dressed in clean white clothes, and laid upon an iron bier. A dog is brought in to take a last look at his inanimate master in order to drive away the evil spirits. This ceremony is called *sogdâd*. A number of priests attend and repeat prayers for the repose of the soul of the departed. All the male friends of the deceased go to the door, bow down, and raise their two hands from the floor to their heads to indicate their respect for the departed. The body, when put upon the bier, is covered over from head to foot. Two attendants bring it out of the house, holding it low in their hands, and deliver it to four pall-bearers, called *nasasalâr*, clad in well-washed, white clothes. A procession is formed by the male friends of the deceased, headed by a number of priests in full dress, to follow the body to the *dakhma*, or "tower of silence." In Bombay these towers are erected in a beautiful garden on the highest point of Malabar Hill, amid trees swarming with vultures; they are constructed of stone, and rise some 25 ft. high, with a small door at the side for the entrance of the body. Upon arriving at the "tower of silence" the bier is laid down, and prayers are said in the *sogrî*, or house of prayer, containing a fire-sanctuary, which is erected near the entrance to the garden. The attendants then raise the body to its final resting-place, lay it upon its stony bed, and retire. A round pit about 6 ft. deep is surrounded by an annular stone pavement about 7 ft. wide, on which the body is exposed to the vultures, where it is soon denuded of flesh, and the bones fall through an iron grating into a pit beneath, from which they are afterwards removed into a subterranean entrance prepared for their reception. On the third day after death an assemblage of the relatives and friends of the deceased takes place at his late residence, and thence proceed to the *Atish-bahrâm*, or "fire-temple." The priests stand before the urns in which the celestial fire is kept burning, and recite prayers for the soul of the departed. The son or adopted son of the deceased kneels before the high-priest, and promises due performance of all the religious duties and obsequies to the dead. The relatives and friends then hand the priest a list of the contributions and charities which have been subscribed in memory of the deceased, which concludes the ceremony of "rising from mourning," or "the resurrection of the dead." On each successive anniversary of the death of a Parsee funeral ceremonies are performed in his memory. An iron framework is erected in the house, in which shrubs are planted and flowers cultivated to bloom in memory of the departed. Before the frame, on iron stands, are placed copper or silver vases, filled with water and covered with flowers. Prayers are said before these iron frames two or three times a day. These ceremonies are called *mûklad*, or "ceremonies of departed souls."

The Parsees of India are divided into two sects, the Shenshahis and the Kadmis. They do not differ on any point of faith; the dispute is confined to a quarrel as to the correct chronological date for the computation of the era of Yazdegerd, the last king of the Sassanian dynasty, who was dethroned by the caliph Omar about A.D. 640. The difference has been productive of no other inconvenience than arises from the variation of a month in the celebration of the festivals. The Parsees compute time from the fall of Yazdegerd. Their calendar is divided into twelve months of thirty days each; the other five days, being added for holy days, are not counted. Each day is named after some particular angel of bliss, under whose special protection it is passed. On feast days a division of five watches is made under the protection of five different divinities. In midwinter a feast of six days is held in commemoration of the six periods of creation. About the 21st of March, the vernal equinox, a festival is held in honour of agriculture, when planting begins. In the middle of April a feast is held to celebrate the creation of trees, shrubs and flowers. On the fourth day of the sixth month a feast is held in honour of Sahrêvar, the deity presiding over mountains and mines. On the sixteenth day of the seventh month a feast is held in honour of Mithra, the deity presiding over and directing the course of the sun, and also a festival to celebrate truth and friendship. On the tenth day of the eighth month a festival is held in honour of Farvardin, the deity who presides over the departed souls of men. This day is especially set apart for the performance of ceremonies for the dead. The people attend on the hills where the "towers of silence" are situated, and perform in the *sogrîs* prayers for the departed souls. The Parsee scriptures require the last ten days of the year to be spent in doing deeds of charity, and in prayers of thanksgiving to Ahurâ-Mazdâ. On the day of Yazdegerd, or New Year's Day, the Parsees emulate the western world in rejoicing and social intercourse. They rise early, and after having performed their prayers and ablutions dress themselves in a new suit of clothes, and sally forth to the "fire-temples," to worship the emblem of their divinity, the sacred fire, which is perpetually burning on the altar. Unless they duly perform this ceremony they believe their souls will not be allowed to pass the bridge "Chinvad," leading to heaven. After they have performed their religious services they visit their relations and friends, when the ceremony of *hamijur*, or joining hands, is performed. The ceremony is a kind of greeting by which they wish each other "a happy new year." Their relatives and friends are invited to dinner, and they spend the rest of the day in feasting and rejoicing; alms are given to the poor, and new suits of clothes are presented to servants and dependants.

There are only two distinct classes among the Parsees—the priests (*dastûrs*, or high priests; *mobeds*, or the middle order; and *herbads*, or the lowest order) and the people (*behadîn*, *behdîn*, or "followers of the best religion"). The priestly office is hereditary, and no one can become a priest who was not born such; but the son of a priest may become a layman.

The secular affairs of the Parsees are managed by an elective committee, or *panchâyat*, composed of six *dastûrs* and twelve *mobeds*, making a council of eighteen. Its functions resemble the Venetian council of ten, and its objects are to preserve unity, peace and justice amongst the followers of Zoroaster. One law of the *panchâyat* is singular in its difference from the custom of any other native community in Asia; nobody who has a wife living shall marry another, except under peculiar circumstances, such as the barrenness of the living wife, or her immoral conduct. Recently a serious difference arose among the Parsees of Bombay on the question of proselytism. A Parsee had married a French lady, who took the necessary steps to adopt the religion of her husband. But it was decided by the High Court, after prolonged argument, that, though the creed of Zoroaster theoretically admitted proselytes, their admission was not consistent with the practice of the Parsees in India.

Their religion teaches them benevolence as the first principle, and no people practise it with more liberality. A beggar among the Parsees is unknown, and would be a scandal to the society. The sagacity, activity and commercial enterprise of the Parsees are proverbial in the East, and their credit as merchants is almost unlimited. In this connexion may be mentioned the well-known names of Sir Jamsetjee Jeejeebhoy and Sir Dinshaw Petit, both baronets, and also of J. N. Tata, founder of the Institute of Scientific Research at Bangalore.

The Parsees have shown themselves most desirous of receiving the benefits of an English education; and their eagerness to embrace the science and literature of the West has been conspicuous in the wide spread of female education, and in the activity shown in studying their sacred writings in critical texts. In recent years many have taken to the professions of law and medicine, and a Parsee barrister was appointed a judge of the High Court at Bombay in 1906. Two Parsees have also been the only natives of India elected to the House of Commons.

See Menant, *Les Parsis* (Paris, 1898); Dosabhai Framji Karaka, *History of the Parsees* (London, 1884); Seervai and Patel, *Gujarat Parsees from the Earliest Times* (Bombay, 1898).

PARSIFAL BELL-INSTRUMENT (Ger. *Parsifal 'Klavier Instrument*), a stringed instrument ingeniously constructed by Schweisgut, of Carlsruhe, from Dr Mottl's design, as a substitute for the church bells in Wagner's *Parsifal*. This instrument has been constructed somewhat on the principle of the grand piano; the massive frame is shaped like a billiard table. There are five notes, each with six strings, three in unison giving the fundamental note and three an octave higher. The strings are struck by large hammers, covered with cotton-wool, which the performer sets in motion by a strong elastic blow from his fist. The hammers are attached to arms 22 in. long, screwed to a strong wooden span bridge placed horizontally above the strings at about two-fifths of the length from the front. On the point of the arm is the name of the note, and behind this the felt ledge struck by the fist. Two belly bridges and two wrest-plank bridges, one set for each octave, determine the vibrating length of the strings, and the belly bridge, as in other stringed instruments, is the medium through which the vibrations of the strings are communicated to the soundboard. The arrangement of pegs and wrest-pins is much the same as on the piano.

The realism demanded by modern dramatic music taxes the resources of the orchestra to the utmost when the composer aims at reproducing on the stage the effect of church bells, as, for instance, in the *Golden Legend*, *Cavalleria rusticana*, *Pagliacci*, *Rienzi* and *Parsifal*. The most serious difficulty of all arose in the last-mentioned drama, where the solemnity of the scene and its deep religious significance demand a corresponding atmosphere on the stage. Real church bells for the notes Wagner has scored in the familiar chime would overpower the orchestra. All substitutes for bells were tried in vain; no other instrument, leaving aside the question of pitch, gave a tone in the least similar to that of the bell. Independently of the rich harmonics composing the clang, the bell has two distinct simultaneous notes, first the *tap* tone, which gives the pitch, and the *hum* tone or lower accompanying note. On the interval separating the hum from the tap tone depend the dignity and beauty of the bell tone and the emotional atmosphere produced. A stringed instrument, similar to the one here described but with four notes only, was used at Bayreuth for the first performance of *Parsifal*, and with it tam-tams or gongs, but after many trials the following combination was adopted as the best makeshift: (1) the stringed instrument with four keys; (2) four tam-tams or gongs tuned to the pitch of the four notes composing the chime; (3) a bass-tuba, which plays the notes staccato in quavers to help make them more distinct; (4) a fifth tam-tam, on which a roll is executed with a drumstick.

The special peal of hemispherical bells constructed for Sir A. Sullivan's *Golden Legend* is the only other successful substitute known to the writer; the lowest of these bells is a minor tenth higher than the lowest note required for *Parsifal*, and the aggregate weight of the four bells is 11 cwt. The bells are struck with mallets and have both tap and hum tone.   (K. S.)

PARSIMONY, LAW OF (Lat. *parsimonia*, from *parcere*, to save), the name given to William of Occam's principle "Entia non sunt multiplicanda praeter necessitatem," *i.e.* that it is scientifically unsound to set up more than one hypothesis at once to explain a phenomenon. This principle is known as "Occam's razor" (see OCCAM, WILLIAM OF).

PARSLEY, a hardy biennal herb known botanically as *Petroselinum sativum* (natural order Umbelliferae), the leaves of which are much used for garnishing and flavouring. It occurs as a garden escape in waste places in Britain and it is doubtful if it is known anywhere as a truly wild plant; A. de Candolle, however (*Origin of Cultivated Plants*) considers it to be wild in the Mediterranean region. It grows best in a partially shaded position, in good soil of considerable depth and not too light; a thick dressing of manure should be given before sowing. For a continuous supply three sowings should be made, as early in February as the weather permits, in April or early in May and in July—the last for the winter supply in a sheltered position with southern exposure. Sow thinly in drills from 12 to 15 in. apart and about 1 in. deep; thin out to 3 in. and finally to 6 in. each. In winter the plants should be protected by frames or hand-glasses. The curled and mossy-leaved varieties are preferable. The Hamburg or turnip-rooted variety is grown for the root, which is cut up and used for flavouring.

PARSNIP, botanically known as *Pastinaca sativa* (or *Peucedanum sativum*), a member of the natural order Umbelliferae, found wild in roadsides and waste places in England and throughout Europe and temperate Asia, and as an introduced plant in North America. It has been cultivated since the time of the Romans for the sake of its long fleshy whitish root, which has a peculiar but agreeable flavour. It succeeds best on a free sandy

loam, which should be trenched and manured in the previous autumn, the manure being well buried. The seed should be sown thinly in March, in rows 15 to 18 in. apart, and finally thinned out to 1 ft. apart. The leaves will decay in October or November, when a portion of the roots may be taken up and stored in dryish sand for immediate use, the rest being left in the ground, to be taken up as required, but the whole should be removed by February to a dry cool place, or they will begin to grow. The best sorts are the Hollow-crowned, the Maltese and the Student. Dusting the ground with soot when sowing the seed and again when the leaves appear will keep the plants free from pests.

PARSON, a technical term in English law for the clergyman of the parish. It is a corruption of *persona*, the parson being, as it were, the *persona ecclesiae*, or representative of the Church in the parish. Parson imparsonee (*persona impersonata*) is he that as rector is in possession of a church parochial, and of whom the church is full, whether it be presentative or impropriate (Coke upon Littleton, 300 *b*). The word parson is properly used only of a rector. A parson must be in holy orders; hence a lay rector could not be called a parson. There are four requisites to the appointment of a parson, viz. holy orders, presentation, institution and induction. The parson is tenant for life of the parsonage house, the glebe, the tithes and other dues, so far as they are not appropriated.

See also RECTOR; VICAR; BENEFICE; and TITHES.

PARSONS (or PERSONS), **ROBERT** (1546–1610), English Jesuit and political agitator, son of a blacksmith, was born at Nether Stowey, Somerset, on the 24th of June 1546. The vicar of the parish gave him instruction and procured his entrance in 1563 as an exhibitioner to Balliol College, Oxford. He graduated B.A. in 1568, and M.A. in 1572. He was fellow, bursar and dean of his college, but in 1574 he resigned or was dismissed his fellowship and offices, for reasons which have been disputed, some alleging improprieties of conduct, and others suspected disloyalty. Soon after his resignation he went to London, and thence in June to Louvain, where he entered the Roman Catholic Church and spent some time in the company of Father William Good, a Jesuit. In July 1575 he entered the Jesuit Society at Rome. In 1580 he was selected, along with Edmund Campion, a former associate at Oxford, and others, to undertake a secret religious and political mission to England. The two emissaries engaged in political intrigue in England and on the Continent. In 1581 Campion was arrested, but Parsons made his escape to Rouen, whence he returned to Rome, where he continued to direct the English mission. In 1588 he went to Spain, where he remained for nine years, founding seminaries for the training of English priests at Valladolid, Lucar, Seville, Lisbon and St Omer. On the death of Cardinal Allen in 1594 he made strenuous efforts to be appointed his successor. He failed in this, but was made rector of the English college at Rome in 1597, and died there on the 18th of April 1610

Parsons was the author of over 30 polemical writings, mostly tracts. Among the more important are *Certayne Reasons why Catholiques refuse to goe to Church* (Douai, 1580), *A Christian Directorie guiding Men to their Saluation* (London, 1583–1591, 2 parts), *A Conference about the Next Succession to the Crowne of England* (1594), *Treatise of the Three Conversions of England* (1603–1604, 3 parts), an answer to Foxe's *Acts and Monuments*. For portrait, see *Gentleman's Magazine*, lxiv.

PARSONS, THEOPHILUS (1750–1813), American jurist, was born in Byfield, Massachusetts, on the 24th of February 1750, the son of a clergyman. He graduated from Harvard College in 1769, was a schoolmaster at Falmouth (now Portland), Maine, in 1770–1773, studied law, and was admitted to the bar in 1774. In 1800 he removed to Boston. He was chief justice of the supreme court of Massachusetts from 1806 until his death in Boston on the 30th of October 1813. In politics he took an active part as one of the Federalist leaders in the state. He was a member of the Essex County convention of 1778, called to protest against the proposed state constitution, and as a member of the "Essex Junto" was probably the author of *The Essex*

Result, which helped to secure the rejection of the constitution at the polls. He was a member of the state constitutional convention of 1779-1780, and one of the committee of twenty-six which drafted the constitution; he was also a delegate to the state convention of 1788 which ratified the Federal Constitution; and according to tradition was the author of the famous " Conciliatory Resolutions," or proposed amendments to the constitution, which did much to win over Samuel Adams and John Hancock to the side of ratification. His *Commentaries on the Laws of the United States* (1836) contains some of his more important legal opinions.

His son THEOPHILUS PARSONS (1797-1882), who was Dane professor of law at Harvard from 1848 to 1870, is remembered chiefly as the author of a series of useful legal treatises, and some books in support of Swedenborgian doctrines; he wrote a life of his father (Boston, 1859).

PARSONS, a city of Labette county, in south-eastern Kansas, U.S.A., situated at the junction of the Big and Little Labette creeks, about 138 m. S. by W. of Kansas City. Pop. (1890), 6736; (1900), 7682, of whom 807 were negroes; (1905), 11,720; (1910), 12,463. It is served by the Kansas City, Fort Scott & Memphis (St Louis & San Francisco system) and the Missouri Kansas & Texas railways. The city has large machine shops of the Missouri Kansas & Texas railway and various manufactures. Natural gas is utilized for light and heat. The first settlement on the site of the city was made in 1869 and was called Mendota (" place of meeting "—*i.e.* of the creeks). In 1871 the city was chartered, and in 1910 government by commission went into effect. It was named in honour of Levi Parsons (1822-1887), the first president of the Missouri Kansas and Texas railway.

PARTABGARH, or PERTABGARH, a native state of India, in the Rajputana agency. Area, 886 sq. m.; pop. (1901), 52,025, showing a decrease of 40% in the decade, owing to the effects of famine. The inhabitants are mostly Bhils and other aboriginal tribes. Estimated revenue, £12,000. The town of Partabgarh (pop., 9819) is connected by a metalled road (20 m.) with the station of Mandasor on the Rajputana railway. It has a reputation for a special kind of enamelled jewelry.

PARTABGARH, PERTABGARH, or PRATAPGARH, a district of British India in the Fyzabad division of the United Provinces. The administrative headquarters are at Bela. Area, 1442 sq. m.; pop. (1901), 912,848. The Ganges forms the south-western boundary line, while the Gumti forms the eastern boundary for a few miles. The only mineral products are salt, saltpetre and *kankar* or nodular limestone. The principal crops are rice, barley, pulse, millets, sugar-cane and poppy. The district is traversed by the branch of the Oudh & Rohilkhand railway from Rae Bareilly to Benares, opened in 1898. There are manufactures of sugar and a little silk; and grain, opium, oil-seeds, hemp and hides are exported.

See *Partabgarh District Gazetteer* (Allahabad, 1904).

PARTERRE, a term, taken from the French phrase *par terre, i.e.* on the surface of the ground, and used of an arrangement in a garden of beds of flowers with gravel or other paths and plots of grass; also of that part of the auditorium of a theatre which is occupied by the orchestra stalls.

PARTHENAY, a town of western France, capital of an arrondissement in the department of Deux-Sèvres, 27 m. N.N.E. of Niort, on the railway between that town and Saumur. Pop. (1906), 5615. The town retains considerable portions of its fine 13th-century ramparts, including the Porte St Jacques, a fortified gateway guarding an old bridge over the Thouet. Amongst ancient buildings of interest are the church of Ste Croix, of the 12th century, restored in 1885, with a 15th-century belfry; the church of St Laurent, also restored in modern times, portions of whose walls date from the 11th century; the ruined Romanesque portal of Notre-Dame de la Couldre; and 1 m. south-west of the town the ancient church (12th century) of Parthenay-le-Vieux. The manufacture of woollen goods and wool-spinning are the principal local industries.

PARTHENIUS, of Nicaea in Bithynia, Greek grammarian and poet. He was taken prisoner in the Mithradatic War and

carried to Rome (72 B.C.); subsequently he visited Neapolis, where he taught Virgil Greek. Parthenius was a writer of elegies, especially dirges, and of short epic poems. The pseudo-Virgilian *Moretum* and *Ciris* were imitated from his Μυττωτός and Μεταμορφώσεις. His Ἐρωτικὰ παθήματα is still extant, containing a collection of 36 love-stories which ended unhappily, taken from different historians and poets. As Parthenius generally quotes his authorities, these stories are valuable as affording information on the Alexandrian poets and grammarians.

See E. Martini in *Mythographi graeci*, vol. ii. (1902, in Teubner Series); poetical fragments in A. Meineke, *Analecta alexandrina* (1843).

PARTHENON (Παρθενών), the name generally given, since the 4th century B.C., to the chief temple of Athena on the Acropolis at Athens (*e.g.* Demosthenes, *c. Androt.* 13, 76). The name is applied in the official inventories of the 5th and early 4th centuries to one compartment of the temple, and this was probably its original meaning. It is certainly to be associated with the cult of Athena Parthenos, "the Virgin," though it is not clear why the name was given to this particular chamber.

The most convenient position for a temple upon the natural rock-platform of the Acropolis was occupied by the early temple of Athena. When it was decided to supersede this by a larger and more magnificent temple, it was necessary to provide a site for this new temple by means of a great substructure, which is on its south side about 40 ft. high. This substructure was not

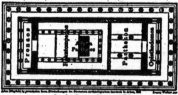

built for the present temple, but for an earlier one, which was longer and narrower in shape; there has been much discussion as to the date of this earlier temple; F. C. Penrose maintained that it was the work of Peisistratus. Some have thought that it dated from the time immediately after the Persian wars; but the fact that portions of its columns and entablature, damaged by fire, were built into the north wall of the Acropolis by Themistocles seems to prove that it dates from the 6th century, whether it be the work of the tyrants or of the renewed democracy under Cleisthenes.

The extant temple was the chief among the buildings with which Pericles adorned the Acropolis. The supervision of the whole work was in the hands of Pheidias, and the architects of the temple were Ictinus and Callicrates. The actual building was not begun until 447 B.C., though the decision to build was made ten years earlier (Keil, *Anonymus argentorensis*). The temple must have been structurally complete by the year 438 B.C., in which the gold and ivory statue of Athena Parthenos was dedicated; but the work of decoration and finish was still going on in 433 B.C. The temple as designed by Ictinus was about 15 ft. shorter and about 6 ft. wider than the building for which the foundations were intended; it thus obtained a proportion of length to breadth of exactly 9:4. It is the most perfect example of the Doric order (see ARCHITECTURE: *Greek*). The plan of the temple was peculiar. The cella, which was exactly 100 ft. long, kept the name and traditional measurement of the old Hecatompedon. It was surrounded on three sides by a Doric colonnade, and in the middle of it was the great basis on which the statue was erected. This cella was probably lighted only by the great doorway and by the light that filtered through the marble tiles. The common notion that there was a hypaethral opening is erroneous. At the back of the cella was a square chamber, not communicating with it, but entered from the west end of the temple; this was the Parthenon in the narrower sense. It seems to have been used only as a store-house, though it may have been originally intended for a more important purpose. The Prodomus and the Opisthodomus were enclosed by bronze gratings fixed between the columns, and were thus adapted to contain valuable offerings and other treasures. We have inventories on marble of the contents of these four compartments of the temple. The opisthodomus, in particular, probably served as a treasury for sacred and other money, though it has been disputed whether the opisthodomus mentioned in the inscriptions is part of the Parthenon or another building.

For the sculptures decorating the Parthenon and the statue by Pheidias in the cella, see article GREEK ART. The metopes over the outer colonnade were all sculptured, and represented on the east the battle of gods and giants, on the west, probably, the battle of Greeks and Amazons, on the south Greeks and Centaurs; those on the north are almost lost. The east pediment represented the birth of Athena, the west pediment her contest with Poseidon for the land of Attica. The frieze, which was placed above the cella wall at the sides, represented the Panathenaic procession, approaching on three sides the group of gods seated in the middle of the east side. These sculptures are all of them admirably adapted to their position on the building, and are, in themselves, the most perfect works that sculpture has ever produced.

The Parthenon probably remained intact until the 5th century of our era, when the colossal statue was removed, and the temple is said to have been transformed into a church dedicated to St Sophia. In the 6th century it was dedicated to the Virgin Mother of God (Θεοτόκος). The adaptation of the building as a church involved the removal of the inner columns and roof, the construction of an apse at the east end, and the opening of a door between the cella and the chamber behind it. These alterations involved some damage to the sculptures. In 1456 Athens was captured by the Turks, and the Parthenon was consequently changed into a mosque, apparently without any serious structural alterations except the addition of a minaret. In this state it was described by Spon and Wheler in 1676 and the sculpture was drawn by the French artist Carrey in 1674. In 1687 the Turks used the building as a powder magazine during the bombardment of the Acropolis by a Venetian army under Morosini, and a shell caused the explosion which blew out the middle of the temple and threw down the columns at the sides. Still further damage to the sculptures was done by Morosini's unsuccessful attempt to lower from the west pediment the chariot of Athena. Later a small mosque was constructed in the midst of the ruins; but nothing except gradual damage is to be recorded during the succeeding century except the visits of various travellers, notably of James Stuart (1713-1788) and Nicholas Revett (1720-1804), whose splendid drawings are the best record of the sculpture as it existed in Athens. In 1801 Lord Elgin obtained a firman authorizing him to make casts and drawings, and to pull down extant buildings where necessary, and to remove sculpture from them. He caused all the remains of the sculpture to be found on the ground or in Turkish houses, and a certain amount—notably the metopes—that was still on the temple, to be transported to England. Some fault has been found with his methods or those of his workmen; but there is no doubt that the result was the preservation of much that would otherwise have been lost. The Elgin marbles were bought by the British government in 1816, and are now in the British Museum. Certain other sculptures from the Parthenon are in the Louvre, Copenhagen or elsewhere, and much is still in Athens, either still on the temple or in the Acropolis museum.

The most accurate measurements of the temple, showing the exactness of its construction and the subtlety of the curvature of all its lines, was made by F. C. Penrose.

AUTHORITIES.—A. Michaelis, der Parthenon (Leipzig, 1871); J. Stuart and N. Revett, Antiquities of Athens (London, 1762-1815); F. C. Penrose, Principles of Athenian Architecture (London, 1851 and 1888); A. S. Murray; The Sculptures of the Parthenon (London, 1903); British Museum, Catalogue of Sculpture, vol. 1. See also GREEK ART. ·   (E. GR.)

PARTHIA, the mountainous country S.E. of the Caspian Sea, which extends from the Elburz chain eastwards towards Herat, and is bounded on the N. by the fertile plain of Hyrcania (about Astrabad) at the foot of the mountains in the corner of the Caspian and by the Turanian desert; on the S. by the great salt desert of central Iran. It corresponds to the modern Khorasan. It was inhabited by an Iranian tribe, the Parthava of the inscriptions of Darius; the correct Greek form is Παρθυαῖοι. Parthia became a province of the Achaemenian and then of the Macedonian Empire. Seleucus I. and Antiochus I. founded Greek towns: Soteira, Charis, Achaea, Calliope (Appian, Syr. 57; Plin. vi. 15; cf. Strabo xi. 516); the capital of Parthia is known only by its Greek name Hecatompylos (" The Hundred-gated ") from the many roads which met there (Polyb. x. 28), and was, according to Appian, founded by Seleucus I. (cf. Curtius vii. 2). In 208 many Greek inhabitants are found in the towns of Parthia and Hyrcania (Polyb. x. 31, 11).

When about 255 B.C. Diodotus had made himself king of Bactria (q.v.) and tried to expand his dominions, the chieftain of a tribe of Iranian nomads (Dahan Scyths) east of the Caspian, the Parni or Aparni, who bore the Persian name Arsaces, fled before him into Parthia.[1] Here the satrap Andragoras appears to have shaken off the Seleucid supremacy, as he struck gold and silver coins in his own name, on which he wears the diadem, although not the royal title (Gardner, Numism. Chronicle, 1879-1881). In Justin xii. 4, 12, Andragoras is wrongly made satrap of Alexander, of Persian origin, and ancestor of Arsaces. He was slain by Arsaces (Justin xli. 4), who occupied Parthia and became the founder of the Parthian kingdom. The date 248 B.C. given by the list of the Olympionicae in Euseb. Chron. i. 207; and in his Canon, ii. 120 (cf. Appian, Syr. 65; Justin, xli. 4, gives wrongly 256 B.C.), is confirmed by numerous Babylonian tablets dated simultaneously by the Seleucid and Arsacid eras (cf. Mahler, in Wiener Zeitschrift für die Kunde des Morgenlands, 1901, xv. 57 sqq.; Lehmann Haupt in Beiträge zur alten Geschichte, 1905, v. 128 sqq.). The origin and early history of the Parthian kingdom, of which we possess only very scanty information, is surrounded by fabulous legends, narrated by Arrian in his Parthica (preserved in Photius, cod. 58, and Syncellus, p. 539 seq.). Here Arsaces and his brother Tiridates are derived from the royal house of the Achaemenids, probably from Artaxerxes II.; the young Tiridates is insulted by the prefect Agathocles or Pherecles; in revenge the brothers with five companions (corresponding to the seven Persians of Darius) slay him, and Arsaces becomes king. He is killed after two years and succeeded by his brother Tiridates, who reigns 37 years. There is scarcely anything historical in this account, perhaps not even the name Tiridates, for, according to the older tradition, Arsaces himself ruled for many years. The troubles of the Seleucid empire, and the war of Seleucus II. against Ptolemy III. and his own brother Antiochus Hierax, enabled him not only to maintain himself in Parthia, but also to conquer Hyrcania; but he was constantly threatened by Diodotus of Bactria (Justin xli. 4). When, about 238 B.C., Seleucus II. was able to march into the east, Arsaces fled to the nomadic tribe of the Aspasiacae (Strabo xi. 513; cf. Polyb. x. 48). But Seleucus was soon recalled by a rebellion in Syria, and Arsaces returned victorious to Parthia; " the day of this victory is celebrated by the Parthians as the beginning of their independence " (Justin xli. 4). Arsaces was proclaimed king at Asaak in the district of Astauene, now Kuchan in the upper Atrek (Attruck) valley (Isidor. Charac.), and built his residence Dara on a rock in a fertile valley in Apavarktikene (Justin xli. 5; Plin. vi. 46), now Kelat still farther eastward; the centre of his power evidently lay on the borders of eastern Khorasan and the Turanian desert. The principal institutions of the Parthian kingdom

[1] Strabo xi. 515; cf. Justin xli. 4; the Parni are said by Strabo [ibid.] to have immigrated from southern Russia, a tradition wrongly transferred to the Parthians themselves by Justin xli. 1, and Arrian ap. Phot. cod. 58.

were created by him (cf. Justin xli. 1). The Scythian nomads became the ruling race; they were invested with large landed property, and formed the council of the king, who appointed the successor. They were archers fighting on horseback, and in their cavalry consisted the strength of the Parthian army; the infantry were mostly slaves, bought and trained for military service, like the janissaries and mamelukes. But these Scythians soon amalgamated with the Parthian peasants. They adopted the Iranian religion of Zoroaster (in the royal town Asaak an eternal fire was maintained), and " their language was a mixture of Scythian and Median " (i.e., Iranian). Therefore their language and writing are called by the later Persians " Pehlevi," i.e. Parthian (Pehlevi is the modern form of Parthawu) and the magnates themselves Pehlevans, i.e. " Parthians," a term transferred by Firdousí to the heroes of the old Iranian legend. But the Arsacid kingdom never was a truly national state; with the Scythian and Parthian elements were united some elements of Greek civilisation. The successors of Arsaces I. even founded some Greek towns, and when they had conquered Babylonia and Mesopotamia they all adopted the epithet " Philhellen."

To Arsaces I. probably belong the earliest Parthian coins; the oldest simply bear the name Arsaces; others, evidently struck after the coronation in Asaak, have the royal title (βασιλέως Ἀρσάκου). The reverse shows the seated archer, or occasionally an elephant; the head of the king is beardless and wears a helmet and a diadem; only from the third or fourth king they begin to wear a beard after the Iranian fashion. In honour of the founder of the dynasty all his successors, when they came to the throne, adopted his name and officially (e.g. on the coins) are almost always called Arsaces, whereas the historians generally use their individual names.

Of the successors of Arsaces I. we know very little. His son, Arsaces II., was attacked by Antiochus III., the Great, in 209, who conquered the Parthian and Hyrcanian towns but at last granted a peace. The next king, whom Justin calls Priapatius, ruled 15 years (about 190-175); his successor, Phraates I., subjected the mountainous tribe of the Mardi (in the Elburz). He died early, and was succeeded not by one of his sons but by his brother, Mithradates I., who became the founder of the Parthian empire. Mithradates I. (c. 170-138) had to fight hard with the Greeks of Bactria, especially with Eucratides (q.v.); at last he was able to conquer a great part of eastern Iran. Soon after the death of Antiochus IV. Epiphanes (163) he conquered Media, where he refounded the town of Rhagae (Rai near Teherān) under the name of Arsacia; and about 141 he invaded Babylonia. He and his son Phraates II. defeated the attempts of Demetrius II. (139) and Antiochus VII. (129) to regain the eastern provinces, and extended the Arsacid dominion to the Euphrates.

For the later history of the Parthian empire reference should be made to PERSIA: Ancient History, and biographical articles on the kings. The following is a list of the kings, as far as it is possible to establish their succession.

The names of pretenders not generally acknowledged are put in brackets.

Arsaces I.	248-c. 211
(perhaps Tiridates I.)	
Arsaces II. . . .	.c. 211-190
Priapatius	.c. 190-175
Phraates I. . . .	.c. 175-170
Mithradates I. . .	.c. 170-138
Phraates II. . . .	.c. 138-127
Artabanus I. . . .	.c. 127-124
Mithradates II. the	
Great	.c. 124-88 [1]
Sanatruces I. . . .	. 76-70
Phraates III. . . .	. 70-57
Orodes I. . . .	. 57-37
(Mithradates III. .	. 57-54)
Phraates IV. . . .	. 37-2
(Tiridates II. . 32-31 and 26)
Phraates V. (Phra-	
taces) . . . .2 B.C.-A.D. 5
Orodes II. . . . . A.D. 5-7

Vonones I. . . .	8-11
Artabanus II. . .	. c. 10-40
(Tiridates III. . .	. 36)
(Cinnamus . . .	. 38)
(Vardanes I. . .	. 40-45)
Gotarzes . . .	. 40-51
Vonones II. . . .	. 51
Vologaeses I. . .	. 51-77
(Vardanes II. . .	. 55)
Vologaeses II. . 77-79; 111-147
Pacorus . . .	. 78-c. 105
Artabanus III. . .	. 80-81)
Osroes . . .	106-129
(Mithradates IV. and his son
Sanatruces II. 115; Partha-
maspates, 116-117; and other
pretenders.)
Mithradates V. . . c. 129-147
Vologaeses III. . . 147-191

Vologaeses IV.	.	191-209	Artabanus IV. . . 209-229
(Vologaeses V.	.	209-c. 222)	

AUTHORITIES.—Persian tradition knows very little about the Arsacids, who by it are called Ashkanians (from Ashak, the modern form of Arsaces.) Of modern works on the history of the Parthians (besides the numismatic literature) the most important are: G. Rawlinson, The Sixth Oriental Monarchy (1873), and A. von Gutschmid, Geschichte Irans und seine Nachbarländer von Alexander d. Gr. bis zum Untergang der Arsaciden (1888).

The principal works on the Arsacid coinage are (after the earlier publications of Longpérier, Prokesch-Ostan, &c.): Percy Gardner, The Parthian Coinage (London, 1877), and especially W. Wroth, Catalogue of the Coins of Parthia in the British Museum (London, 1903), who carefully revised the statements of his predecessors. Cf. also Petrowicz, Arsacidenmünzen (Vienna, 1904), and Allotte de la Fuye, " Classement des monnaies arsacides," in Revue numismatique, 4 série, vol. viii., 1904.

(ED. M.)

PARTICK (formerly Perdyc or Perthick), a municipal and police burgh of the parish of Govan, Lanarkshire, Scotland. Pop. (1891), 36,558; (1901), 54,298. It lies on the north bank of the Clyde, and is continuous with Glasgow, from which it is separated by the Kelvin, and of which it is a large and wealthy residential suburb. Shipbuilding yards are situated in the burgh, which has also industries of paper-staining, flour-milling, hydraulic-machine making, weighing-machine making, brass-founding and galvanizing. The tradition is that the flour-mills and granaries —the Bunhouse Mills—as they are called locally, were given by the Regent Moray to the bakers of Glasgow for their public spirit in supplying his army with bread at the battle of Langside in 1568. Victoria Park contains a grove of fossil trees which were discovered in a quarry. The town forms the greater part of the Partick division of Lanarkshire, which returns one member to Parliament. Though it remained a village till the middle of the 19th century, it is an ancient place. Morken, the Pictish king who persecuted St Kentigern, is believed to have dwelt here and, in 1136, David I. gave the lands of Partick to the see of Glasgow. The bishop's palace stood by the side of the Kelvin, and was occupied—or a mansion erected for him on its site—by George Hutcheson (1580-1639), founder of the Hutcheson Hospital in the city.

PARTISAN, or PARTIZAN. (1) A thoroughgoing " party " man or adherent, usually in a depreciatory sense of one who puts his party before principles; (2) an irregular combatant or guerrilla soldier; (3) a weapon with a long shaft and a broad bladed head, of a type intermediate between the spear and the halberd (q.v.). In senses (1) and (2) the word is derived through the Fr. from Ital. partigiano, from parteggiare, to share, take part in, Lat. pars, part. The name for the weapon has also been attributed to the same origin, as being that used by " partisans," but there is no historical evidence for this. The form which the word now takes in French, pertuisane, has given rise to a connexion with " pertuis, hole; Lat. pertusus, pertundere, to strike through. But the most probable derivation is from the Teutonic parta, barta, axe, which forms the last part of " halberd."

PARTITION, in law, the division between several persons of land or goods belonging to them as co-proprietors. It was a maxim of Roman law, followed in modern systems, that in communione vel societate nemo potest invitus detineri. Partition was either voluntary or was obtained by the actio communi dividendo. In English law the term partition applies only to the division of lands, tenements and hereditaments, or of chattels real between coparceners, joint tenants or tenants in common. It is to be noticed that not all hereditaments are capable of partition. There can be no partition of homage, fealty, or common of turbary, or of an inheritance of dignity, such as a peerage. Partition is either voluntary or compulsory. Voluntary partition is effected by mutual conveyances, and can only be made where all parties are sui juris. Since the Real Property Act 1845, § 3, it must be made by deed, except in the case of copyholds. Compulsory partition is effected by private act of parliament, by judicial process, or through the inclosure commissioners. At common law none but coparceners were entitled to partition against the will of the rest of the proprietors, but the Acts of 31 Henry VIII. c. 1 and 32 Henry VIII. c. 32 gave a compulsory process to joint tenants and tenants in common of

---

[1] The names of the following kings are not known; that one of them was called Artabanus II. is quite conjectural.

freeholds, whether in possession or in reversion, by means of the writ of partition. In the reign of Elizabeth the court of chancery began to assume jurisdiction in partition, and the writ of partition, after gradually becoming obsolete, was finally abolished by the Real Property Limitation Act 1833. The court of chancery could not decree partition of copyholds until the passing of the Copyholds Act 1841. This act was repealed by the Copyholds Act 1894, which empowers the alienation of ancient tenements with the licence of the lord. By the Judicature Act 1873, § 34, partition is one of the matters specially assigned to the chancery division. An order for partition is a matter of right, subject to the discretion vested in the court by the Partition Act 1868 (amended by the Partition Act 1876). By § 3 of the act of 1868 the court may, on the request of a party interested, direct a sale instead of a partition, if a sale would be more beneficial than a partition. By § 12 a county court has jurisdiction in partition where the property does not exceed £500 in value. Under the powers of the Inclosure Act 1845, and the acts amending it, the Inclosure commissioners have power of enforcing compulsory partition among the joint owners of any inclosed lands. An order of the inclosure commissioners or a private act vests the legal estate, as did also the old writ of partition. But an order of the chancery division only declares the rights, and requires to be perfected by mutual conveyances so as to pass the legal estate. Where, however, all the parties are not *sui juris*, the court may make a vesting order under the powers of the Trustee Act 1850, § 30.

Partition is not a technical term of Scots law. In Scotland division of common property is effected either extra-judicially, or by action of declarator and division or division and sale in the court of session, or (to a limited extent) in the sheriff courts. Rights of common are not divisible in English law without an act of parliament or a decree of the inclosure commissioners, but in Scotland the act of 1695, c. 38, made all commonties, except those belonging to the king or royal burghs, divisible, on the application of any having interest, by action in the court of session. By the Sheriff Courts (Scotland) Act 1877, § 8, the action for division of common property or commonty is competent in the sheriff court, when the subject in dispute does not exceed in value £50 by the year, or £1000 value. Runrig lands, except when belonging to corporations, were made divisible by the act of 1695, c. 23. A decree of division of commonty, common property, or runrig lands has the effect of a conveyance by the joint proprietors to the several participants (Conveyancing [Scotland] Act 1874, § 35).

In the United States, "it is presumed," says Chancellor Kent, (4 *Comm.*, lect. liv.), "that the English statutes of 31 & 32 Henry VIII. have been generally re-enacted and adopted, and probably with increased facilities for partition." In a large majority of the states, partition may be made by a summary method of petition to the courts of common law. In the other states the courts of equity have exclusive jurisdiction. As between heirs and devisees the probate courts may in some states award partition. The various state laws with regard to partition will be found in Washburn, *Real Property*, bk. i. ch. xiii., § 7.

PARTNERSHIP (earlier forms, *partener*, *parcener*, from Late Lat. *partionarius* for *partitionarius*, from *partitio*, sharing, *pars*, part), in general, the voluntary association of two or more persons for the purpose of gain, or sharing in the work and profits of any enterprise. This general definition, however, requires to be further restricted, in law, according to the account given below.

The partnership of modern legal systems is based upon the *societas* of Roman law. *Societas* was either *universorum bonorum*, a complete communion of property; *negotiationis alicujus*, for the purpose of a single transaction; *vectigalis*, for the collection of taxes; or *rei unius*, joint ownership of a particular thing. The prevailing form was *societas universorum quae ex quaestu veniunt*, or trade partnership, from which all that did not come under the head of trade profit (*quaestus*) was excluded. This kind of *societas* was presumed to be contemplated in the absence of proof that any other kind was intended. *Societas* was a consensual contract, and rested nominally on the consent of the parties—really, no doubt (though this was not in terms acknowledged by the Roman jurists), on the fact of valuable consideration moving from each partner. No formalities were necessary for the constitution of a *societas*. Either property or labour must be contributed by the *socius*; if one

party contributed neither property nor labour, or if one partner was to share in the loss but not in the profit (*leonina societas*), there was no true *societas*. Societas was dissolved on grounds substantially the same as those of English law (see below). The only ground peculiar to Roman law was change of *status* (*capitis deminutio*). Most of the Roman law on the subject of *societas* is contained in *Dig.* xvii. tit. 2, *Pro socio*.

Though the English law of partnership is based upon Roman law, there are several matters in which the two systems differ. (1) There was no limit to the number of partners in Roman law. (2) In *societas* one partner could generally bind another only by express *mandatum*; one partner was not regarded as the implied agent of the others. (3) The debts of a *societas* were apparently joint, and not joint and several. (4) The *heres* of a deceased partner could not succeed to the rights of the deceased, even by express stipulation. There is no such disability in England. (5) In actions between partners in Roman law, the *beneficium competentiae* applied—that is, the privilege of being condemned only in such an amount as the partner could pay without being reduced to destitution. (6) The Roman partner was in some respects more strictly bound by his fiduciary position than is the English partner. For instance, a Roman partner could not retire in order to enjoy alone a gain which he knew was awaiting him. (7) There was no special tribunal to which matters arising out of *societas* were referred.

Previous to the Partnership Act 1890 the English law of partnership was to be found only in legal decisions and in textbooks. It was mostly the result of judge-made law, and as distinguished from the law of joint stock companies was affected by comparatively few acts of parliament.

In 1890 the Partnership Act of that year was passed to declare and amend the law of partnership; the act came into operation on the 1st of January 1891. With one important exception (§ 23), it applies to the whole United Kingdom. It is not a complete code of partnership law; it contains no provisions regulating the administration of partnership assets in the event of death or bankruptcy, and is silent on the subject of goodwill. The existing rules of equity and common law continue in force, except so far as they are inconsistent with the express provisions of the act. Indeed, the act of 1890 has to be read in the light of the decisions which have built up these rules. On all points specifically dealt with by the act it is now the one binding authority. The act has made no important changes in the law, except in respect of the mode of making a partner's share of the partnership assets available for payment of his separate debts. This change does not affect Scotland. The act is divided into the four main divisions mentioned below.

I. *Nature of Partnership.*—Partnership is defined to be the "relation which subsists between persons carrying on a business in common with a view of profit." From this definition corporations and companies, such as joint-stock companies and cost-book mining companies, which differ from ordinary partnerships in many important respects, are expressly excluded. The act also contains several subsidiary rules for determining the existence of a partnership. These rules are of a fragmentary nature, and for the most part are expressed in a negative form; they have not introduced any change in the law. Co-ownership of property does not of itself create a partnership, nor does the sharing of gross returns. The sharing of profits, though not of itself sufficient to create a partnership, is prima facie evidence of one. This means that if all that is known is that two persons are sharing profits, the inference is that such persons are partners; but if the participation in profits is only one amongst other circumstances, all the circumstances must be considered, and the participation in profits must not be treated as raising a presumption of partnership, which has to be rebutted. To illustrate the rule that persons may share profits without being partners, the act gives statutory expression to the decision in *Cox v. Hickman* (1860, 8 H.L.C., 268), viz. that the receipt by a person of a debt or other fixed sum by instalments, or otherwise, out of the accruing profits of a business does not of itself make him a partner; and it re-enacts with some slight modification the repealed provisions of Bovill's Act (28 & 29 Vict. c. 86), which was passed to remove certain difficulties arising from the decision in *Cox v. Hickman*. Whenever the question of partnership or no partnership arises, it must not be forgotten (though this is not stated in the act) that partnership is a relation arising out of a contract; regard must be paid to the true contract and intention of the parties as appearing from the whole facts of the case. If a partnership be the legal consequence of the true agreement, the parties thereto will be partners, though they may have intended to avoid this consequence (*Adam v. Newbigging*, 1888, L.R. 13 App. Cas. 315). Partners are called collectively a "firm"; the name under which they carry on business is called the firm name. Under English law the firm is not a corporation, nor is it recognized as distinct from the members composing it; any change amongst them destroys the identity of the firm. In Scotland a firm is a legal person distinct from its members, but each partner can be compelled to pay its debts.

At common law there is no limit to the number of partners, but by the Companies Act 1862 (25 & 26 Vict. c. 89, § 4), not more than ten persons can carry on the business of bankers, and not more than twenty any other business, unless (with some exceptions) they conform to the provisions of the act. (See COMPANY, and also *Limited Partnerships* below.)

II. *Relations of Partners to Persons dealing with them.*— Every partner is an agent of the firm and of his co-partners for the purpose of the partnership business; if a partner does an act for carrying on the partnership business in the usual way in which businesses of a like kind are carried on—in other words, if he acts within his apparent authority—he thereby prima facie binds his firm. The partners may by agreement between themselves restrict the power of any of their number to bind the firm. If there be such an agreement, no act done in contravention of it is binding on the firm with respect to persons who have notice of the agreement. Such an agreement does not affect persons who have no notice of it, unless indeed they do not know or believe the person with whom they are dealing to be a partner; in that case he has neither real, nor, so far as they are concerned, apparent authority to bind his firm, and his firm will not be bound. If a partner does an act, *e.g.* pledges the credit of the firm, for a purpose apparently not connected with the firm's ordinary course of business, he is not acting in pursuance of his apparent authority, and whatever liability he may personally incur, his partners will not be bound unless he had in fact authority from them.

Apart from any general rule of law relating to the execution of deeds or negotiable instruments, a firm and all the partners will be bound by any act relating to the business of the firm, and done in the firm name, or in any other manner showing an intention to bind the firm; by any person thereto authorised. An admission or representation by a partner, acting within his apparent authority, is evidence against his firm. Notice to an acting partner of any matter relating to the partnership affairs is, apart from fraud, notice to his firm.

A firm is liable for loss or injury caused to any person not a partner, or for any penalty incurred by any wrongful act or omission of a partner acting in the ordinary course of the partnership business, or with the authority of his co-partners; the extent of his liability is the same as that of the individual partner. The firm is also liable to make good the loss (a) where one partner, acting within his apparent authority, receives money or property of a third person and misapplies it; and (b) where a firm in the course of its business receives money or property of a third person, and such money or property while in the custody of the firm is misapplied by a partner. It is not sufficient, in order to fix innocent partners with liability for the misapplication of money belonging to a third party, merely to show that such money was employed in the business of the partnership, otherwise all the members

of a firm would in all cases be liable to those beneficially interested therein for trust money improperly employed in this manner by one partner. This is not the case. To fix the other partners with liability, notice of the breach of trust must be brought home to them individually.

The liability of partners for the debts and obligations of their firm arising *ex contractu*, is joint, and in Scotland several also; the estate of a deceased partner is also severally liable in a due course of administration, but subject, in England or Ireland, to the prior payment of his separate debt. The liability of partners for the obligations of their firm arising *ex delicto*, is joint and several.

The authority of a partner to bind his co-partners commences with the partnership. A person therefore who enters into a partnership does not thereby become liable to the creditors of his partners for anything done before he became a partner. But a partner who retires from a firm does not thereby cease to be liable for debts or obligations incurred before his retirement. He may be discharged from existing liabilities by an agreement to that effect between himself and the members of the firm as newly constituted and the creditors. This agreement may be either express or inferred as a fact from the course of dealing between the creditors and the new firm. The other ways in which a partner may be freed from partnership liabilities incurred before his retirement are not peculiar to partnership liabilities, and are not therefore dealt with by the Partnership Act.

A continuing guaranty given to a firm, or in respect of the transactions of a firm, is, in the absence of agreement to the contrary, revoked as to the future by a change in the firm. The reason is that such a change destroys its identity.

Any person, not a partner in the firm, who represents himself (or, as the phrase is, "holds himself out"), or knowingly suffers himself to be represented, as a partner, is liable as a partner to any person who has given credit to the firm on the faith of the representation. The representation may be by words spoken or written, or by conduct. The liability will attach, although the person who makes the representation does not know that the person who has acted on it knew of it. The continued use of a deceased partner's name does not impose liability on his estate.

III. *Relations of Partners to one another.*—The mutual rights and duties of partners depend upon the agreement between them. Many of these rights and duties are stated in the Partnership Act; but, whether stated in the act or ascertained by agreement, they may be varied by the consent of all the partners; such consent may be express or inferred from conduct. Subject to any agreement, partners share equally in the capital and profits of their business, and must contribute equally to losses, whether of capital or otherwise; they are entitled to be indemnified by their firm against liabilities incurred in the proper and ordinary conduct of the partnership business, and for anything necessarily done for its preservation; they are entitled to interest at 5 % on their advances to the firm, but not on their capital. Every partner may take part in the management of the partnership business, but no partner is entitled to remuneration for so doing. The majority can bind the minority in ordinary matters connected with the partnership business, but cannot change its nature nor expel a partner, unless expressly authorized so to do. No partner may be introduced into the firm without the consent of all the partners. The partnership books must be kept at the principal place of business, and every partner may inspect and copy them. Partners must render to each other true accounts and full information of all things affecting the partnership. A partner may not make use of anything belonging to his firm for his private purposes, nor may he compete with it in business. If he does so he must account to his firm for any profit he may make.

Partners may agree what shall and what shall not be partnership property, and can by agreement convert partnership property into the separate property of the individual partners, and vice versa. Subject to any such agreement, all property originally brought into the partnership stock, or acquired on account of the firm or for the purposes and in the course of its business, is declared by the act to be partnership property. Property bought with money of the firm is prima facie bought on account of the firm. Partnership property must be applied exclusively for partnership purposes and in accordance with the partnership agreement. Co-owners of land may be partners in the profits of the land without the land being partnership property; if such co-owners purchase other lands out of the profits, these lands will also belong to them (in the absence of any agreement to the contrary) as co-owners and not as partners. The legal estate in partnership land devolves according to the general law, but in trust for the persons beneficially interested therein. As between partners, and as between the heirs of a deceased partner and his executors or administrators, such land is treated as personal or movable estate, unless a contrary intention appears.

When no fixed term has been agreed upon for the duration of the partnership, it is at will, and may be determined by notice at any time by any partner. If a partnership for a fixed term is continued after the term has expired without any express new agreement, the rights and duties of the partners remain as before, so far as they are consistent with a partnership at will.

A partner may assign his share in the partnership either absolutely or by way of mortgage. The assignee does not become a partner; during the continuance of the partnership he has the right to receive the share of profits to which his assignor would have been entitled, but he has no right to interfere in the partnership business, or to require any accounts of the partnership transactions, or to inspect the partnership books. On a dissolution he is entitled to receive the share of the partnership assets to which his assignor is entitled as between himself and his partners, and for this purpose to an account as from the date of dissolution.

Since the act came into operation no writ of execution may issue in England or Ireland against any partnership property, except on a judgment against the firm. If in either of these countries a judgment creditor of a partner wishes to enforce his judgment against that partner's share in the partnership, he must obtain an order of court charging such share with payment of his debt and interest. The court may appoint a receiver of the partner's share, and may order a sale of such share. If a sale be ordered the other partners may buy the share; they may also at any time redeem the charge. The mode of making a partner's share liable for his separate debts in Scotland has not been altered by the act.

IV. *Dissolution of Partnership.*—A partnership for a fixed term, or for a single adventure, is dissolved by the expiration of the term or the termination of the adventure. A partnership for an undefined time is dissolved by notice of dissolution, which may be given at any time by any partner. The death or bankruptcy of any partner dissolves the partnership as between all its members. If a partner suffers his share in the partnership to be charged under the act for his separate debts, his partners may dissolve the partnership. The foregoing rules are subject to any agreement there may be between the partners. A partnership is in every case dissolved by any event which makes the partnership or its business unlawful. The court may order a dissolution in any of the following cases, viz.: When a partner is found lunatic or is of permanently unsound mind, or otherwise permanently incapable of performing his duties as a partner; when a partner has been guilty of conduct calculated to injure the partnership business, or wilfully or persistently breaks the partnership agreement, or so conducts himself in partnership matters that it is not reasonably practicable for his partners to carry on business with him; when the partnership can only be carried on at a loss; and lastly, whenever a dissolution appears to the court to be just and equitable. The act is silent as to the effect of the assignment by a partner of his share in the partnership as a cause of dissolution; probably it is now no more than a circumstance enabling the court, if it thinks fit, to grant a dissolution on the ground that it is just

and equitable to do so. A dissolution usually is not complete as against persons who are not partners, until notice of it has been given; until then such persons may treat all apparent partners as still members of the firm. Consequently, if notice is not given when it is necessary, a partner may be made liable for partnership debts contracted after he ceased to be a partner. Notice is not necessary to protect the estate of a dead or bankrupt partner from partnership debts contracted after his death or bankruptcy; nor is notice necessary when a person not known to be a partner leaves a firm. If a person not generally known to be a partner is known to be so to certain individuals, notice must be given to them. Notice in the *Gazette* is sufficient as regards all persons who were not previously customers of the firm; notice in fact must be given to old customers. On a dissolution, or the retirement of a partner, any partner may notify the fact and require his co-partners to concur in doing so.

After a dissolution, the authority of each partner (unless he be a bankrupt) to bind the firm, and the other rights and obligations of the partners, continue so far as may be necessary to wind up the partnership affairs and to complete unfinished transactions. The partners are entitled to have the partnership property applied in payment of the debts of the firm, and to have any surplus divided between them. Before a partner can receive any part of the surplus, he must make good whatever may be due from him as a partner to the firm. To enforce these rights, any partner or his representatives may apply to the court to wind up the partnership business. It was well established before the act, and is still law, that in the absence of special agreement the right of each partner is to have the partnership property—including the goodwill of its business, if it be saleable—realized by a sale. The value of the goodwill depends largely on the right of the seller to compete with the purchaser after the sale. The act makes no mention of goodwill, but the rights of a seller in this respect were fully discussed in the House of Lords in *Trego* v. *Hunt* (L.R. 1896, App. Cas. 7). In the absence of special agreement, the seller may set up business in competition with, and in the immediate neighbourhood of, the purchaser, and advertise his business and deal with his former customers, but may not represent himself as carrying on his former business, nor canvass his former customers. The purchaser may advertise himself as carrying on the former business, canvass its customers, and trade under the old name, unless that name is or contains the name of the vendor, and the purchaser by using it without qualification would expose the vendor to the liability of being sued as a partner in the business. If, on a dissolution or change in the constitution of a firm, the goodwill belongs under the partnership agreement exclusively to one or more of the partners, the partner who is entitled to the goodwill has the rights of a seller, and those to whom the goodwill does not belong have the rights of a purchaser.

When a partner has paid a premium on entering into a partnership for a fixed term, and the partnership is determined before the expiration of the term, the court may, except in certain cases, order a return of the premium or of some part of it. In the absence of fraud or misrepresentation, the court cannot make such an order when the partnership was at will, or, being for a fixed term, has been terminated by death or by reason of the misconduct of the partner who paid the premium; nor can it do so if terms of dissolution have been agreed upon, and the agreement makes no provision for the return of premium.

When a person is induced by the fraud or misrepresentation of others to become a partner with them, the court will rescind the contract at his instance (*Adam* v. *Newbigging*, 1888, R. 13 App. Cas. 308). Inasmuch as such a person is under the same liability to third parties for liabilities of the firm incurred before rescission as he would have been under had the contract been valid, he is entitled on the rescission to be indemnified by the person guilty of the fraud or making the representation against these liabilities. He is also entitled, without prejudice to any other rights; to receive out of the surplus assets of the partnership, after satisfying the partnership liabilities, any money he may have paid as a premium or contributed as capital, and to stand in the place of the creditors of the firm for any payments made by him in respect of the partnership liabilities.

If a partner ceases to be a member of a firm, and his former partners continue to carry on business with the partnership assets without any final settlement of accounts, he, or, if he be dead, his estate, is, in the absence of agreement, entitled to such part of the subsequent profits as can be attributed to the use of his share of the partnership assets, or, if he or his representatives prefer it, to interest at 5% on the amount of his share. If his former partners have by agreement an option to purchase his share, and exercise the option and comply with its terms, he is not entitled to any further or other share in profits than that given him by the agreement. If, however, his former partners, assuming to exercise such an option, do not comply with its terms, they are liable to account for subsequent profits or interest to the extent mentioned above. Subject to any agreement between the partners, the amount due from the surviving or continuing partners to an outgoing partner, or the representatives of a deceased partner, in respect of his share in the partnership, is a debt accruing at the date of the dissolution or death.

In the absence of any special agreement on a final settlement of accounts between partners, losses (including losses of capital) are paid first out of profits, next out of capital, and lastly by the partners in the proportions in which they share profits. The assets of the firm, including all sums contributed to make up losses of capital, are applied in paying the debts and liabilities of the firm to persons who are not partners; then in paying to each partner rateably what is due from the firm to him, first for advances and next in respect of capital; and the ultimate residue (if any) is divisible among the partners in the proportion in which profits are divisible.

Limited Partnerships.—In the law of partnership as set out above, the Limited Partnership Act 1907 introduced a considerable innovation. By that act power was given to form limited partnerships, like the French *société en commandite*—that is, a partnership consisting not only of general partners, but of others whose liability is limited to the amount contributed to the concern. Such a limited partnership must not consist, in the case of a partnership carrying on the business of banking, of more than ten persons, and in the case of any other partnership of more than twenty persons. There must be one or more persons called general partners who are liable for all the debts and obligations of the firm, and limited partners, who on entering into partnership contribute a certain sum or property valued at a stated amount, beyond which they are not liable. Limited partners cannot withdraw or receive back any of their contributions; any withdrawal brings liability for the debts and obligations of the firm up to the amount withdrawn. A body corporate may be a limited partner. No limited partner can take part in the management of a partnership business; if he does so he becomes liable in the same way as a general partner, but he can at all times inspect the books of the firm and examine into the state and prospects of the business. Every limited partnership must be registered with the registrar of joint stock companies, and the following particulars must be given: (*a*) the firm name; (*b*) the general nature of the business; (*c*) the principal place of business; (*d*) the full name of each of the partners; (*e*) the term, if any, for which the partnership is entered into and the date of its commencement; (*f*) a statement that the partnership is limited, and the description of every limited partner as such; (*g*) the sum contributed by each limited partner, and whether paid in cash or how otherwise. If any change occurs in these particulars, a statement signed by the firm and specifying the nature of the change, must be sent within seven days to the registrar. An advertisement must also be inserted in the gazette of any arrangement by which a general partner becomes a limited partner or under

which the share of a limited partner is assigned. Any person making a false return for the purpose of registration commits a misdemeanour and is liable to imprisonment with hard labour for a term not exceeding two years. The law of private partnership applies to limited partners except where it is inconsistent with the express provisions of the Limited Partnership Act.

See Sir Nathaniel [Lord] Lindley, *A Treatise on the Law of Partnership* (7th ed., London, 1905); Sir Frederick Pollock, *A Digest of the Law of Partnership, incorporating the Partnership Act 1890* (8th ed., London, 1905); also article on "Partnership" in the *Encyclopaedia of the Laws of England*.

Scots Law.—The law of Scotland as to partnership agrees in the main with the law of England. The principal difference is that Scots law recognizes the firm as an entity distinct from the individuals composing it. The firm of the company is either proper or descriptive. A proper or personal firm is a firm designated by the name of one or more of the partners.[1] A descriptive firm does not introduce the name of any of the partners. The former may sue and be sued under the company name; the latter only with the addition of the names of three at least (if there are so many) of the partners. A consequence of this view of the company as a separate person is that an action cannot be maintained against a partner personally without application to the company in the first instance, the individual partners being in the position of cautioners for the company rather than of principal debtors. The provisions of the Mercantile Law Amendment Act 1856 (19 & 20 Vict. c. 60, § 8), do not affect the case of partners. But, though the company must first be discussed, diligence must necessarily be directed against the individual partners. Heritable property cannot be held in the name of a firm; it can only stand in the name of individual partners. Notice of the retirement of even a dormant partner is necessary. The law of Scotland draws a distinction between joint adventure and partnership. Joint adventure or joint trade is a partnership confined to a particular adventure or speculation, in which the partners, whether latent or unknown, use no firm or social name, and incur no responsibility beyond the limits of the adventure. In the rules applicable to cases of insolvency and bankruptcy of a company and partners, Scots law differs in several respects from English. Thus a company can be made bankrupt without the partners being made so as individuals. And, when both company and partners are bankrupt, the company creditors are entitled to rank on the separate estates of the partners for the balance of their debts equally with the separate creditors. But in sequestration, by the Bankruptcy Scotland Act 1856, § 66, the creditor of a company, in claiming upon the sequestrated estate of a partner, must deduct from the amount of his claim the value of his right to draw payment from the company's funds, and he is ranked as creditor only for the balance. (See Erskine's *Inst.* bk. iii. tit. iii.; Bell's *Comm.* ii. 500-562; Bell's *Principles*, §§ 350-403.)

United States.—In the United States the English common law is the basis of the law. Most states have, however, their own special legislation on the subject. The law in the United States permits the existence of limited partnerships, corresponding to the *sociétés en commandite* established in France by the ordinance of 1673, and those legalized in England under the act of 1907 (see above). The State of New York was the first to introduce this kind of partnership by legislative enactment. The provisions of the New York Act have been followed by most of the other states. In many states there can be no limited partnerships in banking and insurance. In this form of partnership one or more persons responsible *in solido* are associated with one or more dormant partners liable only to the extent of the funds supplied by them. In Louisiana such partnerships are called partnerships *in commendam* (Civil Code, art. 2810).

[1] In France, it is to be noted, the style of a firm must contain no names other than those of actual partners. In Germany it must, upon the first constitution of the firm, contain the name of at least one actual partner, and must not contain the name of any one who is not a partner; when once established the style of the firm may be continued notwithstanding changes.

In New York the responsible partners are called *general* partners, the others *special* partners. Such partnerships must, by the law of most states, be registered. In Louisiana universal partnerships (the *societates universorum bonorum* of Roman law) must be created in writing and registered (Civil Code, art. 2800). In some states the English law as it stood before *Cox v. Hickman* is followed, and participation in profits is still regarded as the test of partnership, *e.g. Leggett v. Hyde* (58 New York Rep. 272). In some states nominal partners are not allowed. Thus in New York, where the words "and Company" or "and Co." are used, they must represent an actual partner or partners. A breach of this rule subjects offenders to penalties. In most states claims against the firm after the death of a partner must, in the first instance, be made to the survivors. The creditors cannot, as in England, proceed directly against the representatives of the deceased. An ordinary partnership between miners for working a mine is not dissolved by the death of one of the partners, nor by the transfer by one of his interest in the concern. Contract is not deemed the basis of the relation between the partners, but rather a common property and co-operation in its exploitation (Parsons, *Principles of Partnership*, § 15). A corporation cannot become a partner in any mercantile adventure, unless specially authorized by charter or general statute. If it could, the management of its affairs would no longer be exclusively in the hands of its directors, to whom the law has entrusted it. Hence, corporations cannot associate for the formation of a "trust" to be managed by the associated partners.

See 3 Kent's *Comm.*, lect. xliii.; Story, *On Partnership*; Bates, *Law of Partnership* (1888); Burdick, *Law of Partnership* (1899).

PARTON, JAMES (1822–1891), American biographer, was born in Canterbury, England, on the 9th of February 1822. He was taken to the United States when he was five years old, studied in New York City and White Plains, New York, and was a schoolmaster in Philadelphia and then in New York. He removed (1875) to Newburyport, Massachusetts, where he died on the 17th of October 1891. Parton was the most popular biographer of his day in America. His most important books are *Life of Horace Greeley* (1855), *Life and Times of Aaron Burr* (1857), *Life of Andrew Jackson* (1859–1860), *Life and Times of Benjamin Franklin* (1864), *Life of Thomas Jefferson* (1874), and *Life of Voltaire* (1881). Among his other publications are *General Butler in New Orleans* (1863), *Famous Americans of Recent Times* (1867), *The People's Book of Biography* (1868); *Noted Women of Europe and America* (1883), and *Captains of Industry* (two series, 1884 and 1891, for young people. His first wife, Sara (1811–1872), sister of N. P. Willis, and widow of Charles H. Eldredge (d. 1846), attained considerable popularity as a writer under the pen-name "Fanny Fern." (See James Parton's *Fanny Fern: a Memorial Volume*, 1873). They were married in 1856. Her works include the novels, *Ruth Hall* (1854), reminiscent of her own life, and *Rose Clark* (1857); and several volumes of sketches and stories. In 1876 Parton married Ethel Eldredge, his first wife's daughter by her first husband.

PARTONOPEÜS DE BLOIS, hero of romance. The French romance of *Partonopeus de Blois* dates from the 12th century, and has been assigned, on the strength of an ambiguous passage in the prologue to his *Vie saint Edmund le rei* to Denis Piramus. The tale is, in its essence a variation of the legend of Cupid and Psyche. Partonopeus is represented as having lived in the days of Clovis, king of France. He was seized while hunting in the Ardennes, and carried off to a mysterious castle, the inhabitants of which were invisible. Melior, empress of Constantinople, came to him at night, stipulating that he must not attempt to see her for two years and a half. After successful fighting against the "Saracens," led by Sornegur, king of Denmark; he returned to the castle, armed with an enchanted lantern which broke the spell. The consequent misfortunes have a happy termination. The tale had a continuation giving the adventures of Fursin or Anselet, the nephew of Sornegur. The name of Partonopeus or Partonopex is generally assumed to be a corruption of Parthenopaeus; one of the seven against

Thebes. It has been suggested that the word might be derived from Partenay, a supposition coloured by the points of similarity between this story and the legend of Mélusine (see JEAN D'ARRAS) attached to the house of Lusignan, as the lords of these two places were connected.

BIBLIOGRAPHY.—The French romance was edited by G. A. Crapelet, with an introduction by A. C. M. Robert, as Partonopeus de Blois (2 vols., 1834); an English *Partonope of Blois*, by W. E. Buckley for the Roxburghe Club (London, 1862), and another fragment for the same learned society in 1873; the German *Partonopier und Melior* of Konrad von Würzburg by K. Bartsch (Vienna, 1871); the Icelandic *Partalópa saga* by O. Klockhoff in *Upsala Universitets Artskrift* for 1887. See also H. L. Ward, *Catalogue of Romances*, (i. 689, &c.); E. Kölbing, *Die verschiedenen Gestaltungen der Partono-peus-Sage*, in German. *Stud.* (vol. ii., Vienna, 1875), in which the Icelandic version is compared with the Danish poem *Persenober* and the Spanish prose *Historia del conde Partinobles*; E. Pfeiffer, "Über die HSS des Part. de Blois" in Stengel's *Ausg. in Abh. vom phil.* (No. 25, Marburg, 1885).

PARTRIDGE, JOHN BERNARD (1861–　), British artist, was born in London, son of Professor Richard Partridge, F.R.S., president of the Royal College of Surgeons, and nephew of John Partridge (1790–1872), portrait-painter extraordinary to Queen Victoria. He was educated at Stonyhurst College, and after matriculating at London University entered the office of Dunn & Hansom, architects. He then joined for a couple of years a firm of stained-glass designers (Lavers, Barraud & Westlake), learning drapery and ornament; and then studied and executed church ornament under Philip Westlake, 1880–1884. He began illustration for the press and practised water-colour painting, but his chief success was derived from book illustration. In 1892 he joined the staff of *Punch*. He was elected a member of the Royal Institute of Painters in Water-colours and of the Pastel Society. For some years he was well known as an actor under the name of "Bernard Gould."

PARTRIDGE, WILLIAM ORDWAY (1861–　), American sculptor, was born at Paris, France, on the 11th of April 1861. He received his training as a sculptor in Florence (under Galli), in Rome (under Welonski), and in Paris. He became a lecturer and writer, chiefly on art subjects, and from 1894 to 1897 was professor of fine arts in Columbian University (now the George Washington University), Washington, D.C. Among his publications are: *Art for America* (1894), *The Song Life of a Sculptor* (1894), *The Technique of Sculpture* (1895), *The Angel of Clay* (1900), a novel, and *Nathan Hale, the Ideal Patriot* (1902). His sculptural works consist largely of portraiture.

PARTRIDGE (Du. *Patrijs*, Fr. *perdrix*, from Lat. *perdix*, apparently onomatopoeic from the call of the bird), a game-bird, whose English name properly denotes the only species indigenous to Britain, often nowadays called the grey partridge, the *Perdix cinerea* of ornithologists. The excellence of its flesh at table has been esteemed from the time of Martial. For the sport of partridge-shooting see SHOOTING.

The common red-legged partridge of Europe, generally called the French partridge, *Caccabis rufa*, seems to be justifiably considered the type of a separate group. This bird was introduced into England in the last quarter of the 18th century, and has established itself in various parts of the country, notwithstanding a widely-spread, and in some respects unreasonable, prejudice against it. It has certainly the habit of trusting

The grey partridge has doubtless largely increased in numbers in Great Britain since the beginning of the 19th century, when so much down, heath, and moorland was first brought under the plough, for its partiality to an arable country is very evident. It has been observed that the birds which live on gravel lands or heather only are apt to be smaller and darker in colour than the average; but in truth the species when adult is subject to a much greater variation in plumage than is commonly supposed; and the well-known chestnut horse-shoe mark, generally considered distinctive of the cock, is very often absent. In Asia the grey partridge seems to be unknown, but in the temperate parts of Eastern Siberia its place is taken by a very nearly allied form, *P. barbata*, and in Tibet there is a bird, *P. hodgsoniae*, which can hardly with justice be generically separated from it.

nearly as much to its legs as to its wings, and thus incurred the obloquy of old-fashioned sportsmen, whose dogs it vexatiously kept at a running point; but, when it was also accused of driving away the grey partridge, the charge only showed the ignorance of those who brought it, for as a matter of fact the French partridge rather prefers ground which the common species avoids—such as the heaviest clay-soils or the most infertile heaths. The French partridge has several congeners, all with red legs and plumage of similar character. In Africa north of the Atlas there is the Barbary partridge, *C. petrosa*; in southern Europe another, *C. saxatilis*, which extends eastward till it is replaced by *C. chukar*, which reaches India, where it is a well-known bird. Two very interesting desert-forms, supposed to be allied to *Caccabis*, are the *Ammoperdix heyi* of North Africa and Palestine and the *A. bonhami* of Persia; but the absence of the metatarsal knob, or incipient spur, suggests (in our ignorance of their other osteological characters) an alliance rather to the genus *Perdix*. On the other hand the groups of birds known as Francolins and Snow-Partridges are generally furnished with strong but blunt spurs, and therefore probably belong to the Caccabine group. Of the former, containing many species, there is only room here to mention the francolin, which used to be found in many parts of the south of Europe, *Francolinus vulgaris*, which also extends to India, where it is known as the black partridge. This seems to have been the *Attagas* or *Attagen* of classical authors,[1] a bird so celebrated for its exquisite flavour, the strange disappearance of which from all or nearly all its European haunts still remains inexplicable. It is possible that this bird has been gradually vanishing for several centuries, and if so to this cause may be attributed the great uncertainty attending the determination of the *Attagen*—it being a common practice among men in all countries to apply the name of a species that is growing rare to some other that is still abundant. Of the snow-partridges, *Tetraogallus*, it is only to be said here that they are the giants of their kin, and that nearly every considerable range of mountains in Asia seems to possess its specific form.

By English colonists the name Partridge has been very loosely applied, and especially so in North America. Where a qualifying word is prefixed no confusion is caused, but without it there is sometimes a difficulty at first to know whether the Ruffed Grouse (*Bonasa umbellus*) or the Virginia Quail (*Ortyx virginianus*) is intended. In South America the name is given to various Tinamous (*q.v.*). (A. N.)

PARTY WALL, a building term which, in England, apart from special statutory definitions, may be used in four different legal senses (*Watson v. Gray*, 1880, 14 Ch. D. 192). It may mean (1) a wall of which the adjoining owners are tenants in common; (2) a wall divided longitudinally into two strips, one belonging to each of the neighbouring owners; (3) a wall which belongs entirely to one of the adjoining owners, but is subject to an easement or right in the other to have it maintained as a dividing wall between the two tenements; (4) a wall divided longitudinally into two moieties, each moiety being subject to a cross easement, in favour of the owner of the other moiety. Outside London the rights and liabilities of adjoining owners of party walls are subject to the rules of common law. In London they are governed by the London Building Act 1894. A tenant in common of a party wall is entitled to have a partition vertically and longitudinally, so as to hold separately (*Mayfair Property Co. v. Johnston*, 1894, 1 Ch. 508); each owner can then use only his own part of the wall. By the London Building Act 1894, § 5 (16) the expression "party wall" means—(*a*) a wall forming part of a building and used or constructed to be used for separation of adjoining buildings belonging to different owners, or occupied or constructed or adapted to be occupied by different persons; or (*b*) a wall forming part of a building, and standing to a greater extent than the projection of the footings on lands of different owners. Section 87 regulates the rights

of owners of adjoining lands to erect party walls on the line of junction. Sections 88–90 determine the rights of building owners to deal with party walls by underpinning, repairing or rebuilding. The act also contains provisions for settling disputes (§§ 91–92), and for bearing and recovering expenses (§§ 95–102). Part VI. of the act regulates the structure and thickness, height, &c., of party walls.

See A. R. Rudall, *Party Walls* (1907).

PARUTA, PAOLO (1540–1598), Venetian historian. After studying at Padua he served the Venetian republic in various political capacities, including that of secretary to one of the Venetian delegates at the Council of Trent. In 1579 he published a work entitled *Della Perfezione della vita politica*, and the same year he was appointed official historian to the republic, in succession to Luigi Contarini. He took up the narrative from where Cardinal Bembo had left it, in 1513, and brought it down to 1551. He was made *provveditore* to the Chamber of Loans in 1580, *savio del gran consiglio* in 1590, and governor of Brescia in the following year. In 1596 he was appointed *provveditore* of St Mark, and in 1597 superintendent of fortifications. He died a year later. His history, which was at first written in Latin and subsequently in Italian, was not published until after his death—in 1599. Among his other works may be mentioned a history of the War of Cyprus (1579–72?), and a number of political orations.

See Apostolo Zeno's edition of Paruta's history (in the series *Degli Istorici delle cose veneziane*, Venice, 1718), and C. Monzani's edition of Paruta's political works (Florence, 1852).

PARVIS, PARVISE, or **PARVYSE,** an open space surrounded by an enceinte or stone parapet in front of buildings, particularly cathedrals or large churches; probably first used to keep the people from pressing on and confusing the marshalling of processions. The word "parvis" is French and is a corruption of Lat. *paradisus*, an enclosed garden or paradise (*q.v.*), which is sometimes also used instead of "parvis." The Lat. *paradisus* is defined by Du Cange (*Glossarium*, s.v.) as *atrium porticibus circumdatum ante aedes sacras*. At St Paul's in London the "parvis" was a place where lawyers met for consultation.

PARYSATIS, daughter of Artaxerxes I., married to her brother Ochus (Ctesias, *Pers.* 44), who in 424 B.C. became king of Persia under the name of Darius II. (*q.v.*). She had great influence over her husband, whom she helped by perfidy in the suppression of his brothers Secydianus, who was king before him, and Arsites, who rebelled against him (Ctes. *Pers.* 48–51). Her favourite son was Cyrus the Younger, whom she assisted as far as possible in his attempt to gain the throne. But when he was slain at Cunaxa (401) she nevertheless gained absolute dominion over the victorious Artaxerxes II. She was the evil genius of his reign. By a series of intrigues she was able to inflict the most atrocious punishment on all those who had taken part in the death of Cyrus. (Ed. M.)

PASADENA, a city in the San Gabriel valley of Los Angeles county, in southern California, U.S.A., about 9 m. N.E. of Los Angeles and about 20 m. from the Pacific Ocean. Pop. (1880) 391; (1890) 4882; (1900) 9117, of whom 1278 were foreign-born; (1910 census) 30,291. Area about 11 sq. m. It is served by the Southern Pacific, the Santa Fé, and the San Pedro, Los Angeles & Salt Lake railway systems, and by interurban electric lines. The city lies at an altitude of 750–1000 ft., about 5 m. from the base of the Sierra Madre range. Some half-dozen mountain peaks in the immediate environs rise to heights of 3100 to more than 6000 ft., notably Mt Wilson (6666 ft.), whose base is about 5 m. north-east of Pasadena, Echo mountain (4016 ft.), and Mt Lowe (6100 ft.) From Rubio canyon, near Pasadena, to the summit of Echo mountain, runs a steep cable railway, 1000 yds. long. On Echo mountain is the Lowe Observatory (3500 ft.), with a 16-in. equatorial telescope, and on Mt Wilson is the Solar Observatory (5886 ft.) of the Carnegie Institution of Washington, equipped with a 60-in. reflecting telescope and other instruments for stellar photography, a horizontal telescope for solar photography,

---

[1] Many naturalists have held a different opinion, some making it a woodcock, a godwit, or even the hazel-hen or grouse; see the discussion by Lord Lilford in *Ibis* (1862), pp. 352–356.

a 60-ft. tower telescope (completed in 1907), and a second tower telescope of 150 ft. focal length (under construction in 1910). At this observatory important researches in solar and stellar spectroscopy have been carried on under the direction of George Ellery Hale (b. 1868), the inventor of the spectroheliograph. The physical laboratory, computers' offices and instrument construction shops of the Solar Observatory are in Pasadena. About 5 m. south-east of Pasadena, in the township of San Gabriel (pop. 2501 in 1900), is the Mission (monastery) de San Gabriel Arcangel, founded in 1771. Pasadena is one of the most beautiful places in southern California. Fruits and flowers and sub-tropical trees and small plants grow and bloom the year round in its gardens. On the first of January of every year a flower carnival, known as the "Tournament of Roses," is held. Among the principal public buildings are a handsome Romanesque public library, which in 1909 contained about 28,500 volumes, an opera house of considerable architectural merit, high school, and several fine churches. The surrounding country was given over to sheep ranges until 1874, when a fruit-growing colony, organized in 1873, was established, from which the city was developed. The sale of town lots began in 1882. Pasadena was first chartered as a city in 1886; by a clause in the present special free-holders' charter, adopted in 1901, saloons are prohibited in the city.

PASARGADAE, a city of ancient Persia, situated in the modern plain of Murghab, some 30 m. N.E. of the later Parsepolis. The name originally belonged to one of the tribes of the Persians, which included the clan of the Achaemenidae, from which sprang the royal family of Cyrus and Darius (Herod. I. 125; a Pasargadian Badres is mentioned, Herod. iv. 167). According to the account of Ctesias (preserved by Anaximenes of Lampsacus in *Steph. Byz. s.v.* Πασαργάδαι; Strabo xv. 730, cf. 729; Nicol. Damasc. fr. 66, 68 sqq.; Polyaen. vii. 6, 1. q. 45, 2), the last battle of Cyrus against Astyages, in which the Persians were incited to a desperate struggle by their women, was fought here. After the victory Cyrus built a town, with his palace and tomb, which was named Pasargadae after the tribe (cf. Curt. v. 6, 10; x. 1, 22). Every Persian king was, at his accession, invested here, in the sanctuary of a warlike goddess (Anaitis?), with the garb of Cyrus, and received a meal of figs and terebinths with a cup of sour milk (Plut. *Artax.* 3); and whenever he entered his native country he gave a gold piece to every woman of Pasargadae in remembrance of the heroic intervention of their ancestors in the battle (Nic. Damasc. *loc. cit.*; Plut. *Alex.* 69). According to a fragment of the same tradition, preserved by Strabo (xv. 729), Pasargadae lay "in the hollow Persis (*Coele Persis*) on the bank of the river Cyrus, which formerly changed his name, which was formerly Atradates" (in Nic. Damasc. this is the name of his father). The river Cyrus is the Kur of the Persians, now generally named Bandamir; the historians of Alexander call it Araxes, and give to its tributary, the modern Pulwar, which passes by the ruins of Murghab and Persepolis, the name Medos (Strabo xv. 729; Curt. v. 4, 7). The capital of Cyrus was soon supplanted by Persepolis, founded by Darius; but in Pasargadae remained a great treasury, which was surrendered to Alexander in 336 after his conquest of Persis (Arrian iii. 18, 20; Curt. v. 6, 10). After his return from India he visited Pasargadae on the march from Carmania to Persepolis, found the tomb of Cyrus plundered, punished the malefactors, and ordered Aristobulus to restore it (Arrian vi. 29; Strabo xv. 730). Aristobulus' description agrees exactly with the ruins of Murghab on the Bandamir, about 30 m. upwards from Persepolis; and all the other references in the historians of Cyrus and Alexander indicate the same place. Nevertheless, some modern authors[1] have doubted the identity of the ruins of Murghab with Pasargadae, as Ptolemy (vi. 4, 7), places Pasargada or Pasarrcha south-eastwards of Persepolis, and mentions a tribe Pasargadae in Carmania on the sea (vi. 8, 12); and Pliny, *Nat. hist.* vi. 99, names a Persian

[1] E.g. Weissbach in *Zeitschr. d. d. morgenl. Ges.*, 48, pp. 653 sqq.; for the identification cf. Stolze, *Persepolis*, ii. 269 sqq.; Curzon, *Persia*, ii. 71 sqq.

river Sitioganus "on which one navigates in seven days to Pasargadae."[2] But it is evident that these accounts are erroneous. The conjecture of Oppert, that Pasargadae is identical with Pishiyauvâda, where (on a mountain Arakadri) the usurper Gaumâta (Smerdis) proclaimed himself king, and where his successor, the second false Smerdis Vahyazdâta, gathered an arm (inscrip. of Behistun, i. 11; iii. 41), is hardly probable.

The principal ruins of the town of Pasargadae at Murghab are a great terrace like that of Persepolis, and the remainders of three buildings, on which the building inscription of Cyrus, "I Cyrus the king the Achaemenid" (*sc.* "have built this "), occurs five times in Persian, Susian and Babylonian. They were built of bricks, with a foundation of stones and stone door-cases, like the palaces at Persepolis; and on these fragments of a procession of tribute-bearers and the figure of a winged demon (wrongly considered as a portrait of Cyrus) are preserved. Outside the town are two tombs in the form of towers and the tomb of Cyrus himself, a stone house on a high substruction which rises in seven great steps, surrounded by a court with columns; at its side the remains of a guardhouse, in which the officiating Magians lived, are discernible. The ruins of the tomb absolutely correspond to the description of Aristobulus.

See Sir W. Gore-Ouseley, *Travels in Persia* (1811); Morier, Ker Porter, Rich and others; Texier, *Description de l'Armenie et la Perse*; Flandin and Coste, *Voyage en Perse*, vol. ii.; Stolze, *Persepolis*; Dieulafoy, *L'Art antique de la Perse*; and E. Herzfeld, "Pasargadae," in *Beiträge zur alten Geschichte*, vol. viii. (1908), who has in many points corrected and enlarged the earlier descriptions and has proved that the buildings as well as the sculptures are earlier than those of Persepolis, and are, therefore, built by Cyrus the Great. New photographs of the monuments are published by Fr. Sarre, *Iranische Felsreliefs* (unter Mitwirkung von E. Herzfeld, Berlin, 1908). (ED. M.)

PASCAL, BLAISE (1623–1662), French religious philosopher and mathematician, was born at Clermont Ferrand on the 19th of June 1623. His father was Étienne Pascal, president of the Court of Aids at Clermont; his mother's name was Antoinette Bégon. The Pascal family were Auvergnats by extraction as well as residence, had for many generations held posts in the civil service, and were ennobled by Louis XI. in 1478, but did not assume the *de*. The earliest anecdote of Pascal is one of his being bewitched and freed from the spell by the witch with strange ceremonies. His mother died when he was about four years old, and left him with two sisters—Gilberte, who afterwards married M. Perier, and Jacqueline. Both sisters are of importance in their brother's history, and both are said to have been beautiful and accomplished. When Pascal was about seven years old his father gave up his official post at Clermont, and betook himself to Paris. It does not appear that Blaise, who went to no school, but was taught by his father, was at all forced, but rather the contrary. Nevertheless he has a distinguished place in the story of precocious children, and in the much more limited chapter of children whose precocity has been followed by great performance at maturity, though he never became what is called a learned man, perhaps did not know Greek, and was pretty certainly indebted for most of his miscellaneous reading to Montaigne.

The Pascal family, some years after settling in Paris, had to go through a period of adversity. Étienne Pascal, who had bought some of the hôtel-de-ville *rentes*, protested against Richelieu's reduction of the interest, and to escape the Bastille had to go into hiding. He was, according to the story (told by Jacqueline herself), restored to favour owing to the good acting and graceful appearance of his daughter Jacqueline in a representation of Scudéry's *Amour tyrannique* before Richelieu. Mme d'Aiguillon's intervention in the matter was perhaps as powerful as Jacqueline's acting, and Richelieu gave Étienne Pascal (in 1641) the important and lucrative

[2] In vi. 116, he places "the Castle of Frasargida, where is the tomb of Cyrus, and which is occupied by the Magi "—*i.e.* the guard of Magians mentioned by Aristobulus, which had to protect the tomb—eastwards of Persepolis, and by a curious confusion joins it to Ecbatana.

though somewhat troublesome intendancy of Rouen. The family accordingly removed to the Norman capital, though Gilberte Pascal shortly after, on her marriage, returned to Clermont. At Rouen they became acquainted with Corneille, and Blaise pursued his studies with such vehemence that he already showed signs of an injured constitution. Nothing, however, of importance happened till the year 1646. Then Pascal the elder was confined to the house by the consequences of an accident on the ice, and was visited by certain gentlemen of the neighbourhood who had come under the influence of Saint-Cyran and the Jansenists. It does not appear that up to this time the Pascal family had been contemners of religion, but they now eagerly embraced the creed, or at least the attitude of Jansenism, and Pascal himself showed his zeal by informing against the supposed unorthodoxy of a Capuchin, the Père Saint-Ange.

His bodily health was at this time very far from satisfactory, and he appears to have suffered, not merely from acute dyspepsia, but from a kind of paralysis. He was, however, indefatigable in his mathematical work. In 1647 he published his *Nouvelles expériences sur le vide*, and in the next year the famous experiment with the barometer on the Puy de Dome was carried out for him by his brother-in-law Perier, and repeated on a smaller scale by himself at Paris, to which place by the end of 1647 he and his sister Jacqueline had removed, to be followed shortly by their father. In a letter of Jacqueline's, dated the 27th of September, an account of a visit paid by Descartes to Pascal is given, which, like the other information on the relations of the two, give strong suspicion of mutual jealousy. Descartes, however, gave Pascal the very sensible advice to stay in bed as long as he could (it may be remembered that the philosopher himself never got up till eleven) and to take plenty of beef-tea. As early as May 1648 Jacqueline Pascal was strongly drawn to Port Royal, and her brother frequently accompanied her to its church. She desired indeed to join the convent, but her father, who returned to Paris with the dignity of counsellor of state, disapproved of the plan, and took both brother and sister to Clermont, where Pascal remained for the greater part of two years. E. Fléchier, in his account of the *Grands Jours* at Clermont many years after, speaks of a "belle savante" in whose company Pascal frequently been—a trivial mention on which, as on many other trivial points of scantily known lives, the most childish structures of comment and conjecture have been based. It is sufficient to say that at this time, despite the Rouen "conversion," there is no evidence to show that Pascal was in any way a recluse, an ascetic, or in short anything but a young man of great intellectual promise and performance, not indifferent to society, but of weak health. He, his sister and their father returned to Paris in the late autumn of 1650, and in September of the next year Étienne Pascal died. Almost immediately afterwards Jacqueline fulfilled her purpose of joining Port Royal—a proceeding which led to some soreness, finally healed, between herself and her brother and sister as to the disposal of her property. It has sometimes been supposed that Pascal, from 1651 or earlier to the famous accident of 1654, lived a dissipated, extravagant, worldly, luxurious (though admittedly not vicious) life with his friend the duc de Roannes and others. His *Discours sur les passions de l'amour*, a striking and characteristic piece, not very long since discovered and printed, has also been assigned to this period, and has been supposed to indicate a hopeless passion for Charlotte de Roannes, the duke's sister. But this is sheer romancing. The extant letters of Pascal to the lady show no trace of any affection (stronger than friendship) between them. It is, however, certain that in the autumn of 1654 Pascal's second "conversion" took place, and that it was lasting. He betook himself at first to Port Royal, and began to live a recluse and austere life there. Mme Perier simply says that Jacqueline persuaded him to abandon the world. Jacqueline represents the retirement as the final result of a long course of dissatisfaction with mundane life. But there are certain anecdotic embellishments of the act which are too famous to

be passed over, though they are in part apocryphal. It seems that Pascal in driving to Neuilly was run away with by the horses, and would have been plunged in the river but that the traces fortunately broke. To this, which seems authentic, is usually added the tradition (due to the abbé Boileau) that afterwards he used at times to see an imaginary precipice by his bedside, or at the foot of the chair on which he was sitting. Further, from the 23rd of November 1654 dates the singular document usually known as "Pascal's amulet," a parchment slip which he wore constantly about him, and which bears the date followed by some lines of incoherent and strongly mystical devotion.

It must be noted that, though he lived much at Port Royal, and partly at least observed its rule, he never actually became one of its famous solitaries. But for what it did for him (and for a time his health as well as his peace of mind seems to have been improved) he very soon paid an ample and remarkable return. At the end of 1655 Arnauld, the chief light of Port Royal, was condemned by the Sorbonne for heretical doctrine, and it was thought important by the Jansenist and Port Royal party that steps should be taken to disabuse the popular mind. Arnauld would have undertaken the task himself, but his wiser friends knew that his style was anything but popular, and overruled him. It is said that he personally suggested to Pascal to try his hand, and that the first of the famous *Provinciales* (*Provincial Letters*, properly *Lettres écrites par Louis de Montalte à un provincial de ses amis*) was written in a few days, or, less probably, in a day. It was printed without the real author's name on the 23rd of January 1656, and, being immensely popular, and successful, was followed by others to the number of eighteen.

Shortly after the appearance of the *Provinciales*, on the 24th of May 1656, occurred the miracle of the Holy Thorn, a fragment of the crown of Christ preserved at Port Royal, which cured the little Marguerite Perier of a fistula lacrymalis. The Jesuits were much mortified by this Jansenist miracle, which, as it was officially recognized, they could not openly deny. Pascal and his friends rejoiced in proportion. The details of his later years after this incident are somewhat scanty. For years before his death we hear only of acts of charity and of, as it seems to modern ideas, extravagant asceticism. Thus Mme Perier tells us that he disliked to see her caress her children, and would not allow the beauty of any woman to be talked of in his presence. What may be called his last illness began as early as 1658, and as the disease progressed it was attended with more and more pain, chiefly in the head. In June 1662, having given up his own house to a poor family who were suffering from small-pox, he went to his sister's house to be nursed, and never afterwards left it. His state was, it seems, mistaken by his physicians, so much so that the offices of the Church were long put off. He was able, however, to receive the Eucharist, and soon afterwards died in convulsions on the 19th of August. A post mortem examination was held, which showed not only grave derangement in the stomach and other organs, but a serious lesion of the brain.

Eight years after Pascal's death appeared what purported to be his *Pensées*, and a preface by his nephew Perier gave the world to understand that these were fragments of a great projected apology for Christianity which the author had, in conversation with his friends, planned out years before. The editing of the book was peculiar. It was submitted to a committee of influential Jansenists, with the duc de Roannes at their head, and, in addition, it bore the imprimatur of numerous unofficial approvers who testified to its orthodoxy. It does not appear that there was much suspicion of the garbling which had been practised—garbling not unusual at the time, and excused in this case by the fact of a lull in the troubles of Port Royal and a great desire on the part of its friends to do nothing to disturb that lull. But as a matter of fact no more entirely factitious book ever issued from the press. The fragments which it professed to give were in themselves confused and incoherent enough, nor is it easy to believe that they all formed part of any such single and coherent design as that referred to above. But the editors omitted, altered, added, separated, combined and so forth entirely at their pleasure, actually making some changes which seem to have been thought improvements of style. This rifacimento remained the standard text with a few unimportant additions for nearly two centuries, except that, by a truly comic revolution of public taste, Condorcet in 1776 published, after study of the original, which remained accessible in manuscript, another garbling, conducted this time in the interests of unorthodoxy. It was not till 1842 that Victor Cousin drew attention to the absolutely untrustworthy condition of the text, nor till 1844 that A. P. Faugère edited that text from the MS. In something like a condition of purity, though, as subsequent editions have shown, not with absolute fidelity. But even in its spurious condition the book had been recognized as remarkable and almost unique. Its contents, as was to be expected, are of a very chaotic character—of a character so chaotic indeed that the reader is almost at the mercy of the arrangement, perforce an arbitrary arrangement, of the editors. But the subjects dealt with concern more or less all the great problems of thought on what may be called the theological side of metaphysics—the sufficiency of reason, the trustworthiness of experience, the admissibility of revelation, free will, foreknowledge, and the rest. The peculiarly disjointed and fragmentary condition of the sentiments expressed by Pascal aggravates the appearance of universal doubt which is present in the *Pensées*, just as the completely unfinished condition of the work, from the literary point of view, constantly causes slighter or graver doubts as to the actual meaning which the author wished to express. Accordingly the *Pensées* have always been a favourite exploring ground, not to say a favourite field of battle, to persons who take an interest in their problems. Speaking generally, their tendency is towards the combating of scepticism by a deeper scepticism, or, as Pascal himself calls it, Pyrrhonism, which occasionally goes the length of denying the possibility of any natural theology. Pascal explains all the contradictions and difficulties of human life and thought by the doctrine of the Fall, and relies on faith and revelation alone to justify each other.

Excluding here his scientific attainments (see below), Pascal presents himself for comment in two different lights, the second of which is, if the expression be permitted, a composite one. The first exhibits him as a man of letters, the second as a philosopher, a theologian, and sim ! a man, for in no one is the colour of the theology and the philosophy more distinctly personal. Yet his character as a man is not very distinct. The accounts of his sister and niece have the defect of all hagiology; they are obviously written rather with a view to the ideas and the wishes of the writers than with a view to the actual and absolute personality of the subject. Except from these interesting but somewhat tainted sources, we know little or nothing about him. Hence conjecture, or at least inference, must always enter largely into any estimate of Pascal, except a purely literary one.

On that side, fortunately, there is no possibility of doubt or difficulty to any competent inquirer. The *Provincial Letters* are the first example of French prose which is at once considerable in bulk, varied and important in matter, perfectly finished in form. They owe not a little to Descartes, for Pascal's indebtedness to his predecessor is unquestionable from the literary side, whatever may be the case with the scientific. But Descartes had had neither the opportunity, nor the desire, nor probably the power, to write anything of the literary importance of the *Provinciales*. The first example of polite controversial irony since Lucian, the *Provinciales* have continued to be the best example of it during more than two centuries in which the style has been sedulously practised, and in which they have furnished a model to generation after generation. The unfailing freshness and charm of the contrast between the importance, the gravity, in some cases the dry and abstruse nature, of their subjects, and the lightness, sometimes almost

approaching levity in its special sense, of the manner in which these subjects are attacked is a triumph of literary art of which no familiarity dims the splendour, and which no lapse of time can ever impair. Nor perhaps is this literary art really less evident in the *Pensées*, though it is less clearly displayed, owing to the fragmentary, or rather chaotic condition of the work, and partly also to the nature of the subject. The vividness and distinction of Pascal's phrase, his singular faculty of inserting without any loss of dignity in the gravest and most impassioned meditation what may be almost called quips of thought and diction, the intense earnestness of meaning weighting but not confusing the style, all appear here.

No such positive statements as these are, however, possible as to the substance of the *Pensées* and the attitude of their author. Hitherto the widest differences have been manifested in the estimate of Pascal's opinions on the main questions of philosophy, theology and human conduct. He has been represented as a determined apologist of intellectual orthodoxy animated by an almost fanatical "hatred of reason," and possessed with a purpose to overthrow the appeal to reason; as a sceptic and pessimist of a far deeper dye than Montaigne, anxious chiefly to show how any positive decision on matters beyond the range of experience is impossible; as a nervous believer clinging to conclusions which his clearer and better sense showed to be indefensible; as an almost ferocious ascetic and paradoxer affecting the *credo quia impossibile* in intellectual matters and the *odi quia amabile* in matters moral and sensuous; as a wanderer in the regions of doubt and belief, alternately bringing a vast though vague power of thought and an unequalled power of expression to the expression of ideas incompatible and irreconcilable. An unbiased study of the scanty facts of his history, and of the tolerably abundant but scattered and chaotic facts of his literary production, ought to enable any one to steer clear of these exaggerations, while admitting at the same time that it is impossible to give a complete and final account of his attitude towards the riddles of this world and others. He certainly was no mere advocate of orthodoxy; he as certainly was no mere victim of terror at scepticism; least of all was he a freethinker in disguise. He appears, as far as can be judged from the fragments of his *Pensées*, to have seized firmly and fully the central idea of the difference between reason and religion. Where the difficulty rises respecting him is that most thinkers since his day, who have seen this difference with equal clearness, have advanced from it to the negative side, while he advanced to the positive. In other words, most men since his day who have not been contented with a mere concordat, have let religion go and contented themselves with reason. Pascal, equally discontented with the concordat, held fast to religion and continued to fight out the questions of difference with reason. Surveying these positions, we shall not be astonished to find much that is surprising and some things that are contradictory in Pascal's utterances on "les grands sujets." The influence exercised on him by Montaigne is the one fact regarding him which has not been and can hardly be exaggerated, and his well-known *Entretien* with Sacy on the subject (the restoration of which to its proper form is one of the most valuable results of modern criticism) leaves no doubt possible as to the source of his "Pyrrhonian" method. But it is impossible for anyone who takes Pascal's *Pensées* simply as he finds them in connexion with the facts of Pascal's history to question his theological orthodoxy, understanding by theological orthodoxy the acceptance of revelation and dogma; it is equally impossible for any one in the same condition to declare him absolutely content with dogma and revelation. It is of the essence of an active mind like Pascal's to explore and state all the arguments which are for or make against the conclusion it is investigating.

To sum up, the *Pensées* are excursions into the great unknown made with a full acknowledgment of the greatness of that unknown. From the point of view that belief and knowledge, based on experience or reasoning, are separate domains with an unexplored sea between and round them. Pascal is perfectly comprehensible, and he need not be taken as a deserter from one region to the other. To those who hold that all intellectual exercise outside the sphere of religion is impious or that all intellectual exercise inside that sphere is futile, he must remain an enigma.

There are few writers who are more in need than Pascal of being fully and competently edited. The chief nominally complete edition at present in existence is that of Bossut (1779, 5 vols., and since reprinted), which not only appeared before any attempt had been made to restore the true text of the *Pensées*, but is in other respects quite inadequate. The edition of Lahure, 1858, is not much better, though the *Pensées* appear in their more genuine form. An edition promised for the excellent collection of *Les Grands Écrivains de la France* by A. P. Faugère has been executed as far as the *Pensées* go by Léon Brunschvig (3 vols., 1904), who has also issued a one-volume edition. The *Œuvres complètes* appeared in three volumes (Paris, 1889). Meanwhile, with the exception of the *Provinciales* (of which there are numerous editions, no one much to be preferred to any other, for the text is undisputed and the book itself contains almost all the exegesis of its own contents necessary), Pascal can be read only at a disadvantage. There are five chief editions of the true *Pensées* earlier than Brunschvig's: that of Faugère (1844), the *editio princeps*; that of Havet (1852, 1867 and 1881), on the whole the best; that of Victor Rochet (1873), good, but arranged and edited with the deliberate intention of making Pascal first of all an orthodox apologist; that of Molinier (1877-1879), a carefully edited and interesting text, the important corrections of which have been introduced into Havet's last edition and that of G. Michelaut (Freiburg, 1896). Unfortunately, none of these can be said to be exclusively satisfactory. The minor works must chiefly be sought in Bossut or reprints of him. Works on Pascal are innumerable: Sainte-Beuve's *Port Royal*, Cousin's writings on Pascal and his *Jacqueline Pascal*, and the essays of the editors of the *Pensées* just mentioned are the most noteworthy. Principal Tulloch contributed a useful little monograph to the series of *Foreign Classics for English Readers* (Edinburgh and London, 1878). Recent handlings are, in French, E. Boutroux's *Pascal* (Paris, 1903) and, in English, an article in the *Quarterly Review* (No. 407), for April 1906. (G. Sa.)

Pascal as Natural Philosopher and Mathematician.—Great as is Pascal's reputation as a philosopher and man of letters, it may be fairly questioned whether his claim to be remembered by posterity as a mathematician and physicist is not even greater. In his two former capacities all will admire the form of his work, while some will question the value of his results; but in his two latter capacities no one will dispute either. He was a great mathematician in an age which produced Descartes, Fermat, Huygens, Wallis and Roberval. There are wonderful stories on record of his precocity in mathematical learning, which is sufficiently established by the well-attested fact that he had completed before he was sixteen years of age a work on the conic sections, in which he had laid down a series of propositions, discovered by himself, of such importance that they may be said to form the foundations of the modern treatment of that subject. Owing partly to the youth of the author, partly to the difficulty in publishing scientific works in those days, and partly no doubt to the continual struggle on his part to devote his mind to what appeared to his conscience more important labour, this work (like many others by the same master hand) was never published. We know something of what it contained from a report by Leibnitz, who had seen it in Paris, and from a *résumé* of its results published in 1640 by Pascal himself, under the title *Essai pour les coniques*. The method which he followed was that introduced by his contemporary Girard Desargues, viz. the transformation of geometrical figures by conical or optical projection. In this way he established the famous theorem that the intersections of the three pairs of opposite sides of a hexagon inscribed in a conic are collinear. This proposition, which he called the mystic hexagram, he made the keystone of his theory; from it alone he deduced more than 400 corollaries; embracing, according to his own account, the conics of Apollonius, and other results innumerable.

Pascal also distinguished himself by his skill in the infinitesimal calculus, then in the embryonic form of Cavalieri's method of indivisibles. The cycloid was a famous curve in those days; it had been discussed by Galileo, Descartes, Fermat, Roberval and Torricelli, who had in turn exhausted their skill upon it. Pascal solved the hitherto refractory problem of the general quadrature of the cycloid, and proposed and solved a variety of others relating to the centre of gravity of the curve and its segments, and to the volume and centre of gravity of solids of revolution generated in various ways by means of it. He published a number of these theorems without demonstration as a challenge to contemporary mathematicians. Solutions were furnished by Wallis, Huygens, Wren and others; and Pascal published his own in the form of letters from Amos Dettonville (his assumed name as challenger) to Pierre de Carcavy. There has been some discussion as to the fairness of the treatment accorded by Pascal to his rivals, but no question of the fact that his initiative led to a great extension of our knowledge of the properties of the cycloid, and indirectly hastened the progress of the differential calculus.

In yet another branch of pure mathematics Pascal ranks as a founder. The mathematical theory of probability and the allied theory of the combinatorial analysis were in effect created by the correspondence between Pascal and Fermat, concerning certain questions as to the division of stakes in games of chance, which had been propounded to the former by the gaming philosopher De Méré. A complete account of this interesting correspondence would surpass our present limits; but the reader may be referred to Todhunter's *History of the Theory of Probability* (Cambridge and London, 1865), pp. 7-21. It appears that Pascal contemplated publishing a treatise *De aleos geometriæ*; but all that actually appeared was a fragment on the arithmetical triangle (*Traité du triangle arithmétique*, "Properties of the Figurate Numbers"), printed in 1654; but not published till 1665, after his death.

Pascal's work as a natural philosopher was not less remarkable than his discoveries in pure mathematics. His experiments and his treatise (written before 1651, published 1663) on the equilibrium of fluids entitle him to rank with Galileo and Stevinus as one of the founders of the science of hydrodynamics. The idea of the pressure of the air and the invention of the instrument for measuring it were both new when he made his famous experiment, showing that the height of the mercury column in a barometer decreases when it is carried upwards through the atmosphere. This experiment was made by himself in a tower at Paris, and was carried out on a grand scale under his instructions by his brother-in-law Florin Périer on the Puy de Dôme in Auvergne. Its success greatly helped to break down the old prejudices, and to bring home to the minds of ordinary men the truth of the new ideas propounded by Galileo and Torricelli.

Whether we look at his pure mathematical or at his physical researches we receive the same impression of Pascal; we see the strongest marks of a great original genius creating new ideas, and seizing upon, mastering, and pursuing farther everything that was fresh and unfamiliar in his time. We can still point to much in exact science that is absolutely his; and we can indicate infinitely more which is due to his inspiration.
(G. Ch.)

PASCAL, JACQUELINE (1625-1661), sister of Blaise Pascal, was born at Clermont-Ferrand, France, on the 4th of October 1625. She was a genuine infant prodigy, composing verses when only eight years, and a five-act comedy at eleven. In 1646 the influence of her brother converted her to Jansenism. In 1652, she took the veil, despite the strong opposition of her brother, and subsequently was largely instrumental in the latter's own final conversion. She vehemently opposed the attempt to compel the assent of the nuns to the Papal bulls condemning Jansenism, but was at last compelled to yield her own. This blow, however, hastened her death, which occurred at Paris on the 4th of October 1661.

PASCHAL (Paschalis), the name of two popes, and one anti-pope.

PASCHAL I., pope from 817 to 824, a native of Rome, was raised to the pontificate by the acclamation of the clergy, shortly after the death of Stephen IV., and before the sanction of the emperor (Louis the Pious) had been obtained—a circumstance for which it was one of his first cares to apologise. His relations with the imperial house, however, never became cordial; and he was also unsuccessful in winning the sympathy of the Roman nobles. He died in Rome while the imperial commissioners were investigating the circumstances under which two important Roman personages had been seized at the Lateran, blinded and afterwards beheaded; Paschal had shielded the murderers but denied all personal complicity in their crime. The Roman people refused him the honour of burial within the church of St Peter, but he now holds a place in the Roman calendar (May 16). The church of St Cecilia in Trastevere was restored and St Maria in Dominica rebuilt by him; he also built the church of St Prassede. The successor of Paschal I. was Eugenius II.

(L. D.°)

PASCHAL II. (Ranieri), pope from the 13th of August 1099 to the 21st of January 1118, was a native of Bieda, near Viterbo, and a monk of the Cluniac order. He was created cardinal-priest of S. Clemente by Gregory VII. about 1076, and was consecrated pope in succession to Urban II. on the 14th of August 1099. In the long struggle with the emperors over investiture, he zealously carried on the Hildebrandine policy, but with only partial success. In 1104 Paschal succeeded in instigating the emperor's second son to rebel against his father, but soon found Henry V. even more persistent in maintaining the right of investiture than Henry IV. had been. The imperial Diet at Mains invited (Jan. 1106) Paschal to visit Germany and settle the trouble, but the pope in the Council of Guastalla (Oct. 1106) simply renewed the prohibition of investiture. In the same year he brought to an end the investiture struggle in England, in which Anselm, archbishop of Canterbury, had been engaged with King Henry I., by retaining himself exclusive right to invest with the ring and crozier, but recognizing the royal nomination to vacate benefices and oath of fealty for temporal domains. He went to France at the close of 1106 to seek the mediation of King Philip and Prince Louis in the imperial struggle, but, his negotiations remaining without result, he returned to Italy in September 1107. When Henry V. advanced with an army into Italy in order to be crowned, the pope agreed to a compact (Feb. 1111), by the terms of which the Church should surrender all the possessions and royalties it had received of the empire and kingdom of Italy since the days of Charlemagne, while Henry on his side should renounce lay investiture. Preparations were made for the coronation on the 12th of February 1111, but the Romans rose in revolt against the compact, and Henry retired taking with him pope and curia. After sixty-one days of harsh imprisonment, Paschal yielded and guaranteed investiture to the emperor. Henry was then crowned in St Peter's on the 13th of April, and after exacting a promise that no revenge would be taken for what had passed withdrew beyond the Alps. The Hildebrandine party was aroused to action, however; a Lateran council of March 1112 declared null and void the concessions extorted by violence; a council held at Vienna in October actually excommunicated the emperor, and Paschal sanctioned the proceeding. Towards the end of the pontificate trouble began anew in England, Paschal complaining (1115) that councils were held and bishops translated without his authorization, and threatening Henry I. with excommunication. On the death of the countess Matilda, who had bequeathed all her territories to the Church (1115), the emperor at once laid claim to them as imperial fiefs and forced the pope to flee from Rome. Paschal returned after the emperor's withdrawal at the beginning of 1118, but died within a few days on the 21st of January 1118. His successor was Gelasius II.

The principal sources for the life of Paschal II. are his Letters in the *Monumenta Germaniae historica. Epistolae*, vols. 3, 6, 7. 13, 17, 20-23, 25, and the *Vita* by Petrus Pisanus in the *Liber pontificalis*, ed. Duchesne (Paris, 1892). Important bulls are in J. A. G. von Pflugk-Harttung, *Die Bullen der Päpste bis zum Ende des zwölften Jahrhunderts* (Gotha, 1901), and a valuable digest in Jaffé-Wattenbach, *Regesta pontif. roman.* (1885–1888).
See J. Langen, *Geschichte der römischen Kirche von Gregor VII. bis Innocenz III.* (Bonn, 1893); K. J. von Hefele, *Conciliengeschichte*, vol. v. (2nd ed., 1873–1890); E. Franz, *Papst Paschalis II.* (Breslau,

1877); W. Schum, *Die Politik Papst Paschals II. gegen Kaiser Heinrich V. im Jahre 1112* (Erfurt, 1877); I. Rönkens, *Heinrich V. und Paschalis II.* (Essen, 1885); C. Gernandt, *Die erste Romfahrt Heinrich V.* (Heidelberg, 1890); G. Peiser, *Der deutsche Investiturstreit unter Kaiser Heinrich V. bis zu dem päpstlichen Privileg vom 3 April 1111* (Berlin, 1883); and B. Monod, *Essai sur les rapports de Pascal II. avec Philippe I.* (Paris, 1907). There is an exhaustive bibliography with an excellent article by Carl Mirbt in Herzog-Hauck, *Realencyklopädie* (3rd ed., 1904).

(C. H. HA.)

PASCHAL III., anti-pope from 1164 to 1168, was elected the successor of Victor IV. on the 22nd of April 1164. He was an aged aristocrat, Guido of Crema. Recognized at once by the emperor Frederick I. he soon lost the support of Burgundy, but the emperor crushed opposition in Germany, and gained the co-operation of Henry II. of England. Supported by the victorious imperial army, Paschal was enthroned at St Peter's on the 22nd of July 1167, and Pope Alexander III., became a fugitive. Sudden imperial reverses, however, made Paschal glad in the end to hold so much as the quarter on the right bank of the Tiber, where he died on the 20th of September 1168. He was succeeded by the anti-pope Callixtus III.

See A. Hauck, *Kirchengeschichte Deutschlands*, Bd. IV. (Leipzig, 1903, 259-276); H. Böhmer in Herzog-Hauck, *Realencyklopädie*, Bd. XIV. 724 seq.; and Lobkowitz, *Statistik der Päpste* (Freiburg, i, B. 1905).

(W. W. R.°)

PASCHAL CHRONICLE (Chronicon Paschale, also Chronicum Alexandrinum or Constantinopolitanum, or Fasti Siculi), so called from being based upon the Easter canon, an outline of chronology from Adam down to A.D. 629, accompanied by numerous historical and theological notes. The work, which is imperfect at the beginning and end (breaking off in the year 627), is preceded by an introduction on the Christian methods of reckoning time and the Easter cycle. It was written during the reign of Heraclius (610–641), and is generally attributed to an unknown Byzantine cleric and friend of the patriarch Sergius, who is specially alluded to as responsible for the introduction of certain ritual innovations. The so-called Byzantine or Roman era (which continued in use in the Greek Church until its liberation from Turkish rule) was adopted in the *Chronicum* for the first time as the foundation of chronology, in accordance with which the date of the creation is given as the 21st of March, 5507. The author is merely a compiler from earlier works, except in the history of the last thirty years, which has the value of a contemporary record.

The chief authorities used were: Julius Sextus Africanus (3rd century); the consular *Fasti*; the *Chronicle* and *Church History* of Eusebius; John Malalas; the *Acta martyrum*; the treatise of Epiphanius, bishop of Constantia (the old Salamis) in Cyprus (fl. 4th century), on *Weights and Measures*. Editions: L. Dindorf (1832) in *Corpus scriptorum hist. byzantinae*, with Du Cange's preface and commentary; J. P. Migne, *Patrologia graeca*, xcii.; see also C. Wachsmuth, *Einleitung in das Studium der alten Geschichte* (1895); H. Gelzer, *Sextus Julius Africanus und die byzantinische Chronographie*, ii. 1 (1885); J. van der Hagen, *Observationes in Heraclii imperatoris methodum paschalem* (1736, but still considered indispensable); E. Schwartz in Pauly-Wissowa, *Realencyklopädie*, iii., pt. 2 (1899); C. Krumbacher, *Geschichte der byzantinischen Literatur* (1897).

PAS-DE-CALAIS, a maritime department of northern France, formed in 1790 of nearly the whole of Artois and the northern maritime portion of Picardy including Boulonnais, Calaisis, Ardrésis, and the districts of Langle and Bredenarde, and bounded N. by the Straits of Dover (" Pas de Calais "), E. by the department of Nord, S. by that of Somme, and W. by the English Channel. Pop. (1906), 1,012,466; Area 2606 sq. m. Except in the neighbourhood of Boulogne-sur-Mer with its *côtes de fer* or " iron coasts," the seaboard of the department, which measures 65 m., consists of dunes. From the mouth of the Aa (the limit towards Nord) it trends west-south-west to Gris Nez, the point of France nearest to England; in this section lie the port of Calais, Cape Blanc Nez, rising 440 ft. above the sandy shores, and the port of Wissant (Wishant). The seaside resorts include Boulogne, Berck-sur-Mer, Paris-Plage, Wimereux, &c. Beyond Gris Nez the direction is due south; in this section are the small port of Ambleteuse, Boulogne at the mouth of the Liane, and the two bays formed by the estuaries of the Canche and the Authie (the limit towards Somme). The highest point in the department (700 ft.) is in the west, between Boulogne and St Omer. From the uplands in which it is situated the Lys and Scarpe flow east to the Scheldt, the Aa north to the German Ocean, and the Slack, Wimereux and Liane to the Channel. Farther south are the valleys of the Canche and the Authie, running E.S.E. and W.N.W., and thus parallel with the Somme. Vast plains, open and monotonous, but extremely fertile and well cultivated, occupy most of the department. To the north of the hills running between St Omer and Boulogne, to the south of Gravelines and the south-east of Calais, lies the district of the Wattergands, fens now drained by means of canals and dikes, and turned into highly productive land. The climate is free from extremes of heat and cold, but damp and changeable. At Arras the mean annual temperature is 47°; on the coast it is higher. The rainfall varies from 24 to 32 in., though at Cape Gris Nez the latter figure is much exceeded. Cereals are largely grown and give good yields to the acre; the other principal crops are potatoes, sugar-beet, forage, oil-plants and tobacco. Market gardening flourishes in the Wattergands. The rearing of livestock and poultry is actively carried on, and the horses of the Boulonnais are specially esteemed.

The department is the chief in France for the production of coal, its principal coal-basin, which is a continuation of that of Valenciennes, centring round Béthune. The manufacture of beetroot-sugar, oil and alcohol distilling, iron-working, dyeing, brewing, paper-making, and various branches of the textile manufacture, are foremost among the industries of the department. Boulogne, Calais and Étaples fit out a considerable number of vessels for the cod, herring and mackerel fisheries. Calais and Boulogne are important ports of passenger-transit for England; and Boulogne also carries on a large export trade in the products of the department. The canal system comprises part of the Aa, the Lys, the Scarpe, the Deûle (a tributary of the Lys passing by Lille), the Lawe (a tributary of the Lys passing by Béthune), and the Sensée (an affluent of the Scheldt), as well as the canals of Aire to Bauvin, Neuffossé, Calais, Calais to Ardres, &c., and in this way a line of communication is formed from the Scheldt to the sea by Béthune, St Omer and Calais, with branches to Gravelines and Dunkirk. The department is served by the Northern railway.

Pas-de-Calais forms the diocese of Arras (archbishopric of Cambrai), belongs to the district of the I. army corps, the educational division (académie) of Lille and the circumscription of the appeal court of Douai. There are six arrondissements (Arras, Béthune, Boulogne, Montreuil-sur-Mer, St Omer and St Pol-sur-Ternoise). The more noteworthy places are Arras, the capital, Boulogne, Calais, St Omer, Béthune, Lens, Montreuil-sur-Mer, Bruay, Berck, Étaples and Aire-sur-la-Lys, which are noticed separately. Besides some of the towns mentioned, Liévin (22,070), Hénin-Liétard (13,384), in the neighbourhood of Lens, are large centres of population. Other places of some importance are: Lillers (pop. 5341), which carries on bootmaking and has a fine Romanesque church of the 12th century; Hesdin, which owes its regular plan to Charles V., by whom it was built; and St Pol, which has the remains of medieval fortifications and castles and gave its name to the famous counts of St Pol.

PASDELOUP, JULES ÉTIENNE (1819–1887), French conductor, was born in Paris, and educated in music at the conservatoire. He founded in 1851 a "société des jeunes artistes du conservatoire," and, as conductor of its concerts, did much to popularise the best new compositions of the time. His "popular concerts" at the Cirque d'hiver, from 1861 till 1884, had also a great effect in promoting French taste in music.

PASEWALK, a town of Germany, in the Prussian province of Pomerania, on the Ucker, 26 m. N.W. from Stettin by the railway to Strassburg. Pop. (1905), 10,519. Pasewalk became a town during the 12th century and was soon a member of the Hanseatic League. In 1359 it passed to the duke of Pomerania. Frequently ravaged during the wars which devastated the

district, it was plundered several times by the imperialists during the Thirty Years' War; in 1657 it was burnt by the Poles and in 1713 by the Russians. By the peace of Westphalia in 1648 it was given to Sweden, but in 1676 it was conquered by Brandenburg, and in 1720, by the peace of Stockholm, it was definitely assigned to Brandenburg-Prussia.

See Hückstädt, *Geschichte der Stadt Pasewalk* (Pasewalk, 1883).

PASHA, also written "pacha" and formerly "pashaw," &c., a Turkish title, superior to that of bey (q.v.), borne by persons of high rank and placed after the name. It is in the gift of the sultan of Turkey and, by delegation, of the khedive of Egypt. The title appears, originally, to have been bestowed exclusively upon military commanders, but it is now given to any high official, and also to unofficial persons whom it is desired to honour. It is conferred indifferently upon Moslems and Christians, and is frequently given to foreigners in the service of the Turks or Egyptians. Pashas are of three grades, formerly distinguished by the number of horse-tails (three, two and one respectively) which they were entitled to display as symbols of authority when on campaign. A pashalik is a province governed by or under the jurisdiction of a pasha.

The word is variously derived from the Persian *pádsháh*, Turkish *pádishah*, equivalent to king or emperor, and from the Turkish *bash*, in some dialects *pash*, a head, chief, &c. In old Turkish there was no fixed distinction between *b* and *p*. As first used in western Europe the title was written with the initial *b*. The English forms bashaw, bassaw, bucha, &c., general in the 16th and 17th centuries, were derived through the med. Lat. and Ital. *bassa*.

PASIG, a town and the capital of the province of Rizal, Luzon, Philippine Islands, about 6 m. E.S.E. of Manila. Pop. (1903), 11,287. The town, which covers a considerable area, is traversed by the Pasig river and its tributary, the Mariquino river, and for a short distance borders on Laguna de Bay. In the south-western part is Fort McKinley. Although built on low ground, Pasig is fairly healthy. It was formerly an important commercial centre, the inhabitants being largely engaged in a carrying and forwarding trade between Manila and the lake ports; but this trade was lost after the establishment of direct rail and steamboat service between these ports. The principal industries are rice-farming, the manufacture of a cheap red pottery, and fishing. The language is Tagalog.

PASITELES, the most important member of the Neo-Attic school of sculpture in the time of Julius Caesar. At that period there was a demand for copies of, or variations on, noted works of Greek sculpture: the demand was met by the workshops of Pasiteles and his pupils Stephanus and Menelaus and others, several of whose statues are extant. In working from early Dorian models they introduced refinements of their own, with the result that they produced beautiful, but somewhat vapid and academic types. Pasiteles is said by Pliny (*Nat. Hist.* xxxvi. 39) to have been a native of Magna Graecia, and to have been granted the Roman citizenship.

PASKEVICH, IVAN FEDOROVICH (1782–1856), count of Erivan, prince of Warsaw, Russian field marshal, descended from an old and wealthy family, was born at Poltava on the 19th (8th) of May 1782. He was educated at the imperial institution for pages, where his progress was rapid, and in 1800 received his commission in the Guards and was named aide-de-camp to the tsar. His first active service was in 1805, in the auxiliary army sent to the assistance of Austria against France, when he took part in the battle of Austerlitz. From 1807 to 1812 he was engaged in the campaigns against Turkey; and distinguished himself by many brilliant and daring exploits, being made a general officer in his thirtieth year. During the French War of 1812–14 he was present, in command of the 26th division of infantry, at all the most important engagements; at the battle of Leipzig he won promotion to the rank of lieutenant-general. On the outbreak of war with Persia in 1826 he was appointed second in command, and, succeeding in the following year to the chief command, gained rapid and brilliant successes which compelled the shah to sue for peace in February

1818. In reward of his services he was named by the emperor count of Erivan, and received a million of roubles and a diamond-mounted sword. From Persia he was sent to Turkey in Asia, and, having captured in rapid succession the principal fortresses, he was at the end of the campaign made a field marshal at the age of forty-seven. In 1830 he subdued the mountaineers of Daghestan. In 1831 he was entrusted with the command of the army sent to suppress the revolt of Poland, and after the fall of Warsaw, which gave the death-blow to Polish independence, he was raised to the dignity of prince of Warsaw, and created viceroy of the kingdom of Poland. On the outbreak of the insurrection of Hungary in 1848 he was appointed to the command of the Russian troops sent to the aid of Austria, and finally compelled the surrender of the Hungarians at Világos. In April 1854 he again took the field in command of the army of the Danube, but on the 9th of June, at Silistria, where he suffered defeat, he received a contusion which compelled him to retire from active service. He died on the 13th (1st) of February 1856 at Warsaw, where in 1869 a memorial was erected to him. He held the rank of field marshal in the Prussian and Austrian armies as well as in his own service.

See Tolstoy, *Essai biographique et historique sur le feld-maréchal Prince de Varsovie* (Paris, 1835); *Notice biographique sur le Maréchal Paskévitch* (Leipzig, 1856); and Prince Stcherbatov's *Life* (St Petersburg, 1888-1894).

PASLEY, SIR CHARLES WILLIAM (1780-1861), British soldier and military engineer, was born at Eakdale Muir, Dumfriesshire, on the 8th of September 1780. In 1796 he entered the Royal Military Academy, Woolwich; a year later he gained his commission in the Royal Artillery, and in 1798 he was transferred to the Royal Engineers. He was present in the defence of Gaëta, the battle of Maida and the siege of Copenhagen. In 1807, being then a captain, he went to the Peninsula, where his knowledge of Spanish led to his employment on the staff of Sir David Baird and Sir John Moore. He took part in the retreat to Corunna and the Walcheren Expedition, and received a severe wound while gallantly leading a storming party at Flushing. During his tedious recovery he employed himself in learning German. He saw no further active service, the rest of his life being devoted to the foundation of a complete science of military engineering and to the thorough organization and training of the corps of Royal Engineers. He was so successful that, though only a captain, he was allowed to act for two years as commanding royal engineer at Plymouth and given a special grant. The events of the Peninsular War having emphasized the need of a fully trained engineer corps, Pasley's views were adopted by the war office, and he himself placed at the head of the new school of military engineering at Woolwich. This was in 1812, and Pasley was at the same time gazetted brevet major. He became brevet lieutenant-colonel in 1813 and substantive lieutenant-colonel in 1814. The first volume of his *Military Instruction* appeared in 1814, and contained a course of practical geometry which he had framed for his company at Plymouth. Two other volumes completing the work appeared by 1817, and dealt with the science and practice of fortification, the latter comprising rules for construction. He published a work on *Practical Architecture*, and prepared an important treatise on *The Practical Operations of a Siege* (1829-1832), which was translated into French (1847). He became brevet colonel in 1830 and substantive colonel in 1831. From 1831-1834 the subject that engaged his leisure was that of standardization of coins, weights and measures, and he published a book on this in 1834. In 1838 he was presented with the freedom of the city of London for his services in removing sunken vessels from the bed of the Thames near Gravesend; and from 1839 to 1844 he was occupied with clearing away the wrecks of H.M.S. "Royal George " from Spithead and H.M.S. "Edgar " from St Helens. All this work was subsidiary to his great work of creating a comprehensive art of military engineering. In 1841 on promotion to the rank of major-general he was made inspector-general of railways. In 1846 on vacating this appointment he was made a K.C.B., and thenceforward up to 1855 was chiefly concerned with the East India Company's military academy at Addiscombe. He was promoted lieutenant-general in 1851, made colonel commandant of the Royal Engineers in 1853, and general in 1860. He died in London on the 19th of April 1861. His eldest son, Major-General Charles Pasley (1824-1890), was a distinguished Royal Engineer officer.

Amongst Pasley's works, besides those mentioned, were separate editions of his *Practical Geometry Method* (1822) and of his *Course of Elementary Fortification* (1822), both of which formed part of his *Military Instruction; Rules for Escalading Fortifications not having Palisaded Covered Ways* (1822; new eds. 1845 and 1854); descriptions of a semaphore invented by himself in 1804 (1822 and 1823); *A Simple Practical Treatise on Field Fortification* (1823); and *Exercise of the Newdeched Pontoons invented by Lieutenant-Colonel Pasley* (1823).

PASQUIER, ÉTIENNE (1529-1615), French lawyer and man of letters, was born at Paris, on the 7th of June 1529 by his own account, according to others a year earlier. He was called to the Paris bar in 1549. In 1558 he became very ill through eating poisonous mushrooms, and did not recover fully for two years. This compelled him to occupy himself by literary work, and in 1560 he published the first book of his *Recherches de la France*. In 1565, when he was thirty-seven, his fame was established by a great speech still extant, in which he pleaded the cause of the university of Paris against the Jesuits, and won it. Meanwhile he pursued the *Recherches* steadily, and published from time to time much miscellaneous work. His literary and his legal occupations coincided in a curious fashion at the Grands Jours of Poitiers in 1579. These Grands Jours (an institution which fell into desuetude at the end of the 17th century, with bad effects on the social and political welfare of the French provinces) were a kind of irregular assize in which a commission of the parlement of Paris, selected and despatched at short notice by the king, had full power to hear and determine all causes, especially those in which seignorial rights had been abused. At the Grands Jours of Poitiers of the date mentioned, and at those of Troyes in 1583, Pasquier officiated; and each occasion has left a curious literary memorial of the jests with which he and his colleagues relieved their graver duties. The Poitiers work was the celebrated collection of poems on a flea (see Southey's *Doctor*). In 1585 Pasquier was appointed by Henry III. advocate-general at the Paris cours des comptes, an important body having political as well as financial and legal functions. Here he distinguished himself particularly by opposing, sometimes successfully, the mischievous system of selling hereditary places and offices, which more perhaps than any single thing was the curse of the older French monarchy. The civil wars compelled Pasquier to leave Paris and for some years he lived at Tours, working steadily at his great book, but he returned to Paris in Henry IV.'s train in March 1594. He continued until 1604 at his work in the chambre des comptes; then he retired. He survived this retirement more than ten years, producing much literary work, and died after a few hours' illness on the 1st of September 1615.

In so long and so laborious a life Pasquier's work was naturally considerable, and it has never been fully collected or indeed printed. The standard edition is that of Amsterdam (2 vols. fol., 1723). But for ordinary readers the selections of Léon Feugère, published at Paris (2 vols. 8vo, 1849), with an elaborate introduction, are most accessible. As a poet Pasquier is chiefly interesting as a minor member of the Pléiade movement. As a prose writer he is of much more account. The three chief divisions of his prose work are his *Recherches*, his letters and his professional speeches. The letters are of much biographical interest and historical importance, and the *Recherches* contain in a somewhat miscellaneous fashion invaluable information on a vast variety of subjects, literary, political, antiquarian and other.

PASQUIER, ÉTIENNE DENIS, DUKE (1767-1862), French statesman, was born on the 22nd of April 1767. Descended from a family which had long been distinguished at the bar and in connexion with the parlements of France, he was destined for the legal profession and was educated at the college of Juilly. He then became a counsellor of the parlement of Paris, and witnessed many of the incidents that marked the growing hostility between that body and Louis XVI. In the years preceding the outbreak of the French Revolution in 1789. His views were those of a moderate reformer, who desired to renovate but not to end the institutions of the old monarchy; and his memoirs set forth in a favourable light the actions of that parlement, the existence of which was soon to be terminated amid the political storms of the close of the year 1789. For some time, and especially during the Reign of Terror (1793–1794), Pasquier remained in obscurity; but this did not save him from arrest in the year 1794. He was thrown into prison shortly before the *coup d'état* of Thermidor (July 1794) which overthrew Robespierre. In the reaction in favour of ordinary government which ensued Pasquier regained his liberty and his estates. He did not re-enter the public service until the period of 'the Empire, when the arch-chancellor Cambacérès used his influence with Napoleon to procure for him the office of " maître des requetês " to the council of state. In 1809 he became baron of the French Empire, and in February 1810 counsellor of state. Napoleon in 1810 made him prefect of police. The chief event which ruffled the course of his life at that time was the strange conspiracy of the republican general Malet (Oct. 1812), who, giving out that Napoleon had perished in Russia, managed to surprise and capture some of the ministers and other authorities at Paris, among them Pasquier. The collapse of this bold attempt enabled him, however, speedily to regain his liberty. When Napoleon abdicated in April 1814 Pasquier continued to exercise his functions for a few days in order to preserve order, and then resigned the prefecture of police, whereupon Louis XVIII. allotted to him the control of roads and bridges. He took no share in the imperial restoration at the time of the Hundred Days (1815), and after the second entry of Louis XVIII. into Paris he became minister of the interior, but finding it impossible to work with the hot headed royalists of the Chamber of Deputies (*La Chambre introuvable*), he resigned office. Under the more moderate ministers of succeeding years he again held various appointments, but refused to join the reactionary cabinets of the close of the reign of Charles X. After the July Revolution (1830) he became president of the Chamber of Peers —a post which he held through the whole of the reign of Louis Philippe (1830–1848). In 1842 he was elected a member of the French Academy, and in the same year was created a duke. After the overthrow of Louis Philippe in February 1848, Pasquier retired from active life and set to work to compile the notes and reminiscences of his long and active career. He died in 1862.

See *Mémoires du Chancelier Pasquier* (6 vols., Paris, 1893–1895; partly translated into English, 4 vols., London, 1893–1894). Also L. de Vieilcastel, *Histoire de la Restauration*, vols. i.–iv.

(J. Hl. R.)

PASQUINADE, a variety of libel or lampoon, of which it is not easy to give an exact definition, separating it from other kinds. It should, perhaps, more especially deal with public men and public things. The distinction, however, has been rarely observed in practice, and the chief interest in the word is its curious and rather legendary origin. According to the earliest version, given by Mazocchi in 1509, Pasquino was a schoolmaster (others say a cobbler), who had a biting tongue, and lived in the 15th century at Rome. His name, at the end of that century or the beginning of the next, was transferred to a statue which had been dug up in 1501 in a mutilated condition (some say near his shop) and was set up at the corner of the Piazza Navona, opposite the palace of Cardinal Caraffa. To this statue it became the custom to affix squibs on the papal government and on prominent persons. At the beginning of the 16th century Pasquin had a partner provided for him in the shape of another statue found in the Campus Martius, said to represent a river god, and dubbed Marforio, *a foro Martis*. The regulation form of the pasquinade then became one of dialogue, or rather question and answer, in which Marforio usually addressed leading inquiries to his friend. The proceeding soon attained a certain European notoriety, and a printed collection of the squibs due to it (they were long written in Latin verse, with an occasional excursion into Greek) appeared in 1509. In the first book of *Pantagruel* (1533 or thereabouts) Rabelais introduces books by Pasquillus and Marphurius in the catalogue of the library of St Victor,

XX 15*

and later he quotes some utterances of Pasquin's in his letters to the bishop of Maillezais. These, by the way, show that Pasquin was by no means always satirical, but dealt in grave advice and comment. The original Latin pasquinades were collected in 1544, as *Pasquillorum tomi duo*, edited by Caelius Secundus Curio. The vogue of these lampoons now became general, and rose to its height during the pontificate of Sixtus V. (1585–1590). These utterances were not only called pasquinades (*pasquinate*) but simply pasquils (*pasquillus, pasquillo, pasquille*), and this form was sometimes used for the mythical personage himself. It was used in English for purposes of satire by Sir Thomas Elyot, in his *Pasquin the Plain* (1540) and by the anonymous author of *Pasquin in a Trance* (1566); but it was first made popular in England by Thomas Nash, who in 1589 began to sign his violent controversial pamphlets with the pseudonym of Pasquil of England. It continues to occur through the course of 'the Marprelate controversy as the title of the enemy of the Puritans. These English lampoons were in prose. The French pasquils (examples of which may be found in Fournier's *Variétés historiques et littéraires*) were more usually in verse. In Italy itself Pasquin is said not to have condescended to the vernacular till the 18th century. Contemporary comic periodicals, especially in Italy, still occasionally use the Marforio-Pasquino dialogue form. But this survival is purely artificial and literary, and pasquinade has, as noted above, ceased to have any precise meaning.

PASQUINI, BERNARDO (1637–1710), Italian musical composer, was born at Massa in Val di Nievole (Tuscany) on the 8th of December 1637. He was a pupil of Marcantonio Cesti and Loreto Vittori. He came to Rome while still young and entered the service of Prince Borghese; later he became organist of St Maria Maggiore. He enjoyed the protection of Queen Christina of Sweden, in whose honour an opera of his, *Dov' è amore è pietà*, was produced in 1679. During Alessandro Scarlatti's second sojourn in Rome (1703–1708), Pasquini and Corelli were frequently associated with him in musical performances, especially in connexion with the Arcadian Academy, of which all three were members. Pasquini died at Rome on the 22nd of November 1710, and was buried in the church of St Lorenzo in Lucina. He deserves remembrance as a vigorous composer for the harpsichord; and an interesting account of his music for this instrument will be found in J. S. Shedlock's *The Pianoforte Sonata*.

PASSACAGLIA, the name of an old Spanish dance, supposed to be derived from *pasar*, to walk, and *calle*, street, the tune being played by wandering musicians in the streets. It was a slow and rather solemn dance of one or two dancers. The dance tune resembled the " chaconne," and was, like it, constructed on a ground-bass. Brahms's Symphony in E Minor, No. 4, ends with an elaborate passacaglia.

PASSAGLIA, CARLO (1812–1887), Italian divine, was born at Lucca on the 2nd of May 1812. Passaglia was soon destined for the priesthood, and was placed under the care of the Jesuits at the age of fifteen. He became successively doctor in mathematics, philosophy and theology in the university of Rome. In 1844 he was made professor in the Collegio Romano, the well-known Jesuit college in Rome. In 1845 he took the vows as a member of the Jesuit order. In 1848, during the expulsion of the Jesuits from Rome which followed on the revolutionary troubles in the Italian peninsula, he paid a brief visit to England. On his return to Italy he founded, with the assistance of Father Curci and Luigi Taparelli d'Azeglio, the celebrated organ of the Jesuit order entitled the *Civiltà Cattolica*. In 1854 came the decision of the Roman Church on the long-debated question of the Immaculate Conception of the Virgin. Into the agitation for the promulgation of this dogma Passaglia threw himself with great eagerness, and by so doing recommended himself strongly to Pope Pius IX. But his favour with the pope was of short duration. In 1859, when the war between Austria and France (the first step towards the unification of Italy) broke out, Passaglia espoused the popular side. He took refuge at Turin, and under the influence of Cavour he wrote an *Epistola ad*

Episcopus Catholicus pro causa Italica, in which, like Liverani before him, he boldly attacked the temporal power of the pope. For this he was expelled from the order of Jesuits, his book was put on the *Index*, and his figure struck out, by the pope's order, from a picture painted to commemorate the proclamation of the dogma of the Immaculate Conception. A refuge from the anger of the pope was afforded him in the Casa Cavour at Turin, the house in which Cavour was born. There he laboured for Italian unity with indomitable energy in the north of Italy, in conjunction with Cardinal d'Andrea in the south, and he collected the signatures of 9000 priests to an address to the pope in opposition to the temporal power, and in favour of abandoning all resistance to the union of Italy under a king of the House of Savoy. He and the 9000 priests were excommunicated on the 6th of October 1862. Passaglia disregarded his excommunication, and continued his work as professor of moral philosophy at Turin, to which he had been appointed in 1861, and began a series of Advent addresses in the church of San Carlo at Milan. But on arriving in order to preach his second sermon he found himself met by an inhibition on the part of Mgr Caccia, the administrator of the archdiocese of Milan. Elected deputy in the Italian parliament, he still advocated strongly the cause of Italian independence, and at a later period wrote a defence of the rights of the episcopate under the title of *La Causa di sua eminenza il cardinale d'Andrea*. He also (1864) wrote against Renan's *Vie de Jésus*. Eight days before his death he endeavoured to be reconciled to the pope, and made a full retractation. He died at Turin on the 12th of March 1887.

PASSAIC, a city of Passaic county, New Jersey, U.S.A., at the head of navigation on the Passaic river, 5 m. S.S.E. of Paterson. (Pop. (1890), 13,028; (1900), 27,777, of whom 12,900 were foreign-born; (1910 census), 54,773. Passaic is served by the Erie and the Delaware, Lackawana & Western railways. The east part of the city is a plain occupied chiefly by factories, for which water-power is furnished by the river and a canal; the west part, which is almost wholly residential, extends over hills which command excellent views. Among the principal buildings are the city hall, and the Jane Watson Reid Memorial Library. The city's factory products increased in value from $12,804,805 in 1900 to $22,782,725 in 1905, or 77·9%. About one-half of the value in 1905 was in worsteds, cottons and woollens; other important manufactures are rubber goods and electrical supplies. There are large vineyards near the city. A settlement was established here by the Dutch in 1679, and was called Acquackanonk or Paterson Landing until the middle of the 19th century. Passaic was incorporated as a village in 1869, and in 1873 was chartered as a city.

See W. J. Pape and W. W. Scott, *The News History of Passaic* (Passaic, 1899).

PASSAU, a town and episcopal see of Germany, in the kingdom of Bavaria, picturesquely situated at the confluence of the Danube, the Inn and the Ilz, close to the Austrian frontier, 89 m. N.E. from Munich and 74 S.E. of Regensburg by rail. Pop. (1900), 18,003, nearly all being Roman Catholics. Passau consists of the town proper, lying on the rocky tongue of land between the Danube and the Inn, and of four suburbs, Innstadt on the right bank of the Inn, Ilzstadt on the left bank of the Ilz, Anger in the angle between Ilz and the Danube, and St Nikola. It is one of the most beautiful places on the Danube, a fine effect being produced by the way in which the houses are piled up one above another on the heights rising from the river. The best general view is obtained from the Oberhaus, an old fortress, now used as a prison, which crowns a hill 300 ft. high on the left bank of the Danube. Of the eleven churches, the most interesting is the cathedral of St Stephen, a florid, rococo edifice. It was built after a fire in the 17th century on the site of a church said to have been founded in the 5th century; it has two towers, and contains some valuable relics. Other churches are the Gothic church of the Holy Ghost; the churches of St Severin, of St Paul and St Gertrude; the double church of St Salvator; the Romanesque church of the Holy Cross; the pilgrimage church of Our Lady of Succour (Mariahilf); the church of the hospital

of St John; and the Romanesque Votiv Kirché.' The post office occupies the site of a building in which in 1552 the Treaty of Passau was signed between the emperor Charles V. and Maurice, elector of Saxony. The fine Dom Platz contains a statue of the Bavarian king, Maximilian I. The old forts and bastions of the city have been demolished, but the two linked fortresses, the Oberhaus and the Niederhaus, are still extant. The former was built early in the 13th century by the bishop in consequence of a revolt on the part of the citizens; the latter, mentioned as early as 737, is now private property. The chief industries are the manufacture of tobacco, beer, leather, porcelain, machinery and paper. Large quantities of timber are floated down the Ilz. The well-known Passau crucibles are made at the neighbouring village of Obernzell.

Passau is of ancient origin. The first settlement was probably a Celtic one, *Boiudurum*; this was on the site of the present Innstadt. Afterwards the Romans established a colony of Batavian-veterans, the *castra batava* here. It received civic rights in 1225, and soon became a prosperous place, but much of its history consists of broils between the bishops and the citizens. The strong fortress of the Oberhaus was taken by the Austrians in 1742, and again in 1805. The bishopric of Passau was founded by St Boniface in 738. The diocese was a large one, including until 1468 not only much of Bavaria, but practically the whole of the archduchy of Austria. About 1260 the bishop became a prince of the empire. Amongst the earlier bishops was Pilgrim or Piligrim (d. 991), and among the later ones were the Austrian archdukes, Leopold and Leopold William, the former a brother and the latter a son of the emperor Ferdinand II. In 1803 the bishopric was secularized, and in 1805 its lands came into the possession of Bavaria. The area, which was diminished in the 15th, and again in the 18th century, was then about 350 sq. m., and the population about 50,000. A new bishopric of Passau, with ecclesiastical jurisdiction only, was established in 1817.

See Erhart, *Geschichte der Stadt Passau* (Passau, 1862-1864); and Morin, *Passau* (1878). For the history of the bishopric see Schöller, *Die Bischöfe von Passau* (Passau, 1844); and Schrödl, *Passavia sacra. Geschichte des Bistums Passau* (Passau, 1879).

PASSERAT, JEAN (1534-1602), French poet, was born at Troyes, on the 18th of October 1534. He studied at the university of Paris, and is said to have had some curious adventures—at one time working in a mine. He was, however, a scholar by natural taste, and became eventually a teacher at the Collège de Plessis, and on the death of Ramus was made professor of Latin in 1572 in the Collège de France. In the meanwhile Passerat had studied law, and had composed much agreeable poetry in the Pléiade style, the best pieces being his short ode *Du Premier jour de mai*, and the charming villanelle, *J'ai perdu ma tourterelle*. His exact share in the *Satyre ménippée* (Tours, 1594), the great manifesto of the *politique* or Moderate Royalist party when it had declared itself for Henry of Navarre, is differently stated; but it is agreed that he wrote most of the verse, and the harangue of the guerrilla chief Rieux is sometimes attributed to him. The famous lines *Sur la journée de Senlis*, in which he commends the duc d'Aumale's ability in running away, is one of the most celebrated political songs in French. Towards the end of his life he became blind. He died in Paris on the 14th of September 1602.

See a notice by P. Blanchemain prefixed to his edition of Passerat's *Poésies françaises* (1880). Among his Latin works should be noticed *Kalendae januariae et varia quaedam poemata* (2 vols., 1606), addressed chiefly to his friend and patron Henri de Mesmes. For the *Satyre ménippée* see the edition of Charles Read (1876).

PASSION (post-classical Lat. *passio*, formed from *pati, passus*, to suffer, endure), a term which is used in two main senses: (1) the suffering of pain, and (2) feeling or emotion. The first is chiefly used of the sufferings of Jesus Christ, extending from the time of the agony in the garden until his death on the cross. In this sense *passio* was used by the early Christian writers, and the term is also applied to the sufferings and deeds of saints and martyrs, synonymously with *acta* or *gesta*, a book containing such being known as a "passional" (*liber passionalis*) or "passionary" (passionarius).· The order of Passionist Fathers, the full title of which is the " Congregation of the Discalced Clerks of the Most Holy Cross and Passion of our Lord Jesus Christ," was founded by St Paul of the Cross (Paolo della Croce, 1694–1775; canonized 1867) in 1720, but full sanction was not obtained for the order till 1737, when the first monastery was established at Monte Argentario; Orbetello. The secondary sense of " passion " is due to the late use of *passio* to translate the Greek philosophical term *πάθος*, the classical Latin equivalent being *afectus*. The modern use generally restricts the term to strong and uncontrolled emotion..

PASSIONFLOWER (*Passiflora*), the typical genus of the order to which it gives its name. The name passionflower—*flos*

passionis—arose from the supposed resemblance of the corona to the crown of thorns, and of the other parts of the flower to the nails, or wounds, while the five sepals and five petals were taken to symbolize the ten apostles—Peter, who denied, and Judas, who betrayed, being left out of the reckoning.. The species are mostly natives of western ,tropical South America; others are found in various tropical and sub-tropical districts of both hemispheres. The tacsonias, by some considered to form part of this genus, inhabit the Andes at considerable elevations. They are mostly climbing plants (fig. 1) having a woody stock and herbaceous or woody branches, from the sides. of which tendrils are produced which enable the branches to support themselves at little expenditure of tissue. Some few form trees of considerable stature destitute of tendrils, and with broad magnolia-like leaves in place of the more or less palmately-lobed leaves which are most generally met with in the order. The leaf is usually provided at the base of the leaf-stalk with stipules, which are inconspicuous, or large and leafy; and the stalk is also furnished with one or more glandular excrescences, as in some cases are the leaf itself and the bracts. The inflorescence is of a cymose character, the terminal branch being represented by the' tendril, the side branches by flower-stalks, or the inflorescence may be reduced to a single stalk. The bracts on the flower-stalk are either small and scattered or large and leafy, and then placed near the flower, forming a sort of outer calyx or epicalyx. The flower itself (seen in section in fig. 2) consists of a receptacle varying in form from that of a shallow saucer to that of a long cylindrical or trumpet-shaped tube, thin or fleshy in consistence, and giving off from its upper border the five sepals, the five petals (rarely these latter are absent), and the threads or membranous processes constituting the " corona." This coronet forms the most conspicuous and beautiful part of the flower of many species, and consists of outgrowths from the tube formed subsequently to the other parts, and having little morphological significance, but being physiologically useful in favouring the cross-fertilization of the flower by means of insects. Other outgrowths of similar character, but less conspicuous, occur lower down the tube, and their variations afford useful means of discriminating between the species. From the base of the inner part of the tube of the flower, but quite free from it, uprises a cylindrical stalk surrounded below by a small cup-like outgrowth, and bearing above the middle a ring of five flat filaments each attached by a thread-like point to an anther. Above the ring of stamens is the ovary itself, upraised on a prolongation of the same stalk which bears the filaments, or sessile.

FIG. 2.—Flower of Passionflower cut through the centre to show the arrangement of its constituent parts.

The stalk supporting the stamens and ovary is called the " gynophore " or the " gynandrophore," and is a characteristic of the order. The ovary of passionflowers is one-celled with three parietal placentas, and bears at the top three styles, each capped by a large button-like stigma. The ovary ripens into a berry-like, very rarely capsular, fruit with the three groups of seeds arranged in lines along the. walls, but imbedded in a pulpy arillus derived from the stalk of the seed. This succulent berry is· in some cases highly perfumed, and affords a delicate fruit for the dessert-table, as in the case of the " granadilla " (*P. quadrangularis*), *P. edulis*, *P. macrocarpa*, and various species of *Tacsonia* known as " curubas " in Spanish South America; *P. laurifolia* is .the water-lemon, and *P. maliformis* the sweet calabash of the West Indies. The fruits do not usually exceed in size the dimensions of a hen's or of a swan's egg, but that of *P. macrocarpa* is a gourd-like oblong fruit attaining a weight of 7 to 8 ℔.

The tacsonias, which in cultivation are· generally regarded as distinct, differ from *Passiflora* in having a long cylindrical calyx-tube, bearing two crowns, one at the throat, the other near the base; they are stove or greenhouse plants; *T. pinnatistipula*, with pale rose-coloured flowers, a native of Chile and Peru, has long been in cultivation; *T. Van-Volxemii*, with handsome scarlet flowers, is one of the finest species.

PASSION WEEK, the fifth week in. Lent, beginning with Passion Sunday (*dominica passionis* or *de passione domini*), so called from very early times because with it begins the more special commemoration of Christ's passion. Passion week is often incorrectly identified with Holy week (*q.v.*). In the north of England Passion Sunday was formerly known as Carle or Carling Sunday, a name corrupted from " care," in allusion to the sorrowful season which the day heralds. It was the universal custom in medieval England to eat on this Sunday a grey pea steeped and fried in butter, which came to be called from its association " Carling Nut."

PASSOVER, a Hebrew spring festival, celebrated by the Jews in commemoration of the exodus from Egypt by a family feast in the home on the first evening, and by abstaining from leaven during the seven days of the feast. According to tradition, the first Passover ("The Passover of Egypt"), was preordained by Moses at the command of God. The Israelites were commanded to select on the tenth of Abib (Nisan) a he-lamb of the first year, without blemish, to kill it on the eve of the fourteenth and to sprinkle with its blood the lintel and sidepost of the doors of their dwellings so that the Lord should "pass over" them when he went forth to slay the first-born of the Egyptians. The lamb thus drained of blood was to be roasted and entirely consumed by the Israelites, who should be ready with loins girded, shoes on feet and staff in hand so as to be prepared for the exodus. In memory of this the Israelites were for all time to eat unleavened bread (maᶻᶻoth) for seven days, as well as keep the sacrifice of the Passover on the eve between the fourteenth and the fifteenth of Nisan. This evening meal was not to be attended by any stranger or uncircumcised person. "On the morrow of the Sabbath" a wave offering of a sheaf of barley was to be made. Those who were unable to perform the sacrifice of the Passover owing to impurity at the appointed time, were permitted to do so a month later.

Various theories have been from time to time proposed to account for this complex of enactments. J. Spencer in his De legibus Hebraeorum saw in the Passover a practical protest against the Egyptian worship of Apis. Vatke considered it a celebration of the spring solstice, Baur a means of removing the impurity of the old year. Lengerke recognised a double motive: the lamb for atonement, the unleavened bread as a trace of the haste of the early harvest. Ewald regarded the Passover as an original pre-Mosaic spring festival made to serve the interest of purity and atonement.

All these views have, however, been cast in the shade by more recent investigations based on minute literary analysis of the Pentateuch, begun by Graf, continued by Kuenen, and culminating in the work of Wellhausen and Robertson Smith. This view claims to determine the respective ages and relative chronological position of the various passages in which the Passover is referred to in the Pentateuch, and assumes that each successive stratum represents the practice in ancient Israel at the time of composition, laying great stress upon omissions as implying non-existence. The main passages and their contents are arranged chronologically in the following way:—

A. In the Elohist Book of the Covenant (Exod. xxiii.). The feast of unleavened bread to be kept seven days at the time appointed in the month Abib.

B. In the Yahwist Source (Exod. xxxiv. 18-21, 25). The feast of unleavened bread to be kept seven days, &c. All firstlings to be the Lord's. First-born sons to be redeemed; none to appear before the Lord empty; six days' work, seventh day rest, in the harvest; the sacrifice of the Passover shall not remain until the morning.

C. In the Yahwistic History (Exod. xii. 21-27, 29-36, 38-39, xiii. 3-16). Moses summons the elders of Israel and orders them to kill the Passover and besprinkle the lintel and sideposts with a bunch of hyssop dipped in blood so that the Lord will pass over the door. In later days when the children shall ask what this means it shall be said that this is the sacrifice of the Lord's Passover. At midnight all the first-born of the Egyptians are slain and Pharaoh sends the Israelites out of Egypt in haste, and the people took the dough before it was leavened upon kneading troughs upon their shoulders.

D. The Deuteronomist (Deut. xvi. 1-8, 16-17). Observe the month of Abib and keep the Passover because in that month God brought out the Israelites from Egypt. The sacrifice of the Passover of the flock and the herd shall be done in the place where God shall cause His name to dwell. No leaven shall be eaten with it for seven days, and bread of affliction shall be eaten because they came forth from Egypt in haste. Flesh shall not remain until the morning; the sacrifice must not ᶻ within their gates but in the place where the Lord shall cause His name to dwell. It shall be sodden and eaten, and in the morning they should go to their tents. Six days eat unleavened bread, on the seventh a solemn assembly. Reckon seven weeks from the time of putting the sickle to the standing corn.

E. In the Holiness Code (Lev. xxiii. 4-8, 9-14). The 14th of the first month at even is the Passover of the Lord; on the 15th of the same month is the feast of unleavened bread for seven days.

First and seventh days shall be holy assembly, but a re-offering for seven days. On the morrow after the sabbath a wave offering and also a burnt offering of the he-lamb (with the corresponding meal and drink offering). Neither bread nor parched corn nor fresh ears shall be eaten until the oblation is made.

F. In the Priestly History (Exod. xii. 1-20, 28-31, xiii. 1-2). On the 10th day of the month every household shall take a firstling male without blemish, of sheep or goat, and should kill it on the 14th at even, and sprinkle the two sideposts and lintel with the blood, and eat the roasted flesh, not sodden, including head, legs and inwards; all remaining over until the morning to be burnt by fire. It should be eaten with loins girded, shoes on feet, and staff in hand because in haste. It is the Lord's Passover; when He sees the blood He will pass over you and there will be no plague upon you. As a memorial of this you shall eat unleavened bread seven days, on the 14th day at eve until the 21st day at eve; when children shall ask what this service means, you shall say that it is the Passover of the Lord.

G. In the Secondary Sources of the Priestly Code (Exod. xii. 40-41, 43-50, ix. 1-14, xiv. 16-25). No alien, sojourner or hired servant shall eat thereof, but a bought servant, if circumcised. It shall be eaten in haste; none of the flesh shall be carried forth, neither shall a bone be broken. If a sojourner should wish to keep the Passover, all his male shall be circumcised and he will be as one born in the land. The Passover was kept in the first month on the 14th day of the month at even in the wilderness of Sinai; but certain men, unclean by touching a dead body, asked what they should do; they were to keep it on the second month on the 14th day, eating it with unleavened bread and bitter herbs, leaving none of it until the morning, nor breaking a bone. The first month on the 14th day of the month is the Passover; the 15th day of this month shall be a feast; seven days unleavened bread to be eaten; first day a holy assembly, with fire offering; two young bullocks and one lamb and seven firstling he-lambs without blemish, with appropriate meal offering and one he-goat for sin-offering; on the seventh day another holy assembly.

Many discrepancies have been observed among critics in the different portions of this series of enactments. Thus in the Elohist and in Deuteronomy the date of the festival is only vaguely stated to be in the month of Abib, while in the Holiness Code and in the Priestly History the exact date is given. In the Yahwist and Deuteronomist a solemn assembly is to be held on the seventh day, but in the Holiness Code and in the secondary sources of the Priestly Code both the first and the seventh day of the Feast of Unleavened Bread are to be solemn assemblies. In the Deuteronomist the Passover sacrifice can be from either flock or herd, whereas in the Holiness Code only lamb is mentioned, and in the Priestly Code either kid or lamb. In the Deuteronomist the lamb is to be sodden or boiled, whereas in the Priestly Code this is expressly forbidden. A still more vital contrast occurs concerning the place of sacrificing the Passover; as enjoined in Deuteronomy this is to be by the males of the family at Jerusalem, whereas both in the presumably earlier Yahwist and in the later Priestly Code the whole household joins in the festival which can be celebrated wherever the Israelites are settled. These discrepancies however are chiefly of interest in their bearing upon the problem of the Pentateuch, and really throw little light upon the origin of the two feasts connected together under the name of the Passover, to which the present remarks must be mainly confined. It may be observed however that the absence of a definite date in Deuteronomy must be accidental, since a common pilgrimage feast must be on a fixed day, and the reference to the seven weeks elapsing between Passover and Pentecost also implies the fixing of the date. So too even in the Elohist the time is appointed.

Reverting to the origin and the meaning of the feast, modern criticism draws attention to the different nature of the two observances combined with the name Passover, the pastoral sacrifice of the paschal lamb and the agricultural observance of a seven days' abstention from unleavened bread. It is assumed that the former arose during the pastoral period of Israelite history before or during the stay in Egypt, while the latter was adopted from the Canaanites after the settlement in Palestine. Against this may be urged that, according to the latest inquiries into the pastoral life, there is always connected with it some form of agriculture and a use of cereals, while, historically speaking, the Israelites while in Egypt were dependent on its corn. There is, further, the objection that no distinctive crisis in the agricultural era can be associated with the date of the Passover. The beginning of barley harvest is however generally associated with it, while the wheat harvest is connected with Pentecost. The "sheaf of the first-fruits of your harvest," mentioned in Lev. xxiii. 10, is associated in Jewish tradition with the barley harvest (Mishna, Menachoth x.). This, however, is not immediately connected with the Passover, and is of more significance as determining the exact date of Pentecost.

Considering however the two sections of the Passover separately, it is remarkable how many of the ceremonies associated either historically or ceremonially with the Passover have connexion with the idea of a covenant. The folk-etymology of the word Passover given in Exod. xii. 23 seems to connect the original of the feast with a threshold covenant (see Trumbull, *Threshold Covenant*, Philadelphia, 1902); the daubing of the side-posts and lintel with blood at the original Passover, which finds its counterpart in Babylonian custom (Zimmern, *Beit. s. Bab. Rel.* ii. 126–7) and in Arabic usage (Wåkidî, ed. Kremer, p. 38), implies a blood covenant. The communion meal would, according to the views of Robertson Smith, also involve the idea of a covenant; while the fact that no person joining in the meal should be uncircumcised connects the feast with the covenant of Abraham. Finally, the association of the first-born with the festival specially referred to in the texts, and carried out both in Samaritan tradition, which marks the forehead of the first-born with the blood of the lamb, and in Jewish custom, which obliged the first-born to fast on the day preceding Passover, also connects the idea of the feast with the sacro-sanctity of the first-born. The Hebrew tradition further connects the revelation of the sacred name of the God of the Hebrews with this festival, which thus combines, in itself, all the associations connecting the Hebrews with their God. It is not surprising therefore that Hebrew tradition connects it with the Exodus, the beginning of the theocratic life of the nation. It seems easiest to assume that the festival, so far as the Passover itself is concerned, was actually connected historically with the Exodus.

With regard to the abstention from leavened bread, the inquiry is somewhat more complicated. As before remarked, there seems no direct connexion between the paschal sacrifice and what appears to be essentially an agricultural festival; the Hebrew tradition, to some extent, dissociates them by making the sacrifice on the 14th of Nisan and beginning the Feast of Unleavened Bread on the 15th. This seeming casual connexion, to some extent, confirms the historic connexion suggested by the text, that the Jews at the Exodus had to use bread prepared in haste; but not even Hebrew tradition attempts to explain why the abstention should last for seven days. The attempt of modern critics to account for the period as that in which the barley harvest was gathered in, during which the workers in the field could not prepare leavened bread, is not satisfactory. The first-fruits of the barley harvest are to be gathered on the "morrow of the sabbath" (Lev. xxiii. 11). This expression has formed the subject of dispute between Samaritans and other sectaries and the Jews, the former of whom regard it as referring to the first Sunday during the festival, the latter as a special expression for the second day of the festival itself (see Hoffmann, Lev. ii. 159–213). But whichever interpretation is taken, the connexion of the festival with the harvest is only secondary.

The suggestion has been made by Wellhausen and Robertson Smith that the Passover was, in its original form, connected with the sacrifice of the firstlings, and the latter points to the Arabic annual sacrifices called '*Atair*, which some of the lexico-graphers interpret as firstlings. These were presented in the month Rajab, corresponding to Nisan (Smith, *Religion of Semites*, p. 210). But the real Arabic sacrifice of firstlings was called *Fara'*; it might be sacrificed at any time, as was also the case with the Hebrews (Exod. xxii. 30). The paschal lamb was not necessarily a firstling, but only in the first year of its life (Exod. xii. 5). The suggestion of Wellhausen and Robertson Smith confuses the offering of firstlings (Arabic *Fara'*) and that of the first yeanlings of the flock in the spring (Arabic '*Atair*). It is possible that the Passover was originally connected with the latter (cf. Wellhausen, *Reste arab. Heidentums*, pp. 94 seq.). As regards

the Feast of Unleavened Bread, now indissolubly connected with the paschal sacrifice, no satisfactory explanation has been given either of its original intention or of its connexion with the Passover. It has been suggested that it was originally a *hag* or pilgrimage feast to Jerusalem, of which there were three in the year connected with the agricultural festivals (Exod. xxxiv. 17, 18). But the real agricultural occasion was not the eating of unleavened bread but the offering of the first sheaf of the barley harvest on the "morrow of the sabbath" in the Passover week (Lev. xxiii. 10, 11), and this occasion determined the second agricultural festival, the Feast of Weeks, fifty days later (Deut. xvi. 9; Lev. xxiii. 16; see PENTECOST). The suggestion that the eating of cakes of unleavened bread, similar to the Australian "damper," was due to the exigencies of the harvest does not meet the case, since it does not explain the seven days and is incongruous with the fact that the first sheaf of the harvest was put to the sickle not earlier than the third day of the feast. It still remains possible therefore that the seven days' eating of unleavened bread (and bitter herbs) is an historical reminiscence of the incidents of the Exodus, where the normal commissariat did not begin until a week after the first exit. On the other hand, the absence of leaven may recall primitive practice before its introduction as a domestic luxury; sacral rites generally keep alive primitive custom. There was also associated in the Hebrew mind a connexion of impurity and corruption with the notion of leaven which was tabu in all sacrifice (Exod. xxiii. 18; Lev. ii. 11).

According to Robertson Smith, the development of the various institutions connected with the Passover was as follows. In Egypt the Israelites, as a pastoral people, sacrificed the firstlings of their flocks in the spring, and, according to tradition, it was a refusal to permit a general gathering for this purpose that caused the Exodus. When the Israelites settled in Canaan they found there an agricultural festival connected with the beginnings of the barley harvest, which coincided in point of date with the Passover and was accordingly associated with it. At the time of the reformation under Josiah, represented by Deuteronomy, the attempt was made to turn the family thank offering of firstlings into a sacrificial rite performed by the priests in the Temple with the aid of the males of each household, who had to come up to Jerusalem but left the next morning to celebrate the Feast of Unleavened Bread in their homes. During the exile this was found impossible, and the old home ceremonial was revived and was kept up even after the return of the exile. This is a highly ingenious hypothesis to explain the discrepancies of the text, but is, after all, nothing but hypothesis.

There appears to have been originally considerable variety in the mode of keeping the Passover, but the earliest mention in the historical narratives (Josh. v. 11) connects the paschal sacrifice with the eating of unleavened bread. But it is unsafe to assume, from 2 Kings xxiii. 22, that the festival was not kept in the time of the early kings, since Solomon appears to have kept up the three great pilgrimage festivals, 2 Kings ix. 25, and it is possibly referred to in Isa. i. 9. The complex of observances connected with the Passover and the very want of systemization observed in the literary sources would seem to vindicate the primitive character of the feast, which indeed is recognized by all inquirers.

At any rate the Samaritans have, throughout their history, observed the Passover with all its Pentateuchal ceremonial and still observe it down to the present day. They sacrifice the paschal lamb, which is probably the oldest religious rite that has been continuously kept up. In two important points they differ from later Jewish interpretation. The term "between the evenings" (Lev. xxiii. 5) they take as the time between sunset and dark, and the "morrow of the sabbath" (v. 11) they take literally as the first Sunday in the Passover week; wherein they agree with the Sadducees, Boethusians, Karaites and other Jewish sectaries. This would seem to point to a time when the fixing of the sabbath was determined by the age of the moon, so that the first day of the Passover, which is on the 15th of Nisan, would always occur on a sabbath.

During the existence of the Temple there was a double celebration of the Passover, a series of stipulated sacrifices being offered during the seven days in the Temple, details of which are given in Num. xxviii., but the family ceremonial was still kept up and gradually developed a special ritual, which has been retained among orthodox Jews up to the present day. The paschal lamb is no longer eaten but represented by the shank bone of a lamb roasted in the ashes; unleavened bread and bitter herbs (*haroseth*) are eaten; four cups of wine are drunk before and after the repast, and a certain number of Psalms are recited. The family service, termed *Hagada shel Pesach*, includes a description of the Exodus with a running commentary, and is begun by the youngest son of the house asking the father the reason for the difference in Passover customs.

It is stated in the gospels that the Last Supper was the Passover meal, though certain discrepancies between the accounts given in the Synoptics and in John render this doubtful. It is, at any rate, certain that Jesus came up to Jerusalem in order to join in the celebration of the Passover. When the Passover fell upon the sabbath, as occurred during his visit, a difficulty arose about the paschal sacrifice, which might involve work on the sabbath. There appears to have been a difference of practice between the Sadducees and the Pharisees on such occasions, the former keeping to the strict rules of the Law and sacrificing on the Friday, whereas the Pharisees did so on the Thursday. It has been suggested that Jesus followed the pharisaic practice, and ate the Passover meal (the Last Supper) on Thursday evening, which would account for the discrepancies in the gospel narratives (see Chwolson, *Das letzte Passahmal Jesu*, 2nd ed., St Petersburg, 1904). It seems probable in any case that the ritual of the Mass has grown out of that of the Passover service (see Bickell, *Messe und Pascha*, tr. W. F. Skene, Edinburgh, 1891). Up to the Nicene Council the Church kept Easter (*q.v.*) coincident with the Jewish Passover, but after that period took elaborate precautions to dissociate the two.

See the commentaries on Exodus and Leviticus; that of Kalisch on the latter book (vol. ii., London, 1871) anticipates much of the critical position. The article in Winer's *Bibl. Realwörterbuch* gives a succinct account of the older views: A not altogether unsuccessful attempt to defend the Jewish orthodox position is made by Hoffmann in his *Commentary on Leviticus* (Berlin, 1906, ii. 116–224). Wellhausen's views are given in his *Prolegomena*, ch. iii. A critical yet conservative view of the whole question is given by R. Schaefer, *Das Passah-Massoth-Fest* (Gutersloh, 1900) which has been partly followed above. For the general attitude towards the comparative claims of institutional archaeology and literary criticism adopted above see J. Jacobs, *Studies in Biblical Archaeology* (London, 1895).

(J. JA.)

PASSOW, FRANZ LUDWIG CARL FRIEDRICH (1786–1833), German classical scholar and lexicographer, was born at Ludwigslust in Mecklenburg-Schwerin on the 20th of September 1786. In 1807 he was appointed to the professorship of Greek literature at the Weimar gymnasium by Goethe, whose acquaintance he had made during a holiday tour. In 1815 he became professor of ancient literature in the university of Breslau, where he continued to reside until his death on the 11th of March 1833. His advocacy of gymnastic exercises, in which he himself took part, met with violent opposition and caused a quarrel known as the "Breslauer Turnfehde." Passow's great work was his *Handwörterbuch der griechischen Sprache* (1819–1824), originally a revision of J. G. Schneider's lexicon, which appeared in the fourth edition (1831) as an independent work, without Schneider's name (new ed. by Grönert, 1901). It formed the basis of Liddell and Scott's lexicon. Other works by him are *Grundzüge der griech. und röm. Literatur- und Kunstgeschichte* (2nd ed., 1829) and editions of Persius, Longus, Tacitus *Germania*, Dionysius Periegetes, and Musaeus. His miscellaneous writings have been collected in his *Opuscula academica* (1835) and *Vermischte Schriften* (1843).

See *Frans Passow's Leben und Briefe* (1839), by L. and A. Wachler, which contains a full bibliography.

PASSPORT, or safe-conduct in time of war, a document granted by a belligerent power to protect persons and property from the operation of hostilities. In the case of the ship of a neutral power, the passport is a requisition by the government of the neutral state to suffer the vessel to pass freely with the crew, cargo, passengers, &c., without molestation by the belligerents. The requisition, when issued by the civil authorities of the port from which the vessel is fitted out, is called a sea-letter. But the terms passport and sea-letter are often used indiscriminately. A form of sea-letter (*litterae salvi conductus*) is appended to the Treaty of the Pyrenees, 1659. The passport is frequently mentioned in treaties, *e.g.* the Treaty of Copenhagen, 1670, between Great Britain and Denmark. The violation of a passport, or safe conduct, is a grave breach of international law. The offence in the United States is punishable by fine and imprisonment where the passport or safe conduct is granted under the authority of the United States (Act of Congress, April 30, 1790). In its more familiar sense a passport is a document authorizing a person to pass out of or into a country, or a licence or safe-conduct to the person specified therein and authenticating his right to aid and protection. Although most foreign countries may now be entered without passports, the English foreign office recommends travellers to furnish themselves with them, as affording a ready means of identification in case of need. They are usually granted by the foreign office of a state, or by its diplomatic agents abroad. The English Foreign Office charges two shillings for a passport, whatever number of persons may be named in it. Passports granted in England are subject to a stamp duty of sixpence. They may be granted to naturalised as well as natural-born British subjects.

See "The Passport System," by N. W. Sibley, in *Jour. Comp. Leg.* new series, vol. vii. The regulations respecting passports issued by the English Foreign Office as well as the passport requirements of foreign countries will be found in the annual *Foreign Office List*.

PASTE (O. Fr. *paste*, modern *pâte*, Late Lat. *pasta*, whence also in Span., Port. and Ital., from Gr. πάστη or παστά, barley porridge, or salted pottage, πάσσω, to sprinkle with salt), a mixture or composition of a soft plastic consistency. The term is applied to substances used for various purposes, as *e.g.* in cookery, a mixture of flour and water with lard, butter or suet, for making pies and pastry, or of flour and water boiled, to which starch or other ingredients to prevent souring are added, forming an adhesive for the affixing of wall-paper, bill-posting and other purposes. In technical language, the term is also applied to the prepared clay which forms the body in the manufacture of pottery and porcelain (see CERAMICS) and to the specially prepared glass, known also as "strass," from which imitation gems are manufactured. This latter must be the purest, most transparent and most highly refractive glass that can be prepared. These qualities are comprised in the highest degree in a flint glass of unusual density from the large percentage of lead it contains. Among various mixtures regarded as suitable for strass the following is an example: powdered quartz 300 parts, red lead 470, potash (purified by alcohol) 163, borax 22, and white arsenic 1 part by weight. Special precautions are taken in the melting. The finished colourless glass is used for imitation diamonds; and when employed to imitate coloured precious stones the strass is melted up with various metallic oxides. Imitation gems are easily distinguished from real stones by their inferior hardness and by chemical tests; they may generally be detected by the comparatively warm sensation they communicate to the tongue.

PASTEL, the name of a particular method of painting with dry pigments, so called from the "paste" into which they are first compounded. The invention of pastel, which used to be generally called "crayon," has frequently been accredited to Johann Alexander Thiele (1685–1752), landscape-painter and etcher of distinction, as well as to Mme Vernerin and Mlle Heid (1688–1753), both of Danzig. But the claim cannot be substantiated, as drawing in coloured chalks had been practised long before, *e.g.* by Guido Reni (1575–1642), by whom a head and bust in this manner exists in the Dresden Gallery. Thiele was perhaps the first to carry the art to perfection, at least in Germany, where it was extensively exploited in the

17th century; but his contemporary, Rosalba Carriera of Venice (1675–1757), is more completely identified with it, and in her practice of it made a European reputation which to this day is in some measure maintained. The Dresden Museum contains 157 examples of her work in this medium, portraits, subjects and the like. Thiele was followed by Anton Raphael Mengs (1728–1779) and his sister Theresia Mengs (afterwards Maron, 1725–1806), and by Johann Heinrich Schmidt (1749–1829).

When in 1720 Rosalba Carriera accepted an invitation to visit Paris, where she was received with general enthusiasm, she found the art of pastel-painting well established; that is to say, it was used to reproduce local colour with truth. She made it fashionable and combined truth with nature. Nearly a hundred years before Claude Lorrain had used coloured chalks as Dutch and Italian painters had used them, often with high finish, employing mainly red, blue and black, for the sake of prettiness of effect and not with the intention of reproducing with accuracy the actual colours of the head, the figure, or the landscape before them. This method of making drawings—*rehausés*, as they were called—has remained in common use almost to the present day, especially for studies. It is necessary only to cite among many examples the series of heads by Holbein, the highly esteemed studies by Watteau, Boucher and Greuze, and of John Raphael Smith and Sir Thomas Lawrence, to indicate how general has been the employment of the coloured chalk. In 1747 Nattier (1685–1766) showed a pastel portrait of M. Logerot in the Paris Salon, and his son-in-law, Louis Tocqué (1696–1772), soon followed with similar work. Hubert Drouais (1699–1767) had preceded his rival Nattier in the Salon by a single year with five pastel portraits, and Chardin (1699–1779) followed in 1771. This great master set himself to work in emulation of Quentin de la Tour (1704–1788), who in spite of the ability of his rivals may be regarded as the most eminent pastellist France has produced. His portraits of Mme Boucher and himself appeared in the Salon in 1737; his full strength as a portrait-pastellist is to be gauged in the collection of eighty-five of his principal works now in the museum of St Quentin. Then followed Simon Mathurin Lantara (1729–1778), who was one of the first to paint pastel-pictures of landscapes, including sunsets and moonlights, as well as marines, into which the figures were drawn by Joseph Vernet, Casanova and others, and Jean Baptiste Perronneau (1731–1796), the best of whose heads have been often attributed to de la Tour and whose "Jeune fille au chat" in the Louvre, though not the finest, is perhaps the best known of his works, was the last pre-eminent French pastellist of the 18th century. Since then they have been legion; of these it is needful to mention only Girodet and the flower-painters, Jean Saint-Simon and Sprendonck.

Two Swiss painters had considerable influence in spreading the use of pastel—the experimentalist Dietrich Meyer (1572–1658), one of the first to make designs in coloured chalks (and reputed inventor of soft-ground etching), and Jean Étienne Liotard (1701 or 1704–1788), one of the most brilliant pastellists who ever lived. Two of his works are world-famous, "La Belle Chocolatière de Vienne," executed in 1745, now in the Dresden Museum, and "La Belle Liseuse" of the following year at the museum at Amsterdam. The latter is a portrait of his niece, Mlle Lavergne. In 1753, and again in 1772, Liotard visited England, where his brilliant work, portraits and landscapes, produced a great effect, almost equal to that of de la Tour twenty years before. To the Royal Academy between 1773 and 1775 Liotard contributed the portraits of Dr Thomson, himself, Lord Duncannon and General Cholmondely.

Crayon-painting was practised in England at an early date, and John Riley (1646–1691), many of whose finest works are attributed to Sir Peter Lely, produced numerous portraits in that medium. Francis Knapton (1698–1778), court painter, was a more prolific master, and he, with William Hoare of Bath (?1707–1792) who had studied pastel in Italy and made many classic designs in that medium, exhibiting at the Royal Academy his "Boy as Cupid," "Prudence instructing her Pupil," "Diana," "A Zingara," and others, prepared the way for the

triumph of Francis Cotes (?1725–1770). Then for the first time pastel-painting was fully developed by an English hand. Before he became a painter in oil Cotes had worked under Rosalba Carriera, and, although he was rather cold and chalky in his tones, he produced portraits, such as his "Mr and Mrs Joah Bates" and "Lord Hawke," which testify to his high ability. He was, however, far surpassed by his pupil, John Russell, R.A. (1745–1806), who brought the art to perfection, displaying grace and good expression in all his pastel work, whether portrait, fancy picture, historical subject, group, or "conversation-piece." He had brought from Rosalba her four fine pictures representing "The Seasons," and in a great measure founded his style on them. He was strong and brilliant in colour, and when he was at his best his high, smooth finish in no way robbed his work of vigour. Romney (1734–1802) in his single pastel portrait, a likeness of William Cowper the poet, showed that he might have excelled in this medium, which, indeed, was particularly suited to his tender manner. Hugh D. Hamilton (c. 1734–1806) of the Royal Hibernian Academy, produced note-worthy portraits, mainly in grey, red and black, until on the suggestion of Flaxman he abandoned pastel for oil. Ozias Humphry, A.R.A. (1742–1810), painter and miniaturist, is an important figure among the pastellists, commonly believed to be the first in England who made a point of letting his colour strokes be seen (as by Emile Wauters and others in our own day), contrary to the practice of Russell and his predecessors, whose prime effort was to blend all into imperceptible gradations. Richard Cosway, R.A. (1742–1821) was mainly experimental in his pastels, but his portraits, such as that of George prince of Wales, are forcible and brilliant; those of his wife Maria Cosway (1759–1838) are more delicate. Daniel Gardner (?1750–1805), whose pictures in oil have often been mistaken for Reynolds's and Gainsborough's, gave rein to his exuberant fancy and his rather exaggerated taste in compositions which, in his arrangement of children, remind us of Sir Thomas Lawrence in his more fantastic mood. Gardner marked the deterioration of the art, which thereafter declined, Henry Bright (1814–1873) being almost the only pastellist of real power who followed him. Bright's landscapes have probably in their own line never been surpassed. Since 1870 there has been a revival of the art of pastel, the result of a better understanding and appreciation on the part of the public. Grimm's denunciation of it to Diderot—"every one is agreed that pastel is unworthy the notice of a great painter"—which for many years had found general acceptance, is now seen to have been based on forgetfulness or ignorance of the virtues inherent in the method. It was thought that "coloured chalks," as it used to be called in English-speaking countries, promised nothing but sketches of an ephemeral kind, so fragile that they were at the mercy of every chance blow or every touch of dampness. The fact is, that with care no greater than is accorded to every work of art, pastel properly used is not more perishable than the oil-painting or the water-colour. Damp will affect it seriously, but so also will it ruin the water-colour; and rough usage is to be feared for the oil-picture not less than for the pastel. Moreover, pastel possesses advantages that can be claimed by neither oil-painting nor water-colour. That is to say, if pictures in these three mediums be hung side by side for a hundred years in a fair light and in a dry place, the oil-painting will have darkened and very probably have cracked; the water-colour will have faded; but the pastel will remain as bright, fresh, and pure as the day it was painted. If Time and Varnish, which Hogarth and Millais both declared the two greatest of the old masters, will do nothing to "improve" a pastel, neither will they ruin it—time passes it by and varnish must on no account be allowed to approach it. The pastel-painter, therefore, having no adventitious assistance to hope for, or to fear, must secure at once the utmost of which his method is capable.

The advantages of pastel are threefold: those of working, those of results, and those of permanence. The artist has at his command, without necessity of mixing his colours, every hue to be found in nature, so that freshness and luminosity can always be secured without fear of that loss of brilliancy commonly attendant on the mixing of colour on the palette. Moreover, the fact of pastel being dry permits the artist to leave his work and take it up again as he may choose; and he is free from many of the technical troubles and anxieties natural to oil and water-colour painting. Applied with knowledge, pastel, which has been likened for delicacy of beauty to "the coloured dust upon the velvet of butterflies' wings," will not fall off. It can, if desired—though this is hardly necessary or desirable—be "fixed," most commonly by a *fixatif*. If intending so to treat his work, the artist must paint in a somewhat lighter key, as the effect of the fixing medium is slightly to lower the general tone. The *fixatif Lacase* is considered the best, but the general consensus of opinion among artists is against the use of any such device. This preparation has the advantage of leaving the colour unchanged, even though it dulls it; shellac *fixatif* has the effect of darkening the work.

The inherent qualities of pastel are those of charm, of subtlety, softness, exquisite depths of tone, unsurpassable harmonies and unique freshness of colour, sweetness, delicacy, mystery—all the virtues sought for by the artist of daintiness and refinement. Pastel-painting is essentially, therefore, the art of the colourist. Now, these very qualities suggest its limitations. Although it is unfair to relegate it—as fashion has foolishly done for so long—to the bunch of pretty triflings which Carlyle called "Pompadourisms," we must recognize that a medium which suggests the bloom upon the peach is not proper to be employed for rendering "grand," or even genre subjects, or for the covering of large surfaces of canvas. It is inappropriate to the painting of classic compositions, although in point of fact it has been so used, not without success. It is best adapted to the rendering of still life, of landscape and of portraiture. But in these cases it is not advisable to aim at that solidity which is the virtue of oil-painting, if only because oil can bring about a better result. The real reason is that, in securing solidity, pastel tends to forfeit that lightness and grace which constitute its special charm and merit. Strength belongs to oil, tenderness and subtlety to pastel, together with freshness and elegance.

The pre-eminent technical advantage, in addition to those already mentioned, is the permanence of the tones. In water-colours there is an admixture of gum and glycerine which may attract moisture from the air; and, besides, the pigment is used in very thin washes. In oil-painting not only does the oil darken with age but sometimes draws oxygen from a pigment and changes its hue. In pastel the colour is put on without any moist admixture, and can be laid on thick. Moreover, the permanence may arise from the method of manufacture. In a very rare work, *The Excellency of the Pen and Pencil* (1668), a chapter on "how to make pastils" [*sic*] "of several colours, for drawing figure, landskip, architecture, &c., on blew paper," describes the manner of grinding up the pigments with grease. This used to be the secret of pastel—that every grain of colour was separately and securely locked up in grease, and so was secured from any chemical change that might have come about through contact of the colours with one another or with the atmosphere. With pastel nothing of the kind could occur; and the works of Rosalba Carriera in Italy, of Quentin Latour, Peronneau, Watteau, St Jean, Paul Hoin and Chardin in France, and of Russell and Cotes in England—to name no others —testify to the permanency of the colours. Some manufacturers nowadays employ gum as the binding medium; others beeswax (which at one time was more frequently used than it is at present); others, again, a very small proportion of tallow, and sometimes a little soap. But this introduction of binding media is now adopted only in the case of certain colours. Whether the point or edge of the stick be used (as in pastel *drawing*), or the side of it, helped with the tips of the fingers (as in pastel *painting*), the result is equally permanent; and if, when the work is done, it be struck two or three times, and then touched up by hand-crayons, no dropping of colour from the paper need ever occur. The drawing is made on a grained

paper that will hold the chalk, or on a specially manufactured toothed cloth. The French paper known as *gras gris bleuté* is employed by certain of the leading pastellists. The crisp touches of the pastel can be placed side by side, or the "vibrations" which the artist seeks may be obtained by glazes and super-posed tones. It should here be mentioned that about the year 1900 M. Jean-François Raffaelli produced in Paris sticks of oil colours which he claimed would in a great measure replace painting with the brush. Although the system was widely tried and many good pictures painted in this method, it was found that the colours became dull, and such vogue as these "solid paints" enjoyed for a time has to a very great extent disappeared.

The art of pastel, as M. Roger Ballu expressed it, "was slumbering a little," until in 1870 the Société des Pastellistes was founded in France and met with ready appreciation. With many artists it was a matter of "coloured chalks," as, for example, with Millet, Lhermitte and Degas in France, and with Whistler in England. With the majority the full possibilities were seized, and a great number of artists abroad then practised the art for the sake of colour, among whom may be mentioned Adrien Moreau, A. Besnard, Emile Lévy, Machard, Pointelin, Georges Picard, de Nittis, Iwill, René Billotte, Jozan, Nozel, Raffaelli, Brochard (mainly upon vellum) and Lévy-Dhurmer in France; in Belgium Émile Wauters (who has produced a great series of life-sized portraits of both men and women of amazing strength, vitality and completeness) and Fernand Khnopff; in Italy, C. Laurenti, P. Fragiacomo and Giovanni Segantini; in Holland, Josselin de Jong; in Germany, F. von Lenbach, Max Liebermann and Franz Stück; and in Norway, Fritz Thaulow.

In England the revival of pastel dates from 1880, when the first exhibition of the Pastel Society was held in the Grosvenor Gallery. The exhibition was a *succès d'estime*, but after a while the society languished until, in 1899, it was reconstituted, and obtained the adhesion of many of the most distinguished artists practising in the country, as well as of a score of eminent foreign painters. In that year, and since, it has held exhibitions of a high order; and intelligent public appreciation has been directed to the work of the most noteworthy contributors. Among these are E. A. Abbey, R.A.; M'Lure Hamilton, J. M. Swan, R.A.; J. Lorimer, R.S.A.; A. Peppercorn, R. Anning Bell, J. J. Shannon, R.A.; Sir James Guthrie, P.R.S.A.; H. Brabazon, Walter Crane, Melton Fisher, Edward Stott, A.R.A.; S. J. Solomon, R.A.; and W. Rothenstein.

See Karl Robert [Georges Meusnier], *Le Pastel* (Laurens, Paris, 1890); J. L. Sprinck, *A Guide to Pastel Painting* (Rowney, London); Henry Murray, *The Art of Painting and Drawing in Coloured Crayons* (Winsor & Newton, London). Among early works are: John Russell, R.A., *Elements of Painting with Crayons* (1776); M.P.R. de C.C., *Traité de la peinture au pastel avec les moyens de prévenir l'altération des couleurs* (Paris, 1788); Rosalba Carriera, *Diario degli anni 1720 a 1721 scritto di propria mano in Parigia, &c.* (Giovanni Vianelli, Venice, 1793, 410); Girolamo Zanetti, *Elogio di Rosalba Carriera, pittrice* (Venice, 1818, 8vo). See also Henri Lapauze, *Les Pastels de M. Quentin de La Tour à St Quentin*, preface by Gustave Larroumet (Paris); George C. Williamson, *John Russell, R.A.* (London, 1894).   (M. H. S.)

PASTEUR, LOUIS (1822–1895), French chemist, was born, on the 27th of December 1822, at Dôle, Franche-Comté, where his father carried on the business of a tanner. Shortly afterwards the Pasteur family removed to Arbois, where Louis attended the École primaire, and later the collège of that place. Here he apparently did not especially distinguish himself, belonging to the class of *bons ordinaires*. Fortunately at Arbois he came under the influence of an excellent teacher in the person of the director of the collège, who must have discerned in the quiet boy the germs of greatness, as he constantly spoke to him of his future career at the École normale in Paris. In October 1838 Louis set with a friend to the metropolis, to a school in the Quartier Latin, preparatory to the École normale. But he did not remain long in Paris, for, being a nervous and excitable boy, his health broke down, and he yearned for his home in Franche-Comté. "If only I could smell the tannery once more," said he to his companion, "I should feel well." So home he went, though not for long, as his ambition was still to become a *normalien*, and to this end he entered the Royal College of Besançon, "en attendant l'heureux jour où je serais admis à l'école normale." Step by step he attained his end; in 1840 he won his "bachelier ès lettres," and shortly afterwards he received an appointment as assistant mathematical master in the college. Two years later he passed the examination for the "baccalauréat ès sciences" enabling him to become candidate for the École normale. But here something (probably the examiner) was at fault, for a note was attached to Pasteur's diploma stating that he was only "mediocre" in chemistry. In those early days and early trials the dominant note of Pasteur's life was sounded. To his sisters he writes: "Ces trois choses, la volonté, le travail, le succès, se partagent toute l'existence humaine. La volonté ouvre la porte aux carrières brillantes et heureuses; le travail les franchit, et une fois arrivé au terme du voyage, le succès vient couronner l'œuvre." Throughout his life, and to the very end, "work" was his constant inspiration. On his deathbed he turned to the devoted pupils who watched over their master's last hours. "Où en êtes-vous?" he exclaimed. "Que faites-vous?" and ended by repeating his favourite words, "Il faut travailler."

The first incentive to his serious study of chemistry was given by hearing J. B. A. Dumas' lecture at the Sorbonne; and ere long he broke new ground for himself, A. J. Balard having given him an opportunity for chemical work by appointing him to the post of laboratory assistant. A few words of explanation concerning Pasteur's first research are necessary to give the key to all his future work. What was the secret power which enabled him to bring under the domain of scientific laws phenomena of disease which had so far baffled human endeavour? It simply consisted in the application, to the elucidation of these complex problems, of the exact methods of chemical and physical research. Perhaps the most remarkable discovery of modern chemistry is the existence of compounds, which, whilst possessing an identical composition, are absolutely different bodies, judged of by their properties. The first of the numerous cases of isomerism now known was noted, but unexplained, by J. J. Berzelius. It was that of two tartaric acids, deposited from wine-lees. The different behaviour of these two acids to a ray of polarized light was subsequently observed by J. B. Biot. One possessed the power of turning the plane of the polarized ray to the right; the other possessed no rotary power. Still no explanation of this singular fact was forthcoming, and it was reserved for the young chemist from Franche-Comté to solve a problem which had baffled the greatest chemists and physicists of the time. Pasteur proved that the inactivity of the one acid depended upon the fact that it was composed of two isomeric constituents: one the ordinary or dextrorotary acid, and the other a new acid, which possessed an equally powerful left-handed action. The veteran Biot whose acquaintance Pasteur had made, was incredulous. He insisted on the repetition of the experiment in his presence; and when convinced of the truth of the explanation he exclaimed to the discoverer: "Mon cher enfant, j'ai tant aimé les sciences dans ma vie que cela me fait battre le cœur." Thus at one step Pasteur gained a place of honour among the chemists of the day, and was immediately appointed professor of chemistry at the Faculté of Science at Strasburg, where he soon afterwards married Mlle Laurent, who proved herself to be a true and noble helpmeet. Next he sought to prepare the inactive form of the acid by artificial means; and after great and long-continued labour he succeeded, and was led to the commencement of his classical researches on fermentation, by the observation that when the inactive acid was placed in contact with a special form of mould (*Penicillium glaucum*) the right-handed acid alone was destroyed, the left-handed variety remained unchanged. So well was his position as a leading man of science now established that in 1854 he was appointed professor of chemistry and dean of the Faculté des Sciences at Lille. In his inaugural address he used significant words, the truth of which was soon manifested in his case: "In the field of observation chance only favours those who are prepared." The diseases or sicknesses of beer and wine had from time immemorial baffled all attempts at cure. Pasteur one day visited a brewery containing both sound and unsound beer. He examined the yeasts under the microscope, and at once saw that the globules from the sound beer were nearly spherical, whilst those from the sour beer were elongated; and this led him to a discovery, the consequences of which have revolutionized chemical

as well as biological science, inasmuch as it was the beginning of that wonderful series of experimental researches in which he proved conclusively that the notion of spontaneous generation is a chimera. Up to this time the phenomenon of fermentation was considered strange and obscure. Explanations had indeed been put forward by men as eminent as Berzelius and Liebig, but they lacked experimental foundation. This was given in the most complete degree by Pasteur. For he proved that the various changes occurring in the several processes of fermentation—as, for example, in the vinous, where alcohol is the chief product; in the acetous, where vinegar appears; and in the lactic, where milk turns sour—are invariably due to the presence and growth of minute organisms called ferments. Exclude every trace of these organisms, and no change occurs. Brewers' wort remains unchanged for years, milk keeps permanently sweet, and these and other complex liquids remain unaltered when freely exposed to air from which all these minute organisms are removed. "The chemical act of fermentation," writes Pasteur, "is essentially a correlative phenomenon of a vital act beginning and ending with it."

But we may ask, as Pasteur did, Why does beer or milk become sour on exposure to ordinary air? Are these invisible germs which cause fermentation always present in the atmosphere? or are they not generated from the organic, but the non-organized constituents of the fermentable liquid? In other words, are these organisms not spontaneously generated? The controversy on this question was waged with spirit on both sides; but in the end Pasteur came off victorious, and in a series of the most delicate and most intricate experimental researches he proved that when the atmospheric germs are absolutely excluded no changes take place. In the interior of the grape, in the healthy blood, no such germs exist; crush the grape, wound the flesh, and expose them to the ordinary air, then changes, either fermentative or putrefactive, run their course. But place the crushed fruit or the wounded animal under conditions which preclude the presence or destroy the life of the germ, and again no change takes place; the grape juice remains sweet and the wound clean. The application of these facts to surgical operations, in the able hands of Lord Lister, was productive of the most beneficent results, and has indeed revolutionised surgical practice.

Pasteur was now the acknowledged head of the greatest chemical movement of the time, the recipient of honours both from his own country and abroad, and installed at the École normale in Paris in a dignified and important post. Not, however, was it without grave opposition from powerful friends in the Academy that Pasteur carried on his work. Biot—who loved and admired him as a son—publicly announced that his enterprise was chimerical and the problem insoluble; Dumas evidently thought so too, for he advised Pasteur not to spend more of his time on such a subject. Yet he persevered: "Travailler, travailler toujours" was his motto, and his patience was rewarded by results which have not merely rendered his name immortal, but have benefited humanity in a way and to a degree for which no one could have ventured to hope. To begin with a comparatively small, though not unimportant, matter, Pasteur's discoveries on fermentation inaugurated a new era in the brewing and wine-making industries. Empiricism, hitherto the only guide, if indeed a guide at all, was replaced by exact scientific knowledge; the connexion of each phenomenon with a controllable cause was established, and rule-of-thumb and quackery banished for ever by the free gift to the world of the results of his researches.

But his powers of patient research and of quick and exact observation were about to be put to a severe test. An epidemic of a fatal character had ruined the French silk producers. Dumas, a native of the Alais district, where the disease was rampant, urged Pasteur to undertake its investigation. Up to that time he had never seen a silkworm, and hesitated to attempt so difficult a task; but at the reiterated request of his friend he consented, and in June 1865 went to the south of France for the purpose of studying the disease on the spot. In September of the same year he was able to announce results which pointed to the means of securing immunity from the dreaded plague. The history of this research, of the gradual elimination of the unimportant conditions, of the recognition of those which controlled the disease, is one of the most fascinating chapters of scientific discovery. Suffice it here to say that careful experiment and accurate observation succeeded in ascertaining the cause of the disease and in preventing its recurrence, thus bringing back to prosperity the silk trade of France, with all that this entails. "There is no greater charm," says Pasteur, "for the investigator than to make new discoveries; but his pleasure is heightened when he sees that they have a direct application to practical life." Pasteur had the good fortune, and just reward, of seeing the results of his work applied to the benefit both of the human race and of the animal world. It is to him that the world is indebted for the introduction of methods which have already worked wonders, and bid fair to render possible the preventive treatment of all infectious diseases. Just as each kind of fermentation possesses a definite organized ferment, so many diseases are dependent on the presence of a distinct microbe; and just as the gardener can pick out and grow a given plant or vegetable, so the bacteriologist can (in most cases) eliminate the adventitious and grow the special organism—in other words, can obtain a pure cultivation which has the power of bringing about the special disease. But by a process of successive and continued artificial cultures under different conditions, the virus of the organism is found to become attenuated; and when this weakened virus is administered, the animal is rendered immune against further attacks. The first disease investigated by Pasteur was that of chicken cholera, an epidemic which destroyed 10% of the French fowls; after the application of the preventive method the death-rate was reduced to below 1%. Next came the successful attempt to deal with the fatal cattle scourge known as anthrax. This is also caused by the presence of a microbe, of which the virus can also be attenuated, and by inoculation of this weakened virus the animal rendered immune. Many millions of sheep and oxen all over the world have thus been treated, and the rate of mortality reduced from 10 to less than 1%. As to the money value of these discoveries, T. H. Huxley gave it as his opinion that it was sufficient to cover the whole cost of the war indemnity paid by France to Germany in 1870.

The most interesting of Pasteur's investigations in preventive and curative medicine remains to be told. It is no less than a cure for the dread disease of hydrophobia in man and of rabies in animals; and the interest of the achievement is not only that he successfully combated one of the most mysterious and most fell diseases to which man is subject, but also that this was accomplished in spite of the fact that the special microbe causing the disease had not been isolated. To begin with, Pasteur, in studying the malady in dogs, came to the conclusion that the virus had its seat in the nerve centres, and he proved that the injection of a portion of the matter of the spinal column of a rabid dog into the body of a healthy one produces in the latter with certainty the symptoms of rabies. The next step was to endeavour to so modify and weaken the virus as to enable it to be used as a preventive or as an antitoxin. This, after long and serious labour, he effected; the dog thus inoculated proved to be immune when bitten by a rabid animal. But this was not enough. Would the inoculation of the attenuated virus have a remedial effect on an animal already bitten? If so, it might be possible to save the lives of persons bitten by mad dogs. Here again experiment was successful. A number of dogs were inoculated, the same number were untreated, and both sets were bitten by rabid animals. All the treated dogs lived; all the untreated died from rabies. It was, however, one thing to experiment on dogs, and quite another to do so on human beings. Nevertheless Pasteur was bold enough to try. The trial was successful, and by doing so he earned the gratitude of the human race. Then, on the 14th of November 1888, the Institut Pasteur was founded. Thousands of people suffering from bites from rabid animals, from all lands, have been treated in this institute, and the death-rate from this most horrible of all diseases has been reduced to less than 1%. Not only in Paris, but in many cities throughout the world, institutes on the model of the original one have been set up and are doing beneficent work, all arising from the genius and labour of one man. At the inauguration of the institute Pasteur closed his oration with the following words:—

"Two opposing laws seem to me now in contest. The one, a law of blood and death, opening out each day new modes of destruction, forces nations to be always ready for the battle. The other, a law of peace, work and health, whose only aim is to deliver man from the calamities which beset him. The one seeks violent conquests, the other the relief of mankind. The one places a single life above all victories, the other sacrifices hundreds of thousands of lives to the ambition of a single individual. The law of which we are the instruments strives even through the carnage to cure the wounds due to the law of war. Treatment by our antiseptic methods may preserve the lives of thousands of soldiers. Which of these two laws will prevail, God only knows. But of this we may be sure, that science, in obeying the law of humanity, will always labour to enlarge the frontiers of life."

Rich in years and in honours, but simple-minded and affectionate as a child, this great benefactor to his species passed quietly away near St Cloud on the 28th of September 1895.

Mention need only be made of Pasteur's chief works, as follows: Études sur le vin (1866), Études sur le vinaigre (1868), Études sur la maladie des vers à soie (1870), Études sur la bière (1876). He began the practice of inoculation for hydrophobia in 1885.

See Vie de Pasteur, by René Vallery-Radot (Paris, 1900).

(H. E. R.)

PASTICCIO, an Italian word, now often Englished as "pasticche," formed from pasta, paste, for a composition in music, painting or other arts, made up of selections from fragments or imitations of the work of other artists; a medley or pot-pourri. The term has also been applied to a form of musical composition in which selections from various operas, &c., are pieced together to form a consecutive whole, special librettos being sometimes written for them.

PASTO, a city of Colombia and capital of the department of Nariño, about 36 m. from the boundary line with Ecuador, on one of the inland trade routes with that republic, and on a principal line of communication with the great forested regions of the Caquetá (Japurá), Putumayo and Napo. Pop. (1906 estimate), 6000. It stands on an elevated plain, 8347 ft. above the sea, at the eastern foot of the Pasto volcano, which rises above the city to a height of 13,090 ft. Wool is produced to some extent and is woven for the local market in the woollen factories of Pasto.

PASTON LETTERS, an invaluable collection of letters and papers, consisting of the correspondence of members of the Paston family, and others connected with them, between the years 1422 and 1509, and also including some state papers and other important documents. The bulk of the letters and papers were sold by William Paston, 2nd earl of Yarmouth, the last representative of the family, to the antiquary Peter Le Neve early in the 18th century. On Le Neve's death in 1729 they came into the possession of Thomas Martin of Palgrave, who married his widow; and upon Martin's death in 1771 they were purchased by John Worth, a chemist at Diss, whose executors sold them three years later to John Fenn of East Dereham. In 1787 Fenn published a selection of the letters in two volumes, and general interest was aroused by this publication. In 1789 Fenn published two other volumes of letters, and when he died in 1794 he had prepared for the press a fifth volume, which was published in 1823 by his nephew, Serjeant Frere. In 1787 Fenn had received a knighthood, and on this occasion, the 23rd of May, he had presented the originals of his first two volumes to King George III. These manuscripts soon disappeared, and the same fate attended the originals of the three other volumes. In these circumstances it is not surprising that some doubt should have been cast upon the authenticity of the letters. In 1865 their genuineness was impugned by Herman Merivale in the *Fortnightly Review*; but it was vindicated on grounds of internal evidence by James Gairdner in the same periodical; and within a year Gairdner's contention was established by the discovery of the originals of Fenn's fifth volume, together with other letters and papers, by Serjeant Frere's son, Philip Frere, in his house at Dungate, Cambridgeshire. Ten years later the originals of Fenn's third and fourth volumes, with ninety-five unpublished letters, were found at Roydon Hall, Norfolk, the seat of George Frere, the head of the Frere family; and finally in 1889 the originals of the two remaining volumes were discovered at Orwell Park, Ipswich, the residence of Captain E. G. Pretyman. This latter batch of papers are the letters which were presented to George III., and which possibly reached Orwell through Sir George Pretyman Tomline (1750–1827), the tutor and friend of William Pitt.

The papers which had been in the hands of Sir John Fenn did not, however, comprise the whole of the Paston letters which were extant. When the 2nd earl of Yarmouth died in 1732 other letters and documents relating to the Pastons were found at his seat, Oxnead Hall, and some of these came into the hands of the Rev. Francis Blomefield, who failed to carry out a plan to unite his collection with that of Martin. This section of the letters was scattered in various directions, part being acquired by the antiquary John Ives. The bulk of the Paston letters and documents are now in the British Museum; but others are at Orwell Park; in the Bodleian Library, Oxford; at Magdalen College, Oxford; and a few at Pembroke College, Cambridge. ·

Fenn's edition of the *Paston Letters* held the field until 1872, when James Gairdner published the first volume of a new edition. Taking Fenn's work as a basis, the aim of the new editor was to include all the letters which had come to light since this publication, and in his careful and accurate work·in three volumes (London, 1872–1875) he printed over four hundred letters for the first time. Gairdner's edition, with notes and index, also·contained a valuable introduction to each volume, including a survey of the reign of Henry VI.; and he was just completing his task when the discovery of 1875 was made at Roydon. An appendix gave particulars of this discovery, and the unpublished letters were printed as a supplement to subsequent editions. In 1904 a new and complete edition of the *Paston Letters* was edited by Gairdner, and these six volumes, containing 1088 letters and papers, possess a very valuable introduction, which is the chief authority on the subject.

The family of Paston takes its name from a Norfolk village about twenty miles north of Norwich, and the first member of the family about whom anything is known· was living in this village early in the 15th century. This was one Clement Paston (d. 1419), a peasant, holding and cultivating about one hundred acres of land, who gave an excellent education to his son William, and enabled him to study law. Making good use of his opportunities, William Paston (1378–1444), who is described as " a right cunning man in the law," attained an influential position in his profession, and became a justice of the·common pleas. He bought a good deal of land in Norfolk, including some in Paston, and improved his position by his marriage with Agnes (d. 1479), daughter and heiress of Sir Edmund· Berry of Harlingbury, Hertfordshire. Consequently· when he died he left a large and·valuable inheritance to John Paston (1421–1466), the eldest of his five sons, who was already married to Margaret (d. 1484), daughter of John Mauteby of Mauteby. At this time England ·was in a very disturbed condition. A weak king surrounded by turbulent nobles was incapable of discharging the duties of government, and only the strong man armed could hope to keep his goods in peace. A lawyer like his father, Paston spent much time in London, leaving his wife to look after his business in Norfolk; and many of the *Letters* were written by Margaret to her husband, detailing the progress of affairs in the county. It is during the lifetimes of John Paston and his eldest son that the *Letters* are most numerous and valuable, not only for family matters, but also for the history of England. In 1448 Paston's manor of Gresham was seized by Robert Hungerford,

Lord· Moleyns (1431–1464), and ·although it was afterwards recovered, the owner could obtain no redress for the loss and injury he had sustained. More serious troubles, however, were at hand. ·Paston had become very intimate with the wealthy· knight, Sir. John Fastolf, who was probably related · to his wife, and who had employed him· on several matters of business. In 1459 Sir John died without children, leaving his affairs in rather a tangled condition. In accordance with the custom of the ·time, he had conveyed many· of his estates in Norfolk and Suffolk to trustees, among whom were John Paston and his brother William,·retaining the ·revenues for himself, and probably intending his trustees ·after his death to devote· the property to the foundation of a college. However, it was found that a few days before his decease Fastolf had executed a fresh ·will in which he had named ten executors, of whom two only, ·John Paston and another, were to act; and, moreover, that ·he had bequeathed all his lands· in Norfolk and Suffolk to Paston, subject only to the duty.of founding the ·college· at Caister, and paying 4000 marks to the other executors. At once taking possession of the lands, Paston ·soon found his rights challenged. Various estates were claimed by different noblemen; the excluded executors were angry and aggressive; and Paston soon found himself in a· whirlwind of ·litigation, and exposed also to more violent methods of attack. Something like a regular warfare was waged around Drayton and Hellesdon between John de la Pole, duke of Suffolk, and the Pastons under Margaret and her eldest son, John; Caister Castle was seized by John Mowbray, 3rd duke of Norfolk (d.·1461); and similar occurrences took ·place elsewhere. Some compensation, doubtless, was found in the fact that in 1460, and again in 1461, Paston had been returned ·to parliament as a· knight of the shire· for Norfolk, and enjoying the favour of Edward IV. had regained his castle at Caister. But the royal favour was only temporary, and, having been imprisoned on three occasions, Paston died in May 1466, leaving the suit concerning Fastolf's will still proceeding in ·the church courts. John Paston left· at least five sons, the two eldest of whom were, curiously enough, both named John, and the eldest of whom had been knighted during his father's lifetime. Sir John Paston (1442–1479) was frequently at the court of King Edward IV.,· but· afterwards he favoured the Lancastrian party, and, ·with his· brother John, fought for Henry VI.. at the battle· of Barnet. Meanwhile the struggle over Fastolf's estates continued, although·in 1461 the king and council had decided that Paston's ancestors were not bondmen, and consequently that his ·title to his father's ·lands was good. Caister Castle was taken after a regular siege by John Mowbray, 4th duke of ·Norfolk (1444–1476), and then recovered by· the Pastons, and retaken by the duke. But in 1474 an arrangement was made with William Waynflete, bishop of Winchester, the· representative·of the excluded executors, by which some of the estates were· surrendered to the bishop for charitable purposes, while Paston was secured in the possession of others. Two years later ·the· opportune death of the duke of Norfolk paved· the way for the restoration of Caister Castle; but in 1478 a fresh quarrel broke out with the duke of Suffolk. Sir John,·who was a cultured man, had shown great anxiety to recover Caister; but.·in general he had left the conduct of the struggle to his mother and to the younger·John. Owing to his carelessness and extravagance. the family lands were also diminished by sales; but nevertheless when he died unmarried in November 1479 he left a goodly inheritance to ·his brother John. About this time the *Letters* begin to be scanty and less interesting, but the family continued to flourish. The younger John Paston (d. 1503), after quarrelling with his uncle William over the manors of Oxnead and Marlingford, was knighted at the battle of Stoke in 1487. He married Margery, daughter of Sir Thomas Brews, and left a son, William· Paston (c. 1479–1554), who was also knighted, and who was a prominent figure at the court of Henry VIII. Sir William's second son, Clement (c. 1515–1597), served his country with distinction on the sea, and was wounded at the battle of Pinkie. The family was continued by Sir William's eldest son, Erasmus (d. 1540), whose son William succeeded to his grandfather's estates in 1554, and to those of his uncle Clement in 1597. This William (1528–1610) was knighted in 1578. He was the founder of the Paston grammar-school at North Walsham, and made Oxnead Hall, near Norwich, his principal residence. Christopher Paston was Sir William's son and heir, and Christopher's grandson, William (d. 1663), was created a baronet in 1642; being succeeded in the title by his son Robert (1631–1683), who was a member of parliament from 1661 to 1673, and was created earl of Yarmouth in 1679. Robert's son William (1652–1732), who married a natural daughter of Charles II., was the second earl, and, like his father, was in high favour with the Stuarts. When he died in 1732 he left no son, and his titles became extinct, his estates being sold to discharge his debts.

The perturbed state of affairs revealed by the Paston Letters reflects the general condition of England during the period. It was a time of trouble. The weakness of the government had disorganized every branch of the administration; the succession to the crown itself was contested; the great nobles lived in a state of civil war; and the prevailing discontent found expression in the rising of Jack Cade and in the Wars of the Roses. The correspondence reveals the Pastons in a great variety of relations to their neighbours, friendly or hostile; and abounds with illustrations of the course of public events, as well as of the manners and morals of the time. Nothing is more remarkable than the habitual acquaintance of educated persons, both men and women, with the law, which was evidently indispensable to persons of substance.

In addition to the editions of the Paston Letters already mentioned, see F. Blomefield and C. Parkin, History of Norfolk (London, 1805–1810), and the article in Dict. Nat. Biog. (A. W. H.*)

PASTORAL (from Lat. pastor, a shepherd), the name given to a certain class of modern literature in which the "idyll " of the Greeks and the " eclogue " of the Latins are imitated. It was a growth of humanism at the Renaissance, and its first home was Italy. Virgil had been imitated, even in the middle ages, but it was the example of Theocritus (q.v.) that was originally followed in pastoral. Pastoral, as it appeared in Tuscany in the 16th century, was really a developed eclogue, an idyll which had been expanded from a single scene into a drama. The first dramatic pastoral which is known to exist is the Favola di Orfeo of Politian, which was represented at Mantua in 1472. This poem, which has been elegantly translated by J. A. Symonds, was a tragedy, with choral passages, on an idyllic theme, and is perhaps too grave in tone to be considered as a pure piece of pastoral. It led the way more directly to tragedy than to pastoral, and it is the Il Sagrifisio of Agostino Beccari, which was played at the court of Ferrara in 1554, that is always quoted as the first complete and actual dramatic pastoral in European literature.

In the west of Europe there were various efforts made in the direction of non-dramatic pastoral, which it is hard to classify. Early in the 16th century Alexander Barclay, in England, translated the Latin eclogues of Mantuanus, a scholastic writer of the preceding age. Barnabe Googe, a generation later, in 1563, published his Eglogs, Epytaphes and Sonnettes, a deliberate but not very successful attempt to introduce pastoral into English literature. In France it is difficult to deny the title of pastoral to various productions of the poets of the Pléiade, but especially to Rémy Belleau's pretty miscellany of prose and verse in praise of a country life, called La Bergerie (1565). But the final impulse was given to non-dramatic pastoral by the publication, in 1504, of the famous Arcadia of J. Sannazaro, a work which passed through sixty editions before the close of the 16th century, and which was abundantly copied. Torquato Tasso followed Beccari after an interval of twenty years, and by the success of his Aminta, which was performed before the court of Ferrara in 1573, secured the popularity of dramatic pastoral. Most of the existing works in this class may be traced back to the influence either of the Arcadia or of the Aminta. Tasso was immediately succeeded by Alvisio Pasqualigo, who gave a comic turn to pastoral drama, and by Cristoforo Castelletti, in whose hands it grew heroic and romantic, while, finally, Guarini

produced in 1590 his famous Pastor Fido, and Ongaro his fishermen's pastoral of Alceo in 1591. During the last quarter of the 16th century pastoral drama was really a power in Italy. Some of the best poetry of the age was written in this form, to be acted privately on the stages of the little court theatres, that were everywhere springing up. In a short time music was introduced, and rapidly predominated, until the little forms of tragedy, and pastoral altogether, were merged in opera.

With the reign of Elizabeth a certain tendency to pastoral was introduced in England. In Gascoigne and in Whetstone traces have been observed of a tendency towards the form and spirit of eclogue. It has been conjectured that this tendency, combined with the study of the few extant eclogues of Clémont, Marot, led Spenser to the composition of what is the finest example of pastoral in the English language, the Shepherd's Calendar, printed in 1579. This famous work is divided into twelve eclogues, and it is remarkable because of the constancy with which Spenser turns in it from the artificial Latin style of pastoral then popular in Italy, and takes his inspiration direct from Theocritus. It is important to note that this is the first effort made in European literature to bring upon a pastoral stage the actual rustics of a modern country, using their own peasant dialect. That Spenser's attempt was very imperfectly carried out does not militate against the genuineness of the effort, which the very adoption of such names as Willie and Cuddie, instead of the customary Damon and Daphnis, is enough to prove. Having led up to this work, the influence of which was to be confined to England, we return to Sannazaro's Arcadia, which left its mark upon every literature in Europe. This remarkable romance, which was the type and the original of so many succeeding pastorals, is written in rich but not laborious periods of musical prose, into which are inserted at frequent intervals passages of verse, contests between shepherds on the " humile fistula di Coridone," or laments for the death of some beautiful virgin. The characters move in a world of supernatural and brilliant beings; they commune without surprise with " i gloriosi spiriti degli boschi," and reflect with singular completeness their author's longing for an innocent voluptuous existence, with no hell or heaven in the background.

It was in Spain that the influence of the Arcadia made itself most rapidly felt outside Italy. The earliest Spanish eclogues had been those of Juan de Encina, acted in 1492. Gil Vicente, who was also a Portuguese writer, had written Spanish religious pastorals early in the 16th century. But Garcilaso de la Vega is the founder of Spanish pastoral. His first eclogue, El Dulce lamentar de los pastores, is considered one of the finest poems of its kind in ancient or in modern literature. He wrote little, and died early, in 1536. Two Portuguese poets followed him, and composed pastorals in Spanish, Francisco de Sá de Miranda, who imitated Theocritus, and the famous Jorge de Montemayor, whose Diana (1524) was founded on Sannazaro's Arcadia, Gaspar Gil Polo, after the death of Montemayor in 1561, completed his romance, and published in 1564 a Diana enamorada. It will be recollected that both these works are mentioned with respect, in their kind, by Cervantes. The author of Don Quixote himself published an admirable pastoral romance, Galatea, in 1584.

In France there has always been so strong a tendency towards a graceful sort of bucolic literature that it is hard to decide what should and what should not be mentioned here. The charming pastourelles of the 13th century, with their knight on horseback and shepherdess by the roadside, need not detain us further than to hint that when the influence of Italian pastoral began to be felt in France these earlier lyrics gave it a national inclination. We have mentioned the Bergerie of Rémy Belleau, in which the art of Sannazaro seems to join hands with the simple sweetness of the medieval pastourelle. But there was nothing in France that could compare with the school of Spanish pastoral writers which we have just noticed. Even the typical French pastoral, the Astrée of Honoré d'Urfé (1610), has almost more connexion with the knightly romances which Cervantes laughed at than with the pastorals which he praised. The famous Astrée was the result of the study of Tasso's *Aminta* on the one hand and Montemayor's *Diana* on the other, with a strong flavouring of the romantic spirit of the *Amadis*. To remedy the pagan tendency of the *Astrée* a priest, Camus de Pontcarré, wrote a series of Christian pastorals. Racon produced in 1625 a 'pastoral drama, *Les Bergeries*, founded on the *Astrée* of D'Urfé.

In England the movement in favour of Theocritean simplicity which had been introduced by Spenser in the *Shepherd's Calendar*, was immediately, defeated by the success of Sir Philip Sidney's *Arcadia*, a romance closely modelled on the masterpiece of Sannazaro. So far from attempting to sink to colloquial idiom, and adopt a realism in rustic dialect, the tenor of Sidney's narrative is even more grave and stately than it is conceivable that the conversation of the most serious nobles can have ever been. Henceforward, in England, pastoral took one or other of these forms. It very shortly appeared, however, that the Sannazarian form was more suited to the temper of the age, even in England, than the Theocritean. In 1583 a great impetus was given to the former by Robert Greene, who was composing his *Morando*, and still more in 1584 by the publication of two pastoral dramas, the *Gallathea* of Lyly and the *Arraignment of Paris*. of Peele. It is doubtful whether either of these writers knew anything about the *Arcadia* of Sidney, which was posthumously published, but Greene, at all events, became more and more imbued with the Italian spirit of pastoral. His *Menaphon* and his *Never too Late* are pure bucolic romances. While in the general form of his stories, however, he follows Sidney; the verse which he introduces is often, especially in the *Menaphon*, extremely rustic and colloquial. In 1589 Lodge appended some eclogues to his *Scilla's Metamorphosis*, but in his *Rosalynde* (1590) he made a much more important contribution to English literature in general, and to Arcadian poetry in particular. This beautiful and fantastic book is modelled more exactly upon the masterpiece of Sannazaro than any other in our language. The *Sixe Idillia* of 1588, paraphrases of Theocritus, are anonymous, but conjecture has attributed them to Sir Edward Dyer. In 1598 Bartholomew Young published an English version of the *Diana* of Montemayor.

In 1585 Watson published his collection of Latin elegiacal eclogues, entitled *Amyntas*, which was translated into English by Abraham Fraunce in 1587. Watson is also the author of two frigid pastorals, *Meliboeus* (1590) and *Amyntae gaudia* (1592). John Dickenson produced at a date unstated, but probably not later than 1592, a "passionate eclogue" called *The Shepherd's Complaint*, which begins with a harsh burst of hexameters, but which soon settles down into a harmonious prose story, with lyrical interludes. In 1594 the same writer published the romance of *Arisbas*. Drayton is the next pastoral poet in date of publication. His *Idea: Shepherd's Garland* bears the date 1593, but was probably written much earlier. In 1595 the same poet produced an *Endimion and Phoebe*, which was the least happy of his works. He then turned his fluent pen to the other branches of poetic literature; but after more than thirty years, at the very close of his life, he returned to this early love, and published in 1627 two pastorals, *The Quest of Cynthia* and *The Shepherd's Sirena*. The general character of all these pieces is rich, but vague and unimpassioned. The *Queen's Arcadia* of Daniel must be allowed to lie open to the same charge, and to have been written rather in accordance with a fashion than in following of the author's predominant impulse. The singular eclogue by Barnfield, *The Affectionate Shepherd*, printed in 1594, is an exercise on the theme "O crudelis Alexi, nihil mea carmina curas," and, in spite of its juvenility and indiscretion, takes rank as the first really poetical following of Spenser and Virgil, in distinction to Sidney and Sannazaro. Marlowe's pastoral lyric *Come live with Me*, although not printed until 1599, has been attributed to 1589. In 1600 was printed the anonymous pastoral comedy in rhyme, *The Maid's Metamorphosis*, long attributed to Lyly.

With the close of the 16th century pastoral literature was not extinguished in England as suddenly or as completely as it was in Italy and Spain. Throughout the romantic Jacobean age the English love of country life asserted itself under the guise of pastoral sentiment, and the influence of Tasso and Guarini was felt in England just when it had ceased to be active in Italy. In England it became the fashion to publish lyrical eclogues, usually in short measure, a class of poetry peculiar to the nation and to that age. The lighter staves of *The Shepherd's Calendar* were the model after which all these graceful productions were drawn. We must confine ourselves to a brief enumeration of the principal among these Jacobean eclogues. Nicholas Breton came first with his *Passionate Shepherd* in 1604. Wither followed with *The Shepherd's Hunting* in 1615, and Braithwaite, an inferior writer, published *The Poet's Willow* in 1613 and *Shepherd's Tales* in 1621. The name of Wither must recall to our minds that of his friend William Browne, who published in 1613-1616 his beautiful collection of Devonshire idylls called *Britannia's Pastorals*. These were in heroic verse, and less distinctly Spenserian in character than those eclogues recently mentioned. In 1614 Browne, Wither, Christopher Brook and Davies of Hereford united in the composition of a little volume of pastorals entitled *The Shepherd's Pipe*. Meanwhile the composition of pastoral dramas was not entirely discontinued. In 1606 Day dramatized part of Sidney's *Arcadia* in his *Isle of Gulls*, and about 1625 the Rev. Thomas Goffe composed his *Careless Shepherdess*, which Ben Jonson deigned to imitate in the opening lines of his *Sad Shepherd*. In 1610 Fletcher produced his *Faithful Shepherdess* in emulation of the *Aminta* of Tasso. This is the principal pastoral play in the language, and, in spite of its faults in moral taste, it preserves a fascination which has evaporated from most of its fellows. The *Arcades* of Milton is scarcely dramatic; but it is a bucolic ode of great stateliness and beauty. In the *Sad Shepherd*, which was perhaps written about 1635, and in his pastoral masques, we see Ben Jonson not disdaining to follow along the track that Fletcher had pointed out in the *Faithful Shepherdess*. With the *Piscatory Eclogues* of Phineas Fletcher, in 1633, we may take leave of the more studied forms of pastoral in England early in the 17th century.

When pastoral had declined in all the other nations of Europe; it enjoyed a curious recrudescence in Holland. More than a century after date, the *Arcadia* of Sannazaro began to exercise an influence on Dutch literature. Johan van Heemskirk led the way with his popular *Batavische Arcadia* in 1637. In this curious romance the shepherds and shepherdesses move to and fro between Katwijk and the Hague, in a landscape unaffectedly Dutch. Heemskirk had a troop of imitators. Hendrik Zoeteboom published his *Zaanlandsche Arcadia* in 1658, and Lambertus Bos his *Dordtsche Arcadia* in 1662. These local imitations of the suave Italian pastoral were followed by still more crude romances, the *Rotterdamsche Arcadia* of Willem den Elger, the *Walchersche Arcadia* of Gargon, and the *Noordwijker Arcadia* of Jacobus van der Valk. Germany has nothing to offer us of this class, for the *Diana* of Werder (1644) and *Die adriatische Rosamund* of Zesen (1645) are scarcely pastorals even in form.

In England the writing of eclogues of the sub-Spenserian class of Breton and Wither led in another generation to a rich growth of lyrics which may be roughly called pastoral, but are not strictly bucolic. Carew, Lovelace, Suckling, Stanley and Cartwright are lyrists who all contributed to this harvest of country song, but by far the most copious and the most characteristic of the pastoral lyrists is Herrick. He has, perhaps, no rival in modern literature in this particular direction. His command of his resources, his deep originality and observation, his power of concentrating his genius on the details of rural beauty, his interest in recording homely facts of country life, combined with his extraordinary gift of song to place him in the very first rank among pastoral writers; and it is noticeable that in Herrick's hands, for the first time, the pastoral became a real and modern, instead of being an ideal and humanistic thing. From him we date the recognition in poetry of the humble beauty that lies about our doors. His genius and influence were almost instantly obscured by the Restoration. During the final decline of the Jacobean drama a certain number of pastorals were still produced. Of these the only ones which deserve, mention are three dramatic adaptations, Shirley's *Arcadia* (1640), Fanshawe's *Pastor Fido* (1646), and Leonard Willan's *Astraea* (1651). The last pastoral drama in the 17th century was Settle's *Pastor Fido* (1677). The Restoration was extremely unfavourable to this species of literature. Sir Charles Sedley, Aphra Behn and Congreve published eclogues, and the *Pastoral Dialogue between Thirsis and Strephon* of the first-mentioned was much admired. All of these, however, are in the highest degree insipid and unreal, and partook of the extreme artificiality of the age.

Pastoral came into fashion again early in the 18th century. The controversy in the *Guardian*, the famous critique on Ambrose Philips's *Pastorals*, the anger and rivalry of Pope, and the doubt which must always exist as to Steele's share in the mystification, give 1708 a considerable importance in the annals of bucolic writing. Pope had written his idylls first, and it was a source of infinite annoyance to him that Philips contrived to precede him in publication. He succeeded in throwing ridicule on Philips, however, and his own pastorals were greatly admired. Yet there was some nature in Philips, and, though Pope is more elegant and faultless, he is not one whit more genuinely bucolic than his rival. A far better writer of pastoral than either is Gay, whose *Shepherd's Week* was a serious attempt to throw to the winds the ridiculous Arcadian tradition of nymphs and swains, and to copy Theocritus in his simplicity. Gay was far more successful in executing this pleasing and natural cycle of poems than in writing his pastoral tragedy of *Dione* or his "tragi-comico pastoral farce" of *The What d'ye call it?* (1715). He deserves a very high place in the history of English pastoral on the score of his *Shepherd's Week*. Swift proposed to Gay that he should write a Newgate pastoral in which the swains and nymphs should talk and warble in slang. This Gay never did attempt; but a northern admirer of his and Pope's achieved a veritable and lasting success in Lowland Scotch, a dialect then considered no less beneath the dignity of verse. Allan Ramsay's *Gentle Shepherd*, published in 1725, was the last, and remains the most vertebrate and interesting, bucolic drama produced in Great Britain. It remained a favourite, a hundred and fifty years after, among Lowland reapers and milkmaids.

With the *Gentle Shepherd* the chronicle of pastoral in England practically closes. This is at least the last performance which can be described as a developed eclogue of the school of Tasso and Guarini. It is in Switzerland that we find the next important revival of pastoral properly so-called. The taste of the 18th century was very agreeably tickled by the religious idylls of Salomon Gessner, who died in 1787. His *Daphnis und Phillis* and *Der Tod Abels* were read and imitated throughout Europe. In German literature they left but little mark, but in France they were cleverly copied by Arnaud Berquin. A much more important pastoral writer is Jean Pierre Clovis de Florian, who began by imitating the *Galatea* of Cervantes, and continued with an original bucolic romance entitled *Estelle*. It has always been noticeable that pastoral is a form of literature which disappears before a breath of ridicule. Neither Gessner nor his follower Abbt were able to survive the laughter of Herder. Since Florian and Gessner there has been no reappearance of bucolic literature properly so-called. The whole spirit of romanticism was fatal to pastoral. Voss in his *Luise* and Goethe in *Hermann und Dorothea* replaced it by poetic scenes from homely and simple life.

Half a century later something like pastoral reappeared in a totally new form, in the fashion for *Dorfgeschichten*. About 1830 the Danish poet S. S. Blicher, whose work connects the grim studies of George Crabbe with the milder modern strain of pastoral, began to publish his studies of out-door romance among the poor in Jutland. Immermann followed in Germany with his novel *Der Oberhof* in 1839. Auerbach, who has given to the 19th-century idyll its peculiar character, began to publish his *Schwarzwälder Dorfgeschichten* in 1843. Meanwhile George Sand was writing *Jeanne* in 1844, which was followed by *La Mare au Diable* and *François le Champi*, and in England Clough produced in 1848 his remarkable long-vacation pastoral *The*

Bothie of Tober-na-Vuolich. It seems almost certain that these writers followed a simultaneous but independent impulse in this curious return to bucolic life, in which, however, in every case, the old tiresome conventionality and affectation of lady-like airs and graces were entirely dropped. This school of writers was presently enriched in Norway by Björnson, whose *Synnöve Solbakken* was the first of an exquisite series of pastoral romances. But perhaps the best of all modern pastoral romances is Fritz Reuter's *Ut mine Stromtid*, written in the Mecklenburg dialect of German. In England the Dorsetshire poems of William Barnes and the Dorsetshire novels of Thomas Hardy belong to the same class. It will be noticed, of course, that all these recent productions have so much in common with the literature which is produced around them that they almost evade separate classification. It is conceivable that some poet, in following the antiquarian tendency of the age, may enshrine his fancy once more in the five acts of a pure pastoral drama of the school of Tasso and Fletcher, but any great vitality in pastoral is hardly to be looked for in the future.   (E. G.)

PASTORAL EPISTLES, the name given to St Paul's letters to Timothy and Titus. The term seems to have originated with J. A. L. Wegscheider (1771–1849), professor at Halle. The three epistles mentioned are written to men rather than churches, and to men appointed to certain pastoral work. In this respect they differ from the personal and intimate note which Paul wrote to Philemon. They are closely related in origin, style, diction and thought, and occupy so distinct a place in these respects that the Pauline authorship of them has been much questioned. (See TIMOTHY, EPISTLES TO; TITUS, EPISTLE TO.)

PASTORAL LETTER, an open letter addressed by a bishop to the clergy or laity of his diocese, or to both, containing either general admonition, instruction or consolation, or directions for behaviour in particular circumstances. In the Catholic Church such letters are also sent out regularly at particular ecclesiastical seasons, particularly at the beginning of fasts. In the non-episcopal Protestant churches the name "pastoral letter" is given to any open letter addressed by a pastor to his congregation, but more especially to that customarily issued at certain seasons, *e.g.* by the moderator of a Presbyterian assembly or the chairman of a Congregational or Baptist union.

PASTORAL STAFF, in the Christian Church, an ensign of office or dignity. It is some five feet long, ending at the top in a crook (*volute*) bent inwards, and made of metal, ivory or wood. If of metal, it is hollow; if of wood, it is usually covered with metal. The crook is usually richly ornamented; and is divided from the shaft by a boss; the shaft is commonly separated into sections by rings, so that it can be taken to pieces.

The pastoral staff is the ensign proper of cardinals (except cardinal-deacons) and bishops; but the former are entitled to use it only in the churches from which they derive their titles, the latter only in their dioceses. The pope so early as the time of Innocent III. did not carry the pastoral staff, and it would seem never to have been his custom. The *ferula* that the Ordo of Cencius Sabellius (ch. 48) speaks of was not a pastoral staff, but the symbol of authority over the papal palace, with which by its transference he was invested. This *ferula*, mentioned by Luitprand of Cremona in his account of the deposition of Benedict V., and the *baculus aureus* of the *Historia dedicationis ecclesiae cavensis* (*Acta Sanctorum*, 4 March, I. 354) are sceptres. Abbots carry the pastoral staff only when specially empowered by the pope to do so, and then only in the territory under the jurisdiction of their monastery and in the churches subordinated to it. With certain restrictions the pastoral staff is also sometimes conceded to dignitaries of cathedral and collegiate churches, but never to abbesses (*Sacra Congreg. Rit.* 29 Jan. 1656).

The pastoral staff, as its name implies, symbolizes the pastoral office and authority, a symbolism already known to Isidore of Seville (*De ecclesiast. off.* ii. 5). This symbolism is expressed in the words used, at least since the 10th century, by the consecrator, in delivering the pastoral staff at the consecration of a bishop' and the benediction of an abbot. The pastoral staff is carried in the left hand, in order that the right may remain free to give the blessing. The bishop is directed so to hold it (*Cerem. episc.* ii. 8, 25) that the crook is turned towards the people. It is used not only at pontifical High Mass but at all solemn pontifical functions, *e.g.* vespers, consecrations, processions. It is uncertain at what period the use of the pastoral staff was introduced; but the evidence tends to show that it was about the 5th century, in Gaul or Spain. The pastoral staff was certainly in use in Gaul in the 6th century (*Vita S. Caesar. Arelat.* ii. 18), in Spain at least as early as the 7th, and in Ireland also in the 7th; in Italy, so far as the available evidence shows, its introduction was comparatively late. It had originally nothing of its present liturgical character; this was given to it in the post-Carolingian period.

As regards the development of the form of the pastoral staff, there are four principal types: (1) staves with a simple crook,

the oldest form, which survived in Ireland until the 12th century; (2) staves with a ball or knob at the top, a rare form which did not long survive as a pastoral staff; (3) staves with a horizontal crook, so-called Tau-staves, used especially by abbots and surviving until the 13th century; (4) staves with crook bent inwards. These last already appear in miniatures of the 9th century; from the 11th onwards they predominated; and in the 13th century. they ousted all other forms. Originally plain, the crook was from the 11th century onwards often made in the form of a snake (5), which in richer staves encircled the Lamb of God or the representation of a figure. Since the 13th century the snake, under Gothic influence, developed into a boldly designed tendril set with leaves, which usually encircled a figure or group of figures, and the knob dividing shaft and crook into an elegant chapel (6 and 7). Finally, at the close of the middle ages, the lower part of the crook was bent outwards so that the actual volute came over the middle of the knob, the type that remained dominant from that time onwards (8). As a decoration, rather than for practical reasons, a fine folded cloth (*pannisellus, sudarium, velum*, Eng. veil), was from the 14th century onward often suspended from the knob of the pastoral staff. This was done both in the case of bishops' and of abbots' staves, but is now confined to the latter (*Cerem. epiic.* i. 11, 5; *Decr. Alex. VII.* 27 Sept. 1659; *Sacr. Congr. Rit.* 27 Sept. 1847).

From the pastoral staff must be distinguished the staff of the *chorepiscopus* (director of the choir) and cantors, which is still in use here and there. This, which is also known as *bordonus*, was developed out of the choir-staves, originally no more than sticks to lean on during the long services.

The Reformation abolished the pastoral staff almost everywhere.[1] In the Church of England, however, it was retained among the episcopal ornaments prescribed by the first Prayer-book of Edward VI., and, though omitted in the second Prayer-book, its use seemed once more to be enjoined under the Ornaments Rubric of Elizabeth's Prayer-book. Whatever the theoretical value of this injunction may have been, however, in practice the use of the pastoral staff was discontinued until its gradual revival in the last decades of the 19th century.

In the Churches of the East, a pastoral staff (Gr. ῥάβδος, Russ. *posrock, paterissa*, Syr. and Nest. *chutra*, Arm. *gawazan kayra petate*, Copt. *ibol*) is borne among the Syrians only by the patriarch, in all the other rites by all bishops, in the Greek

[1] Among curious exceptions is the pastoral staff still carried by the Lutheran abbot of Lokkum.

Church also by archimandrites and abbots, and in the Armenian Church also by the *vartapeds* (teachers). The staff of Armenian bishops is reminiscent of that of the West, from which it is apparently derived; that of the *vartapeds* is encircled at the upper end by one or two snakes. The Coptic patriarch uses an iron cross-staff. For the rest, the pastoral staff in the Oriental rites is T-shaped. It is of wood inlaid with ivory and mother-of-pearl. A veil is attached to the staff among the Greeks, Armenians and Copts. The bishops of the Coptic, Syrian and Nestorian Uniate Churches have adopted the Roman pastoral staff.

See Ch. Cahier et A. Martin, *Mélanges d'archéologie* (Paris, 1856); iv. 145 seq.; Rohault et Fleury, *La Messe* (Paris, 1889), vii. 75 seq. For the Anglican usage see the Report of the Sub-committee of Convocation on the Ornaments of the Church, &c. (London, 1908). (J. Bra.)

PATAGONIA, the name given to that portion of South America which, to the east of the Andes, lies mainly south of the Rio Negro (41° S.), and, to the west of the Andes, south of the Chilean province of Llanquihué (42° S.). The Chilean portion embraces the two provinces of Chiloe and Magallanes. East of the Andes the Argentine portion of Patagonia is divided into four territories: (1) Neuquen, 42,000 sq. m. approximately, including the triangle between the rivers Limay and Neuquen, and extending southward to the northern shore of Lake Nahuel-Huapi (41° S.) and northward to the Rio Colorado; (2) Rio Negro, 76,000 sq. m. approximately, extending from the Atlantic to the Cordillera of the Andes, to the north of 42° S.; (3) Chubut, 95,000 sq. m. approximately, embracing the region between 42° and 46° S.; and (4) that portion of the province of Santa Cruz which stretches from the last-named parallel as far south as the dividing line with Chile, and between Point Dungeness and the watershed of the Cordillera, an area approximately of 106,000 sq. m.

Physiography.—The general character of the Argentine portion of Patagonia is for the most part a region of vast steppe-like plains, rising in a succession of abrupt terraces about 300 ft. at a time, and covered with an enormous bed of shingle almost bare of vegetation. In the hollows of the plains are ponds or lakes of brackish and fresh water. Towards the Andes the shingle gives place to porphyry, granite and basalt lavas, animal life becomes more abundant and vegetation more luxuriant, acquiring the characteristics of the flora of the western coast, and consisting principally of the beech and conifers.

Among the depressions by which the plateau is intersected transversely, the principal are the Gualichu, south of the Rio Negro, the Maqtinchau and Balcheta (through which previously flowed the waters of lake Nahuel-Huapi, which now feed the river Limay); the Senguerr, the Deseado. Besides these transverse depressions (some of them marking lines of ancient inter-oceanic communication), there are others which were occupied by more or less extensive lakes, such as the Yagagtoo, Musters and Colhuapi, and others situated to the south of Puerto Deseado, in the centre of the country. In the central region volcanic eruptions, which have taken part in the formation of the plateau from the Tertiary period down to the present era, cover a large part with basaltic lava-caps; and in the western third more recent glacial deposits appear above the lava. There, in contact with folded Cretaceous rocks, uplifted by the Tertiary granite, erosion, caused principally by the sudden melting and retreat of the ice, aided by tectonic changes, has scooped out a deep longitudinal depression, which generally separates the plateau from the first lofty hills, the ridges generally called the pre-Cordillera, while on the west of these there is a similar longitudinal depression all along the foot of the snowy Andean Cordillera. This latter depression contains the richest and most fertile land of Patagonia.

The geological constitution is in accordance with the orographic physiognomy. The Tertiary plateau, flat on the east, gradually rising on the west, shows Upper Cretaceous caps at its base. First come Lower Cretaceous hills, raised by granite and dioritic rocks, undoubtedly of Tertiary origin, as in some cases these rocks have broken across the Tertiary beds, so rich in mammal remains; then follow, on the west, metamorphic schists of uncertain age; then quartzites appear, resting directly on the primitive granite and gneiss which form the axis of the Cordillera. Porphyritic rocks occur between the schists and the quartzites. The Tertiary deposits are greatly varied in character, and there is considerable difference of opinion concerning the succession and correlation of the beds. They are divided by Wilckens[2] into the following series (in ascending order):—

1. Pyrotherium-Notostylops beds. Of terrestrial origin, containing remains of mammalia. Eocene and Oligocene.

[2] O. Wilckens, "Die Meeresablagerungen der Kreide- und Tertiär-formation in Patagonien," in *Neues Jahrb. f. Min.*, Beilage-Band XXI. (1906), 98–195.

3. Patagonian Molasse. Partly marine, partly terrestrial. Lower Miocene. Wilckens includes in this series the coal of Punta Arenas, and the marine beds below it.

3. Santa Cruz series. Containing remains of mammals. Middle and Upper Miocene.

4. Paraná series. Sandstones and conglomerates with marine fossils. Pliocene. Confined to the eastern part of the region.

The Upper Cretaceous and Tertiary deposits have revealed a most interesting vertebrate fauna. This, together with the discovery of the perfect cranium of a chelonian of the genus *Myolania*, which may be said to be almost identical with *Myolania oweni* of the Pleistocene age in Queensland, forms an evident proof of the connexion between the Australian and South American continents. The Patagonian *Myolania* belongs to the Upper Chalk, having been found associated with remains of *Dinosauria*. Other specimens of the interesting fauna of Patagonia, belonging to the Middle Tertiary, are the gigantic wingless birds, exceeding in size any hitherto known, and the singular mammal *Pyrotherium*, also of very large dimensions. In the Tertiary marine formation a considerable number of cetaceans has been discovered. In deposits of much later date, formed when the physiognomy of the country did not differ materially from that of the present time, there have been discovered remains of pampean mammals, such as *Glyptodon* and *Macrauchenia*, and in a cave near Last Hope Inlet, a gigantic ground sloth (*Grypotherium listai*), an animal which lived contemporaneously with man, and whose skin, well preserved, showed that its extermination was undoubtedly very recent. With the remains of *Grypotherium* have been found those of the horse (*Onoshippidium*), which are known only from the lower pampas mud, and of the *Arctotherium*, which is found, although not in abundance, in even the most modern Pleistocene deposits in the pampas of Buenos Aires. It would not be surprising if this latter animal were still in existence, for footprints, which may be attributed to it, have been observed on the borders of the rivers Tamango and Pista, affluents of the Las Heras, which run through the eastern foot-hills of the Cordillera in 47° S.

Glaciers occupy the valleys of the main chain and some of the lateral ridges of the Cordillera, and descend to lakes San Martin, Viedma, Argentino and others in the same locality, strewing them with icebergs. In Patagonia an immense ice-sheet extended to the east of the present Atlantic coast during the first ice age, at the close of the Tertiary epoch, while, during the second glacial age in modern times, the terminal moraines have generally stopped, 30 miles in the north and 50 miles in the south, east of the summit of the Cordillera. These ice-sheets, which scooped out the greater part of the longitudinal depressions, and appear to have rapidly retreated to the point where the glaciers now exist, did not, however, in their retirement fill up with their detritus the fjords of the Cordillera, for these are now occupied by deep lakes on the east, and on the west by the Pacific channels, some of which are as much as 250 fathoms in depth, and soundings taken in them show that the fjords are as usual deeper in the vicinity of the mountains than to the west of the islands. Several of the high peaks are still active volcanoes.

In so far as its main characteristics are concerned, Patagonia seems to be a portion of the Antarctic continent, the permanence of which dates from very recent times, as is evidenced by the apparent recent emergence of the islets around Chiloe, and by the general character of the pampean formation. Some of the promontories of Chiloe are still called *huapi*, the Araucanian equivalent for "islands"; and this may perhaps be accepted as perpetuating the recollection of the time when they actually were islands. They are composed of caps of shingle, with great, more or less rounded boulders, sand and volcanic ashes, precisely of the same form as occurs on the Patagonian plateau. From an examination of the pampean formation it is evident that in recent times the land of the province of Buenos Aires extended farther to the east, and that the advance of the sea, and the salt-water deposits left by it when it retired, forming some of the lowlands which occur on the littoral and in the interior of the pampas, are much more recent phenomena; and certain caps of shingle, derived from rocks of a different class from those of the neighbouring hills, which are observed on the Atlantic coasts of the same province, and increase in quantity and size towards the south, seem to indicate that the caps of shingle which now cover such a great part of the Patagonian territory recently extended farther to the east, over land which has now disappeared beneath the sea, while other marine deposits along the same coasts became converted into bays during the subsequent advance of the sea. There are besides, in the neighbourhood of the present coast, deposits of volcanic ashes, and the ocean throws up on its shores blocks of basaltic lava, which in all probability proceed from eruptions of submerged volcanoes now extinct. One fact, however, which apparently demonstrates with greater certainty the existence in recent times of land that is now lost, is the presence of remains of pampean mammals in Pleistocene deposits in the bay of San Julian and in Santa Cruz. The animals undoubtedly reached these localities from the east; it is not at all probable that they advanced from the north southwards across the plateau intersected at that time by great rivers and covered by the ice-sheet. With the exception of the discoveries at the inlet of Ultima Esperanza, which is

in close communication with the Atlantic valley of Gallegos, none of these remains have been discovered in the Andean regions.

On the upper plains of Neuquen territory thousands of cattle can be fed, and the forests around Lakes Traful and Nahuel-Huapi yield large quantities of valuable timber. The Neuquen river is not navigable, but as its waters are capable of being easily dammed in places, large stretches of land in its valley are utilized; but the lands on each side of its lower part are of little commercial value. As the Cordillera is approached the soil becomes more fertile, and suitable districts for the rearing of cattle and other agricultural purposes exist between the regions which surround the Tromen volcano and the first ridges of the Andes. Chos Malal, the capital of the territory, is situated in one of these valleys. More to the west is the mining region, in great part unexplored, but containing deposits of gold, silver, copper and lignite. In the centre of the territory, also in the neighbourhood of the mining districts, are the valleys of Norquin and Las Lajas, the general camp of the Argentine army in Patagonia, with excellent timber in the forest on the Andean slope. The wide valleys occur near Rio Malleco, Lake Huechulafquen, the river Chimehuin, and Vega de Chapelco, near Lake Lacar, where are situated villages of some importance, such as Junin de los Andes and San Martin de los Andes. Close to these are the famous apple orchards supposed to have been planted by the Jesuits in the 17th and 18th centuries. These regions are drained by the river Collon-Cura, the principal affluent of the river Limay. Lake Lacar is now a contributary of the Pacific, its outlet having been changed to the west, owing to a passage having been opened through the Cordillera.

The Rio Negro runs along a wide transverse depression, the middle part of which is followed by the railway which runs to the settlement of Neuquen at the confluence of the rivers Limay and Neuquen. In this depression are several settlements, among them Viedma, the capital of the Rio Negro territory, Pringles, Conesa, Chocle-Choel and Roca. To the south of the Rio Negro the Patagonian plateau is intersected by the depressions of the Gualicho and Maquinchau, which in former times directed the waters of two great rivers (now disappeared) to the gulf of San Matias, the first-named depression draining the network of the Collon-Cura and the second the Nahuel-Huapi lake system. In 42° S. there is a third broad transverse depression, apparently the bed of another great river, now perished, which carried to the Atlantic the waters of a portion of the eastern slope of the Andes, between 41° and 42° 30′ S.

Chubut territory presents the same characteristics as the Rio Negro territory. Rawson, the capital, is situated at the mouth of the river Chubut on the Atlantic (42° 30′ S.). The town was founded in 1865 by a group of colonists from Wales, assisted by the Argentine government; and its prosperity has led to the foundation of other important centres in the valley, such as Trelew and Gaiman, which is connected by railway with Porto Madryn on Bahia Nueva. Here is the seat of the governor of the territory, and by 1895 the inhabitants of this part of the territory, composed principally of Argentines, Welsh and Italians, numbered 2585. The valley has been irrigated and cultivated, and produces the best wheat of the Argentine Republic. Between the Chubut and the Senguerr there are vast stretches of fertile land, spreading over the Andean region to the foot of the Cordillera and the lateral ridges of the Pre-Cordillera, and filling the basins of some desiccated lakes, which have been occupied since 1895, and farms and colonies founded upon them. The chief of these colonies is that of the 16th of October (16 de Octobre), formed in 1886, mainly by the inhabitants of Chubut colony, in the longitudinal valley which extends to the eastern foot of the Cordillera. Other rivers in this territory flow into the Pacific through breaches in the Cordillera, *e.g.* the upper affluents of the Fetaleufu, Palena and Rio Cisnes. The principal affluent of the Palena, the Carrenleufu, carries off the waters of Lake General Paz, situated on the eastern slope of the Cordillera. Rio Pico, an affluent of the same river, receives nearly the whole of the waters of the extensive undulating plain which lies between the Rio Teka and the Rio Senguerr to the east of the Cordillera, while the remainder are carried away by the affluents of Rio Jehua, viz., the Cherque, Omkel and Appeleg. This region contains auriferous drifts, but these, like the auriferous deposits, veins of galena and lignite in the mountains farther west which flank the Cordillera, have not been properly investigated. At Lake Fontana there are auriferous drifts and lignite deposits which abound in fossil plants of the Cretaceous age. The streams which form the rivers Mayo and Chalia join the tributaries of the Rio Aisen, which flows into the Pacific, watering in its course extensive and valuable districts where colonization has been initiated by Argentine settlers. Colonies have also been formed in the basin of Lakes Musters and Colhué; and on the coasts near the Atlantic, along Bahia Camarones and the Gulf of San Jorge, there are extensive farms.

The territory of Santa Cruz is arid along the Atlantic coast and in the central portion between 46° and 50° S. With the exception of certain valleys at Puerto Deseado (Port Desire) and in the transverse basins which occur as far south as Puerto San Julian, and which contain several cattle farms, few spots are capable of cultivation, the pastures being poor, water insufficient and salt lagunas fairly numerous. Puerto Deseado is the outlet for the produce of the Andean region situated between Lakes Buenos Aires and Pueyrredon.

Into this inlet there flowed at the time of the conquest a voluminous river, which subsequently disappeared, but returned again to its ancient bed, owing to the river Fenix, one of its affluents, which had deviated to the west, regaining its original direction. Lake Buenos Aires, the largest lake in Patagonia, measuring 75 m. in length, poured its waters into the Atlantic even in post-Glacial times by means of the river Deseado; and it is so depicted on the maps of the 17th and 18th centuries; and so too did Lake Pueyrredon, which, through the action of erosion, now empties itself westward, through the river Las Heras, into the Calen inlet of the Pacific, in 48° S. San Julian on Puerto San Julian, where Ferdinand Magellan wintered, is the centre of a cattle farming colony, and colonists have pushed into the interior up the valley of a now extinct river which in comparatively recent times carried down to Puerto San Julian the waters of Lakes Volcan, Belgrano, Azara, Nansen, and some other lakes which now drain into the river Mayer and so into Lake San Martin. The valleys of the Rio Chico throughout their whole extent, as well as those of Lake Shehuen, afford excellent grazing, and around Lakes Belgrano, Burmeister and Rio Mayer and San Martin there are spots suitable for cultivation. In the Cretaceous hills, which flank the Cordillera important lignite beds and deposits of mineral oils have been discovered. The Rio Santa Cruz, originally explored by Captain Fitzroy and Charles Darwin, is an important artery of communication between the regions bordering upon the Cordillera and the Atlantic. In Santa Cruz bay an important trade centre has been established. But the present cattle region *par excellence* of Patagonia is the department of Rio Gallegos, the farms extending from the Atlantic to the Cordillera. Puerto Gallegos itself is an important business centre, which bids fair to rival the Chilean colony of Punta Arenas, on the Straits of Magellan. Owing to the produce of the cattle farms established there, the working of coal in the neighbourhood, and the export of timber from the surrounding forests, the town of Punta Arenas is in a flourishing condition. Its population numbers about 4000. But the colonization of the western (Chilean) coast has generally failed, principally owing to the adverse climatic conditions of the Cordillera in those latitudes.

Climate.—The climate is less severe than was supposed by early travellers. The east slope is warmer than the west, especially in summer, as a branch of the southern equatorial current reaches its shores, whereas the west coast is washed by a cold current. At Puerto Montt, on the inlet behind Chiloe Island, the mean annual temperature is 52° F and the average extremes 78° and 29·5°, whereas at Bahia Blanca near the Atlantic coast and just outside the northern confines of Patagonia the annual temperature is 59° and the range much greater. At Punta Arenas, in the extreme south, the mean temperature is 43° and the average extremes 76° and 28°. The prevailing winds are westerly, and the westward slope has a much heavier precipitation than the eastern; thus at Puerto Montt the mean annual precipitation is 97 in., but at Bahia Blanca it is 19 in. At Punta Arenas it is 22 in.

Fauna.—The guanaco, the puma, the zorro or Brazilian fox (*Canis azarae*), the zorrino or *Mephitis patagonica* (a kind of skunk), and the tuco-tuco or *Ctenomys magellanicus* (a rodent) are the most characteristic mammals of the Patagonian plains. The guanaco roam in herds over the country and form with the ostrich (*Rhea americana*, and more rarely *Rhea darwinii*) the chief means of subsistence for the natives, who hunt them on horseback with dogs and bolas. Bird-life is often wonderfully abundant. The carrancha or carrion-hawk (*Polyborus tharus*) is one of the characteristic objects of a Patagonian landscape; the presence of long-tailed green parakeets (*Conurus cyanolysius*) as far south as the shores of the strait attracted the attention of the earlier navigators; and humming-birds may be seen flying amidst the falling snow. Of the many kinds of water-fowl it is enough to mention the flamingo, the upland goose, and in the strait the remarkable steamer duck.

Population.—The natives of Patagonia are nearly extinct. Here and there one may find a Tehuelchian or Gennaken encampment, but natives of pure race are now very scarce, and the two races all told probably do not number more than 100 male individuals. The Tehuelches were the dominant race in Patagonia. These people, from whom the name of Tierra de Patagones was given by Magellan on observing their large footprints, are remarkable for their great stature, having an average height of 6 ft. to 6 ft. 4 in. They are not known to have applied any collective name to their various tribes; Tehuelche is the Araucanian name for them. They have been described as kindly in disposition, though sometimes quarrelsome; skilled in the chase, addicted to gambling and to drinking, though also capable of long endurance of privation. Their religion recognized a Great Spirit, and designated the new moon as an object of worship. The Gennakens differ in type and language from the Tehuelches. The remaining population is composed of Araucanians, a mixture of the Tehuelches and Gennaken. But these are not the only type of people who have dwelt in Patagonia. The ancient burial-places have yielded the bones of other races

quite distinct from the present inhabitants, some of them having greatly resembled the primitive types which are met with more to the north, in the Argentine Chaco and in Brazil; while others, again, strongly resembled certain of the Pacific races, in that they possessed ethnic characteristics which have not been observed elsewhere in South America. Among these remains every type of artificial deformity of the skull hitherto known has been found, while at the present time the natives only practise the occipital deformation which is so common among the western tribes of America.

History.—Patagonia was discovered in 1520 by Ferdinand Magellan, who on his passage along the coast named many of the more striking features—Gulf of San Matias, Cape of 11,000 Virgins (now simply Cape Virgenes), &c. By 1611 the Patagonian god Setebos (Settaboth in Pigafetta) was familiar to the hearers of the *Tempest*. Rodrigo de Isla, despatched inland in 1535 from San Matias by Alcazava Sotomayor (on whom western Patagonia had been conferred by the king of Spain), was the first to traverse the great Patagonian plain, and, but for the mutiny of his men, he would have struck across the Andes to the Chilean side. Pedro de Mendoza, on whom the country was next bestowed, lived to found Buenos Aires, but not to carry his explorations to the south. Alonzo de Camargo (1539), Juan Ladrilleros (1557) and Hurtado de Mendoza (1558) helped to make known the western coasts, and Sir Francis Drake's voyage in 1577 down the eastern coast through the strait and northward by Chile and Peru was memorable for several reasons; but the geography of Patagonia owes more to Pedro Sarmiento de Gamboa (1579–1580), who, devoting himself especially to the south-west region, made careful and accurate surveys. The settlement which he founded at Nombre de Dios and San Felipe were neglected by the Spanish government, and the latter was in such a miserable state when Thomas Cavendish visited it in 1587 that he called it Port Famine. The district in the neighbourhood of Puerto Deseado, explored by John Davis about the same period, was taken possession of by Sir John Narborough in the name of King Charles II. in 1669. In the second half of the 18th century knowledge of Patagonia was augmented by Byron (1764–1765), S. Wallis (1766) and L. A. de Bougainville (1766); Thomas Falkner, a Jesuit who "resided near forty years in those parts," published his *Description of Patagonia* (Hereford, 1774); Francesco Viedma founded El Carmen, and Antonio advanced inland to the Andes (1782); and Basilio Villarino ascended the Rio Negro (1782). The "Adventure" and "Beagle" expeditions under Philip King (1826–1830) and Robert Fitzroy (1832–1836) were of first-rate importance, the latter especially from the participation of Charles Darwin; but of the interior of the country nothing was observed except 200 miles of the course of the Santa Cruz. Captain G. C. Musters in 1869 wandered in company with a band of Tehuelches through the whole length of the country from the strait to the Manzaneros in the north-west, and collected a great deal of information about the people and their mode of life. Since that date explorations have been carried on by F. P. Moreno, Ramon Lista, Carlos M. Moyano, A. Bertrand, H. Steffen, P. Krüger, R. Hauthal, C. Burckhardt, O. Nordenskiöld, J. B. Hatcher, the surveyors of the Argentine and Chilean Boundary Commissions and others.

Bibliographical lists for Patagonia are given in J. Wappäus, *Handbuch der Geogr. u. Stat. des ehemal. span. Mittel- und Süd-Amerika* (Leipzig, 1863–1870); in V, G. Quesada, *La Patagonia y las tierras australes del continente americano* (Buenos Aires, 1875); and in T. Coan, *Adventures in Patagonia* (New York, 1880). See also C. Darwin, *Journal of Researches* (London, 1845), and *Geological Observations on South America* (London, 1846); W. Parker Snow, *A Two Years' Cruise off . . . Patagonia* (London, 1857); G. C. Musters, *At Home with the Patagonians* (London, 1871); R. O. Cunningham, *Nat. Hist. of the Strait of Magellan* (Edinburgh, 1871); F. P. Moreno, *Viaje á la Patagonia austral* (Buenos Aires, 1879); *Rapport préliminaire Néuquen, Chubut, et Rio Negro* (La Plata, 1897); *Apuntes preliminares* (Buenos Aires, 1897); "Explorations in Patagonia " in *Geographical Journal*, xiv. (London, 1800); and "Patagonia " in the *National Geographical Magazine* (Washington, 1897); Lady Florence Dixie, *Across Patagonia* (London, 1880); R. Lista, *Mis exploraciones . . . en la Patagonia* (Buenos Aires, 1880); *Informe oficial ... de la exp. al Rio Negro* (under General Roca, 1879, Buenos Aires, 1882); Giacomo Bove, *Patagonia, Terra del Fuoco* (Genoa, 1883); *La Region central de las tierras magallanicas* (Santiago, 1886); H. Steffen in *Petermanns Mitteilungen*, xl. (1894); *Espedicion exploradora del Rio Palena* (Santiago, 1895); "The Patagonian Cordillera " in *Geographical Journal* (1900); K. Hauthal, in *Globus* (1897–1898); and Roth, Wherti and Burckhardt in *Revista museo de la Plata*, ix. (1898); O. Nordenskiöld, "A Journey in South-Western Patagonia " in *Geog. Journal*, x. (London, 1897); H. Hesketh Prichard, *Through the Heart of Patagonia* (London, 1902); Sir T. H. Holdich, "The Patagonian Andes," in *Geog. Journ.* xxiii. (1904); F. P. Outes, *La Edad de la Piedra en Patagonia* (Buenos Aires, 1905); *Reports* (1903 seq.) of Princeton University expedition to Patagonia.

PATAN (=" city "), the name of two historic cities in India. One of these, known as Anhilwada Patan, was the capital of the last Hindu dynasty of Gujarat, sacked by Mahmud of Ghazni and finally destroyed by the Mahommedans in 1298. Near its ruins, which are not considerable, has sprung up a modern town, in the state of Baroda (pop. 31,402), which contains many Jain temples (with palm-leaf MSS.) and has manufactures of fine cotton and silk textiles. The other Patan, known as Lalita Patan, was the capital of one of the three Newar kingdoms in the valley of Nepal, conquered by the Gurkhas at the end of the 18th century. It is situated close to Katmandu, on the opposite bank of the river Baghmati. The population is estimated at about 30,000, mostly Newars, who are Buddhists; and the buildings consist mainly of old Buddhist shrines and monasteries.

PATARA, an ancient town of Asia Minor, on the Lycian coast, 3 m. E. of the mouth of the Xanthus river (mod. Eshen Chai). It was noted from early times for its temple and oracle of Apollo, and, as the port of Xanthus and other towns of the same valley, had a large trade, and was regarded as the metropolis of Lycia. Enlarged by Ptolemy Philadelphus I. and renamed for a time Arsinoe, it was adorned by Vespasian with baths. St Paul changed there into a " ship of Phoenicia " on his way to Jerusalem in A.D. 60. Patara was the reputed birth-place of St Nicholas. The principal extant monuments are a triple triumphal arch, with inscription, through which ran the road to Xanthus, and the walls, discernible on either hand of it; the theatre, 265 ft. in diameter, built in A.D. 145 (as attested by an inscription) and wonderfully well preserved, though largely filled with drift sand; and the *thermae* built by Vespasian north of the harbour.

PATARENES, or **PATARELLI**, a name apparently first used in Milan about 1058 to denote the extreme opponents of clerical marriages. The party was so called because, under the leadership of Arialdus, a deacon of Milan, its members used to assemble in the Pataria or ragmen's quarter of that city (*pates* being a provincial word for a rag). In the 13th century the name was appropriated by the Cathari, who said it came from *pati* (to suffer), because they endured hardship for their faith. See BOGOMILS.

PATAS MONKEY, a West African species of the guenon monkeys (see GUENON), characterized by its large size, the foxy-red colour of the upper parts, blue face and white belly. Scientifically it is known as *Cercopithecus* (*Erythrocebus*) *patas*, and typifies a section of its genus of which the other representative is the East African nisnas (*C.* [*E.*] *pyrrhonotus*). See PRIMATES.

PATAVIUM (mod. *Padova*, Eng. Padua, *q.v.*), an ancient city of Venetia, Italy, 55 m. E. of Verona by road. Its central position gave it great importance. One road led from it southwest to Ateste, Hostilia (where the Po was crossed) and Bononia; another east-north-east to Altinum and Concordia. It was accessible by canals from the sea, a distance of about 30 m. The old town (40 ft. above sea-level) lay and lies on a peninsula surrounded by the Bacchiglione except on the south, where it was protected by a canal. Of the bridges which cross the canals by which Padua is now intersected, four go back to Roman times. Remains of a public building, possibly belonging to the forum, were found in the centre of the modern city in making the foundations of the Caffè Pedrocchi at the south-west angle of Piazza Cavour—possibly a colonnade of fine Corinthian architecture (see P. Selvatico, *Relazione dello Scavo . . . su la Piazzetta Pedrocchi*. A large mosaic with geometric designs was also

recently discovered in the centre of the city. In imperial times the town spread even farther, as is shown by the position outside the town of the amphitheatre, built of blocks of local stone with brick courses, which was excavated in 1881 (G. Ghirardini in *Notizie degli Scavi*, 1881, 223). It measures 325 by 205 ft., and is the only Roman building of which visible remains exist. A so-called " paletta " (a bronze plate with a handle—possibly a bell or a votive axe or a simple pendant) with a figure of a horse on one side and a votive inscription on the other, belonging to the 5th or 4th century B.C., was found in 1899 at a great depth close to the church of S. Antonio (G. Ghirardini in *Notizie degli Scavi*, 1901, 314). The name of the town is probably connected with Padus (Po). According to the legend it was founded by the Trojan Antenor. The memory of the defeat of the Spartan king Cleonymus by the fleet of Patavium in 302 B.C. was perpetuated by Spartan spoils in the temple of Juno and a yearly sea-fight which took place on the river. On land Patavium was equally powerful (it had been able, we are told, to put 120,000 men into the field), and perpetually made war against its Celtic neighbours. Patavium acquired Roman citizenship with the rest of Gallia Transpadana in 49 B.C. Under Augustus, Strabo tells us, Patavium surpassed all the cities of the north in wealth, and in the number of Roman knights among its citizens in the census of Augustus was only equalled by Gades, which had also 500. Its commercial importance was also great, being especially due to its trade in wool. The numerous inscriptions, however, as Th. Mommsen remarks (*Corp. inscr. latin.* v. 268), show remarkable dignity and simplicity and avoidance of pomposity; to this Pliny the younger and Martial testify. The importance of Patavium as a literary centre was also considerable. Livy, Q. Asconius Pedianus and Thrasea Paetus were natives of the town; and Quintilian speaks of the directness and simplicity of their diction as *Patavinitas*, comparing it with the artificial obscurity of the writers of Rome itself.

After the 2nd century A.D. it is hardly mentioned, and seems to have been outstripped by other cities, such as Milan and Aquileia. It was destroyed by the Lombards with fire and sword, and it was then that it lost practically all its monuments of the Roman period. (T. AS.)

PATEL, FRAMJEE NASARWANJEE (1804–1894), Parsee merchant and philanthropist, was born in 1804, and had a sound vernacular education, with a smattering of English received in Bombay. At the age of fifteen he entered upon a business career, and his pursuit proved so congenial that by 1827 he had worked his way to a partnership in the firm of Frith, Bomanjee & Co. Banking facilities being then exceedingly scanty, such Parsees as had any capital at command acted as bankers and brokers to the rising English firms. Patel's experience enabled him in a few years to raise the status of his compatriots to the higher level of independent merchants, and he founded in 1844 a business house under the name of Wallace & Co., in which he was himself a partner with the English members of the firm. When he retired in 1858 he had amassed a large competence, and in the following year he established a firm on the same lines under the style of Framjee, Sands & Co., of which the members were some of his sons, together with English partners. It was, however, not so much for his success as a merchant, as for his spirit and liberality as an educationist, reformer and philanthropist, that his name is notable in the annals of western India. He entered on his civic labours in 1837, and in all public movements figured prominently as an accredited representative of his community. As a pioneer of education, both for boys and girls, his example inspired the younger men of his time, like Dadabhai Naoroji, at one time M.P. for East Finsbury, and Naoroji Fardoonjee and Sorabjee Shapurjee Bengallee. When Mountstuart Elphinstone, during his governorship, conceived the idea of concentrating the literary and educational activity which had arisen from isolated efforts on the part of men who had themselves been brought into contact with Western culture, among his chief collaborators were Framjee Cowasjee Banajee and Framjee Patel. To their initiative was due the establishment of the Elphinstone Institution, which comprised a high school and, after some years, a college, which continue to hold foremost rank among the similar academies since established in western India. But Mr Patel's most remarkable public service was performed in connexion with the Parsee Law Association, of which he was president. Since their exodus from Persia the domestic affairs of the Parsees had been in a very unsettled state. Matrimonial obligations and the rights of succession in cases of intestacy had fallen into hopeless confusion, and the adjudication of disputes in relation thereto was effected by certain elders of the community, who had neither the knowledge and help of fixed principles to guide their judgments, nor any authority to enforce their decisions. The case of *Ardesir Cursetjee* v. *Peerozebai*, which came up on appeal before the privy council in England, brought to light the strange fact that even the supreme court of Bombay had no jurisdiction over matrimonial and ecclesiastical disputes among Parsees. This state of lawlessness was recognized by that community as intolerable, and the agitation which ensued thereupon led to the appointment of a commission, of which the distinguished jurist, Sir Joseph Arnould, was the president and Framjee Patel the chief Parsee member. The Parsee Law Association, under the guidance of Patel and Sorabjee Bengallee, rendered invaluable help to the commission, and their joint efforts resulted in the passing by the government of India of the Parsee Marriage and Divorce Act and the Parsee Intestate Succession Act (15 and 21 of 1865). These acts form the charter of matrimonial and ecclesiastical status for the Parsees. At the time of his death in 1894, at the ripe age of nearly ninety years, Framjee Patel was the most revered and best beloved of the distinguished natives of India, having during an eventful public life extending over sixty years worked in co-operation with three generations of the most prominent of his compatriots to better the condition of their country. His family surname refers to the title of *patel*, that is, "mayor," of Bombay, conferred on its founder for services rendered to the English in 1692. (M. M. Bh.)

PATEN (through the Fr. from Lat. *patina* or *patena*, Gr. πατάνη, a flat dish), the name of the shallow plate or dish used in the celebration of the Eucharist for the consecrated bread or wafer. The paten has from the first been almost always of a circular shape. There is a rare example of a rectangular one, dating from the 7th century, in the Cabinet des Medailles in Paris. The central portion of the paten is sometimes decorated with the engraved head of the Saviour, or commonly with a group of lobes.

PATENÔTRE DES NOYERS, JULES (1845–   ), French diplomatist, was born at Baye (Marne) on the 20th of April 1845. Educated at the École Normale Supérieure, he taught for some years in the lycée at Algiers before he joined the diplomatic service in 1871. His most important mission was in 1884, when he was sent as French minister to China to regularize the French dominion in Annam. After arranging at Hué with the king of Annam the condition of the French protectorate, he proceeded to Shanghai to settle with China the difficulties which had arisen over the evacuation of Tongking by the Chinese troops. The negotiation failed, and the French admiral resumed hostilities against China in August. Next year Patenôtre signed with Li Hung Chang a treaty of peace at Tien-tsin, by which the French protectorate in Annam and Tongking was recognized, and both parties agreed to remain within their own borders in the future. After serving as minister plenipotentiary in Morocco (1888–1891), M. Patenôtre was sent to Washington, where he was raised to the rank of ambassador in 1893. He was ambassador at Madrid from 1897 to 1902.

Pierre Loti in *Au Maroc* has described his diplomacy in Morocco. M. Patenôtre himself published some reminiscences in the *Revue des deux mondes*.

PATENTS, properly documents conferring some privilege, right, &c., short for "letters patent" (q.v.). Patents for inventions, instruments which formerly bore the great seal of the United Kingdom, are now issued at the Patent Office in London under the seal of that office. By their means inventors obtain a monopoly in their inventions for fourteen years, a term which, if insufficient to remunerate the inventor, can be extended.

This monopoly is founded on exactly the same principle as the copyright enjoyed by authors and artists. There are persons who argue that no such privilege should be permitted; there are others who think that the most trifling exertions of the inventive faculties should be protected. The right: course clearly lies between these extremes. To grant a very long term of exclusive possession might be detrimental to the public, since it would tend to stop the progress of improvement. A limited property must therefore be allowed—large enough to give the inventor an opportunity of reaping a fair reward, but not barring the way for an unreasonable period. And, when this compromise has been decided on, it will be seen how difficult it may be to determine beforehand what is the real merit of an invention, and apportion the time to that merit. Hence it has been found necessary to allot one fixed period for all kinds of inventions falling within the purview of the patent laws.

United Kingdom.—Formerly the reigning prince considered himself entitled, as part of his prerogative, to grant privileges of the nature of monopolies to any one who had gained his favour. These grants became so numerous that they were oppressive and unjust to various classes of the commonwealth; and hence, in the reign of James I., a statute was wrung from that king which declared all monopolies that were grievous and inconvenient to the subjects of the realm to be void. (See LETTERS PATENT; MONOPOLY.) There was, however, a special exception from this enactment of all letters patent and grants of privilege of the "sole working or making of any manner of new manufacture within the realm to the true and first inventor of such manufacture, which others at the time of making such letters patent and grants should not use, so they be not contrary to law, nor mischievous to the state by raising of the prices of commodities at home or hurt of trade or generally inconvenient." Upon these words hangs the whole law of letters patent for inventions. Many statutes were afterwards passed, but these were all repealed by the Patent Act of 1883 (46 & 47 Vict. c. 57), which, besides introducing a new procedure, modified the law in several particulars. Subsequently acts amending the law were passed in 1885, 1886, 1888, 1901, 1902 and 1907. These acts, with the exception of certain sections of the act of 1883, were repealed by a consolidating act, the Patents and Designs Act 1907, which also introduced new provisions into English patent law. Where the law is not expressly laid down by act of parliament, it has to be gathered from the numerous decisions of the courts, for patent law is to no inconsiderable extent "judge-made law."

The inventions for which patents are obtained are chiefly either vendible articles formed by chemical or mechanical operations, such as cloth, alloys, vulcanized india-rubber, &c., or machinery and apparatus, or processes. It may be remarked here that a scientific principle cannot form the subject of a valid patent unless its application to a practical and useful end and object is shown. An abstract notion, a philosophical idea, may be extremely valuable in the realm of science, but before it is allowed to form a sound basis for a patent the world must be shown how to apply it so as to gain therefrom some immediate material advantage. With regard to processes, the language of the statute of James has been strained to bring them within the words "any manner of new manufacture," and judges on the bench have admitted that the exposition of the act has gone much beyond the letter. However, it is undoubted law that a process is patentable; and patents are accordingly obtained for processes every day.

The principal classes of patentable inventions seem to be these: (1) new contrivances applied to new ends, (2) new contrivances applied to old ends, (3) new combinations of old parts, whether relating to material objects or processes, (4) new methods of applying a well-known object.

With regard to a patent for the new application of a well-known object it may be remarked that there must be some display of ingenuity; some amount of invention in making the application, otherwise the patent will be invalid on the ground that the subject-matter is destitute of novelty. For example, a fishplate, used before the introduction of railways to connect wooden beams could not be patented to connect the rails of a railway (*Harwood* v. *Great Northern Railway Co.*, 1860–1865, 11 H. L. C. 654); nor can a spring long used in the rear of a carriage be patented for use in the front (*Morgan* v. *Windover*, 1890, 7 R. P. C. 131). But a small amount of invention will suffice, so long as the improvement is manifest, either as saving time or labour (*Rickmann* v. *Thierry*, 1896, 14 R.P.C. 105; *Patent Exploitation, Ltd.* v. *Siemens & Co.*, 1904, 21 R.P.C. 549).

Whatever be the nature of the invention, it must possess the incidents of· utility and novelty, else any patent obtained in respect of it will be invalid. The degree of utility need not, however, be great. As to novelty, this is the rock upon which most patents split; for, if it can be shown that other persons have used or published the invention before the date of the patent, it will fall to the ground, although the patentee was an independent inventor deriving his ideas from no one else. The difficulty of steering clear of this rock will be apparent at·once. Suppose A in London patents an invention the result of his own ingenuity and patient study, and it afterwards appears that B, in some distant part of the kingdom, had been previously openly using the same thing in his workshop, A's patent is good for nothing. Thus, where the patent sued on was a lock, it was proved that a similar lock had been in use on a gate adjoining a public road for sixteen years prior to the patent, which was accordingly invalidated (*Carpenter* v. *Smith*, 1842, 1 Web. P.C. 540). It is therefore a very frequent subject of inquiry, whether an invention has been previously used to such an extent as to have been publicly used in the sense attached by the courts to this phrase. But whereas "user" in public is sufficient prior publication to invalidate a subsequent patent for the invention so used, publication in books, &c., will not be a bar to novelty unless its effect is to make the invention actually a part of public knowledge; and in dealing with alleged anticipations by patents that have never come into general use the courts will not invalidate a subsequent patent unless a person of ordinary knowledge of the subject, on having the alleged anticipation brought under his notice, would at once perceive, understand, and be able practically to apply the invention without making experiments or seeking for further information. The inventor himself is not allowed to use his invention, either in public or secretly, with a view to profit, before the date of the patent. Thus, if he manufactures an article by some new process, keeping the process an entire secret, but selling the produce, he cannot afterwards obtain a patent in respect of it. If he were allowed to do this he might in many cases easily obtain a monopoly in his invention for a much longer period than that allowed by law (*Morgan* v. *Seaward*, 1837, 1 Web. P.C. 192). The rule that an inventor's use of the invention invalidates a subsequent patent does not, however, apply to cases where the use was only by way of experiment with a view to improve or test the invention (*Elias* v.· *Grosvend Tinplate Co.*, 1890, 7 P.O.R. 466). And it has been repeatedly decided that the· previous experiments of other persons, if incomplete or abandoned before the realization of the discovery, will not have the effect of vitiating a patent. Even the prior discovery of an invention will not prevent another independent discoverer from obtaining a valid patent if the earlier inventor kept the secret to himself, the law holding that he is the " true and first inventor " who first obtains a patent.

The Patents Act 1883 provided that the exhibition of an invention·at an industrial or International exhibition certified as such by the Board of Trade, or the publication of any description of the invention during the period of the holding of the exhibition, or its use for the purpose of the exhibition in the place where it is held, or during the period of the exhibition by any person elsewhere, without the privity or consent of the inventor, should not prejudice the right of the inventor or of his legal personal representative to apply for and obtain a patent, or the validity of any patent granted on the application, provided that two conditions are complied with, viz. (*a*) the exhibitor must, before exhibiting the invention, ·give·the Comptroller-General a prescribed notice of his intention to·do so; and (*b*) the application for the patent must be made before or within six·months from the

date of the opening of the exhibition. · The ·Patents Act 1886, enabled the Sovereign, by order in council, to extend the provision above mentioned to industrial and international exhibitions held out of the United Kingdom. The act of 1907 re-enacted these provisions (§§ 45, 59). When an invention is the joint production of more persons than one, they must all apply for and obtain a joint patent, for a patent is rendered invalid on showing that a material part of the invention was due to some·one not named therein. The mere suggestion of a workman employed by an inventor to carry out his ideas will not, however, require that he should be joined, provided that the former adds nothing substantial to the invention, but merely works out in detail the principle discovered by his employer.

Procedure.—The attributes of novelty and utility being possessed in due degree by an invention, it remains to put in motion the machinery for its protection. The Patents Act 1907, re-enacting former provisions, requires an application to be made in a prescribed form (the forms and stamps are on sale at all postal money order offices in the United Kingdom), and left at or sent by post to the patent office in the prescribed manner. The application must contain a declaration that the applicant is the true and first inventor, and it must be accompanied by either a provisional or complete specification. A provisional specification describes the nature of an invention, and a complete specification particularly describes and ascertains the nature of the invention and the manner in which it is to be performed. Since the introduction of the patent specification, it has been necessary that an invention protected by patent should be accurately described by the inventor. Formerly, when the condition on which letters patent issued was, that the patentee should file a specification completely describing the nature of his invention within a certain time after the grant, the function of giving the necessary preliminary information on the subject was to some extent discharged by the title; at any rate, the validity of the grant was liable to be objected to on the ground of the title being too general. Under the present law the task of preliminary disclosure falls to the provisional specification, introduced by the Patent Law Amendment Act 1852, and continued by the Patents Acts of 1883 and 1907, although a patentee may, under the latter statutes, dispense with a provisional specification if he thinks proper to file a complete one in the first instance. Where however, these two specifications are filed, it becomes of vital moment to an inventor that the true relation between them should be maintained as defined above. The object of the provisional· specification is to secure immediate protection, and to enable a patentee to work at and improve his invention without the risk of his patent being invalidated by premature publication. He is therefore entitled to embody in his complete specification any improved method of working his invention which he may discover in the interval; and he is indeed bound to do so, since, as we have said, the price that a man who desires a patent has to pay to the public for the privilege is that he should make a full disclosure of his invention in his complete specification. But there is a limit to what the patentee may do in this·respect. He must not describe in his complete specification an invention different from that declared in the provisional. If he falls into this error there is said to be a " variance " or " disconformity " between the two specifications. The Patents Act 1883, § 9, made it the duty of the examiners of the Patent Office to consider the question of disconformity between specifications on applications for patents, but the only power the comptroller had, on discovery of disconformity, was to refuse to accept the specification until the disconforming parts had been eliminated. By the act of 1907, § 6, he may now refuse to accept the complete specification until it has been amended to his satisfaction, or (with the consent of the applicant) cancel the provisional specification and treat the application as having been made on the date at which the complete specification was left. Moreover, if the complete specification includes an invention not included in the provisional specification, the application may proceed as a whole, or may be divided, and the claim for the additional invention included in the complete specification be regarded as an application for that invention made on the date at which the complete specification was left. An act of 1902 (which, with the exception of a portion dealing with compulsory licences, came into operation on the 1st of January 1905) provided for an examination or search as to novelty, such investigation dealing with British complete specifications published and dated within fifty years prior to the date of the application. This search was re-enacted by the act of 1907 (§ 7) and power given to the comptroller to refuse the grant of a patent in case in which the invention had been wholly and specifically claimed in specifications to which his search had extended.

The ·term for which a patent is originally granted is fourteen years, but a patentee may, after advertisement according to the rules of the Supreme Court, petition for a further term. The court. in considering its decision, takes regard of the nature and merit of the invention in relation ·to the public, of the profits made ·by the patentee as such, and of all the circumstances of the case. If it appears to the court that the patentee has been inadequately remunerated by his patent, it may extend the term of the patent to a further term not exceeding seven or, in exceptional cases, fourteen years, or may order the grant of a new patent for a certain term, with any restrictions or provisions it may think fit (Act of 1907, § 18).

Patent privileges, like most other rights, can be made the subject of sale. Partial interests can also be carved out of them by means of licences, instruments which empower other persons to exercise the invention, either universally and for the full time of the patent (when they are tantamount to an assignment of the patentee's entire rights), or for a limited time, or within a limited district. By an exclusive licence is meant one that restrains the patentee from granting other licences to any one else. By means of a licence a patentee may derive benefit from his patent without entering into trade and without running the risks of a partnership.

One of the regulations of the act of 1883 was that a patentee could be compelled by the Board of Trade to grant licences to persons who were able to show that the patent was not being worked in the United Kingdom, or that the reasonable requirements of the public with respect to the invention could not be supplied, or that any person was prevented from working or using to the best advantage an invention of which he was possessed. This regulation, however, remained practically a dead letter, for only three applications were made between the years 1883 and 1897, and these never proceeded to a hearing. After 1897 a few petitions were heard, but even so late as in 1908 there was only one petition and that was withdrawn by agreement between the parties. By § 3 of the act of 1902, the hearing of petitions for a grant of compulsory licences was transferred to the judicial committee of the privy council, but the act of 1907 substituted the High Court as the tribunal in the place of the judicial committee. It also laid down that the reasonable requirements of the public should not be deemed to be satisfied: (a) if by reason of the default of the patentee to manufacture to an adequate extent and supply on reasonable terms, the patented article or any parts thereof necessary for its efficient working or to carry on the patented process to an adequate extent or to grant licences on reasonable terms, any existing trade or industry or the establishment of any new trade or industry in the United Kingdom is unfairly prejudiced, or the demand for the patented article is not reasonably met; or (b) if any trade or industry in the United Kingdom is unfairly prejudiced by the conditions attached by the patentee before or after the passing of the act to the purchase, hire or use of the patented article or to the using or working of the patented process. Clause b is an endeavour to remedy an abuse by which patentees bound down purchasers and licences by all kinds of conditions. Section 38 of the act of 1907 contains also a further remedy, making it unlawful in any contract in relation to the sale or lease of, or licence to use or work, any patented article or process to insert conditions prohibiting or restricting the use of the patent or process from using articles supplied by a third person or requiring him to use other articles not protected by the patent. Such conditions are declared " null and void as being in restraint of trade and contrary to public policy."

Another new and very important provision of the act of 1907 is that dealing with the revocation of patents worked outside the United Kingdom. It may be stated here that in the year 1908 out of a total number of 16,284 patentees, 2819 were resident in the United States, 2516 in Germany, 822 in France, 334 in Austria-Hungary, 200 in Switzerland, 166 in the Australian Commonwealth, 159 in Belgium, 155 in Canada, 139 in Sweden and 134 in Italy. It had been a common practice to take out licences in the United Kingdom (especially in the dyeing industry) in order to close the British market to all except the patentees and their licensees, the patented articles or processes being worked entirely abroad. Section 27 of the act of 1907 enacted that at any time not less than four years after the date of a patent and not less than one year after the passing of the act, any person might apply to the comptroller for the revocation of a patent on the ground that the patented article or process is manufactured or carried on exclusively or mainly outside the United Kingdom. The comptroller is given power to make an order revoking the patent forthwith or after a reasonable interval, unless the patentee can show satisfactory reasons. The insertion of this provision resulted in the establishment of many factories in the United Kingdom.

Legal Remedies.—A patentee's remedy for an infringement of his rights is by civil suit, there being no criminal proceedings in such a case. In prosecuting such suit he subjects those rights to a searching examination, for the alleged infringer is at liberty to show that the invention is not new, that the patentee is not the true and first inventor, &c., as well as to prove that the alleged infringement is not really an infringement. But it may here be remarked that a patentee is not bound down (unless he chooses so to be) to the precise mode of carrying the invention into effect described in the specification. If the principle is new, it is not to be expected that he can describe every mode of working it; he will sufficiently secure the principle by giving some illustrations of it; and no person will be permitted to adopt some mode of carrying

the same principle into effect on the ground that such mode has not been described by the patentee. On the other hand, when the principle is not new, a patentee can only secure the particular method which he has invented, and other persons may safely use other methods of effecting the same object. Instances of this occur every day; and it is well known that scores of patents have been taken out for screw-propellers, steam-hammers, water-meters, &c., each of which is limited to the particular construction described, and cannot be extended further. Again, where the invention patented consists of a combination of parts, some old and some new, the whole constituting a new machine or a new process, it is not open to the world to copy the new part and reject the rest. A man is not permitted to allege that the patent is for a combination, and that, the identical combination not having been used, there has been no infringement. If he has borrowed the substance of the invention, it will be held that he has infringed the patent. At common law a person who, alleging that he has a patent, threatens his rivals in trade, is liable to an action for damages, but the plaintiff cannot succeed without showing that the threats were made maliciously. The Patents Act 1883 provided 'another remedy—what is known as " the threats action." This has been incorporated in the act of 1907, § 36. The statute makes the good faith of the patentee threatening legal proceedings no answer to an action brought against him by any person aggrieved by his threats if the acts complained of are not in fact an infringement of the patent, and if the patentee fails with due diligence to commence and prosecute an action for infringement.

Extent and Construction.—The patent when sealed is to have effect in the United Kingdom and the Isle of Man. The act of 1907, unlike the Patent Law Amendment Act of 1852, does not extend the monopoly to the Channel Islands.

The patent business of the United Kingdom is transacted at the Patent Office in London under the superintendence of the comptroller, an officer appointed by the Board of Trade, under whose direction he performs his duties. At this office is kept a register of all patents issued, of assignments of patents, licences granted under them, &c. An illustrated journal of patent inventions is published at the same office, where printed copies of all specifications can also be obtained. The fees payable to government on patents were considerably reduced by an order of the Board of Trade which came into operation on the 1st of October 1892, and may now be paid by convenient annual instalments. The following are the present fees: before the expiration of the 4th year from the date of the patent, £5 instead of £10; of the 5th year, £6 instead of £10; of the 6th year, £7 instead of £10; of the 7th year, £8 instead of £10; of the 8th year, £9 instead of £15; of the 10th year, £11 instead of £20; of the 11th year, £12 instead of £20; of the 12th year, £13 instead of £20; and of the 13th year, £14 instead of £20. The preliminary fees amounting to £4 were left untouched by the order but under the Patent Rules of 1905 an additional fee of £1 is payable on the sealing of the patent. The entire cost of a patent is now reduced from £154 to £100.

A new Patent Office was constructed on the site of the old buildings, the frontage extending from Southampton Buildings into Staple Inn. The number of applications for patents, which sprang from 5993 in 1883 to 17,110 in 1884, culminated in a total of 30,952 for the year 1892, since which date a steady decline set in down to 1900, when the number was 23,924. But the numbers went up again, reaching 30,030 in 1906, but only 28,598 in 1908. The number of patents sealed on application for a given year shows less variation, the minimum being 8775 for 1885 against 16,060 in 1907. The proportion of seals to applications varies from about 46 to 50%. The receipts from patent fees in 1908 were £262,890, against a total expenditure of £179,531.

The official publications of the Patent Office deserve some notice, as, in the absence of official investigation into novelty, the onus of search rests with the applicant or his agent. The procedure has been greatly simplified by the publication, on a uniform system and at a low rate (1s. per volume), of illustrated abridgments of specifications. From 1877 practically to date the searcher obtains a chronological digest of all specifications falling within a given class. To these classes there is a reference index, known as the " abridgment class and index key," which at once directs the searcher to his proper class and index heading.

Patent Agents.—Patents are frequently obtained through the intervention of persons termed patent agents, who devote themselves to this branch of business.' Their position is now regulated by statute. By the Patents Act 1888, it was provided that no person should, after July 1, 1889, be entitled to describe himself (and whoever does so knowingly incurs liability to a maximum penalty of £20) as a patent agent whether by advertisement, description of his place of business or otherwise, without being registered as such in pursuance of the act. But the act preserves the right to registration of every person who, to the satisfaction of the Board of Trade, shows that he had been bona fide practising as a patent agent before it passed. The Board of Trade is empowered by this statute to make from time to time general rules for the purpose of carrying out its provisions, and by rules issued in 1889, and reissued in 1891, the Board of Trade delegated to the Institute of Patent Agents (which obtained a royal charter in

1891) the care of the register of patent agents and the duty of holding the necessary examinations for entrance into the profession.

British Dominions.—The following notes on colonial law give the salient facts. Prior to 1852 British letters patent extended to all the colonies, but the act of 1852 restricted the rights granted to the United Kingdom, Channel Islands and Isle of Man.

Australia.—The Commonwealth Acts are No. 21 of 1903, and No. 19 of 1906. They are founded on the English act of 1883 and amending acts. They provide for a department of patents controlled by a commissioner "under the minister" (§ 10 of 1903). Any person, whether a British subject or not, may apply for a patent (§ 32 of 1903). The term of a patent is 14 years (§ 64 of 1903). The Commonwealth or a state may acquire patents compulsorily (§§ 93, 94 of 1903). The act creates a new class of "patent attorneys" (§ 101, 1903). There is an examination as to novelty (§ 41 of 1903). The renewal fees amount to a sum of £5 before the end of the 4th year, and £5 before the end of the 7th year from the date of the patent.

Bahama Islands.—The law is regulated by the following acts of the colony: 52 Vict. c. 23; 53 Vict. c. 2; 54 Vict. c. 12; and 63 Vict. c. 3. Duration of patent 7 years, with power in governor to renew for another 7 years, and thereafter for a third period of 7 years. The fees are £10 on filing specification, £10 for second renewal and £20 for third. Apparently there is no preliminary examination as to novelty.

Barbados.—Acts of 1903 (No. 31) and of 1908 (No. 10). Duration of patent 14 years. The governor in council has power to grant compulsory licences. Fees are £2, 10s. on filing specification, £50 before the end of the 4th year and £100 before the end of the 7th year. No preliminary examination as to novelty.

Bermuda.—Act of 1902 (No. 51), on the lines of that of Trinidad.

British Guiana.—The law is regulated by ordinance No. 31 of 1902 and is practically the same as the English act of 1883. The fees are $15 on filing specification and $100 before the end of 7 years.

British Honduras.—The law of the 10th of September 1862 has been re-enacted with slight modifications (see supplement to *Patent Laws of the World*, No. 4, 1900). There is no examination as to novelty.

British India.—The law is now governed by Act 5 of 1888, which applies to the whole of British India. Duration of patent 14 years. A preliminary examination into novelty might apparently be ordered. The following taxes are payable: annual sums of Rs. 50 from the 4th to the 8th year, and of Rs. 100 from the 8th to the 13th year of the term.

British New Guinea.—The Queensland Patents Acts, No. 13 of 1884 and No. 5 of 1886, have been adopted. See British New Guinea ordinance No. 6 of 1889, schedule A.

British North Borneo.—Straits Settlements law (No. 12 of 1871), adopted by Patents Proclamation 1887 (No. 1 of 1887).

Canada.—Patent legislation belongs exclusively to the Dominion Parliament [B.N.A. Act 1867, § 91 (22)]. The existing acts are c. 61 of 1886; 55 & 56 Vict. c. 24; 56 Vict. c. 34; and act of 1903. The duration of the patent is 18 years. At the time of application the applicant may pay the full fee required for that term (viz. $60) or the partial fee required for the term of 6 years ($20) or for the term of 12 years ($40). If a partial fee only is paid, the amount is stated in the patent, and the patent ceases at the end of the term covered by such partial payment, unless before the expiration of such term the patentee pays the fee required for the further term of 6 or 12 years, viz. $20 in the former case and $40 in the latter. There is a preliminary examination into novelty by examiners, with an appeal from the decision of the commissioner of patents to the governor in council. The patent is void unless it is worked in Canada within 2 years, or if after the expiration of 12 months, or any authorized extension of either of these periods, the patentee imports the invention into Canada, but conditions may be substituted for condition as to manufacture in Canada, as, for example, a licence to another to manufacture, &c.

Cape of Good Hope.—The law is regulated by act No. 17 of 1860, No. 24 of 1902 and No. 28 of 1904. There is no preliminary examination into novelty, and the act contains no provisions for compulsory working, or as to the importation of patented articles from abroad.

Ceylon.—The law is now regulated by act 15 of 1906. The duration of the patent is 14 years, with power vested in the governor in council to grant extensions of 7 and 14 years. There is a preliminary examination as to novelty, but there are no provisions as to compulsory working or the importation of patented articles from abroad. The renewal fees are Rs. 50 annually from the expiration of the 4th to before the expiration of the 8th year from the filing of the specification, Rs. 100 after the expiration of the 8th and before the expiration of the 9th year, Rs. 150 after the expiration of the 9th and before the expiration of the 10th year, and Rs. 200 annually after the expiration of the 10th year to before the expiration of the 13th year.

Channel Islands.—These are not now included in grant of letters patent. See form of grant, schedule I., form D., Patents Act 1883.

Falkland Islands.—By ordinance No. 2 of 1903 letters patent for any invention may be granted to any person holding in the United Kingdom a valid patent for any invention or to any person to whom all interest in the patent has been assigned. The fee on application is £5.

Fiji Islands.—The law depends on ordinances No. 3 of 1879 and 7 of 1882, and order of December 29, 1890. The duration of the patent is 14 years. There is no preliminary examination, and there are no provisions as to compulsory working or importation from abroad. The patent is not subject to any payment after issue. A fee of 5 guineas is payable on deposit of petition and specification. The fees for provisional protection is 5 guineas; on obtaining letters patent the applicant pays 10 guineas.

Gambia.—An ordinance (No. 5 of 1900) is practically identical with the English act of 1883. No. 5 of 1904 made international arrangements for protection of patents.

Gibraltar.—There is no patent law in Gibraltar, but special ordinances are sometimes passed extending the privileges of British patentees to the dependency for the unexpired residues of the original terms. See as examples No. 5 of 1890, No. 1 of 1896, and No. 1 of 1898.

Gold Coast.—The law is now regulated by the Patents Ordinances 1900 to 1906, which closely resemble the Imperial Act.

Hong-Kong.—The law is regulated by ordinance No. 2 of 1892. The inventor or assignee of any invention patented in England may obtain protection in the colony for the unexpired residue of the original term. If the English patent is extended by the advice of the Judicial Committee, an extension of the colonial patent may be obtained, or a new patent granted for the extended period. A fee of $25 is payable on grant of patent, and another fee of the same amount on grant of extension or original letters in lieu of extension. There is no preliminary examination, and there are no provisions as to compulsory working or importation from abroad.

Jamaica.—The law is still in substance governed by c. 30 of 1857. But under ordinance No. 15 of 1891 the stamp duty on letters patent is now £2 instead of £6, 10s., and there is no longer any fee payable on the reference to the attorney-general. There is no preliminary examination as to novelty, and there are no provisions as to importation from abroad.

Lagos.—Ordinances of 1900 (No. 17) and 1902 (No. 2) introduce substantially the English law.

Leeward Islands.—Act No. 3 of 1906 has adopted the English act of 1883. The fees are on filing specification £2, 10s.; at end of 4th year £20; at end of 7th year £40.

Malta.—The law is governed by ordinance No. 11 of 1899 and No. 7. of 1907, the duration of the patent is 14 years. There is no express provision for a preliminary examination into novelty. Provision is made for compulsory assignation or licence, where the invention has not been put into use within 3 years subsequent to the grant or its working has been suspended for 3 years continuously. The annual fees are £5 before the expiration of the 4th year from the date of the patent; £6 before the expiration of the 5th; £7 and £8 respectively before the expiration of the 6th and 7th years; £9 and £10 before the expiration of the 8th and 9th; and from £11 to £14 before the expiration of the 10th, 11th, 12th and 13th years.

Mauritius.—The law is still regulated by ordinance No. 16 of 1875. There is no preliminary examination as to novelty, and there are no provisions for compulsory working or importation from abroad.

Natal.—The law is still regulated by No. 4 of 1870. But certain details of practice are amended by No. 2 of 1895. There is no preliminary examination as to novelty, and there are no provisions as to compulsory working or importation from abroad.

Newfoundland.—The law is contained in the Consolidated Statutes, t. xii. c. 109. There is no preliminary examination into novelty. In addition to the office fees, the patentee is required to deposit with the colonial secretary the sum of $25, to be paid by him to the receiver-general for the use of the colony.

New Zealand.—The law now depends on No. 12 of 1889, amended in details by No. 8 of 1897. The duration of a patent is 14 years. There is no preliminary examination as to novelty, and there are no provisions as to compulsory working or importation from abroad. The following fees are payable: £2 on obtaining letters patent, £5 before the expiration of the 4th year and £10 before the expiration of the 7th.

Nigeria, Northern.—No. 12 of 1902 introduces practically the English law of 1883.

Orange River Colony.—Up to the outbreak of war in 1899 the law was regulated by ordinance No. 10 of 1888 and no change has yet been made. The term of a patent was 14 years. No preliminary examination as to novelty. Compulsory licences might be obtained. No prohibition of the importation of patented articles. The fee for signing and sealing the patent was not less than £10 nor more than £50. Taxes of £5 and £10 were payable before or at the expiration of the 3rd and 7th years of the term respectively.

Rhodesia, Southern.—Ordinance No. 7 of 1904 adopts practically the English law.

St Helena.—The law is regulated by ordinance No. 3 of 1872. The grantee of an English patent, or his representatives, can have the grant extended to the colony. All cases of doubt and difficulty not provided for by the laws of the colony are governed by the law in force in England. A fee of one guinea is payable on filing copy of letters patent and specification with the registrar of the Supreme Court.

Sierra Leone.—No special regulations exist, but an ordinance practically identical with that of the Gold Coast is being adopted.

Straits Settlements.—The law is prescribed by ordinance No. 12 of 1871. The duration of a patent is 14 years. There is no preliminary examination as to novelty, and there are no provisions as to compulsory working or importation from abroad. There is a stamp duty of $50 on the petition. No renewal fees are payable.

Transvaal Colony.—Proclamations Nos. 22 and 29 of 1902 introduce substantially the English law.

Trinidad and Tobago.—The law is regulated by ordinance No. 10 of 1900 and No. 13 of 1905. The duration of the patent is 14 years. There is no preliminary examination into novelty, and there are no provisions as to compulsory working or importation from abroad. A fee of £10 is payable on application for a patent.

Turks and Caicos Islands.—The law of Jamaica has been extended to these islands by No. 7 of 1897. See supplement to *Patent Laws of the World*, No. 3 of 1900.

Windward Islands.—In the Windward Islands other than Barbados, viz. Grenada, St Lucia and St Vincent, patents for invention were granted until recently only by special ordinances. See, *e.g.* St Lucia, ordinance No. 41 of 1875 (Tooth's patent). A stamp duty of £10 was payable in this island on letters patent for inventions (No. 6 of 1881, schedule). But ordinances based on the Imperial Act have now been passed, St Vincent (No. 5 of 1898), Grenada (No. 4 of 1898) and St Lucia (No. 14 of 1899).

Foreign Patent Laws.—For the text of these see *Patent Laws of the World*, ed. 1899 and supplemental volumes. But the following are the essential facts.

Algeria.—French law applied by decree of June 5, 1850.

Argentine Republic.—The law of October 11, 1864, is still in force. There is no provision as to importation from abroad.

Austria.—A law of January 11, 1897, came into force on January 1, 1899. The principal changes introduced by this measure were these. A strict preliminary examination was made into novelty. The term of the patent was fixed at 15 years, and besides an application fee of 10 florins, annual fees were imposed rising from 20 florins for the 1st year to 340 florins for the 15th. The period for compulsory working was raised from 1 year to 3 years from the date of the publication of the grant of the patent in the patent journal. Provision was made for the conversion of patents under the old law of August 15, 1852 (extended to Hungary by law of June 27, 1878, and to Bosnia and Herzegovina by law of December 20, 1879) into patents under the present law.

Belgium.—The law is still governed by the law of May 24, 1854. Patents are granted, as in France, without guarantee of novelty.

Bolivia.—The patent law depends on a law of May 8, 1858. The duration of the patent is in the case of a patent of invention not less than 10 nor more than 15 years; in the case of an imported invention, 3 years if its establishment requires an outlay of $25,000, if it reaches $50,000, 6 years, and if $100,000 or more, 10 years. The novelty neither of patents for invention nor of patents for imported inventions is guaranteed. The patent lapses unless the invention is put into complete practice within a year and a day from the date of the privilege, unless the omission is excused by justifiable causes according to law.

Brazil.—Patents are granted under the law of October 14, 1882. The patent lapses unless the invention is brought into effective use within 3 years from the date of the grant, or if such use is suspended for more than a year, except by reason of *force majeure* admitted by government to be a sufficient excuse. Besides expenses and fees, patents of invention are subject to an annual and progressive tax, commencing at $20 and increasing at the rate of £10 a year. The patents issued are without guarantee of novelty or utility.

Chile.—The law is regulated by the law of September 9, 1840, decree of August 1, 1851, and laws of July 25, 1872, January 20, 1883, and January 20, 1888. There is a preliminary examination as to novelty and utility. Though the duration of a patent does not ordinarily exceed 10 years, the term may be extended to 20 years by the president of the republic, if the report of the experts on the nature and importance of the invention seem to justify it. There are no provisions as to importation from abroad.

Colombia.—Patents are granted under law No. 35 of 1869 and decree No. 218 of 1900. The term varies from 5 to 20 years at the option of the applicant. There is no preliminary examination as to novelty, and there is no provision as to importation from abroad. A patent for a new industry is void when such industry is idle for a whole year, unless inevitable circumstances have intervened. An applicant pays a sum of 20 pesos, which is forfeited if the patent is refused, and taken in part payment of the patent fee if it is granted. The patent tax is from 5 to 20 pesos a year for every year of the privilege.

Congo.—Patents are issued under a law of October 29, 1886, and a decree of October 30, 1886. They are of three kinds, patents of invention, of importation and of improvement. There is no preliminary examination as to novelty, and the patent expressly mentions that the grant is made without guarantee. The term of a patent of invention is 20 years. A patent of importation or of improvement expires in the former case with the foreign, in the latter with the principal patent. Patents of improvement are not liable to any tax; on other patents a payment of 100 francs is required. There are no provisions as to compulsory working or prohibiting the importation of patented articles.

Costa Rica.—Prior to June 26, 1896, applications for patents had to be made to the Constitutional Congress. The matter is now dealt with by a law of the above-mentioned date. The duration of the term is 20 years. There is apparently no preliminary examination into novelty. The period for compulsory working is 2 years, and a patent which ceases to be worked during any 3 consecutive years becomes public property.

Denmark.—Patents are now granted under a law of March 28, 1894. The duration of the patent is 15 years, and no extension can be granted. There is a preliminary examination into novelty. The patent may, on terms, be appropriated by the state if the public interest demands it. The period for compulsory working is 3 years, and the patent will also lapse if the exercise of the invention is discontinued for more than a year. The patent commission may release the patentee from the obligation of manufacturing the patented article in Denmark, if satisfied that the cost of such manufacture would be unreasonable, on condition that the patented article is always kept on sale in Denmark. The tax is an annual fee of 25 kroner for the first 3 years, 50 kroner for the next 3, 100 for the following 3; then for 3 years 200 kroner yearly, and for the last 3, 300 kroner yearly.

Ecuador.—Patents are granted under a law of October 18, 1880. The provisions are identical with those given for Bolivia.

Finland.—The law is regulated by ordinances of January 21, 1898. The term of the patent is 15 years. There is a preliminary examination into novelty. The period for compulsory working is 3 years, the penalty for non-compliance being an obligation on the part of the patentee to grant compulsory licences. The tax consists of annual fees, commencing with the second year of the patent, and of the following amounts: 20 marks yearly for the 2nd and 3rd years; 40 marks from the 4th to and including the 6th year; 50 marks from the 7th to and including the 9th; 60 marks from the 10th to and including the 12th year; and 70 marks from the 13th to and including the 15th.

France.—The law is still regulated by the law of July 5, 1844. The following additional points should be noted: The term of a patent of invention is 5, or 10, or 15 years, at the option of the patentee. Every such patent is subject to the following taxes, payable by annual instalments of 100 francs: 500 francs for a patent of 5 years, 1000 francs for a patent of 10 years, and 1500 francs for a patent of 15 years. A tax of 20 francs is payable on application for a patent of addition. Patents of addition are not subject to annual taxes. There is no preliminary examination as to novelty. A patentee is not obliged to mark patented articles as such, but, if he does, the words *Sans Garantie du Gouvernement*, or the initial letters of these words—S. G. D. G.—must be added, under liability to a penalty for omission of from 50 francs to 1000 francs. The provisions as to compulsory working (*exploitation*) are in the main so interpreted as to strike only at voluntary and calculated inactivity. The law of July 5, 1844 is applied to the French colonies by a decree of October 21, 1848, to Madagascar by decree of 1902, and as to French Indo-China, see decree of June 24, 1893.

Germany.—Patents (the law as to which is not affected by the civil code of 1900) are granted under a law of April 7, 1891. The duration of the patent is 15 years. There is a strict preliminary examination into novelty. The period for compulsory working is 3 years, but it is sufficient if the patentee has done everything that is necessary to ensure the carrying out of the invention. A tax of 30 marks has to be paid before the grant. In addition to this there has to be paid at the commencement of the second and every following year of the term a tax amounting to 50 marks for the first year and increasing by 50 marks every subsequent year. An act of 1900 regulates the profession of patent agents.

Greece.—No special patent law apparently exists. A private act is required, which can be introduced by a deputy and is treated like any other bill.

Guatemala.—Patents are granted under the law of May 21, 1886 and a decree of December 17, 1897. The term of the patent ranges from 5 to 15 years. An annual tax of 30 pesos is payable. The period for compulsory working is 1 year, and abandonment of working for a year forfeits the patent. There is apparently a preliminary examination as to novelty (see Art. 16 of the decree of Dec. 17, 1897), but there is no prohibition of the importation of patented articles.

Hawaiian Islands.—Patents were issued till 1900 under the civil code (§§ 255, 256) and a law of August 29, 1884, which were not at first affected by the annexation of the islands by the United States. There was a preliminary examination as to novelty.

The maximum duration of the patent was 10 years. On application a fee of $5 was payable, the commissioner of patents received $20 for his examination, and a fee of $5 was payable when the patent was issued. No further payments. Now the United States law applies.

Honduras.—No. 177 of March 10, 1898. Term not to exceed 20 years. Annual tax 5 to 10 *silver* pesos; in the case of foreigners 10 to 50 *gold* pesos.

Hungary.—The law in force is that of July 7, 1895. The duration of the patent is 15 years. The period for compulsory working is ordinarily 3 years. The annual taxes range from 40 kroner for the 1st year to 500 for the 15th.

Italy.—The law is still governed by that of January 31, 1864, extending the Sardinian law of October 30, 1859 to the whole kingdom. There is no preliminary examination into novelty, and there is no provision prohibiting the importation of patented articles. Patents are subject (i.) to a proportional tax of as many times 10 lire as the years for which the patent is applied for, and (ii.) to an annual tax of 40 lire for the first 3 years; 65 lire for the following 3; 90 lire for the 7th, 8th and 9th; 115 lire for the 10th and 11th; and 140 lire for the remaining 3 years.

Japan.—Patents are issued under an act which came into operation on July 16, 1899. The law as to subject matter resembles that of England and the United States. The term of a patent is 15 years from the date of registration. The patent may be annulled if the patentee has not worked his invention within 3 years from the date of the certificate of grant, or if, having discontinued such use for 3 years, he has refused a reasonable request by a third party for an assignment or a licence. An applicant not domiciled in the empire must appoint within 6 months a duly qualified agent by power of attorney. There is apparently a preliminary examination into novelty. The patent owner must affix his mark to the patent. The fees are calculated on a gradually ascending scale.

Liberia.—Patents are issued under a law of December 23, 1864. The maximum term is 20 years. There is a preliminary examination as to novelty. A sum of $25 or $50 is payable on application, according as the applicant is a citizen or an alien. An invention patented by an alien must be put in practical operation within 3 years. There is no prohibition of the importation of patented articles.

Luxemburg (law of June 30, 1880).—The term of the patent is 15 years. There is no preliminary examination as to novelty, and the importation of patented articles is not prohibited. An annual and progressive tax, commencing at 10 francs and increasing by 10 francs annually, is payable in advance. The period for compulsory working is 3 years, and after the expiration of that period compulsory licences may be ordered.

Mexico (law of Oct. 1, 1903).—The duration of a patent is 20 years, with possible extension for another 5 years. The act defines what is patentable and what is not patentable. There is on request of the interested party, an examination without guarantee as to novelty. There are no provisions as to compulsory working (but compulsory licences may be ordered) or prohibiting the importation of patented articles. The tax ranges from $50 to $150. The patentee must also at the end of each 5 years of the grant, in order to keep the patent in force for another 5 years, pay 50 pesos at the end of the first 5 years; 75 pesos at the end of 10 years, and at the end of 15 years, 100 pesos. The Patent Office publishes a special gazette—*La Gaceta Oficial de Patentes y Marcas.*

Nicaragua.—Patents were, as a general rule, until 1899, granted only by special Act of Congress. But see now supplement 720, No. 15, *Patent Laws of the World.*

Norway (law of June 10, 1885).—The term of the patent is 15 years. There is a preliminary examination into novelty. The invention must be worked within 3 years, and the working must not be discontinued for a year on pain of forfeiture. For each patent an annual tax is payable amounting to 10 crowns for the 2nd year and increasing by 5 crowns each year.

Panama.—Law 88 of 1904 adopts the rules prescribed by the laws of Colombia. The fee is an annual one of $20.

Peru (law of Jan. 28, 1869 and law of Jan. 3, 1896).—The maximum term of the patent is 10 years, and the tax is an annual sum of 100 dollars. There is no preliminary examination into novelty. The period for compulsory working is 2 years, and the importation of patented articles from abroad (except models of machinery whose introduction is authorised by the government) is prohibited.

Portugal (law of Dec. 15, 1894).—The maximum term is 15 years. The patent tax is 3000 reis, payable in advance, for each year of the term for which the privilege is granted or renewed. There is no preliminary examination into novelty. The period for compulsory working is 2 years, and discontinuance of working for any 2 years at a stretch forfeits the patent unless the inaction can be justified. The importation of patented articles from abroad is not prohibited.

Russia (law of May 20, 1896).—The maximum term is 15 years; the tax ranges from 15 roubles for the first year to 400 roubles for the fifteenth. There is apparently (see Arts. 3 and 13) a preliminary examination into novelty, but none into utility. The period for compulsory working is 5 years. There is no prohibition of importation of patented articles.

Spain.—Patents are issued under the law of June 7, 1902. There is no preliminary examination as to novelty, and the importation of patented articles is not prohibited. The duration of a patent is 20 years, and it is subject to an annual and progressive tax, as follows: 10 pesetas for the 1st year, 20 for the 2nd, 30 for the 3rd, and so on successively to the 5th or 20th year, for which the tax is respectively 50 and 200 pesetas.

Sweden (law of May 16, 1884).—The term is 15 years. The annual tax is 25 crowns for the 2nd, 3rd, 4th and 5th years; 50 crowns for each of the following 5 years; and 75 crowns for each of the remaining 5 years. There is a preliminary examination as to novelty, the period for compulsory working is 3 years, and discontinuance during any entire year entails forfeiture. There is no prohibition of the importation of patented articles.

Switzerland.—Federal law of June 21, 1907. The term of the patent is 15 years. There is an annual and progressive tax, rising from 20 francs for the 1st year by an annual increase of 10 francs up to 160 francs for the 15th. There is no preliminary examination as to novelty. The patent is forfeited if the invention has not been carried into practice by the end of the 3rd year, or if patented articles are imported from abroad, while at the same time the proprietor has refused applications on equitable terms for Swiss licences.

Tunis (law of 22nd Rabia-et-Tani, 1306; Dec. 26, 1888).—The term is either 5 years (fee 500 piastres) or 10 years (fee 1000 piastres) or 15 years (fee 1500 piastres). There is no preliminary examination as to novelty. The period for compulsory working is 2 years, and two consecutive years' discontinuance of such working, unless justified, forfeits the patent. So also does the importation of patented articles, but the introduction may be authorized (i.) of models of machines, and (ii.) of articles, made abroad, intended for public exhibitions or for trials.

Turkey.—Patents are still granted under the law of the 2nd of March 1880. There is no preliminary examination as to novelty, and a patentee who mentions his title as such without adding the words " without guarantee of government," is liable to a maximum penalty of 45 Turkish pounds.

United States.—The American law may be considered at greater length. The Federal Constitution empowered Congress " to promote the progress of science and useful arts by securing for limited times to . . . inventors the exclusive right to their . . . discoveries." The existing American patent law is based on a series of Acts of Congress passed in virtue of this provision in the constitution, and on the judicial interpretation of these statutes. Between American and English patent law there is, as will appear in the course of this sketch, a considerable degree of similarity. The fact is not surprising when it is remembered that the Statute of Monopolies (21 Jac. I. c. 3) was, except in limiting the maximum duration of letters patent for inventions at fourteen years, only declaratory of the common law, and therefore formed part of the original common law of America. The English and American patent systems further agree in this, that they contain no provision as to compulsory working, and no prohibition of the importation of patented articles. But there are important differences between the two systems, not merely in points of detail, but in matters affecting the theory and practical working of the law. In England the consideration for the grant of a patent has all along been mainly the benefit which the public derives from the introduction of a new manufacture. In America greater emphasis is placed on the right of an inventor to have his merits rewarded. Again, under the Statute of Monopolies an inventor's exclusive privilege arises only in regard to inventions not known or used at the date of the grant, although it should be observed that under the modern Patents Acts the date of a patent, once granted, relates back to the date of the application. In the United States, on the other hand, the right is conferred on inventors to an exclusive privilege in such inventions as were not known or used before their discovery by the patentees. The practical bearing of this difference is explained in an admirable note on " The Statute of Monopolies " in *Ruling Cases, sub tit.*" Patent " (xx. 5): " It shifts the point of view in the important question of novelty. Many good American inventions have been given away in England by the premature publication in America of the inventor's proceedings. He is interviewed, and an article in the New York *Sun*, or some other paper, in due time finds its way to England. This does no harm in America; on the contrary, it is good evidence of the date of the actual invention. But it is fatal to a subsequent application in England."

The definition of patentability in American law is contained in sect. 4886 of the Revised Statutes of the United States as amended by an act of the 3rd of March 1897. In the following passage the amendments are indicated by italics:—

"Any person who has invented or discovered any new and useful art, machine, manufacture or composition of matter, or any new and useful improvement thereof, not known or used by others in this country *before his invention or discovery thereof*, and not patented or described in any printed publication in this or any foreign country before his invention or discovery thereof *or more than two years prior to his application*, and not in public use or on sale for more than two years prior to his application, unless the same is proved to have been abandoned, may, upon payment of the fees required by law and other due proceedings had, obtain a patent therefor."

The effect of the two amendments made by the act of 1897 should first be noted: (i.) The old law failed to state at what time the invention should be known or used by others in America so as to bar a patent; whether before the application or before the invention. This ambiguity is removed by the use of the words "before his invention or discovery thereof." (ii.) Under the old law a foreign patentee could take out a patent in America for the same invention at any time during the life of the foreign patent, provided it had not been in use in America more than two years prior to his application, unless anticipated by a prior invention or publication. The words " or more than two years prior to his application," merely give the same force to a foreign patent or publication that had previously been given to prior use. An invention to be patentable must, according to American law, be both novel and useful. Utility may be evidence of novelty and vice versa, and commercial success is relevant evidence of utility. As in England, a bare principle is not patentable. A " process " is included under the words " useful art " in the above definition of patentability, and is good subject matter for a patent when the term is used to represent a practical method of producing a beneficial result or effect. The word " machine " in the definition includes every mechanical device or combination of devices for producing certain results. Such a device or combination is patentable when it possesses utility and novelty, and produces either a new result or an old result in a better form.

Under the law of 1790, which was exclusively American in spirit, the duty of granting letters patent for inventions was discharged by the secretary of state, the secretary of war and the attorney-general, or any two of them. The law from 1793 to 1836 was exclusively English in spirit, and during that period the duty fell to the secretary of state, subject to the attorney-general's approval. It was in 1837 that the marked divergence between the English and American patent system began. In that year the patent business of the United States had attained to such dimensions that the powers and duties of the secretary of state in regard to patents were transferred to a sub-department of the state department known as the Patent Office. The American Patent Office consists of a commissioner of patents, one assistant commissioner, and three examiners-in-chief, who are appointed by the President of the United States with the advice and consent of the Senate; and also of other examiners, and a staff of officers, clerks and employés, appointed by the secretary of the interior on the nomination of the commissioner of patents. The commissioner of patents, under the direction of the secretary of the interior, is charged with the superintendence or performance of all duties respecting the grant and issue of patents, and has the control and custody of all books, records, papers, &c., belonging to the Patent Office. He is authorized to make, from time to time, regulations not inconsistent with law, for the conduct of proceedings in the Patent Office, and prepares an annual report which is laid before Congress, and which is framed on the same lines as that of the comptroller-general in England. " He is the final judge, so far as the Patent Office is concerned, of all controverted questions arising in the office, and in granting or withholding patents he is not bound by the decisions of his inferiors " (Robinson on Patents, I. 84). The examiners-in-chief are required to be persons of competent legal knowledge and ability. Their duties are: On the written petition of inventors to revise and determine upon the validity of the adverse decisions of subordinate examiners, upon applications for patents, and for reissues of patents, and in interference cases, and when required by the commissioner of patents to hear and report upon claims for extension, and to do such other similar work as he may assign to them. The Patent Office publishes an Official Gazette corresponding to the English Patent Office Illustrated Journal, and discharges similar functions to those of the English Patent Office in regard to the public dissemination of information as to patented inventions. The number of original applications for patents in the period covered by the report of the commissioner of patents for 1906–1907 was 58,762; the number of patents granted was 36,620; the receipts amounted to $1,910,618, the expenditure to $1,631,458, leaving a surplus of $279,160.

The first step in the procedure to obtain a patent is the lodging by the inventor at the Patent Office of a written application, together with a specification of particular written description of his invention, and a claim distinctly pointing out and claiming what he alleges to be his invention or discovery. The specification and claim are signed by the inventor and attested by two witnesses. Drawings, specimens of ingredients, and models may be required to be furnished. On the filing of each original application for a patent, a fee of $15 is payable. The applicant is required to verify his claim to the invention on oath, taken, if he. resides within the United States, before any person authorized by American law to administer oaths; if he resides in a foreign country, before any diplomatic or commercial agent of the United States, or any notary public of the foreign country in which the applicant may

be. The commissioner of patents then causes an examination to be made into the novelty of the invention, and if the result is satisfactory the patent issues. On the issuing of each original patent, a fee of $20 is payable. A patent is issued in the name of the United States of America and under the seal of the Patent Office. It consists of a short title or description of the invention or discovery, correctly indicating its nature and design, and a grant to the patentee, his heirs and assigns. Patents, it may be observed in passing, may be granted and issued or reissued to the assignee of the inventor or discoverer, and every patent or any interest in it is assignable, the assignment being recorded in the Patent Office, for the term of seventeen years, of the exclusive right to make use of and vend the invention or discovery throughout the United States and the territories thereof. The rights of property in patents granted in Cuba, Porto Rico, the Philippines and other ceded territory under Spanish law are to be respected in those territories as if that law were still in force there. A patent is dated as of a day not later than three months from the time at which it was passed, and if the fee is not paid within six months the patent is withheld. In case, however, the issue of a patent has been prevented by a failure to pay the fee within the prescribed period, the application may be renewed within 2 years after the allowance of the original application. But the applicant has no right to damages for any use of the invention in the interval, and on the hearing of the renewed application abandonment may be considered as a question of fact. So far we have followed the procedure to obtain a patent where its course is uninterrupted. A double form of interruption is, however, possible. A claim for a patent may be rejected on the ground of want of novelty in the alleged invention. In this case, the fact of the rejection, together with the reasons for it, is communicated to the applicant by the commissioner; and if he persists in his claim a re-examination is ordered. Or, again, an application may appear to the commissioner to interfere with a pending application,[1] or with any expired patent. In these circumstances, he gives notice to the applicant, and directs the primary examiner to proceed to determine the question of priority of invention. This interruption of the course of the proceedings to obtain a patent is called an " interference." In either of the cases above mentioned an appeal lies, on payment of a fee of $10, from the primary examiner to the board of examiners-in-chief, and, on payment of a fee of $20, from the examiners-in-chief to the commissioner in person. An applicant for a patent, but not a party to an interference, may appeal from the decision of the commissioner to the supreme court of the District of Columbia sitting in banc. In interference cases the appeal lies to the District of Columbia court of appeals. There is an ultimate right of appeal, in cases involving the validity of a patent, to the Supreme Court of the United States. Patents are obtainable by bill in equity, although the commissioner of patents (or, on appeal, the supreme court of the District of Columbia) may have refused them. The circuit courts of the United States have original jurisdiction in all patent suits. Appellate jurisdiction is vested in the circuit court of appeals; and on the certificate of that court, or by certiorari, an appeal may be brought to the Supreme Court of the United States.

Section 4887 of the revised statutes provides that:—

" No person otherwise entitled thereto shall be debarred from receiving a patent for his invention or discovery, nor shall any patent be declared invalid by reason of its having been first patented or caused to be patented by the inventor or his legal representatives or assigns in a foreign country, unless the application for the said foreign patent was filed more than seven months prior to the filing of the application in this country, in which case no patent shall be granted in this country."

The words italicized in the above section were added by an Amending Act of the 3rd of March 1897. In its original form the section provided that no person should be debarred from receiving a patent because the invention was first patented in a foreign country, whether he was otherwise entitled to the patent or not. The words " otherwise entitled to " merely postulate that no other bar to the issue of the patent shall exist. The words " by the inventor or his legal representatives or assigns " safeguard the inventor to some extent against fraud by third parties; while the provision requiring the application in the United States to be filed within seven months of the filing of the foreign patent is intended to carry out the provisions of the International Convention. It should be noted that the duration of an American patent for an invention already patented abroad is no longer limited by that of the prior foreign patent, but is granted for 17 years from the date of issue.

Patented articles are required to be marked as such, either by the word " patented," together with the day and the year the patent was granted, being affixed to them, or, when from the character of the article this cannot be done, by fixing to it, on the package containing one or more of such articles, a label containing the like

---

[1] A citizen of the United States, taken, or an alien who has within the preceding twelve months given notice of his intention to become one, may, by filing in the Patent Office a " caveat," secure for himself notice of possibly conflicting applications.

notice; and in any suit for infringement by a party failing so to mark, no damages shall be recovered by the plaintiff, except on proof that the defendant was duly notified of the infringement, and continued after such notice to make, use or vend the article so patented. A penalty of not less than 100 dollars is attached to falsely marking or labelling articles as patented.

When through inadvertence, accident or mistake, and without fraudulent or deceptive intention, a patentee has claimed more than he is entitled to, his patent is valid for all that part which is truly and justly his own; provided this is a material or substantial part of the thing patented and the patentee, or his heirs or assigns, on payment of the prescribed fee (\$10) disclaim the surplusage. The disclaimer must be in writing, and attested by one or more witnesses; it is recorded in the Patent Office, and is thereafter considered a part of the original specification. But no disclaimer affects any action pending at the time of its being filed, except so far as may relate to the question of unreasonable neglect or delay in filing it.

In the same circumstance, or where a patent is inoperative or invalid by reason of a defective or insufficient specification, the patentee may surrender his patent, and the commissioner of patents may, on the application of the patentee and on payment of a fee of \$30, issue a new patent in accordance with the amended specification.

Uruguay (law of 12th November 1885).—The term is 3, 6 or 9 years, at the option of the applicant. There is an annual tax of \$25 for every year of the privilege. The invention must be worked within a time fixed by the executive, and the working must not be discontinued for a year, on pain of forfeiture. There is no preliminary examination as to novelty.

Venezuela.—A new law was promulgated by a decree of the 19th of March 1900, but revoked in January 1901 and the old law of 1882 substituted. The term is 5, 10 or 15 years. The tax is 80 francs (bolivars) a year if the patent is for an invention or discovery, and 60 francs (bolivars) a year if it relates to an improved process. There is no preliminary examination as to novelty, nor is there any compulsory working.

International Patents.—The International Convention for the protection of industrial property was signed at Paris on the 20th of March 1883; the necessary ratifications were exchanged on the 6th of June 1884, and the Convention came into force a month later. Provision was made by sections 103 and 104 of the Patents Act 1883 for carrying out the Convention in Great Britain by orders in council, applying it from time to time to (*a*) British possessions whose legislatures had made satisfactory arrangements for the protection of inventions patented in Great Britain; (*b*) foreign states with which the sovereign had made arrangements for the mutual protection of inventions. The following governments have signed the international convention: Australia, Austria-Hungary, Belgium, Brazil, Ceylon, Cuba, Denmark, France, Germany, Italy, Japan, Mexico, Netherlands, New Zealand, Norway, Portugal, San Domingo, Servia, Spain, Sweden, Switzerland, Trinidad and Tobago, Tunis and the United States. Under the powers of the Foreign Jurisdiction Act 1890 penalties have been imposed on British subjects committing offences against the Patents, &c., Acts 1883-1888, and the orders in council issued thereunder, in Africa, East Africa, Morocco, Persia, Persian coast and Zanzibar.

An international bureau in connexion with the Convention has been established at Bern, where an official monthly periodical, *La Propriété industrielle*, is published. Conferences were held under the Convention at Rome in April and May 1886, and at Madrid in April 1890. At the latter conference an important article was adopted, under which it is left to each country to define and apply "compulsory working" (*exploitation*) for the purposes of the convention in the sense that it chooses.

AUTHORITIES.—In addition to the works noted incidentally above, see Edmunds, *Patents* (London); Wallace and Williamson, *Patents* (London); Frost, *Patent Law and Practice* (London, 1898); Terrell, *Letters Patent* (London); Cunynghame, *Patents* (London); Lawson, *The Patents, &c., Acts* (London). For the old law, Webster, *Patent Cases* (London, 1844); Hindmarsh, *Patents* (London, 1846); and the very valuable Parliamentary Reports of 1829, 1851, 1865, 1872. Gordon, *Monopolies by Patents* (London, 1897); Gould and Tucker, *Notes on Rev. Stat. of the U.S.*, vol. ii. (1887-1897); Robinson, *Patents* (3 vols., Boston, 1890); Whitman, *Patent Laws* (Washington, 1871); Law, *Copyright and Patent Laws of the United States, 1790-1866* (New York, 1866); Curtis, *Law of Patents* (4th ed., Boston and London, 1873); Campbell, *U. S. Patent System: a History* (Washington, 1891). (A. W. R.; T. A. I.)

PATENTS OF PRECEDENCE. A patent of precedence is a grant to an individual by letters patent (*q.v.*) of a higher social

or professional position than the precedence to which his ordinary rank entitles him. The principal instance in modern times of patents of grants of this description has been the grant of precedence to members of the English bar. In the days when acceptance of the rank of king's counsel not only precluded a barrister from appearing against the Crown, but, if he was a member of parliament, vacated his seat, a patent of precedence was resorted to as a means of conferring similar marks of honour on distinguished counsel without any such disability attached to it. The patents obtained by Mansfield, Erskine, Scott and Brougham were granted on this ground. After the order of the coif lost its exclusive right of audience in the court of common pleas, it became customary to grant patents of precedence to a number of the serjeants-at-law, giving them rank immediately after counsel of the Crown already created and before those of subsequent creation. Mr Justice Phillimore was, on his appointment as a judge of the queen's bench division (in 1897) the only holder of a patent of precedence at the bar, except Serjeant Simon, who died in that year, and who was the last of the serjeants who held such a patent. See also PRECEDENCE.

In Canada patents of precedence are granted both by the governor-general and by the lieutenant-governor of the provinces under provincial legislation which has been declared *intra vires*. (*Att. Gen. for Canada* v. *Att. Gen. for Ontario*, 1898, A.C. p. 247; Todd, *Parliamentary Govt. in Canada*, 2nd ed. p. 333.)

See Pulling's *Order of the Coif.*

PATER, WALTER HORATIO (1839–1894), English man of letters, was born at Shadwell on the 4th of August 1839. He was the second son of Richard Glode Pater, a medical man, of Dutch extraction, born in New York. Jean-Baptiste Pater, the painter, was probably of the same family. Richard Pater moved from Olney to Shadwell early in the century, and continued to practise there among the poorer classes. He died while his son Walter was yet an infant, and the family then moved to Enfield, where the children were brought up. In 1853 Walter Pater was sent to King's School, Canterbury, where he was early impressed by the aesthetic beauties of the cathedral. These associations remained with him through life. As a schoolboy he read *Modern Painters*, and was attracted to the study of art, but he did not make any conspicuous mark in school studies, and showed no signs of the literary taste which he was afterwards to develop. His progress was always gradual. He gained a school exhibition, however, with which he proceeded in 1858 to Queen's College, Oxford. His undergraduate life was unusually uneventful; he was a shy, "reading man," making few friends. Jowett, however, was struck by his promise, and volunteered to give him private tuition. But Pater's class was a disappointment, and he only took a second in literae humaniores in 1862. After taking his degree he settled in Oxford and read with private pupils. As a boy he had cherished the idea of entering the Anglican Church, but, under the influence of his Oxford reading, his faith in Christianity became shaken, and by the time he took his degree he had thoughts of graduating as a Unitarian minister. This project, too, he resigned; and when, in 1864, he was elected to a fellowship at Brasenose, he had settled down easily into a university career. But it was no part of his ambition to sink into academic torpor. With the assumption of his duties as fellow the sphere of his interests widened rapidly; he became acutely interested in literature, and even began to write articles and criticisms himself. The first of these to be printed was a brief essay upon Coleridge, which he contributed in 1866 to the *Westminster Review*. A few months later (January, 1867) appeared in the same review his now well-known essay on Winckelmann, the first expression of his idealism. In the following year his study of "Aesthetic Poetry" appeared in the *Fortnightly Review*, to be succeeded by essays on Leonardo da Vinci, Sandro Botticelli, Pico della Mirandola and Michelangelo. These, with other studies of the same kind, were in 1878 collected in his *Studies in the History of the Renaissance*. Pater was now the centre of a small but very interesting circle in Oxford. Such men as cherished aesthetic tastes were naturally drawn to him; and, though always retiring and, in a sense, remote in manner, he was continually spreading his influence, not only in the university, but among men of letters in London and elsewhere. The little body of Pre-Raphaelites were among his friends, and by the time that *Marius the Epicurean* appeared he had quite a following of disciples to hail it as a gospel. This fine and polished work, the chief of all his contributions to literature, was published early in 1885. In it Pater displays, with perfected fullness and loving elaboration, his ideal of the aesthetic life, his cult of beauty as opposed to bare asceticism, and his theory of the stimulating effect of the pursuit of beauty as an ideal of its own. In 1887 he published *Imaginary Portraits*, a series of essays in philosophic fiction; in 1889, *Appreciations, with an Essay on Style*; in 1893, *Plato and Platonism*; and in 1894, *The Child in the House*. His *Greek Studies* and his *Miscellaneous Studies* were collected posthumously in 1895; his posthumous romance of *Gaston de Latour* in 1896; and his *Essays from the "Guardian"* were privately printed in 1897. A collected edition of Pater's works, was issued in 1901. Pater changed his residence from time to time, living sometimes at Kensington and in different parts of Oxford; but the centre of his work and influence was always his rooms at Brasenose. Here he laboured, with a wonderful particularity of care and choice, upon perfecting the expression of his theory of life and art. He wrote with difficulty, correcting and recorrecting with imperturbable assiduity. His mind, moreover, returned to the religious fervour of his youth, and those who knew him best believed that had he lived longer he would have resumed his boyish intention of taking holy orders. He was cut off, however, in the prime of his powers. Seized with rheumatic fever, he rallied, and sank again, dying on the staircase of his house, in his sister's arms, on the morning of Monday the 30th of July 1894. Pater's nature was so contemplative, and in a way so centred upon reflection, that he never perhaps gave full utterance to his individuality. His peculiar literary style, too, burnished like the surface of hard metal, was too austerely magnificent to be always persuasive. At the time of his death Pater exercised a remarkable and a growing influence among that necessarily restricted class of persons who have themselves something of his own love for beauty and the beautiful phrase. But the cumulative richness and sonorous depth of his language harmonized intimately with his deep and earnest philosophy of life; and those who can sympathize with a nervous idealism will always find inspiration in his sincere and sustained desire to "burn with a hard, gem-like flame," and to live in harmony with the highest.

(A. WA).

Mr Ferris Greenslet's *Walter Pater* (in the "Contemporary Men of Letters" series, 1904) is an interesting piece of criticism. Mr Arthur Benson's study in the "English Men of Letters" series is admirable. See too a sketch in Edmund Gosse's *Critical Kit-Kats*; and an estimate from a Roman Catholic standpoint in Dr William Barry's *Heralds of Revolt*, where Pater is compared with J. Addington Symonds. T. Wright's *Life of Walter Pater* (1907) is an elaborate but unsatisfactory piece of work.

PATERA, the Latin name for a shallow circular vessel used for drinking or for pouring libations. The Greek name for such a vessel was φιάλη. It has no foot or stem underneath, but occasionally a boss rising in the centre inside. The term is sometimes given incorrectly in architecture to a circular disk carved with a conventional rose, which is found in many early styles, the proper term being rosette.

PATERNO, a town of Sicily, in the province of Catania, 11 m. W.N.W. of Catania by rail, at the southern foot of Mt Etna. Pop. (1881), 15,830; (1901), 20,098 (town), 22,857 (commune). The castle, originally erected in 1073, upon the acropolis of the ancient Hybla Minor or Galeatis, has a square tower and a chapel with frescoes belonging to the 14th century. Some mosaic pavements still exist under the houses in the Strada dell' Ospedale, and remains of baths and of an ancient bridge over the Simeto on the road to Centuripa are to be seen in the neighbourhood. The place was unsuccessfully besieged by the Athenian forces in the summer of 415 B.C.

PATERSON, ROBERT (1715-1801), Scottish stone-mason, who suggested to Sir Walter Scott the character of "Old Mortality," was born near Hawick in 1715. Through the patronage of Sir Thomas Kirkpatrick, whose cook he had married, he obtained the lease of a quarry at Gatelawbrig, but in 1745 his house was plundered by the retreating Jacobites, and Paterson himself, a pronounced Cameronian, was carried off a prisoner. He subsequently devoted his life to cutting and erecting stones for the graves of the Covenanters, for 40 years wandering from place to place in the lowlands. He died in poverty in 1801, and a stone to his memory was erected by Scott's publishers in 1869 in Caerlaverock churchyard.

PATERSON, WILLIAM (1658-1719), British writer on finance, founder of the Bank of England and projector of the Darien scheme, was born in April 1658 at the farmhouse of Skipmyre, parish of Tinwald, Dumfriesshire. His parents occupied the farm there, and with them he resided till he was about seventeen. A desire to escape the religious persecution then raging in Scotland, and the immemorial ambition of his race, led him southward. He went through England with a pedlar's pack (" whereof the print may be seen, if he be alive," says a pamphleteer in 1700), settled for some time in Bristol, and then proceeded to America. There he lived chiefly in the Bahamas, and is said by some to have been a predicant or preacher, and by others a buccaneer. In truth his intellectual and moral superiority to his fellow-settlers caused his selection as their spiritual guide, whilst his thirst for knowledge led to intercourse with the buccaneers. It was here he formed that vast design which is known in history as the Darien scheme. On his return to England he was unable to induce the government of James II. to engage in his plan. He went to the continent and pressed it to no purpose in Hamburg, Amsterdam and Berlin, and on his return to London he engaged in trade and rapidly amassed a considerable fortune. About 1690 he was occupied in the formation in the Hampstead Water Company, and in 1694 he founded the Bank of England. The government required money, and the country, rapidly increasing in wealth, required a bank. The subscribers lent their money to the nation, and this debt became the bank stock. The credit of having formulated the scheme and persuaded its adoption is due to Paterson. He was one of the original directors, but in less than a year he fell out with his colleagues, and withdrew from the management. He had already propounded a new plan for an orphan bank (so called because the debt due to the city orphans by the corporation of London was to form the stock). They feared a dangerous rival to their own undertaking, and they felt some distrust for this eager Scotsman whose brain teemed with new plans in endless succession.

At that time the people of the northern kingdom were considering how best to share in that trade which was so rapidly enriching their southern neighbours. Paterson saw his opportunity. He removed to Edinburgh, unfolded his Darien (q.v.) scheme, and soon had the whole nation with him. He is the supposed author of the act of 1695 which formed the "Company of Scotland trading to Africa and the Indies." This company, he arranged, should establish a settlement on the Isthmus of Darien, and " thus hold the key of the commerce of the world." There was to be free trade, the ships of all nations were to find shelter in this harbour not yet erected, differences of race or religion were neglected; but a small tribute was to be paid to the company, and this and other advantages would so act that, at one supreme stroke, Scotland was to be changed from the poorest to the richest of nations.

On the 26th of July 1698 the first ships of the expedition set sail "amidst the tears and prayers and praises of relatives and friends and countrymen." Some financial transactions in which Paterson was concerned, and in which, though he had acted with perfect honesty, the company had lost, prevented his nomination to a post of importance. He accompanied the expedition as a private individual, and was obliged to look idly on whilst what his enemies called his "golden dream" faded away indeed like the "baseless fabric of a vision" before his eyes. His wife and child died, and he was seized with a dangerous illness, "of which, as I afterwards found," he says, "trouble of mind was not the least cause." It was noted that "he hath been so mightily concerned in this sad disaster, so that he looks now more like a skeleton than a man." Still weak and helpless, and yet protesting to the last against the abandonment of Darien, he was carried on board ship, and, after a stormy and terrible voyage, he and the remnant of the ill-fated band reached home in December 1699.

In his native air Paterson soon recovered his strength, and immediately his fertile and eager mind was at work on new schemes. He prepared an elaborate plan for developing Scottish resources by means of a council of trade, and then tried to induce King William, with whom he had frequent interviews, to enter on a new Darien expedition. In 1701 he removed to London, and here by conferences with statesmen, by writing, and by personal persuasion helped on the union. He was much employed in settling the financial relations of the two countries. One of the last acts of the Scots parliament was to recommend him to the consideration of Queen Anne for all he had done and suffered. The United Parliament, to which he was returned as a member for the Dumfries burghs, though he never took his seat, decided that his claim should be settled, but it was not till 1715 that an indemnity of £18,241 was ordered to be paid him. Even then he found considerable difficulty in obtaining his due. His last years were spent in Queen Square, Westminster, but he removed from there shortly before his death on the 22nd of January 1719.

As many as twenty-two works, all of them anonymous, are attributed to Paterson. These are classified by Bannister under six heads, as dealing with (1) finance, (2) legislative union, (3) colonial enterprise, (4) trade, (5) administration, (6) various social and political questions. Of these the following deserve special notice: (1) *Proposals and Reasons for constituting a Council of Trade* (Edinburgh, 1701).[1] This was a plan to develop the resources of his country. A council, consisting of a president and twelve members, was to be appointed. It was to have a revenue collected from a duty on sales, lawsuits, successions, &c. With these funds the council was to revive the Darien scheme, to build workhouses, to employ, relieve and maintain the poor, and to encourage manufactures and fisheries. It was to give loans without interest to companies and shippers, to remove monopolies, to construct all sorts of vast public works. Encouragement was to be given to foreign Protestants and Jews to settle in the kingdom, gold and silver were to be coined free of charge, and money kept up to its nominal standard. All export-duties were to be abolished and import regulated on a new plan. Paterson believed that thus the late disasters would be more than retrieved. (2) A *Proposal to plant a Colony in Darien to protect the Indians against Spain, and to open the Trade of South America to all Nations* (1701). This was the Darien scheme on a new and broader basis. It points out in detail the advantages to be gained: free trade would be advanced over all the world, and Great Britain would largely profit. (3) *Wednesday Club Dialogues upon the Union* (London, 1706). These were imaginary conversations in a club in the city of London about the union with Scotland. Paterson's real opinions were put into the mouth of a speaker called May. Till the Darien business all Scots were for the union, and they were so still if reasonable terms were offered. Such terms ought to include an incorporating union with equal taxes, freedom of trade, and a proportionate representation in parliament. A union with Ireland, "as likewise with other dominions the queen either hath or shall have," is proposed. (4) Along with this another discussion of the same imaginary body, *An Inquiry into the State of the Union of Great Britain and the Trade thereof* (1717), may be taken. This was a consideration of the union, which, now "that its honeymoon was past," was not giving satisfaction in some quarters, and also a discussion as to the best means of paying off the national debt—a subject which occupied a great deal of Paterson's attention during the later years of his life.

Paterson's plans were vast and magnificent, but he was no mere dreamer. Each design was worked out in minute detail,[2] each was possible and practical. The Bank of England was a stupendous success. The Darien expedition failed from hostile attacks and bad arrangements. But the original design was that the English and Dutch should be partakers in it, and, if this had occurred, and the arrangements against many of which Paterson in letter after letter in vain protested, had been different, Darien might have been to Britain another India. Paterson was a zealous almost a fanatic free-trader long before Adam Smith, and his remarks on finance and his argument against an inconvertible paper-currency, though then novel, now hold a place of economic orthodoxy. Paterson's works are excellent in form and matter; they are quite impersonal, for few men who have written so much have said so little about themselves. There is no reference to the scurrilous attacks made on him. They are the true products of a noble and disinterested as well as vigorous mind. There is singular fitness in the motto "Sic vos non vobis" inscribed under the only portrait of him we possess.

See *Life of W. Paterson*, by S. Bannister (Edinburgh, 1858); Paterson's *Works*, by S. Bannister (3 vols., London, 1859); *The Birthplace and Parentage of W. Paterson*, by W. Pagan (Edinburgh, 1865); *Eng. Hist. Review*, xi. 260. The brilliant account of the Darien scheme in the fifth volume of Macaulay's *History* is incorrect and misleading; that in Burton's *Hist. of Scotland* (vol. viii. ch. 84) is much truer. Consult also the memoir in Paul Coq, *La Monnaie de banque* (Paris, 1863), and J. S. Barbour, *A History of William Paterson and the Darien Company* (1907). For a list of fugitive writings on Paterson see Poole's *Index of Periodicals*. (F. WA.)

PATERSON, a city and the county-seat of Passaic county, New Jersey, U.S.A., in the north-eastern part of the state, on the west bank of the Passaic river, and 16 m. N.W. of New York City. Pop. (1880), 51,031; (1890), 78,347; (1900), 105,171; (1906, estimate), 112,801; (1910), 125,600. Of the total in 1900, 38,791 were foreign-born. Paterson is served by the main lines of the Delaware, Lackawanna & Western, the Erie, and the New York, Susquehanna & Western railways, and by a number of interurban electric lines. The Morris Canal was formerly important for shipping freight between Paterson and Jersey City, but has fallen into disuse. The city lies along a bend of the Passaic river, the southern portion being in a plain and the extreme northern part lying among the hills that rise from the stream near the Great Falls. The river has a descent here of about 70 ft. (of which 50 ft. are in a perpendicular fall), and furnishes water-power for manufactures. The principal public buildings are the city-hall, the post office, the county court-house and the Danforth Memorial (public library) building. Paterson is pre-eminently a manufacturing centre. There were, in 1905, 513 factories employing a capital of $53,595,585, and furnishing work for 28,509 employés; and the total factory product was valued at $54,673,083. The city is the centre of silk manufacturing in the United States. In 1905 it contained 100 silk-mills, and the products were valued at $25,433,245. There were also, in 1905, 27 dyeing and finishing establishments, with products valued at $5,609,295; 30 foundries and machine shops, with products valued at $2,317,285; 3 wholesale slaughtering and packing houses, with products valued at $2,206,698; and 3 jute and jute-goods factories, with an output valued at $929,319. Among the machine works are two locomotive shops, with an average capacity of three locomotives per day, and a large steel mill.

Paterson had its origin in an act of the legislature of New Jersey on the 22nd of November 1791, incorporating the Society for Establishing Useful Manufactures, the plan for this society being drawn up by Alexander Hamilton. As the most suitable location for its enterprise the society in the following year selected the Great Falls of the Passaic river, and named the place Paterson, in honour of William Paterson (1745-1806), a member of the state Constitutional Convention in 1776, attorney-general of New Jersey in 1776-1783, a delegate to the Continental Congress in 1780-1781, and to the Constitutional Convention of

[1] This work was attributed to John Law, who borrowed some of his ideas from it. To Law's "system" Paterson was strongly opposed, and it was chiefly due to his influence that it made no way in Scotland.

[2] The books of the Darien Company were kept after a new and very much improved plan, believed to be an invention of Paterson's (Burton's *Hist. Scot.* viii. 36, note).

1787 (where he proposed the famous "New Jersey Plan"), a United States Senator in 1789-1790, governor of the state in 1790-1793, and an associate justice of the United States Supreme Court from 1793 until his death. Paterson was incorporated as a township in 1831, chartered as a city in 1851 and rechartered in 1861. Three great industries—the manufacture of cotton, machinery and silk—were established in Paterson almost contemporaneously with their introduction into the United States. In 1793 the first cotton yarn was spun at Paterson in a mill run by ox-power, and in the next year, when the dams and reservoir were completed, Paterson's first cotton factory began its operations. After 1840 the manufacture of machinery and of silk gradually supplanted that of cotton goods. Although an attempt was made to manufacture machinery in Paterson as early as 1800, there was little progress until after 1825. The building of the "Sandusky," Paterson's first locomotive, in 1837, marked the beginning of a new industry; and before 1860 the city was supplying locomotives to all parts of the United States and to Mexico and South America. By 1840 the silk industry had obtained a footing, and after this date there was a steady advance in the quantity and quality of the product. From 1871 to 1881 inclusive Paterson consumed two-thirds of the raw silk imported into the country.

See L. R. Trumbull, *History of Industrial Paterson* (Paterson, 1882).

PATEY, JANET MONACH (1842-1894), English vocalist, was born in London on the 1st of May 1842, her maiden name being Whytock. She had a fine alto voice, which developed into a contralto, and she studied singing under J. Wass, Pinsuti and Mrs Sims Reeves. Miss Whytock's first appearance, as a child, was made at Birmingham, and her first regular engagement was in 1865, in the provinces. From 1866, in which year she sang at the Worcester festival, and married John Patey, a bass singer, she was recognized as one of the leading contraltos; and on the retirement of Mme Sainton-Dolby in 1870 Mme Patey was without a rival whether in ballad music. She toured in America in 1871, sang in Paris in 1875, and in Australia in 1890. She died at Sheffield on the 28th of February 1894.

PATHAN, the name applied throughout India to the Afghans, especially to those permanently settled in the country and to those dwelling on the borderland. It is apparently derived from the Afghan name for their own language, Pushtu or Pukhtu, and may be traced back to the *Paktues* of Herodotus. In 1901 the total number of Pathans in all India was nearly 3½ millions, but the speakers of Pushtu numbered less than 1½ millions. The name is frequently, but incorrectly, applied to the Mahommedan dynasties that preceded the Moguls at Delhi, and also to the style of architecture employed by them; but of these dynasties only the Lodis were Afghans.

The Pathans of the Indian borderland inhabit the mountainous country on the Punjab frontier, stretching northwards from a line drawn roughly across the southern border of the Dera Ismail Khan district. South of this line are the Baluchis. The Pathans include all the strongest and most warlike tribes of the North-West frontier of India, such as the Afridis, Orakzais, Waziris, Mohmands, Swatis and many other clans. Those in the settled districts of the North-West Frontier Province (in 1901) numbered 883,770, or more than two-fifths of the population. Each of the principal divisions is dealt with separately in this work under its tribal name. The Pathans are split up into different tribes, each tribe into clans, and each clan into sections, so that the nomenclature is often very puzzling. The tribe, clan and section are alike distinguished by patronymics formed from the name of the common ancestor by the addition of the word *sai* or *khel*; *sai* being a corruption of the Pushtu word *soe*, meaning son, while *khel* is an Arabic word meaning an association or company. Both terms are used indifferently for both the larger and smaller divisions. Pathans enlist largely in the native army of India; and since the frontier risings of 1897 they have been formed with increasing frequency into class-regiments and regiments of native militia. They make excellent soldiers. The greater part

of the Pathan country was placed under British political control by the Durand agreement made with the Amir of Afghanistan in 1893.

PATHOLOGY (from Gr. πάθος, suffering), the science dealing with the theory or causation of disease. The term by itself is usually applied to animal or human pathology, rather than to vegetable pathology or Phytopathology (see PLANTS: *Pathology*).

The outstanding feature in the history of pathology during the 19th century, and more particularly of the latter half of it, was the completion of its rescue from the thraldom of abstract philosophy, and its elevation to the dignity of one of the natural sciences. Our forefathers, if one may venture to criticize them, were too impatient. Influenced by the prevailing philosophy of the day, they interpreted the phenomena of disease through its lights, and endeavoured from time to time to reduce the study of pathology to philosophical order when the very elements of philosophical order were wanting. The pathology of the present day is more modest; it is content to labour and to wait. Whatever its faults may be—and it is for our successors to judge of these—there is this to be said in its favour: that it is in nowise dogmatic. The eloquence of facts appeals to the scientific mind nowadays much more than the assertion of crude and unproven principles. The complexity and mystery of action inherent in living matter have probably been accountable for much of the vague philosophy of disease in the past, and have furnished one reason at least why pathology has been so long in asserting its independence as a science. This, indeed, holds good of the study of biology in general. There are other factors, however, which have kept pathology in the background. Its existence as a science could never have been recognized so long as the subjects of physics, chemistry and biology, in the widest acceptation of the term, remained unevolved. Pathology, in fact, is the child of this ancestry; it begins where they end.

Progress in the study of pathology has been greatly facilitated by the introduction of improved methods of technique. The certainty with which tissues can now be fixed in the state they were in when living, and the delicacy *Recent* with which they can be stained differentially, have *Progress.* been the means of opening up a new world of exploration. Experimental pathology has benefited by the use of antiseptic surgery in operations upon animals, and by the adoption of exact methods of recording; while the employment of solid culture media in bacteriology—the product of Koch's fertile genius—is responsible for a great part of the extraordinary development which has taken place in this department of pathological research. The discoveries made in pathological bacteriology, indeed, must be held to be among the most brilliant of the age. Inaugurated by Pasteur's early work, progress in this subject was first marked by the discovery of the parasite of anthrax and of those organisms productive of fowl-cholera and septic disease. Then followed Koch's great revelation in 1882 of the bacillus of tubercle (fig. 22, Pl. II.), succeeded by the isolation of the organisms of typhoid, cholera, diphtheria, actinomycosis, tetanus, &c. The knowledge we now possess of the causes of immunity from contagious disease has resulted from this study of pathological bacteriology: momentous practical issues have also followed upon this study. Amongst these may be mentioned the neutralizing of the toxins in cases of diphtheria, tetanus and poisonous snake-bite; "serum therapeutics"; and treatment by "vaccines." By means of "vaccination" we are enabled to induce an active immunity against infection by certain pathogenic agents. The value of such protective inoculations is demonstrated in the treatment against small-pox (Jenner), cholera, plague (Haffkine) and typhoid (Wright and Semple). Pasteur's inoculation against hydrophobia is on the same principle. "Vaccines" are also used as a method of treatment during the progress of the disease. Sir A. Wright and others, in recent work on opsonins, have shown that, by injecting dead cultures of the causal agent into subjects infected with the organism, there is produced in the body fluids a substance (opsonin) which apparently in favourable conditions unites with the living causal bacteria and so sensitizes them that they are readily taken up and destroyed by the phagocytic cells of tissues. Before the discovery of the bacillus of tubercle, scrofula and tuberculosis were regarded as two distinct diseases, and it was supposed that the scrofulous constitution could be distinguished from the tubercular. It was always felt, however, that there was a close bond of relationship between them. The fact that the tubercle bacillus is to be found in the lesions of both has set at rest any misgiving on the subject, and put beyond dispute the fact that so-called scrofulous affections are simply local manifestations of tuberculosis. A knowledge of the bacteriology of scrofulous affections of bone and joints, such as caries and gelatinous degeneration, has shown that they also are tubercular diseases—that is to say, diseases due to the presence locally of the tubercle bacillus. At a very early period it was held by Virchow that the large cheesy masses found in tuberculosis of the lung are to be regarded as pneumonic infiltrations of the air-vesicles. Their pneumonic nature has been amply substantiated in later times; they are now regarded simply as evidence of pneumonic reaction to the stimulus of the tubercle bacillus. The caseous necrosis of the implicated mass of lung tissue, and indeed of tubercles generally, is held to be, in great measure, the result of the necrotic influence of the secretions from the bacillus. Tubercular pneumonia may thus be looked upon as comparable to pneumonia excited by any other specific agent.

In the "seventies" of the 19th century feeling ran somewhat high over the rival doctrines concerning the origin of pus-corpuscles, Cohnheim and his school maintaining that they were derived exclusively from the blood, that they were leucocytes which had emigrated through the walls of the vessels and escaped into the surrounding tissue-spaces, while Stricker and his followers, although not denying their origin in part from the blood, traced them, in considerable proportion, to the fixed elements, such as fibrous tissues and endothelia. Our present-day knowledge prompts the adoption of a middle course between the two theories. The cells found in an inflamed part are undoubtedly drawn from both sources, but while the blood leucocytes have a great tendency to become fatty and to die, those cells derived from the fixed tissues incline more to organization; the latter are, in fact, the source of the cicatrix which follows upon the cessation of suppuration (fig. 23, Pl. II. and figs. 31 and 32, Pl. III.). Organization and healing have been keenly inquired into, with results which seem to point the lesson that all methods of healing are to be regarded as extensions of the natural phenomena of growth. Normal cytology, of late, has become a science of itself, and has had a direct bearing upon that which is pathological.

At no time has so much been done to advance our knowledge of diseases of the nervous system as during the last thirty years of the 19th century. The localization of function in the cerebral and in the cerebellar cortex has doubtless been the main cause of this progress, and has proceeded pari passu with an extended insight into the structure and connexions of the parts concerned. The pathology of aphasia, as worked out by a combination of the experimental, the pathological and the anatomical lines of inquiry is a favourable example of what has been accomplished. The origin, nature, and propagation of neoplasms of all kinds, especially of those which are malignant, are engaging much attention. Much light has been thrown upon the functions and diseases of the blood-forming tissues. The origin of the corpuscles, previously a matter of so much difference of opinion, is now pretty fairly set at rest, and has proved the key to the interpretation of the pathology of many diseases of the blood, such as the different forms of anaemia, of leucocythaemia, &c.

It is largely to researches on the bone marrow that we owe our present knowledge of the origin and the classification of the different cellular elements of the blood, both erythrocytes or red corpuscles, and the series of granular leucocytes or white corpuscles. Whatever be the ancestral cell from which these cells spring, it is in the bone marrow that we find a differentiation into the various marrow cells from which are developed the mature corpuscles that pass from the marrow into the blood circulation. The healthy bone marrow reacts with remarkable rapidity to the demand for more blood cells which may be required by the organism; its reactions and variations in disease are very striking. If the demand be for the red cells owing to loss from haemorrhage or any of the anaemias,

the fatty marrow is rapidly replaced by cellular elements; this is mainly an active proliferation of the nucleated red cells, and gives rise to the erythroblastic type of marrow. If the white cells be required, as in local suppurating abscess, general septicaemia, acute pneumonia, &c., there is an active proliferation of the myelocytes to form the polymorpho-nuclear leucocytes, so that we have in this condition a leucoblastic transformation of the fatty marrow.

The cytology of bone marrow, with the technique of blood examination, is of great assistance in the diagnosis of different pathological conditions. The deleterious influence of high blood-pressure has engaged the attention of physicians and pathologists in later years, and the conclusion arrived at is, that although it may arise from accidental causes, such as malcomposition of the blood, yet that in many instances it is a hereditary or family defect, and is bound up with the tendency to gout and cirrhotic degeneration of the kidney. The pathology of intra-cardiac and vascular murmurs has also been inquired into experimentally, the general impression being that these abnormal sounds result, in most cases at least, from the production of a sonorous liquid vein. Pneumonia of the croupous type has been proved to be, as a rule, a germ disease, the nature of the germ varying according to circumstances. The structural changes occurring in the bronchi in catarrhal bronchitis have also been ascertained, and, as in the case of pneumonia, have been shown to be frequently excited by the presence of a microphyte. The vexed question of the diagnosis of diphtheria is now a thing of the past. Quite irrespective of the nature of the anatomical lesion, the finding of the diphtheria bacillus on the part affected and the inoculability of this upon a suitable fresh soil are the sole means by which the diagnosis can be made certain.

The part played by the thyroid body in the internal economy of the organism has also received much attention. The gland evidently excretes, or at any rate gets rid of, a certain waste product of a proteid nature, which otherwise tends to accumulate in the tissues and to excite certain nervous and tissue phenomena. It wastes in the disease known as "myxoedema," and the above product gathers in the tissues, in that disease, to such an extent as to give rise to what has been termed a "solid oedema." It is questionable if the substance in question is mucoid. The pituitary body probably subserves a like purpose. When the pancreas is excised in an animal, or when it is destroyed in man by disease, grape-sugar appears in the urine. The gland is supposed to secrete a ferment, which, being absorbed into the portal circulation, breaks up a certain portion at least of the grape-sugar contained in the portal blood, and so prevents this overflowing into the circulation in general. The transplantation of a piece of living pancreas into the tissues of an animal, thus rendered artificially diabetic, is said to restore it to health.

Pathological chemistry has been remarkable chiefly for the knowledge we have obtained of the nature of bacterial poisons. Certain of these are alkaloids, others appear to be albumoses. The publication of Ehrlich's chemical, or rather physical, theory of immunity has thrown much light upon this very intricate and obscure subject.

Pathology is the science of disease in all its manifestations, whether structural or functional, progressive or regressive. In times past it has been the habit to look upon its sphere *Connexion* as lying within that of practical medicine, and *with human medicine Biology.* more particularly; as something tagged on to the treatment of human disease, but unworthy of being studied for its own sake as a branch of knowledge. Such a view can recommend itself to only the narrowest of minds. A bearing, and of course an essential bearing on the study of medicine, it must always have. A system of medicine reared upon anything but a pathological basis would be unworthy of consideration. Yet it may well be asked whether this is the final goal to be aimed at. Our starting-point in this, as in all departments of biological study, must be the biological unit, and it is to the alterations to which this is subject, under varying conditions of nutrition and stimulation, that the science of pathology must apply itself. Man can never be the only object of appeal in this inquiry The human organism is far too complex to enable us to understand the true significance of diseased processes. Our range must embrace a much wider area—must comprise, in fact, all living matter—if we are ever to arrive at a scientific conception of what disease really means. Hence not only must the study of our subject include the diseases peculiar to man and the higher animals, but those of the lowest forms of animal life, and of plant life, must be held equally worthy of attention. Modern research seems to show that living protoplasm, wherever it exists, is subject to certain laws and manifests itself by certain phenomena, and that there is no hard and fast line between what prevails in the two kingdoms. So it is with the diseased conditions to which it is a prey: there is a wonderful community of design, if the term may be used in such a sense, between the diseases of animals and plants, which becomes singularly striking and instructive the more they are inquired into. Utilitarian, or perhaps rather practical, considerations have very little to do with the subject from a scientific point of view—no more so than the science of chemistry has to do with the art of the manufacturing chemist. The practical bearings of a science, it will be granted, are simply, as it were, the summation of its facts, with the legitimate conclusions from them, the natural application of the data ascertained, and have not necessarily any direct relationship to its pursuit. It is when studied on these lines that pathology finds its proper place as a department of biology. Disease as an entity —as something to which all living matter is subject—is what the pathologist has to recognise and to investigate, and the practical application of the knowledge thus acquired follows as a natural consequence.

Since pathology is the science of disease, we are met at the very threshold by the question: What is disease? This may best be answered by defining what we understand by *Health and Disease.* health. What do we mean when we talk of a healthy organism? Our ideas upon the subject are, purely arbitrary, and depend upon our everyday experience. Health is simply *that condition of structure and function which, on examination of a sufficient number of examples, we find to be commonest.* The term, in fact, has the same significance as "the normal." Disease we may define, accordingly, as *any departure from the normal standard of structure or function of a tissue or organ.* If, for instance, we find that instead of the natural number of Malpighian bodies in the kidney there are only half that number, then we are entitled to say that this defect represents disease of structure; and if we find that the organ is excreting a new substance, such as albumen, we can affirm logically that its function is abnormal. Once grant the above definition of disease, and even the most trivial aberrations from the normal must be regarded as diseased conditions, quite irrespective of whether, when structural, they interfere with the function of the part or not. Thus an abortive supernumerary finger may not cause much, if any, inconvenience to the possessor, but nevertheless it must be regarded as a type of disease, which, trivial as it may appear, has a profound meaning in phylogeny and ontogeny.

Classification.—From the foregoing it will be gathered that the problems in pathology are many-sided and require to be attacked from all points of vantage; and the subject falls naturally into certain great divisions, the chief of which are the following:—

      I. Morbid anatomy.
          (a) Naked-eye or macroscopic.
          (b) Morbid histology or microscopic.
      II. Pathological physiology.
      III. Pathogenesis.
      IV. Aetiology.
      V. Pathological chemistry.

The term "pathogenesis" has reference to the generation and development of disease, and that of "aetiology," in its present bearing, has to do with its causes. The use of the term "pathological physiology" may at first appear strange, for if we define physiology as the sum of the normal functions of the body or organism, it may be hard to see how there can be a physiology which is pathological. The difficulty, however, is more apparent than real, and in this sense, that if we start with a diseased organ as our subject of inquiry, we can quite properly, and without committing a solecism, treat of the functions of that organ in terms of its diseased state.

INFLUENCES WORKING FOR EVIL UPON THE ORGANISM.

(1) *Malnutrition.*—When the blood supply is entirely cut off from a tissue the tissue dies; and in the act of dying, or afterwards, it suffers certain alterations dependent upon its surroundings. Thus, when the circulation to an external part is obstructed completely, as in the case of a limb where the main artery has been occluded and where the anastomotic communi-

cations have not sufficed to continue the supply of blood, the part becomes gangrenous (fig. 24, Pl. II.); that is to say, it dies and falls a prey to the organisms which excite putrefaction, just as would happen to any other dead animal tissue were it unconnected with the body. Fermentative changes are set up in it, characterised by the evolution of gas and the formation of products of suboxidation, some of which, being volatile, account for the characteristic odour. In the formation of these the tissues break down, and in course of time lose their characteristic histological features. The blood suffers first; its pigment is dissolved out and soaks into the surroundings, imparting to them the pink hue so diagnostic of commencing gangrene. Muscle and white fibrous tissue follow next in order, while elastic tissue and bone are the last to show signs of disintegration. The oil separates from the fat-cells and is found lying free, while the sulphuretted hydrogen evolved as one of the products of putrefaction reacts upon the iron of the blood and throws down a precipitate of sulphide of iron, which in course of time imparts to the limb a range of colour commencing in green and terminating in black.

The temperature at which the limb is kept, no doubt, favours and hastens the natural process of destruction, so that putrefaction shows itself sooner than would be the case with a dead tissue removed from the body and kept at a lower temperature. Nevertheless, gangrene is nothing more or less than *the putrefactive fermentation of an animal tissue still attached to the body.* If the amount of liquid contained in the tissue be small in quantity the part mummifies, giving rise to what is known as "dry gangrene." If the dead part be protected from the ingress of putrefactive organisms, however, it separates from that which is living without the ordinary evidences of gangrene, and is then known as an "aseptic slough." Should the portion of tissue deprived of its circulation be contained in an internal organ, as is so often the case where the obstruction in the artery is due to embolism, it becomes converted into what is known as an "infarction." These infarcts are most common in organs provided with a terminal circulation, such as prevails in the kidney and spleen. The terminal branches of the arteries supplying these organs are usually described as not anastomosing but many, if not all, of Cohnheim's end-arteries have minute collateral channels; which, however, are usually insufficient to completely compensate for the blocking that may occur in these arteries, therefore, when one of them is obstructed, the area irrigated by it dies from malnutrition. Being protected from the ravages of the organisms which induce putrefaction, however, it does not become gangrenous; it is only where the obstructing agent contains these organisms that a gangrenous slough follows, or, in the case of the contaminating organisms being of a suppurative variety, ends in the formation of a so-called "pyaemic abscess," followed by rapid dissolution of the dead tissue (fig. 24, Pl. II.). In ordinary circumstances, where the artery is obstructed by an agent free from such organismal contamination, the part becomes first red. This is due to intense engorgement of the vessels brought about through these minute existing collateral channels and results in a peripheral congested zone round the infarct. There may be haemorrhage from these vessels into the tissues. This collateral supply not being sufficient to keep up the proper flow of blood through the part the veins tend to become thrombosed, thus increasing the engorgement. The central part of the obstructed area very soon undergoes degenerative changes, and rapidly becomes decolourised. This necrosed area forms the pale infarct. Absorption of this infarcted zone is carried on by means of leucocytes and other phagocytic cells, and by new blood-vessels. If absorption be not complete the mass undergoes caseation and becomes surrounded by a capsule of fibrous tissue—being sharply cut off from the healthy tissue.

Where the malnutrition is the effect of poorness in the quality of the blood, the results are of course more widespread. The muscles suffer at an early period: they fall off in bulk, and later suffer from fatty degeneration, the heart being probably the first muscle to give way. Indeed, all tissues when under-nourished, either locally as the result of an ischaemia, or generally as from some impairment of the blood, such as that prevailing in pernicious anaemia, tend to suffer from fatty degeneration; and at first sight it seems somewhat remarkable that under-nourished tissues should develop fat in their substance (figs. 26 and 27, Pl. II.). The fatty matter, however, it must be borne in mind, is the expression of dissimilation of the actual substance of the proteids of the tissues, not of the splitting up of proteids or other carbonaceous nourishment supplied to them.

A part deprived of its natural nerve-supply sooner or later suffers from the effects of malnutrition. When the trigeminus nerve is divided (Majendie), or when its root is compressed injuriously, say by a tubercular tumour, the cornea begins to show points of ulceration, which, increasing in area, may bring about total disintegration of the eyeball. The earliest interpretation put upon this experiment was that the trophic influence of the nerve having been withdrawn, the tissue failed to nourish itself, and that degeneration ensued as a consequence. The subsequent experiments of Snellen, Senftleben, and, more lately, of Turner, seem to show that if the eyeball be protected from the impingement of foreign particles, an accident to which it is liable owing to its state of anaesthesia, the ulceration may be warded off indefinitely. If the eyeball be kept perfectly clean and no organism be admitted from the outside then ulceration will not follow. If, on the other hand, any pathogenic organisms be present the results are disastrous because the tissue, deprived of its nervous trophic supply, has greatly lessened resistance. The bed-sores which follow paralysis of the limbs are often quoted as proof of the direct trophic action of the nerve-supply upon the tissues, yet even here the evidence is somewhat contradictory. Still, there are facts which, for want of a better explanation, we are almost bound to conclude are to be accounted for on the direct nerve-control theory. The common variety of bed-sore is the result of continuous pressure on and irritation of the skin, the vitality and resisting power of which are lowered by a lesion of the cord cutting off the trophic supply to the skin affected. The acute bed-sore is, in some cases, a true trophic lesion occurring, as it may, on parts not subjected to continuous pressure or irritation. Trophic disturbance in the nutrition of the skin may be so great that a slight degree of external pressure or irritation is sufficient to excite even a gangrenous inflammation. Again, a fractured bone is a paralysed limb often fails to unite, while another in the opposite sound limb unites readily, and an ulcerated surface on a paralysed limb shows little healing reaction. A salivary gland degenerates when its nerve-supply is cut off; and the nerves leading up to the symmetrical sloughs in Raynaud's disease have been found in an advanced state of degeneration (Affleck and Wiglesworth). It is just a question, however, whether, even in instances such as these, the nutritional failure may not be explained upon the assumption of withdrawal of the local vasomotor control. There seems to be little doubt, notwithstanding, that one of the chief functions of the nerve cell is that of the propagation of a trophic influence along its axon. When a nerve-trunk is separated from its central connexion, the distal portion falls into a state of fatty degeneration (Wallerian or secondary degeneration). That special trophic nerves, however, exist throughout the body, seems to be a myth. It is much more likely, as Verworn alleges, that the nerves which influence the characteristic function of any tissue regulate thereby the metabolism of the cells in question—in other words, that every nerve serves as a trophic nerve for the tissues it supplies. It is a significant fact that neoplasms contain very few nerve-fibres, even although growing luxuriantly, and there is a doubt whether the few twigs contained in them may not merely have been dragged into their midst as the tumour mass expanded (Young).

Overwork.—The effect of overwork upon an organ or tissue varies in accordance with (a) the particular organ or tissue concerned, (b) the amount of nourishment conveyed to it, and (c) the power of assimilation possessed by its cells. In the case of muscle, if the available nourishment be sufficient, and if the power of assimilation of the muscle cells remain unimpaired, its bulk increases, that is to say, it becomes hypertrophied.

It may be advisable to define exactly what is meant by "hypertrophy," as the term is often used in a loose and insignificant sense. Mere enlargement of an organ does not imply that it is in a state of hypertrophy, for some of the largest organs met with in morbid anatomy are in a condition of extreme atrophy. Some organs are subject to enlargement from deposition within them of a foreign substance (amyloid, fat, &c.). This, it need hardly be said, has nothing to do with hypertrophy. The term hypertrophy is used when the individual tissue elements become bigger to meet the demands of greater functional activity; hyperplasia, if there is an increase in the number of these elements;

and pseudo-hypertrophy, when the specific tissue element is largely replaced by another tissue.

There are conditions in which we have an abnormal increase in the tissue elements but which strictly should not be defined as hypertrophies, such as new-growths, abnormal enlargements of bones and organs due to syphilis, tuberculosis, osteitis deformans, acromegaly, myxoedema, &c. The enormously long teeth sometimes found in rodents also are not due to hypertrophy, as they are normally endowed with rapid growth to compensate for the constant and rapid attrition which takes place from the opposed teeth. Should one of these teeth be destroyed the opposed one loses its natural means of attrition and becomes a remarkable, curved tusk-like elongation. The nails of the fingers, or the hair of the scalp may grow to an enormous length if not trimmed.

True hypertrophy is commonly found in the hollow muscular organs such as the heart, bladder and alimentary canal. As any obstruction to the outflow of the contents throws an increased amount of work on the walls, in order to overcome the resistance, the intermittent strain, acting on the muscle cells, stimulates them to enlarge and proliferate, fig. 28, Pl. II., and gives rise to adaptive hypertrophy. Should there be much loss of tissue of an organ, the cells of the remaining part will enlarge and undergo an active proliferation (hyperplasia) so that it may be made up to the original amount. Or again, in the case of paired organs, if one be removed by operation, or destroyed by disease, the other at once undertakes to carry on the functions of both. To do so a general enlargement takes place until it may reach the size and weight equal to the original pair. This is known as compensatory hypertrophy.

Examples of physiological hypertrophy are found in the ovaries, uterus and mammary glands, where there is an increased functional activity required at the period of gestation. Local hypertrophy may also be due to stimulation resulting from friction or intermittent pressure, as one may see in the thickening on the skin of the artisan's hands. The extreme development of the muscles in the weight-lifting athlete and in the arm of the blacksmith is the result of increased functional activity with a corresponding increase in the vascular supply; this exercise may produce an over-development so excessive as to be classed as abnormal.

In atrophy we have a series of retrograde processes in organs and tissues, which are usually characterized by a progressive diminution in size which may even end in their complete disappearance (fig. 29, Pl. II.). This wasting may be general or local—continuously from the embryonic period there is this natural process of displacement and decay of tissues going on in the growing organism. The functions of the thymus gland begin to cease after the second year from birth. The gland then slowly shrinks and undergoes absorption. From atrophy of their roots, caused by the pressure of the growing permanent teeth, the "milk teeth" in children become loose and are cast off. The ovaries show atrophic changes after the menopause. In old age there is a natural wearing out of the elements of the various tissues. Their physiological activities gradually fail owing to the constructive processes having become so exhausted from long use that the destructive ones are able to overtake them. As the cell fails and shrinks, so does it become more and more unable to make good the waste due to metabolism. This physiological wasting is termed senile atrophy.

General atrophy or emaciation is brought about by the tissues being entirely or partially deprived of nutriment, as in starvation, or in malignant, tubercular, and other diseases of the alimentary system which interfere with the proper ingestion, digestion or absorption of food material. The toxic actions produced in continued fevers, in certain chronic diseases, and by intestinal parasites largely aid in producing degeneration, emaciation and atrophy.

Atrophy may follow primary arrest of function—disuse atrophy. The loss of an eye will be followed by atrophy of the optic nerve; the tissues in a stump of an amputated limb show atrophic changes; a paralysed limb from long disuse shows much wasting; and one finds at great depths of the sea fishes and marine animals, which have almost completely lost the organs

PATHOLOGY

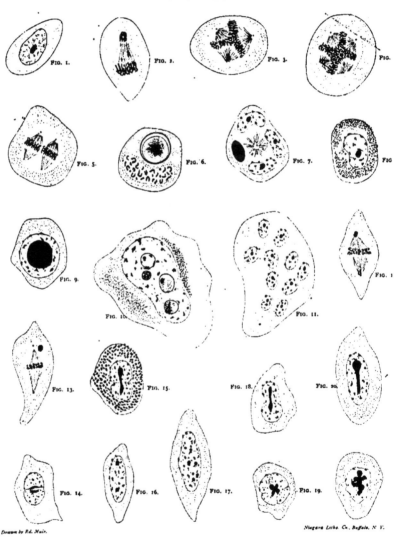

Drawn by Rd. Muir.

Niagara Litho. Co., Buffalo, N.Y.

of sight, having been cut off for long ages from the stimuli (light) essential for these organs, and so brought into an atrophic condition from disuse.

Atrophy may also follow from overwork. Increased work thrown on to a tissue may produce hypertrophy, but, if this excessive function be kept up, atrophy will follow; even the blacksmith's arm breaks down owing to the hypertrophic muscle fibres becoming markedly atrophied.

From these causes a certain shrinkage is liable to occur, more evident in some parts of the body than in others. Thus the brain falls off in bulk, and the muscles become attenuated, and in no muscle is this more notable than in the case of the heart. A tendency to pigmentation also develops in certain tissues of the body, such as the nerve and muscle cells. As a result of these various degenerations the functions of the body deteriorate, the faculties become blunted, and the muscular energy of the body is below what it was in earlier life, while the secreting glands in certain instances become functionally obsolescent.

Continuous Over-pressure.—The tissues of an animal or plant are all under a certain pressure, caused, in the one case, by the expulsive action of the heart and the restraint of the skin and other elastic tissues, and, in the other case, by the force of the rising sap and the restraint of the periderm or bark. Under this normal amount of pressure they can live and grow. But whenever, from any cause, the degree of pressure which they are naturally intended to withstand is surpassed, they fail to nourish themselves, become granular, die, and, failing to pieces, are absorbed.

Deleterious Surroundings.—There can be little doubt that all unnatural and artificial modes of life tend to deterioration of the powers of resistance of the organism to disease. We see it exemplified in plant life in circumstances which are unnatural to the life of the plant, and the prevalence of certain constitutional tendencies among the inhabitants of crowded cities bears evidence to the same law.

Man, like other animals, was naturally intended to lead an outdoor life. He was originally a hunter and a tiller of the ground, breathing a pure atmosphere, living on a frugal diet, and exercising his muscles. Whenever these conditions are infringed his powers of resistance to disease are lessened, and certain tendencies begin to show themselves, which are generally termed constitutional. Thus the liability to tubercular infection is far commoner in the midst of a depraved population than in one fulfilling the primary laws of nature; rickets is a disease of great cities rather than of rural districts; and syphilis is more disastrous and protracted in its course in the depraved in health than in the robust. Cattle kept within-doors in a large proportion of cases tubercular, while those leading an outdoor life are much less liable to infection. The improvement which has taken place in the general health of the inhabitants of cities during recent years, concurrent with hygienic legislation, is ample proof of the above assertions. The diminution in the number of deaths from tuberculosis during the last forty to fifty years of the 19th century of itself points in this direction. Every living organism, animal and vegetable, tends to maintain a normal state of health; it is when the natural laws of health are violated that the liability to disease begins to assert itself. If, in these circumstances, the food supply be also insufficient, the combination of influences is sure, in course of time, to bring about a physical deterioration of the race. Certain avocations have a direct and immediate influence in causing diseased states of body. Thus workers in lead suffer from the effects of this substance as a poison, those who work in phosphorus are liable to necrosis of bone and fatty degeneration of the blood vessels and organs, and the many occupations in which dust is inhaled (coal-mining, stone-dressing, steel-polishing, &c.; fig. 30, Pl. III.) are fraught with the greatest danger, owing to the destructive influence exerted upon the lungs by the inhaled particles. Among the most dangerous of the last class (the pneumokonioses) is perhaps that in which the dust particles take the form of finely divided freestone, as in stone-dressing and the dry-polishing on the grindstone of steel. The particles in this case set up a form of fibrosis of the lung, which, either of itself or by rendering the organ liable to tubercular infection, is extremely fatal. The abuse of alcohol may also be mentioned here as a factor in the production of disease.

Parasitism.—Of all external agents acting for evil, however, probably vegetable and animal micro-organisms with a pathogenic bent are most to be feared. When we consider that tuberculosis, diphtheria, cholera, tetanus, typhoid fever, anthrax, malaria and a host of other contagious diseases have each been proved to be of parasitical origin, an idea may be conveyed of the

range of the subject. The living organism may be regarded as constantly engaged in a warfare with these silent and apparently insignificant messengers of destruction and death, with the result that too often the battle ends in favour of the attacking enemy.

Heredity.—The *tendencies* to disease are in great part hereditary. They probably express a variation which may have occurred in a far-back ancestor, or in one more recent, and render the individual vulnerable to the attacks of parasitic fungi, or, it may be, become manifest as errors of metabolism. The psychopathic, the tubercular, the rickety, and the gouty constitution may all be transmitted through a line of ascendants, and only require the necessary exciting agents to render them apparent. A distinction must be drawn between the above and diseases, like syphilis and small-pox, in which the contagion of, not the tendency to, the disease is transmitted directly to the foetus *in utero*. (See HEREDITY.)

THE CELLULAR DOCTRINE IN PATHOLOGY

The cellular pathology is the pathology of to-day; indeed, protoplasm—its vital characteristics under abnormal influences and its decay—will be regarded most likely as the basis of pathology in all time. According to our present knowledge of physiological and pathological processes, we must regard the cell as the ultimate biological unit—a unit of structure and a unit of function; this was first put forward by Schleiden in 1838, and by Schwann in 1839, but we owe to Virchow the full recognition of the fundamental importance of the living cell in all the processes of life, whether in health or disease. When Virchow wrote, in 1850, " every animal presents itself as a sum of vital unities, every one of which manifests all the characteristics of life," he expressed a doctrine whose sway since then has practically been uninterrupted. The somatic cells represent communities or republics, as it were, which we name organs and tissues, but each cell possesses a certain autonomy and independence of action, and exhibits phenomena which are indicative of vitality.

Still, it must be borne in mind that this alleged autonomy of action is said to be founded upon an erroneous supposition, on the supposition that each cell is structurally, and it may be said functionally, separated from those in its neighbourhood. It is well known that in the vegetable kingdom the protoplasm of one cell frequently overflows into that of cells adjacent—that there is, as it were, a continuous network of protoplasm (idioplasm of Nägeli) prevailing throughout vegetable tissues, rather than an aggregation of isolated units. The same inter-communication prevails between adjacent cells in some animal tissues, and more particularly in those which are pathological, as in the case of the epithelial cells of cancer. Assuming, with Sedgwick and others, this amassed and bound condition of the tissues to be true, it would be necessary to reject the cell-doctrine in pathology altogether, and to regard the living basis of the organism as a continuous substance whose parts are incapable of living independently of the whole. Until, however, further evidence is forthcoming in support of this syncytial theory of structure, it would be unwise to regard it as established sufficiently to constitute a serviceable working hypothesis; hence, for the time being, we must accept the assertion that the cell represents the ultimate tissue-unit. Our present day definition of a cell is a minute portion of living organized substance or protoplasm.

The cells met with in morbid parts which are in a state of active vitality are built up of the same components as those *Structure of* found in normal tissues (Pl. I.).[1] Thus they are pro- *Pathological* vided with a nucleus which is the centre of cell activity; *Cells.* both of the reproductive and chemical (metabolic) processes which occur in the cell protoplasm. The executive centre

[1] DESCRIPTION OF PLATE I.

SERIES OF FIGURES ILLUSTRATIVE OF IRREGULAR DIVISION OF CELLS.

Figs. 1 to 6 are from the epithelial cells of a cancer of the mamma. (*After Galeotti.*)
7 to 21 are from a sarcoma. (*After Trambusti.*)

FIG. 1.—Resting epithelial cell.

varies in shape, but is usually round or oval, and is sharply defined by a nuclear membrane from the cytoplasm in which it lies. The nucleus in its vegetative stage shows a fine network throughout containing in the meshes the so-called nuclear-sap; attached to the network are the chromosomes, in the form of small irregular masses, which have a strong affinity for the "basic dyes." Embedded in the nucleus are one or more nucleoli (plasmosomes) having an affinity for the "acid dyes." The nucleolus shows an unstainable point at the centre known as the endonucleolus or nucleolulus (Auerbach).

The cell body, or cytoplasm, is apparently composed of a fine reticulum or network, containing within the meshes a soft viscid, transparent substance, the cell-sap, or hyaloplasm, which is probably a nutrient material to the living cell. Within the cytoplasm are found manifestations of functional activity, in the form of digestive vacuoles, granules, fat, glycogen, pigment, and foreign bodies. Usually the cytoplasm shows a marked affinity for the acid stains, but the different bodies found in the cell may show great variation in their staining reactions.

The centrosomes which play so important a part in cell division may be found either lying within or at one side of the nucleus in the vegetative condition of the cell. Centrosomes may be single, but usually two are lying close together in the attraction-sphere. When mitosis is about to take place, they separate from one another and pass to the poles of the nucleus, forming the achromatic spindle. After the division and cleavage of the chromosomes of the original nucleus have taken place they pass from the equator to the poles of the spindle, rearranging themselves close to the separated centrosomes to form daughter nuclei.

The cytoplasm of the cell now undergoes division in a line between the two daughter nuclei. When complete separation has taken place, we have two daughter cells formed from the original, each being a perfect cell-unit. Some pathological cells, such as the giant-cells of tumours, of bone, and those of tubercle, are polynucleated; in some instances they may contain as many as thirty or more nuclei. The only evidence we have in pathology of living structures in which apparently a differentiation into cell-body and nucleus does not exist, is in the case of bacteria, but then there comes the question whether they may not possess chromatin distributed through their substance, in the form of metachromatic points, as is the case in some infusoria (Trachelocerca, Gruber).

Although the methods of cell-division prevailing in normal structures are maintained generally in those which are pathological, yet certain modifications of these methods are more noticeable in the latter than in the former. Thus in the neoplasmata cell-division is more the rule than in healthy parts. In actively growing neoplasmata, certainly, the indirect method prevails largely, but seems to go on side by side with the direct.

A curious and interesting modification of the indirect method, known as "asymmetrical division," occurs frequently in epitheliomata, sarcomata, &c. (Hansemann). It consists in an unequal number of chromosomes passing over to each of the daughter nuclei, so that one may become hypochromatic, the other hyperchromatic. When this happens the resulting cleavage of the cytoplasm and nucleus is also unequal. Several explanations have been given of

Fig. 2.—Asymmetrical diaster.
 „   3.—Tripolar division in which the splitting of the loops has commenced.
 „   4.—Tetrapolar karyokinesis.
 „   5.—Another form of tetrapolar division.
 „   6.—Cell in a state of degeneration and chromatolysis; the large rounded body in the cell is a cancer parasite.
 „   7.—Polynucleated cell with nucleli of normal size arising from multiple karyokinetic division.
 „   8.—Pigmented cell with resting nucleus. The attraction-sphere and centrosome lie in the cytoplasm in the neighbourhood of the nucleus.
 „   9.—Hypertrophic nucleolus.
 „ 10.—Large cell with a single nucleus; nucleoli in a state of degeneration.
 „ 11.—Multinucleated giant-cell, the nuclei small and produced amitotically.
 „ 12.—Karyokinetic figure, the one centrosome much larger than the other.
 „ 13.—Cell in process of karyokinetic division with retention of the nucleolus during the division.
 „ 14.—Division of the nucleolus and formation of nuclear plate. The nucleolus is elongated, and its longest measurement lies in the direction of the equatorial plane of the nucleus.
 „ 15.—Division of the nucleolus by elongation, construction, and equilateral division of the nucleus.
 „ 16.—Division of the nucleolus without any evidence of division of the nucleus.
 „ 17.—Nucleus with many nucleoli.
 „ 18.—Direct division of nucleus.
 „ 19.—Multiple direct division of the nucleus.
 „ 20.—Nail-like nucleolus.
 „ 21.—Fragmentation of the nucleus.

the meaning of these irregularly-chromatic cells, but that which most lends itself to the facts of the case seems to be that they represent a condition of abnormal karyorhexis.

In many pathological cells undergoing indirect segmentation, centrosomes appear to be absent, or at any rate do not manifest themselves at the poles of the achromatic spindle. When they are present, that at one end of the spindle may be unusually large, the other of natural size, and they may vary in shape. In pathological cell-division it happens occasionally that the segmentation of the cytoplasm is delayed beyond that of the mitotic network. The daughter nuclei may have arrived at the anaphase stage, and have even gone the length of forming a nuclear membrane, without an equatorial depression having shown itself in the cell-body. Sometimes the equatorial depression fails entirely, and the separation, as in some vegetable cells, takes place through the construction of a cell-plate. Intranuclear plexuses are not usually found in giant-cells, but have been described in the giant-cells of sarcomata by Klebs and Hansemann, and in those of tubercle by Baumgarten. Some of the nuclei within multinucleated cells may occasionally be engaged in mitotic division, the others being in the resting state.

In the earlier accepted notion of direct segmentation, usually known as the schema of Remak, division was described as commencing in the nucleolus, as thereafter spreading to the nucleus, and as ultimately implicating the cell-substance. Trambusti, curiously, finds confirmatory evidence of this in the division of cells in sarcoma. Contrary, however, to the experience of others, he has never found that the attraction-sphere play an important part in direct cell-division, or, indeed, that they exert any influence whatever upon the mechanism of the process. Where pigment was present within the cells (sarcoma), the attraction-spheres were represented by quite clear unpigmented areas, sometimes with a centrosome in their midst.

REPAIR OF INJURIES

In the process of inflammation we have a series of reactions on the part of the tissues, and fluids of the body, to counteract the ill effects of irritation or injury, to get rid of the cause, and to repair its results. Injury and loss of tissue are usually followed by repair, and both the destructive and reparative changes are, as a rule, classified under the term inflammation. The irritants may be bacteria and their toxins, or they may be mechanical, chemical or thermic.

We do not now concur with the old view that inflammation was essentially an injurious process; rather do we look upon it as beneficial to the organism. In the various reactions of the tissues against the exciting cause of the injury we see a striking example of a beautifully organized plan of attack and defence on the part of the organism.

In some of the infective conditions the conflict fortifies the organism against future attacks of the same nature, as for example in the immunity following many of the acute infective diseases. This acquired immunity is brought about by the development of a protective body as a result of the struggle of the cells and fluids of the body with the invading bacteria and their toxins. This resistance may be more or less permanent. If the invasion is due to a pus-producing micro-organism which settles in some local part of the body, the result is an abscess (fig. 25, Pl. II.).

Abscesses.—One can easily demonstrate all the actions and reactions which take place in this form of acute inflammation. In such a conflict one can see the presence of these minute but dangerous foes in the tissues. At once they proceed to make good their hold on the position they have secured by secreting and throwing out toxins which cause more or less injury to the tissues in their immediate neighbourhood. These micro-organisms having found in the tissues everything favourable for their needs, rapidly multiply and very soon produce serious results. At this point one's attention is focused on the wonderful reactions possessed by the healthy tissues to combat these evil influences.

In a very short period—within three or four hours after infection—there appears to have been a message conveyed to the defenders of the body both as to the point of attack and the nature of the invasion. There is thus brought into play a series of processes on the part of the tissues—the vascular inflammatory changes—which is really the first move to neutralize the malign effects. We find at this early stage oedema of the part. This is an increased exudation of fluid from the engorged blood vessels which not only dilutes the toxins, but is supposed to contain substances which in some way act on these living micro-organisms and render them a more easy prey to the polymorpho-nuclear leucocytes (fig. 23, Pl. II.)—cells that are motile and extremely phagocytic to these bacteria. At this stage the rapidity of the blood circulation has become greatly diminished. The polymorpho-nuclear leucocytes are seen in great numbers in the blood vessels.

In health these cells, belonging to our first army of defenders, are found continually circulating in the blood stream in fairly large numbers; they are ever ready to rush to the point of attack, where they at once leave the blood stream by passing through the vessel walls—emigration—into the tissues of the danger zone. There they show marked phagocytosis, attacking and taking up into their interior and destroying the micro-organisms in large numbers. At the same time large numbers of these cells perish in the struggle, but even the death of these cells is of value to the body, as in the process of breaking down there are set free ferments which not only act detrimentally to the bacteria, but also may stimulate the bringing forward of another form of cell defenders—the mononuclear leucocyte.

To replace this cellular destruction there has been a demand for reinforcements on the home centres of the polymorpho-nuclear leucocytes—the bone marrow. This call is immediately answered by an active proliferation and steady maturing of the myelocytes in the marrow to form the polymorpho-nuclear leucocytes. These then pass into the blood stream in very large numbers, and appear to be specially attracted to the point of injury by a positive chemiotactic action. This phenomenon, called *chemiotaxis*, has been studied by several investigators. Leber experimented with several chemical compounds to find what reaction they had on these cells; by using fine glass tubes sealed at the outer end and containing a chemical substance, and by introducing the open end into the blood vessels he found that the leucocytes were attracted—positive chemiotaxis—by the various compounds of mercury, copper, turpentin, and other substances. That quinine, chloroform, glycerin, alcohol, with others, had no attractive influence on them—negative chemiotaxis. It was also found that a weak solution may have a marked positive attraction whilst a strong solution of the same substance will have the opposite effect. It has been proved that the pyo-genic bacterial toxins, if not too concentrated, will attract the polymorpho-nuclear leucocytes, but if concentrated, may have a repelling influence.

Then we have the property of adaptation, in which the negative reaction may be changed into a positive; a given toxin may at first repel the cell, but by a gradual process the cell becomes accustomed to such a toxin and will move towards it.

On reaching the vicinity they leave the blood stream and join in the warfare—many performing their function of phagocytosis (q.v.), others fall ng victims to the toxins. The tissues of the part become disorganized or destroyed, and their place is taken by the mass of warring cellular elements now recognised as pus.

As soon as the fluids and the polymorpho-nuclear leucocytes have succeeded in diminishing the virulence of the micro-organism, the second line of defenders—the large mononuclear leucocytes (fig. 23, Pl. III.) make their appearance at the field of battle in ever increasing numbers. These are amoeboid cells and are extremely phagocytic, their power of digestion being greatly developed. Their principal function is to bring about the removal of foreign, dead or degenerating material. This they take up into their protoplasm, where it is rapidly digested by being acted on by some intracellular digestive ferment (fig. 31, Pl. III.). Where the material is too large to be taken up by an individual cell, the dissolution is brought about by the cells surrounding the material, to which they closely apply themselves, and by the secreting of the ferment, a gradual process of erosion is brought about with ultimate absorption.

If the abscess be deeply situated in some tissue and not able to open on to a free surface so allowing the contents to be drained off, the phagocytic cells play a very prominent part in the resolution of the abscess. They are seen pushing their way right into the field of conflict and greedily ingesting both friends and foes. The first defenders, the polymorpho-nuclear leucocytes, having performed their functions, are of no more use to the organism and are therefore removed by the mono-nuclear phagocytes as useless material (fig. 31, Pl. III.).

The tissues having now mobilised an army that completely surrounds the fighting zone, there is a gradual and general advance made from all sides. The vanguard of the advancing army is composed of a more or less compact layer of the mono-nuclear phagocytes (polyblasts) accompanied by numerous new vessels. These phagocytic cells carry out the complete removal of all the injured warring elements and the damaged tissues of the part. The vessels are only temporary channels by which is brought forward the food supply that is needed by the advancing army if it is successfully to carry on its function; they probably also drain off the deleterious fluid substances formed by the cellular disintegration that has taken place in the part. Closely on the advance of this army of phagocytes or scavenger cells follows the third line of defenders, the connective tissue cells or fibroblasts.

All these cells are probably of local origin and are now stimulated to make good the damage. The connective tissue cells or fibroblasts (fig. 32, Pl. III.) are seen in active proliferation around the phagocytic zone. First they are round or oval in shape; later they become spindle shaped, arranging themselves in layers. Then they develop definite fibrils which differentiate into fibrous laminae forming a zone which shuts off the abscess from the healthy tissue and so prevents the further invasion and injurious effects of the micro-organism. By the ai-1 of the new fibroblasts this fibrous tissue zone gradually encroaches on the pus area and replaces the phagocytic layer of cells as they proceed with the absorption of the pus mass (fig. 33, Pl. III.). When complete removal of the pus mass has been accomplished by the process of absorption, the damaged area is replaced by the new fibrous tissue, which later becomes condensed and forms the cicatricial or scar tissue (fig. 35, Pl. III.)—a healed abscess.

Wounds.—The healing of wounds is brought about by similar processes to that seen in the evolution of an abscess.

If the injury be a small incised wound through the skin and subcutaneous tissues without any septic contamination, there usually follows a minimum of reaction on the part of the tissues. As the edges of the wound are brought into accurate apposition there is little or no blood lodged between them, so that an extremely narrow strip of fibrin glues the cut edges together. This strip is rapidly replaced, mainly by the connective tissue cells of the adjoining tissue growing across the temporary filled breach and firmly uniting the two cut surfaces. The vascular changes are practically absent in healing by first intention.

Healing, by second intention, or granulation, is usually seen where there has been loss of tissue, or extensive damage. The reactions of the tissues vary in degrees according to the nature and severity of the injury. In resenting such insults, a remarkable uniformity and regularity in the processes is brought about by the different cells and fluids of the healthy tissues of the body. Although we have not reached a stage of certainty regarding their origin, function and destiny, recent investigations have brought forward evidence to elucidate the importance of the part played by the different cells in the various types of the inflammatory process.

If there be a loss of tissue brought about by severe injury to the skin and the deeper tissues, there is usually an extravasation of blood from the severed vessels. Along with the exuded serum this fills up the breach in the tissues and the whole is rapidly formed into a fibrinous mass due to the disintegration of the polymorpho-nuclear leucocytes setting free their ferment. The ferment thus set free brings about the coagulation of the serum, which acts as a protective and temporary scaffolding to the injured tissues. Lying between the fibrin mass and the healthy tissues is a zone of injured and degenerated tissue elements, the result of the trauma.

As early as six hours after the injury the polymorpho-nuclear leucocytes are seen passing in large numbers from the dilated and congested blood vessels of the tissues at the margin of the wound into the injured zone, where they carry on an active phagocytosis. It is believed also that they secrete bactericidal substances and ferments which bring about the liquefaction of the fibrin and the damaged tissues—histolysis—and thus assist the process of absorption. They appear to prepare the injured zone for the coming of the next series of cells. Their function being at an end they give way to these cells which carry on the process of absorption.

In a period varying from twenty-four to thirty hours there is marked evidence of the removal of the degenerated cellular elements in the damaged zone by the mono-nuclear phagocytes. Numerous fibroblasts, together with polyblasts, are visible in the fibrin mass, and the vessels at the periphery of the damaged zone are now seen to be sending out offshoots which assist in the process of absorption. These vascular buds grow out in various directions as little solid projections of cells; they then become channelled and form the new but temporary meshwork.

After two to four days these processes are more clearly emphasised. By these processes we reach the stage where the fibrin mass and damaged tissues have been completely removed, and replaced by a temporary vascular and cellular tissue, known as granulation tissue (fig. 34, Pl. III.), which in turn has to give way to the more firm and differentiated fibrous tissue. By this time the skin epithelium may have grown over the wound.

After five to seven days we find the connective tissue cells taking the principal part in the building up of the new permanent tissue, for at this stage there is an active proliferation of the fibroblasts. These cells of various shapes are seen in large numbers, mainly lying in a direction parallel to the new vessels and capillaries, which all run at right angles to the wound surface. The branching processes of these cells apparently anastomose with one another and form a delicate supporting network. It is from these cells that the fine fibrillar substance is formed, and from this stage onwards—eight to fifteen days—there is a steady increase in the new fibrils, giving more density to the new tissue. At the same time there is brought about an alteration in the arrangement of the position of the fibroblasts. These become spindle shaped with their long axis more and more assuming a position at right angles to the vessels (fig. 34, Pl. III.); the two edges of the wound are thus more firmly bound together. As their fibrils become more developed they gradually form fibrous laminae which are laid down first in the deeper part of the wound. When this process has reached a certain stage and all the absorption necessary has occurred the new blood vessels, from the increasing pressure of the successive fibrous layers, gradually dwindle and become obliterated, i.e. at a period corresponding to the condensation of the fibrous laminae and the disappearance of the cellular character of the granulation tissue. Thus is formed in the damaged area a permanent tissue known as scar tissue (fig. 35, Pl. III.).

Fibrosis.—Where a chronic inflammatory process has taken possession of an organ, or, let us say, has been located in periosteum or other fibrous part, there is a great tendency to the production of cicatricial fibrous tissue in mass. Thus it is laid down in large quantity in cirrhosis of the liver, kidney or lung, and reacts upon these organs by contracting and inducing atrophy. The term "cirrhosis" or "fibrosis" is usually applied to such a condition of organs (figs. 36 and 37, Pl. IV.), that of "sclerosis" is used when such a deposition of fibrous tissue occurs within the central nervous system. Gull and Sutton asserted that in particular states of body, and more especially in the condition associated with cirrhotic kidney, such a fibrosis becomes general, running, as they alleged it does, along the adventitia of arteries and spreading to their capillaries. They supposed that it was accompanied by a peculiar hyaline thickening of the arterial wall, usually of the tunica intima, and hence they termed the supposed diseased state "arterio-capillary fibrosis," and gave the fibrous substance the name "hyaline-fibroid." They held that the cirrhotic kidney is simply a local manifestation of a general fibrous disease. Their theory, however, has fallen into disfavour of late years.

TUMOURS OR NEW GROWTHS

The various definitions of the term "new growth" leave us with a definite conception of it as a new formation of tissue which appears to originate and to grow independently. We have already compared the body to a social community, each constituent element of which—the cell—lives its own life but subordinates its individuality to the good of the whole organism. The essential characteristic is that this subordination is lost and the tissue elements, freed from the normal mutual restraint of their interdependence, give way to an abnormal growth. All the hypotheses about the causation of new growths seek to explain the secret of this individuality or "autonomy," as they recognize that the mystery of the origin of the great majority of tumours would be solved if we could trace how or why the tissue elements in which they develop first took on this abnormal growth.

Tumours are divided into two main groups—innocent and malignant. These differ only in degree and there is no hard and fast line between them. Innocent tumours are usually sharply defined from the surrounding tissues, and show no tendency to spread into them or to pass by means of lymphatics and blood-vessels to neighbouring parts (fig. 38, Pl. IV.). Malignant tumours, on the other hand, invade the adjacent tissues and pass by lymphatics and blood vessels to distant parts, where they set up secondary growths (fig. 39, Pl. IV.).

Tumours appear to arise spontaneously, *i.e.* without evident cause; they may develop in association with prolonged irritation or injury (later referred to in more detail). To heredity, as an indirect or predisposing cause, has probably been assigned too great importance, and the many facts brought forward of the relative frequency of cancer in members of one family only justify the conclusion that the tissue-resistance of certain families is lowered.

At the present time we have still before us the question, what is the essential cause of tumours (q.v.)? This, one of the most difficult problems of pathology, is being attacked by many able workers, who are all striving from different standpoints to elucidate the nature of these new formations, which spring from the normal tissues in which they develop and which they destroy. In spite of all the valuable research work that has been done within the last few years, the essential cause of new growths still remains unknown.

To the work carried on apparently by the Imperial Cancer Research Fund in England, and to investigators in other countries, are due the present day scientific efforts made to systematize investigation and clear away many of the hypothetical speculations that have gathered round this most difficult subject. Their investigations on cancers found in the lower animals, and the successful transplantation of such growths into a new host of the same species (mice and rats), have greatly advanced our knowledge of the etiology of this disease.

Many of the hypotheses of the past put forward to explain cancer must be discarded, in view of the facts brought to light by the comparative and experimental research of recent times. According to the hypothesis of Waldeyer and Thiersch there is perfect equilibrium between the normal epithelium and its supporting structure, the connective tissue, but with advancing age this balance is upset owing to the connective tissue gradually losing its restraining power. The epithelial cells are then able to pass from their normal position, in consequence of which they proliferate and at the same time revert to a more primitive type of cell. In this way they give rise to a malignant new growth.

Cohnheim's hypothesis of "embryonic residues" provides that early in the development of the embryo some of the cells, or groups of cells, are separated from their organic continuity during the various foldings that take place in the actively growing embryo. The separated cells become intermingled with other tissue elements amongst which they lie dormant with their inherent power of proliferation in abeyance. At a later date in the life of the individual, by some unknown stimuli, they resume their active power of proliferation and so give rise to new growths.

The "tissue-tension" hypothesis of Ribbert is a combination of the two foregoing. He holds that new growths arise, both before birth or at any subsequent period of life, by the separation of cells or clumps of cells from their normal position, and that in health there is a balance between the various tissues and tissue elements regulated by what he calls the "tissue-tension" of the part, *i.e.* that cells or groups of cells have a restraining power on one another which prevents any physiological over-activity.

From whatever cause the resisting power of the tissue elements is thus weakened, the invasion of other tissue elements is then allowed to take place. These being freed from the normal inhibiting power of the neighbouring elements, multiply and go on to the formation of a new growth. According to Ribbert it is the isolation, together with the latent capacity of isolated cells for unlimited proliferation, that gives rise to new growths.

Hansemann's "anaplasia" hypothesis seeks to find an explanation of the formation of new growths in the absence of the histological differentiation of the cell associated with a corresponding increase in its proliferative power and a suspension, or loss, of its functional activity.

The greater the degree of anaplasia the more the tumour cells conform in character and appearance to the embryonic type of cell and the more malignant is the new growth. A simple fibroma is a growth composed of fully formed fibrous tissue (fig. 40, Pl. IV.). The small round celled sarcoma is a malignant growth, and is composed of the primitive type of cell that goes to form fibrous tissue (fig. 41, Pl. IV.).

Then we have Beard's "germ-cell" hypothesis, in which he holds that many of the germ-cells in the growing embryo fail to reach their proper position—the generative areas—and settle down and become quiescent in some somatic tissue of the embryo. They may at some later date become active in some way, and so give rise to a cellular proliferation that may imitate the structure in which they grow, so giving rise to new growths.

Some workers regard certain appearances in dividing cells found in cancer as evidence of a reversion of the somatic cell to the germ-cell type (heterotypical), otherwise found only in the process which results in the formation of an embryo. These appearances are probably due to a pathological mitosis, commonly found in cancer, in which there is an irregular diminution in the number of chromosomes; some are cast out and become degenerated or some pass over to one of the daughter cells, leaving a reduced number in the other, and thus give rise to asymmetrical mitosis.

From the histological examination of tumour cells there is no evidence to show that they resemble the protozoal unicellular organisms in occasionally passing through a sexual process of reproduction, *i.e.* that nuclear conjugation between cells ever takes place.

In recent years the successful experimental transplantation of new growths, occurring sporadically in white mice and rats, into animals of the same species, has thrown a fresh light on all the features of malignant growths. From these experiments it is shown that cells taken from these growths and introduced into animals of the same species give rise to a cancerous growth, whose cells have acquired unlimited powers of proliferation. They are direct lineal descendants of the cells introduced, and are in no way formed from the tissue cells of the host in which they are placed and grow.

Not only is this true of epithelial cells, but the connective tissue-cells of the supporting structure of cancerous growth, after repeated transplantation, may become so altered that a gradual evolution of apparently normal connective tissue into sarcomatous elements takes place, these giving rise to "mixed tumours." The sarcomatous development may even completely outgrow the epithelial elements and so form and continue to grow as a pure sarcoma.

The fact that it is possible to propagate these cells of one animal for years in other animals of the same species, without any loss of their vegetative vitality, suggests that this continued growth is kept up by a growth-stimulating substance present in the proper species of animal; this substance, however, has not the power of transforming the normal tissue into a cancerous one.

Hauser, Bencke, Adami, Marchand and others have also put forward hypotheses to account for the growth of new tissues. These observers maintain that the cells from some cause lose, or may never have had developed, their functional activity, and thus acquire the activity of growth. The descendants of such cells will become more and more undifferentiated, thereby developing an increased vegetative activity.

Oertel finds an explanation of this want of complete cell-differentiation, loss of function, and acquired vegetative activity in the non-homogeneous character of the nuclear chromatin elements of the cell, and maintains that the different properties of the cell are carried and handed down by the different orders of chromatin loops. We have analogies to this in the two nuclei of some of the protozoa, the one being solely for the purpose of propagation, the other being associated with the functional activities of the cell. Oertel thinks that in man we have these two different functions carried on by the one nucleus containing both chromatin orders. If, from whatever cause, any of the chromatin loops belonging to the functional order be lost the descendants of such a cell, being unable to restore these loops, will be minus the functional attributes associated with the lost elements. These, having the full equipment of the vegetative order, will now develop the inherent power of proliferation to a greater or lesser extent.

The foregoing hypotheses have all sought the origin of new growths in some intrinsic cause which has altered the characters of the cell or cells which gave rise to them, but none of them explain the direct exciting cause. The parasitic hypothesis postulates the invasion of a parasite from without, thus making a new growth an infective process. Many cancer-parasites have been described in cancerous growths, including bacteria, yeasts and protozoa, but the innumerable attempts made to demonstrate the causal infective organism have all completely failed.

It is well known that cancer may develop in places where there has been chronic irritation; an example may be found in cancer of the tongue following on prolonged irritation from a jagged tooth. Clay-pipes may also give rise to cancer of lips in males in England, while cancer of the mouth of both sexes is common in India where chewing a mixture of betel leaves, areca-nut, tobacco and slaked lime is the usual practice. In the case of the squamous epithelial cancer of the anterior abdominal wall found so frequently in the natives of Kashmir, the position of the cancer is peculiar to this people, and is due to the chronic irritation following on repeated burns from using the "kangri"—a small earthenware vessel containing a charcoal fire enclosed in basket-work, and suspended round the waist, to assist in maintaining warmth in the extreme cold of the hills of Kashmir.

The irritant may be chemical, as is seen in the skin cancers that develop in workers in paraffin, petroleum, arsenic and aniline. However close the relationship is between chronic irritation and the starting of cancer, we are not in a position to say that irritation, physical or chemical, by itself can give rise to new growths. It may merely act locally in some way, and so render that part susceptible to unknown tissue stimuli which impart to the cells that extraordinary power of proliferation characteristic of new growth.

At the present time we are quite uncertain what is the ultimate cause of new growths; in all probability there may be one or more aetiological factors at play disturbing that perfect condition of equilibrium of normal tissues. A defect in co-ordination allows the stimulated active vegetative cellular elements, or the more fully differentiated tissue, to over-develop and so form tumours, simple or malignant.

OTHER TISSUE PRODUCTS

Mucoid.—In many pathological conditions we have degenerative products of various kinds formed in the tissues. These substances may be formed in the cells and given out as a secretion, or they may be formed by an intercellular transformation. In the mucinoid conditions, usually termed "mucoid" and "colloid" degenerations, we have closely allied substances which, like the normal mucins of the body, belong to the glucoproteids, and have in common similar physical characters. There is neither any absolute difference nor a constancy in their chemical reactions, and there can be brought about a transition of the "colloid" material into the "mucoid," or conversely. By mucoid is understood a soft gelatinous substance containing mucin, or pseudomucin, which is normally secreted by the epithelial cells of both the mucous membranes and glands. In certain pathological conditions an excessive formation and discharge of such material is usually associated with catarrhal changes in the epithelium. The desquamated cells containing this jelly-like substance become disorganized and blend with the secretion. Should this take place into a closed gland space it will give rise to cysts, which may attain a great size, as is seen in the ovarian adenomata. In some of the adenoid cancers of the alimentary tract this mucoid material is formed by the epithelial cells from which it flows out and infiltrates the

surrounding tissues; both the cells and tissues appear to be transformed into this gelatinous substance, forming the so-called "colloid cancer" (fig. 42, Pl. IV.).

The connective tissue is supplied normally with a certain amount of these mucinoid substances, no doubt acting as a lubricant. In many pathological conditions this tissue is commonly found to undergo mucoid or myxomatous degeneration, which is regarded as a reversion to a closely similar type—that of foetal connective tissue (fig. 43, Pl. IV). These changes are found in senile wasting, in metaplasia of cartilage, in many tumours, especially mixed growths of the parotid gland and testicle, and in various inflammatory granulation ulcers. In the wasting of the thyroid gland in myxoedema, or when the gland is completely removed by operation, myxomatous areas are found in the subcutaneous tissue of the skin, nerve-sheaths, &c.

Colloid.—This term is usually applied to a semi-solid substance of homogeneous and gelatinous consistence, which results partly from excretion and partly from degeneration of cellular structures, more particularly of the epithelial type. These cells become swollen by this translucent substance and are thrown off into the space where they become fused together, forming colloid masses. This substance differs from the mucins by being precipitated by tannic acid but not by acetic acid, and being endowed with a higher proportion of sulphur.

In the normal thyroid there is formed and stored up in the spaces this colloid material. The enlarged cystic goitres show, in the distended vesicles, an abnormal formation and retention of this substance (fig. 44, Pl. V.). Its character is readily changed by the abnormal activities which take place in these glands during some of the acute fevers; the semi-solid consistence may become mucoid or even fluid.

Serous degeneration is met with in epithelial cells in inflammatory conditions and following on burns. The vitality of these cells being altered there is imbibition and accumulation of watery fluid in their cytoplasm, causing swelling and vacuolation of the cells. The bursting of several of these altered cells is the method by which the skin vesicles are formed in certain conditions.

Glycogen is formed by the action of a ferment on the carbohydrates—the starches being converted into sugars. The sugars are taken up from the circulation and stored in a less soluble form—known as "animal starch"—in the liver and muscle cells; they play an important part in the normal metabolism of the body. The significance of glycogen in pathological conditions, or of its absence from the tissues in pathological conditions, is not clearly understood. It is said to be increased in saccharine diabetes and to be greatly diminished in starvation and wasting diseases.

Fat.—Fatty accumulations in the tissues of the body are found in health and in pathological conditions; these are usually recognized and described as fatty infiltrations and fatty degenerations, but there are intermediate conditions which make it difficult to separate sharply these processes.

The fatty accumulations known as infiltrations (figs. 45 and 46, Pl. V.) are undoubtedly the result of excessive ingestion of food material containing more neutral fats than the normal tissues can oxidize, or these, as a result of defective removal owing to enfeebled oxidative capacities on the part of the tissues, become stored up in the tissues.

In acute and chronic alcoholism, in phthisis, and in other diseases this fatty condition may be very extreme, and is commonly found in association with other tissue changes, so that probably we should look on these changes as a degeneration.

Adiposity or obesity occurs when we have an excessive amount of fat stored in the normal connective-tissue areas of adipose tissue. It may be caused by various conditions, e.g. overnutrition with lack of muscular energy, beer-drinking, castration, lactation, disturbed metabolism, some forms of insanity, and may follow on some fevers.

Fatty degeneration is a retrogressive change associated with the deposit of fatty granules or globules in the cytoplasm, and is caused by disorganized cellular activity (figs. 26 and 27, Pl. II.). It is frequently found associated with, or as a sequel to, cloudy swelling in intense or prolonged toxic conditions. Over and above the bacterial intoxications we have a very extreme degree of fatty degeneration, widely distributed throughout the tissues, which is produced by certain organic and inorganic poisons; it is seen especially in phosphorus and chloroform poisoning. The changes are also common in pernicious anaemia, advanced chlorosis, cachexias, and in the later stages of starvation. In diabetes mellitus, in which there is marked derangement in metabolism, extreme fatty changes are occasionally found in the organs, and the blood may be loaded with fat globules. This lipoemic condition may cause embolism, the plugging especially occurring in the lung capillaries.

Fatty degeneration is common to all dead or decaying tissues in the body, and may be followed by calcification.

Autolysis is a disintegration of dead tissues brought about by the action of their own ferments, while degeneration takes place in the still living cell. The study of autolytic phenomena which closely simulates the changes seen in the degenerating cell has thrown much light on these degenerative processes.

These conditions may be purely physiological, e.g. in the mammary gland during lactation or in sebaceous glands, caused by increased functional activity. It may follow a diminished functional activity, as in the atrophying thymus gland and in the muscle cells of the uterus after parturition.

Any of the abnormal conditions that bring about general or local defective nutrition is an important factor in producing fatty degeneration. ·

The part played by fats and closely allied compounds in normal and abnormal metabolism need not here be discussed, as the subject is too complex and the views on it are conflicting. It will be sufficient to state briefly what appears to be the result of recent investigation.

. The neutral fats are composed of fatty acids and glycerin. In the physiological process of intestinal digestion, the precursors of such fats are split up into these two radicles. The free fatty acid radicle then unites with an alkali, and becomes transformed into a soluble soap which is then readily absorbed in this fluid condition by the epithelial cells of the mucous membrane. There it is acted on by ferments (lipases) and converted into neutral fat, which may remain in the cell as such. By the reverse action on the part of the same ferments in the cell, these neutral fats may be redissolved and pass into the lacteals.

Many cells throughout the body contain this ferment. The soluble soaps which are probably conveyed by the blood will be quickly taken up by such cells, synthetized into neutral fats, and stored in a non-diffusible form till required. The fat in this condition is readily recognized by the usual microchemical and staining reactions. As fat is a food element essential to the carrying out of the vital energies of the cell, a certain amount of fatty matter must be present, in a form, however, unrecognizable by our present microchemical and staining methods.

Some investigators hold that the soaps may become combined with albumin, and that on becoming incorporated with the cytoplasm they can no longer be distinguished as fat. If from some cause the cell be damaged in such a way as to produce disintegration of the cytoplasm, there will be a breaking down of that combination, so that the fat will be set free from the complex protein molecule in which it was combined as a soap-albumin, and will become demonstrable by the usual methods as small droplets of oil. This splitting up of the fats previously combined with albumin in the cell by the action of natural ferments—lipases—and the setting free of the fats under the influence of toxins represent the normal and the pathological action in the production of so-called fatty degeneration.

Calcification.—Calcification and calcareous deposits are extremely common in many pathological conditions.

There are few of the connective tissues of the body which may not become affected with deposits of calcareous salts (fig. 47, Pl. V.). This condition is not so frequently seen in the more highly differentiated cells, but may follow necrosis of secreting cells, as is found in the kidney, in corrosive sublimate poisoning and in chronic nephritis. These conditions are quite distinct from the normal process of ossification as is seen in bone.

Many theories have been advanced to explain these processes, and recently the subject has received considerable attention. The old idea of the circulating blood being supersaturated with lime salts which in some way had first become liberated from atrophying bones, and then deposited, to form calcified areas in different tissues will have to be given up, as there is no evidence that this "metastatic" calcification ever takes place. In all probability no excess of soluble lime salts in the blood or lymph can ever be deposited in healthy living tissues.

At the present day both experimental and histological investigations seem to indicate that in the process of calcification there is a combination of the organic substances present in degenerated tissues, or in tissues of low vitality, with the lime salts of the body. From whatever cause the tissues become disorganized and undergo fatty degeneration, the fatty acids may become liberated and combine with the alkalies to form potash and soda soaps.

The potash and soda is then gradually replaced by calcium to form an insoluble calcium soap. The interaction between the soaps, the phosphates and the carbonates which are brought by the blood and lymph to the part results in the weaker fatty acids being replaced by phosphoric and carbonic acid, and thus in the formation of highly insoluble calcium phosphate and carbonate deposits in the disorganized tissues.

Pathological Pigmentations.—These pigmentary changes found in abnormal conditions are usually classified under (1) Albuminoid, (2) Haematogenous, (3) Extraneous.

1. The normal animal pigments and closely allied pigments are usually found in the skin, hair, eye, supra-renal glands, and in certain nerve cells. · These represent the albuminoid series, and are probably elaborated by the cells from albuminous substances through the influence of specific ferments. This pigment is usually intracellular, but may be found lying free in the intercellular substance, and is generally in the form of fine granules of a yellowish-brown or brown-black colour. In the condition known as albinism there is a congenital deficiency or entire absence of pigment. Trophic and nervous conditions sometimes cause localized deficiency of pigment which produces white areas in the skin.

Excessive pigmentation of tissue cells (fig. 48, Pl. V.) is seen in old age, and usually in an accompaniment of certain atrophic processes and functional disorders. Certain degenerative changes in the supra-renal glands may lead to Addison's disease, which is characterized by an excessive pigmentary condition of the skin and mucous membranes. This melanin pigment is found in certain tumour growths, pigmented moles of the skin, and especially in melanatic sarcomata (fig. 49, Pl. V.) and cancer. The action of the sun's rays stimulates the cells of the skin to increase the pigment as a protection to the underlying tissues, e.g. summer bronzing, "freckles," and the skin of the negro.

The coloured fats, or lipochromes, are found normally in some of the cells of the internal organs, and under certain pathological conditions. This pigment is of a light yellow colour, and contains a fatty substance that reacts to the fat-staining reagents. Little is known regarding this class of pigment.

2. Haematogenous pigments are derived from the haemoglobin of the red blood corpuscles. These corpuscles may break down in the blood vessels, and their colouring material (haemoglobin) is set free in the serum. But their disintegration is more commonly brought about by "phagocytosis" on the part of the phagocytic cells in the different organs concerned with the function of haemolysis, i.e. the liver, spleen, haemolymph glands and other tissues.

The haemoglobin may be transformed into haematoidin, a pigment that does not contain iron, or into a pigment which does contain iron, haemosiderin.

The haematoidin pigment may .vary in colour from yellowish or orange-red to a ruby-red, and forms granular masses, rhombic prisms or acicular crystals. It can be formed independently of cell activity, nor does it require oxygen. These crystals are extremely resistant to absorption, are found in old blood clots, and have been known to persist in old cerebral haemorrhages after many years. Haematoidin in normal metabolism is largely excreted by the liver in the form of bilirubin.

Haemosiderin, an iron-containing pigment (probably an hydrated ferrous oxide), is found in more or less loose combination with protein substances in an amorphous form as brownish or black granules. Cellular activity and oxygen appear to be essential for its development; it is found usually in the cells of certain organs, or it may be deposited in the intercellular tissues. Haemosiderin in the normal process of haemolysis is stored up in the cells of certain organs until required by the organism for the formation of fresh haemoglobin. In diseases where haemolysis is extreme, particularly in pernicious anaemia, there are relatively large quantities occasionally as much as ten times the normal amount of haemosiderin deposited in the liver.

In hepatogenous pigmentation (icterus or jaundice) we have the iron-free pigment modified and transformed by the action of the liver cells into bile pigment (bilirubin). If the discharge of this pigment from the liver by the normal channels be prevented, as by obstruction of the main bile ducts, the bile will accumulate until it regurgitates or is absorbed into the lymph and blood vessels, and is carried in a soluble state throughout the tissues, thus producing a general staining—an essential characteristic of jaundice.

3. In extraneous pigmentation we have coloured substances either in a solid or fluid state, gaining entrance into the organism and accumulating in certain tissues. The channels of entrance are usually by the respiratory or the alimentary tract, also by the skin. Pneumonokoniosis is due to the inhalation of minute particles of various substances—such as coal, stone, iron, steel, &c. These foreign particles settle on the lining membranes, and, by the activity of certain cells (fig. 50, Pl. V. and fig. 30, Pl. III.), are carried into the tissues, where they set up chronic irritation of a more or less serious nature according to the nature of the inhaled particles.

Certain metallic poisons give rise to pigmentation of the tissues, e.g. in the blue line on the gums around the roots of the teeth due to the formation of lead sulphide, or in chronic lead poisoning, where absorption may have taken place through the digestive tract, or, in the case of workers in lead and lead paints, through the skin. Prolonged ingestion of arsenic may cause pigmentary changes in the skin. If silver nitrate salts be administered for a long period as a medication, the skin that is exposed to light becomes of a bluish-grey colour, which is extremely persistent. These soluble salts combine with the albumins in the body, and are deposited as minute granules of silver albuminate in the connective tissue of the skin papillae, serous membranes, the intima of arteries and the kidney. This condition is known as argyria.

Various coloured pigments may be deposited in the tissues through damaged skin surface—note, for example, the well-known practice of "tattooing." Many workers following certain occupations show pigmented scars due to the penetration of carbon and other pigments from superficial wounds caused by gunpowder, explosions, &c..

Hyaline.—This term has been applied to several of the transparent homogeneous appearances found in pathological conditions. It is now commonly used to indicate the transparent homogeneous structureless swellings which are found affecting the smaller arteries and the capillaries. The delicate connective-tissue fibrillae of the inner coat of the arterioles are usually first and most affected. The fibrils of the outer coat also show the change to a less extent, while the degeneration very rarely spreads to the middle coat. This swelling of the walls may partly or completely occlude the lumen of the vessels.

Hyaline degeneration is found in certain acute infective conditions; the toxins specially act on these connective-tissue cell elements. It also seems to be brought about by chronic toxaemias, e.g. in subacute and chronic Bright's disease, lead poisoning and other obscure conditions. The hyaline material, unlike the amyloid, does not give the metachromatic staining reactions with methylene-violet or iodine. The chemical constitution is not certain. The substance is very resistant to the action of chemical reagents, to digestion, and possibly belongs to the glyco-proteids.

Amyloid.—The wax-like or amyloid substance has a certain resemblance to the colloid, mucoid and hyaline. It has a firm gelatinous consistence and wax-like lustre, and, microscopically, is found to be homogeneous and structureless, with a translucency like that of ground-glass. Watery solution of iodine imparts to it a deep mahogany-brown colour; iodine and sulphuric acid occasionally, but not always, an azure-blue, methyl-violet, a brilliant rose-pink and methyl-green gives a reaction very much like that of methyl-violet, but not so vivid. The reaction with iodine is seen best by direct light; the reactions with the other substances are visible only by transmitted light. The name "amyloid" was applied to it by Virchow on account of the blue reaction which it gives occasionally with iodine and sulphuric acid, resembling that given with vegetable cellulose. It is now known to have nothing in common with vegetable cellulose, but is regarded as one of the many albuminoid substances existing in the body under pathological conditions. Virchow's conjecture as to the starchy nature of the substance was disproved by Friedrich and Kekule, who confirmed Professor Miller's previous finding as to its albuminous or protein nature. Oddi in 1894 isolated from the amyloid liver a substance

which Schmiedeberg had previously obtained from cartilage and named "chondroitinic-sulphuric acid" (*Chondroitinschwefelsäure*). It also occurs in bones and elastic tissue, but is not present in the normal human liver. Oddi does not regard it as the essential constituent of amyloid, chiefly because the colour reactions are forthcoming in the residuum after the substance has been removed, while the substance itself does not give these reactions. Quite likely the amyloid may be a combination of the substance with a proteid. The soda combination of the acid as obtained from the nasal cartilage of pigs had the composition $C_{18}H_{31}N_2NSO_{17}$.

Krakow in 1897 clearly demonstrated it to be a proteid in firm combination with chrondroitin-sulphuric acid. As probably the protein constituent varies in the different organs, one infers that this will account for the varying results got from the analysis of the substance obtained from different organs in such cases.

This amyloid substance is slowly and imperfectly digested by pepsin—digestion being more complete with trypsin and by autolytic enzymes.

There is no evidence that this material is brought by the circulating blood and infiltrates the tissues. It is believed rather that the condition is due to deleterious toxic substances which act for prolonged periods on the tissue elements and so alter their histon proteins that they combine *in situ* with other protein substances which are brought by the blood or lymph.

Amyloid develops in various organs and tissues and is commonly associated with chronic phthisis, tubercular disease of bone and joints, and syphilis (congenital and acquired). It is known to occur in rheumatism, and has been described in connexion with a few other diseases. A number of interesting experiments, designed to test the relationship between the condition of suppuration and the production of amyloid, have been made of late years. The animal most suitable for experimenting upon is the fowl, but other animals have been found to react. Thus Krakow and Nowak, employing the frequent subcutaneous injection of the usual organisms of suppuration, have induced in the fowl the deposition within the tissues of a homogeneous substance giving the colour reactions of true amyloid. When hardened in spirit, however, the greater part of this experimental amyloid in the fowl vanishes, and the reactions are not forthcoming. They were unable to verify any direct connexion between its production and the organism of tubercle. These observations have been verified in the rabbit, mouse, fowl, guinea-pig and cat by Davidsohn, occasionally in the dog by Lubarsch; and confirmatory observations have also been made by Czerny and Maximoff. Lubarsch succeeded in inducing it merely by the subcutaneous injection of turpentine, which produces its result, it is said, by exciting an abscess. Nowak, however, found later that he could generate it where the turpentine failed to induce suppuration; he believes that it may arise quite apart from the influence of the organisms of suppuration, that it is not a biological product of the micro-organisms of disease, and also that it has nothing to do with emaciation. It is a retrogressive process producing characteristic changes in the fine connective-tissue fibrils. The change appears to begin in the fibrils which lie between the circular muscle fibres of the middle coat of the smaller arterioles and extends both backwards and forwards along the vessels. It spreads forwards, affecting the supporting fibres outside the epithelium of the capillaries, and then passes to the connective-tissue fibrils of the veins. The secreting cells never show this change, although they may become atrophied or destroyed by the pressure and the disturbance of nutrition brought about by the swollen condition of the capillary walls. The circulation is little interfered with, although the walls of the vessels are much thickened by the amyloid material (fig. 51, Pl. V.).

Amyloid Bodies.—These are peculiar bodies which are found in the prostate, in the central nervous system, in the lung, and in other localities, and which get their name from being very like starch-corpuscles, and from giving certain colour reactions closely resembling those of vegetable cellulose or even starch itself. They are minute structures having a round or oval shape, concentrically striated, and frequently showing a small nucleus-like body or cavity in their centre. Iodine gives usually a dark brown reaction, sometimes a deep blue; iodine and sulphuric acid almost always call forth an intense deep blue reaction; and methyl-violet usually a brilliant pink, quite resembling that of true amyloid. They are probably a degeneration-product of cells.

Spurious Amyloid.—If a healthy spinal cord be hung up in spirit for a matter of six months or more, a glassy substance develops within it quite like true amyloid. It further resembles true amyloid in giving all its colour reactions. The reaction with methyl-violet, however, differs from that with true amyloid in being evanescent.

RESPONSE OF TISSUES TO STIMULATION

A stimulus may be defined as every change of the external agencies acting upon an organism; and if a stimulus come in contact with a body possessing the property of irritability, i.e. the capability of reacting to stimuli, the result is stimulation (Verworn). Stimuli comprise chemical, mechanical, thermal, photic and electrical changes in the environment of the organism. A stimulus may act on all sides and induce a general effect without direction of movement, but in the production of movement in a definite direction the stimulus must be applied unilaterally. Stimuli applied generally, not unilaterally, in most cases induce increased divisibility of the cells of the part.

Thus the poison of various insects induces in plants the cellular new formation known as a gall-nut; a foreign body implanted in a limb may become encysted in a capsule of fibrous tissue; septic matter introduced into the abdomen will cause proliferation of the lining endo(epi)thelium; and placing an animal (salamander, Galeotti) in an ambient medium at a higher temperature than that to which it is accustomed naturally, increases the rapidity of cell-division of its epithelium with augmentation of the number of karyokinetic figures. Hair and some other like structures grow luxuriantly on a part to which there is an excessive flux of blood. Bone (e.g. drill-bones) may develop in a soft tissue with no natural bone-forming tendencies, as a result of interrupted pressure, or a fatty tumour may arise in the midst of the natural subcutaneous fat in the same circumstances.

Among stimuli acting unilaterally, perhaps none has proved more interesting, in late times, than what is known as Chemiotaxis. By it is meant the property an organism endowed with the power of movement has to move towards or away from a chemical stimulus applied unilaterally, or, at any rate, where it is applied in a more concentrated state on the one side than on the others, and more particularly where the concentration increases gradually in one direction away from the living organism acted upon. Observed originally by Engelmann in bacteria, by Stahl in myxomycetes, and by Pfeffer in ferns, mosses, &c., it has now become recognized as a widespread phenomenon. The influence of the chemical substance is either that of attraction or repulsion, the one being known as positive, the other as negative chemiotaxis.

The female organs of certain cryptogams, for instance, exert a positive chemiotactic action upon the spermatozoids, and probably, as Pfeffer suggests, the chemical agent which exerts the influence is malic acid. No other substance, at least, with which he experimented had a like effect, and it is possible that in the archegonium which contains the ovum malic acid is present. Massart and Bordet, Leber, Metchnikoff and others have studied the phenomenon in leucocytes, with the result that while there is evidence of their being positively chemiotactic to the toxins of many pathogenic microbes, it is also apparent that they are negatively influenced by such substances as lactic acid.

From a pathological point of view the subject of chemiotaxis must be considered along with that of phagocytosis. Certain free mobile cells within the body, such as blood-leucocytes, as well as others which are fixed, as for instance the endothelium of the hepatic capillaries, have the property of seizing upon some kinds of particulate matter brought within their reach. Within a quarter of an hour after a quantity of cinnabar has been injected into the blood of the frog nearly every particle will be found engulfed by the protoplasm of the leucocytes of the circulating blood. Some bacteria, such as those of anthrax, are seized upon in the same manner, indeed; very much as small algae and other particles are incorporated and devoured by amoeba. Melanine particles formed in the spleen in malaria, which pass along with the blood through the liver, are appropriated by the endothelial cells of the hepatic capillaries, and are found embedded within their substance. If the particle enveloped by the protoplasm be of an organic nature, such as a bacterium, it undergoes digestion, and ultimately becomes destroyed, and accordingly the term "phagocyte" is now in common use to indicate cells having the above properties. This phagocytal action of certain cells of the body is held by Metchnikoff and his followers to

have an important bearing on the pathology of immunity. Phagocytes act as scavengers in ridding the body of noxious particles, and more especially of harmful bacteria.

A further application of the facts of chemiotaxis and phagocytosis has been made by Metchnikoff to the case of Inflammation. It is well known that many attempts to define the process of inflammation have been made from time to time, all of them more or less unsatisfactory. Among the latest is that of Metchnikoff: "Inflammation generally," he says, "must be regarded as a phagocytic reaction on the part of the organism against irritants. This reaction is carried out by the mobile phagocytes sometimes alone, sometimes with the aid of the vascular phagocytes, or of the nervous system." Given a noxious agent in a tissue, such, let us say, as a localized deposit of certain bacteria, the phagocytes swarm towards the locality where the bacteria have taken up their residence. They surround individual bacteria, absorb them into their substance, and ultimately destroy them by digestion. The phagocytes are attracted from the blood vessels and elsewhere towards the noxious focus by the chemiotaxis exerted upon them by the toxins secreted by the bacteria contained within it. The chemiotaxis in this instance is positive, but the toxins from certain other bacteria may act negatively; and such bacteria are fraught with particular danger from the fact that they can spread through the body unopposed by the phagocytes, which may be looked upon as their natural enemies.

NATURAL PROTECTION AGAINST PARASITISM

The living organism is a rich storehouse of the very materials from which parasites, both animal and vegetable, can best derive their nourishment. Some means is necessary, therefore, to protect the one from the encroachments of the other. A plant or animal in perfect health is more resistant to parasitical invasion than one which is ill-nourished and weakly. Of a number of plants growing side by side, those which become infected with moulds are the most weakly, and an animal in low health is more subject to contagious disease than one which is robust. Each organism possesses within itself the means of protection against its parasitical enemies, and these properties are more in evidence when the organism is in perfect health than when it is debilitated.

One chief means employed by nature in accomplishing this object is the investment of those parts of the organism liable to be attacked with an armour-like covering of epidermis, periderm, bark, &c. The grape is proof against the inroads of the yeast-plant so long as the husk is intact, but on the husk being injured the yeast-plant finds its way into the interior and sets up vinous fermentation of its sugar. The root of the French vine is attacked by the Phylloxera, but that of the American vine, whose epidermis is thicker, is protected from it. The larch remains free from parasitism so long as its covering is intact, but as soon as this is punctured by insects, or its continuity interfered with by cracks or fissures, the Peziza penetrates, and before long brings about the destruction of the branch. So long as the epidermis of animals remains sound, disease germs may come in contact with it almost with impunity, but immediately on its being fissured, or a larger wound made through it, the underlying parts, the blood and soft tissues, are attacked by them. A very remarkable instance of an acquired means of protecting a wound against parasitical invasion is to be found in granulations. Should these remain unbroken they constitute a natural barrier to the penetration of most pathogenic and other forms of germ-life into the parts beneath. Bacteria of various kinds which alight upon their surfaces begin to fructify in abundance, but are rapidly destroyed as they burrow deeply. This is accomplished by a twofold agency, for while numbers of them are seized upon by the granulation phagocytes, others are broken up and dissolved by the liquid filling the granulation interspaces (Afanassieff). This latter, or histolytic, property is not confined to the liquid of granulations; normal blood-serum possesses it to a certain extent, and under bacterial influence it may become very much exalted. Jürgelünas makes out that when an animal is rendered immune to a particular micro-organism this histolytic property becomes exalted.

DROPSY

During conditions of health a certain quantity of lymphy liquid is constantly being effused into the tissues and serous cavities of the body, but in the case of the tissues it never accumulates to excess, and in that of the serous cavities it is never more than

PLATE II.

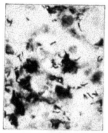

Fig. 22.—Tubercle bacilli in tissues from human lung in a case of acute phthisis. The bacilli are seen lying as short rods, singly and in clumps, in the caseous and degenerated tissues of the lung.

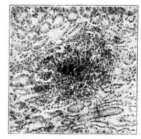

Fig. 25.—Acute abscess in the kidney. A small cellular area formed by emigrated polymorpho-nuclear leucocytes surrounding a central mass of bacteria.

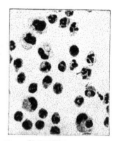

Fig. 23.—Inflammatory cells from acute exudate. Numerous polymorpho-nuclear leucocytes and a few mono-nuclear cells, one of which has taken up a leucocyte into its interior (phagocytosis).

Fig. 28.—Muscle fibre greatly increased in size, from hypertrophied heart.

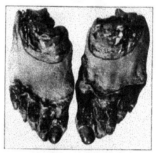

Fig. 24.—Symmetrical gangrene of toes (3 months' duration), showing the sharp "line of demarcation" between the mummified toes and the more healthy tissue.

Fig. 29.—Muscle fibres from atrophied heart. (Contrast Fig. 28.)

Fig. 26.—Fatty degeneration of heart from case of pernicious anæmia. Many of the muscle fibres show numerous droplets of oil seen as dark round granules.

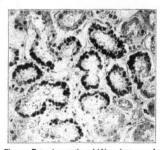

Fig. 27.—Fatty degeneration of kidney from case of starvation. Black droplets of oil are seen in the epithelial cells lining the secreting tubules.

PLATE III.   PATHOLOGY

Fig. 30. — Anthracosis — coal-miner's lung — showing excessive accumulation of carbon pigment in the lymphatic spaces around the vessels of the lung.

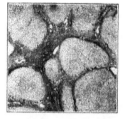

Fig. 36.—Polylobular cirrhosis, or "Gin-drinker's Liver," showing well-formed fibrous overgrowth which has divided up the liver tissue into irregular masses and caused atrophic and degenerative changes in the liver cells.

Fig. 32. — Fibroblasts in young temporary granulation tissue. These are spindle shaped and have long processes. It is from these cells the permanent fibrous tissue is formed.

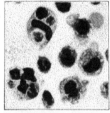

Fig. 31.—Cells from inflammatory exudate showing active phagocytosis. The mono-nuclear cells are ingesting and digesting many of the polymorpho-nuclear leucocytes. Note that these phagocytic cells are pushing out protoplasmic processes (pseudopodia) by which they grasp their victims.

Fig. 35.—Scar tissue in a healed wound. Note the disappearance of blood-vessels and that the cellular character has diminished—the fibroblasts having now developed into well-formed fibrous tissue.

Fig. 33.—Healing abscess showing a wall of young cellular and vascular granulation tissue, which separates the pus area (top of Fig.) from the muscle fibres seen at lower part of Fig.

Fig. 37.—Chronic interstitial myo-carditis, showing the muscle fibres in the heart wall being separated and becoming atrophied by a slow fibrous overgrowth of the connective tissue

Fig. 34. — Granulation tissue showing the character and relation of the cellular elements to the new blood-vessels in the young temporary tissue.

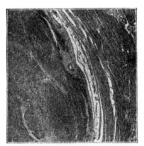

Fig. 38.—Myoma uteri. A simple fibro-myomatous tumour growing in the wall of the uterus Note the sharp line of demarcation between the growth and the tissue in which it is growing.

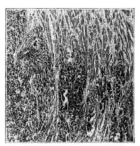

Fig. 39.—Secondary cancerous growth in heart wall. Note that the malignant cells are invading and destroying the muscle fibres of the heart.

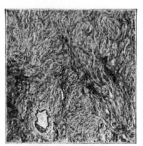

Fig. 40.—Fibroma. A simple tumour composed of well-differentiated fibrous tissue. The fibres are arranged in irregular bundles forming a dense firm tissue.

Fig. 41.—Small round-celled sarcoma. A malignant tumour composed of undifferentiated masses of cells. These cells are readily carried to distant parts and give rise to secondary growths.

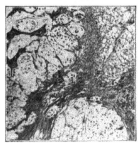

FIG. 42.—"Colloid cancer of stomach" showing the cancer cells in the spaces being transformed into the "colloid material."

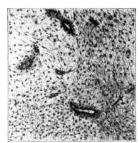

Fig. 43.—Myxoma showing the stellate and branching cells with their processes interlacing and forming a network. The mucinoid substance is contained in the fine meshes.

PLATE V.   PATHOLOGY

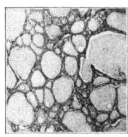

Fig. 44.—Thyroid gland—cystic goitre. The gland spaces vary in size and many may show marked cystic formation. These vesicles are filled with the colloid material.

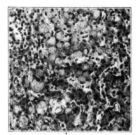

Fig. 45.—Liver. Fatty Infiltration. The liver cells are seen to contain a large globule of fat which pushes the cell nucleus to one side—giving the signet-ring appearance.

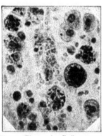

Fig. 50.—Phagocytic cells (in sputum) which have taken into their proto-plasm particles of carbon pigment.

Fig. 47.—Pudic artery showing calcified areas in the muscular coat of the vessel. These degenerated parts are darkly stained owing to the calcareous particles having a strong affinity for the hæmo-toxylin stain.

Fig. 46.—Heart. Fatty Infiltration. The fat cells are increased and infiltrate the connective tissue be-tween the bundles of muscle fibres. These are pressed upon and become atrophied, and may ultimately be replaced by adipose tissue.

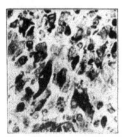

Fig. 49.—Melanotic sarcoma. Many of these malignant cells develop and accumulate in their protoplasm gran-ules of melanin pigment.

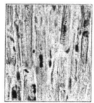

Fig. 48.—Brown atrophy of heart. The muscle fibres show the pig-ment granules, which are of a light yellow colour, situated specially at the poles of the fibre nucleus and extending short distance in the long axis of the fibre.

Fig. 51.—Liver, waxy. The swollen waxy capillaries are pressing on the columns of liver cells and are causing marked atrophy.

sufficient to keep them moist. When any excessive accumulation takes place the condition is known as "hydrops" or "dropsy." A "transudate" is a liquid having a composition resembling that of blood-serum, while the term "exudate" is applied to an effused liquid whose composition approaches that of the blood-plasma in the relationship of its solid and liquid parts, besides in most cases containing numbers of colourless blood-corpuscles. Exudates are poured out under inflammatory conditions, while none of the truly dropsical effusions are of inflammatory origin; and hence the class of exudates, as above defined, may be rejected from the category of liquids we are at present considering. Where the dropsical condition is more or less general the term "anasarca" is applied to it; if the tissues are infiltrated locally the term "oedema" is employed; and various names are applied, with a local significance, to dropsies of individual parts or cavities, such as "hydrothorax," "hydroperitoneum" or "ascites," "hydrocephalus," and so on. In "anasarca" the tissues which suffer most are those which are peculiarly lax, such as the lower eyelids, the scrotum, and the backs of the hands and feet. It is invariably the result of some cause acting generally, such as renal disease, valvular defect of the heart, or an impoverished state of the blood; while a mere oedema is usually dependent upon some local obstruction to the return of blood or lymph, or of both, the presence of parasites within the tissue, such as the filaria sanguinis hominis or trichina spiralis, or the poisonous bites of insects. Dropsy of the serous cavities is very commonly merely part of a general anasarca, although occasionally it may be, as in the case of ascites, the sequel to an obstruction in the venous return. Dropsical liquids are usually pale yellow or greenish, limpid, with a saltish taste and alkaline reaction, and a specific gravity ranging from 1005 to 1024. They all contain albumen and throw down a precipitate with heat and nitric acid. None of them, in man, coagulates spontaneously, although they contain fibrinogen. The addition of some of the liquid squeezed out from a blood-clot, of the squeezed blood-clot itself, or of a little blood-serum, is sufficient to throw down a fibrinous coagulum (Buchanan), evidently by these substances supplying the fibrin-ferment. The proteid constituents are very much like those of blood-serum, although they never come up to them in amount (Runeberg). The quantity of proteid matter in a purely dropsical effusion never amounts to that of an inflammatory exudation (Lassar). Certain peculiar substances, probably degenerative products, some of them reducing copper, are occasionally met with. The liquid of ascites sometimes contains chyle in abundance (hydrops lacteus), the escape having taken place from a ruptured receptaculum chyli.

In a given case of anasarca due to a cause acting generally, it will be found that the liquid of the pleural cavity always contains the highest percentage of proteid, that of the peritoneal cavity comes next, that of the cerebral ventricles follows this, and the liquid of the subcutaneous areolar tissue contains the lowest. The reason of this is apparently that the regular pressure of the pleural, and partly of the peritoneal, cavity tends to aspirate a liquid relatively thicker, so to speak, that that effused where no such extraneous mechanism is at work (James).

The subject of the conditions under which dropsical liquids are poured out opens up a very wide question, and one about which there is the greatest diversity of opinion. It turns in part, but in part only, upon the laws regulating the effusion of lymph, and physiologists are by no means at one in their conclusions on this subject. Thus Ludwig was of opinion that the lymph-flow is dependent upon two factors, first, difference in pressure of the blood in the capillaries and the liquid in the plasma spaces outside; and, secondly, chemical interchanges setting up osmotic currents through the vessel-walls. His results, so far, have been confirmed by Starling, who finds that the amount of lymph-flow from the thoracic duct is dependent upon difference in pressure. It varies with the increase of the intracapillary or decrease of the extracapillary pressure, and is also in part regulated by the greater or lesser permeability of the vessel-walls. Heidenhain, on the other hand, rejected entirely the filtration view of lymph-formation, believing that the passage of lymph across the capillary wall is a true secretion brought about by the secretory function of the endothelial plates. Starling does not accept this view, and cannot regard as an article of faith Heidenhain's dictum that normally filtration plays no part in the formation of lymph. Lazarus-Barlow, again, looks upon the pouring out of lymph as evidence of the demands of the tissue-elements for nutrition. An impulse is communicated to the blood vessels in accordance with this demand, and a greater or smaller outflow is the result. He traces various local dropsies to the starvation from which the tissues are suffering, the liquid accumulating in excess in accordance with the demand for more nourishment. It may be asked, however, whether a dropsical tissue is being held in a high state of nutrition, and whether, on the contrary, the presence of lymph in excess in its interstices does not tend to impair its vitality rather than to lend it support. According to Rogowicz and Heidenhain, certain substances increase the quantity of lymph given off from a part by acting upon the cells of the capillary wall; they hold, in fact, that these substances are true lymphagogues. Heidenhain recognises two classes, first, such substances as peptone, leech extract and crayfish extract; and, secondly, crystalloids such as sugar, salt, &c. Starling sees no reason to believe that members of either class act otherwise than by increasing the pressure in the capillaries or by injuring the endothelial wall. The members of the first class influence the endothelial plates of the capillaries injuriously, inducing thereby increased permeability; those of the second class (sugar, &c.), on injection into the blood, attract water from the tissues and cause a condition of hydraemic plethora with increased capillary pressure. The increased flow of lymph is due to the increased pressure in the abdominal capillaries.

It is now coming to be recognized that increase of blood pressure alone is not sufficient to account for all dropsical effusions. Much more important is the effect of the alteration in the amount of crystalloids in the tissues and blood and therefore of the alteration in the osmotic pressure between these. Loeb found experimentally that increase of metabolic products in muscle greatly raised its osmotic pressure, and so it would absorb water from a relatively concentrated sodium chloride solution. Welch produced oedema of the lungs experimentally by increasing the pressure in the pulmonary vessels by ligature of the aorta and its branches, but this raised the blood pressure only about one-tenth of an atmosphere, while in some of Loeb's experiments the osmotic pressure, due to retained metabolic products, was equal to over thirty atmospheres. Thus differences in osmotic pressure may be much more powerful in producing oedema than mere differences in blood pressure.

Now differences in the amount of crystalloids cause alteration in osmotic pressure while the proteid content affects it but little; and of the crystalloids the chlorides appear to be those most liable to variation.

Widal, Lemierre and other French observers have noted a diminution in the excretion of chlorides in nephritis associated with oedema; Widal and Javal found that a chloride-free diet caused diminution in the oedema and a chloride containing diet an increase of oedema. Oliver and Audibert published some cases of cirrhosis of the liver with ascites in which they got results comparable to those of Widal. Some other observers, however, have not got such good results with a chloride-free diet, and Märishler, Scheel, Limbeck, Dreser and others, dispute Widal's hypothesis of a retention of chlorides as being the cause of oedema, in the case of renal dropsy at all events; they assert that the chlorides are held back in order to keep the osmotic pressure of the fluid, which they assume to have been effused, equal to that of the blood and tissues. Certainly not all cases of renal dropsy show diminution in the excretion of chlorides. Bainbridge suggests that a retention of metabolic products may cause the oedema in renal disease, Bradford having previously shown that loss of a certain amount of renal tissue caused retention of metabolic products in the tissues. As sodium chloride is one of the most permeable of crystalloids it seems strange that damage to the renal tissue should impede its excretion. Cushny has shown experimentally that slowing of the blood-flow through renal tissue causes less sodium chloride to appear in the urine while the excretion of urea and sulphates remains unaffected; apparently the chloride, being more permeable, is reabsorbed and so only appears to be excreted in less quantity.

In the dropsy of cardiac disease, owing to the deficient oxidation from stagnation of blood, metabolic products must accumulate in the tissues; also lymph return must be impeded by the increased pressure in the veins and so dropsy results (Wells).

The local oedema seen in some nervous affections might be explained on the hypothesis of increased metabolic activity in these areas due to some local nervous stimulation.

Thus, while increased pressure in the blood or lymph vessels may be one factor, and increased permeability of the capillary endothelium another, increased osmotic pressure in the tissues and lymph is probably the most important in the production of dropsy. This increased osmotic pressure is again due to accumulation of crystalloids in the tissues, these products of metabolism due to deficient oxidation from alteration in the blood or other cause, or, it may be, as in some cases of nephritis, owing to a retention or reabsorption of chlorides in the tissues.

PRACTICAL APPLICATIONS

Medicine and surgery have never been slow to appropriate and apply the biological facts of pathology, and at no period have they followed more closely in its wake than during the last quarter of the 19th century. When, for instance, the cause of septic infection had been revealed, the prophylaxis of the disease became a possibility. Seldom has it happened, since the discovery of the law of gravity, that so profound an impression has been made upon the scientific world at large as by the revelation of the part played by germ-life in nature; seldom has any discovery been fraught with such momentous issues in so many spheres of science and industry.

The names of Pasteur and Lister will descend to posterity as those of two of the greatest figures in the annals of medical science, and indeed of science in general, during the 19th century. The whole system of treatment of tubercular disease has been altered by the discovery of the tubercle microphyte. Previously consumptive individuals were carefully excluded from contact with fresh air, and were advised to live in rooms almost hermetically sealed and kept at a high temperature. The treatment of the disease has now gone off in the opposite direction. Sanatoria have started up all over Europe and elsewhere for its treatment on the open-air principle. Individuals suffering from pulmonary phthisis are encouraged to live night and day in the open, and with the best results. The rapid diagnosis of diphtheria, by recognizing its bacillus, has enabled the practitioner of medicine to commence the treatment early, and it has also enabled the medical officer of health to step in and insist on the isolation of affected persons before the disease has had time to spread. The discovery of the parasite of malaria by Laveran, and of the method by which it gains entrance to the human body, through the bite of a particular variety of mosquito, by Manson and Ross, promises much in the way of eradication of the disease in the future. One of the most remarkable practical outcomes of germ-pathology, however, has been the production of the immunized sera now employed so extensively in the treatment of diphtheria and other contagious diseases. By the continuous injections under the skin, in increasing doses, of the toxins of certain pathogenic micro-organisms, such as that of diphtheria, an animal—usually the horse—may be rendered completely refractory to the disease. Its serum in course of time is found to contain something (antitoxin) which has the power of neutralizing the toxin secreted by the organism when introduced into the body. This immunity can be transferred to a fresh host (e.g. man) by injecting such serum subcutaneously. The modern system of hygiene is in great part founded upon recent pathology. The recognition of the dangers accompanying the drinking of polluted water or milk, or of those attached to the breathing of a germ-polluted atmosphere, has been the natural sequence of an improved knowledge of pathology in its bacteriological relationships. Skin-grafting and regeneration of bone are among not the least remarkable applications of pathological principles to the combat with disease in recent times; and in this connexion may also be mentioned the daring acts of surgery for the relief of tumours of the brain, rendered practicable by improved methods of localization, as well as operations upon the serous cavities for diseased conditions within them or in their vicinity.

For the special pathological details of various diseases, see the separate articles on PARASITIC DISEASES; NEURO-PATHOLOGY; DIGESTIVE ORGANS; RESPIRATORY SYSTEM; BLOOD: Circulation; METABOLIC DISEASES; FEVER; BLADDER; KIDNEYS; SKIN DISEASES; EYE DISEASES; HEART DISEASE; EAR, &c.; and the articles on different diseases and ailments under the headings of their common names.

AUTHORITIES.—Adami, "Inflammation," Allbutt's System of Med. (London, 1896), vol. ; Afanassieff, "Granulation Tissue and Infection," Centralbl. f. allg. Path. u. path. Anat. (1896), vii. Arnold, "Finer Structure of the Cell," Arch. f. path. Anat. (1879), lxxvii. ; Beyerinck, Beobachtungen üb. d. ersten Entwicklungsphasen einiger Cynipidengallen (Amsterdam, 1882); Bordet, "Phagocytosis," Ann. de l'inst. Pasteur (1895), x. ; Buchner, "Chemiotaxis of Leucocytes," Berl. klin. Wochenschr. (1890), xxvii. 1084; Cancer: synopsis of recent literature. See The Practitioner (1899), vol. ix.; Chatin, "Direct Cellular Division," Compt. rend. acad. d. sc. (1898), cxxvi. 1163; Coats, Manual of Pathology (London, 1895); Cohnheim, Vorlesungen üb. allg. Path. Berlin (1877-1880); Cornil, "Organization of Clot within Vessels," J. de l'anat. et physiol.

(1897), xxxiii. 201; Davidsohn, "Experimental Amyloid," Arch. f. path. Anat. (1897), cl. ; Delage, "Studies in Merogony," Arch. de zool. expér. et gen. ; vii. Ehrlich, "Mastzellen," Arch. f. mik. Anat. (1877), xiii. Engelmann, "Chemiotaxis of Oxygen for Bacteria," Arch. f. d. ges. Physiol. (1881), xxv. Farmer, "Present Position of some Cell Problems," Nature (1898), lviii. ; Flemming, "Studies in Regeneration of the Tissues," Arch. f. mik. Anat. (1885), xxiv. ; Frank, Die Krankheiten der Pflanzen (Breslau, 1895); Galeotti, "Experimental Production of Irregular Karyokinetic Processes," Beitr. z. path. Anat. u. z. allg. Path. (1893), xiv. Gravitz, "Slumber Cells," Arch. f. path. Anat. (1892), cxxvii. Ilahn, "Increase of Natural Resistance by Production of Hyperleucocytosis," Berl. klin. Wochenschr. (1896), xxxiii. ; Hamilton, "Process of Healing," Journ. Anat. Physiol. and Path. (1879), xiii. also "Organization of Sponge," Edin. Med. Journ.(1 ; xxvii. Text-Book of Pathology (London,1894); Hansemann, "Pathological Mitosis," Arch. f. path. Anat. (1891), cxxiii. Hartig, Text-Book of the Diseases of Trees (Eng. trans., London, 1894); Heidenhain, "Action of Poisons on Nerves of Submaxillary Gland," Arch. f. d. ges. Physiol. (1872) v. also, "Question of Lymph Production," ibid. (1891), xlix. also, "Central-Body of Giant-cells," Morph. Arb. (1897), vii. O. Hertwig, Die Zelle u. d. Gewebe (1898, also Eng. trans., 1895); Heubelsen, "Sarcoma and Plastic Inflammation," Arch. f. path. Anat. (1887), cvii. ; Justi, "Unna's Plasma-Cells in Granulations," Arch. f. path. Anat. (1897), cl. ; Jürgelünas, "Protective Action of Granulations." Beiträge z. path. Anat. u. z. allg. Path., Ziegler (1901), xxix. "Histology of Mucoid," Arch. f. path.Anat. (1892), cxxix. ; Krawkow, "Chemistry of Amyloid," Arch. f. exper. Path. u. Pharmakol. (1897) xl. also "Experimental Amyloid." Arch. f. path. Anat. (1898), cliii. Krompecher, "Plasma-Cells," Beitr. z. path. Anat. u. z. allg. Path. (1898), xxiv. ; Labbé, La Cytologie expérimentale (Paris, 1898); Lazarus-Barlow, "Lymph Formation." Journ. Physiol. Cama (1895-1896), xix. also, Manual of General Pathology (London, 1898); Loeb, "Certain Activities of the Epithelial Tissue of Skin of Guinea-pig, &c.," Johns Hopkins Hosp. Bull., Balt. (1898), ix. also "Artificial Production of Normal Larvae," Amer. Journ. Physiol. (1899), iii. ; Löwit, "Relationship of Leucocytes to Bacterial Action," Beitr. z. path. Anat. u. z. allg. Path. (1897), xxii. Lubarsch, "Experimental Amyloid," Arch. f. path. Anat. (1897), cl. ; Lubarsch and Ostertag, Ergebnisse der spec. path. Morphologie u. Physiologie des Menschen (Wiesbaden, 1896); Ludwig, Lehrbuch der Physiol. vol. ii.; Marshall Ward, Timber and some of its Diseases (London, 1889); Massart and Bordet, "Irritability of Leucocytes," Journ. publ. par la soc. des sci. méd. et nat. de Bruxelles (1890), vol. v.; Metchnikoff, Lectures on Comp. Path. of Inflammation (Eng. trans., London, 1893); Notkin, "Nature of Colloid in Thyroid Gland," Arch. f. path. Anat. (1896), cxiv. (Suppl. Hft.); Nowak, "Experimental Researches on Amyloidosis," Arch. f. path. Anat. (1898), cliii. Oddi, "Nature of Amyloid," Arch. f. exp. Path. u. Pharmakol. (1894), xxxiii. Paget, "Address on Healing," Brit. Med. Journ. (1880), ii. ; Pelagatti, "Blastomycetes and Hyaline degeneration," Arch. f. path. Anat. (1897), cl. ; Penzo, "Influence of Temperature on Cellular Regeneration," Archivios per la science medica (1892); Pfeffer, "Chemiotaxis," Unters. aus d. bot. Inst., zu Tübingen (1884), ; ibid. (1888); Pickardt, "Chemistry of Pathological Exudates," Berl. klin. Wochenschr. (1897), xxxiv. ; Plimmer, "Aetiology and Histology of Cancer," Practitioner (1899), ix. Ruffer and Plimmer, "Cancer Bodies," Journ. Path. and Bacteriol. (1892-1893), ; Runeberg, "Filtration of Albuminous Liquids," Arch. f. d. ges. Physiol. (1885), xxxv. also "Diagnostic Value of Proteid in Dropsical Liquids," Deutsch. Arch. f. klin. Med. (1885), xxxiv. ; Russell, "Fuchsin Bodies," Brit Med. Journ. (1890), ii. 1356; Salvioli, "Production of Oedema," Virchow and Hirsch's Jahresbericht (1885), ; Schottländer, "Nuclear and Cell Division in Epithelium of Inflamed Skin," Arch. f. mik. Anat. (1888), xxxi. ; Scrawinska, "Reticular Structure of Nerve-Cells," Compt. rend. acad. d. sc. (1896), cxxiii. ; Senator, "On Transudation," Arch. f. path. Anat. (1888), cxi. ; Shattock," Healing of Incisions in Vegetable Tissues," Journ. Path. and Bacteriol. (1898), v. v. Sicherer, "Chemiotaxis of Leucocytes of Warm-blooded Animals outside the Body," Münch. med. Wochenschr. (1896), xliii. ; Siegert, "Corpora Amylacea," Arch. f. path. Anat. (1892), cxxix. ; Starling, "Mechanical Factors in Lymph Production," Journ. of Physiol. (1894), xvi. ; also a number of other papers bearing upon lymph-production, in same; Thorne, "Endothelia as Phagocytes," Arch. f. mik. Anat. (1898), liii. ; Thoma, Lehrbuch d. allg. Path. (1894), also vol. (Eng. trans., London, 1896); Trambusti, "On Structure and Division of Sarcoma Cells," Beitr. z. path. Anat. u. z. allg. Path. (1897), xxii. ; Verworn, General Physiology (Eng. trans., London, 1899); Weismann, Essays upon Heredity (Eng. trans., Oxford, 1891); also, The Germ Plasm (London, 1893); Welch, "Oedema of Lung," Arch. f. path. Anat. (1878), lxxii. Wilson, The Cell in Development and Inheritance (London, 1896); Ziegler, "Entzündung," in Eulenburg's Real Encyclopädie, also Text-Book of Special Pathological Anatomy (Eng. trans., New York, 1897).

(J. R. Mr.")

PATIALA, or PUTTIALA, a native state of India, within the Punjab. It is the premier state of the Punjab, and chief of the three Sikh Phulkian states—Patiala, Nabha and Jind. It consists of three detached blocks of territory, mostly in the plains, though one portion extends into the hills near Simla. Area 5412 sq. m.; pop. (1901), 1,596,692; estimated revenue, £449,000; military force (including Imperial Service troops), 3429 men. The state was founded by a Sikh chieftain about 1763, and came under British protection, with the other cis-Sutlej states, in 1809. Patiala remained conspicuously loyal to the British during the Mutiny of 1857, Narindar Singh, its ruler, setting an example to the other Sikh states which was of the utmost value. The maharaja, Rajendra Singh, who died in 1900, was devoted to riding and sport. He took part personally in the Tirah campaign of 1897-98, with a battalion of his own Imperial Service Infantry and a field troop of Imperial Service lancers. In recognition of his services on this occasion he received the G.C.S.I. He was succeeded by his son, Bhupindar Singh, who was born in 1891. The town of Patiala has a station on the branch of the North-Western railway from Rajpura to Bhatinda. Pop. (1901), 53,545. It contains several fine modern buildings, including palaces, hospitals and schools.

See *Phulkian States Gazetteer* (Lahore, 1909).

PATIENCE, the name given to certain card-games played by a single person. Although known for centuries, they have seldom been mentioned by writers on playing-cards, and the rules have for the most part been handed down orally. There are two main varieties; in one luck alone prevails, since the player has no choice of play but must follow strict rules; in the other an opportunity is given for the display of skill and judgment, as the player has the choice of several plays at different stages of the game. The usual object is to bring the cards into regular ascending or descending sequences. The starting card is called the "foundation," and the "family" (sequence) is "built" upon it. In other varieties of Patience the object is to make pairs, which are then discarded, the game being brought to a successful conclusion when all the cards have been paired; or to pair cards which will together make certain numbers, and then discard as before. There are hundreds of Patience games, ranging from the simplest to the most complicated.

See Jarbart's *Games of Patience* in De la Rue's series of handbooks (1905); *Patience Games*, by "Cavendish" (London, 1890); *Cyclopaedia of Card and Table Games*, by Professor Hoffmann (London, 1891); *Patience Games*, by Professor Hoffmann (London, 1892); *Games of Patience*, by A. Howard Cady (Spalding's Home Library, New York, 1896); *Dick's Games of Patience*, edited by W. B. and H. B. Dick (New York, 1898); *Games of Patience* (4 series), by Mary E. W. Jones (London, 1898); *Le Livre illustré des patiences*, by "Comtesse de Blanccœur" (Paris, 1898).

PATINA (probably from the Latin word for a flat dish, from *patere*, to lie open; cf. "paten"), a thin coating or incrustation which forms on the surface of bronze after exposure to the air or burial in the ground. It is looked on as a great addition to the beauty of the bronze, especially when it is of the green colour found on antique bronzes (see BRONZE). By extension, the word is applied to the discoloured or incrusted surface of marble, flint, &c., acquired after long burial in the ground or exposure to the air, and also to the special colour given to wood surfaces by time.

PATIÑO, JOSÉ or JOSEF (1666-1736), Spanish statesman, was born at Milan, on the 11th of April 1666. His father, Don Lucas Patiño de Ibarra, Señor de Castelar, who was by origin a Galician, was a member of the privy council and inspector of the troops in the duchy of Milan for the king of Spain, to whom it then belonged. His mother's maiden name was Beatrice de Rosales y Facini. The Patiño family were strong supporters of the Bourbon dynasty in the War of the Spanish Succession. The elder brother Baltasar, afterwards marquis of Castelar, had a distinguished career as a diplomatist, and his son Lucas was a general of some note. José Patiño, who had been intended for the priesthood but adopted a secular career, was granted the reversion of a seat in the senate of Milan on the accession of Phillip V. In 1700, but on the loss of the duchy he was transferred to Spain, and put on the governing body of the military orders in 1707. During the War of Succession he served as intendent of Estremadura, and then of Catalonia from 1711 to 1718. In 1717 he was named intendent of the navy, which had just been reorganized on the French model. His capacity and his faculty for hard work secured him the approval of Alberoni, with whom, however, he was never on very friendly terms in private life. Patiño's Italian education, which affected his Spanish style, and caused him to fall into Italianisms all through his life, may have served to recommend him still further. Patiño profoundly distrusted the reckless foreign policy undertaken by Alberoni under the instigation of the king and his obstinate queen, Elizabeth Farnese. He foretold that it would lead to disaster, but as a public servant he could only obey orders, and he had the chief merit of organizing the various expeditions sent out to Sardinia, Sicily and Ceuta between 1718 and 1720. He became known to the king and queen in the latter year, while he was acting as a species of commissary-general during the disastrous operations against the French troops on the frontier of Navarre. It was not, however, until 1726 that he was fully trusted by the king. He and his brother, the marquis of Castelar, were the chief opponents of the adventurer Ripperdá, who captivated the king and queen for a time. On the fall of this remarkable person, Patiño was named secretary for the navy, the Indies—that is to say the colonies—and for foreign affairs. The war office was added to the other departments at a later date. From the 13th of May 1726 until his death on the 3rd of November 1736 Patiño was in fact prime minister. During the later part of his administration he was much engaged in the laborious negotiations with England in relation to the disputes between the two countries over their commercial and colonial rivalries in America, which after his death led to the outbreak of war in 1739.

In his *Patiño y Campillo* (Madrid, 1882), Don Antonio Rodriguez Villa has collected the dates of the statesman's life, and has published some valuable papers. But the best account of Patiño's administration is to be found in Coxe's *Memoirs of the Kings of Spain of the House of Bourbon* (London, 1815), which is founded on the correspondence of the English ministers at Madrid.

PATIO, the Spanish name for an inner court or enclosed space in a house, which is open to the sky. The "patio" is a common feature in houses in Spain and Spanish America. The word is generally referred to the Lat. *patere*, to lie open; cf. "patent," or to *spatium*, space.

PATKUL, JOHANN REINHOLD (1660-1707), Livonian politician and agitator, was born in prison at Stockholm, where his father lay under suspicion of treason. He entered the Swedish army at an early age and was already a captain when, in 1689, at the head of a deputation of Livonian gentry, he went to Stockholm to protest against the rigour with which the land-recovery project of Charles XI. was being carried out in his native province. His eloquence favourably impressed Charles XI., but his representations were disregarded, and the offensive language with which, in another petition addressed to the king three years later, he renewed his complaints, involved him in a government prosecution. To save himself from the penalties of high treason, Patkul fled from Stockholm to Switzerland, and was condemned in *contumaciam* to lose his right hand and his head. His estates were at the same time confiscated. For the next four years he led a vagabond life, but in 1698, after vainly petitioning the new king, Charles XII., for pardon, he entered the service of Augustus the Strong of Saxony and Poland, with the deliberate intention of wresting from Sweden Livonia, to which he had now no hope of returning so long as that province belonged to the Swedish Crown. The aristocratic republic of Poland was obviously the most convenient suzerain for a Livonian nobleman; so, in 1698, Patkul proceeded to the court of the king-elector at Dresden and bombarded Augustus with proposals for the partition of Sweden. His first plan was a combination against her of Saxony, Denmark and Brandenburg; but, Brandenburg failing him, he was obliged very unwillingly to admit Russia into the partnership. The tsar was to be content with Ingria and Esthonia, while Augustus was to take Livonia, nominally as a fief of Poland, but really as an hereditary possession of the Saxon house. Military operations against Sweden's Baltic provinces were to be begun simultaneously by the Saxons and Russians. After thus forging the first link of the partition treaty, Patkul proceeded to Moscow, and, at a secret conference held at Preobrazhenskoye, easily persuaded Peter the Great to accede to the nefarious league (Nov. 11, 1699). Thoughout the earlier, unluckier days of the Great Northern War, Patkul was the mainstay of the confederates. At Vienna, in 1702, he picked up the Scottish general George Benedict Ogilvie, and enlisted him in Peter's service. The same year, recognizing the unprofitableness of serving such a master as Augustus, he exchanged the Saxon for the Russian service. Peter was glad enough to get a man so famous for his talents and energy, but Patkul speedily belied his reputation. His knowledge was too local and limited. On the 19th of August 1704 he succeeded, at last, in bringing about a treaty of alliance between Russia and the Polish republic to strengthen the hands of Augustus, but he failed to bring Prussia also into the anti-Swedish league because of Frederick I.'s fear of Charles and jealousy of Peter. From Berlin Patkul went on to Dresden to conclude an agreement with the imperial commissioners for the transfer of the Russian contingent from the Saxon to the Austrian service. The Saxon ministers, after protesting against the new arrangement, arrested Patkul and shut him up in the fortress of Sonnenstein (Dec. 19, 1705), altogether disregarding the remonstrances of Peter against such a gross violation of international law. After the peace of Altranstädt (Sept. 24, 1707) he was delivered up to Charles, and at Kazimierz in Poland (Oct. 10, 1707) was broken alive on the wheel, Charles rejecting an appeal for mercy from his sister, the princess Ulrica, on the ground that Patkul, as a traitor, could not be pardoned for example's sake.

See O. Sjögren, *Johan Reinhold Patkul* (Swed.) (Stockholm, 1882); Anton Buchholtz, *Beiträge zur Lebensgeschichte J. R. Patkuls* (Leipzig, 1893). (R. N. B.)

PATMORE, COVENTRY KERSEY DIGHTON (1823–1896), English poet and critic, the eldest son of Peter George Patmore, himself an author, was born at Woodford in Essex, on the 23rd of July 1823. He was privately educated, being his father's intimate and constant companion, and derived from him his early literary enthusiasm. It was his first ambition to become an artist, and he showed much promise, being awarded the silver palette of the Society of Arts in 1838. In the following year he was sent to school in France, where he studied for six months, and began to write poetry. On his return his father contemplated the publication of some of these youthful poems; but in the meanwhile Coventry had evinced a passion for science and the poetry was set aside. He soon, however, returned to literary interests, moved towards them by the sudden success of Tennyson; and in 1844 he published a small volume of *Poems*, which was not without individuality, but marred by inequalities of workmanship. It was widely criticized, both in praise and blame; and Patmore, distressed at its reception, bought up the remainder of the edition and caused it to be destroyed. What chiefly wounded him was a cruel review in *Blackwood*, written in the worst style of unreasoning abuse; but the enthusiasm of private friends, together with their wiser criticism, did much to help him and to foster his talent. Indeed, the publication of this little volume bore immediate fruit in introducing its author to various men of letters, among whom was Dante Gabriel Rossetti, through whose offices Patmore became known to Holman Hunt, and was thus drawn into the eddies of the pre-Raphaelite movement, contributing his poem " The Seasons " to the *Germ*. At this time Patmore's father became involved in financial embarrassments; and in 1846 Monckton Milnes secured for the son an assistant-librarianship in the British Museum, a post which he occupied industriously for nineteen years, devoting his spare time to poetry. In 1847 he married Emily, daughter of Dr Andrews of Camberwell. At the Museum he was austere and remote among his companions, but was nevertheless instrumental in 1852 in starting the Volunteer movement. He

wrote an important letter to *The Times* upon the subject, and stirred up much martial enthusiasm among his colleagues. In the next year he republished, in *Tamerton Church Tower*, the more successful pieces from the *Poems* of 1844, adding several new poems which showed distinct advance, both in conception and treatment; and in the following year (1854) appeared the first part of his best known poem, " The Angel in the House," which was continued in " The Espousals " (1856), " Faithful for Ever " (1860), and " The Victories of Love " (1862). In 1862 he lost his wife, after a long and lingering illness, and shortly afterwards joined the Roman Catholic Church. In 1865 he married again, his second wife being Miss Marianne Byles, second daughter of James Byles of Bowden Hall, Gloucester; and a year later purchased an estate in East Grinstead, the history of which may be read in *How I managed my Estate*, published in 1886. In 1877 appeared *The Unknown Eros*, which unquestionably contains his finest work in poetry, and in the following year *Amelia*, his own favourite among his poems, together with an interesting, though by no means undisputable, essay on *English Metrical Law*. This departure into criticism he continued further in 1879 with a volume of papers, entitled *Principle in Art*, and again in 1893 with *Religio poetae*. Meanwhile his second wife died in 1880, and in the next year he married Miss Harriet Robson. In later years he lived at Lymington, where he died on the 26th of November 1896.

A collected edition of his poems appeared in two volumes in 1886, with a characteristic preface which might serve as the author's epitaph. " I have written little," it runs; " but it is all my best; I have never spoken when I had nothing to say, nor spared time or labour to make my words true. I have respected posterity; and should there be a posterity which cares for letters, I dare to hope that it will respect me." The obvious sincerity which underlies this statement, combined with a certain lack of humour which peers through its naïveté, points to two of the principal characteristics of Patmore's earlier poetry; characteristics which came to be almost unconsciously merged and harmonized as his style and his intention drew together into unity. In the higher flights, to which he arose as his practice in the art grew perfected, he is always noble and often sublime. His best work is found in the volume of odes called *The Unknown Eros*, which is full not only of passages but of entire poems in which exalted thought is expressed in poetry of the richest and most dignified melody. The animating spirit of love, moreover, has here deepened and intensified into a crystalline harmony of earthly passion with the love that is divine and transcending; the outward manifestation is regarded as a symbol of a sentiment at once eternal and quint-essential. Spirituality informs his inspiration; the poetry is of the finest elements, glowing and alive. The magnificent piece in praise of winter, the solemn and beautiful cadences of " Departure," and the homely but elevated pathos of " The Toys," are in their various manners unsurpassed in English poetry for sublimity of thought and perfection of expression. Patmore is one of the few Victorian poets of whom it may confidently be predicted that the memory of his greater achievements will outlive all consideration of occasional lapses from taste and dignity. He wrote, at his best, in the grand manner, melody and thought according with perfection of expression, and his finest poems have that indefinable air of the inevitable which is after all the touchstone of the poetic quality. His son, Henry John Patmore (1860–1883), left a number of poems posthumously printed at Mr Daniell's Oxford Press, which show an unmistakable lyrical quality. (A. WA.)

The standard life of Patmore is the *Memoirs and Correspondence* (1901), edited by Basil Champneys. See also E. W. Gosse, *Coventry Patmore* (1905, " Literary Lives " series), and an essay by Mrs Meynell prefixed to the selection (1905) in the " Muses' Library."

PATMOS, an island in the east of the Aegean Sea, one of the group of the Sporades, about 28 m. S.S.W. of Samos, in 37° 20′ N. lat. and 26° 35′ E. long. Its greatest length from N. to S. is about 10 m., its greatest breadth 6 m., its circumference, owing to the winding nature of the coast, about 37 m. The island, which is volcanic, is bare and rocky throughout; the hills, of which the highest rises to about 800 ft., command magnificent views of the neighbouring sea and islands. The skill of the natives as seamen is proverbial in the archipelago. The deeply indented coast, here falling in huge cliffs sheer into the sea, there retiring to form a beach and a harbour, is favourable to commerce, as in former times it was to piracy. Of the numerous bays and harbours the chief is that of Scala, which, running far into the land on the eastern side, divides the island into two nearly equal portions— a northern and a southern. A narrow isthmus separates Scala from the bay of Merika on the west coast. On the belt of land between the two bays, at the junction between the northern and southern half of the island, stood the ancient town. On the hill above are still to be seen the massive remains of the citadel, built partly in polygonal style. The modern town stands on a hill top in the southern half of the island. A steep paved road leads to it in about twenty minutes from the port of Scala. The town clusters at the foot of the monastery of St John, which, crowning the hill with its towers and battlements, resembles a fortress rather than a monastery. Of the 600 MSS. once possessed by the library of the monastery only 240 are left. The houses of the town are better built than those of the neighbouring islands, but the streets are narrow and winding. The population is about 4000. The port of Scala contains about 140 houses, besides some old well-built magazines and some potteries. Scattered over the island are about 300 chapels.

Patmos is mentioned first by Thucydides (iii. 33) and afterwards by Strabo and Pliny. From an inscription it has been inferred that the name was originally Patnos. Another ancient inscription seems to show that the Ionians settled there at an early date. The chief, indeed the only, title of the island to fame is that it was the place of banishment of St John the Evangelist, who according to Jerome (*De scr. ill.* c. 9) and others, was exiled thither under Domitian in A.D. 95, and released about eighteen months afterwards under Nerva. Here he is said to have written the Apocalypse; to the left of the road from Scala to the town, about half-way up the hill, a grotto is still shown (τὸ σπήλαιον τῆς Ἀποκαλύψεως) in which the apostle is said to have received the heavenly vision. It is reached through a small chapel dedicated to St Anne. The Acts of St John, attributed to Prochorus, narrates the miracles wrought by the apostle during his stay on the island, but, strangely enough, while describing how the Gospel was revealed to him in Patmos, it does not so much as mention the Apocalypse. During the dark ages Patmos seems to have been entirely deserted, probably on account of the pirates. In 1088 the emperor Alexis Comnenus, by a golden bull, which is still preserved, granted the island to St Christodulus for the purpose of founding a monastery. This was the origin of the monastery of St John, which now owns the greater part of the southern half of Patmos, as well as farms in Crete, Samos and other neighbouring islands. The embalmed body of the saintly founder is to be seen to this day in a side chapel of the church. The number of the monks, which amounted to over a hundred at the beginning of the 18th century, is now much reduced. The abbot (ἡγούμενος) has the rank of a bishop, and is subject only to the patriarch of Constantinople. There is a school in connexion with the monastery which formerly enjoyed a high reputation in the Levant. The modern town was recruited by refugees from Constantinople in 1453, and from Crete in 1669, when these places fell into the hands of the Turks. The island is subject to Turkey; the governor is the pasha of Rhodes. The population is Greek. The women are chiefly engaged in knitting cotton stockings, which, along with some pottery, form the chief exports of the island.

See Tournefort, *Relation d'un voyage du Levant* (Lyons, 1717); Walpole, *Memoirs* (relating to Turkey) (London, 1820); Ross, *Reisen auf den griechischen Inseln* (Stuttgart and Halle, 1840–1852); Guérin, *Description de l'île de Patmos* (Paris, 1856); H. F. Tozer, *Islands of the Aegean*, pp. 178–195.

PATNA, a city, district, and division of British India, in the Behar province of Bengal. The city, which is the most important commercial centre in Bengal after Calcutta, lies on the right bank of the Ganges, a little distance below the confluence of the Sone and the Gogra, and opposite the confluence of the Gandak, with a station on the East Indian railway 332 m. N.W. of Calcutta. Municipal area, 6184 acres. Pop. (1901), 134,785. Including the civil station of Bankipur to the west, the city stretches along the river bank for nearly 9 miles. Still farther west is the military cantonment of Dinapur. A government college was founded in 1862. Other educational institutions include the Behar school of engineering organized in 1897.

Patna city has been identified with Pataliputra (the Palibothra of Megasthenes, who came as ambassador from Seleucus Nicator to Chandragupta about 300 B.C.). Megasthenes describes Palibothra as being the capital of India. He adds that its length was 80 stadia, and breadth 15; that it was surrounded by a ditch 30 cubits deep, and that the walls were adorned with 570 towers and 64 gates. According to this account the circumference of the city would be 190 stadia or 25½ miles. Asoka built an outer masonry wall and beautified the city with innumerable stone buildings. The greater part of the ancient city still lies buried in the silt of the rivers under Patna and Bankipur at a depth of from 10 to 20 ft. The two events in the modern history of the district are the massacre of Patna (1763) and the Sepoy Mutiny in 1857. The former occurrence, which may be said to have settled the fate of Mahommedan rule in Bengal, was the result of a quarrel between the nawab, Mir Kasim, and the English authorities regarding transit duties, which ultimately led to open hostilities. The company's sepoys, who had occupied Patna city by the orders of the company's factor, were driven out by the nawab's troops and nearly all killed. The remainder afterwards surrendered, and were put into confinement, together with the European officers and the entire staff of the Cossimbazar factory, who had also been arrested on the first outbreak of hostilities. Mir Kasim was defeated in two pitched battles at Gheria and Udhanala (Oodeynullah) in August and September 1763, and in revenge ordered the massacre of all his prisoners, which was carried out with the help of a renegade in his employment named Walter Reinhardt, (afterwards the husband of the famous Begum Samru). About sixty Englishmen were murdered on this occasion, the bodies being thrown into a well belonging to the house in which they were confined. At the outbreak of the mutiny in May 1857 the three sepoy regiments stationed at Dinapur (the military cantonment of Patna, adjoining the city) were allowed to retain their arms till July, when, on an attempt being made to disarm them, they broke into open revolt. Although many who attempted to cross the Ganges in boats were fired into and run down by a pursuing steamer, the majority crossed by the Sone river into Shahabad, where they joined the rebels under Kuar Singh who were then besieging a small European community at Arrah.

The DISTRICT OF PATNA has an area of 2075 sq. m.; pop. (1901), 1,624,985. Throughout the greater part of its extent the district is a level plain; but towards the south the ground rises into hills. The soil is for the most part alluvial, and the country along the bank of the Ganges is peculiarly fertile. The general line of drainage is from west to east; and high ground along the south of the Ganges forces back the rivers flowing from Gaya district. The result is that during the rains nearly the whole interior of the district south of a line drawn parallel to the Ganges, and 4 or 5 m. from its bank, is flooded. In the south-east are the Rajgir Hills, consisting of two parallel ridges running southwest, with a narrow valley between, intersected by ravines and passes. These hills, which seldom exceed 1000 ft. in height, are rocky and clothed with thick low jungle, and contain some of the earliest memorials of Indian Buddhism. The chief rivers are the Ganges and the Sone. The only other river of any consequence is the Punpun, which is chiefly remarkable for the number of petty irrigation canals which it supplies. So much of the river is thus diverted that only a small portion of its water ever reaches the Ganges at Fatwa. The chief crops are rice, wheat, barley, maize and pulse; poppy and potatoes are also of importance. Apart from the Sone canal, irrigation is largely practised from private channels and also from wells. The district is traversed by the main line of the East Indian railway, with two branches south to Gaya and Bihar.

The DIVISION OF PATNA extended across both sides of the Ganges. It comprised the seven districts of Patna, Gaya, Shahabad, Saran, Champaran, Muzaffarpur and Darbhanga. Total area, 23,748 sq. m.; pop. (1901), 15,514,987. In 1908 the four last districts north of the Ganges were formed into the new division of Tirhut; and the name of Patna division was confined to the three first districts south of the Ganges.

See L. A. Waddell, *Discovery of the Exact Site of Asoka's Classic Capital of Palaliputra* (1892); Vincent Smith, *Asoka* (" Rulers of India " series, 1901); *Patna District Gazetteer* (Calcutta, 1907).

PATNA, one of the Orissa tributary states in Bengal, with an area of 2399 sq. m. It lies in the basin of the Mahanadi river, and is divided by a forest-clad hilly tract into a northern and a southern portion, both of which are undulating and well cultivated. Pop. (1901), 277,748, showing a decrease of 16% in the decade, mainly due to the effects of famine in 1900. Nearly the whole population consists of Oriyas. The capital is Bolangir: pop. (1901), 3706. The principal crop is rice. The maharajas of Patna were formerly heads of a group of states known as the *athara garhjat* or " eighteen forts." They are Chauhban Rajputs, and claim to have been established in Patna for six centuries. Patna was the scene of a rebellion of the Khonds, followed by atrocities on the part of their rulers, in 1869, and, in consequence, came under British management in 1871. The maharaja Ramchandra Singh, installed in 1894, was insane and put an end to his own life in the following year, whereupon his uncle, Lal Dalganjan Singh, became chief, undertaking to administer with the assistance of a diwan or minister appointed by the British government. The powers of this official were extended in 1900 after a serious outbreak of dacoity. Till 1905 the state was included in the Central Provinces.

PATOIS, a French term strictly confined to the dialect of a district or locality in a country which has a common literary language, often used of the form of a common language as spoken by illiterate or uneducated persons, marked by vulgarisms in pronunciation, grammar, &c. The origin of the word is not certain. It has been taken to be a corruption of *patrois*, from Low Lat. *partriensis*, of or belonging to one's *patria*, or native country, fatherland.

PATON, JOHN BROWN (1830–   ), British Nonconformist divine, was born on the 17th of December 1830. He was educated at London, Poole and Spring Hill College, Birmingham; he graduated B.A. at London University in 1849, and was Hebrew and New Testament prizeman in 1850 and gold medallist in philosophy in 1854. He received the honorary degree of doctor of divinity from Glasgow University in 1881. When the Nottingham Congregational Institute was founded in 1863 he became the first principal, a post which he held till 1898, when he was succeeded by James Alexander Mitchell (1849–1905), who from 1903 till his death was general secretary of the Congregational Union. Paton became vice-president of the British and Foreign Bible Society in 1907. He took an active part in the foundation and direction of a number of societies for religious and social work, notably the National Home Reading Union Society and English Land Colonization Society, and was a constant contributor to literary reviews. His publications include *The Two-fold Alternative* (3rd ed., 1900), *The Inner Mission of the Church* (new ed., 1900), and two volumes of collected essays. His son, John Lewis Paton (b. 1863), who headed the Cambridge classical tripos in 1886, became head master of Manchester grammar school in 1903.

PATON, SIR JOSEPH NOEL (1821–1901), British painter, was born, on the 13th of December 1821, in Wooleys Alley, Dunfermline, where his father, a fellow of the Scottish Society of Antiquaries, carried on the trade of a damask manufacturer. He showed strong artistic inclinations in early childhood, but had no regular art training, except a brief period of study in the Royal Academy School in 1843. He gained a prize of £200 in the first Westminster Hall competition, in 1845, for his cartoon " The Spirit of Religion," and in the following year he exhibited at the Royal Scottish Academy his " Quarrel of Oberon and Titania." A companion fairy picture, " The Reconciliation of Oberon and Titania," went to Westminster Hall in 1847, and for it and his picture of " Christ bearing the Cross " he was awarded a prize of £300 by the Fine Arts Commissioners. The two Oberon pictures are in the National Gallery of Scotland, where they have long been a centre of attraction. His first exhibited picture, " Ruth Gleaning," appeared at the Royal Scottish Academy in 1844. He began to contribute to the Royal Academy of London in 1856. Throughout his career his preference was for allegorical, fairy and religious subjects. Among his most famous pictures are " The Pursuit of Pleasure " (1855), " Mors Janua Vitae " (1866), " Oskold and the Elf-maids " (1874), and " In Die Malo " (1882). Sir Noel Paton also produced a certain amount of sculpture, more notable for design than for searching execution. He was elected an associate of the Royal Scottish Academy in 1847, and a full member in 1850; he was appointed Queen's Limner for Scotland in 1866, and received knighthood in 1867. In 1878 the University of Edinburgh conferred upon him the degree of LL.D. He was a poet of distinct merit, as his *Poems by a Painter* (1861) and *Spindrift* (1867) pleasantly exemplified. He was also well known as an antiquary, his hobby, indeed, being the collection of arms and armour. Sir Noel died in Edinburgh on the 26th of December 1901. His eldest son, Diarmid Noel Paton (b. 1859), became regius professor of physiology in Glasgow in 1906; and another son, Frederick Noel Paton (b. 1861), became in 1905 director of commercial intelligence to the government of India.

PATRAS (Gr. *Patrai*), the chief fortified seaport town on the west coast of Greece, and chief town of the province of Achaea and Elis, on a gulf of the same name, 70 m. W.N.W. of Corinth. There are two railway stations, one in the north-east on the line to Athens (via Corinth), the other on the line to Pyrgos. Pop. (1889), 33,529; (1907), 37,401. It has been rebuilt since 1821 (the War of Independence), seat of a Greek archappeal court. chief port reece, from which the great bulk of documents are despatched. The port, formed by a mole and a breakwater, begun in 1836, offers a fair harbour for vessels drawing up to 22 ft. The exports consist of currants, sultanas, valones, tobacco, olive oil, olives in brine, figs, citrons, wine, brandy, cocoons, and lamb, goat, and kid skins. The imports consist chiefly of colonial produce, manufactured goods and sulphate of copper. The two most interesting buildings are the castle, a medieval structure on the site of the ancient acropolis, and the cathedral of St Andrew, which is highly popular as the reputed burial-place of the saint.

The foundation of Patras goes back to prehistoric times, the legendary account being that Eumelus, having been taught by Triptolemus how to grow grain in the rich soil of the Glaucus valley, established three townships, Aroe (i.e. ploughland), Antheia (the flowery), and Mesatis (the middle settlement), which were united by the common worship of Artemis Triclaria at her shrine on the river Meilichus. The Achaeans having strengthened and enlarged Aroe, called it Patrae, as the exclusive residence of the ruling families, and it was recognized as one of the twelve Achaean cities. In 419 B.C. the town was, by the advice of Alcibiades, connected with its harbour by long walls in imitation of those at Athens. The whole armed force was destroyed by Metellus after the defeat of the Achaeans at Scarphela, and many of the remaining inhabitants forsook the city; but after the battle of Actium Augustus restored the ancient name Aroe, introduced a military colony of veterans from the 10th and 12th legions (not, as is usually said, the 22nd), and bestowed the rights of coloni on the inhabitants of Rhypae and Dyme, and all the Locri Ozolae except those of Amphissa. Colonia Augusta Aroe Patraeis became one of the most populous of all the towns of Greece; its colonial coinage extends from Augustus to Gordian III. That the town was the scene of the martyrdom of St Andrew is purely apocryphal, but, like Corinth, it was an early and effective centre of Christianity; its archbishop is mentioned in the lists of the Council of Sardica in 347. In 551 it was laid in ruins by an earthquake. In 807 it was able without external assistance to defeat the Slavonians (Avars), though most of the credit of the victory was assigned to St Andrew, whose church was enriched by the imperial share of the spoils, and whose archbishop was made superior of the bishops of Methone, Lacedaemon and Corone. Captured in 1205 by William of Champlitte and Villehardouin, the city became the capital and its archbishop the primate of the principality of Achaea. In 1387 De Heredia, grand master of the order of the Hospital at Rhodes, endeavoured to make himself master of Achaea and took Patras by storm. At the close of the 15th century the city was governed by the archbishop in the name of the pope; but in 1428 Constantine, son of John VI., managed to get possession of it for a time. Patras was at length, in 1687, surrendered by the Turks to the Venetians, who made it the seat of one of the seven fiscal boards into which they divided the Morea. In 1714 it again fell, with the rest of the Morea, into Turkish hands. It was at Patras that the Greek revolution began in 1821; but the Turks, confined to the citadel, held out till 1828.

PATRIARCH (M.E. and O. Fr. *patriarche*, Lat. *patriarcha*, Gr. πατριάρχης, from πατριά, clan, and ἀρχή, rule), originally the father or chief of a tribe, in this sense now used more especially of the " patriarchs " of the Old Testament, *i.e.* Abraham, Isaac and Jacob, with their forefathers, and the twelve sons of Jacob. In late Jewish history the title " patriarch " (Heb. *nâsî*, prince, chief) was given to the head of the sanhedrim in Palestine, and is sometimes, though wrongly, applied to the " exilarch," a head of the Jewish college at Babylon.

In the early centuries of the Christian Church the designation " patriarch " was applied, like " archbishop," to bishops of the more important sees as a merely honorary style. It developed into a title implying jurisdiction over metropolitans, partly as a result of the organization of the empire into " dioceses," partly owing to the ambition of the greater metropolitan bishops, which had early led them to claim and exercise authority in neighbouring metropolitanates. At the Council of Chalcedon (451) the patriarchs still bore the title of " exarch "; it was not till the 7th century that that of " patriarch " was fixed as proper to the bishops of Constantinople, Alexandria, Antioch and Jerusalem, " exarch " being reserved for those of Ephesus and Caesarea, who had fallen to a lower rank. In the West the only patriarch in the fully developed sense of the Eastern Church has been the bishop of Rome, who is patriarch as well as pope.

PATRICIANS (Lat. *patricius*, an adjectival form from *pater*, father; not, as some say, from *pater* and *ciere*, to call), a term originally applied to the members of the old citizen families of ancient Rome (see I. below). Under the later Roman Empire the name was revived by the Byzantine emperors as the title of a new order of nobility. Subsequently it was used as a personal title of honour for distinguished servants of Constantine I. and his successors, and was conferred on barbarian chiefs (II. below). It was afterwards conferred by the popes on the Frankish kings. In the medieval Italian republics, *e.g.* Genoa and Venice, the term was applied to the hereditary aristocracy (*patrizio*), and in the free cities of the German Empire it was borne by distinguished citizens (*patrizier*). In Italy it is still used for the hereditary nobility. From these specific uses the word has come into general use as a synonym of " aristocrat " or " noble," and implies the possession of such qualities as are generally associated with long descent, hereditary good breeding and the like. In Church history a sect founded by Patricius (c. 387), teacher of Symmachus the Marcionite, are known as the Patricians; they believed that all flesh was made by the devil. The name is also, though rarely, applied to the Roman Catholic body in Ireland regarded as the followers of St Patrick.

I. From the earliest period known to us the free population

of Rome contains two elements, patricians and plebeians, the former class enjoying all political privileges, the latter un-privileged. The derivation and significance of the two names have been established with certainty. The patricians (*patricii*) are those who can point to fathers, *i.e.* those who are members of the clans (*gentes*) whose members originally comprised the whole citizen body. The plebeians (*plebs, plebes*) are the complement (from root *pleo*, fill, see PLEBS) of the noble families possessing a genealogy, and include all the free population other than the patricians. It has been held by T. Mommsen that the plebeian order had its sole origin in the clients who attached themselves in a position of semi-freedom to the heads of patrician houses, and gradually evolved a freedom and citizenship of their own (see PATRON AND CLIENT). The logical consequence of this view is that the *plebs* as an order in the state is of considerably later growth than the beginning of the city, the patricians being originally the only freemen and the only citizens. But this view is untenable on two grounds. First, in the struggle between the two orders for political privilege we find the clients struggling on the side of the patricians against the main body of the plebeians (Livy ii. 56). Again, a method of taking up Roman citizenship which is well attested for a very early period reveals the possibility of a plebeian who does not stand in any relation to a patron. When an immigrant moved to Rome from one of the cities of the Latin league, or any city which enjoyed the *jus commercii* with Rome, and by the exercise of the right of voluntary exile from his own state (*jus exulandi*), claimed Roman citizenship, it is impossible to suppose that it was necessary for him to make application to a Roman patron to represent him in his legal transactions; for the *jus commercii* gave its holder the right of suing and being sued in his own person before Roman courts. Such an immigrant, therefore, must have become at once a free plebeian citizen of Rome. It may therefore be assumed that long before the clients obtained the right to hold land in their own names and appear in the courts in their own persons there was a free *plebs* existing alongside of the patricians enjoying limited rights of citizenship. But it is equally certain that before the time of Servius Tullius the rights and duties of citizenship were practically exercised only by the members of the patrician clans. This is perhaps the explanation of the strange fact that the clients, who through their patrons were attached to these clans, obtained political recognition as early as the plebeians who had no such semi-servile taint. At the time of the Servian reforms both branches of the *plebs* had a plausible claim to recognition as members of the state, the clients as already partial members of the *curia* and the *gens*, the unattached plebeians as equally free with the patricians and possessing clans of their own as solid and united as the recognized *gentes.*

But not only can it be shown that patricians and plebeians coexisted as distinct orders in the Roman state at an earlier date than the evolution of citizenship by the clients. It has further been established on strong archaeological and linguistic evidence that the long struggle between patricians and plebeians in early Rome was the result of a racial difference between them. There is reason to believe that the patricians were a Sabine race which conquered a Ligurian people of whom the plebeians were the survivors (see ROME: *History*). Apart from the definite evidence, the theory of a racial distinction gains probability from the fact that it explains the survival of the distinction between the *patricii*, men with a family and genealogy, and the rest of the citizens, for some time after the latter had acquired the legal status of *patres* and were organized in *gentes* of their own; for on this theory privilege would belong not to all who could trace free descent but only to those who could trace descent to an ancestor of the conquering race. The family organization of the conquering race was probably higher than that of the conquered, and was only gradually attained by the latter. Thus descent from a father would be hereditary in the dominant race to form the title of that race (*patricii*), and when that term had been definitely adopted as the title of a class its persistence in the same sense after the organization of the family and the clan by the unprivileged class would be perfectly natural.

The absurdity of excluding the plebeians from all but a merely theoretical citizenship, based on the negative fact of freedom, seems to have become apparent before the close of the monarchical period. The aim of the reforms associated with the name of Servius Tullius appears to have been the imposition of the duties of citizenship upon the plebeians. Incidentally this involved an extension of plebeian privilege in two directions. First, it was necessary to unify the plebeian order by putting the legal status of the clients on a level with that of the unattached plebeians; and again enrolment in the army involved registration in the tribes and centuries; and as the army soon developed into a legislative assembly meeting in centuries (comitia centuriata), the whole citizen body, including plebeians, now acquired a share of political power, which had hitherto belonged solely to the patricians. At the close of the monarchy, the plebeian possessed the private rights of citizenship in entirety, except for his inability to contract a legal marriage with a patrician, and one of the public rights, that of giving his vote in the assembly.[1] But in the matter of liability to the duties of citizenship, military service and taxation, he was entirely on a level with the patrician. This position was probably tolerable during the monarchy, when the king served to hold the power of the patrician families in check. But when these families had expelled the Tarquins, and formed themselves into an exclusive aristocracy of privilege, the inconsistency between partial privilege and full burdens came to be strongly felt by the plebeians.

The result was the long struggle for entire political equality of the two orders which occupies the first few centuries of the republic (see ROME: History, § II. "The Republic"). The struggle was inaugurated by the plebeians, who in 494 B.C. formed themselves into a separate order with annually elected officers (tribuni plebis) and an assembly of their own, and by means of this machinery forced themselves by degrees into all the magistracies, and obtained the coveted right of intermarriage with the patricians. Admission to the higher magistracies carried with it admission to the senate, and by the close of the struggle (about 300 B.C.) the political privilege of the two orders was equalized, with the exception of certain disabilities which, originally devised to break the political monopoly of the order, continued to be attached to the patricians after the victory of the plebs. They were excluded from the tribunate and the council of the plebs, which had become important instruments of government, and were only eligible for one place in the consulship and censorship, while both were open to plebeians. It is possible, though far from certain (see SENATE), that the powers of the interregnum and the senatorial confirmation (patrum auctoritas) necessary to give validity to decisions of the people, remained the exclusive privileges of the patrician members of the senate. But while the patrician disabilities were of a kind that had gained in importance with the lapse of centuries, these privileges, even if still retained, had become merely formal in the second half of the republican period. Since the plebeian element in the state had an immense numerical preponderance over the patrician these disabilities were not widely spread, and seem generally to have been cheerfully borne as the price of belonging to the families still recognized as the oldest and noblest in Rome. But the adoption of P. Clodius Pulcher into a plebeian family in 59 B.C. with a view to election to the tribunate shows that a rejection of patrician rights (transitio ad plebem) was not difficult to effect by any patrician who preferred actual power to the dignity of ancient descent. It was not so easy to recruit the ranks of the patricians. The traditions of early Rome indeed represent the patricians as receiving the Claudii by a collective act into their body; but the first authenticated instance of the admission of new members to the patriciate is that of the lex Cassia, which authorized Caesar as dictator to create fresh patricians. The same procedure

[1] Cf. the privileges of the Athenians under the Solonian system (see SOLON; ECCLESIA; ARCHON).

was followed by Augustus. Later on, the right of creating patricians came to be regarded as inherent in the principate, and was exercised by Claudius and Vespasian without any legal enactment, apparently in their capacity as censor (Tac. Ann. xi. 25; Vita M. Antonini, i.). Patrician rank seems to have been regarded as a necessary attribute of the princeps; and in two cases we are told that it was conferred upon a plebeian princeps by the senate (Vita Juliani, 3; Macrini, 7). A comparison of this procedure with the original conception of the patriciate as revealed by the derivation of the word, is significant of the history of the conception of nobility at Rome, and illustrative of the tenacity with which the Romans clung to the name and form of an institution which had long lost its significance. After the political equalization of the two orders, noble birth was no longer recognized as constituting a claim to political privilege. Instead of the old hereditary nobility, consisting of the members of the patrician clans, there arose a nobility of office, consisting of all those families, whether patrician or plebeian, which had held curule office. It was now the tenure of office that conferred distinction. In the early days of Rome, office was only open to the member of a patrician gens. In the principate, patrician rank, a sort of abstract conception based upon the earlier state of affairs, was held to be a dignity suitable to be conferred on an individual holder of office. But the conferment of the rank upon an individual as distinct from a whole family (gens) is enough to show how widely the modern conception of patrician rank differed from the ancient. The explanation of this is that the plebeians had long been organized, like the patricians, in gentes, and nothing remained distinctive of the old nobility except a vague sense of dignity and worth. (A.M.CL.)

II. Under Constantine an entirely new meaning was given to the word Patrician. It was used as a personal title of honour conferred for distinguished services. It was a title merely of rank, not of office; its holder ranked next after the emperor and the consul. It naturally happened, however, that the title was generally bestowed upon officials, especially on the chief provincial governors, and even among barbarian chieftains whose friendship was valuable enough to call forth the imperial benediction. Among the former it appears to have become a sort of ex officio title of the Byzantine viceregents of Italy, the exarchs of Ravenna; among the barbarian chiefs who were thus dignified were Odoacer, Theodoric, Sigismund of Burgundy, Clovis, and even in later days princes of Bulgaria, the Saracens, and the West Saxons. The word thus acquired an official connotation. The dignity was not hereditary and belonged only to individuals; thus a patrician family was merely one whose head enjoyed the rank of patricius. Gradually the root sense of "father" came to the front again, and the patricius was regarded as the "father of the emperor" (Ammian Marc. xxix. a). With the word were associated such further titles as eminentia; magnitudo, magnificentia. Those patricians who were purely honorary were called honorarii or codicillarii; those who were still in harness were praesentales. They were all distinguished by a special dress or uniform and in public always drove in a carriage. The emperor Zeno enacted that no one could become patricius who had not been praefectus militum, consul or magister militum, but less careful emperors gave the title to their favourites, however young and undistinguished. The writ in which the title was conferred was called a diploma.

A further change in the meaning of the name is marked by its conferment on Pippin the Frank[2] by Pope Stephen. The idea of this extension originated no doubt in the fact that the Italian patricius of the 6th and 7th centuries had come to be regarded as the defensor, protector, patronus of the Church. At all events, the conferring of the title by a pope was entirely unprecedented; previously its validity had depended on the emperor solely. As a matter of fact it is clear that the patriciate of Pippin was a new office, especially as the title is henceforward generally patricius Romanorum, not patricius alone. It was

[2] The name is used of Charles Martel, but it was not apparently formally conferred upon him.

subsequently conferred on Charlemagne at his coronation, and borne, as we gather from medieval documents, indiscriminately, not only by subsequent emperors, but also by a long line of Burgundian rulers and minor princes of the middle ages generally.[1] On the fall of the Carolingian house the title passed to Alberic II. Subsequently it was held by John Crescentius, and many leading men who received it from Otto III. (e.g. Boleslaw Chabri of Poland). In 1046 it returned to the German Henry III. The emperor Frederick Barbarossa was the last to wear the insignia (in 1167).

BIBLIOGRAPHY.—(1) The Ancient Patricians: Th. Mommsen, Staatsrecht III. passim (3rd ed., Leipzig, 1887); Römische Forsch-ungen I. (Berlin, 1864); P. Willems, Le Droit public romain, pt. i (Louvain, 1888). (2) The Medieval Patricians: J. B. Bury's Later Roman Empire (1889); Bryce, Holy Roman Empire (1904), pp. 40 seq.; Du Cange, Glossarium med. et infim. latinitatis, s.v. "Patricius"; and histories of Charlemagne (q.v.) and his successors. For the Ger-man Patrisiertum see Roth von Schreckenstein, Das Patrisiat in den deutschen Städten, besonders Reichsstädten (2nd ed. Freiburg, 1886); Foltz, Beiträge zur Gesch. des Patrisiats in den deutschen Städten (Marburg, 1899). (J. M. M.)

PATRICK, ST, the patron saint of Ireland,[2] was probably born about the year 389. He was the son of a deacon, Calpurnius, and the grandson of a presbyter named Potitus. His father was a middle-class landed proprietor and a decurion, who is represented as living at a place called Bannauenta. The only place of this name we know is Daventry, but it seems more probable that Patrick's home is to be sought near the Severn, and Rhys con-jectures that one of the three places called Banwen in Glamorgan-shire may be intended. The British name of the future apostle was Sucat, to which Mod. Welsh hygad, "warlike," corresponds. His Roman name has also survived in a hibernicized form, Cothrige, with the common substitution of Irish c for Brythonic p (cf. Irish casc, Lat. pascha). Patrick was doubtless educated as a Christian and was imbued with reverence for the Roman Empire. When about sixteen years of age he was carried off by a band of Irish marauders. The latter were possibly taking part in the raid of the Irish king Niall Noigiallach, who met with his end in Britain in 405. Irish tradition represents the future apostle as tending the herds of a chieftain of the name of Milluce (Milchu), near the mountain called Slemish in county Antrim, but Bury tries to show that the scene of his captivity was Connaught, perhaps in the neighbourhood of Croagh Patrick. His bondage lasted for six years. During this time he became subject to religious emotion and beheld visions which encouraged him to effect his escape. He fled, in all probability to the coast of Wicklow, and encountered a vessel which was engaged in the export of Irish wolf-dogs. After three days at sea the traders landed, possibly on the west coast of Gaul, and journeyed for twenty-eight days through a desert. At the end of two months Patrick parted from his companions and betook himself to the monastery of Lérins, where he probably spent a few years. On leaving the Mediterranean he seems to have returned home. It was doubtless during this stay in Britain that the idea of mission-ary enterprise in Ireland came to him. In a dream he saw a man named Victorious bearing innumerable epistles, one of which he received and read; the beginning of it contained the words "The Voice of the Irish."; whilst repeating these words he says, "I imagined that I heard in my mind the voice of those who were near the wood of Foclut (Fochlad), which is near the western sea, and thus they cried: 'We pray thee, holy youth, to come and walk again amongst us as before.'" The forest of Fochlad was in the neighbourhood of Killala Bay, but it is possible that it extended considerably to the south. Despite

[1] We even find a feminine form, patricissa, for the wife of a patricius. The golden circlet worn on the head by the patricius as a symbol of his dignity was called a patricialis circulus.
[2] His career is involved in considerable obscurity. Widely varying views have been held by modern scholars with regard to his activity, some going so far as to treat all the accounts of his labours as the fictitious creation of a later age. In the present article Bury's reconstruction of the saint's life has been chiefly followed. Apart from its importance in other respects, Bury's treatment of the sub-ject has at any rate the merit of defending the traditional view of St Patrick's career.

his natural diffidence, and opposition on the part of his relatives, Patrick resolved to return to Gaul in order to prepare himself mission. He proceeded to Auxerre—a place which seems for his had a close connexion with Britain and Ireland—and to have ed deacon by Bishop Amator, along with two others who afterwards associated with him in spreading the faith in Ireland. The one was an Irishman called Fith, better known as Iserninus, the other Auxilius. Patrick must have spent at least fourteen years at Auxerre.

It seems not unlikely that Pelagianism had taken root among the Christian communities of Ireland, and it was found necessary to send a bishop to combat the heresy. Pope Celestine's choice fell on the deacon Palladius, who had taken a prominent part in stamping out the doctrine in Britain. The mission of Palladius (431-432), whom Zimmer has endeavoured to identify with Patrick, is obscure. Tradition associates his name with the mountains of Wicklow, and we are told that he retired to the land of the Picts in North Britain, where he died. Patrick probably felt great disappointment when Palladius was sent as the chosen envoy of Rome, but now Germanus seems to have decided that Patrick was the man for the task, and he was consecrated in 432. For the peculiar social conditions with which the Christian missionary would be confronted in Ireland see BREHON LAWS and IRELAND: Early History. Suffice it to say here that the land belonged to the tribes, and that the success of Patrick's undertaking depended entirely on his ability to gain the goodwill of the tribal kings and chiefs of clans. We are totally ignorant as to the extent and number of the pre-Patrician Christian communities in Ireland. It seems probable that they were, largely, if not wholly confined to the south-east of the island. Patrick landed at Inverdea, the mouth of the river Vartry in Wicklow, but we are not informed as to any of his doings in Leinster at this period. According to the story, he immediately proceeded northward to the kingdom of Ulidia (east Ulster), though a certain tradition represents him as going to Meath. Landing on the shores of Strangford Lough, he commenced his labours in the plain on the south-west side of that inlet. A convert chief named Dichu granted him a site for an establish-ment, and a wooden barn is stated to have been utilised for the purpose of worship, whence the modern Saul (Ir. sabull, "barn "). Patrick's activity was bound to bring him sooner or later into conflict with the High-king Loigaire (reigned 428-467), son of Niall Noigiallach. Fedilmid, a brother of the monarch, is represented as having made over his estate at Trim to the saint to found a church, and thus the faith was established within Loigaire's territory. The story in picturesque fashion makes Patrick challenge the royal authority by lighting the Paschal fire on the hill of Slane on the night of Easter Eve. It chanced to be the occasion of a pagan festival at Tara, during which no fire might be kindled until the royal fire had been lit. A number of trials of skill between the Christian missionary and Loigaire's Druids ensue, and the final result seems to have been that the monarch, though unwilling to embrace the foreign creed, under-took to protect the Christian bishop. At a later date the saint was probably invited by Loigaire to take part in the codification of the Senchus Mór in order to represent the interests of the Christian communities. On another occasion Patrick is reported to have overthrown a famous idol known as Cenn Cruaich or Cromm Cruaich in the plain of Mag Slecht (county Cavan). Several churches seem to have been founded in the kingdom of Meath by the saint, but they cannot now be identified. Patrick is stated to have visited Connaught on three different occasions and to have founded churches, one of the most impor-tant being that at Elphin. As regards Ulster our information is very scanty, though we find him establishing churches in the three kingdoms of the province (Ailech, Oriel and Ulidia). Patrick's work is more closely identified with the north of Ireland than with the south. Traces of his mission, however, are to be found in Ossory and Muskerry. But his task in the south was doubtless rather that of an organizer, and a kind of circular letter has come down to us which was addressed by Patrick, Auxilius and Iserninus, to all the clergy of the island. There is some evidence that he made a journey to Rome (441-443) and brought back with him valuable relics. On his return he founded the church and monastery of Armagh, the site of which was granted him by Daire, king of Oriel, and it is probable that the see was intended by him to be specially connected with the supreme ecclesiastical authority. Some years before his death, which took place in 461, Patrick resigned his position as bishop of Armagh to his disciple Benignus, and possibly retired to Saul in Dalaradia, where he spent the remainder of his life. The place of his burial was a matter of dispute in early Ireland, but it seems most likely that he was interred at Saul.

Two highly important documents purporting to have been written by Patrick have come down to us. Although the genuineness of these writings has been impugned on various occasions by different scholars, there seems to be no reason for assuming that they did not emanate from the saint's pen. The one is the Confession, which is contained in an imperfect state in the Book of Armagh (c. 807), but complete copies are found in later MSS. The Confession, written towards the end of his life, gives a general account of his career. Various charges had been brought against him by his enemies, among them that of illiteracy, the truth of which is borne out by the crudeness of his style, and is fully admitted by the writer himself. Before being admitted to deacon's orders he had communicated to a friend some fault which he had committed when about fifteen years of age. This friend had not considered it an obstacle to ordination. Later the secret was betrayed and came to the ears of persons who, as he says, "urged my sins against my laborious episcopate." It is impossible to ascertain who these detractors were—possibly British fellow-workers in Ireland. The other document is the so-called Letter to Coroticus. The soldiers of Coroticus (Ceretic), a British king of Strathclyde, had in the course of a raid in Ireland killed a number of Christian neophytes on the very day of their baptism while still clad in white garments. Others had been carried off into slavery, and a deputation of clergy which Patrick had sent to ask for their release had been subjected to ridicule. In his Letter the saint in very strong language urges the Christian subjects of the British king not to have any dealings with their ruler and his bloodthirsty followers until full satisfaction should have been made. The text of this letter occurs in a number of MSS. but is not contained in the Book of Armagh. It is however certain that it was known in the 7th century. A strange barbaric chant commonly known as the Lorica or Hymn of St Patrick is preserved in the Liber hymnorum. This piece, called in Irish the Faed Fiada or "Cry of the Deer," contains a number of remarkable grammatical forms, and the latest editors are of opinion that it may very well be genuine. From such slender material it is not easy to form a clear conception of the saint's personality. His was evidently an intensely spiritual nature, and in addition to the qualities which go to form a strong man of action he must have possessed an enthusiasm which enabled him to surmount all difficulties. His importance in the history of Ireland and the Irish Church consists in the fact that he brought Ireland into touch with western Europe and more particularly with Rome, and that he introduced Latin into Ireland as the language of the Church. His work consisted largely in organizing the Christian societies which he found in existence on his arrival, and in planting the faith in regions such as the extreme west of Connaught which had not yet come under the sway of the gospel.

AUTHORITIES.—Apart from the Letter and Epistle mentioned above our chief sources of information with regard to the life of St Patrick are contained in the Book of Armagh. The one is the memoir by Tirechán, a bishop who had been the disciple of Bishop Ultan of Ardbraccan in Meath (d. 657). The first part of this memoir, which was probably compiled about 670, deals with the saint's work in Meath, the second with his activity in Connaught. Various additions are appended to this compilation, and there are still further additional notes. The other biography was written towards the end of the 7th century by Muirchu Maccu Machtheni, who dedicated his work to Bishop Aed of Slébte (d. 700). The first portion deals with Patrick's career down to his arrival in Ireland and contains an unvarnished statement of fact. But when the story passes to Ireland Muirchu's narrative becomes full of the mythical

element. The influence of Muirchu's work can be traced in all later biographies. Bury has shown that both Tirechán and Muirchu drew from written material which existed in part at any rate in Irish. Among later lives we may mention the hymn Genair Patraicc, commonly attributed to Fiacc, which is considered by the latest editors to have been originally composed about 800. Three anonymous Latin lives were published by Colgan in his Trias Thaumaturga (Louvain, 1645), and there exists an 11th-century Irish life in three parts published by Whitley Stokes for the Rolls series (1887). A Latin translation of a different copy of this work, now lost, was published by Colgan. Lastly a life by an otherwise unknown Irish writer named Probus occurs in the Basel edition of Bede's works (1563) and was reprinted by Colgan.

See J. B. Bury, The Life of St Patrick and his Place in History (London, 1905); J. H. Todd, St Patrick the Apostle of Ireland (Dublin, 1861); H. Zimmer, article "Keltische Kirche" in Realencyklopädie für protestantische Theologie und Kirche (1901; trans. by Miss Meyer, "The Celtic Church in Britain and Ireland," London, 1902); J. Gwynn, Liber Ardmachanus; Whitley Stokes, The Tripartite Life of St Patrick (London, 1887); N. J. D. White, "The Writings of St Patrick" (critical edition) in Proceedings of the Royal Irish Academy (1904).

(E. C. Q.)

PATRICK, SIMON (1626-1707), English divine, was born at Gainsborough, Lincolnshire, on the 8th of September 1626. He entered Queen's College, Cambridge, in 1644, and after taking orders in 1651 became successively chaplain to Sir Walter St John and vicar of Battersea, Surrey. He was afterwards (1662) preferred to the rectory of St Paul's, Covent Garden, London, where he continued to labour during the plague. He was appointed dean of Peterborough in 1679, and bishop of Chichester in 1689, in which year he was employed, along with others of the new bishops, to settle the affairs of the Church in Ireland. In 1691 he was translated to the see of Ely, which he held until his death on the 31st of May 1707. His sermons and devotional writings, which are very numerous, were long held in high estimation, and his Commentary on the Historical and Poetical Books of the Old Testament, in 10 vols., brought down as far as the Song of Solomon, was reprinted as recently as 1853. His Friendly Debate between a Conformist and a Nonconformist was a controversial tract which excited considerable feeling at the time of its publication in 1668, but he lived long enough to soothe by his moderation and candour the exasperation it had caused. He also contributed to a volume of Poems upon Divine and Moral Subjects (1719).

The first collected edition of his works appeared at Oxford in 1859 (9 vols., 8vo); a small Autobiography was published also at Oxford in 1839.

PATRIZZI, FRANCESCO (FRANCISCUS PATRITIUS) (1529-1597), Italian philosopher and scientist, was born at Clissa, in Dalmatia, and died in Rome. He gained the patronage of the bishop of Cyprus, who brought him to Venice, where his abilities were immediately recognized by his appointment to the chair of philosophy at Ferrara. He was subsequently invited to Rome by Clement VIII. In spite of his almost incessant controversies with the Aristotelians, he found time to make a comprehensive study of contemporary science. He published in 15 books a treatise on the New Geometry (1587), and works on history, rhetoric and the art of war. He studied ancient theories of music, and is said to have invented the thirteen-syllable verse known subsequently as versi martelliani. In his philosophy he was mainly concerned to defend Plato against the followers of Aristotle.

His two great works, Discussionum peripateticorum libri XV. (Basel, 1571), and Nova de universis philosophia (Basel, 1591), developed the view that, whereas Aristotle's teaching was in direct opposition to Christianity, Plato, on the contrary, foreshadowed the Christian revelation and prepared the way for its acceptance. In the earlier treatise he attacks the life and character of Aristotle, impugns the authenticity of almost all his works, and attempts to refute his doctrines from a theological standpoint. In the second and greater work he goes back to the theories and methods of the Ionians and the pre-Socratics generally. His theory of the universe is that, from God there emanated Light which extends throughout space and is the explanation of all development. This Light is not corporeal and yet is the fundamental reality of things. From Light came Heat and Fluidity; these three together with Space make up the elements out of which all things are constructed. This cosmic theory is a curious combination of materialistic and abstract ideas; the influence of his master Telesio (q.v.), generally predominant, is not strong enough to overcome his inherent disbelief in the adequacy of purely scientific explanation.

PATROCLES (*c.* 312–261 B.C.), a Macedonian general and writer on geographical subjects, who lived during the reigns of Seleucus I. and Antiochus I. When in command of the fleet of Seleucus (285) he undertook a voyage of exploration on the Caspian Sea to discover possible trade routes, especially for communication with the peoples of northern India. He came to the conclusion that the Caspian was a gulf or inlet, and that it was possible to enter it by sea from the Indian Ocean. The only information as to his work (even the title is unknown) is derived from Strabo. After the death of Seleucus, Patrocles was sent by his successor Antiochus to put down a revolt in Asia Minor, and lost his life in an engagement with the Bithynians.

See Strabo ii. 68, 74. xi. 508, xv. 689; Diod. Sic. xix. 100; Plutarch, *Demetrius*, 47; Pliny, *Nat. Hist.* vi. 21; Photius, cod. 224 (on Memnon); C. W. Müller, *Fragmenta historicorum graecorum*, ii. 442; E. H. Bunbury, *Hist. of Ancient Geography*, vol. i. (1879); W. W. Tarn, " Patrocles and the Oxo-Caspian Trade Route " in *Journal of Hellenic Studies*, vol. xxi. (1901).

PATROL (Fr. *patrouiller*, connected with *patte*, foot), a verb meaning to move up and down or traverse a specified " round " or " beat " in a district in a town, camp or other place, or on a stretch of water on a river or sea, for the purpose of watching and protecting the same, or for reconnoitring the numbers or positions of an enemy. As a substantive the term is used of the detachment of troops or police employed.

PATRON, a word of which the various meanings in European languages are derived and transferred from that of the Lat. *patronus*, whose position in Roman law and antiquities is treated below (PATRON AND CLIENT). The most general application of the word in these transferred senses is that of an influential supporter or protector. The earliest use of the word in English appears to have been in the special ecclesiastical sense of the holder of an advowson, the right of presentation to a benefice. From this meaning is deduced that of the person in whom lies the right of presenting to public offices, privileges, &c., still surviving in the title of the Patronage Secretary of the Treasury in Great Britain. From the earliest Christian times the saints took the place of the pagan tutelary deities (*Di tutelares*) and were in this capacity called *tutelares* or *patroni*, patron-saints. To them churches and other sacred buildings are dedicated, and they are regarded as the protectors and guardians of countries, towns, professions, trades and the like. Further, a person may have a patron-saint, usually the one on or near whose festival he has been born, or whose name has been taken in baptism.

A full list of saints, with the objects of the peculiar patronage of each, is given in M. E. C. Walcott's *Sacred Archaeology* (1868).

PATRON AND CLIENT (Lat. *patronus*, from *pater*, father; *clientes* or *cluens*, from *cluere*, to obey), in Roman law. Clientage appears to have been an institution of most of the Graeco-Italian peoples in early stages of their history; but it is in Rome that we can most easily trace its origin, progress and decay. Until the reforms of Servius Tullius, the only citizens proper were the members of the patrician and gentile houses; they alone could participate in the solemnities of the national religion, take part in the government and defence of the state, contract quiritarian marriage, hold property, and enjoy the protection of the laws. But alongside of them was a gradually increasing non-citizen population composed partly of slaves, partly of freemen, who were nevertheless not admitted to burgess rights. To the latter class belonged the clients, individuals who had attached themselves in a position of dependence to the heads of patrician houses as their patrons, in order thereby to secure attachment to a *gens*, which would involve a *de facto* freedom. Mommsen held that the *plebs* consisted originally of clients only; but the earliest records of Rome reveal the possibility of a man becoming a plebeian member of the Roman state without assuming the dependent position of clientship (see PATRICIANS); and long before the time of Servius Tullius the clients must be regarded as a section only of the plebeian order, which also contained members unattached to any *patronus*. The relationship of patron and client was ordinarily created by what, from the

client's point of view, was called *adplicatio ad patronum*, from that of the patron, *susceptio clientis*—the client being either a person who had come to Rome as an exile, who had passed through the asylum, or who had belonged to a state which Rome had overthrown. According to Dionysius and Plutarch, it was one of the early cares of Romulus to regulate the relationship, which, by their account of it, was esteemed a very intimate one, imposing upon the patron duties only less sacred than those he owed to his children and his ward, more urgent than any he could be called upon to perform towards his kinsmen, and whose neglect entailed the penalty of death (*Tellumoni sacer esto*). He was bound to provide his client with the necessaries of life; and it was a common practice to make him a grant during pleasure of a small plot of land to cultivate on his own account. Further, he had to advise him in all his affairs; to represent him in any transactions with third parties in which, as a non-citizen, he could not act with effect; and, above all things, to stand by him, or rather be his substitute, in any litigation in which he might become involved. The client in return had not only generally to render his patron the respect and obedience due by a dependant, but, when he was in a position to do so and the circumstances of the patron required it, to render him pecuniary assistance. As time advanced and clients amassed wealth, we find this duty insisted upon in a great variety of forms, as in contributions towards the dowries of a patron's daughters, towards the ransom of a patron or any of his family who had been taken captive, towards the payment of penalties or fines imposed upon a patron, even towards his maintenance when he had become reduced to poverty. Neither might give evidence against the other—a rule we find still in observance well on in the 1st century B.C., when C. Herennius declined to be a witness against C. Marius on the ground that the family of the latter had for generations been clients of the Herennii (Plut. *Mar.* 5). The client was regarded as a minor member (*gentilicius*) of his patron's *gens*; he was entitled to assist in its religious services, and bound to contribute to the cost of them; he had to follow his patron to battle on the order of the *gens*; he was subject to its jurisdiction and discipline, and was entitled to burial in its common sepulchre. And this was the condition, not only of the client who personally had attached himself to a patron, but that also of his descendants; the patronage and the clientage were alike hereditary. The same relationship was held to exist between a freedman and his former owner; for originally a slave did not on enfranchisement become a citizen; it was a *de facto* freedom merely that he enjoyed; his old owner was always called his patron, while he and his descendants were substantially in the position of clients, and often so designated.

In the two hundred years that elapsed before the Servian constitutional reforms, the numerical strength of the clients, whether in that condition by *adplicatio*, enfranchisement or descent, must have become considerable; and it was from time to time augmented by the retainers of distinguished immigrants admitted into the ranks of the patriciate. There seems also to have been during this period a gradual growth of virtual independence on the part of the clients, and it is probable that their precarious tenure of the soil had in many cases come to be practically regarded as ownership, when a patron had not asserted his right for generations. The exact nature of the privileges conferred on the clients by Servius Tullius is not known. Probably this king guaranteed to the whole plebeian order, including the clients, the legal right of private ownership of Roman land. At the same time he imposed upon the whole order the duty of serving in the army, which was now organised on a basis of wealth. The client had previously been liable to military service at the command of the *gens*. Now he was called upon to take his part in it as a member of the state. As a natural corollary to this, all the plebeians seem to have been enrolled in the tribes, and after the institution of the plebeian assembly (*concilium plebis*) the clients, who formed a large part of the order, secured a political influence which steadily increased. It is not certain how soon they acquired the right to litigate in person on their own behalf, but their possession of this right seems to be implied in the XII. Tables, and may have been granted them at an earlier date. At any rate after 449 B.C. there were no disabilities in private law involved in their status. The relation of patron and client, it is true, still remained; the patron could still exact from his client respect, obedience and service, and be and his *gens* had still an eventual right of succession to a deceased client's estate. But the fiduciary duties of the patron were greatly relaxed, and practically little more was expected of him than that he should continue to give his client his advice, and prevent him falling into a condition of indigence; *sacer esto* ceased to be the penalty of protection denied or withheld, its application being limited to *fraus facta*, which in the language of the Tables meant positive injury inflicted or damage done.

So matters remained during the 4th, 3rd and 2nd centuries. In the 2nd and 1st a variety of events contributed still further to modify the relationship. The rapacity of patrons was checked by the lex Cincia (passed by M. Cincius Alimentus, tribune in 204 B.C.), which prohibited their taking gifts of money from their clients; marriages between patron and client gradually ceased to be regarded as unlawful, or as ineffectual to secure to the issue the status of the patron father. At the same time the remaining political disabilities of the clients were removed by their enrolment in all the tribes instead of only the four city tribes, and their admission to the magistracy and the senate. Hereditary clientage ceased when a client attained to a curule dignity; and in the case of the descendants of freedmen enfranchised in solemn forms it came to be limited to the first generation. Gradually but steadily one feature after another of the old institution disappeared, till by the end of the 1st century it had resolved itself into the limited relationship between patron and freedman on the one hand, and the unlimited honorary relationship between the patron who gave gratuitous advice on questions of law and those who came to consult him on the other. To have a large following of clients of this class was a matter of ambition to every man of mark in the end of the republic; it increased his importance, and ensured him a band of zealous agents in his political schemes. But amid the rivalries of parties and with the venality of the lower orders, baser methods had to be resorted to in order to maintain a patron's influence; the favour and support of his clients had to be purchased with something more substantial than mere advice. And so arose that wretched and degrading clientage of the early empire, of which Martial, who was not ashamed to confess himself a first-rate specimen of the breed, has given us such graphic descriptions; gatherings of idlers, sycophants and spendthrifts, at the levees and public appearances of those whom, in their fawning servility, they addressed as lords and masters, but whom they abused behind their backs as close-fisted upstarts—and all for the sake of the *sportula*, the daily dole of a dinner, or of a few pence wherewith to procure one. With the middle empire this disappeared; and when a reference to patron and client occurs in later times it is in the sense of counsel and client, the words patron and advocate being used almost synonymously. It was not so in the days of the great forensic orators. The word advocate, it is said, occurs only once in the singular in the pages of Cicero. But at a later period, when the bar had become a profession, and the qualifications, admission, numbers and fees of counsel had become a matter of state regulation, *advocati* was the word usually employed to designate the pleaders as a class of professional men, each individual advocate, however, being still spoken of as patron in reference to the litigant with whose interest he was entrusted. It is in this limited connexion that patron and client meet under our notice in the latest monuments of Roman law.

LITERATURE.—On the clientage of early Rome see T. Mommsen, "Die römische Clientel," *Röm. Forschungen*, i. 355 (Berlin, 1864); M. Voigt, "Ueber die Clientel und Libertinität," in *Ber. d. phil. histor. Classe d. königl. sächs. Gesellsch. d. Wissenschaften* (1878, pp. 147–219); J. Marquardt, *Privatleben d. Römer*, pp. 196–200 (Leipzig, 1879); M. Voigt, *Die XII. Tafeln*, ii. 667–679 (Leipzig, 1883). Earlier literature is noted in F. Willems, *Le Droit public romain*, 4th ed., p. 26 (Louvain, 1880). On the clientage of the early

empire see W. A. Becker, *Gallus*, vol. ii., Excursus 4 (London, 1849); L. Friedländer, *Sittengeschichte Roms*, i. 200–212 (Leipsig, 1901); Marquardt, *op. cit.* pp. 200–208. On the latest clientage, see T. Grellet-Dumazeau, *Le Barreau romain* (Paris, 1858).
(J. M.†; A. M. CL.)

PATTEN (adapted from Fr. *patin*, in modern usage meaning a "skate"; Med. Lat. *patinus*, Ital. *pattino*, of unknown origin; cf. *patte*, paw), a kind of shoe which, varying in form at different times and places, raised the wearer from the ground in order to keep the feet out of mud or wet. Pattens were necessaries to women of all classes in the uncleaned and unpaved streets of the 16th, 17th and 18th centuries. They may still be found in use in rural parts of England. A wooden shoe or clog, a light strapped shoe with a very thick sole of wood or cork, and, more particularly, an iron ring supporting at a little distance from the ground a wooden sole with a strap through which the foot slips, have all been types which the patten has taken. An extraordinary kind of "patten" was fashionable in Italy and Spain in the 16th or 17th centuries. This was the *chopine*,[1] a loose slipper resting on a very thick sole of cork or wood. During the 17th century at Venice ladies wore "chopines" of exaggerated size. Coryat, in his *Crudities*, 1611 (vol. i. p. 400, ed. 1905), gives a description of these Venetian "chapineys." They were of wood covered with red, white and yellow leather, some gilt or painted, and reached a height sometimes of half a yard. Ladies wearing these exaggerated chopines had to be accompanied by attendants to prevent them falling. There is a 16th century Venetian "chopine" in the British Museum. The "Patten-makers" Company is one of the minor Livery companies of London. The patten-makers were originally joined with the "Pouch and Galoche Makers," and are mentioned as early as 1400. They became a separate fraternity in 1469, but did not obtain a charter till 1670.

PATTER, properly a slang word for the secret or "cant" language used by beggars, thieves, gipsies, &c., hence the fluent plausible talk that a cheap-jack employs to pass off his goods, or a conjuror to cover up his tricks. It is thus used of any rapid manner of talking, and of a "patter-song," in which a very large number of words have to be sung at high speed to fit them to the music. The word, though in some of its senses affected by "patter," to make a series of rapid strokes or pats, as of raindrops, is derived from the quick, mechanical repetition of the *Paternoster*, or Lord's Prayer.

PATTERN, a model, that which serves as an original from which similar objects may be made, or as an example or specimen; in particular an artistic design serving as a sample or model, hence the arrangement or grouping of lines, figures, &c., which make up such a design. The word was taken from Fr. *patron*, Lat. *patronus*, a defender or protector. In medieval Latin *patronus* had the specific meaning of example, and in modern French both meanings of patron and pattern attach to *patron*. "Patron" in the sense of copy, example, began to be pronounced and spelled in England as "pattern" in the 16th century.

PATTESON, JOHN COLERIDGE (1827–1871), English missionary, bishop of Melanesia, was born in London on the 1st of April 1827, the eldest son of Sir John Patteson, justice of the King's Bench, and Frances Duke Coleridge, a near relative of Samuel Taylor Coleridge. He was educated at Ottery St Mary and at Eton, where he distinguished himself on the cricket-field. He entered Balliol College, Oxford, in 1845, graduated B.A. in 1848, and in 1852 became a fellow of Merton College. In 1853 he became curate of Alfington, Devon, and in the following year he was ordained priest. He then joined George Augustus Selwyn, bishop of New Zealand, in his mission to the Melanesian islands. There he laboured with great success, visiting the different islands of the group in the mission ship the "Southern Cross," and by his good sense and devotion winning the esteem and affection of the natives. His linguistic powers were

[1] The word is taken from an obsolete French *chapine* or Spanish *chapin*, and is of doubtful origin. The Spanish *chapa*, flat plate, has been suggested. The word does not occur in Italian, though it is often Italianised in English in such forms as *cioppino*.

exceptional, and he spoke 23 languages with ease. In 1861 he was consecrated bishop of Melanesia, and fixed his headquarters at Mota. He was killed by natives at Nukapu, in the Santa Cruz group, on the 20th of September 1871, the victim of a tragic error. The traders engaged in the nefarious traffic in Kanaka labour for Fiji and Queensland had taken to personating missionaries in order to facilitate their kidnapping; Patteson was mistaken for one of these and killed. His murderers evidently found out their mistake and repented of it, for the bishop's body was found at sea floating in a canoe, covered with a palm fibre matting, and a palm-branch in his hand. He is thus represented in the bas-relief erected in Merton College to his memory.

See *Life* by Charlotte M. Yonge (1873).

PATTI, ADELINA JUANA MARIA [BARONESS CEDERSTRÖM] (1843–   ), the famous vocalist, daughter of an Italian singer, Salvatore Patti, was born at Madrid on the 19th of February 1843. Her mother, also a singer, was Spanish, being known before her marriage as Signora Barili. Both the parents of Adelina went to America, where their daughter was taught singing by Maurice Strakosch, who married Amelia Patti, an elder sister. Gifted with a brilliant soprano voice, Adelina Patti began her public career at the age of seven in the concert halls of New York, where in 1859 she also made her first appearance as Lucia in Donizetti's opera, *Lucia di Lammermoor*. On the 14th of May 1861 she sang as Amina in Bellini's opera *La Sonnambula* at Covent Garden, and from this time she became the leading operatic *prima donna*, her appearances in London, Paris and the other principal musical centres being a long succession of triumphs, and her rôles covering all the great parts in Italian opera. In 1868 she married Henri, marquis de Caux, a member of Napoleon III.'s household, from whom she was divorced in 1885; she then married Nicolini, the tenor, who died in 1898; and in 1899 she became the wife of Baron Cederström, a Swede, who was naturalized as an Englishman. Madame Patti ceased to appear on the operatic stage in public after the 'eighties, but at Craig-y-Nos, her castle in Wales, she built a private theatre, and her occasional appearances at concerts at the Albert Hall continued to attract enthusiastic audiences, her singing of "Home, Sweet Home" becoming peculiarly associated with those events. Partly owing to her fine original training, partly to her splendid method and partly to her avoidance of Wagnerian rôles, Madame Patti wonderfully preserved the freshness of her voice, and she will be remembered as, after Jenny Lind, the greatest soprano of the 19th century.

PATTI, a town and episcopal see of Sicily, in the province of Messina, 42 m. W. by S. of Messina by rail. Pop. (1901), 5473 (town), 10,995 (commune). The cathedral, founded about 1300, has been modernized; it contains the tomb (restored in the 17th century) of Adelasia, widow of Count Roger of Sicily. The abandoned church of San Marco is built into the remains of a Greek temple.

PATTISON, MARK (1813–1884), English author and rector of Lincoln College, Oxford, was born on the 10th of October 1813. He was the son of the rector of Hauxwell, Yorkshire, and was privately educated by his father. In 1832 he matriculated at Oriel College, where he took his B.A. degree in 1836 with second-class honours. After other attempts to obtain a fellowship, he was elected in 1839 to a Yorkshire fellowship at Lincoln, an anti-Puseyite College. Pattison was at this time a Puseyite, and greatly under the influence of J. H. Newman, for whom he worked, helping in the translation of Thomas Aquinas's *Catena Aurea*, and writing in the *British Critic* and *Christian Remembrancer*. He was ordained priest in 1843, and in the same year became tutor of Lincoln College, where he rapidly made a reputation as a clear and stimulating teacher and as a sympathetic friend of youth. The management of the college was practically in his hands, and his reputation as a scholar became high in the university. In 1851 the rectorship of Lincoln became vacant, and it seemed certain that Pattison would be elected, but he lost it by a disagreeable intrigue. The disappointment was acute and his health suffered. In 1855 he resigned the tutorship,

travelled in Germany to investigate Continental systems of education, and began his researches into the lives of Casaubon and Scaliger, which occupied the remainder of his life. In 1861 he was elected rector of Lincoln, marrying in the same year Emilia Francis Strong (afterwards Lady Dilke). The rector contributed largely to various reviews on literary subjects, and took a considerable interest in social science, even presiding over a section at a congress in 1876. The routine of university business he avoided with contempt, and refused the vice-chancellorship. But while living the life of a student, he was fond of society, and especially of the society of women. He died at Harrogate on the 30th of July 1884. His biography of *Isaac Casaubon* appeared in 1875; *Milton*, in Macmillan's English Men of Letters series in 1879. The 18th century, alike in its literature and its theology, was a favourite study, as is illustrated by his contribution (*Tendencies of Religious Thought in England*, 1688–1750) to the once famous *Essays and Reviews* (1860), and by his edition of Pope's *Essay on Man* (1869), &c. His *Sermons and Collected Essays*, edited by Henry Nettleship, were published posthumously (1889), as well as the *Memoirs* (1885), an auto-biography deeply tinged with melancholy and bitterness. His projected *Life of Scaliger* was never finished. Mark Pattison possessed an extraordinary distinction of mind. He was a true scholar, who lived entirely in the things of the intellect. He writes of himself, excusing the composition of his memoirs, that he has known little or nothing of contemporary celebrities, and that his memory is inaccurate: "All my energy was directed upon one end—to improve myself, to form my own mind, to sound things thoroughly, to free myself from the bondage of unreason... If there is anything of interest in my story, it is as a story of mental development" (*Memoirs*, pp. 1, 2). The *Memoirs* is a rather morbid book, and Mark Pattison is merciless to himself throughout. It is evident that he carried rationalism in religion to an extent that seems hardly consistent with his position as a priest of the English Church.

Mark Pattison's tenth and youngest sister was Dorothy Wyndlow Pattison (1832–1878), better known as SISTER DORA, the name she took in 1864 on becoming a member of the Anglican sisterhood of the Good Samaritan at Coatham, Yorkshire. In 1865 she was sent as nurse to their cottage hospital in Walsall, and from 1867 to 1877 she was in charge of a new hospital there. She left the sisterhood in 1874, and their hospital in 1877, to take charge of the municipal epidemic hospital, where the cases were largely small-pox. She had meanwhile qualified herself thoroughly as a nurse and had acquired no mean skill as a surgeon. Her efforts greatly endeared her to those among whom she worked, and after her death a memorial window was erected in the parish church, and a marble portrait statue by F. J. Williamson in the principal square of Walsall.

See Margaret Lonsdale's *Sister Dora* (1887 ed.).

PATTON, FRANCIS LANDEY (1843–   ), American educationalist and theologian, was born in Warwick parish, Bermuda, on the 22nd of January 1843. He studied at Knox College and at the university of Toronto; graduated at Princeton Theological Seminary in 1865; was ordained to the Presbyterian ministry in June 1865; was pastor of the 84th Street Presbyterian Church, New York City, in 1865–1867, of the Presbyterian Church of Nyack, New York, in 1867–1870, of the South Church, Brooklyn, in 1871, and of the Jefferson Park Presbyterian Church, Chicago, in 1874–1881; and in 1872–1881 was professor in McCormick Seminary, Chicago. He was moderator of the General Assembly of the Presbyterian Church in 1878. In 1881–1888 he was Stuart professor "of the relation of philosophy and science to the Christian religion" (a chair founded for him) in Princeton Theological Seminary; in 1888–1902 he was president of the College of New Jersey, which in 1896 became Princeton University; and in 1902 he became president of Princeton Theological Seminary. He brought charges of heresy in 1874 against David Swing, and was prosecuting attorney-at Swing's trial. In 1891 and 1892 he was one of the opponents of Dr Charles A. Briggs at the time of the Briggs heresy case. Dr Patton was an opponent of the revision of the Confession of Faith. He was editor, with Dr Briggs, of the *Presbyterian Review*, in 1880-1888. He wrote *The Inspiration of the Scriptures* (1869), and *Summary of Christian Doctrine* (1874).

PAU, a city of south-western France, chief town of the department of Basses-Pyrénées, 66 m. E.S.E. of Bayonne on the southern railway to Toulouse. Pop. (1906), 30,315. It is situated on the border of a plateau 130 ft. above the right bank of the Gave de Pau (a left-hand affluent of the Adour), at a height of about 620 ft. above the sea. A small stream, the Hédas, flowing in a deep ravine and crossed by several bridges, divides the city into two parts. The modern importance of Pau is due to its climate, which makes it a great winter health-resort. The most striking characteristic is the stillness of the air, resulting from the peculiarly sheltered situation. The average rainfall is about 33 in., and the mean winter temperature is 43°, the mean for the year being 56°.

The town is built on a sandy soil, with the streets running east and west. The Place Royale (in the centre of which stands Nicolas Bernard Raggi's statue of Henry IV., with bas-reliefs by Antoine Etex) is admired for the view over the valley of the Gave and the Pyrenees; it is connected by the magnificent Boulevard des Pyrénées with the castle gardens. Beyond the castle a park of thirty acres planted with beech trees stretches along the high bank of the Gave. Access to the castle is obtained by a stone bridge built under Louis XV.; this leads to the entrance, which gives into a courtyard. On the left of the entrance is the *donjon* or *tour* of Gaston Phœbus. On the right are the *tour neuve*, a modern erection, and the Tour de Montauzet (Monte-Oiseau), the higher storeys of which were reached by ladders; the Tour de Bilhères faces north-west, the Tours de Mazères south-west. Another tower between the castle and the Gave, the Tour de la Monnaie, is in ruins.

In the gardens to the west of the castle stand a statue of Gaston Phœbus, count of Foix, and two porphyry vases presented by Bernadotte king of Sweden, who was born at Pau. On the ground-floor is the old hall of the estates of Béarn, 85 ft. long and 36 ft. wide, adorned with a white marble statue of Henry IV., and magnificent Flemish tapestries ordered by Francis I. Several of the upper chambers are adorned with Flemish, Brussels or Gobelins tapestry, but the most interesting room is that in which Henry IV. is said to have been born, containing his cradle made of a tortoise-shell, and a magnificent carved bed of the time of Louis XII. The churches of St Jacques and St Martin in the Gothic style are both modern. The *lycée* occupies a portion of the buildings of a Jesuit college founded in 1622. The prefecture, the law-court and the hôtel de ville present no remarkable features. Pau is the seat of a court of appeal and a court of assises and has a tribunal of first instance, a tribunal of commerce and a chamber of arts and manufactures. There are training colleges for both sexes, a library, an art museum and several learned societies. Pau owes most of its prosperity to its visitors. The golf club, established 1856, has a course of 18 holes, on the Plaine de Billère, about a mile from the town. Among the industrial establishments are flour-mills, cloth factories and tanneries, and there is a trade in wine, hams, horses and cloth.

Pau derives its name from the word *pal*, in allusion to the stakes which were set up on the site chosen for the town. It was founded probably at the beginning of the 11th century by the viscounts of Béarn. By the erection of the present castle in the latter half of the 14th century, Gaston Phœbus made the town a place of importance and after his death the viscounts of Béarn visited it frequently. Gaston IV. granted a charter to the town in 1464. François Phœbus, grandson and successor of Gaston, became king of Navarre in 1479, and it was not until 1512 that the loss of Spanish Navarre caused the rulers of Béarn to transfer their residence from Pampeluna to Pau, which till 1589 was their seat of government. Margaret of Valois, who married Henri d'Albret, made her court one of the most brilliant of the time. In 1553 her daughter Jeanne d'Albret gave birth to Henry IV. at Pau. It was the residence of Catherine, sister of Henry IV., who governed Béarn in the name of her brother. In 1620

when French Navarre and Béarn were reduced to the rank of province, the intendants took up their quarters there. In the 19th century Abd-el-Kader, during part of his captivity, resided in the castle.

PAUL, "the Apostle of the Gentiles," the first great Christian missionary and theologian. He holds a place in the history of Christianity second only to that of the Founder himself. It was no accident that one who has been styled "the second founder of Christianity" was born and bred a Pharisee. Rather it was through personal proof of the limitations of legal Judaism that he came to distinguish so clearly between it and the Gospel of Christ, and thereby to present Christianity as the universal religion for man as man, not merely a sect of Judaism with proselytes of its own. For this, and nothing less, was the issue involved in the problem of the relation of Christianity to the Jewish Law; and it was Paul who settled it once and for all.

A modern Jew has said, "Jesus seems to expand and spiritualize Judaism; Paul in some senses turns it upside down." The reason of this contrast is their respective attitudes to the Law as the heart of Judaism. Jesus seems never to have breathed the atmosphere of Rabbinic religion.[1] Hence his was a purely positive reinterpretation of the spirit of Old Testament religion as a whole. His attitude to the Law was one of habitual dutifulness to its ordinances, combined with sovereign freedom towards its letter when the interests of its spirit so required (cf. F. J. A. Hort, *Judaistic Christianity*, chap. ii.). . To this the primitive apostles and their converts in the main adhered, without seeing far into their Master's principle in the matter; nor did they feel any great straitening of the spirit by the letter of the Mosaic, rather than the Rabbinic Law. But with Paul it was otherwise. As Saul the Pharisee he had taken the Mosaic *Thorah* as divine Law in the strictest sense, demanding perfect inner and outer obedience; and he had relied on it utterly for the righteousness it was held able to confer. Hence when it gave way beneath him as means of salvation—nay, plunged him ever more deeply into the Slough of Despond by bringing home his inability to be righteous by doing righteousness—he was driven to a *revolutionary* attitude to the Law *as method of justification*. "Through (the) Law" he "died unto (the) Law," that he "might live unto God" (Gal. ii. 19). By this experience not only Pharisaic Judaism, but the legal principle in religion altogether, was turned "upside down" within his own soul; and of this fact his teaching and career as an apostle were the outcome.

But Paul had in him other elements besides the Jewish, though these lay latent till after his conversion. As a native and citizen of Tarsus, he had points of contact with Greek culture and sentiment which help to explain the sympathy and tact with which he adapted his message to the Greek. As a Roman citizen likewise, conscious of membership in a world-wide system of law and order which overrode local and racial differences, he could realize the idea of a universal religious franchise, with a law and order of its own. Both these factors in his training contributed to the moulding of Paul the missionary statesman. In his mind the conception of the Church as something catholic as the Roman Empire first took shape; and through his wonderful labours the foundations of its actual realization were firmly laid. In giving some account of this man and of his teaching, we shall expound the latter mainly as it emerges in the course of his personal career.

Method.—Paul's own letters are our critical basis, as F. C. Baur and the Tübingen school made clear once for all. The book of Acts and other sources of information are to be used only so far as they

[1] This, since the full success of the Maccabaean reaction more than a century before, was determined by the Pharisaic notion of the Law, as a rigorous and technical method of attaining "righteousness" before God by correctness of religious conduct. But this ideal represented only one stream of the religion of the original *Chassidim*, or "pious ones" of the Psalms (see ASSIDEANS). The simpler form in which their piety lived on in less official circles, was that amidst which John the Baptist and Jesus himself were reared. It breathes in the more popular literature of edification represented by the *Testaments of the Twelve Patriarchs*, as well as in Luke i., ii.

are compatible with the letters,[1] as our only strictly contemporary documents. If our results to-day are far more positive than those of the Tübingen critics, this is due partly to the larger number of letters now generally acknowledged as Paul's (some eight or ten), and partly to a fuller knowledge both of Judaism and the Graeco-Roman world. These are seen to have embraced more varieties of religious thought and feeling than used to be assumed. The "particularist" tendency in Judaism was more limited than Baur supposed; while there was even a pre-Christian gnosticism, both Jewish and non-Jewish. Albrecht Ritschl in his *Altkath. Kirche* (2nd ed., 1857) did much to break through the hard-and-fast categories of the school in which he was trained, and in particular showed that Gentile Christians generally were far from Pauline in their modes of conceiving either Law or Gospel.

Chronology.—This has been discussed by Sir W. M. Ramsay in *Pauline and Other Studies* (1907), and by C. H. Turner in Hastings's *Dict. of the Bible* (article "Chronology of New Test."). Their results agree in the main for the period when precision first becomes possible, viz. between Paul's first missionary journey and his arrival in Rome. Here Turner antedates Ramsay by a year throughout. C. Clemen, in his *Paulus* i. 349–410, reaches rather different results. The pivot of the whole is Festus's succession to Felix as procurator, which Turner places in 58 and Ramsay in 59, while they agree in excluding 56 (Blass and Harnack), 57 (Bacon), 60 (Lightfoot, Zahn), as well as yet earlier and later extremes (Clemen argues for 61). On the chronology from Paul's conversion down to the Relief visit (Acts xi. 30), c. 45–47, hardly two scholars agree; but on the whole the tendency is to put his conversion rather earlier than was formerly usual.

I. *Paul's Life.*— "Saul, who is also Paul," was "a Hebrew, of Hebrews" born, *i.e.* of strict Jewish origin, and of the tribe of Benjamin (Phil. iii. 5; cf. 2 Cor. xi. 22). Yet, as his double name suggests, he was not reared on Jewish soil but amid the Dispersion, at Tarsus in Cilicia, the son of a Roman citizen (Acts xxii. 28; cf. xvi. 37, xxiii. 27). "Saul," his Jewish name, was a natural one for a Benjamite to bear, in memory of Israel's first king. "Paul" was his name for the bon-Jewish world, according to a usage seen also in John Mark, Simeon Niger, &c. *Paulus* was not an uncommon name in Syria and eastern Asia Minor (see the *Index nominum* in Boeckh's *Corp. inscr. graec.*), and was a natural one for the son of a Roman citizen. Ramsey develops this point suggestively (*Pauline and Other Studies*, p. 65). "It is as certain that he had a Roman name and spoke the Latin language as it is that he was a Roman citizen. If, for example's sake, we could think of him sometimes as Gaius Julius Paulus—to give him a possible and even not improbable name—how completely would our view of him be transformed. Much of what has been written about him [as a narrow, one-sided Jew] would never have been written *to Tarsus.* if Luke had mentioned his full name." Nor would much of the same sort have been written, if the influences due to his Tarsian citizenship [2] (xxi. 39), viewed in the light of the habits of Jewish life in Asian cities, had been kept in mind. Tarsus, it seems, was peculiarly successful "in producing an amalgamated society in which the Oriental and Occidental spirit in unison attained in some degree to a higher plane of thought and action" (id., *The Cities of St. Paul*, 89). Accordingly it is natural that Paul's letters should bear traces of Hellenic culture up to the level of a man of liberal education. Whether he went beyond this to a first-hand study of philosophy, particularly of the Stoic type for which Tarsus as a university was famous, is open to question.[3] In any case Paul had learnt, when he wrote his epistles, to value Greek "wisdom" at its true worth—the suggestiveness and sanity of its best thoughts,

[1] The method which reverses this relation, using the "we" passages of Acts to discredit the epistles of Paul (as well as the rest of Acts), is a mere *tour de force,* which has received artificial vogue by incorporation in the *Encyclopaedia Biblica,* and to a less degree in the external and partial article "Saul of Tarsus" in the *Jewish Encyclopaedia.* The essential harmony of the epistles and Acts has been shown afresh by A. Harnack, *Die Apostelgeschichte* (1908).

[2] Probably as member of the Jewish "tribe" dating from the Seleucid colony planted there in 171 B.C. (Ramsay).

[3] The main difficulty in deciding on this, as on other points of contact between Paul and Hellenism, is the fact that he certainly got many of his Greek ideas through the medium of Judaeo-Greek or Hellenistic literature, like the *Wisdom of Solomon* (cf. Romans i. 18–ii. fin.). It is clear from the way in which he uses the Greek Bible, even where it diverges wrongly from the original, that he was reared on it rather than on the Hebrew text.

but at the same time its inadequacy to meet the deeper longings of the human spirit. Above all he felt the mental and moral shallowness of the verbal "show of wisdom" which marked current philosophical rhetoric.

Thanks to his letters, we can form some idea of the character and strength of the element in Paul's early life due to Judaism. Looking back, he says (Phil. iii. 4–7), "If any other man thinketh to have confidence in the flesh, I yet *Jewish* more. Circumcised the eighth day, . . . a Hebrew *Training.* of Hebrews; as touching the Law, a Pharisee; as touching the righteousness which is in the Law, found blameless. Howbeit what things were gain to me, these have I counted loss for Christ." He came indeed to regard such inherited advantages as in themselves things of "the flesh," natural rather than spiritual (vv. 4, 9). Yet as advantages, tending to awaken the spirit's thirst for God, he did esteem them, seeing in them part of the preparation vouchsafed by divine providence to himself (Gal. i. 15). Upon the "advantage of the Jew," as "entrusted with the oracles of God" (Rom. iii. 1 seq.), he dwells in Rom. ii. 17 in a way suggestive of his own youthful attitude to "the name of a Jew." Thus we may imagine the eager boy in Tarsus, as developing, under the instructions of a father strictly loyal to the Law, and under the teaching of the synagogue, a typical Jewish consciousness of the more serious and sensitive order.

A good deal depends on the age at which the young Saul passed from Tarsus to Jerusalem and the school of Gamaliel. If he felt his vocation as teacher of the Law at *In* the earliest possible age, this great change may have *Jerusalem.* come soon after his fifteenth year, when Rabbinic studies might begin. This would well accord with the likelihood that he never married. But in any case we must not exaggerate the contrast involved, since he came from a Pharisaic home and passed to sit at the feet of the leader of the more liberal Palestinian Rabbinism. The transition would simply accentuate the legal element in his religious life and outlook. Nor was it mere personal acceptance with God that floated before his soul as the prize of such earnestness. The end of ends was a righteous nation, worthy the fulfilment of the divine promises. But this too could come only by obedience to the Law. Thus all that the young Pharisee cared for most hung upon the Law of his fathers.

Outwardly he obtained the goal of legal blamelessness as few attained it; and for a time he may have felt a measure of self-satisfaction. But if so, a day came when the inner meaning of the Law, as extending to the sphere of desire and motive, came home to him in stern power, and his peace fled (Rom. vii. 9). For sin in his inner, real life was unsubdued; nay, it seemed to grow ever stronger, standing out more clearly and defiantly as insight into the moral life grew by means of the Law. To the Law he had been taught to look for righteousness. In his experience it proved but the means to "knowledge of sin," without a corresponding impulse towards obedience. Not only did it make him realize the latent possibilities of evil desire ("the evil heart," *Yetser hara*), it also made him aware of a subtler evil, the reaction of self-will against the demands of the Law. While one element was in abiding harmony with the will of God, the other was in equal sympathy with "the law of sin." Could the Law achieve the separation, making the moral person "die" to "the flesh" and so escape its sway? No, answered Saul's experience: the Law rather adds power to sin as self-will (1 Cor. xv. 56; Rom. vii. 11, 13). Whence then is deliverance to come? It can only come with the Messianic age and through Messiah. The Law would reign inwardly as outwardly, being "written on the heart" as promised in prophecy.

So may we conceive the position reached by Saul, though not with full consciousness, before he came into contact with Christianity. But as yet he did not realize that *First im-* "through the Law he had died to the Law" (Gal. *pressions as* ii. 19), much less the logical bearing of this fact upon *to Jesus.* the nature and function of the Law. How then would the message, "Jesus is the Messiah," strike such a man? It would seem a blasphemous caricature of things most sacred. It is doubtful whether he had heard Jesus Himself (2 Cor. v. 16 has perhaps another meaning). He may even have been absent from Jerusalem in the first days of apostolic preaching, possibly as a rabbi in Tarsus. But if so, his ardent nature soon brought him on the scene, in time at least to hear Stephen and take part against him (Acts vii. 58, 60). If the simple message of the first witnesses, that one whose life and preaching were largely out of harmony with the Law as Saul understood it, had in fact been raised from the dead by Israel's God and so vindicated—to the condemnation of that generation of God's people—if this seemed to Saul mere madness, what was he to say to Stephen's views as to the Law and the people of the Law, both past and present? (see STEPHEN). Stephen could not be right in the views which still divided them. Perish the thought! Perish too all those who upheld the crucified Nazarene, the accursed of the Law! For His death could mean but one of two things. Either He was accursed of God also, or—awful alternative, yet inevitable to Saul's logical mind—the Law *relative to which He was accursed* was itself set aside. Saul turned from the suggestion as too shocking to his pride alike in his people and in its divine Law, for him seriously to consider its alleged credentials—the Resurrection, and the supernatural power and goodness of Him whose claims it was held to confirm. Why stay to weigh the evidence of Galilean common folk (*Am-ha-arets*), themselves lax in their observance of *Thorah*, when over against it stood the whole weight of immemorial prescription, and the deliberate judgment of the custodians of the Law as to this man as "a deceiver"? No doubt they were self-deceived fanatics. But the logic of the movement had at length declared itself through the mouth of Stephen, and weak toleration must be abandoned.

So Saul was driven to persecute, driven by his acute sense of the radical issue involved, and perhaps hoping to find relief *Saul the* from his own bitter experience in such zeal for the *Persecutor.* Law. Yet the goading of unsatisfied intuitions did not cease. We may even suspect that Stephen's philosophy of Israel's history had made an impression on him, and was undermining his confidence in the infallibility of his nation's religious authorities. If mistaken before, why not again? This granted possible, all turned on the evidence as to the Resurrection of the crucified Prophet of Nazareth. Yet though the joyous mien of His followers, even when confronted with death, seemed to betoken a good conscience before God which could hardly fail to impress him, Saul felt the status of the Law to be too grave an issue to depend on the probabilities of human testimony. So he plunged on, in devotion to what still seemed the cause of God against impugners of His *Thorah*, but not without his own doubts. He was, in fact, finding it "hard to kick against the goad" (Acts xxvi. 14) plied in his deeper consciousness, as he followed his inherited and less personal beliefs. He was, in language which he later applied to his compatriots, loth to "submit himself to the righteousness of God" (Rom. x. 3), when it came in a manner humbling to his feelings. Still he was in the main honest (1 Tim. i. 13), and the hindrances to his belief were exceptional. Direct personal experience on the point on which all hinged, the legal condemnation of Jesus as Messiah following on the legal divine vindication of Jesus as Messiah following on the legal condemnation by the national authorities, was needful to open up a clear exit from his religious *impasse*.

It was at this critical point in his inner history that, as he neared Damascus on a mission of persecution, there was granted *The Vision* him—as he believed ever after in the face of all *at Damas-* challenge—a vision of Jesus, in risen and glorified *cus.* humanity, as objective as those to the original witnesses with which in 1 Cor. xv. he classes it.

As to the sense in which this vision, so momentous in its issues, may be regarded as "objective," the following points deserve notice. On the one hand it is generally agreed (1) that Paul distinguished this appearance of the risen Jesus from his other "visions and revelations of the Lord," such as he refers to in 2 Cor. xii. 1 sqq., and classed it with those to the Twelve and others which first created the belief that Jesus had been "raised from the dead"; (2) that

this belief included for Paul a transformed or spiritualised body (cf. the note of time, "on the third day," and the argument in 1 Cor. xv. 12 sqq., 35 sqq.), his own vision of which seems to colour his conception of the Resurrection body generally (Phil. iii. 21, though he had certain traditional notions on the subject to start with; cf. 2 Cor. v. 1 sqq. with *Apoc. Baruch.* xlix.-li., representing Jewish belief about A.D. 70-100, and see Dr R. H. Charles's ed.). On the other hand, analogies furnished by religious psychology, including a sudden vision amid light and the hearing of a voice as accompaniments of religious crisis in certain cases, affect our ability to take Saul's consciousness in the matter as a simple transcript of objective facts. There is indeed reason to believe that the dazzling light was such a fact, if it blinded Saul temporarily (Acts ix. 8-19) and affected his companions (xxii. 9, xxvi. 14). But beyond this physical prelude to his vision we cannot go critically. Thus the nature of the connexion between the light as an objective antecedent, and the vision subjective to Saul himself, remains doubtful on the plane of history. It is possible to penetrate further only by the aid of faith, with or without speculations based on certain psychical facts more and more establishing themselves to scientific minds. Religious faith, dwelling on the unique issues of the vision in the history of Christianity and arguing from effects to a cause as real as themselves, tends to postulate the objectivity which Saul himself asserts. Some do so in an absolute sense, in spite of the differences between Saul's experience and that of his companions (Acts ix. 7, xxii. 9). Others confine the objectivity to a divine act, producing by special action on Saul's brain a vision not due simply to the antecedents in himself. Thus it was not merely subjective, a mere vision in the sense of hallucination, but an objective vision or genuine revelation of the real, as Paul claimed. Such an objective-subjective revelation, being in this but a special form of what is involved in any real divine revelation, accords in general with modern research as to telepathy and phantasms of distant or deceased persons. But, after all, the main point for Paul's religious history—as well as the basis of all theories of the vision—is the question as to the degree of discontinuity between his thought before and after the event. On this Paul is clear and emphatic; nor can we here go behind the evidence of one whose writings prove him a master in introspective reflection. "There was no possibility that he should by any process of mere thinking come to realize the truth "as to Jesus, so rooted were the prejudices touching things divine which barred the way (see Ramsay, *Pauline and Other Studies*, p. 18).

Important as is the question as to the nature of the vision which changed Saul's career, it is its spiritual content which bears most upon the story of his life. Jesus *Its Spiritual* was, in spite of all, God's Messiah, His Righteous *Content.* One, His Son, the type and ideal of righteousness in man, through spiritual union with whom like righteousness was to be attained, if at all. In a flash Saul's personal problem as to acceptance with God and victory over sin was changed. It became simply a question how spiritual union with the Messiah was to come about. He had vanquished, and "condemned sin in the flesh" by His perfect obedience (Rom. viii. 3, v. 10), of which the Cross was now seen to be the crowning act. As for the Law as means of justification, it was superseded by the very fact that Messiah had realized His righteousness on another principle altogether than that of "works of the Law," and had in consequence been crucified by its action, as one already dead to it *as a dispensational principle*. This meant that those united to Him by faith were themselves sharers in His death to the Law as dispensational master and judge, and so were quit of its claims in that new moral world into which they were raised as sharers also in His Resurrection (Rom. vi. 1-vii. 6). Henceforth they "lived unto God" in and through Messiah, by the self-same Spirit by which He had lived the sinless life (viii. 9).

Here we have at once Paul's mysticism and his distinctive gospel in germ, though the full working out in various directions came only gradually under the stimulus "*All Things* of circumstances. But already the old régime *New.*" had dissolved. His first act was to make explicit, through confession and baptism, his submission and adhesion to Jesus as Messiah implicit in his cry from the ground, "What shall I do, Lord?" Thereby he formally "washed away his sins" (Acts xxii. 16; cf. Rom. x 9). Then with new-born enthusiasm he began boldly to proclaim in the synagogues of Damascus that Jesus, whose followers he had come to root out, was verily the Messianic Son of God (ix. 20; cf. Matt. xvi. 16). Yet ere long he himself felt the need for quiet in which to think out the theory of his new position. He withdrew to some secluded spot in the region south of Damascus, then vaguely called Arabia (Gal. i. 17). Chief among the problems pressing for reinterpretation in the light of his recent experi- *The New* ence was the place of the Law in God's counsels. *Theory of* While the Law could condemn, warn and in some *the Law.* degrees restrain the sinner from overt sins, it could not redeem or save him from the love of sin. In a word, it could not " give life " (Gal. iii. 21). Hence its direct remedial action was quite secondary. Its primary effect, and therefore divine purpose, was to drive men humbly to seek God's grace. It " shut up all unto (realized) disobedience, that God might have mercy upon all " (Rom. xi. 32; Gal. iii. 22). Thus the place of the Law in God's counsels was episodic. The radical egoism of the natural man could be transcended, and self-glorying excluded, not by the law, with its " law (principle) of works," but by the " law of faith " (Rom. iii. 27). In fine, the function of the Law was secondary, preparatory, temporary. The reign of the Law closed when its work in shutting up men to faith in Christ—the perfect form of faith, that of conscious sonship—was accomplished. It had a high place of honour as a dispensation for a limited end and time; but its day was over when Jesus accepted crucifixion at its hands, and so passed on as the inaugurator of a new dispensation marked by a final relation between man and God, the filial, the Spirit of which was already in the hearts of all Christian believers (Gal. iii. 23-iv. 7). Thus the Cross of Jesus was the satisfaction of the claims of Law *as a dispensation* or divinely sanctioned method, which had to be honoured even in the act of being transcended, " that God might be just (*i.e.* dispensationally consistent), while justifying the believer in Jesus " on a fresh basis (Rom. iii. 26). Such a view did but " establish the Law " (v. 31) within its own proper sphere, while pointing beyond it to one in which its final aim found fulfilment.

Here lay the revolutionary element in Paul's thought in relation to Judaism, turning the latter " upside down " and *Its Univ-* marking his gospel off from the form in which Judaeo-*ersal Value.* Christians had hitherto apprehended the salvation in Jesus the Christ. It was the result of profound insight, and, historically, it saved Christianity from being a mere Jewish sect. But as it was conditioned by recoil from an overdriven use of the Law in the circles in which Saul was trained, so there was something one-sided in its emphasis on the pathological workings of the Law upon human nature in virtue of sinful egoism. Saul was the pioneer who secured mankind for ever against bondage to religious legalism. He it was who first detected that specific virus generated by Law in the " natural man," and also discovered the sovereign antidote provided in Christ. Nor is it as though Paul, even in those apologetic writings which present his antitheses to Law in the sharpest form, had the Jewish *Thorah* exclusively in view. He deals with it rather as the classic type of law in religion: it is really law *quâ* law, even the unwritten law in conscience, as determining man's relations to God, that he has in mind in his psychological criticism of its tendencies in the human soul (see Sanday and Headlam, on Rom. ii. 12 seq.): " Nitimur in vetitum cupimusque negata." This is too often overlooked by his Jewish critics. Paul felt nothing but reverence for the *Thorah* in what he took to be its proper place, as secondary to faith and subordinate to Christ. In short, Paul first perceived and set forth the principle of inspiration to God-likeness by a personal ideal in place of obedience to an impersonal Law, as condition of salvation. The former includes the latter, while safeguarding the filial quality of religious obedience.

The above seems to meet part of the criticism directed by modern Jews against Paul's theory of the Law. Other criticisms (cf. C. G. Montefiore, *Jewish Quarterly Review*, vi. 428-474, xiii. 161-217) may just be noted. If Paul supports his theory by bad Scripture exegesis, that is a common Rabbinic failing. If it be said that it is monstrous to hold that God gave the Law mainly for another end than the ostensible one, viz. to lead to life by obedience, this holds so far; but one cannot exclude from the divine purpose the negative effect, viz. promotion of self-knowledge in sinful man and the breaking

down of his self-confidence, conditions essential to a mature filial relation between man and God. Nor did Paul deny the positive or directly beneficent, though limited, function of the Law, so far as it was viewed in the light of the grace of God, as by prophets, psalmists, and others who " walked humbly with God," not as meriting His approval as of right by " works of law." But, objects the modern Jew, the notion of Rabbinic Judaism as generally tainted by " legalism " in any such sense, is a mere figment of Paul's. Nevertheless it is unproven and improbable that Paul unfairly represents the *prevailing tendency in the Pharisaic Judaism of his own day* as " legalistic " in the bad sense. He is really the one extant witness upon the point, as just defined, if we except certain apocalyptic writings (whose evidence modern Jews are anxious to discount), like the *Apocalypse of Baruch* and 4 *Esra*, the latter of which suggests that already the humbling effect of the capture of Jerusalem was being felt. Finally the same liberal Jew who complains that Paul turns Judaism " upside down " by his doctrine of the Law, cites with approval his words, " There is no distinction between Jew and Greek," and adds, " Not till St Paul had written did the prophetic universalism attain its goal." Surely there is a vital connexion between these two things. " Universalism " was the true issue of the higher tendency in Hebraism, as seen in certain of Israel's prophets. But it was attained only through Jesus of Nazareth; and historically the main link between His supra-legal universalism and its actual outcome in the Christian Church was the ex-Pharisee Saul, with his anti-legal gospel.

Saul's conversion left Jesus the Christ as central to his new world as the Law had been to his old. All was summed up in Christ, and Him crucified. This was to him the *The Christ* essence of Christianity as distinct from Judaism. *of Paul.* As, to the Jew, life was lived under the Law or in it as native element, so the Christian life was " in Christ " as element and law of being. Christ simply replaced the Law as form and medium of relations between God and man. In this Paul went far beyond the older apostles, whose simpler attitude to the Law had never suggested the problem of its dispensational relation to Messiah, though in fact they relied on Messiah alone for justification before God. The logic of this, as Paul later urged it on Peter of Antioch (Gal. ii. 15 sqq.), they did not yet perceive. To him it was clear from the first. But the contrast goes farther. The very form in which Jesus was known to Saul by direct experience, namely, as a spiritual being, in a body already glorified in virtue of a regnant " spirit of holiness "—revealed by the Resurrection as the essence of His personality (Rom. i. 4)—determined all his thought about Him. To this even Jesus' earthly life, real as it was, was subordinate. Paul was not indifferent to Jesus' words and deeds, as helping to bring home in detail the spirit of Him who by resurrection was revealed as the Son of God; but apart from insight into His redemptive work, knowledge of these things was of little religious moment. The extent of Paul's knowledge of the historical Jesus has been much debated. Few think that he had seen Jesus in the flesh; some even deny that he knew or cared for more than the bare facts to which he alludes in his epistles—the Davidic birth, the institution of the Supper, the Death and Resurrection. But beyond his express appeals to precepts of " the Lord " in 1 Cor. vii. 10, ix. 14 (cf. Rom. xii. 14), he " shows a marked insight into the character of Jesus as it is described in the Gospels " (see 2 Cor. x. 1; cf. Phil. ii. 5-8). The sources of such knowledge were no doubt oral, *e.g.* Peter (Gal. i. 18), Barnabas, Mark, as well as collections of Jesus' words, along with connected incidents in His life, used in *catechesis*. Thus Saul's attitude to Jesus was fixed by his own experience. The varied theoretic expressions found in his writings as to Christ's relations to God, to mankind, and *His Theology* even to him but corollaries *Rooted in* *Experience.* of this. The most persistent element in his conception of Christ's person, viz. as a heavenly being, who, though God's Son, voluntarily humbled Himself and suffered in fulfilment of God's will, took its start from his own personal experience, although it included the speculative postulate of pre-existence in terms of some current Messianic form of thought. Paul's theory expressed the deeper sense of the all-inclusive significance of Christ, in keeping with his own experience. Hence, too, all his distinctive thoughts on religion, sometimes called

"Paulinism" (see below), were both experimental in origin and capable of statement in terms of his Christ. To him the Death and Resurrection of Christ were not isolated facts, nor yet abstractions. To this man of faith the crucial fact of Christ's Resurrection, in full spiritual humanity, had been brought within his own experience; so that here, and not in any second-hand facts touching Christ's earthly career, lay the real and verified basis of the whole Christian life. This makes his gospel so individual, and at the same time so universal —for those at least who at all share his religious experience.

It is unlikely that Saul began straightway to preach all his ideas or even those most prominent in his epistles, which belong *His Early* only to some ten years at the end of a ministry *Apostolate* of some thirty. In particular his special mission to the Gentiles dawned on him only gradually. No doubt as he looked back in writing Gal. i. 15 sqq., he felt that the final purpose of God in "revealing His Son in him" had been that he "might preach Him among the Gentiles." But this does not prove that he saw it all at once as involved in "the heavenly vision." For one thing the contracted horizon afforded by the hope of a speedy second Advent (*Parousia*) would limit his outlook materially. Then too he was intensely Jewish in feeling; and the probability is that he would begin to declare salvation through Christ alone, apart from "works of the Law," to his compatriots. Only bitter experience convinced him (Rom. ix. 1 sqq., x. 1 sqq.) that the Jews as a people did not share his experience as to the Law, and spurned their proffered birthright in Messiah.

Saul began his preaching in the synagogues of Damascus, and made a deep impression, especially, we may suppose, after his return from Arabia (Acts ix. 22; Gal. i. 17). But finally his Jewish opponents induced him to do away with him, by the connivance of the ethnarch of King Aretas (cf. 2 Cor. xi. 32 seq.). Then came his first visit to Jerusalem since his conversion, in the third year from that event, for the purpose of making the personal acquaintance of Peter (Gal. i. 18), presumably to hear first-hand about Jesus' earthly ministry and teaching, as well as to make the leading apostle directly acquainted with his own remarkable conversion and mission.[1] It was natural that Barnabas should help to break through the suspicion with which the arch-persecutor was at first regarded; also that such preaching as Saul did in Jerusalem should be directed to the Hellenists, *e.g.* his Cilician compatriots (ix. 29; cf. vi. 9). This led to his having to leave suddenly, apparently after a vision in the Temple which brought him fresh light as to the scope of his future ministry. During the ten or eleven years at least "in the regions of Syria and Cilicia" which ensued, it was still primarily to the Jews that he preached; for the news of him which reached "the churches of Judaea" from time to time (ἀκούοντες ἦσαν) was such that they "kept glorifying God" in him (Gal. i. 21-23), as they certainly would not have done had he all along addressed himself largely to Gentiles. His preaching, that is, was for the most part confined to the synagogue and its adherents of non-Jewish origin, whether circumcised or not. Of Saul's actual history, however, during these obscure years we gain only rare glimpses,[2] the first and most important being in connexion with the foundation at Antioch of a mixed Church of Jews and Gentiles. Whatever may have been the first beginnings of this new departure (a question which depends on the alternative readings[3] "Hellenists" and "Greeks" in

[1] Here Galatians (i. 18 sqq.) emphasizes its own special points of interest, in that Saul stayed only a fortnight and saw of the apostolic leaders none save Peter and James the Lord's brother; whereas Acts, in its popular account of the more public side of his visit, conveys a rather different effect, yet one not incompatible with what he himself relates.
[2] It is likely that some at least of the five scourgings in synagogues referred to in 2 Cor. xi. 24, befell him during this period. Many Jews would resent not only the preaching of a crucified Messiah, but also the filching from them of their proselytes.
[3] The present writer now believes that "Hellenists," the better supported reading (see Acts), is yet secondary, being due to assimilation to preceding usage in vi. 1, ix. 29, and possibly also to misinterpretation of the turning to the Gentiles in xiii. 46.

Acts xi. 20), a situation soon arose which Barnabas, who had been sent from Jerusalem to supervise the work begun by certain Hellenist preachers, felt to call for Saul's co-operation. He sought him out in Tarsus; and "for a whole year" the two enjoyed the hospitality of the Antiochene Church and instructed numerous converts—including not a few uncircumcised Gentiles. It is not clear how far Saul continued to reside in Antioch after his first "whole year" of continuous work as colleague of Barnabas. It no doubt remained his headquarters. But we may imagine him evangelizing also in the *His* region between Antioch and Tarsus (Gal. i. 21; cf. *Apostolate* Acts xv. 23, 41). Whilst so engaged, whether at *Expands.* Antioch or elsewhere, he seems to have attained quite a fresh sense of the degree to which Gentiles were destined to form an integral part of that "Israel of God" which was being gathered through faith in Jesus as the Christ (cf. the name "Christians," Acts xi. 26). Writing about summer A.D. 56, he speaks of having had an overpowering revelation some thirteen years previously (2 Cor. xii. 2-4), that is, about 42-43, the very period now in question. He says nothing, it is true, as to its theme; but it can hardly have been unconnected with his central preoccupation, the scope of the Church, as set forth later in Eph. ii. 11, iii. 13.

Saul's relations with the Jerusalem community between his coming to Antioch and his final relinquishing of it as his headquarters about A.D. 50 (a period of some ten years), form a crucial point in his missionary life. The extreme Tübingen theory that Saul was now, and even later, in sharp conflict with the leaders in Judaea, is a thing of the past. But many problems remain, and what follows is offered only on its own merits, as seeming best to unify the relevant data in the light of all we know of Paul as a man and a missionary. Points of divergence from current views will be indicated as far as possible.

Such a new revelation would naturally lead to more definite efforts to win Gentiles as such, and this again to his second visit to Jerusalem, some eleven years after his *Second* former visit (or rather more than thirteen, if the *Visit to* interval in Gal. ii. 1 be reckoned from that visit *Jerusalem.* and not from his conversion). He would come to feel the need of a clear understanding with Jerusalem touching his gospel, "lest perchance he should run in vain or have already so run" (ii. 2). Saul was not the man to wait for a foreseen evil to develop. "In accordance with a revelation" he induced Barnabas to accompany him to a private conference with the leaders in Jerusalem, to lay before them his gospel (ii. 2). The date of this was *c.* 43-45. His aim was to confer solely with leaders (contrast Acts xv. 4, 12) like James and Cephas and John, the "pillars" of the Jerusalem community. But certain persons who showed such a spirit as to make him describe them as "pseudo-brethren," managed to be present and demanded the circumcision of Titus, a Greek whom Saul had taken with him. In this demand he saw a blow at the heart of his gospel for Gentiles, and would not give way. The "pillars" themselves, too, felt that his distinctive mission was bound up with Gentile freedom from obligation to the Mosaic Law as such. They recognized Saul and Barnabas as entrusted with a specific Gentile mission, parallel with their own to Jews. Only, as pledge that the two should not diverge but remain sister branches of Messiah's Ecclesia, until He should return and remove all anomalies, they asked that the Gentile mission should prove the genuineness[4] of its piety by making it a habit to "remember the poor." Here was a proviso which Saul was as eager as they could be to get carried out; and this he was able to prove ere long in the special form of

[4] How essential a mark of true piety such conduct was in the eyes of Jews at this time is well known. A synonym for almsgiving was "righteousness" (cf. Matt. vi. 1 seq.); it is specially praised, in the *Pirke Aboth*, along with *Thorah* and divine worship, as the "three things on which the world rests"; while in *Baba Bathra* 10 b. we read, "As sin-offering makes atonement for Israel, so alms for the Gentiles." In the light of this, confirmed by Acts x. 2, 4, in the case of Cornelius, it seems that the reference in Gal. ii. 10 is to deeds of charity generally, as a token of genuine piety in Messianic proselytes, just as in ordinary Jewish ones; for the primitive Judaeo-Christian community was most earnest on the point: cf. Acts ii. 44 seq., iv. 32-37.

relief to the poor in Judaea, which he and Barnabas fitly administered in person (Acts xi. 30, xii. 25). This relief visit took place about 45-46.[1] Having now reached an understanding with the leaders in Jerusalem, as to his mission to the Gentiles Saul felt anxious to break fresh ground, and probably broached the subject to the local leaders. As they waited on God for guidance, the Spirit through one of the "prophets" directed that Barnabas and Saul be set apart for such an enterprise; and this was done in solemn form (xiii. 1-3). Naturally Barnabas thought of his native Cyprus; and thither they sailed, about spring A.D. 47, with Mark (q.v.) as their assistant. That they had at least one other companion is probable not only from the phrase "Paul and his company" (xiii. 13), but also from the traces of eyewitness in the narrative of Acts (see LUKE). Their work lay at first in synagogues. But at Paphos an unparalleled event occurred, to which due prominence is given. The Roman proconsul, Sergius Paulus, a man whose wide religious interest showed itself in having about his person a Jewish "prophet" with magical pretensions, sent for the new preachers. Barjesus, the magus or wizard (as his surname; Elymas, probably denotes), opposed the rivals to his patron's attention; and this brought Saul decisively to the front. His fitness for his part, as no mere Jew but in a sense Roman facing Roman, is indicated by the pointed description, "Saul, who is also Paulus." His intervention procured the confusion of the magus and the conversion of the proconsul. This incident—so significant of the future in many ways—marked the beginning of a new prominence of Paul in the conduct of the mission (cf. "Paul and his company"). Further, on leaving Cyprus the mission entered the region where Paul, not Barnabas, was most at home. At Perga in Pamphylia a fresh decision was reached as to the route now to be taken, and this led to Mark's withdrawing altogether (see MARK).

It does not seem that the personal factor weighed most with Mark; rather it was the nature of "the work" itself (xv. 38). Perhaps it had been tacitly assumed that the mission would not cross the Taurus range to the different world beyond, but keep to the coast-lands south of that great natural barrier, which were in close relation with Antioch and Syria generally. Accordingly, when Paul at last outlined the larger scheme, which had perhaps lain in principle in his own mind all along, Mark recoiled from its boldness. The natural thing indeed was to evangelize in Pamphylia, a country in close relations with Cilicia and Syria. Why then did Paul insist on pushing inland straight for the Taurus range and the high table-land some 3600 ft. above sea-level ? Not to evangelize Pisidian Antioch, and the other cities in the south of Roman Galatia lying to the east of it; for Paul himself says that his preaching there was due to sickness (Gal. iv. 13), seemingly when on his way to other fields. These would be in the first instance certain cities in the south-east of the Roman province of "Asia," where Jews abounded and had a large Gentile following. Had the great cities of western Asia, and particularly Ephesus (cf. xvi. 6), been his primary aim, he would have taken the easier and more direct route running west-north-west through Laodicea. Sir W. M. Ramsay thinks that Paul sought the Galatian highlands on purpose to get rid of malarial fever, contracted in the lowlands of Pamphylia. But Mark would hardly have left under these conditions. It seems better to suppose that it was only on the arduous journey to Antioch, amid "perils of rivers, perils of robbers," or even after his arrival there, that the malaria (if such it was) so developed as to reduce Paul to the pitiable state, as of one smitten by the wrath of some deity, in which he preached to the Galatians in the first instance (Gal. iv. 13 seq.).

It was in the late summer or autumn of A.D. 46 or 47 that Paul arrived in the Pisidian Antioch, a considerable Roman colony. Its population was typical of the Graeco-Oriental part of the empire. It included the native Anatolian, the Greek, and the Jewish elements,[2] so frequently found together in Asia Minor since the days of the Seleucid kings of the Hellenistic period, who used Jews as colonists attached to their cause. The Anatolian ground-stock had marked affinity with the Semitic peoples, though it was

[1] Sir W. M. Ramsay would identify the visit of Gal. ii. 1-10 with the relief visit itself (a view differing but little in effect from that given above); but most scholars identify it with Acts xv., in spite of Gal. i. 22 seq. compared with Acts xi. 30, xii. 25.

[2] For these, their history and significance in connexion with each of the cities studied, see Sir W. M. Ramsay, The Cities of St Paul (1907).

Hellenized in speech and education. It is in this light that we must view the enthusiasm with which Paul's gospel was received (xiii. 44 sqq.; Gal. iv. 14 seq.), and which marked an epoch in his ministry to the Gentiles. It was here and now that he uttered the memorable exclamation: "It was necessary that the word of God should first be spoken to you: seeing ye thrust it from you, and judge yourselves unworthy of eternal life, lo, we turn to the Gentiles" (xiii. 46). Yet even so he did not here and now give up all hope that the Jews of the Dispersion with their more liberal conception of Judaism, might be won over to a spiritual rather than a national fulfilment of "the promise made to the fathers" by "the voices of the prophets" (xiii. 26-28, 32 seq., 38 seq.). Primarily this "turning to the Gentiles" had for Paul only a local meaning, as he continued to begin in each city with the synagogue.[1] But the emphasis laid on the incident in Acts shows that to one looking back it had a more far-reaching meaning, since henceforth Paul's work was in fact to lie mainly among Gentiles.

Paul's experiences were much the same at Iconium, whither he and Barnabas betook themselves when expelled from Antiochene territory (probably after being scourged by the lictors, 2 Cor. xi. 25). There, too, Jews were at the bottom of the tumult raised against the missionaries ("apostles," xiv. 4, 14), which forced them to flee into the Lycaonian regio of the province. In this district, marked by the native pre-Greek village system, they made Lystra and Derbe successively their headquarters. In the former occurred the healing of the lame man at the word of Paul (cf. Rom. xv. 19; 2 Cor. xii. 12; Gal. iii. 5), with its sequel in the naïve worship offered to the strangers as gods manifest in human form. The story, told in a few graphic touches, sets before us Paul as the tactful missionary, meeting the needs of the simple Lycaonians with an elementary natural theology. Again his work was disturbed by Jews, this time his old foes from Antioch and Iconium, and he barely escaped death—one of those "deaths oft" to which he refers in 2 Cor. xi. 23, a passage which shows how far Acts is from exhausting the tale of Paul's hardships and dangers, either in Galatia or elsewhere (with xiv. 1 cf. 2 Tim. iii. 11). At Derbe, the frontier city of Galatia to the south-east, Paul was within easy reach of Tarsus, his old home. But the needs of his young converts drew him back to face fresh dangers in Lystra, Iconium and Antioch (where, however, new magistrates were now in office), in order to encourage "the disciples." To give them the support of responsible oversight, the apostles procured the election of "elders" in each church, probably on the model of the synagogue: for Paul had a due sense of the corporate life of each local brotherhood (Rom. xii. 4 seq.), and of the value of recognized leaders and pastors (1 Thess. v. 12 seq.; 1 Cor. xvi. 15 seq.; cf. Acts xx. 17, 28). Then, passing through Pamphylia they returned to Antioch, and reported to a church meeting "all that God had done with them, and how he had opened a door of faith unto the Gentiles."

So ended Paul's first missionary journey known to us in detail, the very first wherein his vocation as apostle of the Gentiles took marked effect. So far Gentile believers had been a mere minority, not essentially affecting the Jewish character and atmosphere of the Messianic Ecclesia, any more than the presence of proselytes was thought to affect Judaism even outside Palestine. But all this was menaced by the work accomplished, apparently under divine auspices, in Galatia. There uncircumcised Gentiles formed the majority of the heirs to Messianic salvation; and if expansion continued on these lines, the like would be true of the new Israel as a whole. Nay, a definite check to Jewish conversions would result from the prejudice created by a large influx of men not committed to the Law by their baptism into Christ. Now that the logic of facts was unfolding so as to jeopardize the Law

[1] Naturally Paul would have a regular address which he used with minor variations in beginning his mission in any local synagogue; and this Luke has in substance preserved for us here. For its authenticity, see Sir W. M. Ramsay, op. cit. 303 sqq.; compare A. Sabatier, L'Apôtre Paul (3rd ed., 1896), p. 89, for disproof of dependence on Stephen's speech.

in toto, it could not but appear to many Jewish Christians time to reconsider the situation, and boldly deny the reality of any Gentile's portion in Messianic salvation apart from circumcision (as binding to observance of the Law). So argued the stricter section, those with Pharisaic antecedents, who boldly invaded the headquarters of the liberal mission at Antioch, and began to teach the Gentile converts that circumcision and the Law were matters of life and death to them. Paul and Barnabas took up the gage; and as the judaizers no doubt claimed that they had the Judaean Church at their back, the local church felt that the issue would have to be decided in Jerusalem itself. So they sent up Paul and Barnabas " and certain others of their number " (Acts xv. 2; contrast Gal. ii. 1 seq.) to confer with " the apostles and elders " there. The fact that Paul consented to go at all, to the seeming prejudice of his direct divine commission, is best explained by his prior understanding with " the Pillars " of the Judaean Church itself (Gal. ii. 1–10). His object was twofold: to secure in the centre of Judaeo-Christianity that public vindication of Gentile freedom from " the yoke of the Law " on which he felt he could count, and at the same time to save the Church of Christ from outward schism.

On the main issue there could be no compromise. It was conceded, largely through the influence of Peter and James, that the good pleasure of the Holy Spirit (xv. 28[a]), in possessing Gentile hearts, settled the question. But as to the need of considering age-long Jewish sentiment on points where divergent practice would tend to prevent Jewish Christians from recognizing Gentile believers as brethren, as well as place a needless stumbling-block between Jews and a Messianic society in which unlimited " uncleanness " was tolerated—on this compromise was possible. The compromise was proposed by James (xv. 20 seq.) and accepted by Paul. Indeed he had less to sacrifice than the other side in the concordat. For his Gentile converts had only to limit their freedom a little, in the cause of considerate love; but their Jewish brethren had to surrender a long-standing superiority conferred by divinely instituted national law. For while the law of Moses was still observed by Jewish Christians, in the case of Gentile proselytes to Messianic Judaism it was to be waived, and a *minimum* of proselyte rules, indispensable (xv. 28) to a type of piety[1] essentially common to all " in Christ," taken as sufficient. Of the " abstinences " in question only that touching blood (in its two forms) was really a ritual matter, and it was one on which there was a good deal of scruple outside Judaism. The other two were obvious deductions from fundamental Christian ideas, as well as elements of proselyte piety. On the other hand, security against Gentile liberty undermining Jewish-Christian observance of the Law was felt to exist in the firmly rooted tradition of the synagogues of the Diaspora (xv. 21).

The above is only one reading of the case, though the simplest. Not a few scholars dispute that Paul could have been a party to such a concordat at all, and suppose that the letter embodying it is a fiction, probably composed by the author of Acts. Others hold that, if any such letter were ever sent, it was by James and the Jerusalem Church at a later date, without consulting Paul. In fact it was their solution of the deadlock to which interference with Peter's table-fellowship with Gentiles led in Antioch after the Jerusalem-conference; but the author of Acts unhistorically fused it with the decision of that conference. Finally Harnack (*Die Apostelgeschichte*, 1908, pp. 188 sqq.) maintains that the reference to " things strangled " is an interpolation, not shared by early Western authorities for the text, and that " blood " meant originally homicide. Hence the rules had no reference to food apart from constructive idolatry. This theory—which does not remove the contradiction with Gal. ii. 10, on the assumption that Acts. xv. = Gal. ii. 1–10—seems at once textually improbable (feeling in the East being too anti-Jewish in the sub-apostolic age to allow of such an interpolation) and historically needless.

At no point in his career does Paul's greatness appear more strikingly than now in his relations with Judaeo-Christianity. Equally above the *doctrinaire* temper which cannot see its

favourite principle practically limited by others, and a mere opportunism which snatches at any compromise as the line of least resistance, he acted as a true missionary states- *Paul's Conciliatory Spirit.* man, with his eye both on the larger future and *dilatory* on the limiting present. As he himself obeyed the *Spirit.* principle of loving concern for others good by conforming to certain Jewish forms of piety (1 Cor. ix. 19 seq., 27), as being a Jew by training; so he was ready to enjoin on Gentiles, short of the point of compulsion, abstinence from blood simply as a thing abhorrent to Jewish sentiment. His was the spirit of a strong man, who can afford and loves to be generous for the greater good of all. This is the key to his conduct all along, leading him to interrupt his work on two later occasions simply to keep in touch with Jerusalem by conciliatory visits, as prejudice against him recurred owing to rumours of his free conduct on his Gentile missions.

On the other hand, it was the opposite side of his character; viz. inflexible courage in defence of vital principle, that was called into action soon after, owing to Peter's visit *Peter's* to Antioch (the abrupt reference to which in Gal. *Visit to* ii. 11 probably means that the judaizers were *Antioch.* making capital of it in Galatia). There for a time Peter fell in readily with the local custom whereby Jewish and Gentile Christians ate together. But this was more than was understood even by James to be involved in alliance of the two missions. It was one thing not to force Judaism on Gentile Christians; it was another to sanction table-fellowship between Gentile and Jewish Christians, in consideration for the former as brethren. Let Peter, said James through his friends, remember Judaean feelings as well. Such a step was in advance of their convictions; and in any case it seemed wrong to break with the sentiment of the Mother Church in Judaea for the comfort of Gentile brethren on the spot, whom they had but recently regarded as by nature " unclean."

One man, however, saw further into both the logic and the expediency of the case. Paul saw that by their very reliance on Christ rather than the Law for justification, *Paul's* Jewish Christians had in principle set aside the Law *Protest.* as the divinely appointed means of righteousness: that thereby they had virtually come down from their prerogative standing on the Law and classed themselves with " sinners of the Gentiles "; and finally that they had been led into this by Jesus the Messiah Himself. If that attitude were sinful " then was Christ the minister of sin." If righteousness depend after all on the Law, then why did Christ die? This penetrating analysis (Gal. ii. 14–21) of the implications of Christian faith was unanswerable as regards any legal observance as condition of justification. But was it not possible that the degree of sanctification to be hoped for depended, for Jews at least, upon adhering as closely as possible to the old law of holiness? This was probably the position of Peter and Barnabas and the rest, as it was certainly the theory with which the judaizers " bewitched " the Galatian converts for whose benefit Paul recounts the story (iii. 1–3). But for it too he had an answer, in his doctrine of an evangelical sanctification, homogeneous in nature and motives with the justification out of which it grows, as fruit from root (iii. 5, v. 16–26). But at Antioch he confined his protest to the vital matter of principle, the true relation of Christ and the Law, and the deadly danger of confusing their values and functions if both were to be treated as essential to Christian faith. Thus a higher expediency, for Jews in particular, told against the expediency alleged on the other side; while as for expediency in relation to the Gentiles, it was a matter not only of Antioch and the Jews and Gentiles there involved, but also of the Roman world and the relative numbers of potential converts from either class in it. This point is not made explicit in Gal. ii. 14 sqq.; but it was probably present to Paul's mind and added to the intensity of his feeling touching the gravity of the issue.

The standpoint of the *Epistle to the Galatians* is of great moment in judging of its historical retrospect. What Paul had to establish in the first instance was his independence up to the date of his

---

[1] For this as the spirit of these rules, whatever their exact origin, see Hort, *Judaistic Christianity*, pp. 68 sqq. They thus correspond to the " remembrance of the poor " in the earlier agreement between " the Pillars " and Paul in Gal. ii. 10.

evangelization of the Galatians, which God had obviously blessed (iii. 2, 5). It is therefore natural to regard all related in chapters i.-ii., including his rebuke of Peter, as prior to that cardinal fact. Next the logic of the case, as well as his explicit words in i. 22 sqq., rules out any visit to Jerusalem, including the relief visit to Judaea of Acts xi. 30, xii. 25, between his first visit and that of Gal. ii. 1 sqq. (this tells against the common view that Gal. ii. 1 sqq. = Acts xv.). Finally the reason why no explicit reference is made to the visit of Acts xv. is that it was already familiar to his readers from his own account of it on his second and recent visit to them (Acts xvi. 4-6), and was in fact the starting-point of the judaizers' case. As regards the " Galatians " addressed in this epistle, we assume with the majority of scholars, since Sir W. M. Ramsay's writings on the subject, that they were those evangelized in Acts xiii., xiv., not in xvi. 6. According to the above reading of this epistle it was written in the winter of Paul's first journey to Europe, c. 51-52, say in Corinth (so Rendall, Zahn, Bacon), which would explain not only the " so quickly " of i. 6., but also his inability to hasten to their side (iv. 20). This last condition seems to exclude as place of writing both Antioch on the eve of the second (McGiffert) or third (Ramsay) missionary journey, and Ephesus during Paul's long sojourn there. The one seeming alternative, viz. Antioch on the eve of the conference in Acts xv. (so V. Weber), is preferable only on the assumption that the epistle excludes all knowledge of this event (as the present writer formerly held).

Not long after this episode Paul proposed to Barnabas a visitation of the churches they had jointly founded. But Barnabas, perhaps feeling more than before the *Paul's Second Great Mission Tour.* difference in their attitudes to the Law, made the reinstatement of John Mark as their helper a condition of co-operation. To this Paul demurred on the ground that he could not be relied upon in all emergencies; and the feeling caused by this difference as to Mark's fitness was sufficient to cause Paul and Barnabas to take separate lines. Each went to his own sphere of work, Barnabas to Cyprus and Paul towards Asia Minor, and we never again read of them as together, though Paul continued to refer to his old colleague in kindly terms (1 Cor. ix. 6 and Col. iv. 10). Paul found a colleague in Silas (Silvanus), a " leading " man in the Jerusalem church and a " prophet," but like himself a Roman citizen (Acts xvi. 37, 39); and started, with the goodwill of the Antiochene Church, probably in summer A.D. 50. His way lay through churches of his own foundation, in one of which he found a helper to replace Mark, Timothy of Lystra, who was to be as a son to him up to the very end. Confident in the conciliatory spirit of both sides in the Concordat, and anxious to show how ready he was to consider Jewish feeling where Gentile freedom was not involved, he circumcised this young semi-Jew before taking him as his associate into regions where work would still lie largely among Jews. In a similar spirit he also commended " the resolutions " of the Concordat to the observance of his churches in Galatia, though the circular letter of the conference did not make it apply to more than those of the Syro-Cilician region.

But while the immediate result of this visit was good, the secondary issues were among the bitterest in Paul's life, *Judaizers in South Galatia.* owing to the unscrupulous action of judaizers who, taking advantage of his absence, soon began a vigorous, but subtle, propaganda amongst his converts in this region. They represented Paul as having changed his policy in deference to the Jerusalem authorities, to the extent of allowing that the Law had *some* claim upon Gentile believers in the Jewish Messiah. Otherwise why were the " abstinences " enjoined? Nay, more: these had been put forward as a bare *minimum* of what was expedient, to judge from the practice of those same Judaean authorities. But if so, surely it must at least be· necessary to full Christian piety (Gal. iii. 3; cf. Peter's conduct·at Antioch), though not perhaps to a bare place in the coming kingdom. Had not Paul himself confessed the value of circumcision (v. 11) in the case of Timothy, the son of a Gentile father? As for his earlier policy, it must have been due mainly to a wish to humour his converts' prejudices (i. 10), to begin with. At any rate the gospel they now brought was the authentic Apostolic Gospel, and if Paul's did differ from it, so much the worse for his gospel, since it could·in no case claim to be other than derived from theirs (i. 1-9, 11 seq.). How plausible

must such a plea have seemed to inexperienced Gentile converts, " bewitching " their minds away from the central facts, Christ crucified and the free gift of the spirit through faith in Him. But how disingenuous as regards Paul's real position! Can we wonder at his indignation as he wrote in reply, and that he was goaded on to pass, in his final peroration, a counter-judgment upon their motives too sweepingly severe (vi. 12 seq.)? In any case the gross abuse by the judaizers of Paul's promulgation of the " abstinences " in Galatia fully explains his contrary practice elsewhere.

Paul left his Galatian converts about autumn A.D. 50, bound for the adjacent Asia. But not even yet was he to preach there, being diverted by something in which he saw *Paul enters Europe.* the divine hand. Such as when, on his way northwards through the Phrygian region of Galatia,[1] he tried to enter Bithynia. (where also were cities with a large Jewish element), he was again turned aside by " the Spirit of Jesus " (? a vision in the form of Jesus, xvi. 7, cf. xviii. 9, xxii. 17). Thus his course seemed open only westwards through Mysia (northern " Asia ") to the coast, which was reached at Troas, the chief port in the north-west Aegean for intercourse between Asia and Macedonia. These were but sister provinces, united by the easy pathway of the sea. Yet in sentiment and in conditions of work it was a new departure to which Paul found himself summoned, when in a night-vision " a certain Macedonian " stood as if entreating him: " Come over into Macedonia and· help us." Here was the positive guidance to which two negative divine interventions had been leading up. Paul hesitated not a moment, though the idea was bolder than that of his own frustrated plan. " Straightway," in the words of Luke, " we sought to go forth into Macedonia, concluding that God had called us for to preach the Gospel unto them " (xvi. 10). So, at this crucial point in Paul's mission to the Gentiles, Luke seems to preserve the thrill of emotion which passed from the leader to his companions, by breaking out into the first person plural (see Acts, for the psychological rather than literary reason of this " we," here and later).

The new mission began at Philippi, a Roman *colonia.* Here the Jewish settlement, in which as usual Paul sought first to gain a footing, was a small one, consisting in the *Philippi.* main of women—who enjoyed much freedom in Macedonian society. But the normal extension of his work was cut short by an incident characteristic both of the age and of the way in which the fortunes of the Gospel were affected by the vested interests around it. The story of Paul's imprisonment, with the light it casts on his quiet mastery of any situation, is familiar in its vivid detail.

After being thus " shamefully treated " in Philippi (1 Thess. ii. 2), Paul passed on rapidly to Thessalonica, the real capital of the province and an admirable centre of influence *Thessalonica.* (cf. 1 Thess. i.·8). In this great seaport there was· at least one synagogue; and for three weeks he· there discussed from the scriptures the cardinal points in his· message (cf.·1 Cor. xv. 3 seq.), " that it behoved the Christ to suffer and to rise again from the dead," and that accordingly " this Jesus . . . is the Christ " (xvii. 2 seq.). Some Jews believed, " and of the Godfearing Greeks " (semi-proselytes) a large number, including not a few of the leading women. There was also successful work among those who· turned directly " from idols, to serve a God living and real " (1 Thess. i. 9). This must have occupied several weeks beyond those specified above (cf. 1 Thess. i.-ii.; and the material help received more than once· from Philippi, Phil. iv. 16).

But Jewish jealousy was aroused particularly by the loss of their converts; and at length in alliance with the rabble of the market place, it was able once more to cut short the preachers' work among the Gentiles. The charge made against them had a serious ring, since it involved not only·danger to public order

[1] The region to which some think the Epistle to the Galatians (see I.S.) was addressed—so modifying the older " North Galatian " theory of Bishop Lightfoot and others.

but treason against the emperor (*lassa majestás*). Thus at Thessalonica Paul had experience of the imperial system as *Contrasting* rival to his gospel of the sovereignty of God and of *the Imperial* His Christ, the true king of humanity. Yet it is *Cut.* doubtful if he was thinking of this[1] when he wrote to his converts touching "the mystery of lawlessness," working towards its final conflict with the divine principle also at work in the world. He seems in the whole passage (2 Thess. ii. 3–12) to view the empire in its positive aspect as a system of law and order rather than in its idolatry of its official head, the incarnation of worldly success and power; and he alludes to both emperor and empire (6 seq.) as the force at present restraining "the mystery of lawlessness" (ἀνομία). This phrase itself suggests something more abnormal than the world-principle latent in paganism, such as "the apostasy" of God's own people, the Jewish nation, as once before under Antiochus Epiphanes the prototype of "the man of lawlessness" seated in "the temple of God" (v. 4), of whom the late emperor Caligula might well seem a forerunner. Even so monstrous an issue of Jewish refusal of God's truth, in His Messiah, would be but the climax of so unhallowed an alliance as that which existed at Thessalonica between Jewish unbelief and paganism, seeing that the former was using the very Messianic idea itself to stir up the latter against the followers of Jesus (Acts xvii. 7; cf. 1 Thess. ii. 15 seq.). Paul and Silas withdrew by night, and began work in Beroea, a small city of Thessaly, in the hope of returning when excitement had subsided. But Jewish intriguers from Thessalonica stirred up the populace with the old charges, and Paul, as the prime actor, was forced to retire, first to the coast (whence he may have thought of a secret visit to Thessalonica, 1 Thess. ii. 18; cf. iii. 5), and then by sea to Athens.

At Athens he was consumed with anxiety, and sent word to Silas and Timothy to join him with fresh news about his *Athens.* "orphans" in the faith. While waiting, however, he felt compelled by the signs of idolatry on every hand to preach his gospel. He began discussing in the synagogue with the Jews and their circle, and also in the Agora, after the manner of the place, in informal debate with casual listeners. The scope of his doctrine, the secret of right living, was such as to attract the notice of the Epicureans and Stoics. But its actual contents seemed to them a strange farrago of familiar Greek phrases and outlandish talk about a certain "Jesus" and some power associated with him styled "the Resurrection." To clear up this, the latest intellectual novelty of the Athenian quidnuncs, they carry him off to "the Areopagus," probably the council,[2] so called after its original place of meeting on Mars' Hill. This body seems still to have had in some sense charge of religion and morals in Athens; and before it this itinerant "sophist" seemed most likely to make his exact position plain. A mark of authenticity is the very fruitlessness of his attempt to adapt the gospel of Jesus to Greek "wisdom." One only of his audience, a member of the Areopagus, seems to have been seriously impressed. The real effect of the episode was upon Paul himself and his future ministry among typical Greeks.

Before Timothy's return Paul had moved on to Corinth, where he was to win success and to find material for such experi-*Corinth.* ences, both when present and absent, as developed the whole range of his powers of heart and mind, (see CORINTHIANS, EPISTLES TO THE). Corinth was more typical of the Graeco-Roman world than any other city, certainly of those visited by Paul. In addition to its large Jewish colony, it had Oriental elements of other kinds, especially mystic and ecstatic cults; and its worship of Venus under semi-oriental attributes added to the general sensuality of the moral atmosphere. Over all was a veneer of Greek intellect and polish;

[1] As Sir W. M. Ramsay argues in his *Cities of St Paul*, pp. 425–429.
[2] This is the view favoured by archaeologists like Ernst Curtius (*Expositor*, vii. 4. 436 sqq.) and Sir W. M. Ramsay. On the whole it suits the narrative better than the view which regards the Hill of Ares simply as a good spot for one of those rhetorical " displays " in which Athenians delighted.'

for in its way Corinth prided itself on its culture no less than did Athens. No wonder that Paul's first feeling in this microcosm was one of utter impotence. It was "in weakness, and in fear, and in much trembling," though in dauntless faith, that he began a most fruitful ministry of a year and a half. His guiding principle was to trust solely to the moral majesty of the gospel of the Cross, declared in all simplicity as to its form (1 Cor. ii. 1 sqq.), not heeding its first impression upon the Jew of intolerable humiliation, and on the Greek of utter folly (i. 18 sqq.). Most gladly then would he preach in such a way that "faith should not stand in the wisdom of men, but in the power of God" (ii. 5), "that no flesh should glory before God" (i. 29). How central this was to his gospel, especially as it defined itself over against Greek self-sufficiency of intellect, may be seen from his whole conception of the "spiritual" man in his letters to Corinth (esp. 1 Cor. ii. 1–iv. 7). Before his great work there began, Paul gained two fresh fellow-workers, whose share in parts at least of his later ministry was very great, Aquila, a Jew of Pontus, and his talented wife Priscilla. Probably they were already Christians, and as they too were tent-makers Paul shared their home and their work. That he was often in straitened circumstances is proved by his having to accept aid from Macedonia (2 Cor. xi. 9; cf. Phil. iv. 15). On the arrival of Silas and Timothy from that quarter, he began to preach with yet more intensity, especially to the Jews (xviii. 5). A breach with the synagogue soon followed. The definite turning to the Gentiles met with much success, and Paul was encouraged by a night vision to continue in Corinth for more than a year longer. An attempt of the Jews (cf. 1 Thess. ii. 15 seq; 2 Thess. iii. 1 seq.) to use Gallio, the new proconsul of Achaia, as a tool against him, not only failed but recoiled upon themselves.

It was during his first winter at Corinth, A.D. 51–52,[3] that he wrote his earliest extant missionary letters (see above for Galatians). Paul wrote not as a theologian but as the *First* *Missionary* prince of missionaries. His gospel was always in *Letters.* essence the same; but the form and perspective of its presentation varied with the training, mental and moral, of his hearers or converts. It was no abstract, rigid system, presented uniformly to all. This warns us against hasty inferences from silence, in judging of Paul's own thought at the time represented by any epistle, and so limits our attempt to trace progress in his theology. But it bears also on our estimate of him as a man and an apostle, full of sympathy for others and asking from them only such faith as could be real to them at the time.

His Thessalonian converts had met with much social persecution. The bulk belonged to the working class (iv. 11, 2 Thess. iii. 10–12); and Paul must have endeared himself to them by sharing their lot and plying his own manual industry (Acts xviii. 3). However hard his double toil of teacher and tent-maker might be, no sordid suspicions, such as his Jewish foes were ready to suggest (1 Thess. ii. 9; 2 Thess. iii. 8), should gain any colour from his conduct. He would be to his converts as a father, and an embodiment of the new Christian ethics which he pressed upon his spiritual children as the essential "fruit of the Spirit," and also as a demonstration of the Gospel to " them that were without " (i. 7–12; cf. i. 6, iv. 1 seq.).

The special perspective of his first two epistles is affected by the brevity of his stay at Thessalonica and the severity of persecution there. Owing to the latter fact the Parousia, as a vindication of their cause, so near as reasonably to influence conduct (v. 11), had naturally been prominent in his teaching among them. So in these epistles he deals with it more fully than elsewhere (iv.[4]13 sqq.); and the moral fruits of the new life in the Spirit are here enjoined in a very direct manner (iv. 1–8).

' We need not suppose that Paul himself or his assistants used a set of rules as elaborate as the "Two Ways" (of Life and Death)

[3] This date (and so Ramsay's chronology from this point) is confirmed by a fresh inscription showing that Gallio was proconsul from 52–53 (spring), rather than 51–52; see *Expositor* for May 1909, pp. 467–469.

embodied, e.g. in the *Teaching of the Apostles*.[1] But to judge from these epistles (1 Thess. iv. 1 seq., 6; 2 Thess. ii. 15; iii. 6), and his reference to the " type of teaching " (bearing on " sin, unto death," and " obedience, unto righteousness ") unto which the Roman Christians had been " committed " (Rom. vi. 16 seq.), Paul gave to his converts a fairly full outline of moral instruction, similar at least to that of Judaeo-Christian missionaries (note too the rather uniform lists of vices in Rom. i. 24 seq.; 1 Cor. v. 10 seq.; Gal. v. 19; Col. iii. 5; cf. E. von Dobschütz, *Christian Life in the Primitive Church*, app. 6).

What was distinctive of Paul's ethical teaching was not any lack of positive precepts, but the intimate way in which he, like his Master, infused them with the spirit in which and by which they were to be realized, as aspects of the ideal of love to God and man. He was supremely concerned with the dynamic of conduct, as to which his own experience made him the most inspiring of teachers and the greatest interpreter of the mind of Christ. The master motive on which he relied for all, was the imitation of Christ in a peculiarly inward sense. To the believer Christ was no mere external example, but was already within him as the principle of his own new moral being, in virtue of the Holy Spirit indwelling as the Spirit of Christ. Here lay the secret of the new " power " so characteristic of the Gospel (Rom. i. 16), a power adequate to realize even the enhanced moral ideal revealed in Christ. The wonder of it was that this power annulled the moral past, giving the once vicious an equal freedom with the " virtuous." To this sovereign, emancipating influence of God's Holy Spirit, antagonizing "the flesh" and all its works, Paul confidently entrusted his converts for " sanctification " or progressive transformation (Gal. iii. 3, v. 16 sqq.) into " the image of Christ," the full actuality of the type already latent in Christian faith. Such teaching is implicit in the Thessalonian letters; but it is explicit in the Epistle to the Galatians. Here he announces in the clearest accents the secret of Christian conduct. " Walk by (the) Spirit, and desire of the flesh ye shall not fulfil." " If we live by the Spirit, by the Spirit let us also walk." " On the basis of freedom (from law as external to the conscience) were ye called; only turn not freedom into an opportunity for the flesh, but through love serve one another. For the whole Law stands fulfilled in this, Thou shalt love thy neighbour as thyself " (v. 13 sqq., 25). These are the watchwords of Paul's antinomianism, which had grown out of the soil of his own strict moral discipline, where the ethical ideal had become an instinct and a passion. But how would they be taken by raw Gentiles, say in Corinth, untutored to self-denial whether in the things of sense or spirit? That their egoism often perverted Paul's libertarianism into an apology for libertinism, in keeping with current habits, as well as for selfish individualism in the use of intellect or even " gifts of the Spirit," may be gathered from his letters to Corinth (see CORINTHIANS, EPISTLES TO THE). What here concerns us, however, is the splendidly positive way in which Paul met such abuses, not by falling back upon legalism as a " safeguard " against licence, but by reapplying the laws of spirituality, both in relation to God as source of spiritual gifts, and to God's people as the appointed sphere of their exercise. He does not recede from his way of teaching; he insists that they shall understand it and abide by its real obligations. But while thinking of Paul's work in Corinth, we must note certain special religious conditions affecting both the reception of his gospel and the way in which it was afterwards conceived. Side by side with the religion of the city and of the family, both of them polytheistic and utilitarian in the main, stood the " mysteries " or esoteric cults, which were sought out and participated in by the individual for the satisfaction of essentially personal religious needs   Clearly those trained by such Mysteries would be more drawn than ordinary polytheists to his gospel, with its doctrine of mystical yet real union with the divine in Christ, and would less than others find the Cross, with its message of life through death, to be folly. This being

Paul as Ethical Teacher.

Pauline Anti-nomianism.

[1] Yet compare " the Way " (Acts xix. 9, 23), or " the Way of the Lord " (xviii. 25) as a name for Christianity on its practical side. So Sergius Paulus was " astonished at the Teaching (*didache*) of the Lord," xiii. 12; cf. Tit. i. 8 seq.

so, we shall not be surprised to find, especially at Corinth, traces of the reaction of conceptions proper to the Mysteries upon the ideas and practices of Paul's converts (cf. 1 Cor. xv. 29), and even upon the language in which he set forth his meaning to them (see ii. 6 sqq.). Whether Paul himself was influenced by such ideas, e.g. in relation to the Sacraments, is a further question as to which opinions are divided.[2]

After some eighteen months in Corinth, Paul felt the time had come to break fresh ground now at last perhaps at Ephesus, the key to the province of Asia. With this in view he took with him his fellow-workers Priscilla and Aquila, and left them at Ephesus while he himself visited Syria for ends of his own. That these ends were of high import we may be sure, else he would not have spent on them a period of months when the door seemed already opening in Asia (Acts xviii. 19–21). Acts gives no hint as to their nature, save the statement that " he went up " from Caesarea to Jerusalem, " and saluted the church," before he " went down to Antioch." But Paul's letters enable us to infer that he relied largely on this visit for counteracting rumours which represented him as an apostate from Judaism.[3] After some stay in Antioch Paul started before autumn A.D. 53 for his third great campaign, the centre of which he had already chosen in Ephesus, where Priscilla and Aquila were helping to prepare the ground. Passing through south Galatia, where he further fortified his converts (xviii. 23), he would reach Ephesus before winter closed in. Already his circle of helpers had gained a fresh member of great gifts, the Alexandrine Jew Apollos (q.v.), who had been brought into fuller sympathy with the Pauline gospel by Priscilla and Aquila, and who, learning from them the situation in Corinth, volunteered to try to overcome the prejudices of the Jews there (xviii. 24–28). At first Paul taught in the synagogue, until growing hostility drove him to " separate the disciples " and transfer his headquarters to " the school of Tyrannus." This was a lecture-room such as " sophists " or *rhetors* were wont to hire for their " displays." The change was not only one of place, but also of style of discourse, his appeal now being directly to the Gentiles, who would at first regard Paul as a new lecturer on morals and religion. The influence which went forth from this centre radiated throughout the whole province of Asia, partly through visitors to Ephesus on business or for worship at its great temple, and partly through Paul's lieutenants, such as Timothy and Epaphras (Col. i. 7; iv. 13). Witness to this extensive influence is afforded both by the friendly conduct of certain " Asiarchs " at the time of the riot (xix. 31), and by the fact that Paul later wrote a circular letter to this region, the so-called Epistle to the Ephesians. This result was due not only to Paul's persuasive speech but also to deeds of power,[4] connected with the superhuman gifts with which he felt himself to be endowed by the Spirit of God (Acts xix. 11; cf. Rom. xv. 18 seq.; 2 Cor. xii. 12). Nor can we feel Paul's great greatness unless we remember that he was tried by the searching test of supernormal psychical and physical powers operating through him, and that he came through all with an enhanced sense of the superiority of rational and moral gifts, and of love as the crown and touchstone of all, as well as with a deepened humility. That he suffered much before the final tumult, due to his success affecting trades dependent on the cult of the Ephesian Artemis is implied in his own words, " humanly speaking, I, not proven."[5]

We may doubt whether Paul himself countenanced the practices by which some believed that they drew magical virtue from his person (xviii. 12). But he did perform what he, in common with his age, believed to be the exorcism of evil spirits, as the story of Sceva's sons itself implies (xix. 13 sqq.).

Visit to Jerusalem.

Ephesus.

Strong in Weakness.

[2] The affirmative is maintained by the so-called *Religionsgeschichtliche Schule* in particular. The more general verdict is " not proven."

[3] In this light his polling of his head before embarking at Cenchreae in token of a vow of special self-consecration (to be redeemed at the end of a month in Jerusalem itself; cf. Josephus, *Jewish War*, II. xv. 1), is significant of his feelings as to the critical nature of the visit, including danger from Jewish fanaticism during a voyage probably on the eve of a feast (say Pentecost), for which he went up on his later visit (Acts. xx. 16).

fought the beasts at Ephesus " (1 Cor. xv. 32), which may mean that he was almost torn in pieces by mob fury. It was perhaps on this occasion that Aquila and his wife risked their lives for him (Rom. xvi. 3 seq.). Indeed he lived much of his time in Ephesus as one under daily sentence of death, so constant was his danger (1 Cor. xv. 30 seq.; cf. iv. 9; 2 Cor. i. 9; iv. 9–11). But this almost unbearable strain on his human frailty simply deepened his sense of dependent union with Jesus, both in His death and victorious life, and softened his strong nature into a wonderful gentleness and sympathy with suffering in others (2 Cor. i. 4 sqq.). It is no accident that it was from the midst of his Ephesian experiences that his Hymn of Love (1 Cor. xiii. esp. 6–8a, 13) sounded forth. His own spiritual life seems to have grown in Ephesus more than at any other period since the era of his conversion.

This brings us to the most tragic episode in Paul's career, judged by his own feelings, a psychological crucifixion of which we have the vivid record in his correspondence with the Corinthian church. Reduced to its simplest terms the situation was as follows. The Corinthian church was suffering from the fermentation of ideas and ideals too heterogeneous for their powers of Christian assimilation. Paul had laid the foundation, and others had built on it with materials of varied kind and value (see CORINTHIANS). Specially dangerous was the intellectual and moral reaction of the typically Greek mind, starting from a deep-seated dualism between mind and matter, upon the facts and doctrines of the Gospel. Its issue was an exaggeration of Paul's own religious antithesis between "the flesh" and "the mind " into a metaphysical dualism, so that the conduct of the body, crudely identified with " the flesh," became a thing indifferent for the inner and higher life of the spirit illumined by the Spirit of God. There was not only divergent practice in morals and in religious usage; there was also a spirit of faction threatening to destroy the unity of church life, to which Paul attached the greatest importance. To lead them to realize their unity in Christ and in His spirit of love was the central aim of Paul's first extant letter to this church. He rises sheer above every manifestation of the sectional element in man—whether Jewish, Greek, intellectual, ritual, or ascetic—into the sphere of pure religion, the devotion of the whole personality to God and His ends, as realized once for all in Christ, the second Adam, the archetype of divine sonship. It is his enforcement of this idea, along with firm yet flexible application to the various disorders and errors at Corinth of certain other of his fundamental panciples, such as the indwelling of the Holy Spirit in the individual and the community, that makes this epistle so significant for Paul's biography. Thus, while it gives a more complete picture of a Pauline church than all other sources of knowledge put together, it at the same time illustrates the rare balance of Paul's mind. But neither this letter nor the influence of Timothy (iv. 17), already on his way to Corinth via Macedonia, on collection business (Acts xix. 22; 1 Cor. xvi. 1 seq., 10 seq.)—nor even, as some think, of Paul himself in person (2 Cor. ii. 1; xii. 14, 21; xiii. 1 seq.)—brought about an understanding on certain points involving Paul's authority. In this connexion the presence of interloping Jewish " apostles " with their claims for themselves and their insinuations as to Paul's motives (2 Cor. xii. 14–16), greatly complicated and embittered the situation on both sides.

When next the curtain rises, we gather that Paul had been forced to write a letter of protest in a tone of severity fitted *Paul leaves* to arouse his converts' better selves. It was in *for Mace-* fact an ultimatum[1] that Titus carried to Corinth *donia,* before Paul left Ephesus, his departure hastened by the great tumult. On leaving for Macedonia he " exhorted " the assembled disciples, and perhaps left Timothy to check the tendencies to error which he perceived at work (xx. 1, 1 Tim. i. 3). Then starting from Miletus, the chief port in the vicinity (cf. xx. 15),—where he had to leave Trophimus

[1] On the question whether this letter has been lost (as here assumed), or on the other hand has been partially preserved in 2 Cor. x.–xiii., see CORINTHIANS.

owing to sickness (2 Tim. iv. 20, probably a fragment from a brief note to Timothy written soon after)—he reached Troas. Here he intended to evangelize pending the return of Titus (1. Cor. ii. 12 seq.). But though " a door " of opportunity at once opened to him, growing anxiety as to the reception of his severe letter drove him forward to meet Titus half-way in Macedonia. There " fightings without " were added to " fears within " (vii. 5), until at last his meeting with Titus brought unspeakable relief. The bulk of the Corinthian church, in deep remorse for the way in which they had wounded him who after all was their " father " in Christ (1 Cor. iv. 15), had come out clearly as loyal to him, not only in word but also in discipline on the arch offender, whose contumacious conduct (now repudiated by the church) had so grieved him, but for whom Paul is now the first to bespeak loving treatment, " lest haply he be swallowed up of excessive grief " (ii. 5 sqq.; vii. 12). Accordingly in his next letter his heart overflows with gladness and affection, not so as to blind his clear eye to the roots of danger still remaining in the situation.

The interloping judaizing missionaries (xi. 4, seq., 13, 22; cf. x. 7) are still on the spot, glorying themselves and glorying in their welcome on the field prepared by another's toils (x. 12–18); while in the church itself there are moral abuses yet unredressed, even unacknowledged (xii. 20 seq.), on which Paul felt bound still to press for confession and penitence (xiii. 1 sqq.), in spite of what some might brazenly insinuate, in reliance on his not having acted summarily on his former visit, when the church as a whole was not heartily with him. Hence Paul felt himself bound to act boldly (x. 1–6), if and when on his arrival he found the obedience of the majority full and complete (xii. 6). It is to prepare the way for this (xiii. 10) that Paul, while recognizing in the main the church's loyal affection, writes the second part of his letter (x.–xiii. 10) in so different a key, striving to complete the reaction against his foes, with their taunt as to his not daring openly to take an apostle's support from his converts at Corinth (xi. 12 sqq., xii. 11–18).

The Second Epistle to the Corinthians was written from Philippi or Thessalonica (ix. 2); and Timothy joins in its opening salutation. He had, it seems, been summoned to Paul's side from Ephesus by a hurried note, written after Titus's return from Corinth, in which he is informed that Erastus had remained in Corinth (? as now city-treasurer, Rom. xvi. 13), while Paul had been deprived also of the help of Trophimus, so that Timothy was unexpectedly needed at his side (this is embedded in an alien context in 2 Tim. iv. 20, 21a, see below). One reason at least for Paul's need of Timothy is suggested by the reference to Erastus (cf. Acts xix. 22), viz. the business of the great collection from his churches in Galatia, Asia, Macedonia and Achaia. This had been some time in progress and was to be carried by delegates to Jerusalem on Paul's approaching visit, from which much was hoped in connexion with the unity of Jewish and Gentile Christianity. Another may have been the labour of inspecting the churches in those parts, which now reached at least as far as, if not into, Illyricum (Rom. xv. 19). In any case it was midwinter (56) before Paul became the guest of the hospitable Gaius in Corinth (Rom. xvi. 23)

Touching the resettlement of local church affairs during Paul's three months in Corinth, we know nothing. For us the great event of this visit is the writing of that epistle *The Epistle* which shows that his mind was now bent on the *to the* extension of his mission westwards to the metropolis *Romans.* of the empire itself. To Rome his thoughts had been turned for many a year, but he had time and again checked the impulse to visit it (Rom. xv. 22 seq.) For the city had long been occupied by the Gospel in one form or another; and it was a point of honour with him to preach " where Christ was not named, not to build on others' foundations (xv. 20). But his eye was now fixed on Spain, if not also on south Gaul. It was, then, largely as basis for his mission to the western Mediterranean that Paul viewed Rome. Yet after all Rome was not like other places. It was the focus of the world. Hence Paul could not simply pass by it (i. 11 seq.). Very tactfully does he now offer his preliminary contributions to them—" by way of reminder," at least—emboldened thereto by the consciousness of a divine commission to the Gentiles, proved by what he had been enabled already to accomplish (xv. 15 sqq.).

But how could Paul write at length to a community he had never visited? Not to dwell on what he might have gathered from "Prisca and Aquila," the wonderful list of salutations by name, often with brief characterizations, proves how constant was the flow of Christian life between the capital and provincial centres like Ephesus and Corinth. But, beyond all this, there is the nature of the epistle itself as a great "tract for the times," applicable to the general situation at Rome, but typical also of the hour as reflected in Paul's consciousness. It has therefore a profound biographical significance for Paul himself, summing up all his thought so far, on the basis of his conversion as unfolded by his experiences as an apostle. It is his philosophy of religion and of history, the first worthy of the name, because the first deep-based upon the conception of the unity of humanity, as related to God, its source and the determining factor in its destiny. As such it also includes in broadest outline (viii. 18 sqq.) a philosophy of nature, as related to humanity, its crown and key. Thus it is in effect a universal philosophy in terms of the moral order, which Paul, like every Hebrew, regarded as the most real and significant element in the universe. At the centre of this grand survey stands the Jewish race, the chosen vessel for bearing God's treasure for mankind during the provisional period of human history; and at its spiritual heart, in turn, Jesus, Messiah of Israel, Saviour of mankind, in whom the distinction between the special and general spheres of revelation is transcended, while the law, "the middle wall of partition" between them, is broken down by the Cross.

Into the sweep of this high argument, as it is unfolded step by step, with an organic completeness or exposition peculiar to Romans among his writings (cf. Ephesians), there is wrought not only the problem of the Jew and Gentile (still the burning question of the time), but also the stubborn paradox of the actual rejection of Israel's Messiah by the nation as a whole. This forms a great appendix (ix.-xi.) to the more theoretic part of the epistle, and lays bare Paul's inmost heart, showing how truly a Jewish patriot he was. Even the categories in which he grapples, without formal success, with the problem of divine election and human responsibility, betray the Jew, to whom the final axioms are God's sovereignty and God's righteousness. Further into the contents of this most characteristic writing it is not ours to go (see ROMANS). Suffice it to say, he who apprehends it, as the issue of a real religious experience, already knows Paul as he knew himself and cared to be known. He who masters its thought knows the Pauline theology. Some indeed assume that Paul ceased really to progress beyond the point represented by Romans, and that certain of his later writings, if they be his at all, show a certain enfeeblement of grasp upon principle. But that is to confuse once more Paul's personal theology with the forms of instruction which experience showed him were expedient for the strengthening and development of feeble or undeveloped moral types.

Yet while the horizon of the Roman epistle was so universal in one sense, it was restricted in another. Owing to the foreshortening influence of the parousia hope, even Paul's programme of a world-mission meant simply seizing certain centres of influence, to serve as earnest of Messiah's possession of all mankind on His return to take His great power and reign. Evangelization on the farther side of the parousia was the greater part of the whole. So we gather from this very epistle, as well as from 1 Cor. xv. 23-25 (and yet more clearly from Col. i. 23). In other ways, too, the Christianity of Paul and his age was relative to the parousia, both in theory and in practice (e.g. in its "ascetic" or "other worldly" attitude to life). This difference of perspective, and the ancient view of the world of spirits operating upon human life, are the chief things to be allowed for in reading his epistles.

Thus viewing things, how eagerly Paul must have looked westwards at this time. Yet his heart turned also to Judaea, *Paul's Care for Unity.* where he felt his line of march still threatened by the danger of disunion in the very Body of Christ. At all cost this must be averted. The best hope lay in a practical exhibition of Gentile sympathy with the Mother

XX 16*

Church in Jerusalem, such as would be to it a token of the Holy Spirit as indwelling Paul's churches. The means for such a thankoffering for benefits received ultimately from Jerusalem (Rom. xv. 27) had been collected with much patient labour, and the delegates to accompany Paul with it had already assembled at Corinth (xx. 4). Paul had intended to cross the Aegean from Corinth with his party, by the direct route to Syria. But a Jewish plot, probably to take effect *Last Visit to Jerusalem.* on the voyage, caused him to start earlier by the longer land-route, as far as Philippi, whence, after waiting to observe the Days of the Unleavened Bread,[1] he sailed to join his fellow-almoners at Troas. There is no need to follow all the stages of what follows (see Ramsay, *St Paul the Traveller*). But every personal touch is meant to tell, even Paul's walk from Troas to Assos, perhaps for solitary meditation, away from the crowded ship; and all serves to heighten the feeling that it was the path to death that Paul was already treading (xx. 23). This lies too at the heart of his impressive farewell to the Ephesian elders, a discourse which gives a vivid picture of his past ministry in Ephesus. Its burden, as Luke is at pains to emphasize by his comment upon the actual parting, is that "they should behold his face no more." The scene was repeated at Tyre; while at Caesarea, the last stage of all, the climax was reached, in Agabus's prophetic action and the ensuing dissuasion of all those about him. But Paul, though moved in his feelings, was not to be moved from his purpose. The party went forward, taking the precaution to secure Paul a trusty host on the road to Jerusalem in the person of Mnason, a Hellenist of Cyprus. He entered the holy city in good time to show his loyalty to the Jewish Feast of Pentecost.

He was well received by James and the elders of the church. So far scholars are agreed, since the "we" form of narrative which began again at Philippi (xx. 5), reaches to *Jerusalem.* this point. But as to the historical value of what follows, before "we" reappears with the start for Rome from Caesarea there is large diversity of opinion. The present writer, holding that "we" is no exclusive mark of the eyewitness, sees no reason to doubt the substantial accuracy of the narrative in Acts xxi. 19-xxvi.[2] touching the Jewish outbreak against Paul and its sequel. Its significance for Paul's life is fairly clear, though we are not told what acceptance the Gentile offering of loyal love met with in the Jerusalem church as a whole. But that its general effect upon the comity of the two branches of the Messianic Ecclesia was good seems implied by the serene tone of Paul's later references to the unity of the Body (Eph. ii. 19-22; iii. 5 seq.). What does stand out clearly in Acts is all that bears on Paul's position as between the Jewish and the Roman authorities. Here we observe a gradual shifting of the charge against him, corresponding in part to the changes of venue. The more local elements recede, and those of interest to a Roman court emerge.

To the Jewish mob he is "the man that teacheth all men everywhere against the People, and the Law, and this place; and moreover he brought Greeks also into the Temple" (xxi. 28). Before Felix, Tertullus describes him as "a pestilent fellow, and a mover of tumults among all the Jews throughout the world, and a ringleader of the sect of the Nazarenes, who also tried to profane the Temple" (xxiv. 5 seq.). Similarly among "the many and grievous" offences alleged before Festus (xxv. 7 seq.) we gather that one or more were

[1] This is a valuable datum not only for Paul's own loyalty to the usages of Jewish piety, but also for the chronology of his life, as showing in the light of what follows the day of the week on which Passover fell that year, and so tending to fix the year as 56 or 57 (see above, *Chronology*).

[2] These chapters contain passages as vivid and circumstantial as any in the "we" sections. As to the speeches, their fidelity naturally varies with the circumstances of delivery; but in all there is that which could not be Luke's free composition. The verisimilitude of the demonstration of Paul's personal loyalty to forms of Jewish piety in connexion with the four men under vows (xxi. 23-27) is complete, especially in view of Paul's own vow at Cenchreae and his regard for Jewish feasts; and even Paul's non-recognition of the high priest in what was not a regular session of the Sanhedrin (xxiii. 2-5), is quite probable. Other points hardly merit notice here; see Knowling's *Testimony of St Paul*, lect. xx.

"against Caesar," i.e. treason of one sort or another. Though the others weighed with a procurator like Felix (anxious to humour the Jews cheaply) sufficiently to keep Paul (in the absence of bribes) in prison for two years, it was the last class of charge that was most dangerous, especially when once the case was transferred from the provincial court to the appeal court at Rome. The last words of Agrippa, "This man could have been set at liberty had he not appealed to Caesar," are probably recorded with a touch of tragic irony.

Paul at Caesarea. But what of Paul himself during the two years at Caesarea? Though he must have been in correspondence with his churches, at least through messengers, nothing from his pen has reached us. We can only infer from epistles written later how much this period contributed to his reflective life. The outlook was indeed stimulating to thought. Near at hand Judaea was sliding rapidly down the incline of lawlessness and fanatical resentment of Roman rule, towards a catastrophe which to Paul's eye, trained by Jewish Apocalyptic to regard certain things as signs of the days of Antichrist, would seem to betoken the prelude of the Parousia itself. Then, farther afield, the growing confederacy of Messiah's churches was stepping into the place vacated by "Israel after the flesh," as the people ready for God's Messiah.

The journey to Rome calls for no detailed notice (see Ramsay, *St Paul the Traveller*). Its main interest for us is the impression of nobility, courage and power which Paul conveyed to the centurion Julius and his fellow-passengers generally; while the enthusiasm of the eyewitness[1] himself visibly reaches its climax as dangers thicken and Paul rises above them all. At last Italy is reached, and Paul is met by detachments of "brethren" from Rome, who came as far as thirty and forty miles to welcome him; "whom when Paul saw, he thanked God and took courage."

Rome. From Paul's letters, however, we gather that if he looked for sympathy from the Roman Christians, he looked largely in vain. Whilst some welcomed and most regarded him as indeed a champion of the Gospel whose fearless testimony even in bonds emboldened many, including the judaizing section who wished him no good, to preach Jesus more openly than before; few, if any, really showed him brotherly love or cared for the interests of Christ outside Rome that were still on his heart (Phil. i. 12-17, ii. 21). Such absorption in their own local affairs struck Paul as strangely un-Christian in spirit, and added disappointment to his irksome confinement, chained as he was by one wrist to a praetorian soldier night and day. Yet he rose above it all. Only let "Christ be magnified" in his body, whether by life or death. Then should he not be ashamed, come what might.

The Epistle to Philippians. The letter which makes us aware how things lay is Philippians, the most devotional of all his writings and the most Christlike. It is the perfect expression of personal "Paulinism" in his maturer and more positive manner. It flows from his heart as joyful thanks for tokens of continued mindfulness of him recently received from his old Philippian friends through Epaphroditus, one of their number. Touched and filled with spiritual joy the more that, save for his own personal circle, love was so scant around him, he turns to comfort his friends in their sorrow for him, out of the stores of Divine consolation received through his own fresh sense of need (cf. 2 Cor. i. 3 sqq.). "Rejoice in the Lord" is its recurring note. Here we get the word of the hour, both for Paul and for his converts. The date of Philippians is an open question, English scholars tending to place it early, while most foreign scholars put it late in the "two years" of Acts. The present writer would place it last of those written during the first year, i.e. last of all save 2 Timothy.

Of the remaining imprisonment epistles, the beautiful little note to Philemon touching his slave Onesimus casts fresh light on Paul "the Christian gentleman," by its humour and perfect

[1] That he regarded Paul as endowed with superhuman powers, both of premonition and of healing (as in Malta), is evident, even if in his mind, like that of most ancients, "the line between the miraculous and the providential quite vanishes away"— as B. W. Bacon says (*Story of St Paul*, p. 214) relative to xxviii. 3-5, comparing also the case of Eutychus' "insensibility." But if so, why not apply this to the earthquake at Philippi also?

Letters to Asian Churches. considerateness of tone. The two larger ones do not seem at first sight to reflect his personality so much as his life as the father of churches, and the way in which he extended the lines of his gospel so as to bear on problems raised by ever fresh reactions upon it of the old traditions amid which his Asian converts still lived. Both aspects really blend; for the epistles are addressed to churches which were feeling certain effects of the seeming calamity that had overtaken him whom they in some sense regarded as their founder, and aim at raising them to the writer's own higher standpoint (Eph. iii. 13, vi. 19-22; Col. ii. 1 seq., iv. 8 seq.). It was just here that many of his Asian converts hesitated. They did not realize the all-sufficiency of Christ in the moral sphere; and they viewed their relations with the invisible world of ultimate or heavenly realities in keeping with this fact. They traced the hand of beings belonging to the supernal spheres in their earthly experiences of weal and woe. Hence they dreamed of supplementing what they derived from Christ by help from other spiritual beings. To judge from Colossians (see s.v.) it was largely along the lines of Jewish thought (cf. the *Testaments of the Twelve Patriarchs*), modified by Greek and other Pagan ideas, that this tendency operated. For at Colossae at least it issued in observance of ritual rules connected with the protection of good angels against evil ones, as taught by a sort of theosophy, probably basing itself on a legendary handling of pre-Mosaic Bible history in particular (cf. the Pastorals). Paul does not discuss how far "guardian angels" have any function left them in view of the all-sufficiency of Christ and His Spirit for believers. He obviously (Eph. vi. 11 sqq.) believed in the reality of angelic foes, because this hypothesis explained for him certain moral phenomena; but he had really stripped angelic helpers' of all functions necessary to the Christian. Perhaps he was not sufficiently interested in the matter to think it out fully.

How does Paul deal with this situation of depressed faith and hope as to the power of Christ to confer all needful to the perfecting of the Christian's life on earth, in spite of the hostile forces, visible and invisible? All they need, he says, is to hold fast the Gospel which has already done so much for them—annulling the special privileges of the Jew, and quickening them as Gentiles "dead in sins" and under the full sway of the powers of ill, into a life of filial access to God as Father. Of Christ's ability to achieve God's purpose in all things, the wonderful progress of His Church "in all the world" is already witness (Col. i. 8, 23). Looking then to these things, visible to Christian *gnosis* based on spiritual experience, there is no cause for depression at the sufferings endured for Christ's sake by Christians, and least of all at his own. Both in Colossians and "Ephesians" (really a circular epistle to churches in Asia, including those of the Lycus valley and perhaps most of the Seven Churches of the Apocalypse (see Ephesians), he lays stress on "love, which is the bond of perfectness," and on "unity of the Spirit," as the atmosphere of life worthy the vocation he describes in inspiring terms.

The Biblical supposed Emphasis in Paul's later Epistles. In this respect, as in nearly every other, these epistles exhibit marked affinity with the next group claiming to come from Paul's pen, the so-called Pastoral Epistles, the supposed "moralism" of which is often urged against their authenticity. In both cases the development is quite natural in Paul the missionary, as it answers to growing defects among his churches in the sphere of conduct. Such errors, while twofold in effect, alike sprang from a defective sense for ethics as the essential form of piety (1 Tim. vi. 3-11; 2 Tim. iii. 5; cf. Jas. i. 27) flowing from Christian faith. A merely intellectual faith, instead of the genuinely Pauline type, involving enthusiastic moral devotion to Christ, tended in practice either to a negative and ritual piety, as at Colossae, or to moral laxity. The latter was sometimes defended on a dualistic theory of "flesh" and "spirit," as two realms radically opposed and morally independent.[2]

[2] Of this we have a hint in the "empty words" alluded to in Eph. v. 6 (perhaps also iv. 14), probably of the same sort as in

Paul meets both errors by his doctrine of the "new man," the new moral personality, God's workmanship, "created in Christ Jesus for good works" (Eph. ii. 10), whose nature it is to be fruitful unto holiness and love (cf. Gal. v. 6, vi. 15).

In the so-called Pastoral Epistles the same subject is handled similarly, yet more summarily, as befits one writing instruc-
The Pastoral Epistles. tions to friends familiar with the spirit behind the concrete precepts. Allowing for this, and for the special circumstances presupposed, there is no more "moralism" about the "wholesome instruction" in the Christian walk given in these epistles (1 Tim. i. 10; cf. vi. 3; 2 Tim. iv. 3) than in the other group. "Moralism" is ethical precept divorced from the Christian motive of grateful love, or connected with the notion of salvation as "of works" rather than prevenient grace. But of this there is no real trace in the Pastorals, which are a type of letter by themselves, as regards their recipients and certain of the aspects of church life with which they deal. As dealing with methods of instruction and organization, which must have occupied increasingly the attention of those responsible for the daily course of church life, they contain nothing inappropriate to the last two years of Paul's life, when he was considering how his churches might best be safeguarded from errors in thought and practice in his absence or after his decease.

The main difficulties as to their substance have been imported by anachronistic reading of them, and are falling to the ground with the progress of exegesis and knowledge of the conditions of early church life. Our real difficulties in conceiving the Pastorals as what they purport to be, relate to their form, and " lie in the field of language and of ideas as embodied in language " (Hort, *Jud. Christ.* p. 131). But these, even as regards style and syntax, are reduced to narrow limits, when once due weight is given to the fresh analogies furnished by the now admitted Imprisonment Epistles (see also Ramsay, *Expositor,* 1909). This is specially the case with the use of new words of religious import, like " Saviour " or " Deliverer " (*Soter,* of God and Christ: see Eph. v. 23; Phil. iii. 20)—the idea of which springs naturally from Paul's own outward state, as well as from the trials of his readers; tho " washing " or " laver " of baptism (Eph. v. 26; Tit. iii. 5); the Gospel as a revealed " mystery " (Eph. *passim,* esp. " the mystery " as " great," Eph. v. 32; 1 Tim. iii. 16); and the future " appearing " of Christ (so already in 2 Thess. ii. 8; cf. Col. iii. 4). As to the use of the last term for the incarnation in 2 Tim. i. 10, it has a parallel in the " was manifested " of 1 Tim. iii. 16, itself a fragment of a Christian hymn of praise to Christ, such as is implied in Eph. v. 19, and especially Col. iii. 16. Not only is the fragment in question one in type with that in Eph. v. 14, but may even be part of the same hymn. Nothing could be more natural than for Paul to weave into his epistle to Timothy the religious phraseology actually current among Pauline Christians in Asia, as we see him doing in his repeated citations of the hortatory parts of their hymnology, with the formula " Faithful is the (familiar) saying " (i. 15, iii. 1, 16, iv. 10; cf. 2 Tim. ii. 11 seq.). All this borrowed language, and much more that is virtually the parlance of the Asian churches, helps to explain a comparative lack of the *distinctively* Pauline element even in letters which contain highly characteristic passages. Hence there seem no insuperable difficulties to the authenticity of all three epistles—which most scholars recognize as at least partly from Paul's pen, though they disagree as to the exact limits of the genuine fragments—if only a natural historic setting can be found for them in Paul's life. But there is a general assumption that this cannot be found within the limits allowed by Acts. Accordingly some reject the situations implied in them as on the whole unhistorical, while others postulate a period in Paul's life of which Acts gives no hint, if it does not exclude it. This theory of a release after the " two whole years " with which Acts closes, and of a second imprisonment before the end really came, bases itself partly on the personal notices in the Pastorals (for a suggested itinerary see *e.g.* Lightfoot, *Biblical Essays*), often full of verisimilitude, and partly on tradition. As regards the latter, the only evidence of real weight is the reference in a highly rhetorical passage of the Epistle of Clement (c. A.D. 96) to Paul as having come in his universal ministry, in East and West alike, " to the bound of the West." But, granting that Spain be meant, there is no sign that Clement thought of this visit as following on an imprisonment[1] in Rome,

rather than as falling somewhere in his career, simply on the warrant of Rom. xv. 28: while nowhere do the Pastorals themselves point to any journey west of Rome. Further no early tradition is clear enough to override the almost certain implication of Acts (xx. 25 and 38, read in the light of the closing chapters, and especially of xxvi. 32, which suggests that the appeal to Caesar was a fatal step) that Paul never visited Asia after his farewell at Miletus. Accordingly room for the epistles must be found, if at all, before the spring of 62 in keeping with Acts.[2] The following is an attempt to show how this may be done.

The pastoral epistles reveal certain special aspects of Paul's life and work in Rome during the " two years " of Acts xxviii. *fin.* Addressed to intimate associates, they show him in *Epistle to Titus.* the act of caring for his churches by deputy. In the case of Titus, indeed, the churches in question were apparently not of Paul's own foundation, but those in whose welfare he had become interested while sheltering on his voyage to Rome at Fair Havens in Crete (Acts xxvii. 8 seq.). This spot was nigh to a city named Lasea; and as they were detained " a considerable time," for men eager to be gone, we may well imagine Paul coming into touch with the local Christians and leaving Titus (whose presence is never alluded to in Acts, even when proved by Paul's letters) to set in order the defective conditions prevailing among them (Tit. i. 5). Now, about early summer 60, we seem to see him writing further instructions, on the basis of reports received from Titus. There is no talk of a journey to Spain, and to judge from Paul's plan to winter at Nicopolis (iii. 12) he expects his case to come on too late in autumn to admit of the visit to Asia which he had in mind only shortly before, as it seems, when referring more indefinitely to his hopes in 1 Tim. iii. 14, iv. 13. Possibly his further reference in iii. 13 to Apollos and Zenas " the lawyer " (bearers of the letter), as on a journey of urgency, may mean that a date for his trial was fixed in the interval, and that he was sending to the East to collect counter-evidence to that of the Jews of Asia (Acts xxi. 27; cf. the later plaint in 2 Tim. i. 15, that " all in Asia " had " turned their backs on him ").

Paul's appeal case was not a safe topic for correspondence (cf. Col. iv. 7 seq.), and we gather little directly on the point from his epistles. The long delay in its hearing would be due in part to the accusers' desire to collect evidence sufficient to ensure success even before a tribunal thought to be less amenable to Jewish influence than a procurator's; and, once the first summer was past, the wintry sea (*mare clausum*) would postpone things for another six months. The delay seems to have been unexpected by Paul, and to have led him to mistaken forecasts during his first half year in Rome, in 1 Tim., Titus and Philemon. Somewhat later he expressed himself more guardedly (Phil. ii. 23 seq.; cf. i. 25). As to the charges on which all came to turn, we are left to intrinsic probabilities. They were no doubt those serious from the Roman rather than Jewish standpoint, viz. endangering public law and order by exciting the Jews throughout the world on religious matters, and fostering treason against the imperial cult generally (cf. the charge at Thessalonica). In defence Paul would urge the privileged position of a Jewish monotheist, and the Jews would be at pains to differentiate Christianity from Judaism, and so deprive it of the status of a legally recognized religion (*religio licita*). If they succeeded here, Paul's condemnation was only a matter of time. This is the most probable issue of the case (*pace* Sir W. M. Ramsay and others), both a priori and in the light of later phenomena, *e.g.* 1 Pet. (which in 62–63 seems to imply a recent impulse to persecution for the Name).

The rather earlier but vaguer situation implied in 1 Tim. is as follows. At the moment of Paul's appeal from Caesarea to Rome Timothy was perhaps on duty in Ephesus. *1 Timothy.* There he would receive a message from Paul, possibly through Aristarchus (Acts xxvii. 2, 5 seq.), in terms of good hope as to his appeal. Timothy would in turn send word as to the situation in Ephesus, and at the same time express his desire to hasten to Paul's side. This would lead Paul, in

1 Cor. vi. 12–14, just as the denial by Hymenaeus and Philetus in 2 Tim. ii. 17 seq. of any resurrection, save that of the spirit in conversion (cf. Eph. v. 14), finds its earliest parallel in 1 Cor. xv. 12, 32–34.

2 Add the fact that Clement (ch. vi.) conceives Paul as being *joined* in the place of reward by the Neronian martyrs, and therefore as martyred not later than summer 64. No theory of the Pastorals, therefore, based on Clement's witness, can place Paul's death after this date.

3 Also with 1 Pet., if Dr H. B. Swete (*Comm. on St Mark,* 1898, p. xvii.) is right in saying that it implies Paul's death; for 1 Pet. probably dates from 62–63 (see Dr Hort's *Comm.*).

sending him a letter of encouragement and specific instructions, to open with a sentence (characteristically wanting a grammatical conclusion) in which he recalls a parallel case, where he had exhorted Timothy to "stay on" in Ephesus[1] (i.e. in A.D. 56). Nor was the need less urgent now, owing to Judaic "fables" touching the primitive period of biblical history ("genealogies"), meant to bear on certain parts of the Law (i. 4-7) as of universal religious validity. At Ephesus (as also in Crete) much the same type of Judaism as was re-emerging at Colossae was reacting on local Christianity; while here and there were traces of dualistic antinomian theory (see i. 19 seq.; cf. 2 Tim. ii. 17 seq.). The general need of the hour was wholesome Christian ethics applied all round, supported by firmer organization in church life, especially with a view to check irresponsible teaching (1 Tim. v. 17, vi. 3; Tit. i. 9-11; 2 Tim. ii. 2, iv. 3). To the special local problems Paul addresses himself in this letter, but above all to the bracing of Timothy's somewhat sensitive nature to face the opposition which he must encounter as a Christian leader at such a time (note the similes of the soldier and athlete, both of whom face hardship readily, as part of their profession, i. 18, v. 8 sqq., vi. 12 seq., 20; 2 Tim. ii. 3 sqq., iv. 5). In this connexion occur also certain autobiographic passages, as well as solemn affirmations of his own divine commission (e.g. i. 1, 11 sqq., ii. 7), the aim of which is to reassure his disciple that his gospel will bear all the strain that is being put upon it, or can be in the future (cf. Eph. vi. 19 seq. for all this). Here Paul is answering challenges which he knows are being made in Timothy's hearing on every side, especially now that the apostle seemed less likely to return to Asia. He himself does not flinch, because he knows he had not run save "at the command of God" (i. 1), after being wondrously changed from his former self (i. 12 sqq.). Thus as to the authority of the Gospel "committed to his charge," however much it may be called in question (i. 10 seq., ii. 7), he has no shadow of doubt.

When the curtain rises for the last time, it is on the morrow of the long-expected hearing of Paul's appeal. The case stands *2 Timothy.* adjourned, but he is no longer under any illusion as to its final issue. His one comfort is that by the Lord's support he had been delivered from the greatest danger, "the mouth of the lion" ready to "swallow up" (cf. 1 Pet. v. 8) his soul through craven fear, as he stood solitary before Caesar. From that the Lord had rescued him, and would yet rescue him from every "work of ill" (2 Tim. iv. 16-18). Yet his earthly work is done (iv. 6 seq.). So he writes to Timothy, his "beloved child," whom now he longs to see once more. But lest this should not be granted him, he prefixes to the summons a last will and testament, which may help Timothy to rise above the dismay which his death at the hands of Roman law is bound to cause. Let Timothy take up the Gospel torch as it falls from his own dying hand, and "do the work of an Evangelist," heeding not the hardship. Then after providing for the Gospel, he turns to more personal interests. "Hasten to me with all speed," he says in effect, "for I am all alone, save for Luke. My other trusty friends are away on various missions, and Demas has deserted the sinking ship. Tychicus I had already sent to Ephesus; he will replace you. Pick up Mark and bring him with you—he is so helpful. Bring my cloak, papers and books [copies of the Scriptures], lying in Carpus's hands at Troas"[2]—perhaps since Acts xx. 6 sqq. "Alexander the bronze-worker [an old Jewish foe at Ephesus, Acts xix. 33] did me many a bad turn in my case (his case is in the Lord's hands); be on thy guard against him." Then follow allusions to Paul's "first defence," unsupported by such as might

[1] It is quite likely that Timothy left Ephesus for Rome before receiving 1 Tim., since he was with Paul when Colossians and Philippians were written, the former at least in the summer of 60 (see Philem. 22).

[2] It seems best to take iv. 13-15 as all part of this letter, rather than as part of the note from which iv. 20, 21[b] probably comes (see above). The homely details follow naturally enough on the reference to Mark; while the reference to Alexander is so far borne out by Heb. xiii. 23, which suggests that Timothy was accused on his arrival in Rome.

have appeared on his behalf (especially from Asia; cf. i. 15); and next salutations to Prisca and Aquila, and to the house of Onesiphorus—an Ephesian who had sought Paul out in Rome (i. 16-18).

So the curtain falls for the last time. But Paul's fate is hardly obscure. He himself saw that the charge against him, unrebutted by independent evidence, must bring him to the executioner's sword, the last penalty for a Roman citizen. With this late 2nd-century tradition agrees (Tertullian, *De praescr. haer.* 36), naming the very spot on the Ostian Way, marked by a martyr-memorial (*tropaion*, Caius *ap.* Euseb. ii. 25), probably at the modern Tre Fontane, some three miles from Rome. But the traditional date (June 29) reaches us only on far later authority. Acts simply suggests the first half of A.D. 62; and we may imagine Timothy reaching Rome in time to share Paul's last days (cf. Heb. xiii. 23).

Early Tradition has little to say about Paul. Possibly the earliest reference outside the New Testament is a Christian addition to the *Testament of Benjamin*, xi., which describes a Benjamite as "enlightening with new knowledge the Gentiles." The notice in Clement's epistle (ch. v.) to Paul's having borne bonds "seven times" may be mere rhetoric (perhaps based on 2 Cor. xi. 23). Ignatius refers with reference (cf. Rom. iv. 3) to Paul as his example in martyrdom (*Ad Eph.* xii. 2); similarly Polycarp (*Ad Phil.* iii. 2) deprecates the notion that he, or any other like him, could rival "the wisdom of the blessed and glorious Paul," and refers to his letter(s) to the Philippians. The *Acts of Paul*, composed not long after A.D. 150 by an Asian presbyter, in order to glorify Paul by supplementing Luke's story, is striking evidence of the regard felt for him in certain circles; but it contains (so far as extant in the Coptic, which also enables us to identify other documents as once parts of these Acts) no fresh data, unless the episode dealing with Paul and Thekla echoes an original tradition belonging to Iconium and Pisidian Antioch. Its description of Paul as "a man small in size, bald, bow-legged, sturdy, with eyebrows meeting and a slightly prominent nose, full of grace" in expression, may or may not be based on local memories (see a Cor. x. 10; cf. *Dict. Christ. Antiq.* ii. 1621, for early representations of him). The hostile conception of him lying behind the Simon of our Clementine literature (q.v.) has no historic value; and the same may be said of all traditions not to be traced earlier than the 3rd century (cf. R. A. Lipsius, *Die apokr. Apostelgesch. u.s.w.*, and C. Clemen, *Paulus*, i. 331 sqq.).

Paul's personality is one of the most striking in history. No character of the distant past is known to us more fully, both from within and from without, thanks largely to the self-revealing quality of his letters. His was a deep, complex, many-sided nature, varying widely in mood, yet all so concentrated by moral unity of purpose that the variety of gift and sensibility is apt to escape notice. During his career every faculty comes into play, and we realize how largely human he was. "Even though Paul was an apostle," says Chrysostom, "still he was a man." A true picture of him must preserve the vital unity in which these two aspects appear in our sources. To judge him as we through that vocation which he himself felt to determine all his being, is to fall into unreality. To view him as a mere individual is vain. He cannot be judged entirely by common standards, whether religious or ethical; for owing to his vocation his personality had an universal import which must needs put him out of ordinary human perspective at certain points. Further, we must allow for his limited temporal horizon, shut in for practical purposes by a near Parousia, conceived as bringing ordinary history to an abrupt close, and the hope of which foreshortened all issues. Bearing this in mind, we shall wonder, not so much at any otherworldly spirit or peremptoriness of tone, which were positive duties under such conditions, but rather at the sanity of temper and moral judgment which mark the apostle amid his consuming zeal "by all means to save some" from "the wrath" "soon to be revealed against sin and unrighteousness (1 Thess. i. 10; Rom. i. 18). We must remember too that he lived in an atmosphere of intense "enthusiasm," in the most literal sense, among those who felt that "the powers of the coming age" (Heb. vi. 4 seq.) were already at work in "the saints," men possessed by the divine afflatus and made as it were but organs of the Spirit of God. Viewed in such an environment, Paul is seen to have been a great steadying influence, insisting on character as the normal fruit of the Spirit and the real ground of human worth (1 Cor. xiii. 1-3); insisting also that possession by the Spirit did not supersede responsibility for self-control (xiv. 32 seq.), and that the element of conscious reason was superior to blind ecstasy (xiv. 1 sqq.). He spoke from full personal experience; for he exercised every gift on the list in 1 Cor. xii. 8. Yet with clear and ever-growing emphasis he defined spirituality in moral terms, those of the will informed by love like that of Christ. How great this service was, none can say. It was his balanced attitude to the operations of the Spirit—outwardly the most distinctive thing in Christianity, as compared with Judaism—an attitude at once reverent and reasonable, that saved the Church from fanaticism on the one hand or moralism on the other. It was his own experience as a passionate seeker after righteousness which gave him the key to that reinterpretation of Jesus the Christ as at once moral ideal, master motive and immanent principle of life at work in the soul by the Spirit which was peculiarly his own and may be styled his ethical mysticism. This was his main contribution to Christianity; and as depending on his personal experience, it was bound up closely with his personality—a fact which makes his direct influence, while intense, yet rather limited in its area of appeal.

At the root of Paul's nature lay the Hebrew capacity for personal devotion to the Divine as moral perfection, to an unbounded degree. It found its object in a concrete form, stirring both imagination and affections, in Jesus the Christ, " the image of the invisible God " whose spiritual glory man was created to reflect. This instinct for ideal devotion seems never to have been diverted, even for a season, into a single human channel, in the love of woman. From his early youth his soul was preoccupied by a passion for God and His will in His people. This he came to regard as a special divine gift or vocation (1 Cor. vii. 7), imposing on its possessor, in the face of the world's needs (cf. 29–31), a higher duty than could be fulfilled within the conditions of the closest of human relations (32–35). But the tenderness and chivalrous self-sacrifice which found no vent in the ordinary channel came to pour itself forth in an absorbing love for his churches, which were to him as his own spouse, though his aim was rather to " present them as a pure virgin to Christ " (2 Cor. xi. 2). This educated his human affections, and softened the outlines of a nature inflexibly loyal to principle and absorbed with the divine aspect of life. Thus it was through " the love of Christ " constraining him to look at all, as it were, through Christ's eyes, that Paul came to love men even to the point of a self-forgetfulness that seemed to some hardly sane (2 Cor. v. 13–16²; cf. Mark iii. 21, " He is beside himself "). So too his proud, strong-willed spirit gradually put on " the meekness and conciliatoriness of Christ " to such a degree that during the Corinthian troubles his critics contrasted the vigour of his letters with the seeming feebleness of his outward bearing (2 Cor. x. 1, 10).

There is no good evidence that his presence was physically weak or unimpressive, even if his stature was small, as tradition has it (see above; cf. Acts xiv. 12). Nor is there any sign that he bore habitual traces of those periodic attacks of some nervous affection—allied to epilepsy,¹ but apparently not involving loss of consciousness —to which, as dating from a certain overpowering trance about 42–43, he refers in 2 Cor. xii. 7 sqq. These were most humiliating while they lasted (cf. Gal. iv. 14). But they seem not to have drained his vigour even for great and constant labours of body and mind. His energy indeed was portentous, as he himself felt, when he traced it to the divine power " energizing mightily " in him (1 Cor. xv 10, Col. i. 29), and that most effectively when he felt weakest in himself (2 Cor. xii. 9 seq.).

Not only had Paul a supernatural spiritual force, marked by a rare combination of religious inspiration and reasoning power, which made him impressive both as speaker and writer, he had also a genius for adaptation to varied mental conditions, due partly to his Hellenistic training, but also to the fact that his message was one not of the letter but of spirit and power (cf. 2 Cor. iii. 4 sqq.). This showed itself as tact in relation to individuals and special audiences, and as statesmanlike breadth of view in handling large problems of principle, such as were constantly emerging in relation to the Jewish and Gentile types of Christianity, and again as to the Christian attitude to the pagan state (Rom. xiii. 1 sqq.). He combined grasp with vital flexibility in a degree which made him the prince of missionaries. He was the prophet in the originality of his message; he was the theologian in the reflective interpretation which he gave to it, in terms derived mainly from a profound knowledge of Jewish thought, liberalized by contact with another world, the Graeco-Roman; but above all he was the missionary in the attitude in which he stood to his gospel and to men as its subjects. There was in him nothing doctrinaire: to that, along with the legal attitude, he had been crucified with Christ, for both belonged to " the rudiments of the world " of sense (1 Cor. xiii. 8 sqq.; 2 Cor. x. 4 seq.; Col. ii. 20 seq.; Phil. iv. 7). Accordingly he was great as an organizer of a new order among his Gentile churches, where much was left to local instinct informed by the one Spirit, while yet he jealously cared for such unity in usages as seemed needful to the embodiment of the one life of the Spirit in all, Jew and Gentile alike (1 Cor. iv. 17, xv. 33, 36). In particular he showed his Christian largeness in his exertions to keep in communion the two sections of Christ's people, to the point of risking his life for this end.

In his more personal relations he had the power of feeling and inspiring friendship of the noblest order, a comradeship " in Christ " which fills his letters with delightful touches of loyal affection and trust, even of playfulness on occasion (Philem.). He was a man of heart, with rapid alternations of mood, with nothing of the Stoic

¹ See Lightfoot, Galatians, pp. 183 sqq., who cites King Alfred as a parallel; and Hastings's Dict. Bible, iii. 701. Sir W M. Ramsay, St Paul the Traveller, pp. 94 sqq., prefers " a species of chronic malarial fever," connecting it specially with the attack mentioned in Gal. iv. 13 sqq.

in his self-mastery, which was an acquired grace, rooted in the " peace of God " (Phil. iv. 7, 10–13). Indeed it was in his impetuous, choleric temperament that there lurked " the last infirmity " of his soul, which at times betrayed him into vehemence of expression (Acts xxiii. 4 seq.) and a sweeping harshness of judgment (cf. 2 Cor. vii. 8 seq.), especially where he had detected disingenuous conduct in those who were interfering with his work for Christ or imputing base motives to himself, like the judaizers in Galatia and Corinth (cf. Phil. iii. 2). As to the charge of egoism, based on the emphasis he lays on his own person as medium of Christ's mind and will, it can hold only so far as Paul can be shown to do this gratuitously, and not really in the interests of his vocation. By this latter standard alone can an apostle be judged. Paul is careful, moreover, to distinguish his ordinary and his vocational self (2 Cor. xii. 5), as well as what he says as quoting Christ, as speaking qua apostle (1 Cor. vii. 10, 12), and again as simply one found " faithful " (ib. 25). Such is not the way of egoists or fanatics.

In his Epistles Paul found a fitting vehicle for his personality, whereby to speak not only to his own age but also to kindred souls all down the ages, so coming to spiritual life again and again, when buried under convention and tradition. For the letter is the most spontaneous form of writing, nearest in nature to conversation, and leaving personality most free. No doubt Paul's letters followed current forms (cf. G. A. Deissmann, Bible Studies, 1901, ch. i.). But he transfigured what he used by the new fullness of meaning infused into address, salutation, final messages and benediction. His letters are indeed " the life-blood of a noble spirit," poured forth to nourish its spiritual offspring (cf. 1 Thess. ii. 7 seq.). They are data for his Life and form incidentally an immovable critical basis for historical Christianity, on which the hypercriticism of Van Manen and others (see Ency. biblica, s.v. " Paul ") can make no real impression. On the other hand, as the sources of our knowledge of " Paulinism," they impose by their very form certain limits to our effort to reduce his thought to system. Canon R. J. Knowling's Witness of the Epistles (1892) and The Testimony of St Paul to Christ (1905) contain full summaries of all bearing on Paul's epistles. The history of the collection of Paul's letters into a corpus styled " The Apostle," for reading in Christian worship, is very significant, so far as we can trace it. The reference in 2 Pet. iii. 15 seq. would be of high value, were the date of 2 Pet. itself not so doubtful. The first definite notice we possess of a canon of Pauline epistles is that of the ultra-Pauline Marcion, who used ten Pauline epistles (c. 140). Certain apocryphal Pauline epistles appeared in early times, beginning with one To the Alexandrines, forged in the interests of Marcionism (Canon Murat), and an exchange of letters between the Corinthians and Paul, originally part of the Acta Pauli (ed. C. Schmidt, pp. 145–160). For the forged correspondence between Paul and Seneca, see Lightfoot, Philippians, pp. 329–333.

II. Paulinism.—Of recent years the ambiguity lurking in this term, as used to describe Paul's teaching as a whole, has been fully realized, and efforts have been made to distinguish what is distinctive and essential from what is traditional in form and relative in importance. For Paul, if " the first Christian theologian," was no systematic theologian. His mind was fundamentally semitic. It seized on one truth at a time, penetrating to the underlying principle with extraordinary power and viewing it successively from various sides. But, unlike a Greek thinker, he did not labour to reduce the sum of his principles to formal harmony in a system. In the absence of such critical testing of his thought by Paul himself, we must observe his relative emphasis and the varying causes of this, whether personal conviction or external occasion. Even when this is done it still remains to ask how much represents direct spiritual vision, due to " revelation," and how much traditional forms of thought or imagination, adopted by him as the most natural vehicle of expression occurring to his mind in a given mental environment. That Paul himself was conscious of the limitations here implied, is clear from what he says in 1 Cor. xiii. 9 sqq. as to the transience of the conceptions used by himself and others to body forth divine ideas and relations. After all, his was the theology of a prophet rather than a philosopher. Hence we have to distinguish what may be styled " personal Paulinism," the generalization of his own religious experience, from his apologetic exposition of it over against current Pharisaic Judaism if largely in its terms and also from the speculative setting which it took on in his mind, as his experience enlarged and the thoughts of his converts suggested fresh points of view.

It is mainly in this last sphere that development is traceable in Paulinism. Some idea of its nature and extent has already been given in connexion with Paul's life. If one must attempt to reproduce the Pauline "system" as a whole, it is best to take the form in which it appears in the Epistle to the Romans, and then supplement it with the fresh elements in the later epistles (so far as these seem really to be in terms of the writer's thought, rather than his readers'), instead of constructing an amalgam from the whole range of his epistles taken promiscuously. Paulinism, in the widest sense,[1] includes much that is not distinctively his at all; what can here be given is confined to Paul's specific contribution to Christianity.

i. Paulinism proper springs from an absorbing passion for a righteousness real from the heart outwards, real before God. This could not be satisfied by "works of the Law," i.e. deeds prompted by the categorical imperative of Law, itself viewed as the will of God and supported by sanctions of reward and penalty. Two things hindered: "the flesh," the sensuous element in human nature, positively prone to sin since the first man's trespass introduced an actual bias to evil (Rom. v. 12, 14, 19); and (the) Law itself, a form of divine claim which acted on man's sinful nature as a challenge and irritant to his egoism, so breeding either positive rebellion or self-confident pride, but in neither case real righteousness before God. Thus the main effect of Law was negative: it brought to light the sin latent in "the flesh," i.e. the personality as conditioned by the post-Adamic flesh. From this deliverance could come only by divine interposition or redemption, achieving at once reconciliation and regeneration by the removal of guilt and the creation of a new moral dynamic. Justification, then, or the placing of man in a state in which God could reckon him radically righteous, must be due to "grace" apart altogether from "works of law" and their desert. The medium of such grace was the Christ, in whom the claims of the dispensation of Law, in its typical form as the Jewish *Thorah*, were satisfied by death, while the Resurrection set the seal of God's approval upon Christ's fulfilment of righteousness (Rom. v. 17-19; 1 Cor. xv. 17) on the new and higher plane of filial obedience by love to God as Father.

Thus what the Law could not do, in its weakness in relation to the flesh, had been divinely achieved by God's Son, the Messiah, in virtue of "the Spirit of life" in Him, which annulled "sin and death" in human nature (Rom. viii. 3-4), first in the flesh of Christ Himself as second Adam, and then in the humanity which should be united to Him as spiritual Head (1 Cor. xv. 45). This union was affected by faith, a profound receptivity whereby the new moral personality of the Saviour became as it were the germ of the new moral personality of the believer. He was "in Christ" and Christ "in him" by a mutual spiritual interpenetration, begun on Christ's side by vicarious self-sacrificing love, and consummated on the believer's side by self-surrendering trust under the influence of the Spirit of God and Christ (Gal. ii. 20; Rom. viii. 9, 15 seq.).

Such mystic union by faith (cf. Eph. iii. 16-19) is the very nerve of Paulinism, having two main aspects. In its initial aspect, it is the real basis of justification (as radical sanctification) and regeneration; in its abiding aspect, it is the secret of progressive sanctification or assimilation to the image of Christ, Himself "the image of God." To the one aspect corresponds the initial rite of baptism; to the other the recurring rite of communion in the Lord's Supper. These have both an essentially corporate significance. It is as members of the mystical Body of Christ—or rather of the mystic Christ, consisting of Christ the Head and of His Body, the Church—that believers, already united to the Head by faith, partake in these sacraments (1 Cor. xii. 12 seq., x. 16 seq.).

The keystone of all this is the Christ of God, the glorified Christ who appeared to Paul at his conversion, and in the rays of whose heavenly glory the earthly life of Jesus of Nazareth was ever seen. Here, as elsewhere, the mode of Paul's conversion determined his whole perspective. It differentiated his emphasis from that of the older Judaeo-Christianity, which always started from the earthly manifestation, while it looked fixedly forward to the future manifestation in glory (of which the Resurrection appearances were the fore-gleams). To Paul the glorified Jesus or spirit-Christ (1 Cor. xv. 45; 2 Cor. iii. 18) of his vision became the Christ mystical of permanent, present Christian faith and experience. In union with Him the believer was already essentially "saved," because possessed of Christ's spirit of Sonship (Rom. viii. 9, 14-17, 30), although his redemption was not complete until the body was included, like the soul, in the penetrating "life" of the Spirit (viii. 23-25, 10 seq.). Accordingly he shifted the centre of gravity in Christian faith decisively from the future aspect of the Kingdom, to the present life of righteousness enjoyed by believers through "the first-fruits of the Spirit" in them. Here lay his great advance on Judaeo-Christianity, with its preponderant eschatological emphasis, along with a more external conception of Jesus, as Jewish Messiah, and of relation to Him. To this mode of thought Christ was not the very principle of the new filial righteousness. In a word, while Judaeo-Christianity only implicitly or unconsciously transcended legalism, Paulinism did so explicitly and consciously, thus

safeguarding the future. For Paul's religion was Christocentric in a sense unknown before. Compared with this, his distinctive attitude of soul to Christ, the exact metaphysical conception he formed of Christ's pre-existence was secondary and conditioned by inherited modes of thought. His own specific contribution was his consciousness of Christ's complete religious efficacy, which marked Him as essentially Divine, the Son of God in the highest sense conceivable under human conditions.

ii. *Jesus and Paul.*—In calling Paulinism "Christocentric," one raises the question as to its relation to the Gospel proclaimed by Jesus. That Paul conceived himself as utterly dependent for his gospel upon Jesus the Christ, is not in doubt, but only how far he unconsciously modified the Gospel by making Christ its subject matter rather than its revealer. In one aspect this is but the question as to Paul's attitude to the historic Jesus over again: yet it is more. Granting that Paul felt his gospel to be in essential agreement with the words and deeds of Jesus of Nazareth, as known to him, it remains to ask whether he did not put all into so fresh a perspective as to change the relative emphasis on points central to the teaching of Jesus, and so alter its spirit. A school of writers, by no means unappreciative of Paul as they understand him, of whom W. Wrede may be taken as example, answer that Paul so changed Christianity as to become its "second founder"—the real founder of ecclesiastical Christianity as distinct from the Christianity of Jesus. They say, "either Jesus or Paul: it cannot be both at once." They urge not only that Paulinism is involved in certain "mythological" conceptions, by its view of sin, of redemption and of the pre-existent celestial person of the Redeemer; but also that, apart from the Rabbinic and anti-Rabbinic element in Paul, his whole mystical attitude towards Christ as the medium of redemption (an idea borrowed, they say, not from Jesus Himself but from the religion of the Mysteries) is alien to the sunny and sane teaching of Jesus as to God and man, and their true relations.

The essential issue here is this. Could Jesus the Messiah set forth the Gospel in the same perspective as a devoted disciple of His? Must not the personal embodiment of the life of the Messianic kingdom by Jesus Himself, and so His personality, become the prime medium through which this life in its essential features, and especially in its spirit of devoted love, attains and maintains its hold upon the souls of men? Surely the new life must appear most fully and movingly *sub specie Christi*; and the *imitatio Christi*, in an inner sense which finds in Him the very principle of the new Christian consciousness as to God and man, must be the most direct and morally potent means to the realization of the Christ-type. Thus to say that Paulinism is practically and proximately "Christocentric," is not to deny that it is ultimately and theoretically "Theocentric," if only Christ be regarded as the revealer of God the Father, and that in virtue of a special community of nature with Him as Son. It may be questioned whether Paul attained, or indeed had within his reach in that age, the best intellectual equivalent of his religious intuition of Christ as "mediator between God and man." But it is another intuition or question whether his intuition that the personality of the Christ Himself was the secret of the spiritual power latent in His Gospel, be a true interpretation of the Gospel as it appears even in the Synoptics.[1] Thus the truth seems to lie rather with those who see in Paul "Jesus's most genuine disciple" (H. Weinel), the one who best understood and reproduced His thought. True, Jesus's Gospel is one seen through the sinless consciousness of the Saviour, while Paul's is one seen through the eyes of a conscious sinner. But that is the perspective in which mankind generally has to view the Gospel; and apart from the special intensity of Paul's personal experience of sin, the Gospel as it "found" him may surely be in principle the needful experimental complement to the Gospel as set forth in more ideal form by Jesus Himself. By restoring Jesus's own stress upon "eternal life" as present rather than future, and that on lines other than those of obedience to a divine law, Paul saved Christianity from a Judaizing of the universal and spiritual religion with which Jesus had in fact inspired His personal disciples, but which they had not been able to grasp.

No doubt there is another side to all this, the side of Paul's idiosyncrasy, both religiously and as a thinker. The peculiar depth and form of Paul's religious experience, especially as regards sin, have proved a limitation to his direct and full influence. While "numberless men have discovered themselves in reading Paul," more have not been "found" by him; and of those who have felt the religious appeal of his writings, not a few have gravely misunderstood the theoretic setting of his message. Indeed misunderstanding, one way or another, was Paul's usual lot in the ancient Church,[2] as regards his most distinctive ideas, due partly to the difficult form in which some of those ideas were couched. But to say this is little more than saying that Paulinism is a less universal form of the Gospel than that given it by his Master Jesus Christ. To do full justice

---

[1] One of the best critical summaries of "Pauline Theology" is that by E. Hatch in the *Ency. Brit.* 9th ed.

[1] The whole history of Christianity is proof that the personality of Jesus has counted for more in producing Christians than his teaching *per se*, that is, his Gospel in the narrower sense. And it was Paul, not the older apostles, who first concentrated attention on that personality as the type and pledge of man's potential sonship to God.

[2] See S. Means, *Saint Paul and the ante-Nicene Church* (1903).

to Paulinism in this respect, we must compare it with other interpretations of Jesus and His Gospel in the age immediately ensuing. At the one extreme stands Judaeo-Christianity (so far as uninfluenced by Paul), with its ultra-conservatism and undeveloped spirituality; at the other Gnosticism, with its ultra-spiritualism, born of a rigid dualism and defective sense for historical continuity in revelation. Between these stands Paul, blending the positive ideas of both in a religious unity of immense ethical power and initiative; while the other and intermediate types represented in the New Testament—by 1 Peter, Hebrews and the Johannine writings—all testify to his pervasive influence.

LITERATURE.—For this in anything like its immense range, reference may be made to the articles "Paul" in Hastings's *Dict. Bible*, the *Ency. Bib.*, A. Hauck's *Realencyklopädie* (Zahn); to R. J. Knowling's *Witness of the Epistles* (1892) and *The Testimony of St Paul to Christ* (1905), and C. Clemen, *Paulus* (1904), the footnotes of which are a mine of information on this subject. Besides these, the leading works on New Testament Introduction or theology and on the apostolic age deal largely with Paul, and often contain bibliographies. The following works may be taken as fairly typical :—

1. For Paul's *Life*: A. Neander, *Gesch. der Pflanzung . . . der christl. Kirche*, vol. i. (4th ed., 1847; Eng. trans. in Bohn's Library), and Lives by F. C. Baur (1845, 1866); G. V. Lechler, *Das apost. . . .* *Zeitalter* (1851; 3rd ed., 1885; Eng. trans. 1886); E. Renan (1869); T. Lewin (1851, 1874, rich in archaeology); Conybeare and Howson (1852 and later); H. Ewald, *History of Israel* (vol. vi., 3rd ed., 1868); M. Krenkel (1869); A. Hausrath (2nd ed., 1872); F. W. Farrar (1879); A. Sabatier (2nd ed., 1881); K. Schmidt, *Die Apostelgesch.* (1864); W. Weizsäcker, *Das apost. Zeitalter* (1886; Eng. trans., 1894); W. M. Ramsay, *St Paul the Traveller and Roman Citizen* (1896); A. C. McGiffert, *The Apostolic Age* (1897); O. Cone (1898); C. Clemen (1904); B. W. Bacon (1905). Some of these deal largely with Paul's teaching.

2. For Paul's *Teaching*: L. Usteri, *Die Entwickelung des paulinischen Lehrbegriffs* (1824; 6th ed. 1851); Baur's *Paulus* (1845, 1866); A. Ritschl, *Die Entsteh. d. altkath. Kirche* (2nd ed., 1857); E. Reuss, *Hist. de la théol. chrét. au siècle apostolique*, tome ii. (3rd ed., 1864; Eng. trans., 1872); B. Jowett, essays in his *Epistles of St Paul to the Thess.*, &c. (2nd ed., 1859); C. Holsten, *Zum Evang. d. Paulus u. Petrus* (1868), &c.; B. Lightfoot, dissertations in his *Commentaries*; Matthew Arnold, *St Paul and Protestantism* (1870); O. Pfleiderer, *Der Paulinismus* (1873; Eng. trans. 1877), also Hibbert Lecture (1885) and *Das Urchristentum*, vol. i. (2nd ed., 1902; Eng. trans., 1907); A. Sabatier, *L'Apôtre Paul* (1881); E. Ménégoz, *Le Péché et la rédemption d'après S. Paul* (1882); J. F. Clarke, *The Ideas of the Apostle Paul* (1884); G. B. Stevens, *The Pauline Theology* (1892); A. B. Bruce, *St Paul's Conception of Christianity* (1894); C. C. Everett, *The Gospel of Paul*; G. Matheson, *The Spiritual Development of St Paul*; P. Feine, *Das gesetzfreie Evang. des Paulus* (1899); brief sketches by W. Bousset, H. Weinel, W. Wrede, P. Wernle (also his *Anfänge unserer Religion*, 1901; Eng. trans., 1904), and A. Jülicher (in *Die Kultur der Gegenwart*, 1905, I. iv. i. 69-97); but especially W. Sanday, article "Paul" in *Dict. of Christ and the Gospels* (1908), where the literature bearing on "Jesus and Paul" will be found. For commentaries, see under the several epistles. (J. V. B.)

PAUL (PAULUS), the name of five popes.

PAUL I., pope from 757 to 767, succeeded his brother Stephen III. on the 29th of May 757. His pontificate was chiefly remarkable for his close alliance with Pippin, king of the Franks, to whom he made a present of books highly significant of the intellectual poverty of the times; and for his unsuccessful endeavours to effect a reconciliation with the iconoclastic emperor of the East, Constantine Copronymus. He died on the 28th of June 767. His successor was Stephen IV.

PAUL II. (Pietro Barbo), pope from the 30th of August 1464 to the 26th of July 1471, was born at Venice in 1417. Intended for a business career, he took orders during the pontificate of his uncle, Eugenius IV., and was appointed successively archdeacon of Bologna, bishop of Cervia, bishop of Piacenza, protonotary of the Roman Church, and in 1440 cardinal-deacon of Sta Maria Nuova. He was made cardinal-priest of Sta Cecilia, then of St Marco by Nicholas V., was a favourite of Calixtus III. and was unanimously and unexpectedly elected the successor of Pius II. He immediately declared that election "capitulations," which cardinals had long been in the habit of affirming as rules of conduct for future popes, could affect a new pope only as counsels, not as binding obligations. He opposed with some success the domineering policy of the Venetian government in Italian affairs. His repeated condemnations of the Pragmatic Sanction of Bourges resulted in strained relations with Louis XI. of France. He pronounced excommunication and deposition against King George Podiebrad

on the 23rd of December 1466 for refusal to enforce the Basel agreement against the Utraquists, and prevailed on Matthias Corvinus, king of Hungary, to declare war against him on the 31st of March 1468. Matthias was not particularly successful, but George Podiebrad died on the 22nd of March 1471. The pope carried on fruitless negotiations (1469) with the emperor Frederick III. for a crusade against the Turks. Paul endeavoured to make drastic reforms in the curia, and abolished the college of abbreviators (1466), but this called forth violent protests from the historian Platina, one of their number and subsequently librarian under Sixtus IV., who is responsible for the fiction that Paul was an illiterate persecutor of learning. It is true that the pope suppressed the Roman academy, but on religious grounds. On the other hand he was friendly to Christian scholars; he restored many ancient monuments; made a magnificent collection of antiquities and works of art; built the Palazzo di St Marco, now the Palazzo di Venezia; and probably first introduced printing into Rome. Paul embellished the costume of the cardinals, collected jewels for his own adornment, provided games and food for the Roman people and practically instituted the carnival. He began in 1469 a revision of the Roman statutes of 1363—a work which was not completed until 1490. Paul established the special tax called the *quindennium* in 1470, and by bull of the same year (April 19) announced the jubilee for every twenty-five years. He began negotiations with Ivan III. for the union of the Russian Church with the Roman see. Paul was undoubtedly not a man of quick parts or unusual views, but he was handsome, attractive, strong-willed, and has never been accused of promoting nephews or favourites. He died very suddenly, probably of apoplexy, on the 26th of July, 1471, and was succeeded by Sixtus IV.

The principal contemporary lives of Paul II., including that by Platina, are in L. Muratori, *Rerum ital. scriptores*, iii. pt. 2, and in Raynaldus, *Annales ecclesiastici* (1464-1471). The inventory of his personal effects, published by E. Müntz (*Les Arts*, ii., 1875), is a valuable document for the history of art. See also L. Pastor, *History of the Popes*, vol. iv.; trans. by F. I. Antrobus (London, 1898); M. Creighton, *History of the Papacy*, vol. iv. (London, 1901); F. Gregorovius, *Rome in the Middle Ages*, vol. vii. (trans. by Mrs G. W. Hamilton, London, 1900-1902); H. L'Epinois, *Paul II.*, F. Palacky, *Geschichte von Böhmen*, Bd. IV.-V. (Prague, 1860-1865); *Aus den Annalen-Registern der Päpste Eugen IV., Pius II., Paul II., u. Sixtus IV.*, ed. by K. Hayn (Cologne, 1896). There is an excellent article by C. Benrath in Hauck's *Realencyklopädie* (3rd ed.), vol. xv. (C. H. HA.)

PAUL III. (Alessandro Farnese), pope from 1534 to 1549, was born on the 28th of February 1468, of an old and distinguished family. As a pupil of the famous Pomponius Laetus, and, subsequently, as a member of the circle of Cosmo de' Medici, he received a finished education. From Florence he passed to Rome, and became the father of at least two children, later legitimized. Upon entering the service of the Church, however, he lived more circumspectly. His advancement was rapid. To the liaison between his sister Giulia Farnese Orsini and Alexander VI. he owed his cardinal's hat; but the steady favour which he enjoyed under successive popes was due to his own cleverness and capacity for affairs. His election to the papacy, on the 13th of October 1534, to succeed Clement VII., was virtually without opposition.

The pontificate of Paul III. forms a turning-point in the history of the papacy. The situation at his accession was grave and complex: the steady growth of Protestantism, the preponderant power of the emperor and his prolonged wars with France, the advances of the Turks, the uncertain mind of the Church itself—all conspired to produce a problem involved and delicate. Paul was shrewd, calculating, tenacious; but on the other hand over-cautious, and inclined rather to temporize than to strike at the critical moment. His instincts and ambitions were those of a secular prince of the Renaissance; but circumstances forced him to become the patron of reform. By the promotion to the cardinalate of such men as Contarini, Caraffa, Pole and Morone, and the appointment of a commission to report upon existing evils and their remedy, the way was opened for reform; while by the introduction of the Inquisition into Italy (1542), the establishment of the censorship and the Index (1543), and the approval of the Society of Jesus (1540), most efficient agencies were set on foot for combating heresy.

But in the matter of a general council, so urgently desired by the emperor, Paul showed himself irresolute and procrastinating. Finally on the 13th of December 1545 the Council assembled in Trent; but when the victories of Charles V. seemed to threaten its independence it was transferred to Bologna (March 1547) and not long afterwards suspended (Sept. 1549). He concluded the truce of Nice (1538) between Charles and Francis, and contracted an alliance with each. But the peace of Crespy and the emperor's negotiations with the Protestants (1544) turned him against Charles, and he was suspected of desiring his defeat in the Schmalkaldic War. The most deplorable weakness of Paul was his nepotism. Parma and Piacenza, states of the Church, he bestowed upon his natural son Pier Luigi (1545). But in 1549 Pier Luigi was assassinated by his outraged subjects, and the emperor thereupon claimed the two duchies for his son-in-law Ottavio Farnese, Paul's grandson. This led to a family quarrel which greatly embittered the last days of the pope and hastened his death (Nov. 10, 1549). Parma and Piacenza continued to be a bone of contention for two hundred and fifty years.

Paul was gifted and cultured, a lover and patron of art. He began the famous Farnese Palace; constructed the Sala Regia in the Vatican; commissioned Michelangelo to paint the "Last Judgment," and to resume work upon St Peter's; and otherwise adorned the city. Easy-going, luxurious, worldly-minded, Paul was not in full sympathy with the prevailing influences about him.

See Panvinio, continuator of Platina, De vitis pontiff. rom.; Ciaconius, Vitae et res gestae summorum pontiff. rom. (Rome, 1601–1602, both contemporaries of Paul III.); Quirini, Imago optimi . . . pontif. expressa in gestis Pauli III. (Brixen, 1745); Ranke, Popes (Eng. trans., Austin), i. 243 seq.; v. Reumont, Gesch. der Stadt Rom., iii. 2, 471 seq., 716 seq.; Brosch, Gesch. des Kirchenstaates (1880), i. 163 seq.; Ehses, "Kirchliche Reformarbeiten unter Paul III. vor dem Trienter Konzil," Röm. Quartalschrift (1901), xv. 153 seq.; Capasso, La Politica di papa Paolo III. e l'Italia (Camerino, 1901); and also the extensive bibliography in Herzog-Hauck, Realencyklopädie, s.v. "Paul III."

PAUL IV. (Giovanni Pietro Caraffa), pope from 1555 to 1559, was born on the 28th of June 1476, of a noble Neapolitan family. His ecclesiastical preferment he owed to the influence of an uncle, Cardinal Oliviero Caraffa. Having filled the post of nuncio in England and Spain, he served successive popes as adviser in matters pertaining to heresy and reform. But he resigned his benefices, and, in conjunction with Cajetan, founded the order of the Theatines (1524) with the object of promoting personal piety and of combating heresy by preaching. In 1536 Paul III. made him cardinal-archbishop of Naples and a member of the reform commission. After the failure of Contarini's attempt at reconciliation with the Protestants (1541) the papacy committed itself to the reaction advocated by Caraffa; the Inquisition and censorship were set up (1542, 1543), and the extermination of heresy in Italy undertaken with vigour. Elected pope, on the 23rd of May 1555, in the face of the veto of the emperor, Paul regarded his elevation as the work of God. With his defects of temper, his violent antipathies, his extravagant notion of papal prerogative, his pontificate was filled with strife. Blinded by ungovernable hatred he joined with France (1555) in order to drive the "accursed Spaniards" from Italy. But the victory of Philip II. at St Quentin (1557) and the threatening advance of Alva upon Rome forced him to come to terms and to abandon his French alliance. He denounced the peace of Augsburg as a pact with heresy; nor would he recognise the abdication of Charles V. and the election of Ferdinand. By insisting upon the restitution of the confiscated church-lands, assuming to regard England as a papal fief, requiring Elizabeth, whose legitimacy he aspersed, to submit her claims to him, he raised insuperable obstacles to the return of England to the Church of Rome.

Paul's attitude towards nepotism was at variance with his character as a reformer. An unworthy nephew, Carlo Caraffa,

was made cardinal, and other relatives were invested with the duchies of Paliano and Montebello. It was Paul's hope in this way to acquire a support in his war with the Spaniards. But the defeat of his plans disillusioned him, and he turned to reform. A stricter life was introduced into the papal court; the regular observance of the services of the Church was enjoined; many of the grosser abuses were prohibited. These measures only increased Paul's unpopularity, so that when he died, on the 18th of August 1559, the Romans vented their hatred by demolishing his statue, liberating the prisoners of the Inquisition, and scattering its papers. Paul's want of political wisdom, and his ignorance of human nature aroused antagonisms fatal to the success of his cause.

See Panvinio, continuator of Platina, De vitis pontiff. rom.; Ciaconius, Vitae et res gestas summorum pontiff. rom. (Rome, 1601–1602, both contemporaries of Paul IV.); Caraccioli, De vita Pauli IV. P.M. (Cologne, 1612; for criticism see Hist. Zeitschr., xliv. 460 seq.), whose rich collection of materials was used by Bromata, Vita di Paolo IV. (Ravenna, 1748), and Samm, Une Question ital. au seizième siècle (Paris, 1861). See also Castaldo, Vita del pontifice Paolo Quarto (Modena, 1618); Ranke, Popes (Eng. trans. by Austin), i. 286 seq. (an excellent sketch); v. Reumont, Gesch. der Stadt Rom., iii. 2, 513 seq. and Benrath, "G. P. Caraffa u. d. reformatorische Bewegung seiner Zeit," in Jahrb. für prot. Theol. (1878), vol. i.; Ancel, Disgrace et procès des Caraffa (1909); Riess, Politik Pauls IV. (1909).

PAUL V. (Camillo Borghese), successor of Leo XI., was born in Rome on the 17th of September 1552, of a noble family. He studied in Perugia and Padua, became a canon lawyer, and was vice-legate in Bologna. As a reward of a successful mission to Spain Clement VIII. made him cardinal (1596) and later vicar in Rome and inquisitor. Elevated to the papacy, on the 16th of May 1605, his extreme conception of papal prerogative, his arrogance and obstinacy, his perverse insistence upon the theoretical and disregard of the actual, made strife inevitable. He provoked disputes with the Italian states over ecclesiastical rights. Savoy, Genoa, Tuscany and Naples, wishing to avoid a rupture, yielded; but Venice resisted. The republic stood upon her right to judge all her subjects, and by her demands touching benefices, tithes and papal bulls showed her determination to be supreme in her own territory. Excommunication and interdict (April 17, 1606) were met with defiance. The cause of the republic was brilliantly advocated by Fra Paolo Sarpi, counsellor of state; the defenders of the papal theory were Cardinals Baronius and Bellarmine. The pope talked of coercion by arms; but Spain, to whom he looked for support, refused to be drawn into war, and the quarrel was finally settled by the mediation of France (March 22, 1607). Notwithstanding certain concessions, the victory remained with the republic (see SARPI).

Paul became involved in a quarrel with England also. After the Gunpowder Plot parliament required a new oath of allegiance to the king and a denial of the right of the pope to depose him or release his subjects from their obedience. Paul forbade Roman Catholics to take the oath; but to no purpose, beyond stirring up a literary controversy. By his condemnation of Gallicanism (1613) Paul angered France, and provoked the defiant declaration of the states general of 1614 that the king held his crown from God alone.

Paul encouraged missions, confirmed many new congregations and brotherhoods, authorized a new version of the Ritual, and canonized Carlo Borromeo. His devotion to the interests of his family exceeded all bounds, and they became enormously wealthy. Paul began the famous Villa Borghese; enlarged the Quirinal and Vatican; completed the nave, façade and portico of St Peter's; erected the Borghese Chapel in Sta Maria Maggiore; and restored the aqueduct of Augustus and Trajan ("Acqua Paolina"). He also added to the Vatican library, and began a collection of antiquities. Paul died on the 28th of January 1621, and was succeeded by Gregory XV.

See Bzovius (Bzowski), De vita Pauli V. (Rome, 1625; reprinted in Platina, De vitis pontif. rom.,.ed. 1626), who depicts Paul as a paragon of all public and private virtues; Vitorelli, continuator of Ciaconius, Vitae et res gestae summorum pontiff. rom. (a contemporary of the pope); Goujet, Hist. du pontificat de Paul V.,

(1765); Ranke, *Popes* (Eng. trans. by Austin), ii. 330 seq., iii. 72 seq.; v. Reumont, *Gesch. der Stadt Rom*, iii. 2, 605 seq.; Brosch, *Gesch. des Kirchenstaates* (1880), i. 351 seq. The Venetian version of the quarrel with the pope was written by Sarpi (subsequently translated into English, London, 1626), see also Cornet, *Paolo V et la repub venecia* (Vienna, 1859); and Trollope, *Paul the Pope and Paul the Friar* (London, 1860). An extensive biography will be found in Herzog-Hauck, *Realencyklopädie, s.v.* " Paul V." (T. F. C.)

PAUL I. (1754-1801), emperor of Russia, was born in the Summer Palace in St Petersburg on the 1st of October (N S) —the 20th of September by the Russian calendar—1754. He was the son of the grand duchess, afterwards empress, Catherine. According to a scandalous report his father was not her husband the grand duke Peter, afterwards emperor, but one Colonel Soltykov There is probably no foundation for this story except gossip, and the cynical malice of Catherine. During his infancy he was taken from the care of his mother by the empress Elizabeth, whose ill-judged fondness is believed to have injured his health. As a boy he was reported to be intelligent and good-looking. His extreme ugliness in later life is attributed to an attack of typhus, from which he suffered in 1771. It has been asserted that his mother hated him, and was only restrained from putting him to death while he was still a boy by the fear of what the consequences of another palace crime might be to herself Lord Buckinghamshire, the English ambassador at her court, expressed this opinion as early as 1764. In fact, however, the evidence goes to show that the empress, who was at all times very fond of children, treated Paul with kindness. He was put in charge of a trustworthy governor, Nikita Panin, and of competent tutors. Her dissolute court was a bad home for a boy who was to be the sovereign, but Catherine took great trouble to arrange his first marriage with Wilhelmina of Darmstadt, who was renamed in Russia Nathalie Alexéevna, in 1773. She allowed him to attend the council in order that he might be trained for his work as emperor. His tutor Poroshin complained of him that he was " always in a hurry," acting and speaking without thinking. After his first marriage he began to engage in intrigues. He suspected his mother of intending to kill him, and once openly accused her of causing broken glass to be mingled with his food. Yet, though his mother removed him from the council and began to keep him at a distance, her actions were not unkind. The use made of his name by the rebel Pugachev in 1775 tended no doubt to render his position more difficult. When his wife died in childbirth in that year his mother arranged another marriage with the beautiful Sophia Dorothea of Württemberg, renamed in Russia Maria Feodorovna. On the birth of his first child in 1777 she gave him an estate, Pavlovsk. Paul and his wife were allowed to travel through western Europe in 1781-1782. In 1783 the empress gave him another estate at Gatchina, where he was allowed to maintain a brigade of soldiers whom he drilled on the Prussian model. As Paul grew his character became steadily degraded. He was not incapable of affection nor without generous impulses, but he was flighty, passionate in a childish way, and when angry capable of cruelty. The affection he had for his wife turned to suspicion. He fell under the influence of two of his wife's maids of honour in succession, Nelidov and Lapuknin, and of his barber, a Turkish slave named Korotssov. For some years before Catherine died it was obvious that he was hovering on the border of insanity. Catherine contemplated setting him aside in favour of his son Alexander, to whom she was attached. Paul was aware of his mother's half-intention— for it does not appear to have been more—and became increasingly suspicious of his wife and children, whom he rendered perfectly miserable. No definite step was taken to set him aside, probably because nothing would be effective short of putting him to death, and Catherine shrank from the extreme course. When she was seized with apoplexy he was free to destroy the will by which she left the crown to Alexander, if any such will was ever made. The four and a half years of Paul's rule in Russia were unquestionably the reign of a madman. The excitement of the change from his retired life in Gatchina

to omnipotence drove him below the line of insanity. His conduct of the foreign affairs of Russia plunged the country first into the second coalition against France in 1778, and then into the armed neutrality against Great Britain in 1801. In both cases he acted on personal pique, quarrelling with France because he took a sentimental interest in the Order of Malta, and then with England because he was flattered by Napoleon: But his political follies might have been condoned. What was unpardonable was that he treated the people about him like a shah, or one of the craziest of the Roman emperors. He began by repealing Catherine's law which exempted the free classes of the population of Russia from corporal punishment and mutilation. Nobody could feel himself safe from exile or brutal ill-treatment at any moment. If Russia had possessed any political institution except the tsardom he would have been put under restraint. But the country was not sufficiently civilized to deal with Paul as the Portuguese had dealt with Alphonso VI, a very similar person, in 1667. In Russia as in medieval Europe there was no safe prison for a deposed ruler. A conspiracy was organized, some months before it was executed, by Counts Pahlen and Panin, and a half-Spanish, half-Neapolitan adventurer, Admiral Ribas. The death of Ribas delayed the execution. On the night of the 11th of March 1801 Paul was murdered in his bedroom in the St Michael Palace by a band of dismissed officers headed by General Bennigsen, a Hanoverian in the Russian service. They burst into his bedroom after supping together and when flushed with drink. The conspirators forced him to the table, and tried to compel him to sign his abdication. Paul offered some resistance, and one of the assassins struck him with a sword, and he was then strangled and trampled to death. He was succeeded by his son, the emperor Alexander I, who was actually in the palace, and to whom Nicholas Zubov, one of the assassins, announced his accession.

See, for Paul's early life, K. Waliszewski, *Autour d'un trône* (Paris, 1894), or the English translation, *The Story of a Throne* (London, 1895), and P. Morane, *Paul I. de Russie avant l'avénement* (Paris, 1907). For his reign, T. Schiemann, *Geschichte Russlands unter Nikolaus I.* (Berlin, 1904), vol. i. and *Die Ermordung Pauls*, by the same author (Berlin, 1902).

PAUL OF SAMOSATA, patriarch of Antioch (260-272), was, if we may credit the encyclical letter of his ecclesiastical opponents preserved in Eusebius's *History*, bk. vii. ch. 30, of humble origin. He was certainly born farther east at Samosata, and may have owed his promotion in the Church to Zenobia, queen of Palmyra. The letter just mentioned is the only indisputably contemporary document concerning him and was addressed to Dionysius and Maximus, respectively bishops of Rome and Alexandria, by seventy bishops, priests and deacons, who attended a synod at Antioch in 269 and deposed Paul. Their sentence, however, did not take effect until late in 272, when the emperor Aurelian, having defeated Zenobia and anxious to impose upon Syria the dogmatic system fashionable in Rome, deposed Paul and allowed the rival candidate Domnus to take his place and emoluments. Thus it was a pagan emperor who in this momentous dispute ultimately determined what was orthodox and what was not; and the advanced Christology to which he gave his preference has ever since been upheld as the official orthodoxy of the Church. Aurelian's policy moreover was in effect a recognition of the Roman bishop's pretension to be arbiter for the whole Church in matters of faith and dogma.

Scholars will pay little heed to the charges of rapacity, extortion, pomp and luxury made against Paul by the authors of this letter. It also accuses him not only of consorting himself with two " sisters " of ripe age and fair to look upon; but of allowing his presbyters and deacons also to contract platonic unions with Christian ladies. No actual lapses however from chastity are alleged, and it is only complained that suspicions were aroused, apparently among the pagans.

The real gravamen against Paul seems to have been that he clung to a Christology which was become archaic and had in Rome and Alexandria already fallen into the background.

Paul's heresy lay principally in his insistence on the genuine humanity of Jesus of Nazareth, in contrast with the rising orthodoxy which merged his human consciousness in the divine Logos. It is best to give Paul's beliefs in his own words; and the following sentences are translated from Paul's *Discourses to Sabinus*, of which fragments are preserved in a work against heresies ascribed to Anastasius, and printed by Angelo Mai:—

I. "Having been anointed by the Holy Spirit he received the title of *the anointed* (*i.e.* Christos), suffering in accordance with his nature, working wonders in accordance with grace. For in fixity and resoluteness of character he likened himself to God; and having kept himself free from sin was united with God, and was empowered to grasp as it were the power and authority of wonders. By these he was shown to possess over and above the will, one and the same activity (with God), and won the title of Redeemer and Saviour of our race."

II. "The Saviour became holy and just; and by struggle and hard work overcame the sins of our forefather. By these means he succeeded in perfecting himself, and was through his moral excellence united with God; having attained to unity and sameness of will and *energy* (*i.e.* activity) with Him through his advances in the path of good deeds. This will be preserved inseparable (from the Divine, and so inherited the name which is above all names, the prize of love and affection vouchsafed in grace to him."

III. "The different natures and the different persons admit of union in one way alone, namely in the way of a complete agreement in respect of will, and, thereby is revealed the One (or Monad) in activity in the case of those (wills) which have coalesced in the manner described."

IV. "We do not award praise to beings which submit merely in virtue of their nature; but we do award high praise to beings which submit because their attitude is one of love; and so submitting because their inspiring motive is one and the same, they are confirmed and strengthened by one and the same indwelling power, of which the force ever grows, so that it never ceases to stir. It was in virtue of this love that the Saviour coalesced with God, so as to admit of no divorce from Him, but for all ages to retain one and the same will and activity with Him, an activity perpetually at work in the manifestation of good."

V. "Wonder not that the Saviour had one will with God. For as nature manifests the substance of the many to subsist as one and the same, so the attitude of love produces in the many an unity and sameness of will which is manifested by unity and sameness of approval and well-pleasingness."

From other fairly attested sources we infer that Paul regarded the baptism as a landmark indicative of a great stage in the moral advance of Jesus. But it was a man and not the divine Logos which was born of Mary. Jesus was a man who came to be God, rather than God become man. Paul's Christology therefore was of the Adoptionist type, which we find among the primitive Ebionite Christians of Judæa, in Hermas, Theodotus and Artemon of Rome, and in Archelaus the opponent of Mani, and in the other great doctors of the Syrian Church of the 4th and 5th centuries. Lucian the great exegete of Antioch and his school derived their inspiration from Paul, and he was through Lucian a forefather of Arianism. Probably the Paulicians of Armenia continued his tradition, and hence their name (see PAULICIANS).

Paul of Samosata represented the high-water mark of Christian speculation; and it is deplorable that the fanaticism of his own and of succeeding generations has left us nothing but a few scattered fragments of his writings. Already at the Council of Nicaea in 325 the Pauliani were put outside the Church and condemned to be rebaptized. It is interesting to note that at the synod of Antioch the use of the word *consubstantial* to denote the relation of God the Father to the divine Son or Logos was condemned, although it afterwards became at the Council of Nicaea the watchword of the orthodox faction.

LITERATURE.—Adolph Harnack, *History of Dogma*, vol. iii.; Gieseler's *Compendium of Ecclesiastical History* (Edinburgh, 1834), vol. i.; Routh, *Reliquiae sacrae*, vol. iii.; F. C. Conybeare, *Key of Truth* (Oxford); Hefele, *History of the Christian Councils* (Edinburgh, 1872), vol. i.; Ch. Bigg, *The Origins of Christianity* (Oxford, 1909), ch. xxxv.　　　　(F. C. C.)

PAULDING, JAMES KIRKE (1778–1860), American writer and politician, was born in Dutchess county, New York, on the 22nd of August 1778. After a brief course at a village school, he removed in 1800 to New York City, where in connexion with his brother-in-law, William Irving, and Washington Irving, he began in January 1807 a series of short lightly humorous articles, under the title of *The Salmagundi Papers*. In 1814 he published a political pamphlet, "The United States and England," which attracted the notice of President Madison, who in 1815 appointed him secretary to the board of navy commissioners, which position he held until November 1823. Subsequently Paulding was navy agent in New York City from 1825 to 1837, and from 1837 to 1841 was secretary of the navy in the cabinet of President Van Buren. From 1841 until his death on the 6th of April 1860 he lived near Hyde Park, in Dutchess county, New York. Although much of his literary work consisted of political journalism, he yet found time to write a large number of essays, poems and tales. From his father, an active revolutionary patriot, Paulding inherited strong anti-British sentiments. He was among the first distinctively American writers, and protested vigorously against intellectual thraldom to the mother-country. As a prose writer he is chaste and elegant, generally just, and realistically descriptive. As a poet he is gracefully commonplace, and the only lines by Paulding which survive in popular memory are the familiar—

" Peter Piper picked a peck of pickled peppers:
　　Where is the peck of pickled peppers Peter Piper picked ?"

which may be found in *Koningsmarke*.

The following is a partial list of his writings: *The Diverting History of John Bull and Brother Jonathan* (1812); *The Lay of the Scottish Fiddle* (1813), a good-natured parody on *The Lay of the Last Minstrel*; *Letters from the South* (1817); *The Backwoodsman: a Poem* (1818); *Salmagundi* (2nd series, 1819–1820); *A Sketch of Old England*, by *a New England Man* (1822); *Koningsmarke, the Long Finne* (1823), a quiz on the romantic school of Walter Scott; *John Bull in America; or the New Munchausen* (1824), a broad caricature of the early type of British traveller in America; *The Merry Tales of the Three Wise Men of Gotham* (1826); *Chronicles of the City of Gotham*, from the *Papers of a Retired Common Councilman* (1830); *The Dutchman's Fireside* (1831); *Westward Ho!* (1832); *A Life of Washington* (1835), ably and gracefully written; *Slavery in the United States* (1836), in which he defends slavery as an institution; *The Book of Saint Nicholas* (1837), a series of stories of the old Dutch settlers; *American Comedies* (1847), the joint production of himself and his son William J. Paulding; and *The Puritan and his Daughter* (1849). The same son also published an edition of Paulding's *Select Works* (4 vols., 1867–1868), and a biography called *Literary Life of James K. Paulding* (New York, 1867).

PAULET, POULETT or **POWLETT**, an English family of an ancient Somersetshire stock, taking a surname from the parish of Pawlett near Bridgwater. They advanced themselves by a series of marriages with heirs, acquiring manors and lands in Somersetshire, Wiltshire, Devonshire and Hampshire. A match with a Denebaud early in the 15th century brought the manor of Hinton St George, still the seat of the elder line. the earls Poulett. An ancestor of this branch, Sir Amias Poulett or Paulet (d. 1537), knighted in 1487 after the battle of Stoke, was treasurer of the Middle Temple in 1521, when Wolsey, in revenge for an indignity suffered at the knight's hands when the future chancellor was a young parson at Limington, forbade his leaving London without leave. To propitiate the cardinal, Sir Amias, rebuilding the Middle Temple gate, decorated it with the cardinal's arms and badge. Sir Hugh Poulett, his eldest son, a soldier who had distinguished himself in 1544 at Boulogne in the king's presence, had, in 1551, a patent of the captaincy of Jersey with the governance of Montorgueil Castle. His wisdom and experience in the wars made Queen Elizabeth employ him at Havre in 1562 as adviser to the earl of Warwick. He died in 1572, having married, as his second wife, the wealthy widow of Sir Thomas Pope, founder of Trinity College, Oxford. Sir Amias Poulett (1536–1588), Sir Hugh's son and heir by a first marriage, is famous as the puritan knight into whose charge at Tutbury and Chartley was given the queen of Scots. After his prisoner's sentence at Fotheringhay, he beset Elizabeth's ministers with messages advising her execution, but he firmly withstood " with great grief and bitterness," the suggestion that she should be put to death secretly, saying that God and the law forbade. Sir Anthony Poulett (1562–1600), his eldest surviving son, succeeded him as governor of Jersey and was father of John Poulett (1586-1649) to whom Charles I. in 1627 gave a patent of peerage as Lord Poulett of Hinton St George. In spite of the puritan opinions of his family he declared for the king, raising for the royal army a brigade which he led in Dorsetshire and Devonshire. He was taken prisoner for the second time at the fall of Exeter in 1646 and suffered a heavy fine. His eldest son John, the second Lord Poulett (1615-1665) was taken with his father at Exeter. John, the fourth Lord Poulett (1663-1743), having been a commissioner for the union, was created in 1706 Viscount Hinton of Hinton St George and Earl Poulett. In 1710-1711 he was first lord of the treasury and nominal head of an administration controlled by Harley. A garter was given him in 1712. A moderate Tory, his places were taken from him at the accession of the house of Brunswick. The fifth earl. (d. 1864) re-settled the family estates in 1853 in order to bar the inheritance of one William Turnour Thomas Poulett who, although born in wedlock of the wife of the earl's cousin William Henry Poulett, was repudiated by her husband, afterwards the sixth earl. In 1903 the sixth earl's son by a third marriage established his claim to the peerage, and in 1909 judgment was given against the claim of William Turnour Thomas Poulett, then styling himself Earl Poulett.

A younger line of the Paulets, sprung from William Paulet of Melcombe, serjeant-at-law (d. 1435), reached higher honours than an earldom. William Paulet, by his marriage with Eleanor Delamare (d. 1413), daughter of Philip Delamare and heir of her brother, acquired for his descendants Fisherton Delamare in Wiltshire and Nunney Castle in Somerset. Their son Sir John Paulet married Constance, daughter and coheir of Hugh Poynings, son and heir of Sir Thomas Poynings, Lord St John of Basing. Through this marriage came the lordship and manor of Basing, and the manor of Amport or Ham Port which is still with the descendants of Hugh de Port, its Norman lord at the time of the Domesday Survey. Sir John Paulet of Basing, by his cousin Alice Paulet of the Hinton line (his wife in or before 1467), was father of Sir William Paulet, who, during a very long and supple career as a statesman in four reigns—" I am sprung," he said, " from the willow and not from the oak "—raised his house to a marquessate. Henry VIII. rewarded his diplomatic and judicial services and his campaign against the Pilgrims of Grace with the site and lands of Netley Abbey, the revival of the St John barony, a garter and many high offices. The king's death found him lord president of the council and one of the executors of the famous will of the sovereign. The fall of the protector Somerset gave him the lord treasurership and a patent of the earldom of Wiltshire. He shared the advancement of Northumberland and was created in 1551 marquess of Winchester, but, although he delivered the crown jewels to the Lady Jane in 1553, he was with the lords at Baynard Castle who proclaimed Queen Mary. In spite of his great age he was in the saddle at the proclamation of Mary's successor and was speaker in two Elizabethan parliaments. Only his death in 1572 drove from office this tenacious treasurer, whose age may have been nigh upon a hundred years.

His princely house at Basing was held for King Charles by John, the fifth marquess, whose diamond had scratched " Aimez Loyauté " upon every pane of its windows. Looking on a main road, Basing, with its little garrison of desperate cavaliers, held out for two years against siege and assault, and its shattered walls were in flames about its gallant master when Cromwell himself stormed an entry. The old cavalier marquess died in 1675, his great losses unrecompensed, and his son Charles, a morose extravagant, had the dukedom of Bolton in 1689 for his desertion of the Stuart cause. This new title was taken from the Bolton estates of the Scropes, Lord Winchester having married a natural daughter of Emmanuel, earl of Sunderland, the last Lord Scrope of Bolton. Charles, second duke of Bolton (1661-1722), was made lord-lieutenant of Ireland in 1717. A third Charles, the 3rd duke, is remembered as an opponent of Sir Robert Walpole and as the husband of Lavinia Fenton, the Polly Peachum of Gay's opera. The sixth and last duke of Bolton, an admiral of undistinguished services, died in 1794 without legitimate issue. His dukedom became extinct, and Bolton Castle again passed by bequest to an illegitimate daughter of the fifth duke, upon whom it had been entailed with the greater part of the ducal estates. (O. Ba.)

PAULI, REINHOLD (1823-1882), German historian, was born in Berlin on the 25th of May 1823. He was educated at the universities of Bonn and Berlin, went to England in 1847, and became private secretary to Baron von Bunsen, the Prussian ambassador in London. Returning to Germany in 1855 he was professor of history successively at the universities of Rostock, Tübingen (which he left in 1866 because of his political views), Marburg and Göttingen. He retained his chair at Göttingen until his death at Bremen on the 3rd of June 1882. He was a careful and industrious student of the English records, and his writings are almost wholly devoted to English history.

His first work, *König Aelfred und seine Stellung in der Geschichte Englands* (Berlin, 1851), was followed by monographs on *Bischof Grosseteste und Adam von Marsh* (Tübingen, 1864), and on *Simon von Montfort* (Tübingen, 1867). He continued J. M. Lappenberg's *Geschichte von England* from 1154 to 1509 (Gotha, 1853-1858), and himself wrote a *Geschichte Englands* (Leipzig, 1864-1875), dealing with the period between 1814 and 1852. Two volumes of historical essays, *Bilder aus Alt-England* (Gotha, 1860 and 1876), and *Aufsätze zur englischen Geschichte* (Leipzig, 1869 and 1883), and numerous historical articles in German periodicals came from his pen; and he edited several of the English chroniclers for the *Monumenta Germaniae historica.*

See R. Pauli, *Lebenserinnerungen,* edited by E. Pauli (Halle, 1895), and the sketch of his life prefixed to O. Hartwig's edition of his *Aufsätze* (Leipzig, 1883).

PAULICIANS, an evangelical Christian Church spread over Asia Minor and Armenia from the 5th century onwards. The first Armenian writer who notices them is the patriarch Nerses II. in an encyclical of 553,[1] where he condemns those " who share with Nestorians in belief and prayer, and take their bread-offerings to their shrines and receive communion from them, as if from the ministers of the oblations of the Paulicians." The patriarch John IV. (c. 728)[2] states that Nerses, his predecessor, had chastised the sect, but ineffectually; and that after his death (c. 554) they had continued to lurk in Armenia, where, reinforced by Iconoclasts driven out of Albania of the Caucasus, they had settled in the region of Djirka, probably near Lake Van. In his 31st canon John identifies them with the Messalians, as does the Armenian Gregory of Narek (c. 950). In Albania they were always numerous. We come now to Greek sources. An anonymous account was written perhaps as early as 840 and incorporated in the *Chronicon* of Georgius Monachus. This (known as Esc.) was edited by J. Friedrich in the Munich Academy *Sitzungsberichte* (1896), from a 10th-century Escorial codex (Plut. 1, No. 1). It was also used by Photius (c. 867), bk. I., chs. 1-10 of his *Historia Manicheorum,* who, having held an inquisition of Paulicians in Constantinople was able to supplement Esc. with a few additional details; and by Petrus Siculus (c. 868). The latter visited the Paulician fortress Tephrike to treat for the release of Byzantine prisoners. His *History of the Manicheans* is dedicated to the archbishop of Bulgaria, whither the Paulicians were sending missionaries. Zigabenus (c. 1100), in his *Panoplia,* uses beside Esc. an independent source.

The Paulicians were, according to Esc., Manicheans, so called after Paul of Samosata (q.v.), son of a Manichean woman Callinicé. She sent him and her other son John to Armenia as missionaries, and they settled at the village of Episparis, or " seedplot," in Phanarea. One Constantine, however, of Mananali, a canton on the western Euphrates 60-70 m. west of Erzerüm, was regarded by the Paulicians as their real founder. He based his teaching on the Gospels and the Epistles of Paul, repudiating other scriptures; and taking the Pauline name of Silvanus, organized churches in Castrum Colonias and Cibossa, which he called Macedonia, after Paul's congregation of that

[1] In the Armenian *Letterbook of the Patriarchs* (Tiflis, 1901), p. 73.
[2] *Opera* (Venetiae, 1834), p. 89.

name. His successors were Simeon, called Titus; Gegnesius, an Armenian, called Timotheus; Joseph, called Epaphroditus; Zachariah, rejected by some; Baanes, accused of immoral teaching; lastly Sergius, called Tychicus. As Cibossa, so their other congregations were renamed, Mananali as Achaea, Argaeum and Cynoschōra as Colossae, Mopsuestia as Ephesus, and so on.

Photius and Petrus Siculus supply a few dates and events. Constantine was martyred 684 by Simeon whom Constantine Pogonatus had sent to repress the movement. His victim's death so impressed him that he was converted, became head of the sect, and was martyred in 690 by Justinian II. About 702 Paul the Armenian, who had fled to Episparis, became head of the church. His son Gegnesius in 722 was taken to Constantinople, where he won over to his opinions the Iconoclast emperor, Leo the Isaurian. He died in 745, and was succeeded by Joseph, who evangelized Phrygia and died near Antioch of Pisidia in 775. In 752 Constantine V. transplanted many Paulicians from Germanicia, Doliché, Melitene, and Theodosiu-polis (Erzerûm), to Thrace, to defend the empire from Bulgarians and Sclavonians. Early in the 9th century Sergius, greatest of the leaders, profiting by the tolerance of the emperor Nice-phorus, began that ministry which, in one of the epistles canonized by the sect, but lost, he describes thus: "I have run from east to west, and from north to south, till my knees were weary, preaching the gospel of Christ." The iconoclast emperor Leo V., an Armenian, persecuted the sect afresh, and provoked a rising at Cynoschōra, whence many fled into Saracen territory to Argaeum near Melitene. For the next 50 years they continued to raid the Byzantine empire, although Sergius condemned retaliation. The empress Theodora (842-857) hung, crucified, beheaded or drowned some 100,000 of them, and drove yet more over the frontier, where from Argaeum, Amara, Tephriké and other strongholds their generals Karbeas and Chrysocheir harried the empire, until 873, when the emperor Basil slew Chrysocheir and took Tephriké.

Their sect however continued to spread in Bulgaria, where in 969 John Zimiskes settled a new colony of them at Philippo-polis. Here Frederick Barbarossa found them in strength in 1189. In Armenia they reformed their ranks about 821 at Thonrak (Tendarek) near Diadin, and were numerous all along the eastern Euphrates and in Albania. In this region Smbat, of the great Bagraduni clan, reorganized their Church, and was succeeded during a space of 170 or 200 years by seven leaders, enumerated by the Armenian Grigor Magistros, who as duke of Mesopotamia under Constantine Monomachos harried them about 1140. Fifty years later they were numerous in Syria and Cilicia, according to the Armenian bishops Nerses the Graceful and Nerses of Lambron. In the 10th century Gregory of Narek wrote against them in Armenian, and in the 11th Aristaces of Lastivert and Paul of Taron in the same tongue. During these later centuries their propaganda embraced all Armenia. The crusaders found them everywhere in Syria and Palestine, and corrupted their name to Publicani, under which name, often absurdly conjoined with Sadducaei, we find them during the ages following the crusades scattered all over Europe. After 1200 we can find no notice of them in Armenian writers until the 18th century, when they reappear in their old haunts. In 1828 a colony of them settled in Russian Armenia, bringing with them a book called the *Key of Truth*, which contains their rites of name-giving, baptism and election, compiled from old MSS.,[1] we know not when.

[1] That this is so, is proved by the presence of a doublet in the text of the rite of baptism, the words "But the penitent" on p. 96, as far as "over the person baptized" on p. 97, repeating in substance the words "Next the elect one" on p. 97 to "am well-pleased" on p. 98. This rite therefore was compiled from at least two earlier MSS. In the colophon also the compiler (as he calls himself) excuses the errors of orthography and grammar on the ground that they are not due to himself but to earlier and ig-norant copyists. The division (often inept) of the text into chapters, the references to chapter and verse of a printed N.T., and sundry pious stanzas which interrupt the context, are due to a later editor, perhaps to the copyist of the existing text of 1782. The controversial introduction is later than the Crusades; but the rituals, as far as

Regarding Paulician beliefs we have little except hostile evidence, which needs sifting. Esc. gives these particulars:—

1. They anathematized Mani, yet were dualists and affirmed two principles—one the heavenly Father, who rules not this world but the world to come; the other an evil demiurge, lord and god of this world, who made all flesh. The good god created angels only. The Romans (i.e. the Byzantines) erred in confusing these two first principles. Similarly the Armenian writer Gregory Magistros (c. 1040) accuses the Thonraki of teaching that "Moses saw not God, but the devil," and infers thence that they held Satan to be creator of heaven and earth, as well as of mankind. The *Key of Truth* teaches that after the fall Adam and Eve and their children were slaves of Satan until the advent of the newly created Adam, Jesus Christ. Except Gregory Magistros none of the Armenian sources lays stress on the dualism of the Paulicians. John IV. does not hint at it.

2. They blasphemed the Virgin, allegorizing her as the upper Jerusalem in which the Lord came in and went out, and denying that he was really made flesh of her. John IV. records that in the orthodox Armenian Church of the 7th century many held Christ to have been made flesh in, but not of, the Virgin; and Armenian hymns call the Virgin mother church at once Theotokos and heavenly Jerusalem. It is practically certain that Paulicians held this view.

3. They allegorized the Eucharist and explained away the bread and wine of which Jesus said to His apostles, "Take, eat and drink," as mere words of Christ, and denied that we ought to offer bread and wine as a sacrifice:

Such allegorization meets us already in Origen, Eusebius and other early fathers, and is quite compatible with that use of a material Eucharist which Nerses II. attests among the Paulicians of the early 6th century, and for which the *Key of Truth* provides a form. The Thonraki, according to Gregory Magistros, held that "Jesus in the evening meal, spoke not of an offering of the mass, but of every table." We infer that the Paulicians merely rejected the Eucharistic rites and doctrine of the Greeks. According to Gregory Magistros the Thonraki would say: "We are no worshippers of matter, but of God; we reckon the cross and the church and the priestly robes and the sacrifice of mass all for nothing, and only lay stress on the inner sense."

4. They assailed the cross, saying that Christ is cross, and that we ought not to worship the tree, because it is a cursed instrument. John IV. and other Armenian writers report the same of the Armenian Paulicians or Thonraki, and add that they smashed up crosses when they could.

5. They repudiated Peter, calling him a denier of Christ, and would not accept his repentance and tears.[2] So Gregory

[2] the language is concerned, may belong to the remote age which alone suits the adoptionist Christology of the prayers.

[2] In a fragmentary Syriac homily by Mar Jochanis, found in a Sinai MS. written not later than the 10th century and edited by J. F. Stenning and F. C. Burkitt, *Anecdota oxon*. (Clarendon Press, 1896), the same hostility to Peter is expressed. Compare the following passages: "O Petros, thou wast convicted of fault by Paulos thy colleague. How do men say that upon Petros I have built the church?

"The Lord said not to him, upon thee I build the church, but he said, upon this rock (the which is the body wherewith the Lord was clothed) I build my church. . . . Behold, I have made thee know from the N.T. that that rock was the Messiah.

"O Petros, after that thou didst receive the keys of heaven, and the Lord was seen by thee after he rose from the dead, thou didst let go of the keys, and thy wage is agreed with thy master when thou saidst to him, Behold we have let go of everything and have come after thee. What then shall be to us? And the Lord said to him, Ye shall be sitting on twelve thrones and judging the tribes of Israel. And after all these signs, O Petros, thou wentest away again to the former catching of fish. Wast thou ashamed of me, O Petros?"

Yet the same homilist "concerning the one who is made a priest," writes thus: "Lo, thou seest the priest of the people, with what care the Lord instructed Peter! He said not to him once and stopped, but three times, Feed my sheep." The Syriac text is rendered from a Greek original of unknown age, which from its complete correspondence with the *Key of Truth* may be judged to have been a Paulician writing.

Magistros reports the Thonraki as saying, "We love Paul and excrecrate Peter." But in the *Key of Truth* there is little trace of extreme hostility to Peter. It merely warns us that *all* the apostles constitute the Church universal and not Peter alone; and in the rite of election, *i.e.* of laying on of hands and reception of the Spirit, the reader who is being elected assumes the ritual name of Peter. An identical rite existed among the 12th century Cathars (*q.v.*), and in the Celtic church of Gildas every presbyter was a Peter.

6. The monkish garb was revealed by Satan to Peter at the baptism, when it was the devil, the ruler of this world, who, so costumed, leaned forward and said, This is my beloved son. The same hatred of monkery characterized the Thonraki and inspires the *Key of Truth*. The other statements are nowhere echoed.

7. They called their meetings the Catholic Church, and the places they met in places of prayer, προσευχαί. The Thonraki equally denied the name of church to buildings of wood or stone, and called themselves the Catholic Church.

8. They explained away baptism as "words of the Holy Gospel," citing the text "I am the living water." So the Thonraki taught that the baptismal water of the Church was "mere bath-water," *i.e.* they denied it the character of a reserved sacrament. But there is no evidence that they eschewed water-baptism. The modern Thonraki baptize in rivers, and in the 11th century when Gregory asked them why they did not allow themselves to be baptized, they answered: "Ye do not understand the mystery of baptism; we are in no hurry to be baptized, for baptism is death." They no doubt deferred the baptism which is death to sin, perhaps because, like the Cathars, they held post-baptismal sin to be unforgivable.

9. They permitted external conformity with the dominant Church, and held that Christ would forgive it. The same trait is reported of the Thonraki and of the real Manicheans.

10. They rejected the orders of the Church, and had only two grades of clergy, namely, associate itinerants (συνέκδημοι, Acts xix. 29) and copyists (νοτάριοι). A class of *Astati* (ἄστατοι) is also mentioned by Photius, i. 24, whom Neander regards as elect disciples of Sergius. They called their four original founders apostles and prophets—titles given also in the *Key of Truth* to the elect one. The *Synecdemi* and *Notarii* dressed like other people; the Thonraki also scorned priestly vestments.

11. Their canon included only the "Gospel and Apostle," of which they respected the text, but distorted the meaning. Gregory Magistros, as we have seen, attests their predilection for the apostle Paul, and speaks of their perpetually "quoting the Gospel and the Apostolon." These statements do not warrant us in supposing that they rejected 1 and 2 Peter, though other Greek sources allege it. The "Gospel and Apostle" was a comprehensive term for the whole of the New Testament (except perhaps Revelation), as read in church.

13. Their Christology was as follows: God out of love for mankind called up an angel and communicated to him his desire and counsel; then he bade him go down to earth and be born of woman.... And he bestowed on the angel so commissioned the title of Son, and foretold for him insults, blasphemies, sufferings and crucifixion. Then the angel undertook to do what was enjoined, but God added to the sufferings also death. However, the angel, on hearing of the resurrection, cast away fear and accepted death as well; and came down and was born of Mary, and named himself son of God according to the grace given him from God; and he fulfilled all the command, and was crucified and buried, rose again and was taken up into heaven. Christ was only a creature (κτίσμα), and obtained the title of Christ the Son of God in the reign of Octavius Caesar by way of grace and remuneration for fulfilment of the command.

The scheme of salvation here set forth recurs among the Latin Cathars. It resembles that of the *Key of Truth*, in so far as Jesus is Christ and Son of God by way of grace and reward for faithful fulfilment of God's command. But the *Key* lays more stress on the baptism. "Then, it says, he became Saviour of us sinners, then he was filled with the Godhead; then he was

sealed, then anointed; then was he called by the voice, then he became the loved one." In this scheme therefore the Baptism occupies the same place which the Birth does in the other, but both are adoptionist.

The main difference then between the Greek and Armenian accounts of the Paulicians is that the former make more of their dualism. Yet this did not probably go beyond the dualism of the New Testament itself. They made the most of Paul's antithesis between law and grace, bondage to Satan and freedom of the Spirit. Jesus was a new Adam and a fresh beginning, in so far as he was made flesh in and not of his mother, to whom, as both Esc. and the *Key* insist, Jesus particularly denied blessedness and honour (Mark iii. 31-35), limiting true kinship with himself to those who shall do the will of God. The account of Christ's flesh is torn out of the *Key*, but it is affirmed that it was at the baptism that "he put on that primal raiment of light which Adam lost in the garden." And this view we also meet with in Armenian fathers accounted orthodox.

The Armenian fathers held that Jesus, unlike other men, possessed incorruptible flesh, made of ethereal fire, and so far they shared the main heresy of the Paulicians. In many of their homilies Christ's baptism is also regarded as his regeneration by water and spirit, and this view almost transcends the modest adoptionism of the Thonraki as revealed in the *Key of Truth*.

What was the origin of the name Paulician? The word is of Armenian formation and signifies a son of Paulik or of little Paul; the termination -*ik* must here have originally expressed scorn and contempt. Who then was this Paul? "Paulicians from a certain Paul of Samosata," says Esc. "Here then you see the Paulicians, who got their poison from Paul of Samosata," says Gregory Magistros. They were thus identified with the old party of the *Pauliani*, condemned at the first council of Nice in 325, and diffused in Syria a century later. They called themselves the Apostolic Catholic Church, but hearing themselves nicknamed Paulicians by their enemies, probably interpreted the name in the sense of "followers of St Paul." Certain features of Paulicianism noted by Photius and Petrus Siculus are omitted in Esc. One of these is the Christhood of the fully initiated, who as such ceased to be mere "hearers" (*audientes*) and themselves became vehicles of the Holy Spirit. As Jesus anointed by the Spirit became the Christ, so they became christs. So Gregory of Narck upbraids the Thonraki for their "anthropolatrous apostasy, their self-conferred contemptible priesthood which is a likening of themselves to Satan" (=Christ in Thonraki parlance). And he repeats the taunt which the Arab Emir addressed to Smbat their leader, as he led him to execution: "If Christ rose on the third day, then since you call yourself Christ, I will slay you and bury you; and if you shall come to life again after thirty days, then I will know you are Christ, even though you take so many days over your resurrection." Similarly (in a 10th-century form of renunciation of Bogomil error preserved in a Vienna codex[1]) we hear of Peter "the founder of the heresy of the Messalians or Lycopetrians or Fundaitae and Bogomils who called himself Christ and promised to rise again after death." Of this Peter, Tychichus (? Sergius) is reported in the same document to have been fellow initiate and disciple.

Because they regarded their Perfect or Elect ones as Christs and anointed with the Spirit, the medieval Cathars regularly adored them. So it was with Celtic saints, and Adamnan, in his life of St Columba, i. 37, tells how the brethren after listening to St Baithene, "still kneeling, with joy unspeakable, and with hands spread out to heaven, venerated Christ in the holy and blessed man." So in ch. 44 of the same book we read how a humble stranger "worshipped Christ in the holy man" (*i.e.* St Columba); but such veneration was due to every presbyter. In 1837 we read of how an elect one of the Thonraki sect in Russian Armenia addressed his followers thus: "Lo, I am the cross: on my two hands light tapers, and give me adoration. For I am able to give you salvation, as much as the

---

[1] Cod. theol. gr. 306, fol. 32, edited by Thallóczy, in *Wissensch. Mittheil. aus Bosnien* (Vienna, 1895).

cross and the saints"; and by the light of this we ought perhaps to interpret section ix. of Esc. "They blaspheme the precious cross, saying that the Christ is a cross." The Christ is an elect one, who, as the Cathars (q.v.) put it, having been consoled or become a Paraclete in the flesh, stands in prayer with his hands outspread in the form of a cross, while the congregation of hearers or *audientes* adore the Christ in him. The same idea that the perfect ones are christs as having received the Paraclete is met with in early Christian documents, and still survives among the Syriac-speaking shepherds on the hills north of Mardin. These have their christs, and Dr E. A. Wallis Budge, to whom the present writer owes his information, was shown the stream in which their last christ had been baptized. In modern Russia also survives a sect of Bogomils called *Christowschischina*,[1] because one member of it is adored by the rest as Christ. It was because they believed themselves to have living christs among them that the Paulicians rejected the fetish worship of a material cross, in which orthodox Armenian priests imagined they had by prayers and anointings confined the Spirit of Christ. It is also likely enough that they did not consider sensible matter to be a vehicle worthy to contain divine effluence and holy virtues, and knew that such rites were alien to early Christianity. The former scruple, however, was not confined to Paulicians, for it inspires the answer made by Eusebius, bishop of Thessalonica, to the emperor Maurice, when the latter asked to have relics sent to him of Demetrius the patron saint of that city. It runs thus: " While informing your Reverence of the faith of the Thessalonicans and of the miracles wrought among them, I must yet, in respect of this request of yours, remark that the faith of the city is not of such a kind as that the people desire to worship God and to honour his saints by means of anything sensible. For they have received the faith from the Lord's holy testimonies, to the effect that God is a spirit, and that those who worship him must worship him in spirit and in truth."[2] Manicheans, Bogomils, Cathars and Paulicians for like reasons denied the name of church to material constructions of wood and stone. Among the later Cathars of Europe we find the repudiation of marriage defended on the ground that the only true marriage is of Christ with his bride the Virgin church, and perhaps this is why Paulicians and Thonraki would not make of marriage a religious rite or sacrament.

Did the Paulicians, like the later Cathars (who in so much resembled them), reject water baptism? And must we so interpret clause ix. of Esc? Perhaps they merely rejected the idea that the *numen* or divine grace can be confined by priestly consecration in water and by mere washing be imparted to persons baptized. The *Key of Truth* regards the water as a washing of the body, and sees in the rite no *opus operatum*, but an essentially spiritual rite in which " the king releases certain rulers[3] from the prison of sin, the Son calls them to himself and comforts them with great words, and the Holy Spirit of the king forthwith comes and crowns them, and dwells in them for ever." For this reason the Thonraki adhere to adult baptism, which in ancient wise they confer at thirty years of age or later, and have retained in its primitive significance the rite of giving a Christian name to a child on the eighth day from birth. It is hardly likely that the Thonraki of the 10th century would have rejected water-baptism and yet have retained unction with holy oil; this Gregory Magistros attests they did, but he is an unreliable witness.

[1] "dass einer der Sektierer von den andern als Christus verehrt wer e." K. K. Grass, *Die russischen Sekten* (Leipzig, 1906), Bd. 1, Lief. 3.
[2] From *Monuments of Early Christianity*, by F. C. Conybeare (London, 1894), p. 349.
[3] The term "rulers" appears to be derived from Manichean speculation, or from the same cycle of myth which is reflected in 1 Cor. ii. 6, 8. The title "elect one," used by the Armenia Paulicians also has a Manichean ring. It may be that under stress of common persecution there was a certain fusion in Armenia of Pauliani and Manicheans. The writings and tenets of Mani were widely diffused there. Such a fusion is probably reflected in the *Key of Truth*.

It is then on the whole probable that the Paulicians who appear in Armenian records as early as 550, and were afterwards called Thonraki, by the Greeks by the Armenian name *Pauli-kiani*, were the remains of a primitive adoptionist Christianity, widely dispersed in the east and already condemned under the name of *Pauliani* by the council of Nice in 325. A renegade Armenian Catholicos of the 7th century named Isaac has preserved to us a document which sums up their tenets.[4] He adduces it as a sort of *reductio ad absurdum* of Christians who would model life and cult on Christ and his apostles, unencumbered by later church traditions. It runs thus: (1) Christ was thirty years old when he was baptized. Therefore they baptize no one until he is thirty years of age. (2) Christ, after baptism, was not anointed with myrrh nor with holy oil, therefore let them not be anointed with myrrh or holy oil. (3) Christ was not baptized in a font, but in a river. Therefore, let them not be baptized in a font. (4) Christ, when he was about to be baptized, did not recite the creed of the 318 fathers of Nice, therefore shall they not make profession of it. (5) Christ when about to be baptized, was not first made to turn to the west and renounce the devil and blow upon him, nor again to turn to the east and make a compact with God. For he was himself true God. So let them not impose these things on those to be baptized. (6) Christ, after he had been baptized, did not partake of his own body. Nor let them so partake of it. (7) Christ, after he was baptized, fasted 40 days and only that; and for 120 years such was the tradition which prevailed in the Church. We, however, fast 50 days before Pascha. (8) Christ did not hand down to us the teaching to celebrate the mystery of the offering of bread in church, but in an ordinary house and sitting at a common table. So then let them not offer the sacrifice of bread in churches. (9) It was after supper, when his disciples were sated, that Christ gave them to eat of his own body. Therefore let them first eat meats and be sated, and then let them partake of the mysteries. (10) Christ, although he was crucified for us, yet did not command us to adore the cross, as the Gospel testifies. Let them therefore not adore the cross. (11) The cross was of wood. Let them therefore not adore a cross of gold or silver or bronze or stone. (12) Christ wore neither humeral nor amice nor maniple nor stole nor chasuble. Therefore let them not wear these garments. (13) Christ did not institute the prayers of the liturgy or the Holy Epiphanies, and all the other prayers for every action and every hour. Let them therefore not repeat them, nor be hallowed by such prayers. (14) Christ did not lay hands on patriarchs and metropolitans and bishops and presbyters and deacons and monks, nor ordain their several prayers. Let them therefore not be ordained nor blessed with these prayers. (15) Christ did not enjoin the building of churches and the furnishing of holy tables, and their anointing with myrrh and hallowing with a myriad of prayers. Let them not do it either. (16) Christ did not fast on the fourth day of the week and on the *Paraskevē*. Let them not fast either. (17) Christ did not bid us pray towards the east. Neither shall they pray towards the east.

LITERATURE.—Beside the works mentioned in the text see J. C. L. Gieseler, *Ecclesiastical History*, ii. 208 (Edinburgh, 1848) and " Untersuchungen über die Geschichte der Pauliciner " in *Theol. Studien u. Kritiken*, Heft I. a. 79 (Jahrg., 1829); Neander, *Ecclesiastical History*, vols. v. and vi.; Mosheim's apostles, *Ecclesiastical History*, Century IX. ii. 5; G. Finlay, *History of Greece*, vols. ii. and iii.; Gibbon, *History of the Decline and Fall of the Roman Empire*, ch. liv.; Ign. von Döllinger, *Sektengeschichte des Mittelalters*, chs. I.-iii.; Karapet Ter-Mkhrttschian, *Die Paulikianer* (Leipzig, 1893); Aršak Ter Mikelian, *Die armenische Kirche* (Leipzig, 1892); Basil Sarkisean, *A Study of the Manicheo-Paulician Heresy of the Thomraki* (Venice, San Lazaro, 1893, in Armenian); F. C. Conybeare, *The Key of Truth* (Oxford, 1898). (F. C. C.)

PAULINUS, SAINT, OF NOLA (353–431). Pontius Meropius Anicius Paulinus, who was successively a consul, a monk and a

[4] See Fr. Combefis, *Historia haeretiae monotheliarum* col. 317 (Paris, 1648), col. 317. In the printed text this document, entitled *An Invective Against the Armenians*, is dated 800 years after Constantine, but the author Isaac Catholicos almost certainly belonged to the earlier time.

bishop, was born at Bordeaux in A.D. 353. His father, *praefectus praetorio* in Gaul, was a man of great wealth, who entrusted his son's education, with the best of results, to Ausonius. In 378 Paulinus was raised to the rank of *consul suffectus*, and in the following year he appears to have been sent as *consularis* into Campania. It was at this period, while present at a festival of St Felix of Nola, that he entered upon his lifelong devotion to the cult of that saint. He had married a wealthy Spanish lady named Therasia; this happy union was clouded by the death in infancy of their only child—a bereavement which, combined with the many disasters by which the empire was being visited, did much to foster in them that world-weariness to which they afterwards gave such emphatic expression. From Campania Paulinus returned to his native place and came into correspondence or personal intimacy with men like Martin of Tours and Ambrose of Milan, and ultimately (about 389) he was formally received into the church by bishop Delphinus of Bordeaux, whence shortly afterwards he withdrew with his wife beyond the Pyrenees. The asceticism of Paulinus and his liberality towards the poor soon brought him into great repute; and while he was spending Christmas at Barcelona the people insisted on his being forthwith ordained to the priesthood. The irregularity of this step, however, was resented by many of the clergy, and the occurrence is still passed lightly over by his Roman Catholic panegyrists. In the following year he went into Italy, and after visiting Ambrose at Milan and Siricius at Rome—the latter of whom received him somewhat coldly—he proceeded into Campania, where, in the neighbourhood of Nola, he settled among the rude structures which he had caused to be built around the tomb and relics of his patron saint. With Therasia (now a sister, not a wife), while leading a life of rigid asceticism, he devoted the whole of his vast wealth to the entertainment of needy pilgrims, to payment of the debts of the insolvent, and to public works of utility or ornament; besides building basilicas at Fondi and Nola, he provided the latter place with a much-needed aqueduct. At the next vacancy, not later than 409, he succeeded to the bishopric of Nola, and this office he held with ever-increasing honour until his death, which occurred shortly after that of Augustine, whose friend he was, in 431. He is commemorated by the Church of Rome on the 22nd of June.

The extant writings of Paulinus consist of some fifty *Epistolae*, addressed to Sulpicius Severus, Delphinus, Augustine, Jerome and others; thirty-two *Carmina* in a great variety of metre, including a series of hexameter " natales," begun about 393 and continued annually in honour of the festival of St Felix, metrical epistles to Ausonius and Gestidius, and paraphrases of three psalms; and a *Passio S. Grnesii.* They reveal to us a kindly and cheerful soul, well versed in the literary accomplishments of the period, but without any strength of intellectual grasp and peculiarly prone to superstition.

His works were edited by Rosweyde and Fronton le Duc in 1622 (Antwerp, 8vo), and their text was reprinted in the *Bibl. max. patr.* (1677). The next editor was Le Brun des Marettes (2 vols. 4to, Paris, 1685), whose text was reproduced in substance by Muratori (Verona, 1736), and reprinted by Migne. The poems and letters are edited in the Vienna *Corpus script. eccl. lat.* vol. xxviii. See also P. Reinelt, *Studien über die Briefe d. h. Paulin von Nola* Breslau, 1904) and other literature cited in Herzog-Hauck, *Realencyk. für prot. Theol.* vol. xv.

PAULINUS (d. 644), first bishop of the Northumbrians and archbishop of York, was sent to England by Pope Gregory I. in 601 to assist Augustine in his mission. He was consecrated by Justus of Canterbury in 625 and escorted Æthelberht, daughter of Æthelberht, to the Northumbrian king Edwin (q.v.). In 627 Edwin was baptized and assigned York to Paulinus as his see. It was at Lincoln that he consecrated Honorius as archbishop of Canterbury. In 633 Edwin was slain at Hatfield Chase and Paulinus retired to Kent, where he became bishop of Rochester. The pallium was not sent him until 634, when he had withdrawn from his province. He died in 644.

See Bede, *Historia ecclesiastica* (ed. C. Plummer, Oxford, 1896).

PAULINUS, GAIUS SUETONIUS (1st century A.D.), Roman general. In 42, during the reign of Claudius, he put down a revolt in Mauretania, and was the first of the Romans to cross the Atlas range. He subsequently wrote an account of his experiences. From 59-61 he commanded in Britain, and, after a severe defeat, finally crushed the Iceni under Boadicea (Boudicca). A complaint having been made to the emperor that he was needlessly protracting hostilities, he was recalled, but he was consul (for the second time) in 66. During the civil war he fought on the side of Otho against Vitellius, and obtained a considerable success against Aulus Caecina Alienus (one of the Vitellian generals) near Cremona, but did not follow it up. When Caecina had been joined by Fabius Valens, Paulinus advised his colleagues not to risk a decisive battle, but his advice was disregarded, and Otho (q.v.) was utterly defeated at Bedriacum. After Vitellius had been proclaimed emperor, Paulinus asserted that it was in consequence of his own treachery that Otho's army had been defeated. Vitellius pretended to believe this, and eventually pardoned Paulinus, after which nothing further is heard of him.

See Dio Cassius lxi. 7-12; Tacitus, *Annals,* xiv. 30-39, *Histories,* i. 87, 90, ii. 23-41, 44, 60; Pliny, *Nat. Hist.* v. 1; Plutarch, *Otho.* 7, 8.

PAULSEN, FRIEDRICH (1846-1908), German philosopher and educationalist, was born at Langenhorn (Schleswig) and educated at Erlangen, Bonn and Berlin, where he became extraordinary professor of philosophy and pedagogy in 1878. In 1896 he succeeded Eduard Zeller as professor of moral philosophy at Berlin. He died on the 14th of August 1908. He was the greatest of the pupils of G. T. Fechner, to whose doctrine of panpsychism he gave great prominence by his *Einleitung in die Philosophie* (1892; 7th ed., 1900; Eng. trans., 1895). He went, however, considerably beyond Fechner in attempting to give an epistemological account of our knowledge of the psychophysical. Admitting Kant's hypothesis that by inner sense we are conscious of mental states only, he holds that this consciousness constitutes a knowledge of the " thing-in-itself " —which Kant denies. Soul is, therefore, a practical reality which Paulsen, with Schopenhauer, regards as known by the act of " will." But this " will " is neither rational desire, unconscious irrational will, nor conscious intelligent will, but an instinct, a " will to live " (*Zielstrebigkeit*), often subconscious, pursuing ends, indeed, but without reasoning as to means. This conception of will, though consistent and convenient to the main thesis, must be rigidly distinguished from the ordinary significance of will, *i.e.* rational desire. Paulsen is almost better known for his educational writings than as a pure philosopher. His *German Education, Past and Present* (Eng. trans., by I. Lorenz, 1907) is a work of great value.

Among his other works are: *Versuch einer Entwickelungsgeschichte d. Kantischen Erkenntnistheorie* (Leipzig, 1875); *Im. Kant* (1898, 1899); " Gründung Organization und Lebensordnungen der deutschen Universitäten im Mittelalter " (in Sybel's *Histor. Zeitschr.* vol. xlv. 1881); *Gesch. d. gelehrten Unterrichts auf d. deutschen Schulen und Universitäten* (1885, 1896); *System der Ethik* (1889, 1899; Eng. trans. (partial) 1899); *Das Realgymnasium u. d. humanist. Bildung* (1889); *Kant d. Philos. d. Protestantismus* (1899); *Schopenhauer, Hamlet u. Mephistopheles* (1900); *Philosophia militans* (1900, 1901); *Parteipolitik u. Moral* (1900).

PAULUS, HEINRICH EBERHARD GOTTLOB (1761-1851), German rationalistic theologian, was born at Leonberg, near Stuttgart, on the 1st of September 1761. His father, a Lutheran clergyman at Leonberg, dabbled in spiritualism, and was deprived of his living in 1771. Paulus was educated in the seminary at Tübingen, was three years master in a German school, and then spent two years in travelling through England, Germany, Holland and France. In 1789 he was chosen professor ordinarius of Oriental languages at Jena. Here he lived in close intercourse with Schiller, Goethe, Herder and the most distinguished literary men of the time. In 1793 he succeeded Johann Christoph Döderlein (1745-1792) as professor of exegetical theology. His special work was the exposition of the Old and New Testaments in the light of his great Oriental learning and according to his characteristic principle of "natural explanation." In his explanation of the Gospel narratives Paulus sought to remove what other interpreters regarded as miracles from the Bible by distinguishing between the *fact* related and the author's *opinion* of it, by seeking a naturalistic exegesis of a narrative, *e.g.* that ἐπὶ τῆς θαλάσσῃ (Matt. xiv. 25) means *by the shore* and not *on the sea*, by supplying circumstances omitted by the author, by remembering that the author produces as miracles occurrences which can now be explained otherwise, *e.g.* exorcisms. His *Life of Jesus* (1828) is a synoptical translation of the Gospels, prefaced by an account of the preparation for the Christ and a brief summary of His history, and accompanied by very short explanations interwoven in the translation. The form of the work was fatal to its success, and the subsequent *Exegetisches Handbuch* rendered it quite superfluous. In this *Handbuch* Paulus really contributed much to a true interpretation of the Gospel narratives. In 1803 he became professor of theology and *Consistorialrat* at Würzburg. After this he filled various posts in south Germany—school director at Bamberg (1807), Nuremberg (1808), Ansbach (1810)—until he became professor of exegesis and church history at Heidelberg (1811-1844). He died on the 10th of August 1851.

His chief exegetical works are his *Philologisch-kritischer und historischer Kommentar über das Neue Testament* (4 vols., 1800-1804); *Philologischer Clavis über die Psalmen* (1791); and *Philologischer Clavis über Jesaias* (1793); and particularly his *Exegetisches Handbuch über die drei ersten Evangelien* (3 vols., 1830-1833; 2nd ed., 1841-1842). He also edited a collected small edition of Baruch Spinoza's works (1802-1803), a collection of the most noted Eastern travels (1792-1803), F. W. J. Schelling's *Vorlesungen über die Offenbarung* (1843), and published *Skizzen aus meiner Bildungs- und Lebensgeschichte* (1839). See Karl Reichlin-Meldegg, *H. E. G. Paulus und seine Zeit* (1853), and article in Herzog-Hauck, *Realencyklopädie*; cf. F. Lichtenberger, *History of German Theology in the Nineteenth Century*, pp. 21-24.

PAULUS (older form **PAULLUS**), **LUCIUS AEMILIUS**, surnamed MACEDONICUS (c. 229-160 B.C.), Roman general, a member of a patrician family of the Aemilian gens, son of the consul of the same name who fell at Cannae. As consul for the second time (168) he was entrusted with the command in the Macedonian War, which the incapacity of previous generals had allowed to drag on for three years. He brought the war to a speedy termination by the battle of Pydna, fought on the 22nd of June (Julian calendar) 168. Macedonia was henceforward a Roman province, and Paulus, being on a tour through Greece, with the assistance of ten Roman commissioners arranged the affairs of the country. He enjoyed a magnificent triumph, which lasted three days and was graced by the presence of the captive king Perseus and his three children. He lost his two sons by his second wife, and was thus left without a son to bear his name, his two sons by his first wife having been adopted into the Fabian and Cornelian gentes. Paulus was censor in 164, and died in 160 after a long illness. At the funeral games exhibited in his honour the *Hecyra* of Terence was acted for the second and the *Adelphi* for the first time. An aristocrat to the backbone, he was yet beloved by the people. Of the vast sums brought by him into the Roman treasury from Spain and Macedonia he kept nothing to himself, and at his death his property scarcely sufficed to pay his wife's dowry. As a general he was a strict disciplinarian; as an augur he discharged his duties with care and exactness. He was greatly in sympathy with Greek learning and art, and was a friend of the historian Polybius.

See Plutarch, *Aemilius Paulus*; Livy xliv. 17-xlvi. 41; Polybius xxix.-xxxii.

PAULUS, surnamed SILENTIARIUS (" the silentiary," one of the ushers appointed to maintain silence within the imperial palace), Greek poet, contemporary and friend of Agathias, during the reign of Justinian. In addition to some 80 epigrams, chiefly erotic and panegyric in character, preserved in the Greek Anthology, there is a description by him a description (ἐκφρασις) of the church of St Sophia, and of its pulpit (ἄμβων), in all some 1300 hexameters after the style of Nonnus, with short iambic dedications to Justinian. The poem was recited at the second dedication of the church (A.D. 562), in the episcopal hall of the patriarchate. The poems are of importance for the history of Byzantine art in the 6th century. Another poem (also preserved in the Anthology) on the warm baths of Pythia in Bithynia, written in the Anacreontic rhythm, has sometimes been attributed to him.

BIBLIOGRAPHY.—Ed. of the poems on St Sophia, by I. Bekker in the Bonn *Corpus scriptorum hist. byz.* (1837), including the descriptions of the church by Du Cange and Banduri, and in J. P. Migne, *Patrologia graeca*, lxxxvi.; metrical translations, with commentary, by C. W. Kortüm (1854), and J. J. Kreutzer (1875); poem on the Baths in G. E. Lessing, *Zur Geschichte und Literatur*, i. 5 (1773); see also Merian-Genast, *De Paulo Silentiario* (Leipzig, 1889).

PAULUS DIACONUS, or **WARNEFRIDI**, or **CASINENSIS** (c. 720-c. 800), the historian of the Lombards, belonged to a noble Lombard family and flourished in the 8th century. An ancestor named Leupichis entered Italy in the train of Alboin and received lands at or near Forum Julii (Friuli). During an invasion the Avars swept off the five sons of this warrior into Illyria, but one, his namesake, returned to Italy and restored the ruined fortunes of his house. The grandson of the younger Leupichis was Warnefrid, who by his wife Theodelinda became the father of Paulus. Born between 720 and 725 Paulus received an exceptionally good education, probably at the court of the Lombard king Ratchis in Pavia, learning from a teacher named Flavian the rudiments of Greek. It is probable that he was secretary to the Lombard king Desiderius, the successor of Ratchis; it is certain that this king's daughter Adelperga was his pupil. After Adelperga had married Arichis, duke of Benevento, Paulus at her request wrote his continuation of Eutropius. It is possible that he took refuge at Benevento when Pavia was taken by Charlemagne in 774, but it is much more likely that his residence there was anterior to this event by several years. Soon he entered a monastery on the lake of Como, and before 782 he had become an inmate of the great Benedictine house of Monte Cassino, where he made the acquaintance of Charlemagne. About 776 his brother Arichis had been carried as a prisoner to France, and when five years later the Frankish king visited Rome, Paulus successfully wrote to him on behalf of the captive. His literary attainments attracted the notice of Charlemagne, and Paulus became a potent factor in the Carolingian renaissance. In 787 he returned to Italy and to Monte Cassino, where he died on the 13th of April in one of the years between 794 and 800. His surname Diaconus, or Levita, shows that he took orders as a deacon; and some think he was a monk before the fall of the Lombard kingdom.

The chief work of Paulus is his *Historia gentis Langobardorum*. This incomplete history in six books was written after 787 and deals with the story of the Lombards from 568 to the death of King Liutprand in 747. The story is told from the point of view of a Lombard patriot and is especially valuable for the relations between the Franks and the Lombards. Paulus used the document called the *Origo gentis Langobardorum*, the *Liber pontificalis*, the lost history of Secundus of Trent, and the lost annals of Benevento; he made a free use of Bede, Gregory of Tours and Isidore of Seville. In some respects he suggests a comparison with Jordanes, but in learning and literary honesty is greatly the superior of the Goth. Of the *Historia* there are known a hundred manuscripts extant. It was largely used by subsequent writers, was often continued, and was first printed in Paris in 1514. It has been translated into English, German, French and Italian, the English translation being by W. D. Foulke (Philadelphia, 1807), and the German by O. Abel and R. Jacobi (Leipzig, 1878). Among the editions of the Latin the best is that edited by L. Bethmann and G. Waitz, in the *Monumenta Germaniae historica. Scriptores rerum langobardicarum* (Hanover, 1878).

Cognate with this work is Paulus's *Historia romana*, a continuation of the *Breviarium* of Eutropius. This was compiled between 766 and 771, at Benevento. The story runs that Paulus advised Adelperga to read Eutropius. She did so, but complained that this heathen writer said nothing about ecclesiastical affairs and stopped with the accession of the emperor Valens in 364; consequently Paulus interwove extracts from the Scriptures, from the ecclesiastical historians and from other sources with Eutropius, and added six books, thus bringing the history down to 553. This work has little value, although it was very popular during the middle ages. It has been edited by H Droysen and published in the *Monumenta Germaniae historica. Auctores antiquissimi*, Bd. ii. (1879).

Paulus wrote at the request of Angilram, bishop of Metz (d. 791), a history of the bishops of Metz to 766, the first work of its kind north of the Alps. This *Gesta episcoporum mettensium* is published in Bd. ii. of the *Monumenta Germaniae historica Scriptores*, and has been translated into German (Leipzig, 1880). He also wrote many letters, verses and epitaphs, including those of Duke Arichis and many members of the Carolingian family. Some of the letters are published with the *Historia Langobardorum* in the *Monumenta*; the poems and epitaphs edited by E. Dümmler will be found in the *Poetae latini aevi carolini*, Bd. i. (Berlin, 1881). Fresh material having come to light, a new edition of the poems (*Die Gedichte des Paulus Diaconus*) has been edited by Karl Neff (Munich, 1908). While in France Paulus was requested by Charlemagne to compile a collection of homilies. He executed this after his return to Monte Cassino, and it was largely used in the Frankish churches. A life of Pope Gregory the Great has also been attributed to him.

See C. Cipolla, *Note bibliografiche circa l'odierna condizione degli studi critici sul testo delle opere di Paolo Diacono* (Venice, 1901); the *Atti e memorie del congresso storico tenuto in Cividale* (Udine, 1900); F. Dahn, *Langobardische Studien*, Bd. i. (Leipzig, 1876); W. Wattenbach, *Deutschlands Geschichtsquellen*, Bd. i. (Berlin, 1904); A. Hauck, *Kirchengeschichte Deutschlands*, Bd. ii. (Leipzig, 1898); P. del Giudice, *Studi di storia e diritto* (Milan, 1889); and U. Balzani, *Le Cronache italiane nel medio evo* (Milan, 1884).

PAUL VERONESE (1528–1588), the name ordinarily given to Paolo Caliari, or Cagliari, the latest of the great cycle of painters of the Venetian school, who was born in Verona in 1528 according to Zanetti and others, or in 1532 according to Ridolfi. His father, Gabriele Caliari, a sculptor, began to train Paolo to his own profession. The boy, however, showed more propensity to painting, and was therefore transferred to his uncle, the painter Antonio Badile, whose daughter he eventually married. According to Vasari, he was the pupil of Giovanni Carotto, a painter proficient in architecture and perspective; this statement remains unconfirmed. Paolo, in his early years, applied himself to copying from the engravings of Albert Dürer and the drawings of Parmigiano. He did some work in Verona, but found there little outlet for his abilities, the field being pretty well occupied by Ligozzi, Battista dal Moro, Paolo Farinato, Domenico Riccio, Brussasorci and other artists. Cardinal Ercole Gonzaga took him, when barely twenty years of age, to Mantua, along with the three last-named painters, to execute in the cathedral a picture of the "Temptation of St Anthony "; here Caliari was considered to excel his competitors. Returning to Verona, he found himself exposed to some envy and ill-will. Hence he formed an artistic partnership with Battista Zelotti, and they painted together in the territories of Vicenza and Treviso. Finally Paolo went on to Venice. In this city his first pictures were executed, in 1555, in the sacristy and church of S. Sebastiano, an uncle of his being prior of the monastery. The subjects on the vaulting are taken from the history of Esther; and these excited so much admiration that henceforward Caliari, aged about twenty-eight, ranked almost on a par with Tintoretto, aged about forty-five, or with Titian, who was in his eightieth year. Besides the Esther subjects, these buildings contain his pictures of the "Baptism of Christ," the "Martyrdom of St Marcus and St Marcellinus," the "Martyrdom of St Sebastian," &c. As regards this last-named work, dating towards 1565, there is a vague tradition that Caliari painted it when he had taken refuge in the monastery. He entered into a competition for painting the ceiling of the library of St Mark, and not only obtained the commission but executed it with so much power that his very rivals voted him the golden chain which had been tendered as an honorary distinction. At one time he returned to Verona, and painted the "Banquet in the House of Simon the Pharisee, with Jesus and Mary Magdalene "—a picture now in Turin. In 1560, however, he was in Venice again, working partly in the S. Sebastiano buildings and partly in the ducal palace. He visited Rome in 1563, in the suite of Girolamo Grimani, the Venetian ambassador, and studied the works of Raphael and Michelangelo, and especially the antique. Returning to Venice, he was overwhelmed with commissions. He was compelled to decline an invitation from Philip II. to go to Spain and assist in decorating the Escorial. One of his pictures of this period is the famous "Venice, Queen of the Sea," in the ducal palace. He died in Venice on the 20th (or perhaps 19th) of April 1588, and was buried in the church of S. Sebastiano, a monument being set up to him there by his two sons, Gabriele and Carlo, and his brother, Benedetto, all of them painters.

Beyond his magnificent performances as a painter, the known incidents in the life of Paul Veronese are very few. He was honoured and loved, being kind, amiable, generous and an excellent father. His person is well known from the portraits left by himself and others: he was a dark man, rather good-looking than otherwise, somewhat bald in early middle age, and with nothing to mark an exceptional energy or turn of character In his works the first quality which strikes one is their palatial splendour. The pictorial inspiration is entirely that of the piercing and comprehensive eye and the magical hand—not of the mind. The human form and face are given with decorous comeliness, often with beauty; but of individual apposite expression there is next to none. In fact, Paolo Veronese is pre-eminently a painter working pictorially, and in no wise amenable to a literary or rationalizing standard. He enjoys a sight much as Ariosto enjoys a story, and displays it in form and colour with a zest like that of Ariosto for language and verse. He was supreme in representing, without huddling or confusion, numerous figures in a luminous and diffused atmosphere, while in richness of draperies and transparency of shadows he surpassed all the other Venetians or Italians. In gifts of this kind Rubens alone could be pitted against him. In the moderation of art combined with its profusion he far excelled Rubens; for, dazzling as is the first impression of a great work by Veronese, there is in it, in reality, as much of soberness and serenity as of exuberance. By variety and apposition he produces a most brilliant effect of colour; and yet his hues are seldom bright. He hoards his primary tints and his high lights. He very rarely produced small pictures: the spacious was his element.

Of all Veronese's paintings the one which has obtained the greatest world-wide celebrity is the vast "Marriage-at Cana," now in the Louvre. It contains about a hundred and twenty figures or heads—those in the foreground being larger than life. Several of them are portraits. Among the personages specified (some of them probably without sufficient reason) are the Marquis del Vasto, Queen Eleanor of France, Francis I., Queen Mary, of England, Sultan Soleyman I., Vittoria Colonna, Charles V., Tintoretto, Titian, the elder Bassano, Benedetto Caliari and Paolo Veronese himself (the figure playing the viol). It is impossible to look at this picture without astonishment. The only point of view from which it falls is that of the New Testament narrative; for there is no relation between the Galilean wedding and Veronese's court-banquet. This stupendous performance was executed for the refectory of the monastery of S. Giorgio Maggiore in Venice, the contract for it being signed in June 1562 and the picture completed in September 1563. Its price was 324 silver ducats (= £160), along with the artist's living expenses and a tun of wine. There are five other great banquet-pictures by Caliari, only inferior in scale and excellence to this of Cana. One of them is also in the L·uvre, a "Feast in the House of Simon the Pharisee," painted towards 1570-1575 for the refectory of the Servites in Venice. A different version of the same theme is in the Brera Gallery of Milan. "The Feast of Simon the Leper" (1570) was done for the refectory of the monks of St Sebastian, and the "Feast of Levi" (St Matthew) (1573), now in the Venetian academy, for the refectory of the monks of St John and St Paul. In each instance the price barely exceeded the cost of the materials. The Louvre contains ten other specimens of Veronese, notably the "Susanna and the Elders" and the "Supper at Emmaus." In the National Gallery, London, are ten examples. The most beautiful is "St Helena's Vision of the Cross," founded upon an engraving by Marcantonio after a drawing supposed to be the work of Raphael. Far more famous than this is the "Family of Darius at the Feet of Alexander the Great after the Battle of Issus"—the captives having mistaken Hephaestion for Alexander. It was bought for £13,560, and has even been termed (very unreasonably) the most celebrated of all Veronese's works. The principal figures are portraits of the Pisani family. It is said that Caliari was accidentally detained at the Pisani villa at Este, and there painted this work, and, on quitting, told the family that he had left behind him an equivalent for his courteous entertainment. Another picture in the National Gallery, "Europa and the Bull," is a study for the large painting in the imperial gallery of Vienna, and resembles one in the ducal palace of Venice. The Venetian academy contains fourteen works by Veronese. One of the finest is a comparatively small picture of the Battle of Lepanto, with Christ in heaven pouring light upon the Christian fleet and darkness on the Turkish. In the Uffizi Gallery of Florence are two specimens of exceptional beauty—the "Annunciation" and "Esther Presenting herself to Ahasuerus"; for delicacy and charm this latter work yields to nothing that the master produced. In Verona "St George and St Julian," in Brescia the "Martyrdom of St Afra," and in Padua the "Martyrdom of St Justina" are works of leading renown. Celebrated frescoes by Caliari are in four villas near Venice, more especially the Villa Masiera. His drawings are very fine, and he took pleasure at times in engraving on copper.

The brother and sons of Paolo already mentioned, and Battista Zelotti, were his principal assistants and followers. Benedetto Caliari, the brother, who was about ten years younger than Paolo, is reputed to have had a very large share in the architectural backgrounds which form so conspicuous a feature in Paolo's compositions. If this is not overstated, it must be allowed that a substantial share in Paolo's fame accrues to Benedetto; for not only are the backgrounds admirably schemed and limned, but they govern to a large extent the invention and distribution of the groups. Of the two sons Carlo (or Carletto), the younger, is the better known. He was born in 1570, and was sent to study under Bassano. He produced various noticeable works, and died young in 1596. Gabriele, born in 1568, attended, after Carlo's death, almost entirely to commercial affairs; his works in painting are rare. All three were occupied after the death of Paolo in finishing his pictures left uncompleted.

. See Ridolfi, *Le Meraviglie dell' arte*, &c.; Dal Pozzo, *Vite de' pittori veronesi*, &c.; Zanetti, *Della Pittura veneziana*, &c.; and Lanzi; also, among recent works, the biographies by C. Yriarte (1888); F. H. Meisner (1897); and Mrs Arthur Bell (1904).

(W. M. R.)

PAUMOTU, TUAMOTU, or LOW ARCHIPELAGO, a broad belt of 78 atolls in the Pacific Ocean, belonging to France, between 14° and 24° S., and 131° and 149° W. They trend in irregular lines in a north-west and south-west direction, the major axis of the group extending over 1300 m. The largest atoll, Rangiroa, with a lagoon 45 m. long by 15 wide, is made up of twenty islets. Fakarava, the next in size, consists of fifteen islets, and its oblong lagoon affords the best anchorage in the group. Hau has fifty islets, and its lagoon is dangerously studded with coral. The symmetrically placed eleven islets of Anaa suggested to Captain Cook the name of Chain Island. Heavy storms sometimes greatly alter the form of the atolls. The first discovery of part of the archipelago was made by the Spaniard Pedro Fernandez Quiros in 1606. Many navigators subsequently discovered or rediscovered various parts of the group—among them may be mentioned Jacob Lemaire and Willem Schouten (1616), John Byron (1765), Philip Carteret (1767), Louis Antoine de Bougainville (1768), Captain James Cook (1769), Lieutenant Bligh (1792), Captain Wilson of the "Duff" (1797), Otto von Kotzebue (1815 and 1824), Fabian Gottlieb von Bellingshausen (1819–1820) and Charles Wilkes (1839) who made a detailed survey of the islands. As a result almost all the islands bear alternative names. The dates given are those of first discovery. In the north-west part of the chain are Rangiroa (Vliegen, Deans or Nairsa, this part of the group bearing the name of the Palliser Islands); Fakarava (Witgenstein, 1819), the seat of the French resident; Anaa (Chain, 1769), Makemo (Makima, Phillips, Kutusov, 1803), Hau (Hao, Harp, Bow, 1768). North and east of these are Manihi (Oahe, Waterlandt, 1616), Tikei (Romanzov, 1815), the Disappointment group (1765) of which Napuka is the chief island, Pukapuka (Henuake, Honden, Dog, 1616), Raroia

(Barclay de Tolly, 1820), Angatau (Ahangatu, Arakchev, 1820), Akahaina (Fakaina, Predpriatie, 1824), Tatakoto (Narcissus, Egmont, Clerke, 1774), Pukaruha (Serle, 1797). In the southern part of the archipelago are Hereheretui (Bligh, Santablo, 1606), the Duke of Gloucester group (1767), Tematangi (Bligh Lagoon 1792), Maruroa (Braburgh, Matilda, 1767), the Actaeon or Amphitrite group (discovered by the Tahitian trading vessel "Amphitrite" in 1833), Marutea (Lord Hood, 1791), and the Gambier or Mangareva group (1797), of which Mangareva (Gambier, Peard) is the chief member. To the south again are: Pitcairn (q.v.), Ducie, and a few other islets, which are British and do not properly belong to the Paumotu Archipelago. The Gambier Islands are a cluster of four larger and many smaller volcanic islets, enclosed in one wide reef. The wooded crags of Mangareva, the largest islet, 5 m. in length, rise to a height of 1315 ft. and are covered with a rich vegetation, quite Tahitian in character; but, as in the other Paumotus, there is a dearth of animal life.

The climate of the islands is healthy, and they have a lower mean temperature than Tahiti. The easterly trade winds prevail. Rain and fogs occur even during the dry season. The stormy season lasts from November to March, when devastating hurricanes are not uncommon and a south-westerly swell renders the western shores dangerous. Plants and animals are scantily represented. Coco-nut palms and the pandanus thrive on many of the islets, and the bread-fruit, banana, pine-apple, water-melon and yam have been introduced from Tahiti into the western islands. Mammals are represented by a few rats; among land-birds parakeets, thrushes and doves are noticeable; and of reptiles there are only lizards. Insects are scarce. But the sea and lagoons teem with turtle, fish, molluscs, crustaceans and zoophytes. Coral is luxuriant everywhere. From the abundance of pearl oysters the archipelago gets its traders' name of Pearl Islands.

The Paumotus are sparsely inhabited by a fine strong race of Polynesians, more muscular and mostly darker-skinned than that inhabiting Tahiti. In the west considerable intermixture with other races has taken place. In physique, language, religion and customs the Gambier Islanders closely resemble the Rarotongans. The pearl fisheries in the rocky and surf waters are a source of revenue, the pearls being sold in Tahiti. The best harbour of the group is that of Fakarava, which, together with Mangareva, is open to trade.

The land area of the entire group is about 330 sq. m., and the population is about 6000. The group passed under the protection of France in 1844, and was annexed in 1881, forming part of the dependency of Tahiti.

PAUNCEFOTE, JULIAN PAUNCEFOTE, 1ST BARON (1828–1902), English diplomatist, third son of Robert Pauncefote of Preston Court, Gloucestershire, was born on the 13th of September 1828. He was educated at Marlborough, Paris and Geneva, and called to the bar at the Inner Temple in 1852. He was for a short time secretary to Sir William Molesworth, secretary for the colonies, and in 1862 went out to Hong-Kong, where he was made attorney-general (1865) and then chief justice of the supreme court. He was appointed chief justice of the Leeward Islands in 1873, and, returning to England in the next year; became one of the legal advisers to the colonial office. Two years later he received a similar appointment in the foreign office, and in 1882 was made permanent under-secretary of state for foreign affairs. In 1885 he was one of the delegates to the Suez Canal international commission, and received the G.C.M.G. and the K.C.B. Lord Salisbury departed from precedent in choosing him to succeed Sir Lionel Sackville-West as British minister at Washington in 1889, but the event showed that his knowledge of international law made up for any lack of the ordinary diplomatic training. He did much during his term of office to maintain friendly relations between the two countries, especially during the Venezuelan crisis. The Bering Sea fishery dispute (1890–1892) was successfully negotiated by him; he arranged a draft treaty for Anglo-American arbitration, which was, however, quashed by the Senate; and carried through the revision of the Clayton-Bulwer Treaty on the subject of the Panama Canal. In 1893 the British minister at Washington was raised to the rank of ambassador, and Sir Julian Pauncefote became the doyen of the diplomatic corps. He died on the 26th of May 1902 at Washington. He had been made Baron Pauncefote of Preston in 1899 in recognition of his services at the Peace Conference at the Hague, and he was a member of the Court of Arbitration which resulted from the conference.

PAUPERISM (Lat. *pauper*, poor), a term meaning generally the state of being poor, poverty; but in English usage particularly the condition of being a " pauper," *i.e.* in receipt of relief administered under the poor law. In this sense the word is to be distinguished from "poverty." A person to be relieved under the poor law must be a destitute person, and the moment he has been relieved he becomes a pauper, and as such incurs certain civil disabilities. Statistics dealing with the state of pauperism in this sense convey not the amount of destitution actually prevalent, but the particulars of people in receipt of poor law relief.

PAUSANIAS (5th century B.C.), Spartan regent and commander, of the Agiad family, son of Cleombrotus and nephew of Leonidas, the hero of Thermopylae. Upon the death of the latter in 480 B.C. his son Pleistarchus became king, but as he was still a minor the regency devolved first on Leonidas's brother Cleombrotus, and after his death in 479 on Pausanias. He first distinguished himself as commander of the combined Greek forces in the victory of Plataea. In 478 he was appointed admiral of the Greek fleet, and succeeded in reducing the greater part of Cyprus, the strategic key of the Levant, and in capturing Byzantium from the Persians, thus securing the command of the Bosporus, and of the route by which Darius had invaded Europe. But he entered into treacherous negotiations with the Persian king, and his adoption of Oriental dress and customs, and his haughty behaviour to the Greeks under his command, roused their resentment and suspicion (see DELIAN LEAGUE). Pausanias was recalled by the ephors and, though acquitted on the main charge of Medism, was not again sent out in any official position. He returned to Byzantium, nevertheless, in a ship of Hermione and seized that town and, apparently, Sestos also. He was dislodged from both by the Athenians, to whom the allies had transferred from Sparta the naval hegemony. For some time he lived at Cleonae in the Troad, carrying on negotiations with Xerxes, but was again recalled to Sparta, where he incited the helots to revolt. When his schemes were almost matured, the evidence of a confidential slave led to the discovery of his plot by the ephors. He fled to the sanctuary of Athena Chalcioecus on the Spartan Acropolis: there he was immured, and when starvation and exposure had all but done their work he was dragged out to die. This crime against religion the state subsequently expiated by the burial of his body at the spot where he died and the dedication of two bronze statues. To commemorate Leonidas and Pausanias, a yearly festival was held, at which speeches were made extolling their victories; this was still celebrated when the geographer Pausanias visited Sparta more than six centuries later (Paus. iii. 14). The date of the regent's death probably falls in 471 or 470, though some assign it to a later date on a very doubtful statement of Justin (ix. 1) that Pausanias held Byzantium for seven years.

See Herodotus v. 32, ix. 10–88; Thucydides i. 94–96, 128–134, ii. 71, 72, iii. 58; Diodorus Siculus xi. 30–47, 54; Cornelius Nepos, *Pausanias*; Justin ii. 15, ix. 1, 3; Pausanias iii. 4. 14, 17; Polyaenus viii. 51; Aristodemus ii., iv., vi.–viii.; Athenaeus xii. 535E, 536A; Plutarch, *Cimon* 6, *Themistocles* 23, *Aristides* 11–20, 23; N. Hanske, *Ueber den Königsregenten Pausanias* (Leipzig, 1873). (M. N. T.)

PAUSANIAS, Greek traveller and geographer of the 2nd century A.D., lived in the times of Hadrian, Antoninus Pius and Marcus Aurelius. He was probably a native of Lydia, and was possibly born at Magnesia ad Sipylum; he was certainly interested in Pergamum and familiar with the western coast of Asia Minor; but his travels extended far beyond the limits of Ionia. Before visiting Greece he had been to Antioch, Joppa and

Jerusalem,[1] and to the banks of the river Jordan. In Egypt he had seen the pyramids and had heard the music of the vocal Memnon, while at the temple of Ammon he had been shown the hymn once sent to that shrine by Pindar. He had taken note of the fortifications of Rhodes and Byzantium, had visited Thessaly, and had gazed on the rivulet of " blue water " beside the pass of Thermopylae. In Macedonia he had almost certainly viewed the traditional tomb of Orpheus, while in Epirus he was familiar with the oracular oak of Dodona, and with the streams of Acheron and Cocytus. Crossing over to Italy, he had seen something of the cities of Campania, and of the wonders of Rome.

His *Description of Greece* (περιήγησις τῆς Ἑλλάδος) takes the form of a tour in the Peloponnesus and in part of northern Greece. It is divided into ten books: (i.) Attica and Megara; (ii.) Argolis, including Mycenae, Tiryns and Epidaurus; (iii.) Laconia; (iv.) Messenia; (v.) and (vi.) Elis, including Olympia; (vii.) Achaea; (viii.) Arcadia; (ix.) Boeotia, and (x.) Phocis, including Delphi.

Book i. was written after Herodes Atticus had built the Athenian Stadium (A.D. *c.* 143); but before he had built the Odeum (*c.* 160–161). There is reason to believe that this book was published some years before the rest. The statement in book v. (1, 2), that 217 years had elapsed since the restoration of Corinth (44 B.C.), shows that Pausanias was engaged on his account of Elis in the year A.D. 174, during the reign of Marcus Aurelius. He repeatedly refers to buildings erected by Hadrian, who died in A.D. 138. He had lived in that emperor's time, but had not actually seen that emperor's favourite, Antinoüs, who died about 130. He mentions the wars of Antoninus Pius against the Moors, and of Marcus Aurelius (in and after A.D. 166) against the Germans (viii. 43). The latest event which he records is the incursion of the robber-horde of the Costobocs (A.D. *c.* 176; x. 34, 5). Book i. having been published before 160, and books vi.–x. after 174, the composition of the whole must have extended over more than fourteen years.

The work has no formal preface or conclusion. It suddenly begins with the promontory of Sunium, the first point in Attica that would be seen by the voyager from the shores of Asia Minor, and it ends abruptly with an anecdote of a blind man of Naupactus. The author's general aim may be inferred from his saying at the close of his account of Athens and Attica: " Such (in my opinion) are the *most famous* of the Athenian traditions and *sights*; from the mass of materials I have aimed from the outset at selecting the really *notable* " (i. 39, 3). It is possibly in the hope of giving variety and interest to the topographical details of Athens that the author intersperses them with lengthy historical disquisitions; but the result is that the modern reader is tempted to omit the " history " and to hasten on to the " topography," on which the author is now a primary authority. In the subsequent books he introduces two improvements. His account of each important city begins with a sketch of its history; and, in his subsequent descriptions, he adopts a strictly topographical order. He takes the nearest road from the frontier to the capital; he there makes for the central point, *e.g.* the market-place, and describes in succession the several streets radiating from that centre. Similarly, in the surrounding district, he follows the principal roads in succession, returning to the capital in each case, until, at the end of the last road, he crosses the frontier for the next district. In the later books he supplies us with a few glimpses into the daily life of the inhabitants. He is constantly describing ceremonial rites or superstitious customs. He frequently introduces narratives from the domain of history and of legend and folk-lore; and it is only

[1] The tomb of Helena at Jerusalem; which Pausanias viii. 16, 4–5, compares with the Mausoleum, is mentioned by Josephus, *Ant.* xx. 4, 3; *Bell. Jud.* v. 2, 2; 3, 3; 4, 2; (and Eusebius, *H.E.* ii. 12, 3. Helen, the daughter of Izates, king of Adiabene, sent large supplies of provisions to Rome during the great famine in the time of Claudius (A.D. 44–48). Her tomb is identified by universal consent with the so-called " Tombs of the Kings," half a mile north of the Damascus gate. Cf. Schürer, *Geschichte des jüdischen Volkes*, 3rd ed., iii. 120–122; view of tomb in *Picturesque Palestine*, i. 103.

rarely that he allows us to see something of the scenery. But, happily, he notices the pine-trees on the sandy coast of Elis, the deer and the wild boars in the oak-woods of Phelloë, and the crows amid the giant oak-trees of Alalcomenae. He tells us that " there is no fairer river than the Ladon," " no reeds grow so tall as those in the Boeotian Asopus," and the fact that deluges the fallow plain of Mantinea vanishes into a chasm to rise again elsewhere. It is mainly in the last three books that he touches on the products of nature, the wild strawberries of Helicon, the date-palms of Aulis, and the olive-oil of Tithorea, as well as the bustards of Phocis, the tortoises of Arcadia and the " white blackbirds " of Cyllene. He is rather reticent as to the character of the roads, but he records, with the gratitude of a traveller, the fact that the narrow and perilous cornice of the Scironian way along the coast of Megara had been made w·der and safer by Hadrian. He is inspired by a patriotic interest in the ancient glories of Greece, recognizing in Athens all that was best in the old Greek life, and lamenting the ruin that had befallen the land on the fatal field of Chaeronea. He is most at home in describing the religious art and architecture of Olympia and of Delphi; but, even in the most secluded regions of Greece, he is fascinated by all kinds of quaint and primitive images of the gods, by holy relics and many other sacred and mysterious things. He is interested in visiting the battlefields of Marathon and Plataea, and in viewing the Athenian trophy on the island of Salamis, the grave of Demosthenes at Calauria, of Leonidas at Sparta, of Epaminondas at Mantinea, and the colossal lion guarding the tomb of the Thebans on the Boeotian plain. At Thebes itself he views the shields of those who died at Leuctra, and the ruins of the house of Pindar; the statues of Hesiod and Arion, of Thamyris and Orpheus, in the grove of the Muses on Helicon; the portrait of Corinna at Tanagra, and of Polybius in the cities of Arcadia. At Olympia he takes note of the ancient quoit of Iphitus inscribed with the terms of the Olympic truce, the tablets recording treaties between Athens and other Grecian states, the memorials of the victories of the Greeks at Plataea, of the Spartans at Tanagra, of the Messenians at Naupactus, and even those of Philip at Chaeronea and of Mummius at Corinth. At Delphi, as he climbs the sacred way to the shrine of Apollo, he marks the trophies of the victories of the Athenians at Marathon and on the Eurymedon, of the united Greeks at Artemisium, Salamis and Plataea, of the Spartans at Aegospotami, of the Thebans at Leuctra, and the shields dedicated in memory of the repulse and defeat of the Gauls at Delphi itself. At Athens, he sees pictures of historic battles, portraits of famous poets, orators, statesmen and philosophers, and inscriptions recording the laws of Solon; on the Acropolis, the trophy of the Persian wars, the great bronze statue of Athena; at the entrance to the harbour of the Peiraeus, the grave of Themistocles; and, outside the city, the monuments of Harmodius and Aristogeiton, of Cleisthenes and Pericles, of Conon and Timotheus, and of all the Athenians who fell in battle, except the heroes of Marathon,.." for these, as a meed of valour, were buried on the field."

In the topographical part of his work, he is fond of digressions on the wonders of nature, the signs that herald the approach of an earthquake, the phenomena of the tides, the ice-bound seas of the north, and the noonday sun which at the summer solstice casts no shadow at Syene. While he never doubts the existence of the gods and heroes, he sometimes criticizes the myths and legends relating to them. His main interest is in the *monuments of ancient art*, and he prefers the works of the 5th and 4th centuries B.C. to those of later times. At Delphi he admires the pictures of Polygnotus, closing the seven chapters of his minute description with the appreciative phrase: " so varied and beautiful is the painting of the Thasian artist " (x. 31, 2). In sculpture his taste is no less severe. Even in the " uncouth " work of Daedalus, he recognizes " a touch of the divine " (ii. 4, 5). In architecture, he admires the prehistoric walls of Tiryns, and the " Treasury of Minyas," the Athenian Propylaea, the theatre of Epidaurus, the temples of Bassae and Tegea, the walls of Messene, the Odeum at Patrae, as well as the building

of the same name lately built at Athens by Herodes Atticus (vii. 20, 6), and finally the Stadium which that munificent Athenian had faced with white marble from the quarries of Pentelicus. His descriptions of the monuments of art are plain and unadorned; they bear the impress of reality, and their accuracy is confirmed by the extant remains. He is perfectly frank in his confessions of ignorance. When he quotes a book at second hand he takes pains to say so.

He has been well described by J. G. Frazer as " a man made of common stuff and cast in a common mould; his intelligence and abilities seem to have been little above the average, his opinions not very different from those of his contemporaries." His literary style is " plain and unadorned yet heavy and laboured "; it is not careless or slovenly; the author tried to write well, but his " sentences are devoid of rhythm and harmony " (*Introduction*, pp. xlix., lxix.).

In considering his use of previous writers, we must draw a distinction between the *historical* and the *descriptive* parts of his work. In the former it was necessary for him to depend on written or oral testimony; in the latter it was not. In the historical passages, his principal poetic authority is Homer; he frequently quotes the *Theogony* of Hesiod, and he often refers to Pindar and Aeschylus. His writings are full of echoes of Herodotus, and his debt to Thucydides and Xenophon extends beyond the isolated mention of their names (i. 3, 4; vi. 19, 5). He has carefully studied the Elean register of the Olympic victors; he makes large use of inscriptions, and has generally examined them with care and copied them with accuracy. In the descriptive portion the question arises whether he derived his knowledge from personal observation, or from books, or from both. He does not profess to have seen everything, but he does not acknowledge that he has borrowed any of his descriptions from previous writers. He " cannot commend the men who took the measurements " of the Zeus at Olympia (v. 11, 9). " A certain writer," who states that a particular spring is the source of an Arcadian river, " cannot have seen the spring himself, or spoken with any one who had; I have done both " (viii. 41, 10). There are fifty passages in which he either directly states or implies that he had seen the things that he describes. All of these have been carefully collected and examined by R. Heberdey (1894), who, by using a distinctive type in marking on a map the places " seen " by Pausanias, and by joining those places by lines representing the routes described by him, has shown the large extent of the author's travels in Greece. The complicated coast of Hermionis has, however, been incorrectly described (ii. 34, 8 seq.), and there is some confusion in the account of the three roads leading to the north from Lepreüs, in the extreme south of Elis (v. 5, 3).

A greater difficulty has long been felt in connexion with the " Enneacrunus episode " in the description of Athens (i. 8, 6, and 14, 1-6). In the midst of the account of the market-place, northwest of the Acropolis, the reader is transported to the fountain of Enneacrunus and to some buildings in its neighbourhood, and is suddenly brought back to the market-place. It has been naturally assumed that the Enneacrunus can only be the fountain of that name in the bed of the Ilissus. If so, the description of the fountain is out of place, and its insertion at this point has been ascribed either to some confusion in the author's notes or to a dislocation in the text. On the other hand, it has been suggested that the description may really refer to some other fountain near the market-place, which was shown to Pausanias as the Enneacrunus. Thus it has been held by Dr Dörpfeld that the name Enneacrunus was originally applied to a spring west of the Acropolis, that the old name of this spring, Callirrhoë, had been abandoned from the time when Peisistratus converted it into a " fountain with nine jets," and that the names Callirrhoë and Enneacrunus were afterwards transferred to another fountain in the bed of the Ilissus. The evidence of his own excavations has led him to place the original Enneacrunus near the eastern foot of the hill of the Pnyx, and to identify certain adjacent remains with the buildings mentioned by Pausanias. If this opinion is correct, the account of the Enneacrunus, and the neighbouring buildings, in Pausanias, ceases to be an " episode," and falls into the natural sequence of the narrative. (The " episode " has been fully discussed by the expounders and translators of Pausanias, and by the writers on the topography of Athens. Dr Dörpfeld's views are clearly set forth in Miss J. E. Harrison's *Primitive Athens* (1906). A. Malinin's paper (Vienna,

1906), which assumes a dislocation of the text, has been answered by Dörpfeld (*Wochenschrift für kl Philologie* (1907), p. 940 seq.).

The account of the law courts of Athens and of the altars at Olympia may have been derived from monographs on those subjects. In both cases the author departs from his usual method of following the order of place, and deals with a group of monuments belonging to the same class. But in the extant literature of antiquity (as J. G. Frazer has shown) no passage has been found agreeing in form or substance so closely with the description in Pausanias as to make it probable that he copied it. The theory that Pausanias borrowed largely from Polemon of Ilium, who flourished about 200–177 B.C., and wrote on the Acropolis and the eponymous heroes of Athens, on the treasuries of Delphi, and on other antiquarian topics, was incidentally suggested by Preller in his edition of the fragments (1838), and was revived by Professor von Wilamowitz-Moellendorff in 1877 (*Hermes*, xii. 346). It was subsequently maintained by A. Kalkmann (1886) that Pausanias slavishly copied from Polemon the best part of his descriptions of Athens, Delphi and Olympia, and described those places, not as they were in his own age, but as they had been in that of Polemon, some 300 years before. It is alleged that, in the notices of the monuments on the Acropolis of Athens, and of the sculptors and the athlete-statues of Olympia, the lower limit of Pausanias is practically 150 B.C.; it is inferred that the authority followed by him ended with this date, and it is more than suggested that his sole authority was Polemon. But the comparative neglect of works later than 150 B.C. might also be explained by the fact that the independence of Greece came to an end in 146. And, further, it so happens that Pausanias refers to very few sculptors for the 140 years (296–156 B.C.) *before* the age of his supposed authority, while some of the sculptors represented at Olympia have since been placed *after* that date, and not a few of the Athenian monuments described by Pausanias belong to the period between that date and the accession of Hadrian, or, approximately, the period between about 166 B.C. and A.D. 117 (Gurlitt, *Über Pausanias*, pp. 117 seq., 194 seq., 257–267). More than one hundred extracts from, or reference to, the works of Polemon have come down to us, and it has been shown by Mr Frazer that "the existing fragments hardly justify us in supposing that Pausanias was acquainted with the writings of his learned predecessor; certainly they lend no countenance to the view that he borrowed descriptions of places and monuments from them." Again, it has been urged that his brief description of the Peiraeus is not true of his own time, as it had been burnt by Sulla (86 B.C.), and was still lying desolate in the age of Augustus, but his account of the buildings and monuments has been confirmed by an inscription conjecturally ascribed to the time of Pausanias (Frazer ii. 14 seq.). It has also been stated that the description of Arcadia has been borrowed from far earlier writers, because Strabo (p. 388) says that most of the famous cities of that land had either ceased to exist or had left hardly a trace behind them; but the evidence of coins has proved that at least seven of the eleven cities described by Pausanias were still in existence long after the death of Strabo. It has further been assumed that his account of the temple of Apollo at Delphi is "irreconcilable with the remains of the building" and with the inscriptions recently discovered by the French archaeologists. We are told that Pausanias describes the temple of the 6th century B.C. as if it still existed in his own time. On the contrary, he states that the first sculptures for the gables were executed by a pupil of Calamis, the pupil of a sculptor still at work in 477 B.C., and the shields that he saw suspended on the architrave were captured from the Gauls in 279. Again, his description of New Corinth, built in 44 B.C., more than a century after the time of Polemon, is most minute and systematic, and it is confirmed by coins of the imperial age. In at least one important point Pausanias compares favourably with Strabo. While Strabo erroneously declares that not a vestige of Mycenae remains, Pausanias gives a brief but accurate description of the Lion-gate and the existing circuit-wall of the Acropolis, with a notice of the tombs "within the wall" (ii. 16,

5–7), a notice which led to their discovery by Schliemann. In all parts of Greece the accuracy of his descriptions has been proved by the remains of the buildings which he describes; and a few unimportant mistakes (in v. 10, 6 and 9; viii. 37, 3, and 45, 5), and some slight carelessness in copying inscriptions, do not lend any colour to an imputation of bad faith. It has been stated with perfect justice by Frazer (p. xcv. seq.) that "without him the ruins of Greece would for the most part be a labyrinth without a clue, a riddle without an answer." "His book furnishes the clue to the labyrinth, the answer to many riddles. It will be studied so long as ancient Greece shall continue to engage the attention and awaken the interest of mankind."

EDITIONS.—Siebelis (Leipzig, 1822); Schubart and Walz (1838); Teubner texts, Schubart (1862), and Spiro (1903). Text, Latin translation and index, L. Dindorf (Didot, Paris, 1845); text and German commentary, Hitzig and Blümner, books I.–ix., already published in five parts (Leipzig, 1896–1907). Special edition of *Descriptio arcis Athenarum*, Otto Jahn (Bonn, 1860), 3rd ed., with maps and plans, &c., A. Michaelis (1901). F. Imhoof-Blumer and Percy Gardner, "Numismatic Commentary on Pausanias," first published in *Journal of Hellenic Studies*, vi.–viii. (1885–1887); J. G. Frazer, *Pausanias's Description of Greece*, in six vols., introduction and translation (vol. I.), commentary (vols. ii.–v.), maps and index (vol. vi.) (Macmillan, London, 1898); introduction reprinted in Frazer's *Pausanias and other Greek Sketches* (1900).

SPECIAL LITERATURE.—Wernicke, *De Pausaniae studiis herodoteis* (Berlin, 1884); Wilamowitz, "Thukydideslegende," in *Hermes* (1877), xii. 346; P. Hirt, *De fontibus Pausaniae in Eliacis* (Greifswald, 1878); A. Flasch, in Baumeister's *Denkmäler*, s.v. "Olympia," 90 pp. (1887); A. Kalkmann, *Pausanias der Perieget* (Berlin, 1886), and in *Archäologischer Anzeiger* (1895), p. 12; opposed by W. Gurlitt, *Über Pausanias* (Graz, 1890), 494 pp.; Bencker, *Anteil der Periegese an der Kunstschriftstellerei* (1890), and R. Heberdey, *Die Reisen des Pausanias in Griechenland*, with two maps (Vienna, 1894).

The present writer is much indebted to Gurlitt's comprehensive monograph, and to the admirable Introduction prefixed to J. G. Frazer's excellent Translation and Commentary. See also C. Robert, *Pausanias als Schriftsteller* (Berlin, 1909).   (J. E. S.*)

PAUSIAS, a Greek painter of the 4th century, of the school of Sicyon. He introduced the custom of painting ceilings of houses. His great merit appears to have lain in the better rendering of foreshortening. The words in which Pliny (xxxv. 127) describes a bull painted by him should be quoted: "Wishing to display the length of the bull's body, he painted it from the front, not in profile, and yet fully indicated its measure. Again, while others fill in with white the high lights, and paint in black what is less salient, he painted the whole boll of dark colour, and gave substance to the shadow out of the shadow itself, with great skill making his figures stand out from a flat background, and indicating their shape when foreshortened." This passage well marks the state of painting at the time.

PAVANE, PAVAN or PAVIN, the name of a slow stately dance of the 16th and 17th centuries. The word has been variously derived: (1) from Lat. *pavo*, peacock; the dancers, as they wheel and turn, spread out their long cloaks, which they retained in this dance, like the tail of the bird; (2) from Padovana, *i.e.* of Padua, in Italy; the dance, however, is usually taken to have come from Spain. As an instrumental composition, common in the 16th and 17th centuries, the "pavane" was usually followed by the quick and lively "galliard," as the "gigue" followed the "saraband" in the later suite (see DANCE).

PAVEMENT (Lat. *pavimentum*, a floor beaten or rammed hard, from *pavire*, to beat), a term originally applied to the covering of a road or pathway with some durable material, and so used of the paved footway at the side of a street—the "sidewalk" as opposed to the roadway proper. The term is also extended to the interior floor of churches and public buildings. It is probable that the earliest pavements consisted only of rammed clay, as in the "beehive" tombs of Mycenae, or of cement or stucco decorated with lines in coloured marbles, such as those mentioned in the Book of Esther (vi. 1) in the palace at Susa. W. M. Flinders Petrie discovered at Tell el' Amarna in the palace of Akhenaton the remains of a stucco pavement, decorated with foliage, flowers, birds, &c., and a complete naturalistic treatment. The threshold of the doors of the Assyrian palaces were of stone carved with patterns in imitation of those in a carpet. The pavements of Greek temples were either in stone or marble, and at Olympia the *pronaos* of the temple of Zeus was laid in mosaic representing tritons, and the floor of the *naos* was in coloured marbles. The Roman pavements were invariably in mosaic, sometimes of a very elaborate nature, as in the House of the Faun at Pompeii, where the mosaic represented the battle of Issus between Alexander the Great and Darius III., a reproduction probably of some Greek painting of the period. In Rome the palaces on the Palatine Hill and the thermae were all paved with mosaic, and numerous pavements have been found in Carthage, many of which are in the British Museum, as are also examples from the Roman villas in England. Perhaps the richest Roman pavements outside Italy are those at Trèves in Germany. The Roman tradition was continued by the Byzantine architects, who, throughout the East, paved their churches with mosaics, frequently of the same design and execution as those of the Romans, but with Christian symbols. The churches of the Romanesque, Gothic and Renaissance periods were all paved in marble, but of a different character from those of the earlier period (see Mosaic).

PAVIA (anc. *Ticinum*, q.v.), a town of Lombardy, Italy, capital of the province of Pavia, situated on the Ticino about 2 m. above its junction with the Po, 22½ m. S. of Milan by rail, 253 ft. above sea-level. Pop. (1906), 28,796 (town), 36,424 (commune). On the right bank of the river lies the small suburb of Borgo Ticino, connected with the town by a remarkable covered bridge dating from 1351-1354. In 1872 the city ceased to be a fortress, and the bastions have been transformed into boulevards and public gardens. The church of San Michele Maggiore is one of the finest specimens of the Lombard style in existence, and as it was within its walls that the crown was placed on the head of those "kings of Italy" from whom the house of Savoy claims descent it was by royal decree of 1863 given the title of Basilica Reale. S. Michele (for plan see ARCHITECTURE: § *Romanesque and Gothic in Italy*) was originally constructed under the Lombard kings, but was burnt in 1004, and the present building dates from the latter part of the 11th (crypt, choir and transepts) and the first half of the 12th centuries (façade and nave with two aisles), and was completed in 1155. The lower part of the façade is adorned with three fine portals and with reliefs of a fantastic kind in sandstone, arranged in horizontal bands, and has arcading under the gable. The dome is octagonal. The interior is vaulted and has eight pillars, supporting double round arches. The interior has a mosaic pavement of the 12th-13th centuries. The cathedral church of San Martino is a Renaissance building begun in 1488 by Cristoforo Rocchi; it is a vast "central" structure, finely designed, with four arms, which remained for centuries unfinished until the dome (only surpassed by those of St Peter at Rome and the cathedral at Florence) and façade were completed in 1898 according to Rocchi's still extant model; adjoining the church is the massive Torre Maggiore, 258 ft. high, which is mentioned as early as 1330. The upper part is due to Pellegrino Tibaldi (1583). The cathedral contains the tomb of S. Syrus, first bishop of Pavia (2nd century); an altar-piece (1521), the best work of Giampietino (Rizzi), a pupil of Leonardo da Vinci; and another, the masterpiece of Bernardino Gatti of Parma (1531). The church of S. Pietro in Ciel d'Oro, the origin of which dates from the beginning of the 6th (?) century, but which as it stands was consecrated in 1132, is very similar to S. Michele in respect of its façade (though it has not the elaborate sculptures), dome and mosaic pavements. The use of disks of majolica may be noted in the decoration of the exterior. It has been carefully restored. It served as the burial place of the Lombard king Liutprand (711-744), whose bones were found there in 1896 (R. Majocchi in *Nuovo bullettino d'archeologia cristiana*, 1896, p. 139). The Arca di S. Agostino (after 1362) is a sumptuous tomb containing the relics of S. Augustine of Hippo brought hither by Liutprand from Sardinia. It was only restored to this, its original position, from the cathedral when the church itself was restored.

The church of S. Maria del Carmine is externally one of the

most beautiful of the brick Gothic churches in northern Italy and dates from 1373 (or 1373?). S. Francesco has also a good façade after that of Chiaravalle near Milan. The church of S. Maria di Canepanova with its small dome was designed by Bramante. Near it are three tall, slender brick towers of the Gothic period. S. Teodoro with a 12th-century exterior has frescoes by Bartolommeo Suardi (Bramantino) after 1507. Outside the town on the west lie the churches of S. Salvatore (founded in the 7th century but rebuilt in the 15th and 16th), and of S. Lanfranc (or the Holy Sepulchre, 12th century) with the fine tomb of Bishop Lanfranco Beccari (d. 1189) by Giovanni Antonio Amedeo (1498), one of the best Lombard sculptors and architects of this period (1447-1522) and a native of Pavia, which has a few other works by him. He was for eighteen years in charge of the work at the Certosa. Interesting medieval views of Pavia exist in the churches of S. Teodoro and S. Salvatore; the former dating from 1522 has been published by P. Moiraghi in *Bullettino storico pavese* (1893), i. 41 sqq. (See Magenta, *I Visconti e gli Sforza nel castello di Pavia* (Milan, 1884), for other medieval plans.)

Of the secular buildings the most noteworthy is the university founded by Galeazzo II. in 1361 on the site of a law school probably founded by Lanfranc (d. 1089), though we find Pavia a centre of study as early as A.D. 825. The present imposing building was begun by Lodovico il Moro in 1490; in the library are preserved some of the ashes of Columbus, who was a student here. Volta made here his first electrical experiments. For the maintenance of a number of poor students there are two subsidiary colleges, the Borromeo and the Ghislieri founded by S. Carlo Borromeo (1563) and Pope Pius V. (1569); of the latter a colossal bronze statue has been erected in the piazza before his college. The university of Pavia has long been famous as a medical school, and has the oldest anatomical cabinet in Italy; in addition it has a natural history museum founded under Spallanzini in 1772, a botanical garden, begun in 1774, and excellent geological, palaeontological and mineralogical collections. The old castle of the Visconti built in 1360 for Galeazzo II. is used as barracks. The Museo Civico is housed in the Palazzo Malaspina and contains many interesting national relics and a small picture gallery, with a large collection of offprints on paper from niello plates, including a very fine "Fountain of Love" by Antonio Pollaiuolo; another fine old palace, the Palazzo Mezzabarba, is now used as the Municipio.

Pavia has a number of iron-foundries, military engineering and electrical production works, and other factories, as well as a large covered market, built in 1882. Pavia lies on the main line from Milan to Genoa (which crosses the Ticino by a bridge half a mile long, and shortly afterwards the Po), with several branch lines. Barges from Pavia can pass down the Po to the Adriatic or to Milan by canal. Five miles north of Pavia is the Carthusian monastery of Certosa di Pavia, one of the most magnificent in the world. Its founder Gian Galeazzo Visconti (also the founder of Milan Cathedral) laid the first stone in August 1396, and the nave was then begun in the Gothic style, but was not completed until 1465. However the influence of the Early Renaissance had meanwhile become supreme throughout Italy, and the rest of the church with its external arcaded galleries and lofty pinnacles (including the fine dome) and the cloisters were executed in the new style under Guiniforte Solari (1453-1481) with details in terra-cotta of great beauty and richness. Giovanni Antonio Amedeo was chief architect in 1481-1499, and the lower part of the façade was finished in 1507. It is perhaps the finest piece of elaborate and richly adorned Renaissance architecture in existence, and is the work of a number of different artists. In the south transept of the church is the tomb of the founder; the figure of Galeazzo guarded by angels lies under a marble canopy, with the Madonna in a niche above. It was begun in 1494-1497 by Giovanni Cristoforo Romano and Benedetto Briosco, but was not finished until 1562. In the north transept is the tomb of Lodovico Sforza, Il Moro, and his wife, the figures on which were brought from S. Maria della Grazie in 1564 when the monument of the prince in that church was broken up and sold; these statues are considered to be one of the chief works of Cristoforo Solari. The church contains numerous other works of art. An elegant portal leads from the church into the small cloister, which has a pretty garden in the centre; the terra-cotta ornaments surmounting the slender marble pillars are the work of Rinaldo de Stauris (1463-1478), who executed similar decorations in the great cloister. This cloister is 412 ft. long by 334 ft. wide and contains 24 cells of the monks, pleasant little three-roomed houses each with its own garden. Within the confines of the monastery is the Palazzo Ducale which since 1901 has been occupied by the Certosa museum. The Carthusian monks, to whom the monastery was entrusted by the founder, were bound to employ a certain proportion of their annual revenue in prosecuting the work till its completion, and even after 1542 the monks continued voluntarily to expend large sums on further decoration. The Certosa di Pavia is thus a practical textbook of Italian art for wellnigh three centuries. The Carthusians were expelled in 1782 by the emperor Joseph II., and after being held by the Cistercians in 1784 and the Carmelites in 1789 the monastery was closed in 1810. In 1843 the Certosa was restored to the Carthusians and was exempted from confiscation in 1866, but it has since been declared a national monument.

History.—For earlier period see TICINUM. Under the name Papia (Pavia) the city became, as the capital of the Lombard kingdom, one of the leading cities of Italy. By the conquest of Pavia and the capture of Desiderius in 774 Charlemagne completely destroyed the Lombard supremacy; but the city continued to be the centre of the Carolingian power in Italy, and a royal residence was built in the neighbourhood (Corteolona on the Olona). It was in San Michele Maggiore in Pavia that Berengar of Friuli, and his quasi-regal successors down to Berengar II. and Adalbert II., were crowned "kings of Italy." Under the reign of the first the city was sacked and burned by the Hungarians, and the bishop was among those who perished. At Pavia was celebrated in 951 the marriage of Otto I. and Adelheid (Adelaide), which exercised so important an influence on the relations of the empire and Italy; but, when the succession to the crown of Italy came to be disputed between the emperor Henry II. and Arduin of Ivrea, the city sided strongly with the latter. Laid in ruins by Henry, who was attacked by the citizens on the night after his coronation in 1004, it was none the less ready to close its gates on Conrad the Salic in 1026. In the 11th and 12th centuries we find Pavia called the "Second Rome." The jealousy between Pavia and Milan having in 1056 broken out into open war, Pavia had recourse to the hated emperors, though she seems to have taken no part in the battle of Legnano; and for the most part she remained attached to the Ghibelline party till the latter part of the 14th century. From 1360, when Galeazzo was appointed imperial vicar by Charles IV., Pavia became practically a possession of the Visconti family and in due course formed part of the duchy of Milan. For its insurrection against the French garrison in 1499 it paid a terrible penalty in 1500, and in 1512, after the victory of Ravenna, Pavia presented to Louis XII., as a sign of fidelity, a magnificent standard: this however fell into the hands of Swiss mercenaries and was sent to Fribourg as a trophy of war (it' no longer exists). Having been strongly fortified by Charles V., the city was in 1525 able to bid defiance to Francis I., who was so disastrously beaten in the vicinity, but two years later the French under Lautrec subjected it to a sack of seven days. In 1655 Prince Thomas of Savoy invested Pavia with an army of 20,000 Frenchmen, but had to withdraw after 52 days' siege. The Austrians under Prince Eugène occupied it in 1706, the French in 1733 and the French and Spaniards in 1745; and the Austrians were again in possession from 1746 till 1796. In May of that year it was seized by Napoleon, who to punish it for an insurrection, condemned it to three days' pillage. In 1814 it became Austrian once more. The revolutionary movement of February 1848 was crushed by the Austrians and the university was closed; and, though the Sardinian forces obtained possession in March, the Austrians soon recovered

their ground. It was not till 1859 that Pavia passed with the rest of Lombardy to the Sardinian crown.

At several periods Pavia has been the centre of great intellectual activity. It was according to tradition in a tower which, previous to 1584, stood near the church of the Annunziata that Boethius wrote his *De consolatione philosophiae*; the legal school of Pavia was rendered celebrated in the 11th century by Lanfranc (afterwards archbishop of Canterbury); Petrarch was frequently here as the guest of Galeazzo II., and his grandson died and was buried here. Columbus studied at the university about 1465; and printing was introduced in 1471. Two of the bishops of Pavia were raised to the papal throne as John XIV. and Julius III. Lanfranc, Pope John XIV., Porta the anatomist and Cremona the mathematician were born in the city.

See C. Dell' Acqua, *Guida illustrata di Pavia* (Pavia, 1900), and refs. there given; L. Beltrami, *La Chartreuse de Pavie* (Milan, 1899); *Storia documentata della Certosa di Pavia* (Milan, 1896). (T. As.)

PAVIA Y ALBUQUERQUE, MANUEL (1828-1895), Spanish general, was born at Cadiz on the 2nd of August 1828. He was the son of Admiral Pavia, a naval officer of some note in the early part of the 19th century. He entered the Royal Artillery College at Segovia in 1841; became a lieutenant in 1846, a captain in 1855 and major in 1861. Three years later he joined the staff of Marshal Prim, and took part in the two unsuccessful revolutionary movements concerted by Prim in 1866, and, after two years of exile, in the successful revolution of 1868. Pavia showed much vigour against the republican risings in the southern provinces; the governments of King Amadeus of Savoy, from 1871 to 1873, also showed him much favour. After the abdication of that prince, General Pavia put down the Carlists and the cantonal insurrections of the chief towns of the south. On three occasions during the eventful year 1873, as captain-general of Madrid, he offered his services to put an end to the anarchy that was raging in the provinces and to the disorganization prevalent in the Cortes. To all he used the same arguments, namely, that they had to choose between an Alphonsist restoration or a dictatorial, military and political republic, which would rally round its standard all the most conservative groups that had made the revolution of 1868. This he hoped to realize with Castelar, but the plan was interrupted by the military *pronunciamiento* for the purpose of dissolving the Cortes of 1873. As soon as the federal Cortes had defeated Castelar, Pavia made his *coup d'état* of the 3rd of January 1874, and after the *pronunciamiento* was absolute master of the situation, but having no personal ambition, he sent for Marshal Serrano to form a government with Sagasta, Martos, Ulloa and other Conservatives and Radicals of the revolution. Pavia sat in the Cortes of the Restoration several times, and once defended himself skilfully against Emilio Castelar, who upbraided him for the part he had played on the 3rd of January 1874. He died suddenly on the 4th of January 1895.

PAVILION, properly a tent, a late use of Lat. *papilio*, butterfly, from which the word is derived through the French. The term is chiefly used of a tent with a high pitched roof, a small detached building used as a summer-house, &c., and particularly for a building attached to a recreation ground for the use of players and members. In architecture the term pavilion is specifically applied to a portion of a building which projects from the sides or central part. It is a characteristic of French renaissance architecture. Where the buildings of a large institution are broken up into detached portions, as in St Thomas's Hospital, London, the term is generally applied to such detached buildings.

For the musical instrument known as the Chinese pavilion or Jingling Johnny, see CHINESE PAVILION.

PAVIS, or PAVISE, a large convex shield, some 4 to 5 ft. high and sufficiently broad to cover the entire body, used in medieval warfare, as a protection against arrows and other missiles. The word appears in innumerable forms in Old French, Italian and Medieval Latin, and is probably to be referred to Pavia, in Italy, where such shields were made. The term "pavisade" or "pavesade" was used of a portable screen of hurdles behind which archers might find protection, or of a similar defensive screen formed by linking together "pavises," especially on board a ship of war extending along the bulwarks, and hence in later times of a canvas screen similarly placed to conceal the rowers in a galley or the sailors on other types of ships.

PAVLOVO, a town of Russia, in the government of Nizhniy-Novgorod, 42 m. S.W. of the town of Nizhniy-Novgorod, on the Oka river. Pop. (1897), 12,200. It is the centre of a considerable cutlery, hardware and locksmith trade, which, carried on since the 17th century in cottages and small workshops, engages, besides Pavlovo itself, no less than 120 villages. There are also steel works and cotton, silk, soap and match factories. Pavlovo has a museum of cutlery models and a library.

PAVLOVO POSAD, or VOKHNA, a town of Russia, in the government of Moscow, 41 m. by rail E. of the city of Moscow, on the Klyazma river. Pop. (1897), 10,020. It is the centre of a manufacturing district, with silk, cotton and woollen mills, and dyeing and printing works.

PAVLOVSK, a town of Russia, in the government of St Petersburg 17 m. by rail S. of the city of St Petersburg. Pop. (1897), 4949. It has an imperial castle (1782-1803) standing in a beautiful park and containing a small fine art museum and gallery. In the vicinity are smaller imperial palaces and summer residences of St Petersburg families.

PAWN. (1) A pledge, an object left in the charge of another, as security for the repayment of money lent, for a debt or for the performance of some obligation (see PAWNBROKING). The word is an adaptation of O. Fr. *pan,* pledge, plunder, spoil. This has usually been identified with *pan,* from Lat. *pannus,* piece of cloth. The Teutonic words for pledge—such as Du. *pand,* Ger. *Pfand* have been also traced to the same source; on the other hand these Teutonic forms have been connected with the word which appears in O. Eng. as *pending,* a penny, Ger. *Pfennig,* but this too has been referred to *pannus.* (2) The smallest piece on the chessboard. This, in its early forms, *pown, pown,* &c., is taken from Fr. *poon* or *paon,* variants of *peon,* Med. Lat. *pedo, pedonis,* a foot soldier, from *pes,* foot.

PAWNBROKING (O. Fr. *pan,* pledge, piece, from Lat. *pannus;* for "broking" see BROKER), the business of lending money on the security of goods taken in pledge. If we desire to trace with minuteness the history of pawnbroking, we must go back to the earliest ages of the world, since the business of lending money on portable security (see MONEY-LENDING, and USURY) is one of the most ancient of human occupations. The Mosaic Law struck at the root of pawnbroking as a profitable business, since it forbade the taking of interest from a poor borrower, while no Jew was to pay another for timely accommodation. And it is curious to reflect that, although the Jew was the almost universal usurer and money-lender upon security of the middle ages, it is now very rare in Great Britain to find a Hebrew pawnbroker.

In China the pawnshop was probably as familiar two or three thousand years ago as it is to-day, and its conduct is still regulated quite as strictly as in England. The Chinese conditions, too, are decidedly favourable to the borrower. He may, as a rule, take three years to redeem his property, and he cannot be charged a higher rate than 3% per annum—a regulation which would close every pawnshop in England in a month. Both Rome and Greece were as familiar with the operation of pawning as the modern poor all the world over; indeed, from the Roman jurisprudence most of the contemporary law on the subject is derived. The chief difference between Roman and English law is that under the former certain things, such as wearing apparel, furniture, and instruments of tillage, could not be pledged, whereas there is no such restriction in English legislation. The emperor Augustus converted the surplus arising to the state from the confiscated property of criminals into a *The Pledge System.* fund from which sums of money were lent, without interest, to those who could pledge valuables equal to double the amount borrowed. It was, indeed, in Italy, and in more modern times, that the pledge system which is now almost universal on the continent of Europe arose. In its origin that system was purely benevolent, the early *monts de pièté* established by the authority of the popes lending money to the poor only, without interest, on the sole condition of the advances being covered by the value of the pledges. This was virtually the Augustan system, but it is obvious that an institution which costs money to manage and derives no income from its operations must either limit its usefulness to the extent of the voluntary support it can command, or must come to a speedy end. Thus as early as 1198 something of the kind was started at Freising in Bavaria; while in 1350 a similar endeavour was made at Salins in Franche Comté, where interest at the rate of 7½% was charged. Nor was England backward, for in 1361 Michael Northbury, or de Northborough, bishop of London, bequeathed 1000 silver marks for the establishment of a free pawnshop. These primitive efforts, like the later Italian ones, all failed. The Vatican was therefore constrained to allow the Sacri monti di pietà—no satisfactory derivation of the phrase has yet been suggested—to charge sufficient interest to their customers to enable them to defray expenses. Thereupon a learned and tedious controversy arose upon the lawfulness of charging interest, which was only finally set at rest by Pope Leo X., who, in the tenth sitting of the Council of the Lateran, declared that the pawnshop was a lawful and valuable institution, and threatened with excommunication those who should presume to express doubts on the subject. The Council of Trent inferentially confirmed this decision, and at a somewhat later date we find St Charles Borromeo counselling the establishment of state or municipal pawnshops.

Long before this, however, monti di pietà charging interest for their loans had become common in Italy. The date of their establishment was not later than 1464, when the *Italian Monti di Pietà.* earliest of which there appears to be any record in that country—it was at Orvieto—was confirmed by Pius II. Three years later another was opened at Perugia by the efforts of two Franciscans, Barnabus Interamnensis and Fortunatus de Copolis. They collected the necessary capital by preaching, and the Perugian pawnshop was opened with such success that there was a substantial balance of profit at the end of the first year. The Dominicans endeavoured to preach down the "lending-house," but without avail. Viterbo obtained one of 1469, and Sixtus IV. confirmed another to his native town in Savona in 1479. After the death of Brother Barnabus in 1474, a strong impulse was given to the creation of these establishments by the preaching of another Franciscan, Father Bernardino di Feltre, who was in due course canonized. By his efforts monti di pietà were opened at Assisi, Mantua, Parma, Lucca, Piacenza, Padua, Vicenza, Pavia and a number of places of less importance. At Florence the veiled opposition of the municipality and the open hostility of the Jews prevailed against him, and it was reserved to Savonarola, who was a Dominican, to create the first Florentine pawnshop, after the local theologians had declared that there was "no sin, even venial," in charging interest. The readiness of the popes to give permission for pawnshops all over Italy, makes it the more remarkable that the papal capital possessed nothing of the kind until 1539, and even then owed the convenience to a Franciscan. From Italy the pawnshop spread gradually all over Europe. Augsburg adopted the system in 1591, Nuremberg copied the Augsburg regulations in 1618, and by 1622 it was established at Amsterdam, Brussels, Antwerp and Ghent. Madrid followed suit in 1705, when a priest opened a charitable pawnshop with a capital of fivepence taken from an alms-box.

The institution was, however, very slow in obtaining a footing in France. It was adopted at Avignon in 1577, and at Arras in 1624. The doctors of the once powerful Sorbonne *Introduction in France.* could not reconcile themselves to the lawfulness of interest, and when a pawnshop was opened in Paris in 1626, it had to be closed within a year. Then it was that Jean Boucher published his *Défense des monts de pièté.* Marseilles obtained one in 1695; but it was not until 1777 that the first mont de piété was founded in Paris by royal patent. The statistics which have been preserved relative to the business done in the first few years of its existence show that in the twelve years between 1777 and the Revolution, the average value of the pledges was 42 francs 50 centimes, which is double the present average. The interest charged was 10% per annum, and large profits were made upon the sixteen million livres that were lent every year. The National Assembly, in an evil moment, destroyed the monopoly of the mont de piété, but it struggled on until 1795, when the competition of the money-lenders compelled it to close its doors. So great, however, were the extortions of the usurers that the people began to clamour for its reopening, and in July 1797 it recommenced business with a fund of £20,000 found by five private capitalists. At first it charged interest at the rate of 36% per annum, which was gradually reduced, the gradations being 30, 24, 18, 15, and finally 12% in 1804. In 1806 it fell to 9%, and in 1887 to 7%. In 1806 Napoleon I. re-established its monopoly, while Napoleon III., as prince-president, regulated it by new laws that are still in force. In Paris the pledge-shop is, in effect, a department of the administration; in the French provinces it is a municipal monopoly; and this remark holds goo , with modifications, for most parts of the continent of Europe.

In England the pawnbroker, like so many other distinguished personages, "came in with the Conqueror." From that time, **Great Britain.** indeed, to the famous legislation of Edward I., the Jew money-lender was the only pawnbroker. Yet, despite the valuable services which the class rendered, not infrequently to the Crown itself, the usurer was treated with studied cruelty—Sir Walter Scott's Isaac of York was no mere creation of fiction. These barbarities, by diminishing the number of Jews in the country, had, long before Edward's decree of banishment, begun to make it worth the while of the Lombard merchants to settle in England. It is now as well established as anything of the kind can be that the three golden balls, which have for so long been the trade sign of the pawnbroker, were the symbol which these Lombard merchants hung up in front of their houses, and not, as has often been suggested, the arms of the Medici family. It has, indeed, been conjectured that the golden balls were originally three flat yellow effigies of byzants, or gold coins, laid heraldically upon a sable field, but that they were presently converted into balls the better to attract attention. In 1338 Edward III. pawned his jewels to the Lombards to raise money for his war with France. An equally great king—Henry V.—did much the same in 1415.

The Lombards were not a popular class, and Henry VII. harried them a good deal. In the very first year of James I. "An Act against Brokers" was passed and remained on the statute-book until Queen Victoria had been thirty-five years on the throne. It was aimed at "counterfeit brokers," of whom there were then many in London. This type of broker was evidently regarded as a mere receiver of stolen goods, for the act provided that "no sale or pawn of any stolen jewels, plate or other goods to any pawnbroker in London, Westminster or Southwark shall alter the property therein," and that "pawnbrokers refusing to produce goods to their owner from whom stolen shall forfeit double the value."

In the time of Charles I. there was another act which made it quite clear that the pawnbroker was not deemed to be a very respectable or trustworthy person. Nevertheless a plan was mooted for setting that king up in the business. The Civil War was approaching and supplies were badly needed, when a too ingenious Royalist proposed the establishment of a state "pawnhouse." The preamble of the scheme recited how "the intolerable injuries done to the poore subjects by brokers and usurers that take 30, 40, 50, 60, and more in the hundredth, may be remedied and redressed, the poor thereby greatly relieved and eased, and His Majestie much benefited." That the king would have been "much benefited" is obvious, since he was to enjoy two-thirds of the profits, while the working capital of £100,000 was to be found by the city of London. The reform of what Shakespeare calls "broking pawn" was in the air at that time,

although nothing ever came of it, and in the early days of the commonwealth it was proposed to establish a kind of mont de piété. The idea was emphasized in a pamphlet of 1651 entitled *Observations manifesting the Conveniency and Commodity of Mount Pisteyes, or Public Bancks for Relief of the Poor or Others in Distress, upon Pawns.* No doubt many a ruined cavalier would have been glad enough of some such means of raising money, but this radical change in the principles of English pawnbroking was never brought about. It is said that the Bank of England, under its charter, has power to establish pawnshops; and we learn from *A Short History of the Bank of England,* published in its very early days, that it was the intention of the directors, "for the ease of the poor," to institute "a Lombard" "for small pawns at a penny a pound interest per month."

Throughout both the 17th and 18th centuries the general suspicion of the pawnbroker appears to have been only too well founded. It would appear from the references Fielding makes to the subject in *Amelia,* which was written when George II. was on the throne, that, taken in the mass, he was not a very scrupulous tradesman. Down to about that time it had been customary for publicans to lend money on pledges that their customers might have the means of drinking, but the practice was at last stopped by act of parliament. Nor was respect for the honesty of the business increased by the attempt of "The Charitable Corporation" to conduct pawnbroking on a large scale. Established by charter in 1707, "this nefarious corporation," as Smollett called it, was a swindle on a large scale. The directors gambled wildly with the shareholders' money, and in the end the common council of the city of London petitioned parliament for the dissolution of this dishonest concern, on the ground that "the corporation, by affording an easy method of raising money upon valuables, furnishes the thief and pickpocket with a better opportunity of selling their stolen goods, and enables an intending bankrupt to dispose of the goods he buys on credit for ready money, to the defrauding of his creditors." When the concern collapsed in 1731 its cashier was Mr George Robinson, M.P. for Marlow. In company with another principal official he disappeared, less than £30,000 being left of a capital which had once been twenty times as much.

The pawnbroker's licence dates from 1785, the duty being fixed at £10 in London and £5 in the country; and at the same time the interest chargeable was settled at ⅓% per **Modern** month, the duration of loans being confined to one **Regulations** year. Five years later the interest on advances **in England.** over £2 and under £10 was raised to 15%. The modern history of legislation affecting pawnbroking begins, however, in 1800, when the act of 39 & 40 Geo. III. c. 99 (1800) was passed, in great measure by the influence of Lord Eldon, who never made any secret of the fact that, when he was a young barrister without briefs, he had often been indebted to the timely aid of the pawnshop. The pawnbrokers were grateful, and for many years after Lord Eldon's death they continued to drink his health at their trade dinners. The measure increased the rate of interest to a halfpenny per half-crown per month, or fourpence in the pound per mensem—that is to say, 20% per annum. Loans were to be granted for a year, although pledges might be redeemed up to fifteen months, and the first week of the second month was not to count for interest. The act worked well, on the whole, for three-quarters of a century, but it was thrice found necessary to amend it. Thus in 1815 the licence duties were raised to £15 and £7, 10s. for London and the country respectively; another act of 1840 abolished the reward to the "common informer" for reporting illegal rates of interest; while in 1860 the pawnbroker was empowered to charge a halfpenny for the pawn-ticket when the loan was under five shillings. As time went on, however, the main provisions of the act of 1800 were found to be very irksome, and the Pawnbrokers' National Association and the Pawnbrokers' Defence Association worked hard to obtain a liberal revision of the law. It was argued that the usury laws had been abolished for the whole of the community with the single exception of the pawnbroker who advanced less than £10. The limitations of the act of 1800 interfered so considerably with the pawnbrokers' profits that, it was argued, they could not afford to lend money on bulky articles requiring extensive storage room. In 1870 the House of Commons appointed a Select Committee on Pawnbrokers, and it was stated in evidence before that body that in the previous year 207,780,000 pledges were lodged, of which between thirty and forty millions were lodged in London. The average value of pledges appeared to be about 4s., and the proportion of articles pawned dishonestly was found to be only 1 in 14,000. Later official statistics show that of the forfeited pledges sold in London less than 20 per million are claimed by the police.

The result of the Select Committee was the Pawnbrokers Act of 1872, which repealed, altered and consolidated all previous legislation on the subject, and is still the measure which regulates the relations between the public and the "brokers of pawn." Based mainly upon the Irish law passed by the Union Parliament it put an end to the old irritating restrictions, and reduced the annual tax in London from £15 to the £7, 10s. paid in the provinces. By the provisions of the act (which does not affect loans above £10), a pledge is redeemable within one year, and seven days of grace added to the year. Pledges pawned for 10s. or under and not redeemed in time become the property of the pawnbroker, but pledges above 10s. are redeemable until sale, which must be by public auction. In addition to one halfpenny for the pawn-ticket—which is sometimes not charged for very small pawns—the pawnbroker is entitled to charge as interest one halfpenny per month on every 2s. or part of 2s. lent where the loan is under 40s., and on every 2s. 6d. where the loan is above 40s. "Special contracts" may be made where the loan is above 40s. at a rate of interest agreed upon between lender and borrower. Unlawful pawning of goods not the property of the pawner, and taking in pawn any article from a person under the age of twelve, or intoxicated, or any linen, or apparel or unfinished goods or materials entrusted to wash, make up, &c., are, inter alia, made offences punishable by summary conviction. A new pawnbroker must produce a magistrate's certificate before he can receive a licence; but the permit cannot be refused if the applicant gives sufficient evidence that he is a person of good character. The word "pawnbroker" must always be inscribed in large letters over the door of the shop. Elaborate provisions are made to safeguard the interests of borrowers whose unredeemed pledges are sold under the act. Thus the sales by auction may take place only on the first Monday of January, April, July and October, and on the following days should one not be sufficient. This legislation was, no doubt, favourable to the pawnbroker rather than to the borrower. The annual interest on loans of 2s. had been increased by successive acts of parliament from the 6% at which it stood in 1784 to 25% in 1800, and to 27 in 1860—a rate which was continued by the measure of 1872. The annual interest upon a loan of half-a-crown is now 260%, as compared with 173 in 1860 and 86 in 1784; while the extreme point is reached in the case of a loan of 1s. for three days, in which case the interest is at the rate of 1014% per annum. An English mont de piété was once projected by the Salvation Army, and in 1894 the London County Council considered the practicability of municipal effort on similar lines; but in neither case was anything done.

The growth of pawnbroking in Scotland, where the law as to pledge agrees generally with that of England, is remarkable. Early in the 19th century there was only one pawn-broker in that country, and in 1833 the number reached only 52. Even in 1865 there were no more than 312. It is probable that at the present moment Glasgow and Edinburgh together contain nearly as many as that total. In Ireland the rates for loans are practically identical with those charged in England, but a penny instead of a halfpenny is paid for the ticket. Articles pledged for less than £1 must be redeemed within six months, but nine months are allowed when the amount is between 30s. and £2. For sums over £2 the period is a year, as in England. In Ireland, too,

Scotland and Ireland.

a fraction of a month is calculated as a full month for purposes of interest, whereas in England, after the first month, fortnights are recognized. In 1838 there was an endeavour to establish monts de piété in Ireland, but the scheme was so unsuccessful that in 1841 the eight charitable pawnshops that had been opened had a total adverse balance of £3340. But 1847 only three were left, and eventually they collapsed likewise.

The pawnbroker in the United States is, generally speaking, subject to considerable legal restriction, but violations of the laws and ordinances are frequent. Each state has its own regulations, but those of New York and Massachusetts may be taken as fairly representative. "Brokers of pawn" are usually licensed by the mayors, or by the mayors and aldermen, but in Boston the police commissioners are the licensing authority. In the state of New York permits are renewable annually on payment of $500, and the pawnbroker must file a bond with the mayor, executed by himself and two responsible sureties, in the sum of $10,000. The business is conducted on much the same lines as in England, and the rate of interest is 3% per month for the first six months, and 2% monthly afterwards. Where, however, the loan exceeds $100 the rates are 2 and 1% respectively. To exact higher rates is a misdemeanour. Unredeemed pledges may be sold at the end of a year. Pawnbrokers are not allowed to engage in any kind of second-hand business. New York contains one pawn-shop to every 12,000 inhabitants, and most of the pawnbrokers are Jews. In the state of Massachusetts unredeemed pledges may be sold four months after the date of deposit. The licensing authority may fix the rate of interest, which may vary for different amounts, and in Boston every pawnbroker is bound to furnish to the police daily a list of the pledges taken in during the preceding twenty-four hours, specifying the hour of each transaction and the amount lent.

United States.

The fact that on the continent of Europe monts de piété are almost invariably either a state or a municipal monopoly necessarily places them upon an entirely different footing from the British pawnshop, but, compared with the English system, the foreign is very elaborate and rather cumbersome. Moreover, in addition to being slow in its operation, it is, generally speaking, based upon the supposition that the borrower carries in his pockets "papers" testifying to his identity. On the other hand, it is argued that the English borrower of more than £2 is at the mercy of the pawnbroker in the matter of interest, that sum being the highest for which a legal limit of interest is fixed. The rate of interest upon a "special contract" may be, and often is, high. For the matter of that, indeed, this system of obtaining loans is always expensive, either in actual interest or in collateral disadvantages, whether the lender be a pawnbroker intent upon profit, or the official of a mont de piété. In Paris the rate charged is 7%, and even then the business is conducted at a loss except in regard to long and valuable pledges. Some of the French provincial rates are as high as 12%, but in almost every case they are less than they were prior to the legislation of 1851 and 1852. The French establishments can only be created by decree of the president of the Republic, with the consent of the local conseil communal. In Paris the prefect of the Seine presides over the business; in the provinces the mayor is the president. The administrative council is drawn either each from the conseil communal, the governors of charitable societies, and the townspeople. A large proportion of the capital required for conducting the institutions has to be raised by loan; while some part of the property they possess is the product of gifts and legacies. The profits of the Paris mont de piété are paid over to the "Assistance Publique," the comprehensive term used by France to indicate the body of charitable foundations. Originally this was the rule throughout France, but now many of them are entirely independent of the charitable institutions. Counting the head office, the branches and the auxiliary shops, the Paris establishment has its doors open in some fifty or sixty districts; but the volume of its annual business is infinitely smaller than that transacted by the London pawnbrokers. The amount to be

Municipal Pawnshops.

advanced by a municipal pawnshop is fixed by an official called the *commissaire-priseur*, who is compelled to load the scales against the borrower, since, should the pledge remain unredeemed and be sold for less than was lent upon it, he has to make good the difference. This official is paid at the rate of ½% upon loans and renewals, and 3% on the amount obtained by the sales of forfeited pledges. This is obviously the weakest part of the French system. The Paris mont de piété undertakes to lend four-fifths of the intrinsic value of articles made from the precious metals, and two-thirds of that of other articles. The maximum and minimum that may be advanced are also fixed. The latter varies in different parts of the country from one to three francs, and the former from a very small sum to the 10,000 francs which is the rule in Paris. Loans are granted for twelve months with right of renewal, and unredeemed pledges may then be sold by auction, but the proceeds may be claimed by the borrower at any time within three years. Pledges may be redeemed by instalments.

Somewhere between forty and fifty French towns possess municipal pawnshops, a few of which, like those of Grenoble and Montpellier, having been endowed, charge no interest. Elsewhere the rate varies from nil in some towns, for very small pledges, to 10%. The constant tendency throughout France has been to reduce the rate. The great establishment in Paris obtains part of its working capital—reserves and surplus forming the balance—by borrowing money at a rate varying from 2 to 3% according to the length of time for which the loan is made. Under a law passed in 1891 the Paris mont de piété makes advances upon securities at 6%, plus a duty of 5 centimes upon every hundred francs. The maximum that can be lent in this way is £20. Up to 80% is lent on the face value of government stock and on its own bonds, and 75% upon other securities; but 60% only may be advanced on railway shares. These advances are made for six months. Persons wishing to borrow a larger sum than sixteen francs from the Paris mont de piété have to produce their papers of identity. In every case a numbered metal check is given to the customer, and a duplicate is attached to the article itself. The appraising clerks decide upon the sum that can be lent, and the amount is called out with the number. If the borrower is dissatisfied he can take away his property, but if he accepts the offer he has to give full particulars of his name, address and occupation. The experts calculate that every transaction involving less than twenty-two francs results in a loss to the Paris mont de piété, while it is only those exceeding eighty-five francs which can be counted upon to be invariably profitable. The average loan is under thirty francs.

The borrowing of money on the security of goods deposited has been the subject of minute regulations in the Low Countries *Holland and Belgium.* from an early date. So far back as the year 1600 the "archdukes" Albert and Isabella, governors of the Spanish Netherlands under Philip III., reduced the lawful rate of interest from 32⅔ to 21⅓%; but since extortion continued they introduced the mont de piété in 1618, and, as we have already seen, in the course of a dozen years the institution was established in all the populous Belgian towns, with one or two exceptions. The interest chargeable to borrowers was fixed originally at 15%, but was shortly afterwards reduced, to be again increased to nearly the old level. Meanwhile various towns possessed charitable funds for gratuitous loans, apart from the official institutions. Shortly after the mont de piété was introduced in the Spanish provinces, the prince-bishop of Liége (Ferdinand of Bavaria) followed the example set by the archdukes. He ordained that the net profits were to accumulate, and the interest upon the fund to be used in reduction of the charges. The original rate was 15%, when the Lombard money-lenders had been charging 43; but the prince-bishop's monts de piété were so successful that for many years their rate of interest did not exceed 5%—it was, indeed, not until 1788 that it was increased by one-half. These flourishing institutions, along with those in Belgium proper, were ruined by the French Revolution. They were, however, re-established under French dominion, and for many years the laws governing them were constantly altered by the French, Dutch and Belgian governments in turn. The whole subject is now regulated by a law of 1848, supplemented by a new constitution for the Brussels mont de piété dating from 1891.

The working capital of these official pawnshops is furnished by charitable institutions or the municipalities, but the Brussels one possesses a certain capital of its own in addition. The rate of interest charged in various parts of the country varies from 4 to 16%, but in Brussels it is usually less than half the maximum. The management is very similar to that of the French monts de piété, but the arrangements are much more favourable to the borrower. The ordinary limit of loans is £120. In Antwerp there is an "anonymous" pawnshop, where the customer need not give his name or any other particulars. In Holland private pawnbrokers flourish side by side with the municipal "Banken van Leening," nor are there any limitations upon the interest that may be charged. The rules of the official institutions are very similar to those of the monts de piété in the Latin countries, and unredeemed pledges are sold publicly fifteen months after being pawned. A large proportion of the advances are made upon gold and diamonds; workmen's tools are not taken in pledge, and the amount lent varies from 8d. upwards. On condition of finding such sum of money as may be required for working capital over and above loans from public institutions, and the " caution money " deposited by the city officials, the municipality receives the profits.

Pawnbroking in Germany is conducted at once by the state, by the municipalities, and by private enterprise; but of all these institutions the state loan office in Berlin is the most *Germany and Austria.* interesting. It dates from 1834, and the working capital was found, and still continues to be in part provided, by the Prussian State Bank. The profits are invested, and the interest devoted to charitable purposes. The maximum and minimum rates of interest are fixed, but the rate varies, and often stands at about 12%. Two-thirds of the estimated value is the usual extent of a loan; four-fifths is advanced on silver, and five-sixths on fine gold. State and municipal bonds may be pledged up to a maximum of £250, the advance being 80% of the value, and a fixed interest of 6% is charged upon these securities. The values are fixed by professional valuers, who are liable to make good any loss that may result from over-estimation. The bulk of the loans are under £5, and the state office is used less by the poor than by the middle classes. Loans run for six months, but a further six months' grace is allowed for redemption before the article pledged can be sold by auction. The net annual profit usually amounts to little more than 1% upon the capital employed. The pawnbroking laws of Austria-Hungary are very similar to those which prevail in England. Free trade exists, and the private trader, who does most of the business, has to obtain a government concession and deposit caution-money varying in amount from £80 to £800, according to the size of the town. He has, however, to compete with the monts de piété or Versatzaemter, which are sometimes municipal and sometimes state institutions. The chief of these is the imperial pawn office of Vienna, which was founded with charitable objects by the emperor Joseph I. in 1707, and one-half of the annual surplus has still to be paid over to the Vienna poor fund. Here, as in Berlin, the profits are relatively small. Interest is charged at the uniform rate of 10%, which is calculated in fortnightly periods, however speedily redemption may follow upon pawning. For small loans varying from two to three kronen, 5% only is charged. The Hungarian state and municipal institutions appear, on the whole, to compete somewhat more successfully with the private firms than is the case in Vienna.

In Italy, the "country of origin" of the mont de piété, the institution still flourishes. It is, as a rule, managed by a committee or commission, and the regulations follow *Italy.* pretty closely the lines of the one in Rome, which never lends less than 10d. or more than £40. Four-fifths of the value is lent upon gold, silver and jewels, and two-thirds upon other articles. The interest, which is reckoned monthly, varies with the amount of the loan from 5 to 7%, but no interest is chargeable upon loans up to 5 lire. A loan runs for six months, and may be renewed for similar periods up to a maximum of five years. If the renewal does not take place within a fortnight of the expiration of the ticket, the pledge is sold, any surplus there may be being paid to the pawner. When more than 10 lire is lent there is a charge of 1% for the ticket. Agencies of the mont de piété are scattered about Rome, and carry on their business under the same rules as the central office, with the disadvantage to the borrower that he has to pay an " agent's fee" of 2%, which is deducted from the loan. Private pawn-shops also exist in Italy, under police authority; but they charge very high interest.

The monts de piété in Spain have for a generation past been inseparably connected with the savings banks. We have already **Spain and Portugal.** seen that the institution owes its origin in that country to the charitable exertions of a priest who charged no interest, and the system grew until in 1840 a century after his death, the mont de piété began to receive the sums deposited in the savings bank, which had just been estab-lished, for which it paid 5% interest. In 1869 the two institu-tions were united. This official pawnshop charges 6% upon advances which run for periods varying from four to twelve months, according to the nature of the article pledged, and a further month's grace is allowed before the pledges are sold by auction. Private pawnbrokers are also very numerous, espe-cially in Madrid; but their usual charges amount to about 60% per annum. They appear, however, to derive advantage from making larger advances than their official rivals, and from doing business during more convenient hours. In Portugal the monte pio is an amalgamation of bank, benefit society and pawnshop. Its business consists chiefly in lending money upon marketable securities, but it also makes advances upon plate, jewelry and precious stones, and it employs officially licensed valuers. The rate of interest varies with the bank rate, which it slightly exceeds, and the amount advanced upon each article is about three-fourths of its certified value. There is in Portugal a second class of loan establishment answering exactly to the English pawnshop. The pawnbroker is compelled to deposit a sum, in acceptable securities, equal to the capital he proposes to embark, and the register of his transactions must be sub-mitted quarterly to the chief of the police for examination. As regards small transactions, there appears to be no legal limit to the rate of interest. The sale of unredeemed pledges is governed by the law affecting the "monte pio geral."

In Russia the state maintains two pawnbroking establish-ments, one at St Petersburg and the other at Moscow, but **Russia.** only articles of gold and silver, precious stones and ingots of the precious metals are accepted by them. Advances are made upon such securities at 6% per annum, and the amounts of the loans are officially limited. Loans run for twelve months, with a month's grace before unredeemed pledges are put up to auction. The bulk of this class of business in Russia is, however, conducted by private companies, which advance money upon all descriptions of movable property except stocks and shares. The interest charged is not allowed to exceed 1% per month, but there is an additional charge of ½% per month for "insurance and safe keeping." The loan runs for a year, with two months' grace for redemption before sale. There are also a certain number of pawnshops conducted by individuals, who find it very difficult to compete with the companies. These shops can only be opened by a police permit, which runs for five years, and security, varying from £100 to £700, has to be deposited; 2% per month is the limit of interest fixed, and two months' grace is allowed for redemption after the period for which an article is pledged.

Pawnbroking in Denmark dates from 1753, when the Royal Naval Hospital was granted the monopoly of advancing **Denmark and Norway.** money on pledges and of charging higher interest than the law permitted. The duration of a loan is three months, renewals being allowed. The old law was extended in 1867, and now all pawnbrokers have to be licensed by the municipalities and to pay a small annual licence fee. The rate of interest varies from 6 to 12% according to the amount of the loan, which must not be less than 7d., and unredeemed pledges must be sold by auction. In Sweden there are no special statutes affecting pawnbroking, with the exception of a proclamation by the governor of Stockholm pro-hibiting the lending of money upon articles which may be sus-pected of having been stolen. Individuals still carry on the business on a small scale, but the bulk of it is now conducted by companies, which give general satisfaction. For many years there was in Stockholm a municipal establishment charging 10% for loans paid out of the city funds. The cost of adminis-tration was, however, so great that there was an annual loss upon its working, and the opportunity was taken to abolish it when, in 1880, a private company was formed called the "Pant Aktie Bank," to lend money on furniture and wearing apparel at the rate of 3 öre per krone a month, and 2 öre per krone a month on gold, silver and other valuables: a krone, which equals 1s. 1½d., contains 100 öre. Some years later an opposition was started which charged only half these rates, with the result that the original enterprise reduced its interest to the same level, charging, however, 2 öre per krone per mensem for bulky articles—a figure which is now usual for pledges of that description. The money is lent for three months, and at the end of five months the pledge, if unredeemed, is sold by auction under very carefully prescribed conditions. In Norway a police licence is required for lending money on pawn where the amount advanced does not exceed £4, 10s. Beyond that sum no licence is necessary, but the interest charged must not exceed such a rate as the king may decide.

The fate of pawnbroking in Switzerland appears to be not very dissimilar from that of the Jew who is fabled to have once started in business at Aberdeen. Nevertheless **Switzerland.** the cantons of Bern and Zürich have elaborate laws for the regulation of the business. In Zürich the broker must be licensed by the cantonal government, and the permit can be refused only when the applicant is "known to be a person undeserving of confidence." Regular books have to be kept, which must be at all times open to the inspection of the police, and not more than 1% interest per month must be charged. A loan runs for six months, and unredeemed pledges may be sold by auction a month after the expiration of the fixed period, and then the sale must take place in the parish in which the article was pledged. No more than two persons at a time have ever been licensed under this law, the business being unprofitable owing to the low rate of interest. In the canton of Bern there were once two pawnbrokers. One died and the other put up his shutters. The Zürich cantonal bank, however, conducts a pawnbroking department, which lends nothing under 4s. or over £40 without the special sanction of the bank commission. Loans must not exceed two-thirds of the true value of the pledge, but 80% may be lent upon the intrinsic value of gold and silver articles. The establishment makes practically no profit. The Swiss disinclination to go to the pawnshop is, perhaps, accounted for in some measure by the growing number of dealers in second-hand articles, to whom persons in want of ready money sell outright such things as are usually pledged, in the hope of subsequently buying them back. Since, however, the dealer is at liberty to ask his own price for repurchase, the expectation is often illusory, and can usually be fulfilled only upon ruinous terms.   (J.-P.-B.)

PAWNEE (perhaps from the native word for "horn," in allusion to their scalping lock, which was "dressed" so as to stand straight up), a tribe of North-American Indians of Caddoan stock. They formerly lived on the Platte river in Nebraska. They call themselves *Skihiksihiks* ("men of men"). They were a brave, war-loving tribe, whose history was one of continual strife with their neighbours. In 1823 their village was burned by the Delawares, and in 1838 the tribe suffered severely from small-pox, the death-roll being, it is said, 2000. By treaty in 1833 they had ceded their territory south of the Platte, and in 1858 they surrendered all their remaining land except a strip on the Loup River. Here they lived till 1874, when they moved to a reservation in Indian Territory (now Oklahoma), where they now are.

PAWTUCKET, a city of Providence county, Rhode Island, U.S.A., on the Blackstone river (known below the Pawtucket Falls here as the Pawtucket or Seekonk river), 4 m. N. of Providence, and near the city of Central Falls. Pop. (1905, state census), 43,381, of whom 14,369 were foreign-born, includ-ing 4173 English, 3484 Irish, 2706 French Canadians, and 1198

Scotch: (1910), 51,622. Pawtucket is served by the New York, New Haven & Hartford railroad; and the river is navigable below the falls. The city lies on both sides of the river and its land area in 1906 was nearly 8·6 m. The east bank of the river rises quite abruptly 15–30 ft., but back of this the surface is level or only slightly undulating. On the west side the surface is more diversified. The Blackstone River here makes a picturesque plunge of nearly 50 ft. (Pawtucket Falls) over an irregular mass of rocks, providing a good water-power. The most attractive public building is the Sayles Memorial library, erected (1899–1902) by Frederick Clark Sayles (1835–1902) in memory of his wife. The city has a park of 181 acres in the east end, a park of 55 acres on the west side, three small parks near the business centre, a soldiers' monument, a home for the aged, an emergency hospital, and a state armoury. Manufacturing is the principal industry, and the value of the factory products increased from $19,271,582 in 1900 to $25,846,899 in 1905, or 34·1%. More than one-half the value for 1905 was represented by textiles. Other important manufactures in 1905 were foundry and machine-shop products, packed meats, and electrical machinery, apparatus and supplies. The commerce of the city has been much increased by the deepening and widening of the channel of the Pawtucket river by the United States government. In 1867 the river could not be navigated at low water by boats drawing more than 5 ft. of water, but by March 1905 the government had constructed a channel 100 ft. wide and 22 ft. deep at low water, and Congress had passed an act for increasing the depth to 16 ft.; in 1907 the Federal Congress and the general assembly of the state made appropriations to complete the work.

That portion of Pawtucket which lies east of the river was originally a part of the township of Rehoboth, Massachusetts, but in 1812 the township of Seekonk was set apart from Rehoboth, in 1828 the township of Pawtucket was set apart from Seekonk, and in 1862 almost all of the Massachusetts township of Pawtucket was transferred to Rhode Island. The portion west of the river was taken from the township of North Providence and annexed to the township of Pawtucket in 1874, and in 1885 Pawtucket was chartered as a city. The first settlement within the present city limits was made about 1670 on the west side by Joseph Jenks (c. 1632–1717), a manufacturer of domestic iron implements. His manufactory was destroyed during King Philip's War, but he rebuilt it, and until a century later the industries on the west side were managed largely by his family. In 1790 Samuel Slater reproduced here the Arkwright machinery for the manufacture of cotton goods; this was the first manufactory of the kind that had any considerable success in the United States, and his old mill is still standing in Mill Street.

See R. Grieve, *An Illustrated History of Pawtucket, Central Falls, and Vicinity* (Pawtucket, 1897).

PAX (Lat. for " peace "), the name given in ecclesiastical usage to a small panel or tablet decorated usually with a representation of the Crucifixion, which in the Roman ritual was kissed at the eucharistic service by the celebrating priest, then by the other priests and deacons, and then by the congregation. The " Pax " is also known by the names *osculatorium, tabula pacis* and *pax-bred* (i.e. " pax-board "). The use of the " pax " dates from the 13th century, and it is said to have been first introduced in England in 1250 by Archbishop Walter of York. It took the place of the actual " kiss of peace " (*osculum sanctum*, or *osculum pacis*) which was in the Roman Mass given by the bishop to the priests, and took place after the consecration and before communion. In the Greek Church the kiss (*eiphnh*, ἀσπασμός) takes place at the beginning of the service, and now consists in the celebrating priest kissing the oblation and the deacon kissing his stole (see F. E. Brightman, *Liturgies Eastern and Western*, 1896). Owing to disputes over questions of precedence the kissing of the pax at the service of the Mass was given up. It is still used at times of prayer by religious communities or societies. In the 15th and 16th centuries much artistic skill was lavished on the pax, and beautiful examples of enamelled paxes with chased gold and silver frames

are in the British Museum. Though the Crucifixion is most usually represented, other religious subjects, such as the Virgin and Child, the Annunciation, the figures of patron saints and the like, are found. In the " Inventarie of the Plate, Jewells ... and other Ornaments appertayning to the Cathedrall Churche of Sayncte Paule in London," 1552, we find two paxes mentioned; one " with the ymage of the Crucifix and of Marie and John all gylte with the Sonn alsoe and the Moone, the backsyde whereof is crymosin velvett," and another " with the ymage of our Ladie sett aboughte with x greate stones the backsyde whereof is grene velvett " (*Hierurgia anglicana*, pt. I., 1902).

PAXO [Faxos], one of the Ionian Islands (*q.v.*), about 8 m. S. of the southern extremity of Corfu, is a hilly mass of limestone 5 m. long by 2 broad, and not more than 600 ft. high. Pop. about 5000. Though it has only a single stream and a few springs, and the inhabitants were often obliged, before the Russians and English provided them with cisterns, to bring water from the mainland, Paxo is well clothed with olives, which produce oil of the very highest quality. Gaion (or, less correctly, Gaia), the principal village, lies on the east coast, and has a small harbour. Towards the centre, on an eminence, stands Papandi, the residence of the bishop of Paxo, and throughout the island are scattered a large number of churches, whose belfries add greatly to the picturesqueness of the views. On the west and south-west coasts are some remarkable caverns, of which an account will be found in Davy's *Ionian Islands*, I. 66–71. Ancient writers—Polybius, Pliny, &c.—do not mention Paxos by itself, but apply the plural form Paxi (Παξοί) to Paxos and the smaller island which is now known as Antipaxo (the Propaxos of the *Antonine Itinerary*). Paxos is the scene of the curious legend, recorded in Plutarch's *De defectu oraculorum*, of the cry " Pan is dead " (see PAN).

PAXTON, SIR JOSEPH (1801–1865), English architect and ornamental gardener, was born of humble parents at Milton Bryant, near Woburn, Bedfordshire, on the 3rd of August 1801, and was educated at the grammar school of that town. Having served his apprenticeship as gardener from the age of fifteen, and himself constructed a large lake when gardener to Battlesden in 1821, he was in 1823 employed in the arboretum at Chiswick, the seat of the duke of Devonshire, and eventually became superintendent of the duke's gardens and grounds at Chatsworth, and manager of his Derbyshire estates. In 1836 he began to erect a grand conservatory 300 ft. in length, which was finished in 1840, and formed the model for the Great Exhibition building of 1851. In this year Paxton received the honour of knighthood. Perhaps his most interesting design was that for the mansion of Baron James de Rothschild at Ferrières in France, but he designed many other important buildings. His versatility was shown in his organization of the Army Works Corps which served in the Crimea, his excellent capacity as a man of business in railway management, and his enterprising experiments in floriculture. In 1854 he was chosen M.P. for Coventry, which he continued to represent in the Liberal interest till his death at Sydenham on the 8th of June 1865. Paxton was elected in 1826 a fellow of the Horticultural Society. In the following year he married Sarah Bown. In 1833 he became a fellow of the Linnean Society, and in 1844 he was made a knight of the order of St Vladimir by the emperor of Russia.

He was the author of several contributions to the literature of horticulture, including a *Practical Treatise on the Culture of the Dahlia* (1838), and a *Pocket Botanical Dictionary* (1st ed., 1840). He also edited the *Cottage Calendar*, the *Horticultural Register* and the *Botanical Magazine*.

PAYMASTER-GENERAL, in England, a public officer and a member of the ministry for the time being. The office was, by statutes passed in 1835 and 1848, consolidated with other offices through which moneys voted by parliament were previously paid. The paymaster-general is appointed by sign manual warrant, he is unpaid, and does not require to offer himself for re-election on acceptance of office. The money appropriated by parliament for the various services of the country is placed by order of the Treasury to the account of the paymaster-general, and a communication to that effect made to the comptroller and auditor-general. The paymaster-general then makes all payments required by the various departments in accordance with the parliamentary vote. The duties of the office are carried out by a permanent staff, headed by an assistant paymaster-general, acting on powers granted by the paymaster-general.

PAYMENT (Fr. *paiement*, from *payer*, to pay; Lat. *pacare*, to appease, *pax*, peace), the performance of an obligation, the discharge of a sum due in money or the equivalent of money. In law, in order that payment may extinguish the obligation it is necessary that it should be made at a proper time and place, in a proper manner, and by and to a proper person. If the sum due be not paid at the appointed time, the creditor is entitled to sue the debtor at once, in spite of the readiness of the latter to pay at a later date, subject, in the case of bills and notes, to the allowance of days of grace. In the common case of sale of goods for ready money, a right to the goods vests at once upon sale in the purchaser, a right to the price in the seller; but the seller need not part with the goods till payment of the price.

Payment may be made at any time of the day upon which it falls due, except in the case of mercantile contracts, where the creditor is not bound to wait for payment beyond the usual hours of mercantile business. If no place be fixed for payment, the debtor is bound to find, or to use reasonable means to find, the creditor, unless the latter be abroad. Payment must be made in money which is a legal tender (see below), unless the creditor waive his right to payment in money by accepting some other mode of payment, as a negotiable instrument or a transfer of credit. If the payment be by negotiable instrument, the instrument may operate either as an absolute or as a conditional discharge. In the ordinary case of payment by cheque the creditor accepts the cheque conditionally upon its being honoured; if it be dishonoured, he is remitted to his original rights. If payment be made through the post, in a letter properly directed, and it be lost, the debt is discharged if there was a direction to transmit the money. The creditor has a right to payment in full, and is not bound to accept part payment unless by special agreement. Part payment is sufficient to take the debt out of the Statute of Limitation. It is a technical rule of English law that payment of a smaller sum, even though accepted by the creditor in full satisfaction, is no defence to a subsequent action for the debt. The reason of this rule seems to be that there is no consideration for the creditor foregoing his right to full payment. In order that payment of a smaller sum may satisfy the debt, it must be made by a person other than the person originally liable, or at an earlier date, or at another place, or in another manner than the date, place, or manner contracted for. Thus a bill or note may be satisfied by money to a less amount, or a money debt by a bill or note to a less amount; a debt of £100 cannot be discharged by payment of £90 (unless the creditor execute a release under seal), though it may be discharged by payment of £10 before the day appointed, or by a bill for £10. Payment must in general be made by the debtor or his agent, or by a stranger to the contract with the assent of the debtor. If payment be made by a stranger without the assent of the debtor, it seems uncertain how far English law regards such payment as a satisfaction of the debt. If the debtor ratify the payment, it then undoubtedly becomes a satisfaction. Payment must be made to the creditor or his agent. A bona fide payment to an apparent agent may be good, though he has in fact no authority to receive it. Such payment will usually be good where the authority of the agent has been countermanded without notice to the debtor. The fact of payment may be presumed, as from lapse of time. Thus payment of a testator's debts is generally presumed after twenty years. A written receipt is only presumptive and not conclusive evidence of payment. By the Stamp Act 1891 a duty of one penny is imposed upon a receipt for or upon the payment of money amounting to £2 or upwards, and also a fine of £10 upon any person who, in any case where a receipt would be liable to duty, refuses to give a receipt duly stamped. If payment be made under a mistake of fact, it may be recovered, but it is otherwise if it be made under a mistake of law, for it is a maxim of law that *ignorantia legis neminem excusal*. Money paid under compulsion of law, even though not due, cannot generally be recovered where there has been no fraud or extortion. For appropriation of payments see APPROPRIATION.

Payment Into and Out of Court.—Money is generally paid into court to abide the result of pending litigation, as where litigation has already begun, as security for costs or as a defence or partial defence to a claim. Payment into court does not necessarily (except in actions for libel and slander) operate as an admission of liability. Payment into court is regulated by the *Rules of the Supreme Court*, O. xxii. The fact that money has been paid into court may not be mentioned to a jury. Money may sometimes be paid into court where no litigation is pending, as in the case of trustees. Payment of money out of court is obtained by the order of the court upon petition or summons or otherwise, or simply on the request or the written authority of the person entitled to it.

Payment of Wages.—The payment of wages to labourers and workmen otherwise than in coin is prohibited. See LABOUR LEGISLATION: *Truck*. Domestic or agricultural servants are excepted. Payment of wages in public-houses (except in the case of domestic servants) is illegal.

Tender.—This is payment duly proffered to a creditor, but rendered abortive by the act of the creditor. In order that a tender may be good in law it must as a rule be made under circumstances which would make it a good payment if accepted. The money tendered must be a legal tender, unless the creditor waive his right to a legal tender, as where he objects to the amount and not the mode of tender. Bank of England notes are legal tender for any sum above £5, except by the bank itself. Gold is legal tender to any amount, silver up to 40s., bronze up to 1s. (Coinage Act 1870). Any gold coinage, whether British, colonial or foreign, may be made legal tender by proclamation. The effect of tender is not to discharge the debt, but to enable the debtor, when sued for the debt, to pay the money into court and to get judgment for the costs of his defence.

Scotland.—The law of Scotland as to payment agrees in most points with that of England. Where a debt is constituted by writ payment cannot be proved by witnesses; where it is not constituted by writ, payment to the amount of £100 Scots may be proved by witnesses; beyond that amount it can only be proved by writ or oath of party. The term tender seems to be strictly applied only to a judicial offer of a sum for damages and expenses made by the defender during litigation, not to an offer made by the debtor before litigation. Bank of England notes are not a legal tender in Scotland or in Ireland.

United States.—In the United States the law as a rule does not materially differ from English law. In some states, however, money may be recovered, even when it has been paid under a mistake of law. The question of legal tender has been an important one. In 1862 and 1863 Congress passed acts making treasury notes legal tender (see GREENBACKS). After much litigation, the Supreme Court of the United States decided in 1871 (*Knox v. Lee*) in favour of the constitutionality of these acts, both as to contracts made before and after they were passed. These notes are legal tender for all purposes except duties on imports and interest on the public debt. All gold coins and standard silver dollars are legal tender to any amount. Silver coins below the denomination of a dollar are legal tender up to $10, and cent an 5-cent pieces legal tender to an amount not exceeding 25 cents. It falls exclusively within the jurisdiction of Congress to declare paper or copper money a legal tender. By the constitution of the United States, " no state shall . . . make anything but gold and silver coin a tender in payment of debts " (art. I. § 10). (T. A. I.)

PAYMENT OF MEMBERS. From time to time proposals have been made to reintroduce in the English parliamentary system a practice which is almost universally adopted in other countries, that of paying a state salary to members of the legislative body. In the earlier history of the English parliament the payment of commoners or representatives of the legislative body was for long the practice. They had first been summoned to the great council of the realm in 1265 in the reign of Henry III. The shires and boroughs they represented paid them for their services, and reimbursed the expenses they were put to in journeying to and from the place of meeting. In 1322, by a statute of Edward II., the salary of a knight was fixed at 4s. a day, and that of a citizen or burgher at 2s. a day. These payments could be enforced by writs issued after the dissolution of each parliament, and there are many instances of the issue of such writs down to the reign of Henry VIII.; while the last known instance is that of one Thomas King, who in 1681 obtained a writ for his salary against the corporation of Harwich. The practice of the payment of members of parliament gradually fell into desuetude, and in the second parliament of Charles II. strong disapproval was expressed of the practice. Its gradual abandonment was due first to the difficulty of securing representatives in the early parliaments. Men of business were unwilling to detach themselves from their affairs, as travel was slow and dangerous; in addition to the perils of the journey there was the almost certain knowledge that a safe return from parliament would be followed by the ill will of the member's neighbours, for every meeting of parliament was but a device on the part of the sovereign for inflicting some new form of taxation, and a refusal to vote such taxation was but to incur the royal displeasure. The towns themselves were equally disinclined to bear the burden of their member's maintenance, and some even went so far as to obtain their disfranchisement. In the second place, the growing influence of parliament in the 16th century brought about a revulsion of feeling as to parliamentary services, and the increase in the number of candidates led first to bargaining on their part in the shape of undertaking to accept reduced wages and expenses, and, finally, to forego all. A step further was reached when the constituency bargained as to what it should receive from its representative, resulting in wholesale bribery, which required legislation to end it (see CORRUPT PRACTICES).

In England, the House of Commons has on various occasions carried resolutions in favour of the principle, more especially on the 24th of March 1893 (by 276 votes to 229), and on the 22nd of March 1895 (by 176 to 158). On these occasions the resolutions simply specified an "adequate allowance"; but on the 7th of March 1906 a resolution was carried (by 348 votes to 110) in favour of an allowance "at the rate of £300 per annum."

Appended are the salaries paid to legislators in various countries in 1910.

BRITISH COLONIES

South Africa.—Before the South Africa Act 1909, which brought about the union of Cape Colony, Natal, Orange River Colony and the Transvaal, each colony had its own legislature. For purposes of comparison, the salaries which were paid to the members of these state legislatures are given below. The act of 1909 reduced the colonies to the position of dependent provinces, entrusted only with local administration by means of provincial councils. The act of 1909 (§ 76) enacts that the members of provincial councils shall receive such allowances as shall be determined by the governor-general in council. Members of the new South African legislature receive £400 a year, subject to a deduction of £3 a day for each day's non-attendance.

. *Cape Colony.*—Members of either house were paid 21s. a day, and those residing more than 15 m. from Cape Town an additional 15s. a day, for a period not exceeding 90 days.

Natal.—Members of the legislature were not paid, but those residing more than 2 m. from the seat of government received a travelling allowance of £1 a day during the session.

Orange River Colony.—At the end of the session each member received £150. and an additional £2 for each day of actual attendance, but not more than £300 in all.

Transvaal Colony.—As in the Orange River Colony.

Canada.—Federal government. Members of both houses are paid $2500 per session, but subject to a deduction of $15 a day for each day of non-attendance.

Ontario.—Members of the Legislative Assembly are paid mileage and an allowance of $6 a day for 30 days, with a maximum of $1000.

Quebec.—Members of the Legislative Assembly are paid $6 a day during the session.

Nova Scotia.—Members are paid an indemnity of $500 for the session.

New Brunswick.—Members of the Legislative Assembly receive $500 per session and travelling expenses.

Manitoba.—Members of the Legislative Assembly receive $1000 per session and travelling expenses.

British Columbia.—Members of the Legislative Assembly receive $1200 per session and travelling expenses.

Prince Edward Island.—Members of the Legislative Assembly

¹ Quebec and Nova Scotia have each two chambers. The other Canadian provinces have only one chamber.

receive $160 per annum and travelling expenses, with an additional $12 for postage.

Australian Commonwealth.—Members of parliament receive £600 per annum. .

New South Wales.—Members of the Legislative Assembly receive £300 per annum, and free travel over all government railways and tramways. They are also given official stamped envelopes for their postage purposes.

Victoria.—Members of the Legislative Assembly receive £300 per annum and free passes over all railways.

Queensland.—Members of the Legislative Assembly receive £300 per annum, with travelling expenses.

South Australia.—Members both of the Legislative Council and of the House of Assembly receive £200 per annum and free passes over all government railways.

Western Australia.—Members of the Legislative Council receive £200 a year and free travel on all government railways.

Tasmania.—Members of both houses receive £100 a year and free railway passes.

New Zealand.—Members of the Legislative Council are paid £200 per annum. Members of the House of Representatives are paid £25 a month.

UNITED STATES

Federal Government.—Senators, representatives or delegates receive $7500 a year, and travelling expenses.

Alabama.—There is a session once in four years, such session being limited to 50 days, during which senators and representatives receive $4 a day and mileage.

Arizona Territory.—A biennial session of 60 days' duration, during which members of the council and representatives receive $4 a day and mileage.

Arkansas has a biennial session of 60 days' duration, for which senators and representatives receive $6 a day and mileage.

California's legislature meets biennially, but there is no fixed length for the session. Senators and members of the Assembly receive $1000 and mileage for the term.

Colorado's session is biennial and limited to 90 days. Senators and representatives receive $7 a day and mileage during session.

Connecticut gives senators and representatives $300 and mileage for their term of two years.

Delaware has biennial sessions of 60 days, and may have extra sessions limited to 30 days. Senators and representatives receive $5 a day during sessions.

Florida has biennial sessions of 60 days. Senators and representatives receive $6 a day during the session and mileage.

Georgia has annual sessions limited to 50 days. Senators and representatives receive $4 a day and mileage.

Idaho's senators and representatives receive mileage and $5 a day during the session, which is biennial.

Illinois has a biennial session, for which senators and representatives receive $1000 a year and mileage. For extraordinary sessions they receive $5 a day.

Indiana has biennial sessions limited to 60 days. Senators and representatives receive $6 a day and mileage.

Iowa has biennial sessions of unlimited length. Senators and representatives receive $550 for the session, with mileage.

Kansas has biennial sessions limited to 50 days. Senators and representatives receive $3 a day during the session, with mileage.

Kentucky has biennial sessions limited to 60 days. Senators and representatives receive $5 a day and mileage.

Louisiana has biennial sessions limited to 60 days. Senators and representatives receive $5 a day during the session with mileage.

Maine's senators and representatives receive $300 a year and mileage. Sessions are biennial and of no fixed length.

Maryland has biennial sessions limited to 90 days. Senators and delegates receive $5 a day during the session and mileage.

Massachusetts has an annual session, for which senators and representatives receive each a lump sum of $750 and mileage.

Michigan has biennial sessions not of fixed length, and senators and representatives are paid $800 a year and mileage.

Minnesota has biennial sessions limited to 90 days. Senators and representatives receive $1000 a year besides limited travelling expenses.

Mississippi has a session every four years, unlimited in length. Special sessions, also, limited to 30 days, are held in alternate years. Senators and representatives receive a sum of $400 for each session.

Missouri has biennial sessions of no fixed length. Senators and representatives receive $5 a day for the first 70 days of each session, and $1 a day for each succeeding day.

Montana has biennial sessions limited to 60 days. Senators and representatives receive $12 a day during session.

Nebraska has biennial sessions unlimited in length. Senators and representatives are paid $5 a day and mileage (10 cents a mile) for not more than 60 days of any one session. If extraordinary sessions are held the total days paid for must not exceed 100 during the two years for which they sit.

Nevada has biennial sessions limited to 60 days, but special sessions limited to 20 days may be held. Senators and representatives receive $10 a day and mileage during sessions.

New Hampshire has biennial sessions, which last until prorogued by the governor. The duration is usually about three months. Senators and representatives receive $200 for the session and mileage.

New Jersey has an annual session, unlimited in length. Senators and members of the General Assembly receive $500 a year.

New Mexico has biennial sessions of 60 days. Members of the Council and representatives receive $4 a day.

New York has an annual session. Members of the Senate and of the Assembly receive $1500 a year.

North Carolina has biennial sessions limited to 60 days. Senators and representatives receive $4 a day during the session and mileage.

North Dakota has biennial sessions limited to 60 days. Senators and representatives receive $5 a day during the session and mileage.

Ohio has biennial sessions not limited in length. Senators and representatives receive $1000 a year.

Oklahoma has biennial sessions. Senators and representatives receive $6 a day for the first 60 days—thereafter $2 a day—and mileage (10 cents a mile).

Oregon has biennial sessions limited to 240 days. Senators and representatives receive $3 a day during the session and mileage.

Pennsylvania has biennial sessions. Senators and representatives receive $1500 for the session with mileage, with an extra allowance of $150 for stationery and postage.

Rhode Island has an annual session unlimited in length. Senators and representatives receive $5 a day during the session.

South Carolina has an annual session unlimited in length. Senators and representatives receive $4 a day for the first 40 days.

South Dakota has biennial sessions of 60 days. Senators and representatives receive $5 for each day's attendance, and travelling expenses.

Tennessee has biennial sessions. Senators and representatives receive $4 a day for not more than 75 days a session and mileage (16 cents a mile). If absent they do not receive pay, unless they are physically unable to be present.

Texas has biennial sessions, unlimited in length. Senators and representatives receive mileage and $5 a day for the first 60 days of the session; for succeeding days $2 a day.

Utah has biennial sessions limited to 60 days. Senators and representatives receive $4 a day during the session and mileage.

Vermont has biennial sessions unlimited in length. Senators and representatives receive $4 a day during the session and mileage.

Virginia has biennial sessions limited to 60 days. Senators and delegates receive $500 for the session and mileage.

Washington has biennial sessions limited to 60 days. Senators and representatives receive $5 a day for each day's attendance and travelling expenses.

West Virginia has biennial sessions limited to 45 days, which can be added to by a two-thirds majority. Senators and delegates receive $4 a day during the session and mileage.

Wisconsin has biennial sessions. Senators and members of the Assembly receive $500 for the session, and travelling expenses at the rate of 10 cents a mile.

Wyoming has biennial sessions limited to 40 days. Senators and representatives receive $8 a day during the session and mileage.

FOREIGN COUNTRIES

Argentina.—Both senators (30) and members of the House of Deputies (120) receive £1060 a year.

Austria.—Members of the Lower House (516) receive 16s. 8d. for each day's attendance, with travelling expenses.

Belgium.—Members of the Chamber of Representatives (166) receive £160 a year and a free pass over railways.

Bosnia.—Senators (16) and deputies (69) receive £40 a month during sessions, which last from 60 to 90 days.

Bulgaria.—Members of the Legislature receive 16s. a day during the session, which nominally lasts from the 15th of October to the 15th of December.

Denmark.—Members both of the Landsthing (66) and of the Folkething (114) receive 11s. 1d. a day for the first six months of the session, and 6s. 8d. for each additional day of the session. They receive also second-class free passes on all railways.

France.—Members of both the Senate (300) and of the Chamber of Deputies (584) receive £600 a year.

German Empire.—Members both of the Bundesrat (58) and of the Reichstag (397) receive £150 for the session, but have deducted £1 for each day's absence. They receive also free passes over the German railways during the session.

Baden pays members of its Second Chamber and such members of the Upper Chamber as have not got hereditary seats 12s. a day and travelling expenses, but to those members who reside in the capital 9s. a day only.

Bavaria pays members of the Lower House (163) £180 for a regular session. They are also allowed free travel over the government railways.

Hesse.—Members of the Second Chamber (50) and non-hereditary members of the Upper Chamber who reside more than 1½ m. from the place of meeting receive 9s. a day and 3s. for each night, besides a refund of their travelling expenses.

Prussia.—Members of the Lower Chamber (433) receive travelling expenses and diet money (according to a fixed scale) of 15s. a day.

Saxe-Coburg.—Members of the Second Chamber residing in Coburg or Gotha receive 6s. a day; other members receive 10s. a day and travelling expenses.

Saxony.—Members of the Second Chamber (82) and non-hereditary members of the Upper Chamber receive 12s. a day (6s. a day if they live in the place of meeting) and an allowance for travelling.

Württemberg.—Members of both chambers receive 15s. a day for actual attendance; also free passes over the railways.

Greece.—The members (235) receive £72 for the session, also free passes on railway and steamship lines.

Hungary.—Members of the House of Representatives (453) receive £200 a year, with allowance of £66 13s. for house rent.

Italy.—Members of the Legislature receive no payment, although attempts have been made from 1862 onwards to introduce payment of members. It was last brought forward in 1908, the amount suggested being 24s. for every sitting attended.

Japan.—Members of the House of Representatives (379) and non-hereditary members of the House of Peers receive £210 a year, besides travelling expenses.

Mexico.—Both senators (56) and representatives (340) receive $3000 a year.

Netherlands.—Members of the First Chamber (50) not residing in the Hague receive 16s. 8d. a day during the session; members of the Second Chamber (100) receive £166 a year, besides travelling expenses.

Norway.—Members of the Storting (123) receive 13s. 4d. a day during the session, besides travelling expenses.

Paraguay.—Both senators and deputies receive £200 a year.

Portugal.—Deputies have been unpaid since 1892, but deputies for the colonies, whose homes are in the colonies, receive £20 a month or 13s. 4d. a day during sittings of the Chamber, and £10 a month when the Chamber is not sitting.

Rumania.—Both senators (120) and deputies (183) receive 16s. 8d. for each day of attendance, besides free railway passes.

Russia.—Members of the Duma receive 21s. a day during the session, and travelling expenses.

Servia.—Deputies (120) receive 12s. a day and travelling expenses.

Spain.—Members of the Legislature receive no salary; but deputies on their election receive a railway ticket for 2480 m. travel.

Sweden.—Members of both the First Chamber (150) and the Second Chamber (230) receive £66 for each session of 4 months, besides travelling expenses.

Switzerland.—Members of the State Council are paid by the canton they represent, and their salary varies according to the wealth or liberality of the canton. The salary ranges thus from 12s. 6d. to 25s. a day, the average of the whole being 16s. a day. Members of the National Council (167) are paid from Federal funds. They receive 16s. 8d. a day for each day they are present, with travelling expenses.

(T.A.I.)

END OF TWENTIETH VOLUME.

PRINTED BY R. R. DONNELLEY & SONS COMPANY, CHICAGO, ON "BRITANNICA INDIA PAPER" MANUFACTURED BY S. D. WARREN & COMPANY, BOSTON, MASS. BINDERS, THE J.F. TAPLEY COMPANY, NEW YORK, AND R. R. DONNELLEY & SONS COMPANY, CHICAGO.

Lightning Source UK Ltd.
Milton Keynes UK
UKHW022303070119
334855UK00013BA/2248/P